CW00730441

The Form Book ®

FLAT ANNUAL FOR 2017

THE OFFICIAL FORM BOOK

ALL THE 2016 RETURNS

Complete record of Flat Racing from 1 January to 31 December 2016

Associated Raceform products

The Form Book is updated weekly. Subscribers receive a binder, together with all the early racing. Weekly sections and a new index are threaded into the binder to keep it up to date.

The data contained in *The Form Book Flat Annual for 2017* is available in paper form or on computer disk. The disk serce, Raceform Interactive, contains the same data as The Flat Form Book, and operates on any PC within a 'Windows' environment. The database is designed to allow access to the information in a number of different ways, and is extremely quick and easy to use.

Published in 2017 by Raceform Ltd
27 Kingfisher Court, Hambridge Road, Newbury, Berkshire RG14 5SJ

A catalogue record for this book is available from the British Library

ISBN 978-1-910497-17-3

Printed in the UK by CPI Group (UK) Ltd, Croydon, CR0 4YY
Full details of all Raceform services and publications are available from:

Raceform Ltd, Sanders Road, Wellingborough, Northants NN8 4BX
Tel: 01933 304858 • Fax: 01933 304796
Email: shop@racingpost.com
www.racingpost.com

Cover picture: Postponed (Andrea Atzeni) before winning the Juddmonte International at York.

CONTENTS

Editor: Graham Dench

• Racereaders

Walter Glynn
Richard Lowther
Lee McKenzie
Tim Mitchell
Jonathan Neesom
Darren Owen
Steve Payne
Colin Roberts
Joe Rowntree
Andrew Sheret
Richard Young

The Official Scale of Weight, Age & Distance (Flat)

The following scale should only be used in conjunction with the Official ratings published in this book. Use of any other scale will introduce errors into calculations. The allowances are expressed as the number of pounds that is deemed the average horse in each group falls short of maturity at different dates and distances.

Dist		Jan		Feb		Mar		Apr		May		Jun		Jul		Aug		Sep		Oct		Nov		Dec	
(fur)	Age	1-15	16-31	1-14	15-28	1-15	16-31	1-15	16-30	1-15	16-31	1-15	16-30	1-15	16-31	1-15	16-31	1-15	16-30	1-15	16-31	1-15	16-30	1-15	16-31
5	2	-	-	-	-	-	47	44	41	38	36	34	32	30	28	26	24	22	20	19	18	17	17	16	16
	3	15	15	14	14	13	12	11	10	9	8	7	6	5	4	3	2	1	1	-	-	-	-	-	-
6	2	-	-	-	-	-	-	-	-	44	41	38	36	33	31	28	26	24	22	21	20	19	18	17	17
	3	16	16	15	15	14	13	12	11	10	9	8	7	6	5	4	3	2	2	1	1	-	-	-	-
7	2	-	-	-	-	-	-	-	-	-	-	-	-	38	35	32	30	27	25	23	22	21	20	19	19
	3	18	18	17	17	16	15	14	13	12	11	10	9	8	7	6	5	4	3	2	2	1	1	-	-
8	2	-	-	-	-	-	-	-	-	-	-	-	-	-	-	37	34	31	28	26	24	23	22	21	20
	3	20	20	19	19	18	17	15	14	13	12	11	10	9	8	7	6	5	4	3	3	2	2	1	1
9	3	22	22	21	21	20	19	17	15	14	13	12	11	10	9	8	7	6	5	4	4	3	3	2	2
	4	1	1	-	-	-	-	-	-	-	-	-	-	-	-	-	-	-	-	-	-	-	-	-	-
10	3	23	23	22	22	21	20	19	17	15	14	13	12	11	10	9	8	7	6	5	5	4	4	3	3
	4	2	2	1	1	-	-	-	-	-	-	-	-	-	-	-	-	-	-	-	-	-	-	-	-
11	3	24	24	23	23	22	21	20	19	17	15	14	13	12	11	10	9	8	7	6	6	5	5	4	4
	4	3	3	2	2	1	1	-	-	-	-	-	-	-	-	-	-	-	-	-	-	-	-	-	-
12	3	25	25	24	24	23	22	21	20	19	17	15	14	13	12	11	10	9	8	7	7	6	6	5	5
	4	4	4	3	3	2	2	1	1	-	-	-	-	-	-	-	-	-	-	-	-	-	-	-	-
13	3	26	26	25	25	24	23	22	21	20	19	17	15	14	13	12	11	10	9	8	8	7	7	6	6
	4	5	5	4	4	3	3	2	1	-	-	-	-	-	-	-	-	-	-	-	-	-	-	-	-
14	3	27	27	26	26	25	24	23	22	21	20	19	17	15	14	13	12	11	10	9	9	8	8	7	7
	4	6	6	5	5	4	4	3	2	1	-	-	-	-	-	-	-	-	-	-	-	-	-	-	-
15	3	28	28	27	27	26	25	24	23	22	21	20	19	17	15	14	13	12	11	10	9	8	8	7	7
	4	6	6	5	5	4	4	3	3	2	1	-	-	-	-	-	-	-	-	-	-	-	-	-	-
16	3	29	29	28	28	27	26	25	24	23	22	21	20	19	17	15	14	13	12	11	10	9	9	8	8
	4	7	7	6	6	5	5	4	4	3	2	1	-	-	-	-	-	-	-	-	-	-	-	-	-
18	3	31	31	30	30	29	28	27	26	25	24	23	22	21	20	18	16	14	13	12	11	10	10	9	9
	4	8	8	7	7	6	6	5	5	4	3	2	1	-	-	-	-	-	-	-	-	-	-	-	-
20	3	33	33	32	32	31	30	29	28	27	26	25	24	23	22	20	18	16	14	13	12	11	11	10	10
	4	9	9	8	8	7	7	6	6	5	4	3	2	1	-	-	-	-	-	-	-	-	-	-	-

The Form Book

Welcome to the *The Form Book Flat Annual for 2017,* comprising the complete year's Flat results for 2016.

Race details contain Racing Post Ratings assessing the merit of each individual performance, speed figures for every horse that clocks a worthwhile time, weight-for-age allowances, stall positions for every race and the starting price percentage, in addition to the traditional features.

Race Focus comments are printed below most races, along with the results of stewards' enquiries.

• The official record

THE FORM BOOK records comprehensive race details of every domestic race, every major European Group race and every foreign event in which a British-trained runner participated.

MEETING BACK REFERENCE NUMBER is the Raceform number of the last meeting run at the track and is shown to the left of the course name. Abandoned meetings are signified by a dagger.

THE GOING, The Official going, shown at the head of each meeting, is recorded as follows: Turf: Hard; Firm; Good to firm; Good; Good to soft; Soft; Heavy. All-Weather: Fast; Standard to fast; Standard; Standard to slow; Slow. There may be variations for non-British meetings

Where appropriate, a note is included indicating track bias and any differences to the official going indicated by race times.

THE WEATHER is shown below the date for selected meetings.

THE WIND is given as a strength and direction at the Winning Post, classified as follows:
Strength: gale; v.str; str; fresh; mod; slt; almost nil; nil.
Direction: (half) against; (half) bhd; (half) across from or towards stands.

VISIBILITY is good unless otherwise stated.

RACE NUMBERS for foreign races carry the suffix 'a' in the race header and in the index.

RACE TITLE is the name of the race as shown in the Racing Calendar.

COMPETITIVE RACING CLASSIFICATIONS are shown on a scale from Class 1 to Class 7. All Pattern races are Class 1.

THE RACE DISTANCE is given for all races, and is accompanied by (s) for races run on straight courses and (r) for courses where there is a round track of comparable distance. On All-Weather courses (F) for Fibresand or (P) for Polytrack indicates the nature of the artificial surface on which the race is run.

OFFICIAL RACE TIME as published in the Racing Calendar is followed in parentheses by the time when the race actually started. This is followed by the race class, age restrictions, handicap restrictions and the official rating of the top weight.

PRIZE MONEY shows penalty values down to sixth place (where applicable).

THE POSITION OF THE STARTING STALLS is shown against each race, in the form of: High (H), Centre (C) or Low (L). In keeping with all other major racing nations, stalls are now numbered from the inside rail. If the stalls are placed adjacent to the inside rail they are described as low, if against the outside rail they are described as high. Otherwise they are central.

IN THE RACE RESULT, the figures to the far left of each horse (under FORM) show the most recent form figures. The figure in bold is the finishing position in this race as detailed below.

1...40 - finishing positions first to fortieth; **b** - brought down; **c** - carried out; **f** - fell; **p** - pulled up; **r** - refused; **ro** - ran out; **s** - slipped up; **u** - unseated rider; **v** - void race.

THE OFFICIAL DISTANCES between the horses are shown on the left-hand side immediately after their position at the finish.

NUMBER OF DAYS SINCE PREVIOUS RUN is the superscript figure immediately following the horse name and suffix.

PREVIOUS RACEFORM RACE NUMBER is the boxed figure to the right of the horse's name.

THE HORSE'S AGE is shown immediately before the weight carried.

WEIGHTS shown are actual weights carried.

OFFICIAL RATING is the figure in bold type directly after the horse's name in the race result. This figure indicates the Official BHA rating, at entry, after the following adjustments had been made:
(i) Overweight carried by the rider.
(ii) The number of pounds out of the handicap (if applicable).
(iii) Penalties incurred after the publication of the weights.
However, no adjustments have been made for:
(i) Weight-for-age.
(ii) Riders' claims.

HEADGEAR is shown immediately before the jockey's name and in parentheses and expressed as: **b** (blinkers); **v** (visor); **h** (hood); **e** (eyeshield); **c** (eyecover); **p** (sheepskin cheekpieces); **t** (tongue-tie).

THE JOCKEY is shown for every runner followed, in superscript, by apprentice allowances in parentheses.

APPRENTICE ALLOWANCES The holders of apprentice jockeys' licences under the provisions of Rule 60(iii) are permitted to claim the following allowances in Flat races:
7lb until they have won 20 Flat races run under the Rules of any recognised Turf Authority; thereafter 5lb until they have won 50 such Flat races; thereafter 3lb until they have won 95 such Flat races. These allowances can be claimed in the Flat races set out below, with the exception of races confined to apprentice jockeys:
(a) All handicaps other than those Rated stakes which are classified as listed races.
(b) All selling and claiming races.
(b) All weight-for-age races classified 3, 4, 5, 6 and 7.

THE DRAW for places at the start is shown after each jockey's name.

RACING POST RATINGS, which record the level of performance attained in this race for each horse, appear in the end column after each horse. These are the work of handicappers Simon Turner, Sam Walker and Paul Curtis, who head a dedicated team dealing with Flat races for Raceform and sister publication, the *Racing Post*.

THE TRAINER is shown for every runner.

COMMENT-IN-RUNNING is shown for each horse in an abbreviated form. Details of abbreviations appear later in this section.

STARTING PRICES appear below the jockey in the race result. The favourite indicator appears to the right of the Starting Price;
1 for the favourite, 2 for the second-favourite and 3 for third-favourite. Joint favourites share the same number.

RACE TIMES in Great Britain are official times which are electronically recorded and shown to 100th of a second. Figures in parentheses following the time show the number of seconds faster or slower than the Raceform Median Time for the course and distance.

RACEFORM MEDIAN TIMES are compiled from all races run over the course and distance in the preceding five years. Times equal to the median are shown as (0.00). Times under the median are preceded by minus, for instance, 1.8 seconds under the median would be shown (-1.8). Record times are displayed either referring to the juvenile record (2y crse rec) or to the overall record (course record).

TRACK VARIANT appears against each race to allow for changing conditions of the track and ground. It is shown to a hundredth of a second and indicates the adjustment per furlong against the median time. The going based on the going correction is shown in parentheses and is recorded in the following stages:
Turf: HD (Hard); F (Firm); GF (Good to firm); G (Good); GS (Good to soft); S (Soft); HVY (Heavy). All-Weather: FST (Fast); SF (Standard to fast); STD (Standard); SS (Standard to slow); SLW (Slow)

WEIGHT-FOR-AGE allowances are given where applicable for mixed-age races.

STARTING PRICE PERCENTAGE follows the going correction and weight-for-age details, and gives the total SP percentage of all runners that competed. It precedes the number of runners taking part in the race.

SELLING DETAILS (where applicable) and details of any claim are given. Friendly claims are not detailed.

SPEED RATINGS appear below the race time and going correction. They are the work of time expert Dave Bellingham and differ from conventional ratings systems in that they are an expression of a horse's ability in terms of lengths-per-mile, as opposed to pounds in weight. They are not directly comparable with BHA and Racing Post Ratings.

The ratings take no account of the effect of weight, either historically or on the day, and this component is left completely to the user's discretion. What is shown is a speed rating represented in its purest form, rather than one that has been altered for weight using a mathematical formula that treats all types of horses as if they were the same.

A comparison of the rating achieved with the 'par' figure for the grade of race - the rating that should be achievable by an average winner in that class of race - will both provide an at-a-glance indication of whether or not a race was truly run and also highlight the value of the form from a time perspective.

In theory, if a horse has a best speed figure five points superior to another and both run to their best form in a race over a mile, the first horse should beat the second by five lengths. In a race run over two miles, the margin should be ten lengths and so on.

Before the speed figures can be calculated, it is necessary to establish a set of standard or median times for every distance at every track, and this is done by averaging the times of all winners over a particular trip going back several years. No speed ratings are produced when insufficient races have been run over a distance for a reliable median time to be calculated.

Once a meeting has taken place, a raw unadjusted speed rating is calculated for each winner by calculating how many lengths per mile the winning time was faster or slower than the median for the trip. A difference of 0.2 of a second equals one length. The raw speed ratings of all winners on the card are then compared with the 'par' figure for the class of race. The difference between the 'raw' speed rating and the 'par' figure for each race is then noted, and both the fastest and slowest races are discarded before the rest are averaged to produce the going allowance or track variant. This figure gives an idea as to how much the elements, of which the going is one, have affected the final times of each race.

The figure representing the going allowance is then used to adjust the raw speed figures and produce the final ratings, which represent how fast the winners would have run on a perfectly good surface with no external influences, including the weather. The ratings for beaten horses are worked out by taking the number of lengths they were behind the winner, adjusting that to take into account the distance of the race, and deducting that figure from the winner's rating. The reader is left with a rating which provides an instant impression of the value of a time performance.

The speed 'pars' below act as benchmark with which to compare the speed figures earned by each horse in each race. A horse that has already exceeded the 'par' for the class he is about to run in is of special interest, especially if he has done it more than once, as are horses that have consistently earned higher figures than their rivals.

Class 1 Group One	117
Class 1 Group Two	115
Class 1 Group Three	113
Class 1 Listed	111
Class 2	109
Class 3	107
Class 4	105
Class 5	103
Class 6	101
Class 7	099

Allowances need to be made for younger horses and for fillies. These allowances are as follows.

MONTH	2yo	3yo
Jan / Feb	n/a	-6
Mar / Apr	-11	-5
May / Jun	-10	-4
Jul / Aug	-9	-3
Sep / Oct	-8	-2
Nov / Dec	-7	-1
Races contested by fillies only		-3

Allowances are cumulative. For example, using a combination of the above pars and allowances, the par figure for the Epsom Oaks would be 110. The Group One par is 117, then deduct 4 because the race is confined to three year olds and run in June, then subtract another 3 because the race is confined to fillies.

TOTE prices include £1 stake. Exacta dividends are shown in parentheses. The Computer Straight Forecast dividend is preceded by the letters CSF, Computer Tricast is preceded by CT and Trifecta dividend is preceded by the word Trifecta. Jackpot, Placepot and Quadpot details appear at the end of the meeting to which they refer.

OWNER is followed by the breeder's name and the trainer's location.

STEWARDS' ENQUIRIES are included with the result, and any suspensions and/or fines incurred. Objections by jockeys and officials are included, where relevant.

HISTORICAL FOCUS details occasional points of historical significance.

FOCUS The Focus section helps readers distinguish good races from bad races and reliable form from unreliable form, by drawing together the opinions of handicapper, time expert and paddock watcher and interpreting their views in a punter-friendly manner.

Abbreviations and their meanings

Paddock comments

gd sort - well made, above average on looks
attr - attractive, but not as impressive as good sort
gd bodied - good bodied, well put together
h.d.w - has done well, improved in looks
wl grwn - well grown, has filled to its frame
lengthy - longer than average for its height
tall - tall
rangy - lengthy and tall but in proportion.
cl cpld - close coupled
scope - scope for physical development
str - strong, powerful looking
w'like - workmanlike, ordinary in looks
lt-f - light-framed, not much substance
cmpt - compact
neat - smallish, well put together
leggy - long legs compared with body
angular - unfurnished behind the saddle, not filled to frame
unf - unfurnished in the midriff, not filled to frame
narrow - not as wide as side appearance would suggest
small - lacks any physical scope
nt grwn - not grown
lw - looked fit and well
bkwd - backward in condition
t - tubed
swtg - sweating
b (off fore or nr fore) - bandaged in front
b.hind (off or nr) - bandaged behind

At the start

stdd s - jockey purposely reins back the horse
dwlt - missed the break and left for a short time
s.s - slow to start, left longer than a horse that dwelt
s.v.s - started very slowly
s.i.s - started on terms but took time to get going
ref to r - does not jump off, or travels a few yards then stops
rel to r - tries to pull itself up in mid-race
w.r.s - whipped round start

Position in the race

led - in lead on its own
disp ld - upsides the leader
w ldr - almost upsides the leader

w ldrs - in a line of three or more disputing the lead
prom - on the heels of the leaders, in front third of the field
trckd ldr(s) - just in behind the leaders giving impression that it could lead if asked
chsd ldr - horse in second place
chsd clr ldrs - horse heads main body of field behind two clear leaders
chsd ldrs - horse is in the first four or five but making more of an effort to stay close to the pace than if it were tracking the leaders.
clsd - closed
in tch - close enough to have a chance
hdwy - making ground on the leader
gd hdwy - making ground quickly on the leader, could be a deliberate move
sme hdwy - making some ground but no real impact on the race
w.w - waited with
stdy hdwy - gradually making ground
ev ch - upsides the leaders when the race starts in earnest
rr - at the back of main group but not detached
bhd - detached from the main body of runners
hld up - restrained as a deliberate tactical move
nt rcvr - lost all chance after interference, mistake etc.
wknd - stride shortened as it began to tire
lost tch - had been in the main body but a gap appeared as it tired
lost pl - remains in main body of runners but lost several positions quickly

Riding

effrt - short-lived effort
pushed along - received urgings with hands only, jockey not using legs
rdn - received urgings from saddle, including use of whip
hrd rdn - received maximum assistance from the saddle including use of whip
drvn - received forceful urgings, jockey putting in a lot of effort and using whip
hrd drvn - jockey very animated, plenty of kicking, pushing and reminders

Finishing comments

jst failed - closing rapidly on the winner and probably would have led a stride after the line
r.o - jockey's efforts usually involved to produce an increase in pace without finding an appreciable turn of speed
r.o wl - jockey's efforts usually involved to produce an obvious increase in pace without finding an appreciable turn of speed
unable qckn - not visibly tiring but does not possess a sufficient change of pace
one pce - not tiring but does not find a turn of speed, from a position further out than unable qckn
nt r.o. - did not consent to respond to pressure
styd on - going on well towards the end, utilising stamina
nvr able to chal - unable to produce sufficient to reach a challenging position
nvr nr to chal - in the opinion of the racereader, the horse was never in a suitable position to challenge.
nrst fin - nearer to the winner in distance beaten than at any time since the race had begun in earnest
nvr nrr - nearer to the winner position-wise than at any time since the race had begun in earnest
rallied - responded to pressure to come back with a chance having lost its place
no ex - unable to sustain its run
bttr for r - likely to improve for the run and experience
rn green - inclined to wander and falter through inexperience
too much to do - left with too much leeway to make up

Winning comments

v.easily - a great deal in hand
easily - plenty in hand
comf - something in hand, always holding the others
pushed out - kept up to its work with hands and heels without jockey resorting to whip or kicking along and wins fairly comfortably
rdn out - pushed and kicked out to the line, with the whip employed
drvn out - pushed and kicked out to the line, with considerable effort and the whip employed
all out - nothing to spare, could not have found any more
jst hld on - holding on to a rapidly diminishing lead, could not have found any more if passed
unchal - must either make all or a majority of the running and not be challenged from an early stage

Complete list of abbreviations

a - always
abt - about
a.p - always prominent
appr - approaching
awrdd - awarded
b.b.v - broke blood-vessel
b.d - brought down
bdly - badly
bef - before
bhd - behind
bk - back
blkd - baulked
blnd - blundered
bmpd - bumped
bnd - bend
btn- beaten
bttr - better
c - came
ch - chance
chal - challenged
chse - chase
chsd - chased
chsng - chasing
circ - circuit
cl - close
clr - clear
clsd - closed
comf - comfortably
cpld - coupled
crse - course
ct - caught
def - definite
dismntd - dismounted
disp - disputed
dist - distance
div - division
drvn - driven
dwlt - dwelt
edgd - edged
effrt - effort

ent - entering
ev ch - every chance
ex - extra
f - furlong
fin - finished
fnd - found
fnl - final
fr - from
gd - good
gng - going
gp - group
grad - gradually
grnd - ground
hd - head
hdd - headed
hdwy - headway
hld - held
hmpd - hampered
imp - impression
ins - inside
j.b - jumped badly
j.w - jumped well
jnd - joined
jst - just
kpt - kept
l - length
ld - lead
ldr - leader
lft - left
mod - moderate
m - mile
m.n.s - made no show
mde - made
mid div - mid division
mstke - mistake
n.d - never dangerous
n.g.t - not go through
n.m.r - not much room
nk - neck
no ex - no extra
nr - near
nrr - nearer
nrst fin - nearest finish
nt - not
nvr - never
one pce - one pace
out - from finish
outpcd - outpaced
p.u - pulled up
pce - pace
pckd - pecked
pl - place
plcd - placed
plld - pulled
press - pressure
prog - progress
prom - prominent
qckly - quickly
qckn - quicken
r - race
racd - raced
rch - reach
rcvr - recover
rdn - ridden
rdr - rider
reard - reared
ref - refused
rn - ran
rnd - round
r.o - ran on
rr - rear
rspnse - response
rt - right
s - start
sddle - saddle
shkn - shaken
slt - slight
sme - some
sn - soon
spd- speed
st - straight
stmbld - stumbled
stdd - steadied
stdy - steady
strly - strongly
styd - stayed
styng - staying
s. u - slipped up
swtchd - switched
swvd - swerved
tk - took
t.k.h - took keen hold
t.o - tailed off
tch - touch
thrght - throughout
trbld - troubled
trckd - tracked
u.p - under pressure
u.str.p- under strong pressure
w - with
w.r.s - whipped round start
wd - wide
whn - when
wknd - weakened
wl - well
wnr - winner
wnt - went
1/2-wy - halfway

• Racing Post Ratings

Racing Post Ratings for each horse are shown in the right hand column, headed RPR, and indicate the actual level of performance attained in that race. The figure in the back index represents the BEST public form that Raceform's Handicappers still believe the horse capable of reproducing.

To use the ratings constructively in determining those horses best-in in future events, the following procedure should be followed:

(i) In races where all runners are the same age and are set to carry the same weight, no calculations are necessary. The horse with the highest rating is best-in.

(ii) In races where all runners are the same age but are set to carry different weights, add one point to the Racing Post Rating for every pound less than 10 stone to be carried; deduct one point for every pound more than 10 stone.

For example,

Horse	Age & wt	Adjustment from 10st	Base rating	Adjusted rating
Treclare	3-10-1	-1	78	77
Buchan	3-9-13	+1	80	81
Paper Money	3-9-7	+7	71	78
Archaic	3-8-11	+17	60	77

Therefore Buchan is top-rated (best-in)

(iii) In races concerning horses of different ages the procedure in (ii) should again be followed, but reference must also be made to the Official Scale of Weight-For-Age.

For example,

12 furlongs, July 20th

Horse	Age & wt	Adjustment from 10st	Base rating	Adjusted rating	W-F-A deduct	Final rating
Archaic	5-10-0	0	90	90	Nil	90
Orpheus	4-9-9	+5	88	93	Nil	93
Lemonora	3-9-4	+10	85	95	-12	83
Tamar	4-8-7	+21	73	94	Nil	94

Therefore Tamar is top-rated (best-in)

(A 3-y-o is deemed 12lb less mature than a 4-y-o or older horse on 20th July over 12f. Therefore, the deduction of 12 points is necessary.)

The following symbols are used in conjunction with the ratings:

++: almost certain to prove better

+: likely to prove better

d: disappointing (has run well below best recently)

?: form hard to evaluate

t: tentative rating based on race-time rating may prove unreliable

Weight adjusted ratings for every race are published daily in Raceform Private Handicap.

For subscription terms please contact the Subscription Department on 01933 304858.

Course descriptions

(R.H.) denotes right-hand and (L.H.) left-hand courses.

ASCOT (R.H)

Right-handed triangular track just under 1m 6f in length. The Round course descends from the 1m 4f start into Swinley Bottom, the lowest part of the track. It then turns right-handed and joins the Old Mile Course, which starts on a separate chute. The course then rises to the right-handed home turn over a new underpass to join the straight mile course. The run-in is about 3f, rising slightly to the winning post. The whole course is of a galloping nature with easy turns.

AYR (L.H)

A left-handed, galloping, flat oval track of 1m 4f with a 4f run-in. The straight 6f is essentially flat.

BATH (L.H)

Galloping, left-handed, level oval of 1m 4f 25y, with long, stiff run-in of about 4f which bends to the left. An extended chute provides for races over 5f 11y and 5f 161y.

BEVERLEY (R.H)

A right-handed oval of 1m 3f, generally galloping, with an uphill run-in of two and a half furlongs. The 5f course is very stiff.

BRIGHTON (L.H)

Left-handed, 1m 4f horseshoe with easy turns and a run-in of three and a half furlongs. Undulating and sharp, the track suits handy types.

CARLISLE (R.H)

Right-handed, 1m 4f pear-shaped track. Galloping and undulating with easy turns and a stiff uphill run-in of three and a half furlongs. 6f course begins on an extended chute.

CATTERICK (L.H)

A sharp, left-handed, undulating oval of 1m 180y with a downhill run-in of 3f.

CHELMSFORD CITY (L.H)

Polytrack course: left-handed, two generous, sweeping 2f bends and two roughly 2f straights; chutes for 7f, 1m and 2m starts.

CHEPSTOW (L.H)

A left-handed, undulating oval of about 2m, with easy turns, and a straight run-in of 5f. There is a straight track of 1m 14y.

CHESTER (L.H)

A level, sharp, left-handed, circular course of 1m 73y, with a short run-in of 230y. Chester is a specialists' track which generally suits the sharp-actioned horse.

DONCASTER (L.H)

A left-handed, flat, galloping course of 1m 7f 110y, with a long run-in which extends to a straight mile.

EPSOM (L.H)

Left-handed and undulating with easy turns, and a run-in of just under 4f. The straight 5f course is also undulating and downhill all the way, making it the fastest 5f in the world.

FFOS LAS (L.H)

The track is a 60m wide, basically flat, 1m4f oval with sweeping bends.

GOODWOOD (R.H)

A sharp, undulating, essentially right-handed track with a long run-in. There is also a straight 6f course.

HAMILTON PARK (R.H)

Sharp, undulating, right-handed course of 1m 5f with a five and a half furlong, uphill run-in. There is a straight track of 6f.

HAYDOCK PARK (L.H)

A galloping, almost flat, oval track, 1m 5f round, with a run-in of four and a half furlongs and a straight 6f course.

KEMPTON PARK (R.H)

A floodlit Polytrack circuit opened in March 2006. A 1m 2f outer track accommodates races over 6f, 7f, 1m, 1m 3f, 1m 4f and 2m. The 1m inner track caters for races over 5f and 1m 2f.

LEICESTER (R.H)

Stiff, galloping, right-handed oval of 1m 5f, with a 5f run-in. There is a straight course of 7f.

LINGFIELD PARK (L.H)

Turf Course: A sharp, undulating left-handed circuit, with a 7f 140y straight course.

Polytrack course: left-handed all-weather is 1m 2f round. It is a sharp, level track with a short run-in.

MUSSELBURGH (R.H)

A sharp, level, right-handed oval of 1m 2f, with a run-in of 4f. There is an additional 5f straight course.

NEWBURY (L.H)

Left-handed, oval track of about 1m 7f, with a slightly undulating straight mile. The round course is level and galloping with a four and a half furlong run-in. Races over the round mile and 7f 60y start on the adjoining chute.

NEWCASTLE (L.H)

Tapeta course: galloping, easy, left-handed oval of 1m 6f, with an uphill 4f run-in.

NEWMARKET (R.H)

Rowley Mile Course: There is a straight 1m2f course, which is wide and galloping. Races over 1m4f or more are right-handed. The Rowley course has a long run-in and a stiff finish.

July Course: Races up to a mile are run on the Bunbury course, which is straight. Races over 1m2f or more are right-handed, with a 7f run-in. Like the Rowley course, the July track is stiff.

NOTTINGHAM (L.H)

Left-handed, galloping, oval of about 1m 4f, and a run-in of four and a half furlongs. Flat with easy turns.

PONTEFRACT (L.H)

Left-handed oval, undulating course of 2m 133y, with a short run-in of 2f. It is a particularly stiff track with the last 3f uphill.

REDCAR (L.H)

Left-handed, level, galloping, oval course of 1m 6f with a straight run-in of 5f. There is also a straight 1m.

RIPON (R.H)

A sharp, undulating, right-handed oval of 1m 5f, with a 5f run-in. There is also a 6f straight course.

SALISBURY (R.H)

Right-handed and level, with a run-in of 4f. There is a straight 1m track. The last half mile is uphill, providing a stiff test of stamina.

SANDOWN PARK (R.H)

An easy right-handed oval course of 1m 5f with a stiff straight uphill run-in of 4f. Separate straight 5f track is also uphill. Galloping.

SOUTHWELL (L.H)

Left-handed oval, Fibresand course of 1m 2f with a 3f run-in. There is a straight 5f. Sharp and level, Southwell suits front-runners.

THIRSK (L.H)

Left-handed, oval of 1m 2f with sharp turns and an undulating run-in of 4f. There is a straight 6f track.

WARWICK (L.H)

Left-handed, sharp, level track of 1m 6f 32y in circumference, with a run-in of two and a half furlongs. There is also a 6f chute.

WETHERBY (L.H)

Left-handed, galloping track. Circuit 1m4f. 4f straight, slightly uphill.

WINDSOR (Fig. 8)

Figure eight track of 1m 4f 110y. The course is level and sharp with a long run-in. The 6f course is essentially straight.

WOLVERHAMPTON (L.H)

Left-handed oval, Tapeta course of 1m, with a run-in of 380y. A level track with sharp bends.

YARMOUTH (L.H)

Left-handed, level circuit of 1m 4f, with a run-in of 5f. The straight course is 1m long.

YORK (L.H)

Left-handed, level, galloping track, with a straight 6f. There is also an adjoining chute of 7f.

SOUTHWELL (L-H)

Friday, January 1

OFFICIAL GOING: Fibresand: standard

Wind: Moderate against Weather: Grey cloud

1 DOWNLOAD THE LADBROKES APP H'CAP 1m (F)

12:20 (12:20) (Class 5) (0-75,75) 4-Y-O+ **£3,234** (£962; £481; £240) **Stalls** Low

Form RPR

460- **1** **Moon River (IRE)**[15] 8261 4-8-11 **68**...................... AlistairRawlinson(3) 4 84+
(Michael Appleby) *cl up: led over 3f out: rdn clr over 2f out: readily* **8/1**

452- **2** 3¾ **Clockmaker (IRE)**[10] 8341 10-9-4 **72**.................................. TomEaves 1 77
(Conor Dore) *led: pushed along and hdd over 3f out: rdn wl over 2f out: sn drvn and kpt on: no ch w wnr* **9/2**[2]

600- **3** 4 **Ythan Waters**[27] 8118 4-9-1 **69**..(p) JoeFanning 5 65
(Bryan Smart) *dwlt and in rr: pushed along over 3f out: rdn and hdd over 2f out: drvn wl over 1f out: kpt on same pce* **13/2**

246- **4** 3½ **Best Tamayuz**[15] 8270 5-9-1 **69**....................................(b[1]) KieranO'Neill 3 57
(Scott Dixon) *chsd ldrs on inner: rdn along and outpcd 1/2-way: drvn along wl over 2f out: plugged on fnl f* **13/2**

413- **5** 7 **What Could She Be (IRE)**[17] 8237 4-9-5 **73**...........(p) PaulMulrennan 6 45
(Michael Dods) *chsd ldrs: rdn along 3f out: drvn over 2f out and sn one pce* **9/2**[2]

122- **6** 2¾ **Tiger's Home**[17] 8237 6-8-5 **66**.. KyleCurrie(7) 7 31
(Iain Jardine) *prom on outer: rdn along over 3f out: drvn wl over 2f out: sn wknd* **4/1**[1]

004- **7** nk **Myboydaniel**[96] 6783 4-9-7 **75**... ShaneGray 2 40
(Ivan Furtado) *in tch: hdwy over 3f out: rdn along wl over 2f out: sn drvn and btn* **6/1**[3]

246- **8** ¾ **Kodiac Lady (IRE)**[94] 6837 4-8-2 **63**..............................(e) HollieDoyle(7) 8 26
(Simon West) *dwlt: a in rr* **20/1**

1m 42.43s (-1.27) **Going Correction** -0.05s/f (Stan) **8** Ran SP% **113.2**
Speed ratings (Par 103): **104,100,96,92,85 83,82,81**
CSF £42.84 CT £249.61 TOTE £11.30: £3.20, £1.70, £2.80; EX 58.10 Trifecta £431.20.
Owner Craig Buckingham **Bred** Rockhart Trading Ltd **Trained** Oakham, Rutland

FOCUS
A modest handicap, but the form looks solid for the grade.

2 LADBROKES MOBILE H'CAP 1m (F)

12:55 (12:58) (Class 6) (0-60,60) 4-Y-O+ **£2,587** (£770; £384; £192) **Stalls** Low

Form RPR

440- **1** **Stun Gun**[11] 8335 6-8-10 **49**...(p) TonyHamilton 14 63
(Derek Shaw) *in tch: hdwy over 3f out: led 2f out: rdn clr over 1f out: kpt on strly* **20/1**

/44- **2** 4 **Basingstoke (IRE)**[24] 8146 7-8-12 **51** ow1.......................... RyanClark 6 55
(Simon Hodgson) *midfield: hdwy 3f out: chsd ldrs over 2f out: rdn wl over 1f out: kpt on fnl f* **5/1**[2]

210- **3** nk **Roger Thorpe**[20] 8201 7-9-2 **60**.................................... PaddyPilley(5) 11 64
(Deborah Sanderson) *trckd ldrs: hdwy to ld 3f out: rdn and hdd over 2f out: sn drvn and kpt on same pce* **12/1**

030- **4** 1 **Miss Lillie**[16] 8248 5-9-6 **59**.. AdamBeschizza 7 60
(Roger Teal) *trckd ldrs: hdwy 3f out: rdn over 2f out: drvn over 1f out and kpt on same pce* **8/1**

063- **5** 3¼ **General Tufto**[14] 8278 11-8-8 **47**...................................(b) JoeyHaynes 13 40
(Charles Smith) *sn outpcd and rdn along in rr: hdwy u.p over 2f out: styd on fnl f: nrst fin* **13/2**[3]

303- **6** ½ **Luv U Lucky**[17] 8241 4-9-7 **60**.. AndrewMullen 9 52+
(Michael Appleby) *hld up: hdwy over 2f out: rdn wl over 1f out: kpt on fnl f* **9/1**

221- **7** 1¼ **Excelling Oscar (IRE)**[14] 8278 4-9-7 **60**................(b) PaulMulrennan 10 49
(Conor Dore) *in tch: hdwy to chse ldrs 3f out: rdn along 2f out and ev ch: sn drvn and grad wknd* **7/2**[1]

002- **8** ¾ **Frantical**[5] 8370 4-9-0 **56**.. GeorgeDowning(3) 3 43
(Tony Carroll) *chsd ldrs: rdn along over 3f out: drvn over 2f out and grad wknd* **8/1**

001- **9** 2¾ **Indomitable Spirit**[24] 8145 4-9-2 **58**.............................. TimClark(3) 1 39
(Martin Smith) *slt ld on inner: rdn along and hdd 3f out: drvn over 2f out: grad wknd* **7/1**

400- **10** 6 **Quadriga (IRE)**[20] 8201 6-9-2 **55**.................................... DougieCostello 12 21
(Philip Kirby) *chsd ldrs on outer: rdn along wl over 2f out: sn wknd* **22/1**

655- **11** 2¾ **Rolen Sly**[65] 7567 7-8-9 **48** oh1 ow2...................................... TomEaves 2 8
(Neville Bycroft) *s.i.s: a in rr* **66/1**

000- **12** 1¾ **Madakheel (USA)**[130] 5691 5-8-2 **48**.............................. HollieDoyle(7) 8
(Simon West) *a towards rr* **100/1**

000- **13** 1 **Eeny Mac (IRE)**[101] 6617 9-8-7 **46** oh1............................ BarryMcHugh 4
(John Wainwright) *prom: rdn along wl over 3f out: sn wknd* **66/1**

600- **14** 11 **L'Es Fremantle (FR)**[61] 5000 5-8-4 **46** oh1................... DannyBrock(3) 5
(Michael Chapman) *cl up: rdn along wl over 3f out: sn drvn and wknd* **150/1**

1m 43.27s (-0.43) **Going Correction** -0.05s/f (Stan) **14** Ran SP% **118.4**
Speed ratings (Par 101): **100,96,95,94,91 90,89,88,86,80 77,75,74,63**
CSF £112.60 CT £1314.51 TOTE £19.10: £4.60, £1.60, £4.10; EX 189.20 Trifecta £3410.20 Part won..
Owner John R Saville **Bred** Rothmere Bloodstock **Trained** Sproxton, Leics

FOCUS
A moderate heat, but pretty competitive.

3 UNIBET OFFER DAILY JOCKEY/TRAINER SPECIALS H'CAP 6f (F)

1:30 (1:31) (Class 5) (0-70,76) 3-Y-O **£3,234** (£962; £481; £240) **Stalls** Low

Form RPR

211- **1** **Aguerooo (IRE)**[2] 8391 3-9-7 **76** 12ex...........................(p) HollieDoyle(7) 1 89+
(Richard Hannon) *trckd ldrs: hdwy over 2f out: chal over 1f out: rdn to ld jst ins fnl f: sn hung lft: kpt on* **15/8**[1]

120- **2** 2 **Modest**[55] 7753 3-9-0 **69**.. CallumShepherd(7) 4 75
(Michael Bell) *cl up: rdn along and sltly outpcd 1/2-way: rdn and hdwy on inner over 1f out: ev ch ent fnl f: sn drvn and kpt on same pce* **8/1**

354- **3** 3¼ **Lady McGuffy (IRE)**[14] 8281 3-8-4 **59**.................................. PhilDennis(7) 7 55
(Michael Dods) *prom: cl up 1/2-way: chal over 2f out and sn led: rdn over 1f out: drvn and hdd jst ins fnl f: one pce* **20/1**

226- **4** nk **Sea Of Uncertainty**[10] 8348 3-8-12 **63**.................. AlistairRawlinson(3) 3 58
(Michael Appleby) *trckd ldrs: hdwy over 2f out: rdn wl over 1f out and sn no imp* **6/1**[3]

332- **5** 1½ **Underdressed**[50] 7816 3-9-5 **67**.. JoeFanning 6 57
(Keith Dalgleish) *trckd ldrs: n.m.r and hmpd bnd 3f out: rdn along and n.d after* **11/4**[2]

551- **6** nse **Sarabi**[14] 8282 3-9-2 **64**...(p) KieranO'Neill 5 54
(Scott Dixon) *dwlt: a towards rr* **8/1**

045- **7** nse **Priory**[13] 8306 3-8-6 **57**.. TimClark(3) 2 47
(Martin Smith) *a towards rr* **66/1**

010- **8** ½ **Puteminthetboot (IRE)**[14] 8281 3-8-0 **55** oh4....... JosephineGordon(7) 8 43
(David Evans) *towards rr: rapid hdwy on outer to chse ldng pair 1/2-way: rdn along over 2f out: sn drvn and wknd* **20/1**

204- **9** 1½ **Emerald Bay**[21] 8173 3-8-13 **61**.. TomEaves 9 44
(Ivan Furtado) *led: rdn along wl over 2f out: hdd and drvn wl over 1f out: sn wknd* **20/1**

1m 16.84s (0.34) **Going Correction** -0.05s/f (Stan) **9** Ran SP% **113.7**
Speed ratings (Par 97): **95,92,88,87,85 85,85,84,82**
CSF £16.25 CT £226.51 TOTE £2.60: £1.50, £3.20, £4.90; EX 19.00 Trifecta £279.30.
Owner Middleham Park Racing LXXXVI **Bred** Cooneen Stud **Trained** East Everleigh, Wilts

FOCUS
This proved another comfortable win for the favourite.

4 BET&WATCH EVERY RACE AT UNIBET H'CAP 5f (F)

2:05 (2:05) (Class 3) (0-90,90) 4-Y-O+ **£7,439** (£2,213; £1,106; £553) **Stalls** High

Form RPR

003- **1** **Dungannon**[20] 8200 9-9-6 **89**...(b) OisinMurphy 7 99
(Andrew Balding) *hld up: hdwy in centre to trck ldrs 1/2-way: effrt wl over 1f out: rdn to ld appr fnl f: sn drvn and kpt on wl towards fin* **11/4**[1]

322- **2** ½ **Anonymous John (IRE)**[14] 8288 4-8-13 **89**......... JosephineGordon(7) 3 97
(David Evans) *racd towards far side: trckd ldrs: hdwy and cl up 2f out: rdn to chal over 1f out: sn ev ch tl drvn ins fnl f and no ex nr fin* **11/4**[1]

422- **3** 3¼ **Brother Tiger**[30] 8082 7-9-6 **89**.. TonyHamilton 9 86
(David C Griffiths) *a cl up: rdn and ev ch wl over 1f out: drvn ent fnl f and kpt on same pce* **9/1**

520- **4** ¾ **Desert Command**[17] 8229 6-8-9 **83**.............................(p) AaronJones(5) 2 77
(Robert Cowell) *a cl up: rdn 2f out: drvn and ev ch over 1f out: grad wknd* **22/1**

024- **5** 2 **Apache Storm**[43] 7907 4-9-6 **89**.. AndrewMullen 12 76+
(Michael Appleby) *racd towards stands' rail: chsd ldrs: rdn along 2f out: sn drvn and one pce* **14/1**

044- **6** shd **Come On Dave (IRE)**[20] 8200 7-9-1 **87**...................(b) DanielMuscutt(3) 1 73
(Phil McEntee) *racd towards far side: cl up: led after 2f: rdn along 2f out: drvn and hdd appr fnl f: wknd* **8/1**[3]

210- **7** 2½ **Keep It Dark**[20] 8200 7-8-13 **82**.. BarryMcHugh 4 59
(Tony Coyle) *towards rr: swtchd lft to far side and hdwy 2f out: sn rdn: in tch over 1f out: sn drvn and one pce* **20/1**

005- **8** shd **Oriental Relation (IRE)**[2] 8395 5-9-2 **85**...................(v) JackGarritty 8 62
(James Given) *racd in centre: trckd ldrs: n.m.r and swtchd rt over 2f out: sn rdn and btn* **15/2**[2]

140- **9** ½ **Rita's Boy (IRE)**[20] 8200 4-9-1 **84**..........................(v) DougieCostello 11 59
(K R Burke) *dwlt: a towards rr* **33/1**

360- **10** 4 **Scarborough (IRE)**[20] 8200 5-8-13 **82**.......................... PaulMulrennan 5 43
(Paul Midgley) *racd in centre: led 2f: cl up: rdn along over 2f out: sn wknd* **14/1**

500- **11** 3¼ **Royal Bajan (USA)**[5] 8368 8-9-7 **90**.................................(b) TomEaves 10 39
(James Given) *racd towards stands' rail: chsd ldrs: rdn along over 2f out: sn wknd* **20/1**

59.91s (0.21) **Going Correction** +0.30s/f (Slow) **11** Ran SP% **116.4**
Speed ratings (Par 107): **110,109,104,102,99 99,95,95,94,88 82**
CSF £8.48 CT £59.91 TOTE £3.20: £1.10, £1.60, £2.90; EX 13.40 Trifecta £72.40.
Owner Dr E Harris **Bred** J A E Hobby **Trained** Kingsclere, Hants

FOCUS
A decent handicap in which the first two finished clear.

5 UNIBET OFFER DAILY JOCKEY/TRAINER SPECIALS MEDIAN AUCTION MAIDEN STKS 5f (F)

2:40 (2:40) (Class 6) 3-5-Y-O **£2,587** (£770; £384; £192) **Stalls** High

Form RPR

3- **1** **Bring On A Spinner**[131] 5655 3-8-6 0............................ AaronJones(5) 3 65+
(Stuart Williams) *mde most: shkn up over 1f out: pushed clr ins fnl f: kpt on* **10/11**[1]

555- **2** 2 **Koothrappali**[144] 5218 3-8-11 59.................................... PaulMulrennan 4 58
(David Barron) *cl up: chal over 2f out and sn rdn: drvn over 1f out: kpt on same pce fnl f* **2/1**[2]

045- **3** 6 **Single Summit**[5] 8366 4-9-12 46....................................(v) TonyHamilton 2 42
(J R Jenkins) *cl up: pushed along over 2f out: rdn wl over 1f out: sn one pce* **16/1**

4 2¼ **Red Chatterbox (IRE)** 3-8-6 0.. KieranO'Neill 5 23
(Scott Dixon) *chsd ldrs: pushed along 1/2-way: sn rdn and one pce* **15/2**[3]

00- **5** ¾ **Angel In The Snow**[15] 8266 3-8-11 0.............................. DougieCostello 6 26
(Brian Ellison) *racd nr stands' rail and rdn along sn after s: chsd ldrs to 1/2-way: sn outpcd* **12/1**

400- **6** 7 **Margot Rose**[14] 8290 4-9-7 44.. TomEaves 1
(Alan Berry) *dwlt and wnt lft s: a bhd* **50/1**

1m 1.35s (1.65) **Going Correction** +0.30s/f (Slow)
WFA 3 from 4yo 15lb **6** Ran SP% **113.0**
Speed ratings (Par 101): **98,94,85,81,80 69**
CSF £2.97 TOTE £2.20: £1.50, £1.10; EX 3.90 Trifecta £17.50.
Owner J W Parry **Bred** J W Parry **Trained** Newmarket, Suffolk

FOCUS
A maiden that took little winning, but a gamble was landed.

6 CORAL.CO.UK BEST ODDS GUARANTEED ON RACING CLAIMING STKS 1m 4f (F)

3:15 (3:15) (Class 6) 4-Y-O+ **£2,264** (£673; £336; £168) **Stalls** Low

Form RPR

124- **1** **Yul Finegold (IRE)**[10] 8344 6-9-9 81.............................. PaulMulrennan 2 87
(Conor Dore) *set str pce: rdn along 3f out: drvn over 1f out: kpt on grimly u.p fnl f* **3/1**[3]

/01- **2** 1 **Masterful Act (USA)**[17] 8238 9-8-13 86.........................(vt[1]) SamJames 5 75
(David O'Meara) *rdn along sn after s: chsd ldrs: hdwy to chse ldng pair 4f out: rdn to chse wnr over 2f out: drvn to chal and hung in bhd rival over 1f out and again ins fnl f: kpt on same pce* **2/1**[1]

123- **3** 19 **Bushel (USA)**[17] 8238 6-9-1 76..(p) TomEaves 3 47
(James Given) *prom: chsd wnr 4f out: rdn along 3f out: drvn over 2f out and plugged on one pce* **8/1**

242- **4** nk **Brassbound (USA)**[17] 8238 8-9-3 87.............................. AndrewMullen 1 49
(Michael Appleby) *chsd ldrs on inner: rdn along 4f out: drvn over 3f out and sn outpcd* **5/2**[2]

050- **5** 3 **Monzino (USA)**[6] 3787 8-8-10 50..(t) JoeyHaynes 4 37
(Michael Chapman) *a in rr* **150/1**

464- **6** *hd* **Deep Resolve (IRE)**[26] 7967 5-9-9 67 .... NeilFarley 7 49
(Alan Swinbank) *chsd ldrs: rdn along over 4f out: sn outpcd and bhd* **14/1**

264- **7** *9* **Moshe (IRE)**[14] 8284 5-9-8 79 .... DougieCostello 6 34
(Philip Kirby) *chsd ldrs: rdn along and lost pl 7f out: sn bhd* **11/1**

2m 40.13s (-0.87) **Going Correction** -0.05s/f (Stan) **7** Ran SP% **113.7**
Speed ratings (Par 101): **100,99,86,86,84 84,78**
CSF £9.32 TOTE £4.20: £1.80, £1.70; EX 10.20 Trifecta £49.80.
Owner Mrs Louise Marsh **Bred** Mascara Partnership **Trained** Hubbert's Bridge, Lincs

FOCUS
This was a well-run race and a real test of stamina.

7 CORAL APP DOWNLOAD FROM THE APP STORE H'CAP 1m 3f (F)
3:45 (3:45) (Class 3) (0-90,88) 4-Y-O+ **£7,439** (£2,213; £1,106; £553) **Stalls** Low

Form RPR

003- **1** **The Lock Master (IRE)**[10] 8344 9-8-8 **75** .... (p) AndrewMullen 3 86
(Michael Appleby) *rdn along after s and sn outpcd in rr: detached 1/2-way: hdwy 3f out: rdn over 2f out: drvn to chse ldng pair over 1f out: styd on strly to ld ins fnl f: sn clr* **9/2**[3]

002- **2** *4* **Ralphy Lad (IRE)**[10] 8344 5-8-7 **74** oh4 .... NeilFarley 6 78
(Alan Swinbank) *trckd ldng pair: hdwy to ld 4f out: sn jnd and rdn along 3f out: hdd over 2f out: cl up and drvn: styd on gamely to ld again briefly jst ins fnl f: sn hdd and kpt on same pce* **3/1**[2]

412- **3** *1 3/4* **Ready (IRE)**[42] 7924 6-9-2 **88** .... (p) JustinNewman(5) 5 89+
(Ivan Furtado) *trckd ldrs: smooth hdwy and cl up 4f out: slt ld over 2f out: rdn wl over 1f out: drvn and hdd ent fnl f: kpt on same pce* **6/1**

513- **4** *19* **Countermand**[15] 8272 4-8-11 **81** .... OisinMurphy 2 50
(Andrew Balding) *cl up: led after 3f: hdd and rdn along 4f out: drvn 3f out and sn outpcd* **11/8**[1]

/20- **5** *13* **Taysh (USA)**[25] 8139 4-8-12 **85** .... AlistairRawlinson(3) 4 32
(Michael Appleby) *slt ld 3f: cl up: rdn along over 4f out: sn outpcd and bhd fnl 3f* **8/1**

2m 25.5s (-2.50) **Going Correction** -0.05s/f (Stan)
WFA 4 from 5yo+ 3lb **5** Ran SP% **110.7**
Speed ratings (Par 107): **107,104,102,89,79**
CSF £18.09 TOTE £5.70: £2.80, £3.10; EX 11.30 Trifecta £49.70.
Owner K G Kitchen **Bred** Patrick F Kelly **Trained** Oakham, Rutland

FOCUS
The leaders went off too fast and the winner came from the clouds to score.
T/Plt: £105.80 to a £1 stake. Pool: £43,916.81 - 302.92 winning tickets T/Qpdt: £5.80 to a £1 stake. Pool: £4,571.88 - 579.31 winning tickets **Joe Rowntree**

MEYDAN (L-H)
Friday, January 1

OFFICIAL GOING: Dirt: fast

8a EGA BILLET TROPHY (MAIDEN) (DIRT) 1m (D)
12:00 (12:00) 3-Y-O+ **£13,863** (£4,621; £2,541; £1,386; £693)

RPR

1 **Blue Creek** 3-8-7 .... RichardMullen 9 83
(Charlie Appleby) *slowly away: mid-div: smooth prog 4f out: led 2f out: r.o wl* **1/2**[1]

2 *5* **Tobaco (ARG)**[14] 8301 3-8-11 .... PatDobbs 12 67
(Doug Watson, UAE) *trckd ldrs: led briefly 2f out: sn hdd: r.o wl but no ch w wnr* **9/4**[2]

3 *4* **Brabbham (USA)**[27] 6-9-6 73 .... (bt) HarryBentley 5 59
(A bin Harmash, UAE) *chsd ldrs: r.o same pce fnl 2 1/2f* **16/1**

4 *1 1/2* **Skygazer (IRE)**[14] 8301 4-8-10 57 .... (bt) ManuelFernandes(10) 6 55
(A R Al Rayhi, UAE) *sn led: hdd 2f out: r.o same pce* **50/1**

5 *1 1/2* **Hammerindown (USA)**[29] 8097 5-9-6 .... ChrisHayes 16 52
(D Selvaratnam, UAE) *mid-div: n.d: r.o same pce fnl 2f* **40/1**

6 *10 3/4* **Matador De Toros (SAF)**[14] 8301 7-9-6 55 .... FernandoJara 14 27
(M Al Mheiri, UAE) *mid-div: r.o same pce fnl 2 1/2f* **50/1**

7 *1 1/2* **Gwydir**[14] 8301 5-9-1 53 .... (t) GaryPhillips(5) 1 24
(H Albloushi, UAE) *nvr nr to chal* **100/1**

8 *shd* **Shamal**[43] 7912 6-9-6 .... FrederikTylicki 13 23
(A bin Harmash, UAE) *a mid-div* **33/1**

9 *3/4* **Siberian Height's (USA)** 3-8-7 .... SamHitchcott 4 25
(Doug Watson, UAE) *nvr bttr than mid-div* **25/1**

10 *2* **Junuee (IRE)** 4-9-6 .... WayneSmith 11 17
(M F De Kock, South Africa) *slowly away: nvr nr to chal* **10/1**[3]

11 *nk* **Romosh (IRE)**[21] 8195 4-9-2 .... (b) SMazur 15 12
(R Bouresly, Kuwait) *slowly away: nvr nr to chal but r.o same pce fnl 2f* **66/1**

12 *3* **Lake Hawk (IRE)**[35] 8027 7-9-6 60 .... (t) TadhgO'Shea 10 10
(A R Al Rayhi, UAE) *chsd ldrs tl outpcd 3 1/2f out* **33/1**

13 *7 1/4* **Star Of Broadway**[15] 8274 6-9-6 40 .... RoystonFfrench 3
(H Albloushi, UAE) *nvr bttr than mid-div* **100/1**

14 *2 1/4* **Desert Skywalker (IRE)**[15] 8274 5-9-6 .... (p) DavidProbert 2
(E Charpy, UAE) *trckd ldrs: hrd rdn 4f out: sn btn* **100/1**

15 *34* **Tez**[49] 7851 5-9-1 45 .... (t) GeorgeBuckell(5) 8
(M Ramadan, UAE) *a in rr* **100/1**

1m 38.28s (0.78) **Going Correction** +0.275s/f (Slow)
WFA 3 from 4yo+ 20lb **15** Ran SP% **134.0**
Speed ratings: **107,102,98,96,95 84,82,82,81,79 79,76,69,67,33**
CSF: 1.96.
Owner Godolphin **Bred** Darley **Trained** Newmarket, Suffolk

9 - 11 (Foreign Racing) - See Raceform Interactive

12a EGA CASTHOUSE TROPHY (H'CAP) (DIRT) 1m (D)
2:20 (2:20) (74-89,89) 3-Y-O+ **£16,081** (£5,360; £2,948; £1,608; £804)

RPR

1 **Stormardal (IRE)**[43] 7917 5-9-0 **83** .... WayneSmith 8 88
(Ismail Mohammed) *trckd ldrs: smooth prog 3f out: r.o wl fnl 2f: led 55yds out* **12/1**

2 *1/2* **Muhtaram**[15] 8273 6-8-13 **87** .... (v) GeorgeBuckell(5) 2 91
(M Al Mheiri, UAE) *trckd ldrs: led 2f out: wknd 100yds out: hdd fnl 55yds* **7/1**

3 *2 1/2* **Conquerant**[21] 8191 5-8-13 **82** .... (p) ChrisHayes 10 80
(Ismail Mohammed) *nvr nr to chal but r.o wl fnl 2 1/2f* **12/1**

4 *1 3/4* **Zephuros (IRE)**[323] 532 4-9-6 **89** .... (p) RichardMullen 1 83
(Charlie Appleby) *s.i.s: trckd ldr: ev ch 2 1/2f out: one pce fnl 1 1/2f* **3/1**[1]

5 *2 3/4* **State Law (IRE)**[21] 8191 5-8-11 **80** .... PatDobbs 7 68
(Doug Watson, UAE) *nvr bttr than mid-div* **11/2**

6 *4 1/2* **Colour Guard**[15] 8277 8-8-10 **79** .... (v) FernandoJara 5 57
(M Al Mheiri, UAE) *nvr bttr than mid-div* **7/1**

7 *shd* **Prepared**[29] 8099 7-9-1 **84** .... (bt) TadhgO'Shea 3 61
(A R Al Rayhi, UAE) *s.i.s: trckd ldrs tl outpcd fnl 1 1/2f* **5/1**[3]

8 *9 1/2* **Alareef (SAF)**[315] 643 5-8-13 **82** .... (bt) PaulHanagan 6 37
(M F De Kock, South Africa) *sn led: hdd 2f out: sn btn* **7/2**[2]

9 *3 1/2* **Istinfaar (USA)**[29] 8099 4-8-13 **82** .... (b) FrederikTylicki 9 29
(A bin Harmash, UAE) *a in rr* **33/1**

10 *28* **Active Spirit (IRE)**[21] 8191 5-8-8 **77** .... SamHitchcott 4
(Doug Watson, UAE) *nvr nr to chal* **16/1**

1m 39.02s (1.52) **Going Correction** +0.275s/f (Slow) **10** Ran SP% **128.5**
Speed ratings: **103,102,100,98,95 91,90,81,77,49**
CSF: 102.85; TRICAST: 1089.37.
Owner Sheikh Juma Dalmook Al Maktoum **Bred** Kevin & Meta Cullen **Trained** Newmarket, Suffolk

13 - (Foreign Racing) - See Raceform Interactive

CHELMSFORD (A.W) (L-H)
Saturday, January 2

OFFICIAL GOING: Polytrack: standard
Wind: light, half behind, medium from race 5 Weather: overcast, rain from race 5

14 PLAY SCOOP6SOCCER TODAY FILLIES' H'CAP 1m (P)
12:30 (12:30) (Class 5) (0-70,70) 4-Y-O+ **£5,175** (£1,540; £769; £384) **Stalls** Low

Form RPR

344- **1** **India's Song**[16] 8261 6-9-0 **70** .... (t) SophieKilloran(7) 6 79
(David Simcock) *stdd s: hld up in tch: effrt on inner over 1f out: led jst ins fnl f: sn in command and r.o wl* **6/1**[3]

522- **2** *1 3/4* **Clary (IRE)**[11] 8354 6-9-2 **65** .... PatCosgrave 3 70
(James Unett) *in tch in midfield: wnt 3rd 4f out: effrt u.p and ev ch over 1f out: chsd wnr and styd on same pce ins fnl f* **6/4**[1]

533- **3** *1 1/4* **Venus Grace**[16] 8263 5-8-13 **62** .... (p) AndrewMullen 2 64
(Michael Appleby) *led: rdn wl over 1f out: sn hrd pressed: hdd jst ins fnl f: no ex and outpcd fnl 150yds* **7/2**[2]

050- **4** *nse* **Farletti**[17] 8248 4-9-7 **70** .... (p) OisinMurphy 7 72
(Andrew Balding) *stdd after s: hld up in tch in last pair: hdwy over 1f out: 4th and edgd lft ins fnl f: kpt on but no threat to wnr* **8/1**

034- **5** *1/2* **Caltra Colleen**[18] 8237 4-8-11 **60** .... (bt) JimmyQuinn 4 61
(Gay Kelleway) *t.k.h: stdd bk into midfield after 1f out: rdn and hdwy ent fnl 2f: no imp and one pce fr over 1f out* **8/1**

040- **6** *2 1/2* **Spring Dixie (IRE)**[16] 8261 4-8-9 **58** .... (b[1]) RyanPowell 1 53
(John Ryan) *t.k.h: pressed ldr tl outpcd u.p over 1f out: wknd ins fnl f* **20/1**

035- **7** *3/4* **J'Aspire**[31] 8079 4-9-4 **67** .... [1] MartinHarley 8 60
(Stuart Williams) *stdd s: hld up in tch in rr: effrt 2f out: no imp* **16/1**

620- **8** *4* **Ajig**[17] 8248 5-9-2 **65** .... (p) FergusSweeney 5 49
(Eve Johnson Houghton) *chsd ldng pair tl 1/2-way: lost pl u.p over 1f out: bhd ins fnl f* **10/1**

1m 37.87s (-2.03) **Going Correction** -0.275s/f (Stan) **8** Ran SP% **118.5**
Speed ratings (Par 100): **99,97,96,95,95 92,92,88**
CSF £16.06 CT £37.75 TOTE £8.00: £1.50, £1.10, £2.80; EX 18.80 Trifecta £66.20.
Owner Mrs Julia Annable **Bred** Car Colston Hall Stud **Trained** Newmarket, Suffolk

FOCUS
The track had been power harrowed and then gallop mastered to 2 inches. They was a disputed pace to this fillies' handicap and that set things up for a closer. The first three hugged the inside rail to the turn in.

15 SCOOP6SOCCER HAPPY NEW YEAR MAIDEN STKS 7f (P)
1:05 (1:05) (Class 4) 3-Y-O+ **£8,086** (£2,406; £1,202; £601) **Stalls** Low

Form RPR

1 **Mariee** 3-8-5 0 .... JoeFanning 2 76+
(Mark Johnston) *dwlt: rn green early: chsd ldng pair after 2f: effrt 2f out: wnt between rivals to ld jst ins fnl f: r.o wl* **8/1**[3]

3- **2** *1 1/2* **Town's History (USA)**[28] 8123 3-8-10 0 .... OisinMurphy 5 77
(Saeed bin Suroor) *awkward leaving stalls: sn w ldr and t.k.h: rdn to ld over 1f out: hdd jst ins fnl f: styd on same pce after* **30/100**[1]

323- **3** *2 1/4* **The Commendatore**[24] 8154 3-8-10 71 .... (b) RobertHavlin 1 72
(John Gosden) *led and t.k.h: rdn 2f out: hung lft and hdd over 1f out: wknd ins fnl f: eased cl home* **9/2**[2]

2- **4** *1 1/4* **Figurante (IRE)**[138] 5460 3-8-5 0 .... CathyGannon 3 63
(Jamie Osborne) *chsd ldng pair for 3f: rdn and outpcd in 4th 2f out: kpt on steadily ins fnl f* **20/1**

0- **5** *10* **Voices Of Kings**[35] 8037 3-8-10 0 .... SteveDrowne 4 41
(William Muir) *in tch in rr: rdn 3f out: sn struggling: bhd over 1f out* **66/1**

1m 24.93s (-2.27) **Going Correction** -0.275s/f (Stan) **5** Ran SP% **112.5**
Speed ratings (Par 105): **101,99,96,95,83**
CSF £11.44 TOTE £9.60: £2.50, £1.10; EX 15.70 Trifecta £25.80.
Owner Miss K Rausing **Bred** Miss K Rausing **Trained** Middleham Moor, N Yorks

FOCUS
A fair maiden won by the only newcomer in the line-up.

16 BET SCOOP6SOCCER AT TOTESPORT.COM H'CAP 6f (P)
1:40 (1:40) (Class 4) (0-85,82) 3-Y-O **£8,086** (£2,406; £1,202; £601) **Stalls** Centre

Form RPR

215- **1** **Fast Enough (IRE)**[137] 5485 3-8-13 **77** .... (p) AlistairRawlinson(3) 3 87+
(Saeed bin Suroor) *wl in tch in last pair: effrt on inner 2f out: ev ch 1f out: bmpd and led fnl 100yds: r.o wl* **4/1**[3]

111- **2** *1 3/4* **Kingsley Klarion (IRE)**[13] 8316 3-9-7 **82** .... JoeFanning 5 86+
(Mark Johnston) *chsd ldng pair: clsd and ev ch 2f out: sn rdn: led ent fnl f: hung lft and hdd 100yds out: one pce after* **5/2**[2]

544- **3** *3* **Sir Dudley (IRE)**[3] 8391 3-9-2 **77** .... PaulMulrennan 2 73
(James Given) *led: rdn wl over 1f out: cl up in 3rd but struggling to qckn whn hmpd and snatched up ins fnl f: nt rcvr and one pce after* **10/1**

122- **4** *3/4* **Hearmenow (IRE)**[3] 8391 3-8-2 **70** .... (tp) JosephineGordon(7) 4 62
(J S Moore) *w ldr: rdn and ev ch over 1f out: edgd lft 1f out: unable qck whn squeezed out and swtchd rt ins fnl f: nt rcvr and one pce after* **8/1**

221- **5** *5* **Alshaqee**[26] 8129 3-9-2 **77** .... TomQueally 1 53+
(William Haggas) *wl in tch in last pair: short of room on inner whn bmpd over 2f out: sddle slipped and lost all ch: rdn over 1f out: no imp* **11/8**[1]

1m 11.76s (-1.94) **Going Correction** -0.275s/f (Stan) **5** Ran SP% **110.9**
Speed ratings (Par 99): **101,98,94,93,87**
CSF £14.38 TOTE £4.50: £2.20, £1.60; EX 15.20 Trifecta £88.30.
Owner Godolphin **Bred** Tally-Ho Stud **Trained** Newmarket, Suffolk

The Form Book, Raceform Ltd, Newbury, RG14 5SJ

FOCUS
A fair handicap on paper, but it proved a bit of a messy affair.

17 SCOOP6SOCCER RESULTS AT TOTEPOOLLIVEINFO.COM CONDITIONS STKS (AW CHAMPIONSHIP FAST-TRACK QUAL') 5f (P)
2:15 (2:15) (Class 2) 4-Y-O+
£18,675 (£5,592; £2,796; £1,398; £699; £351) **Stalls** Low

Form RPR
031- **1** **Lancelot Du Lac (ITY)**[38] 7978 6-9-2 109 RobertWinston 7 104
(Dean Ivory) *sn w ldr: rdn to ld ent fnl f: r.o strly: comf* **1/1**[1]
0/0- **2** *1 1/2* **Gamgoom**[41] 5-9-5 101 MartinHarley 1 102
(Mario Hofer, Germany) *chsd ldng pair: rdn 1/2-way: no threat to wnr but kpt on u.p ins fnl f: snatched 2nd last strides* **8/1**[3]
001- **3** *nk* **Lightscameraction (IRE)**[31] 8082 4-9-2 107 (p) AdamKirby 4 98
(Gay Kelleway) *taken down early: led: rdn over 1f out: hdd ent fnl f: no ex and btn fnl 100yds: wknd and lost 2nd last strides* **5/2**[2]
343- **4** *1 1/4* **Magnus Maximus**[49] 7856 5-9-2 90 PatCosgrave 2 93
(Robyn Brisland) *outpcd in last trio: rdn wl over 1f out: wnt 4th 1f out: swtchd rt and kpt on ins fnl f: nvr trbld ldrs* **16/1**
020- **5** *4* **Vimy Ridge**[15] 8288 4-9-2 87 (p) JoeFanning 5 79
(Alan Bailey) *dwlt: hld up on rr: effrt over 1f out: no imp: n.d* **33/1**
014- **6** *3/4* **Meadway**[6] 8368 5-9-2 92 (p) PaulMulrennan 3 76
(Bryan Smart) *chsd ldng trio: rdn 1/2-way: btn and lost 4th 1f out: wknd ins fnl f* **8/1**[3]
1/0- **7** *11* **Likely (GER)**[203] 3160 4-8-11 100 OisinMurphy 6 32
(David Barron) *a in rr: bhd 2f out: sn lost tch and eased fnl f* **9/1**

57.39s (-2.81) **Going Correction** -0.275s/f (Stan) 7 Ran SP% **119.6**
Speed ratings (Par 109): **111,108,108,106,99 98,80**
CSF £11.16 TOTE £2.40: £1.20, £3.00; EX 10.40 Trifecta £23.20.
Owner Michael & Heather Yarrow **Bred** Elektra Di Fausto Martellozzo & C Sas **Trained** Radlett, Herts

FOCUS
A good sprint and the course record was lowered by 0.33sec.

18 BET SCOOP6SOCCER AT BETFRED.COM H'CAP 1m (P)
2:50 (2:51) (Class 3) (0-90,90) 4-Y-O+ **£11,644** (£3,465; £1,731; £865) **Stalls** Low

Form RPR
006- **1** **Lunar Deity**[23] 8168 7-9-7 **90** PatCosgrave 7 101
(Stuart Williams) *hld up in tch: clsd to press ldrs 2f out: rdn to ld over 1f out: r.o strly fnl f: comf* **12/1**
212- **2** *2 1/4* **Bromyard (IRE)**[23] 8169 4-8-11 **80** JamieSpencer 3 86
(David Simcock) *hld up in tch: clsd to chse ldrs and swtchd rt over 1f out: no ch w wnr but kpt on ins fnl f to go 2nd towards fin* **7/4**[1]
1/0- **3** *3/4* **Pearl Spectre (USA)**[17] 8247 5-8-8 **77** OisinMurphy 5 81
(Andrew Balding) *led: rdn ent fnl f: outpcd by wnr and plugged on same pce ins fnl f: lost 2nd towards fin* **5/1**[3]
016- **4** *3* **Dream Spirit (IRE)**[13] 8318 5-9-2 **85** GeorgeBaker 2 82
(Jamie Osborne) *stdd s: hld up in detached last: clsd 1/2-way: swtchd lft and effrt on inner over 1f out: no imp ins fnl f: eased towards fin* **6/1**
200- **5** *3 1/4* **Stetchworth (IRE)**[70] 7470 5-9-2 **85** JoeFanning 1 75
(Mark Johnston) *chsd ldng pair: effrt to go 2nd and swtchd rt over 2f out: lost pl over 1f out: 5th and wknd fnl f* **3/1**[2]
130- **6** *3 1/2* **Starlit Cantata**[14] 8310 5-8-12 **81** FergusSweeney 4 63
(Eve Johnson Houghton) *awkward leaving stalls: in tch towards rr: rdn and no imp over 2f out: sn btn: bhd fnl f* **16/1**
/60- **7** *1* **Dutch Art Dealer**[26] 8132 5-9-5 **88** (b[1]) AdamKirby 6 67
(Paul Cole) *chsd ldr tl drvn and lost pl over 2f out: bhd 1f out* **8/1**

1m 36.61s (-3.29) **Going Correction** -0.275s/f (Stan) 7 Ran SP% **117.0**
Speed ratings (Par 107): **105,102,102,99,95 92,91**
CSF £34.80 TOTE £10.00: £4.50, £1.50; EX 48.10 Trifecta £176.80.
Owner The Morley Family **Bred** Hermes Services Ltd **Trained** Newmarket, Suffolk

FOCUS
A decent enough handicap.

19 SCOOP6SOCCER £1 MILLION FOOTBALL BET H'CAP 1m 5f 66y(P)
3:20 (3:20) (Class 2) (0-105,96) 4-Y-O+
£15,562 (£4,660; £2,330; £1,165; £582; £292) **Stalls** Low

Form RPR
602- **1** **Luv U Whatever**[7] 8359 6-9-9 **95** AndrewMullen 5 101
(Michael Appleby) *mde all: rdn and qcknd jst over 2f out: drvn and hld on gamely ins fnl f: all out* **8/1**
325- **2** *hd* **Intense Tango**[35] 6520 5-9-1 **87** DougieCostello 3 93
(K R Burke) *hld up in tch in midfield: rdn over 2f out: hdwy u.p over 1f out: chsd wnr wl ins fnl f: str chal cl home: jst hld* **7/1**
442- **3** *1/2* **Paddys Motorbike (IRE)**[14] 8308 4-8-3 **87** JosephineGordon(7) 1 92
(David Evans) *chsd ldng pair: effrt 2f out: chsd wnr 1f out: lost 2nd but stl pressing wnr wl ins fnl f: unable qck cl home* **3/1**[2]
202- **4** *1 1/4* **Precision Five**[45] 7893 7-8-13 **85** (p) FergusSweeney 2 88
(Alan King) *hld up in tch in midfield: effrt 2f out: rdn and no imp over 1f out: kpt on ins fnl f: nvr enough pce to chal* **6/1**
233- **5** *3/4* **Percy Veer**[5] 8379 4-8-8 **88** TomMarquand(3) 6 90
(Sylvester Kirk) *chsd wnr: rdn 3f out: lost 2nd 1f out: styd on same pce ins fnl f* **4/1**[3]
212- **6** *3/4* **Ballynanty (IRE)**[28] 8124 4-8-12 **89** OisinMurphy 7 90
(Andrew Balding) *stdd s: hld up in tch in last pair: effrt in centre wl over 1f out: styd on same pce ins fnl f: btn and eased towards fin* **11/4**[1]
500- **7** *17* **Groovejet**[65] 7587 5-9-10 **96** (p) WilliamTwiston-Davies 4 71
(Dave Morris) *stdd s: hld up in tch in rr: rdn ent fnl 2f: no hdwy and btn over 1f out: eased fnl f* **16/1**

2m 50.45s (-3.15) **Going Correction** -0.275s/f (Stan)
WFA 4 from 5yo+ 5lb 7 Ran SP% **115.4**
Speed ratings (Par 109): **98,97,97,96,96 95,85**
CSF £62.25 TOTE £6.80: £2.60, £3.50; EX 66.60 Trifecta £510.30.
Owner Richard and Nicola Hunt **Bred** Richard Hunt **Trained** Oakham, Rutland

FOCUS
A competitive heat on paper, but it was dominated from the front.

20 WELCOME TO 2016 FROM CCR H'CAP 1m 2f (P)
3:55 (3:56) (Class 7) (0-50,52) 4-Y-O+ **£2,587** (£770; £384; £192) **Stalls** Low

Form RPR
003- **1** **Goodwood Moonlight**[12] 8329 4-9-4 **49** AdamKirby 2 59
(Ian Williams) *stmbld leaving stalls: sn led and mde rest: rdn clr over 1f out: styd on strly* **15/8**[1]
046- **2** *3 3/4* **My Tringaling (IRE)**[18] 8231 4-9-5 **50** OisinMurphy 7 53
(Stuart Williams) *chsd wnr thrght: rdn over 2f out: outpcd and btn over 1f out: kpt on same pce fnl f* **5/1**[3]
052- **3** *1 3/4* **Officer In Command (USA)**[12] 8329 10-9-7 **50** (p) JamieSpencer 12 50
(Alan Bailey) *chsd ldng pair thrght: rdn ent 2f out: styd on same pce u.p fnl f* **9/2**[2]
560- **4** *1 3/4* **It's All A Game**[15] 8278 5-9-5 **48** (b) JoeFanning 10 44
(Nigel Tinkler) *in tch in midfield: rdn over 3f out: hdwy u.p over 1f out: kpt on same pce ins fnl f* **20/1**
261- **5** *hd* **Elle Rebelle**[12] 8329 6-9-2 **52** CharlieBennett(7) 11 48
(Mark Brisbourne) *hld up in tch in last trio: rdn and effrt over 2f out: hdwy over 1f out: styd on same pce ins fnl f* **9/2**[2]
054- **6** *4* **Aru Cha Cha**[16] 8264 5-9-5 **48** RobertHavlin 5 36
(Roger Ingram) *chsd ldng trio: rdn ent 2f out: lost pl and btn over 1f out: wknd fnl f* **20/1**
/06- **7** *1* **Mr Morocco**[18] 8040 4-9-0 **48** (bt) EoinWalsh(3) 3 34
(Giles Bravery) *mounted on crse: hld up in last trio: reminder 5f out: bhd and rdn over 2f out: sn btn* **16/1**
605- **8** *1 3/4* **Brean Golf Birdie**[12] 8329 4-9-0 **45** JackMitchell 6 28
(Bill Turner) *hld up in rr: effrt on outer 3f out: sn struggling: bhd over 1f out* **25/1**
604- **9** *3/4* **Strawberryfields**[31] 8079 4-9-2 **47** ShaneKelly 1 29
(Des Donovan, Ire) *in tch in midfield: rdn 4f out: lost pl and drvn over 2f out: bhd over 1f out* **6/1**

2m 6.24s (-2.36) **Going Correction** -0.275s/f (Stan)
WFA 4 from 5yo+ 2lb 9 Ran SP% **121.4**
Speed ratings (Par 97): **98,95,93,92,92 88,88,86,86**
CSF £11.86 CT £38.98 TOTE £2.30: £1.10, £2.10, £1.90; EX 12.40 Trifecta £47.00.
Owner Miss J A Leighs **Bred** Biddestone Stud Ltd **Trained** Portway, Worcs

FOCUS
A moderate affair and the first three finished in the places they occupied heading into the first turn.
T/Jkpt: Not won. Placepot Jackpot: £569.40 to a £1 stake. Pool: £3,697.00 - 4.74 winning tickets T/Plt: £53.20 to a £1 stake. Pool: £52,622.91 - 721.04 winning tickets T/Qpdt: £37.40 to a £1 stake. Pool: £4,045.65 - 79.85 winning tickets **Steve Payne**

[1]SOUTHWELL (L-H)
Saturday, January 2

OFFICIAL GOING: Fibresand: standard
Wind: Moderate against Weather: Grey cloud

21 BET&WATCH EVERY RACE AT UNIBET H'CAP 5f (F)
12:15 (12:15) (Class 5) (0-70,73) 4-Y-O+ **£3,234** (£962; £481; £240) **Stalls** High

Form RPR
031- **1** **Crosse Fire**[4] 8389 4-9-10 **73** 6ex (p) KieranO'Neill 1 86
(Scott Dixon) *racd centre: cl up: led wl over 1f out: rdn ent fnl f: kpt on strly* **6/5**[1]
210- **2** *3* **Excellent Aim**[2] 8408 9-8-9 **65** LuluStanford(7) 6 67
(George Margarson) *trckd ldrs centre: pushed along and sltly outpcd 1/2-way: rdn wl over 1f out: swtchd rt appr fnl f and kpt on wl towards fin* **5/1**[2]
051- **3** *nk* **Shawkantango**[21] 8196 9-8-8 **57** (p) AdamBeschizza 5 58
(Derek Shaw) *s.i.s and bhd: sn swtchd lft towards far rail: rdn along 1/2-way: hdwy wl over 1f out: styd on u.p fnl f: nrst fin* **12/1**
/00- **4** *1 1/4* **Razin' Hell**[205] 3085 5-9-0 **70** (v) CallumShepherd(7) 2 66+
(John Balding) *racd centre: slt ld: rdn along over 2f out: hdd wl over 1f out: sn drvn and wknd appr fnl f* **13/2**[3]
504- **5** *2 1/2* **Monsieur Jamie**[25] 8148 8-9-4 **67** (v) DougieCostello 4 54
(J R Jenkins) *dwlt and sn pushed along towards rr: outpcd and swtchd lft towards far rail over 3f out: sn rdn along: styd on u.p fnl 2f* **16/1**
0/0- **6** *1 1/4* **Seamster**[18] 8242 9-9-5 **68** SamJames 8 51
(David O'Meara) *racd towards stands' rail: chsd ldrs: rdn along over 2f out: sn btn* **20/1**
002- **7** *2* **Fuel Injection**[16] 8271 5-8-11 **60** (b) BarryMcHugh 7 36
(Paul Midgley) *chsd ldrs centre: rdn along 2f out: grad wknd* **7/1**
003- **8** *1/2* **Daring Dragon**[59] 7711 6-8-11 **60** (v) StevieDonohoe 3 34
(Derek Shaw) *chsd ldrs centre: rdn along 2f out: grad wknd* **20/1**
050- **9** *1 3/4* **Emblaze**[50] 7832 4-8-4 **56** oh1 AdamCarter(3) 9 24
(Bryan Smart) *racd nr stands' rail: a in rr* **66/1**

1m 0.31s (0.61) **Going Correction** +0.20s/f (Slow) 9 Ran SP% **112.5**
Speed ratings (Par 103): **103,98,97,95,91 89,86,85,82**
CSF £6.73 CT £46.08 TOTE £2.20: £1.10, £1.50, £3.30; EX 8.00 Trifecta £44.10.
Owner Chappell, Cope, Dixon **Bred** Dr A Gillespie **Trained** Babworth, Notts

FOCUS
A routine sprint handicap in which, as usual, those that raced up the centre of the track dominated, and few got into it. The second and third have been rated close to their recent lesser grade C&D form.

22 UNIBET OFFER DAILY JOCKEY/TRAINER SPECIALS H'CAP 6f (F)
12:50 (12:52) (Class 6) (0-60,58) 4-Y-O+ **£2,587** (£770; £384; £192) **Stalls** Low

Form RPR
006- **1** **Speightowns Kid (USA)**[25] 8149 8-9-1 **57** (be) AnnStokell(5) 3 67
(Ann Stokell) *towards rr: pushed along 2f out: hdwy to chse ldrs over 1f out: swtchd lft and rdn ent fnl f: led last 120yds: styd on wl* **25/1**
004- **2** *1 3/4* **Lucky Mark (IRE)**[25] 8149 7-9-7 **58** (p) LiamKeniry 10 63
(John Balding) *dwlt: sn chsng ldrs: rdn along wl over 1f out: led ent fnl f: sn drvn: hdd and no ex last 120yds* **8/1**[3]
204- **3** *3/4* **Mambo Fever**[37] 8009 5-9-2 **58** (p) JustinNewman(5) 7 61+
(David C Griffiths) *dwlt and in rr: hdwy and wd st: rdn to chse ldrs 2f out: drvn and ev ch ent fnl f: kpt on same pce* **6/4**[1]
066- **4** *1 1/2* **Pancake Day**[21] 8206 4-9-7 **58** BarryMcHugh 8 56
(Jason Ward) *chsd ldrs: hdwy over 2f out: rdn to ld wl over 1f out: drvn and hdd ent fnl f: kpt on same pce* **9/1**
/23- **5** *nk* **Hab Reeh**[297] 858 8-9-5 **56** TomEaves 11 53
(Ruth Carr) *dwlt: sn in tch: hdwy and wd st: rdn to chse ldrs wl over 1f out: drvn appr fnl f: no imp* **50/1**
546- **6** *1* **Ms Eboracum (IRE)**[16] 8265 4-8-2 **46** JaneElliott(7) 4 40
(Michael Appleby) *chsd ldrs on inner: rdn along 2f out: sn one pce* **12/1**
004- **7** *nk* **Devilution (IRE)**[18] 8241 4-8-10 **47** ow1 (v[1]) StevieDonohoe 1 40
(Derek Shaw) *a towards rr* **14/1**
500- **8** *shd* **Loud**[87] 7037 6-8-12 **52** (b) SimonPearce(3) 2 45
(Lydia Pearce) *a towards rr* **11/2**[2]
100- **9** *1/2* **Spirit Of Rosanna**[35] 8035 4-8-13 **50** (tp) AdamBeschizza 5 42
(Steph Hollinshead) *chsd ldrs: rdn along over 2f out: sn drvn and grad wknd* **25/1**

540- **10** *5* **Pull The Pin (IRE)**[25] 8149 7-9-6 **57**...(bt) CharlesBishop 9 34+
(Heather Dalton) *cl up: led 1/2-way: rdn 2f out: sn hdd & wknd* **14/1**

002- **11** *3 1/2* **Perfect Peak**[25] 8149 4-8-12 **56**...(bt) DanielleMooney(7) 6 22+
(Michael Easterby) *slt ld to 1/2-way: cl up: rdn over 2f out: drvn wl over 1f out: sn wknd* **12/1**

1m 16.62s (0.12) **Going Correction** -0.10s/f (Stan) **11** Ran SP% **114.9**
Speed ratings (Par 101): **95,92,91,89,89 87,87,87,86,80 75**
CSF £205.57 CT £502.07 TOTE £34.70: £7.00, £2.80, £1.20; EX 141.00 Trifecta £1153.10.
Owner Geoff Pacey **Bred** Sandyview Farm **Trained** Lincoln, Lincolnshire

FOCUS
A moderate handicap. The leaders went off far too quick and the pair responsible for the breakneck gallop ended up finishing detached from the rest.

23 DOWNLOAD THE LADBROKES APP CLAIMING STKS 1m (F)
1:25 (1:25) (Class 6) 4-Y-O+ **£2,264** (£673; £336; £168) **Stalls** Low

Form RPR
021- **1** **Captain Lars (SAF)**[2] 8411 6-8-2 80...(v) CallumShepherd(7) 1 90
(Michael Bell) *mde most: rdn clr 2f out: easily* **5/4**[1]

460- **2** *7* **Hannington**[13] 8318 5-9-1 80...(p) LiamKeniry 6 79
(Andrew Balding) *hld up: hdwy 3f out: rdn to chse wnr 2f out: sn drvn and no imp* **7/1**

000- **3** *1 1/2* **Kung Hei Fat Choy (USA)**[2] 8412 7-9-9 82...(b) TomEaves 8 84
(James Given) *chsd ldrs on outer: pushed along and sltly outpcd 3f out: swtchd lft and rdn 2f out: kpt on appr fnl f* **12/1**

000- **4** *5* **Subtle Knife**[26] 8132 7-9-0 79... WilliamCarson 3 63
(Giles Bravery) *dwlt: sn trcking ldrs on inner: cl up 1/2-way: rdn along 3f out: drvn over 2f out and sn one pce* **16/1**

510- **5** *7* **Two Moons**[54] 7776 6-9-9 80... RyanClark 7 55
(Daniel Mark Loughnane) *cl up on outer: wd st: rdn along over 2f out: sn drvn and wknd* **3/1**[2]

000- **6** *3/4* **Eutropius (IRE)**[128] 5778 7-9-9 88... NeilFarley 5 53
(Alan Swinbank) *cl up towards outer: rdn along over 3f out: sn wknd* **13/2**[3]

7 *hd* **Silva Samourai**[100] 7-9-1 0...[1] JoeyHaynes 2 45
(Susan Corbett) *dwlt: a in rr* **250/1**

346- **8** *6* **Tartan Trip**[11] 8341 9-8-4 69...(v) RPWalsh(7) 4 26
(Michael Appleby) *prom: rdn along over 3f out: sn wknd* **20/1**

1m 41.36s (-2.34) **Going Correction** -0.10s/f (Stan) **8** Ran SP% **114.0**
Speed ratings (Par 101): **107,100,98,93,86 85,85,79**
CSF £10.85 TOTE £2.20: £1.20, £1.20, £3.00; EX 8.80 Trifecta £45.40.Captain Lars was claimed by D Shaw for £5,000. Hannington was claimed by F. J. Brennan for £8,000.
Owner Wildcard Racing Syndicate **Bred** Klawervlei Stud **Trained** Newmarket, Suffolk

FOCUS
They went a fair pace in this claimer with several disputing the lead in a line across the track down the back straight. However, it ended up a case of the favourite first, the rest nowhere.

24 LADBROKES H'CAP 7f (F)
2:00 (2:00) (Class 4) (0-80,80) 4-Y-O+ **£5,175** (£1,540; £769; £384) **Stalls** Low

Form RPR
635- **1** **Zaeem**[6] 8369 7-9-2 **80**...(p) JustinNewman(5) 5 95
(Ivan Furtado) *trckd ldrs: hdwy and cl up 3f out: led over 2f out: rdn clr wl over 1f out: readily* **7/1**[3]

050- **2** *5* **Captain Revelation**[103] 6593 4-9-3 **76**... RichardKingscote 4 78
(Tom Dascombe) *cl up: effrt over 2f out and ev ch: rdn wl over 1f out: kpt on: no ch w wnr* **6/1**[2]

402- **3** *1* **Assault On Rome (IRE)**[12] 8333 4-9-5 **78**...(b) AdrianNicholls 3 77
(Mark Johnston) *s.i.s and reminders s: sn rdn along and detached in rr: hdwy over 2f out: styd on wl u.p appr fnl f: nrst fin* **14/1**

006- **4** *3 3/4* **Queen Aggie (IRE)**[18] 8242 6-8-3 **69**... CallumShepherd(7) 7 59
(Tony Carroll) *chsd ldrs: wd st: rdn over 2f out: sn drvn and kpt on same pce* **7/1**[3]

122- **5** *1/2* **Shootingsta (IRE)**[16] 8270 4-9-6 **79**...(p) JackGarritty 2 67
(Bryan Smart) *slt ld on inner: rdn along over 2f out: sn hdd: drvn and edgd rt wl over 1f out: wknd* **5/4**[1]

445- **6** *4* **Alpha Tauri (USA)**[15] 8283 10-8-12 **71**... JoeyHaynes 9 49
(Charles Smith) *cl up: rdn along wl over 2f out: sn wknd* **16/1**

22-6 **7** *3* **Tiger's Home**[1] 1 6-8-2 **68** ow2... KyleCurrie(7) 1 38
(Iain Jardine) *a towards rr* **14/1**

000- **8** *6* **Golden Highway (USA)**[165] 4469 4-8-8 **72**... CharlesEddery(5) 6 27
(Michael Appleby) *a in rr* **14/1**

000- **9** *1/2* **Curzon Line**[16] 8270 7-8-9 **68**...(t) TomEaves 8 21
(Michael Easterby) *prom: rdn along over 3f out: sn wknd* **40/1**

1m 27.33s (-2.97) **Going Correction** -0.10s/f (Stan) **9** Ran SP% **112.1**
Speed ratings (Par 105): **112,106,105,100,100 95,92,85,84**
CSF £46.60 CT £566.63 TOTE £7.20: £2.10, £2.10, £2.70; EX 46.70 Trifecta £698.30.
Owner The Giggle Factor Partnership **Bred** Umm Qarn Management Co Ltd **Trained** Wiseton, Nottinghamshire

FOCUS
A fair handicap run at a decent pace thanks to a disputed lead. The level is a bit fluid, but the runner-up has been rated close to form for now.

25 LADBROKES MOBILE H'CAP 7f (F)
2:35 (2:35) (Class 6) (0-60,60) 4-Y-O+ **£2,587** (£770; £384; £192) **Stalls** Low

Form RPR
005- **1** **Falcon's Reign (FR)**[21] 8203 7-8-5 **51**...(p) RPWalsh(7) 3 60
(Michael Appleby) *trckd ldrs on inner: hdwy to chse ldr over 2f out: rdn over 1f out: chal ins fnl f: drvn and kpt on to ld nr fin* **16/1**

210- **2** *3/4* **Danish Duke (IRE)**[18] 8236 5-9-7 **60**... TomEaves 1 67
(Ruth Carr) *led: pushed clr 2f out: rdn over 1f out: drvn ins fnl f: hdd and no ex nr fin* **8/1**[3]

652- **3** *3 1/2* **Royal Rettie**[16] 8268 4-9-6 **59**... CharlesBishop 2 57
(Heather Dalton) *in tch: hdwy to chse ldrs over 2f out: rdn wl over 1f out: kpt on u.p fnl f* **8/1**[3]

006- **4** *1* **Evident (IRE)**[15] 8283 6-9-5 **58**...(p) WilliamCarson 7 53
(Tony Carroll) *cl up: rdn along over 2f out: sn drvn and wknd wl over 1f out* **7/1**[2]

010- **5** *1* **Cadeaux Pearl**[18] 8236 8-9-4 **57**... KieranO'Neill 8 49
(Scott Dixon) *cl up: rdn along 3f out: sn drvn and wknd over 2f out* **10/1**

521- **6** *5* **Grey Destiny**[21] 8203 6-8-12 **58**...(p) MathewStill(7) 6 37
(Antony Brittain) *v.s.a and lost several l s: sn swtchd to outer and rdn along: a bhd* **6/5**[1]

305- **7** *9* **Divertimenti (IRE)**[11] 8346 12-8-4 **48**...(b) AaronJones(5) 4 2
(Roy Bowring) *cl up: rdn along 3f out: sn wknd* **25/1**

335- **8** *10* **Amenable (IRE)**[15] 8278 9-8-9 **51**...(p) ShelleyBirkett(3) 5
(Conor Dore) *towards rr: rdn along and wd st: sn outpcd and bhd* **7/1**[2]

1m 29.52s (-0.78) **Going Correction** -0.10s/f (Stan) **8** Ran SP% **111.5**
Speed ratings (Par 101): **100,99,95,94,92 87,76,65**
CSF £129.00 CT £787.92 TOTE £17.60: £4.50, £2.20, £2.20; EX 144.40 Trifecta £823.90.
Owner W Sewell **Bred** Rabbah Bloodstock Ltd **Trained** Oakham, Rutland

FOCUS
A weak handicap and the second warm favourite on the card to lose his race at the start.

26 32RED MAIDEN FILLIES' STKS 1m 3f (F)
3:10 (3:10) (Class 4) 4-Y-O+ **£4,851** (£1,443; £721; £360) **Stalls** Low

Form RPR
03- **1** **Kuriosa (IRE)**[12] 8327 4-8-11 0... DanielMuscutt(3) 10 82+
(Marco Botti) *trckd ldr: cl up 4f out: led 3f out: rdn and edgd rt over 1f out: drvn ins fnl f: kpt on wl towards fin* **11/8**[1]

52- **2** *2 1/4* **Fair's Fair (IRE)**[56] 7748 4-9-0 0... RichardKingscote 1 77
(Ralph Beckett) *trckd ldrs whn n.m.r and hmpd bnd after 1 1/2f: in tch: hdwy 4f out: effrt over 2f out: rdn to chse wnr wl over 1f out: drvn to chal ent fnl f: ev ch tl edgd rt and no ex last 100yds* **11/4**[2]

3 *8* **Independent Rose** 4-9-0 0...[1] StevieDonohoe 7 63
(Michael Bell) *chsd ldng pair: effrt 3f out: rdn along over 2f out: drvn wl over 1f out: kpt on same pce* **16/1**

4 *6* **Moonshine Ridge (IRE)**[29] 5-9-3 0... NeilFarley 6 53
(Alan Swinbank) *s.i.s and lost several l s: bhd and rdn along 1/2-way: plugged on u.p fnl 3f: nrst fin* **5/1**[3]

5 *1 1/2* **Do It Tomorrow (IRE)**[21] 4-8-11 0... ShelleyBirkett(3) 3 51
(J R Jenkins) *chsd ldrs: rdn along over 3f out: drvn over 2f out: sn one pce* **40/1**

343- **6** *2 1/2* **Spirit Of The Sea (IRE)**[15] 8291 4-8-7 57... KyleCurrie(7) 5 46
(Iain Jardine) *dwlt and a towards rr* **15/2**

000- **7** *6* **Rosie Hall (IRE)**[35] 8040 6-9-3 41...(p) BarryMcHugh 9 36
(John Wainwright) *chsd ldrs whn n.m.r bnd after 1 1/2f: rdn along 4f out: drvn over 3f out: sn outpcd* **250/1**

8 *4 1/2* **Crazy Queen**[17] 4-9-0 0... WilliamCarson 2 29
(Anthony Carson) *led: rdn along 4f out: hdd 3f out: sn wknd* **12/1**

000- **9** *13* **North Bay Lady (IRE)**[77] 7293 4-9-0 34... TomEaves 8 6
(John Wainwright) *a in rr: rdn along over 5f out: sn outpcd and bhd* **250/1**

2m 25.97s (-2.03) **Going Correction** -0.10s/f (Stan)
WFA 4 from 5yo+ 3lb **9** Ran SP% **114.0**
Speed ratings (Par 102): **103,101,95,91,90 88,83,80,71**
CSF £5.12 TOTE £2.50: £1.10, £1.30, £3.90; EX 5.90 Trifecta £56.80.
Owner Mrs Lucie Botti **Bred** Northmore Stud **Trained** Newmarket, Suffolk
■ Stewards' Enquiry : Daniel Muscutt three-day ban: careless riding (16-18 Jan)

FOCUS
An uncompetitive older-fillies' maiden in which the two market leaders pulled clear. The first two have been rated as progressing in line with the better view of their previous runs.

27 32RED.COM AMATEUR RIDERS' H'CAP 2m (F)
3:40 (3:41) (Class 6) (0-65,65) 4-Y-O+ **£2,495** (£774; £386; £193) **Stalls** Low

Form RPR
002- **1** **Vivacissimo (IRE)**[21] 8198 9-9-12 **54**...(tp) MrThomasGreatrex(5) 10 65
(Ivan Furtado) *hld up towards rr: hdwy into midfield 1/2-way: trckd ldrs 4f out: effrt to chse clr ldr wl over 1f out: sn rdn: led ent fnl f: kpt on strly* **5/2**[1]

520- **2** *6* **Ellerina**[15] 8291 4-9-1 **48**... MissBeckySmith(3) 8 52
(Chris Fairhurst) *cl up: led after 5f: rdn clr over 2f out: hung bdly rt to stands' rail jst over 1f out: hdd ent fnl f: kpt on same pce* **7/1**

054- **3** *1* **Dissertation**[13] 8315 4-9-7 **51**... MrRBirkett 6 54
(Julia Feilden) *hld up towards rr: hdwy over 5f out: rdn along 3f out: styd on u.p fnl 2f: nrst fin* **6/1**[3]

432- **4** *1 3/4* **Hall Of Beauty**[16] 8269 4-9-6 **50**... MissSBrotherton 7 51
(Michael Appleby) *trckd ldrs: hdwy to chse ldr over 5f out: rdn along over 2f out: drvn wl over 1f out: sn one pce* **4/1**[2]

030- **5** *17* **Toptempo**[46] 6324 7-10-9 **65**... MissEllaSmith(5) 1 45
(Ralph J Smith) *s.i.s: detached and sn rdn along: wl bhd 1/2-way: plugged on fnl 4f: n.d* **20/1**

060- **6** *3 3/4* **Rock Of Ages**[32] 7871 7-9-12 **52**...(b) MissJodieHughes(3) 9 28
(Steve Flook) *chsd ldrs: rdn along over 3f out: sn drvn and wknd* **16/1**

643- **7** *1 1/2* **Lucie Rie (IRE)**[21] 8198 4-9-8 **52**...(v) MissCWalton 11 26
(K R Burke) *chsd ldrs: rdn along 4f out: wknd over 3f out* **6/1**[3]

003- **8** *3 1/2* **Sign Of The Times**[16] 8269 4-8-10 **47** oh1 ow1.... MrTomFanshawe(7) 2 17
(J R Jenkins) *trckd ldrs on inner: pushed along over 5f out: rdn over 4f out: sn drvn and wknd* **20/1**

041- **9** *34* **Chloe's Image**[252] 1676 6-10-1 **59**... MissJAHeneghan(7) 4
(Philip Kirby) *led 5f: prom tl rdn along over 5f out and sn wknd* **11/1**

000/ **P** **Doctor Of Music (IRE)**[387] 718 10-9-2 **46** oh1...(b[1]) MissHStuckey(7) 3
(Jo Davis) *a in rr: rdn along and bhd 1/2-way: t.o whn p.u over 4f out: lame* **100/1**

3m 44.48s (-1.02) **Going Correction** -0.10s/f (Stan)
WFA 4 from 6yo+ 7lb **10** Ran SP% **114.4**
Speed ratings (Par 101): **98,95,94,93,85 83,82,80,63,**
CSF £19.51 CT £94.21 TOTE £3.20: £1.10, £5.00, £2.30; EX 18.30 Trifecta £107.70.
Owner Richard Ward **Bred** Haras De Bourgeaville **Trained** Wiseton, Nottinghamshire

FOCUS
A moderate race, but a decent test of stamina for both horse and rider. The first four pulled well clear.
T/Plt: £47.10 to a £1 stake. Pool: £57,530.94 - 891.32 winning tickets T/Qpdt: £14.20 to a £1 stake. Pool: £4,638.48 - 241.40 winning tickets **Joe Rowntree**

[14]CHELMSFORD (A.W) (L-H)
Sunday, January 3

OFFICIAL GOING: Polytrack: standard
Wind: moderate 1/2 behind Weather: wet and windy

28 BET SCOOP6SOCCER AT TOTESPORT.COM H'CAP 6f (P)
1:00 (1:00) (Class 5) (0-75,75) 4-Y-O+ **£5,175** (£1,540; £769; £384) **Stalls** Centre

Form RPR
053- **1** **Money Team (IRE)**[17] 8262 5-9-5 **73**... PhillipMakin 1 86
(David Barron) *trckd ldrs: effrt over 2f out: led over 1f out: readily* **7/4**[1]

630- **2** *2 3/4* **For Ayman**[34] 8051 5-8-5 **66**...(t) JosephineGordon(7) 7 70
(Joseph Tuite) *in rr: hdwy whn pushed wd bnd over 2f out: styd on to take 2nd last 75yds* **10/1**

323- **3** 1 **Jacob's Pillow**[16] 8283 5-9-3 **71**....(p) AndrewMullen 5 72
(Michael Appleby) *trckd ldr: effrt over 2f out: kpt on to take 3rd last 50yds* **6/1**

413- **4** 1 1/4 **Bosham**[37] 8011 6-9-0 **75**....(b) NathanEvans(7) 2 72
(Michael Easterby) *led: hdd over 1f out: wknd last 75yds* **5/1**[3]

612- **5** 2 **Spinning Cobblers**[3] 8408 5-8-6 **65**....(v) AaronJones(5) 8 56
(Stuart Williams) *dwlt: swtchd lft after s: bhd: sme hdwy and hung rt over 1f out: nvr a threat* **7/2**[2]

040- **6** shd **Colourbearer (IRE)**[103] 6627 9-9-4 **72**....(t) OisinMurphy 4 62
(Charlie Wallis) *mid-div: effrt over 2f out: nvr a factor* **20/1**

010- **7** 3 1/4 **Cloak And Degas (IRE)**[27] 8131 4-8-13 **67**....(v) KieranO'Neill 3 47
(Scott Dixon) *mid-div: drvn over 2f out: nvr a factor* **12/1**

400- **8** 8 **Oscars Journey**[19] 8240 6-9-2 **70**....(v) AdamKirby 6 24
(J R Jenkins) *trckd ldrs: t.k.h: hung rt thrght: lost pl 2f out: bhd whn eased clsng stages* **16/1**

1m 11.15s (-2.55) **Going Correction** -0.175s/f (Stan) **8** Ran SP% **117.0**
Speed ratings (Par 103): **110,106,102,103,100 100,96,85**
CSF £21.48 CT £89.63 TOTE £2.70: £1.20, £2.90, £2.40; EX 18.90 Trifecta £109.20.
Owner White Rose Racing **Bred** Mrs Claire Doyle **Trained** Maunby, N Yorks

FOCUS
The track had been power harrowed and then gallop mastered to 2 inches. A soundly run race and a cosy success for the favourite.

29 WIN A FOOTBALL FORTUNE WITH SCOOP6SOCCER MAIDEN AUCTION STKS (PLUS 10 RACE) 1m 2f (P)
1:30 (1:30) (Class 4) 3-Y-O **£6,469** (£1,925; £962; £481) **Stalls** Low

Form RPR

333- **1** **Cape Of Glory (IRE)**[38] 7998 3-9-5 75.... AdamKirby 1 84
(James Tate) *chsd ldrs: reminders over 4f out: edgd rt and led over 1f out: styd on wl* **3/1**[2]

05- **2** 3 1/2 **Milrow (IRE)**[38] 7998 3-9-5 0.... FergusSweeney 2 77
(Martyn Meade) *dwlt and wnt rt s: sn trcking ldrs: n.m.r bnd over 2f out: styd on to chse wnr 1f out: no imp* **6/1**

53- **3** 4 1/2 **Ghostwriter (IRE)**[25] 8153 3-9-5 0.... MartinHarley 8 68
(Hugo Palmer) *s.i.s and carried rt s: jnd ldrs after 2f: drvn over 3f out: one pce over 1f out* **9/4**[1]

033- **4** 1/2 **Kelvin Hall**[52] 7810 3-9-0 68.... JoeFanning 3 62
(Mark Johnston) *drvn over 2f out: hdd over 1f out: one pce* **7/2**[3]

0- **5** 3 3/4 **Graceful Lady**[72] 7422 3-9-0 0.... OisinMurphy 5 55
(Robert Eddery) *slowly away: sn mid-div: effrt and chsng ldrs over 2f out: nvr a threat* **33/1**

0- **6** 2 1/2 **Quick Witted**[18] 8246 3-9-0 0.... PatCosgrave 7 50
(Harry Dunlop) *wnt rt s: sn chsng ldrs: drvn over 5f out: lost pl over 2f out* **20/1**

7 nk **Talent To Amuse (IRE)** 3-9-0 0.... JackMitchell 9 49
(Roger Varian) *s.i.s: in rr: drvn 4f out: nvr on terms* **8/1**

36- **8** 1 3/4 **Golden Isles (IRE)**[34] 8048 3-9-0 0.... LiamKeniry 6 45
(J S Moore) *chsd ldrs: lost pl over 2f out* **20/1**

05- **9** 9 **Highburgh Road (IRE)**[16] 8280 3-9-0 0.... AdrianNicholls 4 27
(Mark Johnston) *in rr: sn pushed along: bhd fnl 3f* **50/1**

2m 4.37s (-4.23) **Going Correction** -0.175s/f (Stan) **9** Ran SP% **117.8**
Speed ratings (Par 99): **109,106,102,102,99 97,96,95,88**
CSF £20.67 TOTE £3.70: £1.40, £2.00, £1.50; EX 31.80 Trifecta £90.70.
Owner Saif Ali **Bred** Razza Pallorsi Snc Di Giacomo Gariboldi **Trained** Newmarket, Suffolk

FOCUS
An ordinary maiden.

30 PLAY SCOOP6SOCCER EVERY WEEK FILLIES' H'CAP 1m 5f 66y(P)
2:00 (2:01) (Class 4) (0-80,76) 4-Y-O+ **£8,086** (£2,406; £1,202; £601) **Stalls** Low

Form RPR

440- **1** **Oratorio's Joy (IRE)**[12] 8344 6-9-11 **75**.... WilliamCarson 4 81
(Jamie Osborne) *hld up in rr: hdwy 4f out: led over 1f out: drvn rt out* **15/2**

312- **2** 3/4 **Kelly's Finest (IRE)**[7] 8367 4-8-6 **63**....(p) AndrewMullen 3 68
(Michael Appleby) *chsd ldr: led after 5f: hdd over 1f out: kpt on same pce clsng stages* **4/1**[2]

3 1 3/4 **Crazy (GER)**[867] 7-8-10 **60**.... MartinLane 5 62
(David Dennis) *hld up in rr: hdwy over 3f out: kpt on over 1f out: tk 3rd nr fin* **8/1**

610- **4** hd **Blue Sea Of Ibrox (IRE)**[65] 7597 8-9-9 **76**.... DanielMuscutt(3) 2 78
(John Berry) *trckd ldrs: effrt 4f out: kpt on same pce fnl f* **16/1**

022- **5** nk **Indira**[12] 8353 5-9-7 **71**.... TomQueally 6 73
(John Berry) *chsd ldrs: outpcd over 3f out: hdwy to chse ldrs over 2f out: kpt on same pce fnl f* **9/2**[3]

416- **6** 2 1/2 **Kissy Suzuki**[54] 7784 4-9-0 **69**.... OisinMurphy 8 67
(Hughie Morrison) *hld up towards rr: hdwy over 2f out: edgd lft and one pce fnl f* **5/1**

014- **7** 16 **Taurian**[14] 8319 5-9-4 **68**.... WilliamTwiston-Davies 1 42
(Ian Williams) *t.k.h: led 5f: hung rt and wknd 1f out: sn heavily eased* **10/3**[1]

020- **8** nk **High And Flighty (IRE)**[25] 8159 4-9-6 **75**....(p) SamJames 7 48
(David O'Meara) *chsd ldrs: drvn over 4f out: lost pl over 3f out: sn bhd* **8/1**

2m 51.4s (-2.20) **Going Correction** -0.175s/f (Stan)
WFA 4 from 5yo+ 5lb **8** Ran SP% **117.8**
Speed ratings (Par 102): **99,98,97,97,97 95,85,85**
CSF £38.73 CT £251.22 TOTE £8.10: £2.00, £1.50, £3.00; EX 46.40 Trifecta £478.00.
Owner A F Tait **Bred** R Mahon & J Reilly **Trained** Upper Lambourn, Berks

FOCUS
An open fillies' handicap.

31 BET SCOOP6SOCCER AT BETFRED SHOPS H'CAP 1m 2f (P)
2:30 (2:32) (Class 2) (0-105,105) 4-Y-O+ **£19,407** (£5,775; £2,886; £1,443) **Stalls** Low

Form RPR

211- **1** **Power Game**[104] 6592 4-8-5 **88**.... WilliamCarson 5 98+
(Saeed bin Suroor) *trckd ldrs: pushed v wd and effrt over 1f out: edgd lft and styd on to ld last 100yds* **6/5**[1]

245- **2** 1 **Ansaab**[15] 8308 8-8-7 **88**.... AndrewMullen 3 95
(Michael Appleby) *led: qcknd pce 4f out: hdd last 100yds: styd on same pce* **8/1**

043- **3** nk **Solar Deity (IRE)**[8] 8359 7-9-7 **105**.... MarcMonaghan(3) 4 111
(Marco Botti) *hld up in rr: effrt over 2f out: kpt on same pce to take 3rd nr fin* **8/1**

611- **4** 1/2 **Pactolus (IRE)**[24] 8169 5-8-0 **86** oh8....(t) AaronJones(5) 2 91?
(Stuart Williams) *mid-div: effrt 3f out: hdwy on inner 2f out: kpt on one pce over 1f out* **7/1**[3]

001- **5** 1 **First Mohican**[29] 8124 8-9-7 **102**.... TomQueally 7 105
(Alan King) *trckd ldr: t.k.h: drvn and edgd rt over 1f out: one pce* **5/1**[2]

630/ **6** 1 **Whispering Warrior (IRE)**[414] 7803 7-8-12 **93**.... JamieSpencer 6 94
(David Simcock) *hld up in rr: effrt over 2f out: chsng ldrs over 1f out: kpt on same pce* **5/1**[2]

/00- **7** 1 3/4 **Unex El Greco**[41] 7957 8-8-5 **89**.... TimClark(3) 1 87?
(Martin Smith) *trckd ldrs: effrt over 2f out: fdd appr fnl f* **50/1**

2m 6.7s (-1.90) **Going Correction** -0.175s/f (Stan)
WFA 4 from 5yo+ 2lb **7** Ran SP% **115.5**
Speed ratings (Par 109): **100,99,98,98,97 96,95**
CSF £12.16 TOTE £2.00: £1.60, £3.60; EX 9.30 Trifecta £44.20.
Owner Godolphin **Bred** Darley **Trained** Newmarket, Suffolk

FOCUS
They didn't go that quick and they finished in a heap, but there's no doubt the winner was much the best.

32 BET SCOOP6SOCCER AT BETFRED.COM H'CAP 1m (P)
3:00 (3:00) (Class 6) (0-55,55) 4-Y-O+ **£3,234** (£962; £481; £240) **Stalls** Low

Form RPR

301- **1** **Thello**[12] 8340 4-9-3 **51**.... TonyHamilton 9 58
(Nigel Tinkler) *trckd ldng pair: led over 1f out: drvn out* **5/2**[1]

033- **2** 1/2 **Anjuna Beach (USA)**[17] 8264 6-8-10 **49**.... AnnStokell(5) 5 55
(Ann Stokell) *hld up in rr: hdwy on outer and 4th over 2f out: chsd wnr fnl f: no ex clsng stages* **6/1**

156- **3** 3 1/2 **Ela Goog La Mou**[27] 8134 7-9-4 **55**.... MarcMonaghan(3) 8 52
(Peter Charalambous) *trckd ldrs: effrt over 2f out: kpt on same pce fnl f* **8/1**

005- **4** nse **Hagree (IRE)**[150] 5067 5-9-1 **49**....(tp) OisinMurphy 4 46
(Jose Santos) *w ldr: led over 2f out: hung rt and hdd over 1f out: kpt on one pce* **5/1**[3]

400- **5** 2 **Je T'Aime Encore**[18] 8252 4-9-5 **53**.... AdamKirby 10 45
(Gay Kelleway) *hld up towards rr: hdwy over 2f out: one pce over 1f out* **8/1**

130- **6** 2 3/4 **El Duque**[25] 8160 5-9-3 **54**....(p) PhilipPrince(3) 6 40
(Bill Turner) *led: hdd over 2f out: wknd over 1f out* **4/1**[2]

563- **7** nk **Mr Chocolate Drop (IRE)**[13] 8335 12-8-12 **46**....(vt) JimmyQuinn 3 31
(Mandy Rowland) *in rr: sme hdwy 2f out: nvr a factor* **8/1**

000- **8** 1 **Pipers Piping (IRE)**[79] 7266 10-9-7 **55**.... KieranO'Neill 7 38
(Mandy Rowland) *rr-div: effrt over 2f out: nvr on terms* **20/1**

040- **9** 12 **Blue Melody Girl (IRE)**[160] 4700 4-9-7 **55**.... TomEaves 2 9
(James Given) *chsd ldrs: drvn over 3f out: lost pl over 3f out: sn bhd* **33/1**

1m 39.4s (-0.50) **Going Correction** -0.175s/f (Stan) **9** Ran SP% **120.6**
Speed ratings (Par 101): **95,94,91,90,88 86,85,84,72**
CSF £18.90 CT £108.96 TOTE £3.40: £1.60, £2.50, £2.90; EX 22.80 Trifecta £157.50.
Owner Y T Szeto **Bred** Mickley Stud & Mr W T Whittle **Trained** Langton, N Yorks

FOCUS
The leaders wound things up from some way out here.

33 SCOOP6SOCCER HAPPY NEW YEAR H'CAP 1m 2f (P)
3:30 (3:32) (Class 5) (0-75,76) 4-Y-O+ **£5,175** (£1,540; £769; £384) **Stalls** Low

Form RPR

201- **1** **Buckland Beau**[13] 8336 5-9-8 **76**.... StevieDonohoe 4 85+
(Charlie Fellowes) *hld up in rr: hdwy on wd outside over 2f out: chal 1f out: led post* **5/1**[3]

440- **2** hd **Boonga Roogeta**[13] 8325 7-9-2 **73**.... MarcMonaghan(3) 7 81
(Peter Charalambous) *mid-div: hdwy over 3f out: sn chsng ldrs: led 1f out: edgd rt: hdd post* **8/1**

421- **3** 2 3/4 **Hernando Torres**[20] 8227 8-8-11 **72**....(tp) NathanEvans(7) 5 75
(Michael Easterby) *trckd ldr: led 2f out: hdd 1f out: kpt on same pce* **6/1**

100- **4** 1/2 **Tyrsal (IRE)**[32] 8081 5-8-13 **67**.... JimmyQuinn 9 69
(Clifford Lines) *s.i.s: swtchd lft after s: hld up in rr: effrt over 2f out: swtchd lft and styd on last 150yds* **20/1**

251- **5** 1 **Tatting**[30] 8105 7-9-2 **70**.... ShaneKelly 3 70
(Mark Hoad) *mid-div: drvn and outpcd over 4f out: hdwy on inner over 1f out: kpt on towards fin* **8/1**

01- **6** 2 1/4 **St Patrick's Day (IRE)**[20] 8226 4-9-1 **71**....(v) AdamKirby 2 66
(J R Jenkins) *s.i.s: sn trcking ldrs: drvn over 3f out: wknd over 1f out* **3/1**[1]

610- **7** 1/2 **Cornelious (IRE)**[48] 7875 4-9-4 **74**.... OisinMurphy 1 68
(Robert Eddery) *led: hdd 2f out: wknd appr fnl f* **9/2**[2]

134- **8** 2 **Walk Like A Giant**[13] 8336 5-9-2 **70**....(p) AndrewMullen 8 60
(Michael Appleby) *chsd ldrs: upsides 5f out: wknd over 1f out* **8/1**

024- **9** 16 **El Tel**[215] 2813 4-9-1 **71**.... JackMitchell 6 29
(Roger Varian) *hld up in rr: t.k.h: effrt over 2f out: sn lost pl and bhd: eased clsng stages* **11/2**

2m 4.92s (-3.68) **Going Correction** -0.175s/f (Stan)
WFA 4 from 5yo+ 2lb **9** Ran SP% **127.6**
Speed ratings (Par 103): **107,106,104,104,103 101,101,99,86**
CSF £49.57 CT £256.82 TOTE £6.80: £2.00, £2.40, £2.60; EX 57.00 Trifecta £292.20.
Owner P S McNally **Bred** D G Hardisty Bloodstock **Trained** Newmarket, Suffolk

FOCUS
A modest handicap in which the first two finished clear.
T/Plt: £21.80 to a £1 stake. Pool: £90,485.79 - 3,022.51 winning tickets T/Qpdt: £13.60 to a £1 stake. Pool: £7,785.96 - 422.62 winning tickets **Walter Glynn**

34 (Foreign Racing) - See Raceform Interactive

WOLVERHAMPTON (A.W) (L-H)
Monday, January 4

OFFICIAL GOING: Tapeta: standard

35 DOWNLOAD THE LADBROKES APP H'CAP 7f 32y (Tp)
2:00 (2:01) (Class 6) (0-52,52) 4-Y-O+ **£2,587** (£770; £384; £192) **Stalls** High

Form RPR

043- **1** **Gulland Rock**[13] 8346 5-9-6 **51**.... WilliamCarson 8 56
(Anthony Carson) *led: hdd narrowly 1f out: kpt on to ld nr fin despite sddle slipping* **10/1**

320- **2** hd **Tasaaboq**[18] 8265 5-9-5 **50**....(bt) AdamKirby 4 55
(Phil McEntee) *trckd ldrs: led narrowly 1f out: edgd lft: hdd clsng stages* **11/2**[3]

502- **3** nk **Binky Blue (IRE)**[5] 8406 4-9-2 **47**.... GeorgeBaker 1 51
(Daniel Mark Loughnane) *trckd ldrs: upsides on ins 1f out: crowded and no ex nr fin* **5/4**[1]

005- **4** 3 1/4 **Stanlow**[14] 8334 6-9-6 **51**....(v) TomEaves 9 47
(Michael Mullineaux) *mid-div: effrt over 2f out: one pce over 1f out* **11/1**

503- **5** 4 1/2 **Patron Of Explores (USA)**[5] 8406 5-9-1 **46**.... JackGarritty 5 31+
(Patrick Holmes) *s.i.s: hld up detached in last: t.k.h: hdwy over 2f out: kpt on: nvr on terms* **11/4**[2]

055- **6** *¾* **Rosie Crowe (IRE)**[30] 8119 4-9-7 **52**........................(v) TimmyMurphy 10 35
(Shaun Harris) *trckd ldr: wknd fnl f* **9/1**

006- **7** *1 ½* **Ambitious Rosie**[25] 8172 5-8-12 **46** oh1..............(p) GeorgeDowning(3) 7 25
(Tony Carroll) *in rr: pushed along 4f out: lost pl over 2f out* **50/1**

050- **8** *5* **Red Shadow**[13] 8346 7-9-1 **46** oh1....................................(p) ShaneKelly 3 13
(Alan Brown) *dwlt: mid-div: lost pl over 2f out: sn bhd* **25/1**

500- **9** *6* **Waterloo Dock**[112] 6384 11-8-12 **50**.........................(v) NicolaGrundy(7) 6
(James Unett) *hld up in rr: hdwy over 3f out: lost pl over 2f out: sn bhd* **28/1**

0/0- **10** *43* **Bewdley**[62] 7695 11-8-8 **46** oh1................................. CallumShepherd(7) 2
(Ray Peacock) *mid-div: drvn 3f out: sn lost pl and wl bhd: t.o: b.b.v* **200/1**

1m 29.3s (0.50) **Going Correction** -0.05s/f (Stan) **10** Ran SP% **123.7**
Speed ratings (Par 101): **95,94,94,90,85 84,83,77,70,21**
CSF £66.49 CT £122.25 TOTE £10.40: £2.40, £2.00, £1.20; EX 63.80 Trifecta £256.50.
Owner W H Carson **Bred** Whitsbury Manor Stud **Trained** Newmarket, Suffolk

FOCUS
A modest contest. The gallop wasn't strong, the first three all being handy throughout.

36 LADBROKES H'CAP 7f 32y (Tp)

2:35 (2:36) (Class 5) (0-70,70) 4-Y-O+ **£3,234** (£962; £481; £120; £120) **Stalls** High

Form RPR

661- **1** **Ziggys Star**[14] 8324 4-9-7 **70**... AndrewMullen 7 79
(Michael Appleby) *trckd ldrs: chal 2f out: led over 1f out: hung lft: jst hld on* **3/1**[1]

300- **2** *hd* **Jammy Guest (IRE)**[28] 8131 6-9-7 **70**............................... RyanPowell 3 78+
(George Margarson) *hld up towards rr: hdwy 2f out: styd on wl fnl f: jst failed* **9/2**[2]

634- **3** *¾* **Bogsnog (IRE)**[23] 8206 6-8-13 **62**....................................... ShaneGray 1 68
(Kristin Stubbs) *trckd ldrs: t.k.h: effrt over 1f out: kpt on to take 3rd clsng stages* **14/1**

214- **4** *2 ¼* **Sewn Up**[24] 8179 6-9-1 **64**..(p) JoeFanning 2 67+
(Keith Dalgleish) *in rr-div: hdwy on inner over 2f out: keeping on same pce whn hmpd last 100yds* **6/1**

256- **4** *dht* **Coreczka (IRE)**[24] 8184 5-8-10 **59**................................... TonyHamilton 9 59
(Miss Clare Louise Cannon, Ire) *chsd ldrs: drvn over 2f out: one pce* **13/2**

050- **6** *1 ¼* **Secret Look**[17] 8283 6-9-0 **63**..(p) SeanLevey 11 60
(Ed McMahon) *swtchd lft after s: led hdd over 1f out: one pce* **25/1**

510- **7** *½* **Summerinthecity (IRE)**[27] 8148 9-9-3 **66**........................ MartinHarley 4 61
(Patrick Morris) *trckd ldrs: effrt 2f out: wknd appr fnl f* **16/1**

005- **8** *1 ¼* **Lucky Lodge**[14] 8333 6-9-3 **66**.......................................(b) PJMcDonald 8 58
(Antony Brittain) *mid-div: effrt 2f out: swtchd lft last 150yds: kpt on* **11/2**[3]

005- **9** *1 ¾* **Grandest**[45] 7925 5-9-0 **63**... DougieCostello 6 50
(Brian Ellison) *s.s: in rr: sme hdwy 2f out: nvr a factor* **14/1**

400/ **10** *2 ¾* **Hadaj**[402] 7949 7-9-4 **67**.. TomEaves 10 47
(Michael Herrington) *towards rr: bhd fnl 2f: eased clsng stages* **50/1**

510- **11** *5* **Admirable Art (IRE)**[151] 5074 6-9-0 **63**.......................... WilliamCarson 5 29
(Tony Carroll) *in rr: hdwy over 3f out: lost pl 2f out: bhd whn heavily eased* **20/1**

1m 28.28s (-0.52) **Going Correction** -0.05s/f (Stan) **11** Ran SP% **116.0**
Speed ratings (Par 103): **100,99,98,96,96 94,94,92,90,87 82**
CSF £15.37 CT £165.42 TOTE £3.90: £1.60, £2.40, £3.30; EX 21.50 Trifecta £255.20.
Owner Tariq Al Nisf **Bred** Honeypuddle Stud **Trained** Oakham, Rutland

FOCUS
A fair handicap and the form looks sound. The gallop didn't look overly strong, the tempo only really increasing over 2f out and the prominently ridden winner stealing a bit of a march on the runner-up.

37 LADBROKES (S) STKS 1m 141y (Tp)

3:10 (3:10) (Class 6) 4-Y-O+ **£2,587** (£770; £384; £192) **Stalls** Low

Form RPR

536- **1** **Moonlight Venture**[27] 8147 5-9-1 66..............................(tp) TomEaves 4 70+
(Kevin Ryan) *set stdy pce: qcknd gallop 4f out: styd on wl fnl 2f: unchal* **9/4**[2]

/56- **2** *3 ¾* **Never To Be (USA)**[305] 781 5-9-1 81.........................(t[1]) PatCosgrave 6 63
(Jim Boyle) *trckd ldrs: t.k.h: effrt over 3f out: chsd wnr over 1f out: hung lft and no imp* **6/4**[1]

044- **3** *2* **Oak Bluffs (IRE)**[13] 8341 5-9-1 61.................................. TonyHamilton 2 58
(Richard Fahey) *trckd ldrs: effrt over 3f out: 3rd over 1f out: one pce* **9/2**[3]

611- **4** *½* **Greek Islands (IRE)**[18] 8264 8-9-13 60............................. LiamKeniry 1 69
(Neil Mulholland) *hld up in rr: hdwy over 2f out: kpt on fnl f* **11/1**

000- **5** *8* **The Firm (IRE)**[31] 8105 7-9-0 60..............................(v[1]) RyanHolmes(7) 7 46
(Daniel Mark Loughnane) *s.v.s: hdwy over 5f out: drvn over 2f out: sn lost pl* **33/1**

005- **6** *4 ½* **Become Aware**[21] 8222 4-9-0 40...................................(b) JoeyHaynes 5 31
(Tim Etherington) *sn chsng wnr: drvn 4f out: lost pl wl over 1f out* **125/1**

000- **7** *5* **Al Muheer (IRE)**[31] 8105 11-9-1 65........................(b) RichardKingscote 3 20
(Tom Dascombe) *hld up in rr: drvn over 3f out: lost pl 2f out: bhd whn eased clsng stages* **15/2**

1m 48.32s (-1.78) **Going Correction** -0.05s/f (Stan)
WFA 4 from 5yo+ 1lb **7** Ran SP% **112.8**
Speed ratings (Par 101): **105,101,99,99,92 88,83**
CSF £5.82 TOTE £3.30: £1.90, £1.40; EX 7.80 Trifecta £21.70.
Owner Mrs J Ryan **Bred** G Reed **Trained** Hambleton, N Yorks

FOCUS
A fair effort from the winner, who dominated from the off. He did not need to match the best of last year's form.

38 CORAL CONNECT H'CAP 1m 1f 103y (Tp)

3:40 (3:40) (Class 5) (0-70,70) 4-Y-O+ **£3,234** (£962; £481; £240) **Stalls** Low

Form RPR

445- **1** **Fern Owl**[24] 8176 4-9-4 **68**.. LiamKeniry 9 76
(Hughie Morrison) *trckd ldrs: drvn over 2f out: sn outpcd: styd on over 1f out: edgd lft last 75yds: led nr fin* **7/1**[3]

111- **2** *hd* **Tangramm**[17] 8292 4-9-3 **67**.. PatCosgrave 13 74
(Dean Ivory) *trckd ldrs: led over 1f out: edgd rt last 75yds: hdd nr fin* **9/2**[2]

300- **3** *½* **Mr Red Clubs (IRE)**[19] 8247 7-9-0 **70**............................ JaneElliott(7) 11 76
(Michael Appleby) *mid-div: hdwy over 3f out: chsng ldrs over 1f out: kpt on towards fin* **12/1**

605- **4** *1* **Freud (FR)**[21] 8221 6-9-7 **70**.. TonyHamilton 8 73
(Ian Williams) *t.k.h in rr: hdwy 2f out: kpt on fnl f* **8/1**

003- **5** *nk* **Matraash (USA)**[19] 8252 10-9-2 **65**................................(be) AdamKirby 4 69+
(Daniel Mark Loughnane) *mid-div: hdwy over 2f out: kpt on same pce fnl f: nt clr run and snatched up nr fin* **22/1**

005- **6** *nse* **Archie's Advice**[20] 8238 5-9-7 **70**...................................... JoeFanning 2 74+
(Keith Dalgleish) *hld up in mid-div: hdwy over 2f out: nt clr run fr over 1f out: nt rcvr* **8/1**

260- **7** *½* **Leonard Thomas**[20] 8228 6-9-2 **68**...................... GeorgeDowning(3) 10 70
(Tony Carroll) *in rr: hdwy over 2f out: styd on last 75yds* **33/1**

041- **8** *hd* **Bogardus (IRE)**[20] 8228 5-9-1 **64**.. JoeyHaynes 6 65
(Patrick Holmes) *mid-div: hdwy over 3f out: one pce over 1f out* **4/1**[1]

561- **9** *¾* **Hussar Ballad (USA)**[21] 8221 7-9-4 **67**........................... PJMcDonald 5 67
(Antony Brittain) *sn led: hdd over 1f out: one pce* **8/1**

400- **10** *1* **Innoko (FR)**[24] 8176 6-9-0 **63**... WilliamCarson 1 61
(Tony Carroll) *led early: trckd ldrs: one pce whn n.m.r clsng stages* **100/1**

053- **11** *¾* **Lean On Pete (IRE)**[21] 8221 7-9-7 **70**........................(p) RobertWinston 3 73+
(Ollie Pears) *hld up towards rr: hdwy over 12f out: nt clr run on inner last 150yds: eased nr fin* **10/1**

532- **12** *¾* **Apache Glory (USA)**[26] 8164 8-9-3 **66**.....................(be) StevieDonohoe 7 60
(Daniel Mark Loughnane) *in rr: effrt over 3f out: nvr a factor* **20/1**

450- **13** *13* **The Lampo Genie**[66] 5859 4-8-10 **67**.............................. CliffordLee(7) 12 34
(K R Burke) *sn chsng ldrs: drvn 4f out: sn lost pl: wl bhd fnl 2f* **25/1**

2m 0.98s (0.18) **Going Correction** -0.05s/f (Stan)
WFA 4 from 5yo+ 1lb **13** Ran SP% **117.7**
Speed ratings (Par 103): **97,96,96,95,95 95,94,94,93,93 92,91,80**
CSF £35.55 CT £377.39 TOTE £9.00: £2.80, £1.90, £4.60; EX 47.20 Trifecta £516.10.
Owner Sir Thomas Pilkington **Bred** Sir Thomas Pilkington **Trained** East Ilsley, Berks

FOCUS
They didn't of a much gallop here, resulting in a bunch finish and bit of trouble inside the final furlong, but the bottom line is that a pair of progressive sorts came to the fore and it's still a contest from which a few winners are likely to emerge. THe winner is rated back to his early form.

39 BET £5 GET £20 AT CORAL H'CAP 1m 1f 103y (Tp)

4:10 (4:10) (Class 6) (0-60,60) 4-Y-O+ **£2,587** (£770; £384; £192) **Stalls** Low

Form RPR

452- **1** **Rockwood**[30] 8119 5-9-1 **54**...(v) PaulMulrennan 8 62
(Karen McLintock) *hld up in mid-div: hdwy over 3f out: 3rd over 1f out: styd on to ld last 100yds* **7/2**[2]

013- **2** *nk* **Tijuca (IRE)**[20] 8235 7-9-7 **60**..(tp) KieranO'Neill 9 67
(Ed de Giles) *dwlt: hld up in rr: hdwy 2f out: styd on appr fnl f: tk 2nd nr fin* **5/2**[1]

400- **3** *½* **Cool Music (IRE)**[45] 7923 6-9-2 **55**................................. PJMcDonald 11 61
(Antony Brittain) *in rr: hdwy over 3f out: styng on whn swtchd lft last 100yds: tk 3rd nr fin* **22/1**

363- **4** *1 ¼* **Cahar Fad (IRE)**[31] 8109 4-8-13 **53**.........................(bt) AdamBeschizza 1 57
(Steph Hollinshead) *drvn to ld: hdd 6f out: led over 1f out: hdd and no ex last 100yds* **8/1**[3]

000- **5** *3 ½* **On A Whim**[24] 8178 4-8-6 **46**... JoeFanning 2 43
(Daniel Mark Loughnane) *in rr: drvn over 3f out: hdwy over 2f out: one pce over 1f out* **16/1**

400- **6** *1 ¼* **Lynngale**[28] 8134 5-9-4 **57**.. ShaneGray 12 52
(Kristin Stubbs) *hdwy to trck ldrs after 2f: led 6f out: hdd over 1f out: one pce whn hmpd clsng stages* **9/1**

00/- **7** *2 ¼* **Let Me In (IRE)**[586] 2672 6-9-7 **60**..................................(v) MartinLane 5 50
(Bernard Llewellyn) *mid-div: outpcd over 3f out: kpt on over 1f out* **20/1**

000- **8** *1 ¼* **Time Square (FR)**[20] 8231 9-8-13 **52**................................ JoeyHaynes 4 40
(Tony Carroll) *chsd ldrs: drvn 4f out: one pce fnl 2f* **10/1**

604- **9** *4* **Toymaker**[8] 8370 9-9-7 **60**..(tp) AdamKirby 10 40
(Phil McEntee) *in rr: hdwy over 2f out: wknd over 1f out* **10/1**

042- **10** *1 ¾* **Vivre La Reve**[31] 8109 4-9-6 **60**...................................... PatCosgrave 6 37
(James Unett) *trckd ldrs: drvn over 2f out: wknd over 1f out* **8/1**[3]

006- **11** *35* **Starlight Genie**[24] 8176 4-9-6 **60**........................... WilliamTwiston-Davies 7
(Richard Phillips) *sn chsng ldrs: lost pl over 1f out: sn eased and wl bhd: t.o* **14/1**

000/ **12** *36* **Vermuyden**[571] 3160 7-8-10 **52**.. RobHornby(3) 3
(Pam Sly) *mid-div: drvn 4f out: sn lost pl and bhd: t.o over 2f out: sn eased: eventually completed* **18/1**

1m 59.53s (-1.27) **Going Correction** -0.05s/f (Stan)
WFA 4 from 5yo+ 1lb **12** Ran SP% **128.1**
Speed ratings (Par 101): **103,102,102,101,98 96,94,93,90,88 57,25**
CSF £13.83 CT £180.59 TOTE £3.70: £1.80, £1.60, £8.70; EX 17.60 Trifecta £580.80.
Owner I R Clements **Bred** Norcroft Park Stud **Trained** Ingoe, Northumberland

FOCUS
A run-of-the-mill contest, though it was at least more truly run than some of the other races on the card. A minor pb from the winner.

40 32RED.COM MAIDEN AUCTION STKS 1m 141y (Tp)

4:40 (4:44) (Class 5) 3-Y-O **£3,557** (£1,058; £529; £264) **Stalls** Low

Form RPR

62- **1** **With Pleasure**[59] 7730 3-9-5 0.. RobertHavlin 1 76+
(Simon Crisford) *mde all: drvn and edgd rt fnl f: kpt on wl* **10/11**[1]

2 *1 ¼* **Byres Road** 3-9-5 0... JoeFanning 7 73+
(Mark Johnston) *mid-div: drvn over 5f out: hdwy over 2f out: edgd lft and styd on to take 2nd last 100yds* **11/1**

- **3** *1 ¼* **Fun For All** 3-9-0 0... PatCosgrave 5 65
(James Tate) *chsd ldrs: drvn over 2f out: kpt on same pce appr fnl f* **18/1**

0- **4** *1 ¼* **Young Christian**[21] 8225 3-9-5 0.................................... JamesSullivan 6 67
(Tom Tate) *chsd ldrs: one pce and hung lft appr fnl f* **150/1**

03- **5** *¾* **Dr Drey (IRE)**[76] 7353 3-9-5 0.. TimmyMurphy 2 65
(Jamie Osborne) *mid-div: hdwy to chse ldrs over 2f out: kpt on same pce fnl f* **11/1**

00- **6** *½* **Ice Alert (IRE)**[17] 8285 3-9-2 0.................................. DanielMuscutt(3) 9 64
(Marco Botti) *chsd ldrs: drvn over 2f out: kpt on same pce over 1f out* **16/1**

42- **7** *¾* **Inswing (IRE)**[17] 8285 3-9-0 0.. MartinLane 13 57
(Ralph Beckett) *hld up towards rr: hdwy over 2f out: sn rdn: kpt on fnl f* **7/2**[2]

06- **8** *3 ½* **Toffee Apple (IRE)**[18] 8259 3-9-0 0.................. WilliamTwiston-Davies 4 49+
(Ed Dunlop) *hdwy over 2f out: chsng ldrs over 1f out: wknd fnl f* **100/1**

9 *4* **Avoidable** 3-9-5 0... LiamKeniry 3 45+
(David Simcock) *s.i.s: in rr: bhd fnl 2f* **8/1**[3]

0- **10** *½* **Page Of Wands**[30] 8122 3-9-0 0.................................... PaulMulrennan 8 39
(Karen McLintock) *dwlt: in rr: bhd fnl 3f* **150/1**

63- **11** *¾* **Daybreak Lady**[17] 8285 3-9-0 0.. JoeyHaynes 10 37
(Jo Hughes) *chsd ldrs: lost pl over 2f out: sn bhd* **20/1**

- **12** *nk* **Daisy Bere (FR)** 3-9-0 0.. DougieCostello 12 36
(K R Burke) *s.s: swtchd lft after s: in rr: bhd fnl 3f* **100/1**

1m 49.71s (-0.39) **Going Correction** -0.05s/f (Stan) **12** Ran SP% **121.6**
Speed ratings (Par 97): **99,97,96,95,95 94,93,90,87,86 85,85**
CSF £13.35 TOTE £2.00: £1.10, £3.20, £3.10; EX 14.70 Trifecta £154.00.
Owner Abdullah Saeed Belhab **Bred** Rabbah Bloodstock Limited **Trained** Newmarket, Suffolk

FOCUS
Probably not a maiden with massive depth to it, but the winner did it nicely enough from the front and the second and third both shaped encouragingly on debut. The winner is rated close to his latest form.

41 32RED CASINO FILLIES' H'CAP 5f 216y (Tp)
5:10 (5:10) (Class 5) (0-75,75) 4-Y-0+ **£3,234** (£962; £481; £240) **Stalls** Low

Form RPR
004- **1** **Effusive**[19] 8250 4-9-1 **69**..............................(p) PatCosgrave 2 79
(William Haggas) *led 1f: trckd ldrs: led 2f out: drvn out* **5/1**
214- **2** 1 ½ **Lady Lydia (IRE)**[9] 8357 5-9-4 **75**.............................. DanielMuscutt(3) 5 80
(Conrad Allen) *trckd ldrs: 2nd and hung lft over 1f out: kpt on same pce last 75yds* **11/4**[2]
3U3- **3** ½ **Quite A Story**[135] 5613 4-9-2 **70**.............................. AdamKirby 6 74
(Clive Cox) *s.i.s: hld up in tch on outer: drvn over 3f out: chsng ldrs over 2f out: 3rd over 1f out: kpt on towards fin* **7/4**[1]
101- **4** 2 **Exentricity**[23] 8207 4-9-0 **68**.............................. JoeFanning 1 65
(Mick Channon) *chsd ldrs: kpt on one pce over 1f out* **3/1**[3]
10- **5** ¾ **Ki Ki**[106] 6558 4-8-9 **66**.............................. AdamCarter(3) 3 61
(Bryan Smart) *s.s: t.k.h in rr: outpcd over 2f out: edgd rt over 1f out: kpt on clsng stages* **16/1**
/42- **6** 3 ¼ **Angel Way (IRE)**[233] 2288 7-9-5 **73**.............................. ShaneGray 4 57
(John Gallagher) *led after 1f: hdd 2f out: sn wknd* **12/1**

1m 13.46s (-1.04) **Going Correction** -0.05s/f (Stan) **6** Ran SP% **118.3**
Speed ratings (Par 100): **104,102,101,98,97 93**
CSF £20.32 TOTE £6.80: £3.00, £1.70; EX 21.40 Trifecta £54.00.
Owner Cheveley Park Stud **Bred** Cheveley Park Stud Ltd **Trained** Newmarket, Suffolk

FOCUS
A fair fillies' handicap which was soundly run. The winner is rated to last year's best.
T/Jkpt: not won. JACKPOT PLACEPOT £278.20. Pool: £2,744.71 - 7.20 winning units. T/Plt: £17.10 to a £1 stake. Pool: £81,085.49 - 3442.22 winning units. T/Qpdt: £5.50 to a £1 stake. Pool: £7,417.59 - 993.82 winning units. **Walter Glynn**

LINGFIELD (L-H)
Tuesday, January 5

OFFICIAL GOING: Polytrack: standard
Wind: Light, half behind Weather: Fine but cloudy

42 DOWNLOAD THE NEW UNIBET RACING APP MAIDEN AUCTION STKS 6f 1y(P)
1:00 (1:00) (Class 6) 3-Y-0 **£2,264** (£673; £336; £168) **Stalls** Low

Form RPR
3- **1** **Khameela**[77] 7372 3-9-0 0.............................. JamieSpencer 6 67+
(David Simcock) *trckd ldr: led wl over 1f out: sn drvn and drew clr* **1/2**[1]
303- **2** 3 ½ **Magic Garden (IRE)**[6] 8402 3-9-0 0.............................. LukeMorris 3 56
(Jonathan Portman) *chsd ldrs but sn pushed along: rdn 2f out: kpt on fnl f on inner to take 2nd last strides* **7/2**[2]
0- **3** hd **Rojina (IRE)**[6] 8402 3-9-0 0.............................. JFEgan 1 55
(Joseph Tuite) *led: rdn and hdd wl over 1f out: one pce and lost 2nd last strides* **33/1**
06- **4** 1 **Hey Ben**[32] 8103 3-9-0 0.............................. JordanNason(5) 5 57
(Ronald Thompson) *racd in 5th: shkn up over 2f out: n.d but kpt on fnl f to take 4th last strides* **25/1**
50- **5** nk **Red Ruffian (IRE)**[20] 8246 3-8-12 0.............................. PaulBooth(7) 7 57
(Dean Ivory) *chsd ldng pair to 2f out: wd bnd sn after: one pce and lost 4th last strides* **33/1**
6- **6** 1 **Daydream (IRE)**[103] 6666 3-9-0 0.............................. TimmyMurphy 4 49
(Jamie Osborne) *hld up in 6th: wd bnd 2f out: reminders 1f out: kpt on but nvr involved* **12/1**[3]
7 14 **Still Kicking (IRE)** 3-9-5 0.............................. AdamKirby 2 12
(Phil McEntee) *a last: struggling by 1/2-way: t.o* **16/1**

1m 12.12s (0.22) **Going Correction** -0.05s/f (Stan) **7** Ran SP% **112.2**
Speed ratings (Par 95): **96,91,91,89,89 88,69**
CSF £2.31 TOTE £1.40: £1.10, £1.60; EX 2.60 Trifecta £21.80.
Owner Huckleberry Racing **Bred** C J Mills **Trained** Newmarket, Suffolk

FOCUS
A modest maiden won easily by the well-backed favourite. The field field compressed behind in a slow time.

43 32RED.COM H'CAP 1m 7f 169y(P)
1:30 (1:30) (Class 5) (0-75,74) 4-Y-0+ **£2,911** (£866; £432; £216) **Stalls** Low

Form RPR
222- **1** **Tempuran**[15] 8328 7-9-5 **66**.............................. OisinMurphy 5 74
(David Bridgwater) *mde all: 10 l clr after 4f: rdn over 2f out and stl 6 l ahd: kpt on wl and nvr chal: eased last 50yds* **5/1**
102- **2** 4 **Todd**[20] 8257 6-9-10 **71**.............................. GeorgeBaker 3 73+
(Anabel K Murphy) *hld up in last: stl there over 2f out: prog on outer over 1f out: rdn and r.o to take 2nd last 130yds: too much to do* **11/4**[1]
621- **3** 1 ¼ **Rebel Collins (IRE)**[39] 8014 5-9-6 **74**.............................. JosephineGordon(7) 1 74
(David Evans) *t.k.h: hld up in 6th: prog over 2f out: chal for 2nd fnl f: nvr any ch* **6/1**
310- **4** 2 ¾ **Starcrossed**[27] 8156 4-9-2 **70**.............................. JohnFahy 4 67
(Eve Johnson Houghton) *chsd wnr: rdn 4f out and no imp: lost 2nd over 2f out: no ch after* **9/2**[3]
006- **5** hd **Topaling**[35] 8064 5-9-9 **70**.............................. SaleemGolam 2 67
(Mark H Tompkins) *trckd ldrs in 4th: shkn up over 2f out: no real prog and nvr any ch* **20/1**
200/ **6** ½ **Magic Music Man**[43] 7281 5-9-12 **73**.............................. AdamKirby 7 69
(Alan King) *trckd ldng pair: rdn 4f out: chsd wnr over 2f out: no imp: lost 2nd and wknd last 130yds* **4/1**[2]
433- **7** 13 **Virnon**[17] 7528 5-9-8 **69**.............................. NeilFarley 6 50
(Alan Swinbank) *in tch in rr: wknd jst over 2f out: t.o* **10/1**

3m 23.21s (-2.49) **Going Correction** -0.05s/f (Stan)
WFA 4 from 5yo+ 7lb **7** Ran SP% **109.7**
Speed ratings (Par 103): **104,102,101,100,99 99,93**
CSF £17.52 TOTE £4.50: £2.20, £2.30; EX 11.50 Trifecta £33.30.
Owner David J Smith **Bred** Stiftung Gestut Fahrhof **Trained** Icomb, Gloucs

FOCUS
One-way traffic here, with the winner establishing a big early lead which he was able to defend. He's accorded a shaky pb for this effort.

44 32RED MAIDEN FILLIES' STKS 1m 2f (P)
2:00 (2:00) (Class 5) 3-Y-0+ **£2,911** (£866; £432; £216) **Stalls** Low

Form RPR
44- **1** **Stars At Night (IRE)**[21] 8233 3-8-5 0.............................. NickyMackay 1 69+
(John Gosden) *mde all: shkn up over 2f out: sn drew clr: styd on wl fnl f* **5/4**[1]
4- **2** 4 **O'Connor's Girl**[16] 8320 3-8-5 0.............................. LukeMorris 3 61
(Sir Mark Prescott Bt) *trckd ldrs: rdn over 2f out: wnt 2nd wl over 1f out: one pce and no imp on wnr* **5/1**[3]
0- **3** hd **Genuine Approval (IRE)**[22] 8225 3-8-2 0.............................. DannyBrock(3) 2 60
(Jonathan Portman) *trckd wnr to over 6f out: dropped to 4th and rdn over 2f out: kpt on again fnl f and nrly snatched 2nd* **100/1**
3- **4** 1 ¼ **Rivers Run (IRE)**[31] 8125 4-9-12 0.............................. OisinMurphy 4 61
(Ralph Beckett) *prog to join wnr over 6f out: rdn and nt qckn over 2f out: lost 2nd and one pce wl over 1f out* **6/4**[2]
4/5- **5** nk **Hope You Dance (FR)**[236] 2215 4-9-12 0.............................. JamieSpencer 7 62+
(David Simcock) *hld up in 6th: shkn up over 2f out: keeping on one pce whn nt clr run ins fnl f* **10/1**
0- **6** 3 **Ingen Brave**[6] 8404 3-7-13 0 ow1.............................. JosephineGordon(7) 6 52
(David Evans) *in tch: rdn 3f out and sn outpcd: one pce after* **100/1**
0- **7** 11 **Perusal (IRE)**[20] 8246 3-8-2 0.............................. RyanTate(3) 5 29
(Jonathan Portman) *mostly in last: wknd over 2f out: t.o* **25/1**

2m 5.61s (-0.99) **Going Correction** -0.05s/f (Stan)
WFA 3 from 4yo 23lb **7** Ran SP% **116.0**
Speed ratings (Par 100): **101,97,97,96,96 94,85**
CSF £8.44 TOTE £2.10: £1.10, £2.90; EX 8.50 Trifecta £148.30.
Owner Derrick Smith & Mrs John Magnier & Michael Tabor **Bred** Miarixa Syndicate **Trained** Newmarket, Suffolk

FOCUS
They didn't go that quick early and this turned into a bit of a dash heading to the turn in. The favourite didn't need to improve to win.

45 BET&WATCH EVERY RACE AT UNIBET CONDITIONS STKS (PLUS 10 RACE) 5f 6y(P)
2:30 (2:30) (Class 3) 3-Y-0 **£7,246** (£2,168; £1,084) **Stalls** High

Form RPR
131- **1** **Gracious John (IRE)**[66] 7661 3-9-5 106.............................. JFEgan 1 106
(David Evans) *disp ld tl led 1/2-way: rdn and styd on wl fr over 1f out* **6/4**[2]
423- **2** 2 ¾ **Ornate**[31] 8120 3-9-2 110..............................(t) PatCosgrave 2 93
(William Haggas) *w other pair 1f then restrained: effrt on inner to go 2nd wl over 1f out: sn rdn and nt qckn: no imp after* **4/6**[1]
100- **3** 7 **Adham (IRE)**[88] 7072 3-9-2 90.............................. LukeMorris 3 68
(James Tate) *forced to r wd early: disp ld to over 2f out: edgd rt sn after: lost 2nd wl over 1f out: wknd and eased* **12/1**[3]

57.14s (-1.66) **Going Correction** -0.05s/f (Stan) **3** Ran SP% **107.7**
Speed ratings (Par 101): **111,106,95**
CSF £2.94 TOTE £2.40; EX 2.80 Trifecta £3.20.
Owner Terry Reffell **Bred** Skeaghmore Hill **Trained** Pandy, Monmouths

FOCUS
Only the three runners, but the winner impressed in this conditions race. The race has been rated around the runner-up's previous AW run.

46 UNIBET H'CAP 5f 6y(P)
3:00 (3:00) (Class 7) (0-50,50) 3-Y-0+ **£1,704** (£503; £251) **Stalls** High

Form RPR
000- **1** **Loudly (USA)**[129] 5864 4-9-10 **50**.............................. GeorgeBaker 3 56
(George Peckham) *hld up in last: plenty to do whn prog wl over 1f out: rdn and r.o fnl f to ld post* **7/2**[3]
050- **2** nse **Kuanyao (IRE)**[14] 8346 10-9-0 **45**..............................(be) AnnStokell(5) 8 51
(Ann Stokell) *w ldr tl nudged by her over 3f out: dropped to 3rd 2f out: rdn and kpt on wl fr over 1f out: led nr fin: hdd post* **16/1**
006- **3** ½ **Midnight Destiny (IRE)**[18] 8290 4-9-10 **50**..............................(v) MartinLane 6 54
(Derek Shaw) *chsd ldrs: wnt 2nd 2f out: drvn to chal fnl f: upsides 75yds out: one pce* **7/1**
522- **4** nse **Redalani (IRE)**[6] 8401 6-9-9 **49**..............................(b) ShaneKelly 2 53
(Alan Brown) *mde most: edgd rt over 3f out: urged along over 1f out: hdd and no ex nr fin* **9/4**[1]
405- **5** 3 ½ **Tax Reform (IRE)**[6] 8400 6-9-3 **48**..............................(b) PaddyPilley(5) 7 39
(Natalie Lloyd-Beavis) *hld up in rr: rdn wl over 1f out: fnd nil and sn btn* **3/1**[2]
500- **6** 2 ¼ **Cerulean Silk**[40] 7995 6-8-12 **45**.............................. JosephineGordon(7) 1 28
(Tony Carroll) *chsd ldrs: rdn on inner wl over 1f out: no prog: wknd fnl f* **25/1**
550- **7** 9 **Big City Boy (IRE)**[34] 8071 8-9-10 **50**..............................(vt) AdamKirby 4 1
(Phil McEntee) *a in rr: wknd qckly jst over 1f out: t.o* **8/1**

59.09s (0.29) **Going Correction** -0.05s/f (Stan) **7** Ran SP% **111.3**
Speed ratings (Par 97): **95,94,94,94,88 84,70**
CSF £50.99 CT £359.20 TOTE £4.60: £2.60, £7.40; EX 57.20 Trifecta £442.60.
Owner Fawzi Abdulla Nass **Bred** Timothy Wickes **Trained** Newmarket, Suffolk

FOCUS
A moderate sprint run at a good gallop, but a desperate finish.

47 LADBROKES MAIDEN H'CAP 7f 1y(P)
3:30 (3:30) (Class 6) (0-65,64) 3-Y-0+ **£2,264** (£673; £336; £168) **Stalls** Low

Form RPR
505- **1** **Timia**[20] 8253 3-8-10 **64**.............................. PatCosgrave 1 69+
(Ed Dunlop) *trckd ldrs: gng best 2f out: led on inner 1f out: urged along and in command after* **6/4**[1]
506- **2** 1 ¼ **Ertidaad (IRE)**[76] 7385 4-9-9 **59**..............................(vt[1]) AdamKirby 4 63
(Emma Owen) *led: rdn over 2f out: hdd and one pce 1f out: jst hld on for 2nd* **2/1**[2]
006- **3** shd **Footlight**[14] 8350 3-7-12 **55**.............................. SammyJoBell(3) 3 55
(Richard Fahey) *hld up in tch: rdn over 1f out: styd on ins fnl f and nrly grabbed 2nd* **9/2**[3]
000- **4** ½ **Cross Examine (IRE)**[150] 5149 3-7-7 **54** oh2.............................. SophieKilloran(7) 2 52
(David Simcock) *dwlt: t.k.h and hld up in last: pushed along and tried to cl on inner over 1f out: one pce fnl f* **8/1**

R25- **5** *6* **Thief Of Hearts**[29] 8136 3-8-2 **56**......................................(p) LukeMorris 5 38
(Bill Turner) *s.i.s but sn pressed ldr: rdn 2f out: sn lost 2nd and wknd* **10/1**

1m 26.23s (1.43) **Going Correction** -0.05s/f (Stan)
WFA 3 from 4yo 18lb 5 Ran SP% **111.7**
Speed ratings (Par 101): **89,87,87,86,80**
CSF £4.88 TOTE £2.50: £1.40, £1.30; EX 4.40 Trifecta £11.40.
Owner Ahmed Jaber **Bred** L J Vaessen **Trained** Newmarket, Suffolk

FOCUS
Ordinary form and the winner had a better profile than the others.
T/Plt: £170.70 to a £1 stake. Pool: £56,724.69 - 242.47 winning units. T/Qpdt: £44.70 to a £1 stake. Pool: £5,095.84 - 84.20 winning units. **Jonathan Neesom**

21 SOUTHWELL (L-H)
Tuesday, January 5

OFFICIAL GOING: Fibresand: standard
Wind: Light against Weather: grey cloud

48 32RED H'CAP 1m (F)
12:40 (12:45) (Class 6) (0-55,55) 3-Y-O **£2,587** (£770; £384; £192) **Stalls** Low

Form RPR
030- **1** **Carbutt's Ridge (IRE)**[25] 8177 3-9-0 **48**........................ DougieCostello 6 55
(K R Burke) *dwlt: sn pushed along and trckd ldrs after 2f: effrt and swtchd rt 2f out: rdn to ld 1 1/2f out: clr ins fnl f* **11/4**[1]

605- **2** *3 3/4* **Never Say (IRE)**[40] 8007 3-8-12 **46** oh1............................. PJMcDonald 2 44
(Jason Ward) *chsd ldrs on outer: pushed along and sltly outpcd over 3f out: rdn over 2f out: styd on to chse wnr ins fnl f: no imp* **12/1**

000- **3** *1 1/2* **Boom Junior**[29] 8130 3-8-12 **46** oh1............................... WilliamCarson 7 40
(Tony Carroll) *cl up: slt ld wl over 3f out: rdn over 2f out: hdd 1 1/2f out: sn drvn and kpt on same pce* **25/1**

255- **4** *3/4* **Piccacard**[18] 8281 3-9-1 **52**...................................... AlistairRawlinson(3) 1 45
(Michael Appleby) *slt ld on inner: pushed along and hdd after 3f: sn rdn along and sltly outpcd over 3f out: hdwy on inner to chal 2f out: ev ch tl drvn and wknd over 1f out* **4/1**[2]

000- **5** *8* **Dazeekha**[18] 8285 3-9-7 **55**... RobertHavlin 5 28
(Michael Herrington) *t.k.h: cl up: slt ld after 3f: rdn along and hdd wl over 3f out: cl up tl drvn 2f out and sn wknd* **5/1**

006- **6** *12* **Parisianna**[18] 8287 3-9-0 **48**.. TonyHamilton 9
(Richard Fahey) *a in rr: outpcd and bhd fr wl over 2f out* **5/1**

226- **7** *18* **Bond's Tricks**[18] 8281 3-9-7 **55**...................................... RobertWinston 3
(Ronald Thompson) *towards rr: rdn along wl over 3f out: wknd wl over 2f out: bhd and eased over 1f out* **9/2**[3]

1m 42.47s (-1.23) **Going Correction** -0.325s/f (Stan) 7 Ran SP% **109.7**
Speed ratings (Par 95): **93,89,87,87,79 67,49**
CSF £33.11 CT £618.17 TOTE £3.80: £2.10, £6.00; EX 26.90 Trifecta £382.30.
Owner Ontoawinner 9 & Mrs E Burke **Bred** Thomas Hassett **Trained** Middleham Moor, N Yorks

FOCUS
The opening contest was a very moderate 3yo handicap. They went a respectable gallop on standard Fibresand.

49 DOWNLOAD THE LADBROKES APP H'CAP 1m (F)
1:10 (1:15) (Class 5) (0-75,75) 4-Y-O+ **£3,234** (£962; £481; £240) **Stalls** Low

Form RPR
063- **1** **Patriotic (IRE)**[19] 8270 8-9-7 **75**.............................(p) SilvestreDeSousa 4 84
(Chris Dwyer) *chsd ldrs: pushed along after 2f: hdwy 3f out: rdn to chal 2f out: led 1 1/2f out: drvn and edgd rt ins fnl f: styd on* **10/11**[1]

52-2 **2** *2 1/4* **Clockmaker (IRE)**[4] 1 10-9-4 **72**.................................. TomEaves 1 76
(Conor Dore) *prom: swtchd rt after 2f and sn cl up: slt ld 1/2-way: rdn along wl over 2f out: drvn and hdd 1 1/2f out: kpt on u.p fnl f* **4/1**[2]

000- **3** *5* **Foolaad**[19] 8270 5-8-13 **72**...(t) AaronJones(5) 3 65
(Roy Bowring) *cl up: effrt over 2f out: sn rdn and ev ch: drvn and one pce appr fnl f* **16/1**

105- **4** *4* **Harwoods Star (IRE)**[28] 8148 6-8-9 **63**................(t) RichardKingscote 7 46
(Stuart Williams) *dwlt: hdwy to chse ldrs after 3f: rdn along 3f out: drvn 2f out and sn btn* **11/1**

46-0 **5** *3/4* **Tartan Trip**[3] 23 9-8-12 **69**................................(tp) AlistairRawlinson(3) 6 51
(Michael Appleby) *chsd ldrs: rdn along over 3f out: drvn over 2f out: sn btn* **25/1**

00-3 **6** *6* **Ythan Waters**[4] 1 4-9-1 **69**.. PaulMulrennan 5 37
(Bryan Smart) *dwlt: sn rdn along in rr: detached fr 1/2-way* **11/2**[3]

401- **7** *6* **Princess Peaches**[19] 8268 4-8-7 **61** oh2........................... JoeFanning 2 15
(James Bethell) *led: pushed along and hdd 1/2-way: rdn over 3f out: sn wknd* **20/1**

1m 40.8s (-2.90) **Going Correction** -0.325s/f (Stan) 7 Ran SP% **110.6**
Speed ratings (Par 103): **101,98,93,89,89 83,77**
CSF £4.34 TOTE £1.70: £1.30, £2.00; EX 4.90 Trifecta £39.20.
Owner M M Foulger **Bred** Darley **Trained** Newmarket, Suffolk

FOCUS
A fair handicap and they went a proper gallop. The winner was on a good mark, but is still rated 6lb off last winter's peak.

50 LADBROKES H'CAP 7f (F)
1:40 (1:45) (Class 3) (0-95,93) 4-Y-O **£7,246** (£2,168; £1,084; £542; £270) **Stalls** Low

Form RPR
211- **1** **Philba**[19] 8270 4-8-7 **82** ow1..................................(tp) AlistairRawlinson(3) 1 93
(Michael Appleby) *cl up on inner: slt ld after 2f: styd cl to inner rail home st: rdn 2f out: drvn ent fnl f: kpt on gamely* **4/1**[3]

201- **2** *hd* **Certificate**[27] 8163 5-9-7 **93**.......................................(v) JackMitchell 5 103
(Roger Varian) *cl up on outer: effrt over 2f out and sn chal on wd outside: rdn and edgd rt wl over 1f out: drvn and ev ch ins fnl f: no ex towards fin* **9/4**[1]

000- **3** *1 3/4* **Townsville**[19] 8270 4-8-10 **82**... JoeFanning 2 87
(Keith Dalgleish) *trckd ldrs: styd towards inner home st: rdn wl over 1f out: drvn and ch ent fnl f: kpt on same pce* **33/1**

064- **4** *1 1/4* **Showboating (IRE)**[14] 8342 8-9-3 **89**............................ RobertWinston 7 91
(John Balding) *chsd ldrs: wd st: rdn and hdwy over 2f out: drvn over 1f out: no imp* **16/1**

011- **5** *2 3/4* **Westwood Hoe**[24] 8199 5-9-6 **92**.. TomQueally 4 87
(Tony Coyle) *slt ld 2f: cl up: rdn along over 2f out: drvn wl over 1f out: grad wknd* **11/4**[2]

406- **6** *1* **Al Khan (IRE)**[27] 8163 7-9-7 **93**.. ShaneGray 3 85
(Kevin Ryan) *in tch: rdn along 3f out: drvn over 2f out and no imp* **16/1**

401- **P** **Mr Bossy Boots (IRE)**[76] 7390 5-9-2 **88**..............(t) RichardKingscote 6
(Ralph Beckett) *in tch: pushed along after 2f: sddle slipped 1/2-way: bhd and rn v wd home turn: p.u 2f out: dismntd* **4/1**[3]

1m 26.8s (-3.50) **Going Correction** -0.325s/f (Stan) 7 Ran SP% **112.1**
Speed ratings (Par 107): **107,106,104,103,100 99,**
CSF £12.90 TOTE £5.30: £2.30, £1.40; EX 14.90 Trifecta £375.60.
Owner T Johnson **Bred** T F T F Ltd **Trained** Oakham, Rutland

FOCUS
The feature contest was a decent handicap and they went a good gallop.

51 LADBROKES MAIDEN STKS 1m 4f (F)
2:10 (2:15) (Class 5) 4-Y-O+ **£2,911** (£866; £432; £216) **Stalls** Low

Form RPR
244- **1** **Signed Sealed (USA)**[15] 8327 4-9-3 77........................... RobertHavlin 5 81+
(John Gosden) *trckd ldng pair: cl up over 5f out: slt ld wl over 3f out: rdn clr wl over 1f out: readily* **11/10**[1]

4- **2** *7* **Brave Richard (IRE)**[14] 8343 5-9-7 0.............................. TonyHamilton 1 70
(J R Jenkins) *in rr and niggled along after 3f: rdn along and hdwy 3f out: chsd ldrs over 1f out: swtchd rt ent fnl f: styd on to take modest 2nd last 100yds: fin sltly lame* **25/1**

02- **3** *2* **Kay Sera**[14] 8343 8-9-4 0.. EoinWalsh(3) 2 67
(Tony Newcombe) *trckd ldrs: smooth hdwy over 3f out: chsd wnr over 2f out: rdn wl over 1f out: drvn and edgd lft ent fnl f: lost modest 2nd last 100yds* **6/1**[3]

43- **4** *1 3/4* **Nineteenth Hole (IRE)**[32] 8108 4-9-3 0.................. SilvestreDeSousa 3 64
(Michael Wigham) *t.k.h: trckd ldrs on inner: hdwy over 3f out: rdn to chse ldrs wl over 1f out: sn drvn: edgd rt ent fnl f: kpt on same pce* **8/1**

52- **5** *11* **Starving Faithful**[24] 8202 4-8-12 0............................(p) RichardKingscote 4 42
(Ralph Beckett) *led: rdn along over 4f out: hdd wl over 3f out: drvn over 2f out and sn wknd* **3/1**[2]

6 *7* **Rosette**[66] 4-8-12 0... JoeFanning 6 30
(Alan Swinbank) *prom: pushed along on outer over 4f out: rdn over 3f out: sn lost pl and bhd* **12/1**

2m 35.77s (-5.23) **Going Correction** -0.325s/f (Stan)
WFA 4 from 5yo+ 4lb 6 Ran SP% **109.6**
Speed ratings (Par 103): **104,99,98,96,89 84**
CSF £28.28 TOTE £2.00: £1.10, £6.00; EX 18.40 Trifecta £66.10.
Owner George Strawbridge **Bred** George Strawbridge Jr **Trained** Newmarket, Suffolk

FOCUS
A fair middle-distance maiden, though the winner's task was made easier by a disappointing effort from his market rival. They went a respectable gallop.

52 CORAL H'CAP 1m 3f (F)
2:40 (2:45) (Class 4) (0-80,80) 4-Y-O+ **£5,175** (£1,540; £769; £384) **Stalls** Low

Form RPR
004- **1** **Royal Marskell**[19] 8272 7-9-5 **79**.. TomEaves 1 90
(Gay Kelleway) *trckd ldrs on inner: hdwy and cl up over 2f out: rdn to ld wl over 1f out: drvn clr ent fnl f: readily* **8/1**

02-2 **2** *5* **Ralphy Lad (IRE)**[4] 7 5-9-2 **76**.. JoeFanning 2 79
(Alan Swinbank) *led: pushed along and qcknd 3f out: jnd and rdn 2f out: sn hdd and drvn: kpt on same pce* **15/8**[1]

051- **3** *2 1/4* **Swift Cedar (IRE)**[14] 8344 6-9-0 **77**.............................. PhilipPrince(3) 5 76
(David Evans) *trckd ldrs: cl up 4f out: rdn along over 2f out: sn drvn and kpt on same pce* **5/2**[2]

100- **4** *5* **Ciao Cielo (GER)**[77] 7369 4-9-3 **80**.................................... PhillipMakin 3 70
(David Barron) *t.k.h early: trckd ldrs: hdwy and cl up on outer over 3f out: wd st and sn rdn: drvn wl over 1f out: sn wknd* **11/4**[3]

000- **5** *7* **Gabrial The Terror (IRE)**[178] 4167 6-9-6 **80**.................. TonyHamilton 4 58
(Richard Fahey) *t.k.h early: sn trcking ldr: cl up 5f out: pushed along over 4f out: rdn over 3f out: sn wknd* **9/1**

2m 23.67s (-4.33) **Going Correction** -0.325s/f (Stan)
WFA 4 from 5yo+ 3lb 5 Ran SP% **111.1**
Speed ratings (Par 105): **102,98,96,93,88**
CSF £23.63 TOTE £10.70: £4.20, £1.50; EX 33.40 Trifecta £77.30.
Owner Miss Chantal Wootten **Bred** Miss V Woodward **Trained** Exning, Suffolk

FOCUS
A fair middle-distance handicap. They went a respectable gallop and the winner is rated back to his best..

53 CORAL MOBILE JUST THREE CLICKS TO BET H'CAP 1m 4f (F)
3:10 (3:15) (Class 6) (0-65,65) 4-Y-O+ **£2,264** (£673; £336; £168) **Stalls** Low

Form RPR
501- **1** **Play Nicely**[81] 7258 4-9-4 **63**... PhillipMakin 6 83+
(David Barron) *trckd ldr: led 1/2-way: pushed clr wl over 2f out: unchal* **5/4**[1]

633- **2** *13* **Yulong Xiongba (IRE)**[32] 8107 4-9-5 **64**...................... DougieCostello 2 59
(Julie Camacho) *led to 1/2-way: chsd wnr: rdn along over 3f out: drvn fnl 2f: plugged on* **10/3**[2]

453- **3** *3/4* **Geeaitch**[14] 8345 7-8-13 **54**.. SilvestreDeSousa 1 48
(Peter Hiatt) *trckd ldrs on inner: pushed along 7f out: lost pl and rr 1/2-way: sn swtchd rt to outer and rdn: bhd tl styd on u.p fnl 2f* **10/1**

040- **4** *1/2* **Astra Hall**[42] 7967 7-9-4 **62**...................................(p) AlistairRawlinson(3) 4 55
(Michael Appleby) *hld up: pushed along 1/2-way: rdn in rr over 4f out: plugged on u.p fnl 2f* **14/1**

456- **5** *1* **Vastly (USA)**[21] 8228 7-9-6 **61**......................................(t) AdamBeschizza 3 53
(Julia Feilden) *trckd ldrs: hdwy 5f out: rdn to chse clr ldr 3f out: sn drvn: wknd over 1f out* **7/2**[3]

5- **6** *15* **Social Climber (IRE)**[63] 7686 4-9-2 **64**...............(p) GeorgeDowning(3) 7 32
(Ronald Harris) *t.k.h early: chsd ldng pair: pushed along 1/2-way: sn rdn and lost pl: bhd fr over 3f out* **25/1**

2m 37.0s (-4.00) **Going Correction** -0.325s/f (Stan)
WFA 4 from 7yo 4lb 6 Ran SP% **109.3**
Speed ratings (Par 101): **100,91,90,90,89 79**
CSF £5.27 TOTE £2.20: £1.70, £1.80; EX 6.20 Trifecta £26.90.
Owner Lets Be Lucky Racing 5 **Bred** Susanna Ballinger **Trained** Maunby, N Yorks

FOCUS
A modest middle-distance handicap. They went a decent gallop and the easy winner confirmed the promise of his disqualified run at Redcar.

54 BET&WATCH EVERY RACE AT UNIBET H'CAP 6f (F)
3:40 (3:47) (Class 6) (0-55,55) 4-Y-O+ **£2,726** (£805; £402) **Stalls** Low

Form RPR
532- **1** **Fortinbrass (IRE)**[14] 8346 6-9-5 **53**................................ RobertWinston 7 63
(John Balding) *prom: wd st: rdn to ld 2f out: drvn and kpt on wl fnl f* **11/4**[1]

231- **2** 2 1/4 **Arizona Snow**[7] 8388 4-9-3 **54** 6ex........................(p) GeorgeDowning(3) 5 57
(Ronald Harris) *midfield: hdwy and wd st: effrt on outer over 2f out: rdn to chse ldrs wl over 1f out: kpt on fnl f* **4/1**[2]
002- **3** *nk* **Your Lucky Day**[21] 8241 4-9-7 **55**.............................. SilvestreDeSousa 1 57
(Chris Dwyer) *chsd ldrs on inner: hdwy over 2f out: rdn to chse wnr over 1f out: drvn and no imp fnl f* **11/4**[1]
000- **4** *nk* **Thunderbird**[24] 8203 4-9-1 **49**..(p) KieranO'Neill 8 50
(Scott Dixon) *slt ld: rdn along and hdd 2f out: sn drvn: edgd rt over 1f out: kpt on same pce* **20/1**
500- **5** 2 1/2 **Equilicious**[28] 8145 4-9-4 **52**.. TomEaves 2 46
(Ollie Pears) *chsd ldrs: rdn along and outpcd 1/2-way: kpt on fr over 1f out* **33/1**
066- **6** *hd* **Ciaras Cookie (IRE)**[24] 8196 4-9-2 **50**........................ TonyHamilton 11 43
(Heather Dalton) *chsd ldrs on outer: wd st: rdn over 2f out: sn drvn and kpt on one pce* **16/1**
05-0 **7** 2 1/4 **Divertimenti (IRE)**[3] 25 12-8-9 **48**............................ AaronJones(5) 10 35
(Roy Bowring) *cl up: disp ld 1/2-way: rdn over 2f out: drvn wl over 1f out and grad wknd* **25/1**
/05- **8** 2 1/2 **Tell Me When**[19] 8268 5-8-12 **46** oh1.............................. BarryMcHugh 4 25
(Tony Coyle) *a towards rr* **100/1**
062- **9** 2 3/4 **Artbeat (IRE)**[7] 8388 4-9-1 **49**....................................... AdamBeschizza 3 20+
(Julia Feilden) *s.i.s: a towards rr* **6/1**[3]
00-0 **10** 1 1/2 **Spirit Of Rosanna**[3] 22 4-8-13 **50**..........................(bt1) JackDuern(3) 6 16
(Steph Hollinshead) *a towards rr* **16/1**

1m 15.03s (-1.47) **Going Correction** -0.325s/f (Stan) **10** Ran SP% **111.9**
Speed ratings (Par 101): **96,93,92,92,88 88,85,82,78,76**
CSF £12.56 CT £31.94 TOTE £3.40: £1.10, £2.20, £1.20; EX 13.90 Trifecta £29.00.
Owner Billy Herring **Bred** Tom Wallace **Trained** Scrooby, S Yorks

FOCUS
The concluding contest was a moderate sprint handicap. They went a decent gallop and the winner was fully entitled to take this..
T/Jkpt: £4,733.30. JACKPOT PLACEPOT £260.00. Pool: £2386.37 - 6.70 winning units. T/Plt: £27.70 to a £1 stake. Pool: £67,061.60 - 1764.09 winning units. T/Qpdt: £8.00 to a £1 stake. Pool: £7,357.69 - 677.90 winning units. **Joe Rowntree**

[28]CHELMSFORD (A.W) (L-H)

Wednesday, January 6

OFFICIAL GOING: Polytrack: standard
Wind: virtually nil Weather: overcast

55 TOTEPLACEPOT H'CAP 1m 2f (P)
12:30 (12:30) (Class 6) (0-60,66) 4-Y-O+ **£3,234** (£962; £481; £240) **Stalls** Low

Form RPR
506- **1** **Jethou Island**[19] 8291 5-9-1 **54**..(t) TomEaves 5 60
(David Menuisier) *hld up in tch in midfield: rdn and outpcd over 1f out: rallied to chse clr ldng pair 1f out: styd on to ld wl ins fnl f* **12/1**
415- **2** 1 3/4 **Kristal Hart**[34] 8094 7-9-1 **54**...(p) LiamKeniry 1 57
(Neil Mulholland) *led: jnd and rdn over 2f out: sn kicked clr w rival: edging lft fr over 1f out: hdd and no ex wl ins fnl f* **11/4**[1]
/03- **3** 1/2 **Capelena**[28] 8151 5-9-4 **57**.. StevieDonohoe 2 59
(Miss Joey Ellis) *chsd ldrs: 3rd and outpcd over 2f out: rallied u.p over 1f out: clsng and swtchd rt ins fnl f: kpt on fnl 100yds* **5/1**[3]
006- **4** 1/2 **Sonnythenavigator (USA)**[11] 8360 4-9-2 **57**.............(p) TonyHamilton 9 58
(David Simcock) *hld up in tch in last pair: effrt 2f out: sn drvn and hdwy 1f out: kpt on ins fnl f* **8/1**
001- **5** 1 **Jazri**[10] 8371 5-9-10 **66** 6ex...(b) PhilipPrince(3) 4 65+
(Milton Bradley) *s.i.s: hld up in rr: gd hdwy to join ldr over 3f out: rdn and clr w rival over 2f out: no ex and btn ins fnl f: wknd towards fin* **7/2**[2]
003- **6** 1/2 **Attain**[30] 8134 7-9-4 **60**..(tp) ShelleyBirkett(3) 3 58
(Julia Feilden) *in tch in midfield: outpcd over 2f out: kpt on ins fnl f: no threat to ldrs* **7/2**[2]
/00- **7** 9 **Kuwait Star**[25] 8201 7-9-4 **57**.. LukeMorris 6 38
(Charlie Wallis) *chsd ldr tl over 3f out: rdn and outpcd over 2f out: wknd over 1f out: bhd fnl f* **20/1**
044- **8** 35 **Fen Lady**[15] 8340 4-8-7 **48**... JFEgan 7
(John Berry) *chsd ldrs tl 3f out: lost pl and bhd 2f out: sn eased: t.o* **20/1**
0/0- **P** **Dutchartcollector**[37] 8046 5-9-4 **57**..................................(p) JoeFanning 8
(Tim McCarthy) *in tch in midfield: lost pl over 3f out: sn eased: p.u 2f out* **33/1**

2m 5.06s (-3.54) **Going Correction** -0.325s/f (Stan)
WFA 4 from 5yo+ 2lb **9** Ran SP% **119.0**
Speed ratings (Par 101): **101,99,99,98,98 97,90,62,**
CSF £45.53 CT £194.50 TOTE £17.40: £3.90, £2.00, £2.90; EX 57.00 Trifecta £342.70.
Owner Mrs F A Veasey & Partners **Bred** Mrs F A Veasey **Trained** Pulborough, W Sussex

FOCUS
This was competitive enough for the grade, and the pace was good. The winner was entitled to win this on his best effort for his previous yard.

56 TOTEEXACTA H'CAP 5f (P)
1:00 (1:01) (Class 5) (0-75,75) 4-Y-O+ **£5,175** (£1,540; £769; £384) **Stalls** Low

Form RPR
13-4 **1** **Bosham**[3] 28 6-9-0 **75**...(bt) NathanEvans(7) 7 83
(Michael Easterby) *mde virtually all: rdn over 1f out: hld on wl ins fnl f: all out* **5/1**[3]
030- **2** 1/2 **Saved My Bacon (IRE)**[22] 8242 5-8-13 **67**............. SilvestreDeSousa 3 73
(Chris Dwyer) *blindfold awkward to remove: dwlt and sltly hmpd leaving stalls: outpcd in rr: clsd 1/2-way: swtchd lft and hdwy u.p over 1f out: chsd wnr fnl 100yds: styd on* **9/2**[2]
200- **3** 3/4 **You're Cool**[27] 8170 4-9-5 **73**.. TomEaves 2 76
(James Given) *pushed rt s: in tch in midfield: pushed along 1/2-way: rdn over 1f out: hdwy 1f out: wnt 3rd fnl 100yds: kpt on* **14/1**
010- **4** 1 3/4 **Zipedeedodah (IRE)**[8] 8389 4-9-1 **69**.............................. MartinHarley 1 66
(Joseph Tuite) *wnt rt s: chsd ldrs: unable qck u.p over 1f out: lost 2nd fnl 100yds: wknd towards fin* **8/1**
642- **5** *hd* **Picansort**[18] 8307 9-9-0 **68**... JimmyQuinn 6 64
(Peter Crate) *hld up in last pair: effrt over 1f out: styd on wl u.p ins fnl f: nt rch ldrs* **16/1**
442- **6** *nk* **Borough Boy (IRE)**[8] 8389 6-9-1 **69**............................(v) TonyHamilton 4 64
(Derek Shaw) *wnt lft s: in tch in midfield: effrt on inner over 1f out: no imp and styd on same pce u.p ins fnl f* **2/1**[1]
P33- **7** 1/2 **Mossgo (IRE)**[27] 8170 6-9-5 **73**......................................(t) KierenFox 5 66
(John Best) *in tch in midfield: rdn over 1f out: styd on same pce u.p ins fnl f: nvr trbld ldrs* **8/1**
023- **8** 1 3/4 **Powerful Wind (IRE)**[8] 8389 7-9-7 **75**................................ LukeMorris 8 62
(Charlie Wallis) *racd keenly: chsd ldrs tl no ex u.p over 1f out: wknd ins fnl f* **7/1**

58.37s (-1.83) **Going Correction** -0.325s/f (Stan) **8** Ran SP% **115.5**
Speed ratings (Par 103): **101,100,99,96,95 95,94,91**
CSF £28.01 CT £298.49 TOTE £5.00: £1.30, £1.50, £5.00; EX 31.20 Trifecta £378.90.
Owner Peter Easterby **Bred** Rabbah Bloodstock Limited **Trained** Sheriff Hutton, N Yorks

FOCUS
A competitive handicap run at a sound pace. The winner has been rated to his 6f Wolverhampton win.

57 TOTEQUADPOT H'CAP 5f (P)
1:30 (1:31) (Class 5) (0-75,72) 3-Y-O **£5,175** (£1,540; £769; £384) **Stalls** Low

Form RPR
204- **1** **Dark Side Princess**[30] 8129 3-9-0 **65**....................(p) SilvestreDeSousa 1 74
(Chris Dwyer) *chsd ldrs: effrt and rdn to chse ldr over 1f out: wandered 1f out: sn led and flashed tail u.p: r.o strly: readily* **5/2**[2]
321- **2** 3 3/4 **Krystallite**[16] 8330 3-9-5 **70**.. KieranO'Neill 7 65
(Scott Dixon) *led: rdn wl over 1f out: hdd jst ins fnl f: sn outpcd: hld on for 2nd cl home* **7/2**[3]
102- **3** *hd* **Rosealee (IRE)**[10] 8365 3-9-5 **70**.................................. AdamBeschizza 5 64
(Jeremy Gask) *restless in stalls: dwlt: outpcd in rr: effrt u.p over 1f out: drvn to chse ldng pair 1f out: kpt on but no threat to wnr* **9/4**[1]
153- **4** 3 3/4 **Men United (FR)**[10] 8365 3-9-5 **70**................................ PaulMulrennan 6 51
(James Given) *w ldr tl no ex u.p over 1f out: wknd ins fnl f* **8/1**
364- **5** 1 3/4 **Cool Silk Boy (IRE)**[19] 8282 3-9-7 **72**.................................. TomEaves 3 46
(James Given) *hld up in tch: effrt over 1f out: sn hung lft and btn: bhd ins fnl f* **9/2**

58.97s (-1.23) **Going Correction** -0.325s/f (Stan) **5** Ran SP% **110.9**
Speed ratings (Par 97): **96,90,89,83,80**
CSF £11.53 TOTE £3.10: £2.10, £2.10; EX 8.40 Trifecta £24.20.
Owner M M Foulger **Bred** Qatar Bloodstock Ltd **Trained** Newmarket, Suffolk

FOCUS
The pace was solid for this open handicap and the winner looks progressive.

58 TOTETRIFECTA H'CAP 1m (P)
2:00 (2:01) (Class 4) (0-80,79) 4-Y-O+ **£8,086** (£2,406; £1,202; £601) **Stalls** Low

Form RPR
554- **1** **Loyalty**[10] 8369 9-9-7 **79**..(v) TonyHamilton 5 87
(Derek Shaw) *trckd ldrs and travelled strly: led wl over 1f out: rdn and kpt on fnl f: rdn out* **11/4**[2]
312- **2** 1 **Exceeding Power**[16] 8325 5-9-3 **75**................................ MartinHarley 1 81
(Martin Bosley) *hld up in tch: hdwy 2f out: sn chsng wnr: drvn and kpt on same pce ins fnl f* **5/2**[1]
551- **3** 1 1/4 **Boots And Spurs**[15] 8341 7-9-5 **77**................................(v) LukeMorris 6 80
(Scott Dixon) *chsd ldrs: effrt on inner over 1f out: chsd ldrs and styd on same pce u.p ins fnl f* **6/1**[3]
010- **4** *nk* **Dukes Meadow**[37] 8049 5-8-13 **71**................................... SteveDrowne 7 73
(Roger Ingram) *hld up in tch in last trio: swtchd rt and effrt over 1f out: kpt on ins fnl f: nt rch ldrs* **7/1**
200- **5** 1/2 **Fantasy Gladiator**[16] 8325 10-9-3 **78**.................(p) AlistairRawlinson(3) 3 79
(Michael Appleby) *niggled along in rr: effrt and clsd whn nt clrest of runs ent fnl f: styd on same pce u.p ins fnl f* **10/1**
/06- **6** 4 1/2 **She Loves You**[21] 8247 5-9-0 **72**...................(p) WilliamTwiston-Davies 8 63
(Roger Charlton) *hld up in tch in midfield: effrt and no rspnse over 1f out: wl hld ins fnl f* **14/1**
000- **7** 7 **Baileys En Premier (FR)**[55] 7812 5-8-10 **68**........(b) SilvestreDeSousa 2 43
(Chris Dwyer) *sn bustled along: w ldr tl led 4f out: drvn over 2f out: hdd wl over 1f out: btn and eased ins fnl f* **10/1**
02-3 **8** 20 **Assault On Rome (IRE)**[4] 24 4-9-6 **78**.......................(b) JoeFanning 4 7
(Mark Johnston) *led tl 1/2-way: styd upsides ldr tl over 2f out: sn lost pl: bhd and eased over 1f out: t.o* **7/1**

1m 36.42s (-3.48) **Going Correction** -0.325s/f (Stan) **8** Ran SP% **119.4**
Speed ratings (Par 105): **104,103,101,101,100 96,89,69**
CSF £10.64 CT £38.66 TOTE £2.70: £1.10, £2.00, £2.30; EX 7.60 Trifecta £35.60.
Owner Brian Johnson (Northamptonshire) **Bred** Ecoutila Partnership **Trained** Sproxton, Leics

FOCUS
They went a decent pace for this fair handicap. The form is rated around the second.

59 TOTESWINGER MAIDEN FILLIES' STKS 1m (P)
2:30 (2:31) (Class 4) 3-Y-O+ **£6,469** (£1,925; £962; £481) **Stalls** Low

Form RPR
1 **Nezwaah** 3-8-8 0.. JackMitchell 1 70+
(Roger Varian) *t.k.h: trckd ldrs: pushed along to chal over 1f out: led ins fnl f: r.o wl: pushed out* **8/11**[1]
52- **2** 1 1/2 **Rahyah**[17] 8320 3-8-5 0... NathanAlison(3) 8 67
(William Haggas) *awkward leaving stalls: sn pressing ldr: rdn to ld over 1f out: hdd and styd on same pce ins fnl f* **7/2**[2]
3 3/4 **Capricious Cantor (IRE)** 3-8-8 0........................... SilvestreDeSousa 7 65
(Ed Dunlop) *dwlt: in tch in rr: rdn over 2f out: hdwy on inner over 1f out: pushed along and kpt on wl ins fnl f* **7/1**
02- **4** 3/4 **Primrose Brown**[17] 8314 5-10-0 0....................................... JimmyQuinn 3 68
(Conrad Allen) *hld up in tch: rdn and effrt over 1f out: drvn and kpt on same pce ins fnl f* **33/1**
32- **5** 1 1/4 **Mockinbird (IRE)**[20] 8259 3-8-8 0....................................... LukeMorris 6 61
(Sir Mark Prescott Bt) *chsd ldrs: effrt u.p to chal over 1f out: finding little and hung lft 1f out: wknd fnl 100yds* **9/2**[3]
6 3/4 **Summer Collection (IRE)** 3-8-8 0............................. StevieDonohoe 2 59
(Charles Hills) *hld up in tch in midfield: effrt and unable qck over 1f out: kpt on same pce ins fnl f* **25/1**
7 2 3/4 **Fun Money** 3-8-8 0...[1] NickyMackay 4 53
(Ed Dunlop) *hld up in tch in last pair: rdn and no hdwy over 1f out: styd on same pce and wl hld ins fnl f* **50/1**
4- **8** 14 **Togetherwecan (IRE)**[258] 1612 4-10-0 0............................ JoeFanning 5 24
(Mark Johnston) *led: rdn and hdd over 1f out: sn dropped out and bhd 1f out: wknd fnl f* **33/1**

1m 38.01s (-1.89) **Going Correction** -0.325s/f (Stan)
WFA 3 from 4yo+ 20lb **8** Ran SP% **122.5**
Speed ratings (Par 102): **96,94,93,93,91 91,88,74**
CSF £3.89 TOTE £1.80: £1.10, £1.10, £2.70; EX 4.70 Trifecta £21.30.
Owner Sheikh Ahmed Al Maktoum **Bred** Darley **Trained** Newmarket, Suffolk

FOCUS
A fair maiden run at a steady pace. The winner has the potential to rate higher.

60 TOTEPOOL RACING'S BIGGEST SUPPORTER H'CAP — 7f (P)
3:00 (3:00) (Class 6) (0-55,57) 4-Y-O+ **£3,234** (£962; £481; £240) **Stalls** Low

Form RPR

204- **1** **Mercury**[19] 8292 4-9-7 **55**.....(p) TomEaves 9 61
(Kevin Ryan) *mde all: wnt clr w runner-up over 2f out: drvn and drifted rt fr over 1f out: hld on wl ins fnl f: all out* **8/1**

011- **2** *nk* **Louis Vee (IRE)**[7] 8400 8-9-4 **57** 6ex..... CiaranMckee(5) 7 62
(John O'Shea) *chsd wnr thrght: rdn and wnt clr w wnr over 2f out: drvn and drifting rt fr over 1f out: ev ch ins fnl f: kpt on* **9/2**[3]

445- **3** *1* **Sleet (IRE)**[8] 8388 5-9-3 **51**.....(b) LukeMorris 2 53
(Michael Appleby) *hld up in tch: effrt over 1f out: chsd ldrs and hrd drvn ins fnl f: kpt on* **11/1**

20-2 **4** *hd* **Tasaaboq**[2] 35 5-9-2 **50**.....(bt) SilvestreDeSousa 3 52
(Phil McEntee) *in tch towards rr: hdwy u.p over 1f out: chsd ldrs and swtchd lft 1f out: kpt on* **15/8**[1]

400- **5** *1 ¾* **Little Big Man**[7] 8393 5-9-5 **53**..... StevieDonohoe 4 50
(Brendan Powell) *in tch in midfield: rdn over 2f out: drvn and unable qck over 1f out: styd on same pce ins fnl f* **9/1**

650- **6** *1 ½* **Menelik (IRE)**[7] 8393 7-9-7 **55**.....(bt) KieranO'Neill 8 48
(Des Donovan, Ire) *s.i.s: hld up in rr: effrt on inner over 1f out: no imp ins fnl f: nvr trbld ldrs* **10/1**

422- **7** *¾* **Beggers Luck**[7] 8393 6-9-7 **55**.....(b[1]) KierenFox 5 46
(Eric Wheeler) *chsd ldrs: rdn and outpcd over 2f out: lost 3rd and btn 1f out: wknd fnl f* **4/1**[2]

006- **8** *1* **White Dog (IRE)**[150] 5176 4-9-2 **55**..... AaronJones(5) 6 43
(Eugene Stanford) *niggled along towards rr early: hdwy to chse ldrs 4f out: lost pl 2f out: wknd over 1f out* **20/1**

1m 25.08s (-2.12) **Going Correction** -0.325s/f (Stan) **8 Ran SP% 116.3**
Speed ratings (Par 101): **99,98,97,97,95 93,92,91**
CSF £44.53 CT £403.70 TOTE £9.30: £1.70, £2.10, £2.80; EX 75.40 Trifecta £244.80.
Owner Mrs Angie Bailey **Bred** Park Farm Racing **Trained** Hambleton, N Yorks

FOCUS
A modest handicap. The action unfolded up the centre and the winner posted a minor pb.

61 CELEBRATE ST. PATRICKS DAY AT CCR H'CAP — 1m 5f 66y(P)
3:30 (3:30) (Class 6) (0-65,61) 4-Y-O+ **£3,234** (£962; £481; £240) **Stalls** Low

Form RPR

613- **1** **Coorg (IRE)**[17] 8315 4-8-7 **52**.....(b) SilvestreDeSousa 5 69
(Chris Dwyer) *chsd ldrs: rdn over 6f out: plld lft and rt to keep interested over 5f out: rdn to ld over 3f out: sn clr: eased towards fin* **3/1**[2]

655- **2** *8* **Megara**[28] 8164 4-9-2 **61**.....(p) LukeMorris 1 66
(Sir Mark Prescott Bt) *in tch: rdn over 3f out: chsd clr wnr over 2f out: plugged on but no imp* **6/4**[1]

46-2 **3** *16* **My Tringaling (IRE)**[4] 20 4-8-0 **50**..... AaronJones(5) 2 31
(Stuart Williams) *chsd ldr tl 4f out: sn u.p: 3rd and wknd over 2f out* **10/3**[3]

641- **4** *21* **Coup De Vent**[7] 8397 5-8-13 **58** 6ex..... CiaranMckee(5) 4 8
(John O'Shea) *led tl rdn and hdd over 3f out: sn btn: 4th and wl bhd fnl f: t.o* **9/1**

000- **5** *24* **Heska (IRE)**[11] 8361 5-9-1 **58**.....(tp) AlistairRawlinson(3) 3 +
(Michael Appleby) *v s.i.s and lost many l s: steadily rcvrd and in tch 9f out: rdn 6f out: sn struggling: t.o fnl 3f* **7/1**

2m 47.0s (-6.60) **Going Correction** -0.325s/f (Stan) course record
WFA 4 from 5yo 5lb **5 Ran SP% 110.6**
Speed ratings (Par 101): **107,102,92,79,64**
CSF £8.00 TOTE £2.70: £2.10, £2.30; EX 8.00 Trifecta £16.40.
Owner Mrs C M Goode **Bred** Malih Al Basti **Trained** Newmarket, Suffolk

FOCUS
A moderate staying handicap, but the winner did it well. The first pair came miles clear.
T/Plt: £67.40 to a £1 stake. Pool: £54,833.65 - 593.8 winning units. T/Qpdt: £10.10 to a £1 stake. Pool: £5,748.34 - 418.6 winning units. **Steve Payne**

KEMPTON (A.W) (R-H)
Wednesday, January 6

OFFICIAL GOING: Polytrack: standard

62 32RED CASINO H'CAP — 1m 4f (P)
4:10 (4:11) (Class 6) (0-60,60) 4-Y-O+ **£2,264** (£673; £336; £168) **Stalls** Centre

Form RPR

164- **1** **San Quentin (IRE)**[25] 8209 5-9-10 **60**..... RobertWinston 9 71+
(Dean Ivory) *hld up: pushed along over 2f out: gd hdwy to ld ins fnl f: sn clr* **15/2**

/30- **2** *3 ¼* **Red Dragon (IRE)**[22] 8228 6-9-8 **58**..... MartinHarley 12 63
(Michael Blanshard) *hld up in midfield: hdwy and cl up over 5f out: effrt and ev ch over 1f out to ins fnl f: kpt on: nt pce of wnr* **8/1**

050- **3** *nk* **Master Burbidge**[23] 6412 5-9-0 **50**.....(p) LiamKeniry 3 54+
(Neil Mulholland) *hld up in midfield on ins: effrt and swtchd lft over 2f out: kpt on fnl f: nrst fin* **13/2**[3]

004- **4** *½* **Rennie Mackintosh (IRE)**[18] 8312 4-9-4 **58**..... WilliamCarson 14 62
(John Bridger) *led: rdn and hung lft 2f out: hdd ins fnl f: kpt on same pce* **10/1**

223- **5** *2 ¾* **Bennelong**[7] 8392 10-9-3 **60**.....(b) RhiainIngram(7) 6 59
(Lee Carter) *t.k.h: hld up in tch: rdn over 2f out: hung rt and no ex over 1f out* **6/1**[2]

500- **6** *½* **Toad Corner**[96] 6900 4-9-5 **59**..... TimmyMurphy 7 57
(Mary Hambro) *prom: drvn along over 2f out: no ex over 1f out* **25/1**

0/0- **7** *hd* **Dellbuoy**[42] 4236 7-9-3 **60**.....(t) PaddyBradley(7) 1 58
(Pat Phelan) *hld up: effrt and shkn up over 2f out: kpt on fnl f: nvr nrr* **14/1**

060- **8** *1 ¼* **Pink Lips**[35] 8077 8-8-9 **52**.....(b) CallumShepherd(7) 2 48
(Neil Mulholland) *s.i.s: hld up: rdn over 2f out: sme late hdwy: nvr rchd ldrs* **16/1**

0/0- **9** *2 ½* **Master Dancer**[17] 8317 5-9-7 **60**..... DanielMuscutt(3) 10 52
(Tim Vaughan) *hld up: rdn and effrt on outside over 2f out: sn outpcd: btn over 1f out* **14/1**

032- **10** *4* **Silver Lining (IRE)**[18] 8312 4-9-4 **58**.....(tp) GeorgeBaker 8 44
(Marcus Tregoning) *in tch: effrt and rdn over 2f out: wknd over 1f out* **9/2**[1]

560- **11** *5* **Don Padeja**[15] 8354 6-9-10 **60**..... WilliamTwiston-Davies 5 38
(Ronald Harris) *midfield: drvn and outpcd over 2f out: sn btn* **16/1**

004- **12** *2 ¾* **El Bravo**[16] 8337 10-8-10 **46** oh1..... JFEgan 11 19
(Shaun Harris) *prom: rdn along 3f out: wknd fr 2f out* **20/1**

656- **13** *5* **Tilstarr (IRE)**[20] 7000 6-9-10 **60**.....(p) AdamBeschizza 4 25
(Roger Teal) *hld up in midfield on ins: struggling over 2f out: sn btn* **16/1**

254- **14** *4 ½* **Take Note (IRE)**[21] 8258 4-9-5 **59**.....(p) SteveDrowne 13 17
(Seamus Mullins) *t.k.h early: cl up tl rdn and wknd fr 2f out* **33/1**

2m 35.3s (0.80) **Going Correction** +0.025s/f (Slow)
WFA 4 from 5yo+ 4lb **14 Ran SP% 120.3**
Speed ratings (Par 101): **98,95,95,95,93 93,93,92,90,87 84,82,79,76**
CSF £64.73 CT £418.47 TOTE £8.80: £2.90, £3.00, £2.60; EX 78.60 Trifecta £827.60.
Owner Stephen Louch **Bred** London Thoroughbred Services Ltd **Trained** Radlett, Herts

FOCUS
The track had been power harrowed to a depth of 75mm, returning the surface to standard. A moderate handicap.

63 £10 FREE BET AT 32REDSPORT.COM H'CAP — 1m (P)
4:40 (4:40) (Class 5) (0-70,67) 3-Y-O **£2,911** (£866; £432; £216) **Stalls** Low

Form RPR

064- **1** **Winged Dancer**[9] 8378 3-9-7 **67**..... GeorgeBaker 3 75
(Sylvester Kirk) *hld up in tch: smooth hdwy to ld over 1f out: pushed clr fnl f: comf* **5/1**[2]

520- **2** *3 ¾* **Sky Ferry**[65] 7672 3-8-4 **55**..... PaddyPilley(5) 7 54
(J S Moore) *t.k.h: led: rdn and qcknd over 3f out: hdd over 1f out: kpt on fnl f: nt pce of wnr* **25/1**

540- **3** *nk* **Zoffany's Way (IRE)**[54] 7823 3-8-13 **66**..... GeorgeWood(7) 8 64
(James Fanshawe) *hld up on outside: rdn and hdwy over 2f out: kpt on ins fnl f: nt pce to chal* **17/2**

000- **4** *2* **Night To Remember (IRE)**[28] 8155 3-9-4 **64**.....(b) RichardKingscote 6 58
(Ralph Beckett) *in tch on outside: drvn along over 2f out: rallied: kpt on same pce fnl f* **5/1**[2]

060- **5** *5* **Lady Fontenail**[35] 8076 3-9-3 **63**..... RobertHavlin 2 45
(Rod Millman) *t.k.h: hld up: stdy hdwy over 2f out: effrt and rdn over 1f out: sn outpcd* **50/1**

405- **6** *3* **Weld Al Khawaneej (IRE)**[37] 8055 3-9-4 **64**..... PaulMulrennan 4 39
(Kevin Ryan) *cl up: drvn and outpcd over 2f out: btn over 1f out* **6/1**[3]

000- **7** *1 ¼* **Navajo Storm (IRE)**[28] 8155 3-9-2 **62**..... TonyHamilton 5 34
(Michael Appleby) *t.k.h: hld up in tch: drvn and hung rt over 2f out: sn wknd* **25/1**

1- **8** *11* **Autumn Blossom (USA)**[20] 8266 3-9-7 **67**..... JoeFanning 1 14
(Mark Johnston) *dwlt: t.k.h and sn cl up: rdn over 2f out: wknd qckly wl over 1f out: eased whn btn ins fnl f* **10/11**[1]

1m 40.64s (0.84) **Going Correction** +0.025s/f (Slow) **8 Ran SP% 120.2**
Speed ratings (Par 97): **96,92,91,89,84 81,80,69**
CSF £116.03 CT £1060.19 TOTE £5.90: £1.40, £4.00, £2.50; EX 97.50 Trifecta £1044.10.
Owner J C Smith **Bred** Littleton Stud **Trained** Upper Lambourn, Berks

FOCUS
A modest 3yo handicap, but the winner took it in decisive fashion. The second and third are rated close to form.

64 32RED ON THE APP STORE H'CAP — 1m (P)
5:10 (5:11) (Class 5) (0-70,69) 4-Y-O+ **£2,911** (£866; £432; £216) **Stalls** Low

Form RPR

/26- **1** **Isis Blue**[34] 8092 6-9-2 **69**..... AliceMills(5) 5 78
(Rod Millman) *s.i.s: hld up: smooth hdwy to ld appr fnl f: pushed out* **9/1**

612- **2** *½* **Equleus**[19] 8292 4-9-3 **65**.....(p) MartinLane 4 72
(Jeremy Gask) *prom: drvn and outpcd over 3f out: rallied to chse wnr ins fnl f: kpt on fin* **11/2**

005- **3** *1 ½* **Flying Fantasy**[20] 8263 4-9-4 **66**..... PatCosgrave 2 70
(Stuart Williams) *hld up on ins: stdy hdwy over 2f out: effrt and cl up over 1f out: kpt on same pce ins fnl f* **7/2**[2]

551- **4** *hd* **Exalted (IRE)**[22] 8235 5-8-8 **56**.....(t) JoeFanning 1 60
(William Knight) *t.k.h: sn led: shkn up and rdn 2f out: edgd lft and hdd appr fnl f: kpt on same pce* **11/4**[1]

002- **5** *1 ¾* **Viserion**[23] 8226 4-9-7 **69**.....(p) FergusSweeney 8 69
(David Simcock) *hld up in tch on outside: rdn and outpcd over 2f out: kpt on fnl f: nt pce to chal* **14/1**

621- **6** *13* **Orlando Rogue (IRE)**[28] 8158 4-9-5 **67**.....(p) PaulMulrennan 6 37
(Conor Dore) *sn trcking ldr: rdn over 2f out: wknd over 1f out* **10/1**

044- **7** *10* **Alketios (GR)**[16] 8324 5-9-5 **67**..... GeorgeBaker 3 14
(Gary Moore) *plld hrd: early ldr: cl up tl rdn and wknd qckly over 1f out* **5/1**[3]

323- **8** *1 ¼* **Depth Charge (IRE)**[23] 8226 4-9-6 **68**.....(tp) TonyHamilton 7 12
(Kristin Stubbs) *prom: rdn over 2f out: wknd wl over 1f out* **20/1**

1m 39.4s (-0.40) **Going Correction** +0.025s/f (Slow) **8 Ran SP% 111.5**
Speed ratings (Par 103): **103,102,101,100,99 86,76,74**
CSF £54.54 CT £202.52 TOTE £10.50: £3.00, £1.80, £1.50; EX 69.30 Trifecta £270.70.
Owner Cantay Racing **Bred** Mette Campbell-Andenaes **Trained** Kentisbeare, Devon

FOCUS
A competitive little handicap. The winner was back to his old best.

65 32RED.COM MAIDEN STKS — 1m (P)
5:40 (5:41) (Class 5) 3-Y-O+ **£2,911** (£866; £432; £216) **Stalls** Low

Form RPR

1 **Sam Missile (IRE)** 3-8-5 0..... DanielMuscutt(3) 3 83+
(James Fanshawe) *hld up: rdn over 2f out: gd hdwy to ld appr fnl f: kpt on strly to draw clr fnl f: readily* **3/1**[2]

2 *6* **Bartok (IRE)** 3-8-8 0..... RobertHavlin 7 69+
(John Gosden) *s.i.s: t.k.h and sn in midfield: hdwy over 2f out: rdn and chal briefly appr fnl f: edgd rt: no ch w wnr* **11/8**[1]

04- **3** *1 ¼* **Ubla (IRE)**[20] 8259 3-8-8 0.....(b) FergusSweeney 8 66
(Hugo Palmer) *t.k.h: led: qcknd over 2f out: hdd appr fnl f: kpt on same pce* **7/1**

062- **4** *nk* **Fire And Passion**[25] 8211 4-10-0 73.....(p) MartinLane 4 69
(Jeremy Gask) *chsd ldrs: drvn and outpcd over 2f out: kpt on fnl f: no imp* **6/1**[3]

300- **5** *7* **Debit**[29] 8148 5-10-0 62..... RyanClark 2 53
(Simon Hodgson) *t.k.h early: cl up: rdn over 2f out: wknd over 1f out* **100/1**

6 *nse* **Betsalottie** 3-8-8 0..... WilliamCarson 6 49
(John Bridger) *hld up: shkn up and outpcd over 2f out: no imp after* **100/1**

6- **7** *6* **Spinning Rose**[28] 8151 4-9-9 0..... PatCosgrave 1 34
(Dean Ivory) *s.i.s: t.k.h on ins: outpcd 3f out: btn fnl 2f* **16/1**

0- **8** *1 ¾* **Eljaddaaf (IRE)**[53] 7864 5-9-7 0..... PaulBooth(7) 10 35
(Dean Ivory) *t.k.h: cl up tl rdn and wknd fr 2f out* **100/1**

0- **9** *8* **Dynamo (IRE)**[28] 8151 5-10-0 0..... TimmyMurphy 5 17
(Richard Hughes) *s.i.s: bhd and sn detached: nvr on terms* **66/1**

10 *33* **Blanco (USA)** 3-8-8 0....................(t) LukeMorris 11
(Paul Cole) *hld up: pushed along over 3f out: wknd fnl 2f: t.o* **8/1**

1m 39.26s (-0.54) **Going Correction** +0.025s/f (Slow)
WFA 3 from 4yo+ 20lb **10** Ran SP% **115.3**
Speed ratings (Par 103): **103,97,95,95,88 88,82,80,72,39**
CSF £7.42 TOTE £4.00: £1.40, £1.10, £2.70; EX 9.00 Trifecta £40.30.
Owner Apple Tree Stud **Bred** Barronstown Stud **Trained** Newmarket, Suffolk

FOCUS
An ordinary maiden on paper, and lacking depth, but the winner looks useful.

66 32REDSPORT.COM H'CAP 1m 4f (P)
6:10 (6:13) (Class 4) (0-85,84) 4-Y-O+ **£4,690** (£1,395; £697; £348) **Stalls** Centre

Form RPR
062- **1** **Giantstepsahead (IRE)**[17] 8318 7-9-5 **82**................ DanielMuscutt(3) 2 91
(Brian McMath) *led at modest gallop: rdn and hdd over 1f out: rallied and regained ld ins fnl f: hld on gamely* **16/1**
054- **2** *nk* **Jolievitesse (FR)**[28] 8157 4-8-9 **73**.................... JoeyHaynes 8 81
(K R Burke) *t.k.h: hld up in tch: hdwy to dispute ld over 1f out: rdn and kpt on fnl f: hld nr fin* **6/1**[3]
414/ **3** *1 ¼* **Music Man (IRE)**[690] 623 6-9-3 **77**.................... SeanLevey 3 83
(Jo Crowley) *hld up in midfield: rdn and hdwy to ld over 1f out: hdd ins fnl f: no ex towards fin* **33/1**
612- **4** *3 ¼* **Cahill (IRE)**[36] 8064 4-8-8 **79**....................(p) GeorgiaCox(7) 4 80
(Alan King) *prom on ins: drvn and outpcd 3f out: edgd lft and rallied fnl f: nt rch first three* **13/2**
512- **5** *nk* **Robins Pearl (FR)**[23] 8227 4-8-11 **75**.................... LukeMorris 7 75
(Harry Dunlop) *hld up: rdn along over 2f out: hdwy over 1f out: no imp ins fnl f* **12/1**
000- **6** *2* **Spiritoftomintoul**[49] 7893 7-9-5 **79**....................(t) TomQueally 12 76
(Tony Carroll) *s.i.s: hld up in rr: hdwy on outside over 2f out: no imp fr over 1f out* **25/1**
352- **7** *½* **Royal Warranty**[28] 8157 5-9-8 **82**.................... OisinMurphy 10 78
(Andrew Balding) *hld up: rdn along over 2f out: sme hdwy over 1f out: nvr able to chal* **9/2**[2]
342- **8** *2 ½* **Troopingthecolour**[23] 8222 10-9-0 **77**....................(tp) RobHornby(3) 9 69
(Steve Gollings) *hld up: drvn and outpcd on outside wl over 2f out: n.d after* **16/1**
651- **9** *1* **Jamhoori**[23] 8222 8-9-4 **78**.................... MartinLane 11 69
(Jeremy Gask) *prom: drvn and lost pl over 2f out: sn wknd* **25/1**
2U1- **10** *hd* **U S Navy Seal (USA)**[16] 8327 4-9-6 **84**.................... AdamKirby 5 74
(J R Jenkins) *t.k.h: hld up in midfield: effrt and hdwy over 2f out: wknd over 1f out* **9/2**[2]
363- **11** *3 ¼* **Serena Grae**[34] 8093 5-9-8 **82**.................... GeorgeBaker 6 67
(Marcus Tregoning) *cl up: rdn over 2f out: wknd wl over 1f out* **7/2**[1]
1/0- **12** *28* **Yeats Magic (IRE)**[236] 2240 4-9-6 **84**.................... RobertHavlin 1 24
(Ronald Harris) *prom: drvn along over 2f out: sn wknd: eased whn btn fnl f* **50/1**

2m 32.73s (-1.77) **Going Correction** +0.025s/f (Slow)
WFA 4 from 5yo+ 4lb **12** Ran SP% **118.3**
Speed ratings (Par 105): **106,105,104,102,102 101,100,99,98,98 96,77**
JACKPOT: Not won. Pool of £2,480 carried forward. JACKPOT PLACEPOT: £159.00. Pool: £2,679 - 12.3 winning units. CSF £105.28 CT £3141.38 TOTE £9.90: £2.30, £2.60, £9.80; EX 148.70 Trifecta £5502.40 Part won..
Owner K Hills **Bred** Darragh O'Reilly **Trained** Newmarket, Suffolk

FOCUS
The first three finished nicely clear in this fair handicap and another personal best from the winner.

67 GOOD LUCK ON YOUR ADVENTURE GREG H'CAP 7f (P)
6:40 (6:40) (Class 5) (0-75,75) 4-Y-O+ **£1,888** (£1,888; £432; £216) **Stalls** Low

Form RPR
546- **1** **Light From Mars**[16] 8331 11-9-4 **72**....................(p) LukeMorris 8 79
(Ronald Harris) *hld up in midfield: hdwy 2f out: rdn to ld ins fnl f: kpt on: jnd on line* **10/1**
231- **1** *dht* **Dutch Golden Age (IRE)**[35] 8075 4-9-6 **74**....................(t) GeorgeBaker 4 81+
(Gary Moore) *hld up on ins: effrt and hdwy 2f out: drvn and kpt on wl fnl f to dead-heat on line* **5/2**[1]
1/0- **3** *1 ¼* **Rightway (IRE)**[360] 125 5-9-4 **75**.................... GeorgeDowning(3) 3 79
(Tony Carroll) *checked s: hld up: pushed along and outpcd over 2f out: gd hdwy fnl f: nrst fin* **33/1**
423- **4** *hd* **Alhella**[21] 8248 4-9-6 **74**.................... MartinHarley 7 77
(William Knight) *led: rdn over 2f out: hdd ins fnl f: kpt on same pce* **15/2**
050- **5** *hd* **Robero**[37] 8049 4-8-13 **72**.................... PaddyPilley(5) 1 74
(John E Long) *t.k.h early: cl up: rdn over 2f out: kpt on same pce ins fnl f* **6/1**[2]
454- **6** *1* **Brazen Spirit**[54] 7828 4-9-6 **74**.................... AdamKirby 10 74
(Clive Cox) *cl up: rdn over 2f out: edgd lft and no ex ins fnl f* **10/1**
402- **7** *2 ¼* **Mac's Power (IRE)**[9] 8376 10-8-7 **61**.................... JFEgan 5 55
(Willie Musson) *hld up in tch: effrt and edgd rt 2f out: outpcd fnl f* **7/1**[3]
204- **8** *3* **Shamlan (IRE)**[16] 8333 4-9-4 **72**.................... StevieDonohoe 9 58
(Kevin Frost) *bhd: struggling and detached 1/2-way: kpt on fnl f: nvr on terms* **14/1**
236- **9** *2 ¼* **Hercullian Prince**[16] 8336 4-9-5 **73**....................(p) PaulMulrennan 6 53
(Conor Dore) *prom: rdn and edgd rt over 2f out: wknd over 1f out* **8/1**
400- **10** *nk* **First Experience**[21] 8247 5-9-4 **72**.................... CathyGannon 2 51
(Lee Carter) *hmpd s: bhd and pushed along: struggling over 2f out: sn btn* **11/1**

1m 26.32s (0.32) **Going Correction** +0.025s/f (Slow) **10** Ran SP% **114.4**
Speed ratings (Par 103): **99,99,97,97,97 95,93,89,87,87**
WIN: 1.60 Dutch Golden Age, 4.40 Light From Mars; PL: 6.80 Rightway, 3.10 Dutch Golden Age, 3.00 Light From Mars; EX: 16.60, 22.50; CSF: 14.02, 17.26; TC: 336.16, 412.27; TF: 316.80, 580.50;.
Owner Mrs N Macauley **Bred** Harts Farm And Stud **Trained** Earlswood, Monmouths
Owner R A Green **Bred** Denis Bergin **Trained** Lower Beeding, W Sussex

FOCUS
There was a bunched finish to this fair handicap and the judge couldn't split the first two.

68 RACING UK ANYWHERE H'CAP 6f (P)
7:10 (7:10) (Class 6) (0-65,65) 4-Y-O+ **£2,264** (£673; £336; £168) **Stalls** Low

Form RPR
003- **1** **Chetan**[34] 8095 4-9-0 **58**....................(tp) LukeMorris 7 66
(Charlie Wallis) *trckd ldrs: rdn over 2f out: led ins fnl f: kpt on strly* **5/1**[1]
360- **2** *1 ¼* **Gold Beau (FR)**[37] 8051 6-9-7 **65**....................(p) CathyGannon 3 69
(Kristin Stubbs) *in tch: rdn over 2f out: hdwy and ev ch ins fnl f: sn chsng wnr: kpt on* **11/1**[3]
454- **3** *nk* **Welease Bwian (IRE)**[21] 8254 7-9-0 **65**....................(be) MillyNaseb(7) 5 68
(Stuart Williams) *t.k.h: in tch: hdwy on outside to ld 2f out: edgd rt and hdd ins fnl f: no ex* **5/1**[1]
050- **4** *½* **Nasri**[72] 7513 10-9-3 **61**.................... TomQueally 8 63
(Emma Owen) *disp ld to 2f out: sn rdn: kpt on same pce ins fnl f* **16/1**
515- **5** *1* **Only Ten Per Cent (IRE)**[22] 8236 8-9-1 **62**......... AlistairRawlinson(3) 4 61
(J R Jenkins) *dwlt: hld up: pushed along and hdwy whn n.m.r briefly over 1f out: kpt on ins fnl f: no imp* **15/2**[2]
165- **6** *shd* **Divine Call**[78] 7363 9-9-2 **60**....................(b) PatCosgrave 1 59+
(Milton Bradley) *hld up on ins: drvn and outpcd 1/2-way: hdwy fnl f: nrst fin* **5/1**[1]
000- **7** *nse* **Rialto Magic**[15] 8351 4-9-0 **58**....................(p) TimmyMurphy 9 56
(Jamie Osborne) *dwlt: hld up on outside: drvn and outpcd over 2f out: plugged on fnl f: no imp* **33/1**
314- **8** *1* **Blackthorn Stick (IRE)**[35] 8078 7-8-13 **57**.................... JimmyQuinn 6 52
(Paul Burgoyne) *hld up: pushed along and effrt 2f out: no imp fnl f* **5/1**[1]
122- **9** *nk* **Triple Dream**[21] 8255 11-9-1 **62**.................... PhilipPrince(3) 2 57
(Milton Bradley) *slt ld to 2f out: sn rdn: wknd ins fnl f* **5/1**[1]
000- **10** *3 ¾* **Sakhee's Rose**[21] 8248 6-9-7 **65**....................(b) SeanLevey 12 48
(Ed McMahon) *t.k.h: hld up: pushed along and shortlived effrt 2f out: wknd fnl f* **16/1**

1m 12.56s (-0.54) **Going Correction** +0.025s/f (Slow) **10** Ran SP% **118.1**
Speed ratings (Par 101): **104,102,101,101,99 99,99,98,98,93**
CSF £62.85 CT £292.21 TOTE £5.30: £1.70, £3.60, £2.20; EX 55.80 Trifecta £282.00.
Owner Roger & Val Miles, Tony Stamp **Bred** Andrew W Robson **Trained** Ardleigh, Essex

FOCUS
An open sprint.
T/Jkpt: Not won. JACKPOT PLACEPOT: £159.00. Pool: £2,679.00 - 12.3 winning units. T/Plt: £1,429.30 to a £1 stake. Pool: £81,847.28 - 41.80 winning units. T/Qpdt: £28.70 to a £1 stake. Pool: £12,354.12 - 317.80 winning units. **Richard Young**

[35]WOLVERHAMPTON (A.W) (L-H)
Wednesday, January 6

OFFICIAL GOING: Tapeta: standard
Wind: light 1/2 behind Weather: fine

69 £10 FREE AT 32RED.COM APPRENTICE H'CAP 1m 4f 50y (Tp)
12:50 (12:50) (Class 6) (0-65,64) 3-Y-O **£2,716** (£808; £404; £202) **Stalls** Low

Form RPR
053- **1** **Whitecliff Park (IRE)**[26] 8177 3-8-11 **59**................ CallumShepherd(5) 1 64
(Brian Ellison) *trckd ldng pair: effrt over 3f out: 2nd over 1f out: led 1f out: drvn out* **1/1**[1]
004- **2** *1 ½* **Frivolous Prince (IRE)**[26] 8177 3-8-0 **46**.................... NoelGarbutt(3) 4 49
(David Evans) *t.k.h: trckd ldr: shkn up over 4f out: led briefly over 1f out: kpt on same pce* **7/4**[2]
020- **3** *3 ¾* **Lady President (IRE)**[26] 8177 3-8-0 **48**............... JosephineGordon(5) 2 45
(J S Moore) *set stdy pce: qcknd gallop over 3f out: hdd over 1f out: grad wknd* **13/2**[3]
0- **4** *3* **Rajapur**[15] 8349 3-9-0 **64**.................... RossTurner(7) 3 56
(Philip Kirby) *rrd s: racd in last but wl in tch: outpcd over 3f out: one pce fnl 2f* **11/1**

2m 44.45s (3.65) **Going Correction** 0.0s/f (Stan) **4** Ran SP% **108.0**
Speed ratings (Par 95): **87,86,83,81**
CSF £3.00 TOTE £1.70; EX 2.50 Trifecta £4.00.
Owner D Gilbert, M Lawrence, A Bruce **Bred** Rosetown Bloodstock Ltd **Trained** Norton, N Yorks

FOCUS
The opening contest was a modest apprentice riders' 3yo middle-distance handicap. They went an ordinary gallop until about 3f out on standard Tapeta. The winner looks ready to rate a bit higher.

70 32RED CASINO H'CAP 1m 1f 103y (Tp)
1:20 (1:20) (Class 5) (0-75,74) 3-Y-O **£3,234** (£962; £481; £240) **Stalls** Low

Form RPR
443- **1** **Artful Mind**[23] 8224 3-9-1 **68**.................... GrahamLee 6 73+
(James Unett) *hld up in rr: hdwy over 2f out: led over 1f out: pushed clr: readily* **9/2**[3]
036- **2** *3 ¼* **Repeat Offender (IRE)**[35] 8080 3-8-10 **70**........(p) JosephineGordon(7) 4 69
(J S Moore) *chsd ldr: drvn over 3f out: kpt on same pce fnl f* **14/1**
546- **3** *nk* **Trespassed (IRE)**[22] 8234 3-9-2 **69**....................(p) PatCosgrave 3 67
(William Haggas) *chsd ldrs: reminders over 2f out: one pce over 1f out* **13/8**[1]
601- **4** *¾* **Sark (IRE)**[64] 7692 3-9-5 **72**.................... AdamKirby 5 68
(David Evans) *chsd ldrs: shkn up 6f out and over 4f out: swtchd rt over 1f out: kpt on towards fin* **3/1**[2]
135- **5** *½* **Holiday Henry (USA)**[11] 8358 3-8-9 **62**....................(v) BarryMcHugh 2 57
(Richard Fahey) *led: qcknd pce over 3f out: edgd rt and hdd over 1f out: one pce* **6/1**
015- **6** *1 ¼* **Khismet**[35] 8080 3-9-2 **74**....................(p) CharlesEddery(5) 1 67
(Rae Guest) *s.s: hld up in rr: t.k.h: drvn 3f out: chsng ldrs over 1f out: one pce: n.m.r and eased towards fin* **16/1**

2m 1.42s (0.62) **Going Correction** 0.0s/f (Stan) **6** Ran SP% **108.1**
Speed ratings (Par 97): **97,94,93,93,92 91**
CSF £53.42 TOTE £4.20: £2.50, £5.80; EX 58.70 Trifecta £187.50.
Owner Northern Line Racing Ltd **Bred** Mill House Stud **Trained** Wolverhampton, West Midlands

FOCUS
A fair 3yo handicap. They went a muddling gallop and the level of the form is set around the third.

71 32REDSPORT.COM H'CAP 2m 119y (Tp)
1:50 (1:50) (Class 6) (0-60,65) 4-Y-O+ **£2,587** (£770; £384; £192) **Stalls** Low

Form RPR
01- **1** **Mr Boss Man (IRE)**[7] 8403 8-10-4 **65** 6ex.................... PatCosgrave 6 72
(Adrian McGuinness, Ire) *hld up in mid-div: hdwy 8f out: 2nd over 1f out: hung rt: styd on to ld nr fin* **7/4**[1]
310/ **2** *½* **Pass The Time**[25] 278 7-9-8 **55**....................(p) AdamKirby 9 61
(Neil Mulholland) *chsd ldr: led over 2f out: hdd and no ex nr fin* **11/4**[2]
443- **3** *2* **Maple Stirrup (IRE)**[21] 8249 4-8-8 **55**.................... PaulaMuir(7) 8 59
(Patrick Holmes) *dwlt: hld up in rr: hdwy 5f out: styd on over 1f out: tk 3rd nr fin* **9/1**
000- **4** *nk* **Sail With Sultana**[71] 7543 5-9-5 **52**.................... GrahamLee 1 56
(Mark Rimell) *dwlt: in rr: hdwy over 2f out: kpt on same pce to take 4th last 100yds* **33/1**
660- **5** *2 ¾* **Yorkshireman (IRE)**[32] 8121 6-9-4 **51**.................... JoeyHaynes 3 51
(Lynn Siddall) *chsd ldrs: drvn 4f out: one pce fnl 2f* **9/1**

/05- **6** 2 **Lord Aratan (GER)**[15] 8343 9-9-0 **47** JackGarritty 2 45
(Patrick Holmes) *s.i.s: hld up in rr: hdwy 5f out: n.m.r on inner 2f out: sn wknd* **50/1**

053- **7** 4 1/2 **Castle Talbot (IRE)**[8] 8385 4-9-5 **59** (p) ShaneKelly 5 52
(Richard Hughes) *led: hdd over 2f out: lost pl over 1f out: lame* **10/3**[3]

000- **8** 2 3/4 **Madrasa (IRE)**[81] 7293 8-9-5 **55** (b) RobHornby(3) 4 44
(Tony Forbes) *mid-div: hdwy to trck ldrs 8f out: drvn over 2f out: wknd over 1f out* **25/1**

400- **9** 59 **Harps Of Bretagne**[7] 8403 4-8-0 **45** ShirleyTeasdale(5) 7
(Lisa Williamson) *chsd ldrs: pushed along over 5f out: lost pl over 4f out: sn wl bhd: t.o over 2f out: eventually completed* **200/1**

3m 42.13s (-1.57) **Going Correction** 0.0s/f (Stan)
WFA 4 from 5yo+ 7lb **9** Ran SP% **115.4**
Speed ratings (Par 101): **103,102,101,101,100 99,97,96,68**
CSF £6.54 CT £32.03 TOTE £2.40: £1.02, £1.90, £2.60; EX 6.60 Trifecta £45.70.
Owner Camillus Slevin **Bred** W Tanner **Trained** Lusk, Co Dublin

FOCUS
A modest staying handicap. They went a respectable gallop. The winner stepped up on his recent course win.

72 EBF 32RED.COM FILLIES' H'CAP 1m 141y (Tp)
2:20 (2:20) (Class 3) (0-95,91) 4-Y-O+ **£10,396** (£3,111; £1,555; £778; £387) **Stalls** Low

Form RPR

341- **1** **Oakley Girl**[54] 7826 4-9-0 **82** OisinMurphy 6 98
(Stuart Williams) *hld up in rr: hdwy 3f out: drvn to ld over 1f out: forged wl clr: eased towards fin* **9/4**[1]

003- **2** 6 **Stosur (IRE)**[21] 8256 5-9-0 **81** (b) GrahamLee 4 83
(Gay Kelleway) *led after 1f: hdd over 2f out: kpt on to take modest 2nd clsng stages* **11/1**

40-2 **3** nk **Boonga Roogeta**[3] 33 7-7-13 **73** JosephineGordon(7) 5 74
(Peter Charalambous) *chsd ldrs: led over 2f out: hdd over 1f out: kpt on same pce* **5/2**[2]

200- **4** 1 1/2 **Maiden Approach**[30] 8140 5-8-12 **79** JackGarritty 2 77
(Richard Fahey) *led 1f: chsd ldrs: drvn over 3f out: one pce fnl 2f* **25/1**

032- **5** 1/2 **Kalon Brama (IRE)**[10] 8369 5-8-6 **76** ow2 MarcMonaghan(3) 1 73
(Peter Charalambous) *in rr: drvn 4f out: kpt on over 1f out: nvr a factor* **9/1**

000- **6** 1 **Amaze Me**[53] 7857 4-9-9 **91** AdamKirby 8 85
(Robyn Brisland) *in rr: pushed along over 4f out: kpt on fnl 150yds: nvr on terms* **12/1**

1/1- **7** 1/2 **Miss Understood (IRE)**[20] 8261 4-8-9 **77** MartinLane 3 70
(David Simcock) *chsd ldrs: effrt over 3f out: lost pl over 1f out* **7/2**[3]

1m 48.1s (-2.00) **Going Correction** 0.0s/f (Stan)
WFA 4 from 5yo+ 1lb **7** Ran SP% **111.4**
Speed ratings (Par 104): **108,102,102,101,100 99,99**
CSF £25.72 CT £63.16 TOTE £2.90: £2.50, £5.10; EX 20.30 Trifecta £59.70.
Owner The Parry's **Bred** Mrs Sarah Hamilton **Trained** Newmarket, Suffolk

FOCUS
The feature contest was a decent fillies' handicap won by an unexposed type. They went an even gallop.

73 CORAL.CO.UK H'CAP 1m 1f 103y (Tp)
2:50 (2:50) (Class 4) (0-85,86) 4-Y-O+ **£4,851** (£1,443; £721; £360) **Stalls** Low

Form RPR

634- **1** **Perfect Cracker**[47] 7924 8-9-7 **83** AdamKirby 6 92
(Clive Cox) *hld up in mid-div: t.k.h: hdwy to trck ldrs over 2f out: led over 1f out: edgd lft and styd on: drvn out* **7/2**[1]

403- **2** 3/4 **Off The Pulse**[16] 8336 6-8-13 **75** (p) GrahamLee 3 82
(John Mackie) *trckd ldrs: t.k.h: kpt on same pce fnl 100yds* **9/2**[3]

115- **3** 3/4 **Idol Deputy (FR)**[40] 8016 10-8-9 **76** (p) RachealKneller(5) 8 82
(James Bennett) *in rr: effrt 3f out: hdwy on outside over 1f out: hung lft and kpt on wl fnl 150yds* **9/1**

560- **4** 1 1/4 **Gabrial The Duke (IRE)**[137] 5630 6-9-6 **82** (b) JackGarritty 7 85
(Richard Fahey) *s.i.s: in rr: styd on appr fnl f: nt rch ldrs* **8/1**

000- **5** 1/2 **Lawyer (IRE)**[7] 8405 5-9-1 **77** PhillipMakin 1 79
(David Barron) *t.k.h: led: hdd over 1f out: fdd last 75yds* **4/1**[2]

005- **6** 1 **Lostock Hall (IRE)**[17] 8318 4-8-10 **73** (p) JoeyHaynes 9 73
(K R Burke) *jnd ldr after 1f: drvn 3f out: fdd fnl 100yds* **4/1**[2]

060- **7** 5 **Tee It Up Tommo (IRE)**[23] 7908 7-8-11 **73** (t) ShaneKelly 2 63
(Sheena West) *mid-div: drvn 3f out: wknd appr fnl f* **25/1**

306- **8** 5 **Mr Frankie**[32] 8118 5-8-10 **72** ShaneGray 4 51
(Richard Phillips) *chsd ldrs: drvn over 3f out: lost pl over 2f out* **12/1**

2m 0.9s (0.10) **Going Correction** 0.0s/f (Stan)
WFA 4 from 5yo+ 1lb **8** Ran SP% **113.1**
Speed ratings (Par 105): **99,98,97,96,96 95,90,86**
CSF £18.94 CT £127.73 TOTE £3.90: £1.50, £2.30, £3.10; EX 10.50 Trifecta £91.00.
Owner Mildmay Racing **Bred** Mildmay Bloodstock Ltd **Trained** Lambourn, Berks

FOCUS
Another decent handicap with the first two both on good marks. They went a slightly muddling gallop.

74 LADBROKES MEDIAN AUCTION MAIDEN STKS 7f 32y (Tp)
3:20 (3:22) (Class 6) 3-5-Y-O **£2,587** (£770; £384; £192) **Stalls** High

Form RPR

202- **1** **Bank Of Gibraltar**[16] 8327 4-9-12 80 ShaneKelly 2 86
(Richard Hughes) *mde all: t.k.h: increased pce over 3f out: drvn clr over 1f out: edgd rt: unchal* **6/5**[1]

2- **2** 3 3/4 **Andaz**[22] 8232 3-8-3 0 ShaneGray 1 67
(Roger Varian) *s.i.s: t.k.h: sn trcking ldrs: 2nd 3f out: sn drvn: no imp* **6/5**[1]

665- **3** 8 **Zebedee's Girl (IRE)**[19] 8287 3-7-10 65 JosephineGordon(7) 3 45
(David Evans) *in rr but wl in tch: drvn 3f out: clr 3rd over 1f out: one pce* **8/1**[2]

4- **4** 2 1/4 **Sayeuri**[20] 8268 4-9-7 0 (t) SaleemGolam 5 43
(Rae Guest) *in rr but wl in tch: drvn over 3f out: wknd appr fnl f* **25/1**[3]

0- **5** 29 **Womble**[19] 8287 3-8-3 0 NoelGarbutt(3) 6
(Laura Young) *uns rdr and rn loose bef s: racd wd: t.k.h: sn trcking ldrs: drvn over 3f out: lost pl and bhd over 2f out: sn t.o* **250/1**

1m 28.23s (-0.57) **Going Correction** 0.0s/f (Stan)
WFA 3 from 4yo 18lb **5** Ran SP% **106.3**
Speed ratings (Par 101): **103,98,89,87,53**
CSF £2.57 TOTE £2.00: £1.30, £1.10; EX 3.10 Trifecta £4.80.
Owner Richard Hughes **Bred** Haras D'Haspel **Trained** Upper Lambourn, Berkshire

FOCUS
A fair maiden, but basically a match. They went a decent gallop.

75 DOWNLOAD THE NEW UNIBET RACING APP H'CAP 5f 20y (Tp)
3:50 (3:50) (Class 6) (0-65,65) 4-Y-O+ **£2,587** (£770; £384; £192) **Stalls** Low

Form RPR

654- **1** **Ohsosecret**[18] 8307 4-9-3 **61** (t) SaleemGolam 7 67
(Stuart Williams) *chsd ldr: edgd rt and kpt on fnl f: led last 50yds: all out* **9/4**[1]

622- **2** hd **Major Muscari (IRE)**[21] 8254 8-9-4 **62** GrahamLee 8 67
(Shaun Harris) *trckd ldrs: effrt over 1f out: styd on wl to take 2nd last 50yds: jst failed* **7/2**[2]

634- **3** 1 **Frank The Barber (IRE)**[19] 8289 4-8-7 **54** (bt) JackDuern(3) 4 56
(Steph Hollinshead) *led early: trckd ldrs: swtchd lft and chal on bit appr fnl f: shkn up and kpt on same pce fnl 100yds* **9/2**[3]

214- **4** nse **Fine 'n Dandy (IRE)**[20] 8271 5-9-7 **65** DougieCostello 5 67
(J R Jenkins) *sn led: hung rt over 1f out: hdd last 50yds: no ex* **5/1**

300- **5** 2 **Your Gifted (IRE)**[7] 8399 9-9-5 **63** (v) RaulDaSilva 3 57
(Lisa Williamson) *s.i.s: in rr: kpt on fnl f: nvr a factor* **12/1**

050- **6** 2 **Seraphima**[7] 8401 6-8-2 **51** oh6 (p) ShirleyTeasdale(5) 6 38
(Lisa Williamson) *in rr: nvr a factor* **40/1**

603- **7** 1 1/2 **Give Us A Belle (IRE)**[7] 8399 7-8-12 **59** (vt) EoinWalsh(3) 2 41
(Christine Dunnett) *mid-div: drvn and outpcd over 3f out: lost pl over 1f out* **11/2**

1m 1.54s (-0.36) **Going Correction** 0.0s/f (Stan) **7** Ran SP% **113.4**
Speed ratings (Par 101): **102,101,100,100,96 93,91**
CSF £10.11 CT £31.21 TOTE £3.70: £2.80, £1.10; EX 13.20 Trifecta £44.80.
Owner The Secretly Hopeful Partnership **Bred** Park Farm Racing **Trained** Newmarket, Suffolk

FOCUS
The concluding contest was a modest sprint handicap. They went a proper gallop and the principals are rated close to their recent best.
T/Plt: £52.40 to a £1 stake. Pool: £37,784.27 - 526.07 winning units. T/Qpdt: £3.60 to a £1 stake. Pool: £5,912.31 - 1190.84 winning units. **Walter Glynn**

[55]CHELMSFORD (A.W) (L-H)
Thursday, January 7

OFFICIAL GOING: Polytrack: standard
Wind: medium. half behind Weather: dry

76 PLAY SCOOP6SOCCER EVERY WEEK CLASSIFIED CLAIMING STKS 6f (P)
5:10 (5:10) (Class 6) 4-Y-O+ **£3,234** (£962; £481; £240) **Stalls** Centre

Form RPR

303- **1** **Ocean Legend (IRE)**[22] 8250 11-8-11 70 CathyGannon 2 73
(Tony Carroll) *chsd ldrs: effrt on inner over 1f out: rdn to ld ent fnl f: styd on wl* **3/1**[2]

000- **2** 1/2 **Swiss Cross**[7] 8412 9-8-8 72 JosephineGordon(7) 3 75
(Phil McEntee) *in tch in midfield: effrt to press ldrs and edging lft over 1f out: chsd wnr ins fnl f: kpt on* **5/1**

643- **3** 2 1/4 **Elusivity (IRE)**[10] 8382 8-9-3 72 JFEgan 1 70
(Conor Dore) *led: rdn over 1f out: hdd ent fnl f: no ex and outpcd fnl 75yds* **7/2**[3]

005- **4** 1 3/4 **Galvanize**[16] 8351 5-8-9 59 (be[1]) BarryMcHugh 5 57
(Noel Wilson) *blindfold stuck in blinkers and s.i.s: in tch: effrt over 1f out: no ex u.p 1f out: kpt on same pce fnl 100yds* **33/1**

036- **5** 2 1/2 **Thataboy (IRE)**[17] 8333 5-9-3 72 TomQueally 4 57
(Tom Dascombe) *chsd ldr tl over 1f out: hung lft and wknd ins fnl f* **5/2**[1]

000- **6** 3 1/2 **Grosmont**[30] 8148 4-8-8 62 (p) TomEaves 6 36
(James Given) *a in rr: rdn and outpcd 1/2-way: n.d after* **20/1**

000- **7** 1 1/4 **New Leyf (IRE)**[17] 8331 10-8-7 72 (b) MartinLane 7 31
(Jeremy Gask) *a in rr: rdn and outpcd 1/2-way: n.d after* **6/1**

1m 10.88s (-2.82) **Going Correction** -0.35s/f (Stan) **7** Ran SP% **114.4**
Speed ratings (Par 101): **104,103,100,98,94 90,88**
CSF £18.36 TOTE £2.90: £1.50, £3.10; EX 16.60 Trifecta £60.50.
Owner W McLuskey **Bred** Mark Commins **Trained** Cropthorne, Worcs

FOCUS
They went a sound pace in this ordinary claimer.

77 SCOOP6SOCCER THE £1 MILLION FOOTBALL BET MEDIAN AUCTION MAIDEN STKS 6f (P)
5:40 (5:41) (Class 5) 3-5-Y-O **£5,175** (£1,540; £769; £384) **Stalls** Centre

Form RPR

364- **1** **Invade (IRE)**[151] 5176 4-9-4 61 (t) AaronJones(5) 8 67
(Stuart Williams) *racd in last trio: clsd over 1f out: swtchd rt ins fnl f: str run fnl 100yds: led on post* **14/1**

2-4 **2** nse **Figurante (IRE)**[5] 15 3-8-7 0 CathyGannon 5 63
(Jamie Osborne) *chsd ldrs: effrt 2f out: drvn and chsd ldr jst ins fnl f: styd on to ld cl home: hdd on post* **3/1**[2]

232- **3** 1/2 **Burmese Whisper**[9] 8387 3-8-12 67 LiamKeniry 6 66
(Andrew Balding) *led: rdn over 1f out: drvn fnl f: hdd and no ex cl home* **2/1**[1]

62- **4** 3/4 **Don't Blame Me**[22] 8244 3-8-12 0 JohnFahy 2 64
(Clive Cox) *trckd ldrs: effrt to press ldrs on inner 1f out: styd on same pce ins fnl f* **7/2**[3]

2- **5** 3/4 **Tilsworth Micky**[11] 8366 4-10-0 0 JFEgan 4 65
(J R Jenkins) *w ldr tl ent fnl 2f: no ex u.p and lost 2nd jst ins fnl f: wknd towards fin* **6/1**

6 6 **On The Clock** 3-8-7 0 LukeMorris 7 37
(James Tate) *dwlt: outpcd in last pair: effrt and sme hdwy u.p over 1f out: wknd ins fnl f* **10/1**

4- **7** 1 1/4 **Zephyr Breeze**[279] 1167 3-8-12 0 DougieCostello 3 38
(Noel Wilson) *t.k.h: hld up in tch in midfield: rdn and no ex over 1f out: wknd ins fnl f* **16/1**

00- **8** 11 **Admirals Choice**[21] 8259 3-8-12 0 JackMitchell 1
(Robert Eddery) *broke okay but sn dropped to rr and outpcd: lost tch over 1f out* **50/1**

1m 11.55s (-2.15) **Going Correction** -0.35s/f (Stan)
WFA 3 from 4yo 16lb **8** Ran SP% **118.4**
Speed ratings (Par 103): **100,99,99,98,97 89,87,72**
CSF £57.99 TOTE £14.70: £3.30, £1.50, £1.30; EX 65.90 Trifecta £325.10.
Owner Happy Valley Racing & Breeding Limited **Bred** Ballylinch Stud **Trained** Newmarket, Suffolk

The Form Book, Raceform Ltd, Newbury, RG14 5SJ

FOCUS
A moderate sprint maiden.

78 WIN A FOOTBALL FORTUNE WITH SCOOP6SOCCER H'CAP 2m (P)
6:10 (6:12) (Class 4) (0-85,84) 4-Y-O+ **£8,086** (£2,406; £1,202; £601) **Stalls** Low

Form RPR
142- **1** **Flashman**[45] 7960 7-10-0 **84**....(b) GeorgeBaker 5 94
(Gary Moore) *hld up in tch: smooth hdwy to ld 2f out: rdn over 1f out: styd on wl: rdn out* **9/4**[2]

406- **2** ¾ **Glan Y Gors (IRE)**[12] 8359 4-9-5 **82**.... MartinLane 2 91
(David Simcock) *hld up in rr: travelling wl but stuck bhd horses over 2f out: hdwy on inner over 1f out: 3rd and hung rt 1f out: styd on to go 2nd last strides* **5/1**[3]

413- **3** *hd* **Scarlet Minstrel**[29] 8156 4-8-13 **76**.... OisinMurphy 6 84
(Andrew Balding) *in tch in midfield: effrt to chse ldrs over 2f out: pressed wnr and drvn over 1f out: kpt on but a hld ins fnl f: lost 2nd last strides* **2/1**[1]

/45- **4** 4 ½ **Laser Blazer**[18] 8319 8-9-1 **71**....(v) FergusSweeney 1 74
(Alan King) *hld up in tch in midfield: effrt over 2f out: wnt 4th ins fnl f: no imp* **6/1**

5/3- **5** 8 **Mick Duggan**[22] 8257 6-9-6 **76**.... LukeMorris 3 69
(Michael Blake) *chsd ldrs: rdn over 3f out: wknd over 1f out* **12/1**

003- **6** 1 ¾ **Villa Royale**[20] 8284 7-10-0 **84**.... GrahamLee 8 75
(Michael Appleby) *chsd ldr tl led after 2f: rdn and hdd 2f out: no ex and wknd over 1f out* **9/1**

/04- **7** 16 **Russian Bolero (GER)**[33] 8125 5-9-8 **78**.... DougieCostello 7 50
(David Dennis) *s.i.s: hdwy into midfield after 3f: pressed ldr over 4f out tl over 2f out: sn dropped out: lost tch over 1f out* **50/1**

405- **8** 18 **Arcamante (ITY)**[41] 7436 5-9-1 **71**.... JoeyHaynes 4 22
(K R Burke) *led for 2f: chsd ldr tl over 4f out: sn dropped out u.p: t.o over 1f out* **20/1**

3m 25.65s (-4.35) **Going Correction** -0.35s/f (Stan)
WFA 4 from 5yo+ 7lb **8** Ran SP% **119.5**
Speed ratings (Par 105): **96,95,95,93,89 88,80,71**
CSF £14.88 CT £26.19 TOTE £3.40: £1.50, £2.10, £1.10; EX 18.20 Trifecta £61.50.
Owner Andrew Bradmore **Bred** Avenue Farm Stud **Trained** Lower Beeding, W Sussex

FOCUS
The form of this modest staying handicap is solid with the market leaders coming clear.

79 BET SCOOP6SOCCER AT BETFRED SHOPS H'CAP 1m (P)
6:40 (6:41) (Class 7) (0-50,50) 4-Y-O+ **£2,587** (£770; £384; £192) **Stalls** Low

Form RPR
030- **1** **Gunner Moyne**[219] 2812 4-9-7 **50**....(t) GeorgeBaker 3 61+
(Gary Moore) *hld up in tch: hdwy 2f out: sn chalng: led ent fnl f: asserted wl ins fnl f: r.o* **7/2**[3]

33-2 **2** ¾ **Anjuna Beach (USA)**[4] 32 6-9-1 **49**.... AnnStokell(5) 2 58
(Ann Stokell) *stdd s: t.k.h: hld up in last pair: hdwy over 2f out: rdn to chal over 1f out: no ex and btn fnl 75yds* **11/4**[2]

/00- **3** 7 **Zarliman (IRE)**[17] 8335 6-9-2 **45**....(p) LiamKeniry 9 37
(Neil Mulholland) *in tch: hdwy to press ldr 1/2-way: led wl over 1f out: sn rdn and hrd pressed: hdd and no ex ent fnl f: wknd fnl 150yds* **6/4**[1]

546- **4** 3 ¾ **Kingston Sassafras**[16] 8340 4-9-4 **47**.... LukeMorris 6 30
(Phil McEntee) *chsd ldrs: 3rd and outpcd u.p over 2f out: 4th and wl btn 1f out: wknd* **25/1**

005- **5** *shd* **Let It Go**[43] 7976 4-9-2 **45**....[1] JoeyHaynes 1 28
(Tony Carroll) *hld up in last pair: swtchd rt and effrt over 2f out: no imp and wl hld over 1f out: plugged on ins fnl f* **50/1**

020- **6** 1 ¼ **Little Indian**[27] 8178 6-9-7 **50**.... FergusSweeney 4 30
(J R Jenkins) *in tch in midfield: effrt and swtchd rt 2f out: sn no imp and wl hld whn n.m.r jst ins fnl f* **6/1**

056- **7** 2 ¾ **Nifty Kier**[21] 8264 7-9-2 **48**....(p) DannyBrock(3) 8 22
(Phil McEntee) *dwlt: rcvrd to ld over 6f out: drvn and hdd wl over 1f out: sn btn: wknd 1f out* **16/1**

05-0 **8** 45 **Brean Golf Birdie**[5] 20 4-9-2 **45**....(p) JackMitchell 5
(Bill Turner) *led tl over 6f out: chsd ldr tl dropped out u.p 3f out: t.o fnl f* **25/1**

1m 37.93s (-1.97) **Going Correction** -0.35s/f (Stan) **8** Ran SP% **118.7**
Speed ratings (Par 97): **95,94,87,83,83 82,79,34**
CSF £13.94 CT £20.25 TOTE £4.40: £1.10, £1.70, £1.10; EX 16.00 Trifecta £33.80.
Owner G L Moore **Bred** Five Horses Ltd **Trained** Lower Beeding, W Sussex

FOCUS
There was no hanging about in this bottom-drawer handicap, which suited the closers, and the runner-up is the benchmark.

80 BET SCOOP6SOCCER AT BETFRED.COM FILLIES' H'CAP 7f (P)
7:10 (7:11) (Class 5) (0-75,74) 4-Y-O+ **£5,175** (£1,540; £769; £384) **Stalls** Low

Form RPR
04-3 **1** **Mambo Fever**[5] 22 5-8-5 **58**....[1] LukeMorris 1 66
(David C Griffiths) *sn led and mde virtually all: rdn over 1f out: drvn ins fnl f: hld on cl home* **9/4**[1]

360- **2** *nk* **Quite Smart (IRE)**[36] 8084 4-9-0 **67**....(v[1]) GrahamLee 3 74
(Robert Cowell) *chsd wnr: drvn over 1f out: kpt on wl u.p towards fin: nvr quite getting to wnr* **11/1**

352- **3** 2 ¼ **Ixelles Diamond (IRE)**[7] 8411 5-9-3 **70**.... JFEgan 6 71
(Andrew Reid) *t.k.h: hld up in tch: clsd and bmpd wl over 1f out: nt clr run and swtchd lft over 1f out: hdwy to chse ldrs ins fnl f: styd on same pce after* **6/1**

252- **4** 2 **Be Royale**[22] 8248 6-9-7 **74**.... RobertWinston 7 70
(Michael Appleby) *hld up in tch in rr: effrt to chse ldrs and bmpd wl over 1f out: no ex jst ins fnl f: wknd fnl 75yds* **5/2**[2]

035- **5** 1 **Birdie Queen**[43] 7984 6-9-7 **74**.... GeorgeBaker 4 67
(Gary Moore) *t.k.h: hld up in tch: effrt over 1f out: no imp 1f out: wknd ins fnl f* **8/1**

316- **6** *shd* **Crystal Malt (IRE)**[31] 8140 4-9-5 **72**.... SeanLevey 2 65
(Richard Hannon) *bustled along leaving stalls: chsd ldrs: rdn 2f out: no ex and btn 1f out: wknd ins fnl f* **4/1**[3]

310- **7** 2 **Mrs Bubbles (IRE)**[17] 8338 4-8-5 **65**.... JosephineGordon(7) 5 52
(J S Moore) *t.k.h: in tch in midfield: rdn and lost pl whn squeezed for room and hmpd wl over 1f out: no imp after: wknd ins fnl f* **14/1**

1m 24.28s (-2.92) **Going Correction** -0.35s/f (Stan) **7** Ran SP% **119.7**
Speed ratings (Par 100): **102,101,99,96,95 95,93**
CSF £29.18 TOTE £3.10: £1.60, £5.00; EX 30.70 Trifecta £207.20.
Owner Norcroft Park Stud **Bred** Norcroft Park Stud **Trained** Bawtry, S Yorks

FOCUS
A moderate but competitive fillies' handicap. A small personal-best from the winner.

81 BET SCOOP6SOCCER AT TOTESPORT.COM H'CAP 5f (P)
7:40 (7:42) (Class 6) (0-55,51) 3-Y-O **£3,234** (£962; £481; £240) **Stalls** Low

Form RPR
000- **1** **Yisty**[49] 7895 3-9-1 **45**....(v) TonyHamilton 3 49
(Derek Shaw) *mde all: rdn over 1f out: styd on and asserted ins fnl f: rdn out* **14/1**

000- **2** 1 ¼ **Freeze A Crowd (IRE)**[106] 6651 3-9-1 **45**....(t) GrahamLee 2 44
(Ben Haslam) *chsd wnr thrght: swtchd rt over 1f out: drvn and pressing wnr 1f out: no ex and one pce fnl 100yds* **2/1**[2]

420- **3** *nk* **Romancingthestone**[16] 8348 3-9-0 **51**....(p) JosephineGordon(7) 1 49
(J S Moore) *chsd ldrs: rdn over 2f out: swtchd lft over 1f out: styd on same pce u.p ins fnl f* **13/8**[1]

006- **4** *shd* **E Fourteen**[56] 7808 3-9-1 **45**.... JackMitchell 4 43
(Robyn Brisland) *t.k.h: hld up in tch in last pair: rdn over 2f out: no imp tl styd on u.p fnl 100yds* **5/1**[3]

030- **5** 2 ¾ **Memyselfie (IRE)**[51] 7877 3-9-2 **46**.... StevieDonohoe 5 34
(Derek Shaw) *s.i.s and wnt lft after s: a in rr: rdn over 2f out: sme prog over 1f out: no imp ins fnl f: eased cl home* **5/1**[3]

59.21s (-0.99) **Going Correction** -0.35s/f (Stan) **5** Ran SP% **111.4**
Speed ratings (Par 95): **93,91,90,90,85**
CSF £42.59 TOTE £9.30: £3.30, £1.60; EX 27.00 Trifecta £64.80.
Owner Paddy Barrett **Bred** P E Barrett **Trained** Sproxton, Leics

FOCUS
A very weak 3yo sprint handicap.

82 TOTEPOOL H'CAP 7f (P)
8:10 (8:10) (Class 4) (0-80,79) 4-Y-O+ **£8,086** (£2,406; £1,202; £601) **Stalls** Low

Form RPR
162- **1** **Gentlemen**[21] 8263 5-8-9 74.... JosephineGordon(7) 3 87
(Phil McEntee) *dwlt: niggled along in rr early: travelling bttr after 2f: hdwy u.p over 1f out: chsd ldr ins fnl f: styd on wl to ld last strides* **5/2**[1]

532- **2** *hd* **Welliesinthewater (IRE)**[17] 8324 6-8-7 65 oh1....(v) MartinLane 7 77
(Derek Shaw) *led: rdn over 1f out: kpt on wl u.p tl hdd and no ex last strides* **10/1**

320- **3** 3 ½ **Nortron (IRE)**[38] 8050 4-9-7 79....(v[1]) OisinMurphy 5 82
(Andrew Balding) *chsd ldrs: clsd to join ldr 2f out: drvn over 1f out: 3rd and btn 1f out: wknd fnl 100yds* **4/1**[2]

420- **4** 2 ½ **Crack Shot (IRE)**[7] 8412 4-9-7 79.... LukeMorris 2 75
(James Tate) *in tch in midfield: nt clr run 2f out: gap opened and effrt u.p over 1f out: 4th no imp 1f out: wknd ins fnl f* **4/1**[2]

433- **5** 2 ¼ **Excellent Guest**[17] 8325 9-9-6 78.... RyanPowell 4 69
(George Margarson) *hld up in tch in midfield: effrt u.p over 1f out: no imp 1f out: wknd ins fnl f* **4/1**[2]

666- **6** ½ **Woofie (IRE)**[29] 8161 4-9-4 76....(p) TomQueally 1 65
(Laura Mongan) *in tch in midfield: effrt u.p but little rspnse over 1f out: wknd ins fnl f* **16/1**

600- **7** 4 ½ **Run With Pride (IRE)**[16] 8342 6-9-5 77.... TonyHamilton 6 55
(Derek Shaw) *hld up in rr: swtchd rt and effrt wl over 1f out: no imp: wknd fnl f* **8/1**[3]

550- **8** 2 ½ **Dana's Present**[31] 8132 7-9-5 77.... RichardKingscote 8 48
(Tom Dascombe) *led rdrless to post: s.i.s: bustled along and rcvrd to chse ldr after 1f tl 2f out: sn lost pl: bhd fnl f* **16/1**

1m 23.67s (-3.53) **Going Correction** -0.35s/f (Stan) **8** Ran SP% **120.5**
Speed ratings (Par 105): **106,105,101,98,96 95,90,87**
CSF £30.93 CT £101.81 TOTE £4.00: £1.40, £2.30, £1.70; EX 17.40 Trifecta £109.10.
Owner Eventmaker Racehorses **Bred** Mrs Eleanor Kent **Trained** Newmarket, Suffolk

FOCUS
This modest handicap was run at a decent pace and rather fell apart at the furlong marker. The winner continues to progress on the AW.
T/Jkpt: Pool of £4733.30 to a £1 stake. Pool of £5306.40 - 1.50 winning units. JACKPOT PLACEPOT: £28.00 to a £1 stake. Pool of £2650.03 - 68.90 winning units. T/Plt: £89.90 to a £1 stake. Pool of £95619.76 - 775.60 winning tickets. T/Qpdt: £17.30 to a £1 stake. Pool of £10136.55 - 431.85 winning tickets. **Steve Payne**

[42]LINGFIELD (L-H)
Thursday, January 7

OFFICIAL GOING: Polytrack: standard
Wind: Strong, half against Weather: Cloudy becoming fine

83 DAILY PRICE BOOSTS AT UNIBET MEDIAN AUCTION MAIDEN STKS 5f 6y(P)
1:20 (1:20) (Class 6) 3-5-Y-O **£2,264** (£673; £336) **Stalls** High

Form RPR
66- **1** **Pink Martini (IRE)**[86] 7191 3-8-6 0.... JFEgan 2 74
(Joseph Tuite) *mde virtually all: shkn up and drew clr over 1f out: in n.d fnl f* **5/2**[2]

3- **2** 4 **K'Gari Spirit**[17] 8330 3-8-6 0.... NickyMackay 4 60
(Jeremy Gask) *chsd other pair: urged along over 2f out: kpt on one pce to take 2nd ins fnl f: n.d* **4/6**[1]

023- **3** 1 **Deer Song**[22] 8244 3-8-11 64....(b) WilliamCarson 3 61
(John Bridger) *w wnr to 1/2-way: rdn 2f out: hanging and fnd nil over 1f out: lost 2nd ins fnl f* **5/1**[3]

58.69s (-0.11) **Going Correction** 0.0s/f (Stan) **3** Ran SP% **105.2**
Speed ratings (Par 101): **100,93,92**
CSF £4.57 TOTE £3.90; EX 3.80 Trifecta £3.80.
Owner Lawrence Eke **Bred** E Ryan **Trained** Lambourn, Berks

FOCUS
An uncompetitive maiden run at an honest pace. The form is taken at something like face value.

84 32RED.COM H'CAP 1m 5f (P)
1:50 (1:50) (Class 6) (0-55,55) 4-Y-O+ **£2,264** (£673; £336; £168) **Stalls** Low

Form RPR
004- **1** **Smugglers Lane (IRE)**[8] 8403 4-8-11 **50**.... PatCosgrave 3 56
(David Evans) *hld up towards rr: prog to chse ldrs over 2f out: drvn to cl over 1f out: led ins fnl f: kpt on wl* **13/2**

042- **2** *nk* **Little Flo**[17] 8337 5-9-3 **51**.... RyanPowell 7 57
(William Stone) *trckd ldng pair: wnt 2nd over 3f out: carried wd bnd 2f out: drvn to chal jst over 1f out: pressed wnr ins fnl f: jst hld* **7/1**

002- **3** 1 ½ **Shirataki (IRE)**[22] 8258 8-8-8 **49**.... LuluStanford(7) 1 52
(Peter Hiatt) *dwlt: hld up in rr: prog over 2f out: lft w ch whn ldrs rn wd bnd sn after: urged along and kpt on to take 3rd last stride* **8/1**

000- **4** *shd* **Lucky Dottie**[36] 8077 5-9-4 **52**........................ JFEgan 4 57
(Pat Phelan) *rrd s: nt gng wl in last early: rdn and prog on inner 2f out: kpt on fnl f to press for 3rd nr fin* **9/2**[2]

552- **5** *nse* **Fieldmouse**[23] 8231 4-9-0 **53**........................ TomQueally 2 56
(Eve Johnson Houghton) *led: rn wd bnd 2f out and sn drvn: hdd and one pce ins fnl f: lost 2 pls last strides* **11/2**[3]

500- **6** *1 1/4* **Weardiditallgorong**[61] 7749 4-9-2 **55**........................(b) OisinMurphy 9 56
(Des Donovan, Ire) *dwlt: wl in rr: taken wd bnd 2f out: sn rdn: no prog tl styd on last 150yds: nrst fin* **7/1**

606- **7** *1* **Fleetwood Poppy**[19] 8312 4-8-7 **46** oh1........................ LukeMorris 12 46
(Michael Attwater) *chsd ldng pair: disp 2nd over 3f out tl carried wd bnd 2f out: fdd fnl f* **25/1**

353- **8** *3/4* **Ron Waverly (IRE)**[23] 8231 6-8-13 **47**........................(tp) WilliamCarson 10 46
(Paddy Butler) *settled in midfield: sme prog over 2f out: lft w ch whn ldrs rn wd sn after: wknd fnl f* **14/1**

664/ **9** *19* **Witch From Rome**[348] 3471 5-8-11 **52**........................ JosephineGordon(7) 13 23
(Nick Lampard) *chsd ldr to over 3f out: wknd qckly: t.o* **25/1**

012- **10** *9* **Street Art (IRE)**[20] 8291 4-9-0 **53**........................(t) ShaneKelly 8 11
(Mike Murphy) *a towards rr: rdn and wknd over 3f out: t.o* **4/1**[1]

2m 48.0s (2.00) **Going Correction** 0.0s/f (Stan)
WFA 4 from 5yo+ 5lb **10** Ran SP% **117.4**
Speed ratings (Par 101): **93,92,91,91,91 91,90,89,78,72**
CSF £51.82 CT £367.61 TOTE £6.40: £2.00, £2.70, £2.70; EX 57.90 Trifecta £487.40.
Owner Mrs I M Folkes **Bred** Tally-Ho Stud **Trained** Pandy, Monmouths
■ Stewards' Enquiry : Josephine Gordon three-day ban: careless riding (Jan 21-23)
Pat Cosgrave three-day ban: careless riding (Jan 21-23)
Ryan Powell caution: careless riding

FOCUS
They went a steady pace for this open handicap. It was quite messy with a few taken very wide off the home bend.

85 32RED CASINO H'CAP 1m 2f (P)
2:20 (2:20) (Class 5) (0-75,75) 3-Y-O **£2,911** (£866; £432; £216) **Stalls** Low

Form RPR

450- **1** **Kalkrand (IRE)**[23] 8234 3-8-13 **67**........................ RobertHavlin 5 74
(John Gosden) *hld up in last: prog 3f out and gng bttr than rest: trckd ldr 2f out: shkn up to ld over 1f out: styd on: readily* **11/4**[2]

031- **2** *1 3/4* **Mayasa (IRE)**[20] 8280 3-9-7 **75**........................(b) LukeMorris 2 78
(James Tate) *drvn vigorously to ld: hrd rdn over 2f out: hdd over 1f out: kpt on wl but readily hld* **8/1**

46-3 **3** *7* **Trespassed (IRE)**[1] 70 3-9-1 **69**........................(p) PatCosgrave 3 58
(William Haggas) *cl up: chsd ldr 6f out to over 4f out: drvn 3f out: fdd fnl 2f* **7/2**[3]

065- **4** *2* **The Plough (IRE)**[54] 7863 3-8-12 **66**........................(b[1]) FergusSweeney 4 51
(Martyn Meade) *hld up: prog to chse ldr over 4f out: drvn 3f out: lost 2nd 2f out: sn btn* **6/4**[1]

660- **5** *7* **Fast And Hot (IRE)**[36] 8076 3-8-9 **63**........................ KieranO'Neill 1 34
(Richard Hannon) *chsd ldr to 6f out: rdn over 4f out: dropped to last and wl btn over 3f out* **10/1**

2m 4.89s (-1.71) **Going Correction** 0.0s/f (Stan) **5** Ran SP% **109.1**
Speed ratings (Par 97): **106,104,99,97,91**
CSF £22.00 TOTE £3.90: £1.60, £2.50; EX 19.20 Trifecta £34.40.
Owner Godolphin **Bred** Ballylinch Stud **Trained** Newmarket, Suffolk

FOCUS
A trappy handicap with the first two unexposed.

86 DAILY UNIBET EARLY PRICES FROM 9AM H'CAP 6f 1y(P)
2:50 (2:52) (Class 3) (0-95,93) 4-Y-O- **£7,246** (£2,168; £1,084; £542; £270) **Stalls** Low

Form RPR

252- **1** **Mythmaker**[8] 8395 4-9-5 **91**........................ PaulMulrennan 5 100
(Bryan Smart) *pressed ldr: rdn to ld over 1f out: kpt on wl* **2/1**[1]

112- **2** *3/4* **Seychelloise**[31] 8140 4-9-4 **90**........................(b) LukeMorris 6 96+
(Sir Mark Prescott Bt) *pressed ldng pair but racd on outer: wd bnd 2f out and lost grnd: sn drvn: styd on fnl f to take 2nd nr fin* **3/1**[2]

065- **3** *3/4* **Russian Realm**[19] 8311 6-9-7 **93**........................ ShaneKelly 4 97
(Richard Hughes) *settled in last pair: off the pce and pushed along 1/2-way: stl in last pair 1f out: rdn and r.o wl to take 3rd last strides* **7/1**

346- **4** *nk* **Ballista (IRE)**[20] 8288 8-9-2 **88**........................ RichardKingscote 1 91
(Tom Dascombe) *fast away: led: drvn and hdd over 1f out: hld whn hanging rt and lost pls nr fin* **7/2**[3]

466- **5** *3/4* **Normal Equilibrium**[11] 8368 6-9-4 **90**........................(p) PatCosgrave 3 90
(Robert Cowell) *chsd ldng trio: shkn up and no imp over 1f out: kpt on last 100yds but lost 4th nr fin* **25/1**

050- **6** *2 1/2* **Trojan Rocket (IRE)**[16] 8342 8-9-4 **90**........................(p) GeorgeBaker 2 82
(Michael Wigham) *hmpd on inner after 100yds: a in last pair after: pushed along fr 1/2-way: nvr involved* **8/1**

450- **7** *1 1/4* **Taajub (IRE)**[23] 8229 9-8-11 **83**........................ JimmyQuinn 7 71
(Peter Crate) *racd off the pce in 5th: nt on terms over 2f out: no prog on inner over 1f out* **25/1**

1m 10.43s (-1.47) **Going Correction** 0.0s/f (Stan) **7** Ran SP% **111.9**
Speed ratings (Par 107): **109,108,107,106,105 102,100**
CSF £7.77 TOTE £2.70: £1.50, £1.60; EX 8.60 Trifecta £31.30.
Owner Crossfields Racing **Bred** Crossfields Bloodstock Ltd **Trained** Hambleton, N Yorks

FOCUS
A competitive handicap run at a sound pace. The winner looked well in.

87 LADBROKES H'CAP 7f 1y(P)
3:20 (3:20) (Class 7) (0-50,50) 3-Y-O+ **£1,704** (£503; £251) **Stalls** Low

Form RPR

02-3 **1** **Binky Blue (IRE)**[3] 35 4-9-9 **47**........................ GeorgeBaker 12 59
(Daniel Mark Loughnane) *hld up in last trio: gd prog on inner fr 2f out: led ins fnl f: sn in command* **2/1**[1]

002- **2** *1* **Kristoff (IRE)**[28] 8166 3-7-11 **46**........................ RhiainIngram(7) 5 51
(Jim Boyle) *mde most: rdn 2f out: hdd ins fnl f: styd on* **4/1**[2]

/64- **3** *1 3/4* **Comadoir (IRE)**[40] 8035 10-9-10 **48**........................(p) OisinMurphy 7 52
(Jo Crowley) *w ldr: rdn and upsides 2f out: lost 2nd and one pce fnl f* **10/1**

403- **4** *1/2* **Fairy Mist (IRE)**[8] 8393 9-9-12 **50**........................(b) WilliamCarson 11 53
(John Bridger) *hld up in last: prog over 1f out: chsd ldrs ins fnl f: kpt on same pce nr fin* **8/1**[3]

200- **5** *3/4* **Chandrayaan**[8] 8393 9-9-7 **45**........................(v) RobertHavlin 6 46
(John E Long) *racd in 7th: rdn and nt qckn 2f out: n.d after: styd on ins fnl f* **16/1**

000- **6** *hd* **Paradise Spectre**[8] 8406 9-9-10 **48**........................(v) FergusSweeney 2 48
(Zoe Davison) *in tch: sme prog 2f out to chse ldrs 1f out: one pce after* **66/1**

500- **7** *1 3/4* **Bohemian Origin (IRE)**[28] 8166 3-8-3 **45**........................(p) KieranO'Neill 8 37
(J S Moore) *t.k.h: chsd ldng pair: shkn up wl over 2f out: wknd over 1f out* **33/1**

606- **8** *1 1/2* **Ashford Island**[119] 6236 3-8-8 **50**........................ ShaneKelly 3 38
(Mike Murphy) *s.i.s: prog fr rr on outer 1/2-way: shkn up over 2f out: sn lost pl and btn* **4/1**[2]

000- **9** *2 3/4* **Justice (IRE)**[194] 3638 3-8-3 **45**........................ JimmyQuinn 10 25
(Dean Ivory) *plld hrd on outer: chsd ldrs: wknd fr 2f out* **25/1**

/06- **10** *1 1/4* **Fleetwood Bella**[10] 8381 5-9-7 **45**........................ KierenFox 4 26
(Michael Attwater) *chsd ldng pair: wknd 2f out* **33/1**

050- **11** *8* **Busta Nellie**[50] 7887 3-8-3 **45**........................ NickyMackay 1
(Simon Dow) *dwlt: a in rr: t.o* **16/1**

1m 24.92s (0.12) **Going Correction** 0.0s/f (Stan)
WFA 3 from 4yo+ 18lb **11** Ran SP% **116.5**
Speed ratings (Par 97): **99,97,95,95,94 94,92,90,87,85 76**
CSF £9.25 CT £65.03 TOTE £2.80: £1.50, £1.60, £2.80; EX 10.70 Trifecta £50.90.
Owner Mrs C Loughnane **Bred** Gerard & Anne Corry **Trained** Baldwin's Gate, Staffs

FOCUS
A good race for the lowly grade.

88 CORAL H'CAP (FOR LADY AMATEUR RIDERS) 1m 2f (P)
3:50 (3:50) (Class 5) (0-75,75) 4-Y-O+ **£2,807** (£870; £435; £217) **Stalls** Low

Form RPR

040- **1** **Black Dave (IRE)**[17] 8333 6-9-9 **70**........................ MissEMacKenzie(7) 8 77
(David Evans) *t.k.h on outer: prog to ld after 3f: clr over 4f out: 5 l up over 2f out: pushed along and hld on wl* **10/1**

405- **2** *nk* **Tower Power**[22] 8256 5-10-0 **75**........................ MissMBishop-Peck(7) 1 81
(Phil McEntee) *rrd s: sn in tch: prog to chse clr wnr 3f out: grad clsd fr 2f out: jst failed* **20/1**

555- **3** *2 3/4* **Cosmic Halo**[21] 8261 7-9-6 **67**........................ MissEmilyBullock(7) 5 68
(Richard Fahey) *dwlt: hld up in last: prog over 2f out: chsd clr ldng pair over 1f out: kpt on but nvr able to threaten* **6/1**[3]

010- **4** *3 3/4* **Estibdaad (IRE)**[24] 8221 6-9-12 **69**........................(t) MissMBryant(3) 2 62
(Paddy Butler) *led 3f: sn in 3rd: outpcd fr 3f out: one pce after* **8/1**

264- **5** *5* **Commissar**[23] 8238 7-9-13 **72**........................(tp) MissAmyTaylor(5) 3 55
(Heather Dalton) *hld up in rr: no prog on outer over 3f out: plugged on fr over 1f out* **5/1**[2]

162- **6** *3* **Captain Felix**[24] 8221 4-10-5 **75**........................ MissHayleyMoore 7 52
(Gay Kelleway) *t.k.h: trckd ldrs: outpcd over 3f out: hung rt bnd 2f out: wl btn after* **11/10**[1]

220- **7** *1* **Mediate**[18] 8318 5-9-9 **68**........................ MissTWorsley(5) 4 43
(Richard Rowe) *sn lost prom pl: toiling in rr 3f out* **33/1**

014- **8** *shd* **Power Up**[11] 8371 5-9-3 **62**........................ MissGFriswell(5) 6 37
(Robert Eddery) *mostly chsd ldr to 3f out: wknd qckly* **8/1**

2m 6.45s (-0.15) **Going Correction** 0.0s/f (Stan)
WFA 4 from 5yo+ 2lb **8** Ran SP% **117.6**
Speed ratings (Par 103): **100,99,97,94,90 88,87,87**
CSF £183.97 CT £1308.52 TOTE £12.90: £3.20, £4.20, £1.90; EX 233.60 Trifecta £989.40.
Owner Mrs E Evans & J Smith **Bred** Richard Frayne **Trained** Pandy, Monmouths
■ A winner for Ellie MacKenzie on her first ride under rules.

FOCUS
A fair handicap for lady riders, and rather muddling. The form is unconvincing.
T/Plt: £498.20 to a £1 stake. Pool of £61882.90 - 90.66 winning tickets. T/Qpdt: £53.80 to a £1 stake. Pool of £6320.0 - 86.90 winning tickets. **Jonathan Neesom**

AQUEDUCT (L-H)
Thursday, January 7

OFFICIAL GOING: Dirt: fast

89a ALLOWANCE RACE (4YO+ FILLIES & MARES) (DIRT) 1m 110y
8:50 (8:50) 4-Y-O+
£27,346 (£9,115; £4,557; £2,278; £1,367; £227)

RPR

1 **Jules N Rome (USA)** 4-8-11 0........................(b) KendrickCarmouche 5
(Danny Gargan, U.S.A) **49/10**[2]

2 *1 1/4* **Rachel's Temper (USA)**[28] 5-8-9 0........................ MichaelLuzzi 1
(David Cannizzo, U.S.A) **158/10**

3 *4* **High Ridge Road (USA)**[56] 4-8-11 0........................ IradOrtizJr 6
(Chad C Brown, U.S.A) **3/4**[1]

4 *2 1/4* **Flick Of An Eye (USA)**[108] 4-8-11 0........................(b[1]) GabrielSaez 9
(Danny Gargan, U.S.A) **43/1**

5 *nk* **Theresas Candyrose (USA)** 5-8-9 0........................ JuniorAlvarado 4
(Robert Barbara, U.S.A) **106/10**

6 *5 1/2* **Milaya (USA)**[180] 4-8-4 0........................(b) EricCancel 2
(Michael Dilger, U.S.A) **44/5**

7 *2* **Kathy's Humor (USA)**[375] 4-8-11 0........................(b) AaronTGryder 7
(Richard Violette Jr, U.S.A) **143/10**

8 *2* **Defoe Street (USA)** 6-8-9 0........................ ChristopherPDeCarlo 3
(Gregory DiPrima, U.S.A) **53/1**

9 *3/4* **Wickedly Smart (USA)**[69] 7603 4-8-11 0........................ ManuelFranco 8
(Jeremy Noseda) *a towards rr: rdn 3f out: no imp in st: wknd and dropped to last* **84/10**[3]

Owner Midwest Thoroughbreds Inc **Bred** Harry L Landry, Constancia Farm & Dunkirk Syndicat **Trained** North America

[8]MEYDAN (L-H)
Thursday, January 7

OFFICIAL GOING: Dirt: fast; turf: good

90a LONGINES CONQUEST CLASSIC GENTS MOON PHASES (H'CAP) (DIRT) 6f (D)
3:35 (3:35) (95-108,108) 3-Y-O+
£44,897 (£14,965; £7,482; £3,741; £2,244; £1,496)

RPR

1 **Nawwaar (USA)**[41] 8031 7-8-10 98........................ TadhgO'Shea 3 105+
(A R Al Rayhi, UAE) *trckd ldng duo: led 1f out: r.o wl* **14/1**

2 *1 1/4* **Kifaah**[21] 8276 5-8-7 95........................ PaulHanagan 4 98
(A R Al Rayhi, UAE) *sn led: hdd 1f out but r.o same pce* **9/4**[2]

3 1 ½ **My Catch (IRE)**[49] 7913 5-9-3 105 PatDobbs 5 103
(Doug Watson, UAE) *trckd ldr: ev ch 1 1/2f out: one pce fnl f* **13/8**[1]

4 1 ¼ **Royal Ridge (SAF)**[313] 740 7-8-8 96 (bt) WayneSmith 1 90
(M F De Kock, South Africa) *settled in rr: chsd ldr 2 1/2f out: r.o same pce fnl 1 1/2f* **12/1**

5 3 **Cheongu (USA)**[46] 4-8-8 96 (b) RoystonFfrench 2 81
(I Seo, Korea) *s.i.s: nvr nr to chal* **10/1**

6 ¾ **Rafeej**[21] 8276 7-9-6 108 DaneO'Neill 6 90
(M Al Mheiri, UAE) *trckd ldng trio tl wknd fnl 2f* **7/1**[3]

7 2 ¼ **Frank Lloyd Wright (SWE)**[56] 5-8-13 100 (t) WilliamBuick 8 76
(Niels Petersen, Norway) *nvr bttr than mid-div* **20/1**

8 3 ½ **Unforgiving Minute**[152] 5132 5-9-1 102 JamesDoyle 7 67
(Barry Brennan) *a in rr* **20/1**

1m 11.61s (0.01) **Going Correction** +0.175s/f (Slow) **8 Ran SP% 114.3**
Speed ratings: **106,104,102,100,96 95,92,88**
CSF: 45.85; TRICAST: 80.11.
Owner Hamdan Al Maktoum **Bred** Shadwell Farm LLC **Trained** UAE

FOCUS
TRAKUS: 2nd -1, 3rd +4, 4th 0, 5th +4, 6th +4, 7th +8, 8th +10. The second and third took each other on through fractions of 23.92 (400m) and 22.58 (800m) and that set the race up for the winner, who finished in 24.94.

91a LONGINES DOLCE VITA COLLECTION (H'CAP) (TURF) 5f (T)
4:10 (4:10) (100-113,109) 3-Y-O+
£48,979 (£16,326; £8,163; £4,081; £2,448; £1,632)

RPR

1 **Ertijaal (IRE)**[313] 741 5-9-5 108 PaulHanagan 12 118+
(A R Al Rayhi, UAE) *sn led: kicked clr 2f out: easily* **7/2**[1]

2 4 **Divine (IRE)**[89] 7117 5-9-0 102 WilliamBuick 5 99
(Mick Channon) *mid-div: r.o fnl 2 1/2f but no ch w wnr* **11/1**

3 ¾ **Speed Hawk (USA)**[76] 7449 5-9-3 106 (p) JamesDoyle 8 99
(Robert Cowell) *trckd ldng pair: r.o fnl 2f but no ch w wnr* **5/1**[2]

4 ½ **Roi De Vitesse (IRE)**[306] 822 9-9-4 107 (v) DavidProbert 10 98
(Ali Jan, Qatar) *in rr of main gp: r.o fnl 2f: nrst fin* **25/1**

5 nk **Ajeeb (NZ)**[336] 443 6-9-6 109 RichardMullen 13 99
(S Seemar, UAE) *in rr of main gp: nvr a threat* **18/1**

6 1 ¼ **Demora**[75] 7461 7-8-11 100 AndrewMullen 4 86
(Michael Appleby) *trckd ldr: outpcd 2f out but r.o same pce* **11/1**

7 hd **Green Door (IRE)**[107] 6614 5-9-2 105 (p) JamieSpencer 14 90
(Robert Cowell) *trckd ldng pair: r.o same pce fnl 2f* **7/1**[3]

8 1 ¼ **Fityaan**[55] 7850 8-9-1 104 FernandoJara 7 85
(M Al Mheiri, UAE) *in rr of main gp: nvr bttr than mid-div* **14/1**

9 nk **Morawij**[69] 7620 6-8-11 100 ChrisHayes 1 80
(D Selvaratnam, UAE) *wl away: trckd ldng pair: ev ch 2f out: outpcd fnl 1 1/2f* **9/1**

10 hd **Banaadeer (AUS)**[306] 822 4-9-5 108 DaneO'Neill 3 87
(M F De Kock, South Africa) *s.i.s: nvr nr to chal* **8/1**

11 1 ¼ **Dux Scholar**[649] 1179 8-9-3 106 (b) PatDobbs 11 81
(Doug Watson, UAE) *a in rr* **20/1**

12 1 ¾ **Ahlan Emarati (IRE)**[202] 3343 4-9-2 105 (bt) MickaelBarzalona 6 74
(S Seemar, UAE) *s.i.s: nvr nr to chal* **25/1**

13 12 ½ **Foxy Forever (IRE)**[116] 6358 6-8-11 100 (b) ColmO'Donoghue 9 24
(Michael Wigham) *nvr bttr than mid-div* **9/1**

56.9s (-0.20) **Going Correction** +0.20s/f (Good) **13 Ran SP% 123.6**
Speed ratings: **109,102,101,100,100 98,97,96,95,95 93,90,70**
CSF: 43.48; TRICAST: 202.70.
Owner Hamdan Al Maktoum **Bred** Shadwell Estate Co Ltd **Trained** UAE

FOCUS
TRAKUS: 2nd -2, 3rd 0, 4th -1, 5th -1, 6th -1, 7th 0, 8th 0, 9th -1, 10th 0, 11th -1, 12th -1, 13th 0. A visually impressive and smart performance from the winner.

92a AL MAKTOUM CHALLENGE R1 PRESENTED BY LONGINES DOLCE VITA COLLECTION (GROUP 2) (DIRT) 1m (D)
4:45 (4:45) 3-Y-O+
£102,040 (£34,013; £17,006; £8,503; £5,102; £3,401)

RPR

1 **Le Bernardin (USA)**[21] 8273 7-9-0 113 (t) TadhgO'Shea 11 111
(A R Al Rayhi, UAE) *trckd ldr: led 3f out: r.o wl* **3/1**[1]

2 hd **Layl (USA)**[21] 8273 6-9-0 109 (v) PatDobbs 8 111+
(Doug Watson, UAE) *s.i.s: settled in rr: r.o fnl 2f: nrst fin* **10/1**

3 hd **Prayer For Relief (USA)**[285] 1091 8-9-0 110 (b) ChristopheSoumillon 10 110+
(M F De Kock, South Africa) *mid-div: r.o fnl 2f: nrst fin* **14/1**

4 hd **Faulkner**[35] 8098 6-9-0 102 SamHitchcott 1 110
(Doug Watson, UAE) *s.i.s: settled in rr: r.o fnl 2f but no ch w wnr* **16/1**

5 3 **Surfer (USA)**[285] 1091 7-9-0 112 (t) RichardMullen 2 103
(S Seemar, UAE) *trckd ldr: ev ch 2 1/2f out: wknd fnl 1 1/12f* **9/2**[2]

6 2 ¼ **Special Fighter (IRE)**[21] 8275 5-9-0 107 FernandoJara 7 98
(M Al Mheiri, UAE) *racd in rr: n.d but r.o fnl 1 1/2f* **12/1**

7 ¾ **Haatheq (USA)**[21] 8275 9-9-0 108 PaulHanagan 13 96
(A R Al Rayhi, UAE) *a in mid-div* **20/1**

8 1 ½ **Top Clearance (USA)**[158] 4921 4-9-0 100 (t) ChrisHayes 5 92
(D Selvaratnam, UAE) *nvr bttr than mid-div* **25/1**

9 2 ¾ **Gold City (IRE)**[21] 8273 7-9-0 110 (bt) HectorCrouch 6 86
(S Seemar, UAE) *nvr bttr than mid-div* **20/1**

10 6 **Pearl Nation (USA)**[26] 8199 7-9-0 102 AndrewMullen 4 72
(Michael Appleby) *sn led: hdd 3f out: sn btn* **25/1**

11 nk **Frankyfourfingers (FR)**[285] 1091 6-9-0 111 MickaelBarzalona 9 72
(S bin Ghadayer, UAE) *trckd ldrs tl wknd fnl 2 1/2f* **6/1**[3]

12 2 ¼ **Free Wheeling (AUS)**[285] 1091 7-9-0 109 (t) JamesDoyle 12 66
(Saeed bin Suroor) *wl away: trckd ldr tl outpcd 3f out* **10/1**

13 23 **Long River (USA)**[285] 1098 6-9-0 110 (bt) RoystonFfrench 3 13
(S bin Ghadayer, UAE) *a in rr* **40/1**

1m 37.12s (-0.38) **Going Correction** +0.175s/f (Slow) **13 Ran SP% 115.5**
Speed ratings: **108,107,107,107,104 102,101,99,97,91 90,88,65**
CSF: 29.42.
Owner Sheikh Ahmed bin Mohammed Al Maktoum **Bred** Mike G Rutherford **Trained** UAE

FOCUS
TRAKUS: 2nd -7, 3rd +8, 4th -7, 5th -9, 6th +4, 7th +3, 8th 0, 9th -1, 10th -1, 11th 0, 12th +4, 13th -2. Ordinary form for a Group 2 but really competitive, and the pace was strong: 25.02, 22.74, 23.82 and the winner finished in 25.54.

93a LONGINES MASTER COLLECTION (H'CAP) (TURF) 1m 2f
5:20 (5:20) (95-113,113) 3-Y-O+
£61,224 (£20,408; £10,204; £5,102; £3,061; £2,040)

RPR

1 **Star Empire (SAF)**[285] 1092 9-9-3 110 SamHitchcott 10 113
(M F De Kock, South Africa) *settled in rr: r.o wl fnl 1 1/2f: led fnl 110yds* **20/1**

2 1 ¼ **Elleval (IRE)**[117] 6336 6-8-13 106 (p) PatDobbs 8 106
(David Marnane, Ire) *settled in rr: smooth prog 2 1/2f out: led 1f out: hdd fnl 110yds* **8/1**

3 4 **Sanshaawes (SAF)**[298] 927 6-9-0 107 (b) ChristopheSoumillon 11 99
(M F De Kock, South Africa) *mid-div: chsd ldrs 3f out: ev ch 1f out: one pce fnl 110yds* **9/2**[2]

4 1 **Start Right**[279] 9-8-7 100 RichardMullen 16 90
(S Seemar, UAE) *mid-div: r.o same pce fnl 2f* **20/1**

5 2 ½ **Zambucca (SAF)**[306] 824 7-8-6 106 (b) HectorCrouch[(7)] 13 91
(S Seemar, UAE) *trckd ldrs: led briefly 1 1/2f out: sn hdd & wknd* **25/1**

6 nk **Atomic Rush (SAF)**[313] 744 5-8-10 104 WayneSmith 12 87
(M F De Kock, South Africa) *in rr: r.o fnl 2 1/2f but nvr nr to chal* **25/1**

7 2 ½ **Antinori (IRE)**[32] 10-8-8 101 (b) TadhgO'Shea 2 80
(S Seemar, UAE) *nvr bttr than mid-div* **25/1**

8 ¾ **Code Of Honor**[447] 7243 6-8-7 100 (v) WilliamBuick 7 78
(Saeed bin Suroor) *mid-div: chsd ldrs 2 1/2f out: one pce fnl 1 1/2f* **7/2**[1]

9 2 ½ **Earnshaw (USA)**[285] 1096 5-9-6 113 (bt) MickaelBarzalona 14 86
(S bin Ghadayer, UAE) *trckd ldr: led 6f out: hdd & wknd fnl 1 1/2f* **8/1**

10 hd **Zen Zansai Zaid (SWE)**[71] 7-8-7 100 (bt) ChrisHayes 1 73
(Tommy Gustafsson, Sweden) *nvr nr to chal* **33/1**

11 1 ¾ **Paene Magnus (IRE)**[20] 8302 7-8-9 102 (tp) FrederikTylicki 3 71
(A bin Harmash, UAE) *sn led: hdd 6f out: sn btn* **33/1**

12 4 **Bayrir (FR)**[76] 7-8-9 102 ow2 (t) DaneO'Neill 15 63
(N Al Mandeel, Saudi Arabia) *nvr bttr than mid-div* **40/1**

13 3 ¼ **Pilote (IRE)**[306] 824 6-8-13 106 (p) RoystonFfrench 4 61
(S bin Ghadayer, UAE) *nvr bttr than mid-div* **14/1**

14 9 ½ **Bancnuanaheireann (IRE)**[63] 7718 9-8-11 105 AndrewMullen 6 40
(Michael Appleby) *s.i.s: nvr nr to chal* **9/1**

15 ¾ **Vaasa (IRE)**[285] 1092 5-8-7 100 FernandoJara 5 34
(A bin Harmash, UAE) *trckd ldrs but hanging: wknd fnl 3f* **50/1**

16 11 ½ **Hasanour (USA)**[116] 6365 6-8-10 104 JamieSpencer 9 14
(M Halford, Ire) *nvr nr to chal* **11/2**[3]

2m 1.59s (-1.11) **Going Correction** +0.20s/f (Good) **16 Ran SP% 126.0**
Speed ratings: **112,111,107,107,105 104,102,102,100,100 98,95,92,85,84 75**
CSF: 162.41; TRICAST: 870.74.
Owner Mohd Khaleel Ahmed **Bred** Sydney A Muller, F M Ratner & L M Salzman **Trained** South Africa

FOCUS
TRAKUS: 2nd -1, 3rd 0, 4th -3, 5th -3, 6th +8, 7th -8, 8th +2, 9th -8, 10th -8, 11th -3, 12th +2, 13th -11, 14th -4, 15th -6, 16th -5. The early pace was too strong - 25.72, 22.5, 23.98, 24.56, winner home in 23.83 - and here are the positions of the first six after 800m: 16th, 15th, 6th, 11th, 4th, 14th.

94a LONGINES CONQUEST CLASSIC LADIES (H'CAP) (DIRT) 1m 1f 110y(D)
5:55 (5:55) (95-108,106) 3-Y-O+
£44,897 (£14,965; £7,482; £3,741; £2,244; £1,496)

RPR

1 **One Man Band (IRE)**[35] 8098 5-9-4 106 PatDobbs 5 110
(Doug Watson, UAE) *wl away: sn led: kicked clr 3f out: r.o: comf* **4/5**[1]

2 1 ½ **Emirates Flyer**[313] 742 5-9-1 102 JamesDoyle 4 104
(Saeed bin Suroor) *trckd ldr: r.o but no ch w wnr* **6/1**[2]

3 ¾ **Hunting Ground (USA)**[350] 257 6-9-2 104 MickaelBarzalona 8 103+
(S bin Ghadayer, UAE) *settled in rr: r.o fnl 2f but n.d* **12/1**

4 ½ **Artigiano (USA)**[322] 616 6-9-2 104 (b) WilliamBuick 2 102
(Charlie Appleby) *trckd ldr: ev ch 3f out: one pce fnl 2f* **7/1**[3]

5 9 ¼ **Mawhub**[20] 8302 7-9-1 102 (b) RichardMullen 9 82
(S Seemar, UAE) *s.i.s: nvr nr to chal* **12/1**

6 3 ½ **Romansh (USA)**[293] 987 6-9-2 104 (bt) RoystonFfrench 7 76
(S bin Ghadayer, UAE) *trckd ldrs tl outpcd fnl 3f* **20/1**

7 1 ¾ **Alabaster (USA)**[172] 4-8-10 100 (v) DaneO'Neill 6 69
(Saeed bin Suroor) *slowly away: a in rr* **16/1**

8 10 **Beach Bar (IRE)**[64] 7709 5-8-13 100 FrederikTylicki 3 49
(Brendan Powell) *s.i.s: trckd ldrs tl wknd 3f out* **40/1**

9 6 ¼ **Majeed**[103] 6734 6-8-13 100 JamieSpencer 1 36
(David Simcock) *a in rr* **8/1**

1m 57.85s (-0.95) **Going Correction** +0.175s/f (Slow)
WFA 4 from 5yo+ 1lb **9 Ran SP% 121.9**
Speed ratings: **110,108,108,107,100 97,96,88,83**
CSF: 6.61; TRICAST: 38.46.
Owner Sheikh Saeed Bin Mohammed Al Maktoum **Bred** Richard A Pegum **Trained** United Arab Emirates

FOCUS
TRAKUS: 2nd +8, 3rd +19, 4th +2, 5th +25, 6th +15, 7th +17, 8th +13, 9th +10. The top weight went the shortest route and made all through the following splits: 26.52 (400m), 23.55 (800m), 24.27 (1200m), 24.32 (1600m). Sound form.

95a LONGINES MASTER COLLECTION (H'CAP) (TURF) 7f
6:30 (6:30) (100-113,111) 3-Y-O+
£48,979 (£16,326; £8,163; £4,081; £2,448; £1,632)

RPR

1 **Ghaamer (USA)**[32] 6-8-11 102 (t) TadhgO'Shea 15 108
(A R Al Rayhi, UAE) *sn led: kicked clr 3f out: r.o gamely* **25/1**

2 1 ¼ **Eastern Rules (IRE)**[117] 6340 8-8-11 102 JamesDoyle 16 105+
(M Halford, Ire) *s.i.s: settled in rr: r.o wl fnl 2f: nrst fin* **8/1**

3 hd **Majestic Mount**[96] 6-8-10 101 (t) RichardMullen 12 103
(S Seemar, UAE) *nvr able to chal but r.o fnl 2f* **33/1**

4 shd **Anaerobio (ARG)**[306] 826 8-9-3 108 (t) WayneSmith 5 110
(M F De Kock, South Africa) *mid-div: r.o fnl 2f: nrst fin* **16/1**

5 hd **B Fifty Two (IRE)**[75] 7466 7-8-10 101 MickaelBarzalona 3 103
(Charles Hills) *nvr able to chal but r.o fnl 2f* **12/1**

6 shd **Encipher (USA)**[278] 7-8-9 100 SamHitchcott 8 101
(A R Al Rayhi, UAE) *trckd ldr: ev ch 2 1/2f out: r.o one pce fnl 2f* **33/1**

7 ½ **Merhee (AUS)**[21] 8276 7-8-4 **101**............................(b) HectorCrouch(6) 11 101
(S Seemar, UAE) *mid-div: wd: ev ch fnl 2f: one pce fnl 1 1/2f* **16/1**
8 ½ **Dark Emerald (IRE)**[101] 6817 6-9-3 **108**..........................(v) PatDobbs 14 107
(Brendan Powell) *chsd ldr: one pce fnl 2f* **5/2**[1]
9 1 **Glory Awaits (IRE)**[90] 7074 6-9-0 **105**.......................... JamieSpencer 4 101
(David Simcock) *slowly away: nvr nr to chal but r.o fnl 2 1/2f* **18/1**
10 shd **Bossy Guest (IRE)**[139] 5599 4-9-3 **108**....................... CharlesBishop 13 104
(Mick Channon) *s.i.s: a in rr* **6/1**[2]
11 1 ¼ **Whistle Stop (SAF)**[322] 618 5-8-10 **101**.......................... DaneO'Neill 7 93
(M F De Kock, South Africa) *nvr bttr than mid-div* **20/1**
12 1 **Battle Of Marathon (USA)**[141] 5537 4-8-7 **102** ow1 GeorgeBuckell(5) 10 92
(John Ryan) *nvr nr to chal* **25/1**
13 1 ¼ **Mashaaref**[27] 8192 8-8-10 **101**.. PaulHanagan 6 87
(M Al Mheiri, UAE) *trckd ldr tl outpcd fnl 1 1/2f* **6/1**[2]
14 2 ¾ **Heavy Metal**[32] 6-8-13 **104**.. RoystonFfrench 9 83
(S bin Ghadayer, UAE) *nvr bttr than mid-div* **25/1**
15 ½ **United Color (USA)**[21] 8276 7-8-13 **104**.........................(t) ChrisHayes 1 81
(D Selvaratnam, UAE) *mid-div on rail: rdn 3 1/2f out: sn btn* **33/1**
16 2 ¼ **Zahee (NZ)**[313] 741 6-9-6 **111**............................ ChristopheSoumillon 2 82
(M F De Kock, South Africa) *nvr bttr than mid-div* **7/1**[3]

1m 23.61s (-0.49) **Going Correction** +0.20s/f (Good) **16** Ran SP% **130.6**
Speed ratings: **110,108,108,108,108 107,107,106,105,105 104,102,101,98,97 95**
CSF: 214.41; TRICAST: 3,736.37.
Owner Hamdan Al Maktoum **Bred** Shadwell Farm LLC **Trained** UAE

FOCUS
TRAKUS: 2nd +5, 3rd +5, 4th 0, 5th +2, 6th +4, 7th +8, 8th +8, 9th +1, 10th +4, 11th +7, 12th +12, 13th -1, 14th +6, 15th -3, 16th -1. The winner got across from a wide draw and made all - 25.03, 23.08, 23.24, 12.26 - to complete an unbelievable four-timer for Ali Al Raihe. This was also a third winner on the night for Tadhg O'Shea, who is enjoying a fantastic season.

[83]LINGFIELD (L-H)
Friday, January 8

OFFICIAL GOING: Polytrack: standard
Wind: Fresh, behind, moderating from race 4 Weather: Cloudy, raining races 4/5

96 32RED.COM MAIDEN STKS 1m 4f (P)
1:05 (1:05) (Class 5) 3-Y-O **£2,911** (£866; £432; £216) **Stalls** Low

Form RPR
523- **1** **Epsom Day (IRE)**[43] 7999 3-9-5 67..............................(b[1]) TomQueally 6 74+
(John Gosden) *dwlt: led after 1f: mde rest: drew clr 2f out: easily* **10/11**[1]
0- **2** 6 **Tartan Bute**[69] 7638 3-9-5 0..(b) AdrianNicholls 5 61
(Mark Johnston) *chsd ldrs but pushed along at various stages: rdn 4f out: kpt on to take 2nd jst over 1f out: no ch w wnr* **16/1**
60- **3** ½ **Skylark Lady (IRE)**[23] 8253 3-9-0 0.................................... ChrisCatlin 2 55
(Rae Guest) *settled in last pair: rdn 3f out: prog to dispute 2nd jst over 1f out: kpt on same pce after* **25/1**
4 4 ½ **Regina Cordium (IRE)** 3-9-0 0...................................... RobertHavlin 1 48
(John Gosden) *disp 4th pl and in tch: trapped bhd struggling rivals and dropped to last over 3f out and sn urged along: sme prog 2f out: n.d* **11/4**[2]
5 4 ½ **Royal Beekeeper** 3-9-5 0...[1] AdamKirby 3 46
(George Scott) *dwlt: rcvrd to chse wnr 8f out: rdn 3f out: lost 2nd and wknd qckly jst over 1f out* **9/2**[3]
000- **6** 1 ¾ **Mooizo (IRE)**[24] 8233 3-9-0 23.. ShaneKelly 7 38
(Paul D'Arcy) *hld up in last pair: prog over 3f out to chse ldng pair over 2f out: hanging and wknd rapidly over 1f out* **100/1**
7 7 **Monet's Sky (IRE)** 3-9-5 0.. FergusSweeney 4 32
(Lucy Wadham) *led 1f: chsd wnr to 8f out: rdn 4f out: wknd rapidly 3f out: t.o* **12/1**

2m 32.58s (-0.42) **Going Correction** -0.10s/f (Stan) **7** Ran SP% **115.6**
Speed ratings (Par 97): **97,93,92,89,86 85,80**
CSF £19.36 TOTE £1.90: £1.50, £8.30; EX 26.20 Trifecta £234.50.
Owner Mohamed Obaida **Bred** Rabbah Bloodstock Limited **Trained** Newmarket, Suffolk

FOCUS
A very weak maiden behind the winner, who set a modest standard.

97 DOWNLOAD THE LADBROKES APP H'CAP 1m 1y(P)
1:35 (1:38) (Class 6) (0-60,60) 4-Y-O+ **£2,264** (£673; £336; £168) **Stalls** High

Form RPR
034- **1** **Bookmaker**[23] 8252 6-9-5 **58**..(b) WilliamCarson 9 65
(John Bridger) *trckd ldr: rdn to chal 2f out: narrow ld fnl f: hld on wl* **5/1**[3]
400- **2** hd **Trending (IRE)**[17] 8351 7-9-3 **56**....................................(t) GeorgeBaker 2 63
(Jeremy Gask) *led at decent pce: rdn and jnd 2f out: narrowly hdd fnl f: kpt on wl but jst hld* **10/1**
063- **3** 1 ¾ **Pyroclastic (IRE)**[11] 8376 4-9-7 **60**............................(p) PatCosgrave 11 62
(Jim Boyle) *hld up in last pair fr wd draw: prog over 2f out: rdn to chse ldng pair fnl f and looked a threat: edgd lft and nt qckn* **7/2**[2]
3/0- **4** 1 ¼ **First Summer**[121] 6222 4-9-4 **57**.. JFEgan 7 56
(Shaun Harris) *trckd ldrs: rdn to chse ldng pair 2f out to 1f out: one pce* **6/1**
045- **5** ½ **Scot Daddy (USA)**[17] 8354 4-9-7 **60**........................... FergusSweeney 5 58
(David Dennis) *reluctant to post: hld up in tch: prog to chse ldng pair 3f out to 2f out: rdn and no rspnse over 1f out* **9/4**[1]
/00- **6** 2 **Star Pursuits**[30] 8158 4-8-11 **50**.. KieranO'Neill 10 43
(Jimmy Fox) *wl in rr: shkn up 3f out: stl wl in rr 2f out: rdn and kpt on one pce fr over 1f out* **16/1**
000- **7** 3 ¼ **Rezwaan**[21] 8278 9-9-4 **57**...(b) ShaneKelly 1 43
(Murty McGrath) *a towards rr: shkn up 3f out: sn struggling* **16/1**
004- **8** 7 **Indus Valley (IRE)**[23] 8255 9-9-3 **56**............................(v) RobertWinston 8 25
(Lee Carter) *dwlt: mostly in last: urged along 1/2-way: sn bhd* **12/1**
406- **9** 4 **Cyflymder (IRE)**[87] 7190 10-8-11 **55**........................ JustinNewman(5) 4 14
(David C Griffiths) *chsd ldng pair to 3f out: wknd qckly* **8/1**

1m 36.77s (-1.43) **Going Correction** -0.10s/f (Stan) **9** Ran SP% **123.6**
Speed ratings (Par 101): **103,102,101,99,99 97,94,87,83**
CSF £57.77 CT £204.60 TOTE £6.70: £1.70, £1.90, £1.80; EX 51.70 Trifecta £166.30.
Owner T Wallace & J J Bridger **Bred** Benjamin Newton And Graycroft Farm **Trained** Liphook, Hants
■ Kubeba was withdrawn. Price at time of withdrawal 3-1. Rule 4 applies to bets placed prior to withdrawal, but not to SP bets - deduction 25p in the pound. New market formed.

FOCUS
A moderate handicap, weakened further when the well-backed Kubeba was withdrawn at the start. Despite a decent pace, few ever got into this with the first two holding those positions throughout.

98 UNIBET OFFER DAILY JOCKEY AND TRAINER SPECIALS H'CAP 5f 6y(P)
2:10 (2:10) (Class 6) (0-60,60) 4-Y-O+ **£2,264** (£673; £336; £168) **Stalls** High

Form RPR
423- **1** **Rocket Rob (IRE)**[8] 8413 10-9-6 **59**.................................... TomQueally 3 66
(Willie Musson) *hld up off the pce: prog on inner wl over 1f out: chsd ldr ins fnl f: drvn and styd on to ld last 50yds* **3/1**[2]
030- **2** ½ **Boxing Shadows**[171] 4489 6-9-7 **60**.............................. RobertWinston 4 65
(Les Eyre) *pressed ldr: rdn to ld over 1f out: kpt on but hdd last 50yds* **2/1**[1]
005- **3** 1 **Secret Millionaire (IRE)**[65] 7712 9-9-4 **57**................................ JFEgan 1 59
(Shaun Harris) *in tch: trckd ldng pair 3f out: rdn over 1f out: tried to cl fnl f but nt qckn last 100yds* **5/1**[3]
016- **4** ¾ **Go Charlie**[9] 8399 5-8-9 **48**.. ShaneKelly 5 47
(Lisa Williamson) *taken down early: dwlt: urged along in last pair after 2f: no prog tl styd on ins fnl f* **8/1**
665- **5** nk **Burnt Cream**[8] 8413 9-9-4 **57**..(t) RobertHavlin 6 55
(Martin Bosley) *dwlt: hld up in last: pushed along 2f out: no prog tl shkn up and kpt on ins fnl f: nvr involved* **8/1**
5/0- **6** ¾ **Frozen Princess**[37] 8071 4-9-5 **58**.. AdamKirby 2 53
(Jamie Osborne) *led to over 1f out: wknd ins fnl f* **14/1**
201- **7** ½ **Rat Catcher (IRE)**[21] 8289 6-8-12 **54**..........................(b) RobHornby(3) 8 47
(Lisa Williamson) *racd on outer: pressed ldng pair 2f: rdn and fdd over 1f out* **8/1**

58.1s (-0.70) **Going Correction** -0.10s/f (Stan) **7** Ran SP% **115.0**
Speed ratings (Par 101): **101,100,98,97,96 95,94**
CSF £9.57 CT £27.76 TOTE £4.50: £2.10, £1.80; EX 10.30 Trifecta £40.90.
Owner W J Musson **Bred** Mrs Marita Rogers **Trained** Newmarket, Suffolk

FOCUS
A moderate sprint handicap, but run at a decent pace.

99 CORAL H'CAP 1m 4f (P)
2:45 (2:45) (Class 2) (0-105,102) 4-Y-O+
£11,827 (£3,541; £1,770; £885; £442; £222) **Stalls** Low

Form RPR
021- **1** **Barye**[20] 8308 5-9-7 **98**.. ShaneKelly 2 107+
(Richard Hughes) *trckd ldrs: clsd over 2f out: plenty of room on inner and led over 1f out: pushed out: comf* **1/1**[1]
01-5 **2** 1 ¼ **First Mohican**[5] 31 8-9-11 **102**... TomQueally 3 108
(Alan King) *dwlt: hld up in 5th in slowly run r: pushed along 2f out: prog on inner over 1f out: drvn and kpt on to take 2nd last 100yds: unable to chal* **5/1**
004- **3** ½ **Blue Surf**[132] 5846 7-9-8 **99**... AdamKirby 6 104
(Amanda Perrett) *sn led at sedate pce: sed dash for home jst over 3f out: hdd over 1f out: one pce and lost 2nd last 100yds* **9/2**[3]
136- **4** 2 ¼ **The Steward (USA)**[20] 8308 5-9-2 **93**.............................(p) ChrisCatlin 5 95
(Sir Mark Prescott Bt) *sn trckd ldr: rdn whn pce lifted jst over 3f out: lost 2nd and one pce fnl 2f* **4/1**[2]
0/0- **5** 1 ½ **Winterlude (IRE)**[100] 5597 6-9-5 **96**................................ GeorgeBaker 1 95
(Jennie Candlish) *hld up in last in slowly run r: effrt and shkn up wl over 1f out: no prog and no ch to play a part* **25/1**
250- **6** 5 **Masterpaver**[187] 3930 5-9-3 **94**....................................(v) RobertWinston 4 85
(Alan Bailey) *trckd ldrs on outer: rdn 3f out: wd bnd 2f out and sn wknd* **25/1**

2m 35.04s (2.04) **Going Correction** -0.10s/f (Stan) **6** Ran SP% **112.5**
Speed ratings (Par 109): **89,88,87,86,85 82**
CSF £6.56 TOTE £1.80: £1.20, £2.70; EX 4.60 Trifecta £12.30.
Owner Anthony Hogarth **Bred** Miss K Rausing **Trained** Upper Lambourn, Berkshire

FOCUS
A decent handicap, but they went no pace and it developed into something of a 3f sprint. The winner was better than the bare form.

100 UNIBET.CO.UK DAILY ENHANCED PLACE TERMS H'CAP 6f 1y(P)
3:15 (3:16) (Class 5) (0-70,70) 4-Y-O+ **£2,911** (£866; £432; £216) **Stalls** Low

Form RPR
00-2 **1** **Jammy Guest (IRE)**[4] 36 6-9-7 **70**.. AdamKirby 3 79
(George Margarson) *hld up in 4th: shkn up over 1f out: clsd qckly to ld last 125yds: sn clr* **4/9**[1]
000- **2** 1 ¾ **Bush Warrior (IRE)**[81] 7345 5-9-7 **70**..........................(v) GeorgeBaker 1 73
(Anabel K Murphy) *led: rdn over 1f out: hdd and one pce last 125yds* **5/1**[2]
320- **3** 1 **Time Medicean**[74] 7514 10-8-1 **57**......................... JosephineGordon(7) 5 57
(Tony Carroll) *s.i.s: hld up in last pair: shkn up 2f out: hanging over 1f out: styd on fnl f to take 3rd last strides* **12/1**
600- **4** nk **Wahaab (IRE)**[23] 8250 5-9-0 **63**.. ShaneKelly 4 62
(Richard Hughes) *t.k.h: in tch: chsd ldr over 2f out to 1f out: fdd* **8/1**[3]
006- **5** 1 ½ **Ask The Guru**[20] 8307 6-9-4 **67**......................................(v) RobertHavlin 6 61
(Michael Attwater) *chsd ldr to over 2f out: stl wl in tch 1f out: wknd* **20/1**
0- **6** 10 **Whip Up A Frenzy (IRE)**[22] 8262 4-9-2 **65**................. AdamBeschizza 2 27
(Richard Rowe) *a in last pair: shkn up and wknd 2f out: t.o* **33/1**

1m 11.2s (-0.70) **Going Correction** -0.10s/f (Stan) **6** Ran SP% **112.4**
Speed ratings (Par 103): **100,97,96,95,93 80**
CSF £3.12 TOTE £1.40: £1.20, £2.20; EX 3.00 Trifecta £12.50.
Owner John Guest Racing **Bred** Robert Power Bloodstock Ltd **Trained** Newmarket, Suffolk

FOCUS
This was about as uncompetitive as the lopsided betting market suggested it would be. The winner probably only had to his recent form.

101 CORAL.CO.UK APPRENTICE H'CAP 1m 4f (P)
3:50 (3:50) (Class 5) (0-70,70) 4-Y-O+ **£2,911** (£866; £432; £216) **Stalls** Low

Form RPR
113- **1** **Saint Honore**[36] 8092 4-9-5 **67**.. PaddyBradley 6 75+
(Pat Phelan) *hld up in last trio: prog on outer over 3f out to chse ldr 2f out: sn rdn and looked hld: styd on wl fnl f to ld narrowly last 50yds* **3/1**[2]
001- **2** shd **Classic Mission**[19] 8317 5-9-9 **67**.............................(b) CharlieBennett 3 74
(Jonathan Portman) *trckd ldrs: clsd to ld over 2f out and sent for home: kpt on but hdd and jst hld fnl 50yds* **5/4**[1]
336- **3** 5 **Percella**[21] 8292 4-8-9 **62**.. PaulBooth(5) 5 61
(Ian Williams) *hld up in last trio: trying to make prog whn n.m.r 2f out: hdwy over 1f out to chse ldng pair fnl f: styd on but no ch to threaten* **16/1**
6/0- **4** 2 **Rising Breeze (FR)**[65] 2642 5-9-12 **70**.................... JosephineGordon 8 66
(Tony Carroll) *mostly in last and pushed along at times: stl in last over 2f out: rdn and prog over 1f out: kpt on to take 4th ins fnl f* **12/1**

300- **5** 2 3/4 **Munsarim (IRE)**[23] 8252 9-9-1 **62**....(b) RhiainIngram(3) 1 53
(Lee Carter) *trckd ldrs: gng easily 3f out: shkn up over 2f out: fnd nil and sn btn* **14/1**
134- **6** 3 3/4 **Mary Le Bow**[28] 8176 5-9-0 **63**....(t) MitchGodwin(5) 7 48
(Victor Dartnall) *disp 2nd pl: led on outer over 3f out to over 2f out: wknd over 1f out* **6/1**[3]
000- **7** 4 **Salient**[23] 8249 12-8-12 **56**.... AdamMcLean 4 35
(Michael Attwater) *disp 2nd pl: chal over 3f out: sn rdn: wknd qckly 2f out* **20/1**
0/3- **8** 19 **My Lord**[13] 262 8-9-10 **68**....(b1) CharlesEddery 2 17
(Jim Best) *t.k.h: sn led: hdd and rdn over 3f out: wknd rapidly over 2f out: t.o* **16/1**

2m 30.48s (-2.52) **Going Correction** -0.10s/f (Stan)
WFA 4 from 5yo+ 4lb **8** Ran SP% **114.6**
Speed ratings (Par 103): **104,103,100,99,97 94,92,79**
CSF £7.12 CT £47.14 TOTE £3.60: £1.20, £1.30, £3.70; EX 9.50 Trifecta £59.60.
Owner William Bocking **Bred** The Lavington Stud **Trained** Epsom, Surrey
■ Stewards' Enquiry : Charlie Bennett two-day ban; used his whip above the permitted level (22nd-23rd Jan)

FOCUS
A modest apprentice event and the two favourites pulled clear.
T/Plt: £14.60 to a £1 stake. Pool: £61,555.29 - 3,069.09 winning tickets T/Qpdt: £2.80 to a £1 stake. Pool: £7,124.53 - 1,819.45 winning tickets **Jonathan Neesom**

69 WOLVERHAMPTON (A.W) (L-H)
Friday, January 8

OFFICIAL GOING: Tapeta: standard
Wind: Light behind Weather: Cloudy

102 32RED CASINO MAIDEN FILLIES' STKS 5f 216y (Tp)
4:15 (4:16) (Class 5) 3-Y-O+ **£3,234** (£962; £481; £240) **Stalls** Low

Form RPR
- **1** **Cocoa Beach (IRE)** 3-8-10 0.... LukeMorris 8 77+
(Sir Mark Prescott Bt) *mid-div: hdwy over 2f out: shkn up to ld ins fnl f: r.o wl* **9/4**[2]
2 1 1/4 **Semra (USA)** 3-8-7 0.... DanielMuscutt(3) 7 72+
(Marco Botti) *a.p: rdn and ev ch ins fnl f: styd on same pce* **10/1**[3]
54- **3** 2 **Miss Goldsmith (IRE)**[17] 8350 3-8-7 0....[1] SammyJoBell(3) 2 66
(Richard Fahey) *hld up: hdwy over 1f out: r.o to go 3rd nr fin* **14/1**
42- **4** 1/2 **Mondial (IRE)**[17] 8350 3-8-10 0.... MartinLane 5 64
(Charlie Appleby) *led: rdn and hdd ins fnl f: no ex* **1/1**[1]
5 4 **Fearbuster (IRE)** 3-8-10 0.... MartinHarley 10 52
(Hugo Palmer) *chsd ldrs: pushed along over 2f out: wknd ins fnl f* **20/1**
6 1/2 **Bemusement** 3-8-10 0.... JoeFanning 6 50
(Mark Johnston) *sn chsng ldr: rdn and ev ch over 1f out: wknd ins fnl f* **12/1**
00- **7** 1/2 **Rip Van Suzy (IRE)**[9] 8402 3-8-7 0.... PhilipPrince(3) 9 48
(David Evans) *hld up: shkn up over 2f out: nvr on terms* **33/1**
00- **8** 8 **Trulove**[17] 8350 3-8-3 0.... VitorSantos(7) 1 23
(John David Riches) *prom 4f* **150/1**
9 3/4 **Lillyput (IRE)** 3-8-10 0.... CathyGannon 3 20
(Mick Channon) *hld up: pushed along over 2f out: sn wknd* **66/1**
10 8 **Bethellie Pride**[44] 6-9-12 0.... JoeyHaynes 4
(Lynn Siddall) *s.s: sn pushed along in rr: wknd over 2f out* **200/1**

1m 13.69s (-0.81) **Going Correction** -0.10s/f (Stan)
WFA 3 from 6yo 16lb **10** Ran SP% **114.6**
Speed ratings (Par 100): **101,99,96,96,90 90,89,78,77,67**
CSF £23.35 TOTE £3.90: £1.10, £2.70, £3.50; EX 24.80 Trifecta £224.60.
Owner Donald R Dizney **Bred** Rockfield Farm **Trained** Newmarket, Suffolk

FOCUS
Some interesting newcomers were on show in this opener and there's a suspicion that the winner is above average.The form is rated around the third.

103 32RED.COM H'CAP 1m 5f 194y (Tp)
4:45 (4:45) (Class 5) (0-75,75) 4-Y-O+ **£3,234** (£962; £481; £240) **Stalls** Low

Form RPR
0/0- **1** **Zakatal**[17] 8353 10-9-2 **65**.... PJMcDonald 4 74
(Rebecca Menzies) *hld up: hdwy over 2f out: rdn to ld 1f out: edgd lft: styd on wl* **8/1**
516/ **2** 1 3/4 **Lucky Jim**[65] 6981 5-9-5 **68**.... MartinLane 3 74
(David Dennis) *chsd ldrs: rdn over 3f out: styd on same pce ins fnl f* **7/1**
004- **3** 2 1/4 **Kiwayu**[38] 8064 7-9-4 **67**....(p) PhillipMakin 1 70
(Philip Kirby) *hld up: pushed along over 3f out: hdwy and nt clr run over 2f out: styd on to go 3rd nr fin* **9/2**[2]
000- **4** nk **Arthurs Secret**[13] 8361 6-8-13 **69**....(b) CallumShepherd(7) 8 72
(John Quinn) *led: hdd over 11f out: chsd ldr tl led again over 2f out: sn rdn: hdd 1f out: no ex ins fnl f* **11/1**
211- **5** 2 **With Hindsight (IRE)**[25] 8223 8-9-7 **70**.... LukeMorris 9 70
(Steve Gollings) *chsd ldrs: led over 11f out: qcknd over 3f out: rdn and hdd over 2f out: wknd ins fnl f* **15/8**[1]
02- **6** 2 1/4 **Wildomar**[27] 8209 7-8-12 **61**.... StevieDonohoe 2 58
(Peter Hiatt) *dwlt: hld up: rdn over 3f out: nt clr run over 2f out: nvr on terms* **5/1**[3]
205- **7** 2 1/4 **Heart Locket**[49] 7920 4-8-6 **68**.... DanielleMooney(7) 7 61
(Michael Easterby) *hld up: racd keenly: pushed along over 2f out: sn wknd* **10/1**
5/0- **8** 5 **Desert Recluse (IRE)**[17] 8353 9-9-0 **63**.... DougieCostello 5 49
(Henry Oliver) *chsd ldrs tl rdn and wknd over 2f out* **28/1**

3m 2.26s (-2.54) **Going Correction** -0.10s/f (Stan)
WFA 4 from 5yo+ 6lb **8** Ran SP% **114.1**
Speed ratings (Par 103): **103,102,100,100,99 98,96,93**
CSF £61.89 CT £283.19 TOTE £11.20: £3.30, £3.00, £1.90; EX 56.00 Trifecta £259.90.
Owner David Furman & John Sugarman **Bred** H H The Aga Khan's Studs Sc **Trained** Mordon, Co. Durham

FOCUS
A fair race for the grade, in which the favourite was bidding for a C&D hat-trick. It was steadily run and developed into a sprint. The winner was on a good mark on back form.

104 32REDSPORT.COM H'CAP 5f 216y (Tp)
5:15 (5:15) (Class 6) (0-60,60) 3-Y-O **£2,587** (£770; £384; £192) **Stalls** Low

Form RPR
453- **1** **Madame Barker (IRE)**[17] 8348 3-9-0 **60**.... PhilDennis(7) 8 68
(Bryan Smart) *led early: chsd ldr tl led over 2f out: rdn clr and hung lft over 1f out: styd on* **9/2**[1]
060- **2** 2 1/4 **Israfel**[27] 8204 3-8-10 **49**.... CathyGannon 10 50
(Jamie Osborne) *s.i.s: hld up: pushed along 1/2-way: nt clr run over 2f out: r.o ins fnl f: nt rch wnr* **11/1**
455- **3** nk **Cool Crescendo**[17] 8348 3-9-4 **57**.... PJMcDonald 3 57
(Rebecca Menzies) *chsd ldrs: rdn over 1f out: styd on same pce* **15/2**[3]
004- **4** 1/2 **Espoir**[21] 8287 3-9-2 **55**.... JackGarritty 6 54
(Richard Fahey) *a.p: rdn and hung rt fr over 1f out: styd on same pce* **9/1**
232- **5** 1/2 **Rupert Boy (IRE)**[24] 8239 3-8-10 **49**....(b) KieranO'Neill 1 46
(Scott Dixon) *sn led: rdn and hdd over 2f out: no ex fnl f* **6/1**[2]
040- **6** 1/2 **Matilda Gleam**[28] 8173 3-9-7 **60**.... OisinMurphy 5 56
(Lisa Williamson) *sn pushed along in rr: rdn over 2f out: r.o ins fnl f: nvr nrr* **6/1**[2]
200- **7** 1 1/2 **Ormanumps (IRE)**[28] 8173 3-8-7 **46**.... LukeMorris 4 37
(Daniel Mark Loughnane) *hld up: hmpd over 2f out: hdwy u.p and nt clr run over 1f out: n.m.r ins fnl f: styd on same pce* **9/1**
445- **8** 3/4 **Castlerea Tess**[28] 8173 3-8-7 **46** oh1.... JamesSullivan 7 35
(Sarah Hollinshead) *mid-div: rdn and hung lft over 2f out: no ex fnl f* **14/1**
004- **9** 4 1/2 **Royal Display**[97] 6940 3-9-0 **53**....(b) TomEaves 2 28
(Kevin Ryan) *s.i.s: hld up: rdn and wknd over 1f out* **9/2**[1]

1m 14.23s (-0.27) **Going Correction** -0.10s/f (Stan) **9** Ran SP% **111.7**
Speed ratings (Par 95): **97,94,93,92,92 91,89,88,82**
CSF £51.98 CT £356.90 TOTE £3.30: £1.20, £5.70, £3.10; EX 52.10 Trifecta £366.90.
Owner Middleham Park Racing XLII & The Barkers **Bred** Ballyhane Stud **Trained** Hambleton, N Yorks

FOCUS
This was turned into a procession by the seemingly exposed Madame Barker. Fair form for the grade.

105 £10 FREE AT 32RED.COM H'CAP 7f 32y (Tp)
5:45 (5:45) (Class 6) (0-60,60) 3-Y-O **£2,587** (£770; £384; £192) **Stalls** High

Form RPR
053- **1** **Inaam (IRE)**[21] 8281 3-9-6 **59**.... DavidNolan 9 64
(Richard Fahey) *prom: n.m.r and lost pl over 4f out: nt clr run over 2f out: swtchd rt and hdwy over 1f out: r.o to ld wl ins fnl f* **11/2**[3]
005- **2** 1 3/4 **La Manga (IRE)**[37] 8073 3-9-3 **56**.... TimmyMurphy 4 57
(Jamie Osborne) *hmpd sn after s: hld up: hdwy over 1f out: r.o: nt rch wnr* **12/1**
400- **3** shd **Opera Buffa (IRE)**[23] 8253 3-9-5 **58**.... JoeFanning 10 58
(Mark Johnston) *racd keenly: sn w ldr: rdn to ld and hung lft fr over 1f out: hdd and unable qck wl ins fnl f* **11/1**
000- **4** 1 1/2 **The Big Guy**[17] 8349 3-9-5 **58**.... CathyGannon 1 57
(Mick Channon) *prom: hmpd and lost pl over 6f out: nt clr run over 2f out: hdwy over 1f out: r.o* **9/1**
005- **5** 1/2 **Englishwoman**[17] 8349 3-9-7 **60**.... SeanLevey 8 58
(David Evans) *led: rdn and hdd over 1f out: no ex wl ins fnl f* **5/1**[2]
403- **6** 1/2 **Intimately**[24] 8239 3-9-2 **55**....(b1) LukeMorris 5 49
(Jonathan Portman) *plld hrd and prom: n.m.r and pushed along 3f out: rdn over 1f out: no ex ins fnl f* **9/2**[1]
660- **7** 3 3/4 **Coral Island**[21] 8281 3-8-8 **50**.... ShelleyBirkett(3) 2 35
(David O'Meara) *mid-div: hmpd and lost pl over 6f out: nt clr run over 2f out: hdwy and nt clr run over 1f out: nt trble ldrs* **28/1**
505- **8** 1 1/4 **Cappy Brown**[64] 7715 3-9-1 **54**....(p) SaleemGolam 3 36
(Alan Bailey) *chsd ldrs: rdn over 2f out: hung lft and wknd over 1f out* **7/1**
340- **9** 1 1/4 **I T Guru**[17] 8348 3-9-4 **57**.... BarryMcHugh 11 36
(Noel Wilson) *plld hrd and prom: lost pl over 3f out: rdn over 2f out: nt clr run and wknd over 1f out* **33/1**
000- **10** 1 1/4 **Mikro Polemistis (IRE)**[55] 7861 3-8-9 **55**.... CallumShepherd(7) 6 31
(Brian Ellison) *in rr: drvn along 1/2-way: wknd over 2f out* **16/1**
560- **11** 7 **Dalalah**[17] 8348 3-9-5 **58**.... JFEgan 7 17
(Richard Guest) *hld up: racd keenly: pushed along and hdwy on outer 1/2-way: eased over 1f out* **7/1**

1m 29.9s (1.10) **Going Correction** -0.10s/f (Stan) **11** Ran SP% **113.5**
Speed ratings (Par 95): **89,87,86,85,84 84,79,78,76,75 67**
CSF £67.17 CT £709.83 TOTE £6.40: £2.50, £3.30, £4.60; EX 56.10 Trifecta £406.70.
Owner Yorkshire Connections Ltd **Bred** John Doyle **Trained** Musley Bank, N Yorks

FOCUS
Some mainly disappointing sorts featured in this very ordinary handicap. The easy winner was making it tenth time lucky.

106 DOWNLOAD THE NEW UNIBET RACING APP H'CAP 5f 20y (Tp)
6:15 (6:15) (Class 4) (0-85,85) 4-Y-O+ **£5,175** (£1,540; £769; £384) **Stalls** Low

Form RPR
123- **1** **Pensax Lad (IRE)**[9] 8395 5-9-3 **84**.... GeorgeDowning(3) 2 93
(Ronald Harris) *mid-div: hdwy over 1f out: rdn to ld ins fnl f: r.o* **15/2**
212- **2** 3/4 **Hoofalong**[22] 8262 6-9-7 **85**....(b) PhillipMakin 1 94+
(Michael Easterby) *a.p: nt clr run over 1f out: sn rdn: r.o* **5/1**[3]
021- **3** hd **Jebediah Shine**[24] 8229 4-9-2 **85**.... JoshDoyle(5) 6 91
(David O'Meara) *chsd ldr: led over 1f out: rdn and hdd ins fnl f: kpt on* **10/1**
414- **4** 1/2 **Burning Thread (IRE)**[24] 8229 9-9-7 **85**....(b) OisinMurphy 9 89
(David Elsworth) *hld up in tch: rdn over 1f out: r.o* **18/1**
111- **5** 1 1/2 **Miracle Garden**[39] 8058 4-8-10 **74**....(p) TomEaves 10 72
(Roy Brotherton) *chsd ldrs: rdn over 1f out: styd on same pce ins fnl f* **14/1**
053- **6** nse **Stocking**[12] 8368 4-9-6 **84**.... JackMitchell 7 82
(Roger Varian) *s.i.s: hld up: hdwy and nt clr run over 1f out: sn swtchd lft: rdn and no ex ins fnl f* **3/1**[2]
/22- **7** nk **Royal Birth**[24] 8229 5-9-5 **83**....(t) SaleemGolam 8 80+
(Stuart Williams) *dwlt: hld up: racd keenly: rdn over 1f out: nt rch ldrs* **2/1**[1]
116- **8** 1/2 **Quality Art (USA)**[267] 1432 8-8-5 **72**.... RobHornby(3) 5 67
(Simon Hodgson) *prom: rdn and nt clr run over 1f out: no ex ins fnl f* **33/1**
600- **9** 2 1/4 **Pearl Noir**[32] 8137 6-8-7 **71** oh3....(b) KieranO'Neill 4 58
(Scott Dixon) *led: rdn and hdd over 1f out: wknd ins fnl f* **40/1**
106- **10** 3 1/4 **Agerzam**[154] 5090 6-8-12 **76**....(b) LukeMorris 3 52
(Ronald Harris) *in rr: nt clr run 2f out: wknd fnl f* **20/1**

1m 0.15s (-1.75) **Going Correction** -0.10s/f (Stan) **10** Ran SP% **117.9**
Speed ratings (Par 105): **110,108,108,107,105 105,104,103,100,95**
CSF £44.49 CT £390.04 TOTE £10.40: £3.00, £2.00, £2.90; EX 45.60 Trifecta £317.90.
Owner S & A Mares **Bred** Seamus And James McMullan **Trained** Earlswood, Monmouths

FOCUS
Easily the strongest and most competitive race on the card. It was run at a good pace and rates as solid handicap form, the winner to his best.

107 CORAL CONNECT H'CAP 1m 1f 103y (Tp)
6:45 (6:45) (Class 6) (0-55,55) 4-Y-O+ **£2,587** (£770; £384; £192) **Stalls** Low

Form RPR

63-4 **1** **Cahar Fad (IRE)**[4] 39 4-9-4 **53** (bt) AdamBeschizza 8 60
(Steph Hollinshead) *mid-div: hdwy 1/2-way: led 2f out: rdn and hung rt ins fnl f: styd on* **5/1**[2]

515- **2** *3/4* **Les Gar Gan (IRE)**[9] 8397 5-9-7 **55** StevieDonohoe 6 61
(Daniel Mark Loughnane) *sn pushed along into mid-div: hdwy over 2f out: rdn to chse wnr over 1f out: r.o* **14/1**

061- **3** *hd* **Foylesideview (IRE)**[18] 8335 4-9-1 **50** CathyGannon 4 55
(Harry Chisman) *s.i.s: hld up: hdwy over 1f out: r.o* **13/2**[3]

040- **4** *3 1/4* **Celtic Artisan (IRE)**[18] 8335 5-8-11 **52** (p) DanielleMooney[(7)] 9 51
(Rebecca Menzies) *hld up: hdwy and hung lft fr over 1f out: nt rch ldrs* **28/1**

234- **5** *hd* **Trigger Park (IRE)**[18] 8334 5-8-13 **47** LukeMorris 13 46
(Ronald Harris) *hld up: hdwy over 2f out: rdn over 1f out: styd on same pce fnl f* **11/1**

404- **6** *3 1/2* **Warden Bond**[18] 8335 8-9-6 **54** (p) RyanPowell 12 46
(William Stone) *prom: rdn over 1f out: wknd fnl f* **18/1**

000- **7** *nse* **Thrtypointstothree (IRE)**[105] 6715 5-8-12 **46** oh1 (b) OisinMurphy 3 38+
(Nikki Evans) *prom: chsd ldr over 6f out: led over 2f out: sn rdn and hdd: wknd fnl f* **25/1**

533- **8** *4* **Quite Sparky**[13] 8360 9-8-8 **47** (b) RachelRichardson[(5)] 5 31
(Lucinda Egerton) *prom: rdn over 2f out: wknd over 1f out* **9/1**

005- **9** *hd* **Cookie Ring (IRE)**[13] 8360 5-8-12 **46** oh1 DougieCostello 11 30
(Patrick Holmes) *s.i.s: hld up: hdwy over 2f out: rdn over 1f out: wknd fnl f* **14/1**

300- **10** *5* **Sexy Secret**[39] 8044 5-9-4 **55** (p) SimonPearce[(3)] 2 29+
(Lydia Pearce) *led 1f: chsd ldrs: hmpd and wknd 2f out* **14/1**

056- **11** *1* **Zubaidah**[21] 8278 4-9-6 **55** (p[1]) SaleemGolam 7 28
(Heather Dalton) *s.i.s: hld up: rdn over 3f out: wknd over 2f out* **28/1**

03-1 **12** *1 1/4* **Goodwood Moonlight**[6] 20 4-9-6 **55** 6ex SeanLevey 10 25+
(Ian Williams) *led after 1f: rdn and hdd over 2f out: sn wknd* **9/4**[1]

1m 59.59s (-1.21) **Going Correction** -0.10s/f (Stan)
WFA 4 from 5yo+ 1lb **12** Ran SP% **115.1**
Speed ratings (Par 101): **101,100,100,97,97 93,93,90,90,85 84,83**
CSF £68.95 CT £454.08 TOTE £5.30: £1.80, £4.60, £2.40; EX 69.60 Trifecta £244.00.
Owner D Hodson, K Meredith, N Sweeney **Bred** Tally-Ho Stud **Trained** Upper Longdon, Staffs

FOCUS
A moderate finale in which the short-priced favourite ran well below expectations. Three broke nicely clear., each coming from the rear.
T/Jkpt: not won. JACKPOT PLACEPOT £544.00. Pool £2,646.00 - 3.55 winning units. T/Plt: £579.10 to a £1 stake. Pool: £92,427.45 - 116.51 winning tickets T/Qpdt: £42.70 to a £1 stake. Pool: £12,746.65 - 220.70 winning tickets **Colin Roberts**

108 - 120a (Foreign Racing) - See Raceform Interactive

[96]LINGFIELD (L-H)
Saturday, January 9

OFFICIAL GOING: Polytrack: standard
Wind: Strong, behind Weather: Overcast, raining race 1

121 CORAL H'CAP 1m 2f (P)
12:10 (12:10) (Class 3) (0-90,90) 4-Y-**£7,246** (£2,168; £1,084; £542; £270) **Stalls** Low

Form RPR

324- **1** **Aleator (USA)**[33] 8139 4-9-5 **88** (b[1]) LukeMorris 6 94
(Sir Mark Prescott Bt) *pushed up to ld after 1f: mde rest: rdn 2f out: hrd pressed fnl f: drvn and hld on* **7/4**[1]

012- **2** *1/2* **Sheila's Buddy**[24] 8256 7-8-13 **80** LiamKeniry 3 85
(J S Moore) *dwlt: sn in 4th: prog to chse wnr over 2f out: drvn to chal fnl f: kpt on but nt qckn nr fin* **4/1**[3]

040- **3** *1* **Warfare**[10] 8405 7-8-13 **80** BarryMcHugh 1 83
(Tim Fitzgerald) *racd mostly in 3rd: rdn over 2f out: kpt on fr over 1f out: cl enough on inner but nvr pce to chal seriously* **10/1**

431- **4** *3/4* **Modernism**[20] 8318 7-9-3 **84** DavidNolan 4 86
(Richard Fahey) *led 1f: chsd wnr to over 2f out: nt qckn and sn wl hld in 4th: kpt on nr fin* **3/1**[2]

405- **5** *1 1/4* **Swing Easy**[45] 7985 6-9-4 **85** (b) FergusSweeney 2 84
(Gary Moore) *hld up in last pair: shkn up and no prog over 2f out: n.d after but kpt on nr fin* **5/1**

351/ **6** *26* **Cai Shen (IRE)**[646] 1268 8-9-9 **90** StevieDonohoe 5 37
(Grace Harris) *a in last pair: wknd over 3f out: t.o* **25/1**

2m 3.28s (-3.32) **Going Correction** -0.05s/f (Stan)
WFA 4 from 6yo+ 2lb **6** Ran SP% **111.0**
Speed ratings (Par 107): **111,110,109,109,108 87**
CSF £8.85 TOTE £2.50: £1.80, £3.40; EX 8.60 Trifecta £58.30.
Owner W E Sturt - Osborne House II **Bred** Kirsten Rausing **Trained** Newmarket, Suffolk

FOCUS
Just an ordinary 0-90. The first two are rated to form.

122 32RED.COM MEDIAN AUCTION MAIDEN STKS 1m 1y(P)
12:45 (12:45) (Class 6) 3-Y-O **£2,264** (£673; £336; £168) **Stalls** High

Form RPR

3- **1** **Singyoursong (IRE)**[25] 8232 3-9-0 0 JamieSpencer 8 75+
(David Simcock) *awkward s: in tch: wnt 3rd over 3f out: rdn to cl on ldng pair over 2f out: led over 1f out: styd on wl and sn clr* **1/1**[1]

64- **2** *3* **Lord Huntingdon**[24] 8251 3-9-5 0 OisinMurphy 1 72
(Andrew Balding) *led: rdn 2f out: hdd over 1f out and edgd lft: one pce and sn btn* **7/2**[3]

5- **3** *1 1/4* **Zeehan**[22] 8285 3-9-0 0 AdamKirby 7 64
(Clive Cox) *awkward s: chsd ldr after 2f: rdn over 2f out: sn lost 2nd and nt qckn: pushed along and kpt on same pce fnl f* **5/2**[2]

0- **4** *10* **Harry's Endeavour**[31] 8153 3-9-5 0 SteveDrowne 6 46
(Seamus Mullins) *hld up: in tch to 3f out: sn lft bhd and poor 4th over 2f out* **100/1**

5 *1* **Smirnova (IRE)** 3-8-7 0 EvaMoscrop[(7)] 4 39
(Marco Botti) *hld up in last: pushed along and outpcd fr 3f out: no ch after* **25/1**

06- **6** *5* **Little Salamanca**[24] 8245 3-9-2 0 RyanTate[(3)] 5 32
(Clive Cox) *chsd ldrs: urged along bef 1/2-way: wknd 3f out* **20/1**

0- **7** *1/2* **Ice Cristal (IRE)**[40] 8047 3-9-0 0 JackMitchell 2 26
(Sylvester Kirk) *chsd ldr: sn pushed along: wknd over 3f out* **100/1**

1m 38.33s (0.13) **Going Correction** -0.05s/f (Stan) **7** Ran SP% **111.4**
Speed ratings (Par 95): **97,94,92,82,81 76,76**
CSF £4.53 TOTE £1.70: £1.10, £3.20; EX 5.10 Trifecta £8.00.
Owner Mohammed Jaber **Bred** Rabbah Bloodstock Limited **Trained** Newmarket, Suffolk

FOCUS
This maiden only concerned three runners. Tricky form to assess, with the potential to rate higher.

123 32RED H'CAP 1m 1y(P)
1:20 (1:20) (Class 4) (0-85,85) 3-Y-O **£4,690** (£1,395; £697; £348) **Stalls** High

Form RPR

631- **1** **Hombre Rojo (IRE)**[24] 8251 3-8-13 **77** JimCrowley 2 87
(Simon Dow) *led 3f: w ldr tl led again 2f out: rdn clr fr over 1f out* **10/11**[1]

033- **2** *6* **Strawberry Sorbet**[25] 8234 3-8-4 **71** RyanTate[(3)] 1 67
(Clive Cox) *chsd ldrs: rdn to go 3rd over 2f out: nt qckn and no imp over 1f out: kpt on to take 2nd last stride* **9/2**[2]

311- **3** *shd* **Threebagsue (IRE)**[12] 8378 3-8-2 **73** (b) JosephineGordon[(7)] 4 69
(J S Moore) *w wnr: led after 3f to 2f out: btn over 1f out: fdd and lost 2nd last stride* **7/1**

303- **4** *1 1/4* **Manhattan Skyline (IRE)**[21] 8309 3-9-7 **85** LiamKeniry 5 78
(J S Moore) *hld up in last: gng bttr than sme but stl last 3f out: prog to go 4th over 1f out: rdn and fnd nil sn after* **33/1**

321- **5** *11* **Shypen**[9] 8410 3-8-9 **73** RyanPowell 3 41
(George Margarson) *t.k.h early: trckd ldrs: shkn up 3f out: wknd 2f out* **6/1**[3]

001- **6** *1 1/2* **Silk Gem (IRE)**[23] 8259 3-8-11 **78** (p) NathanAlison[(3)] 6 42
(William Haggas) *t.k.h early: racd on outer: trckd ldrs: shkn up 3f out: wknd 2f out* **8/1**

1m 35.76s (-2.44) **Going Correction** -0.05s/f (Stan) **6** Ran SP% **111.4**
Speed ratings (Par 99): **110,104,103,102,91 90**
CSF £5.23 TOTE £1.80: £1.30, £1.40; EX 6.10 Trifecta £21.50.
Owner Robert Moss **Bred** Helen Lyons **Trained** Ashtead, Surrey

FOCUS
The winner was much and scored in a good time. The next two ran to their marks.

124 BET NOW WITH THE LADBROKES APP H'CAP 7f 1y(P)
1:55 (1:56) (Class 5) (0-70,70) 4-Y-O+ **£2,911** (£866; £432; £216) **Stalls** Low

Form RPR

005- **1** **Twin Point**[24] 8250 5-9-4 **67** (t) MartinLane 4 78
(Charlie Fellowes) *mde all: upped the pce fr 3f out: rdn to assert over 1f out: in n.d after* **7/4**[1]

355- **2** *3* **Perfect Alchemy (IRE)**[24] 8248 5-9-6 **69** OisinMurphy 1 73
(Patrick Chamings) *trckd ldrs: rdn to chse wnr wl over 1f out: kpt on but no imp* **3/1**[2]

143- **3** *2 3/4* **The Happy Hammer (IRE)**[86] 7242 10-9-0 **63** RobertTart 2 59
(Eugene Stanford) *in tch: rdn in 5th whn hit rail then stmbld over 2f out: rallied over 1f out: kpt on to take 3rd last stride* **14/1**

360- **4** *shd* **Whaleweigh Station**[25] 8242 5-9-7 **70** (p) AdamKirby 7 66
(J R Jenkins) *chsd wnr: rdn 3f out: lost 2nd wl over 1f out: one pce after: lost 3rd last stride* **7/1**[3]

550- **5** *1 3/4* **Autumn Tonic (IRE)**[31] 8158 4-8-8 **57** LukeMorris 10 48
(Simon Dow) *stdd s and hld up in last fr wd draw: gng wl but stl last whn hmpd over 2f out: nt clr run over 1f out: shkn up and r.o fnl f: no ch to be involved* **12/1**

2/0- **6** *1 1/2* **Poppet Rocket (IRE)**[223] 2742 4-9-4 **67** PaulMulrennan 3 54
(Brian Meehan) *hld up in last pair: effrt on outer over 2f out: shkn up and no prog wl over 1f out* **8/1**

500- **7** *3/4* **Satchville Flyer**[24] 8250 5-9-4 **67** JackMitchell 5 52
(Brett Johnson) *plld hrd early: hld up in midfield: rdn 3f out: struggling after: wknd over 1f out* **10/1**

046- **8** *1 1/4* **West Leake (IRE)**[10] 8396 10-8-11 **60** (p) LiamKeniry 6 42
(Paul Burgoyne) *t.k.h early: trckd ldrs on outer: shkn up 3f out: wknd 2f out: eased fnl f* **10/1**

1m 24.0s (-0.80) **Going Correction** -0.05s/f (Stan) **8** Ran SP% **117.5**
Speed ratings (Par 103): **102,98,95,95,93 91,90,89**
CSF £7.25 CT £54.44 TOTE £3.20: £1.50, £1.02, £2.90; EX 7.90 Trifecta £48.10.
Owner F J Perry **Bred** V I Araci **Trained** Newmarket, Suffolk

FOCUS
A modest handicap, lacking depth.

125 LADBROKES CONDITIONS STKS 1m 1y(P)
2:30 (2:30) (Class 2) 4-Y-O+ **£11,827** (£3,541; £1,770; £885; £442) **Stalls** High

Form RPR

113- **1** **Lamar (IRE)**[21] 8310 5-9-1 100 LukeMorris 5 108
(James Tate) *trckd ldr at mod pce: led over 2f out: shkn up and clr over 1f out: rdn out* **2/1**[2]

554- **2** *3* **Captain Cat (IRE)**[105] 6733 7-9-3 107 JamieSpencer 3 103+
(Roger Charlton) *stdd and awkward s: hld up in last in slowly run r: effrt and wd bnd 2f out: urged along and prog to take 2nd ins fnl f: no ch w wnr and no imp either* **7/4**[1]

546- **3** *1* **Complicit (IRE)**[143] 5542 5-9-3 105 GrahamLee 1 101
(Paul Cole) *trckd ldng pair: rdn over 2f out: disp 2nd briefly 1f out but already outpcd by wnr: one pce* **7/2**[3]

025- **4** *2 1/4* **Capo Rosso (IRE)**[118] 6348 6-9-3 97 RichardKingscote 2 96
(Tom Dascombe) *led at mod pce: kicked on 3f out: hdd over 2f out: fdd fnl f* **10/1**

400- **5** *2 1/4* **Grey Mirage**[28] 8199 7-9-3 101 (p) MartinHarley 4 90
(Marco Botti) *t.k.h: hld up in 4th: shkn up over 2f out: no rspnse over 1f out and wl btn after* **7/1**

1m 38.96s (0.76) **Going Correction** -0.05s/f (Stan) **5** Ran SP% **113.5**
Speed ratings (Par 109): **94,91,90,87,85**
CSF £6.16 TOTE £3.40: £2.90, £1.02; EX 6.00 Trifecta £13.30.
Owner Saif Ali **Bred** Rabbah Bloodstock Limited **Trained** Newmarket, Suffolk

FOCUS
The pace was muddling and the time was slower than the maiden and much slower than the Class 4 at this trip. The winner coulsd be rated to a pb at face value.

126 BET&WATCH EVERY RACE AT UNIBET MAIDEN STKS 6f 1y(P)
3:05 (3:05) (Class 5) 3-Y-O **£2,911** (£866; £432; £216) **Stalls** Low

Form RPR

23-3 **1** **The Commendatore**[7] 15 3-9-5 71 (b) RobertHavlin 4 74
(John Gosden) *trckd ldrs: wnt 2nd on inner wl over 1f out: drvn to ld ins fnl f: kpt on* **2/1**[1]

230- **2** *3/4* **Cee Jay**[31] 8155 3-9-5 70 (v[1]) JimCrowley 2 71
(Jeremy Noseda) *led: drvn wl over 1f out: hdd ins fnl f: kpt on* **5/2**[2]

3- **3** *1/2* **Rococoa (IRE)**[20] 8320 3-9-0 0.. LukeMorris 7 65
(Ed Walker) *trckd ldrs: nt clr run briefly wl over 1f out: sn drvn: tk 3rd ins fnl f: kpt on but a hld* **9/2**

623- **4** *1/2* **Phantom Flipper**[12] 8378 3-9-5 70................................ KieranO'Neill 3 68
(Richard Hannon) *trckd ldr: hanging rt bnd 2f out: sn lost 2nd: kpt on same pce fnl f* **3/1**[3]

06- **5** *1* **Kestrel Call (IRE)**[18] 8349 3-9-5 0................................(t) MartinLane 8 65
(Simon Crisford) *hld up in 6th: tried to make prog on inner over 1f out: shkn up and one pce fnl f* **16/1**

0- **6** *6* **Evening Starlight**[24] 8253 3-8-11 0.............................. PhilipPrince(3) 6 41
(Ron Hodges) *in tch: effrt on outer over 2f out: wknd wl over 1f out* **200/1**

7 *3 1/2* **Music Major** 3-9-5 0.. AdamBeschizza 1 34
(Kevin Morgan) *s.s: a detached in last* **100/1**

1m 11.3s (-0.60) **Going Correction** -0.05s/f (Stan) **7** Ran SP% **112.5**
Speed ratings (Par 97): **102,101,100,99,98 90,85**
CSF £7.04 TOTE £2.50: £1.20, £1.90; EX 7.20 Trifecta £28.00.
Owner M Tabor & Rachel Hood **Bred** J K Beckitt & Son **Trained** Newmarket, Suffolk

FOCUS
A typically ordinary sprint maiden, but it was at least competitive enough. The form makes sense.

127 32RED CASINO FILLIES' H'CAP 1m 2f (P)

3:40 (3:41) (Class 5) (0-75,73) 4-Y-0+ **£2,911** (£866; £432; £216) **Stalls** Low

Form RPR

331- **1** **Wavelet**[31] 8162 4-9-6 69... JamieSpencer 7 75
(David Simcock) *trckd ldrs: pushed along 3f out: drvn to chal over 1f out: edgd rt but forced ahd last 75yds: hld on* **11/4**[1]

345- **2** *nk* **Miss Giler**[19] 8327 4-9-7 70.. RobertHavlin 1 75
(John Gosden) *hld up in 6th in modly run r: prog on outer wl over 1f out: drvn and r.o fnl f: tk 2nd last strides: too much to do* **3/1**[2]

441- **3** *hd* **Chefchaouen (IRE)**[10] 8398 4-8-1 57................(p) JosephineGordon(7) 3 62
(J S Moore) *trckd ldrs in 5th: rdn over 2f out: clsd on inner to chal over 1f out: led briefly ins fnl f: kpt on but lost 2nd last strides* **7/2**[3]

/40- **4** *1 1/2* **Colourfilly**[155] 5105 4-8-13 62.................................. RichardKingscote 4 64
(Tom Dascombe) *trckd ldr: led 2f out: drvn and hdd ins fnl f: fdd nr fin* **10/1**

102- **5** *2* **Actonetaketwo**[19] 8334 6-8-4 54 oh1.............................. PhilipPrince(3) 6 52
(Ron Hodges) *hld up in last pair: shkn up 2f out: stl last over 1f out: r.o fnl f: no ch* **16/1**

6 *3* **Annakrista (GER)**[9] 7139 8-9-5 66................................(bt) LukeMorris 5 58
(Zoe Davison) *t.k.h: trckd ldrs: rdn 3f out: wknd over 1f out* **66/1**

040- **7** *3 1/2* **Tea Gown (IRE)**[60] 7784 5-9-12 73................................(p) ShaneGray 2 58
(Ed de Giles) *dwlt: hld up in last pair: tried to make prog over 1f out: sn no hdwy and wknd* **8/1**

252- **8** *8* **Chella Thriller (SPA)**[31] 8165 7-8-9 63.......................... RhiainIngram(7) 8 32
(Ralph J Smith) *sn led and set mod pce: kicked on 4f out: hdd 2f out: wknd qckly* **6/1**

2m 7.65s (1.05) **Going Correction** -0.05s/f (Stan)
WFA 4 from 5yo+ 2lb **8** Ran SP% **115.8**
Speed ratings (Par 100): **93,92,92,91,89 87,84,78**
CSF £11.43 CT £28.76 TOTE £3.20: £1.10, £2.40, £2.10; EX 11.00 Trifecta £35.30.
Owner Miss K Rausing **Bred** Miss K Rausing **Trained** Newmarket, Suffolk

FOCUS
A modest fillies' handicap. The winner found a bit on recent maiden form.
T/Plt: £8.10 to a £1 stake. Pool: £48,885.54 - 4372.27 winning units. T/Qpdt: £3.40 to a £1 stake. Pool: £4,716.41 - 1026.05 winning units. **Jonathan Neesom**

DEAUVILLE (R-H)
Saturday, January 9

OFFICIAL GOING: Polytrack: standard

128a PRIX DU PHARE (CLAIMER) (3YO) (POLYTRACK) 7f 110y

1:45 (12:00) 3-Y-O **£7,352** (£2,941; £2,205; £1,470; £735)

RPR

1 **Accord D'Argent (FR)**[13] 3-8-10 0.............................. LukasDelozier(6) 1 65
(Y Barberot, France) **2/1**[1]

2 *1 1/4* **Beret (FR)**[29] 8177 3-8-11 0... ThierryThulliez 6 57
(Harry Dunlop) *trckd ldr: rdn to chal over 1f out: led ins fnl f: kpt on but hdd towards fin and no match for wnr* **9/1**

3 *nk* **Sing Something**[81] 7370 3-9-4 0...............................(b) TheoBachelot 13 63
(P Monfort, France) **49/10**[2]

4 *2* **Princess Emma (FR)**[13] 3-8-11 0.................................. EddyHardouin 7 51
(S Jesus, France) **106/10**

5 *1 1/4* **Place Des Ternes (FR)**[24] 3-8-8 0............................(p) JohanVictoire 11 45
(M Boutin, France) **35/1**

6 *nse* **Mathison (FR)**[12] 3-8-8 0... IoritzMendizabal 8 45
(D De Waele, France) **143/10**

7 *hd* **Lipsie (FR)**[40] 3-8-8 0...(p) CristianDemuro 10 45
(Gianluca Bietolini, Italy) **163/10**

8 *3/4* **Dark Redeemer**[23] 3-8-13 0.......................................(b) AdrienMoreau(5) 3 53
(N Caullery, France) **77/10**

9 *3/4* **Bishnoi (FR)**[6] 3-8-5 0... EmmanuelEtienne(3) 5 41
(G Doleuze, France) **92/1**

10 *2 1/2* **Limeta (FR)**[12] 3-8-8 0... AlexisBadel 9 35
(D De Waele, France) **63/10**[3]

11 *3* **Mirroronthewall (FR)**[62] 7765 3-9-7 0...................... MathieuPelletan(5) 2 46
(Gianluca Bietolini, Italy) **78/10**

12 *8* **Queveda De Lopa**[23] 3-8-11 0...................................... MichaelCadeddu 4 10
(Yasmin Almenrader, Germany) **91/1**

13 *4* **Texas Holdem (FR)**[197] 3-8-13 0................................ LudovicBoisseau(5) 15 7
(Mlle S Delaroche, France) **106/1**

Owner Carim Joomun **Bred** H H Sheikh Abdulla Bin Khalifa Al Thani **Trained** France SF: 23.60

129 - (Foreign Racing) - See Raceform Interactive

[48]SOUTHWELL (L-H)
Sunday, January 10

OFFICIAL GOING: Fibresand: standard
Wind: fresh 1/2 behind Weather: fine and sunny but cold and breezy

130 UNIBET.CO.UK DAILY ENHANCED PLACE TERMS H'CAP 6f (F)

12:40 (12:41) (Class 6) (0-60,62) 4-Y-0+ **£2,587** (£770; £384; £192) **Stalls** Low

Form RPR

06-1 **1** **Speightowns Kid (USA)**[8] 22 8-9-4 62..................(be) AnnStokell(5) 6 73
(Ann Stokell) *chsd ldrs: led 2f out: forged clr fnl f* **7/1**[3]

32-1 **2** *2 3/4* **Fortinbrass (IRE)**[5] 54 6-9-6 59 6ex.......................... RobertWinston 9 62
(John Balding) *sn chsng ldrs: effrt on outside over 2f out: 2nd 1f out: kpt on: no imp* **5/4**[1]

46-6 **3** *1 1/2* **Ms Eboracum (IRE)**[8] 22 4-8-7 46 oh1...................[1] AndrewMullen 3 45
(Michael Appleby) *w ldr: led briefly over 2f out: kpt on same pce fnl f* **12/1**

66-4 **4** *1/2* **Pancake Day**[8] 22 4-8-13 57.................................. CallumShepherd(5) 5 54
(Jason Ward) *in rr: hdwy over 2f out: kpt on one pce fnl f* **7/1**[3]

04-2 **5** *2* **Lucky Mark (IRE)**[8] 22 7-9-6 59..............................(p) LiamKeniry 10 50
(John Balding) *sn chsng ldrs: rdn over 2f out: one pce* **9/2**[2]

533- **6** *1/2* **Leith Bridge**[20] 8332 4-9-7 60... OisinMurphy 8 50
(Mark Usher) *chsd ldrs: lost pl over 2f out: hdwy on outside over 2f out: one pce* **14/1**

00-0 **7** *2 1/4* **Madakheel (USA)**[9] 2 5-8-7 46 oh1...........................(t) JoeyHaynes 1 29
(Simon West) *sn drvn along in rr: outpcd: sme hdwy over 1f out: nvr a factor* **100/1**

050- **8** *4 1/2* **Little**[119] 6344 4-8-11 53.. JackDuern(3) 4 22
(Steph Hollinshead) *dwlt: hdwy on ins over 2f out: sn chsng ldrs: wknd appr fnl f* **22/1**

30- **9** *2 1/4* **Amis Reunis**[11] 8400 7-9-0 53 ow3............................. PaulMulrennan 7 16
(Alan Berry) *chsd ldrs: lost pl over 1f out* **66/1**

/03- **10** *3/4* **Show Boat**[277] 1254 4-9-6 59.. PJMcDonald 2 19
(Ann Duffield) *led: hdd over 2f out: wknd over 1f out* **14/1**

1m 17.2s (0.70) **Going Correction** -0.075s/f (Stan) **10** Ran SP% **115.5**
Speed ratings (Par 101): **92,88,86,85,83 82,79,73,70,69**
CSF £15.81 CT £108.39 TOTE £9.10: £2.70, £1.10, £3.80; EX 14.90 Trifecta £178.00.
Owner Geoff Pacey **Bred** Sandyview Farm **Trained** Lincoln, Lincolnshire

FOCUS
A moderate sprint handicap. The winner was fully entitled to win this on last year's form from this time of year.

131 DAILY PRICE BOOSTS AT UNIBET H'CAP 6f (F)

1:10 (1:10) (Class 4) (0-85,86) 3-Y-O **£5,175** (£1,540; £769; £384) **Stalls** Low

Form RPR

20-2 **1** **Modest**[9] 3 3-8-2 73.. JosephineGordon(7) 6 78
(Michael Bell) *t.k.h: mde all: edgd rt over 1f out: hld on wl clsng stages* **11/2**[3]

11-1 **2** *1* **Aguerooo (IRE)**[9] 3 3-9-1 86.....................................(p) HollieDoyle(7) 2 87
(Richard Hannon) *sn trcking ldrs: 2nd over 2f out: swtchd lft over 1f out: styd on to press ldr last 50yds* **13/8**[1]

106- **3** *4* **Rantan (IRE)**[11] 8391 3-9-0 78.. PhillipMakin 4 66
(David Barron) *chsd ldrs: outpcd over 2f out: kpt on appr fnl f: tk modest 3rd last 100yds* **15/2**

11-2 **4** *1 3/4* **Kingsley Klarion (IRE)**[8] 16 3-9-6 84.............................. JoeFanning 3 67
(Mark Johnston) *chsd wnr: effrt over 2f out: fdd fnl f* **9/4**[2]

110- **5** *4 1/2* **Bahamian Sunshine**[40] 8065 3-8-1 68........................ SammyJoBell(3) 5 36
(Richard Fahey) *dwlt: sn chsng ldrs on outer: drvn and outpcd over 2f out: lost pl over 1f out* **8/1**

1m 15.99s (-0.51) **Going Correction** -0.075s/f (Stan) **5** Ran SP% **107.1**
Speed ratings (Par 99): **100,98,93,91,85**
CSF £14.13 TOTE £7.10: £3.30, £1.40; EX 15.30 Trifecta £76.20.
Owner T Hyde and David Graham **Bred** Cheveley Park Stud Ltd **Trained** Newmarket, Suffolk

FOCUS
A fair 3yo handicap. The winner reversed C&D form with the second.

132 CORAL H'CAP 1m 4f (F)

1:40 (1:40) (Class 5) (0-75,75) 4-Y-0+ **£3,234** (£962; £481; £240) **Stalls** Low

Form RPR

1/0- **1** **Muhtaris (IRE)**[71] 7015 6-9-10 75.................................. TimmyMurphy 7 87
(James Evans) *hld up: t.k.h: hdwy to trck ldrs over 7f out: effrt and 3rd over 2f out: 2nd over 1f out: led last 100yds: kpt on* **20/1**

01-1 **2** *1 1/4* **Play Nicely**[5] 53 4-9-0 69 6ex.. PhillipMakin 1 79
(David Barron) *trckd ldr: led 5f out: edgd rt 2f out: hdd and no ex last 100yds* **2/5**[1]

456- **3** *6* **Percys Princess**[19] 8344 5-9-5 73........................ AlistairRawlinson(3) 2 73
(Michael Appleby) *chsd ldrs: drvn and 2nd over 4f out: one pce over 1f out* **25/1**

232- **4** *5* **Northside Prince (IRE)**[12] 8383 10-9-5 70............................ NeilFarley 4 62
(Alan Swinbank) *led: hdd 5f out: sn drvn: wknd over 1f out* **8/1**[3]

031- **5** *2 1/2* **Dark Diamond (IRE)**[19] 8345 6-9-3 68......................(v) AdamBeschizza 5 56
(Julia Feilden) *chsd ldrs: drvn over 8f out: lost pl over 1f out* **5/1**[2]

336- **6** *19* **Mr Snoozy**[33] 8150 7-9-5 70..(p) DougieCostello 6 28
(Mark Walford) *in rr and sn pushed along: bhd 8f out: t.o 5f out* **40/1**

2m 38.04s (-2.96) **Going Correction** -0.075s/f (Stan)
WFA 4 from 5yo+ 4lb **6** Ran SP% **110.3**
Speed ratings (Par 103): **106,105,101,97,96 83**
CSF £28.25 TOTE £17.20: £5.20, £1.10; EX 43.30 Trifecta £293.00.
Owner The Cheltenham Boys Racing Club 1 **Bred** Rabbah Bloodstock Limited **Trained** Broadwas, Worcs

FOCUS
An uncompetitive handicap but the favourite was still turned over. The first pair finished clear.

133 UNIBET OFFER DAILY JOCKEY/TRAINER SPECIALS H'CAP 6f (F)

2:10 (2:10) (Class 5) (0-75,72) 4-Y-0+ **£3,234** (£962; £481; £240) **Stalls** Low

Form RPR

551- **1** **Boolass (IRE)**[26] 8241 4-8-8 64...........................(b) CallumShepherd(5) 5 74+
(Brian Ellison) *s.i.s: bhd and sn drvn along: hdwy on outer over 2f out: sn edgd lft: styd on to ld last 100yds* **11/4**[1]

45-6 **2** *1 1/4* **Alpha Tauri (USA)**[8] 24 10-9-4 69.................................. MartinLane 9 75
(Charles Smith) *mid-div: hdwy over 2f out: chsng ldrs over 1f out: led briefly last 100yds: no ex* **8/1**

43-3 **3** *2 1/2* **Elusivity (IRE)**[3] 76 8-9-7 72..................................... PaulMulrennan 4 70
(Conor Dore) *w ldr: led over 2f out: hdd last 150yds: kpt on same pce* **4/1**[3]

240- 4 3/4 **Spowarticus**[34] 8142 7-8-13 **64**........(v) KieranO'Neill 6 60
(Scott Dixon) *chsd ldrs: edgd rt 2f out: one pce* **8/1**

210- 5 3 1/4 **Age Of Innocence**[12] 8389 5-9-3 **68**........(v) DougieCostello 7 53
(Derek Shaw) *fractious in stalls: dwlt: hdwy on outside 3f out: nvr a threat: tk modest 5th post* **10/3**[2]

100- 6 hd **Coiste Bodhar (IRE)**[26] 8242 5-8-8 **62**........(p) TimClark(3) 3 47
(Scott Dixon) *chsd ldrs: drvn over 2f out: wknd last 150yds* **16/1**

215- 7 9 **Bapak Bangsawan**[12] 8389 6-9-1 **71**........(v) AnnStokell(5) 2 27
(Ann Stokell) *t.k.h: led: hdd over 2f out: wknd qckly 1f out* **12/1**

0/3- 8 7 **Perfect Fit (IRE)**[13] 8381 4-9-3 **68**........(v1) BarryMcHugh 1 21
(Tony Coyle) *s.s: sn detached in last and drvn along* **12/1**

1m 16.13s (-0.37) **Going Correction** -0.075s/f (Stan) **8** Ran SP% **113.2**
Speed ratings (Par 103): **99,97,94,93,88 88,76,75**
CSF £24.78 CT £86.93 TOTE £3.30: £1.10, £2.40, £1.60; EX 21.90 Trifecta £98.10.
Owner Mrs J A Martin **Bred** Roland H Alder **Trained** Norton, N Yorks

FOCUS
The leaders went too hard. The winner built on his maiden win.

134 LADBROKES H'CAP 1m (F)
2:40 (2:40) (Class 3) (0-95,90) 4-Y-O+ **£7,561** (£2,263; £1,131; £566; £282) **Stalls** Low

Form RPR

51-3 1 **Boots And Spurs**[4] 58 7-8-8 **77**........(v) KieranO'Neill 4 86
(Scott Dixon) *led 1f: drvn over 4f out: styd on to ld appr fnl f: kpt on wl* **13/2**[3]

11-1 2 2 **Philba**[5] 50 4-9-1 **87** 6ex........(tp) AlistairRawlinson(3) 7 91
(Michael Appleby) *trckd ldrs: led over 3f out: hdd appr fnl f: kpt on same pce* **15/8**[1]

64-4 3 nk **Showboating (IRE)**[5] 50 8-9-6 **89**........ RobertWinston 2 92
(John Balding) *chsd ldrs: effrt on outer over 3f out: sn outpcd: styd on fnl f: tk 3rd last 50yds* **12/1**

21-1 4 2 1/2 **Captain Lars (SAF)**[8] 23 6-8-13 **87**........(v) CallumShepherd(5) 5 85
(Derek Shaw) *trckd ldrs: effrt over 2f out: hung lft: wknd clsng stages* **8/1**

35-1 5 1 1/4 **Zaeem**[8] 24 7-9-2 **90**........(p) JustinNewman(5) 6 85
(Ivan Furtado) *trckd ldrs: effrt over 2f out: one pce* **2/1**[2]

440- 6 3/4 **Cordite (IRE)**[19] 8342 5-9-4 **87**........(p) AndrewMullen 3 80
(Michael Appleby) *w ldr: led after 1f: hdd over 3f out: fdd fnl f* **20/1**

003- 7 6 **Dubai Hills**[19] 8342 10-9-4 **87**........(v) SamJames 1 66
(David O'Meara) *sn drvn along in last: bhd fnl 4f* **14/1**

1m 41.85s (-1.85) **Going Correction** -0.075s/f (Stan) **7** Ran SP% **111.7**
Speed ratings (Par 107): **106,104,103,101,99 99,93**
CSF £18.24 TOTE £9.80: £3.70, £1.80; EX 21.30 Trifecta £154.30.
Owner S Chappell **Bred** Miss G Abbey **Trained** Babworth, Notts

FOCUS
A fair handicap. The form could be rated a little higher.

135 DAILY UNIBET EARLY PRICES FROM 9AM (S) STKS 6f (F)
3:10 (3:10) (Class 6) 4-Y-O+ **£2,587** (£770; £384; £192) **Stalls** Low

Form RPR

23-3 1 **Jacob's Pillow**[7] 28 5-9-6 71........(p) AndrewMullen 4 77
(Michael Appleby) *w ldr: led over 3f out: drvn clr 1f out* **1/1**[1]

153- 2 5 **Spitfire**[66] 7719 11-9-6 64........(t) JoeFanning 3 62
(J R Jenkins) *dwlt: hdwy 4f out: kpt on to take modest 2nd 1f out: no ch w wnr* **6/1**[3]

300- 3 3 3/4 **Molly Approve (IRE)**[76] 7521 4-8-12 52 ow3........ DougieCostello 5 43
(Tony Coyle) *chsd ldrs: outpcd over 4f out: hdwy and hung lft over 1f out: kpt on to take modest 3rd nr fin* **66/1**

40-0 4 1/2 **Pull The Pin (IRE)**[8] 22 7-9-0 55........(bt) SaleemGolam 1 43
(Heather Dalton) *led: hdd over 3f out: fdd fnl f* **25/1**

230- 5 1/2 **Abi Scarlet (IRE)**[23] 8283 7-9-1 73........(b) KieranO'Neill 2 43
(Scott Dixon) *chsd ldng pair: outpcd over 4f out: kpt on fnl 2f: nvr a threat* **7/4**[2]

066- 6 1 1/2 **Plunder**[11] 8401 6-9-0 46........ JackGarritty 6 37
(Alan Berry) *outpcd and lost pl over 4f out: sn detached in rr: nvr on terms* **66/1**

1m 15.65s (-0.85) **Going Correction** -0.075s/f (Stan) **6** Ran SP% **107.5**
Speed ratings (Par 101): **102,95,90,89,89 87**
CSF £6.81 TOTE £1.70: £1.10, £2.80; EX 6.60 Trifecta £61.50.Jacob's Pillow was bought by Rebecca Bastiman for 6,750gns
Owner L A Hill & C L Bacon **Bred** Lael Stables **Trained** Oakham, Rutland

FOCUS
The second favourite flopped and there was little depth to this seller. The winner is rated right up to his recent success.

136 BET & WATCH EVERY AT UNIBET AWT "HANDS AND HEELS" APPRENTICE SERIES H'CAP 5f (F)
3:40 (3:41) (Class 6) (0-55,55) 4-Y-O+ **£2,587** (£770; £384; £192) **Stalls** Centre

Form RPR

606- 1 **Very First Blade**[96] 7010 7-9-0 **55**........(be) MrLewisStones(7) 10 61
(Michael Mullineaux) *hld up towards stands' side: hdwy 2f out: edgd lft and styd on to ld nr fin* **12/1**

000- 2 hd **Sir Geoffrey (IRE)**[24] 8271 10-9-5 **53**........(b) SophieKilloran 2 58
(Scott Dixon) *w ldr: drvn over 2f out: led 1f out: hdd and no ex nr fin* **7/2**[2]

320- 3 1/2 **Charlie Lad**[11] 8400 4-9-7 **55**........(b) PaddyBradley 1 58
(Daniel Mark Loughnane) *led: edgd rt and hdd 1f out: kpt on same pce last 50yds* **5/4**[1]

340- 4 2 **Azerelle (IRE)**[11] 8401 4-8-8 **49**........(b1) AdamMcNamara(7) 3 45
(Tim Easterby) *dwlt: sn chsng ldrs: edgd lft over 1f out: kpt on one pce* **9/1**

/43- 5 1/2 **Wattaboutsteve**[12] 8388 5-8-12 **46**........ RhiainIngram 8 40
(Ralph J Smith) *chsd ldrs: one pce over 1f out: b.b.v* **8/1**[3]

500- 6 1 1/4 **Red Flute**[24] 8265 4-8-9 **46**........(v) PatrickVaughan(3) 9 36
(Denis Quinn) *chsd ldrs: one pce fnl 2f* **40/1**

006- 7 3/4 **Abonos (IRE)**[24] 8271 4-9-4 **52**........(e) HollieDoyle 7 39
(Simon West) *dwlt: in rr: sme hdwy over 1f out: nvr a factor* **12/1**

000- 8 1 3/4 **Incomparable**[33] 8149 11-9-2 **55**........(p) CliffordLee(5) 4 36
(Scott Dixon) *in rr: sn drvn along: nvr on terms* **10/1**

350- 9 2 1/4 **Red Forever**[23] 8289 5-8-5 **46**........ NicolaGrundy(7) 12 19
(Alan Berry) *dwlt: sn drvn along in rr: nvr on terms* **80/1**

59.68s (-0.02) **Going Correction** +0.025s/f (Slow) **9** Ran SP% **115.9**
Speed ratings (Par 101): **101,100,99,96,95 93,92,89,86**
CSF £54.06 CT £91.76 TOTE £12.50: £2.60, £1.70, £1.30; EX 65.20 Trifecta £224.20.
Owner Ogwen Valley Racing **Bred** L R Owen **Trained** Alpraham, Cheshire
■ The first winner for Lewis Stones.

FOCUS
A moderate sprint handicap with not much to take forward.

T/Jkpt: Not won.JACKPOT PLACEPOT £40.70. Pool: £3155.87 - 56.60 winning units. T/Plt: £13.30 to a £1 stake. Pool: £98,581.29 - 5373.33 winning units. T/Qpdt: £6.90 to a £1 stake. Pool: £8632.69 - 917.96 winning units. **Walter Glynn**

137 (Foreign Racing) - See Raceform Interactive

62 KEMPTON (A.W) (R-H)
Monday, January 11

OFFICIAL GOING: Polytrack: standard
Wind: Moderate, across (away from stands) Weather: Cloudy, raining race 3

138 RACINGUK.COM/ANYWHERE H'CAP 2m (P)
2:00 (2:05) (Class 5) (0-70,70) 4-Y-O+ **£3,234** (£962; £481; £240) **Stalls** Low

Form RPR

065- 1 **Tarakkom (FR)**[30] 8197 4-8-2 **51** oh5........ CathyGannon 8 58
(Peter Hiatt) *wnt lft s: sn disp 4th: rdn and prog to chse ldr over 3f out: clsd to ld over 2f out: drvn and kpt on after* **66/1**

206- 2 3 1/2 **Shalambar (IRE)**[47] 7973 10-10-0 **70**........(v) LukeMorris 9 73
(Tony Carroll) *dwlt and hmpd s: disp 6th: rdn 4f out: racd awkwardly but prog fr 3f out to chse wnr 2f out: one pce and no imp* **14/1**

300- 3 2 3/4 **Guards Chapel**[36] 7140 8-9-13 **69**........(v) GeorgeBaker 2 69
(Gary Moore) *dwlt: hld up in detached last: prog on inner 3f out: rdn to dispute 2nd over 1f out: one pce after* **9/2**[2]

605- 4 1 1/4 **Four Nations (USA)**[56] 7871 8-9-10 **66**........(p) PatCosgrave 4 64
(George Baker) *dwlt: hld up in 8th: rdn 3f out: kpt on fnl 2f but n.d* **8/1**

00- 5 1 3/4 **Jezza**[34] 8150 10-8-13 **60**........(bt) CallumShepherd(5) 3 56
(Victor Dartnall) *in tch disputing 6th: rdn 3f out: plugged on one pce fnl 2f: n.d* **20/1**

215- 6 6 **Maison Brillet (IRE)**[26] 8257 9-9-11 **67**........(p) WilliamCarson 5 56
(Clive Drew) *chsd ldrs disputing 4th: rdn and tried to cl over 2f out: wknd over 1f out* **12/1**

303- 7 4 **Ledbury (IRE)**[20] 8343 4-9-3 **66**........ AdamKirby 7 50
(Lee Carter) *led: racd awkwardly and hung lft 6f out: tried to go for home 4f out: hdd & wknd qckly over 2f out* **11/2**[3]

160/ 8 37 **Honourable Knight (IRE)**[475] 6632 8-9-4 **60**........ LiamKeniry 1
(Mark Usher) *chsd ldr: rdn 4f out: wknd qckly jst over 3f out: t.o* **33/1**

322- 9 31 **Flighty Filia (IRE)**[22] 8315 4-9-2 **65**........(b1) JimCrowley 6
(Amanda Perrett) *chsd ldr: rdn and wknd rapidly 4f out: sn t.o: eased* **11/10**[1]

3m 31.43s (1.33) **Going Correction** +0.075s/f (Slow)
WFA 4 from 8yo+ 7lb **9** Ran SP% **115.9**
Speed ratings (Par 103): **99,97,95,95,94 91,89,70,55**
CSF £784.50 CT £4959.43 TOTE £39.10: £9.40, £2.80, £1.30; EX 583.80 Trifecta £5263.40.
Owner Phil Kelly **Bred** Shadwell Farm **Trained** Hook Norton, Oxon

FOCUS
Quite a shock in this weak staying handicap. The form is rated negatively through the runner-up.

139 RACING UK 3 DEVICES 1 PRICE MEDIAN AUCTION MAIDEN STKS 1m 4f (P)
2:30 (2:35) (Class 5) 3-4-Y-O **£3,234** (£962; £481; £240) **Stalls** Centre

Form RPR

236- 1 **Jazzy (IRE)**[13] 8384 3-8-7 64........ CathyGannon 2 69
(Martin Keighley) *awkward s: t.k.h early: hld up in last: urged along over 3f out: prog on outer to ld wl over 1f out: rdn and kpt on wl* **9/1**[3]

4-2 2 3 1/4 **O'Connor's Girl**[6] 44 3-8-2 0........ LukeMorris 4 59
(Sir Mark Prescott Bt) *led at mod pce: shkn up and hdd 2f out: nt qckn and sn outpcd in 3rd: kpt on to take 2nd last 100yds* **8/13**[1]

3 2 **Playful Dude (USA)** 3-8-7 0........ WilliamCarson 3 61+
(David Simcock) *trckd ldr after 2f: moved up to ld 2f out gng easily: immediately rn green and sn hdd: one pce and lost 2nd last 100yds* **2/1**[2]

00- 4 6 **Fateh (IRE)**[37] 8122 3-8-7 0........ MartinLane 1 51
(David Dennis) *chsd ldr 2f: in tch after: pushed along over 3f out: cl enough 2f out: sn wknd* **40/1**

2m 40.78s (6.28) **Going Correction** +0.075s/f (Slow) **4** Ran SP% **107.7**
Speed ratings (Par 103): **82,79,78,74**
CSF £15.52 TOTE £9.00; EX 13.30 Trifecta £17.70.
Owner Jazz Summers Racing **Bred** Ballyhane Stud **Trained** Condicote, Gloucs

FOCUS
They went a steady early pace before sprinting up the straight. The form has an unreliable look to it.

140 RACINGUK.COM/WINTERSEASONTICKET H'CAP 1m (P)
3:05 (3:10) (Class 6) (0-60,60) 3-Y-O **£2,264** (£673; £336; £168) **Stalls** Low

Form RPR

414- 1 **Fable Of Arachne**[32] 8166 3-9-3 **56**........(t) OisinMurphy 5 62
(Stuart Williams) *settled in midfield: prog to ld 2f out: sn rdn: hrd pressed fr over 1f out: hld on wl* **8/1**

360- 2 hd **Clive Clifton (IRE)**[27] 8234 3-9-7 **60**........ PatCosgrave 6 65
(David Evans) *trckd ldrs: rdn to chal 2f out: pressed wnr fr over 1f out: gd battle but nt qckn and jst hld ins fnl f* **9/2**[3]

324- 3 4 1/2 **Romantic Comedy (IRE)**[13] 8384 3-9-6 **59**........(p) LukeMorris 8 53
(James Tate) *trckd ldng pair: led briefly jst over 2f out: lft bhd by ldng pair over 1f out: jst hld on for 3rd* **8/1**

606- 4 shd **Miss Fortune**[31] 8177 3-8-5 **49**........ CallumShepherd(5) 3 43
(Mark Usher) *towards rr: rdn 3f out: kpt on fr over 1f out: nrly snatched 3rd* **40/1**

000- 5 nk **Faster Company (IRE)**[11] 8409 3-8-13 **52**........(p) MartinLane 1 45
(J S Moore) *settled in rr: rdn and prog over 2f out: chal for 3rd fnl f: one pce nr fin* **12/1**

005- 6 shd **You're A Goat**[25] 8259 3-9-6 **59**........ AdamKirby 2 53+
(Gary Moore) *s.i.s and urged along early in last pair: drvn 3f out: no real prog tl styd on fnl f: nrst fin* **5/2**[1]

05-2 7 4 1/2 **La Manga (IRE)**[3] 105 3-8-12 **56**........ LucyKBarry(5) 10 38
(Jamie Osborne) *chsd ldrs but racd out wd: rdn and hanging over 2f out: sn btn* **4/1**[2]

000- 8 1 1/2 **Cla Rock (IRE)**[46] 7996 3-9-7 **60**........(b1) MartinHarley 11 39
(William Haggas) *sn chsd ldr: lost 2nd over 2f out: sltly impeded sn after: wknd* **10/1**

000- 9 1 1/2 **Pour Pavot (IRE)**[165] 4790 3-9-7 **60**........ GeorgeBaker 4 35
(Gary Moore) *slowly away: t.k.h early: hld up in last: pushed along on inner over 2f out and only limited prog: wknd fnl f* **8/1**

040- 10 3 1/2 **Mullover**[11] 8410 3-8-11 **50**........ KierenFox 9 17
(John Best) *led to jst over 2f out: edgd lft and wknd qckly* **25/1**

050- **11** *19* **Daioni**[39] 8091 3-9-2 **55**........ JimCrowley 7
(Simon Dow) *in tch in midfield: rdn over 3f out: wknd rapidly wl over 2f out: t.o* **50/1**

1m 41.42s (1.62) **Going Correction** +0.075s/f (Slow) **11** Ran SP% **125.1**
Speed ratings (Par 95): **94,93,89,89,88 88,84,82,81,77 58**
CSF £46.32 CT £310.49 TOTE £7.00: £2.30, £2.00, £2.30; EX 50.10 Trifecta £185.70.
Owner D A Shekells **Bred** Old Mill Stud And S C Williams **Trained** Newmarket, Suffolk

FOCUS
The first two drew clear in this moderate handicap. A definite step up from the winner.

141 RACING UK WINTER SEASON TICKET H'CAP 1m (P)
3:40 (3:45) (Class 5) (0-70,69) 4-Y-O+ **£3,234** (£962; £481; £240) **Stalls** Low

Form RPR

51-4 **1** **Exalted (IRE)**[5] 64 5-8-8 **56**........(t) MartinLane 3 68
(William Knight) *mde all: sent for home 3f out: drvn over 1f out: kpt on wl u.p* **15/8**[1]

003- **2** *1 ¾* **Gracious George (IRE)**[39] 8089 6-9-2 **64**........ AdamKirby 9 72
(Jimmy Fox) *urged along early in last pair: rdn and prog over 2f out: drvn to chse wnr over 1f out and tried to cl: kpt on but no imp last 150yds* **10/3**[2]

402- **3** *2 ½* **Napoleon Solo**[52] 7919 4-9-3 **65**........[1] WilliamTwiston-Davies 6 67
(Dave Morris) *trckd ldrs: rdn to chse wnr 2f out to over 1f out: one pce after* **13/2**[3]

366- **4** *2 ½* **Stormbound (IRE)**[142] 5616 7-7-9 **69**........(b) LukeMorris 7 65
(Paul Cole) *t.k.h early: hld up in rr: rdn 2f out: prog to take 4th ins fnl f: no ch to threaten* **9/1**

/00- **5** *1 ¼* **The Tichborne (IRE)**[11] 8414 8-9-6 **68**........ GeorgeBaker 4 61
(Roger Teal) *chsd wnr to 2f out: steadily wknd* **16/1**

413- **6** *nk* **Spirit Of Gondree (IRE)**[15] 8370 8-9-0 **62**........(b) PatCosgrave 2 54
(Milton Bradley) *t.k.h early: prom: rdn to dispute 2nd jst over 2f out: wknd over 1f out* **8/1**

044- **7** *¾* **Abertillery**[79] 7464 4-9-3 **65**........ MartinHarley 8 55
(Michael Blanshard) *nvr bttr than midfield: shkn up and no prog over 2f out: sn btn* **33/1**

50-4 **8** *½* **Farletti**[9] 14 4-9-7 **69**........(v[1]) OisinMurphy 5 58
(Andrew Balding) *chsd ldrs: rdn over 2f out: wknd wl over 1f out* **10/1**

000- **9** *4 ½* **Embankment**[73] 7598 7-9-7 **69**........ RyanPowell 1 47
(Michael Attwater) *s.v.s and lft abt 10 l: ct up after 3f: wknd over 2f out* **16/1**

1m 39.4s (-0.40) **Going Correction** +0.075s/f (Slow) **9** Ran SP% **116.1**
Speed ratings (Par 103): **105,103,100,98,97 96,95,95,90**
CSF £8.01 CT £32.97 TOTE £2.80: £1.30, £1.70, £1.90; EX 9.90 Trifecta £45.60.
Owner N J Roach **Bred** Rathbarry Stud **Trained** Patching, W Sussex
■ Stewards' Enquiry : William Twiston-Davies two-day ban: used whip above permitted level (Jan 25-26)

FOCUS
This was dominated from the front by the favourite. There was little depth behind.

142 RACING UK 3 DEVICES 1 PRICE H'CAP 6f (P)
4:10 (4:15) (Class 4) (0-85,84) 4-Y-O+ **£5,175** (£1,540; £769; £384) **Stalls** Low

Form RPR

006- **1** **Searchlight**[27] 8229 5-9-7 **84**........ PatCosgrave 6 91
(Jim Boyle) *hld up in rr: stdy prog over 2f out: shkn up over 1f out: clsd to ld ins fnl f: drvn and hld on* **10/1**

061- **2** *nk* **Royal Normandy**[26] 8250 4-8-6 **72**........(b) RobHornby[(3)] 2 78+
(Andrew Balding) *trckd ldrs: effrt on inner 2f out: rdn and styd on to take 2nd last 100yds: kpt on wl but jst hld* **3/1**[1]

440- **3** *¾* **Glastonberry**[97] 7017 8-9-5 **82**........ GeorgeBaker 8 86
(Geoffrey Deacon) *stdd s: hld up in last: prog 2f out: rdn and r.o fnl f to take 3rd last strides: too much to do* **20/1**

015- **4** *¾* **Foreign Diplomat**[16] 8357 4-9-5 **82**........ DanielTudhope 1 84
(David O'Meara) *prom: chsd ldr over 2f out: rdn to ld 1f out: hdd and one pce ins fnl f* **5/1**[3]

46-1 **5** *shd* **Light From Mars**[5] 67 11-9-1 **78** 6ex........(p) LukeMorris 9 79
(Ronald Harris) *settled in rr: rdn and struggling 2f out: styd on wl fnl f: nrst fin* **12/1**

304- **6** *1* **Stellarta**[46] 8000 5-9-1 **78**........ MartinHarley 7 76
(Michael Blanshard) *trckd ldrs: shkn up 2f out: nt qckn over 1f out: no imp after* **7/2**[2]

424- **7** *½* **Doctor Parkes**[20] 8347 10-9-1 **78**........ OisinMurphy 3 74
(Stuart Williams) *t.k.h: chsd ldr to over 2f out: lost pl over 1f out: sn wl btn* **9/1**

316- **8** *1 ½* **Archie Stevens**[11] 8412 6-8-9 **77**........ CallumShepherd[(5)] 5 69
(David Evans) *t.k.h: led: rdn 2f out: hdd & wknd 1f out* **12/1**

200- **9** *2 ½* **Yeeoow (IRE)**[25] 8262 7-8-12 **80**........(p) JustinNewman[(5)] 4 64
(K R Burke) *racd on outer: chsd ldrs: rdn over 2f out: wknd over 1f out* **6/1**

1m 12.45s (-0.65) **Going Correction** +0.075s/f (Slow) **9** Ran SP% **117.4**
Speed ratings (Par 105): **107,106,105,104,104 103,102,100,97**
CSF £40.87 CT £606.26 TOTE £12.20: £2.50, £1.70, £4.60; EX 57.20 Trifecta £673.10.
Owner Elite Racing Club **Bred** Elite Racing Club **Trained** Epsom, Surrey

FOCUS
A competitive sprint handicap, and they finished in a bit of a heap. The winner is rated back to form.

143 RACING UK DAY PASS JUST £10 H'CAP 6f (P)
4:40 (4:45) (Class 6) (0-55,55) 4-Y-O+ **£2,264** (£673; £336; £168) **Stalls** Low

Form RPR

540- **1** **Invectus Hero**[30] 8203 4-9-6 **54**........ MartinLane 2 63
(Derek Shaw) *chsd ldng pair: rdn on inner 2f out: styd on fnl f to ld nr fin* **10/3**[1]

465- **2** *nk* **Blue Bounty**[40] 8078 5-9-7 **55**........(p) SaleemGolam 8 63
(Mark H Tompkins) *chsd ldr: rdn 2f out: hd at awkward angle but led 100yds out: hdd nr fin* **9/1**

6/5- **3** *1 ½* **Bridge Builder**[47] 7982 6-8-12 **49**........(p) RobHornby[(3)] 4 53
(Peter Hedger) *led: rdn over 1f out: hdd and no ex last 100yds* **4/1**[2]

05-5 **4** *1 ½* **Tax Reform (IRE)**[6] 46 6-8-8 **47**........(b) PaddyPilley[(5)] 6 46
(Natalie Lloyd-Beavis) *chsd ldng trio: hanging and racd v awkwardly whn asked to cl fr 2f out: cajoled along and hld on to 4th fnl f but no imp* **25/1**

454- **5** *1 ¼* **Jolly Red Jeanz (IRE)**[12] 8399 5-9-7 **55**........(b) CathyGannon 3 50+
(Daniel Mark Loughnane) *t.k.h: hld up in midfield: rdn and nt qckn 2f out: no imp after* **9/2**[3]

31-2 **6** *shd* **Arizona Snow**[6] 54 4-9-4 **52**........(p) LukeMorris 7 47+
(Ronald Harris) *racd in midfield: drvn and no prog 2f out: wl hld over 1f out* **4/1**[2]

554- **7** *hd* **Glenbuck Lass (IRE)**[30] 8196 4-8-13 **47**........ OisinMurphy 10 41+
(Alan Bailey) *hld up in rr: sltly impeded after 1f: wl off the pce whn shkn up over 2f out: styd on fnl f: nvr nrr* **20/1**

365- **8** *½* **Assertive Agent**[12] 8401 6-9-6 **54**........ JimCrowley 9 47+
(Tony Carroll) *dropped in fr wd draw: hld up in last and detached: reminder over 2f out: styd on fnl f: nvr involved* **16/1**

023- **9** *1* **Bold Max**[12] 8401 5-9-5 **53**........(v) MartinHarley 1 43+
(Zoe Davison) *hmpd on inner after 1f: a in rr after: reminders and no prog wl over 1f out* **9/1**

230- **10** *6* **Mon Petit Fleur**[45] 8013 4-9-3 **54**........ SimonPearce[(3)] 5 26
(Lydia Pearce) *nvr beyond midfield: hanging over 2f out: sn btn* **20/1**

1m 13.01s (-0.09) **Going Correction** +0.075s/f (Slow) **10** Ran SP% **120.5**
Speed ratings (Par 101): **103,102,100,98,96 96,96,95,94,86**
CSF £34.41 CT £129.12 TOTE £4.30: £1.40, £3.00, £1.80; EX 36.50 Trifecta £168.00.
Owner Brian Johnson (Northamptonshire) **Bred** Poulton Farm Stud **Trained** Sproxton, Leics
■ Stewards' Enquiry : Saleem Golam two-day ban: used whip above permitted level (Jan 25-26)

FOCUS
The pace held up in this moderate sprint, albeit the first three swapped places in the closing stages. The winner has the scope to do a bit better.
T/Jkpt: Not won. JACKPOT PLACEPOT: £939.20 to a £1 stake. Pool of £2,766.30 - 2.15 winning units. T/Plt: £1,858.10 to a £1 stake. Pool of £77990.99 - 30.64 winning tickets. T/Qpdt: £32.00 to a £1 stake. Pool of £10530.99- 243.43 winning tickets. **Jonathan Neesom**

[102]WOLVERHAMPTON (A.W) (L-H)
Monday, January 11

OFFICIAL GOING: Tapeta: standard
Wind: Light behind Weather: Sunny spells

144 LADBROKES APPRENTICE H'CAP 7f 32y (Tp)
12:45 (12:46) (Class 6) (0-65,64) 4-Y-O+ **£2,587** (£770; £384; £192) **Stalls** High

Form RPR

001- **1** **Pacolita (IRE)**[14] 8376 4-9-6 **63**........ RyanClark 2 72
(Sylvester Kirk) *s.i.s: sn prom: lost pl 1/2-way: hdwy over 1f out: r.o to ld wl ins fnl f* **12/1**

14-4 **2** *¾* **Sewn Up**[7] 36 6-9-7 **64**........(p) JoeyHaynes 1 71
(Keith Dalgleish) *a.p: rdn to ld over 1f out: hdd wl ins fnl f: kpt on* **6/1**[3]

600- **3** *½* **Al's Memory (IRE)**[11] 8414 7-9-6 **63**........ PhilipPrince 10 69
(David Evans) *chsd ldrs: rdn over 1f out: r.o* **15/2**

041- **4** *1 ¼* **Believe It (IRE)**[20] 8352 4-8-7 **57**........ ChrisKelly[(7)] 7 63+
(Richard Hughes) *s.i.s: hld up: r.o ins fnl f: nt rch ldrs* **13/8**[1]

200- **5** *½* **Black Truffle (FR)**[14] 8376 6-9-2 **64**........ JosephineGordon[(5)] 4 66
(Mark Usher) *hld up: nt clr run wl over 1f out: r.o ins fnl f: nt rch ldrs* **14/1**

46-0 **6** *1 ¾* **Kodiac Lady (IRE)**[10] 1 4-8-13 **61**........(e) HollieDoyle[(5)] 6 60
(Simon West) *hld up: hdwy and nt clr run over 1f out: styd on same pce ins fnl f* **25/1**

050- **7** *½* **Top Offer**[11] 8408 7-8-13 **63**........ NicolaGrundy[(7)] 12 59
(Patrick Morris) *prom: chsd ldr 5f out: led over 2f out: rdn and hdd over 1f out: wknd wl ins fnl f* **40/1**

34-3 **8** *½* **Bogsnog (IRE)**[7] 36 6-9-5 **62**........ ShaneGray 9 57
(Kristin Stubbs) *hld up in tch: rdn over 1f out: wknd ins fnl f* **5/1**[2]

6/3- **9** *½* **The Fenland Man**[30] 8211 5-9-3 **60**........ RobHornby 3 54
(James Unett) *chsd ldr 2f: remained handy: rdn over 2f out: wknd ins fnl f* **25/1**

010- **10** *1* **Beauty's Forte (IRE)**[20] 8352 5-8-8 **58**........ LeeByrne[(7)] 5 49
(Declan Carroll) *sn pushed along in rr: effrt over 1f out: wknd fnl f* **50/1**

201- **11** *3 ¼* **Dandys Perier (IRE)**[20] 8351 5-9-4 **61**........ GeorgeDowning 8 44
(Ronald Harris) *sn pushed along to ld: hdd over 2f out: wknd ins fnl f* **16/1**

400- **12** *5* **Munaawib**[27] 8236 8-9-0 **64**........(bt) BenSanderson[(7)] 11 35
(Deborah Sanderson) *s.i.s: hld up: pushed along on outer 3f out: wknd 2f out* **25/1**

1m 27.63s (-1.17) **Going Correction** -0.20s/f (Stan) **12** Ran SP% **117.0**
Speed ratings (Par 101): **98,97,96,95,94 92,92,91,90,89 86,80**
CSF £76.83 CT £594.58 TOTE £10.20: £3.20, £2.20, £2.60; EX 59.70 Trifecta £684.00.
Owner G Dolan & P Wheatley **Bred** Ms Clara O'Reilly **Trained** Upper Lambourn, Berks

FOCUS
A moderate handicap, confined to apprentice riders. There was something of an uneven pace on but the form makes sense.

145 32RED.COM MAIDEN STKS 7f 32y (Tp)
1:15 (1:18) (Class 5) 3-Y-O **£3,557** (£1,058; £529; £264) **Stalls** High

Form RPR

2- **1** **War Glory (IRE)**[20] 8349 3-9-5 0........ SeanLevey 3 85+
(Richard Hannon) *trckd ldrs: racd keenly: shkn up to ld over 1f out: rdn and edgd lft ins fnl f: styd on* **4/11**[1]

0- **2** *¾* **Eskandari (IRE)**[34] 8144 3-9-5 0........ RobertHavlin 9 83
(Simon Crisford) *chsd ldr: led 3f out: rdn and hdd over 1f out: styd on* **14/1**

34- **3** *6* **Pirate's Treasure**[26] 8245 3-9-5 0........ JamieSpencer 2 67
(James Tate) *chsd ldrs: rdn over 1f out: edgd lft and no ex fnl f* **9/2**[2]

03- **4** *3* **Joyful Day (IRE)**[25] 8266 3-9-5 0........ JoeFanning 5 59
(Robert Cowell) *led 4f: sn rdn: wknd fnl f* **8/1**[3]

4- **5** *2* **Falcon's Fire (IRE)**[13] 8387 3-9-5 0........ PhillipMakin 8 54
(Keith Dalgleish) *mid-div: rdn over 2f out: wkng whn hung lft over 1f out* **33/1**

6 *1 ¼* **Pensax Lady (IRE)** 3-9-0 0........ SteveDrowne 12 46
(Daniel Mark Loughnane) *s.s: in rr tl sme hdwy over 1f out: sn wknd* **66/1**

60- **7** *2 ½* **Dark Illustrator**[20] 8350 3-8-9 0........ JoshDoyle[(5)] 6 39
(David O'Meara) *mid-div: rdn over 2f out: wknd over 1f out* **80/1**

8 *1 ¾* **Keep The Silence (IRE)** 3-8-11 0........ EoinWalsh[(3)] 7 35
(James Tate) *mid-div: rdn over 2f out: sn wknd: hung lft over 1f out* **18/1**

6- **9** *20* **Golden Cape**[77] 7512 3-9-0 0........ TomEaves 1
(Michael Mullineaux) *sn outpcd* **66/1**

0- **10** *3 ½* **Sharp Jack**[24] 8287 3-9-5 0........ RichardKingscote 10
(Tom Dascombe) *rn wout declared tongue strap: sn pushed along and prom: rdn and wknd over 2f out* **12/1**

11 *3* **Millady Percy** 3-9-0 0........[1] PaulMulrennan 4
(Roy Brotherton) *s.s: outpcd* **100/1**

0-5 **12** *½* **Womble**[5] 74 3-9-0 0........[1] NoelGarbutt[(5)] 11
(Laura Young) *hld up: pushed along 5f out: bhd fnl 4f* **100/1**

1m 27.61s (-1.19) **Going Correction** -0.20s/f (Stan) **12** Ran SP% **131.4**
Speed ratings (Par 97): **98,97,90,86,84 83,80,78,55,51 48,47**
CSF £9.95 TOTE £1.40: £1.10, £3.30, £1.60; EX 11.20 Trifecta £51.00.
Owner Mohamed Saeed Al Shahi **Bred** Pier House Stud **Trained** East Everleigh, Wilts

FOCUS
A modest 3yo maiden in which the first two came clear. The winner set a good standard and built on that.

146 32RED CASINO FILLIES' H'CAP 5f 216y (Tp)
1:50 (1:50) (Class 5) (0-75,75) 4-Y-O+ **£3,557** (£1,058; £529; £264) **Stalls** Low

Form RPR
322- **1** **By Rights**[12] 8399 5-8-9 **65** GeorgeDowning(3) 3 73
(Tony Carroll) *mde all: rdn over 1f out: styd on* **6/1**[3]
400- **2** 1 ¾ **Lady Gemini**[45] 8011 4-9-2 **69** (p) JoeyHaynes 2 71
(Jo Hughes) *a.p: chsd wnr over 2f out: rdn over 1f out: styd on same pce ins fnl f* **14/1**
04-1 **3** 3 ¼ **Effusive**[7] 41 4-9-8 **75** 6ex (p) JoeFanning 6 67
(William Haggas) *chsd ldrs: lost pl over 3f out: hdwy over 1f out: styd on same pce fnl f* **11/10**[1]
300- **4** ½ **Loumarin (IRE)**[21] 8331 4-8-12 **65** AndrewMullen 5 55
(Michael Appleby) *hld up: rdn over 2f out: r.o ins fnl f: nvr nrr* **9/1**
U04- **5** ¾ **Dilgura**[14] 8382 6-9-7 **74** ShaneKelly 1 62
(Stuart Kittow) *hld up: hdwy over 2f out: rdn over 1f out: wknd ins fnl f* **4/1**[2]
006- **6** 6 **Gower Princess**[11] 8413 5-8-5 **58** KieranO'Neill 4 26
(Ronald Harris) *sn pushed along to chse wnr: rdn and lost 2nd over 2f out: wknd over 1f out* **33/1**
10-5 **7** 4 ½ **Ki Ki**[7] 41 4-8-10 **66** AdamCarter(3) 7 20
(Bryan Smart) *pushed along in rr early: hdwy over 4f out: rdn over 2f out: sn wknd* **11/1**

1m 12.73s (-1.77) **Going Correction** -0.20s/f (Stan) **7** Ran SP% **109.8**
Speed ratings (Par 100): **103,100,96,95,94 86,80**
CSF £74.12 TOTE £5.10: £2.00, £4.30; EX 81.40 Trifecta £272.70.
Owner Last Day Racing Partnership **Bred** Grove Farm Stud **Trained** Cropthorne, Worcs

FOCUS
An ordinary fillies' sprint handicap in which two came clear. The first two are rated similar to last year's best.

147 32REDSPORT.COM (S) STKS 1m 141y (Tp)
2:20 (2:20) (Class 6) 3-Y-O **£2,587** (£770; £384; £192) **Stalls** Low

Form RPR
030- **1** **Frivolous Lady (IRE)**[25] 8267 3-8-7 66 (v) JFEgan 2 58
(David Evans) *led early: chsd ldrs: pushed along over 4f out: sn lost pl: rallied over 2f out: rdn to ld and hung lft fr over 1f out: styd on* **8/1**
20-2 **2** 2 ¼ **Sky Ferry**[5] 63 3-8-5 55 JosephineGordon(7) 3 58
(J S Moore) *chsd ldr 8f out tl over 6f out: remained handy: nt clr run over 1f out: rdn to chse wnr fnl f: styd on* **5/2**[2]
00-0 **3** 4 ½ **Bohemian Origin (IRE)**[4] 87 3-8-12 43 (p) KieranO'Neill 4 49
(J S Moore) *prom: chsd ldr over 6f out tl led over 2f out: rdn and hdd over 1f out: wknd ins fnl f* **40/1**
020- **4** nk **Global Avenger (IRE)**[32] 8166 3-8-12 60 (b) JoeFanning 5 48
(Ed Dunlop) *s.i.s: hld up: hdwy over 4f out: rdn over 2f out: sn outpcd* **4/1**[3]
320- **5** 3 ½ **Southern Seas**[34] 8143 3-8-7 64 PJMcDonald 6 36
(Ann Duffield) *sn led: rdn and hdd over 2f out: wknd fnl f* **13/8**[1]
016- **6** 2 ¼ **Q Ten Girl (IRE)**[28] 8224 3-9-5 67 (v) AndrewMullen 1 43
(James Unett) *hld up: hdwy u.p over 1f out: wknd fnl f* **9/1**

1m 50.4s (0.30) **Going Correction** -0.20s/f (Stan) **6** Ran SP% **110.2**
Speed ratings (Par 95): **90,88,84,83,80 78**
CSF £27.22 TOTE £8.80: £4.30, £1.60; EX 40.00 Trifecta £559.10.
Owner B Drew & W Clifford **Bred** Rory O'Brien **Trained** Pandy, Monmouths

FOCUS
There was no hanging about early on in this moderate 3yo seller. The time and the third hardly inspire confidence in the form.

148 £10 FREE AT 32RED.COM H'CAP 1m 1f 103y (Tp)
2:55 (2:55) (Class 6) (0-60,60) 3-Y-O **£2,587** (£770; £384; £192) **Stalls** Low

Form RPR
000- **1** **Kalamata**[42] 8047 3-9-5 **58** JackMitchell 6 63+
(Roger Varian) *hld up in tch: rdn over 2f out: sn outpcd: rallied fnl f: edgd lft and r.o to ld towards fin* **3/1**[2]
000- **2** ½ **Schoolboy Error (IRE)**[38] 8102 3-9-2 **55** (b[1]) TimmyMurphy 2 59
(Jamie Osborne) *plld hrd and prom: rdn to chse ldr ins fnl f: hung rt and ev ch towards fin: styd on* **11/2**[3]
650- **3** 1 ¼ **First Party**[42] 8055 3-9-6 **59** JoeFanning 8 61
(Mark Johnston) *chsd ldr after 1f: led over 2f out: rdn and hung lft fr over 1f out: hdd towards fin* **12/1**
560- **4** 1 **Herridge (IRE)**[34] 8143 3-9-0 **60** MeganNicholls(7) 3 61
(Richard Hannon) *chsd ldrs: rdn and nt clr run over 1f out: styd on* **14/1**
04-2 **5** hd **Frivolous Prince (IRE)**[5] 69 3-8-7 **46** (v[1]) JFEgan 5 45
(David Evans) *sn pushed along to ld: rdn over 2f out: hdd over 1f out: hmpd sn after: styd on same pce* **6/5**[1]
064- **6** 3 **Secret Sinner (IRE)**[42] 8057 3-8-0 **46** oh1 JosephineGordon(7) 1 40
(Jamie Osborne) *s.i.s: hld up: hdwy over 3f out: rdn and outpcd over 2f out: n.d after* **33/1**
000- **7** 5 **Rosecomb (IRE)**[157] 5113 3-9-2 **55** [1] JamieSpencer 4 39
(Michael Bell) *s.i.s: a in rr: rdn and wknd over 2f out* **11/1**
000- **8** 7 **It's A Stitch Up**[11] 8410 3-8-11 **50** (b) MartinDwyer 7 21
(Brian Meehan) *hld up: pushed along over 5f out: rdn and wknd over 2f out* **40/1**

2m 0.06s (-0.74) **Going Correction** -0.20s/f (Stan) **8** Ran SP% **113.9**
Speed ratings (Par 95): **95,94,93,92,92 89,85,79**
CSF £19.74 CT £170.19 TOTE £3.60: £1.80, £1.10, £3.10; EX 24.30 Trifecta £144.60.
Owner Nurlan Bizakov **Bred** Hesmonds Stud Ltd **Trained** Newmarket, Suffolk
■ Stewards' Enquiry : J F Egan caution: careless riding

FOCUS
They went hard early on in this weak 3yo handicap and it saw changing fortunes in the final furlong, with slow closing fractions. The runner-up has the scope to do a lot better.

149 BET IN PLAY AT CORAL H'CAP 1m 1f 103y (Tp)
3:25 (3:26) (Class 6) (0-60,60) 4-Y-O+ **£2,587** (£770; £384; £192) **Stalls** Low

Form RPR
13-2 **1** **Tijuca (IRE)**[7] 39 7-9-7 **60** (tp) KieranO'Neill 11 68
(Ed de Giles) *hld up: hdwy u.p and hung lft fr over 1f out: styd on to ld wl ins fnl f: sn clr* **5/2**[2]
050- **2** 2 ¼ **Mfiftythreedotcom (IRE)**[16] 8360 5-9-0 **53** (b[1]) JackGarritty 7 56
(Richard Fahey) *chsd ldr: rdn to ld 1f out: edgd lft and hdd wl ins fnl f* **11/1**
05-4 **3** nk **Stanlow**[7] 35 6-8-12 **51** (v) RobertHavlin 2 54
(Michael Mullineaux) *mid-div: nt clr run over 2f out: hdwy over 1f out: styd on same pce wl ins fnl f* **14/1**
515- **4** 3 ½ **Incurs Four Faults**[30] 8201 5-9-3 **56** (b[1]) JoeFanning 6 52
(Keith Dalgleish) *s.i.s and hmpd s: hld up: hdwy over 2f out: rdn over 1f out: no ex fnl f* **5/1**[3]
121- **5** hd **Roman De Brut (IRE)**[16] 8360 4-9-5 **59** TomEaves 4 54
(Ronald Thompson) *prom: rdn over 2f out: no ex fnl f* **9/4**[1]
025- **6** 1 ½ **Little Choosey**[21] 8335 6-8-6 **50** (t) AaronJones(5) 3 42
(Roy Bowring) *sn led: rdn and hdd 1f out: wknd wl ins fnl f* **16/1**
060- **7** 2 ½ **Star Links (USA)**[12] 8396 10-8-13 **52** (bt) ShaneKelly 10 40
(Sylvester Kirk) *s.s: in rr: rdn 3f out: sn outpcd* **16/1**
330- **8** 23 **Medal Of Valour (JPN)**[21] 8334 8-9-1 **54** PaulMulrennan 1
(Roy Brotherton) *prom: rdn over 3f out: wknd over 1f out* **66/1**
000- **9** 1 **Rizal Park (IRE)**[39] 8089 5-9-7 **60** (b[1]) TimmyMurphy 9 2
(James Evans) *plld hrd and prom: rdn over 2f out: sn wknd* **9/1**
200- **10** 42 **Bella Blur**[33] 8164 4-9-4 **58** JamieSpencer 8
(Michael Bell) *a in rr: rdn and wknd 3f out: eased* **25/1**

1m 58.84s (-1.96) **Going Correction** -0.20s/f (Stan)
WFA 4 from 5yo+ 1lb **10** Ran SP% **118.1**
Speed ratings (Par 101): **100,98,97,94,94 93,90,70,69,32**
CSF £31.01 CT £327.97 TOTE £3.40: £1.60, £3.30, £2.70; EX 45.20 Trifecta £561.90.
Owner E B De Giles **Bred** M Kennelly **Trained** Ledbury, H'fords

FOCUS
A moderate handicap, run at a sound pace. Straightforward form, rated around the second and third.

150 DOWNLOAD THE CORAL APP H'CAP 1m 4f 50y (Tp)
4:00 (4:01) (Class 6) (0-55,55) 4-Y-O+ **£2,587** (£770; £384; £192) **Stalls** Low

Form RPR
/1- **1** **Little Stampy (IRE)**[24] 8291 5-9-7 **55** (p) ShaneGray 10 63
(D Broad, Ire) *s.i.s: hld up: hdwy over 2f out: rdn to ld ins fnl f: styd on* **2/1**[1]
006- **2** 1 ¼ **Pinotage**[40] 6062 8-9-7 **55** (p) JamesSullivan 5 61
(Peter Niven) *mid-div: hdwy over 3f out: led over 2f out: rdn and hdd ins fnl f: styd on same pce* **9/1**
61-5 **3** 1 ½ **Elle Rebelle**[9] 20 6-9-4 **52** JamieSpencer 4 56
(Mark Brisbourne) *hld up: hdwy over 2f out: rdn over 1f out: styd on to go 3rd post* **10/1**
004- **4** hd **Missandei**[24] 8291 4-8-10 **51** (t) JackDuern(3) 2 54
(Steph Hollinshead) *hld up: hdwy over 3f out: chsd ldr over 2f out: sn rdn and ev ch: no ex wl ins fnl f* **12/1**
/00- **5** 3 ½ **Toboggan's Gift**[47] 4443 4-8-9 **47** PJMcDonald 6 45
(Ann Duffield) *hld up: rdn over 3f out: hdwy over 1f out: sn hung lft: no ex ins fnl f* **100/1**
030- **6** 1 ¼ **Castanea**[21] 8337 4-8-8 **46** oh1 KieranO'Neill 7 42
(Ronald Harris) *hld up: rdn over 4f out: hdwy over 1f out: nvr trbld ldrs* **11/1**
000- **7** ½ **Renewing**[27] 8231 5-9-0 **48** PaulMulrennan 3 43
(Roy Brotherton) *sn chsng ldr: lost 2nd 9f out: chsd ldr again over 5f out tl rdn over 2f out: wknd fnl f* **16/1**
044- **8** 7 **Different Scenario**[30] 8197 5-9-7 **55** AndrewMullen 1 39
(Antony Brittain) *prom: rdn over 3f out: wknd 2f out* **6/1**[3]
04-0 **9** ½ **El Bravo**[5] 62 10-8-12 **46** oh1 JFEgan 9 29
(Shaun Harris) *prom: rdn over 2f out: wknd over 1f out* **33/1**
030- **10** 1 ½ **Ballyfarsoon (IRE)**[24] 8291 5-9-2 **53** (t) GeorgeDowning(3) 8 33
(Ian Williams) *s.i.s: sn pushed along and a in rr* **14/1**
642- **11** 11 **Cool Beans**[13] 8385 4-8-11 **54** (p) AaronJones(5) 12 17
(Roy Bowring) *sn led: clr over 6f out tl over 3f out: rdn and hdd over 2f out: wknd over 1f out* **9/2**[2]
40-0 **12** 50 **Blue Melody Girl (IRE)**[8] 32 4-9-3 **55** (b[1]) TomEaves 11
(James Given) *chsd ldrs: wnt 2nd 9f out tl over 5f out: rdn and wknd over 3f out* **80/1**

2m 37.72s (-3.08) **Going Correction** -0.20s/f (Stan)
WFA 4 from 5yo+ 4lb **12** Ran SP% **118.6**
Speed ratings (Par 101): **102,101,100,100,97 96,96,91,91,90 83,49**
CSF £20.88 CT £150.53 TOTE £3.10: £1.40, £3.00, £2.80; EX 24.00 Trifecta £97.60.
Owner A Broad **Bred** John Lyons **Trained** Summerhill, Co Meath
■ Stewards' Enquiry : J F Egan caution: careless riding; one-day ban; failed to ride to draw (Jan 25)

FOCUS
A weak handicap, rated around the third and fourth.
T/Plt: £195.50 to a £1 stake. Pool of £81312.26 - 303.58 winning tickets. T/Qpdt: £74.40 to a £1 stake. Pool of £8370.19 - 83.20 winning tickets. **Colin Roberts**

[121]LINGFIELD (L-H)
Tuesday, January 12

OFFICIAL GOING: Polytrack: standard
Wind: Strong, across (towards stands) Weather: Cloudy

151 DOWNLOAD THE NEW UNIBET RACING APP H'CAP 5f 6y(P)
1:10 (1:15) (Class 6) (0-60,60) 3-Y-O+ **£2,264** (£673; £336; £168) **Stalls** High

Form RPR
445- **1** **More Spice (IRE)**[26] 8271 4-9-8 **54** (v[1]) JamieSpencer 4 60
(Robert Cowell) *mde all: hld together over 1f out: drvn whn pressed last 150yds: a looked in command* **6/4**[1]
05-3 **2** ½ **Secret Millionaire (IRE)**[4] 98 9-9-11 **57** (p) LukeMorris 3 61
(Shaun Harris) *chsd wnr: drvn to chal over 1f out: kpt on but a hld* **7/4**[2]
/0-6 **3** 2 ½ **Frozen Princess**[4] 98 4-9-7 **58** LucyKBarry(5) 2 53
(Jamie Osborne) *t.k.h: hld up in 4th: rdn over 1f out: tk 3rd ins fnl f: kpt on one pce and no imp* **10/1**
403- **4** 1 ¼ **Nidnod**[36] 8136 3-8-13 **60** WilliamCarson 5 45
(John Bridger) *chsd ldng pair on outer: rdn over 2f out: lost 3rd and fdd ins fnl f* **16/1**
50-2 **5** ½ **Kuanyao (IRE)**[7] 46 10-8-9 **46** oh1 (be) AnnStokell(5) 1 42
(Ann Stokell) *awkward s: a last and urged along after 2f: detached 2f out: styd on nr fin* **7/2**[3]

58.13s (-0.67) **Going Correction** -0.10s/f (Stan)
WFA 3 from 4yo+ 15lb **5** Ran SP% **113.6**
Speed ratings (Par 101): **101,100,96,94,93**
CSF £4.64 TOTE £2.00: £1.10, £1.60; EX 5.00 Trifecta £18.50.
Owner Khalifa Dasmal & Partner **Bred** K A Dasmal **Trained** Six Mile Bottom, Cambs

FOCUS
The winner got away with setting steady fractions in this moderate sprint handicap. The second is the best guide.

152 UNIBET 90PLUS INJURY TIME INSURANCE IS BACK H'CAP 6f 1y(P)
1:40 (1:45) (Class 5) (0-75,75) 3-Y-O **£2,911** (£866; £432; £216) **Stalls** Low

Form RPR
21- **1** **Summer Chorus**[60] 7824 3-9-5 **73** JimCrowley 1 80+
(Andrew Balding) *taken down early: trckd ldrs: wnt 2nd 2f out: led over 1f out: rdn whn pressed ins fnl f: styd on wl* **7/2**[2]
651- **2** ¾ **Discreet Hero (IRE)**[112] 6629 3-9-6 **74** (t) RobertHavlin 3 78+
(Simon Crisford) *patiently rdn in 6th: prog 2f out: tk 2nd 1f out and sn chalng: drvn and styd on but wnr had first run* **11/10**[1]
100- **3** 2 **Abberley Dancer (IRE)**[209] 3275 3-8-10 **71** JosephineGordon(7) 6 69
(J S Moore) *in tch: pushed along 1/2-way: rdn and prog over 1f out: tk 3rd ins fnl f: no ch w ldng pair* **16/1**
640- **4** 2½ **Ten Rocks**[13] 8402 3-8-6 **67** (b1) JordanUys(7) 2 57
(Brian Meehan) *taken down early: led: more than 2 l ahd over 2f out: hdd & wknd over 1f out* **50/1**
220- **5** 1½ **Lightsome**[25] 8286 3-9-7 **75** OisinMurphy 8 60
(Clive Cox) *chsd ldrs but trapped out wd: lost pl and rdn 2f out: btn sn after* **7/1**
653- **6** 4 **Toledo**[15] 8377 3-9-5 **73** SeanLevey 5 45
(Richard Hannon) *chsd ldr to 2f out: shkn up briefly over 1f out: wknd qckly fnl f* **5/1**[3]
533- **7** 1¾ **Port Gaverne (IRE)**[251] 1988 3-8-12 **73** TylerSaunders(7) 7 40
(Marcus Tregoning) *hld up in 7th: lost tch over 4f out: sn wl bhd: pushed along and no hdwy after* **25/1**
100- **8** 11 **Fishergate**[25] 8286 3-9-5 **73** AdamBeschizza 4 5
(Richard Rowe) *s.i.s: outpcd and t.o after 1f* **33/1**

1m 10.34s (-1.56) **Going Correction** -0.10s/f (Stan) **8** Ran SP% **113.6**
Speed ratings (Par 97): **106,105,102,99,97 91,89,74**
CSF £7.56 CT £50.21 TOTE £3.80: £1.50, £1.10, £3.10; EX 8.50 Trifecta £60.60.
Owner Sheikh Juma Dalmook Al Maktoum **Bred** Genesis Green Stud Ltd And Thurso Ltd **Trained** Kingsclere, Hants
■ Stewards' Enquiry : Adam Beschizza two-day ban: careless riding (26-27 Jan)

FOCUS
A fair little sprint featuring some unexposed types, with the first two progressing. The level is set around the fourth.

153 32RED.COM MAIDEN STKS 1m 2f (P)
2:10 (2:15) (Class 5) 3-Y-O **£2,911** (£866; £432; £216) **Stalls** Low

Form RPR
232- **1** **King Of Dreams**[13] 8404 3-9-5 73 JamieSpencer 1 79+
(David Simcock) *led: hdd and drvn over 1f out: styd on wl fnl f: hung rt but led last 75yds* **5/4**[1]
56- **2** ¾ **Cachao**[38] 8122 3-9-5 0 RobertTart 4 77
(John Gosden) *trckd wnr to over 3f out: nipped through on inner to ld over 1f out: drvn fnl f: hdd last 75yds* **9/4**[2]
3 6 **Muaither (IRE)** 3-9-5 0 RobertHavlin 3 65+
(John Gosden) *dwlt: rn green and pushed along at various times: lost tch 4f out: no ch after: picked up and styd on to take 3rd ins fnl f* **11/4**[3]
05- **4** 3¾ **Silca Wings**[28] 8232 3-9-0 0 ShaneKelly 2 53
(James Fanshawe) *t.k.h: trckd ldng pair tl pressed wnr on outer over 3f out: lost 2nd and wknd wl over 1f out* **14/1**

2m 6.03s (-0.57) **Going Correction** -0.10s/f (Stan) **4** Ran SP% **108.5**
Speed ratings (Par 97): **98,97,92,89**
CSF £4.35 TOTE £1.90; EX 4.90 Trifecta £7.20.
Owner Khalifa Dasmal **Bred** Brightwalton Stud **Trained** Newmarket, Suffolk

FOCUS
They went steady in the early stages before the pace picked up running down the hill. Not straightforward to assess, the second the best guide.

154 LADBROKES CONDITIONS STKS (PLUS 10 RACE) 1m 1y(P)
2:40 (2:45) (Class 3) 3-Y-O **£7,439** (£2,213; £1,106; £553) **Stalls** High

Form RPR
31-1 **1** **Hombre Rojo (IRE)**[3] 123 3-9-2 77 JimCrowley 3 92
(Simon Dow) *mde all: kicked on 3f out: drvn over 1f out: edgd rt fnl f but styd on wl* **3/1**[2]
126- **2** 1 **Lazzam**[85] 7339 3-8-13 91 DanielMuscutt(3) 1 90
(Marco Botti) *trckd ldng pair: wnt 2nd wl over 1f out: drvn to chal fnl f: nt qckn last 100yds* **8/1**
421- **3** 2½ **Special Season**[24] 8309 3-9-2 100 (p) PatCosgrave 4 84
(William Haggas) *trckd wnr: trying to mount a chal whn hung rt bnd 2f out: sn lost 2nd and one pce after* **8/13**[1]
1- **4** 1¾ **Red Rannagh (IRE)**[46] 8023 3-9-2 0 (t) JamieSpencer 2 80
(David Simcock) *dwlt: hld up in last: shkn up and outpcd over 2f out: no ch after: kpt on nr fin* **7/1**[3]

1m 38.37s (0.17) **Going Correction** -0.10s/f (Stan) **4** Ran SP% **110.5**
Speed ratings (Par 101): **95,94,91,89**
CSF £21.24 TOTE £3.60; EX 19.60 Trifecta £38.20.
Owner Robert Moss **Bred** Helen Lyons **Trained** Ashtead, Surrey

FOCUS
A fair conditions event, billed as something of a trial for the UAE 2,000 Guineas. The winner confirmed his recent improved form, although he got an easy lead.

155 CORAL H'CAP 1m 2f (P)
3:10 (3:16) (Class 7) (0-50,50) 3-Y-O+ **£1,704** (£503; £251) **Stalls** Low

Form RPR
050- **1** **Clock On Tom**[57] 7264 6-9-9 **45** LukeMorris 1 53+
(Denis Quinn) *in tch in midfield: pushed along over 3f out: waiting for room tl gap appeared on inner 2f out: prog over 1f out: hrd rdn to ld last 100yds: hld on* **6/1**[3]
00-3 **2** ½ **Zarliman (IRE)**[5] 79 6-9-9 **45** (p) LiamKeniry 13 52
(Neil Mulholland) *hld up towards rr: prog 3f out: clsd on ldrs over 1f out: chal and upsides 100yds: jst hld* **4/1**[1]
402- **3** ½ **One Last Dream**[13] 8398 7-9-10 **46** FergusSweeney 8 52
(Ron Hodges) *trckd ldr 2f: styd prom: rdn to chal over 1f out: nrly on terms last 100yds: nt qckn* **14/1**
535- **4** nk **Happy Jack (IRE)**[22] 8337 5-9-11 **47** (b) ShaneKelly 7 53
(Michael Wigham) *prom: wnt 2nd 3f out: gng easily 2f out: led over 1f out: fnd nil and hdd last 100yds* **6/1**[3]
664- **5** 2½ **Charlie's Star**[13] 8398 4-9-12 **50** JamieSpencer 4 51
(Laura Mongan) *chsd ldrs: rdn 3f out: tried to cl over 1f out: hrd drvn and no imp fnl f* **10/1**
006- **6** 1½ **Plover**[13] 8397 6-9-10 **46** KierenFox 5 44
(Michael Attwater) *hld up towards rr: taken wd over 3f out: lost grnd bnd 2f out: rdn on fnl f: no ch* **20/1**
643- **7** hd **Solveig's Song**[13] 8398 4-9-8 **47** oh1 (p) WilliamCarson 10 44
(Steve Woodman) *nvr bttr than midfield: shkn up 3f out: no prog tl styd on ins fnl f* **12/1**
453- **8** 1 **Sudden Wish (IRE)**[13] 8397 7-10-0 **50** (p) JimmyQuinn 12 46
(Paul Burgoyne) *hld up in last trio: shkn up 3f out: modest prog fr over 1f out: no threat* **12/1**
050- **9** ½ **Sixties Queen**[22] 8334 6-9-6 **45** (p) TimClark(3) 6 40
(Lisa Williamson) *hld up in rr: nt clr run on inner 3f out to 2f out: kpt on one pce after and n.d* **100/1**
003- **10** 1¾ **Fast Approach (IRE)**[23] 8314 4-9-10 **48** (v1) OisinMurphy 11 39
(Andrew Balding) *led fr wd draw: hdd & wknd qckly over 1f out* **9/2**[2]
000- **11** 2 **Querido (GER)**[13] 8398 12-9-2 **45** (tp) DanielleMooney(7) 3 33
(Paddy Butler) *awkward s: mostly in last pair: v modest late prog* **100/1**
450- **12** 2 **Movie Magic**[26] 8264 5-9-3 **46** (v) JosephineGordon(7) 14 30
(Mark Hoad) *trckd ldr after 2f tl 3f out: wknd 2f out* **33/1**
13 4½ **Pao De Acuca (IRE)**[76] 7574 4-9-0 **47** oh2 (tp) CharlieBennett(7) 9 20
(Jose Santos) *dwlt: prog arnd rivals fr rr to go prom 6f out but sn pushed along: wknd over 2f out* **8/1**
006- **14** 6 **Fine Share (IRE)**[27] 8251 3-8-0 **45** (vt) CathyGannon 2 6
(John Bridger) *a in last pair: struggling sn after 1/2-way* **20/1**

2m 5.51s (-1.09) **Going Correction** -0.10s/f (Stan)
WFA 3 from 4yo 23lb 4 from 5yo+ 2lb **14** Ran SP% **123.5**
Speed ratings (Par 97): **100,99,99,98,96 95,95,94,94,93 91,89,86,81**
CSF £29.60 CT £333.46 TOTE £7.60: £2.90, £1.50, £2.60; EX 34.30 Trifecta £433.40.
Owner John Mangan **Bred** Kingwood Bloodstock **Trained** Newmarket, Suffolk

FOCUS
A low-grade handicap. Straightforward form behind the winner, who was well treated on his recent hurdling form.

156 CORAL.CO.UK H'CAP (FOR GENTLEMAN AMATEUR RIDERS) 1m 4f (P)
3:40 (3:50) (Class 6) (0-65,65) 4-Y-O+ **£2,183** (£677; £338; £169) **Stalls** Low

Form RPR
36-3 **1** **Percella**[4] 101 4-10-7 **65** ow3 MrRyanBird(3) 9 71
(Ian Williams) *hld up in last pair: gd prog on inner wl over 1f out: rdn to ld jst ins fnl f: kpt on wl* **3/1**[2]
020- **2** 1¼ **Ruzeiz (USA)**[29] 8052 7-10-10 **61** (p) MrThomasGreatrex 5 65
(Peter Hedger) *t.k.h: w ldr: gng easily over 2f out: rdn and nt qckn over 1f out: chal again fnl f: one pce last 100yds* **7/2**[3]
/65- **3** shd **Obboorr**[17] 8361 7-10-10 **61** KaineWood 7 65
(Tim Fitzgerald) *hld up towards rr: waiting for room 2f out: rapid prog and hrd rdn jst over 1f out: styd on but too late to chal* **9/4**[1]
026- **4** ½ **Opera Buff**[280] 1243 7-10-9 **65** (p) MrWillPettis(5) 1 68
(Jose Santos) *t.k.h: mde most: urged along 3f out: hdd and one pce jst ins fnl f* **7/1**
005- **5** 1½ **Game Mascot**[70] 7681 6-9-9 **51** oh5 AidenBlakemore(5) 10 52
(Shaun Harris) *hld up in last pair: urged along 3f out: no prog tl kpt on ins fnl f* **33/1**
035- **6** nse **Comedy House**[23] 8317 8-10-5 **63** (v) MrLFMadgwick(7) 3 64
(Michael Madgwick) *s.s: sn in tch: rdn 2f out: chsd ldrs jst over 1f out: one pce after* **10/1**
360- **7** ½ **Golden Thread**[45] 8039 6-10-11 **65** MrMJPKendrick(3) 8 65
(Neil King) *t.k.h: trckd ldrs: urged along over 2f out: lost pl over 1f out: btn after* **14/1**
0/-0 **8** 1¼ **Let Me In (IRE)**[8] 39 6-10-9 **60** (v) MrRhysHughes 2 58
(Bernard Llewellyn) *t.k.h: trckd ldng pair: rdn and wknd over 1f out* **25/1**

2m 37.59s (4.59) **Going Correction** -0.10s/f (Stan)
WFA 4 from 5yo+ 4lb **8** Ran SP% **113.0**
Speed ratings (Par 101): **80,79,79,78,77 77,77,76**
CSF £13.62 CT £26.53 TOTE £3.90: £1.70, £1.50, £1.30; EX 16.00 Trifecta £42.10.
Owner Ian Williams **Bred** Mr & Mrs A E Pakenham **Trained** Portway, Worcs
■ Premier Jack's (100-1) was withdrawn. Rule 4 does not apply.

FOCUS
A modest contest. The winner rates a minor pb.
T/Jkpt: £14,642.70 to a £1 stake. Pool: £30,935.00 - 1.50 winning tickets. JACKPOT PLACEPOT: £23.00 to a £1 stake. Pool of £2,741.00 - 86.90 winning units. T/Plt: £67.40 to a £1 stake. Pool: £84,814.44 - 918.19 winning tickets. T/Qpdt: £33.50 to a £1 stake. Pool: £5,350.65 - 118.05 winning tickets. **Jonathan Neesom**

[76]CHELMSFORD (A.W) (L-H)
Wednesday, January 13

OFFICIAL GOING: Polytrack: standard
Wind: light, behind Weather: dry, bright spells

157 TOTEPLACEPOT RACING'S FAVOURITE BET H'CAP 2m (P)
1:25 (1:26) (Class 6) (0-65,71) 4-Y-O+ **£3,234** (£962; £481; £240) **Stalls** Low

Form RPR
13-1 **1** **Coorg (IRE)**[7] 61 4-8-11 **58** 6ex (b) EoinWalsh(3) 7 73+
(Chris Dwyer) *dwlt and bustled along early: sn rcvrd to chse ldr: led over 3f out and sn rdn clr: in command fnl 2f: easily* **13/8**[1]
/0-1 **2** 7 **Zakatal**[5] 103 10-10-6 **71** 6ex PJMcDonald 6 78
(Rebecca Menzies) *hld up in last pair: effrt over 3f out: 3rd and drvn over 2f out: chsd clr wnr over 1f out: styd on but no ch w wnr* **5/2**[2]
3 **3** 7 **Crazy (GER)**[10] 30 7-9-9 **60** (v1) MartinLane 3 58
(David Dennis) *chsd ldrs: rdn to chse wnr 3f out: no imp: lost 2nd and wknd over 1f out* **7/2**[3]
02-1 **4** 6 **Vivacissimo (IRE)**[11] 27 9-9-8 **59** (tp) TomEaves 8 50
(Ivan Furtado) *hld up in midfield: effrt 3f out: no ch w wnr but styd on u.p ins fnl f: snatched modest 4th last stride* **6/1**
000- **5** shd **Noor Al Haya (IRE)**[28] 8249 6-9-5 **56** KierenFox 2 47
(Laura Mongan) *t.k.h: hld up in last pair: plenty to do and effrt 2f out: modest 4th and no imp 1f out: lost 4th last stride* **25/1**
004- **6** 8 **Zip Wire (IRE)**[15] 8383 7-9-5 **56** AndrewMullen 4 37
(Donald McCain) *in tch in midfield: reminder 5f out: drvn and outpcd 3f out: wl bhd and swtchd lft over 1f out* **16/1**
005- **7** 1¾ **Cascadia (IRE)**[15] 8385 5-8-8 **52** JosephineGordon(7) 1 31
(Ivan Furtado) *led tl hdd and rdn over 3f out: 4th and wl btn 2f out: drifted rt and wknd over 1f out* **12/1**

3m 25.73s (-4.27) **Going Correction** -0.15s/f (Stan)
WFA 4 from 5yo+ 7lb **7** Ran SP% **120.6**
Speed ratings (Par 101): **104,100,97,94,93 89,89**
CSF £6.45 CT £12.65 TOTE £2.40: £1.60, £1.60; EX 6.90 Trifecta £24.60.
Owner Mrs C M Goode **Bred** Malih Al Basti **Trained** Newmarket, Suffolk

FOCUS
Three last-time-out winners took their chance in this modest staying handicap.

158 BET SCOOP6SOCCER AT BETFRED SHOPS APPRENTICE H'CAP 1m (P)
1:55 (1:56) (Class 6) (0-60,60) 4-Y-O+ **£3,234** (£962; £481; £240) **Stalls** Low

Form RPR
505- **1** **Hierarch (IRE)**[23] 8324 9-9-4 **60**....(p) SophieKilloran(3) 2 66
(David Simcock) *chsd ldng pair: effrt to chal over 1f out: rdn to ld ins fnl f: pushed out* **5/1**[3]
040- **2** *1* **Schottische**[27] 8264 6-8-9 **53**....(p) LuluStanford(5) 6 57
(Alan Bailey) *off the pce in last trio: clsd to chse ldrs 4f out: effrt over 1f out: chsd ldng pair 1f out: kpt on to go 2nd last strides* **8/1**
45-5 **3** *nk* **Scot Daddy (USA)**[5] 97 4-9-7 **60**....(t) PaddyBradley 4 63
(David Dennis) *chsd ldr tl led jst over 2f out: rdn and hrd pressed over 1f out: hdd and one pce ins fnl f: lost 2nd last strides* **7/4**[1]
34-5 **4** *2 3/4* **Caltra Colleen**[11] 14 4-9-0 **58**....(bt) JaneElliott(5) 7 54
(Gay Kelleway) *stdd s: t.k.h: hld up in rr: clsd 4f out: effrt and hdwy over 1f out: kpt on u.p ins fnl f: no threat to wnr* **3/1**[2]
050- **5** *1* **Beat The Blues**[35] 8158 4-8-13 **57**.... JackOsborn(5) 3 51
(Miss Joey Ellis) *off the pce in last trio: clsd and in tch 4f out: rdn and outpcd 3f out: rallied 1f out: kpt on but no threat to wnr ins fnl f* **11/1**
006- **6** *1 1/2* **Jonnie Skull (IRE)**[17] 8370 10-8-13 **52**....(vt) JosephineGordon 1 42
(Phil McEntee) *led: rdn and hdd jst over 2f out: wknd ent fnl f* **6/1**
1m 38.81s (-1.09) **Going Correction** -0.15s/f (Stan) **6** Ran SP% **111.8**
Speed ratings (Par 101): **99,98,97,94,93 92**
CSF £41.40 TOTE £4.90: £2.50, £4.50; EX 35.80 Trifecta £117.40.
Owner Tick Tock Partnership **Bred** Castlemartin Stud And Skymarc Farm **Trained** Newmarket, Suffolk

FOCUS
An apprentice handicap which took very little winning.

159 TOTEPOOLLIVEINFO.COM H'CAP 6f (P)
2:25 (2:26) (Class 5) (0-75,80) 4-Y-O+ **£5,175** (£1,540; £769; £384) **Stalls** Centre

Form RPR
62-1 **1** **Gentlemen**[6] 82 5-9-5 **80** 6ex.... JosephineGordon(7) 7 88+
(Phil McEntee) *dwlt and hmpd sn after s: in tch in rr: effrt on inner over 1f out: str run ins fnl f to ld towards fin* **3/1**[2]
536- **2** *3/4* **Saint Pois (FR)**[90] 7233 5-9-1 **72**.... GeorgeDowning(3) 5 77
(Tony Carroll) *chsd ldr: effrt over 1f out: kpt on u.p: ev ch ins fnl f: no ex towards fin* **8/1**
53-1 **3** *shd* **Money Team (IRE)**[10] 28 5-9-11 **79** 6ex.... PhillipMakin 4 84
(David Barron) *ducked as stalls opened and blindfold off late: in tch in midfield: effrt over 1f out: chsd ldrs 1f out: kpt on u.p: wnt 3rd nr fin* **1/1**[1]
361- **4** *nk* **Encapsulated**[13] 8408 6-8-2 **63**.... RhiainIngram(7) 2 67
(Roger Ingram) *taken down early and led to post: rdn and kicked clr ent fnl 2f: worn down ins fnl f: hdd and lost 3 pls towards fin* **14/1**
30-2 **5** *2 1/4* **For Ayman**[10] 28 5-8-5 **66**....(t) SeanMooney(7) 8 63
(Joseph Tuite) *swtchd lft after s: hld up in last pair: effrt over 1f out: pushed along and styd on same pce ins fnl f* **4/1**[3]
300- **6** *7* **Classic Flyer**[28] 8250 4-8-7 **66**....(v) JoshDoyle(5) 6 40
(David O'Meara) *t.k.h: chsd ldrs: rdn and unable qck 2f out: sn lost pl: wknd fnl f* **25/1**
000- **7** *2 3/4* **Malaysian Boleh**[23] 8325 6-9-7 **75**.... LukeMorris 3 41
(Shaun Lycett) *dwlt: in tch in rr: hdwy to chse ldrs 3f out: unable qck u.p over 1f out: wknd fnl f* **10/1**
1m 11.0s (-2.70) **Going Correction** -0.15s/f (Stan) **7** Ran SP% **125.7**
Speed ratings (Par 103): **112,111,110,110,107 98,94**
CSF £30.12 CT £41.11 TOTE £3.50: £1.50, £4.00; EX 32.00 Trifecta £84.10.
Owner Eventmaker Racehorses **Bred** Mrs Eleanor Kent **Trained** Newmarket, Suffolk
■ Stewards' Enquiry : Sean Mooney two-day ban: careless riding (Jan 27-28)

FOCUS
A fair sprint handicap, with a strong favourite, where they went a good clip. The winner continues to progress.

160 TOTEQUADPOT RACING'S FOUR LEGGED FRIEND H'CAP 1m 2f (P)
2:55 (2:55) (Class 4) (0-85,88) 4-Y-O- **£7,876** (£2,357; £1,178; £590; £293) **Stalls** Low

Form RPR
023- **1** **Coillte Cailin (IRE)**[14] 8405 6-9-3 **78**.... AdamKirby 8 84
(Daniel Mark Loughnane) *hld up in tch: effrt wl over 1f out: str run u.p ins fnl f to ld last strides* **5/1**[2]
11-4 **2** *hd* **Pactolus (IRE)**[10] 31 5-8-12 **78**....(t) AaronJones(5) 2 84
(Stuart Williams) *t.k.h: chsd ldrs: rdn to chal over 1f out: led 150yds out: r.o u.p: hdd last strides* **4/5**[1]
051- **3** *nk* **Berlusca (IRE)**[14] 8405 7-9-7 **82**.... DanielTudhope 3 87
(David O'Meara) *taken down early: stdd after s: hld up in tch in last pair: effrt over 1f out: swtchd rt 1f out: styd on wl fnl 100yds* **7/1**[3]
010- **4** *nse* **Excellent Puck (IRE)**[32] 8208 6-9-3 **78**.... FergusSweeney 6 83
(Shaun Lycett) *led: rdn ent fnl 2f: drvn over 1f out: hdd 150yds: kpt on same pce after* **16/1**
03-2 **5** *1 3/4* **Stosur (IRE)**[7] 72 5-9-6 **81**....(b) LukeMorris 1 83
(Gay Kelleway) *chsd ldr: rdn over 2f out: drvn and unable qck over 1f out: kpt on same pce ins fnl f* **8/1**
443- **6** *nk* **Cottesloe (IRE)**[24] 8319 7-9-1 **76**....(b) JFEgan 5 77
(John Berry) *stdd s: hld up in tch: effrt over 1f out: unable qck and kpt on same pce ins fnl f* **5/1**[2]
2m 7.23s (-1.37) **Going Correction** -0.15s/f (Stan)
WFA 4 from 5yo+ 2lb **6** Ran SP% **118.4**
Speed ratings (Par 105): **99,98,98,98,97 96**
CSF £10.14 CT £28.95 TOTE £5.70: £3.40, £1.10; EX 13.10 Trifecta £64.80.
Owner Peter J Moran **Bred** Whisperview Trading Ltd **Trained** Baldwin's Gate, Staffs

FOCUS
A fair field turned up to compete for the good prize-money on offer. It proved a bit messy, though, and an uneven gallop led to a close finish. The form is rated around the fourth.

161 TOTEEXACTA PICK THE 1ST AND 2ND MEDIAN AUCTION MAIDEN STKS 1m 2f (P)
3:25 (3:25) (Class 6) 4-6-Y-O **£3,234** (£962; £481; £240) **Stalls** Low

Form RPR
032- **1** **Chorlton House**[85] 7374 4-9-5 61.... AdamKirby 1 66
(Ian Williams) *trckd ldrs: swtchd rt and rdn to ld over 1f out: asserted u.p 150yds: r.o wl* **11/10**[1]
35-0 **2** *1* **J'Aspire**[11] 14 4-8-9 63....(tp) AaronJones(5) 2 59
(Stuart Williams) *t.k.h: hld up in tch in last pair: effrt and hdwy over 1f out: chsd wnr fnl 75yds: styd on wl but nvr getting to wnr* **9/2**[3]
050- **3** *1 1/2* **Rose Above**[168] 4767 4-9-0 65.... PhillipMakin 3 56
(Andrew Balding) *t.k.h: hld up in tch in midfield: effrt and chal u.p over 1f out: no ex ins fnl f: lost 2nd and one pce fnl 75yds* **3/1**[2]
5 **4** *2* **Do It Tomorrow (IRE)**[11] 26 4-8-11 0.... AlistairRawlinson(3) 6 52
(J R Jenkins) *t.k.h early: chsd ldr tl led 2f out: rdn and hdd over 1f out: wknd ins fnl f* **20/1**
5- **5** *2 1/4* **Black Hole Sun**[30] 8226 4-9-0 0.... CathyGannon 4 48
(Tony Carroll) *hld up in tch in last pair: rdn over 2f out: outpcd and kpt on same pce fr over 1f out* **33/1**
63- **6** *3 3/4* **Tseo**[35] 8162 4-9-5 0.... PatCosgrave 5 46
(David Brown) *led: rdn and hdd 2f out: lost pl over 1f out: wknd fnl f* **5/1**
2m 8.21s (-0.39) **Going Correction** -0.15s/f (Stan) **6** Ran SP% **115.2**
Speed ratings: **95,94,93,91,89 86**
CSF £6.88 TOTE £2.20: £1.30, £2.50; EX 8.20 Trifecta £20.70.
Owner Ian Williams Racing Club **Bred** Mrs P A Cave **Trained** Portway, Worcs

FOCUS
A typically weak maiden for older horses. They were a second slower than the preceding Class 4 handicap and a horse rated 61 was good enough to take it.

162 SCOOP6SOCCER £1 MILLION FOOTBALL BET H'CAP 5f (P)
3:55 (3:55) (Class 5) (0-75,73) 4-Y-O+ **£5,175** (£1,540; £769; £384) **Stalls** Low

Form RPR
54-3 **1** **Welease Bwian (IRE)**[7] 68 7-8-6 **65**....(be) MillyNaseb(7) 1 73
(Stuart Williams) *hld up in last pair: effrt on inner over 1f out: rdn to chal 1f out: led ins fnl f: r.o wl* **6/4**[1]
00-3 **2** *1 1/4* **You're Cool**[7] 56 4-9-7 **73**.... TomEaves 4 76
(James Given) *chsd ldr: rdn and ev ch over 1f out: hdd and no ex ins fnl f* **9/2**[3]
055- **3** *nk* **Secret Asset (IRE)**[18] 8356 11-9-4 **73**....(p) RobHornby(3) 6 75
(Lisa Williamson) *in tch: shkn up over 1f out: chsd ldrs and r.o same pce u.p fnl 100yds* **7/1**
10-4 **4** *2 1/4* **Zipedeedodah (IRE)**[7] 56 4-9-3 **69**....(t) JFEgan 3 61
(Joseph Tuite) *led: rdn over 1f out: hdd 1f out: no ex and wknd fnl 75yds* **3/1**[2]
142- **5** *1 3/4* **State Of The Union (IRE)**[16] 8382 4-9-6 **72**.... CathyGannon 2 58
(Lee Carter) *t.k.h: chsd ldrs: rdn and unable qck over 1f out: awkward hd carriage and wknd ins fnl f* **5/1**
42-6 **6** *3 3/4* **Angel Way (IRE)**[9] 41 7-9-7 **73**....[1] ShaneGray 5 45
(John Gallagher) *hld up in last pair: rdn 1/2-way: struggling over 1f out: sn wknd* **20/1**
58.62s (-1.58) **Going Correction** -0.15s/f (Stan) **6** Ran SP% **117.1**
Speed ratings (Par 103): **106,104,103,99,96 90**
CSF £9.30 TOTE £2.40: £1.30, £2.20; EX 7.00 Trifecta £30.60.
Owner W E Enticknap **Bred** Nils Koop **Trained** Newmarket, Suffolk

FOCUS
A trappy handicap to close the card, and the strong pace proved important in the way this played out. Straightforward form.
T/Plt: £124.90 to a £1 stake. Pool: £57,959.70 - 338.72 winning units. T/Qpdt: £14.40 to a £1 stake. Pool: £6,374.00 - 327.50 winning units. **Steve Payne**

[138]KEMPTON (A.W) (R-H)
Wednesday, January 13

OFFICIAL GOING: Polytrack: standard
Wind: virtually nil Weather: fine, cloudy

163 32RED ON THE APP STORE MAIDEN FILLIES' STKS 7f (P)
4:35 (4:35) (Class 5) 3-Y-O+ **£2,911** (£866; £432; £216) **Stalls** Low

Form RPR
2- **1** **Shaan (IRE)**[44] 8047 3-8-10 0.... SeanLevey 7 80+
(Richard Hannon) *wnt lft s: chsd ldr: rdn over 2f out: led 1f out: gng away at fin* **5/6**[1]
5- **2** *1 1/2* **Australian Queen**[44] 8047 3-8-10 0.... JamieSpencer 4 76+
(David Elsworth) *dwlt: rousted along and sn led: rdn over 2f out: strly pressed and hdd 1f out: hld after* **5/4**[2]
44- **3** *8* **Southern Storm (IRE)**[213] 3198 4-9-9 0.... PatrickO'Donnell(5) 5 58+
(Ralph Beckett) *in rr: pushed along 3f out: styd on ins fnl f to take 3rd: improver* **14/1**[3]
0/ **4** *1 1/4* **Royal Roman**[637] 1504 4-9-11 0.... NathanAlison(3) 1 55
(Kevin Frost) *chsd ldrs: pushed along 3f out: no ex fnl f* **100/1**
0-6 **5** *4 1/2* **Quick Witted**[10] 29 3-8-10 0.... MartinLane 3 39
(Harry Dunlop) *racd on inner in mid-div: pushed along to hold position 4f out: no ex fr 2f out* **50/1**
63- **6** *shd* **Miss Buckaroo (IRE)**[27] 8268 4-10-0 0.... JimCrowley 6 43
(James Given) *racd in mid-div: pushed along 3f out: sn no ex and wknd fr 1 1/2f out* **66/1**
1m 26.33s (0.33) **Going Correction** 0.0s/f (Stan)
WFA 3 from 4yo 18lb **6** Ran SP% **110.1**
Speed ratings (Par 100): **98,96,87,85,80 80**
CSF £2.01 TOTE £1.50: £1.10, £1.30; EX 2.20 Trifecta £4.50.
Owner Al Shaqab Racing **Bred** J F Tuthill **Trained** East Everleigh, Wilts
■ Stewards' Enquiry : Sean Levey one-day ban: careless riding (Jan 27)

FOCUS
The market made this a two-horse race and that's how it turned out. The first three can all rate higher.

164 32RED CASINO H'CAP 1m 3f (P)
5:10 (5:12) (Class 5) (0-70,70) 4-Y-O+ **£2,911** (£866; £432; £216) **Stalls** Low

Form RPR
044- **1** **Dakota City**[56] 7886 5-9-7 **70**....(v) AdamBeschizza 5 79
(Julia Feilden) *in tch in mid-div: cl up and gng wl over 2f out: rdn 2f out: led fnl f: rdn out* **8/1**[3]
623- **2** *1 1/4* **Karnage (IRE)**[29] 8228 4-9-3 **69**.... LukeMorris 8 76
(Daniel Kubler) *pressed ldr: rdn over 2f out: led 2f out: hdd fnl f: kpt on* **11/8**[1]
045- **3** *1 1/2* **I'm Harry**[29] 8228 7-9-6 **69**....(vt) LiamKeniry 12 73
(George Baker) *hmpd s: rousted along and settled on inner in mid-div: rdn 2f out: kpt on wl to hold 3rd nr fin* **14/1**
120- **4** *hd* **Fair Comment**[113] 6626 6-8-11 **60**.... RobertHavlin 1 64
(Michael Blanshard) *t.k.h in mid-div: ev ch over 2f out: rdn along on inner 2f out: kpt on to press 3rd nr fin* **25/1**
0/0- **5** *5* **Altaira**[123] 5-9-0 **66**.... GeorgeDowning(3) 3 61
(Tony Carroll) *broke wl and led early: settled bhd ldrs: rdn along 2f out: wknd ins fnl f* **20/1**

4- **6** nse **Bamako Du Chatelet (FR)**^{16} [8381] 5-8-10 **59** ow1........ JimCrowley 10 54
(Ian Williams) *wnt lft s: mid-div: rdn 3f out: one pce fr over 2f out: wknd ins fnl f* **5/2**^{2}
460- **7** 2 **Several (USA)**^{47} [8014] 4-9-3 **69**.................................... StevieDonohoe 4 60
(Kevin Frost) *hld up in midfield: rapid prog to chse ldr over 6f out to over 2f out: wknd* **25/1**
040- **8** shd **Fearless Lad (IRE)**^{63} [7797] 6-9-0 **63**.................................... KierenFox 2 54
(John Best) *hld up in rr: rdn over 1f out: wknd* **9/1**
4- **9** ½ **Put The Boot In (IRE)**^{63} [5971] 4-8-10 **69**.................. CharlieBennett$^{(7)}$ 6 59
(Barry Brennan) *missed break: in rr: pushed along over 4f out: nvr involved* **66/1**
216- **10** 1½ **Thane Of Cawdor (IRE)**^{17} [8371] 7-8-13 **62**................. JamieSpencer 7 49
(Joseph Tuite) *hld up in rr: rdn over 2f out: nvr gng pce to chal* **8/1**^{3}
000- **11** 4 **Bertie Moon**^{86} [7348] 6-9-3 **69**.. TimClark$^{(3)}$ 9 49
(Polly Gundry) *pushed along fr wd draw to ld: rdn and hdd over 2f out: wknd qckly fr 2f out* **33/1**
000/ **12** 6 **Vedani (IRE)**^{36} [4948] 7-8-11 **60**.................................... WilliamCarson 11 29
(Tony Carroll) *in rr: nvr involved* **66/1**

2m 22.26s (0.36) **Going Correction** 0.0s/f (Stan)
WFA 4 from 5yo+ 3lb **12** Ran SP% **127.9**
Speed ratings (Par 103): **98,97,96,95,92 92,90,90,90,89 86,81**
CSF £19.89 CT £169.28 TOTE £8.80: £2.30, £1.30, £4.50; EX 23.60 Trifecta £206.90.
Owner Good Company Partnership **Bred** Juddmonte Farms Ltd **Trained** Exning, Suffolk

FOCUS
They went steady early and it developed into a bit of a sprint from the turn in. The winner found a bit more improvement.

165 £10 FREE BET AT 32REDSPORT.COM H'CAP (FOR AMATEUR RIDERS) 1m 4f (P)
5:40 (5:40) (Class 4) (0-85,85) 4-Y-O+ **£4,523** (£1,402; £701; £350) **Stalls** Centre

Form RPR
514- **1** **Sunblazer (IRE)**^{32} [8210] 6-10-7 **85**................................(t) MrJMorris$^{(7)}$ 5 92
(Kim Bailey) *awkward s: hld up in last trio and wl off the pce: clsd 3f out: hrd rdn fnl 2f: led ins fnl f: styd on u.str.p* **8/1**
22- **2** ¾ **Ballyglasheen (IRE)**^{94} [4473] 6-9-7 **71** oh1...... MissIsabelWilliams$^{(7)}$ 10 77
(Evan Williams) *hld up off the pce in midfield: clsd 3f out: pushed along fnl 2f: kpt on to take 2nd wl ins fnl f: nt rch wnr* **16/1**
550- **3** ¾ **Albahar (FR)**^{94} [7140] 5-10-7 **78**.. MrSWalker 4 83
(Chris Gordon) *restrained s but sn chsd clr ldrs in 4th: clsd qckly 4f out: led wl over 2f out: sn hung lft: hdd and no ex ins fnl f* **12/1**
352- **4** 3 **Cotton Club (IRE)**^{16} [8379] 5-10-13 **84**............................ MrPMillman 6 84
(Rod Millman) *hld up off the pce in last trio: clsd 3f out: cl enough 2f out: fdd fnl f* **11/2**^{3}
100- **5** 7 **Phyllis Maud (IRE)**^{25} [8310] 4-10-2 **77**...................... MissSBrotherton 1 66
(Simon Crisford) *chsd clr ldng pair: clsd qckly over 4f out: led over 3f out to wl over 2f out: sn btn* **9/2**^{2}
603- **6** 3¼ **Breakheart (IRE)**^{13} [8411] 9-9-8 **72**...................(b) MissMNash-Steer$^{(7)}$ 3 56
(Andrew Balding) *hld up off the pce in midfield: clsd 3f out: urged along and no imp 2f out: wknd* **50/1**
016- **7** 9 **Top Diktat**^{35} [8157] 8-9-13 **77**.. MrCJewell$^{(7)}$ 8 46
(Gary Moore) *awkward s: hld up in last trio and off the pce: clsd 3f out: wknd qckly 2f out* **16/1**
0/1- **8** 19 **Good Judge (USA)**^{74} [7640] 4-10-1 **79**.................. MrAlexFerguson$^{(3)}$ 7 18
(Saeed bin Suroor) *pressed ldr at overly str pce: led over 4f out to over 3f out: wknd rapidly: t.o* **11/10**^{1}
225- **9** 35 **Secular Society**^{245} [2175] 6-10-1 **77**..............................(p) MrBJames$^{(5)}$ 2
(George Baker) *led at furious pce but pressed: hdd & wknd rapidly over 4f out: wl t.o* **33/1**

2m 32.72s (-1.78) **Going Correction** 0.0s/f (Stan)
WFA 4 from 5yo+ 4lb **9** Ran SP% **116.7**
Speed ratings (Par 105): **105,104,104,102,97 95,89,76,53**
CSF £126.26 CT £1526.62 TOTE £11.10: £2.50, £2.40, £4.30; EX 107.40 Trifecta £2371.10.
Owner Norman Carter **Bred** Michael G Daly **Trained** Andoversford, Gloucs
■ The first winner for Joey Morris.
■ Stewards' Enquiry : Mr J Morris four-day ban: used whip above permitted level (Jan 29,Feb 1,9,13)

FOCUS
The leaders took each other on in front, went far too fast, and the race was set up for the closers. The form is rated around the third.

166 32RED CONDITIONS STKS 6f (P)
6:10 (6:10) (Class 2) 4-Y-O+ **£12,291** (£3,657; £1,827; £913) **Stalls** Low

Form RPR
141- **1** **Chookie Royale**^{18} [8356] 8-9-2 109...................................(p) TomEaves 3 111
(Keith Dalgleish) *missed break: pushed along to ld after 1f: 3 l ld at 1/2-way: kicked 2f out: ld dwindling nr fin: hld on wl* **5/6**^{1}
325- **2** hd **Intransigent**^{23} [8326] 7-9-2 103.................................. JamieSpencer 6 110
(Andrew Balding) *led 1f: chsd ldr: rdn 2f out: kpt on wl ins fnl f to press wnr cl home: jst hld* **7/1**^{3}
224- **3** 2¼ **Alben Star (IRE)**^{137} [5837] 8-9-2 107.................................. JackGarritty 1 103+
(Richard Fahey) *t.k.h in rr: gng wl over 3f out: pushed along 2f out: kpt on wout troubling ldng pair* **9/1**
162- **4** nk **Sir Maximilian (IRE)**^{18} [8356] 7-9-7 112.............................. AdamKirby 5 107
(Ian Williams) *settled bhd ldrs: rdn 2f out: no ex and wknd ins fnl f* **5/1**^{2}
306- **5** ½ **Hallelujah**^{49} [7978] 8-8-11 97.. ShaneKelly 4 95
(James Fanshawe) *settled in rr: rdn 3f out: no rspnse tl ins fnl f: kpt on* **8/1**
420- **6** 1¼ **Horsted Keynes (FR)**^{18} [8356] 6-9-2 98...................(b) JimCrowley 2 96
(David Simcock) *settled bhd ldrs: rdn and wknd fr over 1f out* **16/1**

1m 11.56s (-1.54) **Going Correction** 0.0s/f (Stan) **6** Ran SP% **110.7**
Speed ratings (Par 109): **110,109,106,106,105 104**
CSF £7.03 TOTE £1.70: £1.20, £2.50; EX 6.40 Trifecta £25.60.
Owner Raeburn Brick Limited **Bred** D And J Raeburn **Trained** Carluke, S Lanarks

FOCUS
A decent little conditions race. The winner was the form pick and the form is rated around the second.

167 32RED.COM H'CAP 6f (P)
6:40 (6:43) (Class 6) (0-65,65) 4-Y-O+ **£2,264** (£673; £336; £168) **Stalls** Low

Form RPR
50-4 **1** **Nasri**^{7} [68] 10-9-3 **61**... JamieSpencer 2 68
(Emma Owen) *chsd ldrs on inner: pushed along 3f out bhd ldrs: rdn through gap to ld fnl 100yds: kpt on* **7/1**^{3}
03-1 **2** ½ **Chetan**^{7} [68] 4-9-6 **64** 6ex..(tp) LukeMorris 7 70
(Charlie Wallis) *racd in mid-div: rdn over 2f out on rail: kpt on wl but hld nr fin* **4/1**^{2}
60-2 **3** nk **Gold Beau (FR)**^{7} [68] 6-9-7 **65**.................................(p) CathyGannon 10 70
(Kristin Stubbs) *settled in mid-div on outer: gd prog 3f out to take ld ent fnl f: hdd 100yds out: kpt on* **11/1**
15-5 **4** 2 **Only Ten Per Cent (IRE)**^{7} [68] 8-9-1 **62**........... AlistairRawlinson$^{(3)}$ 4 61
(J R Jenkins) *s.s: in rr: rdn and hdwy on outer over 2f out: nvr nrr* **11/1**
335- **5** ½ **New Rich**^{28} [8254] 6-9-4 **62**..(b) JohnFahy 5 59
(Eve Johnson Houghton) *reluctant to load: in rr: prog to chse ldrs on inner over 2f out: wknd ins fnl f* **7/1**^{3}
122- **6** 1½ **Compton Prince**^{14} [8400] 7-8-13 **57**...............................(b) JimCrowley 11 50
(Milton Bradley) *early pce to chse ldrs: pressed ldr fr 1/2-way: rdn 2f out: wknd ins fnl f* **16/1**
105- **7** ½ **Duke Of North (IRE)**^{13} [8408] 4-9-7 **65**.........................(p) PatCosgrave 1 56
(Jim Boyle) *in rr: rdn over 3f out: drifted lft over 2f out: kpt on* **3/1**^{1}
304- **8** shd **Rigolleto (IRE)**^{13} [8408] 8-9-5 **63**.. AdamKirby 8 54
(Anabel K Murphy) *pushed along fr stalls to ld early: rdn and hdd fnl f: wknd qckly* **12/1**
110- **9** ½ **Burauq**^{32} [8207] 4-9-1 **59**..(b) RobertHavlin 9 48
(Milton Bradley) *racd in mid-div: wknd fr over 2f out* **14/1**
162- **10** 5 **Emperors Warrior (IRE)**^{41} [8096] 4-9-2 **60**................(b) GeorgeBaker 12 34
(Gary Moore) *chsd ldrs: lost pl and wknd fr over 2f out* **8/1**

1m 12.18s (-0.92) **Going Correction** 0.0s/f (Stan) **10** Ran SP% **118.0**
Speed ratings (Par 101): **106,105,104,102,101 99,98,98,98,91**
CSF £35.61 CT £317.91 TOTE £7.30: £2.20, £1.70, £3.80; EX 35.10 Trifecta £363.90.
Owner Miss Emma L Owen **Bred** Lady Hardy **Trained** Bicester, Oxon
■ This was Emma Owen's first winner since she took over the licence on the death of her partner Pat Eddery.

FOCUS
A modest sprint handicap. The first four home had taken each other on over the C&D seven days earlier, but the placings were different this time.

168 JUMP RACING HERE ON 25.01.16 H'CAP 7f (P)
7:10 (7:10) (Class 7) (0-50,50) 4-Y-O+ **£1,940** (£577; £288; £144) **Stalls** Low

Form RPR
/5-3 **1** **Bridge Builder**^{2} [143] 6-9-3 **49**....................................(p) RobHornby$^{(3)}$ 4 63
(Peter Hedger) *mde all: shkn up and drew rt away wl over 1f out: in n.d after* **5/4**^{1}
000- **2** 6 **Blistering Dancer (IRE)**^{41} [8095] 6-8-13 **45**........... GeorgeDowning$^{(3)}$ 1 43
(Tony Carroll) *dwlt: tk fierce hold early: sn chsd ldrs on inner: prog over 2f out: chsd clr wnr jst over 1f out: no imp* **16/1**
004- **3** nse **Lutine Charlie (IRE)**^{14} [8406] 9-9-2 **45**........................(p) JamieSpencer 5 43
(Emma Owen) *chsd wnr to 2f out: sn rdn: kpt on again fnl f to press for 2nd* **7/1**^{3}
04-0 **4** nk **Devilution (IRE)**^{11} [22] 4-9-2 **45**................................. StevieDonohoe 7 42
(Derek Shaw) *wl in rr: rdn over 2f out: prog over 1f out: kpt on to press for a pl nr fin* **14/1**
060- **5** 1½ **Alfie The Pug**^{121} [6380] 4-9-2 **45**..(t) JFEgan 11 38
(Pat Phelan) *wl in rr: rdn and prog on inner wl over 1f out: kpt on one pce* **16/1**
404- **6** ½ **Purford Green**^{14} [8393] 7-9-3 **46**...(p) KierenFox 3 37
(Michael Attwater) *chsd ldrs: rdn and no prog 2f out: one pce after* **20/1**
03-4 **7** hd **Fairy Mist (IRE)**^{6} [87] 9-9-7 **50**..............................(b) WilliamCarson 8 41
(John Bridger) *nvr bttr than midfield: rdn and no prog over 2f out* **8/1**
006- **8** 5 **Sinema**^{15} [8388] 4-9-7 **50**...(b) AdamBeschizza 2 27
(Christine Dunnett) *t.k.h: prom: chsd wnr 2f out to jst over 1f out: wknd qckly* **25/1**
000- **9** 2¼ **Gladsome**^{32} [8203] 8-9-3 **46**... LukeMorris 10 17
(Charlie Wallis) *a towards rr on outer: struggling 2f out* **33/1**
4- **10** nk **Diamond Sam**^{46} [8036] 4-9-3 **46**.......................................(t) ShaneKelly 6 17
(Sylvester Kirk) *chsd ldrs on outer: wknd qckly 2f out* **5/1**^{2}
000- **11** 2¾ **District Twelve (FR)**^{26} [8289] 4-9-2 **45**.............................. JimCrowley 9 8
(Tony Carroll) *restrained into last but stl plld v hrd: pushed along and no prog over 2f out* **66/1**

1m 26.07s (0.07) **Going Correction** 0.0s/f (Stan) **11** Ran SP% **116.2**
Speed ratings (Par 97): **99,92,92,91,90 89,89,83,80,80 77**
CSF £23.01 CT £107.08 TOTE £2.30: £1.10, £4.40, £2.20; EX 25.00 Trifecta £132.50.
Owner P C F Racing Ltd **Bred** D J And Mrs Deer **Trained** Hook, Hampshire
■ Stewards' Enquiry : Kieren Fox two-day ban: used whip above permitted level (Jan 27-28)
Jim Crowley jockey said filly ran too free

FOCUS
A moderate handicap, taken apart by the well-backed favourite.
T/Jkpt: not won. JACKPOT PLACEPOT £73.60. Pool: £3,018.59 - 29.93 winning units. T/Plt: £130.20 to a £1 stake. Pool: £82,396.30 - 461.65 winning units. T/Qpdt: £58.90 to a £1 stake. Pool: £7,919.08 - 99.45 winning units. **Cathal Gahan**

157 CHELMSFORD (A.W) (L-H)
Thursday, January 14

OFFICIAL GOING: Polytrack: standard
Wind: fresh, across Weather: dry, cold wind

169 BET TOTEPLACEPOT APPRENTICE H'CAP 7f (P)
5:10 (5:10) (Class 5) (0-75,80) 4-Y-O+ **£5,175** (£1,540; £769; £384) **Stalls** Low

Form RPR
040- **1** **Until Midnight (IRE)**^{24} [8325] 6-8-12 **73**........................ LuluStanford$^{(7)}$ 4 85
(Eugene Stanford) *chsd ldrs: hdwy to go 2nd over 2f out: rdn to ld over 1f out: hrd pressed fnl f: hld up wl fnl 100yds* **5/1**
32-2 **2** nk **Welliesinthewater (IRE)**^{7} [82] 6-8-10 **64**....................(p) NoelGarbutt 6 75
(Derek Shaw) *pressed ldrs: rdn 2f out: hdwy to press wnr over 1f out: drvn and ev ch fnl f: edgd lft and one pce towards fin* **2/1**^{1}
216- **3** 7 **Justice First**^{14} [8414] 4-8-12 **73**.. LukeCarson$^{(7)}$ 3 65
(Ed Dunlop) *stdd s: hld up in rr: clsd 2f out: nt clr run and hmpd over 1f out: swtchd rt ent fnl f: styd on to go 3rd last stride: no ch w ldrs* **7/2**^{3}
00-2 **4** shd **Swiss Cross**^{7} [76] 9-8-12 **69**........................... JosephineGordon$^{(3)}$ 7 61
(Phil McEntee) *in tch: rdn over 2f out: plugged on to chse clr ldng pair 150yds out: no imp: lost 3rd last stride* **10/1**
31-1 **5** 2¾ **Dutch Golden Age (IRE)**^{8} [67] 4-9-9 **80** 6ex........(t) PaddyBradley$^{(3)}$ 8 64
(Gary Moore) *hld up in tch but wd: drvn and unable qck 2f out: outpcd and wl btn over 1f out* **3/1**^{2}
33-3 **6** ½ **Venus Grace**^{12} [14] 5-8-0 **61**..(v^{1}) JaneElliott$^{(7)}$ 1 44
(Michael Appleby) *w ldr on inner tl led 3f out: rdn and hdd over 1f out: sn btn: wknd ins fnl f* **9/1**

40-1 **7** *2* **Black Dave (IRE)**[7] 88 6-9-1 **76** 6ex............................ RyanTimby[(7)] 2 54
(David Evans) *mde most tl 3f out: lost pl u.p over 1f out: bhd and wknd fnl f* **7/1**

1m 23.94s (-3.26) **Going Correction** -0.325s/f (Stan) **7** Ran SP% **128.8**
Speed ratings (Par 103): **105,104,96,96,93 92,90**
CSF £17.88 CT £43.14 TOTE £8.60: £4.70, £1.10; EX 21.30 Trifecta £90.90.
Owner newmarketracingclub.co.uk **Bred** Rathbarry Stud **Trained** Newmarket, Suffolk

FOCUS
The opening contest was a fair apprentice riders' handicap, in which they went a respectable gallop on standard Polytrack. The winner is rated back to his best.

170 TOTEPOOLLIVEINFO.COM H'CAP 1m 5f 66y(P)
5:40 (5:40) (Class 6) (0-60,66) 4-Y-O+ **£3,234** (£962; £481; £240) **Stalls** Low

Form RPR
64-1 **1** **San Quentin (IRE)**[8] 62 5-9-13 **66** 6ex...................... RobertWinston 4 75
(Dean Ivory) *hld up in tch: pushed along and hdwy over 2f out: rdn to chse ldr jst over 1f out: led 150yds out: styd on wl and gng away at fin* **11/8**[1]

224- **2** *2* **Bracken Brae**[40] 7543 4-8-11 **55**..................................... SaleemGolam 6 60
(Mark H Tompkins) *chsd ldr: rdn to ld wl over 1f out: drvn and hrd pressed 1f out: sn hdd and styd on same pce after* **5/1**[3]

/04- **3** *3 ½* **Sylvette**[24] 8328 4-9-2 **60**..(tp) JackMitchell 3 60
(Roger Varian) *trckd ldrs: effrt 2f out: drvn and kpt on same pce fr over 1f out: snatched 3rd last strides* **10/1**

043- **4** *hd* **Cosmic Statesman**[15] 8403 4-9-2 **60**................................ JackGarritty 1 60
(Richard Fahey) *sn led: rdn and hdd wl over 1f out: no ex u.p over 1f out: wknd ins fnl f: lost 3rd last strides* **7/2**[2]

32-4 **5** *2 ¼* **Hall Of Beauty**[12] 27 4-7-12 **49**... RPWalsh[(7)] 2 46
(Michael Appleby) *t.k.h: hld up in tch in midfield: effrt u.p 2f out: no imp over 1f out: wl hld whn hung lft ins fnl f* **12/1**

04-1 **6** *1 ¾* **Smugglers Lane (IRE)**[7] 84 4-8-11 **55** 6ex.................. PatCosgrave 9 49
(David Evans) *hld up in last pair: effrt 3f out: no imp over 1f out: nvr trbld ldrs* **11/1**

545- **7** *1 ½* **Easydoesit (IRE)**[15] 8403 8-9-1 **54**................................. CathyGannon 8 46
(Tony Carroll) *hld up in last pair: effrt 3f out: plugging on but no ch whn nt clr run and hmpd ins fnl f* **33/1**

000- **8** *15* **Glasgow Central**[18] 8370 5-9-7 **60**..................................... AdamKirby 7 31
(Phil McEntee) *chsd ldng trio: drvn over 4f out: lost pl and bhd over 2f out: wknd wl over 1f out* **8/1**

00-0 **9** *17* **North Bay Lady (IRE)**[12] 26 4-8-2 **46** oh1..............(b[1]) JimmyQuinn 5
(John Wainwright) *dwlt: hld up in tch in midfield: rdn and dropped to rr 3f out: sn lost tch: t.o fnl f* **66/1**

2m 50.36s (-3.24) **Going Correction** -0.325s/f (Stan)
WFA 4 from 5yo+ 5lb **9** Ran SP% **121.7**
Speed ratings (Par 101): **96,94,92,92,91 90,89,79,69**
CSF £9.23 CT £52.97 TOTE £1.80: £1.10, £2.40, £5.10; EX 10.10 Trifecta £75.60.
Owner Stephen Louch **Bred** London Thoroughbred Services Ltd **Trained** Radlett, Herts

FOCUS
A modest staying handicap. They went an ordinary gallop. The form is rated as straightforward.

171 BET TOTEQUADPOT H'CAP 7f (P)
6:10 (6:12) (Class 5) (0-75,75) 3-Y-O **£5,175** (£1,540; £769; £384) **Stalls** Low

Form RPR
460- **1** **Secret Insider (USA)**[120] 6428 3-9-0 **68**........................ MartinHarley 10 74+
(Hugo Palmer) *hld up in tch towards rr of main gp: swtchd rt and gd hdwy over 1f out: led 150yds: r.o wl and sn in command: comf* **9/1**

13- **2** *1 ¼* **Ice Royal (IRE)**[36] 8155 3-9-6 **74**................................... TimmyMurphy 3 77+
(Jamie Osborne) *chsd ldrs: snatched up bnd 4f out: effrt over 1f out: drvn to press ldrs jst ins fnl f: kpt on u.p to go 2nd towards fin* **2/1**[1]

165- **3** *¾* **Silver Springs (IRE)**[18] 8365 3-8-9 **63**........................ StevieDonohoe 2 64
(David Evans) *led: drvn over 1f out: hdd 150yds: no ex and styd on same pce after: lost 2nd towards fin* **25/1**

44-3 **4** *2 ¼* **Sir Dudley (IRE)**[12] 16 3-9-7 **75**....................................... TomEaves 8 70
(James Given) *chsd ldr: rdn over 1f out: no ex u.p jst ins fnl f: wknd fnl 75yds* **12/1**

032- **5** *½* **Ilzam (IRE)**[14] 8409 3-9-5 **73**..(t) SaleemGolam 5 67
(Marco Botti) *taken down early: hld up in tch in midfield: effrt over 1f out: nt clrest of runs ent fnl f: kpt on same pce and wl hld after* **9/2**[2]

14- **6** *¾* **Lucymai**[202] 3587 3-9-7 **75**.. RobertWinston 9 67
(Dean Ivory) *stdd after s: hld up in tch towards rr but stuck wd: effrt 2f out: kpt on steadily ins fnl f: no threat to ldrs* **12/1**

003- **7** *1* **Vallance Road**[61] 7852 3-9-4 **72**...(b) JFEgan 6 61
(Robyn Brisland) *dwlt: sn rcvrd and chsd ldrs but stuck wd: unable qck u.p and hung lft over 1f out: btn and n.m.r ins fnl f: wknd fnl 100yds* **8/1**

241- **8** *½* **Murdanova (IRE)**[15] 8402 3-9-5 **73**.................................... JohnFahy 1 61
(Kevin Frost) *chsd ldrs: drvn and no ex over 1f out: wknd ins fnl f* **6/1**[3]

162- **9** *6* **Mollie's Girl (IRE)**[16] 8384 3-8-12 **66**........................... AndrewMullen 7 38
(Michael Appleby) *s.i.s: sn bustled along: a in rr of main gp: struggling over 2f out: bhd over 1f out* **12/1**

61- **10** *nk* **Strictly Art (IRE)**[51] 7965 3-8-10 **67**............................... EoinWalsh[(3)] 4 39
(Alan Bailey) *broke in midfield: sn u.p and dropped to rr: nvr travelling wl and detached last 1/2-way* **20/1**

1m 24.51s (-2.69) **Going Correction** -0.325s/f (Stan) **10** Ran SP% **118.6**
Speed ratings (Par 97): **102,100,99,97,96 95,94,94,87,86**
CSF £27.81 CT £463.33 TOTE £11.10: £3.80, £1.10, £6.80; EX 30.80 Trifecta £1289.30.
Owner Sheikh Juma Dalmook Al Maktoum **Bred** KatieRich Farms **Trained** Newmarket, Suffolk

FOCUS
A fair 3yo handicap. They went a decent gallop and the form is rated around the third.

172 TOTETRIFECTA H'CAP 1m (P)
6:40 (6:41) (Class 4) (0-85,85) 4-Y-O+ **£8,086** (£2,406; £1,202; £601) **Stalls** Low

Form RPR
001- **1** **Bold Prediction (IRE)**[14] 8414 6-9-4 **82**........................... LukeMorris 5 90
(Ed Walker) *mde all: rdn over 1f out: drvn and hld on wl ins fnl f: gamely* **7/1**

045- **2** *nk* **Abbey Angel (IRE)**[15] 8405 4-8-13 **77**............................... JackGarritty 4 84
(Richard Fahey) *chsd ldng pair: effrt on inner over 1f out: ev ch ins fnl f: styd on wl but hld towards fin* **9/1**

045- **3** *hd* **Dance Of Fire**[188] 4091 4-9-0 **81**.................................... RobHornby[(3)] 1 88+
(Andrew Balding) *hld up wl in tch in midfield: effrt over 1f out: wnt 3rd and swtchd rt ins fnl f: kpt on wl towards fin* **6/1**[3]

331- **4** *1 ¼* **Steal The Scene (IRE)**[45] 8050 4-9-6 **84**........................ KieranO'Neill 3 88
(Richard Hannon) *chsd ldng trio: effrt over 1f out: edgd lft u.p 1f out: styd on same pce ins fnl f* **5/2**[1]

121- **5** *3 ¼* **Brasted (IRE)**[28] 8260 4-8-11 **75**..(t) JFEgan 8 71
(Paul Cole) *hld up in tch: hdwy 3f out: swtchd rt and effrt u.p over 1f out: no imp 1f out: nvr trbld ldrs* **16/1**

520- **6** *¾* **Spiritual Star (IRE)**[17] 8380 7-9-7 **85**..........................(t) WilliamCarson 6 79
(Anthony Carson) *stdd after s: t.k.h: hld up in last pair: effrt on inner over 1f out: no imp 1f out: nvr trbld ldrs* **12/1**

113- **7** *shd* **New Strategy (IRE)**[131] 6095 4-9-4 **85**.............(t[1]) AlistairRawlinson[(3)] 9 79
(Saeed bin Suroor) *dwlt: hld up in tch: effrt over 1f out: drvn ent fnl f: no imp: nvr trbld ldrs* **11/4**[2]

103- **7** *dht* **Street Force (USA)**[19] 8357 5-9-3 **81**..........................(t) AndrewMullen 7 75
(Michael Appleby) *chsd ldr tl no ex u.p and lost pl jst over 1f out: wknd ins fnl f* **8/1**

220/ **9** *7* **Icebuster**[546] 4349 8-9-0 **78**... RobertHavlin 2 56
(Rod Millman) *s.i.s: hld up in rr: effrt and no rspnse over 1f out: bhd fnl f* **33/1**

1m 37.8s (-2.10) **Going Correction** -0.325s/f (Stan) **9** Ran SP% **119.7**
Speed ratings (Par 105): **97,96,96,95,92 91,91,91,84**
CSF £70.42 CT £408.19 TOTE £9.30: £3.20, £2.90, £2.90; EX 85.00 Trifecta £577.90.
Owner John Nicholls (Trading) & Matthew Cottis **Bred** Mountarmstrong Stud **Trained** Upper Lambourn, Berks

FOCUS
The feature contest was a decent handicap. The winner set a respectable gallop and the form is rated around the runner-up.

173 SCOOP6SOCCER THE £1 MILLION FOOTBALL BET H'CAP 1m 2f (P)
7:10 (7:10) (Class 6) (0-65,65) 4-Y-O+ **£3,234** (£962; £481; £240) **Stalls** Low

Form RPR
000- **1** **Moonday Sun (USA)**[85] 7388 7-9-5 **64**..........................(p) AdamKirby 6 75
(Phil McEntee) *hld up in tch: swtchd rt and hdwy 3f out: rdn and clsd on ldrs over 1f out: led 1f out: styd on: rdn out* **4/1**[2]

206- **2** *1 ¼* **What A Dandy (IRE)**[24] 8325 5-8-13 **65**..................(p) RhiainIngram[(7)] 3 74
(Jim Boyle) *chsd ldrs: rdn and outpcd in 3rd over 2f out: rallied and pressed ldrs 1f out: wnt 2nd and kpt on same pce ins fnl f* **7/1**

052- **3** *3 ¼* **Weld Arab (IRE)**[18] 8371 5-9-4 **63**.................................... PatCosgrave 5 66
(Michael Blake) *chsd ldr: rdn and kicked clr w ldr over 2f out: drvn to ld over 1f out: hdd 1f out: no ex: wknd ins fnl f* **5/1**[3]

01-5 **4** *2 ¾* **Jazri**[8] 55 5-9-5 **64**..(b) LukeMorris 1 62
(Milton Bradley) *dwlt and bustled along early: hdwy into midfield after 2f: rdn 3f out: outpcd over 1f out: plugged on same pce fnl f* **5/1**[3]

612- **5** *¾* **Le Deluge (FR)**[51] 7962 6-9-4 **63**................................(t) SaleemGolam 2 59
(Heather Dalton) *taken down early: led: rdn and kicked clr w rival over 2f out: hdd over 1f out: 4th and btn 1f out: wknd ins fnl f* **9/1**

005- **6** *2* **Brave Decision**[29] 8252 9-9-2 **61**.................................... KieranO'Neill 4 53
(Brett Johnson) *chsd ldr: 4th and outpcd u.p over 2f out: wknd over 1f out* **20/1**

433- **7** *7* **Koreen (IRE)**[25] 8317 5-9-5 **64**..(t) JFEgan 9 43
(John Berry) *hld up in last trio: outpcd over 2f out: n.d but sme hdwy u.p over 1f out: n.d* **3/1**[1]

342- **8** *1* **Thou Swell (IRE)**[15] 8394 4-8-11 **63**............................ JustinNewman[(5)] 8 40
(Shaun Harris) *s.i.s: nvr gng wl in rr: outpcd over 2f out: n.d after* **7/1**

332- **9** *7* **Mops Angel**[19] 8360 5-9-0 **62**.............................(p) AlistairRawlinson[(3)] 11 26
(Michael Appleby) *in tch in midfield: outpcd u.p over 2f out: wl bhd 1f out* **14/1**

103- **10** *6* **Nouvelle Ere**[18] 8371 5-8-13 **61**.............................. GeorgeDowning[(3)] 10 13
(Tony Carroll) *chsd ldrs: lost pl u.p over 3f out: wl bhd 1f out* **16/1**

100- **11** *1 ½* **Automotive**[31] 8221 8-8-13 **61**.................................... ShelleyBirkett[(3)] 7 11
(Julia Feilden) *hld up in last pair: outpcd and rdn over 2f out: wl bhd fnl f* **25/1**

2m 4.48s (-4.12) **Going Correction** -0.325s/f (Stan)
WFA 4 from 5yo+ 2lb **11** Ran SP% **134.5**
Speed ratings (Par 101): **103,102,99,97,96 95,89,88,83,78 77**
CSF £37.63 CT £154.84 TOTE £6.60: £2.50, £2.80, £2.00; EX 47.60 Trifecta £357.10.
Owner Power Geneva Ltd **Bred** Juddmonte Farms Inc **Trained** Newmarket, Suffolk

FOCUS
Another modest handicap run at an even gallop. The winner was thrown in on the best of last year's form.

174 BET SCOOP6SOCCER AT BETFRED.COM H'CAP 6f (P)
7:40 (7:40) (Class 7) (0-50,50) 3-Y-O+ **£2,587** (£770; £384; £192) **Stalls** Centre

Form RPR
06-4 **1** **E Fourteen**[7] 81 3-7-12 **45**.. PaddyPilley[(5)] 10 49
(Robyn Brisland) *t.k.h: chsd ldrs: rdn to chse ldr jst over 1f out: led 150yds out: jst hld on: all out* **6/1**[2]

000/ **2** *shd* **Camdora (IRE)**[463] 7037 4-9-5 **45**................................ TimmyMurphy 8 53
(Jamie Osborne) *s.i.s: bhd: plenty to do but hdwy on inner over 1f out: str run to press ldrs wl ins fnl f: r.o: jst failed* **10/1**

0-24 **3** *½* **Tasaaboq**[8] 60 5-9-10 **50**..(tp) AdamKirby 7 57
(Phil McEntee) *sn bhd: hdwy into midfield over 3f out: forced to switch rt arnd horses over 1f out: hdwy u.p and ev ch ins fnl f: no ex towards fin* **2/1**[1]

654- **4** *2 ¼* **Multi Quest**[28] 8265 4-9-7 **47**.......................................(b) RobertHavlin 2 47
(John E Long) *t.k.h: chsd ldrs: rdn over 1f out: kpt on same pce u.p ins fnl f* **6/1**[2]

100- **5** *hd* **Salvado (IRE)**[15] 8406 6-9-5 **48**.............................. GeorgeDowning[(3)] 1 47
(Tony Carroll) *taken down early and led to post: t.k.h: hld up in tch in midfield: swtchd rt and effrt over 1f out: kpt on ins fnl f: no threat to ldrs* **7/1**[3]

006- **6** *1 ¼* **Seamoor Secret**[15] 8400 4-9-5 **45**................................(t) KieranO'Neill 3 40
(Alex Hales) *chsd ldrs: rdn ent fnl 2f no ex u.p ent fnl f: wknd fnl 100yds* **20/1**

00-0 **7** *1 ¾* **Justice (IRE)**[7] 87 3-8-3 **45**.. JimmyQuinn 4 31
(Dean Ivory) *t.k.h: led: rdn over 1f out: hdd 150yds: sn wknd* **16/1**

66-6 **8** *½* **Ciaras Cookie (IRE)**[9] 54 4-9-10 **50**..........................[1] SaleemGolam 11 39
(Heather Dalton) *stdd s: hld up towards rr: effrt over 1f out: no imp fnl f: nvr trbld ldrs* **20/1**

006- **9** *2* **Black Vale (IRE)**[14] 8411 5-9-0 **47**..................(bt) JosephineGordon[(7)] 12 30
(Phil McEntee) *sn pushed along in midfield: nvr threatened ldrs* **10/1**

004- **10** *nse* **Harpers Ruby**[15] 8400 6-9-5 **45**.. JackGarritty 5 28
(Lynn Siddall) *t.k.h: chsd ldr tl lost pl u.p over 1f out: wknd ins fnl f* **7/1**[3]

/00- **11** *16* **Celestial Vision (USA)**[28] 8264 4-9-7 **50**................... ShelleyBirkett[(3)] 6
(Miss Joey Ellis) *midfield tl dropped to rr over 3f out: sn struggling: t.o over 1f out* **50/1**

1m 11.99s (-1.71) **Going Correction** -0.325s/f (Stan)
WFA 3 from 4yo+ 16lb **11** Ran SP% **122.5**
Speed ratings (Par 97): **98,97,97,94,93 92,89,89,86,86 65**
CSF £65.78 CT £165.01 TOTE £8.00: £1.30, £3.90, £1.10; EX 21.90 Trifecta £276.50.

Owner Franconson Partners **Bred** D Curran **Trained** Newmarket, Suffolk

■ The first winner as a trainer for Robyn Brisland, who has taken over the licence from Nick Littmoden.

FOCUS

A low-grade sprint handicap run at a respectable gallop. Not many positives to take from the form.

175 TOTEPOOL H'CAP 1m (P)

8:10 (8:10) (Class 7) (0-50,56) 4-Y-O+ **£2,587** (£770; £384; £192) **Stalls** Low

Form				RPR
30-1	1		**Gunner Moyne**[7] 79 4-9-13 **56** 6ex..........................(t) FergusSweeney 1 (Gary Moore) *in tch in midfield: effrt and swtchd rt over 1f out: rdn to ld jst ins fnl f: styd on wl: rdn out* **10/11**[1]	64
3-22	2	1 ½	**Anjuna Beach (USA)**[7] 79 6-9-1 **49**............................ AnnStokell(5) 7 (Ann Stokell) *stdd s: t.k.h: hld up in last pair: effrt u.p on inner over 1f out: chsd wnr ins fnl f: no ex and one pce fnl 100yds* **7/2**[2]	53
00-0	3	1	**Rosie Hall (IRE)**[12] 26 6-9-2 **45**....................................(b[1]) TomEaves 4 (John Wainwright) *in tch in midfield: effrt over 1f out: drvn and kpt on ins fnl f: wnt 3rd fnl 75yds* **33/1**	47
45-3	4	1 ¼	**Sleet (IRE)**[8] 60 5-9-7 **50**..(b) LukeMorris 3 (Michael Appleby) *chsd ldr for 1f: chsd ldrs tl drvn to chal over 1f out: no ex jst ins fnl f: wknd fnl 100yds* **7/2**[2]	49
00-0	5	2	**Loud**[12] 22 6-9-4 **50**..(b) SimonPearce(3) 8 (Lydia Pearce) *sn led: rdn over 1f out: hdd and no ex jst ins fnl f: wknd fnl 100yds* **12/1**[3]	44
600-	6	2 ¾	**Suni Dancer**[47] 8040 5-8-13 **45**................................ GeorgeDowning(3) 2 (Tony Carroll) *hld up in tch in midfield: no imp u.p over 1f out: wknd ins fnl f* **20/1**	33
46-4	7	nse	**Kingston Sassafras**[7] 79 4-9-4 **47**................................(p) AdamKirby 5 (Phil McEntee) *chsd ldr after 1f tl lost pl u.p over 1f out: wknd fnl f* **20/1**	34
230-	8	3	**Daniel Thomas (IRE)**[24] 8329 14-9-2 **45**...................(tp) SaleemGolam 6 (Heather Dalton) *s.i.s: a bhd* **33/1**	25

1m 39.44s (-0.46) **Going Correction** -0.325s/f (Stan) 8 Ran SP% **119.9**

Speed ratings (Par 97): **89,87,86,85,83 80,80,77**

CSF £4.40 CT £58.77 TOTE £1.80: £1.10, £1.10, £4.80; EX 5.00 Trifecta £103.90.

Owner G L Moore **Bred** Five Horses Ltd **Trained** Lower Beeding, W Sussex

FOCUS

The concluding contest was another moderate handicap. They went an ordinary gallop. The winner took a further step forward.

T/Plt: £245.60 to a £1 stake. Pool of £89118.08 - 264.79 winning tickets. T/Qpdt: £57.80 to a £1 stake. Pool of £10469.94 - 133.82 winning tickets. **Steve Payne**

130 SOUTHWELL (L-H)

Thursday, January 14

OFFICIAL GOING: Fibresand: standard

Wind: Very strong behind Weather: Driving rain and sleet showers clearing after 1.30 race

176 DAILY PRICE BOOSTS AT UNIBET APPRENTICE CLASSIFIED CLAIMING STKS 5f (F)

12:30 (12:33) (Class 6) 4-Y-O+ **£2,587** (£770; £384; £192) **Stalls** Centre

Form				RPR
252-	1		**Jaarih (IRE)**[34] 8174 4-8-8 70................................(t) JosephineGordon(5) 8 (George Scott) *cl up: led 2f out: rdn clr over 1f out: kpt on strly* **7/2**[3]	77
00-0	2	2 ¾	**Oscars Journey**[11] 28 6-9-1 70............................(v) AlistairRawlinson 5 (J R Jenkins) *slt ld: rdn along and hdd 2f out: chsd wnr and drvn over 1f out: no imp* **16/1**	70
04-5	3	1 ¼	**Monsieur Jamie**[12] 21 8-8-8 65............................(v) CharlieBennett(5) 6 (J R Jenkins) *cl up: pushed along 3f out: hung rt to stands' rail over 2f out: sn rdn and kpt on fnl f* **12/1**	63
05-4	4	1	**Harwoods Star (IRE)**[9] 49 6-8-8 63..........................(t) AaronJones(3) 4 (Stuart Williams) *chsd ldrs: rdn along after 1f: sn outpcd and towards rr: rdn 1/2-way: styd on appr fnl f* **5/2**[2]	57
5-62	5	3 ½	**Alpha Tauri (USA)**[4] 133 10-8-13 69................................ ShaneGray 1 (Charles Smith) *chsd ldrs on outer: rdn along 1/2-way: sn drvn and one pce* **13/8**[1]	47
50-0	6	½	**Emblaze**[12] 21 4-8-6 52.. PhilDennis(5) 2 (Bryan Smart) *chsd ldrs: rdn along over 2f out: sn one pce* **40/1**	43
51-3	7	4 ½	**Shawkantango**[12] 21 9-8-2 57................................(p) JackOsborn(7) 7 (Derek Shaw) *s.i.s: a bhd* **8/1**	25

57.73s (-1.97) **Going Correction** -0.45s/f (Stan) 7 Ran SP% **116.0**

Speed ratings (Par 101): **97,92,90,89,83 82,75**

CSF £55.37 TOTE £3.30: £1.30, £8.90; EX 55.50 Trifecta £224.40.The winner was claimed for £8000 by C Marsh.

Owner J R Boughey **Bred** Dean Harron & Ciaran Conroy **Trained** Newmarket, Suffolk

FOCUS

A fair claimer featuring several multiple course winners, but the least exposed runner in the field proved totally dominant. Tricky form to assess. There was a strong following wind and the winning time was 0.27sec under Racing Post standard.

177 BET&WATCH EVERY RACE AT UNIBET MAIDEN STKS 5f (F)

1:00 (1:01) (Class 5) 3-Y-O+ **£3,234** (£962; £481; £240) **Stalls** Centre

Form				RPR
43-	1		**James Bond Girl (USA)**[18] 8366 4-9-9 65.....................(p) GrahamLee 3 (Robert Cowell) *chsd ldng pair: hdwy 1/2-way: rdn to chal over 1f out: led ins fnl f: styd on* **5/1**[3]	72
4-	2	1 ½	**Eleuthera**[224] 2852 4-9-9 0.. PatrickO'Donnell(5) 4 (Kevin Ryan) *cl up: led after 2f: rdn along nr stands' rail and jnd over 1f out: drvn and hdd ins fnl f: kpt on same pce* **5/2**[2]	71
330-	3	2 ¼	**Iconic Figure (IRE)**[38] 8129 3-8-13 74................................ SamJames 1 (David O'Meara) *slt ld: hdd after 2f and cl up: rdn along over 2f out: drvn wl over 1f out: grad wknd* **11/8**[1]	57
	4	½	**Graceful Favour** 3-8-8 0... JoeFanning 2 (David Barron) *dwlt and towards rr: hdwy on outer 1/2-way: rdn to chse ldrs wl over 1f out: kpt on same pce fnl f* **12/1**	50
5/5-	5	4	**Grandad Chunk (IRE)**[16] 8386 5-10-0 0...................... DougieCostello 5 (Tracy Waggott) *towards rr: rdn along and sme hdwy over 2f out: sn no imp* **33/1**	47
060-	6	1 ¾	**Mighty Bond**[16] 8388 4-9-7 49... PhilDennis(7) 6 (Tracy Waggott) *a towards rr* **50/1**	41
0-3	7	1 ¼	**Rojina (IRE)**[9] 42 3-8-1 0...................................... JosephineGordon(7) 7 (Joseph Tuite) *prom: rdn along wl over 2f out: sn drvn and wknd* **9/1**	25

58.71s (-0.99) **Going Correction** -0.45s/f (Stan)

WFA 3 from 4yo+ 15lb 7 Ran SP% **109.9**

Speed ratings (Par 103): **89,86,83,82,75 73,71**

CSF £16.49 TOTE £6.70: £3.20, £1.70; EX 17.50 Trifecta £41.90.

Owner Ecurie La Boetie **Bred** Capital Bloodstock **Trained** Six Mile Bottom, Cambs

FOCUS

Just an ordinary maiden, with a disappointing favourite. The form is rated cautiously.

178 UNIBET OFFER DAILY JOCKEY/TRAINER SPECIALS H'CAP 6f (F)

1:30 (1:31) (Class 6) (0-65,65) 4-Y-O+ **£2,587** (£770; £384; £192) **Stalls** Low

Form				RPR
000-	1		**Sartori**[28] 8271 5-9-5 **63**..(p) DanielTudhope 5 (Marjorie Fife) *mde most: rdn along 2f out: drvn over 1f out: kpt on wl fnl f* **12/1**	71
40-4	2	1 ¾	**Spowarticus**[4] 133 7-9-6 **64**..(v) KieranO'Neill 2 (Scott Dixon) *cl up: rdn 2f out: drvn over 1f out: kpt on same pce fnl f* **4/1**[2]	67
406-	3	hd	**Great Expectations**[17] 8376 8-9-1 **62**...............(vt) AlistairRawlinson(3) 3 (J R Jenkins) *trckd ldrs: hdwy over 2f out: rdn and ch wl over 1f out: drvn and kpt on same pce fnl f* **6/1**	64
23-5	4	3 ¼	**Hab Reeh**[12] 22 8-8-11 **55**.. JamesSullivan 1 (Ruth Carr) *trckd ldrs on inner: hdwy over 2f out: rdn wl over 1f out: sn drvn and one pce* **16/1**	47
10-5	5	1 ¼	**Cadeaux Pearl**[12] 25 8-8-13 **57**...............................(v) LukeMorris 6 (Scott Dixon) *chsd ldrs effrt on outer over 2f out: sn rdn and one pce* **15/2**	46
4-25	6	3 ¾	**Lucky Mark (IRE)**[4] 130 7-9-1 **59**.................................(p) LiamKeniry 7 (John Balding) *dwlt and towards rr: hdwy 1/2-way: chsd ldrs whn sddle slipped over 2f out: no prog after* **5/1**[3]	51+
323-	7	3 ¼	**Tellovoi (IRE)**[30] 8236 8-9-2 **65**.............................(v) CharlesEddery(5) 4 (Richard Guest) *rdn along sn aftetr s: trckd ldrs: shkn up 3f out: sn rdn and wknd: bhd whn hung lft wl over 1f out* **15/8**[1]	33

1m 16.34s (-0.16) **Going Correction** -0.05s/f (Stan) 7 Ran SP% **111.1**

Speed ratings (Par 101): **99,96,96,92,90 85,81**

CSF £55.67 TOTE £17.10: £6.80, £1.40; EX 70.60 Trifecta £376.20.

Owner R W Fife **Bred** D R Tucker **Trained** Stillington, N Yorks

FOCUS

A modest handicap in which the favourite ran no race at all. The pace held up and the winner was near his best turf form.

179 LADBROKES H'CAP 1m (F)

2:00 (2:00) (Class 5) (0-70,70) 4-Y-O+ **£3,234** (£962; £481; £240) **Stalls** Low

Form				RPR
222-	1		**Billy Bond**[14] 8414 4-8-8 **60**..(v) SammyJoBell(3) 5 (Richard Fahey) *awkward s and sn chsd along: smooth hdwy to trck ldrs 1/2-way: effrt to ld wl over 2f out: sn rdn clr: easily* **6/4**[1]	76
05-6	2	13	**Archie's Advice**[10] 38 5-9-7 **70**.. TomEaves 7 (Keith Dalgleish) *in tch on outer: wd st and sn pushed along: hdwy over 2f out: sn rdn: styd on to take remote 2nd ins fnl f* **3/1**[2]	56
020-	3	1 ¾	**Shearian**[113] 6656 6-9-3 **66**.. DougieCostello 2 (Tracy Waggott) *trckd ldng pair: hdwy to ld over 3f out: sn rdn and hdd wl over 2f out: drvn and kpt on one pce fnl 2f: lost remote 2nd ins fnl f* **20/1**	48
53-0	4	6	**Lean On Pete (IRE)**[10] 38 7-9-7 **70**........................(p) PaulMulrennan 4 (Ollie Pears) *in rr: pushed along over 3f out: rdn over 2f out: plugged on one pce fnl 2f* **13/2**	38
03-6	5	3	**Luv U Lucky**[13] 2 4-8-8 **57**... AndrewMullen 3 (Michael Appleby) *chsd ldrs: rdn along over 3f out: sn wknd* **6/1**[3]	18
130-	6	2 ¼	**Llewellyn**[30] 8242 8-8-11 **67**.. PhilDennis(7) 6 (Declan Carroll) *slt ld: rdn along 4f out: hdd over 3f out and sn wknd* **10/1**	23
00-0	7	30	**Curzon Line**[12] 24 7-9-0 **63**.. GrahamGibbons 1 (Michael Easterby) *cl up on inner: rdn along wl over 3f out: sn wknd and bhd fr over 2f out* **20/1**	

1m 42.49s (-1.21) **Going Correction** -0.05s/f (Stan) 7 Ran SP% **111.2**

Speed ratings (Par 103): **104,91,89,83,80 78,48**

CSF £5.69 CT £54.75 TOTE £2.30: £1.90, £1.10; EX 6.90 Trifecta £58.70.

Owner Mr & Mrs P Ashton **Bred** Mr & Mrs P Ashton **Trained** Musley Bank, N Yorks

FOCUS

An uncompetitive handicap and the winner bolted in. He's set for a big rise.

180 CORAL.CO.UK BEST ODDS GUARANTEED ON RACING MEDIAN AUCTION MAIDEN STKS 1m 3f (F)

2:30 (2:30) (Class 5) 4-6-Y-O **£3,234** (£962; £481; £240) **Stalls** Low

Form				RPR
022-	1		**Step On It (IRE)**[41] 8107 4-9-5 65..................................(p) LukeMorris 3 (Daniel Mark Loughnane) *trckd ldrs: hdwy and n.m.r 4f out: led 3f out: sn rdn wl clr: heavily eased last 120yds* **4/6**[1]	76+
6-23	2	2 ¾	**My Tringaling (IRE)**[8] 61 4-9-0 50.......................... GrahamGibbons 6 (Stuart Williams) *prom: effrt and cl up 4f out: rdn to dispute ld over 3f out: chsd wnr and drvn over 2f out: sn one pce* **9/1**	54
4	3	1	**Moonshine Ridge (IRE)**[12] 26 5-9-3 0.......................... JoeFanning 5 (Alan Swinbank) *sn led: rdn along 4f out: sn jnd: hdd 3f out and sn drvn: plugged on one pce* **11/2**[3]	52
/60-	4	nk	**Art Charter (FR)**[26] 8312 4-9-0 54................................ DougieCostello 2 (K R Burke) *in rr: outpcd and bhd 1/2-way: rdn along over 3f out: kpt on u.p fnl 2f* **25/1**	52
3	5	19	**Independent Rose**[12] 26 4-9-0 0................................ JamieSpencer 4 (Michael Bell) *trckd ldr on inner: pushed along over 4f out: lost pl over 3f out: sn bhd* **4/1**[2]	19

2m 31.29s (3.29) **Going Correction** -0.05s/f (Stan)

WFA 4 from 5yo 3lb 5 Ran SP% **109.2**

Speed ratings: **86,84,83,83,69**

CSF £7.32 TOTE £1.70: £1.10, £3.40; EX 6.60 Trifecta £22.20.

Owner The Batham Boys **Bred** Newtown Anner Stud **Trained** Baldwin's Gate, Staffs

FOCUS

Little depth to this maiden and another facile winner on the card. There's a chance the eased winner improved again.

181 UNIBET.CO.UK DAILY ENHANCED PLACE TERMS H'CAP 5f (F)

3:05 (3:09) (Class 6) (0-65,65) 3-Y-O **£2,587** (£770; £384; £192) **Stalls** Centre

Form				RPR
3-1	1		**Bring On A Spinner**[13] 5 3-9-2 **65**.......................... AaronJones(5) 6 (Stuart Williams) *trckd ldrs: hdwy to ld jst over 2f out: shkn up jst over 1f out: pushed out* **11/8**[1]	77+
30-5	2	2	**Memyselfie (IRE)**[7] 81 3-8-1 **52** oh5 ow1.............(v[1]) JackOsborn(7) 8 (Derek Shaw) *racd towards stands' rail: chsd ldrs: hdwy over 2f out: rdn to chal over 1f out: kpt on same pce fnl f* **33/1**	53

51-6 **3** 3 3/4 **Sarabi**[13] 3 3-9-6 **64**........(p) KieranO'Neill 5 52
(Scott Dixon) *dwlt and in rr: rdn along 1/2-way: hdwy wl over 1f out: kpt on fnl f* **8/1**

55-2 **4** 1 1/2 **Koothrappali**[13] 5 3-9-1 **59**........ GrahamGibbons 3 41
(David Barron) *chsd ldrs: rdn along and outpcd 1/2-way: kpt on u.p appr fnl f* **9/2**[2]

006- **5** 1 **Scottish Command**[18] 8365 3-9-1 **59**........(v[1]) SeanLevey 1 38+
(Richard Hannon) *dwlt: sn prom on outer: rdn along and cl up over 2f out: sn rdn and wknd over 1f out* **9/2**[2]

503- **6** 1 1/4 **Fiftytintsofsilver (IRE)**[16] 8387 3-8-11 **55**........ LukeMorris 7 29
(Gay Kelleway) *prom: rdn along over 2f out: grad wknd* **20/1**

014- **7** 7 **Young Windsor (IRE)**[83] 7438 3-9-6 **64**........(p) PJMcDonald 2 13
(Ann Duffield) *in tch on wd outside: rdn along 1/2-way: sn wknd* **7/1**[3]

045- **8** 1/2 **Lady Elizabeth (IRE)**[27] 8282 3-9-1 **59**........(p) TomEaves 4 6
(Scott Dixon) *slt ld: rdn along 1/2-way: sn hdd: drvn and wknd* **25/1**

57.49s (-2.21) **Going Correction** -0.45s/f (Stan) **8** Ran SP% **113.6**
Speed ratings (Par 95): **99,95,89,87,85 83,72,71**
CSF £60.02 CT £275.88 TOTE £1.90: £1.10, £8.10, £2.20; EX 56.10 Trifecta £393.00.
Owner J W Parry **Bred** J W Parry **Trained** Newmarket, Suffolk

FOCUS
This modest handicap proved a good opportunity for the unexposed winner, who scored in a decent time.

182 32RED H'CAP 1m 3f (F)
3:40 (3:40) (Class 5) (0-75,81) 3-Y-O **£3,234** (£962; £481; £240) **Stalls** Low

Form RPR

33-1 **1** **Cape Of Glory (IRE)**[11] 29 3-9-13 **81** 6ex........ LukeMorris 3 91+
(James Tate) *chsd ldng pair: pushed along 7f out: reminders over 4f out: swtchd rt and hdwy over 3f out: sn cl up: rdn to ld 2f out: drvn and edgd lft over 1f out: hung rt to inner rail ins fnl f: drvn out* **10/11**[1]

000- **2** 1 1/2 **Jarir**[133] 6018 3-8-11 **65**........ SeanLevey 1 71
(Richard Hannon) *cl up: disp ld 4f out: led 3f out: sn rdn and hdd 2f out: drvn and carried lft over 1f out: no ex last 120yds* **7/2**[2]

311- **3** 16 **Masqueraded (USA)**[28] 8267 3-9-5 **73**........(p) PaulMulrennan 4 52
(Gay Kelleway) *led: rdn along 4f out: hdd 3f out: sn drvn and kpt on one pce* **4/1**[3]

15-6 **4** 2 1/2 **Khismet**[8] 70 3-9-1 **74**........(p) CharlesEddery[(5)] 5 49
(Rae Guest) *chsd ldrs: hdwy 4f out: rdn along 3f out: sn drvn and outpcd fnl 2f* **25/1**

051- **5** 10 **Luath**[16] 8384 3-8-10 **64**........ NickyMackay 2 22
(David Brown) *in rr and sn detached: hdwy to take cl order 4f out: rdn 3f out: sn drvn and outpcd fnl 2f* **8/1**

2m 27.2s (-0.80) **Going Correction** -0.05s/f (Stan) **5** Ran SP% **109.6**
Speed ratings (Par 97): **100,98,87,85,78**
CSF £4.33 TOTE £1.90: £1.30, £1.20; EX 5.00 Trifecta £9.50.
Owner Saif Ali **Bred** Razza Pallorsi Snc Di Giacomo Gariboldi **Trained** Newmarket, Suffolk

FOCUS
The first two pulled well clear off a good pace in an uncompetitive handicap. The winner can rate higher.
T/Plt: £130.40 to a £1 stake. Pool of £56239.41 - 314.66 winning tickets. T/Qpdt: £11.50 to a £1 stake. Pool of £6139.18 - 393.60 winning tickets. **Joe Rowntree**

[90]MEYDAN (L-H)
Thursday, January 14
OFFICIAL GOING: Dirt: fast turf: good

183a MINA RASHID (H'CAP) (DIRT) 1m (D)
3:00 (3:00) (78-94,94) 3-Y-O+
£24,489 (£8,163; £4,081; £2,040; £1,224; £816)

RPR

1 **Tiz Now Tiz Then (USA)**[301] 11-9-5 93........(bt) RichardMullen 2 100
(S Seemar, UAE) *mid-div: smooth prog 2 1/2f out: led 1f out: r.o wl* **16/1**

2 2 **Nathr (USA)**[56] 7917 5-8-9 83........ PaulHanagan 8 85+
(Doug Watson, UAE) *mid-div: chsd ldrs 2 1/2f out: ev ch 1f out: nt qckn fnl 110yds* **6/4**[1]

3 3/4 **Alareef (SAF)**[13] 12 5-8-6 79........(b) SamHitchcott 3 80
(M F De Kock, South Africa) *sn led: kicked clr 3f out: hdd 1f out: r.o same pce* **9/1**

4 2 1/2 **Muhtaram**[13] 12 6-9-2 89........(v) FernandoJara 4 85
(M Al Mheiri, UAE) *trckd ldr: ev ch 3f out: one pce fnl 2f* **9/2**[2]

5 1/2 **Prepared**[6] 116 7-8-8 82........(bt) TadhgO'Shea 5 75
(A R Al Rayhi, UAE) *s.i.s: nvr nr to chal but r.o fnl 2 1/2f* **9/1**

6 12 **Stormardal (IRE)**[13] 12 5-9-0 87........ WayneSmith 7 54
(Ismail Mohammed) *trckd ldrs tl outpcd 3f out: wknd fnl 2 1/2f* **6/1**[3]

7 1 3/4 **Bluff (USA)**[163] 4-9-6 94........ ChrisHayes 1 56
(D Selvaratnam, UAE) *wl away: sn dropped in rr: n.d* **14/1**

8 dist **Filfil (USA)**[13] 11 6-9-0 93........(b) HectorCrouch[(5)] 6
(S Seemar, UAE) *slowly away: a in rr* **8/1**

1m 36.94s (-0.56) **Going Correction** +0.15s/f (Slow) **8** Ran SP% **116.1**
Speed ratings: **108,106,105,102,102 90,88,**
CSF: 41.29.
Owner Zabeel Racing International, Corp **Bred** WinStar Farm LLC **Trained** United Arab Emirates

FOCUS
A non-carnival event to start. There was no Trakus information available.

184a UAE 1000 GUINEAS TRIAL SPONSORED BY DP WORLD UAE REGION (CONDITIONS RACE) (FILLIES (DIRT) 7f (D)
3:35 (3:35) 3-Y-O
£30,612 (£10,204; £5,102; £2,551; £1,530; £1,020)

RPR

1 **Polar River (USA)**[42] 8097 3-8-8 95........ PatDobbs 4 106+
(Doug Watson, UAE) *trckd ldr: smooth prog 3f out: led 1f out* **11/8**[1]

2 4 3/4 **Promising Run (USA)**[97] 7075 3-8-13 107........ JamesDoyle 6 96
(Saeed bin Suroor) *wl away: sn led: hdd 1f out: r.o but no ch w wnr* **9/4**[2]

3 4 1/4 **Pure Diamond**[106] 6852 3-8-8 91........ WilliamBuick 1 82
(Saeed bin Suroor) *slowly away: settled in rr: r.o fnl 2 1/2f but nvr nr to chal* **5/1**

4 1 1/4 **Kabaw (IRE)**[42] 8097 3-8-8 73........ RichardMullen 5 76
(S Seemar, UAE) *mid-div: chsd ldrs 3f out: r.o same pce fnl 2f* **100/1**

5 2 3/4 **Dolly Dagger (SWE)**[112] 3-8-8 88........ TadhgO'Shea 8 69
(Fredrik Reuterskiold, Sweden) *trckd ldr tl wknd 2f out* **33/1**

6 6 **Almashooqa (AUS)**[194] 3921 3-9-4 104........(b) PaulHanagan 2 55
(M F De Kock, South Africa) *s.i.s: trckd ldr: t.k.h: wknd 3f out* **4/1**[3]

7 2 **Burnt Pavlova (USA)**[100] 6995 3-8-8 60........ FrederikTylicki 7 47
(A bin Harmash, UAE) *a in rr* **150/1**

8 1 1/4 **High Start (USA)**[27] 8301 3-8-8........ SamHitchcott 3 44
(Doug Watson, UAE) *s.i.s: sn rdn in rr* **100/1**

1m 24.26s (-0.84) **Going Correction** +0.15s/f (Slow) **8** Ran SP% **115.1**
Speed ratings: **110,104,99,98,95 88,86,84**
CSF: 4.77.
Owner Valentin Bukhtoyarov & Evgeny Kappushev **Bred** Bob McCann Mark Kelder Doug Richards **Trained** United Arab Emirates

FOCUS
There was again no Trakus data, but Polar River was visually impressive and the final time was 1.29secs quicker than the following 2000 Guineas Trial.

185a UAE 2000 GUINEAS TRIAL SPONSORED BY DP WORLD UAE REGION (CONDITIONS RACE) (DIRT) 7f (D)
4:10 (4:10) 3-Y-O
£30,612 (£10,204; £5,102; £2,551; £1,530; £1,020)

RPR

1 **Steady Pace**[110] 6754 3-9-0 112........ JamesDoyle 1 100
(Saeed bin Suroor) *trckd ldr: t.k.h: rdn 2 1/2f out: led 110yds out: r.o wl: jst hld on* **4/5**[1]

2 nse **Rouleau**[110] 6754 3-9-2 104........ WilliamBuick 7 102
(Charlie Appleby) *trckd ldr: rdn 3f out: r.o fnl 2f: jst failed* **5/2**[2]

3 2 1/4 **Calder Prince (IRE)**[68] 7745 3-9-0 98........ RichardKingscote 8 94
(Tom Dascombe) *sn led: rdn 3f out: hdd 110yds out: r.o* **6/1**[3]

4 1 1/2 **Market Rally (USA)**[159] 3-9-0 93........(t) ChrisHayes 2 90
(D Selvaratnam, UAE) *trckd ldrs: outpcd 3f out: r.o fnl 1 1/2f* **8/1**

5 6 1/4 **Illegally Blonde (IRE)**[17] 8378 3-8-9 90........ PatDobbs 4 68
(Jamie Osborne) *slowly away: settled in rr: smooth prog 3f out: one pce fnl 2f* **12/1**

6 5 **Prince Jai**[27] 8301 3-9-0 58........ RichardMullen 3 60
(S Seemar, UAE) *s.i.s: nvr nr to chal* **100/1**

7 nk **Atta Alla** 3-9-0........ CSanchez 6 59
(R Bouresly, Kuwait) *v.s.a: a in rr* **100/1**

8 3 **Follow The Rules**[203] 3552 3-8-8........ HectorCrouch[(6)] 5 51
(S Seemar, UAE) *nvr bttr than mid-div* **100/1**

1m 25.55s (0.45) **Going Correction** +0.15s/f (Slow) **8** Ran SP% **120.2**
Speed ratings: **103,102,100,98,91 85,85,82**
CSF: 3.27.
Owner Godolphin **Bred** T G Roddick **Trained** Newmarket, Suffolk

FOCUS
A one-two for Godolphin but this trip looked to stretch both of these speedy horses, so they'd have to be doubtful stayers at 1m, and it will be interesting to see if the owners are tempted into running their impressive maiden winner Blue Creek in the UAE 2000 Guineas. The time was over a second slower than the preceding fillies' trial and the winner didn't need to hit his mark.

186a DUBAWI STKS SPONSORED BY DP WORLD UAE REGION (LISTED RACE) (DIRT) 6f (D)
4:45 (4:45) 3-Y-O+
£61,224 (£20,408; £10,204; £5,102; £3,061; £2,040)

RPR

1 **Reynaldothewizard (USA)**[336] 533 10-9-0 113....(bt) RichardMullen 8 112
(S Seemar, UAE) *trckd ldr: rdn 2f out: led 110yds out: r.o wl* **7/2**[2]

2 2 3/4 **Cool Cowboy (USA)**[28] 8276 5-9-0 106........ PatDobbs 9 103
(Doug Watson, UAE) *rn wout declared visor: settled in rr: smooth prog 3f out: r.o fnl 1 1/2f but no ch w wnr* **25/1**

3 1 **Let'sgoforit (IRE)**[98] 8-9-2 109........(bt) OliverWilson 1 104+
(Bodil Hallencreutz, Sweden) *sn led: kicked clr 3f out: hdd 1f out: wknd fnl 110yds* **25/1**

4 4 1/2 **Krypton Factor**[292] 1095 8-9-0 106........(b) FrederikTylicki 10 85
(Fawzi Abdulla Nass, Bahrain) *settled in rr: nvr able to chal but r.o fnl 2f* **16/1**

5 4 **Muarrab**[28] 8276 7-9-0 113........ PaulHanagan 2 73
(M Al Mheiri, UAE) *trckd ldr tl wknd fnl 1 1/2f* **4/7**[1]

6 shd **Indianapolis (USA)**[28] 8276 5-9-0 105........(bt) FernandoJara 5 72
(S Seemar, UAE) *nvr bttr than mid-div* **25/1**

7 4 1/4 **Speed Hawk (USA)**[7] 91 5-9-0 106........(p) JamesDoyle 6 59
(Robert Cowell) *nvr bttr than mid-div* **7/1**[3]

8 12 **Price Is Truth (USA)**[28] 8276 6-9-0 100........(bt) HectorCrouch 3 20
(S Seemar, UAE) *chsd ldrs tl outpcd 3f out* **50/1**

9 5 1/4 **Intibaah**[75] 7662 6-9-0 100........ WilliamBuick 4 3
(George Baker) *s.i.s: a in rr* **33/1**

1m 10.97s (-0.63) **Going Correction** +0.15s/f (Slow) **9** Ran SP% **120.7**
Speed ratings: **110,106,105,99,93 93,87,71,64**
CSF: 87.89.
Owner Zabeel Racing International, Corp **Bred** Gibraltar Group Lp **Trained** United Arab Emirates

FOCUS
No Trakus info, but the pace looked way too hot.

187a SINGSPIEL STKS SPONSORED BY MINA JEBEL ALI (LISTED RACE) (TURF) 1m 1f (T)
5:20 (5:20) 3-Y-O+
£61,224 (£20,408; £10,204; £5,102; £3,061; £2,040)

RPR

1 **More Aspen (USA)**[39] 5-8-9 99........ RichardMullen 9 103
(S Seemar, UAE) *trckd ldrs: rdn 3f out: r.o fnl 2f: led fnl 110yds* **11/1**

2 1 **Big Baz (IRE)**[57] 7891 6-9-0 113........ WilliamBuick 6 106
(William Muir) *trckd ldr: led 1f out: hdd fnl 110yds* **11/4**[2]

3 nk **Mujaarib (AUS)**[320] 744 7-9-0 110........ PaulHanagan 3 105+
(M F De Kock, South Africa) *settled in rr: r.o fnl 2f: nrst fin* **4/1**

4 2 **Limario (GER)**[39] 6-9-0 112........ PatDobbs 5 101+
(Doug Watson, UAE) *settled in rr: r.o fnl 2f but nvr nr to chal* **7/2**[3]

5 shd **Zamaam**[48] 8029 6-9-0 99........(t) DavidProbert 7 101
(E Charpy, UAE) *trckd ldr: led 2f out: hdd 1f out: wknd fnl 110yds* **40/1**

6 1 1/2 **Maid Of The Glens (IRE)**[42] 8099 5-8-9 91........ SamHitchcott 4 93+
(S Seemar, UAE) *s.i.s: nvr nr to chal* **50/1**

7 hd **Excilly**[126] 6242 4-8-8 102........ TadhgO'Shea 8 92+
(Tom Dascombe) *s.i.s: settled in rr: nvr nr to chal* **14/1**

The Form Book, Raceform Ltd, Newbury, RG14 5SJ

8 3 3/4 **Farraaj (IRE)**[27] 8302 7-9-0 115 .... ChrisHayes 1 90
(D Selvaratnam, UAE) *sn led: rdn 3f out: hdd & wknd 2f out* **5/2**[1]

1m 49.8s (0.70) **Going Correction** +0.125s/f (Good)
WFA 4 from 5yo+ 1lb 8 Ran SP% **116.9**
Speed ratings: **101,100,99,98,97 96,96,93**
CSF: 42.43.

Owner Mohamed Albousi Alghufli **Bred** Barry Weisbord **Trained** United Arab Emirates

FOCUS
Turf track out 4m from the inside line. A weak Listed race in which most of the runners were below their peak.

188a MINA AL HAMRIYA (H'CAP) (DIRT) 1m 2f (D)
5:55 (5:55) (95-108,106) 3-Y-O+
£44,897 (£14,965; £7,482; £3,741; £2,244; £1,496)

RPR

1 **Munaaser**[145] 5643 5-9-1 **100** .... PaulHanagan 4 104
(A R Al Rayhi, UAE) *s.i.s: trckd ldrs: led 1f out: r.o wl: jst hld on* **12/1**

2 *shd* **Good Contact (USA)**[110] 6739 4-8-11 **99** .... OisinMurphy 6 102+
(Saeed bin Suroor) *slowly away: settled in rr: r.o wl fnl 2f out: jst failed* **11/1**

3 *1 1/4* **Think Ahead**[106] 6868 5-9-3 **102** .... (p) JamesDoyle 2 103
(Saeed bin Suroor) *sn led: hdd 1f out: r.o same pce* **4/1**[3]

4 *3/4* **Farrier (USA)**[28] 8275 8-9-4 **104** .... (b) RichardMullen 9 103
(S Seemar, UAE) *s.i.s: settled in rr: smooth prog 5f out: ev ch 1 1/2f out* **11/1**

5 *1/2* **Hunting Ground (USA)**[7] 94 6-9-4 **104** .... MickaelBarzalona 7 102
(S bin Ghadayer, UAE) *mid-div: nvr able to chal but r.o fnl 2f* **3/1**[2]

6 *2* **Pit Stop (IRE)**[300] 987 5-8-9 **95** .... RoystonFfrench 1 89
(S bin Ghadayer, UAE) *settled in rr: nvr able to chal but mod prog fnl 2 2/2f* **33/1**

7 *6 3/4* **Flag War (GER)**[145] 5633 5-9-0 **99** .... (p) FrederikTylicki 10 80
(Saeed bin Suroor) *settled in rr: nvr able to chal* **14/1**

8 *4* **Jutland**[27] 8302 9-9-4 **104** .... PatDobbs 5 76
(Doug Watson, UAE) *trckd ldrs tl wknd fnl 3f* **20/1**

9 *13* **Cat O'Mountain (USA)**[468] 6909 6-9-6 **106** .... (b) WilliamBuick 3 52
(Charlie Appleby) *wl away: trckd ldr tl wknd fnl 3f* **7/4**[1]

10 *39* **Probably (IRE)**[120] 6-8-13 **98** .... CarlosLopez 8
(Rune Haugen) *mid-div: wknd qckly 4 1/2f out* **50/1**

2m 4.64s (-0.06) **Going Correction** +0.15s/f (Slow)
WFA 4 from 5yo+ 2lb 10 Ran SP% **122.1**
Speed ratings: **106,105,104,104,103 102,96,93,83,52**
CSF: 138.95 TRICAST: 633.15.

Owner Hamdan Al Maktoum **Bred** Shadwell Estate Co Ltd **Trained** UAE

FOCUS
The first three were trying dirt for the first time and this form is nothing out of the ordinary by carnival standards. The first five are close to their marks.

189a FUJAIRAH CONTAINER TERMINAL (H'CAP) (TURF) 1m
6:30 (6:30) (95-108,105) 3-Y-O+
£44,897 (£14,965; £7,482; £3,741; £2,244; £1,496)

RPR

1 **Forries Waltz (SAF)**[343] 440 4-9-5 **104** .... ChristopheSoumillon 4 110+
(M F De Kock, South Africa) *mid-div: smooth prog 2 1/2f out: led 1 1/2f out: r.o wl* **7/1**[3]

2 *nk* **Flash Fire (IRE)**[145] 5627 4-9-3 **101** .... MickaelBarzalona 3 107+
(Charlie Appleby) *mid-div: chsd ldrs 2 1/2f out: led briefly: hdd 1 1/2f out but r.o wl* **14/1**

3 *1 1/4* **Musaddas**[89] 7282 6-9-4 **102** .... (p) JamesDoyle 11 105
(Saeed bin Suroor) *trckd ldrs: ev ch 1f out: one pce fnl 110yds* **9/4**[1]

4 *1 1/4* **Boomshackerlacker (IRE)**[138] 5845 6-9-2 **100** .... SamHitchcott 9 101
(George Baker) *mid-div: r.o fnl 2f nrst fin* **20/1**

5 *1 1/2* **Beach Bar (IRE)**[7] 94 5-9-2 **100** .... RichardKingscote 2 97
(Brendan Powell) *trckd ldrs: ev ch 1 1/2f out: one pce fnl f* **40/1**

6 *nk* **Belgian Bill**[89] 7282 8-9-5 **104** .... (tp) PatDobbs 8 99
(George Baker) *settled in rr: nvr able to chal but r.o fnl 2f* **7/1**[3]

7 *nse* **Wychwood Warrior (IRE)**[148] 5537 4-9-4 **102** .... TadhgO'Shea 10 98
(M Halford, Ire) *a in mid-div* **12/1**

8 *nk* **Battle Of Marathon (USA)**[7] 95 4-8-13 **102** ......(v) GeorgeBuckell(5) 7 98
(John Ryan) *nvr bttr than mid-div* **12/1**

9 *1 1/4* **Emirates Skycargo (IRE)**[180] 4394 4-9-4 **102** .... WilliamBuick 15 95
(Charlie Appleby) *in rr: nvr nr to chal* **12/1**

10 *1/2* **El Tren (IRE)**[159] 5-9-4 **102** .... ChrisHayes 13 94
(Michael Attwater) *nvr bttr than mid-div* **40/1**

11 *1 1/4* **Scotland Forever (IRE)**[39] 6-9-2 **100** .... RichardMullen 1 89
(S Seemar, UAE) *trckd ldrs tl wknd fnl 2f* **33/1**

12 *1/2* **Giftorm (USA)**[116] 6-9-4 **102** .... OisinMurphy 12 90
(Fredrik Reuterskiold, Sweden) *s.i.s: at rr: nvr nr to chal* **25/1**

13 *nk* **Rock Cocktail (AUS)**[336] 531 6-9-5 **104** .... (b) WayneSmith 14 90
(M F De Kock, South Africa) *sn led: rdn 2 1/2f out: hdd & wknd 1 1/2f out* **25/1**

14 *2* **Heavy Metal**[7] 95 6-9-2 **100** .... RoystonFfrench 16 82
(S bin Ghadayer, UAE) *nvr bttr than mid-div* **40/1**

15 *1 1/4* **Mustadeem (IRE)**[123] 6348 4-9-6 **105** .... PaulHanagan 5 83
(A R Al Rayhi, UAE) *trckd ldrs tl wknd 2f out* **7/2**[2]

16 *4 1/2* **Tarbawi (IRE)**[392] 8216 6-9-2 **100** .... FrederikTylicki 6 69
(A bin Harmash, UAE) *s.i.s: nvr bttr than mid-div* **25/1**

1m 36.39s (-1.11) **Going Correction** +0.125s/f (Good) 16 Ran SP% **134.3**
Speed ratings: **110,109,108,107,105 105,105,105,103,103 102,101,101,99,98 93**
CSF: 101.62. TRICAST: 310.64. Placepot: £89.40 to a £1 stake. Pool of £6431.07 - 52.5 winning tickets. Quadpot: £18.70 to a £1 stake. Pool of £382.80 - 15.1 winning tickets..

Owner Sh Mohd Khalifa Al Maktoum, Gerber, De Kock **Bred** Wicklow Stud **Trained** South Africa

FOCUS
There was no Trakus data but the winner's stablemate, Rock Cocktail, looked to set a strong gallop.

[151] LINGFIELD (L-H)
Friday, January 15

OFFICIAL GOING: Polytrack: standard
Wind: light against Weather: sunny

190 LADBROKES H'CAP (DIV I) 1m 1y(P)
1:00 (1:05) (Class 6) (0-65,65) 4-Y-O+ **£2,264** (£673; £336; £168) **Stalls** High

Form RPR

315- 1 **Etaad (USA)**[25] 8324 5-9-7 **65** .... (b) GeorgeBaker 9 72
(Gary Moore) *hld up: rdn and hdwy on inner over 1f out: drvn ent fnl f: kpt on: led 110yds out* **1/1**[1]

044- 2 *1* **Skidby Mill (IRE)**[143] 5712 6-9-5 **63** .... JimCrowley 8 67
(Laura Mongan) *led: hdd over 6f out: trckd ldr: rdn and ev ch over 1f out: kpt on* **16/1**

63-3 3 *3/4* **Pyroclastic (IRE)**[7] 97 4-9-3 **61** .... (v[1]) PatCosgrave 3 63
(Jim Boyle) *trckd ldr on inner racing keenly: rdn to ld narrowly wl over 1f out: hdd 110yds out: no ex* **3/1**[2]

003- 4 *1 1/2* **Hawk Moth (IRE)**[37] 8165 8-9-0 **58** .... (b) LukeMorris 1 56
(John Spearing) *midfield: rdn wl over 2f out: one pce* **10/1**[3]

000- 5 *1* **Palace Moon**[16] 8396 11-9-4 **62** .... (t) KierenFox 7 58
(Michael Attwater) *hld up in tch: rdn 2f out: kpt on fnl f* **25/1**

/00- 6 *2 1/2* **Ali Bin Nayef**[25] 8336 4-9-6 **64** .... (b[1]) NickyMackay 6 54
(Michael Wigham) *dwlt: rapid hdwy on outer to ld over 6f out: rdn whn hdd wl over 1f out: sn wknd* **16/1**

110- 7 *3/4* **Goolagong Girl (IRE)**[19] 8370 4-9-2 **63** .... DannyBrock(3) 4 51
(Jane Chapple-Hyam) *midfield: rdn over 3f out: wknd ins fnl f* **14/1**

000- 8 *1 3/4* **Not Your Call (IRE)**[15] 8408 5-9-0 **58** .... CathyGannon 5 42
(Lee Carter) *stdd s: hld up in rr: rdn over 2f out: sn btn* **25/1**

0/3- 9 *12* **Nubar Boy**[16] 8396 9-9-4 **65** .... (p) NathanAlison(3) 2 20
(Ronald Thompson) *chsd ldrs on outer: rdn over 2f out: wknd over 1f out* **12/1**

1m 37.38s (-0.82) **Going Correction** -0.075s/f (Stan) 9 Ran SP% **117.9**
Speed ratings (Par 101): **101,100,99,97,96 94,93,91,79**
CSF £21.35 CT £39.06 TOTE £1.70: £1.10, £3.70, £1.50; EX 16.40 Trifecta £56.30.

Owner John Ansell & Ian J Herbert **Bred** Shadwell Farm LLC **Trained** Lower Beeding, W Sussex

FOCUS
They went quite steady early and the winner proved different class. Straightforward form.

191 LADBROKES H'CAP (DIV II) 1m 1y(P)
1:30 (1:35) (Class 6) (0-65,65) 4-Y-O+ **£2,264** (£673; £336; £168) **Stalls** High

Form RPR

00-3 1 **Al's Memory (IRE)**[4] 144 7-9-5 **63** .... AdamKirby 5 71
(David Evans) *mde all: rdn 2f out: edgd rt ins fnl f: kpt on* **6/4**[1]

01-1 2 *1* **Pacolita (IRE)**[4] 144 4-8-12 **63** .... PaddyBradley(7) 9 68
(Sylvester Kirk) *slowly away: hld up: rdn and hdwy on outer 2f out: kpt on* **5/2**[2]

005- 3 *shd* **Rakaan (IRE)**[16] 8396 9-9-1 **59** .... (p) CathyGannon 3 64
(Brendan Powell) *s.i.s: hld up: rdn and hdwy appr fnl f: kpt on* **10/1**

20-0 4 *1* **Ajig**[13] 14 5-9-5 **63** .... (tp) JohnFahy 6 66
(Eve Johnson Houghton) *trckd ldr: rdn 2f out: swtchd lft ins fnl f: one pce* **25/1**

240- 5 *1* **Welsh Inlet (IRE)**[16] 8396 8-8-13 **57** .... WilliamCarson 4 57
(John Bridger) *trckd ldr: rdn 2f out: wknd fnl 110yds* **16/1**

054- 6 *3 1/4* **Texas Scramble**[34] 8211 4-9-0 **58** .... JimCrowley 2 51
(Michael Wigham) *hld up in tch: rdn 2f out: wknd fnl f* **7/1**[3]

562- 7 *shd* **Diletta Tommasa (IRE)**[16] 8396 6-9-6 **64** .... (p) LukeMorris 8 57+
(Daniel Mark Loughnane) *dwlt: t.k.h in midfield: hdwy to go prom 4f out: rdn over 2f out: wknd appr fnl f* **8/1**

1m 37.7s (-0.50) **Going Correction** -0.075s/f (Stan) 7 Ran SP% **111.0**
Speed ratings (Par 101): **99,98,97,96,95 92,92**
CSF £4.98 CT £22.91 TOTE £2.00: £1.50, £1.60; EX 5.30 Trifecta £32.80.

Owner Mrs Rachel Barnes **Bred** Brian Miller **Trained** Pandy, Monmouths

FOCUS
The slower of the two divisions by 0.32sec, and once again the market got it right. The winner was a fraction better than he was earlier in the week.

192 DAILY PRICE BOOSTS AT UNIBET CLAIMING STKS 6f 1y(P)
2:00 (2:07) (Class 6) 4-Y-O+ **£2,264** (£673; £336; £168) **Stalls** Low

Form RPR

00-0 1 **Yeeoow (IRE)**[4] 142 7-9-1 80 .... DougieCostello 6 86
(K R Burke) *mde all: rdn over 1f out: jnd jst ins fnl f: hld on gamely* **10/1**

24-0 2 *nk* **Doctor Parkes**[4] 142 10-8-6 78 .... AaronJones(5) 1 81
(Stuart Williams) *hld up in tch: rdn and hdwy on inner over 1f out: chal strly ins fnl f: hld nr fin* **6/1**

260- 3 *1* **Showtime Star**[34] 8205 6-9-3 84 .... LukeMorris 5 85
(Gay Kelleway) *in tch on outer: pushed along 1/2-way: briefly snatched up 2f out: drvn over 1f out: kpt on ins fnl f* **11/4**[2]

160- 4 *hd* **Majestic Myles (IRE)**[69] 7754 8-8-12 90 .... JackGarritty 2 79
(Richard Fahey) *trckd ldrs: rdn over 1f out: one pce ins fnl f* **11/8**[1]

/10- 5 *1* **Peace Seeker**[116] 6591 8-8-10 88 .... (t) CathyGannon 3 74
(Ronald Harris) *hld up in tch: rdn 2f out: one pce and nvr threatened* **5/1**[3]

10-0 6 *1/2* **Mrs Bubbles (IRE)**[8] 80 4-7-13 65 .... JosephineGordon(7) 4 68
(J S Moore) *chsd ldr: rdn over 2f out: wknd fnl f* **33/1**

06-0 7 *2 1/4* **Agerzam**[7] 106 6-8-10 76 .... (p[1]) KieranO'Neill 7 65
(Ronald Harris) *wnt rt s and s.i.s: sn pushed along in rr: a bhd* **50/1**

1m 10.48s (-1.42) **Going Correction** -0.075s/f (Stan) 7 Ran SP% **113.7**
Speed ratings (Par 101): **106,105,104,104,102 102,99**
CSF £66.48 TOTE £13.80: £5.50, £1.80; EX 68.10 Trifecta £340.30.

Owner Ontoawinner 7 & Mrs E Burke **Bred** Arctic Tack Stud **Trained** Middleham Moor, N Yorks

■ Stewards' Enquiry : Dougie Costello two-day ban: careless riding (29-30 Jan)

FOCUS
A decent claimer, with six of the seven runners officially rated between 76 and 90.The winner is rated to the best of this winter's form.

193 BET & WATCH EVERY RACE AT UNIBET MAIDEN STKS 5f 6y(P)
2:30 (2:35) (Class 5) 3-Y-O **£2,911** (£866; £432; £216) **Stalls** High

Form RPR

302- 1 **Gorokai (IRE)**[20] 8355 3-9-5 72 .... JimCrowley 4 74
(David Simcock) *mde all: rdn appr fnl f: kpt on* **10/11**[1]

300- 2 *2 1/4* **Yeah Baby Yeah (IRE)**[124] 6364 3-9-0 0 .... LukeMorris 5 61
(Gay Kelleway) *chsd ldr: rdn 2f out: drvn appr fnl f: one pce and sn no ch w wnr* **11/4**[2]

026- **3** ½ **Belle Mare Plage**[39] 8129 3-8-9 70 .... AaronJones(5) 2 59
(Stuart Williams) *in tch: rdn 2f out: kpt on same pce* **11/4**[2]

00- **4** 3¾ **Kiringa**[18] 8377 3-9-0 0 .... PatCosgrave 1 46
(William Knight) *chsd ldr: rdn 2f out: wknd fnl f* **33/1**[3]

56- **5** 1¼ **Oak Forest**[118] 6546 3-9-5 0 .... KierenFox 3 46
(Michael Attwater) *hld up: rdn over 2f out: wknd fnl f* **66/1**

59.31s (0.51) **Going Correction** -0.075s/f (Stan) 5 Ran SP% **110.2**
Speed ratings (Par 97): **92,88,87,81,79**
CSF £3.75 TOTE £1.70: £1.10, £2.30; EX 3.80 Trifecta £4.90.

Owner Mrs Fitri Hay **Bred** Tally-Ho Stud **Trained** Newmarket, Suffolk

FOCUS
A weak maiden, and the third race in a row in which the winner made all. He's rated to a length pb.

194 CORAL CONDITIONS STKS 1m 4f (P)
3:00 (3:05) (Class 3) 4-Y-O+ **£7,246** (£2,168; £1,084; £542; £270) **Stalls** Low

Form RPR
412/ **1** **Arch Villain (IRE)**[637] 1556 7-9-2 93 .... JimCrowley 2 103
(Amanda Perrett) *trckd ldr: rdn over 2f out: styd on fr over 1f out: led towards fin* **5/1**[3]

215- **2** 1¼ **Super Kid**[34] 8208 4-8-12 95 .... MartinHarley 1 101
(Saeed bin Suroor) *hld up in tch: rapid hdwy to ld over 2f out: sn qcknd 3 1/2 l clr: reduced advantage ins fnl f: wknd and hdd towards fin* **11/10**[1]

25-2 **3** 4 **Intense Tango**[13] 19 5-8-11 88 .... DougieCostello 4 90
(K R Burke) *trckd ldr: rdn over 3f out: outpcd over 2f out: plugged on fr appr fnl f* **7/1**

035- **4** 1½ **Castillo Del Diablo (IRE)**[90] 7295 7-9-2 93 .... (p) AdamKirby 5 92
(David Simcock) *dwlt: hld up: rdn over 3f out: nvr threatened* **9/2**[2]

434- **5** ½ **Plutocracy (IRE)**[113] 6681 6-9-2 92 .... GeorgeBaker 3 91
(Gary Moore) *led: rdn whn hdd over 2f out: wknd appr fnl f* **5/1**[3]

2m 29.37s (-3.63) **Going Correction** -0.075s/f (Stan)
WFA 4 from 5yo+ 4lb 5 Ran SP% **111.6**
Speed ratings (Par 107): **109,108,105,104,104**
CSF £11.26 TOTE £6.30: £4.00, £1.10; EX 12.10 Trifecta £53.60.

Owner Mr & Mrs F Cotton, Mr & Mrs P Conway **Bred** Summerhill Bloodstock **Trained** Pulborough, W Sussex

FOCUS
The first two finished nicely clear in this conditions race. The form is taken at face value.

195 32RED.COM H'CAP 1m 7f 169y(P)
3:30 (3:35) (Class 6) (0-65,61) 4-Y-O+ **£2,264** (£673; £336; £168) **Stalls** Low

Form RPR
55-2 **1** **Megara**[9] 61 4-9-7 61 .... (p) LukeMorris 1 71+
(Sir Mark Prescott Bt) *in tch: pushed along and hdwy to chse ldr 3f out: rdn to ld wl over 1f out: drvn fnl f: hld on wl* **11/8**[1]

551- **2** nk **Golly Miss Molly**[30] 8249 5-10-0 61 .... (b) GeorgeBaker 5 68
(Jeremy Gask) *hld up: smooth hdwy over 2f out: rdn to chse ldr appr fnl f: kpt on but a jst hld* **4/1**[3]

442- **3** 2½ **Helmsman (IRE)**[158] 5224 4-8-11 58 .... JosephineGordon(7) 2 62
(J S Moore) *trckd ldr: rdn over 2f out: kpt on same pce* **10/1**

050- **4** 1½ **Delagoa Bay (IRE)**[16] 8403 8-8-12 45 .... CathyGannon 4 47
(Sylvester Kirk) *led: rdn over 2f out: hdd wl over 1f out: wknd ins fnl f* **33/1**

201- **5** 1½ **Mighty Thor**[44] 8085 6-9-11 58 .... SteveDrowne 3 58
(Lydia Richards) *hld up: rdn over 2f out: one pce and nvr threatened* **7/2**[2]

441- **6** 17 **Grand Facile**[26] 8315 4-8-13 53 .... (v) KierenFox 7 33
(Gary Moore) *trckd ldr: rdn and lost pl 3f out: wknd fnl 2f: eased ins fnl f* **8/1**

356- **P** **Feb Thirtyfirst**[30] 8249 7-9-11 58 .... (b) MattieBatchelor 6
(Sheena West) *in tch on outside: pushed along 10f out: sn lost pl: bhd fnl 5f: sn t.o: p.u over 1f out* **25/1**

3m 22.31s (-3.39) **Going Correction** -0.075s/f (Stan)
WFA 4 from 5yo+ 7lb 7 Ran SP% **111.3**
Speed ratings (Par 101): **105,104,103,102,102 93,**
CSF £6.66 TOTE £1.70: £1.60, £2.00; EX 6.80 Trifecta £38.10.

Owner Bluehills Racing Limited **Bred** Bluehills Racing Limited **Trained** Newmarket, Suffolk

■ Stewards' Enquiry : Mattie Batchelor eight-day ban: failed to pull up horse quick enough (29-30 Jan, 16 Feb)

FOCUS
A moderate heat but solid form for the level. A minor step up from the winner.

196 UNIBET OFFER DAILY JOCKEY & TRAINER SPECIALS APPRENTICE H'CAP 5f 6y(P)
4:00 (4:05) (Class 6) (0-65,65) 4-Y-O+ **£2,264** (£673; £336; £168) **Stalls** High

Form RPR
30-2 **1** **Boxing Shadows**[7] 98 6-8-13 60 .... HarryBurns(3) 2 66
(Les Eyre) *trckd ldr: jnd ldr 1/2-way: led over 1f out: sn rdn: reduced advantage nr fin but nvr in danger* **7/4**[1]

10-2 **2** ½ **Excellent Aim**[13] 21 9-9-2 65 .... DarylMcLaughlin(5) 3 69
(George Margarson) *in tch: rdn over 1f out: wnt 2nd 75yds out: kpt on* **11/4**[2]

211- **3** 1½ **Roy's Legacy**[15] 8413 7-9-0 63 .... JordanUys(5) 4 62
(Shaun Harris) *led: jnd 1/2-way: rdn whn hdd over 1f out: lost 2nd 75yds out: no ex* **3/1**[3]

220- **4** 1¾ **Tidal's Baby**[44] 8078 7-9-1 59 .... RhiainIngram 1 52
(Lee Carter) *s.i.s: hld up: in tch by 1/2-way: rdn 2f out: one pce* **5/1**

160- **5** 3¼ **Bubbly Bailey**[59] 7882 6-9-0 63 .... (v) CameronNoble(5) 5 44
(J R Jenkins) *chsd ldr on outer: rdn 1/2-way: wknd over 1f out* **10/1**

58.97s (0.17) **Going Correction** -0.075s/f (Stan) 5 Ran SP% **113.8**
Speed ratings (Par 101): **95,94,91,89,83**
CSF £7.15 TOTE £2.20: £1.10, £2.80; EX 6.10 Trifecta £9.90.

Owner Billy Parker **Bred** Catridge Farm Stud **Trained** Catwick, N Yorks

FOCUS
A moderate sprint handicap.

T/Plt: £27.60 to a £1 stake. Pool: £70,454.81 - 1,856.85 winning tickets T/Qpdt: £13.30 to a £1 stake. Pool: £4,866.76 - 270.40 winning tickets **Andrew Sheret**

[144] WOLVERHAMPTON (A.W) (L-H)
Friday, January 15

OFFICIAL GOING: Tapeta: standard
Wind: Fresh half-behind Weather: Showers

197 DOWNLOAD THE NEW UNIBET RACING APP H'CAP 5f 216y (Tp)
4:15 (4:16) (Class 6) (0-60,60) 4-Y-O+ **£2,587** (£770; £384; £192) **Stalls** Low

Form RPR
302- **1** **Kyllach Me (IRE)**[63] 7833 4-9-0 60 .... (b) PhilDennis(7) 5 66
(Bryan Smart) *mid-div: hdwy over 2f out: rdn and edgd rt 1f out: r.o to ld last strides* **10/3**[1]

013- **2** nk **Fujin**[16] 8400 5-9-7 60 .... (b) PaulMulrennan 8 65
(Shaun Harris) *sn led: rdn over 1f out: hdd last strides* **15/2**[3]

334- **3** ½ **Top Cop**[15] 8413 7-9-4 57 .... (be) WilliamTwiston-Davies 2 61
(Ronald Harris) *a.p: rdn to chse ldr over 1f out: styd on u.p* **11/1**

400- **4** hd **Reginald Claude**[42] 8104 8-9-0 58 .... RachealKneller(5) 4 62+
(Mark Usher) *hld up: nt clr run and swtchd lft ins fnl f: r.o wl towards fin: nt rch ldrs* **11/1**

65-6 **5** shd **Divine Call**[9] 68 9-9-7 60 .... (b) RobertHavlin 6 63+
(Milton Bradley) *s.i.s: hld up: hdwy over 1f out: sn rdn: styd on* **8/1**

023- **6** ½ **John Coffey (IRE)**[24] 8351 7-9-5 58 .... AndrewMullen 12 59
(Michael Appleby) *mid-div: rdn over 2f out: hdwy over 1f out: edgd lft ins fnl f: r.o* **7/1**[2]

11-2 **7** 1 **Louis Vee (IRE)**[9] 60 8-8-13 57 .... (p) CiaranMckee(5) 10 55
(John O'Shea) *s.i.s: hld up: rdn over 1f out: r.o ins fnl f: nt rch ldrs* **10/1**

150- **8** ½ **Prigsnov Dancer (IRE)**[63] 7832 11-8-12 56 .... (p) PaddyPilley(5) 3 53
(Deborah Sanderson) *led early: chsd ldr tl over 3f out: remained handy: rdn over 1f out: styd on same pce ins fnl f* **25/1**

300- **9** 2¼ **Gilmer (IRE)**[24] 8352 5-8-11 55 .... (t) NoelGarbutt(5) 13 48
(Laura Young) *racd wd: mid-div: rdn over 2f out: nt clr run over 1f out: nvr on terms* **100/1**

131- **10** 2¼ **Hamis Al Bin (IRE)**[16] 8401 7-9-6 59 .... (bt) TomEaves 7 48+
(Milton Bradley) *chsd ldrs: rdn whn nt clr run over 1f out: wknd ins fnl f* **9/1**

000- **11** nk **Insolenceofoffice (IRE)**[29] 8271 8-9-0 60 .... (p) CallumRodriguez(7) 1 42
(Richard Ford) *mid-div: lost pl over 3f out: rdn over 1f out: wknd fnl f* **25/1**

350- **12** 1¼ **Zebs Lad (IRE)**[15] 8408 4-9-6 59 .... (p) StevieDonohoe 9 40
(Nikki Evans) *s.i.s: sn pushed along into mid-div: hmpd and lost pl over 3f out: in rr whn nt clr run over 1f out* **20/1**

150- **13** 1½ **Smart Dj**[34] 8206 5-9-5 58 .... MartinDwyer 11 32
(Sarah Hollinshead) *plld hrd and sn prom: wnt 2nd over 3f out tl rdn over 1f out: wknd fnl f* **12/1**

1m 14.68s (0.18) **Going Correction** 0.0s/f (Stan) 13 Ran SP% **115.3**
Speed ratings (Par 101): **98,97,96,96,96 95,94,93,90,87 87,85,83**
CSF £24.95 CT £255.07 TOTE £3.90: £1.30, £3.50, £2.80; EX 28.50 Trifecta £248.00.
Owner The Smart Stoneacre Sarah Partnership **Bred** Tally-Ho Stud **Trained** Hambleton, N Yorks

FOCUS
A competitive handicap for the grade run at a sound pace. It's hard to rate the form any higher but the winner can do better here.

198 DAILY PRICE BOOSTS AT UNIBET H'CAP 5f 216y (Tp)
4:45 (4:48) (Class 4) (0-85,84) 4-Y-O+ **£5,498** (£1,636; £817; £408) **Stalls** Low

Form RPR
601- **1** **Nuno Tristan (USA)**[92] 7239 4-9-1 81 .... SammyJoBell(3) 2 91+
(Richard Fahey) *a.p: chsd ldr 2f out: rdn to ld over 1f out: r.o* **9/4**[1]

005- **2** 1¼ **Clubland (IRE)**[29] 8270 7-8-12 78 .... RobHornby(3) 9 84
(Roy Bowring) *sn prom: lost pl over 3f out: hdwy over 1f out: r.o* **40/1**

05-0 **3** nk **Oriental Relation (IRE)**[14] 4 5-9-6 83 .... (v) TomEaves 1 88
(James Given) *sn led: rdn and hdd over 2f out: styng on same pce whn hung rt towards fin* **20/1**

005- **4** ¾ **Dominium (USA)**[18] 8382 9-9-0 77 .... (b) AdamBeschizza 5 80
(Jeremy Gask) *pushed along in rr early: rdn over 1f out: r.o ins fnl f: nt rch ldrs* **25/1**

100- **5** ¾ **Classic Seniority**[90] 7288 4-9-3 80 .... DanielTudhope 8 80
(Marjorie Fife) *chsd ldrs: rdn over 2f out: styd on same pce fnl f* **16/1**

155- **6** nk **Kingscroft (IRE)**[15] 8412 8-8-13 83 .... (b) PatrickVaughan(7) 10 82
(Tom Dascombe) *dwlt: hld up: rdn and n.m.r over 1f out: r.o ins fnl f: nt trble ldrs* **25/1**

545- **7** ½ **Rich Again (IRE)**[24] 8347 7-8-10 73 .... (b) PJMcDonald 6 71
(James Bethell) *dwlt: hld up: shkn up over 2f out: hdwy over 1f out: styd on same pce ins fnl f* **5/1**[2]

216- **8** shd **Renounce (IRE)**[18] 8382 4-9-0 77 .... RobertHavlin 11 74
(Jeremy Noseda) *sn pushed along in rr: rdn and r.o ins fnl f: nvr nrr* **12/1**

105- **9** 1½ **Musharrif**[34] 8205 4-9-1 78 .... JoeFanning 4 71
(Declan Carroll) *hld up in tch: racd keenly: rdn and nt clr run over 1f out: styd on same pce* **7/1**[3]

600- **10** 1¼ **Billyoakes (IRE)**[42] 8106 4-9-5 82 .... PhillipMakin 13 71
(David Barron) *sn pushed along in rr: nt clr run 3f out: nvr on terms* **16/1**

336- **11** ¾ **Guishan**[29] 8262 6-9-4 84 .... AlistairRawlinson(3) 3 70
(Michael Appleby) *prom: nt clr run over 2f out: rdn over 1f out: wknd fnl f* **16/1**

060- **12** 2¼ **Dark Side Dream**[34] 8200 4-9-5 82 .... IrineuGoncalves 12 61
(Chris Dwyer) *prom on outer: rdn over 1f out: wknd fnl f* **18/1**

012- **13** ¾ **Mighty Zip (USA)**[39] 8131 4-9-3 80 .... (b) GrahamLee 7 57
(Kevin Ryan) *chsd ldr tl rdn over 2f out: wknd fnl f* **15/2**

1m 13.42s (-1.08) **Going Correction** 0.0s/f (Stan) 13 Ran SP% **117.2**
Speed ratings (Par 105): **107,105,104,103,102 102,101,101,99,98 97,94,93**
CSF £124.73 CT £1520.85 TOTE £2.50: £1.10, £12.20, £6.40; EX 109.00 Trifecta £1141.30.
Owner R A Fahey **Bred** Galleria Bloodstock & Samac **Trained** Musley Bank, N Yorks

FOCUS
A fair handicap run at a decent pace. The winner is on the up.

199 32RED.COM H'CAP 1m 5f 194y (Tp)
5:15 (5:17) (Class 6) (0-65,65) 4-Y-O+ **£2,587** (£770; £384; £192) **Stalls** Low

Form RPR
06-2 **1** **Pinotage**[4] 150 8-9-2 55 .... (p) JamesSullivan 6 67
(Peter Niven) *hld up: hdwy over 3f out: shkn up to ld and hung rt over 1f out: styd on wl* **3/1**[1]

456- **2** 4½ **Moulin Rouge (DEN)**[217] 2443 5-9-4 57 .... StevieDonohoe 5 63
(Kevin Frost) *dwlt: hld up: hdwy over 2f out: rdn to chse wnr over 1f out: no ex ins fnl f* **33/1**

602- 3 2 1/4 **Medieval Bishop (IRE)**16 8403 7-9-4 **60**..................(p) RobHornby(3) 8 63
(Tony Forbes) *hld up: hdwy over 5f out: outpcd over 2f out: hung lft over 1f out: styd on to go 3rd post* **6/1**

2/3- 4 nse **Favorite Girl (GER)**17 7182 8-9-12 **65**.......................... AndrewMullen 3 67
(Michael Appleby) *hld up in tch: rdn over 3f out: no ex ins fnl f* **8/1**

204- 5 3 3/4 **Tidal Way (IRE)**32 8223 7-9-12 **65**..........................(p) FergusSweeney 7 62
(Shaun Lycett) *chsd ldrs: rdn over 2f out: ev ch over 1f out: edgd lft and wknd ins fnl f* **5/1**3

262- 6 1 1/2 **Shirls Son Sam**77 7604 8-8-11 **50**.................................. JoeFanning 1 45
(Chris Fairhurst) *prom: chsd ldr 9f out tl led over 2f out: rdn and hdd over 1f out: wknd ins fnl f* **10/1**

533- 7 3 **Flying Power**24 8353 8-9-11 **64**.................................. PaulMulrennan 9 55
(John Norton) *w ldr tl led over 10f out: rdn and hdd over 2f out: wknd fnl f* **9/2**2

261- 8 3/4 **Bernisdale**58 5989 8-9-2 **58**...................................... DanielMuscutt(3) 4 48
(John Flint) *led: hdd over 10f out: remained handy: rdn over 3f out: wknd fnl f* **33/1**

550- 9 10 **Surround Sound**134 6022 6-9-6 **64**...................(t) RachelRichardson(5) 2 40
(Tim Easterby) *s.s: hld up: shkn up over 3f out: sn wknd* **15/2**

4/0- 10 36 **Mr Vendman (IRE)**55 7947 6-8-7 **46** oh1........................ RyanPowell 10
(Ian Williams) *sn pushed along and prom: lost pl over 5f out: bhd fnl 4f* **66/1**

3m 4.0s (-0.80) **Going Correction** 0.0s/f (Stan) **10** Ran SP% **113.5**
Speed ratings (Par 101): **102,99,98,98,95 95,93,92,87,66**
CSF £107.85 CT £558.38 TOTE £3.00: £1.10, £6.60, £3.30; EX 78.00 Trifecta £845.50.
Owner S Bowett **Bred** Hellwood Stud Farm **Trained** Barton-le-Street, N Yorks

FOCUS
An open handicap but the winner did it well to build on this week's earlier run.

200 BET IN PLAY AT CORAL H'CAP 1m 4f 50y (Tp)
5:45 (5:45) (Class 5) (0-75,75) 4-Y-O+ **£3,557** (£1,058; £529; £264) **Stalls** Low

Form RPR

05-2 1 **Tower Power**8 88 5-9-7 **75**.................................. MarcMonaghan(3) 2 83
(Phil McEntee) *chsd ldr over 3f: remained handy: shkn up to ld 1f out: r.o* **13/2**

560- 2 3/4 **The Kid**131 6134 5-9-7 **72**..(p) PhillipMakin 5 79
(John Quinn) *hld up in tch: rdn and hung lft fr over 1f out: r.o* **6/1**

- 3 2 **Lady Fandango (IRE)**51 7992 4-8-8 **63**............................ LiamKeniry 7 67
(Gordon Elliott, Ire) *s.i.s: hld up: pushed along and hdwy over 1f out: rdn and hung lft ins fnl f: styd on* **5/1**3

206- 4 3/4 **Archipeligo**11 8062 5-9-6 **71**.. MartinDwyer 1 74
(Iain Jardine) *hld up: hdwy u.p over 1f out: styd on* **9/2**2

15- 5 1 1/4 **Horseguardsparade**24 8353 5-9-5 **70**............ WilliamTwiston-Davies 8 71
(Nigel Twiston-Davies) *sn led at stdy pce: qcknd 3f out: sn rdn: hdd 1f out: no ex* **11/4**1

141- 5 dht **Bayan Kasirga (IRE)**20 8361 6-8-11 **69**................ NatalieHambling(7) 3 70+
(Richard Fahey) *dwlt: hld up: rdn over 2f out: r.o ins fnl f: nt rch ldrs* **5/1**3

/00- 7 1 1/2 **Thimaar (USA)**20 8361 8-9-2 **72**............................ PatrickO'Donnell(5) 6 70
(Sarah Hollinshead) *prom: chsd ldr over 8f out tl rdn 2f out: wknd ins fnl f* **33/1**

521/ 8 6 **Looking On**18 6207 8-9-7 **75**... RobHornby(3) 4 64
(Edward Bevan) *prom: rdn over 3f out: wknd over 2f out* **33/1**

2m 45.74s (4.94) **Going Correction** 0.0s/f (Stan)
WFA 4 from 5yo+ 4lb **8** Ran SP% **111.7**
Speed ratings (Par 103): **83,82,81,80,79 79,78,74**
CSF £42.75 CT £206.88 TOTE £8.90: £3.00, £1.90, £2.70; EX 56.60 Trifecta £264.70.
Owner Miss M Bishop-Peck **Bred** Sir Eric Parker **Trained** Newmarket, Suffolk

FOCUS
The pace was steady for this fair handicap. The first two are rated to form.

201 LADBROKES H'CAP 7f 32y (Tp)
6:15 (6:15) (Class 6) (0-60,60) 4-Y-O+ **£2,587** (£770; £384; £192) **Stalls** High

Form RPR

0/4- 1 **National Service (USA)**35 8184 5-9-1 **54**....................(tp) LiamKeniry 3 61
(Gordon Elliott, Ire) *s.i.s: hld up: n.m.r 3f out: hdwy over 2f out: shkn up to ld ins fnl f: sn rdn: jst hld on* **6/1**2

153- 2 nk **Moonbi Creek (IRE)**24 8351 9-8-9 **55**...............(t) CallumRodriguez(7) 4 61
(Richard Ford) *s.i.s: hld up: rdn: hung lft and r.o ins fnl f: nt quite get there* **8/1**

00-0 3 1 3/4 **Rialto Magic**9 68 4-9-5 **58**......................................(p) TimmyMurphy 9 60
(Jamie Osborne) *s.i.s: hdwy 3f out: rdn to ld ins fnl f: sn hdd and unable qck* **40/1**

334- 4 2 1/4 **Zed Candy Girl**24 8352 6-9-4 **57**..............................(p) StevieDonohoe 10 53
(Daniel Mark Loughnane) *in rr: rdn and r.o ins fnl f: nt rch ldrs* **14/1**

056- 5 3/4 **Smalljohn**24 8352 10-9-2 **58**......................................(v) AdamCarter(3) 11 53
(Bryan Smart) *sn led: rdn over 1f out: hdd and no ex ins fnl f* **25/1**

004/ 6 1 **Malvesi**1528 7338 7-8-10 **49**.. JoeFanning 5 41
(Mark Johnston) *chsd ldrs: rdn over 2f out: wknd ins fnl f* **12/1**

41-4 7 1/2 **Believe It (IRE)**4 144 4-8-11 **57**.. ChrisKelly(7) 1 50+
(Richard Hughes) *hld up in tch racd keenly: nt clr run and lost pl over 2f out: n.d after* **11/8**1

502- 8 hd **Caledonia Laird**24 8352 5-9-6 **59**....................................... JoeyHaynes 8 49
(Jo Hughes) *prom: rdn over 2f out: wknd ins fnl f* **7/1**3

340- 9 hd **Bionic Indian**16 8406 4-8-3 **49**.................................. NathanEvans(7) 6 39
(Michael Easterby) *chsd ldr tl rdn over 1f out: wknd ins fnl f* **14/1**

600- 10 1 **My Bubba**25 8334 4-9-0 **53**................................ WilliamTwiston-Davies 7 41
(Michael Blanshard) *hld up: n.m.r over 3f out: rdn over 2f out: nvr on terms* **33/1**

10-0 11 hd **Beauty's Forte (IRE)**4 144 5-8-12 **58**..........................(v) LeeByrne(7) 2 45
(Declan Carroll) *hld up: effrt and nt clr run over 2f out: n.m.r over 1f out: wknd ins fnl f* **25/1**

42-0 12 12 **Vivre La Reve**11 39 4-9-7 **60**...............................(v1) AndrewMullen 12 18
(James Unett) *chsd ldrs: rdn over 2f out: wknd over 1f out: eased* **50/1**

1m 28.24s (-0.56) **Going Correction** 0.0s/f (Stan) **12** Ran SP% **116.1**
Speed ratings (Par 101): **103,102,100,98,97 96,95,95,95,93 93,79**
CSF £49.16 CT £1778.20 TOTE £8.20: £2.20, £2.40, £9.90; EX 65.50 Trifecta £1603.20.
Owner T Howley Jnr **Bred** Three Chimneys Farm Llc **Trained** Longwood, Co Meath

FOCUS
A modest handicap run at a decent pace. The winner was on a fair mark on the pick of his recent Irish form.

202 LADBROKES MEDIAN AUCTION MAIDEN STKS 1m 141y (Tp)
6:45 (6:45) (Class 6) 3-4-Y-O **£2,587** (£770; £384; £192) **Stalls** Low

Form RPR

62- 1 **Dwight D**25 8323 3-8-7 0.. JoeFanning 4 84+
(William Haggas) *mde all: shkn up and c readily clr fr over 1f out: easily* **1/5**1

00- 2 9 **Dream Revival**16 8404 3-8-2 0.. AndrewMullen 6 58
(James Unett) *plld hrd and prom: rdn to chse wnr over 2f out: outpcd fr over 1f out* **66/1**

3 7 **Song Lark** 3-8-2 0.. JimmyQuinn 7 43
(David Simcock) *pushed along to chse wnr after 1f tl rdn over 2f out: wknd over 1f out* **9/2**2

02/ 4 3 1/2 **Tatawu (IRE)**451 7354 4-9-9 0...................................... CiaranMckee(5) 2 45
(Peter Hiatt) *dwlt: hld up: rdn and wknd over 2f out* **12/1**3

5 5 **Blue Vision (FR)** 3-8-7 0.. NeilFarley 1 30
(Alan Swinbank) *pushed along in rr thrght: rdn and wknd 3f out* **16/1**

56- 6 3 1/2 **Oasis Rose (FR)**25 8332 4-9-9 0.................................. AdamBeschizza 5 22
(Jeremy Gask) *chsd wnr 1f: remained handy tl rdn and wknd over 2f out* **40/1**

1m 49.67s (-0.43) **Going Correction** 0.0s/f (Stan)
WFA 3 from 4yo 22lb **6** Ran SP% **119.0**
Speed ratings (Par 101): **101,93,86,83,79 76**
CSF £27.04 TOTE £1.10: £1.10, £22.30; EX 25.80 Trifecta £70.70.
Owner W J and T C O Gredley **Bred** Whitley Stud **Trained** Newmarket, Suffolk

FOCUS
An uncompetitive maiden run at a steady pace. Easy for the winner, who stood up beforehand.
T/Jkpt: £10,650.00 to a £1 stake. Jackpot placepot: £330.90 Pool: £2,697.00 - 5.95 winning tickets T/Plt: £228.40 to a £1 stake. Pool: £94,329.42 - 301.41 winning tickets T/Qpdt: £21.70 to a £1 stake. Pool: £10,439.67 - 354.90 winning tickets **Colin Roberts**

203 - 207a (Foreign Racing) - See Raceform Interactive

108 DUNDALK (A.W) (L-H)
Friday, January 15

OFFICIAL GOING: Polytrack: standard

208a DUNDALK STADIUM ON FACEBOOK H'CAP 2m (P)
8:30 (8:33) 4-Y-O+ **£11,470** (£3,352; £1,588; £529)

RPR

1 **Saga Bolton (IRE)**7 112 4-8-9 **75**..................................(b) RoryCleary 7 81+
(Anthony Mullins, Ire) *chsd ldrs early: 7th 1/2-way: hdwy bhd ldrs 3f out: gng wl on outer 1 1/2f out: disp ins fnl f and rdn to ld narrowly: all out cl home where jnd: prevailed on line* **9/2**3

2 shd **Duchess Of Marmite (IRE)**37 8156 4-9-1 **81**.............(b) ShaneKelly 13 87+
(Richard Hughes) *w.w and racd keenly early: clsr in 9th at 1/2-way: gng wl in 9th into st and prog far side 1 1/2f out to chse ldrs: qcknd between horses ins fnl f to dispute under hands and heels cl home: hdd on line* **9/4**1

3 1 1/4 **Bittern (IRE)**49 8020 4-8-12 **78**... WayneLordan 3 83
(Emmet Mullins, Ire) *chsd ldrs: 3rd 1/2-way: tk clsr order and on terms fr 2f out: led u.p over 1f out: sn jnd and hdd ins fnl 100yds: no ex in 3rd cl home* **13/2**

4 1 3/4 **Pivot Bridge**97 6510 8-9-1 **74**... ConnorKing 6 77
(Adrian McGuinness, Ire) *on toes befhand: hld up: 8th 1/2-way: tk clsr order over 2f out and impr to chse ldrs over 1f out: kpt on same pce in 4th wl ins fnl f* **33/1**

5 3/4 **Jan Van Eyck (USA)**24 8353 6-8-7 **71**........................(bt) GaryHalpin(5) 1 73
(Gerard O'Leary, Ire) *chsd ldrs: n.m.r on inner after 1f and checked sltly: 5th at 1/2-way: rdn far side 2f out and tk clsr order bhd ldrs: no ex disputing 2nd ins fnl f: wknd clsng stages* **14/1**

6 nk **Taglietelle**27 7928 7-9-10 **83**..(b) PatSmullen 12 85
(Gordon Elliott, Ire) *hld up in tch: 6th 1/2-way: impr bhd ldrs 4f out: pushed along in 4th into st: sn rdn and no imp on ldrs over 1f out: one pce after* **5/1**

7 3 1/2 **Wither Hills (IRE)**20 8020 10-8-12 **71**........................(p) RonanWhelan 4 69
(Dermot Anthony McLoughlin, Ire) *chsd ldrs: 4th 1/2-way: disp ld briefly fr 6f out: rdn to ld 2f out: sn jnd and hdd u.p: wknd 1f out* **40/1**

8 1/2 **Asian Wing (IRE)**97 7124 7-9-0 **76**........................ RobbieDowney(3) 10 73
(John James Feane, Ire) *hld up towards rr: rdn over 2f out and sn no imp: kpt on one pce in 8th ins fnl f* **20/1**

9 4 1/2 **Modem**77 7493 6-9-3 **81**..(p) SeanCorby(5) 2 73
(Mrs John Harrington, Ire) *led and disp: in front bef 1/2-way: 2 l clr at 1/2-way: jnd briefly fr 6f out: rdn and hdd 2f out: sn wknd* **11/4**2

10 7 **Pacelli Road (IRE)**78 1534 7-8-9 **73**.........................(tp) TomMadden(5) 9 57
(J P Broderick, Ire) *hld up: 10th 1/2-way: rdn and no imp in rr appr st: one pce fnl 2f* **50/1**

11 3/4 **Egyptian Warrior (IRE)**261 6349 7-9-2 **80**..................(t) AnaO'Brien(5) 8 64
(A P O'Brien, Ire) *dwlt sltly: settled in 2nd bef 1/2-way: pushed along in 3rd over 4f out and wknd into st: eased 1 1/2f out* **25/1**

12 1 3/4 **Back Off Mate (IRE)**75 6510 8-9-3 **76**............................. ColinKeane 11 58
(A L T Moore, Ire) *dwlt and settled towards rr: last at 1/2-way: pushed along in 10th into st and no imp: eased fnl f* **40/1**

3m 27.07s (207.07)
WFA 4 from 6yo+ 7lb **12** Ran SP% **130.7**
CSF £15.79 CT £72.16 TOTE £5.70: £2.00, £1.70, £2.00; DF 21.90 Trifecta £97.20.
Owner Jean-Mary Saguin **Bred** Michael Kelly & Intense Focus Syndicate **Trained** Gowran, Co Kilkenny
■ Cardinal Palace was withdrawn. Price at time of withdrawal 16-1. Rule 4 does not apply.

FOCUS
There were some flops here but the first two are really progressive. It was a classy staying event. It's been rated around the balance of the first six.

209 - 210a (Foreign Racing) - See Raceform Interactive

^{169}CHELMSFORD (A.W) (L-H)

Saturday, January 16

OFFICIAL GOING: Polytrack: standard

Wind: Virtually nil Weather: dry, chilly

211 TOTEPLACEPOT MEDIAN AUCTION MAIDEN STKS 6f (P)

1:00 (1:02) (Class 5) 3-5-Y-O **£5,175** (£1,540; £769; £384) **Stalls** Centre

Form RPR

2-42 **1** **Figurante (IRE)**^{9} [77] 3-8-7 64 CathyGannon 1 65
(Jamie Osborne) *dwlt: in tch in last pair: hdwy 1/2-way: rdn and chal 1f out: led ins fnl f: styd on wl: rdn out* **7/4**^{2}

3-3 **2** ¾ **Rococoa (IRE)**^{7} [126] 3-8-7 0 LukeMorris 5 63
(Ed Walker) *chsd ldrs: swtchd rt and effrt over 1f out: hrd drvn and ev ch ins fnl f: styd on same pce fnl 75yds* **11/10**^{1}

40-4 **3** ½ **Ten Rocks**^{4} [152] 3-8-5 67 (b) JordanUys$^{(7)}$ 2 66
(Brian Meehan) *bustled along and sn led: rdn over 1f out: hdd ins fnl f: styd on same pce fnl 100yds* **16/1**

65-3 **4** 1½ **Zebedee's Girl (IRE)**^{10} [74] 3-8-0 62 (v^{1}) JosephineGordon$^{(7)}$ 4 56
(David Evans) *chsd ldr tl no ex u.p over 1f out: wknd ins fnl f* **10/1**

2-5 **5** 29 **Tilsworth Micky**^{9} [77] 4-10-0 0 AdamBeschizza 3
(J R Jenkins) *dwlt: sn niggled along and outpcd in rr: lost tch over 1f out: eased ins fnl f: burst blood vessel* **8/1**^{3}

1m 11.6s (-2.10) **Going Correction** -0.30s/f (Stan)
WFA 3 from 4yo 16lb **5** Ran SP% **110.1**
Speed ratings (Par 103): **102,101,100,98,59**
CSF £4.03 TOTE £2.60: £1.20, £1.10; EX 4.10 Trifecta £29.90.
Owner The Hon A Blyth **Bred** Mount Coote Stud **Trained** Upper Lambourn, Berks

FOCUS
The opening contest was an ordinary maiden. They went a decent gallop on standard Polytrack. The runner-up has been rated close to form.

212 TOTEPOOLLIVEINFO.COM H'CAP 1m 2f (P)

1:35 (1:36) (Class 5) (0-75,75) 4-Y-O+ **£5,175** (£1,540; £769; £384) **Stalls** Low

Form RPR

05-4 **1** **Freud (FR)**^{12} [38] 6-8-13 70 GeorgeDowning$^{(3)}$ 2 78+
(Ian Williams) *stdd s: t.k.h: hld up in tch: clsd to chse ldrs and rdn over 1f out: led 150yds out: r.o wl: rdn out* **9/4**^{1}

120- **2** ¾ **Comanche Chieftain (CAN)**^{50} [8017] 4-8-10 66 (p) AndrewMullen 5 72
(Michael Appleby) *led: rdn over 2f out: hdd 1f out: kpt on u.p ins fnl f* **14/1**

261- **3** ½ **Enriching (USA)**^{70} [7749] 8-8-7 68 JosephineGordon$^{(7)}$ 6 73
(Robyn Brisland) *chsd ldr: rdn and ev ch over 2f out: drvn to ld 1f out: sn hdd and no ex fnl 150yds* **8/1**

00-4 **4** 1 **Tyrsal (IRE)**^{13} [33] 5-8-12 66 JimmyQuinn 4 69
(Clifford Lines) *stdd s: hld up in tch in last trio: effrt and hdwy over 1f out: styd on u.p ins fnl f: nt rch ldrs* **16/1**

152- **5** nse **Pink Ribbon (IRE)**^{52} [7973] 4-8-12 68 (p) LukeMorris 1 71
(Sylvester Kirk) *t.k.h: chsd ldrs: rdn and unable qck over 2f out: hrd drvn and rallied 1f out: swtchd rt and kpt on wl ins fnl f* **4/1**^{2}

352- **6** 2 **Marmalad (IRE)**^{36} [8176] 4-8-8 69 CallumShepherd$^{(5)}$ 3 68
(Shaun Lycett) *in tch in midfield: effrt u.p over 1f out: kpt on same pce and no imp ins fnl f* **10/1**

0-23 **7** 2½ **Boonga Roogeta**^{10} [72] 7-9-4 75 MarcMonaghan$^{(3)}$ 8 69
(Peter Charalambous) *hld up in tch in last trio: effrt over 1f out: kpt on but no real imp: nvr trbld ldrs* **5/1**^{3}

600- **8** 8 **First Sargeant**^{89} [7338] 6-8-11 70 (p) PatrickO'Donnell$^{(5)}$ 9 48
(Lawrence Mullaney) *in tch in midfield: dropped to last trio but stl in tch 5f out: rdn over 2f out: sn btn: lost tch over 1f out* **10/1**

350- **9** 1 **Topamichi**^{45} [8081] 6-9-6 74 SaleemGolam 7 50
(Mark H Tompkins) *stdd s: t.k.h: hdwy to chse ldrs after 2f: rdn and lost pl over 2f out: bhd over 1f out* **8/1**

2m 4.41s (-4.19) **Going Correction** -0.30s/f (Stan)
WFA 4 from 5yo+ 2lb **9** Ran SP% **120.4**
Speed ratings (Par 103): **104,103,103,102,102 100,98,92,91**
CSF £38.49 CT £224.87 TOTE £4.00: £1.60, £4.90, £2.70; EX 43.80 Trifecta £419.40.
Owner J Tredwell **Bred** E Puerari, Oceanic Bloodstock Et Al **Trained** Portway, Worcs

FOCUS
A fair handicap. They went a respectable gallop. Muddling form, with the first two closely matched on November C&D form, and the fourth rated close to his C&D latest.

213 TOTEQUADPOT H'CAP 5f (P)

2:10 (2:11) (Class 3) (0-95,94) 4-Y-O+ **£10,350** (£3,080; £1,539; £769) **Stalls** Low

Form RPR

22-0 **1** **Royal Birth**^{8} [106] 5-8-10 83 (t) PatCosgrave 7 93
(Stuart Williams) *rrd as stalls opened and slowly away: t.k.h: hld up in tch in last trio: hdwy and swtchd rt 1f out: str run ins fnl f to ld fnl 75yds: sn in command* **5/1**^{3}

653- **2** ¾ **Dynamo Walt (IRE)**^{54} [7958] 5-9-3 90 (v) MartinLane 6 97
(Derek Shaw) *in tch in midfield: effrt over 1f out: nt clr run and swtchd rt ent fnl f: ev ch ins fnl f: wnt 2nd and kpt on same pce fnl 50yds* **7/1**

005- **3** 1 **Pearl Acclaim (IRE)**^{45} [8072] 6-8-9 82 AdrianNicholls 8 85
(David Nicholls) *w ldr: rdn 2f out: drvn to ld over 1f out: drifted rt u.p 1f out: hdd and no ex fnl 75yds* **20/1**

/01- **4** ½ **Judicial (IRE)**^{66} [7791] 4-9-7 94 (e) LukeMorris 4 96
(Julie Camacho) *taken down early: dwlt: sn rcvrd and wl in tch in midfield: effrt over 1f out: ev ch ins fnl f: no ex fnl 75yds* **7/2**^{1}

20-5 **5** 1 **Vimy Ridge**^{14} [17] 4-8-7 87 (p) LuluStanford$^{(7)}$ 1 85
(Alan Bailey) *in tch in midfield: rdn and hdwy on inner over 1f out: pressing ldrs ins fnl f: no ex and outpcd fnl 100yds* **14/1**

22-3 **6** hd **Brother Tiger**^{15} [4] 7-9-2 89 MartinHarley 3 86
(David C Griffiths) *taken down early: chsd ldrs: rdn over 1f out: drvn and unable qck 1f out: wknd fnl 100yds* **9/2**^{2}

512- **7** shd **Stake Acclaim (IRE)**^{119} [6540] 4-9-0 87 RobertWinston 10 84
(Dean Ivory) *chsd ldrs: rdn and unable qck over 1f out: wknd ins fnl f* **5/1**^{3}

001- **8** ¾ **Seve**^{25} [8347] 4-9-4 91 RichardKingscote 2 85
(Tom Dascombe) *taken down early: led: rdn 2f out: hdd and no ex over 1f out: wknd ins fnl f* **8/1**

561- **9** 1½ **Red Stripes (USA)**^{20} [8368] 4-8-7 87 JordanUys$^{(7)}$ 5 76
(Brian Meehan) *sn outpcd in last trio: hdwy but hanging lft over 1f out: kpt on same pce ins fnl f: nvr trbld ldrs* **12/1**

025- **10** 1¾ **It Must Be Faith**^{20} [8368] 6-9-0 87 AndrewMullen 9 70
(Michael Appleby) *in tch in midfield: effrt over 1f out: keeping on same pce whn hmpd 1f out: nt rcvr and wknd ins fnl f: burst blood vessel* **25/1**

620- **11** 1 **Air Of York (IRE)**^{17} [8395] 4-8-8 88 GeorgiaCox$^{(7)}$ 12 67
(David Evans) *swtchd lft after s: bhd: wnt bdly rt bnd over 3f out: nvr on terms after* **50/1**

58.04s (-2.16) **Going Correction** -0.30s/f (Stan) **11** Ran SP% **122.3**
Speed ratings (Par 107): **105,103,102,101,99 99,99,98,95,92 91**
CSF £40.83 CT £661.00 TOTE £9.90: £2.00, £3.60, £8.80; EX 51.20 Trifecta £2320.80.
Owner The Morley Family **Bred** Old Mill Stud & S Williams & J Parry **Trained** Newmarket, Suffolk

FOCUS
A decent sprint handicap. They went a proper gallop. A small pb from the runner-up.

214 TOTEEXACTA FILLIES' CONDITIONS STKS (ALL-WEATHER CHAMPIONSHIP FAST TRACK QUALIFIER) 7f (P)

2:45 (2:46) (Class 2) 4-Y-O+

£18,675 (£5,592; £2,796; £1,398; £699; £351) **Stalls** Low

Form RPR

214- **1** **Volunteer Point (IRE)**^{20} [8374] 4-9-0 98 GrahamGibbons 3 104
(Mick Channon) *stdd after s: hld up in tch in rr: shkn up 2f out: clsd to chse ldrs and swtchd rt over 1f out: r.o wl ins fnl f to ld cl home* **7/1**^{3}

121- **2** nk **My Call**^{35} [8205] 4-9-0 95 MartinHarley 2 103
(Saeed bin Suroor) *chsd ldrs: swtchd rt wl over 1f out: sn rdn to chal: drvn to ld 150yds out: kpt on u.p tl hdd and no ex cl home* **2/1**^{2}

13-1 **3** 1 **Lamar (IRE)**^{7} [125] 5-9-3 106 LukeMorris 6 103
(James Tate) *chsd ldr: rdn over 2f out: drvn to ld over 1f out: hdd 150yds out: no ex and styd on same pce after* **4/5**^{1}

353- **4** 6 **Secret Hint**^{40} [8140] 5-9-0 90 LiamKeniry 4 85
(Andrew Balding) *hld up in tch: rdn whn carried rt and hmpd wl over 1f out: no imp u.p over 1f out: wknd 1f out* **20/1**

004- **5** 1 **Maggie Pink**^{40} [8140] 7-9-0 87 AndrewMullen 1 82
(Michael Appleby) *led: rdn ent fnl 2f: hdd and no ex over 1f out: sn btn: wknd fnl f* **33/1**

40- **6** 3½ **Spicy Jam**^{29} [8288] 4-9-6 94 PatCosgrave 5 79
(Marco Botti) *t.k.h: hld up in tch: effrt but forced wd bnd wl over 1f out: sn bhd and wknd over 1f out* **20/1**

1m 23.23s (-3.97) **Going Correction** -0.30s/f (Stan) course record **6** Ran SP% **113.9**
Speed ratings (Par 96): **110,109,108,101,100 96**
CSF £21.31 TOTE £7.50: £3.40, £1.30; EX 16.90 Trifecta £26.60.
Owner Box 41 **Bred** G Strawbridge & London Thoroughbred Services Ltd **Trained** West Ilsley, Berks

■ Stewards' Enquiry : Martin Harley two-day ban; careless riding (30th Jan - 1st Feb)

FOCUS
A good-quality fillies' conditions contest. They went a decent gallop and the course-record time was lowered. A pb from the winner, with the third a bit off.

215 WILLIAM HILL DOWNLOAD THE APP H'CAP 1m 2f (P)

3:20 (3:20) (Class 2) (0-105,101) 4-Y-O+

£18,675 (£5,592; £2,796; £1,398; £699; £351) **Stalls** Low

Form RPR

002- **1** **Our Channel (USA)**^{28} [8311] 5-9-4 95 (p) PatCosgrave 7 106
(William Haggas) *taken down early: trckd ldng pair: clsd and travelling best whn swtchd rt wl over 1f out: led over 1f out: rdn and r.o wl ins fnl f* **7/1**^{3}

204- **2** 1¾ **Afonso De Sousa (USA)**^{21} [8359] 6-9-9 100 DanielTudhope 6 107
(David O'Meara) *in tch in midfield: effrt to chse ldrs and nudged rt wl over 1f out: pressed wnr over 1f out: kpt on same pce ins fnl f* **5/1**^{2}

30/6 **3** 3¼ **Whispering Warrior (IRE)**^{13} [31] 7-9-2 93 TomEaves 3 94
(David Simcock) *stdd s: hld up in rr: clsd over 2f out: swtchd lft and rdn to chse ldrs over 1f out: 3rd and btn 1f out: wknd ins fnl f* **3/1**^{1}

000- **4** 6 **Sirius Prospect (USA)**^{175} [4618] 8-9-10 101 RobertWinston 5 90
(Dean Ivory) *stdd s: t.k.h: hld up in 5th: clsd over 2f out: rdn whn pushed lft over 1f out: 4th and btn 1f out: wknd ins fnl f* **7/1**^{3}

02-1 **5** 4 **Luv U Whatever**^{14} [19] 6-9-6 97 AndrewMullen 2 78
(Michael Appleby) *led: rdn over 2f out: hdd over 1f out: sn btn: wknd fnl f* **3/1**^{1}

/0-3 **6** 1½ **Pearl Spectre (USA)**^{14} [18] 5-8-5 82 oh5 CathyGannon 4 60
(Andrew Balding) *w ldr: rdn over 2f out: btn over 1f out: wknd fnl f* **5/1**^{2}

62-6 **7** 46 **Captain Felix**^{9} [88] 4-8-3 82 oh7 LukeMorris 1
(Gay Kelleway) *hld up in last pair: strrugling whn hung rt over 3f out: sn lost tch and eased: t.o* **16/1**

2m 2.4s (-6.20) **Going Correction** -0.30s/f (Stan)
WFA 4 from 5yo+ 2lb **7** Ran SP% **114.2**
Speed ratings (Par 109): **112,110,108,103,100 98,62**
CSF £41.20 TOTE £4.90: £1.50, £2.70; EX 40.50 Trifecta £112.20.
Owner Abdulla Al Mansoori **Bred** Bluegrass Hall Llc **Trained** Newmarket, Suffolk

FOCUS
A good handicap. They went another decent gallop. The first two have been rated close to their best.

216 CORAL.CO.UK H'CAP 1m (P)

3:55 (3:55) (Class 6) (0-55,54) 4-Y-O+ **£3,234** (£962; £481; £240) **Stalls** Low

Form RPR

0/0- **1** **De Lesseps (USA)**^{18} [8388] 8-8-5 45 VitorSantos$^{(7)}$ 6 55
(John David Riches) *stdd and dropped in bhd after s: hld up in rr: hdwy and swtchd rt jst over 1f out: str run to ld fnl 100yds: sn clr: readily* **33/1**

56-3 **2** 2½ **Ela Goog La Mou**^{13} [32] 7-9-3 53 MarcMonaghan$^{(3)}$ 2 57
(Peter Charalambous) *hld up in tch in midfield: hdwy u.p to chse ldrs over 1f out: kpt on ins fnl f to go 2nd cl home* **5/1**^{2}

542- **3** nk **Hold Firm**^{30} [8264] 4-9-2 54 CallumShepherd$^{(5)}$ 1 57
(Mark H Tompkins) *chsd ldrs: cl 3rd and swtchd rt 2f out: drvn and ev ch over 1f out: led 150yds out: sn hdd and styd on same pce after: lost 2nd cl home* **6/4**^{1}

00-5 **4** nse **Je T'Aime Encore**^{13} [32] 4-9-4 51 LukeMorris 3 54
(Gay Kelleway) *in tch in midfield: effrt and swtchd lft over 1f out: kpt on u.p ins fnl f* **8/1**^{3}

40-2 **5** ¾ **Schottische**^{3} [158] 6-8-13 53 (p) LuluStanford$^{(7)}$ 9 54
(Alan Bailey) *chsd ldrs: wnt 2nd 1/2-way: lost 2nd over 1f out but stl pressing ldr: no ex u.p ins fnl f: wknd towards fin* **5/1**^{2}

50-6 **6** ¾ **Menelik (IRE)**^{10} [60] 7-9-5 52 (bt) LiamKeniry 8 52
(Des Donovan, Ire) *t.k.h: led: rdn over 1f out: hdd 150yds out: no ex and btn whn short of room wl ins fnl f: wknd towards fin* **12/1**

06-0 **7** 2¾ **Ambitious Rosie**^{12} [35] 5-8-9 45 (p) GeorgeDowning$^{(3)}$ 5 38
(Tony Carroll) *hld up in tch in last trio: effrt over 1f out: no imp 1f out: wknd ins fnl f* **50/1**

00-0 **8** 2¼ **Waterloo Dock**^{12} [35] 11-8-5 45 (v) NicolaGrundy$^{(7)}$ 4 33
(James Unett) *hld up in tch in last pair: effrt towards inner over 1f out: no imp 1f out: wknd ins fnl f* **40/1**

43-1 **9** 1 ½ **Gulland Rock**[12] 35 5-8-13 **53**.................................. RhiainIngram(7) 7 37
(Anthony Carson) *chsd ldr tl 1/2-way: lost pl over 2f out: no imp u.p over 1f out: wknd ins fnl f* **5/1**[2]

644- **10** 6 **Marmooz**[18] 8388 4-8-12 **45**.. AndrewMullen 10 15
(Michael Appleby) *in tch in midfield: rdn and struggling 2f out: lost pl and bhd over 1f out: wknd* **20/1**

1m 38.74s (-1.16) **Going Correction** -0.30s/f (Stan) **10** Ran SP% **120.9**
Speed ratings (Par 101): **93,90,90,90,89 88,85,83,82,76**
CSF £192.80 CT £422.91 TOTE £64.50: £14.80, £3.10, £1.10; EX 508.60 Trifecta £1960.70.
Owner J W Barrett **Bred** Darley **Trained** Pilling, Lancashire

FOCUS
A moderate handicap. They went a respectable gallop. The winner has been rated to his 2014 level, with the form straightforward in behind.

217 CHELMSFORD CITY RACECOURSE 1ST ANNIVERSARY H'CAP 5f (P)
4:25 (4:25) (Class 7) (0-50,50) 4-Y-O+ **£2,587** (£770; £384; £192) **Stalls** Low

Form RPR

00-6 **1** **Red Flute**[6] 136 4-9-0 **46**..(v) TimClark(3) 7 51
(Denis Quinn) *led: rdn over 1f out: hdd ins fnl f: kpt on: led again on post* **16/1**

300- **2** nse **Spray Tan**[17] 8400 6-9-5 **48**...(b) LukeMorris 3 53
(Tony Carroll) *chsd ldrs: swtchd rt and effrt to chse ldr over 1f out: led ins fnl f: sn hung bdly rt: hdd on post* **5/1**[3]

066/ **3** ¾ **Rutterkin (USA)**[482] 6580 8-8-9 **45**.................................. VitorSantos(7) 1 47
(John David Riches) *dwlt: hld up in midfield: hdwy to chse ldrs over 1f out: kpt on same pce ins fnl f* **25/1**

50-6 **4** ½ **Seraphima**[10] 75 6-8-11 **45**.................................(p) ShirleyTeasdale(5) 8 45
(Lisa Williamson) *hld up in midfield: shkn up and sltly impeded over 1f out: hdwy ent fnl f: swtchd lft ins fnl f: kpt on: nt rch ldrs* **16/1**

06-0 **5** 1 ¼ **Black Vale (IRE)**[2] 174 5-8-11 **47**....................(bt) JosephineGordon(7) 6 43
(Phil McEntee) *dwlt: towards rr: hdwy u.p ent fnl f: kpt on: no threat to ldrs* **9/4**[2]

45-3 **6** 1 ¼ **Single Summit**[15] 5 4-9-3 **46**...............................(v) AdamBeschizza 9 37
(J R Jenkins) *sn pushed along in last trio: drvn and hdwy ent fnl f: kpt on: nvr trbld ldrs* **10/1**

006- **7** 3 **Willow Spring**[152] 5440 4-9-4 **47**.. TomEaves 5 28
(Conrad Allen) *stdd s: t.k.h: hld up in rr: rdn and hdwy on inner over 1f out: no imp ins fnl f: wknd fnl 75yds* **20/1**

204- **8** ¾ **Anfield**[108] 6848 5-9-2 **45**.. PatCosgrave 2 23
(Mick Quinn) *w wnr: hung rt bnd over 3f out: lost pl and rdn over 1f out: no ex: wknd ins fnl f* **8/1**

06-3 **9** 5 **Midnight Destiny (IRE)**[11] 46 4-9-7 **50**......................(v) MartinLane 4 10
(Derek Shaw) *chsd ldrs: lost pl u.p and swtchd lft over 1f out: wknd fnl f: burst blood vessel* **2/1**[1]

59.74s (-0.46) **Going Correction** -0.30s/f (Stan) **9** Ran SP% **121.3**
Speed ratings (Par 97): **91,90,89,88,86 84,80,78,70**
CSF £98.63 CT £2053.27 TOTE £18.80: £3.90, £2.10, £6.10; EX 156.80 Trifecta £296.50.
Owner Tariq Al Nisf **Bred** D R Tucker **Trained** Newmarket, Suffolk
■ Stewards' Enquiry : Tim Clark two-day ban; used whip above the permitted level (31st Jan - 1st Feb)

FOCUS
The concluding contest was another moderate sprint handicap. They went a respectable gallop. Weak form.
T/Jkpt: Not won. Jackpot placepot: Part won. £2,457.90 to a £1 stake. Pool of £3,367.11 - 0.30 winning units. T/Plt: £150.40 to a £1 stake. Pool: £54,884.34 - 266.26 winning tickets T/Qpdt: £55.80 to a £1 stake. Pool: £4,777.72 - 63.30 winning tickets **Steve Payne**

190 LINGFIELD (L-H)
Saturday, January 16

OFFICIAL GOING: Polytrack: standard
Wind: Light; across Weather: Fine

218 CORAL.CO.UK CLASSIFIED (S) STKS 1m 4f (P)
1:10 (1:11) (Class 6) 4-6-Y-O **£2,264** (£673; £336; £168) **Stalls** Low

Form RPR

06-4 **1** **Sonnythenavigator (USA)**[10] 55 4-9-3 56..........(p) FergusSweeney 5 62
(David Simcock) *hld up in last: stl there over 2f out as ldrs kicked for home: urged along and prog over 1f out but making heavy weather of it: rdn and r.o fnl f to ld last 75yds* **3/1**[2]

302- **2** 1 ¼ **What A Party (IRE)**[31] 8252 4-9-3 58..............................(v) AdamKirby 4 60
(Gay Kelleway) *trckd ldr: rdn to ld over 2f out: kpt on u.p but hdd and outpcd last 75yds* **4/1**

561- **3** 3 **Turnbury**[31] 8252 5-9-7 60...(p) KierenFox 2 55
(Laura Mongan) *led at mod pce: kicked on 3f out: hdd over 2f out: lost 2nd and fdd jst ins fnl f* **7/4**[1]

605- **4** 1 ½ **Isabella Liberty (FR)**[35] 2570 5-9-7 64..........................(tp) JoeFanning 3 53
(Gordon Elliott, Ire) *trckd ldrs: rdn 3f out: outpcd over 2f out: no imp after* **10/1**

436- **5** nse **Sacred Square (GER)**[27] 8238 6-9-7 70......................(p) GeorgeBaker 1 53
(Conor Dore) *trckd ldrs: urged along and no great rspnse over 2f out: wl hld after: one pce* **7/2**[3]

2m 34.56s (1.56) **Going Correction** -0.125s/f (Stan)
WFA 4 from 5yo+ 4lb **5** Ran SP% **112.7**
Speed ratings: **89,88,86,85,85**
CSF £15.27 TOTE £4.90: £2.60, £2.20; EX 17.50 Trifecta £48.90.There was no bid for the winner
Owner Oliver Brendon **Bred** Runnymede Farm Inc & Catesby W Clay **Trained** Newmarket, Suffolk

FOCUS
A moderate seller. Weak form.

219 32RED.COM MAIDEN STKS 1m 1y(P)
1:45 (1:47) (Class 5) 3-Y-O **£2,911** (£866; £432; £216) **Stalls** High

Form RPR

0- **1** **Telegram**[116] 6628 3-9-5 0.. SeanLevey 4 84
(Richard Hannon) *trckd ldrs: cl up over 2f out: shkn up to ld over 1f out: sn clr* **16/1**

2 5 **Ragner** 3-9-5 0.. FergusSweeney 9 73
(David Simcock) *settled in midfield: prog over 2f out but nt on terms w ldng quartet: shkn up over 1f out: styd on steadily to take 2nd last 75yds* **14/1**

2 **3** 1 ¼ **Byres Road**[12] 40 3-9-5 0.. JoeFanning 6 70
(Mark Johnston) *led to over 3f out: sn shkn up: led again briefly wl over 1f out: sn btn: lost 2nd last 75yds* **7/4**[1]

00- **4** 1 ¼ **Assisted**[25] 8349 3-9-5 0.. StevieDonohoe 2 67
(George Peckham) *chsd ldrs: rdn over 3f out: clsd on outer 2f out: ch of 2nd pl 1f out: fdd* **100/1**

334- **5** 6 **Broadway Icon**[16] 8410 3-9-5 80.............................(v[1]) TimmyMurphy 3 53
(Jeremy Noseda) *trckd ldr: led over 3f out gng easily: rdn 2f out: fnd nil and sn hdd: wknd qckly* **9/4**[2]

0- **6** 1 **Mischief Maisy (IRE)**[16] 8410 3-9-0 0............................ RobertHavlin 11 46
(Amanda Perrett) *chsd ldrs: rdn and lft bhd fr 3f out: no ch after* **50/1**

6 **7** ¾ **Betsalottie**[10] 65 3-9-5 0.. WilliamCarson 8 49
(John Bridger) *hld up in last: long way off the pce 3f out: pushed along and fin to sme effect fnl f* **100/1**

0- **8** shd **Milyaar (IRE)**[33] 8225 3-9-5 0... GeorgeBaker 5 49
(Roger Teal) *a towards rr: outpcd over 3f out: pushed along and nvr on terms after* **33/1**

9 3 ¼ **Attitude Rocks** 3-9-5 0.. AdamKirby 7 42
(Clive Cox) *slowly away: nvr able to make any significant grnd: rdn and lft bhd fr over 3f out* **4/1**[3]

10 10 **Plymouth Mo** 3-9-0 0.. AliceMills(5) 10 19
(Rod Millman) *dwlt: racd on outer: struggling fr 1/2-way: t.o* **66/1**

1m 35.91s (-2.29) **Going Correction** -0.125s/f (Stan) **10** Ran SP% **108.1**
Speed ratings (Par 97): **106,101,99,98,92 91,90,90,87,77**
CSF £179.38 TOTE £19.60: £2.90, £2.60, £1.10; EX 211.70 Trifecta £1135.60.
Owner Mohamed Saeed Al Shahi **Bred** Langton Stud **Trained** East Everleigh, Wilts
■ Beleave was withdrawn. Price at time of withdrawal 10-1. Rule 4 applies to all bets - deduction 5p in the pound.
■ Stewards' Enquiry : Joe Fanning one-day ban; did not keep straight from the stalls (30th Jan)

FOCUS
Not a strong maiden but a nice performance from the winner. The winner has been rated as taking a big step up, but the form is a bit fluid in behind. The third has been rated close to his debut form.

220 UNIBET.CO.UK DAILY ENHANCED PRICE TERMS H'CAP 6f 1y(P)
2:20 (2:20) (Class 3) (0-95,94) 4-Y-O **£7,246** (£2,168; £1,084; £542; £270) **Stalls** Low

Form RPR

12- **1** **Hold Tight**[79] 7588 4-9-0 **90**.................................... AlistairRawlinson(3) 5 101+
(Saeed bin Suroor) *nt that wl away: hld up in last pair: stl last over 2f out: prog between rivals over 1f out: rdn to ld ins fnl f: styd on wl and a holding runner-up* **8/13**[1]

011- **2** nk **Boomerang Bob (IRE)**[17] 8395 7-9-7 **94**...................... WilliamCarson 2 104
(Jamie Osborne) *hld up in last pair: clsd 2f out: rdn to ld jst over 1f out: hdd ins fnl f: styd on wl but a hld* **3/1**[2]

601- **3** 3 ½ **Luis Vaz De Torres (IRE)**[19] 8382 4-8-9 **82**..................... JackGarritty 1 81
(Richard Fahey) *trckd ldrs: effrt on inner to chal over 1f out: easily lft bhd by ldng pair fnl f* **8/1**[3]

66-5 **4** 1 ½ **Normal Equilibrium**[9] 86 6-9-1 **88**..............................(p) AdamKirby 6 82
(Robert Cowell) *fast away fr wd draw: led: hdd & wknd jst over 1f out* **20/1**

24-5 **5** 1 **Apache Storm**[15] 4 4-9-0 **87**... LiamJones 4 78
(Michael Appleby) *t.k.h: sn trckd ldr: rdn to chal 2f out: wknd jst over 1f out* **16/1**

333- **6** 3 ½ **Sandfrankskipsgo**[25] 8347 7-8-12 **85**................................ ShaneKelly 3 65
(Peter Crate) *t.k.h: trckd ldrs: cl up whn wdst of all bnd 2f out and dropped to last: nudged along and wknd* **25/1**

1m 9.95s (-1.95) **Going Correction** -0.125s/f (Stan) **6** Ran SP% **112.5**
Speed ratings (Par 107): **108,107,102,100,99 94**
CSF £2.71 TOTE £1.70: £1.40, £1.30; EX 3.20 Trifecta £8.20.
Owner Godolphin **Bred** Manor Farm Stud (rutland) **Trained** Newmarket, Suffolk

FOCUS
The winner and second settled better than most but this is still decent form and they need keeping on side. The runner-up has been rated back to last year's best.

221 LADBROKES H'CAP 1m 1y(P)
2:55 (2:55) (Class 2) (0-105,97) 4-Y-O **£11,971** (£3,583; £1,791; £896; £446) **Stalls** High

Form RPR

031- **1** **Forceful Appeal (USA)**[38] 8161 8-8-9 **88**.......................... JackDuern(3) 1 96
(Simon Dow) *hld up in rr: prog wl over 1f out and urged along: clsd fnl f: rdn to ld last 50yds: kpt on wl* **7/1**

326- **2** nk **Mutawathea**[133] 6089 5-9-7 **97**......................................(p) RobertHavlin 5 104
(Simon Crisford) *trckd ldr after 2f: shkn up 2f out: led 1f out: hdd fnl 50yds: kpt on but jst hld* **5/2**[2]

2/6- **3** ½ **Truth Or Dare**[134] 6041 5-9-0 **90**.. MartinDwyer 7 96
(William Muir) *hld up in last: urged along and prog over 1f out: nt clr run briefly ins fnl f: styd on but nvr quite rchd ldng pair* **25/1**

403- **4** nk **Melvin The Grate (IRE)**[19] 8380 6-9-2 **92**......................... AdamKirby 6 97
(Andrew Balding) *dwlt: hld up in rr: shkn up over 2f out: prog over 1f out: rdn and kpt on fnl f but nvr able to chal* **7/4**[1]

025- **5** 1 ½ **Robert The Painter (IRE)**[40] 8139 8-8-7 **83**...............(v) JoeFanning 4 85
(Lee Carter) *led at gd pce: rdn and hdd 1f out: wknd* **16/1**

451- **6** 3 ¾ **Intrude**[124] 6389 4-9-0 **90**... FergusSweeney 2 83
(David Simcock) *chsd ldrs: rdn and no prog over 2f out: wknd over 1f out* **4/1**[3]

11-5 **7** hd **Westwood Hoe**[11] 50 5-9-2 **92**.................................... DougieCostello 3 85
(Tony Coyle) *chsd ldr 2f: rdn 3f out: wknd over 1f out* **14/1**

305- **8** 16 **Athletic**[21] 8359 7-8-9 **85**...(v) JFEgan 8 41
(Andrew Reid) *dwlt: t.k.h: racd on outer in midfield: rdn over 3f out: wknd over 2f out: t.o* **25/1**

1m 35.02s (-3.18) **Going Correction** -0.125s/f (Stan) **8** Ran SP% **117.7**
Speed ratings (Par 109): **110,109,109,108,107 103,103,87**
CSF £25.69 CT £416.91 TOTE £8.70: £3.50, £1.10, £9.50; EX 26.20 Trifecta £223.00.
Owner Mark McAllister **Bred** Juddmonte Farms Inc **Trained** Ashtead, Surrey

FOCUS
A decent, competitive handicap. Sound form, with the winner and runner-up rated back to their best.

222 CORAL H'CAP 1m 2f (P)
3:30 (3:31) (Class 6) (0-60,60) 4-Y-O+ **£2,264** (£673; £336; £168) **Stalls** Low

Form RPR

03-6 **1** **Attain**[10] 55 7-9-3 **59**...(t) ShelleyBirkett(3) 6 66
(Julia Feilden) *trckd ldrs and a wl plcd: shkn up and clsd over 1f out: led ins fnl f: styd on wl* **7/1**

000- **2** 1 **Runaiocht (IRE)**[32] 8228 6-9-3 **56**.................................(b) JimmyQuinn 1 61
(Paul Burgoyne) *trckd ldrs: effrt on inner wl over 1f out: drvn and styd on fnl f to take 2nd last 75yds: unable to chal* **7/1**

0/6- **3** 1 **Black Minstrel (IRE)**[27] 8317 7-9-2 **60**.................(p) CiaranMckee(5) 11 63
(John O'Shea) *dwlt: rcvrd to chse ldr after 2f: rdn 2f out: led over 1f out tl ins fnl f: one pce and lost 2nd sn after* **20/1**

234- **4** 1/2 **Tommys Geal**[32] 8228 4-9-3 **58** AdamKirby 2 60
(Michael Madgwick) *hld up in midfield: drvn over 2f out: clsd on ldrs u.p over 1f out: one pce fnl f* **5/1**[2]
04-4 **5** 3/4 **Rennie Mackintosh (IRE)**[10] 62 4-9-3 **58** WilliamCarson 3 59
(John Bridger) *trckd ldr 2f: styd prom: rdn over 2f out: cl up bhd ldrs 1f out: one pce after* **6/1**[3]
11- **6** nk **Dove Mountain (IRE)**[8] 111 5-9-7 **60** (tp) TimmyMurphy 8 62
(Gordon Elliott, Ire) *stdd s: hld up in last trio: stl there over 2f out: effrt over 1f out but sed to hang once rdn: styd on nr fin: no ch* **7/4**[1]
000- **7** nk **Engai (GER)**[17] 8398 10-8-13 **52** DougieCostello 5 54
(David Bridgwater) *hld up towards rr: trying to make prog on inner whn nt clr run over 1f out and lost all ch: styd on fnl 100yds* **66/1**
052- **8** 2 **Malih**[17] 8397 7-8-13 **52** JoeyHaynes 12 48
(Eric Wheeler) *in tch in midfield: rdn over 2f out: kpt on fr over 1f out but nvr able to threaten* **16/1**
206- **9** 1 3/4 **Daring Indian**[17] 7983 8-9-3 **56** (p) GeorgeBaker 4 49
(Roger Teal) *stdd s: hld up in last pair: stl there 2f out: pushed along and no real prog: nvr involved* **25/1**
006- **10** hd **Understory (USA)**[17] 8398 9-9-0 **53** (b) JoeFanning 10 45
(Tim McCarthy) *led: rdn over 2f out: hdd & wknd over 1f out* **16/1**
205- **11** 1 **Rainford Glory (IRE)**[58] 7909 6-9-6 **59** (p) DavidNolan 7 49
(Tim Fitzgerald) *chsd ldrs: rdn 3f out: no prog 2f out: wknd over 1f out* **16/1**
00-5 **12** 3 1/2 **Little Big Man**[10] 60 5-8-11 **50** StevieDonohoe 9 34
(Brendan Powell) *s.s: t.k.h early: hld up in last pair: pushed along and wknd over 2f out* **25/1**

2m 4.41s (-2.19) **Going Correction** -0.125s/f (Stan)
WFA 4 from 5yo+ 2lb **12** Ran SP% **123.9**
Speed ratings (Par 101): **103,102,101,101,100 100,99,98,96,96 95,93**
CSF £55.68 CT £960.25 TOTE £10.00: £4.10, £3.80, £5.10; EX 69.90 Trifecta £2144.10.
Owner Newmarket Equine Tours Racing Club **Bred** Millsec Limited **Trained** Exning, Suffolk

FOCUS
A moderate handicap. The runner-up has been rated near his best from last year.

223 32RED.COM FILLIES' H'CAP 1m 1y(P)
4:00 (4:01) (Class 5) (0-75,73) 4-Y-O+ **£2,911** (£866; £432; £216) **Stalls** High

Form RPR
60-2 **1** **Quite Smart (IRE)**[9] 80 4-9-4 **70** (v) AdamKirby 2 76
(Robert Cowell) *mde all: kicked on wl over 2f out and sn had rest at full stretch: drvn over 1f out: kpt on wl* **7/2**[2]
036- **2** 1 1/2 **Free Running (IRE)**[141] 5826 4-9-6 **72** [1] RobertHavlin 5 74
(Simon Crisford) *t.k.h: trckd wnr: rdn over 2f out: nt qckn and no real imp over 1f out: kpt on* **4/6**[1]
52-3 **3** hd **Ixelles Diamond (IRE)**[9] 80 5-9-4 **70** JFEgan 4 72
(Andrew Reid) *hld up in 4th: shkn up wl over 2f out: no prog tl r.o fnl f to press for 2nd nr fin* **7/1**[3]
360- **4** 1 3/4 **Cascading Stars (IRE)**[31] 8248 4-9-7 **73** LiamJones 3 71
(J S Moore) *chsd ldng pair: rdn to dispute 2nd wl over 1f out tl ins fnl f: wknd last 100yds* **8/1**
/3-0 **5** 1 **Perfect Fit (IRE)**[6] 133 4-9-2 **68** (p[1]) DougieCostello 1 64
(Tony Coyle) *s.s: a in last: pushed along fr 3f out: nvr any prog: kpt on nr fin* **20/1**

1m 37.65s (-0.55) **Going Correction** -0.125s/f (Stan) **5** Ran SP% **110.6**
Speed ratings (Par 100): **97,95,95,93,92**
CSF £6.34 TOTE £3.90: £2.00, £1.20; EX 7.10 Trifecta £16.80.
Owner Abdulla Al Mansoori **Bred** Rathbarry Stud **Trained** Six Mile Bottom, Cambs

FOCUS
An exhibition in front-running riding from Adam Kirby, who set a steady pace on the winner, and most of those in behind raced keenly, so not form to take too seriously. It's been rated around the winner.
T/Plt: £71.80 to a £1 stake. Pool: £54,843.65 - 557.39 winning units T/Qpdt: £13.70 to a £1 stake. Pool: £4,544.63 - 245.10 winning units **Jonathan Neesom**

224 - 228a (Foreign Racing) - See Raceform Interactive

[183]MEYDAN (L-H)
Saturday, January 16

OFFICIAL GOING: Dirt: fast; turf: good

229a MEYDAN SOBHA TROPHY (H'CAP) (TURF) 1m
2:55 (2:55) (84-99,98) 3-Y-O+ **£18,299** (£6,099; £3,354; £1,829; £914)

RPR
1 **Udododontu (IRE)**[212] 3304 4-9-1 **94** HarryBentley 8 102
(Saeed bin Suroor) *trckd ldr: led 1 1/2f out: easily* **1/3**[1]
2 3 1/4 **Need To Know (SAF)**[8] 117 7-9-1 **94** (bt) TadhgO'Shea 9 95
(A R Al Rayhi, UAE) *s.i.s: trckd ldr: wd: led 4f out: hdd fnl f* **10/1**[3]
3 3/4 **Pupil (IRE)**[8] 117 5-8-10 **89** (p) RichardMullen 2 88
(S Seemar, UAE) *trckd ldr: r.o same pce fnl 3f* **14/1**
4 2 **Hoarding (USA)**[940] 3485 6-8-11 **90** RoystonFfrench 3 85
(S bin Ghadayer, UAE) *s.i.s: nvr nr to chal but r.o fnl 2 1/2f* **25/1**
5 1 **Marching Time**[30] 8277 10-9-1 **94** PaulHanagan 7 80
(Doug Watson, UAE) *nvr bttr than mid-div* **7/1**[2]
6 shd **Shebebi (USA)**[50] 8030 6-9-0 **93** DaneO'Neill 10 79
(Doug Watson, UAE) *nvr nr to chal* **20/1**
7 10 **Idler (IRE)**[34] 8220 7-8-11 **90** FrederikTylicki 5 53
(A bin Harmash, UAE) *a in rr* **12/1**
8 9 **Sadeek's Song (USA)**[436] 7695 8-9-2 **95** SamHitchcott 6 37
(M Al Subouse, UAE) *sn led: hdd 4f out: wknd fnl 3f* **66/1**
9 2 1/2 **Not A Given (USA)**[8] 117 7-8-3 **91** (t) ManuelFernandes[(10)] 4 28
(A R Al Rayhi, UAE) *missed break totally: a in rr* **25/1**
D 2 3/4 **Sea Shanty (USA)**[492] 6257 6-9-5 **98** (b) OisinMurphy 1 86
(M Al Subouse, UAE) *a mid-div* **33/1**

1m 37.17s (-0.33) **Going Correction** +0.20s/f (Good) **10** Ran SP% **127.9**
Speed ratings: **109,105,105,103,99 99,89,80,77,100**
CSF: 5.34; TRICAST 31.89. Placepot: £39.50 to a £1 stake. Pool of £2,845.95 - 52.55 winning units. Quadpot: £22.00 to a £1 stake. Pool of £146.20 - 4.90 winning units..
Owner Godolphin **Bred** Minch Bloodstock **Trained** Newmarket, Suffolk

[163]KEMPTON (A.W) (R-H)
Sunday, January 17

OFFICIAL GOING: Polytrack: standard
Wind: light, half against Weather: dry, cold

230 WATCH RACING UK ON 3 DEVICES H'CAP 6f (P)
1:00 (1:10) (Class 6) (0-55,60) 4-Y-O+ **£2,264** (£673; £336; £168) **Stalls** Low

Form RPR
/4-1 **1** **National Service (USA)**[2] 201 5-9-12 **60** 6ex (tp) TimmyMurphy 7 72+
(Gordon Elliott, Ire) *hld up in last trio: clsd and travelling strly 2f out: chsd ldng trio over 1f out: effrt to chse ldr ins fnl f: r.o wl to ld nr fin* **11/4**[2]
65-2 **2** nk **Blue Bounty**[6] 143 5-9-7 **55** (p) SaleemGolam 6 66
(Mark H Tompkins) *chsd ldr: upsides 2f out: rdn to ld ent fnl f: clr ins fnl f: kpt on tl hdd and no ex nr fin* **9/4**[1]
00-1 **3** 2 1/4 **Loudly (USA)**[12] 46 4-9-4 **52** LukeMorris 3 56
(George Peckham) *chsd ldrs and travelled strly: effrt u.p over 1f out: unable qck ins fnl f: 3rd and outpcd fnl 100yds* **9/2**[3]
034- **4** 1 1/4 **First Rebellion**[18] 8401 7-9-1 **52** (b) GeorgeDowning[(3)] 5 53
(Tony Carroll) *led: rdn and jnd 2f out: hdd and no ex ent fnl f: wknd fnl 150yds* **16/1**
50-0 **5** 1/2 **Red Shadow**[13] 35 7-8-12 **46** oh1 (v[1]) ShaneKelly 2 45
(Alan Brown) *restless in stalls: hld up in rr: rdn and hdwy over 1f out: swtchd lft and kpt on ins fnl f: nvr trbld ldrs* **33/1**
304- **6** 3/4 **Dream Ally (IRE)**[51] 8012 6-9-6 **54** MartinLane 10 51
(John Weymes) *in tch in midfield: rdn and unable qck 2f out: outpcd over 1f out: wl hld and plugged on same pce fnl f* **12/1**
5-54 **7** 2 **Tax Reform (IRE)**[6] 143 6-8-9 **46** (b) PhilipPrince[(3)] 8 37
(Natalie Lloyd-Beavis) *in tch in midfield: rdn over 2f out: unable qck and wl hld over 1f out: wknd fnl f* **20/1**
00-6 **8** 1 **Paradise Spectre**[10] 87 9-8-12 **46** oh1 (v) FergusSweeney 9 34
(Zoe Davison) *hld up in last trio: effrt jst over 2f out: no imp and wl hld over 1f out* **25/1**
050- **9** 1 1/4 **Two Turtle Doves (IRE)**[45] 8095 10-8-12 **46** oh1 RobertHavlin 12 30
(Michael Mullineaux) *chsd ldrs: rdn ent fnl 2f: 5th and outpcd over 1f out: wknd fnl f* **66/1**

1m 11.9s (-1.20) **Going Correction** -0.10s/f (Stan) **9** Ran SP% **102.2**
Speed ratings (Par 101): **104,103,100,98,98 97,94,93,91**
CSF £7.09 CT £16.98 TOTE £3.40: £1.10, £1.40, £1.70; EX 8.90 Trifecta £27.80.
Owner T Howley Jnr **Bred** Three Chimneys Farm Llc **Trained** Longwood, Co Meath
■ Jolly Red Jeanz (6-1). Rule 4 applies to all bets. Deduction - 10p in the pound.

FOCUS
A low-grade sprint.

231 RACING UK PROFITS RETURNED TO RACING H'CAP 7f (P)
1:30 (1:36) (Class 5) (0-70,74) 4-Y-O+ **£2,911** (£866; £432; £216) **Stalls** Low

Form RPR
0-21 **1** **Jammy Guest (IRE)**[9] 100 6-9-11 **74** AdamKirby 8 85
(George Margarson) *dwlt and short of room leaving stalls: hld up in midfield: hdwy to chse ldrs and rdr looking arnd over 1f out: rdn to ld ins fnl f: sn in command: r.o wl* **3/1**[2]
034- **2** 2 **Lupo D'Oro (IRE)**[17] 8414 7-9-2 **65** KierenFox 3 71
(John Best) *midfield: rdn over 2f out: hdwy to chse ldr wl over 1f out tl ent fnl f: outpcd by wnr ins fnl f: wnt 2nd again towards fin* **8/1**
05-1 **3** 1/2 **Twin Point**[8] 124 5-9-11 **74** (t) MartinLane 10 78
(Charlie Fellowes) *mounted on crse: led: rdn and wnt clr ent fnl 2f: drvn over 1f out: hdd and no ex ins fnl f: lost 2nd towards fin* **15/8**[1]
043- **4** 1 3/4 **Bailiwick**[52] 8002 5-9-0 **63** RichardKingscote 2 63
(Daniel Kubler) *midfield: effrt ent fnl 2f: kpt on same pce u.p ins fnl f* **6/1**[3]
365- **5** hd **Muzaahim (IRE)**[21] 8370 5-8-12 **61** ShaneKelly 1 60
(Kevin Morgan) *rrd as stalls opened: hld up in last pair: rdn and hdwy over 1f out: kpt on same pce ins fnl f* **14/1**
050- **6** 3 3/4 **Soaring Spirits (IRE)**[46] 8084 6-9-2 **65** (b) PatCosgrave 7 54
(Dean Ivory) *wnt lft s: sn rcvrd to chse clr ldng pair: lost pl u.p over 1f out: wknd ins fnl f* **14/1**
640- **7** 2 3/4 **Youm Jamil (USA)**[22] 5039 9-8-10 **59** (t) LukeMorris 6 40
(Tony Carroll) *hld up off the pce in rr: effrt 2f out: no imp: n.d* **33/1**
10-0 **8** 8 **Admirable Art (IRE)**[13] 36 6-8-11 **60** WilliamCarson 4 20
(Tony Carroll) *w ldr tl jst over 2f out: lost 2nd wl over 1f out and sn lost pl: bhd fnl f* **66/1**
03-1 **9** 1/2 **Ocean Legend (IRE)**[10] 76 11-9-7 **70** CathyGannon 9 28
(Tony Carroll) *midfield: rdn and lost pl over 2f out: bhd fnl f* **10/1**

1m 24.09s (-1.91) **Going Correction** -0.10s/f (Stan) **9** Ran SP% **112.0**
Speed ratings (Par 103): **106,103,103,101,100 96,93,84,83**
CSF £26.12 CT £54.69 TOTE £3.50: £1.40, £1.20, £1.60; EX 24.10 Trifecta £58.00.
Owner John Guest Racing **Bred** Robert Power Bloodstock Ltd **Trained** Newmarket, Suffolk
■ Stewards' Enquiry : Kieren Fox ban; used his whip above the permitted level (tba)

FOCUS
The leaders took each other on and this was set up nicely for a closer.

232 RACINGUK.COM/WINTERSEASONTICKET H'CAP (DIV I) 1m 4f (P)
2:00 (2:05) (Class 6) (0-55,58) 4-Y-O+ **£2,264** (£673; £336; £168) **Stalls** Centre

Form RPR
1 **Cartographic (USA)**[67] 7805 4-9-2 **54** AdamKirby 5 61+
(David Evans) *stdd s: hld up in rr: clsd and swtchd rt 2f out: drvn to chse ldr 1f out: r.o u.p to ld last strides* **8/11**[1]
04- **2** hd **Feelthenrhythm (IRE)**[18] 8397 5-8-12 **46** oh1 (p) ShaneKelly 3 52
(Des Donovan, Ire) *hld up in tch: rdn and hdwy to ld over 1f out: sn drifted rt: drvn and kpt on ins fnl f: hdd and no ex last strides* **7/1**[3]
054- **3** 2 1/4 **Claude Greenwood**[27] 8329 6-8-12 **46** oh1 (b) RobertHavlin 1 48
(Linda Jewell) *led: rdn and hdd over 1f out: sltly hmpd 1f out: styd on same pce ins fnl f* **20/1**
550- **4** 1 1/4 **Heurtevent (FR)**[32] 8249 7-9-1 **52** GeorgeDowning[(3)] 6 52
(Tony Carroll) *chsd ldrs: swtchd rt and effrt wl over 1f out: drvn and unable qck 1f out: outpcd ins fnl f* **66/1**
560- **5** nse **Citisonsmith (IRE)**[230] 2778 4-8-8 **46** oh1 WilliamCarson 8 46
(Tony Carroll) *chsd ldr: rdn over 2f out: unable qck over 1f out: outpcd ins fnl f* **66/1**
350- **6** 1 **Athenian Garden (USA)**[18] 8398 9-8-8 **49** DanielleMooney[(7)] 4 50
(Paddy Butler) *stdd s: t.k.h: hld up in last pair: shkn up and hdwy over 1f out: keeping on but no threat to ldng pair whn squeezed for room and snatched up ins fnl f: nt rcvr* **33/1**

066- **7** *nk* **Anginola (IRE)**[20] 8337 7-9-0 **48**........................(b) MartinLane 2 46
(David Dennis) *in tch in midfield: rdn over 2f out: unable qck and btn over 1f out: kpt on again ins fnl f: no threat to ldrs* **25/1**

06-1 **8** *shd* **Jethou Island**[11] 55 5-9-10 **58**........................(t) TomEaves 9 56
(David Menuisier) *chsd ldrs: effrt 2f out: unable qck and struggling whn sltly hmpd ent fnl f: wknd* **9/1**

031- **9** *4* **Lady D's Rock (IRE)**[45] 8094 4-8-13 **51**........................(t) LukeMorris 10 43
(Clive Cox) *stdd s: hld up in tch towards rr: rdn and swtchd lft ent fnl 2f: no hdwy: wknd over 1f out* **3/1**[2]

2m 36.49s (1.99) **Going Correction** -0.10s/f (Stan)
WFA 4 from 5yo+ 4lb **9** Ran SP% **119.9**
Speed ratings (Par 101): **89,88,87,86,86 85,85,85,82**
CSF £6.71 CT £60.16 TOTE £1.70: £1.20, £1.10, £5.20; EX 6.10 Trifecta £65.70.
Owner Mrs I M Folkes **Bred** Curtis Sampson **Trained** Pandy, Monmouths

FOCUS
The leader was able to slow things right down heading into the back straight and the race then developed into a bit of a sprint from the turn in.

233 RACINGUK.COM/WINTERSEASONTICKET H'CAP (DIV II) 1m 4f (P)
2:35 (2:40) (Class 6) (0-55,55) 4-Y-O+ **£2,264** (£673; £336; £168) **Stalls** Centre

Form RPR

02-3 **1** **Shirataki (IRE)**[10] 84 8-8-8 **49**........................ LuluStanford(7) 2 55
(Peter Hiatt) *s.i.s: detached in last: clsd and in tch 8f out: rdn and effrt jst over 2f out: hdwy over 1f out: styd on to ld fnl 100yds: rdn out* **6/1**[2]

060- **2** *nk* **Awesome Rock (IRE)**[18] 8397 7-8-12 **46** oh1........................ MartinLane 3 52
(Roger Ingram) *hld up in tch in last trio: hdwy over 2f out: rdn to ld over 1f out: hdd fnl 100yds: kpt on but a hld after* **8/1**

111- **3** *1* **Mrs Burbidge**[27] 8337 6-9-1 **49**........................(tp) LiamKeniry 6 53
(Neil Mulholland) *chsd ldrs: effrt over 2f out: rdn and ev ch over 1f out: styd on same pce ins fnl f* **7/4**[1]

5/ **4** *shd* **Akinspirit (IRE)**[32] 2263 12-9-0 **48**........................(t) StevieDonohoe 5 52
(Nikki Evans) *stdd s: hld up in tch: swtchd rt and hdwy 2f out: drvn to chse ldrs 1f out: styd on same pce ins fnl f* **14/1**

500- **5** *½* **Indian Scout**[27] 8337 8-8-12 **46** oh1........................(p) LukeMorris 7 49
(Anabel K Murphy) *in tch in midfield: effrt u.p to press ldrs over 1f out: styd on same pce ins fnl f* **25/1**

530- **6** *2* **Epsom Flyer**[76] 3402 6-8-12 **46**........................ JFEgan 9 46
(Pat Phelan) *chsd ldr: rdn to ld 2f out: hdd over 1f out and sn no ex: wknd wl ins fnl f* **13/2**[3]

500- **7** *4 ½* **Standing Strong (IRE)**[18] 8398 8-9-3 **51**........................(v) RobertHavlin 4 44
(Zoe Davison) *hld up in tch in midfield: swtchd rt and effrt u.p 2f out: sn drvn and no imp: wknd ins fnl f* **12/1**

245- **8** *1 ½* **Investissement**[18] 8392 10-9-0 **55**........................(tp) DanielleMooney(7) 1 45
(Paddy Butler) *hld up in last trio: effrt but stl plenty to do whn hmpd and swtchd lft wl over 1f out: nt rcvr and no imp after* **16/1**

544- **9** *1* **Ocean Bentley (IRE)**[188] 4209 4-8-8 **46** oh1........................ RyanPowell 8 35
(Tony Carroll) *chsd ldrs: lost pl u.p over 1f out: wknd fnl f* **8/1**

0/0- **10** *19* **Norphin**[22] 7979 6-8-5 **46** oh1........................(b[1]) RhiainIngram(7) 10 4+
(Simon Hodgson) *led and sn clr: hdd 2f out: sn dropped out: wl bhd fnl f* **66/1**

2m 34.44s (-0.06) **Going Correction** -0.10s/f (Stan)
WFA 4 from 6yo+ 4lb **10** Ran SP% **111.8**
Speed ratings (Par 101): **96,95,95,95,94 93,90,89,88,76**
CSF £50.92 CT £116.07 TOTE £7.10: £2.40, £2.80, £1.40; EX 50.00 Trifecta £172.10.
Owner P W Hiatt **Bred** Deerfield Farm **Trained** Hook Norton, Oxon

FOCUS
This was run at a better early gallop than the first division and it suited the hold-up horses. The time was 2.05sec faster.

234 RACINGUK.COM/ANYWHERE H'CAP 2m (P)
3:10 (3:15) (Class 5) (0-75,74) 4-Y-O+ **£2,911** (£866; £432; £216) **Stalls** Low

Form RPR

504- **1** **Haines**[22] 8361 5-9-10 **73**........................ RobHornby(3) 4 83+
(Andrew Balding) *hld up in midfield: effrt to chse ldrs 2f out: rdn to ld 1f out: r.o strly: readily* **5/2**[1]

16/2 **2** *3 ¾* **Lucky Jim**[9] 103 5-9-9 **69**........................ MartinLane 10 74
(David Dennis) *led for 4f: chsd ldr tl led again 3f out: rdn over 2f out: hdd and no ex 1f out: styd on same pce ins fnl f* **7/1**[3]

02-2 **3** *nk* **Todd**[12] 43 6-9-11 **71**........................ GeorgeBaker 2 76
(Anabel K Murphy) *hld up in tch: clsd and wl in tch 3f out: rdn and hdwy over 1f out: wnt 3rd ins fnl f: kpt on: no threat to wnr* **3/1**[2]

21-3 **4** *2 ¼* **Rebel Collins (IRE)**[12] 43 5-10-0 **74**........................ AdamKirby 3 76
(David Evans) *in tch in midfield: swtchd lft and effrt over 2f out: 3rd and no imp u.p over 1f out: lost 3rd and wknd ins fnl f* **15/2**

021- **5** *¾* **King Olav (UAE)**[27] 8328 11-9-3 **66**........................ GeorgeDowning(3) 8 67
(Tony Carroll) *hld up in tch towards rr: effrt over 2f out: hdwy 1f out: kpt on steadily ins fnl f: no threat to wnr* **16/1**

06-5 **6** *1 ¼* **Topaling**[12] 43 5-9-8 **68**........................ SaleemGolam 7 68
(Mark H Tompkins) *hld up in tch: swtchd lft and effrt over 2f out: swtchd bk rt and hdwy 2f out: sn no imp: wl hld fnl f* **25/1**

040/ **7** *3* **Ordensritter (GER)**[18] 2482 8-9-12 **72**........................(bt) PatCosgrave 1 68
(Chris Down) *chsd ldrs: rdn over 2f out: outpcd u.p and btn over 1f out: wknd fnl f* **12/1**

100- **8** *½* **Coup De Grace (IRE)**[36] 7436 7-9-8 **68**........................ ShaneKelly 9 63
(Pat Phelan) *in tch in midfield: rdn and struggling over 2f out: wknd over 1f out* **11/1**

360- **9** *10* **Kirkman (IRE)**[103] 7007 5-8-12 **58**........................ WilliamCarson 5 41
(Peter Hiatt) *chsd ldr for 4f: styd chsng ldrs: clsd to press ldrs 3f out: rdn and btn ent fnl 2f: fnl f: bhd and eased ins fnl f* **20/1**

050- **10** *35* **Emilio Largo**[32] 7474 8-9-9 **69**........................ TimmyMurphy 6 10
(Mark Pitman) *t.k.h: chsd ldrs: hdwy to ld after 4f: hdd 3f out: sn dropped out: t.o over 1f out* **33/1**

3m 26.79s (-3.31) **Going Correction** -0.10s/f (Stan) **10** Ran SP% **111.3**
Speed ratings (Par 103): **104,102,101,100,100 99,98,98,93,75**
CSF £18.71 CT £51.53 TOTE £2.90: £1.30, £2.40, £1.60; EX 19.20 Trifecta £54.70.
Owner Bow River Racing **Bred** Spring Bloodstock Ltd **Trained** Kingsclere, Hants

FOCUS
A fair staying handicap.

235 WATCH RACING UK ON 3 DEVICES CONDITIONS STKS (AW CHAMPIONSHIP FAST-TRACK QUALIFIER) (PLUS 10 RACE) 6f (P)
3:40 (3:45) (Class 2) 3-Y-O **£12,291** (£3,657; £1,827; £913) **Stalls** Low

Form RPR

31-1 **1** **Gracious John (IRE)**[12] 45 3-9-5 **106**........................ JFEgan 1 109
(David Evans) *mde all: rdn and 2 l clr over 1f out: hld on wl fnl f* **4/9**[1]

522- **2** *1 ½* **Field Of Vision (IRE)**[100] 7072 3-9-2 **106**........................ GeorgeBaker 3 101
(Joseph Tuite) *chsd wnr thrght: rdn ent fnl 2f: kpt on u.p ins fnl f* **3/1**[2]

200- **3** *5* **Thatsallimsaying (IRE)**[121] 6495 3-8-11 **95**........................ CathyGannon 2 80
(David Evans) *stdd after s: a 3rd: rdn and rdr dropped whip jst over 2f out: 3rd and plugged on same pce fr over 1f out* **20/1**

3-1 **4** *1 ½* **Khameela**[12] 42 3-8-11 **75**........................ PatCosgrave 4 75
(David Simcock) *stdd s: t.k.h: hld up in tch in last: effrt ent fnl 2f: sn outpcd and wl hld over 1f out* **10/1**[3]

1m 10.93s (-2.17) **Going Correction** -0.10s/f (Stan) **4** Ran SP% **108.1**
Speed ratings (Par 103): **110,108,101,99**
CSF £2.04 TOTE £1.40; EX 2.10 Trifecta £6.90.
Owner Terry Reffell **Bred** Skeaghmore Hill **Trained** Pandy, Monmouths

FOCUS
Another fine performance from the up-and-coming winner.

236 100% RACINGUK PROFITS RETURNED TO RACING H'CAP 6f (P)
4:10 (4:15) (Class 5) (0-75,75) 4-Y-O+ **£2,911** (£866; £432; £216) **Stalls** Low

Form RPR

U26- **1** **Noble Deed**[32] 8250 6-9-0 **68**........................ KierenFox 2 76
(Michael Attwater) *chsd ldrs: rdn to press ldr over 1f out: sustained battle w rival fnl f: led fnl 75yds: jst prevailed* **9/1**

006- **2** *nse* **Desert Strike**[19] 8389 10-9-7 **75**........................(p) JFEgan 3 83
(Conor Dore) *taken down early: led: rdn and hrd pressed over 1f out: hdd fnl 75yds: battled bk gamely u.p: jst hld* **16/1**

610- **3** *½* **Quintus Cerialis (IRE)**[37] 8179 4-9-6 **74**........................(p) AdamKirby 9 80
(Clive Cox) *in tch in midfield: effrt to chse ldrs over 1f out: kpt on wl u.p ins fnl f: nt quite rch ldrs* **5/1**[2]

053- **4** *hd* **Pour La Victoire (IRE)**[32] 8247 6-9-5 **73**........................(b) LukeMorris 10 78
(Tony Carroll) *stdd and swtchd rt after s: hld up towards rr: rdn and hdwy over 1f out: kpt on wl u.p ins fnl f: nt quite rch ldrs* **6/1**[3]

50/- **5** *2* **Mezmaar**[511] 5727 7-9-4 **72**........................ ShaneKelly 8 71
(Kevin Morgan) *stdd and swtchd rt s: hld up in last: shkn up and outpcd 2f out: rallied and swtchd rt ins fnl f: styd on strly: nt rch ldrs* **33/1**

61-2 **6** *nk* **Royal Normandy**[6] 142 4-9-1 **72**........................(b) RobHornby(3) 6 70
(Andrew Balding) *chsd ldr: rdn and little rspnse over 1f out: styd on same pce ins fnl f* **11/8**[1]

00-0 **7** *¾* **New Leyf (IRE)**[10] 76 10-9-2 **70**........................(b) MartinLane 4 66
(Jeremy Gask) *in tch in midfield: rdn and little rspnse 2f out: styd on same pce fr over 1f out* **16/1**

030- **8** *½* **Generalyse**[32] 8250 7-9-0 **68**........................(b) PatCosgrave 1 62
(Anabel K Murphy) *in tch in midfield: unable qck 2f out: lost pl u.p over 1f out: kpt on same pce fnl f* **33/1**

330- **9** *2* **Indian Affair**[78] 7639 6-9-2 **70**........................(bt) WilliamCarson 5 58
(Milton Bradley) *in tch in midfield: rdn ent fnl 2f: sn outpcd: wl hld and one pce fr over 1f out* **20/1**

441/ **10** *2* **Summersault (IRE)**[391] 8256 5-9-0 **68**........................ TimmyMurphy 11 49
(Jamie Osborne) *hld up in tch in midfield: pushed along ent fnl 2f: sn lost pl: bhd fnl f* **25/1**

200- **11** *2* **Lucky Di**[27] 8333 6-9-4 **72**........................ RobertHavlin 7 47
(Peter Hedger) *v awkward and rrd as stalls opened: lost many l: clsd and in tch after 2f: outpcd ent fnl 2f: bhd over 1f out* **20/1**

1m 11.23s (-1.87) **Going Correction** -0.10s/f (Stan) **11** Ran SP% **114.1**
Speed ratings (Par 103): **108,107,107,107,104 103,102,102,99,96 94**
CSF £123.84 CT £812.66 TOTE £9.60: £1.30, £4.30, £2.30; EX 135.70 Trifecta £914.50.
Owner Canisbay Bloodstock **Bred** Cheveley Park Stud Ltd **Trained** Epsom, Surrey
■ Stewards' Enquiry : Kieren Fox four-day ban; used whip above the permitted level (1st-4th Feb)

FOCUS
Not too many got into this.

237 RACING UK WINTER SEASON TICKET H'CAP 7f (P)
4:40 (4:45) (Class 6) (0-52,55) 4-Y-O+ **£2,264** (£673; £336; £168) **Stalls** Low

Form RPR

605- **1** **Celtic Ava (IRE)**[18] 8393 4-9-5 **50**........................ JFEgan 8 61
(Pat Phelan) *chsd ldrs: effrt to press ldr 2f: rdn and ev ch over 1f out: styd on wl u.p to ld fnl 50yds: rdn out* **7/1**[3]

5-31 **2** *½* **Bridge Builder**[4] 168 6-9-7 **55** 6ex........................(p) RobHornby(3) 3 64+
(Peter Hedger) *led: pressed and rdn over 1f out: hdd and no ex fnl 50yds* **1/2**[1]

00-6 **3** *2 ¾* **Star Pursuits**[9] 97 4-9-3 **48**........................(p) KieranO'Neill 1 50
(Jimmy Fox) *chsd ldrs: effrt 2f out: wnt 3rd 1f out: styd on but no imp on ldng pair* **14/1**

450- **4** *¾* **Wedgewood Estates**[18] 8400 5-9-7 **52**........................ AdamKirby 5 52
(Tony Carroll) *hld up in tch in last quartet: hdwy into 5th and drvn over 1f out: kpt on ins fnl f: no threat to ldng pair* **10/1**

04-3 **5** *½* **Lutine Charlie (IRE)**[4] 168 9-9-1 **46** oh1........................ FergusSweeney 2 45
(Emma Owen) *chsd ldrs: rdn and unable qck over 1f out: lost 3rd and btn 1f out: wknd ins fnl f* **13/2**[2]

54-0 **6** *7* **Glenbuck Lass (IRE)**[6] 143 4-8-9 **47**........................ LuluStanford(7) 7 27
(Alan Bailey) *taken down early: stdd and rrd as stalls opened: plld hrd and sn dashed up into midfield: rdn 2f out: sn btn: wknd over 1f out* **16/1**

00-5 **7** *1 ½* **Chandrayaan**[10] 87 9-9-1 **46** oh1........................(v) RobertHavlin 11 22
(John E Long) *swtchd rt sn after s: hld up in last pair: effrt and swtchd rt wl over 1f out: sn hung rt and no hdwy: wknd* **33/1**

364/ **8** *1* **My Scat Daddy (USA)**[245] 1015 7-9-1 **46** oh1........(t) StevieDonohoe 10 19
(Nikki Evans) *in tch in midfield: rdn over 2f out: lost pl 2f out: sn wknd* **66/1**

000- **9** *hd* **As A Dream (IRE)**[13] 3614 4-9-2 **50**........................ RyanTate(3) 9 22
(Nikki Evans) *t.k.h: hld up in midfield: pushed lft after 2f and dropped to last quartet: rdn 2f out: sn btn: bhd fnl f* **50/1**

06-0 **10** *nk* **Fleetwood Bella**[10] 87 5-9-1 **46** oh1........................ KierenFox 4 18
(Michael Attwater) *chsd ldr tl 2f out: sn struggling and wl btn 6th over 1f out: wknd fnl f* **66/1**

0/0- **11** *¾* **My Time**[86] 7437 7-9-1 **46**........................ TomEaves 6 16
(Michael Mullineaux) *stdd s: hld up in last pair: effrt 2f out: no hdwy: bhd fnl f* **50/1**

1m 26.19s (0.19) **Going Correction** -0.10s/f (Stan) **11** Ran SP% **124.0**
Speed ratings (Par 101): **94,93,90,89,88 80,79,78,77,77 76**
CSF £11.34 CT £58.15 TOTE £9.90: £2.10, £1.20, £2.50; EX 18.40 Trifecta £115.30.
Owner Celtic Contractors Limited **Bred** Castletown Bloodstock Ltd **Trained** Epsom, Surrey

FOCUS
A moderate affair.

T/Jkpt: Not won. JACKPOT PLACEPOT: £50.20 to a £1 stake. Pool of £7,053.00 - 102.45 winning units. T/Plt: £6.20 to a £1 stake. Pool: £8,6606.50 - 10,180.06 winning tickets. T/Qpdt: £3.70 to a £1 stake. Pool: £6,175.14 - 1,229.45 winning tickets. **Steve Payne**

238 - (Foreign Racing) - See Raceform Interactive

197 WOLVERHAMPTON (A.W) (L-H)

Monday, January 18

OFFICIAL GOING: Tapeta: standard

Wind: Light behind Weather: Overcast

239 LADBROKES CLASSIFIED CLAIMING STKS 7f 32y (Tp)

2:00 (2:02) (Class 5) 4-Y-O+ **£2,587** (£770; £384; £192) **Stalls** High

Form				RPR
23-0	1		**Depth Charge (IRE)**[12] 64 4-9-4 65 (vt) RobertHavlin 2 (Kristin Stubbs) *s.i.s: hld up: hdwy over 1f out: shkn up to ld wl ins fnl f: r.o: comf* **33/1**	76
36-0	2	1 1/4	**Hercullian Prince**[12] 67 4-8-10 71 (p) JFEgan 9 (Conor Dore) *hdwy to chse ldr over 5f out: rdn to ld over 1f out: hdd and unable qck wl ins fnl f* **8/1**	65
030-	3	1 1/4	**Jimmy's Hall**[21] 8382 4-8-10 74 (b) JosephineGordon(5) 6 (J S Moore) *sn led: rdn and hdd over 1f out: styd on same pce ins fnl f* **9/2**[2]	66
4-42	4	1	**Sewn Up**[7] 144 6-8-11 64 (p) JoeyHaynes 1 (Keith Dalgleish) *hld up: rdn over 2f out: hdwy over 1f out: styd on: nt rch ldrs* **9/2**[2]	60
300-	5	hd	**Logans Lad (IRE)**[58] 7949 6-8-12 71 (bt) FrannyNorton 3 (Daniel Mark Loughnane) *hld up: racd keenly: hmpd over 5f out: rdn over 2f out: styd on fr over 1f out: nrst fin* **5/1**[3]	60
000-	6	3/4	**Mujazif (IRE)**[27] 8341 6-8-13 70 JustinNewman(5) 5 (David Nicholls) *s.i.s: sn prom: lost pl over 5f out: rdn over 2f out: nt clr run over 1f out: nt trble ldrs* **7/1**	66
56-2	7	1 1/2	**Never To Be (USA)**[14] 37 5-8-8 75 (t) LukeMorris 4 (Jim Boyle) *chsd ldrs: rdn over 2f out: wknd ins fnl f* **3/1**[1]	50
6-05	8	nk	**Tartan Trip**[13] 49 9-8-7 65 (vt) AndrewMullen 7 (Michael Appleby) *chsd ldrs: rdn over 1f out: wknd ins fnl f* **18/1**	48
00-0	9	1 3/4	**Sakhee's Rose**[12] 68 6-8-9 62 (b) SeanLevey 8 (Ed McMahon) *hld up: hdwy 2f out: sn rdn and wknd* **33/1**	45

1m 29.16s (0.36) **Going Correction** 0.0s/f (Stan) 9 Ran SP% **112.8**

Speed ratings (Par 103): **97,95,94,93,92 91,90,89,87**

CSF £268.58 TOTE £29.90: £5.20, £2.50, £2.10; EX 105.30 Trifecta £513.50.

Owner Paramount Racing III **Bred** Budget Stable **Trained** Norton, N Yorks

FOCUS

The opening contest was a fair claimer. They went a respectable gallop at best on standard Tapeta. The shock winner was badly in and has improved a stone plus on face value, but it's probbably not that straightforward given the grade. The level is a bit fluid.

240 LADBROKES H'CAP 1m 141y (Tp)

2:30 (2:30) (Class 3) (0-95,85) 4-Y-O- **£7,246** (£2,168; £1,084; £542; £270) **Stalls** Low

Form				RPR
45-2	1		**Abbey Angel (IRE)**[4] 172 4-8-12 77 (p) JackGarritty 7 (Richard Fahey) *a.p: chsd ldr and hung lft fr over 1f out: rdn to ld ins fnl f: r.o* **9/2**[3]	87
204-	2	2 1/4	**Best Example (USA)**[33] 8247 4-9-6 85 MartinHarley 4 (Saeed bin Suroor) *s.i.s: sn prom: rdn and nt clr run over 1f out: r.o to go 2nd nr fin* **2/1**[1]	89
415-	3	hd	**Jodies Jem**[40] 8161 6-9-5 83 GrahamLee 5 (William Jarvis) *chsd ldr tl led over 2f out: rdn over 1f out: hdd ins fnl f: styd on same pce* **12/1**	87
16-4	4	hd	**Dream Spirit (IRE)**[16] 18 5-9-6 84 GeorgeBaker 3 (Jamie Osborne) *stdd s: hld up: nt clr run over 1f out: rdn and r.o ins fnl f: nt rch ldrs* **9/1**	88
03-0	5	2 1/2	**Street Force (USA)**[4] 172 5-9-3 81 (t) AndrewMullen 1 (Michael Appleby) *hld up: rdn over 1f out: styd on same pce fnl f* **10/1**	79
00-5	6	1 3/4	**Stetchworth (IRE)**[16] 18 5-9-5 83 JoeFanning 6 (Mark Johnston) *hld up: racd keenly: rdn over 1f out: nvr trbld ldrs* **12/1**	77
332-	7	6	**Big Time (IRE)**[40] 8161 5-9-7 85 AdrianNicholls 2 (David Nicholls) *led: rdn and hdd over 2f out: wknd fnl f* **7/2**[2]	65

1m 48.24s (-1.86) **Going Correction** 0.0s/f (Stan)

WFA 4 from 5yo+ 1lb 7 Ran SP% **108.2**

Speed ratings (Par 107): **108,106,105,105,103 101,96**

CSF £12.39 TOTE £4.90: £2.40, £1.60; EX 14.40 Trifecta £166.50.

Owner Richard Fahey Ebor Racing Club Ltd **Bred** Paul Hyland **Trained** Musley Bank, N Yorks

FOCUS

A decent handicap. They went a respectable gallop. The winner has been rated close to her best.

241 DOWNLOAD THE NEW UNIBET RACING APP H'CAP 5f 20y (Tp)

3:00 (3:00) (Class 6) (0-55,55) 3-Y-O+ **£2,587** (£770; £384; £192) **Stalls** Low

Form				RPR
516-	1		**Quantum Dot (IRE)**[47] 8071 5-9-10 55 (b) KieranO'Neill 10 (Ed de Giles) *mde all: rdn over 1f out: edgd lft ins fnl f: jst hld on* **16/1**	61
01-0	2	nk	**Rat Catcher (IRE)**[10] 98 6-9-6 54 (b) RobHornby(3) 3 (Lisa Williamson) *chsd wnr: rdn over 1f out: nt clr run and swtchd rt ins fnl f: r.o* **10/1**	59
660-	3	3/4	**Cockle Town Boy**[46] 8089 4-9-3 48 StevieDonohoe 8 (Brendan Powell) *s.i.s: hld up: rdn over 1f out: r.o wl ins fnl f: nt rch ldrs* **11/2**[2]	50
34-3	4	3/4	**Frank The Barber (IRE)**[12] 75 4-9-5 53 (bt) JackDuern(3) 7 (Steph Hollinshead) *chsd ldrs: rdn and hung lft ins fnl f: no ex* **15/2**	53
04-0	5	3/4	**Harpers Ruby**[4] 174 6-9-1 46 oh1 JackGarritty 2 (Lynn Siddall) *prom: n.m.r and lost pl over 4f out: hmpd 3f out: r.o ins fnl f: nvr trbld ldrs* **22/1**	43
20-3	6	nk	**Charlie Lad**[8] 136 4-9-5 55 (b) CallumShepherd(5) 9 (Daniel Mark Loughnane) *s.i.s: hld up: hdwy over 1f out: sn rdn: styd on same pce ins fnl f* **13/2**[3]	51
16-4	7	3/4	**Go Charlie**[10] 98 5-9-2 47 ShaneKelly 5 (Lisa Williamson) *s.i.s: hld up: hdwy nt clr run and swtchd lft over 1f out: hmpd sn aftr: nt trblo ldrs* **8/1**	44
02-3	8	1 1/2	**Your Lucky Day**[13] 54 4-9-5 55 JosephineGordon(5) 6 (Chris Dwyer) *chsd ldrs: rdn and hung lft over 1f out: wknd ins fnl f* **13/8**[1]	43
/60-	9	10	**Steel Rain**[140] 5931 8-9-10 55 JFEgan 1 (Nikki Evans) *prom: rdn 1/2-way: hmpd and eased over 1f out* **66/1**	7

1m 2.31s (0.41) **Going Correction** 0.0s/f (Stan) 9 Ran SP% **110.5**

Speed ratings (Par 101): **96,95,94,93,91 91,90,87,71**

CSF £154.30 CT £960.88 TOTE £15.20: £3.70, £2.40, £2.40; EX 81.70 Trifecta £1274.20.

Owner Mrs Yvonne Fleet **Bred** R N Auld **Trained** Ledbury, H'fords

FOCUS

A moderate sprint handicap. They went a proper gallop. The fourth helps pin the level.

242 32RED CASINO H'CAP 5f 216y (Tp)

3:30 (3:31) (Class 6) (0-65,65) 3-Y-O **£2,587** (£770; £384; £192) **Stalls** Low

Form				RPR
450-	1		**Wishsong**[60] 7895 3-8-13 62 AnnaHesketh(5) 3 (David Nicholls) *prom: lost pl 4f out: hdwy over 1f out: r.o to ld wl ins fnl f* **16/1**	70+
644-	2	1 1/4	**Custard The Dragon**[40] 8154 3-9-2 65 PatrickO'Donnell(5) 8 (Ralph Beckett) *mid-div: hdwy over 1f out: n.m.r sn after: r.o to go 2nd nr fin: nt trble wnr* **4/1**[1]	69
051-	3	3/4	**Hold On Magnolia**[27] 8348 3-9-7 65 (p) DavidNolan 6 (Richard Fahey) *pushed along in rr: hdwy u.p over 1f out: r.o* **9/2**[2]	67
26-4	4	shd	**Sea Of Uncertainty**[17] 3 3-9-1 62 AlistairRawlinson(3) 2 (Michael Appleby) *a.p: rdn over 1f out: edgd rt: styd on* **8/1**	64
20-3	5	1/2	**Romancingthestone**[11] 81 3-8-1 50 (p) JosephineGordon(5) 10 (J S Moore) *chsd ldrs: rdn over 1f out: styd on* **25/1**	50
232-	6	shd	**Mysterious Look**[27] 8348 3-9-5 63 SeanLevey 4 (Ed McMahon) *led: pushed clr over 1f out: rdn: hdd and no ex wl ins fnl f* **8/1**	63
366-	7	1/2	**Justice Rock**[46] 8090 3-9-6 64 (b[1]) TomQueally 5 (David Elsworth) *plld hrd and prom: stdd and lost pl 5f out: rdn: edgd lft and r.o ins fnl f: nvr on terms* **11/1**	62
025-	8	1 1/2	**The Lillster**[19] 8391 3-9-0 65 JordanUys(7) 7 (Brian Meehan) *s.i.s: hdwy over 3f out: rdn and edgd rt over 2f out: no ex ins fnl f* **8/1**	59
504-	9	1	**Port Paradise**[22] 8365 3-8-13 62 [1] CallumShepherd(5) 1 (William Jarvis) *mid-div: lost pl 4f out: n.d after* **13/2**[3]	53
00-3	10	3 1/2	**Opera Buffa (IRE)**[10] 105 3-9-0 58 JoeFanning 11 (Mark Johnston) *chsd ldr tl over 3f out: rdn 2f out: wknd fnl f* **10/1**	38
200-	11	3/4	**Tevershams**[153] 5485 3-9-7 65 (b) IrineuGoncalves 12 (Chris Dwyer) *prom: chsd ldr over 3f out tl rdn over 1f out: wknd fnl f* **50/1**	43
034-	12	10	**David's Beauty (IRE)**[104] 7005 3-9-4 62 TomEaves 9 (Brian Baugh) *hld up: rdn over 2f out: sn wknd* **40/1**	10

1m 14.65s (0.15) **Going Correction** 0.0s/f (Stan) 12 Ran SP% **116.4**

Speed ratings (Par 95): **99,97,96,96,95 95,94,92,91,86 85,72**

CSF £76.64 CT £350.60 TOTE £22.30: £5.50, £2.80, £2.40; EX 176.60 Trifecta £1037.10.

Owner R F H Partnership 1 **Bred** Rockcliffe Stud **Trained** Sessay, N Yorks

FOCUS

A modest 3yo sprint handicap. They went an even gallop. The winner was fairly treated on her best 2yo run and this rates a bit better.

243 32RED.COM H'CAP 1m 141y (Tp)

4:00 (4:00) (Class 5) (0-75,75) 3-Y-O **£3,234** (£962; £481; £240) **Stalls** Low

Form				RPR
560-	1		**Zainat (IRE)**[92] 7309 3-8-13 67 DougieCostello 6 (K R Burke) *hld up: hdwy over 1f out: shkn up to ld and edgd lft wl ins fnl f: sn clr: comf* **14/1**	75+
64-1	2	2 1/2	**Winged Dancer**[12] 63 3-9-7 75 LukeMorris 2 (Sylvester Kirk) *chsd ldrs: rdn to ld 1f out: hdd and unable qck wl ins fnl f* **9/4**[1]	77
36-2	3	1 3/4	**Repeat Offender (IRE)**[12] 70 3-8-11 70 (p) JosephineGordon(5) 3 (J S Moore) *chsd ldrs: rdn over 2f out: styd on same pce fnl f* **14/1**	68
523-	4	1 1/4	**Clodianna (IRE)**[18] 8409 3-9-3 71 GeorgeBaker 4 (Roger Charlton) *led: rdn and hung lft over 1f out: sn hdd: no ex ins fnl f* **5/2**[2]	66
301-	5	1/2	**Frap**[97] 7180 3-8-4 61 SammyJoBell(3) 8 (Richard Fahey) *s.s: hld up: rdn over 2f out: styd on ins fnl f: nvr nrr* **11/2**[3]	55
101-	6	nk	**Sahalin**[35] 8224 3-8-9 66 MarcMonaghan(3) 5 (Marco Botti) *chsd ldrs: rdn over 1f out: wknd ins fnl f* **7/1**	59
065-	7	2 1/4	**Lulworth (IRE)**[21] 8377 3-8-11 65 ShaneKelly 7 (William Jarvis) *plld hrd: trckd ldr: rdn and ev ch over 2f out: wknd ins fnl f* **12/1**	53
00-0	8	1/2	**Navajo Storm (IRE)**[12] 63 3-8-7 61 oh1 (p) AndrewMullen 1 (Michael Appleby) *s.i.s: hld up: rdn over 3f out: wknd fnl f* **50/1**	48

1m 50.04s (-0.06) **Going Correction** 0.0s/f (Stan) 8 Ran SP% **110.2**

Speed ratings (Par 97): **100,97,96,95,94 94,92,91**

CSF £42.56 CT £436.36 TOTE £18.40: £3.40, £1.10, £2.90; EX 67.20 Trifecta £598.50.

Owner Hassan Al Abdulmalik **Bred** H A A M Al-Abdulmalik **Trained** Middleham Moor, N Yorks

FOCUS

A fair 3yo handicap. They went a respectable gallop at best. It's been rated around the third.

244 CORAL H'CAP 1m 4f 50y (Tp)

4:30 (4:30) (Class 3) (0-95,95) 4-Y-O- **£7,246** (£2,168; £1,084; £542; £270) **Stalls** Low

Form				RPR
42-3	1		**Paddys Motorbike (IRE)**[16] 19 4-8-7 87 JosephineGordon(5) 4 (David Evans) *led 1f: chsd ldrs: rdn to ld over 1f out: edgd lft: styd on* **6/5**[1]	95+
/0-5	2	1 1/2	**Winterlude (IRE)**[10] 99 6-9-8 93 GeorgeBaker 3 (Jennie Candlish) *hld up: swtchd lft and hdwy over 1f out: rdn to chse wnr ins fnl f: kpt on* **9/1**	99
000-	3	1 3/4	**Communicator**[21] 8379 8-9-0 85 (p) LiamKeniry 1 (Andrew Balding) *a.p: rdn over 2f out: styd on same pce ins fnl f* **8/1**[3]	88
02-4	4	1 3/4	**Precision Five**[16] 19 7-9-0 85 (p) FergusSweeney 9 (Alan King) *led after 1f: hdd over 5f out: rdn over 2f out: led over 1f out: sn hdd: no ex ins fnl f* **8/1**[3]	85
040-	5	1	**Stencive**[30] 8308 7-9-1 86 LukeMorris 2 (Charlie Wallis) *hld up in tch: rdn over 2f out: styd on same pce fnl f* **11/1**	85
143/	6	1 1/4	**Sizzler**[580] 3321 6-9-10 95 GrahamGibbons 5 (Ralph Beckett) *awkward s: hld up: hdwy over 1f out: wknd fnl f* **6/1**[2]	92
/36-	7	shd	**Kashmir Peak (IRE)**[38] 6520 7-8-12 88 CallumShepherd(5) 8 (John Quinn) *plld hrd and prom: wnt 2nd over 8f out tl led over 5f out: rdn and hdd over 1f out: wknd ins fnl f* **12/1**	85
4/0-	8	3 3/4	**Shwaiman (IRE)**[216] 3252 6-9-7 92 TomQueally 6 (William Jarvis) *chsd ldrs: rdn over 3f out: wknd fnl f* **25/1**	83
51/6	9	18	**Cai Shen (IRE)**[9] 121 8-9-0 85 StevieDonohoe 7 (Grace Harris) *hld up: bhd fnl 7f* **50/1**	47

2m 37.66s (-3.14) **Going Correction** 0.0s/f (Stan)

WFA 4 from 6yo+ 4lb 9 Ran SP% **113.8**

Speed ratings (Par 107): **110,109,107,106,106 105,105,102,90**

CSF £12.65 CT £60.95 TOTE £2.10: £1.30, £3.10, £2.60; EX 14.80 Trifecta £144.30.

Owner Walters Plant Hire Ltd Egan Waste Ltd **Bred** Peter And Jackie Grimes **Trained** Pandy, Monmouths

FOCUS
The feature contest was a good middle-distance handicap. They went an ordinary gallop.

245 CORAL CONNECT MAIDEN STKS 1m 1f 103y (Tp)
5:00 (5:01) (Class 5) 3-Y-O+ **£3,234** (£962; £481; £240) **Stalls** Low

Form RPR
342- **1** **Mitre Peak**20 8386 4-9-7 80 DavidNolan 5 73+
(Richard Fahey) *trckd ldrs: led over 1f out: c clr ins fnl f: readily* **7/2**2
0- **2** 4 1/2 **Amazement (GER)**28 8323 3-8-5 0 LukeMorris 7 63
(James Tate) *led: rdn and hdd over 1f out: hung lft and no ex ins fnl f* **11/10**1
3 *hd* **Project Bluebook (FR)** 3-8-5 0 JamesSullivan 9 63+
(John Quinn) *s.s: hld up: hdwy over 1f out: styd on* **33/1**
0-2 **4** *shd* **Tartan Bute**10 96 3-8-5 0 (b) JoeFanning 6 63
(Mark Johnston) *hld up: hdwy over 6f out: rdn over 1f out: styd on same pce ins fnl f* **8/1**3
36- **5** *nk* **L'Amiral David (FR)**44 8125 6-9-13 0 FergusSweeney 8 67
(Alan King) *prom: rdn over 1f out: styd on same pce fnl f* **12/1**
6 3/4 **Force Of Destiny (GER)** 4-9-12 0 SteveDrowne 1 65
(Mrs Ilka Gansera-Leveque) *hld up: hdwy over 1f out: edgd lft and styd on same pce fnl f* **16/1**
322- **7** 1 1/4 **Miro (IRE)**21 8381 4-9-5 75 GeorgeWood(7) 12 63
(James Fanshawe) *chsd ldrs: rdn over 1f out: wknd fnl f* **7/2**2
0-6 **8** *1* **Ingen Brave**13 44 3-8-0 0 CathyGannon 11 51
(David Evans) *chsd ldr: rdn over 3f out: wknd fnl f* **66/1**
6-0 **9** 1 3/4 **Spinning Rose**12 65 4-9-7 0 1 TomQueally 10 52
(Dean Ivory) *hld up: rdn over 2f out: nvr on terms* **40/1**
0- **10** *1* **Stonecoldsoba**42 8138 3-8-5 0 FrannyNorton 4 50
(Paul Morgan) *prom tl rdn and wknd over 2f out* **100/1**
0-0 **11** *7* **Dynamo (IRE)**12 65 5-9-6 0 StephanieJoannides(7) 2 40
(Richard Hughes) *s.s: a bhd* **100/1**
/6- **12** *12* **Sea Silk**37 8211 4-9-12 0 1 RenatoSouza 3 15
(Dean Ivory) *hld up: rdn and wknd over 2f out* **20/1**

2m 0.94s (0.14) **Going Correction** 0.0s/f (Stan)
WFA 3 from 4yo 22lb 4 from 5yo+ 1lb **12 Ran SP% 130.4**
Speed ratings (Par 103): **99,95,94,94,94 93,92,91,90,89 83,72**
CSF £8.33 TOTE £4.00: £1.60, £1.10, £6.70; EX 13.20 Trifecta £222.20.
Owner R A Fahey **Bred** Juddmonte Farms Ltd **Trained** Musley Bank, N Yorks
■ Stewards' Enquiry : Stephanie Joannides ten-day ban: failed to take all reasonable and permissable measures to obtain best possible placing (Feb 1-10)

FOCUS
The concluding contest was a fair maiden. They went a steady gallop. The level is a bit fluid level, rated around the fourth and fifth.
T/Jkpt: not won. JACKPOT PLACEPOT £472.20. Pool: £1,983.00 - 4.20 winning units. T/Plt: £862.60 to a £1 stake. Pool: £72,497.43 - 61.35 winning units. T/Qpdt: £60.90 to a 31 stake. Pool: £9,903.92 - 120.20 winning units. **Colin Roberts**

176 SOUTHWELL (L-H)
Tuesday, January 19

OFFICIAL GOING: Fibresand: standard
Wind: Virtually nil Weather: Cloudy

246 LADBROKES H'CAP 7f (F)
1:10 (1:10) (Class 6) (0-65,70) 4-Y-O+ **£2,587** (£770; £384; £192) **Stalls** Low

Form RPR
144- **1** **Afkar (IRE)**28 8354 8-8-12 61 (p) JosephineGordon(5) 8 72
(Ivan Furtado) *slt ld: pushed along and hdd narrowly over 2f out: rdn to ld again wl over 1f out: kpt on strly fnl f* **13/2**3
/54- **2** 1 3/4 **Dutch Garden**21 8386 4-9-7 65 (v1) SeanLevey 9 71
(David Brown) *cl up: chal 3f out: rdn to take narrow ld over 2f out: hdd wl over 1f out: sn drvn and kpt on same pce* **16/1**
05-1 **3** *1* **Falcon's Reign (FR)**17 25 7-8-5 56 (p) RPWalsh(7) 6 60
(Michael Appleby) *trckd ldrs: hdwy on outer 3f out: rdn and ch whn edgd lft wl over 1f out: sn drvn and kpt on same pce* **11/1**
51-1 **4** *shd* **Boolass (IRE)**9 133 4-9-7 70 6ex (b) CallumShepherd(5) 12 73
(Brian Ellison) *towards rr: pushed along 1/2-way: hdwy and wd st: rdn to chse ldrs wl over 1f out: drvn and no imp fnl f* **11/4**1
652- **5** 1 1/2 **Monsieur Jimmy**35 8236 4-9-7 65 DanielTudhope 1 64
(Declan Carroll) *trckd ldrs on inner: effrt wl over 2f out: sn rdn along and no imp fr over 1f out* **10/1**
10-2 **6** *2* **Danish Duke (IRE)**17 25 5-9-5 63 JamesSullivan 5 57
(Ruth Carr) *in tch: hdwy to chse ldrs over 2f out: sn rdn: drvn and no imp fr over 1f out* **7/1**
02-3 **7** 1/2 **Napoleon Solo**8 141 4-9-7 65 WilliamTwiston-Davies 11 58
(Dave Morris) *towards rr tl styd on fnl 2f* **9/2**2
6-11 **8** *6* **Speightowns Kid (USA)**9 130 8-9-5 68 6ex (be) AnnStokell(5) 10 44
(Ann Stokell) *a towards rr* **11/1**
2-60 **9** *5* **Tiger's Home**17 24 6-8-13 64 KyleCurrie(7) 4 27
(Iain Jardine) *a towards rr* **20/1**
010- **10** 3/4 **Scarlet Bounty (IRE)**22 8376 4-9-4 62 DavidNolan 2 23
(Richard Fahey) *t.k.h: trckd ldrs: shkn up 3f out: sn rdn and wknd qckly* **20/1**

1m 30.58s (0.28) **Going Correction** +0.175s/f (Slow) **10 Ran SP% 111.8**
Speed ratings (Par 101): **105,103,101,101,100 97,97,90,84,83**
CSF £99.90 CT £1106.28 TOTE £7.10: £2.40, £3.50, £2.40; EX 126.50 Trifecta £2356.50.
Owner Dallas Racing **Bred** Jaykayenn Syndicate **Trained** Wiseton, Nottinghamshire

FOCUS
The track had been worked overnight. A moderate handicap, but competitive enough with a few of these coming into the race in good form. However, it proved crucial to race handily with the first two holding those positions throughout. It's been rated a tad positively.

247 DOWNLOAD THE LADBROKES APP H'CAP 1m (F)
1:45 (1:46) (Class 6) (0-60,60) 4-Y-O+ **£2,587** (£770; £384; £192) **Stalls** Low

Form RPR
504- **1** **Master Of Song**38 8201 9-8-10 52 (p) RobHornby(3) 6 62
(Roy Bowring) *midfield: smooth hdwy to trck ldrs over 3f out: effrt 2f out: rdn to ld appr fnl f: kpt on strly* **9/2**2
10-3 **2** 2 1/2 **Roger Thorpe**18 2 7-9-2 60 PaddyPilley(5) 2 64
(Deborah Sanderson) *led 1f: trckd ldr: effrt over 2f out: rdn wl over 1f out: sn drvn and kpt on same pce* **12/1**
402- **3** 2 1/4 **Eium Mac**32 8278 7-8-12 51 (b) RaulDaSilva 11 50
(Neville Bycroft) *cl up on outer: led after 1f: pushed along 2f out: rdn over 1f out: hdd appr fnl f: kpt on one pce* **11/2**3
21-0 **4** *nk* **Excelling Oscar (IRE)**18 2 4-9-7 60 (b) PaulMulrennan 1 58
(Conor Dore) *trckd ldrs on inner: hdwy 3f out: rdn along 2f out: drvn and one pce fr over 1f out* **11/1**
63-5 **5** *5* **General Tufto**18 2 11-8-8 47 (b) MartinLane 9 33
(Charles Smith) *sn rdn along and outpcd in rr: detached 1/2-way: hdwy over 2f out: swtchd lft to inner wl over 1f out: kpt on fnl f: n.d* **8/1**
310- **6** 1/2 **Candesta (USA)**63 7884 6-9-3 56 (t) AdamBeschizza 8 41
(Julia Feilden) *cl up: rdn along wl over 3f out: drvn over 2f out: sn wknd* **8/1**
15-4 **7** *hd* **Incurs Four Faults**8 149 5-9-3 56 (b) JoeFanning 5 40
(Keith Dalgleish) *dwlt and awkward s: in rr: rdn along and hdwy over 3f out: plugged on u.p fnl 2f: nvr a factor* **8/1**
01-1 **8** 4 1/2 **Thello**16 32 4-9-3 56 PhillipMakin 4 29
(Nigel Tinkler) *dwlt: in tch 1/2-way: rdn along over 3f out: sn btn* **10/3**1
000- **9** 2 1/4 **Monsieur Valentine**21 8046 4-9-1 57 GeorgeDowning(3) 10 25
(Tony Carroll) *chsd ldrs on outer: rdn along 3f out: sn drvn and wknd* **22/1**
00-3 **10** 1 3/4 **Molly Approve (IRE)**9 135 4-8-13 52 DougieCostello 7 16
(Tony Coyle) *chsd ldrs on outer: rdn along over 3f out: sn wknd* **40/1**
000- **11** *8* **Mac Tiernan (IRE)**21 8385 9-9-1 54 JoeyHaynes 12
(Philip Kirby) *a towards rr: outpcd and bhd fr over 3f out* **66/1**
000- **12** 3 1/4 **Solid Justice (IRE)**28 8346 5-8-6 52 (b) KyleCurrie(7) 3
(Kenny Johnson) *a towards rr: outpcd and bhd fnl 3f* **100/1**

1m 44.57s (0.87) **Going Correction** +0.175s/f (Slow) **12 Ran SP% 115.3**
Speed ratings (Par 101): **102,99,97,96,91 91,91,86,84,82 74,71**
CSF £54.28 CT £307.70 TOTE £4.60: £1.60, £3.80, £1.30; EX 62.90 Trifecta £736.80.
Owner S R Bowring **Bred** S R Bowring **Trained** Edwinstowe, Notts

FOCUS
Another moderate handicap. Straightforward form, with the runner-up rated to his recent form.

248 32RED.COM H'CAP 7f (F)
2:20 (2:20) (Class 6) (0-60,60) 3-Y-O **£2,587** (£770; £384; £192) **Stalls** Low

Form RPR
205- **1** **Specialv (IRE)**21 8384 3-9-2 60 CallumShepherd(5) 5 70
(Brian Ellison) *trckd ldrs: hdwy over 2f out: swtchd lft and rdn wl over 1f out: led ent fnl f: sn drvn: edgd rt and hld on wl towards fin* **7/1**
32-5 **2** *hd* **Rupert Boy (IRE)**11 104 3-8-9 48 (b) KieranO'Neill 2 57
(Scott Dixon) *led: rdn along 2f out: drvn and hdd over 1f out: drvn and rallied wl ins fnl f: sn ev ch: n.m.r nr fin* **16/1**
051- **3** *hd* **Kemsing (IRE)**32 8281 3-8-13 55 ShelleyBirkett(3) 9 64
(Julia Feilden) *trckd ldrs on outer: hdwy over 2f out: sn chal: rdn to ld and edgd lft over 1f out: drvn and ev ch whn edgd lft ins fnl f: no ex towards fin* **7/4**1
24-3 **4** *4* **Romantic Comedy (IRE)**8 140 3-9-6 59 (b1) LukeMorris 7 57
(James Tate) *cl up: effrt and ev ch over 2f out: rdn wl over 1f out and grad wknd* **5/1**3
33U- **5** *1* **Leitrim Traveller (USA)**50 8045 3-8-11 50 (b) WilliamCarson 6 45+
(Jamie Osborne) *s.i.s and lost several l s: hdwy 1/2-way: rdn along 3f out: kpt on u.p fnl 2f: nrst fin* **4/1**2
06-3 **6** 1/2 **Footlight**14 47 3-9-1 54 JackGarritty 8 48
(Richard Fahey) *cl up: rdn along 3f out: drvn 2f out and grad wknd* **8/1**
026- **7** *7* **Ada Misobel (IRE)**54 8007 3-8-5 51 (p) CliffordLee(7) 4 26
(K R Burke) *trckd ldrs: hdwy on inner 3f out: rdn along 2f out: sn wknd* **40/1**
300- **8** *6* **Rainbow Lad (IRE)**125 6430 3-8-9 51 AlistairRawlinson(3) 3 10
(Michael Appleby) *towards rr and swtchd rt to outer after 1f: rdn along 1/2-way: nvr a factor* **16/1**
046- **9** 1 3/4 **Burning Love (IRE)**219 3192 3-9-7 60 WilliamTwiston-Davies 1 14
(Dave Morris) *a in rr* **33/1**

1m 31.25s (0.95) **Going Correction** +0.175s/f (Slow) **9 Ran SP% 113.8**
Speed ratings (Par 95): **101,100,100,95,94 94,86,79,77**
CSF £108.54 CT £280.61 TOTE £6.60: £2.10, £3.80, £1.30; EX 100.70 Trifecta £359.80.
Owner D Gilbert, M Lawrence, A Bruce **Bred** Peter & Hugh McCutcheon **Trained** Norton, N Yorks

FOCUS
A moderate handicap for 3yos, but a thrilling finish between the first three. The third has been rated as finding a bit on his recent C&D win.

249 BET & WATCH EVERY RACE AT UNIBET MAIDEN FILLIES' STKS 6f (F)
2:50 (2:50) (Class 5) 3-Y-O+ **£3,881** (£1,155; £577; £288) **Stalls** Low

Form RPR
64- **1** **Undertow (IRE)**32 8285 3-8-8 0 JoeyHaynes 3 64+
(K R Burke) *cl up: led wl over 1f out: rdn ent fnl f: green and sn edgd lft: kpt on wl towards fin* **9/2**3
535- **2** 1/2 **Best New Show (IRE)**19 8410 3-8-8 67 JFEgan 5 61
(David Evans) *cl up: effrt wl over 2f out: pushed along and swtchd lft over 1f out: drvn and ev ch ins fnl f: no ex towards fin* **6/4**1
52-3 **3** 3/4 **Royal Rettie**17 25 4-9-10 58 SaleemGolam 6 63
(Heather Dalton) *trckd ldrs: effrt wl over 2f out: swtchd lft wl over 1f out: sn rdn: styd on fnl f* **12/1**
4 **4** 2 1/2 **Red Chatterbox (IRE)**18 5 3-8-8 0 KieranO'Neill 2 51
(Scott Dixon) *slt ld on inner: rdn along over 2f out: hdd wl over 1f out: sn drvn and kpt on same pce* **50/1**
54-3 **5** 2 3/4 **Miss Goldsmith (IRE)**11 102 3-8-5 67 SammyJoBell(3) 7 42
(Richard Fahey) *cl up on outer: wd st: rdn along 2f out: sn drvn and wknd over 1f out* **9/4**2
6 1 1/2 **Xceedingly Xcited (IRE)** 3-8-8 0 LiamJones 4 37
(Marco Botti) *dwlt: green and sn rdn along towards rr: effrt 1/2-way: rdn and green over 2f out: n.d* **10/1**
6-6 **7** *7* **Daydream (IRE)**14 42 3-8-8 0 WilliamCarson 1 15
(Jamie Osborne) *a in rr: outpcd and bhd fnl 2f* **25/1**

1m 17.94s (1.44) **Going Correction** +0.175s/f (Slow)
WFA 3 from 4yo 16lb **7 Ran SP% 111.5**
Speed ratings (Par 100): **97,96,95,92,88 86,77**
CSF £11.09 TOTE £7.30: £3.90, £1.50; EX 13.40 Trifecta £85.60.
Owner Middleham Park Racing CXVII & Mrs Burke **Bred** J C Bloodstock **Trained** Middleham Moor, N Yorks

FOCUS
A modest fillies' maiden, but a decent pace thanks to a disputed lead. It's been rated around the third.

250 UNIBET.CO.UK DAILY ENHANCED PLACE TERMS H'CAP 5f (F)
3:25 (3:25) (Class 4) (0-85,85) 4-Y-O+ **£5,175** (£1,540; £769; £384) **Stalls** Centre

Form RPR
360- **1** **Uptight (FR)**22 8382 4-8-9 73 (bt1) ShaneGray 1 85
(Kevin Ryan) *dwlt: racd towards far rail and sn chsng ldrs on outer: cl up 1/2-way: led 1 1/2f out: rdn clr ent fnl f: kpt on strly* **8/1**

20-4 **2** *2 1/2* **Desert Command**[18] 4 6-9-4 **82**........................(p) DanielTudhope 2 85
(Robert Cowell) *prom towards far rail: effrt 2f out: rdn over 1f out: drvn to chse wnr ins fnl f: no imp* **4/1**[2]

31-1 **3** *1/2* **Crosse Fire**[17] 21 4-9-3 **81**........................(p) KieranO'Neill 8 82
(Scott Dixon) *racd in centre: prom: rdn to chse wnr over 1f out: sn drvn and kpt on same pce* **4/1**[2]

606- **4** *3 1/2* **Among Angels**[120] 6598 4-9-7 **85**........................ StevieDonohoe 5 74
(Kevin Frost) *towards rr in centre: rdn along bef 1/2-way: hdwy 2f out: swtchd rt and drvn over 1f out: kpt on fnl f* **20/1**

5-03 **5** *1* **Oriental Relation (IRE)**[4] 198 5-9-5 **83**........................(v) TomEaves 3 68
(James Given) *prom centre: rdn along 1/2-way: drvn 2f out: sn wknd* **15/8**[1]

42-6 **6** *hd* **Borough Boy (IRE)**[13] 56 6-8-7 **71**........................(v) MartinLane 7 55
(Derek Shaw) *dwlt: a towards rr* **17/2**

15-0 **7** *2 3/4* **Bapak Bangsawan**[9] 133 6-8-5 **74** ow3........................(v) AnnStokell(5) 6 48
(Ann Stokell) *racd centre: led: rdn along over 2f out: hdd 1 1/2f out: sn wknd* **25/1**

004- **8** *2* **Sleepy Blue Ocean**[21] 8389 10-8-11 **75**........................(p) LukeMorris 4 42
(John Balding) *chsd ldrs in centre: rdn bef along 1/2-way: drvn and wknd 2f out* **15/2**[3]

1m 0.5s (0.80) **Going Correction** +0.30s/f (Slow) **8** Ran SP% **116.8**
Speed ratings (Par 105): **105,101,100,94,93 92,88,85**
CSF £40.87 CT £150.11 TOTE £11.90: £3.10, £2.00, £2.10; EX 52.70 Trifecta £270.10.
Owner Matt & Lauren Morgan **Bred** Madame Antonia Devin **Trained** Hambleton, N Yorks

FOCUS
Not a bad sprint handicap with half the field having previously scored over C&D at least twice. They went a strong pace and, as is often the case, the centre of the track was the place to be with stall one beating stall two. A length pb from the winner.

251 CORAL APP DOWNLOAD FROM THE APP STORE H'CAP 1m 4f (F)
4:00 (4:00) (Class 6) (0-60,60) 4-Y-O+ **£2,587** (£770; £384; £192) **Stalls** Low

Form RPR

2- **1** **Edgar (GER)**[211] 3465 6-9-7 **58**........................(p) WilliamTwiston-Davies 7 70+
(David Bridgwater) *prom: cl up 1/2-way: led 3f out: rdn clr over 1f out: eased towards fin* **5/1**[2]

600- **2** *2* **Celestial Dancer (FR)**[21] 8385 4-8-5 **46** oh1........................ AndrewMullen 9 48
(Michael Appleby) *chsd ldrs: hdwy 4f out: rdn over 2f out: chsd wnr and drvn over 1f out: no imp* **20/1**

636- **3** *nk* **A Little Bit Dusty**[18] 7296 8-9-7 **58**........................(p) PaulMulrennan 14 60
(Conor Dore) *sn led: rdn along and hdd 3f out: drvn wl over 1f out: kpt on u.p fnl f* **9/2**[1]

53-3 **4** *nse* **Geeaitch**[14] 53 7-9-1 **52**........................ LukeMorris 5 54
(Peter Hiatt) *chsd ldrs: pushed along 1/2-way: rdn 4f out: wd st: drvn and kpt on same pce fnl 2f* **11/2**[3]

42-0 **5** *3/4* **Cool Beans**[8] 150 4-8-10 **54**........................ RobHornby(3) 10 55
(Roy Bowring) *hld up towards rr: stdy hdwy 5f out: chsd ldrs and rdn over 2f out: drvn and kpt on same pce fr over 1f out* **9/2**[1]

40-4 **6** *1 1/2* **Astra Hall**[14] 53 7-9-6 **60**........................ AlistairRawlinson(3) 12 58
(Michael Appleby) *trckd ldrs on outer: effrt over 3f out: rdn along over 2f out: drvn over 1f out and kpt on same pce* **12/1**

55-0 **7** *1/2* **Rolen Sly**[18] 2 7-8-10 **47** oh1 ow1........................ TomEaves 4 45
(Neville Bycroft) *hld up towards rr: stdy hdwy over 3f out: chsd ldrs 2f out: sn swtchd rt and rdn: drvn and kpt on same pce fr over 1f out* **40/1**

620- **8** *7* **Amazing Blue Sky**[21] 8385 10-8-12 **49**........................(v) JamesSullivan 8 35
(Ruth Carr) *dwlt and towards rr: hdwy over 3f out: wd st and rdn over 2f out: n.d* **12/1**

400- **9** *2 3/4* **Lady Knight (IRE)**[63] 6810 5-8-13 **50**........................ JoeyHaynes 11 32
(Sally Randell) *a towards rr* **33/1**

43-6 **10** *2 3/4* **Spirit Of The Sea (IRE)**[17] 26 4-9-2 **57**........................ JoeFanning 1 35
(Iain Jardine) *midfield on inner: rdn along 4f out: sn outpcd* **12/1**

063- **11** *14* **Sober Up**[49] 8067 4-8-5 **46** oh1........................ RaulDaSilva 2 1
(Ivan Furtado) *prom: rdn along on inner over 4f out: drvn over 3f out: sn wknd* **8/1**

600/ **12** *3/4* **Mcvicar**[426] 7175 7-9-4 **55**........................ PhillipMakin 6 9
(John Davies) *in tch: hdwy 4f out: rdn along over 3f out: wd st and sn wknd* **25/1**

1/0- **13** *64* **Magic Empress (IRE)**[364] 220 4-8-12 **53**........................ DougieCostello 3
(Tony Coyle) *in rr: rdn along 1/2-way: outpcd and bhd fr wl over 3f out* **25/1**

2m 44.77s (3.77) **Going Correction** +0.175s/f (Slow)
WFA 4 from 5yo+ 4lb **13** Ran SP% **120.4**
Speed ratings (Par 101): **94,92,92,92,91 90,90,85,84,82 72,72,29**
CSF £108.38 CT £489.89 TOTE £6.80: £2.80, £7.40, £2.20; EX 146.70 Trifecta £1517.60.
Owner K J McCourt & Partners **Bred** Gestut Brummerhof **Trained** Icomb, Gloucs

FOCUS
A moderate middle-distance handicap outside of the winner, who bolted up.
T/Plt: £484.10 to a £1 stake. Pool: £73,817.98 - 111.29 winning units. T/Qpdt: £30.30 to a £1 stake. Pool: £11,136.20 - 271.90 winning units. **Joe Rowntree**

[230]KEMPTON (A.W) (R-H)
Wednesday, January 20

OFFICIAL GOING: Polytrack: standard
Wind: Nil Weather: Clear, crisp

252 RACING UK ANYWHERE H'CAP 1m (P)
4:40 (4:42) (Class 7) (0-50,50) 4-Y-O+ **£1,940** (£577; £288; £144) **Stalls** Low

Form RPR

3-40 **1** **Fairy Mist (IRE)**[7] 168 9-9-6 **49**........................(b) WilliamCarson 13 56
(John Bridger) *t.k.h: dropped in fr wd draw and hld up in last: gd prog rt on inner fr 2f out: urged along hands and heels fnl f: led last strides* **20/1**

05-4 **2** *hd* **Hagree (IRE)**[17] 32 5-8-11 **47**........................(tp) CharlieBennett(7) 4 53
(Jose Santos) *urged along in rr early: rchd midfield and pushed along 1/2-way: drvn and gd prog 2f out to ld 1f out: kpt on but hdd last strides* **8/1**[3]

20-6 **3** *1 3/4* **Little Indian**[13] 79 6-9-5 **48**........................ AdamKirby 6 49
(J R Jenkins) *hld up towards rr: gd prog on wd outside fr 2f out to chal fnl f: kpt on one pce after: lft in 3rd last strides* **8/1**[3]

553- **4** *nse* **Dreaming Again**[30] 8334 6-9-6 **49**........................ KieranO'Neill 1 51
(Jimmy Fox) *chsd ldrs: shkn up over 2f out: prog to chal over 1f out: hrd rdn and kpt on same pce: 3rd whn short of room and snatched up nr fin* **7/2**[1]

/00- **5** *shd* **Hoofithully**[22] 8388 4-8-9 **45**........................(b[1]) NathanEvans(7) 14 46
(Michael Easterby) *t.k.h: prog on outer to ld after 2f: drvn 2f out: hdd and one pce 1f out* **20/1**

505- **6** *nk* **Crowning Star (IRE)**[20] 8411 7-9-2 **45**........................ JFEgan 3 45
(Steve Woodman) *dwlt: wl in rr: rdn over 2f out: kpt on fr over 1f out: nrst fin but unable to threaten* **10/1**

000- **7** *3/4* **Haames (IRE)**[36] 8235 9-9-7 **50**........................ ShaneKelly 10 49
(Kevin Morgan) *dropped in fr wd draw and hld up wl in rr: gd prog on inner over 2f out: tried to chal over 1f out: one pce fnl f: short of room nr fin* **16/1**

02-3 **8** *1/2* **One Last Dream**[8] 155 7-9-3 **46**........................ FergusSweeney 7 43
(Ron Hodges) *prom: chsd ldr 5f out to wl over 1f out: fdd fnl f* **6/1**[2]

4-04 **9** *hd* **Devilution (IRE)**[7] 168 4-9-2 **45**........................ MartinLane 5 44
(Derek Shaw) *wl in tch: rdn whn hmpd and dropped to last over 2f out: no ch after: styd on ins fnl f* **10/1**

34-5 **10** *1* **Trigger Park (IRE)**[12] 107 5-9-4 **47**........................ LukeMorris 9 43
(Ronald Harris) *in tch in midfield: urged along over 2f out: drvn and no prog whn hmpd and swtchd lft over 1f out: kpt on same pce after* **10/1**

644- **11** *3 3/4* **Endless Seas**[188] 4315 5-9-2 **45**........................ CathyGannon 8 30
(Pat Phelan) *led after 1f tl after 2f: styd prom: drvn over 2f out: wknd over 1f out* **16/1**

006- **12** *1* **Fridge Kid**[34] 8260 4-9-0 **48**........................ PaddyPilley(5) 12 31
(Dr Jon Scargill) *chsd ldrs: rdn over 2f out: wknd over 1f out* **33/1**

504- **13** *1/2* **Top Pocket**[31] 8314 4-9-7 **50**........................ TomQueally 2 34
(Michael Madgwick) *led 1f: lost pl after 3f but stl handy: shkn up over 2f out: no prog and btn whn hmpd over 1f out: wknd* **12/1**

1m 39.8s **Going Correction** -0.05s/f (Stan) **13** Ran SP% **117.9**
Speed ratings (Par 97): **98,97,96,96,95 95,94,94,94,93 89,88,87**
CSF £166.62 CT £1450.34 TOTE £23.70: £5.90, £3.10, £2.50; EX 288.20 Trifecta £1712.10.
Owner J J Bridger **Bred** Sandro Garavelli **Trained** Liphook, Hants
■ Stewards' Enquiry : Charlie Bennett two-day ban: careless riding (Feb 3-4)

FOCUS
An ordinary contest in which they went a fair pace and the first three came from the back of the field.

253 32RED.COM H'CAP (LONDON MILE SERIES QUALIFIER) 1m (P)
5:10 (5:10) (Class 5) (0-70,70) 3-Y-O **£2,911** (£866; £432; £216) **Stalls** Low

Form RPR

36-1 **1** **Jazzy (IRE)**[9] 139 3-9-7 **70** 6ex........................ TomQueally 11 77
(Martin Keighley) *mde all: kicked for home 2f out: drvn over 1f out: styd on wl and in n.d fnl f* **10/1**

056- **2** *2 1/2* **Redmane**[20] 8410 3-9-4 **67**........................ TimmyMurphy 9 68+
(Jamie Osborne) *chsd ldrs: rdn and prog fr 2f out: chsd ldng pair over 1f out: styd on to take 2nd nr fin* **16/1**

104- **3** *1/2* **Jassur**[55] 7999 3-9-0 **63**........................(p) OisinMurphy 4 63
(Marco Botti) *chsd wnr 3f and again 3f out: nt qckn 2f out: racd awkwardly fnl f: lost 2nd nr fin* **13/2**

430- **4** *1* **Rubis**[31] 8320 3-8-13 **62**........................ JackGarritty 12 60+
(Richard Fahey) *dropped in fr wd draw and hld up in last: nt clr run 2f out and again over 1f out whn trying to make prog: styd on fnl f: nrst fin* **20/1**

631- **5** *2 1/2* **Frozen Force (IRE)**[36] 8234 3-9-6 **69**........................(b) FrannyNorton 6 61
(Amanda Perrett) *in tch: rdn over 2f out: one pce and no imp on ldrs over 1f out* **4/1**[2]

52-2 **6** *1 1/2* **Rahyah**[14] 59 3-9-7 **70**........................(p) PatCosgrave 8 58
(William Haggas) *t.k.h early: racd wd: chsd ldrs: rdn over 2f out: fdd over 1f out* **3/1**[1]

653- **7** *3/4* **Adventure Zone (IRE)**[34] 8267 3-8-8 **64**........................ MitchGodwin(7) 1 50
(Richard Hannon) *s.i.s: wl in rr: rdn over 2f out: one pce and no great prog* **20/1**

04-3 **8** *3/4* **Ubla (IRE)**[14] 65 3-9-7 **70**........................(b) LukeMorris 5 54
(Hugo Palmer) *t.k.h: trckd ldrs: wknd fr over 1f out w jockey looking down* **9/2**[3]

40-3 **9** *1 3/4* **Zoffany's Way (IRE)**[14] 63 3-8-10 **66**........................ GeorgeWood(7) 7 46
(James Fanshawe) *a in rr: rdn and no prog over 2f out* **6/1**

030- **10** *9* **Sacrament (IRE)**[24] 8365 3-9-4 **67**........................(v[1]) AdamKirby 10 26
(David Evans) *prom: chsd wnr 5f out to 3f out: wknd u.p: t.o* **33/1**

1m 38.98s (-0.82) **Going Correction** -0.05s/f (Stan) **10** Ran SP% **118.2**
Speed ratings (Par 97): **102,99,99,98,95 94,93,92,90,81**
CSF £153.06 CT £1155.77 TOTE £10.30: £3.10, £4.20, £2.10; EX 154.00 Trifecta £975.70.
Owner Jazz Summers Racing **Bred** Ballyhane Stud **Trained** Condicote, Gloucs

FOCUS
The pace was controlled by the winner in this modest handicap. It's been rated around the third.

254 32RED/EBF STALLIONS BREEDING FILLIES' H'CAP 1m (P)
5:40 (5:40) (Class 3) (0-95,91) 4-Y-O+ **£10,673** (£3,176; £1,587; £793) **Stalls** Low

Form RPR

44-1 **1** **India's Song**[18] 14 6-7-11 **74**........................(t) SophieKilloran(7) 7 82
(David Simcock) *hld up in last pair: gd prog fr jst over 2f out: led jst over 1f out: rdn and styd on wl* **8/1**[3]

41-1 **2** *1 3/4* **Oakley Girl**[14] 72 4-9-7 **91**........................ OisinMurphy 3 95
(Stuart Williams) *trckd ldrs: shkn up 2f out: tried to chal on outer over 1f out: tk 2nd fnl f but no imp on wnr* **8/13**[1]

00-4 **3** *1/2* **Maiden Approach**[14] 72 5-8-4 **77**........................(p) SammyJoBell(3) 4 80
(Richard Fahey) *led: kicked on over 3f out: hdd over 2f out but styd on terms: stl nrly upsides jst over 1f out: one pce after* **10/1**

00-4 **4** *1/2* **Subtle Knife**[18] 23 7-8-7 **77**........................ WilliamCarson 2 79
(Giles Bravery) *prom: rdn to ld narrowly 2f out to jst over 1f out: fdd* **16/1**

100- **5** *3/4* **Lady Marl**[156] 5463 5-9-0 **84**........................ FergusSweeney 8 84
(Gary Moore) *dropped in fr wd draw and hld up in last pair: pushed along over 2f out: hdwy and rdn fnl f: kpt on but nvr involved* **12/1**

350- **6** *1/2* **Pretty Bubbles**[24] 8369 7-8-12 **82**........................(p) JimCrowley 6 81
(J R Jenkins) *nvr beyond midfield: shkn up over 2f out: one pce and no prog fnl f* **9/1**

60-1 **7** *3 1/4* **Moon River (IRE)**[19] 1 4-8-8 **78**........................ LukeMorris 5 69
(Michael Appleby) *trckd ldr: shkn up over 3f out: led briefly over 2f out: wknd over 1f out* **7/1**[2]

-232 **8** *3/4* **My Tringaling (IRE)**[6] 180 4-7-9 **72** oh22........................ MillyNaseb(7) 1 61?
(Stuart Williams) *nvr beyond midfield: shkn up and wknd 2f out* **50/1**

1m 38.07s (-1.73) **Going Correction** -0.05s/f (Stan) **8** Ran SP% **120.2**
Speed ratings (Par 104): **106,104,103,103,102 102,98,98**
CSF £14.08 CT £57.30 TOTE £11.90: £2.40, £1.10, £2.20; EX 20.90 Trifecta £109.30.
Owner Mrs Julia Annable **Bred** Car Colston Hall Stud **Trained** Newmarket, Suffolk

FOCUS
Not a bad fillies' handicap. Muddling form, though, and it's been rated a bit cautiously.

255 £10 FREE BET AT 32REDSPORT.COM H'CAP 1m 4f (P)
6:10 (6:10) (Class 6) (0-55,60) 4-Y-O+ **£2,264** (£673; £336; £168) **Stalls** Centre

Form RPR
0-32 **1** **Zarliman (IRE)**[8] 155 6-8-12 **45**....(p) LiamKeniry 8 53+
(Neil Mulholland) *t.k.h: prom in chsng gp: gng easily whn clsd 3f out: led jst over 2f out: shkn up and asserted over 1f out: kpt on wl* **5/4**[1]
1-53 **2** *2 ¼* **Elle Rebelle**[9] 150 6-9-5 **52**.... LukeMorris 3 56
(Mark Brisbourne) *wl in tch in chsng gp: drvn over 2f out: kpt on to take 2nd 1f out: no ch w wnr* **6/1**[2]
30-6 **3** *¾* **Castanea**[9] 150 4-8-8 **45**.... KieranO'Neill 9 48
(Ronald Harris) *hld up in rr: shkn up and no prog over 2f out: drvn over 1f out: r.o to take 3rd last 75yds* **9/1**
52-5 **4** *1 ½* **Fieldmouse**[13] 84 4-9-2 **53**.... ShaneKelly 11 54
(Eve Johnson Houghton) *chsd clr ldr: clsd to ld briefly over 2f out: lost 2nd wl over 1f out: one pce* **8/1**[3]
635- **5** *shd* **Well Owd Mon**[33] 8291 6-9-4 **54**....(p) RobHornby(3) 4 55
(Sarah Hollinshead) *hld up in last: shkn up over 3f out: prog over 1f out: kpt on one pce fnl f* **14/1**
040- **6** *1 ¼* **Lily Edge**[21] 8397 7-9-2 **49**....(b) WilliamCarson 7 48
(John Bridger) *prom in chsng gp: prog to chse wnr wl over 1f out to 1f out: wknd* **12/1**
04-4 **7** *1* **Missandei**[9] 150 4-8-11 **51**....(t) JackDuern(3) 5 48
(Steph Hollinshead) *in tch in chsng gp: rdn over 3f out: struggling and no prog over 2f out* **8/1**[3]
64-5 **8** *¾* **Charlie's Star**[8] 155 4-8-13 **50**.... KierenFox 1 46
(Laura Mongan) *in tch in chsng gp: rdn 3f out: no imp on ldrs 2f out: fdd* **14/1**
0 **9** *45* **Pao De Acuca (IRE)**[8] 155 4-8-8 **45**....(tp) RaulDaSilva 2
(Jose Santos) *t.k.h: led and sn wl clr: racd wd in bk st: hung lft fr 5f out: hdd over 2f out: wknd rapidly and sn t.o* **25/1**

2m 34.44s (-0.06) **Going Correction** -0.05s/f (Stan)
WFA 4 from 6yo+ 4lb 9 Ran SP% **115.8**
Speed ratings (Par 101): **98,96,96,95,94 94,93,92,62**
CSF £8.92 CT £47.84 TOTE £2.10: £1.30, £1.40, £2.60; EX 11.10 Trifecta £60.90.
Owner M Cahill **Bred** His Highness The Aga Khan's Studs S C **Trained** Limpley Stoke, Wilts
FOCUS
A moderate heat. The leader went off too fast and was largely ignored by the chasing pack.

256 32RED CASINO H'CAP 1m 3f (P)
6:40 (6:40) (Class 5) (0-75,75) 4-Y-O+ **£2,911** (£866; £432; £216) **Stalls** Low

Form RPR
061- **1** **Whinging Willie (IRE)**[21] 8392 7-9-5 **73**....(v) GeorgeBaker 9 81
(Gary Moore) *trckd ldr to 7f out and again 2f out gng easily: led jst over 1f out: shkn up and wl on top fnl f* **8/1**
41-0 **2** *1 ¼* **Bogardus (IRE)**[16] 38 5-8-10 **64**.... JoeyHaynes 11 72+
(Patrick Holmes) *t.k.h: hld up in rr: sat bhd rivals waiting for an opening fr over 2f out to over 1f out: rapid prog fnl f: r.o wl to take 2nd last strides: too much to do* **6/1**[2]
020- **3** *1* **The Ginger Berry**[106] 7015 6-8-7 **66**.... PaddyPilley(5) 10 70
(Dr Jon Scargill) *hld up in last pair: gd prog on inner jst over 2f out: urged along to chse wnr ins fnl f: one pce after and lost 2nd last strides* **20/1**
641- **4** *nk* **Vale Of Iron (IRE)**[32] 8312 4-8-10 **67**.... KierenFox 4 70+
(John Best) *hld up in tch: t.k.h and plld way through to ld 6f out: hdd and no ex jst over 1f out* **7/2**[1]
55-3 **5** *¾* **Cosmic Halo**[13] 88 7-8-13 **67**.... JackGarritty 3 69
(Richard Fahey) *hld up in midfield: rdn and prog 2f out: kpt on one pce fr over 1f out: nvr able to chal* **12/1**
122- **6** *nk* **Alshan Fajer**[21] 8392 6-9-7 **75**.... AdamKirby 13 79+
(J R Jenkins) *hld up in last: nt clr run over 2f out to over 1f out: styd on wl fnl f: no ch to threaten* **13/2**[3]
300- **7** *nk* **Dragoon Guard (IRE)**[29] 8344 5-9-4 **72**....(t) LukeMorris 8 73
(Anthony Honeyball) *chsd ldrs: rdn over 2f out: tried to cl over 1f out: one pce after* **16/1**
555- **8** *3 ¼* **Occult**[31] 8314 4-8-11 **68**.... JimCrowley 2 64
(Simon Dow) *prom: rdn over 2f out: steadily wknd jst over 1f out* **14/1**
/0-3 **9** *hd* **Rightway (IRE)**[14] 67 5-9-4 **75**.... GeorgeDowning(3) 6 70
(Tony Carroll) *nvr bttr than midfield: rdn and no imp on ldrs fr 2f out* **10/1**
00-3 **10** *hd* **Mr Red Clubs (IRE)**[16] 38 7-8-9 **70**.... JaneElliott(7) 7 65
(Michael Appleby) *t.k.h: hld up in midfield: rdn on outer over 2f out: no prog* **12/1**
530- **11** *3 ¼* **Barren Brook**[90] 6615 9-9-6 **74**.... TomQueally 1 63
(Laura Mongan) *led to 6f out: chsd ldr to 2f out: wknd* **16/1**
/62- **12** *¾* **Shimba Hills**[25] 8361 5-9-5 **73**.... WilliamTwiston-Davies 12 61
(Lawney Hill) *nvr bttr than midfield: shkn up over 2f out: wl btn whn short of room jst over 1f out: eased* **14/1**
40-0 **13** *1* **Tea Gown (IRE)**[11] 127 5-9-4 **72**....(p) ShaneGray 5 58
(Ed de Giles) *a towards rr: rdn and no prog over 2f out* **40/1**

2m 21.19s (-0.71) **Going Correction** -0.05s/f (Stan)
WFA 4 from 5yo+ 3lb 13 Ran SP% **117.7**
Speed ratings (Par 103): **100,99,98,98,97 97,97,94,94,94 92,91,90**
CSF £54.54 CT £935.81 TOTE £6.80: £3.20, £2.20, £6.00; EX 54.40 Trifecta £1049.20.
Owner P B Moorhead **Bred** Joe Rogers **Trained** Lower Beeding, W Sussex
FOCUS
The early pace wasn't strong but it picked up when the favourite pulled his way to the front. Muddling form. The third has been rated to his 1m4f effort here off a similar break.

257 32RED ON THE APP STORE H'CAP 7f (P)
7:10 (7:14) (Class 6) (0-55,60) 4-Y-O+ **£2,264** (£673; £336; £168) **Stalls** Low

Form RPR
05-0 **1** **Cookie Ring (IRE)**[12] 107 5-8-5 **46** oh1....(v[1]) PaulaMuir(7) 6 55
(Patrick Holmes) *hld up in rr: prog jst over 2f out: shkn up over 1f out: r.o wl fnl f to ld last 75yds* **33/1**
14-0 **2** *1* **Blackthorn Stick (IRE)**[14] 68 7-9-7 **55**.... JimmyQuinn 3 61
(Paul Burgoyne) *hld up in rr: smooth prog over 2f out: rdn to take 2nd over 1f out: clsd on idling ldr fnl f: got there jst as wnr flashed past 75yds out* **8/1**[3]
-312 **3** *1 ¾* **Bridge Builder**[3] 237 6-9-4 **55** 6ex....(p) RobHornby(3) 10 57
(Peter Hedger) *led after 1f: sn stretched field: clr 2f out: idled bdly fnl f: hdd last 75yds* **15/8**[1]
036- **4** *nse* **Clement (IRE)**[21] 8393 6-9-2 **55**....(b) CiaranMckee(5) 11 56
(John O'Shea) *prom: chsd ldr after 2f: rdn and no imp over 2f out: kpt on one pce but lost 2nd over 1f out* **8/1**[3]
60-5 **5** *9* **Alfie The Pug**[7] 168 4-8-12 **46** oh1....(t) JFEgan 1 23
(Pat Phelan) *led 1f: urged along in 3rd pl over 4f out: readily lft bhd fr 2f out* **14/1**
40-1 **6** *3 ¼* **Invectus Hero**[9] 143 4-9-12 **60** 6ex.... MartinLane 7 28
(Derek Shaw) *chsd ldrs over 2f out: sn btn and wknd* **2/1**[2]
030- **7** *1 ¼* **Stamp Of Approval (IRE)**[21] 8393 4-9-5 **53**.... GeorgeBaker 2 18
(Chris Wall) *t.k.h: hld up bhd ldrs: nudged along and wknd 2f out: eased* **12/1**
50-0 **8** *4* **Little**[10] 130 4-9-2 **53**.... JackDuern(3) 4 7
(Steph Hollinshead) *nvr bttr than midfield: wknd wl over 2f out* **50/1**
60-0 **9** *6* **Don Padeja**[14] 62 6-9-7 **55**....(p) WilliamTwiston-Davies 5
(Ronald Harris) *sn drvn and struggling in last pair: t.o* **40/1**
000- **10** *nse* **Just Marion (IRE)**[30] 8335 4-9-6 **54**....(v) SteveDrowne 9
(James Grassick) *sn drvn and outpcd in last: t.o* **66/1**

1m 25.35s (-0.65) **Going Correction** -0.05s/f (Stan) 10 Ran SP% **113.5**
Speed ratings (Par 101): **101,99,97,97,87 83,82,77,70,70**
CSF £265.91 CT £764.61 TOTE £38.20: £8.20, £2.70, £1.30; EX 414.60 Trifecta £2028.80.
Owner Mrs Ailsa Stirling **Bred** Gerard Brady **Trained** Middleham, N Yorks
FOCUS
This was run at a strong pace and set up nicely for a couple of the closers.
T/Jkpt: JACKPOT PLACEPOT £5,128.80. Pool: £5642.00 - 1.10 winning units. T/Plt: £452.00 to a £1 stake. Pool: £76,229.41 - 123.09 winning units. T/Qpdt: £6.30 to a £1 stake. Pool: £13,204.57 - 1544.01 winning units. **Jonathan Neesom**

218 LINGFIELD (L-H)
Wednesday, January 20

OFFICIAL GOING: Polytrack: standard
Wind: virtually nil Weather: sunny and bright, chilly

258 DAILY UNIBET EARLY PRICES FROM 9AM MAIDEN FILLIES' STKS 5f 6y(P)
12:30 (12:30) (Class 5) 3-Y-O+ **£2,911** (£866; £432; £216) **Stalls** High

Form RPR
26-3 **1** **Belle Mare Plage**[5] 193 3-8-13 70.... OisinMurphy 6 57
(Stuart Williams) *sn bustled along: in tch: pushed along and chsd ldrs 2f out: rdn and ev ch ent fnl f: styd on wl to ld wl ins fnl f* **6/4**[1]
545- **2** *½* **Guapo Bay**[36] 8230 3-8-13 58.... KieranO'Neill 5 55
(Richard Hannon) *dwlt and bustled along early: in tch: effrt on inner to chal over 1f out: drvn to ld 1f out: hdd and styd on same pce wl ins fnl f* **9/1**[3]
5 **3** *½* **Fearbuster (IRE)**[12] 102 3-8-13 0.... LukeMorris 2 53
(Hugo Palmer) *chsd ldrs: shkn up 2f out: drvn to ld over 1f out: hdd 1f out: kpt on same pce ins fnl f* **6/4**[1]
60- **4** *3 ¼* **Ready Steady (USA)**[29] 8350 3-8-13 0.... SeanLevey 7 42
(Richard Hannon) *s.i.s: outpcd in detached last: swtchd rt over 1f out: kpt on ins fnl f: no threat to ldrs* **20/1**
04-0 **5** *¾* **Anfield**[4] 217 5-10-0 45.... WilliamCarson 1 45
(Mick Quinn) *led: hung rt bnd 2f out: sn rdn and hdd: wknd ins fnl f* **100/1**
05- **6** *3 ½* **Aksum**[29] 8350 3-8-13 0.... TomQueally 3 26
(Emma Owen) *chsd ldr tl lost pl and hmpd over 1f out: wknd fnl f* **9/2**[2]

1m 0.5s (1.70) **Going Correction** +0.10s/f (Slow)
WFA 3 from 5yo 15lb 6 Ran SP% **113.9**
Speed ratings (Par 100): **90,89,88,83,82 76**
CSF £17.24 TOTE £2.70: £1.40, £5.60; EX 11.20 Trifecta £30.10.
Owner J W Parry **Bred** Bba 2010 Ltd **Trained** Newmarket, Suffolk
FOCUS
A moderate fillies' sprint maiden. The winner's official rating of 70 set the standard. The winner sets the standard, with the runner-up close to her AW best.

259 CORAL MEDIAN AUCTION MAIDEN STKS 1m 4f (P)
1:00 (1:00) (Class 6) 4-6-Y-O **£2,264** (£673; £336; £168) **Stalls** Low

Form RPR
1 **Byron Flyer**[257] 5-9-9 0.... AdamKirby 5 76+
(Ian Williams) *hld up in tch: swtchd rt and rdn to ld over 2f out: drvn 3 l clr 2f out: in n.d over 1f out: eased towards fin* **3/1**[3]
04-0 **2** *4* **Russian Bolero (GER)**[13] 78 5-9-9 74....(p) MartinLane 1 70
(David Dennis) *stdd s: hld up in tch in rr: cl 4th but trapped on inner and hmpd as wnr kicked clr jst over 2f out: swtchd rt and rallied over 1f out: chsd clr wnr 150yds: kpt on but no threat* **11/8**[1]
5-02 **3** *3* **J'Aspire**[7] 161 4-8-9 63....(tp) AaronJones(5) 2 60
(Stuart Williams) *chsd ldrs: wnt 2nd 3f out: sn swtchd rt and rdn: chsd clr wnr wl over 1f out: no imp: 3rd and wl hld fnl 150yds* **11/4**[2]
4 *3 ¼* **Rhythm Star**[45] 6-9-4 0....(b) WilliamCarson 3 55
(Jamie Snowden) *sn pushed up to ld: rdn and hdd over 2f out: sn outpcd: 4th and wl btn 1f out* **10/1**
4- **5** *8* **Hank Williams**[41] 8171 4-9-5 0.... CathyGannon 6 47
(Kristin Stubbs) *chsd ldr: rdn 4f out: losing pl whn squeezed for room and hmpd jst over 2f out: sn wknd* **20/1**
0- **6** *15* **Glimmer Of Hope**[42] 8162 5-9-9 0.... WilliamTwiston-Davies 4 23
(Mark Hoad) *in tch in last pair: rdn and struggling over 4f out: lost tch 3f out: t.o* **200/1**

2m 33.58s (0.58) **Going Correction** +0.10s/f (Slow)
WFA 4 from 5yo+ 4lb 6 Ran SP% **108.1**
Speed ratings: **102,99,97,95,89 79**
CSF £6.94 TOTE £3.50: £2.90, £2.00; EX 7.00 Trifecta £9.90.
Owner Anchor Men **Bred** Barton Stud **Trained** Portway, Worcs
■ Stewards' Enquiry : Aaron Jones caution: careless riding
FOCUS
A moderate maiden, though a couple of these were interesting for various reasons. The pace was modest, but they still came home at wide intervals and the race was notable for yet another example of the Kirby Kick.

260 LADBROKES H'CAP 7f 1y(P)
1:35 (1:35) (Class 4) (0-85,84) 4-Y-O+ **£4,690** (£1,395; £697; £348) **Stalls** Low

Form RPR
250- **1** **Fleckerl (IRE)**[31] 8318 6-9-1 **78**....(p) LiamKeniry 8 85
(Conor Dore) *stdd s: hld up in tch in last pair: hdwy over 1f out: chsng ldrs and clsng whn forced to switch rt ins fnl f: str run fnl 100yds: led on post* **20/1**
31-4 **2** *nse* **Steal The Scene (IRE)**[6] 172 4-9-7 **84**.... KieranO'Neill 4 91+
(Richard Hannon) *in tch in midfield: effrt to chse clr ldr jst over 2f out: clsng u.p but forced to switch rt ins fnl f: styd on to ld cl home: hdd on post* **6/5**[1]

20-3 **3** *nk* **Nortron (IRE)**[13] 82 4-9-1 **78**......................................(v) OisinMurphy 2 84
(Andrew Balding) *led: rdn and kicked 3 l clr 2f out: drvn and edgd lft 1f out: hdd and no ex cl home* **11/4**[2]

112- **4** *1* **Corporal Maddox**[20] 8412 9-9-4 **81**................................(p) LukeMorris 3 84
(Ronald Harris) *in tch in midfield: effrt u.p to chse ldrs over 1f out: kpt on ins fnl f: nvr quite enough pce to chal* **9/2**[3]

52-4 **5** *5* **Be Royale**[13] 80 6-8-10 **73**...(p) CathyGannon 7 63
(Michael Appleby) *t.k.h: hld up in tch in midfield: effrt 2f out: sn outpcd: wl hld and plugged on same pce fnl f* **16/1**

2-30 **6** *2 3/4* **Assault On Rome (IRE)**[14] 58 4-9-1 **78**................(b) AdrianNicholls 1 60
(Mark Johnston) *chsd ldrs tl lost pl qckly wl over 1f out: sn wknd* **20/1**

60-2 **7** *1/2* **Hannington**[18] 23 5-8-10 **80**................................(tp) CharlieBennett(7) 5 61
(Barry Brennan) *s.i.s: in tch in last pair: rdn over 2f out: no imp: wl hld over 1f out* **33/1**

460- **8** *1/2* **Maverik**[151] 5636 8-9-1 **78**.. JimCrowley 6 58
(Ali Stronge) *chsd ldr tl jst over 2f out: lost pl u.p wl over 1f out: wknd over 1f out* **20/1**

1m 23.96s (-0.84) **Going Correction** +0.10s/f (Slow) **8** Ran SP% **113.4**
Speed ratings (Par 105): **108,107,107,106,100 97,97,96**
CSF £42.72 CT £93.56 TOTE £5.30: £5.10, £1.10, £1.40; EX 70.20 Trifecta £329.80.
Owner Andrew Page **Bred** Yeguada De Milagro Sa **Trained** Hubbert's Bridge, Lincs

FOCUS
A decent handicap run at a good pace, but a lopsided betting market with them betting 16-1 bar three. A thrilling finish, but the feeling is that the best horse didn't win. The third has been rated to form.

261 32RED.COM H'CAP 1m 5f (P)
2:10 (2:12) (Class 6) (0-65,67) 4-Y-O+ **£2,264** (£673; £336; £168) **Stalls** Low

Form RPR

6-31 **1** **Percella**[8] 156 4-9-4 **67** 6ex...................................... GeorgeDowning(3) 2 72
(Ian Williams) *chsd ldng trio: effrt 2f out: clsd to press ldrs and pushed rt 1f out: chal ins fnl f: styd on wl u.p to ld last strides* **6/1**[3]

424- **2** *hd* **Peeps**[55] 8001 4-8-11 **57**.. SaleemGolam 4 62
(Mark H Tompkins) *s.i.s: sn rcvrd and in tch in midfield: clsd to chse ldrs and nt clr run over 1f out: swtchd rt and squeezed through 1f out: drvn to chal ins fnl f: styd on to ld cl home: hdd last strides* **10/1**

525- **3** *nk* **Thomas Blossom (IRE)**[37] 8223 6-9-10 **65**..................(t) GeorgeBaker 6 69
(Ali Stronge) *hld up in tch in midfield: hdwy 2f out: clsd to chse ldrs and pushed rt 1f out: kpt on wl u.p fnl 100yds: wnt 3rd last strides* **6/1**[3]

340- **4** *nk* **Furiously Fast (IRE)**[53] 8039 4-9-5 **65**............................. DavidNolan 3 69
(Richard Fahey) *chsd ldr: upsides over 2f out: rdn to ld 2f out: hrd pressed and drvn over 1f out: hdd 1f out: battled bk to ld again ins fnl f: hdd and lost 3 pls cl home* **7/2**[2]

002- **5** *hd* **Harlestone Hopes**[41] 8171 4-9-5 **65**..............................(p) AdamKirby 8 69
(Ed Dunlop) *chsd ldrs: swtchd rt and effrt over 2f out: drvn and ev ch over 1f out: led 1f out: hdd ins fnl f: no ex towards fin* **3/1**[1]

000- **6** *nk* **Hiorne Tower (FR)**[67] 7858 5-9-2 **57**................................. KierenFox 10 60
(John Best) *stdd after s: hld up in tch in last trio: effrt 2f out: chsng ldrs whn sltly impeded 1f out: rallied ins fnl f: kpt on wl towards fin* **16/1**

2-31 **7** *hd* **Shirataki (IRE)**[3] 233 8-8-7 **55** 6ex.............................. LuluStanford(7) 5 60
(Peter Hiatt) *s.i.s: in tch in last trio: effrt ent fnl 2f: clsd to chse ldrs 1f out: stuck bhd a wall of horses nvr anywhere to go thrght fnl f: one pce* **8/1**

003/ **8** *5* **Running Wolf (IRE)**[36] 4536 5-9-3 **58**..........................(t) KieranO'Neill 1 53
(Alex Hales) *led: rdn and joied over 2f out: hdd 2f out: wknd ins fnl f* **10/1**

500- **9** *3 3/4* **Star Anise (FR)**[110] 6899 5-9-7 **62**................................. MartinLane 7 52
(Paddy Butler) *s.i.s: hld up in tch in last trio: shkn up and outpcd over 2f out: sn btn: bhd fnl f* **50/1**

000- **10** *16* **Shadow Rock (IRE)**[48] 8092 4-9-5 **65**..........................(b) SeanLevey 9 31
(Richard Hannon) *in tch in midfield: rdn 4f out: lost pl and dropped to last over 2f out: lost tch over 1f out* **20/1**

2m 48.73s (2.73) **Going Correction** +0.10s/f (Slow)
WFA 4 from 5yo+ 5lb **10** Ran SP% **117.7**
Speed ratings (Par 101): **95,94,94,94,94 94,94,91,88,78**
CSF £65.11 CT £378.94 TOTE £6.80: £2.50, £3.90, £2.40; EX 42.10 Trifecta £370.30.
Owner Ian Williams **Bred** Mr & Mrs A E Pakenham **Trained** Portway, Worcs

FOCUS
A moderate staying handicap and a messy contest, with only a couple of lengths covering the first seven at the line.

262 BET AND WATCH EVERY RACE AT UNIBET H'CAP 5f 6y(P)
2:45 (2:45) (Class 2) (0-105,96) 3-Y-O **£12,291** (£3,657; £1,827; £913) **Stalls** High

Form RPR

022- **1** **Kadrizzi (FR)**[31] 8316 3-9-7 **96**...................................... RobertWinston 2 102
(Dean Ivory) *mde virtually all: edgd rt u.p but forged ahd over 1f out: stl drifting rt but styd on wl ins fnl f* **2/1**[1]

1-24 **2** *3/4* **Kingsley Klarion (IRE)**[10] 131 3-8-9 **84**.......................... JoeFanning 5 87
(Mark Johnston) *chsd ldrs: effrt over 1f out: clsd and swtchd lft ins fnl f: styd on wl to go 2nd cl home: no serious threat to wnr* **6/1**[3]

1-12 **3** *nk* **Aguerooo (IRE)**[10] 131 3-8-11 **86**.................................(p) KieranO'Neill 1 88
(Richard Hannon) *trckd ldrs: effrt: swtchd lft and effrt on inner over 1f out: chsd wnr ins fnl f: kpt on but no imp: lost 2nd cl home* **3/1**[2]

21-5 **4** *2* **Alshaqee**[18] 16 3-8-2 **77**... LukeMorris 4 72
(William Haggas) *racd keenly: w ldr: rdn and sltly outpcd whn swtchd lft 1f out: sn lost 2nd and wknd wl ins fnl f* **2/1**[1]

58.91s (0.11) **Going Correction** +0.10s/f (Slow) **4** Ran SP% **106.0**
Speed ratings (Par 103): **103,101,101,98**
CSF £12.30 TOTE £3.20; EX 15.20 Trifecta £32.20.
Owner A Chapman & Wentdale Limited **Bred** Simon Urizzi & Yann Loizeau **Trained** Radlett, Herts

FOCUS
Just the four remaining runners for this valuable 3yo sprint handicap, though all of them could be given a chance. A small pb from the winner, with the runner-up rated to form.

263 BET NOW WITH THE LADBROKES APP H'CAP 1m 1y(P)
3:20 (3:20) (Class 5) (0-75,75) 4-Y-O+ **£2,911** (£866; £432; £216) **Stalls** High

Form RPR

300- **1** **Charlies Mate**[30] 8325 5-9-5 **73**... KierenFox 6 81
(John Best) *hld up in tch: effrt over 1f out: hdwy u.p to chse ldr ins fnl f: led fnl 75yds: r.o strly: readily* **4/1**[3]

033- **2** *1 3/4* **Chelwood Gate (IRE)**[20] 8414 6-9-6 **74**.......................(v) OisinMurphy 2 78
(Patrick Chamings) *chsd ldrs: rdn to ld over 1f out: drvn and hdd 75yds: no ex and sn outpcd* **9/4**[1]

000- **3** *1 1/4* **Freddy With A Y (IRE)**[42] 8161 6-9-7 **75**....................(p) GeorgeBaker 8 76
(Gary Moore) *chsd ldr tl over 1f out: chsd wnr again briefly 1f out: 3rd and plugged on same pce ins fnl f* **10/1**

400- **4** *hd* **Gabrial The Thug (FR)**[29] 8354 6-8-4 **61**.................(t) SammyJoBell(3) 3 62
(Richard Fahey) *hld up in tch in last pair: rdn and hdwy over 1f out: nt clrest of runs and swtchd lft ins fnl f: styd on towards fin: no threat to wnr* **16/1**

03-6 **5** *1/2* **Breakheart (IRE)**[7] 165 9-9-1 **72**..................................(b) RobHornby(3) 4 72
(Andrew Balding) *in tch in midfield: effrt towards inner over 1f out: kpt on ins fnl f: nvr enough pce to threaten ldrs* **10/1**

123- **6** *3 1/4* **Wink Oliver**[54] 8016 4-9-7 **75**..(p) MartinLane 1 67
(David Dennis) *stdd s: hld up in tch in last pair: effrt and wd bnd wl over 1f out: no hdwy and wl hld fnl f* **11/4**[2]

24-0 **7** *1 1/2* **El Tel**[17] 33 4-9-1 **69**..[1] JackMitchell 7 58
(Roger Varian) *led: rdn and hdd over 1f out: lost 2nd 1f out: fdd ins fnl f* **10/1**

1m 37.71s (-0.49) **Going Correction** +0.10s/f (Slow) **7** Ran SP% **110.6**
Speed ratings (Par 103): **106,104,103,102,102 99,97**
CSF £12.51 CT £76.24 TOTE £4.90: £2.90, £2.40; EX 14.60 Trifecta £101.20.
Owner Mrs Jackie Jones **Bred** J H Mayne **Trained** Oad Street, Kent

FOCUS
An ordinary handicap. It's been rated a bit cautiously.

264 DOWNLOAD THE LADBROKES APP APPRENTICE H'CAP 7f 1y(P)
3:55 (3:55) (Class 6) (0-60,66) 4-Y-O+ **£2,264** (£673; £336; £168) **Stalls** Low

Form RPR

1-41 **1** **Exalted (IRE)**[9] 141 5-9-9 **62** 6ex..................................(t) PaddyBradley 3 69
(William Knight) *chsd ldr: upsides and rdn wl over 1f out: forged ahd wl ins fnl f: rdn out* **4/6**[1]

34-4 **2** *1/2* **First Rebellion**[3] 230 7-8-10 **52**................................(v) GeorgiaCox(3) 2 58
(Tony Carroll) *taken down early: chsd ldng pair: swtchd rt and effrt over 1f out: kpt on ins fnl f: wnt 2nd cl home* **12/1**

04-1 **3** *1/2* **Mercury**[14] 60 4-9-5 **58**...(b) PhilDennis 1 62
(Kevin Ryan) *racd keenly: led: jnd and rdn 2f out: hdd and no ex wl ins fnl f: wknd and lost 2nd cl home* **4/1**[2]

05-1 **4** *1 1/4* **Hierarch (IRE)**[7] 158 9-9-10 **66** 6ex.....................(p) SophieKilloran(3) 4 67
(David Simcock) *broke wl: sn restrained and in tch in 4th: shkn up and effrt over 1f out: kpt on ins fnl f: nvr enough pce to chal* **5/1**[3]

06-6 **5** *1/2* **Jonnie Skull (IRE)**[7] 158 10-8-13 **52**.....................(t) JosephineGordon 5 52
(Phil McEntee) *hld up in tch in rr: effrt on inner over 1f out: styd on but nvr enough pce to chal* **20/1**

1m 25.26s (0.46) **Going Correction** +0.10s/f (Slow) **5** Ran SP% **109.1**
Speed ratings (Par 101): **101,100,99,98,97**
CSF £9.44 TOTE £1.40: £1.10, £4.10; EX 8.20 Trifecta £21.70.
Owner N J Roach **Bred** Rathbarry Stud **Trained** Patching, W Sussex

FOCUS
A moderate apprentice handicap, though three of the five runners had been successful in their most recent starts. The majority also normally like to force it, so at least a couple had to change tactics.
T/Plt: £55.10 to a £1 stake. Pool: £46935.61 - 621.8 winning tickets T/Qpdt: £17.70 to a £1 stake. Pool: £6083.18 - 253.8 winning tickets **Steve Payne**

211 CHELMSFORD (A.W) (L-H)
Thursday, January 21

OFFICIAL GOING: Polytrack: standard
Wind: light, half behind Weather: dry

265 TOTEPLACEPOT RACING'S FAVOURITE BET H'CAP 1m 2f (P)
5:10 (5:11) (Class 6) (0-60,60) 3-Y-O **£3,234** (£962; £481; £240) **Stalls** Low

Form RPR

60-3 **1** **Skylark Lady (IRE)**[13] 96 3-9-4 **57**.................................... ChrisCatlin 5 64
(Rae Guest) *s.i.s: niggled for 2f: in tch in rr: nt clr run over 2f out: hdwy on inner over 1f out: swtchd rt and chsd ldr ins fnl f: led fnl 75yds: r.o wl* **5/1**

05-6 **2** *1/2* **You're A Goat**[10] 140 3-9-5 **58**.. AdamKirby 1 64
(Gary Moore) *hld up in last trio: effrt and stl plenty to do over 2f out: hdwy and edgd lft u.p over 1f out: sn chsng clr ldr: pressed wnr fnl 75yds: kpt on* **2/1**[2]

00-2 **3** *1 1/2* **Schoolboy Error (IRE)**[10] 148 3-9-2 **55**...................(b) TimmyMurphy 3 58
(Jamie Osborne) *racd keenly: led: wnt clr 3f out: 3 l clr 2f out: rdn ent fnl f: hdd fnl 75yds: sn btn and wknd towards fin* **15/8**[1]

60-2 **4** *4 1/2* **Clive Clifton (IRE)**[10] 140 3-9-4 **60**............................. PhilipPrince(3) 2 55
(David Evans) *chsd ldrs: rdn 5f out: drvn over 2f out: chsd clr ldr briefly over 1f out: 4th and no imp 1f out: wknd* **7/2**[3]

006- **5** *3 3/4* **Diamondsaretrumps (IRE)**[32] 8320 3-9-1 **57**.... MichaelJMMurphy(3) 7 48
(Charles Hills) *chsd ldrs: over 2f out: struggling whn squeezed for room and hmpd over 1f out: sn wknd* **33/1**

460- **6** *9* **Modello (IRE)**[52] 8055 3-9-4 **60**...................................... EoinWalsh(3) 4 33
(Giles Bravery) *rdn along early: sn chsng ldr: rdn 3f out and sn outpcd: losing pl and hmpd wl over 1f out: sn wknd* **20/1**

20-4 **7** *2* **Global Avenger (IRE)**[10] 147 3-9-7 **60**.....................(b) OisinMurphy 6 27
(Ed Dunlop) *hld up in last trio: u.p and struggling over 2f out: bhd over 1f out* **20/1**

2m 5.94s (-2.66) **Going Correction** -0.25s/f (Stan) **7** Ran SP% **119.5**
Speed ratings (Par 95): **100,99,98,94,91 84,83**
CSF £16.07 TOTE £6.80: £3.20, £1.50; EX 21.30 Trifecta £66.00.
Owner C J Murfitt **Bred** David Fenlon **Trained** Newmarket, Suffolk

FOCUS
A weak handicap, run at a strong pace and it saw the principals come clear.

266 TOTEPOOLLIVEINFO.COM CLAIMING STKS 1m 2f (P)
5:40 (5:41) (Class 6) 4-Y-O+ **£3,234** (£962; £481; £240) **Stalls** Low

Form RPR

444- **1** **Quest Of Colour (IRE)**[113] 6860 5-8-7 64.......................... ShaneGray 3 74
(Richard Fahey) *chsd ldrs: effrt on inner over 1f out: ev ch ins fnl f: styd on wl to ld towards fin* **16/1**

034- **2** *hd* **Gaelic Silver (FR)**[32] 8318 10-8-13 85.....................(p) PaddyBradley(7) 5 87
(Gary Moore) *in tch in midfield: clsd to press ldrs 2f out: rdn to ld jst ins fnl f: hdd and no ex towards fin* **5/4**[1]

23-3 **3** *1 1/4* **Bushel (USA)**[20] 6 6-8-10 75..................................(p) JamesSullivan 2 74
(James Given) *led: rdn and edgd rt over 1f out: hdd jst ins fnl f: no ex and outpcd fnl 100yds* **10/1**

20-6 **4** *3/4* **Spiritual Star (IRE)**[7] 172 7-9-6 85............................(t) WilliamCarson 1 83
(Anthony Carson) *stdd s: t.k.h: hld up in tch in rr: hdwy over 1f out: wnt 4th and rdr dropped rein jst ins fnl f: styd on same pce fnl 100yds* **7/2**[2]

43-6 **5** *1* **Cottesloe (IRE)**[8] 160 7-9-4 76.. JFEgan 4 79
(John Berry) *stdd s: hld up in tch: effrt wl over 1f out: swtchd rt and kpt on same pce u.p ins fnl f* **8/1**

 The Form Book, Raceform Ltd, Newbury, RG14 5SJ

660- **6** *1* **Dominandros (FR)**[43] 8157 5-9-4 80................................ LukeMorris 8 77
(Gay Kelleway) *chsd ldr: rdn ent fnl 2f: unable qck ent fnl f: outpcd fnl f* **16/1**

100- **7** *4* **Monsieur Chevalier (IRE)**[22] 8405 9-9-0 80.................(p) JimCrowley 7 65
(James Given) *hld up in tch in last trio: rdn over 2f out: dropped to rr over 1f out: wknd ins fnl f* **5/1**[3]

2m 9.42s (0.82) **Going Correction** -0.25s/f (Stan) 7 Ran SP% **115.3**
Speed ratings (Par 101): **86,85,84,84,83 82,79**
CSF £37.39 TOTE £12.50: £4.70, £1.60; EX 39.10 Trifecta £154.90.Bushel was claimed by N. A. Lloyd Beavis for £4000.
Owner Havelock Racing 2 **Bred** Awbeg Stud **Trained** Musley Bank, N Yorks

FOCUS
They went steadily in this modest claimer and it saw a muddling finish.

267 TOTEQUADPOT RACING'S FOUR LEGGED FRIEND H'CAP 1m 2f (P)

6:10 (6:13) (Class 4) (0-85,84) 4-Y-O+ **£8,086** (£2,406; £1,202; £601) **Stalls** Low

Form RPR

5-41 **1** **Freud (FR)**[5] 212 6-8-10 76 6ex.............................. GeorgeDowning(3) 6 84+
(Ian Williams) *t.k.h: chsd ldrs: rdn and effrt on inner to ld 1f out: r.o wl: eased cl home* **5/2**[1]

520- **2** *½* **Mountain Rescue (IRE)**[85] 7556 4-8-12 77.................... OisinMurphy 1 83
(Roger Charlton) *t.k.h: wl in tch in midfield: effrt over 1f out: swtchd rt ent fnl f: wnt 2nd fnl 75yds: r.o wl* **5/1**

653- **3** *½* **One Pekan (IRE)**[25] 8369 6-9-6 83.................................. JackMitchell 3 88+
(Roger Varian) *stdd s: t.k.h: hld up in tch in last trio: clsd over 1f out: nt clr run and swtchd rt 1f out: styd on wl u.p fnl 100yds* **10/3**[2]

U1-0 **4** *½* **U S Navy Seal (USA)**[15] 66 4-9-5 84.............................. AdamKirby 8 88
(J R Jenkins) *stdd s: hld up in tch in last trio: swtchd rt and effrt wl over 1f out: sme hdwy and bmpd 1f out: reminder and wandered ins fnl f: kpt on wl under hands and heels riding fnl 100yds* **6/1**

0-43 **5** *¾* **Maiden Approach**[1] 254 5-9-0 77............................(p) JamesSullivan 9 80
(Richard Fahey) *sn led: rdn over 1f out: hdd 1f out: no ex: lost 2nd 75yds out: wknd towards fin* **16/1**

/05- **6** *2 ¼* **Art Scholar (IRE)**[43] 8157 9-8-13 76.............................. AndrewMullen 7 74
(Michael Appleby) *hld up in tch in midfield: effrt wl over 1f out: keeping on but struggling to qckn whn bmpd 1f out: wknd ins fnl f* **12/1**

40-3 **7** *3 ¾* **Warfare**[12] 121 7-9-3 80.. JimCrowley 2 71
(Tim Fitzgerald) *sn chsng ldr: rdn 2f out: unable qck and lost pl whn n.m.r jst over 1f out: wknd ins fnl f* **9/2**[3]

113- **8** *nse* **All The Winds (GER)**[182] 4544 11-9-0 77.......................(t) LukeMorris 4 67
(Shaun Lycett) *stdd s: t.k.h: hld up in tch in rr: rdn over 2f out: no imp and outpcd over 1f out: bhd ins fnl f* **25/1**

2m 5.48s (-3.12) **Going Correction** -0.25s/f (Stan)
WFA 4 from 5yo+ 2lb 8 Ran SP% **118.2**
Speed ratings (Par 105): **102,101,101,100,100 98,95,95**
CSF £16.05 CT £42.59 TOTE £3.50: £1.10, £1.80, £1.70; EX 23.60 Trifecta £92.60.
Owner J Tredwell **Bred** E Puerari, Oceanic Bloodstock Et Al **Trained** Portway, Worcs
■ Stewards' Enquiry : Jack Mitchell two-day ban: careless riding (Feb 4-5)

FOCUS
They went a fair pace in this competitive handicap and the form is sound. The second, third and fourth have been rated close to their marks in a straightforward looking race.

268 TOTEEXACTA PICK THE 1ST AND 2ND MEDIAN AUCTION MAIDEN STKS 6f (P)

6:40 (6:42) (Class 5) 3-5-Y-O **£5,175** (£1,540; £769; £384) **Stalls** Centre

Form RPR

6- **1** **Princess Cookie**[34] 8285 3-8-4 0.................................. DannyBrock(3) 1 77+
(Philip McBride) *trckd ldng pair: swtchd rt and clsd over 1f out: rdn to ld ent fnl f: in command and r.o wl ins fnl f* **6/1**[2]

23-4 **2** *2 ½* **Phantom Flipper**[12] 126 3-8-12 70..............................(p) KieranO'Neill 2 72
(Richard Hannon) *led: rdn and drifted rt over 1f out: hdd and outpcd ent fnl f: no ch w wnr and plugged on same pce ins fnl f* **5/2**[1]

00- **3** *4* **Santiburi Spring**[56] 7997 3-8-7 0.. KierenFox 7 54
(John Best) *midfield: outpcd and dropped to last pair 4f out: sme hdwy u.p over 1f out: styd on to go 3rd fnl 75yds: nvr trbld ldrs* **10/1**[3]

32-3 **4** *3* **Burmese Whisper**[14] 77 3-8-12 67.............................. OisinMurphy 6 50
(Andrew Balding) *restless in stalls: w ldr: rdn and ev ch whn carried rt over 1f out: 3rd and btn 1f out: wknd ins fnl f* **5/2**[1]

5 *nse* **Summer Music (IRE)** 3-8-7 0.. LukeMorris 4 44
(Robert Cowell) *dwlt: rn green and sn rdn along in last trio: hdwy into midfield over 3f out: 4th and u.p 2f out: no hdwy and hung lft 1f out: wknd ins fnl f* **5/2**[1]

0 **6** *10* **Music Major**[12] 126 3-8-12 0...................................... AdamBeschizza 5 17
(Kevin Morgan) *restless in stalls: in tch in midfield: 5th and outpcd 2f out: wknd over 1f out* **50/1**

7 *9* **Shirocco Cloud** 4-9-9 0.. SteveDrowne 3
(Mrs Ilka Gansera-Leveque) *sn bhd and pushed along: rdn and struggling 1/2-way: wl bhd over 1f out* **25/1**

1m 10.96s (-2.74) **Going Correction** -0.25s/f (Stan)
WFA 3 from 4yo 16lb 7 Ran SP% **114.9**
Speed ratings (Par 103): **108,104,99,95,95 81,69**
CSF £21.62 TOTE £8.00: £4.10, £1.50; EX 21.00 Trifecta £134.60.
Owner Howard J Cooke **Bred** J W Mitchell **Trained** Newmarket, Suffolk

FOCUS
There was a messy start in this ordinary maiden and the leaders didn't hang about.

269 SCOOP6SOCCER THE £1 MILLION FOOTBALL BET FILLIES' H'CAP 6f (P)

7:10 (7:12) (Class 5) (0-70,70) 4-Y-O+ **£5,175** (£1,540; £769; £384) **Stalls** Centre

Form RPR

06-4 **1** **Queen Aggie (IRE)**[19] 24 6-9-2 68...................... GeorgeDowning(3) 4 76
(Tony Carroll) *taken down early: stdd s: hld up in tch in rr: swtchd rt and effrt over 1f out: n.m.r tl gap opened ins fnl f: str run u.p fnl 100yds to ld last stride* **8/1**

503- **2** *shd* **Barbs Princess**[93] 7356 6-9-7 70...................................... JimCrowley 1 77
(Charles Hills) *led: rdn over 1f out: kpt on u.p ins fnl f: hdd last stride* **4/1**[2]

2-33 **3** *nk* **Royal Rettie**[2] 249 4-8-6 58.. DannyBrock(3) 3 64
(Heather Dalton) *taken down early: t.k.h: hld up in tch: effrt jst over 1f out: hdwy u.p ins fnl f: styd on wl* **5/1**[3]

4-31 **4** *¾* **Mambo Fever**[14] 80 5-8-13 62...................................... LukeMorris 6 66
(David C Griffiths) *restless in stalls: chsd ldr: rdn and ev ch 2f out: unable qck and hrd drvn ins fnl f: lost 2nd and one pce fnl 75yds* **5/2**[1]

54-1 **5** *½* **Ohsosecret**[15] 75 4-9-0 63...(t) SaleemGolam 7 65
(Stuart Williams) *chsd ldng pair: effrt u.p over 1f out: styd on same pce ins fnl f* **7/1**

30-2 **6** *½* **Saved My Bacon (IRE)**[15] 56 5-9-3 69........................ EoinWalsh(3) 2 70
(Chris Dwyer) *taken down early: restless in stalls: hld up in tch: effrt over 1f out: nt clrest of runs 1f out: kpt on same pce ins fnl f* **5/2**[1]

1m 12.48s (-1.22) **Going Correction** -0.25s/f (Stan) 6 Ran SP% **117.4**
Speed ratings (Par 100): **98,97,97,96,95 95**
CSF £41.25 TOTE £9.90: £5.00, £2.20; EX 43.50 Trifecta £178.90.
Owner Shropshire Wolves 4 **Bred** Mrs Marion Daly **Trained** Cropthorne, Worcs

FOCUS
The fillies were pretty much still upsides half a furlong out in this moderate sprint handicap. The runner up has been rated to her Polytrack best.

270 WIN A FOOTBALL FORTUNE WITH SCOOP6SOCCER H'CAP 7f (P)

7:40 (7:40) (Class 7) (0-50,50) 4-Y-O+ **£2,587** (£770; £384; £192) **Stalls** Low

Form RPR

00/2 **1** **Camdora (IRE)**[7] 174 4-9-2 45.................................... TimmyMurphy 2 55
(Jamie Osborne) *stdd s: hld up in tch in last pair: swtchd lft and clsd over 1f out: nt clr run ent fnl f: gap opened and qcknd to ld ins fnl f: sn in command: comf* **4/5**[1]

0-05 **2** *1 ¾* **Loud**[7] 175 6-9-4 50..(b) SimonPearce(3) 1 53
(Lydia Pearce) *led: sn hdd and chsd ldr tl 3f out: rdn to ld and edgd lft over 1f out: hdd and one pce ins fnl f* **5/1**[2]

55-6 **3** *1 ¼* **Rosie Crowe (IRE)**[17] 35 4-9-7 50.............................(p) LukeMorris 7 50
(Shaun Harris) *chsd ldrs tl wnt 2nd 3f out: rdn and ev ch over 1f out tl unable qck ins fnl f: outpcd fnl 100yds* **5/1**[2]

6-60 **4** *2 ¼* **Ciaras Cookie (IRE)**[7] 174 4-9-5 48.......................... CharlesBishop 6 42
(Heather Dalton) *stdd s: hld up in tch in rr: rdn over 2f out: unable qck u.p over 1f out: plugged on same pce ins fnl f* **25/1**

00-5 **5** *½* **Salvado (IRE)**[7] 174 6-9-2 48................................ GeorgeDowning(3) 5 40
(Tony Carroll) *taken down early and led to s: t.k.h: hld up in rr: effrt and swtchd rt 1f out: kpt on same pce u.p ins fnl f: nvr trbld ldrs* **8/1**[3]

260- **6** *2 ½* **Tamarin**[35] 8265 4-8-12 48....................................(b) NatalieHambling(7) 8 34
(Lisa Williamson) *sn led: rdn and hdd over 1f out: sn btn: wknd ins fnl f* **33/1**

6-05 **7** *3 ¼* **Black Vale (IRE)**[5] 217 5-9-1 47..............................(bt) DannyBrock(3) 4 24
(Phil McEntee) *in tch in midfield: effrt over 1f out: sn outpcd and btn whn nt clr run 1f out: wknd fnl f* **8/1**[3]

1m 26.21s (-0.99) **Going Correction** -0.25s/f (Stan) 7 Ran SP% **117.9**
Speed ratings (Par 97): **95,93,91,89,88 85,81**
CSF £5.65 CT £13.27 TOTE £2.00: £1.20, £2.50; EX 7.00 Trifecta £19.10.
Owner Lady Blyth **Bred** Bernard Cooke **Trained** Upper Lambourn, Berks

FOCUS
An uncompetitive bottom-drawer handicap, rated around the third.

271 TOTEPOOL H'CAP 6f (P)

8:10 (8:11) (Class 6) (0-65,65) 4-Y-O+ **£3,234** (£962; £481; £240) **Stalls** Centre

Form RPR

10-0 **1** **Summerinthecity (IRE)**[17] 36 9-9-0 65............ AdamMcNamara(7) 2 75
(Richard Fahey) *hld up in tch in midfield: effrt on inner over 1f out: rdn to chse ldr and swtchd lft 1f out: r.o wl to ld wl ins fnl f: rdn out* **8/1**

/0-6 **2** *1 ¼* **Seamster**[19] 21 9-9-7 65...(vt) DanielTudhope 1 71
(David O'Meara) *broke fast: led: rdn over 1f out: kpt on tl hdd and no ex wl ins fnl f* **11/4**[1]

31-0 **3** *3* **Hamis Al Bin (IRE)**[6] 197 7-9-1 59..............................(bt) LukeMorris 5 56
(Milton Bradley) *chsd ldrs: rdn to chse ldr over 1f out tl 1f out: 3rd and no ex 1f out: wknd fnl 100yds* **11/1**

5-65 **4** *1* **Divine Call**[6] 197 9-9-1 59..(b) FrannyNorton 3 53
(Milton Bradley) *dwlt: hld up in tch in rr: effrt on inner over 1f out: wnt 4th and kpt on u.p ins fnl f: kpt on but no threat to ldrs* **4/1**[2]

440- **5** *2* **Humour (IRE)**[21] 8408 5-9-6 64.. KierenFox 8 52
(Christine Dunnett) *in tch in midfield but stuck wd: effrt u.p over 1f out: no imp and styd on same pce fnl f* **7/1**

4-30 **6** *hd* **Bogsnog (IRE)**[10] 144 6-9-6 64.................................... CathyGannon 6 52
(Kristin Stubbs) *in tch in midfield: n.m.r and shuffled bk wl over 1f out: kpt on same pce and no imp u.p fnl f* **6/1**[3]

00/0 **7** *1 ¼* **Hadaj**[17] 36 7-9-5 63.. TomEaves 7 47
(Michael Herrington) *in tch in last pair: rdn over 2f out: no imp over 1f out: wl hld and plugged on same pce ins fnl f* **20/1**

00-0 **8** *1 ¼* **Satchville Flyer**[12] 124 5-9-7 65.............................(v[1]) JimCrowley 4 45
(Brett Johnson) *chsd ldr tl lost pl u.p over 1f out: wknd ins fnl f* **4/1**[2]

1m 11.53s (-2.17) **Going Correction** -0.25s/f (Stan) 8 Ran SP% **117.7**
Speed ratings (Par 101): **104,102,98,97,94 94,92,90**
CSF £31.28 CT £250.42 TOTE £7.70: £2.10, £1.90, £2.10; EX 43.40 Trifecta £429.30.
Owner Dr Marwan Koukash **Bred** J Costello **Trained** Musley Bank, N Yorks

FOCUS
A wide-open looking sprint handicap. A low draw proved a real advantage.
T/Plt: £185.30 to a £1 stake. Pool of £65700.65 - 258.72 winning tickets. T/Qpdt: £31.00 to £1 stake. Pool of £9181.19 - 218.95 winning tickets. **Steve Payne**

246 SOUTHWELL (L-H)

Thursday, January 21

OFFICIAL GOING: Fibresand: standard
Wind: Virtually nil Weather: Grey cloud

272 DAILY UNIBET EARLY PRICES FROM 9AM H'CAP 6f (F)

12:40 (12:40) (Class 6) (0-60,60) 4-Y-O+ **£2,587** (£770; £384; £192) **Stalls** Low

Form RPR

13-2 **1** **Fujin**[6] 197 5-9-7 60...(b) PaulMulrennan 5 75
(Shaun Harris) *mde all: pushed along wl over 1f out: clr ins fnl f: readily* **8/11**[1]

2-12 **2** *3* **Fortinbrass (IRE)**[11] 130 6-9-1 59........................ CallumShepherd(5) 2 63
(John Balding) *a chsng wnr: rdn along 2f out: drvn appr fnl f: no imp* **10/3**[2]

06-2 **3** *2* **Ertidaad (IRE)**[16] 47 4-9-5 58.....................................(vt) TomQueally 1 56
(Emma Owen) *trckd ldng pair on inner: hdwy wl over 2f out: rdn wl over 1f out: drvn over 1f out: kpt on same pce* **7/1**[3]

1-26 **4** *¾* **Arizona Snow**[10] 143 4-9-1 54.................................(p) KieranO'Neill 3 50
(Ronald Harris) *t.k.h early: in tch: hdwy to trck ldrs 1/2-way: effrt 2f out: sn rdn: drvn over 1f out and sn btn* **17/2**

440- **5** *6* **Diamond Vine (IRE)**[35] 8265 8-8-7 46 oh1...............(p) WilliamCarson 4 24
(Ronald Harris) *chsd ldrs on outer: rdn along 1/2-way: sn drvn and wknd* **33/1**

1m 19.23s (2.73) **Going Correction** +0.40s/f (Slow) 5 Ran SP% **107.0**
Speed ratings (Par 101): **97,93,90,89,81**
CSF £3.12 TOTE £1.80: £1.40, £1.10; EX 3.30 Trifecta £5.40.
Owner Mrs S L Robinson **Bred** Juddmonte Farms Ltd **Trained** Carburton, Notts

FOCUS
This proved straightforward for the favourite.

273 CORAL H'CAP 1m 4f (F)
1:10 (1:12) (Class 5) (0-75,75) 4-Y-O+ **£3,234** (£962; £481; £240) **Stalls** Low

Form RPR
33-0 **1** **Virnon**[16] 43 5-8-13 **67** JoeFanning 2 78
(Alan Swinbank) *trckd ldrs: cl up 1/2-way: led wl over 3f out: pushed clr over 2f out: kpt on strly* **10/1**
063- **2** 5 **Kingscombe (USA)**[15] 503 7-9-4 **72** RobertHavlin 6 75
(Linda Jewell) *prom: pushed along over 4f out: effrt 3f out and sn chsng wnr: rdn over 2f out: drvn wl over 1f out: no imp* **25/1**
001- **3** ¾ **Honeymoon Cocktail (FR)**[36] 8258 5-9-0 **71** RobHornby(3) 9 73
(David Pipe) *hld up and bhd: hdwy over 4f out: chsd ldrs wl over 2f out: sn rdn: chsd ldng pair wl over 1f out: sn drvn and kpt on same pce* **9/4**[1]
13-5 **4** 9 **What Could She Be (IRE)**[20] 1 4-8-12 **70** (p) PaulMulrennan 8 58
(Michael Dods) *hld up in tch: hdwy 4f out: rdn along on outer to chse ldrs 3f out: drvn over 2f out: sn one pce* **12/1**
56-3 **5** 2 ½ **Percys Princess**[11] 132 5-9-5 **73** LiamJones 5 57
(Michael Appleby) *reminders s: sn pushed along to chse ldrs: rdn along 1/2-way: drvn 4f out: sn outpcd* **12/1**
15-5 **6** 8 **Horseguardsparade**[6] 200 5-9-2 **70** WilliamTwiston-Davies 3 41
(Nigel Twiston-Davies) *trckd ldrs on inner: pushed along over 4f out: rdn along to chse ldrs 3f out: drvn over 2f out and sn outpcd* **9/2**[3]
050- **7** 25 **Jacobs Son**[30] 8344 8-9-7 **75** (p) DanielTudhope 4 6
(John Balding) *chsd ldrs: rdn along over 4f out: sn lost pl: bhd whn eased over 1f out* **16/1**
6- **8** 9 **Dunquin (IRE)**[22] 8405 4-9-0 **72** GrahamLee 7
(John Mackie) *in rr: swtchd rt to outer and pushed along 1/2-way: rdn 5f out: sn lost pl and bhd* **11/4**[2]
000- **9** 4 ½ **Sov (IRE)**[30] 8344 5-8-8 **62** (p) ShaneGray 1
(John Balding) *led: rdn along 4f out: sn hdd: drvn 3f out and sn wknd* **66/1**

2m 46.27s (5.27) **Going Correction** +0.40s/f (Slow)
WFA 4 from 5yo+ 4lb **9** Ran SP% **111.3**
Speed ratings (Par 103): **98,94,94,88,86 81,64,58,55**
CSF £211.57 CT £738.75 TOTE £13.30: £3.50, £6.50, £1.10; EX 260.70 Trifecta £794.60.
Owner Jack Pearce **Bred** World Racing Network **Trained** Melsonby, N Yorks

FOCUS
They finished well strung out in this fair middle-distance handicap. There's little solid about the form.

274 32RED.COM H'CAP 1m (F)
1:45 (1:46) (Class 6) (0-60,60) 3-Y-O **£2,587** (£770; £384; £192) **Stalls** Low

Form RPR
51-3 **1** **Kemsing (IRE)**[2] 248 3-8-13 **55** ShelleyBirkett(3) 8 66+
(Julia Feilden) *hld up: smooth hdwy to trck ldrs 3 1/2f out: chal on outer 2f out: shkn up to ld 1 1/2f out: rdn and edgd lft jst ins fnl f: sn clr* **11/8**[1]
05-2 **2** 3 ½ **Never Say (IRE)**[16] 48 3-8-2 **46** (p) CallumShepherd(5) 1 49
(Jason Ward) *trckd ldrs on inner: pushed along and lost pl after 3f: sn rdn along in rr and swtchd rt to outer: wd st: hdwy on outer 2f out: drvn and styd on fnl f* **20/1**
30-1 **3** 1 ¼ **Carbutt's Ridge (IRE)**[16] 48 3-9-2 **55** DougieCostello 3 55
(K R Burke) *hld up in tch: hdwy on inner to trck ldng pair 3f out: rdn 2f out: chsd wnr 1f out: sn drvn and kpt on same pce* **5/1**[3]
400- **4** 6 **Granita (USA)**[84] 7585 3-9-7 **60** [1] TedDurcan 9 46
(George Scott) *dwlt: sn trcking ldrs: hdwy on outer to chal 3f out: rdn to ld 2f out: sn drvn and hdd 1 1/2f out: wknd* **4/1**[2]
000- **5** 4 ½ **Regal Galaxy**[91] 7412 3-8-7 **46** oh1 JoeFanning 7 21
(Mark H Tompkins) *in tch: rdn along 3f out: sn wknd* **25/1**
422- **6** nk **Pivotal Dream (IRE)**[41] 8177 3-8-6 **52** CharlieBennett(7) 2 26
(Mark Brisbourne) *cl up: led after 1f: rdn along 3f out: hdd 2f out: sn drvn and wknd* **9/1**
440- **7** 4 ½ **Window Shopping (IRE)**[34] 8281 3-8-7 **46** oh1 (p) KieranO'Neill 4 9
(Mark Usher) *slt ld 1f: cl up: rdn along after 3f: sn lost pl and bhd* **66/1**
006- **8** 1 ¼ **Mumbles Magic (IRE)**[183] 4517 3-8-7 **46** JoeyHaynes 5 6
(Jo Hughes) *cl up: rdn along 3f out: drvn and wknd over 2f out* **25/1**
350- **9** 3 ½ **Rockliffe**[21] 8409 3-9-7 **60** TomEaves 6 12
(Mick Channon) *cl up: rdn along over 3f out: sn wknd* **8/1**

1m 48.09s (4.39) **Going Correction** +0.40s/f (Slow) **9** Ran SP% **113.8**
Speed ratings (Par 95): **94,90,89,83,78 78,73,72,69**
CSF £35.94 CT £111.32 TOTE £3.10: £1.40, £4.60, £2.10; EX 28.60 Trifecta £98.20.
Owner Miss J Feilden **Bred** D Dwan **Trained** Exning, Suffolk

FOCUS
There was plenty of competition for the lead and the principals all came from off the pace.

275 32RED CASINO MAIDEN AUCTION STKS 1m (F)
2:20 (2:23) (Class 5) 3-Y-O **£3,234** (£962; £481; £240) **Stalls** Low

Form RPR
-0 **1** **Daisy Bere (FR)**[17] 40 3-9-0 0 JoeyHaynes 9 71
(K R Burke) *chsd ldrs on outer: wd st: hdwy and cl up 2f out: rdn to chal over 1f out: drvn: green and edgd lft ins fnl f: kpt on wl to ld nr fin* **66/1**
05- **2** hd **Rain In The Face**[36] 8246 3-9-5 0 GrahamGibbons 1 75
(Ralph Beckett) *slt ld: pushed along over 2f out: sn jnd and rdn: drvn ent fnl f: hdd and no ex nr fin* **10/1**
6- **3** 6 **Kaisan**[100] 7175 3-9-5 0 JamieSpencer 11 61
(Michael Bell) *cl up on outer: wd st: rdn whn n.m.r and swtchd lft wl over 1f out: sn drvn and kpt on same pce* **5/4**[1]
034- **4** 1 ½ **Powered (IRE)**[35] 8267 3-9-5 65 (p) DavidNolan 3 57
(Jo Hughes) *chsd ldrs: rdn along over 2f out: drvn wl over 1f out: kpt on same pce* **11/1**
002- **5** ½ **Kadooment Day (IRE)**[120] 6655 3-9-5 72 DougieCostello 7 56
(K R Burke) *t.k.h: trckd ldrs whn n.m.r after 1f: hdwy over 3f out: rdn to chse ldrs over 2f out: drvn wl over 1f out and grad wknd* **8/1**[3]
33-4 **6** 3 **Kelvin Hall**[18] 29 3-9-0 67 JoeFanning 4 44
(Mark Johnston) *cl up: rdn along wl over 2f out: drvn wl over 1f out: grad wknd* **5/1**[2]
300- **7** 1 ½ **Canford Thompson**[36] 8246 3-9-2 68 DanielMuscutt(3) 2 45
(Marco Botti) *trckd ldrs on inner: hdwy 1/2-way: green and rdn along wl over 2f out: sn wknd* **14/1**
- **8** 1 ½ **Mossy's Lodge** 3-9-0 0 WilliamCarson 8 36
(Anthony Carson) *towards rr: smooth hdwy on inner and cl up 3f out: rdn along over 2f out: sn wknd* **8/1**[3]
050- **9** 21 **Let There Be Light**[87] 7507 3-9-5 62 PaulMulrennan 6
(Gay Kelleway) *sn rdn along and outpcd in rr: bhd fr 1/2-way* **33/1**

10 7 **Compromise** 3-9-2 0 EoinWalsh(3) 5
(Conor Dore) *s.i.s: green and a bhd* **66/1**

1m 47.72s (4.02) **Going Correction** +0.40s/f (Slow) **10** Ran SP% **113.4**
Speed ratings (Par 97): **95,94,88,87,86 83,82,80,59,52**
CSF £611.71 TOTE £58.80: £9.60, £3.00, £1.20; EX 538.40 Trifecta £1246.00.
Owner Mrs Elaine M Burke **Bred** S N C Regnier & San Gabriel Inv Inc **Trained** Middleham Moor, N Yorks

FOCUS
The first two came clear in this maiden and there was quite a turn-up. The fourth has been rated in line with the better view of her latest C&D effort.

276 LADBROKES (S) STKS 7f (F)
2:55 (2:56) (Class 6) 4-Y-O+ **£2,911** (£866; £432; £216) **Stalls** Low

Form RPR
36-1 **1** **Moonlight Venture**[17] 37 5-9-4 67 (tp) KeaganLatham 4 75
(Kevin Ryan) *chsd ldng trio: hdwy over 2f out: swtchd wd and effrt wl over 1f out: rdn and edgd lft over 1f out: drvn and hung rt and lft ins fnl f: styd on to ld last 75yds* **4/1**[3]
061- **2** ½ **Greyfriarschorista**[44] 8148 9-9-10 73 (bt) PaulMulrennan 7 80
(Giles Bravery) *cl up: led after 1f: jnd over 2f out and sn rdn: drvn over 1f out: hdd and no ex last 75yds* **15/8**[1]
52-5 **3** 5 **Monsieur Jimmy**[2] 246 4-9-1 65 DanielTudhope 5 58
(Declan Carroll) *chsd ldng pair: hdwy and cl up over 2f out: rdn to chal wl over 1f out: ev ch tl drvn and one pce ent fnl f* **7/2**[2]
44-3 **4** 1 ½ **Oak Bluffs (IRE)**[17] 37 5-9-4 60 DavidNolan 3 57
(Richard Fahey) *dwlt: hdwy on inner 3f out: rdn over 2f out: sn drvn and one pce* **14/1**
30-5 **5** 1 ½ **Abi Scarlet (IRE)**[11] 135 7-9-5 73 (p) KieranO'Neill 6 54
(Scott Dixon) *in rr: rdn along and wd st: sn drvn and n.d* **14/1**
00-3 **6** 1 ½ **Kung Hei Fat Choy (USA)**[19] 23 7-9-10 82 (b) TomEaves 2 55
(James Given) *led 1f: chsd ldr: rdn along over 2f out: drvn wl over 1f out and sn btn* **9/2**

1m 32.15s (1.85) **Going Correction** +0.40s/f (Slow) **6** Ran SP% **108.5**
Speed ratings (Par 101): **105,104,98,97,95 93**
CSF £11.12 TOTE £6.40: £3.30, £2.00; EX 12.30 Trifecta £34.10.There was no bid for the winner.
Owner Mrs J Ryan **Bred** G Reed **Trained** Hambleton, N Yorks

FOCUS
The leaders went off a bit quick and that set things up for a closer.

277 LADBROKES H'CAP 1m (F)
3:30 (3:31) (Class 6) (0-65,66) 4-Y-O+ **£2,587** (£770; £384; £192) **Stalls** Low

Form RPR
00-5 **1** **The Firm (IRE)**[17] 37 7-8-12 **58** (be) RobHornby(3) 4 65
(Daniel Mark Loughnane) *chsd ldrs: swtchd rt and hdwy on outer 2f out: rdn and edgd lft over 1f out: styd on to ld ins fnl f* **25/1**
30-4 **2** 1 ¾ **Miss Lillie**[20] 2 5-9-1 **58** (p) GrahamLee 8 61
(Roger Teal) *cl up: chal over 2f out: rdn wl over 1f out: slt ld jst over 1f out: sn drvn and edgd lft: hdd ins fnl f* **15/2**[2]
40-1 **3** 2 **Stun Gun**[20] 2 6-9-0 **57** (p) MartinLane 1 55
(Derek Shaw) *led: rdn along over 2f out: drvn and hdd jst over 1f out: kpt on same pce* **9/1**[3]
541- **4** 3 **Limerick Lord (IRE)**[40] 8201 4-9-3 **63** (p) ShelleyBirkett(3) 5 54
(Julia Feilden) *t.k.h: cl up: effrt over 2f out: rdn wl over 1f out: drvn and one pce appr fnl f* **3/1**[1]
055- **5** 11 **Bunker Hill Lass**[30] 8340 4-8-1 **51** (p) JaneElliott(7) 2 15
(Michael Appleby) *chsd ldrs: rdn along over 3f out: sn outpcd* **28/1**
560- **6** 3 ¼ **Humphry Repton**[112] 6886 4-8-10 **53** JoeFanning 6 10
(Mark H Tompkins) *chsd ldrs: rdn along 3f out: sn wknd* **28/1**
/0-6 **7** 1 ¼ **Poppet Rocket (IRE)**[12] 124 4-9-0 **64** JordanUys(7) 3 18
(Brian Meehan) *a in rr* **20/1**

1m 46.05s (2.35) **Going Correction** +0.40s/f (Slow) **7** Ran SP% **62.3**
Speed ratings (Par 101): **104,102,100,97,86 83,81**
CSF £58.87 CT £266.78 TOTE £14.70: £5.70, £3.30; EX 67.90 Trifecta £125.30.
Owner Amazing Racing **Bred** Sir E J Loder **Trained** Baldwin's Gate, Staffs
■ Billy Bond was withdrawn. Price at time of withdrawal 4/5F. Rule 4 applies to all bets - deduct 55p in the pound.

FOCUS
There was another shock result here.

278 DOWNLOAD THE LADBROKES APP H'CAP 7f (F)
4:05 (4:05) (Class 5) (0-75,75) 4-Y-O+ **£3,234** (£962; £481; £240) **Stalls** Low

Form RPR
30-6 **1** **Llewellyn**[7] 179 8-8-6 **67** (b) PhilDennis(7) 3 76
(Declan Carroll) *mde all: qcknd clr wl over 1f out: readily* **14/1**
31- **2** 1 ½ **Final**[328] 720 4-9-5 **73** JoeFanning 1 78+
(Mark Johnston) *sn pushed along in rr: bhd 1/2-way: hdwy over 2f out: rdn over 1f out: styd on wl fnl f* **6/1**[3]
505- **3** 1 ¼ **Burning Blaze**[37] 8242 6-9-1 **74** CallumShepherd(5) 8 76
(Brian Ellison) *towards rr: pushed along and hdwy on outer 3f out: wd st: rdn 2f out: chsd clr ldr over 1f out: kpt on same pce* **3/1**[2]
-625 **4** ½ **Alpha Tauri (USA)**[7] 176 10-9-1 **69** MartinLane 2 69
(Charles Smith) *trckd ldrs on inner: effrt over 2f out: rdn wl over 1f out: sn drvn and kpt on same pce* **10/1**
000- **5** 7 **Golden Spun (USA)**[200] 3935 4-9-1 **69** PaulMulrennan 6 50
(Michael Dods) *trckd wnr: effrt 3f out: rdn along 2f out: sn drvn and wknd* **7/1**
61-1 **6** 3 **Ziggys Star**[17] 36 4-9-7 **75** LiamJones 5 48
(Michael Appleby) *chsd ldrs: pushed along 3f out: rdn over 2f out: sn btn* **15/8**[1]
3-33 **7** shd **Elusivity (IRE)**[11] 133 8-9-4 **72** TomEaves 4 45
(Conor Dore) *hld up towards rr: hdwy on inner 3f out: rdn over 2f out: sn wknd* **12/1**
300- **8** 8 **Ypres**[117] 6760 7-9-0 **68** PJMcDonald 7 19
(Jason Ward) *prom: rdn along over 2f out: sn drvn and wknd* **25/1**

1m 31.24s (0.94) **Going Correction** +0.40s/f (Slow) **8** Ran SP% **113.9**
Speed ratings (Par 103): **110,108,106,106,98 94,94,85**
CSF £93.86 CT £325.66 TOTE £15.50: £4.10, £2.00, £1.10; EX 54.90 Trifecta £545.80.
Owner Mrs Sarah Bryan **Bred** Elite Racing Club **Trained** Malton, N Yorks

FOCUS
This was dominated from the front by the winner. The third has been rated to his latest form.
T/Plt: £664.30 to a £1 stake. Pool of £52053.26 - 57.20 winning tickets. T/Qpdt: £181.00 to a £1 stake. Pool of £6973.23 - 28.50 winning tickets. **Joe Rowntree**

224 MEYDAN (L-H)

Thursday, January 21

OFFICIAL GOING: Dirt: fast; turf: good

279a DISTRICT ONE VILLAS (H'CAP) (DIRT) 1m 1f 110y(D)

3:00 (3:00) (78-94,94) 3-Y-O+

£24,489 (£8,163; £4,081; £2,040; £1,224; £816)

RPR

1 **Respect Me**[49] 8099 6-9-5 **93**.....(b) WayneSmith 2 98
(Ismail Mohammed) *mid-div: chsd ldrs 2f out: r.o wl: led fnl 55yds* **12/1**

2 1 1/4 **Etijaah (USA)**[13] 116 6-9-4 **91**..... PaulHanagan 4 94
(Doug Watson, UAE) *settled in rr: chsd ldr 2 1/2f out: led briefly 110yds out: hdd fnl 55yds* **11/4**[1]

3 nk **Grand Argentier (FR)**[34] 8302 4-9-5 **94**.....(v) SamHitchcott 1 96+
(Doug Watson, UAE) *s.i.s: rdn to ld: kicked clr 3 1/2f out: reeled in tl hdd 110yds out* **8/1**

4 2 **Enery (IRE)**[13] 119 7-8-7 **80**..... FernandoJara 3 78
(M Al Mheiri, UAE) *nvr nr to chal but r.o fnl 2 1/2f* **6/1**

5 5 1/4 **Zephuros (IRE)**[20] 12 4-8-13 **87**.....(b) WilliamBuick 5 76
(Charlie Appleby) *trckd ldrs tl outpcd fnl 2f* **9/2**[3]

6 3 3/4 **Ormindo (USA)**[307] 986 6-8-10 **84**..... FrederikTylicki 7 63
(A bin Harmash, UAE) *nvr bttr than mid-div* **7/1**

7 3 3/4 **Street Act (USA)**[20] 13 9-8-6 **79**.....(bt) TadhgO'Shea 6 51
(A R Al Rayhi, UAE) *s.i.s: nvr nr to chal* **7/2**[2]

8 5 1/4 **Invincible Strike (IRE)**[4] 238 5-8-6 **79**..... RichardMullen 8 40
(S Seemar, UAE) *trckd ldr tl wknd fnl 4 1/2f* **25/1**

1m 58.35s (-0.45) **Going Correction** +0.15s/f (Slow)
WFA 4 from 5yo+ 1lb 8 Ran SP% **116.5**
Speed ratings: **107,106,105,104,99 96,93,89**
CSF: 46.08 TRICAST: 288.64.

Owner Sheikh Majid bin Mohammed Al Maktoum **Bred** Darley **Trained** Newmarket, Suffolk

FOCUS
TRAKUS (metres travelled compared to winner): 2nd +9, 3rd +1, 4th +13, 5th +14, 6th +14, 7th +18, 8th +9. A non-carnival handicap run at a strong pace.

280a DISTRICT ONE (H'CAP) (TURF) 5f (T)

3:35 (3:35) (100-113,110) 3-Y-O+

£48,979 (£16,326; £8,163; £4,081; £2,448; £1,632)

RPR

1 **Roicead (USA)**[83] 7620 9-9-1 105.....(t) WayneSmith 4 108
(D Selvaratnam, UAE) *trckd ldng pair: rdn 3f out: led 1 1/2f out: r.o wl* **25/1**

2 2 **Saayerr**[378] 84 5-9-0 104..... ChrisHayes 3 100
(D Selvaratnam, UAE) *s.i.s: settled in rr: r.o fnl 2f nrst fin* **10/1**

3 nk **Caspian Prince (IRE)**[109] 6971 7-9-2 106..... RobertWinston 2 101
(Dean Ivory) *wl away: sn led: hdd 1 1/2f out: r.o same pce* **4/1**[2]

4 1 **Green Door (IRE)**[14] 91 5-9-1 105.....(v) AndreaAtzeni 1 96
(Robert Cowell) *trckd ldr: ev ch 1 1/2f out: one pce fnl 1f* **3/1**[1]

5 3/4 **Stepper Point**[109] 6971 7-9-6 110.....(p) JamesDoyle 5 98
(William Muir) *trckd ldng pair tl outpcd fnl 2f* **11/2**[3]

6 1/2 **Fityaan**[14] 91 8-8-13 102..... DaneO'Neill 6 90
(M Al Mheiri, UAE) *s.i.s: a in rr* **12/1**

7 hd **Banaadeer (AUS)**[14] 91 4-9-3 107.....(b) PaulHanagan 8 93
(M F De Kock, South Africa) *settled in rr: nvr nr to chal* **4/1**[2]

8 2 **Demora**[14] 91 7-8-7 100..... AlistairRawlinson(3) 7 79
(Michael Appleby) *trckd ldng pair tl wknd fnl 2 1/2f* **11/2**[3]

56.94s (-0.16) **Going Correction** +0.25s/f (Good) 8 Ran SP% **116.4**
Speed ratings: **111,107,107,105,104 103,103,100**
CSF: 251.81 TRICAST: 1222.79.

Owner Michael Gerard Daly & Dhruba Selvaratnam **Bred** Michael Daly **Trained** United Arab Emirates

FOCUS
TRAKUS: 2nd 0, 3rd 0, 4th 0, 5th 0, 6th 0, 7th 0, 8th 0. The rail on the turf course was out 12 metres. All of these had something to prove and the race seemed to fall apart a bit, the outsider of the lot a decisive winner. The splits were 23.75, 21.71 before the winner clocked a slowing 11.98 to the line.

281a MEYDAN SOBHA (H'CAP) (DIRT) 1m 1f 110y(D)

4:10 (4:10) (100-123,110) 3-Y-O+

£48,979 (£16,326; £8,163; £4,081; £2,448; £1,632)

RPR

1 **Special Fighter (IRE)**[14] 92 5-9-4 **107**..... FernandoJara 4 112+
(M Al Mheiri, UAE) *mid-div: chsd ldrs 3 1/2f out: led 1 1/2f out: r.o comf* **4/1**[2]

2 5 **Plantagenet (SPA)**[67] 9-8-11 **100**..... Per-AndersGraberg 5 95
(Niels Petersen, Norway) *settled in rr: nvr nr to chal but r.o fnl 2 1/2f* **40/1**

3 1 3/4 **Romansh (USA)**[14] 94 6-8-13 **101**..... RoystonFfrench 3 93
(S bin Ghadayer, UAE) *trckd ldng pair: ev ch 3f out: one pce fnl 2f* **40/1**

4 3/4 **Storm Belt (USA)**[35] 8275 7-9-5 **108**..... SamHitchcott 2 98
(Doug Watson, UAE) *trckd ldr: rdn 4 1/2f out: sn btn but r.o same pce fnl 2f* **11/1**

5 3/4 **Let's Go (USA)**[68] 7857 4-9-6 **110**..... JamesDoyle 6 99
(Saeed bin Suroor) *settled in rr: t.k.h: nvr nr to chal* **4/7**[1]

6 3 **Footbridge (USA)**[327] 742 6-9-6 **109**..... WilliamBuick 1 91
(Charlie Appleby) *sn led: hdd & wknd 1 1/2f out* **11/2**[3]

1m 57.39s (-1.41) **Going Correction** +0.15s/f (Slow)
WFA 4 from 5yo+ 1lb 6 Ran SP% **112.2**
Speed ratings: **111,107,105,105,104 102**
CSF: 102.41.

Owner Sheikh Mansoor bin Mohammed al Maktoum **Bred** Darley **Trained** UAE

FOCUS
TRAKUS: 2nd -16, 3rd +1, 4th -8, 5th -1, 6th -13. This was another race that fell apart - only six runners and there were a couple of notable disappointments, but the winner is decent. The opening 1200m were run 1.10secs slower than the first race on this card but the final time 0.96sec quicker - the fastest time yet from 17 races over C&D.

282a AL FAHIDI FORT SPONSORED BY MEYDAN SOBHA (GROUP 2) (TURF) 7f

4:45 (4:45) 3-Y-O+

£102,040 (£34,013; £17,006; £8,503; £5,102; £3,401)

RPR

1 **Safety Check (IRE)**[131] 6313 5-9-0 116..... WilliamBuick 7 116+
(Charlie Appleby) *mid-div: smooth prog 2f out: led 1f out: r.o wl* **4/6**[1]

2 1 3/4 **Harry's Son (AUS)**[299] 4-9-0 113.....(t) PStrydom 1 111
(P V Lafferty, South Africa) *led chsng gp: r.o wl fnl 2f nrst fin* **11/1**

3 1 **Mastermind (SAF)**[329] 704 4-9-0 100..... WayneSmith 4 108
(M F De Kock, South Africa) *s.i.s: trckd ldr: rdn 3f out: led 1 1/2f out: hdd fnl 1f* **20/1**

4 1/2 **Anaerobio (ARG)**[14] 95 8-9-0 108.....(t) ChristopheSoumillon 8 107
(M F De Kock, South Africa) *mid-div: r.o fnl 2f but nvr nr to chal* **9/1**[3]

5 3 1/4 **Royal Ridge (SAF)**[14] 90 7-9-0 101.....(bt) RichardMullen 3 98
(M F De Kock, South Africa) *a mid-div* **50/1**

6 1 1/4 **Eastern Rules (IRE)**[14] 95 8-9-0 102..... JamesDoyle 9 95
(M Halford, Ire) *nvr nr to chal* **16/1**

7 2 **Zarwaan**[110] 6932 5-9-0 107..... PaulHanagan 5 89
(Doug Watson, UAE) *settled in rr: nvr able to chal* **9/2**[2]

8 1 **Ghaamer (USA)**[14] 95 6-9-0 106.....(t) DaneO'Neill 2 87
(A R Al Rayhi, UAE) *sn led: hdd & wknd fnl 1 1/2f* **16/1**

9 hd **Tellina (SAF)**[201] 3923 6-9-0 112..... SamHitchcott 6 86
(M F De Kock, South Africa) *s.i.s: a in rr* **33/1**

1m 22.77s (-1.33) **Going Correction** +0.25s/f (Good) 9 Ran SP% **117.9**
Speed ratings: **117,115,113,113,109 108,105,104,104**
CSF: 9.59.

Owner Godolphin **Bred** Malih Al Basti **Trained** Newmarket, Suffolk

FOCUS
TRAKUS: 2nd - 3, 3rd +1, 4th +2, 5th -3, 6th +1, 7th -3, 8th -3, 9th -3. The third running of the Al Fahidi Fort as a 7f contest and last year's winner repeated the trick. Two horses raced clear of the others for much of the way, but the pace was sensible and one of them finished third. Here are the splits: 25.10, 22.82, 23.24, before the winner finished in 11.49. The winner has been rated in line with last year's C&D seasonal debut figure.

283a DISTRICT ONE TROPHY (H'CAP) (TURF) 1m 2f

5:20 (5:20) (100-113,107) 3-Y-O+

£48,979 (£16,326; £8,163; £4,081; £2,448; £1,632)

RPR

1 **Sanshaawes (SAF)**[14] 93 6-9-6 **107**..... ChristopheSoumillon 3 110
(M F De Kock, South Africa) *trckd ldrs: rdn to ld 1f out: r.o wl: comf* **7/2**[3]

2 3/4 **Whistle Stop (SAF)**[14] 95 5-9-0 **100**..... PaulHanagan 5 103
(M F De Kock, South Africa) *mid-div: rdn 2 1/2f out: r.o wl fnl 1 1/2f: nrst fin* **12/1**

3 1 1/2 **Elleval (IRE)**[14] 93 6-9-6 **107**.....(p) PatSmullen 4 106
(David Marnane, Ire) *settled in rr: nvr able to chal but r.o fnl 2 1/2f* **4/1**

4 shd **Elhaame (IRE)**[82] 7645 6-9-5 **106**..... JamesDoyle 10 104+
(Saeed bin Suroor) *settled in rr: r.o fnl 2f: nrst fin* **3/1**[2]

5 shd **Pilote (IRE)**[14] 93 6-9-3 **104**..... RoystonFfrench 1 102+
(S bin Ghadayer, UAE) *nvr nr to chal but r.o fnl 2f* **33/1**

6 shd **Zambucca (SAF)**[14] 93 7-8-13 **105**.....(b) HectorCrouch(5) 9 104
(S Seemar, UAE) *trckd ldr: ev ch 1 1/2f out: one pce fnl 110yds* **25/1**

7 1 1/4 **Fearless Hunter (GER)**[123] 6576 6-9-4 **105**..... CarlosLopez 2 100+
(Rune Haugen) *nvr nr to chal* **33/1**

8 1 1/4 **Start Right**[14] 93 9-9-0 **100**..... RichardMullen 6 94+
(S Seemar, UAE) *nvr bttr than mid-div* **14/1**

9 3 1/4 **Tha'ir (IRE)**[138] 6128 6-9-5 **106**..... WilliamBuick 7 92
(Saeed bin Suroor) *sn led: rdn 3f out: hdd & wknd 1f out* **11/4**[1]

10 5 1/4 **Bancnuanaheireann (IRE)**[14] 93 9-9-1 **105**..... AlistairRawlinson(3) 8 81
(Michael Appleby) *trckd ldrs: wd: t.k.h: wknd fnl 2f* **28/1**

2m 4.48s (1.78) **Going Correction** +0.25s/f (Good) 10 Ran SP% **121.4**
Speed ratings: **102,101,100,100,100 99,98,97,95,91**
CSF: 44.39 TRICAST: 177.53.

Owner Sh Ahmed bin Mohd bin Khalifa Al Maktoum **Bred** Oldlands Stud **Trained** South Africa

FOCUS
TRAKUS: 2nd +3, 3rd +5, 4th +5, 5th -1, 6th +2, 7th 0, 8th +7, 9th -1, 10th +7. This was steadily run; 27.84 (400m), 24.27 (800m), 24.62 (1200m), 24.12 (1600m) before the winner quickened up in 23.4. The first three have been rated to their marks.

284a DISTRICT ONE MANSIONS (H'CAP) (DIRT) 1m (D)

5:55 (5:55) (95-118,107) 3-Y-O+

£44,897 (£14,965; £7,482; £3,741; £2,244; £1,496)

RPR

1 **Top Clearance (USA)**[14] 92 4-9-0 **100**.....(t) ChrisHayes 8 101
(D Selvaratnam, UAE) *trckd ldrs: rdn 2 1/2f out: r.o wl to ld fnl 55yds* **9/2**[2]

2 1 **American Hope (USA)**[218] 3278 5-9-0 **100**..... JamesDoyle 11 99
(Saeed bin Suroor) *trckd ldr: led 1f out: hdd fnl 55yds* **11/2**[3]

3 1 1/4 **Success Story (KOR)**[60] 5-9-0 **100**..... TadhgO'Shea 4 96
(Jang G Min, Korea) *sn led: rdn 3 1/2f out: hdd 1f out: r.o same pce* **10/1**

4 1 **Mind That Boy (IRE)**[116] 6801 4-9-6 **107**..... MickaelBarzalona 2 100+
(S bin Ghadayer, UAE) *s.i.s: settled in rr: r.o fnl 2 1/2f but nvr nr to chal* **16/1**

5 1 1/4 **Tiz Now Tiz Then (USA)**[7] 183 11-8-10 **97**.....(bt) RichardMullen 5 87+
(S Seemar, UAE) *mid-div: n.m.r after 3f: r.o same pce fnl 2f* **7/2**[1]

6 nse **Energia Colonial (BRZ)**[78] 8-9-2 **102**.....(t) Per-AndersGraberg 3 93+
(Niels Petersen, Norway) *settled in rr: r.o fnl 2f: nrst fin* **25/1**

7 6 1/4 **Fox Trotter (IRE)**[138] 6075 4-8-13 **99**..... PatSmullen 1 75+
(Brian Meehan) *nvr bttr than mid-div* **20/1**

8 hd **Silver Ocean (USA)**[95] 8-9-4 **105**..... RoystonFfrench 7 80+
(Niels Petersen, Norway) *nvr nr to chal* **33/1**

9 1 1/4 **Secret Brief (IRE)**[139] 6040 4-9-0 **100**..... WilliamBuick 6 73+
(Charlie Appleby) *a in rr* **7/1**

10 2 1/4 **Bannock (IRE)**[69] 7848 7-8-8 **95**..... FrederikTylicki 13 62+
(A bin Harmash, UAE) *mid-div: wd: wknd fnl 2 1/2f* **33/1**

11 5 1/2 **Royal Navy Ship (USA)**[158] 5426 4-9-2 **102**.....(tp) PStrydom 9 57+
(P V Lafferty, South Africa) *s.i.s: a in rr* **9/1**

12 3 1/2 **Vortex (NOR)**[71] 7-9-0 **100**.....(b) CarlosLopez 14 47
(Rune Haugen) *trckd ldrs tl wknd fnl 3f* **20/1**

13 *8* **Unforgiving Minute**^{14} 90 5-9-2 **102** SamHitchcott 10 31
(Barry Brennan) *trckd ldrs tl outpcd 3 1/2f out* **33/1**
14 *8 1/2* **Mustadeem (IRE)**^{7} 189 4-9-2 **102** PaulHanagan 12 11+
(A R Al Rayhi, UAE) *nvr bttr than mid-div* **10/1**

1m 38.14s (0.64) **Going Correction** +0.15s/f (Slow) **14** Ran SP% **124.5**
Speed ratings: **102,101,99,98,97 97,91,91,89,87 82,78,70,62**
CSF: 27.75 TRICAST: 244.91.
Owner Sheikh Ahmed Al Maktoum **Bred** Gary & Mary West Stables Inc **Trained** United Arab Emirates

FOCUS
TRAKUS: 2nd +2, 3rd -5, 4th -4, 5th +6, 6th -5, 7th -4, 8th +7, 9th +7, 10th +12, 11th +9, 12th +8, 13th +4, 14th +5 The early pace was fast - 25.19 (400m from standing start), 22.49 (800m), 24.73 (1200m), before the winner clocked 25,73 - yet few got involved and this isn't form to be too strong on.

285a MOHAMMED BIN RASHID AL MAKTOUM CITY - DISTRICT ONE (H'CAP) (TURF) 1m 4f 38y(T)

6:30 (6:30) (95-111,111) 3-Y-O+

£61,224 (£20,408; £10,204; £5,102; £3,061; £2,040)

RPR

1 **Haafaguinea**^{327} 744 6-9-6 **111** WilliamBuick 10 111
(Saeed bin Suroor) *trckd ldrs: rdn to ld fnl 1/2f* **6/1**^{3}
2 *1/2* **Al Saham**^{343} 534 7-9-1 **106** JamesDoyle 3 105
(Saeed bin Suroor) *trckd ldr: ev ch 1f out: one pce fnl 110yds* **9/4**^{1}
3 *shd* **Quarterback (GER)**^{22} 4-8-10 **105** (p) DaneO'Neill 13 104
(Rune Haugen) *sn led: r.o wl but hdd fnl 110yds* **16/1**
4 *nk* **Dormello (IRE)**^{55} 8029 8-8-13 **104** ChrisHayes 8 103+
(D Selvaratnam, UAE) *mid-div: n.m.r bhd ldrs 1f out: r.o once clr: nrst fin* **20/1**
5 *shd* **Paene Magnus (IRE)**^{14} 93 7-8-9 **100** (t) FrederikTylicki 1 98+
(A bin Harmash, UAE) *settled in rr: nvr nr to chal but r.o v wl fnl 1 1/2f* **66/1**
6 *1/2* **Tannaaf (IRE)**^{22} 4-8-10 **105** ChristopheSoumillon 14 103+
(M F De Kock, South Africa) *a in mid-div* **3/1**^{2}
7 *nk* **Sugar Boy (IRE)**$^{/96}$ 7927 6-8-9 **106** (p) HectorCrouch$^{(6)}$ 2 103
(S Seemar, UAE) *trckd ldrs: t.k.h: ev ch 1f out: wknd fnl 110yds* **50/1**
8 *shd* **Zen Zansai Zaid (SWE)**^{14} 93 7-8-9 **100** (bt) TadhgO'Shea 7 97+
(Tommy Gustafsson, Sweden) *nvr bttr than mid-div* **66/1**
9 *1* **Majeed**^{14} 94 6-8-9 **100** PaulHanagan 5 95+
(David Simcock) *s.i.s: nvr nr to chal* **16/1**
10 *nk* **Antinori (IRE)**^{14} 93 10-8-10 **101** (b) RichardMullen 6 96+
(S Seemar, UAE) *v.s.a: a in rr* **33/1**
11 *nk* **Spend The Cash (IRE)**^{116} 6798 5-9-0 **105** WayneSmith 9 99+
(W Mongil, Germany) *a in rr* **33/1**
12 *1 1/4* **Certerach (IRE)**^{116} 6796 8-8-13 **104** (p) PatSmullen 11 96+
(M Halford, Ire) *nvr bttr than mid-div* **10/1**
13 *2 1/2* **Keep In Line (GER)**^{104} 7076 4-8-6 **100** (p) DavidProbert 4 89+
(Saeed bin Suroor) *a in rr* **8/1**
14 *2 3/4* **Rio Tigre (IRE)**^{299} 1092 5-9-3 **108** MickaelBarzalona 12 92+
(S bin Ghadayer, UAE) *nvr bttr than mid-div* **14/1**

2m 35.06s (3.26) **Going Correction** +0.25s/f (Good)
WFA 4 from 5yo+ 4lb **14** Ran SP% **124.3**
Speed ratings: **99,98,98,98,98 98,97,97,97,96 96,95,94,92**
CSF: 19.50 TRICAST: 216.18.Placepot: £411.40 to a £1 stake. Pool of £7383.37 - 13.10 winning units. Quadpot: £40.90 to a £1 stake. Pool of £420.10 - 7.60 winning units..
Owner Sheikh Rashid Dalmook Al Maktoum **Bred** Bishop Wilton Stud **Trained** Newmarket, Suffolk

FOCUS
TRAKUS: 2nd 0, 3rd -6, 4th -7, 5th -11, 6th +11, 7th -11, 8th -2, 9th +3, 10th +1, 11th -3, 12th +7, 13th +5, 14th +8. The pace was slow - 27.16 (400m) 25.86 (800m), 25.97 (1200m), 26.49 (1600m), 24.36 (2000m) - and there was a bunched finish.

^{258}LINGFIELD (L-H)

Friday, January 22

OFFICIAL GOING: Polytrack: standard
Wind: Half behind, moderate becoming light Weather: Raining until after race 4

286 DOWNLOAD THE NEW UNIBET RACING APP H'CAP 5f 6y(P)

12:50 (12:55) (Class 6) (0-65,65) 3-Y-O **£2,264** (£673; £336; £168) **Stalls** High

Form RPR

356- **1** **Jess**^{159} 5415 3-9-7 **65** ShaneGray 5 67
(Kevin Ryan) *chsd ldr: clsd over 1f out: narrow ld ins fnl f: jst prevailed* **11/4**^{2}
6-41 **2** *nse* **E Fourteen**^{8} 174 3-8-2 **51** 6ex PaddyPilley$^{(5)}$ 1 53
(Robyn Brisland) *dwlt: sn chsd ldrs: clsd over 1f out: chal towards inner fnl f: w wnr last 100yds: jst pipped* **4/1**^{3}
66-0 **3** *1* **Justice Rock**^{4} 242 3-9-6 **64** (b) TomQueally 2 62
(David Elsworth) *wl away: led: 2 l up 2f out: hrd rdn over 1f out: edgd lft and hdd ins fnl f: nt qckn* **9/4**^{1}
042- **4** *3/4* **Hot Stuff**^{42} 8173 3-9-5 **63** LukeMorris 4 62
(Tony Carroll) *dwlt: racd in 4th: rdn 2f out: clsng on ldrs whn nowhere to go jst ins fnl f: kpt on but nt rcvr* **11/4**^{2}
400- **5** *7* **Little Pebbles**^{130} 6385 3-8-11 **55** WilliamCarson 3 25
(Jamie Osborne) *dwlt: a in last and outpcd bef 1/2-way* **16/1**

59.02s (0.22) **Going Correction** +0.05s/f (Slow) **5** Ran SP% **110.0**
Speed ratings (Par 95): **100,99,98,97,85**
CSF £13.68 TOTE £4.00: £1.90, £3.00; EX 13.50 Trifecta £30.60.
Owner Mrs J Ryan **Bred** Cecil And Miss Alison Wiggins **Trained** Hambleton, N Yorks
■ Stewards' Enquiry : Tom Queally one-day ban; careless riding (5th Feb)

FOCUS
Following the abandonment of the jumps fixture at Chepstow, the off times for each of the first six races on this card were put back five minutes. A low-grade opener, though, it was run at a brisk pace and provided an exciting finish. The winner can replicate her best figure in the coming weeks.

287 32RED CASINO MAIDEN STKS 1m 2f (P)

1:25 (1:30) (Class 5) 3-Y-O **£2,911** (£866; £432; £216) **Stalls** Low

Form RPR

1 **Barton Lodge (IRE)** 3-9-5 0 JamieSpencer 8 78+
(David Simcock) *dwlt: hld up in last trio: prog over 2f out: gd hdwy to ld ins fnl f: v green but kpt on* **7/1**
006- **2** *3/4* **Cat Royale (IRE)**^{23} 8404 3-9-2 65 (p) DannyBrock$^{(3)}$ 7 73
(Jane Chapple-Hyam) *trckd ldr: chal 2f out but on outside of trio: chsd new ldr over 1f out to ins fnl f: kpt on u.p* **25/1**
05-2 **3** *nk* **Milrow (IRE)**^{19} 29 3-9-5 79 FergusSweeney 2 72
(Martyn Meade) *trckd ldng pair: rdn to ld 2f out: idled and hanging 1f out: hdd and fnd little ins fnl f* **6/4**^{1}
3 **4** *2 3/4* **Muaither (IRE)**^{10} 153 3-9-5 0 RobertHavlin 5 67+
(John Gosden) *stl green: chsd ldng trio: urged along 1/2-way: outpcd over 2f out: kpt on one pce fnl f* **11/4**^{2}
5 *1/2* **The Magic Pencil (IRE)** 3-9-5 0 TomEaves 6 66+
(Kevin Ryan) *s.s: sn in tch in last: outpcd over 2f out but gng wl enough: shkn up over 1f out: kpt on fnl f* **16/1**
6 *1* **Our Little Sister (IRE)** 3-9-0 0 LiamKeniry 4 59+
(Hughie Morrison) *mostly in last trio: nudged by rival 3f out: outpcd sn after: no ch fnl 2f: plugged on* **25/1**
0- **7** *1* **Norse Castle**^{79} 7701 3-9-5 0 TomQueally 1 62
(David Elsworth) *dwlt: t.k.h early: wl in tch: outpcd over 2f out: fdd fnl f* **10/1**
220- **8** *1/2* **Canford Crossing (IRE)**^{27} 8358 3-9-5 72 SeanLevey 3 61
(Richard Hannon) *t.k.h: led: rdn and hdd 2f out: fnd nil and dropped away qckly fnl f* **6/1**^{3}

2m 7.59s (0.99) **Going Correction** +0.05s/f (Slow) **8** Ran SP% **116.1**
Speed ratings (Par 97): **98,97,97,94,94 93,92,92**
CSF £155.08 TOTE £6.00: £1.60, £7.70, £1.50; EX 157.90 Trifecta £455.70.
Owner Steffen Norris **Bred** Queen Cleopatra Syndicate **Trained** Newmarket, Suffolk

FOCUS
It's unlikely the favourite ran up to his official mark in this maiden and it was Barton Lodge, one of three newcomers in the line-up, that comfortably came out on top. Muddling form.

288 UNIBET H'CAP 6f 1y(P)

2:00 (2:05) (Class 2) (0-105,101) 4-Y-O+

£11,827 (£3,541; £1,770; £885; £442; £222) **Stalls** Low

Form RPR

101- **1** **Spring Loaded (IRE)**^{35} 8288 4-8-9 **89** ShaneKelly 5 97
(Paul D'Arcy) *in tch in midfield: prog on outer over 1f out: drvn and r.o to ld last 100yds* **5/1**^{2}
11-2 **2** *1/2* **Boomerang Bob (IRE)**^{6} 220 7-9-0 **94** WilliamCarson 2 100+
(Jamie Osborne) *hld up in rr: prog wl over 1f out: drvn and styd on fnl f: tk 2nd last stride* **5/2**^{1}
231- **3** *shd* **Barracuda Boy (IRE)**^{129} 6422 6-9-4 **98** RichardKingscote 4 104
(Tom Dascombe) *led: hrd rdn over 1f out: hdd last 100yds: kpt on but lost 2nd last stride* **10/1**
030- **4** *nk* **Boom The Groom (IRE)**^{125} 6517 5-9-3 **97** LukeMorris 9 102
(Tony Carroll) *chsd ldr to 1/2-way: styd prom: chal on inner over 1f out: upsides ins fnl f: no ex* **10/1**
333- **5** *1* **Steelriver (IRE)**^{107} 7036 6-8-13 **93** SeanLevey 1 95+
(David Barron) *c out of stall slowly: hld up in last: prog on inner over 1f out: pushed along and tk 5th ins fnl f: nvr involved* **10/1**
005- **6** *nk* **Justice Good (IRE)**^{84} 7595 4-9-7 **101** (t) TomQueally 10 102
(David Elsworth) *prom: chsd ldr 1/2-way: drvn over 1f out: lost 2nd and fdd fnl f* **25/1**
22-2 **7** *1* **Anonymous John (IRE)**^{21} 4 4-8-13 **93** GrahamGibbons 3 91
(David Evans) *trckd ldrs: lost pl 1/2-way and sn in midfield: shkn up over 1f out: no imp on ldrs: eased nr fin* **10/1**
0-55 **8** *1* **Vimy Ridge**^{6} 213 4-8-0 **87** (p) LuluStanford$^{(7)}$ 6 81
(Alan Bailey) *in tch in midfield: shkn up 2f out: no prog over 1f out: one pce* **25/1**
655- **9** *1/2* **Upavon**^{46} 8132 6-8-8 **88** (t) OisinMurphy 7 81
(Stuart Williams) *rrd s: sltly hmpd after 150yds: a in rr: drvn on wd outside bnd 2f out: no prog* **6/1**^{3}
43-4 **10** *2* **Magnus Maximus**^{20} 17 5-8-13 **93** JamieSpencer 11 79
(Robyn Brisland) *chsd ldrs: chal on outer 1/2-way: wknd wl over 1f out* **14/1**
12-2 **11** *1 1/4* **Hoofalong**^{14} 106 6-8-7 **87** (b) JamesSullivan 8 69
(Michael Easterby) *blindfold off late and dwlt: bdly hmpd after 150yds: rdn on outer 2f out: no prog* **14/1**

1m 11.62s (-0.28) **Going Correction** +0.05s/f (Slow) **11** Ran SP% **116.9**
Speed ratings (Par 109): **103,102,102,101,100 100,98,97,96,94 92**
CSF £17.71 CT £118.11 TOTE £5.60: £1.90, £1.50, £3.60; EX 20.80 Trifecta £165.00.
Owner Rowley Racing **Bred** Swordlestown Little **Trained** Newmarket, Suffolk

FOCUS
Arguably one of the most competitive 6f handicaps of the winter so far. The form horses came to the fore. The third has been rated to last winter's C&D form.

289 32RED.COM CLASSIFIED CLAIMING STKS 1m 5f (P)

2:30 (2:36) (Class 5) 4-Y-O+ **£2,911** (£866; £432; £216) **Stalls** Low

Form RPR

06-2 **1** **Shalambar (IRE)**^{11} 138 10-9-5 70 (b^{1}) LukeMorris 2 61
(Tony Carroll) *trckd ldr after 2f: led over 2f out and sn sent for home: drvn and kpt on fr over 1f out* **4/7**^{1}
6 **2** *2 1/4* **Annakrista (GER)**^{13} 127 8-8-10 62 (bt) FergusSweeney 3 48
(Zoe Davison) *trckd ldr 2f: styd cl up: rdn over 2f out: chsd wnr 1f out: no imp after* **14/1**^{3}
0/0- **3** *nk* **Boston Blue**^{25} 1110 9-9-1 49 TomQueally 4 53
(Tony Carroll) *dropped to last after 4f: urged along fr 5f out and racd awkwardly after: rousted over 1f out and chsd ldng pair fnl f: effrt flattened out sn after* **16/1**
00-5 **4** *3 1/4* **Munsarim (IRE)**^{14} 101 9-8-13 62 (b) ShaneKelly 5 45
(Lee Carter) *rel to r and lft 10 l: t.k.h and sn in tch: prog on outer to chse wnr 2f out: hung bdly rt fr over 1f out and sn lost 2nd: nt run on* **11/4**^{2}
/46- **5** *2* **Vertueux (FR)**^{27} 6379 11-8-12 43 (p) WilliamCarson 1 41
(Tony Carroll) *led: urged along over 3f out: hdd over 2f out: sn btn* **16/1**

2m 49.15s (3.15) **Going Correction** +0.05s/f (Slow) **5** Ran SP% **108.8**
Speed ratings (Par 103): **92,90,90,88,86**
CSF £9.56 TOTE £1.30: £1.10, £3.80; EX 7.50 Trifecta £38.70.
Owner B J Millen **Bred** His Highness The Aga Khan's Studs S C **Trained** Cropthorne, Worcs

FOCUS
A very weak claimer, in which trainer Tony Carroll was responsible for three of the five runners.

290 LADBROKES H'CAP 7f 1y(P)

3:05 (3:12) (Class 2) 4-Y-O+

£28,012 (£8,388; £4,194; £2,097; £1,048; £526) **Stalls** Low

Form RPR

612- **1** **Realize**^{32} 8326 6-9-10 **98** (t) SeanLevey 4 107
(Stuart Williams) *chsd ldrs: drvn and prog over 1f out: clsd to ld 120yds out and edgd lft: styd on* **11/4**^{1}

004- **2** *nk* **Shyron**[23] 8395 5-8-13 **87** RyanPowell 3 95+
(George Margarson) *hld up in last pair: rapid prog over 1f out: drvn and r.o to take 2nd nr fin: jst too late to chal* **7/1**[2]
126- **3** *nk* **Arnold Lane (IRE)**[32] 8326 7-9-1 **89** TomEaves 10 96
(Mick Channon) *led: drvn for home wl over 1f out: hdd 120yds out: lost 2nd nr fin* **14/1**
01-P **4** *1/2* **Mr Bossy Boots (IRE)**[17] 50 5-9-0 **88** (t) GrahamGibbons 8 94
(Ralph Beckett) *nt that wl away but sn in tch: hrd rdn and prog over 1f out: clsd on ldrs fnl f: kpt on same pce nr fin* **8/1**[3]
001 **5** *1* **Bertiewhittle**[41] 8205 8-9-2 **90** JackMitchell 1 93
(David Barron) *hld up towards rr: urged along on inner and prog over 1f out: kpt on fnl f but nvr cl enough to chal* **8/1**[3]
060- **6** *nk* **Have A Nice Day**[14] 108 6-9-2 **90** LeighRoche 7 94+
(Sabrina J Harty, Ire) *prom: rdn to chse ldr 2f out: cl enough 1f out: jst lost 2nd whn hmpd ins fnl f: nt rcvr* **14/1**
050- **7** *nk* **Baddilini**[58] 7978 6-9-9 **97** (v) JimCrowley 11 98
(Alan Bailey) *chsd ldrs on outer: rdn wl over 1f out: styd on ins fnl f: n.d* **25/1**
65-3 **8** *shd* **Russian Realm**[15] 86 6-9-5 **93** ShaneKelly 9 94
(Richard Hughes) *hld up in rr: shkn up over 1f out: kpt on fnl f: nvr nr to chal* **8/1**[3]
06-1 **9** *nse* **Lunar Deity**[20] 18 7-9-7 **95** JamieSpencer 14 96
(Stuart Williams) *towards rr on outer: effrt wl over 1f out: kpt on fnl f: nrst fin but no ch* **8/1**[3]
06-6 **10** *1* **Al Khan (IRE)**[17] 50 7-9-2 **90** (p) ShaneGray 12 88
(Kevin Ryan) *dropped in fr wd draw and hld up in last pair: urged along over 1f out: kpt on fnl f but nvr involved* **25/1**
000- **11** *hd* **Primrose Valley**[104] 7117 4-9-9 **97** OisinMurphy 2 95
(Ed Vaughan) *chsd ldrs: rdn 2f out: wknd fnl f* **10/1**
50-6 **12** *1/2* **Trojan Rocket (IRE)**[15] 86 8-8-13 **87** (p) TomQueally 5 83
(Michael Wigham) *chsd ldr to 3f out: hmpd on inner over 2f out: fdd over 1f out* **50/1**
20-6 **13** *3 1/4* **Horsted Keynes (FR)**[9] 166 6-9-3 **98** (p) SophieKilloran(7) 6 86
(David Simcock) *prom: chsd ldr 3f out to 2f out: wknd qckly fnl f* **20/1**

1m 22.91s (-1.89) **Going Correction** +0.05s/f (Slow) **13** Ran SP% **120.5**
Speed ratings (Par 109): **112,111,111,110,109 109,108,108,108,107 107,106,103**
CSF £20.25 CT £243.32 TOTE £3.80: £1.90, £3.50, £3.60; EX 25.00 Trifecta £322.40.
Owner JKB Racing **Bred** M J Watson **Trained** Newmarket, Suffolk
■ Stewards' Enquiry : Sophie Killoran one-day ban; careless riding (5th Feb)
Sean Levey three-day ban; careless riding (5th-7th Feb)

FOCUS
A hotly contested feature, representing solid form for the grade. It's been rated around the front-running third.

291 32REDSPORT.COM H'CAP 7f 1y(P)
3:40 (3:45) (Class 6) (0-65,65) 3-Y-O **£2,264** (£673; £336; £168) **Stalls** Low

Form RPR
664- **1** **World's Greatest (USA)**[27] 8355 3-9-6 **64** SeanLevey 8 67+
(Stuart Williams) *hld up in 7th: rdn and prog on outer over 1f out: drvn and r.o to ld last 100yds: hld on* **7/2**[2]
5-34 **2** *nk* **Zebedee's Girl (IRE)**[6] 211 3-9-4 **62** TomQueally 6 64
(David Evans) *hld up in 8th: drvn and prog on inner over 1f out: chal ins fnl f: styd on but jst hld* **8/1**
250- **3** *nk* **Refulgence (FR)**[88] 7507 3-9-4 **62** OisinMurphy 3 63
(Marco Botti) *prom: pressed ldr 3f out: led 2f out and sn drvn: hdd last 100yds: kpt on* **10/1**
00-4 **4** *1* **The Big Guy**[14] 105 3-9-0 **58** CharlesBishop 1 56
(Mick Channon) *wl in tch: chsd ldrs 2f out: cl enough 1f out: styd on but nvr quite pce to chal* **7/1**[3]
53-1 **5** *1* **Inaam (IRE)**[14] 105 3-9-6 **64** DavidNolan 9 60
(Richard Fahey) *in tch in midfield: n.m.r 2f out: trying to make prog whn nt clr run over 1f out: keeping on but hld whn nowhere to go ins fnl f* **11/4**[1]
06-4 **6** *1 1/4* **Hey Ben**[17] 42 3-9-7 **65** JohnFahy 4 57
(Ronald Thompson) *led: rdn and hdd 2f out: fdd ins fnl f* **7/1**[3]
05-0 **7** *nse* **Cappy Brown**[14] 105 3-8-0 **51** (p) LuluStanford(7) 7 43
(Alan Bailey) *hld up in last: shkn up and hanging over 1f out: kpt on last 100yds: no ch* **12/1**
03-2 **8** *3/4* **Magic Garden (IRE)**[17] 42 3-9-4 **65** RyanTate(3) 2 55
(Jonathan Portman) *cl up: rdn 2f out: sing to lose pl whn short of room ins fnl f: fdd* **10/1**
50-5 **9** *2 1/4* **Red Ruffian (IRE)**[17] 42 3-9-0 **65** PaulBooth(7) 5 49
(Dean Ivory) *t.k.h: racd on outer: chsd ldr to 3f out: wknd over 1f out* **16/1**

1m 26.18s (1.38) **Going Correction** +0.05s/f (Slow) **9** Ran SP% **116.8**
Speed ratings (Par 95): **94,93,93,92,91 89,89,88,86**
CSF £32.04 CT £258.62 TOTE £3.10: £1.10, £2.70, £3.60; EX 39.90 Trifecta £261.30.
Owner D A Shekells **Bred** Darley **Trained** Newmarket, Suffolk

FOCUS
Plenty were open to improvement in this modest handicap, none more so than Godolphin cast-off World's Greatest, who continued the excellent recent form of trainer Stuart Williams.

292 UNIBET OFFER DAILY TRAINER & JOCKEY SPECIALS H'CAP 5f 6y(P)
4:10 (4:11) (Class 6) (0-60,60) 4-Y-O+ **£2,264** (£673; £336; £168) **Stalls** High

Form RPR
0-21 **1** **Boxing Shadows**[7] 196 6-9-0 **60** HarryBurns(7) 3 69
(Les Eyre) *awkward s: trckd ldrs: clsd on inner over 1f out: shkn up to ld ins fnl f: pushed out* **6/4**[1]
5-32 **2** *3/4* **Secret Millionaire (IRE)**[10] 151 9-8-12 **56** (p) JustinNewman(5) 7 62
(Shaun Harris) *prom: chsd ldr 1/2-way: rdn to chal 1f out: kpt on but nt gng pce of wnr last 100yds* **6/1**[3]
460- **3** *1 1/2* **Blue Amazon (IRE)**[50] 8095 4-9-5 **58** OisinMurphy 5 59
(Lee Carter) *mde most: rdn over 1f out: hdd and one pce ins fnl f* **8/1**
02-0 **4** *1/2* **Fuel Injection**[20] 21 5-9-7 **60** (b) TomQueally 1 59
(Paul Midgley) *mostly in 6th: rdn over 1f out: styd on ins fnl f but n.d* **8/1**
132- **5** *1/2* **Prominna**[22] 8413 6-9-5 **58** WilliamCarson 8 55
(Tony Carroll) *chsd ldrs: rdn in 5th and in tch 2f out: no hdwy over 1f out* **4/1**[2]
0-63 **6** *2 3/4* **Frozen Princess**[10] 151 4-8-11 **55** LucyKBarry(5) 4 42
(Jamie Osborne) *pressed ldr to 1/2-way: wknd jst over 1f out* **14/1**
65-5 **7** *hd* **Burnt Cream**[14] 98 9-9-2 **55** (t) WilliamTwiston-Davies 9 42
(Martin Bosley) *dropped in fr wd draw and hld up in last: rdn over 1f out: no prog* **16/1**
225- **8** *nk* **Warm Order**[148] 5782 5-8-8 **54** RhiainIngram(7) 6 40
(Tony Carroll) *dwlt: a in last pair: shkn up and no prog over 1f out* **16/1**

58.52s (-0.28) **Going Correction** +0.05s/f (Slow) **8** Ran SP% **114.9**
Speed ratings (Par 101): **104,102,100,99,98 94,94,93**
CSF £10.97 CT £54.44 TOTE £2.50: £1.10, £1.20, £2.50; EX 12.20 Trifecta £45.60.
Owner Billy Parker **Bred** Catridge Farm Stud **Trained** Catwick, N Yorks

FOCUS
This concluding sprint lacked depth and proved easy pickings for the resurgent favourite.
T/Plt: £37.40 to a £1 stake. Pool: £58,159.35 - 1,133.33 winning tickets T/Qpdt: £10.60 to a £1 stake. Pool: £8,284.31 - 578.10 winning tickets **Jonathan Neesom**

[239] WOLVERHAMPTON (A.W) (L-H)
Friday, January 22

OFFICIAL GOING: Tapeta: standard
Wind: Fine Weather: virtually nil

293 DOWNLOAD THE NEW UNIBET RACING APP H'CAP 5f 20y (Tp)
4:35 (4:35) (Class 5) (0-70,70) 4-Y-O+ **£3,396** (£1,010; £505; £252) **Stalls** Low

Form RPR
00-5 **1** **Your Gifted (IRE)**[16] 75 9-8-12 **61** (v) RaulDaSilva 1 69
(Lisa Williamson) *chsd ldr: rdn 2f out: led jst ins fnl f: kpt on* **20/1**
4-34 **2** *1 1/4* **Frank The Barber (IRE)**[4] 241 4-8-4 **56** oh3 (bt) JackDuern(3) 9 59
(Steph Hollinshead) *in tch towards outer: rdn appr fnl f: kpt on: wnt 2nd towards fin* **8/1**
141- **3** *nk* **Summer Isles**[23] 8399 6-9-4 **67** PaulMulrennan 4 69
(Paul Midgley) *led: rdn over 1f out: hdd jst ins fnl f: edgd lft: no ex fnl 110yds and lost 2nd towards fin* **9/2**[1]
223- **4** *hd* **Oil Strike**[36] 8271 9-8-11 **67** (t) NathanEvans(7) 7 68
(Michael Easterby) *hld up in tch: rdn and sme hdwy over 1f out: one pce fnl f* **5/1**[2]
16-0 **5** *3/4* **Quality Art (USA)**[14] 106 8-9-4 **70** RobHornby(3) 2 69
(Simon Hodgson) *in tch: rdn 2f out: one pce fnl f* **9/2**[1]
460- **6** *1/2* **Point North (IRE)**[57] 8004 9-9-4 **67** (b) DanielTudhope 8 64
(John Balding) *hld up: rdn 2f out: kpt on ins fnl f: nvr threatened* **11/2**[3]
206- **7** *2 1/4* **Extreme Supreme**[134] 6231 5-9-2 **65** (v) MartinLane 6 54
(Derek Shaw) *rrd s: hld up: rdn 2f out: nvr threatened* **8/1**
510- **8** *1/2* **Camanche Grey (IRE)**[171] 4960 5-8-7 **56** AndrewMullen 3 43
(Ben Haslam) *s.i.s: hld up: rdn 2f out: nvr threatened* **16/1**
11-3 **9** *5* **Roy's Legacy**[7] 196 7-9-0 **63** JFEgan 5 32
(Shaun Harris) *chsd ldr: rdn 3f out: wknd over 1f out* **15/2**

1m 1.67s (-0.23) **Going Correction** +0.025s/f (Slow) **9** Ran SP% **113.0**
Speed ratings (Par 103): **102,100,99,99,98 97,93,92,84**
CSF £166.57 CT £858.56 TOTE £18.80: £4.50, £2.30, £1.50; EX 94.70 Trifecta £636.10.
Owner Anthony Thomas Sykes **Bred** Rathasker Stud **Trained** Saighton, Cheshire

FOCUS
The track had been harrowed to a depth of 4 inches on Monday after racing and reinstated with a gallop master finish. A modest but competitive sprint. The winner is rated to a better view of last year's form.

294 DAILY PRICE BOOSTS AT UNIBET H'CAP 1m 1f 103y (Tp)
5:10 (5:12) (Class 7) (0-50,50) 4-Y-O+ **£2,264** (£673; £336; £168) **Stalls** Low

Form RPR
00-5 **1** **On A Whim**[18] 39 4-9-1 **45** JoeFanning 2 55
(Daniel Mark Loughnane) *chsd ldrs: rdn over 2f out: styd on wl: led 75yds out* **7/1**[3]
640- **2** *1 3/4* **Overrider**[38] 8235 6-8-11 **45** (bt) CallumShepherd(5) 5 52
(Shaun Lycett) *prom: rdn to ld over 2f out: kpt on: hdd 75yds out* **16/1**
00-0 **3** *4* **Thrtypointstothree (IRE)**[14] 107 5-9-2 **45** (b) JFEgan 6 44
(Nikki Evans) *led: rdn whn hdd over 2f out: sn outpcd in 3rd: plugged on fr over 1f out* **12/1**
625- **4** *hd* **Tamujin (IRE)**[23] 8398 8-9-2 **50** GaryMahon(5) 11 49+
(Ken Cunningham-Brown) *midfield on outside: rdn 3f out: kpt on fr over 1f out* **8/1**
00-5 **5** *1 1/4* **Hoofithully**[2] 252 4-8-8 **45** (b) NathanEvans(7) 4 42
(Michael Easterby) *in tch: bit tight for room as ldng pair qcknd clr 2f out: rdn over 1f out: one pce* **11/2**[2]
240- **6** *1/2* **Riverlynx (IRE)**[240] 2604 4-9-1 **45** (p) DougieCostello 8 43
(Ben Haslam) *hld up: rdn 2f out: swtchd rt ins fnl f: kpt on: nvr threatened* **33/1**
33-0 **7** *1 1/4* **Quite Sparky**[14] 107 9-8-12 **46** (b) RachelRichardson(5) 9 39
(Lucinda Egerton) *hld up: rdn over 2f out: nvr threatened* **14/1**
046- **8** *3/4* **Supa Seeker (USA)**[32] 8329 10-8-13 **45** GeorgeDowning(3) 12 37
(Tony Carroll) *swtchd lft s: hld up: bit short of room over 2f out: nvr involved* **25/1**
626- **9** *2* **Right Madam (IRE)**[62] 7951 4-9-6 **50** (p) ChrisCatlin 1 38
(Sarah Hollinshead) *trckd ldrs: rdn over 2f out: wknd over 1f out* **12/1**
52-3 **10** *3/4* **Officer In Command (USA)**[20] 20 10-9-7 **50** (tp) LiamKeniry 3 37
(Giles Bravery) *midfield: rdn over 2f out: wknd over 1f out* **11/2**[2]
5-43 **11** *4 1/2* **Stanlow**[11] 149 6-9-7 **50** RobertHavlin 13 28
(Michael Mullineaux) *hld up: bit short of room over 2f out: sn rdn: wknd over 1f out: eased* **4/1**[1]
60-4 **12** *hd* **It's All A Game**[20] 20 5-9-4 **47** (b) AndrewMullen 7 25
(Nigel Tinkler) *chsd ldrs: rdn and lost pl over 3f out: sn wknd* **18/1**

2m 1.39s (0.59) **Going Correction** +0.025s/f (Slow)
WFA 4 from 5yo+ 1lb **12** Ran SP% **114.4**
Speed ratings (Par 97): **98,96,92,92,91 91,90,89,87,86 82,82**
CSF £109.41 CT £1313.97 TOTE £8.70: £2.60, £5.80, £4.50; EX 151.80 Trifecta £4069.10 Part won..
Owner R M Brilley **Bred** Minster Stud **Trained** Baldwin's Gate, Staffs
■ Poor Duke was withdrawn. Price at time of withdrawal 16-1. Rule 4 does not apply.

FOCUS
It paid to race close to the pace in this ordinary handicap.

295 DOWNLOAD THE CORAL APP H'CAP 1m 4f 50y (Tp)
5:45 (5:45) (Class 6) (0-65,71) 4-Y-O+ **£2,587** (£770; £384; £192) **Stalls** Low

Form RPR
535- **1** **Whisky Marmalade (IRE)**[58] 4962 4-8-8 **53** RaulDaSilva 5 59
(Ben Haslam) *hld up in midfield: stl fair bit to do whn swtchd rt to outside over 1f out: styd on wl: edgd lft ins fnl f: led towards fin* **33/1**
211- **2** *3/4* **Lions Charge (USA)**[27] 8077 9-9-7 **62** (tp) LiamKeniry 2 67
(Neil Mulholland) *chsd ldrs: rdn over 2f out: led jst ins fnl f: kpt on: hdd towards fin* **5/1**[3]
00-0 **3** *1 3/4* **Innoko (FR)**[18] 38 6-9-3 **61** GeorgeDowning(3) 4 63
(Tony Carroll) *in tch: rdn and outpcd 3f out: styd on fr appr fnl f: wnt 3rd post* **12/1**
106- **4** *nk* **Nolecce**[31] 8353 9-9-2 **60** RobHornby(3) 3 62
(Tony Forbes) *prom: rdn to ld 2f out: hdd jst ins fnl f: no ex* **12/1**
343- **5** *1 3/4* **Robben**[50] 6982 4-9-1 **60** (v) GrahamLee 10 59
(John Mackie) *hld up: rdn 3f out: styd on fnl f: nvr threatened* **8/1**

34-6 **6** 7 **Mary Le Bow**[14] 101 5-9-2 **62**..............................(t) CallumShepherd[(5)] 6 50
(Victor Dartnall) *midfield: rdn over 2f out: wknd fnl f* **12/1**
655- **7** 7 **Who'sthedaddy**[35] 8292 4-9-5 **64**.................................. TimmyMurphy 7 40
(Daniel Kubler) *led: rdn whn hdd 2f out: sn wknd* **20/1**
023- **8** 2 1/2 **Baker**[72] 7797 4-9-6 **65**.. JoeFanning 1 37
(Robyn Brisland) *dwlt: racd keenly in midfield: rdn over 2f out: wknd over 1f out: eased ins fnl f* **4/1**[2]
000- **9** 2 1/2 **Filament Of Gold (USA)**[49] 8105 5-9-7 **62**..............(p) PaulMulrennan 9 30
(Roy Brotherton) *hld up: rdn over 3f out: sn wknd* **18/1**
22-1 **P** **Step On It (IRE)**[8] 180 4-9-12 **71** 6ex....................................(p) JFEgan 8
(Daniel Mark Loughnane) *trckd ldr: wnt wrong and p.u over 10f out: fatally injured* **9/4**[1]

2m 40.19s (-0.61) **Going Correction** +0.025s/f (Slow)
WFA 4 from 5yo+ 4lb **10** Ran SP% **114.6**
Speed ratings (Par 101): **103,102,101,101,99 95,90,88,87,**
CSF £188.11 CT £2121.95 TOTE £21.70: £5.60, £2.10, £3.30; EX 172.00 Trifecta £4423.70 Part won..
Owner Middleham Park Racing LXX & Partner **Bred** T S Palin & M Prince **Trained** Middleham Moor, N Yorks

FOCUS
A modest affair, but it was run at a sound gallop.

296 32RED.COM H'CAP 7f 32y (Tp)
6:15 (6:15) (Class 4) (0-80,78) 3-Y-O **£5,175** (£1,540; £769; £384) **Stalls** High

Form RPR
1 **1** **Mariee**[20] 15 3-9-3 **74**... JoeFanning 3 83+
(Mark Johnston) *dwlt: sn in tch: pushed along and hdwy on outer 2f out: led jst ins fnl f: pushed out: drew clr fnl 110yds: comf* **4/5**[1]
504- **2** 1 3/4 **Dose**[22] 8409 3-8-2 **62**.. SammyJoBell[(3)] 2 65
(Richard Fahey) *trckd ldr: rdn over 2f out: ev ch over 1f out: kpt on but no ch w wnr fnl 110yds* **11/2**[2]
416- **3** 3/4 **Outback Blue**[25] 8378 3-9-7 **78**..................................... DanielTudhope 1 79
(David Evans) *hld up: rdn over 1f out: kpt on ins fnl f: wnt 3rd post* **11/1**
133- **4** hd **Hide Your Fires (IRE)**[35] 8286 3-9-0 **74**.................. DanielMuscutt[(3)] 4 74
(Marco Botti) *trckd ldr: rdn to chal strly 2f out: led narrowly appr fnl f: hdd jst ins fnl f: edgd lft: sn no ex* **8/1**[3]
140- **5** 4 1/2 **Mostashreqah**[22] 8409 3-9-2 **73**...................................(p) RobertHavlin 6 61
(Simon Crisford) *led: rdn and strly pressed 2f out: hdd appr fnl f: wknd* **12/1**
1- **6** 2 1/4 **Sweet Temptation (IRE)**[43] 8167 3-9-0 **76**.................. AaronJones[(5)] 5 58
(Stuart Williams) *racd keenly in tch: rdn over 2f out: sn btn* **8/1**[3]

1m 29.18s (0.38) **Going Correction** +0.025s/f (Slow) **6** Ran SP% **109.2**
Speed ratings (Par 99): **98,96,95,94,89 87**
CSF £5.16 TOTE £1.80: £1.60, £1.10; EX 5.80 Trifecta £23.00.
Owner Miss K Rausing **Bred** Miss K Rausing **Trained** Middleham Moor, N Yorks

FOCUS
The early gallop wasn't particularly strong and it turned into something of a sprint from the turn in. There's more to come from the unexposed winner, with the runner-up close to his best form.

297 LADBROKES H'CAP 7f 32y (Tp)
6:45 (6:45) (Class 6) (0-60,62) 4-Y-O+ **£2,587** (£770; £384; £192) **Stalls** High

Form RPR
2-31 **1** **Binky Blue (IRE)**[15] 87 4-9-1 **54**..................................... LukeMorris 3 63
(Daniel Mark Loughnane) *chsd ldng pair: rdn to ld over 1f out: drvn and kpt on wl* **7/2**[2]
03-4 **2** 2 1/4 **Hawk Moth (IRE)**[7] 190 8-9-5 **58**................................(b) GrahamLee 10 61
(John Spearing) *hld up in rr: pushed along and sme hdwy on inner over 1f out: swtchd rt appr fnl f: kpt on wl: wnt 2nd towards fin* **8/1**
06-4 **3** 1/2 **Evident (IRE)**[20] 25 6-9-4 **57**...(p) JFEgan 8 59
(Tony Carroll) *chsd ldng pair: rdn and outpcd over 2f out: kpt on fr over 1f out* **6/1**
0-30 **4** nk **Molly Approve (IRE)**[3] 247 4-8-13 **52**.....................(p) DougieCostello 2 54
(Tony Coyle) *prom: rdn over 2f out: one pce* **33/1**
53-2 **5** 1/2 **Moonbi Creek (IRE)**[7] 201 9-8-9 **55**.................(t) CallumRodriguez[(7)] 5 55
(Richard Ford) *dwlt: hld up towards inner: rdn and hdwy over 1f out: one pce fnl f* **2/1**[1]
23-6 **6** 1 **John Coffey (IRE)**[7] 197 7-9-5 **58**..................................... LiamJones 1 56
(Michael Appleby) *led: rdn over 2f out: hdd over 1f out: wknd fnl 110yds* **9/2**[3]
00-5 **7** shd **Debit**[16] 65 5-9-7 **60**.. RyanClark 6 58
(Simon Hodgson) *hld up: rdn over 3f out: nvr threatened* **25/1**
23-0 **8** 1/2 **Bold Max**[11] 143 5-9-0 **53**...(v) AdamBeschizza 7 49
(Zoe Davison) *hld up: rdn over 3f out: nvr threatened* **20/1**
000- **9** 3/4 **Chester Deelyte (IRE)**[23] 8400 8-8-2 **46** oh1......(b) ShirleyTeasdale[(5)] 4 41
(Lisa Williamson) *midfield: rdn over 2f out: wknd fnl f* **16/1**

1m 28.9s (0.10) **Going Correction** +0.025s/f (Slow) **9** Ran SP% **116.6**
Speed ratings (Par 101): **100,97,96,96,95 94,94,94,93**
CSF £30.89 CT £164.78 TOTE £3.30: £1.10, £3.70, £2.00; EX 26.50 Trifecta £113.40.
Owner C Loughnane & C Austin **Bred** Gerard & Anne Corry **Trained** Baldwin's Gate, Staffs

FOCUS
A moderate affair, but the winner confirmed her current well-being.

298 LADBROKES MAIDEN STKS 7f 32y (Tp)
7:15 (7:18) (Class 5) 3-Y-O+ **£3,396** (£1,010; £505; £252) **Stalls** High

Form RPR
1 **Misty Lord (IRE)** 3-8-7 0.. DanielMuscutt[(3)] 12 71+
(Marco Botti) *trckd ldng pair: pushed along and rn green over 1f out: swtchd lft ins fnl f: r.o wl: led post* **6/1**[2]
2 **2** hd **Bartok (IRE)**[16] 65 3-8-10 0.. RobertHavlin 7 70
(John Gosden) *trckd ldr: pushed along to ld narrowly over 1f out: drvn ins fnl f: kpt on same pce: hdd post* **1/2**[1]
3 1/2 **Rocket Power** 3-8-10 0.. LukeMorris 8 69
(James Tate) *led narrowly: rdn over 2f out: hdd over 1f out: edgd rt ins fnl f: kpt on* **7/1**[3]
0 **4** 2 1/4 **Keep The Silence (IRE)**[11] 145 3-8-5 0...................... KieranO'Neill 11 58
(James Tate) *pressed ldr: rdn 2f out: edgd lft and no ex ins fnl f* **28/1**
5 7 **Win Lose Draw (IRE)** 4-10-0 0.................................... AndrewMullen 4 49+
(Michael Appleby) *hld up in rr: pushed along appr fnl f: kpt on* **40/1**
6 5 **Virtuous Belle** 3-8-5 0.. JoeFanning 9 25
(Daniel Kubler) *midfield towards outer: pushed along over 2f out: nvr threatened* **40/1**
4-5 **7** 1/2 **Falcon's Fire (IRE)**[11] 145 3-8-11 0 ow1.................. DougieCostello 1 30
(Keith Dalgleish) *hld up: pushed along over 3f out: nvr threatened* **16/1**
8 1 1/4 **Somepink (IRE)** 3-8-5 0.. FrannyNorton 2 20
(Daniel Mark Loughnane) *slowly away: hld up: nvr threatened* **40/1**
0- **9** 2 1/4 **Autre Princess (IRE)**[35] 8287 3-8-5 0.................................... NeilFarley 5 14
(Eric Alston) *midfield on inner: rdn over 2f out: wknd over 1f out* **66/1**
0 **10** 4 **Bethellie Pride**[14] 102 6-9-4 0... JoshDoyle[(5)] 10 9
(Lynn Siddall) *midfield: rdn 3f out: sn wknd* **150/1**

1m 32.42s (3.62) **Going Correction** +0.025s/f (Slow)
WFA 3 from 4yo+ 18lb **10** Ran SP% **112.3**
Speed ratings (Par 103): **80,79,79,76,68 62,62,60,58,53**
CSF £8.83 TOTE £10.10: £1.80, £1.02, £1.70; EX 13.70 Trifecta £46.30.
Owner Fabfive **Bred** Skymarc Farm **Trained** Newmarket, Suffolk

FOCUS
A weak maiden lacking depth, and run in a slow time. The first four pulled clear but the form has been rated cautiously.
T/Jkpt: Not won. Jackpot placepot: £457.30 - Pool: £3,321.00 - 5.3 winning tickets. T/Plt: £399.60 to a £1 stake. Pool: £89,587.00 - 163.61 winning tickets T/Qpdt: £13.50 to a £1 stake. Pool: £12,714.00 - 694.56 winning tickets **Andrew Sheret**

299 - 308 (Foreign Racing) - See Raceform Interactive

116 JEBEL ALI (L-H)
Friday, January 22

OFFICIAL GOING: Dirt: fast

309a JEBEL ALI MILE SPONSORED BY DERRINSTOWN STUD (GROUP 3) (DIRT) 1m
11:30 (11:30) 3-Y-O+
£63,770 (£21,256; £10,628; £5,314; £3,188; £2,125)

RPR
1 **Sefri (USA)**[14] 117 6-9-0 97...(b) PaulHanagan 3 105
(E Charpy, UAE) *mid-div: smooth prog to ld 2 1/2f out: r.o wl* **20/1**
2 3/4 **Forjatt (IRE)**[14] 117 8-9-0 112... ChrisHayes 4 103
(D Selvaratnam, UAE) *settled in rr: smooth prog 2 1/2f out: rdn 1 1/2f out: r.o: nrst fin* **4/9**[1]
3 1 **Ennobled Friend (USA)**[14] 117 6-9-0 102..............(bt) FrederikTylicki 2 101
(A bin Harmash, UAE) *trckd ldr: ev ch 2f out: one pce fnl f* **20/1**
4 nse **Interpret (USA)**[308] 987 8-9-0 106...........................(v) FernandoJara 10 101
(M Al Mheiri, UAE) *trckd ldr: outpcd 3f out: r.o fnl 1 1/2f* **10/1**
5 nse **Mawhub**[15] 94 7-9-0 101..(b) RichardMullen 5 100
(S Seemar, UAE) *s.i.s: mid-div: r.o fnl 2f but nvr nr to chal* **16/1**
6 1/2 **Shamaal Nibras (USA)**[42] 8192 7-9-0 100........................(v) PatDobbs 7 99
(Doug Watson, UAE) *s.i.s: settled in rr: n.m.r 2 1/2f out: r.o fnl 1 1/2f but nvr nr to chal* **7/1**[3]
7 1 3/4 **Jayed Jidan (IRE)**[14] 117 6-9-0 95...................................... CSanchez 1 95
(R Bouresly, Kuwait) *mid-div: t.k.h: ev ch 2f out: one pce fnl f* **33/1**
8 9 **Silver Galaxy**[336] 642 5-9-2 105.....................................(v) JamesDoyle 9 77
(M Al Mheiri, UAE) *sn led: hdd 2 1/2f out: wknd fnl 2f* **6/1**[2]
9 4 1/4 **Grand Salute (BRZ)**[14] 118 5-9-0 104...........................(t) WayneSmith 6 65
(D Selvaratnam, UAE) *nvr bttr than mid-div* **40/1**
10 4 **Fauvism (USA)**[708] 7-9-0 95.. DaneO'Neill 8 56
(R Bouresly, Kuwait) *nvr bttr than mid-div* **66/1**

1m 38.06s (98.06) **10** Ran SP% **127.4**
CSF: 31.20.
Owner Hamdan Al Maktoum **Bred** Shadwell Farm LLC **Trained** United Arab Emirates

310 - 312a (Foreign Racing) - See Raceform Interactive

286 LINGFIELD (L-H)
Saturday, January 23

OFFICIAL GOING: Polytrack: standard
Wind: light, across Weather: cloudy

313 LADBROKES H'CAP 1m 1y(P)
12:35 (12:35) (Class 4) (0-85,82) 4-Y-O+ **£4,690** (£1,395; £697; £348) **Stalls** High

Form RPR
12-2 **1** **Bromyard (IRE)**[21] 18 4-9-5 **80**...................................... JamieSpencer 2 89+
(David Simcock) *trckd ldrs: wnt 2nd and swtchd rt 2f out: rdn hands and heels to chal over 1f out: edging lft and leaning into runner-up tl led ins fnl f: sn asserted: eased cl home* **11/8**[1]
25-5 **2** 1 1/4 **Robert The Painter (IRE)**[7] 221 8-9-7 **82**..................(v) JoeFanning 1 88
(Lee Carter) *led: rdn and drifted rt over 1f out: hdd ins fnl f: styd in same pce after* **6/1**[3]
543- **3** 3/4 **Franco's Secret**[34] 8318 5-9-2 **77**...............................(p) CharlesBishop 6 81
(Peter Hedger) *stdd s: hld up in tch: effrt to chse ldrs 2f out: cl enough in 3rd and drvn 1f out: swtchd rt and kpt on wl ins fnl f* **6/1**[3]
012- **4** nse **Presumido (IRE)**[47] 8141 6-9-2 **80**................................ JackDuern[(3)] 4 84
(Simon Dow) *stdd after s: hld up in tch in rr: hdwy on inner over 1f out: rdn to chse ldrs 1f out: kpt on same pce fnl 100yds* **6/1**[3]
3-25 **5** 3 3/4 **Stosur (IRE)**[10] 160 5-9-5 **80**..(b) LukeMorris 8 75
(Gay Kelleway) *chsd ldr tl 2f out: sn lost pl u.p: 5th and wl hld fnl f* **20/1**
225- **6** 2 **Berrahri (IRE)**[105] 7125 5-9-1 **76**.. KierenFox 5 66
(John Best) *hld up in tch: rdn ent fnl 2f: sn outpcd: wl hld and plugged on same pce fr over 1f out* **9/2**[2]
/0-0 **7** 6 **Yeats Magic (IRE)**[17] 66 4-9-4 **79**................................... RobertHavlin 3 55
(Ronald Harris) *t.k.h: in tch in midfield: lost pl and drvn wl over 1f out: sn wknd* **66/1**

1m 36.71s (-1.49) **Going Correction** -0.075s/f (Stan) **7** Ran SP% **109.4**
Speed ratings (Par 105): **104,102,102,101,98 96,90**
CSF £9.14 CT £32.32 TOTE £2.10: £1.10, £3.10; EX 8.40 Trifecta £32.60.
Owner Mrs Ann Simcock **Bred** Brian Gallivan **Trained** Newmarket, Suffolk

FOCUS
This was run at a fair pace despite the leader having his own way out in front. There should be more to come from the winner. The second is rated to his winter AW best.

314 DOWNLOAD THE LADBROKES APP MAIDEN STKS 1m 1y(P)
1:10 (1:21) (Class 5) 3-Y-O+ **£2,911** (£866; £432; £216) **Stalls** High

Form RPR
0- **1** **Sea Of Flames**[184] 4546 3-8-7 0... OisinMurphy 2 80+
(David Elsworth) *chsd ldrs: effrt to inner to ld over 1f out: hld on wl ins fnl f: rdn out* **5/1**
024- **2** nk **Blacklister**[28] 8358 3-8-7 77.. JFEgan 6 79
(Mick Channon) *chsd ldng trio: swtchd rt and effrt 2f out: chal ins fnl f: r.o wl u.p but a hld fnl 100yds* **7/2**[3]

043- **3** *2 1/2* **Pictograph (USA)**[32] 8349 3-8-7 78 MartinLane 5 76+
(Charlie Appleby) *chsd ldr: rdn and chse wnr over 1f out: 3rd and outpcd whn squeezed for room ins fnl f: no ex* **13/8**[1]

5- **4** *2* **Jintshi**[212] 3559 3-8-7 0 JoeFanning 1 68+
(Mark Johnston) *hld up in tch in midfield: swtchd lft to inner over 2f out: effrt to chse ldrs over 1f out: no imp and one pce fnl f* **3/1**[2]

4- **5** *2 3/4* **Pearly Prince**[24] 8394 4-9-13 0[1] RobertHavlin 11 67
(Peter Hedger) *s.i.s: in tch in rr of main gp: rdn wl over 1f out: no imp and wl hld fnl f* **33/1**

00- **6** *2 3/4* **Justice Ears (IRE)**[94] 7395 3-8-7 0 WilliamCarson 3 55
(David Elsworth) *t.k.h: hld up in tch in midfield: swtchd rt and wd over 2f out: pushed along and outpcd bnd 2f out: wknd over 1f out* **25/1**

0-0 **7** *3/4* **Eljaddaaf (IRE)**[17] 65 5-9-8 0 CharlesEddery(5) 4 58
(Dean Ivory) *racd keenly: led and sn clr: rdn and hdd over 1f out: sn btn: wknd fnl f* **66/1**

8 *26* **Allen's Folly** 3-7-13 0 ShelleyBirkett(3) 8
(Peter Hiatt) *s.i.s: a struggling in rr: lost tch 3f out: t.o fnl 2f* **100/1**

00- **9** *15* **Drumlin**[23] 8410 3-8-2 0 PaddyPilley(5) 9
(Geoffrey Deacon) *sn towards rr: last and struggling u.p over 4f out: lost tch and t.o over 2f out* **200/1**

1m 36.58s (-1.62) **Going Correction** -0.075s/f (Stan)
WFA 3 from 4yo+ 20lb **9** Ran SP% **111.8**
Speed ratings (Par 103): **105,104,102,100,97 94,93,67,52**
Brevet and Harry Holland were withdrawn. Prices at time of withdrawal 25-1 & 20-1 respectively.
CSF £21.46 TOTE £6.50: £1.50, £1.30, £1.10; EX 23.60 Trifecta £56.80.
Owner J C Smith **Bred** Littleton Stud **Trained** Newmarket, Suffolk

FOCUS
Fair maiden form, rated around the second and third.

315 32RED CASINO H'CAP 7f 1y(P)
1:45 (1:49) (Class 3) (0-95,84) 3-Y-O **£7,246** (£2,168; £1,084; £542; £270) **Stalls** Low

Form RPR

51- **1** **Cape Speed (FR)**[33] 8323 3-9-5 **82** JoeFanning 5 89+
(Mark Johnston) *pressed ldr: shkn up 2f out: rdn over 1f out: sustained effrt to ld ins fnl f: styd on wl: rdn out* **9/4**[2]

113- **2** *3/4* **Take The Helm**[28] 8358 3-9-7 **84** PaulMulrennan 2 89
(Brian Meehan) *led: rdn wl over 1f out: hdd ins fnl f: no ex and one pced fnl 100yds* **3/1**[3]

-1 **3** *2 1/4* **Cocoa Beach (IRE)**[15] 102 3-8-13 **76** LukeMorris 6 75
(Sir Mark Prescott Bt) *stdd and dropped in bhd after s: hld up in tch in rr: effrt on inner over 1f out: outpcd by ldng pair 1f out: wnt 3rd and kpt on same pce ins fnl f* **7/4**[1]

006- **4** *nk* **War Department (IRE)**[100] 7235 3-9-3 **80** (p) JamieSpencer 1 78
(Michael Bell) *trckd ldrs: swtchd rt and effrt over 1f out: little rspnse to press and outpcd 1f out: kpt on same pce and lost 3rd ins fnl f* **8/1**

03-4 **5** *2 1/4* **Manhattan Skyline (IRE)**[14] 123 3-9-7 **84** LiamKeniry 3 76
(J S Moore) *in tch in midfield: sltly impeded and outpcd over 1f out: wl hld 5th and styd on same pce ins fnl f* **25/1**

11-3 **6** *2 1/4* **Threebagsue (IRE)**[14] 123 3-8-5 **73** (b) PaddyPilley(5) 4 59
(J S Moore) *dwlt: sn rcvrd and in tch in midfield but stuck wd: rdn and lost pl bnd wl over 1f out: bhd fnl f* **14/1**

1m 24.18s (-0.62) **Going Correction** -0.075s/f (Stan) **6** Ran SP% **113.8**
Speed ratings (Par 101): **100,99,96,96,93 91**
CSF £9.67 TOTE £2.80: £1.70, £2.50; EX 10.70 Trifecta £18.50.
Owner Kingsley Park 3 - Originals **Bred** Famille Niarchos **Trained** Middleham Moor, N Yorks

FOCUS
Few got into this, with the two up front dominating throughout. There's more to come from the unexposed winner.

316 CORAL.CO.UK H'CAP 1m 2f (P)
2:20 (2:20) (Class 6) (0-65,67) 4-Y-O+ **£2,264** (£673; £336; £168) **Stalls** Low

Form RPR

00-2 **1** **Trending (IRE)**[15] 97 7-9-1 **59** (t) RichardKingscote 3 66
(Jeremy Gask) *trckd ldrs: swtchd rt and effrt over 1f out: qcknd to ld ins fnl f: r.o wl* **14/1**

00-2 **2** *1/2* **Runaiocht (IRE)**[7] 222 6-8-13 **57** (b) JimmyQuinn 5 63
(Paul Burgoyne) *taken down early: in tch in midfield: squeezed for room bnd after 1f: nt clr run ent fnl 2f: swtchd rt and hdwy over 1f out: chsd wnr wl ins fnl f: r.o: nt rch wnr* **9/2**[1]

50-2 **3** *1 1/2* **Mfiftythreedotcom (IRE)**[12] 149 5-8-10 **54** (b) JackGarritty 13 57
(Richard Fahey) *chsd ldr tl 5f out: styd prom: rdn and ev ch 2f out tl unable qck jst ins fnl f: kpt on same pce fnl 100yds* **10/1**

32-0 **4** *3/4* **Apache Glory (USA)**[19] 38 8-9-7 **65** (p) StevieDonohoe 4 67
(Daniel Mark Loughnane) *taken down early in tch in midfield: effrt over 1f out: kpt on wl u.p ins fnl f: nt rch ldrs* **8/1**

60-0 **5** *1/2* **Leonard Thomas**[19] 38 6-9-4 **65** GeorgeDowning(3) 11 67
(Tony Carroll) *s.i.s: wl off the pce in rr: clsd and in tch 6f out: swtchd lft and effrt over 1f out: styd on wl ins fnl f: nt rch ldrs* **8/1**

03-5 **6** *1/2* **Matraash (USA)**[19] 38 10-9-7 **65** (be) AdamKirby 8 66
(Daniel Mark Loughnane) *off the pce in last quintet: clsd and in tch 6f out: n.m.r over 2f out: hdwy over 1f out: kpt on wl u.p ins fnl f: nt rch ldrs* **5/1**[2]

06-2 **7** *1 1/2* **What A Dandy (IRE)**[9] 173 5-9-2 **67** (p) RhiainIngram(7) 10 64
(Jim Boyle) *chsd ldrs: wnt 2nd 5f out tl led over 3f out: rdn 2f out: hdd ins fnl f: sn wknd* **6/1**[3]

34-1 **8** *1 3/4* **Bookmaker**[15] 97 6-9-3 **61** (b) WilliamCarson 7 55
(John Bridger) *in tch on midfield: effrt to chse ldrs over 2f out: no ex u.p ent fnl f: wknd fnl 150yds* **12/1**

1-54 **9** *1 1/4* **Jazri**[9] 173 5-9-6 **64** (b) FrannyNorton 1 55
(Milton Bradley) *dwlt and pushed along in rr early: hdwy into midfield 6f out: rdn and no hdwy over 1f out: wknd fnl f* **10/1**

14-0 **10** *10* **Power Up**[16] 88 5-9-3 **61** OisinMurphy 2 33
(Robert Eddery) *in tch in midfield: lost pl u.p and bhd 2f out: sn wknd* **20/1**

/0-4 **11** *6* **First Summer**[15] 97 4-8-10 **56** JoeFanning 6 21
(Shaun Harris) *hld up off the pce in last quintet: clsd and in tch 6f out: effrt wd over 2f out: wl btn and eased over 1f out* **10/1**

5-6 **12** *15* **Social Climber (IRE)**[18] 53 4-9-0 **60** (b) WilliamTwiston-Davies 12
(Ronald Harris) *racd freely: led: rdn and hdd over 3f out: dropped out and bhd 2f out: lost tch and eased ins fnl f: t.o* **33/1**

460- **13** *16* **Satin And Lace (IRE)**[14] 7983 4-9-2 **62** (vt[1]) LiamKeniry 9
(Michael Madgwick) *s.i.s: nvr travelling in rr: lost tch over 3f out: t.o over 1f out* **66/1**

2m 4.72s (-1.88) **Going Correction** -0.075s/f (Stan)
WFA 4 from 5yo+ 2lb **13** Ran SP% **122.2**
Speed ratings (Par 101): **104,103,102,101,101 101,99,98,97,89 84,72,59**
CSF £76.53 CT £681.44 TOTE £16.00: £4.90, £1.10, £3.70; EX 106.20 Trifecta £950.90.
Owner The Twitterati **Bred** Thomas Hassett **Trained** Stockbridge, Hants

FOCUS
A modest but competitive heat, and straightforward form.

317 32RED.COM CONDITIONS STKS (ALL-WEATHER CHAMPIONSHIP FAST-TRACK QUALIFIER) 1m 7f 169y(P)
2:55 (2:56) (Class 2) 4-Y-O+ **£11,971** (£3,583; £1,791; £896; £446) **Stalls** Low

Form RPR

222- **1** **Anglophile**[42] 8210 5-9-2 102 MartinLane 4 101
(Charlie Appleby) *in tch in midfield: effrt ent fnl 2f: drvn to chse ldr over 1f out: led ins fnl f: styd on: rdn out* **2/1**[2]

12-6 **2** *1/2* **Ballynanty (IRE)**[21] 19 4-8-9 89 (t) OisinMurphy 2 100
(Andrew Balding) *hld up in tch in last pair: effrt whn squeezed out and snatched up wl over 1f out: swtchd rt and sn rallied: chsd wnr wl ins fnl f: r.o wl: nvr getting to wnr* **10/1**

151- **3** *1* **Pinzolo**[262] 2000 5-9-5 108 (p) AdamKirby 7 102
(Charlie Appleby) *chsd ldrs tl led after 3f: rdn and kicked 2 l clr whn drifted rt bnd 2f out: drvn over 1f out: hdd and one pce ins fnl f* **13/8**[1]

04-3 **4** *nk* **Blue Surf**[15] 99 7-9-2 99 TomQueally 5 99
(Amanda Perrett) *hld up in tch in last pair: pushed along and effrt on outside bnd 2f out: drvn over 1f out: hdwy ins fnl f: chsd ldrs and nt clr run ins fnl f: keeping on but hld whn squeezed for room again towards fin* **14/1**

603- **5** *nk* **Pearl Castle (IRE)**[22] 8308 6-9-2 90 DougieCostello 1 98
(K R Burke) *in tch in midfield: rdn and dropped to rr but stl in tch 2f out: rallied u.p 1f out: kpt on ins fnl f* **16/1**

122- **6** *3/4* **Hamelin (IRE)**[59] 7977 6-9-2 102 StevieDonohoe 6 98
(George Scott) *chsd ldrs: wnt 2nd after 3f: rdn over 2f out: unable qck 1f out: styd on same pce and lost 2 pls ins fnl f* **6/1**[3]

42-1 **7** *6* **Flashman**[16] 78 7-9-2 88 (b) GeorgeBaker 3 90
(Gary Moore) *led for 3f: stdd bk and trckd ldng pair after: rdn and lost pl 2f out: wknd 1f out* **20/1**

3m 20.4s (-5.30) **Going Correction** -0.075s/f (Stan)
WFA 4 from 5yo+ 7lb **7** Ran SP% **112.1**
Speed ratings (Par 109): **110,109,109,109,108 108,105**
CSF £21.05 TOTE £3.60: £2.00, £3.80; EX 22.40 Trifecta £55.60.
Owner Godolphin **Bred** Darley **Trained** Newmarket, Suffolk

FOCUS
A good race run at a pretty sound gallop. The winner did not need to match his best.

318 CORAL MAIDEN STKS 1m 4f (P)
3:30 (3:30) (Class 5) 4-Y-O+ **£2,911** (£866; £432; £216) **Stalls** Low

Form RPR

23-2 **1** **Karnage (IRE)**[10] 164 4-8-10 71 (b[1]) LukeMorris 2 75+
(Daniel Kubler) *t.k.h: chsd ldr for 2f: styd handy: wnt 2nd again and gng best over 2f out: rdn to ld over 1f out: sn clr: eased wl ins fnl f* **2/1**[2]

5- **2** *4 1/2* **Handsome Dan (IRE)**[57] 8014 10-9-0 0 DougieCostello 3 65
(Sarah Hollinshead) *s.i.s: off the pce in last pair: clsd and in tch 7f out: pushed along and nt clr run over jst over 2f out: swtchd rt and chal for placings 1f out: chsd clr wnr fnl 150yds: kpt on but no ch* **25/1**

3 *1 3/4* **Court Minstrel (IRE)**[63] 9-9-0 0 JamieSpencer 7 62
(Evan Williams) *v.s.a: detached in last: clsd and in tch 7f out: rdn 3f out: no ch w wnr over 1f out: plugged on into modest 3rd ins fnl f* **4/7**[1]

5-5 **4** *2* **Black Hole Sun**[10] 161 4-8-5 0 WilliamCarson 4 54
(Tony Carroll) *led for 2f: chsd ldr tl 8f out: styd prom: rdn over 2f out: outpcd and wl btn over 1f out: 4th and heavily eased towards fin* **66/1**

36-5 **5** *4 1/2* **L'Amiral David (FR)**[5] 245 6-9-0 0 WilliamTwiston-Davies 5 52
(Alan King) *chsd ldrs: wnt 2nd 8f out tl led over 2f out: sn rdn: hdd over 1f out and immediately btn: lost 2nd and wknd ins fnl f* **10/1**[3]

6 *9* **Executive Order**[23] 7-8-11 0 TimClark(3) 6 37
(Martin Smith) *dwlt: hdwy to ld 10f out: rdn and hdd over 2f out: sn dropped out: no ch whn wnt rt ins fnl f* **100/1**

7 *16* **Jeans Lady**[48] 7-8-4 0 PatrickO'Donnell(5) 1 7
(John Gallagher) *in tch in midfield: dropped to last trio and pushed along 8f out: last and u.p over 2f out: lost tch 2f out: t.o* **100/1**

2m 31.84s (-1.16) **Going Correction** -0.075s/f (Stan)
WFA 4 from 6yo+ 4lb **7** Ran SP% **113.4**
Speed ratings (Par 103): **100,97,95,94,91 85,74**
CSF £37.33 TOTE £3.20: £1.20, £4.80; EX 37.80 Trifecta £68.90.
Owner Keep Racing **Bred** Richard Murphy **Trained** Lambourn, Berks

FOCUS
With the favourite losing many lengths at the start this probably didn't take much winning. It's doubtful the winner had to improve.

319 DAILY UNIBET EARLY PRICES FROM 9AM H'CAP 6f 1y(P)
4:05 (4:06) (Class 5) (0-70,72) 4-Y-O+ **£2,911** (£866; £432; £216) **Stalls** Low

Form RPR

203- **1** **Elusive Ellen (IRE)**[93] 7418 6-9-3 **66** JimmyQuinn 4 76
(Brendan Powell) *hld up in tch in midfield: nt clr run and hmpd bnd 2f out: hdwy to chse ldr 1f out: swtchd rt and clsd to ld fnl 75yds: r.o wl: readily* **8/1**[3]

502- **2** *1 3/4* **Head Space (IRE)**[38] 8250 8-9-7 **70** DougieCostello 10 74+
(Brian Barr) *awkward as stalls opened and s.i.s: hld up in last pair: trying to cl and nt clr run over 1f out: hdwy jst ins fnl f: r.o strly to snatch 2nd last strides: no threat to wnr* **8/1**[3]

52-1 **3** *nk* **Jaarih (IRE)**[9] 176 4-9-9 **72** JFEgan 6 75+
(Conor Dore) *taken down early: led: rdn over 1f out: hdd and no ex fnl 75yds: styd on same pce after: lost 2nd last strides* **11/4**[1]

22-2 **4** *1* **Major Muscari (IRE)**[17] 75 8-9-0 **63** LukeMorris 11 63
(Shaun Harris) *stdd s: hld up in tch in last quartet: hmpd on inner bnd 2f out: hdwy 1f out: styd on wl ins fnl f: no threat to wnr* **8/1**[3]

066- **5** *3/4* **Secret Witness**[71] 7828 10-9-2 **65** (b) WilliamTwiston-Davies 5 62
(Ronald Harris) *in tch in midfield: effrt u.p over 1f out: styd on same pce ins fnl f* **14/1**

/50- **6** *nk* **Johnny Splash (IRE)**[350] 468 7-9-7 **70** (v) RobertWinston 2 66
(Roger Teal) *chsd ldrs: unable qck u.p over 1f out: wknd fnl 100yds* **16/1**

60-4 **7** *1 3/4* **Whaleweigh Station**[14] 124 5-9-5 **68** (v) AdamKirby 9 59
(J R Jenkins) *sn chsng ldr on outer: rdn and unable qck over 1f out: wknd ins fnl f* **5/1**[2]

00-2 **8** *1 1/4* **Bush Warrior (IRE)**[15] 100 5-9-7 **70** (v) GeorgeBaker 7 57
(Anabel K Murphy) *chsd ldng trio: unable qck over 1f out: wknd ins fnl f* **5/1**[2]

42-5 **9** *3 3/4* **Picansort**[17] 56 9-9-4 **67** ShaneKelly 12 42
(Peter Crate) *hld up in last pair: effrt and wd bnd 2f out: no imp: bhd fnl f* **14/1**

40-6 **10** 2½ **Colourbearer (IRE)**[20] 28 9-9-7 **70**.............................(t) OisinMurphy 8 37
(Charlie Wallis) *taken down early: stdd s: hld up in tch in last quartet: effrt jst over 2f out: no prog: bhd ins fnl f* **10/1**

1m 11.4s (-0.50) **Going Correction** -0.075s/f (Stan) **10** Ran SP% **121.6**
Speed ratings (Par 103): **100,97,97,95,94 94,92,90,85,82**
CSF £73.54 CT £230.27 TOTE £11.50: £4.10, £2.90, £1.10; EX 109.90 Trifecta £581.90.
Owner B G Powell **Bred** Mrs Chris Harrington **Trained** Upper Lambourn, Berks

FOCUS
This was run at a good gallop and suited those ridden with a bit of patience. The winner seems to have improved.
T/Plt: £57.70 to a £1 stake. Pool: £49,843.94 - 629.57 winning tickets T/Qpdt: £25.30 to a £1 stake. Pool: £41,86.97 - 122.10 winning tickets **Steve Payne**

265 CHELMSFORD (A.W) (L-H)

Sunday, January 24

OFFICIAL GOING: Polytrack: standard
Wind: light, half behind Weather: dry, sunny spells

320 BET TOTEPLACEPOT APPRENTICE H'CAP 6f (P)
1:10 (1:11) (Class 6) (0-60,62) 4-Y-O+ **£3,234** (£962; £481; £240) **Stalls** Centre

Form RPR
1-20 **1** **Louis Vee (IRE)**[9] 197 8-9-4 **59**..................................(p) GeorgiaCox(2) 1 65
(John O'Shea) *sn pushed up to chse ldr: rdn to chal and wnt clr in ldng trio 2f out: led 1f out: hld on wl ins fnl f* **7/2**[2]

22-6 **2** ½ **Compton Prince**[11] 167 7-9-4 **57**...........................(b) CallumShepherd 4 62
(Milton Bradley) *t.k.h: hld up wl in tch in midfield: hdwy to chse ldrs and wnt clr in ldng trio 2f out: ev ch 1f out: kpt on wl but a jst hld* **6/1**[3]

005- **3** 1¼ **Mountain Man**[25] 8399 4-9-5 **58**.................................(bt) NathanEvans 2 59
(Michael Easterby) *led: rdn and drew clr w 2 rivals 2f out: hdd 1f out: no ex: wknd fnl 75yds* **8/1**

10-0 **4** 2 **Burauq**[11] 167 4-9-5 **58**..(b) PaddyBradley 6 53
(Milton Bradley) *hld up in rr: stl last 2f out: rdn and hdwy on inner over 1f out: styd on wl u.p ins fnl f: nvr trbld ldrs* **8/1**

02-1 **5** ½ **Kyllach Me (IRE)**[9] 197 4-9-9 **62**....................................(b) PhilDennis 7 55
(Bryan Smart) *in tch towards rr: pushed along 4f out: 6th and drvn 2f out: chsd clr ldng trio 1f out: 5th and kpt on fnl 100yds: nvr threatened ldrs* **6/4**[1]

33-6 **6** 4½ **Leith Bridge**[14] 130 4-9-0 **57**....................................(p) MitchGodwin(4) 3 37
(Mark Usher) *chsd ldrs: rdn and outpcd 2f out: wknd over 1f out* **10/1**

50-0 **7** 4½ **Prigsnov Dancer (IRE)**[9] 197 11-8-9 **54**................ BenSanderson(6) 5 20+
(Deborah Sanderson) *rrd as stalls opened and s.i.s: t.k.h: hld up in tch: hdwy on inner 3f out: outpcd 2f out: rdn and wknd over 1f out* **14/1**

030- **8** 1¼ **Mary Ann Bugg (IRE)**[24] 8413 4-8-13 **52**.............(t) JosephineGordon 8 15
(Phil McEntee) *in tch in midfield: lost pl and u.p in 7th 2f out: bhd over 1f out* **12/1**

1m 11.69s (-2.01) **Going Correction** -0.225s/f (Stan) **8** Ran SP% **122.2**
Speed ratings (Par 101): **104,103,101,99,98 92,86,84**
CSF £26.73 CT £162.53 TOTE £4.80: £1.70, £1.90, £2.70; EX 25.40 Trifecta £169.40.
Owner Quality Pipe Supports (Q P S) Ltd **Bred** Rev James Browne **Trained** Elton, Gloucs

FOCUS
A moderate apprentice handicap in which it paid to be handy and the first three came widest up the home straight.

321 TOTEPOOLLIVEINFO.COM H'CAP 7f (P)
1:45 (1:45) (Class 6) (0-65,65) 4-Y-O+ **£3,234** (£962; £481; £240) **Stalls** Low

Form RPR
43-3 **1** **The Happy Hammer (IRE)**[15] 124 10-8-12 **63**.......... LuluStanford(7) 6 69
(Eugene Stanford) *swtchd lft sn after s: hld up in tch in rr: hdwy u.p over 1f out: drvn and ev ch ins fnl f: led wl ins fnl f: hld on wl* **9/1**

622- **2** hd **Misu Pete**[33] 8351 4-8-12 **56**... OisinMurphy 7 61
(Mark Usher) *in tch in rr: rdn over 3f out: struggling in last 3f out: gd hdwy u.p over 1f out: ev ch ins fnl f: r.o wl: jst hld* **7/1**

013/ **3** ¾ **Mr Shekells**[495] 6436 4-9-4 **65**....................................... DannyBrock(3) 2 68
(Philip McBride) *t.k.h: chsd ldrs: rdn to ld over 1f out: sn drifting rt: drvn and hdd wl ins fnl f: styd on same pce after: burst blood vessel* **6/1**[3]

34-2 **4** 2½ **Lupo D'Oro (IRE)**[7] 231 7-9-7 **65**...................................... KierenFox 4 62
(John Best) *pressed ldr: rdn ent fnl 2f: unable qck u.p over 1f out: styd on same pce u.p ins fnl f* **5/2**[1]

0-03 **5** hd **Rialto Magic**[9] 201 4-9-0 **58**.......................................(p) TimmyMurphy 5 54
(Jamie Osborne) *hld up in tch: effrt and swtchd lft over 1f out: kpt on same pce and no imp ins fnl f* **16/1**

226- **6** nse **Wild Flower (IRE)**[52] 8095 4-8-7 **51** oh1........................(p) KieranO'Neill 3 47
(Jimmy Fox) *led: rdn: drifted rt and hdd over 1f out: outpcd ent fnl f: wknd ins fnl f* **8/1**

43-4 **7** ½ **Bailiwick**[7] 231 5-9-5 **63**...(b[1]) RichardKingscote 8 58
(Daniel Kubler) *in tch: hdwy to chse ldrs 5f out: lost pl and rdn over 2f out: styd on same pce and no imp fr over 1f out* **7/2**[2]

-243 **8** hd **Tasaaboq**[10] 174 5-8-7 **51**...(tp) LukeMorris 1 45
(Phil McEntee) *niggled along early: in tch in midfield and racing keenly 5f out: effrt to chal and carried rt over 1f out: no ex 1f out: wknd ins fnl f* **8/1**

1m 25.64s (-1.56) **Going Correction** -0.225s/f (Stan) **8** Ran SP% **115.7**
Speed ratings (Par 101): **99,98,97,95,94 94,94,93**
CSF £70.52 CT £414.85 TOTE £7.60: £2.30, £2.10, £2.60; EX 48.90 Trifecta £375.40.
Owner newmarketracingclub.co.uk **Bred** Rathbarry Stud **Trained** Newmarket, Suffolk

FOCUS
A moderate handicap in which the early pace was modest, with a couple taking a hold as a result. The contrast with the opening contest couldn't have been greater, with the first two coming from the back of the field and the first three home racing closest to the rail starting up the straight, though the leading pair did hang right late on.

322 BET TOTEQUADPOT H'CAP 5f (P)
2:15 (2:16) (Class 4) (0-85,85) 3-Y-O **£8,086** (£2,406; £1,202; £601) **Stalls** Low

Form RPR
02-1 **1** **Gorokai (IRE)**[9] 193 3-8-9 **73**.. MartinDwyer 6 78
(David Simcock) *stdd s: hld up towards rr: hdwy to chse ldrs 2f out: drvn to chal and drifted lft 1f out: led fnl 100yds: drvn out* **11/4**[2]

04-1 **2** ½ **Dark Side Princess**[18] 57 3-8-8 **75**.........................(p) EoinWalsh(3) 4 78
(Chris Dwyer) *in tch in midfield: lost pl and rdn 1/2-way: swtchd rt over 1f out: hdwy whn nt clr run and swtchd rt ins fnl f: flashed tail u.p but r.o strly fnl 100yds: snatched 2nd last strides* **11/4**[2]

1-54 **3** hd **Alshaqee**[4] 262 3-8-13 **77**... TomQueally 1 79
(William Haggas) *t.k.h: hld up in tch towards rr: clsd 1/2-way: hdwy u.p over 1f out: ev ch and drvn ins fnl f: kpt on: lost 2nd last strides* **2/1**[1]

00-3 **4** 1½ **Adham (IRE)**[19] 45 3-9-7 **85**...(b[1]) LukeMorris 5 82
(James Tate) *racd keenly: led tl hung rt and hdd on bnd over 3f out: styd w ldr: rdn to ld and edgd lft over 1f out: hdd ins fnl f: wknd towards fin* **10/1**[3]

0-21 **5** 1 **Modest**[14] 131 3-8-7 **78**... PhilDennis(7) 7 71
(Michael Bell) *s.i.s: bhd: sme hdwy u.p 1f out: kpt on same pce ins fnl f* **12/1**

53-4 **6** 1¼ **Men United (FR)**[18] 57 3-8-1 **68**.............................. SammyJoBell(3) 3 57
(James Given) *led: rdn and hdd over 1f out: no ex 1f out: wknd ins fnl f* **14/1**

64-5 **7** 7 **Cool Silk Boy (IRE)**[18] 57 3-8-6 **70**.......................(v[1]) JamesSullivan 2 34
(James Given) *t.k.h: chsd ldng pair: awkward hd carriage u.p and lost pl over 1f out: wknd fnl f* **16/1**

58.97s (-1.23) **Going Correction** -0.225s/f (Stan) **7** Ran SP% **116.0**
Speed ratings (Par 99): **100,99,98,96,94 92,81**
CSF £11.13 TOTE £4.20: £2.30, £2.30; EX 15.00 Trifecta £34.20.
Owner Mrs Fitri Hay **Bred** Tally-Ho Stud **Trained** Newmarket, Suffolk

FOCUS
A decent 3yo sprint handicap with three of the seven runners having won their last starts. The pace was strong, which favoured those held up.

323 BET TOTETRIFECTA H'CAP 5f (P)
2:50 (2:50) (Class 4) (0-85,87) 4-Y-O+ **£8,086** (£2,406; £1,202; £601) **Stalls** Low

Form RPR
21-3 **1** **Jebediah Shine**[16] 106 4-9-2 **85**.................................... JoshDoyle(5) 3 94
(David O'Meara) *chsd clr ldng trio: clsd 1/2-way: effrt on inner over 1f out: led u.p 150yds out: sn edgd rt: styd on wl* **5/1**[3]

05-3 **2** 1¼ **Pearl Acclaim (IRE)**[8] 213 6-9-4 **82**.............................. AdrianNicholls 7 87
(David Nicholls) *midfield: clsd to chse ldrs 2f out: swtchd rt and effrt in centre over 1f out: styd on u.p to chse wnr wl ins fnl f: kpt on* **11/4**[1]

3-41 **3** 1¼ **Bosham**[18] 56 6-8-8 **79**...(bt) NathanEvans(7) 2 79
(Michael Easterby) *led and sn clr w rival: rdn over 1f out: hdd 1f out: stl ev ch tl no ex 100yds out: wknd towards fin* **7/1**

0-32 **4** shd **You're Cool**[11] 162 4-8-9 **73**.. TomEaves 1 73
(James Given) *anticipated s and s.i.s: off the pce in 5th: effrt u.p over 1f out: kpt on u.p fnl 100yds: no threat to wnr* **6/1**

44-6 **5** nse **Come On Dave (IRE)**[23] 4 7-9-4 **85**..................(b) DanielMuscutt(3) 4 84
(Phil McEntee) *taken down early: w ldr and sn clr: rdn over 1f out: led 1f out: sn hdd and no ex: wknd towards fin* **5/1**[3]

06-1 **6** 1½ **Searchlight**[13] 142 5-9-9 **87**... AdamKirby 5 81
(Jim Boyle) *off the pce in last pair: drvn and effrt over 1f out: no real imp: n.d* **7/2**[2]

200- **7** hd **Diamond Charlie (IRE)**[53] 8082 8-9-2 **80**............................ LukeMorris 6 73
(Simon Dow) *s.i.s: a in rr: drvn and effrt on inner over 1f out: no imp: n.d* **14/1**

57.9s (-2.30) **Going Correction** -0.225s/f (Stan) **7** Ran SP% **115.7**
Speed ratings (Par 105): **109,107,105,104,104 102,102**
CSF £19.62 TOTE £4.70: £1.70, £2.50; EX 20.00 Trifecta £102.10.
Owner Sterling Racing **Bred** Whatton Manor Stud **Trained** Upper Helmsley, N Yorks

FOCUS
A decent sprint handicap and a strong pace was always likely with a few in here that like to force it. The winning time was around half a second outside the course record.

324 SCOOP6SOCCER THE £1 MILLION FOOTBALL BET FILLIES' H'CAP 1m (P)
3:25 (3:26) (Class 5) (0-75,75) 4-Y-O+ **£5,175** (£1,540; £577; £577) **Stalls** Low

Form RPR
32-5 **1** **Kalon Brama (IRE)**[18] 72 5-9-7 **75**.................................. MartinLane 4 81
(Peter Charalambous) *led for 1f: chsd ldr tl 6f out: styd prom: rdn to chal over 1f out: led fnl 100yds: styd on wl: rdn out* **3/1**[1]

02-4 **2** ¾ **Primrose Brown**[18] 59 5-8-11 **65**.................................. JimmyQuinn 1 69
(Conrad Allen) *stdd s: t.k.h: hld up in tch in last pair: swtchd rt and effrt over 1f out: styd on wl u.p ins fnl f: snatched 2nd last strides* **9/1**[3]

400- **3** hd **Hollie Point**[29] 8357 4-9-6 **74**.. ShaneKelly 3 78
(Sylvester Kirk) *stdd s: hld up in last pair: swtchd rt and hdwy to chse ldr 6f out: rdn to ld over 1f out: drvn 1f out: hdd fnl 100yds: styd on same pce towards fin* **12/1**

22-2 **3** dht **Clary (IRE)**[22] 14 6-8-6 **65**.................................... JosephineGordon(5) 6 69
(James Unett) *stdd s: hld up in tch in rr: swtchd lft and nt clr run over 1f out: hdwy 1f out: kpt on wl u.p ins fnl f* **3/1**[1]

351- **5** ½ **Desert Morning (IRE)**[28] 8366 4-8-5 **59**............................ WilliamCarson 2 62
(Anthony Carson) *in tch in midfield: nt clr run 2f out: effrt to chse ldrs over 1f out: styd on same pce u.p ins fnl f* **7/1**[2]

64-1 **6** ¾ **Invade (IRE)**[17] 77 4-8-6 **65**.....................................(t) AaronJones(5) 5 66
(Stuart Williams) *in tch in midfield: effrt in centre over 1f out: styd on same pce u.p ins fnl f* **3/1**[1]

6-32 **7** 9 **Ela Goog La Mou**[8] 216 7-8-2 **56** oh3................................. LukeMorris 7 36
(Peter Charalambous) *led after 1f: rdn ent fnl 2f: lost pl and bhd 1f out: wknd fnl f* **10/1**

1m 38.31s (-1.59) **Going Correction** -0.225s/f (Stan) **7** Ran SP% **114.3**
Speed ratings (Par 100): **98,97,97,97,96 95,86**
CSF £31.56 TOTE £3.90: £1.70, £4.80; EX 29.30 Trifecta £59.70.
Owner pcracing.co.uk **Bred** Tally-Ho Stud **Trained** Newmarket, Suffolk

FOCUS
An ordinary fillies' handicap. They went a modest pace and there wasn't much covering the front six at the line.

325 PLAY SCOOP6SOCCER EVERY WEEK MAIDEN FILLIES' STKS 1m 2f (P)
3:55 (3:56) (Class 4) 3-Y-O+ **£6,469** (£1,925; £962; £481) **Stalls** Low

Form RPR
1 **Mighty Lady** 3-8-5 0.. JimmyQuinn 3 73
(Robyn Brisland) *s.i.s and rn green early: hld up in last trio and t.k.h after 2f: swtchd rt and gd hdwy wl over 1f out: chsd ldng pair 1f out: led fnl 100yds: r.o wl* **50/1**

46-2 **2** 1¼ **Miss Gilor**[15] 127 4-9-12 71.. RobertHavlin 2 74
(John Gosden) *rdn along leaving stalls: hld up in tch in midfield: clsd to chse ldr 2f out: rdn to chse ldr over 1f out: led ins fnl f: sn hdd and styd on same pce after* **2/1**[2]

-3 **3** 1¼ **Fun For All**[20] 40 3-8-5 0.. LukeMorris 7 68
(James Tate) *t.k.h: led: rdn and fnd ex over 1f out: drvn and hrd pressed 1f out: hdd ins fnl f: no ex* **11/8**[1]

0-5 **4** 5 **Graceful Lady**[21] 29 3-8-5 0.. WilliamCarson 9 58
(Robert Eddery) *chsd ldrs: rdn to chse ldr 2f out tl over 1f out: 4th and btn 1f out: wknd ins fnl f* **20/1**

54 **5** 1 3/4 **Do It Tomorrow (IRE)**[11] 161 4-9-9 0 DannyBrock(3) 8 58
(J R Jenkins) *hld up in last quartet: shkn up and swtchd rt wl over 1f out: styd on ins fnl f: nvr trbld ldrs* **33/1**

0- **6** 2 1/4 **Muhazwara (IRE)**[127] 6526 4-9-12 0 StevieDonohoe 12 54
(George Peckham) *hld up in last trio: rdn 2f out: styd on to pass btn horses ins fnl f: nvr trbld ldrs* **33/1**

00- **7** nk **Orangecherie (IRE)**[40] 8232 3-8-5 0 KieranO'Neill 1 49
(Mike Murphy) *chsd ldr for 2f: styd chsng ldrs tl outpcd u.p over 1f out: wknd fnl f* **66/1**

8 1 **Haunted (IRE)** 3-8-5 0 MartinDwyer 11 47
(David Simcock) *s.i.s: rn green in detached last: clsd but stl in last 4f out: rdn ent fnl 2f: sn outpcd: swtchd lft and plugged on same pce fnl f* **9/2**3

0 **9** 1/2 **Fun Money**[18] 59 3-8-5 0 NickyMackay 5 46
(Ed Dunlop) *stdd after s: t.k.h: hld up in tch in midfield: clsd and nt clr run over 2f out: sn swtchd rt and rdn: fnd little and sn outpcd: wknd over 1f out* **14/1**

66- **10** 4 **Reverent (IRE)**[85] 7640 4-9-12 0 (p) AdamKirby 10 42
(James Tate) *pushed along early: chsd ldr after 2f tl rdn and lost pl 2f out: sn btn bhd and eased ins fnl f* **16/1**

26- **11** 21 **Teputina**[25] 8394 4-9-9 0 ShelleyBirkett(3) 6
(Julia Feilden) *hld up in midfield: squeezed for room bnd after 2f: rdn and lost pl over 2f out: bhd and lost tch over 1f out: t.o: burst bllod vessel* **25/1**

2m 6.42s (-2.18) **Going Correction** -0.225s/f (Stan)
WFA 3 from 4yo 23lb **11** Ran SP% **124.1**
Speed ratings (Par 102): **99,98,97,93,91 89,89,88,88,85 68**
CSF £151.66 TOTE £22.40: £7.40, £1.30, £1.10; EX 215.50 Trifecta £997.50.
Owner Franconson Partners **Bred** D Curran **Trained** Newmarket, Suffolk

FOCUS
A modest fillies' maiden in which the betting was dominated by two half-sisters. It looked as though the finish would be fought out between them until a big-price debutante came out of the clouds to nail the pair.

326 CHELMSFORDCITYRACECOURSE.COM H'CAP 1m 2f (P)
4:25 (4:28) (Class 6) (0-55,55) 4-Y-O+ **£3,234** (£962; £481; £240) **Stalls** Low

Form RPR

00-0 **1** **Sexy Secret**[16] 107 5-9-2 **53** (p) SimonPearce(3) 2 58
(Lydia Pearce) *mde virtually all: rdn 2f out: forged ahd 1f out: hld on wl u.p: all out: gamely* **10/1**

-222 **2** hd **Anjuna Beach (USA)**[10] 175 6-9-0 **53** AnnStokell(5) 8 58
(Ann Stokell) *taken down early: stdd and swtchd lft s: t.k.h in rr: effrt over 1f out: r.o strly ins fnl f: snatched 2nd on post: nt quite rch wnr* **5/1**3

530- **3** nse **Queen Zain (IRE)**[109] 7037 4-9-3 **53** StevieDonohoe 5 58
(Charlie Fellowes) *in tch in midfield: effrt on inner over 1f out: styd on u.p and ev ch wl ins fnl f: wnt 2nd towards fin: kpt on: lost 2nd on post* **10/3**2

3-10 **4** nk **Goodwood Moonlight**[16] 107 4-9-5 **55** AdamKirby 3 59
(Ian Williams) *chsd ldrs: effrt over 1f out: hrd drvn and ev ch ins fnl f: unable qck cl home* **7/4**1

06-0 **5** 1 **Understory (USA)**[8] 222 9-9-1 **52** (b) ShelleyBirkett(3) 4 54
(Tim McCarthy) *w wnr: rdn 2f out: drvn and no ex ins fnl f: wknd towards fin* **8/1**

05-5 **6** 3 1/4 **Game Mascot**[12] 156 6-8-13 **47** LukeMorris 6 43
(Shaun Harris) *hld up in last trio: rdn over 2f out: sn outpcd: hrd drvn and rallied 1f out: kpt on: no threat to ldrs* **8/1**

006- **7** 1/2 **Follow The Faith**[153] 5683 4-9-2 **52** CharlesBishop 7 47
(Mick Channon) *hld up in last trio: rdn over 2f out: sn outpcd: rallied and kpt on again ins fnl f: no threat to ldrs* **16/1**

2m 6.4s (-2.20) **Going Correction** -0.225s/f (Stan)
WFA 4 from 5yo+ 2lb **7** Ran SP% **113.3**
Speed ratings (Par 101): **99,98,98,98,97 95,94**
CSF £57.35 CT £203.12 TOTE £10.30: £4.60, £2.10; EX 53.00 Trifecta £336.00.
Owner R G Thurston **Bred** W G H Barrons **Trained** Newmarket, Suffolk
■ Simon Pearce's first winner since 2014.

FOCUS
A moderate handicap run at a modest pace, but this was a thriller with four in a line across the track at the finish.
T/Jkpt: Not won. Jackpot Placepot: £1,572.50 to a £1 stake. Pool: £3,554.00 - 1.65 winning tickets T/Plt: £263.30 to a £1 stake. Pool: £94,890.33 - 263.02 winning tickets T/Qpdt: £16.20 to a £1 stake. Pool: £12,919.74 - 587.67 winning tickets **Steve Payne**

293 WOLVERHAMPTON (A.W) (L-H)
Monday, January 25

OFFICIAL GOING: Tapeta: standard
Wind: moderate 1/2 behind, becoming fresh last 3 Weather: overcast, light shower after race 6 (5.05)

327 £10 FREE AT 32RED.COM H'CAP (DIV I) 7f 32y (Tp)
2:20 (2:25) (Class 6) (0-55,55) 3-Y-O **£2,587** (£770; £384; £192) **Stalls** High

Form RPR

004- **1** **Nouvelli Dancer (IRE)**[108] 7084 3-8-12 **46** oh1 OisinMurphy 10 57+
(Ivan Furtado) *trckd ldrs: 2nd over 1f out: rdn to ld 1f out: styd on strly: eased clsng stages* **7/1**3

135- **2** 2 **Secret Interlude (IRE)**[49] 8130 3-9-7 **55** JoeFanning 4 58
(Jamie Osborne) *mid-div: effrt over 1f out: edgd lft: styd on to take 2nd last 100yds: no imp* **11/4**1

00-0 **3** hd **Ormanumps (IRE)**[17] 104 3-8-5 **46** oh1 RyanHolmes(7) 8 49
(Daniel Mark Loughnane) *rrd s: in rr: hdwy 2f out: kpt on fnl f: tk 3rd clsng stages* **12/1**

06-0 **4** 1 1/2 **Ashford Island**[18] 87 3-9-0 **48** ShaneKelly 1 47
(Mike Murphy) *sn led: hdd 1f out: hung rt: one pce* **8/1**

300- **5** 2 **Candy Banter (USA)**[34] 8350 3-9-4 **52** (p) RaulDaSilva 3 46
(Kevin Ryan) *chsd ldr: reminders over 3f out: fdd fnl f* **8/1**

03-6 **6** hd **Intimately**[17] 105 3-9-5 **53** LukeMorris 11 46
(Jonathan Portman) *in rr: effrt over 2f out: kpt on fnl f: nvr a factor* **11/2**2

40-0 **7** 1 1/4 **Window Shopping (IRE)**[4] 274 3-8-7 **46** oh1 CallumShepherd(5) 2 36
(Mark Usher) *in rr: hdwy on ins over 1f out: sn hmpd: nvr a threat* **28/1**

5-00 **8** 1 1/4 **Cappy Brown**[3] 291 3-9-3 **51** (v1) GrahamGibbons 7 38
(Alan Bailey) *dwlt: sn mid-div: hung lft over 1f out: nvr a factor* **8/1**

0-35 **9** 1 1/4 **Romancingthestone**[7] 242 3-8-11 **50** (p) JosephineGordon(5) 9 34
(J S Moore) *led early: chsd ldrs: drvn over 3f out: lost pl over 1f out* **7/1**3

1m 29.82s (1.02) **Going Correction** +0.10s/f (Slow) **9** Ran SP% **111.5**
Speed ratings (Par 95): **98,95,95,93,91 91,89,88,86**
CSF £25.27 CT £223.29 TOTE £9.10: £2.40, £1.40, £4.20; EX 26.50 Trifecta £284.50.
Owner S Laffan **Bred** Colin Kennedy **Trained** Wiseton, Nottinghamshire
■ Stewards' Enquiry : Callum Shepherd caution; careless riding
Ryan Holmes caution: careless riding

FOCUS
The opening contest was the first division of a moderate 3yo handicap. They went a decent gallop and the placed horses help set the level.

328 £10 FREE AT 32RED.COM H'CAP (DIV II) 7f 32y (Tp)
2:50 (2:57) (Class 6) (0-55,55) 3-Y-O **£2,587** (£770; £384; £192) **Stalls** High

Form RPR

60-2 **1** **Israfel**[17] 104 3 9 1 **49** CathyGannon 5 53
(Jamie Osborne) *chsd ldrs: drvn over 3f out: styd on fnl f: edgd rt 100yds out: led nr fin* **3/1**1

02-2 **2** hd **Kristoff (IRE)**[18] 87 3-8-9 **50** RhiainIngram(7) 8 54
(Jim Boyle) *w ldrs: led narrowly over 1f out: edgd lft ins fnl f: hdd nr fin* **5/1**3

000- **3** 1 1/4 **More Kudos (USA)**[131] 6433 3-9-2 **50** DougieCostello 1 50
(John Quinn) *hld up in mid-div: effrt over 2f out: chsng ldrs over 1f out: styng on at fin* **7/2**2

0-22 **4** 1 **Sky Ferry**[14] 147 3-9-2 **55** JosephineGordon(5) 2 53
(J S Moore) *led: hdd over 1f out: keeping on same pce whn sltly hmpd 100yds out* **7/2**2

040- **5** 1 **Ryan The Giant**[39] 8267 3-9-5 **53** (b1) SeanLevey 6 49
(Richard Hannon) *trckd ldrs: effrt 2f out: kpt on one pce fnl f* **12/1**

500- **6** 3/4 **Edith Weston**[46] 8166 3-8-12 **46** oh1 (p) JimmyQuinn 10 40
(Robert Cowell) *s.i.s: in rr: hdwy 2f out: keeping on whn n.m.r clsng stages* **33/1**

00-4 **7** 1 1/2 **Cross Examine (IRE)**[20] 47 3-9-4 **52** JamieSpencer 3 44+
(David Simcock) *slowly away and wnt lft s: t.k.h in rr: hdwy over 2f out: wknd appr fnl f* **5/1**3

050- **8** 7 **Miss Victory (IRE)**[38] 8281 3-8-7 **46** oh1 (p) CallumShepherd(5) 7 19
(Mark Usher) *chsd ldrs: drvn over 3f out: lost pl 2f out* **50/1**

554- **9** 12 **Mistaken Lady**[187] 4518 3-8-12 **46** oh1 (b) JoeyHaynes 4
(Jo Hughes) *in rr: sme hdwy over 4f out: sn drvn: lost pl over 2f out: eased whn bhd clsng stages* **50/1**

1m 31.29s (2.49) **Going Correction** +0.10s/f (Slow) **9** Ran SP% **117.3**
Speed ratings (Par 95): **89,88,87,86,85 84,82,74,60**
CSF £18.60 CT £54.32 TOTE £4.50: £1.50, £1.70, £1.40; EX 18.30 Trifecta £58.70.
Owner Mrs R D Peacock **Bred** Mrs R D Peacock **Trained** Upper Lambourn, Berks

FOCUS
The second division of a moderate 3yo handicap. The winning time was over two seconds slower.

329 32RED CASINO H'CAP 1m 5f 194y (Tp)
3:25 (3:30) (Class 5) (0-75,74) 4-Y-O+ **£2,911** (£866; £432; £216) **Stalls** Low

Form RPR

0-12 **1** **Zakatal**[12] 157 10-9-9 **71** PJMcDonald 4 79
(Rebecca Menzies) *hld up in rr: effrt over 3f out: gd hdwy on outer over 2f out: led over 1f out: drvn out* **9/2**

14- **2** 1 1/4 **Innish Man (IRE)**[34] 8353 4-9-0 **68** FrannyNorton 2 74
(John Mackie) *trckd ldrs: effrt over 3f out: chsd wnr fnl f: styd on same pce* **7/2**3

6-21 **3** 1 1/2 **Pinotage**[10] 199 8-8-13 **61** (p) JamesSullivan 8 65
(Peter Niven) *hld up in rr: hdwy over 2f out: styd on same pce fnl f* **3/1**2

1/0- **4** 3/4 **Dovils Date**[227] 2515 7-9-5 **74** GeorgeBlackwell(7) 6 77
(Tim Vaughan) *w ldr: drvn over 2f out: kpt on same pce over 1f out* **20/1**

025- **5** hd **Flambeuse**[44] 8213 5-9-10 **72** LukeMorris 5 75
(Harry Dunlop) *led: t.k.h: hdd over 1f out: kpt on same pce* **9/4**1

320- **6** 1/2 **Next Edition (IRE)**[34] 8353 8-8-6 **61** PhilDennis(7) 1 63
(Philip Kirby) *s.i.s: t.k.h: sn trcking ldrs: nt clr run on ins jst over 2f out: chsng ldrs over 1f out: one pce* **10/1**

304- **7** 3 3/4 **Symbolist (IRE)**[125] 6630 4-8-8 **62** AdamBeschizza 3 59
(John Norton) *in rr: drvn 4f out: lost pl fnl 2f* **33/1**

21/0 **8** 18 **Looking On**[10] 200 8-9-5 **70** RobHornby(3) 7 42
(Edward Bevan) *mid-div: hdwy on outer over 5f out: drvn over 3f out: lost pl over 2f out: sn bhd* **50/1**

3m 5.37s (0.57) **Going Correction** +0.10s/f (Slow)
WFA 4 from 5yo+ 6lb **8** Ran SP% **114.9**
Speed ratings (Par 103): **102,101,100,100,99 99,97,87**
CSF £20.34 CT £54.03 TOTE £6.60: £1.90, £1.30, £1.10; EX 20.90 Trifecta £59.90.
Owner David Furman & John Sugarman **Bred** H H The Aga Khan's Studs Sc **Trained** Mordon, Co. Durham

FOCUS
A fair staying handicap. They went an ordinary gallop. The winner is edging closer to his old form, the less-exposed runner-up earned a small pb, with the third confrming back to best.

330 32RED.COM H'CAP 1m 4f 50y (Tp)
4:00 (4:05) (Class 4) (0-80,80) 4-Y-O+ **£4,568** (£1,367; £683; £342; £170) **Stalls** Low

Form RPR

51-0 **1** **Jamhoori**[19] 66 8-9-2 **75** MartinLane 7 82+
(Jeremy Gask) *hld up towards rr: t.k.h: effrt 3f out: hdwy to chse ldrs over 1f out: edgd lft: edgd rt and styd on to ld nr fin* **9/2**3

210- **2** hd **Golden Jubilee (USA)**[87] 7593 7-9-6 **79** (p) WilliamTwiston-Davies 2 85
(Nigel Twiston-Davies) *trckd ldr: upsides 5f out: led over 1f out: crowded: hdd and no ex clsng stages* **13/2**

13-0 **3** 1 3/4 **All The Winds (GER)**[4] 267 11-9-4 **77** (t) LukeMorris 4 80
(Shaun Lycett) *s.i.s: hld up in rr: hdwy to chse ldrs over 3f out: kpt on same pce fnl f* **14/1**

600- **4** hd **Lady Clitico (IRE)**[35] 8336 5-8-13 **72** (p) PJMcDonald 6 75
(Rebecca Menzies) *trckd ldrs: t.k.h: effrt over 2f out: one pce appr fnl f* **25/1**

023- **5** 1 **Miss Minuty**[45] 8175 4-9-0 **80** RobHornby(3) 5 81
(Tony Newcombe) *trckd ldrs: upsides over 1f out: wknd last 150yds* **2/1**1

400- **6** nk **Sharp Sword (IRE)**[165] 3000 5-9-3 **76** LiamKeniry 1 77
(Neil Mulholland) *s.s: t.k.h in last: hdwy over 2f out: one pce over 1f out* **9/1**

00-5 **7** 3 **Gabrial The Terror (IRE)**[20] 52 6-9-4 **77** (p) DavidNolan 3 73
(Richard Fahey) *led: hdd over 1f out: wknd fnl f* **10/3**2

2m 43.52s (2.72) **Going Correction** +0.10s/f (Slow)
WFA 4 from 5yo+ 4lb **7** Ran SP% **108.4**
Speed ratings (Par 105): **94,93,92,92,91 91,89**
CSF £29.66 TOTE £6.10: £3.10, £2.40; EX 31.00 Trifecta £213.90.
Owner Guy Carstairs & Horses First Racing **Bred** Minster Enterprises Ltd **Trained** Stockbridge, Hants

FOCUS
A muddling handicap.

331 32REDSPORT.COM MAIDEN AUCTION STKS 1m 1f 103y (Tp)
4:30 (4:36) (Class 5) 3-Y-O £2,911 (£866; £432; £216) Stalls Low

Form RPR

6- **1** **Jive Time**[40] 8246 3-9-5 0 LukeMorris 10 74+
(James Tate) *mid-div: drvn over 1f out: hdwy on inner over 1f out: styd on to ld last 50yds: jst hld on* **11/4**[2]

5-3 **2** *hd* **Zeehan**[16] 122 3-9-0 0 JohnFahy 9 68
(Clive Cox) *trckd ldrs: edgd lft over 1f out: styd on wl clsng stages: jst denied* **8/1**

5-23 **3** *½* **Milrow (IRE)**[3] 287 3-9-5 79 (p) FergusSweeney 2 72
(Martyn Meade) *trckd ldrs: 2nd over 2f out: led over 1f out: edgd rt: hdd and no ex last 50yds* **9/4**[1]

0-4 **4** *½* **Young Christian**[21] 40 3-9-5 0 JamesSullivan 6 70
(Tom Tate) *w ldr: led briefly after 1f: chsd ldrs: kpt on same pce fnl f* **11/1**

0 **5** *¾* **Avoidable**[21] 40 3-9-5 0 JamieSpencer 3 69+
(David Simcock) *chsd ldrs: drvn and outpcd over 3f out: hdwy 2f out: swtchd lft and styd on same pce fnl f* **6/1**[3]

6 *hd* **Feel This Moment (IRE)** 3-9-2 0 DanielMuscutt(3) 5 69+
(Marco Botti) *mid-div: hdwy to chse ldrs over 2f out: n.m.r over 1f out: kpt on same pce* **12/1**

7 *4 ½* **Flying Lesson (IRE)** 3-9-5 0 JoeFanning 1 59
(Mark Johnston) *led 1f: led over 7f out: hdd over 1f out: wknd and eased fnl f* **10/1**

8 *10* **You'll Do** 3-9-5 0 RyanClark 8 38
(Jonathan Portman) *hld up in rr: drvn 4f out: bhd fnl 2f* **33/1**

0 **9** *28* **Millady Percy**[14] 145 3-9-0 0 TomEaves 4
(Roy Brotherton) *s.s: bhd and drvn along 6f out: t.o over 2f out* **125/1**

00- **10** *¾* **Carr Lane**[39] 8267 3-8-7 0 DanielleMooney(7) 7
(Michael Easterby) *in rr: sn drvn along: wl bhd fnl 4f: t.o whn eased over 1f out* **125/1**

2m 0.98s (0.18) **Going Correction** +0.10s/f (Slow) **10** Ran SP% **112.5**
Speed ratings (Par 97): **103,102,102,101,101 101,97,88,63,62**
CSF £24.00 TOTE £3.70: £1.50, £2.40, £1.30; EX 23.20 Trifecta £56.20.
Owner Saeed Manana **Bred** Bearstone Stud Ltd **Trained** Newmarket, Suffolk

FOCUS
A fair 3yo maiden. They went a respectable gallop. There wasn't much between the front six at the line and it has been rated around the well-placed fourth.

332 DOWNLOAD THE CORAL APP STORE H'CAP 1m 1f 103y (Tp)
5:00 (5:05) (Class 5) (0-75,75) 4-Y-O+ £2,911 (£866; £432; £216) Stalls Low

Form RPR

06-4 **1** **Archipeligo**[10] 200 5-9-3 71 MartinDwyer 2 78
(Iain Jardine) *up in mid-div: hdwy over 2f out: upsides over 1f out: led 1f out: edgd rt: hld on towards fin* **8/1**

12-5 **2** *½* **Robins Pearl (FR)**[19] 66 4-9-5 74 LukeMorris 5 80
(Harry Dunlop) *w ldrs: upsides over 1f out: no ex clsng stages* **5/2**[1]

20- **3** *¾* **Toga Tiger (IRE)**[25] 8414 9-9-7 75 SeanLevey 7 80
(Kevin Frost) *dwlt: hld up in rr: effrt and outpcd over 2f out: styd on fnl f: tk 3rd towards fin* **8/1**

21-3 **4** *½* **Hernando Torres**[22] 33 8-8-10 71 (tp) NathanEvans(7) 3 75
(Michael Easterby) *led after 1f: hdd 1f out: fdd clsng stages* **9/2**[3]

050- **5** *nk* **L'Inganno Felice (FR)**[73] 7837 6-9-2 70 ShaneKelly 8 73
(John Mackie) *hld up in mid-div: hdwy to chse ldrs over 2f out: kpt on same pce fnl f* **7/2**[2]

112/ **6** *1* **Elysian Prince**[419] 7998 5-9-6 74 (t) DougieCostello 4 75
(Neil King) *dwlt: hld up in rr: effrt: outpcd and hung lft over 2f out: kpt on fnl f* **12/1**

52-6 **7** *1 ½* **Marmalad (IRE)**[9] 212 4-8-9 69 CallumShepherd(5) 6 67
(Shaun Lycett) *w ldrs: upsides over 1f out: fdd fnl 150yds* **9/1**

305- **8** *10* **Big Storm Coming**[34] 8344 6-8-12 66 (b[1]) StevieDonohoe 1 43
(David C Griffiths) *led 1f: chsd ldrs: reminders 3f out: sn lost pl: bhd whn eased clsng stages* **22/1**

1m 59.42s (-1.38) **Going Correction** +0.10s/f (Slow)
WFA 4 from 5yo+ 1lb **8** Ran SP% **113.2**
Speed ratings (Par 103): **110,109,108,108,108 107,105,97**
CSF £27.81 CT £166.00 TOTE £8.40: £2.90, £1.90, £3.30; EX 31.50 Trifecta £249.00.
Owner Tapas Partnership **Bred** Dachel Stud **Trained** Carrutherstown, D'fries & G'way

FOCUS
An ordinary handicap. They went a decent gallop. The winner is rated back to something like his best.

333 CORAL CONDITIONS STKS 1m 1f 103y (Tp)
5:30 (5:36) (Class 2) 4-Y-O+ £11,827 (£3,541; £1,770; £885; £442) Stalls Low

Form RPR

43-3 **1** **Solar Deity (IRE)**[22] 31 7-9-4 105 LukeMorris 2 104
(Marco Botti) *trckd ldrs: effrt over 2f out: chsd ldr fnl f: edgd lft: led clsng stages* **15/8**[1]

015- **2** *nk* **Basil Berry**[38] 8288 5-9-4 98 EoinWalsh 1 103
(Chris Dwyer) *led 2f: trckd ldrs: drvn over 2f out: led narrowly over 1f out: hdd and no ex clsng stages* **8/1**

04-2 **3** *1 ½* **Afonso De Sousa (USA)**[9] 215 6-9-4 102 (p) DanielTudhope 4 100
(David O'Meara) *w ldr: led after 2f: drvn over 2f out: hdd over 1f out: kpt on same pce* **3/1**[3]

410- **4** *1 ½* **Man Of Harlech**[37] 8310 5-9-4 100 OisinMurphy 3 97
(Andrew Balding) *trckd ldrs: t.k.h: drvn to chal over 2f out: fdd fnl 100yds* **9/4**[2]

520- **5** *2 ½* **Starboard**[89] 7548 7-9-4 92 DarylMcLaughlin 5 91
(David Simcock) *wnt rt s: hdwy to trck ldrs over 6f out: drvn over 2f out: wknd appr fnl f* **16/1**

2m 0.09s (-0.71) **Going Correction** +0.10s/f (Slow) **5** Ran SP% **107.5**
Speed ratings (Par 109): **107,106,105,104,101**
CSF £15.48 TOTE £3.50: £1.90, £3.40; EX 14.00 Trifecta £40.30.
Owner G Manfredini & A Tinkler **Bred** Castlemartin Stud And Skymarc Farm **Trained** Newmarket, Suffolk

FOCUS
The feature contest was a good quality conditions race but they went a muddling gallop and there are doubts about the form.

334 LADBROKES H'CAP 1m 141y (Tp)
6:00 (6:05) (Class 6) (0-55,55) 4-Y-O+ £2,264 (£673; £336; £168) Stalls Low

Form RPR

15-2 **1** **Les Gar Gan (IRE)**[17] 107 5-9-7 55 (be) StevieDonohoe 9 61
(Daniel Mark Loughnane) *dwlt: in rr: drvn over 2f out: gd hdwy on wd outside over 1f out: styd on to ld post* **11/2**[3]

00-6 **2** *nse* **Lynngale**[21] 39 5-9-7 55 ShaneGray 6 61
(Kristin Stubbs) *mid-div: hdwy over 2f out: swtchd lft over 1f out: styd on to ld last 50yds: hdd post* **4/1**[2]

04/6 **3** *1* **Malvesi**[10] 201 7-8-13 47 JoeFanning 4 51
(Mark Johnston) *chsd ldr: led over 2f out: hdd last 75yds: no ex* **6/1**

355- **4** *nse* **La Havrese (FR)**[101] 7266 5-9-2 55 JoshDoyle(5) 7 59
(Lynn Siddall) *dwlt: hld up in rr: hdwy over 2f out: nt clr run over 1f out: styd on wl fnl 150yds* **9/1**

63-0 **5** *nk* **Mr Chocolate Drop (IRE)**[22] 32 12-8-12 46 (vt) KieranO'Neill 3 49
(Mandy Rowland) *chsd ldrs: led briefly last 75yds: kpt on same pce* **16/1**

00-0 **6** *½* **Pipers Piping (IRE)**[22] 32 10-9-2 53 RobHornby(3) 10 55
(Mandy Rowland) *chsd ldrs: effrt over 2f out: kpt on same pce fnl f* **20/1**

61-3 **7** *1 ¼* **Foylesideview (IRE)**[17] 107 4-9-1 50 CathyGannon 13 49+
(Harry Chisman) *mid-div: t.k.h: hdwy on outer to trck ldrs over 4f out: hung lft and wknd appr fnl f* **5/2**[1]

02-5 **8** *4* **Actonetaketwo**[16] 127 6-9-2 53 PhilipPrince(3) 1 44
(Ron Hodges) *slowly away and stmbld sn after s: bhd: drvn over 4f out: kpt on over 1f out: nvr on terms* **10/1**

356- **9** *hd* **John Potts**[172] 5039 11-8-13 47 TomEaves 12 38+
(Brian Baugh) *mid-div: jnd ldrs 6f out: lost pl over 1f out* **20/1**

/00- **10** *3 ¼* **Honey Required**[89] 7567 4-9-5 54 GrahamGibbons 2 38
(Alan Bailey) *mid-div: effrt over 2f out: sn lost pl* **40/1**

600- **11** *5* **Rocky Hill Ridge**[34] 8346 5-8-12 46 oh1 (v) LiamKeniry 11 19
(John Balding) *led: hdd over 2f out: sn lost pl and bhd: eased clsng stages* **50/1**

1m 51.38s (1.28) **Going Correction** +0.10s/f (Slow)
WFA 4 from 5yo+ 1lb **11** Ran SP% **117.1**
Speed ratings (Par 101): **98,97,97,97,96 96,95,91,91,88 84**
CSF £26.47 CT £137.86 TOTE £6.00: £1.70, £2.40, £2.40; EX 33.90 Trifecta £133.30.
Owner John P Evitt **Bred** Sean O'Sullivan **Trained** Baldwin's Gate, Staffs

FOCUS
The concluding contest was a moderate handicap. They finished in a bit of a heap.
T/Jkpt: Not Won. JACKPOT PLACEPOT: £30.00 to a £1 stake. Pool: £3581.00 - 87 winning tickets. T/Plt: £43.30 to a £1 stake. Pool: £87358.14 - 1470.79 winning tickets T/Qpdt: £12.10 to a £1 stake. Pool: £8531.64 - 517.77 winning tickets **Walter Glynn**

272 SOUTHWELL (L-H)
Tuesday, January 26

OFFICIAL GOING: Fibresand: standard
Wind: Very strong across Weather: Grey cloud

335 32RED MAIDEN H'CAP 1m (F)
1:30 (1:30) (Class 6) (0-65,64) 3-Y-O £2,587 (£770; £384; £192) Stalls Low

Form RPR

53-0 **1** **Adventure Zone (IRE)**[6] 253 3-9-7 64 (p) SeanLevey 3 68
(Richard Hannon) *mde all: jnd and rdn 2f out: drvn jst over 1f out: kpt on wl fnl f* **7/2**[3]

6-44 **2** *¾* **Sea Of Uncertainty**[8] 242 3-9-2 62 AlistairRawlinson(3) 6 64
(Michael Appleby) *trckd wnr: hdwy and cl up over 2f out: sn chal and rdn: drvn over 1f out: ev ch tl no ex last 100yds* **10/3**[2]

30-4 **3** *2 ¼* **Rubis**[6] 253 3-9-5 62 DavidNolan 2 59
(Richard Fahey) *trckd ldrs: hdwy to chse ldng pair over 3f out: wd st: rdn along over 2f out: drvn over 1f out: kpt on same pce* **6/5**[1]

00-0 **4** *6* **Mikro Polemistis (IRE)**[18] 105 3-8-3 51 ow1 CallumShepherd(5) 1 33
(Brian Ellison) *dwlt and bhd: rdn along over 3f out: kpt on u.p fnl 2f: n.d* **33/1**

20-5 **5** *6* **Southern Seas**[15] 147 3-9-5 62 (p) PJMcDonald 5 30
(Ann Duffield) *chsd ldng pair: rdn along over 3f out: drvn wl over 2f out and sn wknd* **10/1**

60-6 **6** *1* **Modello (IRE)**[5] 265 3-9-0 60 (b[1]) EoinWalsh(3) 4 25
(Giles Bravery) *chsd ldrs on inner: rdn along over 3f out: sn wknd* **14/1**

1m 46.62s (2.92) **Going Correction** +0.125s/f (Slow) **6** Ran SP% **109.5**
Speed ratings (Par 95): **90,89,87,81,75 74**
CSF £14.65 TOTE £5.60: £2.10, £3.00; EX 12.80 Trifecta £27.50.
Owner R Hannon **Bred** Lynn Lodge Stud **Trained** East Everleigh, Wilts

FOCUS
The track had not been worked since the previous meeting as there had been no frosts, and clerk of the course Roderick Duncan said it walked a lot better than it did that day. The first two had it between them from early in the straight in this modest handicap. The winner earned a small pb on the surface.

336 LADBROKES H'CAP 1m (F)
2:05 (2:05) (Class 6) (0-60,60) 4-Y-O+ £2,587 (£770; £384; £192) Stalls Low

Form RPR

032- **1** **Berkshire Beauty**[35] 8340 4-9-0 53 OisinMurphy 7 64+
(Andrew Balding) *cl up: led 3f out: rdn wl over 1f out: drvn and kpt on wl fnl f* **4/1**[2]

52-1 **2** *3* **Rockwood**[22] 39 5-9-5 58 (v) GrahamLee 8 62
(Karen McLintock) *trckd ldrs: hdwy over 3f out: cl up wl over 2f out: rdn to chal over 1f out: ev ch tl drvn and no ex ins fnl f* **9/2**[3]

0-32 **3** *6* **Roger Thorpe**[7] 247 7-9-2 60 PaddyPilley(5) 6 49
(Deborah Sanderson) *cl up: pushed along 3f out: rdn over 2f out: sn drvn and kpt on one pce* **3/1**[1]

3-55 **4** *1 ¼* **General Tufto**[7] 247 11-8-8 47 (b) MartinLane 4 33
(Charles Smith) *sn swtchd rt to outer and rdn along and outpcd in rr: bhd 1/2-way: styd on u.p fr over 2f out: n.d* **12/1**

0-42 **5** *2 ¾* **Miss Lillie**[5] 277 5-9-5 58 (p) RobertWinston 1 38
(Roger Teal) *trckd ldrs on inner: slt ld bnd at 1/2-way: n.m.r: sltly hmpd and lost pl bnd jst over 3f out: sn swtchd rt and rdn along: sn wknd* **11/2**

00-0 **6** *2 ½* **Rizal Park (IRE)**[15] 149 5-9-7 60 TimmyMurphy 3 34
(James Evans) *in tch: rdn along wl over 3f out: sn outpcd* **16/1**

1-04 **7** *2 ¼* **Excelling Oscar (IRE)**[7] 247 4-9-7 60 (b) JFEgan 2 32
(Conor Dore) *slt ld to 1/2-way: rdn along and edgd lft over 3f out: rdn wl over 2f out and sn wknd* **13/2**

00-5 **8** *32* **Heska (IRE)**[20] 61 5-9-0 **56**..............................(p) AlistairRawlinson[(3)] 9 +
(Michael Appleby) *v.s.a and lost 30 l s: a t.o* **20/1**

1m 44.14s (0.44) **Going Correction** +0.125s/f (Slow) 8 Ran SP% **110.2**
Speed ratings (Par 101): **102,99,93,91,89 86,84,52**
CSF £20.63 CT £56.11 TOTE £4.00: £1.02, £2.90, £1.90; EX 13.10 Trifecta £60.80.
Owner Berkshire Parts & Panels Ltd **Bred** J H Widdows **Trained** Kingsclere, Hants

FOCUS
An ordinary contest, but the runner-up is in form and the winner is improving. This could be rated a bit higher.

337 CORAL.CO.UK H'CAP 1m 4f (F)
2:40 (2:40) (Class 3) (0-90,88) 4-Y-O+ **£7,439** (£2,213; £1,106; £553) **Stalls** Low

Form RPR

311- **1** **Gang Warfare**[129] 6549 5-9-11 **88**.................................... RobertHavlin 1 99+
(Simon Crisford) *trckd ldrs: smooth hdwy over 3f out: chsd ldng pair 2f out: shkn up to ld appr fnl f: pushed out* **6/1**[2]

2-22 **2** *2* **Ralphy Lad (IRE)**[21] 52 5-8-13 **76**.................................... NeilFarley 6 82
(Alan Swinbank) *chsd clr ldr: tk clsr order 5f out: led wl over 3f out: rdn over 2f out: drvn over 1f out: hdd appr fnl f: kpt on same pce* **8/1**[3]

03-1 **3** *¾* **The Lock Master (IRE)**[25] 7 9-9-3 **80**..................(p) AndrewMullen 7 85
(Michael Appleby) *trckd ldrs: pushed along and hdwy over 3f out: rdn to chse ldng pair 2f out: drvn and kpt on same pce fnl f* **8/1**[3]

51-3 **4** *2¼* **Swift Cedar (IRE)**[21] 52 6-8-9 **77**...................... JosephineGordon[(5)] 9 78
(David Evans) *hld up in rr: hdwy 3f out: rdn 2f out: styd on wl appr fnl f: nrst fin* **8/1**[3]

00-6 **5** *¾* **Spiritoftomintoul**[20] 66 7-9-0 **77**................................(t) TomQueally 2 77
(Tony Carroll) *hld up in rr: hdwy over 3f out: swtchd lft to inner 2f out: sn rdn to chse ldrs: drvn and kpt on same pce fnl f* **16/1**

04-1 **6** *5* **Royal Marskell**[21] 52 7-9-8 **85**.. TomEaves 5 77
(Gay Kelleway) *dwlt and reminders s: sn chsng ldng pair: chsd ldr 3f out: rdn over 2f out: drvn wl over 1f out and sn one pce* **8/1**[3]

426- **7** *2* **Brandon Castle**[46] 8175 4-9-2 **83**................................. OisinMurphy 10 72
(Andrew Balding) *trckd ldrs: pushed along and outpcd over 3f out: sn rdn: drvn and plugged on one pce fnl 2f* **9/2**[1]

00-6 **8** *10* **Eutropius (IRE)**[24] 23 7-9-8 **85**.. BenCurtis 8 58
(Alan Swinbank) *in tch on outer: hdwy to chse ldrs over 4f out: rdn along 3f out: sn wknd* **25/1**

24-1 **9** *9* **Yul Finegold (IRE)**[25] 6 6-9-6 **83**.. JFEgan 4 41
(Conor Dore) *sn led and clr at gd pce: pushed along over 4f out: rdn and hdd over 3f out: sn wknd* **9/2**[1]

006- **10** *11* **Dark Ruler (IRE)**[119] 6826 7-9-4 **81**.................................... JoeFanning 3 22
(Alan Swinbank) *chsd ldrs on inner: pushed along bef 1/2-way: sn rdn along and lost pl: bhd fnl 4f sn bhd* **9/1**

2m 39.39s (-1.61) **Going Correction** +0.125s/f (Slow)
WFA 4 from 5yo+ 4lb 10 Ran SP% **114.8**
Speed ratings (Par 107): **110,108,108,106,106 102,101,94,88,81**
CSF £52.42 CT £386.06 TOTE £4.80: £2.00, £3.10, £3.30; EX 35.80 Trifecta £239.00.
Owner The Hassiakos & Manasseh Partnership **Bred** West Stow Stud Ltd **Trained** Newmarket, Suffolk

FOCUS
This was run at a strong gallop and that suited the winner, who stays much further and continues to progress.

338 DAILY PRICE BOOSTS AT UNIBET H'CAP 5f (F)
3:10 (3:10) (Class 2) (0-105,95) 4-Y-O+ **£12,291** (£3,657; £1,827; £913) **Stalls** Centre

Form RPR

1-13 **1** **Crosse Fire**[7] 250 4-8-7 **81**..(p) KieranO'Neill 6 90
(Scott Dixon) *slt ld: rdn wl over 1f out: drvn and edgd lft jst over 1f out: kpt on strly fnl f* **10/1**

063- **2** *½* **Sir Billy Wright (IRE)**[75] 7819 5-8-5 **82**........................ PhilipPrince[(3)] 2 89
(David Evans) *racd towards far rail: chsd ldrs: hdwy 2f out: swtchd rt and rdn over 1f out: chsd wnr ins fnl f: sn drvn and no imp towards fin* **8/1**[3]

60-3 **3** *¾* **Showtime Star**[11] 192 6-8-9 **83**....................................(b[1]) LukeMorris 1 87
(Gay Kelleway) *disp ld 2f: cl up: rdn and edgd lft wl over 1f out: drvn ent fnl f: kpt on same pce* **12/1**

502- **4** *½* **Mappin Time (IRE)**[45] 8200 8-8-12 **91**...........(be) RachelRichardson[(5)] 4 93
(Tim Easterby) *trckd ldrs: effrt 2f out: rdn and n.m.r over 1f out: kpt on u.p fnl f* **3/1**[1]

042- **5** *nk* **Waseem Faris (IRE)**[30] 8368 7-8-12 **91**................. CallumShepherd[(5)] 8 92
(Joseph Tuite) *racd towards stands' rail: prom: rdn and edgd lft 2f out: drvn and hung lft over 1f out: kpt on same pce u.p fnl f* **16/1**

03-1 **6** *1¾* **Dungannon**[25] 4 9-9-7 **95**...(b) OisinMurphy 3 90
(Andrew Balding) *towards rr: hdwy over 2f out: rdn and n.m.r whn swtchd rt over 1f out: drvn and no imp fnl f* **3/1**[1]

53-2 **7** *3¼* **Dynamo Walt (IRE)**[10] 213 5-9-5 **93**.............................(v) MartinLane 7 76
(Derek Shaw) *chsd ldrs: rdn along 2f out: sn drvn and wknd* **8/1**[3]

2-20 **8** *10* **Anonymous John (IRE)**[4] 288 4-9-0 **93**................ JosephineGordon[(5)] 5 40
(David Evans) *dwlt: sn rdn along in rr: outpcd and bhd fr 1/2-way* **9/2**[2]

59.09s (-0.61) **Going Correction** +0.075s/f (Slow) 8 Ran SP% **113.1**
Speed ratings (Par 109): **107,106,105,104,103 100,95,79**
CSF £84.07 CT £978.49 TOTE £8.30: £1.60, £3.00, £3.10; EX 131.60 Trifecta £856.30.
Owner Chappell, Cope, Dixon **Bred** Dr A Gillespie **Trained** Babworth, Notts

FOCUS
A decent sprint in which the pace held up pretty well. The second is rated to form and the winner was reversing placings from their November meeting despite being 11lb worse off.

339 BET&WATCH EVERY RACE AT UNIBET (S) STKS 5f (F)
3:45 (3:45) (Class 6) 4-Y-O+ **£2,726** (£805; £402) **Stalls** Centre

Form RPR

506- **1** **Wild Tobacco**[68] 7897 4-9-0 57.. SeanLevey 1 55
(Richard Hannon) *chsd ldng pair: hdwy 2f out: rdn to ld jst over 1f out: kpt on wl* **4/1**[2]

046- **2** *2* **Imjin River (IRE)**[118] 6848 9-9-6 46..................................(tp) BenCurtis 2 54
(William Stone) *slt ld: rdn along 2f out: drvn and hdd jst over 1f out: kpt on same pce* **33/1**

-322 **3** *4½* **Secret Millionaire (IRE)**[4] 292 9-8-9 57.........(p) JosephineGordon[(5)] 5 32
(Shaun Harris) *cl up: rdn along 2f out: drvn over 1f out and sn one pce* **9/2**[3]

10-5 **4** *3½* **Peace Seeker**[11] 192 8-9-6 85..(t) LukeMorris 4 30
(Ronald Harris) *dwlt: in rr and sn pushed along: rdn bef 1/2-way: drvn over 2f out and sn btn* **1/2**[1]

59.78s (0.08) **Going Correction** +0.075s/f (Slow) 4 Ran SP% **107.8**
Speed ratings (Par 101): **102,98,91,86**
CSF £49.08 TOTE £4.00; EX 34.90 Trifecta £72.90.
Owner R Hannon **Bred** Rockcliffe Stud **Trained** East Everleigh, Wilts

FOCUS
With the favourite running miles below form this took little winning. The runner-up is key to the level.

340 UNIBET OFFER DAILY JOCKEY/TRAINER SPECIALS H'CAP 6f (F)
4:20 (4:20) (Class 6) (0-60,60) 4-Y-O+ **£2,587** (£770; £384; £192) **Stalls** Low

Form RPR

00-2 **1** **Sir Geoffrey (IRE)**[16] 136 10-9-1 **54**..............................(b) LukeMorris 6 62
(Scott Dixon) *cl up: chal 2f out: rdn to ld over 1f out: drvn out* **5/1**[2]

0-04 **2** *2½* **Pull The Pin (IRE)**[16] 135 7-8-13 **52**.....................(bt) CharlesBishop 4 53
(Heather Dalton) *led: rdn along 2f out: hdd and drvn over 1f out: kpt on same pce* **7/1**[3]

-256 **3** *¾* **Lucky Mark (IRE)**[12] 178 7-9-6 **59**................................(p) LiamKeniry 1 57
(John Balding) *trckd ldrs on inner: hdwy over 2f out: rdn wl over 1f out: kpt on same pce* **8/1**

3-54 **4** *¾* **Hab Reeh**[12] 178 8-9-0 **53**... JamesSullivan 8 49
(Ruth Carr) *chsd ldrs on outer: rdn along over 2f out: sn swtchd lft to inner and kpt on one pce* **5/1**[2]

06-1 **5** *1* **Very First Blade**[16] 136 7-9-4 **57**...............................(be) RobertHavlin 3 50
(Michael Mullineaux) *trckd ldrs: hdwy wl over 2f out: rdn wl over 1f out: sn drvn and no imp* **5/1**[2]

00-5 **6** *2* **Equilicious**[21] 54 4-8-11 **50**...(p) TomEaves 7 37
(Ollie Pears) *dwlt: a towards rr* **8/1**

00-6 **7** *4* **Coiste Bodhar (IRE)**[16] 133 5-9-7 **60**........................(b) KieranO'Neill 5 35
(Scott Dixon) *chsd ldng pair: rdn along wl over 2f out: sn drvn and wknd wl over 1f out* **7/2**[1]

00-0 **8** *5* **Insolenceofoffice (IRE)**[11] 197 8-9-4 **57**.....................(p) GrahamLee 2 17
(Richard Ford) *sn rdn along and outpcd: a bhd* **10/1**

1m 17.2s (0.70) **Going Correction** +0.125s/f (Slow) 8 Ran SP% **116.0**
Speed ratings (Par 101): **100,96,95,94,93 90,85,78**
CSF £40.13 CT £278.97 TOTE £5.40: £2.60, £2.50, £3.50; EX 34.40 Trifecta £369.00.
Owner General Sir Geoffrey Howlett **Bred** P Rabbitte **Trained** Babworth, Notts

FOCUS
The pace was controlled and the first two had it between them up the straight.
T/Jkpt: not won. JACKPOT PLACEPOT £2,483.60. Pool: £3,402.20 - 0.60 winning units. T/Plt: £1,605.80 to a £1 stake. Pool: £62,608.28 - 28.46 winning units. T/Qpdt: £426.00 to a £1 stake. Pool: £6,564.19 - 11.40 winning units. **Joe Rowntree**

[252]KEMPTON (A.W) (R-H)
Wednesday, January 27

OFFICIAL GOING: Polytrack: standard
Wind: fresh, across Weather: overcast

341 DECLAN'S FOUR LEGGED VOLLEY BALL H'CAP 6f (P)
4:40 (4:41) (Class 7) (0-50,50) 4-Y-O+ **£1,940** (£577; £288; £144) **Stalls** Low

Form RPR

300- **1** **Lizzy's Dream**[28] 8401 8-9-2 **45**.................................... DanielTudhope 7 50
(Rebecca Bastiman) *in rr: effrt on outer 2f out: str run over 1f out: kpt on wl to ld last strides* **13/2**

4-0 **2** *nk* **Diamond Sam**[14] 168 4-9-3 **46**.. ShaneKelly 2 50
(Sylvester Kirk) *chsd ldrs: rdn to ld over 1f out: kpt on ins fnl f: hdd last strides* **6/1**[3]

4-35 **3** *2* **Lutine Charlie (IRE)**[10] 237 9-9-2 **45**..........................(p) TomQueally 4 43
(Emma Owen) *mid-div: nt clr run 2f out: rdn over 1f out: kpt on wl for 3rd wout troubling ldrs* **5/1**[2]

5-00 **4** *shd* **Divertimenti (IRE)**[22] 54 12-9-0 **46**..................(b) RobHornby[(3)] 11 44
(Roy Bowring) *in rr: effrt 2f out: ev ch ins fnl f: wknd and lost 3rd cl home* **14/1**

00-6 **5** *1* **Cerulean Silk**[22] 46 6-8-13 **45**.........................(p) GeorgeDowning[(3)] 1 40
(Tony Carroll) *in rr: effrt on inner 2f out: plugged on ins fnl f* **33/1**

0-05 **6** *1½* **Red Shadow**[10] 230 7-9-2 **45**...(p) BenCurtis 5 35
(Alan Brown) *in rr: rdn over 2f out: kpt on ins fnl f* **7/1**

260- **7** *5* **Dark Phantom (IRE)**[28] 8406 5-9-3 **46**......................... GeorgeBaker 10 21+
(Geoffrey Deacon) *pressed ldr: rdn and wknd fr 2f out* **11/4**[1]

330- **8** *2* **We Have A Dream**[62] 7995 11-9-5 **48**.........................(tp) SaleemGolam 3 17+
(Heather Dalton) *led: rdn and hdd over 1f out: sn wknd* **16/1**

060/ **9** *hd* **Shikari**[522] 5683 5-9-3 **46**..................................... WilliamTwiston-Davies 8 15+
(Rebecca Bastiman) *chsd ldrs: effrt 2f out: sn wknd* **25/1**

000- **10** *9* **Sammy's Choice**[55] 8096 4-9-7 **50**................................(b[1]) JimmyQuinn 6
(Paul Burgoyne) *hld up in rr: no prog fr 2f out: t.o* **16/1**

000- **11** *3* **Danzoe (IRE)**[124] 6717 9-9-6 **49**..(v) AdamKirby 9
(Christine Dunnett) *in rr: rdn over 2f out: sn wknd and eased ins fnl f: t.o* **12/1**

1m 13.59s (0.49) **Going Correction** +0.075s/f (Slow) 11 Ran SP% **116.4**
Speed ratings (Par 97): **99,98,95,95,94 92,85,83,82,70 66**
CSF £44.79 CT £216.26 TOTE £8.30: £2.60, £2.40, £2.00; EX 52.10 Trifecta £268.30.
Owner Mrs P Bastiman **Bred** Sheikh Abdulla Bin Isa Al-Khalifa **Trained** Cowthorpe, N Yorks

FOCUS
A low-grade sprint run at a strong pace. The well-ridden winner hasn't rated this high since April 2014.

342 32RED.COM MAIDEN STKS 1m 4f (P)
5:10 (5:11) (Class 5) 4-Y-O+ **£3,072** (£914; £456; £228) **Stalls** Centre

Form RPR

3-4 **1** **Rivers Run (IRE)**[22] 44 4-9-0 0.............................. GrahamGibbons 7 65+
(Ralph Beckett) *chsd ldrs in 3rd: rdn 2f out: swtchd lft off ins 1f out: gd prog between horses ins fnl f: led 150yds out: kpt on* **9/4**[1]

03- **2** *¾* **Start Seven**[28] 8394 4-9-5 0... JFEgan 1 69
(Joseph Tuite) *led: rdn over 2f out: kpt on same pce ins fnl f: hdd 150yds fr home: kpt on* **12/1**

466- **3** *nk* **Competent**[32] 8361 4-9-5 68.. ShaneKelly 3 68
(Kristin Stubbs) *chsd ldr: rdn 2f out: ev ch fr over 1f out: kpt on same pce ins fnl f* **12/1**

/5-5 **4** *½* **Hope You Dance (FR)**[22] 44 4-9-0 67...................... FergusSweeney 4 62
(David Simcock) *chsd ldrs: rdn 2f out: kpt on ins fnl f* **4/1**[3]

4-02 **5** *hd* **Russian Bolero (GER)**[7] 259 5-9-9 74.........................(p) MartinLane 2 67
(David Dennis) *in rr: ct on heels turning into st: rdn 2f out: kpt on wl ins fnl f: nvr nrr* **3/1**[2]

6 *2* **Antonio Joli (IRE)**[54] 4-9-5 0....................................... DougieCostello 5 63
(Jo Hughes) *in rr: effrt over 2f out on inner: kpt on: nrst fin* **12/1**

60- **7** *9* **Giveagirlachance (IRE)**[61] 8014 7-9-4 0.................... SteveDrowne 6 44
(Seamus Mullins) *in rr: rdn 2f out: no prog* **33/1**

00/- **8** *1¼* **Alhamareer (IRE)**[48] 7730 4-9-5 0...............................[1] WilliamCarson 8 47
(Paul Webber) *mid-div: rdn over 2f out: wknd ins fnl f* **33/1**

5- **9** *50* **Samson**[48] 8171 5-9-9 0 OisinMurphy 9
(Hughie Morrison) *mid-div: rdn to hold pl over 4f out: wknd qckly in st: ease fr 2f out: t.o* **12/1**

2m 37.47s (2.97) **Going Correction** +0.075s/f (Slow)
WFA 4 from 5yo+ 4lb **9** Ran SP% **112.4**
Speed ratings (Par 103): **93,92,92,91,91 90,84,83,50**
CSF £29.78 TOTE £2.70: £1.20, £3.20, £3.20; EX 25.80 Trifecta £246.60.
Owner Ballymore Sterling Syndicate **Bred** Quiet Waters Syndicate **Trained** Kimpton, Hants

FOCUS
An ordinary maiden, and they finished in a heap. It's rated around the third for now.

343 32RED ON THE APP STORE H'CAP 1m 4f (P)
5:40 (5:40) (Class 5) (0-70,70) 4-Y-O+ **£2,911** (£866; £432; £216) **Stalls** Centre

Form RPR
11-2 **1** **Tangramm**[23] 38 4-9-1 **68** (p) RobertWinston 2 74
(Dean Ivory) *racd in 3rd: rdn 2f out: kpt on wl ins to ld last 100yds* **2/1**[2]

45-1 **2** *hd* **Fern Owl**[23] 38 4-9-3 **70** LiamKeniry 4 75
(Hughie Morrison) *chsd ldr: t.k.h: gng wl over 2f out: sn rdn and led 2f out: hdd last 100yds: kpt on* **11/8**[1]

/0-4 **3** *1* **Rising Breeze (FR)**[19] 101 5-9-1 **67** GeorgeDowning(3) 3 70
(Tony Carroll) *hld up in last: rdn over 2f out: kpt on ins fnl f: nvr nrr* **12/1**

446- **4** *3/4* **Midtech Star (IRE)**[32] 6743 4-9-3 **70** AdamKirby 1 72
(Ian Williams) *led: rdn and hdd over 2f out: wknd cl home* **10/3**[3]

2m 38.24s (3.74) **Going Correction** +0.075s/f (Slow)
WFA 4 from 5yo 4lb **4** Ran SP% **106.2**
Speed ratings (Par 103): **90,89,89,88**
CSF £4.97 TOTE £2.70; EX 3.90 Trifecta £5.90.
Owner John Marsden **Bred** W G H Barrons **Trained** Radlett, Herts

FOCUS
This developed into another duel between Tangramm and Fern Owl, and this time it was the Dean Ivory-trained gelding who came out narrowly on top. The front two are rated to the form of their latest Wolverhampton runs.

344 32RED H'CAP 6f (P)
6:10 (6:11) (Class 4) (0-85,83) 3-Y-O **£4,690** (£1,395; £697; £348) **Stalls** Low

Form RPR
-242 **1** **Kingsley Klarion (IRE)**[7] 262 3-9-7 **83** JoeFanning 1 90
(Mark Johnston) *mde all: rdn 2f out: kpt on wl and a holding on* **3/1**[2]

410- **2** *1/2* **Dream Mover (IRE)**[161] 5529 3-9-4 **80** LukeMorris 4 85
(Marco Botti) *chsd ldrs: rdn 2f out: tk 2nd ins fnl f: kpt on but a hld* **13/8**[1]

21- **3** *1 1/2* **Go On Go On Go On**[36] 8350 3-9-2 **78** AdamKirby 6 78
(Clive Cox) *chsd wnr: t.k.h: gng wl 2f out: rdn over 1f out: lost 2nd and one pce ins fnl f* **4/1**[3]

02-3 **4** *2 1/2* **Rosealee (IRE)**[21] 57 3-8-8 **70** MartinLane 8 62
(Jeremy Gask) *t.k.h: hld up in last pair: prog on outer 2f out: wknd fnl f* **9/2**

616- **5** *3/4* **Fashionata (IRE)**[99] 7361 3-8-11 **73** GrahamGibbons 7 63
(Kristin Stubbs) *in tch: rdn 2f out: no imp over 1f out: fdd* **25/1**

660- **6** *3/4* **Silver Wings (IRE)**[28] 8391 3-8-7 **76** RhiainIngram(7) 2 63
(Roger Ingram) *chsd ldrs: effrt 2f out: wknd fr 1f out* **33/1**

556- **7** *3 1/2* **Katie Canford**[188] 4552 3-8-3 **65** WilliamCarson 5 41
(John Bridger) *towards rr: rdn 2f out: wknd* **33/1**

00-0 **8** *1 1/4* **Fishergate**[15] 152 3-8-7 **69** AdamBeschizza 3 41
(Richard Rowe) *in rr: nt gng wl fr 4f out: sn rdn: wknd fr 2f out* **66/1**

1m 13.14s (0.04) **Going Correction** +0.075s/f (Slow) **8** Ran SP% **112.5**
Speed ratings (Par 99): **102,101,99,96,95 94,89,87**
CSF £7.90 CT £18.12 TOTE £3.90: £1.30, £1.10, £1.50; EX 9.80 Trifecta £21.30.
Owner Paul Dean **Bred** Pier House Stud & Martinstown **Trained** Middleham Moor, N Yorks

FOCUS
A good little 3yo sprint which should throw up a winner or two.

345 32RED CASINO H'CAP 1m (P)
6:40 (6:41) (Class 6) (0-55,55) 3-Y-O **£2,264** (£673; £336; £168) **Stalls** Low

Form RPR
04-1 **1** **Nouvelli Dancer (IRE)**[2] 327 3-9-4 **51** 6ex OisinMurphy 2 64+
(Ivan Furtado) *hld up in rr: rdn on outer over 1f out: led 1f out: hung rt but drew clr ins fnl f: easily* **6/4**[1]

006- **2** *4* **Clevedon Court**[42] 8253 3-9-7 **55** ShaneKelly 7 55
(Gary Moore) *chsd ldrs: led briefly over 1f out: hdd 1f out: kpt on same pce* **8/1**

00-5 **3** *2* **Faster Company (IRE)**[16] 140 3-9-2 **50** (p) GeorgeBaker 5 46
(J S Moore) *in rr: n.m.r fr 3f out: rdn 2f out: kpt on ins fnl f: nvr nrr* **5/1**[2]

-224 **4** *2 1/4* **Sky Ferry**[2] 328 3-9-2 **55** JosephineGordon(5) 9 45
(J S Moore) *led after 1f: rdn 2f out: hdd over 1f out: wknd* **5/1**[2]

06-4 **5** *1 1/2* **Miss Fortune**[16] 140 3-9-0 **48** KieranO'Neill 8 34
(Mark Usher) *chsd ldrs: rdn 3f out: wknd fr 2f out* **16/1**

560- **6** *2 3/4* **Fenner Hill Neasa (IRE)**[42] 8243 3-9-2 **50** JFEgan 3 30
(Pat Phelan) *chsd ldrs: rdn 3f out: wknd fr over 1f out* **6/1**[3]

000- **7** *1 1/2* **Totzo (IRE)**[113] 7011 3-9-3 **51** [1] LukeMorris 6 27
(Paul D'Arcy) *in rr: rdn to stay in tch 4f out: a bhd* **33/1**

00-5 **8** *3/4* **Angel In The Snow**[26] 5 3-9-5 **53** DougieCostello 1 27
(Brian Ellison) *in rr: rdn 3f out: wknd fr 2f out* **25/1**

00-3 **9** *7* **Boom Junior**[22] 48 3-8-12 **46** oh1 WilliamCarson 4 3
(Tony Carroll) *broke wl and led for 1f: settled bhd ldrs: rdn 3f out: wknd fr 2f out: eased* **16/1**

1m 40.15s (0.35) **Going Correction** +0.075s/f (Slow) **9** Ran SP% **117.3**
Speed ratings (Par 95): **101,97,95,92,91 88,87,86,79**
CSF £14.81 CT £50.38 TOTE £2.30: £1.10, £2.20, £2.20; EX 15.00 Trifecta £68.10.
Owner S Laffan **Bred** Colin Kennedy **Trained** Wiseton, Nottinghamshire

FOCUS
This proved pretty uncompetitive, with the penalised winner drawing clear to win well. This could be rated a bit higher.

346 ROA/RACING POST OWNERS JACKPOT H'CAP (DIV I) 1m (P)
7:10 (7:10) (Class 6) (0-55,58) 4-Y-O+ **£2,264** (£673; £336; £168) **Stalls** Low

Form RPR
000- **1** **Giovanni Di Bicci**[237] 2868 4-9-7 **55** (t[1]) AdamKirby 1 73+
(Jim Boyle) *cl up in chsng pack on inner: led 2f out: sn clr: rdn out* **7/1**

53-4 **2** *4 1/2* **Dreaming Again**[7] 252 6-9-1 **49** KieranO'Neill 9 54
(Jimmy Fox) *hld up wl in rr: rdn over 2f out: kpt on wl fr over 1f out: tk 2nd ins fnl f: no ch w wnr* **4/1**[2]

136- **3** *3/4* **Gavarnie Encore**[50] 8146 4-9-3 **51** RobertHavlin 4 54
(Michael Blanshard) *in rr: rdn 2f out: kpt on fr over 1f out to go 3rd ins fnl f* **9/2**[3]

04-6 **4** *1 3/4* **Warden Bond**[19] 107 8-9-5 **53** (p) GeorgeBaker 3 52
(William Stone) *in rr: rdn and prog over 2f out: chsd wnr 1f out: one pce and lost 2 pls ins fnl f* **5/1**

6-40 **5** *6* **Kingston Sassafras**[13] 175 4-8-12 **46** oh1 (p) LukeMorris 8 31
(Phil McEntee) *cl up in chsng pack: rdn 3f out: wknd over 1f out* **25/1**

04-1 **6** *1 1/4* **Master Of Song**[8] 247 9-9-7 **58** 6ex (p) RobHornby(3) 5 40
(Roy Bowring) *in rr: rdn 2f out: wknd over 1f out* **11/4**[1]

00-0 **7** *6* **Not Your Call (IRE)**[12] 190 5-9-6 **54** CathyGannon 7 21
(Lee Carter) *slowly away: tk hold in rr: rdn 2f out: sn wknd* **14/1**

00-0 **8** *2* **Rezwaan**[19] 97 9-9-7 **55** (be) ShaneKelly 6 17
(Murty McGrath) *in rr: rdn and struggling fr 4f out* **14/1**

05-5 **9** *12* **Let It Go**[20] 79 4-8-12 **46** oh1 WilliamCarson 2
(Tony Carroll) *chsd ldr: rdn 3f out: sn lost pl and wknd fr 2f out: t.o* **25/1**

260- **10** *28* **Blackadder**[44] 5039 4-8-11 **50** RyanWhile(5) 10 +
(Mark Gillard) *led: sn 5 l clr of chsng pack: rdn over 3f out: hdd and stopped to walk over 2f out: t.o* **33/1**

1m 39.13s (-0.67) **Going Correction** +0.075s/f (Slow) **10** Ran SP% **118.0**
Speed ratings (Par 101): **106,101,100,99,93 91,85,83,71,43**
CSF £34.87 CT £146.06 TOTE £5.80: £2.20, £1.10, £2.30; EX 34.10 Trifecta £174.00.
Owner Epsom Equine Spa Partnership **Bred** Vimal And Gillian Khosla **Trained** Epsom, Surrey

FOCUS
This was run at a good gallop (time was 1.64sec faster than the second division) and they finished well strung out behind the gambled-on, improved winner.

347 ROA/RACING POST OWNERS JACKPOT H'CAP (DIV II) 1m (P)
7:40 (7:40) (Class 6) (0-55,56) 4-Y-O+ **£2,264** (£673; £336; £168) **Stalls** Low

Form RPR
05-1 **1** **Celtic Ava (IRE)**[10] 237 4-9-1 **56** 6ex PaddyBradley(7) 5 64+
(Pat Phelan) *mostly in last trio: prog gng wl over 2f out: str run on outer over 1f out: got up on line* **13/8**[1]

0-50 **2** *nse* **Little Big Man**[11] 222 5-9-1 **49** StevieDonohoe 4 57
(Brendan Powell) *led: rdn over 2f out: kpt on wl tl hdd on line* **14/1**

0-63 **3** *1* **Star Pursuits**[10] 237 4-9-0 **48** (p) KieranO'Neill 3 53
(Jimmy Fox) *cl up: wnt 2nd and chal jst over 2f out tl ins fnl f: one pce nr fin* **9/1**

006- **4** *hd* **McDelta**[170] 5216 6-9-7 **55** GeorgeBaker 1 64+
(Geoffrey Deacon) *settled in mid-div: rdn on inner 2f out: n.m.r on inner over 1f out: swtchd lft and kpt on ins fnl f* **11/4**[2]

04-0 **5** *1/2* **Top Pocket**[7] 252 4-9-2 **50** LiamKeniry 8 54+
(Michael Madgwick) *hld up in rr: rn in snatches: kpt on wl ins fnl f: nvr nrr* **25/1**

506- **6** *2 1/4* **Mariners Moon (IRE)**[140] 6200 5-9-7 **55** DanielTudhope 9 53+
(Patrick Holmes) *hld up in rr: rdn over 2f out: kpt on at same pce* **8/1**[3]

6/0- **7** *hd* **Rectitude**[28] 8397 5-9-1 **52** EoinWalsh(3) 2 50
(Henry Tett) *chsd ldrs: rdn and wknd over 1f out* **33/1**

56-0 **8** *2 1/4* **Zubaidah**[19] 107 4-9-5 **53** (bt) SaleemGolam 6 46
(Heather Dalton) *chsd ldrs: rdn 2f out: wknd ins fnl f* **16/1**

05-6 **9** *6* **Crowning Star (IRE)**[7] 252 7-8-12 **46** oh1 (p) JFEgan 7 24
(Steve Woodman) *racd in mid-div: rdn 3f out: sn wknd* **8/1**[3]

1m 40.77s (0.97) **Going Correction** +0.075s/f (Slow) **9** Ran SP% **116.3**
Speed ratings (Par 101): **98,97,96,96,96 94,93,91,85**
CSF £27.31 CT £162.82 TOTE £2.70: £1.10, £3.50, £2.00; EX 28.80 Trifecta £195.20.
Owner Celtic Contractors Limited **Bred** Castletown Bloodstock Ltd **Trained** Epsom, Surrey

FOCUS
A moderate, messy heat, and the slower of the two divisions by 1.64sec.

348 £10 FREE BET AT 32REDSPORT.COM H'CAP 1m 4f (P)
8:10 (8:10) (Class 6) (0-60,60) 4-Y-O+ **£2,264** (£673; £336; £168) **Stalls** Centre

Form RPR
604- **1** **Authorized Spirit**[139] 6226 4-8-12 **52** KierenFox 10 59
(John Best) *hld up in last pair: gd prog over 2f out on inner: chsd ldr 1f out: drvn to ld last 100yds: styd on wl* **25/1**

20-4 **2** *1 1/4* **Fair Comment**[14] 164 6-9-10 **60** RobertHavlin 11 65
(Michael Blanshard) *trckd ldng quartet: smooth prog to ld 2f out: rdn over 1f out: hdd and one pce last 100yds* **14/1**

11-3 **3** *2 1/4* **Mrs Burbidge**[10] 233 6-8-13 **49** (tp) LiamKeniry 2 50
(Neil Mulholland) *trckd ldng pair: wnt 2nd 3f out: chal 2f out: chsd new ldr tl 1f out: one pce* **6/1**[2]

1 **4** *1 1/4* **Cartographic (USA)**[10] 232 4-9-6 **60** 6ex AdamKirby 7 60
(David Evans) *hld up in midfield: looked to be gng wl whn nt clr run 2f out and swtchd lft: sn drvn: kpt on fr over 1f out but nvr gng pce to threaten* **6/4**[1]

60-2 **5** *4* **Awesome Rock (IRE)**[10] 233 7-8-3 **46** oh1 RhiainIngram(7) 1 39
(Roger Ingram) *hld up in rr: drvn over 2f out on outer: kpt on one pce fr over 1f out: n.d* **12/1**

4-45 **6** *1/2* **Rennie Mackintosh (IRE)**[11] 222 4-9-3 **57** WilliamCarson 9 49
(John Bridger) *trckd ldng trio: rdn over 2f out: lost pl and btn over 1f out: fdd* **9/1**

41-3 **7** *1* **Chefchaouen (IRE)**[18] 127 4-8-13 **58** (p) JosephineGordon(5) 8 49
(J S Moore) *hld up in midfield: rdn and fnd nil over 2f out: sn btn* **14/1**

2-54 **8** *2 1/4* **Fieldmouse**[7] 255 4-8-13 **53** (b[1]) ShaneKelly 5 40
(Eve Johnson Houghton) *pushed up to ld and set gd pce: hdd & wknd 2f out* **14/1**

60/0 **9** *1 3/4* **Honourable Knight (IRE)**[16] 138 8-9-7 **57** SteveDrowne 4 41
(Mark Usher) *wl in rr: brief effrt on inner 2f out: sn wknd* **33/1**

03-3 **10** *5* **Capelena**[21] 55 5-9-4 **57** ShelleyBirkett(3) 6 33
(Miss Joey Ellis) *chsd ldr to 3f out: sn wknd* **7/1**[3]

000- **11** *1/2* **Saint Helena (IRE)**[56] 8077 8-9-3 **58** (b) RyanWhile(5) 3 33
(Mark Gillard) *rel to r: a in last: nvr figured* **33/1**

2m 34.03s (-0.47) **Going Correction** +0.075s/f (Slow)
WFA 4 from 5yo+ 4lb **11** Ran SP% **114.2**
Speed ratings (Par 101): **104,103,101,100,98 97,97,95,94,91 90**
CSF £323.79 CT £2364.18 TOTE £27.60: £6.30, £4.00, £1.80; EX 276.80 Trifecta £3586.90.
Owner Stapleford Racing Ltd **Bred** Stapleford Racing **Trained** Oad Street, Kent

FOCUS
This was run at a good gallop and the form is straightforward.

T/Jkpt: Not won. PLACEPOT £2,923.40 to a £1 stake. Pool: £5,806.93. 1.45 winning tickets. T/Plt: £28.00 to a £1 stake. Pool: £55,880.14. 1,972.12 winning tickets. T/Qpdt: £6.40 to a £1 stake. Pool: £10,680.29. 1,223.77 winning tickets. **Cathal Gahan**

[313]LINGFIELD (L-H)

Wednesday, January 27

OFFICIAL GOING: Polytrack: standard

Wind: strong, half behind Weather: rain until race 5, windy

349 DOWNLOAD THE LADBROKES APP H'CAP — 1m 1y(P)

1:00 (1:01) (Class 5) (0-75,75) 4-Y-0+ **£2,911** (£866; £432; £216) **Stalls** High

Form RPR

0-10 **1** **Black Dave (IRE)**[13] 169 6-9-7 **75** AdamKirby 1 81
(David Evans) *chsd ldr: drvn ent fnl 2f: swtchd rt over 1f out: hrd drvn and styd on wl ins fnl f: led towards fin: jst hld on* **7/1**

21-5 **2** *shd* **Brasted (IRE)**[13] 172 4-9-5 **73** (t) LukeMorris 5 78
(Paul Cole) *hld up in tch: effrt but wd bnd 2f out: hdwy 1f out: styd on strly fnl 100yds: jst failed* **6/1**[3]

00-0 **3** *½* **Malaysian Boleh**[14] 159 6-8-13 **72** (p) CallumShepherd(5) 3 76
(Shaun Lycett) *s.i.s: hld up in tch in rr: hdwy over 1f out: swtchd rt ins fnl f: styd on strly fnl 75yds: snatched 3rd last strides* **16/1**

001- **4** *nk* **Tabla**[56] 8079 4-8-13 **67** JoeFanning 7 70
(Lee Carter) *chsd ldr: rdn and ev ch wl over 1f out: kpt on wl u.p: unable qck towards fin* **4/1**[2]

025- **5** *shd* **Pool House**[72] 7873 5-9-4 **72** TedDurcan 4 75
(Mike Murphy) *in tch in midfield: effrt to chse ldr over 1f out: drvn and ev ch ins fnl f: led 75yds out: sn hdd and no ex* **8/1**

16-3 **6** *nse* **Justice First**[13] 169 4-9-5 **73** GeorgeBaker 9 76
(Ed Dunlop) *stdd after s: hld up in rr: hdwy over 1f out: kpt on u.p fnl 100yds: nt quite rch ldrs* **11/4**[1]

00-0 **7** *1¼* **First Experience**[21] 67 5-9-2 **70** CathyGannon 10 70
(Lee Carter) *led: rdn 2f out: hrd pressed and drvn 1f out: hdd 75yds: no ex and wknd towards fin* **16/1**

23-4 **8** *4* **Alhella**[21] 67 4-8-13 **74** PaddyBradley(7) 2 64
(William Knight) *wl in tch in midfield: unable qck u.p over 1f out: wknd ins fnl f* **7/1**

6-02 **9** *2¼* **Herculian Prince**[9] 239 4-9-3 **71** (p) JFEgan 6 56
(Conor Dore) *chsd ldrs: lost pl u.p over 1f out: bhd fnl f* **7/1**

1m 38.67s (0.47) **Going Correction** +0.025s/f (Slow) **9** Ran SP% **121.3**
Speed ratings (Par 103): **98,97,97,97,97 96,95,91,89**
CSF £51.10 CT £666.73 TOTE £7.50: £2.40, £2.30, £5.10; EX 39.70 Trifecta £389.60.
Owner Mrs E Evans & J Smith **Bred** Richard Frayne **Trained** Pandy, Monmouths

FOCUS
Wet and windy conditions, although the wind possibly helped the horses on the downhill run to the home turn. A trademark Lingfield blanket finish to this modest handicap. The fourth and fifth set the standard.

350 CORAL.CO.UK MAIDEN AUCTION STKS — 7f 1y(P)

1:30 (1:30) (Class 6) 3-Y-O **£2,264** (£673; £336; £168) **Stalls** Low

Form RPR

0- **1** **Trodero**[76] 7816 3-8-11 0 JimmyQuinn 1 69+
(Dr Jon Scargill) *dwlt: hld up in tch in rr: shkn up and hdwy 2f out: chsd ldng pair over 1f out: styd on to ld fnl 100yds: styd on: rdn out* **25/1**

00-2 **2** *½* **Yeah Baby Yeah (IRE)**[12] 193 3-8-11 85 LukeMorris 6 68
(Gay Kelleway) *hld up in tch in midfield: clipped heels and stmbld over 5f out: drvn bnd 2f out: hdwy 1f out: chsd wnr wl ins fnl f: kpt on wl* **7/4**[1]

0-43 **3** *2¾* **Ten Rocks**[11] 211 3-8-9 67 (b) JordanUys(7) 5 66
(Brian Meehan) *t.k.h: led: 3 l clr 3f out: rdn over 1f out: hdd fnl 100yds: sn btn and wknd towards fin* **5/1**

33-0 **4** *1¼* **Port Gaverne (IRE)**[15] 152 3-9-2 70 MartinDwyer 4 62
(Marcus Tregoning) *t.k.h: chsd ldng pair: effrt 2f out: chsd clr ldr over 1f out tl ins fnl f: plugged on same pce after* **3/1**[2]

5 *5* **Pickering** 3-9-2 0 AdamKirby 7 49
(Denis Quinn) *dwlt: sn rcvrd to chse ldr: rdn 3f out: lost 2nd 2f out and sn btn: wknd 1f out* **7/2**[3]

0- **6** *7* **Palmina**[74] 7861 3-8-11 0 [1] RenatoSouza 3 41
(Dean Ivory) *t.k.h: hld up in last pair: rdn wl over 1f out: sn wknd* **8/1**

1m 26.05s (1.25) **Going Correction** +0.025s/f (Slow) **6** Ran SP% **115.2**
Speed ratings (Par 95): **93,92,89,87,82 81**
CSF £71.59 TOTE £24.00: £10.10, £1.50; EX 62.50 Trifecta £934.90.
Owner Kingree Bloodstock **Bred** Mervyn Stewkesbury **Trained** Newmarket, Suffolk

FOCUS
Pretty ordinary maiden form, far from convincing and the level is fluid.

351 EBF STALLIONS/32RED FILLIES' H'CAP — 7f 1y(P)

2:00 (2:00) (Class 3) (0-90,87) 4-Y-O **£10,396** (£3,111; £1,555; £778; £387) **Stalls** Low

Form RPR

0-44 **1** **Subtle Knife**[7] 254 7-8-11 **77** WilliamCarson 5 85
(Giles Bravery) *stdd s: hld up off the pce in 4th: effrt and stl plenty to do 2f out: clsd u.p 1f out: led wl ins fnl f: r.o wl* **5/1**

411- **2** *1¼* **Russian Radiance**[58] 8054 4-9-1 **81** RichardKingscote 4 86
(Jonathan Portman) *racd off the pce in 3rd: effrt and stl plenty to do 2f out: clsd u.p 1f out: styd on wl to go 2nd fnl 50yds: no threat to wnr* **6/4**[1]

203- **3** *¾* **Elis Eliz (IRE)**[46] 8205 4-9-7 **87** GeorgeBaker 3 90
(Michael Wigham) *chsd clr ldr: rdn wl over 1f out: clsd u.p lost 2nd ins fnl f: kpt on* **5/2**[2]

04-5 **4** *¾* **Maggie Pink**[11] 214 7-9-4 **87** AlistairRawlinson(3) 1 88
(Michael Appleby) *taken down early: led and sn allowed to go clr: 6 l clr and rdn 2f out: hdd and no ex wl ins fnl f: lost 2 pls fnl 50yds* **9/2**[3]

40-3 **5** *3* **Glastonberry**[16] 142 8-9-2 **82** TimmyMurphy 2 74
(Geoffrey Deacon) *stdd after s: hld up wl off the pce in last: stl 12 l off the pce and rdn over 1f out: kpt on ins fnl f: nvr a threat* **8/1**

1m 24.64s (-0.16) **Going Correction** +0.025s/f (Slow) **5** Ran SP% **114.5**
Speed ratings (Par 104): **101,99,98,97,94**
CSF £13.60 TOTE £7.10: £2.80, £1.40; EX 18.20 Trifecta £68.90.
Owner D B Clark **Bred** Mrs F Bravery **Trained** Newmarket, Suffolk

FOCUS
The fourth set a reasonable gallop in this decent fillies' handicap. The winner is rated to form.

352 BET AND WATCH EVERY RACE AT UNIBET MAIDEN STKS — 6f 1y(P)

2:35 (2:36) (Class 5) 3-Y-O **£2,911** (£866; £432; £216) **Stalls** Low

Form RPR

326- **1** **He's A Dreamer (IRE)**[75] 7835 3-9-5 82 JamieSpencer 1 81+
(David Simcock) *mde all: rdn and drifted rt bnd 2f out: hrd pressed 1f out: kpt on wl and asserted wl ins fnl f: rdn out* **2/1**[2]

2 *1* **Steam Ahead** 3-9-5 0 GrahamGibbons 2 78+
(Ralph Beckett) *chsd ldng pair: effrt to chse wnr over 1f out: rdn and ev ch jst ins fnl f: no ex and one pce wl ins fnl f* **6/4**[1]

34-5 **3** *1½* **Broadway Icon**[11] 219 3-9-5 80 (v) JimCrowley 5 73
(Jeremy Noseda) *chsd ldr: ev ch and carried rt bnd 2f out: unable qck over 1f out: 3rd and styd on same pce ins fnl f* **3/1**[3]

4 *4* **Lucky Louie** 3-9-5 0 RobertWinston 6 60
(Roger Teal) *chsd ldng trio: rdn 2f out: sn outpcd and no ch w ldrs 1f out: kpt on same pce after* **20/1**

5 *1* **Rhythm And Blues** 3-9-5 0 AdamKirby 7 57+
(Clive Cox) *in tch: rdn over 4f out: outpcd and drvn ent fnl 2f: wl hld and kpt on same pce fnl f* **14/1**

6 *1* **Indigo Princess** 3-9-0 0 AndrewMullen 3 49
(Michael Appleby) *rn green: sn wl outpcd in last pair and rdn along: hdwy 1f out: styd on wl to pass btn horses ins fnl f: nvr trbld ldrs* **50/1**

0-6 **7** *¾* **Evening Starlight**[18] 126 3-8-11 0 PhilipPrince(3) 9 46
(Ron Hodges) *hld up in tch in midfield: effrt but outpcd by ldng trio 2f out: wl hld and battling for 4th over 1f out: wknd ins fnl f* **66/1**

03- **8** *½* **King Of Spin**[32] 8355 3-9-5 0 MartinDwyer 4 50
(William Muir) *rdr lost iron leaving stalls and outpcd in last trio early: clsd to rr of main gp and in tch 3f out: rdn and outpcd wl over 1f out: wknd ins fnl f* **12/1**

9 *1* **Little Miss Kodi (IRE)** 3-9-0 0 SteveDrowne 8 42
(Daniel Mark Loughnane) *in tch in midfield but stuck wd: rdn over 2f out: outpcd wl over 1f out: wknd fnl f* **33/1**

10 *32* **Stylish Queen** 3-8-11 0 SimonPearce(3) 10
(Lydia Pearce) *s.i.s and swtchd lft after s: a bhd: lost tch 1/2-way: t.o* **50/1**

1m 12.11s (0.21) **Going Correction** +0.025s/f (Slow) **10** Ran SP% **125.8**
Speed ratings (Par 97): **99,97,95,90,89 87,86,86,84,42**
CSF £5.72 TOTE £4.10: £1.80, £1.20, £1.10; EX 7.50 Trifecta £24.60.
Owner Mrs A J Jackson **Bred** Jeddah Bloodstock **Trained** Newmarket, Suffolk

FOCUS
The first three dominated this maiden. The winner is rated to form.

353 CORAL H'CAP — 1m 2f (P)

3:10 (3:10) (Class 2) (0-105,93) 4-Y-O **£11,971** (£3,583; £1,791; £896; £446) **Stalls** Low

Form RPR

0-52 **1** **Winterlude (IRE)**[9] 244 6-9-9 **93** GeorgeBaker 7 101+
(Jennie Candlish) *stdd s: hld up in rr: clsd over 2f out: hdwy to chse ldrs over 1f out: rdn to ld fnl 75yds: r.o wl* **5/1**[3]

0/63 **2** *¾* **Whispering Warrior (IRE)**[11] 215 7-9-8 **92** JimCrowley 3 98
(David Simcock) *in tch in midfield: hdwy u.p over 1f out: ev ch ins fnl f: kpt on to go 2nd towards fin* **6/1**

45-2 **3** *½* **Ansaab**[24] 31 8-9-4 **88** BenCurtis 6 93
(Michael Appleby) *chsd ldr: rdn over 2f out: hdwy to ld over 1f out: sn hrd pressed: hdd and one pce fnl 75yds* **14/1**

020- **4** *1¾* **Brocklebank (IRE)**[32] 8359 7-9-1 **88** JackDuern(3) 8 90
(Simon Dow) *stdd after s: hld up in last trio: hdwy over 1f out: wnt 4th ins fnl f: kpt on same pce towards fin* **16/1**

50-6 **5** *1¼* **Masterpaver**[19] 99 5-9-8 **92** (v) AdamKirby 9 91
(Alan Bailey) *hld up in last trio: bhd and rdn over 1f out: styd on ins fnl f: nt rch ldrs* **33/1**

24-1 **6** *¾* **Aleator (USA)**[18] 121 4-9-4 **90** (b) LukeMorris 2 88
(Sir Mark Prescott Bt) *led: 4 l clr 4f out: rdn over 2f out: hung lft and hdd over 1f out: wknd ins fnl f* **4/1**[2]

-411 **7** *1* **Freud (FR)**[6] 267 6-8-4 **79** 6ex CallumShepherd(5) 10 75
(Ian Williams) *dwlt: sn rcvrd to chse ldrs: rdn over 2f out: unable qck 1f out: wknd ins fnl f* **10/1**

401- **8** *3* **Franklin D (USA)**[71] 7881 4-9-7 **93** JamieSpencer 1 83+
(Michael Bell) *hld up in tch in midfield: swtchd lft and effrt to press ldrs whn squeezed for room and snatched up over 1f out: nt rcvr and wl hld fnl f* **11/8**[1]

30-6 **9** *2½* **Starlit Cantata**[25] 18 5-8-10 **80** JohnFahy 4 65
(Eve Johnson Houghton) *chsd ldrs: rdn over 2f out: no ex and lost pl over 1f out: wknd ins fnl f* **25/1**

2m 3.97s (-2.63) **Going Correction** +0.025s/f (Slow)
WFA 4 from 5yo+ 2lb **9** Ran SP% **121.5**
Speed ratings (Par 109): **111,110,110,108,107 107,106,103,101**
CSF £37.04 CT £404.39 TOTE £7.80: £2.50, £3.10, £1.90; EX 38.60 Trifecta £299.10.
Owner Brian Verinder & Alan Baxter **Bred** Darley **Trained** Basford Green, Staffs
■ Stewards' Enquiry : Jamie Spencer caution: careless riding

FOCUS
Not a particularly strong race for the grade, but still a good handicap and the pace was decent. It's rated around the third.

354 32RED CASINO H'CAP — 1m 7f 169y(P)

3:45 (3:47) (Class 6) (0-60,60) 4-Y-O+ **£2,264** (£673; £336; £168) **Stalls** Low

Form RPR

6-41 **1** **Sonnythenavigator (USA)**[11] 218 4-9-1 **58** (p) FergusSweeney 10 66
(David Simcock) *stdd after s: hld up in last trio: hdwy on outer over 1f out: str run ins fnl f to ld nr fin* **7/1**

003- **2** *nk* **Ruler Of The Nile**[53] 8121 4-9-3 **60** LukeMorris 7 67
(Robert Stephens) *in tch in midfield: nt clr run jst over 2f out: hdwy to chse ldrs 1f out: styd on strly u.p ins fnl f: ev ch towards fin: snatched 2nd last strides* **4/1**[2]

50-3 **3** *nk* **Master Burbidge**[21] 62 5-9-0 **50** (p) LiamKeniry 9 56+
(Neil Mulholland) *trckd ldrs: clsd to press ldr and travelling strly over 2f out: rdn to ld over 1f out: kpt on u.p ins fnl f: hdd and lost 2 pls cl home* **3/1**[1]

43-4 **4** *1* **Cosmic Statesman**[13] 170 4-8-13 **59** SammyJoBell(3) 5 64
(Richard Fahey) *in tch in midfield: n.m.r jst over 2f out: chsd ldrs 1f out: kpt on ins fnl f: nvr quite enough pce to chal* **7/1**

532- **5** *2¾* **Activation**[42] 8249 4-7-13 **49** CharlieBennett(7) 1 51
(Hughie Morrison) *sn led: rdn and hrd pressed over 2f out: hdd over 1f out: no ex ins fnl f: wknd fnl 100yds* **14/1**

403- **6** *½* **Broughtons Berry (IRE)**[37] 8337 5-8-12 **48** RichardKingscote 12 51
(Willie Musson) *hld up in tch in midfield: shuffled bk and nt clr run jst over 2f out: sme hdwy and nt clr run jst over 1f out: kpt on ins fnl f: no threat to ldrs* **20/1**

/0-0 **7** *2¾* **Dellbuoy**[21] 62 7-9-1 **58** (t) PaddyBradley(7) 3 58
(Pat Phelan) *hld up in tch: dropped to rr and stuck bhd a wall of horses over 2f out: rdn and effrt over 1f out: kpt on ins fnl f: no threat to ldrs* **10/1**

50-4 **8** *½* **Delagoa Bay (IRE)**[12] 195 8-8-10 **46** oh1 MartinDwyer 6 43
(Sylvester Kirk) *hld up in tch in last trio: hdwy to press ldrs 7f out: rdn 4f out: styd handy tl no ex jst over 1f out: wknd ins fnl f* **25/1**

01-5 **9** 1 3/4 **Mighty Thor**[12] 195 6-9-8 **58**.......... SteveDrowne 11 53
(Lydia Richards) *hld up in tch in last pair: effrt and wd bnd 2f out: no imp: wknd fnl f* **16/1**

65-1 **10** 1 1/4 **Tarakkom (FR)**[16] 138 4-8-13 **56**.......... CathyGannon 4 54
(Peter Hiatt) *chsd ldrs: nt clr run on inner and shuffled bk over 2f out: trying to rally whn squeezed for room and hmpd over 1f out: nt rcvr and wl hld fnl f* **5/1**[3]

240- **11** 3 1/4 **Black Iceman**[91] 6468 8-8-8 **47**.......... SimonPearce(3) 8 37
(Lydia Pearce) *mostly chsd ldr tl over 2f out: u.p and no ex 2f out: sn lost pl: wknd fnl f* **33/1**

3m 25.47s (-0.23) **Going Correction** +0.025s/f (Slow)
WFA 4 from 5yo+ 7lb **11** Ran SP% **119.9**
Speed ratings (Par 101): **101,100,100,100,98 98,97,96,96,95 93**
CSF £35.02 CT £104.42 TOTE £7.70: £2.30, £1.90, £1.80; EX 41.70 Trifecta £191.40.
Owner Oliver Brendon **Bred** Runnymede Farm Inc & Catesby W Clay **Trained** Newmarket, Suffolk

FOCUS
This was competitive for the grade, and the gallop was a sound one. Straightforward form.

355 BET NOW WITH THE LADBROKES APP APPRENTICE H'CAP 7f 1y(P)
4:15 (4:15) (Class 6) (0-55,60) 4-Y-O+ **£2,264** (£673; £336; £168) **Stalls** Low

Form RPR

36-4 **1** **Clement (IRE)**[7] 257 6-9-10 **55**.......... (v) GeorgiaCox 4 67+
(John O'Shea) *in tch in midfield: effrt to chse ldr over 1f out: led 1f out: r.o wl: rdn out* **13/8**[2]

-311 **2** 2 **Binky Blue (IRE)**[5] 297 4-9-10 **60** 6ex.......... RyanHolmes(5) 2 66
(Daniel Mark Loughnane) *hld up in tch in last pair: clsd over 2f out: chsd ldrs 1f out: chsd wnr 150yds: edgd lft and r.o same pce after* **11/10**[1]

2-50 **3** 3 3/4 **Actonetaketwo**[2] 334 6-9-5 **53**.......... PatrickVaughan(3) 1 48
(Ron Hodges) *bhd: effrt on inner over 1f out: nt clrest of runs and swtchd lft jst ins fnl f: sn 3rd and kpt on: no threat to ldrs* **16/1**

22-0 **4** 3 1/4 **Beggers Luck**[21] 60 6-9-5 **55**.......... MitchGodwin(5) 3 42
(Eric Wheeler) *in tch in midfield: rdn ent fnl 2f: swtchd rt over 1f out: sn no ex: wknd ins fnl f* **14/1**

00-2 **5** 1/2 **Blistering Dancer (IRE)**[14] 168 6-9-1 **46** oh1.......... RhiainIngram 6 31
(Tony Carroll) *led: rdn and hdd over 1f out: wknd ins fnl f* **14/1**

-050 **6** 1 3/4 **Black Vale (IRE)**[6] 270 5-9-1 **46** oh1.......... (t) JoshQuinn 7 27
(Phil McEntee) *chsd ldr tl over 1f out: sn lost pl: wknd fnl f* **25/1**

2430 **7** 1 **Tasaaboq**[3] 321 5-9-1 **51**.......... (bt) CliffordLee(5) 5 29
(Phil McEntee) *chsd ldrs: u.p and wd bnd 2f out: sn lost pl: wknd fnl f* **7/1**[3]

1m 24.48s (-0.32) **Going Correction** +0.025s/f (Slow) **7** Ran SP% **121.3**
Speed ratings (Par 101): **102,99,95,91,91 89,88**
CSF £4.12 TOTE £2.90: £1.90, £1.30; EX 6.00 Trifecta £29.40.
Owner K W Bell **Bred** P Kelly **Trained** Elton, Gloucs

FOCUS
A very moderate event. This could be rated a bit higher.
T/Plt: £162.40 to a £1 stake. Pool: £64,541.43. 290.08 winning tickets. T/Qpdt: £14.40 to a £1 stake. Pool: £8,515.53. 436.02 winning tickets. **Steve Payne**

320 CHELMSFORD (A.W) (L-H)
Thursday, January 28

OFFICIAL GOING: Polytrack: standard
Wind: light, half behind Weather: dry

356 BETFRED TV H'CAP 7f (P)
5:00 (5:00) (Class 6) (0-60,60) 4-Y-O+ **£3,234** (£962; £481; £240) **Stalls** Low

Form RPR

061- **1** **Honiton Lace**[49] 8172 5-8-8 **52**.......... (tp) JosephineGordon(5) 6 58
(Phil McEntee) *hld up in tch in last pair: rdn over 2f out: hdwy to chal over 1f out: sustained effrt fnl f: led cl home* **11/1**

-333 **2** hd **Royal Rettie**[7] 269 4-9-5 **58**.......... SaleemGolam 2 63
(Heather Dalton) *taken down early: trckd ldng pair: swtchd rt and rdn to ld over 1f out: sustained duel w wnr fnl f: hdd and no ex cl home* **11/4**[2]

6-23 **3** 2 1/4 **Ertidaad (IRE)**[7] 272 4-9-5 **58**.......... (b[1]) TomQueally 3 57
(Emma Owen) *chsd ldr tl over 1f out: sn hung lft and hmpd: stl edging lft and kpt on same pce ins fnl f: wnt 3rd last stride* **7/2**[3]

-201 **4** shd **Louis Vee (IRE)**[4] 320 8-9-1 **59**.......... (p) CiaranMckee(5) 1 58
(John O'Shea) *led: rdn and hdd over 1f out: 3rd and no ex 1f out: kpt on same pce after: lost 3rd last stride* **6/4**[1]

00-6 **5** 9 **Ali Bin Nayef**[13] 190 4-9-7 **60**.......... (b) NickyMackay 4 34
(Michael Wigham) *stdd s: hld up in rr: pushed along over 2f out: wknd over 1f out: eased ins fnl f* **9/2**

1m 25.83s (-1.37) **Going Correction** -0.15s/f (Stan) **5** Ran SP% **115.4**
Speed ratings (Par 101): **101,100,98,98,87**
CSF £42.28 TOTE £6.50: £3.00, £1.80; EX 22.80 Trifecta £73.30.
Owner Eventmaker Racehorses **Bred** Mrs P De W Johnson **Trained** Newmarket, Suffolk

FOCUS
A moderate affair.

357 BETFRED RACING FOLLOW US ON TWITTER H'CAP 1m 5f 66y(P)
5:30 (5:30) (Class 5) (0-75,75) 4-Y-O+ **£5,175** (£1,540; £769; £384) **Stalls** Low

Form RPR

532- **1** **Daisy Boy (IRE)**[57] 8081 5-9-5 **75**.......... (t) AaronJones(5) 1 82
(Stuart Williams) *sn led: rdn and fnd ex wl over 1f out: styd on wl ins fnl f: rdn out* **11/8**[1]

534- **2** 1 **Scrafton**[43] 8257 5-9-0 **68**.......... GeorgeDowning(3) 5 73
(Tony Carroll) *stdd s: hld up in rr: clsd and wl in tch 4f out: rdn and effrt over 1f out: styd on to chse wnr wl ins fnl f: kpt on* **9/2**

4-11 **3** 3/4 **San Quentin (IRE)**[14] 170 5-9-7 **72**.......... RobertWinston 2 76
(Dean Ivory) *stdd s: hld up in 4th: hdwy to chse ldr 6f out: effrt wl over 1f out: styd on same pce and lost 2nd wl ins fnl f* **11/4**[2]

011- **4** 1 1/4 **Aumerle**[32] 8367 4-8-13 **74**.......... CallumShepherd(5) 4 77
(Shaun Lycett) *chsd ldr tl 6f out: cl 3rd and rdn jst over 2f out: 4th and kpt on same pce ins fnl f: hld and eased cl home* **7/2**[3]

051- **5** 3 1/2 **Artistic Flight (IRE)**[76] 7830 4-8-3 **66**.......... (p) RhiainIngram(7) 6 63
(Jim Boyle) *t.k.h: hld up in 3rd tl 6f out: styd in tch in last pair: dropped to last and rdn over 2f out: wknd ins fnl f* **10/1**

2m 50.74s (-2.86) **Going Correction** -0.15s/f (Stan)
WFA 4 from 5yo 5lb **5** Ran SP% **118.3**
Speed ratings (Par 103): **102,101,100,100,98**
CSF £8.81 TOTE £2.50: £1.10, £3.30; EX 11.20 Trifecta £28.80.
Owner G Johnson **Bred** Shadwell Estate Company Limited **Trained** Newmarket, Suffolk

FOCUS
A fair race featuring a number of in-form horses. The winner was given a fine front-running ride. The pick of his turf foem last year could be rated this high.

358 BETFRED JANUARY SALE H'CAP 2m (P)
6:05 (6:05) (Class 5) (0-70,70) 4-Y-O+ **£5,175** (£1,540; £769; £384) **Stalls** Low

Form RPR

3-11 **1** **Coorg (IRE)**[15] 157 4-9-4 **67**.......... GeorgeBaker 1 81+
(Chris Dwyer) *dwlt and niggled along leaving stalls: in tch in last pair: swtchd rt and hdwy to ld 4f out: mde rest: rdn clr over 1f out and in command after: eased cl home: comf* **1/1**[1]

5-21 **2** 3 3/4 **Megara**[13] 195 4-9-2 **65**.......... (p) LukeMorris 5 74
(Sir Mark Prescott Bt) *wnt rt s: a 2nd: chsd wnr after 4f: drvn over 4f out: wl hld by wnr and battling for 2nd fr over 1f out: kpt on same pce* **11/4**[2]

22-1 **3** 1/2 **Tempuran**[23] 43 7-10-0 **70**.......... OisinMurphy 2 78
(David Bridgwater) *t.k.h: hld up in tch: cl 3rd and rdn over 2f out: outpcd by wnr and battling for 2nd fr over 1f out: kpt on same pce* **7/1**

4-6 **4** 7 **Bamako Du Chatelet (FR)**[15] 164 5-8-12 **57**.......... GeorgeDowning(3) 6 57
(Ian Williams) *pushed rt s: dropped in bhd and hld up in tch in rr: swtchd rt and hdwy to chse ldng trio 5f out: rdn over 3f out: wknd over 1f out* **5/1**[3]

6/0- **5** 28 **Tawseef (IRE)**[20] 112 8-9-11 **67**.......... (p) TimmyMurphy 4 33
(Colin Bowe, Ire) *chsd ldrs tl stdd bk into last pair after 4f: rdn over 4f out: sn btn: lost tch 3f out: t.o* **16/1**

006- **6** 3 1/2 **Arsenale (GER)**[13] 8269 5-9-0 **56**.......... AndrewMullen 3 18
(Michael Appleby) *led for 4f: chsd ldng pair after tl lost pl u.p 5f out: 5th and lost tch 3f out: t.o* **33/1**

3m 25.06s (-4.94) **Going Correction** -0.15s/f (Stan)
WFA 4 from 5yo+ 7lb **6** Ran SP% **114.7**
Speed ratings (Par 103): **106,104,103,100,86 84**
CSF £4.13 TOTE £1.90: £1.20, £1.60; EX 4.70 Trifecta £11.60.
Owner Mrs K W Sneath **Bred** Malih Al Basti **Trained** Newmarket, Suffolk

FOCUS
The winner confirmed himself a progressive stayer with another improved run.

359 BETFRED HOME OF GOALS GALORE H'CAP 5f (P)
6:40 (6:40) (Class 4) (0-85,91) 4-Y-O+ **£8,086** (£2,406; £1,202; £601) **Stalls** Low

Form RPR

-413 **1** **Bosham**[4] 323 6-8-8 **79**.......... (bt) NathanEvans(7) 2 88
(Michael Easterby) *sn led and mde rest: rdn over 1f out: styd on wl fnl f: rdn out* **5/1**[3]

0-26 **2** 3/4 **Saved My Bacon (IRE)**[7] 269 5-8-7 **71** oh2.......... LukeMorris 7 77
(Chris Dwyer) *taken down early: dwlt: in tch in rr: hdwy over 1f out: drvn and chsd wnr 1f out: kpt on wl but hld fnl 100yds* **7/1**

4-55 **3** 1 1/4 **Apache Storm**[12] 220 4-9-7 **85**.......... AndrewMullen 5 87
(Michael Appleby) *in tch in midfield: effrt on inner over 1f out: styd on ins fnl f to go 3rd wl ins fnl f: no threat to wnr* **6/1**

4-65 **4** 1/2 **Come On Dave (IRE)**[4] 323 7-9-4 **85**.......... (be) DanielMuscutt(3) 4 85
(Phil McEntee) *taken down early: pressed ldr: rdn over 1f out: 3rd and unable qck 1f out: lost 3rd and wknd wl ins fnl f* **8/1**

1-31 **5** 3/4 **Jebediah Shine**[4] 323 4-9-8 **91** 6ex.......... JoshDoyle(5) 6 88
(David O'Meara) *broke fast: sn hdd and grad stdd bk into last pair after 1f: nt clr run and swtchd rt over 1f out: sn rdn and no imp tl styd on wl ins fnl f: no threat to ldrs* **3/1**[2]

5-32 **6** 1/2 **Pearl Acclaim (IRE)**[4] 323 6-8-13 **82**.......... JustinNewman(5) 8 77
(David Nicholls) *dwlt: racd keenly: hdwy to chse ldrs over 3f out: pressed ldr 1/2-way: rdn and outpcd over 1f out: hld and kpt on same pce fnl f* **7/4**[1]

57.92s (-2.28) **Going Correction** -0.15s/f (Stan) **6** Ran SP% **115.9**
Speed ratings (Par 105): **112,110,108,108,106 106**
CSF £39.27 CT £215.14 TOTE £3.80: £2.60, £2.90; EX 22.80 Trifecta £203.00.
Owner Peter Easterby **Bred** Rabbah Bloodstock Limited **Trained** Sheriff Hutton, N Yorks

FOCUS
On paper this looked likely to be run at a strong gallop, but the jockeys knew that as well and several were keen to restrain their mounts. As a consequence the pace was not as fierce as expected. A length pb from the winner, with the second running to her best.

360 BETFRED LOTTO H'CAP 1m (P)
7:10 (7:11) (Class 4) (0-85,85) 4-Y-O+ **£8,086** (£2,406; £1,202; £601) **Stalls** Low

Form RPR

32-0 **1** **Big Time (IRE)**[10] 240 5-9-7 **85**.......... (p) FrannyNorton 4 91
(David Nicholls) *t.k.h: chsd ldrs: nt clr run over 2f out: swtchd lft and effrt on inner over 1f out: styd on to ld fnl 75yds: rdn out* **9/2**[3]

6-44 **2** 1/2 **Dream Spirit (IRE)**[10] 240 5-9-6 **84**.......... GeorgeBaker 3 89
(Jamie Osborne) *stdd s: hld up in tch in rr: shkn up and effrt over 1f out: styd on wl u.p fnl 100yds: wnt 2nd last strides* **11/4**[1]

1-34 **3** hd **Hernando Torres**[3] 332 8-8-0 **71**.......... (tp) NathanEvans(7) 7 75
(Michael Easterby) *in tch in midfield: hdwy to chse ldrs over 2f out: rdn and ev ch over 1f out: kpt on u.p to ld 100yds out: sn hdd and one pce: lost 2nd last strides* **8/1**

033- **4** 3/4 **Van Huysen (IRE)**[28] 8412 4-8-9 **76**.......... DannyBrock(3) 5 79
(Dominic Ffrench Davis) *t.k.h: mostly chsd ldr: rdn and ev ch over 1f out: drvn to ld 1f out: hdd 100yds: no ex towards fin* **9/2**[3]

/00- **5** 1 **Publilia**[50] 8163 4-9-4 **82**.......... JoeFanning 1 82
(Mark Johnston) *awkward leaving stalls: sn rcvrd and led: hrd pressed and drvn over 1f out: hdd 1f out: stl ev ch tl no ex and wknd towards fin* **16/1**

12-2 **6** nk **Exceeding Power**[22] 58 5-8-12 **76**.......... LukeMorris 6 75
(Martin Bosley) *hld up wl in tch in midfield: effrt over 1f out: chsng ldrs whn nt clr run and swtchd rt ins fnl f: kpt on towards fin* **4/1**[2]

1-14 **7** 1 **Captain Lars (SAF)**[18] 134 6-9-2 **85**.......... (v) CallumShepherd(5) 2 82
(Derek Shaw) *plld hrd: hld up in tch in last pair: effrt on inner over 1f out: drvn and styd on same pce ins fnl f: sddle slipped* **6/1**

1m 40.01s (0.11) **Going Correction** -0.15s/f (Stan) **7** Ran SP% **114.3**
Speed ratings (Par 105): **93,92,92,91,90 90,89**
CSF £17.28 TOTE £5.40: £2.70, £1.90; EX 19.80 Trifecta £94.60.
Owner Mrs C C Regalado-Gonzalez **Bred** Highfort Stud **Trained** Sessay, N Yorks

FOCUS
They went no pace and this turned into a sprint from the turn in. Pretty ordinary form.

361 BETFRED 1400 SHOPS NATIONWIDE MAIDEN AUCTION STKS 1m (P)
7:40 (7:40) (Class 5) 3-Y-O **£5,175** (£1,540; £769; £384) **Stalls** Low

Form RPR

23 **1** **Byres Road**[12] 219 3-9-5 0.......... JoeFanning 1 79+
(Mark Johnston) *mde all: pushed along and qcknd clr over 1f out: eased wl ins fnl f: easily* **5/4**[1]

 The Form Book, Raceform Ltd, Newbury, RG14 5SJ

24-2 **2** 3 1/4 **Blacklister**[5] 314 3-9-5 77 JFEgan 2 69
(Mick Channon) *hld up in tch in midfield: rdn and effrt jst over 2f out: chsd clr wnr 1f out: kpt on but no imp* **11/8**[2]

3 1 1/4 **Cold Fusion (IRE)** 3-9-0 0 OisinMurphy 7 61
(Ed Vaughan) *s.i.s: hld up in tch in last pair: hdwy into 4th over 1f out: kpt on steadily to go 3rd wl ins fnl f: no ch w wnr* **25/1**

0-30 **4** 3/4 **Zoffany's Way (IRE)**[8] 253 3-8-12 66 (p) GeorgeWood[(7)] 5 64
(James Fanshawe) *chsd wnr: rdn and unable qck over 1f out: 3rd and wl hld 1f out: plugged on same pce and lost 3rd wl ins fnl f* **25/1**

5 2 **West Coast Flyer** 3-9-5 0 FergusSweeney 3 59+
(David Simcock) *s.i.s: rn green in rr: rdn over 2f out: stl green and no imp over 1f out tl kpt on steadily ins fnl f: n.d* **7/1**[3]

- **6** hd **Dilly Daydream (IRE)**[102] 7319 3-9-0 64 SaleemGolam 6 54
(Giles Bravery) *in tch in midfield: rdn over 2f out: 5th and wl hld 1f out: plugged on same pce fnl f* **14/1**

50-0 **7** 14 **Let There Be Light**[7] 275 3-9-5 62 (v[1]) LukeMorris 4 25
(Gay Kelleway) *t.k.h: chsd ldrs tl lost pl jst over 2f out: wknd over 1f out: wl bhd and eased ins fnl f* **33/1**

1m 41.08s (1.18) **Going Correction** -0.15s/f (Stan) 7 Ran SP% **116.3**
Speed ratings (Par 97): **88,84,83,82,80 80,66**
CSF £3.28 TOTE £1.90: £1.10, £1.80; EX 3.10 Trifecta £21.80.
Owner Robin Holleyhead **Bred** Usk Valley Stud **Trained** Middleham Moor, N Yorks

FOCUS
This proved rather straightforward for the favourite, who had the run of the race and won easily. This is rated around the fourth to his recent handicap form.

362 BOOK TICKETS AT CHELMSFORDCITYRACECOURSE.COM H'CAP 1m 2f (P)
8:10 (8:10) (Class 7) (0-50,50) 4-Y-O+ **£2,587** (£770; £384; £192) **Stalls** Low

Form RPR

50-1 **1** **Clock On Tom**[16] 155 6-9-5 48 LukeMorris 5 55
(Denis Quinn) *hld up in tch in last pair: clsd and swtchd lft over 1f out: sn drvn to chal: led 150yds out and edgd rt: styd on: rdn out* **7/4**[1]

35-4 **2** 1 1/4 **Happy Jack (IRE)**[16] 155 5-9-5 48 (b) ShaneKelly 6 54
(Michael Wigham) *hld up in tch in rr: clsd over 1f out: chsd ldrs and rdn 1f out: pressing ldrs whn squeezed for room and hmpd 100yds out: sn swtchd lft and chsd wnr: kpt on but no threat* **9/4**[2]

00-0 **3** 1 3/4 **Time Square (FR)**[24] 39 9-9-4 50 GeorgeDowning[(3)] 1 51
(Tony Carroll) *t.k.h: chsd ldr tl 7f out: styd prom: rdn over 1f out: kpt on same pce ins fnl f: wnt 3rd last strides* **4/1**[3]

440- **4** hd **Ferryview Place**[189] 4563 7-9-7 50 (tp) RyanPowell 2 51
(Ian Williams) *t.k.h: hld up in tch in midfield: hdwy to chse ldrs over 2f out: rdn to chal over 1f out: led ent fnl f: sn hdd and edgd lft: wknd towards fin* **8/1**

50-0 **5** 5 **Sixties Queen**[16] 155 6-8-13 45 (p) TimClark[(3)] 3 36
(Lisa Williamson) *hld up in tch in midfield: nt clr run and hmpd over 2f out: effrt on inner over 1f out: no imp fnl f* **25/1**

0-54 **6** 1 1/4 **Je T'Aime Encore**[12] 216 4-9-5 50 AdamKirby 8 39
(Gay Kelleway) *t.k.h: chsd ldrs: wnt 2nd 7f out: rdn to ld over 1f out: hdd ent fnl f: sn wknd* **8/1**

000- **7** 20 **Soliana**[61] 8035 4-9-0 45 (p) FergusSweeney 7
(John O'Shea) *led: rdn and hdd over 2f out: sn lost pl: bhd over 1f out: eased ins fnl f* **25/1**

2m 6.72s (-1.88) **Going Correction** -0.15s/f (Stan)
WFA 4 from 5yo+ 2lb 7 Ran SP% **117.0**
Speed ratings (Par 97): **101,100,98,98,94 93,77**
CSF £6.19 CT £12.34 TOTE £2.70: £1.70, £1.80; EX 5.00 Trifecta £18.60.
Owner John Mangan **Bred** Kingwood Bloodstock **Trained** Newmarket, Suffolk
■ Stewards' Enquiry : Tim Clark two-day ban: used whip above permitted level (Feb 11-12)
Luke Morris two-day ban: careless riding (Feb 11-12)

FOCUS
A moderate heat run at a leisurely early pace.
T/Plt: £137.40 to a £1 stake. Pool of £69662.05 - 370.0 winning tickets. T/Qpdt: £25.30 to a £1 stake. Pool of £9720.91 - 283.81 winning tickets. **Steve Payne**

[335]SOUTHWELL (L-H)
Thursday, January 28

OFFICIAL GOING: Standard
Wind: Fresh across Weather: Cloudy

363 UNIBET OFFER DAILY JOCKEY/TRAINER SPECIALS MAIDEN STKS 5f (F)
1:35 (1:36) (Class 5) 3-Y-O+ **£3,234** (£962; £481; £240) **Stalls** Centre

Form RPR

4-2 **1** **Eleuthera**[14] 177 4-9-7 0 PatrickO'Donnell[(5)] 2 78+
(Kevin Ryan) *cl up: slt ld 1/2-way: rdn over 1f out: kpt on* **5/4**[1]

235- **2** 1 1/4 **Kyllukey**[93] 7531 3-8-8 72 MichaelJMMurphy[(3)] 8 68
(Charles Hills) *prom: cl up 1/2-way: rdn and ev ch over 1f out: drvn and kpt on same pce fnl f* **2/1**[2]

440- **3** 8 **Rampers (IRE)**[128] 6629 3-8-11 63 CathyGannon 5 39
(Jamie Osborne) *dwlt and in rr: pushed along and hdwy 1/2-way: rdn 2f out: styd on appr fnl f: n.d* **11/2**[3]

4-05 **4** 2 **Anfield**[8] 258 5-9-7 43 WilliamCarson 7 33
(Mick Quinn) *led: hdd 1/2-way: sn rdn along and one pce* **66/1**

04- **5** 1 1/2 **Oh What A Species (IRE)**[29] 8402 3-8-6 0 (t) BarryMcHugh 6 21
(Alan Berry) *chsd ldrs: rdn along over 2f out: grad wknd* **18/1**

6 1 3/4 **Giant Bradley** 3-8-11 0 AndrewMullen 1 20
(Michael Appleby) *dwlt and wnt lft s: in tch in wd outside: rdn along 1/2-way: sn edgd lft and wknd* **16/1**

7 1 1/4 **Bomber Etches** 3-8-11 0 KieranO'Neill 9 15
(Scott Dixon) *towards rr: rdn along 1/2-way: sn outpcd* **28/1**

59.09s (-0.61) **Going Correction** -0.075s/f (Stan)
WFA 3 from 4yo+ 15lb 7 Ran SP% **109.2**
Speed ratings (Par 103): **101,99,86,83,80 77,75**
CSF £3.49 TOTE £2.30: £1.20, £1.40; EX 3.70 Trifecta £9.10.
Owner Guy Reed Racing **Bred** G Reed **Trained** Hambleton, N Yorks

FOCUS
A very modest maiden that lacked depth, the first two finishing well clear.

364 DAILY PRICE BOOSTS AT UNIBET H'CAP 5f (F)
2:10 (2:10) (Class 5) (0-75,79) 4-Y-O+ **£3,234** (£962; £481; £240) **Stalls** Centre

Form RPR

2-13 **1** **Jaarih (IRE)**[5] 319 4-9-4 72 JFEgan 2 81
(Conor Dore) *prom: cl up 2f out: rdn jst over 1f out: led ins fnl f: kpt on wl towards fin* **5/2**[2]

04-0 **2** 1/2 **Sleepy Blue Ocean**[9] 250 10-9-7 75 (p) DanielTudhope 1 82
(John Balding) *chsd ldrs on outer: hdwy over 2f out: cl up over 1f out: sn rdn and ev ch tl drvn ins fnl f and no ex last 50yds* **9/1**

23-0 **3** 1 3/4 **Powerful Wind (IRE)**[22] 56 7-9-6 74 LukeMorris 3 75
(Charlie Wallis) *cl up: led after 1f: jnd and rdn wl over 1f out: drvn and hdd jst ins fnl f: kpt on same pce* **6/1**[3]

0-02 **4** 3 3/4 **Oscars Journey**[14] 176 6-8-10 67 (v) AlistairRawlinson[(3)] 8 54
(J R Jenkins) *chsd ldrs: cl up 1/2-way: rdn along over 2f out: grad wknd* **33/1**

5-00 **5** 1 1/2 **Bapak Bangsawan**[9] 250 6-8-11 70 [1] AnnStokell[(5)] 4 52
(Ann Stokell) *in rr and sn swtchd lft towards far rail: rdn along 1/2-way: n.d* **20/1**

60-1 **6** 4 **Uptight (FR)**[9] 250 4-9-6 79 6ex (bt) JosephineGordon[(5)] 7 46
(Kevin Ryan) *racd towards stands' rail: chsd ldrs: rdn along 2f out: sn edgd rt and wknd* **6/4**[1]

03-2 **7** nse **Barbs Princess**[7] 269 6-8-13 70 MichaelJMMurphy[(3)] 5 37
(Charles Hills) *chsd ldrs: rdn along 1/2-way: sn wknd* **12/1**

00-0 **8** 2 1/4 **Pearl Noir**[20] 106 6-8-13 67 (b) KieranO'Neill 6 26
(Scott Dixon) *led 1f: chsd ldrs: rdn along bef 1/2-way: sn lost pl and bhd* **25/1**

58.77s (-0.93) **Going Correction** -0.075s/f (Stan) 8 Ran SP% **112.1**
Speed ratings (Par 103): **104,103,100,94,92 85,85,81**
CSF £23.50 CT £112.35 TOTE £3.20: £1.10, £2.40, £2.80; EX 25.20 Trifecta £126.00.
Owner Chris Marsh **Bred** Dean Harron & Ciaran Conroy **Trained** Hubbert's Bridge, Lincs

FOCUS
Modest handicap form. The first three came clear and the winner has the potential to rate higher.

365 BET&WATCH EVERY RACE AT UNIBET H'CAP 6f (F)
2:40 (2:46) (Class 6) (0-65,68) 3-Y-O **£2,587** (£770; £384; £192) **Stalls** Low

Form RPR

06-5 **1** **Kestrel Call (IRE)**[19] 126 3-9-7 65 (t) RobertHavlin 2 80+
(Simon Crisford) *t.k.h: trckd ldrs: smooth hdwy 1/2-way and sn cl up: chal 2f out: led wl over 1f out: rdn clr ent fnl f* **2/1**[1]

05-5 **2** 3 3/4 **Englishwoman**[20] 105 3-9-0 58 JFEgan 1 60
(David Evans) *slt ld on inner: rdn along over 2f out: hdd wl over 1f out: sn drvn and kpt on same pce appr fnl f* **9/1**

45-2 **3** 3 1/4 **Guapo Bay**[8] 258 3-9-0 58 (p) SeanLevey 5 50
(Richard Hannon) *dwlt and in rr: hdwy on inner over 3f out: rdn to chse ldrs 2f out: sn drvn and kpt on same pce* **9/1**

2-52 **4** 1 **Rupert Boy (IRE)**[9] 248 3-8-4 48 (v[1]) KieranO'Neill 3 37
(Scott Dixon) *cl up: rdn along wl over 2f out: drvn wl over 1f out and grad wknd* **5/2**[2]

50-1 **5** 6 **Wishsong**[10] 242 3-9-5 68 6ex AnnaHesketh[(5)] 8 39
(David Nicholls) *dwlt and in rr: hdwy wl over 2f out: rdn to chse ldrs whn hung lft wl over 1f out: sn no imp* **7/2**[3]

34-0 **6** 8 **David's Beauty (IRE)**[10] 242 3-9-4 62 TomEaves 6 9
(Brian Baugh) *cl up on outer: rdn along wl over 2f out: grad wknd* **66/1**

225- **7** 2 1/2 **Anagallis (IRE)**[30] 8387 3-9-1 64 (t) CallumShepherd[(5)] 7 4
(John Balding) *dwlt: a towards rr* **25/1**

626- **8** 3 3/4 **Roman Times (IRE)**[33] 8355 3-8-12 56 GrahamLee 4
(Alan Berry) *prom: rdn along wl over 3f out: sn wknd* **50/1**

1m 15.87s (-0.63) **Going Correction** -0.075s/f (Stan) 8 Ran SP% **111.4**
Speed ratings (Par 95): **101,96,91,90,82 71,68,63**
CSF £19.58 CT £127.36 TOTE £2.60: £1.10, £2.10, £2.40; EX 21.80 Trifecta £119.00.
Owner Sheikh Rashid Dalmook Al Maktoum **Bred** W J Kennedy **Trained** Newmarket, Suffolk

FOCUS
A moderate handicap in which the favourite, who like the runner-up is by Acclamation, proved much too good.

366 32RED H'CAP 1m (F)
3:15 (3:15) (Class 4) (0-80,77) 3-Y-O **£5,175** (£1,540; £769; £384) **Stalls** Low

Form RPR

016- **1** **Ritasun (FR)**[33] 8358 3-8-13 69 (p) KieranO'Neill 5 77+
(Richard Hannon) *trckd ldrs: smooth hdwy on outer 3f out: led 2f out: rdn over 1f out: kpt on strly* **9/2**[3]

13-2 **2** 1 1/4 **Ice Royal (IRE)**[14] 171 3-9-6 76 TimmyMurphy 2 79
(Jamie Osborne) *cl up on inner tl n.m.r and lost pl bnd at 1/2-way: rr tl hdwy on inner over 2f out: sn rdn and edgd rt: chsd wnr over 1f out: sn drvn and no imp* **3/1**[2]

502- **3** 4 **Lilbourne Prince (IRE)**[33] 8358 3-9-6 76 JFEgan 1 70
(David Evans) *in rr and sn pushed along: tk clsr order after 3f: trckd ldrs 3f out: effrt over 2f out: sn rdn and n.m.r wl over 1f out: kpt on same pce* **15/2**

1-0 **4** 2 3/4 **Autumn Blossom (USA)**[22] 63 3-8-11 67 FrannyNorton 3 54
(Mark Johnston) *cl up: slt ld 3f out: sn rdn and hdd 2f out: drvn wl over 1f out and grad wknd* **5/1**

62-1 **5** 3/4 **With Pleasure**[24] 40 3-9-7 77 RobertHavlin 4 63
(Simon Crisford) *slt ld on outer: pushed along and hdd 3f out: rdn over 2f out: drvn and wknd over 1f out* **7/4**[1]

1m 43.54s (-0.16) **Going Correction** -0.075s/f (Stan) 5 Ran SP% **108.0**
Speed ratings (Par 99): **97,95,91,89,88**
CSF £17.28 TOTE £6.90: £2.80, £1.70; EX 17.20 Trifecta £69.30.
Owner Middleham Park Racing CX **Bred** Peter Brauer **Trained** East Everleigh, Wilts

FOCUS
An interesting handicap which was run at a reasonable gallop. The level of the form is a bit fluid.

367 LADBROKES H'CAP 1m (F)
3:50 (3:50) (Class 5) (0-75,73) 4-Y-O+ **£3,234** (£962; £481; £240) **Stalls** Low

Form RPR

01-6 **1** **St Patrick's Day (IRE)**[25] 33 4-9-4 70 (v) DougieCostello 6 79+
(J R Jenkins) *dwlt: hdwy and cl up after 3f: effrt to chal 2f out: rdn to ld ent fnl f: kpt on wl towards fin* **16/1**

64-6 **2** 1 1/2 **Deep Resolve (IRE)**[27] 6 5-8-13 65 BenCurtis 4 70
(Alan Swinbank) *dwlt and towards rr: hdwy over 3f out: chsd ldrs 2f out: sn rdn: styd on to chse wnr ins fnl f: no imp towards fin* **8/1**

436- **3** 1 1/4 **Red Unico (IRE)**[96] 7457 4-8-11 66 AlistairRawlinson[(3)] 5 68
(Michael Appleby) *cl up: led wl over 2f out: rdn along wl over 1f out: drvn and hdd ent fnl f: kpt on same pce* **13/2**[3]

2-22 **4** 2 1/2 **Clockmaker (IRE)**[23] 49 10-9-6 72 TomEaves 7 68
(Conor Dore) *slt ld: pushed along 3f out: sn hdd and rdn: drvn over 1f out and kpt on one pce* **11/4**[2]

31-2 **5** 8 **Final**[7] 278 4-9-7 73 JoeFanning 1 51
(Mark Johnston) *chsd ldrs on inner: sn pushed along: lost pl after 2f and sn bhd: rdn over 3f out and n.d* **11/8**[1]

6254 **6** 3 1/2 **Alpha Tauri (USA)**[7] 278 10-9-4 70 MartinLane 2 40
(Charles Smith) *chsd ldrs on inner: rdn along over 3f out: sn wknd* **20/1**

040- **7** *20* **Solarmaite**[231] 3087 7-9-1 **70**.......................................(p) RobHornby(3) 3
(Roy Bowring) *promient: rdn along 1/2-way: sn lost pl and bhd* **16/1**
1m 42.46s (-1.24) **Going Correction** -0.075s/f (Stan) **7** Ran SP% **109.7**
Speed ratings (Par 103): **103,101,100,97,89 86,66**
CSF £122.45 TOTE £11.90: £4.80, £4.10; EX 171.30 Trifecta £587.70.
Owner Miss A Finn **Bred** Lorgnette Bloodstock **Trained** Royston, Herts

FOCUS
This was 1.08secs quicker than the preceding Class 4 handicap. This is rated around the runner-up.

368 CORAL H'CAP 1m 4f (F)
4:20 (4:21) (Class 6) (0-55,55) 4-Y-O+ **£2,587** (£770; £384; £192) **Stalls** Low

Form RPR
051- **1** **Major Rowan**[47] 8197 5-9-7 **52**... PhillipMakin 3 64
(John Davies) *dwlt and hld up in rr: hdwy and wd st: str run to ld wl over 1f out: rdn clr appr fnl f: kpt on strly* **7/2**[1]
00-5 **2** *5* **Toboggan's Gift**[17] 150 4-8-11 **46** oh1.......................... JimmyQuinn 12 50
(Ann Duffield) *trckd ldrs: hdwy over 3f out: rdn 2f out: chsd wnr over 1f out: drvn and no imp fnl f* **16/1**
00/0 **3** *1 1/2* **Mcvicar**[9] 251 7-9-10 **55**.. DanielTudhope 7 57
(John Davies) *hld up towards rr: stdy hdwy 4f out: chsd ldrs over 2f out: sn cl up: rdn wl over 1f out: kpt on same pce* **50/1**
5-40 **4** *1 1/4* **Incurs Four Faults**[9] 247 5-9-10 **55**........................... DougieCostello 1 55
(Keith Dalgleish) *hld up towards rr: hdwy on inner 5f out: rdn to chse ldrs over 2f out: kpt on same pce* **14/1**
62-6 **5** *3/4* **Shirls Son Sam**[13] 199 8-9-5 **50**.................................... JoeyHaynes 13 48
(Chris Fairhurst) *midfield: hdwy on wd outside to chse ldrs 7f out: cl up over 3f out: rdn and ev ch over 2f out: sn drvn and wknd* **12/1**
060- **6** *2* **X Raise (IRE)**[30] 8385 4-8-12 **47**....................................... GrahamLee 9 42
(David Brown) *sn led: rdn along over 3f out: hdd wl over 2f out: sn drvn and grad wknd* **25/1**
3-34 **7** *nk* **Geeaitch**[9] 251 7-9-7 **52**.. WilliamCarson 11 47
(Peter Hiatt) *chsd ldrs: rdn along on outer and wd st: drvn and one pce fnl 2f* **10/1**
336- **8** *3 1/4* **Noble Reach**[51] 5496 5-8-12 **48**.................................... JordanNason(5) 8 38
(Ronald Thompson) *chsd ldrs: pushed along and lost pl 1/2-way and sn in rr: plugged on fnl 3f* **25/1**
42-2 **9** *nse* **Little Flo**[21] 84 5-9-8 **53**.. RyanPowell 4 42
(William Stone) *chsd ldrs on inner: rdn along 5f out: sn wknd* **7/1**
00-2 **10** *2 1/2* **Celestial Dancer (FR)**[9] 251 4-8-11 **46** oh1.. WilliamTwiston-Davies 5 31
(Michael Appleby) *trckd ldrs: hdwy over 3f out: chal over 2f out: sn rdn and wknd* **12/1**
034- **11** *1/2* **Sofias Number One (USA)**[30] 8385 8-9-4 **52**............(p) RobHornby(3) 6 37
(Roy Bowring) *a in rr: bhd fnl 4f* **9/2**[2]
04-2 **12** *2 1/2* **Feeltherhythm (IRE)**[11] 232 5-9-1 **46** oh1.....................(p) ShaneKelly 2 27
(Des Donovan, Ire) *midfield: rdn along on inner 1/2-way: sn outpcd and bhd* **6/1**[3]
040- **13** *20* **Kyllachykov (IRE)**[30] 8385 8-9-1 **46** oh1........................(p) TomEaves 14
(Rebecca Bastiman) *cl up: rdn along over 4f out: sn wknd* **33/1**
44-0 **14** *1/2* **Fen Lady**[22] 55 4-8-11 **46**.. JFEgan 10
(John Berry) *in rr: pushed along and sme hdwy 1/2-way: rdn over 4f out and sn outpcd* **33/1**
2m 40.33s (-0.67) **Going Correction** -0.075s/f (Stan)
WFA 4 from 5yo+ 4lb **14** Ran SP% **119.7**
Speed ratings (Par 101): **99,95,94,93,93 92,91,89,89,87 87,85,72,72**
CSF £58.23 CT £2405.52 TOTE £4.90: £2.50, £5.50, £5.90; EX 72.90 Trifecta £4916.40.
Owner David H Cox **Bred** David H Cox **Trained** Piercebridge, Durham

FOCUS
This low-grade handicap looked competitive enough on paper, but the favourite won easily.
T/Jkpt: £60946.00 to a £1 stake. Pool of £171678.94 - 2.00 winning units. JACKPOT PLACEPOT: £188.40 to a £1 stake. Pool of £3922.95 - 15.20 winnin units. T/Plt: £975.20 to a £1 stake. Pool of £54375.17 - 40.70 winning tickets. T/Qpdt: £343.70 to a £1 stake. Pool of £4413.17 - 9.50 winning tickets. **Joe Rowntree**

[279]MEYDAN (L-H)
Thursday, January 28
OFFICIAL GOING: Dirt: fast; turf: good

369a AL FORSAN AT BAB AL SHAMS (H'CAP) (DIRT) 7f (D)
3:00 (3:00) (78-94,93) 3-Y-O+
£24,489 (£8,163; £4,081; £2,040; £1,224; £816)

RPR
1 **Alareef (SAF)**[14] 183 5-8-6 79......................................(b) PaulHanagan 4 89
(M F De Kock, South Africa) *trckd ldng pair: rdn 3f out: r.o to ld fnl 110yds* **11/4**[1]
2 *1 1/4* **State Law (IRE)**[12] 226 5-8-13 86.....................................(v) PatDobbs 8 93
(Doug Watson, UAE) *sn led: rdn 2f out: hdd fnl 110yds* **11/4**[1]
3 *2 3/4* **Stunned**[20] 119 5-9-0 87..(v) SamHitchcott 7 86
(Doug Watson, UAE) *s.i.s: trckd ldr: ev ch 2f out: one pce fnl 1 1/2f* **7/1**[2]
4 *1 1/4* **Beachy Head (IRE)**[20] 119 5-9-5 93............................ TadhgO'Shea 1 88
(A R Al Rayhi, UAE) *nvr nr to chal: r.o fnl 2f* **11/4**[1]
5 *1 1/4* **Long Water (USA)**[487] 5-8-6 84 ow4.......................... HectorCrouch(5) 3 77
(H Al Alawi, UAE) *a mid-div* **28/1**
6 *2 1/2* **Al Razi (USA)**[20] 118 9-9-2 89..................................(bt) RichardMullen 5 75
(S Seemar, UAE) *s.i.s: a in rr* **11/1**[3]
7 *shd* **Modern History (IRE)**[12] 227 8-8-7 86 ow2........... GeorgeBuckell(5) 6 71
(M Al Mheiri, UAE) *trckd ldng pair tl outpcd fnl 2 1/2f* **20/1**
8 *1 1/2* **Resolute Response (IRE)**[41] 8304 6-8-8 82.............(tp) FernandoJara 2 62
(M Al Mheiri, UAE) *a in rr* **14/1**
1m 25.04s (-0.06) **Going Correction** +0.20s/f (Slow) **8** Ran SP% **115.7**
Speed ratings: **108,106,103,102,100 97,97,95**
CSF: 10.15 TRICAST: 47.06.
Owner Hamdan Al Maktoum **Bred** Shadwell Stud **Trained** South Africa

FOCUS
TRAKUS (metres travelled compared to winner): 2nd -1, 3rd +4, 4th -1, 5th +13, 6th +7, 7th +5, 8th +7. The early pace was fast but few got into it. The runner-up took them along in 24.70 (400m from standing start), 23.35 (800m), 24.27 (1200m), before the winner came home in a slowing 12.46.

370a SHIBA AT THE MEYDAN HOTEL (H'CAP) (TURF) 6f
3:35 (3:35) (95-108,108) 3-Y-O+
£44,897 (£14,965; £7,482; £3,741; £2,244; £1,496)

RPR
1 **Jungle Cat (IRE)**[223] 3343 4-9-4 **106**............................... WilliamBuick 8 114+
(Charlie Appleby) *trckd ldr: led 1 1/2f out: r.o wl* **6/1**[2]
2 *3 3/4* **Ashaadd (IRE)**[84] 7724 6-8-7 **100**............................. GeorgeBuckell(6) 2 97
(D Selvaratnam, UAE) *s.i.s: trckd ldr: r.o fnl 1 1/2f: nrst fin* **33/1**
3 *1/2* **Jamesie (IRE)**[48] 8186 8-8-13 **100**.....................................(t) PatSmullen 9 95
(David Marnane, Ire) *mid-div: r.o fnl 1 1/2f: nrst fin* **6/1**[2]
4 *nse* **Divine (IRE)**[21] 91 5-9-1 **102**............................. ChristopheSoumillon 5 97
(Mick Channon) *trckd ldrs: ev ch 1f out: one pce fnl 110yds* **2/1**[1]
5 *hd* **Fityaan**[7] 280 8-8-13 **100**..(v) DaneO'Neill 1 95
(M Al Mheiri, UAE) *trckd ldrs: ev ch 1 1/2f out: one pce fnl f* **25/1**
6 *2 3/4* **Liber**[130] 6-8-13 **100**.. JamieSpencer 4 86
(Bent Olsen, Denmark) *sn led: hdd 1 1/2f out: r.o same pce fnl f* **33/1**
7 *nk* **Roi De Vitesse (IRE)**[21] 91 9-9-5 **107**......................... AdriedeVries 13 91+
(Ali Jan, Qatar) *settled in rr: r.o fnl 2f: nvr nr to chal* **12/1**
8 *2 1/2* **B Fifty Two (IRE)**[21] 95 7-9-0 **101**......................... MickaelBarzalona 7 78
(Charles Hills) *trckd ldrs tl outpcd fnl 1 1/2f* **15/2**[3]
9 *hd* **Seanie (IRE)**[41] 8297 7-8-10 **98**....................................(t) SamHitchcott 16 73+
(David Marnane, Ire) *nvr nr to chal* **25/1**
10 *nk* **Kanaf (IRE)**[20] 118 9-9-1 **102**......................................(v) PaulHanagan 14 77+
(M Al Mheiri, UAE) *nvr nr to chal* **9/1**
11 *1* **Ahlan Emarati (IRE)**[21] 91 4-8-11 **105**.................(b) HectorCrouch(6) 3 76
(S Seemar, UAE) *trckd ldr: ev ch 2f out: outpcd fnl 1 1/2f* **40/1**
12 *3/4* **Ajeeb (NZ)**[21] 91 6-9-6 **108**....................................(bt) RichardMullen 11 77+
(S Seemar, UAE) *s.i.s: nvr nr to chal* **12/1**
13 *3/4* **Winklemann (IRE)**[137] 4-9-0 **101**.................................. WayneSmith 10 68+
(M F De Kock, South Africa) *nvr nr to chal* **33/1**
14 *1* **Dux Scholar**[21] 91 8-9-4 **106**...(b) PatDobbs 15 69+
(Doug Watson, UAE) *a in rr* **20/1**
15 *dist* **Intibaah**[14] 186 6-8-13 **100**...(v) TadhgO'Shea 12 +
(George Baker) *nvr bttr than mid-div* **25/1**
1m 9.65s (0.65) **Going Correction** +0.40s/f (Good) **15** Ran SP% **126.6**
Speed ratings: **111,106,105,105 101,100,97,97,96 95,94,93,92,**
CSF: 189.20 TRICAST: 1129.87.
Owner Godolphin **Bred** Darley **Trained** Newmarket, Suffolk
■ Sholaan was withdrawn at the start under stewards' orders. Price at time of withdrawal 12/1. Rule 4 applies to all bets - deduction 5p in the pound.

FOCUS
Turf track on inside line. TRAKUS: 2nd -2, 3rd -2, 4th -2, 5th -1, 6th -3, 7th -1, 8th -2, 9th -3, 10th -1, 11th -1, 12th -1, 13th -2, 14th 0, 15th +2. There was a short delay after Sholaan burst out the front of his stall, before being caught by the excellent outriders and withdrawn. Considering the stable's second string was runner-up, Sholaan may have gone close had he behaved himself. There were three groups early on, but they all merged middle to far side in the closing stages and there was no obvious major bias.

371a PRIME AT THE MEYDAN HOTEL (H'CAP) (DIRT) 6f (D)
4:10 (4:10) (95-118,105) 3-Y-O+
£44,897 (£14,965; £7,482; £3,741; £2,244; £1,496)

RPR
1 **Kifaah**[21] 90 5-8-13 97.. PaulHanagan 5 104+
(A R Al Rayhi, UAE) *trckd ldr: rdn 3f out: led 110yds out: r.o wl* **15/8**[1]
2 *2* **My Catch (IRE)**[21] 90 5-9-6 105.. PatDobbs 4 105
(Doug Watson, UAE) *sn led: rdn 2 1/2f out: hdd 110yds out* **5/2**[2]
3 *3 3/4* **Krypton Factor**[14] 186 8-9-6 105...............................(b) FrederikTylicki 2 93
(Fawzi Abdulla Nass, Bahrain) *settled in rr: chsd ldrs 3f out: r.o same pce fnl 2f* **11/2**[3]
4 *1 1/4* **Rafeej**[21] 90 7-9-6 105...(t) DaneO'Neill 3 89
(M Al Mheiri, UAE) *nvr nr to chal: r.o same pce fnl 2f* **9/1**
5 *3 1/2* **Roicead (USA)**[7] 280 9-9-6 105.......................................(t) ChrisHayes 6 78
(D Selvaratnam, UAE) *nvr bttr than mid-div* **11/2**[3]
6 *1 1/2* **Muharaaj (IRE)**[137] 6367 5-9-6 105........................... MickaelBarzalona 7 73
(Mme Pia Brandt, France) *nvr bttr than mid-div* **16/1**
1m 11.52s (-0.08) **Going Correction** +0.20s/f (Slow) **6** Ran SP% **110.0**
Speed ratings: **108,105,100,98,94 92**
CSF: 6.47.
Owner Hamdan Al Maktoum **Bred** Shadwell Estate Co Ltd **Trained** UAE
■ Over The Ocean was withdrawn at the start under stewards' orders. Price at time of withdrawal 22/1. No Rule 4 applied

FOCUS
TRAKUS: 2nd -5, 3rd -6, 4th -1, 5th +3, 6th +6. Kifaah and My Catch didn't take each other on up front like they had when fading into second and third respectively over C&D last time, the former happy to take a lead off his old rival this time, and that meant a more sensible pace. Here are those opening splits, with the January 7 meeting in brackets: 24.8 (23.92) through 400m, 47.49 (46.50) for 800m. The final time was almost identical.

372a AL RASHIDIYA SPONSORED BY MEYDAN GROUP (GROUP 2) (TURF) 1m 1f (T)
4:45 (4:45) 3-Y-O+
£81,632 (£27,210; £13,605; £6,802; £4,081; £2,721)

RPR
1 **Forries Waltz (SAF)**[14] 189 4-9-1 108............. ChristopheSoumillon 13 114
(M F De Kock, South Africa) *mid-div: smooth prog 2 1/2f out: rdn 2f out: led fnl f: r.o wl* **9/4**[1]
2 *1 1/4* **Ertijaal (AUS)**[243] 4-9-1 110... PaulHanagan 4 111
(M F De Kock, South Africa) *trckd ldng trio: rdn 3f out: led 1 1/2f out: hdd fnl f* **5/2**[2]
3 *2 3/4* **Earnshaw (USA)**[21] 93 5-9-1 111......................(bt) MickaelBarzalona 6 105
(S bin Ghadayer, UAE) *mid-div: r.o fnl 2f: nt pce of first two* **10/1**
4 *shd* **Mujaarib (AUS)**[14] 187 7-9-1 110.. DaneO'Neill 9 105+
(M F De Kock, South Africa) *settled in rr: r.o fnl 2f: nrst fin* **9/1**
5 *1 1/4* **Battle Of Marathon (USA)**[14] 189 4-9-0 101...........(v) DavidProbert 14 102
(John Ryan) *trckd ldr: led 2f out: hdd 1 1/2f out: wknd fnl f* **50/1**
6 *1* **Limario (GER)**[14] 187 6-9-1 112.. PatDobbs 5 100
(Doug Watson, UAE) *mid-div: chsd ldrs: ev ch 2 1/2f out: one pce fnl 1 1/2f* **12/1**

7 hd **Calling Out (FR)**40 8311 5-9-1 104 JamieSpencer 2 100
(David Simcock) *trckd ldng trio: ev ch 3f out: one pce fnl 2f* **20/1**

8 2 ¾ **Zamaam**14 187 6-9-1 100 (t) TadhgO'Shea 7 94
(E Charpy, UAE) *s.i.s: nvr nr to chal* **50/1**

9 2 **Tarbawi (IRE)**14 189 6-9-1 100 AdriedeVries 12 90
(A bin Harmash, UAE) *nvr nr to chal* **50/1**

10 hd **Moohaarib (IRE)**145 6081 5-9-1 110 PatSmullen 10 89
(Marco Botti) *s.i.s: a in rr* **10/1**

11 3 ¼ **Bossy Guest (IRE)**21 95 4-9-0 108 CharlesBishop 1 83+
(Mick Channon) *slowly away: a in rr* **10/1**

12 3 ½ **Ennobled Friend (USA)**6 309 6-9-1 102 (bt) FrederikTylicki 11 75
(A bin Harmash, UAE) *sn led: hdd & wknd 2f out* **50/1**

13 2 ¼ **El Tren (IRE)**14 189 5-9-1 102 ChrisHayes 3 71
(Michael Attwater) *trckd ldr: rdn 3f out: wknd fnl 2f* **66/1**

14 dist **Big Baz (IRE)**14 187 6-9-1 113 WilliamBuick 8
(William Muir) *nvr nr to chal* **7/1**3

1m 47.85s (-1.25) **Going Correction** +0.15s/f (Good)
WFA 4 from 5yo+ 1lb 14 Ran SP% **130.9**
Speed ratings: **111,109,107,107,106 105,105,102,100,100 97,94,92,**
CSF: 8.38.
Owner Sh Mohd Khalifa Al Maktoum, Gerber, De Kock **Bred** Wicklow Stud **Trained** South Africa

FOCUS
TRAKUS: 2nd +1, 3rd -6, 4th 0, 5th -2, 6th 0, 7th -5, 8th -6, 9th -1, 10th -5, 11th -3, 12th -5, 13th -5, 14th +7. An eighth win in this race for Mike De Kock, his fifth in succession and the third time he's had the one-two - he almost had the third as well. There wasn't a great deal of depth to this despite the big field, but two smart horses pulled clear. The pace was sensible.

373a BAB AL SHAMS DESERT RESORT AND SPA (H'CAP) (TURF) 7f
5:20 (5:20) (100-113,107) 3-Y-O+
£48,979 (£16,326; £8,163; £4,081; £2,448; £1,632)

RPR

1 **Anaerobio (ARG)**7 282 8-9-6 **107** (t) ChristopheSoumillon 2 107+
(M F De Kock, South Africa) *trckd ldrs: rdn 2 1/2f out: r.o wl: led last strides* **4/1**2

2 shd **Banaadeer (AUS)**7 280 4-9-4 **105** (b) PaulHanagan 6 105
(M F De Kock, South Africa) *sn led: kicked clr 2f out: hdd on line* **20/1**

3 ¾ **Royal Ridge (SAF)**7 282 7-9-0 **100** (bt) DaneO'Neill 12 99+
(M F De Kock, South Africa) *s.i.s: settled in rr: r.o fnl 2f: nrst fin* **25/1**

4 1 **Flash Fire (IRE)**14 189 4-9-3 **104** WilliamBuick 1 99
(Charlie Appleby) *trckd ldr: ev ch 2f out: one pce fnl 1 1/2f* **7/4**1

5 ½ **Fils Anges (IRE)**334 741 6-9-6 **107** AdriedeVries 9 101+
(Ali Jan, Qatar) *settled in rr: r.o fnl 2f: nrst fin* **14/1**

6 1 ½ **Yaa Wayl (IRE)**62 8030 9-9-1 **101** (t) ChrisHayes 3 92+
(D Selvaratnam, UAE) *s.i.s: settled in rr: nvr able to chal: r.o fnl 2f* **25/1**

7 1 ¼ **Majestic Mount**21 95 6-9-1 **101** (t) RichardMullen 10 89
(S Seemar, UAE) *trckd ldr tl outpcd fnl 2f* **20/1**

8 ½ **Eastern Rules (IRE)**7 282 8-9-2 **102** PatSmullen 8 88+
(M Halford, Ire) *nvr nr to chal* **6/1**3

9 shd **Jallota**117 6919 5-9-4 **105** MickaelBarzalona 11 90+
(Charles Hills) *nvr nr to chal* **16/1**

10 ¾ **Boomshackerlacker (IRE)**14 189 6-9-0 **100** SamHitchcott 7 84+
(George Baker) *nvr bttr than mid-div* **8/1**

11 1 **Glory Awaits (IRE)**21 95 6-9-4 **105** JamieSpencer 4 85+
(David Simcock) *nvr bttr than mid-div* **12/1**

12 23 **Anfitrion Sale (ARG)**332 4-9-3 **104** TadhgO'Shea 5 22+
(Y Al Blooshi, UAE) *nvr bttr than mid-div* **20/1**

1m 23.13s (-0.97) **Going Correction** +0.15s/f (Good) 12 Ran SP% **124.0**
Speed ratings: **111,110,110,108,108 106,105,104,104,103 102,76**
CSF: 89.83 TRICAST: 1813.43.
Owner Mohd Khaleel Ahmed **Bred** Haras La Madrugada **Trained** South Africa

FOCUS
TRAKUS: 2nd -1, 3rd +6, 4th -5, 5th -1, 6th -4, 7th +2, 8th +7, 9th +2, 10th +6, 11th -3, 12th +1. The runner-up set a solid pace - 24.88, 22.89, 23.02 - and the winner was home in 11.91. A one-two-three for Mike De Kock after his one-two-four in the preceding race, and a treble on the night for the stable.

374a TERRACE BRUNCH AT MEYDAN RACECOURSE (H'CAP) (DIRT) 7f (D)
5:55 (5:55) (100-123,109) 3-Y-O+
£48,979 (£16,326; £8,163; £4,081; £2,448; £1,632)

RPR

1 **Cool Cowboy (USA)**14 186 5-9-3 **106** PatDobbs 9 108+
(Doug Watson, UAE) *mid-div: smooth prog 3f out: led fnl f: r.o wl* **11/4**1

2 1 ¾ **Giftorm (USA)**14 189 6-8-11 **100** FernandoJara 7 97
(Fredrik Reuterskiold, Sweden) *mid-div: chsd ldr 4 1/2f out: led 3f out: hdd fnl f: r.o same pce* **10/1**

3 nse **Encipher (USA)**21 95 7-8-11 **100** TadhgO'Shea 4 97
(A R Al Rayhi, UAE) *mid-div: r.o fnl 2f: nrst fin* **7/2**2

4 ¾ **Ross (IRE)**47 8212 4-8-11 **100** AdriedeVries 1 95+
(P Schiergen, Germany) *mid-div: r.o fnl 2 1/2f: nrst fin* **8/1**

5 4 **Free Wheeling (AUS)**21 92 7-9-6 **109** (t) FrederikTylicki 8 93
(Saeed bin Suroor) *trckd ldrs: ev ch 3 1/2f out: one pce fnl 2f* **10/1**

6 7 ½ **Frank Lloyd Wright (SWE)**21 90 5-8-11 **100**(t) Per-AndersGraberg 3 64
(Niels Petersen, Norway) *mid-div: wknd 3 1/2f out* **33/1**

7 nse **Emirates Skycargo (IRE)**14 189 4-9-0 **102** WilliamBuick 2 67
(Charlie Appleby) *slowly away: nvr nr to chal* **4/1**3

8 3 ¾ **Almargo (IRE)**343 618 5-8-11 **100** MickaelBarzalona 6 54
(S bin Ghadayer, UAE) *nvr nr to chal* **25/1**

P **Muaanid**327 823 6-9-0 **102** PaulHanagan 5
(Doug Watson, UAE) *sn led: hdd & wknd 2f out: p.u* **11/2**

1m 24.45s (-0.65) **Going Correction** +0.20s/f (Slow) 9 Ran SP% **120.4**
Speed ratings: **111,109,108,108,103 94,94,90,**
CSF: 33.13 TRICAST: 102.10.
Owner Zaur Sekrekov **Bred** Columbiana Farm **Trained** United Arab Emirates

FOCUS
TRAKUS: 2nd -1, 3rd -1, 4th -8, 5th -3, 6th -4, 7th +3, 8th 0. They went 0.58secs faster through the opening 800m than the earlier lower-class race over C&D and the final time was 0.59secs quicker.

375a THE MEYDAN HOTEL (H'CAP) (TURF) 1m
6:30 (6:30) (100-113,112) 3-Y-O+
£48,979 (£16,326; £8,163; £4,081; £2,448; £1,632)

RPR

1 **Fanciful Angel (IRE)**123 6801 4-9-0 106 DaneO'Neill 8 108
(Marco Botti) *slowly away: mid-div: smooth prog: led fnl 55yds* **12/1**

2 nk **Dark Emerald (IRE)**21 95 6-9-2 108 (v) RichardMullen 12 109
(Brendan Powell) *mid-div: wd: rdn 2f out: led 2f out: hdd cl home* **3/1**2

3 1 ¼ **Farraaj (IRE)**14 187 7-9-5 111 ChrisHayes 9 109
(D Selvaratnam, UAE) *mid-div: r.o wl fnl 2f: nrst fin* **14/1**

4 shd **Beach Bar (IRE)**14 189 5-8-8 100 TadhgO'Shea 1 98
(Brendan Powell) *sn led: rdn 3f out: hdd 1f out: r.o same pce* **14/1**

5 ½ **Liquid Mercury (SAF)**215 4-8-8 100 SamHitchcott 3 97
(M F De Kock, South Africa) *s.i.s: nvr nr to chal but r.o fnl 2f* **10/1**

6 1 ½ **Vortex (NOR)**7 284 7-8-8 100 (b) DavidProbert 11 93
(Rune Haugen) *trckd ldr: ev ch 3f out: one pce fnl 2f* **33/1**

7 ¾ **Wychwood Warrior (IRE)**14 189 4-8-10 102 PatSmullen 4 94
(M Halford, Ire) *trckd ldrs tl one pce fnl 2f* **8/1**

8 2 ½ **Vin Chaud (FR)**145 6120 4-9-6 112 (t) ChristopheSoumillon 7 98
(F Rohaut, France) *nvr bttr than mid-div* **9/2**3

9 1 ¼ **Avon Pearl**102 7-8-10 102 (vt) CarlosLopez 2 85
(Rune Haugen) *trckd ldrs tl wknd fnl 1 1/2f* **25/1**

10 nk **Iguazu Falls (USA)**385 88 11-9-4 110 (t) FrederikTylicki 5 92
(A bin Harmash, UAE) *slowly away: nvr bttr than mid-div* **33/1**

11 nk **Mutamakkin (AUS)**334 4-8-8 100 PaulHanagan 10 82
(M F De Kock, South Africa) *a in rr* **5/2**1

P **Rock Cocktail (AUS)**14 189 6-8-10 102 (b) WayneSmith 6
(M F De Kock, South Africa) *sn struggling in rr: virtually p.u 4 1/2f out* **14/1**

1m 36.21s (-1.29) **Going Correction** +0.15s/f (Good) 12 Ran SP% **129.4**
Speed ratings: **112,111,110,110,109 108,107,105,103,103 103,**
CSF: 51.66 TRICAST: 541.85. Placepot: £93.50 to a £1 stake. Pool of £6816.82 - 53.22 winning units. Quadpot: £23.90 to a £1 stake. Pool of £379.19 - 11.71 winning units..
Owner Scuderia Blueberry SRL **Bred** Berjis Desai **Trained** Newmarket, Suffolk

FOCUS
TRAKUS: 2nd +7, 3rd +4, 4th -4, 5th -2, 6th +1, 7th -2, 8th 0, 9th -4, 10th +2, 11th +4. They went a fair gallop; 25.55, 22.85, 23.55, before the winner clocked 23.78 to the line.

349 LINGFIELD (L-H)
Friday, January 29
OFFICIAL GOING: Polytrack: standard
Wind: very strong, half behind Weather: Overcast, drizzly

376 32RED.COM H'CAP 1m 1y(P)
1:15 (1:15) (Class 6) (0-65,65) 3-Y-O **£2,264** (£673; £336; £168) **Stalls** High

Form RPR

42-0 1 **Inswing (IRE)**25 40 3-9-2 **65** (p) PatrickO'Donnell(5) 3 77
(Ralph Beckett) *trckd ldrs: clsd over 2f out: led wl over 1f out: sn clr: rdn out* **5/1**3

062- 2 2 ¾ **Gabster (IRE)**73 7879 3-9-6 **64** AdamKirby 2 70
(Amanda Perrett) *settled in 6th: rdn and prog 2f out: chsd wnr 1f out: styd on but no imp* **12/1**

14-1 3 3 **Fable Of Arachne**18 140 3-9-3 **61** (t) OisinMurphy 8 60
(Stuart Williams) *settled towards rr: swtchd off rail and rdn jst over 2f out: prog over 1f out: styd on to take 3rd last 75yds: n.d* **5/1**3

35-5 4 1 ¼ **Holiday Henry (USA)**23 70 3-9-4 **62** (b1) TonyHamilton 6 58
(Richard Fahey) *hld up in last pair: pushed along 3f out: rdn and prog over 1f out: styd on to take 4th last stride: nvr involved* **7/1**

0-23 5 nse **Schoolboy Error (IRE)**8 265 3-9-0 **58** (b) TimmyMurphy 1 54+
(Jamie Osborne) *dwlt: rcvrd to ld after 2f: hdd wl over 1f out: wknd fnl f* **4/1**1

532- 6 3 ¼ **Home Again**122 6825 3-9-7 **65** RobertWinston 9 54
(Lee Carter) *hld up in last trio: effrt on outer over 2f out: hanging and nt qckn wl over 1f out: nvr a factor* **16/1**

504- 7 1 ¼ **Fastnet Prince (IRE)**186 4705 3-9-7 **65** RobertHavlin 5 51
(Roger Ingram) *chsd ldng pair: rdn over 3f out: stl on terms 2f out: wknd qckly fnl f* **9/2**2

000- 8 2 **Ahraam (IRE)**85 7716 3-9-0 **58** JamieSpencer 7 39
(Peter Chapple-Hyam) *dropped in s and hld up in last pair: effrt on outer over 2f out: hanging and nvr any real prog* **20/1**

05-6 9 1 ¼ **Weld Al Khawaneej (IRE)**23 63 3-9-4 **62** (p) KeaganLatham 11 40+
(Kevin Ryan) *prog on outer to press ldr after 2f to 2f out: wknd qckly* **20/1**

00-0 10 nse **Pour Pavot (IRE)**18 140 3-8-13 **57** FergusSweeney 10 35
(Gary Moore) *t.k.h: led 2f: stdd bhd ldrs: nudged along and steadily wknd fr 2f out* **22/1**

0-44 11 2 ¼ **The Big Guy**7 291 3-9-0 **58** CathyGannon 4 31
(Mick Channon) *pushed along in midfield bef 1/2-way: wknd over 2f out* **14/1**

1m 37.84s (-0.36) **Going Correction** -0.025s/f (Stan) 11 Ran SP% **118.1**
Speed ratings (Par 95): **100,97,94,93,92 89,88,86,85,85 82**
CSF £61.62 CT £324.40 TOTE £5.50: £2.10, £2.90, £1.80; EX 64.60 Trifecta £341.20.
Owner The Millennium Madness Partnership **Bred** Martin Kraft **Trained** Kimpton, Hants
■ Stewards' Enquiry : Timmy Murphy two-day ban: use of whip (12-13 Feb)

FOCUS
There was a strong wind half-behind the runners up the straight. A moderate 3yo handicap in which it looked hard to make up ground from the back of the field.

377 32RED CASINO MAIDEN STKS 1m 2f (P)
1:50 (1:51) (Class 5) 3-Y-O **£2,911** (£866; £432; £216) **Stalls** Low

Form RPR

1 **High Grounds (IRE)** 3-9-5 0 RobertWinston 1 91+
(Charles Hills) *hld up in tch: n.m.r and bmpd 3f out: prog 2f out: led over 1f out: pushed along and qckly drew clr* **3/1**3

56-2 2 6 **Cachao**17 153 3-9-5 78 (b1) RobertHavlin 2 76
(John Gosden) *led 2f: t.k.h once hdd: styd cl up: chsd ldr over 2f out to wl over 1f out: hanging and nt qckn but tk 2nd again fnl f* **4/1**

2 3 1 ¾ **Ragner**13 219 3-9-5 0 JamieSpencer 4 73
(David Simcock) *mostly trckd ldr tl led 3f out: drvn and hdd over 1f out: outpcd and wl btn after: lost 2nd fnl f* **7/4**1

0-0 4 3 ¾ **Norse Castle**7 287 3-9-5 0 TomQueally 7 65
(David Elsworth) *dwlt: t.k.h: led after 2f: hdd 3f out: wknd wl over 1f out* **25/1**

5 7 **The New Master** 3-9-5 0 OisinMurphy 6 59
(David Elsworth) *dwlt: plld hrd and trapped out wd to 1/2-way: in tch to over 2f out: sn btn* **11/4**2

2m 6.95s (0.35) **Going Correction** -0.025s/f (Stan) 5 Ran SP% **111.9**
Speed ratings (Par 97): **97,92,90,87,82**
CSF £15.15 TOTE £3.50: £2.60, £1.90; EX 11.80 Trifecta £27.50.
Owner A M Shead, Cavendish Inv Ltd, J Hanson **Bred** Lynch Bages, Camas Park & Brittas House **Trained** Lambourn, Berks
■ Celestra (33-1) was withdrawn. Rule 4 does not apply.

FOCUS
An ordinary 3yo maiden, though a couple had already shown ability and were up against a couple of Derby entries making their racecourse debut. The early pace was steady and a few fought for their heads as a result, but the winner was still impressive.

378 32REDSPORT.COM (S) H'CAP — 1m 7f 169y(P)
2:20 (2:21) (Class 6) (0-60,55) 4-Y-O+ £2,264 (£673; £336; £168) Stalls Low

Form RPR
45-0 1 **Easydoesit (IRE)**[15] 170 8-9-2 52 (p) GeorgiaCox(7) 2 59
(Tony Carroll) *trckd ldng pair: wnt 2nd over 2f out: shkn up to ld over 1f out: pushed along and kpt on steadily* 4/1[3]
00-5 2 1 ¾ **Indian Scout**[12] 233 8-9-2 45 (b) KieranO'Neill 4 50
(Anabel K Murphy) *trckd ldr: led over 3f out and committed for home: hdd over 1f out: kpt on but readily hld by wnr* 14/1
4-16 3 4 **Smugglers Lane (IRE)**[15] 170 4-9-3 53 AdamKirby 6 53
(David Evans) *hld up in 5th: rdn and prog over 2f out but no imp on ldrs: tk 3rd fnl f but n.d* 7/4[1]
-310 4 ½ **Shirataki (IRE)**[9] 261 8-9-5 55 6ex LuluStanford(7) 3 56
(Peter Hiatt) *hld up in last pair: sweeping move on outer over 3f out to chse ldng pair 2f out: urged along and no imp sn after: lost 3rd fnl f* 7/2[2]
000- 5 2 ¼ **Sawwala**[122] 6735 6-9-2 45 OisinMurphy 8 42
(John E Long) *settled in last trio: urged along 5f out: outpcd fr 3f out: tk modest 5th over 1f out* 20/1
50-0 6 3 ¼ **Movie Magic**[17] 155 5-9-2 45 ShaneKelly 5 38
(Mark Hoad) *hld up in 6th: trying to make prog whn squeezed out over 2f out: rdn and one pce after* 16/1
540- 7 3 ¾ **Teide Peak (IRE)**[42] 8291 7-9-8 51 (tp) StevieDonohoe 9 39
(Grace Harris) *t.k.h: hld up in last pair: ldrs already gone whn shkn up over 2f out: no prog and nvr in it* 10/1
00-0 8 9 **Lady Knight (IRE)**[10] 251 5-9-7 50 (v1) WilliamTwiston-Davies 1 28
(Sally Randell) *shoved along to ld: hdd over 3f out: wknd over 2f out* 25/1
66-0 9 11 **Anginola (IRE)**[12] 232 7-9-5 48 (v) MartinLane 7 12
(David Dennis) *chsd ldng pair: rdn over 4f out: wknd 3f out: t.o* 16/1
3m 27.34s (1.64) **Going Correction** -0.025s/f (Stan)
WFA 4 from 5yo+ 7lb 9 Ran SP% **114.7**
Speed ratings (Par 101): **94,93,91,90,89 88,86,81,76**
CSF £57.47 CT £130.66 TOTE £5.50: £2.40, £2.60, £1.10; EX 50.20 Trifecta £293.90.There was no bid for the winner.
Owner Six Pack **Bred** Tinnakill Bloodstock & Alan Byrne **Trained** Cropthorne, Worcs
FOCUS
A moderate staying selling handicap with the two market leaders unproven over this far.

379 £10 FREE AT 32RED.COM H'CAP — 1m 2f (P)
2:50 (2:50) (Class 5) (0-75,72) 3-Y-O £2,911 (£866; £432; £216) Stalls Low

Form RPR
00-2 1 **Jarir**[15] 182 3-9-1 66 SeanLevey 4 77
(Richard Hannon) *mde all: drew clr sn after 1/2-way: nvr c bk to field: rdn over 2f out: kpt on: unchal* 11/4[2]
03-5 2 4 ½ **Dr Drey (IRE)**[25] 40 3-9-3 68 TimmyMurphy 1 70
(Jamie Osborne) *chsd ldrs: rdn 3f out: tk 2nd wl over 1f out: kpt on but nvr able to threaten* 12/1
50-1 3 3 **Kalkrand (IRE)**[22] 85 3-9-6 71 RobertHavlin 2 67
(John Gosden) *t.k.h early: hld up in last: stl there as wnr wnt clr 4f out: urged along 3f out: prog on outer 2f out: tk 3rd fnl f: no ch* 10/11[1]
64-2 4 1 ¾ **Lord Huntingdon**[20] 122 3-9-2 67 OisinMurphy 3 60
(Andrew Balding) *unruly bef ent stall: t.k.h: hld up in last pair: outpcd 4f out: shkn up over 2f out: modest prog and no ch* 6/1[3]
01-4 5 5 **Sark (IRE)**[23] 70 3-9-7 72 (v1) AdamKirby 6 55
(David Evans) *chsd wnr after 2f: rdn and outpcd fr 4f out: lost 2nd and wknd wl over 1f out* 16/1
6-23 6 4 **Repeat Offender (IRE)**[11] 243 3-9-2 70 (p) RobHornby(3) 5 45
(J S Moore) *chsd wnr 2f: styd prom: outpcd fr 4f out: wknd qckly 2f out* 25/1
2m 4.09s (-2.51) **Going Correction** -0.025s/f (Stan) 6 Ran SP% **110.8**
Speed ratings (Par 97): **109,105,103,101,97 94**
CSF £31.69 TOTE £5.40: £2.10, £3.70; EX 26.10 Trifecta £65.10.
Owner Al Shaqab Racing **Bred** Deerfield Farm **Trained** East Everleigh, Wilts
FOCUS
A modest 3yo handicap, though a couple of these were entitled to improve now handicapping/stepping up in trip. It resulted in a well-judged front-running ride from the winning jockey, though.

380 LADBROKES CLAIMING STKS — 7f 1y(P)
3:25 (3:25) (Class 6) 3-Y-O £2,264 (£673; £336; £168) Stalls Low

Form RPR
44-2 1 **Custard The Dragon**[11] 242 3-9-6 65 GrahamGibbons 6 70
(Ralph Beckett) *led after 1f and maintained modest pce: jnd and kicked on 3f out: rn wd bnd 2f out: drvn to assert over 1f out: kpt on* 10/11[1]
244- 2 1 ½ **Broughtons Fancy**[38] 8349 3-9-5 70 AdamKirby 3 65
(David Evans) *led at modest pce 1f: chsd wnr: chal and upsides fr 3f out: carried wd bnd 2f out: drvn and nt qckn over 1f out: hld fnl f* 11/10[2]
03-4 3 nk **Nidnod**[17] 151 3-8-8 57 ShelleyBirkett(3) 2 56
(John Bridger) *t.k.h: hld up in tch: outpcd by ldng pair over 2f out but lft w ch as they wnt wd bnd sn after: edgd rt and one pce fr over 1f out* 14/1[3]
0 4 17 **Still Kicking (IRE)**[24] 42 3-8-13 0 DannyBrock(3) 1 15
(Phil McEntee) *t.k.h: hld up in tch: wknd wl over 2f out: t.o* 66/1
1m 29.17s (4.37) **Going Correction** -0.025s/f (Stan) 4 Ran SP% **108.2**
Speed ratings (Par 95): **74,72,71,52**
CSF £2.18 TOTE £1.70; EX 2.70 Trifecta £3.40.
Owner Mr & Mrs Kevan Watts **Bred** Mr & Mrs Kevan Watts **Trained** Kimpton, Hants
FOCUS
A moderate claimer and a two-horse race according to the market.

381 UNIBET OFFER DAILY JOCKEY AND TRAINER SPECIALS H'CAP — 6f 1y(P)
4:00 (4:00) (Class 6) (0-52,52) 4-Y-O+ £2,264 (£673; £336; £168) Stalls Low

Form RPR
0-25 1 **Kuanyao (IRE)**[17] 151 10-8-10 46 (be) AnnStokell(5) 9 53
(Ann Stokell) *mde all: rdn over 1f out: hld on wl nr fin* 14/1
500- 2 ½ **Presto Boy**[51] 8165 4-9-7 52 ShaneKelly 2 58
(Richard Hughes) *trckd ldng trio: rdn and prog to chse wnr over 1f out: wobbled u.p and nt qckn: grad clsd nr fin* 13/8[1]
0-00 3 2 ¼ **Little**[9] 257 4-9-2 50 JackDuern(3) 1 49
(Steph Hollinshead) *s.i.s: in last pair tl prog on inner 2f out: chsd ldng pair over 1f out: one pce fnl f* 16/1
4-42 4 2 ¾ **First Rebellion**[9] 264 7-9-0 52 (v) GeorgiaCox(7) 5 43
(Tony Carroll) *chsd wnr to over 1f out: wknd fnl f* 9/4[2]
54-4 5 nk **Multi Quest**[15] 174 4-9-1 46 (b) OisinMurphy 11 36
(John E Long) *chsd ldng pair: wd bnd 2f out and sn lft bhd: no ch after: kpt on nr fin* 6/1[3]
60-6 6 2 **Tamarin**[8] 270 4-8-10 48 (b) NatalieHambling(7) 4 32
(Lisa Williamson) *hld up disputing 4th: rdn and no prog over 2f out: wl btn after* 10/1
30-0 7 4 **Mon Petit Fleur**[18] 143 4-9-4 52 SimonPearce(3) 6 24
(Lydia Pearce) *sn rdn: outpcd and a last* 14/1
1m 11.22s (-0.68) **Going Correction** -0.025s/f (Stan) 7 Ran SP% **111.5**
Speed ratings (Par 101): **103,102,99,95,95 92,87**
CSF £35.48 CT £370.72 TOTE £9.70: £4.30, £1.80; EX 39.00 Trifecta £580.90.
Owner Geoff Pacey **Bred** Newlands House Stud **Trained** Lincoln, Lincolnshire
FOCUS
A poor 46-52 sprint handicap, with a 14-race maiden sent off a warm favourite.

382 CORAL AMATEUR RIDERS' H'CAP — 1m 4f (P)
4:30 (4:30) (Class 5) (0-75,79) 4-Y-O+ £2,807 (£870; £435; £217) Stalls Low

Form RPR
65-3 1 **Obboorr**[17] 156 7-9-11 63 ow2 KaineWood(5) 12 71
(Tim Fitzgerald) *cl up bhd ldng trio and sn wl clr of rest: dropped off them 5f out: clsd again over 2f out: drvn to ld 1f out: hld on* 8/1
61-1 2 hd **Whinging Willie (IRE)**[9] 256 7-10-13 79 6ex..(v) MissHayleyMoore(5) 1 86
(Gary Moore) *trckd ldng pair: chal on outer fr 2f out: chsd wnr fnl f: styd on nr fin: jst failed* 9/2[3]
544- 3 1 ½ **Noguchi (IRE)**[33] 8367 11-10-0 68 (p) MissEBushe(7) 8 73
(Chris Dwyer) *led at gd pce and had field strung out: pressed fr 1/2-way: kpt on but hdd and one pce fnl f* 20/1
506- 4 4 ½ **Heezararity**[50] 8169 8-10-4 68 ChrisMeehan(3) 9 65
(Jonathan Geake) *pressed ldr in spreadeagled field: upsides over 3f out to over 1f out: wknd fnl f* 14/1
22-2 5 ¾ **Ballyglasheen (IRE)**[16] 165 6-10-4 72 MissIsabelWilliams(7) 7 68
(Evan Williams) *hld up in 5th and wl off the pce: pushed along and no real inroads 3f out: kpt on fr over 1f out: no ch* 13/8[1]
01-2 6 8 **Classic Mission**[21] 101 5-10-4 70 (b) MrJHarding(5) 3 53+
(Jonathan Portman) *hld up in last and a long way off the pce: stl last 3f out and t.o: shkn up and styd on after: no ch to be involved* 4/1[2]
20-2 7 nk **Ruzeiz (USA)**[17] 156 7-9-7 61 (p) MrTBenjamin(7) 6 44
(Peter Hedger) *wl off the pce in rr gp: wnt 6th over 4f out but no imp on ldrs after* 14/1
41-5 8 8 **Bayan Kasirga (IRE)**[14] 200 6-10-1 69 MrMEnnis(7) 5 39
(Richard Fahey) *dwlt: a wl off the pce in rr gp: bhd fnl 2f* 14/1
50-6 9 10 **Athenian Garden (USA)**[12] 232 9-9-8 62 oh12 ow1 MissMBryant(7) 11 16
(Paddy Butler) *a off the pce in rr gp: wknd over 2f out and sn bhd* 50/1
45-0 10 3 **Investissement**[12] 233 10-9-7 61 oh6 (tp) MissJMOlliver(7) 10 10
(Paddy Butler) *a wl off the pce in rr gp: bhd fnl 2f* 50/1
2m 31.98s (-1.02) **Going Correction** -0.025s/f (Stan) 10 Ran SP% **116.1**
Speed ratings (Par 103): **102,101,100,97,97 92,91,86,79,77**
CSF £43.05 CT £695.48 TOTE £9.50: £2.50, £2.10, £5.60; EX 53.50 Trifecta £521.20.
Owner Dukes Racing 1 **Bred** Darley **Trained** Norton, N Yorks
■ Stewards' Enquiry : Mr J Harding 14-day ban: failed to obtain the best possible placing (TBC)
FOCUS
Four horses soon skipped clear in this modest amateurs' handicap and nothing could get into the race from behind.
T/Plt: £124.10 to a £1 stake. Pool: £54,268.56 - 319.03 winning tickets. T/Qpdt: £27.20 to a £1 stake. Pool: £5,584.20 - 151.50 winning tickets. **Jonathan Neesom**

327 WOLVERHAMPTON (A.W) (L-H)
Friday, January 29

OFFICIAL GOING: Tapeta: standard
Wind: strong, behind Weather: overcast, rain race from 5

383 BET IN PLAY AT CORAL APPRENTICE H'CAP — 1m 1f 103y (Tp)
4:45 (4:45) (Class 6) (0-55,55) 4-Y-O+ £2,587 (£770; £384; £192) Stalls Low

Form RPR
0-51 1 **On A Whim**[7] 294 4-8-13 51 6ex PaddyBradley(3) 6 60
(Daniel Mark Loughnane) *chsd ldng trio: wnt 3rd 4f out: clsd to chse ldr over 2f out: rdn to ld over 1f out: styd on wl: rdn out* 7/4[1]
40-4 2 1 ¼ **Celtic Artisan (IRE)**[21] 107 5-8-12 51 (b) DanielleMooney(5) 2 57
(Rebecca Menzies) *hld up towards rr: clsd whn nt clr run over 2f out: swtchd rt over 1f out: styd on wl to go 2nd towards fin: no threat to wnr* 11/2[3]
25-6 3 ½ **Little Choosey**[18] 149 6-9-0 48 (tp) AaronJones 5 52
(Roy Bowring) *w ldr and wnt clr 6f out: led over 2f out: sn rdn: hdd over 1f out: styd on same pce ins fnl f: lost 2nd towards fin* 17/2
060- 4 ½ **Anniversarie**[31] 8385 4-9-2 54 (t) PhilDennis(3) 7 57
(John Norton) *hld up towards rr: hdwy over 3f out: rdn to chse ldrs over 1f out: styd on same pce u.p ins fnl f* 22/1
30-3 5 3 ½ **Queen Zain (IRE)**[5] 326 4-9-1 53 CallumShepherd(3) 3 49
(Charlie Fellowes) *chsd ldng pair tl 4f out: rdn and lost pl over 2f out: plugged on same pce fnl f* 5/2[2]
540- 6 2 ¾ **Heat Storm (IRE)**[109] 7168 5-9-7 55 PaddyPilley 4 46
(James Unett) *stdd after s: hld up in rr: rdn over 3f out: no imp: wl hld and plugged on same pce fr over 1f out* 14/1
-430 7 hd **Stanlow**[7] 294 6-9-3 51 (v) JordanNason 8 41
(Michael Mullineaux) *hld up towards rr: effrt u.p ent fnl 2f: sn no imp: wl hld and swtchd lft jst ins fnl f* 9/1
30-0 8 32 **Medal Of Valour (JPN)**[18] 149 8-9-4 52 (bt) CiaranMckee 1
(Roy Brotherton) *led: wnt clr w rival 6f out: rdn and hdd over 2f out: sn dropped out: eased ins fnl f: t.o* 40/1
2m 0.45s (-0.35) **Going Correction** -0.025s/f (Stan)
WFA 4 from 5yo+ 1lb 8 Ran SP% **114.3**
Speed ratings (Par 101): **100,98,98,98,94 92,92,63**
CSF £11.93 CT £63.36 TOTE £2.70: £1.10, £1.60, £3.00; EX 11.70 Trifecta £51.80.
Owner R M Brilley **Bred** Minster Stud **Trained** Baldwin's Gate, Staffs
FOCUS
A modest handicap run at a fair pace.

384 32REDSPORT.COM MAIDEN FILLIES' STKS — 1m 141y (Tp)
5:15 (5:19) (Class 5) 3-Y-O+ £3,234 (£962; £481; £240) Stalls Low

Form RPR
1 **Toumar** 3-8-5 0 JoeFanning 7 74+
(Roger Varian) *trckd ldrs: cl 4th and wnt clr of field over 2f out: pushed along to ld jst ins fnl f: sn in command and r.o wl: comf* 5/6[1]

6 **2** 3 **Our Little Sister (IRE)**[7] 287 3-7-13 0 ow1............ CharlieBennett(7) 4 66
(Hughie Morrison) *pressed ldr: wnt clr in ldng quartet rdn and ev ch over 2f out: drvn over 1f out: outpcd by wnr ins fnl f: kpt on to go 2nd wl ins fnl f* **14/1**

0- **3** 1 1/4 **Logarithm (USA)**[57] 8091 3-8-5 0.................................. NickyMackay 1 62
(John Gosden) *led: rdn and drew clr w 3 rivals over 2f out: drvn over 1f out: hdd jst ins fnl f: sn outpcd: lost 2nd wl ins fnl f* **7/1**[3]

6 **4** 2 3/4 **Pensax Lady (IRE)**[18] 145 3-8-5 0.................................. LukeMorris 3 56
(Daniel Mark Loughnane) *s.i.s and bustled along leaving stalls: sn rcvrd and in tch in midfield: effrt over 2f out: chsd clr ldng quartet wl over 1f out: kpt on but no imp* **20/1**

05- **5** 1/2 **Tombe Girl**[80] 7787 3-8-5 0.. JoeyHaynes 11 55+
(Keith Dalgleish) *stuck v wd: chsd ldrs: pressed ldng pair and clr in ldng quartet over 2f out: 4th and btn over 1f out: wknd ins fnl f* **14/1**

6 2 **Margoesque** 3-8-5 0.. MartinDwyer 12 50+
(William Muir) *s.i.s: rn green and sn wl off the pce in last pair: stl bhd and swtchd rt over 2f out: hdwy over 1f out: no ch but styd on ins fnl f* **5/1**[2]

5 **7** 2 3/4 **Smirnova (IRE)**[20] 122 3-8-5 0.. LiamJones 5 44
(Marco Botti) *chsd ldrs: rdn and getting outpcd whn edgd lft over 2f out: 6th and btn wl over 1f out: wknd fnl f* **22/1**

34- **8** 1 **Chesham Rose (IRE)**[42] 8280 3-8-5 0....................... AdamBeschizza 8 42
(Dave Roberts) *hld up in tch in midfield: rdn and sme hdwy 3f out: sn outpcd: wknd over 1f out* **33/1**

9 hd **Regent's Rock**[41] 4-9-12 0.. GrahamLee 6 46
(Peter Niven) *s.i.s: wl off the pce in rr: hmpd wl over 2f out: sme late hdwy: n.d* **40/1**

0 **10** 7 **Shirocco Cloud**[8] 268 4-9-12 0.................................... SteveDrowne 10 30
(Mrs Ilka Gansera-Leveque) *stdd after s: hld up in tch towards rr of main gp: rdn over 3f out: sn struggling: bhd over 1f out* **66/1**

11 7 **Suzu** 3-8-5 0... RaulDaSilva 2 9
(Ivan Furtado) *chsd ldrs: losing pl and hmpd on inner over 2f out: bhd fnl f* **20/1**

12 2 **Cafe Nervosa (IRE)** 3-8-0 0... PaddyPilley(5) 9 5
(James Unett) *s.i.s: t.k.h in rr: swtchd rt and hdwy into midfield 5f out: rdn over 3f out: sn lost pl: bhd over 1f out: burst blood vessel* **40/1**

1m 50.19s (0.09) **Going Correction** -0.025s/f (Stan)
WFA 3 from 4yo 22lb **12** Ran SP% **120.2**
Speed ratings (Par 100): **98,95,94,91,91 89,87,86,86,79 73,71**
CSF £13.30 TOTE £1.80: £1.10, £3.20, £2.30; EX 12.70 Trifecta £64.60.
Owner Nurlan Bizakov **Bred** Hesmonds Stud Ltd **Trained** Newmarket, Suffolk

FOCUS
Not a strong maiden.

385 32RED.COM H'CAP — 2m 119y (Tp)
5:45 (5:45) (Class 4) (0-85,92) 4-Y-O+ £5,175 (£1,540; £769; £384) Stalls Low

Form RPR

36-4 **1** **The Steward (USA)**[21] 99 5-10-3 **92**...........................(p) LukeMorris 2 100
(Sir Mark Prescott Bt) *prom in main gp: clsd to trck ldng pair 9f out: nt clr run over 2f out: gap opened and rdn to ld over 1f out: drvn 1f out: hrd pressed 100yds out: fnd ex and hld runner-up towards fin* **15/8**[1]

06-2 **2** nk **Glan Y Gors (IRE)**[22] 78 4-9-3 **85**.................................... LiamKeniry 1 92
(David Simcock) *stdd s: hld up in last pair: clsd and in tch 9f out: travelling wl over 2f out: effrt on outer over 1f out: chsd wnr and edgd lft jst ins fnl f: str chal fnl 100yds: r.o but hld towards fin* **5/2**[2]

646- **3** 3 1/4 **Winter Spice (IRE)**[51] 8156 5-9-0 **78**.............................(b) RyanTate(3) 6 81
(Clive Cox) *stdd s: hld up in rr: clsd and in tch 1/2-way: effrt on inner over 1f out: styd on u.p ins fnl f: wnt 3rd nr fin: no threat to ldng pair* **8/1**

214- **4** 1/2 **Grand Meister**[32] 8379 5-9-4 **79**....................................(p) PhillipMakin 5 81
(John Quinn) *chsd ldrs tl clsd and ldr and wnt 2nd 9f out: ev ch and rdn 2f out: 3rd and outpcd jst ins fnl f: kpt on same pce: lost 3rd nr fin* **3/1**[3]

03-6 **5** 1 1/4 **Villa Royale**[22] 78 7-9-8 **83**......................................(p[1]) AndrewMullen 4 84
(Michael Appleby) *taken down early: sn pushed up to ld: clr tl 9f out: rdn over 3f out: hdd over 1f out: sn no ex: wknd ins fnl f* **20/1**

40-1 **6** nse **Oratorio's Joy (IRE)**[26] 30 6-9-2 **77**......................... WilliamCarson 3 78
(Jamie Osborne) *led: sn hdd: chsd ldr tl 9f out: styd wl in tch in midfield: rdn over 3f out: drvn and dropped to rr 2f out: wl hld but kpt on ins fnl f* **14/1**

3m 40.08s (-3.62) **Going Correction** -0.025s/f (Stan)
WFA 4 from 5yo+ 7lb **6** Ran SP% **110.9**
Speed ratings (Par 105): **107,106,105,105,104 104**
CSF £6.63 TOTE £2.40: £1.50, £2.10; EX 6.90 Trifecta £27.30.
Owner Donald R Dizney **Bred** Fairway Thoroughbreds **Trained** Newmarket, Suffolk

FOCUS
A fair staying handicap run at a stop-start pace.

386 32RED CASINO CLASSIFIED CLAIMING STKS — 1m 5f 194y (Tp)
6:15 (6:16) (Class 5) 4-Y-O+ £3,234 (£962; £481; £240) Stalls Low

Form RPR

21-5 **1** **King Olav (UAE)**[12] 234 11-8-9 66........................ GeorgeDowning(3) 6 67
(Tony Carroll) *chsd ldr: jnd ldr and pce qckning 4f out: pushed into ld over 2f out: r.o wl and a doing enough ins fnl f* **2/1**[1]

0-46 **2** 1 1/4 **Astra Hall**[10] 251 7-8-10 60.. BenCurtis 1 62
(Michael Appleby) *chsd ldrs: nt clr run on inner and shuffled bk over 2f out: swtchd rt and rdn to chse wnr wl over 1f out: kpt on wl on u.p fnl f: a hld* **11/1**

420- **3** 5 **Hallstatt (IRE)**[91] 7250 10-9-0 70......................................(t) GrahamLee 3 59
(John Mackie) *hld up in tch: nt clr run 4f out: pushed along over 2f out: drvn and unable qck 2f out: wnt 3rd 150yds: kpt on but no ch w ldng pair* **3/1**[3]

05-4 **4** 1 1/4 **Four Nations (USA)**[18] 138 8-8-12 64..........................(p) LiamKeniry 2 55
(George Baker) *s.i.s: t.k.h: hld up in rr: hdwy on outer 5f out: rdn over 3f out: dropped to rr and outpcd u.p 2f out: wl hld and plugged on same pce after* **9/4**[2]

00-0 **5** 3 1/2 **Thimaar (USA)**[14] 200 8-9-3 68..........................(p) PatrickO'Donnell(5) 4 60
(Sarah Hollinshead) *led and set stdy gallop: jnd and qckning pce 4f out: rdn and hdd over 2f out: outpcd over 1f out: wknd ins fnl f* **9/1**

3m 10.5s (5.70) **Going Correction** -0.025s/f (Stan)
WFA 4 from 7yo+ 6lb **5** Ran SP% **107.4**
Speed ratings (Par 103): **82,81,78,77,75**
CSF £20.61 TOTE £2.50: £1.10, £3.40; EX 13.70 Trifecta £38.40.
Owner Cover Point Racing **Bred** Darley **Trained** Cropthorne, Worcs

FOCUS
The pace was steady for this open claimer.

387 BET NOW WITH LADBROKES APP H'CAP — 7f 32y (Tp)
6:45 (6:47) (Class 6) (0-65,71) 4-Y-O+ £2,587 (£770; £384; £192) Stalls High

Form RPR

54-2 **1** **Dutch Garden**[10] 246 4-9-7 **65**...(v) TomEaves 8 78
(David Brown) *mde all: sn clr: rdn and 3 l clr 2f out: in command and drifted rt ins fnl f: kpt on: unchal* **7/2**[2]

00-5 **2** 2 1/2 **Black Truffle (FR)**[18] 144 6-9-0 **63**......................... RachealKneller(5) 3 69
(Mark Usher) *chsd clr ldng trio: effrt over 1f out: chsd clr wnr ins fnl f: kpt on but no imp* **5/1**[3]

50-0 **3** 1/2 **Top Offer**[18] 144 7-9-3 **61**.. GrahamLee 4 66
(Patrick Morris) *hld up in midfield: effrt over 1f out: styd on u.p to go 3rd fnl 75yds: kpt on: no threat to wnr* **10/1**

0-25 **4** 2 **For Ayman**[16] 159 5-9-0 **65**..(t) SeanMooney(7) 6 65
(Joseph Tuite) *chsd ldng pair: wnt 2nd but wnr 3 l clr 2f out: no imp: lost 2nd ins fnl f: wknd fnl 75yds* **8/1**

02-0 **5** shd **Mac's Power (IRE)**[23] 67 10-9-4 **62**................................ LukeMorris 5 61+
(Willie Musson) *awkward leaving stalls and squeezed for room sn after s: hld up in last quartet: swtchd rt and hdwy over 1f out: styd on u.p ins fnl f: nvr trbld ldrs* **10/1**

3-01 **6** nk **Depth Charge (IRE)**[11] 239 4-9-8 **71** 6ex.......(vt) PatrickO'Donnell(5) 11 69+
(Kristin Stubbs) *stdd after s: t.k.h: hld up off the pce in last pair: swtchd rt and effrt over 1f out: styd on u.p ins fnl f: nvr trbld ldrs* **3/1**[1]

566- **7** 1 **First Excel**[204] 4053 4-8-11 **60**..................................... AaronJones(5) 2 56
(Roy Bowring) *midfield but nvr on terms w ldrs: effrt on inner over 1f out: kpt on ins fnl f: nvr trbld ldrs* **25/1**

000- **8** shd **Mambo Spirit (IRE)**[32] 8376 12-9-1 **62**.......................... EoinWalsh(3) 1 57
(Tony Newcombe) *chsd clr ldr tl 2f out: sn drvn and no ex: wknd ins fnl f* **14/1**

040- **9** hd **Foie Gras**[93] 7551 6-9-6 **64**.. JoeFanning 7 59+
(Chris Dwyer) *t.k.h: hld up in last quartet: effrt and wd bnd wl over 1f out: kpt on fnl f: nvr trbld ldrs* **12/1**

6-06 **10** 1/2 **Kodiac Lady (IRE)**[18] 144 4-9-2 **60**..............................(e) JoeyHaynes 9 54+
(Simon West) *stdd s: t.k.h: hld up in rr: effrt on inner 2f out: sme hdwy but no threat to ldrs 1f out: wknd ins fnl f* **16/1**

1m 28.04s (-0.76) **Going Correction** -0.025s/f (Stan) **10** Ran SP% **117.3**
Speed ratings (Par 101): **103,100,99,97,97 96,95,95,95,94**
CSF £21.61 CT £164.22 TOTE £4.30: £1.60, £2.00, £3.90; EX 21.10 Trifecta £184.60.
Owner J C Fretwell **Bred** Coln Valley Stud **Trained** Averham Park, Notts

FOCUS
A competitive contest for the grade.

388 DOWNLOAD THE LADBROKES APP H'CAP — 1m 141y (Tp)
7:15 (7:15) (Class 7) (0-50,50) 4-Y-O+ £2,587 (£770; £384; £192) Stalls Low

Form RPR

40-2 **1** **Overrider**[7] 294 6-8-11 **45**.................................(bt) CallumShepherd(5) 3 56
(Shaun Lycett) *chsd ldrs: rdn to chse ldr 3f out: sn led and kicked clr 2f out: kpt on u.p: rdn out* **7/2**[2]

5-42 **2** 2 1/2 **Hagree (IRE)**[9] 252 5-8-11 **47**.................................(tp) CharlieBennett(7) 4 53
(Jose Santos) *reminder sn after s: in tch in midfield: swtchd rt and effrt ent fnl 2f: chsd clr wnr 1f out: kpt on but no threat to wnr* **11/4**[1]

000- **3** 1/2 **Music Hall (FR)**[89] 6617 6-8-11 **45**............................ JustinNewman(5) 1 50
(Shaun Harris) *hld up in tch in midfield: effrt in 5th 2f out: wnt 3rd 1f out: kpt on u.p but no threat to wnr* **28/1**

60-0 **4** 1 1/4 **Star Links (USA)**[18] 149 10-9-6 **49**................................(bt) SeanLevey 7 51
(Sylvester Kirk) *led to post: hdd and rdn over 2f out: sn outpcd: lost btn 2nd 1f out: plugged on same pce fnl f* **4/1**[3]

00-0 **5** 2 3/4 **Eeny Mac (IRE)**[28] 2 9-9-2 **45**.......................................(v) TomEaves 11 42
(John Wainwright) *hld up in last trio: effrt into midfield but nt on terms w ldrs 2f out: kpt on: nvr trbld ldrs* **33/1**

4-50 **6** nk **Trigger Park (IRE)**[9] 252 5-9-4 **47**...............................(b[1]) LukeMorris 6 43
(Ronald Harris) *chsd ldr tl 6f out: styd prom: wnt 2nd again 3f out tl 3f out: sn outpcd u.p: wl hld and plugged on fr over 1f out* **13/2**

005- **7** 4 1/2 **Poor Duke (IRE)**[30] 8406 6-9-6 **49**................................ RobertHavlin 2 35
(Michael Mullineaux) *dwlt: hld up in midfield: effrt over 2f out: no imp and wl hld over 1f out: wknd fnl f* **12/1**

-604 **8** 1 **Ciaras Cookie (IRE)**[8] 270 4-9-3 **47**........................(t[1]) CharlesBishop 9 31
(Heather Dalton) *stdd s: hld up in rr: rdn over 1f out: no imp: n.d* **22/1**

0-00 **9** 4 **Madakheel (USA)**[19] 130 5-9-2 **45**...............................(t) JoeyHaynes 13 21
(Simon West) *v wd early: hdwy to chse ldr 6f out tl over 3f out: sn u.p and lost pl: bhd fnl f* **66/1**

/00- **10** 6 **Cabbies Lou**[263] 2133 4-8-13 **50**.......................... CallumRodriguez(7) 10 13
(Richard Ford) *in tch in midfield: rdn over 2f out: sn btn and dropped out: bhd fnl f* **50/1**

U/0- **11** 8 **Victor's Beach (IRE)**[39] 8337 6-9-4 **47**..........................(tp) LiamKeniry 8
(Mark Michael McNiff, Ire) *stdd s: t.k.h: hld up in last trio: pushed along over 3f out: no rspnse: lost tch over 1f out: eased ins fnl f* **11/1**

0-00 **12** 17 **Waterloo Dock**[13] 216 11-9-2 **45**.. GrahamLee 5
(James Unett) *in tch in midfield: reminder and dropped towards rr 5f out: last and lost tch over 2f out: t.o and eased ins fnl f* **25/1**

1m 49.27s (-0.83) **Going Correction** -0.025s/f (Stan)
WFA 4 from 5yo+ 1lb **12** Ran SP% **116.3**
Speed ratings (Par 97): **102,99,99,98,95 95,91,90,87,81 74,59**
CSF £12.23 CT £212.75 TOTE £4.20: £1.50, £1.40, £6.30; EX 12.60 Trifecta £323.40.
Owner L & M Atkins **Bred** P M Cunningham **Trained** Clapton-on-the-Hill, Gloucs

FOCUS
A modest handicap.
T/Plt: £14.10 to a £1 stake. Pool: £77,558.00 - 4,003.71 winning tickets. T/Qpdt: £6.60 to a £1 stake. Pool: £8,073.00 - 893.01 winning tickets. **Steve Payne**

389 - 397a (Foreign Racing) - See Raceform Interactive

376 LINGFIELD (L-H)
Saturday, January 30

OFFICIAL GOING: Polytrack: standard
Wind: strong, across Weather: bright and breezy

398 UNIBET.CO.UK DAILY ENHANCED PLACE TERMS H'CAP — 6f 1y(P)
1:40 (1:42) (Class 6) (0-65,70) 4-Y-O+ £2,587 (£770; £384; £192) Stalls Low

Form RPR

0-62 **1** **Seamster**[9] 271 9-9-9 **67**..(vt) DanielTudhope 11 75
(David O'Meara) *led for 1f: chsd ldr tl rdn to ld again over 1f out: kpt on: all out* **8/1**

013- **2** *nk* **Ghost Train (IRE)**[30] 8408 7-9-4 **62**................................(p) LukeMorris 10 69
(Tim McCarthy) *chsd ldng pair: swtchd rt and effrt jst over 1f out: chsd wnr wl ins fnl f: styd on towards fin: nvr quite getting to wnr* **14/1**

61-4 **3** *1* **Encapsulated**[17] 159 6-8-12 **63**.................................. RhiainIngram(7) 1 67
(Roger Ingram) *taken down early and led to post: sn bustled along to go prom: led after 1f: rdn and hdd over 1f out: styd on same pce ins fnl f: lost 2nd wl ins fnl f* **6/1**[3]

1-03 **4** *1 1/4* **Hamis Al Bin (IRE)**[9] 271 7-9-0 **58**..........................(bt) FrannyNorton 12 58
(Milton Bradley) *chsd ldng trio: effrt and unable qck over 1f out: styd on same pce ins fnl f* **25/1**

23-1 **5** *2 3/4* **Rocket Rob (IRE)**[22] 98 10-9-4 **62**................................ TomQueally 6 54+
(Willie Musson) *t.k.h: hld up in midfield: effrt over 1f out: styd on ins fnl f: nvr trbld ldrs* **14/1**

0-01 **6** *nk* **Summerinthecity (IRE)**[9] 271 9-9-5 **70**.............. AdamMcNamara(7) 3 61
(Richard Fahey) *in tch in midfield: swtchd rt: wd and lost pl bnd 2f out: rallied and styd on ins fnl f: no threat to ldrs* **4/1**[1]

66-5 **7** *1/2* **Secret Witness**[7] 319 10-9-5 **63**..................................(b) MartinHarley 8 53+
(Ronald Harris) *hld towards rr: hdwy into midfield whn carried rt: v wd and lost pl bnd 2f out: rallied and kpt on ins fnl f: no threat to ldrs* **12/1**

4-15 **8** *1* **Ohsosecret**[9] 269 4-9-5 **63**...(t) SaleemGolam 4 50
(Stuart Williams) *chsd ldrs: 5th and hit rail jst over 2f out: sn u.p and unable qck: wknd ins fnl f* **12/1**

50-6 **9** *hd* **Soaring Spirits (IRE)**[13] 231 6-9-5 **63**....................(vt[1]) RenatoSouza 2 49
(Dean Ivory) *in tch in midfield: shkn up over 2f out: 6th and no imp u.p 2f out: wknd ins fnl f* **8/1**

05-0 **10** *1 3/4* **Duke Of North (IRE)**[17] 167 4-9-6 **64**.........................(p) GeorgeBaker 5 45+
(Jim Boyle) *s.i.s: hld up in last trio: effrt over 1f out: no imp: n.d* **9/2**[2]

000- **11** *4* **Spellmaker**[33] 8382 7-9-3 **64**... EoinWalsh(3) 7 33+
(Tony Newcombe) *hld up in last trio: effrt u.p on inner over 1f out: no prog: bhd and wknd ins fnl f* **8/1**

1m 10.95s (-0.95) **Going Correction** -0.075s/f (Stan) **11** Ran SP% **118.4**
Speed ratings (Par 101): **103,102,101,99,95 95,94,93,93,90 85**
CSF £114.96 CT £738.46 TOTE £8.70: £3.10, £3.10, £2.30; EX 90.40 Trifecta £1103.30.
Owner P Bamford **Bred** D G Hardisty Bloodstock **Trained** Upper Helmsley, N Yorks

FOCUS
A moderate sprint handicap. It was completely dominated by those that raced handily and being ridden that way negated a wide draw for three of the first four home.

399 CORAL H'CAP 1m 4f (P)
2:15 (2:15) (Class 3) (0-90,85) 4-Y-O **£7,246** (£2,168; £1,084; £542; £270) **Stalls** Low

Form RPR

22-6 **1** **Alshan Fajer**[10] 256 6-8-10 **75**.. OisinMurphy 2 82
(J R Jenkins) *chsd ldng pair: effrt jst over 2f out: hdwy to chal 1f out: led wl ins fnl f: hld on towards fin: drvn out* **7/2**[2]

62-1 **2** *nk* **Giantstepsahead (IRE)**[24] 66 7-9-3 **85**................ DanielMuscutt(3) 6 91
(Brian McMath) *led: jnd and rdn over 2f out: hdd wl ins fnl f: kpt on u.p but hld towards fin* **11/8**[1]

60-4 **3** *1 1/2* **Gabrial The Duke (IRE)**[24] 73 6-9-3 **82**..................(b) TonyHamilton 3 86
(Richard Fahey) *dwlt and urged along early: travelling bttr after 1f and hld up in last: rdn 4f out: outpcd 3f out: chsd clr ldng trio 2f out: hung lft u.p over 1f out: hdwy ins fnl f: styd on to go 3rd nr fin* **6/1**

44-1 **4** *1/2* **Dakota City**[17] 164 5-8-9 **74**.....................................(v) AdamBeschizza 1 77
(Julia Feilden) *hld up in tch in 4th: hdwy to join ldr and gng best* **9/2**[3]

5-21 **5** *15* **Tower Power**[15] 200 5-9-0 **79**... LukeMorris 5 58
(Phil McEntee) *chsd ldr: rdn 4f out: lost pl over 2f out: dropped to last 2f out: sn lost tch* **8/1**

2m 29.7s (-3.30) **Going Correction** -0.075s/f (Stan) **5** Ran SP% **107.9**
Speed ratings (Par 107): **108,107,106,106,96**
CSF £8.42 TOTE £4.20: £1.50, £1.40; EX 11.70 Trifecta £47.60.
Owner Glynn Linder & Wendy Jenkins **Bred** Jeddah Bloodstock **Trained** Royston, Herts
■ Stewards' Enquiry : Oisin Murphy two-day ban: use of whip (13-14 Feb)

FOCUS
Not the most competitive of 0-90 handicaps and they only went a modest pace.

400 LADBROKES MEDIAN AUCTION MAIDEN STKS 1m 1y(P)
2:50 (2:50) (Class 6) 3-5-Y-O **£2,587** (£770; £384; £192) **Stalls** High

Form RPR

4- **1** **Beleave**[45] 8253 3-8-1 0... KieranO'Neill 7 66+
(Luke Dace) *taken down early and led to s: dwlt: sn rcvrd and in tch in midfield: hdwy to chse ldr 2f out: rdn to ld 1f out: rn green in front but a doing enough ins fnl f: styd on* **3/1**[2]

553- **2** *1 1/4* **Pickapocket (IRE)**[68] 7955 3-8-7 68 ow1.......................(p) OisinMurphy 3 69
(Andrew Balding) *hld up in tch in midfield: effrt jst over 2f out: drvn to chse wnr fnl 100yds: r.o same pce and a hld after* **11/8**[1]

0- **3** *3/4* **Heads You Win**[31] 8402 3-8-1 0...................................... CathyGannon 6 61
(Jamie Osborne) *hld up in tch in last quartet: hdwy and chsng ldrs 2f out: rdn over 1f out: swtchd lft ins fnl f: kpt on to go 3rd towards fin* **16/1**

4- **4** *1/2* **Evidence (FR)**[170] 5309 3-8-1 0.. LukeMorris 8 60
(Harry Dunlop) *chsd ldr tl rdn to ld jst over 2f out: hdd 1f out: no ex and one-pced after: lost 2 pls fnl 100yds* **4/1**[3]

0- **5** *2 3/4* **Mulled Wine**[115] 7032 3-8-6 0... MartinDwyer 5 58
(John Best) *hld up in last trio: sme hdwy in 7th 2f out: pushed along and kpt on steadily ins fnl f: no threat to ldrs* **25/1**

0-4 **6** *3/4* **Harry's Endeavour**[21] 122 3-8-6 0.................................... CamHardie 1 57
(Seamus Mullins) *chsd ldrs: rdn jst over 2f out: no ex u.p 1f out: wknd ins fnl f* **25/1**

0- **7** *16* **Kimbelle**[30] 8410 3-8-1 0.. RyanPowell 4 13
(Mark Usher) *led: rdn and hdd jst over 2f out: lost pl over 1f out: fdd* **66/1**

050- **8** *3/4* **Links Bar Marbella (IRE)**[99] 7435 3-8-6 53..................... JoeyHaynes 9 16
(Eric Wheeler) *hld up towards rr: carried wd and hdwy bnd 4f out: rdn over 2f out: sn btn: wl bhd fnl f* **33/1**

0-0 **9** *2 1/2* **Milyaar (IRE)**[14] 219 3-8-1 0................................. JosephineGordon(5) 2 10
(Roger Teal) *chsd ldrs: rdn and losing pl whn hung rt bnd 4f out: wl bhd fnl 2f* **20/1**

10 *1 1/2* **Big Toms Girl** 4-9-0 0.. JackDuern(3) 10 3
(Simon Dow) *s.i.s: sn swtchd lft: t.k.h and rn green in rr: lost tch over 2f out* **14/1**

1m 37.95s (-0.25) **Going Correction** -0.075s/f (Stan)
WFA 3 from 4yo 20lb **10** Ran SP% **116.5**
Speed ratings (Par 101): **98,96,96,95,92 92,76,75,72,71**
CSF £7.00 TOTE £3.40: £1.80, £1.60, £3.30; EX 8.30 Trifecta £64.30.
Owner Richard L Page **Bred** Copped Hall Farm & Stud **Trained** Pulborough, W Sussex
■ Stewards' Enquiry : Josephine Gordon jockey said that the colt hung right-handed throughout

FOCUS
A moderate and uncompetitive maiden in which they bet 14-1 bar three.

401 LADBROKES H'CAP 1m 1y(P)
3:25 (3:26) (Class 3) (0-95,90) 4-Y-O **£7,246** (£2,168; £1,084; £542; £270) **Stalls** High

Form RPR

025- **1** **Si Senor (IRE)**[120] 6891 5-9-4 **87**... AdamKirby 5 95
(Ed Vaughan) *chsd ldrs tl chsd clr ldr over 3f out: 3 l down and u.p 2f out: pressing ldr 1f out: styd on to ld towards fin* **9/4**[1]

245- **2** *1/2* **Solo Hunter**[119] 6928 5-9-0 **88**...........................(b) JosephineGordon(5) 3 95
(Martyn Meade) *dwlt: sn rcvrd to ld: wnt clr fr 1/2-way: 3 l clr 2f out: sn rdn: kpt on u.p tl hdd and no ex towards fin* **12/1**

000- **3** *1/2* **Brigliadoro (IRE)**[176] 5118 5-9-4 **87**................................. DanielTudhope 2 93
(Philip McBride) *hld up in midfield: outpcd over 3f out: trying to cl whn nt clr run and swtchd rt over 2f out: effrt in 4th 2f out: styd on wl u.p ins fnl f: wnt 3rd last strides: nvr quite getting to ldng pair* **8/1**

0-64 **4** *hd* **Spiritual Star (IRE)**[9] 266 7-8-13 **82**..........................(t) WilliamCarson 1 87
(Anthony Carson) *hld up in midfield: effrt in 3rd 2f out: swtchd rt and pressing ldng pair 1f out: kpt on same pce u.p fnl 100yds: lost 3rd last strides* **10/1**

31-1 **5** *2 1/2* **Forceful Appeal (USA)**[14] 221 8-9-7 **90**.......................... JimCrowley 4 89
(Simon Dow) *hld up in last pair: 6th and plenty to do over 2f out: effrt on inner over 1f out: kpt on ins fnl f: nvr trbld ldrs* **3/1**[2]

51-6 **6** *hd* **Intrude**[14] 221 4-9-7 **90**.. JamieSpencer 6 89
(David Simcock) *chsd ldr tl over 2f out: lost pl and drvn wl over 2f out: styd on same pce u.p fr over 1f out* **9/2**[3]

001- **7** *19* **Jack Of Diamonds (IRE)**[88] 7693 7-9-3 **86**................ RobertWinston 8 39
(Roger Teal) *hld up in midfield: effrt and pushed wd over 2f out: v wd bnd 2f out and lost all ch: sn eased* **12/1**

\- **8** *14* **Rail Dancer**[272] 4-9-4 **87**.. AdamBeschizza 7
(Richard Rowe) *stdd s: hld up in rr: outpcd over 3f out: lost tch over 2f: t.o* **50/1**

1m 36.6s (-1.60) **Going Correction** -0.075s/f (Stan) **8** Ran SP% **111.5**
Speed ratings (Par 107): **105,104,104,103,101 101,82,68**
CSF £28.84 CT £177.83 TOTE £3.80: £1.80, £3.40, £2.40; EX 34.20 Trifecta £163.10.
Owner A M Pickering **Bred** Hascombe And Valiant Studs **Trained** Newmarket, Suffolk
■ Stewards' Enquiry : Adam Kirby two-day ban: use of whip (13-14 Feb)

FOCUS
A decent handicap run at a strong pace with a thrilling finish. Five of the eight runners were returning from absences of three months or longer, including the first three home.

402 DOWNLOAD THE LADBROKES APP MAIDEN STKS 7f 1y(P)
4:00 (4:01) (Class 5) 3-Y-O+ **£3,234** (£962; £481; £240) **Stalls** Low

Form RPR

02- **1** **Bear Faced**[214] 3747 3-8-9 0.. LukeMorris 9 76+
(Sir Mark Prescott Bt) *chsd ldrs: clsd to press ldr whn carried rt bnd 2f out: sn rdn and chalng: led ins fnl f: r.o wl: comf* **1/1**[1]

0- **2** *1 1/4* **Whistle (IRE)**[58] 8091 3-8-4 0....................................... FrannyNorton 2 68
(Martyn Meade) *led: pressed and hung rt bnd 2f out: hdd and styd on same pce ins fnl f* **6/1**[3]

53- **3** *1 1/2* **Sandacres**[45] 8245 3-8-9 0.. OisinMurphy 8 69
(Jo Crowley) *in tch in midfield: effrt in 5th 2f out: chsd ldng pair and drvn over 1f out: kpt on same pce ins fnl f* **11/4**[2]

4 *4* **Dor's Law** 3-8-4 0.. JimmyQuinn 6 53
(Dean Ivory) *hld up in midfield: effrt in 6th 2f out: styd on to chse clr ldng trio ins fnl f: kpt on but no imp* **25/1**

60-4 **5** *1/2* **Ready Steady (USA)**[10] 258 3-8-4 57............................ KieranO'Neill 3 52
(Richard Hannon) *chsd ldr: ev ch whn carried rt bnd 2f out: sn lost 2nd and swtchd lft: outpcd and btn 1f out: wknd ins fnl f* **16/1**

00- **6** *1 3/4* **Horatia The Fleet**[30] 8410 3-8-4 0................................ CathyGannon 4 47
(Willie Musson) *hld up in tch towards rr: effrt in 7th but outpcd 2f out: wl hld and kpt on same pce fr over 1f out* **66/1**

0- **7** *nk* **Tamara Love (IRE)**[249] 2579 3-8-4 0........................(t) AdamBeschizza 5 46+
(Stuart Williams) *restless in stalls: hld up in last pair: pushed rt 3f out: plenty to do and rdn along over 1f out: kpt on same pce ins fnl f: n.d* **16/1**

8 *2 1/2* **Desafinado (IRE)** 4-9-8 0... StevieDonohoe 7 45
(Miss Joey Ellis) *s.i.s: sn rcvrd and in tch in rr: swtchd rt over 2f out: sn outpcd: bhd over 1f out* **14/1**

9 *3/4* **Two Many Words (IRE)**[18] 4-9-8 0................................ RyanWhile(5) 1 48
(Bill Turner) *dwlt: sn rcvrd to chse ldrs: rdn and outpcd 2f out: sn btn: wknd fnl f* **33/1**

1m 25.84s (1.04) **Going Correction** -0.075s/f (Stan)
WFA 3 from 4yo 18lb **9** Ran SP% **117.7**
Speed ratings (Par 103): **91,89,87,83,82 80,80,77,76**
CSF £7.77 TOTE £1.80: £1.10, £2.40, £1.50; EX 8.00 Trifecta £20.70.
Owner The Barkers & Chris Jenkins **Bred** The Kathryn Stud **Trained** Newmarket, Suffolk

FOCUS
Another uncompetitive maiden.

403 BET NOW WITH THE LADBROKES APP APPRENTICE H'CAP 7f 1y(P)
4:30 (4:31) (Class 6) (0-60,65) 4-Y-O+ **£2,587** (£770; £384; £192) **Stalls** Low

Form RPR

6-41 **1** **Clement (IRE)**[3] 355 6-9-5 **61** 6ex..............................(v) GeorgiaCox(2) 3 80+
(John O'Shea) *dwlt: sn rcvrd to chse ldrs: wnt 2nd 4f out: rdn to chal 2f out: led over 1f out: r.o strly and drew clr fnl f: readily* **6/5**[1]

-411 **2** *5* **Exalted (IRE)**[10] 264 5-9-10 **64**....................................(t) PaddyBradley 2 70
(William Knight) *led: rdn and jnd 2f out: hdd over 1f out: sn no ex and btn: wknd fnl 100yds* **7/4**[2]

20-4 **3** *1* **Tidal's Baby**[15] 196 7-9-4 **58**... AdamMcLean 1 61
(Lee Carter) *stdd s: t.k.h: hld up in tch in midfield: effrt to chse clr ldng pair: kpt on but no imp: drifted rt ins fnl f* **25/1**

00-5 **4** *3/4* **Palace Moon**[15] 190 11-9-5 **59**................................(t) CallumShepherd 5 60
(Michael Attwater) *hld up in midfield: wnt 3rd 3f out tl 4th and outpcd u.p 2f out: wl hld and kpt on same pce after* **16/1**

4-02 **5** *1* **Blackthorn Stick (IRE)**[10] 257 7-9-3 **59**........................ JoshQuinn(2) 6 57
(Paul Burgoyne) *taken down early: stdd s: t.k.h: hld up in last pair: n.m.r over 2f out: sn outpcd: wl hld and kpt on same pce fr over 1f out* **6/1**[3]

46-0 **6** *1* **West Leake (IRE)**[21] 124 10-9-5 **59**............................. CharlieBennett 8 55
(Paul Burgoyne) *stdd s: hld up in rr: outpcd over 2f out: plugged on same pce fr over 1f out: n.d* **20/1**

000- **7** *20* **Chevise (IRE)**[33] 8376 8-9-2 **56**...............................(b) JosephineGordon 7
(Steve Woodman) *chsd ldr tl 4f out: sn rdn: lost pl 3f out: bhd over 1f out* **33/1**

1m 23.53s (-1.27) **Going Correction** -0.075s/f (Stan) **7** Ran SP% **113.5**
Speed ratings (Par 101): **104,98,97,96,95 94,71**
CSF £3.40 CT £26.35 TOTE £1.80: £1.50, £1.50; EX 3.70 Trifecta £36.70.
Owner K W Bell **Bred** P Kelly **Trained** Elton, Gloucs

FOCUS
The betting for this moderate apprentice handicap was dominated by two horses who had recently won similar events under today's riders over C&D. The pair had the race to themselves from some way out.
T/Plt: £22.70 to a £1 stake. Pool: £69965.3 - 2247.16 winning tickets T/Qpdt: £3.50 to a £1 stake. Pool: £5467.14 - 1150.12 winning tickets **Steve Payne**

404 - 406a (Foreign Racing) - See Raceform Interactive

369 MEYDAN (L-H)
Saturday, January 30

OFFICIAL GOING: Dirt: fast; turf: good

407a AL NABOODAH CARGO TROPHY (H'CAP) (DIRT) 1m (D)
1:10 (1:10) (70-87,87) 3-Y-O+ **£14,417** (£4,805; £2,643; £1,441; £720)

RPR
1 **Active Spirit (IRE)**[29] 12 5-9-4 **77**....(v) PatDobbs 2 85+
(Doug Watson, UAE) *sn led: rdn 3f out: comf* **33/1**
2 1 ¾ **Blue Creek**[29] 8 3-8-10 **87**.... WilliamBuick 3 88+
(Charlie Appleby) *s.i.s: in rr: rdn 4f out: r.o fnl 1 1/2f: nrst fin* **2/11**[1]
3 1 ½ **Taqneen (IRE)**[178] 5022 5-9-4 **77**.... DaneO'Neill 5 78
(A R Al Rayhi, UAE) *s.i.s: trckd ldr tl outpcd fnl 3f* **14/1**
4 3 ¾ **Conquerant**[14] 225 5-9-6 **79**....(p) WayneSmith 6 71
(Ismail Mohammed) *a mid-div* **11/1**[3]
5 5 ½ **Marching Time**[14] 229 10-9-6 **79**.... PaulHanagan 4 58
(Doug Watson, UAE) *nvr nr to chal* **16/1**
6 1 **Entifaadha**[14] 225 7-9-4 **77**....(t) FernandoJara 8 54
(M Al Mheiri, UAE) *nvr bttr than mid-div* **25/1**
7 17 **Hammurabi (IRE)**[8] 311 6-9-3 **76**....(bt) RichardMullen 7 14
(S Seemar, UAE) *s.i.s: in rr: r.o same pce fnl 3f* **9/1**[2]
1m 38.29s (0.79) **Going Correction** +0.35s/f (Slow)
WFA 3 from 5yo+ 20lb **7** Ran SP% **122.3**
Speed ratings: **110,108,106,103,97 96,79**
CSF: 43.93; TRICAST: 167.02.
Owner EERC (Mngr: Mrs Rebecca Byrne) **Bred** Darley **Trained** United Arab Emirates

408 - 411a (Foreign Racing) - See Raceform Interactive

341 KEMPTON (A.W) (R-H)
Monday, February 1

OFFICIAL GOING: Polytrack: standard
Wind: Fresh, across away from stands Weather: Cloudy

412 RACINGUK.COM/ANYWHERE H'CAP 1m (P)
2:15 (2:20) (Class 7) (0-50,50) 4-Y-O+ **£1,940** (£577; £288; £144) **Stalls** Low

Form RPR
-502 1 **Little Big Man**[5] 347 5-9-6 49.... StevieDonohoe 8 58
(Brendan Powell) *led tl over 2f out: rallied to dispute ld ins fnl f: jst prevailed* **3/1**[2]
-353 2 nse **Lutine Charlie (IRE)**[5] 341 9-9-2 45....(p) TomQueally 4 54
(Emma Owen) *prom: slt ld over 2f out tl jnd ins fnl f: r.o: jst denied* **7/2**[3]
0-63 3 3 ½ **Little Indian**[12] 252 6-9-5 48.... JoeFanning 7 48
(J R Jenkins) *t.k.h: cl up on outer: rdn and styd on same pce fnl 2f* **11/4**[1]
6-00 4 3 ¾ **Ambitious Rosie**[16] 216 5-8-11 45....(p) CallumShepherd[(5)] 3 36
(Tony Carroll) *in tch: rdn over 3f out: btn over 2f out* **40/1**
5-34 5 nk **Sleet (IRE)**[18] 175 5-9-7 50....(b) LiamJones 1 41
(Michael Appleby) *in tch: rdn 4f out: btn over 2f out* **8/1**
46-0 6 1 ¼ **Supa Seeker (USA)**[10] 294 10-8-13 45....(p) GeorgeDowning[(3)] 9 33
(Tony Carroll) *outpcd in rr: passed btn horses fnl 2f* **16/1**
40-6 7 6 **Lily Edge**[12] 255 7-9-4 47....(b) WilliamCarson 5 20
(John Bridger) *a towards rr: drvn along and n.d fnl 2f* **15/2**
0-50 8 2 ¾ **Chandrayaan**[15] 237 9-8-13 45....(v) ShelleyBirkett[(3)] 2 12
(John E Long) *prom tl hung rt and wknd over 2f out* **16/1**
00-0 9 5 **Soliana**[4] 362 4-9-2 45....(v) CathyGannon 6
(John O'Shea) *outpcd towards rr: no ch fnl 3f* **25/1**
1m 40.84s (1.04) **Going Correction** +0.20s/f (Slow) **9** Ran SP% **114.8**
Speed ratings (Par 97): **102,101,98,94,94 93,87,84,79**
CSF £13.88 CT £31.26 TOTE £4.00: £1.50, £1.40, £1.10; EX 16.40 Trifecta £52.30.
Owner Teamchoochoo & Partners **Bred** Paul Merritt **Trained** Upper Lambourn, Berks
FOCUS
The first pair came clear in this bottom-drawer handicap. The winner backed up last week's run.

413 RACING UK DEVICES 1 PRICE MAIDEN FILLIES' STKS 1m (P)
2:50 (2:55) (Class 5) 3-Y-O+ **£3,234** (£962; £481; £240) **Stalls** Low

Form RPR
44-3 1 **Southern Storm (IRE)**[19] 163 4-9-9 0.... PatrickO'Donnell[(5)] 4 81
(Ralph Beckett) *chsd ldrs: led over 1f out: pushed clr* **11/10**[1]
3-46 2 6 **Kelvin Hall**[11] 275 3-8-9 67.... JoeFanning 3 62
(Mark Johnston) *chsd ldr: led over 2f out tl over 1f out: sn btn* **2/1**[2]
256- 3 2 ½ **Highest Quality (IRE)**[36] 8366 4-9-9 62....(t[1]) AaronJones[(5)] 6 61
(Stuart Williams) *s.i.s: bhd: hdwy into 3rd over 1f out: nt rch ldrs* **20/1**
00 4 2 ¼ **Fun Money**[8] 325 3-8-9 0.... MartinLane 5 51
(Ed Dunlop) *disp modest 4th most of way: no hdwy fnl 2f* **20/1**
0 5 1 **Haunted (IRE)**[8] 325 3-8-9 0.... MartinDwyer 1 49
(David Simcock) *disp modest 4th most of way: btn over 2f out* **11/2**[3]
05-0 6 7 **Highburgh Road (IRE)**[29] 29 3-8-9 39.... LiamJones 2 33
(Mark Johnston) *pushed along to ld at gd pce: hdd & wknd over 2f out* **40/1**
1m 40.74s (0.94) **Going Correction** +0.20s/f (Slow)
WFA 3 from 4yo 19lb **6** Ran SP% **108.3**
Speed ratings (Par 100): **103,97,94,92,91 84**
CSF £3.15 TOTE £1.80: £1.10, £1.70; EX 4.00 Trifecta £16.00.
Owner Christopher McHale **Bred** Chris & James McHale **Trained** Kimpton, Hants
FOCUS
A moderate fillies' maiden and not the most solid form.

414 RACINGUK.COM/WINTERSEASONTICKET H'CAP 1m (P)
3:25 (3:30) (Class 5) (0-75,75) 4-Y-O+ **£3,234** (£962; £481; £240) **Stalls** Low

Form RPR
1-16 1 **Ziggys Star**[11] 278 4-9-7 75.... LiamJones 6 83
(Michael Appleby) *t.k.h in 5th: effrt and edgd rt over 2f out: led over 1f out: drvn out* **11/2**[3]
53-4 2 nk **Pour La Victoire (IRE)**[15] 236 6-9-2 73....(b) GeorgeDowning[(3)] 1 80
(Tony Carroll) *dwlt: hld up in rr: swtchd lft and hdwy over 1f out: styd on: clsng at fin* **5/2**[1]
33-2 3 ¾ **Chelwood Gate (IRE)**[12] 263 6-9-6 74....(v) JoeFanning 5 79
(Patrick Chamings) *chsd ldrs: hmpd over 2f out: rdn to press wnr ins fnl f: unable qck nr fin* **3/1**[2]
305- 4 5 **Light Rose (IRE)**[61] 8084 6-8-13 67.... MartinLane 3 60
(Jeremy Gask) *prom: rdn 3f out: wknd jst over 1f out* **8/1**
0-03 5 1 **Malaysian Boleh**[5] 349 6-8-13 72....(p) CallumShepherd[(5)] 2 63
(Shaun Lycett) *s.s: nvr trbld ldrs* **11/2**[3]
62-0 6 hd **Shimba Hills**[12] 256 5-9-5 73.... WilliamTwiston-Davies 4 63
(Lawney Hill) *led tl over 1f out: wknd fnl f* **12/1**
60-0 7 3 ¼ **Maverik**[12] 260 8-9-7 75....(bt[1]) TomQueally 7 58
(Ali Stronge) *chsd ldr tl over 2f out: sn wknd* **16/1**
1m 40.07s (0.27) **Going Correction** +0.20s/f (Slow) **7** Ran SP% **109.0**
Speed ratings (Par 103): **106,105,104,99,98 98,95**
CSF £17.78 CT £43.03 TOTE £4.90: £2.30, £2.20; EX 19.70 Trifecta £49.00.
Owner Tariq Al Nisf **Bred** Honeypuddle Stud **Trained** Oakham, Rutland
FOCUS
The principals were clear at the finish and this is not bad form for the class. The winner resumed his progress.

415 RACING UK WINTER SEASON TICKET FILLIES' H'CAP 7f (P)
3:55 (4:00) (Class 5) (0-75,74) 4-Y-O+ **£3,234** (£962; £481; £240) **Stalls** Low

Form RPR
55-2 1 **Perfect Alchemy (IRE)**[23] 124 5-9-2 69.... JoeFanning 3 76
(Patrick Chamings) *in tch: slt ld 1f out: rdn along and hld on wl fnl f* **9/4**[1]
00-3 2 shd **Hollie Point**[8] 324 4-9-7 74.... ShaneKelly 2 80
(Sylvester Kirk) *hld up towards rr: hdwy over 1f out: pressed wnr ins fnl f: r.o: jst failed* **5/1**[2]
2-45 3 nk **Be Royale**[12] 260 6-9-5 72.... RobertWinston 6 77
(Michael Appleby) *chsd ldrs: drvn to chal over 1f out: kpt on* **7/1**
-314 4 1 **Mambo Fever**[11] 269 5-8-4 62.... CallumShepherd[(5)] 4 64
(David C Griffiths) *dwlt: sn chsng ldrs on outer: unable qck ins fnl f* **11/2**[3]
6-41 5 nk **Queen Aggie (IRE)**[11] 269 6-9-1 71.... GeorgeDowning[(3)] 1 73
(Tony Carroll) *bhd: rdn over 2f out: nrest at fin* **6/1**
60-4 6 1 ¼ **Cascading Stars (IRE)**[16] 223 4-9-5 72....(p) LiamJones 7 70
(J S Moore) *t.k.h: sn led: hdd and no ex 1f out* **10/1**
2-33 7 2 ¾ **Ixelles Diamond (IRE)**[16] 223 5-9-2 69.... JimCrowley 5 60
(Andrew Reid) *chsd ldr tl 2f out: sn outpcd* **13/2**
1m 27.76s (1.76) **Going Correction** +0.20s/f (Slow) **7** Ran SP% **112.0**
Speed ratings (Par 100): **97,96,96,95,95 93,90**
CSF £13.00 TOTE £3.00: £1.50, £4.10; EX 14.30 Trifecta £83.40.
Owner The Perfect Partnership & D H Caslon **Bred** W Maxwell Ervine **Trained** Baughurst, Hants
FOCUS
A modest fillies' handicap that produced a tight finish. Muddling form.

416 RACING UK DEVICES 1 PRICE H'CAP 6f (P)
4:30 (4:35) (Class 4) (0-85,82) 4-Y-O+ **£5,175** (£1,540; £769; £384) **Stalls** Low

Form RPR
4-02 1 **Doctor Parkes**[17] 192 10-8-11 77.... AaronJones[(5)] 4 83
(Stuart Williams) *trckd ldrs gng wl: effrt over 1f out: r.o to ld fnl 75yds: rdn out* **8/1**
02-2 2 nk **Head Space (IRE)**[9] 319 8-8-10 71.... CathyGannon 3 76
(Brian Barr) *hmpd s and missed break: towards rr: hdwy over 1f out: pressed wnr ins fnl f: r.o* **3/1**[2]
0-01 3 ½ **Yeeoow (IRE)**[17] 192 7-9-2 82.... JustinNewman[(5)] 5 85
(K R Burke) *led: hld on gamely tl hdd fnl 75yds: kpt on* **11/2**[3]
54-6 4 1 **Brazen Spirit**[26] 67 4-8-10 74....(v[1]) RyanTate[(3)] 7 74
(Clive Cox) *hld up in rr: rdn over 2f out: hdwy over 1f out: kpt on fnl f* **13/2**
00- 5 nk **Bouclier (IRE)**[47] 8247 6-8-9 70.... WilliamCarson 6 69
(Tony Carroll) *t.k.h in 5th: outpcd 3f out: styd on fnl f* **14/1**
36-2 6 1 ½ **Saint Pois (FR)**[19] 159 5-8-9 73.... GeorgeDowning[(3)] 2 67
(Tony Carroll) *bmpd and stmbld s: hdwy to press ldr after 1f tl over 1f out: no ex* **9/4**[1]
030- 7 2 ½ **Cool Strutter (IRE)**[144] 6238 4-9-0 75.... JimCrowley 1 61
(Andrew Balding) *wnt lft s: t.k.h: prom tl hrd rdn and wknd over 1f out* **9/1**
1m 13.02s (-0.08) **Going Correction** +0.20s/f (Slow) **7** Ran SP% **112.3**
Speed ratings (Par 105): **108,107,106,105,105 103,99**
CSF £30.99 TOTE £9.00: £4.10, £1.80; EX 38.30 Trifecta £94.50.
Owner The Doctor Parkes Partnership **Bred** Joseph Heler **Trained** Newmarket, Suffolk
FOCUS
There was just an ordinary pace on in this modest sprint handicap and it saw a messy finish. The form is rated cautiously.

417 RACING UK DAY PASS JUST £10 H'CAP 2m (P)
5:00 (5:05) (Class 6) (0-60,64) 4-Y-O+ **£2,587** (£770; £384; £192) **Stalls** Low

Form RPR
-411 1 **Sonnythenavigator (USA)**[5] 354 4-9-9 64 6ex....(p) MartinLane 6 69
(David Simcock) *stdd s: patiently rdn in rr: rdn 3f out and carried hd to lft: rapid hdwy over 1f out: str run to ld fnl 30yds* **5/6**[1]
30-6 2 1 **Epsom Flyer**[15] 233 6-8-5 45.... CallumShepherd[(5)] 4 49
(Pat Phelan) *hld up in 5th: hdwy over 1f out: pressed ldr fnl f: kpt on* **7/2**[2]
50-4 3 nk **Heurtevent (FR)**[15] 232 7-8-12 50.... GeorgeDowning[(3)] 1 54
(Tony Carroll) *in tch: hrd rdn over 2f out: pressed ldrs fnl f: kpt on* **16/1**
00/0 4 ¾ **Vedani (IRE)**[19] 164 7-9-6 55....(t) WilliamCarson 7 58
(Tony Carroll) *led: qcknd and kicked 2 l ahd 3f out: hdd and no ex fnl 30yds* **25/1**
0-06 5 2 **Movie Magic**[3] 378 5-8-10 45.... ShaneKelly 5 45
(Mark Hoad) *prom: chsd ldr over 2f out tl over 1f out: no ex* **14/1**
435- 6 2 **Galuppi**[41] 8345 5-9-9 58....(b) JoeFanning 2 56
(J R Jenkins) *towards rr: rdn 3f out: nvr able to chal* **7/1**[3]
62 7 nk **Annakrista (GER)**[10] 289 8-9-7 59....(bt) RobHornby[(3)] 8 57
(Zoe Davison) *chsd ldr tl over 2f out: wknd wl over 1f out* **25/1**
/0-3 8 14 **Boston Blue**[10] 289 9-9-3 52.... TomQueally 3 33
(Tony Carroll) *a towards rr: outpcd and struggling 3f out* **10/1**
3m 38.82s (8.72) **Going Correction** +0.20s/f (Slow)
WFA 4 from 5yo+ 6lb **8** Ran SP% **118.6**
Speed ratings (Par 101): **86,85,85,84,83 82,82,75**
CSF £4.12 CT £24.36 TOTE £2.00: £1.10, £1.60, £3.00; EX 5.00 Trifecta £47.30.
Owner Oliver Brendon **Bred** Runnymede Farm Inc & Catesby W Clay **Trained** Newmarket, Suffolk
FOCUS
This moderate staying handicap was run at an uneven tempo and suited those racing handily, so the winner did well. Very ordinary form, rated around the placed horses.
T/Plt: £13.80 to a £1 stake. Pool: £54,757.27 - 2888.60 winning units. T/Qpdt: £11.60 to a £1 stake. Pool: £4,305.36 - 273.90 winning units. **Lee McKenzie**

[383]WOLVERHAMPTON (A.W) (L-H)

Monday, February 1

OFFICIAL GOING: Tapeta: standard

Wind: Strong behind Weather: Cloudy

418 DOWNLOAD THE NEW UNIBET RACING APP AMATEUR RIDERS' H'CAP 5f 216y (Tp)

2:00 (2:00) (Class 6) (0-55,55) 4-Y-O+ **£2,495** (£774; £386; £193) **Stalls** Low

Form RPR

1- **1** **Fairy Foxglove (IRE)**[33] 8406 6-10-11 **52**.......................... MrSWalker 6 62
(P J F Murphy, Ire) *a.p: chsd ldr over 2f out: rdn over 1f out: led and edgd lft ins fnl f: styd on* **11/10**[1]

6-44 **2** 1 ½ **Pancake Day**[22] 130 4-10-9 **55**..............................(p) MrHHunt(5) 4 60
(Jason Ward) *a.p: shkn up over 1f out: styd on* **7/1**[3]

-544 **3** ¾ **Hab Reeh**[6] 340 8-10-12 **53**.............................. MissSBrotherton 1 56
(Ruth Carr) *chsd ldr tl led 1/2-way: rdn and hdd ins fnl f: styd on same pce* **6/1**[2]

20-3 **4** ¾ **Time Medicean**[24] 100 10-10-7 **55**.............................. MissSAColl(7) 10 56+
(Tony Carroll) *hld up: hdwy over 1f out: edgd lft ins fnl f: r.o: nt rch ldrs* **14/1**

-304 **5** 2 ½ **Molly Approve (IRE)**[10] 297 4-10-6 **50**..................(p) KaineWood(3) 12 43
(Tony Coyle) *hld up: hdwy over 1f out: r.o: nt trble ldrs* **22/1**

04-6 **6** 3 ¼ **Dream Ally (IRE)**[15] 230 6-10-8 **52**.................... MissBeckySmith(3) 11 35+
(John Weymes) *s.i.s: hld up: r.o ins fnl f: nvr nrr* **6/1**[2]

25-0 **7** 1 **Warm Order**[10] 292 5-10-11 **52**.............................. MissJoannaMason 7 32
(Tony Carroll) *chsd ldrs: rdn over 2f out: wknd fnl f* **25/1**

050- **8** 1 **Upper Lambourn (IRE)**[183] 4903 8-10-0 **46** oh1............ MrMEnnis(5) 8 23
(Christopher Kellett) *broke wl enough: sn pushed along and lost pl: rdn over 2f out: wknd over 1f out* **100/1**

0-0 **9** 1 ¾ **Amis Reunis**[22] 130 7-10-7 **48**.............................. MissMMullineaux 3 20
(Alan Berry) *in rr: pushed along over 3f out: wknd over 2f out* **66/1**

000- **10** hd **Novabridge**[61] 8071 8-10-12 **53**..............................(p) BrodieHampson 2 24
(Phil McEntee) *hld up: a in rr: no ch whn nt clr run over 1f out* **33/1**

66-6 **11** nse **Plunder**[22] 135 6-10-0 **46** oh1..........................(b) KatherineGlenister(5) 9 17
(Alan Berry) *mid-div: rdn over 2f out: sn wknd* **80/1**

-042 **12** 7 **Pull The Pin (IRE)**[6] 340 7-10-6 **52**..................(bt) MissAmyTaylor(5) 5 2
(Heather Dalton) *sn pushed along to ld: hung rt over 3f out: sn hdd: wknd over 1f out* **17/2**

1m 14.85s (0.35) **Going Correction** +0.025s/f (Slow) **12** Ran SP% **120.7**

Speed ratings (Par 101): **98,96,95,94,90 86,85,83,81,81 81,71**

CSF £8.95 CT £36.37 TOTE £2.30: £1.10, £2.20, £2.00; EX 10.40 Trifecta £35.60.

Owner Brian Mullen **Bred** John I O'Byrne **Trained** Castlecomer, Co Kilkenny

FOCUS

A moderate contest, and not many got into it with pace holding up. The winner is getting closer to her back form.

419 £10 FREE AT 32RED.COM CLAIMING STKS 5f 216y (Tp)

2:35 (2:35) (Class 6) 3-Y-O **£2,587** (£770; £384; £192) **Stalls** Low

Form RPR

53-6 **1** **Toledo**[20] 152 3-9-11 72.. SeanLevey 2 71
(Richard Hannon) *a.p: rdn to ld and edgd lft ins fnl f: r.o* **4/1**[3]

10-5 **2** 1 ¾ **Bahamian Sunshine**[22] 131 3-9-3 65..............................(p) DavidNolan 5 58
(Richard Fahey) *sn led: rdn over 1f out: hdd ins fnl f: styd on same pce* **8/1**

0-40 **3** 2 ¼ **Cross Examine (IRE)**[7] 328 3-8-2 51...................... SophieKilloran(7) 6 43+
(David Simcock) *s.i.s: hld up: rdn over 1f out: r.o ins fnl f: wnt 3rd nr fin: nt rch ldrs* **16/1**

534- **4** nk **Jeanie's Place**[43] 8316 3-9-2 71.............................. TonyHamilton 4 49
(Richard Fahey) *prom: chsd ldr over 4f out: rdn over 2f out: no ex fnl f* **5/4**[1]

006- **5** nse **Master Pekan**[42] 8330 3-8-8 23.............................. CiaranMckee(5) 1 46
(Roy Brotherton) *s.i.s: hld up: rdn over 1f out: nt trble ldrs* **200/1**

316- **6** 3 ½ **Zeeoneandonly (IRE)**[32] 8409 3-9-6 74..........................(v) AdamKirby 3 42
(David Evans) *chsd ldr tl over 4f out: remained handy: rdn over 2f out: wknd fnl f* **2/1**[2]

1m 14.6s (0.10) **Going Correction** +0.025s/f (Slow) **6** Ran SP% **115.3**

Speed ratings (Par 95): **100,97,94,94,94 89**

CSF £35.01 TOTE £4.30: £2.10, £2.70; EX 35.20 Trifecta £259.80.Toledo was claimed by Mrs Marjorie Fife for £12,000

Owner Rockcliffe Stud **Bred** Rockcliffe Stud **Trained** East Everleigh, Wilts

FOCUS

With a couple of the market principals running below form and the rank outsider finishing fairly close up, this probably didn't take much winning. The fifth highlights obvious limitations to the form.

420 32REDSPORT.COM FILLIES' H'CAP 1m 4f 50y (Tp)

3:10 (3:10) (Class 5) (0-75,73) 4-Y-O+ **£3,234** (£962; £481; £240) **Stalls** Low

Form RPR

363- **1** **Celestial Bay**[37] 8361 7-9-10 **73**.............................. LukeMorris 4 80
(Sylvester Kirk) *led 1f: chsd ldrs: wnt 2nd again 3f out: rdn to ld over 1f out: edgd lft: styd on* **7/1**

31-1 **2** ¾ **Wavelet**[23] 127 4-9-5 **71**.............................. JamieSpencer 5 77
(David Simcock) *hld up: hdwy to chse ldr over 9f out tl led over 3f out: rdn and hdd over 1f out: kpt on* **3/1**[1]

22-5 **3** 2 ¼ **Indira**[29] 30 5-9-7 **70**.. JFEgan 7 72
(John Berry) *prom: racd keenly: lost pl after 1f: hdwy 10f out: hdwy over 2f out: rdn over 1f out: styd on same pce fnl f* **5/1**[3]

/3-4 **4** hd **Favorite Girl (GER)**[17] 199 8-8-10 **64**................ JosephineGordon(5) 6 66
(Michael Appleby) *trckd ldrs: racd keenly: outpcd 3f out: rallied over 1f out: r.o* **10/1**

5-35 **5** 3 ¾ **Cosmic Halo**[12] 256 7-9-3 **66**.............................. TonyHamilton 3 62
(Richard Fahey) *hld up: nt clr run and swtchd rt over 2f out: sn rdn: nt trble ldrs* **9/1**

3-21 **6** ½ **Tijuca (IRE)**[21] 149 7-9-3 **66**..............................(tp) KieranO'Neill 2 61
(Ed de Giles) *hld up: nt clr run over 2f out: effrt over 1f out: n.d* **11/2**

-3 **7** 1 **Lady Fandango (IRE)**[17] 200 4-8-11 **63**.............................. LiamKeniry 1 56
(Gordon Elliott, Ire) *hld up in tch: plld hrd: rdn over 1f out: wknd fnl f* **7/2**[2]

066- **8** 12 **Cosette (IRE)**[106] 7308 5-9-4 **67**.............................. TimmyMurphy 8 41
(Bernard Llewellyn) *led at stdy pce after 1f: hdd over 3f out: wknd over 2f out* **40/1**

2m 42.25s (1.45) **Going Correction** +0.025s/f (Slow)

WFA 4 from 5yo+ 3lb **8** Ran SP% **113.3**

Speed ratings (Par 100): **96,95,94,93,91 91,90,82**

CSF £27.78 CT £114.24 TOTE £8.10: £2.40, £1.40, £1.70; EX 33.10 Trifecta £105.10.

Owner Homebred Racing **Bred** Chris Wall **Trained** Upper Lambourn, Berks

FOCUS

They went a fairly steady early gallop in this fillies' handicap. Muddling form.

421 32RED CASINO H'CAP 1m 141y (Tp)

3:40 (3:40) (Class 5) (0-75,75) 3-Y-O **£3,234** (£962; £481; £240) **Stalls** Low

Form RPR

1 **1** **Nezwaah**[26] 59 3-9-5 **73**.. JackMitchell 3 86+
(Roger Varian) *s.i.s: hld up: hdwy over 2f out: qcknd to ld over 1f out: pushed out: readily* **4/5**[1]

16-1 **2** 3 ½ **Ritasun (FR)**[4] 366 3-9-7 **75** 6ex..............................(p) KieranO'Neill 1 77
(Richard Hannon) *trckd ldrs: rdn over 1f out: styd on same pce fnl f* **4/1**[3]

33-2 **3** 1 ¼ **Strawberry Sorbet**[23] 123 3-9-3 **71**.............................. AdamKirby 4 70
(Clive Cox) *led: rdn over 2f out: hdd over 1f out: no ex fnl f* **12/1**

60-1 **4** nk **Zainat (IRE)**[14] 243 3-9-7 **75**.............................. DougieCostello 2 73
(K R Burke) *hld up: rdn and hung lft fr over 1f out: nt trble ldrs* **7/2**[2]

56-2 **5** 6 **Redmane**[12] 253 3-9-0 **68**.............................. TimmyMurphy 5 53
(Jamie Osborne) *chsd ldr: rdn over 2f out: wknd fnl f* **8/1**

1m 50.62s (0.52) **Going Correction** +0.025s/f (Slow) **5** Ran SP% **116.6**

Speed ratings (Par 97): **98,94,93,93,88**

CSF £4.86 TOTE £1.90: £1.20, £2.10; EX 5.30 Trifecta £20.50.

Owner Sheikh Ahmed Al Maktoum **Bred** Darley **Trained** Newmarket, Suffolk

FOCUS

Not a bad little handicap, and a good performance from the winner. It has been rated around the third.

422 EBF 32RED.COM FILLIES' H'CAP 1m 141y (Tp)

4:10 (4:10) (Class 2) (0-105,91) 4-Y-O+

£16,807 (£5,032; £2,516; £1,258; £629; £315) **Stalls** Low

Form RPR

5-21 **1** **Abbey Angel (IRE)**[14] 240 4-9-1 **82**..............................(p) TonyHamilton 3 90
(Richard Fahey) *chsd ldrs: rdn to ld ins fnl f: r.o* **9/4**[2]

4-11 **2** ½ **India's Song**[12] 254 6-8-5 **79**..............................(t) SophieKilloran(7) 5 86
(David Simcock) *hld up: hdwy over 1f out: r.o* **7/1**

1-12 **3** ½ **Oakley Girl**[12] 254 4-9-10 **91**.............................. OisinMurphy 4 97
(Stuart Williams) *hld up: hdwy on outer over 2f out: rdn to ld over 1f out: hdd ins fnl f: styd on same pce* **15/8**[1]

42-1 **4** 1 ¼ **Mitre Peak**[14] 245 4-8-10 **80**.............................. SammyJoBell(3) 8 83
(Richard Fahey) *chsd ldrs: nt clr run and lost pl over 2f out: effrt and nt clr run over 1f out: styd on* **4/1**[3]

-306 **5** 7 **Assault On Rome (IRE)**[12] 260 4-8-10 **77**..............(b) AdrianNicholls 2 64
(Mark Johnston) *s.i.s: hld up: rdn over 1f out: wknd fnl f* **25/1**

00-5 **6** 4 **Lady Marl**[12] 254 5-9-3 **84**.............................. AdamKirby 1 62
(Gary Moore) *led: rdn and hdd over 1f out: wknd fnl f* **12/1**

50-6 **7** ½ **Pretty Bubbles**[12] 254 7-8-13 **80**..............................(p) DougieCostello 7 56
(J R Jenkins) *hld up: a in rr: rdn and wknd over 1f out* **28/1**

2320 **8** 3 ¾ **My Tringaling (IRE)**[12] 254 4-8-5 **72** oh19.............. AdamBeschizza 6 40
(Stuart Williams) *pushed along to chse ldr over 7f out: rdn over 3f out: wknd over 1f out* **100/1**

1m 47.85s (-2.25) **Going Correction** +0.025s/f (Slow) **8** Ran SP% **114.0**

Speed ratings (Par 96): **111,110,110,109,102 99,98,95**

CSF £17.95 CT £33.87 TOTE £3.20: £1.10, £1.80, £1.30; EX 20.20 Trifecta £37.00.

Owner Richard Fahey Ebor Racing Club Ltd **Bred** Paul Hyland **Trained** Musley Bank, N Yorks

■ Stewards' Enquiry : Sophie Killoran two-day ban: used whip in incorrect place (Feb 15-16)

Adam Beschizza one-day ban: weighed-in with girth (Feb 15)

FOCUS

Not as good a race as the conditions would suggest, with the top-weight weighing in a stone below the ceiling, but nevertheless it featured some in-form fillies. The winner is rated back to her best.

423 LADBROKES MAIDEN STKS 7f 32y (Tp)

4:45 (4:46) (Class 5) 3-Y-O+ **£3,234** (£962; £481; £240) **Stalls** High

Form RPR

35-2 **1** **Best New Show (IRE)**[13] 249 3-8-0 66 ow1....... JosephineGordon(5) 9 67
(David Evans) *towards rr: pushed along and hdwy 1/2-way: carried rt and led ins fnl f: r.o wl* **2/1**[1]

2 1 ½ **Grecian King** 3-8-9 0..............................(p) LukeMorris 5 67+
(James Tate) *trckd ldrs: shkn up to ld over 1f out: sn hung rt: rdn and hdd ins fnl f: styd on same pce* **11/4**[2]

02-5 **3** 3 **Kadooment Day (IRE)**[11] 275 3-8-2 72.................... CliffordLee(7) 4 59
(K R Burke) *led 6f out: pushed along 1/2-way: rdn and hdd over 1f out: hmpd sn after: no ex ins fnl f* **5/1**[3]

4 1 ¼ **Torreon (IRE)** 5-9-12 0.. AdamKirby 6 61+
(Phil McEntee) *hld up: plld hrd: swtchd rt over 2f out: hdwy over 1f out: sn rdn: no ex ins fnl f* **12/1**

0 **5** 3 ½ **Plymouth Mo**[16] 219 3-8-4 0.............................. AliceMills(5) 7 47
(Rod Millman) *hld up in tch: rdn over 1f out: wknd fnl f* **80/1**

6 **6** 4 ½ **On The Clock**[25] 77 3-8-4 0.............................. FrannyNorton 8 30
(James Tate) *chsd ldrs: shkn up over 1f out: wknd fnl f* **6/1**

7 2 **Monpazier (IRE)** 3-8-9 0.............................. JoeyHaynes 10 30
(K R Burke) *s.s: hld up: hmpd over 2f out: sn wknd* **10/1**

005- **8** 1 ½ **Sun In His Eyes**[35] 8381 4-9-12 30.............................. KieranO'Neill 3 31
(Ed de Giles) *prom: racd keenly: nt clr run and lost pl 3f out: hmpd over 2f out: sn wknd* **100/1**

9 3 ½ **Always Endeavour** 3-8-4 0.............................. JimmyQuinn 2 12
(Daniel Mark Loughnane) *s.s: outpcd* **33/1**

0/4 **10** 2 **Royal Roman**[19] 163 4-9-4 0.............................. NathanAlison(3) 1 12
(Kevin Frost) *led 1f: chsd ldr tl rdn 1/2-way: wknd over 2f out* **25/1**

1m 30.24s (1.44) **Going Correction** +0.025s/f (Slow)

WFA 3 from 4yo+ 17lb **10** Ran SP% **116.7**

Speed ratings (Par 103): **92,90,86,85,81 76,74,72,68,66**

CSF £7.38 TOTE £2.40: £1.30, £1.60, £1.90; EX 8.50 Trifecta £31.20.

Owner Peter O'Callaghan **Bred** Mrs C Hartery **Trained** Pandy, Monmouths

FOCUS

Modest, muddling maiden for, rated around the winner.

424 LADBROKES H'CAP 7f 32y (Tp)

5:15 (5:17) (Class 5) (0-70,70) 4-Y-O+ **£3,234** (£962; £481; £240) **Stalls** High

Form RPR

00-5 **1** **Logans Lad (IRE)**[14] 239 6-9-7 **70**..............................(vt) LukeMorris 8 80
(Daniel Mark Loughnane) *pushed along early in rr: swtchd rt and hdwy over 1f out: rdn to ld and hung lft 1f out: r.o* **11/2**[3]

4-11 **2** 2 **National Service (USA)**[15] 230 5-9-1 **64**..............(tp) TimmyMurphy 3 69
(Gordon Elliott, Ire) *hld up: hdwy over 2f out: ev ch 1f out: sn rdn: styd on same pce* **7/4**[1]

21-6 **3** *4* **Orlando Rogue (IRE)**[26] 64 4-9-4 **67**..........................(p) LiamKeniry 1 61
(Conor Dore) *hld up: rdn over 1f out: r.o to go 3rd nr fin: nt rch ldrs* **14/1**
U3-3 **4** *½* **Quite A Story**[28] 41 4-9-7 **70**.................................. AdamKirby 9 63
(Clive Cox) *trckd ldrs: plld hrd: rdn over 1f out: no ex ins fnl f* **5/1**[2]
0-00 **5** *nse* **Admirable Art (IRE)**[15] 231 6-8-9 **58**...................................... JFEgan 5 51
(Tony Carroll) *prom: chsd ldr over 4f out: pushed along 1/2-way: rdn and ev ch over 1f out: wknd ins fnl f* **25/1**
6-11 **6** *1 ¾* **Moonlight Venture**[11] 276 5-9-5 **68**..............................(p) TomEaves 10 56
(Conor Dore) *s.i.s: hld up: rdn over 1f out: nvr on terms* **8/1**
0-31 **7** *nk* **Al's Memory (IRE)**[17] 191 7-9-0 **66**.............................. PhilipPrince(3) 2 54
(David Evans) *led 1f: chsd ldrs: pushed along 1/2-way: wknd fnl f* **5/1**[2]
000- **8** *¾* **Marmarus**[42] 8333 5-9-7 **70**.. FrannyNorton 7 56
(David Nicholls) *hld up in tch: rdn over 1f out: wknd fnl f* **16/1**
63- **9** *nk* **Picks Pinta**[170] 5372 5-9-0 **70**.. VitorSantos(7) 6 55
(John David Riches) *hld up: nt clr run over 2f out: nvr nr to chal* **16/1**
41/0 **10** *¾* **Summersault (IRE)**[15] 236 5-9-3 **66**........................... JamieSpencer 12 49
(Jamie Osborne) *led 6f out: rdn and hdd 1f out: sn hung lft and wknd* **14/1**
-050 **11** *9* **Tartan Trip**[14] 239 9-9-2 **65**..(vt) AndrewMullen 4 25
(Michael Appleby) *hld up: rdn over 2f out: wknd over 1f out* **28/1**

1m 27.74s (-1.06) **Going Correction** +0.025s/f (Slow) **11** Ran SP% **128.6**
Speed ratings (Par 103): **107,104,100,99,99 97,97,96,95,95 84**
CSF £17.04 CT £142.52 TOTE £6.70: £2.30, £1.60, £3.30; EX 29.50 Trifecta £350.50.
Owner Ian O'Connor **Bred** Tally-Ho Stud **Trained** Baldwin's Gate, Staffs

FOCUS
There was plenty of pace on here and that set things up for the closers. The winner could have been rated higher.
T/Jkpt: £14,778.60 to a £1 stake. Pool: £7,190.90 - 0.5 winning units. T/Plt: £26.10 to a £1 stake. Pool: £72,568.15 - 2023.76 winning units. T/Qpdt: £2.30 to a £1 stake. Pool: £9,230.52 - 2922.40 winning units. **Colin Roberts**

363 SOUTHWELL (L-H)
Tuesday, February 2

OFFICIAL GOING: Fibresand: standard
Wind: Fresh half behind Weather: Cloudy

425 32RED.COM H'CAP 1m 6f (F)
2:00 (2:00) (Class 5) (0-70,70) 4-Y-O+ **£3,234** (£962; £481; £240) **Stalls** Low

Form RPR
2-1 **1** **Edgar (GER)**[14] 251 6-9-8 **66**........................(p) WilliamTwiston-Davies 1 77+
(David Bridgwater) *led 2f: cl up: led again 3f out: rdn wl over 1f out: drvn and kpt on strly fnl f* **5/1**[2]
32-4 **2** *1 ½* **Northside Prince (IRE)**[23] 132 10-9-12 **70**........................ BenCurtis 6 76
(Alan Swinbank) *hld up in tch: hdwy over 3f out: wd st and rdn 2f out: drvn over 1f out: styd on wl fnl f* **7/2**[1]
42-0 **3** *nk* **Thou Swell (IRE)**[19] 173 4-9-0 **63**.................................... LukeMorris 8 68
(Shaun Harris) *trckd ldrs: effrt and hdwy 4f out: rdn along 3f out: drvn 2f out: kpt on same pce u.p* **17/2**
11-5 **4** *1 ¼* **With Hindsight (IRE)**[25] 103 8-9-7 **70**........................... JoshDoyle(5) 9 74
(Steve Gollings) *cl up: led after 2f: pushed along 4f out: sn rdn and hdd 3f out: drvn 2f out: grad wknd* **6/1**[3]
523- **5** *4* **Singzak**[35] 8383 8-9-5 **63**.. OisinMurphy 7 61
(David C Griffiths) *towards rr: hdwy 1/2-way: chsd ldrs over 3f out: rdn wl over 2f out: drvn and no imp fr wl over 1f out* **7/1**
02-3 **6** *2* **Kay Sera**[28] 51 8-9-8 **69**.. EoinWalsh(3) 10 64
(Tony Newcombe) *towards rr: hdwy 1/2-way chsd ldrs 4f out: rdn to chse ldng pair 3f out: drvn over 2f out and grad wknd* **10/1**
00-4 **7** *2* **Arthurs Secret**[25] 103 6-9-10 **68**..................................(b) PhillipMakin 3 61
(John Quinn) *hld up in rr: hdwy 1/2-way: in tch and rdn along over 3f out: n.d* **15/2**
06-6 **8** *16* **Arsenale (GER)**[5] 358 5-8-12 **56**..............................(p) AndrewMullen 5 26
(Michael Appleby) *chsd ldng pair on inner: rdn along 4f out: sn wknd* **50/1**
6-56 **9** *22* **Topaling**[16] 234 5-9-7 **65**... SaleemGolam 2
(Mark H Tompkins) *chsd ldrs: rdn along over 5f out: sn lost pl and bhd* **16/1**
33-0 **10** *61* **Koreen (IRE)**[19] 173 5-9-3 **64**.................................... DanielMuscutt(3) 4
(John Berry) *midfield: rdn along over 5f out: sn lost pl and bhd* **12/1**

3m 12.76s (4.46) **Going Correction** +0.35s/f (Slow)
WFA 4 from 5yo+ 5lb **10** Ran SP% **112.6**
Speed ratings (Par 103): **101,100,99,99,96 95,94,85,72,38**
CSF £21.97 CT £142.99 TOTE £4.20: £1.80, £2.00, £3.30; EX 23.00 Trifecta £171.90.
Owner K J McCourt & Partners **Bred** Gestut Brummerhof **Trained** Icomb, Gloucs

FOCUS
A fair handicap won by a progressive horse who beat a fair yardstick in the runner-up. The winner was value for a bit extra.

426 DAILY UNIBET EARLY PRICES FROM 9AM H'CAP 6f (F)
2:30 (2:33) (Class 5) (0-75,71) 4-Y-O+ **£3,234** (£962; £481; £240) **Stalls** Low

Form RPR
00-4 **1** **Razin' Hell**[31] 21 5-9-5 **69**..(v) BenCurtis 5 85+
(John Balding) *chsd ldrs: hdwy on outer over 2f out: rdn and hung lft over 1f out: kpt on to ld ins fnl f: drvn out* **5/1**[2]
3-31 **2** *2 ½* **Jacob's Pillow**[23] 135 5-9-7 **71**.................................... DanielTudhope 1 79
(Rebecca Bastiman) *trckd ldrs on inner: hdwy over 2f out: rdn to ld jst over 1f out: drvn and hdd ins fnl f: kpt on same pce* **11/2**[3]
-330 **3** *2 ¼* **Elusivity (IRE)**[12] 278 8-9-5 **69**......................................(p) TomEaves 6 70
(Conor Dore) *sn led: rdn along over 2f out: drvn over 1f out: hdd appr fnl f: kpt on same pce* **20/1**
2-66 **4** *1 ½* **Borough Boy (IRE)**[14] 250 6-9-6 **70**..........................(v) TonyHamilton 9 66
(Derek Shaw) *cl up on outer: rdn 2f out and ev ch tl drvn and one pce fr jst over 1f out* **10/1**
30-0 **5** *½* **Indian Affair**[16] 236 6-9-4 **68**......................................(bt) FrannyNorton 3 62
(Milton Bradley) *in tch on inner: rdn along 1/2-way: drvn 2f out and sn no imp* **20/1**
0-42 **6** *3 ¼* **Spowarticus**[19] 178 7-9-0 **64**..(v) KieranO'Neill 7 48
(Scott Dixon) *cl up: rdn and ev ch over 2f out: drvn wl over 1f out: hld whn n.m.r appr fnl f* **8/1**
3-21 **7** *3* **Fujin**[12] 272 5-9-4 **68**..(b) AdamKirby 2 42
(Shaun Harris) *towards rr: effrt and wd st: rdn over 2f out: sn no hdwy* **9/2**[1]
06-3 **8** *1 ¼* **Great Expectations**[19] 178 8-8-12 **62**..........................(vt) JoeFanning 8 40
(J R Jenkins) *dwlt: a in rr* **16/1**
00-5 **9** *½* **Golden Spun (USA)**[12] 278 4-9-3 **67**.......................... AndrewMullen 4 36
(Michael Dods) *a towards rr* **10/1**
525- **10** *nse* **Pennine Warrior**[68] 8004 5-9-7 **71**..................................(b) LukeMorris 11 40
(Scott Dixon) *sn rdn along on outer: a towards rr* **8/1**
0-60 **11** *hd* **Colourbearer (IRE)**[10] 319 9-9-3 **67**............................(t) OisinMurphy 10 35
(Charlie Wallis) *dwlt: hdwy and in tch 1/2-way: wd st: sn rdn and wknd* **12/1**

1m 17.74s (1.24) **Going Correction** +0.35s/f (Slow) **11** Ran SP% **113.7**
Speed ratings (Par 103): **105,101,98,96,96 91,87,86,85,85 85**
CSF £31.49 CT £505.78 TOTE £5.50: £2.60, £1.90, £6.10; EX 29.30 Trifecta £533.10.
Owner Timms, Timms & McCabe **Bred** Alan J McCabe **Trained** Scrooby, S Yorks

FOCUS
This should prove solid enough form for the level, the winner finding some more improvement on just his second start for John Balding. The form is rated around the runner-up.

427 LADBROKES CLAIMING STKS 1m (F)
3:00 (3:00) (Class 6) 4-Y-O+ **£2,587** (£770; £384; £192) **Stalls** Low

Form RPR
60-6 **1** **Dominandros (FR)**[12] 266 5-8-3 77........................(b[1]) RhiainIngram(7) 3 81
(Gay Kelleway) *trckd ldr: cl up 1/2-way: pushed along and sltly outpcd 3f out: sn cl up again: rdn to chal over 1f out: led ins fnl f: styd on wl towards fin* **13/2**[3]
0-60 **2** *2 ¼* **Eutropius (IRE)**[7] 337 7-9-2 85..................................... BenCurtis 5 82
(Alan Swinbank) *set stdy pce: qcknd 3f out: jnd 2f out and sn rdn: drvn over 1f out: hdd ins fnl f: kpt on same pce* **7/2**[2]
63-1 **3** *2 ¼* **Patriotic (IRE)**[28] 49 8-9-5 80..................................(p) LukeMorris 1 79
(Chris Dwyer) *trckd ldng pair: pushed along 3f out: rdn 2f out: drvn over 1f out: sn one pce* **8/15**[1]
003- **4** *hd* **Red Touch (USA)**[90] 5167 4-8-7 68.............................. AdamBeschizza 2 67
(Dave Roberts) *hld up in rr: hdwy on inner to chse ldr 3f out: styd nr inner rail and rdn over 2f out: sn drvn and one pce* **12/1**

1m 46.38s (2.68) **Going Correction** +0.35s/f (Slow) **4** Ran SP% **108.5**
Speed ratings (Par 101): **100,97,95,95**
.Dominandros (FR) was the subject of a friendly claim for £6,000.\n\x\x Red Touch (USA) was claimed by Mr Michael Appleby £3,000.
Owner Winterbeck Manor Stud & Partners **Bred** S C E A Haras De La Perelle **Trained** Exning, Suffolk

FOCUS
With the favourite clearly below par this was a claimer which probably didn't take much winning. The form could conceibvably be rated up to 8lb better. The pace was on the steady side.

428 LADBROKES MAIDEN STKS 1m (F)
3:30 (3:32) (Class 5) 3-Y-O+ **£3,234** (£962; £481; £240) **Stalls** Low

Form RPR
1 **Flymetothestars** 3-8-8 0.. LukeMorris 1 85
(Sir Mark Prescott Bt) *trckd ldrs: hdwy over 3f out: chsd ldr wl over 2f out: chal wl over 1f out and sn rdn: drvn ent fnl f: styd on wl u.p to ld nr fin* **5/1**[3]
3- **2** *nk* **Hermitage Bay (USA)**[55] 8152 3-8-8 0.............................. RobertTart 9 84
(John Gosden) *cl up: led 1/2-way: rdn along over 2f out and sn jnd: slt ld and drvn ent fnl f: hdd and no ex nr fin* **8/13**[1]
0 **3** *12* **Flying Lesson (IRE)**[8] 331 3-8-8 0.................................... JoeFanning 2 56
(Mark Johnston) *trckd ldrs: hdwy 3f out: rdn along over 2f out: drvn wl over 1f out and sn one pce* **10/1**
3 **4** *shd* **Playful Dude (USA)**[22] 139 3-8-8 0................................ OisinMurphy 8 56
(David Simcock) *in tch: hdwy over 3f out: rdn to chse ldng pair wl over 1f out: sn drvn and kpt on one pce* **7/2**[2]
0- **5** *9* **Almutamarred (USA)**[264] 2207 4-9-13 0.......................... TimmyMurphy 7 40
(Kevin Morgan) *towards rr and swtchd rt to outer after 1f: bhd tl sme late hdwy* **40/1**
6- **6** *shd* **Ronaldjamessach (IRE)**[47] 8266 3-8-8 0............................. ShaneGray 6 35
(James Bethell) *prom: pushed along 1/2-way: sn rdn and wknd over 3f out* **33/1**
44 **7** *nk* **Red Chatterbox (IRE)**[14] 249 3-8-3 0............................. KieranO'Neill 4 29
(Scott Dixon) *slt ld on inner: hdd 1/2-way: cl up: rdn along 3f out: drvn over 2f out and sn wknd* **33/1**
43 **8** *2 ½* **Moonshine Ridge (IRE)**[19] 180 5-9-8 0............................. BenCurtis 5 28
(Alan Swinbank) *dwlt: a in rr* **20/1**
9 *hd* **Indibeau** 4-9-8 0.. AndrewMullen 3 28
(Garry Moss) *cl up: rdn along wl over 3f out: sn outpcd* **66/1**
0-00 **10** *19* **Dynamo (IRE)**[15] 245 5-9-13 0.. ShaneKelly 10
(Richard Hughes) *dwlt: a in rr* **66/1**

1m 44.63s (0.93) **Going Correction** +0.35s/f (Slow)
WFA 3 from 4yo+ 19lb **10** Ran SP% **126.0**
Speed ratings (Par 103): **109,108,96,96,87 87,87,84,84,65**
CSF £8.93 TOTE £9.90: £2.60, £1.10, £2.50; EX 11.30 Trifecta £55.60.
Owner Lady Bamford **Bred** Lady Bamford **Trained** Newmarket, Suffolk

FOCUS
Clearly not a maiden with much depth to it but probably still best to view the leading pair in a positive light, particularly the winner who overcome greenness to strike on debut. The time was relatively good.

429 DOWNLOAD THE LADBROKES APP H'CAP 1m (F)
4:00 (4:01) (Class 6) (0-65,65) 4-Y-O+ **£2,587** (£770; £384; £192) **Stalls** Low

Form RPR
0-51 **1** **The Firm (IRE)**[12] 277 7-9-1 **62**..................................(be) RobHornby(3) 4 70
(Daniel Mark Loughnane) *hld up in tch: hdwy wl over 2f out: chsd ldrs and nt clr run over 1f out: swtchd lft and rdn ent fnl f: styd on wl to ld nr fin* **10/1**[3]
0-13 **2** *shd* **Stun Gun**[12] 277 6-8-13 **57**...(p) TonyHamilton 2 63
(Derek Shaw) *trckd ldrs on inner: hdwy over 2f out: led wl over 1f out: rdn and hung rt ins fnl f: hdd and no ex towards fin* **20/1**
100- **3** *1 ¼* **Golden Wedding (IRE)**[49] 8228 4-9-7 **65**......................(p) ShaneKelly 7 68
(Eve Johnson Houghton) *prom: rdn over 2f out: sn ev ch: drvn over 1f out: kpt on same pce fnl f* **14/1**
4-62 **4** *6* **Deep Resolve (IRE)**[5] 367 5-9-7 **65**................................ BenCurtis 10 54
(Alan Swinbank) *s.i.s: hdwy on outer to join ldrs after 3f: rdn along over 2f out: drvn over 1f out: sn edgd lft and wknd* **2/1**[2]
32-1 **5** *3 ¼* **Berkshire Beauty**[7] 336 4-9-1 **59** 6ex.............................. OisinMurphy 9 40
(Andrew Balding) *towards rr: pushed along 1/2-way: rdn and outpcd over 3f out: hdwy 2f out: kpt on appr fnl f: n.d* **5/4**[1]
600- **6** *1 ¾* **Response**[76] 7886 6-9-7 **65**...(p) AndrewMullen 1 42
(Michael Appleby) *cl up on inner: slt ld after 3f: hdd 3f out and sn rdn: wknd wl over 1f out* **33/1**
1/0- **7** *4* **Colour My World**[290] 1504 6-9-4 **62**.................................. JoeFanning 6 29
(Ed McMahon) *slt ld 3f: cl up: led again 3f out: rdn over 2f out: hdd and drvn wl over 1f out: sn wknd* **50/1**

200- **8** 1/2 **Prayer Time**^{222} 3568 4-9-7 **65** .... SaleemGolam 8 31
(Mark H Tompkins) *a towards rr* **12/1**

100- **9** 2 1/2 **Dovil's Duel (IRE)**^{53} 8176 5-9-2 **63** .... EoinWalsh$^{(3)}$ 5 23
(Tony Newcombe) *hld up: hdwy to chse ldrs over 3f out: sn rdn along: drvn over 2f out and n.d* **33/1**

20-3 **10** 10 **Shearian**^{19} 179 6-9-6 **64** .... DougieCostello 3
(Tracy Waggott) *prom: rdn along wl over 3f out: sn wknd* **28/1**

06-0 **11** 11 **Cyflymder (IRE)**^{25} 97 10-8-11 **55** .... StevieDonohoe 11
(David C Griffiths) *chsd ldrs towards outer: pushed along 1/2-way: rdn and lost pl over 3f out: wd st and bhd* **66/1**

1m 46.25s (2.55) **Going Correction** +0.35s/f (Slow) **11** Ran SP% **118.8**
Speed ratings (Par 101): **101,100,99,93,90 88,84,84,81,71 60**
CSF £189.64 CT £2831.66 TOTE £11.00: £3.50, £4.50, £12.00; EX 110.30 Trifecta £1703.60.
Owner Amazing Racing **Bred** Sir E J Loder **Trained** Baldwin's Gate, Staffs

FOCUS
A run-of-the-mill affair, the two market leaders not in anything like the same form as they were here last week. The pace was sound and the first three were clear.

430 BET NOW WITH THE LADBROKES APP H'CAP 7f (F)
4:30 (4:32) (Class 6) (0-60,60) 4-Y-O+ **£2,587** (£770; £384; £192) **Stalls** Low

Form RPR

040- **1** **Trust Me Boy**^{68} 8008 8-9-7 **60** .... FrannyNorton 2 66
(John E Long) *slt ld on inner: edgd rt to centre in st: rdn along over 2f out: hdd briefly 1 1/2f out: drvn and rallied to ld jst over 1f out and sn hung rt: kpt on* **8/1**

01-0 **2** 3/4 **Princess Peaches**^{28} 49 4-9-5 **58** .... DanielTudhope 7 62
(James Bethell) *trckd ldrs: hdwy over 3f out: wd st and chal 2f out: rdn to ld briefly 1 1/2f out: sn hdd and swtchd lft ent fnl f: kpt on same pce* **11/1**

-233 **3** 1 1/2 **Ertidaad (IRE)**^{5} 356 4-9-4 **57** ....(b) TonyHamilton 8 57
(Emma Owen) *trckd ldrs on outer: wd st: hdwy 2f out: rdn wl over 1f out: kpt on u.p fnl f* **9/2**^{2}

0-55 **4** 3/4 **Cadeaux Pearl**^{19} 178 8-9-2 **55** .... LukeMorris 6 53
(Scott Dixon) *trckd ldrs: hdwy 3f out and sn rdn along: drvn wl over 1f out: kpt on fnl f* **11/1**

21-6 **5** 1/2 **Grey Destiny**^{31} 25 6-8-12 **58** ....(p) MathewStill$^{(7)}$ 3 55
(Antony Brittain) *s.i.s and bhd: hdwy wl over 2f out: rdn wl over 1f out: styd on to chse ldrs fnl f: nrst fin* **11/2**^{3}

5-13 **6** 1/2 **Falcon's Reign (FR)**^{14} 246 7-8-10 **56** ....(p) RPWalsh$^{(7)}$ 9 51
(Michael Appleby) *cl up: chal on outer 3f out: sn rdn and ev ch tl drvn wl over 1f out and grad wknd* **7/2**^{1}

34-4 **7** 4 **Zed Candy Girl**^{18} 201 6-9-3 **56** ....(p) AdamKirby 1 40
(Daniel Mark Loughnane) *towards rr and swtchd rt to outer after 1f: wd st: a towards rr* **8/1**

5-63 **8** 6 **Rosie Crowe (IRE)**^{12} 270 4-8-11 **50** ....(v) ShaneGray 4 18
(Shaun Harris) *cl up: rdn along 3f out: drvn over 2f out and sn wknd* **14/1**

-040 **9** 1 3/4 **Devilution (IRE)**^{13} 252 4-8-7 **46** oh1 ....(v) MartinLane 5 9
(Derek Shaw) *cl up: rdn along 3f out: sn wknd* **8/1**

1m 32.61s (2.31) **Going Correction** +0.35s/f (Slow) **9** Ran SP% **112.5**
Speed ratings (Par 101): **100,99,97,96,96 95,90,84,82**
CSF £88.54 CT £444.03 TOTE £9.50: £2.90, £4.00, £1.70; EX 110.20 Trifecta £554.20.
Owner R Pearson & J Pearson **Bred** S & Mrs M Bayless **Trained** Royston, Herts

FOCUS
A modest handicap, and straightforward form.
T/Jkpt: Not won. T/Plt: £1,620.90 to a £1 stake. Pool: £96,966.56 - 43.67 winning tickets. T/Qpdt: £304.20 to a £1 stake. Pool: £7,946.15 - 19.32 winning tickets. **Joe Rowntree**

412 KEMPTON (A.W) (R-H)
Wednesday, February 3

OFFICIAL GOING: Polytrack: standard
Wind: virtually nil Weather: dry

431 ROBERT DYAS H'CAP 7f (P)
5:05 (5:05) (Class 7) (0-50,50) 4-Y-O+ **£1,940** (£577; £288; £144) **Stalls** Low

Form RPR

646- **1** **Yard Of Ale**^{50} 8235 5-9-2 **48** ....(b^{1}) TimClark$^{(3)}$ 7 53
(Martin Smith) *s.i.s and rdn along leaving stalls: racd off the pce in last pair: swtchd lft and effrt ent fnl 2f: str run u.p ins fnl f: to ld cl home* **9/1**

-633 **2** nk **Little Indian**^{2} 412 6-9-5 **48** .... AdamKirby 4 52
(J R Jenkins) *hld up off the pce in last quartet: clsd and swtchd rt over 1f out: hdwy u.p to chse ldrs 1f out: r.o to ld wl ins fnl f: hdd and no ex cl home* **11/4**^{1}

0-25 **3** 1/2 **Blistering Dancer (IRE)**^{7} 355 6-8-13 **45** .... GeorgeDowning$^{(3)}$ 6 48
(Tony Carroll) *led: clr 1/2-way: rdn over 1f out: tired ins fnl f: hdd and lost 2 pls wl ins fnl f* **20/1**

26-6 **4** nse **Wild Flower (IRE)**^{10} 321 4-9-7 **50** ....(b) KieranO'Neill 1 53
(Jimmy Fox) *chsd ldr: effrt and hung rt 2f out: kpt on u.p and pressing wnr ins fnl f: styd on same pce fnl 100yds* **5/1**^{3}

450- **5** 3/4 **Affectionate Lady (IRE)**^{135} 6580 5-9-3 **49** ......(v^{1}) NataliaGemelova$^{(3)}$ 9 50
(Keith Reveley) *s.i.s: hld up off the pce in last quartet: rdn and gd hdwy to chse ldrs 1f out: kpt on same pce ins fnl f* **20/1**

02/ **6** 3/4 **Tsar Paul (IRE)**^{5} 391 11-8-13 **47** ....(t) AnaO'Brien$^{(5)}$ 8 46+
(J A Nash, Ire) *hld up off the pce in last quartet: rdn and effrt 2f out: hdwy and hung rt 1f out: styd on wl u.p ins fnl f: nt rch ldrs* **9/2**^{2}

-345 **7** 1 **Sleet (IRE)**^{2} 412 5-9-7 **50** ....(b) LukeMorris 5 46
(Michael Appleby) *jostled leaving stalls: hld up in tch in midfield: swtchd rt and effrt u.p 2f out: sn chsng ldrs: no ex 1f out: wknd fnl 100yds* **8/1**

04-6 **8** 1 1/4 **Purford Green**^{21} 168 7-8-11 **45** ....(p) CallumShepherd$^{(5)}$ 10 38
(Michael Attwater) *wl in tch in midfield: effrt over 2f out: sn struggling to qckn: wknd ins fnl f* **40/1**

00-0 **9** 3/4 **My Bubba**^{19} 201 4-9-7 **50** .... WilliamTwiston-Davies 11 41
(Michael Blanshard) *taken down early: hld up in tch in midfield: rdn and unable qck over 2f out: wl hld and kpt on same pce fnl f* **25/1**

4-02 **10** 2 1/4 **Diamond Sam**^{7} 341 4-9-3 **46** .... ShaneKelly 13 30
(Sylvester Kirk) *t.k.h: chsd ldrs tl no ex u.p over 1f out: wknd ins fnl f* **8/1**

-052 **11** 4 **Loud**^{13} 270 6-9-4 **50** ....(b) SimonPearce$^{(3)}$ 12 24
(Lydia Pearce) *chsd ldrs: rdn ent fnl 2f: sn struggling: wknd over 1f out* **16/1**

56-6 **12** 5 **Oasis Rose (FR)**^{19} 202 4-9-3 **46** ....(p) MartinLane 3 6
(Jeremy Gask) *chsd ldrs: rdn 2f out: sn lost pl: wknd fnl f* **20/1**

00-0 **13** 3 3/4 **Just Marion (IRE)**^{14} 257 4-9-7 **50** .... SteveDrowne 2
(James Grassick) *in tch in midfield: rdn over 2f out: sn lost pl: bhd fnl f* **100/1**

1m 25.52s (-0.48) **Going Correction** -0.05s/f (Stan) **13** Ran SP% **121.2**
Speed ratings (Par 97): **100,99,99,99,98 97,96,94,93,91 86,81,76**
CSF £31.59 CT £502.89 TOTE £9.20: £3.00, £2.40, £5.10; EX 45.90 Trifecta £620.70.
Owner Martin Smith **Bred** The Hon Mrs E J Wills **Trained** Newmarket, Suffolk

FOCUS
A low-grade handicap run at a good gallop. Those close up set the level.

432 32RED ON THE APP STORE MEDIAN AUCTION MAIDEN STKS 6f (P)
5:40 (5:40) (Class 5) 3-5-Y-O **£2,911** (£866; £432; £216) **Stalls** Low

Form RPR

1 **Buying Trouble (USA)** 3-8-8 0 .... AndrewMullen 2 80+
(David Evans) *dwlt: in tch in rr of main gp: effrt ent fnl 2f: qcknd to ld over 1f out: r.o strly: readily* **10/3**^{2}

5- **2** 5 **Cultured Knight**^{49} 8243 3-8-13 0 .... ShaneKelly 5 69+
(Richard Hughes) *t.k.h: trckd ldrs: swtchd lft to press ldr and stl hld onto 2f out: rdn as wnr hit the front over 1f out: nvr gng pce of wnr but clr fnl f* **11/8**^{1}

5 **3** 2 3/4 **Summer Music (IRE)**^{13} 268 3-8-8 0 .... LukeMorris 7 55
(Robert Cowell) *dwlt and swtchd lft after s: in tch in rr of main gp: rdn jst over 2f out: outpcd over 1f out: plugged on into modest 3rd ins fnl f* **9/2**^{3}

0-30 **4** 2 1/2 **Rojina (IRE)**^{20} 177 3-8-8 60 .... JFEgan 1 47
(Joseph Tuite) *led: rdn 2f out: hdd and outpcd over 1f out: wknd fnl f* **10/1**

050- **5** 1 **Porcupine Creek (IRE)**^{102} 7453 3-8-13 55 .... DougieCostello 4 49
(Daniel Mark Loughnane) *chsd ldrs tl dropped to rr of main gp but stl wl in tch 1/2-way: outpcd u.p over 1f out: wknd fnl f* **6/1**

5-36 **6** 16 **Single Summit**^{18} 217 4-10-0 44 ....(v) AdamKirby 6
(J R Jenkins) *w ldr tl over 2f out: sn lost pl: bhd fnl f* **33/1**

7 8 **My Shootin Star** 3-8-5 0 .... RobHornby$^{(3)}$ 3
(Peter Hedger) *s.i.s: a detached in last: hung lft fr 4f out: t.o* **33/1**

1m 12.15s (-0.95) **Going Correction** -0.05s/f (Stan)
WFA 3 from 4yo 15lb **7** Ran SP% **112.6**
Speed ratings (Par 103): **104,97,93,90,89 67,57**
CSF £8.05 TOTE £4.40: £2.20, £1.30; EX 11.30 Trifecta £41.60.
Owner Mrs I M Folkes **Bred** Flaxman Holdings Limited **Trained** Pandy, Monmouths

FOCUS
An ordinary maiden, but there was plenty to like about the way the winner drew clear in the closing stages. The level is fluid.

433 32RED.COM H'CAP 7f (P)
6:10 (6:10) (Class 4) (0-85,85) 4-Y-O+ **£4,690** (£1,395; £697; £348) **Stalls** Low

Form RPR

0/-5 **1** **Mezmaar**^{17} 236 7-8-7 **71** oh1 .... JoeFanning 4 81
(Kevin Morgan) *taken down early: chsd ldrs: effrt to chse ldr 2f out: chal 1f out: sustained battle w runner-up tl forged ahd towards fin: drvn out* **8/1**^{3}

044- **2** 1/2 **Dutiful Son (IRE)**^{37} 8380 6-9-7 **85** .... JamieSpencer 3 93
(Simon Dow) *hld up in tch in midfield: swtchd rt and effrt wl over 1f out: led 1f out: sustained battle w wnr after: hdd and no ex towards fin* **11/4**^{1}

104- **3** 2 1/4 **Mystical Sapphire**^{34} 8412 6-9-0 **78** .... OisinMurphy 7 80
(Jo Crowley) *hld up in tch in midfield: effrt 2f out: hdwy 1f out: styd on wl ins fnl f to snatch 3rd on post: nvr threatened ldng pair* **9/1**

-211 **4** nse **Jammy Guest (IRE)**^{17} 231 6-9-2 **80** .... AdamKirby 12 82+
(George Margarson) *hld up off the pce in last trio: stl plenty to do and hdwy jst over 1f out: gd hdwy to chse clr ldng pair fnl 100yds: kpt on but no threat: lost 3rd on post* **7/2**^{2}

54-1 **5** 1/2 **Loyalty**^{28} 58 9-9-4 **82** ....(v) TonyHamilton 11 82
(Derek Shaw) *chsd ldr tl 2f out: 3rd and outpcd over 1f out: no threat to ldrs and styd on same pce ins fnl f* **16/1**

3-05 **6** 1 1/4 **Street Force (USA)**^{16} 240 5-9-2 **80** ....(tp) AndrewMullen 1 77
(Michael Appleby) *taken down early: in tch in midfield: effrt u.p 2f out: no imp over 1f out: styd on same pce fnl f* **20/1**

064- **7** 1/2 **Fever Few**^{48} 8262 7-8-13 **77** .... MartinHarley 5 73
(Chris Wall) *led: rdn over 1f out: hdd and no ex 1f out: lost 3rd fnl 100yds: wknd towards fin* **20/1**

3-42 **8** hd **Pour La Victoire (IRE)**^{2} 414 6-8-9 **73** ....(b) LukeMorris 14 68
(Tony Carroll) *stdd s: t.k.h: hld up in midfield and stuck wd: effrt 2f out: kpt on ins fnl f: nvr threatened ldrs* **14/1**

50-1 **9** 1/2 **Fleckerl (IRE)**^{14} 260 6-9-2 **80** ....(p) LiamKeniry 6 74
(Conor Dore) *stdd s: hld up in midfield: swtchd rt and effrt 2f out: no imp ent fnl f: wknd fnl 150yds* **8/1**^{3}

400- **10** nk **Multitask**^{37} 8382 6-8-11 **75** .... WilliamCarson 8 68
(Michael Madgwick) *stdd s: hld up off the pce in last: swtchd lft and effrt 2f: sme modest late hdwy: nvr trbld ldrs* **16/1**

206- **11** 3/4 **Ambitious Boy**^{65} 8050 7-8-6 **75** .... JosephineGordon$^{(5)}$ 2 66
(Sarah Hollinshead) *sn niggled along in midfield: dropped to last trio 4f out: no imp u.p 2f out: nvr trbld ldrs* **50/1**

05-0 **12** nk **Athletic**^{18} 221 7-8-13 **80** ....(v) DannyBrock$^{(3)}$ 10 70
(Andrew Reid) *hld up in tch in midfield: rdn and effrt 2f out: unable qck and btn 1f out: wl hld and kpt on same pce fnl f* **25/1**

16-0 **13** 6 **Renounce (IRE)**^{19} 198 4-8-11 **75** .... JimCrowley 13 49
(Jeremy Noseda) *wl in tch in midfield: u.p and unable qck over 2f out: lost pl over 1f out: wknd fnl f* **16/1**

01-3 **14** 1 1/4 **Luis Vaz De Torres (IRE)**^{18} 220 4-9-4 **82** .... JackGarritty 9 53
(Richard Fahey) *t.k.h: hld up in tch in midfield: rdn and edgd rt jst over 2f out: sn btn: bhd fnl f* **20/1**

1m 23.91s (-2.09) **Going Correction** -0.05s/f (Stan) **14** Ran SP% **125.5**
Speed ratings (Par 105): **109,108,105,105,105 103,103,103,102,102 101,100,94,92**
CSF £29.23 CT £214.86 TOTE £13.20: £5.00, £1.80, £3.20; EX 53.30 Trifecta £613.30.
Owner Roemex Ltd **Bred** Denford Stud Ltd **Trained** Gazeley, Suffolk

FOCUS
A good, competitive handicap, but the early gallop wasn't hectic. Sound form, with the runner-up rated to his best.

434 32RED H'CAP (LONDON MILE SERIES QUALIFIER) 1m (P)
6:40 (6:40) (Class 3) (0-95,88) 3-Y-O **£7,439** (£2,213; £1,106; £553) **Stalls** Low

Form RPR

51-1 **1** **Cape Speed (FR)**^{11} 315 3-9-7 **88** .... JoeFanning 3 95+
(Mark Johnston) *dwlt: sn rcvrd to chse ldr: shkn up to ld wl over 1f out: asserted ins fnl f: r.o wl and gng away at fin* **4/5**^{1}

131- **2** 1 1/2 **Nokhada (IRE)**^{39} 8358 3-9-3 **84** .... JamieSpencer 1 86
(David Simcock) *chsd ldng pair: swtchd rt and effrt 2f out: chalng and drvn 1f out: no ex and kpt on same pce fnl 100yds* **3/1**^{2}

4-12 **3** 2 **Winged Dancer**^{16} 243 3-8-11 **78** .... LukeMorris 2 75
(Sylvester Kirk) *awkward leaving stalls: hld up wl in tch in last pair: effrt wl over 1f out: drvn and battling for 3rd 1f out: kpt on to go 3rd wl ins fnl f: no threat to ldrs* **7/1**^{3}

324- **4** 1/2 **Peak Hill**^{138} 6492 3-8-10 **77** .... JFEgan 4 73
(David Evans) *t.k.h: led and set stdy gallop: rdn and hdd 2f out: 3rd and outpcd 1f out: kpt on same pce after: lost 3rd wl ins fnl f* **10/1**

02-3 **5** *2 ¼* **Lilbourne Prince (IRE)**[6] 366 3-8-4 **76**.............. JosephineGordon(5) 5 66
(David Evans) *t.k.h: hld up wl in tch in last pair: effrt 2f out: no imp and wl hld fnl f* **9/1**

1m 39.89s (0.09) **Going Correction** -0.05s/f (Stan) **5** Ran SP% **112.1**
Speed ratings (Par 101): **97,95,93,93,90**
CSF £3.55 TOTE £1.80: £1.20, £1.60; EX 4.10 Trifecta £6.40.
Owner Kingsley Park 3 - Originals **Bred** Famille Niarchos **Trained** Middleham Moor, N Yorks

FOCUS
The top weight was rated 7lb below the ceiling for the race, and this was a bit of a tactical affair, but the winner is progressive and would have been more superior with a faster pace. The third has been rated to his penultimate C&D form.

435 £10 FREE BET AT 32REDSPORT.COM H'CAP 1m 4f (P)
7:10 (7:11) (Class 6) (0-65,65) 4-Y-O+ **£2,264** (£673; £336; £168) **Stalls** Centre

Form RPR

1/ **1** **Kalahari (IRE)**[254] 7-9-6 **64**...(p) MartinHarley 8 72+
(Lucy Wadham) *stdd s: hld up in tch in midfield: clsd and gng wl over 2f out: rdn and qcknd to ld wl over 1f out: sn drifting rt: in command and r.o wl fnl f* **9/4**[1]

52-3 **2** *1 ¼* **Weld Arab (IRE)**[20] 173 5-9-5 **63**...................................... LukeMorris 5 69
(Michael Blake) *t.k.h: chsd ldrs: rdn ent fnl 2f: kpt on u.p to chse wnr ins fnl f: no imp but kpt on for clr 2nd* **6/1**[3]

30-2 **3** *1 ¼* **Red Dragon (IRE)**[28] 62 6-9-0 **58**................................... MartinLane 7 62
(Michael Blanshard) *chsd ldrs: effrt on inner to chal 2f out: 2nd and unable qck w wnr wl over 1f out: kpt on same pce and lost 2nd ins fnl f* **6/1**[3]

004/ **4** *2* **Bramshill Lass**[603] 3078 7-9-4 **62**....................................(t) JimCrowley 1 63
(Amanda Perrett) *chsd ldrs: rdn ent fnl 2f: kpt on same pce u.p ins fnl f* **20/1**

0-03 **5** *nk* **Innoko (FR)**[12] 295 6-9-3 **61**... WilliamCarson 4 61
(Tony Carroll) *hld up in tch in midfield: shuffled bk towards rr over 3f out: hdwy u.p over 1f out: styd on same pce ins fnl f* **6/1**[3]

0-54 **6** *nse* **Munsarim (IRE)**[12] 289 9-9-2 **60**.................................(b) ShaneKelly 11 60
(Lee Carter) *s.i.s: hld up in rr: hdwy on outer 4f out: rdn and no hdwy over 1f out: kpt on same pce ins fnl f* **33/1**

4-0 **7** *3 ½* **Put The Boot In (IRE)**[21] 164 4-8-11 **65**................. CharlieBennett(7) 6 60
(Barry Brennan) *hld up in tch towards rr: rdn over 2f out: sme hdwy over 1f out: kpt on same pce ins fnl f: nvr trbld ldrs* **66/1**

260- **8** *nse* **Unex Modigliani (IRE)**[28] 7679 7-9-1 **59**.................(tp) TonyHamilton 12 54
(Derek Shaw) *s.i.s: t.k.h in rr: stl last and rdn over 2f out: no ch but styd on ins fnl f: nvr trbld ldrs* **14/1**

60-0 **9** *½* **Several (USA)**[21] 164 4-9-4 **65**.................................... DougieCostello 2 59
(Kevin Frost) *hld up in tch in last quartet: effrt on inner 2f out: sn no imp u.p: nvr trbld ldrs* **25/1**

/0-5 **10** *3* **Altaira**[21] 164 5-9-7 **65**... AdamKirby 9 54
(Tony Carroll) *led tl 7f out: chsd ldr tl clsd to ld over 2f out: hdd and unable qck wl over 1f out: wknd fnl f* **11/2**[2]

4-00 **11** *14* **El Tel**[14] 263 4-9-3 **64**... JackMitchell 10 31
(Roger Varian) *stdd s: t.k.h: hld up in trio: swtchd lft and hdwy over 8f out: led 7f out tl rdn and hdd over 2f out: dropped out rapidly over 1f out: wl bhd and eased ins fnl f* **16/1**

2m 36.83s (2.33) **Going Correction** -0.05s/f (Stan)
WFA 4 from 5yo+ 3lb **11** Ran SP% **114.6**
Speed ratings (Par 101): **90,89,88,87,86 86,84,84,84,82 72**
CSF £14.39 CT £70.68 TOTE £4.40: £2.40, £2.90, £1.10; EX 21.50 Trifecta £111.40.
Owner Dai Griffiths **Bred** Summerhill Bloodstock **Trained** Newmarket, Suffolk

FOCUS
A modest handicap run at a stop-start pace and won comfortably by the well-backed favourite.

436 32RED CASINO H'CAP 6f (P)
7:40 (7:41) (Class 6) (0-55,55) 3-Y-O **£2,264** (£673; £336; £168) **Stalls** Low

Form RPR

3U-5 **1** **Leitrim Traveller (USA)**[15] 248 3-9-1 **49**.................(b) WilliamCarson 8 55
(Jamie Osborne) *taken down early: sn bustled up to ld and mde virtually all: rdn and wnt clr 2f out: 4 l clr and drvn over 1f out: tiring but a holding on ins fnl f: rdn out* **15/2**

3-66 **2** *1 ½* **Intimately**[9] 327 3-9-5 **53**.. OisinMurphy 5 56
(Jonathan Portman) *chsd wnr: rdn and unable qck 2f out: kpt on u.p ins fnl f but nvr getting to wnr* **13/2**

6-04 **3** *2 ¼* **Ashford Island**[9] 327 3-9-0 **48**.......................................(p) TedDurcan 4 43+
(Mike Murphy) *hld up in midfield: effrt 2f out: kpt on ins fnl f to go 3rd cl home: no ch w wnr* **6/1**[3]

2-22 **4** *nk* **Kristoff (IRE)**[9] 328 3-9-2 **50**.. AdamKirby 7 44
(Jim Boyle) *chsd ldrs: 3rd and outpcd u.p 2f out: wl hld but battled on in wl btn 3rd tl lost 3rd cl home* **7/4**[1]

00-4 **5** *½* **Kiringa**[19] 193 3-9-2 **50**.. LukeMorris 1 42
(William Knight) *chsd ldrs: rdn and outpcd 2f out: battling for wl hld 3rd after: kpt on same pce u.p fnl f* **16/1**

03-6 **6** *2 ½* **Fiftytintsofsilver (IRE)**[20] 181 3-9-4 **52**................(p) AdamBeschizza 3 37
(Gay Kelleway) *stdd s: hld up towards rr: effrt on inner 2f out: no imp and wl hld over 1f out* **33/1**

25-5 **7** *nk* **Thief Of Hearts**[29] 47 3-9-2 **55**...............................(b[1]) RyanWhile(5) 2 39
(Bill Turner) *dwlt and short of room leaving stalls: in rr: rdn over 2f out: no imp: n.d* **33/1**

06-2 **8** *hd* **Clevedon Court**[7] 345 3-9-7 **55**... ShaneKelly 9 41
(Gary Moore) *hld up in last pair: clipped heels and stmbld after 1f: swtchd lft and effrt over 2f out: no hdwy* **4/1**[2]

56-5 **9** *2 ¾* **Oak Forest**[19] 193 3-8-13 **50**................................... RobHornby(3) 6 25
(Michael Attwater) *hld up in tch: heels clipped and lost action briefly 4f out: rdn over 2f out: no hdwy* **33/1**

0-00 **10** *nk* **Justice (IRE)**[20] 174 3-8-12 **46** oh1.............................. JimmyQuinn 10 20
(Dean Ivory) *t.k.h: hld up wl in tch in midfield: rdn jst over 2f out: sn btn: wknd over 1f out* **50/1**

1m 13.49s (0.39) **Going Correction** -0.05s/f (Stan) **10** Ran SP% **112.4**
Speed ratings (Par 95): **95,93,90,89,88 85,85,84,81,80**
CSF £51.59 CT £309.99 TOTE £7.00: £2.40, £2.40, £2.30; EX 80.00 Trifecta £495.20.
Owner Chris Watkins And David N Reynolds **Bred** Mill Ridge Farm Ltd **Trained** Upper Lambourn, Berks

FOCUS
A moderate sprint and not the deepest even allowing for the grade.
T/Jkpt: Not won. T/Plt: £90.90 to a £1 stake. Pool: £80,959.72 - 649.85 winning units. T/Qpdt: £20.50 to a £1 stake. Pool: £9,701.94 - 349.03 winning units. **Steve Payne**

[356] CHELMSFORD (A.W) (L-H)
Thursday, February 4

OFFICIAL GOING: Polytrack: standard
Wind: virtually nil Weather: dry

437 FIND NEW CUSTOMER OFFERS AT SIGNUPBONUSES.CO.UK APPRENTICE H'CAP 1m (P)
5:10 (5:10) (Class 5) (0-70,70) 4-Y-O+ **£5,175** (£1,540; £769; £384) **Stalls** Low

Form RPR

00-1 **1** **Giovanni Di Bicci**[8] 346 4-8-5 **61** 6ex.......................(t) LuluStanford(7) 8 74+
(Jim Boyle) *stdd s: hld up in last pair: stl plenty to do and effrt on outer 2f out: 4th and clsng 1f out: edging lft and pressing ldrs 100yds out: led fnl 50yds: r.o* **15/8**[1]

606- **2** *nk* **Pyla (IRE)**[84] 7813 4-8-10 **64**.. EvaMoscrop(5) 9 70
(Denis Quinn) *led: rdn and kicked clr of field w rival 2f out: kpt on wl u.p tl hdd and no ex fnl 50yds* **25/1**

004/ **3** *¾* **Anton Chigurh**[492] 6841 7-9-0 **68**................................ PaddyBradley(5) 5 72
(Philip McBride) *chsd ldr: rdn to press ldr and kicked clr of field 2f out: kpt on but unable qck ins fnl f: lost 2nd fnl 75yds* **14/1**

0-30 **4** *1 ¾* **Mr Red Clubs (IRE)**[15] 256 7-9-0 **70**............................. JaneElliott(7) 2 70
(Michael Appleby) *in tch in midfield: effrt ent fnl 2f out: chsd clr ldng pair 1f out: kpt on: squeezed of room fnl 100yds: 4th and kpt on same pce after* **9/2**[2]

621- **5** *2 ¾* **Pendo**[36] 8396 5-9-5 **68**... CamHardie 4 62
(Paul Cole) *taken down early: chsd ldng pair: rdn and outpcd over 2f out: lost btn 3rd 1f out: wknd ins fnl f* **6/1**[3]

000- **6** *1 ¼* **Little Lord Nelson**[45] 8325 4-8-9 **65**............................(t) MillyNaseb(7) 6 56
(Stuart Williams) *hld up in rr: stl plenty to do and effrt over 1f out: no real imp fnl f: nvr trbld ldrs* **8/1**

00-4 **7** *1 ¾* **Gabrial The Thug (FR)**[15] 263 6-8-11 **60**..................(t) SammyJoBell 1 47
(Richard Fahey) *in tch in midfield: rdn over 2f out: lost pl and btn over 1f out* **7/1**

166- **8** *½* **Theydon Bois**[223] 3603 4-8-11 **65**..................(v[1]) JosephineGordon(5) 10 51
(Peter Charalambous) *dwlt: sn bustled and steadily rcvrd: 4th 1/2-way: rdn and outpcd over 2f out: lost pl and btn over 1f out* **20/1**

13/3 **9** *1* **Mr Shekells**[11] 321 4-9-2 **65**.. DannyBrock 7 49
(Philip McBride) *in tch in midfield: rdn over 2f out: lost pl over 1f out: bhd fnl f* **10/1**

1m 37.86s (-2.04) **Going Correction** -0.25s/f (Stan) **9** Ran SP% **115.2**
Speed ratings (Par 103): **100,99,98,97,94 93,91,90,89**
CSF £56.23 CT £521.65 TOTE £2.60: £1.20, £4.60, £3.50; EX 53.00 Trifecta £523.50.
Owner Epsom Equine Spa Partnership **Bred** Vimal And Gillian Khosla **Trained** Epsom, Surrey

FOCUS
The early pace wasn't that strong, which suited the runner-up and third, who were up there throughout. Credit goes to the winner, who came from well back. The form is rated around the third.

438 SCOOP6SOCCER THE £1 MILLION FOOTBALL BET H'CAP 1m 2f (P)
5:40 (5:40) (Class 5) (0-70,68) 4-Y-O+ **£5,175** (£1,540; £769; £384) **Stalls** Low

Form RPR

500- **1** **Biff Johnson (IRE)**[115] 7164 4-9-5 **67**............................(p) PhillipMakin 1 82
(Keith Dalgleish) *hld up in tch in midfield: 4th and travelling wl whn nt clr run over 2f out: rdn and hdwy to ld over 1f out: r.o strly: easily* **9/4**[1]

20-2 **2** *4 ½* **Comanche Chieftain (CAN)**[19] 212 4-9-5 **67**.........(p) AndrewMullen 5 73
(Michael Appleby) *led: 6 l clr 1/2-way: pressed and rdn over 2f out: hdd over 1f out: no ch w wnr fnl f: kpt on to hold 2nd* **10/3**[2]

05-3 **3** *1 ¾* **Flying Fantasy**[29] 64 4-9-3 **65**...................................... SaleemGolam 6 68
(Stuart Williams) *stdd s: t.k.h: hld up in midfield: clsd and in tch 3f out: swtchd lft and effrt over 1f out: wnt 3rd 150yds: kpt on: no ch w wnr* **4/1**[3]

36-5 **4** *½* **Sacred Square (GER)**[19] 218 6-9-4 **65**.........................(p) LiamKeniry 7 67
(Conor Dore) *stdd s: hld up in last trio: plenty to do and effrt on inner over 1f out: kpt on wl to go 4th fnl 100yds: nvr trbld ldrs* **33/1**

61-3 **5** *2 ¾* **Enriching (USA)**[19] 212 8-9-7 **68**.............................. StevieDonohoe 2 64
(Robyn Brisland) *chsd ldrs: clsd and cl 3rd 3f out: unable qck u.p over 1f out: wknd fnl f* **9/2**

442- **6** *3 ¼* **Ifan (IRE)**[135] 5716 8-9-7 **68**.. AdamKirby 10 58
(Tim Vaughan) *chsd ldr tl fnd little for press over 1f out: sn lost pl: wknd fnl f* **8/1**

6-10 **7** *1 ¾* **Jethou Island**[18] 232 5-8-11 **58**....................................(t) ShaneKelly 9 44
(David Menuisier) *in tch in midfield: rdn ent fnl 2f: sn outpcd: wl hld 1f out* **14/1**

20-0 **8** *1* **Mediate**[28] 88 5-9-4 **65**.. AdamBeschizza 4 49
(Richard Rowe) *hld up in last trio: rdn 2f out: sn btn* **33/1**

300- **9** *nk* **Voice Of A Leader (IRE)**[45] 8336 5-9-4 **65**.................. WilliamCarson 8 48
(Andi Brown) *taken down early: stdd s: t.k.h: hld up in last trio: effrt and sme hdwy on outer 3f out: sn btn: bhd 1f out* **25/1**

2m 5.51s (-3.09) **Going Correction** -0.25s/f (Stan)
WFA 4 from 5yo+ 1lb **9** Ran SP% **119.5**
Speed ratings (Par 103): **102,98,97,96,94 91,90,89,89**
CSF £10.07 CT £27.89 TOTE £3.00: £1.10, £1.60, £2.10; EX 12.30 Trifecta £49.20.
Owner Ronnie Docherty **Bred** Frank Dunne **Trained** Carluke, S Lanarks

FOCUS
The leader set a good gallop and this proved a true test. The winner could do better again.

439 PLAY SCOOP6SOCCER THIS SATURDAY H'CAP 5f (P)
6:10 (6:10) (Class 4) (0-80,85) 4-Y-O+ **£8,086** (£2,406; £1,202; £601) **Stalls** Low

Form RPR

4131 **1** **Bosham**[7] 359 6-9-6 **85** 6ex.......................................(bt) NathanEvans(7) 3 100
(Michael Easterby) *racd keenly: mde all: rdn over 1f out: in command and styd on wl fnl f* **3/1**[2]

-262 **2** *2 ¼* **Saved My Bacon (IRE)**[7] 359 5-8-6 **69**.............. JosephineGordon(5) 5 76
(Chris Dwyer) *in tch in 4th: effrt 2f out: styd on same pce ins fnl f: wnt 2nd last strides* **2/1**[1]

55-3 **3** *hd* **Secret Asset (IRE)**[22] 162 11-8-12 **73**......................(v[1]) RobHornby(3) 2 79
(Lisa Williamson) *chsd ldng pair: effrt to chse wnr over 1f out: styd on same pce ins fnl f: lost 2nd last strides* **8/1**

4-31 **4** *1 ¾* **Welease Bwian (IRE)**[22] 162 7-8-4 **69**....................(be) MillyNaseb(7) 1 69
(Stuart Williams) *hld up in tch in last pair: effrt over 1f out: no imp fnl f* **3/1**[2]

6-26 **5** *hd* **Saint Pois (FR)**[3] 416 5-8-12 **73**............................ GeorgeDowning(3) 4 72
(Tony Carroll) *awkward as stalls opened and s.i.s: hld up in rr: effrt u.p over 1f out: no imp fnl f* **5/1**[3]

06-2 **6** *nk* **Desert Strike**[18] 236 10-9-4 **76**..........(p) JFEgan 6 74
(Conor Dore) *chsd wnr tl lost pl u.p over 1f out: wknd ins fnl f* **8/1**

58.01s (-2.19) **Going Correction** -0.25s/f (Stan) **6** Ran SP% **122.2**
Speed ratings (Par 105): **107,103,103,100,99 99**
CSF £10.54 TOTE £4.30: £1.90, £1.50; EX 7.80 Trifecta £67.90.
Owner Peter Easterby **Bred** Rabbah Bloodstock Limited **Trained** Sheriff Hutton, N Yorks

FOCUS
This was all about the winner, who made all once again. The time was good. The third has been rated to his C&D latest.

440 WIN A FOOTBALL FORTUNE WITH SCOOP6SOCCER H'CAP 1m 6f (P)
6:40 (6:40) (Class 4) (0-85,84) 4-Y-O+ **£8,086** (£2,406; £1,202; £601) **Stalls** Low

Form RPR
52-4 **1** **Cotton Club (IRE)**[22] 165 5-9-11 **84**.......... RyanTate(3) 4 92
(Rod Millman) *hld up in tch in last trio: effrt wd 2f out: hdwy over 1f out: styd on to ld fnl 75yds: rdn out* **6/1**[3]

0-16 **2** *1* **Oratorio's Joy (IRE)**[6] 385 6-9-7 **77**.......... WilliamCarson 1 83
(Jamie Osborne) *in tch in midfield: effrt on inner over 1f out: ev ch ins fnl f: styd on same pce fnl 75yds: wnt 2nd last stride* **20/1**

13-3 **3** *shd* **Scarlet Minstrel**[28] 78 4-9-3 **78**.......... OisinMurphy 5 84
(Andrew Balding) *t.k.h: chsd ldr tl 1/2-way: styd prom: effrt 2f out: rdn to ld over 1f out: hdd and no ex fnl 75yds: lost 2nd last stride* **4/1**[2]

11-2 **4** *½* **Duchess Of Marmite (IRE)**[20] 208 4-9-8 **83**..........(b) ShaneKelly 9 89+
(Richard Hughes) *stdd s: hld up in last: clsd but stl last whn nt clr run over 1f out: swtchd lft and effrt ent fnl f: no imp tl styd on towards fin: nvr gng to rch ldrs* **7/4**[1]

2-44 **5** *nk* **Precision Five**[17] 244 7-9-9 **84**..........(p) JosephineGordon(5) 2 89
(Alan King) *in tch in midfield: effrt over 2f out: hdwy over 1f out: chsd ldrs ins fnl f: no ex and one pce wl ins fnl f* **8/1**

341- **6** *nk* **Cotillion**[13] 8257 10-8-10 **69**..........(p) GeorgeDowning(3) 8 73
(Ian Williams) *s.i.s: hld up in last pair: effrt over 1f out: sn swtchd lft: chsd ldrs and kpt on same pce fnl 100yds* **6/1**[3]

425- **7** *2* **Treasure The Ridge (IRE)**[38] 8379 7-9-13 **83**..........(b) JFEgan 7 85
(Andrew Reid) *chsd ldng trio: effrt 2f out: swtchd rt over 1f out: no ex jst ins fnl f: outpcd fnl 100yds* **10/1**

42-4 **8** *4* **Brassbound (USA)**[34] 6 8-10-0 **84**.......... AndrewMullen 3 80
(Michael Appleby) *chsd ldrs tl wnt 2nd 1/2-way: ev ch and rdn over 2f out: no ex 1f out: sn wknd* **16/1**

550- **9** *11* **Dabadiyan (IRE)**[65] 8064 6-9-7 **77**..........(v) GeorgeBaker 6 58
(Gary Moore) *led and set stdy gallop: rdn and hdd over 1f out: sn outpcd: bhd and eased ins fnl f* **11/1**

2m 59.66s (-3.54) **Going Correction** -0.25s/f (Stan)
WFA 4 from 5yo+ 5lb **9** Ran SP% **124.1**
Speed ratings (Par 105): **100,99,99,99,98 98,97,95,89**
CSF £123.11 CT £549.30 TOTE £14.40: £3.90, £3.70, £1.60; EX 126.60 Trifecta £683.70.
Owner The Links Partnership **Bred** Patrick Gleeson **Trained** Kentisbeare, Devon

FOCUS
Not a bad handicap, but they finished in a bit of a heap after a steady pace. The form is rated through the second.

441 BET SCOOP6SOCCER AT BETFRED.COM MAIDEN FILLIES' STKS 6f (P)
7:10 (7:10) (Class 5) 3-Y-O+ **£5,175** (£1,540; £769; £384) **Stalls** Centre

Form RPR
2 **1** **Semra (USA)**[27] 102 3-8-10 0.......... DanielMuscutt(3) 1 69+
(Marco Botti) *mde virtually all: rdn hands and heels and asserted ent fnl f: r.o wl: comf* **8/15**[1]

-0 **2** *2 ¼* **Mossy's Lodge**[14] 275 3-8-13 0.......... WilliamCarson 2 62+
(Anthony Carson) *broke wl: sn stdd bk and chsd ldng pair: rdn over 2f out: swtchd rt over 1f out: kpt on to go 2nd wl ins fnl f: no ch w wnr and sn eased* **14/1**[3]

5- **3** *1* **Paradise Palm**[36] 8402 3-8-10 0.......... DannyBrock(3) 4 59
(Philip McBride) *w wnr: rdn over 2f out: unable qck u.p jst over 1f out: kpt on same pce ins fnl f* **20/1**

0- **4** *2 ¼* **Serendib's Glory (IRE)**[66] 8048 3-8-13 0.......... AdamBeschizza 3 52
(Julia Feilden) *chsd ldrs: effrt 2f out: unable qck and carried rt over 1f out: sn outpcd: wl hld 4th fnl f* **66/1**

66- **5** *2* **Al Kirana (IRE)**[118] 7089 3-8-13 0.......... KieranO'Neill 5 45
(Richard Hannon) *t.k.h: hld up wl in tch: rdn 2f out: outpcd and swtchd lft over 1f out: wl btn ins fnl f* **11/4**[2]

04 **6** *1 ½* **Keep The Silence (IRE)**[13] 298 3-8-10 0.......... EoinWalsh(3) 6 41
(James Tate) *a in rr: rdn 1/2-way: n.d* **16/1**

1m 12.14s (-1.56) **Going Correction** -0.25s/f (Stan) **6** Ran SP% **110.7**
Speed ratings (Par 100): **100,97,95,92,90 88**
CSF £9.64 TOTE £1.30: £1.10, £4.90; EX 9.40 Trifecta £70.80.
Owner Sheikh Mohammed Bin Khalifa Al Maktoum **Bred** Brushwood Stable **Trained** Newmarket, Suffolk

■ Stewards' Enquiry : William Carson caution: careless riding

FOCUS
This weak maiden looked a good opportunity for the favourite and she won with the minimum of fuss. She didn't need to improve.

442 BET SCOOP6SOCCER AT BETFRED SHOPS H'CAP 6f (P)
7:40 (7:40) (Class 6) (0-60,60) 4-Y-O+ **£3,234** (£962; £481; £240) **Stalls** Centre

Form RPR
2-62 **1** **Compton Prince**[11] 320 7-9-4 **57**..........(b) FrannyNorton 10 64
(Milton Bradley) *in tch in midfield: clsd to trck ldrs 2f out: wnt between horses and rdn to ld over 1f out: drvn ins fnl f: kpt on: all out cl home* **5/1**[3]

0-00 **2** *nk* **Eljaddaaf (IRE)**[12] 314 5-9-4 **57**.......... AdamKirby 8 64+
(Dean Ivory) *in rr: rdn and hdwy over 1f out: wnt 3rd 150yds out: styd on to chse wnr wl ins fnl f: clsng at fin but nvr quite getting to wnr* **7/2**[2]

3332 **3** *½* **Royal Rettie**[7] 356 4-8-13 **59**.......... PaddyBradley(7) 1 64
(Heather Dalton) *taken down early: t.k.h: hld up in tch in midfield: clsd and swtchd rt over 1f out: chsd wnr jst ins fnl f: lost 2nd wl ins fnl f: kpt on towards fin* **10/3**[1]

0-04 **4** *6* **Burauq**[11] 320 4-9-5 **58**..........(b) JoeFanning 2 45
(Milton Bradley) *wnt lft and hmpd s: t.k.h: sn switching to outer and hld up in tch: effrt over 1f out: styd on into 4th ins fnl f to snatch 4th last stride: nvr trbld ldrs* **8/1**

62-0 **5** *nse* **Emperors Warrior (IRE)**[22] 167 4-9-6 **59**..........(b) GeorgeBaker 7 46
(Gary Moore) *chsd ldr: drvn and ev ch over 1f out: no ex 1f out: sn dropped to 4th and wknd ins fnl f: lost 4th last stride* **10/1**

0420 **6** *¾* **Pull The Pin (IRE)**[3] 418 7-8-10 **52**..........(bt) DannyBrock(3) 11 37
(Heather Dalton) *led: rdn ent fnl 2f: hdd over 1f out: sn btn: wknd fnl f* **14/1**

00-4 **7** *nk* **Wahaab (IRE)**[27] 100 5-9-7 **60**.......... KieranO'Neill 6 44
(Richard Hughes) *t.k.h: hld up in last pair: effrt over 1f out: no imp: wl btn fnl f* **7/2**[2]

6-63 **8** *½* **Ms Eboracum (IRE)**[25] 130 4-8-7 **46** oh1.......... AndrewMullen 3 28
(Michael Appleby) *chsd ldng pair: drvn and unable qck over 2f out: btn over 1f out: sn wknd* **16/1**

060- **9** *1 ¼* **Blackasyourhat (IRE)**[135] 6633 4-8-13 **55**..........(t) RobHornby(3) 4 33
(Michael Attwater) *in tch in midfield: rdn over 2f out: lost pl and bhd over 1f out: wknd fnl f* **33/1**

1m 11.92s (-1.78) **Going Correction** -0.25s/f (Stan) **9** Ran SP% **119.9**
Speed ratings (Par 101): **101,100,99,91,91 90,90,89,88**
CSF £23.85 CT £68.36 TOTE £7.20: £1.90, £2.00, £1.30; EX 33.40 Trifecta £133.20.
Owner E A Hayward **Bred** Whitsbury Manor Stud **Trained** Sedbury, Gloucs

FOCUS
The first three finished nicely clear in this moderate handicap, and the form is sound.

443 BET SCOOP6SOCCER AT TOTESPORT.COM H'CAP 7f (P)
8:10 (8:10) (Class 6) (0-65,68) 3-Y-O **£3,234** (£962; £481; £240) **Stalls** Low

Form RPR
00-0 **1** **Teversham**[17] 242 3-9-3 **60**.......... IrineuGoncalves 9 65
(Chris Dwyer) *s.i.s: rcvrd to chse ldng pair after 1f: rdn over 1f out: styd on to chal wl ins fnl f: led last strides* **66/1**

65-3 **2** *hd* **Silver Springs (IRE)**[21] 171 3-9-4 **64**.......... PhilipPrince(3) 12 68
(David Evans) *led tl over 3f out: styd pressing ldrs: ev ch u.p over 1f out: battled on u.p to ld 100yds: hdd last strides* **6/1**[3]

6-36 **3** *shd* **Footlight**[16] 248 3-8-7 **53**.......... SammyJoBell(3) 10 57
(Richard Fahey) *in tch in midfield: effrt u.p over 1f out: hdwy to press ldrs fnl 100yds: kpt on wl towards fin* **9/1**

020- **4** *nse* **Sunbaked (IRE)**[66] 8045 3-9-3 **60**..........(p) ShaneKelly 6 64
(Eve Johnson Houghton) *in tch in midfield: effrt over 1f out: styd on and ev ch ins fnl f: kpt on* **8/1**

3-01 **5** *¾* **Adventure Zone (IRE)**[9] 335 3-9-4 **68** 6ex..........(p) MeganNicholls(7) 2 70
(Richard Hannon) *sn chsng ldr tl led over 3f out: rdn and drifted rt over 1f out: hdd 100yds: no ex and wknd towards fin* **3/1**[1]

050- **6** *¾* **Packing (IRE)**[54] 8204 3-9-4 **61**.......... TimmyMurphy 1 61
(Jamie Osborne) *sn stdd and bk and hld up in last quartet: pushed along and hdwy over 1f out: chsd ldrs and rdn ins fnl f: no imp towards fin and eased cl home* **6/1**[3]

50-3 **7** *¾* **Refulgence (FR)**[13] 291 3-9-5 **62**.......... OisinMurphy 4 60
(Marco Botti) *hld up in tch in last quartet: rdn over 2f out: hdwy u.p 1f out: kpt on ins fnl f: nvr enough pce to rch ldrs* **5/1**[2]

04-4 **8** *½* **Espoir**[27] 104 3-8-11 **54**.......... TonyHamilton 11 51
(Richard Fahey) *broke wl and chsd ldr early: sn stdd and in tch in 5th: unable qck u.p over 1f out: hld and styd on same pce ins fnl f* **11/1**

60-0 **9** *3 ¼* **Dark Illustrator**[24] 145 3-9-0 **57**.......... DanielTudhope 3 45
(David O'Meara) *hld up in tch in midfield: n.m.r on inner ent fnl 2f: effrt on inner over 1f out: sn no imp: wknd ins fnl f* **12/1**

3-20 **10** *½* **Magic Garden (IRE)**[13] 291 3-9-5 **62**.......... RyanClark 8 49
(Jonathan Portman) *chsd ldrs: rdn over 2f out: no ex u.p 1f out: wknd ins fnl f* **16/1**

60-5 **11** *1 ¼* **Lady Fontenail**[29] 63 3-9-3 **60**.......... LiamKeniry 5 43
(Rod Millman) *a in rr: rdn and no hdwy over 1f out: n.d* **33/1**

0-30 **12** *20* **Opera Buffa (IRE)**[17] 242 3-9-1 **58**.......... JoeFanning 7
(Mark Johnston) *hld up in last pair: lost tch 2f out: eased ins fnl f: t.o* **12/1**

1m 25.84s (-1.36) **Going Correction** -0.25s/f (Stan) **12** Ran SP% **125.4**
Speed ratings (Par 95): **97,96,96,96,95 94,94,93,89,89 87,64**
CSF £453.01 CT £2693.52 TOTE £29.80: £8.00, £1.10, £5.80; EX 619.60 Trifecta £2018.10.
Owner Strawberry Fields Stud **Bred** G & J Equestrian Of Newmarket **Trained** Newmarket, Suffolk

FOCUS
A moderate contest and a shock result. Pace held up and there was a blanket finish.
T/Plt: £20.00 to a £1 stake. Pool of £79496.19 - 2899.26 winning tickets. T/Qpdt: £6.00 to a £1 stake. Pool of £8951.39 - 1089.39 winning tickets. **Steve Payne**

425 SOUTHWELL (L-H)
Thursday, February 4

OFFICIAL GOING: Fibresand: standard
Wind: Fresh behind Weather: Cloudy

444 UNIBET OFFER DAILY JOCKEY/TRAINER SPECIALS H'CAP 5f (F)
1:50 (1:50) (Class 6) (0-65,65) 4-Y-O+ **£2,587** (£770; £384; £192) **Stalls** Centre

Form RPR
14-4 **1** **Fine 'n Dandy (IRE)**[29] 75 5-9-6 **64**.......... TonyHamilton 9 82
(J R Jenkins) *cl up: led 1/2-way: pushed clr appr fnl f: readily* **8/1**

5-22 **2** *3 ¾* **Blue Bounty**[18] 230 5-9-0 **58**..........(p) SaleemGolam 4 62
(Mark H Tompkins) *chsd ldng pair: rdn wl over 1f out: drvn to chse wnr ins fnl f: no imp* **7/2**[2]

2-24 **3** *1 ½* **Major Muscari (IRE)**[12] 319 8-9-0 **63**..........(p) JustinNewman(5) 2 62
(Shaun Harris) *dwlt and sn pushed along: hdwy on outer over 2f out and sn rdn: kpt on u.p appr fnl f* **4/1**[3]

0-21 **4** *nk* **Sir Geoffrey (IRE)**[9] 340 10-9-2 **60** 6ex..........(b) TomEaves 7 58+
(Scott Dixon) *slt ld: hdd 1/2-way and sn rdn along: drvn over 1f out and grad wknd* **6/1**

2-04 **5** *hd* **Fuel Injection**[13] 292 5-9-1 **59**..........(b) BarryMcHugh 5 56+
(Paul Midgley) *dwlt and outpcd in rr: hdwy u.p wl over 1f out: kpt on fnl f* **9/1**

06-0 **6** *¾* **Extreme Supreme**[13] 293 5-9-5 **63**..........(v) MartinLane 3 57
(Derek Shaw) *chsd ldrs: rdn along 2f out: sn drvn and btn over 1f out* **5/2**[1]

00-0 **7** *4 ½* **Incomparable**[25] 136 11-8-7 **51**..........(p) KieranO'Neill 8 29
(Scott Dixon) *chsd ldrs: rdn along 1/2-way: sn outpcd* **28/1**

59.37s (-0.33) **Going Correction** -0.025s/f (Stan) **7** Ran SP% **109.6**
Speed ratings (Par 101): **101,95,92,92,91 90,83**
CSF £33.00 CT £118.77 TOTE £5.40: £2.80, £2.20; EX 23.60 Trifecta £177.40.
Owner Miss A Finn **Bred** G Flannery Developments **Trained** Royston, Herts

FOCUS
The stalls for this event were in the centre, as they have been for 5f races here since January 10th. The pace was down the middle of the track. Straightforward form, and it's doubtful this flatters the winner.

445 CORAL.CO.UK H'CAP 1m 4f (F)
2:20 (2:21) (Class 6) (0-65,64) 4-Y-O+ **£2,587** (£770; £384; £192) **Stalls** Low

Form RPR
300- **1** **Weald Of Kent (USA)**[49] 8272 4-9-9 **64**..........(v) LiamJones 4 77
(Michael Appleby) *chsd ldng pair: hdwy to ld 4f out: rdn clr wl over 2f out: kpt on strly* **7/2**[1]

The Form Book, Raceform Ltd, Newbury, RG14 5SJ

100- **2** 7 **Star Ascending (IRE)**[31] 7258 4-9-4 **59** .... JoeFanning 1 63
(Jennie Candlish) *hld up in tch: smooth hdwy to trck ldrs 4f out: chsd wnr wl over 2f out and sn rdn: drvn wl over 1f out: sn no imp* **8/1**

-340 **3** 3 1/2 **Geeaitch**[7] 368 7-9-0 **52** ....(b) BarryMcHugh 6 48
(Peter Hiatt) *trckd ldrs on outer: effrt 4f out: rdn along 3f out: drvn 2f out and sn one pce* **6/1**

36-3 **4** 2 1/2 **A Little Bit Dusty**[16] 251 8-9-6 **58** ....(p) TomEaves 3 50
(Conor Dore) *slt ld: rdn along and hdd 4f out: drvn along 3f out: sn outpcd* **4/1**[2]

-040 **5** 7 **Excelling Oscar (IRE)**[9] 336 4-9-4 **59** .... KieranO'Neill 2 40
(Conor Dore) *chsd ldrs on inner: rdn along over 3f out: sn wknd* **11/2**

24-2 **6** 16 **Peeps**[15] 261 4-9-2 **57** .... SaleemGolam 8 12
(Mark H Tompkins) *s.i.s: a bhd* **5/1**[3]

6-00 **7** 15 **Spinning Rose**[17] 245 4-9-0 **55** .... TomQueally 7
(Dean Ivory) *cl up: rdn along 5f out: lost pl 4f out and sn bhd* **7/1**

2m 41.59s (0.59) **Going Correction** +0.05s/f (Slow)
WFA 4 from 5yo+ 3lb 7 Ran SP% **112.2**
Speed ratings (Par 101): **100,95,93,91,86 76,66**
CSF £30.05 CT £159.70 TOTE £4.40: £1.80, £2.80; EX 23.20 Trifecta £195.40.
Owner Tariq Al Nisf **Bred** Juddmonte Farms Inc **Trained** Oakham, Rutland

FOCUS
This very moderate handicap was run at a fair gallop. A minor pb from the winner, who was down in grade.

446 DOWNLOAD THE CORAL APP H'CAP 1m 3f (F)
2:50 (2:53) (Class 5) (0-75,75) 4-Y-O+ **£3,234** (£962; £481; £240) **Stalls** Low

Form RPR

602- **1** **Blades Lad**[31] 7815 7-9-0 **67** ....(p) TomEaves 8 76
(Peter Niven) *led after 1f: pushed along 3f out: rdn wl over 1f out: drvn ent fnl f: kpt on gamely* **5/1**[3]

50-5 **2** nk **L'Inganno Felice (FR)**[10] 332 6-9-3 **70** .... GrahamLee 3 78
(John Mackie) *trckd ldrs: smooth hdwy 4f out: cl up 3f out: chal 2f out: rdn over 1f out: drvn and ev ch ent fnl f tl carried hd high and no ex towards fin* **15/8**[1]

-224 **3** 3 3/4 **Clockmaker (IRE)**[7] 367 10-9-5 **72** .... JoeFanning 2 74
(Conor Dore) *stmbld s and in rr: swtchd to outer after 3f: hdwy 5f out: cl up 3f out: rdn 2f out and ev ch tl drvn appr fnl f and kpt on same pce* **5/1**[3]

3-04 **4** 3 1/2 **Lean On Pete (IRE)**[21] 179 7-9-1 **68** ....(e[1]) GrahamGibbons 1 64
(Ollie Pears) *in tch: pushed along 5f out: rdn along and outpcd 4f out: sn in rr and rdn along: styd on fnl 2f* **14/1**

05-6 **5** 1 3/4 **Art Scholar (IRE)**[14] 267 9-9-5 **75** .... AlistairRawlinson[(3)] 6 68
(Michael Appleby) *hld up towards rr: hdwy 5f out: chsd ldrs 4f out: rdn along 3f out: sn drvn and wknd* **4/1**[2]

63-2 **6** 9 **Kingscombe (USA)**[14] 273 7-9-5 **72** ....(p) SteveDrowne 5 50
(Linda Jewell) *prom: pushed along 4f out: rdn along over 3f out: sn wknd* **8/1**

000- **7** 14 **Hydrant**[145] 6308 10-9-6 **73** ....(e[1]) JasonHart 7 27
(Richard Guest) *led 1f: prom: rdn along over 4f out: lost pl over 3f out and sn bhd* **25/1**

2m 27.38s (-0.62) **Going Correction** +0.05s/f (Slow) 7 Ran SP% **109.7**
Speed ratings (Par 103): **104,103,101,98,97 90,80**
CSF £13.59 CT £43.86 TOTE £4.30: £2.30, £2.50; EX 15.00 Trifecta £63.30.
Owner Crown Select **Bred** David Holgate **Trained** Barton-le-Street, N Yorks

FOCUS
An ordinary handicap, run at a solid pace. The winner is rated to his old C&D best.

447 CORAL H'CAP 1m 4f (F)
3:25 (3:25) (Class 4) (0-85,85) 4-Y-O+ **£5,175** (£1,540; £769; £384) **Stalls** Low

Form RPR

1-12 **1** **Play Nicely**[25] 132 4-8-13 **77** .... GrahamGibbons 2 88+
(David Barron) *cl up: led over 3f out: rdn 2f out and sn clr: kpt on strly* **5/2**[1]

1-04 **2** 2 1/2 **U S Navy Seal (USA)**[14] 267 4-9-6 **84** ....(v[1]) TomQueally 4 88
(J R Jenkins) *hld up in rr: hdwy and wd st: sn chsng ldng pair: rdn wl over 1f out: drvn to chse wnr ent fnl f: no imp* **5/1**

36-0 **3** 1 **Kashmir Peak (IRE)**[17] 244 7-9-10 **85** .... DougieCostello 5 87
(John Quinn) *trckd ldrs: hdwy 4f out: chsd wnr wl over 2f out and sn rdn: drvn wl over 1f out and kpt on same pce* **14/1**

10-2 **4** 1 **Golden Jubilee (USA)**[10] 330 7-9-4 **79** ......(p) WilliamTwiston-Davies 3 80
(Nigel Twiston-Davies) *trckd ldng pair: pushed along 4f out: rdn 3f out: drvn and kpt on same pce fnl 2f* **10/1**

3-13 **5** 1 1/4 **The Lock Master (IRE)**[9] 337 9-9-2 **80** ....(p) AlistairRawlinson[(3)] 6 79
(Michael Appleby) *trckd ldrs: pushed along over 4f out: rdn over 3f out: lost pl and drvn 2f out: sn one pce* **3/1**[2]

3-01 **6** 13 **Virnon**[14] 273 5-9-0 **75** .... JoeFanning 1 53
(Alan Swinbank) *led: jnd and pushed along over 4f: rdn and hdd over 3f out: drvn over 2f out: sn wknd and eased over 1f out* **7/2**[3]

2m 42.07s (1.07) **Going Correction** +0.05s/f (Slow)
WFA 4 from 5yo+ 3lb 6 Ran SP% **108.2**
Speed ratings (Par 105): **98,96,95,95,94 85**
CSF £14.04 TOTE £3.80: £2.70, £3.10; EX 15.60 Trifecta £98.50.
Owner Lets Be Lucky Racing 5 **Bred** Susanna Ballinger **Trained** Maunby, N Yorks

FOCUS
A fair handicap, run in a time half a second slower than the earlier Class 6 event. The winner added to his good record here, while the runner-up has been rated as running a small pb.

448 LADBROKES H'CAP 1m (F)
4:00 (4:00) (Class 5) (0-70,76) 4-Y-O+ **£3,234** (£962; £481; £240) **Stalls** Low

Form RPR

1-61 **1** **St Patrick's Day (IRE)**[7] 367 4-9-13 **76** 6ex............(v) DougieCostello 4 88
(J R Jenkins) *dwlt and towards rr: hdwy over 3f out: chsd ldng pair wl over 1f out: sn rdn: drvn to chal jst ins fnl f: sn led and kpt on strly* **9/4**[1]

060- **2** 4 1/2 **Sooqaan**[45] 8333 5-9-3 **66** .... TonyHamilton 3 68
(Antony Brittain) *slt ld 2f: cl up on inner: effrt to chal over 2f out: rdn wl over 1f out and ev ch: drvn ent fnl f: kpt on same pce* **7/1**

2-53 **3** 3/4 **Monsieur Jimmy**[14] 276 4-9-1 **64** ....(b) DanielTudhope 5 64
(Declan Carroll) *cl up: slt ld after 2f: rdn along 2f out: drvn over 1f out: hdd jst ins fnl f: kpt on same pce* **10/1**

-116 **4** 3 **Moonlight Venture**[3] 424 5-9-5 **68** ....(p) TomEaves 7 61
(Conor Dore) *chsd ldrs on outer: effrt 3f out: rdn along over 2f out: drvn wl over 1f out: kpt on one pce* **9/2**[3]

231- **5** 1/2 **Nosey Barker (IRE)**[36] 8394 4-9-7 **70** ....(p) KieranO'Neill 2 62
(Richard Hannon) *reminders s: chsd ldrs on inner: rdn along 3f out: sn drvn and wknd* **3/1**[2]

-554 **6** 6 **General Tufto**[9] 336 11-8-0 **56** oh10............(b) RPWalsh[(7)] 1 34
(Charles Smith) *sn rdn along and outpcd in rr: bhd fr 1/2-way* **40/1**

41-4 **7** 1/2 **Limerick Lord (IRE)**[14] 277 4-9-0 **63** ....(p) TomQueally 6 40
(Julia Feilden) *trckd ldrs: hdwy over 3f out: rdn along wl over 2f out: drvn 2f out and sn wknd* **13/2**

1m 43.47s (-0.23) **Going Correction** +0.05s/f (Slow) 7 Ran SP% **111.3**
Speed ratings (Par 103): **103,98,97,94,94 88,87**
CSF £17.50 CT £124.15 TOTE £3.40: £1.90, £4.00; EX 19.50 Trifecta £137.30.
Owner Miss A Finn **Bred** Lorgnette Bloodstock **Trained** Royston, Herts

FOCUS
This was run at a sound pace. The winner is improving, while the third has been rated to his latest form.

449 LADBROKES APPRENTICE H'CAP 7f (F)
4:35 (4:35) (Class 5) (0-75,74) 4-Y-O+ **£3,234** (£962; £481; £240) **Stalls** Low

Form RPR

2-22 **1** **Welliesinthewater (IRE)**[21] 169 6-9-2 **70** ....(v) NoelGarbutt[(3)] 7 80
(Derek Shaw) *chsd ldng pair: hdwy on outer 3f out: rdn to chal over 1f out: drvn ins fnl f: kpt on to ld nr fin* **2/1**[1]

44-1 **2** nk **Afkar (IRE)**[16] 246 8-9-1 **66** ....(p) MichaelJMMurphy 5 75
(Ivan Furtado) *cl up: chal over 2f out: rdn wl over 1f out: slt ld ent fnl f and sn drvn: hdd and no ex* **5/2**[2]

0-26 **3** 2 1/4 **Danish Duke (IRE)**[16] 246 5-8-12 **63** .... JackGarritty 2 66
(Ruth Carr) *led: pushed along over 2f out: rdn wl over 1f out: drvn and hdd ent fnl f: kpt on same pce* **15/2**

0-61 **4** 6 **Llewellyn**[14] 278 8-9-1 **73** ....(b) LeeByrne[(7)] 1 60
(Declan Carroll) *chsd ldrs on inner: rdn along over 2f out: sn one pce* **11/1**

05-3 **5** 1 3/4 **Burning Blaze**[14] 278 6-9-4 **74** .... JoshDoyle[(5)] 3 56
(Brian Ellison) *dwlt and reminders s: sn swtchd to outer: sme hdwy and wd st: rdn 2f out and no imp* **3/1**[3]

00-0 **6** 2 **Munaawib**[24] 144 8-8-4 **62** ....(tp) BenSanderson[(7)] 6 39
(Deborah Sanderson) *dwlt: a in rr* **20/1**

1m 29.28s (-1.02) **Going Correction** +0.05s/f (Slow) 6 Ran SP% **111.8**
Speed ratings (Par 103): **107,106,104,97,95 92**
CSF £7.20 TOTE £2.40: £1.10, £1.80; EX 8.30 Trifecta £24.00.
Owner The Whiteman Partnership **Bred** Brendan Ryan **Trained** Sproxton, Leics

FOCUS
The first three finished clear in this very ordinary event. The winner rates better than ever.
T/Plt: £146.80 to a £1 stake. Pool of £55633.71- 276.60 winning tickets. T/Qpdt: £8.30 to a £1 stkae. Pool of £5305.19 - 467.47 winning tickets. **Joe Rowntree**

[405]MEYDAN (L-H)
Thursday, February 4

OFFICIAL GOING: Dirt: fast; turf: good

450a EGA BILLET TROPHY (H'CAP) (TURF) 5f (T)
3:35 (3:35) (100-113,113) 3-Y-O+
£48,979 (£16,326; £8,163; £4,081; £2,448; £1,632)

RPR

1 **Ertijaal (IRE)**[28] 91 5-9-6 113............ PaulHanagan 16 120+
(A R Al Rayhi, UAE) *trckd ldr: led 1 1/2f out: r.o wl: comf* **1/1**[1]

2 2 **Fityaan**[7] 370 8-8-7 100............(v) TadhgO'Shea 10 100
(M Al Mheiri, UAE) *mid-div: r.o fnl 2f: no ch w wnr* **25/1**

3 3/4 **Roi De Vitesse (IRE)**[7] 370 9-8-11 105............(v) PatSmullen 9 101+
(Ali Jan, Qatar) *settled in rr: r.o fnl 2 1/2f: nrst fin* **20/1**

4 hd **Naadirr (IRE)**[110] 7278 5-9-2 109............(p) ChristopheSoumillon 5 105+
(Marco Botti) *s.i.s: nvr nr to chal: r.o fnl 2 1/2f: nrst fin* **6/1**[2]

5 hd **Speed Hawk (USA)**[21] 186 5-8-13 106............(v) JamesDoyle 4 102
(Robert Cowell) *mid-div: r.o same pce fnl 2f* **16/1**

6 1 1/4 **Sir Maximilian (IRE)**[22] 166 7-9-1 108............ PatDobbs 2 99
(Ian Williams) *trckd ldr tl outpcd fnl 1 1/2f* **16/1**

7 nk **Mubtaghaa (IRE)**[151] 6132 4-8-11 105............ DaneO'Neill 8 94
(M Al Mheiri, UAE) *settled in rr: nvr nr to chal* **12/1**

8 nse **Caspian Prince (IRE)**[14] 280 7-8-13 106............ RobertWinston 15 96
(Dean Ivory) *sn led: hdd 1 1/2f out: r.o same pce* **9/1**[3]

9 1 1/4 **Foxy Forever (IRE)**[28] 91 6-8-7 100............(b) RichardMullen 7 85
(Michael Wigham) *trckd ldr: ev ch 2 1/2f out: one pce fnl 2f* **33/1**

10 shd **Green Door (IRE)**[14] 280 5-8-10 104............ AndreaAtzeni 11 88
(Robert Cowell) *nvr bttr than mid-div* **20/1**

11 shd **Liber**[7] 370 6-8-7 100............ WayneSmith 14 85
(Bent Olsen, Denmark) *nvr bttr than mid-div* **25/1**

12 1/2 **Saayerr**[14] 280 5-8-10 104............ ChrisHayes 3 86
(D Selvaratnam, UAE) *trckd ldr tl outpcd 2 1/2f out* **14/1**

13 3 1/4 **Muharaaj (IRE)**[7] 371 5-8-11 105............ MickaelBarzalona 1 75
(Mme Pia Brandt, France) *a in rr* **50/1**

14 3/4 **Over The Ocean (USA)**[201] 6-8-10 104............(t) WilliamBuick 13 71
(Niels Petersen, Norway) *nvr nr to chal* **40/1**

15 2 **Hototo**[263] 2316 6-9-3 110............(v) LukeMorris 6 71
(Fawzi Abdulla Nass, Bahrain) *slowly away: a in rr* **16/1**

57.28s (0.18) **Going Correction** +0.30s/f (Good) 15 Ran SP% **130.8**
Speed ratings: **110,106,105,105,104 102,102,102,100,100 100,99,94,92,89**
CSF: 41.65 TRICAST: 403.13.
Owner Hamdan Al Maktoum **Bred** Shadwell Estate Co Ltd **Trained** UAE

FOCUS
TRAKUS (metres travelled compared to winner): 2nd -1, 3rd 0, 4th 0, 5th +1, 6th 0, 7th +1, 8th -1, 9th 0, 10th +1, 11th -1, 12th 0, 13th 0, 14th -1, 15th +1. Rail movement narrowed the course and the main speed was with the high numbers, so the action unfolded stands' side and those draw low were not favoured. The winner was probably helped by his draw but was different class.

451a CAPE VERDI SPONSORED BY EGA (GROUP 2) (F&M) (TURF) 1m
4:10 (4:10) 3-Y-O+
£81,632 (£27,210; £13,605; £6,802; £3,401; £3,401)

RPR

1 **Very Special (IRE)**[78] 7891 4-9-4 104............ JamesDoyle 7 109+
(Saeed bin Suroor) *sn led: rdn 2f out: r.o wl: easily* **13/8**[1]

2 3 **Excilly**[21] 187 4-9-4 102............ RichardKingscote 1 102
(Tom Dascombe) *s.i.s: mid-div: r.o fnl 1 1/2f: no ch w wnr* **20/1**

3 1/2 **More Aspen (USA)**[21] 187 5-9-4 104............ RichardMullen 6 101
(S Seemar, UAE) *led chsng gp: rdn 3f out: r.o same pce fnl 2f* **7/2**[2]

4 2 1/4 **Si Luna (GER)**[95] 7667 7-9-4 108............ ChristopheSoumillon 5 96+
(W Mongil, Germany) *a mid-div* **4/1**[3]

5 2 **Malka (FR)**[39] 8374 5-9-4 102............ MickaelBarzalona 3 91+
(Mme Pia Brandt, France) *a in rr* **33/1**

5 dht **Icecapada (IRE)**[109] 4-9-4 102 .... WilliamBuick 4 91+
(Niels Petersen, Norway) *a in rr* **16/1**

7 2 1/2 **Almashooqa (AUS)**[21] 184 3-8-11 104 .... PaulHanagan 2 78
(M F De Kock, South Africa) *mid-div: rdn 3 1/2f out: sn btn* **11/2**

1m 37.88s (0.38) **Going Correction** +0.30s/f (Good)
WFA 3 from 4yo+ 19lb **7** Ran SP% **109.3**
Speed ratings: **110,107,106,104,102 102,99**
CSF: 33.26.
Owner Godolphin **Bred** Ballylinch Stud **Trained** Newmarket, Suffolk

FOCUS
TRAKUS: 2nd -2, 3rd -2, 4th +1, 5th -2, 6th +1, 7th -2. This looked a weak Group 2 beforehand and the way it unfolded was farcical, the free-running winner given a few lengths head start despite setting a slow pace. Very Special posted the following splits: 27.10, 24.15, 23.9, 22.73. The standard is set by the second and third.

452a AL MAKTOUM CHALLENGE R2 SPONSORED BY EGA (GROUP 2) (DIRT) 1m 1f 110y(D)

4:45 (4:45) 3-Y-O+

£102,040 (£34,013; £17,006; £8,503; £5,102; £3,401)

RPR

1 **Frosted (USA)**[96] 7657 4-9-0 120 .... (b) WilliamBuick 5 119+
(Kiaran McLaughlin, U.S.A) *trckd ldr: smooth prog 2 1/2f out: led 1 1/2f out: easily* **10/11**[1]

2 5 **Gold City (IRE)**[28] 92 7-9-1 108 .... (bt) RichardMullen 4 109
(S Seemar, UAE) *s.i.s: trckd ldr: ev ch 1 1/2f out: r.o same pce fnl f* **50/1**

3 2 3/4 **Faulkner**[28] 92 6-9-1 108 .... PatDobbs 6 103
(Doug Watson, UAE) *settled in rr: r.o fnl 2f but no ch w first two* **10/1**

4 shd **Munaaser**[21] 188 5-9-1 104 .... PaulHanagan 1 103
(A R Al Rayhi, UAE) *sn led: hdd 1 1/2f out: wknd fnl 110yds* **25/1**

5 hd **Prayer For Relief (USA)**[28] 92 8-9-1 110 ....(b) ChristopheSoumillon 7 102
(M F De Kock, South Africa) *trckd ldrs: ev ch 3f out: one pce fnl 2 1/2f* **9/2**[2]

6 4 **Special Fighter (IRE)**[14] 281 5-9-1 111 .... FernandoJara 8 94
(M Al Mheiri, UAE) *nvr bttr than mid-div* **5/1**[3]

7 1/2 **Layl (USA)**[28] 92 6-9-1 109 .... (v) SamHitchcott 9 93
(Doug Watson, UAE) *s.i.s: a in rr* **9/1**

8 3 3/4 **Mind That Boy (IRE)**[14] 284 4-9-0 107 .... MickaelBarzalona 2 86
(S bin Ghadayer, UAE) *a in rr* **33/1**

9 2 3/4 **Elnaawi (USA)**[35] 6-9-1 104 .... (v) DaneO'Neill 3 80
(Kiaran McLaughlin, U.S.A) *nvr bttr than mid-div* **25/1**

1m 56.67s (-2.13) **Going Correction** +0.175s/f (Slow) **9** Ran SP% **118.9**
Speed ratings: **115,111,108,108,108 105,104,101,99**
CSF: 76.82.
Owner Godolphin **Bred** Darley **Trained** USA

FOCUS
TRAKUS: 2nd -13, 3rd -7, 4th -8, 5th +10, 6th +14, 7th +12, 8th 0, 9th -3. This was run at an even pace: 26.14 (400m, allow about two seconds for standing start), 23.87 (800m), 23.87 (1200m), 24.16 (1600m). The course record was lowered - it was only the 18th race over this trip on dirt here but it was a smart time. The first two help set the level.

453a EGA POTLINES TROPHY (H'CAP) (TURF) 1m 6f 11y

5:20 (5:20) (95-113,113) 3-Y-O+

£61,224 (£20,408; £10,204; £5,102; £3,061; £2,040)

RPR

1 **Battersea**[146] 6270 5-8-5 98 .... AndreaAtzeni 3 102+
(Roger Varian) *t.k.h in rr: smooth prog 3f out: rdn to ld fnl strides* **9/4**[1]

2 shd **Paene Magnus (IRE)**[14] 285 7-8-8 100 ow1 .... (t) FrederikTylicki 5 105
(A bin Harmash, UAE) *trckd ldrs: led 2f out: r.o wl: hdd nr line* **10/1**

3 1 **Famous Kid (USA)**[54] 8210 5-9-3 110 .... JamesDoyle 2 112+
(Saeed bin Suroor) *mid-div: r.o fnl 2f: nrst fin* **3/1**[2]

4 1 3/4 **Rio Tigre (IRE)**[14] 285 5-8-11 105 .... MickaelBarzalona 9 104
(S bin Ghadayer, UAE) *settled in rr: r.o wl fnl 2f: nrst fin* **16/1**

5 shd **Star Empire (SAF)**[28] 93 9-9-6 113 .... ChristopheSoumillon 8 113
(M F De Kock, South Africa) *mid-div: smooth prog 5f out: r.o same pce fnl 3f* **4/1**[3]

6 4 **Topclas (FR)**[685] 1061 10-8-5 97 .... (p) XavierZiani 13 92
(A bin Harmash, UAE) *nvr nr to chal: r.o fnl 2f* **40/1**

7 nk **Semeen**[321] 7-8-5 96 .... LukeMorris 12 92
(Fawzi Abdulla Nass, Bahrain) *trckd ldng duo: ev ch 2 1/2f out: one pce fnl 2f* **25/1**

8 5 1/2 **Layali Al Andalus**[48] 8302 9-8-5 95 .... RichardMullen 6 84
(S Seemar, UAE) *s.i.s: nvr nr to chal* **50/1**

9 3 3/4 **Eye In The Sky (IRE)**[137] 6576 5-8-11 105 .... (t) WilliamBuick 7 85
(Niels Petersen, Norway) *trckd ldrs: ev ch 2f out: one pce fnl 1 1/2f* **16/1**

10 3/4 **Keep In Line (GER)**[14] 285 4-8-5 100 .... (p) DavidProbert 1 83
(Saeed bin Suroor) *sn led: hdd & wknd 2f out* **14/1**

11 5 1/4 **Certerach (IRE)**[14] 285 8-8-10 104 .... (p) PatSmullen 4 76
(M Halford, Ire) *slowly away: nvr nr to chal* **12/1**

12 nk **Jeeraan (USA)**[49] 8275 6-8-6 99 .... PaulHanagan 11 71
(Doug Watson, UAE) *nvr bttr than mid-div* **20/1**

13 25 **Bedale**[161] 3597 5-8-5 95 .... DDavid 10 35
(Ernst Oertel, UAE) *trckd ldr tl outpcd 3 1/2f out* **50/1**

2m 57.91s (-1.49) **Going Correction** +0.30s/f (Good)
WFA 4 from 5yo+ 5lb **13** Ran SP% **126.0**
Speed ratings: **116,115,115,114,114 112,111,108,106,106 103,102,88**
CSF: 26.67 TRICAST: 72.94.
Owner H R H Sultan Ahmad Shah **Bred** Newsells Park Stud **Trained** Newmarket, Suffolk

FOCUS
TRAKUS: 2nd +1, 3rd +3, 4th +10, 5th +12, 6th +14, 7th +15, 8th +1, 9th +21, 10th +1, 11th +12, 12th +20, 13th +11. A decent staying handicap run at a sensible pace. The second, fourth and fifth have been rated close to their best.

454a FIREBREAK STKS SPONSORED BY EGA (GROUP 3) (DIRT) 1m (D)

5:55 (5:55) 3-Y-O+

£81,632 (£27,210; £13,605; £6,802; £4,081; £2,721)

RPR

1 **Confrontation (USA)**[230] 6-9-0 107 .... WilliamBuick 1 109
(Kiaran McLaughlin, U.S.A) *trckd ldng pair: rdn to ld fnl 55yds* **11/2**

2 2 **One Man Band (IRE)**[28] 94 5-9-0 110 .... PatDobbs 6 104+
(Doug Watson, UAE) *sn led: rdn 2f out: r.o but hdd fnl strides* **9/2**[3]

3 shd **Watershed (USA)**[40] 8364 4-9-0 102 .... JamesDoyle 3 104
(Kiaran McLaughlin, U.S.A) *s.i.s: nvr nr to chal: r.o fnl 2f* **10/1**

4 3/4 **Le Bernardin (USA)**[28] 92 7-9-3 113 .... (t) TadhgO'Shea 5 105+
(A R Al Rayhi, UAE) *trckd ldrs: ev ch 1 1/2f out: one pce fnl f* **7/2**[2]

5 1 1/2 **Mubtaahij (IRE)**[243] 2956 4-9-0 119 .... ChristopheSoumillon 4 99
(M F De Kock, South Africa) *settled in rr: rdn 3f out: r.o same pce fnl 2f* **1/1**[1]

6 1/2 **Long River (USA)**[28] 92 6-9-0 104 .... (v) RoystonFfrench 2 97
(S bin Ghadayer, UAE) *a in rr* **66/1**

7 10 **Indianapolis (USA)**[21] 186 5-9-0 102 .... (vt) RichardMullen 7 74
(S Seemar, UAE) *nvr bttr than mid-div* **66/1**

1m 37.37s (-0.13) **Going Correction** +0.175s/f (Slow) **7** Ran SP% **117.9**
Speed ratings: **107,105,104,104,102 102,92**
CSF: 31.57.
Owner Godolphin **Bred** W S Farish **Trained** USA

FOCUS
TRAKUS: 2nd +1, 3rd +7, 4th +5, 5th +5, 6th +4, 7th +10. The last two winners of this went on to land the Godolphin Mile, Tamarkuz last year in the first season of dirt racing at Meydan. This year's race was quite decent. The runner-up set a strong pace - 25.54, 23.78, 23.46 and the winner finished less slowly, 24.16 compared to 25.00 for the second. The winner and third set the standard.

455a EGA CASTHOUSE TROPHY (H'CAP) (TURF) 1m 2f

6:30 (6:30) (100-111,111) 3-Y-O+

£71,428 (£23,809; £11,904; £5,952; £3,571; £2,380)

RPR

1 **Think Ahead**[21] 188 5-8-11 102 .... (p) JamesDoyle 10 104
(Saeed bin Suroor) *trckd ldrs: led 1 1/2f out: r.o wl* **10/3**[1]

2 1/2 **Elleval (IRE)**[14] 283 6-9-1 106 .... (p) PatSmullen 5 107+
(David Marnane, Ire) *mid-div: chsd ldrs 3f out: r.o fnl 2f: nrst fin* **5/1**[2]

3 shd **Zamaam**[7] 372 6-8-9 100 .... (t) DaneO'Neill 3 101+
(E Charpy, UAE) *mid-div: r.o fnl 2f nrst fin* **33/1**

4 1 **Sanshaawes (SAF)**[14] 283 6-9-6 111 .... SamHitchcott 9 110
(M F De Kock, South Africa) *wl away: sn led: rdn 3f out: hdd 1 1/2f out: wknd fnl f* **7/1**[3]

5 1/2 **Meadow Creek**[97] 5-8-13 104 .... PatDobbs 7 102+
(Doug Watson, UAE) *settled rr: r.o fnl 2f but nvr able to chal* **25/1**

6 1/2 **Tellina (SAF)**[14] 282 6-9-5 110 .... (b) WayneSmith 1 107
(M F De Kock, South Africa) *trckd ldng pair: t.k.h: ev ch 1 1/2 out: one pce fnl f* **7/1**[3]

7 1 **Zambucca (SAF)**[14] 283 7-8-11 102 .... (b) RichardMullen 11 97+
(S Seemar, UAE) *nvr bttr than mid-div* **33/1**

8 1/2 **Majeed**[14] 285 6-8-9 100 .... AndreaAtzeni 2 94+
(David Simcock) *s.i.s: nvr nr to chal* **10/1**

9 2 **Mustadeem (IRE)**[14] 284 4-8-8 100 .... (t) TadhgO'Shea 6 90
(A R Al Rayhi, UAE) *trckd ldrs: ev ch 2 1/2f out: wknd fnl 1 1/2f* **40/1**

10 nk **Bayrir (FR)**[28] 93 7-8-9 100 .... (t) MickaelBarzalona 8 89+
(N Al Mandeel, Saudi Arabia) *nvr nr to chal* **50/1**

11 nk **Tannaaf (IRE)**[14] 285 4-8-13 105 .... ChristopheSoumillon 14 94+
(M F De Kock, South Africa) *nvr bttr than mid-div* **10/3**[1]

12 3 3/4 **Hasanour (USA)**[28] 93 6-8-13 104 .... WilliamBuick 12 85+
(M Halford, Ire) *nvr nr to chal* **14/1**

13 16 **Nolohay (IRE)**[49] 8273 5-9-3 108 .... (v) PaulHanagan 13 57
(M Al Mheiri, UAE) *trckd ldng pair tl outpcd fnl 3f* **20/1**

2m 2.77s (0.07) **Going Correction** +0.30s/f (Good)
WFA 4 from 5yo+ 1lb **13** Ran SP% **122.5**
Speed ratings: **111,110,110,109,109 108,108,107,106,105 105,102,89**
CSF: 18.76, TRICAST: 483.67. Placepot: £78.80 to a £1 stake. Pool: £5367.84 - 49.69 winning tickets. Quadpot: £12.60 to a £1 stake. Pool: £330.40 - 19.30 winning tickets..
Owner Godolphin **Bred** Lordship Stud **Trained** Newmarket, Suffolk

FOCUS
TRAKUS: 2nd -5, 3rd -8, 4th -5, 5th -5, 6th -6, 7th -4,8th -7, 9th -3, 10th 0, 11th +1, 12th +2, 13th +5. A standard carnival handicap run at ordinary tempo; 26.52, 23.86, 24.33, 24.15, before the winner finished in 23.87. The fourth has been rated to his latest effort.

[398]LINGFIELD (L-H)

Friday, February 5

OFFICIAL GOING: Polytrack: standard
Wind: strong, half behind Weather: overcast

456 32RED.COM FILLIES' H'CAP 1m 1y(P)

2:00 (2:00) (Class 5) (0-75,73) 4-Y-O+ **£2,911** (£866; £432; £216) **Stalls** High

Form RPR

141- 1 **Slovak (IRE)**[106] 7418 4-9-7 73 .... GeorgeBaker 1 80+
(James Tate) *fast away: mde all: rdn whn pressed over 1f out: sn asserted: ld dwindled nr fin* **5/4**[1]

36-2 2 nk **Free Running (IRE)**[20] 223 4-9-6 72 .... RobertHavlin 3 78
(Simon Crisford) *t.k.h: hld up in midfield: pushed along in 4th over 2f out and no prog: drvn fnl f: r.o to take 2nd nr fin and cl on wnr: too much to do* **11/4**[2]

44-2 3 3/4 **Skidby Mill (IRE)**[21] 190 6-8-12 64 .... OisinMurphy 7 68
(Laura Mongan) *trckd wnr: rdn over 2f out: nt qckn over 1f out: kpt on same pce* **8/1**[3]

40-4 4 1/2 **Colourfilly**[27] 127 4-8-10 62 .... JimCrowley 2 65
(Tom Dascombe) *trckd ldng pair: rdn to chal on inner over 1f out: nt qckn fnl f* **10/1**

000- 5 4 1/2 **Two In The Pink (IRE)**[122] 7014 6-8-10 67 .... PaddyPilley[(5)] 5 60
(Ralph J Smith) *hld up in last pair: shkn up 3f out: brief effrt over 1f out: sn wknd* **25/1**

0-46 6 3 1/4 **Cascading Stars (IRE)**[4] 415 4-9-6 72 .... LiamJones 6 57
(J S Moore) *hld up in midfield: rdn over 2f out: wknd wl over 1f out* **12/1**

540- 7 4 **Precast**[284] 1726 4-8-4 63 .... SophieKilloran[(7)] 4 39
(David Simcock) *t.k.h: hld up in last pair: pushed along and no prog over 2f out: sn wknd* **12/1**

1m 38.07s (-0.13) **Going Correction** 0.0s/f (Stan) **7** Ran SP% **110.5**
Speed ratings (Par 100): **100,99,98,98,93 90,86**
CSF £4.36 TOTE £2.00: £1.10, £2.30; EX 4.90 Trifecta £12.40.
Owner Saeed Manana **Bred** John Grogan **Trained** Newmarket, Suffolk

FOCUS
An ordinary fillies' handicap and not many got into it. Another step up from the winner, with the third setting the standard.

457 DOWNLOAD THE LADBROKES APP CLAIMING STKS 7f 1y(P)
2:35 (2:35) (Class 6) 4-Y-O+ **£2,264** (£673; £336; £168) **Stalls** Low

Form RPR
60-4 **1** **Majestic Myles (IRE)**[21] 192 8-9-10 88........................ TonyHamilton 5 83
(Richard Fahey) *mde all: rdn over 1f out: clr fnl f: nvr seriously threatened* **1/1**[1]
00-5 **2** *2* **The Tichborne (IRE)**[25] 141 8-9-0 65........................(b[1]) JackMitchell 2 68
(Roger Teal) *dwlt: hld up in 5th: prog and rdn wl over 1f out: styd on to take 2nd nr fin: no ch to threaten* **8/1**[3]
6-20 **3** *½* **Never To Be (USA)**[18] 239 5-8-7 70........................(t) LuluStanford[(7)] 4 67
(Jim Boyle) *t.k.h: trckd wnr: rdn and hanging over 1f out: no imp after: lost 2nd nr fin* **5/1**[2]
30-3 **4** *nk* **Jimmy's Hall**[18] 239 4-9-3 73........................(b) PaddyPilley[(5)] 1 74
(J S Moore) *trckd ldng pair: pushed along on inner 2f out: rdn and kpt on same pce fnl f* **8/1**[3]
060- **5** *3* **Straits Of Malacca**[109] 7342 5-9-10 70........................ JimCrowley 7 68
(Kevin Ryan) *hld up in 6th: rdn and wd bnd 2f out: no prog after* **16/1**
05-3 **6** *¾* **Rakaan (IRE)**[21] 191 9-9-0 59........................(p) StevieDonohoe 6 56
(Brendan Powell) *dwlt: mostly in last: pushed along and no prog over 2f out: no ch over 1f out* **14/1**
640- **7** *nse* **Ravenous**[78] 7908 5-9-3 74........................ JoshQuinn[(7)] 3 66
(Luke Dace) *chsd ldng trio: urged along 2f out: wknd jst over 1f out* **8/1**[3]
1m 25.45s (0.65) **Going Correction** 0.0s/f (Stan) 7 Ran SP% **112.5**
Speed ratings (Par 101): **96,93,93,92,89 88,88**
CSF £9.45 TOTE £1.60: £1.10, £5.50; EX 10.60 Trifecta £47.20.
Owner Richard Fahey Ebor Racing Club Ltd **Bred** Arctic Tack Stud **Trained** Musley Bank, N Yorks

FOCUS
A modest claimer featuring a few who have seen better days and another all-the-way winner.

458 32REDSPORT.COM MEDIAN AUCTION MAIDEN STKS 1m 2f (P)
3:05 (3:05) (Class 6) 3-Y-O **£2,264** (£673; £336; £168) **Stalls** Low

Form RPR
0-3 **1** **Genuine Approval (IRE)**[31] 44 3-8-11 0........................ DannyBrock[(3)] 1 72
(Jonathan Portman) *led 1f: sn chsd ldng pair: rdn over 2f out: chal on inner over 1f out: led last 100yds: hung rt but styd on* **8/1**
4- **2** *1* **Sabaani**[53] 8225 3-9-5 0........................ GeorgeBaker 7 75
(James Tate) *led after 1f: upped the pce 3f out: rdn wl over 1f out: rn green and hung rt: hdd last 100yds: one pce* **9/4**[1]
3 **3** *1 ½* **Project Bluebook (FR)**[18] 245 3-9-5 0........................ KeaganLatham 3 72+
(John Quinn) *dwlt: hld up in last pair: lft bhd whn pce qcknd 3f out: rdn and prog 2f out: styd on to take 3rd last strides: far too much to do* **11/4**[2]
4-24 **4** *hd* **Lord Huntingdon**[7] 379 3-9-5 67........................ LiamKeniry 5 72
(Andrew Balding) *trckd ldr after 2f: poised to chal 2f out: drvn over 1f out: hanging and fnd nil: sn lost 2nd and btn* **9/2**[3]
5 *6* **Il Sassicaia** 3-9-5 0........................ LiamJones 6 60
(Marco Botti) *dwlt: sn in tch: urged along sn after 1/2-way: outpcd fr 3f out: no ch after* **25/1**
3 **6** *hd* **Song Lark**[21] 202 3-9-0 0........................ OisinMurphy 2 55
(David Simcock) *hld up in midfield: outpcd and pushed along over 2f out: no prog after: fdd fnl f* **14/1**
7 *2* **Ms Gillard** 3-9-0 0........................ JimCrowley 4 51+
(David Simcock) *hld up in last pair: pushed along sn after 1/2-way: outpcd 3f out: rn green and hanging on outer 2f out: wl btn after* **5/1**
2m 7.44s (0.84) **Going Correction** 0.0s/f (Stan) 7 Ran SP% **113.9**
Speed ratings (Par 95): **96,95,94,93,89 88,87**
CSF £26.21 TOTE £16.60: £7.10, £1.20; EX 52.80 Trifecta £152.60.
Owner The Genuine Partnership **Bred** Rossenarra Bloodstock Limited **Trained** Upper Lambourn, Berks

FOCUS
An ordinary 3yo maiden in which the pace only really picked up inside the last 3f. The level is fluid.

459 LADBROKES APPRENTICE H'CAP 7f 1y(P)
3:40 (3:40) (Class 3) (0-95,88) 3-Y-O **£7,246** (£2,168; £1,084; £542; £270) **Stalls** Low

Form RPR
0-1 **1** **Sea Of Flames**[13] 314 3-8-5 77........................ AdamMcLean[(5)] 5 91+
(David Elsworth) *mde virtually all: shkn up over 1f out: stretched clr fnl f: v readily* **7/4**[1]
13-2 **2** *4* **Take The Helm**[13] 315 3-9-0 88........................ JordanUys[(7)] 4 91
(Brian Meehan) *mostly chsd wnr: rdn over 1f out: easily lft bhd and hung lft ins fnl f* **2/1**[2]
242- **3** *¾* **Theos Lolly (IRE)**[77] 7921 3-8-8 75........................ SammyJoBell 6 76
(Richard Fahey) *sn in 4th: shkn up 2f out: kpt on one pce fnl f: no ch* **8/1**
1-36 **4** *1* **Threebagsue (IRE)**[13] 315 3-7-12 72........................(b) HollieDoyle[(7)] 2 72
(J S Moore) *mostly chsd ldng pair: rdn 2f out: wl hld whn hmpd ins fnl f and lost 3rd sn after* **14/1**
00-3 **5** *½* **Abberley Dancer (IRE)**[24] 152 3-8-1 71........................ PaddyPilley[(3)] 1 68
(J S Moore) *hld up in last pair: pushed along on inner 2f out: reminder and nt clr run 1f out: nvr involved but kpt on* **5/1**[3]
051- **6** *3 ½* **Foxinthehenhouse**[47] 8320 3-8-0 70........................ NoelGarbutt[(3)] 3 58
(J R Jenkins) *hld up in last: shkn up over 2f out: no prog and sn btn* **16/1**
1m 23.98s (-0.82) **Going Correction** 0.0s/f (Stan) 6 Ran SP% **110.0**
Speed ratings (Par 101): **104,99,98,97,96 92**
CSF £5.27 TOTE £2.30: £1.10, £1.70; EX 6.50 Trifecta £21.40.
Owner J C Smith **Bred** Littleton Stud **Trained** Newmarket, Suffolk
■ Stewards' Enquiry : Jordan Uys 1-day ban; carless riding (19th Feb)

FOCUS
The third winner on the card to make all. Not the strongest race for the grade with the top weight 7lb below the race ceiling and the other five runners 18lb or more below it, but the favourite was still impressive. The runner-up has been rated to form.

460 DAILY UNIBET EARLY PRICES FROM 9AM MAIDEN STKS 5f 6y(P)
4:10 (4:10) (Class 5) 3-Y-O+ **£2,911** (£866; £432; £216) **Stalls** High

Form RPR
1 **Justice Lady (IRE)** 3-8-9 0........................ MartinLane 1 64+
(David Elsworth) *slowly away: chsd ldng pair after 2f: pushed along and clsd fr over 1f out: urged into ld last 75yds: on top at fin* **11/10**[1]
42-4 **2** *¾* **Hot Stuff**[14] 286 3-9-0 63........................ JimCrowley 3 66
(Tony Carroll) *sn chsd ldr: shkn up 1/2-way: clsd over 1f out: rdn to ld ins fnl f: hdd last 75yds: kpt on* **7/4**[2]
60-3 **3** *3* **Blue Amazon (IRE)**[14] 292 4-9-2 57........................(v[1]) PaddyBradley[(7)] 4 56
(Lee Carter) *led: clr after 2f: 4 l up 2f out: wknd and hdd ins fnl f* **12/1**
45- **4** *2* **Showdaisy**[41] 8355 3-8-9 0........................(t[1]) OisinMurphy 5 43
(Andrew Balding) *dwlt: off the pce in last: hanging and racd awkwardly bnd 2f out: kpt on fnl f: no ch* **8/1**[3]
2-55 **5** *15* **Tilsworth Micky**[20] 211 4-9-11 63........................ AlistairRawlinson[(3)] 2
(J R Jenkins) *sn hld up: off the pce fr 1/2-way: hanging bnd 2f out: wknd and t.o* **8/1**[3]
58.53s (-0.27) **Going Correction** 0.0s/f (Stan)
WFA 3 from 4yo 14lb 5 Ran SP% **113.9**
Speed ratings (Par 103): **102,100,96,92,68**
CSF £3.45 TOTE £1.80: £1.10, £2.20; EX 3.40 Trifecta £12.10.
Owner Robert Ng **Bred** Miss Audrey F Thompson **Trained** Newmarket, Suffolk

FOCUS
A moderate sprint maiden run at a decent pace, though the winner is open to improvement. The third has been rated close to her C&D latest.

461 32RED CASINO H'CAP 1m 5f (P)
4:40 (4:40) (Class 6) (0-65,65) 4-Y-O+ **£2,264** (£673; £336; £168) **Stalls** Low

Form RPR
0-21 **1** **Trending (IRE)**[13] 316 7-9-4 62........................(t) RichardKingscote 8 72
(Jeremy Gask) *plld hrd: led after 3f: mde rest in handy ld: stl 4 l up 2f out: drvn over 1f out: tired fnl f but a holding on* **7/2**[2]
35-6 **2** *1 ¼* **Galuppi**[4] 417 5-8-11 58........................(b) AlistairRawlinson[(3)] 9 64
(J R Jenkins) *s.s: hld up in last pair: gng bttr than most 3f out: prog over 2f out: rdn over 1f out: styd on to take 2nd nr fin and cl on wnr: too much to do* **10/1**
00-4 **3** *nk* **Lucky Dottie**[29] 84 5-8-8 52........................ KieranO'Neill 5 58
(Pat Phelan) *settled in 6th: hung rt sing fnl circ over 9f out: rdn and prog 3f out: chsd wnr over 1f out: steadily clsd but lost 2nd nr fin* **5/1**[3]
26-4 **4** *5* **Opera Buff**[24] 156 7-9-7 65........................(p) GeorgeBaker 4 64
(Jose Santos) *chsd ldr 2f: racd in 3rd after: rdn over 3f out: no imp 2f out* **7/2**[2]
620 **5** *½* **Annakrista (GER)**[4] 417 8-9-1 59........................(bt) WilliamCarson 6 57
(Zoe Davison) *led 3f: chsd wnr and clr of rest: rdn over 3f out: lost 2nd and wknd over 1f out* **50/1**
00-6 **6** *1 ¼* **Hiorne Tower (FR)**[16] 261 5-8-13 57........................ MartinDwyer 2 53
(John Best) *stdd s: hld up in last trio: rdn wl over 2f out: one pce and no threat* **11/4**[1]
2-20 **7** *3 ¼* **Little Flo**[8] 368 5-8-9 53........................ RyanPowell 7 45
(William Stone) *chsd ldrs: rdn to dispute 3rd 3f out: wknd 2f out* **10/1**
00-0 **8** *1 ¼* **Star Anise (FR)**[16] 261 5-9-1 59........................ MartinLane 3 49
(Paddy Butler) *stdd s: hld up in last: shkn up 3f out: no prog* **25/1**
30-5 **9** *nk* **Toptempo**[34] 27 7-9-4 62........................ JimmyQuinn 1 51
(Ralph J Smith) *in tch: urged along 4f out: wknd over 2f out* **25/1**
2m 45.12s (-0.88) **Going Correction** 0.0s/f (Stan) 9 Ran SP% **115.6**
Speed ratings (Par 101): **102,101,101,97,97 96,94,94,93**
CSF £37.11 CT £174.83 TOTE £4.20: £1.90, £3.50, £2.20; EX 36.50 Trifecta £217.80.
Owner The Twitterati **Bred** Thomas Hassett **Trained** Stockbridge, Hants

FOCUS
A moderate staying handicap, but another remarkable effort from the winner.
T/Plt: £20.90 to a £1 stake. Pool: £52,463.38 - 1,831.76 winning tickets. T/Qpdt: £9.50 to a £1 stake. Pool: £3,982.31 - 308.1 winning tickets. **Jonathan Neesom**

418 WOLVERHAMPTON (A.W) (L-H)
Friday, February 5

OFFICIAL GOING: Tapeta: standard
Wind: Strong behind Weather: Overcast

462 DOWNLOAD THE NEW UNIBET RACING APP H'CAP 5f 20y (Tp)
5:15 (5:15) (Class 5) (0-75,78) 4-Y-O+ **£2,975** (£885; £442; £221) **Stalls** Low

Form RPR
45-0 **1** **Rich Again (IRE)**[21] 198 7-9-5 71........................(b) TedDurcan 8 83
(James Bethell) *hld up: swtchd lft and hdwy over 1f out: rdn to ld wl ins fnl f: r.o* **3/1**[2]
11-5 **2** *1 ½* **Miracle Garden**[28] 106 4-9-7 73........................(p) TomEaves 4 80
(Roy Brotherton) *led 4f out: hrd rdn and hdd wl ins fnl f: edgd lft: styd on same pce* **2/1**[1]
6-05 **3** *1 ¼* **Quality Art (USA)**[14] 293 8-9-0 69........................ RobHornby[(3)] 3 71
(Simon Hodgson) *hld up in tch: shkn up over 1f out: styd on* **18/1**
36-5 **4** *nk* **Thataboy (IRE)**[29] 76 5-9-4........................ GrahamGibbons 2 72
(Tom Dascombe) *chsd ldrs: rdn over 1f out: styng on same pce whn n.m.r wl ins fnl f* **8/1**
43-1 **5** *2* **James Bond Girl (USA)**[22] 177 4-9-2 68........................(p) GrahamLee 6 62
(Robert Cowell) *prom: hmpd and lost pl sn after s: rdn over 1f out: styd on same pce* **10/1**
0-44 **6** *shd* **Zipedeedodah (IRE)**[23] 162 4-9-1 67........................(t) AdamKirby 5 60
(Joseph Tuite) *led 1f: chsd ldr: rdn and ev ch over 1f out: no ex ins fnl f* **14/1**
-131 **7** *nk* **Jaarih (IRE)**[8] 364 4-9-12 78 6ex........................ JFEgan 7 70
(Conor Dore) *chsd ldrs: edgd lft sn after s: rdn over 1f out: no ex fnl f* **7/2**[3]
200- **8** *½* **Dusty Blue**[70] 8011 4-8-11 66........................ GeorgeDowning[(3)] 1 56
(Tony Carroll) *s.i.s: rdn 1/2-way: nvr on terms* **50/1**
1m 1.09s (-0.81) **Going Correction** -0.05s/f (Stan) 8 Ran SP% **114.6**
Speed ratings (Par 103): **104,101,99,99,95 95,95,94**
CSF £9.45 CT £88.41 TOTE £4.40: £1.60, £1.10, £4.80; EX 12.10 Trifecta £103.30.
Owner Richard T Vickers **Bred** Mrs Sandra Maye **Trained** Middleham Moor, N Yorks

FOCUS
An ordinary sprint handicap. The third has been rated similar to his latest effort.

463 CORAL CONNECT APPRENTICE H'CAP 1m 1f 103y (Tp)
5:45 (5:45) (Class 6) (0-60,60) 4-Y-O+ **£2,328** (£693; £346; £173) **Stalls** Low

Form RPR
/6-3 **1** **Black Minstrel (IRE)**[20] 222 7-9-4 60........................(p) PatrickVaughan[(3)] 7 67
(John O'Shea) *s.i.s: sn prom: rdn to ld and edgd lft ins fnl f: r.o* **3/1**[1]
0-50 **2** *1 ¼* **Debit**[14] 297 5-9-4 57........................ RhiainIngram 11 62
(Simon Hodgson) *hld up: hdwy over 2f out: rdn over 1f out: edgd lft ins fnl f: r.o* **33/1**
0-42 **3** *¾* **Celtic Artisan (IRE)**[7] 383 5-8-12 51........................(b) DanielleMooney 8 54
(Rebecca Menzies) *led: racd keenly: rdn over 1f out: hdd ins fnl f: styd on same pce* **7/2**[2]
00-0 **4** *1 ¼* **Glasgow Central**[22] 170 5-8-11 57........................ GeorgeWood[(7)] 3 58
(Phil McEntee) *chsd ldrs: rdn over 2f out: nt clr run and swtchd lft ins fnl f: kpt on* **25/1**
40-0 **5** *hd* **Teide Peak (IRE)**[7] 378 7-8-7 51........................(tp) MitchGodwin[(5)] 5 51
(Grace Harris) *prom: rdn over 1f out: styd on same pce ins fnl f* **20/1**

000- **6** nse **Kicking The Can (IRE)**100 7557 5-9-5 **58**.......................... HarryBurns 9 58
(David Thompson) *chsd ldr: rdn and ev ch over 1f out: no ex ins fnl f* **33/1**
360- **7** ½ **Evacusafe Lady**67 8044 5-9-0 **58**..............................(t) CliffordLee(5) 4 57
(John Ryan) *hld up: pushed along 1/2-way: nvr trbld ldrs* **10/1**
04-3 **8** ¾ **Sylvette**22 170 4-9-1 **59**..(vt1) CameronNoble(5) 2 60
(Roger Varian) *prom: pushed along over 2f out: styng on whn hmpd wl ins fnl f* **8/1**3
0-23 **9** ¾ **Mfiftythreedotcom (IRE)**13 316 5-8-10 **54**.....(b) AdamMcNamara(5) 6 51
(Richard Fahey) *chsd ldrs: rdn over 1f out: no ex ins fnl f* **3/1**1
55-0 **10** 3 **Who'sthedaddy**14 295 4-9-0 **60**................(b1) KimberleyVanderVegt(7) 1 51
(Daniel Kubler) *s.s: a in rr* **16/1**

2m 0.2s (-0.60) **Going Correction** -0.05s/f (Stan) **10** Ran SP% **112.8**
Speed ratings (Par 101): **100,98,98,97,96 96,96,95,95,92**
CSF £109.15 CT £356.40 TOTE £4.40: £1.90, £8.60, £1.10; EX 104.80 Trifecta £467.80.
Owner Red & Black Racing **Bred** Corduff Stud Ltd **Trained** Elton, Gloucs
■ Stewards' Enquiry : George Wood 2-day ban; careless riding (19th-20th Feb)
Danielle Mooney jockey said gelding hung left-handed in the home straight
Kimberley Van der Vegt jockey said gelding missed the break

FOCUS
A moderate handicap restricted to apprentice jockeys.

464 BET IN PLAY AT CORAL CLAIMING STKS 1m 1f 103y (Tp)
6:15 (6:15) (Class 5) 4-Y-O+ **£2,975** (£885; £442; £221) **Stalls** Low

Form RPR
56-5 **1** **Vastly (USA)**31 53 7-8-12 60................................(bt) AdamBeschizza 5 69
(Julia Feilden) *mde all: set stdy pce tl qcknd over 2f out: rdn over 1f out: styd on* **12/1**
3-56 **2** 1 **Matraash (USA)**13 316 10-8-12 64.............................(be) JoeFanning 1 67
(Daniel Mark Loughnane) *chsd wnr: rdn over 1f out: edgd lft ins fnl f: styd on* **8/1**3
51-5 **3** 1 **Tatting**33 33 7-9-0 69...................................... WilliamTwiston-Davies 2 67
(Mark Hoad) *chsd ldrs: rdn over 3f out: hung lft fr over 1f out: kpt on* **11/2**2
110- **4** 6 **Field Of Dream**60 8132 9-9-3 89.......................................(p) AdamKirby 3 57
(Jamie Osborne) *hld up: rdn over 1f out: nvr trbld ldrs* **1/2**1
050- **5** nse **Evervescent (IRE)**121 7045 7-8-9 65.............................. EoinWalsh(3) 4 52
(Graeme McPherson) *rrd s: hld up: rdn over 1f out: nvr on terms* **25/1**
210- **6** 1 **Rio Falls (IRE)**37 8405 4-8-13 72...................................... GrahamLee 6 51
(Jennie Candlish) *hld up: rdn over 1f out: n.d* **10/1**

2m 1.37s (0.57) **Going Correction** -0.05s/f (Stan) **6** Ran SP% **113.8**
Speed ratings (Par 103): **95,94,93,87,87 86**
CSF £98.37 TOTE £14.80: £3.50, £2.90; EX 88.90 Trifecta £243.20.Tatting was claimed by C. Dore for £7,000.
Owner The Sultans of Speed **Bred** Juddmonte Farms Inc **Trained** Exning, Suffolk

FOCUS
A muddling claimer in which the first four home raced 1-2-3-4 more or less the whole round, in single file for much of the journey. The time was much the slowest of three races at the trip. The winner has been rated back to the level of his C&D maiden win, but with little confidence given he had the run of the race.

465 DOWNLOAD THE CORAL APP H'CAP 1m 1f 103y (Tp)
6:45 (6:45) (Class 4) (0-85,85) 4-Y-O+ **£5,175** (£1,540; £769; £384) **Stalls** Low

Form RPR
23-1 **1** **Coillte Cailin (IRE)**23 160 6-9-2 **80**................................ GrahamLee 7 90
(Daniel Mark Loughnane) *s.i.s: hld up: hdwy over 2f out: rdn to ld ins fnl f: r.o* **12/1**
34-1 **2** 1 **Perfect Cracker**30 73 8-9-7 **85**.. AdamKirby 9 93
(Clive Cox) *hld up in tch: chsd ldr over 2f out: led over 1f out: rdn and hdd ins fnl f: styd on same pce* **13/2**
03-2 **3** 1 ¼ **Off The Pulse**30 73 6-8-11 **75**............................(p) GrahamGibbons 12 80
(John Mackie) *chsd ldrs: led over 2f out: rdn and hdd over 1f out: styd on same pce ins fnl f* **8/1**
51-3 **4** 2 **Berlusca (IRE)**23 160 7-9-4 **82**................................... DanielTudhope 8 83
(David O'Meara) *hld up: racd wd arnd the fnl bnd: hdwy over 1f out: rdn and swtchd lft ins fnl f: styd on same pce* **9/2**2
301- **5** ¾ **Corton Lad**56 8175 6-9-7 **85**..(tp) PhillipMakin 10 85
(Keith Dalgleish) *mid-div: hdwy over 3f out: rdn over 1f out: styd on same pce fnl f* **4/1**1
312- **6** 1 ¼ **Sbraase**302 1284 5-9-7 **85**... RobertHavlin 6 82
(James Tate) *hld up: hdwy over 1f out: sn rdn: styd on same pce ins fnl f* **7/1**
134- **7** 4 ½ **Qasser (IRE)**30 2362 7-8-9 **73**... JoeFanning 5 61
(Harry Whittington) *chsd ldr tl over 3f out: nt clr run and lost pl over 2f out: sn rdn: wknd and eased fnl f* **11/2**3
15-3 **8** ½ **Idol Deputy (FR)**30 73 10-8-7 **76**.....................(p) RachealKneller(5) 2 62
(James Bennett) *chsd ldrs: nt clr run and lost pl over 2f out: wknd fnl f* **16/1**
143- **9** 3 ¼ **Peterhouse (USA)**147 6275 4-9-4 **82**.................................. BenCurtis 3 62
(Jason Ward) *hld up: pushed along 4f out: in rr whn hmpd 3f out: sn wknd* **10/1**
040- **10** 23 **Spes Nostra**230 3386 8-9-7 **85**...(b) TomEaves 4 16
(Iain Jardine) *led: rdn and hdd over 2f out: sn wknd* **28/1**

1m 57.4s (-3.40) **Going Correction** -0.05s/f (Stan) **10** Ran SP% **116.6**
Speed ratings (Par 105): **113,112,111,109,108 107,103,103,100,79**
CSF £87.86 CT £669.96 TOTE £18.90: £4.20, £2.10, £2.90; EX 78.40 Trifecta £436.40.
Owner Peter J Moran **Bred** Whisperview Trading Ltd **Trained** Baldwin's Gate, Staffs

FOCUS
A fair, competitive handicap. The runner-up has been rated as running a small pb.

466 32RED.COM MAIDEN STKS 1m 141y (Tp)
7:15 (7:16) (Class 5) 3-Y-O **£2,975** (£885; £442; £221) **Stalls** Low

Form RPR
5-4 **1** **Jintshi**13 314 3-9-5 0.. JoeFanning 3 78+
(Mark Johnston) *chsd ldr tl led over 2f out: shkn up over 1f out: styd on wl* **5/2**2
45- **2** 2 ½ **Carry Me Home**108 7357 3-9-5 0............................... GrahamGibbons 1 70
(Charles Hills) *a.p: rdn to chse wnr over 1f out: edgd lft and styd on same pce ins fnl f* **13/2**
032- **3** 6 **Rivers Of Asia**125 6929 3-9-5 78................................(t) DanielTudhope 2 56
(Philip McBride) *led: rdn and hdd over 2f out: hung lft fr over 1f out: wknd ins fnl f* **3/1**3
3- **4** 3 **Dangerous Thought (USA)**51 8251 3-9-5 0................. RobertHavlin 5 49
(John Gosden) *prom: rdn over 2f out: wknd over 1f out* **11/8**1
5 4 **New Legend (IRE)** 3-9-5 0... GrahamLee 4 40
(Robert Cowell) *s.i.s: sn pushed along in rr: rdn and wknd over 2f out* **28/1**

1m 48.55s (-1.55) **Going Correction** -0.05s/f (Stan) **5** Ran SP% **112.5**
Speed ratings (Par 97): **104,101,96,93,90**
CSF £18.15 TOTE £3.80: £1.50, £3.20; EX 15.80 Trifecta £33.10.
Owner Sheikh Hamdan bin Mohammed Al Maktoum **Bred** Trg Vestey **Trained** Middleham Moor, N Yorks

FOCUS
The favourite flopped and there wasn't much depth to this maiden. The level is a bit fluid, with the third and fourth disappointing.

467 LADBROKES H'CAP 1m 141y (Tp)
7:45 (7:45) (Class 5) (0-70,70) 4-Y-O+ **£2,975** (£885; £442) **Stalls** Low

Form RPR
123- **1** **Jumbo Prado (USA)**45 8354 7-9-2 **65**..............................(b) AdamKirby 5 70
(Daniel Mark Loughnane) *mde all: set stdy pce tl qcknd over 2f out: rdn over 1f out: r.o* **2/5**1
04-0 **2** 3 ¾ **Toymaker**32 39 9-8-10 **59** ow1.................................(t) GrahamGibbons 1 55
(Phil McEntee) *hld up in tch: rdn to chse wnr over 1f out: no ex ins fnl f* **7/2**2
02/4 **3** hd **Tatawu (IRE)**21 202 4-9-2 **70**.. CiaranMckee(5) 3 66
(Peter Hiatt) *chsd wnr: rdn over 2f out: lost 2nd over 1f out: styd on same pce* **7/1**3

1m 51.21s (1.11) **Going Correction** -0.05s/f (Stan) **3** Ran SP% **106.2**
Speed ratings (Par 103): **93,89,89**
CSF £2.04 TOTE £1.30; EX 1.80 Trifecta £1.70.
Owner J T Stimpson **Bred** Mr & Mrs Foreman Hardy **Trained** Baldwin's Gate, Staffs

FOCUS
A poor turnout even allowing for two non-runners and it was straightforward for the odds-on jolly. The winner has been rated to form.
T/Jkpt: Not won. T/Plt: £543.60 to a £1 stake. Pool: £89,437.56 - 120.09 winning tickets. T/Qpdt: £104.60 to a £1 stake. Pool: £8,318.77 - 58.82 winning tickets. **Colin Roberts**

468 - 481a (Foreign Racing) - See Raceform Interactive

456LINGFIELD (L-H)
Saturday, February 6

OFFICIAL GOING: Polytrack: standard
Wind: strong, behind Weather: overcast, windy

482 BET NOW WITH THE LADBROKES APP H'CAP 7f 1y(P)
1:10 (1:10) (Class 5) (0-70,72) 4-Y-O+ **£3,234** (£962; £481; £240) **Stalls** Low

Form RPR
-411 **1** **Clement (IRE)**7 403 6-9-2 **72**.....................................(v) GeorgiaCox(7) 2 86
(John O'Shea) *in tch in midfield: effrt and gd hdwy to ld 2f out: sn clr and in command: r.o wl: readily* **9/4**1
4-34 **2** 4 **Oak Bluffs (IRE)**16 276 5-8-11 **60**................................ TonyHamilton 10 64
(Richard Fahey) *hld up in midfield: stl travelling wl but nt clr run over 2f out tl swtchd lft and hdwy on inner over 1f out: chsd clr wnr ins fnl f: r.o but no ch w wnr* **20/1**
225- **3** 1 ¼ **Polar Kite (IRE)**40 8376 8-8-11 **63**.............................. RobHornby(3) 11 64
(Michael Attwater) *hld up off the pce in last trio: stl plenty to do whn swtchd rt over 1f out: gd hdwy to go 3rd fnl 100yds: styd on: nvr trbld ldrs* **20/1**
620- **4** 2 ¼ **Veeraya**131 6816 6-9-4 **67**...(t) AdamBeschizza 7 62
(Julia Feilden) *in tch in midfield: rdn and effrt whn hung rt bnd 2f out: no ch w wnr and styd on same pce fr over 1f out* **33/1**
4-13 **5** hd **Mercury**17 264 4-8-9 **58**... TomEaves 5 52
(Kevin Ryan) *led: rdn and hdd 2f out: sn outpcd: lost 2nd 150yds out: wknd wl ins fnl f* **12/1**
15-1 **6** 1 ¾ **Etaad (USA)**22 190 5-9-6 **69**...(b) GeorgeBaker 9 59
(Gary Moore) *hld up off the pce in last trio: swtchd lft and effrt over 1f out: sme hdwy but nvr on terms w ldrs: 6th and wl hld whn eased towards fin* **9/4**1
50-5 **7** 4 ½ **Autumn Tonic (IRE)**28 124 4-8-8 **57**................................ LukeMorris 6 35
(Simon Dow) *in tch in midfield: effrt and sme hdwy over 2f out: no imp and btn over 1f out: sn wknd* **20/1**
400- **8** nk **For Shia And Lula (IRE)**98 7639 7-9-7 **70**...................... AdamKirby 3 47
(Daniel Mark Loughnane) *chsd ldr tl losing pl u.p over 2f out: wknd over 1f out* **10/1**3
5-00 **9** 4 **Duke Of North (IRE)**7 398 4-8-9 **63**..............(t1) JosephineGordon(5) 8 30
(Jim Boyle) *v.s.a: nvr on terms* **16/1**
/55- **10** 2 ½ **Lady Maesmor**15 305 4-9-3 **66**.. LeighRoche 1 26
(D J Bunyan, Ire) *chsd ldrs tl lost pl over 2f out: wl btn and eased 1f out* **20/1**
3-33 **11** 3 ½ **Pyroclastic (IRE)**22 190 4-8-5 **61**...........................(b) RhiainIngram(7) 4 12
(Jim Boyle) *chsd ldrs on outer: 3rd and rdn and 2f out: fdd and wl bhd fnl f* **8/1**2

1m 23.59s (-1.21) **Going Correction** +0.025s/f (Slow) **11** Ran SP% **117.3**
Speed ratings (Par 103): **107,102,101,98,98 96,91,90,86,83 79**
CSF £58.46 CT £744.86 TOTE £3.40: £1.70, £4.50, £4.80; EX 51.90 Trifecta £757.00.
Owner K W Bell **Bred** P Kelly **Trained** Elton, Gloucs

FOCUS
The improving winner showed himself better than this level and his rivals couldn't live with him, recording a time quicker than the later Class 2. The second and third have been rated close to their recent form.

483 UNIBET CLEVES STKS (ALL-WEATHER CHAMPIONSHIP FAST-TRACK QUALIFIER) (LISTED RACE) 6f 1y(P)
1:45 (1:46) (Class 1) 4-Y-O+
£25,519 (£9,675; £4,842; £2,412; £1,210; £607) **Stalls** Low

Form RPR
055- **1** **Rivellino**73 7978 6-9-0 100... DougieCostello 5 108
(K R Burke) *chsd ldr: rdn 2f out: styd on u.p ins fnl f: led last strides* **7/1**3
/0-2 **2** nk **Gamgoom**35 17 5-9-3 101... MartinHarley 12 110
(Mario Hofer, Germany) *broke fast to ld and crossed to rail: rdn and fnd ex 2f out: clr over 1f out: drvn fnl f: worn down and hdd last strides* **33/1**
41- **3** 1 ½ **Cold As Ice (SAF)**47 8326 4-8-9 110................................. JoeFanning 4 97+
(William Haggas) *taken down early: dwlt and short of room sn after s: hld up towards rr: effrt but stl plenty to do over 1f out: r.o v strly ins fnl f: snatched 3rd last strides: nvr gng to rch ldrs* **9/4**1

01-3 **4** *nk* **Lightscameraction (IRE)**[35] 17 4-9-0 107..................(p) LukeMorris 9 101
(Gay Kelleway) *chsd ldrs: rdn and outpcd by ldng pair 2f out: battling for 3rd and hrd drvn 1f out: kpt on u.p but nvr enough pce to get bk on terms w ldng pair* **33/1**

1-22 **5** *nse* **Boomerang Bob (IRE)**[15] 288 7-9-0 97....................... WilliamCarson 1 101
(Jamie Osborne) *taken down early: in tch in midfield: rdn in 6th and outpcd 2f out: rallied 1f out: styd on strly u.p ins fnl f: nvr gng to rch ldrs* **20/1**

05-6 **6** *nk* **Justice Good (IRE)**[15] 288 4-9-0 100...........................(t) TomQueally 3 100
(David Elsworth) *in tch in midfield: 5th and outpcd u.p 2f out: rallied 1f out: wnt 3rd towards fin: kpt on but lost 3 pls cl home* **25/1**

41-1 **7** *1/2* **Chookie Royale**[24] 166 8-9-0 109...................................(p) TomEaves 2 99
(Keith Dalgleish) *taken down early: chsd ldrs: 3rd and outpcd u.p 2f out: kpt on but nvr getting bk on terms w ldrs: lost 4 pls wl ins fnl f* **4/1**[2]

000- **8** *1 1/2* **Golden Steps (FR)**[91] 7755 5-9-0 101.......................... AndreaAtzeni 6 94
(Marco Botti) *taken down early: taken down early: hld up in midfield: hmpd 5f out and in last quartet after: rdn over 1f out: kpt on but nvr a threat* **12/1**

21-2 **9** *nk* **My Call**[21] 214 4-8-9 100...(p) WilliamBuick 10 88
(Saeed bin Suroor) *hld up in tch in midfield: effrt whn wd and outpcd bnd 2f out: no imp after* **8/1**

24-3 **10** *2 1/4* **Alben Star (IRE)**[24] 166 8-9-0 107.............................. TonyHamilton 11 86
(Richard Fahey) *stdd and dropped in bhd after s: hld up in rr: hmpd 5f out: plenty to do and effrt on inner over 1f out: no imp: n.d* **12/1**

25-2 **11** *1 3/4* **Intransigent**[24] 166 7-9-0 104... OisinMurphy 7 80
(Andrew Balding) *hld up in last trio: plenty to do and effrt wl over 1f out: no imp: n.d* **16/1**

061- **12** *3 3/4* **Angelic Lord (IRE)**[217] 3892 4-9-0 108.................... RichardKingscote 8 68
(Tom Dascombe) *s.i.s: a off the pce in last trio: effrt 2f out: sn wl btn* **8/1**

1m 10.64s (-1.26) **Going Correction** +0.025s/f (Slow) **12** Ran SP% **121.2**
Speed ratings (Par 111): **109,108,106,106,106 105,105,103,102,99 97,92**
CSF £228.83 TOTE £9.20: £3.20, £5.80, £1.10; EX 250.10 Trifecta £906.70.

Owner Mrs Melba Bryce **Bred** Castlemartin Sky & Skymarc Farm **Trained** Middleham Moor, N Yorks

■ Stewards' Enquiry : Martin Harley one-day ban; careless riding (20th Feb)

FOCUS
A repeat of the 2015 running, the same winner who again came into this fresh and once more benefited from a handy ride in a modestly run race. The winner has been rated to form.

484 DAILY PRICE BOOSTS AT UNIBET H'CAP 5f 6y(P)
2:20 (2:20) (Class 4) (0-85,85) 4-Y-O+ **£5,175** (£1,540; £769; £384) **Stalls** High

Form RPR

50-0 **1** **Taajub (IRE)**[30] 86 9-9-2 80.. ShaneKelly 1 89
(Peter Crate) *in tch in 6th but on and off the bridle: clsd over 1f out: gap opened and qcknd to ld ins fnl f: sn in command: r.o* **5/1**[3]

14-4 **2** *2 1/4* **Burning Thread (IRE)**[29] 106 9-9-7 85.......................(b) OisinMurphy 4 86
(David Elsworth) *in tch in midfield: effrt on inner to chal 1f out: chsd wnr and styd on same pce fnl 100yds* **11/4**[1]

16-0 **3** *1 1/4* **Archie Stevens**[26] 142 6-8-7 76.......................... JosephineGordon(5) 2 73
(David Evans) *led: rdn over 1f out: sn drifted rt: hdd ins fnl f: no ex and wknd fnl 100yds* **4/1**[2]

0-42 **4** *1 1/4* **Desert Command**[18] 250 6-9-4 82...........................(p) DanielTudhope 5 74
(Robert Cowell) *trckd ldrs and travelled strly: effrt and little rspnse over 1f out: wl hld and styd on same pce ins fnl f* **11/4**[1]

00-0 **5** *1 3/4* **Diamond Charlie (IRE)**[13] 323 8-8-13 77...................... JimCrowley 6 63
(Simon Dow) *pressed wnr: unable qck and carried rt ent fnl f: sn no ex: wknd ins fnl f* **12/1**

12-0 **6** *1* **Mighty Zip (USA)**[22] 198 4-9-1 79..................................(b) TomEaves 7 61
(Kevin Ryan) *sn bustled along to press ldrs on outer: lost pl u.p bnd 2f out: wknd fnl f* **8/1**

011- **7** *6* **Secret Glance**[185] 5032 4-9-3 81................................ AdamBeschizza 3 42
(Richard Rowe) *stdd s: a detached in last: n.d* **16/1**

57.97s (-0.83) **Going Correction** +0.025s/f (Slow) **7** Ran SP% **114.7**
Speed ratings (Par 105): **107,103,101,99,96 95,85**
CSF £19.27 TOTE £5.60: £2.60, £1.70; EX 20.00 Trifecta £88.90.

Owner Peter Crate **Bred** Rabbah Bloodstock Limited **Trained** Newdigate, Surrey

FOCUS
There was a three-way battle for the lead and a couple of closers finished one-two. The winner has been rated to the best of his form over the past two years.

485 CORAL.CO.UK WINTER DERBY TRIAL STKS (ALL-WEATHER CHAMPIONSHIP FAST-TRACK QUALIFIER) (LISTED) 1m 2f (P)
2:55 (2:55) (Class 1) 4-Y-O+
£25,519 (£9,675; £4,842; £2,412; £1,210; £607) **Stalls** Low

Form RPR

522- **1** **Grendisar (IRE)**[49] 8310 6-9-0 108..................................(p) AdamKirby 6 112
(Marco Botti) *hld up in tch in midfield: clsd to trck ldrs 2f out: swtchd lft and rdn to chal jst over 1f out: drvn to ld 150yds: styd on wl* **4/1**[2]

641- **2** *1/2* **Festive Fare**[56] 8208 4-8-13 108.. WilliamBuick 5 111
(Charlie Appleby) *in tch in midfield: hdwy and pushed along to press ldr 2f out: ev ch over 1f out: drvn fnl f: kpt on: wnt 2nd last strides* **1/1**[1]

3-13 **3** *nk* **Lamar (IRE)**[21] 214 5-8-12 105... LukeMorris 3 108
(James Tate) *chsd ldng trio: wnt 2nd 3f out tl rdn to ld 2f out: hrd pressed and drvn over 1f out: hdd 150yds out: styd on same pce after: lost 2nd last strides* **8/1**

54-2 **4** *shd* **Captain Cat (IRE)**[28] 125 7-9-0 107.............................. JamieSpencer 4 110
(Roger Charlton) *stdd s: hld up in last trio: clsd and wl in tch over 2f out: wd bnd 2f out: rdn and effrt to press ldrs 1f out: kpt on same pce u.p fnl 100yds* **6/1**[3]

404- **5** *3 3/4* **Watersmeet**[141] 6500 5-9-0 103... JoeFanning 1 102
(Mark Johnston) *chsd ldrs: nt clr run over 2f out: swtchd rt 2f out: sn rdn and ev ch: no ex and btn ins fnl f: wknd fnl 100yds* **12/1**

46-3 **6** *6* **Complicit (IRE)**[28] 125 5-9-0 102.................................... GrahamLee 8 90
(Paul Cole) *chsd ldr tl led over 3f out: rdn and hdd 2f out: sn outpcd and btn: wknd fnl f* **20/1**

2-14 **7** *26* **Mitre Peak**[5] 422 4-8-8 80... SammyJoBell 2 33
(Richard Fahey) *led tl over 3f out: sn u.p and lost pl 3f out: lost tch 2f out: t.o* **66/1**

20-4 **8** *45* **Brocklebank (IRE)**[10] 353 7-9-0 88................ WilliamTwiston-Davies 9
(Simon Dow) *stdd s: hld up in last pair: rdn over 3f out: sn lost tch: eased 2f out: t.o* **100/1**

342- **P** **Charles Camoin (IRE)**[56] 8208 8-9-0 97.......................... MartinDwyer 7
(Sylvester Kirk) *stdd s: hld up in last pair: rdn over 3f out: sn lost tch: wl btn whn hung lft jst over 2f out: lost action and sn eased: p.u and dismntd 1f out* **33/1**

2m 3.68s (-2.92) **Going Correction** +0.025s/f (Slow)
WFA 4 from 5yo+ 1lb **9** Ran SP% **113.3**
Speed ratings (Par 111): **112,111,111,111,108 103,82,46,**
CSF £8.00 TOTE £4.20: £1.60, £1.10, £2.10; EX 9.90 Trifecta £25.00.

Owner Mohamed Albousi Alghufli **Bred** Old Carhue & Graeng Bloodstock **Trained** Newmarket, Suffolk

■ Stewards' Enquiry : William Buick two-day ban; used his whip down the shoulder in the forehand (20th, 22nd Feb)

FOCUS
A solid trial for the Winter Derby and the principals, bar Lamar, will presumably be back for the main event at the end of the month, but it's not difficult to imagine Sloane Avenue proving in a different league if he shows up. The winner has been rated to form.

486 LADBROKES H'CAP 7f 1y(P)
3:30 (3:36) (Class 2) 4-Y-O+
£28,012 (£6,291; £6,291; £2,097; £1,048; £526) **Stalls** Low

Form RPR

12-1 **1** **Realize**[15] 290 6-9-10 101..(t) OisinMurphy 10 109
(Stuart Williams) *chsd ldrs: effrt in 3rd 2f out: drvn and ev ch 1f out: sustained chal to ld wl ins fnl f: kpt on: all out* **6/1**[2]

01-2 **2** *nk* **Certificate**[32] 50 5-9-5 96..(b[1]) AndreaAtzeni 14 103
(Roger Varian) *led: rdn wl over 1f out: sustained battled w wnr fr 1f out: hdd wl ins fnl f: kpt on wl but a jst hld after* **8/1**

04-2 **2** *dht* **Shyron**[15] 290 5-8-12 89.. RyanPowell 3 96
(George Margarson) *hld up in last quartet: hdwy on inner over 1f out: chsng ldrs 100yds: hung rt but r.o wl towards fin: nt quite rch wnr* **5/1**[1]

2114 **4** *nk* **Jammy Guest (IRE)**[3] 433 6-8-0 80.......................... DannyBrock(3) 4 86+
(George Margarson) *hld up in last quartet: stl in last and effrt whn edgd lft over 1f out: hdwy 1f out: str run ins fnl f: gng on wl at fin: nt quite rch ldrs* **8/1**

00-5 **5** *1* **Grey Mirage**[28] 125 7-9-6 97..(p) AdamKirby 2 101+
(Marco Botti) *hld up in tch in midfield: effrt over 1f out: sn nt clr run: swtchd rt and hdwy u.p ins fnl f: chsng ldrs whn nt clr run and eased wl ins fnl f* **7/1**[3]

44-2 **6** *shd* **Dutiful Son (IRE)**[3] 433 6-8-8 85..................................... LukeMorris 5 88
(Simon Dow) *in tch in midfield: effrt 2f out: no imp 1f out: hrd drvn and rallied 1f out: kpt on same pce fnl 100yds* **5/1**[1]

5-30 **7** *1 1/4* **Russian Realm**[15] 290 6-9-1 92.. ShaneKelly 9 92
(Richard Hughes) *w ldr: rdn and ev ch over 1f out: 3rd and no ex 1f out: btn whn pushed rt wl ins fnl f* **16/1**

26-3 **8** *3/4* **Arnold Lane (IRE)**[15] 290 7-8-13 90.................................. TomEaves 1 88
(Mick Channon) *chsd ldrs: rdn 2f out: unable qck 1f out: keeping on same pce and btn whn pushed rt wl ins fnl f* **10/1**

6-10 **9** *3/4* **Lunar Deity**[15] 290 7-9-4 95... JamieSpencer 7 95+
(Stuart Williams) *hld up in midfield: hmpd 5f out: effrt and rdn over 1f out: swtchd rt and no imp jst ins fnl f: hld whn nt clr run and eased wl ins fnl f* **10/1**

6-60 **10** *nk* **Al Khan (IRE)**[15] 290 7-8-11 88.................................(b[1]) GrahamLee 12 83
(Kevin Ryan) *s.i.s: in tch in last quartet: effrt 2f out: kpt on ins fnl f: nvr trbld ldrs* **33/1**

220- **11** *1* **Justice Well**[56] 8199 4-9-9 100... TomQueally 6 92
(David Elsworth) *s.i.s: in rr: rdn 1/2-way: sme late prog: nvr trbld ldrs* **14/1**

04-5 **12** *hd* **Bertiewhittle**[15] 290 8-8-13 90... JackMitchell 11 82
(David Barron) *s.i.s: in tch towards rr: sme hdwy u.p into midfield 2f out: no imp and one pce fnl f* **25/1**

06-5 **13** *2 1/2* **Hallelujah**[24] 166 8-9-1 95... DanielMuscutt(3) 13 80
(James Fanshawe) *in tch in midfield: rdn 1/2-way: lost pl and towards rr 2f out: bhd fnl f* **33/1**

1m 23.85s (-0.95) **Going Correction** +0.025s/f (Slow) **13** Ran SP% **122.8**
Speed ratings (Par 109): **106,105,105,105,104 104,102,101,100,100 99,99,96**
PL: 2.40 Shyron, 2.10 Realize, 2.90 Certificate; EX: R&S: 14.50, R&C: 18.00; R&C £27.04, R&S £18.24: Tricast: R&C&S £134.87, R&S&C: £126.9 TOTE £6.70.

Owner JKB Racing **Bred** M J Watson **Trained** Newmarket, Suffolk

■ Stewards' Enquiry : Ryan Powell caution; careless riding

FOCUS
A good, well-contested handicap. Another pb from the winner.

487 CORAL MAIDEN STKS 1m 4f (P)
4:05 (4:11) (Class 5) 4-Y-O+ **£3,234** (£962; £481; £240) **Stalls** Low

Form RPR

40- **1** **Midnight Whistler (USA)**[135] 6672 4-9-5 0................ PaulMulrennan 4 76+
(Martyn Meade) *t.k.h: led for 1f: chsd ldrs after tl rdn to chse ldr 3f out: led over 1f out: clr ins fnl f: styd on: rdn out* **5/4**[1]

0/ **2** *2* **Medicean Queen (IRE)**[604] 3142 5-9-3 0.......................... LukeMorris 6 68+
(James Tate) *hld up in tch: effrt in cl 3rd 2f out: drvn to chse clr wnr 150yds out: kpt on same pce after* **5/1**[3]

50-3 **3** *2 3/4* **Rose Above**[24] 161 4-9-0 62.. OisinMurphy 3 64
(Andrew Balding) *t.k.h early: in tch: effrt in 4th 2f out: sn outpcd: kpt on same pce after: wnt 3rd cl home* **8/1**

5-22 **4** *nk* **Miss Giler**[13] 325 4-9-0 71.. RobertHavlin 1 63
(John Gosden) *hld up in midfield: swtchd rt after 1f and hdwy to ld 9f out: rdn and hdd over 1f out: no ex: wknd ins fnl f: lost 3rd cl home* **13/8**[2]

6 **5** *27* **Executive Order**[14] 318 7-9-5 0.. TimClark(3) 2 25
(Martin Smith) *t.k.h: led after 1f tl 9f out: chsd ldr after tl 3f out: sn struggling and wknd 2f out: t.o* **66/1**

00 **6** *1* **Shirocco Cloud**[8] 384 4-9-0 0.. SteveDrowne 5 18
(Mrs Ilka Gansera-Leveque) *hld up in last pair: hmpd after 1f out: rdn 4f out: lost tch 3f out: t.o* **50/1**

0 **7** *7* **Jeans Lady**[14] 318 7-9-0 0...............................(b[1]) MichaelJMMurphy(3) 7 7
(John Gallagher) *wnt rt s and s.i.s: early reminders and rdn early: in tch in last pair after 2f: rdn 4f out: lost tch 3f out: t.o* **100/1**

2m 32.77s (-0.23) **Going Correction** +0.025s/f (Slow)
WFA 4 from 5yo+ 3lb **7** Ran SP% **114.8**
Speed ratings (Par 103): **101,99,97,97,79 78,74**
CSF £8.28 TOTE £2.00: £1.40, £4.20; EX 8.30 Trifecta £38.70.

Owner Calypso Bloodstock and Partners **Bred** Kirk Wycoff & Deby Wycoff **Trained** Newmarket, Suffolk

■ Stewards' Enquiry : Robert Havlin one-day ban; carelss riding (20th Feb)

FOCUS
A weak maiden. It's been rated around the fourth.

488 DOWNLOAD THE LADBROKES APP H'CAP 1m 7f 169y(P)
4:35 (4:36) (Class 5) (0-75,75) 4-Y-0+ **£2,911** (£866; £432; £216) **Stalls** Low

Form RPR
-212 **1** **Megara**[9] 358 4-8-12 **66**....................(p) LukeMorris 7 79+
(Sir Mark Prescott Bt) *chsd ldr: upsides 3f out: rdn to ld 2f and sn kicked clr: styd on strly and in n.d after: eased towards fin* **7/4**[1]

13-1 **2** *6* **Saint Honore**[29] 101 4-9-3 **71**.................... TedDurcan 1 75
(Pat Phelan) *stdd s: hld up off the pce in rr: clsd and in tch 1/2-way: effrt as wnr kicked clr 2f out: sn rdn: chsd clr wnr ins fnl f: kpt on but no ch* **7/2**[2]

6/22 **3** *nk* **Lucky Jim**[20] 234 5-9-8 **70**.................... MartinLane 3 73
(David Dennis) *led: jnd 3f out: sn rdn: hdd 2f out and immediately outpcd: kpt on same pce after: lost 2nd ins fnl f* **9/2**[3]

405- **4** *½* **Burning Desire (IRE)**[12] 8383 5-9-5 **67**....................(tp) ShaneKelly 2 70
(Richard Hughes) *chsd ldng pair: rdn over 3f out: outpcd jst over 2f out: no ch w wnr and kpt on same pce after* **12/1**

3-65 **5** *hd* **Cottesloe (IRE)**[16] 266 7-9-13 **75**.................... JFEgan 5 78
(John Berry) *stdd s: hld up off the pce in last pair: clsd and in tch 1/2-way: nt clrest of runs as wnr kicked clr 2f out: styd on same pce u.p ins fnl f: nt clr run and swtchd rt towards fin* **8/1**

51-2 **6** *½* **Golly Miss Molly**[22] 195 5-9-2 **64**....................(b) RichardKingscote 4 66
(Jeremy Gask) *chsd ldng trio: rdn over 3f out: outpcd over 2f out: no ch w wnr and kpt on same pce fr over 1f out* **9/2**[3]

3m 26.01s (0.31) **Going Correction** +0.025s/f (Slow)
WFA 4 from 5yo+ 6lb **6** Ran SP% **113.8**
Speed ratings (Par 103): **100,97,96,96,96 96**
CSF £8.29 TOTE £2.10: £1.60, £1.70; EX 7.50 Trifecta £24.40.
Owner Bluehills Racing Limited **Bred** Bluehills Racing Limited **Trained** Newmarket, Suffolk

FOCUS
Nothing could live with the improving winner when he kicked into a clear lead off the final bend. It's been rated around the third.

T/Jkpt: Not won. T/Plt: £38.30 to a £1 stake. Pool: £84,006.09 - 1,597.48 winning tickets T/Qpdt: £11.70 to a £1 stake. Pool: £7,917.52 - 500.00 winning tickets **Steve Payne**

489 - 490a (Foreign Racing) - See Raceform Interactive

[437]CHELMSFORD (A.W) (L-H)
Sunday, February 7

OFFICIAL GOING: Polytrack: standard
Wind: medium, half behind Weather: overcast, bright spells

491 TOTEPLACEPOT H'CAP 1m 2f (P)
2:10 (2:10) (Class 5) (0-70,73) 4-Y-0+ **£5,175** (£1,540; £769; £384) **Stalls** Low

Form RPR
00-1 **1** **Biff Johnson (IRE)**[3] 438 4-9-9 **73** 6ex....................(p) PhillipMakin 6 79
(Keith Dalgleish) *led early: sn stdd and chsd ldrs: effrt over 1f out: drvn to chal ins fnl f: led wl ins fnl f: styd on* **4/5**[1]

-304 **2** *¾* **Mr Red Clubs (IRE)**[3] 437 7-9-7 **70**.................... LiamJones 1 74
(Michael Appleby) *bmpd s: pushed along and sn swtchd rt: chsd ldrs after 1f out: wnt 3rd 5f out: rdn to chal 3f out: led 2f out: hrd pressed and battled on wl ins fnl f: hdd and no ex wl ins fnl f* **7/1**[3]

0-22 **3** *nse* **Runaiocht (IRE)**[15] 316 6-8-10 **59**....................(b) JimmyQuinn 2 63
(Paul Burgoyne) *bmpd s: t.k.h: trckd ldrs: effrt and drifted rt over 1f out: hrd drvn jst ins fnl f: styd on strly towards fin* **5/1**[2]

02-5 **4** *shd* **Viserion**[32] 64 4-9-4 **68**....................(p) MartinLane 9 72
(David Simcock) *sn niggled along in last quartet: drvn and swtchd lft over 1f out: continued shifting lft tl on rail ins fnl f: styd on strly towards fin* **10/1**

16-0 **5** *nk* **Thane Of Cawdor (IRE)**[25] 164 7-8-7 **61**........(b[1]) PatrickO'Donnell[(5)] 4 64
(Joseph Tuite) *stdd s: t.k.h: hld up in rr: rdn and hdwy over 1f out: chsd ldrs 1f out: kpt on same pce fnl 100yds* **25/1**

1-35 **6** *hd* **Enriching (USA)**[3] 438 8-9-0 **68**.................... JosephineGordon[(5)] 3 71
(Robyn Brisland) *sn bustled along: led after 1f: rdn and hdd 2f out: kpt on and ev ch after tl no ex and outpcd wl ins fnl f* **12/1**

45-3 **7** *4 ½* **I'm Harry**[25] 164 7-9-6 **69**....................(vt) LiamKeniry 5 63
(George Baker) *dwlt: sn swtchd lft: in tch in last trio: effrt and shifting lft over 1f out: no ex 1f out: wknd ins fnl f* **10/1**

00-0 **8** *3 ¼* **Baileys En Premier (FR)**[32] 58 5-9-4 **67**....................(b) JoeFanning 7 54
(Chris Dwyer) *sn w ldr: rdn in cl 3rd 2f out: unable qck and lost pl over 1f out: wknd fnl f* **33/1**

3-65 **9** *4 ½* **Breakheart (IRE)**[18] 263 9-9-3 **69**....................(b) RobHornby[(3)] 8 47
(Andrew Balding) *in tch in midfield: dropped to last pair 7f out: lost tch over 1f out* **33/1**

2m 5.0s (-3.60) **Going Correction** -0.35s/f (Stan)
WFA 4 from 5yo+ 1lb **9** Ran SP% **120.3**
Speed ratings (Par 103): **100,99,99,99,99 98,95,92,89**
CSF £7.37 CT £19.12 TOTE £1.70: £1.20, £2.00, £1.70; EX 10.80 Trifecta £47.50.
Owner Ronnie Docherty **Bred** Frank Dunne **Trained** Carluke, S Lanarks

FOCUS
There was a blanket finish to this modest handicap. It's hard to be confident about the level.

492 TOTEEXACTA H'CAP 5f (P)
2:40 (2:41) (Class 3) (0-95,95) 4-Y-0+ **£9,703** (£2,887; £1,443; £721) **Stalls** Low

Form RPR
2-36 **1** **Brother Tiger**[22] 213 7-8-13 **87**.................... JFEgan 1 97
(David C Griffiths) *taken down early: wnt rt s: mde all: rdn over 1f out: styd on wl fnl f: unchal* **6/1**[3]

-553 **2** *2* **Apache Storm**[10] 359 4-8-5 **84**.................... JosephineGordon[(5)] 2 87
(Michael Appleby) *squeezed for room sn after s: in tch in midfield: effrt in 3rd 2f out: chsd wnr ins fnl f: kpt on* **7/1**

2-01 **3** *½* **Royal Birth**[22] 213 5-9-1 **89**....................(t) AdamKirby 7 90+
(Stuart Williams) *taken down early: stdd s: hld up in rr: hdwy on inner over 1f out: clsng and swtchd rt ins fnl f: styd on to go 3rd wl ins fnl f: no threat to wnr* **5/2**[1]

3-20 **4** *½* **Dynamo Walt (IRE)**[12] 338 5-9-5 **93**....................(v) MartinLane 6 92
(Derek Shaw) *stdd s: hld up in last pair: effrt u.p over 1f out: styd on wl fnl 100yds: nvr trbld ldrs* **8/1**

6-54 **5** *¾* **Normal Equilibrium**[22] 220 6-8-7 **86**....................(p) AaronJones[(5)] 8 83
(Robert Cowell) *chsd ldng pair tl 2f out: outpcd and swtchd rt ent fnl f: styd on same pce after* **14/1**

12-0 **6** *nse* **Stake Acclaim (IRE)**[22] 213 4-8-13 **87**.................... RobertWinston 4 83
(Dean Ivory) *chsd wnr: rdn wl over 1f out: no imp u.p: lost 2nd ins fnl f: wknd towards fin* **3/1**[2]

23-1 **7** *2 ¾* **Pensax Lad (IRE)**[30] 106 5-8-11 **88**.................... GeorgeDowning[(3)] 3 74
(Ronald Harris) *in tch in midfield: u.p and no imp over 1f out: wknd fnl f* **7/1**

3-16 **8** *7* **Dungannon**[12] 338 9-9-7 **95**....................(b) OisinMurphy 5 56
(Andrew Balding) *taken down early: in tch in midfield: dropped to rr and u.p over 1f out: sn wknd* **14/1**

57.3s (-2.90) **Going Correction** -0.35s/f (Stan) course record **8** Ran SP% **117.3**
Speed ratings (Par 107): **109,105,105,104,103 102,98,87**
CSF £48.36 CT £133.75 TOTE £7.30: £1.70, £2.90, £1.50; EX 60.30 Trifecta £234.10.
Owner Norcroft Park Stud **Bred** Norcroft Park Stud **Trained** Bawtry, S Yorks

FOCUS
A fairly decent sprint, but the winner got away well and was able to dictate throughout. A small pb from the winner.

493 TOTEQUADPOT CONDITIONS STKS (PLUS 10 RACE) (ALL-WEATHER CHAMPIONSHIP FAST-TRACK QUALIFIER) 5f (P)
3:10 (3:10) (Class 2) 3-Y-O **£19,407** (£5,775; £2,886; £1,443) **Stalls** Low

Form RPR
22-1 **1** **Kadrizzi (FR)**[18] 262 3-9-3 100.................... RobertWinston 3 104
(Dean Ivory) *bmpd s: chsd ldng pair: lft cl up 3f out: ev ch 2f out: rdn to ld 1f out: kpt on and a doing enough ins fnl f* **7/2**[3]

22-2 **2** *½* **Field Of Vision (IRE)**[21] 235 3-9-3 106.................... GeorgeBaker 1 102
(Joseph Tuite) *broke fast: led: jnd 1/2-way: rdn over 1f out: hdd 1f out: rallied u.p wl ins fnl f but a hld* **3/1**[2]

1-11 **3** *½* **Gracious John (IRE)**[21] 235 3-9-6 109.................... JFEgan 2 103+
(David Evans) *wnt rt and bmpd wnr s: chsd ldr but hanging rt: rdr struggling to steer and wnt v wd bnd over 3f out: sn dropped to last: rallied in 3rd 1f out: kpt on towards fin but unable to rcvr: fin lame* **4/6**[1]

00-3 **4** *8* **Thatsallimsaying (IRE)**[21] 235 3-8-12 90.................... JosephineGordon 4 66
(David Evans) *dwlt: sn rcvrd and lft 2nd 3f out: 3rd and u.p 2f out: dropped to last and wknd 1f out* **33/1**

57.89s (-2.31) **Going Correction** -0.35s/f (Stan) **4** Ran SP% **110.2**
Speed ratings (Par 103): **104,103,102,89**
CSF £13.68 TOTE £4.10; EX 11.30 Trifecta £20.70.
Owner A Chapman & Wentdale Limited **Bred** Simon Urizzi & Yann Loizeau **Trained** Radlett, Herts

FOCUS
A good little sprint, most notable for the performance of the third, who would have won had he not hung so badly around the bend. The runner-up has been rated to form.

494 TOTETRIFECTA H'CAP 1m (P)
3:40 (3:40) (Class 4) (0-85,86) 4-Y-0+ **£8,086** (£2,406; £1,202; £601) **Stalls** Low

Form RPR
156- **1** **Supersta**[42] 8369 5-8-13 **77**....................(p) MartinLane 1 86
(Michael Appleby) *stdd s: t.k.h: hld up in last pair: swtchd rt and effrt wl over 1f out: edging lft but str run to ld fnl 100yds: sn in command* **5/1**[3]

53-3 **2** *1 ½* **One Pekan (IRE)**[17] 267 6-9-5 **83**.................... JackMitchell 7 89
(Roger Varian) *chsd ldr: rdn and ev ch over 1f out: led jst ins fnl f: hdd and one pce fnl 100yds* **5/1**[3]

12-4 **3** *¾* **Presumido (IRE)**[15] 313 6-9-1 **79**.................... AdamKirby 6 83
(Simon Dow) *awkward leaving stalls: in tch in midfield: effrt 2f out: drvn over 1f out: kpt on same pce ins fnl f: wnt 3rd last strides* **8/1**

2-01 **4** *hd* **Big Time (IRE)**[10] 360 5-9-8 **86**....................(p) FrannyNorton 3 90
(David Nicholls) *t.k.h: led: rdn wl over 1f out: hdd jst ins fnl f: no ex: wknd wl ins fnl f* **3/1**[1]

2-11 **5** *2* **Gentlemen**[25] 159 5-9-1 **84**.................... JosephineGordon[(5)] 4 83
(Phil McEntee) *taken down early: s.i.s: hld up in rr: effrt over 2f out: drvn over 1f out: kpt on fnl f: nvr trbld ldrs* **10/3**[2]

2-51 **6** *1 ¼* **Kalon Brama (IRE)**[14] 324 5-8-11 **78**.................... DanielMuscutt[(3)] 2 74
(Peter Charalambous) *t.k.h: chsd ldrs: rdn ent fnl 2f out: no ex u.p over 1f out: wknd ins fnl f* **9/1**

-644 **7** *26* **Spiritual Star (IRE)**[8] 401 7-9-4 **82**....................(t) WilliamCarson 5 19
(Anthony Carson) *broke fast: sn stdd into midfield and t.k.h: dropped to rr and swtchd rt over 1f out: sn lost tch: eased ins fnl f: t.o: burst blood vessel* **8/1**

1m 37.5s (-2.40) **Going Correction** -0.35s/f (Stan) **7** Ran SP% **113.6**
Speed ratings (Par 105): **98,96,95,95,93 92,66**
CSF £29.45 TOTE £5.80: £3.10, £2.90; EX 39.50 Trifecta £193.40.
Owner Rod In Pickle Partnership **Bred** Cheveley Park Stud Ltd **Trained** Oakham, Rutland

FOCUS
A competitive handicap. The form is set around the runner-up to his penultimate C&D form.

495 TOTESWINGER H'CAP 1m (P)
4:10 (4:10) (Class 4) (0-80,80) 3-Y-O **£8,086** (£2,406; £1,202; £601) **Stalls** Low

Form RPR
164- **1** **Theydon Grey**[133] 6775 3-9-1 **77**.................... DanielMuscutt[(3)] 5 87
(Peter Charalambous) *stdd after s: hld up in last pair: smooth hdwy to trck ldrs 2f out: swtchd rt and effrt over 1f out: rdn and qcknd to ld jst ins fnl f: edging lft but sn in command: readily* **8/1**[3]

3-22 **2** *2 ¾* **Ice Royal (IRE)**[10] 366 3-9-6 **79**.................... TimmyMurphy 7 83
(Jamie Osborne) *led: rdn over 1f out: hdd jst ins fnl f: sn outpcd: kpt on to hold 2nd after* **10/1**

11 **3** *½* **Mariee**[16] 296 3-9-7 **80**.................... JoeFanning 1 83
(Mark Johnston) *chsd ldr: rdn and ev ch over 1f out tl outpcd jst ins fnl f: kpt on same pce after* **5/6**[1]

2-01 **4** *6* **Inswing (IRE)**[9] 376 3-8-9 **73**....................(p) PatrickO'Donnell[(5)] 2 62
(Ralph Beckett) *t.k.h: chsd ldrs: 3rd and rdn over 2f out: struggling whn sltly hmpd over 1f out: ins wknd fnl f* **4/1**[2]

43-1 **5** *1 ½* **Artful Mind**[32] 70 3-8-12 **74**.................... RobHornby[(3)] 4 60
(James Unett) *hld up in tch in midfield: swtchd rt and effrt u.p over 1f out: no imp: wknd ins fnl f* **10/1**

03-0 **6** *3 ¼* **Vallance Road**[24] 171 3-8-6 **70**....................(b) JosephineGordon[(5)] 6 48
(Robyn Brisland) *s.i.s: in tch in rr: rdn over 2f out: sn struggling: wl btn over 1f out* **25/1**

05-1 **7** *¾* **Timia**[33] 47 3-8-7 **66**.................... MartinLane 3 42
(Ed Dunlop) *hld up in tch in midfield: effrt ent fnl 2f: no ex and btn over 1f out: wknd fnl f* **16/1**

1m 37.33s (-2.57) **Going Correction** -0.35s/f (Stan) **7** Ran SP% **113.6**
Speed ratings (Par 99): **98,95,94,88,87 84,83**
CSF £79.83 TOTE £8.10: £2.90, £2.20; EX 46.40 Trifecta £87.30.
Owner E O'Riordan **Bred** Pinnacle Bloodstock Ltd **Trained** Newmarket, Suffolk

FOCUS
A good performance by the winner, who is clearly at home on this track.

496 MYTOTEPOOL.COM MAIDEN STKS 6f (P)
4:40 (4:42) (Class 4) 3-Y-O+ **£5,175** (£1,540; £769; £384) **Stalls** Centre

Form RPR
3-2 **1** **Town's History (USA)**[36] 15 3-8-13 0.......................... OisinMurphy 1 80+
(Saeed bin Suroor) *wnt lft s: hld up in 3rd: effrt on inner over 1f out: rdn to ld ent fnl f: drew clr ins fnl f: comf* **2/9**[1]
3-42 **2** *2* **Phantom Flipper**[17] 268 3-8-13 70............................(p) AdrianNicholls 2 72
(David Nicholls) *led: rdn jst over 2f out: hdd ent fnl f: wl hld and styd on same pce ins fnl f* **7/2**[2]
0- **3** *6* **Emily Goldfinch**[99] 7629 3-8-10 0 ow2................................ RobertTart 3 50
(Phil McEntee) *chsd ldr: rdn over 2f out: dropped to 3rd and outpcd over 1f out: wknd fnl f* **25/1**[3]
06 **4** *8* **Music Major**[17] 268 3-8-13 0... LiamJones 4 27
(Kevin Morgan) *a in last: rdn 1/2-way: struggling 2f out: wknd and bhd 1f out* **40/1**
1m 11.62s (-2.08) **Going Correction** -0.35s/f (Stan) **4** Ran SP% **110.3**
Speed ratings (Par 105): **99,96,88,77**
CSF £1.42 TOTE £1.20; EX 1.30 Trifecta £3.50.
Owner Godolphin **Bred** Darley **Trained** Newmarket, Suffolk

FOCUS
Not a particularly competitive maiden. The runner-up has been rated to his C&D latest.
T/Plt: £295.00 to a £1 stake. Pool of £77835.28 - 192.58 winning tickets. T/Qpdt: £58.70 to a £1 stake. Pool of £5253.42 - 66.17 winning tickets. **Steve Payne**

497 - (Foreign Racing) - See Raceform Interactive

[462]WOLVERHAMPTON (A.W) (L-H)
Monday, February 8

OFFICIAL GOING: Tapeta: standard
Wind: Strong behind Weather: Overcast

498 32RED CASINO ALL WEATHER "HANDS AND HEELS" APPRENTICE SERIES H'CAP 1m 5f 194y (Tp)
2:10 (2:11) (Class 6) (0-60,60) 4-Y-O+ **£2,587** (£770; £384; £192) **Stalls** Low

Form RPR
4-40 **1** **Missandei**[19] 255 4-8-9 **50**...(t) JoshQuinn 7 56
(Steph Hollinshead) *mid-div: hdwy over 2f out: shkn up to ld ins fnl f: styd on* **12/1**
02-3 **2** *½* **Medieval Bishop (IRE)**[24] 199 7-9-10 **60**................(p) PaddyBradley 4 65
(Tony Forbes) *chsd ldr after 1f: led over 3f out: pushed along and hdd 2f out: ev ch ins fnl f: kpt on* **9/2**[2]
-462 **3** *¾* **Astra Hall**[10] 386 7-9-7 **60**.. PatrickVaughan[(3)] 3 64
(Michael Appleby) *chsd ldrs: pushed along over 2f out: ev ch ins fnl f: edgd lft: styd on same pce* **10/1**
0-40 **4** *1* **Delagoa Bay (IRE)**[12] 354 8-8-5 **46** oh1................. BenSanderson[(5)] 8 49
(Sylvester Kirk) *hld up: pushed along on outer over 2f out: r.o ins fnl f: nt rch ldrs* **16/1**
20-6 **5** *nk* **Next Edition (IRE)**[14] 329 8-9-5 **60**.............................. RossTurner[(5)] 6 63
(Philip Kirby) *s.i.s: hld up: nt clr run over 2f out: r.o ins fnl f: nvr nrr* **11/2**[3]
5-10 **6** *nk* **Tarakkom (FR)**[12] 354 4-9-1 **56**................................... LuluStanford 10 58
(Peter Hiatt) *led: hdd over 3f out: led again 2f out: hdd and no ex ins fnl f* **11/2**[3]
5-01 **7** *8* **Easydoesit (IRE)**[10] 378 8-9-6 **56**..................................(p) GeorgiaCox 2 47
(Tony Carroll) *chsd ldrs: pushed along over 2f out: wknd fnl f* **4/1**[1]
525- **8** *7* **Stoneham**[19] 5929 5-9-6 **59**... KyleCurrie[(3)] 11 40
(Iain Jardine) *prom: pushed along over 3f out: wknd over 1f out* **6/1**
50/- **9** *7* **Secret Dancer (IRE)**[42] 5031 11-9-10 **60**....................(bt[1]) HarryBurns 9 31
(John Flint) *s.s: hld up: bhd fnl 5f* **25/1**
40-6 **10** *5* **Heat Storm (IRE)**[10] 383 5-9-3 **53**.............................. SophieKilloran 5 17
(James Unett) *s.s: hld up: pushed along over 7f out: bhd fnl 6f* **28/1**
3m 4.85s (0.05) **Going Correction** -0.125s/f (Stan)
WFA 4 from 5yo+ 5lb **10** Ran SP% **113.2**
Speed ratings (Par 101): **94,93,93,92,92 92,87,83,79,76**
CSF £63.39 CT £564.25 TOTE £13.30: £4.30, £1.80, £3.00; EX 81.50 Trifecta £1769.20.
Owner Mrs Veronica Gilbert **Bred** Immobiliare Casa Paola SRL **Trained** Upper Longdon, Staffs
■ Stewards' Enquiry : Paddy Bradley four-day ban: careless riding (Feb 22-25)
Kyle Currie seven-day ban: used whip contrary to race conditions (tbn)

FOCUS
Not many got involved in this moderate handicap for apprentices, which was pretty slowly run for the first half of the race. The winner improved a fraction on her recent form.

499 32RED.COM H'CAP 2m 119y (Tp)
2:40 (2:41) (Class 2) (0-105,99) 4-Y-O+
£11,827 (£3,541; £1,770; £885; £442; £222) **Stalls** Low

Form RPR
14-1 **1** **Sunblazer (IRE)**[26] 165 6-9-1 **88**...................(t) WilliamTwiston-Davies 2 98+
(Kim Bailey) *a.p: shkn up to ld on outer over 2f out: sn rdn clr* **6/1**
04-1 **2** *1 ¼* **Haines**[22] 234 5-8-4 **80**... RobHornby[(3)] 1 87+
(Andrew Balding) *hld up: hdwy over 2f out: nt clr run and swtchd rt over 1f out: hung lft and r.o to go 2nd wl ins fnl f: nt rch wnr* **15/2**
4-34 **3** *2 ½* **Blue Surf**[16] 317 7-9-12 **99**... AdamKirby 3 103
(Amanda Perrett) *chsd ldrs: rdn over 2f out: edgd lft and styd on same pce ins fnl f* **4/1**[3]
35-4 **4** *4 ½* **Castilo Del Diablo (IRE)**[24] 194 7-9-6 **93**................(p) JamieSpencer 6 92
(David Simcock) *hld up: rdn over 3f out: styd on ins fnl f: nvr nrr* **7/2**[2]
2-15 **5** *¾* **Luv U Whatever**[23] 215 6-9-10 **97**..................................... LiamJones 5 95
(Michael Appleby) *hld up: hdwy to ld over 3f out: rdn and hdd over 2f out: wknd fnl f* **10/1**
2-31 **6** *3 ¾* **Paddys Motorbike (IRE)**[21] 244 4-8-8 **92**.......... JosephineGordon[(5)] 4 85
(David Evans) *led at stdy pce: qcknd over 4f out: rdn and hdd over 3f out: wknd fnl f* **9/4**[1]
0-65 **7** *7* **Masterpaver**[12] 353 5-9-4 **91**..................................... GrahamGibbons 7 76
(Alan Bailey) *chsd ldr after 1f: rdn over 3f out: wknd over 2f out* **16/1**
3m 36.68s (-7.02) **Going Correction** -0.125s/f (Stan)
WFA 4 from 5yo+ 6lb **7** Ran SP% **114.0**
Speed ratings (Par 109): **111,110,109,107,106 105,101**
CSF £48.62 TOTE £7.40: £2.70, £3.20; EX 26.40 Trifecta £160.60.
Owner Norman Carter **Bred** Michael G Daly **Trained** Andoversford, Gloucs

FOCUS
A good staying handicap, but the pace was rather steady, only lifting with half a mile left, and as a result the form may not prove entirely reliable. The winner is better than ever, with the race rated around the third.

500 DOWNLOAD THE CORAL APP STORE MAIDEN STKS 1m 1f 103y (Tp)
3:10 (3:10) (Class 5) 4-Y-O+ **£3,234** (£962; £481; £240) **Stalls** Low

Form RPR
1 **Appeared**[316] 1117 4-9-7 0.. AndreaAtzeni 9 84+
(Roger Varian) *chsd ldr tl led wl over 1f out: pushed clr fnl f: easily* **1/2**[1]
0- **2** *½* **Faiseur De Miracle**[269] 2229 4-9-7 0................................ GrahamLee 6 81
(Micky Hammond) *disp ld 3f: chsd wnr: rdn and ev ch over 1f out: styd on* **9/1**
3 *shd* **Sarmadee (IRE)** 4-9-7 0... CharlesBishop 5 80
(Mick Channon) *a.p: rdn and swtchd lft over 1f out: styd on* **9/2**[2]
4-0 **4** *9* **Togetherwecan (IRE)**[33] 59 4-9-2 0................................ JoeFanning 2 56
(Mark Johnston) *chsd ldrs: rdn over 2f out: wknd over 1f out* **14/1**
6 **5** *1* **Force Of Destiny (GER)**[21] 245 4-9-7 0...................... SteveDrowne 4 59
(Mrs Ilka Gansera-Leveque) *disp ld 3f: chsd ldrs: rdn over 2f out: wknd over 1f out* **5/1**[3]
6 *23* **Thiepval**[99] 4-9-4 0... RobHornby[(3)] 8 11
(Jason Ward) *s.s: hld up: a in rr: rdn and wknd over 2f out* **80/1**
7 *9* **Lmntrix** 4-9-7 0...[1] JimmyQuinn 7
(George Margarson) *s.s: a in rr: rdn and wknd over 3f out* **28/1**
0 **8** *20* **Two Many Words (IRE)**[9] 402 4-9-2 0........................... RyanWhile[(5)] 3
(Bill Turner) *hld up: rdn and wknd over 3f out* **100/1**
1m 59.14s (-1.66) **Going Correction** -0.125s/f (Stan) **8** Ran SP% **132.2**
Speed ratings (Par 103): **102,101,101,93,92 72,64,46**
CSF £6.61 TOTE £1.40: £1.10, £3.40, £1.10; EX 7.60 Trifecta £23.30.
Owner Sheikh Mohammed Obaid Al Maktoum **Bred** Darley **Trained** Newmarket, Suffolk

FOCUS
There was little depth to this older-horse maiden, which saw three finish clear. The winner stood out on 2yo debut form in Ireland, but it's hard to know quite what he achieved here. The level is fluid for now.

501 LADBROKES CONDITIONS STKS 1m 141y (Tp)
3:40 (3:40) (Class 2) 4-Y-O+ **£11,827** (£3,541; £1,770; £885) **Stalls** Low

Form RPR
113- **1** **Mindurownbusiness (IRE)**[68] 8083 5-9-0 111................. JimCrowley 4 114+
(Roger Varian) *chsd ldr tl led wl over 1f out: pushed clr fnl f: easily* **1/2**[1]
00-4 **2** *3* **Sirius Prospect (USA)**[23] 215 8-9-0 101.................... RobertWinston 3 104
(Dean Ivory) *hld up: rdn over 2f out: edgd lft and r.o to go 2nd wl ins fnl f: no ch w wnr* **9/1**[3]
200- **3** *1 ¾* **Lat Hawill (IRE)**[145] 6451 5-9-0 101.................................. LukeMorris 2 100
(Marco Botti) *s.i.s: sn chsng ldrs: rdn over 2f out: no ex fnl f* **14/1**
15-2 **4** *6* **Basil Berry**[14] 333 5-9-0 103.. JoeFanning 1 95
(Chris Dwyer) *led: rdn and hdd wl over 1f out: wknd and eased fnl f* **10/3**[2]
1m 46.3s (-3.80) **Going Correction** -0.125s/f (Stan) **4** Ran SP% **106.4**
Speed ratings (Par 109): **111,108,106,101**
CSF £5.29 TOTE £1.30; EX 3.90 Trifecta £16.70.
Owner A D Spence **Bred** Laundry Cottage Stud Farm **Trained** Newmarket, Suffolk

FOCUS
The wind had picked up considerably by now and was in their faces down the back. A classy little conditions event, run at a sound pace in a time just outside standard. The winner was the clear standout and is rated close to his best, but the level is fluid.

502 DOWNLOAD THE LADBROKES APP CLASSIFIED (S) STKS 7f 32y (Tp)
4:10 (4:10) (Class 6) 3-Y-O+ **£2,587** (£770; £384; £192) **Stalls** High

Form RPR
0-03 **1** **Top Offer**[10] 387 7-9-5 61.. ShaneKelly 5 72
(Patrick Morris) *s.i.s: hld up: hdwy 2f out: rdn to ld 1f out: styd on* **11/1**
3112 **2** *¾* **Binky Blue (IRE)**[12] 355 4-9-5 64...................................... LukeMorris 3 70
(Daniel Mark Loughnane) *chsd ldrs: rdn to ld over 1f out: sn hdd: styd on same pce ins fnl f* **11/4**[2]
3-10 **3** *2 ¼* **Ocean Legend (IRE)**[22] 231 11-9-5 68.......................... AdamKirby 8 65
(Tony Carroll) *hld up: hdwy over 1f out: sn rdn: styd on same pce ins fnl f* **7/2**[3]
4-30 **4** *1 ¼* **Ubla (IRE)**[19] 253 3-8-4 70 ow2...................................(b) AndreaAtzeni 1 59+
(Hugo Palmer) *chsd ldr: led 2f out: rdn and hdd over 1f out: edgd lft and no ex fnl f* **9/4**[1]
54-3 **5** *1* **Lady McGuffy (IRE)**[38] 3 3-7-12 58 ow1................... PaddyPilley[(5)] 6 55
(Brian Barr) *chsd ldrs: rdn over 1f out: wknd ins fnl f* **22/1**
-020 **6** *3* **Hercullian Prince**[12] 349 4-9-5 69.......................................(p) JFEgan 4 52
(Conor Dore) *s.i.s: hld up: rdn 1/2-way: n.d* **5/1**
0-00 **7** *4 ½* **Satchville Flyer**[18] 271 5-9-5 62.................................... KieranO'Neill 2 41
(Brett Johnson) *led: racd keenly: rdn and hdd 2f out: wknd fnl f* **16/1**
1m 27.87s (-0.93) **Going Correction** -0.125s/f (Stan)
WFA 3 from 4yo+ 17lb **7** Ran SP% **114.9**
Speed ratings (Par 101): **100,99,96,95,94 90,85**
CSF £41.76 TOTE £14.90: £5.60, £1.90; EX 61.90 Trifecta £132.10.The winner was bought in for 6,000gns.
Owner Matt Watkinson **Bred** Juddmonte Farms Ltd **Trained** Prescot, Merseyside

FOCUS
A moderate seller, but the pace appeared honest. The could arguably be rated a bit higher.

503 LADBROKES H'CAP 7f 32y (Tp)
4:40 (4:40) (Class 3) (0-95,95) 4-Y-O **£7,246** (£2,168; £1,084; £542; £270) **Stalls** High

Form RPR
010- **1** **Peril**[149] 6316 5-9-3 **91**.. RobertHavlin 1 101
(Simon Crisford) *mid-div: hdwy over 1f out: rdn to ld wl ins fnl f: r.o* **3/1**[2]
055- **2** *¾* **Crazy Chic (IRE)**[42] 8380 5-9-3 **91**................................. AndreaAtzeni 7 99
(Marco Botti) *trckd ldrs: rdn to ld ins fnl f: sn edgd lft and hdd: styd on* **11/4**[1]
006- **3** *1 ¾* **Mange All**[131] 6868 5-9-0 **88**.. JimCrowley 2 91
(Charlie Wallis) *s.i.s: hld up: rdn over 1f out: r.o ins fnl f: nt rch ldrs* **28/1**
064- **4** *hd* **Hillbilly Boy (IRE)**[61] 8163 6-9-1 **89**........................ RichardKingscote 6 92
(Tom Dascombe) *led: rdn and edgd rt over 1f out: hdd and unable qck ins fnl f* **6/1**
12-2 **5** *shd* **Seychelloise**[32] 86 4-9-2 **90**..(b) LukeMorris 4 92
(Sir Mark Prescott Bt) *chsd ldr: rdn over 2f out: hung lft and lost 2nd over 1f out: styd on same pce* **4/1**[3]
115- **6** *¾* **Capelita**[48] 8341 5-8-8 **82**..[1] LiamJones 9 82
(Michael Appleby) *dwlt: hld up: rdn and r.o ins fnl f: nvr nrr* **25/1**
20-0 **7** *1 ¾* **Air Of York (IRE)**[23] 213 4-8-8 **87**....................... JosephineGordon[(5)] 3 83
(David Evans) *chsd ldrs: rdn over 2f out: no ex fnl f* **22/1**

50-0 **8** *shd* **Baddilini**[17] 290 6-9-7 **95**..........(v) GrahamGibbons 8 90
(Alan Bailey) *broke wl: sn stdd and lost pl: rdn over 2f out: n.d* **8/1**
0-60 **9** *8* **Horsted Keynes (FR)**[17] 290 6-9-7 **95**.......... JamieSpencer 5 69
(David Simcock) *hld up: rdn over 1f out: nvr on terms* **22/1**
1m 27.36s (-1.44) **Going Correction** -0.125s/f (Stan) **9** Ran SP% **113.1**
Speed ratings (Par 107): **103,102,100,99,99 98,96,96,87**
CSF £10.72 CT £185.01 TOTE £3.70: £1.40, £1.50, £7.20; EX 11.70 Trifecta £147.00.
Owner Saeed H Al Tayer **Bred** Juddmonte Farms Ltd **Trained** Newmarket, Suffolk

FOCUS
A decent handicap run at a solid gallop thanks to the fourth, who is rated close to his Lingfield latest.

504 DOWNLOAD THE NEW UNIBET RACING APP H'CAP 5f 20y (Tp)
5:10 (5:11) (Class 6) (0-60,59) 4-Y-O+ **£2,587** (£770; £384; £192) **Stalls** Low

Form RPR
3223 **1** **Secret Millionaire (IRE)**[13] 339 9-9-6 **58**..........(p) LukeMorris 2 65
(Shaun Harris) *trckd ldrs: rdn to ld wl ins fnl f: r.o* **11/1**
0-64 **2** *¾* **Seraphima**[23] 217 6-8-2 **45**..........(p) JosephineGordon(5) 4 49
(Lisa Williamson) *mid-div: hdwy over 1f out: led ins fnl f: sn hdd: styd on* **20/1**
-342 **3** *1½* **Frank The Barber (IRE)**[17] 293 4-9-4 **56**..........(bt) AdamBeschizza 1 55
(Steph Hollinshead) *chsd ldrs: led over 1f out: rdn and hdd ins fnl f: styd on same pce* **9/1**
05-3 **4** *½* **Mountain Man**[15] 320 4-8-12 **57**..........(bt) NathanEvans(7) 8 54
(Michael Easterby) *hld up: hdwy over 1f out: r.o: nt rch ldrs* **13/2**[2]
03-0 **5** *½* **Give Us A Belle (IRE)**[33] 75 7-9-6 **58**..........(vt) AdamKirby 11 53
(Christine Dunnett) *led 4f out: rdn: hung rt and hdd over 1f out: styd on same pce ins fnl f* **14/1**
-045 **6** *1* **Fuel Injection**[4] 444 5-9-7 **59**..........(p) BarryMcHugh 7 50
(Paul Midgley) *prom: pushed along 2f out: nt clr run wl over 1f out: styd on same pce* **14/1**
1-02 **7** *nse* **Rat Catcher (IRE)**[21] 241 6-9-0 **55**..........(b) RobHornby(3) 3 46
(Lisa Williamson) *hld up: rdn over 1f out: nt trble ldrs* **8/1**
45-1 **8** *nk* **More Spice (IRE)**[27] 151 4-9-5 **57**..........(v) JamieSpencer 5 47
(Robert Cowell) *led 1f: chsd ldr tl rdn and hung rt over 1f out: no ex fnl f* **2/1**[1]
6-15 **9** *nk* **Very First Blade**[13] 340 7-9-5 **57**..........(be) RobertHavlin 10 46
(Michael Mullineaux) *hld up: rdn over 1f out: nt trble ldrs* **40/1**
16-1 **10** *5* **Quantum Dot (IRE)**[21] 241 5-9-5 **57**..........(b) KieranO'Neill 6 28
(Ed de Giles) *chsd ldrs: pushed along 1/2-way: rdn and nt clr run over 1f out: wknd fnl f* **7/1**[3]
50-0 **11** *1½* **Smart Dj**[24] 197 5-9-5 **57**.......... DougieCostello 9 23
(Sarah Hollinshead) *s.i.s: a in rr* **20/1**
1m 1.08s (-0.82) **Going Correction** -0.125s/f (Stan) **11** Ran SP% **113.9**
Speed ratings (Par 101): **101,99,97,96,95 94,94,93,93,85 82**
CSF £207.31 CT £1352.59 TOTE £9.20: £3.20, £5.30, £2.90; EX 108.70 Trifecta £1216.70.
Owner Wilf Hobson **Bred** James Delaney **Trained** Carburton, Notts
■ Stewards' Enquiry : Luke Morris two-day ban: used whip above shoulder height (Feb 22-23)
Adam Kirby jockey said gelding hung right-handed in the home straight
Kieran O'Neill jockey said gelding was unsuited by being taken on for the lead and therefore unable to dominate
Jamie Spencer jockey said gelding hung right-handed throughout

FOCUS
Moderate sprint handicap form.
T/Jkpt: Part won. T/Plt: £71.20 to a £1 stake. Pool: £81,441.68 - 834.13 winning tickets T/Qpdt: £7.90 to a £1 stake. Pool: £6,520.66 - 608.10 winning tickets **Colin Roberts**

444 SOUTHWELL (L-H)
Tuesday, February 9

OFFICIAL GOING: Fibresand: standard
Wind: Fresh half behind Weather: Fine & dry

505 CORAL.CO.UK AMATEUR RIDERS' H'CAP 1m 3f (F)
2:10 (2:11) (Class 6) (0-52,52) 4-Y-O+ **£2,183** (£677; £338; £169) **Stalls** Low

Form RPR
54-3 **1** **Claude Greenwood**[23] 232 6-10-1 **46** oh1..........(b) MissFPullar(7) 1 57
(Linda Jewell) *sn trcking ldrs: hdwy on inner to chse ldr 3f out: led wl over 1f out: rdn appr fnl f: kpt on strly* **10/1**
653- **2** *2¼* **Henry Smith**[103] 7583 4-10-5 **48**..........(be) KaineWood(3) 7 55
(Garry Moss) *trckd ldrs: hdwy over 3f out: chal wl over 1f out: sn rdn and ev ch: kpt on same pce fnl f* **5/1**[2]
006- **3** *4½* **Skywards Miles (IRE)**[41] 8403 4-10-5 **50**.......... MissHDukes(5) 10 50
(Tim Fitzgerald) *hld up in midfield: hdwy over 3f out: rdn to chse ldrs 2f out: kpt on fnl f* **14/1**
065- **4** *nk* **Magnolia Ridge (IRE)**[56] 7951 6-10-5 **50**..........(p) MrHJKinder(7) 14 50
(Mark Walford) *hld up in midfield: hdwy over 3f out: rdn along to chse ldrs 2f out: kpt on appr fnl f* **12/1**
604- **5** *hd* **Storytale**[181] 5259 4-10-9 **49**.......... MrAlexEdwards 13 48
(Dave Roberts) *chsd ldrs: rdn along over 3f out: drvn 2f out and grad wknd* **16/1**
00-0 **6** *1¾* **Engai (GER)**[24] 222 10-10-8 **51**.......... MissPBridgwater(5) 5 48
(David Bridgwater) *led: rdn along 3f out: hdd wl over 1f out: grad wknd* **9/1**
3403 **7** *1* **Geeaitch**[5] 445 7-10-8 **51**.......... MissMollyKing(5) 3 46
(Peter Hiatt) *towards rr tl styd on fr over 2f out: n.d* **4/1**[1]
5-56 **8** *8* **Game Mascot**[16] 326 6-10-3 **46**.......... AidenBlakemore(5) 9 28
(Shaun Harris) *a towards rr* **8/1**[3]
0-11 **9** *7* **Clock On Tom**[12] 362 6-10-7 **52**.......... MrWDegnan(7) 12 23
(Denis Quinn) *chsd ldrs: hdwy 5f out: rdn along 3f out: sn drvn and wknd* **5/1**[2]
53-0 **10** *6* **Ron Waverly (IRE)**[33] 84 6-10-3 **46**..........(tp) MissMBryant(5) 6 7
(Paddy Butler) *a towards rr: bhd fnl 3f* **20/1**
000- **11** *9* **Rockweiller**[58] 8040 9-10-1 **46**.......... MissJWelch(7) 4
(Shaun Harris) *a towards rr: bhd fnl 3f* **25/1**
5/0- **12** *2¼* **Premier Jack's**[69] 517 5-10-1 **46** oh1.......... MrMichaelPalmer(7) 11
(Nikki Evans) *prom: cl up 1/2-way: rdn along over 4f out: sn lost pl and bhd* **66/1**
400- **13** *1¼* **Opus Too (IRE)**[126] 6999 5-10-3 **46** oh1.......... MrBJames(5) 8
(John Ryan) *prom: pushed along 6f out: rdn over 4f out: sn lost pl and bhd* **20/1**
/ **14** *43* **Streele (USA)**[79] 4331 6-10-3 **46** oh1.......... KatherineGlenister(5) 2
(Ken Wingrove) *a in rr: detached 1/2-way: t.o fr over 3f out* **125/1**
2m 28.54s (0.54) **Going Correction** +0.05s/f (Slow)
WFA 4 from 5yo+ 2lb **14** Ran SP% **119.4**
Speed ratings (Par 101): **100,98,95,94,94 93,92,86,81,77 70,69,68,37**
CSF £55.85 CT £715.15 TOTE £11.30: £3.60, £2.20, £4.80; EX 98.90 Trifecta £1275.10.
Owner Valence Racing **Bred** Mrs J A Rawding **Trained** Sutton Valence, Kent
■ A first winner on her first ride under rules for Frankie Pullar.

FOCUS
They went a good gallop and they were quite well strung out from an early stage. The winner is rated back to his 2015 best, and this could even be a bit higher.

506 CORAL H'CAP 1m 4f (F)
2:45 (2:45) (Class 5) (0-70,70) 4-Y-O+ **£3,234** (£962; £481; £240) **Stalls** Low

Form RPR
00-1 **1** **Weald Of Kent (USA)**[5] 445 4-9-4 **70** 6ex..........(v) LiamJones 5 78+
(Michael Appleby) *dwlt and swtchd rt to outer s: reminders and hdwy to ld after 2f: rdn clr and wd st: edgd rt wl over 1f out: drvn and kpt on gamely fnl f* **15/8**[1]
1-54 **2** *¾* **With Hindsight (IRE)**[7] 425 8-9-2 **70**.......... JoshDoyle(5) 6 75
(Steve Gollings) *led 2f: trckd ldng pair: hdwy to chse wnr 4f out: rdn along 2f out: styd on and ch ins fnl f: sn drvn and kpt on same pce towards fin* **4/1**[2]
31-5 **3** *1¼* **Dark Diamond (IRE)**[30] 132 6-9-4 **67**..........(b[1]) LukeMorris 3 70
(Julia Feilden) *cl up 2f: chsd wnr: pushed along 4f out: rdn over 3f out: drvn wl over 1f out: kpt on same pce* **9/2**[3]
2-53 **4** *3½* **Indira**[8] 420 5-9-2 **70**.......... JosephineGordon(5) 1 67
(John Berry) *chsd ldrs: effrt over 3f out: rdn along wl over 2f out: drvn and no imp fr wl over 1f out* **12/1**
0-05 **5** *hd* **Thimaar (USA)**[11] 386 8-9-3 **66**..........(p) KieranO'Neill 7 63
(Sarah Hollinshead) *in tch: rdn along wl over 3f out: drvn 2f out: kpt on one pce* **28/1**
200- **6** *5* **Moon Arc (IRE)**[18] 5111 4-8-11 **63**..........(p) JoeFanning 4 52
(Keith Dalgleish) *a towards rr* **12/1**
042/ **7** *29* **Sir Pitt**[90] 6631 9-9-2 **65**..........(tp) OisinMurphy 2
(David Bridgwater) *dwlt: a in rr: bhd fnl 4f* **5/1**
2m 40.07s (-0.93) **Going Correction** +0.05s/f (Slow)
WFA 4 from 5yo+ 3lb **7** Ran SP% **108.5**
Speed ratings (Par 103): **105,104,103,101,101 97,78**
CSF £8.37 TOTE £2.70: £1.50, £1.80; EX 8.30 Trifecta £24.70.
Owner Tariq Al Nisf **Bred** Juddmonte Farms Inc **Trained** Oakham, Rutland
■ Stewards' Enquiry : Liam Jones two-day ban: used whip above permitted level (Feb 23-24)

FOCUS
A tight little handicap on paper and the form of the first three makes sense.

507 NEW UNIBET RACING APP DOWNLOAD MAIDEN STKS 6f (F)
3:15 (3:16) (Class 5) 3-Y-O+ **£2,911** (£866; £432; £216) **Stalls** Low

Form RPR
322- **1** **White Bullet**[204] 4445 3-8-7 87..........(p) LukeMorris 4 68
(Sir Mark Prescott Bt) *dwlt and sn pushed along: hdwy to chse ldrs 1/2-way: wd st: rdn to chal 2f out: drvn and edgd lft over 1f out: styd on gamely u.p fnl f to ld nr line* **4/6**[1]
-422 **2** *shd* **Phantom Flipper**[2] 496 3-8-12 70..........(p) AdrianNicholls 2 72
(David Nicholls) *qckly away: led: jnd 2f out and sn rdn: drvn ins fnl f: hdd and no ex nr line* **15/8**[2]
53 **3** *7* **Fearbuster (IRE)**[20] 258 3-8-7 0.......... OisinMurphy 6 45
(Hugo Palmer) *cl up: rdn over 2f out: ev ch tl drvn over 1f out and sn one pce* **10/1**[3]
0 **4** *4* **Bomber Etches**[12] 363 3-8-12 0.......... KieranO'Neill 5 37
(Scott Dixon) *chsd ldrs: rdn along wl over 2f out: drvn wl over 1f out: kpt on one pce* **80/1**
6 **5** *nk* **Giant Bradley**[12] 363 3-8-12 0.......... LiamJones 1 36
(Michael Appleby) *chsd ldrs on inner: rdn along wl over 2f out: sn drvn and kpt on one pce* **33/1**
0 **6** *nk* **Suzu**[11] 384 3-8-7 0.......... RaulDaSilva 7 30
(Ivan Furtado) *chsd ldrs on outer: rdn along and wd st: sn drvn and wknd* **33/1**
0-50 **7** *50* **Womble**[29] 145 3-8-7 0.......... NoelGarbutt(5) 3
(Laura Young) *a outpcd in rr: bhd fr 1/2-way* **250/1**
1m 16.44s (-0.06) **Going Correction** +0.05s/f (Slow) **7** Ran SP% **111.4**
Speed ratings (Par 103): **102,101,92,87,86 86,19**
CSF £1.97 TOTE £1.60: £1.10, £1.40; EX 2.60 Trifecta £4.60.
Owner Mrs Olivia Hoare **Bred** A Parker & New England Stud **Trained** Newmarket, Suffolk

FOCUS
Not much depth to this maiden and the front two, who dominated the betting, pulled well clear.

508 UNIBET OFFER DAILY JOCKEY/TRAINER SPECIALS H'CAP 6f (F)
3:50 (3:50) (Class 4) (0-85,85) 4-Y-O+ **£5,175** (£1,540; £769; £384) **Stalls** Low

Form RPR
05-2 **1** **Clubland (IRE)**[25] 198 7-8-13 **80**.......... RobHornby(3) 2 89
(Roy Bowring) *trckd ldrs: hdwy wl over 1f out: effrt and n.m.r ent fnl f: sn swtchd rt and rdn: styd on wl to ld nr fin* **5/1**[3]
000- **2** *½* **Addictive Dream (IRE)**[113] 7342 9-9-0 **78**..........(be[1]) PJMcDonald 4 85
(Garry Moss) *cl up: led 2f out: rdn over 1f out: drvn and hung lft ent fnl f: hdd and no ex towards fin* **25/1**
63-2 **3** *1* **Sir Billy Wright (IRE)**[14] 338 5-9-1 **84**.......... JosephineGordon(5) 6 88
(David Evans) *in tch: wd st and hdwy 2f out: rdn over 1f out: drvn and kpt on fnl f* **9/4**[1]
0-33 **4** *1* **Showtime Star**[14] 338 6-9-5 **83**..........(b) LukeMorris 8 84
(Gay Kelleway) *hld up in rr: wd st: hdwy over 2f out: rdn wl over 1f out: drvn and kpt on same pce fnl f* **7/2**[2]
06-4 **5** *1½* **Among Angels**[21] 250 4-9-5 **83**.......... StevieDonohoe 1 79
(Kevin Frost) *slt ld on inner: hdd after 2f: cl up: rdn along 3f out and grad wknd* **14/1**
36-0 **6** *¾* **Guishan**[25] 198 6-9-1 **82**.......... AlistairRawlinson(3) 3 76
(Michael Appleby) *cl up: led after 2f: rdn and hdd 2f out: sn drvn and wknd over 1f out* **8/1**
00-0 **7** *¾* **Billyoakes (IRE)**[25] 198 4-9-1 **79**.......... GrahamGibbons 7 70
(David Barron) *a towards rr* **10/1**
-140 **8** *3½* **Captain Lars (SAF)**[12] 360 6-9-7 **85**..........(v) TonyHamilton 5 65
(Derek Shaw) *awkward s: sn cl up: rdn along wl over 2f out: sn wknd* **13/2**
1m 15.33s (-1.17) **Going Correction** +0.05s/f (Slow) **8** Ran SP% **113.7**
Speed ratings (Par 105): **109,108,107,105,103 102,101,97**
CSF £110.77 CT £356.18 TOTE £5.10: £1.50, £6.00, £1.60; EX 152.10 Trifecta £608.50.
Owner L P Keane **Bred** Mrs Sharon Slattery **Trained** Edwinstowe, Notts

FOCUS
A decent little handicap run at what looked a reasonable gallop and the winner is better than ever.

509 32RED MAIDEN H'CAP 1m (F)
4:20 (4:21) (Class 6) (0-55,53) 3-Y-O **£2,587** (£770; £384; £192) **Stalls** Low

Form RPR
-524 **1** **Rupert Boy (IRE)**[12] 365 3-9-6 **52**...(b) KieranO'Neill 4 63
(Scott Dixon) *slt ld: jnd and rdn over 2f out: hdd and drvn 1 1/2f out: rallied to ld again jst ins fnl f: kpt on wl* **11/4**[1]
000- **2** *2* **Divine Touch**[141] 6589 3-8-13 **45**... JackMitchell 2 50
(Robert Eddery) *hld up in tch: hdwy wl over 2f out: rdn wl over 1f out: styd on wl fnl f* **7/2**[3]
5-22 **3** *3 1/4* **Never Say (IRE)**[19] 274 3-9-1 **47**...(p) PJMcDonald 7 44
(Jason Ward) *cl up: hdwy to chal over 2f out: rdn to ld 1 1/2f out: drvn and edge lft ent fnl f: sn hdd and one pce* **3/1**[2]
00-6 **4** *2* **Edith Weston**[15] 328 3-8-13 **45**...(p) JimmyQuinn 1 37
(Robert Cowell) *chsd ldrs on inner: rdn along over 2f out: drvn wl over 1f out: kpt on one pce* **28/1**
40-5 **5** *shd* **Ryan The Giant**[15] 328 3-9-5 **51**...(b) TomEaves 6 43
(Keith Dalgleish) *cl up: rdn along 3f out: sn drvn and wknd* **9/1**
00-0 **6** *4* **Rainbow Lad (IRE)**[21] 248 3-9-2 **48**... BenCurtis 8 31
(Michael Appleby) *chsd ldrs: rdn along wl over 2f out: sn wknd* **25/1**
060- **7** *1/2* **Simply Clever**[167] 5754 3-8-13 **45**...(v[1]) OisinMurphy 3 26
(David Brown) *dwlt: sn swtchd rt to outer and t.k.h: hdwy to chse ldrs after 2f: rdn along over 3f out: sn wknd* **8/1**
06-0 **8** *6* **Toffee Apple (IRE)**[36] 40 3-9-7 **53**... MartinLane 5 20
(Ed Dunlop) *a in rr* **15/2**
1m 45.64s (1.94) **Going Correction** +0.05s/f (Slow) **8** Ran SP% **114.1**
Speed ratings (Par 95): **92,90,86,84,84 80,80,74**
CSF £12.59 CT £29.83 TOTE £3.10: £1.10, £2.20, £1.50; EX 17.70 Trifecta £38.60.
Owner J Radford **Bred** Sinead Bishop **Trained** Babworth, Notts

FOCUS
A weak event in which most looked in major trouble by the home turn as the front two began to pull clear. The winner posted an effort in keeping with his good 7f run two runs back.

510 DAILY PRICE BOOSTS AT UNIBET H'CAP 5f (F)
4:50 (4:53) (Class 6) (0-60,59) 3-Y-O **£2,587** (£770; £384; £192) **Stalls** Centre

Form RPR
5-52 **1** **Englishwoman**[12] 365 3-9-1 **58**... JosephineGordon[(5)] 3 72+
(David Evans) *cl up: led 1/2-way: rdn clr over 1f out: readily* **6/4**[1]
40-3 **2** *3 3/4* **Rampers (IRE)**[12] 363 3-9-7 **59**... TimmyMurphy 1 59
(Jamie Osborne) *in tch: hdwy on outer 1/2-way: rdn to chse wnr wl over 1f out: drvn and kpt on same pce fnl f* **8/1**
0-52 **3** *4 1/2* **Memyselfie (IRE)**[26] 181 3-9-1 **53**...(v) MartinLane 5 37
(Derek Shaw) *cl up: led over 3f out: hdd 1/2-way and sn rdn along: drvn wl over 1f out and sn one pce* **9/2**[3]
00-1 **4** *2 3/4* **Yisty**[33] 81 3-8-11 **49**...(v) TonyHamilton 4 23
(Derek Shaw) *led 1 1/2f: cl up: rdn along over 2f out: sn wknd* **12/1**
504- **5** *1/2* **Amy Blair**[124] 7056 3-9-4 **56**... PhillipMakin 2 28
(Keith Dalgleish) *a in rr* **11/4**[2]
300- **6** *nk* **Comparinka**[143] 6523 3-9-7 **59**... LukeMorris 6 30
(Scott Dixon) *chsd ldrs on outer: rdn along bef 1/2-way: sn outpcd* **16/1**
58.82s (-0.88) **Going Correction** -0.30s/f (Stan) **6** Ran SP% **109.5**
Speed ratings (Par 95): **95,89,81,77,76 76**
CSF £13.40 TOTE £2.10: £1.50, £3.80; EX 12.60 Trifecta £36.00.
Owner R Kent **Bred** Peter Winkworth **Trained** Pandy, Monmouths

FOCUS
A modest sprint handicap in which they finished quite well strung out. It's not easy to set the level but this could be rated a bit higher.
T/Jkpt: £64,818.40 to a £1 stake. Pool: £136,940.32 - 1.50 winning units. T/Plt: £29.60 to a £1 stake. Pool: £77,260.36 - 1899.14 winning units. T/Qpdt: £2.90 to a £1 stake. Pool: £7,438.12 - 1888.71 winning units. **Joe Rowntree**

CHANTILLY (R-H)
Tuesday, February 9

OFFICIAL GOING: Polytrack: standard

511a PRIX DE CHASSELOUP (MAIDEN) (3YO) (POLYTRACK) 6f 110y
1:05 (12:00) 3-Y-O **£9,191** (£3,676; £2,757; £1,838; £919)

RPR
1 **Yeah Baby Yeah (IRE)**[13] 350 3-9-0 0 ow1..(p) Pierre-CharlesBoudot 7 81
(Gay Kelleway) *trckd ldr: rdn to chal over 1f out: led ent fnl f: kpt on wl and asserted: pushed out* **17/10**[1]
2 *1 1/2* **Never Compromise (FR)** 3-9-2 0... AntoineHamelin 4 78
(Henk Grewe, Germany) **15/1**
3 *shd* **Range Of Knowledge (IRE)**[32] 3-9-2 0...(b) CristianDemuro 3 78
(E J O'Neill, France) **16/5**[2]
4 *1 1/2* **Great Trip (USA)**[82] 3-8-13 0... MaximeGuyon 8 71
(F Head, France) **33/10**[3]
5 *3/4* **Kekko (IRE)**[55] 3-9-2 0... UmbertoRispoli 2 71
(Gianluca Bietolini, Italy) **71/1**
6 *2 1/2* **Shiver In The River (FR)**[11] 3-8-5 0... PierreBazire[(8)] 5 61
(G Botti, France) **32/5**
7 *3 1/2* **Strategic Way (FR)** 3-8-11 0... EddyHardouin 6 49
(G E Mikhalides, France) **68/1**
8 *10* **Kingbowl Menantie (FR)** 3-8-11 0... AlexisBadel 9 20
(C Bauer, France) **269/10**
9 *nk* **Ayguemorte (FR)**[5] 3-9-2 0... GerardRivases 1 24
(P-L Guerin, France) **195/1**
Owner Winterbeck Manor Stud & Sheila Bailey **Bred** Mr And Mrs P McEnery **Trained** Exning, Suffolk

512a PRIX DU CARREFOUR MIRA (CLAIMER) (5YO+) (POLYTRACK) 1m 1f 110y
2:40 (12:00) 5-Y-O+ **£5,514** (£2,205; £1,654; £1,102; £551)

RPR
1 **Caesaria (IRE)**[11] 6-8-11 0...(b) NathanKasztelan 7 51
(N Branchu, France) **162/10**
2 *3/4* **Dominandros (FR)**[7] 427 5-9-6 0...(b) JohanVictoire 1 58
(Gay Kelleway) *prom on inner: angled out and rdn 2f out: effrt to chal fnl f: styd on wl for 2nd: nt quite pce of wnr* **13/10**[1]
3 *hd* **Pleasant Flight (FR)**[22] 5-9-2 0... MathieuBreand 4 54
(D Windrif, France) **36/1**
4 *3/4* **River Prince (FR)**[11] 6-8-11 0... FrankPanicucci 6 48
(P Adda, France) **33/1**
5 *3/4* **Snow Tigress (FR)**[31] 5-8-13 0...(p) LudovicProietti 12 48
(Mme J Proietti, France) **134/10**
6 *1 1/2* **Night Of Paris (FR)**[314] 7-8-8 0... MlleZoePfeil 10 40
(S Morineau, France) **269/10**
7 *3* **Cuevo Especial (FR)**[31] 7-8-11 0...(p) AnthonyCaramanolis 13 37
(N Branchu, France) **52/1**
8 *nk* **Bridjnaia (FR)**[55] 7-8-8 0...(p) CesarPasserat 5 33
(C Bauer, France) **48/1**
9 *hd* **Airley (FR)**[22] 5-8-13 0...(p) FlavienMasse 8 38
(R Labit, France) **26/1**
10 *3* **Cool Star (FR)**[55] 11-8-11 0...(b) ErwannLebreton 2 30
(A Bonin, France) **28/1**
11 *1 1/4* **Blyde River (IRE)**[423] 5-8-11 0...(p) ThibaultSpeicher 14 27
(F-X De Chevigny, France) **142/10**
12 *nse* **Panama (FR)**[11] 6-8-11 0... JeremyCrocquevieille 16 27
(D Windrif, France) **117/10**[3]
13 *1 1/4* **Monte Napoleone (FR)**[22] 7-9-6 0... WilliamsSaraiva 15 33
(G Pannier, France) **27/10**[2]
14 *1 3/4* **Fortuna Do Brasil (FR)** 5-8-13 0... ThomasMessina 3 23
(W Delalande, France) **72/1**
15 *6* **Friliad (FR)**[31] 5-8-11 0...(p) YohannBourgois 17 8
(M Cesandri, France) **57/1**
16 *15* **Gold Knight (FR)**[50] 6-8-11 0... StephaneBreux 11
(J Chapel, France) **236/1**
17 *snk* **Sol Car (FR)**[22] 5-9-1 0 ow2... CedricSagot 9
(A Sagot, France) **96/1**
Owner Haras De Bernesq **Bred** Haras De Bernesq
Trained in France
WIN (incl. 1 euro stake): 17.20. PLACES: 4.80, 1.70, 4.80. DF: 29.70. SF: 99.90

431 KEMPTON (A.W) (R-H)
Wednesday, February 10

OFFICIAL GOING: Polytrack: standard
Wind: Moderate, half against, becoming almost nil Weather: Cloudy

513 RACING UK FREE TRIAL H'CAP 5f (P)
4:55 (4:55) (Class 7) (0-50,50) 4-Y-O+ **£1,940** (£577; £288; £144) **Stalls** Low

Form RPR
00-1 **1** **Lizzy's Dream**[14] 341 8-9-5 **48**... DanielTudhope 9 56
(Rebecca Bastiman) *hld up off the pce in 7th: prog over 1f out: clsd qckly to ld ins fnl f: pushed out: comf* **7/2**[1]
46-2 **2** *1 1/2* **Imjin River (IRE)**[15] 339 9-9-5 **48**...(tp) GeorgeBaker 6 50
(William Stone) *settled in 8th and wl off the pce: rdn and prog jst over 1f out: clsd to take 2nd last 100yds: styd on but no imp on wnr* **4/1**[2]
0-65 **3** *1 1/2* **Cerulean Silk**[14] 341 6-9-2 **45**...(p) AdamKirby 7 42
(Tony Carroll) *wl off the pce in last: swtchd lft and prog 1f out: r.o to take 3rd nr fin* **25/1**
4-06 **4** *3/4* **Glenbuck Lass (IRE)**[24] 237 4-9-2 **45**... SaleemGolam 4 39
(Alan Bailey) *chsd ldng quartet: rdn over 1f out: kpt on same pce as others wnt by: tk 4th nr fin* **10/1**
0-61 **5** *shd* **Red Flute**[25] 217 4-9-3 **49**...(v) TimClark[(3)] 8 43
(Denis Quinn) *t.k.h: disp ld at str pce: def advantage over 1f out: hdd & wknd ins fnl f* **8/1**
06-6 **6** *1 1/4* **Seamoor Secret**[27] 174 4-9-2 **45**...(vt[1]) KieranO'Neill 1 34
(Alex Hales) *disp ld to over 1f out: wknd ins fnl f* **5/1**[3]
00-2 **7** *3/4* **Spray Tan**[25] 217 6-9-4 **50**...(b) GeorgeDowning[(3)] 3 37
(Tony Carroll) *chsd ldng pair: rdn over 1f out: wknd fnl f* **5/1**[3]
-366 **8** *2* **Single Summit**[7] 432 4-9-2 **45**...(b[1]) TonyHamilton 5 25
(J R Jenkins) *nvr bttr than midfield: rdn 1/2-way: lost pl jst over 1f out* **9/1**
06-0 **9** *2 1/4* **Willow Spring**[25] 217 4-9-2 **45**...(b[1]) TomEaves 2 16
(Conrad Allen) *dwlt: sn trckd ldng pair: effrt on inner whn nt clr run over 1f out: wknd qckly fnl f* **25/1**
59.9s (-0.60) **Going Correction** -0.075s/f (Stan) **9** Ran SP% **113.4**
Speed ratings (Par 97): **101,98,96,95,94 92,91,88,84**
CSF £17.14 CT £291.87 TOTE £4.70: £1.90, £1.60, £3.40; EX 20.60 Trifecta £247.50.
Owner Mrs P Bastiman **Bred** Sheikh Abdulla Bin Isa Al-Khalifa **Trained** Cowthorpe, N Yorks

FOCUS
An extremely moderate sprint handicap got the twilight card under way. They went a strong pace, which collapsed and those held-up early occupied the places.

514 RACING UK ANYWHERE H'CAP 1m 2f (P)
5:25 (5:25) (Class 7) (0-50,50) 4-Y-O+ **£1,940** (£577; £288; £144) **Stalls** Low

Form RPR
0-04 **1** **Star Links (USA)**[12] 388 10-9-5 **48**...(bt) MartinHarley 7 55
(Sylvester Kirk) *rdn to ld but hdd after 1f and in 3rd after 3f: chsd ldr 3f out: drvn to ld 1f out: jst hld on* **7/1**[2]
4-05 **2** *shd* **Top Pocket**[14] 347 4-9-4 **48**... LiamKeniry 5 55
(Michael Madgwick) *hld up in midfield: gng bttr than most fr 3f out: prog to chse ldng pair wl over 1f out: drvn to chse wnr ins fnl f: kpt on nr fin: jst failed* **16/1**
06-0 **3** *2 1/2* **White Dog (IRE)**[35] 60 4-9-3 **50**... DannyBrock[(3)] 4 52
(Sarah Humphrey) *sltly impeded after 100yds: racd on outer: in tch: wd on bnd 3f out to 2f out: drvn and kpt on fnl f to take 3rd last stride* **50/1**
43-0 **4** *shd* **Solveig's Song**[29] 155 4-9-2 **46**...(p) WilliamCarson 10 48
(Steve Woodman) *led after 1f: drvn 2f out: hdd and fdd 1f out* **20/1**
5-42 **5** *nk* **Happy Jack (IRE)**[13] 362 5-9-7 **50**...(b) GeorgeBaker 9 51
(Michael Wigham) *stdd s: hld up in last: prog over 2f out: tried to cl on ldrs over 1f out but only one pce whn rdn and nvr able to threaten* **5/2**[1]
000/ **6** *7* **Seven Summits (IRE)**[345] 2511 9-9-7 **50**... ShaneKelly 6 38
(Sophie Leech) *stdd s: hld up in last quartet: drvn over 2f out: no great prog and sn btn: plodded on* **5/2**[1]
-540 **7** *1 3/4* **Tax Reform (IRE)**[24] 230 6-9-2 **45**... JFEgan 2 30
(Natalie Lloyd-Beavis) *sltly impeded after 100yds: dropped to rr of midfield sn after: effrt whn nt clr run briefly wl over 1f out: no hdwy after* **66/1**
5-63 **8** *2 1/2* **Little Choosey**[12] 383 6-9-2 **48**...(bt) RobHornby[(3)] 1 28
(Roy Bowring) *chsd ldng quartet: rdn to go 3rd briefly 2f out: sn wknd qckly* **10/1**
0-63 **9** *1* **Castanea**[21] 255 4-9-1 **45**... KieranO'Neill 3 23
(Ronald Harris) *hld up in last pair: racd awkwardly over 4f out and detached in last: modest late prog* **8/1**[3]
0-03 **10** *hd* **Time Square (FR)**[13] 362 9-9-7 **50**...(t) AdamKirby 11 28
(Tony Carroll) *chsd ldr after 3f to 3f out: wknd qckly: eased fnl f* **8/1**[3]

53-0 **11** 1/2 **Sudden Wish (IRE)**29 **155** 7-9-7 **50**..............................(p) SeanLevey 8 27
(Michael Attwater) *chsd ldng trio: rdn over 3f out: wknd qckly 2f out* **16/1**

4-50 **12** 1 3/4 **Charlie's Star**21 **255** 4-8-12 **49**..........................(p) MeganNicholls(7) 12 23
(Laura Mongan) *nvr bttr than midfield on outer: rdn over 3f out: sn wknd* **25/1**

06-0 **13** 3/4 **Follow The Faith**17 **326** 4-9-6 **50**.............................. CharlesBishop 13 22
(Mick Channon) *a in rr: drvn and dropped to last pair over 2f out: bhd after* **33/1**

2m 6.26s (-1.74) **Going Correction** -0.075s/f (Stan)
WFA 4 from 5yo+ 1lb **13** Ran SP% **127.7**
Speed ratings (Par 97): **103,102,100,100,100 95,93,91,90,90 90,88,88**
CSF £114.63 CT £5206.88 TOTE £8.10: £2.40, £4.60, £10.60; EX 142.10 Trifecta £7357.70 Part won..
Owner Gerry Dolan **Bred** Shell Bloodstock **Trained** Upper Lambourn, Berks

FOCUS
A poor race, notable for the gamble on the joint-favourite Seven Summits, the first of three of Shane Kelly's Kempton mounts which had been shortened significantly by bookmakers during the day. A race to rate on recent form.

515 32RED.COM H'CAP 5f (P)
5:55 (5:56) (Class 5) (0-75,73) 3-Y-O **£2,911** (£866; £432; £216) **Stalls** Low

Form RPR

6-1 **1** **Princess Cookie**20 **268** 3-9-4 **73**................................ DannyBrock(3) 9 79+
(Philip McBride) *chsd ldrs but trapped out wd: rdn to cl over 1f out: drvn into narrow ld 75yds out: hld on wl* **5/1**3

2-34 **2** *nk* **Rosealee (IRE)**14 **344** 3-9-3 **69**.. MartinLane 3 74
(Jeremy Gask) *trckd ldrs: clsd to ld 1f out: drvn and hdd last 75yds: kpt on but jst hld* **9/4**1

033- **3** 3/4 **Gorgeous Geezer**56 **8243** 3-9-5 **71**............................. RobertWinston 2 73
(Martin Smith) *dwlt: t.k.h in midfield: nt clr run briefly over 1f out: prog fnl f: drvn and kpt on to take 3rd nr fin* **7/2**2

32-6 **4** *hd* **Mysterious Look**23 **242** 3-8-7 **62**................................ RobHornby(3) 8 64
(Ed McMahon) *hld up in midfield: pushed along and prog over 1f out: clsd on ldng pair fnl f but little room between them: lost 3rd nr fin* **9/1**

021- **5** 3/4 **Miss Phillyjinks (IRE)**42 **8402** 3-9-0 **66**.........................(b) ShaneKelly 7 65
(Paul D'Arcy) *s.i.s: hld up in last pair: shkn up over 1f out: styd on fnl f: nrst fin but nvr able to chal* **5/1**3

66-1 **6** *hd* **Pink Martini (IRE)**34 **83** 3-9-6 **72**.. JFEgan 4 70
(Joseph Tuite) *mde most to 1f out: one pce and lost pls after* **8/1**

60-6 **7** 4 **Silver Wings (IRE)**14 **344** 3-9-0 **73**.......................... RhiainIngram(7) 1 57
(Roger Ingram) *cl up on inner: disp 2nd briefly over 1f out: wknd qckly fnl f* **16/1**

1- **8** 1 1/4 **Feelin Dicky**99 **7685** 3-9-5 **71**.. TomEaves 6 50
(James Given) *w ldr to over 1f out: wknd qckly* **9/1**

56-0 **9** 7 **Katie Canford**14 **344** 3-8-10 **62**.................................. WilliamCarson 5 16
(John Bridger) *a in last pair: struggling 1/2-way: t.o* **66/1**

1m 0.05s (-0.45) **Going Correction** -0.075s/f (Stan) **9** Ran SP% **124.8**
Speed ratings (Par 97): **100,99,98,98,96 96,90,88,76**
CSF £18.17 CT £47.24 TOTE £5.50: £2.30, £1.50, £1.50; EX 20.10 Trifecta £75.20.
Owner Howard J Cooke **Bred** J W Mitchell **Trained** Newmarket, Suffolk

FOCUS
A 3yo sprint handicap featuring four last-time-out winners. They were slightly slower than the earlier Class 7 and finished in a bit of a heap, but some of these should be able to improve on this bare form.

516 32RED ON THE APP STORE MAIDEN FILLIES' STKS 7f (P)
6:25 (6:25) (Class 5) 3-Y-O+ **£2,911** (£866; £432; £216) **Stalls** Low

Form RPR

56-3 **1** **Highest Quality (IRE)**9 **413** 4-10-0 62........................(t) PatCosgrave 3 70
(Stuart Williams) *awkward s but sn led: set stdy pce tl sent for home wl over 2f out: clr over 1f out: jst hld on* **8/1**

5- **2** *nse* **Ruby Wednesday**168 **5753** 3-8-11 0.............................. MartinDwyer 2 65+
(John Best) *dwlt: chsd ldng trio: rdn once pce lifted wl over 2f out: stl green but prog over 1f out: tk 2nd ins fnl f: clsd on wnr after: needed one more stride* **5/1**3

3 2 3/4 **Ventura Falcon (IRE)** 3-8-11 0.. SeanLevey 1 57
(Richard Hannon) *prom: chsd wnr over 2f out: rdn and no imp over 1f out: lost 2nd ins fnl f* **15/8**1

4 2 1/2 **Deep Dream** 3-8-11 0.. LiamKeniry 8 51+
(Andrew Balding) *dwlt: hld up in last trio: no ch once pce had lifted wl over 2f out: pushed along and prog wl over 1f out: reminder fnl f: kpt on to take 4th last strides* **5/2**2

0-3 **5** 1 **Logarithm (USA)**12 **384** 3-8-11 0.................................. RobertHavlin 6 48
(John Gosden) *chsd wnr to over 2f out: steadily fdd* **11/2**

0- **6** 5 **Pacabag**52 **8320** 3-8-11 0.. CharlesBishop 5 34
(Peter Hedger) *stdd s: t.k.h in last trio: no ch once pce had lifted wl over 2f out: nvr on terms* **66/1**

6- **7** *nk* **Cloud Nine (FR)**56 **8244** 3-8-11 0................................ WilliamCarson 9 34
(Tony Carroll) *t.k.h: a in last trio: no ch once pce had lifted wl over 2f out: nvr on terms* **50/1**

8 9 **Shift The Blame** 3-8-11 0... KieranO'Neill 4 9
(Jimmy Fox) *chsd ldrs: wknd over 2f out: t.o* **50/1**

1m 28.09s (2.09) **Going Correction** -0.075s/f (Stan)
WFA 3 from 4yo 17lb **8** Ran SP% **111.9**
Speed ratings (Par 100): **85,84,81,78,77 72,71,61**
CSF £45.07 TOTE £10.40: £3.70, £1.10, £1.10; EX 58.90 Trifecta £189.30.
Owner D A Shekells **Bred** Darley **Trained** Newmarket, Suffolk

FOCUS
A couple of well-bred debutantes in a modest fillies' maiden, but disappointingly they couldn't beat an exposed 60-rated horse.

517 £10 FREE BET AT 32REDSPORT.COM H'CAP 1m 4f (P)
6:55 (6:55) (Class 6) (0-65,62) 3-Y-O **£2,264** (£673; £336; £168) **Stalls** Centre

Form RPR

00-1 **1** **Kalamata**30 **148** 3-9-6 **61**.. JackMitchell 3 68+
(Roger Varian) *trckd ldr to over 4f out and again 3f out: led wl over 1f out: shkn up and styd on fnl f: readily* **5/4**1

-235 **2** 1 **Schoolboy Error (IRE)**12 **376** 3-9-3 **58**........................ GeorgeBaker 4 60
(Jamie Osborne) *t.k.h: hld up in tch: smooth prog over 2f out: chsd wnr over 1f out: sn rdn and nt qckn: kpt on same pce* **7/2**2

53-1 **3** *nk* **Whitecliff Park (IRE)**35 **69** 3-9-7 **62**............................... BenCurtis 7 64
(Brian Ellison) *dwlt: hld up in last pair: prog jst over 2f out: drvn to take 3rd jst over 1f out: kpt on same pce* **4/1**3

64-6 **4** 1 1/2 **Secret Sinner (IRE)**30 **148** 3-8-4 **45**.......................... WilliamCarson 8 44
(Jamie Osborne) *stdd s: hld up in last pair: prog jst over 2f out: pressed for 3rd fr jst over 1f out: one pce fnl f* **40/1**

0-31 **5** 1 1/2 **Skylark Lady (IRE)**20 **265** 3-9-6 **61**.................................. ChrisCatlin 6 58
(Rae Guest) *chsd ldrs: rdn over 2f out: sn outpcd: kpt on again ins fnl f* **9/2**

0-65 **6** 3 1/2 **Quick Witted**28 **163** 3-9-2 **57**... FrannyNorton 5 48
(Harry Dunlop) *chsd ldng pair: wnt 2nd over 4f out to 3f out: wknd 2f out* **20/1**

0-60 **7** 2 1/4 **Ingen Brave**23 **245** 3-9-5 **60**... AdamKirby 2 48
(David Evans) *led at v modest pce: tried to kick on 3f out but limited rspnse: hdd & wknd wl over 1f out* **14/1**

2m 39.89s (5.39) **Going Correction** -0.075s/f (Stan) **7** Ran SP% **118.7**
Speed ratings (Par 95): **79,78,78,77,76 73,72**
CSF £6.32 CT £13.89 TOTE £2.40: £1.60, £2.00; EX 7.90 Trifecta £28.20.
Owner Nurlan Bizakov **Bred** Hesmonds Stud Ltd **Trained** Newmarket, Suffolk

FOCUS
Just a modest handicap run at a funereal pace, but it featured three last-time-out winners and the winner has scope to do better.

518 32RED H'CAP 1m (P)
7:25 (7:26) (Class 4) (0-80,79) 4-Y-O+ **£4,690** (£1,395; £697; £348) **Stalls** Low

Form RPR

6-36 **1** **Justice First**14 **349** 4-9-1 **73**... PatCosgrave 6 82
(Ed Dunlop) *chsd clr ldrs in 5th: prog to go 3rd over 2f out: drvn to cl over 1f out: looked hld but kpt on fnl f to ld last stride* **14/1**

43-3 **2** *hd* **Franco's Secret**18 **313** 5-9-5 **77**..........................(p) CharlesBishop 4 86
(Peter Hedger) *dwlt: hld up off the pce disputing 6th: prog over 2f out: drvn to cl over 1f out: led 150yds out: idled in front and hdd last stride* **6/1**

532- **3** *hd* **Mystical Spirit (FR)**144 **6537** 4-9-2 **79**.............. JosephineGordon(5) 3 87
(Martyn Meade) *led at str pce and stretched field: drvn 2f out: c bk to rivals and hdd 150yds out: kpt on* **3/1**1

00-1 **4** 1 1/4 **Charlies Mate**21 **263** 5-9-6 **78**... MartinDwyer 2 83
(John Best) *chsd clr ldng trio: rdn over 2f out: tried to cl over 1f out: kpt on same pce* **11/2**3

00-3 **5** 3 1/4 **Foolaad**36 **49** 5-8-8 **69**..(t) RobHornby(3) 1 67
(Roy Bowring) *chsd ldr at str pce: drvn over 2f out: lost 2nd over 1f out: fdd* **12/1**

00-0 **6** 1 **Embankment**30 **141** 7-8-10 **68**..................................... RobertHavlin 10 63
(Michael Attwater) *s.s: hld up in last pair and wl off the pce: shkn up over 2f out: modest late prog and n.d* **33/1**

620- **7** 1 **Merhoob (IRE)**117 **7257** 4-9-6 **78**.. AdamKirby 9 71
(John Ryan) *chsd clr ldng pair to over 2f out: wknd over 1f out* **12/1**

2-26 **8** 2 3/4 **Exceeding Power**13 **360** 5-9-4 **76**................................ MartinHarley 7 63
(Martin Bosley) *hld up off the pce disputing 8th: rdn over 2f out: no prog* **9/1**

0-20 **9** 2 1/2 **Hannington**21 **260** 5-8-13 **78**..........................(p) CharlieBennett(7) 5 59
(Barry Brennan) *hld up off the pce disputing 6th: pushed along whn sltly impeded over 2f out: wknd* **40/1**

340- **10** 7 **My Son Max**111 **6417** 8-9-3 **75**..(v) JFEgan 11 40
(Nikki Evans) *blanket on and jockey off for stall entry: s.v.s: tk little interest and a wl in rr: t.o* **50/1**

26-1 **U** **Isis Blue**35 **64** 6-8-10 **73**.. AliceMills(5) 8
(Rod Millman) *dwlt: hld up off the pce disputing 8th: sing to make prog on inner whn hit rail: stmbld and uns rdr over 2f out* **9/2**2

23-6 **U** **Wink Oliver**21 **263** 4-9-2 **74**..(p) MartinLane 12
(David Dennis) *dwlt: hld up wl off the pce in 10th: trying to make prog whn hmpd and uns rdr over 2f out* **25/1**

1m 37.3s (-2.50) **Going Correction** -0.075s/f (Stan) **12** Ran SP% **116.1**
Speed ratings (Par 105): **109,108,108,107,104 103,102,99,96,89 ,**
CSF £91.16 CT £324.06 TOTE £13.90: £4.10, £2.30, £1.70; EX 105.50 Trifecta £397.00.
Owner Robert Ng **Bred** Whitsbury Manor Stud & Rangefield Bld **Trained** Newmarket, Suffolk

FOCUS
A fair, competitive handicap. They were well strung out from an early stage in an incident-packed race. The second chucked this away by idling late, rates up to best, with winner back to Chelmsford win.

519 32RED CASINO H'CAP 7f (P)
7:55 (7:56) (Class 5) (0-75,75) 3-Y-O **£2,911** (£866; £432; £216) **Stalls** Low

Form RPR

100- **1** **Willsy**113 **7361** 3-9-1 **69**.. JFEgan 4 73
(Mick Channon) *trckd ldrs: prog 2f out to ld over 1f out: drvn and jnd nr fin: fnd ex to cling on* **33/1**

00-3 **2** *hd* **Santiburi Spring**20 **268** 3-8-8 **62**................................... MartinDwyer 1 65
(John Best) *trckd ldrs on inner: prog to chal over 1f out: chsd wnr after: upsides nr fin: jst hld* **16/1**

14-6 **3** 2 **Lucymai**27 **171** 3-9-7 **75**... RobertWinston 5 76+
(Dean Ivory) *dwlt: hld up in last trio: tried to make prog on inner fr over 2f out but repeatedly nowhere to go: hdwy and bmpd fnl f: styd on to take 3rd last strides* **10/1**

000- **4** *nk* **Highwayman**103 **7592** 3-8-11 **65**.. ShaneKelly 2 62
(William Jarvis) *led: drvn 2f out: hdd over 1f out: racd awkwardly after: hung lft ins fnl f: one pce* **11/2**3

0-1 **5** 3/4 **Trodero**14 **350** 3-9-4 **72**.. JimmyQuinn 9 67
(Dr Jon Scargill) *hld up towards rr: prog gng strly over 2f out into midfield: nt clr run briefly wl over 1f out: sn rdn and one pce* **25/1**

354- **6** *nk* **Stone Quercus (IRE)**140 **6655** 3-8-9 **63**...................... FrannyNorton 11 57
(James Given) *dwlt: hld up in last trio: shkn up and no prog over 2f out: drvn over 1f out: styd on last 150yds: nrst fin* **16/1**

4-34 **7** *shd* **Sir Dudley (IRE)**27 **171** 3-9-5 **73**....................................... TomEaves 7 67
(James Given) *prom: drvn to try to chal 2f out: nt qckn over 1f out: one pce after* **14/1**

254- **7** *dht* **Boycie**63 **8155** 3-9-4 **72**.. KieranO'Neill 6 66
(Richard Hannon) *chsd ldr: cl 2f out: sn drvn and lost 2nd: one pce after* **9/2**2

64-1 **9** *shd* **Undertow (IRE)**22 **249** 3-8-13 **67**.................................... JoeyHaynes 3 61
(K R Burke) *prom on inner: drvn 2f out: hld whn short of room briefly 1f out: one pce and lost pls nr fin* **10/1**

60-1 **10** *hd* **Secret Insider (USA)**27 **171** 3-9-6 **74**.......................... MartinHarley 8 67+
(Hugo Palmer) *hld up in last trio: nvr clrest of runs whn trying to make prog fr 2f out: nvr any ch but kpt on nr fin* **13/8**1

51-3 **11** 1 3/4 **Hold On Magnolia**23 **242** 3-8-12 **66**......................(p) TonyHamilton 10 55
(Richard Fahey) *nvr bttr than midfield: struggling in rr 2f out: n.d after* **20/1**

3-04 **12** 5 **Port Gaverne (IRE)**14 **350** 3-8-7 **68**...................... TylerSaunders(7) 12 43
(Marcus Tregoning) *trapped out wd in midfield: wknd over 2f out* **66/1**

1m 25.51s (-0.49) **Going Correction** -0.075s/f (Stan) **12** Ran SP% **121.3**
Speed ratings (Par 97): **99,98,96,96,95 94,94,94,94,94 92,86**
CSF £482.16 CT £5586.49 TOTE £37.60: £7.80, £5.20, £3.80; EX 735.80 Trifecta £6205.10 Part won..
Owner E & R Bastian **Bred** R Bastian **Trained** West Ilsley, Berks

The Form Book, Raceform Ltd, Newbury, RG14 5SJ

FOCUS
An interesting race as a number of these were pretty unexposed. There was a bit of an turn up though, with a number of bad luck stories in behind. This could prove a bit better than rated.
T/Jkpt: Not won. T/Plt: £111.20 to a £1 stake. Pool: £83,166.91 - 545.96 winning units. T/Qpdt: £6.60 to a £1 stake. Pool: £12,418.86 - 1382.43 winning units. **Jonathan Neesom**

[505] SOUTHWELL (L-H)
Wednesday, February 10

OFFICIAL GOING: Fibresand: standard
Wind: Moderate behind Weather: Fine & dry

520 NEW UNIBET RACING APP DOWNLOAD H'CAP — 6f (F)
1:10 (1:11) (Class 5) (0-70,75) 4-Y-O+ **£3,234** (£962; £481; £240) **Stalls** Low

Form RPR
-664 **1** **Borough Boy (IRE)**[8] 426 6-9-7 **70**............................(v) TonyHamilton 2 84
(Derek Shaw) *hld up in tch: smooth hdwy on inner 1/2-way: led over 1f out: sn pushed clr: readily* **10/1**
-210 **2** *5* **Fujin**[8] 426 5-9-5 **68**..(b) PaulMulrennan 4 66
(Shaun Harris) *sn led: rdn over 2f out: drvn and hdd over 1f out: kpt on same pce* **8/1**[3]
000- **3** *1 1/2* **Viva Verglas (IRE)**[104] 7581 5-9-6 **69**.............................. OisinMurphy 1 62
(Daniel Mark Loughnane) *trckd ldrs: hdwy over 2f out: rdn wl over 1f out: drvn and kpt on fnl f* **9/2**[2]
00-1 **4** *1 1/4* **Sartori**[27] 178 5-9-4 **67**...(p) DanielTudhope 3 56
(Marjorie Fife) *cl up: pushed along 3f out: rdn over 2f out: drvn wl over 1f out and kpt on one pce* **8/1**[3]
3303 **5** *1 1/2* **Elusivity (IRE)**[8] 426 8-9-6 **69**..(p) TomEaves 9 53
(Conor Dore) *chsd ldrs: wd st: rdn along wl over 2f out: sn one pce* **14/1**
-110 **6** *1* **Speightowns Kid (USA)**[22] 246 8-9-1 **69**................(be) AnnStokell[(5)] 8 50
(Ann Stokell) *in tch: rdn along over 2f out: sn one pce* **16/1**
0-41 **7** *shd* **Razin' Hell**[8] 426 5-9-12 **75** 6ex...(v) BenCurtis 5 56
(John Balding) *trckd ldrs: hdwy and wd st: sn chal: rdn 2f out and ev ch: drvn over 1f out and sn wknd* **6/4**[1]
-214 **8** *3 3/4* **Sir Geoffrey (IRE)**[6] 444 10-8-10 **59**..............................(b) LukeMorris 6 28
(Scott Dixon) *chsd ldrs: wd st: rdn along over 2f out: sn wknd* **12/1**
00-0 **9** *4 1/2* **Marmarus**[9] 424 5-9-7 **70**..(v[1]) FrannyNorton 7 24
(David Nicholls) *dwlt: a bhd* **16/1**

1m 15.08s (-1.42) **Going Correction** -0.10s/f (Stan) **9** Ran SP% **115.6**
Speed ratings (Par 103): **105,98,96,94,92 91,91,86,80**
CSF £86.98 CT £413.37 TOTE £12.70: £3.20, £1.90, £1.60; EX 88.10 Trifecta £574.20.
Owner Brian Johnson (Northamptonshire) **Bred** E Kopica And M Rosenfeld **Trained** Sproxton, Leics

FOCUS
This was run at a good pace and suited those ridden with a bit of patience. This was a pb from the winner.

521 32RED.COM H'CAP — 2m (F)
1:40 (1:42) (Class 6) (0-60,60) 4-Y-O+ **£2,587** (£770; £384; £192) **Stalls** Low

Form RPR
10/2 **1** **Pass The Time**[11] 71 7-9-7 **57**.......................................(p) LiamKeniry 6 66
(Neil Mulholland) *trckd ldng pair: smooth hdwy and cl up over 4f out: slt ld wl over 2f out: rdn along wl over 1f out: drvn clr ins fnl f* **6/4**[1]
32-5 **2** *4* **Activation**[14] 354 4-8-0 **49**.. CharlieBennett[(7)] 7 53
(Hughie Morrison) *led: jnd and pushed along over 4f out: rdn 3f out: sn hdd and drvn: stl cl up and ch appr fnl f: kpt on same pce* **12/1**
20-2 **3** *3 3/4* **Ellerina**[39] 27 4-8-6 **48**.. JoeyHaynes 5 48
(Chris Fairhurst) *trckd ldrs: hdwy to chse ldng pair 6f out: rdn along over 3f out: drvn over 2f out and kpt on one pce* **6/1**[3]
20-0 **4** *12* **Amazing Blue Sky**[22] 251 10-8-12 **48**.......................... JamesSullivan 2 33
(Ruth Carr) *dwlt and in rr: pushed along after 4f: hdwy 5f out: rdn along wl over 3f out: drvn over 2f out: plugged on one pce* **50/1**
54-3 **5** *5* **Dissertation**[39] 27 4-8-8 **50**.. AdamBeschizza 4 29
(Julia Feilden) *chsd ldrs: reminders after 5f: rdn along 7f out: drvn over 4f out: sn outpcd* **12/1**
60-0 **6** *99* **Kirkman (IRE)**[24] 234 5-9-6 **56**.. LukeMorris 8
(Peter Hiatt) *prom: rdn along 1/2-way: sn lost pl and bhd: t.o over 4f out: virtually p.u over 3f out: walked home* **20/1**
2-14 **S** **Vivacissimo (IRE)**[28] 157 9-9-9 **59**.............................(tp) OisinMurphy 3
(Ivan Furtado) *chsd ldrs: rdn along over 4f out: sn drvn and outpcd whn slipped up on bnd 3f out: fatally injured* **9/2**[2]

3m 43.3s (-2.20) **Going Correction** -0.10s/f (Stan)
WFA 4 from 5yo+ 6lb **7** Ran SP% **94.6**
Speed ratings (Par 101): **101,99,97,91,88 39,**
CSF £13.33 CT £35.76 TOTE £2.50: £1.70, £3.10; EX 16.30 Trifecta £40.50.
Owner Dajam Ltd **Bred** M Burbidge **Trained** Limpley Stoke, Wilts

FOCUS
An ordinary staying handicap. The stewards held an enquiry to establish the circumstances behind the withdrawal at the start of Feeltherhythm. Shane Kelly reported that on arrival at the start he was unhappy with the mare and asked the vet to examine her. The vet confirmed that after concerns expressed by Kelly that he thought the mare was unsound, and having trotted her up at the start, found the mare to be slightly lame and advised for her to be withdrawn. The vet reported that when initially leaving the racecourse, she observed that the mare was lame, however, on subsequent examination back at the stable yard, and having trotted her up without saddle or rider, Feeltherhythm appeared to be sound. The stewards noted their explanations.

522 32RED H'CAP — 1m (F)
2:10 (2:12) (Class 5) (0-75,74) 3-Y-O **£3,234** (£962; £481; £240) **Stalls** Low

Form RPR
34-3 **1** **Pirate's Treasure**[30] 145 3-9-1 **68**................................. LukeMorris 2 78
(James Tate) *trckd ldrs: smooth hdwy on inner 3f out: chal 2f out: sn rdn: carried hd high and hung rt: drvn and hung bdly rt ent fnl f: led nr fin* **11/8**[1]
-01 **2** *nk* **Daisy Bere (FR)**[20] 275 3-9-2 **69**.................................... JoeyHaynes 1 78
(K R Burke) *slt ld: pushed along and jnd 2f out: sn rdn and slt ld whn carried rt and bmpd jst over 1f out: drvn and stl slt ld whn carried bdly rt to stands' rail and n.m.r ins fnl f: hdd nr fin* **2/1**[2]
61-0 **3** *13* **Strictly Art (IRE)**[27] 171 3-8-11 **64**............................... FrannyNorton 4 43
(Alan Bailey) *chsd ldng pair: pushed along and outpcd after 2f: rdn along on rr over 3f out: drvn over 2f out: sn no imp* **7/1**
11-3 **4** *11* **Masqueraded (USA)**[27] 182 3-8-10 **70**...............(v[1]) RhiainIngram[(7)] 5 24
(Gay Kelleway) *cl up: rdn along 3f out: drvn over 2f out: sn wknd* **4/1**[3]

1m 41.27s (-2.43) **Going Correction** -0.10s/f (Stan) **4** Ran SP% **107.9**
Speed ratings (Par 97): **108,107,94,83**
CSF £4.37 TOTE £2.10; EX 4.30 Trifecta £10.70.
Owner Saif Ali **Bred** Meon Valley Stud **Trained** Newmarket, Suffolk

■ Stewards' Enquiry : Luke Morris two-day ban: careless riding (Feb 24-25)

FOCUS
The first two finished well clear and look ones to keep on side. The level is fluid for now but it could be rated higher.

523 LADBROKES H'CAP — 7f (F)
2:45 (2:45) (Class 5) (0-75,74) 4-Y-O+ **£3,234** (£962; £481; £240) **Stalls** Low

Form RPR
61-2 **1** **Greyfriarschorista**[20] 276 9-9-3 **73**..........................(vt) SladeO'Hara[(3)] 3 83
(Giles Bravery) *dwlt: sn trcking ldrs: smooth hdwy on inner 3f out: led 2f out: rdn over 1f out: kpt on strly* **5/2**[1]
2546 **2** *2 1/2* **Alpha Tauri (USA)**[13] 367 10-9-1 **68**.................................... BenCurtis 7 72
(Charles Smith) *chsd ldrs on outer: rdn along and sltly outpcd over 2f out: kpt on u.p fnl f* **14/1**
413- **3** *1/2* **Royal Holiday (IRE)**[50] 8341 9-9-7 **74**..........................(p) SamJames 4 76
(Marjorie Fife) *slt ld: pushed along 1/2-way: hdd 3f out and sn rdn: drvn wl over 1f out: kpt on same pce* **9/2**
-453 **4** *1/2* **Be Royale**[9] 415 6-9-5 **72**.. LukeMorris 6 73
(Michael Appleby) *trckd ldng pair: pushed along 3f out: rdn to chal and ev ch 2f out: sn drvn and kpt on same pce* **4/1**[3]
-533 **5** *1 3/4* **Monsieur Jimmy**[6] 448 4-8-11 **64**...............................(b) PJMcDonald 5 60
(Declan Carroll) *cl up: slt ld 3f out: rdn and hdd 2f out: sn drvn and wknd over 1f out* **7/2**[2]
644- **6** *9* **Khajaaly (IRE)**[86] 7873 9-9-5 **72**..................................(t) StevieDonohoe 2 45
(Daniel Mark Loughnane) *towards rr: rdn along after 3f: sn outpcd and bhd* **10/1**
000- **7** *4 1/2* **Samsonite (IRE)**[110] 7427 4-9-6 **73**.................................. BarryMcHugh 1 34
(Tony Coyle) *dwlt: rdn along and in tch on inner: lost pl after 3f: sn outpcd and bhd* **10/1**

1m 29.04s (-1.26) **Going Correction** -0.10s/f (Stan) **7** Ran SP% **113.8**
Speed ratings (Par 103): **103,100,99,99,97 86,81**
CSF £37.44 TOTE £3.00: £1.80, £4.60; EX 35.10 Trifecta £195.70.
Owner Future Electrical Services Ltd **Bred** Castlemartin Stud And Skymarc Farm **Trained** Newmarket, Suffolk

FOCUS
A modest affair run at a sound gallop. The winner is rated in line with better view of his recent C&D run.

524 LADBROKES MEDIAN AUCTION MAIDEN STKS — 1m (F)
3:20 (3:25) (Class 5) 3-5-Y-O **£3,234** (£962; £481; £240) **Stalls** Low

Form RPR
2- **1** **Wings Of Esteem (IRE)**[54] 8280 3-8-4 0........................... JoeyHaynes 4 75
(K R Burke) *cl up: led wl over 2f out and sn rdn: clr over 1f out: edgd rt to stands' rail ins fnl f: kpt on* **9/2**[2]
032- **2** *1 1/2* **Mystic Blaze (IRE)**[76] 8006 3-8-9 77............................... OisinMurphy 2 75
(Andrew Balding) *slt ld on inner: rdn along and hdd wl over 2f out: drvn wl over 1f out: edgd rt and kpt on same pce fnl f* **30/100**[1]
0-24 **3** *15* **Clive Clifton (IRE)**[20] 265 3-8-9 64............................. StevieDonohoe 3 41
(David Evans) *prom: rdn along and outpcd wl over 3f out: styd nr far rail in st: kpt on u.p to take remote 3rd fnl f* **16/1**
5 **4** *1 1/4* **Blue Vision (FR)**[26] 202 3-8-9 0... JoeFanning 1 38
(Alan Swinbank) *dwlt and towards rr: pushed along and hdwy over 3f out: rdn wl over 2f out: plugged on one pce* **50/1**
6 **5** *3 1/2* **Indigo Princess**[14] 352 3-8-4 0.. LukeMorris 5 25
(Michael Appleby) *prom on outer: rdn along to chse ldng pair over 3f out: drvn wl over 2f out: wknd wl over 1f out* **14/1**[3]
6 *26* **Shulammite Man (IRE)** 3-8-9 0... BenCurtis 6
(Alan Swinbank) *dwlt: sn pushed along in rr: green and rdn bef 1/2-way: sn outpcd and bhd* **25/1**

1m 42.01s (-1.69) **Going Correction** -0.10s/f (Stan) **6** Ran SP% **113.5**
Speed ratings (Par 103): **104,102,87,86,82 56**
CSF £6.36 TOTE £5.70: £1.90, £1.10; EX 7.10 Trifecta £22.80.
Owner M Nelmes-Crocker & Mrs E Burke **Bred** Knocktoran Stud **Trained** Middleham Moor, N Yorks

FOCUS
Only two mattered from the turn out of the back straight in this weak maiden. The runner-up is rated to his improved C&D latest.

525 BET NOW WITH THE LADBROKES APP H'CAP — 7f (F)
3:55 (3:59) (Class 6) (0-52,52) 4-Y-O+ **£2,587** (£770; £384; £192) **Stalls** Low

Form RPR
0-06 **1** **Emblaze**[27] 176 4-9-0 **52**.. PhilDennis[(7)] 4 60
(Bryan Smart) *mde all: rdn wl over 1f out: kpt on wl fnl f* **8/1**
40-0 **2** *2 3/4* **Bionic Indian**[26] 201 4-9-2 **47**.. BarryMcHugh 8 48
(Michael Easterby) *prom: effrt to chal 2f out: sn rdn and ev ch: drvn ent fnl f: kpt on same pce* **3/1**[1]
0-56 **3** *1 1/4* **Equilicious**[15] 340 4-9-3 **48**.. PJMcDonald 9 45
(Ollie Pears) *cl up on outer: pushed along 3f out: rdn 2f out: kpt on fnl f* **8/1**
-000 **4** *3/4* **Madakheel (USA)**[12] 388 5-9-1 **46** oh1..........................(t) JoeyHaynes 7 41
(Simon West) *in tch towards rr: pushed along and outpcd in rr 1/2-way: rdn wl over 2f out: swtchd rt to outer and drvn over 1f out: kpt on fnl f* **33/1**
6040 **5** *1/2* **Ciaras Cookie (IRE)**[12] 388 4-9-1 **46** oh1................(t) DougieCostello 1 40
(Heather Dalton) *cl up on inner: rdn and ev ch 2f out: sn drvn and kpt on same pce appr fnl f* **16/1**
63-6 **6** *1* **Miss Buckaroo (IRE)**[28] 163 4-9-7 **52**........................... JamesSullivan 6 43
(James Given) *towards rr and swtchd lft to inner after 3f: hdwy to chse ldrs over 2f out and sn rdn: drvn over 1f out and kpt on one pce* **16/1**
036- **7** *nse* **Machiavelian Storm (IRE)**[42] 8406 4-9-1 **46** oh1....(p) PaulMulrennan 2 37
(Michael Herrington) *trckd ldrs: hdwy wl over 2f out: rdn wl over 1f out: sn drvn and wknd* **6/1**[3]
0520 **8** *hd* **Loud**[7] 431 6-9-2 **50**...(b) SimonPearce[(3)] 5 40
(Lydia Pearce) *dwlt and bhd tl styd on fnl 2f* **9/2**[2]
44-0 **9** *14* **Marmooz**[25] 216 4-9-1 **46** oh1.. LukeMorris 3
(Michael Appleby) *chsd ldrs: rdn along 1/2-way: sn wknd* **11/1**
62-0 **10** *1* **Artbeat (IRE)**[36] 54 4-9-6 **51**................................(b[1]) AdamBeschizza 10 +
(Julia Feilden) *s.i.s and bhd: sme hdwy on outer 1/2-way: rdn 3f out and sn outpcd* **13/2**

1m 30.15s (-0.15) **Going Correction** -0.10s/f (Stan) **10** Ran SP% **116.1**
Speed ratings (Par 101): **96,92,91,90,90 88,88,88,72,71**
CSF £32.07 CT £206.31 TOTE £5.80: £4.10, £1.40, £3.20; EX 53.90 Trifecta £484.10.
Owner Crossfields Racing **Bred** Crossfields Bloodstock Ltd **Trained** Hambleton, N Yorks

FOCUS
A moderate handicap.

526 LADBROKES MOBILE H'CAP 1m (F)
4:25 (4:26) (Class 6) (0-52,52) 4-Y-O+ **£2,587** (£770; £384; £192) **Stalls** Low

Form RPR

02-3 **1** **Eium Mac**[22] 247 7-9-5 **50**....(b) RaulDaSilva 2 57
(Neville Bycroft) *mde all: rdn 2f out: drvn over 1f out: kpt on wl fnl f* **3/1**[2]

44-2 **2** *2 1/4* **Basingstoke (IRE)**[40] 2 7-9-7 **52**.... LukeMorris 3 55
(Daniel Mark Loughnane) *prom: trckd wnr 1/2-way: cl up 3f out: chal 2f out: rdn and edgd lft jst over 1f out: sn drvn and kpt on same pce* **1/1**[1]

00-3 **3** *3 1/4* **Music Hall (FR)**[12] 388 6-8-10 **46** oh1....(p) JustinNewman(5) 5 40
(Shaun Harris) *dwlt and in rr: hdwy over 3f out: wd st: rdn to chse ldng pair wl over 1f out: sn drvn and no imp* **12/1**

5546 **4** *1 1/2* **General Tufto**[6] 448 11-9-1 **46**....(b) JoeyHaynes 7 36
(Charles Smith) *in tch: rdn along and outpcd over 3f out: drvn over 2f out: styd on fnl f* **10/1**

-546 **5** *3/4* **Je T'Aime Encore**[13] 362 4-9-4 **49**....(e1) AdamBeschizza 1 37
(Gay Kelleway) *chsd ldrs on inner: rdn along 3f out: drvn over 2f out and sn wknd* **25/1**

510- **6** *2 1/2* **Hazel Blue (IRE)**[51] 8334 5-9-6 **51**.... DavidNolan 4 33
(David Loughnane) *cl up: wd st and sn rdn along: wknd wl over 1f out* **9/1**[3]

/00- **7** *25* **Show Me Baileys (FR)**[280] 1998 4-9-5 **50**....(b1) PaulMulrennan 8
(James Given) *chsd ldrs on outer: rdn along 1/2-way: sn outpcd and bhd* **16/1**

1m 43.72s (0.02) **Going Correction** -0.10s/f (Stan) 7 Ran SP% **111.5**
Speed ratings (Par 101): **95,92,89,88,87 84,59**
CSF £6.01 CT £26.07 TOTE £4.40: £1.80, £1.20; EX 7.40 Trifecta £31.50.
Owner N Bycroft **Bred** N Bycroft **Trained** Norton, N Yorks

FOCUS
The early pace wasn't strong in this low-grade handicap. The winner repeated his recent C&D form in better race, with the runner-up to his recent level.
T/Plt: £127.00 to a £1 stake. Pool: £63,233.59 - 363.46 winning units. T/Qpdt: £9.30 to a £1 stake. Pool: £7,645.28 - 604.02 winning units. **Joe Rowntree**

491 CHELMSFORD (A.W) (L-H)
Thursday, February 11

OFFICIAL GOING: Polytrack: standard
Wind: virtually nil Weather: dry, chilly

527 TOTEPOOLLIVEINFO.COM APPRENTICE H'CAP 1m 2f (P)
5:10 (5:10) (Class 6) (0-55,55) 4-Y-O+ **£3,234** (£962; £481; £240) **Stalls** Low

Form RPR

-423 **1** **Celtic Artisan (IRE)**[6] 463 5-9-4 **52**....(b) DanielleMooney 8 59
(Rebecca Menzies) *hld up in tch in rr of main gp: nt clr run on inner over 2f out: rdn and gd hdwy over 1f out: styd on strly to ld ins fnl f: sn in command* **4/1**[2]

045/ **2** *1 3/4* **Barnaby Brook (CAN)**[632] 2443 6-9-0 **53**....(b) SamuelClarke(5) 3 57
(Robyn Brisland) *t.k.h: chsd ldr tl led over 3f out: 2 l clr 2f out: rdn over 1f out: hdd and styd on same pce ins fnl f* **9/2**[3]

036- **3** *3* **Oakley Star**[86] 7884 4-9-6 **55**.... LuluStanford 10 53
(Gay Kelleway) *stdd and dropped in bhd after s: sn detached in last: clsd and in tch but stl last 3f: hdwy on outer 2f out: chsd ldng pair and shifted lft jst ins fnl f: styd on wl but nvr a threat* **8/1**

-110 **4** *7* **Clock On Tom**[2] 505 6-9-4 **52**.... PatrickVaughan 6 37+
(Denis Quinn) *in tch in midfield: hdwy to chse ldr over 2f out: rdn and pressed ldr wl over 1f out: sn outpcd: 3rd and btn 1f out: wknd ins fnl f* **5/2**[1]

-320 **5** *2 1/2* **Ela Goog La Mou**[18] 324 7-8-12 **53**.... GeorgeWood(7) 7 33
(Peter Charalambous) *slowly into tch: sn rcvrd and in tch in midfield: effrt u.p to chse ldrs 2f out: outpcd and btn whn sltly hmpd 1f out: wknd fnl f* **12/1**

3200 **6** *1 3/4* **My Tringaling (IRE)**[10] 422 4-8-13 **53**.... MillyNaseb(5) 9 30
(Stuart Williams) *dwlt: sn in tch in rr of main gp: effrt over 2f out: sn struggling: wknd over 1f out* **8/1**

0-05 **7** *5* **Sixties Queen**[14] 362 6-8-5 **46** oh1....(p) ChrisKelly(7) 4 13
(Lisa Williamson) *t.k.h: chsd ldrs tl 3f out: sn rdn and lost pl: bhd over 1f out* **25/1**

3-65 **8** *12* **Luv U Lucky**[28] 179 4-9-1 **55**.... MitchGodwin(5) 1
(Michael Appleby) *led tl over 3f out: rdn and lost pl over 2f out: wknd and bhd 1f out* **5/1**

2m 5.84s (-2.76) **Going Correction** -0.20s/f (Stan)
WFA 4 from 5yo+ 1lb 8 Ran SP% **117.2**
Speed ratings (Par 101): **103,101,99,93,91 90,86,76**
CSF £22.99 CT £138.31 TOTE £4.50: £1.20, £2.10, £2.70; EX 26.60 Trifecta £181.40.
Owner EPDS Racing Partnership 11 **Bred** Fortbarrington Stud **Trained** Mordon, Co. Durham

FOCUS
A moderate handicap run at a good gallop. The winner seems to be heading back towards his best.

528 FOLLOW @TOTEPOOL ON TWITTER H'CAP 6f (P)
5:40 (5:41) (Class 6) (0-52,52) 4-Y-O+ **£3,234** (£962; £481; £240) **Stalls** Centre

Form RPR

0/21 **1** **Camdora (IRE)**[21] 270 4-9-7 **52**.... TimmyMurphy 3 67+
(Jamie Osborne) *outpcd in last trio: 7th and plenty to do whn rdn over 2f out: gd hdwy over 1f out: led ins fnl f: sn gng clr and r.o strly: readily* **5/4**[1]

4-45 **2** *3 1/2* **Multi Quest**[13] 381 4-9-1 **46** oh1....(b) RobertHavlin 1 49
(John E Long) *pressed ldrs on inner: led over 3f out: rdn over 1f out: hdd ins fnl f: sn brushed aside by wnr but kpt on for 2nd* **12/1**

3-00 **3** *1 1/4* **Bold Max**[20] 297 5-9-7 **52**....(v) LiamJones 4 51
(Zoe Davison) *in tch in midfield: rdn 3f out: hdwy u.p 1f out: kpt on wl to go 3rd towards fin: no threat to wnr* **16/1**

-251 **4** *1 1/4* **Kuanyao (IRE)**[13] 381 10-8-13 **49**....(be) AnnStokell(5) 9 45
(Ann Stokell) *w ldrs: led 4f out: sn hdd but styd upsides ldr: rdn 2f out: outpcd by wnr ins fnl f: wknd fnl 75yds* **8/1**

4-66 **5** *2 3/4* **Dream Ally (IRE)**[10] 418 6-9-7 **52**.... JamieSpencer 5 39
(John Weymes) *led tl 4f out: chsd ldrs: rdn over 2f out: outpcd u.p over 1f out: wknd fnl f* **5/1**[3]

66/3 **6** *2 1/4* **Rutterkin (USA)**[26] 217 8-8-8 **46** oh1.... VitorSantos(7) 8 27
(John David Riches) *taken down early: chsd ldrs: rdn over 2f out: outpcd and btn over 1f out: wknd fnl f* **25/1**

00-2 **7** *hd* **Presto Boy**[13] 381 4-9-0 **52**....(tp) StephanieJoannides(7) 2 32
(Richard Hughes) *awkward leaving stalls and s.i.s: sn rcvrd to chse ldrs: rdn over 2f out: outpcd and btn over 1f out: wknd fnl f* **9/2**[2]

30-0 **8** *1/2* **Stamp Of Approval (IRE)**[22] 257 4-9-6 **51**....[1] GeorgeBaker 7 29
(Chris Wall) *restless in stalls: stdd s: sn detacehed in last: nvr on terms* **8/1**

135- **9** *13* **Brean Splash Susie**[128] 7002 5-9-2 **52**.... RyanWhile(5) 6
(Bill Turner) *sn outpcd in last pair and nvr on terms: rdn 4f out: wl bhd and eased ins fnl f* **25/1**

1m 11.98s (-1.72) **Going Correction** -0.20s/f (Stan) 9 Ran SP% **122.8**
Speed ratings (Par 101): **103,98,96,95,91 88,88,87,70**
CSF £20.46 CT £174.82 TOTE £2.20: £1.40, £3.30, £2.80; EX 21.90 Trifecta £290.10.
Owner Lady Blyth **Bred** Bernard Cooke **Trained** Upper Lambourn, Berks

FOCUS
This was run at a sound gallop and the winner showed herself to still be well handicapped. Straightforward form in behind.

529 TOTEPOOL BETTING ON ALL UK RACING H'CAP 6f (P)
6:10 (6:10) (Class 3) (0-95,94) 4-Y-O+ **£9,703** (£2,887; £1,443; £721) **Stalls** Centre

Form RPR

1311 **1** **Bosham**[7] 439 6-8-8 **88** 6ex....(bt) NathanEvans(7) 5 99
(Michael Easterby) *mde all: pushed along over 1f out: 2 l clr 150yds: kpt on and a holding on* **6/1**[2]

01-1 **2** *3/4* **Nuno Tristan (USA)**[27] 198 4-9-0 **87**.... TonyHamilton 3 96
(Richard Fahey) *t.k.h: hld up in tch in midfield: swtchd rt and effrt over 1f out: chsd wnr ins fnl f: kpt on wl u.p but nvr getting to wnr* **7/4**[1]

3-40 **3** *1 3/4* **Magnus Maximus**[20] 288 5-9-3 **90**.... JFEgan 2 93
(Robyn Brisland) *chsd wnr: rdn 3f out: drvn and no imp on wnr over 1f out: lost 2nd and kpt on same pce ins fnl f* **7/1**[3]

40-6 **4** *1/2* **Spicy Jam**[26] 214 4-9-5 **92**.... AndreaAtzeni 1 93
(Marco Botti) *chsd ldng trio: rdn over 2f out: hrd drvn over 1f out: styd on same pce ins fnl f* **8/1**

436- **5** *hd* **Varsovian**[61] 8205 6-9-0 **87**.... RenatoSouza 6 88
(Dean Ivory) *dwlt and hmpd sn after s: sn swtchd lft and in tch in midfield: effrt over 1f out: 5th and trying to cl whn nt clrest of runs 1f out: kpt on same pce ins fnl f* **9/1**

066- **6** *2 1/2* **Zac Brown (IRE)**[43] 8395 5-9-5 **92**.... DanielTudhope 4 85
(Charlie Wallis) *in tch in midfield: swtchd rt and effrt u.p over 1f out: 6th and no imp fnl f* **14/1**

6-16 **7** *2 1/2* **Searchlight**[18] 323 5-9-0 **87**.... PatCosgrave 9 72
(Jim Boyle) *hld up in tch in rr: sme hdwy u.p over 1f out: no imp and wl hld fnl f* **25/1**

03-3 **8** *1* **Elis Eliz (IRE)**[15] 351 4-9-0 **87**.... AdamKirby 8 69
(Michael Wigham) *hmpd sn after s: in tch in last trio: effrt and no imp over 1f out: wl hld fnl f* **14/1**

-550 **9** *1 1/4* **Vimy Ridge**[20] 288 4-8-11 **84**....(p) CathyGannon 11 62
(Alan Bailey) *in tch in last trio: hung rt bnd 2f out: sn u.p and no imp: wl hld fnl f* **33/1**

-035 **10** *3/4* **Oriental Relation (IRE)**[23] 250 5-8-11 **84**....(v) TomEaves 7 59
(James Given) *bmpd sn after s: chsd ldrs tl no ex u.p over 1f out: wknd fnl f* **25/1**

52-1 **U** **Mythmaker**[35] 86 4-9-7 **94**.... PaulMulrennan 10
(Bryan Smart) *broke wl but wnt lft: bmpd rival and uns rdr sn after s* **6/1**[2]

1m 10.34s (-3.36) **Going Correction** -0.20s/f (Stan) 11 Ran SP% **122.5**
Speed ratings (Par 107): **114,113,110,110,109 106,103,101,100,99**
CSF £17.25 CT £79.78 TOTE £6.20: £2.80, £1.70, £2.00; EX 23.90 Trifecta £231.10.
Owner Peter Easterby **Bred** Rabbah Bloodstock Limited **Trained** Sheriff Hutton, N Yorks

FOCUS
A good sprint handicap. It's possible Mythmaker would have pressed the winner for the lead, but his early mishap left Bosham to his own devices up front and the winner was better than ever.

530 TOTEPOOL H'CAP 1m 2f (P)
6:40 (6:41) (Class 2) (0-105,102) 4-Y-O+ **£12,938** (£3,850; £1,924; £962) **Stalls** Low

Form RPR

45-3 **1** **Dance Of Fire**[28] 172 4-8-4 **83**.... CathyGannon 4 91
(Andrew Balding) *t.k.h: mde all and set stdy gallop: rdn and qcknd wl over 1f out: r.o wl and in command ins fnl f: rdn out* **4/1**[2]

1-42 **2** *1 1/4* **Pactolus (IRE)**[29] 160 5-8-5 **83** oh1....(t) AdamBeschizza 1 88
(Stuart Williams) *hld up in tch in midfield: effrt to chse ldrs over 1f out: swtchd rt ins fnl f: r.o to go 2nd wl ins fnl f* **7/1**

4-23 **3** *nk* **Afonso De Sousa (USA)**[17] 333 6-9-10 **102**....(p) DanielTudhope 2 106
(David O'Meara) *chsd wnr: rdn and drifted rt over 1f out: styd on same pce ins fnl f: lost 2nd wl ins fnl f* **5/1**[3]

34-5 **4** *1 3/4* **Plutocracy (IRE)**[27] 194 6-9-0 **92**.... AdamKirby 5 93
(Gary Moore) *stdd s: hld up in last pair: effrt on inner over 1f out: styd on same pce ins fnl f* **14/1**

-521 **5** *hd* **Winterlude (IRE)**[15] 353 6-9-5 **97**.... GeorgeBaker 6 97
(Jennie Candlish) *stdd s: hld up in midfield: swtchd rt and effrt over 1f out: styd on same pce ins fnl f* **3/1**[1]

/632 **6** *4 1/2* **Whispering Warrior (IRE)**[15] 353 7-9-1 **93**.... JamieSpencer 7 84
(David Simcock) *stdd s: hld up in last pair: effrt over 1f out: rdn and no imp 1f out: wl hld and eased towards fin* **5/1**[3]

/02- **7** *3* **Latin Charm (IRE)**[289] 1775 5-8-11 **89**....(p) AndreaAtzeni 3 74
(Marco Botti) *chsd ldrs: rdn 3f out: struggling and lost pl over 1f out: bhd ins fnl f* **5/1**[3]

2m 9.95s (1.35) **Going Correction** -0.20s/f (Stan)
WFA 4 from 5yo+ 1lb 7 Ran SP% **114.2**
Speed ratings (Par 109): **86,85,84,83,83 79,77**
CSF £31.32 TOTE £4.80: £3.50, £4.20; EX 30.20 Trifecta £193.70.
Owner J C Smith **Bred** Littleton Stud **Trained** Kingsclere, Hants

FOCUS
A decent race on paper, but nothing wanted to go on and the winner was handed an uncontested lead.

531 TOTEPOOL LIKE US ON FACEBOOK MAIDEN STKS 5f (P)
7:10 (7:10) (Class 4) 3-4-Y-O **£8,086** (£2,406; £1,202; £601) **Stalls** Low

Form RPR

5-2 **1** **Cultured Knight**[8] 432 3-9-0 0.... ShaneKelly 3 64+
(Richard Hughes) *mde virtually all: pushed along over 1f out: drvn wl ins fnl f: kpt on* **4/6**[1]

036- **2** *nk* **Strictly Carter**[62] 8173 3-9-0 62.... SaleemGolam 7 63
(Alan Bailey) *chsd ldrs: effrt over 1f out: ev ch ins fnl f: kpt on wl u.p towards fin* **6/1**[3]

6- **3** *1* **One Big Surprise**[363] 538 4-9-2 0.... StephenCummins(7) 2 60+
(Richard Hughes) *stdd s: hld up in rr: detached after 2f: clsd qckly on inner 2f out: nt clr run over 1f out: swtchd rt ins fnl f: nvr enough room after: wnt 3rd cl home* **14/1**

6-03 **4** 3/4 **Justice Rock**[20] 286 3-8-9 62............................(b) JosephineGordon(5) 1 57
(Phil McEntee) *w wnr: rdn and ev ch 2f out: no ex ins fnl f: wknd fnl 50yds* **7/2**[2]
5 3/4 **Birrafun (IRE)** 3-8-9 0.. PJMcDonald 4 49
(Ann Duffield) *off the pce in 5th: swtchd rt and hdwy wl over 1f out: chsd ldrs and drvn 1f out: no ex and wknd fnl 75yds* **14/1**
004- **6** 3 1/2 **Sirdaab (USA)**[46] 8366 4-9-9 52.. AnnStokell(5) 6 47
(Ann Stokell) *taken down early: chsd ldrs: effrt over 1f out: no ex ins fnl f: wknd* **33/1**

59.56s (-0.64) **Going Correction** -0.20s/f (Stan)
WFA 3 from 4yo 14lb **6** Ran SP% **112.8**
Speed ratings (Par 105): **97,96,94,93,92 86**
CSF £5.39 TOTE £1.60: £1.10, £2.70; EX 5.80 Trifecta £34.80.
Owner Don Churston & Ray Greatorex **Bred** Lookout Partnership **Trained** Upper Lambourn, Berkshire

FOCUS
A weak maiden rated around the runner-up.

532 SCOOP6SOCCER THE £1 MILLION FOOTBALL BET H'CAP 1m (P)
7:40 (7:41) (Class 5) (0-70,70) 4-Y-O+ **£5,175** (£1,540; £769; £384) **Stalls** Low

Form RPR
03-2 **1** **Gracious George (IRE)**[31] 141 6-9-2 **65**........................ KieranO'Neill 3 73
(Jimmy Fox) *hld up in tch in midfield: hdwy to chse ldrs 1/2-way: rdn over 2f out: swtchd rt wl over 1f out: styd on to ld fnl 100yds: hld on cl home* **9/2**[2]
/0-1 **2** *hd* **De Lesseps (USA)**[26] 216 8-8-0 **56** oh4....................... VitorSantos(7) 9 63+
(John David Riches) *stdd s and dropped in bhd: hld up in rr: nt clr run over 2f out: rdn and hdwy over 1f out: clsng and squeezed between horses 1f out: chsd wnr fnl 75yds: styd on wl* **14/1**
5-14 **3** 1 1/4 **Hierarch (IRE)**[22] 264 9-8-6 **62**...............................(p) SophieKilloran(7) 1 66
(David Simcock) *broke wl: steadily lost pl and in last pair after 2f: hdwy to chse ldrs 1f out: kpt on same pce ins fnl f: wnt 3rd last strides* **10/1**
555- **4** *hd* **Fingal's Cave (IRE)**[248] 3003 4-9-7 **70**............................ GeorgeBaker 4 74
(Mick Channon) *stdd s: t.k.h in last trio: swtchd rt and hdwy to ld over 6f out: rdn wl over 1f out: hdd fnl 100yds: no ex and wknd towards fin* **7/1**[3]
4-02 **5** 1 1/2 **Toymaker**[6] 467 9-8-4 **58**.....................................(t) JosephineGordon(5) 5 58
(Phil McEntee) *chsd ldrs: effrt over 2f out: unable qck u.p 1f out: wknd wl ins fnl f* **25/1**
3-36 **6** 2 3/4 **Venus Grace**[28] 169 5-8-11 **60**...(p) LiamJones 8 54
(Michael Appleby) *t.k.h: led and set stdy gallop tl over 6f out: pressed ldr after: rdn wl over 1f out: struggling to qckn and swtchd lft 1f out: sn btn and wknd ins fnl f* **14/1**
-221 **7** 4 **Welliesinthewater (IRE)**[7] 449 6-9-2 **70**..................(v) NoelGarbutt(5) 2 55
(Derek Shaw) *awkward leaving stalls and s.i.s: t.k.h in rr: swtchd rt and hdwy on outer after 2f: rdn and lost pl 3f out: bhd over 1f out* **11/8**[1]
3-31 **8** 2 **The Happy Hammer (IRE)**[18] 321 10-8-10 **66**.......... LuluStanford(7) 7 46
(Eugene Stanford) *in tch in midfield but stuck wd: rdn wl over 2f out: sn struggling: bhd and wknd 1f out* **12/1**
2-42 **9** 3 **Primrose Brown**[18] 324 5-9-3 **66**.................................... JimmyQuinn 6 39
(Conrad Allen) *chsd ldr for 1f: chsd ldrs tl lost pl over 3f out: rdn and struggling wl over 2f out: bhd fnl f* **8/1**

1m 38.2s (-1.70) **Going Correction** -0.20s/f (Stan) **9** Ran SP% **117.9**
Speed ratings (Par 103): **100,99,98,98,96 94,90,88,85**
CSF £66.14 CT £607.34 TOTE £6.70: £1.60, £2.80, £2.90; EX 82.90 Trifecta £893.50.
Owner Mrs Barbara Fuller **Bred** D Fuller **Trained** Collingbourne Ducis, Wilts
■ Stewards' Enquiry : Kieran O'Neill two-day ban: used whip above permitted level (Feb 25-26)

FOCUS
Modest handicap form with the winner building on his recent efforts.

533 CELEBRATE ST. PATRICKS DAY ON 17TH MARCH H'CAP 1m 2f (P)
8:10 (8:13) (Class 6) (0-60,60) 3-Y-O **£3,234** (£962; £481; £240) **Stalls** Low

Form RPR
5-62 **1** **You're A Goat**[21] 265 3-9-7 **60**.. AdamKirby 1 65
(Gary Moore) *chsd ldrs: nt clr run on inner over 2f out: effrt and drvn to chal over 1f out: led ins fnl f: drvn out* **11/8**[1]
50-0 **2** 1/2 **Rockliffe**[21] 274 3-9-4 **57**.. TomEaves 6 61
(Mick Channon) *led: rdn over 2f out: drvn over 1f out: hdd ins fnl f: kpt on but hld fnl 75yds* **20/1**
4-25 **3** 1 1/4 **Frivolous Prince (IRE)**[31] 148 3-8-7 **46**................................... JFEgan 4 48
(David Evans) *hld up in tch in last pair: rdn and hdwy 3f out: drvn to chse ldr 2f out tl over 1f out: 3rd and styd on same pce ins fnl f* **6/1**[2]
0-53 **4** 5 **Faster Company (IRE)**[15] 345 3-8-5 **49**............ JosephineGordon(5) 2 42
(J S Moore) *in tch in 4th: hung rt bnd 3f out tl 2f out: no ex u.p over 1f out: wknd ins fnl f* **10/1**[3]
4-50 **5** 1/2 **Falcon's Fire (IRE)**[20] 298 3-9-5 **58**................................ PhillipMakin 7 50
(Keith Dalgleish) *chsd ldr: rdn: lost 2nd and jostled 2f out: no ex u.p over 1f out: wknd ins fnl f* **6/1**[2]
0-00 **6** 90 **Milyaar (IRE)**[12] 400 3-9-4 **57**...(t) GeorgeBaker 5
(Roger Teal) *hld up in last pair: reminder 6f out: dropped to last 4f out: lost tch 2f out: eased over 1f out* **25/1**

2m 6.45s (-2.15) **Going Correction** -0.20s/f (Stan) **6** Ran SP% **88.4**
Speed ratings (Par 95): **100,99,98,94,94 22**
CSF £16.69 CT £43.71 TOTE £2.10: £1.10, £5.90; EX 17.20 Trifecta £58.00.
Owner Power Geneva Ltd **Bred** Mrs James Wigan **Trained** Lower Beeding, W Sussex
■ Divine Touch was withdrawn. Price at time of withdrawal 3/1. Rule 4 applies to all bets - deduct 25p in the pound.

FOCUS
Ordinary form.
T/Plt: £103.10 to a £1 stake. Pool of £80261.39 - 568.18 winning tickets. T/Qpdt: £31.80 to a £1 stake. Pool of £10749.45 - 249.85 winning tickets. **Steve Payne**

450 MEYDAN (L-H)
Thursday, February 11

OFFICIAL GOING: Dirt: fast; turf: good

534a UAE 1000 GUINEAS SPONSORED BY FRIDAY (LISTED RACE) (DIRT) 1m (D)
3:00 (3:00) 3-Y-O **£102,721** (£34,693; £17,687; £9,183; £5,782)

RPR
1 **Polar River (USA)**[28] 184 3-9-0 107.. PatDobbs 5 112+
(Doug Watson, UAE) *trckd ldng pair: smooth prog 4f out: led 2f out: r.o wl: easily* **2/9**[1]
2 13 **Promising Run (USA)**[28] 184 3-9-0 107.......................... JamesDoyle 1 82
(Saeed bin Suroor) *trckd ldr: rdn 4f out: r.o fnl 2 1/2f but no ch w wnr* **5/1**[2]
3 2 1/2 **Kabaw (IRE)**[28] 184 3-9-0 82.. RichardMullen 2 76
(S Seemar, UAE) *slowly away: nvr bttr than mid-div* **100/1**
4 1 **Dubai Fashion (IRE)**[103] 7631 3-9-0 85.......................... PaulHanagan 4 74
(Saeed bin Suroor) *slowly away: racd in rr: nvr able to chal* **13/2**[3]
5 1/2 **Dolly Dagger (SWE)**[28] 184 3-9-0 86.............................. FernandoJara 3 73
(Fredrik Reuterskiold, Sweden) *sn led: hdd & wknd fnl 2f* **100/1**

1m 37.09s (-0.41) **Going Correction** +0.20s/f (Slow) **5** Ran SP% **113.8**
Speed ratings: **110,97,94,93,93**
CSF: 2.07.
Owner Valentin Bukhtoyarov & Evgeny Kappushev **Bred** Bob McCann Mark Kelder Doug Richards **Trained** United Arab Emirates

FOCUS
TRAKUS (metres travelled compared to winner): 2nd -1, 3rd -7, 4th +3, 5th -6. Another wildly impressive performance from the winner. The splits were 26.17, 23.03, 24.16, 23.73, and the final time was the quickest of three races at this distance on the card, including 0.99secs faster than the similarly run UAE 2000 Guineas.

535a XPRESS (H'CAP) (DIRT) 1m (D)
3:35 (3:35) (78-94,94) 3-Y-O+
£24,489 (£8,163; £4,081; £2,040; £1,224; £816)

RPR
1 **Grand Argentier (FR)**[12] 408 4-9-6 94.......................(v) SamHitchcott 2 103
(Doug Watson, UAE) *s.i.s: rdn to ld: kicked clr 2f out: r.o wl* **9/2**[3]
2 4 1/4 **Dornoch (USA)**[41] 11 5-9-3 90.. PatDobbs 1 90
(Doug Watson, UAE) *trckd ldr: rdn 3f out: r.o fnl 2f: no ch w wnr* **7/4**[1]
3 5 1/4 **Ormindo (USA)**[21] 279 6-8-10 84...............................(b) FrederikTylicki 8 71
(A bin Harmash, UAE) *mid-div: r.o fnl 2f: no ch w wnr* **12/1**
4 2 3/4 **Alareef (SAF)**[14] 369 5-8-13 86....................................(b) PaulHanagan 7 68
(M F De Kock, South Africa) *trckd ldr: ev ch 3 1/2f out: one pce fnl 2 1/2f* **9/4**[2]
5 3/4 **Innocuous**[12] 405 9-8-6 79... FernandoJara 3 59
(M Al Mheiri, UAE) *s.i.s: nvr nr to chal* **40/1**
6 3 1/4 **Long Water (USA)**[6] 480 5-8-6 84 ow4..................(b) HectorCrouch(5) 6 57
(H Al Alawi, UAE) *s.i.s: nvr bttr than mid-div* **14/1**
7 7 1/4 **Beachy Head (IRE)**[14] 369 5-9-5 93............................ TadhgO'Shea 4 48
(A R Al Rayhi, UAE) *nvr nr to chal* **7/1**
8 4 1/2 **Greatest Hits (USA)**[6] 480 4-8-11 85............................ FrankieDettori 5 29
(Y Al Blooshi, UAE) *slowly away: a in rr* **20/1**

1m 37.41s (-0.09) **Going Correction** +0.20s/f (Slow) **8** Ran SP% **119.4**
Speed ratings: **108,103,98,95,95 91,84,80**
CSF: 13.45 TRICAST: 90.84.
Owner EERC (Mngr: Mrs Rebecca Byrne) **Bred** Claude Lambert **Trained** United Arab Emirates

FOCUS
TRAKUS: 2nd +2, 3rd +11, 4th +5, 5th 0, 6th +13, 7th +6, 8th +9. The winner galloped these into submission, setting a fast pace that seemingly took an unconvincing bunch of rivals out of their comfort zone: 25.65, 22.66, 24.06, 25.04.

536a MEYDAN CLASSIC TRIAL SPONSORED BY GULF NEWS CLASSIFIEDS (CONDITIONS RACE) (TURF) 7f
4:10 (4:10) 3-Y-O
£30,612 (£10,204; £5,102; £2,551; £1,530; £1,020)

RPR
1 **Comicas (USA)**[203] 4539 3-9-0 88.................................(p) WilliamBuick 9 95+
(Charlie Appleby) *trckd ldr: smooth prog to ld 1 1/2f out: r.o wl: comf* **10/3**[2]
2 3/4 **Pure Diamond**[28] 184 3-8-9 91...................................... FrederikTylicki 4 88+
(Saeed bin Suroor) *slowly away: settled in rr: r.o wl fnl 2f: nrst fin* **10/1**
3 2 3/4 **Ajwad**[12] 406 3-9-0.. DavidProbert 1 86
(R Bouresly, Kuwait) *sn led: hdd 1 1/2f out: r.o same pce* **66/1**
4 3/4 **Lytham St Annes (IRE)**[134] 6869 3-9-0 88........................ PatDobbs 12 84
(Doug Watson, UAE) *trckd ldr: ev ch 1 1/2f out: r.o one pce fnl f* **9/1**[3]
5 3 3/4 **Illegally Blonde (IRE)**[28] 185 3-8-9 90............................ DaneO'Neill 2 68
(Jamie Osborne) *s.i.s: nvr nr to chal but r.o fnl 2f* **10/1**
6 1 3/4 **Calder Prince (IRE)**[28] 185 3-9-0 98.................. RichardKingscote 11 69
(Tom Dascombe) *mid-div: r.o same pce fnl 2f* **10/3**[2]
7 *nk* **Taexali (IRE)**[264] 2519 3-9-0 89...................................... RichardMullen 8 68
(S Seemar, UAE) *s.i.s: nvr nr to chal but r.o fnl 2f* **16/1**
8 1 1/4 **Start Time (IRE)**[110] 7468 3-9-0 95................................(v) JamesDoyle 10 65
(Saeed bin Suroor) *trckd ldrs tl outpcd fnl 2f* **2/1**[1]
9 5 1/4 **Follow The Rules**[28] 185 3-8-8 ....(b) HectorCrouch(6) 5 50
(S Seemar, UAE) *nvr bttr than mid-div* **100/1**
10 *nk* **Ruler Of Course (IRE)**[116] 3-9-0 94..........................(t) FrankieDettori 7 50
(Niels Petersen, Norway) *nvr bttr than mid-div* **16/1**
11 1 1/4 **Burnt Pavlova (USA)**[28] 184 3-8-9 60.......................(p) TadhgO'Shea 14 41
(A bin Harmash, UAE) *trckd ldrs tl outpcd 3f out* **150/1**
12 3 1/2 **Redstaroverchina (IRE)**[125] 7097 3-8-9 89..................... PatSmullen 13 32
(M Halford, Ire) *nvr bttr than mid-div* **16/1**
13 1 1/4 **Al Yaboob (IRE)** 3-8-10 .... MarcMonaghan(4) 6 33
(Ali Jan, Qatar) *a in rr* **100/1**
14 9 1/4 **High Start (USA)**[28] 184 3-8-9 .... SamHitchcott 3 3
(Doug Watson, UAE) *a in rr* **150/1**

1m 24.46s (0.36) **Going Correction** +0.40s/f (Good) **14** Ran SP% **130.1**
Speed ratings: **113,112,109,108,103 101,101,100,94,93 92,88,86,76**
CSF: 40.79.
Owner Godolphin **Bred** Darley **Trained** Newmarket, Suffolk

FOCUS
TRAKUS: 2nd +2, 3rd -2, 4th +2, 5th -2, 6th +6, 7th +7, 8th +4, 9th +4, 10th -1, 11th +7, 12th +4, 13th +3, 14th -2. A trial for the Meydan Classic, a Listed race to be run over C&D on March 3. The third, a huge outsider, set fractions of 25.19 (400m from standing start), 23.26 (800m) and 23.66 (1200m) and almost nicked this, before the winner finished in 12.06. The rail on the turf course was out 12 metres. The third, fifth and ninth help set the level.

537a AL SHINDAGHA SPRINT SPONSORED BY GULFNEWS.COM (GROUP 3) (DIRT) 6f (D)
4:45 (4:45) 3-Y-O+
£81,632 (£27,210; £13,605; £6,802; £4,081; £2,721)

RPR
1 **Rich Tapestry (IRE)**[60] 8217 8-9-0 112.........................(b) GeraldMosse 9 118
(C W Chang, Hong Kong) *sn led: rdn clr 2f out: styd on* **7/1**[3]
2 1 1/2 **Muarrab**[28] 186 7-9-0 112.. PaulHanagan 7 113
(M Al Mheiri, UAE) *trckd ldrs: ev ch 2f out: nt qckn fnl 1 1/2f* **7/1**[3]

3 *2* **Reynaldothewizard (USA)**[28] 186 10-9-0 113.......(bt) RichardMullen 8 107
(S Seemar, UAE) *mid-div: r.o fnl 2f: nrst fin* **10/3**[2]
4 *1 1/2* **My Catch (IRE)**[14] 371 5-9-0 105.......................... PatDobbs 1 102
(Doug Watson, UAE) *trckd ldr: ev ch 2 1/2f out: one pce fnl 1 1/2f* **22/1**
5 *1 1/4* **Krypton Factor**[14] 371 8-9-0 102..............................(b) FrederikTylicki 6 98+
(Fawzi Abdulla Nass, Bahrain) *nvr able to chal but r.o fnl 2 1/2f* **33/1**
6 *3/4* **Kifaah**[14] 371 5-9-0 104.. DaneO'Neill 4 95
(A R Al Rayhi, UAE) *nvr bttr than mid-div* **20/1**
7 *7 1/4* **Let'sgoforit (IRE)**[28] 186 8-9-2 109............................(vt) OliverWilson 5 74
(Bodil Hallencreutz, Sweden) *broke awkwardly: a in rr* **12/1**
8 *2 1/4* **Anfitrion Sale (ARG)**[14] 373 4-9-0 104...................... FrankieDettori 10 65
(Y Al Blooshi, UAE) *chsd ldr tl outpcd fnl 2 1/2f* **50/1**
9 *2 3/4* **Scotland Forever (IRE)**[12] 410 6-9-0 95..................(b) SamHitchcott 3 56
(S Seemar, UAE) *s.i.s: a in rr* **100/1**
U **Marking (USA)**[47] 8364 4-9-0 109...................................... JamesDoyle 2
(Kiaran McLaughlin, U.S.A) *stmbld and uns rdr s* **4/5**[1]

1m 10.88s (-0.72) **Going Correction** +0.20s/f (Slow) **10** Ran SP% **126.3**
Speed ratings: **112,110,107,105,103 102,93,90,86,**
CSF: 56.17.
Owner Silas Yang Siu Shun, Wong Tak Wai Et Al **Bred** Moyglare Stud Farm Ltd **Trained** Hong Kong

FOCUS
TRAKUS: 2nd +7, 3rd +11, 4th +1, 5th +10, 6th +5, 7th +4, 8th +6, 9th +4. The winner made all through comfortable enough fractions: 24.04, 23.12, 23.72. The winner is rated back to his best.

538a GULF NEWS SPORT (H'CAP) (TURF) 1m 4f 38y(T)
5:20 (5:20) (100-110,110) 3-Y-O+
£71,428 (£23,809; £11,904; £5,952; £3,571; £2,380)

RPR
1 **Liquid Mercury (SAF)**[14] 375 4-8-13 **103** ow3.. ChristopheSoumillon 2 102+
(M F De Kock, South Africa) *trckd ldng pair: rdn 2 1/2f out: led fnl f: r.o wl* **4/5**[1]
2 *1 1/2* **Code Of Honor**[35] 93 6-8-11 **101** ow1........................(v) JamesDoyle 3 100+
(Saeed bin Suroor) *mid-div: r.o fnl 2 1/2f nrst fin* **11/2**[2]
3 *1 3/4* **Sugar Boy (IRE)**[21] 285 6-8-10 **106**.......................(p) HectorCrouch(6) 1 103
(S Seemar, UAE) *sn led: clr 3f out: rdn 2f out: hdd fnl f: r.o gamely* **25/1**
4 *hd* **Pilote (IRE)**[21] 283 6-8-13 **102**................................ MickaelBarzalona 6 100
(S bin Ghadayer, UAE) *nvr bttr than mid-div* **8/1**
5 *nk* **Quarterback (GER)**[21] 285 4-8-13 **105**.............................. PatDobbs 8 102
(Rune Haugen) *trckd ldr: rdn 3f out: wknd fnl 1 1/2f* **8/1**
6 *hd* **Antinori (IRE)**[21] 285 10-8-11 **101**.............................(b) RichardMullen 9 97+
(S Seemar, UAE) *nvr nr to chal but r.o fnl 2f* **50/1**
7 *7 3/4* **Snow Squall**[348] 744 5-8-10 **100**................................(t) FrederikTylicki 7 84
(A bin Harmash, UAE) *nvr nr to chal* **20/1**
8 *4* **Spend The Cash (IRE)**[21] 285 5-9-1 **105**...................... WayneSmith 4 82
(W Mongil, Germany) *nvr bttr than mid-div* **33/1**
9 *24* **Mujaarib (AUS)**[14] 372 7-9-6 **110**................................. PaulHanagan 5 49
(M F De Kock, South Africa) *s.i.s: a in rr* **13/2**[3]

2m 34.42s (2.62) **Going Correction** +0.40s/f (Good)
WFA 4 from 5yo+ 3lb **9** Ran SP% **120.0**
Speed ratings: **107,106,104,104,104 104,99,96,80**
CSF: 5.62 TRICAST 66.79.
Owner Sheikh Mohammed Bin Khalifa Al Maktoum **Bred** Drakenstein Stud **Trained** South Africa

FOCUS
TRAKUS: 2nd -2, 3rd -3, 4th -2, 5th +1, 6th +6, 7th +6, 8th +10, 9th +5. This was a weak carnival handicap and the early pace was modest: 27.52 (400m), 25.74 (800m), 25.23 (1200m), 25.39 (1600m), 24.07 (2000m). The third and sixth help set the level. The rail was out 12 metres.

539a UAE 2000 GUINEAS SPONSORED BY GULF NEWS (GROUP 3) (DIRT) 1m (D)
5:55 (5:55) 3-Y-O
£102,040 (£34,013; £17,006; £8,503; £5,102; £3,401)

RPR
1 **Market Rally (USA)**[28] 185 3-9-0 95................................ ChrisHayes 1 106
(D Selvaratnam, UAE) *sn led: rdn 3f out: r.o wl: comf* **5/1**
2 *6* **Lazzam**[30] 154 3-9-0 91...................................(b) ChristopheSoumillon 4 92
(Marco Botti) *mid-div: smooth prog 3f out: r.o fnl 2f but no ch w wnr* **12/1**
3 *7* **Hombre Rojo (IRE)**[30] 154 3-9-0 93................................ JimCrowley 7 76+
(Simon Dow) *mid-div: r.o same pce fnl 2f* **6/1**
4 *3/4* **Steady Pace**[28] 185 3-9-0 112... JamesDoyle 5 74
(Saeed bin Suroor) *nvr bttr than mid-div* **11/4**[2]
5 *7 1/4* **Qurbaan (USA)**[134] 3-9-0 95.. PaulHanagan 3 58
(F Rohaut, France) *slowly away: nvr nr to chal* **4/1**[3]
6 *3 1/4* **Rouleau**[28] 185 3-9-0 105.. WilliamBuick 2 66
(Charlie Appleby) *trckd ldr: rdn 4f out: sn btn* **7/4**[1]
7 *11 1/2* **Busy Earning (FR)**[97] 3-9-0 90.......................................(t) PatDobbs 6 24
(Niels Petersen, Norway) *nvr nr to chal* **40/1**

1m 38.08s (0.58) **Going Correction** +0.20s/f (Slow) **7** Ran SP% **124.1**
Speed ratings: **105,99,92,91,84 80,69**
CSF: 65.67.
Owner Sheikh Ahmed Al Maktoum **Bred** Ashview Farm Llc, Colts Neck Stables Llc & Unbridl **Trained** United Arab Emirates

FOCUS
TRAKUS: 2nd 0, 3rd +8, 4th +2, 5th +4, 6th +5, 7th +6. The two Godolphin horses did not run to form and the 'interesting' French runner failed to go a yard, so the front-running winner had little to beat. Here are his splits with the earlier 1000 Guineas in brackets: 25.79 (26.17), 23.15 (23.03), 24.01 (24.16), 25.13 (23.73). In contrast to Polar River, who didn't go quite as hard but had a wider trip, Market Rally was slowing down in the closing stages and the final time was 0.99secs slower.

540a GULF NEWS TABLOID (H'CAP) (TURF) 1m 1f (T)
6:30 (6:30) (95-108,108) 3-Y-O+
£44,897 (£14,965; £7,482; £3,741; £2,244; £1,496)

RPR
1 **Musaddas**[28] 189 6-9-1 **102**..(p) JamesDoyle 9 107
(Saeed bin Suroor) *trckd ldr: led 2f out: r.o wl* **7/4**[1]
2 *1 1/2* **Dormello (IRE)**[21] 285 8-9-2 **104**.................................... ChrisHayes 11 105
(D Selvaratnam, UAE) *mid-div: smooth prog 3f out: ev ch 1 1/2f out: r.o same pce fnl f* **10/1**
3 *1 1/4* **Golden Soul (USA)**[194] 6-9-1 **102**................................... WayneSmith 3 101
(M F De Kock, South Africa) *trckd ldrs: ev ch 3f out: r.o same pce fnl 2f* **16/1**
4 *hd* **Fearless Hunter (GER)**[21] 283 6-9-3 **105**................. FrankieDettori 14 103+
(Rune Haugen) *in rr: r.o fnl 2f: nrst fin* **16/1**
5 *1/2* **Shamaal Nibras (USA)**[20] 309 7-8-13 **100**.......................(v) PatDobbs 5 98
(Doug Watson, UAE) *s.i.s: in rr: nvr able to chal but r.o fnl 2f* **16/1**
6 *1 1/4* **Slumdogmillionaire (SAF)**[364] 531 7-9-1 **102**.........(b) SamHitchcott 6 97
(Doug Watson, UAE) *sn led: hdd 2f out: wknd fnl 1 1/2f* **20/1**
7 *1 1/2* **Battle Of Marathon (USA)**[14] 372 4-9-1 **102**.............(v) DavidProbert 8 94
(John Ryan) *trckd ldrs: ev ch 3 1/2f out: one pce fnl 2f* **14/1**
8 *1 1/4* **Rogue Runner (GER)**[43] 4-9-3 **105**.......................(p) EduardoPedroza 4 93
(Mario Hofer, Germany) *nvr bttr than mid-div* **12/1**
9 *1/2* **Royal Navy Ship (USA)**[21] 284 4-9-1 **102**............(tp) RoystonFfrench 1 90
(P V Lafferty, South Africa) *nvr bttr than mid-div* **25/1**
10 *nk* **Belgian Bill**[28] 189 8-9-2 **104**.......................................(tp) JimCrowley 2 91
(George Baker) *s.i.s: nvr nr to chal* **7/1**[2]
11 *2* **Tandem**[139] 6728 7-8-13 **100**.. PatSmullen 12 83
(D K Weld, Ire) *nvr bttr than mid-div* **7/1**[2]
12 *3 1/4* **Moohaarib (IRE)**[14] 372 5-9-6 **108**................(b) ChristopheSoumillon 13 84
(Marco Botti) *nvr bttr than mid-div* **17/2**[3]
13 *4* **El Estruendoso (ARG)**[348] 738 6-9-1 **102**.............(b) RichardMullen 10 70
(S Seemar, UAE) *trckd ldrs tl one pce fnl 2 1/2f* **25/1**
14 *9 1/4* **Bancnuanaheireann (IRE)**[21] 283 9-8-13 **100**.......... FrederikTylicki 7 49
(Michael Appleby) *trckd ldrs tl one pce fnl 2 1/2f* **33/1**

1m 50.03s (0.93) **Going Correction** +0.40s/f (Good) **14** Ran SP% **128.4**
Speed ratings: **111,109,108,108,107 106,105,104,103,103 101,99,95,87**
CSF: 20.50; TRICAST: 244.35. Placepot: £110.10 to a £1 stake. Pool of £7,192.78 - 47.65 winning units. Quadpot: £69.50 to a £1 stake. Pool of £422.80 - 4.50 winning units..
Owner Sheikh Juma Dalmook Al Maktoum **Bred** Highbury Stud Ltd **Trained** Newmarket, Suffolk

FOCUS
TRAKUS: 2nd +6, 3rd -3, 4th +4, 5th -3, 6th -5, 7th +1, 8th +2, 9th -3, 10th +1, 11th +6, 12th +21, 13th +6, 14th -1. There was a muddling pace: 25.89 (400m), 22.92 (800m), 24.3 (1200m), 23.86 (1600m). The rail was out 12 metres.

[498] WOLVERHAMPTON (A.W) (L-H)
Friday, February 12

OFFICIAL GOING: Tapeta: standard
Wind: Light against Weather: Cloudy

541 BET AND WATCH EVERY RACE AT UNIBET H'CAP 5f 20y (Tp)
5:15 (5:15) (Class 6) (0-65,70) 4-Y-O+ **£2,587** (£770; £384; £192) **Stalls** Low

Form RPR
60-6 **1** **Point North (IRE)**[21] 293 9-9-7 **65**..........................(b) DanielTudhope 6 73+
(John Balding) *a.p: shkn up over 1f out: rdn to ld wl ins fnl f: edgd lft: r.o* **12/1**
3423 **2** *3/4* **Frank The Barber (IRE)**[4] 504 4-8-12 **56**..............(t) AdamBeschizza 9 61
(Steph Hollinshead) *hld up: hdwy and nt clr run over 1f out: sn rdn: r.o* **9/1**
033- **3** *1/2* **Frangarry (IRE)**[98] 7735 4-9-2 **60**................................ SaleemGolam 3 63
(Alan Bailey) *pushed along to chse ldrs: rdn to ld ins fnl f: sn hdd: styd on same pce* **9/2**[3]
662- **4** *hd* **Ancient Cross**[66] 8148 12-9-0 **65**..............................(t) NathanEvans(7) 5 67
(Michael Easterby) *hld up: hdwy over 1f out: r.o* **6/1**
0-51 **5** *1* **Your Gifted (IRE)**[21] 293 9-9-7 **65**................................(p) RaulDaSilva 2 64
(Lisa Williamson) *chsd ldr: rdn over 1f out: styd on same pce ins fnl f* **16/1**
4-41 **6** *nk* **Fine 'n Dandy (IRE)**[8] 444 5-9-12 **70** 6ex.................... TonyHamilton 1 68
(J R Jenkins) *led: rdn and hdd ins fnl f: styd on same pce* **10/3**[1]
3-15 **7** *hd* **Rocket Rob (IRE)**[13] 398 10-9-4 **62**........................ RobertWinston 4 59
(Willie Musson) *hld up: shkn up over 1f out: nt clr run and r.o wl ins fnl f: nvr nrr* **12/1**
40-5 **8** *hd* **Humour (IRE)**[22] 271 5-9-5 **63**.. AdamKirby 7 59
(Christine Dunnett) *prom: rdn over 1f out: styd on same pce* **4/1**[2]
00-0 **9** *nk* **Ypres**[22] 278 7-9-7 **65**... BenCurtis 8 60
(Jason Ward) *sn pushed along in rr: r.o ins fnl f: nvr on terms* **25/1**
462- **10** *1* **Eland Ally**[53] 8331 8-9-3 **61**.......................................(b) KieranO'Neill 10 53
(Anabel K Murphy) *s.i.s: hld up: rdn over 1f out: n.d* **20/1**

1m 1.14s (-0.76) **Going Correction** -0.075s/f (Stan) **10** Ran SP% **115.4**
Speed ratings (Par 101): **103,101,101,100,99 98,98,97,97,95**
CSF £113.95 CT £576.45 TOTE £12.10: £3.50, £2.80, £2.10; EX 108.00 Trifecta £809.80.
Owner Billy Herring **Bred** Barronstown Stud **Trained** Scrooby, S Yorks

FOCUS
A typically competitive race of its type. They went hard up front and it paid to come from off the pace. The second and third have been rated to form.

542 DOWNLOAD THE NEW UNIBET RACING APP H'CAP (DIV I) 5f 216y (Tp)
5:45 (5:46) (Class 6) (0-60,64) 4-Y-O+ **£2,587** (£770; £384; £192) **Stalls** Low

Form RPR
3-10 **1** **Gulland Rock**[27] 216 5-9-0 **53**..................................(p) WilliamCarson 10 62
(Anthony Carson) *chsd ldr tl over 4f out: wnt 2nd again over 2f out: sn rdn: r.o to ld wl ins fnl f* **6/1**[2]
00-0 **2** *3/4* **Mambo Spirit (IRE)**[14] 387 12-9-4 **60**.......................... EoinWalsh(3) 7 66
(Tony Newcombe) *s.i.s: hld up: hdwy over 1f out: r.o* **25/1**
1-1 **3** *2 1/4* **Fairy Foxglove (IRE)**[11] 418 6-9-5 **58** 6ex.................... TonyHamilton 4 57+
(P J F Murphy, Ire) *s.i.s: hld up: nt clr run and swtchd rt over 1f out: r.o u.p ins fnl f: nt rch ldrs* **5/4**[1]
0-00 **4** *3/4* **Prigsnov Dancer (IRE)**[19] 320 11-8-7 **51**...............(p) PaddyPilley(5) 13 47+
(Deborah Sanderson) *sn led: rdn over 1f out: hdd and no ex wl ins fnl f* **25/1**
-034 **5** *hd* **Hamis Al Bin (IRE)**[13] 398 7-9-4 **57**..........................(bt) PatCosgrave 9 52
(Milton Bradley) *broke wl: sn stdd and lost pl: hdwy over 2f out: rdn over 1f out: styd on same pce fnl f* **7/1**
000- **5** *dht* **Krazy Paving**[165] 5933 4-9-4 **57**...................................... KieranO'Neill 8 52
(Anabel K Murphy) *prom: rdn over 2f out: styd on same pce fnl f* **25/1**
00-4 **7** *1* **Reginald Claude**[28] 197 8-9-0 **58**............................ RachealKneller(5) 11 50+
(Mark Usher) *in rr: racd wd fr 1/2-way: styd on ins fnl f: nvr nrr* **13/2**[3]
0-66 **8** *1/2* **Tamarin**[14] 381 4-8-2 **46**....................................(p) JosephineGordon(5) 2 37
(Lisa Williamson) *prom: pushed along and lost pl wl over 3f out: rallied over 1f out: no ex fnl f* **33/1**
0456 **9** *hd* **Fuel Injection**[4] 504 5-9-6 **59**....................................... PaulMulrennan 3 49
(Paul Midgley) *hld up: hdwy wl over 2f out: nt clr run and sn lost pl: n.d after* **8/1**
0-00 **10** *3/4* **Beauty's Forte (IRE)**[28] 201 5-8-11 **57**..........................(b) LeeByrne(7) 6 45
(Declan Carroll) *hld up: rdn over 1f out: nvr on terms* **25/1**
/0-0 **11** *1 1/4* **My Time**[26] 237 7-8-9 **48** oh1 ow2....................................[1] RobertHavlin 1 32
(Michael Mullineaux) *mid-div: nt clr run fr over 2f out tl over 1f out: nvr trbld ldrs* **100/1**

06-6 **12** *5* **Gower Princess**[32] 146 5-9-3 **56**................(b[1]) WilliamTwiston-Davies 5 24
(Ronald Harris) *prom: chsd ldr over 4f out tl rdn and hung lft fr over 2f out: wknd and eased over 1f out* **40/1**

1m 14.17s (-0.33) **Going Correction** -0.075s/f (Stan) **12** Ran SP% **117.4**
Speed ratings (Par 101): **99,98,95,94,93 93,92,91,91,90 88,82**
CSF £146.48 CT £306.78 TOTE £8.80: £2.20, £6.10, £1.20; EX 131.60 Trifecta £785.10.
Owner W H Carson **Bred** Whitsbury Manor Stud **Trained** Newmarket, Suffolk

FOCUS
This revolved around the hat-trick chasing favourite, who was penalised for her win over C&D earlier this month. However, plenty went wrong for her in a rough race and she had to settle for minor honours. The winner has been rated to last year's form.

543 DOWNLOAD THE NEW UNIBET RACING APP H'CAP (DIV II) 5f 216y (Tp)
6:15 (6:17) (Class 6) (0-60,60) 4-Y-O+ **£2,587** (£770; £384; £192) **Stalls** Low

Form RPR
-002 **1** **Eljaddaaf (IRE)**[8] 442 5-9-2 **55**.................................. RobertWinston 12 68+
(Dean Ivory) *hld up: hdwy over 1f out: rdn and r.o to ld wl ins fnl f* **11/8**[1]

6/0- **2** *1* **Lewisham**[377] 365 6-8-13 **57**................................ JosephineGordon(5) 4 66
(J R Jenkins) *a.p: chsd ldr over 2f out: rdn to ld over 1f out: hdd and unable qck wl ins fnl f* **13/2**[2]

0-00 **3** *½* **Sakhee's Rose**[25] 239 6-9-7 **60**.................................(b) GeorgeBaker 5 67
(Ed McMahon) *s.i.s: hld up: hdwy over 1f out: r.o* **20/1**

-035 **4** *1* **Rialto Magic**[19] 321 4-8-13 **57**................................(p) LucyKBarry(5) 11 61
(Jamie Osborne) *in rr: pushed along 1/2-way: rdn and r.o ins fnl f: nt rch ldrs* **16/1**

-003 **5** *1 ¾* **Little**[14] 381 4-8-9 **48**...(p) AdamBeschizza 8 47
(Steph Hollinshead) *s.i.s: hld up: effrt and nt clr run over 1f out: styd on towards fin: nt trble ldrs* **33/1**

-654 **6** *shd* **Divine Call**[22] 271 9-9-5 **58**...(b) RobertHavlin 1 56
(Milton Bradley) *prom: rdn over 1f out: styd on same pce fnl f* **10/1**

34-3 **7** *shd* **Top Cop**[28] 197 7-9-4 **57**...........................(be) WilliamTwiston-Davies 13 55
(Ronald Harris) *prom: sn lost pl: rdn over 1f out: styd on ins fnl f: nt rch ldrs* **12/1**

54-5 **8** *shd* **Jolly Red Jeanz (IRE)**[32] 143 5-9-0 **53**.....................(b) CathyGannon 6 51
(Daniel Mark Loughnane) *sn w ldr: led over 4f out: rdn and hdd over 1f out: no ex ins fnl f* **10/1**

-122 **9** *nse* **Fortinbrass (IRE)**[22] 272 6-9-6 **59**............................ DanielTudhope 10 56
(John Balding) *led early: chsd ldrs: rdn over 2f out: no ex fnl f* **9/1**[3]

0/00 **10** *1 ½* **Hadaj**[22] 271 7-9-5 **58**.. TomEaves 3 51
(Michael Herrington) *sn led: hdd over 4f out: chsd ldr tl rdn over 2f out: wknd ins fnl f* **18/1**

0- **11** *¾* **Lady Mandeville (IRE)**[28] 207 4-8-7 **46** oh1.............(b[1]) KieranO'Neill 9 36
(Adrian McGuinness, Ire) *broke wl: sn stdd and lost pl: rdn and nt clr run over 1f out: wknd ins fnl f* **40/1**

4-05 **12** *hd* **Harpers Ruby**[25] 241 6-8-1 **40** oh1 ow1...................... NathanEvans(7) 7 37
(Lynn Siddall) *prom: rdn over 2f out: wknd over 1f out* **25/1**

1m 13.69s (-0.81) **Going Correction** -0.075s/f (Stan) **12** Ran SP% **116.4**
Speed ratings (Par 101): **102,100,100,98,96 96,96,95,95,93 92,92**
CSF £9.13 CT £126.37 TOTE £2.00: £1.10, £2.60, £4.90; EX 10.60 Trifecta £208.30.
Owner Wentdale Ltd & Mrs L A Ivory **Bred** Shadwell Estate Company Limited **Trained** Radlett, Herts

■ Spellmaker was withdrawn. Price at time of withdrawal 22/1. Rule 4 does not apply.

FOCUS
Few could be seriously fancied in this low-grade handicap and it was the well punted Eljaddaaf who came home strongly to land the spoils. Sound form, with the fourth rated to her winter form.

544 DAILY PRICE BOOSTS AT UNIBET MEDIAN AUCTION MAIDEN STKS 5f 216y (Tp)
6:45 (6:47) (Class 6) 3-5-Y-O **£2,587** (£770; £384; £192) **Stalls** Low

Form RPR
0- **1** **Big Amigo (IRE)**[52] 8349 3-8-12 0............................ RichardKingscote 6 73+
(Tom Dascombe) *sn w ldr: rdn to ld over 1f out: edgd lft: hung rt ins fnl f: r.o* **4/6**[1]

53-3 **2** *2 ¼* **Sandacres**[13] 402 3-8-12 70.. SeanLevey 2 60
(Jo Crowley) *sn led: rdn and hdd over 1f out: styd on same pce ins fnl f* **9/4**[2]

45-0 **3** *2 ¼* **Castlerea Tess**[35] 104 3-8-7 43...................................... KieranO'Neill 3 48
(Sarah Hollinshead) *plld hrd: w ldr tl settled after 100yds: rdn over 2f out: styd on same pce fr over 1f out* **25/1**

4 *2 ¼* **Thatsthewaytodoit (IRE)** 3-8-7 0.............................. StevieDonohoe 8 41
(Kevin Frost) *mid-div: rdn over 2f out: styd on same pce* **13/2**[3]

0-0 **5** *10* **Autre Princess (IRE)**[21] 298 3-8-7 0............................(p) JasonHart 10 9
(Eric Alston) *broke wl: sn drvn along and outpcd: nvr on terms afterwards* **40/1**

04- **6** *hd* **Max Beddow (IRE)**[58] 8243 3-8-7 0...................... JosephineGordon(5) 9 13
(Geoffrey Deacon) *hld up: rdn and wknd 1/2-way* **16/1**

7 *1 ¼* **Secret Shot** 4-9-13 0.. DougieCostello 4 13
(David Dennis) *s.i.s: sn pushed along in rr: wknd 1/2-way* **14/1**

- **8** *42* **Lowrie** 3-8-0 0.. VitorSantos(7) 1 +
(John David Riches) *s.i.s: plld hrd and sn prom: sddle slipped 5f out: wknd and eased over 2f out* **66/1**

1m 14.38s (-0.12) **Going Correction** -0.075s/f (Stan)
WFA 3 from 4yo 15lb **8** Ran SP% **124.4**
Speed ratings (Par 101): **97,94,91,88,74 74,72,16**
CSF £2.68 TOTE £1.60: £1.10, £1.10, £4.80; EX 2.60 Trifecta £21.40.
Owner Laurence Bellman **Bred** Kildaragh Stud **Trained** Malpas, Cheshire

FOCUS
This maiden lacked depth and was dominated by the pair at the top of the market. The third is the key to the form.

545 32RED.COM H'CAP 1m 5f 194y (Tp)
7:15 (7:15) (Class 5) (0-75,75) 4-Y-O+ **£3,557** (£1,058; £529; £264) **Stalls** Low

Form RPR
0-65 **1** **Spiritoftomintoul**[17] 337 7-9-9 **75**........................(t) GeorgeDowning(3) 8 85
(Tony Carroll) *hld up: hdwy over 1f out: rdn to ld wl ins fnl f: r.o* **11/2**[2]

01-1 **2** *1 ½* **Mr Boss Man (IRE)**[37] 71 8-9-5 **68**................................ PatCosgrave 4 76
(Adrian McGuinness, Ire) *hld up: hdwy over 2f out: rdn to chse ldr over 1f out: led ins fnl f: sn hdd: styd on same pce* **11/2**[2]

-121 **3** *1 ¾* **Zakatal**[18] 329 10-9-12 **75**... PJMcDonald 5 82
(Rebecca Menzies) *hld up: hdwy and nt clr run over 2f out: rdn over 1f out: styd on* **9/2**[1]

05-0 **4** *1* **Heart Locket**[35] 103 4-8-12 **66**..............................(b[1]) GrahamGibbons 1 70
(Michael Easterby) *led after 1f: clr 6f out: rdn over 1f out: hdd ins fnl f: styd on same pce* **12/1**

-113 **5** *2* **San Quentin (IRE)**[15] 357 5-9-9 **72**............................ RobertWinston 9 73
(Dean Ivory) *hld up: hdwy over 1f out: sn rdn and edgd lft: no ex ins fnl f* **12/1**

2-23 **6** *2 ¾* **Todd**[26] 234 6-9-9 **72**.. GeorgeBaker 3 70
(Anabel K Murphy) *led 1f: chsd ldrs who wnt clr 10f out: rdn to chse ldr who was stl clr over 3f out: rdn over 2f out: wknd ins fnl f* **10/1**

60-2 **7** *1 ¾* **The Kid**[28] 200 5-9-11 **74**..(p) PhillipMakin 10 69
(John Quinn) *hld up: hdwy u.p 2f out: nt clr run over 1f out: wknd fnl f* **8/1**[3]

13-0 **8** *8* **Asian Wing (IRE)**[28] 208 7-9-12 **75**.........................(tp) DanielTudhope 7 59
(John James Feane, Ire) *chsd ldrs: rdn over 2f out: wknd over 1f out* **9/2**[1]

02-6 **9** *16* **Wildomar**[35] 103 7-8-12 **61**.. StevieDonohoe 11 22
(Peter Hiatt) *hld up: rdn and wknd over 4f out* **28/1**

00/6 **10** *12* **Magic Music Man**[38] 43 5-9-8 **71**.................................. AdamKirby 12 16
(Alan King) *hld up: rdn over 6f out: wknd 4f out* **16/1**

0-50 **11** *25* **Gabrial The Terror (IRE)**[18] 330 6-9-11 **74**............(p) TonyHamilton 6
(Richard Fahey) *chsd ldr after 1f: wnt clr of rivals 10f out: lost grnd on ldr 6f out: rdn and wknd over 3f out* **12/1**

3m 0.33s (-4.47) **Going Correction** -0.075s/f (Stan)
WFA 4 from 5yo+ 5lb **11** Ran SP% **119.7**
Speed ratings (Par 103): **109,108,107,106,105 103,102,98,89,82 68**
CSF £36.58 CT £150.40 TOTE £7.40: £3.00, £2.20, £2.00; EX 38.80 Trifecta £361.70.
Owner The Sunday Players **Bred** Barry Walters Farms **Trained** Cropthorne, Worcs

FOCUS
This featured a number of in-form individuals and represents solid form for this level. The complexion of the race changed dramatically late on as the aggressively ridden Heart Locket ran out of steam. The fourth has been rated similar to her penultimate C&D form.

546 LADBROKES H'CAP 7f 32y (Tp)
7:45 (7:46) (Class 4) (0-85,84) 4-Y-O+ **£5,498** (£1,636; £817; £204; £204) **Stalls** High

Form RPR
56-1 **1** **Supersta**[5] 494 5-9-6 **83** 6ex..(p) GeorgeBaker 2 93
(Michael Appleby) *a.p: shkn up to ld wl ins fnl f: r.o* **3/1**[2]

121- **2** *¾* **Dougan**[43] 8412 4-9-4 **81**.. AdamKirby 7 89
(David Evans) *chsd ldrs: edgd lft wl over 1f out: qcknd to ld sn after: rdn and hdd wl ins fnl f* **7/4**[1]

-016 **3** *3* **Depth Charge (IRE)**[14] 387 4-8-9 **72** ow1.................(vt) RobertHavlin 6 72
(Kristin Stubbs) *hld up: hdwy over 1f out: sn rdn: styd on* **14/1**

12-4 **4** *nk* **Corporal Maddox**[23] 260 9-9-4 **81**...............(p) WilliamTwiston-Davies 5 80
(Ronald Harris) *hld up in tch: rdn over 1f out: styd on same pce fnl f* **12/1**[3]

-101 **4** *dht* **Black Dave (IRE)**[16] 349 6-8-8 **78**.................................. AledBeech(7) 1 77
(David Evans) *sn led: clr 5f out tl pushed along over 2f out: hdd over 1f out: styd on same pce insidse fnl f* **22/1**

0-10 **6** *¾* **Fleckerl (IRE)**[9] 433 6-9-3 **80**..(p) LiamKeniry 9 77
(Conor Dore) *s.i.s: hld up: rdn over 1f out: nt trble ldrs* **16/1**

621- **7** *nse* **My Target (IRE)**[48] 8357 5-9-7 **84**.. TomEaves 8 81
(Michael Wigham) *hld up: effrt and nt clr run over 1f out: nt trble ldrs* **3/1**[2]

600/ **8** *¾* **Common Touch (IRE)**[525] 6097 8-9-3 **80**........................ RobertWinston 4 75
(Willie Musson) *trckd ldr: racd keenly: hmpd wl over 1f out: eased fnl f* **33/1**

1m 28.24s (-0.56) **Going Correction** -0.075s/f (Stan) **8** Ran SP% **113.9**
Speed ratings (Par 105): **100,99,95,95,95 94,94,93**
CSF £8.57 CT £59.74 TOTE £5.30: £2.00, £1.80, £3.20; EX 10.70 Trifecta £74.80.
Owner Rod In Pickle Partnership **Bred** Cheveley Park Stud Ltd **Trained** Oakham, Rutland

FOCUS
A fair feature handicap, involving four last-time-out winners. Two pulled nicely clear. Another pb from the winner.

547 DOWNLOAD THE LADBROKES APP H'CAP 7f 32y (Tp)
8:15 (8:15) (Class 7) (0-50,50) 4-Y-O+ **£2,587** (£770; £384; £192) **Stalls** High

Form RPR
6332 **1** **Little Indian**[9] 431 6-9-4 **48**... AdamKirby 4 55
(J R Jenkins) *hld up: hdwy over 2f out: rdn to ld ins fnl f: r.o* **9/2**[3]

0-02 **2** *1 ½* **Bionic Indian**[2] 525 4-9-3 **47**...............................(b[1]) GrahamGibbons 12 50
(Michael Easterby) *w ldr: rdn to ld over 1f out: hdd ins fnl f: styd on same pce* **11/2**

00-0 **3** *shd* **As A Dream (IRE)**[26] 237 4-9-3 **47**............................[1] StevieDonohoe 3 49
(Nikki Evans) *plld hrd and prom: rdn over 1f out: styd on* **50/1**

0/0- **4** *½* **Tom Dooley (IRE)**[105] 7612 5-9-5 **49**.......................(p) PaulMulrennan 10 50
(John James Feane, Ire) *hld up: hdwy over 1f out: sn rdn and edgd lft: styd on* **9/4**[1]

3045 **5** *¾* **Molly Approve (IRE)**[11] 418 4-9-6 **50**.....................(p) DougieCostello 1 49
(Tony Coyle) *chsd ldrs: rdn 3f out: styd on u.p* **18/1**

4/63 **6** *1* **Malvesi**[18] 334 7-9-3 **47**.. JoeFanning 7 44
(Mark Johnston) *s.i.s: hld up: hdwy and nt clr run over 1f out: nt rch ldrs* **4/1**[2]

6-64 **7** *1* **Wild Flower (IRE)**[9] 431 4-9-5 **49**................................(b) KieranO'Neill 5 43
(Jimmy Fox) *led: rdn and hdd over 1f out: no ex ins fnl f* **15/2**

-020 **8** *shd* **Diamond Sam**[9] 431 4-9-4 **48**.. GeorgeBaker 6 41
(Sylvester Kirk) *hld up: rdn over 1f out: nvr on terms* **12/1**

030- **9** *8* **Spoken Words**[44] 8406 7-8-9 **46**...............................(b) VitorSantos(7) 9 18
(John David Riches) *s.i.s: a in rr* **33/1**

06-0 **10** *½* **Sinema**[30] 168 4-9-3 **47**.. LiamKeniry 2 17
(Christine Dunnett) *hld up: rdn over 2f out: wknd over 1f out* **40/1**

1m 28.95s (0.15) **Going Correction** -0.075s/f (Stan) **10** Ran SP% **116.4**
Speed ratings (Par 97): **96,94,94,93,92 91,90,90,81,80**
CSF £29.08 CT £1113.92 TOTE £5.40: £1.40, £2.10, £13.90; EX 25.90 Trifecta £689.90.
Owner Two Little Indians **Bred** D R Tucker **Trained** Royston, Herts

■ Stewards' Enquiry : Vitor Santos five-day ban: use of whip (26, 26, 29, 1-2 Mar)

FOCUS
A weak finale was won in convincing fashion by Little Indian, who'd been knocking at the door in similar company at Kempton of late. The runner-up has been rated close to his best. The runner-up has been rated close to his best.

T/Jkpt: Not won. T/Plt: £21.10 to a £1 stake. Pool: £108,921.01 - 3,764.58 winning tickets. T/Qpdt: £4.10 to a £1 stake. Pool: £11,245.80 - 2,028.74 winning tickets. **Colin Roberts**

548 - 555a (Foreign Racing) - See Raceform Interactive

[482]LINGFIELD (L-H)

Saturday, February 13

OFFICIAL GOING: Polytrack: standard

Wind: light, across Weather: light rain after a wet morning, mainly dry from race 2

556 CORAL H'CAP — 1m 4f (P)

1:25 (1:25) (Class 4) (0-85,85) 4-Y-O+ **£4,690** (£1,395; £697; £348) **Stalls** Low

Form / RPR

4-16 **1** **Royal Marskell**[18] 337 7-9-7 **85** .... LukeMorris 1 — 92
(Gay Kelleway) *mde all: rdn 2f out: styd on wl ins fnl f: drvn out* **14/1**

000- **2** 1 ¼ **Kings Bayonet**[38] 5597 9-9-5 **83** .... TomQueally 5 — 88
(Alan King) *hld up in tch in last pair: effrt to chse ldrs on inner over 1f out: drvn 1f out: chsd wnr fnl 75yds: no imp* **5/1**[3]

34-2 **3** ¾ **Gaelic Silver (FR)**[23] 266 10-9-6 **84** ....(p) GeorgeBaker 2 — 88
(Gary Moore) *chsd ldrs: wnt 2nd and swtchd rt 2f out: shkn up over 1f out: rdn and unable qck 1f out: lost 2nd fnl 75yds: wknd towards fin* **6/1**

1-01 **4** nse **Jamhoori**[19] 330 8-8-13 **77** .... RichardKingscote 6 — 81
(Jeremy Gask) *hld up in last pair: shkn up over 1f out: hdwy on inner 1f out: rdn and kpt on fnl 100yds: no threat to wnr* **8/1**

2-61 **5** 1 ¼ **Alshan Fajer**[14] 399 6-9-0 **78** .... AndreaAtzeni 4 — 80
(J R Jenkins) *in tch in 4th: rdn 2f out: drvn and unable qck over 1f out: wl hld and kpt on same pce ins fnl f* **9/4**[1]

00-3 **6** 1 ¾ **Communicator**[26] 244 8-9-7 **85** ....(v[1]) JimCrowley 3 — 84
(Andrew Balding) *chsd wnr tl 2f out: drvn and outpcd over 1f out: lost pl and bhd ins fnl f* **5/2**[2]

2m 32.94s (-0.06) **Going Correction** -0.025s/f (Stan) **6** Ran SP% **108.1**
Speed ratings (Par 105): **99,98,97,97,96 95**
CSF £73.83 TOTE £14.50: £5.50, £2.10; EX 110.50 Trifecta £658.90.

Owner Miss Chantal Wootten **Bred** Miss V Woodward **Trained** Exning, Suffolk

FOCUS
A fair handicap, but they only went a modest pace and the tempo didn't really increase until inside the last half-mile, which was to the advantage of the all-the-way winner.

557 32RED.COM MAIDEN STKS — 1m 1y(P)

2:00 (2:01) (Class 5) 3-Y-O **£2,911** (£866; £432; £216) **Stalls** High

Form / RPR

4-22 **1** **Blacklister**[16] 361 3-9-5 75 .... GeorgeBaker 2 — 71+
(Mick Channon) *broke fast and led for over 1f: trckd ldrs after: rdn and wnt between rivals to ld jst ins fnl f: r.o wl* **6/4**[1]

2 ¾ **Lastmanlastround (IRE)** 3-9-5 0 .... ChrisCatlin 1 — 69+
(Rae Guest) *rn green in last pair: pushed along and hdwy on inner over 1f out: r.o u.p hands and heels riding to chse wnr wl ins fnl f: nvr gng to rch wnr but gng on wl at fin* **20/1**

32-5 **3** 1 ½ **Ilzam (IRE)**[30] 171 3-9-5 73 ....(t) AndreaAtzeni 8 — 65
(Marco Botti) *chsd ldr: rdn and ev ch over 1f out tl outpcd by wnr 100yds out: kpt on same pce and lost 2nd wl ins fnl f* **7/4**[2]

0- **4** ½ **Daring Knight**[206] 4526 3-9-5 0 .... RobertWinston 4 — 64
(Martin Smith) *t.k.h: chsd ldrs: rdn and sltly outpcd wl over 1f out: kpt on again ins fnl f: no threat to wnr* **7/1**

-233 **5** hd **Milrow (IRE)**[19] 331 3-9-5 75 ....(p) RobertHavlin 5 — 63
(Martyn Meade) *dwlt: rcvrd and hdwy to ld over 6f out: rdn and hrd pressed over 1f out: hdd jst ins fnl f: wknd towards fin* **9/2**[3]

00- **6** 1 **Red Hot Chilly (IRE)**[222] 3964 3-9-5 0 .... JFEgan 6 — 61
(Joseph Tuite) *t.k.h: hld up in last pair: hdwy on outer over 2f out: no imp and styd on same pce fr over 1f out* **66/1**

4- **7** 3 ¾ **Straduff (IRE)**[260] 2656 3-9-5 0 .... LiamJones 3 — 52
(J S Moore) *in tch in midfield: rdn and outpcd over 1f out: wknd fnl f* **33/1**

0 **8** 8 **Compromise**[23] 275 3-9-2 0 .... EoinWalsh[(3)] 7 — 33
(Conor Dore) *t.k.h: hld up in tch in last pair: rdn and racd awkwardly over 3f out: bhd over 1f out: wknd fnl f* **100/1**

1m 38.05s (-0.15) **Going Correction** -0.025s/f (Stan) **8** Ran SP% **117.2**
Speed ratings (Par 97): **99,98,96,96,96 95,91,83**
CSF £33.89 TOTE £1.90: £1.10, £4.50, £1.30; EX 29.40 Trifecta £81.60.

Owner Box 41 Racing **Bred** Aston House Stud **Trained** West Ilsley, Berks

FOCUS
A routine 3yo maiden and not the most competitive of races. The pace was only fair.

558 32RED.COM FILLIES' H'CAP — 7f 1y(P)

2:35 (2:35) (Class 5) (0-75,75) 4-Y-O+ **£2,911** (£866; £432; £216) **Stalls** Low

Form / RPR

5-21 **1** **Perfect Alchemy (IRE)**[12] 415 5-9-4 **72** .... JoeFanning 5 — 80
(Patrick Chamings) *hld up in tch: effrt over 1f out: hung lft and chsd wnr 1f out: str run under hands and heels riding to ld fnl 50yds: eased cl home* **9/4**[1]

00-0 **2** ½ **Lucky Di**[27] 236 6-9-4 **72** .... CharlesBishop 4 — 78
(Peter Hedger) *stdd s: hld up in tch in last pair: nt clr run and swtchd rt over 1f out: hdwy u.p 1f out: r.o wl to go 2nd towards fin: nvr gng to rch wnr* **14/1**

14-2 **3** ¾ **Lady Lydia (IRE)**[40] 41 5-9-4 **75** .... DanielMuscutt[(3)] 2 — 79
(Conrad Allen) *led: rdn wl over 1f out: kpt on u.p tl hdd and no ex fnl 50yds: lost 2nd towards fin* **7/2**[3]

0-00 **4** 2 ¾ **First Experience**[17] 349 5-9-2 **70** .... CathyGannon 3 — 67
(Lee Carter) *chsd ldr: drvn over 1f out: struggling to qckn whn squeezed for room and hmpd 1f out: no unable to rcvr and btn after: wknd fnl 75yds* **5/1**

150- **5** ½ **Caius College Girl (IRE)**[59] 8248 4-9-4 **72** .... AdamKirby 6 — 67
(Patrick Chamings) *awkward leaving stalls: in tch in rr: rdn 2f out: no imp tl kpt on wl ins fnl f: nvr trbld ldrs* **8/1**

3144 **6** ¾ **Mambo Fever**[12] 415 5-8-8 **62** ....(p[1]) LukeMorris 1 — 55
(David C Griffiths) *dwlt: sn rcvrd and chsd ldrs: rdn 2f out: drvn and struggling to qckn whn squeezed for room and hmpd 1f out: nt rcvr: wknd ins fnl f* **11/4**[2]

1m 24.25s (-0.55) **Going Correction** -0.025s/f (Stan) **6** Ran SP% **114.1**
Speed ratings (Par 100): **102,101,100,97,96 96**
CSF £32.83 TOTE £2.70: £1.70, £2.40; EX 18.30 Trifecta £67.40.

Owner The Perfect Partnership & D H Caslon **Bred** W Maxwell Ervine **Trained** Baughurst, Hants

FOCUS
An ordinary fillies' handicap with few coming into it in much form. The pace was no more than fair.

559 32RED CASINO H'CAP — 6f 1y(P)

3:10 (3:10) (Class 3) (0-95,88) 3-Y-O **£7,246** (£2,168; £1,084; £542; £270) **Stalls** Low

Form / RPR

-123 **1** **Aguerooo (IRE)**[24] 262 3-8-12 **86** ....(p) HollieDoyle[(7)] 1 — 92
(Richard Hannon) *hld up in tch in rr: effrt over 1f out: hdwy to chse ldr jst ins fnl f: r.o wl u.p to ld nr fin* **5/1**

2421 **2** nk **Kingsley Klarion (IRE)**[17] 344 3-9-7 **88** .... JoeFanning 4 — 93
(Mark Johnston) *led: rdn and fnd ex over 1f out: drvn ins fnl f: kpt on wl tl hdd and no ex nr fin* **4/1**[2]

2-11 **3** 1 ½ **Gorokai (IRE)**[20] 322 3-8-9 **76** .... JamieSpencer 2 — 76
(David Simcock) *hld up in tch: effrt u.p on inner over 1f out: kpt on same pce ins fnl f* **9/2**[3]

51-2 **4** ¾ **Discreet Hero (IRE)**[32] 152 3-8-12 **79** ....(t) RobertHavlin 3 — 77
(Simon Crisford) *chsd ldr tl over 4f out: effrt and 2nd again 2f out: drvn over 1f out: no imp: lost 2nd and no ex ins fnl f* **5/2**[1]

21-1 **5** 3 ½ **Summer Chorus**[32] 152 3-8-13 **80** .... JimCrowley 5 — 67
(Andrew Balding) *taken down early: dwlt: t.k.h: hdwy to chse ldr over 4f out tl drifted rt and lost pl bnd 2f out: sn bhd: wknd ins fnl f* **5/2**[1]

1m 11.28s (-0.62) **Going Correction** -0.025s/f (Stan) **5** Ran SP% **112.0**
Speed ratings (Par 101): **103,102,100,99,94**
CSF £24.57 TOTE £7.40: £2.90, £2.30; EX 23.80 Trifecta £67.10.

Owner Middleham Park Racing LXXXVI **Bred** Cooneen Stud **Trained** East Everleigh, Wilts

FOCUS
A decent 3yo sprint handicap with all five having shown decent form on the AW this winter. Despite the small field the pace was solid.

560 LADBROKES H'CAP — 1m 1y(P)

3:45 (3:47) (Class 2) (0-105,98) 4-Y-O+
£11,827 (£3,541; £1,770; £885; £442; £222) **Stalls** High

Form / RPR

-100 **1** **Lunar Deity**[7] 486 7-9-4 **95** .... PatCosgrave 3 — 103
(Stuart Williams) *stdd after s: hld up in tch in midfield: effrt 2f out: str run u.p 1f out: led 100yds out: r.o wl: rdn out* **5/1**

25-1 **2** nk **Si Senor (IRE)**[14] 401 5-8-12 **89** .... LukeMorris 1 — 96
(Ed Vaughan) *chsd ldrs: effrt to chse wnr 2f out: sn hrd drvn: ev ch ins fnl f: r.o wl but a jst hld fnl 100yds* **4/1**[3]

462- **3** ¾ **Bravo Zolo (IRE)**[47] 8380 4-9-5 **96** .... GeorgeBaker 5 — 102
(Jeremy Noseda) *stdd s: hld up in tch in rr: effrt to chse ldrs 1f out: swtchd rt ins fnl f: r.o wl towards fin: nt rch ldrs* **2/1**[1]

/6-3 **4** ½ **Truth Or Dare**[28] 221 5-8-13 **90** .... MartinDwyer 2 — 94
(William Muir) *dwlt: t.k.h: hld up in tch: effrt on inner over 1f out: chsd ldrs and drvn 1f out: kpt on* **6/1**

26-2 **5** shd **Mutawathea**[28] 221 5-9-7 **98** ....(p) RobertHavlin 4 — 102
(Simon Crisford) *led: rdn wl over 1f out: drvn and hdd 100yds out: no ex* **3/1**[2]

25-4 **6** 6 **Capo Rosso (IRE)**[35] 125 6-8-13 **97** ....(v) PatrickVaughan[(7)] 7 — 87
(Tom Dascombe) *chsd ldr tl 2f out: sn u.p and lost pl: wknd fnl f* **25/1**

20-5 **7** 7 **Starboard**[19] 333 7-9-1 **92** .... JamieSpencer 6 — 66
(David Simcock) *taken down early: hld up in tch in last trio: swtchd rt and effrt over 1f out: sn btn and eased ins fnl f* **25/1**

1m 35.68s (-2.52) **Going Correction** -0.025s/f (Stan) **7** Ran SP% **117.0**
Speed ratings (Par 109): **111,110,109,109,109 103,96**
CSF £26.14 TOTE £7.90: £2.70, £2.20; EX 32.40 Trifecta £74.90.

Owner The Morley Family **Bred** Hermes Services Ltd **Trained** Newmarket, Suffolk

FOCUS
A warm handicap, but despite a fair pace there wasn't much covering the front five at the line. The form looks solid.

561 UNIBET OFFER DAILY JOCKEY AND TRAINER SPECIALS H'CAP — 6f 1y(P)

4:20 (4:22) (Class 5) (0-75,74) 4-Y-O+ **£2,911** (£866; £432; £216) **Stalls** Low

Form / RPR

26-1 **1** **Noble Deed**[27] 236 6-9-3 **70** .... JoeFanning 6 — 80
(Michael Attwater) *taken down early: chsd ldng pair: rdn and effrt 2f out: chal 1f out: styd on u.p to ld wl ins fnl f: rdn out* **8/1**

-621 **2** ½ **Seamster**[14] 398 9-9-3 **70** ....(vt) DanielTudhope 3 — 78
(David O'Meara) *led: rdn wl over 1f out: battled on wl under hdd and kpt on same pce wl ins fnl f* **3/1**[2]

10-3 **3** 1 ¼ **Quintus Cerialis (IRE)**[27] 236 4-9-7 **74** ....(p) AdamKirby 1 — 78+
(Clive Cox) *hld up in midfield: effrt in 5th over 1f out: styd on u.p to go 3rd wl ins fnl f: nvr trbld ldrs* **9/4**[1]

50-5 **4** 1 ½ **Robero**[38] 67 4-9-0 **72** .... PaddyPilley[(5)] 7 — 72
(John E Long) *pressed ldr: rdn and ev ch 2f out: 3rd and btn 1f out: wknd ins fnl f* **12/1**

221- **5** shd **Picket Line**[64] 8174 4-9-6 **73** .... TimmyMurphy 5 — 72
(Geoffrey Deacon) *midfield: effrt to chse clr ldng trio 2f out: kpt on but nvr threatened ldrs* **14/1**

00-0 **6** nk **Multitask**[10] 433 6-9-6 **73** .... LiamKeniry 10 — 71+
(Michael Madgwick) *stdd and dropped in bhd after s: hld up in last: hdwy but stl plenty to do over 1f out: r.o strly ins fnl f: nvr trbld ldrs* **7/1**[3]

35-5 **7** ½ **Birdie Queen**[37] 80 6-9-5 **72** .... GeorgeBaker 11 — 69
(Gary Moore) *stdd and dropped in bhd after s: hld up in last trio: hdwy but stl plenty to do over 1f out: r.o wl ins fnl f: nvr trbld ldrs* **16/1**

440- **8** shd **Maymyo (IRE)**[59] 8250 5-9-1 **68** ....(t) LukeMorris 2 — 64
(Sylvester Kirk) *t.k.h: hld up in last quartet: effrt over 1f out: styd on ins fnl f: nvr trbld ldrs* **8/1**

30-0 **9** 2 ¼ **Cool Strutter (IRE)**[12] 416 4-9-2 **72** .... RobHornby[(3)] 4 — 61
(Andrew Balding) *stdd s: hld up in last trio: effrt on inner over 1f out: kpt on: nvr trbld ldrs* **20/1**

42-5 **10** 1 ½ **State Of The Union (IRE)**[31] 162 4-9-3 **70** .... CathyGannon 9 — 54
(Lee Carter) *hld up in midfield: rdn and no hdwy over 1f out: wknd fnl f* **33/1**

30-0 **11** 12 **Generalyse**[27] 236 7-8-8 **66** ....(b) JosephineGordon[(5)] 8 — 12
(Anabel K Murphy) *chsd clr ldng trio tl 2f out: sn u.p and lost pl qckly: wl bhd fnl f* **33/1**

1m 10.85s (-1.05) **Going Correction** -0.025s/f (Stan) **11** Ran SP% **121.4**
Speed ratings (Par 103): **106,105,103,101,101 101,100,100,97,95 79**
CSF £32.66 CT £74.82 TOTE £10.50: £3.30, £2.40, £1.20; EX 34.90 Trifecta £87.80.

Owner Canisbay Bloodstock **Bred** Cheveley Park Stud Ltd **Trained** Epsom, Surrey

FOCUS
A modest sprint handicap and not many got into it.

562 BET&WATCH EVERY RACE AT UNIBET MEDIAN AUCTION MAIDEN STKS 5f 6y(P)
4:50 (4:51) (Class 6) 3-Y-O **£2,264** (£673; £336; £168) **Stalls** High

Form RPR
1 **Equijade** 3-9-0 0 .... LukeMorris 4 68+
(Robert Stephens) *dwlt: in tch in last: effrt on outer 2f out: chsd wnr over 1f out: led 1f out: r.o wl: readily* **11/8**[2]
-304 2 4 **Rojina (IRE)**[10] 432 3-9-0 56 .... JFEgan 1 50
(Joseph Tuite) *led: rdn over 1f out: hdd 1f out: sn outpcd by wnr: plugged on* **5/4**[1]
0-0 3 1 1/4 **Kimbelle**[14] 400 3-8-9 0 .... RachealKneller(5) 2 46
(Mark Usher) *t.k.h: trckd ldng pair: swtchd rt and effrt jst over 1f out: sn outpcd: 3rd and plugged on same pce ins fnl f* **10/1**
0- 4 6 **Sand By Me**[117] 7344 3-9-5 0 .... GeorgeBaker 3 29
(Peter Crate) *chsd ldr tl dropped to last over 1f out: sn btn: bhd and eased wl ins fnl f* **6/1**[3]
1m 0.22s (1.42) **Going Correction** -0.025s/f (Stan) 4 Ran SP% **109.9**
Speed ratings (Par 95): **87,80,78,69**
CSF £3.53 TOTE £1.80; EX 2.90 Trifecta £10.00.
Owner D J Deer **Bred** D J And Mrs Deer **Trained** Penhow, Newport
FOCUS
There won't be many weaker maidens than this in 2016, though all four earned prize-money. The runner-up sets the standard.
T/Plt: £270.20 to a £1 stake. Pool: £66,871.02 - 180.64 winning units. T/Qpdt: £18.50 to a £1 stake. Pool: £6,182.39 - 247.10 winning units. **Steve Payne**

541 WOLVERHAMPTON (A.W) (L-H)
Saturday, February 13
OFFICIAL GOING: Tapeta: standard
Wind: Light against Weather: Fine

563 LADBROKES AMATEUR RIDERS' H'CAP 1m 141y (Tp)
6:15 (6:16) (Class 6) (0-60,60) 4-Y-O+ **£2,651** (£822; £410; £205) **Stalls** Low

Form RPR
0-25 1 **Schottische**[28] 216 6-10-0 53 .... (p) MissCBanham(7) 11 60
(Alan Bailey) *a.p: chsd ldr over 2f out: led over 1f out: pushed out* **14/1**
-425 2 1 **Miss Lillie**[18] 336 5-10-5 58 .... (p) HarryTeal(7) 7 63
(Roger Teal) *mid-div: hdwy over 2f out: rdn over 1f out: edgd lft ins fnl f: styd on* **13/2**[2]
300- 3 1 1/4 **Lendal Bridge**[81] 7962 5-10-3 52 .... KaineWood(3) 8 54
(Tony Coyle) *a.p: rdn and ev ch over 1f out: styd on same pce ins fnl f* **11/1**
56-0 4 1/2 **John Potts**[19] 334 11-10-0 46 .... (p) MissSBrotherton 4 47
(Brian Baugh) *w ldr tl led 7f out: rdn and hdd over 1f out: no ex ins fnl f* **8/1**[3]
-060 5 1 1/2 **Kodiac Lady (IRE)**[15] 387 4-10-7 58 .... (be) MissPBridgwater(5) 3 56
(Simon West) *hld up: hdwy over 1f out: styd on: nt rch ldrs* **16/1**
4300 6 1 **Stanlow**[15] 383 6-10-4 50 .... (v) MissMMullineaux 2 45
(Michael Mullineaux) *mid-div: pushed along over 3f out: hdwy over 1f out: no ex ins fnl f* **22/1**
5-21 7 3/4 **Les Gar Gan (IRE)**[19] 334 5-10-12 58 .... (be) MrSWalker 6 52+
(Daniel Mark Loughnane) *hld up: hdwy on outer over 2f out: rdn over 1f out: edgd lft and no ex fnl f* **2/1**[1]
-503 8 2 **Actonetaketwo**[17] 355 6-9-12 51 .... MrCJewell(7) 5 40
(Ron Hodges) *s.i.s: hld up: nvr nrr* **16/1**
060- 9 1/2 **All Or Nothin (IRE)**[286] 1919 7-10-4 55 .... MissMBryant(5) 12 43
(Paddy Butler) *hld up in tch: racd keenly: effrt over 2f out: nt clr run wl over 1f out: wknd fnl f* **66/1**
00-0 10 shd **Automotive**[30] 173 8-11-0 60 .... (p) MrRBirkett 13 48
(Julia Feilden) *hld up: sme hdwy over 1f out: wknd fnl f* **22/1**
2-00 11 7 **Vivre La Reve**[29] 201 4-10-7 60 .... MrADean(7) 10 31
(James Unett) *led: hdd 7f out: chsd ldrs: wnt 2nd over 3f out tl rdn over 2f out: wknd over 1f out* **50/1**
0/0- 12 1 1/4 **Johnnys Legacy (IRE)**[75] 8052 9-10-0 49 .... (p) MissPFuller(3) 9 18
(Ken Wingrove) *prom: chsd ldr over 6f out tl rdn over 3f out: wknd over 2f out* **125/1**
1m 50.88s (0.78) **Going Correction** -0.075s/f (Stan) 12 Ran SP% **97.5**
Speed ratings (Par 101): **93,92,91,90,89 88,87,85,85,85 79,78**
Lynngale was withdrawn. Price at time of withdrawal 4-1. Rule 4 applies to all bets - deduction 20p in the pound. CSF £63.96 CT £544.85 TOTE £13.00: £2.80, £1.90, £2.40; EX 67.80 Trifecta £1034.70.
Owner AB Racing Limited **Bred** Mrs M L Parry & P M Steele-Mortimer **Trained** Newmarket, Suffolk
FOCUS
An ordinary handicap for amateur riders which the original second favourite Lynngale became upset in the stalls and was withdrawn. The pace was no more than fair and there were four in line a furlong out. The winner has been rated to form.

564 32RED.COM FILLIES' H'CAP 7f 32y (Tp)
6:45 (6:45) (Class 5) (0-75,76) 4-Y-O+ **£3,881** (£1,155; £577; £288) **Stalls** High

Form RPR
-415 1 **Queen Aggie (IRE)**[12] 415 6-9-0 71 .... GeorgeDowning(3) 6 79
(Tony Carroll) *hld up: hdwy over 1f out: rdn to ld wl ins fnl f: r.o: comf* **9/2**[2]
0-44 2 1 1/2 **Colourfilly**[8] 456 4-8-8 62 ow1 .... (p) RichardKingscote 8 66
(Tom Dascombe) *sn led: hdd over 5f out: chsd ldr tl led again wl over 1f out: rdn and hdd wl ins fnl f: styd on same pce* **9/2**[2]
4534 3 1/2 **Be Royale**[3] 523 6-9-5 73 .... RobertWinston 2 76
(Michael Appleby) *hld up: nt clr run fr over 2f out tl ins fnl f: r.o to go 3rd nr fin* **7/2**[1]
4-16 4 nk **Invade (IRE)**[20] 324 4-8-11 65 .... (t) SaleemGolam 1 67
(Stuart Williams) *a.p: rdn over 1f out: styd on same pce ins fnl f* **8/1**
0-32 5 1/2 **Hollie Point**[12] 415 4-9-5 76 .... TomMarquand(3) 5 76
(Sylvester Kirk) *hld up in tch: rdn and edgd lft over 1f out: styd on same pce ins fnl f* **9/2**[2]
310- 6 2 **The Dukkerer (IRE)**[128] 7067 5-8-6 60 .... JamesSullivan 3 55
(James Given) *sn pushed along in rr: effrt over 1f out: edgd lft ins fnl f: nt trble ldrs* **16/1**
306- 7 1 1/2 **Deep Blue Sea**[156] 6250 4-9-6 74 .... KieranO'Neill 4 65
(Anthony Carson) *trckd ldrs: plld hrd: shkn up over 2f out: wknd fnl f* **5/1**[3]
-366 8 6 **Venus Grace**[2] 532 5-8-6 60 .... (p) LiamJones 7 35
(Michael Appleby) *s.i.s: hdwy to ld over 5f out: rdn and hdd wl over 1f out: sn wknd* **9/1**
1m 27.41s (-1.39) **Going Correction** -0.075s/f (Stan) 8 Ran SP% **120.4**
Speed ratings (Par 100): **104,102,101,101,100 98,96,89**
CSF £26.54 CT £81.25 TOTE £4.90: £1.90, £2.30, £2.50; EX 33.00 Trifecta £131.60.
Owner Shropshire Wolves 4 **Bred** Mrs Marion Daly **Trained** Cropthorne, Worcs
FOCUS
A fair handicap for fillies with an open market. The pace was sound. The winner has been rated back to the level of her C&D win in September.

565 32RED CASINO (S) STKS 7f 32y (Tp)
7:15 (7:17) (Class 6) 3-Y-O **£2,749** (£818; £408; £204) **Stalls** High

Form RPR
44-2 1 **Broughtons Fancy**[15] 380 3-8-2 68 .... NoelGarbutt(5) 1 61
(David Evans) *mde all: rdn over 1f out: styd on wl* **13/8**[1]
01-6 2 2 3/4 **Sahalin**[26] 243 3-9-2 66 .... DanielMuscutt(3) 2 66
(Marco Botti) *sn pushed along and prom: chsd wnr 3f out: rdn over 1f out: styd on same pce ins fnl f* **5/2**[2]
5-60 3 1/2 **Weld Al Khawaneej (IRE)**[15] 376 3-8-12 60 .... (p) ShaneGray 6 57
(Kevin Ryan) *hld up: hdwy over 2f out: rdn over 1f out: styd on same pce ins fnl f* **13/2**
46-0 4 nse **Burning Love (IRE)**[25] 248 3-8-7 57 .... JackMitchell 3 52
(Dave Morris) *hld up: hdwy over 2f out: sn rdn: styd on* **16/1**
5-3 5 9 **Paradise Palm**[9] 441 3-8-4 0 .... DannyBrock(3) 8 28
(Philip McBride) *prom: rdn over 2f out: wknd over 1f out* **4/1**[3]
26-0 6 1 1/2 **Bond's Tricks**[39] 48 3-8-7 53 .... JordanNason(5) 4 29
(Ronald Thompson) *chsd wnr 4f: sn rdn: wknd over 1f out* **40/1**
1m 28.12s (-0.68) **Going Correction** -0.075s/f (Stan) 6 Ran SP% **108.3**
Speed ratings (Par 95): **100,96,96,96,85 84**
CSF £5.42 TOTE £2.40: £1.60, £1.60; EX 5.90 Trifecta £19.00.
Owner Lynn Cullimore & Mrs E Evans **Bred** Michael E Broughton **Trained** Pandy, Monmouths
FOCUS
An ordinary conditions seller in which the winner was the clear pick on adjusted official ratings, though she came into the race an 11-race maiden. The pace was no more than fair. The runner-up has been rated to form.

566 BEST ODDS GUARANTEED AT CORAL H'CAP 1m 4f 50y (Tp)
7:45 (7:45) (Class 5) (0-75,75) 4-Y-O+ **£3,881** (£1,155; £577; £288) **Stalls** Low

Form RPR
4-14 1 **Dakota City**[14] 399 5-9-6 74 .... (v) AdamBeschizza 4 82
(Julia Feilden) *prom: hmpd and lost pl after 1f: hdwy over 5f out: rdn to ld ins fnl f: r.o* **7/2**[2]
20/0 2 1 1/4 **Icebuster**[30] 172 8-9-7 75 .... DanielTudhope 11 81
(Rod Millman) *s.i.s: hdwy 10f out: chsd ldr over 4f out: led over 2f out: rdn over 1f out: hdd ins fnl f: kpt on* **25/1**
006- 3 nse **Dalaki (IRE)**[26] 7901 5-8-13 67 .... (b) KieranO'Neill 5 73
(Des Donovan, Ire) *sn pushed along to chse ldr: lost 2nd over 4f out: remained handy: rdn and ev ch fr over 2f out: kpt on* **16/1**
6-41 4 shd **Archipeligo**[19] 332 5-9-5 73 .... MartinDwyer 12 79
(Iain Jardine) *chsd ldrs: rdn and ev ch fr over 1f out: unable qck towards fin* **13/2**[3]
254- 5 1 1/4 **Paddys Runner**[82] 7597 4-9-2 73 .... WilliamTwiston-Davies 8 77+
(Alan King) *hld up: hdwy u.p over 2f out: edgd lft ins fnl f: kpt on* **13/8**[1]
1-50 6 1 **Bayan Kasirga (IRE)**[15] 382 6-9-0 68 .... TonyHamilton 1 70
(Richard Fahey) *prom: hmpd after 1f: lost pl over 9f out: nt clr run over 2f out: hdwy over 1f out: sn rdn: nt rch ldrs* **10/1**
0-43 7 1 **Rising Breeze (FR)**[17] 343 5-8-10 67 .... GeorgeDowning(3) 2 68
(Tony Carroll) *s.i.s: hld up: styd on u.p fr over 1f out: nt trble ldrs* **12/1**
10-4 8 2 1/4 **Blue Sea Of Ibrox (IRE)**[41] 30 8-9-4 75 .... DanielMuscutt(3) 3 72
(John Berry) *hld up: rdn over 2f out: nvr nrr* **16/1**
00-0 9 hd **Hydrant**[9] 446 10-9-2 70 .... JasonHart 7 67
(Richard Guest) *hld up: hdwy over 3f out: rdn over 2f out: edgd lft over 1f out: sn wknd* **66/1**
1-34 10 2 1/2 **Swift Cedar (IRE)**[18] 337 6-9-0 75 .... RyanTimby(7) 10 68
(David Evans) *s.i.s: hld up: nvr on terms* **11/1**
66-0 11 1/2 **Cosette (IRE)**[12] 420 5-8-11 65 .... LiamKeniry 6 57
(Bernard Llewellyn) *prom: rdn over 4f out: wknd over 2f out* **66/1**
42-6 12 6 **Ifan (IRE)**[9] 438 8-8-13 67 .... DougieCostello 9 49
(Tim Vaughan) *led: rdn and hdd over 2f out: wknd over 1f out* **33/1**
2m 39.91s (-0.89) **Going Correction** -0.075s/f (Stan)
WFA 4 from 5yo+ 3lb 12 Ran SP% **120.3**
Speed ratings (Par 103): **99,98,98,98,97 96,95,94,94,92 92,88**
CSF £95.38 CT £1255.32 TOTE £4.60: £1.60, £6.00, £5.50; EX 92.00 Trifecta £1250.90.
Owner Good Company Partnership **Bred** Juddmonte Farms Ltd **Trained** Exning, Suffolk
FOCUS
Quite a competitive handicap run at a fair gallop.

567 CORAL.CO.UK MAIDEN STKS 1m 4f 50y (Tp)
8:15 (8:15) (Class 5) 4-Y-O+ **£3,396** (£1,010; £505; £252) **Stalls** Low

Form RPR
- 1 **Walpole (IRE)**[132] 4-9-5 0 .... JamieSpencer 1 79+
(Hugo Palmer) *trckd ldrs: racd keenly: shkn up to ld over 1f out: styd on wl: eased nr fin* **1/1**[1]
5-2 2 1 1/2 **Handsome Dan (IRE)**[21] 318 10-9-8 0 .... DanielTudhope 3 74
(Sarah Hollinshead) *hld up: hdwy 2f out: nt clr run over 1f out: sn rdn: styd on to go 2nd ins fnl f* **9/1**
5- 3 1 1/4 **Be My Sea (IRE)**[47] 7380 5-9-8 69 .... WilliamCarson 9 72
(Tony Carroll) *prom: rdn over 2f out: led wl over 1f out: sn hdd: styd on same pce ins fnl f* **11/2**[3]
0- 4 3 1/4 **Alphabetical Order**[70] 8125 8-9-8 0 .... SamJames 2 67
(David O'Meara) *hld up: hdwy over 1f out: sn rdn: no ex ins fnl f* **28/1**
556- 5 2 1/4 **Singular Quest**[161] 6093 4-9-2 74 .... DanielMuscutt(3) 4 63
(Kevin Frost) *chsd ldrs: rdn over 2f out: wknd over 1f out* **15/2**
6 nk **Never Never (IRE)**[43] 6-9-8 0 .... PaulMulrennan 8 63
(Iain Jardine) *chsd ldr: rdn over 3f out: led over 2f out: hdd wl over 1f out: wknd ins fnl f* **28/1**
7 3/4 **Mr Caffrey**[49] 7052 4-9-5 74 .... LiamKeniry 7 62
(Robert Stephens) *led: rdn and hdd over 2f out: wknd ins fnl f* **11/4**[2]
6 8 1 1/2 **Antonio Joli (IRE)**[17] 342 4-9-5 0 .... DougieCostello 6 59
(Jo Hughes) *hld up: rdn over 3f out: a in rr* **20/1**

9 8 **Magna Cartor**[119] 6-9-3 0 .... JordanNason(5) 5 46
(Ronald Thompson) *dwlt: bhd: hdwy over 3f out: rdn over 2f out: sn wknd* **66/1**

2m 40.3s (-0.50) **Going Correction** -0.075s/f (Stan)
WFA 4 from 5yo+ 3lb 9 Ran SP% **127.0**
Speed ratings (Par 103): **98,97,96,94,92 92,91,90,85**
CSF £12.89 TOTE £2.10: £1.30, £2.20, £1.80; EX 16.20 Trifecta £65.40.
Owner Roldvale Limited **Bred** Roundhill Stud **Trained** Newmarket, Suffolk

FOCUS

A moderately-run maiden so the form should be treated with a degree of caution, but the winner won in good style. Muddling form.

568 CORAL CONNECT H'CAP (DIV I) 1m 1f 103y (Tp)
8:45 (8:45) (Class 6) (0-60,65) 4-Y-O+ £2,749 (£818; £408; £204) Stalls Low

Form RPR
55-4 1 **La Havrese (FR)**[19] 334 5-8-11 **55** .... JoshDoyle(5) 5 66
(Lynn Siddall) *hld up: hdwy on outer over 2f out: rdn to ld wl ins fnl f: r.o* **8/1**

/-00 2 2 1/4 **Let Me In (IRE)**[32] 156 6-9-0 **56** .... (v) DanielMuscutt(3) 1 62
(Bernard Llewellyn) *chsd ldrs: led over 2f out: rdn and hdd wl ins fnl f* **25/1**

32-0 3 1 **Silver Lining (IRE)**[38] 62 4-9-5 **58** .... (t) GeorgeBaker 8 62
(Marcus Tregoning) *hld up: hdwy over 2f out: rdn over 1f out: styd on to go 3rd wl ins fnl f* **5/1**[2]

26-0 4 1 1/2 **Right Madam (IRE)**[22] 294 4-8-10 **49** .... (p) KieranO'Neill 2 50
(Sarah Hollinshead) *hld up in tch: racd keenly: rdn and edgd lft over 1f out: no ex ins fnl f* **33/1**

14 5 3/4 **Cartographic (USA)**[17] 348 4-8-12 **58** .... [1] RyanTimby(7) 3 57
(David Evans) *hld up and bhd: rdn over 1f out: styd on ins fnl f: nvr nrr* **11/2**[3]

6-31 6 10 **Black Minstrel (IRE)**[8] 463 7-9-7 **65** .... (p) CiaranMckee(5) 9 43+
(John O'Shea) *s.i.s: rcvrd to chse ldr 7f out: led 5f out: rdn and hdd over 2f out: wknd fnl f* **9/4**[1]

21-5 7 1 3/4 **Roman De Brut (IRE)**[33] 149 4-9-1 **59** .... JordanNason(5) 7 34
(Ronald Thompson) *chsd ldrs: rdn over 2f out: wknd over 1f out* **7/1**

5-53 8 nk **Scot Daddy (USA)**[31] 158 4-9-6 **59** .... (t) DougieCostello 6 33
(David Dennis) *prom: rdn over 2f out: wknd over 1f out* **9/1**

60-6 9 1 1/4 **X Raise (IRE)**[16] 368 4-8-8 **47** ow1 .... (p) RichardKingscote 10 19
(David Brown) *sn led: hdd 5f out: chsd ldr: rdn over 2f out: wknd over 1f out* **22/1**

60-4 10 1 3/4 **Anniversarie**[15] 383 4-8-8 **54** .... (t) PhilDennis(7) 4 22
(John Norton) *s.i.s: hld up: rdn over 3f out: wknd 2f out* **14/1**

1m 59.33s (-1.47) **Going Correction** -0.075s/f (Stan) 10 Ran SP% **114.2**
Speed ratings (Par 101): **103,101,100,98,98 89,87,87,86,84**
CSF £186.84 CT £1096.50 TOTE £7.90: £2.80, £5.50, £2.00; EX 163.90 Trifecta £833.00.
Owner Jimmy Kay **Bred** S C A Elevage De La Croix De Place **Trained** Colton, N Yorks
■ Stewards' Enquiry : Daniel Muscutt two-day ban: use of whip (27 and 29 Feb)

FOCUS

A modest handicap in which the leaders kicked for home a long way out which suited the closers so the overall form should be treated with a degree of caution. The third has been rated close to his 1m4f form.

569 CORAL CONNECT H'CAP (DIV II) 1m 1f 103y (Tp)
9:15 (9:16) (Class 6) (0-60,60) 4-Y-O+ £2,749 (£818; £408; £204) Stalls Low

Form RPR
2-12 1 **Rockwood**[18] 336 5-9-5 **58** .... (v) PaulMulrennan 3 71+
(Karen McLintock) *s.i.s: hld up: hdwy over 2f out: led 1f out: r.o wl* **6/4**[1]

3-41 2 3 **Cahar Fad (IRE)**[36] 107 4-9-2 **55** .... (bt) AdamBeschizza 5 62
(Steph Hollinshead) *hld up: hdwy over 3f out: rdn over 1f out: sn ev ch: styd on same pce fnl f* **3/1**[2]

4-30 3 4 1/2 **Sylvette**[8] 463 4-9-5 **58** .... (bt[1]) JackMitchell 10 56
(Roger Varian) *sn pushed along to chse ldr: led over 3f out: clr over 2f out: rdn and hdd 1f out: wknd ins fnl f* **15/2**

40-4 4 1 1/4 **Ferryview Place**[16] 362 7-8-8 **50** .... (p) GeorgeDowning(3) 6 45
(Ian Williams) *hld up in tch: chsd ldr 3f out: rdn over 1f out: wknd ins fnl f* **9/2**[3]

2-30 5 1 **One Last Dream**[24] 252 7-8-8 **47** ow1 .... RichardKingscote 2 40
(Ron Hodges) *prom: lost pl over 3f out: n.d after* **12/1**

545 6 1/2 **Do It Tomorrow (IRE)**[20] 325 4-9-4 **57** .... TonyHamilton 1 49
(J R Jenkins) *hld up: rdn over 2f out: nvr on terms* **20/1**

040- 7 3 1/4 **Rossington**[54] 8335 7-8-7 **46** oh1 .... JamesSullivan 9 31
(John Wainwright) *hld up: rdn over 2f out: a in rr* **33/1**

41-4 8 shd **Coup De Vent**[38] 61 5-9-1 **54** .... TimmyMurphy 4 39
(John O'Shea) *hld up: rdn over 2f out: wknd over 1f out* **22/1**

00-0 9 19 **Filament Of Gold (USA)**[22] 295 5-9-1 **59** .... (b[1]) CiaranMckee(5) 8 4
(Roy Brotherton) *prom: rdn over 2f out: wknd over 1f out* **25/1**

/00- 10 6 **Announcement**[66] 7973 5-9-2 **60** .... (t) JordanNason(5) 7
(Ronald Thompson) *sn led: hdd over 3f out: wknd over 2f out* **50/1**

1m 59.07s (-1.73) **Going Correction** -0.075s/f (Stan) 10 Ran SP% **120.5**
Speed ratings (Par 101): **104,101,97,96,95 94,92,91,75,69**
CSF £5.77 CT £26.15 TOTE £3.20: £1.40, £1.30, £1.70; EX 7.40 Trifecta £33.50.
Owner I R Clements & Dr L G Parry **Bred** Norcroft Park Stud **Trained** Ingoe, Northumberland
■ Stewards' Enquiry : Timmy Murphy jockey said that the mare hung left throughout

FOCUS

A modest handicap but the pace was strong and the first two both came from well off the pace. The runner-up has been rated to his latest C&D win.

T/Plt: £212.20 to a £1 stake. Pool: £108,479.57 - 373.11 winning units. T/Qpdt: £19.10 to a £1 stake. Pool: £10,782.53 - 416.84 winning units. **Colin Roberts**

570 - 576a (Foreign Racing) - See Raceform Interactive

[520]SOUTHWELL (L-H)
Sunday, February 14

OFFICIAL GOING: Fibresand: standard
Wind: Fresh across Weather: Bright & dry

577 CORAL (S) H'CAP 1m 4f (F)
1:50 (1:50) (Class 6) (0-60,57) 4-Y-O+ £2,587 (£770; £384; £192) Stalls Low

Form RPR
0-52 1 **Toboggan's Gift**[17] 368 4-8-7 **46** .... JimmyQuinn 2 55
(Ann Duffield) *chsd clr ldr: hdwy 4f out: cl up on inner 3f out: rdn to chal over 1f out: led jst ins fnl f: drvn out* **9/4**[2]

401- 2 1 1/4 **Mazovian (USA)**[9] 8385 8-9-3 **53** .... (p) LiamKeniry 3 60
(Neil Mulholland) *trckd ldng pair: hdwy 4f out: cl up 3f out: led 2f out: rdn over 1f out: hdd jst ins fnl f: sn drvn and kpt on same pce* **5/4**[1]

6-34 3 18 **A Little Bit Dusty**[10] 445 8-9-7 **57** .... (b) PaulMulrennan 1 35
(Conor Dore) *dwlt and hld up in rr: effrt and pushed along 4f out: rdn 3f out: plugged on to take remote 3rd ins fnl f* **3/1**[3]

6-60 4 3/4 **Arsenale (GER)**[12] 425 5-9-2 **52** .... (p) LukeMorris 4 29
(Michael Appleby) *sn led and clr: pushed along over 4f out: rdn over 3f out: hdd 2f out and sn wknd* **12/1**

2m 43.79s (2.79) **Going Correction** +0.075s/f (Slow)
WFA 4 from 5yo+ 3lb 4 Ran SP% **107.9**
Speed ratings (Par 101): **93,92,80,79**
CSF £5.46 TOTE £3.40; EX 5.30 Trifecta £7.10.
Owner T P McMahon and D McMahon **Bred** D McMahon **Trained** Constable Burton, N Yorks

FOCUS

A weak selling handicap, especially after the two non-runners, and the two at the head of the market dominated.

578 UNIBET OFFER DAILY JOCKEY/TRAINER SPECIALS H'CAP 6f (F)
2:20 (2:21) (Class 6) (0-60,64) 3-Y-O £2,587 (£770; £384; £192) Stalls Low

Form RPR
-521 1 **Englishwoman**[5] 510 3-9-6 **64** 6ex .... JosephineGordon(5) 1 78
(David Evans) *trckd ldng pair on inner: smooth hdwy and cl up 2f out: sn led: pushed clr ent fnl f: readily* **1/2**[1]

5-23 2 7 **Guapo Bay**[17] 365 3-9-1 **57** .... (p) TomMarquand(3) 2 47
(Richard Hannon) *in rr: pushed along over 3f out: rdn and hdwy on inner 2f out: kpt on u.p fnl f: no ch w wnr* **8/1**[3]

U-51 3 1 1/4 **Leitrim Traveller (USA)**[11] 436 3-9-2 **55** .... (b) WilliamCarson 3 41
(Jamie Osborne) *sn trcking ldr: cl up 1/2-way: rdn along 2f out: sn drvn and kpt on same pce* **7/2**[2]

440 4 3 **Red Chatterbox (IRE)**[12] 428 3-9-2 **55** .... KieranO'Neill 5 31
(Scott Dixon) *led: rdn along 3f out and sn jnd: drvn 2f out: sn hdd and grad wknd* **22/1**

0-45 5 1/2 **Ready Steady (USA)**[15] 402 3-9-4 **57** .... DavidNolan 4 32
(David Loughnane) *dwlt: chsd ldrs on outer: rdn along 1/2-way: drvn over 2f out: sn outpcd* **20/1**

1m 16.92s (0.42) **Going Correction** +0.075s/f (Slow) 5 Ran SP% **109.1**
Speed ratings (Par 95): **100,90,89,85,84**
CSF £5.14 TOTE £1.40: £1.10, £2.50; EX 4.50 Trifecta £5.70.
Owner R Kent **Bred** Peter Winkworth **Trained** Pandy, Monmouths

FOCUS

Four fillies against one gelding in this uncompetitive 3yo sprint handicap and every bit as easy for the odds-on favourite as the betting suggested it would be.

579 DAILY PRICE BOOSTS AT UNIBET CLASSIFIED CLAIMING STKS 5f (F)
2:50 (2:50) (Class 6) 4-Y-O+ £2,264 (£673; £336; £168) Stalls Centre

Form RPR
3035 1 **Elusivity (IRE)**[4] 520 8-9-1 67 .... (p) PaulMulrennan 1 70
(Conor Dore) *cl up: slt ld after 1f: rdn wl over 1f out: drvn and kpt on wl fnl f* **11/8**[1]

6-22 2 3 1/4 **Imjin River (IRE)**[4] 513 9-8-12 48 .... (tp) BenCurtis 2 54
(William Stone) *slt ld 1f: cl up: rdn along and sltly outpcd bef 1/2-way: kpt on u.p to chse wnr jst over 1f out: sn no imp* **11/2**[3]

-024 3 1 **Oscars Journey**[17] 364 6-8-13 65 .... (v) AlistairRawlinson(3) 5 54
(J R Jenkins) *cl up: effrt over 2f out: sn rdn and ev ch: drvn wl over 1f out and grad wknd* **2/1**[2]

000- 4 1 1/4 **Special Code (IRE)**[82] 7968 4-8-10 54 .... DannyBrock(3) 3 47
(Heather Dalton) *dwlt and rdn along in rr: swtchd rt to stands' rail over 3f out: hdwy u.p to chse ldrs 2f out: sn drvn and btn* **14/1**

4-53 5 5 **Monsieur Jamie**[31] 176 8-9-1 64 .... (v) TonyHamilton 4 31
(J R Jenkins) *towards rr and sn pushed along: rdn 3f out: sn outpcd and bhd* **11/2**[3]

59.78s (0.08) **Going Correction** +0.10s/f (Slow) 5 Ran SP% **112.9**
Speed ratings (Par 101): **103,97,96,94,86**
CSF £9.64 TOTE £2.20: £1.10, £2.60; EX 8.50 Trifecta £23.90.
Owner Mrs Louise Marsh **Bred** J Costello **Trained** Hubbert's Bridge, Lincs

FOCUS

A moderate classified claimer.

580 NEW UNIBET RACING APP DOWNLOAD H'CAP 5f (F)
3:20 (3:20) (Class 3) (0-90,87) 4-Y-O+ £7,439 (£2,213; £1,106; £553) Stalls Centre

Form RPR
2-20 1 **Hoofalong**[23] 288 6-9-7 **87** .... (b) PhillipMakin 1 98
(Michael Easterby) *chsd ldrs on outer: hdwy 2f out: rdn to chal over 1f out: led ins fnl f: jst hld on* **7/1**

1- 2 nse **Flowers On Venus (IRE)**[55] 8332 4-9-0 **80** .... CathyGannon 7 91+
(David Evans) *racd towards stands' rail: chsd ldrs: rdn along 2f out: drvn over 1f out: styd on wl u.p towards fin: jst failed* **9/2**[3]

-131 3 2 **Crosse Fire**[19] 338 4-9-5 **85** .... (p) KieranO'Neill 3 89
(Scott Dixon) *dwlt: racd towards centre: sn chsng ldrs: rdn wl over 1f out: drvn ins fnl f: kpt on same pce* **7/2**[2]

46-4 4 shd **Ballista (IRE)**[38] 86 8-9-7 **87** .... RichardKingscote 4 90
(Tom Dascombe) *racd centre: slt ld: rdn wl over 1f out: drvn and hdd ins fnl f: kpt on same pce* **11/2**

5532 5 1/2 **Apache Storm**[7] 492 4-8-13 **84** .... JosephineGordon(5) 5 85
(Michael Appleby) *chsd ldrs: rdn along 2f out: drvn over 1f out: sn drvn and no imp* **10/3**[1]

4-02 6 hd **Sleepy Blue Ocean**[17] 364 10-8-11 **77** .... (p) LukeMorris 10 78
(John Balding) *racd nr stands' rail: chsd ldrs: rdn along over 2f out: drvn wl over 1f out: grad wknd* **20/1**

-416 7 3 1/2 **Fine 'n Dandy (IRE)**[2] 541 5-8-9 **75** .... TonyHamilton 8 63
(J R Jenkins) *cl up centre: effrt 2f out: sn rdn and ev ch tl drvn and wknd ent fnl f* **8/1**

1310 8 4 1/2 **Jaarih (IRE)**[9] 462 4-8-10 **76** .... LiamKeniry 6 48
(Conor Dore) *chsd ldrs: rdn along 2f out: sn drvn and btn* **8/1**

59.53s (-0.17) **Going Correction** +0.10s/f (Slow) 8 Ran SP% **118.4**
Speed ratings (Par 107): **105,104,101,101,100 100,94,87**
CSF £39.85 CT £132.13 TOTE £7.70: £2.80, £1.50, £2.40; EX 33.40 Trifecta £322.20.
Owner A Chandler, L Westwood, D & Y Blunt **Bred** D F Spence **Trained** Sheriff Hutton, N Yorks

FOCUS

A decent sprint handicap predictably run at a strong pace.

581 DOWNLOAD THE LADBROKES APP H'CAP 7f (F)
3:50 (3:50) (Class 4) (0-80,84) 4-Y-O+ £5,175 (£1,540; £769; £384) Stalls Low

Form RPR
0-10 1 **Moon River (IRE)**[25] 254 4-9-5 **78** .... BenCurtis 8 92
(Michael Appleby) *cl up: led after 1f: rdn clr wl over 1f out: kpt on strly* **7/1**

 The Form Book, Raceform Ltd, Newbury, RG14 5SJ

50-2 **2** 3 3/4 **Captain Revelation**[43] 24 4-9-3 **76**........................ RichardKingscote 4 80
(Tom Dascombe) *hld up in tch: hdwy on inner 3f out: styd towards inner rail st: rdn 2f out: kpt on u.p fnl f: no ch w wnr* **3/1**[1]

0-55 **3** 3/4 **Abi Scarlet (IRE)**[24] 276 7-8-11 **70**..............................(b) KieranO'Neill 1 72
(Scott Dixon) *cl up on inner: pushed along 3f out: rdn over 2f out: chsd wnr and drvn over 1f out: kpt on same pce* **33/1**

546- **4** 1 **Bognor (USA)**[263] 2603 5-9-6 **79**.. LukeMorris 5 78
(Michael Appleby) *trckd ldrs: hdwy over 2f out and sn rdn: drvn wl over 1f out: kpt on same pce* **8/1**

00-5 **5** 1 **Lawyer (IRE)**[39] 73 5-9-3 **76**....................................... PaulMulrennan 7 73
(David Barron) *cl up: rdn along wl over 2f out: drvn wl over 1f out: kpt on one pce* **12/1**

0-00 **6** 3/4 **Billyoakes (IRE)**[5] 508 4-9-6 **79**...................................... PhillipMakin 10 74
(David Barron) *chsd ldrs: effrt on outer wl over 2f out: sn rdn: drvn wl over 1f out: no imp* **16/1**

1164 **7** 1/2 **Moonlight Venture**[10] 448 5-8-8 **67**...............................(b) ShaneGray 6 61
(Conor Dore) *a towards rr* **16/1**

4-12 **8** 1 1/4 **Afkar (IRE)**[10] 449 8-8-5 **69**................................(p) JosephineGordon(5) 3 59
(Ivan Furtado) *slt ld 1f: cl up: rdn along 3f out: drvn 2f out and sn wknd* **6/1**[3]

3-13 **9** 1 1/4 **Patriotic (IRE)**[12] 427 8-9-7 **80**...............................(p) IrineuGoncalves 9 67
(Chris Dwyer) *a in rr* **10/1**

-611 **10** 2 **St Patrick's Day (IRE)**[10] 448 4-9-11 **84**.................(v) DougieCostello 2 66
(J R Jenkins) *dwlt: a in rr* **4/1**[2]

0-60 **11** 3 1/4 **Pretty Bubbles**[13] 422 7-9-5 **78**..............................(p) TonyHamilton 11 51
(J R Jenkins) *dwlt: a in rr* **14/1**

1m 29.59s (-0.71) **Going Correction** +0.075s/f (Slow) **11** Ran SP% **121.1**
Speed ratings (Par 105): **107,102,101,100,99 98,98,96,95,93 89**
CSF £29.12 CT £681.50 TOTE £9.70: £3.50, £1.40, £7.60; EX 36.90 Trifecta £1035.50.
Owner Craig Buckingham **Bred** Rockhart Trading Ltd **Trained** Oakham, Rutland

FOCUS
A good handicap, but few ever got into it.

582 LADBROKES MAIDEN STKS 7f (F)
4:20 (4:20) (Class 5) 3-Y-O+ **£3,234** (£962; £481; £240) **Stalls** Low

Form RPR
3 **1** **Rocket Power**[23] 298 3-8-10 0.. LukeMorris 6 79
(James Tate) *trckd ldrs: hdwy and cl up on outer 1/2-way: wd st: rdn to chal 2f out and sn edgd rt to stands' rail: led over 1f out: clr ins fnl f* **2/1**[2]

4222 **2** 4 1/2 **Phantom Flipper**[5] 507 3-8-10 70.............................(p) AdrianNicholls 5 67
(David Nicholls) *cl up: slt ld 3f out: wd st: rdn 2f out: hdd and drvn over 1f out: kpt on same pce* **1/1**[1]

00- **3** 1/2 **Deben**[116] 7394 3-8-10 0.. RaulDaSilva 1 66
(Kevin Ryan) *slt ld on inner: pushed along and hdd 3f out: cl up and rdn over 2f out: drvn over 1f out: kpt on same pce* **22/1**

044- **4** 2 3/4 **Bonjour Baby**[138] 6834 3-8-5 65... JoeyHaynes 2 54
(K R Burke) *chsd ldrs on inner: pushed along 3f out: rdn over 2f out: kpt on one pce* **10/1**

20-0 **5** 5 **Canford Crossing (IRE)**[23] 287 3-8-7 71.............. TomMarquand(3) 8 46
(Richard Hannon) *t.k.h: in tch: effrt and hdwy 3f out: wd st: rdn to chse ldrs over 2f out: sn drvn and btn* **8/1**[3]

0/- **6** 3/4 **Muhtadim (IRE)**[498] 6935 4-9-6 0... RPWalsh(7) 3 49
(Charles Smith) *chsd ldrs on inner: rdn along wl over 2f out: sn wknd* **50/1**

0-5 **7** 6 **Almutamarred (USA)**[12] 428 4-9-13 0........................ TimmyMurphy 7 33
(Kevin Morgan) *dwlt: a in rr* **33/1**

5 **8** 1 3/4 **Win Lose Draw (IRE)**[23] 298 4-9-10 0............... AlistairRawlinson(3) 4 28
(Michael Appleby) *s.i.s: green and a in rr* **12/1**

1m 30.77s (0.47) **Going Correction** +0.075s/f (Slow)
WFA 3 from 4yo 17lb **8** Ran SP% **120.5**
Speed ratings (Par 103): **100,94,94,91,85 84,77,75**
CSF £4.55 TOTE £3.20: £1.40, £1.10, £6.50; EX 5.20 Trifecta £52.30.
Owner Saeed Manana **Bred** Crossfields Bloodstock Ltd **Trained** Newmarket, Suffolk

FOCUS
An uncompetitive maiden.

583 32RED H'CAP 2m (F)
4:50 (4:50) (Class 5) (0-70,74) 4-Y-O+ **£3,234** (£962; £481; £240) **Stalls** Low

Form RPR
03-2 **1** **Ruler Of The Nile**[18] 354 4-8-10 **62**............................ AdamBeschizza 1 79+
(Robert Stephens) *trckd ldrs: smooth hdwy on inner to ld 3f out and sn pushed wl clr: heavily eased fnl f* **11/1**

2-42 **2** 7 **Northside Prince (IRE)**[12] 425 10-9-10 **70**......................... BenCurtis 4 71
(Alan Swinbank) *hld up: hdwy to trck ldrs 4f out: effrt on outer 3f out and sn rdn along drvn 2f out and plugged on to take modest 2nd ins fnl f* **6/1**[2]

2121 **3** 1 1/4 **Megara**[8] 488 4-9-8 **74**...(p) LukeMorris 6 74
(Sir Mark Prescott Bt) *trckd ldr: cl up 4f out: effrt 3f out and sn pushed along: rdn to chse wnr wl over 2f out: sn drvn and plugged on one pce: lost modest 2nd ins fnl f* **8/11**[1]

12-2 **4** 8 **Kelly's Finest (IRE)**[42] 30 4-8-11 **63**...........................(p) LiamJones 2 53
(Michael Appleby) *led: pushed along and jnd 4f out: rdn and hdd 3f out: sn drvn and outpcd* **16/1**

5/3- **5** 4 1/2 **Argot**[15] 1576 5-9-6 **66**...(p) DavidNolan 3 51
(Charlie Longsdon) *trckd ldrs: pushed along 1/2-way: rdn along over 5f out: drvn wl over 3f out and sn outpcd* **7/1**[3]

2-03 **6** 23 **Thou Swell (IRE)**[12] 425 4-8-11 **63**............................ PaulMulrennan 5 20
(Shaun Harris) *trckd ldrs: pushed along 5f out: rdn wl over 3f out: sn outpcd* **6/1**[2]

3m 45.59s (0.09) **Going Correction** +0.075s/f (Slow)
WFA 4 from 5yo+ 6lb **6** Ran SP% **113.2**
Speed ratings (Par 103): **102,98,97,93,91 80**
CSF £72.86 TOTE £7.30: £2.30, £2.40; EX 28.20 Trifecta £98.50.
Owner Threes Company **Bred** Stephen Hillen & Highbank Syndicate **Trained** Penhow, Newport

FOCUS
An ordinary staying handicap which turned into a one-horse race, though not the horse most people would have thought of.
T/Jkpt: Not won. T/Plt: £51.40 to a £1 stake. Pool: £81,150.94 - 1,151.12 winning tickets. T/Qpdt: £12.70 to a £1 stake. Pool: £7,612.94 - 443.55 winning tickets. **Joe Rowntree**

584 - 585a (Foreign Racing) - See Raceform Interactive

ST MORITZ (R-H)
Sunday, February 14

OFFICIAL GOING: Snow: frozen

586a PREIS WROCLAW EUROPEAN CAPITAL OF CULTURE & WHITE TURF JOCKEY CLUB (CONDITIONS) (5YO+) (SNOW) 4f
11:35 (12:00) 5-Y-O+ **£5,714** (£2,857; £2,040; £1,360; £680)

RPR
1 **Mateur (FR)**[1065] 7-9-13 0.. FXWeissmeier
(Meret Kaderli, Switzerland) **23/5**[1]

2 2 **Sword Of The Lord**[48] 5976 6-10-3 0.................................. MissAEStirling
(Nigel Twiston-Davies) *chsd ldrs: rdn to go 2nd 1/2-way: nt pce to chal wnr*

3 1/2 **Egisto (FR)** 8-9-11 0...(p) RaphaelLingg(6)
(P Schaerer, Switzerland)

4 3 **Tenor Des Neiges (FR)**[1361] 9-9-6 0.......................... AurelienRousse(7)
(A Schaerer, Switzerland)

5 nse **Vicomte Alco (FR)**[812] 7-10-3 0...................................(p) AnthonyLecordier
(A Schaerer, Switzerland)

\n\x\x PARI-MUTUEL (all including 1 chf stakes): WIN 6.60; PLACE 1.30, 1.20, 1.20;
Owner Rene Kaderli **Bred** Gfa Haras Du Hoguenet **Trained** Switzerland

587a GRAND PRIX PRESTIGE (CONDITIONS) (4YO+) (SNOW) 4f
12:05 (12:00) 4-Y-O+ **£4,897** (£1,959; £1,469; £979)

RPR
1 **Vale Of Iron (IRE)**[25] 256 4-9-12 0................................... RobertHavlin 2
(John Best) *mde virtually all: drvn clr fr wl over 1f out: comf* **11/5**[1]

2 3 1/2 **Buddhist Monk**[1470] 444 11-9-0 0...................................(b) TimBurgin(4) 4
(Dagmar Geissmann, Switzerland)

3 2 **Dandys Perier (IRE)**[34] 144 5-9-13 0.......................... MaximPecheur 7
(Ronald Harris) *chsd ldr: rdn and no imp 1 1/2f out: readily lft bhd fnl f*

4 3/4 **Gild Master**[36] 8092 4-8-13 0 ow2.............................. AlexanderPietsch 3
(C Von Der Recke, Germany)

\n\x\x PARI-MUTUEL (all including 1 chf stakes): WIN 3.20; PLACE 1.10, 1.10, 1.10;
Owner White Turf Racing Club UK **Bred** Knockainey Stud & Storway Ltd **Trained** Oad Street, Kent

588a GRAND PRIX CHRISTOFFEL BAU TROPHY (CONDITIONS) (4YO+) (SNOW) 4f
2:20 (12:00) 4-Y-O+
£5,714 (£2,857; £2,040; £1,360; £680; £408)

RPR
1 **Zarras (GER)**[357] 659 7-8-11 0.. RaphaelLingg 9
(P Schaerer, Switzerland) **9/2**[1]

2 1 **Soundtrack (IRE)**[543] 5557 5-8-11 0.................................. DanielePorcu 8
(P Schaerer, Switzerland)

3 1 3/4 **Berrahri (IRE)**[22] 313 5-9-8 0.. RobertHavlin 4
(John Best) *a cl up: scrubbed along to chse ldr fr 1/2-way: nvr able to get on terms and hld fnl f*

4 1 1/4 **Renny Storm (CZE)**[446] 6-8-13 0 ow2.......................... AlexanderPietsch 7
(C Von Der Recke, Germany)

5 hd **Lacan (IRE)**[66] 8168 5-9-6 0.. GrahamGibbons 6
(Ralph Beckett) *outpcd in rr: rdn along to chse ldrs bef 1/2-way: sltly impeded over 1f out: one pce u.p fnl f*

6 hd **Footprintinthesand (IRE)**[357] 659 6-9-6 0.................. OlivierPlacais 3
(M Weiss, Switzerland)

7 8 **Tweet Lady**[1250] 6151 7-8-6 0...................................... FrauRebeccaDanz 10
(Bernhard J Friesdorf, Germany)

8 1 1/2 **Kakapuka**[153] 6381 9-8-11 0 ow2... TimBurgin 5
(Anabel K Murphy) *scrubbed along towards rr: wl bhd fr 1/2-way*

9 nk **Cahill (IRE)**[39] 66 4-8-11 0.......................................(p) MaximPecheur 1
(Ronald Harris) *outpcd and rousted along: a bhd*

\n\x\x PARI-MUTUEL (all including 1 chf stakes): WIN 5.50; PLACE 2.50, 6.80, 3.30;
Owner Scuderia Del Clan **Bred** Gestut Auenquelle **Trained** Switzerland

563 WOLVERHAMPTON (A.W) (L-H)
Monday, February 15

OFFICIAL GOING: Tapeta: standard
Wind: Fresh across Weather: Fine

589 DOWNLOAD THE NEW UNIBET RACING APP H'CAP 5f 20y (Tp)
1:50 (1:50) (Class 6) (0-55,55) 4-Y-O+ **£2,587** (£770; £384; £192) **Stalls** Low

Form RPR
00-0 **1** **Novabridge**[14] 418 8-9-3 **51**...(b) AdamKirby 8 56
(Phil McEntee) *mde all: rdn over 1f out: all out* **9/2**[3]

60-3 **2** nse **Cockle Town Boy**[28] 241 4-9-0 **48**........................... StevieDonohoe 3 53
(Brendan Powell) *hld up: hdwy over 1f out: rdn and swtchd rt wl ins fnl f: r.o* **7/2**[2]

-442 **3** nse **Pancake Day**[14] 418 4-9-7 **55**......................................(v) BenCurtis 2 60
(Jason Ward) *chsd ldrs: rdn and ev ch ins fnl f: r.o* **3/1**[1]

0-34 **4** 1/2 **Time Medicean**[14] 418 10-9-3 **54**......................... GeorgeDowning(3) 4 57+
(Tony Carroll) *hld up: pushed along 1/2-way: hdwy over 1f out: rdn and nt clr run ins fnl f: r.o* **13/2**

-020 **5** 1 1/4 **Rat Catcher (IRE)**[7] 504 6-9-4 **55**.............................(b) RobHornby(3) 5 54
(Lisa Williamson) *hld up: pushed along on outer 2f out: r.o towards fin: nt rch ldrs* **7/1**

0-11 **6** 3/4 **Lizzy's Dream**[5] 513 8-9-6 **54** 6ex.................................. DanielTudhope 6 50
(Rebecca Bastiman) *prom: rdn 1/2-way: edgd lft and styd on same pce ins fnl f* **7/2**[2]

5-00 **7** 3/4 **Warm Order**[14] 418 5-9-1 **49**.....................................(b) WilliamCarson 11 45
(Tony Carroll) *sn chsng wnr: rdn and ev ch over 1f out: styng on same pce whn hmpd and eased wl ins fnl f* **20/1**

060- **8** 3/4 **Bilash**[154] 6387 9-9-3 **51**.. PaulQuinn 9 41
(Sarah Hollinshead) *prom: rdn over 1f out: styd on same pce* **50/1**

1m 1.65s (-0.25) **Going Correction** -0.125s/f (Stan) **8** Ran SP% **120.2**
Speed ratings (Par 101): **97,96,96,96,94 92,91,90**
CSF £21.85 CT £56.19 TOTE £7.80: £2.60, £1.50, £1.40; EX 38.40 Trifecta £160.50.

Owner Power Geneva Ltd **Bred** Bishopswood Bloodstock & Trickledown Stud **Trained** Newmarket, Suffolk

■ Stewards' Enquiry : Stevie Donohoe five-day ban: careless riding (Feb 29-Mar 4)

FOCUS

The opening contest was a moderate sprint handicap. They went a decent gallop on standard Tapeta. The winner has been rated back to form.

590 LADBROKES H'CAP 7f 32y (Tp)

2:20 (2:21) (Class 6) (0-60,60) 4-Y-O+ **£2,587** (£770; £384; £192) **Stalls** High

Form RPR

02-0 **1** **Caledonia Laird**[31] 201 5-9-6 **59** JoeyHaynes 9 69
(Jo Hughes) *a.p: rdn to ld ins fnl f: edgd rt: r.o* **18/1**

4-40 **2** *nk* **Zed Candy Girl**[13] 430 6-9-2 **55** (p) StevieDonohoe 4 64
(Daniel Mark Loughnane) *a.p: rdn and swtchd rt over 1f out: r.o* **12/1**

316- **3** *3/4* **Mr Christopher (IRE)**[55] 8351 4-9-7 **60** RichardKingscote 5 67
(Tom Dascombe) *chsd ldr 4f: rdn over 1f out: edgd rt ins fnl f: styd on* **3/1**[2]

3-40 **4** *1/2* **Bailiwick**[22] 321 5-9-7 **60** (b) GeorgeBaker 3 66
(Daniel Kubler) *chsd ldrs: rdn over 1f out: styd on same pce wl ins fnl f* **9/2**[3]

3-42 **5** *1/2* **Hawk Moth (IRE)**[24] 297 8-9-4 **57** (p) LukeMorris 12 61
(John Spearing) *hld up: hdwy over 1f out: r.o* **14/1**

0-06 **6** *hd* **Pipers Piping (IRE)**[21] 334 10-8-10 **52** RobHornby(3) 7 56
(Mandy Rowland) *hld up: rdn and r.o ins fnl f: nt rch ldrs* **22/1**

-005 **7** *3/4* **Admirable Art (IRE)**[14] 424 6-9-4 **57** (p) AdamKirby 11 59
(Tony Carroll) *hld up: pushed along over 2f out: styd on u.p ins fnl f: nt trble ldrs* **11/2**

1-13 **7** *dht* **Fairy Foxglove (IRE)**[3] 542 6-9-5 **58** TonyHamilton 10 60
(P J F Murphy, Ire) *chsd ldrs: wnt 2nd 3f out: rdn and ev ch over 1f out: no ex ins fnl f* **11/4**[1]

-135 **9** *1 1/4* **Mercury**[9] 482 4-9-5 **58** (b) KeaganLatham 1 56
(Kevin Ryan) *led: rdn over 1f out: hdd and no ex ins fnl f* **7/1**

2-05 **10** *1/2* **Mac's Power (IRE)**[17] 387 10-9-7 **60** (b[1]) TomQueally 2 57
(Willie Musson) *hld up: racd keenly: rdn over 1f out: styd on same pce ins fnl f* **16/1**

40-6 **11** *1/2* **Riverlynx (IRE)**[24] 294 4-8-7 **46** oh1 (p) JoeFanning 8 42
(Ben Haslam) *hld up: rdn over 2f out: n.d* **33/1**

1m 27.64s (-1.16) **Going Correction** -0.125s/f (Stan) **11** Ran SP% **130.5**
Speed ratings (Par 101): **101,100,99,99,98 98,97,97,96,95 95**
CSF £239.67 CT £850.69 TOTE £29.20: £7.00, £3.50, £1.60; EX 367.50 Trifecta £2917.90.
Owner Isla & Colin Cage **Bred** Mrs I M Cage And Mr C J Cage **Trained** Lambourn, Berks

FOCUS

Another moderate handicap. They went a decent gallop. A surprise pb from the winner.

591 32RED CASINO MAIDEN FILLIES' STKS 1m 141y (Tp)

2:50 (2:51) (Class 5) 3-Y-O+ **£3,557** (£1,058; £529; £264) **Stalls** Low

Form RPR

1 **Beauly** 3-8-5 0 LukeMorris 5 75+
(Charles Hills) *chsd ldrs: shkn up to ld over 1f out: rdn and edgd rt ins fnl f: styd on: wnt lft towards fin* **5/6**[1]

0- **2** *1 3/4* **Divine Joy**[77] 8048 3-8-5 0 LiamJones 9 71
(Marco Botti) *chsd ldr over 7f out: led over 2f out: hdd over 1f out: styd on same pce ins fnl f* **10/1**

50- **3** *3 1/4* **Rock 'n Red (IRE)**[147] 6589 3-8-5 0 JoeFanning 1 64
(Ed Dunlop) *prom: hmpd over 7f out: rdn over 1f out: styd on same pce* **16/1**

5- **4** *3/4* **Asafoetida (IRE)**[95] 7810 3-8-5 0 WilliamCarson 4 62
(Peter Chapple-Hyam) *sn led: hdd over 7f out: chsd ldrs: swtchd rt over 3f out: sn rdn: styd on same pce fr over 1f out* **7/2**[2]

3-05 **5** *6* **Perfect Fit (IRE)**[30] 223 4-9-7 67 PatrickO'Donnell(5) 2 54
(Tony Coyle) *chsd ldrs: led over 7f out: rdn and hdd over 2f out: wknd over 1f out* **14/1**

62 **6** *1 1/2* **Our Little Sister (IRE)**[17] 384 3-7-12 0 CharlieBennett(7) 8 45
(Hughie Morrison) *prom and sn pushed along: lost pl over 6f out: n.d after* **9/2**[3]

0 **7** *7* **Regent's Rock**[17] 384 4-9-12 0 PJMcDonald 7 35
(Peter Niven) *s.i.s: hld up: a in rr* **50/1**

0-0 **8** *24* **Ice Cristal (IRE)**[37] 122 3-8-5 0 MartinDwyer 6
(Sylvester Kirk) *bhd fnl 6f* **100/1**

1m 48.64s (-1.46) **Going Correction** -0.125s/f (Stan)
WFA 3 from 4yo 21lb **8** Ran SP% **119.6**
Speed ratings (Par 100): **101,99,96,95,90 89,83,61**
CSF £11.86 TOTE £2.10: £1.10, £2.50, £2.70; EX 12.00 Trifecta £91.00.
Owner R A Bartlett **Bred** New England, Mount Coote & P Barrett **Trained** Lambourn, Berks

FOCUS

An ordinary fillies' maiden. They went a respectable gallop. It's been rated loosely around the fourth close to her debut run.

592 32REDSPORT.COM H'CAP 2m 119y (Tp)

3:20 (3:20) (Class 6) (0-60,63) 4-Y-O+ **£2,587** (£770; £384; £192) **Stalls** Low

Form RPR

/1-1 **1** **Little Stampy (IRE)**[35] 150 5-9-10 **60** (p) ShaneGray 7 69+
(D Broad, Ire) *hld up in tch: chsd ldr over 2f out: led wl over 1f out: sn rdn clr: eased nr fin* **15/8**[1]

60-0 **2** *2 1/2* **Unex Modigliani (IRE)**[12] 435 7-9-7 **57** (p) TonyHamilton 5 61
(Derek Shaw) *dwlt: hld up: hdwy over 2f out: rdn over 1f out: styd on same pce ins fnl f: wnt 2nd nr fin* **14/1**

645- **3** *hd* **Iguacu**[154] 5989 12-8-10 **46** oh1 JoeFanning 3 49
(Richard Price) *dwlt: hld up: hdwy over 3f out: rdn over 1f out: styd on same pce ins fnl f* **80/1**

60-5 **4** *2* **Yorkshireman (IRE)**[40] 71 6-9-0 **50** (v) JoeyHaynes 2 51
(Lynn Siddall) *prom: lost pl 4f out: rallied over 1f out: rdn and swtchd rt ins fnl f: styd on same pce* **8/1**[3]

0/21 **5** *3* **Pass The Time**[5] 521 7-9-13 **63** 6ex (p) LiamKeniry 9 60
(Neil Mulholland) *w ldr tl led over 5f out: rdn and hdd wl over 1f out: wknd ins fnl f* **15/8**[1]

04-0 **6** *6* **Symbolist (IRE)**[21] 329 4-9-4 **60** (t) AdamBeschizza 1 50
(John Norton) *hld up: rdn and wknd over 2f out* **66/1**

0-43 **7** *1* **Heurtevent (FR)**[14] 417 7-9-0 **50** (t) LukeMorris 4 39
(Tony Carroll) *prom: chsd ldr over 4f out tl rdn and lost 2nd over 2f out: wknd over 1f out* **14/1**

2-32 **8** *1/2* **Medieval Bishop (IRE)**[7] 498 7-9-3 **60** (p) PaddyBradley(7) 8 48
(Tony Forbes) *chsd ldrs: rdn over 2f out: sn wknd* **13/2**[2]

0-52 **9** *73* **Indian Scout**[17] 378 8-8-10 **46** (b) KieranO'Neill 6
(Anabel K Murphy) *led: hdd over 5f out: sn rdn: wknd over 3f out: eased* **20/1**

3m 36.79s (-6.91) **Going Correction** -0.125s/f (Stan)
WFA 4 from 5yo+ 6lb **9** Ran SP% **114.8**
Speed ratings (Par 101): **111,109,109,108,107 104,104,103,69**
CSF £32.32 CT £1547.42 TOTE £3.10: £1.40, £2.90, £8.60; EX 27.90 Trifecta £867.50.
Owner A Broad **Bred** John Lyons **Trained** Summerhill, Co Meath

FOCUS

A modest staying handicap. They went an even gallop. The winner has been rated back to her old best.

593 32RED.COM H'CAP 1m 1f 103y (Tp)

3:50 (3:50) (Class 5) (0-70,69) 3-Y-O **£3,557** (£1,058; £529; £264) **Stalls** Low

Form RPR

055- **1** **Space Mountain**[140] 6809 3-9-7 **69** JoeFanning 1 75+
(Mark Johnston) *mde virtually all: rdn and edgd rt over 1f out: styd on* **3/1**[2]

62-2 **2** *1 1/4* **Gabster (IRE)**[17] 376 3-9-4 **66** AdamKirby 4 68
(Amanda Perrett) *hld up: rdn over 2f out: hdwy over 1f out: styd on to go 2nd wl ins fnl f: nt rch wnr* **4/1**[3]

3-52 **3** *1 1/2* **Dr Drey (IRE)**[17] 379 3-9-6 **68** TimmyMurphy 3 67
(Jamie Osborne) *chsd ldrs: pushed along over 3f out: rdn to chse wnr on outer over 2f out: no ex ins fnl f* **5/4**[1]

01-5 **4** *6* **Frap**[28] 243 3-8-13 **61** TonyHamilton 2 47
(Richard Fahey) *chsd ldrs: rdn over 2f out: wknd fnl f* **8/1**

666- **5** *13* **Ressurreto (IRE)**[240] 3383 3-8-10 **58** PJMcDonald 5 17
(Keith Dalgleish) *racd keenly: wnt 2nd over 7f out tl rdn over 2f out: wknd over 1f out* **12/1**

1m 59.57s (-1.23) **Going Correction** -0.125s/f (Stan) **5** Ran SP% **108.2**
Speed ratings (Par 97): **100,98,97,92,80**
CSF £14.35 TOTE £3.60: £2.00, £1.50; EX 12.80 Trifecta £28.40.
Owner J M Brown **Bred** Qatar Bloodstock Ltd **Trained** Middleham Moor, N Yorks

FOCUS

A modest 3yo handicap. They went a respectable gallop. The runner-up has been rated to her Lingfield latest.

594 CORAL H'CAP 1m 1f 103y (Tp)

4:20 (4:20) (Class 2) (0-105,105) 4-Y-O+

£11,827 (£3,541; £1,770; £885; £442; £222) **Stalls** Low

Form RPR

1-66 **1** **Intrude**[16] 401 4-8-5 **89** MartinDwyer 1 97
(David Simcock) *hld up and bhd: hdwy over 1f out: rdn to ld wl ins fnl f: r.o* **12/1**

261- **2** *nk* **Razor Wind (IRE)**[296] 1651 5-9-2 **100** AdamKirby 4 107
(Charlie Appleby) *trckd ldrs: nt clr run 2f out: rdn to ld 1f out: hdd wl ins fnl f: r.o u.p* **5/4**[1]

222- **3** *1 1/4* **Mont Ras (IRE)**[67] 8168 9-8-10 **94** ShaneGray 2 98
(David Loughnane) *chsd ldrs: rdn over 1f out: styd on* **16/1**

3-31 **4** *hd* **Solar Deity (IRE)**[21] 333 7-9-4 **105** DanielMuscutt(3) 3 109
(Marco Botti) *hld up: hdwy over 1f out: sn rdn: kpt on* **13/2**

5-31 **5** *1 1/4* **Dance Of Fire**[4] 530 4-8-5 **89** 6ex CathyGannon 7 90
(Andrew Balding) *racd keenly: disp ld tl wnt on over 7f out: rdn and hdd 1f out: styd on same pce* **7/2**[2]

01-0 **6** *nk* **Jack Of Diamonds (IRE)**[16] 401 7-8-2 **86** CamHardie 6 86
(Roger Teal) *s.i.s: hld up: rdn on outer over 2f out: styd on ins fnl f: nt trble ldrs* **33/1**

6326 **7** *1 1/2* **Whispering Warrior (IRE)**[4] 530 7-8-9 **93** SeanLevey 5 90
(David Simcock) *disp ld tl settled to trck ldr over 7f out: rdn over 2f out: no ex fnl f* **11/2**[3]

1m 58.53s (-2.27) **Going Correction** -0.125s/f (Stan) **7** Ran SP% **111.9**
Speed ratings (Par 109): **105,104,103,103,102 102,100**
CSF £26.46 TOTE £12.60: £4.40, £1.30; EX 43.20 Trifecta £523.40.
Owner Happy Valley Racing & Breeding Limited **Bred** Wallace Holmes & Partners **Trained** Newmarket, Suffolk

■ Stewards' Enquiry : Daniel Muscutt two-day ban: used whip above permitted level (Mar 1-2)

FOCUS

The feature contest was a good quality handicap. They went an even gallop. The third helps set the standard.

595 CORAL.CO.UK H'CAP 1m 1f 103y (Tp)

4:50 (4:51) (Class 4) (0-80,80) 4-Y-O+ **£5,175** (£1,540; £769; £384) **Stalls** Low

Form RPR

5-30 **1** **Idol Deputy (FR)**[10] 465 10-8-11 **75** (p) RachealKneller(5) 5 82
(James Bennett) *hld up: hdwy over 1f out: r.o to ld and edgd lft wl ins fnl f* **8/1**

330- **2** *3/4* **Sands Chorus**[143] 6716 4-8-13 **72** PJMcDonald 8 77
(James Given) *chsd clr ldr: tk clsr order over 2f out: led over 1f out: rdn and hdd wl ins fnl f* **8/1**

-255 **3** *1* **Stosur (IRE)**[23] 313 5-9-4 **77** (b) AdamKirby 6 80
(Gay Kelleway) *hld up: hdwy over 2f out: rdn and ev ch over 1f out: styd on same pce ins fnl f* **6/1**[3]

12/6 **4** *3/4* **Elysian Prince**[21] 332 5-9-1 **74** (t) LiamJones 4 76
(Neil King) *chsd ldrs: rdn over 1f out: styd on* **7/2**[2]

23-5 **5** *3 3/4* **Miss Minuty**[21] 330 4-9-4 **80** RobHornby(3) 3 74
(Tony Newcombe) *hld up: hdwy on outer over 1f out: no ex fnl f* **8/1**

50-0 **6** *3/4* **Dana's Present**[39] 82 7-9-0 **73** RichardKingscote 2 65
(Tom Dascombe) *led and sn clr: c bk to the field over 2f out: rdn and hdd over 1f out: wknd ins fnl f* **9/1**

1-53 **7** *2 1/2* **Tatting**[10] 464 7-8-8 **67** ShaneGray 1 54
(Conor Dore) *chsd ldrs: rdn over 3f out: wknd fnl f* **8/1**

0-3 **8** *2 3/4* **Toga Tiger (IRE)**[21] 332 9-9-2 **75** SeanLevey 7 56
(Kevin Frost) *hld up: rdn over 2f out: sn wknd* **3/1**[1]

1m 58.03s (-2.77) **Going Correction** -0.125s/f (Stan) **8** Ran SP% **116.0**
Speed ratings (Par 105): **107,106,105,104,101 100,98,96**
CSF £70.29 CT £413.73 TOTE £10.00: £2.80, £1.90, £1.80; EX 87.50 Trifecta £339.00.
Owner Miss J C Blackwell **Bred** Sheikh Sultan Bin Khalifa Al Nayan **Trained** Letcombe Bassett, Oxon

FOCUS

The concluding race was a fairly decent handicap. The free front-runner set this up for a closer. It's possible the race could be rated higher, but the winner is not an obvious improver.

T/Jkpt: Not won. T/Plt: £87.80 to a £1 stake. Pool: £77,467.04 - 643.73 winning units. T/Qpdt: £17.90 to a £1 stake. Pool: £6,950.19 - 286.74 winning units. **Colin Roberts**

577 SOUTHWELL (L-H)

Tuesday, February 16

OFFICIAL GOING: Fibresand: standard

Wind: Strong across Weather: Fine & dry

596 UNIBET OFFER DAILY JOCKEY/TRAINER SPECIALS H'CAP 6f (F)

2:00 (2:01) (Class 6) (0-55,55) 4-Y-O+ **£2,587** (£770; £384; £192) **Stalls** Low

Form RPR

66-0 **1** **First Excel**[18] 387 4-9-2 **55**........................ AaronJones(5) 2 62
(Roy Bowring) *sn rdn along and outpcd in rr: hdwy 3f out: chsd ldrs 2f out: rdn to chal and edgd rt ent fnl f: kpt on wl to ld last 100yds* **4/1**[2]

-264 **2** *hd* **Arizona Snow**[26] 272 4-9-5 **53**........................ LukeMorris 6 59
(Ronald Harris) *chsd ldrs on outer: wd st: hdwy over 2f out: rdn to ld and edgd lft wl over 1f out: drvn and hung lft ent fnl f: hdd last 100yds: kpt on* **3/1**[1]

5443 **3** *1 3/4* **Hab Reeh**[15] 418 8-9-4 **52**........................ JamesSullivan 7 53
(Ruth Carr) *prom: cl up 1/2-way: rdn 2f out and ev ch: n.m.r and hmpd ent fnl f: kpt on same pce* **4/1**[2]

0405 **4** *1/2* **Ciaras Cookie (IRE)**[6] 525 4-8-9 **46** oh1........................(t) DannyBrock(3) 5 45
(Heather Dalton) *cl up: led after 2f: rdn along wl over 2f out: hdd wl over 1f out: sn drvn and kpt on same pce fnl f* **8/1**

-064 **5** *hd* **Glenbuck Lass (IRE)**[6] 513 4-8-12 **46** oh1........................ SaleemGolam 3 44
(Alan Bailey) *trckd ldrs: effrt over 2f out and sn rdn: drvn over 1f out: kpt on same pce* **9/2**[3]

50-0 **6** *3* **Upper Lambourn (IRE)**[15] 418 8-8-12 **46** oh1........................ JoeFanning 4 35
(Christopher Kellett) *slt ld on inner 2f: rdn along 1/2-way: drvn wl over 1f out and sn wknd* **12/1**

062/ **7** *1/2* **Ripon Rose**[540] 5767 4-9-3 **51**........................ PaulMulrennan 9 38
(Paul Midgley) *cl up: wd st: rdn over 2f out: sn wknd* **22/1**

4-00 **8** *5* **Marmooz**[6] 525 4-8-12 **46** oh1........................(v1) LiamJones 10 17
(Michael Appleby) *racd wd: in tch: rdn along and wd st: sn outpcd* **16/1**

1m 18.79s (2.29) **Going Correction** +0.25s/f (Slow) 8 Ran SP% **112.2**
Speed ratings (Par 101): **94,93,91,90,90 86,85,79**
CSF £15.77 CT £49.68 TOTE £4.70: £1.50, £1.70, £1.60; EX 17.00 Trifecta £82.50.
Owner S R Bowring **Bred** S R Bowring **Trained** Edwinstowe, Notts

FOCUS
Despite a very cold night, the track had not been worked. A very moderate handicap to start and a few still held a chance coming to the last furlong. The runner-up has been rated to his best.

597 32RED H'CAP 1m (F)

2:35 (2:35) (Class 6) (0-65,63) 3-Y-O **£2,587** (£770; £384; £192) **Stalls** Low

Form RPR

1-31 **1** **Kemsing (IRE)**[26] 274 3-9-3 **62**........................ ShelleyBirkett(3) 2 71+
(Julia Feilden) *broke wl: restrained and hld up in rr: smooth hdwy on inner over 3f out and sn trcking ldrs: swtchd rt 2f out: shkn up to chal and edgd lft over 1f out: drvn and edgd lft ins fnl f: kpt on to ld last 50yds* **6/5**[1]

00-4 **2** *1/2* **Granita (USA)**[26] 274 3-8-10 **57**........................ JosephineGordon(5) 6 63
(George Scott) *cl up: led 2f out: rdn over 1f out: drvn ins fnl f: hdd and no ex last 50yds* **8/1**

05-5 **3** *4* **Tombe Girl**[18] 384 3-9-3 **59**........................ JoeFanning 5 56
(Keith Dalgleish) *slt ld: hdd 2f out and sn rdn: drvn appr fnl f and kpt on same pce* **7/1**

0-13 **4** *4* **Carbutt's Ridge (IRE)**[26] 274 3-8-13 **55**........................ DougieCostello 3 43
(K R Burke) *chsd ldrs: rdn along and sltly outpcd 3f out: wd st: drvn on outer 2f out: sn one pce* **5/1**[3]

-442 **5** *7* **Sea Of Uncertainty**[21] 335 3-9-7 **63**........................(v) BenCurtis 4 35
(Michael Appleby) *cl up on outer: rdn along wl over 2f out: drvn wl over 1f out: sn wknd* **4/1**[2]

-455 **6** *16* **Ready Steady (USA)**[2] 578 3-9-1 **57**........................ ShaneGray 1
(David Loughnane) *chsd ldrs: rdn along wl over 3f out: sn outpcd and bhd* **40/1**

1m 45.99s (2.29) **Going Correction** +0.25s/f (Slow) 6 Ran SP% **108.2**
Speed ratings (Par 95): **98,97,93,89,82 66**
CSF £10.62 TOTE £2.00: £1.10, £3.30; EX 9.30 Trifecta £42.10.
Owner Miss J Feilden **Bred** D Dwan **Trained** Exning, Suffolk

FOCUS
A moderate 3yo handicap, but another tight finish. The runner-up has been rated close to her debut figure, with the third to her maiden form.

598 DOWNLOAD THE LADBROKES APP H'CAP 7f (F)

3:05 (3:12) (Class 5) (0-75,72) 4-Y-O+ **£3,234** (£962; £481; £240) **Stalls** Low

Form RPR

1640 **1** **Moonlight Venture**[2] 581 5-9-2 **67**........................(b) LiamKeniry 6 79
(Conor Dore) *chsd ldrs on outer: hdwy over 2f out: led 1 1/2f out: sn rdn clr: readily* **9/1**

36-3 **2** *7* **Red Unico (IRE)**[19] 367 4-9-0 **65**........................ BenCurtis 2 59
(Michael Appleby) *chsd ldrs on inner: hdwy over 2f out: rdn wl over 1f out: sn drvn and kpt on same pce* **6/1**[3]

46-4 **3** *nk* **Best Tamayuz**[46] 1 5-9-2 **67**........................(p) LukeMorris 9 60
(Scott Dixon) *prom: rdn along and outpcd 3f out: styd on u.p appr fnl f: fin wl* **6/1**[3]

624- **4** *hd* **Make On Madam (IRE)**[126] 7190 4-8-13 **64**........................ JasonHart 8 57
(Les Eyre) *t.k.h: chsd ldrs: n.m.r after 3f and sn lost pl: in rr and rdn 3f out: hdwy on inner rail over 2f out: sn drvn to chse ldrs: kpt on same pce* **16/1**

-614 **5** *2* **Llewellyn**[12] 449 8-9-7 **72**........................(b) DanielTudhope 1 59
(Declan Carroll) *qckly away and led: rdn along over 2f out: hdd 1 1/2f out: grad wknd* **12/1**

-132 **6** *nk* **Stun Gun**[14] 429 6-8-9 **60**........................(p) TonyHamilton 3 47
(Derek Shaw) *towards rr: pushed along 1/2-way: hdwy on outer 2f out: kpt on u.p fnl f: nrst fin* **8/1**

04/3 **7** *1 1/4* **Anton Chigurh**[12] 437 7-9-0 **68**........................ DannyBrock(3) 7 51
(Philip McBride) *cl up: rdn along over 2f out: sn drvn and wknd* **11/2**[2]

-511 **8** *1 3/4* **The Firm (IRE)**[14] 429 7-8-12 **66**........................(be) RobHornby(3) 4 45
(Daniel Mark Loughnane) *dwlt: a in rr* **5/1**[1]

2243 **9** *1 1/2* **Clockmaker (IRE)**[12] 446 10-9-7 **72**........................ PaulMulrennan 5 47
(Conor Dore) *dwlt: a in rr* **13/2**

5462 **10** *3/4* **Alpha Tauri (USA)**[6] 523 10-9-3 **68**........................ ShaneGray 11 41
(Charles Smith) *dwlt: sn prom: chsd ldr 3f out: sn rdn and wknd 2f out* **11/1**

1m 30.08s (-0.22) **Going Correction** +0.25s/f (Slow) 10 Ran SP% **117.0**
Speed ratings (Par 103): **111,103,102,102,100 99,98,96,94,93**
CSF £62.34 CT £362.52 TOTE £11.00: £3.20, £2.60, £2.10; EX 80.50 Trifecta £711.40.
Owner Mrs Jennifer Marsh **Bred** G Reed **Trained** Hubbert's Bridge, Lincs

FOCUS
An ordinary, albeit open handicap containing a few who normally like to be up there, so a decent pace was always likely. The winner hosed up and has been rated back to his old best.

599 LADBROKES H'CAP 7f (F)

3:40 (3:45) (Class 3) (0-95,94) 4-Y-O+ **£7,439** (£2,213; £1,106; £553) **Stalls** Low

Form RPR

1-12 **1** **Philba**[37] 134 4-8-11 **87**........................(tp) AlistairRawlinson(3) 9 99
(Michael Appleby) *cl up on outer: effrt 2f out: led wl over 1f out: rdn clr and edgd lft appr fnl f: styd on strly* **7/2**[2]

101- **2** *1 3/4* **Ian's Memory (USA)**[56] 8342 5-9-7 **94**........................(b) LukeMorris 1 101
(Jeremy Noseda) *trckd ldrs on inner: pushed along 3f out: rdn 2f out: drvn over 1f out: styd on wl fnl f* **5/2**[1]

-014 **3** *hd* **Big Time (IRE)**[9] 494 5-8-13 **86**........................(p) FrannyNorton 6 92
(David Nicholls) *cl up: effrt over 2f out and ev ch: rdn wl over 1f out: drvn over 1f out: kpt on same pce* **13/2**

1-50 **4** *1 1/4* **Westwood Hoe**[31] 221 5-9-4 **91**........................ BenCurtis 7 94
(Tony Coyle) *in tch: pushed along and hdwy on outer over 2f out: rdn to chse ldrs wl over 1f out: sn drvn and no imp fnl f* **8/1**

5-52 **5** *1 1/4* **Robert The Painter (IRE)**[24] 313 8-8-9 **82**........................(v) JoeFanning 3 82
(Lee Carter) *led: rdn along over 2f out: hdd wl over 1f out: sn drvn and grad wknd* **14/1**

4-50 **6** *3 1/4* **Bertiewhittle**[10] 486 8-9-1 **88**........................ GrahamGibbons 5 79
(David Barron) *dwlt and in rr: hdwy and wd st: rdn 2f out: n.d* **14/1**

1-P4 **7** *5* **Mr Bossy Boots (IRE)**[25] 290 5-8-10 **88**........................(t) PatrickO'Donnell(5) 4 66
(Ralph Beckett) *trckd ldrs: pushed along over 3f out: rdn wl over 2f out: sn drvn and btn* **4/1**[3]

03-0 **8** *3/4* **Dubai Hills**[37] 134 10-8-12 **85**........................(v) SamJames 2 61
(David O'Meara) *in tch on inner: pushed along 1/2-way: rdn 3f out: sn outpcd and bhd* **33/1**

1m 30.56s (0.26) **Going Correction** +0.25s/f (Slow) **8** Ran SP% **111.5**
Speed ratings (Par 107): **108,106,105,104,102 99,93,92**
CSF £12.01 CT £51.21 TOTE £3.80: £1.60, £1.40, £2.00; EX 11.70 Trifecta £62.90.
Owner T Johnson **Bred** T F T F Ltd **Trained** Oakham, Rutland

FOCUS
A warm handicap and a strong pace was always likely with at least a couple in here that like to force it. The third helps set the standard.

600 LADBROKES MAIDEN STKS 1m (F)

4:15 (4:23) (Class 5) 3-Y-O+ **£2,911** (£866; £432; £216) **Stalls** Low

Form RPR

23- **1** **Hutton (IRE)**[61] 8259 3-8-9 0........................ TonyHamilton 8 75
(Richard Fahey) *cl up: chal 2f out: rdn to ld ent fnl f: kpt on wl towards fin* **8/1**

05-2 **2** *1/2* **Rain In The Face**[26] 275 3-8-9 73........................ GrahamGibbons 5 74
(Ralph Beckett) *led: pushed along over 2f out: rdn wl over 1f out: hdd ent fnl f: sn drvn and kpt on* **6/5**[1]

3 *1 1/2* **Four Mile Beach** 3-8-9 0........................ JoeFanning 6 70
(Mark Johnston) *dwlt: sn cl up on outer: pushed along 3f out and wd st: rdn: green and sltly outpcd wl over 1f out: edgd lft and kpt on fnl f* **9/2**[3]

4 *hd* **Mr Boomer (USA)** 4-10-0 0........................(v1) LukeMorris 4 76
(Jeremy Noseda) *trckd ldng pair on inner: bmpd bnd at 1/2-way: effrt over 2f out and sn rdn: drvn over 1f out: kpt on same pce fnl f* **10/3**[2]

5 *hd* **Sir Runs A Lot** 4-10-0 0........................ PaulMulrennan 7 75
(David Barron) *trckd ldrs: smooth hdwy 3f out: effrt whn n.m.r and green wl over 1f out: sn rdn and kpt on same pce fnl f* **25/1**

6 *13* **Masterful Man (IRE)** 3-8-9 0........................ BenCurtis 3 40
(K R Burke) *s.i.s: green and sn rdn along in rr: a outpcd* **12/1**

7 *38* **Eddy Mercs** 4-10-0 0........................ RaulDaSilva 2
(Ivan Furtado) *in tch: hdwy on inner and cl up whn nt clr run and hmpd bnd after 4f: nt rcvr and sn bhd* **33/1**

1m 45.59s (1.89) **Going Correction** +0.25s/f (Slow)
WFA 3 from 4yo 19lb 7 Ran SP% **112.3**
Speed ratings (Par 103): **100,99,98,97,97 84,46**
CSF £17.47 TOTE £8.90: £4.70, £1.10; EX 16.60 Trifecta £73.30.
Owner David W Armstrong **Bred** Patrick Byrnes **Trained** Musley Bank, N Yorks
■ Basil Bear was withdrawn. Price at time of withdrawal 66/1. Rule 4 does not apply.

FOCUS
This maiden had gone to a 3yo nine times in the previous ten years and that trend continues, with the first two the only ones with previous experience. It's been rated a bit cautiously, with the runner-up a bit off his C&D latest.

601 CORAL H'CAP 1m 4f (F)

4:50 (4:55) (Class 6) (0-65,64) 4-Y-O+ **£2,587** (£770; £384; £192) **Stalls** Low

Form RPR

1 **Lifting Me Higher (IRE)**[18] 395 4-8-8 **54**........................ JFEgan 7 65
(W P Browne, Ire) *led: pushed along and jnd 3f out: rdn 2f out: rdr dropped whip wl over 1f out: hdd over 1f out: rallied gamely ins fnl f to ld again last 100yds* **10/11**[1]

00-2 **2** *1 1/4* **Star Ascending (IRE)**[12] 445 4-8-13 **59**........................ JoeFanning 3 68
(Jennie Candlish) *trckd ldng pair: hdwy to trck wnr 7f out: cl up 3f out: sn chal: rdn wl over 1f out: led appr fnl f: sn drvn: hdd and no ex last 100yds* **3/1**[2]

635/ **3** *9* **Thankyou Very Much**[300] 6865 6-9-7 **64**........................(p) PJMcDonald 6 59
(James Bethell) *trckd ldrs: hdwy over 4f out: rdn to chse ldng pair wl over 2f out: sn drvn and kpt on same pce* **10/1**

0/03 **4** *1 1/2* **Mcvicar**[19] 368 7-8-10 **53**........................ SamJames 8 45
(John Davies) *hld up in tch: hdwy 4f out: rdn along 3f out: sn drvn and plugged on same pce* **13/2**[3]

-604 **5** *2 3/4* **Arsenale (GER)**[2] 577 5-8-9 **52**........................(p) LukeMorris 5 40
(Michael Appleby) *chsd ldrs: rdn along over 3f out: drvn 2f out: sn one pce* **20/1**

055- **6** *17* **Chauvelin**[61] 8269 5-9-1 **58**........................(e) JasonHart 4 19
(Richard Guest) *hld up in rr: swtchd rt to outer and pushed along over 5f out: sn outpcd and bhd* **12/1**

300- **7** *19* **Oracle Boy**[147] 6630 5-9-5 **62**........................(p) JoeyHaynes 1
(Michael Chapman) *prom: rdn along 1/2-way: sn lost pl and bhd* **66/1**

2m 44.58s (3.58) **Going Correction** +0.25s/f (Slow)
WFA 4 from 5yo+ 3lb 7 Ran SP% **113.8**
Speed ratings (Par 101): **98,97,91,90,88 77,64**
CSF £3.73 CT £14.49 TOTE £1.90: £1.10, £1.90; EX 4.80 Trifecta £25.40.
Owner Mrs Paul Shanahan **Bred** Mrs C Regalado-Gonzalez **Trained** Fethard, Co Tipperary

FOCUS
A moderate handicap in which the first two pulled clear, but there was a little bit of drama. The runner-up has been rated back to his best.
T/Plt: £8.70 to a £1 stake. Pool: £90,065.89 - 7,534.07 winning tickets. T/Qpdt: £5.40 to a £1 stake. Pool: £7,434.96 - 1,001.45 winning tickets. **Joe Rowntree**

[513]KEMPTON (A.W) (R-H)

Wednesday, February 17

OFFICIAL GOING: Polytrack: standard

Wind: light 1/2 behind Weather: raining and cold

602 HAPPY 80TH BIRTHDAY CLIVE MARK MARKLEY APPRENTICE H'CAP 1m 2f (P)

5:20 (5:20) (Class 7) (0-50,54) 4-Y-O+ **£1,940** (£577; £288; £144) **Stalls** Low

Form RPR

-030 **1** **Time Square (FR)**[7] 514 9-9-2 **50**....(t) MitchGodwin(5) 8 60
(Tony Carroll) *sn led: clr over 2f out: drvn out* **10/1**

0-44 **2** *3 ¼* **Ferryview Place**[4] 569 7-9-2 **50**....(tp) PaulBooth(5) 4 54
(Ian Williams) *hld up in rr: t.k.h: hdwy and hung tight over 2f out: chsd wnr 1f out: no imp* **9/2**[3]

3-04 **3** *½* **Solveig's Song**[7] 514 4-9-2 **46**....(p) JosephineGordon 10 49
(Steve Woodman) *chsd ldrs: effrt over 2f out: kpt on same pce appr fnl f* **4/1**[2]

00-0 **4** *1 ¾* **Standing Strong (IRE)**[31] 233 8-9-1 **49**....(p) SophieKilloran(5) 2 48+
(Zoe Davison) *s.s: hld up in rr: hdwy over 2f out: kpt on fnl f* **16/1**

06-6 **5** *1 ¾* **Plover**[36] 155 6-8-13 **45**.... CallumShepherd(3) 11 41
(Michael Attwater) *sn chsng ldrs: hung rt 2f out: wknd over 1f out* **10/1**

-041 **6** *2* **Star Links (USA)**[7] 514 10-9-4 **54** 6ex....(t) BenSanderson(7) 6 46+
(Sylvester Kirk) *s.i.s: hdwy after 2f: sn trcking ldrs: effrt 2f out: wknd over 1f out* **3/1**[1]

3-00 **7** *nk* **Ron Waverly (IRE)**[8] 505 6-8-12 **46**....(t) DanielleMooney(5) 1 37
(Paddy Butler) *rr-div: effrt 2f out: n.m.r: kpt on fnl f: nvr a factor* **14/1**

0-05 **8** *2 ¼* **Eeny Mac (IRE)**[19] 388 9-8-11 **45**....(p) HarryBurns(5) 5 31
(John Wainwright) *chsd ldrs: 2nd over 2f out: wknd over 1f out* **10/1**

-004 **9** *hd* **Ambitious Rosie**[16] 412 5-8-11 **45**....(p) RhiainIngram(5) 3 31
(Tony Carroll) *led early: trckd ldrs: wknd 2f out* **33/1**

0-00 **10** *1 ¾* **North Bay Lady (IRE)**[34] 170 4-8-10 **45**....(b) HollieDoyle(5) 12 28
(John Wainwright) *in rr: drvn 4f out: nvr on terms* **100/1**

000- **11** *5* **Wowee**[79] 8044 5-9-3 **49**....(t) GeorgiaCox(3) 9 22
(Tony Carroll) *trckd ldrs: drvn 4f out: lost pl over 1f out: eased clsng stages* **7/1**

2m 7.89s (-0.11) **Going Correction** -0.025s/f (Stan)
WFA 4 from 5yo+ 1lb **11** Ran SP% **119.4**
Speed ratings (Par 97): **99,96,96,94,93 91,91,89,89,88 84**
CSF £55.50 CT £215.49 TOTE £14.60: £3.60, £1.90, £2.00; EX 85.00 Trifecta £753.00.
Owner M S Cooke **Bred** Mme Therese Bouche & Isabelle Roussel **Trained** Cropthorne, Worcs

FOCUS
A low-grade handicap in which the winner was let loose on the lead. The third has been rated close to his recent form.

603 32RED.COM MAIDEN STKS 1m 2f (P)

5:50 (5:52) (Class 5) 3-4-Y-O **£3,072** (£914; £456; £228) **Stalls** Low

Form RPR

06-2 **1** **Cat Royale (IRE)**[26] 287 3-8-4 72....(p) DannyBrock(3) 11 75
(Jane Chapple-Hyam) *chsd ldrs: drvn 3f out: led over 1f out: hld on clsng stages* **12/1**

2 *¾* **Angelical Dancer (FR)** 3-8-7 0.... AndreaAtzeni 1 73+
(Marco Botti) *t.k.h early: trckd ldrs: drvn 3f out: edgd lft over 1f out: styd on to take 2nd clsng stages* **12/1**

3 *nk* **Isharah (USA)** 3-8-7 0.... JoeFanning 7 73+
(Mark Johnston) *hmpd s: sn chsng ldrs: drvn 3f out: styd on wl fnl f: tk 3rd nr fin* **6/4**[1]

3P- **4** *¾* **Air Of Astana (IRE)**[198] 4947 4-10-0 0.... MartinHarley 3 76
(Hugo Palmer) *led: hdd over 1f out: wknd last 50yds* **9/2**[2]

5 **5** *½* **The Magic Pencil (IRE)**[26] 287 3-8-7 0.... ShaneGray 4 71
(Kevin Ryan) *hld up in mid-div: hdwy 4f out: hung rt and kpt on same pce over 1f out: n.m.r clsng stages* **10/1**

5 *dht* **Shoofly (IRE)** 3-7-9 0.... HollieDoyle(7) 5 65
(Martyn Meade) *hmpd s: mid-div: hdwy 5f out: kpt on same pce over 1f out* **16/1**

34 **7** *2 ¼* **Muaither (IRE)**[26] 287 3-8-7 0....(b[1]) WilliamCarson 6 66
(John Gosden) *awkward leaving stalls: in rr: hdwy over 2f out: kpt on fnl f* **8/1**

8 *6* **Rockery (IRE)** 3-8-2 0.... JoeyHaynes 2 49
(Ed Dunlop) *trckd ldrs: effrt over 2f out: sn lost pl* **25/1**

420- **9** *1* **Darebin (GER)**[33] 4821 4-9-9 78.... CallumShepherd(5) 12 57
(Gary Moore) *in rr: bhd fnl 2f* **13/2**[3]

0/ **10** *4* **Pandora's Pyx**[483] 7377 4-9-9 0.... RichardKingscote 13 44
(Gary Moore) *wnt lft s and slowly away: sn drvn along in rr: bhd fnl 2f* **100/1**

0 **11** *25* **Lmntrix**[9] 500 4-9-7 0.... LuluStanford(7) 10
(George Margarson) *mid-div: t.k.h: rn v wd bnd 4f out: sn t.o* **100/1**

2m 6.94s (-1.06) **Going Correction** -0.025s/f (Stan)
WFA 3 from 4yo 22lb **11** Ran SP% **118.8**
Speed ratings (Par 103): **103,102,102,101,101 101,99,94,93,90 70**
CSF £147.33 TOTE £12.60: £3.80, £3.10, £1.20; EX 156.20 Trifecta £807.90.
Owner Bryan Hirst Ltd & S&G Refurbishments Ltd **Bred** Kellsgrange Stud & Ruskerne Ltd **Trained** Dalham, Suffolk

FOCUS
A fair maiden. They finished in a bit of a heap, but the winner and fourth made the decisive move when quickening on the turn in. It's been rated around the first four.

604 32RED ON THE APP STORE H'CAP 5f (P)

6:20 (6:21) (Class 5) (0-75,75) 4-Y-O+ **£2,911** (£866; £432; £216) **Stalls** Low

Form RPR

1-52 **1** **Miracle Garden**[12] 462 4-9-6 **74**....(p) AdamKirby 1 84
(Roy Brotherton) *trckd ldrs: led on ins jst ins fnl f: edgd lft: drvn out* **15/8**[1]

0-05 **2** *1 ¼* **Diamond Charlie (IRE)**[11] 484 8-9-7 **75**.... JoeFanning 4 80
(Simon Dow) *n.m.r s: towards rr: hdwy over 1f out: keeping on to take 2nd nr fin* **11/2**[3]

33-0 **3** *nk* **Mossgo (IRE)**[42] 56 6-9-4 **72**....(t) WilliamCarson 2 76
(John Best) *led: hdd jst ins fnl f: kpt on same pce* **4/1**[2]

06-5 **4** *1* **Ask The Guru**[40] 100 6-8-10 **64**....(v) RobertHavlin 3 64
(Michael Attwater) *chsd ldrs: kpt on same pce last 150yds* **16/1**

3-03 **5** *¾* **Powerful Wind (IRE)**[20] 364 7-9-5 **73**.... RichardKingscote 7 71
(Charlie Wallis) *hld up in rr: hdwy and n.m.r over 1f out: kpt on clsng stages* **10/1**

130- **6** *½* **Temple Road (IRE)**[57] 8347 8-9-4 **72**....(bt) FrannyNorton 6 68
(Milton Bradley) *s.s: in rr: hdwy on outside over 1f out: kpt on: nt rch ldrs* **14/1**

6-03 **7** *1 ¼* **Archie Stevens**[11] 484 6-9-4 **75**.... PhilipPrince(3) 5 66
(David Evans) *w ldr: drvn over 2f out: wknd fnl 150yds* **7/1**

50-6 **8** *2 ½* **Johnny Splash (IRE)**[25] 319 7-9-0 **68**....(v) RobertWinston 9 50
(Roger Teal) *in rr: nvr a factor: b.b.v* **25/1**

1-30 **9** *hd* **Roy's Legacy**[26] 293 7-8-8 **62**.... ShaneGray 8 44
(Shaun Harris) *w ldrs: lost pl after 2f: bhd fnl 2f* **20/1**

59.01s (-1.49) **Going Correction** -0.025s/f (Stan) **9** Ran SP% **112.9**
Speed ratings (Par 103): **110,108,107,105,104 103,101,97,97**
CSF £11.91 CT £35.93 TOTE £2.30: £1.40, £2.20, £1.50; EX 13.10 Trifecta £54.90.
Owner M A Geobey **Bred** W And R Barnett Ltd **Trained** Elmley Castle, Worcs

FOCUS
The market leaders dominated here. The third has been rated close to his best.

605 32RED H'CAP 1m 2f (P)

6:50 (6:50) (Class 4) (0-85,83) 4-Y-O+ **£4,690** (£1,395; £697; £348) **Stalls** Low

Form RPR

01-1 **1** **Buckland Beau**[45] 33 5-9-3 **79**.... StevieDonohoe 2 86+
(Charlie Fellowes) *hld up in rr: t.k.h: hdwy to trck ldrs over 3f out: styd on to ld last 100yds* **9/4**[2]

631- **2** *nk* **Fit The Bill (IRE)**[63] 8256 4-9-4 **81**.... LukeMorris 3 87
(James Tate) *sn trcking ldr: drvn over 2f out: led and edgd rt over 1f out: hdd and no ex last 100yds* **11/10**[1]

16-0 **3** *3 ¼* **Top Diktat**[35] 165 8-9-1 **77**.... AdamKirby 1 76
(Gary Moore) *trckd ldng pair: n.m.r on inner over 1f out: one pce fnl f* **9/1**

230- **4** *3 ½* **Aldeburgh**[68] 8093 7-9-7 **83**.... WilliamTwiston-Davies 4 75
(Nigel Twiston-Davies) *led: hdd and n.m.r over 1f out: wknd fnl f: eased clsng stages* **9/2**[3]

2m 6.91s (-1.09) **Going Correction** -0.025s/f (Stan)
WFA 4 from 5yo+ 1lb **4** Ran SP% **106.6**
Speed ratings (Par 105): **103,102,100,97**
CSF £5.02 TOTE £2.30; EX 5.90 Trifecta £11.50.
Owner P S McNally **Bred** D G Hardisty Bloodstock **Trained** Newmarket, Suffolk

FOCUS
A bit of a messy, tactical race which turned into a dash in the straight. The second has been rated as running a pb.

606 RACING UK 3 DEVICES 1 PRICE H'CAP 1m 4f (P)

7:20 (7:20) (Class 6) (0-65,65) 4-Y-O+ **£2,264** (£673; £336; £168) **Stalls** Centre

Form RPR

2-32 **1** **Weld Arab (IRE)**[14] 435 5-9-7 **65**.... LukeMorris 7 73
(Michael Blake) *led after 1f: set stdy pce: qcknd gallop over 2f out: rdn and edgd lft over 1f out: hld on clsng stages* **2/1**[1]

160- **2** *½* **Sandy Cove**[120] 7359 5-9-4 **65**.... RyanTate(3) 2 72
(James Eustace) *sn trcking wnr: upsides over 4f out: no ex clsng stages* **9/2**[2]

3104 **3** *1 ¾* **Shirataki (IRE)**[19] 378 8-8-3 **54**.... LuluStanford(7) 5 58+
(Peter Hiatt) *hld up in rr: hdwy over 1f out: styd on same pce to take 3rd towards fin* **11/1**

0-42 **4** *¾* **Fair Comment**[21] 348 6-9-4 **62**.... RobertHavlin 1 65
(Michael Blanshard) *led early: trckd ldrs: t.k.h: effrt 2f out: kpt on same pce to take 4th last 75yds* **5/1**[3]

0-05 **5** *2* **Leonard Thomas**[25] 316 6-9-3 **64**.... GeorgeDowning(3) 9 64+
(Tony Carroll) *s.s: in rr: drvn over 2f out: kpt on clsng stages* **8/1**

55-0 **6** *¾* **Occult**[28] 256 4-9-4 **65**.... JimCrowley 3 64
(Simon Dow) *dwlt: t.k.h towards rr: effrt over 2f out: hdwy on ins over 1f out: nvr a threat* **8/1**

-540 **7** *1 ¾* **Jazri**[25] 316 5-9-5 **63**....(b) FrannyNorton 4 59
(Milton Bradley) *mid-div: t.k.h: effrt 2f out: nvr a threat* **14/1**

23-5 **8** *1 ¼* **Bennelong**[42] 62 10-8-8 **59**....(b) RhiainIngram(7) 6 53
(Lee Carter) *sn led: hdd after 1f: chsd ldrs: wknd appr fnl f* **12/1**

2m 37.09s (2.59) **Going Correction** -0.025s/f (Stan)
WFA 4 from 5yo+ 3lb **8** Ran SP% **113.1**
Speed ratings (Par 101): **90,89,88,88,86 86,85,84**
CSF £10.62 CT £76.02 TOTE £2.50: £1.10, £1.70, £3.20; EX 11.90 Trifecta £79.50.
Owner The Moonlighters **Bred** Shadwell Estate Company Limited **Trained** Trowbridge, Wilts

FOCUS
They went no pace here and the two up front had it between them from the turn in. The third has been rated just off his recent best.

607 £10 FREE BET AT 32REDSPORT.COM H'CAP (DIV I) 7f (P)

7:50 (7:51) (Class 6) (0-65,65) 4-Y-O+ **£2,264** (£673; £336; £168) **Stalls** Low

Form RPR

3-12 **1** **Chetan**[35] 167 4-9-7 **65**....(tp) LukeMorris 5 72
(Charlie Wallis) *trckd ldrs: drvn over 2f out: led narrowly 1f out: rdr dropped rt rein: all out* **5/1**[2]

0-04 **2** *nse* **Ajig**[33] 191 5-9-4 **62**....(tp) JohnFahy 3 68
(Eve Johnson Houghton) *trckd ldrs: led briefly over 1f out: kpt on wl: jst failed* **14/1**

0-41 **3** *¾* **Nasri**[35] 167 10-9-6 **64**.... TomQueally 4 68
(Emma Owen) *led 2f: drvn over 2f out: styd on same pce clsng stages* **8/1**[3]

5-54 **4** *hd* **Only Ten Per Cent (IRE)**[35] 167 8-9-0 **61**.... AlistairRawlinson(3) 2 64+
(J R Jenkins) *s.i.s: in rr: hdwy over 1f out: styd on wl clsng stages* **14/1**

6-06 **5** *1 ¼* **West Leake (IRE)**[18] 403 10-8-13 **57**.... LiamKeniry 7 57
(Paul Burgoyne) *hld up in mid-div: t.k.h: effrt over 2f out: edgd rt: kpt on one pce appr fnl f: hld whn n.m.r nr fin* **16/1**

051- **6** *1* **Captain Kendall (IRE)**[49] 8393 7-8-7 **51**....(p) CathyGannon 6 48
(Harry Chisman) *w ldr: led after 2f: hdd over 1f out: fdd clsng stages* **11/1**

65-5 **7** *2 ½* **Muzaahim (IRE)**[31] 231 5-9-1 **59**.... JoeFanning 1 50
(Kevin Morgan) *trckd ldrs: t.k.h: wkng whn n.m.r jst ins fnl f* **4/1**[1]

000- **8** *½* **Showtime Blues**[51] 8376 4-9-5 **63**....(b) AdamKirby 8 55
(Jim Boyle) *mid-div: drvn over 2f out: chsng ldrs over 1f out: sn wknd* **4/1**[1]

560- **9** *nse* **Pike Corner Cross (IRE)**[84] 7974 4-9-7 **65**.... GeorgeBaker 9 54
(Gary Moore) *hld up in rr: t.k.h: effrt over 2f out: wknd over 1f out* **8/1**[3]

25-3 **10** *10* **Polar Kite (IRE)**[11] 482 8-9-2 **63**.... RobHornby(3) 10 25
(Michael Attwater) *in rr: gd hdwy on outer 2f out: lost pl over 1f out: bhd whn eased clsng stages: b.b.v* **10/1**

1m 26.04s (0.04) **Going Correction** -0.025s/f (Stan) **10** Ran SP% **115.5**
Speed ratings (Par 101): **98,97,97,96,95 94,91,90,90,79**
CSF £71.69 CT £551.91 TOTE £4.70: £1.90, £4.40, £4.50; EX 75.10 Trifecta £410.00.
Owner Roger & Val Miles, Tony Stamp **Bred** Andrew W Robson **Trained** Ardleigh, Essex

FOCUS
A modest contest, and the slower of the two divisions by 0.5sec. The second and third have been rated to form.

608 **£10 FREE BET AT 32REDSPORT.COM H'CAP (DIV II)** **7f (P)**
8:20 (8:20) (Class 6) (0-65,65) 4-Y-O+ **£2,264** (£673; £336; £168) **Stalls** Low

Form RPR
4-10 **1** **Bookmaker**[25] 316 6-9-3 **61**..(b) WilliamCarson 8 67
(John Bridger) *chsd ldr: drvn over 2f out: led and edgd lft appr fnl f: hld on clsng stages* **9/1**
0-23 **2** 1/2 **Gold Beau (FR)**[35] 167 6-9-7 **65**................................(p) CathyGannon 4 69
(Kristin Stubbs) *trckd ldrs: t.k.h: drvn over 2f out: hung rt: n.m.r over 1f out: styd on clsng stages* **11/4**[1]
5-01 **3** nse **Cookie Ring (IRE)**[28] 257 5-8-1 **52**............................(v) PaulaMuir[(7)] 7 56+
(Patrick Holmes) *dwlt: in rr: hdwy 2f out: styd on wl fnl 150yds* **6/1**[2]
-025 **4** 1/2 **Blackthorn Stick (IRE)**[18] 403 7-9-1 **59**........................ JimmyQuinn 6 62
(Paul Burgoyne) *mid-div: hdwy over 3f out: chsng ldrs over 1f out: kpt on same pce last 50yds* **13/2**[3]
40-0 **5** 1 1/4 **Foie Gras**[19] 387 6-9-5 **63**.. IrineuGoncalves 1 63
(Chris Dwyer) *in rr: effrt over 2f out: styd on fnl f* **14/1**
2-05 **6** hd **Emperors Warrior (IRE)**[13] 442 4-8-13 **57**........(b) RichardKingscote 5 56
(Gary Moore) *led: hdd appr fnl f: wknd last 50yds* **11/1**
0-52 **7** 1 1/4 **Black Truffle (FR)**[19] 387 6-9-1 **64**.................... RachealKneller[(5)] 2 60
(Mark Usher) *hld up in mid-div: hdwy 2f out: kpt on same pce fnl f* **6/1**[2]
045- **8** 1/2 **Deluxe**[70] 8158 4-8-12 **63**... PaddyBradley[(7)] 9 57
(Pat Phelan) *trckd ldrs: t.k.h: effrt 2f out: one pce appr fnl f* **10/1**
-243 **9** 16 **Major Muscari (IRE)**[13] 444 8-9-4 **62**.......................(p) MartinHarley 3 13
(Shaun Harris) *in rr: drvn over 2f out: lost pl over 1f out: eased whn bhd* **8/1**

1m 25.54s (-0.46) **Going Correction** -0.025s/f (Stan) **9** Ran SP% **113.8**
Speed ratings (Par 101): **101,100,100,99,98 98,96,96,77**
CSF £33.49 CT £163.38 TOTE £12.30: £3.10, £1.10, £2.70; EX 41.30 Trifecta £229.50.
Owner T Wallace & J J Bridger **Bred** Benjamin Newton And Graycroft Farm **Trained** Liphook, Hants

FOCUS
An open handicap and the faster of the two divisions by 0.5sec. The winner has been rated to form.

609 **32RED CASINO H'CAP** **1m (P)**
8:50 (8:51) (Class 6) (0-55,55) 4-Y-O+ **£2,264** (£673; £336; £168) **Stalls** Low

Form RPR
-402 **1** **Zed Candy Girl**[2] 590 6-9-0 **55**................................(p) PaddyBradley[(7)] 6 63
(Daniel Mark Loughnane) *in rr-div: hdwy on outside 2f out: styd on wl: led nr fin* **5/1**[2]
06-4 **2** nk **McDelta**[21] 347 6-9-7 **55**.. GeorgeBaker 1 62
(Geoffrey Deacon) *sn trcking ldrs: led jst ins fnl f: hdd and no ex nr fin* **7/4**[1]
36-3 **3** 3/4 **Gavarnie Encore**[21] 346 4-9-3 **51**.................................. RobertHavlin 7 56
(Michael Blanshard) *chsd ldrs: edgd lft 2f out:styd on same pce last 150yds* **9/1**[3]
5021 **4** nk **Little Big Man**[16] 412 5-9-5 **53**...................................... StevieDonohoe 8 57
(Brendan Powell) *led: hdd jst ins fnl f: no ex* **9/1**[3]
1-30 **5** 1/2 **Foylesideview (IRE)**[23] 334 4-9-2 **50**........................... CathyGannon 4 53+
(Harry Chisman) *s.i.s: effrt whn nt clr run 2f out: styd on wl fnl f* **9/1**[3]
-422 **6** 1 3/4 **Hagree (IRE)**[19] 388 5-8-12 **49**.................................(t) KevinStott[(3)] 10 48
(Jose Santos) *mid-div: effrt over 2f out: one pce appr fnl f* **14/1**
50-5 **7** nk **Affectionate Lady (IRE)**[14] 431 5-8-12 **49**.....(v) NataliaGemelova[(3)] 12 47
(Keith Reveley) *mid-div: hdwy over 2f out: kpt on one pce appr fnl f* **25/1**
-401 **8** 3/4 **Fairy Mist (IRE)**[28] 252 9-9-4 **52**...........................(b) WilliamCarson 13 49
(John Bridger) *swtchd rt after s: bhd: effrt whn hmpd 2f out: styd on fnl f* **33/1**
10-6 **9** 1/2 **Candesta (USA)**[29] 247 6-9-7 **55**...........................(t) AdamBeschizza 5 51
(Julia Feilden) *s.i.s: bhd and sn drvn along: kpt on over 1f out: nvr a factor* **14/1**
06-6 **10** nk **Mariners Moon (IRE)**[21] 347 5-8-13 **54**.......................... PaulaMuir[(7)] 14 49
(Patrick Holmes) *mid-div: effrt over 2f out: wknd over 1f out* **33/1**
6-43 **11** 4 **Evident (IRE)**[26] 297 6-9-7 **55**...(p) AdamKirby 9 41
(Tony Carroll) *chsd ldrs: hmpd and lost pl 2f out: eased whn bhd clsng stages* **10/1**
00-0 **12** 4 1/2 **Haames (IRE)**[28] 252 9-9-1 **49**..................................(be[1]) JoeFanning 11 24
(Kevin Morgan) *w ldrs: lost pl 2f out: eased whn bhd clsng stages* **20/1**
/0-0 **13** 4 **Rectitude**[21] 347 5-8-13 **50**.. EoinWalsh[(3)] 3 16
(Henry Tett) *chsd ldrs: wknd 2f out: eased whn bhd clsng stages* **100/1**

1m 39.22s (-0.58) **Going Correction** -0.025s/f (Stan) **13** Ran SP% **120.9**
Speed ratings (Par 101): **101,100,99,99,97 97,97,96,95,95 91,87,83**
CSF £13.49 CT £79.86 TOTE £8.20: £2.30, £1.30, £3.20; EX 17.30 Trifecta £162.50.
Owner J T Stimpson **Bred** H H L Bloodstock **Trained** Baldwin's Gate, Staffs

FOCUS
A moderate handicap but it featured some in-form horses. The form is set around the third and fourth.
T/Jkpt: Not won. T/Plt: £52.10 to a £1 stake. Pool: £73,827.47 - 1034.31 winning units. T/Qpdt: £11.70 to a £1 stake. Pool: £8,615.97 - 542.62 winning units. **Walter Glynn**

556 LINGFIELD (L-H)
Wednesday, February 17

OFFICIAL GOING: Polytrack: standard
Wind: light, behind Weather: overcast

610 **32RED CASINO H'CAP** **7f 1y(P)**
1:30 (1:30) (Class 6) (0-65,65) 3-Y-O **£2,264** (£673; £336; £168) **Stalls** Low

Form RPR
3-15 **1** **Inaam (IRE)**[26] 291 3-9-6 **64**.. DavidNolan 7 70
(Richard Fahey) *t.k.h: chsd ldng pair: effrt and hung lft over 1f out: swtchd rt 1f out: str run ins fnl f to ld towards fin* **4/1**[1]
5-32 **2** 3/4 **Silver Springs (IRE)**[13] 443 3-9-6 **64**............................... AdamKirby 11 68
(David Evans) *sn led and crossed to inner: rdn and fnd ex 2f out: drvn 1f out: hdd and no ex towards fin* **9/2**[2]
-224 **3** 1 1/4 **Kristoff (IRE)**[14] 436 3-8-2 **53**...................................... RhiainIngram[(7)] 3 54
(Jim Boyle) *chsd ldr: rdn and sltly outpcd 2f out: tried to rally 1f out: lost 2nd and styd on same pce fnl 100yds* **7/1**[3]
50-6 **4** nse **Packing (IRE)**[13] 443 3-9-2 **60**.. TimmyMurphy 5 60+
(Jamie Osborne) *hld up in tch in midfield: effrt 2f out: edging lft over 1f out: hdwy ins fnl f: styd on: eased last strides* **7/1**[3]
6-60 **5** 1 **Daydream (IRE)**[29] 249 3-8-10 **59**..............................(t) LucyKBarry[(5)] 4 57
(Jamie Osborne) *chsd ldng pair: effrt on inner but unable qck over 1f out: kpt on same pce ins fnl f* **16/1**
00-3 **6** 1 1/4 **More Kudos (USA)**[23] 328 3-8-6 **50**................................ FrannyNorton 9 44
(John Quinn) *in tch in midfield: rdn ent fnl 2f: unable qck and styd on same pce after* **4/1**[1]
20-4 **7** 2 **Sunbaked (IRE)**[13] 443 3-9-2 **60**...................................(p) TomQueally 1 49+
(Eve Johnson Houghton) *awkward leaving stalls and slowly away: in tch in midfield: rdn and no imp wl over 1f out* **7/1**[3]
066- **8** nk **Ron's Ballad**[193] 5149 3-8-2 **46** oh1.................................. KieranO'Neill 8 34+
(Michael Madgwick) *in tch in last trio: effrt 2f out: no imp: nvr trbld ldrs* **66/1**
130- **9** 1/2 **Multigifted**[120] 7361 3-9-2 **60**.. LiamKeniry 10 47+
(Michael Madgwick) *s.i.s: rn in snatches: pushed along and hdwy on outer over 4f out: lost pl 3f out: no hdwy u.p 2f out* **16/1**
32-6 **10** 1 **Home Again**[19] 376 3-9-7 **65**.. AmirQuinn 2 49+
(Lee Carter) *s.i.s: a in rr: n.d* **10/1**

1m 25.74s (0.94) **Going Correction** +0.025s/f (Slow) **10** Ran SP% **118.0**
Speed ratings (Par 95): **95,94,92,92,91 90,87,87,86,85**
CSF £22.24 CT £126.67 TOTE £4.70: £2.00, £1.20, £2.40; EX 16.10 Trifecta £79.40.
Owner Yorkshire Connections Ltd **Bred** John Doyle **Trained** Musley Bank, N Yorks

FOCUS
A moderate handicap to start. The runner-up has been rated to form.

611 **£10 FREE AT 32RED.COM MEDIAN AUCTION MAIDEN FILLIES' STKS** **6f 1y(P)**
2:00 (2:01) (Class 6) 3-5-Y-O **£2,587** (£770; £384; £192) **Stalls** Low

Form RPR
-02 **1** **Mossy's Lodge**[13] 441 3-8-8 0.. WilliamCarson 2 62+
(Anthony Carson) *trckd ldrs: wnt 2nd 4f out: effrt wl over 1f out: drvn to chal 1f out: kpt on u.p to ld wl ins fnl f* **7/4**[1]
340- **2** 1/2 **Lady Lloyd**[48] 8409 3-8-8 63...(p) LukeMorris 3 60
(Phil McEntee) *led: rdn 2f out: hrd pressed and drvn 1f out: hdd and styd on same pce wl ins fnl f* **6/1**
0- **3** 1 3/4 **Heathfield Park (IRE)**[57] 8350 3-8-3 0................ JosephineGordon[(5)] 1 54
(William Stone) *chsd ldr tl 4f out: trckd ldng pair tl rdn and sltly outpcd 2f out: rallied 1f out: styd on same pce ins fnl f* **33/1**
3 **4** 3 **Ventura Falcon (IRE)**[7] 516 3-8-1 0............................. HollieDoyle[(7)] 5 45
(Richard Hannon) *restless in stalls: hld up in tch in last pair: rdn and outpcd 2f out: wknd ins fnl f* **2/1**[2]
320- **5** 1 3/4 **Pouliche**[128] 7167 3-8-8 68... FrannyNorton 4 39
(Harry Dunlop) *hld up in tch in last pair: struggling over 2f out: bhd and wl hld over 1f out* **7/2**[3]

1m 14.08s (2.18) **Going Correction** +0.025s/f (Slow) **5** Ran SP% **109.1**
Speed ratings (Par 98): **86,85,83,79,76**
CSF £12.05 TOTE £2.40: £1.20, £2.60; EX 12.90 Trifecta £77.80.
Owner MacAttack **Bred** N Poole And A Franklin **Trained** Newmarket, Suffolk

FOCUS
A modest fillies' maiden, though four of the five runners had already been placed on the AW. The runner-up has been rated to form.

612 **32RED.COM H'CAP** **6f 1y(P)**
2:35 (2:35) (Class 4) (0-80,79) 3-Y-O **£4,690** (£1,395; £697; £348) **Stalls** Low

Form RPR
1 **1** **Buying Trouble (USA)**[14] 432 3-9-7 **79**........................... AdamKirby 5 86+
(David Evans) *restless in stalls: in tch in last pair: hdwy on outer 2f out: effrt over 1f out: r.o to chal and rdn ins fnl f: led towards fin* **5/4**[1]
-340 **2** shd **Sir Dudley (IRE)**[7] 519 3-9-1 **73**...................................... JimCrowley 6 76
(James Given) *chsd ldr: rdn and ev ch over 1f out: led ins fnl f: kpt on tl hdd and no ex towards fin* **4/1**[3]
16-5 **3** 2 1/4 **Fashionata (IRE)**[21] 344 3-9-0 **72**............................. GrahamGibbons 2 68
(Kristin Stubbs) *trckd ldng pair: effrt on inner and ev ch over 1f out: no ex 100yds out: sn wknd* **16/1**
56-1 **4** 1/2 **Jess**[26] 286 3-8-9 **67**.. ShaneGray 3 61
(Kevin Ryan) *led: rdn over 1f out: hdd and no ex ins fnl f: wknd fnl 75yds: drifted rt towards fin* **7/1**
06-4 **5** 1 **War Department (IRE)**[25] 315 3-9-7 **79**...................(p) WilliamCarson 1 70
(Michael Bell) *s.i.s: hld up in tch in last pair: effrt over 1f out: swtchd rt and rdn jst ins fnl f: no imp and wl hld whn carried rt towards fin* **11/4**[2]
0-00 **6** 6 **Fishergate**[21] 344 3-8-7 **65**.. AdamBeschizza 4 37
(Richard Rowe) *in tch in midfield: rdn and dropped to last over 1f out: wknd over 1f out* **100/1**

1m 11.67s (-0.23) **Going Correction** +0.025s/f (Slow) **6** Ran SP% **110.5**
Speed ratings (Par 99): **102,101,98,98,96 88**
CSF £6.42 TOTE £2.40: £1.40, £1.70; EX 6.30 Trifecta £42.60.
Owner Mrs I M Folkes **Bred** Flaxman Holdings Limited **Trained** Pandy, Monmouths

FOCUS
An interesting 3yo sprint handicap won by a nice prospect. The runner-up has been rated to his winter form.

613 **32RED CASINO CLAIMING STKS** **1m 2f (P)**
3:10 (3:12) (Class 6) 3-Y-O **£2,264** (£673; £336; £168) **Stalls** Low

Form RPR
30-1 **1** **Frivolous Lady (IRE)**[37] 147 3-8-7 65 ow1.........................(v) JFEgan 6 58
(David Evans) *mde all: dictated stdy gallop tl rdn over 3f out: drvn over 1f out: hld on wl ins fnl f* **4/1**
1-34 **2** 3/4 **Masqueraded (USA)**[7] 522 3-9-2 70..............................(p) LukeMorris 4 66
(Gay Kelleway) *t.k.h: chsd wnr thrght: rdn over 3f out: swtchd rt 2f out and sn drvn: kpt on u.p: a hld ins fnl f* **7/2**[3]
5-64 **3** nk **Khismet**[34] 182 3-8-6 72...(p) CharlesEddery[(5)] 5 60
(Rae Guest) *stdd s: trckd ldrs: clsd and pressed ldrs on outer over 4f out: rdn over 3f out: styd on same pce u.p fnl f* **9/4**[1]
5 **4** 1/2 **Il Sassicaia**[12] 458 3-9-1 0.. DanielMuscutt[(3)] 1 66?
(Marco Botti) *restless in stalls: s.i.s: in tch in last pair: rdn over 3f out: sme hdwy 1f out: styd on same pce ins fnl f* **6/1**
-015 **5** 2 1/4 **Adventure Zone (IRE)**[13] 443 3-8-11 67.............(p) MeganNicholls[(7)] 3 61
(Richard Hannon) *stdd s: hld up in tch in rr: rdn over 3f out: styd on same pce and no imp fnl f* **3/1**[2]

2m 10.45s (3.85) **Going Correction** +0.025s/f (Slow) **5** Ran SP% **112.3**
Speed ratings (Par 95): **85,84,84,83,81**
CSF £18.20 TOTE £3.20: £1.70, £2.20; EX 7.00 Trifecta £17.10.
Owner B Drew & W Clifford **Bred** Rory O'Brien **Trained** Pandy, Monmouths

FOCUS
A moderate 3yo claimer, though four of the five runners were previous winners. They went very steadily which played into the hands of the winner.

614 32RED CONDITIONS STKS 1m 7f 169y(P)
3:45 (3:45) (Class 2) 4-Y-O+ **£11,971** (£3,583; £1,791; £896; £446) **Stalls** Low

Form RPR
12/1 **1** **Arch Villain (IRE)**[33] 194 7-9-2 98 JimCrowley 6 103
(Amanda Perrett) *chsd ldr: rdn 3f out: drvn over 1f out and stdy on to chal ins fnl f: led cl home* **5/4**[1]
000- **2** *hd* **John Reel (FR)**[179] 5641 7-9-2 97 JFEgan 5 102
(David Evans) *led: rdn 3f out: drvn ent fnl f: kpt on u.p tl hdd and no ex cl home* **5/1**[3]
003- **3** *1 ½* **Notarised**[147] 6640 5-9-2 100 JoeFanning 4 100+
(Mark Johnston) *in tch in midfield: effrt in 3rd 2f out: styd on same pce u.p ins fnl f* **7/2**[2]
455- **4** *1 ½* **Monaleen (IRE)**[84] 7977 5-8-11 91 RichardKingscote 3 93+
(Ian Williams) *stdd s: hld up in tch in rr: effrt on inner over 1f out: chsd ldng trio 1f out: styd on same pce u.p ins fnl f* **7/1**
5-44 **5** *1 ¾* **Castilo Del Diablo (IRE)**[9] 499 7-9-2 93 (b) AdamKirby 2 96
(David Simcock) *hld up in tch in last trio: effrt over 2f out: drvn and no imp over 1f out* **10/1**
-155 **6** *3 ¼* **Luv U Whatever**[9] 499 6-9-2 97 LiamJones 1 92
(Michael Appleby) *chsd ldrs: rdn wl over 2f out: lost pl 2f out: wknd fnl f* **20/1**
111- **7** *2 ¼* **Frosty Berry**[61] 8284 7-8-11 82 ShaneGray 7 85
(Ed de Giles) *hld up in tch in last pair: rdn wl over 2f out: no imp and swtchd rt wl over 1f out: bhd fnl f* **25/1**

3m 20.42s (-5.28) **Going Correction** +0.025s/f (Slow) **7** Ran SP% **113.5**
Speed ratings (Par 109): **114,113,113,112,111 109,108**
CSF £7.79 TOTE £1.90: £1.40, £2.30; EX 10.30 Trifecta £32.40.
Owner Mr & Mrs F Cotton, Mr & Mrs P Conway **Bred** Summerhill Bloodstock **Trained** Pulborough, W Sussex

FOCUS
A fascinating staying conditions event, but they only went an ordinary pace and it didn't pick up until the last half-mile. The runner-up has been rated close to his best.

615 BET AND WATCH EVERY RACE AT UNIBET H'CAP 6f 1y(P)
4:20 (4:20) (Class 6) (0-65,64) 4-Y-O+ **£2,587** (£770; £384; £192) **Stalls** Low

Form RPR
35-5 **1** **New Rich**[35] 167 6-9-4 61 (b) JohnFahy 3 68
(Eve Johnson Houghton) *wnt rt and bmpd s: detached in last pair: rdn and hdwy on inner over 1f out: str run to ld fnl 100yds: sn in command: r.o wl* **7/2**[2]
22- **2** *1 ¼* **Copper Cavalier**[145] 6717 5-8-12 55 (p) RobertHavlin 2 58
(Michael Blanshard) *in tch in midfield: nt clr run over 2f out: rdn and hdwy over 1f out: ev ch jst ins fnl f: 2nd and outpcd by wnr fnl 100yds* **8/1**
13-2 **3** *½* **Ghost Train (IRE)**[18] 398 7-9-7 64 (p) LukeMorris 5 65
(Tim McCarthy) *chsd ldr tl over 3f out: effrt u.p over 1f out: ev ch jst ins fnl f: 3rd and one-pced fnl 100yds* **6/4**[1]
055- **4** *¾* **Perfect Bounty**[88] 7940 4-9-4 61 AdamKirby 4 60
(Patrick Chamings) *bmpd s: sn rcvrd and led: rdn 2f out: drvn over 1f out: hdd ins fnl f: outpcd fnl 100yds* **6/1**
0-50 **5** *¾* **Autumn Tonic (IRE)**[11] 482 4-8-12 55 (b[1]) JimCrowley 6 56+
(Simon Dow) *hld up in tch: clsd to trck ldrs whn nt clr run ent fnl f: nvr enough room thrght fnl f and unable to chal* **9/2**[3]
-044 **6** *3 ¼* **Buraug**[13] 442 4-8-13 56 (b) FrannyNorton 7 42
(Milton Bradley) *hmpd after 1f: in tch in midfield: effrt and wd 2f out: sn no imp: wknd ins fnl f* **7/1**
60-0 **7** *2 ¼* **Blackasyourhat (IRE)**[13] 442 4-8-6 52 (t) RobHornby[(3)] 9 31
(Michael Attwater) *hdwy to press ldrs after 1f: wnt 2nd over 3f out tl lost pl u.p wl over 1f out: wknd fnl f* **33/1**
0-6 **8** *7* **Whip Up A Frenzy (IRE)**[40] 100 4-9-3 60 AdamBeschizza 8 17
(Richard Rowe) *a in rr: rdn 2f out: wl bhd ins fnl f* **50/1**

1m 11.51s (-0.39) **Going Correction** +0.025s/f (Slow) **8** Ran SP% **123.2**
Speed ratings (Par 101): **103,101,100,99,98 94,91,82**
CSF £34.15 CT £60.53 TOTE £4.60: £1.90, £1.80, £1.10; EX 28.20 Trifecta £62.10.
Owner Eden Racing Club **Bred** Whitsbury Manor Stud And Mrs M E Slade **Trained** Blewbury, Oxon

FOCUS
A moderate sprint handicap in which few came into the race in much form, but the pace was decent. The winner has been rated to form, while the third has been rated a bit off his recent form.

616 CORAL H'CAP 1m 2f (P)
4:55 (4:55) (Class 5) (0-75,75) 4-Y-O+ **£2,911** (£866; £432; £216) **Stalls** Low

Form RPR
2/64 **1** **Elysian Prince**[2] 595 5-9-6 74 (t) LiamJones 4 83
(Neil King) *mde all: rdn and fnd ex 2f out: 2 l clr over 1f out: styd on wl: rdn out* **7/2**[2]
1-52 **2** *2 ½* **Brasted (IRE)**[21] 349 4-9-6 75 (t) LukeMorris 1 79
(Paul Cole) *chsd ldrs: effrt wl over 1f out: drvn to chse clr wnr 1f out: kpt on but no imp ins fnl f* **3/1**[1]
2-06 **3** *¾* **Shimba Hills**[16] 414 5-9-4 72 (p) WilliamTwiston-Davies 7 75
(Lawney Hill) *in tch in midfield: effrt u.p to chse ldrs 2f out: styd on same pce ins fnl f: wnt 3rd fnl 100yds* **16/1**
00-3 **4** *½* **Golden Wedding (IRE)**[15] 429 4-8-10 65 (p) LiamKeniry 9 67
(Eve Johnson Houghton) *chsd wnr: rdn ent fnl 2f: unable qck and lost 2nd 1f out: styd on same pce ins fnl f* **7/1**
40-0 **5** *hd* **Ravenous**[12] 457 5-9-5 73 KieranO'Neill 5 74
(Luke Dace) *chsd ldng trio: effrt u.p wl over 1f out: 5th and no imp 1f out: kpt on same pce after* **20/1**
-310 **6** *1 ¼* **Al's Memory (IRE)**[16] 424 7-8-12 66 JFEgan 3 65
(David Evans) *broke wl: sn stdd and hld up in tch in midfield: effrt over 1f out: kpt on but no imp ins fnl f* **7/1**
0-00 **7** *½* **Maverik**[16] 414 8-9-2 70 CharlesBishop 8 68
(Ali Stronge) *t.k.h: hld up in tch in midfield: effrt over 1f out: styd on same pce ins fnl f* **50/1**
2-54 **8** *nse* **Viserion**[10] 491 4-8-13 68 (p) MartinDwyer 10 66
(David Simcock) *off the pce in last trio: pushed along 7f out: clsd and reminder over 4f out: rdn 3f out: hung lft and no imp over 1f out: wl hld and eased towards fin* **9/2**[3]
00-3 **9** *¾* **Freddy With A Y (IRE)**[28] 263 6-9-6 74 (p) GeorgeBaker 11 70
(Gary Moore) *s.i.s: dropped in bhd after s: hld up in rr: effrt but stl plenty to do wl over 1f out: kpt on ins fnl f: nvr trbld ldrs* **8/1**
100/ **10** *13* **Maria's Choice (IRE)**[68] 89 7-9-7 75 TimmyMurphy 6 45
(Jim Best) *bmpd sn after: a last trio: rdn 4f out: lost tch 2f out* **33/1**

2m 4.11s (-2.49) **Going Correction** +0.025s/f (Slow)
WFA 4 from 5yo+ 1lb **10** Ran SP% **117.1**
Speed ratings (Par 103): **110,108,107,107,106 105,105,105,104,94**
CSF £14.22 CT £147.83 TOTE £4.50: £1.50, £1.80, £4.70; EX 17.30 Trifecta £173.30.
Owner D S Lee **Bred** D S Lee **Trained** Barbury Castle, Wiltshire

FOCUS
An ordinary handicap. The third and fourth have been rated close to form.
T/Plt: £18.40 to a £1 stake. Pool: £50925.62 - 2013.02 winning tickets T/Qpdt: £3.90 to a £1 stake. Pool: £4223.66 - 790.08 winning tickets **Steve Payne**

527 CHELMSFORD (A.W) (L-H)
Thursday, February 18

OFFICIAL GOING: Polytrack: standard
Wind: virtually nil Weather: dry, cold

617 BETFRED TV H'CAP 7f (P)
5:35 (5:36) (Class 6) (0-52,58) 4-Y-O+ **£3,234** (£962; £481; £240) **Stalls** Low

Form RPR
-013 **1** **Cookie Ring (IRE)**[1] 608 5-9-0 52 (v) PaulaMuir[(7)] 6 61
(Patrick Holmes) *s.i.s: hld up in rr: clsd and in tch 4f out: effrt and hdwy over 1f out: ev ch 1f out: drifting lft and led ins fnl f: r.o wl* **5/1**[3]
/211 **2** *nk* **Camdora (IRE)**[7] 528 4-9-13 58 6ex TimmyMurphy 3 66
(Jamie Osborne) *in tch in midfield: effrt over 1f out: led 1f out: hdd ins fnl f: kpt on wl but a jst hld after* **8/13**[1]
-003 **3** *3* **Bold Max**[7] 528 5-9-7 52 (v) LiamJones 2 52
(Zoe Davison) *led: rdn and hung bdly rt over 1f out: hdd 1f out: sn outpcd: kpt on same pce fnl 150yds* **20/1**
5200 **4** *1 ½* **Loud**[8] 525 6-9-0 48 (b) TimClark[(3)] 5 44
(Lydia Pearce) *dwlt and urged along early: in tch in last trio: effrt u.p on inner over 1f out: wnt 4th ins fnl f: kpt on but nvr threatened ldrs* **14/1**
0-00 **5** *nk* **Not Your Call (IRE)**[22] 346 5-9-7 52 ShaneKelly 8 47
(Lee Carter) *t.k.h early: hld up in tch in last trio: effrt over 1f out: sn drvn and no rspnse: edging lft and one pce fnl f* **4/1**[2]
-630 **6** *3 ¼* **Ms Eboracum (IRE)**[14] 442 4-8-10 46 oh1 JosephineGordon[(5)] 4 32
(Michael Appleby) *chsd ldr: rdn over 2f out: lost pl over 1f out: wknd fnl f* **20/1**
6-65 **7** *5* **Jonnie Skull (IRE)**[29] 264 10-9-6 51 (vt) LukeMorris 1 24
(Phil McEntee) *chsd ldrs tl lost pl over 1f out: bhd fnl f* **10/1**

1m 25.27s (-1.93) **Going Correction** -0.20s/f (Stan) **7** Ran SP% **123.9**
Speed ratings (Par 101): **103,102,99,97,97 93,87**
CSF £9.39 CT £59.55 TOTE £5.30: £2.10, £1.30; EX 9.40 Trifecta £61.50.
Owner Mrs Ailsa Stirling **Bred** Gerard Brady **Trained** Middleham, N Yorks

FOCUS
The track was power harrowed to 4 inches and gallop master finished to 2 inches for racing. A moderate contest run at a fair pace. The winner quikcly build on good run 24 hours earlier.

618 BETFRED RACING FOLLOW US ON TWITTER MEDIAN AUCTION MAIDEN STKS 1m (P)
6:10 (6:10) (Class 5) 3-5-Y-O **£5,175** (£1,540; £769; £384) **Stalls** Low

Form RPR
4-2 **1** **Sabaani**[13] 458 3-8-9 0 LukeMorris 3 76
(James Tate) *chsd ldng pair: effrt over 1f out: chal 1f out: led ins fnl f: drifted lft but styd on wl fnl 100yds: rdn out* **9/4**[2]
252- **2** *1* **Bernie's Boy**[52] 8377 3-8-9 81 JimCrowley 2 74
(Andrew Balding) *t.k.h: led: hdd and rdn 2f out: led again 1f out: sn hdd: carried lft and kpt on same pce fnl 100yds* **8/15**[1]
32-3 **3** *1* **Rivers Of Asia**[13] 466 3-8-6 78 DannyBrock[(3)] 7 71
(Philip McBride) *w ldr: rdn to ld 2f out: awkward hd carriage u.p: hdd and hung rt 1f out: 3rd and styd on same pce ins fnl f* **10/1**[3]
4 *3 ½* **Shining Romeo**[20] 4-10-0 0 LemosdeSouza 6 69
(Denis Quinn) *t.k.h: hld up in tch in last trio: effrt 2f out: kpt on to go 4th wl ins fnl f: no threat to ldrs* **33/1**
0-4 **5** *1 ¼* **Serendib's Glory (IRE)**[14] 441 3-8-1 0 ShelleyBirkett[(3)] 1 55
(Julia Feilden) *in tch in 4th: rdn 2f out: outpcd and btn 1f out: wknd ins fnl f* **40/1**
6 *1 ¼* **Tudor Icon** 3-8-9 0[1] ChrisCatlin 5 57
(Rae Guest) *stdd s: hld up in tch in last pair: effrt on inner over 1f out: no prog* **33/1**
4-4 **7** *7* **Sayeuri**[43] 74 4-9-9 0 AdamKirby 4 41
(David Evans) *stdd s: hld up in tch in rr: pushed along over 2f out: c wd wl over 1f out: sn btn and bhd fnl f* **33/1**

1m 39.3s (-0.60) **Going Correction** -0.20s/f (Stan)
WFA 3 from 4yo 19lb **7** Ran SP% **116.4**
Speed ratings (Par 103): **95,94,93,89,88 87,80**
CSF £3.84 TOTE £3.40: £1.30, £1.10; EX 4.10 Trifecta £8.50.
Owner Saif Ali **Bred** Rabbah Bloodstock Limited **Trained** Newmarket, Suffolk

FOCUS
A fair maiden in which the market principals came to the fore. Muddling form. The winner has been rated as taking another step forward, but maybe not as much as it seems at face value. The third has been rated close to form.

619 BETFRED HOME OF GOALS GALORE H'CAP 2m (P)
6:40 (6:41) (Class 4) (0-85,84) 4-Y-O+ **£8,086** (£2,406; £1,202; £601) **Stalls** Low

Form RPR
50-3 **1** **Albahar (FR)**[24] 165 5-9-8 78 (p) JimCrowley 9 88
(Chris Gordon) *in tch in midfield: clsd to trck ldng pair and gng wl over 2f out: gap opened and qcknd to ld jst over 1f out: in command and r.o wl fnl f: rdn out* **7/1**[3]
1213 **2** *1 ¼* **Zakatal**[6] 545 10-9-5 75 PJMcDonald 5 83
(Rebecca Menzies) *stdd s: hld up in rr: rdn 4f out: swtchd rt wl over 1f out: hdwy over 1f out: styd on u.p to chse wnr fnl 100yds: kpt on but nvr a serious threat* **4/1**[2]
210- **3** *2 ½* **Duke Street (IRE)**[102] 5639 4-9-7 83 LukeMorris 2 88
(Dr Richard Newland) *chsd ldng pair: wnt 2nd and pressing ldr over 3f out: rdn to ld over 1f out: sn hdd and unable qck: kpt on same pce and lost 2nd fnl 100yds* **4/1**[2]
10-4 **4** *¾* **Excellent Puck (IRE)**[36] 160 6-9-3 78 CallumShepherd[(5)] 10 82
(Shaun Lycett) *hld up in tch in last trio: hdwy to chse ldrs but nt clr run on inner over 2f out: rdn and followed wnr through gap over 1f out: styd on same pce ins fnl f* **16/1**

32-1 **5** *1* **Daisy Boy (IRE)**[21] [357] 5-9-2 **77**................................(t) AaronJones(5) 6 80
(Stuart Williams) *led: rdn over 2f out: hdd over 1f out and sn no ex: wknd ins fnl f* **11/4**[1]

-042 **6** *12* **U S Navy Seal (USA)**[14] [447] 4-9-8 **84**...........................(v) AdamKirby 7 73
(J R Jenkins) *stdd s: hld up in tch in last trio: effrt and hdwy to chse ldrs over 2f out: no ex u.p and btn 1f out: sn wknd and eased ins fnl f* **4/1**[2]

2-40 **7** *8* **Brassbound (USA)**[14] [440] 8-9-12 **82**................................ LiamJones 4 61
(Michael Appleby) *chsd ldrs: rdn 6f out: clsd to press ldrs but stuck wd over 3f out: sn struggling: bhd 2f out: sn wknd: eased ins fnl f* **16/1**

1-51 **8** *14* **King Olav (UAE)**[20] [386] 11-8-3 **66**.............................. RhiainIngram(7) 8 28
(Tony Carroll) *chsd ldr tl over 3f out: sn u.p and struggling: lost pl and bhd 2f out: sn lost tch and eased ins fnl f: t.o* **20/1**

3m 24.73s (-5.27) **Going Correction** -0.20s/f (Stan)
WFA 4 from 5yo+ 6lb **8** Ran SP% **115.7**
Speed ratings (Par 105): **105,104,103,102,102 96,92,85**
CSF £35.53 CT £128.23 TOTE £9.00: £2.10, £1.40, £2.50; EX 37.10 Trifecta £187.20.
Owner Mrs Kate Digweed **Bred** Julien Leaunes **Trained** Morestead, Hampshire

FOCUS
A competitive staying handicap. The fourth has been rated close to form.

620 BETFRED LOTTO H'CAP 1m (P)
7:10 (7:13) (Class 4) (0-85,89) 4-Y-0+ **£8,086** (£2,406; £1,202; £601) **Stalls** Low

Form RPR

4-15 **1** **Loyalty**[15] [433] 9-9-4 **82**..(v) TonyHamilton 6 89
(Derek Shaw) *sn pushed up to press ldr: swtchd rt and effrt over 1f out: flashed tail a edgd lft u.p ins fnl f: led 75yds out: drvn out* **11/1**

01-1 **2** *nk* **Bold Prediction (IRE)**[35] [172] 6-9-7 **85**........................ GeorgeBaker 3 91
(Ed Walker) *led and set stdy gallop: rdn and fnd ex over 1f out: drvn 1f out: bmpd and hdd fnl 75yds: kpt on but hld towards fin* **7/2**[3]

6-11 **3** *nk* **Supersta**[6] [546] 5-9-11 **89** 12ex.......................................(p) JimCrowley 9 97+
(Michael Appleby) *stdd after s: t.k.h: hld up in tch in rr: swtchd rt and effrt wl over 1f out: hdwy 1f out: str run and edging lft fnl 100yds: nt quite rch ldrs* **5/2**[1]

15-3 **4** *hd* **Jodies Jem**[31] [240] 6-9-5 **83**.. CharlesBishop 2 88
(William Jarvis) *chsd ldrs: effrt over 1f out: drvn and ev ch 1f out: no ex and one pce wl ins fnl f: lost 3rd last strides* **7/1**

21-0 **5** *hd* **My Target (IRE)**[6] [546] 5-9-6 **84**... AdamKirby 1 88
(Michael Wigham) *in tch in midfield: effrt over 1f out: drvn and chsd ldrs 1f out: kpt on but unable qck towards fin* **3/1**[2]

-106 **6** *3 ¾* **Fleckerl (IRE)**[6] [546] 6-9-2 **80**...(p) LiamKeniry 5 75
(Conor Dore) *stdd s: t.k.h: hld up in tch in last trio: n.m.r over 1f out: swtchd rt and effrt 1f out: sn no imp: wknd fnl 100yds* **22/1**

3-32 **7** *2* **One Pekan (IRE)**[11] [494] 6-8-12 **83**......................(p) CameronNoble(7) 8 74
(Roger Varian) *in tch in midfield: effrt and unable qck over 1f out: wknd ins fnl f* **6/1**

-0 **8** *24* **Rail Dancer**[19] [401] 4-9-4 **82**...................................... AdamBeschizza 4 15
(Richard Rowe) *dwlt: in tch in last trio: rdn 3f out: sn dropped to last: lost tch over 1f out* **100/1**

20-4 **U** **Crack Shot (IRE)**[42] [82] 4-8-13 **77**.................................... LukeMorris 7
(James Tate) *in tch in midfield: effrt in cl 5th 2f out: drvn and unable qck over 1f out: wknd jst ins fnl f: wl hld whn lost action, stmbld and uns rdr towards fin: fatally injured* **16/1**

1m 37.05s (-2.85) **Going Correction** -0.20s/f (Stan) **9** Ran SP% **122.1**
Speed ratings (Par 105): **106,105,105,105,105 101,99,75,**
CSF £52.36 CT £132.20 TOTE £11.50: £3.30, £1.70, £1.40; EX 55.50 Trifecta £237.40.
Owner Brian Johnson (Northamptonshire) **Bred** Ecoutila Partnership **Trained** Sproxton, Leics

FOCUS
The early pace wasn't strong and it paid to race handily. They finished in a heap. The fourth helps set the standard.

621 BETFRED 1400 SHOPS NATIONWIDE H'CAP 1m (P)
7:40 (7:43) (Class 6) (0-65,65) 4-Y-0+ **£3,234** (£962; £481; £240) **Stalls** Low

Form RPR

121- **1** **Bridge Of Sighs**[53] [8370] 4-9-2 **60**....................................... AdamKirby 9 68
(Martin Smith) *racd in last quartet: hdwy over 1f out: edging lft but clsd to chse ldrs 1f out: hrd drvn to ld 150yds out: sustained duel after: hld on wl: all out* **2/1**[1]

00-6 **2** *nse* **Little Lord Nelson**[14] [437] 4-9-4 **62**............................(t) SaleemGolam 3 70
(Stuart Williams) *in tch in midfield: swtchd rt and effrt over 1f out: drvn and ev ch jst ins fnl f: sustained duel w wnr fnl 150yds: r.o: jst hld* **8/1**

13-6 **3** *1 ¾* **Spirit Of Gondree (IRE)**[38] [141] 8-9-4 **62**.................(b) FrannyNorton 1 68
(Milton Bradley) *hld up in last quartet: hdwy u.p over 1f out: swtchd lft 1f out: cl 4th and styng on whn nt clr run and snatched up 100yds out: sn swtchd rt but unable to rcvr: wnt 3rd towards fin* **14/1**

06-2 **4** *¾* **Pyla (IRE)**[14] [437] 4-9-7 **65**..(p) LemosdeSouza 7 67
(Denis Quinn) *t.k.h: chsd ldrs: wnt 2nd 5f out tl led over 2f out: drvn over 1f out: hdd 150yds out: no ex: wknd and lost 3rd towards fin* **6/1**[3]

2-30 **5** *5* **Napoleon Solo**[30] [246] 4-9-5 **63**...................... WilliamTwiston-Davies 2 53
(Dave Morris) *chsd ldr tl 5f out: effrt u.p over 2f out: wnt 2nd again briefly over 1f out: no ex 1f out: wknd ins fnl f* **5/1**[2]

1-40 **6** *2 ¼* **Limerick Lord (IRE)**[14] [448] 4-9-1 **62**.................(p) ShelleyBirkett(3) 4 47
(Julia Feilden) *chsd ldrs: drvn over 2f out: unable qck over 1f out: btn whn sltly hmpd and swtchd rt jst ins fnl f: wknd fnl 150yds* **11/1**

40-0 **7** *½* **Youm Jamil (USA)**[32] [231] 9-8-6 **57**..........................(t) GeorgiaCox(7) 10 40
(Tony Carroll) *stdd s: hld up in rr: effrt over 1f out: sme hdwy and swtchd rt jst ins fnl f: nvr trbld ldrs* **33/1**

0-60 **8** *2 ¼* **Soaring Spirits (IRE)**[19] [398] 6-9-2 **60**......................(tp) RenatoSouza 6 38
(Dean Ivory) *in tch in midfield: rdn over 2f out: unable qck and lost pl over 1f out: wknd fnl f* **20/1**

00-0 **9** *2* **Voice Of A Leader (IRE)**[14] [438] 5-9-4 **62**...................... MartinHarley 5 35
(Andi Brown) *led: rdn and hdd over 2f out: lost 2nd and btn over 1f out: wknd qckly fnl f* **25/1**

11-4 **10** *1 ½* **Greek Islands (IRE)**[45] [37] 8-9-6 **64**.............................. LiamKeniry 8 34
(Neil Mulholland) *stdd s: hld up in tch in midfield: effrt 2f out: sn rdn and btn: wknd over 1f out* **8/1**

00-0 **11** *37* **Golden Highway (USA)**[47] [24] 4-9-7 **65**.................(vt[1]) JimCrowley 11
(Michael Appleby) *a towards rr: dropped to last and struggling over 2f out: lost tch and eased over 1f out: t.o* **20/1**

1m 38.17s (-1.73) **Going Correction** -0.20s/f (Stan) **11** Ran SP% **117.8**
Speed ratings (Par 101): **100,99,98,97,92 90,89,87,85,83 46**
CSF £17.38 CT £183.48 TOTE £2.30: £2.60, £2.40, £3.40; EX 21.90 Trifecta £267.10.
Owner SN Racing VI **Bred** S Nunn **Trained** Newmarket, Suffolk

FOCUS
A modest handicap run at a fairly decent gallop. Quite straightforward form.

622 COLLECT TOTEPOOL WINNINGS AT BETFRED SHOPS H'CAP 1m 5f 66y(P)
8:10 (8:12) (Class 6) (0-60,57) 4-Y-0+ **£3,234** (£962; £481; £240) **Stalls** Low

Form RPR

24-2 **1** **Bracken Brae**[35] [170] 4-9-3 **57**....................................... SaleemGolam 7 69+
(Mark H Tompkins) *chsd clr ldng pair: grad clsd 4f out: wnt 2nd over 2f out: rdn to ld over 1f out and sn clr: eased towards fin* **6/4**[1]

6-03 **2** *7* **White Dog (IRE)**[8] [514] 4-8-7 **50**.................................. DannyBrock(3) 8 50
(Sarah Humphrey) *pressed ldr and clr of field: rdn to ld over 2f out: hdd and brushed aside by wnr over 1f out: wknd but hld on to 2nd cl home* **7/1**[3]

163 **3** *hd* **Smugglers Lane (IRE)**[20] [378] 4-8-6 **53**........................ AledBeech(7) 6 53
(David Evans) *hld up in midfield: clsd 4f out: 3rd and rdn 2f out: no ch w wnr and kpt on same pce ins fnl f* **7/1**[3]

40-0 **4** *½* **Black Iceman**[22] [354] 8-8-6 **45**................................. SimonPearce(3) 2 44
(Lydia Pearce) *hld up in midfield: clsd 4f out: effrt in 5th and hung lft over 1f out: no ch w wnr but kpt on wl ins fnl f* **16/1**

2006 **5** *1 ½* **My Tringaling (IRE)**[7] [527] 4-8-8 **53**........................... AaronJones(5) 5 50
(Stuart Williams) *midfield: clsd and in tch 4f out: effrt in 4th 2f out: no ch w wnr and styd on same pce ins fnl f* **8/1**

0-04 **6** *12* **Glasgow Central**[13] [463] 5-9-7 **57**..................................(v) AdamKirby 3 37
(Phil McEntee) *stdd s: hld up in last pair: pushed along 6f out: rdn over 3f out: wknd 2f out: wl bhd and eased ins fnl f* **5/1**[2]

06-0 **7** *3 ¼* **Daring Indian**[33] [222] 8-9-4 **54**.......................................(p) GeorgeBaker 4 30
(Roger Teal) *stdd s: hld up in last pair: swtchd rt and effrt wl over 1f out: sn btn: eased fnl f* **7/1**[3]

6205 **8** *1 ¼* **Annakrista (GER)**[13] [461] 8-9-5 **55**..............................(bt) LiamKeniry 1 29
(Zoe Davison) *racd keenly: led and clr w rival tl hdd over 2f out: sn btn: lost action and eased over 1f out* **16/1**

2m 50.38s (-3.22) **Going Correction** -0.20s/f (Stan)
WFA 4 from 5yo+ 4lb **8** Ran SP% **117.0**
Speed ratings (Par 101): **101,96,96,96,95 87,85,85**
CSF £13.05 CT £58.07 TOTE £2.30: £1.10, £1.90, £2.40; EX 12.00 Trifecta £54.90.
Owner David P Noblett **Bred** Dullingham Park Stud & Mr D Noblett **Trained** Newmarket, Suffolk

FOCUS
An ordinary handicap and a straightforward success for the favourite. Weak form behind the winner.
T/Jkpt: £30,374.20 to a £1 stake. Pool: £45,561.00 - 1.5 winning tickets. T/Plt: £12.00 to a £1 stake. Pool: £84,563.11 - 5,114.48 winning tickets. T/Qpdt: £9.60 to a £1 stake. Pool: £8,066.19 - 620.71 winning tickets. **Steve Payne**

571 MEYDAN (L-H)
Thursday, February 18

OFFICIAL GOING: Dirt: fast; turf: good

623a RANGE ROVER (H'CAP) (TURF) 7f
3:35 (3:35) (100-110,110) 3-Y-0+
£71,428 (£23,809; £11,904; £5,952; £3,571; £2,380)

RPR

1 **Fils Anges (IRE)**[21] [373] 6-9-3 107........................... MickaelBarzalona 1 110
(Ali Jan, Qatar) *settled in rr: smooth prog 2 1/2f out: led 110yds out: r.o wl* **9/2**[2]

2 *¾* **Kanaf (IRE)**[4] 9-8-11 101...(v) DaneO'Neill 9 102
(M Al Mheiri, UAE) *s.i.s: nvr nr to chal but r.o fnl 2f nrst fin* **33/1**

3 *nk* **Mastermind (SAF)**[28] [282] 4-9-4 108............................ PaulHanagan 8 108
(M F De Kock, South Africa) *sn led: hdd 6f out: led again 2f out: hdd 110yds out: wknd fnl 55yds* **9/4**[1]

4 *½* **Dark Emerald (IRE)**[21] [375] 6-9-6 110........................(v) RichardMullen 7 109
(Brendan Powell) *settled in rr: rdn 3f out: r.o fnl 2f: nrst fin* **9/4**[1]

5 *1 ¼* **Glory Awaits (IRE)**[21] [373] 6-8-13 102......................(b) FrederikTylicki 2 98
(David Simcock) *trckd ldr: led 6f out: hdd 2f out: r.o same pce* **16/1**

6 *1 ½* **Ashaadd (IRE)**[21] [370] 6-8-10 100................................ ChrisHayes 3 91
(D Selvaratnam, UAE) *trckd ldrs: ev ch 3f out: one pce fnl 2 1/2f* **8/1**[3]

7 *nk* **Jallota**[21] [373] 5-8-13 102.. JamieSpencer 4 94
(Charles Hills) *nvr bttr than mid-div* **12/1**

8 *4 ¼* **Art Wave (IRE)**[27] [312] 5-8-10 100..............................(v) FernandoJara 6 79
(M Al Mheiri, UAE) *trckd ldrs tl outpcd fnl 2 1/2f* **25/1**

9 *3* **Redbrook (IRE)**[147] 5-8-10 100.. PatDobbs 5 71
(Doug Watson, UAE) *s.i.s: a in rr* **18/1**

1m 23.51s (-0.59) **Going Correction** +0.125s/f (Good) **9** Ran SP% **116.5**
Speed ratings: **108,107,106,106,104 103,102,97,94**
CSF: 133.43 TRICAST: 420.68.
Owner Mohammae Mahran Jamsheer **Bred** Yeomanstown Stud **Trained** Qatar

FOCUS
TRAKUS (metres travelled compared to winner): 2nd +2, 3rd +1, 4th +3, 5th -4, 6th +1, 7th -3, 8th +5, 9th -4. There were a lack of unexposed runners, but solid enough handicap form. The went a solid pace; 25.39 (400m from standing start), 22.8 (800m), 23.05 (1200m), and the winner finished in 12.17. The standard is set by the placed horses.

624a RANGE ROVER SPORT (H'CAP) (DIRT) 1m (D)
4:10 (4:10) (100-123,110) 3-Y-0+
£48,979 (£16,326; £8,163; £4,081; £2,040; £2,040)

RPR

1 **Maftool (USA)**[165] [6152] 4-9-5 **109**.................................. DaneO'Neill 1 111
(M Al Mheiri, UAE) *s.i.s: mid-div: chsd ldrs 1 1/2f out: led 110yds out: r.o wl* **11/1**

2 *½* **Cool Cowboy (USA)**[21] [374] 5-9-6 **110**.............................. PatDobbs 11 111
(Doug Watson, UAE) *trckd ldng pair: ev ch 1 1/2f out: r.o same pce fnl f* **4/1**[2]

3 *nk* **Prayer For Relief (USA)**[14] [452] 8-9-5 **109**....(b) ChristopheSoumillon 9 109+
(M F De Kock, South Africa) *mid-div: r.o fnl 2f nrst fin* **4/1**[2]

4 *hd* **American Hope (USA)**[28] [284] 5-8-13 **102**..................... WilliamBuick 3 103
(Saeed bin Suroor) *mid-div: t.k.h: rdn 4f out: chsd ldrs 2 1/2f out: r.o same pce fnl 1 1/2f* **7/2**[1]

5 *hd* **Munaaser**[14] [452] 5-9-1 **105**... PaulHanagan 12 104
(A R Al Rayhi, UAE) *trckd ldr: led 2 1/2f out: hdd & wknd 110yds out* **7/1**

5 *dht* **Footbridge (USA)**[28] [281] 6-9-2 **106**...........................(b) RichardMullen 6 105
(Charlie Appleby) *settled in rr: r.o fnl 1 1/2f: nrst fin* **25/1**

7 *1 ¼* **Ross (IRE)**[21] [374] 4-8-10 **100**....................................... AndraschStarke 4 97
(P Schiergen, Germany) *nvr nr to chal* **9/2**[3]

8 4 1/2 **Krypton Factor**[7] 537 8-8-13 **102**................................(b) TadhgO'Shea 10 89
(Fawzi Abdulla Nass, Bahrain) *wl away: sn led: hdd 2 1/2f out: sn btn* **25/1**

9 5 1/4 **Energia Colonial (BRZ)**[28] 284 8-8-13 **102**......(t) Per-AndersGraberg 8 77
(Niels Petersen, Norway) *a in rr* **50/1**

10 2 1/2 **Pylon (SAF)**[327] 1091 7-9-1 **105**....................................(b) WayneSmith 5 73
(M F De Kock, South Africa) *a in rr* **40/1**

11 1 1/4 **Mind That Boy (IRE)**[14] 452 4-9-1 **105**.................. MickaelBarzalona 2 70
(S bin Ghadayer, UAE) *s.i.s: nvr nr to chal* **20/1**

12 4 1/4 **Pearl Nation (USA)**[42] 92 7-8-13 **102**......................... FrederikTylicki 7 59
(Michael Appleby) *nvr bttr than mid-div* **25/1**

1m 37.15s (-0.35) **Going Correction** +0.075s/f (Slow) **12** Ran SP% **121.9**
Speed ratings: **104,103,103,103,102 102,101,97,91,89 88,83**
CSF: 52.06 TRICAST: 216.19.

Owner Hamdan Al Maktoum **Bred** C Kidder & J K & Linda Griggs **Trained** UAE

FOCUS

TRAKUS: 2nd +7, 3rd +11, 4th +1, 5th +8, 6th +7, 7th -1, 8th 0, 9th +3, 10th +13, 11th +6, 12th +12. A good, competitive dirt handicap. The early pace was strong; 25.07, 22.8, 24.02 and the winner was home in a slowing 24.75.

625a DUBAI MILLENNIUM STKS SPONSORED BY AL TAYER MOTORS (GROUP 3) (TURF) 1m 2f

4:45 (4:45) 3-Y-O+

£81,632 (£27,210; £13,605; £6,802; £4,081; £2,721)

RPR

1 **Tryster (IRE)**[145] 6733 5-9-1 113....................................(p) WilliamBuick 5 117+
(Charlie Appleby) *slowly away: settled in rr: smooth prog 2 1/2f out: led 1f out: easily* **7/2**[2]

2 2 3/4 **Haafaguinea**[28] 285 6-9-1 113.. FrederikTylicki 2 111
(Saeed bin Suroor) *sn led: hdd 1f out but r.o wl* **15/8**[1]

3 nk **Meadow Creek**[14] 455 5-9-1 104.. PatDobbs 9 110
(Doug Watson, UAE) *trckd ldrs: ev ch 1 1/2f out: r.o wl but no ch w wnr* **7/1**

4 nk **Sanshaawes (SAF)**[14] 455 6-9-1 111................. ChristopheSoumillon 7 110
(M F De Kock, South Africa) *trckd ldr: n.m.r 2 1/2f out: r.o fnl 1 1/2f* **4/1**[3]

5 nk **Belgian Bill**[7] 540 8-9-1 102... JamieSpencer 10 109
(George Baker) *s.i.s: mid-div: chsd ldrs 2f out: r.o same pce fnl 1 1/2f* **33/1**

6 1 **Zamaam**[14] 455 6-9-1 100...(t) PaulHanagan 3 107
(E Charpy, UAE) *nvr bttr than mid-div* **20/1**

7 shd **Tellina (SAF)**[14] 455 6-9-1 109.....................................(b) WayneSmith 8 107
(M F De Kock, South Africa) *nvr nr to chal* **10/1**

8 1 1/2 **Earnshaw (USA)**[21] 372 5-9-1 111......................(bt) MickaelBarzalona 4 104
(S bin Ghadayer, UAE) *nvr bttr than mid-div* **8/1**

9 1 1/2 **Vale Do Sol (IRE)**[5] 574 4-9-0 95.................................... DavidProbert 6 101
(Fawzi Abdulla Nass, Bahrain) *a in rr* **50/1**

10 8 3/4 **Zambucca (SAF)**[14] 455 7-9-1 99.............................(b) RichardMullen 1 84
(S Seemar, UAE) *trckd ldr tl wknd 2 1/2f out* **80/1**

2m 4.79s (2.09) **Going Correction** +0.125s/f (Good)
WFA 4 from 5yo+ 1lb **10** Ran SP% **120.6**
Speed ratings: **96,93,93,93,93 92,92,91,89,82**
CSF: 10.61.

Owner Godolphin **Bred** Herbertstown House Stud **Trained** Newmarket, Suffolk

FOCUS

TRAKUS: 2nd -9, 3rd -5, 4th -9, 5th -3, 6th -11, 7th -1, 8th -3, 9th -10, 10th -11. The first running of this as a Group 3, upgraded from Listed status. It was not a deep race but there was a very smart winner who quickened exceptionally off a slow pace; 28.59 (400m), 25.42 (800m), 24.74 (1200m), 23.73 (1600m), with Tryster to the line in 21.79. The sixth, along with the fifth and ninth potentially limit the form, but the rest have been rated pretty close to their marks.

626a JAGUAR F-TYPE (H'CAP) (TURF) 5f (T)

5:20 (5:20) (100-111,111) 3-Y-O+

£71,428 (£23,809; £11,904; £5,952; £3,571; £2,380)

RPR

1 **Sir Maximilian (IRE)**[14] 450 7-9-3 **108**............................. PatDobbs 14 111
(Ian Williams) *settled in rr: smooth prog 2 1/2f out on nr side: led 1f out: r.o wl* **13/2**[3]

2 1 1/4 **Roicead (USA)**[21] 371 9-9-4 **109**....................................(t) ChrisHayes 3 108+
(D Selvaratnam, UAE) *settled in rr: smooth prog on far side: r.o wl fnl 1 1/2f: led far gp* **16/1**

3 nk **Roi De Vitesse (IRE)**[14] 450 9-9-0 **105**...............(v) MickaelBarzalona 7 102
(Ali Jan, Qatar) *settled in rr: r.o wl fnl 1 1/2f far side: nrst fin* **10/1**

4 nk **Caspian Prince (IRE)**[14] 450 7-9-0 **105**....................(t) TadhgO'Shea 13 101
(Dean Ivory) *led nr side: hdd 1f out: r.o same pce* **8/1**

5 nk **Toscanini (IRE)**[130] 7149 4-9-6 **111**.................................. WilliamBuick 6 106
(M Halford, Ire) *s.i.s: swtchd nr side: nvr able to chal but r.o fnl 2f* **9/2**[1]

6 3/4 **Stepper Point**[28] 280 7-9-4 **109**...................................(b) MartinDwyer 5 102
(William Muir) *led after 2f: ev ch 1f out: wknd fnl 110yds* **12/1**

7 3/4 **Medicean Man**[87] 7958 10-9-3 **108**...........................(tp) RichardMullen 4 98
(Jeremy Gask) *nvr bttr than mid-div* **8/1**

8 1/2 **Fityaan**[14] 450 8-8-9 **100**..(v) PaulHanagan 12 88
(M Al Mheiri, UAE) *nvr nr to chal* **6/1**[2]

9 3/4 **Mirza**[137] 6971 9-9-3 **108**..(p) DavidProbert 9 93
(Rae Guest) *nvr nr to chal* **14/1**

10 1 **Speed Hawk (USA)**[14] 450 5-9-0 **105**.......................(v) SamHitchcott 8 87
(Robert Cowell) *chsd ldrs tl outpcd fnl 1 1/2f* **16/1**

11 1 1/2 **Green Door (IRE)**[14] 450 5-8-11 **102**........................(v) JamieSpencer 1 78
(Robert Cowell) *nvr nr to chal* **20/1**

12 3/4 **Demora**[28] 280 7-8-9 **100**..(p) FrederikTylicki 10 74
(Michael Appleby) *led in centre for 2f: hdd 3f out: one pce fnl 1 1/2f* **20/1**

13 1 1/4 **Mubtaghaa (IRE)**[14] 450 4-9-0 **105**.................................... DaneO'Neill 2 74
(M Al Mheiri, UAE) *s.i.s: nvr nr to chal* **12/1**

14 1/2 **Hototo**[14] 450 6-9-3 **108**..(v) WayneSmith 11 75
(Fawzi Abdulla Nass, Bahrain) *nvr nr to chal* **33/1**

57.57s (0.47) **Going Correction** +0.375s/f (Good) **14** Ran SP% **123.4**
Speed ratings: **111,109,108,108,107 106,105,104,103,101 99,97,95,95**
CSF: 106.17 TRICAST: 1078.12.

Owner Paul Wildes **Bred** Holborn Trust Co **Trained** Portway, Worcs

FOCUS

TRAKUS: 2nd +4, 3rd 0, 4th +1, 5th +1, 6th +3, 7th +1, 8th +1, 9th +1, 10th +1, 11th +1, 12th +1, 13th +2, 14th +1. The field split into two groups but there was no obvious bias, with the winner near side and the runner-up far side. The first four have been rated close to their recent form.

627a LAND ROVER DISCOVERY SPORT (H'CAP) (DIRT) 1m 1f 110y(D)

5:55 (5:55) (95-118,111) 3-Y-O+

£44,897 (£14,965; £7,482; £3,741; £2,244; £1,496)

RPR

1 **Faulkner**[14] 452 6-9-3 **108**... PatDobbs 3 110
(Doug Watson, UAE) *trckd ldng duo: led 1f out: r.o wl* **10/3**[2]

2 nk **Tiz Now Tiz Then (USA)**[28] 284 11-8-6 **97**..............(bt) RichardMullen 4 98
(S Seemar, UAE) *sn led: rdn 3f out: hdd 1f out but r.o wl* **14/1**

3 7 3/4 **Let's Go (USA)**[28] 281 4-9-4 **110**...............................(v) FrederikTylicki 8 95+
(Saeed bin Suroor) *s.i.s: nvr nr to chal but r.o fnl 2 1/2f* **7/1**[3]

4 shd **Long River (USA)**[14] 454 6-8-13 **104**.......................(v) RoystonFfrench 2 89+
(S bin Ghadayer, UAE) *mid-div: r.o fnl 2f but no ch w first two* **33/1**

5 2 3/4 **Top Clearance (USA)**[28] 284 4-8-13 **105**...................(t) ChrisHayes 13 85+
(D Selvaratnam, UAE) *mid-div: rdn 3f out: ev ch 2 1/2f out: one pce fnl 2f* **15/2**

6 1/2 **Artigiano (USA)**[42] 94 6-8-11 **102**.......................(b) MickaelBarzalona 9 81+
(Charlie Appleby) *nvr nr to chal* **10/1**

7 2 1/4 **Plantagenet (SPA)**[28] 281 9-8-9 **100**................. Per-AndersGraberg 10 74
(Niels Petersen, Norway) *nvr bttr than mid-div* **40/1**

8 shd **Prince Alzain (USA)**[392] 259 7-8-10 **101**....................... SamHitchcott 6 75
(Doug Watson, UAE) *s.i.s: nvr bttr than mid-div* **40/1**

9 1 1/2 **Respect Me**[28] 279 6-8-6 **97**......................................(b) WayneSmith 14 68
(Ismail Mohammed) *nvr nr to chal* **22/1**

10 1 1/2 **Vortex (NOR)**[21] 375 7-8-9 **100**...................................(b) TadhgO'Shea 5 68
(Rune Haugen) *trckd ldr tl wknd 3f out* **66/1**

11 4 3/4 **Cat O'Mountain (USA)**[35] 188 6-9-1 **106**..................(b) WilliamBuick 11 64
(Charlie Appleby) *nvr nr to chal* **10/1**

12 5 1/4 **Ertijaal (AUS)**[21] 372 4-9-6 **111**.. PaulHanagan 7 58
(M F De Kock, South Africa) *trckd ldng duo: rdn 4f out: sn btn* **13/8**[1]

13 6 3/4 **Semeen**[14] 453 7-8-6 **96** ow1..(v) DavidProbert 1 30
(Fawzi Abdulla Nass, Bahrain) *s.i.s: nvr bttr than mid-div* **66/1**

14 9 **Bedale**[14] 453 5-8-5 **95**... JoseSantiago 12 11
(Ernst Oertel, UAE) *a in rr* **100/1**

1m 56.72s (-2.08) **Going Correction** +0.075s/f (Slow) **14** Ran SP% **126.4**
Speed ratings: **111,110,104,104,102 101,100,100,98,97 93,89,84,77**
CSF: 50.04 TRICAST: 324.63.

Owner Sheikh Ahmed bin Mohammed Al Maktoum **Bred** Darley **Trained** United Arab Emirates

FOCUS

TRAKUS: 2nd +2, 3rd +18, 4th +1, 5th +22, 6th +8, 7th +10, 8th +16, 9th +26, 10th +8, 11th +23, 12th +12, 13th +1, 14th +14. Another decent, competitive dirt handicap, although the runner-up set ordinary fractions - 26.18 (400m), 24.27 (800m), 24.3 (1200m), 24.01 (1600m) - and the winner was always close up, and nothing much else got into it. The second and third have been rated in line with their recent best.

628a JAGUAR XF (H'CAP) (TURF) 1m

6:30 (6:30) (95-108,107) 3-Y-O+

£44,897 (£14,965; £7,482; £3,741; £2,244; £1,496)

RPR

1 **Carry On Deryck**[245] 3304 4-9-1 **101**................................ DavidProbert 6 107
(Saeed bin Suroor) *mid-div: smooth prog 2 1/2f out: rdn to ld cl home* **8/1**[3]

2 1/2 **Udododontu (IRE)**[33] 229 4-9-2 **102**.......................... FrederikTylicki 5 107
(Saeed bin Suroor) *trckd ldrs: 1f out: hdd fnl 55yds* **11/8**[1]

3 1 1/4 **Secret Brief (IRE)**[28] 284 4-9-0 **100**...................... MickaelBarzalona 14 102
(Charlie Appleby) *s.i.s: in rr: r.o fnl 2f: nrst fin* **16/1**

4 nk **Flash Fire (IRE)**[21] 373 4-9-3 **104**..................................... WilliamBuick 7 104
(Charlie Appleby) *trckd ldrs: ev ch 1 1/2f out: one pce fnl f* **7/2**[2]

5 1 1/4 **Boomshackerlacker (IRE)**[21] 373 6-9-0 **100**........... RichardMullen 11 98
(George Baker) *mid-div: r.o same pce fnl 2f* **20/1**

6 nse **Beach Bar (IRE)**[21] 375 5-9-0 **100**................................ TadhgO'Shea 12 98
(Brendan Powell) *sn led: rdn clr 3f out: hdd 2f out: r.o same pce* **25/1**

7 2 1/2 **Avon Pearl**[21] 375 7-9-1 **101**..(vt) PatDobbs 15 94
(Rune Haugen) *in rr: nvr able to chal but r.o fnl 2f* **50/1**

8 hd **Sahaafy (USA)**[181] 5602 4-8-13 **99**................................... FernandoJara 1 91
(M Al Mheiri, UAE) *s.i.s: trckd ldr: ev ch 2 1/2f out: one pce fnl 2f* **20/1**

9 shd **Yaa Wayl (IRE)**[21] 373 9-9-1 **101**....................................(t) ChrisHayes 10 93
(D Selvaratnam, UAE) *in rr: n.d* **28/1**

10 nk **Nafaqa (IRE)**[145] 6755 4-9-3 **104**...(t) DaneO'Neill 8 94
(E Charpy, UAE) *nvr bttr than mid-div* **25/1**

11 2 **Calling Out (FR)**[21] 372 5-9-2 **102**................................. JamieSpencer 4 89
(David Simcock) *nvr bttr than mid-div* **14/1**

12 1 3/4 **Fox Trotter (IRE)**[28] 284 4-8-13 **99**................................ SamHitchcott 13 82
(Brian Meehan) *slowly away: a in rr* **33/1**

13 3/4 **Zarwaan**[28] 282 5-9-6 **107**... PaulHanagan 2 87
(Doug Watson, UAE) *nvr bttr than mid-div* **9/1**

14 nk **Ennobled Friend (USA)**[21] 372 6-8-13 **102**......(bt) MarcMonaghan(3) 3 82
(A bin Harmash, UAE) *nvr nr to chal* **66/1**

15 2 **Moohaarib (IRE)**[7] 540 5-9-4 **105**....................(b) ChristopheSoumillon 9 80
(Marco Botti) *trckd ldr: ev ch 2 1/2f out: wknd fnl 1 1/2f* **14/1**

16 11 **Silver Ocean (USA)**[28] 284 8-9-2 **102**................ Per-AndersGraberg 16 52
(Niels Petersen, Norway) *trckd ldrs tl wknd 3f out* **66/1**

1m 36.14s (-1.36) **Going Correction** +0.125s/f (Good) **16** Ran SP% **133.2**
Speed ratings: **111,110,109,108,107 107,105,104,104,104 102,100,100,99,97 86**
CSF: 19.14 TRICAST: 205.57. Placepot: £76.90 to a £1 stake. Pool of £6,929.99 - 65.78 winning units. Quadpot: £12.30 to a £1 stake. Pool of £483.20 - 28.90 winning units..

Owner Godolphin **Bred** Landmark Racing Limited **Trained** Newmarket, Suffolk

FOCUS

TRAKUS: 2nd -3, 3rd +3, 4th +2, 5th +1, 6th -7, 7th -5, 8th -7, 9th +2, 10th +1, 11th -6, 12th -4, 13th -6, 14th -1, 15th -6, 16th -1. The early pace was good, until they slowed up a touch on the turn - 25.29, 23.03, 23.84 - and the winner finished in 23.18. This is quite strong handicap form, with last year's Britannia Stakes fourth defeating the runner-up from that race and both still unexposed. It was a one-two for Saeed Bin Suroor and a one-two-three-four for Godolphin. The first two are improving.

[610]LINGFIELD (L-H)

Friday, February 19

OFFICIAL GOING: Polytrack: standard

Wind: light, half behind Weather: bright becoming cloudy, rain from race 5

629 LADBROKES H'CAP 1m 1y(P)

2:20 (2:21) (Class 5) (0-75,75) 4-Y-0+ **£2,911** (£866; £432; £216) **Stalls** High

Form RPR

0-52 **1** **The Tichborne (IRE)**[14] 457 8-8-13 **67**........................(b) JackMitchell 9 75
(Roger Teal) *mde all: sn allowed to go clr: c bk to field 3f out: rdn 2f out: kpt on u.p and a holding runner-up ins fnl f: rdn out* **12/1**[3]

33-4 **2** *nk* **Van Huysen (IRE)**[22] 360 4-9-4 **75**.............................. DannyBrock(3) 2 82
(Dominic Ffrench Davis) *chsd ldng pair: clsd 3f out: wnt 2nd wl over 1f out: rdn to chal 1f out: kpt on but a jst hld ins fnl f* **9/4**[1]

3-23 **3** *1 ½* **Chelwood Gate (IRE)**[18] 414 6-9-6 **74**.......................(v) GeorgeBaker 8 78+
(Patrick Chamings) *s.i.s: hld up in last pair: clsd 3f out: nt clr run and swtchd lft over 1f out: hdwy 1f out: styd on wl to go 3rd towards fin: nvr gng to rch ldrs* **9/4**[1]

10-4 **4** *nk* **Dukes Meadow**[44] 58 5-9-3 **71**..................................... RobertHavlin 7 74
(Roger Ingram) *stdd after s: hld up in last pair: clsd and in tch 3f out: effrt on inner over 1f out: hdwy u.p to go 3rd wl ins fnl f: kpt on but nvr threatening ldrs: lost 3rd towards fin* **11/2**[2]

3-6U **5** *¾* **Wink Oliver**[9] 518 4-9-6 **74**...(p) TimmyMurphy 1 75
(David Dennis) *s.i.s: hld up in midfield: clsd and in tch 3f out: effrt u.p to chse clr ldng pair over 1f out: no imp: lost 2 pls wl ins fnl f* **14/1**

-035 **6** *1 ¼* **Malaysian Boleh**[18] 414 6-9-0 **73**.......................(p) CallumShepherd(5) 3 71
(Shaun Lycett) *hld up in midfield: clsd and in tch 3f out: nt clr run over 1f out: kpt on ins fnl f: nvr trbld ldrs* **12/1**[3]

1-63 **7** *nk* **Orlando Rogue (IRE)**[18] 424 4-8-12 **66**........................(p) LiamKeniry 6 64
(Conor Dore) *stdd after s: midfield: clsd and in tch 3f out: rdn and unable qck 2f out: lost pl 1f out: wl hld and one pce ins fnl f* **16/1**

061- **8** *nse* **Seek The Fair Land**[72] 8160 10-9-1 **69**............................(v) ShaneKelly 5 66
(Lee Carter) *chsd clr wnr: clsd 3f out: lost 2nd and rdn wl over 1f out: little rspnse and btn 1f out: wknd ins fnl f* **12/1**[3]

1m 37.78s (-0.42) **Going Correction** +0.05s/f (Slow) 8 Ran SP% **112.5**

Speed ratings (Par 103): **104,103,102,101,101 99,99,99**

CSF £38.13 CT £84.58 TOTE £18.00: £3.90, £1.90, £1.10; EX 63.30 Trifecta £157.40.

Owner Chris Simpson & Mick Waghorn **Bred** Ms Alyson Flower And Chris Simpson **Trained** Great Shefford, Berks

FOCUS

The wind was blowing across the track into the stand. With nothing else wanting to go on the winner was able to dictate a pace to suit himself.

630 CORAL MAIDEN STKS 1m 4f (P)

2:55 (2:55) (Class 5) 4-Y-0+ **£2,911** (£866; £432; £216) **Stalls** Low

Form RPR

-224 **1** **Miss Giler**[13] 487 4-9-0 71.. RobertHavlin 3 69
(John Gosden) *hld up in tch: clsd and chsd ldrs 5f out: wnt 2nd jst over 2f out: rdn to ld over 1f out: styd on: rdn out* **4/1**[3]

03-2 **2** *2* **Start Seven**[23] 342 4-9-5 69... JFEgan 7 71
(Joseph Tuite) *chsd ldr tl led 3f out: sn rdn: hdd ent fnl f: kpt on same pce after* **7/2**[2]

4-26 **3** *hd* **Peeps**[15] 445 4-9-0 57..(b[1]) SaleemGolam 5 65
(Mark H Tompkins) *t.k.h: chsd ldrs: effrt in cl 3rd 2f out: styd on same pce u.p fnl f* **10/1**

4 *10* **Oscar Hill (IRE)**[297] 10-9-8 0.......................... WilliamTwiston-Davies 2 54
(David Bridgwater) *led: rdn and hdd jst over 2f out: sn dropped to 4th and struggling: wknd over 1f out* **6/1**

600- **5** *18* **Bickershaw**[128] 7215 4-8-12 45................................... RhiainIngram(7) 6 25
(Roger Ingram) *midfield tl dropped to last pair 7f out: rdn and struggling over 3f out: lost tch over 2f out* **100/1**

6 *32* **Anglo Paddy (IRE)**[85] 7-9-3 0.......................................(b[1]) LiamKeniry 1
(Neil Mulholland) *v.s.a and early reminders: a in rr: rdn over 3f out: lost tch over 2f out: t.o* **66/1**

P **Claret Cloak (IRE)**[146] 9-9-8 0...................................... TimmyMurphy 4
(Emma Lavelle) *hld up towards rr: hdwy to chse ldrs 9f out: lost action and eased 3f out: p.u over 2f out: fatally injured* **11/10**[1]

2m 31.48s (-1.52) **Going Correction** +0.05s/f (Slow)

WFA 4 from 7yo+ 3lb 7 Ran SP% **115.7**

Speed ratings (Par 103): **107,105,105,98,86 65,**

CSF £18.84 TOTE £5.00: £2.00, £2.20; EX 13.80 Trifecta £52.00.

Owner Rachel Hood & Elaine Lawlor **Bred** Sir Eric Parker **Trained** Newmarket, Suffolk

FOCUS

A modest maiden.

631 32REDSPORT.COM FILLIES' H'CAP 1m 2f (P)

3:30 (3:30) (Class 5) (0-70,67) 4-Y-0+ **£2,911** (£866; £432; £216) **Stalls** Low

Form RPR

34-4 **1** **Tommys Geal**[34] 222 4-8-9 **58**.................................. DanielMuscutt(3) 7 66
(Michael Madgwick) *hld up in tch in midfield: effrt to chal over 1f out: led 1f out: kpt on u.p: jst hld on* **9/2**

-355 **2** *nse* **Cosmic Halo**[18] 420 7-9-3 **65**...................................... SammyJoBell(3) 6 72
(Richard Fahey) *stdd s: hld up in tch in rr: effrt and swtchd rt wl over 1f out: hdwy u.p ins fnl f: str chal towards fin: jst failed* **7/2**[3]

02-2 **3** *1 ½* **What A Party (IRE)**[34] 218 4-8-11 **57**.....................(v) AdamBeschizza 5 61
(Gay Kelleway) *taken down early: s.i.s: sn rdn and hdwy to ld after 1f: rdn 2f out: hdd 1f out: stl ev ch tl no ex and outpcd fnl 75yds* **8/1**

01-4 **4** *¾* **Tabla**[23] 349 4-9-7 **67**.. AmirQuinn 1 70
(Lee Carter) *t.k.h: led for 1f: chsd ldrs after: effrt and ev ch over 1f out: no ex jst ins fnl f: one pce after* **3/1**[2]

234- **5** *hd* **Lady Lunchalot (USA)**[51] 8392 6-9-5 **64**......................(p) GeorgeBaker 3 66
(Laura Mongan) *chsd ldrs: wnt 2nd 7f out tl over 2f out: nvr much room and kpt on same pce ins fnl f* **9/4**[1]

005- **6** *¾* **Vivo Per Lei (IRE)**[262] 2812 4-8-8 **54**.............................. JimmyQuinn 4 55
(Dr Jon Scargill) *hld up in tch in last pair: rdn 2f out: no imp and styd on same pce fr over 1f out* **25/1**

2m 6.64s (0.04) **Going Correction** +0.05s/f (Slow)

WFA 4 from 6yo+ 1lb 6 Ran SP% **111.1**

Speed ratings (Par 100): **101,100,99,99,99 98**

CSF £19.96 TOTE £8.60: £2.40, £2.50; EX 26.70 Trifecta £104.70.

Owner Recycled Products Limited **Bred** Recycled Products Limited **Trained** Denmead, Hants

FOCUS

A modest but competitive fillies' event.

632 EBF STALLIONS BREEDING WINNERS/32RED FILLIES' H'CAP 7f 1y(P)

4:00 (4:03) (Class 3) (0-90,90) 4-Y-0+ **£10,396** (£3,111; £1,555; £778; £387) **Stalls** Low

Form RPR

040- **1** **Saucy Minx (IRE)**[72] 8163 6-9-7 **90**................................. JimCrowley 3 98
(Amanda Perrett) *t.k.h: hld up in tch: pushed along and effrt over 1f out: rdn to press ldrs and edging lft ins fnl f: led fnl 100yds: r.o wl* **9/4**[1]

41-1 **2** *1 ¼* **Slovak (IRE)**[14] 456 4-8-7 **76**... RobertHavlin 1 81
(James Tate) *led: rdn jst over 2f out: drvn over 1f out: sn edgd rt and hdd 100yds: sn carried lft and styd on same pce towards fin* **3/1**[2]

4151 **3** *shd* **Queen Aggie (IRE)**[6] 564 6-8-1 **77** 6ex........................ LuluStanford(7) 5 81
(Tony Carroll) *taken down early: hld up in tch in midfield: effrt over 1f out: hdwy to chse ldrs ins fnl f: carried lft wl ins fnl f: kpt on* **7/1**

15-6 **4** *1* **Capelita**[11] 503 5-8-13 **82**... LiamJones 8 84
(Michael Appleby) *led to s: s.i.s and rdn along early: hdwy to chse ldr after 1f: rdn jst over 2f out: stl pressing ldrs whn squeezed for room and snatched up jst ins fnl f: swtchd rt and rallied wl fnl 75yds* **6/1**[3]

-441 **5** *hd* **Subtle Knife**[23] 351 7-8-13 **82**... WilliamCarson 2 83
(Giles Bravery) *chsd ldr for 1f: styd chsng ldrs: rdn jst over 2f out: drvn and ev ch jst ins fnl f: no ex and hld whn carried lft and hmpd wl ins fnl f* **7/1**

-230 **6** *½* **Boonga Roogeta**[34] 212 7-8-5 **74**..................................(v) JimmyQuinn 6 72
(Peter Charalambous) *hld up in tch in last trio: rdn over 2f out: no imp tl styd on ins fnl f: nvr trbld ldrs* **12/1**

4-23 **7** *¾* **Lady Lydia (IRE)**[6] 558 5-8-3 **75**.............................. DanielMuscutt(3) 7 75
(Conrad Allen) *t.k.h: hld up in tch in last trio: hdwy on inner over 1f out: chsd ldrs 1f out: no ex and wknd wl ins fnl f* **10/1**

0-35 **8** *5* **Glastonberry**[23] 351 8-8-13 **82**...................................... TimmyMurphy 9 66
(Geoffrey Deacon) *stdd s: t.k.h: hld up in rr: effrt over 1f out: sn no imp: wknd ins fnl f* **25/1**

1m 23.94s (-0.86) **Going Correction** +0.05s/f (Slow) 8 Ran SP% **115.7**

Speed ratings (Par 104): **106,104,104,103,103 101,102,95**

CSF £9.20 CT £39.53 TOTE £3.70: £1.40, £1.20, £1.60; EX 11.40 Trifecta £72.00.

Owner Mr & Mrs F Cotton, Mr & Mrs P Conway **Bred** Summerhill & J Osborne **Trained** Pulborough, W Sussex

FOCUS

A fairly decent fillies' handicap.

633 32RED CASINO MAIDEN AUCTION STKS 1m 1y(P)

4:35 (4:37) (Class 6) 3-Y-0 **£2,264** (£673; £336; £168) **Stalls** High

Form RPR

42-3 **1** **Theos Lolly (IRE)**[14] 459 3-9-5 74.................................... DavidNolan 2 72
(Richard Fahey) *mde all: rdn ent fnl 2f: drvn ins fnl f: all out towards fin* **5/2**[2]

2 *hd* **Aid To Africa (IRE)** 3-9-5 0.. WilliamCarson 4 71
(Michael Bell) *chsd ldrs: effrt to chse wnr over 1f out: drvn ins fnl f: styd on wl fnl 100yds: nt quite getting to wnr* **20/1**

45-2 **3** *¾* **Carry Me Home**[14] 466 3-9-5 67.................................. DarryllHolland 6 69
(Charles Hills) *in tch in midfield: effrt and wd bnd 2f out: lost pl and looked hld in 4th 1f out: styd on wl fnl 100yds: gng on at fin* **11/10**[1]

3 **4** *¾* **Cold Fusion (IRE)**[22] 361 3-9-0 0..................................... TedDurcan 5 62
(Ed Vaughan) *chsd wnr tl unable qck u.p over 1f out: styd on same pce ins fnl f* **9/2**[3]

0-3 **5** *¾* **Heads You Win**[20] 400 3-9-0 0.. TimmyMurphy 7 60
(Jamie Osborne) *wl in tch in midfield: pushed along ent fnl f: kpt on same pce fnl 150yds* **16/1**

32- **6** *3 ¼* **Ede's The Mover**[136] 6995 3-9-0 0.................................. KieranO'Neill 3 52
(Pat Phelan) *hld up in tch: effrt on inner over 1f out: no imp: wknd ins fnl f* **14/1**

7 *¾* **Melendez (USA)** 3-9-0 0... LucyKBarry(5) 1 56
(Jamie Osborne) *s.i.s: detached in last: effrt over 1f out: no imp* **66/1**

1m 39.49s (1.29) **Going Correction** +0.05s/f (Slow) 7 Ran SP% **113.2**

Speed ratings (Par 95): **95,94,94,93,92 89,88**

CSF £46.30 TOTE £2.90: £1.40, £9.30; EX 49.90 Trifecta £162.10.

Owner M J Macleod **Bred** Mrs Claire Doyle **Trained** Musley Bank, N Yorks

FOCUS

An ordinary maiden and they finished in a bit of a bunch. The winner is rated to the balance of his recent form.

634 £10 FREE AT 32RED.COM AMATEUR RIDERS' H'CAP 1m 7f 169y(P)

5:05 (5:06) (Class 6) (0-60,60) 4-Y-0+ **£2,183** (£677; £338; £169) **Stalls** Low

Form RPR

00 **1** **Pao De Acuca (IRE)**[30] 255 4-9-3 **46** oh1.................(t) MrWillPettis(5) 6 60
(Jose Santos) *w ldr and a wl clr of field: led 10f out: rdn 2f out: kpt on fnl f: rdn out* **66/1**

0-33 **2** *1 ¼* **Master Burbidge**[23] 354 5-9-12 **51**.....................(p) MissRWaterson(7) 1 64
(Neil Mulholland) *led and sn wl clr w wnr: hdd 10f out but styd clr w wnr: nudged along over 1f out: wanting to hang lft and styd on same pce fnl f* **11/8**[1]

-404 **3** *11* **Delagoa Bay (IRE)**[11] 498 8-10-0 **46** oh1............ MrThomasGreatrex 2 45+
(Sylvester Kirk) *midfield but nvr on terms: rdn over 3f out: no ch and wd bnd 2f out: styd on to go modest 3rd wl ins fnl f* **3/1**[2]

5-62 **4** *2 ¾* **Galuppi**[14] 461 5-10-8 **59**.......................................(b) MrBMLinehan(5) 10 55+
(J R Jenkins) *hld up in rr: effrt u.p over 2f out: modest 5th 2f out: plugged on: nvr trbld ldrs* **6/1**[3]

0/04 **5** *¾* **Vedani (IRE)**[18] 417 7-10-5 **54**..(t) MrHHunt(3) 11 49+
(Tony Carroll) *hld up in midfield but nt on terms: effrt in 4th over 2f out: wnt modest 3rd over 1f out: no imp: plugged on and lost 3rd wl ins fnl f* **8/1**

00-0 **6** *7* **Opus Too (IRE)**[10] 505 5-9-9 **46** oh1.............................. MrBJames(5) 9 33
(John Ryan) *chsd clr ldng pair but nvr on terms: rdn and no imp over 2f out: lost modest 3rd and wknd over 1f out* **50/1**

0-30 **7** *¾* **Boston Blue**[18] 417 9-9-12 **51**.. MissSAColl(7) 7 37+
(Tony Carroll) *hld up wl off the pce in last: sme hdwy over 1f out: kpt on ins fnl f: n.d* **33/1**

41-6 **8** *5* **Grand Facile**[35] 195 4-9-8 **53**..............................(v) MissBeckyButler(7) 8 33+
(Gary Moore) *midfield but nvr on terms w ldrs: wknd over 2f out: wl bhd over 1f out* **10/1**

5/0- **9** *1 ¾* **Green Du Ciel (FR)**[51] 3021 11-10-2 **53**.........................(t) MissHHeal(5) 3 31+
(Carroll Gray) *midfield but nvr on terms: rdn over 2f out: 6th and no prog 2f out: wknd over 1f out: eased ins fnl f* **66/1**

35-6 **10** *14* **Comedy House**[38] 156 8-10-7 **60**...........................(p) MrLFMadgwick(7) 5 21+
(Michael Madgwick) *stdd s: hld up in rr: hdwy into midfield 1/2-way but nvr on terms w ldrs: rdn and wknd over 2f out: t.o* **12/1**

0/0- **11** 3/4 **Hawk Gold (IRE)**[79] 8085 12-9-11 **46** oh1................(b) MissMBryant(3) 4
(Paddy Butler) *chsd clr ldng pair but nvr on terms: wknd over 2f out: t.o*
100/1

3m 26.52s (0.82) **Going Correction** +0.05s/f (Slow)
WFA 4 from 5yo+ 6lb **11** Ran SP% **118.2**
Speed ratings (Par 101): **99,98,92,91,91 87,87,84,83,76 76**
CSF £158.63 CT £396.19 TOTE £50.70: £6.40, £1.30, £1.20; EX 270.80 Trifecta £1486.20.
Owner Jose Santos **Bred** Derrick Fisher **Trained** Upper Lambourn, Berks
■ Stewards' Enquiry : Miss S A Coll 12-day ban; failing to take all reasonable and permissible measures to obtain the best possible placing (tba)

FOCUS
A moderate affair. The first two pulled clear of the others in the early stages and nothing else ever got into it.
T/Plt: £28.60 to a £1 stake. Pool: £65,430.75 - 1,668.41 winning tickets T/Qpdt: £8.60 to a £1 stake. Pool: £4,486.66 - 384.10 winning tickets **Steve Payne**

589 WOLVERHAMPTON (A.W) (L-H)

Friday, February 19

OFFICIAL GOING: Tapeta: standard
Wind: Fresh behind Weather: Cloudy

635 DOWNLOAD THE NEW UNIBET RACING APP H'CAP 5f 20y (Tp)
5:20 (5:20) (Class 6) (0-60,70) 3-Y-O **£2,587** (£770; £384; £192) **Stalls** Low

Form RPR

5211 **1** **Englishwoman**[5] 578 3-9-12 **70** 12ex.................. JosephineGordon(5) 1 78
(David Evans) *chsd ldrs: shkn up to ld over 1f out: r.o* **4/5**[1]

024- **2** 1 1/4 **La Asomada**[164] 6189 3-9-7 **60**.................................... GrahamGibbons 5 62+
(David Barron) *hld up: hdwy over 1f out: sn rdn: r.o* **9/1**[3]

4-06 **3** 1 1/4 **David's Beauty (IRE)**[22] 365 3-9-5 **58**....................(p) DougieCostello 3 55
(Brian Baugh) *led: rdn and hdd over 1f out: styd on same pce ins fnl f*
40/1

0-32 **4** 3/4 **Rampers (IRE)**[10] 510 3-9-6 **59**... AdamKirby 7 53
(Jamie Osborne) *prom: rdn over 1f out: edgd lft and styd on same pce*
3/1[2]

000- **5** 4 **Cuban Queen (USA)**[165] 6162 3-8-13 **52**.............(p) RichardKingscote 9 32
(Jeremy Gask) *sn chsng ldr: rdn and ev ch over 1f out: edgd lft and wknd ins fnl f* **10/1**

6-50 **6** 2 3/4 **Oak Forest**[16] 436 3-8-5 **47**... RobHornby(3) 6 17
(Michael Attwater) *prom: lost pl 4f out: hdwy over 1f out: sn rdn and wknd* **50/1**

466- **7** 3 1/4 **Passionateprincess (IRE)**[84] 8010 3-8-7 **46**............... PJMcDonald 11 4
(Ann Duffield) *s.i.s and swtchd lft sn after s: hld up: rdn and wknd over 1f out* **22/1**

3042 **8** 1 **Rojina (IRE)**[6] 562 3-8-10 **56**....................................... SeanMooney(7) 4 11
(Joseph Tuite) *in rr: nt clr run wl over 2f out: wknd over 1f out* **25/1**

0-14 **9** 4 1/2 **Yisty**[10] 510 3-8-10 **49**...(v) TonyHamilton 10
(Derek Shaw) *chsd ldrs: rdn 1/2-way: sn wknd* **22/1**

1m 1.5s (-0.40) **Going Correction** -0.175s/f (Stan) **9** Ran SP% **116.6**
Speed ratings (Par 95): **96,94,92,90,84 80,74,73,66**
CSF £8.48 CT £169.04 TOTE £1.60: £1.10, £2.30, £8.30; EX 8.00 Trifecta £106.30.
Owner R Kent **Bred** Peter Winkworth **Trained** Pandy, Monmouths

FOCUS
A modest 3yo sprint handicap.The winner is better than this grade.

636 32RED CASINO FILLIES' H'CAP 1m 4f 50y (Tp)
5:50 (5:51) (Class 5) (0-75,75) 4-Y-O+ **£3,234** (£962; £481; £240) **Stalls** Low

Form RPR

-506 **1** **Bayan Kasirga (IRE)**[6] 566 6-9-3 **68**........................... TonyHamilton 3 75
(Richard Fahey) *chsd ldrs: pushed along over 3f out: rdn to ld over 1f out: hung lft ins fnl f: styd on* **5/1**[3]

5-54 **2** 1/2 **Hope You Dance (FR)**[23] 342 4-8-12 **66**....................... MartinDwyer 4 72
(David Simcock) *hld up: hdwy over 1f out: rdn to chse wnr and hung lft fnl f: styd on* **13/2**

63-1 **3** 3 1/2 **Celestial Bay**[18] 420 7-9-10 **75**... LukeMorris 2 75
(Sylvester Kirk) *chsd ldrs: nt clr run over 2f out: rdn over 1f out: styd on same pce fnl f* **3/1**[2]

6-35 **4** 1/2 **Percys Princess**[29] 273 5-9-5 **73**...................... AlistairRawlinson(3) 6 73
(Michael Appleby) *led: rdn over 2f out: hdd over 1f out: no ex ins fnl f* **7/1**

-311 **5** 1 3/4 **Percella**[30] 261 4-9-0 **68**.. AdamKirby 1 65
(Ian Williams) *hld up: rdn over 2f out: nt clr run wl over 1f out: n.d* **5/1**[3]

3-41 **6** 3/4 **Rivers Run (IRE)**[23] 342 4-9-4 **72**........................... GrahamGibbons 5 68
(Ralph Beckett) *prom: chsd ldr over 10f out: rdn and ev ch over 2f out: wknd fnl f* **11/4**[1]

2m 37.52s (-3.28) **Going Correction** -0.175s/f (Stan)
WFA 4 from 5yo+ 3lb **6** Ran SP% **110.8**
Speed ratings (Par 100): **103,102,100,100,98 98**
CSF £34.79 TOTE £6.80: £2.60, £4.10; EX 41.60 Trifecta £180.80.
Owner Stephen Humphreys **Bred** Lynn Lodge Stud **Trained** Musley Bank, N Yorks

FOCUS
An ordinary fillies' handicap. The winner is rated back to her 2014 form.

637 32REDSPORT.COM H'CAP 1m 5f 194y (Tp)
6:20 (6:24) (Class 6) (0-65,65) 4-Y-O+ **£2,587** (£770; £384; £192) **Stalls** Low

Form RPR

334- **1** **Consortium (IRE)**[69] 6673 4-9-7 **65**..................................(p) AdamKirby 1 71
(Neil King) *hld up: hdwy over 8f out: pushed along 6f out: rdn over 2f out: led and hung lft ins fnl f: styd on u.p* **3/1**[2]

4623 **2** 1 1/2 **Astra Hall**[11] 498 7-9-7 **60**.. LukeMorris 3 64
(Michael Appleby) *led 2f: chsd ldrs: led over 2f out: rdn over 1f out: hdd and hmpd ins fnl f: styd on same pce* **10/1**

43-5 **3** 3/4 **Robben**[28] 295 4-9-1 **59**...(v) PJMcDonald 6 62
(John Mackie) *s.i.s: hld up: hdwy over 7f out: rdn over 1f out: styd on* **6/1**

60-0 **4** 1 1/4 **Golden Thread**[38] 156 6-9-10 **63**................................ CharlesBishop 5 64
(Neil King) *s.i.s: hld up: hdwy u.p over 1f out: styd on same pce ins fnl f* **20/1**

-213 **5** 4 **Pinotage**[25] 329 8-9-8 **61**...(p) JamesSullivan 8 57
(Peter Niven) *trckd ldrs: plld hrd: lost pl 8f out: nt clr run over 2f out: hdwy over 1f out: wknd ins fnl f* **11/4**[1]

23-5 **6** 19 **Singzak**[17] 425 8-9-9 **62**.. MartinDwyer 7 31+
(David C Griffiths) *led 12f out: hdd over 2f out: eased over 1f out* **9/2**[3]

2-65 **7** 11 **Shirls Son Sam**[22] 368 8-8-10 **49**... JoeyHaynes 2 3
(Chris Fairhurst) *racd keenly: w ldr 2f: remained handy: rdn over 3f out: wknd over 2f out* **20/1**

3m 3.95s (-0.85) **Going Correction** -0.175s/f (Stan)
WFA 4 from 5yo+ 5lb **7** Ran SP% **102.7**
Speed ratings (Par 101): **95,94,93,93,90 79,73**
CSF £25.31 CT £119.23 TOTE £4.10: £2.70, £4.60; EX 23.70 Trifecta £115.10.
Owner Govier & Brown & Neil King **Bred** Mrs Celine Collins **Trained** Barbury Castle, Wiltshire
■ Moulin Rouge was withdrawn. Price at time of withdrawal 17/2. Rule 4 applies to all bets - deduction 10p in the pound.

FOCUS
A moderate staying event run a modest gallop. A straightforward feel to the form.

638 32RED.COM H'CAP 7f 32y (Tp)
6:50 (6:53) (Class 4) (0-85,85) 3-Y-O **£4,851** (£1,443; £721; £360) **Stalls** High

Form RPR

10-2 **1** **Dream Mover (IRE)**[23] 344 3-9-5 **83**............................. AndreaAtzeni 2 87
(Marco Botti) *chsd ldr: rdn over 2f out: r.o to ld wl ins fnl f: jst hld on* **10/11**[1]

510- **2** shd **The Supreme (FR)**[184] 5529 3-9-5 **83**........................ FrannyNorton 4 86
(Mick Channon) *plld hrd and prom: rdn over 1f out: r.o wl* **4/1**[3]

02-1 **3** 1 1/4 **Bear Faced**[20] 402 3-9-7 **85**... LukeMorris 1 85
(Sir Mark Prescott Bt) *led: qcknd over 2f out: rdn over 1f out: hdd wl ins fnl f: styd on same pce* **3/1**[2]

0-35 **4** 3/4 **Abberley Dancer (IRE)**[14] 459 3-8-2 **71**........... JosephineGordon(5) 5 69
(J S Moore) *hld up: pushed along over 2f out: hdwy over 1f out: styd on* **22/1**

16-3 **5** 2 1/4 **Outback Blue**[28] 296 3-9-0 **78**... AdamKirby 3 70
(David Evans) *hld up in tch: rdn over 2f out: no ex fnl f* **8/1**

1m 27.38s (-1.42) **Going Correction** -0.175s/f (Stan) **5** Ran SP% **112.8**
Speed ratings (Par 99): **101,100,99,98,96**
CSF £5.15 TOTE £1.40: £1.02, £3.00; EX 3.00 Trifecta £14.00.
Owner Team Valor **Bred** D G Iceton **Trained** Newmarket, Suffolk

FOCUS
A fair 3yo handicap rated around the front-running second.

639 LADBROKES MAIDEN STKS 7f 32y (Tp)
7:20 (7:24) (Class 5) 3-Y-O+ **£2,911** (£866; £432; £216) **Stalls** High

Form RPR

24- **1** **Ikerrin Road (IRE)**[169] 6017 3-8-9 0............................ DougieCostello 5 80+
(John Quinn) *mde all: rdn over 1f out: r.o* **13/8**[1]

4 **2** 1 1/4 **Torreon (IRE)**[18] 423 5-9-12 0... AdamKirby 11 83
(John Ryan) *chsd wnr 6f out: rdn over 1f out: styd on same pce ins fnl f* **20/1**

3 4 1/2 **Rosenborg Rider (IRE)** 3-8-9 0............................... GrahamGibbons 2 64+
(Ralph Beckett) *s.i.s: sn rcvrd into mid-div: shkn up over 2f out: r.o to go 3rd ins fnl f: nt trble ldrs* **11/4**[2]

4 1/2 **Justice Grace (IRE)** 3-8-4 0................................ PatrickO'Donnell(5) 3 63+
(Ralph Beckett) *mid-div: pushed along over 2f out: r.o ins fnl f: nvr nrr* **25/1**

2 **5** 3 **Grecian King**[18] 423 3-8-9 0...(p) LukeMorris 1 55+
(James Tate) *plld hrd and prom: rdn over 1f out: wknd fnl f* **3/1**[3]

4 **6** 1 3/4 **Lucky Louie**[23] 352 3-8-9 0.. StevieDonohoe 8 50
(Roger Teal) *s.i.s: hld up: hung lft fr 1/2-way: styd on ins fnl f: nvr nrr* **25/1**

0-2 **7** nk **Whistle (IRE)**[20] 402 3-8-4 0.. FrannyNorton 12 44
(Martyn Meade) *plld hrd and prom: rdn over 2f out: wknd over 1f out* **14/1**

00 **8** 1/2 **Regent's Rock**[4] 591 4-9-7 0.. PJMcDonald 6 49
(Peter Niven) *hld up: rdn over 2f out: nvr on terms* **150/1**

9 1 3/4 **Harry Holland** 4-9-12 0... MartinDwyer 7 49
(William Muir) *mid-div: shkn up over 2f out: sn wknd* **20/1**

06 **10** 2 1/2 **Suzu**[10] 507 3-8-4 0.. RaulDaSilva 4 32
(Ivan Furtado) *chsd ldrs: rdn 1/2-way: wknd 2f out* **125/1**

11 11 **Dandy Star (IRE)** 3-8-9 0..(t) AndreaAtzeni 10 7
(Marco Botti) *s.i.s: hld up: rdn and wknd over 2f out* **25/1**

1m 27.83s (-0.97) **Going Correction** -0.175s/f (Stan)
WFA 3 from 4yo+ 17lb **11** Ran SP% **118.9**
Speed ratings (Par 103): **98,96,91,90,87 85,85,84,82,79 67**
CSF £41.89 TOTE £2.50: £1.10, £5.10, £1.70; EX 40.90 Trifecta £172.00.
Owner Mrs S Quinn **Bred** Gerard Kerin **Trained** Settrington, N Yorks

FOCUS
The first two raced one-two pretty much throughout, but fair form and a couple of Ralph Beckett newcomers kept on nicely behind them. The winner is rated to his debut form.

640 CORAL.CO.UK H'CAP 1m 4f 50y (Tp)
7:50 (7:52) (Class 5) (0-70,70) 4-Y-O+ **£3,234** (£962; £481; £240) **Stalls** Low

Form RPR

1-21 **1** **Tangramm**[23] 343 4-9-4 **70**.......................................(p) RobertWinston 1 78+
(Dean Ivory) *hld up in tch: shkn up to ld 1f out: sn rdn: jst hld on* **7/2**[2]

46-4 **2** nk **Midtech Star (IRE)**[23] 343 4-9-3 **69**............................(v^1) AdamKirby 5 76
(Ian Williams) *a.p: rdn to chse ldr 3f out: styd on wl u.p* **11/2**[3]

-044 **3** nk **Lean On Pete (IRE)**[15] 446 7-9-3 **66**.....................(e) GrahamGibbons 2 73
(Ollie Pears) *hld up: hdwy over 1f out: sn rdn: r.o* **10/1**

5-31 **4** 1/2 **Obboorr**[21] 382 7-9-2 **65**... BarryMcHugh 3 71
(Tim Fitzgerald) *chsd ldrs: rdn over 3f out: r.o* **7/2**[2]

-211 **5** nk **Trending (IRE)**[14] 461 7-9-4 **67**.......................(t) RichardKingscote 7 73
(Jeremy Gask) *led: rdn over 2f out: hdd 1f out: no ex towards fin* **3/1**[1]

500- **6** 6 **Ring Eye (IRE)**[111] 7636 8-8-4 **58**.......................... PatrickO'Donnell(5) 9 54
(John O'Shea) *hld up: hdwy over 2f out: rdn over 1f out: wknd ins fnl f* **50/1**

50-0 **7** 1 **Surround Sound**[35] 199 6-8-13 **62**...............................(t) JamesSullivan 8 56
(Tim Easterby) *hld up: hung lft over 2f out: rdn over 1f out: nt trble ldrs* **28/1**

110- **8** 8 **Ninepointsixthree**[131] 7140 6-9-0 **68**.......................... CiaranMckee(5) 4 50
(John O'Shea) *s.s: hld up: hmpd 2f out: a in rr* **25/1**

1-26 **9** 10 **Classic Mission**[21] 382 5-9-0 **70**...................(b) Pierre-LouisJamin(7) 6 36
(Jonathan Portman) *prom tl rdn and wknd over 2f out* **8/1**

2/43 **10** 2 1/4 **Tatawu (IRE)**[14] 467 4-9-2 **68**... LukeMorris 10 30
(Peter Hiatt) *chsd ldr tl rdn 3f out: sn wknd* **16/1**

2m 36.3s (-4.50) **Going Correction** -0.175s/f (Stan)
WFA 4 from 5yo+ 3lb **10** Ran SP% **120.2**
Speed ratings (Par 103): **108,107,107,107,107 103,102,97,90,88**
CSF £23.58 CT £180.06 TOTE £3.60: £1.10, £2.20, £3.20; EX 23.60 Trifecta £153.30.
Owner John Marsden **Bred** W G H Barrons **Trained** Radlett, Herts

FOCUS
A modest but competitive handicap run 1.22secs faster than the earlier fillies' 0-75. Solid form for the level, with more to come from the winner perhaps.

T/Plt: £223.60 to a £1 stake. Pool: £80,730.00 - 263.48 winning tickets. T/Qpdt: £30.90 to a £1 stake. Pool: £11,400.00 - 272.54 winning tickets. **Colin Roberts**

641 - 643a (Foreign Racing) - See Raceform Interactive

548 DUNDALK (A.W) (L-H)

Friday, February 19

OFFICIAL GOING: Polytrack: standard

644a 32RED CASINO RACE (ALL-WEATHER CHAMPIONSHIPS FAST-TRACK QUALIFIER) 7f (P)

7:35 (7:35) 3-Y-O **£11,948** (£3,492; £1,654; £551)

RPR

1 **Roman Impero**[42] 109 3-9-4 87 ConorHoban 1 85
(M Halford, Ire) *disp early tl restrained and settled in 3rd: tk clsr order under 2f out: effrt in 2nd over 1f out and clsd u.p to ld ins fnl 150yds: kpt on wl* **7/4**[2]

2 1 ¼ **Turbine (IRE)**[90] 7938 3-9-4 91 JoeFanning 4 82
(Mark Johnston) *disp early tl sn settled bhd ldr in 2nd: impr to ld under 2f out: strly pressed ins fnl f and hdd u.p ins fnl 150yds: no ex* **4/7**[1]

3 hd **More Than Munny (USA)**[28] 302 3-8-11 80 DenisLinehan(7) 3 81
(J P Murtagh, Ire) *settled in rr of quartet: pushed along appr st: rdn into cl 3rd ins fnl f and kpt on same pce: nt trble wnr* **16/1**[3]

4 1 **Lex Talionis (IRE)**[121] 7403 3-8-7 75 (p) DonaghO'Connor(7) 2 75
(J F Levins, Ire) *hooded to load: disp early and sn led: over 1 l clr at 1/2-way: rdn and pressed clly 2f out: sn hdd and no ex in 3rd over 1f out: dropped to rr ins fnl f and kpt on one pce* **16/1**[3]

1m 25.84s (85.84) **4** Ran SP% **111.8**
CSF £3.26 TOTE £2.50; DF 3.00 Trifecta £4.90.
Owner Eric Koh **Bred** Theakston Stud **Trained** Doneany, Co Kildare

FOCUS
They seemed to go a reasonable enough gallop in this race and there were no excuses for anything. The winner is certainly an improver and one would imagine there's more to come. The winner and third have been rated as running fair personal bests.

645 - 652a (Foreign Racing) - See Raceform Interactive

629 LINGFIELD (L-H)

Saturday, February 20

OFFICIAL GOING: Polytrack: standard
Wind: strong, half behind Weather: light rain until race 3 and again race 7

653 CORAL.CO.UK H'CAP 1m 4f (P)

1:25 (1:25) (Class 6) (0-55,54) 4-Y-O+ **£2,264** (£673; £336; £168) **Stalls** Low

Form RPR

06-0 1 **Fleetwood Poppy**[44] 84 4-8-9 45 RobertHavlin 9 51
(Michael Attwater) *midfield: effrt in 4th 2f out: styd on wl u.p ins fnl f: led last strides* **12/1**

3-00 2 hd **Sudden Wish (IRE)**[10] 514 7-9-2 49 JimCrowley 4 55
(Michael Attwater) *chsd ldrs: wnt 2nd 5f tl jst over 2f out: drvn to ld over 1f out: kpt on and forged ahd ins fnl f: hdd and no ex last strides* **8/1**

0-25 3 2 ½ **Awesome Rock (IRE)**[24] 348 7-8-7 47 RhiainIngram(7) 7 49
(Roger Ingram) *in tch in midfield: effrt to chse ldr jst over 2f out: ev ch over 1f out: 3rd and no ex ins fnl f: wknd towards fin* **5/1**[3]

-000 4 1 ¼ **Dynamo (IRE)**[18] 428 5-8-13 46 (t) ShaneKelly 2 46
(Richard Hughes) *chsd ldr tl led 10f out: rdn 2f out: hdd over 1f out: no ex u.p and wknd ins fnl f* **9/2**[2]

1043 5 ¾ **Shirataki (IRE)**[3] 606 8-9-0 54 LuluStanford(7) 6 53
(Peter Hiatt) *s.i.s: bhd: stl last whn nt clr run and swtchd lft over 2f out: stl nt clr run and swtchd rt wl over 1f out: hdwy 1f out: styd on wl ins fnl f: nt rch ldrs* **5/2**[1]

5-00 6 1 **Investissement**[22] 382 10-9-0 52 (bt[1]) CallumShepherd(5) 8 49
(Paddy Butler) *hld up in last trio: rdn over 3f out: kpt on u.p fnl 2f: nvr enough pce to threaten ldrs* **16/1**

44-0 7 6 **Ocean Bentley (IRE)**[34] 233 4-8-9 45 RyanPowell 3 33
(Tony Carroll) *plld hrd: chsd ldrs: rdn and struggling over 2f out: wknd over 1f out* **20/1**

52-0 8 2 ¾ **Malih**[35] 222 7-9-5 52 JoeyHaynes 5 35
(Eric Wheeler) *s.i.s: hld up in tch in last trio: rdn 4f out: 6th and no hdwy 2f out: wknd over 1f out* **6/1**

60-5 9 18 **Citisonsmith (IRE)**[34] 232 4-8-9 45 WilliamCarson 1
(Tony Carroll) *led for 2f: chsd ldrs tl 5f out: lost pl u.p 3f out: lost tch 2f out* **12/1**

2m 30.74s (-2.26) **Going Correction** -0.15s/f (Stan)
WFA 4 from 5yo+ 3lb **9** Ran SP% **114.8**
Speed ratings (Par 101): **101,100,99,98,97 97,93,91,79**
CSF £103.11 CT £546.55 TOTE £11.20: £2.90, £2.40, £1.40; EX 69.10 Trifecta £594.60.
Owner Canisbay Bloodstock **Bred** Canisbay Bloodstock Ltd **Trained** Epsom, Surrey

FOCUS
A weak affair. The winner is rated back to his best form of last year.

654 32RED MAIDEN FILLIES' STKS (PLUS 10 RACE) 1m 1y(P)

2:00 (2:00) (Class 5) 3-Y-O **£2,911** (£866; £432; £216) **Stalls** High

Form RPR

5-2 1 **Australian Queen**[38] 163 3-9-0 0 JamieSpencer 5 73+
(David Elsworth) *chsd ldr: upsides and gng best whn awkward and hung rt bnd 2f out: rallied u.p 1f out: led fnl 100yds: styd on: rdn out* **4/11**[1]

2 ¾ **Dazzling Rose** 3-9-0 0 RobertHavlin 4 71+
(John Gosden) *in tch in 4th: shkn up and rn green bnd 2f out: hdwy to go 3rd and swtchd lft 1f out: kpt on wl to go 2nd last stride* **8/1**[3]

3-23 3 shd **Strawberry Sorbet**[19] 421 3-9-0 71 AdamKirby 3 70
(Clive Cox) *led: rdn wl over 2f out: lft clr bnd 2f out: drvn ent fnl f: hdd and kpt on same pce fnl 100yds: lost 2nd last stride* **5/1**[2]

- 4 3 ¾ **Harikiri (IRE)** 3-9-0 0 DarryllHolland 1 61
(Charles Hills) *chsd ldng pair: rdn over 2f out: lost 3rd and no ex 1f out: wknd ins fnl f* **16/1**

5 1 ¼ **Topalova** 3-9-0 0 SaleemGolam 2 58
(Mark H Tompkins) *s.i.s: in tch in rr: rdn over 2f out: no ex ent fnl f: wknd ins fnl f* **50/1**

1m 37.87s (-0.33) **Going Correction** -0.15s/f (Stan) **5** Ran SP% **108.9**
Speed ratings (Par 94): **95,94,94,90,89**
CSF £3.87 TOTE £1.10: £1.10, £2.10; EX 2.40 Trifecta £3.80.
Owner J C Smith **Bred** Littleton Stud **Trained** Newmarket, Suffolk

FOCUS
A fair maiden. The first two look likely types to progress and the third is rated to form.

655 DAILY PRICE BOOSTS AT UNIBET H'CAP 5f 6y(P)

2:35 (2:35) (Class 4) (0-85,85) 4-Y-O+ **£4,690** (£1,395; £697; £348) **Stalls** High

Form RPR

33-6 1 **Sandfrankskipsgo**[35] 220 7-9-6 84 GeorgeBaker 9 93
(Peter Crate) *broke v fast: mde all: rdn over 1f out: kpt on wl: rdn out* **8/1**

5500 2 1 ¼ **Vimy Ridge**[9] 529 4-9-3 81 (p) SaleemGolam 1 86
(Alan Bailey) *midfield: effrt over 1f out: hdwy u.p 1f out: chsd wnr ins fnl f: styd on but nvr threatened wnr* **7/1**

-654 3 1 ¼ **Come On Dave (IRE)**[23] 359 7-9-5 83 (v) AdamKirby 4 83+
(John Butler) *taken down early: chsd ldng trio: stmbld after 1f: styd in 4th: rdn over 1f out: kpt on ins fnl f: no threat to wnr* **3/1**[1]

0-01 4 ½ **Taajub (IRE)**[14] 484 9-9-7 85 ShaneKelly 7 83
(Peter Crate) *midfield and niggled along at times: hdwy on inner over 1f out: drvn and styd on same pce ins fnl f* **6/1**[3]

-021 5 hd **Doctor Parkes**[19] 416 10-8-11 80 AaronJones(5) 8 77
(Stuart Williams) *off the pce in last trio: effrt over 1f out: r.o strly fnl 100yds: nt rch ldrs* **8/1**

4-42 6 shd **Burning Thread (IRE)**[14] 484 9-9-0 85 (b) AdamMcLean(7) 6 82
(David Elsworth) *midfield: c wd and effrt over 1f out: styd on u.p ins fnl f: nt rch ldrs* **10/1**

30-6 7 ½ **Temple Road (IRE)**[3] 604 8-8-8 72 (bt) FrannyNorton 10 67
(Milton Bradley) *chsd wnr: rdn over 1f out: lost 2nd ins fnl f: wknd towards fin* **12/1**

6-26 8 shd **Desert Strike**[16] 439 10-8-12 76 (p) LiamKeniry 3 71
(Conor Dore) *taken down early: chsd ldng pair: unable qck u.p over 1f out: btn whn n.m.r and swtchd lft wl ins fnl f* **20/1**

-334 9 1 **Showtime Star**[11] 508 6-9-5 83 (p) JimCrowley 5 74
(Gay Kelleway) *dwlt: a towards rr: effrt over 1f out: keeping on same pce and wl hld whn carried lft and nt clr run wl ins fnl f: burst blood vessel* **5/1**[2]

00-5 10 1 ¼ **Classic Seniority**[36] 198 4-9-1 79 RobertWinston 2 66
(Marjorie Fife) *s.i.s: a bhd* **10/1**

56.95s (-1.85) **Going Correction** -0.15s/f (Stan) **10** Ran SP% **121.3**
Speed ratings (Par 105): **108,106,104,103,102 102,101,101,100,98**
CSF £65.59 CT £215.12 TOTE £8.00: £2.30, £3.20, £1.70; EX 89.70 Trifecta £546.90.
Owner Peter Crate **Bred** Peter Crate **Trained** Newdigate, Surrey

FOCUS
A good, competitive sprint handicap on paper, but very few got into it. The time was quick and the winner is rated close to his old best.

656 CORAL H'CAP 1m 2f (P)

3:10 (3:10) (Class 3) (0-95,93) 4-Y-O **£7,246** (£2,168; £1,084; £542; £270) **Stalls** Low

Form RPR

12-2 1 **Sheila's Buddy**[42] 121 7-8-9 81 LiamKeniry 2 88
(J S Moore) *s.i.s: hld up in tch in last pair: pushed along and swtchd lft over 2f out: swtchd rt and edging lft over 1f out: str run u.p to ld cl home* **14/1**

-422 2 nk **Pactolus (IRE)**[9] 530 5-8-7 84 (t) AaronJones(5) 5 90
(Stuart Williams) *chsd ldrs: effrt ent fnl 2f: drvn and styd on to chal jst ins fnl f: led wl ins fnl f: hdd and no ex cl home* **6/1**[3]

2-12 3 ¾ **Giantstepsahead (IRE)**[21] 399 7-8-12 87 DanielMuscutt(3) 4 92
(Brian McMath) *led: hdd and rdn 2f out: sn led again: drvn 1f out: hdd and styd on same pce wl ins fnl f* **9/2**[2]

-300 4 nk **Russian Realm**[14] 486 6-9-5 91 ShaneKelly 1 95
(Richard Hughes) *hld up in tch in midfield: clsd to trck ldrs 2f out: effrt over 1f out: drvn and styd on same pce ins fnl f* **8/1**

01-0 5 nk **Franklin D (USA)**[24] 353 4-9-6 93 JamieSpencer 6 96
(Michael Bell) *hld up in tch in midfield: 5th and rdn over 2f out: hung lft bnd 2f out: hdwy to chse ldrs ins fnl f: styd on same pce fnl 100yds* **6/4**[1]

5-23 6 3 **Ansaab**[24] 353 8-9-2 88 BenCurtis 3 85
(Michael Appleby) *chsd ldr: rdn to ld 2f out: sn hdd but stl ev ch tl no ex jst ins fnl f: wknd fnl 100yds* **9/2**[2]

0-30 7 17 **Warfare**[30] 267 7-8-8 80 ow1 BarryMcHugh 7 43
(Tim Fitzgerald) *s.i.s: sn rcvrd to chse ldrs: rdn over 3f out: lost pl and wl btn 2f out: wknd over 1f out* **25/1**

2m 2.78s (-3.82) **Going Correction** -0.15s/f (Stan)
WFA 4 from 5yo+ 1lb **7** Ran SP% **112.3**
Speed ratings (Par 107): **109,108,108,107,107 105,91**
CSF £89.94 TOTE £10.30: £4.10, £3.20; EX 50.00 Trifecta £165.60.
Owner Ray Styles **Bred** Mrs Anita R Dodd **Trained** Upper Lambourn, Berks

FOCUS
Not a bad handicap, but they finished in a heap. Muddling form, with an unlikely pb from the winner.

657 UNIBET H'CAP 6f 1y(P)

3:45 (3:45) (Class 2) (0-105,99) 4-Y-**£11,971** (£3,583; £1,791; £896; £446) **Stalls** Low

Form RPR

01-1 1 **Spring Loaded (IRE)**[29] 288 4-9-1 93 ShaneKelly 2 100+
(Paul D'Arcy) *hld up in tch in last pair: effrt and n.m.r over 1f out: gap opened ins fnl f: r.o wl under hands and heels riding to ld last strides* **9/4**[1]

31-3 2 hd **Barracuda Boy (IRE)**[29] 288 6-9-7 99 RichardKingscote 1 105
(Tom Dascombe) *led: rdn 2f out: drvn and pressed 1f out: kpt on tl hdd and no ex last strides* **4/1**[2]

0-00 3 ¾ **Baddilini**[12] 503 6-9-2 94 (p) SaleemGolam 3 98
(Alan Bailey) *chsd ldrs: effrt 2f out: drvn and pressing ldr 1f out: kpt on same pce ins fnl f* **14/1**

-403 4 shd **Magnus Maximus**[9] 529 5-8-12 90 JFEgan 4 93
(Robyn Brisland) *chsd ldr: rdn over 2f out: stl pressing ldr and drvn 1f out: lost 2nd and styd on same pce ins fnl f* **7/1**[3]

1-12 5 1 ¼ **Nuno Tristan (USA)**[9] 529 4-8-13 91 TonyHamilton 5 90
(Richard Fahey) *in tch in 4th: effrt over 1f out: no imp: outpcd fnl 100yds* **9/4**[1]

00-0 6 8 **Primrose Valley**[29] 290 4-9-4 96 AdamKirby 6 70
(Ed Vaughan) *dropped in bhd after s: a last: rdn and no hdwy 2f out: wknd fnl f* **7/1**[3]

1m 9.87s (-2.03) **Going Correction** -0.15s/f (Stan) **6** Ran SP% **113.2**
Speed ratings (Par 109): **107,106,105,105,103 93**
CSF £11.77 TOTE £2.70: £1.20, £2.90; EX 12.70 Trifecta £103.60.
Owner Rowley Racing **Bred** Swordlestown Little **Trained** Newmarket, Suffolk

FOCUS
There was a tight finish to this good handicap, masking the winner's authority. He confirmed C&D form with the second despite worse terms.

658 UNIBET OFFER DAILY JOCKEY & TRAINER SPECIALS H'CAP 6f 1y(P)
4:20 (4:20) (Class 6) (0-65,65) 4-Y-O+ **£2,264** (£673; £336; £168) **Stalls** Low

Form RPR

04-0 **1** **Rigolleto (IRE)**[38] 167 8-9-4 **62**....(p) GeorgeBaker 2 69
(Anabel K Murphy) *broke fast: mde all: rdn over 1f out: drvn and kpt on wl ins fnl f* **5/1**

450- **2** *¾* **Pharoh Jake**[151] 6633 8-9-0 **58**.... WilliamTwiston-Davies 6 63
(John Bridger) *in tch in midfield: effrt over 1f out: drvn 1f out: styd on u.p to go 2nd cl home: nvr getting to wnr* **25/1**

0-40 **3** *shd* **Whaleweigh Station**[28] 319 5-9-7 **65**....(p) RaulDaSilva 7 69
(J R Jenkins) *hld up in rr: effrt on inner over 1f out: styd on wl ins fnl f: wnt 3rd cl home: nvr gong to rch wnr* **12/1**

-621 **4** *nk* **Compton Prince**[16] 442 7-9-2 **60**....(b) FrannyNorton 1 64
(Milton Bradley) *chsd ldrs: effrt over 1f out: chsd wnr 1f out: kpt on same pce ins fnl f: lost 2 pls cl home* **3/1**[2]

1-43 **5** *hd* **Encapsulated**[21] 398 6-8-12 **63**.... RhiainIngram(7) 5 66
(Roger Ingram) *taken down early: hld up in tch: swtchd rt and effrt over 1f out: kpt on wl u.p ins fnl f: nt rch ldrs* **4/1**[3]

520- **6** *3* **Best Trip (IRE)**[67] 8240 9-9-6 **64**.... RobertWinston 4 58
(Marjorie Fife) *chsd ldr rdn 2f out: lost 2nd and no ex 1f out: wknd ins fnl f* **10/1**

-505 **7** *shd* **Autumn Tonic (IRE)**[3] 615 4-8-11 **55**....(v[1]) JimCrowley 8 53
(Simon Dow) *hld up in tch: effrt whn hmpd and snatched up over 1f out: unable to rcvr and kpt on same pce fnl f* **11/4**[1]

00-0 **8** *11* **Dusty Blue**[15] 462 4-9-6 **64**.... AdamKirby 3 25
(Tony Carroll) *s.i.s: in tch in last trio: hdwy on outer into midfield over 3f out: lost pl on bnd and drvn 2f out: sn bhd: eased wl ins fnl f* **16/1**

1m 10.85s (-1.05) **Going Correction** -0.15s/f (Stan) **8** Ran SP% **114.8**
Speed ratings (Par 101): **101,100,99,99,99 95,95,80**
CSF £112.49 CT £1425.72 TOTE £6.10: £2.00, £5.50, £3.30; EX 82.30 Trifecta £1018.30.
Owner All The Kings Horses **Bred** Michael O'Mahony **Trained** Wilmcote, Warwicks

FOCUS
A modest sprint where the winner had the run of things in front. A blanket finish.

659 UNIBET.CO.UK DAILY ENHANCED PLACE TERMS MAIDEN STKS 5f 6y(P)
4:55 (4:55) (Class 5) 3-Y-O+ **£2,911** (£866; £432; £216) **Stalls** High

Form RPR

-222 **1** **Blue Bounty**[16] 444 5-9-5 58....(p) SaleemGolam 4 70
(Mark H Tompkins) *mde all: pushed along and wnt clr over 1f out: kpt on* **9/2**[2]

034- **2** *1 ¾* **Sadie Babes (IRE)**[91] 7945 3-7-11 65....[1] SammyJoBell(3) 6 53
(Richard Fahey) *taken down early: chsd wnr: rdn and outpcd over 1f out: kpt on same pce ins fnl f* **6/1**[3]

33-3 **3** *¾* **Gorgeous Geezer**[10] 515 3-8-2 71.... TimClark(3) 5 55
(Martin Smith) *in tch: effrt to chse ldrs 2f out: drvn and kpt on same pce fnl f* **4/7**[1]

5 **4** *7* **Birrafun (IRE)**[9] 531 3-8-0 0.... JoeyHaynes 1 25
(Ann Duffield) *hld up in tch: rdn and struggling to qckn 2f out: sn outpcd: wknd fnl f* **14/1**

0-4 **5** *hd* **Sand By Me**[7] 562 3-8-5 0.... JimmyQuinn 3 29
(Peter Crate) *bustled along early: chsd ldrs after 1f tl lost pl 1/2-way: bhd 2f out: sn wknd* **33/1**

620- **6** *1 ¾* **Just A Groove (IRE)**[98] 7859 3-8-5 70.... FrannyNorton 7 23+
(Ann Duffield) *chsd ldrs: rein broke and wnt v wd bnd after 1f: styd prom tl v wd again and dropped to rr bnd 2f out: no ch after* **8/1**

58.07s (-0.73) **Going Correction** -0.15s/f (Stan)
WFA 3 from 5yo 14lb **6** Ran SP% **116.8**
Speed ratings (Par 103): **99,96,95,83,83 80**
CSF £31.90 TOTE £5.30: £2.20, £2.20; EX 20.80 Trifecta £44.40.
Owner Raceworld **Bred** Pollards Stables **Trained** Newmarket, Suffolk
■ Dutch Archer was withdrawn. Price at time of withdrawal 16-1. Rule 4 does not apply.

FOCUS
A moderate maiden. The winner is rated back to his best.
T/Jkpt: Not won. T/Plt: £720.30 to a £1 stake. Pool: £61,648.01 - 62.47 winning tickets T/Qpdt: £157.80 to a £1 stake. Pool: £6,450.29 - 30.24 winning tickets **Steve Payne**

[584] CAGNES-SUR-MER
Saturday, February 20
OFFICIAL GOING: Polytrack: standard

660a PRIX SAONOIS (LISTED RACE) (4YO+) (POLYTRACK) 1m (F)
2:40 (12:00) 4-Y-O+ **£19,117** (£7,647; £5,735; £3,823; £1,911)

RPR

1 **Incahoots**[109] 7696 4-8-9 0.... MaximeGuyon 5 98
(F Head, France) **26/5**

2 *2* **Skaters Waltz (IRE)**[32] 5-8-13 0....(b) CesarPasserat 8 97
(X Nakkachdji, France) *fin 3rd: plcd 2nd* **7/1**

3 *1 ¾* **Il Segreto (FR)**[32] 4-8-13 0.... Pierre-CharlesBoudot 1 93
(C Delcher-Sanchez, France) *fin 4th: plcd 3rd* **9/5**[1]

4 *nk* **Sharpalo (FR)**[81] 8070 4-8-13 0....(b[1]) FranckBlondel 4 93
(Y Durepaire, France) *fin 5th: plcd 4th* **111/10**

5 *hd* **Toungi (IRE)**[32] 4-9-0 0.... CristianDemuro 2 93
(F Rossi, France) *fin 6th: plcd 5th* **49/10**[3]

6 *nk* **Almorox**[32] 4-8-13 0.... JulionAugo 6 92
(C Ferland, France) *fin 2nd: disqualified and plcd 6th* **5/2**[2]

7 *¾* **Netsuke (IRE)**[32] 5-8-9 0.... OlivierPlacais 3 86
(Mlle L-L Rohn-Pelvin, France) **38/1**

8 *½* **Yonna (FR)**[35] 5-8-9 0.... TonyPiccone 7 85
(E Lellouche, France) **147/10**

1m 34.01s (94.01) **8** Ran SP% **127.1**
WIN (incl. 1 euro stake): 6.20. PLACES: 2.50, 1.80, 1.40. DF: 36.10. SF: 68.90.
Owner Wertheimer & Frere **Bred** George Strawbridge **Trained** France

661 - 662a (Foreign Racing) - See Raceform Interactive

[586] ST MORITZ (R-H)
Sunday, February 21
OFFICIAL GOING: Snow: frozen

663a GRAND PRIX MOYGLARE STUD (CONDITIONS) (4YO+) (SNOW) 4f
11:40 (12:00) 4-Y-O+
£8,571 (£4,285; £3,061; £2,040; £1,020; £612)

RPR

1 **High Duty**[281] 5-9-0 0 ow3.... DennisSchiergen 1
(Karin Suter-Weber, Switzerland) **37/10**

2 *nse* **Boomerang Bob (IRE)**[15] 483 7-9-4 0.... WilliamCarson 3
(Jamie Osborne) *prom: rdn to chal and led after 1/2-way: kpt on but worn down towards fin and hdd post* **7/2**[3]

3 *1 ¾* **Zarras (GER)**[7] 588 7-9-2 0.... RaphaelLingg 8
(P Schaerer, Switzerland) **23/10**[1]

4 *2* **Footprintinthesand (IRE)**[7] 588 6-9-4 0.... RobertHavlin 6
(M Weiss, Switzerland) **53/10**

5 *1* **Renny Storm (CZE)**[7] 588 6-8-11 0.... AlexanderPietsch 7
(C Von Der Recke, Germany) **57/10**

6 *1* **Vale Of Iron (IRE)**[7] 587 4-9-2 0.... KierenFox 4
(John Best) *sn rdn and outpcd in rr: n.d after* **31/10**[2]

7 *2 ½* **Dandys Perier (IRE)**[7] 587 5-8-11 0.... RonanWhelan 2
(Ronald Harris) *sn rdn and outpcd in rr: n.d after* **103/10**

8 *nk* **Kakapuka**[7] 588 9-8-9 0.... RobertTart 5
(Anabel K Murphy) *prom: rdn 1/2-way: sn no ex: wknd* **141/10**

Owner Meile & Weiss **Bred** Ammerland Verwaltung Gmbh & Co Kg **Trained** Switzerland

664a GUBELIN 77TH GROSSER PREIS VON ST MORITZ (CONDITIONS) (4YO+) (SNOW) 1m 1f 165y
12:45 (12:00) 4-Y-O+
£31,745 (£15,872; £11,337; £7,558; £3,778; £2,267)

RPR

1 **Jungleboogie (GER)** 4-9-3 0.... RenePiechulek 8
(C Von Der Recke, Germany) **66/10**

2 *2* **Soundtrack (IRE)**[7] 588 5-8-11 0.... DanielePorcu 2
(P Schaerer, Switzerland) **7/1**

3 *2* **Berrahri (IRE)**[7] 588 5-9-2 0.... KierenFox 1
(John Best) *sn prom: led 1/2-way: rdn and hdd into st: readily outpcd by wnr: dropped to 3rd fnl f and hld* **48/10**[3]

4 *1 ¼* **Interior Minister**[235] 3780 6-8-11 0.... AlexanderPietsch 7
(C Von Der Recke, Germany) **68/10**

5 *½* **Simba**[119] 5-8-11 0.... JozefBojko 4
(C Von Der Recke, Germany) **41/5**

6 *5* **Cap Sizun (FR)**[364] 660 7-8-11 0.... AndreBest 9
(Frau M Muller, Switzerland) **3/1**[1]

7 *hd* **Runaway (GER)**[147] 6804 9-9-4 0....(p) OlivierPlacais 10
(Frau M Muller, Switzerland) **99/10**

8 *5* **High Strung (IRE)**[95] 7894 5-8-10 0.... DarrenMoffatt 5
(J D Hillis, Germany) **169/10**

9 *¾* **Arable**[378] 492 5-8-11 0....(p) FreddyDiFede 6
(P Schaerer, Switzerland) **26/5**

10 *dist* **Vermont (IRE)**[34] 6-9-2 0.... ClementL'Heureux 3
(A Schaerer, Switzerland) **18/5**[2]

Owner Stall Nizza **Bred** Jurgen Imm **Trained** Weilerswist, Germany

665a GRAND PRIX SCHLOSSATELIER (CONDITIONS) (4YO+) (SNOW) 4f
2:00 (12:00) 4-Y-O+
£4,285 (£2,142; £1,530; £1,020; £510; £306)

RPR

1 **Eagle Valley (IRE)**[72] 8181 4-9-3 0.... RonanWhelan 2
(Tracey Collins, Ire) *mde most: rdn 1/2-way: r.o wl and asserted: readily* **19/10**[1]

2 *1 ¼* **Duchess Andorra (IRE)**[239] 3668 5-9-5 0.... ConnorKing 6
(J P Murtagh, Ire) *in tch: rdn 1/2-way: kpt on wl for 2nd but nt pce of wnr* **2/1**[2]

3 *nk* **Semilla (FR)**[168] 5-8-6 0.... KarinZwahlen 7
(A Schaerer, Switzerland) **5/1**

4 *3* **Sword Of The Lord**[7] 586 6-9-2 0.... KierenFox 5
(Nigel Twiston-Davies) *in tch: sn rdn: outpcd and wl hld fnl f* **37/10**[3]

5 *½* **Lacan (IRE)**[7] 588 5-9-11 0.... WilliamCarson 3
(Ralph Beckett) *in rr early: in tch whn rdn 1/2-way: sn outpcd* **74/10**

6 *2 ½* **Tweet Lady**[7] 588 7-8-6 0.... FrauRebeccaDanz 4
(Bernhard J Friesdorf, Germany) **67/10**

7 *5* **From Frost**[209] 4711 5-8-11 0 ow2.... AlexanderPietsch 1
(C Von Der Recke, Germany) **59/10**

Owner Micheal D Ryan **Bred** Micheal D Ryan **Trained** The Curragh, Co Kildare

666 - (Foreign Racing) - See Raceform Interactive

[653] LINGFIELD (L-H)
Monday, February 22
OFFICIAL GOING: Polytrack: standard
Wind: Moderate, across (towards stands) Weather: Overcast

667 32RED FILLIES' H'CAP 1m 1y(P)
2:20 (2:20) (Class 5) (0-75,74) 4-Y-O+ **£2,911** (£866; £432; £216) **Stalls** High

Form RPR

51-5 **1** **Desert Morning (IRE)**[29] 324 4-8-6 59.... ShaneGray 3 73
(Anthony Carson) *dwlt: hld up in last: rapid prog arnd rivals 3f out to ld wl over 1f out: drifted towards nr side rail but rdn wl clr fnl f* **4/1**[3]

-330 **2** *6* **Ixelles Diamond (IRE)**[21] 415 5-8-12 68.... DannyBrock(3) 5 69
(Andrew Reid) *chsd ldrs: shkn up 3f out: kpt on u.p fr over 1f out to take 2nd nr fin: no ch* **7/1**

24-4 **3** *nk* **Make On Madam (IRE)**[6] 598 4-8-11 64.... JasonHart 6 64
(Les Eyre) *broke wl: led 100yds but restrained: in tch: rdn to chal on inner over 1f out: sn outpcd: lost 2nd nr fin* **9/2**

-442 **4** *nk* **Colourfilly**[9] 564 4-8-10 63...(p) JimCrowley 4 62
(Tom Dascombe) *led briefly after 100yds: trckd ldr: shkn up to ld 2f out: sn hdd: wl outpcd fnl f* **9/4**[1]

210- **5** *3* **Sheer Honesty**[133] 7171 4-9-4 74.................................. SladeO'Hara(3) 1 66
(Gay Kelleway) *hld up: dropped to last and outpcd 3f out: urged along and one pce over 1f out* **16/1**

1-44 **6** *2* **Tabla**[3] 631 4-8-7 67..(v[1]) RhiainIngram(7) 2 55
(Lee Carter) *t.k.h: led after 100yds: hdd 2 out: wknd fnl f* **3/1**[2]

1m 36.58s (-1.62) **Going Correction** -0.025s/f (Stan) **6** Ran SP% **112.3**
Speed ratings (Par 100): **107,101,100,100,97 95**
CSF £30.60 TOTE £4.30: £2.20, £2.60; EX 32.50 Trifecta £190.20.
Owner W H Carson **Bred** Breeding Capital **Trained** Newmarket, Suffolk

FOCUS
Modest handicap form, although it was run at a fair gallop and produced a clear-cut winner who recorded a personal best.

668 BET AND WATCH EVERY RACE AT UNIBET MAIDEN STKS 6f 1y(P)
2:55 (2:55) (Class 5) 3-Y-O+ **£2,911** (£866; £432; £216) **Stalls** Low

Form RPR

35-2 **1** **Kyllukey**[25] 363 3-8-13 70... DarryllHolland 3 73
(Charles Hills) *trckd ldr: chal 2f out: rdn to take narrow ld jst over 1f out: jst hld on* **9/2**[2]

2222 **2** *shd* **Phantom Flipper**[8] 582 3-8-13 70.............................(p) AdrianNicholls 1 72
(David Nicholls) *pushed up to ld: drvn 2f out: narrowly hdd jst over 1f out: kpt on wl nr fin: jst failed* **6/1**[3]

2 **3** *hd* **Steam Ahead**[26] 352 3-8-13 0... JimCrowley 4 71
(Ralph Beckett) *hld up: wd bnd 4f out: waiting for a gap 2f out: swtchd to ins over 1f out: drvn to chal fnl f: nt qckn nr fin* **4/11**[1]

0P/ **4** *9* **Ince Moss**[482] 7503 4-9-6 0... SammyJoBell(3) 2 42
(Richard Fahey) *in tch: rdn 2f out: wknd qckly jst over 1f out* **33/1**

1m 12.45s (0.55) **Going Correction** -0.025s/f (Stan)
WFA 3 from 4yo 15lb **4** Ran SP% **108.7**
Speed ratings (Par 103): **95,94,94,82**
CSF £25.61 TOTE £5.20; EX 15.00 Trifecta £27.20.
Owner R J Tufft **Bred** Whatton Manor Stud **Trained** Lambourn, Berks
■ Darryll Holland's first winner in Britain since 2012, following a spell riding abroad.

FOCUS
A muddling maiden, with little between the front three and the heavy odds-on favourite managing only third. The race has been rated around the runner-up.

669 UNIBET H'CAP 5f 6y(P)
3:25 (3:25) (Class 6) (0-60,58) 4-Y-O+ **£2,587** (£770; £384; £192) **Stalls** High

Form RPR

32-5 **1** **Prominna**[31] 292 6-9-3 57... GeorgeDowning(3) 1 64
(Tony Carroll) *t.k.h: hld up in tch: plld out 2f out: rdn and clsd jst over 1f out: led ins fnl f: sn clr* **9/4**[2]

-000 **2** *1 3/4* **Warm Order**[7] 589 5-8-5 49.......................................(b) LuluStanford(7) 5 50
(Tony Carroll) *sn led: rdn 2f out: hdd and outpcd ins fnl f* **12/1**

50-2 **3** *shd* **Pharoh Jake**[2] 658 8-9-7 58............................ WilliamTwiston-Davies 4 58
(John Bridger) *broke wl but sn in 3rd: rdn and tried to chal on inner 1f out: kpt on same pce* **11/10**[1]

0-55 **4** *3 1/4* **Salvado (IRE)**[32] 270 6-8-2 46..................................... MitchGodwin(7) 3 35
(Tony Carroll) *t.k.h early: hld up: lugged rt bnd after 1f: wd bnd 2f out and lost grnd: nvr on terms after* **10/1**

0-33 **5** *13* **Blue Amazon (IRE)**[17] 460 4-8-11 55.....................(v) RhiainIngram(7) 2
(Lee Carter) *sn chsd ldr: rdn and lost action over 1f out: wknd rapidly* **9/2**[3]

58.9s (0.10) **Going Correction** -0.025s/f (Stan) **5** Ran SP% **113.4**
Speed ratings (Par 101): **98,95,95,89,69**
CSF £25.61 TOTE £2.60: £1.30, £4.30; EX 23.80 Trifecta £56.20.
Owner Mayden Stud **Bred** Mayden Stud, J A And D S Dewhurst **Trained** Cropthorne, Worcs

FOCUS
Moderate sprinting form.

670 LADBROKES H'CAP 7f 1y(P)
4:00 (4:00) (Class 4) (0-80,79) 4-Y-O+ **£4,851** (£1,443; £721; £360) **Stalls** Low

Form RPR

1066 **1** **Fleckerl (IRE)**[4] 620 6-9-7 79...(p) JimCrowley 8 88
(Conor Dore) *hld up in last: stl there 2f out: gd prog towards inner over 1f out: led jst ins fnl f: sn drvn clr: convincingly* **5/2**[1]

513- **2** *1 3/4* **Diamond Lady**[77] 8131 5-9-2 79..................................... AaronJones(5) 3 82
(William Stone) *pressed ldr: led over 1f out: hdd jst ins fnl f and sn outpcd: kpt on* **10/1**

0-22 **3** *nk* **Captain Revelation**[8] 581 4-8-11 76...................... PatrickVaughan(7) 5 78
(Tom Dascombe) *led: rdn over 2f out: hdd over 1f out: outpcd fnl f but kpt on* **9/2**[2]

0-34 **4** *hd* **Jimmy's Hall**[17] 457 4-9-1 73...(b) LiamJones 1 75
(J S Moore) *trckd ldng pair: urged along over 2f out: kpt on same pce fr over 1f out* **16/1**

210- **5** *nse* **Russian Reward (IRE)**[77] 8141 4-9-5 77........................(t) MartinHarley 2 79
(Paul Cole) *hld up in tch: effrt and nt clr run briefly 2f out: drvn over 1f out: styd on same pce fnl f* **5/1**[3]

1513 **6** *nk* **Queen Aggie (IRE)**[3] 632 6-9-2 77......................... GeorgeDowning(3) 4 78
(Tony Carroll) *taken down early: hld up in last trio: wd bnd 2f out: nvr on terms after: shkn up and kpt on fnl 150yds* **5/1**[3]

322- **7** *nk* **Johnny B Goode (IRE)**[197] 5173 4-8-8 73........... AdamMcNamara(7) 6 73
(Richard Fahey) *trckd ldrs on outer: rdn over 1f out: nt clr run briefly 1f out: kpt on same pce after* **7/1**

0-12 **8** *1 1/4* **De Lesseps (USA)**[11] 532 8-8-4 65 oh6................ ShelleyBirkett(3) 7 62
(John David Riches) *dwlt: hld up in last pair: effrt on inner wl over 1f out: no prog fnl f: fdd nr fin* **10/1**

1m 25.03s (0.23) **Going Correction** -0.025s/f (Stan) **8** Ran SP% **116.7**
Speed ratings (Par 105): **97,95,94,94,94 94,93,92**
CSF £29.61 CT £109.12 TOTE £3.40: £1.60, £1.80, £1.90; EX 35.20 Trifecta £174.60.
Owner Andrew Page **Bred** Yeguada De Milagro Sa **Trained** Hubbert's Bridge, Lincs

FOCUS
Plenty had their chance in this with little separating them in behind the winner, who was much too good.

671 UNIBET OFFER DAILY JOCKEY AND TRAINER SPECIALS H'CAP 6f 1y(P)
4:30 (4:31) (Class 5) (0-70,70) 4-Y-O+ **£2,911** (£866; £432; £216) **Stalls** Low

Form RPR

0-20 **1** **Bush Warrior (IRE)**[30] 319 5-9-5 68.............................(v) MartinHarley 6 78
(Anabel K Murphy) *mde all at str pce: 3 l clr over 1f out: kpt on wl: unchal* **5/1**[3]

-016 **2** *1 1/2* **Summerinthecity (IRE)**[23] 398 9-9-0 70............ AdamMcNamara(7) 1 75
(Richard Fahey) *chsd ldng pair: rdn 2f out: tk 2nd 1f out: kpt on but unable to threaten wnr* **4/1**[1]

-103 **3** *nk* **Ocean Legend (IRE)**[14] 502 11-9-1 67................ GeorgeDowning(3) 3 71
(Tony Carroll) *chsd ldng pair: rdn 2f out: clsd to chal for 2nd 1f out: kpt on same pce* **9/2**[2]

61-0 **4** *1/2* **Seek The Fair Land**[3] 629 10-9-6 69..............................(v) AmirQuinn 2 71
(Lee Carter) *hld up in 5th: gng wl enough over 2f out: shkn up over 1f out and hanging: drvn and styd on fnl f to take 4th last strides* **5/1**[3]

-101 **5** *1/2* **Gulland Rock**[10] 542 5-8-7 56..(p) ShaneGray 5 57
(Anthony Carson) *chsd wnr: rdn and no imp over 2f out: lost 2nd and one pce fnl f* **9/2**[2]

2014 **6** *5* **Louis Vee (IRE)**[25] 356 8-8-8 62.............................(p) CiaranMckee(5) 4 47
(John O'Shea) *s.i.s: a in last pair: shkn up 2f out: no prog over 1f out: fdd* **8/1**

-000 **7** *4* **Duke Of North (IRE)**[16] 482 4-8-13 62.......................... JimCrowley 7 34
(Jim Boyle) *s.v.s and lost abt 10 l: jst in tch in last 1/2-way: effrt on inner 2f out: no prog over 1f out: eased whn no ch* **6/1**

1m 10.54s (-1.36) **Going Correction** -0.025s/f (Stan) **7** Ran SP% **115.1**
Speed ratings (Par 103): **108,106,105,104,104 97,92**
CSF £25.50 TOTE £6.10: £3.20, £2.30; EX 32.40 Trifecta £167.00.
Owner Ridgeway Racing Club **Bred** Vincent Dunne **Trained** Wilmcote, Warwicks

FOCUS
No hanging around here, the winner stretching them from an early stage and maintaining the gallop. He has been rated back to last year's C&D win.

672 CORAL H'CAP 1m 2f (P)
5:05 (5:05) (Class 5) (0-70,65) 4-Y-O+ **£2,911** (£866; £432; £216) **Stalls** Low

Form RPR

5-11 **1** **Celtic Ava (IRE)**[26] 347 4-8-13 58...................................... LiamJones 3 66
(Pat Phelan) *trckd ldrs: shkn up over 2f out: clsd on outer over 1f out: led jst ins fnl f: drvn out* **5/1**[3]

3552 **2** *1/2* **Cosmic Halo**[3] 631 7-9-4 65.. SammyJoBell(3) 2 72
(Richard Fahey) *v awkward s and slowly away: hld up in last: waiting for room over 2f out whn gng wl: prog on inner over 1f out: chal fnl f: styd on but a hld* **9/4**[1]

3-61 **3** *3/4* **Attain**[37] 222 7-9-1 62..(t) ShelleyBirkett(3) 6 67
(Julia Feilden) *t.k.h: hld up: nt wl plcd out wd over 2f out: nt qckn over 1f out: rdn and r.o fnl f to take 3rd last strides: nrst fin* **11/4**[2]

6-05 **4** *1/2* **Understory (USA)**[29] 326 9-8-4 51.................................(p) RyanTate(3) 1 55
(Tim McCarthy) *cl up: wnt 2nd 3f out: rdn to ld over 1f out: hdd and one pce jst ins fnl f* **8/1**

0301 **5** *1 1/4* **Time Square (FR)**[5] 602 9-8-0 51 oh2...................... MitchGodwin(7) 4 53
(Tony Carroll) *led: rdn over 2f out: hdd over 1f out: fdd ins fnl f* **7/1**

0-04 **6** *13* **Standing Strong (IRE)**[5] 602 8-8-1 52 oh2 ow1.(p) MeganNicholls(7) 5 28
(Zoe Davison) *prog fr rr to chse ldrs on outer 1/2-way: rdn over 2f out: sn lost pl: wknd qckly over 1f out* **16/1**

0-50 **7** *98* **Altaira**[19] 435 5-9-1 62.. GeorgeDowning(3) 7
(Tony Carroll) *chsd ldr to 3f out: wknd rapidly: virtually p.u fnl f* **8/1**

2m 4.1s (-2.50) **Going Correction** -0.025s/f (Stan)
WFA 4 from 5yo+ 1lb **7** Ran SP% **114.7**
Speed ratings (Par 103): **109,108,108,107,106 96,17**
CSF £16.81 TOTE £3.80: £2.30, £1.80; EX 18.30 Trifecta £50.90.
Owner Celtic Contractors Limited **Bred** Castletown Bloodstock Ltd **Trained** Epsom, Surrey

FOCUS
A couple of these like to lead and the race was set up for those who tracked/sat off the speed.
T/Plt: £599.00 to a £1 stake. Pool: £50,693.82 - 61.78 winning tickets T/Qpdt: £17.60 to a £1 stake. Pool: £6,102.19 - 255.14 winning tickets **Jonathan Neesom**

635 WOLVERHAMPTON (A.W) (L-H)
Monday, February 22

OFFICIAL GOING: Tapeta: standard
Wind: Fresh across Weather: Cloudy with sunny spells

673 BET IN PLAY AT CORAL AMATEUR RIDERS' H'CAP (DIV I) 1m 4f 50y (Tp)
2:10 (2:11) (Class 6) (0-52,52) 4-Y-O+ **£2,620** (£812; £406; £203) **Stalls** Low

Form RPR

001 **1** **Pao De Acuca (IRE)**[3] 634 4-10-5 **51** 6ex.................(t) MrWillPettis(5) 3 71
(Jose Santos) *chsd ldr tl led over 3f out: sn pushed clr: rdn out* **2/1**[1]

00-5 **2** *16* **Sawwala**[14] 378 6-10-1 **46** oh1... MrMBurge(7) 4 40
(J R Jenkins) *hld up: hdwy over 5f out: rdn and nt clr run 3f out: sn outpcd: wnt mod 2nd ins fnl f* **20/1**

006- **3** *3 1/2* **Goldmadchen (GER)**[62] 8345 8-11-0 **52**........................... MrSWalker 5 40
(James Given) *prom: rdn over 3f out: chsd wnr who was clr over 2f out: sn wknd: lost 2nd ins fnl f* **3/1**[2]

65-4 **4** *1 1/2* **Magnolia Ridge (IRE)**[13] 505 6-10-4 **49**................(b) MrHJKinder(7) 10 35
(Mark Walford) *mid-div: hdwy 8f out: chsd wnr over 3f out tl rdn over 2f out: sn wknd* **7/1**[3]

-000 **5** *1* **Ron Waverly (IRE)**[5] 602 6-10-3 **46** oh1..................(t) MissMBryant(5) 7 30
(Paddy Butler) *hld up: rdn over 2f out: n.d* **20/1**

64/0 **6** *3 1/2* **Witch From Rome**[46] 84 5-10-4 **49**............................. MrsDScott(7) 1 28
(Nick Lampard) *chsd ldrs: lost pl 8f out: n.d after* **40/1**

06-3 **7** *2 3/4* **Skywards Miles (IRE)**[13] 505 4-10-3 **49**................... MissHDukes(5) 9 23
(Tim Fitzgerald) *hld up: rdn over 2f out: nvr on terms* **7/1**[3]

402/ **8** *1 3/4* **Deadline Day (IRE)**[291] 2026 5-10-13 **51**...............(p) MissMMullineaux 2 23
(Michael Mullineaux) *mid-div: nt clr run and lost pl 8f out: n.d after* **14/1**

0/5- **9** *1* **Prairie Hawk (USA)**[66] 7947 11-10-3 **46** oh1.......(t) MrSeanHoulihan(5) 6 16
(Adrian Wintle) *hld up: rdn along over 3f out: sn wknd* **15/2**

/0-0 **10** *6* **Johnnys Legacy (IRE)**[9] 563 9-10-1 **46** oh1........(tp) MissJWelch(7) 11 6
(Ken Wingrove) *hld up: bhd fnl 5f* **150/1**

500- **11** *nk* **Felice (IRE)**[18] 8198 6-10-3 **46**...................................(p) MrKLocking(5) 12 6
(Scott Dixon) *led and sn clr: c bk to the field over 6f out: rdn and hdd over 3f out: wknd over 2f out* **33/1**

0- **12** *28* **Molans Mare (IRE)**[31] 300 6-10-1 **46** oh1.......................[1] HarryTeal(7) 8
(Emmet Michael Butterly, Ire) *mid-div: hdwy 8f out: pushed along 5f out: sn wknd* **22/1**

2m 38.98s (-1.82) **Going Correction** -0.05s/f (Stan)
WFA 4 from 5yo+ 3lb **12** Ran SP% **121.7**
Speed ratings (Par 101): **104,93,91,90,89 87,85,84,83,79 79,60**
CSF £52.40 CT £125.64 TOTE £3.20: £2.50, £4.20, £1.50; EX 48.70 Trifecta £272.90.
Owner Jose Santos **Bred** Derrick Fisher **Trained** Upper Lambourn, Berks
■ Stewards' Enquiry : Mr Will Pettis two-day ban: used whip when clearly winning (Mar 23,30)

FOCUS
The winner showed himself better than this grade, with 16l the second longest margin of victory on Tapeta at Wolverhampton and the time 1.85sec faster than the second division.

674 BET IN PLAY AT CORAL AMATEUR RIDERS' H'CAP (DIV II) 1m 4f 50y (Tp)
2:45 (2:45) (Class 6) (0-52,52) 4-Y-O+ **£2,620** (£812; £406; £203) **Stalls** Low

Form RPR
04-5 **1** **Storytale**[13] 505 4-10-7 **48**.......................(p) MrAlexEdwards 8 53
(Dave Roberts) *hld up: hdwy over 3f out: rdn and hung lft over 1f out: styd on to ld nr fin* **11/1**
0-20 **2** ½ **Celestial Dancer (FR)**[25] 368 4-10-5 **46**.............. MissSBrotherton 12 51
(Michael Appleby) *a.p: chsd ldr over 2f out: rdn to ld wl ins fnl f: hdd nr fin* **16/1**
-521 **3** 1 **Toboggan's Gift**[8] 577 4-10-11 **52** 6ex...................... MrPMillman 7 55
(Ann Duffield) *trckd ldr: plld hrd: led 4f out: rdn over 1f out: hdd and unable qck wl ins fnl f* **4/1**[2]
0-33 **4** 2 ¾ **Music Hall (FR)**[12] 526 6-10-3 **46** oh1.............. AidenBlakemore(5) 5 45
(Shaun Harris) *chsd ldrs: hmpd over 3f out: sn pushed along: rdn over 1f out: styd on same pce ins fnl f* **11/1**
6/0- **5** 3 ½ **Stynes (IRE)**[63] 8329 6-10-5 **46** oh1..............(t) MrJoshuaNewman(3) 6 39
(Ali Stronge) *mid-div: hdwy over 1f out: sn rdn: wknd ins fnl f* **14/1**
6 1 ¼ **Universal Mind (IRE)**[24] 395 9-10-3 **46**..................(b) MrHHunt(5) 4 37
(R McGlinchey, Ire) *hld up: hdwy and nt clr run over 1f out: sn rdn: wknd ins fnl f* **10/3**[1]
0-05 **7** 4 ½ **Teide Peak (IRE)**[17] 463 7-10-9 **50**.....................(tp) MrRyanBird(3) 2 34
(Grace Harris) *hld up: hdwy over 2f out: rdn and wknd over 1f out* **13/2**[3]
5/4 **8** nk **Akinspirit (IRE)**[19] 233 12-10-3 **48**....................(t) MissRDagge(7) 10 31
(Nikki Evans) *hld up: plld hrd: hdwy 6f out: chsd ldr over 3f out tl over 2f out: wknd over 1f out* **20/1**
0-60 **9** 2 ½ **Athenian Garden (USA)**[24] 382 9-10-5 **48**.............. MissMBryant(5) 9 27
(Paddy Butler) *hld up: rdn over 2f out: n.d* **33/1**
000- **10** 1 ¼ **Tinseltown**[190] 4509 10-11-0 **52**................................... MissHBethell 1 29
(Harriet Bethell) *led 8f: rdn and wknd 2f out* **20/1**
400/ **11** 2 ½ **Endorser**[2008] 5389 8-10-1 **46** oh1..............................(b) HarryTeal(7) 3 19
(Emmet Michael Butterly, Ire) *mid-div: hmpd 10f out: rdn and wknd over 3f out* **9/1**
4-35 **12** 4 ½ **Dissertation**[12] 521 4-10-8 **49**...................................(b) MrRBirkett 11 15
(Julia Feilden) *prom: pushed along at various stages: rdn over 4f out: wknd 3f out: eased* **12/1**

2m 40.83s (0.03) **Going Correction** -0.05s/f (Stan)
WFA 4 from 6yo+ 3lb **12** Ran SP% **115.8**
Speed ratings (Par 101): **97,96,96,94,91 91,88,87,86,85 83,80**
CSF £165.36 CT £827.56 TOTE £14.60: £3.70, £3.70, £1.60; EX 174.10 Trifecta £1334.30.
Owner D B Roberts **Bred** Worksop Manor Stud **Trained** Kenley, Shropshire
■ The first winner on the Flat for trainer Dave Roberts.
■ Stewards' Enquiry : Mr Alex Edwards two-day ban: used whip without giving gelding time to respond (Mar 23,30)

FOCUS
A moderate contest with the winning time 1.85sec slower than the first division. The winner has been rated a minor improver.

675 CORAL CONNECT MAIDEN STKS 1m 1f 103y (Tp)
3:15 (3:16) (Class 5) 3-Y-O+ **£3,234** (£962; £481; £240) **Stalls** Low

Form RPR
0-2 **1** **Faiseur De Miracle**[14] 500 4-10-0 0.......................... GrahamLee 4 82
(Micky Hammond) *mde all: qcknd over 2f out: c readily clr fnl f* **9/4**[2]
-33 **2** 6 **Fun For All**[29] 325 3-8-2 0.. LukeMorris 11 58
(James Tate) *prom: chsd wnr over 7f out: rdn over 2f out: styd on same pce fnl f* **13/8**[1]
46- **3** 1 ½ **Carolinae**[62] 8343 4-9-9 0..[1] TomQueally 10 61+
(Charlie Fellowes) *hld up: racd keenly: nt clr run over 3f out: rdn over 1f out: r.o to go 3rd wl ins fnl f: nvr nrr* **17/2**[3]
0-4 **4** 1 **Alphabetical Order**[9] 567 8-10-0 0................................. SamJames 5 64
(David O'Meara) *chsd ldrs: rdn over 2f out: no ex fnl f* **10/1**
64 **5** 2 ½ **Pensax Lady (IRE)**[24] 384 3-8-2 0................................ JimmyQuinn 7 48
(Daniel Mark Loughnane) *hld up: hdwy u.p over 2f out: styd on same pce fr over 1f out* **12/1**
00- **6** nk **Esspeegee**[88] 8006 3-8-7 0... FrannyNorton 1 52
(Alan Bailey) *hld up: hdwy over 2f out: sn rdn: styd on same pce fr over 1f out* **80/1**
304- **7** nk **High Intensity**[111] 7686 4-10-0 67..............................(p) BenCurtis 3 57
(Scott Dixon) *chsd ldrs: rdn over 3f out: wknd fnl f* **16/1**
8 3 ¼ **Super Seer** 3-8-7 0.. KieranO'Neill 2 45
(Philip Hide) *prom: rdn over 2f out: wknd over 1f out* **22/1**
65 **9** 8 **Executive Order**[16] 487 7-9-11 0................................. TimClark(3) 9 34
(Martin Smith) *dwlt: a in rr* **200/1**
10 nk **Zac Courageous (IRE)** 4-9-9 0.......................... RachealKneller(5) 6 33
(James Bennett) *prom: pushed along 1/2-way: wknd over 2f out* **80/1**
11 22 **Nordenfelt (IRE)** 3-8-7 0... JoeFanning 8
(Ed Dunlop) *s.i.s: rn green in rr: pushed along over 5f out: wknd over 3f out* **22/1**

2m 1.1s (0.30) **Going Correction** -0.05s/f (Stan)
WFA 3 from 4yo+ 21lb **11** Ran SP% **113.7**
Speed ratings (Par 103): **96,90,89,88,86 85,85,82,75,75 55**
CSF £5.75 TOTE £2.70: £1.30, £1.10, £2.60; EX 6.30 Trifecta £34.10.
Owner The Faiseur De Miracle Partnership **Bred** Newsells Park Stud **Trained** Middleham, N Yorks

FOCUS
An uncompetitive maiden with the first two holding those positions throughout.

676 BEST ODDS GUARANTEED AT CORAL H'CAP 1m 1f 103y (Tp)
3:50 (3:51) (Class 6) (0-65,65) 4-Y-O+ **£2,587** (£770; £384; £192) **Stalls** Low

Form RPR
4-66 **1** **Mary Le Bow**[31] 295 5-8-12 **61**......................(t) CallumShepherd(5) 13 67
(Victor Dartnall) *hld up: hdwy: nt clr run and swtchd lft over 1f out: rdn to ld wl ins fnl f: r.o* **12/1**
33-2 **2** ½ **Yulong Xiongba (IRE)**[48] 53 4-9-6 **64**.................... DougieCostello 2 69
(Julie Camacho) *led at stdy pce tl qcknd over 2f out: rdn and hdd wl ins fnl f* **11/1**
1-6 **3** ¾ **Dove Mountain (IRE)**[37] 222 5-9-2 **60**..................(tp) TomQueally 12 65
(Gordon Elliott, Ire) *hld up: nt clr run and lost pl over 2f out: r.o ins fnl f: nt rch ldrs* **11/4**[1]
6-05 **4** ½ **Thane Of Cawdor (IRE)**[15] 491 7-8-12 **61**.......(b) PatrickO'Donnell(5) 1 64
(Joseph Tuite) *hld up: hdwy over 1f out: sn rdn: styd on* **16/1**
50-5 **5** ½ **Evervescent (IRE)**[17] 464 7-9-4 **62**............................ LiamKeniry 11 64
(Graeme McPherson) *chsd ldrs: rdn over 1f out: styd on same pce ins fnl f* **50/1**
644- **6** ½ **Cherry Street**[107] 7749 7-8-12 **59**................................ KevinStott(3) 3 60
(John Berry) *prom: rdn to chse wnr over 1f out tl no ex ins fnl f* **7/1**[2]
-216 **7** ½ **Tijuca (IRE)**[21] 420 7-9-7 **65**................................(tp) KieranO'Neill 7 65
(Ed de Giles) *hld up: rdn over 2f out: styd on ins fnl f: nt trble ldrs* **7/1**[2]
62-0 **8** nse **Diletta Tommasa (IRE)**[38] 191 6-9-5 **63**................(p) StevieDonohoe 5 66
(Daniel Mark Loughnane) *hld up: hdwy and hmpd over 1f out: r.o towards fin* **12/1**
32-0 **9** nse **Mops Angel**[39] 173 5-9-4 **62**.......................................(p) LukeMorris 10 62
(Michael Appleby) *prom: rdn over 3f out: styd on u.p* **28/1**
32-1 **10** hd **Chorlton House**[40] 161 4-9-5 **63**................................ TonyHamilton 9 62
(Ian Williams) *chsd ldr: rdn over 2f out: lost 2nd over 1f out: no ex ins fnl f* **11/1**
6-51 **11** 2 **Vastly (USA)**[17] 464 7-9-6 **64**..............................(bt) AdamBeschizza 4 59
(Julia Feilden) *prom: rdn over 2f out: wknd ins fnl f* **15/2**[3]
-562 **12** 17 **Matraash (USA)**[17] 464 10-9-5 **63**...............................(be) JoeFanning 6 26
(Daniel Mark Loughnane) *hld up: hdwy 1/2-way: rdn and wknd over 2f out: eased* **15/2**[3]

1m 59.51s (-1.29) **Going Correction** -0.05s/f (Stan) **12** Ran SP% **118.5**
Speed ratings (Par 101): **103,102,101,101,101 100,100,100,100,99 98,82**
CSF £137.45 CT £472.23 TOTE £14.20: £4.40, £4.30, £2.00; EX 149.30 Trifecta £1029.70.
Owner Mrs J Scrivens **Bred** Mr & Mrs A E Pakenham **Trained** Brayford, Devon
■ Stewards' Enquiry : Callum Shepherd three-day ban: careless riding (Mar 7-9)

FOCUS
A moderate handicap run at a steady early pace.

677 DOWNLOAD THE NEW UNIBET RACING APP H'CAP 5f 20y (Tp)
4:20 (4:22) (Class 2) 4-Y-O+
£28,012 (£8,388; £4,194; £2,097; £1,048; £526) **Stalls** Low

Form RPR
30-4 **1** **Boom The Groom (IRE)**[31] 288 5-9-8 **97**.................. WilliamCarson 7 106
(Tony Carroll) *a.p: chsd ldr 1/2-way: rdn to ld wl ins fnl f: r.o* **7/2**[1]
000- **2** ½ **Fast Track**[156] 6515 5-9-4 **93**................................... GrahamGibbons 6 100
(David Barron) *chsd ldrs: rdn over 1f out: r.o* **16/1**
-013 **3** hd **Royal Birth**[15] 492 5-9-0 **89**.......................................(t) PatCosgrave 2 95
(Stuart Williams) *s.i.s: hld up: hdwy over 1f out: sn rdn: r.o wl* **4/1**[2]
-201 **4** nse **Hoofalong**[8] 580 6-9-4 **93** 6ex.................................(b) PhillipMakin 5 99
(Michael Easterby) *mid-div: hdwy over 1f out: sn rdn: r.o* **14/1**
66-6 **5** hd **Zac Brown (IRE)**[11] 529 5-9-1 **90**............................ DanielTudhope 4 95
(Charlie Wallis) *plld hrd and prom: rdn over 1f out: r.o* **12/1**
3111 **6** ½ **Bosham**[11] 529 6-8-13 **95**..................................(bt) NathanEvans(7) 9 99
(Michael Easterby) *led: rdn and hdd wl ins fnl f: no ex* **10/1**
33-5 **7** 1 **Steelriver (IRE)**[31] 288 6-9-4 **93**............................... GeorgeBaker 10 93
(David Barron) *s.i.s: hld up: rdn and hung lft over 1f out: running on wl whn nt clr run and eased towards fin* **8/1**
01-0 **8** 1 ¼ **Seve**[37] 213 4-9-2 **91**.. RichardKingscote 8 87
(Tom Dascombe) *chsd ldr to 1/2-way: rdn over 1f out: no ex ins fnl f* **16/1**
01-4 **9** hd **Judicial (IRE)**[37] 213 4-9-5 **94**..................................(e) LukeMorris 1 90
(Julie Camacho) *hmpd sn after s: hld up: pushed along 1/2-way: hdwy over 1f out: sn rdn: styd on same pce ins fnl f* **6/1**[3]
5-66 **10** 3 ¼ **Justice Good (IRE)**[16] 483 4-9-3 **99**...................(t) AdamMcLean(7) 3 84
(David Elsworth) *sn pushed along in rr: rdn 1/2-way: sn wknd* **15/2**
-204 **11** nk **Dynamo Walt (IRE)**[15] 492 5-9-3 **92**......................(v) TonyHamilton 11 76
(Derek Shaw) *hld up: rdn and wknd over 1f out* **28/1**

59.39s (-2.51) **Going Correction** -0.05s/f (Stan) course record **11** Ran SP% **118.0**
Speed ratings (Par 109): **118,117,116,116,116 115,114,112,111,106 106**
CSF £61.27 CT £240.58 TOTE £5.40: £2.90, £5.10, £1.90; EX 69.20 Trifecta £474.70.
Owner Gary Attwood **Bred** John Foley **Trained** Cropthorne, Worcs
■ Stewards' Enquiry : William Carson three-day ban: careless riding (Mar 7-9)

FOCUS
A good, competitive sprint handicap and the time was the fastest to date from 134 races over this trip on the Tapeta here.

678 32RED CASINO H'CAP 1m 141y (Tp)
4:55 (4:55) (Class 5) (0-75,72) 3-Y-O **£3,557** (£1,058; £529; £264) **Stalls** Low

Form RPR
4-31 **1** **Pirate's Treasure**[12] 522 3-9-6 **71**................................ LukeMorris 3 75+
(James Tate) *trckd ldrs: racd keenly: nt clr run over 2f out: r.o u.p to ld wl ins fnl f* **13/8**[1]
656- **2** hd **Manjaam (IRE)**[127] 7309 3-9-2 **67**................................ PatCosgrave 2 70+
(Ed Dunlop) *hld up: hdwy u.p over 1f out: r.o wl* **9/1**
560- **3** nk **Albert Boy (IRE)**[76] 8143 3-8-9 **60**................................ BenCurtis 4 62
(Scott Dixon) *led: rdn over 1f out: hdd wl ins fnl f* **40/1**
-364 **4** ¾ **Threebagsue (IRE)**[17] 459 3-9-1 **71**..............(b) JosephineGordon(5) 1 71
(J S Moore) *chsd ldr: rdn and ev ch ins fnl f: no ex nr fin* **17/2**
54-0 **5** 2 ½ **Boycie**[12] 519 3-9-7 **72**... KieranO'Neill 6 67
(Richard Hannon) *trckd ldrs: racd keenly: rdn over 1f out: no ex ins fnl f* **8/1**[3]
0-43 **6** 2 ¾ **Rubis**[27] 335 3-8-9 **60**.. TonyHamilton 5 48
(Richard Fahey) *hld up: rdn over 1f out: n.d* **9/1**
64-1 **7** 2 ¾ **World's Greatest (USA)**[31] 291 3-9-1 **66**.............. GrahamGibbons 8 48
(Stuart Williams) *hld up: effrt over 2f out: rdn and wknd over 1f out* **3/1**[2]
4-1 **R** **Beleave**[23] 400 3-9-1 **66**.. DougieCostello 7
(Luke Dace) *hood was stl on whn the stalls opened: filly rrd and ref to come out of the stalls* **8/1**[3]

1m 49.84s (-0.26) **Going Correction** -0.05s/f (Stan) **8** Ran SP% **118.3**
Speed ratings (Par 97): **99,98,98,97,95 93,90,**
CSF £18.39 CT £432.32 TOTE £2.60: £2.80, £2.50, £5.90; EX 17.20 Trifecta £315.40.
Owner Saif Ali **Bred** Meon Valley Stud **Trained** Newmarket, Suffolk

FOCUS
An unconvincing bunch and they went a muddling pace.

679 32RED.COM MAIDEN FILLIES' STKS 7f 32y (Tp)
5:25 (5:29) (Class 5) 3-Y-O+ **£3,557** (£1,058; £529; £264) **Stalls** High

Form RPR
565- **1** **Alyaa (IRE)**[93] 7937 3-8-7 75..................................... MartinDwyer 6 73
(Conrad Allen) *mde all: set stdy pce tl qcknd over 2f out: rdn ins fnl f: all out* **6/1**
0 **2** hd **Little Miss Kodi (IRE)**[26] 352 3-8-7 0.......................... LukeMorris 8 72
(Daniel Mark Loughnane) *chsd wnr: rdn over 2f out: nt clr run and swtchd lft over 1f out: ev ch ins fnl f: r.o* **33/1**
3 1 ½ **Bint Arcano (FR)**[183] 3-8-7 0.................................... JamesSullivan 12 68+
(Julie Camacho) *hld up: r.o ins fnl f: nt rch ldrs* **12/1**
2- **4** hd **Spirit Glance**[24] 390 3-8-7 66.................................... PJMcDonald 7 67
(Tim Easterby) *a.p: rdn over 2f out: styd on same pce fnl f* **4/1**[3]
5 ¾ **Sonnet (IRE)** 3-8-7 0... FrannyNorton 3 65
(Charles Hills) *hld up in tch: shkn up over 2f out: styd on: nt rch ldrs* **3/1**[2]

2-2 **6** *1* **Andaz**[47] 74 3-8-7 0 JackMitchell 2 62
(Roger Varian) *s.i.s: hld up: hdwy and nt clr run over 1f out: swtchd lft: sn rdn: no imp ins fnl f* **13/8**[1]

65 **7** *1 1/4* **Indigo Princess**[12] 524 3-8-0 0 RPWalsh(7) 5 59
(Michael Appleby) *hld up: rdn and hung lft fr over 1f out: nvr on terms* **50/1**

34 **8** *2 1/2* **Ventura Falcon (IRE)**[5] 611 3-8-0 0 HollieDoyle(7) 9 52
(Richard Hannon) *chsd ldrs: rdn over 2f out: wknd over 1f out* **16/1**

0 **9** *7* **Always Endeavour**[21] 423 3-8-7 0 JimmyQuinn 11 33
(Daniel Mark Loughnane) *s.s: a in rr* **100/1**

6-0 **10** *1* **Golden Cape**[42] 145 3-8-7 0 JoeyHaynes 1 31
(Michael Mullineaux) *chsd ldrs: pushed along 1/2-way: wknd 2f out* **100/1**

00 **11** *55* **Bethellie Pride**[31] 298 6-9-5 0 JoshDoyle(5) 4
(Lynn Siddall) *hld up: rdn and wknd over 2f out* **150/1**

1m 29.19s (0.39) **Going Correction** -0.05s/f (Stan) 11 Ran SP% **118.5**
WFA 3 from 6yo 17lb
Speed ratings (Par 100): **95,94,93,92,91 90,89,86,78,77 14**
CSF £181.22 TOTE £8.30: £2.90, £5.00, £3.00; EX 180.60 Trifecta £1004.30.
Owner A Al Kathiri **Bred** N Hartery **Trained** Newmarket, Suffolk

FOCUS
The first two raced one-two throughout, with the winner left alone in front in this modest fillies' maiden.

680 LADBROKES H'CAP 7f 32y (Tp)
5:55 (5:57) (Class 5) (0-70,70) 4-Y-0+ **£3,234** (£962; £481; £240) **Stalls** High

Form RPR

55-4 **1** **Fingal's Cave (IRE)**[11] 532 4-9-7 **70** GeorgeBaker 5 81+
(Mick Channon) *hld up: hdwy over 1f out: rdn to ld ins fnl f: r.o* **15/8**[1]

-031 **2** *1 3/4* **Top Offer**[14] 502 7-9-4 **67** ShaneKelly 10 72
(Patrick Morris) *s.i.s: hld up: hdwy and nt clr run over 1f out: rdn and hung lft ins fnl f: r.o* **9/1**

0-05 **3** *hd* **Indian Affair**[20] 426 6-9-4 **67** (bt) FrannyNorton 8 71
(Milton Bradley) *chsd ldr 2f: remained handy: wnt 2nd again over 2f out: rdn to ld over 1f out: hdd ins fnl f: styd on same pce* **11/1**

-112 **4** *nk* **National Service (USA)**[17] 469 5-9-5 **68** (tp) TimmyMurphy 2 72
(Gordon Elliott, Ire) *a.p: rdn and n.m.r over 1f out: no ex towards fin* **5/1**[2]

522- **5** *3* **Tango Sky (IRE)**[147] 6816 7-9-5 **68** PaulMulrennan 9 64
(Paul Midgley) *hld up: r.o ins fnl f: nt rch ldrs* **11/1**

0206 **6** *1/2* **Hercullian Prince**[14] 502 4-9-5 **68** (p) LiamKeniry 1 62
(Conor Dore) *chsd ldrs: rdn over 1f out: no ex fnl f* **28/1**

00-0 **7** *2* **For Shia And Lula (IRE)**[16] 482 7-9-6 **69** LukeMorris 11 58
(Daniel Mark Loughnane) *chsd ldrs: rdn over 2f out: wknd fnl f* **12/1**

44-6 **8** *nse* **Khajaaly (IRE)**[12] 523 9-9-3 **69** (vt) RobHornby(3) 4 58
(Daniel Mark Loughnane) *hld up: hdwy and nt clr run over 1f out: sn rdn: wknd ins fnl f* **18/1**

63-0 **9** *1 1/4* **Picks Pinta**[21] 424 5-9-0 **70** VitorSantos(7) 12 55
(John David Riches) *s.i.s: hdwy to ld 5f out: rdn and hdd over 1f out: wknd ins fnl f* **33/1**

3/30 **10** *3/4* **Mr Shekells**[18] 437 4-9-2 **65** DanielTudhope 6 48
(Philip McBride) *hld up: rdn over 2f out: n.d* **8/1**[3]

-426 **11** *3* **Spowarticus**[20] 426 7-9-1 **64** (v) KieranO'Neill 3 39
(Scott Dixon) *led 2f: chsd ldr tl rdn over 2f out: wknd ins fnl f* **16/1**

1m 27.15s (-1.65) **Going Correction** -0.05s/f (Stan) 11 Ran SP% **114.5**
Speed ratings (Par 103): **107,105,104,104,101 100,98,98,96,95 92**
CSF £18.59 CT £146.12 TOTE £2.70: £1.30, £2.70, £3.10; EX 19.30 Trifecta £165.10.
Owner The Motley Cru I **Bred** Rathasker Stud **Trained** West Ilsley, Berks

FOCUS
The winner, second and fourth all travelled strongly into contention under hold-up rides. The form looks sound.
T/Jkpt: Not won. T/Plt: £28.40 to a £1 stake. Pool: £69,855.14 - 1,792.67 winning tickets T/Qpdt: £7.20 to a £1 stake. Pool: £8,402.32 - 860.17 winning tickets **Colin Roberts**

673 WOLVERHAMPTON (A.W) (L-H)
Tuesday, February 23

OFFICIAL GOING: Tapeta: standard
Wind: Fresh across Weather: Cloudy with sunny spells

681 LADBROKES H'CAP (DIV I) 7f 32y (Tp)
1:50 (1:51) (Class 6) (0-60,65) 4-Y-0+ **£2,587** (£770; £384; £192) **Stalls** High

Form RPR

060- **1** **Eastern Dragon (IRE)**[85] 8046 6-9-1 **54** MartinHarley 7 66+
(Seamus Durack) *hld up: hdwy over 1f out: rdn to ld ins fnl f: r.o wl: comf* **15/8**[1]

2-01 **2** *1 1/2* **Caledonia Laird**[8] 590 5-9-12 **65** 6ex JoeyHaynes 2 71
(Jo Hughes) *a.p: rdn to ld and hung rt over 1f out: hdd ins fnl f: styd on same pce* **3/1**[2]

-425 **3** *3* **Hawk Moth (IRE)**[8] 590 8-9-4 **57** (b) WilliamCarson 5 56
(John Spearing) *hld up: hdwy u.p over 1f out: styd on same pce ins fnl f* **9/2**[3]

56-5 **4** *1* **Smalljohn**[39] 201 10-8-10 **56** (v) PhilDennis(7) 8 52
(Bryan Smart) *chsd ldr: rdn and ev ch whn hmpd over 1f out: no ex ins fnl f* **6/1**

-554 **5** *2* **Cadeaux Pearl**[21] 430 8-9-1 **54** BenCurtis 4 45
(Scott Dixon) *chsd ldrs: rdn over 2f out: wknd ins fnl f* **11/1**

/0-0 **6** *2 1/2* **Colour My World**[21] 429 6-9-7 **60** JoeFanning 6 45
(Ed McMahon) *led: rdn: edgd rt and hdd over 1f out: wknd ins fnl f* **14/1**

0/40 **7** *9* **Royal Roman**[22] 423 4-9-7 **60** DougieCostello 1 23
(Kevin Frost) *hld up: rdn 1/2-way: wknd 2f out* **80/1**

050- **8** *16* **Cerise Firth**[144] 6898 4-8-7 **46** oh1 (t) AdamBeschizza 3 +
(Steph Hollinshead) *rrd s: a wl bhd* **50/1**

1m 27.2s (-1.60) **Going Correction** -0.125s/f (Stan) 8 Ran SP% **110.4**
Speed ratings (Par 101): **104,102,98,97,95 92,82,64**
CSF £6.96 CT £19.21 TOTE £2.60: £1.30, £1.20, £1.50; EX 7.90 Trifecta £23.30.
Owner Miss Rosie Leena Kim Kavanagh **Bred** James Mahon **Trained** Upper Lambourn, Berkshire

FOCUS
A moderate handicap, but run at a good pace and the form looks strong for the grade.

682 LADBROKES H'CAP (DIV II) 7f 32y (Tp)
2:20 (2:22) (Class 6) (0-60,60) 4-Y-0+ **£2,587** (£770; £384; £192) **Stalls** High

Form RPR

16-3 **1** **Mr Christopher (IRE)**[8] 590 4-9-7 **60** (p) RichardKingscote 6 72
(Tom Dascombe) *mde all: rdn over 1f out: edgd rt: styd on* **1/1**[1]

4-22 **2** *1 1/2* **Basingstoke (IRE)**[13] 526 7-9-1 **54** (b[1]) StevieDonohoe 1 62
(Daniel Mark Loughnane) *trckd ldrs: plld hrd: wnt 2nd 3f out: rdn over 1f out: styd on same pce ins fnl f* **4/1**[2]

1-02 **3** *3* **Princess Peaches**[21] 430 4-9-7 **60** PJMcDonald 4 61
(James Bethell) *prom: pushed along 1/2-way: styd on same pce fnl f* **8/1**[3]

626- **4** *1* **Ted's Brother (IRE)**[120] 7514 8-9-7 **60** (e) JasonHart 3 59
(Richard Guest) *hld up: pushed along 1/2-way: nt clr run over 2f out: hdwy over 1f out: no imp fnl f* **22/1**

-530 **5** *3/4* **Scot Daddy (USA)**[10] 568 4-9-5 **58** DougieCostello 5 55
(David Dennis) *hld up: rdn over 2f out: nt trble ldrs* **10/1**

0-40 **6** *1/2* **Reginald Claude**[11] 542 8-8-13 **57** RachealKneller(5) 9 52+
(Mark Usher) *hld up: swtchd lft sn after s: swtchd rt wl over 1f out: nvr nrr* **10/1**

0035 **7** *4* **Little**[11] 543 4-8-8 **47** (p) AdamBeschizza 2 33
(Steph Hollinshead) *hld up: pushed along and hdwy over 2f out: rdn over 1f out: wknd fnl f* **22/1**

-000 **8** *3/4* **Beauty's Forte (IRE)**[11] 542 5-9-2 **55** (b) DanielTudhope 8 39
(Declan Carroll) *sn prom: rdn over 2f out: wknd over 1f out* **12/1**

-660 **9** *nk* **Tamarin**[11] 542 4-8-2 **46** oh1 (p) JosephineGordon(5) 7 29
(Lisa Williamson) *chsd wnr tl rdn 3f out: wknd over 1f out* **66/1**

1m 27.29s (-1.51) **Going Correction** -0.125s/f (Stan) 9 Ran SP% **117.2**
Speed ratings (Par 101): **103,101,97,96,95 95,90,89,89**
CSF £4.99 CT £20.98 TOTE £1.90: £1.20, £1.70, £2.50; EX 6.00 Trifecta £18.90.
Owner Mrs M C Antrobus **Bred** Denis McDonnell **Trained** Malpas, Cheshire

FOCUS
Marginally the slower of the two divisions. The winner had the run of the race out in front.

683 DOWNLOAD THE LADBROKES APP H'CAP 1m 141y (Tp)
2:55 (2:55) (Class 5) (0-70,73) 4-Y-0+ **£3,234** (£962; £481; £240) **Stalls** Low

Form RPR

-121 **1** **Rockwood**[10] 569 5-9-2 **65** (v) PaulMulrennan 12 74
(Karen McLintock) *hld up: hdwy on outer over 2f out: rdn to ld wl ins fnl f: edgd lft: styd on* **3/1**[1]

66-4 **2** *1/2* **Stormbound (IRE)**[43] 141 7-9-4 **67** (b) MartinHarley 8 75
(Paul Cole) *hld up: hdwy over 1f out: rdn and ev ch whn hung lft ins fnl f: kpt on* **8/1**

3042 **3** *nk* **Mr Red Clubs (IRE)**[16] 491 7-9-7 **70** LiamJones 9 77
(Michael Appleby) *a.p: rdn on outer over 2f out: led over 1f out: hdd wl ins fnl f* **7/1**[3]

2-60 **4** *2* **Marmalad (IRE)**[29] 332 4-9-0 **68** (b[1]) CallumShepherd(5) 4 71
(Shaun Lycett) *hld up in tch: rdn over 1f out: no ex ins fnl f* **9/1**

-530 **5** *nk* **Tatting**[8] 595 7-9-4 **67** LiamKeniry 7 69
(Conor Dore) *hld up: hdwy u.p over 1f out: nt rch ldrs* **14/1**

000- **6** *nk* **Almanack**[242] 3611 6-9-7 **70** (t) GeorgeBaker 6 71
(Daniel Mark Loughnane) *broke wl: sn stdd and lost pl: hld up: hdwy over 1f out: nt trble ldrs* **8/1**

5-33 **7** *2 1/4* **Flying Fantasy**[19] 438 4-9-2 **65** SaleemGolam 11 61
(Stuart Williams) *prom: nt clr run 2f out: sn rdn: wknd ins fnl f* **9/1**

400- **7** *dht* **Ellaal**[112] 7694 7-8-10 **59** JamesSullivan 3 55
(Ruth Carr) *chsd ldr tl led over 2f out: rdn and hdd over 1f out: wknd ins fnl f* **25/1**

641- **9** *3* **Outlaw Torn (IRE)**[123] 7443 7-9-2 **65** (e) JasonHart 13 54
(Richard Guest) *chsd ldrs: rdn over 2f out: wknd over 1f out* **22/1**

640- **10** *11* **Dutch S**[246] 3463 5-9-0 **66** RyanTate(3) 10 30
(Clive Cox) *hld up: rdn and wknd over 1f out* **18/1**

04-0 **11** *3/4* **Shamlan (IRE)**[48] 67 4-9-7 **70** StevieDonohoe 5 32
(Kevin Frost) *hld up: rdn over 3f out: sn lost tch* **18/1**

143/ **12** *4 1/2* **Rochelle (IRE)**[495] 7225 5-8-4 **58** ow1 CiaranMckee(5) 2 10
(Roy Brotherton) *hld up: rdn and wknd over 2f out* **66/1**

6401 **13** *10* **Moonlight Venture**[7] 598 5-9-10 **73** 6ex (b) TomEaves 1 2
(Conor Dore) *led: rdn and hdd over 2f out: wknd over 1f out* **13/2**[2]

1m 47.87s (-2.23) **Going Correction** -0.125s/f (Stan) 13 Ran SP% **119.9**
Speed ratings (Par 103): **104,103,103,101,101 100,98,98,96,86 85,81,72**
CSF £26.09 CT £159.24 TOTE £4.10: £2.20, £3.20, £2.30; EX 24.40 Trifecta £97.90.
Owner I R Clements & Dr L G Parry **Bred** Norcroft Park Stud **Trained** Ingoe, Northumberland

FOCUS
A modest but competitive handicap, rated around the third and fourth.

684 BET IN PLAY AT CORAL H'CAP 1m 4f 50y (Tp)
3:30 (3:30) (Class 6) (0-60,60) 4-Y-0+ **£2,587** (£770; £384; £192) **Stalls** Low

Form RPR

0-22 **1** **Star Ascending (IRE)**[7] 601 4-9-3 **59** JoeFanning 7 65
(Jennie Candlish) *chsd ldr: rdn over 1f out: led and edgd rt ins fnl f: all out* **4/1**[3]

-035 **2** *hd* **Innoko (FR)**[20] 435 6-9-7 **60** WilliamCarson 2 66
(Tony Carroll) *hld up in tch: rdn over 2f out: r.o* **8/1**

1-63 **3** *nk* **Dove Mountain (IRE)**[1] 676 5-9-7 **60** (tp) TomQueally 8 65+
(Gordon Elliott, Ire) *s.v.s: bhd: hdwy over 1f out: nt clr run ins fnl f: swtchd lft: r.o* **11/4**[1]

6232 **4** *shd* **Astra Hall**[4] 637 7-9-7 **60** BenCurtis 1 65
(Michael Appleby) *led: rdn and edgd rt over 1f out: hdd ins fnl f: unable qck nr fin* **6/1**

2- **5** *1 3/4* **Gold Not Silver (IRE)**[18] 475 7-8-9 **53** (b) GaryHalpin(5) 4 55
(Adrian Brendan Joyce, Ire) *chsd ldrs: rdn over 2f out: styd on same pce ins fnl f* **3/1**[2]

1633 **6** *5* **Smugglers Lane (IRE)**[5] 622 4-8-4 **53** AledBeech(7) 5 47
(David Evans) *prom: rdn over 3f out: outpcd over 2f out: rallied and wnt lft over 1f out: wknd ins fnl f* **22/1**

35-1 **7** *8* **Whisky Marmalade (IRE)**[32] 295 4-9-1 **57** RaulDaSilva 9 38
(Ben Haslam) *hld up: rdn over 3f out: sn wknd* **15/2**

0-04 **8** *shd* **Amazing Blue Sky**[13] 521 10-8-8 **47** JamesSullivan 3 28
(Ruth Carr) *prom: hmpd after 1f: rdn over 3f out: wknd over 2f out* **50/1**

/02- **9** *4 1/2* **Sir Dylan**[282] 1795 7-8-9 **51** TimClark(3) 10 25
(Polly Gundry) *hld up: rdn and wknd 3f out* **33/1**

0-00 **10** *1 1/2* **Star Anise (FR)**[18] 461 5-8-13 **57** CallumShepherd(5) 6 29
(Paddy Butler) *hld up: rdn and wknd over 2f out: hung rt over 1f out* **33/1**

2m 37.72s (-3.08) **Going Correction** -0.125s/f (Stan) 10 Ran SP% **121.0**
WFA 4 from 5yo+ 3lb
Speed ratings (Par 101): **105,104,104,104,103 100,94,94,91,90**
CSF £35.94 CT £104.62 TOTE £5.30: £1.90, £2.60, £1.20; EX 36.70 Trifecta £196.80.
Owner Paul Wright-Bevans **Bred** Philip Gilligan & Anne Gilligan **Trained** Basford Green, Staffs
■ Stewards' Enquiry : Joe Fanning three-day ban: careless riding (Mar 8-10)

FOCUS
There was a bunched finish to this ordinary handicap with the winner close to his recent Fibresand form.

685 UNIBET.CO.UK DAILY ENHANCED PLACE TERMS CLASSIFIED (S) STKS 5f 216y (Tp)
4:00 (4:00) (Class 5) 3-Y-0+ **£3,234** (£962; £481; £240) **Stalls** Low

Form RPR
1124 **1** **National Service (USA)**[1] 680 5-9-4 68..................(tp) TimmyMurphy 3 75
(Gordon Elliott, Ire) *hld up: hdwy on bit to ld over 1f out: easily* **13/8**[2]
-030 **2** *2* **Archie Stevens**[6] 604 6-9-1 75.................................. PhilipPrince(3) 4 68
(David Evans) *led: rdn over 2f out: hdd over 1f out: styd on same pce wl ins fnl f* **6/5**[1]
2231 **3** *nse* **Secret Millionaire (IRE)**[15] 504 9-8-13 62..........(p) JustinNewman(5) 2 68
(Shaun Harris) *chsd ldr: rdn over 2f out: styd on* **8/1**
6-00 **4** *3/4* **Agerzam**[39] 192 6-9-4 70.......................................(b) RichardKingscote 1 66
(Ronald Harris) *prom: rdn and ev ch over 1f out: no ex wl ins fnl f* **7/1**[3]
1m 14.12s (-0.38) **Going Correction** -0.125s/f (Stan) **4** Ran SP% **107.2**
Speed ratings (Par 103): **97,94,94,93**
CSF £3.90 TOTE £2.60; EX 3.60 Trifecta £7.20.
Owner T Howley Jnr **Bred** Three Chimneys Farm Llc **Trained** Longwood, Co Meath

FOCUS
This proved straightforward for the winner in this muddling seller.

686 DOWNLOAD THE NEW UNIBET RACING APP H'CAP 5f 20y (Tp)
4:35 (4:35) (Class 4) (0-85,87) 3-Y-O **£5,822** (£1,732; £865; £432) **Stalls** Low

Form RPR
531- **1** **Wolowitz (IRE)**[56] 8387 3-9-7 85.................................. GrahamGibbons 5 97
(David Barron) *chsd ldr: shkn up to ld ins fnl f: edgd lft: r.o* **13/8**[1]
21-2 **2** *2 1/4* **Krystallite**[48] 57 3-8-6 70.. BenCurtis 6 74
(Scott Dixon) *led: rdn over 1f out: hdd and unable qck ins fnl f* **8/1**
-113 **3** *1 1/4* **Gorokai (IRE)**[10] 559 3-8-12 76.................................. JamieSpencer 2 76
(David Simcock) *chsd ldrs: rdn over 1f out: styd on same pce ins fnl f* **3/1**[2]
005- **4** *1 1/4* **Silk Bow**[206] 4877 3-9-3 81.. TomEaves 1 76
(James Given) *hld up: hdwy u.p over 1f out: no ex ins fnl f* **11/2**[3]
4-12 **5** *1 1/2* **Dark Side Princess**[30] 322 3-8-8 77.........................(p) AaronJones(5) 3 67+
(Chris Dwyer) *sn pushed along in rr: nt clr run wl over 1f out: n.d* **13/2**
0-34 **6** *2 1/4* **Thatsallimsaying (IRE)**[16] 493 3-9-4 87........... JosephineGordon(5) 7 69
(David Evans) *chsd ldrs: rdn 1/2-way: wknd over 1f out* **40/1**
521- **7** *nse* **Fruit Salad**[90] 7972 3-8-5 69.. JoeFanning 4 50
(James Bethell) *hld up: rdn and wknd over 1f out* **18/1**
1m 0.45s (-1.45) **Going Correction** -0.125s/f (Stan) **7** Ran SP% **110.6**
Speed ratings (Par 99): **106,102,100,98,96 92,92**
CSF £14.44 TOTE £2.30: £1.40, £4.40; EX 14.10 Trifecta £48.20.
Owner Mrs Christine Barron **Bred** Jerry O'Sullivan **Trained** Maunby, N Yorks

FOCUS
Very few got into this, but the winner produced an eyecatching performance.

687 32RED.COM MAIDEN AUCTION STKS 1m 4f 50y (Tp)
5:10 (5:10) (Class 5) 3-Y-O **£3,234** (£962; £481; £240) **Stalls** Low

Form RPR
5 **1** **West Coast Flyer**[26] 361 3-9-5 0.................................. TomEaves 1 73+
(David Simcock) *hld up: hdwy on outer 3f out: rdn over 2f out: hung lft over 1f out: r.o to ld wl ins fnl f* **6/4**[1]
0- **2** *1 1/2* **My Isla**[164] 6319 3-9-0 0.. MartinHarley 3 66
(James Tate) *led 1f: chsd ldr tl over 7f out: wnt 2nd again 5f out: led over 2f out: rdn over 1f out: hdd and unable qck wl ins fnl f* **17/2**
6-3 **3** *3/4* **Kaisan**[33] 275 3-9-5 0.. JamieSpencer 5 69
(Michael Bell) *led after 1f: rdn and hdd over 2f out: hung lft 1f out: styd on same pce* **9/4**[2]
323- **4** *nk* **Zio Gianni (USA)**[75] 8167 3-9-5 72.................................. TimmyMurphy 4 69
(Jamie Osborne) *stdd and hung rt s: hld up: nt clr run over 2f out: hdwy over 1f out: styd on* **3/1**[3]
5 *7* **Nightmare (IRE)** 3-9-0 0.. LucyKBarry(5) 2 58
(Jamie Osborne) *prom: chsd ldr over 7f out tl 5f out: rdn over 2f out: sn wknd* **25/1**
2m 42.52s (1.72) **Going Correction** -0.125s/f (Stan) **5** Ran SP% **110.1**
Speed ratings (Par 97): **89,88,87,87,82**
CSF £14.25 TOTE £2.40: £1.30, £2.70; EX 11.90 Trifecta £29.50.
Owner Ali Saeed **Bred** Miss K Rausing **Trained** Newmarket, Suffolk

FOCUS
A modest maiden run at a fairly steady pace and the form may not be reliable.

688 32RED CASINO H'CAP 1m 141y (Tp)
5:40 (5:40) (Class 6) (0-55,55) 3-Y-O **£2,587** (£770; £384; £192) **Stalls** Low

Form RPR
000- **1** **Big Shoes (IRE)**[168] 6180 3-9-3 51.................................. DarrylHolland 8 54
(Charles Hills) *chsd ldr over 7f out: rdn over 1f out: styd on to ld wl ins fnl f* **4/1**[2]
0-00 **2** *3/4* **Dark Illustrator**[19] 443 3-9-5 53.................................. DanielTudhope 9 54
(David O'Meara) *sn led: rdn over 1f out: hdd wl ins fnl f* **16/1**
-253 **3** *hd* **Frivolous Prince (IRE)**[12] 533 3-8-12 46..........................(v) JFEgan 4 47
(David Evans) *trckd ldrs: racd keenly: rdn over 2f out: styd on* **11/4**[1]
-363 **4** *hd* **Footlight**[19] 443 3-9-5 53.. TonyHamilton 1 53
(Richard Fahey) *chsd ldrs: rdn over 2f out: edgd lft over 1f out: kpt on* **9/2**[3]
-505 **5** *1/2* **Falcon's Fire (IRE)**[12] 533 3-9-7 55.............................(p) PhillipMakin 6 54+
(Keith Dalgleish) *hld up: racd keenly: hdwy over 2f out: rdn over 1f out: styd on* **9/2**[3]
-223 **6** *nk* **Never Say (IRE)**[14] 509 3-8-8 47.......................(p) CallumShepherd(5) 5 45+
(Jason Ward) *hld up: rdn over 2f out: r.o ins fnl f: nvr nrr* **6/1**
0-64 **7** *2 1/2* **Edith Weston**[14] 509 3-8-12 46 oh1.............................(p) JimmyQuinn 2 39
(Robert Cowell) *prom: rdn over 1f out: no ex ins fnl f* **20/1**
6-45 **8** *1 1/2* **Miss Fortune**[27] 345 3-8-12 46.. LiamKeniry 7 36
(Mark Usher) *hld up: rdn over 1f out: wknd fnl f* **22/1**
5-50 **9** *3 1/2* **Thief Of Hearts**[20] 436 3-8-13 52.............................(b) RyanWhile(5) 3 35
(Bill Turner) *hld up: plld hrd: rdn over 1f out: sn wknd* **66/1**
1m 51.86s (1.76) **Going Correction** -0.125s/f (Stan) **9** Ran SP% **113.8**
Speed ratings (Par 95): **87,86,86,85,85 85,83,81,78**
CSF £61.14 CT £204.64 TOTE £4.90: £1.90, £6.10, £1.30; EX 69.10 Trifecta £397.60.
Owner Gary and Linnet Woodward & Partner **Bred** Declan Johnson **Trained** Lambourn, Berks

FOCUS
There was a bunched finish to this steadily run handicap in which the pace held up.
T/Jkpt: Not won. T/Plt: £27.10 to a £1 stake. Pool: £68,318.00 - 1839.59 winning units. T/Qpdt: £21.30 to a £1 stake. Pool: £4,994.78 - 173.42 winning units. **Colin Roberts**

689a (Foreign Racing) - See Raceform Interactive

[602]KEMPTON (A.W) (R-H)
Wednesday, February 24

OFFICIAL GOING: Polytrack: standard
Wind: Light, across Weather: Fine, cold

690 DGS MORTGAGE SOLUTIONS ALL WEATHER "HANDS AND HEELS" APPRENTICE SERIES H'CAP 1m (P)
5:40 (5:42) (Class 7) (0-50,50) 4-Y-O+ **£1,940** (£577; £288; £144) **Stalls** Low

Form RPR
3532 **1** **Lutine Charlie (IRE)**[23] 412 9-9-6 49......................(p) SophieKilloran 10 54
(Emma Owen) *trckd ldr 2f and again over 2f out: led over 1f out: kpt on* **9/2**[2]
5-60 **2** *1 1/4* **Crowning Star (IRE)**[28] 347 7-8-13 45......................(p) CliffordLee(3) 1 47
(Steve Woodman) *led to over 1f out: kpt on same pce* **25/1**
5400 **3** *nk* **Tax Reform (IRE)**[14] 514 6-9-2 45.................................. HollieDoyle 4 46
(Natalie Lloyd-Beavis) *dwlt: wl in rr: prog over 2f out: tk 3rd jst over 1f out: kpt on and pressed for 2nd nr fin* **11/1**
03-5 **4** *1/2* **Patron Of Explores (USA)**[51] 35 5-8-13 45............... PaulaMuir(3) 6 45
(Patrick Holmes) *dwlt: plld hrd and prog to press ldr after 2f: lost 2nd over 2f out: one pce after* **9/2**[2]
3-42 **5** *1 3/4* **Dreaming Again**[28] 346 6-9-1 49.................................. TinaSmith(5) 9 45
(Jimmy Fox) *racd on outer: pushed along in midfield bef 1/2-way: nvr gng wl enough to make any imp on ldrs: one pce* **15/8**[1]
54-6 **6** *8* **Aru Cha Cha**[53] 20 5-9-4 47.. RhiainIngram 3 24
(Roger Ingram) *chsd ldrs to over 2f out: wknd qckly* **15/2**[3]
00-0 **7** *3 1/4* **Wowee**[7] 602 5-9-6 49.. GeorgiaCox 2 18
(Tony Carroll) *sn in rr: no prog over 2f out: bhd after* **8/1**
6-06 **8** *1 3/4* **Supa Seeker (USA)**[23] 412 10-8-11 45................(p) BenSanderson(5) 8 10
(Tony Carroll) *dwlt: a in rr: v wd bnd 3f out: bhd after* **16/1**
1m 40.06s (0.26) **Going Correction** 0.0s/f (Stan) **8** Ran SP% **112.1**
Speed ratings (Par 97): **98,96,96,95,94 86,82,81**
CSF £97.72 CT £1158.18 TOTE £4.30: £1.60, £5.80, £3.50; EX 66.10 Trifecta £510.70.
Owner Miss Emma L Owen **Bred** Patrice O'Connell **Trained** Bicester, Oxon

FOCUS
No better than plating form and not many got into it with a slow-motion finish.

691 32RED ON THE APP STORE MAIDEN STKS 1m (P)
6:10 (6:11) (Class 5) 3-Y-O+ **£2,911** (£866; £432; £216) **Stalls** Low

Form RPR
00- **1** **Papou Tony**[173] 6051 3-8-9 0.. TedDurcan 4 70+
(George Baker) *broke wl but restrained bhd ldrs: clsd gng easily over 2f out: shkn up to ld over 1f out: rdn out and on top fnl f* **16/1**
2 *1 1/4* **I Can't Stop** 3-8-4 0.. RyanPowell 5 62
(Chris Wall) *hld up and sn in last pair: gd prog jst over 2f out: clsd on ldrs 1f: rn green and swtchd but styd on to take 2nd last 100yds: unable to chal* **40/1**
4 **3** *1* **Dor's Law**[25] 402 3-8-4 0.. JimmyQuinn 3 60
(Dean Ivory) *hld up but sn in midfield: clsd on inner 2f out: chsd wnr 1f out to last 100yds: one pce* **20/1**
32-2 **4** *1/2* **Mystic Blaze (IRE)**[14] 524 3-8-9 75.................................. LiamKeniry 1 64+
(Andrew Balding) *mde most 2f: chsd ldr: drvn over 2f out: nt qckn and sn lost 2nd: one pce over 1f out* **8/11**[1]
5 *1/2* **Haabis (USA)** 3-8-9 0.. StevieDonohoe 6 62
(George Peckham) *s.i.s: mostly in last pair: prog 2f out: shoved along and no imp on ldrs jst over 1f out: styd on again ins fnl f: nrst fin* **25/1**
6- **6** *hd* **Howardian Hills (IRE)**[77] 8154 3-8-6 0.................. TomMarquand(3) 11 62
(Richard Hannon) *t.k.h early: w ldrs 2f: chsng after: rdn over 3f out: struggling to stay on terms after: one pce* **11/2**[3]
7 *1 1/4* **Bunbury** 4-10-0 0.. ShaneKelly 10 65+
(Richard Hughes) *nt that wl away but quick prog to ld after 2f: hdd & wknd over 1f out* **5/1**[2]
0 **8** *1/2* **Attitude Rocks**[39] 219 3-8-9 0.. JohnFahy 7 58
(Clive Cox) *chsd ldrs: rdn over 3f out: no prog over 2f out: fdd* **7/1**
60 **9** *9* **Betsalottie**[39] 219 3-8-9 0.. WilliamCarson 8 36
(John Bridger) *t.k.h and hld up in rr: c wd bnd 3f out: bhd after* **100/1**
10 *3 3/4* **Montycristo** 3-8-9 0.. JoeFanning 9 27
(Philip Hide) *a towards rr: hung lft bnd 3f out: bhd after* **50/1**
1m 38.59s (-1.21) **Going Correction** 0.0s/f (Stan)
WFA 3 from 4yo 19lb **10** Ran SP% **122.3**
Speed ratings (Par 103): **106,104,103,103,102 102,101,100,91,88**
CSF £519.28 TOTE £28.20: £4.80, £6.70, £3.40; EX 695.30 Trifecta £8127.70.
Owner PJL, Clark & Moore **Bred** Litex Commerce **Trained** Manton, Wilts

FOCUS
A modest maiden, which totally changed complexion in the straight with the leaders possibly going off too quick. They went nearly a second and a half quicker than the preceding Class 7 event.

692 32RED CONDITIONS STKS (ALL-WEATHER CHAMPIONSHIP FAST-TRACK QUALIFIER) 1m (P)
6:40 (6:41) (Class 2) 4-Y-O+ **£11,827** (£3,541; £1,770; £885) **Stalls** Low

Form RPR
4-24 **1** **Captain Cat (IRE)**[18] 485 7-9-2 107.................................. JamieSpencer 5 112
(Roger Charlton) *mde all: set stdy pce tl past 1/2-way: sent for home over 2f out: hrd pressed over 1f out: cajoled along and styd on wl* **11/4**[2]
1/2- **2** *1* **Sloane Avenue (USA)**[333] 1091 5-9-2 112........................ JimCrowley 4 110
(Jeremy Noseda) *disp 2nd pl: rdn to chal fr 2f out: pressed wnr fnl f: styd on but a hld* **4/6**[1]
0-42 **3** *4 1/2* **Sirius Prospect (USA)**[16] 501 8-9-2 101..................... RobertWinston 1 99
(Dean Ivory) *t.k.h: disp 2nd pl: tried to chal jst over 2f out: sn btn off: wl hld in 3rd fr over 1f out* **16/1**
-314 **4** *2 1/4* **Solar Deity (IRE)**[9] 594 7-9-2 105..............................(p) AndreaAtzeni 3 93
(Marco Botti) *restrained s: hld up in last: drvn whn pce lifted over 2f out and no prog* **7/1**[3]
1m 38.35s (-1.45) **Going Correction** 0.0s/f (Stan) **4** Ran SP% **105.0**
Speed ratings (Par 109): **107,106,101,99**
CSF £4.79 TOTE £3.80; EX 4.40 Trifecta £12.10.
Owner Seasons Holidays **Bred** Azienda Agricola Mediterranea **Trained** Beckhampton, Wilts

The Form Book, Raceform Ltd, Newbury, RG14 5SJ

FOCUS
A small but select field, with all four runners possessing official marks in three figures. The winner was allowed an easy lead.

693 £10 FREE BET AT 32REDSPORT.COM H'CAP 1m 4f (P)
7:10 (7:11) (Class 5) (0-75,75) 4-Y-O+ **£2,911** (£649; £649; £216) **Stalls** Centre

Form RPR

5-12 **1** **Fern Owl**[28] 343 4-9-0 **71**........................ JimCrowley 2 78
(Hughie Morrison) *a cl up in slowly run event: rdn to chse ldr on inner over 2f out: drvn ahd last 120yds: styd on* **7/2**[2]

2-60 **2** *1* **Wildomar**[12] 545 7-8-7 **61** oh2........................ WilliamCarson 1 66
(Peter Hiatt) *in tch: shkn up on inner over 2f out: prog over 1f out: nvr gng pce to chal but styd on to dead-heat for 2nd last stride* **33/1**

0-11 **2** *dht* **Biff Johnson (IRE)**[17] 491 4-9-4 **75**........................(p) PhillipMakin 9 80
(Keith Dalgleish) *led: set mod pce: fnlly kicked for home over 2f out: drvn and hdd 120yds out: jnd for 2nd on line* **7/2**[2]

3-12 **4** *½* **Saint Honore**[18] 488 4-9-1 **72**........................ JFEgan 10 76
(Pat Phelan) *trckd ldrs: prog and prom over 3f out: drvn to chse ldr over 2f out to over 1f out: one pce* **10/1**

324/ **5** *½* **Charlie Wells (IRE)**[441] 8096 5-9-7 **75**........................ JohnFahy 7 78
(Eve Johnson Houghton) *t.k.h: trckd ldr 2f: styd handy: hanging bdly whn asked for effrt wl over 2f out: kpt on fnl f: n.d* **9/1**[3]

1/1 **6** *¾* **Kalahari (IRE)**[21] 435 7-9-2 **70**........................(p) MartinHarley 6 72
(Lucy Wadham) *t.k.h: hld up in last pair: stl there whn pce qcknd over 2f out and swtchd lft: tried to make prog over 1f out but no ch of getting involved* **11/8**[1]

6-00 **7** *1* **Cosette (IRE)**[11] 566 5-8-8 **62**........................ JimmyQuinn 5 63
(Bernard Llewellyn) *trckd ldr after 2f to over 2f out: steadily lost pl* **100/1**

00-6 **8** *1¼* **Sharp Sword (IRE)**[30] 330 5-9-7 **75**........................ LiamKeniry 8 74
(Neil Mulholland) *stdd s: plld hrd in last: prog over 4f out into midfield: no hdwy 2f out: fdd* **25/1**

254/ **9** *5* **Stand Guard**[606] 3710 12-9-1 **72**........................ DanielMuscutt[(3)] 4 63
(John Butler) *in tch: dropped to last pair over 3f out: wknd over 2f out* **66/1**

2m 38.87s (4.37) **Going Correction** 0.0s/f (Stan)
WFA 4 from 5yo+ 3lb **9** Ran SP% **114.9**
Speed ratings (Par 103): **85,84,84,84,83 83,82,81,78**
PL: Wildomar 7.70, Biff Johnson 1.40; EX: FO-BJ 8.30, FO-W 68.90; CSF: FO-BJ 7.87, FO-W 54.29; TC: FO-BJ-W 170.08, FO-W-BJ 216.55; TF: FO-BJ-W 121.80, FO-W-BJ 337.00 TOTE £4.50: £1.40.
Owner Sir Thomas Pilkington **Bred** Sir Thomas Pilkington **Trained** East Ilsley, Berks

FOCUS
A fair race, with a number of these coming into the race in good form. They went an extremely sedate gallop, though, and it was a sprint in the straight.

694 32RED.COM H'CAP 6f (P)
7:40 (7:42) (Class 4) (0-85,85) 4-Y-O+ **£4,690** (£1,395; £697; £348) **Stalls** Low

Form RPR

0-60 **1** **Trojan Rocket (IRE)**[33] 290 8-9-6 **84**........................(p) GeorgeBaker 3 94
(Michael Wigham) *chsd clr ldng trio and clr of rest early: lost pl sltly over 2f out: rdn and prog on outer over 1f out: drvn to ld last 100yds: styd on wl* **4/1**[3]

5-01 **2** *1* **Rich Again (IRE)**[19] 462 7-8-13 **77**........................(b) TedDurcan 4 84
(James Bethell) *hld up off the pce in last trio: gd prog on inner jst over 2f out: clsd over 1f out: led briefly ins fnl f: kpt on* **7/2**[2]

1-21 **3** *½* **Greyfriarschorista**[14] 523 9-8-13 **80**........................(vt) SladeO'Hara[(3)] 6 85
(Giles Bravery) *hld up off the pce in rr: rdn and prog over 1f out: styd on to take 3rd nr fin* **16/1**

/-51 **4** *½* **Mezmaar**[21] 433 7-8-11 **75**........................ ShaneKelly 10 79
(Kevin Morgan) *stdd s: hld up off the pce in rr: sme prog over 1f out: drvn and styd on fnl f: nvr rchd ldrs* **11/4**[1]

6641 **5** *hd* **Borough Boy (IRE)**[14] 520 6-9-1 **79**........................(v) TonyHamilton 5 82
(Derek Shaw) *hld up in last and off the pce: clsr but stl wl in rr 2f out: drvn over 1f out: styd on fnl f but no ch* **25/1**

542- **6** *1½* **Plucky Dip**[221] 4399 5-9-6 **84**........................ RyanPowell 12 82
(John Ryan) *off the pce in midfield: rdn over 2f out: no prog but kpt on ins fnl f* **25/1**

0-00 **7** *nk* **Air Of York (IRE)**[16] 503 4-9-4 **85**........................ PhilipPrince[(3)] 7 82
(David Evans) *w.w off the pce in midfield: clsr over 1f out but stl nt on terms: pushed along fnl f: no imp after* **50/1**

0350 **8** *shd* **Oriental Relation (IRE)**[13] 529 5-9-4 **82**........................(b) TomEaves 2 79
(James Given) *rdn to ld: set str pce and had field strung out: hdd & wknd ins fnl f* **11/1**

1400 **9** *½* **Captain Lars (SAF)**[15] 508 6-9-0 **83**........................(p) CallumShepherd[(5)] 8 78
(Derek Shaw) *stdd s: hld up off the pce in last trio: shkn up 2f out: kpt on fnl f: nvr really involved* **50/1**

5-21 **10** *¾* **Clubland (IRE)**[15] 508 7-9-2 **83**........................ RobHornby[(3)] 1 76
(Roy Bowring) *hld up off the pce in midfield: prog into 3rd over 2f out: clsd on ldng pair over 1f out: wknd qckly last 150yds* **14/1**

2-06 **11** *3¾* **Stake Acclaim (IRE)**[17] 492 4-9-7 **85**........................ RobertWinston 11 66
(Dean Ivory) *chsd ldr and clr of rest: drvn and tried to chal over 2f out: lost 2nd and wknd rapidly jst over 1f out* **15/2**

2-06 **12** *¾* **Mighty Zip (USA)**[18] 484 4-8-13 **77**........................(b) JamieSpencer 9 56
(Kevin Ryan) *chsd ldng pair and clr of rest: rdn and hung lft over 2f out: sn wknd* **20/1**

1m 11.05s (-2.05) **Going Correction** 0.0s/f (Stan) **12** Ran SP% **117.9**
Speed ratings (Par 105): **113,111,111,110,110 108,107,107,106,105 100,99**
CSF £17.14 CT £201.13 TOTE £4.30: £1.80, £1.50, £2.70; EX 23.10 Trifecta £279.70.
Owner G Linder, D Hassan, R Warner **Bred** J G F Fox **Trained** Newmarket, Suffolk

FOCUS
No more than a fair handicap and probably not as competitive as it looked on paper. They went quick and the pace collapsed late on.

695 32RED CASINO H'CAP 2m (P)
8:10 (8:15) (Class 6) (0-60,60) 4-Y-O+ **£2,264** (£673; £336; £168) **Stalls** Low

Form RPR

-332 **1** **Master Burbidge**[5] 634 5-9-1 **51**........................(p) LiamKeniry 7 57
(Neil Mulholland) *trckd ldr after 1f: led wl over 2f out: sn rdn: pressed and looked vulnerable over 1f out: kpt on u.p* **4/6**[1]

00-5 **2** *nk* **Jezza**[44] 138 10-9-7 **57**........................(bt) GeorgeBaker 2 63
(Victor Dartnall) *hld up in last quartet: gd prog on inner over 2f out: chsd wnr over 1f out: chal fnl f: nt qckn last 75yds* **14/1**

1-50 **3** *¾* **Mighty Thor**[28] 354 6-9-7 **57**........................ CharlesBishop 4 62
(Lydia Richards) *trckd ldrs: drvn wl over 2f out: no real imp on outer over 1f out: kpt on again fnl f to take 3rd last stride* **33/1**

/64- **4** *nse* **Newtown Cross (IRE)**[371] 594 6-9-2 **52**........................ TedDurcan 14 57
(Jimmy Fox) *hld up in last quartet: drvn over 2f out: prog over 1f out: styd on wl fnl f: nrly snatched 3rd* **25/1**

4043 **5** *shd* **Delagoa Bay (IRE)**[5] 634 8-8-7 **46** oh1........................ TomMarquand[(3)] 5 51
(Sylvester Kirk) *walked to post after rest had arrived: reversed into stall: hld up in midfield: rdn over 2f out: kpt on wl fnl f: nrst fin* **16/1**

630- **6** *2* **Toretto (IRE)**[299] 1844 8-9-4 **54**........................(b) JimmyQuinn 9 57
(Bernard Llewellyn) *hld up in midfield: rdn over 2f out: clsd on ldrs over 1f out: fdd ins fnl f* **66/1**

03-6 **7** *hd* **Broughtons Berry (IRE)**[28] 354 5-8-12 **48**........................ RichardKingscote 1 50
(Willie Musson) *trckd ldrs: clsd to dispute 2nd wl over 1f out and tried to chal: fdd ins fnl f* **14/1**

0-62 **8** *nse* **Epsom Flyer**[23] 417 6-8-10 **46** oh1........................ JFEgan 10 48
(Pat Phelan) *led 1f: styd cl up: drvn 3f out: disp 2nd wl over 1f out and ch: fdd ins fnl f* **10/1**[3]

00-5 **9** *1¼* **Noor Al Haya (IRE)**[42] 157 6-9-4 **54**........................ TomQueally 3 59+
(Laura Mongan) *hld up in last quartet: waiting for a gap over 2f out: trying to make prog whn nt clr run and swtchd rt over 1f out: no ch after* **33/1**

0-02 **10** *1* **Unex Modigliani (IRE)**[9] 592 7-9-7 **57**........................(tp) TonyHamilton 13 57
(Derek Shaw) *t.k.h: hld up in last: rdn and no rspnse over 2f out: no ch after: plugged on* **7/1**[2]

60-0 **11** *2½* **Giveagirlachance (IRE)**[28] 342 7-9-5 **55**........................ SteveDrowne 6 52
(Seamus Mullins) *t.k.h: pressed ldrs: drvn over 2f out: wknd over 1f out* **16/1**

4-00 **12** *3¼* **Put The Boot In (IRE)**[21] 435 4-8-11 **60**........................ CharlieBennett[(7)] 11 53
(Barry Brennan) *led after 1f: hdd wl over 2f out: lost 2nd and wknd wl over 1f out* **50/1**

00-4 **13** *39* **Sail With Sultana**[49] 71 5-9-2 **52**........................ JamieSpencer 8
(Mark Rimell) *hld up in midfield: prog to go 3rd 1/2-way: rdn 6f out: wknd 4f out: t.o* **12/1**

3m 31.32s (1.22) **Going Correction** 0.0s/f (Stan)
WFA 4 from 5yo+ 6lb **13** Ran SP% **127.6**
Speed ratings (Par 101): **96,95,95,95,95 94,94,94,93,93 91,90,70**
CSF £12.82 CT £214.78 TOTE £1.70: £1.10, £2.80, £6.80; EX 16.30 Trifecta £242.20.
Owner Dajam Ltd **Bred** M Burbidge **Trained** Limpley Stoke, Wilts

FOCUS
A moderate staying handicap with a bunched finish.
T/Plt: £2,566.60 to a £1 stake. Pool: £79,284.96. 22.55 winning tickets. T/Qpdt: £19.40 to a £1 stake. Pool: £10,969.32. 417.86 winning tickets. **Jonathan Neesom**

[667] LINGFIELD (L-H)
Wednesday, February 24

OFFICIAL GOING: Polytrack: standard
Wind: virtually nil Weather: sunny, cold

696 LADBROKES H'CAP 7f 1y(P)
2:20 (2:20) (Class 6) (0-60,60) 4-Y-O+ **£2,264** (£673; £336; £168) **Stalls** Low

Form RPR

1-40 **1** **Believe It (IRE)**[40] 201 4-9-4 **57**........................ ShaneKelly 6 65
(Richard Hughes) *chsd ldrs: wnt 2nd 5f out: pushed along to chal 2f out: led 1f out: forged ahd u.p ins fnl f: styd on and gng away at fin* **11/10**[1]

-330 **2** *1¼* **Pyroclastic (IRE)**[18] 482 4-9-7 **60**........................(p) PatCosgrave 3 65
(Jim Boyle) *chsd ldr tl 5f out: styd trcking ldrs tl effrt on inner to chal over 1f out: drvn 1f out: no ex and outpcd fnl 100yds* **7/2**[2]

3321 **3** *½* **Little Indian**[12] 547 6-9-0 **53**........................ DougieCostello 1 57
(J R Jenkins) *dwlt: sn rcvrd and in tch in midfield: rdn over 2f out: drvn and outpcd over 1f out: rallied ins fnl f: styd on wl to snatch 3rd last strides* **5/1**[3]

-424 **4** *hd* **First Rebellion**[26] 381 7-8-10 **52**........................(v) GeorgeDowning[(3)] 5 55
(Tony Carroll) *led: rdn and hrd pressed wl over 1f out: hdd 1f out: no ex and hld whn n.m.r ins fnl f: kpt on same pce: lost 3rd last strides* **12/1**

0-43 **5** *3¾* **Tidal's Baby**[25] 403 7-9-4 **57**........................ AmirQuinn 7 50
(Lee Carter) *s.i.s: in tch in last pair: effrt over 2f out: no imp: wknd fnl f* **8/1**

-500 **6** *3¾* **Chandrayaan**[23] 412 9-8-2 **46** oh1........................(v) AaronJones[(5)] 8 29
(John E Long) *s.i.s: in tch in last pair: rdn over 2f out: sn struggling: wknd over 1f out* **33/1**

4-60 **7** *6* **Purford Green**[21] 431 7-8-7 **46** oh1........................(p) JoeFanning 4 13
(Michael Attwater) *in tch in midfield: rdn and struggling over 2f out: bhd over 1f out* **25/1**

1m 23.98s (-0.82) **Going Correction** -0.025s/f (Stan) **7** Ran SP% **112.1**
Speed ratings (Par 101): **103,101,101,100,96 92,85**
CSF £4.85 CT £12.29 TOTE £2.40: £1.60, £1.80; EX 6.40 Trifecta £17.80.
Owner Richard Hughes **Bred** The Kathryn Stud **Trained** Upper Lambourn, Berkshire

FOCUS
An ordinary handicap with the winner a bit of a standout on profile.

697 DOWNLOAD THE LADBROKES APP MAIDEN STKS 7f 1y(P)
2:50 (2:50) (Class 5) 3-Y-O+ **£3,234** (£962; £481; £240) **Stalls** Low

Form RPR

1 **Mukaabra** 3-8-4 0........................ AndreaAtzeni 2 76+
(James Tate) *in tch in midfield: effrt and wd bnd 2f out: chsd clr wnr jst over 1f out: qcknd under hands and heels riding and str run to ld towards fin: wl in command at fin* **8/11**[1]

20-0 **2** *½* **Merhoob (IRE)**[14] 518 4-9-12 76........................ RyanPowell 3 75
(John Ryan) *led after 1f: rdn and kicked clr 2f out: 4 l clr 1f out: kpt on u.p: hdd and one pce towards fin* **13/8**[2]

3 *6* **Red Rose Riot (IRE)** 3-7-11 0........................ MitchGodwin[(7)] 4 48
(David Menuisier) *s.i.s: rn green in rr early: swtchd lft and gd hdwy on inner over 1f out: wnt 3rd ent fnl f: no imp* **25/1**

4 **4** *¾* **Shining Romeo**[6] 618 4-9-12 0........................ LemosdeSouza 5 57
(Denis Quinn) *hld up in tch: nt clrest of runs ent fnl 2f: hdwy into 4th 1f out: no imp fnl f* **10/1**[3]

05 **5** *¾* **Plymouth Mo**[23] 423 3-8-6 0........................ RyanTate[(3)] 6 49
(Rod Millman) *hld up in tch: effrt 2f out: wl hld 5th and plugged on same pce fnl f* **25/1**

00 **6** *6* **Compromise**[11] 557 3-8-6 0........................ EoinWalsh[(3)] 1 33
(Conor Dore) *led for 1f: chsd ldr tl 5f out: styd handy: rdn to chse ldr again but outpcd 2f out: lost 2nd jst over 1f out: sn wknd* **100/1**

0/0 **7** *4* **Pandora's Pyx**[7] 603 4-9-7 0........................ GeorgeBaker 7 23
(Gary Moore) *dwlt and pushed along early: hdwy to chse ldr 5f out: lost 2nd 2f out and sod outpcd u.p: wknd and bhd ins fnl f* **50/1**

1m 24.15s (-0.65) **Going Correction** -0.025s/f (Stan)
WFA 3 from 4yo 17lb **7** Ran SP% **115.7**
Speed ratings (Par 103): **102,101,94,93,92 86,81**
CSF £2.13 TOTE £1.60: £1.10, £1.30; EX 2.70 Trifecta £17.10.

Owner Sheikh Juma Dalmook Al Maktoum **Bred** Biddestone Stud Ltd **Trained** Newmarket, Suffolk
FOCUS
A modest maiden lacking depth, but a nice performance from the winner.

698 32REDSPORT.COM H'CAP 1m 7f 169y(P)
3:20 (3:22) (Class 5) (0-70,68) 4-Y-O+ **£2,911** (£866; £432; £216) **Stalls** Low

Form RPR
22-0 **1** **Flighty Filia (IRE)**[44] 138 4-9-2 **65** JimCrowley 6 71
(Amanda Perrett) *in tch in midfield: swtchd rt and effrt wl over 1f out: styd on wl ins fnl f to ld fnl 50yds* **5/1**[2]
25-3 **2** ½ **Thomas Blossom (IRE)**[35] 261 6-9-8 **65** (tp) GeorgeBaker 5 70
(Ali Stronge) *stdd after s: hld up in tch in rr: clsd and nt clrest of runs over 1f out: swtchd lft 1f out: styd on wl u.p to go 2nd towards fin* **5/1**[2]
2/0- **3** nk **Amanto (GER)**[90] 7436 6-9-4 **68** (b) MeganNicholls(7) 9 72
(Paul Nicholls) *s.i.s: sn rcvrd to chse ldr after 1f: upsides and gng best 3f out: rdn over 1f out: drifted rt 1f out: kpt on same pce fnl 100yds* **7/1**[3]
3-21 **4** hd **Ruler Of The Nile**[10] 583 4-9-5 **68** 6ex AdamBeschizza 1 72
(Robert Stephens) *trckd ldrs tl led on inner wl over 1f out: sn hrd drvn: hdd fnl 50yds: no ex and one pce after: lost 2 pls towards fin* **5/6**[1]
603- **5** ¾ **Takeitfromalady (IRE)**[100] 5968 7-9-7 **64** (v) AmirQuinn 3 67
(Lee Carter) *hld up in tch: effrt on inner over 1f out: hrd drvn and chsd ldrs 1f out: no ex and one pce fnl 100yds* **25/1**
-560 **6** 1¼ **Topaling**[22] 425 5-9-7 **64** SaleemGolam 8 66
(Mark H Tompkins) *taken down early: hld up in tch: nt clrest of runs ent fnl 2f: swtchd rt and effrt wl over 1f out: kpt on same pce ins fnl f* **16/1**
6-44 **7** ½ **Opera Buff**[19] 461 7-9-4 **64** (v[1]) KevinStott(3) 7 65
(Jose Santos) *hld up in tch: hdwy into midfield 3f out: wd and lost pl bnd 2f out: styd on same pce fnl f* **10/1**
8 6 **The Scourge (IRE)**[153] 3870 5-9-4 **64** DannyBrock(3) 2 58
(Sarah Humphrey) *led: rdn 3f out: drvn over 2f out: hdd wl over 1f out: sn lost pl: bhd fnl f* **50/1**

3m 25.08s (-0.62) **Going Correction** -0.025s/f (Stan)
WFA 4 from 5yo+ 6lb **8 Ran SP% 121.2**
Speed ratings (Par 103): **100,99,99,99,99 98,98,95**
CSF £32.09 CT £179.93 TOTE £6.10: £1.60, £2.30, £1.60; EX 38.30 Trifecta £125.90.
Owner Cotton, Conway **Bred** The Lavington Stud **Trained** Pulborough, W Sussex
FOCUS
There was a tight finish to this staying handicap run at a steady pace.

699 32RED.COM MAIDEN FILLIES' STKS (PLUS 10 RACE) 1m 2f (P)
3:55 (3:56) (Class 5) 3-Y-O **£2,911** (£866; £432; £216) **Stalls** Low

Form RPR
5- **1** **Golden Chapter**[71] 8233 3-9-0 0 GrahamGibbons 4 67+
(Ralph Beckett) *t.k.h: trckd ldrs: swtchd rt and effrt to chal 1f out: rdn to ld ins fnl f: kpt on and jst hld on: rdn out* **10/11**[1]
2 nse **Celestra** 3-9-0 0 WilliamTwiston-Davies 2 66+
(Alan King) *in tch in midfield: rdn 3f out: clsd and nt clr run over 1f out: gap opened and hdwy under hands and heels riding ins fnl f: chsd wnr wl ins fnl f: r.o wl: jst failed* **20/1**
-462 **3** 1 **Kelvin Hall**[23] 413 3-9-0 65 JoeFanning 3 64
(Mark Johnston) *chsd ldrs: effrt on outer bnd 2f out: kpt on u.p ins fnl f* **6/1**[3]
5-4 **4** nk **Asafoetida (IRE)**[9] 591 3-9-0 0 WilliamCarson 6 63
(Peter Chapple-Hyam) *led: rdn wl over 1f out: hdd ins fnl f: kpt on same pce after: lost 2 pls towards fin* **12/1**
5 nse **Bellotta** 3-9-0 0 RichardKingscote 7 63+
(Jonathan Portman) *s.i.s: in tch in rr: shkn up and effrt on inner over 1f out: pushed along and swtchd rt ins fnl f: kpt on wl towards fin* **33/1**
00- **6** ½ **Spinning Pearl (IRE)**[98] 7890 3-9-0 0 JohnFahy 5 62+
(Eve Johnson Houghton) *hld up in tch: rdn and rn green whn hung rt bnd 2f out: rallied 1f out: styd on wl towards fin* **66/1**
7 ½ **Malhama** 3-9-0 0 AndreaAtzeni 8 61
(Roger Varian) *chsd ldr: rdn and ev ch over 1f out tl no ex ins fnl f: wknd towards fin* **11/8**[2]

2m 6.38s (-0.22) **Going Correction** -0.025s/f (Stan) **7 Ran SP% 125.7**
Speed ratings (Par 94): **99,98,98,97,97 97,97**
CSF £25.00 TOTE £1.80: £1.30, £6.40; EX 31.20 Trifecta £97.50.
Owner Sutong Pan **Bred** Arbib Bloodstock Partnership **Trained** Kimpton, Hants
■ Belle Of Seville was withdrawn. Price at time of withdrawal 66-1. Rule 4 does not apply.
FOCUS
They went pretty steady in this maiden and the result was a dash to the line and a bunched finish.

700 32RED CASINO APPRENTICE H'CAP 1m 2f (P)
4:25 (4:25) (Class 6) (0-55,55) 3-Y-O **£2,587** (£770; £384; £192) **Stalls** Low

Form RPR
006- **1** **New Abbey Angel (IRE)**[119] 7545 3-9-5 **55** LuluStanford(5) 8 63+
(Gay Kelleway) *t.k.h: hld up in tch: nt clrest of runs over 2f out: hdwy to chse ldr wl over 1f out: sn chalng and rn green: rdn to ld ins fnl f: r.o wl and gng away at fin* **11/4**[2]
4-64 **2** 1¾ **Secret Sinner (IRE)**[14] 517 3-9-1 **46** oh1 LucyKBarry 7 49
(Jamie Osborne) *chsd ldrs tl hdwy to ld 8f out: rdn wl over 1f out: sn hrd pressed: hdd and styd on same pce ins fnl f* **5/1**[3]
0-50 **3** 7 **Lady Fontenail**[20] 443 3-9-7 **55** CallumShepherd(3) 2 45
(Rod Millman) *hld up in tch: effrt over 2f out: no ch w ldng pair and swtchd lft 1f out: wnt modest 3rd ins fnl f: spooked and hung bdly rt fnl 50yds* **12/1**
0-30 **4** 2¾ **Boom Junior**[28] 345 3-8-10 **46** oh1 MitchGodwin(5) 1 30
(Tony Carroll) *led for 2f: chsd ldr tl wl over 1f out: sn outpcd and btn 1f out: lost 3rd ins fnl f: no ch whn hmpd towards fin* **20/1**
06-5 **5** ¾ **Diamondsaretrumps (IRE)**[34] 265 3-9-10 **55** NoelGarbutt 4 38
(Denis Quinn) *chsd ldrs: rdn 4f out: lost pl ent fnl 2f: sn outpcd and wl btn 1f out* **12/1**
-534 **6** 3¼ **Faster Company (IRE)**[13] 533 3-9-3 **48** (b[1]) AaronJones 5 25
(J S Moore) *hld up in tch: rdn and struggling whn hung rt and wd bnd 2f out: sn wknd* **6/4**[1]
0-00 **7** 42 **Pour Pavot (IRE)**[26] 376 3-9-9 **54** (e[1]) CiaranMckee 6
(Gary Moore) *v.s.a and lost arnd 30 l s: grad clsd and in tch 5f out: rdn 4f out: sn btn: eased over 1f out: t.o* **7/1**

2m 6.53s (-0.07) **Going Correction** -0.025s/f (Stan) **7 Ran SP% 116.0**
Speed ratings (Par 95): **99,97,92,89,89 86,53**
CSF £17.40 CT £141.02 TOTE £3.70: £2.30, £2.20; EX 16.00 Trifecta £122.70.
Owner A G MacLennan **Bred** Yeomanstown Stud **Trained** Exning, Suffolk
FOCUS
The first two pulled well clear in this moderate contest.

701 CORAL AMATEUR RIDERS' H'CAP 1m 2f (P)
5:00 (5:00) (Class 6) (0-60,60) 4-Y-O+ **£2,183** (£677; £338; £169) **Stalls** Low

Form RPR
4252 **1** **Miss Lillie**[11] 563 5-10-6 **59** (p) HarryTeal(7) 4 65
(Roger Teal) *taken down early: t.k.h: hld up in tch in midfield: hdwy over 2f out: swtchd lft and chalng over 1f out: sn led: kpt on: rdn out* **5/1**[3]
0-06 **2** 1¼ **Engai (GER)**[15] 505 10-9-12 **49** MissPBridgwater(5) 7 54
(David Bridgwater) *s.i.s: sn rcvrd and in tch: chsd ldr 5f out tl led 3f out: carried wd by loose horse bnd 2f out and hdd over 1f out: rallied to chse wnr ins fnl f: no imp towards fin* **7/1**
-502 **3** shd **Debit**[19] 463 5-10-6 **59** MrMSBastyan(7) 10 62
(Simon Hodgson) *hld up in tch in last quartet: clsd and nt clr run jst over 2f out: hdwy and rdn to chse ldrs 1f out: kpt on u.p* **14/1**
-442 **4** nk **Ferryview Place**[7] 602 7-10-3 **49** (tp) MrRyanBird 3 52
(Ian Williams) *t.k.h: chsd ldrs: hmpd over 5f out: effrt and lft in ld over 1f out: sn unable qck 1f out: styd on same pce ins fnl f* **10/3**[1]
241- **5** 2¼ **Storm Runner (IRE)**[77] 8165 8-10-11 **60** MissKMargarson(3) 5 62+
(George Margarson) *stdd after s: hld up in rr: hdwy on outer over 3f out: swtchd rt and v wd bnd 2f out: rallied and hdwy 1f out: kpt on: unable to rcvr* **7/1**
656/ **6** 2 **Hollywood All Star (IRE)**[11] 3852 7-9-9 **46** oh1 TobyEley(5) 12 41
(Graeme McPherson) *hld up in tch: clsd towards inner over 2f out: rdn and unable qck over 1f out: wknd ins fnl f* **8/1**
0-0 **7** 4 **Evacusafe Lady**[19] 463 5-10-6 **57** (t) MrBJames(5) 2 44
(John Ryan) *taken down early: t.k.h: chsd ldr early: styd wl in tch: hmpd over 5f out: rdn and wd bnd 2f out: lost pl and n.d after: plugged on* **16/1**
0/0- **8** ¾ **Mildmay Arms**[287] 2177 4-9-11 **51** MrLFerguson(7) 1 37
(Simon Hodgson) *t.k.h: led tl 3f out: sn rdn: lost pl wl over 1f out: sn wknd* **66/1**
502/ **9** nk **Kudu Country (IRE)**[70] 7343 10-10-7 **60** MissIsabelWilliams(7) 6 45
(Evan Williams) *chsd ldr after 1f: hmpd over 5f out and sn lost 2nd: styd chsng ldrs tl over 2f out: wknd over 1f out* **8/1**
050- **10** 3½ **Spice Boat**[56] 8397 4-9-9 **49** MissJMOlliver(7) 13 28
(Paddy Butler) *hld up in tch in last quartet: hdwy on inner 3f out: no ex over 1f out: wknd fnl f* **66/1**
03-0 **U** **Nouvelle Ere**[41] 173 5-11-0 **60** (t) MrThomasGreatrex 8
(Tony Carroll) *awkward leaving stalls and uns rdr* **4/1**[2]

2m 9.7s (3.10) **Going Correction** -0.025s/f (Stan)
WFA 4 from 5yo+ 1lb **11 Ran SP% 122.5**
Speed ratings (Par 101): **86,85,84,84,82 81,78,77,77,74**
CSF £41.86 CT £470.25 TOTE £5.60: £2.00, £5.20, £2.90; EX 50.20 Trifecta £457.70.
Owner The Rat Racers **Bred** Newsells Park Stud & Cannon Bloodstock **Trained** Great Shefford, Berks
■ Harry Teal's first winner.
FOCUS
Nouvelle Ere unseated his rider soon after the start, but the loose horse still played a part in deciding the outcome of the race.
T/Jkpt: £5,362.40 to a £1 stake. Pool: £33,987.11 - 4.50 winning tickets. T/Plt: £105.00 to a £1 stake. Pool: £63,710.73 - 442.70 winning tickets. T/Qpdt: £41.60 to a £1 stake. Pool: £5,261.49 - 93.58 winning tickets. **Steve Payne**

617 CHELMSFORD (A.W) (L-H)
Thursday, February 25

OFFICIAL GOING: Polytrack: standard
Wind: nil Weather: dry, cold

702 TOTEPLACEPOT H'CAP 1m 2f (P)
5:40 (5:40) (Class 6) (0-55,55) 4-Y-O+ **£3,234** (£962; £481; £240) **Stalls** Low

Form RPR
45/2 **1** **Barnaby Brook (CAN)**[14] 527 6-9-5 **53** (b) MartinHarley 7 59
(Robyn Brisland) *t.k.h: chsd ldr: clsd 3f out: c centre and rdn to ld over 1f out: in command and styd on fnl f: comf* **2/1**[1]
1104 **2** 1¾ **Clock On Tom**[14] 527 6-9-4 **52** LukeMorris 2 55
(Denis Quinn) *chsd ldrs: effrt over 2f out: drvn to chse ldr over 1f out: clr 2nd but styd on same pce ins fnl f* **5/1**[3]
-425 **3** 4 **Happy Jack (IRE)**[15] 514 5-9-2 **50** (b) PaulMulrennan 5 45
(Michael Wigham) *squeezed for room leaving stalls: hld up in last pair: clsd 3f out: effrt over 1f out: wnt 3rd ins fnl f: kpt on but no ch w ldng pair* **7/2**[2]
4231 **4** 1¾ **Celtic Artisan (IRE)**[14] 527 5-9-0 **55** (b) DanielleMooney(7) 6 47
(Rebecca Menzies) *hld up in last pair: clsd 3f out: sn rdn: no ch w ldng pair and plugged on same pce fr over 1f out* **2/1**[1]
-104 **5** ¾ **Goodwood Moonlight**[32] 326 4-9-3 **55** GeorgeDowning(3) 3 45
(Ian Williams) *led: clr 1/2-way tl over 2f out: rdn and hdd over 1f out: sn btn: wknd ins fnl f* **8/1**

2m 6.22s (-2.38) **Going Correction** -0.175s/f (Stan)
WFA 4 from 5yo+ 1lb **5 Ran SP% 116.7**
Speed ratings (Par 101): **102,100,97,96,95**
CSF £13.15 TOTE £2.30: £1.30, £2.00; EX 13.90 Trifecta £39.80.
Owner Franconson Partners **Bred** Adena Springs **Trained** Newmarket, Suffolk
FOCUS
A moderate handicap. They went a respectable gallop at best.

703 TOTEPLACEPOT RACING'S FAVOURITE BET H'CAP 6f (P)
6:10 (6:11) (Class 5) (0-75,75) 4-Y-O+ **£5,175** (£1,540; £769; £384) **Stalls** Centre

Form RPR
4-21 **1** **Eleuthera**[28] 363 4-9-0 **73** PatrickO'Donnell(5) 6 86+
(Kevin Ryan) *in tch in midfield and travelled strly: swtchd lft and effrt over 1f out: sn rdn: led ins fnl f: r.o wl and gng away at fin: readily* **3/1**[1]
2102 **2** 2 **Fujin**[15] 520 5-8-13 **67** (b) TomEaves 9 72
(Shaun Harris) *led: rdn wl over 1f out: drifted rt and hdd 1f out: chsd wnr wl ins fnl f: kpt on but no imp* **20/1**
-312 **3** nse **Jacob's Pillow**[23] 426 5-9-6 **74** PaulMulrennan 1 79
(Rebecca Bastiman) *taken down early: chsd ldr tl 1/2-way: styd prom: effrt over 1f out: drvn 1f out: kpt on same pce ins fnl f* **5/1**[2]
-314 **4** ¾ **Welease Bwian (IRE)**[21] 439 7-8-8 **69** MillyNaseb(7) 12 72+
(Stuart Williams) *s.i.s: hld up in last pair: shkn up over 1f out: rdn and styd on strly ins fnl f: no threat to wnr* **12/1**
64-0 **5** shd **Fever Few**[22] 433 7-9-6 **74** MartinHarley 8 76
(Chris Wall) *chsd ldrs: wnt 2nd 1/2-way: rdn and ev ch over 1f out: led 1f out: hdd ins fnl f: no ex: wknd towards fin* **6/1**[3]

-232 **6** *hd* **Gold Beau (FR)**[8] 608 6-8-11 **65**..........(p) CathyGannon 3 67
(Kristin Stubbs) *hld up in last trio: rdn and hdwy on inner over 1f out: styd on same pce ins fnl f* **6/1**[3]

6212 **7** *3/4* **Seamster**[12] 561 9-9-5 **73**..........(vt) DanielTudhope 5 72
(David O'Meara) *chsd ldrs: rdn over 1f out: stl handy but struggling to qckn whn bdly hmpd and swtchd rt 1f out: nt rcvr and kpt on same pce ins fnl f* **5/1**[2]

0-54 **8** *1/2* **Robero**[12] 561 4-9-3 **71**.......... TomQueally 4 69
(John E Long) *s.i.s: sn swtchd towards outer and in tch in midfield: effrt in centre wl over 1f out: no imp and kpt on same pce ins fnl f* **10/1**

-424 **9** *nk* **Sewn Up**[38] 239 6-8-11 **65** ow1..........(p) PhillipMakin 11 62
(Keith Dalgleish) *taken down early: rdn along early: in tch in midfield: rdn and unable qck 2f out: kpt on but no imp fnl f* **14/1**

000- **10** *3 1/2* **City Of Angkor Wat (IRE)**[127] 7388 6-9-0 **68**..........(p) LiamKeniry 2 53
(Conor Dore) *in tch in midfield: effrt wl over 1f out: little rspnse and sn btn: bhd fnl f* **20/1**

000- **11** *3 3/4* **Holland Park**[129] 7345 4-8-13 **67**..........(p) ShaneGray 7 40
(Conor Dore) *s.i.s: a bhd* **50/1**

1m 11.29s (-2.41) **Going Correction** -0.175s/f (Stan) **11** Ran SP% **121.8**
Speed ratings (Par 103): **109,106,106,105,105 104,103,103,102,98 93**
CSF £72.85 CT £308.12 TOTE £3.60: £1.40, £5.00, £2.10; EX 75.80 Trifecta £438.50.
Owner Guy Reed Racing **Bred** G Reed **Trained** Hambleton, N Yorks

FOCUS
An ordinary sprint handicap and the winner was starting off a fair mark. They went a decent gallop.

704 TOTEPLACEPOT AVAILABLE AT ALL UK MEETINGS H'CAP 1m 6f (P)
6:40 (6:42) (Class 4) (0-85,80) 4-Y-O+ **£8,086** (£2,406; £1,202; £601) **Stalls** Low

Form RPR

021/ **1** **Knight's Parade (IRE)**[119] 4711 6-9-4 **73**..........(t) DannyBrock(3) 3 80
(Sarah Humphrey) *hld up in tch: rdn over 3f out: hdwy on inner to ld ent fnl f: kpt on u.p: drvn out* **16/1**

14-4 **2** *nk* **Grand Meister**[27] 385 5-9-13 **79**..........(p) IanBrennan 6 85
(John Quinn) *hld up in tch: effrt to chal and hung lft ent fnl f: racd awkwardly and hung bk rt ins fnl f: styd on towards fin but nvr looked like passing wnr* **5/2**[2]

060- **3** *4 1/2* **Mirsaale**[155] 6656 6-9-8 **74**.......... PhillipMakin 2 74
(Keith Dalgleish) *led tl 9f out: styd chsng ldrs: nt clr run 2f out tl rdn to chal over 1f out: outpcd 1f out: wknd ins fnl f* **7/4**[1]

10-0 **4** *hd* **Ninepointsixthree**[6] 640 6-8-11 **68**..........(p) CiaranMckee(5) 1 67
(John O'Shea) *taken down early: v.s.a: detached in last tl clsd and in tch 8f out: effrt over 2f out: no ch w ldng pair and plugged on same pce ins fnl f* **25/1**

-135 **5** *1/2* **The Lock Master (IRE)**[21] 447 9-10-0 **80**..........(p) AndrewMullen 5 79
(Michael Appleby) *chsd ldr tl led 9f out: rdn over 2f out: hdd ent fnl f and sn bmpd and outpcd: wl hld and plugged on ins fnl f* **12/1**[3]

11-4 **6** *7* **Aumerle**[28] 357 4-9-3 **74**.......... LukeMorris 4 63
(Shaun Lycett) *chsd ldrs tl wnt 2nd 8f out: rdn and ev ch 2f out: drvn and no ex over 1f out: sn wknd: bhd and eased ins fnl f* **5/2**[2]

2m 59.62s (-3.58) **Going Correction** -0.175s/f (Stan)
WFA 4 from 5yo+ 5lb **6** Ran SP% **110.9**
Speed ratings (Par 105): **103,102,100,100,99 95**
CSF £54.50 TOTE £12.80: £5.80, £2.90; EX 73.00 Trifecta £307.60.
Owner Mrs S J Humphrey **Bred** E Heary **Trained** West Wratting, Cambs

FOCUS
A fair staying handicap. They went an ordinary gallop until the tempo increased over 5f out.

705 TOTEPLACEPOT SIX PLACES IN SIX RACES H'CAP 1m (P)
7:10 (7:12) (Class 3) (0-95,91) 3-Y-O **£9,703** (£2,887; £1,443; £721) **Stalls** Low

Form RPR

421- **1** **Ennaadd**[80] 8138 3-9-7 **91**.......... AndreaAtzeni 4 100+
(Roger Varian) *stdd s: t.k.h: hld up in rr: clsd and swtchd rt over 1f out: shkn up and qcknd to chal but hung lft 1f out: bmpd runner-up and led ins fnl f: sn in command and eased cl home: comf* **10/11**[1]

-222 **2** *1 1/4* **Ice Royal (IRE)**[18] 495 3-8-10 **80**.......... JamieSpencer 2 84
(Jamie Osborne) *chsd ldng pair tl over 3f out: rdn: hung lft and hdwy to ld over 1f out: bmpd and hdd ins fnl f: one pce fnl 100yds* **11/1**

64-1 **3** *shd* **Theydon Grey**[18] 495 3-8-12 **85**.......... DanielMuscutt(3) 5 89
(Peter Charalambous) *stdd after s: hld up in tch: hdwy to trck ldng pair over 3f out: pressing ldrs over 1f out: rdn ent fnl f: r.o same pce fnl 100yds* **4/1**[3]

24-4 **4** *6* **Peak Hill**[22] 434 3-8-7 **77**.......... JFEgan 3 67
(David Evans) *t.k.h: led and set stdy gallop: rdn ent fnl 2f: hdd over 1f out: 4th and btn 1f out: wknd ins fnl f* **25/1**

5-41 **5** *7* **Jintshi**[20] 466 3-8-4 **74**.......... JoeFanning 1 48
(Mark Johnston) *t.k.h: chsd ldr: rdn wl over 2f out: sn struggling and outpcd: bhd and wknd fnl f* **11/4**[2]

1m 38.5s (-1.40) **Going Correction** -0.175s/f (Stan) **5** Ran SP% **111.2**
Speed ratings (Par 101): **100,98,98,92,85**
CSF £11.98 TOTE £1.50: £1.10, £2.90; EX 8.50 Trifecta £21.00.
Owner Sheikh Ahmed Al Maktoum **Bred** Darley **Trained** Newmarket, Suffolk

FOCUS
The feature contest was a decent little 3yo handicap and a smart effort from the winner. They went an ordinary gallop.

706 PLAY SCOOP6SOCCER EVERY WEEK MEDIAN AUCTION MAIDEN FILLIES' STKS 1m (P)
7:40 (7:42) (Class 5) 3-5-Y-O **£5,175** (£1,540; £769; £384) **Stalls** Low

Form RPR

045- **1** **Bocking End (IRE)**[117] 7630 3-8-9 72..........[1] JamieSpencer 2 62
(Michael Bell) *mde virtually: rdn 2f out: wnt rt and drvn over 1f out: hld on towards fin: all out* **11/8**[1]

5-2 **2** *shd* **Ruby Wednesday**[15] 516 3-8-9 0.......... KierenFox 3 61
(John Best) *t.k.h: pressed wnr tl over 5f out: rdn to press wnr again over 1f out: ev ch ins fnl f: r.o: jst hld* **6/4**[2]

0 **3** *1* **Ms Gillard**[20] 458 3-8-9 0.......... LukeMorris 1 59
(David Simcock) *in tch in 4th: effrt over 2f out: chsd ldng pair 1f out: styd on same pce u.p ins fnl f* **8/1**[3]

50 **4** *1/2* **Smirnova (IRE)**[27] 384 3-8-2 0.......... EvaMoscrop(7) 4 58
(Marco Botti) *hld up in tch: hdwy to press ldrs 2f out: styd on same pce u.p ins fnl f* **20/1**

0-0 **5** *3/4* **Tamara Love (IRE)**[26] 402 3-8-9 0..........(t) SaleemGolam 6 56
(Stuart Williams) *broke fast: sn stdd bk and hld up in tch in rr: effrt over 1f out: kpt on same pce ins fnl f* **33/1**

-6 **6** *1 3/4* **Dilly Daydream (IRE)**[28] 361 3-8-2 60.......... LuluStanford(7) 5 52
(Giles Bravery) *nt best away: t.k.h and sn chsng ldrs: jnd wnr over 5f out tl lost pl over 1f out: wknd ins fnl f* **10/1**

1m 39.91s (0.01) **Going Correction** -0.175s/f (Stan) **6** Ran SP% **110.0**
Speed ratings (Par 100): **92,91,90,90,89 87**
CSF £3.53 TOTE £1.60: £1.10, £3.00; EX 3.00 Trifecta £9.30.
Owner W J and T C O Gredley **Bred** Howard Barton Stud **Trained** Newmarket, Suffolk

FOCUS
An ordinary fillies' maiden with a bunch finish. They went just a respectable gallop.

707 BET SCOOP6SOCCER AT TOTESPORT.COM H'CAP 1m (P)
8:10 (8:11) (Class 6) (0-55,55) 4-Y-O+ **£3,234** (£962; £481; £240) **Stalls** Low

Form RPR

42-3 **1** **Hold Firm**[40] 216 4-9-6 **54**.......... SaleemGolam 3 60
(Mark H Tompkins) *hld up in tch in last trio: hdwy and swtchd lft over 1f out: rdn to chse ldr jst ins fnl f: r.o wl to ld towards fin* **4/1**[2]

-633 **2** *1/2* **Star Pursuits**[29] 347 4-8-13 **47**..........(b[1]) LukeMorris 2 52
(Jimmy Fox) *t.k.h: chsd ldng trio: effrt wl over 1f out: drvn to ld jst over 1f out: kpt on u.p tl hdd and no ex towards fin* **4/1**[2]

-022 **3** *1 1/4* **Bionic Indian**[13] 547 4-9-0 **48**..........(b) GrahamGibbons 6 50
(Michael Easterby) *chsd ldrs: wnt 2nd over 2f out: drvn and ev ch over 1f out tl no ex jst ins fnl f: one pce after* **4/1**[2]

-650 **4** *1 1/4* **Jonnie Skull (IRE)**[7] 617 10-9-0 **51**..........(tp) DannyBrock(3) 8 50
(Phil McEntee) *sn led: rdn wl over 1f out: hdd jst over 1f out: no ex and outpcd fnl 150yds* **25/1**

3205 **5** *nk* **Ela Goog La Mou**[14] 527 7-9-1 **52**.......... DanielMuscutt(3) 7 50
(Peter Charalambous) *in tch in midfield: drvn over 1f out: kpt on same pce and no imp after* **12/1**

0-00 **6** *3 1/2* **Rezwaan**[29] 346 9-9-5 **53**..........(p) ShaneKelly 5 43
(Murty McGrath) *hld up in tch in last trio: effrt over 1f out: sn btn: wknd ins fnl f* **20/1**

/636 **7** *6* **Malvesi**[13] 547 7-8-13 **47**.......... JoeFanning 1 22
(Mark Johnston) *t.k.h: chsd ldr tl over 2f out: sn rdn: lost pl over 1f out: sn wknd* **3/1**[1]

50-5 **8** *5* **Beat The Blues**[43] 158 4-9-4 **55**.......... ShelleyBirkett(3) 9 18
(Miss Joey Ellis) *in tch in midfield: rdn and lost pl over 2f out: bhd over 1f out* **20/1**

3-54 **U** **Patron Of Explores (USA)**[1] 690 5-8-5 **46** oh1.......... PaulaMuir(7) 4
(Patrick Holmes) *s.i.s: t.k.h: hld up in rr: clipped heels: stmbld bdly and uns rdr wl over 4f out* **7/1**[3]

1m 39.07s (-0.83) **Going Correction** -0.175s/f (Stan) **9** Ran SP% **118.6**
Speed ratings (Par 101): **97,96,95,94,93 90,84,79,**
CSF £20.38 CT £69.25 TOTE £7.30: £3.70, £2.60, £2.20; EX 21.60 Trifecta £72.20.
Owner Raceworld **Bred** Richard W Farleigh **Trained** Newmarket, Suffolk

FOCUS
Another moderate handicap. They went just a respectable gallop and a marginal step forward fom the winner.

708 BOOK SIMPLY RED TICKETS AT CHELMSFORDCITYRACECOURSE.COM H'CAP 1m 2f (P)
8:40 (8:42) (Class 5) (0-75,75) 4-Y-O+ **£5,175** (£1,540; £769; £384) **Stalls** Low

Form RPR

323- **1** **Barsanti (IRE)**[190] 5519 4-9-6 **75**.......... AndreaAtzeni 4 88+
(Roger Varian) *rn green: hld up in tch: clsd to chse ldrs and pushed along 2f out: swtchd lft and squeezed between horses 1f out: sn led and wnt clr: in command and pricked ears ins fnl f: easily* **11/10**[1]

34-0 **2** *3 1/4* **Qasser (IRE)**[20] 465 7-9-4 **72**.......... LukeMorris 5 77
(Harry Whittington) *chsd ldrs: wnt 2nd 1/2-way: rdn and ev ch over 1f out: led and edgd lft ent fnl f: hdd jst ins fnl f: sn brushed aside by wnr: kpt on to hold 2nd* **5/1**[2]

-316 **3** *nk* **Black Minstrel (IRE)**[12] 568 7-8-6 **65**..........(p) CiaranMckee(5) 2 69
(John O'Shea) *t.k.h: chsd ldr tl 1/2-way: styd handy: rdn and ev ch on inner over 1f out: struggling to qckn whn bmpd and hmpd 1f out: no ch w wnr and kpt on same pce after* **12/1**

0-22 **4** *1 1/2* **Comanche Chieftain (CAN)**[21] 438 4-8-12 **67**.......(p) AndrewMullen 7 70
(Michael Appleby) *led: rdn ent fnl 2f: hdd ent fnl f: struggling to qckn whn bmpd and bdly hmpd 1f out: no ch w wnr and kpt on same pce after* **5/1**[2]

-356 **5** *2 1/4* **Enriching (USA)**[18] 491 8-8-6 **67**.......... LuluStanford(7) 3 64
(Robyn Brisland) *in tch in midfield: rdn over 2f out: 5th and no imp over 1f out: plugged on same pce after* **10/1**

5-62 **6** *3/4* **Archie's Advice**[42] 179 5-9-2 **70**.......... PhillipMakin 6 65
(Keith Dalgleish) *stdd s: hld up in tch in last pair: effrt on outer 2f out: sn rdn and outpcd: wl hld fnl f* **6/1**[3]

6-54 **7** *3* **Sacred Square (GER)**[21] 438 6-8-9 **63**..........(p) LiamKeniry 1 52
(Conor Dore) *stdd s: hld up in tch in last pair: nt clr run on inner over 2f out: effrt over 1f out: sn no imp: bhd and wknd fnl f* **25/1**

2m 5.06s (-3.54) **Going Correction** -0.175s/f (Stan)
WFA 4 from 5yo+ 1lb **7** Ran SP% **115.9**
Speed ratings (Par 103): **107,104,104,102,101 100,98**
CSF £7.24 TOTE £1.80: £1.30, £2.00; EX 6.90 Trifecta £76.40.
Owner Sheikh Mohammed Obaid Al Maktoum **Bred** Glenvale Stud **Trained** Newmarket, Suffolk

FOCUS
Another ordinary handicap, but the winner has the potential to do even better. They went a modest gallop.

T/Jkpt: Not won. T/Plt: £32.50 to a £1 stake. Pool: £67,314.22 - 1509.49 winning units. T/Qpdt: £4.60 to a £1 stake. Pool: £9,059.65 - 1439.14 winning units. **Steve Payne**

[696]LINGFIELD (L-H)
Thursday, February 25

OFFICIAL GOING: Standard
Wind: Fresh, half against Weather: Fine

709 DOWNLOAD THE LADBROKES APP H'CAP 1m 1y(P)
2:00 (2:00) (Class 6) (0-65,65) 4-Y-O+ **£2,458** (£731; £365; £182) **Stalls** High

Form RPR

4-23 **1** **Skidby Mill (IRE)**[20] 456 6-9-6 **64**.......... JimCrowley 7 70
(Laura Mongan) *mde all: set modest pce: qcknd and carried v wd by loose horse into st: hld on wl* **11/4**[2]

0-11 **2** *1* **Gunner Moyne**[42] 175 4-9-4 **62**..........(t) GeorgeBaker 4 66
(Gary Moore) *disp 2nd: chsd wnr 2f out: styd on inner and ch fr wl over 1f out: kpt on* **5/4**[1]

-065 **3** *2 1/4* **West Leake (IRE)**[8] 607 10-8-13 **57**.......... LiamKeniry 5 55
(Paul Burgoyne) *t.k.h in 4th: rdn and one pce fnl 2f* **5/1**[3]

160- 4 nk **Bloodsweatandtears**[118] 7599 8-9-5 **63** AmirQuinn 3 60
(William Knight) *disp 2nd tl 2f out: no ex over 1f out* **12/1**
44-0 5 shd **Abertillery**[45] 141 4-9-2 **60** RobertHavlin 1 57
(Michael Blanshard) *hld up in 5th: effrt 2f out: no imp* **10/1**
0-54 U **Palace Moon**[26] 403 11-8-7 **56** (t) CallumShepherd(5) 6
(Michael Attwater) *rrd and uns rdr leaving stalls* **16/1**
1m 38.55s (0.35) **Going Correction** -0.075s/f (Stan) **6** Ran SP% **110.4**
Speed ratings (Par 101): **95,94,91,91,91**
CSF £6.35 TOTE £3.40: £2.30, £1.10; EX 6.70 Trifecta £16.70.
Owner Charlie's Starrs **Bred** Michael O'Mahony **Trained** Epsom, Surrey
FOCUS
A modest handicap and not form to treat too seriously, but drama at the start when Palace Moon fly-jumped exiting the stalls and gave his rider a nasty-looking fall. The loose horse then gave the remaining runners a lead.

710 BET NOW WITH THE LADBROKES APP MEDIAN AUCTION MAIDEN STKS 1m 1y(P)
2:35 (2:35) (Class 6) 4-6-Y-O **£2,587** (£770; £384; £192) **Stalls** High

Form RPR
62- 1 **Esteemable**[185] 5695 4-8-11 0 DanielMuscutt(3) 1 68
(James Fanshawe) *disp 2nd: shkn up and led jst over 1f out: pushed out: comf* **5/4**[2]
4-5 2 ½ **Pearly Prince**[33] 314 4-9-5 0 RobertHavlin 3 71
(Peter Hedger) *stdd s: hld up in 4th: effrt over 1f out: r.o wl to take 2nd fnl 100yds: a hld* **10/1**[3]
3 3 1¾ **Sarmadee (IRE)**[17] 500 4-9-5 0 CharlesBishop 2 67
(Mick Channon) *led tl jst over 1f out: one pce* **5/6**[1]
00 4 3¼ **Lmntrix**[8] 603 4-9-5 0 RyanPowell 4 59?
(George Margarson) *disp 2nd tl 2f out: sn outpcd* **100/1**
1m 37.2s (-1.00) **Going Correction** -0.075s/f (Stan) **4** Ran SP% **109.1**
Speed ratings: **102,101,99,96**
CSF £11.64 TOTE £2.10; EX 8.70 Trifecta £9.40.
Owner Mrs C R Philipson **Bred** Mrs M L Parry & P M Steele-Mortimer **Trained** Newmarket, Suffolk
■ Stewards' Enquiry : Charles Bishop one-day ban: did not keep straight from the start
FOCUS
An uncompetitive maiden and something of a tactical affair. The form is rated cautiously.

711 32RED.COM H'CAP 6f 1y(P)
3:10 (3:10) (Class 6) (0-60,58) 3-Y-O **£2,458** (£731; £365; £182) **Stalls** Low

Form RPR
0-60 1 **Evening Starlight**[29] 352 3-8-13 **53** PhilipPrince(3) 7 62+
(Ron Hodges) *sluggish s: sn led and crossed fr wd stall: mde rest: rdn clr over 2f out: easily* **14/1**
064 2 5 **Music Major**[18] 496 3-8-8 **45** AdamBeschizza 2 39
(Kevin Morgan) *s.s: bhd: hdwy over 1f out: r.o u.p to take 2nd fnl 50yds* **25/1**
-232 3 nk **Guapo Bay**[11] 578 3-8-13 **57** (p) TinaSmith(7) 3 50
(Richard Hannon) *chsd ldrs: squeezed on 1st bnd: rdn to dispute 2nd over 1f out: one pce* **6/1**[3]
-200 4 nk **Magic Garden (IRE)**[21] 443 3-9-0 **58** CharlieBennett(7) 6 50
(Jonathan Portman) *sn bhd: rdn 3f out: r.o fr over 1f out: nvr nrr* **7/1**
-513 5 2½ **Leitrim Traveller (USA)**[11] 578 3-9-4 **55** (b) WilliamCarson 1 40
(Jamie Osborne) *walked to post: chsd wnr tl wknd ins fnl f* **7/4**[1]
-662 6 9 **Intimately**[22] 436 3-9-4 **55** RichardKingscote 4 13+
(Jonathan Portman) *chsd ldrs: hmpd on 1st bnd: wknd 2f out* **9/4**[2]
300- 7 ¾ **Wicked Woo**[202] 5128 3-9-2 **58** DannyBurton(5) 5 13
(Jo Hughes) *chsd ldrs on outer: lost pl over 3f out: sn struggling* **20/1**
1m 11.26s (-0.64) **Going Correction** -0.075s/f (Stan) **7** Ran SP% **109.2**
Speed ratings (Par 95): **101,94,93,93,90 78,77**
CSF £250.06 TOTE £13.70: £5.20, £6.10; EX 246.80 Trifecta £3792.40.
Owner Miss R Dobson **Bred** Worksop Manor Stud **Trained** Charlton Mackrell, Somerset
■ Stewards' Enquiry : Philip Prince four-day ban: careless riding (10-12 & 15 March)
FOCUS
A moderate 3yo sprint handicap containing only one previous winner. It soon turned into a rough race and the handicap debutants filled the first two places. The form does look a bit suspect.

712 LADBROKES H'CAP 1m 1y(P)
3:45 (3:46) (Class 4) (0-85,84) 4-Y-O+ **£5,822** (£1,732; £865; £432) **Stalls** High

Form RPR
3-32 1 **Franco's Secret**[15] 518 5-9-1 **78** (v) CharlesBishop 4 86
(Peter Hedger) *dwlt: hld up towards rr: hdwy over 1f out: r.o to ld fnl strides* **5/2**[2]
1-05 2 shd **My Target (IRE)**[7] 620 5-9-7 **84** AdamKirby 5 91
(Michael Wigham) *chsd ldrs: led over 1f out: kpt on u.p fnl f: hdd fnl strides* **2/1**[1]
0-14 3 1 **Charlies Mate**[15] 518 5-9-1 **78** KierenFox 7 83
(John Best) *chsd ldr: chal over 1f out: kpt on* **4/1**[3]
-361 4 1 **Justice First**[15] 518 4-8-13 **76** PatCosgrave 1 78
(Ed Dunlop) *chsd ldrs: hrd rdn over 1f out: one pce ins fnl f* **6/1**
5-00 5 1¾ **Athletic**[22] 433 7-8-9 **75** DannyBrock(3) 3 73
(Andrew Reid) *dwlt: t.k.h in 5th: hdwy on inner over 1f out: no ex ins fnl f* **12/1**
00-5 6 1¾ **Publilia**[28] 360 4-9-3 **80** JoeFanning 6 74
(Mark Johnston) *led tl over 1f out: wknd fnl f* **12/1**
00/0 7 7 **Maria's Choice (IRE)**[8] 616 7-8-12 **75** TimmyMurphy 2 53
(Jim Best) *sn bhd* **100/1**
1m 36.7s (-1.50) **Going Correction** -0.075s/f (Stan) **7** Ran SP% **112.6**
Speed ratings (Par 105): **104,103,102,101,100 98,91**
CSF £7.66 TOTE £3.90: £2.30, £1.50; EX 9.20 Trifecta £29.60.
Owner P C F Racing Ltd **Bred** J J Whelan **Trained** Hook, Hampshire
FOCUS
A fair handicap run at an even pace with three of these having met in a strongly run event at Kempton 15 days ago. The 1-2-4 from there finished 4-1-3 here.

713 32RED CASINO FILLIES' H'CAP 6f 1y(P)
4:20 (4:22) (Class 5) (0-75,74) 4-Y-O+ **£3,234** (£962; £481; £240) **Stalls** Low

Form RPR
100- 1 **Heartsong (IRE)**[128] 7363 7-9-0 **70** MichaelJMMurphy(3) 3 76
(John Gallagher) *stdd s: hld up towards rr: hdwy 2f out: drvn to ld ins fnl f: jst hld on* **16/1**
-164 2 shd **Invade (IRE)**[12] 564 4-8-6 **64** (t) AaronJones(5) 1 69
(Stuart Williams) *chsd ldrs: hrd rdn over 1f out: r.o wl fnl 150yds: clsng at fin: jst failed* **3/1**[1]
0-02 3 nk **Lucky Di**[12] 558 6-9-7 **74** CharlesBishop 8 78+
(Peter Hedger) *hld up in rr: shkn up over 1f out: fin wl* **7/1**[3]
460- 4 hd **Potternello (IRE)**[128] 7355 4-8-12 **65** JFEgan 2 68
(Mick Channon) *led tl over 1f out: kpt on u.p* **5/1**[2]
5-50 5 hd **Birdie Queen**[12] 561 6-9-3 **70** GeorgeBaker 6 73
(Gary Moore) *t.k.h in 6th: hdwy on outer 3f out: led over 1f out tl ins fnl f: no ex* **3/1**[1]
3-15 6 1¾ **James Bond Girl (USA)**[20] 462 4-9-0 **67** (p) PatCosgrave 7 64
(Robert Cowell) *hld up in tch: n.m.r 4f out: no imp fnl 2f* **10/1**
04-5 7 ¾ **Dilgura**[45] 146 6-9-5 **72** ShaneKelly 5 67
(Stuart Kittow) *chsd ldrs tl outpcd 2f out* **8/1**
406/ 8 ¾ **Brindle**[486] 7497 4-8-9 **62** ow1 TonyHamilton 4 54
(Richard Fahey) *prom: squeezed and lost pl over 2f out: sn btn* **8/1**
1m 11.65s (-0.25) **Going Correction** -0.075s/f (Stan) **8** Ran SP% **116.4**
Speed ratings (Par 100): **98,97,97,97,96 94,93,92**
CSF £64.97 CT £381.00 TOTE £17.10: £4.90, £1.30, £2.20; EX 80.50 Trifecta £382.00.
Owner J & L Wetherald - M & M Glover **Bred** Gerry And John Rowley **Trained** Chastleton, Oxon
FOCUS
An ordinary fillies' handicap with little covering the first five at the line.

714 UNIBET OFFER DAILY JOCKEY & TRAINER SPECIALS H'CAP 5f 6y(P)
4:55 (4:55) (Class 5) (0-75,75) 4-Y-O+ **£3,234** (£962; £481; £240) **Stalls** High

Form RPR
5-33 1 **Secret Asset (IRE)**[21] 439 11-9-5 **73** (v) GeorgeBaker 6 81
(Lisa Williamson) *prom: chsd ldr 3f out: drvn to ld ins fnl f* **6/1**[3]
0-60 2 1¼ **Temple Road (IRE)**[5] 655 8-9-4 **72** (bt) FrannyNorton 8 76
(Milton Bradley) *hld up in 6th: shkn up over 1f out: r.o wl to take 2nd nr fin* **7/1**
6-54 3 shd **Ask The Guru**[8] 604 6-8-10 **64** (v) RobertHavlin 2 67
(Michael Attwater) *prom: drvn to chal 1f out: r.o* **4/1**[1]
010- 4 nse **King Crimson**[120] 7565 4-9-7 **75** CharlesBishop 1 78
(Mick Channon) *led at str pce tl ins fnl f: no ex nr fin* **7/1**
-052 5 ¾ **Diamond Charlie (IRE)**[8] 604 8-9-7 **75** JimCrowley 10 75
(Simon Dow) *dwlt: bhd: rdn over 1f out: fin wl* **6/1**[3]
3-03 6 ½ **Mossgo (IRE)**[8] 604 6-9-4 **72** (t) KierenFox 7 70
(John Best) *in tch: hrd rdn over 1f out: kpt on fnl f* **5/1**[2]
-053 7 nse **Quality Art (USA)**[20] 462 8-8-11 **68** RobHornby(3) 3 66
(Simon Hodgson) *chsd ldrs: rdn and one pce appr fnl f* **7/1**
250- 8 ½ **Pucon**[188] 5584 7-9-4 **72** (p) AdamKirby 4 68
(Roger Teal) *a abt same pl: nvr able to chal* **20/1**
006- 9 5 **Dishy Guru**[92] 7984 7-9-2 **70** (b) WilliamTwiston-Davies 5 48
(Michael Blanshard) *s.v.s: a bhd* **14/1**
57.69s (-1.11) **Going Correction** -0.075s/f (Stan) **9** Ran SP% **114.2**
Speed ratings (Par 103): **105,103,102,102,101 100,100,99,91**
CSF £46.85 CT £188.17 TOTE £6.00: £2.10, £2.20, £1.70; EX 54.30 Trifecta £226.80.
Owner Simon&JeanettePierpoint/Dave&WendyHughes **Bred** Mrs C Hartery **Trained** Saighton, Cheshire
FOCUS
A modest sprint handicap in which four of these met at Kempton the previous week and the 2-3-4-6 from there finished 5-6-3-2 here. This was a race where it paid to be handy.
T/Plt: £1,207.40 to a £1 stake Pool: £50663.84 - 30.63 winning tickets T/Qpdt: £586.70 to a £1 stake. Pool: £4281.81 - 5.4 winning tickets **Lee McKenzie**

511 CHANTILLY (R-H)
Thursday, February 25
OFFICIAL GOING: Polytrack: standard

715a PRIX DE LA ROUTE D'AUMONT (CLAIMER) (5YO+) (POLYTRACK) 1m
12:30 (12:00) 5-Y-O+ **£6,617** (£2,647; £1,985; £1,323; £661)

RPR
1 **Silverheels (IRE)**[78] 8161 7-9-8 0 (b) JohanVictoire 3 77
(Paul Cole) *a cl up: shkn up to ld 2f out: hdd 1 1/2f out: rdn and rallied 1f out: regained ld fnl 100yds: drvn out* **17/10**[2]
2 ¾ **Lykastos (IRE)**[21] 6-9-5 0 (b) CesarPasserat 9 72
(X Nakkachdji, France) **8/5**[1]
3 1¼ **Winitall**[6] 5-9-2 0 (b) ThomasMessina 7 66
(J-M Baudrelle, France) **186/10**
4 hd **Tostaky Blue (FR)**[6] 7-9-1 0 (p) YohannBourgois 8 65
(A Spanu, France) **63/10**[3]
5 1¾ **Belango (GER)**[38] 10-9-6 0 FrankPanicucci 1 66
(Frau R Weissmeier, Germany) **17/2**
6 10 **My Delight (FR)**[38] 9-9-4 0 CedricSagot 6 41
(A Sagot, France) **230/1**
7 1¾ **Statu Quo (FR)**[631] 7-8-11 0 MlleJohannaHeitz 5 29
(E Schepens, Belgium) **219/1**
8 hd **See Dex (GER)**[21] 6-9-8 0 MathieuBreand 2 40
(D Windrif, France) **29/1**
9 dist **Mutinne (IRE)**[252] 5-8-11 0 VincentVion 4
(Y Gourraud, France) **159/10**
R **Dream Tune**[21] 7-9-4 0 JimmyTastayre 11
(Mlle M Henry, France) **195/10**
Owner P F I Cole Ltd **Bred** Castlemartin Stud And Skymarc Farm Trained Paul Cole, Wantage
WIN (incl. 1 euro stake): 2.70. PLACES: 1.20, 1.30, 2.50. DF: 2.60. SF: 5.50

716a PRIX DE LA CROIX VAILLANT (MAIDEN) (3YO FILLIES) (POLYTRACK) 1m 1f 110y
1:05 (12:00) 3-Y-O **£9,191** (£3,676; £2,757; £1,838; £919)

RPR
1 **Pakora (FR)** 3-8-11 0 Pierre-CharlesBoudot 5 74
(P Sogorb, France) **37/10**[3]
2 3½ **Valenka (GER)** 3-8-6 0 EmmanuelEtienne(5) 4 67
(M Munch, Germany) **79/1**
3 nk **Evidence (FR)**[26] 400 3-9-2 0 TonyPiccone 1 71
(Harry Dunlop) *wnt lft s and bmpd rival: w.w cl up: 4th and nudged along 2 1/2f out: rdn to chse ldr over 1 1/2f out: styd on fnl f but readily outpcd by wnr* **18/5**[2]
4 hd **So Funny (USA)** 3-8-11 0 MaximeGuyon 2 66
(F Head, France) **23/5**
5 ½ **Amalina (FR)**[75] 3-9-2 0 AnthonyCrastus 7 70
(N Caullery, France) **32/1**
6 ½ **Zappeuse (FR)**[27] 3-9-2 0 JeremyCrocquevieille 9 69
(Y Barberot, France) **125/10**
7 ½ **La Valkyrie**[53] 3-9-2 0 TheoBachelot 10 68
(P Van De Poele, France) **13/5**[1]

The Form Book, Raceform Ltd, Newbury, RG14 5SJ

8 3/4 **Queen Agdal (IRE)**[205] 3-9-2 0 .... StephanePasquier 8 66
(M Delcher Sanchez, France) **115/10**
9 1 **No Taboo (FR)** 3-8-11 0 .... RonanThomas 3 59
(Robert Collet, France) **27/1**
10 1 1/2 **Bien Nommee (FR)**[170] 3-9-2 0 .... (p) UmbertoRispoli 11 61
(F Doumen, France) **55/1**
11 3 **Dame D'Id (FR)** 3-8-6 0 .... PierreBazire(5) 12 50
(A Lyon, France) **70/1**
12 1/2 **Waki Delight (FR)**[16] 3-9-2 0 .... CedricSagot 6 54
(A Sagot, France) **134/1**
\n\x\x WIN (incl. 1 euro stake): 4.70. PLACES: 2.50, 12.40, 2.30. DF: 156.50. SF:
Owner Guy Pariente **Bred** Guy Pariente Holding **Trained** France

623 MEYDAN (L-H)
Thursday, February 25
OFFICIAL GOING: Dirt: fast; turf: good

717a AL NABOODAH NATIONAL CONTRACTING ABU DHABI TROPHY (H'CAP) (DIRT) 7f (D)
3:00 (3:00) (100-123,110) 3-Y-0+
£48,979 (£16,326; £8,163; £4,081; £2,448; £1,632)

RPR
1 **One Man Band (IRE)**[21] 454 5-9-6 110 .... SamHitchcott 4 115
(Doug Watson, UAE) *sn led: kicked clr 3f out: r.o wl: easily* **4/7**[1]
2 6 **Heavy Metal**[42] 189 6-9-0 104 .... (b) MickaelBarzalona 1 93
(S bin Ghadayer, UAE) *mid-div: rdn 4f out: r.o same pce fnl 2 1/2f: no ch w wnr* **25/1**
3 1/2 **Over The Ocean (USA)**[21] 450 6-9-0 104 .... (t) RichardMullen 3 92
(Niels Petersen, Norway) *trckd ldr: rdn 4f out: outpcd 3f out: r.o fnl 1 1/2f* **33/1**
4 1 1/2 **Giftorm (USA)**[28] 374 6-8-10 100 .... FernandoJara 2 84
(Fredrik Reuterskiold, Sweden) *s.i.s: racd in rr: nvr nr to chal* **7/2**[2]
5 1 1/2 **Encipher (USA)**[11] 7-8-10 100 .... TadhgO'Shea 5 80
(A R Al Rayhi, UAE) *trckd ldrs tl outpcd 3f out* **6/1**[3]
6 2 3/4 **Nolohay (IRE)**[21] 455 5-9-1 105 .... (v) PaulHanagan 6 77
(M Al Mheiri, UAE) *a in rr* **9/1**
1m 23.55s (-1.55) **Going Correction** +0.175s/f (Slow) **6** Ran SP% **116.9**
Speed ratings: **115,108,107,105,104 101**
CSF:19.87.
Owner Sheikh Saeed Bin Mohammed Al Maktoum **Bred** Richard A Pegum **Trained** United Arab Emirates

FOCUS
TRAKUS (metres travelled compared to winner): 2nd +3, 3rd 0, 4th +4, 5th +1, 6th +5. An uncompetitive handicap but a smart performance from the winner, who forced a strong early pace; 24.44 (400m from standing start), 22.57 (800m), 23.69 (1200m), before finishing in a slowing 12.85. He missed the track record - which was set by Mashaaref in this race last year - by 0.01secs.

718a AL NABOODAH HSE TROPHY (H'CAP) (DIRT) 1m 2f (D)
3:35 (3:35) (78-94,91) 3-Y-0+
£24,489 (£8,163; £4,081; £2,040; £1,224; £816)

RPR
1 **Brabbham (USA)**[26] 409 6-8-6 79 .... (t) MickaelBarzalona 4 87+
(A bin Harmash, UAE) *trckd ldrs: rdn 3 1/2f out: led 1 1/2f out: r.o wl* **10/3**[2]
2 1 3/4 **Active Spirit (IRE)**[12] 575 5-9-3 90 .... (v) SamHitchcott 5 93
(Doug Watson, UAE) *sn led: hdd 1 1/2f out: r.o gamely* **7/4**[1]
3 hd **Etijaah (USA)**[35] 279 6-9-4 91 .... PaulHanagan 8 94+
(Doug Watson, UAE) *mid-div: rdn 4f out: r.o fnl 2 1/2f* **7/2**[3]
4 5 3/4 **Enery (IRE)**[12] 575 7-8-6 79 .... FernandoJara 6 70+
(M Al Mheiri, UAE) *nvr nr to chal: r.o one pce fnl 2 1/2f* **6/1**
5 3 1/2 **Mustahdaf (USA)**[4] 5-8-8 82 .... (p) TadhgO'Shea 3 65+
(M Al Mheiri, UAE) *mid-div: rdn 5f out: sn btn* **20/1**
6 3 **Tanfeeth**[6] 649 8-9-0 87 .... (vt) DaneO'Neill 1 65+
(M Al Mheiri, UAE) *s.i.s: nvr nr to chal* **16/1**
7 3 1/2 **Pupil (IRE)**[6] 649 5-9-2 89 .... (p) RichardMullen 2 60+
(S Seemar, UAE) *trckd ldng pair: rdn 5f out: sn btn* **16/1**
8 4 1/4 **Indiana Jones (ARG)**[26] 409 6-8-6 79 .... (v) DavidProbert 7 42+
(M Al Mheiri, UAE) *s.i.s: a in rr* **66/1**
2m 4.27s (-0.43) **Going Correction** +0.175s/f (Slow) **8** Ran SP% **114.0**
Speed ratings: **108,106,106,101,99 96,93,90**
CSF: 9.50 TRICAST: 20.46.
Owner Sheikh Ahmed bin Mohammed Al Maktoum **Bred** Nancy S Dillman **Trained** United Arab Emirates

FOCUS
TRAKUS: 2nd -9, 3rd +5, 4th +8, 5th -6, 6th +10, 7th -8, 8th +4. The runner-up set a strong, gradually slowing gallop; 25.82 (400m from standing start), 23.98 (800m), 23.93 (1200m), 24.9 (1600m), and the winner was home in 25.51.

719a AL NABOODAH NATIONAL PLANT TROPHY (H'CAP) (DIRT) 6f (D)
4:10 (4:10) (95-118,109) 3-Y-0+
£44,897 (£14,965; £7,482; £3,741; £2,244; £1,496)

RPR
1 **Marking (USA)**[14] 537 4-9-6 **109** .... WilliamBuick 5 114+
(Kiaran McLaughlin, U.S.A) *broke awkwardly: trckd ldng trio: rdn 2 1/2f out: led 110yds out: comf* **2/5**[1]
2 2 **Kifaah**[14] 537 5-9-1 **104** .... (t) PaulHanagan 1 103
(A R Al Rayhi, UAE) *sn led: kicked clr 2 1/2f out: hdd 110yds out* **8/1**[2]
3 3 1/2 **Kasb (IRE)**[12] 576 4-8-6 **95** .... (t) TadhgO'Shea 7 83
(A R Al Rayhi, UAE) *trckd ldr: ev ch 3f out: r.o same pce fnl 2f* **14/1**
4 2 1/4 **Shaishee (USA)**[6] 652 6-9-6 **109** .... (v) DavidProbert 8 90
(M Al Mheiri, UAE) *s.i.s: mid-div: r.o same pce fnl 2f* **16/1**
5 2 1/2 **Krypton Factor**[7] 624 8-8-11 **100** .... (b) FrederikTylicki 4 73
(Fawzi Abdulla Nass, Bahrain) *trckd ldr: ev ch 3f out: one pce fnl 2f* **12/1**[3]
6 2 **The Taj (USA)**[434] 8214 6-9-1 **104** .... DaneO'Neill 10 70
(Doug Watson, UAE) *a in mid-div* **16/1**
7 1 3/4 **Saayerr**[21] 450 5-9-1 **104** .... ChrisHayes 9 65
(D Selvaratnam, UAE) *trckd ldng trio tl wknd 3f out* **33/1**
8 2 1/4 **Let'sgoforit (IRE)**[14] 537 8-9-3 **106** .... (bt) RichardMullen 3 59
(Bodil Hallencreutz, Sweden) *slowly away: a in rr* **14/1**
9 3/4 **Cheongu (USA)**[49] 90 4-8-7 **96** .... (b) RoystonFfrench 2 47
(I Seo, Korea) *a in rr* **20/1**
10 nk **Taayel (IRE)**[90] 8031 6-8-8 **97** .... FernandoJara 6 47
(M Al Mheiri, UAE) *a in rr* **40/1**
1m 10.86s (-0.74) **Going Correction** +0.175s/f (Slow) **10** Ran SP% **125.5**
Speed ratings: **111,108,103,100,97 94,92,89,88,87**
CSF: 4.95 TRICAST: 28.87.
Owner Godolphin **Bred** Darley **Trained** USA

FOCUS
TRAKUS: 2nd -1, 3rd +9, 4th +5, 5th +3, 6th +15, 7th +10, 8th +7, 9th +2, 10th +12. They went a rapid early pace - 23.92 from a standing start for the first 400m, with 800m in 46.75 (22.83) and the winner to the line in 23.73.

720a ZABEEL MILE SPONSORED BY AL NABOODAH CONSTRUCTION GROUP (GROUP 2) (TURF) 1m
4:45 (4:45) 3-Y-0+
£102,040 (£34,013; £17,006; £8,503; £5,102; £3,401)

RPR
1 **Safety Check (IRE)**[35] 282 5-9-4 116 .... WilliamBuick 4 112+
(Charlie Appleby) *mid-div: smooth prog 2 1/2f out: r.o fnl 1 1/2f: led on line* **5/6**[1]
2 shd **Ghaamer (USA)**[11] 6-9-1 109 .... (t) PaulHanagan 8 109
(A R Al Rayhi, UAE) *sn led: hdd 1 1/2f out: led again fnl 55yds: hdd on line* **25/1**
3 1 **Zahee (NZ)**[11] 6-9-1 109 .... (t) WayneSmith 3 107
(M F De Kock, South Africa) *trckd ldr: led 1 1/2f out: hdd fnl 55yds* **33/1**
4 1 1/4 **Harry's Son (AUS)**[35] 282 4-9-1 113 .... (t) RichardMullen 2 104+
(P V Lafferty, South Africa) *trckd ldng pair: ev ch 1f out: one pce fnl 110yds* **7/2**[2]
5 1 1/4 **Forjatt (IRE)**[11] 8-9-1 109 .... ChrisHayes 6 101+
(D Selvaratnam, UAE) *slowly away: nvr nr to chal: r.o one pce fnl 2f* **25/1**
6 hd **Big Baz (IRE)**[28] 372 6-9-1 112 .... MartinDwyer 9 100+
(William Muir) *nvr nr to chal* **20/1**
7 1 **Fanciful Angel (IRE)**[28] 375 4-9-1 110 .... DaneO'Neill 10 98+
(Marco Botti) *slowly away: nvr able to chal: r.o same pce fnl 2 1/2f* **9/1**[3]
8 3 **Johann Strauss**[355] 826 5-9-1 109 .... ChristopheSoumillon 5 91+
(M F De Kock, South Africa) *nvr nr to chal* **12/1**
9 4 **Bossy Guest (IRE)**[28] 372 4-9-1 108 .... PatSmullen 1 82+
(Mick Channon) *trckd ldng pair tl wknd 3f out* **33/1**
10 18 **Championship (IRE)**[26] 410 5-9-1 104 .... FrederikTylicki 7 41+
(A bin Harmash, UAE) *mid-div: rdn 3 1/2f out: sn btn* **10/1**
1m 36.45s (-1.05) **Going Correction** +0.20s/f (Good) **10** Ran SP% **121.9**
Speed ratings: **113,112,111,110,109 109,108,105,101,83**
CSF: 35.64.
Owner Godolphin **Bred** Malih Al Basti **Trained** Newmarket, Suffolk

FOCUS
TRAKUS: 2nd +1, 3rd 0, 4th +2, 5th -2, 6th -2, 7th +6, 8th +4, 9th -4, 10th +6. Not a strong Group 2. The runner-up, pursued by the third, set just a modest, even pace - 25.43, 23.52, 23.6 - and only the penalised winner made significant ground, home in 23.5.

721a AL NABOODAH COMMERCIAL DIVISION TROPHY (H'CAP) (TURF) 1m 2f
5:20 (5:20) (100-113,111) 3-Y-0+
£48,979 (£16,326; £8,163; £4,081; £2,448; £1,632)

RPR
1 **Basateen (IRE)**[187] 5633 4-8-8 **100** .... DaneO'Neill 5 107+
(Doug Watson, UAE) *s.i.s: settled in rr: smooth prog 2 1/2f out* **10/1**
2 4 1/4 **Think Ahead**[21] 455 5-9-0 **105** .... (p) WilliamBuick 8 104+
(Saeed bin Suroor) *trckd ldng pair: led 2f out: hdd 1 1/2f out: r.o but no ch w wnr* **5/4**[1]
3 1 3/4 **Zamaam**[7] 625 6-8-9 **100** .... (t) PaulHanagan 7 95
(E Charpy, UAE) *mid-div: chsd ldrs 2 1/2f out: ev ch 1 1/2f out: one pce fnl f* **9/2**[3]
4 3 1/4 **Slumdogmillionaire (SAF)**[14] 540 7-8-11 **102** .... (v) SamHitchcott 6 91
(Doug Watson, UAE) *trckd ldr: ev ch 2 1/2f out: one pce fnl 1 1/2f* **16/1**
5 1 1/4 **Royal Navy Ship (USA)**[14] 540 4-8-8 **100** .... (tp) RoystonFfrench 2 86
(P V Lafferty, South Africa) *s.i.s: sn led: hdd 2f out: wknd fnl f* **33/1**
6 4 1/4 **Fearless Hunter (GER)**[14] 540 6-9-0 **105** .... DavidProbert 1 83
(Rune Haugen) *nvr bttr than mid-div* **8/1**
7 shd **Farraaj (IRE)**[28] 375 7-9-6 **111** .... ChrisHayes 3 88
(D Selvaratnam, UAE) *settled in rr: nvr nr to chal* **10/3**[2]
2m 1.9s (-0.80) **Going Correction** +0.20s/f (Good)
WFA 4 from 5yo+ 1lb **7** Ran SP% **114.7**
Speed ratings: **111,107,106,103,102 99,99**
CSF: 23.26 TRICAST: 66.84.
Owner Hamdan Al Maktoum **Bred** Forenaghts Stud **Trained** United Arab Emirates

FOCUS
TRAKUS: 2nd -2, 3rd -1, 4th -1, 5th -4, 6th -5, 7th -5. An uncompetitive race and Basateen, a new kid on the block, bolted up. This was a decent enough test - 26.12, 22.98, 23.75, 24.76 - and the winner finished in 24.06.

722a TRANS GULF ELECTROMECHANICAL TROPHY (H'CAP) (DIRT) 1m 2f (D)
5:55 (5:55) (95-121,121) 3-Y-0+
£61,224 (£20,408; £10,204; £5,102; £3,061; £2,040)

RPR
1 **California Chrome (USA)**[46] 137 5-9-6 **121** .... (vt) VictorEspinoza 1 125+
(Art Sherman, U.S.A) *trckd ldng pair: smooth prog 3f out: led 1 1/2f out: r.o wl: easily* **1/3**[1]
2 2 **Storm Belt (USA)**[35] 281 7-8-5 **105** .... SamHitchcott 3 104+
(Doug Watson, UAE) *mid-div: rdn 4f out: r.o fnl 2 1/2f but no ch w wnr* **16/1**
3 2 1/4 **Success Story (KOR)**[35] 284 5-8-5 **100** .... (e) TadhgO'Shea 4 100
(Jang G Min, Korea) *sn led: hdd 1 1/2f out: r.o same pce* **10/1**[3]
4 nk **Hunting Ground (USA)**[42] 188 6-8-6 **102** ow1 .... MickaelBarzalona 8 100
(S bin Ghadayer, UAE) *trckd ldr: ev ch 2f out: outpcd fnl 1 1/2f: r.o same pce* **11/1**
5 5 **Pit Stop (IRE)**[42] 188 5-8-5 **95** .... RoystonFfrench 5 89
(S bin Ghadayer, UAE) *nvr nr to chal* **80/1**
6 2 1/4 **Good Contact (USA)**[42] 188 4-7-13 **101** .... EdwardGreatrex(6) 6 85
(Saeed bin Suroor) *s.i.s: a in rr* **7/2**[2]
7 5 3/4 **Plantagenet (SPA)**[7] 627 9-8-5 **98** .... RichardMullen 7 73
(Niels Petersen, Norway) *nvr bttr than mid-div* **80/1**

8 22 **El Tren (IRE)**[28] 372 5-8-5 **100**..(b) ChrisHayes 2 29
(Michael Attwater) *nvr nr to chal* **100/1**
2m 4.24s (-0.46) **Going Correction** +0.175s/f (Slow)
WFA 4 from 5yo+ 1lb **8** Ran SP% **124.0**
Speed ratings: **108,106,104,104,100 98,93,76**
CSF: 10.36 TRICAST: 34.25.
Owner California Chrome LLC **Bred** Perry Martin & Steve Coburn **Trained** USA
FOCUS
TRAKUS: 2nd -1, 3rd -9, 4th -3, 5th +4, 6th +13, 7th +11, 8th -10. This wasn't a true test - here are the splits were the earlier low-grade handicap, won by Brabbham, who carried 14lb less than California Chrome, in brackets: 25.86 (25.82), 51.00 (49.80), 1:14.92 (1:13.73), 1:39.36 (1:38.63), and the final time was only 0.03secs quicker. All of the winner's rivals were out of the handicap. Curlin won the equivalent running of this race at Nad Al Sheba in 2008 ahead of his World Cup victory.

723a AL NABOODAH CIVILS DIVISION TROPHY (H'CAP) (TURF) 6f
6:30 (6:30) (100-109,109) 3-Y-O+
£71,428 (£23,809; £11,904; £5,952; £3,571; £2,380)

RPR
1 **Baccarat (IRE)**[495] 7272 7-9-1 **104**.................................... WilliamBuick 2 112+
(Charlie Appleby) *s.i.s: in rr: smooth prog 2f out: led 55yds out: comf* **7/1**
2 1 3/4 **Naadirr (IRE)**[21] 450 5-9-6 **109**..........................(p) ChristopheSoumillon 9 111
(Marco Botti) *trckd ldr: led 1f out: r.o but no ch w wnr* **13/8**[1]
3 1 **Jamesie (IRE)**[28] 370 8-8-11 **100**..........................(t) PatSmullen 3 99
(David Marnane, Ire) *trckd ldr: led 1 1/2f out: hdd 1f out: r.o* **7/1**
4 4 1/4 **Fityaan**[7] 626 8-8-11 **100**..(v) DaneO'Neill 4 87
(M Al Mheiri, UAE) *trckd ldr: ev ch 2f out: one pce fnl 1 1/2f* **16/1**
5 1 1/4 **Almashooqa (AUS)**[21] 451 3-8-8 **100**............................. WayneSmith 6 84
(M F De Kock, South Africa) *s.i.s: trckd ldrs tl outpcd 1 1/2f out* **25/1**
6 1 **Caspian Prince (IRE)**[7] 626 7-9-2 **105**......................... TadhgO'Shea 7 83
(Dean Ivory) *sn led: hdd 1 1/2f out: one pce fnl f* **14/1**
7 1 **Banaadeer (IRE)**[12] 576 5-9-0 **102**................................ PaulHanagan 5 78
(Doug Watson, UAE) *nvr nr to chal* **6/1**[2]
8 1/2 **Sholaan (IRE)**[48] 118 7-9-1 **104**.. ChrisHayes 1 78
(D Selvaratnam, UAE) *s.i.s: a in rr* **10/1**
9 2 3/4 **Majestic Mount**[11] 6-9-0 **102**......................................(t) RichardMullen 10 68
(S Seemar, UAE) *nvr bttr than mid-div* **16/1**
10 3/4 **Winklemann (IRE)**[28] 370 4-8-13 **101**......................(e) SamHitchcott 11 64+
(M F De Kock, South Africa) *racd alone nrside: nvr involved* **50/1**
11 7 1/2 **Divine (IRE)**[28] 370 5-9-0 **102**.................................... MickaelBarzalona 8 41
(Mick Channon) *a in rr* **13/2**[3]
1m 10.43s (1.43) **Going Correction** +0.525s/f (Yiel)
WFA 3 from 4yo+ 15lb **11** Ran SP% **124.0**
Speed ratings: **111,108,107,101,100 98,97,96,93,92 82**
CSF: 19.76 TRICAST: 90.69. PLACEPOT: £2.90 to a £1 stake. Pool: £5929.10 - 1458.70 winning tickets. QUADPOT: £2.30 to a £1 stake. Pool: £376.90 - 116.70 winning tickets.
Owner Godolphin **Bred** Twelve Oaks Stud **Trained** Newmarket, Suffolk
FOCUS
TRAKUS: 2nd +1, 3rd 0, 4th 0, 5th 0, 6th +1, 7th 0, 8th 0, 9th -1, 10th 0, 11th 0. A decent sprint handicap in which the front three finished clear. The main action unfolded far side, with only Winklemann stands' side.

709 LINGFIELD (L-H)
Friday, February 26
OFFICIAL GOING: Polytrack: standard
Wind: light, half behind Weather: mainly cloudy, brighter spells

724 CORAL.CO.UK H'CAP 1m 4f (P)
2:00 (2:00) (Class 6) (0-65,65) 4-Y-O+ **£2,264** (£673; £336; £168) **Stalls** Low

Form RPR
2-04 1 **Apache Glory (USA)**[34] 316 8-9-8 **65**............................(p) LukeMorris 3 72
(Daniel Mark Loughnane) *taken down early: hld up in last pair: clsd and nt clr run jst over 2f out: squeezed for room over 1f out: hdwy 1f out: str run u.p to ld fnl 50yds* **8/1**
145 2 1 **Cartographic (USA)**[13] 568 4-8-12 **58**.................................... JFEgan 1 62
(David Evans) *hld up in tch in midfield: nt clr run jst over 2f out: rdn and hdwy to chse clr ldr over 1f out: lost 2nd but kpt on u.p ins fnl f: regained 2nd last stride* **11/4**[1]
4-64 3 shd **Bamako Du Chatelet (FR)**[29] 358 5-8-9 **55**........ GeorgeDowning(3) 6 59
(Ian Williams) *chsd ldrs tl wnt 2nd 7f out: pushed into ld 3f out: rdn and kicked 2 l clr 2f out: hdd and no ex fnl 50yds: lost 2nd last stride* **9/2**
04-1 4 2 **Authorized Spirit**[30] 348 4-8-11 **57**....................................... KierenFox 2 58
(John Best) *in tch in rr: niggled along fr 7f out: nt clr run on inner jst over 2f out: hdwy u.p to chse ldrs over 1f out: styd on same pce ins fnl f* **7/2**[2]
-223 5 1 **Runaiocht (IRE)**[19] 491 6-9-2 **59**...................................(b) JimmyQuinn 7 58
(Paul Burgoyne) *taken down early: t.k.h: hld up in tch in midfield: bmpd jst over 2f out: u.p and bmpd again over 1f out: kpt on ins fnl f: no threat to ldrs* **4/1**[3]
-065 6 2 3/4 **Movie Magic**[25] 417 5-8-3 **51** oh6.................................. AaronJones(5) 8 46
(Mark Hoad) *led: hdd 3f out and sn rdn: lost pl over 1f out: wknd ins fnl f* **100/1**
0-20 7 1 3/4 **Ruzeiz (USA)**[28] 382 7-9-4 **61**....................................(v[1]) CharlesBishop 5 53
(Peter Hedger) *chsd ldr tl 7f out: chsd ldrs: rdn and bmpd jst over 2f out: wnt 2nd 2f out tl over 1f out: sn lost pl: bhd ins fnl f* **10/1**
2m 29.75s (-3.25) **Going Correction** -0.125s/f (Stan)
WFA 4 from 5yo+ 3lb **7** Ran SP% **108.3**
Speed ratings (Par 101): **105,104,104,102,102 100,99**
CSF £27.05 CT £97.93 TOTE £7.00: £3.50, £1.70; EX 27.60 Trifecta £97.10.
Owner J T Stimpson **Bred** Malih Al Basti **Trained** Baldwin's Gate, Staffs
FOCUS
A moderate middle-distance handicap and the pace was ordinary.

725 32RED H'CAP 1m 1y(P)
2:30 (2:31) (Class 6) (0-65,68) 3-Y-O **£2,264** (£673; £336; £168) **Stalls** High

Form RPR
-243 1 **Clive Clifton (IRE)**[16] 524 3-9-5 **62**...............................(v[1]) AdamKirby 2 68
(David Evans) *led tl over 6f out: chsd ldrs: rdn 2f out: sn lft in ld: drvn and wnt rt 1f out: styd on ins fnl f: drvn out* **12/1**
0-32 2 1 1/2 **Santiburi Spring**[16] 519 3-9-7 **64**.. KierenFox 1 66
(John Best) *hld up in tch in midfield: effrt over 1f out: chsd ldr 1f out: hung rt and styd on same pce ins fnl f* **7/2**[2]

0-30 3 1 **Refulgence (FR)**[22] 443 3-9-5 **62**.. LiamJones 3 62
(Marco Botti) *pushed along leaving stalls: in tch towards rr: hdwy on inner over 1f out: wnt 3rd and kpt on same pce ins fnl f* **20/1**
3-43 4 1/2 **Nidnod**[28] 380 3-9-0 **57**... WilliamCarson 6 56
(John Bridger) *chsd ldrs: lft 2nd and drvn wl over 1f out: lost 2nd 1f out and kpt on same pce fnl f* **50/1**
30-0 5 1/2 **Multigifted**[9] 610 3-9-3 **60**...[1] LiamKeniry 7 58
(Michael Madgwick) *rdn along leaving stalls: in tch towards rr: carried rt bnd 2f out: trying to rally and nt clr run over 1f out: hdwy 1f out: kpt on ins fnl f: nvr threatened ldrs* **50/1**
00-4 6 3/4 **Highwayman**[16] 519 3-9-7 **64**... ShaneKelly 4 60
(William Jarvis) *t.k.h: chsd ldr tl led over 6f out: rdn and hung rt bnd 2f out: sn hdd and no ex u.p over 1f out: wl hld and plugged on same pce fnl f* **5/1**[3]
04-2 7 1 1/4 **Dose**[35] 296 3-8-12 **62**... AdamMcNamara(7) 9 55
(Richard Fahey) *in tch in midfield: effrt and carried wd bnd 2f out: no imp u.p over 1f out: wl hld fnl f* **5/1**[3]
54-6 8 3/4 **Stone Quercus (IRE)**[16] 519 3-9-4 **61**............................... TomEaves 5 57+
(James Given) *stdd s: hld up in rr: squeezed for room and hmpd bnd 5f out: drvn and no rspnse over 1f out: nvr trbld ldrs* **10/3**[1]
-311 9 nk **Kemsing (IRE)**[10] 597 3-9-8 **68** 6ex............................ ShelleyBirkett(3) 8 60
(Julia Feilden) *s.i.s: rcvrd to chse ldr 5f out: rdn ent fnl 2f: lost pl and btn whn squeezed for room and hmpd jst ins fnl f: wknd* **5/1**[3]
1m 38.56s (0.36) **Going Correction** -0.125s/f (Stan) **9** Ran SP% **111.7**
Speed ratings (Par 95): **93,91,90,90,89 88,87,86,86**
CSF £51.28 CT £643.13 TOTE £9.80: £2.60, £1.10, £5.70; EX 29.10 Trifecta £415.10.
Owner Paul Clifton & P D Evans **Bred** Tally-Ho Stud **Trained** Pandy, Monmouths
■ Stewards' Enquiry : Liam Keniry caution: careless riding
Kieren Fox jockey said that the filly hung badly right in the straight
FOCUS
A modest 3yo handicap and rather a messy race. A minor personal best from the winner.

726 BET&WATCH EVERY RACE AT UNIBET H'CAP 5f 6y(P)
3:00 (3:00) (Class 5) (0-70,80) 3-Y-O **£2,911** (£866; £432; £216) **Stalls** High

Form RPR
6-16 1 **Pink Martini (IRE)**[16] 515 3-9-2 **70**........................ PatrickO'Donnell(5) 1 76
(Joseph Tuite) *chsd ldrs: effrt and rdn to ld over 1f out: r.o wl: rdn out* **9/2**[3]
21-5 2 1 1/4 **Miss Phillyjinks (IRE)**[16] 515 3-9-3 **66**..........................(b) ShaneKelly 3 67
(Paul D'Arcy) *t.k.h: w ldr on inner tl led 2f out: hdd over 1f out and sn hung rt: styd on same pce ins fnl f* **7/2**[2]
1 3 1 1/4 **Equijade**[13] 562 3-9-5 **68**.. LukeMorris 6 65
(Robert Stephens) *in tch in midfield: effrt to chse ldng pair 1f out: no imp and one pce fnl f* **10/1**
0-52 4 1 3/4 **Bahamian Sunshine**[25] 419 3-8-7 **63**...............(p) AdamMcNamara(7) 5 53
(Richard Fahey) *led tl 2f out: lost pl over 1f out and sltly impeded jst over 1f out: wknd ins fnl f* **8/1**
240- 5 3/4 **Pacches (IRE)**[223] 4391 3-9-7 **70**.................................. CharlesBishop 2 58
(Mick Channon) *hld up in tch in last pair: effrt on inner over 1f out: no imp ins fnl f: nvr trbld ldrs* **8/1**
2111 6 1/2 **Englishwoman**[7] 635 3-9-10 **80** 12ex............................ GeorgiaCox(7) 4 66
(David Evans) *restless in stalls: sn dropped to rr and niggled along: rdn 2f out: no imp: nvr trbld ldrs* **13/8**[1]
59.28s (0.48) **Going Correction** -0.125s/f (Stan) **6** Ran SP% **109.8**
Speed ratings (Par 97): **91,89,87,84,83 82**
CSF £19.47 TOTE £4.90: £2.00, £5.10; EX 24.30 Trifecta £217.10.
Owner Pulse.Aero Partnership **Bred** E Ryan **Trained** Lambourn, Berks
FOCUS
One colt against five fillies in this ordinary 3yo sprint handicap. With the favourite running so poorly it remains to be seen how strong the form is.

727 LADBROKES H'CAP 7f 1y(P)
3:35 (3:35) (Class 3) (0-90,90) 4-Y-O **£7,246** (£2,168; £1,084; £542; £270) **Stalls** Low

Form RPR
-420 1 **Pour La Victoire (IRE)**[23] 433 6-7-12 **76** oh2 ow1...(b) PaddyPilley(5) 4 84
(Tony Carroll) *t.k.h: hld up in tch in rr: gd hdwy on inner to ld jst over 1f out: r.o strly: eased towards fin* **8/1**
40-1 2 2 **Until Midnight (IRE)**[43] 169 6-8-6 **80**........................... WilliamCarson 3 82+
(Eugene Stanford) *in tch in midfield: nt clr run and swtchd rt over 1f out: rdn and kpt on wl ins fnl f to go 2nd fnl 50yds: no ch w wnr* **5/1**[3]
4111 3 hd **Clement (IRE)**[20] 482 6-8-2 **83**...................................(v) GeorgiaCox(7) 2 87+
(John O'Shea) *s.i.s: hld up in tch in last trio: hdwy whn nt clr run: hmpd and swtchd rt 1f out: trying to rally whn nt clr run and swtchd rt again ins fnl f: r.o strly fnl 100yds: no threat to wnr* **3/1**[2]
6-30 4 3/4 **Arnold Lane (IRE)**[20] 486 7-9-2 **90**.................................... TomEaves 6 89
(Mick Channon) *pressed ldr tl rdn to ld wl over 1f out: hdd ent fnl f: sn outpcd by wnr: kpt on same pce after: lost 2 pls fnl 50yds* **2/1**[1]
-525 5 1/2 **Robert The Painter (IRE)**[10] 599 8-8-8 **82**....................(v) KierenFox 7 80
(Lee Carter) *chsd ldrs tl hdwy to ld over 3f out: rdn over 2f out: hdd over 1f out: no ex and styd on same pce ins fnl f* **8/1**
0-41 6 nse **Majestic Myles (IRE)**[21] 457 8-8-7 **88**................. AdamMcNamara(7) 1 86
(Richard Fahey) *led tl over 3f out: styd handy: rdn 2f out: drvn over 1f out: outpcd by wnr and kpt on same pce ins fnl f* **10/1**
0215 7 shd **Doctor Parkes**[6] 655 10-8-1 **80**.................................... AaronJones(5) 8 77
(Stuart Williams) *hld up in tch in last trio: effrt over 1f out: kpt on u.p ins fnl f: nvr trbld ldrs* **16/1**
200- 8 1 **Bravo Echo**[196] 5348 10-9-0 **88**.. RobertHavlin 5 83
(Michael Attwater) *in tch in midfield: outpcd u.p over 1f out: bhd and one pce ins fnl f* **25/1**
1m 23.06s (-1.74) **Going Correction** -0.125s/f (Stan) **8** Ran SP% **116.0**
Speed ratings (Par 107): **104,101,101,100,100 100,99,98**
CSF £48.25 CT £148.49 TOTE £8.80: £2.00, £2.00, £1.60; EX 37.30 Trifecta £238.40.
Owner Curry House Corner **Bred** L Fox **Trained** Cropthorne, Worcs
FOCUS
A decent handicap run at just a fair pace and a clear winner, but a couple of these didn't enjoy the smoothest of trips.

728 CORAL MAIDEN STKS 1m 4f (P)
4:05 (4:05) (Class 5) 4-Y-O+ **£2,911** (£866; £432; £216) **Stalls** Low

Form RPR
0- 1 **Kawartha**[99] 7906 4-9-0 0.. TomQueally 5 67+
(Robert Stephens) *off the pce in last trio early: clsd and in tch 5f out: hdwy into 4th jst over 2f out: clsd to join ldr on bit 1f out: pushed into ld fnl 100yds: sn rdn and asserted: comf* **25/1**

65 **2** *1 1/4* **Force Of Destiny (GER)**[18] 500 4-9-5 0........................ SteveDrowne 6 64
(Mrs Ilka Gansera-Leveque) *w ldr and clr of field tl 5f out: led over 4f out: rdn wl over 1f out: jnd by cruising wnr 1f out: hdd fnl 100yds: sn outpcd* **9/2**

3 *1* **Demographic (USA)**[133] 7-9-8 0.................................. TimmyMurphy 3 62
(Emma Lavelle) *v.s.a: wl off the pce in rr: clsd and in tch 5f out: effrt in 5th 2f out: styd on ins fnl f to go 3rd fnl 50yds: no threat to wnr* **14/1**

0 **4** *1/2* **Mr Caffrey**[13] 567 4-9-5 72.. LiamKeniry 2 61
(Robert Stephens) *midfield: clsd and in tch 5f out: 3rd and drvn 2f out: kpt on ins fnl f: nvr showing enough pce to rch ldrs* **7/4**[1]

5 *nk* **Earthwindorfire**[88] 5-9-5 0...................................... AlistairRawlinson(3) 4 60
(Geoffrey Deacon) *off the pce in last trio: clsd and in tch 5f out: rdn in 6th 6f out: hdwy on inner 1f out: kpt on ins fnl f: no threat to wnr* **25/1**

-043 **6** *1 1/4* **Solveig's Song**[9] 602 4-9-0 46..................................(p) WilliamCarson 7 54
(Steve Woodman) *chsd clr ldrs: clsd and wl in tch 5f out: 3rd and drvn 2f out: no ex and btn 1f out: wknd ins fnl f* **4/1**[3]

7 *27* **Makday** 4-9-5 0.. LukeMorris 8 16
(Robert Stephens) *off the pce in midfield: clsd and in tch 5f out: struggling u.p over 2f out: lost tch over 1f out: t.o* **7/2**[2]

4 **8** *4* **Oscar Hill (IRE)**[7] 630 10-9-8 0........................ WilliamTwiston-Davies 1 9
(David Bridgwater) *led and clr w rival tl 5f out: sn hdd and rdn: dropped to last 3f out: lost tch 2f out: t.o* **10/1**

2m 30.23s (-2.77) **Going Correction** -0.125s/f (Stan)
WFA 4 from 5yo+ 3lb **8** Ran SP% **120.2**
Speed ratings (Par 103): **104,103,102,102,101 101,83,80**
CSF £139.96 TOTE £35.90: £6.00, £1.40, £2.80; EX 172.20 Trifecta £3906.00 Part won..
Owner D J Deer **Bred** D J And Mrs Deer **Trained** Penhow, Newport

FOCUS
A weak middle-distance maiden. Two soon scampered off into a clear lead, but the tempo had eased by halfway.

729 CORAL H'CAP 1m 4f (P)
4:40 (4:40) (Class 4) (0-80,76) 3-Y-O **£4,568** (£1,367; £683; £342; £170) **Stalls** Low

Form RPR

-523 **1** **Dr Drey (IRE)**[11] 593 3-9-1 **68**... AdamKirby 9 73
(Jamie Osborne) *chsd ldr for 2f: styd chsng ldrs: drvn to chal 2f out: led 1f out: styd on: drvn out* **8/1**

0-11 **2** *3/4* **Kalamata**[16] 517 3-8-13 **66**.. JackMitchell 4 69
(Roger Varian) *hld up in tch: effrt in midfield over 2f out: hdwy 1f out: kpt on wl u.p to go 2nd wl ins fnl f: nvr gng to rch wnr* **6/1**[3]

2335 **3** *shd* **Milrow (IRE)**[13] 557 3-9-6 **73**..(p) RobertHavlin 8 76
(Martyn Meade) *stdd and dropped in bhd after s: t.k.h: hld up in last trio: clsd and nt clr run over 1f out: hdwy between horses 1f out: r.o wl u.p ins fnl f: nvr gng to rch wnr* **25/1**

0-21 **4** *3/4* **Jarir**[28] 379 3-9-3 **73**.. TomMarquand(3) 3 75
(Richard Hannon) *sn led: rdn over 2f out: hdd 1f out: sn no ex: styd on same pce after: lost 2 pls wl ins fnl f* **11/10**[1]

-315 **5** *3/4* **Skylark Lady (IRE)**[16] 517 3-8-3 **61**........................ CharlesEddery(5) 2 62
(Rae Guest) *hld up in rr: effrt over 1f out: hdwy and swtchd rt jst ins fnl f: r.o strly fnl 100yds: nvr trbld ldrs* **33/1**

23-1 **6** *shd* **Epsom Day (IRE)**[49] 96 3-9-9 **76**.................................(b) TomQueally 7 76
(John Gosden) *hdwy to press ldr 10f out: rdn and ev ch 2f out: 3rd and no ex 1f out: wknd wl ins fnl f* **5/1**[2]

1-45 **7** *1 1/2* **Sark (IRE)**[28] 379 3-9-4 **71**... JFEgan 6 69
(David Evans) *chsd ldrs: 4th and outpcd u.p 2f out: wknd ins fnl f* **33/1**

2352 **8** *1* **Schoolboy Error (IRE)**[16] 517 3-8-6 **59**........................ WilliamCarson 1 55
(Jamie Osborne) *hld up in last trio: effrt on inner over 1f out: no imp ins fnl f* **20/1**

2-22 **9** *1/2* **Gabster (IRE)**[11] 593 3-8-13 **66**... LukeMorris 5 62
(Amanda Perrett) *in tch in midfield: effrt wl over 1f out: sn lost pl: bhd ins fnl f* **10/1**

2m 30.27s (-2.73) **Going Correction** -0.125s/f (Stan) **9** Ran SP% **113.3**
Speed ratings (Par 99): **104,103,103,102,102 102,101,100,100**
CSF £51.03 CT £1135.56 TOTE £9.00: £2.40, £2.00, £3.50; EX 66.90 Trifecta £755.80.
Owner George Popov **Bred** Austin Curran **Trained** Upper Lambourn, Berks

FOCUS
A good 3yo middle-distance handicap and the majority of these had already met each other at least once so far this year. The pace was fair.
T/Plt: £1,241.70 to a £1 stake. Pool: £66,967.13 - 39.37 winning tickets T/Qpdt: £250.60 to a £1 stake. Pool: £6,502.94 - 19.20 winning tickets **Steve Payne**

681 WOLVERHAMPTON (A.W) (L-H)
Friday, February 26

OFFICIAL GOING: Tapeta: standard
Wind: Light across Weather: Overcast

730 UNIBET OFFER DAILY JOCKEY/TRAINER SPECIALS APPRENTICE H'CAP 5f 216y (Tp)
5:45 (5:45) (Class 7) (0-50,50) 3-Y-O+ **£2,587** (£770; £384; £192) **Stalls** Low

Form RPR

0-00 **1** **Stamp Of Approval (IRE)**[15] 528 4-9-3 **48**.............. SamuelClarke(5) 2 53
(Chris Wall) *s.i.s: hld up: hdwy over 1f out: rdn and r.o to ld nr fin* **9/1**

-253 **2** *nk* **Blistering Dancer (IRE)**[23] 431 6-9-2 **45**................ MitchGodwin(3) 13 49
(Tony Carroll) *a.p: chsd ldr over 2f out: rdn to ld and edgd lft over 1f out: hdd nr fin* **3/1**[1]

40-5 **3** *nk* **Diamond Vine (IRE)**[36] 272 8-9-0 **45**...................(p) CameronNoble(5) 8 48
(Ronald Harris) *s.i.s: pushed along in rr: rdn and r.o ins fnl f: nt quite rch ldrs* **12/1**

-653 **4** *1 3/4* **Cerulean Silk**[16] 513 6-9-5 **45**.....................................(p) LuluStanford 7 43
(Tony Carroll) *mid-div: hdwy 1/2-way: rdn over 1f out: styd on same pce ins fnl f* **11/1**

00-2 **5** *1/2* **Freeze A Crowd (IRE)**[50] 81 3-8-4 **45**.............................(t) HollieDoyle 4 37
(Ben Haslam) *chsd ldrs: hmpd wl over 3f out: sn pushed along: nt clr run 1f out: sn swtchd rt: styd on same pce wl ins fnl f* **9/2**[2]

630- **6** *1 3/4* **Natalia**[183] 5783 7-9-6 **46**...(v) NatalieHambling 9 37
(Sarah Hollinshead) *sn pushed along in rr: hung lft over 1f out: r.o towards fin: nvr nrr* **11/1**

-004 **7** *1* **Prigsnov Dancer (IRE)**[14] 542 11-9-3 **50**..........(p) BenSanderson(7) 12 38
(Deborah Sanderson) *led early: chsd ldr tl led again over 4f out: rdn and hdd over 1f out: wknd ins fnl f* **10/1**

000- **8** *1/2* **Barnsdale**[92] 8007 3-7-11 **45**.................................. MeganEllingworth(7) 5 28
(John Holt) *prom: edgd lft wl over 3f out: rdn over 1f out: wknd ins fnl f* **33/1**

0-00 **9** *shd* **My Time**[14] 542 7-8-12 **45**.. GeorgeWood(7) 1 31
(Michael Mullineaux) *in rr: pushed along over 2f out: nvr on terms* **33/1**

66-0 **10** *3 3/4* **Passionateprincess (IRE)**[7] 635 3-8-5 **46**..............(p) SophieKilloran 6 17
(Ann Duffield) *sn led: hdd over 4f out: chsd ldr tl over 2f out: wknd fnl f* **16/1**

-630 **11** *10* **Rosie Crowe (IRE)**[24] 430 4-9-8 **48**..............................(v) RhiainIngram 3
(Shaun Harris) *prom: sn pushed along and lost pl: no ch whn hmpd over 2f out* **5/1**[3]

1m 14.92s (0.42) **Going Correction** -0.025s/f (Stan)
WFA 3 from 4yo+ 15lb **11** Ran SP% **115.1**
Speed ratings (Par 97): **96,95,95,92,92 89,88,87,87,82 69**
CSF £35.29 CT £330.09 TOTE £9.90: £2.70, £1.50, £3.90; EX 42.00 Trifecta £432.80.
Owner Induna Racing Partners Two **Bred** Bishop Wilton Stud **Trained** Newmarket, Suffolk
■ Stewards' Enquiry : Megan Ellingworth two-day ban: careless riding (11-12 Mar)

FOCUS
This featured a host of disappointing individuals and isn't a race to dwell on. It was run at a stern early pace and suited those played late.

731 32RED CASINO H'CAP 1m 5f 194y (Tp)
6:15 (6:15) (Class 6) (0-60,63) 4-Y-O+ **£2,587** (£770; £384; £192) **Stalls** Low

Form RPR

4-21 **1** **Bracken Brae**[8] 622 4-9-8 **63** 6ex.................................. SaleemGolam 1 69
(Mark H Tompkins) *chsd ldr tl shkn up to ld over 2f out: rdn over 1f out: styd on u.p* **5/6**[1]

3-53 **2** *1 1/4* **Robben**[7] 637 4-9-4 **59**..(v) PJMcDonald 4 63
(John Mackie) *s.i.s: hld up: hdwy over 6f out: rdn over 1f out: styd on* **9/2**[2]

505- **3** *1* **Cantankerous**[154] 6714 5-8-10 **46** oh1.......................(p) StevieDonohoe 7 49
(Daniel Mark Loughnane) *s.i.s: hld up: hdwy over 2f out: rdn over 1f out: styd on same pce ins fnl f* **33/1**

06-4 **4** *1 1/2* **Nolecce**[35] 295 9-9-6 **59**.. RobHornby(3) 5 60
(Tony Forbes) *hld up: rdn over 2f out: hdwy over 1f out: nt rch ldrs* **14/1**

-401 **5** *nse* **Missandei**[18] 498 4-8-4 **52**...(t) JoshQuinn(7) 9 52
(Steph Hollinshead) *hld up: hdwy u.p over 1f out: nt rch ldrs* **8/1**[3]

-010 **6** *1/2* **Easydoesit (IRE)**[18] 498 8-9-3 **56**.....................(p) GeorgeDowning(3) 3 56
(Tony Carroll) *prom: rdn over 2f out: styd on same pce fr over 1f out* **28/1**

0-65 **7** *1* **Next Edition (IRE)**[18] 498 8-9-3 **60**.............................. PhilDennis(7) 2 58
(Philip Kirby) *trckd ldrs: plld hrd: rdn over 2f out: no ex fnl f* **8/1**[3]

61-3 **8** *2* **Turnbury**[41] 218 5-9-10 **60**...(p) DarryllHolland 6 57
(Nikki Evans) *led: clr 11f out tl 7f out: rdn and hdd over 2f out: wknd and eased ins fnl f* **22/1**

340- **9** *3 1/2* **Crakehall Lad (IRE)**[115] 7678 5-9-4 **54**.........................(v) NeilFarley 8 45
(Andrew Crook) *hld up: rdn and wknd over 2f out* **50/1**

3m 4.25s (-0.55) **Going Correction** -0.025s/f (Stan)
WFA 4 from 5yo+ 5lb **9** Ran SP% **114.3**
Speed ratings (Par 101): **100,99,98,97,97 97,96,95,93**
CSF £4.36 CT £65.20 TOTE £1.70: £1.10, £1.50, £6.60; EX 4.90 Trifecta £70.80.
Owner David P Noblett **Bred** Dullingham Park Stud & Mr D Noblett **Trained** Newmarket, Suffolk

FOCUS
Three of these had already won this year and it represents fair form for the grade, with the winner well in after her Chelmsford romp.

732 DOWNLOAD THE NEW UNIBET RACING APP H'CAP 5f 20y (Tp)
6:45 (6:46) (Class 6) (0-55,55) 3-Y-O+ **£2,587** (£770; £384; £192) **Stalls** Low

Form RPR

-050 **1** **Harpers Ruby**[14] 543 6-9-1 **46** oh1.................................... JackGarritty 6 57
(Lynn Siddall) *mde all: rdn over 1f out: r.o wl* **22/1**

0-36 **2** *2* **Charlie Lad**[39] 241 4-9-10 **55**.. GeorgeBaker 1 59
(Daniel Mark Loughnane) *trckd wnr: plld hrd: lost 2nd over 3f out: rdn over 1f out: wnt 2nd ins fnl f: styd on* **2/1**[1]

0-20 **3** *hd* **Spray Tan**[16] 513 6-9-2 **50**...............................(b) GeorgeDowning(3) 4 53
(Tony Carroll) *hld up: hdwy over 1f out: r.o* **22/1**

0-0 **4** *1 1/4* **Camanche Grey (IRE)**[35] 293 5-9-7 **52**......................... JoeFanning 10 51
(Ben Haslam) *hld up: rdn 1/2-way: r.o ins fnl f: nvr nrr* **9/1**

4423 **5** *1/2* **Pancake Day**[11] 589 4-9-5 **55**............................(b[1]) CallumShepherd(5) 9 52
(Jason Ward) *prom: chsd ldr over 3f out: rdn over 1f out: no ex ins fnl f* **5/1**[3]

642 **6** *nk* **Seraphima**[18] 504 6-8-8 **46**..(p) PhilDennis(7) 7 42
(Lisa Williamson) *s.i.s: hld up: rdn over 1f out: nt trble ldrs* **9/1**

-523 **7** *nk* **Memyselfie (IRE)**[17] 510 3-8-9 **54** ow2......................(v) TonyHamilton 2 43
(Derek Shaw) *sn pushed along in to mid-div: hdwy u.p over 1f out: no ex ins fnl f* **4/1**[2]

0205 **8** *nk* **Rat Catcher (IRE)**[11] 589 6-9-7 **55**.........................(b) RobHornby(3) 3 49
(Lisa Williamson) *chsd ldrs: rdn over 1f out: no ex fnl f* **15/2**

60-0 **9** *5* **Steel Rain**[39] 241 8-9-7 **52**.. DarryllHolland 8 28
(Nikki Evans) *s.i.s: a in rr: wknd over 1f out* **66/1**

1m 1.43s (-0.47) **Going Correction** -0.025s/f (Stan)
WFA 3 from 4yo+ 14lb **9** Ran SP% **112.0**
Speed ratings (Par 101): **102,98,98,96,95 95,94,94,86**
CSF £63.30 CT £1011.46 TOTE £21.70: £5.10, £1.60, £4.90; EX 79.10 Trifecta £2300.80.
Owner Jimmy Kay **Bred** Select Bloodstock **Trained** Colton, N Yorks

FOCUS
Regular winners were very thin on the ground in this weak sprint handicap and the winner left her previous form well behind.

733 DAILY PRICE BOOSTS AT UNIBET H'CAP 5f 20y (Tp)
7:15 (7:16) (Class 6) (0-65,65) 4-Y-O+ **£2,587** (£770; £384; £192) **Stalls** Low

Form RPR

3-05 **1** **Give Us A Belle (IRE)**[18] 504 7-8-8 **57**.....................(bt) PaddyPilley(5) 7 63
(Christine Dunnett) *led: rdn and hdd wl ins fnl f: rallied to ld last strides* **16/1**

4-50 **2** *hd* **Jolly Red Jeanz (IRE)**[14] 543 5-8-9 **53** ow1.........(be) StevieDonohoe 9 58
(Daniel Mark Loughnane) *chsd ldrs: rdn over 1f out: sn edgd lft: led towards fin: hdd last strides* **14/1**

6-06 **3** *nk* **Extreme Supreme**[22] 444 5-9-2 **60**.......................(v) TonyHamilton 10 64
(Derek Shaw) *mid-div: racd wd: rdn over 1f out: r.o wl* **20/1**

100- **4** *nk* **Captain Scooby**[105] 7833 10-8-13 **57**..............................(b) JasonHart 5 60
(Richard Guest) *sn pushed along in rr: r.o wl ins fnl f: nt quite rch ldrs* **40/1**

-515 **5** *1/2* **Your Gifted (IRE)**[14] 541 9-9-7 **65**.............................(v) RaulDaSilva 6 66
(Lisa Williamson) *hld up: rdn over 1f out: r.o towards fin: nvr nrr* **22/1**

4232 **6** *hd* **Frank The Barber (IRE)**[14] 541 4-8-13 **57**............(t) AdamBeschizza 8 57
(Steph Hollinshead) *hld up: nt clr run over 1f out: swtchd lft and qcknd to ld wl ins fnl f: sn rdn and hdd: edgd lft and no ex* **8/1**

-211 **7** *nk* **Boxing Shadows**[35] 292 6-9-0 **65**................................ HarryBurns(7) 3 69+
(Les Eyre) *plld hrd and prom: hmpd after 1f: effrt: hmpd and lost pl ins fnl f: r.o towards fin* **2/1**[1]

62-0 **8** nk **Eland Ally**[14] 541 8-9-2 **60**........(v1) JoeFanning 4 58
(Anabel K Murphy) *chsd ldr: rdn over 1f out: n.m.r and no ex ins fnl f* **6/1**
33-3 **9** 3/4 **Frangarry (IRE)**[14] 541 4-9-2 **60**........ SaleemGolam 1 56
(Alan Bailey) *prom: nt clr run and lost pl 4f out: hdwy over 1f out: nt clr run and no ex ins fnl f* **7/2**[2]
5-34 **10** 1/2 **Mountain Man**[18] 504 4-8-12 **56**........(bt) GrahamGibbons 2 50
(Michael Easterby) *sn rdn to chse ldrs: effrt over 1f out: styng on same pce whn nt clr run towards fin* **4/1**[3]

1m 1.55s (-0.35) **Going Correction** -0.025s/f (Stan) **10** Ran SP% **125.1**
Speed ratings (Par 101): **101,100,100,99,98 98,98,97,96,95**
CSF £226.48 CT £2758.90 TOTE £16.10: £4.20, £4.00, £3.10; EX 214.50 Trifecta £5808.00 Part won..
Owner F Butler & Mrs C Dunnett **Bred** Audrey Frances Stynes **Trained** Hingham, Norfolk
■ Stewards' Enquiry : Adam Beschizza one-day ban: careless riding (11 Mar)

FOCUS
This revolved around the hat-trick seeking favourite. It was run at a good pace and produced a thrilling blanket finish.

734 CORAL CONNECT H'CAP 1m 1f 103y (Tp)
7:45 (7:46) (Class 4) (0-85,84) 4-Y-O+ **£5,175** (£1,540; £769; £384) **Stalls** Low

Form RPR
40-0 **1** **Spes Nostra**[21] 465 8-9-6 **83**........(b) TomEaves 4 93
(Iain Jardine) *led over 8f out: rdn over 1f out: r.o wl: eased nr fin* **28/1**
3-11 **2** 2 **Coillte Cailin (IRE)**[21] 465 6-9-7 **84**........ GeorgeBaker 7 90+
(Daniel Mark Loughnane) *hld up: hdwy over 1f out: r.o to go 2nd wl ins fnl f: no ch w wnr* **2/1**[1]
0423 **3** 3/4 **Mr Red Clubs (IRE)**[3] 683 7-8-7 **70**........ AndrewMullen 1 74
(Michael Appleby) *prom: lost pl over 6f out: hdwy u.p over 1f out: styd on* **6/1**
3-23 **4** shd **Off The Pulse**[21] 465 6-8-12 **75**........(p) GrahamGibbons 5 79
(John Mackie) *hld up: hdwy over 6f out: nt clr run over 2f out: rdn over 1f out: styd on* **7/2**[2]
0-52 **5** 1 1/4 **L'Inganno Felice (FR)**[22] 446 6-8-9 **72**........ ShaneKelly 8 73
(John Mackie) *s.i.s: sn prom: chsd wnr over 7f out: rdn over 1f out: no ex ins fnl f* **7/1**
-140 **6** hd **Mitre Peak**[20] 485 4-9-3 **80**........ TonyHamilton 6 81
(Richard Fahey) *hld up: hdwy over 1f out: styd on same pce ins fnl f* **11/2**[3]
1014 **7** 4 **Black Dave (IRE)**[14] 546 6-8-8 **78**........ AledBeech(7) 3 71
(David Evans) *chsd ldrs: hung rt over 6f out: rdn over 2f out: wknd over 1f out* **10/1**
4-10 **8** nk **Yul Finegold (IRE)**[31] 337 6-9-6 **83**........ PaulMulrennan 2 75
(Conor Dore) *led 1f: chsd ldrs: rdn over 2f out: wknd over 1f out* **16/1**

1m 58.28s (-2.52) **Going Correction** -0.025s/f (Stan) **8** Ran SP% **116.1**
Speed ratings (Par 105): **110,108,107,107,106 106,102,102**
CSF £85.72 CT £403.26 TOTE £30.70: £7.90, £1.50, £1.70; EX 140.00 Trifecta £485.00.
Owner James A Cringan **Bred** James A Cringan **Trained** Carrutherstown, D'fries & G'way

FOCUS
Tactics played a big part in the result of this feature handicap as Tom Eaves stole it off the front end aboard Spes Nostra.

735 32RED.COM MAIDEN STKS 1m 141y (Tp)
8:15 (8:15) (Class 5) 3-Y-O **£3,881** (£1,155; £577; £288) **Stalls** Low

Form RPR
1 **Ultimate Star** 3-9-5 0........ JamieSpencer 7 77+
(David Simcock) *hld up: hdwy over 1f out: shkn up to ld and hung lft wl ins fnl f: comf* **13/8**[2]
3 **2** 3/4 **Four Mile Beach**[10] 600 3-9-5 0........ JoeFanning 5 70
(Mark Johnston) *s.i.s: sn prom: chsd ldr over 7f out: shkn up to ld over 1f out: sn rdn: hung lft and hdd wl ins fnl f* **6/4**[1]
5 **3** 2 1/4 **New Legend (IRE)**[21] 466 3-9-5 0........ GrahamGibbons 4 65
(Robert Cowell) *led: rdn and hdd over 1f out: no ex ins fnl f* **28/1**
4 3/4 **Skara Mae (IRE)** 3-9-0 0........ DarryllHolland 2 58
(Charles Hills) *chsd ldrs: shkn up over 2f out: styd on same pce fnl f* **5/1**[3]
00- **5** 4 1/2 **Pursuit Of Time**[225] 4292 3-9-0 0........ AndrewMullen 1 48
(Michael Appleby) *hld up: rdn over 2f out: wknd over 1f out* **66/1**
66- **6** 3/4 **King Oswald (USA)**[60] 8377 3-9-5 0........ ShaneKelly 6 51
(James Unett) *chsd ldrs tl rdn and wknd over 1f out* **10/1**
000- **7** 7 **Selena Rose**[150] 6836 3-9-0 38........ RichardKingscote 3 30
(Ronald Harris) *hld up: rdn over 2f out: sn wknd* **100/1**

1m 51.57s (1.47) **Going Correction** -0.025s/f (Stan) **7** Ran SP% **109.8**
Speed ratings (Par 97): **92,91,89,88,84 84,77**
CSF £4.00 TOTE £2.50: £1.10, £1.50; EX 4.60 Trifecta £48.20.
Owner Qatar Racing Limited **Bred** The Pocock Family **Trained** Newmarket, Suffolk

FOCUS
This lacked depth and the finish was predictably fought out by those at the head of the market. The form has been rated around the runner-up.
T/Plt: £287.80 to a £1 stake. Pool: £85,188.88 - 216.07 winning tickets T/Qpdt: £182.70 to a £1 stake. Pool: £9,236.83 - 37.41 winning tickets **Colin Roberts**

736 - 743a (Foreign Racing) - See Raceform Interactive

DOHA
Friday, February 26
OFFICIAL GOING: Turf: good

744a IRISH THOROUGHBRED MARKETING CUP (CONDITIONS) (3YO+) (TURF) 1m
4:45 (12:00) 3-Y-O+ **£77,551** (£29,931; £14,965; £8,163; £5,442)

RPR
1 **Baltic Knight (IRE)**[193] 5441 6-9-6 0........ DuranFentiman 1 103
(B Al Abed, Bahrain)
2 nk **Roman Legend (IRE)**[295] 5-9-6 0........(t) HarryBentley 5 102
(Jassim Al Ghazali, Qatar)
3 1 1/2 **Moheet (IRE)**[210] 4816 4-9-6 0........ FrankieDettori 9 99
(Richard Hannon) *t.k.h: hld up in midfield: 8th but n.m.r 2f out: swtchd outside and styd on fr 1 1/2f out: angled ins again 1f out: wnt 3rd cl home but nvr matching pce of front two*
4 nk **Bretherton**[316] 5-9-6 0........(p) AlbertoSanna 8 98
(Jassim Al Ghazali, Qatar)
5 nk **Itorio (IRE)**[58] 4-9-6 0........(b) StephaneLadjadj 12 97
(Jassim Al Ghazali, Qatar)
6 1/2 **Bartack (IRE)**[322] 6-9-6 0........(b1) AndreaAtzeni 14 96
(Abdulla Kuwaiti, Bahrain)
7 shd **Third Dimension**[139] 7130 5-9-6 0........ RichardMullen 2 96
(Jassim Al Ghazali, Qatar)
8 3 1/2 **Anaerobio (ARG)**[29] 373 8-9-6 0........(t) WayneSmith 6 88
(M F De Kock, South Africa)
9 1/2 **Hearts Of Stone (IRE)**[101] 6-9-6 0........(tp) J-PGuillambert 3 87
(Ahmed Kobeissi, Qatar)
10 shd **Quatorze (FR)**[101] 6-9-6 0........ OlivierPeslier 7 87
(A De Mieulle, Arabia)
11 1 1/2 **Crescent (IRE)**[58] 4-9-6 0........(p) SebSanders 10 83
(Ahmed Kobeissi, Qatar)
12 nk **Convergence (IRE)**[58] 4-9-6 0........(p) DarrenWilliams 4 82
(Debbie Mountain, Qatar)
13 1/2 **Pearl Bridge**[8] 6-9-6 0........ MarvinSuerland 11 81
(Zuhair Mohsen, Qatar)
14 1 1/2 **Primitorio (IRE)**[881] 6825 5-9-6 0........(b) AlanMunro 15 78
(O Al Dhafa, Qatar)
15 2 **Al Rayyan (IRE)**[87] 4-9-6 0........(tp) PierantonioConvertino 13 73
(Majed Seifeddine, Qatar)
16 1 3/4 **Dubawi King**[752] 9-9-6 0........(t) IssaAlBalushi 16 69
(Isa Bin Ismail Al Baloch, Oman)

Owner Elbrahim Al Afoo **Bred** Henry O'Callaghan **Trained** Bahrain

724 LINGFIELD (L-H)
Saturday, February 27
OFFICIAL GOING: Polytrack: standard
Wind: light, half against Weather: overcast, chilly

745 UNIBET HEVER SPRINT STKS (ALL-WEATHER CHAMPIONSHIP FAST-TRACK QUALIFIER) (LISTED RACE) 5f 6y(P)
1:45 (1:46) (Class 1) 4-Y-O+
£25,519 (£9,675; £4,842; £2,412; £1,210; £607) **Stalls** High

Form RPR
1-34 **1** **Lightscameraction (IRE)**[21] 483 4-9-0 106........(b) LukeMorris 2 112
(Gay Kelleway) *chsd ldr: drvn to ld 1f out: kpt on wl and maintained narrow advantage fnl f: all out* **6/1**[2]
301- **2** nk **Take Cover**[127] 7449 9-9-3 109........ AndreaAtzeni 10 114
(David C Griffiths) *taken down early and led to post: led: rdn over 1f out: hdd 1f out: kpt on u.p and ev thrght fnl f: a jst hld* **6/1**[2]
163- **3** 1/2 **Muthmir (IRE)**[146] 6971 6-9-7 115........ PatCosgrave 1 116
(William Haggas) *hld up in tch in midfield: swtchd lft and effrt over 1f out: ev ch jst ins fnl f: r.o but hld fnl 100yds* **11/4**[1]
205- **4** 1/2 **Line Of Reason (IRE)**[158] 6614 6-9-3 110........ PaulMulrennan 8 110
(Paul Midgley) *stdd after s: hld up in tch in last quartet: swtchd rt over 1f out: hdwy u.p 1f out: styd on strly ins fnl f: nt rch ldrs* **12/1**
015- **5** nk **Move In Time**[146] 6971 8-9-5 112........ DavidNolan 4 111
(David O'Meara) *hld up in tch in midfield: effrt over 1f out: kpt on u.p fnl f: nvr gng pce to chal ldrs* **8/1**
0-41 **6** 1 **Boom The Groom (IRE)**[5] 677 5-9-0 97........ WilliamCarson 6 103
(Tony Carroll) *taken down early: t.k.h: chsd ldrs tl nt clr run and shuffled bk ent fnl 2f: rallied 1f out: kpt on same pce and no imp fnl 100yds* **10/1**
4-30 **7** 1 **Alben Star (IRE)**[21] 483 8-9-0 105........ TonyHamilton 9 99
(Richard Fahey) *taken down early: dwlt: hld up in last quartet: hdwy on outer 1/2-way: wd and lost pl bnd 2f out: rallied and sme prog ins fnl f: no threat to ldrs* **12/1**
2/6- **8** nk **Abstraction (IRE)**[258] 3206 6-9-0 97........ GaryCarroll 3 98
(Miss Natalia Lupini, Ire) *hld up in tch in last quartet: effrt on inner over 1f out: hdwy u.p 1f out: kpt on same pce and no imp ins fnl f* **33/1**
0-22 **9** hd **Gamgoom**[21] 483 5-9-3 107........ MartinHarley 7 100
(Mario Hofer, Germany) *chsd ldng pair tl rdn and lost pl over 1f out: wknd ins fnl f* **7/1**[3]
006- **10** 3/4 **Russian Soul (IRE)**[8] 642 8-9-0 100........(p) ConorHoban 5 95
(M Halford, Ire) *taken down early: s.i.s: hld up in rr: effrt wl over 1f out: no imp* **12/1**

57.9s (-0.90) **Going Correction** -0.025s/f (Stan) **10** Ran SP% **114.0**
Speed ratings (Par 111): **106,105,104,103,103 101,100,99,99,98**
CSF £40.86 TOTE £6.70: £1.80, £2.00, £1.40; EX 41.80 Trifecta £195.70.
Owner LCA Lights Camera Action Ltd **Bred** Timmy & Michael Hillman **Trained** Exning, Suffolk

FOCUS
A Fast-Track Qualifier for the Unibet All-Weather Sprint Championship over 6f here on Good Friday and a hot Listed sprint in its own right, featuring four Group-race winners and two Listed winners. The pace was decent, though by no means frantic, and the first two were always up there. Lightscameraction is rated to form.

746 LADBROKES MAIDEN STKS 1m 1y(P)
2:15 (2:15) (Class 5) 3-Y-O+ **£2,911** (£866; £432; £216) **Stalls** High

Form RPR
0 **1** **Harry Holland**[8] 639 4-10-0 0........ GeorgeBaker 1 83
(William Muir) *mde all: rdn and fnd ex over 1f out: in command and styd on wl ins fnl f: rdn out* **16/1**
5 **2** 1 1/4 **The New Master**[29] 377 3-8-9 0........ ShaneKelly 4 73
(David Elsworth) *stdd s: hld up in tch in last pair: effrt over 1f out: rdn and hdwy 1f out: styd on steadily to go 2nd wl ins fnl f: no threat to wnr* **4/1**[3]
23 **3** 1/2 **Ragner**[29] 377 3-8-9 0........ TomEaves 5 72
(David Simcock) *chsd ldr: rdn and edgd lft over 1f out: styd on same pce ins fnl f: lost 2nd wl ins fnl f* **13/8**[1]
2 **4** 1 1/2 **Aid To Africa (IRE)**[8] 633 3-8-9 0........ WilliamCarson 2 69
(Michael Bell) *dwlt: in tch in rr: rdn and hdwy on inner over 1f out: one pce and no imp ins fnl f* **9/4**[2]
0-05 **5** 1 **Canford Crossing (IRE)**[13] 582 3-8-6 68........(p) TomMarquand(3) 8 66
(Richard Hannon) *t.k.h: in tch in midfield: effrt in cl 3rd jst over 2f out: unable qck and lost pl over 1f out: hld and kpt on same pce fnl f* **12/1**
50-3 **6** 1/2 **Rock 'n Red (IRE)**[12] 591 3-8-4 64........ JoeFanning 3 61
(Ed Dunlop) *trckd ldrs: 4th and effrt 2f out: struggling to qckn whn squeezed for room and hmpd jst over 1f out: hld and one pce after* **10/1**

1m 37.07s (-1.13) **Going Correction** -0.025s/f (Stan)
WFA 3 from 4yo 19lb **6** Ran SP% **111.5**
Speed ratings (Par 103): **104,102,102,100,99 99**
CSF £76.08 TOTE £16.60: £7.10, £2.40; EX 106.60 Trifecta £201.70.
Owner Muir Racing Partnership - Windsor **Bred** Mrs F M Gordon **Trained** Lambourn, Berks

The Form Book, Raceform Ltd, Newbury, RG14 5SJ

FOCUS
A modest maiden with the form pair both disappointing, bit the form is taken at face value.

747 CORAL.CO.UK H'CAP 1m 4f (P)
2:45 (2:45) (Class 3) (0-95,94) 4-Y-O- **£7,246** (£2,168; £1,084; £542; £270) **Stalls** Low

Form RPR

4-11 **1** **Sunblazer (IRE)**[19] 499 6-9-7 **94**...................(t) WilliamTwiston-Davies 4 102+
(Kim Bailey) *hld up in midfield: rdn and effrt in 5th jst over 2f out: hdwy over 1f out: styd on to ld 100yds out: hld on wl: all out* **5/1**[3]

-161 **2** *nse* **Royal Marskell**[14] 556 7-9-1 **88**.. LukeMorris 3 95
(Gay Kelleway) *chsd ldr for 2f: styd chsng ldrs: effrt 2f out: hrd drvn and styd on to chal ins fnl f: r.o wl: jst hld* **8/1**

-316 **3** *2 1/4* **Paddys Motorbike (IRE)**[19] 499 4-9-2 **92**............................. JFEgan 6 95
(David Evans) *t.k.h: chsd ldrs tl stdd bk into midfield after 2f: rdn 3f out: 5th and no imp over 1f out: styd on wl u.p fnl 100yds: snatched 3rd last stride* **4/1**[2]

4-54 **4** *shd* **Plutocracy (IRE)**[16] 530 6-9-4 **91**...................................... AdamKirby 5 94
(Gary Moore) *stdd s: hld up in last trio tl hdwy to chse ldr after 2f: rdn to chal ent fnl 2f: drvn to ld 1f out: hdd 100yds out: no ex and wknd cl home* **3/1**[1]

-650 **5** *shd* **Masterpaver**[19] 499 5-9-1 **88**.. MartinHarley 8 91
(Alan Bailey) *hld up in last trio: effrt in 6th but stl plenty to do 2f out: swtchd lft and hdwy over 1f out: styd on wl ins fnl f: nvr trbld ldrs* **16/1**

520- **6** *1 1/2* **Be Perfect (USA)**[162] 6496 7-9-1 **88**..............................(p) PJMcDonald 9 89
(Ruth Carr) *led: rdn and jnd ent fnl 2f: hdd 1f out: sn no ex: wknd fnl 100yds* **12/1**

036- **7** *nk* **Ridgeway Storm (IRE)**[61] 8379 6-9-2 **89**......................... TomQueally 1 89+
(Alan King) *niggled along leaving stalls: hld up in rr: effrt and plenty to do 2f out: styd on ins fnl f: nvr trbld ldrs* **6/1**

43/6 **8** *1 1/4* **Sizzler**[40] 244 6-9-7 **94**.. GrahamGibbons 2 92
(Ralph Beckett) *in tch in midfield: rdn over 2f out: sn struggling: wknd over 1f out* **14/1**

02-0 **9** *18* **Latin Charm (IRE)**[16] 530 5-9-0 **87**..............................(p) AndreaAtzeni 7 56
(Marco Botti) *stdd s: hld up in rr: rdn and no rspnse over 2f out: lost tch over 1f out* **8/1**

2m 30.9s (-2.10) **Going Correction** -0.025s/f (Stan)
WFA 4 from 5yo+ 3lb **9** Ran SP% **118.4**
Speed ratings (Par 107): **106,105,104,104,104 103,103,102,90**
CSF £45.71 CT £177.47 TOTE £5.00: £1.90, £2.80, £2.40; EX 35.90 Trifecta £73.90.
Owner Norman Carter **Bred** Michael G Daly **Trained** Andoversford, Gloucs

FOCUS
A decent handicap and a thrilling finish, but a few of these are better known as stayers and the ordinary pace wouldn't have suited many of them. Another pb from the winner.

748 CORAL WINTER DERBY (ALL-WEATHER CHAMPIONSHIP FAST-TRACK QUALIFIER) (GROUP 3) 1m 2f (P)
3:20 (3:20) (Class 1) 4-Y-O+
£56,710 (£21,500; £10,760; £5,360; £2,690; £1,350) **Stalls** Low

Form RPR

22-1 **1** **Grendisar (IRE)**[21] 485 6-9-0 109..................................(p) AdamKirby 7 115
(Marco Botti) *stdd s: hld up in tch in last: clsd and travelling wl 2f out: shkn up to chal over 1f out: rdn to ld ins fnl f: sn in command: r.o* **11/4**[2]

006- **2** *1 1/4* **Maverick Wave (USA)**[105] 7857 5-9-0 110......................... RobertTart 6 112
(John Gosden) *led: rdn 2f out: drvn and hdd jst ins fnl f: styd on same pce after* **7/1**[3]

3 *1 1/4* **Furia Cruzada (CHI)**[302] 4-8-11 110.............................. RobertHavlin 4 107
(John Gosden) *stdd s: hld up in tch in last pair: followed wnr through on inner over 1f out: wnt 3rd and styd on same pce ins fnl f* **8/1**

41-2 **4** *1* **Festive Fare**[21] 485 4-8-13 108..................................(p) AndreaAtzeni 3 108
(Charlie Appleby) *chsd ldrs: wnt 2nd 6f out: rdn and ev ch 2f out: fnd little for press over 1f out: wknd ins fnl f* **7/4**[1]

506- **5** *1* **Tullius (IRE)**[111] 7767 8-9-5 113...................................... JimmyFortune 2 111
(Andrew Balding) *hld up in tch in midfield: clsd and rdn jst over 2f out: outpcd over 1f out: rallied and kpt on ins fnl f: no threat to ldrs* **8/1**

401- **6** *1/2* **Fire Fighting (IRE)**[94] 7977 5-9-0 108........................(b) PaulMulrennan 5 105
(Mark Johnston) *r.o snatches: in tch in midfield: rdn 3f out: outpcd u.p over 1f out: kpt on same pce fnl f* **8/1**

6-36 **7** *4 1/2* **Complicit (IRE)**[21] 485 5-9-0 100...................................... LukeMorris 8 96
(Paul Cole) *in tch in midfield: n.m.r over 2f out: drvn and outpcd wl over 1f out: wknd fnl f* **20/1**

0050 **8** *6* **Battle Of Marathon (USA)**[16] 540 4-8-13 102...........(p) MartinHarley 9 84
(John Ryan) *chsd ldr tl 7f: styd chsng ldrs: rdn 2f out: sn outpcd and btn whn sltly hmpd over 1f out: bhd ins fnl f* **33/1**

2m 1.05s (-5.55) **Going Correction** -0.025s/f (Stan)
WFA 4 from 5yo+ 1lb **8** Ran SP% **116.6**
Speed ratings (Par 113): **121,120,119,118,117 117,113,108**
CSF £22.88 TOTE £3.10: £1.40, £2.00, £2.20; EX 20.70 Trifecta £139.80.
Owner Mohamed Albousi Alghufli **Bred** Old Carhue & Graeng Bloodstock **Trained** Newmarket, Suffolk

FOCUS
With Easter falling in March this year, this season's Winter Derby was much earlier than usual, providing a four-week gap until the Coral Easter Classic on Good Friday, for which this was a Fast-Track Qualifier. This season's renewal featured the second and fourth-placed horses from last year and, despite a smaller field than usual, they went a proper pace which was very much in the winner's favour.

749 DOWNLOAD THE LADBROKES APP H'CAP 1m 1y(P)
3:55 (3:55) (Class 3) (0-95,92) 4-Y-O- **£7,246** (£2,168; £1,084; £542; £270) **Stalls** High

Form RPR

1-12 **1** **Bold Prediction (IRE)**[9] 620 6-9-1 **86**.............................. LukeMorris 4 94
(Ed Walker) *led: rdn and fnd ex 2f out: hrd pressed 1f out: hdd briefly 100yds out: sn led again and hld on: all out* **6/1**[3]

5-12 **2** *hd* **Si Senor (IRE)**[14] 560 5-9-2 **92**.......................... PaddyPilley[(5)] 6 99
(Ed Vaughan) *t.k.h: hld up in tch in midfield: effrt over 1f out: chal 1f out and struck on nose by winning rdrs flailing whip: led 100yds out: sn hdd and hld towards fin* **9/4**[1]

-151 **3** *1* **Loyalty**[9] 620 9-8-8 **84**..(v) CallumShepherd[(5)] 5 89
(Derek Shaw) *awkward leaving stalls and dwlt: in tch but stuck wd: nt clrest of runs over 1f out: swtchd rt jst ins fnl f: r.o strly fnl 100yds: wnt 3rd cl home: nt rch ldrs* **8/1**

0143 **4** *1/2* **Big Time (IRE)**[11] 599 5-9-1 **86**..................................(p) FrannyNorton 1 90
(David Nicholls) *in tch in midfield: effrt to chse ldrs 1f out: styd on same pce ins fnl f: lost 3rd cl home* **6/1**[3]

013- **5** *1* **Illusive (IRE)**[153] 6777 5-9-1 **89**..............................(t) TomMarquand[(3)] 8 91
(George Scott) *stdd s: hld up in tch in rr: clsd and nt clr run over 1f out: sn swtchd lft and hdwy 1f out: kpt on ins fnl f: nvr enough pce to chal* **8/1**

000- **6** *1/2* **Moonlightnavigator (USA)**[182] 5840 4-9-1 **86**................. JoeFanning 7 86
(John Quinn) *chsd wnr tl lost pl u.p over 1f out: hld and styd on same pce ins fnl f* **5/1**[2]

-211 **7** *3/4* **Abbey Angel (IRE)**[26] 422 4-9-1 **86**..........................(p) TonyHamilton 2 85
(Richard Fahey) *chsd ldrs: effrt on inner to chse wnr briefly over 1f out: no ex 1f out: wknd fnl 100yds* **5/1**[2]

-200 **8** *2 3/4* **Anonymous John (IRE)**[32] 338 4-9-7 **92**............................. JFEgan 3 84
(David Evans) *dwlt and pushed along early: racd keenly after 2f: hdwy into midfield 3f out: lost pl over 1f out: bhd ins fnl f* **25/1**

1m 35.58s (-2.62) **Going Correction** -0.025s/f (Stan) **8** Ran SP% **118.7**
Speed ratings (Par 107): **112,111,110,110,109 108,108,105**
CSF £20.78 CT £111.74 TOTE £5.20: £1.50, £1.20, £2.70; EX 24.30 Trifecta £120.70.
Owner John Nicholls (Trading) & Matthew Cottis **Bred** Mountarmstrong Stud **Trained** Upper Lambourn, Berks

FOCUS
A decent handicap and a game front-running performance by the winner. He's edging closer to his old form.

750 DAILY PRICE BOOSTS AT UNIBET MAIDEN AUCTION STKS 5f 6y(P)
4:30 (4:30) (Class 5) 3-Y-O **£2,911** (£866; £432; £216) **Stalls** High

Form RPR

-324 **1** **Rampers (IRE)**[8] 635 3-9-5 58.. GeorgeBaker 2 64
(Jamie Osborne) *hld up in tch in last: smooth hdwy on outer to join ldrs jst over 1f out: pushed into ld ins fnl f: sn clr: comf* **9/4**[2]

25 **2** *1 3/4* **Grecian King**[8] 639 3-9-5 0...(p) LukeMorris 1 58
(James Tate) *chsd ldng pair: effrt over 1f out: pressed ldrs and wnt between horses jst ins fnl f: outpcd by wnr and wnt 2nd fnl 75yds: kpt on same pce* **10/11**[1]

40-2 **3** *1/2* **Lady Lloyd**[10] 611 3-9-1 63 ow1......................................(p) AdamKirby 4 52
(Phil McEntee) *chsd ldr: rdn and ev ch over 1f out: drvn to ld 1f out: hdd and sn brushed aside by wnr ins fnl f: lost 2nd and one pce fnl 75yds* **4/1**[3]

006- **4** *2 1/2* **Frank Sandatra**[131] 7344 3-9-5 51.................................... ShaneKelly 3 47
(Peter Crate) *led: rdn over 1f out: hdd 1f out: dropped to last and btn 100yds out: eased and swtchd rt towards fin* **16/1**

1m 0.49s (1.69) **Going Correction** -0.025s/f (Stan) **4** Ran SP% **109.0**
Speed ratings (Par 97): **85,82,81,77**
CSF £4.77 TOTE £3.00; EX 5.10 Trifecta £7.00.
Owner Fromthestables.com Racing **Bred** T Boylan **Trained** Upper Lambourn, Berks

FOCUS
A weak 3yo sprint maiden with a bit of doubt over the form.
T/Plt: £181.90 to a £1 stake. Pool: £80,643.66 - 323.57 winning tickets T/Qpdt: £18.90 to a £1 stake. Pool: £6,533.04 - 254.45 winning tickets **Steve Payne**

751 - 754a (Foreign Racing) - See Raceform Interactive

744 DOHA
Saturday, February 27

OFFICIAL GOING: Turf: good

755a KATARA SPRINT CUP SPONSORED BY ATTHERACES (CONDITIONS) (3YO+) (TURF) 6f
11:05 (12:00) 3-Y-O+ **£96,938** (£37,414; £18,707; £10,204; £6,802)

RPR

1 **Izzthatright (IRE)**[245] 3663 4-9-6 0................................ RichardMullen 7 106
(Jassim Al Ghazali, Qatar)

2 *1 1/4* **Roi De Vitesse (IRE)**[9] 626 9-9-6 0.............................(v) AdriedeVries 4 102
(Ali Jan, Qatar)

3 *2* **Golden Steps (FR)**[21] 483 5-9-6 0.............................. FrankieDettori 14 95
(Marco Botti) *hld up in last: rdn into st: r.o wl towards fin and wnt 3rd post: nvr nrr*

4 *shd* **Sandbetweenourtoes (IRE)**[352] 7-9-6 0..................(b) HarryBentley 12 95
(Jassim Al Ghazali, Qatar)

5 *nk* **My Sharona**[368] 676 7-9-2 0......................................(b) J-PGuillambert 5 90
(Jassim Al Ghazali, Qatar)

6 *1/2* **Rivellino**[21] 483 6-9-6 0.. DougieCostello 2 92
(K R Burke) *prom: rdn into st: kpt on same pce: nvr able to chal*

7 *3/4* **Qatar Light (IRE)**[102] 4-9-6 0..........................(b) PierantonioConvertino 8 90
(Majed Seifeddine, Qatar)

8 *shd* **Lupie (IRE)**[352] 4-9-6 0..(b) StephaneLadjadj 9 90
(Mohammed Jassim Ghazali, Qatar)

9 *1/2* **Victory Laurel (IRE)**[368] 676 6-9-6 0..............................(t) AlanMunro 13 88
(Ibrahim Al Malki, Qatar)

10 *nk* **Bazaruto**[352] 9-9-6 0.. GeraldAvranche 6 87
(Abduljabar Ali, Qatar)

11 *1 1/4* **Chilworth Icon**[189] 5634 6-9-6 0................................ DarrenWilliams 15 83
(Debbie Mountain, Qatar)

12 *nk* **Collect Art (IRE)**[368] 676 9-9-6 0..............................(b) AlbertoSanna 16 82
(Mohammed Jassim Ghazali, Qatar)

13 *hd* **Baitha Alga (IRE)**[203] 5134 4-9-6 0............................ MarvinSuerland 11 82
(Jassim Al Ghazali, Qatar)

14 *1 1/2* **Complimentor (IRE)**[174] 6149 6-9-6 0.............................. BrettDoyle 10 77
(Hilal Kobeissi, Qatar)

Owner Injaaz Stud **Bred** Patrick Cummins **Trained** Qatar

756a AL BIDDAH LAFFAN MILE SPONSORED BY NBK (CONDITIONS) (3YO) (TURF) 1m
12:10 (12:00) 3-Y-O **£96,938** (£37,414; £18,707; £10,204; £6,802)

RPR

1 **Opera Baron**[23] 3-9-2 0.. J-PGuillambert 6 94
(Jassim Al Ghazali, Qatar)

2 *1/2* **Flying Empress**[23] 3-8-11 0.. AdriedeVries 7 88
(Jassim Al Ghazali, Qatar)

3 *1 1/4* **French Encore**[23] 3-9-2 0.. DarrenWilliams 2 90
(Debbie Mountain, Qatar)

4 *1* **Tony Curtis**[126] 7463 3-9-2 0.. SeanLevey 4 88
(Richard Hannon) *midfield: rdn 2f out: kpt on in st but nt pce to chal*

5 *1/2* **Perkunas (IRE)**[60] 8390 3-9-2 0.................................... FrankieDettori 10 87
(Brian Meehan) *midfield: niggled to hold position early: rdn bef st: kpt on fnl f and wnt 5th cl home: nt pce to chal*

6 *nk* **Rasikh (IRE)**[23] 3-9-2 0 .... EduardoPedroza 1 86
(Zuhair Mohsen, Qatar)
7 *nk* **Greyscape (IRE)**[23] 3-9-2 0 ....(t) EvertPheiffer 3 85
(Ibrahim Al Malki, Qatar)
8 *5* **Black Beach**[16] 3-9-2 0 .... RichardMullen 16 74
(Jassim Al Ghazali, Qatar)
9 *nk* **Ard San Aer (IRE)**[23] 3-9-2 0 .... GeraldAvranche 12 73
(M Al Attiya, Qatar)
10 *½* **Astley Hall**[23] 3-9-2 0 .... HarryBentley 9 72
(Mohammed Jassim Ghazali, Qatar)
11 *hd* **Gerrard's Quest**[60] 8390 3-9-2 0 ....(b) JulienAuge 5 71
(Mohammed Hussain, Qatar)
12 *2½* **Secret Tale (IRE)**[23] 3-8-11 0 .... SebSanders 13 61
(Ahmed Kobeissi, Qatar)
13 *6* **Spongy (IRE)**[16] 3-9-2 0 ....(p) AlbertoSanna 14 52
(Mohammed Jassim Ghazali, Qatar)
14 *2* **Shaka Zulu (IRE)**[16] 3-9-2 0 .... AlanMunro 8 47
(Ibrahim Al Malki, Qatar)
15 *nk* **Binzart (IRE)**[16] 3-9-2 0 ....(tp) PierantonioConvertino 11 47
(Majed Seifeddine, Qatar)
16 *3½* **Ocean Jive**[118] 7666 3-9-2 0 .... JimCrowley 15 39
(Brian Meehan) *dwlt slt and hld up: a in rr: rdn and wl btn in st: no factor*

1m 33.5s (93.50) **16** Ran

Owner Khalifa Bin Sheail Al Kuwari **Bred** Littleton Stud **Trained** Qatar

757a H H THE EMIRS TROPHY PRESENTED BY LONGINES (LOCAL GROUP 1) (3YO+) (TURF) 1m 4f

1:15 (12:00) 3-Y-O+ **£387,755** (£149,659; £74,829; £40,816; £27,210)

RPR
1 **The Blue Eye**[23] 4-9-3 0 .... HarryBentley 1 109+
(Jassim Al Ghazali, Qatar)
2 *4* **Billabong (MOR)**[132] 7330 7-9-6 0 .... CristianDemuro 7 103
(P Bary, France)
3 *shd* **Fort Moville (FR)**[23] 4-9-3 0 ....(p) MarvinSuerland 13 103
(Ahmed Kobeissi, Qatar)
4 *1½* **Agent Murphy**[133] 7277 5-9-6 0 .... JimCrowley 4 100
(Brian Meehan) *t.k.h: midfield: rdn into st: styd on into 4th but wl hld*
5 *nk* **Hall Of Fame (IRE)**[531] 6373 4-9-3 0 ....(t) GeraldAvranche 3 100
(M Al Attiya, Qatar)
6 *shd* **Tannaaf (IRE)**[23] 455 4-9-3 0 .... WayneSmith 14 100
(M F De Kock, South Africa)
7 *shd* **Extremis (IRE)**[170] 6261 4-9-3 0 .... RichardMullen 5 100
(Mohammed Jassim Ghazali, Qatar)
8 *shd* **Canndal (FR)**[23] 4-9-3 0 ....(tp) SebSanders 15 99
(Ahmed Kobeissi, Qatar)
9 *¾* **Ponfeigh (IRE)**[23] 5-9-6 0 ....(p) DarrenWilliams 12 98
(Debbie Mountain, Qatar)
10 *nk* **Ningara**[23] 6-9-6 0 .... AlbertoSanna 2 98
(Jassim Al Ghazali, Qatar)
11 *½* **Right To Dream (IRE)**[23] 7-9-6 0 .... AlanMunro 9 97
(Ibrahim Al Malki, Qatar)
12 *¾* **Al Waab (IRE)**[44] 6-9-6 0 ....(bt) PierantonioConvertino 11 96
(Majed Seifeddine, Qatar)
13 *hd* **Tashaar (IRE)**[155] 6712 4-9-3 0 .... FrankieDettori 8 95
(Richard Hannon) *in tch: rdn into st: sn outpcd: btn and wknd fnl f*
14 *¾* **Afonso De Sousa (USA)**[16] 530 6-9-6 0 .... DanielTudhope 10 94
(David O'Meara) *midfield: rdn into st: outpcd and btn fnl f: wknd*
15 *5* **Rogue Runner (GER)**[16] 540 4-9-3 0 ....(p) EduardoPedroza 16 86
(Mario Hofer, Germany)
16 *3* **Peter Anders**[9] 7-9-6 0 .... AdriedeVries 6 81
(Zuhair Mohsen, Qatar)

2m 25.85s (145.85)
WFA 4 from 5yo+ 3lb **16** Ran

Owner Khalifa Bin Sheail Al Kuwari **Bred** Aleyrion Bloodstock Ltd **Trained** Qatar

758 - 762a (Foreign Racing) - See Raceform Interactive

730 WOLVERHAMPTON (A.W) (L-H)

Monday, February 29

OFFICIAL GOING: Tapeta: standard
Wind: Fresh half-behind Weather: Overcast

763 BET&WATCH EVERY RACE AT UNIBET H'CAP 5f 20y (Tp)

1:50 (1:50) (Class 6) (0-60,60) 3-Y-O **£2,749** (£818; £408; £204) **Stalls** Low

Form RPR
015- 1 **Powerful Dream (IRE)**[214] 4781 3-9-6 **59** .... LukeMorris 2 66+
(Ronald Harris) *sn pushed along towards rr: hung rt 1/2-way: hdwy 2f out: swtchd rt over 1f out: shkn up to ld and edgd lft ins fnl f: r.o* **7/1**[2]
24-2 2 *1¼* **La Asomada**[10] 635 3-9-7 **60** .... GrahamGibbons 3 63
(David Barron) *chsd ldrs: rdn and ev ch ins fnl f: styd on same pce: eased whn hld nr fin* **5/6**[1]
-063 3 *1¼* **David's Beauty (IRE)**[10] 635 3-9-4 **57** ....(p) TomEaves 5 55
(Brian Baugh) *led 1f: chsd ldr: rdn over 1f out: nt clr run ins fnl f: styd on same pce fnl f* **17/2**[3]
400- 4 *nk* **Bertie Buoy**[126] 7517 3-8-4 **46** oh1 ....(v) PhilipPrince[(3)] 4 43
(Richard Guest) *led 4f out: rdn over 1f out: hdd and no ex ins fnl f* **25/1**
06-5 5 *5* **Master Pekan**[28] 419 3-8-7 **46** oh1 .... BenCurtis 1 25
(Roy Brotherton) *n.m.r sn after s: swtchd rt: hld up: hung rt over 2f out: wknd over 1f out* **12/1**
651- 6 *2¼* **Name That Toon**[114] 7744 3-8-10 **49** ....(v) TonyHamilton 7 20
(Derek Shaw) *chsd ldrs: rdn 1/2-way: wknd over 1f out* **7/1**[2]
000- 7 *1¼* **Taroneesh**[195] 5471 3-8-7 **46** oh1 ....(v[1]) AdamBeschizza 9 12
(Derek Shaw) *s.i.s: sn pushed along in rr: rdn and wknd over 1f out* **22/1**
-000 8 *nk* **Justice (IRE)**[26] 436 3-8-7 **46** oh1 ....(p) JimmyQuinn 6 11
(Dean Ivory) *s.i.s: hld up: rdn and wknd over 1f out* **10/1**

1m 1.38s (-0.52) **Going Correction** -0.15s/f (Stan) **8** Ran SP% **115.1**
Speed ratings (Par 95): **98,96,94,93,85 81,79,79**
CSF £13.34 CT £51.81 TOTE £6.80: £3.10, £1.02, £2.30; EX 14.10 Trifecta £48.20.
Owner Ridge House Stables Ltd **Bred** Ballyhane Stud **Trained** Earlswood, Monmouths

FOCUS
A moderate sprint handicap. A clear pb from the winner.

764 DOWNLOAD THE NEW UNIBET RACING APP H'CAP 5f 20y (Tp)

2:20 (2:20) (Class 5) (0-75,75) 4-Y-O+ **£3,234** (£962; £481; £240) **Stalls** Low

Form RPR
500- 1 **Something Lucky (IRE)**[140] 7170 4-9-7 **75** .... ShaneGray 3 84
(Kristin Stubbs) *hld up: hdwy over 1f out: led and hung lft wl ins fnl f: r.o* **9/1**
301- 2 *¾* **Bahango (IRE)**[210] 4937 4-9-5 **73** ....(p) FrannyNorton 1 79
(Patrick Morris) *hld up: hdwy 2f out: rdn and ev ch whn hung rt wl ins fnl f: styd on* **16/1**
3100 3 *1½* **Jaarih (IRE)**[15] 580 4-9-6 **74** ....(p) PaulMulrennan 7 77
(Conor Dore) *chsd ldrs: rdn to ld and hung lft ins fnl f: hdd and hmpd sn after: no ex* **8/1**
0356 4 *¾* **Malaysian Boleh**[10] 629 6-8-13 **72** ....(b) CallumShepherd[(5)] 6 70
(Shaun Lycett) *s.i.s: sn pushed along in rr: nt clr run ins fnl f: r.o wl towards fin: nt rch ldrs* **11/2**[3]
305- 5 *1¼* **Mutafaakir (IRE)**[143] 7080 7-9-4 **72** .... PJMcDonald 2 66
(Ruth Carr) *chsd ldrs: rdn over 1f out: styng on same pce whn hmpd ins fnl f* **4/1**[1]
0302 6 *shd* **Archie Stevens**[6] 685 6-9-2 **73** .... PhilipPrince[(3)] 9 69
(David Evans) *sn pushed along and prom: chsd ldr over 3f out: led 1/2-way: rdn and edgd lft over 1f out: hdd and hmpd ins fnl f: no ex* **9/1**
-035 7 *1* **Powerful Wind (IRE)**[12] 604 7-9-4 **72** .... LukeMorris 4 61
(Charlie Wallis) *plld hrd and prom: nt clr run over 3f out: rdn over 1f out: styd on same pce* **9/2**[2]
-324 8 *nse* **You're Cool**[36] 323 4-9-5 **73** .... TomEaves 8 62
(John Balding) *hld up: rdn over 1f out: nvr trbld ldrs* **6/1**
0-00 9 *¾* **Pearl Noir**[32] 364 6-8-7 **64** ....(b) TimClark[(3)] 5 51
(Scott Dixon) *sn led: rdn and hdd 1/2-way: ev ch over 1f out: wknd ins fnl f* **14/1**

1m 0.72s (-1.18) **Going Correction** -0.15s/f (Stan) **9** Ran SP% **111.5**
Speed ratings (Par 103): **103,101,99,98,96 96,94,94,93**
CSF £133.49 CT £1180.76 TOTE £12.80: £2.40, £3.00, £2.20; EX 178.20 Trifecta £1224.00.
Owner Paul & Linda Dixon **Bred** Rathasker Stud **Trained** Norton, N Yorks

FOCUS
This was run at a good gallop. The winner has been rated back to lasy year's handicap best.

765 UNIBET OFFER DAILY JOCKEY/TRAINER SPECIALS MAIDEN STKS 5f 216y (Tp)

2:50 (2:51) (Class 5) 3-Y-O+ **£3,234** (£962; £481; £240) **Stalls** Low

Form RPR
5 1 **Rhythm And Blues**[33] 352 3-8-12 0 .... JohnFahy 6 73
(Clive Cox) *chsd ldrs: rdn over 1f out: r.o to ld towards fin* **13/2**[2]
2-4 2 *nk* **Spirit Glance**[7] 679 3-8-7 66 .... AndrewMullen 10 67
(Tim Easterby) *hld up in tch: rdn and ev ch ins fnl f: r.o* **8/1**[3]
30-2 3 *nk* **Cee Jay**[51] 126 3-8-12 70 ....(v) JimCrowley 12 71
(Jeremy Noseda) *led early: chsd ldr tl led over 1f out: rdn and hdd towards fin* **10/11**[1]
54 4 *5* **Birrafun (IRE)**[9] 659 3-8-7 0 .... PJMcDonald 2 50
(Ann Duffield) *chsd ldrs: rdn over 1f out: no ex fnl f* **66/1**
5 *¾* **Bromley Cross (IRE)** 3-8-12 0 .... TonyHamilton 4 53
(Richard Fahey) *sn led: rdn: hung lft and hdd over 1f out: wknd ins fnl f* **9/1**
6 *1* **Dutch Archer** 3-8-12 0 .... SteveDrowne 5 49
(Jeremy Gask) *s.i.s: hld up: styd on fr over 1f out: nt trble ldrs* **22/1**
4 7 *1½* **Graceful Favour**[46] 177 3-8-7 0 .... JoeFanning 9 40
(David Barron) *mid-div: rdn over 2f out: n.d* **16/1**
5 8 *½* **Pickering**[33] 350 3-8-12 0 ....(t) AntonioFresu 7 43
(Denis Quinn) *prom: rdn over 2f out: wknd over 1f out* **25/1**
4 9 *1* **Thatsthewaytodoit (IRE)**[17] 544 3-8-4 0 .... TimClark[(3)] 3 35
(Kevin Frost) *sn pushed along in rr: nt clr run over 1f out: nvr nrr* **22/1**
366- 10 *2¼* **Amor Invicto (IRE)**[167] 6403 3-8-5 0 .... KimberleyVanderVegt[(7)] 1 33
(Daniel Kubler) *prom: lost pl over 5f out: n.d after* **20/1**
11 *nk* **Nine Carat (IRE)**[899] 6369 5-9-13 0 .... ShaneGray 8 36
(Keith Henry Clarke, Ire) *hld up: racd keenly: shkn up over 2f out: nvr on terms* **125/1**
33- 12 *7* **Luvly**[308] 1734 3-8-12 0 .... TomEaves 11 9
(Brian Baugh) *unruly in stalls: s.i.s: outpcd* **33/1**

1m 13.97s (-0.53) **Going Correction** -0.15s/f (Stan)
WFA 3 from 5yo 15lb **12** Ran SP% **115.2**
Speed ratings (Par 103): **97,96,96,89,88 87,85,84,83,80 79,70**
CSF £50.91 TOTE £5.90: £1.50, £1.50, £1.80; EX 49.30 Trifecta £122.30.
Owner A D Spence **Bred** Bearstone Stud Ltd **Trained** Lambourn, Berks

FOCUS
Modest maiden form. The third has been rated to form.

766 DOWNLOAD THE CORAL APP H'CAP 1m 4f 50y (Tp)

3:25 (3:25) (Class 5) (0-75,75) 4-Y-O+ **£3,234** (£962; £481; £240) **Stalls** Low

Form RPR
-112 1 **Biff Johnson (IRE)**[5] 693 4-9-4 **75** ....(p) GrahamLee 3 86+
(Keith Dalgleish) *a.p: rdn to ld ins fnl f: r.o* **15/8**[1]
0/02 2 *2¼* **Icebuster**[16] 566 8-9-7 **75** .... DanielTudhope 9 81
(Rod Millman) *a.p: chsd ldr over 6f out tl led over 3f out: rdn over 1f out: hdd ins fnl f: styd on same pce* **5/1**[3]
6-0 3 *1¼* **Dunquin (IRE)**[39] 273 4-9-1 **72** .... FrannyNorton 1 76
(John Mackie) *hld up: hdwy over 1f out: r.o: nt rch ldrs* **13/2**
2-36 4 *1¾* **Kay Sera**[27] 425 8-8-10 **67** .... EoinWalsh[(3)] 4 68
(Tony Newcombe) *hld up: hdwy over 1f out: nt trble ldrs* **14/1**
60-2 5 *hd* **Sandy Cove**[12] 606 5-8-12 **66** .... LukeMorris 2 67
(James Eustace) *trckd ldrs: wnt 2nd over 2f out: rdn over 1f out: no ex ins fnl f* **4/1**[2]
-354 6 *6* **Percys Princess**[10] 636 5-8-13 **70** .... AlistairRawlinson[(3)] 7 61
(Michael Appleby) *hld up: hdwy over 5f out: rdn over 3f out: wknd over 1f out* **8/1**
04-0 7 *6* **High Intensity**[7] 675 4-8-10 **67** .... BenCurtis 5 49
(Scott Dixon) *hld up: rdn over 3f out: sn wknd* **22/1**
2-60 8 *2* **Ifan (IRE)**[16] 566 8-8-11 **65** .... DougieCostello 6 43
(Tim Vaughan) *led: hdd over 3f out: sn rdn: wknd over 1f out* **66/1**
50-0 9 *5* **Jacobs Son**[39] 273 8-9-4 **72** ....(v) JoeyHaynes 8 42
(John Balding) *racd keenly: trckd ldr after 1f tl over 6f out: rdn and wknd over 2f out* **40/1**

2m 38.07s (-2.73) **Going Correction** -0.15s/f (Stan)
WFA 4 from 5yo+ 3lb **9** Ran SP% **110.8**
Speed ratings (Par 103): **103,101,100,99,99 95,91,90,86**
CSF £10.48 CT £46.10 TOTE £2.70: £1.40, £1.40, £2.00; EX 10.10 Trifecta £43.30.

The Form Book, Raceform Ltd, Newbury, RG14 5SJ

Owner Ronnie Docherty **Bred** Frank Dunne **Trained** Carluke, S Lanarks

FOCUS

The early gallop wasn't strong and plenty raced keenly. It's been rated around the runner-up to his C&D latest.

767 CORAL H'CAP 1m 1f 103y (Tp)

4:00 (4:00) (Class 2) (0-105,105) 4-Y-O+ **£11,971** (£3,583; £1,791; £896; £446) **Stalls** Low

Form RPR

62-3 **1** **Bravo Zolo (IRE)**[16] 560 4-8-13 **97** JimCrowley 5 105+
(Jeremy Noseda) *racd keenly: led after 1f: rdn over 1f out: styd on u.p* **7/4**[1]

4-12 **2** *½* **Perfect Cracker**[24] 465 8-7-13 **86** RyanTate(3) 4 94+
(Clive Cox) *hld up: hdwy and nt clr run over 1f out: n.m.r ins fnl f: r.o* **7/1**[3]

02-1 **3** *hd* **Our Channel (USA)**[44] 215 5-9-2 **100** (p) PatCosgrave 3 106
(William Haggas) *chsd ldrs: rdn over 1f out: ev ch ins fnl f: styd on* **3/1**[2]

230- **4** *nk* **Tempus Temporis (USA)**[107] 7857 4-9-2 **100** (b) RobertHavlin 7 105
(John Gosden) *a.p: rdn over 1f out: unable qck towards fin* **15/2**

4222 **5** *2* **Pactolus (IRE)**[9] 656 5-8-2 **86** oh1 (t) JoeFanning 8 87
(Stuart Williams) *hld up: shkn up over 1f out: hung lft ins fnl f: nt trble ldrs* **9/1**

22-3 **6** *¾* **Mont Ras (IRE)**[14] 594 9-8-10 **94** BenCurtis 1 94
(David Loughnane) *hld up: rdn over 1f out: styd on same pce fnl f* **20/1**

00-3 **7** *2¾* **Lat Hawill (IRE)**[21] 501 5-9-2 **100** [1] LukeMorris 6 94
(Marco Botti) *led 1f: chsd wnr: rdn over 2f out: wknd fnl f* **11/1**

1m 56.96s (-3.84) **Going Correction** -0.15s/f (Stan) course record **7 Ran SP% 108.7**
Speed ratings (Par 109): **111,110,110,110,108 107,105**
CSF £13.01 CT £29.50 TOTE £2.60: £2.20, £1.40; EX 12.50 Trifecta £44.40.

Owner Marc Keller **Bred** Tipper House Stud **Trained** Newmarket, Suffolk

FOCUS

A good handicap, but a bit of a messy race. The third has been rated to his Chelmsford win.

768 32RED.COM MAIDEN STKS 1m 1f 103y (Tp)

4:30 (4:30) (Class 5) 3-Y-O **£3,396** (£1,010; £505; £252) **Stalls** Low

Form RPR

3 **1** **Isharah (USA)**[12] 603 3-9-5 0 JoeFanning 1 75
(Mark Johnston) *led after 1f: rdn over 1f out: jst hld on* **30/100**[1]

2 *shd* **Clayton Hall (IRE)** 3-9-5 0 TonyHamilton 5 74
(Richard Fahey) *chsd ldrs: rdn over 2f out: r.o wl towards fin* **16/1**[3]

3 *½* **Proven Point (IRE)** 3-9-5 0 BarryMcHugh 2 73
(Tony Coyle) *led 1f: w wnr: rdn over 1f out: unable qck nr fin* **20/1**

05 **4** *17* **Avoidable**[35] 331 3-9-5 0 TomEaves 7 37
(David Simcock) *chsd ldrs: lost pl 4f out: wknd over 2f out* **5/1**[2]

5 *nk* **Peggy Joyce** 3-9-0 0 GrahamGibbons 6 31
(David Barron) *prom: rdn over 3f out: wknd over 2f out* **16/1**[3]

5- **6** *6* **Mr Grumpy**[162] 6560 3-9-5 0 JasonHart 4 24
(Keith Dalgleish) *s.i.s: hld up: rdn and wknd over 2f out* **33/1**

0- **7** *4½* **Don't Tell Nik (IRE)**[136] 7251 3-9-0 0 BenCurtis 3 9
(David Loughnane) *s.i.s: hld up: rdn and wknd over 2f out* **100/1**

1m 58.7s (-2.10) **Going Correction** -0.15s/f (Stan) **7 Ran SP% 114.0**
Speed ratings (Par 97): **103,102,102,87,87 81,77**
CSF £6.97 TOTE £1.40: £1.50, £2.80; EX 5.90 Trifecta £44.10.

Owner Abdulla Al Mansoori **Bred** M Buckley, M Buckley & K L Ramsey **Trained** Middleham Moor, N Yorks

FOCUS

The short-priced favourite was given a real scare in this maiden. The level is a bit fluid.

769 LADBROKES H'CAP 1m 141y (Tp)

5:00 (5:00) (Class 6) (0-60,60) 4-Y-O+ **£2,911** (£866; £432; £216) **Stalls** Low

Form RPR

336- **1** **Lord Of The Storm**[370] 673 8-9-6 **59** KierenFox 7 69
(Michael Attwater) *a.p: rdn to chse ldr 1f out: r.o to ld nr fin* **16/1**

00-6 **2** *¾* **Kicking The Can (IRE)**[24] 463 5-9-4 **57** BarryMcHugh 10 65
(David Thompson) *sn led: rdn over 1f out: hdd nr fin* **16/1**

5-41 **3** *1* **La Havrese (FR)**[16] 568 5-9-2 **60** JoshDoyle(5) 5 66+
(Lynn Siddall) *hld up: hdwy and nt clr run over 1f out: r.o: nt rch ldrs* **7/2**[1]

-025 **4** *1* **Toymaker**[18] 532 9-9-3 **56** (t) TomEaves 12 60
(Phil McEntee) *a.p: rdn over 1f out: styd on* **22/1**

-404 **5** *½* **Bailiwick**[14] 590 5-9-7 **60** (b) LukeMorris 2 63
(Daniel Kubler) *a.p: rdn to chse ldr over 2f out tl 1f out: no ex ins fnl f* **4/1**[2]

3660 **6** *shd* **Venus Grace**[16] 564 5-9-4 **57** AndrewMullen 4 60+
(Michael Appleby) *hld up in tch: rdn over 2f out: styd on* **25/1**

-210 **7** *hd* **Les Gar Gan (IRE)**[16] 563 5-9-5 **58** (be) ShaneKelly 8 61+
(Daniel Mark Loughnane) *hld up: rdn over 2f out: hdwy over 1f out: nt rch ldrs* **8/1**

00-0 **8** *¾* **Dovil's Duel (IRE)**[27] 429 5-9-4 **60** EoinWalsh(3) 1 61+
(Tony Newcombe) *hld up: hdwy over 1f out: styd on same pce ins fnl f* **12/1**

00-3 **9** *nk* **Lendal Bridge**[16] 563 5-8-13 **52** (p) BenCurtis 6 52
(Tony Coyle) *chsd ldr tl rdn over 2f out: no ex ins fnl f* **10/1**

6-42 **10** *¾* **McDelta**[12] 609 6-9-1 **57** GeorgeDowning(3) 9 56+
(Geoffrey Deacon) *hld up: rdn over 1f out: nvr on terms* **11/2**[3]

0605 **11** *½* **Kodiac Lady (IRE)**[16] 563 4-8-11 **57** (be) HollieDoyle(7) 13 55+
(Simon West) *hld up: racd keenly: hdwy over 5f out: styd on same pce fnl 2f* **16/1**

0-65 **12** *1½* **Ali Bin Nayef**[32] 356 4-9-4 **57** RobertHavlin 11 52+
(Michael Wigham) *hld up: shkn up over 1f out: nvr on terms* **25/1**

-251 **13** *6* **Schottische**[16] 563 6-9-3 **56** (p) SaleemGolam 3 38+
(Alan Bailey) *hld up: rdn over 2f out: sn wknd* **14/1**

1m 49.95s (-0.15) **Going Correction** -0.15s/f (Stan) **13 Ran SP% 121.9**
Speed ratings (Par 101): **94,93,92,91,91 91,90,90,89,89 88,87,82**
CSF £248.25 CT £1107.31 TOTE £21.50: £6.00, £5.70, £2.20; EX 368.50 Trifecta £4919.50.

Owner Mrs M S Teversham **Bred** Mrs Monica Teversham **Trained** Epsom, Surrey

FOCUS

A moderate handicap. It's been rated around the winner.

T/Jkpt: Not won. T/Plt: £42.40 to a £1 stake. Pool of £62155.23 - 1069.88 winning tickets. T/Qpdt: £3.40 to a £1 stake. Pool of £6879.16 - 1494.66 winning tickets. **Colin Roberts**

745 LINGFIELD (L-H)

Tuesday, March 1

OFFICIAL GOING: Polytrack: standard

Wind: medium, half behind Weather: overcast, after a wet morning

770 32RED CASINO MAIDEN STKS 7f 1y(P)

2:10 (2:10) (Class 5) 3-Y-O **£2,911** (£866; £432; £216) **Stalls** Low

Form RPR

545- **1** **Easter Mate (IRE)**[130] 7421 3-9-5 80 (p) GrahamGibbons 4 79
(Ralph Beckett) *mde all: rdn 2f out: styd on wl u.p and in command fnl f* **6/4**[1]

2 *2¼* **Abareeq** 3-9-5 0 JoeFanning 6 74+
(Mark Johnston) *restless in stalls: s.i.s: sn rcvrd and in tch in midfield: wnt 2nd and shkn up over 1f out: sn rn green and hung lft: kpt on same pce after: eased towards fin* **15/8**[2]

3 *1½* **Major Assault** 3-9-5 0 AdamKirby 5 70+
(Clive Cox) *chsd wnr: rdn over 2f out: 3rd and unable qck over 1f out: styd on same pce ins fnl f* **3/1**[3]

4-0 **4** *7* **Straduff (IRE)**[17] 557 3-9-5 0 LiamJones 3 54
(J S Moore) *in tch in midfield: rdn over 2f out: wnt 4th but outpcd by ldng trio 2f out: wl hld and plugged on same pce after* **25/1**

5 *nk* **Dalavand (IRE)** 3-9-5 0 TimmyMurphy 7 53+
(Jamie Osborne) *s.i.s and wnt rt s: rn green and detached in last: clsd and jst in tch 1/2-way: outpcd over 2f out: no ch after: urged along and pressing for modest 4th ins fnl f* **16/1**

05 **6** *3¼* **Haunted (IRE)**[29] 413 3-9-0 0 FrannyNorton 2 41
(Milton Bradley) *in tch in rr of main gp: rdn over 2f out: sn struggling and bmpd 2f out: wl btn over 1f out* **66/1**

0 **7** *24* **My Shootin Star**[27] 432 3-9-0 0 CharlesBishop 1
(Peter Hedger) *t.k.h: chsd ldng pair: rdn over 2f out: losing pl whn bmpd 2f out: sn bhd: eased ins fnl f: t.o* **100/1**

1m 23.71s (-1.09) **Going Correction** -0.05s/f (Stan) **7 Ran SP% 112.0**
Speed ratings (Par 98): **104,101,99,91,91 87,60**
CSF £4.36 TOTE £2.70: £2.80, £1.10; EX 5.30 Trifecta £8.60.

Owner Robert Ng **Bred** J Hanly **Trained** Kimpton, Hants

FOCUS

A fair maiden. The winner has been rated to form.

771 DAILY PRICE BOOSTS AT UNIBET H'CAP 6f 1y(P)

2:40 (2:41) (Class 3) (0-95,94) 4-Y-O- **£7,246** (£2,168; £1,084; £542; £270) **Stalls** Low

Form RPR

0661 **1** **Fleckerl (IRE)**[8] 670 6-8-12 **85** 6ex (p) JimCrowley 6 93
(Conor Dore) *stdd after s: hld up in last pair: gd hdwy on inner over 1f out: chal ins fnl f: r.o wl u.p to ld wl ins fnl f: hld on cl home* **6/1**[3]

-160 **2** *shd* **Searchlight**[19] 529 5-8-13 **86** PatCosgrave 3 93
(Jim Boyle) *in tch in midfield: effrt over 1f out: drvn and ev ch ins fnl f: kpt on wl: snatched 2nd last stride* **14/1**

414- **3** *shd* **Patrick (IRE)**[215] 4792 4-9-1 **88** TonyHamilton 1 95
(Richard Fahey) *taken down early: trckd ldng pair: effrt to press ldr over 1f out: rdn and ev ch 1f out: led 100yds out: hdd wl ins fnl f: kpt on but a jst hld: lost 2nd last stride* **5/2**[1]

2014 **4** *1* **Hoofalong**[8] 677 6-9-4 **91** (b) GrahamGibbons 10 94+
(Michael Easterby) *rdr struggling to remove hood and slowly away: sn swtchd lft and hld up in rr: c wd and effrt wl over 1f out: styd on strly ins fnl f: nt rch ldrs* **6/1**[3]

-003 **5** *nse* **Baddilini**[10] 657 6-9-7 **94** (p) SaleemGolam 9 97
(Alan Bailey) *in tch in midfield: hdwy to chse ldrs over 4f out: swtchd rt and effrt over 1f out: kpt on same pce ins fnl f* **6/1**[3]

36-5 **6** *½* **Varsovian**[19] 529 6-8-13 **86** RenatoSouza 4 88
(Dean Ivory) *chsd ldrs early: stdd bk and in tch in midfield after 1f: effrt wl over 1f out: nvr enough room and kpt on same pce ins fnl f* **9/2**[2]

1-30 **7** *nk* **Luis Vaz De Torres (IRE)**[27] 433 4-8-5 **81** SammyJoBell(3) 2 82
(Richard Fahey) *led: rdn over 1f out: hdd 100yds: no ex and wknd towards fin* **7/1**

621- **8** *½* **Iseemist (IRE)**[142] 7143 5-9-3 **90** ShaneGray 7 89
(John Gallagher) *pressed ldr tl unable qck and lost pl over 1f out: hld and styd on same pce ins fnl f* **14/1**

5325 **9** *nk* **Apache Storm**[16] 580 4-8-11 **84** AndrewMullen 5 85
(Michael Appleby) *in tch in midfield: effrt over 1f out: hld and keeping on same pce whn nt clr run and swtchd lft wl ins fnl f* **8/1**

11-0 **10** *7* **Secret Glance**[24] 484 4-8-7 **78** AdamBeschizza 8 56
(Richard Rowe) *hld up in tch in last trio: effrt and no rspnse over 1f out: wknd ins fnl f* **100/1**

1m 10.23s (-1.67) **Going Correction** -0.05s/f (Stan) **10 Ran SP% 127.5**
Speed ratings (Par 107): **109,108,108,107,107 106,106,105,105,95**
CSF £94.49 CT £277.76 TOTE £7.90: £2.60, £4.50, £1.50; EX 119.90 Trifecta £760.20.

Owner Andrew Page **Bred** Yeguada De Milagro Sa **Trained** Hubbert's Bridge, Lincs

FOCUS

A competitive sprint and a tight finish. The runner-up has been rated close to his old form.

772 32REDSPORT.COM H'CAP 1m 5f (P)

3:10 (3:10) (Class 5) (0-70,70) 4-Y-O+ **£2,911** (£866; £432; £216) **Stalls** Low

Form RPR

5-04 **1** **Heart Locket**[18] 545 4-9-0 **66** GrahamGibbons 3 74
(Michael Easterby) *chsd ldr after 1f tl over 7f out: styd handy: effrt jst over 2f out: hdwy to ld ent fnl f: styd on wl: rdn out* **5/4**[1]

-263 **2** *2* **Peeps**[11] 630 4-8-8 **60** (b) SaleemGolam 2 65
(Mark H Tompkins) *t.k.h: trckd ldr for 1f: styd handy: effrt 2f out: chsd wnr ins fnl f: kpt on but no imp* **6/1**

34-2 **3** *1½* **Scrafton**[33] 357 5-9-2 **68** GeorgeDowning(3) 4 70
(Tony Carroll) *stdd after s: hld up in tch in last: hdwy to press ldr over 7f out tl rdn to ld 2f out: hdd ent fnl f: styd on same pce after: lost 2nd ins fnl f* **9/4**[2]

-542 **4** *3½* **With Hindsight (IRE)**[21] 506 8-9-7 **70** LukeMorris 1 67
(Steve Gollings) *led: rdn wl over 2f out: hdd 2f out: no ex ent fnl f: wknd ins fnl f* **7/2**[3]

2m 46.69s (0.69) **Going Correction** -0.05s/f (Stan)
WFA 4 from 5yo+ 3lb **4 Ran SP% 111.7**
Speed ratings (Par 103): **95,93,92,90**
CSF £8.89 TOTE £2.20; EX 9.80 Trifecta £18.60.

Owner A Chandler & L Westwood **Bred** Juddmonte Farms Ltd **Trained** Sheriff Hutton, N Yorks

FOCUS
A modest handicap run at a steady early gallop. The winner has been rated to her best.

773 CORAL H'CAP 1m 2f (P)
3:40 (3:41) (Class 5) (0-70,70) 4-Y-O+ **£2,911** (£866; £432; £216) **Stalls** Low

Form RPR
06-4 **1** **Heezararity**[32] 382 8-9-4 **67**.. JimmyFortune 2 74
(Jonathan Geake) *mde all: rdn ent fnl 2f: edgd rt ins fnl f: hld on wl u.p* **6/1**[3]

5-30 **2** ½ **I'm Harry**[23] 491 7-9-6 **69**..............................(vt) PatCosgrave 3 75
(George Baker) *chsd wnr: rdn and effrt wl over 1f out: pressing wnr 1f out: stl ev ch whn carried rt and hld wl ins fnl f* **8/1**

00-1 **3** *hd* **Moonday Sun (USA)**[47] 173 7-9-7 **70**.............................. AdamKirby 5 76
(John Butler) *hld up in tch in midfield: effrt wl over 1f out: pressed ldng pair and drvn ins fnl f: kpt on u.p towards fin* **11/8**[1]

5522 **4** 1 **Cosmic Halo**[8] 672 7-9-1 **67**.................................... SammyJoBell(3) 4 71
(Richard Fahey) *stdd after s: hld up in tch in rr: clsd on inner 2f out: hdwy and switching rt over 1f out: chsng ldrs and keeping on whn squeezed for room towards fin* **9/2**[2]

-055 **5** ½ **Leonard Thomas**[13] 606 6-8-10 **62**........................ GeorgeDowning(3) 1 65
(Tony Carroll) *hld up in tch in midfield: effrt u.p to chse ldrs over 1f out: kpt on same pce ins fnl f* **7/1**

45-0 **6** 2½ **Deluxe**[13] 608 4-8-12 **61**.. ShaneKelly 6 59
(Pat Phelan) *stdd after s: hld up in tch in last pair: swtchd rt and effrt over 1f out: no imp* **12/1**

5400 **7** ½ **Jazri**[13] 606 5-8-13 **62**..(b) FrannyNorton 8 59
(Milton Bradley) *dwlt: sn rcvrd and wl in tch in midfield: rdn over 2f out: lost pl over 1f out: wl hld and one pce fnl f* **16/1**

5/0- **8** 1 **Purple 'n Gold (IRE)**[122] 4774 7-9-7 **70**.....................(p) DougieCostello 7 65
(David Pipe) *chsd ldrs: drvn 2f out: unable qck and lost pl over 1f out: wknd ins fnl f* **25/1**

2m 5.84s (-0.76) **Going Correction** -0.05s/f (Stan) **8** Ran SP% **115.6**
Speed ratings (Par 103): **101,100,100,99,99 97,96,96**
CSF £53.12 CT £102.30 TOTE £12.10: £1.20, £2.50, £1.20; EX 58.30 Trifecta £211.00.
Owner Miss E J Tanner **Bred** D J Weston **Trained** East Kennett, Wilts

FOCUS
A modest handicap dominated by the leader. The winner has been rated to his old best.

774 BRITISH STALLION STUDS/32RED EBF FILLIES' CONDITIONS STKS 1m 1y(P)
4:10 (4:11) (Class 2) 4-Y-O+ **£16,807** (£5,032; £2,516; £1,258; £629) **Stalls** High

Form RPR
14-1 **1** **Volunteer Point (IRE)**[45] 214 4-9-0 102.................. GrahamGibbons 2 90+
(Mick Channon) *t.k.h: trckd ldr: effrt wl over 1f out: rdn to ld jst ins fnl f: r.o and a doing enough after* **1/3**[1]

064- **2** ¾ **Bint Dandy (IRE)**[85] 8132 5-9-0 88.........................(p) IrineuGoncalves 5 88
(Chris Dwyer) *sn led: rdn wl over 1f out: hdd jst ins fnl f: kpt on but a hld after* **12/1**

5-64 **3** ½ **Capelita**[11] 632 5-9-0 82.. AndrewMullen 4 87
(Michael Appleby) *taken down early: stdd s: hld up in tch in rr: effrt on inner and chsd ldng pair over 1f out: swtchd rt and kpt on towards fin* **10/1**[3]

-112 **4** 1¼ **India's Song**[29] 422 6-9-0 82......................................(t) JamieSpencer 3 84
(David Simcock) *hld up in tch: wnt 3rd 5f out tl rdn and sltly outpcd over 1f out: styd on same pce ins fnl f* **7/1**[2]

2553 **5** 2¼ **Stosur (IRE)**[15] 595 5-9-0 76..(b) LukeMorris 1 79
(Gay Kelleway) *chsd ldng pair tl 5f out: 4th and drvn over 2f out: dropped to rr and carried rt over 1f out: bhd and kpt on same pce ins fnl f* **20/1**

1m 37.44s (-0.76) **Going Correction** -0.05s/f (Stan) **5** Ran SP% **109.1**
Speed ratings (Par 96): **101,100,99,98,96**
CSF £5.22 TOTE £1.40: £1.10, £3.40; EX 5.70 Trifecta £14.60.
Owner Box 41 **Bred** G Strawbridge & London Thoroughbred Services Ltd **Trained** West Ilsley, Berks

FOCUS
The winner was favoured by the conditions of the race but she was made to work for her victory. The form is set around the third, fourth and fifth.

775 UNIBET OFFER DAILY JOCKEY & TRAINER SPECIALS H'CAP 5f 6y(P)
4:40 (4:41) (Class 6) (0-65,65) 4-Y-O+ **£2,264** (£673; £336; £168) **Stalls** High

Form RPR
5-10 **1** **More Spice (IRE)**[22] 504 4-8-13 **57**........................(b[1]) JamieSpencer 3 72+
(Robert Cowell) *mde all and sn arnd 2 l clr: rdn wl over 1f out: kpt on strly: nvr seriously chal* **9/2**[3]

-543 **2** 2 **Ask The Guru**[5] 714 6-9-5 **63**......................................(v) RobertHavlin 2 71
(Michael Attwater) *chsd ldng trio but nt on terms w wnr: effrt 2f out: styd on u.p to snatch 2nd last strides: no threat to wnr* **7/2**[2]

2221 **3** *nk* **Blue Bounty**[10] 659 5-9-2 **60**.......................................(p) SaleemGolam 1 67
(Mark H Tompkins) *chsd ldng pair: effrt to chse wnr over 1f out: rdn and no imp fnl f: lost 2nd last strides* **2/1**[1]

2313 **4** ½ **Secret Millionaire (IRE)**[7] 685 9-9-4 **62**.....................(p) LukeMorris 4 67
(Shaun Harris) *off the pce in midfield: 5th and rdn ent fnl 2f: drvn over 1f out: kpt on u.p fnl 100yds: no threat to wnr* **6/1**

-150 **5** *hd* **Rocket Rob (IRE)**[18] 541 10-9-3 **61**................................ TomQueally 5 65
(Willie Musson) *short of room sn after s: off the pce in last pair: hdwy on inner over 1f out: kpt on ins fnl f: no threat to wnr* **20/1**

0-50 **6** 2¼ **Humour (IRE)**[18] 541 5-9-3 **61**.. AdamKirby 6 57
(Christine Dunnett) *off the pce in last quartet: rdn 1/2-way: kpt on but no imp fnl f: nvr trbld ldrs* **8/1**

2-50 **7** 1¾ **Picansort**[38] 319 9-9-7 **65**..(v) ShaneKelly 7 55+
(Peter Crate) *squeezed out and bdly hmpd sn after s: wl off the pce in last pair: c wd and effrt wl over 1f out: no hdwy: n.d* **14/1**

-300 **8** 1¼ **Roy's Legacy**[13] 604 7-9-2 **60**.. JFEgan 9 45
(Shaun Harris) *chsd wnr: rdn 2f out: lost pl and btn over 1f out: btn and eased fnl 100yds* **33/1**

0-60 **9** 2 **Johnny Splash (IRE)**[13] 604 7-9-2 **65**................(v) RachealKneller(5) 8 43
(Roger Teal) *short of room sn after s: a off the pce last quartet and wd: rdn wl over 1f out: no hdwy and wl hld whn swtchd bk lft ent fnl f* **25/1**

57.62s (-1.18) **Going Correction** -0.05s/f (Stan) **9** Ran SP% **117.4**
Speed ratings (Par 101): **107,103,103,102,102 98,95,93,90**
CSF £20.51 CT £41.14 TOTE £4.20: £1.10, £1.80, £1.60; EX 23.60 Trifecta £73.80.
Owner Khalifa Dasmal & Partner **Bred** K A Dasmal **Trained** Six Mile Bottom, Cambs

FOCUS
An ordinary sprint, but the time was good and it was won by a lightly raced 4yo with more to offer. Sound form, with the winner improving significantly, the runner-up dropping in class and the third and fourth in good form of late.

776 LADBROKES APPRENTICE H'CAP 1m 1y(P)
5:10 (5:10) (Class 6) (0-55,60) 4-Y-O+ **£2,264** (£673; £336; £168) **Stalls** High

Form RPR
60-1 **1** **Eastern Dragon (IRE)**[7] 681 6-10-2 **60** 6ex.............. PatrickVaughan 1 71
(Seamus Durack) *in tch: hdwy to trck ldrs 6f out: clsd on inner and rdn to ld over 1f out: r.o wl: comf* **4/5**[1]

-222 **2** 2¾ **Basingstoke (IRE)**[7] 682 7-9-5 **54**........................(p) RyanHolmes(5) 6 58
(Daniel Mark Loughnane) *led: rdn 2f out: hdd and unable qck over 1f out: styd on same pce ins fnl f* **2/1**[2]

0-60 **3** 1¼ **Candesta (USA)**[13] 609 6-9-6 **55**..............................(bt) MillyNaseb(5) 4 56
(Julia Feilden) *dwlt: in tch in rr: effrt in 4th 2f out: kpt on ins fnl f: wnt 3rd last strides: no threat to wnr* **8/1**[3]

360- **4** *nk* **Powerfulstorm**[326] 1320 4-9-8 **55**................................ MitchGodwin(3) 5 55
(Michael Appleby) *chsd ldr: rdn 2f out: 3rd and unable qck over 1f out: kpt on same pce after: lost 3rd last strides* **16/1**

-050 **5** 13 **Sixties Queen**[19] 527 6-8-10 **47** oh2..........................(p) ChrisKelly(7) 3 16
(Lisa Williamson) *in tch: pushed along 4f out: rdn and struggling in last pair 2f out: sn wknd* **50/1**

00-5 **6** 2¾ **Bickershaw**[11] 630 4-9-3 **47** oh2..............................(v[1]) RhiainIngram 2 9
(Roger Ingram) *in tch: rdn 4f out: struggling in last pair 2f out: sn wknd* **50/1**

1m 37.16s (-1.04) **Going Correction** -0.05s/f (Stan) **6** Ran SP% **109.8**
Speed ratings (Par 101): **103,100,99,98,85 82**
CSF £2.43 TOTE £1.80: £1.10, £1.20; EX 2.80 Trifecta £6.10.
Owner Miss Rosie Leena Kim Kavanagh **Bred** James Mahon **Trained** Upper Lambourn, Berkshire

FOCUS
A moderate handicap. Straightforward form.
T/Plt: £15.20 to a £1 stake. Pool: £54,288.08 - 2598.16 winning units. T/Qpdt: £5.40 to a £1 stake. Pool: £5,227.04 - 713.08 winning units. **Steve Payne**

690 KEMPTON (A.W) (R-H)
Wednesday, March 2

OFFICIAL GOING: Polytrack: standard
Weather: cold, fresh across

777 WATCH RACING UK ON 3 DEVICES H'CAP 1m (P)
5:45 (5:52) (Class 6) (0-65,67) 4-Y-O+ **£2,264** (£673; £336; £168) **Stalls** Low

Form RPR
6-33 **1** **Gavarnie Encore**[14] 609 4-8-7 **51**................................ AndrewMullen 6 61
(Michael Blanshard) *chsd ldrs: rdn on inner over 1f out: sn led: kpt on wl* **8/1**

60-0 **2** 2¾ **Pike Corner Cross (IRE)**[14] 607 4-9-4 **62**.................. GeorgeBaker 1 65
(Gary Moore) *hld up in rr: stl in rr whn rdn over 1f out: gd hdwy ins fnl f to take 2nd: nvr nrr* **9/1**

4-41 **3** ½ **Tommys Geal**[12] 631 4-8-13 **60**................................ DanielMuscutt(3) 3 62
(Michael Madgwick) *hld up in mid-div: cl up 2f out: rdn and kpt on over 1f out* **9/1**

0-06 **4** 1 **Embankment**[21] 518 7-9-7 **65**.. RobertHavlin 9 65
(Michael Attwater) *missed break and in rr: clsr over 3f out: kpt on ins fnl f: nvr nrr* **6/1**[2]

6-31 **5** ½ **Mr Christopher (IRE)**[8] 682 4-9-4 **67** 6ex..............(p) AnnaHesketh(5) 5 66
(Tom Dascombe) *hld up in rr: n.m.r over 2f out: swtchd to inner and kpt on under hands and heels* **4/1**[1]

6-24 **6** ½ **Pyla (IRE)**[13] 621 4-9-7 **65**......................................(p) LemosdeSouza 11 62
(Denis Quinn) *racd in mid-div: effrt over 1f out: hdwy and sltly snatched up: fdd* **8/1**

44-0 **7** 1½ **Alketios (GR)**[56] 64 5-9-2 **65**................................ HectorCrouch(5) 10 59
(Gary Moore) *chsd ldrs: led briefly over 1f out: sn rdn and wknd* **16/1**

-042 **8** ¾ **Ajig**[14] 607 5-9-2 **65**..(tp) EdwardGreatrex(5) 7 57
(Eve Johnson Houghton) *chsd ldrs: rdn over 1f out: no ex* **13/2**[3]

0-00 **9** *nk* **Youm Jamil (USA)**[13] 621 9-8-5 **56**............................ GeorgiaCox(7) 2 47
(Tony Carroll) *in rr: sme hdwy fr 2f out* **20/1**

0254 **10** *nk* **Blackthorn Stick (IRE)**[14] 608 7-9-1 **59**..................(p) JimmyQuinn 13 50
(Paul Burgoyne) *hld up in rr: nvr involved* **16/1**

-101 **10** *dht* **Bookmaker**[14] 608 6-9-6 **64**.......................................(b) WilliamCarson 4 55
(John Bridger) *led for 6f tl hdd: rdn over 1f out: wknd* **13/2**[3]

550- **12** *nk* **Lucky Leyf**[177] 6169 4-9-2 **60**.. ShaneKelly 12 50
(Philip Hide) *prom: led 6f: rdn and hdd over 1f out: wknd* **50/1**

1m 40.1s (0.30) **Going Correction** +0.025s/f (Slow) **12** Ran SP% **121.7**
Speed ratings (Par 101): **99,96,95,94,94 93,92,91,91,90 90,90**
CSF £80.30 CT £684.81 TOTE £7.90: £2.80, £3.40, £3.00; EX 95.30 Trifecta £987.20.
Owner Hill, Price & Blanshard **Bred** Shinko Foods International Ltd **Trained** Upper Lambourn, Berks

FOCUS
The track had been cultivated to a depth of 100mm, compressed and returned to standard. A modest handicap. The winner has been rated near his best.

778 32RED ON THE APP STORE MAIDEN STKS 1m (P)
6:15 (6:17) (Class 5) 3-Y-O+ **£2,911** (£866; £432; £216) **Stalls** Low

Form RPR
1 **Burcan (FR)** 4-10-0 0.. LukeMorris 4 83
(Jeremy Noseda) *hld up in rr: pushed along 2f out: str run ins fnl f to ld post* **7/2**[2]

020- **2** *shd* **California Lad**[235] 4130 3-8-10 71.................................. JimCrowley 5 76
(Harry Dunlop) *racd in mid-div: gng wl over 1f out: rdn 1f out: led 55yds out: hdd post* **7/2**[2]

00- **3** 1½ **River Thames**[252] 3518 3-8-10 0...................................... JoeFanning 2 72
(Mark Johnston) *sn led: rdn over 1f out: hdd fnl 55yds: wkng nr fin* **7/2**[2]

0-4 **4** 2¼ **Daring Knight**[18] 557 3-8-7 0.................................... TimClark(3) 8 67
(Martin Smith) *chsd ldr: pushed along 4f out: rdn 2f out: kpt on same pce fr over 1f out* **7/1**[3]

62-4 **5** 2 **Fire And Passion**[56] 65 4-10-0 70.............................. GeorgeBaker 3 68
(Jeremy Gask) *chsd ldrs: rdn over 1f out: wknd* **11/4**[1]

0-0 **6** 8 **Stonecoldsoba**[44] 245 3-8-10 0...................................... ShaneKelly 1 43
(Paul Morgan) *mid-div: rdn 2f out: wknd ins fnl f* **66/1**

0 **7** 5 **Secret Shot**[19] 544 4-9-11 0................................ GeorgeDowning(3) 7 37
(David Dennis) *a bhd* **66/1**

8 10 **Flashy King (IRE)** 3-8-3 0 SeanMooney(7) 6 7
(Joseph Tuite) *a in rr* **33/1**
1m 39.36s (-0.44) **Going Correction** +0.025s/f (Slow)
WFA 3 from 4yo 18lb **8** Ran SP% **111.8**
Speed ratings (Par 103): **103,102,101,99,97 89,84,74**
CSF £15.33 TOTE £4.40: £1.50, £1.10, £2.10; EX 14.60 Trifecta £73.20.
Owner Raed El Youssef **Bred** S F Bloodstock LLC **Trained** Newmarket, Suffolk

FOCUS
There was a tight finish to this modest maiden. It's been rated around the second, third and fourth.

779 £10 FREE BET AT 32REDSPORT.COM H'CAP (LONDON MIDDLE DISTANCE SERIES QUALIFIER) 1m 3f (P)
6:45 (6:45) (Class 4) (0-85,84) 4-Y-O+ **£4,690** (£1,395; £697; £348) **Stalls** Low

Form RPR
361- **1** **Two Jabs**[40] 7893 6-9-5 **82** AndrewMullen 2 90
(Michael Appleby) *led: rdn and hdd 2f out: battled bk in sustained duel w runner-up ins fnl f: jst got bk up* **9/2**[2]
14/3 **2** *nse* **Music Man (IRE)**[56] 66 6-9-0 **77** SeanLevey 5 85
(Jo Crowley) *mid-div: clsr over 2f out: rdn and led 2f out: kpt on wl in sustained duel w wnr: hdd post* **10/3**[1]
123- **3** *1 1/4* **Quality Song (USA)**[79] 8223 4-8-10 **74** ShaneKelly 4 80+
(Richard Hughes) *in rr: swtchd to inner and rdn over 2f out: kpt on wl ins fnl f wout matching front pair* **13/2**
-143 **4** *nk* **Charlies Mate**[6] 712 5-9-1 **78** KierenFox 1 83
(John Best) *chsd ldrs: rdn 2f out: kpt on* **6/1**[3]
-615 **5** *4* **Alshan Fajer**[18] 556 6-8-12 **78** AlistairRawlinson(3) 6 76
(J R Jenkins) *chsd ldrs: rdn over 2f out: one pce* **16/1**
1-11 **6** *hd* **Buckland Beau**[14] 605 5-9-4 **81** GeorgeBaker 3 79
(Charlie Fellowes) *hld up in rr: nt clr run 3f out: rdn over 1f out: kpt on same pce* **9/2**[2]
43-0 **7** *1 1/2* **Peterhouse (USA)**[26] 465 4-9-3 **81** RobertHavlin 11 76
(Jason Ward) *racd in mid-div: rdn over 2f out: no ex and wknd* **33/1**
1- **8** *2 1/4* **Closer To Home (IRE)**[14] 5652 4-9-6 **84** (b) AdamKirby 7 75
(David Pipe) *in rr: nvr involved* **25/1**
4-23 **9** *1 1/4* **Gaelic Silver (FR)**[18] 556 10-9-2 **84** (p) HectorCrouch(5) 10 73
(Gary Moore) *hld up in rr: t.k.h and sme prog on outer over 3f out: sn rdn and wknd* **20/1**
40-5 **10** *5* **Stencive**[44] 244 7-9-7 **84** LukeMorris 9 65
(Charlie Wallis) *a bhd* **10/1**
2m 19.47s (-2.43) **Going Correction** +0.025s/f (Slow)
WFA 4 from 5yo+ 1lb **10** Ran SP% **113.6**
Speed ratings (Par 105): **109,108,108,107,104 104,103,102,101,97**
CSF £18.80 CT £95.57 TOTE £6.40: £2.10, £1.40, £2.70; EX 24.70 Trifecta £122.00.
Owner The Horse Watchers **Bred** Paramount Bloodstock **Trained** Oakham, Rutland
■ Stewards' Enquiry : Andrew Mullen two-day ban: used whip above permitted level (Mar 16-17)

FOCUS
A fair handicap, and a good finish. The winner has been rated to his best.

780 32RED/EBF STALLIONS BREEDING FILLIES' H'CAP 7f (P)
7:15 (7:15) (Class 3) (0-95,93) 4-Y-O+
£10,271 (£3,075; £1,537; £768; £384; £193) **Stalls** Low

Form RPR
236- **1** **Three Gracez**[24] 4-8-5 **82** PaddyPilley(5) 3 89
(C Gourdain, France) *cl up: pushed along 2f out: r.o wl on outer ins fnl f: led post* **9/1**
04-3 **2** *nse* **Mystical Sapphire**[28] 433 6-8-4 **76** JoeFanning 2 83
(Jo Crowley) *chsd ldrs: gng wl 3f out: rdn and led over 1f out: kpt on and hdd post* **2/1**[1]
3-30 **3** *1* **Elis Eliz (IRE)**[20] 529 4-9-1 **87** AdamKirby 4 91
(Michael Wigham) *led: hdd over 1f out: kpt on* **8/1**
5343 **4** *nk* **Be Royale**[18] 564 6-7-9 **74** oh1 RPWalsh(7) 1 77
(Michael Appleby) *awkward s: in rr and t.k.h: swtchd to ins over 1f out: rdn and one pce ins fnl f* **10/1**
11-2 **5** *hd* **Russian Radiance**[35] 351 4-8-11 **83** LukeMorris 5 85
(Jonathan Portman) *in rr: rdn over 2f out: kpt on* **5/2**[2]
4415 **6** *1/2* **Subtle Knife**[12] 632 7-8-10 **82** WilliamCarson 8 83
(Giles Bravery) *in rr: rdn over 2f out: one pce* **16/1**
0-06 **7** *2* **Primrose Valley**[11] 657 4-9-7 **93** (p) GeorgeBaker 6 89
(Ed Vaughan) *chsd ldr: rdn and wknd qckly ins fnl f* **7/1**[3]
1m 28.04s (2.04) **Going Correction** +0.025s/f (Slow) **7** Ran SP% **110.5**
Speed ratings (Par 104): **89,88,87,87,87 86,84**
CSF £25.60 CT £143.24 TOTE £8.90: £3.70, £1.60; EX 43.20 Trifecta £332.10.
Owner Neil Hormann **Bred** Barton Stud **Trained** France
■ A winner with his first runner in Britain for French-based Charles Gourdain.

FOCUS
The early pace wasn't strong and it turned into a bit of a dash from 2f out. It's been rated around the runner-up and third.

781 32RED CASINO H'CAP 1m 4f (P)
7:45 (7:45) (Class 6) (0-65,62) 4-Y-O+ **£2,264** (£673; £336; £168) **Stalls** Centre

Form RPR
0-33 **1** **Rose Above**[25] 487 4-9-5 **62** JimCrowley 6 73
(Andrew Balding) *chsd ldr: rdn and led 2f out: readily drew clr ins fnl f* **9/2**[3]
0-04 **2** *6* **Golden Thread**[12] 637 6-9-6 **61** CharlesBishop 4 62
(Neil King) *mid-div: rdn over 2f out: kpt on ins fnl f: no ch w easy wnr* **4/1**[2]
0352 **3** *1 1/4* **Innoko (FR)**[8] 684 6-9-5 **60** WilliamCarson 5 59
(Tony Carroll) *hld up in rr: mod prog fr over 1f out* **2/1**[1]
-424 **4** *3* **Fair Comment**[14] 606 6-9-7 **62** RobertHavlin 3 57
(Michael Blanshard) *led: hdd 2f out: wknd ins fnl f* **9/2**[3]
05-6 **5** *3 1/2* **Vivo Per Lei (IRE)**[12] 631 4-8-9 **52** JimmyQuinn 1 41
(Dr Jon Scargill) *mid-div: rdn and wknd fr 2f out* **25/1**
330/ **6** *6* **Castlemorris King**[512] 7016 8-9-7 **62** LukeMorris 8 41
(Brian Barr) *mid-div: rdn 3f out: sn hld and wknd* **10/1**
0435 **7** *7* **Shirataki (IRE)**[11] 653 8-8-10 **54** TimClark(3) 2 22
(Peter Hiatt) *dropped in rr: rdn 2f out: nvr involved* **8/1**
2m 34.64s (0.14) **Going Correction** +0.025s/f (Slow)
WFA 4 from 6yo+ 2lb **7** Ran SP% **113.7**
Speed ratings (Par 101): **100,96,95,93,90 86,82**
CSF £22.47 CT £46.04 TOTE £5.70: £1.70, £2.90; EX 31.00 Trifecta £105.00.
Owner Sir Roger Buckley, Gerald Oury **Bred** Sir R J Buckley & G Oury **Trained** Kingsclere, Hants

FOCUS
An ordinary handicap, but it was run at a solid pace and the winner showed improved form. A step up from the winner.

782 32RED.COM H'CAP 6f (P)
8:15 (8:15) (Class 5) (0-75,75) 4-Y-O+ **£2,911** (£866; £432; £216) **Stalls** Low

Form RPR
11- **1** **The Big Lad**[93] 8051 4-9-6 **74** ShaneKelly 10 85+
(Richard Hughes) *c across fr wd draw and hmpd two rivals: t.k.h in mid-div: hanging on bnds: gng wl over 1f out: rdn to chse ldr ins fnl f: pushed out to ld cl home: progive* **11/8**[1]
0-33 **2** *3/4* **Quintus Cerialis (IRE)**[18] 561 4-9-6 **74** (p) AdamKirby 12 82
(Clive Cox) *chsd ldrs: rdn and led 2f out: kpt on wl: hd cl home* **8/1**[3]
-233 **3** *2 3/4* **Chelwood Gate (IRE)**[12] 629 6-9-6 **74** (v) GeorgeBaker 5 73+
(Patrick Chamings) *hld up wl in rr: pushed along and gd prog ins fnl f: nvr nrr* **4/1**[2]
2-22 **4** *hd* **Head Space (IRE)**[30] 416 8-9-5 **73** LukeMorris 6 72+
(Brian Barr) *hmpd sn after s and in rr: clsr 2f out: rdn over 1f and kpt on* **11/1**
143- **5** *nse* **Major Valentine**[156] 6807 4-8-13 **72** CiaranMckee(5) 3 70
(John O'Shea) *mid-div: rdn 3f out: kpt on* **14/1**
054- **6** *1/2* **Honcho (IRE)**[124] 7595 4-9-1 **74** LucyKBarry(5) 2 71
(John Ryan) *chsd ldr: rdn 2f out: no ex* **33/1**
4-64 **7** *1/2* **Brazen Spirit**[30] 416 4-9-3 **74** (v) RyanTate(3) 8 69
(Clive Cox) *hmpd s and in rr: rdn 2f out: one pce over 1f out* **10/1**
12-5 **8** *2 3/4* **Spinning Cobblers**[59] 28 5-9-0 **68** (v) SaleemGolam 4 54
(Stuart Williams) *in rr: checked in run over 3f out: nvr involved* **11/1**
-265 **9** *1/2* **Saint Pois (FR)**[27] 439 5-9-1 **72** GeorgeDowning(3) 1 57
(Tony Carroll) *chsd ldrs: ev ch over 1f out: wknd qckly ins fnl f* **12/1**
-260 **10** *3* **Desert Strike**[11] 655 10-9-7 **75** (p) JimCrowley 9 50
(Conor Dore) *led: rdn and hdd 2f out: wknd qckly ins fnl f* **16/1**
1m 12.67s (-0.43) **Going Correction** +0.025s/f (Slow) **10** Ran SP% **122.2**
Speed ratings (Par 103): **103,102,98,98,98 97,96,93,92,88**
CSF £14.08 CT £40.42 TOTE £2.50: £1.60, £2.50, £1.40; EX 15.20 Trifecta £69.80.
Owner Don Churston & Ray Greatorex **Bred** Lookout Partnership **Trained** Upper Lambourn, Berkshire
■ Stewards' Enquiry : Shane Kelly six-day ban: careless riding (Mar 16-19,22-23)

FOCUS
A bit of a messy race but the winner impressed once again.

783 RACINGUK.COM/ANYWHERE H'CAP 6f (P)
8:45 (8:45) (Class 6) (0-65,63) 3-Y-O **£2,264** (£673; £336; £168) **Stalls** Low

Form RPR
0-01 **1** **Teversham**[27] 443 3-9-5 **61** IrineuGoncalves 1 66+
(Chris Dwyer) *hld up in rr: nt clr run and swtchd to outer over 2f out: rdn over 1f out: led ins fnl f* **6/1**[3]
-524 **2** *1* **Bahamian Sunshine**[5] 726 3-9-0 **63** (p) AdamMcNamara(7) 6 65
(Richard Fahey) *led: rdn and hdd 2f out: kpt on again ins fnl f to take 2nd nr fin* **11/2**[2]
430- **3** *nk* **Naziba (IRE)**[176] 6189 3-8-13 **62** MitchGodwin(7) 7 63
(David Menuisier) *in rr: rdn and clsr on inner over 1f out: kpt on* **20/1**
1 **4** *nk* **Justice Lady (IRE)**[26] 460 3-8-13 **62** AdamMcLean(7) 4 62+
(David Elsworth) *hld up in rr: tk fierce hold and sn pressed ldr: led 2f out: hdd ins fnl f and wknd out of contention* **11/10**[1]
000- **5** *2 1/4* **Arizona Sunrise**[96] 8010 3-9-1 **62** AaronJones(5) 2 55
(David Brown) *in rr: prog past btn horse ins fnl f* **20/1**
40-6 **6** *nk* **Matilda Gleam**[54] 104 3-9-3 **59** LemosdeSouza 3 52
(Lisa Williamson) *chsd ldrs in mid-div: t.k.h: effrt 2f out: sn wknd* **16/1**
4-35 **7** *3 1/2* **Lady McGuffy (IRE)**[23] 502 3-9-1 **57** LukeMorris 9 39
(Brian Barr) *chsd ldrs: rdn 3f out: wknd fr 2f out* **14/1**
120- **8** *7* **Tahiti One**[143] 7142 3-9-5 **61** AdamKirby 8 22
(Tony Carroll) *in rr: rn wd bnd: sn bhd* **6/1**[3]
1m 13.53s (0.43) **Going Correction** +0.025s/f (Slow) **8** Ran SP% **113.6**
Speed ratings (Par 96): **98,96,96,95,92 92,87,78**
CSF £38.24 CT £620.45 TOTE £8.70: £2.60, £2.30, £5.80; EX 46.60 Trifecta £355.70.
Owner Strawberry Fields Stud **Bred** G & J Equestrian Of Newmarket **Trained** Newmarket, Suffolk

FOCUS
The early gallop wasn't strong and plenty of these took a real tug. The runner-up and those close up suggest this is a sensible level.
T/Plt: £129.50 to a £1 stake. Pool: £77,589.18 - 437.22 winning tickets. T/Qpdt: £15.60 to a £1 stake. Pool: £9,127.37 - 430.50 winning tickets. **Cathal Gahan**

763 WOLVERHAMPTON (A.W) (L-H)
Wednesday, March 2

OFFICIAL GOING: Tapeta: standard
Wind: Strong across Weather: Showers

784 DOWNLOAD THE NEW UNIBET RACING APP H'CAP 5f 20y (Tp)
2:20 (2:20) (Class 5) (0-70,74) 4-Y-O+ **£3,234** (£962; £481; £240) **Stalls** Low

Form RPR
0-61 **1** **Point North (IRE)**[19] 541 9-9-7 **69** (b) DanielTudhope 5 79+
(John Balding) *hld up: hdwy over 1f out: rdn to ld ins fnl f: r.o* **4/1**[2]
-201 **2** *1 1/2* **Bush Warrior (IRE)**[9] 671 5-9-12 **74** 6ex (v) JoeFanning 8 78
(Anabel K Murphy) *hld up: pushed along 1/2-way: hdwy over 1f out: r.o to go 2nd wl ins fnl f* **7/1**
0351 **3** *1/2* **Elusivity (IRE)**[17] 579 8-9-5 **67** (p) PaulMulrennan 7 69
(Conor Dore) *chsd ldrs: rdn 1/2-way: styd on* **8/1**
00-3 **4** *nse* **Viva Verglas (IRE)**[21] 520 5-9-5 **67** [1] LukeMorris 3 69
(Daniel Mark Loughnane) *a.p: rdn 1/2-way: styd on u.p* **5/2**[1]
-000 **5** *3/4* **Pearl Noir**[2] 764 6-8-13 **64** (b) TimClark(3) 4 63
(Scott Dixon) *s.i.s: hdwy over 3f out: rdn over 1f out: ev ch ins fnl f: styd on same pce* **22/1**
504- **6** *1 1/2* **Orient Class**[214] 4867 5-9-7 **69** GrahamLee 6 63
(Paul Midgley) *hld up: shkn up and nt clr run over 1f out: nvr on terms* **9/1**
6-54 **7** *hd* **Thataboy (IRE)**[26] 462 5-9-7 **69** RichardKingscote 1 62
(Tom Dascombe) *sn led: rdn over 1f out: hdd and no ex ins fnl f* **9/2**[3]
503- **8** *10* **Lydiate Lady**[140] 7224 4-8-13 **61** JFEgan 2 18
(Paul Green) *chsd ldr: rdn 1/2-way: wknd and eased fnl f* **16/1**
1m 0.5s (-1.40) **Going Correction** +0.075s/f (Slow) **8** Ran SP% **110.6**
Speed ratings (Par 103): **114,111,110,110,109 107,106,90**
CSF £29.68 CT £200.36 TOTE £3.90: £1.50, £2.10, £2.80; EX 18.90 Trifecta £117.10.
Owner Billy Herring **Bred** Barronstown Stud **Trained** Scrooby, S Yorks

FOCUS
A modest sprint handicap run at a true gallop. The third has been rated close to his recent form.

785 32RED CASINO H'CAP 7f 32y (Tp)
2:55 (2:57) (Class 6) (0-60,60) 3-Y-O **£2,587** (£770; £384; £192) **Stalls** High

Form RPR
0-40 **1** **Sunbaked (IRE)**[14] 610 3-9-7 **60**..............................(p) RobertWinston 3 64
(Eve Johnson Houghton) *a.p: nt clr run and swtchd rt over 1f out: rdn to ld wl ins fnl f: r.o* **15/2**
0-21 **2** *1* **Israfel**[37] 328 3-9-0 **53**...................................... CathyGannon 7 57
(Jamie Osborne) *chsd ldrs: nt clr run and hmpd over 1f out: swtchd lft ins fnl f: r.o to go 2nd towards fin* **11/2**[3]
60-3 **3** *1/2* **Albert Boy (IRE)**[9] 678 3-9-7 **60**...................................... BenCurtis 2 61
(Scott Dixon) *chsd ldrs: rdn over 1f out: styd on same pce ins fnl f* **7/2**[2]
5-53 **4** *shd* **Tombe Girl**[15] 597 3-9-4 **57**...................................... GrahamLee 6 58
(Keith Dalgleish) *led: rdn and edgd rt over 1f out: hdd and unable qck wl ins fnl f* **3/1**[1]
-043 **5** *6* **Ashford Island**[28] 436 3-8-8 **47**..............................(p) TedDurcan 10 33+
(Mike Murphy) *s.i.s: hld up: r.o ins fnl f: nvr nrr* **8/1**
50-5 **6** *1/2* **Porcupine Creek (IRE)**[28] 432 3-9-2 **55**................. GrahamGibbons 9 42
(Daniel Mark Loughnane) *chsd ldr: rdn and hmpd over 1f out: wknd ins fnl f* **10/1**
00-0 **7** *2 1/4* **Rip Van Suzy (IRE)**[54] 102 3-9-3 **59**........................ PhilipPrince(3) 5 46+
(David Evans) *in rr and pushed along at various stages: nt clr run over 2f out: nvr on terms* **7/2**[2]
000- **8** *2* **Teepee Time**[155] 6825 3-8-11 **50**...................................... TomEaves 8 24
(Brian Baugh) *mid-div: drvn along over 2f out: wknd over 1f out* **150/1**
00-0 **9** *hd* **Trulove**[54] 102 3-8-4 **46** oh1...................................... TimClark(3) 12 20+
(John David Riches) *s.i.s: hld up: plld hrd: rdn over 2f out: wknd over 1f out* **66/1**
66-5 **10** *1 3/4* **Ressurreto (IRE)**[16] 593 3-9-4 **57**............................... PJMcDonald 11 26+
(Keith Dalgleish) *s.i.s: a in rr* **50/1**
0-05 **11** *10* **Autre Princess (IRE)**[19] 544 3-8-7 **46** oh1.......................... NeilFarley 1
(Eric Alston) *mid-div: rdn 1/2-way: wknd 2f out* **100/1**

1m 29.18s (0.38) **Going Correction** +0.075s/f (Slow) **11** Ran SP% **121.9**
Speed ratings (Par 96): **100,98,98,98,91 90,88,85,85,83 72**
CSF £50.29 CT £174.49 TOTE £9.70: £2.80, £1.90, £1.50; EX 53.90 Trifecta £179.90.
Owner Miss E Johnson Houghton **Bred** Tally-Ho Stud **Trained** Blewbury, Oxon

FOCUS
A moderate 3yo handicap containing just one previous winner. Few ever got into this and it was also quite a rough race up the home straight.

786 32RED.COM H'CAP 2m 119y (Tp)
3:30 (3:30) (Class 5) (0-75,74) 4-Y-O+ **£3,234** (£962; £481; £240) **Stalls** Low

Form RPR
-650 **1** **Next Edition (IRE)**[5] 731 8-8-5 **60**.............................. PhilDennis(7) 9 67
(Philip Kirby) *hld up: hdwy over 1f out: edgd lft and r.o to ld wl ins fnl f* **14/1**
34-1 **2** *1 3/4* **Consortium (IRE)**[12] 637 4-9-1 **68**..............................(p) LiamJones 10 73
(Neil King) *plld hrd and prom: rdn over 2f out: led 1f out: edgd lft and hdd wl ins fnl f* **9/4**[1]
04-5 **3** *1 3/4* **Tidal Way (IRE)**[47] 199 7-8-11 **64**.......................(p) CallumShepherd(5) 4 67
(Shaun Lycett) *chsd ldr tl led wl over 1f out: rdn: edgd rt and hdd 1f out: styng on same pce whn hung lft ins fnl f* **5/1**[3]
/00- **4** *nk* **Hyperlink (IRE)**[136] 7307 7-9-2 **64**.............................. CharlesBishop 2 66
(Heather Dalton) *chsd ldrs: rdn over 1f out: styd on same pce ins fnl f* **33/1**
20-3 **5** *nk* **Hallstatt (IRE)**[33] 386 10-9-7 **69**..............................(t) PaulMulrennan 3 71
(John Mackie) *hld up: nt clr run over 2f out: rdn over 1f out: styd on: nt trble ldrs* **12/1**
2135 **6** *1 1/2* **Pinotage**[12] 637 8-8-13 **61**..............................(p) JamesSullivan 8 61
(Peter Niven) *hld up: rdn over 2f out: hdwy over 1f out: edgd lft and no ex ins fnl f* **5/1**[3]
2-11 **7** *nk* **Edgar (GER)**[29] 425 6-9-9 **71**..............................(p) DougieCostello 6 71
(David Bridgwater) *led at stdy pce tl qcknd over 3f out: rdn and hdd wl over 1f out: no ex ins fnl f* **5/2**[2]
5/0- **8** *1* **Storm Hawk (IRE)**[400] 298 9-8-4 **59**...................(be) SophieKilloran(7) 5 58
(Emma Owen) *hld up: plld hrd: rdn over 1f out: wknd ins fnl f* **25/1**

3m 48.01s (4.31) **Going Correction** +0.075s/f (Slow)
WFA 4 from 6yo+ 5lb **8** Ran SP% **113.8**
Speed ratings (Par 103): **92,91,90,90,90 89,89,88**
CSF £45.43 CT £184.70 TOTE £18.80: £3.50, £1.10, £2.00; EX 59.70 Trifecta £322.30.
Owner The Dibble Bridge Partnership **Bred** Manister House Stud **Trained** East Appleton, N Yorks

FOCUS
An ordinary staying handicap and having dawdled on the first circuit, the eight runners were still within a couple of lengths of each other passing the furlong pole. The form may not be that reliable as a result. A minor step up from the winner, with the runner-up rated similar to his win last time out.

787 BET NOW WITH THE LADBROKES APP H'CAP 1m 141y (Tp)
4:05 (4:05) (Class 7) (0-50,50) 4-Y-O+ **£2,587** (£770; £384; £192) **Stalls** Low

Form RPR
3-66 **1** **Miss Buckaroo (IRE)**[21] 525 4-9-5 **48**........................... TomEaves 13 54
(James Given) *chsd ldrs: rdn over 2f out: hung lft ins fnl f: r.o to ld post* **25/1**
-305 **2** *shd* **Foylesideview (IRE)**[14] 609 4-9-6 **49**........................... CathyGannon 2 55
(Harry Chisman) *hld up: hdwy over 1f out: r.o* **9/4**[1]
5465 **3** *nse* **Je T'Aime Encore**[21] 526 4-9-5 **48**.......................(b[1]) AdamBeschizza 9 54
(Gay Kelleway) *chsd ldrs: led over 1f out: rdn ins fnl f: hdd post* **10/1**
000- **4** *1/2* **Anneani (IRE)**[110] 7838 4-9-7 **50**...................................... JFEgan 11 55
(Paul Green) *hld up: rdn over 2f out: hdwy over 1f out: edgd lft ins fnl f: r.o* **14/1**
6-04 **5** *nk* **John Potts**[18] 563 11-9-2 **45**..............................(p) TonyHamilton 7 49
(Brian Baugh) *hld up in tch: rdn over 1f out: r.o* **7/1**[3]
5030 **6** *1 1/2* **Actonetaketwo**[18] 563 6-9-4 **50**........................... PhilipPrince(3) 3 51
(Ron Hodges) *hld up: rdn over 1f out: r.o ins fnl f: nvr nrr* **12/1**
5321 **7** *3/4* **Lutine Charlie (IRE)**[7] 690 9-8-13 **49**...................(p) SophieKilloran(7) 5 48
(Emma Owen) *prom: rdn over 2f out: no ex ins fnl f* **4/1**[2]
6/36 **8** *1/2* **Rutterkin (USA)**[20] 528 8-8-11 **45**..................(b[1]) CallumShepherd(5) 12 43
(John David Riches) *s.i.s: hld up: rdn over 1f out: r.o ins fnl f: nvr nrr* **25/1**
0-00 **9** *1/2* **Rectitude**[14] 609 5-8-13 **45**.. EoinWalsh(3) 6 42
(Henry Tett) *hld up: rdn over 2f out: hdwy and hung lft fr over 1f out: nvr trbld ldrs* **50/1**
000 **10** *2* **Regent's Rock**[12] 639 4-9-7 **50**.. GrahamLee 4 43
(Peter Niven) *chsd ldr: rdn and ev ch over 1f out: wknd ins fnl f* **9/1**
060- **11** *2 1/4* **Farrah's Choice**[110] 7838 4-9-5 **48**.............................. TimmyMurphy 1 36
(James Grassick) *led: shkn up over 2f out: hdd over 1f out: wknd fnl f* **100/1**
0455 **12** *7* **Molly Approve (IRE)**[19] 547 4-9-6 **49**....................(v[1]) DougieCostello 8 21
(Tony Coyle) *hld up: hdwy over 5f out: wknd 2f out* **14/1**

1m 49.88s (-0.22) **Going Correction** +0.075s/f (Slow) **12** Ran SP% **114.0**
Speed ratings (Par 97): **103,102,102,102,102 100,100,99,99,97 95,89**
CSF £76.65 CT £633.25 TOTE £18.70: £6.30, £1.20, £2.10; EX 132.90 Trifecta £1555.40.
Owner Buckhurst Chevaliers **Bred** P Kavanagh & P O'Donovan **Trained** Willoughton, Lincs

FOCUS
This 45-50 handicap is about as low as it gets, though a thrilling finish with barely a length covering the first five. Those close up set the level.

788 LADBROKES H'CAP 1m 141y (Tp)
4:40 (4:41) (Class 4) (0-85,85) 4-Y-O+ **£5,175** (£1,540; £769; £384) **Stalls** Low

Form RPR
1-06 **1** **Jack Of Diamonds (IRE)**[16] 594 7-9-2 **85**......... CallumShepherd(5) 10 93
(Roger Teal) *hld up: hdwy 5f out: chsd ldr over 1f out: shkn up to ld ins fnl f: edgd lft: r.o* **7/2**[2]
46-4 **2** *3/4* **Bognor (USA)**[17] 581 5-9-1 **79**.. TomEaves 3 85
(Michael Appleby) *chsd ldr tl led over 2f out: rdn over 1f out: hdd ins fnl f: styd on* **14/1**
313- **3** *nk* **Beautiful Stranger (IRE)**[266] 3028 5-8-7 **71**................(p) PJMcDonald 8 76
(Keith Dalgleish) *hld up: hdwy over 1f out: sn rdn: r.o* **11/2**[3]
0163 **4** *nk* **Depth Charge (IRE)**[19] 546 4-8-7 **71**............................(vt) ShaneGray 9 75+
(Kristin Stubbs) *hld up: swtchd rt over 1f out: r.o wl ins fnl f: nt rch ldrs* **8/1**
-301 **5** *shd* **Idol Deputy (FR)**[16] 595 10-8-9 **78**.......................(p) RachealKneller(5) 4 82
(James Bennett) *prom: swtchd lft and shkn up ins fnl f: styd on* **6/1**
4-31 **6** *1 1/2* **Southern Storm (IRE)**[30] 413 4-8-8 **77**................ PatrickO'Donnell(5) 2 78
(Ralph Beckett) *chsd ldrs: rdn over 1f out: no ex wl ins fnl f* **5/2**[1]
006- **7** *3 1/4* **Auspicion**[134] 7363 4-9-1 **79**... JamesSullivan 5 72
(Tom Tate) *hld up in tch: plld hrd: lost pl 4f out: n.d after* **20/1**
0-06 **8** *hd* **Dana's Present**[16] 595 7-8-9 **73**.. LiamJones 1 66
(Tom Dascombe) *dwlt: hld up: plld hrd: nvr on terms* **12/1**
112- **9** *1 1/4* **Pick A Little**[210] 5001 8-9-1 **79**.. TimmyMurphy 7 69
(Michael Blake) *led: rdn and hdd over 2f out: wknd fnl f* **33/1**
-00 **10** *2 3/4* **Rail Dancer**[13] 620 4-8-11 **75**...................................... AdamBeschizza 11 59
(Richard Rowe) *s.i.s: hld up: nvr on terms* **150/1**

1m 51.37s (1.27) **Going Correction** +0.075s/f (Slow) **10** Ran SP% **114.3**
Speed ratings (Par 105): **97,96,96,95,95 94,91,91,90,87**
CSF £49.15 CT £268.63 TOTE £3.60: £1.20, £3.80, £2.00; EX 51.00 Trifecta £395.90.
Owner Inside Track Racing Club **Bred** Gigginstown House Stud **Trained** Great Shefford, Berks

FOCUS
A fair handicap and a fine ride from the winning jockey. The decent early pace slowed right down before halfway. The runner-up has been rated close to his Southwell form.

789 BEST ODDS GUARANTEED AT CORAL MEDIAN AUCTION MAIDEN STKS 1m 4f 50y (Tp)
5:15 (5:15) (Class 5) 3-5-Y-O **£3,234** (£962; £481; £240) **Stalls** Low

Form RPR
33 **1** **Project Bluebook (FR)**[26] 458 3-8-8 0 ow2..................... IanBrennan 6 68+
(John Quinn) *a.p: rdn to chse ldr over 1f out: r.o to ld wl ins fnl f* **5/6**[1]
66-3 **2** *nk* **Competent**[35] 342 4-9-12 68...................................... GrahamGibbons 1 70
(Kristin Stubbs) *led: rdn over 2f out: hdd wl ins fnl f* **5/1**[2]
3 *1 1/2* **Wishing Well**[25] 7451 4-9-7 64.. PJMcDonald 8 63
(Micky Hammond) *hld up: hdwy over 1f out: sn rdn: r.o* **20/1**
6 **4** *1 3/4* **Tudor Icon**[13] 618 3-8-5 0... AdamBeschizza 2 62
(Rae Guest) *hld up: hdwy over 4f out: rdn and edgd lft ins fnl f: styd on same pce* **16/1**
5 *1* **Cosmic Tigress**[96] 5-9-9 0... KeaganLatham 3 59+
(John Quinn) *hld up: hdwy over 1f out: nt clr run ins fnl f: nt rch ldrs* **11/2**[3]
626 **6** *1* **Our Little Sister (IRE)**[16] 591 3-8-0 67.......................... CamHardie 10 54
(Hughie Morrison) *chsd ldr tl rdn over 1f out: hung lft and no ex ins fnl f* **8/1**
54 **7** *5* **Il Sassicaia**[14] 613 3-8-5 0.. LiamJones 7 51
(Marco Botti) *prom: rdn over 2f out: wknd wl over 1f out* **16/1**
0 **8** *hd* **Melendez (USA)**[12] 633 3-8-5 0.................................... CathyGannon 4 50
(Jamie Osborne) *hld up: nvr on terms* **20/1**
6-55 **9** *1 1/4* **Diamondsaretrumps (IRE)**[7] 700 3-7-9 55................ NoelGarbutt(5) 9 43
(Denis Quinn) *chsd ldrs: rdn over 3f out: wknd over 2f out* **66/1**

2m 41.67s (0.87) **Going Correction** +0.075s/f (Slow)
WFA 3 from 4yo 23lb 4 from 5yo 2lb **9** Ran SP% **120.5**
Speed ratings (Par 103): **100,99,98,97,96 96,92,92,92**
CSF £5.50 TOTE £2.00: £1.10, £2.10, £3.30; EX 8.90 Trifecta £58.90.
Owner Ross Harmon **Bred** S C E A Haras De La Perelle **Trained** Settrington, N Yorks
■ Stewards' Enquiry : Ian Brennan three-day ban: weighed in 2.5lb heavy (Mar 16-18)

FOCUS
A modest middle-distance maiden, but a couple caught the eye. The runner-up sets the standard.
T/Jkpt: Not won. T/Plt: £74.80 to a £1 stake. Pool: £75,274.99 - 733.94 winning tickets. T/Qpdt: £9.70 to a £1 stake. Pool: £7,530.36 - 570.0 winning tickets. **Colin Roberts**

702 CHELMSFORD (A.W) (L-H)
Thursday, March 3

OFFICIAL GOING: Polytrack: standard
Wind: virtually nil Weather: dry

790 CRAWFORDS & MASSEY FERGUSON H'CAP 6f (P)
6:05 (6:06) (Class 6) (0-52,51) 4-Y-O+ **£3,234** (£962; £481; £240) **Stalls** Centre

Form RPR
-452 **1** **Multi Quest**[21] 528 4-9-1 **45**..............................(b) FrannyNorton 1 51
(John E Long) *mde all: rdn over 1f out: forged in front 1f out: hrd pressed and hld on gamely cl home* **7/2**[3]
50-4 **2** *hd* **Wedgewood Estates**[46] 237 5-9-7 **51**............................ LukeMorris 2 56
(Tony Carroll) *chsd ldrs: swtchd lft and effrt over 1f out: wnt 2nd and hrd drvn 150yds: sn ev ch: kpt on wl: hld towards fin* **3/1**[1]
4300 **3** *1* **Tasaaboq**[36] 355 5-9-6 **50**..............................(vt) AdamKirby 7 52
(Phil McEntee) *t.k.h: hld up in last pair: effrt over 1f out: drvn to chse ldrs 1f out: kpt on u.p to go 3rd wl ins fnl f: nvr enough pce to threaten ldrs* **4/1**
0-20 **4** *1 1/2* **Presto Boy**[21] 528 4-9-7 **51**..............................(b[1]) ShaneKelly 5 49
(Richard Hughes) *t.k.h: chsd ldr: rdn and ev ch 2f out tl no ex 1f out: lost 3rd and wknd wl ins fnl f* **10/3**[2]

566- **5** 1 1/4 **Senor Firecracker (IRE)**[233] 4237 4-9-1 **45**................(v[1]) JimCrowley 4 39
(Brett Johnson) *taken down early: in tch in midfield: unable qck u.p over 1f out: wl hld and plugged on same pce fnl f* **8/1**

4054 **6** 1/2 **Ciaras Cookie (IRE)**[16] 596 4-8-12 **45**......................(t) DannyBrock(3) 6 37
(Heather Dalton) *stdd s: t.k.h: hld up in last pair: effrt over 1f out: no imp* **12/1**

1m 12.16s (-1.54) **Going Correction** -0.20s/f (Stan) **6** Ran SP% **109.1**
Speed ratings (Par 101): **102,101,100,98,96 96**
CSF £13.50 TOTE £4.20: £2.00, £1.90; EX 12.20 Trifecta £48.00.
Owner Martin J Gibbs **Bred** Mrs C Lloyd **Trained** Royston, Herts

FOCUS
The track had been power harrowed to 4 inches and gallop mastered to 2 inches for racing. The gallop masters went round after the 3rd race. This was a weak event considering the lack of wins between them.

791 TOTEEXACTA MAIDEN FILLIES' STKS 6f (P)
6:40 (6:40) (Class 5) 3-Y-O+ **£5,175** (£1,540; £769; £384) **Stalls** Centre

Form RPR

2- **1** **Doeadeer (IRE)**[196] 5551 3-9-0 0....................................... GrahamLee 6 66
(Keith Dalgleish) *taken down early: sn w ldr tl led 1/2-way: rdn over 1f out: hld on wl ins fnl f: rdn out* **1/1**[1]

200- **2** *nk* **Basma**[142] 7191 3-9-0 71... PatCosgrave 5 65
(Owen Burrows) *t.k.h: broke wl: sn stdd and trckd ldrs: swtchd lft and effrt over 1f out: str chal 1f out: r.o u.p: hld towards fin* **5/1**[3]

53 **3** 1 1/4 **Summer Music (IRE)**[29] 432 3-9-0 0............................... LukeMorris 8 61
(Robert Cowell) *sn led: hdd 1/2-way but styd upsides ldr: rdn over 1f out: cl 3rd and drvn 1f out: kpt on same pce ins fnl f* **9/2**[2]

0-3 **4** *shd* **Emily Goldfinch**[25] 496 3-8-11 0....................................... TimClark(3) 3 60
(Phil McEntee) *t.k.h: hld up in tch: rdn and hdwy on inner over 1f out: chsd ldrs 1f out: kpt on* **20/1**

6-3 **5** *4* **One Big Surprise**[21] 531 4-9-7 0......................... StephenCummins(7) 7 52
(Richard Hughes) *racd keenly: chsd ldrs: rdn and unable qck over 1f out: sn btn: wknd ins fnl f* **9/2**[2]

6 *8* **Prophetess** 3-9-0 0... WilliamCarson 9 22
(Giles Bravery) *s.i.s: sn rcvrd and in tch in midfield: rdn over 2f out: sn outpcd: wknd over 1f out* **33/1**

7 *2* **Just Over** 3-9-0 0... AdamBeschizza 4 16
(Robert Cowell) *s.i.s and wnt lft s: rn green and pushed along in rr: rdn and clsd over 2f out: wknd over 1f out* **33/1**

1m 12.64s (-1.06) **Going Correction** -0.20s/f (Stan)
WFA 3 from 4yo 14lb **7** Ran SP% **113.7**
Speed ratings (Par 100): **99,98,96,96,91 80,78**
CSF £6.31 TOTE £1.80: £1.30, £3.00; EX 7.60 Trifecta £18.20.
Owner Weldspec Glasgow Limited **Bred** Liam Wright **Trained** Carluke, S Lanarks

FOCUS
The track had been power harrowed to 4 inches and gallop mastered to 2 inches for racing. The gallop masters went round after the 3rd race. This looked a fair maiden, but its doubtful this it will be strong form in the coming weeks. The form is a bit shaky.

792 TOTEQUADPOT H'CAP 1m (P)
7:10 (7:10) (Class 5) (0-70,70) 4-Y-O+ **£5,175** (£1,540; £769; £384) **Stalls** Low

Form RPR

3-21 **1** **Gracious George (IRE)**[21] 532 6-9-6 **69**........................ KieranO'Neill 3 76
(Jimmy Fox) *racd in midfield: clsd over 2f out: effrt on inner to press ldrs 1f out: drvn to ld wl ins fnl f: r.o* **7/2**[3]

2430 **2** *nk* **Clockmaker (IRE)**[16] 598 10-9-7 **70**................................ JimCrowley 1 76
(Conor Dore) *taken down early: led: clr 6f out tl 2f out: sn rdn and hrd pressed over 1f out: hdd and kpt on same pce wl ins fnl f* **10/3**[2]

3-63 **3** 1/2 **Spirit Of Gondree (IRE)**[14] 621 8-8-13 **62**...............(b) FrannyNorton 6 67
(Milton Bradley) *stdd after s: t.k.h: hld up in 5th: clsd over 2f out: pressed ldrs and rdn 1f out: kpt on same pce fnl 100yds* **10/1**

1-51 **4** *1* **Desert Morning (IRE)**[10] 667 4-9-2 **65** 6ex................ WilliamCarson 2 68
(Anthony Carson) *chsd ldr: clsd over 2f out: drvn and ev ch over 1f out: no ex ins fnl f: wknd towards fin* **11/4**[1]

0131 **5** *shd* **Cookie Ring (IRE)**[14] 617 5-8-0 **56**.............................(v) PaulaMuir(7) 5 60+
(Patrick Holmes) *v.s.a: bhd but steadily rcvrd: clsd and in tch 2f out: effrt over 1f out: chsng ldrs 1f out: nvr enough room thrght fnl f and nvr able to make a chal* **9/2**

2066 **6** *21* **Hercullian Prince**[10] 680 4-9-5 **68**.................................(p) AdamKirby 4 22
(Conor Dore) *chsd ldrs: drvn 3f out: sn lost pl and hung rt: bhd and lost tch over 1f out: eased ins fnl f* **8/1**

1m 38.41s (-1.49) **Going Correction** -0.20s/f (Stan) **6** Ran SP% **110.4**
Speed ratings (Par 103): **99,98,98,97,97 76**
CSF £14.91 TOTE £3.40: £2.20, £1.50; EX 15.40 Trifecta £99.40.
Owner Mrs Barbara Fuller **Bred** D Fuller **Trained** Collingbourne Ducis, Wilts

FOCUS
The track had been power harrowed to 4 inches and gallop mastered to 2 inches for racing. The gallop masters went round after the 3rd race. A competitive race that produced a tight finish. The runner-up has been rated close to his winter best.

793 TOTETRIFECTA CONDITIONS STKS (ALL-WEATHER CHAMPIONSHIPS FAST-TRACK QUALIFIER) 2m (P)
7:40 (7:40) (Class 2) 4-Y-O+ **£16,172** (£4,812; £2,405; £1,202) **Stalls** Low

Form RPR

03-3 **1** **Notarised**[15] 614 5-9-3 100.. JoeFanning 1 106
(Mark Johnston) *chsd ldrs: effrt to chse ldr wl over 1f out: rdn to ld 1f out: in command and styd on wl fnl 150yds* **6/1**

00-2 **2** *2* **John Reel (FR)**[15] 614 7-9-3 98.. JFEgan 6 104
(David Evans) *led: rdn over 2f out: drvn and hdd 1f out: styd on same pce and comf hld after* **5/1**[3]

03-5 **3** *5* **Pearl Castle (IRE)**[25] 317 6-9-3 95............................ DougieCostello 3 98
(K R Burke) *hld up in tch: pushed along over 3f out: rdn 3f out: chsd clr ldng pair 1f out: no imp* **14/1**

51-3 **4** 4 1/2 **Pinzolo**[40] 317 5-9-6 108...(p) AdamKirby 2 96
(Charlie Appleby) *chsd ldr: rdn over 2f out: fnd little and btn over 1f out: wknd fnl f* **11/8**[1]

230- **5** *6* **Tommy Docc (IRE)**[218] 4743 4-8-12 94............................ GrahamLee 4 85
(Keith Dalgleish) *dwlt: in tch in rr: rdn 5f out: struggling and btn over 2f out: lost tch over 1f out* **10/1**

21-1 **6** *20* **Barye**[55] 99 5-9-3 103.. ShaneKelly 5 61
(Richard Hughes) *hld up in tch: rdn 3f out: sn struggling and btn 2f out: eased fr over 1f out: t.o: fin lame* **3/1**[2]

3m 22.37s (-7.63) **Going Correction** -0.20s/f (Stan) course record
WFA 4 from 5yo+ 5lb **6** Ran SP% **113.8**
Speed ratings (Par 109): **111,110,107,105,102 92**
CSF £35.66 TOTE £5.60: £2.30, £2.70; EX 31.30 Trifecta £290.00.
Owner Hugh Hart **Bred** Mrs P Hart **Trained** Middleham Moor, N Yorks

FOCUS
The track had been power harrowed to 4 inches and gallop mastered to 2 inches for racing. The gallop masters went round after the 3rd race. A good-quality staying contest, which resulted in a course record. The form makes sense with the first three rated close to their marks.

794 TOTESWINGER H'CAP 1m (P)
8:10 (8:11) (Class 6) (0-60,60) 3-Y-O **£3,234** (£962; £481; £240) **Stalls** Low

Form RPR

630- **1** **Whitstable Pearl (IRE)**[223] 4580 3-8-11 **50**........................ KierenFox 11 55
(John Best) *sn chsng ldr: lost 2nd over 3f out but styd handy: rdn to chse ldr again wl over 1f out: looked hld tl styd on wl fnl 75yds to ld last strides* **25/1**

-605 **2** *nk* **Daydream (IRE)**[15] 610 3-8-12 **56**...............................(t) LucyKBarry(5) 1 60
(Jamie Osborne) *led: rdn over 1f out: almost 2 l clr 1f out: wknd towards fin and hdd last strides* **14/1**

60-0 **3** *1* **Simply Clever**[23] 509 3-8-2 **46** oh1................................ AaronJones(5) 2 48
(David Brown) *hld up in midfield: clsd on inner and n.m.r 2f out: hdwy into 5th 1f out: styd on strly wl ins fnl f to snatch 3rd last strides: nvr quite getting to ldrs* **50/1**

-002 **4** *nk* **Dark Illustrator**[9] 688 3-9-0 **53**................................ DanielTudhope 3 54
(David O'Meara) *taken down early: chsd ldrs: effrt u.p in 3rd over 1f out: kpt on u.p but nvr enough pce to rch ldr: lost 3rd last strides* **6/1**[3]

1-54 **5** *shd* **Frap**[17] 593 3-9-0 **60**.. AdamMcNamara(7) 4 61
(Richard Fahey) *hld up in last trio: clsd 2f out: rdn and hdwy over 1f out: chsd ldng trio 1f out: kpt on wl u.p ins fnl f: nvr quite getting to ldrs* **7/1**

046 **6** 2 3/4 **Keep The Silence (IRE)**[28] 441 3-9-6 **59**......................... LukeMorris 7 53
(James Tate) *in tch in midfield: rdn 3f out: hdwy over 1f out: kpt on ins fnl f: nvr enough pce to threaten ldrs* **6/1**[3]

0-36 **7** 2 1/4 **More Kudos (USA)**[15] 610 3-8-11 **50**............................(t) IanBrennan 5 39
(John Quinn) *wl in tch in midfield: effrt and unable qck over 1f out: wknd ins fnl f* **8/1**

000- **8** 1 1/2 **Packing Empire (IRE)**[66] 8377 3-8-11 **50**.................... WilliamCarson 9 35+
(Jamie Osborne) *s.i.s: bhd: rdn wl over 1f out: no imp* **22/1**

00-2 **9** *nse* **Divine Touch**[23] 509 3-8-10 **49**...................................... JackMitchell 6 34
(Robert Eddery) *t.k.h: in tch in midfield: hdwy to chse ldr over 3f out tl rdn and lost pl over 1f out: wknd fnl f* **4/1**[1]

0-42 **10** *nk* **Granita (USA)**[16] 597 3-9-4 **60**................................ TomMarquand(3) 8 44
(George Scott) *in tch in midfield: pushed along over 5f out: drvn and c wd 2f out: sn no imp: wknd fnl f* **9/2**[2]

5055 **11** *shd* **Falcon's Fire (IRE)**[9] 688 3-9-2 **55**.............................(p) GrahamLee 10 39
(Keith Dalgleish) *a towards rr: rdn over 2f out: no imp* **7/1**

1m 39.49s (-0.41) **Going Correction** -0.20s/f (Stan) **11** Ran SP% **119.7**
Speed ratings (Par 96): **94,93,92,92,92 89,87,85,85,85 85**
CSF £337.27 CT £16368.20 TOTE £16.60: £4.80, £4.10, £12.10; EX 232.80 Trifecta £4157.60 Part won..
Owner Bruce Woodward & Mark Wellbelove **Bred** Tally-Ho Stud **Trained** Oad Street, Kent

FOCUS
The track had been power harrowed to 4 inches and gallop mastered to 2 inches for racing. The gallop masters went round after the 3rd race. Probably just moderate form.

795 TOTEPOOL BETTING ON ALL UK RACING H'CAP 7f (P)
8:40 (8:40) (Class 5) (0-75,76) 4-Y-O+ **£5,175** (£1,540; £769; £384) **Stalls** Low

Form RPR

4-21 **1** **Dutch Garden**[34] 387 4-9-5 **73**...(v) SeanLevey 4 82+
(David Brown) *taken down early: led and set stdy gallop tl hdd 5f out: chsd ldr tl rdn to ld again over 1f out: sustained duel w runner-up fnl f: r.o wl u.p* **9/4**[1]

030- **2** 1/2 **Smokethatthunders (IRE)**[143] 7170 6-9-7 **75**................ PatCosgrave 6 82
(James Unett) *t.k.h early: chsd ldrs: effrt on inner to chal jst over 1f out: sustained effrt fnl f: r.o but a jst hld* **20/1**

-342 **3** *2* **Oak Bluffs (IRE)**[26] 482 5-8-5 **62**............................ SammyJoBell(3) 8 64
(Richard Fahey) *t.k.h early: hld up in midfield: effrt over 1f out: hdwy 1f out: wnt 3rd wl ins fnl f: styd on but no threat to ldng pair* **8/1**[3]

3-42 **4** 3/4 **Van Huysen (IRE)**[13] 629 4-9-4 **75**............................ DannyBrock(3) 7 75+
(Dominic Ffrench Davis) *dwlt: hld up in tch in last pair: effrt wl over 1f out: kpt on wl u.p ins fnl f: nt rch ldrs* **4/1**[2]

5-41 **5** *nse* **Fingal's Cave (IRE)**[10] 680 4-9-8 **76** 6ex.................... GeorgeBaker 3 75+
(Mick Channon) *t.k.h: chsd ldrs tl hdwy to ld 5f out: rdn and hdd over 1f out: 3rd and btn 1f out: wknd ins fnl f* **9/4**[1]

-6U5 **6** 1 1/4 **Wink Oliver**[13] 629 4-9-5 **73**.......................................(p) TimmyMurphy 1 69
(David Dennis) *hld up in tch in midfield: effrt to chse ldrs over 1f out: no ex u.p in 4th 1f out: wknd ins fnl f* **11/1**

0-24 **7** *1* **Swiss Cross**[49] 169 9-9-2 **70**... LukeMorris 5 63
(Phil McEntee) *broke wl and t.k.h early: stdd bk to chse ldrs after 2f: rdn over 2f out: no ex over 1f out: wknd ins fnl f* **18/1**

303- **8** *nse* **Red Invader (IRE)**[73] 8331 6-8-13 **67**.............................. ShaneKelly 2 60
(Paul D'Arcy) *hld up in tch in last pair: effrt over 1f out: no imp* **20/1**

1m 25.41s (-1.79) **Going Correction** -0.20s/f (Stan) **8** Ran SP% **115.8**
Speed ratings (Par 103): **102,101,99,98,98 96,95,95**
CSF £52.10 CT £306.50 TOTE £3.50: £2.50, £4.00, £2.30; EX 50.10 Trifecta £557.20.
Owner J C Fretwell **Bred** Coln Valley Stud **Trained** Averham Park, Notts

FOCUS
The track had been power harrowed to 4 inches and gallop mastered to 2 inches for racing. The gallop masters went round after the 3rd race. A decent race for the level. The runner-up helps set the standard.

796 TOTEPOOLLIVEINFO.COM H'CAP 1m 5f 66y(P)
9:10 (9:10) (Class 6) (0-52,52) 4-Y-O+ **£3,234** (£962; £481; £240) **Stalls** Low

Form RPR

505- **1** **Eurato (FR)**[135] 7358 6-9-7 **52**...(p) LukeMorris 14 59+
(Steve Gollings) *hld up in midfield: swtchd rt and effrt on outer 2f out: chsd ldrs and lugging lft 1f out: led and hung lft u.p ins fnl f: rdn out* **9/4**[1]

-002 **2** *1* **Sudden Wish (IRE)**[12] 653 7-9-6 **51**................................ JimCrowley 1 56
(Michael Attwater) *hld up in last quartet: gd hdwy on inner over 2f out: rdn and chsd ldrs over 1f out: ev ch 1f out: unable qck wl ins fnl f* **6/1**

422- **3** 1 1/2 **Lorelei**[190] 5756 4-9-3 **51**.. GeorgeBaker 3 55
(William Muir) *trckd ldrs and travelled strly: wnt 2nd over 2f out: rdn to ld over 1f out: hdd ins fnl f: stl cl but no ex whn bdly hmpd and snatched up wl ins fnl f: one pce after* **4/1**[2]

0004 **4** 1/2 **Dynamo (IRE)**[12] 653 5-9-1 **46** oh1...............................(t) ShaneKelly 7 49
(Richard Hughes) *stdd after s: hld up in rr: hdwy 2f out: swtchd rt and rdn to chse ldrs jst over 1f out: cl 4th and keeping on whn bdly hmpd wl ins fnl f: one pce after* **5/1**[3]

344- **5** *5* **Yourholidayisover (IRE)**[181] 6069 9-8-11 **49**................ PaulaMuir(7) 6 44
(Patrick Holmes) *hld up in tch in last quartet: swtchd rt and hdwy over 1f out: kpt on ins fnl f: no threat to ldrs* **12/1**

0-04 **6** *2 1/2* **Black Iceman**[14] 622 8-8-12 **46** oh1 SimonPearce(3) 13 37
(Lydia Pearce) *rdn along leaving stalls: in tch in midfield: hdwy and rdn to chse ldrs over 2f out: outpcd over 1f out: wknd ins fnl f* **16/1**

-200 **7** *3* **Little Flo**[27] 461 5-9-7 **52** (t) AdamKirby 2 39
(William Stone) *in tch in midfield: rdn over 3f out: hdwy on inner to chse ldrs over 2f out: outpcd over 1f out: wknd fnl f* **7/1**

0-50 **8** *5* **Citisonsmith (IRE)**[12] 653 4-8-12 **46** oh1 (p) WilliamCarson 8 26
(Tony Carroll) *led: rdn and hdd over 1f out: sn btn and wknd fnl f* **40/1**

4-00 **9** *3* **Ocean Bentley (IRE)**[12] 653 4-8-12 **46** oh1[1] RyanPowell 5 22
(Tony Carroll) *t.k.h: wl in tch in midfield: rdn 6f out: losing pl and hmpd over 2f out: bhd over 1f out* **25/1**

500- **10** *hd* **Everywish**[190] 5758 5-8-8 **46** oh1 CharlieBennett(7) 12 22
(Jonathan Portman) *chsd ldrs: rdn over 2f out: sn btn and lost pl 2f out: bhd fnl f* **33/1**

600- **11** *17* **Hoonose**[171] 6379 7-9-1 **46** oh1 (b) TomQueally 10
(Emma Owen) *s.i.s: hld up in last pair: swtchd rt and shortlived effrt wl over 2f out: wl bhd 1f out: t.o* **25/1**

0-06 **12** *20* **Opus Too (IRE)**[13] 634 5-8-10 **46** oh1 CallumShepherd(5) 9
(John Ryan) *chsd ldr: rdn over 4f out: lost pl over 2f out: dropped to rr wl over 1f out: sn lost tch and eased: t.o* **40/1**

2m 51.06s (-2.54) **Going Correction** -0.20s/f (Stan)
WFA 4 from 5yo+ 3lb **12** Ran SP% **123.3**
Speed ratings (Par 101): **99,98,97,97,94 92,90,87,85,85 75,62**
CSF £15.87 CT £53.18 TOTE £3.60: £1.50, £2.60, £1.80; EX 19.60 Trifecta £54.30.
Owner Northern Bloodstock Racing **Bred** Wertheimer & Frere **Trained** Scamblesby, Lincs

FOCUS
The track had been power harrowed to 4 inches and gallop mastered to 2 inches for racing. The gallop masters went round after the 3rd race. A weak race, in which four came nicely clear.
T/Plt: £3,156.90 to a £1 stake. Pool of £76111.96 - 17.60 winning tickets. T/Qpdt: £1,069.40 to a £1 stake. Pool of £8526.83 - 5.90 winning tickets. **Steve Payne**

596 SOUTHWELL (L-H)
Thursday, March 3

OFFICIAL GOING: Fibresand: standard
Wind: Moderate behind Weather: Cloudy

797 UNIBET.CO.UK DAILY ENHANCED PLACE TERMS H'CAP 5f (F)
1:45 (1:45) (Class 5) (0-75,75) 3-Y-O **£3,234** (£962; £481; £240) **Stalls** Centre

Form RPR

2-64 **1** **Mysterious Look**[22] 515 3-8-5 **62** RobHornby(3) 3 69
(Ed McMahon) *cl up: effrt 2f out: rdn to chal over 1f out: kpt on to ld last 100yds* **14/1**

5-21 **2** *1* **Cultured Knight**[21] 531 3-9-1 **72** RyanTate(3) 4 75
(Richard Hughes) *prom: effrt 2f out and sn rdn: kpt on u.p fnl f* **7/1**[2]

4-50 **3** *1/2* **Cool Silk Boy (IRE)**[39] 322 3-8-13 **67** PaulMulrennan 6 69
(James Given) *sn led: rdn wl over 1f out: edgd lft and drvn ent fnl f: hdd and no ex last 100yds* **8/1**[3]

6-14 **4** *1* **Jess**[15] 612 3-8-13 **67** ShaneGray 1 65
(Kevin Ryan) *pushed along s and sn chsng ldrs on outer: rdn along 2f out: drvn over 1f out and kpt on same pce* **12/1**

321- **5** *1 1/2* **Twentysvnthlancers**[177] 6189 3-9-1 **69** GrahamLee 8 62
(Paul Midgley) *racd towards stands' rail: chsd ldrs: rdn along 2f out: sn drvn and no imp* **20/1**

6-51 **6** *2 1/4* **Kestrel Call (IRE)**[35] 365 3-9-7 **75** (t) RobertHavlin 7 60
(Simon Crisford) *dwlt and towards rr: pushed along 3f out: rdn and sme hdwy over 2f out: sn drvn and n.d* **4/5**[1]

3-46 **7** *2* **Men United (FR)**[39] 322 3-8-9 **66** AlistairRawlinson(3) 2 43
(Roy Bowring) *dwlt: sn chsng ldrs towards outer: rdn along over 2f out: sn wknd* **8/1**[3]

1-0 **8** *3 1/4* **Feelin Dicky**[22] 515 3-9-1 **69** TomEaves 5 35
(James Given) *chsd ldrs: pushed along 3f out: rdn 1/2-way and sn outpcd in rr* **18/1**

59.35s (-0.35) **Going Correction** -0.05s/f (Stan) **8** Ran SP% **114.7**
Speed ratings (Par 98): **100,98,97,96,93 90,86,81**
CSF £107.31 CT £844.15 TOTE £16.80: £5.10, £1.80, £2.60; EX 109.50 Trifecta £1010.20.
Owner S L Edwards **Bred** S L Edwards **Trained** Lichfield, Staffs

FOCUS
An ordinary 3yo sprint handicap which went to the only maiden in the field. The form looks a little suspect, though, with the red-hot favourite running so poorly. It's been rated around the runner-up.

798 DAILY PRICE BOOSTS AT UNIBET MAIDEN STKS 5f (F)
2:15 (2:15) (Class 5) 3-Y-O+ **£3,234** (£962; £481; £240) **Stalls** Centre

Form RPR

6- **1** **Berlios (IRE)**[156] 6842 3-9-1 69 GrahamGibbons 3 76
(David Barron) *cl up: slt ld after 2f: rdn over 1f out: drvn and edgd lft ins fnl f: kpt on* **11/10**[1]

2222 **2** *1* **Phantom Flipper**[10] 668 3-9-1 70 (p) AdrianNicholls 2 72
(David Nicholls) *cl up: rdn and ev ch over 1f out: drvn ins fnl f: kpt on same pce towards fin* **6/4**[2]

3 *2 1/2* **Spice Mill (IRE)** 3-9-1 0 LukeMorris 4 63
(Robert Cowell) *dwlt: green and sn wnt lft: sn pushed along and in tch after 1 1/2f: rdn along on outer to chse ldng pair 2f out: drvn over 1f out: kpt on same pce fnl f* **8/1**[3]

4 *5* **Aegean Boy** 3-9-1 0 AndrewMullen 5 45
(Michael Appleby) *in tch: green and pushed along 3f out: hdwy to chse ldrs 2f out: sn rdn and edgd lft wl over 1f out: sn one pce* **8/1**[3]

04-6 **5** *7* **Sirdaab (USA)**[21] 531 4-9-9 50 AnnStokell(5) 6 26
(Ann Stokell) *slt ld: hdd 3f out: sn rdn along and wknd* **50/1**

04 **6** *2* **Bomber Etches**[23] 507 3-9-1 0 BenCurtis 7 13
(Scott Dixon) *towards rr: rdn along bef 1/2-way: sn outpcd and bhd* **66/1**

7 *13* **Temujins Quest (IRE)** 3-9-1 0 AdamBeschizza 1
(Derek Shaw) *s.i.s and lost several l s: a bhd* **33/1**

59.35s (-0.35) **Going Correction** -0.05s/f (Stan)
WFA 3 from 4yo 13lb **7** Ran SP% **116.2**
Speed ratings (Par 103): **100,98,94,86,75 72,51**
CSF £3.08 TOTE £2.60: £1.50, £1.10; EX 2.90 Trifecta £10.00.
Owner Lets Be Lucky Racing 6 **Bred** John Malone **Trained** Maunby, N Yorks

FOCUS
A moderate sprint maiden dominated by the two form horses. The runner-up has been rated to form.

799 UNIBET OFFER DAILY JOCKEY & TRAINER SPECIALS H'CAP 6f (F)
2:50 (2:50) (Class 6) (0-65,65) 4-Y-O+ **£2,587** (£770; £384; £192) **Stalls** Low

Form RPR

5335 **1** **Monsieur Jimmy**[22] 523 4-9-4 **62** (b) DanielTudhope 9 71
(Declan Carroll) *trckd ldrs: wd st: hdwy to chal 2f out: rdn to ld over 1f out: kpt on wl fnl f* **9/2**[1]

4260 **2** *1 3/4* **Spowarticus**[10] 680 7-9-3 **64** (b) AlistairRawlinson(3) 6 68
(Scott Dixon) *slt ld: rdn 2f out: drvn and hdd over 1f out: kpt on fnl f* **8/1**

2140 **3** *1 1/2* **Sir Geoffrey (IRE)**[22] 520 10-8-13 **57** (b) BenCurtis 11 56
(Scott Dixon) *cl up: wd st: rdn 2f out: drvn and edgd lft whn ev ch over 1f out: kpt on same pce fnl f* **16/1**

540- **4** *3/4* **New Lease Of Life**[121] 7683 7-9-7 **65** (p) JasonHart 1 62
(Keith Dalgleish) *trckd ldrs on inner: hdwy over 2f out: rdn and ev ch over 1f out: sn drvn and kpt on same pce* **25/1**

1220 **5** *shd* **Fortinbrass (IRE)**[20] 543 6-9-0 **58** RobertWinston 3 55
(John Balding) *chsd ldrs: rdn along 2f out: drvn over 1f out: no imp fnl f* **9/2**[1]

53-2 **6** *1 1/2* **Spitfire**[53] 135 11-9-4 **62** (t) JoeFanning 10 54
(J R Jenkins) *dwlt and towards rr: wd st: rdn and hdwy 2f out: styd on fnl f* **15/2**[3]

62-4 **7** *1 1/2* **Ancient Cross**[20] 541 12-9-0 **65** (t) NathanEvans(7) 4 53
(Michael Easterby) *towards rr: wd st: hdwy 2f out: sn rdn and no imp* **6/1**[2]

-600 **8** *1* **Colourbearer (IRE)**[30] 426 9-9-7 **65** (t) LukeMorris 8 50
(Charlie Wallis) *cl up: rdn along over 2f out: drvn over 1f out: wknd ent fnl f* **11/1**

2430 **9** *1* **Major Muscari (IRE)**[15] 608 8-8-12 **61** (p) JustinNewman(5) 2 43
(Shaun Harris) *dwlt: a towards rr* **20/1**

-413 **10** *2 1/4* **Nasri**[15] 607 10-9-7 **65** TomQueally 7 40
(Emma Owen) *a in rr* **6/1**[2]

05-4 **11** *1 3/4* **Galvanize**[56] 76 5-9-1 **59** BarryMcHugh 5 29
(Noel Wilson) *a in rr* **25/1**

1m 17.12s (0.62) **Going Correction** +0.05s/f (Slow) **11** Ran SP% **114.5**
Speed ratings (Par 101): **97,94,92,91,91 89,87,86,84,81 79**
CSF £38.18 CT £528.50 TOTE £5.00: £1.10, £4.10, £5.20; EX 44.30 Trifecta £551.20.
Owner Ray Flegg & H J Bousfield **Bred** J P Repard **Trained** Malton, N Yorks

FOCUS
A moderate sprint handicap and race where you just had to be handy.

800 CORAL H'CAP 1m 4f (F)
3:25 (3:25) (Class 4) (0-85,85) 4-Y-O+ **£5,175** (£1,540; £769; £384) **Stalls** Low

Form RPR

-121 **1** **Play Nicely**[28] 447 4-9-5 **85** GrahamGibbons 6 96+
(David Barron) *trckd ldr: hdwy and cl up 4f out: rdn to chal whn carried sltly rt 2f out: sn swtchd lft and rdn: drvn to ld ins fnl f: kpt on wl towards fin* **5/4**[1]

0-11 **2** *hd* **Weald Of Kent (USA)**[23] 506 4-8-7 **73** (v) LiamJones 3 82
(Michael Appleby) *led: pushed along 4f out: rdn and edgd rt 2f out: sn drvn: hdd ins fnl f: sn drvn and kpt on wl towards fin* **11/2**

633- **3** *6* **Karam Albaari (IRE)**[289] 2358 8-8-10 **77** AlistairRawlinson(3) 2 76
(J R Jenkins) *hld up in rr: hdwy 4f out: chsd ldng pair and swtchd lft 2f out: sn rdn: kpt on same pce fnl f* **33/1**

1355 **4** *hd* **The Lock Master (IRE)**[7] 704 9-9-2 **80** (p) AndrewMullen 5 79
(Michael Appleby) *in tch: pushed along 4f out: rdn 3f out: drvn and kpt on same pce fnl 2f* **9/2**[3]

-222 **5** *1 1/4* **Ralphy Lad (IRE)**[37] 337 5-8-13 **77** BenCurtis 1 74
(Alan Swinbank) *chsd ldr on inner: rdn along over 3f out: drvn wl over 2f out and sn wknd* **5/2**[2]

2m 40.44s (-0.56) **Going Correction** +0.05s/f (Slow)
WFA 4 from 5yo+ 2lb **5** Ran SP% **109.5**
Speed ratings (Par 105): **103,102,98,98,97**
CSF £8.47 TOTE £1.90: £1.10, £3.00; EX 6.20 Trifecta £41.30.
Owner Lets Be Lucky Racing 5 **Bred** Susanna Ballinger **Trained** Maunby, N Yorks
■ Stewards' Enquiry : Liam Jones caution: careless riding

FOCUS
A good middle-distance handicap with the finish fought out between two horses who have been in cracking form around here already this year. The pace looked ordinary. A pb from the runner-up.

801 CORAL.CO.UK RACING H'CAP 1m 3f (F)
4:00 (4:01) (Class 6) (0-65,65) 4-Y-O+ **£2,587** (£770; £384; £192) **Stalls** Low

Form RPR

5305 **1** **Tatting**[9] 683 7-9-7 **65** PaulMulrennan 10 79+
(Conor Dore) *hld up in rr: smooth hdwy on outer to trck ldrs 4f out: led 2f out: sn pushed clr: readily* **9/2**[3]

00-0 **2** *4 1/2* **Prayer Time**[30] 429 4-9-4 **63** SaleemGolam 11 69
(Mark H Tompkins) *trckd ldrs: chsd ldr 6f out: hdwy 4f out: led 3f out: rdn and hdd 2f out: sn drvn: kpt on but no ch w wnr* **20/1**

340- **3** *2* **Frosty The Snowman (IRE)**[181] 6067 5-8-7 **51** oh2 JamesSullivan 1 54
(Ruth Carr) *prom on inner: hdwy over 3f out: rdn 2f out: sn drvn and kpt on same pce* **10/1**

0-34 **4** *8* **Golden Wedding (IRE)**[15] 616 4-9-6 **65** (p) RobertWinston 4 55
(Eve Johnson Houghton) *trckd ldrs: hdwy over 3f out: rdn along over 2f out: drvn wl over 1f out: sn one pce* **11/4**[1]

35/3 **5** *1 3/4* **Thankyou Very Much**[16] 601 6-9-5 **63** (p) PJMcDonald 5 50
(James Bethell) *in rr: rdn along 1/2-way: hdwy wl over 2f out: kpt on appr fnl f: nrst fin* **16/1**

-036 **6** *3 3/4* **Thou Swell (IRE)**[18] 583 4-8-13 **63** JustinNewman(5) 2 44
(Shaun Harris) *towards rr: rdn along and bhd 1/2-way: plugged on fnl 3f* **16/1**

2324 **7** *nk* **Astra Hall**[9] 684 7-9-2 **60** AndrewMullen 7 41
(Michael Appleby) *in tch: chsd ldrs over 4f out: rdn along over 3f out: sn drvn and wknd* **9/1**

110- **8** *1 3/4* **Rosie Royale (IRE)**[143] 7164 4-8-13 **61** RobHornby(3) 12 39
(Roger Teal) *chsd ldrs on outer: rdn along 4f out: sn wknd* **16/1**

6-30 **9** *nse* **Skywards Miles (IRE)**[10] 673 4-8-6 **51** oh2 ShaneGray 3 29
(Tim Fitzgerald) *dwlt and in rr: pushed along and hdwy into midfield on inner after 3f: rdn along over 5f out: sn lost pl and bhd* **33/1**

4-31 **10** *nse* **Claude Greenwood**[23] 505 6-8-9 **53** (b) RobertHavlin 9 31
(Linda Jewell) *trckd ldrs: hdwy and cl up 3f out: rdn over 2f out: sn wknd* **3/1**[2]

0000 **11** *6* **Beauty's Forte (IRE)**[9] [682] 5-8-11 **55**....................(b) GrahamGibbons 6 23
(Declan Carroll) *led and sn clr: pushed along 4f out: hdd 3f out and sn wknd* **66/1**
2m 27.13s (-0.87) **Going Correction** +0.05s/f (Slow)
WFA 4 from 5yo+ 1lb **11** Ran SP% **115.8**
Speed ratings (Par 101): **105,101,100,94,93 90,90,88,88,88 84**
CSF £91.41 CT £855.68 TOTE £4.60: £1.70, £4.90, £2.80; EX 100.20 Trifecta £644.60.
Owner Mrs Jennifer Marsh **Bred** Darley **Trained** Hubbert's Bridge, Lincs
FOCUS
A moderate handicap, but run at a decent pace. They finished well spread out and the winner bolted up.

802 LADBROKES APPRENTICE H'CAP 1m (F)
4:35 (4:35) (Class 5) (0-75,75) 4-Y-O+ **£2,911** (£866; £432; £216) **Stalls** Low

Form RPR
-223 **1** **Captain Revelation**[10] [670] 4-9-4 **75**....................... PatrickVaughan[(3)] 9 85
(Tom Dascombe) *prom: cl up 1/2-way: led wl over 2f out: rdn over 1f out: kpt on wl fnl f* **7/2**[1]
6-43 **2** *4* **Best Tamayuz**[16] [598] 5-8-8 **67**.....................................(p) JaneElliott[(5)] 5 68
(Scott Dixon) *led: rdn along 3f out: sn hdd: chsd wnr: drvn over 1f out: kpt on same pce* **7/2**[1]
1-25 **3** *1* **Final**[35] [367] 4-9-6 **74**... CallumShepherd 3 73+
(Mark Johnston) *sn outpcd in rr and swtchd wd after 1f: detached after 3f: wd st: rdn and hdwy over 2f out: drvn and hung rt ent fnl f: kpt on: tk 3rd nr fin* **6/1**
604- **4** *1/2* **Shaw Ting**[80] [8222] 4-8-4 **63**... MitchGodwin[(5)] 10 60
(Mark Appleby) *cl up: rdn along wl over 2f out: drvn wl over 1f out: kpt on same pce fnl f* **9/1**
0-55 **5** *3/4* **Lawyer (IRE)**[18] [581] 5-9-5 **73**.. NathanEvans 7 69
(David Barron) *trckd ldrs: effrt 3f out: rdn over 2f out: sn drvn and one pce* **9/2**[3]
-624 **6** *1/2* **Deep Resolve (IRE)**[30] [429] 5-8-12 **66**....................... MeganNicholls 6 60
(Alan Swinbank) *dwlt and towards rr: hdwy 3f out: rdn 2f out: sn no imp* **4/1**[2]
40-0 **7** *15* **Solarmaite**[35] [367] 7-8-13 **67**.......................................(b) CharlesEddery 8 27
(Roy Bowring) *trckd ldrs: rdn along wl over 3f out: sn wknd and bhd* **25/1**
460- **8** *7* **Powderonthebonnet (IRE)**[15] [7012] 8-8-4 **65**............ SeanMooney[(7)] 2 9
(Richard Phillips) *a in rr: rdn along over 3f out: sn outpcd and bhd* **50/1**
1m 43.12s (-0.58) **Going Correction** +0.05s/f (Slow) **8** Ran SP% **112.7**
Speed ratings (Par 103): **104,100,99,98,97 97,82,75**
CSF £15.40 CT £69.59 TOTE £3.90: £1.70, £1.40, £2.40; EX 18.70 Trifecta £63.50.
Owner Cheshire Racing **Bred** Downfield Cottage Stud **Trained** Malpas, Cheshire
■ Stewards' Enquiry : Jane Elliott four-day ban: used whip above permitted level (Mar 17-19,22)
FOCUS
An ordinary apprentice handicap and another race dominated by those who raced prominently. It's been rated around the winner.
T/Plt: £274.50 to a £1 stake. Pool of £56238.48 - 149.54 winning tickets. T/Qpdt: £46.60 to a £1 stake. Pool of £7119.55 - 113.0 winning tickets. **Joe Rowntree**

803 - 806a (Foreign Racing) - See Raceform Interactive

[717] MEYDAN (L-H)
Thursday, March 3
OFFICIAL GOING: Dirt: fast; turf: good

807a MEYDAN CLASSIC SPONSORED BY SKYWARDS (LISTED RACE) (TURF) 7f
3:35 (3:35) 3-Y-O
£51,020 (£17,006; £8,503; £4,251; £2,551; £1,700)

RPR
1 **Pure Diamond**[21] [536] 3-8-5 91.. HarryBentley 1 103+
(Saeed bin Suroor) *mid-div: smooth prog 3f out: led 1f out: comf* **7/2**[3]
2 *4 1/2* **Comicas (USA)**[21] [536] 3-8-9 95...................................(p) WilliamBuick 6 95
(Charlie Appleby) *mid-div: chsd ldrs 2 1/2f out: r.o but no ch w wnr* **11/8**[1]
3 *1 1/4* **Taexali (IRE)**[21] [536] 3-8-9 89.. RichardMullen 7 92
(S Seemar, UAE) *trckd ldr: ev ch 1 1/2f out: r.o same pce fnl f* **50/1**
4 *2* **Ajwad**[21] [536] 3-8-9 87.. FrederikTylicki 4 86
(R Bouresly, Kuwait) *sn led: hdd 1f out: r.o same pce* **40/1**
5 *nk* **Dubai Fashion (IRE)**[21] [534] 3-8-5 85............................ DavidProbert 5 81
(Saeed bin Suroor) *s.i.s: nvr nr to chal but r.o fnl 2 1/2f* **16/1**
6 *1/2* **First Selection (SPA)**[151] [6968] 3-8-9 109.......................... RyanMoore 2 84
(Simon Crisford) *mid-div: t.k.h: chsd ldrs 3f out: ev ch 2f out: wknd fnl 1 1/2f* **2/1**[2]
7 *1/2* **Calder Prince (IRE)**[21] [536] 3-8-9 98...................... RichardKingscote 9 83
(Tom Dascombe) *nvr bttr than mid-div* **20/1**
8 *1 1/4* **Almashooqa (AUS)**[7] [723] 3-9-0 97............................... PaulHanagan 3 78
(M F De Kock, South Africa) *s.i.s: a in rr* **12/1**
9 *8 1/2* **Ruler Of Course (IRE)**[21] [536] 3-8-9 90.......................(t) TadhgO'Shea 8 56
(Niels Petersen, Norway) *a in rr* **66/1**
1m 23.55s (-0.55) **Going Correction** +0.15s/f (Good) **9** Ran SP% **121.9**
Speed ratings: **109,103,102,100,99 99,98,97,87**
CSF: 9.08.
Owner Godolphin **Bred** Darley **Trained** Newmarket, Suffolk
FOCUS
TRAKUS (metres travelled compared to winner): 2nd +4, 3rd 0, 4th +4, 5th +2, 6th +1, 7th +6, 8th +8, 9th +6. The rail on the turf course was out 12 metres. Not a strong Listed race but Pure Diamond belatedly showed why she was sent off a short-priced favourite for a Group 2 in Britain last season. The splits were 25.36, 23.38, 23.4, with the winner home in 11.41. The third, fourth and fifth help set the standard.

808a UAE OAKS SPONSORED BY EMIRATES (GROUP 3) (FILLIES) (DIRT) 1m 1f 110y(D)
4:10 (4:10) 3-Y-O **£102,040** (£34,013; £17,006)

RPR
1 **Polar River (USA)**[21] [534] 3-8-9 112..................................... PatDobbs 3 112+
(Doug Watson, UAE) *trckd ldr: led 2 1/2f out: clr 1 1/2f out: coasted home* **1/14**[1]
2 *3/4* **Vale Dori (ARG)**[307] 3-9-5 108......................... ChristopheSoumillon 1 111
(M F De Kock, South Africa) *sn led: hdd 2 1/2f out: r.o but no ch w wnr* **10/1**[2]
3 *18 1/4* **Dolly Dagger (SWE)**[21] [534] 3-8-9 85........................... FernandoJara 2 71
(Fredrik Reuterskiold, Sweden) *settled in 3rd: rdn 4f out: sn btn* **66/1**[3]
2m 0.57s (1.77) **Going Correction** +0.325s/f (Slow) **3** Ran SP% **104.0**
Speed ratings: **105,104,89**
CSF: 1.14.
Owner Valentin Bukhtoyarov & Evgeny Kappushev **Bred** Bob McCann Mark Kelder Doug Richards **Trained** United Arab Emirates
FOCUS
TRAKUS: 2nd -5, 3rd -3. Not the fireworks most were expecting from Polar River. The early pace was slow and gradually picked up: 27.73 (400m), 25.63 (800m), 24.67 (1200m), 23.66 (1600m). This was the joint-smallest field ever for a race at Meydan, the only other three-runner contest coming when Allybar defeated Presvis and Zulu Chief in a handicap in 2010.

809a BALANCHINE SPONSORED BY SKYWARDS (GROUP 2) (F&M) (TURF) 1m 1f (T)
4:45 (4:45) 3-Y-O+
£81,632 (£27,210; £13,605; £6,802; £4,081; £2,721)

RPR
1 **Very Special (IRE)**[28] [451] 4-9-3 110................................ JamesDoyle 4 113
(Saeed bin Suroor) *sn led: kicked clr 3f out: r.o wl: comf* **7/4**[2]
2 *2 1/2* **Euro Charline**[173] [6338] 5-9-0 113....................................... RyanMoore 3 105+
(Marco Botti) *s.i.s: mid-div: t.k.h: r.o fnl 2f but no ch w wnr* **1/1**[1]
3 *4 1/2* **Excilly**[28] [451] 4-9-0 104.. RichardKingscote 6 95
(Tom Dascombe) *s.i.s: nvr nr to chal but r.o fnl 2 1/2f* **16/1**
4 *1 3/4* **Icecapada (IRE)**[28] [451] 4-9-0 102.................................... WilliamBuick 5 92
(Niels Petersen, Norway) *nvr nr to chal but r.o fnl 2f* **33/1**
5 *10* **More Aspen (USA)**[28] [451] 5-9-0 104.......................... RichardMullen 7 71
(S Seemar, UAE) *trckd ldrs tl outpcd 3f out* **16/1**
6 *5* **Malka (FR)**[28] [451] 5-9-0 102.. GeraldMosse 1 60
(Mme Pia Brandt, France) *s.i.s: trckd ldr tl outpcd 3f out* **50/1**
7 *15* **Si Luna (GER)**[28] [451] 7-9-0 108........................ ChristopheSoumillon 2 29
(W Mongil, Germany) *mid-div tl wknd fnl 3f* **9/1**[3]
1m 48.85s (-0.25) **Going Correction** +0.15s/f (Good) **7** Ran SP% **113.0**
Speed ratings: **107,104,100,99,90 85,72**
CSF: 3.71.
Owner Godolphin **Bred** Ballylinch Stud **Trained** Newmarket, Suffolk
FOCUS
TRAKUS: 2nd 0, 3rd -1, 4th +3, 5th +5, 6th -2, 7th +3. The rail on the turf course was out 12 metres. This is the latest the Balanchine has been staged since 2004 and its new position in the calendar, around two weeks later than the last five renewals, makes no obvious sense. It essentially denies any top fillies, like Very Special, the chance to contest both this race and the Jebel Hatta (run two days later this year). It's particularly odd considering Sajjhaa won both races only in 2013. The winner and third help set the level.

810a EMIRATES HOLIDAYS (H'CAP) (TURF) 7f
5:20 (5:20) (100-113,112) 3-Y-O+
£48,979 (£16,326; £8,163; £4,081; £2,448; £1,632)

RPR
1 **American Hope (USA)**[14] [624] 5-8-10 **102**..................... JamesDoyle 10 109+
(Saeed bin Suroor) *mid-div: smooth prog 2f out: led 55yds out: r.o wl* **4/1**[2]
2 *1* **Championship (IRE)**[7] [720] 5-8-11 **104**...................(t) FrederikTylicki 12 107
(A bin Harmash, UAE) *mid-div: rdn 1 1/2f out: led 1f out: hdd 55yds out* **20/1**
3 *3/4* **Jamesie (IRE)**[7] [723] 8-8-8 **100**......................................(t) SamHitchcott 7 102+
(David Marnane, Ire) *mid-div: r.o wl fnl 1 1/2f: nrst fin* **8/1**
4 *2* **Yaa Wayl (IRE)**[14] [628] 9-8-8 **100**....................................(t) ChrisHayes 8 97
(D Selvaratnam, UAE) *mid-div: r.o fnl 1 1/2f: nrst fin* **33/1**
5 *nk* **Vin Chaud (FR)**[35] [375] 4-9-6 **112**.....................(t) ChristopheSoumillon 1 108
(F Rohaut, France) *mid-div: r.o fnl 2f but nvr able to chal* **14/1**
6 *nse* **Kanaf (IRE)**[14] [623] 9-8-7 **104** ow3.........................(v) GeorgeBuckell[(5)] 6 97
(M Al Mheiri, UAE) *s.i.s: settled in rr: r.o fnl 2f but nvr able to chal* **16/1**
7 *1 3/4* **Banaadeer (AUS)**[35] [373] 4-9-0 **106**............................(b) DaneO'Neill 13 97
(M F De Kock, South Africa) *sn led: hdd & wknd 1f out* **12/1**
8 *1/2* **Mastermind (SAF)**[14] [623] 4-9-2 **108**........................... PaulHanagan 11 98
(M F De Kock, South Africa) *trckd ldr tl wknd fnl 1 1/2f* **5/1**[3]
9 *2 1/2* **Dark Emerald (IRE)**[14] [623] 6-9-3 **109**.....................(v) RichardMullen 14 92
(Brendan Powell) *trckd ldr tl wknd fnl 1 1/2f* **7/1**
10 *nk* **Redbrook (IRE)**[14] [623] 5-8-8 **100**.................................. PatDobbs 9 82
(Doug Watson, UAE) *s.i.s: nvr nr to chal* **33/1**
11 *1 1/2* **Decathlete (USA)**[378] [616] 5-8-8 **100**.......................(t) RoystonFfrench 3 78
(S bin Ghadayer, UAE) *s.i.s: a in rr* **50/1**
12 *nse* **Fils Anges (IRE)**[14] [623] 6-9-3 **109**..................................... PatSmullen 4 87
(Ali Jan, Qatar) *settled in rr: nvr nr to chal* **10/3**[1]
13 *3 1/2* **Muharaaj (IRE)**[28] [450] 5-8-9 **101**.................................. MartinDwyer 5 69
(Mme Pia Brandt, France) *a in rr* **50/1**
14 *3 3/4* **Mutamakkin (AUS)**[35] [375] 4-8-8 **100**..........................(b) WayneSmith 2 58
(M F De Kock, South Africa) *mid-div: tl wknd 2f out* **12/1**
1m 23.5s (-0.60) **Going Correction** +0.15s/f (Good) **14** Ran SP% **125.9**
Speed ratings: **109,107,107,104,104 104,102,101,98,98 96,96,92,88**
CSF: 92.09; TRICAST: 632.30.
Owner Godolphin **Bred** Liberty Road Stables **Trained** Newmarket, Suffolk
FOCUS
TRAKUS: 2nd +5, 3rd -1, 4th +5, 5th -4, 6th +4, 7th -1, 8th +1, 9th +11, 10th -1, 11th -4, 12th +2, 13th +3, 14th -4. The rail on the turf course was out 12 metres. A competitive handicap run at a good, gradually slowing pace; 24.79 (400m from standing start), 23.03 (800m), 23.5 (1200m), with the winner to the line in 12.16.

811a NAD AL SHEBA TROPHY SPONSORED BY SKYCARGO (GROUP 3) (TURF) 1m 6f 11y
5:55 (5:55) 3-Y-O+
£81,632 (£27,210; £13,605; £5,442; £5,442; £2,721)

RPR
1 **Sheikhzayedroad**[137] [7335] 7-9-0 111.................................. MartinHarley 3 113+
(David Simcock) *mid-div: smooth prog: led 1 1/2f out: r.o wl: easily* **4/1**[3]
2 *3 3/4* **Certerach (IRE)**[28] [453] 8-9-0 101...............................(b) TadhgO'Shea 13 107
(M Halford, Ire) *slowly away: sn led: rdn 4f out: hdd 1 1/2f out but r.o gamely* **25/1**
3 *nk* **Star Empire (SAF)**[28] [453] 9-9-0 113................ ChristopheSoumillon 12 107
(M F De Kock, South Africa) *s.i.s: mid-div: chsd ldrs 2f out: nt qckn fnl f* **3/1**[2]
4 *1/2* **Meadow Creek**[14] [625] 5-9-0 104.. PatDobbs 5 106
(Doug Watson, UAE) *mid-div: r.o same pce fnl 2 1/2f* **9/1**
4 *dht* **Battersea**[28] [453] 5-9-0 101... AndreaAtzeni 7 106
(Roger Varian) *mid-div: r.o fnl 2f but nvr nr to chal* **11/4**[1]
6 *3/4* **Tellina (SAF)**[14] [625] 6-9-0 107.. RyanMoore 9 105
(M F De Kock, South Africa) *settled in rr: r.o fnl 2 1/2f but nvr able to chal* **9/1**
7 *1 1/2* **Quarterback (GER)**[21] [538] 4-8-9 104...........................(p) DaneO'Neill 1 102
(Rune Haugen) *trckd ldr tl wknd 2f out* **25/1**

8 nk **Rio Tigre (IRE)**[28] 453 5-9-0 105 RoystonFfrench 11 103
(S bin Ghadayer, UAE) *s.i.s: nvr nr to chal* **12/1**
9 3/4 **Wasir (GER)**[144] 7154 4-8-9 101 EduardoPedroza 2 101
(A Wohler, Germany) *nvr bttr than mid-div* **20/1**
10 shd **Paene Magnus (IRE)**[28] 453 7-9-0 102 (t) FrederikTylicki 6 102
(A bin Harmash, UAE) *nvr bttr than mid-div* **12/1**
11 4 1/2 **Zambucca (SAF)**[14] 625 7-9-0 98 HarryBentley 10 96
(S Seemar, UAE) *nvr nr to chal* **50/1**
12 4 1/4 **Eye In The Sky (IRE)**[28] 453 5-9-2 105 (t) WilliamBuick 14 92
(Niels Petersen, Norway) *nvr bttr than mid-div* **40/1**
13 1 **Antinori (IRE)**[21] 538 10-9-0 100 (b) RichardMullen 8 89
(S Seemar, UAE) *slowly away: a in rr* **50/1**
14 2 1/4 **Respect Me**[14] 627 6-9-0 97 (b) WayneSmith 86
(Ismail Mohammed) *racd in 3rd tl wknd 3f* **66/1**

2m 57.19s (-2.21) **Going Correction** +0.15s/f (Good)
WFA 4 from 5yo+ 4lb **14** Ran SP% **127.4**
Speed ratings: **112,109,109,109,109 108,108,107,107,107 104,102,101,100**
CSF: 111.09.
Owner Mohammed Jaber **Bred** Rabbah Bloodstock Limited **Trained** Newmarket, Suffolk

FOCUS
TRAKUS: 2nd 0, 3rd +8, 4th -2, 5th 0, 6th +1, 7th +3, 8th +7, 9th +10, 10th +8, 11th +12, 12th +10, 13th +2, 14th -2. The rail on the turf course was out 12 metres. The runner-up set a modest pace to suit - 1:44.07 for the first 1m - and few got into this. The runner-up, fourth and ninth limit the form.

812a ARABIAN ADVENTURES (H'CAP) (TURF) 1m 2f
6:30 (6:30) (95-108,108) 3-Y-O+
£44,897 (£14,965; £7,482; £3,741; £2,244; £1,496)

RPR
1 **Dormello (IRE)**[21] 540 8-9-2 **104** ChrisHayes 14 106
(D Selvaratnam, UAE) *mid-div: smooth prog 2f out to ld 110yds out: comf* **12/1**
2 2 3/4 **Beach Bar (IRE)**[14] 628 5-8-13 **100** TadhgO'Shea 11 98
(Brendan Powell) *sn led: clr 4f out: hdd 110yds out: r.o* **33/1**
3 1 1/4 **Avon Pearl**[14] 628 7-8-13 **100** (vt) AdriedeVries 10 95
(Rune Haugen) *settled in rr: chsd ldr 2f out: r.o same pce fnl 1 1/2f* **50/1**
4 3/4 **Nolohay (IRE)**[7] 717 5-8-13 **100** (v) FernandoJara 2 94
(M Al Mheiri, UAE) *s.i.s: in rr: r.o fnl 2f nrst fin* **25/1**
5 hd **Artigiano (USA)**[14] 627 6-9-0 **101** (b) WilliamBuick 5 94
(Charlie Appleby) *trckd ldrs: ev ch 1 1/2f out: nt qckn fnl f* **9/1**
6 nk **Khusoosy (USA)**[11] 4-8-13 **100** (t) PaulHanagan 9 93
(A R Al Rayhi, UAE) *mid-div: r.o same pce fnl 2f* **7/1**[3]
7 3 1/4 **Elleval (IRE)**[28] 455 6-9-4 **106** (tp) PatSmullen 1 91
(David Marnane, Ire) *trckd ldrs: t.k.h: ev ch 1 1/2f out: wknd fnl f* **9/2**[2]
8 3/4 **Shamaal Nibras (USA)**[21] 540 7-8-13 **100** (v) PatDobbs 7 85
(Doug Watson, UAE) *nvr nr to chal* **10/1**
9 12 1/2 **Night Run (FR)**[103] 7952 4-8-7 **100** ow1 GeorgeBuckell(5) 58
(Y Al Blooshi, UAE) *slowly away: nvr nr to chal* **25/1**
10 1 1/2 **Pilote (IRE)**[21] 538 6-9-0 **101** (p) RoystonFfrench 8 58
(S bin Ghadayer, UAE) *nvr nr to chal* **16/1**
11 1 1/2 **Snow Squall**[21] 538 5-8-13 **100** (t) FrederikTylicki 6 54
(A bin Harmash, UAE) *trckd ldr tl wknd fnl 2f* **28/1**
12 2 3/4 **Musaddas**[21] 540 6-9-5 **107** (p) JamesDoyle 4 54
(Saeed bin Suroor) *trckd ldr: rdn 3f out: sn btn* **9/4**[1]
13 1 1/4 **Limario (GER)**[35] 372 6-9-6 **108** SamHitchcott 3 53
(Doug Watson, UAE) *trckd ldrs tl wknd 2 1/2f out* **8/1**
14 8 **Nafaqa (IRE)**[14] 628 4-9-2 **104** (t) DaneO'Neill 13 33
(E Charpy, UAE) *mid-div: wknd 3f out* **12/1**

2m 2.67s (-0.03) **Going Correction** +0.15s/f (Good) **14** Ran SP% **129.0**
Speed ratings: **106,103,102,102,102 101,99,98,88,87 86,84,83,76**
CSF: 377.42, TRICAST: 17456.83. Placepot: £45.40 to a £1 stake. Pool of £6824.50 - 109.60 winning units. Quadpot: £9.10 to a £1 stake. Pool of £477.80 - 38.80 winning units..
Owner Sheikh Ahmed Al Maktoum **Bred** Grundy Bloodstock Srl **Trained** United Arab Emirates

FOCUS
TRAKUS: 2nd -1, 3rd -3, 4th +4, 5th +6, 6th +10, 7th 0, 8th +3, 9th +9, 10th +6, 11th +2, 12th +5, 13th +3, 14th +12. The rail on the turf course was out 12 metres. This was a strange sort of race, as the runner-up set a good early pace before slowing it down, (25.72, 22.94, 24.5, 24.62, winner finished in 24.12), and opened up a clear advantage, and it seemed those who chased him early got burnt, with the others involved in the finish staying on from some way back. Whatever way you look it, it's not strong carnival form.

770 LINGFIELD (L-H)
Friday, March 4

OFFICIAL GOING: Polytrack: standard
Wind: Moderate, across (towards stands) Weather: Bright, crisp

813 32RED.COM FILLIES' H'CAP 1m 1y(P)
2:00 (2:00) (Class 5) (0-75,74) 4-Y-O+ **£2,911** (£866; £432; £216) **Stalls** High

Form RPR
-231 1 **Skidby Mill (IRE)**[8] 709 6-9-3 **70** 6ex JimCrowley 4 74
(Laura Mongan) *mde all: set stdy pce early as rest t.k.h: jnd over 4f out: sent for home and def advantage over 1f out: drvn out* **4/1**[2]
3302 2 1 **Ixelles Diamond (IRE)**[11] 667 5-8-12 **68** DannyBrock(3) 5 70
(Andrew Reid) *dwlt: t.k.h: hld up in last: rdn and no prog over 2f out: hdwy to take 2nd ins fnl f: no imp on wnr nr fin* **8/1**
6-22 3 nk **Free Running (IRE)**[28] 456 4-9-7 **74** RobertHavlin 3 75
(Simon Crisford) *t.k.h: trckd wnr: upsides over 4f out tl rdn and nt qckn wl over 1f out: kpt on same pce after* **1/1**[1]
6606 4 nse **Venus Grace**[4] 769 5-8-4 **57** AndrewMullen 1 58
(Michael Appleby) *t.k.h: hld up bhd ldrs: rdn over 2f out: tk 2nd on inner briefly jst ins fnl f: one pce last 100yds* **7/1**
2521 5 1 1/2 **Miss Lillie**[9] 701 5-8-7 **65** 6ex (p) CallumShepherd(5) 2 63
(Roger Teal) *stdd s: t.k.h: hld up in tch: rdn over 2f out: one pce and nvr able to chal* **5/1**[3]

1m 39.28s (1.08) **Going Correction** -0.075s/f (Stan) **5** Ran SP% **110.3**
Speed ratings (Par 100): **91,90,89,89,88**
CSF £31.67 TOTE £3.50: £2.10, £2.90; EX 23.20 Trifecta £44.30.
Owner Charlie's Starrs **Bred** Michael O'Mahony **Trained** Epsom, Surrey

FOCUS
An ordinary fillies' handicap and a tactical event with the early pace a modest one, but the race was won by an admirable mare. There are doubts over the form.

814 £10 FREE AT 32RED.COM MAIDEN FILLIES' STKS (PLUS 10 RACE) 1m 1y(P)
2:30 (2:30) (Class 5) 3-Y-O **£2,911** (£866; £432; £216) **Stalls** High

Form RPR
-233 1 **Strawberry Sorbet**[13] 654 3-9-0 71 AdamKirby 2 68
(Clive Cox) *led after 2f: mde rest: hrd drvn fr over 1f out: hld on* **3/1**[2]
0- 2 1/2 **Performer**[268] 3048 3-9-0 0 SeanLevey 3 67+
(Richard Hannon) *chsd ldng pair: effrt over 2f out: rdn to chse wnr over 1f out: kpt on but a hld fnl f* **10/11**[1]
3 3 1/2 **Flinty Fell (IRE)** 3-9-0 0 PatCosgrave 9 58+
(Ed Dunlop) *dwlt: hld up wl in rr and off the pce: stdy prog fr 3f out: pushed along over 1f out: styd on to snatch 3rd last stride: shaped w promise* **16/1**
6-00 4 shd **Katie Canford**[23] 515 3-9-0 57 WilliamCarson 10 58
(John Bridger) *led 2f: chsd wnr: rdn over 2f out: lost 2nd over 1f out: lost 3rd last stride* **66/1**
5 shd **Dangerous Secret** 3-9-0 0 JimmyQuinn 5 58+
(Dr Jon Scargill) *dwlt: wl in rr and off the pce: gng wl enough 3f out: shkn up wl over 1f out: kpt on wl to press for 3rd last strides: shaped w promise* **50/1**
34 6 nse **Cold Fusion (IRE)**[14] 633 3-9-0 0 TedDurcan 4 58
(Ed Vaughan) *chsd ldng quartet but nt on terms: pushed along over 2f out: rdn and kpt on fr over 1f out to press for 3rd last strides* **10/1**
4623 7 1 1/2 **Kelvin Hall**[9] 699 3-9-0 65 FrannyNorton 1 54
(Mark Johnston) *chsd ldng pair: rdn 2f out: fdd and lost pls ins fnl f* **7/1**[3]
8 6 **Lemon Thyme** 3-8-7 0 [1] KevinLundie(7) 7 40
(Mike Murphy) *dwlt: detached in last after 3f: nvr a factor* **100/1**
9 3/4 **Mon Petite Etoile (FR)** 3-9-0 0 TomQueally 6 38
(David Elsworth) *dwlt: sn in 6th: shkn up on outer 3f out: no prog* **20/1**
10 1/2 **Amazing Moon** 3-8-11 0 RyanTate(3) 8 37
(Richard Hughes) *a in rr and off the pce: shkn up and no prog 3f out* **20/1**

1m 37.24s (-0.96) **Going Correction** -0.075s/f (Stan) **10** Ran SP% **118.8**
Speed ratings (Par 95): **101,100,97,96,96 96,95,89,88,88**
CSF £5.93 TOTE £3.50: £1.40, £1.30, £2.70; EX 6.70 Trifecta £34.10.
Owner Cheveley Park Stud **Bred** Aislabie Bloodstock Ltd **Trained** Lambourn, Berks

FOCUS
An interesting 3yo fillies' maiden and the pace looked decent. The winner set the benchmark and is rated close to form.

815 CORAL CLASSIFIED CLAIMING STKS 1m 2f (P)
3:05 (3:05) (Class 5) 4-Y-O+ **£2,911** (£866; £432; £216) **Stalls** Low

Form RPR
5620 1 **Matraash (USA)**[11] 676 10-8-13 63 (be) AndrewMullen 5 69
(Daniel Mark Loughnane) *hld up in last pair: sweeping prog on outer fr 3f out to ld 2f out: rdn fnl f: jst hld on* **8/1**
0-30 2 nk **Freddy With A Y (IRE)**[16] 616 6-9-3 73 (p) GeorgeBaker 3 72
(Gary Moore) *led 4f: styd cl up on inner: rdn to chse wnr 1f out: kpt on and grad clsd nr fin* **13/8**[1]
2-23 3 2 **What A Party (IRE)**[14] 631 4-8-10 57 (v) LukeMorris 7 61
(Gay Kelleway) *early reminder and urged along into midfield: drvn and no prog over 2f out: kpt on u.p to take 3rd nr fin* **6/1**[3]
30-0 4 3/4 **Barren Brook**[44] 256 9-8-4 73 MeganNicholls(7) 4 61
(Laura Mongan) *plld hrd: hld up tl led after 4f: hdd 2f out: fdd fnl f* **6/1**[3]
0-05 5 1 1/4 **Ravenous**[16] 616 5-9-4 72 (v[1]) KieranO'Neill 8 65
(Luke Dace) *prom: trckd ldr 5f out to 2f out: rdn and fnd nil wl over 1f out: fdd* **9/2**[2]
-00 6 3 **Evacusafe Lady**[9] 701 5-8-6 57 (t) RyanPowell 6 47
(John Ryan) *hld up in last pair: rdn and struggling wl over 2f out: n.d* **20/1**
5-06 7 2 3/4 **Occult**[16] 606 4-9-4 62 JimCrowley 1 54
(Simon Dow) *in tch: rdn 2f out: wknd over 1f out* **8/1**

2m 4.62s (-1.98) **Going Correction** -0.075s/f (Stan) **7** Ran SP% **111.8**
Speed ratings (Par 104): **104,103,102,101,100 98,95**
CSF £20.55 TOTE £9.00: £3.60, £1.80; EX 28.90 Trifecta £134.80.
Owner Over The Moon Racing **Bred** Shadwell Farm LLC **Trained** Baldwin's Gate, Staffs

FOCUS
A moderate classified claimer with recent winning form thin on the ground. Muddling form.

816 LADBROKES H'CAP 7f 1y(P)
3:40 (3:40) (Class 2) (0-105,101) 4-Y-O+
£11,827 (£3,541; £1,770; £885; £442; £222) **Stalls** Low

Form RPR
4-22 1 **Shyron**[27] 486 5-8-10 **90** RyanPowell 2 97+
(George Margarson) *w.w disputing 5th: prog to chse ldr 1f out: rdn to ld last 100yds: styd on and a holding on* **11/4**[1]
100- 2 nk **Majestic Moon (IRE)**[153] 6919 6-9-4 **101** MichaelJMMurphy(3) 7 107
(John Gallagher) *led: drvn for home 2f out: hdd last 100yds: kpt on* **33/1**
6-25 3 hd **Mutawathea**[20] 560 5-9-4 **98** (p) RobertHavlin 6 103+
(Simon Crisford) *trckd ldng trio: drvn on outer wl over 1f out: styd on fnl f to press for 2nd nr fin* **5/1**[3]
2252 4 3/4 **Boomerang Bob (IRE)**[12] 663 7-9-3 **97** WilliamCarson 5 100
(Jamie Osborne) *hld up in last pair: rdn and prog jst over 1f out: styd on but nt gng pce to chal* **8/1**
050- 5 hd **Lexington Times (IRE)**[127] 7588 4-8-13 **96** TomMarquand(3) 1 99
(Richard Hannon) *hld up in last pair: pushed along on inner fr over 1f out: rdn and kpt on same pce fnl f: no threat* **10/1**
0-55 6 1/2 **Grey Mirage**[27] 486 7-9-3 **97** (p) AntonioFresu 3 99
(Marco Botti) *trckd ldrs: disp 2nd briefly over 1f out: sn rdn and nt qckn: one pce and lost pl ins fnl f* **5/1**[3]
1113 7 3/4 **Clement (IRE)**[7] 727 6-7-13 **84** ow1 (v) PaddyPilley(5) 8 84
(John O'Shea) *t.k.h: trckd ldr: rdn 2f out: lost 2nd and fdd over 1f out* **9/2**[2]
4-26 8 1 1/4 **Dutiful Son (IRE)**[27] 486 6-8-7 **87** LukeMorris 4 83
(Simon Dow) *hld up in disputing 5th: rdn over 1f out: keeping on but nvr gng pce to chal whn short of room and eased last 100yds* **6/1**

1m 22.19s (-2.61) **Going Correction** -0.075s/f (Stan) **8** Ran SP% **115.6**
Speed ratings (Par 109): **111,110,110,109,109 108,107,106**
CSF £94.55 CT £439.96 TOTE £3.80: £1.40, £4.50, £2.00; EX 84.70 Trifecta £522.30.
Owner F Butler & Mrs Connie Taylor **Bred** F Butler **Trained** Newmarket, Suffolk

FOCUS
A decent handicap and the pace was good without being anything out of the ordinary. Solid form, the first two to their best.

817 32REDSPORT.COM H'CAP 7f 1y(P)
4:10 (4:10) (Class 5) (0-70,70) 3-Y-O £2,911 (£866; £432; £216) Stalls Low

Form RPR
4-1R **1** **Beleave**[11] 678 3-9-3 **66**........ KieranO'Neill 3 70
(Luke Dace) *taken down early: trckd ldng pair: wnt 2nd on inner over 1f out and sn chalng: rdn to ld jst ins fnl f: styd on* **3/1**[2]

-151 **2** *1* **Inaam (IRE)**[16] 610 3-9-6 **69**........ DavidNolan 7 70
(Richard Fahey) *t.k.h: trckd ldr: rdn and lost 2nd over 1f out: chsd wnr ins fnl f: styd on same pce* **7/4**[1]

061- **3** *1* **Ginger Joe**[99] 8007 3-9-4 **67**........ SeanLevey 4 65
(David Brown) *led: rdn over 1f out: hdd jst ins fnl f: one pce* **7/2**[3]

0-15 **4** *nk* **Trodero**[23] 519 3-9-7 **70**........ JimmyQuinn 5 67
(Dr Jon Scargill) *s.i.s: sn trckd ldng trio: rdn over 1f out: one pce and nvr able to chal* **6/1**

-643 **5** *shd* **Khismet**[16] 613 3-9-2 **70**........(p) CharlesEddery(5) 1 67
(Rae Guest) *awkward s and slowly away: in tch in last: drvn over 1f out: styd on last 100yds: gaining at fin* **12/1**

0-45 **6** *nse* **Serendib's Glory (IRE)**[15] 618 3-8-5 **61**........ MillyNaseb(7) 2 58
(Julia Feilden) *hld up in 6th: pushed along on inner 2f out: one pce and nvr able to chal* **20/1**

1m 25.57s (0.77) **Going Correction** -0.075s/f (Stan) **6** Ran SP% **110.3**
Speed ratings (Par 98): **92,90,89,89,89 89**
CSF £8.36 TOTE £4.20: £2.20, £1.20; EX 10.60 Trifecta £34.80.
Owner Richard L Page **Bred** Copped Hall Farm & Stud **Trained** Pulborough, W Sussex

FOCUS
A modest 3yo handicap. They went no pace early and there wasn't much covering the six runners at the line. The form makes sense around the first four.

818 32RED CASINO MAIDEN STKS 1m 4f (P)
4:45 (4:46) (Class 5) 3-Y-O £2,911 (£866; £432; £216) Stalls Low

Form RPR
1 **Pechora (IRE)** 3-9-0 0........ RobertHavlin 9 66+
(John Gosden) *s.s: hld up in last pair: prog on outer fr 3f out: chsd ldr 2f out: rdn to ld jst over 1f out: styd on wl* **3/1**[3]

23-4 **2** *1* **Zio Gianni (USA)**[10] 687 3-9-5 72........ GeorgeBaker 1 69
(Jamie Osborne) *hld up in last: prog on outer 2f out: drvn over 1f out: chsd wnr ins fnl f: kpt on but too much to do* **2/1**[1]

3 *½* **Hongkong Adventure** 3-9-5 0........ SeanLevey 6 68
(Rae Guest) *wl in tch: shkn up over 2f out: tried to cl over 1f out: kpt on same pce fnl f* **8/1**

55 **4** *2 ¼* **The Magic Pencil (IRE)**[16] 603 3-9-5 0........ ShaneGray 3 65
(Kevin Ryan) *slowly away: sn trckd ldng pair: led on outer over 2f out: drvn and hdd jst over 1f out: wknd ins fnl f* **9/4**[2]

5 **5** *1* **Nightmare (IRE)**[10] 687 3-9-5 0........(b[1]) TimmyMurphy 2 63
(Jamie Osborne) *trckd ldrs: nudged along and outpcd fr 2f out: reminders fnl f and kpt on same pce* **50/1**

0-06 **6** *¾* **Rainbow Lad (IRE)**[24] 509 3-9-5 43........ AndrewMullen 4 62?
(Michael Appleby) *disp ld to over 2f out: steadily wknd* **66/1**

0- **7** *1 ¼* **Jamaica Inn (IRE)**[80] 8233 3-9-0 0........(p) JimmyQuinn 5 55
(John Gosden) *in tch in rr: rdn and dropped to last 3f out: detached 2f out: plugged on u.p* **14/1**

-656 **8** *12* **Quick Witted**[23] 517 3-9-0 54........(v[1]) PatCosgrave 8 47
(Harry Dunlop) *disp ld to over 2f out: wknd qckly over 1f out: eased* **33/1**

2m 32.02s (-0.98) **Going Correction** -0.075s/f (Stan) **8** Ran SP% **113.3**
Speed ratings (Par 98): **100,99,99,97,96 96,95,87**
CSF £9.21 TOTE £3.30: £1.30, £1.30, £1.90; EX 9.80 Trifecta £33.70.
Owner Godolphin **Bred** Sunderland Holdings Inc **Trained** Newmarket, Suffolk

FOCUS
A modest 3yo middle-distance maiden and despite an ordinary pace, the front pair came from the very back of the field. There is some doubt over the form horses running to their marks.
T/Plt: £48.10 to a £1 stake. Pool: £55,064.76 - 835.36 winning tickets T/Qpdt: £6.70 to a £1 stake. Pool: £5,402.79 - 591.74 winning tickets **Jonathan Neesom**

784 WOLVERHAMPTON (A.W) (L-H)
Friday, March 4

OFFICIAL GOING: Tapeta: standard
Wind: Fresh half-against Weather: Showers

819 BET IN PLAY AT CORAL APPRENTICE H'CAP 1m 4f 50y (Tp)
5:45 (5:46) (Class 6) (0-55,59) 4-Y-O+ £2,587 (£770; £384; £192) Stalls Low

Form RPR
330- **1** **Yasir (USA)**[16] 1125 8-8-13 **51**........ SophieKilloran(3) 3 61
(Sophie Leech) *hld up: hdwy over 4f out: led wl over 1f out: sn rdn clr* **25/1**

35-5 **2** *5* **Well Owd Mon**[44] 255 6-9-4 **53**........(p) AdamMcLean 5 55
(Sarah Hollinshead) *s.i.s: hld up: hdwy over 1f out: styd on to go 2nd wl ins fnl f: nt trble wnr* **10/1**

53-2 **3** *nk* **Henry Smith**[24] 505 4-8-13 **50**........(be) PhilDennis 9 52
(Garry Moss) *led: hdd over 9f out: remained handy: rdn over 3f out: styng on same pce whn hung lft ins fnl f* **5/1**[2]

00-6 **4** *2 ¾* **Ring Eye (IRE)**[14] 640 8-9-6 **55**........ GeorgiaCox 4 52
(John O'Shea) *plld hrd and prom: jnd ldr over 3f out: rdn and ev ch 2f out: wknd ins fnl f* **9/1**

36-3 **5** *½* **Oakley Star**[22] 527 4-9-0 **54**........ RhiainIngram(3) 1 50
(Gay Kelleway) *prom: nt clr run and lost pl 6f out: outpcd 3f out: hung lft over 1f out: styd on towards fin* **8/1**[3]

02/0 **6** *1 ½* **Deadline Day (IRE)**[11] 673 5-8-9 **51**........ GeorgeWood(7) 6 45
(Michael Mullineaux) *sn pushed along and prom: rdn and lost pl over 3f out: wknd over 2f out* **40/1**

0/ **7** *nk* **That's Ours (USA)**[91] 8114 8-8-11 **46** oh1........(b) NathanEvans 10 39
(E Sheehy, Ire) *chsd ldr tl led over 9f out: rdn and hdd wl over 1f out: wknd fnl f* **20/1**

0011 **8** *7* **Pao De Acuca (IRE)**[11] 673 4-9-1 **59** 6ex........(t) ChrisKelly(7) 8 41
(Jose Santos) *s.i.s: hdwy 10f out: chsd ldr over 6f out tl rdn over 3f out: wknd over 2f out* **2/5**[1]

2m 39.09s (-1.71) **Going Correction** -0.20s/f (Stan)
WFA 4 from 5yo+ 2lb **8** Ran SP% **129.3**
Speed ratings (Par 101): **97,93,93,91,91 90,90,85**
CSF £271.24 CT £1487.33 TOTE £22.90: £4.70, £3.40, £1.70; EX 158.70 Trifecta £1085.10.
Owner Mike Harris Racing Club **Bred** Shadwell Farm LLC **Trained** Elton, Gloucs

FOCUS
The track had been harrowed to a depth of 3.5 inches and had been reinstated with a gallop master finish. There was a shock winner in this apprentice handicap, which was run at a stop-start gallop. The form is rated as straightforward.

820 32RED.COM H'CAP 5f 216y (Tp)
6:15 (6:17) (Class 6) (0-55,55) 3-Y-O £2,587 (£770; £384; £192) Stalls Low

Form RPR
00-4 **1** **Bertie Buoy**[4] 763 3-8-9 **46** oh1........(v) PhilipPrince(3) 8 61
(Richard Guest) *mde all: rdn clr over 1f out: comf* **15/2**

00-6 **2** *5* **Comparinka**[24] 510 3-9-7 **55**........ BenCurtis 2 55
(Scott Dixon) *sn pushed along to chse ldrs: rdn over 2f out: chsd wnr fnl f: no imp* **25/1**

-212 **3** *1* **Israfel**[2] 785 3-9-5 **53**........ CathyGannon 6 50
(Jamie Osborne) *hld up: rdn over 2f out: styd on to go 3rd ins fnl f: nt trble ldrs* **5/4**[1]

0-03 **4** *nk* **Ormanumps (IRE)**[39] 327 3-8-12 **46** oh1........ ShaneKelly 1 42
(Daniel Mark Loughnane) *hld up: plld hrd: swtchd lft and hdwy over 1f out: nt trble ldrs* **4/1**[2]

533 **5** *¾* **Fearbuster (IRE)**[24] 507 3-9-7 **55**........ JackMitchell 7 49
(Hugo Palmer) *jnd wnr 5f out tl rdn over 2f out: wknd fnl f* **11/2**[3]

060- **6** *1 ½* **Bushwise (IRE)**[115] 7783 3-8-12 **46** oh1........(p) RaulDaSilva 4 35
(Milton Bradley) *prom: racd keenly: rdn over 2f out: wknd fnl f* **22/1**

5230 **7** *1* **Memyselfie (IRE)**[7] 732 3-9-4 **52**........(v) TonyHamilton 5 38
(Derek Shaw) *hld up: rdn over 2f out: nvr on terms* **12/1**

5-03 **8** *6* **Castlerea Tess**[21] 544 3-9-2 **50**........ DougieCostello 3 18
(Sarah Hollinshead) *s.i.s: hdwy over 3f out: rdn over 2f out: wknd over 1f out* **16/1**

1m 14.02s (-0.48) **Going Correction** -0.20s/f (Stan) **8** Ran SP% **113.4**
Speed ratings (Par 96): **95,88,87,86,85 83,82,74**
CSF £160.42 CT £386.38 TOTE £8.10: £2.80, £7.60, £1.90; EX 166.00 Trifecta £527.70.
Owner ColinWing,MichaelCook&StephenHodgkinson **Bred** S D Bevan **Trained** Ingmanthorpe, W Yorks

FOCUS
A moderate contest but a nice front-running performance from the winner, who's clearly much improved.

821 DOWNLOAD THE NEW UNIBET RACING APP CONDITIONS STKS (PLUS 10 RACE) (AW CSHIP FAST-TRACK QUALIFIER) 5f 20y (Tp)
6:45 (6:45) (Class 2) 3-Y-O £11,971 (£3,583; £1,791; £896; £446) Stalls Low

Form RPR
31-1 **1** **Wolowitz (IRE)**[10] 686 3-9-0 85........ GrahamGibbons 9 96+
(David Barron) *chsd ldrs: swtchd lft over 3f out: rdn to ld and edgd lft ins fnl f: r.o* **5/2**[2]

2-11 **2** *nk* **Kadrizzi (FR)**[26] 493 3-9-0 104........ RobertWinston 2 95+
(Dean Ivory) *sn pushed along in mid-div: hdwy over 1f out: rdn and ev ch ins fnl f: r.o* **11/8**[1]

003- **3** *2 ¾* **Shadow Hunter (IRE)**[147] 7072 3-8-12 99........ ShaneKelly 3 84
(Paul D'Arcy) *hld up: hdwy over 1f out: styd on to go 3rd wl ins fnl f* **11/2**

1-22 **4** *1 ¼* **Krystallite**[10] 686 3-8-9 70........ BenCurtis 4 76
(Scott Dixon) *led: rdn over 1f out: hdd and no ex ins fnl f* **33/1**

2-22 **5** *nk* **Field Of Vision (IRE)**[26] 493 3-9-0 102........(p) JFEgan 5 80
(Joseph Tuite) *chsd ldr: rdn 1/2-way: no ex ins fnl f* **5/1**[3]

200- **6** *nk* **Glenrowan Rose (IRE)**[167] 6514 3-8-9 93........ JasonHart 8 74
(Keith Dalgleish) *s.i.s: outpcd: styd on fr over 1f out: nt trble ldrs* **20/1**

4-0 **7** *1 ¾* **Zephyr Breeze**[57] 77 3-9-0 0........ BarryMcHugh 1 73
(Noel Wilson) *hld up: pushed along 1/2-way: sme hdwy over 1f out: wknd ins fnl f* **200/1**

3402 **8** *½* **Sir Dudley (IRE)**[16] 612 3-9-0 75........ JamesSullivan 7 71
(James Given) *broke wl enough: sn lost pl: hung rt over 3f out: n.d after* **40/1**

05-4 **9** *9* **Silk Bow**[10] 686 3-8-9 81........ TomEaves 6 33
(James Given) *chsd ldrs: pushed along 1/2-way: wknd over 1f out* **20/1**

59.77s (-2.13) **Going Correction** -0.20s/f (Stan) course record **9** Ran SP% **118.1**
Speed ratings (Par 104): **109,108,104,102,101 101,98,97,83**
CSF £6.17 TOTE £3.10: £1.10, £1.30, £1.80; EX 8.10 Trifecta £25.40.
Owner Mrs Christine Barron **Bred** Jerry O'Sullivan **Trained** Maunby, N Yorks

FOCUS
A decent contest run at a good gallop. The front0running fourth is the key to the form.

822 BEST ODDS GUARANTEED AT CORAL H'CAP 1m 1f 103y (Tp)
7:15 (7:16) (Class 6) (0-55,60) 4-Y-O+ £2,587 (£770; £384; £192) Stalls Low

Form RPR
4424 **1** **Ferryview Place**[9] 701 7-8-13 **50**........(tp) GeorgeDowning(3) 9 56
(Ian Williams) *hld up: nt clr run over 2f out: hdwy over 1f out: r.o to ld wl ins fnl f* **11/1**

-511 **2** *1 ¼* **On A Whim**[35] 383 4-9-1 **56** ow1........ PaddyBradley(7) 5 60
(Daniel Mark Loughnane) *a.p: rdn over 2f out: ev ch over 1f out: styd on* **4/1**[2]

-334 **3** *nk* **Music Hall (FR)**[11] 674 6-8-12 **46** oh1........ DougieCostello 3 49
(Shaun Harris) *hld up: hdwy over 2f out: rdn over 1f out: r.o* **10/1**

0-11 **4** *nk* **Eastern Dragon (IRE)**[3] 776 6-9-5 **60** 6ex........ PatrickVaughan(7) 6 62
(Seamus Durack) *hld up: nt clr run over 2f out: hdwy over 1f out: sn rdn: r.o* **5/4**[1]

10-6 **5** *shd* **Hazel Blue (IRE)**[23] 526 5-9-3 **51**........ BenCurtis 12 53
(David Loughnane) *hld up: rdn over 2f out: hdwy over 1f out: r.o* **20/1**

2-05 **6** *½* **Cool Beans**[45] 251 4-9-2 **53**........(b) RobHornby(3) 1 54
(Roy Bowring) *chsd ldrs: rdn to ld over 1f out: edgd lft: hdd and no ex wl ins fnl f* **12/1**

003/ **7** *½* **Appease**[119] 7739 7-9-5 **53**........(b[1]) GrahamGibbons 10 53
(E Sheehy, Ire) *prom: chsd ldr over 6f out tl led 2f out: rdn and hdd over 1f out: no ex ins fnl f* **6/1**[3]

0-03 **8** *3* **Thrtypointstothree (IRE)**[42] 294 5-8-12 **46** oh1........(b) JFEgan 7 41
(Nikki Evans) *sn led: rdn and hdd 2f out: wknd and eased wl ins fnl f* **22/1**

450- **9** *1 ¼* **Notts So Blue**[65] 8398 5-8-12 **46** oh1........(b) AdamBeschizza 2 38
(Shaun Harris) *chsd ldrs: rdn over 2f out: wknd over 1f out* **66/1**

3-00 **10** *3 ¾* **Quite Sparky**[28] 294 9-8-7 **46** oh1........(b) RachelRichardson(5) 4 31
(Lucinda Egerton) *hld up: plld hrd: rdn over 2f out: nvr trbld ldrs* **40/1**

245- **11** *nse* **Don't Tell Louise**[150] 7021 4-9-4 **52**........ TomEaves 13 37
(Brian Baugh) *hld up: rdn over 1f out: n.d* **40/1**

600- **12** *9* **Strictly Glitz (IRE)**[64] 8201 5-9-5 **53**........(p) CathyGannon 11 21
(Clare Ellam) *s.i.s: hld up: rdn over 2f out: a in rr* **66/1**

050- **13** *4* **Vicarage Gold**[296] 2178 4-8-7 **46**.............................. CallumShepherd(5) 8 6
(Shaun Lycett) *hld up: pushed along and hdwy over 4f out: rdn and wknd over 2f out: eased fnl f* **100/1**

1m 59.17s (-1.63) **Going Correction** -0.20s/f (Stan) **13** Ran SP% **121.8**
Speed ratings (Par 101): **99,97,97,97,97 96,96,93,92,89 89,81,77**
CSF £53.33 CT £470.89 TOTE £14.90: £3.90, £1.50, £2.60; EX 90.40 Trifecta £446.10.
Owner Vendman **Bred** Bishopswood Bloodstock & Trickledown Stud **Trained** Portway, Worcs

FOCUS
An ordinary handicap. The pace picked up from a fair way out. The winner is rated close to his win here this time last year.

823 DOWNLOAD THE CORAL APP H'CAP 1m 1f 103y (Tp)
7:45 (7:46) (Class 5) (0-75,75) 4-Y-O+ **£3,881** (£1,155; £577; £288) **Stalls** Low

Form RPR
-211 **1** **Tangramm**[14] 640 4-9-5 **73**..(p) RobertWinston 5 84+
(Dean Ivory) *hld up: hdwy: nt clr run and swtchd rt over 1f out: r.o to ld wl ins fnl f: sn clr* **5/2**[1]

-234 **2** *2* **Off The Pulse**[7] 734 6-9-7 **75**..................................(p) GrahamGibbons 6 81
(John Mackie) *hld up: hdwy 5f out: swtchd rt over 2f out: shkn up to ld ins fnl f: sn rdn and hdd: styd on same pce* **5/2**[1]

400- **3** *1/2* **Sakhalin Star (IRE)**[87] 8147 5-9-0 **68**..................................(e) JasonHart 3 73
(Richard Guest) *a.p: racd keenly: rdn over 1f out: styd on same pce ins fnl f* **25/1**

30-2 **4** *1/2* **Sands Chorus**[18] 595 4-9-4 **72**.. TomEaves 2 76
(James Given) *led: rdn over 1f out: hdd and no ex ins fnl f* **5/1**[3]

3-22 **5** *2 1/4* **Yulong Xiongba (IRE)**[11] 676 4-8-10 **64**.................... DougieCostello 1 63
(Julie Camacho) *unruly in stalls: chsd ldr 1f: remained handy: shkn up over 3f out: wnt 2nd again 2f out: sn rdn: no ex ins fnl f* **10/1**

026- **6** *1* **Peak Storm**[156] 6414 7-8-13 **72**... CiaranMckee(5) 4 69
(John O'Shea) *hld up: rdn over 1f out: nvr trbld ldrs* **28/1**

250- **7** *1/2* **All You (IRE)**[270] 2988 4-9-5 **73**...................................... DanielTudhope 7 69
(David O'Meara) *hld up: rdn over 2f out: nt clr run and wknd ins fnl f* **9/2**[2]

00-0 **8** *2* **Samsonite (IRE)**[23] 523 4-9-5 **73**..................................(p) BarryMcHugh 8 65
(Tony Coyle) *chsd ldr after 1f tl rdn 2f out: wknd fnl f* **28/1**

1m 57.9s (-2.90) **Going Correction** -0.20s/f (Stan) **8** Ran SP% **111.8**
Speed ratings (Par 103): **104,102,101,101,99 98,98,96**
CSF £8.13 CT £115.38 TOTE £3.00: £1.30, £1.40, £5.80; EX 9.50 Trifecta £141.30.
Owner John Marsden **Bred** W G H Barrons **Trained** Radlett, Herts

FOCUS
A fair handicap rated around the second and fourth.

824 LADBROKES MEDIAN AUCTION MAIDEN STKS 7f 32y (Tp)
8:15 (8:16) (Class 5) 3-5-Y-O **£3,881** (£1,155; £577; £288) **Stalls** High

Form RPR
3 **1** **Bint Arcano (FR)**[11] 679 3-8-6 0.................................... JamesSullivan 8 73
(Julie Camacho) *hld up: hdwy over 1f out: rdn and r.o to ld towards fin* **11/4**[2]

2 *3/4* **Magical Path (IRE)** 3-8-6 0.. JFEgan 5 71+
(Hugo Palmer) *led 1f: chsd ldrs: shkn up to ld over 2f out: rdn over 1f out: hdd towards fin* **12/1**

3 *2* **Bond Trader** 3-8-11 0.. JohnFahy 2 71
(Clive Cox) *chsd ldrs: lost pl over 5f out: hdwy over 2f out: shkn up over 1f out: styd on same pce ins fnl f* **9/1**

3- **4** *1 1/2* **Philadelphia (IRE)**[133] 7423 3-8-11 0.......................... JackMitchell 7 67+
(Roger Varian) *prom: chsd ldr over 5f out: rdn over 2f out: hung lft over 1f out: no ex ins fnl f* **4/7**[1]

5 *8* **Ksenia (IRE)** 3-7-13 0... KieranSchofield(7) 4 40
(Nigel Tinkler) *s.i.s: hld up: rdn and wknd over 2f out* **33/1**

00-3 **6** *shd* **Deben**[19] 582 3-8-11 69.. RaulDaSilva 6 45+
(Kevin Ryan) *plld hrd: led 5f out: rdn and hdd over 2f out: sn hung rt: nt clr run over 1f out: wknd ins fnl f* **5/1**[3]

7 *5* **Sunshine Quest** 4-9-3 0... RachelRichardson(5) 3 32
(Lucinda Egerton) *sn prom: rdn and wknd over 2f out* **80/1**

006 **8** *nk* **Compromise**[9] 697 3-8-8 0... EoinWalsh(3) 1 30
(Conor Dore) *hld up: rdn and wknd over 2f out* **50/1**

1m 27.3s (-1.50) **Going Correction** -0.20s/f (Stan)
WFA 3 from 4yo 16lb **8** Ran SP% **130.8**
Speed ratings (Par 103): **100,99,96,95,86 85,80,79**
CSF £39.63 TOTE £4.10: £1.70, £5.00, £2.30; EX 47.70 Trifecta £168.90.
Owner G B Turnbull Ltd **Bred** Rabbah Bloodstock Limited **Trained** Norton, N Yorks

FOCUS
A modest maiden run at a fair pace. Not a great deal to go on when rating the race.
T/Plt: £83.80 to a £1 stake. Pool: £78,473.56 - 683.20 winning tickets T/Qpdt: £10.80 to a £1 stake. Pool: £11,530.63 - 783.26 winning tickets **Colin Roberts**

825 - 827a (Foreign Racing) - See Raceform Interactive

[736]DUNDALK (A.W) (L-H)
Friday, March 4

OFFICIAL GOING: Polytrack: standard

828a BIG BAD BOB RACE 7f (P)
7:30 (7:30) 3-Y-O **£7,610** (£1,764; £772; £441)

RPR
1 **Bear Faced**[14] 638 3-9-4 85.................................... DeclanMcDonogh 1 85+
(Sir Mark Prescott Bt) *led but sn hdd: travelled wl in 2nd tl led under 2f out: sn pushed clr: styd on wl* **7/4**[2]

2 *2 1/4* **Proud Sky**[126] 7592 3-9-1 88.. KevinManning 2 76+
(J S Bolger, Ire) *t.k.h early in 3rd: rdn over 2f out: prog to chse wnr in 2nd appr fnl f: nvr on terms* **8/15**[1]

3 *1 3/4* **Helvic (IRE)**[28] 470 3-9-1 0... ColinKeane 4 71
(John Joseph Murphy, Ire) *sn led: strly pressed 2f out and sn hdd: no ex in 3rd appr fnl f* **12/1**[3]

4 *8* **Modh Coinniolach (IRE)** 3-9-1 0...................................... PBBeggy 3 50
(Dermot Anthony McLoughlin, Ire) *a in rr and nvr a factor: adrift over 2f out* **66/1**

1m 27.0s (87.00) **4** Ran SP% **110.8**
CSF £3.15 TOTE £2.00; DF 3.20 Trifecta £3.10.
Owner The Barkers & Chris Jenkins **Bred** The Kathryn Stud **Trained** Newmarket, Suffolk

FOCUS
This looked a match and the market got it completely wrong. The third and fourth potentially limit the form.

829a CORAL.IE RACE (ALL-WEATHER CHAMPIONSHIPS FAST-TRACK QUALIFIER) 1m 2f 150y(P)
8:00 (8:00) 4-Y-O+ **£11,948** (£3,492; £1,654; £551)

RPR
1 **Watersmeet**[27] 485 5-9-2 103... JoeFanning 2 99+
(Mark Johnston) *led and sn clr: rdn under 2f out: strly pressed ins fnl f: rallied wl to sn reassert: kpt on wl* **10/11**[1]

2 *1/2* **Political Policy (IRE)**[21] 553 5-9-2 98......................(tp) RonanWhelan 5 98+
(Gavin Cromwell, Ire) *chsd ldrs in 3rd: rdn to press ldrs over 1f out: almost on terms ins fnl f: kpt on wl: no imp on wnr cl home* **7/1**[3]

3 *1/2* **Mandatario**[14] 643 5-9-2 95..(t) KevinManning 3 97+
(J S Bolger, Ire) *chsd clr ldr in 2nd: rdn in cl 3rd appr fnl f: kpt on wl: no ex cl home* **3/1**[2]

4 *4 3/4* **Shalaman (IRE)**[14] 643 7-9-2 100..................................(tp) ConnorKing 4 88+
(David Marnane, Ire) *v.s.a and sn detached: clsr after 2f: wnt 4th under 2f out: sn rdn and no imp appr fnl f: kpt on one pce* **7/1**[3]

5 *4 1/2* **Vivat Rex (IRE)**[310] 1801 5-9-2 95................................(tp) GaryCarroll 1 79
(John James Feane, Ire) *hld up in 4th: dropped to rr under 2f out: sn no ex* **11/1**

2m 18.15s (138.15) **5** Ran SP% **110.7**
CSF £7.95 TOTE £1.70: £1.20, £2.50; DF 7.80 Trifecta £11.50.
Owner J Barson **Bred** Stetchworth & Middle Park Studs **Trained** Middleham Moor, N Yorks

FOCUS
An interesting conditions race witnessed a good tough performance by Watersmeet, a second British-trained winner on the night. The form mkaes sense around the second and third.

830 - 831a (Foreign Racing) - See Raceform Interactive

[813]LINGFIELD (L-H)
Saturday, March 5

OFFICIAL GOING: Polytrack: standard
Wind: Moderate against Weather: Overcast with occasional heavy showers

832 CORAL H'CAP 1m 4f (P)
1:55 (1:55) (Class 5) (0-70,70) 4-Y-O+ **£2,911** (£866; £432; £216) **Stalls** Low

Form RPR
6-42 **1** **Midtech Star (IRE)**[15] 640 4-9-5 **70**.................................(v) AdamKirby 3 83
(Ian Williams) *led for 1f: trckd ldr: rdn to ld 2f out: styd on wl: drew clr fnl f* **9/4**[1]

-302 **2** *5* **I'm Harry**[4] 773 7-9-6 **69**..(vt) PatCosgrave 6 74
(George Baker) *in tch: rdn over 2f out: kpt on: wnt 2nd ins fnl f: no threat wnr* **9/2**

2115 **3** *4* **Trending (IRE)**[15] 640 7-9-4 **67**..............................(t) RichardKingscote 5 66
(Jeremy Gask) *racd keenly: led after 1f: rdn whn hdd 2f out: wknd fnl f* **7/2**[3]

-430 **4** *1 1/4* **Rising Breeze (FR)**[21] 566 5-9-0 **66**...................... GeorgeDowning(3) 2 63
(Tony Carroll) *in tch: rdn over 2f out: no imp* **8/1**

15-6 **5** *2 1/4* **Maison Brillet (IRE)**[54] 138 9-9-2 **65**..........................(p) RobertHavlin 4 58
(Clive Drew) *hld up: rdn 4f out: sn btn* **20/1**

-041 **6** *dist* **Apache Glory (USA)**[8] 724 8-9-5 **68**..............................(p) LukeMorris 1
(Daniel Mark Loughnane) *hld up: rdn along over 4f out: eased fr over 2f out w rdr looking down: lame* **3/1**[2]

2m 29.14s (-3.86) **Going Correction** -0.025s/f (Stan)
WFA 4 from 5yo+ 2lb **6** Ran SP% **112.0**
Speed ratings (Par 103): **111,107,105,104,102**
CSF £12.66 TOTE £3.30: £1.60, £3.70; EX 13.10 Trifecta £39.30.
Owner Midtech **Bred** Denis McDonnell **Trained** Portway, Worcs
■ Stewards' Enquiry : Luke Morris five-day ban; continued riding when it was contrary to the mare's welfare (22nd-25th March)

FOCUS
A modest middle-distance handicap. They initially went quite steadily but an even gallop broke out after about 1f on standard Polytrack. This was not the most robust field but the winner is progressive on the AW.

833 LADBROKES H'CAP 1m 1y(P)
2:30 (2:31) (Class 2) (0-105,102) 4-Y-O+ **£11,971** (£3,583; £1,791; £896; £446) **Stalls** High

Form RPR
260- **1** **Mister Universe**[154] 6919 4-9-7 **102**................................... JoeFanning 8 112
(Mark Johnston) *mde all: set stdy pce: qcknd pce over 1f out: rdn and kpt on fnl f* **6/1**

0-00 **2** *1 1/2* **Unforgiving Minute**[44] 284 5-8-9 **90**................................ ShaneKelly 7 96
(Gary Moore) *trckd ldr: rdn over 1f out: kpt on but a hld* **6/1**

1001 **3** *1 1/2* **Lunar Deity**[21] 560 7-9-4 **99**... PatCosgrave 5 102
(Stuart Williams) *racd keenly: trckd ldr: rdn over 1f out: one pce* **5/2**[1]

0-55 **4** *nk* **Lacan (IRE)**[13] 665 5-8-9 **90**...................................... GrahamGibbons 2 92
(Ralph Beckett) *racd keenly in tch: rdn over 1f out: one pce* **9/2**[2]

-506 **5** *1/2* **Bertiewhittle**[18] 599 8-8-6 **87**.. SamJames 3 88
(David Barron) *hld up in rr: nudged along appr fnl f: r.o fnl 110yds: nrst fin* **16/1**

1-15 **6** *nse* **Forceful Appeal (USA)**[35] 401 8-8-9 **90**......................... JimCrowley 4 91
(Simon Dow) *midfield: rdn over 1f out: kpt on same pce* **5/1**[3]

5-24 **7** *1 1/4* **Basil Berry**[26] 501 5-9-7 **102**...................................... IrineuGoncalves 6 100
(Chris Dwyer) *dwlt: sn in tch on outside racing keenly: rdn over 1f out: wknd ins fnl f* **12/1**

344- **8** *3/4* **Emell**[145] 7163 6-9-5 **100**...(p) KieranO'Neill 1 96
(Richard Hannon) *hld up: rdn 2f out: no imp* **10/1**

1m 35.6s (-2.60) **Going Correction** -0.025s/f (Stan) **8** Ran SP% **114.7**
Speed ratings (Par 109): **112,110,109,108,108 108,106,106**
CSF £41.67 CT £112.68 TOTE £5.70: £1.70, £2.60, £1.20; EX 45.10 Trifecta £246.00.
Owner Abdulla Al Mansoori **Bred** Car Colston Hall Stud **Trained** Middleham Moor, N Yorks

FOCUS
A good handicap in which the winner set a modest gallop. A pb from the winner.

834 UNIBET MAIDEN STKS 6f 1y(P)
3:05 (3:05) (Class 5) 3-Y-O+ **£2,911** (£866; £432; £216) **Stalls** Low

Form RPR
0-02 **1** **Merhoob (IRE)**[10] 697 4-9-10 77.. AdamKirby 3 82
(John Ryan) *pressed ldr: pushed along to ld 2f out: rdn and kpt on fnl f* **4/7**[1]

3-4 **2** *2 1/4* **Dangerous Thought (USA)**[29] 466 3-8-10 0................ RobertHavlin 4 71
(John Gosden) *trckd ldng pair: pushed along over 2f out: rdn to go 2nd 1f out: kpt on but a hld* **5/2**[2]

0-23 **3** 3 1/4 **Lady Lloyd**[7] 750 3-8-5 60 (p) LukeMorris 2 55
(Phil McEntee) *led narrowly: rdn whn hdd 2f out: wknd fnl f* **14/1**
4 1/2 **Polly's Serenade** 3-8-5 0 JimmyQuinn 1 54
(Richard Hughes) *trckd ldng pair: pushed along and outpcd 2f out: one pce fnl f* **10/1**[3]
5 1 1/4 **Secret Sonnet** 3-8-5 0 KieranO'Neill 6 50+
(Stuart Williams) *slowly away: sn pushed along and rn green towards rr: sme hdwy over 1f out: nvr threatened* **33/1**
060- **6** 4 1/2 **Island Express (IRE)**[312] 1778 9-9-5 47 (tp) AnnStokell(5) 5 44
(Ann Stokell) *hld up: rdn over 2f out: sn btn* **100/1**
1m 12.7s (0.80) **Going Correction** -0.025s/f (Stan)
WFA 3 from 4yo+ 14lb 6 Ran SP% **111.9**
Speed ratings (Par 103): **93,90,85,85,83 77**
CSF £2.20 TOTE £1.70: £1.40, £1.10; EX 2.90 Trifecta £7.50.
Owner Gerry McGladery **Bred** Airlie Stud **Trained** Newmarket, Suffolk
FOCUS
An ordinary maiden with little form to go on. They went an honest gallop.

835 UNIBET H'CAP 5f 6y(P)
3:40 (3:42) (Class 2) (0-105,105) 4-Y-0+ **£11,971** (£3,583; £1,791; £896; £446) **Stalls** High

Form RPR
0133 **1** **Royal Birth**[12] 677 5-8-1 **90** (t) AaronJones(5) 8 101+
(Stuart Williams) *hld up in midfield: pushed along 2f out: r.o strly on outside fr appr fnl f: led 75yds out* **11/4**[1]
00-2 **2** 1 1/4 **Fast Track**[12] 677 5-8-10 **94** GrahamGibbons 7 100
(David Barron) *chsd ldng pair: rdn over 2f out: kpt on: wnt 2nd post* **3/1**[2]
1116 **3** hd **Bosham**[12] 677 6-8-3 **94** (b) NathanEvans(7) 4 99
(Michael Easterby) *led: rdn over 1f out: hdd 75yds out: one pce: lost 2nd post* **5/1**[3]
3-61 **4** 1 1/4 **Sandfrankskipsgo**[14] 655 7-8-5 **89** LukeMorris 2 90
(Peter Crate) *prom: rdn 2f out: no ex fnl 110yds* **5/1**[3]
2040 **5** 1 1/4 **Dynamo Walt (IRE)**[12] 677 5-8-6 **90** (v) AdamBeschizza 9 86
(Derek Shaw) *hld up: rdn 2f out: kpt on ins fnl f* **25/1**
-014 **6** 1 **Taajub (IRE)**[14] 655 9-8-2 **86** oh1 JimmyQuinn 5 78
(Peter Crate) *midfield: rdn over 1f out: edgd lft and no imp* **16/1**
-160 **7** 1 1/2 **Dungannon**[27] 492 9-8-4 **93** (b) EdwardGreatrex(5) 6 80
(Andrew Balding) *hld up: pushed along over 1f out: nvr threatened* **16/1**
140- **8** 1 1/4 **Desert Law (IRE)**[178] 6210 8-9-7 **105** PaulMulrennan 3 88
(Paul Midgley) *chsd ldng pair: rdn 2f out: wknd fnl f* **5/1**[3]
57.32s (-1.48) **Going Correction** -0.025s/f (Stan) 8 Ran SP% **117.3**
Speed ratings (Par 109): **110,108,107,105,103 102,99,97**
CSF £11.61 CT £39.02 TOTE £3.60: £1.30, £2.50, £1.60; EX 14.50 Trifecta £51.70.
Owner The Morley Family **Bred** Old Mill Stud & S Williams & J Parry **Trained** Newmarket, Suffolk
FOCUS
A good sprint handicap run at a decent gallop. The form is rated around the second, third and fourth.

836 32RED SPRING CUP STKS (ALL-WEATHER CHAMPIONSHIP FAST-TRACK QUALIFIER) (LISTED RACE) 7f 1y(P)
4:15 (4:16) (Class 1) 3-Y-O
£25,519 (£9,675; £4,842; £2,412; £1,210; £607) **Stalls** Low

Form RPR
126- **1** **Haalick (IRE)**[163] 6677 3-9-1 101 JackMitchell 3 103
(Roger Varian) *hld up in midfield: pushed and gd hdwy appr fnl f: rdn to ld ins fnl f: kpt on* **8/1**
244- **2** 1 1/4 **Tutu Nguru (USA)**[148] 7073 3-8-10 98 PatCosgrave 11 95
(William Haggas) *hld up: rdn and gd hdwy appr fnl f: wnt 2nd 110yds out: kpt on* **14/1**
10-2 **3** 1 **The Supreme (FR)**[15] 638 3-9-1 85 JFEgan 6 99+
(Mick Channon) *trckd ldng pair: n.m.r over 1f out: short of room again 1f out: kpt on wl fnl 110yds: wnt 3rd nr fin* **20/1**
111- **4** nk **Race Day (IRE)**[105] 7938 3-9-1 100 (p) OisinMurphy 5 96
(Saeed bin Suroor) *led: rdn 2f out: hdd ins fnl f: hung rt: no ex* **3/1**[2]
3-22 **5** nse **Take The Helm**[29] 459 3-9-1 89 PaulMulrennan 10 96
(Brian Meehan) *dwlt: hld up in rr: hdwy into midfield over 3f out: rdn over 2f out: kpt on* **33/1**
123- **6** 1 1/4 **Above N Beyond**[67] 8390 3-9-1 96 RichardKingscote 7 93
(Tom Dascombe) *prom: rdn over 2f out: keeping on whn hmpd ins fnl f: short of room again nr fin* **25/1**
105- **7** hd **Great Page (IRE)**[162] 6709 3-9-0 105 KieranO'Neill 1 91
(Richard Hannon) *midfield: rdn hdwy on inner to chse ldr over 1f out: wknd fnl 110yds* **16/1**
0-11 **8** 1 1/4 **Sea Of Flames**[29] 459 3-9-1 87 TomQueally 2 89
(David Elsworth) *trckd ldng pair: rdn 2f out: one pce whn hmpd ins fnl f* **6/1**[3]
462- **9** 2 **Squash**[127] 7594 3-8-10 104 LukeMorris 8 79+
(Philip McBride) *half-rrd s: hld up in midfield: rdn 3f out: clipped heels and stmbld 2f out: no ch after* **20/1**
13- **10** 1/2 **Abe Lincoln (USA)**[105] 7938 3-9-1 95 JimCrowley 4 99+
(Jeremy Noseda) *midfield: pushed along and hdwy whn hmpd 1f out: no ch after and eased* **11/4**[1]
335- **11** 1 **Adventurous (IRE)**[147] 7114 3-9-1 107 JoeFanning 9 90+
(Mark Johnston) *chsd ldng pair: rdn 2f out: wkng whn hmpd ins fnl f: eased* **7/1**
1m 22.28s (-2.52) **Going Correction** -0.025s/f (Stan) 11 Ran SP% **118.4**
Speed ratings (Par 106): **113,111,110,110,110 108,108,106,104,104 102**
CSF £107.26 TOTE £11.60: £3.10, £4.80, £8.00; EX 147.60 Trifecta £1861.40.
Owner Sheikh Ahmed Al Maktoum **Bred** Storway Limited **Trained** Newmarket, Suffolk
FOCUS
A good quality 3yo Listed race won in 2014 by the very smart sprinter Ertijaal. They went a decent gallop but it was a rough race from over 1f out. The race is rated around the second.

837 BET&WATCH EVERY RACE AT UNIBET H'CAP 5f 6y(P)
4:50 (4:52) (Class 6) (0-55,55) 4-Y-O+ **£2,264** (£673; £336; £168) **Stalls** High

Form RPR
-362 **1** **Charlie Lad**[8] 732 4-9-7 **55** LukeMorris 4 64
(Daniel Mark Loughnane) *w ldr: rdn to ld 2f out: drvn and kpt on wl fnl f* **5/2**[1]
2514 **2** 1 1/2 **Kuanyao (IRE)**[23] 528 10-8-11 **48** ow2 (be) AnnStokell(5) 6 54
(Ann Stokell) *led narrowly: rdn whn hdd 2f out: kpt on* **8/1**
0-01 **3** 1 1/2 **Novabridge**[19] 589 8-9-4 **52** (b) AdamKirby 1 50
(John Butler) *in tch on inner: rdn to chse ldng pair 2f out: one pce and hld in 3rd fnl 110yds* **11/4**[2]
0506 **4** nk **Black Vale (IRE)**[38] 355 5-8-9 **46** oh1 (t) DannyBrock(3) 2 43
(Phil McEntee) *hld up in tch: rdn 2f out: kpt on ins fnl f: nvr threatened* **10/1**
000- **5** 1/2 **Nelson's Pride**[136] 7385 5-8-5 **46** oh1 RhiainIngram(7) 7 41
(Roger Ingram) *midfield on outer: rdn 2f out: kpt on ins fnl f* **33/1**
-502 **6** 3/4 **Jolly Red Jeanz (IRE)**[8] 733 5-9-6 **54** (be) CathyGannon 5 47
(Daniel Mark Loughnane) *chsd ldng pair: rdn 2f out: wknd ins fnl f* **4/1**[3]
0-00 **7** nse **Blackasyourhat (IRE)**[17] 615 4-8-12 **49** (t[1]) RobHornby(3) 3 41
(Michael Attwater) *dwlt: hld up in rr: pushed along 1/2-way: minor late hdwy* **10/1**
0002 **8** 2 1/2 **Warm Order**[12] 669 5-8-12 **49** (b) GeorgeDowning(3) 8 32
(Tony Carroll) *chsd ldng pair: rdn 2f out: wknd fnl f* **16/1**
58.73s (-0.07) **Going Correction** -0.025s/f (Stan) 8 Ran SP% **113.4**
Speed ratings (Par 101): **99,96,94,93,92 91,91,87**
CSF £22.66 CT £58.10 TOTE £2.70: £1.20, £2.80, £1.80; EX 23.40 Trifecta £79.10.
Owner S & A Mares & C Loughnane **Bred** Willie Musson Racing Ltd **Trained** Baldwin's Gate, Staffs
FOCUS
A moderate sprint handicap run at an honest gallop. A small step up from the winner on his latest form with the second to recent form.

838 32RED.COM ALL WEATHER "HANDS AND HEELS" APPRENTICE SERIES FINAL H'CAP (EXCELLENCE INITIATIVE) 1m 7f 169y(P)
5:25 (5:25) (Class 4) (0-85,82) 4-Y-O+ **£6,301** (£1,886; £943; £472; £235) **Stalls** Low

Form RPR
0-43 **1** **Gabrial The Duke (IRE)**[35] 399 6-9-5 **82** (b) AdamMcNamara(3) 4 85
(Richard Fahey) *in tch: hdwy to press ldr over 4f out: pushed along 2f out: led ins fnl f: kpt on* **7/4**[1]
-236 **2** 3/4 **Todd**[22] 545 6-8-12 **72** (p) PaddyBradley 2 74
(Anabel K Murphy) *in tch: hdwy to press ldr over 4f out: pushed along and sltly outpcd 2f out: kpt on ins fnl f: wnt 2nd nr fin* **3/1**[3]
-542 **3** nk **Hope You Dance (FR)**[15] 636 4-8-3 **68** SophieKilloran 3 69
(David Simcock) *racd keenly: trckd ldr: pushed along over 2f out: kpt on fnl f* **2/1**[2]
040- **4** hd **Mister Fizz**[124] 7140 8-9-5 **79** (p) HollieDoyle 5 80
(Miss Imogen Pickard) *led at slow pce: jnd over 4f out: pushed along 2f out: hdd ins fnl f: no ex and lost 2 pls towards fin* **12/1**
0-04 **5** 1 1/4 **Ninepointsixthree**[9] 704 6-8-8 **68** oh1 (p) GeorgiaCox 1 67
(John O'Shea) *v.s.a: hld up: pushed along over 2f out: one pce and nvr threatened* **10/1**
3m 46.57s (20.87) **Going Correction** -0.025s/f (Stan)
WFA 4 from 6yo+ 5lb 5 Ran SP% **111.5**
Speed ratings (Par 105): **46,45,45,45,44**
CSF £7.47 TOTE £2.00: £1.30, £1.80; EX 6.30 Trifecta £9.70.
Owner Dr Marwan Koukash **Bred** Old Carhue & Graeng Bloodstock **Trained** Musley Bank, N Yorks
FOCUS
A fairly decent little apprentice riders' staying handicap. They went a farcical pace until the tempo increased about 4f out. Shaky form.
T/Plt: £75.30 to a £1 stake. Pool: £64,925.52 - 629.24 winning tickets T/Qpdt: £16.90 to a £1 stake. Pool: £5,410.75 - 235.98 winning tickets **Andrew Sheret**

807 MEYDAN (L-H)
Saturday, March 5

OFFICIAL GOING: Dirt: fast; turf: good

839a AL BASTAKIYA SPONSORED BY EMIRATES SKYWARDS (LISTED RACE) (DIRT) 1m 1f 110y(D)
12:00 (12:00) 3-Y-O **£102,040** (£34,013; £17,006; £8,503)

RPR
1 **Market Rally (USA)**[23] 539 3-9-0 107 PatSmullen 4 104+
(D Selvaratnam, UAE) *sn led: tk v t.k.h: rdn 2 1/2f out: r.o wl: comf* **8/13**[1]
2 4 3/4 **Lazzam**[23] 539 3-9-1 95 ow1 (b) ChristopheSoumillon 3 94
(Marco Botti) *s.i.s: settled in rr: smooth prog 3f out: r.o fnl 2f but no ch w wnr* **16/1**
3 hd **Blue Creek**[35] 407 3-9-0 87 (p) WilliamBuick 2 94
(Charlie Appleby) *s.i.s: trckd ldr: rdn 4f out: outpcd 3f out but r.o fnl 1 1/2f* **2/1**[2]
4 8 1/2 **Hombre Rojo (IRE)**[23] 539 3-9-0 93 HarryBentley 1 76
(Simon Dow) *trckd ldr: rdn 3 1/2f out: outpcd fnl 2 1/2f* **14/1**[3]
1m 58.52s (-0.28) **Going Correction** +0.10s/f (Slow) 4 Ran SP% **107.8**
Speed ratings: **105,101,101,94**
CSF: 10.15.
Owner Sheikh Ahmed Al Maktoum **Bred** Ashview Farm Llc, Colts Neck Stables Llc & Unbridl **Trained** United Arab Emirates
FOCUS
TRAKUS (metres travelled compared to winner): 2nd +10, 3rd +9, 4th -4. The middle leg of the UAE Triple Crown but it was a desperate race, two of the beaten runners finishing with physical issues and the unconvincing winner allowed to set a slow, muddling pace; 27.5 (400m), 23.9 (800m), 24.58 (1200m), 24.01 (1600m).

840a MAHAB AL SHIMAAL SPONSORED BY EMIRATES SKYWARDS (GROUP 3) (DIRT) 6f (D)
12:35 (12:35) 3-Y-O+
£81,632 (£27,210; £13,605; £6,802; £4,081; £2,721)

RPR
1 **Muarrab**[23] 537 7-9-0 112 PaulHanagan 1 117+
(M Al Mheiri, UAE) *sn led: kicked clr 2 1/2f out: r.o wl: easily* **7/4**[2]
2 5 1/4 **Kifaah**[9] 719 5-9-0 104 (t) DaneO'Neill 5 100+
(A R Al Rayhi, UAE) *mid-div: r.o fnl 2f but no ch w wnr* **9/1**[3]
3 1 1/4 **Rich Tapestry (IRE)**[23] 537 8-9-0 115 (b) GeraldMosse 3 96
(C W Chang, Hong Kong) *trckd ldr: ev ch 3f out: r.o one pce fnl 2f* **10/11**[1]
4 3/4 **Shaishee (USA)**[9] 719 6-9-0 107 (v) TadhgO'Shea 4 94
(M Al Mheiri, UAE) *s.i.s: mid-div: rdn 4f out: r.o same pce fnl 3f* **16/1**
5 5 1/2 **Sweet Swap (USA)**[14] 7-9-0 104 (t) FrankieDettori 2 76
(K Al Subaie, Saudi Arabia) *a in rr* **40/1**
6 2 1/4 **Anfitrion Sale (ARG)**[23] 537 4-9-0 100 SamHitchcott 6 69
(Y Al Blooshi, UAE) *s.i.s: a in rr* **100/1**
1m 10.2s (-1.40) **Going Correction** +0.10s/f (Slow) 6 Ran SP% **108.1**
Speed ratings: **113,106,104,103,96 93**
CSF: 15.86.
Owner Hamdan Al Maktoum **Bred** Stratford Place Stud **Trained** UAE

FOCUS
TRAKUS: 2nd +6, 3rd +3, 4th +2, 5th +2, 6th +5. The winner got his way in front, covered less ground than any of his rivals on a fast track and broke the course record - set by Secret Circle in last year's Golden Shaheen - by 0.44secs. The splits were 24.09, 22.63, 23.48.

841a MEYDAN SPRINT SPONSORED BY ARABIAN ADVENTURES (GROUP 3) (TURF) 5f (T)
1:10 (1:10) 3-Y-O+

£71,428 (£23,809; £11,904; £5,952; £3,571; £2,380)

			RPR
1		**Fityaan**[9] 723 8-9-0 98 (v) PaulHanagan 11 (M Al Mheiri, UAE) *trckd ldrs: rdn 2 1/2f out: r.o wl: led nr line* **50/1**	110
2	*nse*	**Jungle Cat (IRE)**[37] 370 4-9-0 112 WilliamBuick 8 (Charlie Appleby) *trckd ldr: led 2f out: r.o wl but hdd cl home* **3/1**[1]	110
3	*shd*	**Sole Power**[83] 8217 9-9-0 118 RyanMoore 3 (Edward Lynam, Ire) *settled in rr: r.o wl fnl 1 1/2f: jst failed* **11/2**[3]	109+
4	*2 1/4*	**Sir Maximilian (IRE)**[16] 626 7-9-0 112 PatDobbs 10 (Ian Williams) *s.i.s: mid-div: r.o fnl 2f* **4/1**[2]	101
5	*1/2*	**Krypton Factor**[9] 719 8-9-0 97 (b) FrankieDettori 6 (Fawzi Abdulla Nass, Bahrain) *sn led: hdd 2f out: r.o same pce* **50/1**	100
6	*3/4*	**Medicean Man**[16] 626 10-9-0 108 (tp) HarryBentley 2 (Jeremy Gask) *a in mid-div* **16/1**	97
7	*shd*	**Goldream**[153] 6971 7-9-0 116 (p) MartinHarley 9 (Robert Cowell) *trckd ldr tl one pce fnl 2f* **4/1**[2]	97
8	*1 1/4*	**Taayel (IRE)**[9] 719 6-9-0 95 DaneO'Neill 4 (M Al Mheiri, UAE) *slowly away: last most of way: r.o fnl 2f but nvr involved* **100/1**	92+
9	*1/2*	**Mirza**[16] 626 9-9-0 108 (p) DavidProbert 1 (Rae Guest) *a in rr* **25/1**	90
10	*shd*	**Toscanini (IRE)**[16] 626 4-9-0 111 (p) JamesDoyle 7 (M Halford, Ire) *trckd ldr tl wknd 2 1/2f out* **11/2**[3]	90
11	*1/2*	**Stepper Point**[16] 626 7-9-0 108 (b) MartinDwyer 5 (William Muir) *trckd ldr tl outpcd 2f out* **14/1**	88

57.07s (-0.03) **Going Correction** +0.325s/f (Good) **11** Ran SP% **117.1**
Speed ratings: **113,112,112,109,108 107,107,105,104,104 103**
CSF: 194.12.
Owner Hamdan Al Maktoum **Bred** Usk Valley Stud **Trained** UAE

FOCUS
TRAKUS: 2nd -1, 3rd -1, 4th +1, 5th 0, 6th -1, 7th -1, 8th 0, 9th -1, 10th -1, 11th 0. The rail on the turf course was out four metres. A result that makes a lot of sense, if you take out the winner, who, at the age of eight and fully exposed, improved a fair whack on his previous best.

842a BURJ NAHAAR SPONSORED BY EMIRATES HOLIDAYS (GROUP 3) (DIRT) 1m (D)
1:45 (1:45) 3-Y-O+

£81,632 (£27,210; £13,605; £6,802; £4,081; £2,721)

			RPR
1		**Cool Cowboy (USA)**[16] 624 5-9-0 111 PatDobbs 3 (Doug Watson, UAE) *wl away: sn led: rdn 2 1/2f out: r.o wl: comf* **2/1**[2]	111
2	*3 3/4*	**Ross (IRE)**[16] 624 4-9-0 100 AdriedeVries 1 (P Schiergen, Germany) *trckd ldng pair: r.o fnl 2f but no ch w wnr* **20/1**	102
3	*1/2*	**Le Bernardin (USA)**[30] 454 7-9-0 111 (t) TadhgO'Shea 8 (A R Al Rayhi, UAE) *trckd ldr: rdn 4f out: outpcd 2 1/2f out: lost 2nd cl home* **5/4**[1]	101
4	*1/2*	**Long River (USA)**[16] 627 6-9-0 101 (b) RoystonFfrench 7 (S bin Ghadayer, UAE) *nvr nr to chal but r.o fnl 2 1/2f* **33/1**	100+
5	*3/4*	**Layl (USA)**[30] 452 6-9-0 109 SamHitchcott 2 (Doug Watson, UAE) *s.i.s: nvr able to chal but r.o fnl 2 1/2f* **11/2**[3]	98
6	*5 1/4*	**Top Clearance (USA)**[16] 627 4-9-0 105 (t) PatSmullen 9 (D Selvaratnam, UAE) *trckd ldng pair tl outpcd 3f out* **11/1**	86
7	*1*	**Mind That Boy (IRE)**[16] 624 4-9-0 102 MickaelBarzalona 6 (S bin Ghadayer, UAE) *s.i.s: a in rr* **33/1**	84
8	*14*	**Over The Ocean (USA)**[9] 717 6-9-0 101 (t) DaneO'Neill 4 (Niels Petersen, Norway) *slowly away: mid-div tl wknd 4f out* **66/1**	52

1m 36.43s (-1.07) **Going Correction** +0.10s/f (Slow) **8** Ran SP% **113.6**
Speed ratings: **109,105,104,104,103 98,97,83**
CSF: 41.41.
Owner Zaur Sekrekov **Bred** Columbiana Farm **Trained** United Arab Emirates

FOCUS
TRAKUS: 2nd -3, 3rd +5, 4th +8, 5th +3, 6th +7, 7th +7, 8th +13. On a fast track, the winner made all through the following fractions; 25.94, 23.23, 23.46, 23.8. Tamarkuz won this last year and followed up in the Godolphin Mile.

843a DUBAI CITY OF GOLD SPONSORED BY SKYCARGO (GROUP 2) (TURF) 1m 4f 11y(T)
2:20 (2:20) 3-Y-O+

£102,040 (£34,013; £17,006; £8,503; £5,102; £3,401)

			RPR
1		**Postponed (IRE)**[174] 6371 5-9-0 121 AndreaAtzeni 6 (Roger Varian) *mid-div: smooth prog 3f out: led 1 1/2f out: easily* **11/10**[1]	119+
2	*3*	**Dariyan (FR)**[83] 8216 4-8-11 117 ChristopheSoumillon 4 (A De Royer-Dupre, France) *settled in rr: chsd wnr 2f out: nt qckn fnl 1 1/2f* **15/8**[2]	113+
3	*1*	**Haafaguinea**[16] 625 6-9-0 112 JamesDoyle 1 (Saeed bin Suroor) *trckd ldr: rdn 3f out: ev ch 2f out: r.o same pce fnl 1 1/2f* **11/1**	112
4	*5 1/4*	**Balios (IRE)**[199] 5530 4-8-11 113 JamieSpencer 5 (David Simcock) *settled in rr: nvr nr to chal* **8/1**[3]	103
5	*2 1/4*	**Sanshaawes (SAF)**[16] 625 6-9-0 110 RyanMoore 2 (M F De Kock, South Africa) *wl away: mid-div tl wknd 3 1/2f out* **16/1**	100
6	*8 3/4*	**Captain Morley**[175] 6315 5-9-0 100 MartinHarley 8 (David Simcock) *sn led: rdn 4f out: hdd & wknd 1 1/2f out* **40/1**	86

2m 27.9s (-3.90) **Going Correction** +0.10s/f (Good)
WFA 4 from 5yo+ 2lb **6** Ran SP% **110.2**
Speed ratings: **117,115,114,110,109 103**
CSF: 31.19.
Owner Sheikh Mohammed Obaid Al Maktoum **Bred** St Albans Bloodstock Llp **Trained** Newmarket, Suffolk

FOCUS
TRAKUS: 2nd +2, 3rd -6, 4th 0, 5th -5, 6th 0. The rail on the turf course was out four metres. The splits were 27.11, 24.58, 24.71, 24.38, 23.71, and the winner came home in 23.42. This went pretty much to form and the winner set himself up nicely for World Cup night.

844a AL MAKTOUM CHALLENGE R3 SPONSORED BY EMIRATES (GROUP 1) (DIRT) 1m 2f (D)
2:55 (2:55) 3-Y-O+

£163,265 (£54,421; £27,210; £13,605; £8,163; £5,442)

			RPR
1		**Special Fighter (IRE)**[30] 452 5-9-0 110 FernandoJara 6 (M Al Mheiri, UAE) *sn led: kicked clr 2 1/2f out: r.o wl: easily* **14/1**	115
2	*4 1/2*	**Gun Pit (AUS)**[28] 5-9-0 115 (bt) JoaoMoreira 1 (C Fownes, Hong Kong) *trckd ldr: t.k.h: r.o fnl 3f but no ch w wnr* **8/1**	106
3	*2 3/4*	**Faulkner**[16] 627 6-9-0 110 PatDobbs 8 (Doug Watson, UAE) *trckd ldr: rdn 3f out: r.o but no ch w wnr* **7/1**	101
4	*nk*	**Mubtaahij (IRE)**[30] 454 4-9-0 119 ChristopheSoumillon 4 (M F De Kock, South Africa) *trckd ldng trio: rdn 3 1/2f out: outpcd 2 1/2f out: r.o same pce* **9/4**[1]	100+
5	*1/2*	**Munaaser**[16] 624 5-9-0 105 PaulHanagan 2 (A R Al Rayhi, UAE) *settled in rr: chsd ldrs 3f out: r.o same pce fnl 2f* **12/1**	99+
6	*2 3/4*	**Watershed (USA)**[30] 454 4-9-0 109 JamesDoyle 3 (Kiaran McLaughlin, U.S.A) *s.i.s: nvr nr to chal* **6/1**[3]	93+
7	*1*	**Keen Ice (USA)**[28] 490 4-9-0 122 (t) RyanMoore 11 (Dale Romans, U.S.A) *s.i.s: trckd ldng trio: rdn and outpcd 4f out: r.o same pce fnl 3f* **3/1**[2]	91+
8	*2 1/2*	**Storm Belt (USA)**[9] 722 7-9-0 104 (v) SamHitchcott 10 (Doug Watson, UAE) *nvr bttr than mid-div* **33/1**	86+
9	*2 1/2*	**Haatheq (USA)**[15] 649 9-9-0 106 DaneO'Neill 5 (A R Al Rayhi, UAE) *trckd ldng trio tl wknd 3 1/2f out* **25/1**	81+
10	*1 3/4*	**Pylon (SAF)**[16] 624 7-9-0 102 (b) RoystonFfrench 12 (M F De Kock, South Africa) *nvr bttr than mid-div* **100/1**	78+
11	*2 3/4*	**Gold City (IRE)**[30] 452 7-9-0 109 (bt) RichardMullen 7 (S Seemar, UAE) *s.i.s: nvr nr to chal* **33/1**	72+
12	*19*	**Golden Soul (USA)**[23] 540 6-9-0 102 WayneSmith 9 (M F De Kock, South Africa) *s.i.s: a in rr* **40/1**	34+

2m 3.09s (-1.61) **Going Correction** +0.10s/f (Slow) **12** Ran SP% **121.2**
Speed ratings: **110,106,104,103,103 101,100,98,96,95 92,77**
CSF: 119.14.
Owner Sheikh Mansoor bin Mohammed al Maktoum **Bred** Darley **Trained** UAE

FOCUS
TRAKUS: 2nd -7, 3rd +8, 4th 0, 5th -2, 6th 0, 7th +16, 8th +9, 9th +4, 10th +20, 11th +9, 12th +18. Dubai Millennium (2000), Street Cry (2002) and Electrocutionist (2006) won this at Nad Al Sheba before landing the Dubai World Cup. But four of the six World Cup winners at Meydan were beaten when prepping in this race, including Prince Bishop (2nd) in the first season on dirt here last year. The best thing you could do with the form of this latest running is totally ignore it. The winner, whose trainer was completing a quite unbelievable Group-race treble, got an uncontested lead and, on a track that was riding extremely fast, set slow fractions before sprinting home - 26.09, 25.4, 25.13, 23.78, 22.69. The other three dirt races on this card were also won from the front and this was the second track record on the day, 0.15secs quicker than Prince Bishop's World Cup. The runner-up and third were never out of the front three either.

845a JEBEL HATTA SPONSORED BY EMIRATES (GROUP 1) (TURF) 1m 1f (T)
3:30 (3:30) 3-Y-O+

£122,448 (£40,816; £20,408; £10,204; £6,122; £4,081)

			RPR
1		**Tryster (IRE)**[16] 625 5-9-0 113 (p) WilliamBuick 8 (Charlie Appleby) *settled in rr: smooth prog 2f out: led 1f out: easily* **4/9**[1]	110+
2	*1 1/2*	**Farrier (USA)**[15] 649 8-9-0 104 (p) RichardMullen 6 (S Seemar, UAE) *mid-div: chsd ldrs 2f out: r.o but no ch w wnr* **40/1**	105
3	*1 1/2*	**Ertijaal (AUS)**[16] 627 4-9-0 111 PaulHanagan 3 (M F De Kock, South Africa) *sn led: rdn 2 1/2f out: hdd 1f out: r.o same pce* **9/2**[2]	102
4	*nk*	**Harry's Son (AUS)**[9] 720 4-9-0 111 (t) HarryBentley 4 (P V Lafferty, South Africa) *trckd ldng trio: ev ch 1 1/2f out: r.o same pce fnl f* **14/1**[3]	101
5	*nk*	**Zahee (NZ)**[9] 720 6-9-0 110 (t) WayneSmith 1 (M F De Kock, South Africa) *mid-div: chsd ldrs 2f out: r.o fnl 1 1/2f* **25/1**	101
6	*2 3/4*	**Earnshaw (USA)**[16] 625 5-9-0 109 (bt) MickaelBarzalona 5 (S bin Ghadayer, UAE) *s.i.s: nvr nr to chal* **33/1**	95
7	*1 1/2*	**Johann Strauss**[9] 720 5-9-0 109 ChristopheSoumillon 2 (M F De Kock, South Africa) *trckd ldr: rdn 3f out: wknd fnl 2f* **14/1**[3]	92
8	*1*	**Prayer For Relief (USA)**[16] 624 8-9-0 109 (b) RyanMoore 9 (M F De Kock, South Africa) *a in rr* **16/1**	90
9	*2 1/4*	**Sefri (USA)**[15] 649 6-9-0 105 (b) DaneO'Neill 7 (E Charpy, UAE) *trckd ldr tl outpcd 2f out* **40/1**	85

1m 48.71s (-0.39) **Going Correction** +0.10s/f (Good) **9** Ran SP% **118.3**
Speed ratings: **105,103,102,102,101 99,98,97,95**
CSF: 36.49. Placepot: £78.60 to a £1 stake. Pool of £4898.26 - 45.45 winning units. Quadpot: £11.80 to a £1 stake. Pool of £367.60 - 22.90 winning units..
Owner Godolphin **Bred** Herbertstown House Stud **Trained** Newmarket, Suffolk

FOCUS
TRAKUS: 2nd 0, 3rd -4, 4th -4, 5th -2, 6th -4, 7th -4, 8th 0, 9th 0. The rail on the turf course was out four metres. The splits were 26.03, 23.81, 24.55, and the winner came home in 23.04 and 11.29. Not a strong Group 1, but another good performance from the winner, who set himself up nicely for a clash with Solow in the Dubai Turf.

846 - 855a (Foreign Racing) - See Raceform Interactive

819 WOLVERHAMPTON (A.W) (L-H)
Monday, March 7

OFFICIAL GOING: Tapeta: standard
Wind: Fresh across Weather: Fine

856 DOWNLOAD THE NEW UNIBET RACING APP H'CAP (DIV I) 5f 216y (Tp)
2:20 (2:20) (Class 5) (0-70,70) 4-Y-O+ **£3,234** (£962; £481; £240) **Stalls** Low

Form				RPR
00-0	1		**City Of Angkor Wat (IRE)**[11] 703 6-9-2 65 (p) LiamKeniry 7 (Conor Dore) *hld up: hdwy over 2f out: rdn to ld wl ins fnl f: r.o* **12/1**	75
602-	2	*1 1/4*	**Lackaday**[80] 8283 4-9-7 70 (p) JasonHart 6 (Mark Walford) *chsd ldrs: rdn over 1f out: ev ch ins fnl f: styd on same pce* **4/1**[2]	76
6546	3	*1 1/4*	**Divine Call**[24] 543 9-8-8 57 (v) FrannyNorton 3 (Milton Bradley) *hld up: hdwy over 1f out: sn rdn: styd on same pce ins fnl f* **6/1**[3]	59

312 **4** 1 3/4 **Top Offer**[14] 680 7-9-5 **68** ShaneKelly 5 64
(Patrick Morris) *s.i.s: hld up: rdn over 2f out: hung lft over 1f out: r.o: nt rch ldrs* **5/2**[1]

0146 **5** *nk* **Louis Vee (IRE)**[14] 671 8-8-5 **61** GeorgiaCox(7) 2 56
(John O'Shea) *sn led: rdn over 2f out: hdd and no ex wl ins fnl f* **8/1**

0-00 **6** 3/4 **Generalyse**[23] 561 7-9-0 **63** (p) KieranO'Neill 8 56
(Anabel K Murphy) *chsd ldr tl rdn over 1f out: styd on same pce fnl f* **20/1**

0530 **7** 1 1/4 **Quality Art (USA)**[11] 714 8-9-1 **67** RobHornby(3) 9 56
(Simon Hodgson) *prom: rdn over 1f out: wknd ins fnl f* **10/1**

0-00 **8** 3/4 **Ypres**[24] 541 7-8-13 **62** (p) BenCurtis 1 49
(Jason Ward) *prom: rdn over 2f out: wknd fnl f* **11/1**

2-50 **9** 1 1/4 **State Of The Union (IRE)**[23] 561 4-9-4 **67** [1] CathyGannon 4 50
(Lee Carter) *hld up: racd keenly: shkn up over 1f out: nvr on terms* **12/1**

1m 13.23s (-1.27) **Going Correction** -0.075s/f (Stan) **9** Ran SP% **111.5**
Speed ratings (Par 103): **105,103,101,99,98 97,96,95,93**
CSF £56.77 CT £316.94 TOTE £13.30: £3.20, £1.70, £2.70; EX 63.90 Trifecta £533.90.
Owner Mrs Louise Marsh **Bred** T Jones **Trained** Hubbert's Bridge, Lincs

FOCUS
A modest sprint handicap, faster by 0.49sec than division two. The pace was sound.

857 DOWNLOAD THE NEW UNIBET RACING APP H'CAP (DIV II) 5f 216y (Tp)
2:50 (2:52) (Class 5) (0-70,68) 4-Y-O+ **£3,234** (£962; £481; £240) **Stalls** Low

Form RPR

-053 **1** **Indian Affair**[14] 680 6-9-6 **67** (bt) FrannyNorton 7 74
(Milton Bradley) *chsd ldrs: pushed along over 2f out: rdn to ld ins fnl f: r.o* **7/2**[1]

4240 **2** 1/2 **Sewn Up**[11] 703 6-9-2 **63** (p) GrahamLee 8 68
(Keith Dalgleish) *sn pushed along in mid-div: hdwy over 1f out: swtchd lft ins fnl f: r.o* **9/2**[2]

-004 **3** 1 1/4 **Agerzam**[13] 685 6-9-6 **67** (b) LukeMorris 1 68
(Ronald Harris) *s.i.s: hld up: plld hrd: hdwy over 1f out: hung lft ins fnl f: r.o* **16/1**

2-00 **4** 1/2 **Eland Ally**[10] 733 8-8-12 **59** (v) KieranO'Neill 6 59
(Anabel K Murphy) *chsd ldr: rdn and ev ch over 1f out: styd on same pce ins fnl f* **25/1**

-306 **5** *nk* **Bogsnog (IRE)**[46] 271 6-9-1 **62** TonyHamilton 4 61
(Kristin Stubbs) *led: rdn over 1f out: hdd and no ex ins fnl f* **7/2**[1]

1-04 **6** *nse* **Seek The Fair Land**[14] 671 10-9-7 **68** (v) AmirQuinn 5 67
(Lee Carter) *s.i.s: racd keenly and sn hld up in tch: nt clr run wl over 1f out: sn rdn: styd on same pce ins fnl f* **9/1**

-630 **7** *nk* **Orlando Rogue (IRE)**[17] 629 4-9-4 **65** (p) LiamKeniry 3 63
(Conor Dore) *s.i.s: hld up: hdwy over 1f out: nt trble ldrs* **8/1**

-000 **8** 2 1/4 **Satchville Flyer**[28] 502 5-8-12 **62** PhilipPrince(3) 9 53
(David Evans) *hld up: plld hrd: swtchd lft over 2f out: swtchd rt over 1f out: hung lft ins fnl f: nt trble ldrs* **12/1**

3-66 **P** **John Coffey (IRE)**[45] 297 7-8-10 **57** LiamJones 2
(Michael Appleby) *sn pushed along to chse ldrs: wknd over 1f out: p.u and dismntd wl ins fnl f: lame* **15/2**[3]

1m 13.72s (-0.78) **Going Correction** -0.075s/f (Stan) **9** Ran SP% **112.9**
Speed ratings (Par 103): **102,101,99,99,98 98,98,95,**
CSF £18.63 CT £218.14 TOTE £4.00: £1.60, £2.00, £3.70; EX 16.40 Trifecta £107.00.
Owner J M Bradley **Bred** Mette Campbell-Andenaes **Trained** Sedbury, Gloucs

FOCUS
This looked competitive, but it was the slower of the two divisions by 0.49sec. Preety ordinary form, the winner rated to his best.

858 UNIBET OFFER DAILY JOCKEY/TRAINER SPECIALS MAIDEN STKS 5f 216y (Tp)
3:20 (3:22) (Class 5) 3-Y-O+ **£3,234** (£962; £481; £240) **Stalls** Low

Form RPR

42 **1** **Torreon (IRE)**[17] 639 5-9-12 0 AdamKirby 5 82+
(John Ryan) *chsd ldr tl led wl over 1f out: sn rdn: r.o: comf* **11/8**[1]

2 3 **Intense Starlet (IRE)** 5-9-7 0 SamJames 6 65
(Marjorie Fife) *got loose on the way to post: a.p: rdn over 1f out: styd on same pce ins fnl f* **40/1**

2-42 **3** *nk* **Spirit Glance**[7] 765 3-8-7 70 AndrewMullen 4 60
(Tim Easterby) *chsd ldrs: rdn over 1f out: styd on same pce ins fnl f* **11/4**[2]

-342 **4** 3 1/2 **Zebedee's Girl (IRE)**[45] 291 3-8-7 63 JFEgan 3 49
(David Evans) *hld up: rdn over 2f out: hung lft over 1f out: nt trble ldrs* **10/1**

40 **5** *nk* **Thatsthewaytodoit (IRE)**[7] 765 3-8-7 0 LiamJones 2 48
(Kevin Frost) *prom: rdn over 1f out: wknd fnl f* **66/1**

6 *shd* **Inner Knowing (IRE)**[24] 551 3-8-7 68 JoeFanning 1 48
(Ross O'Sullivan, Ire) *sn led: rdn and hdd wl over 1f out: wknd ins fnl f* **7/2**[3]

0 **7** 21 **Monpazier (IRE)**[35] 423 3-8-12 0 JoeyHaynes 7
(K R Burke) *sn pushed along in rr: bhd fr 1/2-way* **16/1**

1m 13.59s (-0.91) **Going Correction** -0.075s/f (Stan)
WFA 3 from 5yo 14lb **7** Ran SP% **109.9**
Speed ratings (Par 103): **103,99,98,93,93 93,65**
CSF £52.89 TOTE £2.10: £1.20, £9.70; EX 47.40 Trifecta £204.00.
Owner Marco Sanna **Bred** Blue Bloodstock Ltd **Trained** Newmarket, Suffolk

FOCUS
A fair performance from the winner, who proved a good bit better than his modest rivals. The form could be rated a bit higher.

859 32RED.COM FILLIES' H'CAP 7f 32y (Tp)
3:50 (3:52) (Class 5) (0-75,67) 4-Y-O+ **£3,234** (£962; £481; £240) **Stalls** High

Form RPR

1122 **1** **Binky Blue (IRE)**[28] 502 4-9-5 **65** LukeMorris 5 72
(Daniel Mark Loughnane) *chsd ldrs: rdn to ld ins fnl f: r.o* **5/1**[3]

6050 **2** 1/2 **Kodiac Lady (IRE)**[7] 769 4-8-4 **57** (be) HollieDoyle(7) 6 62
(Simon West) *hld up: hdwy over 1f out: sn rdn: r.o* **16/1**

231- **3** *shd* **Mallymkun**[136] 7440 4-9-7 **67** FrannyNorton 3 72+
(K R Burke) *hld up: hdwy and nt clr run over 1f out: swtchd rt: r.o* **7/2**[1]

2112 **4** 1/2 **Camdora (IRE)**[18] 617 4-9-1 **61** TimmyMurphy 1 65
(Jamie Osborne) *hld up: plld hrd: hdwy over 1f out: sn rdn: styd on* **7/2**[1]

2-00 **5** *nk* **Mops Angel**[14] 676 5-8-12 **61** (p) AlistairRawlinson(3) 2 64
(Michael Appleby) *chsd ldrs: rdn to ld over 1f out: hdd ins fnl f: styd on same pce* **8/1**

60-4 **6** 1/2 **Potternello (IRE)**[11] 713 4-9-5 **65** SilvestreDeSousa 4 67
(Mick Channon) *led: rdn and hdd over 1f out: styd on same pce ins fnl f* **4/1**[2]

4-04 **7** 2 3/4 **Togetherwecan (IRE)**[28] 500 4-8-10 **56** JoeFanning 8 50
(Mark Johnston) *s.i.s: sn prom: rdn over 1f out: no ex ins fnl f* **11/1**

4-43 **8** 3/4 **Make On Madam (IRE)**[14] 667 4-9-4 **64** (p) DarryllHolland 7 56
(Les Eyre) *sn chsng ldr: rdn and lost 2nd over 2f out: wknd fnl f* **16/1**

1m 28.47s (-0.33) **Going Correction** -0.075s/f (Stan) **8** Ran SP% **112.3**
Speed ratings (Par 100): **98,97,97,96,96 95,92,91**
CSF £75.43 CT £312.09 TOTE £4.80: £1.60, £4.80, £1.80; EX 76.90 Trifecta £400.70.
Owner B Dunn, C Loughnane & C Austin **Bred** Gerard & Anne Corry **Trained** Baldwin's Gate, Staffs

FOCUS
A competitive fillies' handicap, but not as good a race as the conditions suggested, with the top weight rated 8lb below the ceiling for the race. Ordinary, sound form.

860 DOWNLOAD THE LADBROKES APP CLAIMING STKS 1m 141y (Tp)
4:20 (4:20) (Class 6) 4-Y-O+ **£2,587** (£770; £384; £192) **Stalls** Low

Form RPR

23-1 **1** **Jumbo Prado (USA)**[31] 467 7-9-2 67 (b) AdamKirby 6 70
(Daniel Mark Loughnane) *chsd ldr tl led over 2f out: rdn over 1f out: r.o* **10/3**[2]

00-6 **2** 1 1/2 **Almanack**[13] 683 6-9-2 68 (t) LukeMorris 5 67
(Daniel Mark Loughnane) *a.p: rdn over 2f out: styd on to go 2nd wl ins fnl f: nt trble wnr* **9/2**

36-0 **3** 3/4 **Machiavelian Storm (IRE)**[26] 525 4-8-0 42 (p) KieranO'Neill 1 49
(Michael Herrington) *a.p: rdn to chse wnr and swtchd lft over 1f out: styd on same pce ins fnl f* **66/1**

000- **4** 1 1/4 **Viewpoint (IRE)**[145] 7222 7-9-10 89 LiamJones 2 70
(Michael Appleby) *hld up: rdn over 2f out: styd on fr over 1f out: nvr on terms* **5/2**[1]

5255 **5** 4 1/2 **Robert The Painter (IRE)**[10] 727 8-9-10 82 (v) AmirQuinn 4 60
(Lee Carter) *led at stdy pce tl qckned over 3f out: rdn and hdd over 2f out: wknd fnl f* **7/2**[3]

10-4 **6** 92 **Field Of Dream**[31] 464 9-8-12 84 (p) AdrianNicholls 8
(David Nicholls) *hld up: shkn up over 3f out: wknd and eased over 2f out* **4/1**

1m 49.09s (-1.01) **Going Correction** -0.075s/f (Stan) **6** Ran SP% **113.5**
Speed ratings (Par 101): **101,99,99,97,93 12**
CSF £18.77 TOTE £6.00: £2.30, £2.40; EX 16.00 Trifecta £135.10.
Owner J T Stimpson **Bred** Mr & Mrs Foreman Hardy **Trained** Baldwin's Gate, Staffs
■ Stewards' Enquiry : Luke Morris two-day ban: used whip above shoulder height approaching final furlong (Mar 26-27)

FOCUS
A modest claimer most notable for an alarming drift on the morning favourite Field Of Dream, who ended up trailing in a distant last. The pace was steady and there were doubts over the form.

861 CORAL.CO.UK H'CAP 1m 4f 50y (Tp)
4:50 (4:50) (Class 2) (0-105,102) 4-Y£01,971 (£3,583; £1,791; £896; £446) **Stalls** Low

Form RPR

5215 **1** **Winterlude (IRE)**[25] 530 6-9-4 **96** GeorgeBaker 8 102+
(Jennie Candlish) *hld up: hdwy over 1f out: rdn and edgd lft ins fnl f: r.o to ld towards fin* **7/2**[1]

0-01 **2** 1/2 **Spes Nostra**[10] 734 8-8-10 **88** (b) TomEaves 4 93
(Iain Jardine) *chsd ldr tl led over 2f out: rdn over 1f out: hdd towards fin* **14/1**

6505 **3** *nk* **Masterpaver**[9] 747 5-8-10 **88** FrannyNorton 6 93
(Alan Bailey) *a.p: rdn to chse ldr over 1f out: styd on: nt clr run towards fin* **12/1**

-445 **4** *nk* **Castilo Del Diablo (IRE)**[19] 614 7-9-0 **92** (p) SophieKilloran 5 96
(David Simcock) *hld up: rdn over 1f out: r.o ins fnl f: nt rch ldrs* **13/2**[3]

12-6 **5** 1 **Sbraase**[31] 465 5-8-6 **84** LukeMorris 3 86
(James Tate) *hld up: hdwy u.p over 1f out: nt clr run ins fnl f: styd on same pce* **9/2**[2]

1-52 **6** 1/2 **First Mohican**[59] 99 8-9-10 **102** TomQueally 1 106+
(Alan King) *hld up: hdwy and nt clr run fr over 1f out: nvr trbld ldrs* **7/2**[1]

3163 **7** 1 **Paddys Motorbike (IRE)**[9] 747 4-8-7 **92** JosephineGordon(5) 2 92
(David Evans) *trckd ldrs: racd keenly: rdn and nt clr run over 1f out: no ex ins fnl f* **8/1**

510- **8** 3 3/4 **Wordiness**[149] 7115 8-8-10 **88** SilvestreDeSousa 7 82
(David Evans) *led: rdn and hdd over 2f out: wknd fnl f* **7/1**

2m 36.86s (-3.94) **Going Correction** -0.075s/f (Stan)
WFA 4 from 5yo+ 2lb **8** Ran SP% **113.9**
Speed ratings (Par 109): **110,109,109,109,108 108,107,105**
CSF £52.47 CT £526.16 TOTE £3.70: £1.60, £4.00, £3.90; EX 56.90 Trifecta £496.10.
Owner Brian Verinder & Alan Baxter **Bred** Darley **Trained** Basford Green, Staffs

FOCUS
A decent handicap but a bunch finish and pretty ordinary form for the grade.

862 BET IN PLAY AT CORAL H'CAP 1m 1f 103y (Tp)
5:20 (5:21) (Class 6) (0-65,65) 4-Y-O+ **£2,587** (£770; £384; £192) **Stalls** Low

Form RPR

612- **1** **The Way You Dance (IRE)**[136] 7443 4-9-5 **63** (p) LiamKeniry 5 71
(Neil Mulholland) *a.p: rdn to chse ldr over 1f out: r.o to ld post* **11/4**[1]

-002 **2** *nk* **Let Me In (IRE)**[23] 568 6-8-13 **57** (v) JimmyQuinn 3 64
(Bernard Llewellyn) *chsd ldrs: nt clr run 2f out: rdn to ld wl ins fnl f: hdd nr fin: r.o* **7/1**[3]

2100 **3** *shd* **Les Gar Gan (IRE)**[7] 769 5-9-0 **58** (be) LukeMorris 11 65
(Daniel Mark Loughnane) *hld up: hdwy over 1f out: rdn to ld nr fin: hdd post* **14/1**

0-55 **4** 3/4 **Evervescent (IRE)**[14] 676 7-9-0 **61** EoinWalsh(3) 2 67
(Graeme McPherson) *hld up: hdwy over 3f out: rdn over 1f out: r.o* **16/1**

6-32 **5** *nse* **Red Unico (IRE)**[20] 598 4-9-7 **65** BenCurtis 9 71
(Michael Appleby) *a.p: chsd ldr over 7f out tl led 3f out: rdn over 1f out: hdd wl ins fnl f* **8/1**

-412 **6** 1 **Cahar Fad (IRE)**[23] 569 4-8-13 **57** (bt) AdamBeschizza 12 62
(Steph Hollinshead) *hld up: n.m.r 2f out: hdwy over 1f out: sn rdn: nt clr run wl ins fnl f: styd on same pce* **6/1**[2]

105- **7** 1 **Senor George (IRE)**[194] 5737 9-9-3 **64** RobHornby(3) 1 66
(Simon Hodgson) *hld up: hdwy over 1f out: rdn and hung lft ins fnl f: nt rch ldrs* **66/1**

2160 **8** 7 **Tijuca (IRE)**[14] 676 7-9-6 **64** (tp) KieranO'Neill 7 53
(Ed de Giles) *hld up: shkn up over 1f out: nvr on terms* **9/1**

/3-0 **9** 2 1/4 **My Lord**[59] 101 8-9-0 **65** RyanTimby(7) 6 49
(David Evans) *hld up: pushed along and hdwy on outer over 2f out: wknd fnl f* **25/1**

3163 **10** 2 **Black Minstrel (IRE)**[11] 708 7-9-0 **65** PatrickVaughan(7) 8 46
(John O'Shea) *prom: rdn over 2f out: wknd over 1f out* **7/1**[3]

0-00 **11** 5 **Several (USA)**[33] 435 4-9-2 **60** DougieCostello 4 31
(Kevin Frost) *led 1f: chsd ldrs: rdn over 3f out: wknd over 2f out* **33/1**

41-0 **12** 1/2 **Outlaw Torn (IRE)**[13] 683 7-9-7 **65** (e) JasonHart 13 35
(Richard Guest) *led after 1f: hdd 3f out: rdn and wknd wl over 1f out* **14/1**

-540 **13** 3 3/4 **Sacred Square (GER)**[11] 708 6-9-2 **60**................(p) PaulMulrennan 10 23
(Conor Dore) *hld up: shkn up over 3f out: sn lost tch* **33/1**

1m 58.07s (-2.73) **Going Correction** -0.075s/f (Stan) **13** Ran SP% **117.5**
Speed ratings (Par 101): **109,108,108,107,107 107,106,99,97,96 91,91,87**
CSF £20.19 CT £231.72 TOTE £3.50: £2.10, £2.60, £3.20; EX 25.00 Trifecta £256.40.
Owner BG Racing Partnership **Bred** Grangemore Stud **Trained** Limpley Stoke, Wilts

FOCUS
There was a bunched finish to this modest heat. A small step up from the winner.

863 CORAL CONNECT MAIDEN STKS 1m 1f 103y (Tp)
5:50 (5:54) (Class 5) 3-Y-O+ **£3,234** (£962; £481; £240) **Stalls** Low

Form RPR

1 **Pivotal Flame (IRE)** 3-8-2 0.. LukeMorris 8 66+
(James Tate) *hld up: pushed along and hdwy over 2f out: rdn to ld and edgd lft wl ins fnl f: styd on* **7/2**[3]

536- **2** 1/2 **Farham (USA)**[78] 8319 4-9-13 71.................................... TonyHamilton 9 76
(Richard Fahey) *led after 1f: rdn over 1f out: hung lft and hdd wl ins fnl f: styd on* **11/4**[2]

32 **3** 3 **Four Mile Beach**[10] 735 3-8-7 0...................................... JoeFanning 4 64
(Mark Johnston) *pushed along to ld: hdd after 1f: chsd ldrs: rdn over 1f out: hung lft and no ex ins fnl f* **1/1**[1]

0- **4** 4 1/2 **Tred Softly (IRE)**[158] 6874 3-8-7 0.............................. JamesSullivan 10 54+
(John Quinn) *hld up: hdwy over 1f out: nt rch ldrs* **33/1**

00- **5** 1/2 **Fairy Pools**[76] 8343 5-9-8 0..(b[1]) JimmyQuinn 7 54?
(Les Eyre) *prom: chsd ldr over 6f out: rdn over 2f out: wknd fnl f* **66/1**

0- **6** 2 **Chookie Valentine**[133] 7516 3-8-7 0.................................. JasonHart 1 49
(Keith Dalgleish) *prom: rdn over 2f out: wknd over 1f out* **12/1**

6 **7** 7 **Thiepval**[28] 500 4-9-13 0... BenCurtis 11 40
(Jason Ward) *hld up: rdn over 2f out: nvr on terms* **66/1**

8 nk **Up North (IRE)**[19] 4-9-6 0.. PhilDennis(7) 6 40
(Micky Hammond) *mid-div: hdwy over 5f out: rdn over 2f out: wknd wl over 1f out* **20/1**

004- **9** 5 **Cay Location (IRE)**[176] 6352 3-8-7 0............................ KieranO'Neill 3 23
(Ed de Giles) *plld hrd and prom: lost pl 7f out: n.d after* **50/1**

0 **10** 2 **Zac Courageous (IRE)**[14] 675 4-9-8 0................. RachealKneller(5) 5 25
(James Bennett) *chsd ldrs: pushed along over 3f out: sn wknd* **100/1**

0/ **11** 3 3/4 **Dutch Barney**[891] 6824 6-9-6 0.............................. BeckyBrisbourne(7) 2 17
(Mark Brisbourne) *hld up: hdwy over 4f out: wknd over 2f out* **100/1**

2m 0.12s (-0.68) **Going Correction** -0.075s/f (Stan)
WFA 3 from 4yo+ 20lb **11** Ran SP% **121.2**
Speed ratings (Par 103): **100,99,96,92,92 90,84,84,79,77 74**
CSF £13.65 TOTE £6.10: £3.20, £1.10, £1.10; EX 13.80 Trifecta £24.50.
Owner Saeed Manana **Bred** Rabbah Bloodstock Limited **Trained** Newmarket, Suffolk

FOCUS
A modest maiden with little depth, but a pleasing debut from the winner. The form is rated around the second.
T/Jkpt: Not won. T/Plt: £526.20 to a £1 stake. Pool: £78415.37 - 108.77 winning tickets T/Qpdt: £61.20 to a £1 stake. Pool: £8532.59 - 103.04 winning tickets **Colin Roberts**

[797] SOUTHWELL (L-H)
Tuesday, March 8

OFFICIAL GOING: Fibresand: standard
Wind: Moderate across Weather: Cloudy

864 32RED H'CAP 1m 6f (F)
2:20 (2:20) (Class 5) (0-75,77) 4-Y-O+ **£3,234** (£962; £481; £240) **Stalls** Low

Form RPR

5-3 **1** **Be My Sea (IRE)**[24] 567 5-9-4 **69**...................................... LukeMorris 2 80+
(Tony Carroll) *trckd ldr: hdwy and cl up over 3f out: chal over 2f out and sn rdn: drvn to ld appr fnl f: styd on* **3/1**[2]

5-56 **2** 2 **Horseguardsparade**[47] 273 5-9-3 **68**.........(p) WilliamTwiston-Davies 6 76
(Nigel Twiston-Davies) *hld up: hdwy 4f out: chsd ldrs 3f out: styd nr inner rail st: sn rdn: styd on wl fnl f* **10/1**

-112 **3** 3 **Weald Of Kent (USA)**[5] 800 4-9-4 **73**...........................(v) LiamJones 1 77
(Michael Appleby) *cl up: led after 1 1/2f: pushed along 3f out: sn jnd and rdn: drvn over 1f out: hdd appr fnl f: kpt on same pce* **6/4**[1]

-016 **4** 7 **Virnon**[33] 447 5-9-10 **75**.. BenCurtis 5 69
(Alan Swinbank) *slt ld 1 1/2f: prom: pushed along 4f out: rdn over 3f out: drvn over 2f out: plugged on one pce* **6/1**[3]

0443 **5** 1 **Lean On Pete (IRE)**[18] 640 7-9-2 **67**.......................(e) GrahamGibbons 4 60
(Ollie Pears) *trckd ldrs: hdwy over 3f out: rdn along over 2f out: plugged on same pce* **8/1**

100- **6** 2 1/4 **Lexington Bay (IRE)**[70] 8383 8-9-0 **72**.........................(p) PhilDennis(7) 7 61
(Philip Kirby) *hld up in tch: hdwy on inner over 3f out: rdn along over 2f out: sn drvn and no imp* **16/1**

0/0- **7** 8 **Weapon Of Choice (IRE)**[357] 496 8-9-9 **77** ow2 MissEmmaSayer(3) 3 55
(Dianne Sayer) *chsd ldrs: rdn along over 4f out: sn outpcd and bhd* **66/1**

54/0 **8** 22 **Stand Guard**[13] 693 12-9-0 **68**................................ DanielMuscutt(3) 9 15
(John Butler) *a in rr: rdn along 4f out: sn outpcd and bhd* **28/1**

3m 6.05s (-2.25) **Going Correction** -0.10s/f (Stan)
WFA 4 from 5yo+ 4lb **8** Ran SP% **110.3**
Speed ratings (Par 103): **102,100,99,95,94 93,88,76**
CSF £30.20 CT £56.15 TOTE £3.80: £1.70, £2.90, £1.10; EX 32.60 Trifecta £102.20.
Owner Gary Attwood **Bred** Sunderland Holdings Inc **Trained** Cropthorne, Worcs

FOCUS
A modest staying handicap with a few of these having stamina to prove. The pace was solid and they finished well spread out. The winner is open to progress.

865 DOWNLOAD THE CORAL APP H'CAP 1m 4f (F)
2:55 (2:55) (Class 6) (0-65,71) 4-Y-O+ **£2,587** (£770; £384; £192) **Stalls** Low

Form RPR

3051 **1** **Tatting**[5] 801 7-9-13 **71** 6ex.. PaulMulrennan 5 84
(Conor Dore) *hld up in rr: swtchd to outer and tk clsr order 1/2-way: smooth hdwy to trck ldrs over 3f out: hdwy and cl up wl over 2f out: rdn to ld 1 1/2f out: sn clr: readily* **9/4**[1]

1 **2** 2 1/4 **Lifting Me Higher (IRE)**[21] 601 4-9-0 **60**...........................(p) JFEgan 7 68
(W P Browne, Ire) *trckd ldng pair: hdwy and cl up 4f out: led wl over 2f out: sn rdn: drvn and hdd 1 1/2f out: kpt on same pce* **9/4**[1]

-221 **3** 3 1/2 **Star Ascending (IRE)**[14] 684 4-9-2 **62**......................... TimmyMurphy 8 64
(Jennie Candlish) *in tch: trckd ldrs after 4f: effrt and cl up 3f out: rdn over 2f out: drvn wl over 1f out: kpt on same pce* **9/2**[3]

310- **4** 3 1/2 **Frightened Rabbit (USA)**[46] 5555 4-9-2 **62**...................... GrahamLee 2 59+
(Keith Dalgleish) *in tch: pushed along and outpcd over 4f out: rdn and bhd whn wd st: styd on fnl 2f* **7/2**[2]

6336 **5** 3 3/4 **Smugglers Lane (IRE)**[14] 684 4-8-6 **52**................. SilvestreDeSousa 1 43
(David Evans) *trckd ldrs: effrt on inner to trck ldrs 4f out: rdn along 3f out: drvn over 2f out and sn one pce* **20/1**

-055 **6** 1/2 **Thimaar (USA)**[28] 506 8-9-5 **63**...................................(p) KieranO'Neill 3 53
(Sarah Hollinshead) *trckd ldr: rdn along 4f out: sn drvn and wknd* **20/1**

40-0 **7** 14 **Rossington**[24] 569 7-8-7 **51** oh6..................................... JamesSullivan 4 19
(John Wainwright) *led: pushed along 4f out: rdn over 3f out: drvn and hdd wl over 2f out and sn wknd* **100/1**

00-0 **P** **Oracle Boy**[21] 601 5-8-6 **57**...................................... RhiainIngram(7) 6
(Michael Chapman) *a in rr: rdn along over 4f out: sn outpcd and bhd whn p.u and dismntd jst over 3f out* **100/1**

2m 38.5s (-2.50) **Going Correction** -0.10s/f (Stan)
WFA 4 from 5yo+ 2lb **8** Ran SP% **113.4**
Speed ratings (Par 101): **104,102,100,97,95 95,85,**
CSF £7.14 CT £19.11 TOTE £3.40: £1.10, £1.30, £1.50; EX 8.80 Trifecta £21.30.
Owner Mrs Jennifer Marsh **Bred** Darley **Trained** Hubbert's Bridge, Lincs

FOCUS
A moderate handicap, though three of the eight runners had won their most recent starts and the race was dominated by the market principals. The winner is rated back to his peak 2015 level.

866 LADBROKES H'CAP 1m (F)
3:30 (3:30) (Class 4) (0-85,82) 4-Y-O+ **£5,175** (£1,540; £769; £384) **Stalls** Low

Form RPR

2231 **1** **Captain Revelation**[5] 802 4-9-0 **75**........................ RichardKingscote 2 85+
(Tom Dascombe) *slt ld on inner: rdn over 2f out: drvn and clr over 1f out: kpt on strly* **7/4**[1]

-602 **2** 1 1/2 **Eutropius (IRE)**[35] 427 7-9-5 **80**.. BenCurtis 8 86
(Alan Swinbank) *cl up: effrt over 2f out: sn chsng wnr: rdn wl over 1f out: drvn and kpt on fnl f* **33/1**

-130 **3** nk **Patriotic (IRE)**[23] 581 8-9-3 **78**............................(p) SilvestreDeSousa 9 83
(Chris Dwyer) *hld up towards rr: hdwy on outer and wd st: rdn over 2f out: chsd ldng pair over 1f out: styd on fnl f* **7/1**[3]

6-42 **4** 7 **Bognor (USA)**[6] 788 5-9-4 **79**....................................... AndrewMullen 4 68
(Michael Appleby) *towards rr and swtchd rt to outer after 2f: hdwy on outer to trck ldrs 4f out: pushed along 3f out: rdn over 2f out: sn drvn and one pce* **15/2**

1-31 **5** 2 **Boots And Spurs**[58] 134 7-9-7 **82**................................(v) LukeMorris 7 66
(Scott Dixon) *trckd ldrs on inner: effrt 3f out: rdn wl over 2f out: sn drvn and wknd* **7/2**[2]

-432 **6** 2 3/4 **Best Tamayuz**[5] 802 5-8-7 **68** oh1..............................(p) KieranO'Neill 3 46
(Scott Dixon) *cl up: rdn along over 3f out: drvn wl over 2f out: grad wknd* **12/1**

0140 **7** 34 **Black Dave (IRE)**[11] 734 6-8-11 **77**..................... JosephineGordon(5) 5
(David Evans) *towards rr: rdn along over 3f out: sn drvn: outpcd and bhd fnl 2f* **20/1**

/30- **8** 9 **Illusive Force (IRE)**[410] 267 4-8-9 **70**.......................... TonyHamilton 1
(Derek Shaw) *dwlt: a in rr: outpcd and bhd fnl 3f* **66/1**

3-00 **P** **Dubai Hills**[21] 599 10-9-7 **82**.. DanielTudhope 10
(David O'Meara) *in tch: hdwy over 3f out: effrt to chse ldng pair 2f out: stmbld bdly and p.u 1 1/2f out: fatally injured* **17/2**

1m 42.1s (-1.60) **Going Correction** -0.10s/f (Stan) **9** Ran SP% **110.3**
Speed ratings (Par 105): **104,102,102,95,93 90,56,47,**
CSF £68.22 CT £309.60 TOTE £2.80: £1.60, £7.50, £1.10; EX 44.40 Trifecta £269.10.
Owner Cheshire Racing **Bred** Downfield Cottage Stud **Trained** Malpas, Cheshire

FOCUS
A decent handicap run at a solid pace and the front three pulled well clear. The winner is rated to his C&D best.

867 DOWNLOAD THE LADBROKES APP H'CAP 7f (F)
4:00 (4:05) (Class 6) (0-52,52) 4-Y-O+ **£2,587** (£770; £384; £192) **Stalls** Low

Form RPR

-000 **1** **My Time**[11] 730 7-9-1 **46** oh1....................................(be[1]) RobertHavlin 3 51
(Michael Mullineaux) *trckd ldrs: hdwy wl over 2f out: rdn to ld over 1f out: drvn and hld on wl fnl f* **66/1**

3003 **2** 1/2 **Tasaaboq**[5] 790 5-9-2 **50**......................................(vt) DannyBrock(3) 7 54
(Phil McEntee) *dwlt and bhd: swtchd rt to outer after 2f: hdwy 3f out: swtchd lft and rdn wl over 1f out ev ch ins fnl f: drvn and no ex towards fin* **9/2**[2]

00-0 **3** nk **Quadriga (IRE)**[67] 2 6-9-7 **52**.................................... DougieCostello 11 55
(Philip Kirby) *in tch on outer: hdwy and wd st: rdn to ld 2f out: drvn and hdd over 1f out: kpt on fnl f* **9/4**[1]

62/0 **4** 2 3/4 **Ripon Rose**[21] 596 4-9-3 **48**... GrahamLee 5 44
(Paul Midgley) *midfield: pushed along wl over 2f out: rdn wl over 1f out: kpt on fnl f: nrst fin* **20/1**

000- **5** 1 **Great Demeanor (USA)**[124] 3953 6-9-1 **46** oh1............(vt) TomEaves 12 39
(Dianne Sayer) *prom on outer: effrt and hdwy wl over 2f out: rdn wl over 1f out: ev ch tl drvn and wknd ent fnl f* **16/1**

-563 **6** 4 **Equilicious**[27] 525 4-9-2 **47**.. PJMcDonald 8 29
(Ollie Pears) *slt ld: hdd 1/2-way and sn rdn along: drvn 2f out and sn wknd* **9/2**[2]

504- **7** 7 **Eye Glass (IRE)**[53] 207 4-9-5 **50**....................................(v[1]) BenCurtis 1 13
(T G McCourt, Ire) *chsd ldrs on inner: rdn along 3f out: drvn and wknd 2f out* **10/1**

-506 **8** 3 1/2 **Trigger Park (IRE)**[39] 388 5-9-1 **46** oh1.......................(b) LukeMorris 6
(Ronald Harris) *cl up: led 1/2-way: rdn and hdd 2f out: sn wknd* **7/1**[3]

0004 **9** 4 **Madakheel (USA)**[27] 525 5-9-1 **46** oh1.......................(t) JoeyHaynes 4
(Simon West) *a towards rr* **14/1**

0/0- **10** 16 **Kwanto**[171] 6544 6-8-12 **46** oh1....................................(p) RobHornby(3) 10
(Ken Wingrove) *dwlt: a bhd* **150/1**

6-00 **10** dht **Sinema**[25] 547 4-9-1 **46** oh1... LiamKeniry 2
(Christine Dunnett) *cl up on inner: disp ld over 3f out: rdn wl over 2f out: sn wknd* **28/1**

000/ **12** 8 **Excellent Addition (IRE)**[887] 6980 6-9-7 **52**...............(t) JamesSullivan 9
(Lee James) *a towards rr* **50/1**

1m 31.04s (0.74) **Going Correction** -0.10s/f (Stan) **12** Ran SP% **113.6**
Speed ratings (Par 101): **91,90,90,86,85 81,73,69,64,46 46,37**
CSF £326.09 CT £990.55 TOTE £52.70: £12.20, £1.80, £2.50; EX 549.50 Trifecta £3565.10.
Owner Mark Kilner **Bred** John Heywood & Michael Mullineaux **Trained** Alpraham, Cheshire

FOCUS
This is about as bad as it gets with only three of these having won a race before and the 12 runners having a record of 6-200 on the Flat between them. The SP of the winner says it all and this isn't form to be taking forward. A surprise result but no fluke.

868 DAILY UNIBET EARLY PRICES FROM 9AM H'CAP 5f (F)
4:30 (4:30) (Class 5) (0-70,68) 4-Y-O+ **£3,234** (£962; £481; £240) **Stalls** Centre

Form RPR
3513 **1** **Elusivity (IRE)**[6] 784 8-9-6 **67**....................(p) PaulMulrennan 4 76
(Conor Dore) *mde all: rdn over 1f out: drvn and edgd lft ins fnl f: kpt on strly* **13/8**[1]
113- **2** *1* **Hit The Lights (IRE)**[195] 5732 6-8-4 **58**................(v) DanielleMooney(7) 2 63
(David Nicholls) *trckd ldng pair: hdwy 2f out: sn rdn to chal: drvn and edgd lft ins fnl f: kpt on same pce* **12/1**
-063 **3** *1 ¼* **Extreme Supreme**[11] 733 5-8-13 **60**..........................(v) TonyHamilton 3 61
(Derek Shaw) *dwlt: sn chsng ldrs on outer: pushed along and hdwy 1/2-way: chsd ldng pair wl over 1f out: sn swtchd rt and drvn: kpt on same pce* **2/1**[2]
0243 **4** *1 ¾* **Oscars Journey**[23] 579 6-8-13 **63**....................(v) AlistairRawlinson(3) 7 57
(J R Jenkins) *in tch: hdwy over 2f out: rdn to chse ldrs over 1f out: sn drvn and no imp* **7/1**[3]
-150 **5** *2 ¼* **Very First Blade**[29] 504 7-8-9 **56**...............................(be) RobertHavlin 8 42
(Michael Mullineaux) *racd towards stands' side: in tch: rdn along over 2f out: sn drvn and one pce* **16/1**
00-0 **6** *4* **Holland Park**[12] 703 4-9-1 **62**.......................................(p) LiamKeniry 5 34
(Conor Dore) *dwlt and sn hung lft towards far rail: in rr and outpcd 1/2-way: n.d* **25/1**
-005 **7** *3 ½* **Bapak Bangsawan**[40] 364 6-9-2 **68**....................(v) AnnStokell(5) 6 27
(Ann Stokell) *cl up: disp ld 1/2-way: sn rdn and wknd wl over 1f out* **15/2**

59.68s (-0.02) **Going Correction** +0.075s/f (Slow) **7** Ran SP% **113.1**
Speed ratings (Par 103): **103,101,99,96,93 86,81**
CSF £21.56 CT £40.41 TOTE £2.50: £2.20, £4.30; EX 22.50 Trifecta £60.40.
Owner Mrs Louise Marsh **Bred** J Costello **Trained** Hubbert's Bridge, Lincs

FOCUS
A modest sprint handicap with all seven runners sporting some sort of headgear and a two-horse race according to the market. The winner matched his best form since November.

869 UNIBET OFFER DAILY JOCKEY/TRAINER SPECIALS H'CAP 6f (F)
5:00 (5:00) (Class 6) (0-60,60) 4-Y-O+ **£2,587** (£770; £384; £192) **Stalls** Low

Form RPR
5-44 **1** **Harwoods Star (IRE)**[54] 176 6-9-7 **60**..........................(be[1]) JFEgan 2 73
(John Butler) *trckd ldrs: hdwy over 2f out: rdn to ld wl over 1f out: sn edgd rt: drvn and styd on wl fnl f* **4/1**[3]
02-0 **2** *2 ¾* **Perfect Peak**[66] 22 4-8-10 **56**..........................(vt[1]) NathanEvans(7) 4 61
(Michael Easterby) *prom on outer: cl up 1/2-way: effrt over 2f out: rdn and ev ch over 1f out: drvn and kpt on fnl f* **10/1**
2563 **3** *3* **Lucky Mark (IRE)**[42] 340 7-9-5 **58**..........................(p) DanielTudhope 1 54
(John Balding) *slt ld on inner: rdn along over 2f out: hdd wl over 1f out: swtchd lft and drvn appr fnl f: kpt on one pce* **3/1**[2]
1403 **4** *1 ¼* **Sir Geoffrey (IRE)**[5] 799 10-9-4 **57**..........................(b) LukeMorris 3 49
(Scott Dixon) *cl up: disp ld 1/2-way: rdn along over 2f out: drvn and wknd over 1f out* **9/4**[1]
/30- **5** *½* **Mclovin Riverdance**[88] 8185 4-8-7 **46** oh1..........................(p) BenCurtis 6 37
(T G McCourt, Ire) *chsd ldrs on outer: wd st: rdn along 2f out: sn drvn and wknd* **16/1**
-535 **6** *½* **Monsieur Jamie**[23] 579 8-9-7 **60**..........................(v) DougieCostello 5 49
(J R Jenkins) *dwlt and towards rr: rdn and hdwy 2f out: drvn and kpt on fnl f: nrst fin* **16/1**
00-4 **7** *2 ½* **Captain Scooby**[11] 733 10-9-4 **57**..........................(be) JasonHart 8 39
(Richard Guest) *dwlt: a in rr* **10/1**
535- **8** *5* **Under Approval**[154] 7009 5-8-9 **53**..........................(v) GemmaTutty(5) 7 20
(Karen Tutty) *dwlt: a in rr* **11/1**

1m 15.68s (-0.82) **Going Correction** -0.10s/f (Stan) **8** Ran SP% **114.0**
Speed ratings (Par 101): **101,97,93,91,91 90,87,80**
CSF £42.62 CT £135.09 TOTE £5.20: £1.50, £1.70, £1.40; EX 39.00 Trifecta £176.60.
Owner Jameson Racing Ltd **Bred** Barronstown Stud **Trained** Newmarket, Suffolk

FOCUS
A moderate handicap and another race with plenty of headgear about. Those that raced up with the pace dominated and the form looks straightforward.
T/Jkpt: Not won. T/Plt: £24.60 to a £1 stake. Pool: £72,320.46 - 2145.90 winning units. T/Qpdt: £14.40 to a £1 stake. Pool: £6,534.67 - 335.14 winning units. **Joe Rowntree**

777 KEMPTON (A.W) (R-H)
Wednesday, March 9

OFFICIAL GOING: Polytrack: standard
Wind: Light, half against Weather: Overcast with frequent showers

870 STAR LINKS 100TH RUN H'CAP 1m 2f (P)
5:40 (5:43) (Class 6) (0-55,55) 4-Y-O+ **£2,264** (£673; £336; £168) **Stalls** Low

Form RPR
0436 **1** **Solveig's Song**[12] 728 4-8-12 **46**..........................(p) JackMitchell 9 55
(Steve Woodman) *trckd ldng trio: pushed along over 3f out: clsd to ld wl over 1f out: drvn out and kpt on wl* **8/1**
-006 **2** *1 ½* **Rezwaan**[13] 707 9-9-3 **51**..........................(b) ShaneKelly 1 57
(Murty McGrath) *hld up in 7th: trckd ldrs over 2f out gng wl: rdn and hanging over 1f out: sn chsd wnr but no imp fnl f* **5/1**[2]
-052 **3** *shd* **Top Pocket**[28] 514 4-9-3 **51**.......................... LiamKeniry 6 57
(Michael Madgwick) *hld up in 8th: rdn over 2f out: prog on outer over 1f out: styd on to press for 2nd nr fin* **9/2**[1]
3015 **4** *1 ½* **Time Square (FR)**[16] 672 9-9-0 **55**.......................... MitchGodwin(7) 11 58
(Tony Carroll) *trckd ldng pair: cl up on inner 2f out: shkn up and nt qckn over 1f out: one pce after* **16/1**
0416 **5** *½* **Star Links (USA)**[21] 602 10-9-4 **52**..........................(bt) MartinHarley 5 55
(Sylvester Kirk) *led to post and bked into stall: trckd ldrs in 5th: nt clr run on inner over 1f out: lost pl and swtchd lft: kpt on ins fnl f* **5/1**[2]
0-40 **6** *¾* **First Summer**[46] 316 4-9-2 **55**.......................... JustinNewman(5) 2 57
(Shaun Harris) *hld up in 9th: trying to make prog on inner whn nt clr run over 1f out: kpt on fnl f: no ch* **12/1**
-600 **7** *¾* **Athenian Garden (USA)**[16] 674 9-8-12 **46**.................. CathyGannon 8 45
(Paddy Butler) *slow out of stall: hld up in last trio: stl there over 2f out: pushed along and kpt on quite wl fr over 1f out: nvr involved* **33/1**
-054 **8** *2 ½* **Understory (USA)**[16] 672 9-9-0 **51**..........................(p) RyanTate(3) 12 46+
(Tim McCarthy) *pushed up fr wd draw but unable to ld: pressed ldr: led over 2f out to wl over 1f out: wknd fnl f* **9/1**
-030 **9** *½* **Thrtypointstothree (IRE)**[5] 822 5-8-12 **46** oh1.......(t) StevieDonohoe 7 40+
(Nikki Evans) *pushed up to ld: hdd over 2f out: wknd over 1f out* **25/1**
4010 **10** *1 ¼* **Fairy Mist (IRE)**[21] 609 9-9-4 **52**..................(b) WilliamTwiston-Davies 3 43
(John Bridger) *t.k.h in 6th: rdn 3f out: no prog and sn struggling* **20/1**
00/6 **11** *nk* **Seven Summits (IRE)**[28] 514 9-9-0 **48**.......................... TomQueally 10 39
(Sophie Leech) *slow out of stall: hld up in last and wl off the pce: no ch whn rdn 2f out* **16/1**
1042 **12** *3* **Clock On Tom**[13] 702 6-9-4 **52**.......................... JFEgan 13 37
(Denis Quinn) *hld up in last quartet: rdn and no prog over 3f out* **7/1**[3]
04-0 **13** *11* **Strawberryfields**[67] 20 4-8-12 **46**.......................... DavidProbert 4 10
(Des Donovan, Ire) *a in rr: wknd 3f out: t.o* **33/1**

2m 6.48s (-1.52) **Going Correction** -0.10s/f (Stan) **13** Ran SP% **119.1**
Speed ratings (Par 101): **102,100,100,99,99 98,97,95,95,94 94,91,83**
CSF £45.47 CT £204.20 TOTE £8.90: £1.20, £3.00, £2.20; EX 67.50 Trifecta £398.80.
Owner Sally Woodman D Mortimer **Bred** Mrs Sally Woodman & Mr D Mortimer **Trained** East Lavant, W Sussex

FOCUS
This was run at a strong gallop and was a good race for the grade.

871 32RED H'CAP 1m 2f (P)
6:10 (6:10) (Class 2) (0-105,110) 4-Y-O+ **£12,291** (£3,657; £1,827; £913) **Stalls** Low

Form RPR
2-13 **1** **Our Channel (USA)**[9] 767 5-8-9 **100**..........................(p) GeorgiaCox(7) 6 107
(William Haggas) *trckd ldrs in 4th: pushed along and clsd over 1f out: led last 150yds: rdn and hld on* **6/1**
6-34 **2** *nk* **Truth Or Dare**[25] 560 5-8-6 **90**.......................... MartinDwyer 4 97
(William Muir) *t.k.h: hld up in 5th: forced to wait briefly for a passage over 1f out: hrd rdn and r.o fnl f: tk 2nd and clsd on wnr nr fin* **9/2**[3]
0-22 **3** *¾* **John Reel (FR)**[6] 793 7-9-0 **98**.......................... JFEgan 2 103
(David Evans) *led: rdn 2f out: hdd last 150yds: styd on same pce* **8/1**
06-2 **4** *1 ¼* **Maverick Wave (USA)**[11] 748 5-9-12 **110**.................. JamesDoyle 7 113
(John Gosden) *trckd ldr: shkn up over 2f out: nt qckn over 1f out: lost pl sn after and wl hld* **2/1**[1]
-315 **5** *½* **Dance Of Fire**[23] 594 4-8-2 **86**.......................... CathyGannon 1 89
(Andrew Balding) *t.k.h: trckd ldng pair: pushed along to dispute 2nd whn nowhere to go on inner fr over 1f out to ins fnl f: fdd nr fin* **12/1**
3004 **6** *¾* **Russian Realm**[18] 656 6-8-4 **91**.......................... RyanTate(3) 3 91
(Richard Hughes) *broke wl but sn restrained into 6th: shuffled along fr over 2f out: no imp on ldrs and nvr involved* **14/1**
61-2 **7** *½* **Razor Wind (IRE)**[23] 594 5-9-4 **102**.......................... WilliamBuick 5 101
(Charlie Appleby) *hld up in last but nvr really gng wl and pushed along at various times: rdn and no prog 2f out: one pce* **11/4**[2]

2m 4.44s (-3.56) **Going Correction** -0.10s/f (Stan) **7** Ran SP% **117.9**
Speed ratings (Par 109): **110,109,109,108,107 107,106**
CSF £34.35 TOTE £5.60: £2.50, £3.00; EX 36.30 Trifecta £238.40.
Owner Abdulla Al Mansoori **Bred** Bluegrass Hall Llc **Trained** Newmarket, Suffolk

FOCUS
This very classy handicap was won last year by Tryster, who added the Winter Derby and the Easter Classic on his next two starts. The pace was decent and the time was just over two seconds quicker than that for the opening 46-55 handicap. A minor pb with the rider's claim for the winner.

872 32RED.COM H'CAP (DIV I) 6f (P)
6:40 (6:41) (Class 6) (0-65,65) 4-Y-O+ **£2,264** (£673; £336; £168) **Stalls** Low

Form RPR
0021 **1** **Eljaddaaf (IRE)**[26] 543 5-9-3 **61**.......................... RobertWinston 11 72+
(Dean Ivory) *dropped in fr wdst draw: hld up in last and wl off the pce: stl in last whn forced to check arnd rival wl over 1f out: rdn and prog on outer after: drvn and styd on to ld last 100yds* **6/4**[1]
65-0 **2** *¾* **Assertive Agent**[58] 143 6-8-9 **53**.......................... DavidProbert 1 59
(Tony Carroll) *hld up towards rr: prog as ldrs faltered fr 2f out: drvn to ld jst ins fnl f: hdd and one pce last 100yds* **20/1**
5463 **3** *½* **Divine Call**[2] 856 9-8-13 **57**..........................(v) FrannyNorton 6 62
(Milton Bradley) *hld up off the pce in last trio: prog as ldrs faltered fr 2f out: drvn to chal fnl f: one pce last 100yds* **13/2**[3]
4130 **4** *nk* **Nasri**[6] 799 10-9-7 **65**.......................... TomQueally 8 69
(Emma Owen) *pressed ldng pair: tried to chal u.p 2f out: nt qckn over 1f out: kpt on fnl f* **12/1**
100- **5** *1 ½* **Catalinas Diamond (IRE)**[113] 7883 8-9-4 **62**...............(t) SteveDrowne 9 61
(Pat Murphy) *hld up off the pce in last trio: prog wl over 1f out: drvn and kpt on fnl f: nt gng pce to chal* **66/1**
-006 **6** *nk* **Generalyse**[2] 856 7-9-5 **63**..........................(p) GeorgeBaker 2 61
(Anabel K Murphy) *led at brisk pce but pressed: kpt on whn chal on all sides tl hdd and fdd jst ins fnl f* **8/1**
-330 **7** *1 ¼* **Flying Fantasy**[15] 683 4-9-6 **64**.......................... OisinMurphy 10 58
(Stuart Williams) *racd wd in midfield: struggling whn hung lft 2f out: no ch after: passed wkng rivals nr fin* **6/1**[2]
520- **8** *shd* **Noverre To Go (IRE)**[100] 8051 10-9-7 **65**..................(p) LukeMorris 5 59
(Ronald Harris) *hld up in midfield: rdn and tried to cl on ldrs over 1f out: wknd ins fnl f* **25/1**
3134 **9** *2 ¾* **Secret Millionaire (IRE)**[8] 775 9-8-13 **62**............(p) JustinNewman(5) 4 48
(Shaun Harris) *t.k.h: pressed ldr to 2f out: sn wknd* **20/1**
55-4 **10** *3 ¾* **Perfect Bounty**[21] 615 4-8-13 **60**.......................... RyanTate(3) 3 35
(Patrick Chamings) *pushed along in midfield bef 1/2-way: effrt on inner 2f out: wknd over 1f out* **9/1**
60-5 **11** *¾* **Bubbly Bailey**[54] 196 6-9-3 **61**..........................(v) DarryllHolland 7 33
(J R Jenkins) *chsd ldng pair: drvn to try to chal wl over 1f out: wknd rapidly jst over 1f out* **50/1**

1m 11.95s (-1.15) **Going Correction** -0.10s/f (Stan) **11** Ran SP% **113.2**
Speed ratings (Par 101): **103,102,101,100,98 98,96,96,93,88 87**
CSF £39.62 CT £156.32 TOTE £2.10: £1.30, £5.80, £2.10; EX 34.70 Trifecta £162.70.
Owner Wentdale Ltd & Mrs L A Ivory **Bred** Shadwell Estate Company Limited **Trained** Radlett, Herts
■ Stewards' Enquiry : Darryll Holland £140 fine: failed to report gelding had lost its action

FOCUS
A modest, truly run sprint handicap. The pace collapsed and the first three and the fifth all came from the rear. Straightforward form and the winner can rate higher.

873 32RED.COM H'CAP (DIV II) 6f (P)
7:10 (7:11) (Class 6) (0-65,65) 4-Y-O+ **£2,264** (£673; £336; £168) **Stalls** Low

Form RPR
4-01 **1** **Rigolleto (IRE)**[18] 658 8-9-7 **65**..........................(p) GeorgeBaker 1 77
(Anabel K Murphy) *mde all: 3 l clr and gng bttr than rest 2f out: rdn out fnl f: unchal* **9/2**[2]

5-51 **2** 3 1/4 **New Rich**[21] 615 6-9-7 **65**......(b) JohnFahy 5 67
(Eve Johnson Houghton) *hld up in 6th: rdn and prog 2f out: chsd wnr jst over 1f out: no imp* **7/2**[1]

6-50 **3** hd **Secret Witness**[39] 398 10-9-3 **61**......(b) LukeMorris 9 63
(Ronald Harris) *dwlt: hld up in last trio: rdn and tried to make prog 2f out: drvn and kpt on fnl f to take 3rd nr fin* **9/1**

0446 **4** 1 **Burauq**[21] 615 4-8-10 **54**......(b) FrannyNorton 4 53
(Milton Bradley) *prom: rdn over 2f out: nvr gng pce to threaten but kpt on fnl f* **11/1**

0-23 **5** hd **Pharoh Jake**[16] 669 8-9-0 **58**...... WilliamTwiston-Davies 3 56
(John Bridger) *t.k.h: prom: chsd wnr over 2f out to jst over 1f out: one pce* **9/1**

-544 **6** 1 **Only Ten Per Cent (IRE)**[21] 607 8-9-1 **62**......(p) AlistairRawlinson(3) 7 57
(J R Jenkins) *w.w in 5th: shkn up on outer over 2f out: little rspnse to press and no hdwy* **6/1**[3]

1505 **7** nk **Rocket Rob (IRE)**[8] 775 10-9-3 **61**...... TomQueally 2 55
(Willie Musson) *dwlt: hld up in last trio: effrt on inner 2f out: sn no prog: one pce fnl f* **12/1**

531- **8** 1 **Posh Bounty**[127] 7680 5-9-3 **61**...... JFEgan 6 52
(Joseph Tuite) *taken down early: sn in last: rdn and detached over 2f out: kpt on ins fnl f* **11/1**

-435 **9** shd **Encapsulated**[18] 658 6-8-11 **62**...... RhiainIngram(7) 10 53
(Roger Ingram) *walked to post: racd wd: chsd wnr to over 2f out: steadily fdd* **7/1**

1m 11.9s (-1.20) **Going Correction** -0.10s/f (Stan) **9** Ran SP% **111.5**
Speed ratings (Par 101): **104,99,99,98,97 96,96,94,94**
CSF £19.59 CT £131.32 TOTE £4.80: £2.20, £2.00, £3.50; EX 22.00 Trifecta £186.90.
Owner All The Kings Horses **Bred** Michael O'Mahony **Trained** Wilmcote, Warwicks

FOCUS
Marginally the quicker of the two divisions. The winner was allowed the run of things up front and is rated to his best form of the past two years.

874 £10 FREE BET AT 32REDSPORT.COM MAIDEN AUCTION STKS 1m (P)
7:40 (7:41) (Class 5) 3-Y-O **£2,911** (£866; £432; £216) **Stalls** Low

Form RPR

52-2 **1** **Bernie's Boy**[20] 618 3-9-2 81...... RobHornby(3) 3 69
(Andrew Balding) *sddle slipped sltly forward s: mde all: pushed along and hung lft fr 2f out: kpt on fnl f* **1/4**[1]

00-6 **2** 1 1/4 **Red Hot Chilly (IRE)**[25] 557 3-9-5 69...... JFEgan 5 66
(Joseph Tuite) *hld up in 4th: prog to press wnr jst over 2f out: carried lft after tl swtchd rt 1f out: no imp last 100yds* **4/1**[2]

600 **3** 4 1/2 **Betsalottie**[14] 691 3-9-5 54...... WilliamTwiston-Davies 4 55
(John Bridger) *trckd wnr to jst over 2f out: fdd over 1f out* **33/1**

4 19 **Russian Ranger (IRE)** 3-9-5 0...... RyanClark 1 10
(Jonathan Portman) *s.i.s: rn green in last: wknd over 2f out: t.o* **8/1**[3]

0 **5** 7 **Flashy King (IRE)**[7] 778 3-9-5 0...... LiamKeniry 2
(Joseph Tuite) *in tch to over 2f out: wknd rapidly: t.o* **50/1**

1m 39.17s (-0.63) **Going Correction** -0.10s/f (Stan) **5** Ran SP% **116.0**
Speed ratings (Par 98): **99,97,93,74,67**
CSF £1.95 TOTE £1.20: £1.02, £2.10; EX 2.30 Trifecta £8.50.
Owner B P McGuire **Bred** Mrs Eleanor Kent **Trained** Kingsclere, Hants
■ Stewards' Enquiry : Rob Hornby caution: careless riding

FOCUS
A weak maiden, the winner making hard work of it.

875 32RED CASINO APPRENTICE H'CAP (LONDON MILE SERIES QUALIFIER) 1m (P)
8:10 (8:10) (Class 5) (0-75,73) 4-Y-O+ **£2,911** (£866; £432; £216) **Stalls** Low

Form RPR

0-11 **1** **Giovanni Di Bicci**[34] 437 4-8-8 **65**......(t) RhiainIngram(5) 4 77+
(Jim Boyle) *trckd ldrs: prog to ld jst over 2f out: pushed along and sn firmly in control: pushed out* **15/8**[1]

10-4 **2** 1 3/4 **Estibdaad (IRE)**[62] 88 6-9-3 **69**......(t) JosephineGordon 6 74
(Paddy Butler) *led: rdn and hdd jst over 2f out: jnd for 2nd over 1f out: kpt on wl fnl f* **25/1**

6-42 **3** 1/2 **Stormbound (IRE)**[15] 683 7-9-2 **68**......(b) EdwardGreatrex 5 72
(Paul Cole) *hld up in midfield: drvn over 2f out: prog to dispute 2nd over 1f out: one pce fnl f* **11/4**[2]

650- **4** 1 1/4 **Makhfar (IRE)**[148] 7189 5-8-8 **60**......(v1) NoelGarbutt 7 61
(Kevin Morgan) *t.k.h: hld up in rr on outer: rdn over 2f out: kpt on fr over 1f out to take 4th nr fin* **14/1**

1033 **5** 1/2 **Ocean Legend (IRE)**[16] 671 11-9-1 **67**...... PaddyPilley 1 67
(Tony Carroll) *t.k.h: hld up towards rr: pushed along and prog 2f out: disp 2nd over 1f out: fdd ins fnl f* **10/1**

444- **6** 1 3/4 **Buckleberry**[226] 4707 4-9-4 **73**...... CharlieBennett(3) 9 68
(Jonathan Portman) *chsd ldng pair: disp 2nd 1/2-way: sn pushed along: lost pl 3f out: n.d after* **17/2**[3]

304- **7** 2 1/2 **Dark Amber**[137] 7474 6-9-7 **73**...... JennyPowell 8 62
(Brendan Powell) *s.i.s: prog on outer fr 6f out: chsd ldr 1/2-way to over 2f out: sn wknd* **16/1**

100- **8** 4 1/2 **Paladin (IRE)**[144] 6237 7-8-13 **70**...... MitchGodwin(5) 2 49
(Michael Blake) *chsd ldr to 1/2-way: styd prom tl wknd qckly 2f out* **10/1**

-650 **9** hd **Breakheart (IRE)**[31] 491 9-8-7 **66**......(v) WilliamCox(7) 3 44
(Andrew Balding) *hld up in last: lost tch 1/2-way: rdn and no prog over 2f out* **16/1**

1m 39.88s (0.08) **Going Correction** -0.10s/f (Stan) **9** Ran SP% **112.4**
Speed ratings (Par 103): **95,93,92,91,91 89,86,82,82**
CSF £50.72 CT £127.04 TOTE £2.70: £1.70, £5.50, £1.02; EX 35.90 Trifecta £123.80.
Owner Epsom Equine Spa Partnership **Bred** Vimal And Gillian Khosla **Trained** Epsom, Surrey

FOCUS
This ordinary handicap was run in a slightly slower time than the preceding maiden. The winner was value for a bit extra with the second setting the level.

876 32RED ON THE APP STORE H'CAP 1m (P)
8:40 (8:41) (Class 7) (0-50,50) 4-Y-O+ **£1,940** (£577; £288; £144) **Stalls** Low

Form RPR

5006 **1** **Chandrayaan**[14] 696 9-9-2 **45**......(v) RobertHavlin 11 51
(John E Long) *sn hld up in rr: rdn and prog on outer 2f out: edgd rt over 1f out: styd on fnl f to ld nr fin* **25/1**

-425 **2** 1/2 **Dreaming Again**[14] 690 6-9-6 **49**...... KieranO'Neill 9 54
(Jimmy Fox) *dwlt: hld up in rr: waiting for room over 2f out: rdn and prog over 1f out: styd on to take 2nd last strides* **3/1**[2]

0-50 **3** hd **Affectionate Lady (IRE)**[21] 609 5-9-2 **48**......(b) NataliaGemelova(3) 6 53
(Keith Reveley) *rn wout declared tongue-strap: slowly away: sn in midfield on inner: nt clr run over 2f out: prog against far rail wl over 1f out: rdn to ld ins fnl f: hdd nr fin* **8/1**[3]

040- **4** nse **Play The Blues (IRE)**[134] 7538 9-9-4 **50**......(t) EoinWalsh(3) 4 55
(Henry Tett) *jockey had trble removing blindfold and slowly away: hld up in last pair: trapped bhd rivals over 2f out tl swtchd lft over 1f out: gd prog fnl f: gaining at fin* **20/1**

4653 **5** 1 **Je T'Aime Encore**[7] 787 4-9-5 **48**......(b) LukeMorris 3 52
(Gay Kelleway) *wl in tch: gng strly over 3f out: rdn and no rspnse over 2f out: kpt on same pce fr over 1f out: nvr able to chal* **5/2**[1]

4003 **6** shd **Tax Reform (IRE)**[14] 690 6-9-2 **45**...... JFEgan 2 47
(Natalie Lloyd-Beavis) *prom: trckd ldng pair over 3f out: rdn to ld over 1f out: hdd and fdd ins fnl f* **8/1**[3]

6045 **7** 1 1/4 **Arsenale (GER)**[22] 601 5-9-4 **47**...... AndrewMullen 1 46
(Michael Appleby) *chsd ldng pair to over 3f out but sn urged along: hrd rdn and stl in w ch over 1f out: fdd fnl f* **16/1**

0-03 **8** 2 1/2 **As A Dream (IRE)**[26] 547 4-9-5 **48**...... StevieDonohoe 5 43
(Nikki Evans) *t.k.h: pressed ldr: hung lft bnd over 4f out: lost 2nd 2f out: btn whn short of room ins fnl f: eased* **14/1**

60-0 **9** 1 1/4 **Farrah's Choice**[7] 787 4-9-5 **48**...... TimmyMurphy 7 38
(James Grassick) *led to over 1f out: wknd fnl f* **66/1**

-602 **10** 1 **Crowning Star (IRE)**[14] 690 7-8-9 **45**......(p) CliffordLee(7) 10 40
(Steve Woodman) *pressed ldrs: rdn over 2f out: sing to lose pl whn bdly hmpd over 1f out and nrly fell: nt rcvr* **8/1**[3]

-050 **11** 1 **Eeny Mac (IRE)**[21] 602 9-9-2 **45**......(v) TomEaves 8 30
(John Wainwright) *a towards rr: struggling over 2f out* **25/1**

/0-0 **12** 21 **Mildmay Arms**[14] 701 4-9-2 **48**......(p) RobHornby(3) 13
(Simon Hodgson) *stdd s: t.k.h: hld up in last: wknd over 2f out: t.o* **40/1**

1m 40.44s (0.64) **Going Correction** -0.10s/f (Stan) **12** Ran SP% **115.8**
Speed ratings (Par 97): **92,91,91,91,90 90,88,86,85,84 83,62**
CSF £93.11 CT £685.49 TOTE £27.30: £8.00, £1.40, £1.50; EX 158.10 Trifecta £3204.00.
Owner R D John **Bred** Whatton Manor Stud **Trained** Royston, Herts
■ Stewards' Enquiry : Natalia Gemelova 13-day ban: used whip above permitted level and in the incorrect place (Mar 23-Apr 5)

FOCUS
The principals came from the back in this basement handicap, which had a compressed finish. Straightforward form.
T/Jkpt: Not won. T/Plt: £34.80 to a £1 stake. Pool: £85,753.59 - 1,795.05 winning tickets T/Qpdt: £2.40 to a £1 stake. Pool: £10,020.73 - 3,049.1 winning tickets **Jonathan Neesom**

832 LINGFIELD (L-H)
Wednesday, March 9

OFFICIAL GOING: Polytrack: standard
Wind: virtually nil Weather: showers after a very wet night and morning

877 LADBROKES H'CAP 1m 1y(P)
2:10 (2:15) (Class 6) (0-65,65) 4-Y-O+ **£2,264** (£673; £336; £168) **Stalls** High

Form RPR

-54U **1** **Palace Moon**[13] 709 11-8-12 **56**......(t) KierenFox 10 61
(Michael Attwater) *chsd ldng trio: effrt wl over 1f out: sn ev ch: led ins fnl f: kpt on wl: rdn out* **20/1**

0653 **2** nk **West Leake (IRE)**[13] 709 10-8-12 **56**...... LiamKeniry 9 60
(Paul Burgoyne) *stdd s: t.k.h: hld up in tch in last trio: effrt over 1f out: r.o strly ins fnl f: wnt 2nd cl home: nvr quite getting to wnr* **14/1**

-303 **3** hd **Sylvette**[25] 569 4-8-13 **57**......(bt) AndreaAtzeni 3 61
(Roger Varian) *chsd ldng pair: effrt wl over 1f out: ev ch ins fnl f: kpt on: no ex cl home and lost 2nd last strides* **5/1**[3]

4253 **4** shd **Hawk Moth (IRE)**[15] 681 8-8-13 **57**......(b) LukeMorris 1 60
(John Spearing) *in tch in midfield: swtchd lft and drvn to chal over 1f out: kpt on: no ex cl home* **12/1**

005- **5** 1/2 **Surewecan**[141] 7355 4-9-7 **65**...... JimCrowley 6 67
(Mark Johnston) *chsd ldrs: rdn to ld over 1f out: hdd ins fnl f: styd on same pce u.p fnl 100yds* **3/1**[1]

-112 **6** nk **Gunner Moyne**[13] 709 4-9-6 **64**......(t) GeorgeBaker 2 67
(Gary Moore) *dwlt: hld up in last trio: clsd and swtchd rt 2f out: sn n.m.r: rdn and hdwy 1f out: r.o wl ins fnl f: nvr gng to rch ldrs* **3/1**[1]

41-5 **7** 1 1/2 **Storm Runner (IRE)**[14] 701 8-9-2 **60**...... OisinMurphy 5 58
(George Margarson) *in tch in midfield: effrt on inner over 1f out: hdwy 1f out: kpt on same pce ins fnl f* **4/1**[2]

60-4 **8** nk **Bloodsweatandtears**[13] 709 8-9-4 **62**...... AmirQuinn 8 59
(William Knight) *dwlt and bustled along early: sn rcvrd and in tch in midfield: unable qck and lost pl over 1f out: styd on same pce fnl f* **25/1**

-403 **9** 1/2 **Whaleweigh Station**[18] 658 5-9-7 **65**......(p) RaulDaSilva 7 61
(J R Jenkins) *stdd after s: t.k.h: hld up in last trio: effrt on outer 2f out: no imp over 1f out* **8/1**

100/ **10** 1/2 **Mr Lando**[104] 7961 7-8-13 **57**...... JimmyQuinn 4 52
(Luke Dace) *taken down early: led: rdn over 2f out: hdd over 1f out and lost pl 1f out: wknd ins fnl f* **33/1**

1m 37.3s (-0.90) **Going Correction** -0.075s/f (Stan) **10** Ran SP% **123.7**
Speed ratings (Par 101): **101,100,100,100,99 99,98,97,97,96**
CSF £280.36 CT £1681.33 TOTE £28.60: £6.20, £3.80, £2.10; EX 329.30 Trifecta £1287.50.
Owner Canisbay Bloodstock **Bred** Miss B Swire **Trained** Epsom, Surrey

FOCUS
There was a messy and compressed finish to this moderate handicap. Straightforward form.

878 UNIBET 90PLUS INJURY TIME INSURANCE IS BACK CLAIMING STKS 6f 1y(P)
2:40 (2:45) (Class 6) 4-Y-O+ **£2,264** (£673; £336) **Stalls** Low

Form RPR

2-44 **1** **Corporal Maddox**[26] 546 9-9-9 80......(p) LukeMorris 2 86
(Ronald Harris) *dwlt: in tch in 3rd: rdn 2f out: drvn to chse wnr jst ins fnl f: styd on to ld fnl 50yds* **4/1**[3]

6-44 **2** 1/2 **Ballista (IRE)**[24] 580 8-9-12 85...... RichardKingscote 3 88
(Tom Dascombe) *led: drifted rt and rdn over 1f out: drvn ins fnl f: hdd fnl 50yds: no ex* **6/4**[1]

-416 **3** 1/2 **Majestic Myles (IRE)**[12] 727 8-9-4 85...... TomEaves 5 78
(Richard Fahey) *chsd ldr: rdn wl over 1f out: unable qck and lost 2nd jst ins fnl f: kpt on again wl ins fnl f* **2/1**[2]

1m 11.02s (-0.88) **Going Correction** -0.075s/f (Stan) **3** Ran SP% **93.3**
Speed ratings (Par 101): **102,101,100**
CSF £7.50 TOTE £3.80; EX 5.80 Trifecta £3.60.Majestic Myles was claimed by Mr L. A. Carter for £7,000.
Owner S & A Mares & Ridge House Stables Ltd **Bred** Theobalds Stud **Trained** Earlswood, Monmouths
■ Silver Rainbow was withdrawn. Price at time of withdrawal 5/1. Rule 4 applies to all bets - deduction 15p in the pound.

FOCUS
The three runners were covered by around a length at the finish in this ordinary claimer. Straightforward form, the winner to his recent best.

879 DOWNLOAD THE NEW UNIBET RACING APP H'CAP — 6f 1y(P)
3:10 (3:15) (Class 4) (0-85,90) 4-Y-O+ **£4,690** (£1,395; £697; £348) **Stalls** Low

Form RPR

04-6 **1** **Stellarta**[58] 142 5-9-0 **77** .... DavidProbert 8 83
(Michael Blanshard) *midfield and niggled along early: rdn over 1f out: hdwy u.p ins fnl f: r.o wl to ld towards fin* **5/2**[2]

500- **2** *nk* **Bertie Blu Boy**[165] 6760 8-9-5 **82** .... (v) GeorgeBaker 2 87
(Lisa Williamson) *led: rdn over 1f out: hdd jst ins fnl f: rallied gamely u.p and ev ch wl ins fnl f: kpt on* **8/1**

6611 **3** *shd* **Fleckerl (IRE)**[8] 771 6-9-13 **90** 6ex .... (p) JimCrowley 10 95
(Conor Dore) *stdd and dropped in after s: hld up off the pce in last: clsd 2f out: swtchd lft over 1f out: hdwy u.p 1f out: ev ch wl ins fnl f: kpt on* **9/4**[1]

4201 **4** *½* **Pour La Victoire (IRE)**[12] 727 6-9-0 **82** .... (b) PaddyPilley(5) 3 85
(Tony Carroll) *chsd clr ldng pair: effrt on inner wl over 1f out: rdn to ld jst ins fnl f: hdd and no ex wl ins fnl f* **4/1**[3]

-060 **5** *2 ¾* **Mighty Zip (USA)**[14] 694 4-8-12 **75** .... (b) TomEaves 6 69
(Kevin Ryan) *taken down early: chsd ldr and clr of field: rdn and lost 2nd over 1f out: wknd ins fnl f* **16/1**

350- **6** *1* **Midnight Rider (IRE)**[152] 7093 8-9-6 **83** .... OisinMurphy 7 74
(Rod Millman) *squeezed for room sn after s: racd off the pce in last pair: hdwy u.p over 1f out: no imp ins fnl f* **14/1**

-521 **7** *2 ¾* **The Tichborne (IRE)**[19] 629 8-8-7 **70** oh2 .... (b) JackMitchell 5 52
(Roger Teal) *midfield: rdn over 2f out: no imp and lost pl over 1f out: wknd ins fnl f* **8/1**

1m 10.89s (-1.01) **Going Correction** -0.075s/f (Stan) 7 Ran SP% **114.1**
Speed ratings (Par 105): **103,102,102,101,98 96,93**
CSF £22.40 CT £50.05 TOTE £3.70: £2.30, £4.10; EX 22.70 Trifecta £71.70.
Owner Vincent Ward **Bred** Whitsbury Manor Stud & Pigeon House Stud **Trained** Upper Lambourn, Berks

FOCUS
A modest sprint handicap diluted by the non-runners. There was no hanging about. The winner has a length better to his name last year.

880 32RED CASINO MAIDEN STKS — 1m 2f (P)
3:40 (3:48) (Class 5) 3-Y-O **£2,911** (£866; £432; £216) **Stalls** Low

Form RPR

5-23 **1** **Carry Me Home**[19] 633 3-9-5 70 .... DarryllHolland 7 79
(Charles Hills) *mde all: rdn and wnt 2 l clr 2f out: styd on and a doing enough fnl f: rdn out* **5/2**[2]

5 **2** *1* **Shoofly (IRE)**[21] 603 3-9-0 0 .... DavidProbert 2 72
(Martyn Meade) *chsd ldng pair: swtchd rt and effrt to chse wnr over 1f out: kpt on u.p but a hld fnl f* **9/2**[3]

252- **3** *4 ½* **Templier (IRE)**[138] 7442 3-9-5 79 .... SilvestreDeSousa 5 68
(Mark Johnston) *chsd wnr: rdn to press wnr but nt travelling as wl 3f out: outpcd and lost 2nd whn sltly hmpd over 1f out: hung lft and wknd ins fnl f* **11/8**[1]

6-6 **4** *2 ½* **Howardian Hills (IRE)**[14] 691 3-9-5 0 .... SeanLevey 4 63
(Richard Hannon) *in tch: rdn 4f out: 4th and outpcd 2f out: wl hld and plugged on same pce fr over 1f out* **8/1**

5 **5** *2 ½* **Topalova**[18] 654 3-9-0 0 .... SaleemGolam 8 53
(Mark H Tompkins) *s.i.s: sn rcvrd and in tch in midfield: rdn over 2f out: 5th and outpcd 2f out: wknd over 1f out* **10/1**

50 **6** *15* **Pickering**[9] 765 3-9-5 0 .... (p) AntonioFresu 6 28
(Denis Quinn) *v.s.a: sn rcvrd and in tch in last: shkn up 3f out: sn btn: lost tch 2f out* **100/1**

2m 4.32s (-2.28) **Going Correction** -0.075s/f (Stan) 6 Ran SP% **110.1**
Speed ratings (Par 98): **106,105,101,99,97 85**
CSF £13.41 TOTE £3.30: £1.60, £1.60; EX 11.90 Trifecta £19.60.
Owner Gary And Linnet Woodward **Bred** Gary Woodward **Trained** Lambourn, Berks
■ Montycristo was withdrawn. Price at time of withdrawal 100/1. Rule 4 does not apply.

FOCUS
An ordinary 3yo maiden and straightforward enough form rated around the 1-2. There was little depth.

881 DAILY UNIBET EARLY PRICES FROM 9AM H'CAP — 5f 6y(P)
4:10 (4:16) (Class 3) (0-95,90) 3-Y-O **£7,246** (£2,168; £1,084; £542) **Stalls** High

Form RPR

1231 **1** **Aguerooo (IRE)**[25] 559 3-9-0 **90** .... (p) HollieDoyle(7) 1 95
(Richard Hannon) *hld up wl in tch in rr: effrt over 1f out: rdn to chal 1f out: sn led and drifted rt: r.o wl and sn in command* **15/8**[2]

301- **2** *1 ¼* **Furiant**[134] 7523 3-9-2 **85** .... SilvestreDeSousa 3 85
(Mark Johnston) *sn led: rdn ent fnl 2f: drvn 1f out: sn hdd and styd on same pce ins fnl f* **6/4**[1]

-161 **3** *shd* **Pink Martini (IRE)**[12] 726 3-8-2 **76** oh1 .... JosephineGordon(5) 2 76
(Joseph Tuite) *pressed ldr for 1f: styd handy: swtchd lft and effrt to chal over 1f out: kpt on same pce ins fnl f* **7/1**

2-55 **4** *nk* **Illegally Blonde (IRE)**[27] 536 3-9-6 **89** .... AdamKirby 4 88
(Jamie Osborne) *pressed ldr after 1f: rdn and ev ch over 1f out: unable qck whn carried rt and hmpd 100yds out: one pce after* **7/2**[3]

59.23s (0.43) **Going Correction** -0.075s/f (Stan) 4 Ran SP% **109.5**
Speed ratings (Par 102): **93,91,90,90**
CSF £5.14 TOTE £2.60; EX 5.20 Trifecta £14.60.
Owner Middleham Park Racing LXXXVI **Bred** Cooneen Stud **Trained** East Everleigh, Wilts
■ Stewards' Enquiry : Hollie Doyle one-day ban: careless riding (Mar 23); two-day ban: used whip above permitted level (Mar 24-25)

FOCUS
A fair little 3yo sprint handicap. Sound AW form, taken at face value.

882 32RED H'CAP — 1m 7f 169y(P)
4:40 (4:45) (Class 5) (0-75,73) 4-Y-O+ **£2,911** (£866; £432; £216) **Stalls** Low

Form RPR

-331 **1** **Rose Above**[7] 781 4-9-2 **68** 6ex .... JimCrowley 3 76+
(Andrew Balding) *chsd ldr for 2f: trckd ldrs after tl wnt 2nd again 6f out: upsides ldr and gng best over 2f out: rdn to ld over 1f out: in command and styd on wl fnl f: eased cl home* **11/8**[1]

521- **2** *1 ¼* **Danglydontask**[143] 7307 5-8-11 **58** .... LukeMorris 2 63
(David Arbuthnot) *in tch in midfield: rdn over 4f out: drvn over 2f out: chsd wnr ent fnl f: styd on same pce after* **8/1**

5-32 **3** *½* **Thomas Blossom (IRE)**[14] 698 6-9-5 **66** .... (tp) GeorgeBaker 6 70
(Ali Stronge) *hld up in last pair: effrt and n.m.r jst over 2f out: swtchd rt wl over 1f out: hdwy u.p 1f out: wnt 3rd 100yds out: kpt on but no threat to wnr* **3/1**[2]

030- **4** *2 ½* **Westerly**[102] 8039 5-9-4 **65** .... KieranO'Neill 1 66
(Luke Dace) *led for 5f: chsd ldr tl 6f out: styd handy: rdn over 2f out: no ex u.p 1f out: wknd ins fnl f* **25/1**

1-46 **5** *1 ½* **Aumerle**[13] 704 4-9-7 **73** .... AdamKirby 7 73
(Shaun Lycett) *hld up in tch in last pair: swtchd rt and effrt u.p 3f out: chsd ldrs 2f out: no ex and btn 1f out: wknd ins fnl f* **8/1**

/0-3 **6** *hd* **Amanto (GER)**[14] 698 6-9-0 **68** .... (b) MeganNicholls(7) 8 67
(Paul Nicholls) *dwlt: t.k.h and hdwy to press ldr after 2f: led after 5f: rdn over 2f out: hdd and no ex over 1f out: wknd ins fnl f* **5/1**[3]

5606 **7** *24* **Topaling**[14] 698 5-9-1 **62** .... (p) SaleemGolam 5 33
(Mark H Tompkins) *taken down early: in tch in midfield: reminders 9f out: rdn 4f out: wknd over 2f out: wl bhd and eased ins fnl f* **12/1**

3m 21.35s (-4.35) **Going Correction** -0.075s/f (Stan)
WFA 4 from 5yo+ 5lb 7 Ran SP% **117.5**
Speed ratings (Par 103): **107,106,106,104,104 104,92**
CSF £14.24 CT £30.02 TOTE £2.40: £1.60, £3.90; EX 13.00 Trifecta £30.20.
Owner Sir Roger Buckley, Gerald Oury **Bred** Sir R J Buckley & G Oury **Trained** Kingsclere, Hants

FOCUS
A moderate staying handicap, run at a fair enough gallop. The winner can do better than this.

883 DAILY PRICE BOOSTS AT UNIBET H'CAP — 5f 6y(P)
5:10 (5:16) (Class 6) (0-65,65) 3-Y-O **£2,264** (£673; £336; £168) **Stalls** High

Form RPR

15-1 **1** **Powerful Dream (IRE)**[9] 763 3-9-7 **65** 6ex .... LukeMorris 4 73+
(Ronald Harris) *t.k.h: chsd ldr for over 1f: trckd ldrs after: effrt over 1f out: hdwy and rdn to ld ins fnl f: r.o wl: readily* **7/4**[2]

2-42 **2** *1 ¾* **Hot Stuff**[33] 460 3-9-5 **63** .... AdamKirby 5 65
(Tony Carroll) *chsd ldrs: wnt 2nd over 3f out: rdn and ev ch over 1f out: led 1f out: sn drvn and hdd ins fnl f: sn brushed aside and one pce after* **11/10**[1]

-034 **3** *hd* **Justice Rock**[27] 531 3-8-13 **62** .... (v[1]) JosephineGordon(5) 7 63
(Phil McEntee) *taken down early: broke fast and led: jnd and rdn 2f out: hdd over 1f out: styd on same pce u.p ins fnl f* **6/1**[3]

0-45 **4** *1* **Sand By Me**[18] 659 3-8-2 **46** oh1 .... JimmyQuinn 6 44
(Peter Crate) *dwlt: rn green in 5th: effrt in 4th over 1f out: kpt on same pce u.p ins fnl f* **25/1**

0-66 **5** *¾* **Matilda Gleam**[7] 783 3-9-1 **59** .... LemosdeSouza 1 54+
(Lisa Williamson) *taken down early: restless in stalls: s.i.s: t.k.h in rr: effrt and wd wl over 1f out: no real imp: n.d* **8/1**

00-0 **6** *1* **Barnsdale**[12] 730 3-7-9 **46** oh1 .... MeganEllingworth(7) 3 37
(John Holt) *in tch in 4th: swtchd rt over 3f out: lost 4th and outpcd over 1f out: wl hld and styd on same pce after* **66/1**

59.62s (0.82) **Going Correction** -0.075s/f (Stan) 6 Ran SP% **114.7**
Speed ratings (Par 96): **90,87,86,85,84 82**
CSF £4.17 CT £7.40 TOTE £2.60: £1.60, £1.10; EX 4.30 Trifecta £7.30.
Owner Ridge House Stables Ltd **Bred** Ballyhane Stud **Trained** Earlswood, Monmouths

FOCUS
A weak 3yo sprint handicap, rated around the placed horses. The winner confirmed she is on an upward curve.
T/Plt: £4,187.40 to a £1 stake. Pool: £74,170.24 - 12.93 winning tickets T/Qpdt: £86.10 to a £1 stake. Pool: £8,226.69 - 70.7 winning tickets **Steve Payne**

790 CHELMSFORD (A.W) (L-H)
Thursday, March 10

OFFICIAL GOING: Polytrack: standard
Wind: virtually nil Weather: dry

884 PLAY SCOOP6SOCCER EVERY WEEK APPRENTICE FILLIES' H'CAP — 1m 5f 66y(P)
5:50 (5:52) (Class 5) (0-75,75) 4-Y-O+ **£5,175** (£1,540; £769; £384) **Stalls** Low

Form RPR

-211 **1** **Bracken Brae**[13] 731 4-8-12 **66** .... CallumShepherd(4) 2 71
(Mark H Tompkins) *broke wl: sn stdd and chsd ldr: rdn to ld ent fnl 2f: edging sltly lft over 1f out: hld on wl u.p ins fnl f: rdn out* **5/6**[1]

2-24 **2** *nk* **Kelly's Finest (IRE)**[25] 583 4-8-11 **63** .... (p) JosephineGordon(2) 5 67
(Michael Appleby) *led and dictated stdy gallop: rdn over 2f out: hdd but stl ev ch over 1f out: kpt on wl u.p: a jst hld ins fnl f* **5/1**[2]

3115 **3** *hd* **Percella**[20] 636 4-9-4 **68** .... GeorgeDowning 3 72
(Ian Williams) *hld up in tch in last: effrt over 2f out: styd on wl u.p ins fnl f: nt quite rch ldrs* **6/1**[3]

3-13 **4** *½* **Celestial Bay**[20] 636 7-10-0 **75** .... TomMarquand 4 78
(Sylvester Kirk) *hld up in tch in 4th: effrt in 3rd over 2f out: styd on same pce ins fnl f: lost 3rd towards fin* **5/1**[2]

0-40 **5** *1 ¼* **Blue Sea Of Ibrox (IRE)**[26] 566 8-9-12 **73** .... DanielMuscutt 1 74
(John Berry) *chsd ldng pair: rdn over 3f out: lost pl but stl wl in tch whn swtchd rt over 1f out: keeping on same pce and hld whn nt clrest of runs ins fnl f* **12/1**

2m 55.21s (1.61) **Going Correction** -0.125s/f (Stan)
WFA 4 from 7yo+ 3lb 5 Ran SP% **109.9**
Speed ratings (Par 100): **90,89,89,89,88**
CSF £5.35 TOTE £1.60: £1.10, £1.80; EX 5.40 Trifecta £12.70.
Owner David P Noblett **Bred** Dullingham Park Stud & Mr D Noblett **Trained** Newmarket, Suffolk

FOCUS
The early gallop wasn't strong and it turned into something of a dash from the turn in. It's hard to take the race too seriously.

885 SCOOP6SOCCER THE £1 MILLION FOOTBALL BET MEDIAN AUCTION MAIDEN STKS — 6f (P)
6:20 (6:20) (Class 5) 3-5-Y-O **£5,175** (£1,540; £769; £384) **Stalls** Centre

Form RPR

4- **1** **False Id**[182] 6249 3-9-0 0 .... WilliamCarson 5 68
(Robert Eddery) *in tch in midfield: effrt to chal and bumping match w rival over 1f out: rdn to ld ins fnl f: r.o and a holding runner-up towards fin: rdn out* **7/4**[1]

0- **2** *nk* **Saeedan (IRE)**[182] 6227 3-9-0 0 .... AndreaAtzeni 3 67
(Marco Botti) *hld up in tch in midfield: swtchd rt and effrt over 1f out: str run u.p ins fnl f: pressing wnr and clsng at fin: nvr quite getting up* **9/2**[3]

233 **3** *1 ¼* **Lady Lloyd**[5] 834 3-8-9 60 .... (v[1]) SilvestreDeSousa 7 58
(Phil McEntee) *chsd ldrs: rdn to chal and bumping w wnr over 1f out: sn led: edgd lft and hdd jst ins fnl f: outpcd fnl 75yds* **7/1**

0-6 **4** 1¼ **Palmina**[43] 350 3-8-9 0 RenatoSouza 6 54
(Dean Ivory) *led: rdn: wnt rt and bmpd rival over 1f out: sn hdd and outpcd u.p 1f out: hld and kpt on same pce ins fnl f* **33/1**

252 **5** shd **Grecian King**[12] 750 3-9-0 67 (p) LukeMorris 1 61
(James Tate) *stdd after s: chsd ldng pair: effrt on inner to press ldrs over 1f out: struggling to qckn whn squeezed for room and sltly hmpd jst ins fnl f: one pce after* **11/4**[2]

3 **6** hd **Red Rose Riot (IRE)**[15] 697 3-8-9 0 DavidProbert 4 53
(David Menuisier) *s.i.s: hld up in tch in last pair: effrt over 1f out: styd on wl ins fnl f: no threat to ldrs* **8/1**

44 **7** 1¼ **Shining Romeo**[15] 697 4-10-0 0 LemosdeSouza 2 58
(Denis Quinn) *t.k.h: hld up in tch in rr: shkn up over 1f out: nt clr run and swtchd rt ins fnl f: eased wl ins fnl f* **12/1**

1m 14.0s (0.30) **Going Correction** -0.125s/f (Stan)
WFA 3 from 4yo 14lb **7** Ran SP% **115.5**
Speed ratings (Par 103): **93,92,90,89,89 88,87**
CSF £10.30 TOTE £2.90: £1.70, £2.40; EX 11.10 Trifecta £56.70.
Owner Edwin Phillips & Mrs Pamela Aitken **Bred** N E Poole And George Thornton **Trained** Newmarket, Suffolk

FOCUS
Modest maiden form, with a slow time. The 1-2 are entitled to do better than the bare form.

886 WIN A FOOTBALL FORTUNE WITH SCOOP6SOCCER H'CAP 1m (P)
6:50 (6:51) (Class 3) (0-95,89) 4-Y-O+ **£9,703** (£2,887; £1,443; £721) **Stalls** Low

Form RPR

110- **1** **Revolutionist (IRE)**[117] 7855 4-9-6 88 SilvestreDeSousa 5 99+
(Mark Johnston) *hdwy to ld after 1f: mde rest: rdn ent fnl 2f: hrd pressed and hld on wl u.p fnl 150yds: gamely* **6/4**[1]

00-3 **2** ½ **Brigliadoro (IRE)**[40] 401 5-9-5 87 DanielTudhope 3 97
(Philip McBride) *hld up in tch in rr: swtchd rt and hdwy over 1f out: drvn and str chal 150yds out: r.o u.p but a jst hld* **7/2**[2]

5-34 **3** 3 **Jodies Jem**[21] 620 6-9-1 83 CharlesBishop 8 86
(William Jarvis) *chsd wnr over 6f out: rdn wl over 1f out: no ex jst ins fnl f: outpcd fnl 100yds* **12/1**

2110 **4** ½ **Abbey Angel (IRE)**[12] 749 4-9-4 86 (p) TonyHamilton 2 88
(Richard Fahey) *led for 1f: chsd ldrs after: effrt on inner over 1f out: no ex jst ins fnl f: outpcd fnl 100yds* **10/1**

1513 **5** ½ **Loyalty**[12] 749 9-8-11 84 (v) CallumShepherd(5) 1 87
(Derek Shaw) *hld up in tch in last pair: rdn over 2f out: hdwy whn nt clr run on inner and swtchd rt over 1f out: trying to rally whn squeezed for room and swtchd rt ins fnl f: kpt on: no ch w ldrs* **9/2**[3]

06-3 **6** ½ **Mange All**[31] 503 5-9-4 86 JimCrowley 4 86
(Charlie Wallis) *in tch in midfield: effrt u.p to chse ldrs over 1f out: no ex 1f out: outpcd ins fnl f* **5/1**

1m 36.66s (-3.24) **Going Correction** -0.125s/f (Stan) **6** Ran SP% **113.9**
Speed ratings (Par 107): **111,110,107,107,106 106**
CSF £7.15 CT £43.02 TOTE £2.00: £1.30, £1.90; EX 8.60 Trifecta £47.80.
Owner Sheikh Hamdan bin Mohammed Al Maktoum **Bred** Darley **Trained** Middleham Moor, N Yorks

FOCUS
A good handicap, and the first two finished nicely clear. The winner is entitled to do better.

887 BET SCOOP6SOCCER AT BETFRED SHOPS H'CAP 1m (P)
7:20 (7:20) (Class 4) (0-85,85) 3-Y-O **£8,086** (£2,406; £1,202; £601) **Stalls** Low

Form RPR

56-2 **1** **Manjaam (IRE)**[17] 678 3-8-5 69 LukeMorris 3 75
(Ed Dunlop) *in tch in midfield: effrt to chal and awkward hd carriage over 1f out: rdn to ld 1f out: r.o wl: rdn out* **7/2**[3]

2222 **2** nk **Ice Royal (IRE)**[14] 705 3-9-2 80 JamieSpencer 4 85
(Jamie Osborne) *stdd s: hld up in tch in rr: clsd 2f out: effrt over 1f out: str chal jst ins fnl f: r.o wl u.p: a jst hld* **4/1**

1 **3** 3¼ **Toumar**[41] 384 3-8-13 77 AndreaAtzeni 6 75
(Roger Varian) *chsd ldr: rdn over 1f out: unable qck ent fnl f: wnt 3rd but no ch w ldng pair fnl 75yds: no imp* **6/4**[1]

4-13 **4** hd **Theydon Grey**[14] 705 3-9-4 85 RosieJessop(3) 2 83+
(Peter Charalambous) *t.k.h: trckd ldng pair: trapped on inner and nt clr run over 1f out: swtchd rt ins fnl f: battling for 3rd but no ch w ldng pair wl ins fnl f: kpt on* **11/4**[2]

2-31 **5** 1½ **Theos Lolly (IRE)**[20] 633 3-8-10 74 TonyHamilton 5 68
(Richard Fahey) *racd keenly: led: rdn over 1f out: hdd and no ex 1f out: wknd ins fnl f* **20/1**

-221 **6** hd **Blacklister**[26] 557 3-8-8 77 PaddyPilley(5) 1 71
(Mick Channon) *stdd s: hld up in tch: effrt and swtchd rt over 1f out: sn rdn and no imp: bhd ins fnl f* **12/1**

1m 38.39s (-1.51) **Going Correction** -0.125s/f (Stan) **6** Ran SP% **121.3**
Speed ratings (Par 100): **102,101,98,98,96 96**
CSF £19.41 TOTE £4.00: £1.30, £2.70; EX 15.10 Trifecta £53.90.
Owner Mohammed Jaber **Bred** Ballylinch Stud **Trained** Newmarket, Suffolk

FOCUS
A competitive little handicap. The winner built on his reappearance promise.

888 BET SCOOP6SOCCER AT BETFRED.COM H'CAP 1m 2f (P)
7:50 (7:50) (Class 4) (0-85,85) 4-Y-O+ **£8,086** (£2,406; £1,202; £601) **Stalls** Low

Form RPR

2225 **1** **Pactolus (IRE)**[10] 767 5-9-7 85 (t) OisinMurphy 8 93
(Stuart Williams) *wnt lft s: t.k.h: chsd ldrs: effrt over 1f out: drvn and ev ch 1f out: sustained duel w rival and styd on wl u.p to ld last strides* **9/2**[3]

0-56 **2** hd **Stetchworth (IRE)**[52] 240 5-9-2 80 SilvestreDeSousa 2 87
(Mark Johnston) *chsd ldr: rdn to chal 2f out: drvn to ld over 1f out: hrd pressed 1f out: kpt on wl u.p and sustained duel w wnr: hdd last strides* **7/2**[1]

-112 **3** ½ **Coillte Cailin (IRE)**[13] 734 6-9-7 85 AndreaAtzeni 5 91
(Daniel Mark Loughnane) *hld up in tch: hdwy over 2f out: swtchd rt and effrt u.p over 1f out: chsd ldrs 1f out: kpt on wl towards fin* **4/1**[2]

4110 **4** 1¼ **Freud (FR)**[43] 353 6-8-12 79 GeorgeDowning(3) 1 83
(Ian Williams) *t.k.h: hld up in tch: effrt u.p to chse ldrs over 1f out: drvn and unable qck 1f out: outpcd fnl 75yds* **4/1**[2]

0-44 **5** 2 **Dukes Meadow**[20] 629 5-8-0 71 RhiainIngram(7) 6 71
(Roger Ingram) *stdd s: hld up in tch in rr: effrt over 1f out: kpt on ins fnl f: nvr threatened ldrs* **8/1**

01-5 **6** nse **Corton Lad**[34] 465 6-9-7 85 (tp) TomEaves 4 84
(Keith Dalgleish) *led: clr 1/2-way: pressed and rdn 2f out: hdd and no ex u.p over 1f out: wknd fnl 100yds* **14/1**

-100 **7** 2¼ **Yul Finegold (IRE)**[13] 734 6-9-4 82 PaulMulrennan 3 77
(Conor Dore) *t.k.h: chsd ldrs: rdn and unable qck over 1f out: sn lost pl: wknd ins fnl f* **20/1**

31-2 **8** 4 **Fit The Bill (IRE)**[22] 605 4-9-3 81 LukeMorris 7 68
(James Tate) *bmpd s: in tch in midfield: effrt over 1f out: sn btn: bhd fnl f* **9/2**[3]

2m 4.65s (-3.95) **Going Correction** -0.125s/f (Stan) **8** Ran SP% **121.1**
Speed ratings (Par 105): **110,109,109,108,106 106,105,101**
CSF £22.04 CT £70.08 TOTE £6.70: £2.00, £1.70, £1.60; EX 23.60 Trifecta £106.30.
Owner T W Morley & Mrs J Morley **Bred** Tom McDonald **Trained** Newmarket, Suffolk

FOCUS
An open handicap. The winner rates a small pb.

889 BET SCOOP6SOCCER AT TOTESPORT.COM H'CAP 6f (P)
8:20 (8:21) (Class 6) (0-60,60) 4-Y-O+ **£3,234** (£962; £481; £240) **Stalls** Centre

Form RPR

0354 **1** **Rialto Magic**[27] 543 4-8-13 57 (p) LucyKBarry(5) 1 63
(Jamie Osborne) *s.i.s: sn pushed along and outpcd in rr: clsd 2f out: drvn to chse ldrs ins fnl f: styd on wl to ld nr fin* **5/1**

6214 **2** ½ **Compton Prince**[19] 658 7-9-7 60 (b) FrannyNorton 5 65
(Milton Bradley) *chsd clr ldng pair: clsd and travelling wl 2f out: upsides ldr jst over 1f out: drvn ins fnl f: led fnl 75yds: hdd and no ex towards fin* **9/4**[1]

640- **3** ½ **Swendab (IRE)**[190] 5986 8-9-2 60 (b) CiaranMckee(5) 7 63+
(John O'Shea) *sn pushed along to press ldr and clr of field: led 2f out: sn rdn: hrd pressed and drvn 1f out: hdd and one pce fnl 75yds* **25/1**

1015 **4** ½ **Gulland Rock**[17] 671 5-9-3 56 (p) WilliamCarson 6 58
(Anthony Carson) *outpcd in 5th: rdn over 2f out: clsd u.p over 1f out: chsd ldrs ins fnl f: styd on* **3/1**[2]

0345 **5** 1¼ **Hamis Al Bin (IRE)**[27] 542 7-9-2 55 (bt) LukeMorris 2 53
(Milton Bradley) *racd in 4th: clsd 2f out: swtchd rt and effrt over 1f out: fnd little for press and wknd fnl 100yds* **7/2**[3]

6-10 **6** 12 **Quantum Dot (IRE)**[31] 504 5-9-4 57 (b) KieranO'Neill 4 19+
(Ed de Giles) *led and sn clr w rival: rdn and hdd 2f out: btn over 1f out: fdd fnl f* **10/1**

-051 **7** 5 **Give Us A Belle (IRE)**[13] 733 7-9-1 59 (bt) PaddyPilley(5) 8 6
(Christine Dunnett) *sn outpcd in last pair: rdn 4f out: wl bhd over 1f out* **12/1**

1m 12.43s (-1.27) **Going Correction** -0.125s/f (Stan) **7** Ran SP% **115.3**
Speed ratings (Par 101): **103,102,101,101,99 83,76**
CSF £16.99 CT £255.05 TOTE £4.80: £2.10, £1.70; EX 18.50 Trifecta £221.10.
Owner Fromthestables.Com & Partner **Bred** The Manjri Stud Farm PVT Ltd **Trained** Upper Lambourn, Berks

FOCUS
The two leaders took each other on, the pace was strong and the winner came from well back.
T/Plt: £57.00 to a £1 stake. Pool of £77201.92 - 987.49 winning units. T/Qpdt: £12.60 to a £1 stake. Pool of £9097.02 - 532.78 winning units. **Steve Payne**

864 SOUTHWELL (L-H)
Thursday, March 10

OFFICIAL GOING: Standard
Wind: Light half behind Weather: Cloudy

890 CORAL.CO.UK APPRENTICE H'CAP 1m 3f (F)
2:10 (2:15) (Class 5) (0-75,75) 4-Y-O+ **£3,234** (£962; £481; £240) **Stalls** Low

Form RPR

-340 **1** **Swift Cedar (IRE)**[26] 566 6-9-0 75 AledBeech(7) 3 83
(David Evans) *hld up towards rr: smooth hdwy 4f out: trckd ldrs 3f out: effrt to chal over 1f out: rdn to ld ins fnl f: kpt on strly* **6/1**[3]

1- **2** 1½ **Busy Street**[79] 8343 4-9-6 75 PatrickVaughan 6 80+
(Alan Swinbank) *trckd ldrs: hdwy 4f out: cl up 3f out: rdn to ld 1 1/2f out: hdd ins fnl f: kpt on same pce* **9/4**[1]

0-02 **3** 4 **Prayer Time**[7] 801 4-8-8 63 JoshQuinn 5 62
(Mark H Tompkins) *trckd ldng pair: hdwy over 3f out: sn cl up: rdn 2f out: kpt on same pce* **4/1**[2]

-224 **4** 2 **Comanche Chieftain (CAN)**[14] 708 4-8-8 66 (p) MitchGodwin(3) 9 61
(Michael Appleby) *half-rrd s: t.k.h and chsd ldrs on outer whn rn v wd bnd after 1 1/2f and sn bhd: pushed along 1/2-way: hdwy 4f out: rdn to chse ldrs 2f out: no imp appr fnl f* **15/2**

506- **5** 3¾ **Moojaned (IRE)**[84] 8272 5-9-0 68 RhiainIngram 4 57
(David Evans) *led: rdn along over 3f out: drvn over 2f out: hdd 1 1/2f out and sn wknd* **28/1**

5061 **6** 1¾ **Bayan Kasirga (IRE)**[20] 636 6-9-4 72 NatalieHambling 2 58
(Richard Fahey) *chsd ldrs on inner: n.m.r and pushed along 4f out: rdn and styd nr inner rail over 2f out: sn outpcd* **20/1**

60-3 **7** nk **Mirsaale**[14] 704 6-9-5 73 (p) HarryBurns 1 58
(Keith Dalgleish) *rdn along sn after s: a bhd* **12/1**

4302 **8** 6 **Clockmaker (IRE)**[7] 792 10-8-11 70 CameronNoble(5) 8 45
(Conor Dore) *chsd ldrs: cl up after 3f: rdn along 4f out: drvn 3f out: sn wknd* **10/1**

61-0 **9** 21 **Hussar Ballad (USA)**[66] 38 7-8-8 67 MathewStill(5) 7 6
(Antony Brittain) *chsd ldng pair: pushed along 4f out: rdn over 3f out: sn wknd* **10/1**

2m 23.93s (-4.07) **Going Correction** -0.10s/f (Stan)
WFA 4 from 5yo+ 1lb **9** Ran SP% **110.9**
Speed ratings (Par 103): **110,108,106,104,101 100,100,95,80**
CSF £18.66 CT £57.12 TOTE £6.40: £2.00, £1.50, £1.90; EX 21.80 Trifecta £102.50.
Owner J E Abbey **Bred** Carlingford Breeding Syndicate **Trained** Pandy, Monmouths
■ Aled Beech's first winner.
■ Stewards' Enquiry : Patrick Vaughan two-day ban: used whip above permitted level (Mar 24-25)

FOCUS
They went a decent gallop in this modest handicap, and the principals came centre to stands side up the straight. The winner is rated back to form.

891 DOWNLOAD THE CORAL APP (S) STKS 1m 4f (F)
2:45 (2:50) (Class 6) 4-Y-O+ **£2,587** (£770; £384; £192) **Stalls** Low

Form RPR

-400 **1** **Brassbound (USA)**[21] 619 8-9-5 79 AndrewMullen 1 86
(Michael Appleby) *trckd ldr: cl up over 3f out: rdn to ld over 2f out: edgd lft 1 1/2f out: styd on* **2/1**[2]

-422 **2** 3½ **Northside Prince (IRE)**[25] 583 10-8-13 70 BenCurtis 4 74
(Alan Swinbank) *led: pushed along and increased pce 4f out: jnd and rdn 3f out: hdd over 2f out: carried sltly lft 1 1/2f out: sn swtchd rt and drvn: kpt on same pce* **10/11**[1]

3/0- **3** 10 **Swinging Hawk (GER)**[96] 8124 10-8-10 72 GeorgeDowning(3) 5 58
(Ian Williams) *hld up in rr: hdwy 4f out: chsd ldng pair over 2f out: sn rdn and no imp* **4/1**[3]

 The Form Book, Raceform Ltd, Newbury, RG14 5SJ

50-5 **4** 2 1/2 **Monzino (USA)**[69] 6 8-8-6 50........................ RhiainIngram[(7)] 3 54
(Michael Chapman) *chsd ldng pair: pushed along 4f out: rdn 3f out: sn one pce* **100/1**

2m 40.23s (-0.77) **Going Correction** -0.10s/f (Stan) **4** Ran SP% **106.7**
Speed ratings (Par 101): **98,95,89,87**
CSF £4.13 TOTE £2.20; EX 4.00 Trifecta £3.70.There was no bid for the winner.
Owner Ferrybank Properties Limited **Bred** Darley **Trained** Oakham, Rutland

FOCUS
This very modest event was run at just a moderate initial gallop. Not sure what the form is worth but the winner is definitely this good on his day.

892 LADBROKES MOBILE MEDIAN AUCTION MAIDEN STKS 1m (F)
3:15 (3:20) (Class 5) 3-5-Y-O **£3,234** (£962; £481; £240) **Stalls** Low

Form RPR
-244 **1** **Lord Huntingdon**[34] 458 3-8-10 67........................ OisinMurphy 3 74
(Andrew Balding) *trckd ldng pair: cl up 1/2-way: chal 3f out: led over 2f out: rdn clr appr fnl f* **11/4**[2]
5-22 **2** 5 **Rain In The Face**[23] 600 3-8-10 75........................ GrahamGibbons 2 67
(Ralph Beckett) *slt ld: jnd and rdn along 3f out: hdd over 2f out: drvn wl over 1f out and sn one pce* **8/15**[1]
54 **3** 2 **Blue Vision (FR)**[29] 524 3-8-10 0........................ BenCurtis 5 56
(Alan Swinbank) *towards rr: wd st: hdwy over 2f out: sn rdn and kpt on one pce* **25/1**
4 4 **Star Of Kheleyf** 3-8-10 0........................ AndrewMullen 4 47
(Michael Appleby) *dwlt and sn rdn along: hdwy on inner over 3f out: rdn wl over 2f out: sn no imp* **12/1**[3]
5 **5** 2 1/4 **Peggy Joyce**[10] 768 3-8-5 0........................ SamJames 1 37
(David Barron) *cl up: rdn along wl over 3f out: sn wknd* **25/1**
56- **6** 6 **Joaldo**[225] 4757 4-9-7 0........................ MathewStill[(7)] 6 34
(Antony Brittain) *plld hrd: chsd ldrs on outer: chsd ldng pair over 3f out: styd towards inner rail in st and sn wknd* **66/1**

1m 43.32s (-0.38) **Going Correction** -0.10s/f (Stan)
WFA 3 from 4yo 18lb **6** Ran SP% **108.8**
Speed ratings (Par 103): **97,92,90,86,83 77**
CSF £4.27 TOTE £3.70: £1.50, £1.10; EX 4.30 Trifecta £20.20.
Owner Kingsclere Racing Club **Bred** Kingsclere Stud **Trained** Kingsclere, Hants

FOCUS
Only two really counted in this, and the form is weak with the faavourite disappointing. The time was modest.

893 LADBROKES H'CAP 7f (F)
3:50 (3:56) (Class 5) (0-70,70) 4-Y-O+ **£3,234** (£962; £481; £240) **Stalls** Low

Form RPR
03-4 **1** **Red Touch (USA)**[37] 427 4-9-2 68........................ AlistairRawlinson[(3)] 8 86+
(Michael Appleby) *in tch: n.m.r and lost pl bnd after 3f: sn pushed along: hdwy 3f out: rdn wl over 1f out: chsd clr ldr appr fnl f: styd on strly to ld last 120yds: sn clr* **15/8**[1]
100- **2** 3 1/2 **Azrur (IRE)**[146] 7255 6-9-4 67........................ PhillipMakin 1 74
(Keith Dalgleish) *chsd clr ldr: rdn and hdwy over 2f out: drvn over 1f out: kpt on fnl f* **16/1**
-263 **3** 1 1/2 **Danish Duke (IRE)**[35] 449 5-9-0 63........................(p) JamesSullivan 11 66
(Ruth Carr) *qckly away and set str pce: sn clr: rdn wl over 1f out: drvn and edgd lft ent fnl f: hdd & wknd last 120yds* **11/2**[2]
000- **4** hd **Star Of The Stage**[71] 8396 4-9-0 63........................(p) AdamBeschizza 9 65
(Julia Feilden) *dwlt and towards rr: swtchd lft towards inner and hdwy wl over 2f out: sn rdn: styd on wl u.p fnl f: nrst fin* **14/1**
0-00 **5** nk **Cool Strutter (IRE)**[26] 561 4-9-6 69........................[1] OisinMurphy 2 71
(Andrew Balding) *chsd ldrs on inner: rdn along over 2f out: sn drvn and kpt on same pce* **16/1**
40-1 **6** 2 1/4 **Trust Me Boy**[37] 430 8-9-1 64........................ FrannyNorton 4 60
(John E Long) *prom: rdn along wl over 2f out: sn drvn and grad wknd* **7/1**[3]
4620 **7** 4 1/2 **Alpha Tauri (USA)**[23] 598 10-9-2 68........................ RobHornby[(3)] 6 51
(Charles Smith) *prom: hdwy to chse ldng pair wl over 2f out: rdn wl over 2f out: sn drvn and wknd* **16/1**
06-0 **8** 1/2 **Mr Frankie**[64] 73 5-9-7 70........................ GrahamGibbons 7 52
(Richard Phillips) *dwlt and sltly hmpd s: a towards rr* **16/1**
002- **9** 4 1/2 **Cliff (IRE)**[146] 7256 6-9-5 68........................ JasonHart 10 38
(Nigel Tinkler) *in tch: edgd rt and hdwy bnd after 3f: wd st: rdn to chse ldrs over 2f out: sn drvn and wknd* **8/1**
/60- **10** 7 **Mayfield Boy**[241] 4196 5-8-8 64........................ MathewStill[(7)] 5 15
(Antony Brittain) *a towards rr* **25/1**
-553 **11** 7 **Abi Scarlet (IRE)**[25] 581 7-9-6 69........................(b) BenCurtis 3
(Scott Dixon) *sn rdn along: a towards rr* **12/1**

1m 28.24s (-2.06) **Going Correction** -0.10s/f (Stan) **11** Ran SP% **115.5**
Speed ratings (Par 103): **107,103,101,101,100 98,93,92,87,79 71**
CSF £34.98 CT £145.82 TOTE £2.70: £1.40, £4.10, £1.70; EX 29.70 Trifecta £154.90.
Owner Racing Daily **Bred** Dark Hollow Farm, Dorsey Brown Et Al **Trained** Oakham, Rutland

FOCUS
A modest handicap run at a brisk tempo, and won by the well backed favourite. He can go in again.

894 DAILY UNIBET EARLY PRICES FROM 9AM H'CAP 5f (F)
4:25 (4:31) (Class 4) (0-85,85) 4-Y-O+ **£5,175** (£1,540; £769; £384) **Stalls** Centre

Form RPR
1313 **1** **Crosse Fire**[25] 580 4-9-7 85........................(p) KieranO'Neill 2 93
(Scott Dixon) *cl up: effrt 2f out: rdn to ld ent fnl f: drvn and kpt on wl towards fin* **7/2**[2]
500- **2** 1/2 **Rusty Rocket (IRE)**[127] 7710 7-9-2 80........................ JFEgan 7 86
(Paul Green) *qckly away and led 1 1/2f: chsd ldrs: rdn over 1f out: styd on and ch ins fnl f: nt qckn towards fin* **50/1**
4160 **3** 1 1/4 **Fine 'n Dandy (IRE)**[25] 580 5-8-8 72........................ FrannyNorton 8 74
(J R Jenkins) *cl up: slt ld 2f out: sn rdn: hdd ent fnl f: kpt on same pce* **9/1**
004- **4** 1 **Vallarta (IRE)**[153] 7082 6-9-1 79........................ JamesSullivan 6 77
(Ruth Carr) *chsd ldrs: rdn wl over 1f out: kpt on same pce* **5/1**[3]
3-23 **5** 1/2 **Sir Billy Wright (IRE)**[30] 508 5-9-6 84........................ AndrewMullen 4 80
(David Evans) *towards rr: pushed along 1/2-way: swtchd rt and rdn over 1f out: kpt on towards fin* **10/3**[1]
-424 **6** 2 1/4 **Desert Command**[33] 484 6-9-2 80........................(v) GrahamGibbons 5 68
(Robert Cowell) *cl up: slt ld over 3f out: rdn and hdd 2f out: sn drvn and wknd appr fnl f* **7/1**
-026 **7** 1 1/2 **Sleepy Blue Ocean**[25] 580 10-8-11 75........................(p) ShaneGray 1 58
(John Balding) *dwlt: in tch on outer: hdwy to chse ldrs over 2f out: sn rdn and wknd over 1f out* **9/1**

3340 **8** 1 1/4 **Showtime Star**[19] 655 6-9-4 82........................(b) PatCosgrave 3 60
(Gay Kelleway) *dwlt and sn rdn along: a in rr* **7/1**

58.68s (-1.02) **Going Correction** -0.075s/f (Stan) **8** Ran SP% **108.9**
Speed ratings (Par 105): **105,104,102,100,99 96,93,91**
CSF £124.63 CT £1313.92 TOTE £4.20: £1.50, £6.10, £3.40; EX 99.30 Trifecta £710.00.
Owner Paul J Dixon & Darren Lucas **Bred** Dr A Gillespie **Trained** Babworth, Notts
■ Stewards' Enquiry : Kieran O'Neill two-day ban: used whip above permitted level (Mar 24-25)

FOCUS
A fair sprint handicap in which the principals were always to the fore.

895 DAILY PRICE BOOSTS AT UNIBET H'CAP 6f (F)
5:00 (5:05) (Class 6) (0-52,52) 4-Y-O+ **£2,587** (£770; £384; £192) **Stalls** Low

Form RPR
0546 **1** **Ciaras Cookie (IRE)**[7] 790 4-8-12 46 oh1........................(t) DannyBrock[(3)] 2 54
(Heather Dalton) *chsd ldrs on inner: hdwy 3f out: chal over 2f out: rdn 1 1/2f out: sn led: drvn and edgd rt ins fnl f: drvn out* **16/1**
4244 **2** 2 **First Rebellion**[15] 696 7-9-7 52........................(v) JFEgan 6 54
(Tony Carroll) *trckd ldrs: hdwy over 2f out: rdn over 1f out: drvn and ev ch ins fnl f: no ex towards fin* **11/2**[3]
4433 **3** 1/2 **Hab Reeh**[23] 596 8-9-7 52........................ JamesSullivan 3 53
(Ruth Carr) *hld up: hdwy on inner wl over 2f out: rdn wl over 1f out: sn drvn and kpt on same pce* **11/2**[3]
0033 **4** nk **Bold Max**[21] 617 5-9-5 50........................(v) LiamJones 7 50
(Zoe Davison) *chsd ldrs on outer: wd st: rdn to chse ldrs 2f out: sn drvn and kpt on same pce fnl f* **15/2**
0350 **5** nk **Little**[16] 682 4-9-1 46 oh1........................(b[1]) AdamBeschizza 4 45
(Steph Hollinshead) *chsd ldr: rdn along wl over 2f out: drvn wl over 1f out: edgd rt and wknd fnl f* **14/1**
35-0 **6** nk **Amenable (IRE)**[68] 25 9-9-0 50........................(be) AnnStokell[(5)] 5 48
(Ann Stokell) *in rr: rdn along 1/2-way: kpt on fnl 2f: n.d* **9/1**
5064 **7** 2 1/4 **Black Vale (IRE)**[5] 837 5-9-1 46 oh1........................(t) AndrewMullen 8 37
(Phil McEntee) *dwlt: sn chsng ldrs on wd outside: rdn over 2f out: swtchd lft and drvn over 1f out: sn wknd* **9/2**[2]
4206 **8** 1 3/4 **Pull The Pin (IRE)**[35] 442 7-8-13 51 ow1........................(bt) PaddyBradley[(7)] 9 37
(Heather Dalton) *qckly away and led: jnd and rdn over 2f out: drvn wl over 1f out: sn hdd & wknd qckly* **11/4**[1]

1m 16.2s (-0.30) **Going Correction** -0.10s/f (Stan) **8** Ran SP% **109.9**
Speed ratings (Par 101): **98,95,94,94,93 93,90,88**
CSF £93.18 CT £521.42 TOTE £20.80: £5.80, £1.80, £1.70; EX 117.40 Trifecta £834.70.
Owner Stephen Arnold **Bred** River Downs Stud **Trained** Childs Ercall, Shropshire

FOCUS
A weak sprint handicap which went to the outsider of the field. The form does make sense, however.

896 32RED H'CAP 1m (F)
5:35 (5:40) (Class 6) (0-55,54) 3-Y-O **£2,587** (£770; £384; £192) **Stalls** Low

Form RPR
3634 **1** **Footlight**[16] 688 3-8-13 53........................ AdamMcNamara[(7)] 9 62
(Richard Fahey) *chsd ldrs: rdn along 2f out: hdwy and swtchd rt ent fnl f: led last 120yds: styd on wl* **5/1**[2]
2236 **2** 3 **Never Say (IRE)**[16] 688 3-9-0 47........................(p) BenCurtis 5 49
(Jason Ward) *chsd ldrs: hdwy to chse ldr 3f out: led 2f out: clr whn rdn and hung lft ent fnl f: hdd and no ex last 120yds* **5/1**[2]
26-0 **3** 1/2 **Ada Misobel (IRE)**[51] 248 3-8-13 49........................(b[1]) AlistairRawlinson[(3)] 1 50
(Roy Bowring) *led: jnd and rdn 3f out: hdd 2f out: drvn and edgd lft appr fnl f: kpt on u.p towards fin* **33/1**
00-1 **4** 1 1/2 **Big Shoes (IRE)**[16] 688 3-9-7 54........................ DarryllHolland 7 51+
(Charles Hills) *dwlt and sn pushed along: towards rr and rdn along after 2f: swtchd to inner 1/2-way: rdn over 2f out: sme late hdwy* **11/8**[1]
-304 **5** nk **Boom Junior**[15] 700 3-8-12 45........................ StevieDonohoe 4 41
(Tony Carroll) *prom: cl up over 3f out: rdn over 2f out: sn drvn and grad wknd* **16/1**
00-5 **6** 2 **Pursuit Of Time**[13] 735 3-9-7 54........................ AndrewMullen 8 46
(Michael Appleby) *towards rr: rdn along 3f out: sme late hdwy* **14/1**
2533 **7** 8 **Frivolous Prince (IRE)**[16] 688 3-8-13 46........................(v) JFEgan 2 18
(David Evans) *in tch: rdn along over 3f out: sn outpcd* **6/1**[3]
606- **8** 2 1/4 **Mozimba**[209] 5327 3-8-5 45........................(b) MathewStill[(7)] 6 12
(Antony Brittain) *dwlt: a bhd* **50/1**
000- **9** 5 **Threeinoneday (IRE)**[120] 7794 3-9-5 52........................(v) JasonHart 3 7
(Nigel Tinkler) *prom on inner: chsd ldr 1/2-way: rdn along 3f out: sn wknd* **28/1**

1m 43.56s (-0.14) **Going Correction** -0.10s/f (Stan) **9** Ran SP% **110.6**
Speed ratings (Par 96): **96,93,92,91,90 88,80,78,73**
CSF £27.97 CT £701.77 TOTE £7.00: £2.70, £1.90, £4.90; EX 27.50 Trifecta £674.60.
Owner Mrs P B E P Farr **Bred** Worksop Manor Stud **Trained** Musley Bank, N Yorks

FOCUS
A low-grade handicap run in only a slightly slower time than the earlier maiden.
T/Jkpt: Not won. T/Plt: £54.20 to a £1 stake. Pool of £69775.97 -938.85 winning tickets. T/Qpdt: £14.00 to a £1 stake. Pool of £7046.77 - 369.90 winning tickets. **Joe Rowntree**

897 - (Foreign Racing) - See Raceform Interactive

[884]CHELMSFORD (A.W) (L-H)
Friday, March 11

OFFICIAL GOING: Polytrack: standard
Wind: nil Weather: dry

898 TOTEPLACEPOT H'CAP 1m 2f (P)
5:45 (5:47) (Class 6) (0-60,60) 4-Y-O+ **£3,234** (£962; £481; £240) **Stalls** Low

Form RPR
5-2 **1** **Kristal Hart**[65] 55 7-9-2 55........................(p) LiamKeniry 7 61
(Neil Mulholland) *sn led and mde rest: rdn 2f out: kpt on wl ins fnl f: rdn out* **7/1**[3]
3-0U **2** 3/4 **Nouvelle Ere**[16] 701 5-9-4 60........................(t) GeorgeDowning[(3)] 2 65
(Tony Carroll) *chsd wnr for 2f: styd chsng ldrs: effrt u.p over 1f out: ev ch jst over 1f out: styd on same pce wl ins fnl f* **12/1**
30-1 **3** 1 1/4 **Yasir (USA)**[7] 819 8-8-5 51........................ SophieKilloran[(7)] 9 57
(Sophie Leech) *stdd s: hld up in rr: rdn and clsng whn nt clr run over 1f out tl eventually managed to switch rt ins fnl f: r.o strly fnl 100yds: snatched 3rd last stride* **4/1**[2]
10-6 **4** nse **The Dukkerer (IRE)**[27] 564 5-9-7 60........................ PaulMulrennan 5 62
(James Given) *wl in tch in midfield: effrt ent fnl 2f: pressed ldng pair 1f out: styd on same pce u.p ins fnl f* **11/1**
2235 **5** 3/4 **Runaiocht (IRE)**[14] 724 6-6-9 59........................(b) JimmyQuinn 8 60
(Paul Burgoyne) *taken down early: t.k.h: hdwy to chse wnr after 2f: drvn and unable qck over 1f out: 4th and btn 1f out: wknd ins fnl f* **7/2**[1]

44-6 **6** 2 1/2 **Cherry Street**[18] 676 7-9-2 **58**........ KevinStott(3) 6 54
(John Berry) *hld up in tch in midfield: effrt over 2f out: swtchd rt over 1f out: no imp and hung lft ins fnl f* **7/1**[3]

5456 **7** 1/2 **Do It Tomorrow (IRE)**[27] 569 4-9-2 **55**........ TonyHamilton 1 50
(J R Jenkins) *hld up in tch in midfield: effrt 2f out: no imp u.p 1f out: wknd ins fnl f: fin lame* **25/1**

6-65 **8** shd **Plover**[23] 602 6-8-8 **47** oh1 ow1........ KierenFox 3 42
(Michael Attwater) *t.k.h: hld up in tch in last trio: effrt on inner over 1f out: no imp 1f out: wknd ins fnl f* **16/1**

2-03 **9** 2 3/4 **Silver Lining (IRE)**[27] 568 4-9-5 **58**........(t) ShaneKelly 4 48
(Mark Hoad) *hld up in tch in last trio: hdwy on outer into midfield 5f out: rdn over 2f out: lost pl over 1f out: wknd fnl f* **10/1**

0223 **10** 7 **Bionic Indian**[15] 707 4-8-9 **48**........ SilvestreDeSousa 10 24
(Michael Easterby) *t.k.h: hld up in tch in midfield: dropped to rr and u.p 3f out: wknd over 1f out* **4/1**[2]

2m 5.74s (-2.86) **Going Correction** -0.275s/f (Stan) **10** Ran SP% **122.1**
Speed ratings (Par 101): **100,99,98,98,97 95,95,95,93,87**
CSF £91.62 CT £388.92 TOTE £5.00: £1.40, £3.30, £2.40; EX 61.60 Trifecta £452.10.
Owner The White Hart Racing Syndicate **Bred** Carmel Stud **Trained** Limpley Stoke, Wilts

FOCUS
They didn't go a strong gallop and the leader was able to hang on. The third is rated as finishing alongside the winner.

899 TOTEEXACTA H'CAP 1m 2f (P)
6:15 (6:16) (Class 5) (0-75,79) 4-Y-O+ **£5,175** (£1,540; £769; £384) **Stalls** Low

Form RPR

2111 **1** **Tangramm**[7] 823 4-9-11 **79** 6ex........(p) RobertWinston 9 88+
(Dean Ivory) *swtchd lft after s: hld up in midfield: effrt over 1f out: rdn and hdwy to chal ins fnl f: r.o wl to ld towards fin* **11/8**[1]

141- **2** 1/2 **My Mo (FR)**[139] 7457 4-9-1 **69**........ SilvestreDeSousa 8 77
(David Dennis) *led: rdn ent fnl 2f: drvn and battled on gamely fr over 1f out: hdd and no ex towards fin* **7/1**

3-21 **3** 1 **Karnage (IRE)**[48] 318 4-9-5 **73**........(b) RichardKingscote 6 79
(Daniel Kubler) *chsd ldr: upsides and travelling bttr ent fnl 2f: drvn over 1f out: no ex ins fnl f: wknd towards fin* **11/4**[2]

/022 **4** nk **Icebuster**[11] 766 8-9-7 **75**........ DanielTudhope 1 80
(Rod Millman) *hld up in last pair: effrt over 1f out: 5th 1f out: pushed along ins fnl f: kpt on wl towards fin: snatched 4th last strides: no threat to ldrs* **6/1**[3]

4233 **5** nk **Mr Red Clubs (IRE)**[14] 734 7-9-2 **70**........ AndrewMullen 4 74
(Michael Appleby) *chsd ldrs: rdn over 2f out: styd on same pce and edgd lft ins fnl f* **7/1**

0-60 **6** 5 **Sharp Sword (IRE)**[16] 693 5-9-5 **73**........ LiamKeniry 3 67
(Neil Mulholland) *stdd s: hld up off the pce in rr: effrt over 2f out: no imp: wl btn 1f out* **16/1**

4-52 **7** nk **Pearly Prince**[15] 710 4-9-2 **70**........ RobertHavlin 5 64
(Peter Hedger) *stdd s: t.k.h: hld up in midfield: effrt over 1f out: sn btn: wknd fnl f* **12/1**

2m 5.22s (-3.38) **Going Correction** -0.275s/f (Stan) **7** Ran SP% **121.6**
Speed ratings (Par 103): **102,101,100,100,100 96,96**
CSF £13.23 CT £25.67 TOTE £2.40: £1.70, £2.10; EX 11.60 Trifecta £26.40.
Owner John Marsden **Bred** W G H Barrons **Trained** Radlett, Herts

FOCUS
Another win for one of the stars of this winter's AW season, who continues on the upgrade. The form reads sound.

900 TOTEQUADPOT H'CAP 1m (P)
6:45 (6:45) (Class 4) (0-80,79) 4-Y-O+ **£8,086** (£2,406; £1,202; £601) **Stalls** Low

Form RPR

204- **1** **Craftsmanship (FR)**[144] 7348 5-9-6 **78**........ SilvestreDeSousa 4 89
(Robert Eddery) *s.i.s: in tch in rr: effrt and swtchd rt wl over 1f out: hdwy u.p to chal 1f out: led 150yds out: r.o strly: readily* **11/2**

3614 **2** 3 3/4 **Justice First**[15] 712 4-9-4 **76**........ PatCosgrave 6 78
(Ed Dunlop) *hld up in midfield: effrt to chse ldrs over 1f out: ev ch 1f out: clr 2nd but outpcd by wnr fnl 150yds* **3/1**[1]

-633 **3** 1 1/4 **Berrahri (IRE)**[19] 664 5-9-3 **75**........ KierenFox 8 75
(John Best) *chsd ldrs: rdn to chse ldr 2f out: wandered rt and lft u.p over 1f out: outpcd by wnr and one pce ins fnl f* **7/2**[2]

-056 **4** nk **Street Force (USA)**[37] 433 5-9-7 **79**........(tp) AndrewMullen 2 78
(Michael Appleby) *in tch in midfield: effrt over 1f out: outpcd and n.m.r ent fnl f: kpt on fnl 100yds: no ch w wnr* **5/1**

2306 **5** nk **Boonga Roogeta**[21] 632 7-8-12 **73**........(v) RosieJessop(3) 7 71
(Peter Charalambous) *led: clr 5f out: rdn 2f out: hdd ins fnl f: sn outpcd and wknd fnl 100yds* **7/1**

-012 **6** 4 1/2 **Caledonia Laird**[17] 681 5-8-9 **67**........ JoeyHaynes 1 55
(Jo Hughes) *chsd ldr tl 2f out: lost pl u.p over 1f out: wknd ins fnl f* **4/1**[3]

-200 **7** 7 **Hannington**[30] 518 5-8-12 **77**........(p) CharlieBennett(7) 3 49
(Barry Brennan) *dwlt: racd in last pair: last and struggling u.p over 2f out: bhd over 1f out* **33/1**

1m 36.38s (-3.52) **Going Correction** -0.275s/f (Stan) **7** Ran SP% **114.7**
Speed ratings (Par 105): **106,102,101,100,100 95,88**
CSF £22.49 CT £65.63 TOTE £6.30: £2.90, £2.10; EX 20.30 Trifecta £80.30.
Owner Trisha Keane & Julia Rayment **Bred** Haras Du Logis Saint Germain **Trained** Newmarket, Suffolk

FOCUS
This was a solidly run handicap. The winner is probably the best guide.

901 TOTETRIFECTA H'CAP 6f (P)
7:15 (7:15) (Class 4) (0-80,80) 4-Y-O+ **£8,086** (£2,406; £1,202; £601) **Stalls** Centre

Form RPR

3500 **1** **Oriental Relation (IRE)**[16] 694 5-9-0 **80**........(v) PhilDennis(7) 1 90
(James Given) *broke wl: sn settled bk into 4th: effrt to chal and carried rt wl over 1f out: drvn to ld jst over 1f out: styd on wl: rdn out* **7/2**[1]

431- **2** 1/2 **Under Siege (IRE)**[153] 7104 4-8-11 **77**........ SophieKilloran(7) 12 85+
(David Simcock) *in tch in midfield: swtchd lft and effrt over 1f out: wnt 2nd and pressing wnr 150yds out: kpt on but hld fnl 75yds* **7/2**[1]

2150 **3** 1 **Doctor Parkes**[14] 727 10-9-1 **79**........ AaronJones(5) 3 84
(Stuart Williams) *in tch in last quartet: effrt and swtchd rt over 1f out: hdwy 1f out: r.o strly ins fnl f: nt rch ldrs* **10/1**

3564 **4** 1/2 **Malaysian Boleh**[11] 764 6-8-7 **71**........(b) CallumShepherd(5) 9 75
(Shaun Lycett) *in tch in last quartet: effrt and drifted lft over 1f out: hdwy 1f out: styd on strly ins fnl f: nt rch ldrs* **16/1**

10-5 **5** nse **Russian Reward (IRE)**[18] 670 4-9-3 **76**........(tp) JimCrowley 4 79
(Paul Cole) *in tch in midfield: effrt on inner over 1f out: chsd ldrs 1f out: styd on same pce u.p fnl 100yds* **7/1**

6415 **6** hd **Borough Boy (IRE)**[16] 694 6-9-6 **79**........(v) TonyHamilton 7 82
(Derek Shaw) *t.k.h: hld up in tch in midfield: effrt whn sltly hmpd over 1f out: hdwy 1f out: kpt on u.p ins fnl f: nt rch ldrs* **16/1**

140- **7** 1/2 **Penny Dreadful**[154] 7079 4-9-0 **73**........(p) KieranO'Neill 6 74
(Scott Dixon) *chsd ldr tl led 2f: sn rdn and drifted rt u.p: hdd jst over 1f out: lost 2nd and wknd ins fnl f* **33/1**

050- **8** 3/4 **Sunraider (IRE)**[154] 7093 9-9-7 **80**........ GrahamLee 11 80+
(Paul Midgley) *s.i.s: in tch in rr: hdwy 1f out: kpt on ins fnl f: nvr trbld ldrs* **50/1**

6-11 **9** 3/4 **Noble Deed**[27] 561 6-9-2 **75**........ KierenFox 5 75+
(Michael Attwater) *taken down early: hld up in tch in last quartet: effrt and sme hdwy whn squeezed for room over 1f out: kpt on but no threat to ldrs ins fnl f* **5/1**[2]

3-13 **10** 1 1/2 **Money Team (IRE)**[58] 159 5-9-2 **80**........ JosephineGordon(5) 10 72
(David Barron) *hood removed late: in tch in midfield: rdn 1/2-way: no imp and btn over 1f out: wl ins hld fnl f* **6/1**[3]

023- **11** 1/2 **Inshaa**[73] 8386 4-8-13 **72**........ SilvestreDeSousa 13 62
(Michael Herrington) *wl in tch in midfield: rdn and lost pl 2f out: btn over 1f out: wl hld and eased ins fnl f* **14/1**

2120 **12** 4 1/2 **Seamster**[15] 703 9-8-9 **73**........(vt) JoshDoyle(5) 14 49
(David O'Meara) *chsd ldrs: rdn over 1f out: sn struggling and lost pl: fdd ins fnl f* **25/1**

0-16 **13** 7 **Uptight (FR)**[43] 364 4-9-7 **80**........(bt) ShaneGray 8 33
(Kevin Ryan) *sn led: hdd and rdn 2f out: losing pl whn hmpd over 1f out: sn wknd: bhd ins fnl f* **22/1**

1m 10.92s (-2.78) **Going Correction** -0.275s/f (Stan) **13** Ran SP% **128.5**
Speed ratings (Par 105): **107,106,105,104,104 104,103,102,101,99 98,92,83**
CSF £15.60 CT £123.57 TOTE £5.20: £2.30, £1.90, £4.70; EX 30.00 Trifecta £231.00.
Owner The Cool Silk Partnership **Bred** Brendan Laffan & Michael McCormick **Trained** Willoughton, Lincs

■ Stewards' Enquiry : Callum Shepherd two-day ban; careless riding (25th-26th Mar)
Sophie Killoran two-day ban; used whip above the permitted level (25th-26th Mar)

FOCUS
A competitive handicap. The third and fourth help with the standard.

902 JON QUARMBY MEMORIAL MAIDEN STKS 5f (P)
7:45 (7:50) (Class 5) 3-Y-O+ **£5,175** (£1,540; £769; £384) **Stalls** Low

Form RPR

2- **1** **Dominance**[90] 8204 3-8-10 0........ SilvestreDeSousa 4 71
(Rae Guest) *racd freely: led: rdn and fnd ex over 1f out: styd on strly fnl f: readily* **9/4**[2]

0343 **2** 3 3/4 **Justice Rock**[2] 883 3-8-10 62........(v) JosephineGordon(5) 7 62
(Phil McEntee) *chsd ldng pair: effrt over 2f out: drvn and unable qck over 1f out: chsd clr wnr and styd on same pce ins fnl f* **14/1**[3]

0-23 **3** 2 **Cee Jay**[11] 765 3-9-1 70........(v) JimCrowley 1 55
(Jeremy Noseda) *s.i.s: off the pce in 5th: rdn and clsd 1/2-way: drvn and no imp over 1f out: plugged on into 3rd ins fnl f: no ch w wnr* **8/13**[1]

0000 **4** 1 1/2 **Justice (IRE)**[11] 763 3-8-5 42........ CharlesEddery(5) 3 44
(Dean Ivory) *chsd wnr: rdn and no ex over 1f out: lost 2nd ins fnl f and sn wknd* **66/1**

0- **5** 4 **Storming Ambition**[129] 7689 3-9-1 0........ MartinDwyer 2 35
(Conrad Allen) *s.i.s: clsd and in tch 1/2-way: rdn and struggling whn hung lft over 1f out: sn wknd* **25/1**

60-6 **6** 15 **Island Express (IRE)**[6] 834 9-9-9 47........(tp) AnnStokell(5) 5
(Ann Stokell) *v.s.a: a t.o* **80/1**

59.23s (-0.97) **Going Correction** -0.275s/f (Stan)
WFA 3 from 9yo 13lb **6** Ran SP% **105.9**
Speed ratings (Par 103): **96,90,86,84,78 54**
CSF £23.97 TOTE £3.20: £1.20, £3.00; EX 16.50 Trifecta £19.40.
Owner The Storm Again Syndicate **Bred** Brook Stud Bloodstock Ltd **Trained** Newmarket, Suffolk

■ Corridor Kid was withdrawn. Price at time of withdrawal 12-1. Rule 4 applies to all bets - deduction 5p in the pound.

FOCUS
A very modest maiden. The form is taken at face value.

903 TOTESWINGER H'CAP 5f (P)
8:15 (8:16) (Class 5) (0-75,75) 4-Y-O+ **£5,175** (£1,540; £769; £384) **Stalls** Low

Form RPR

3144 **1** **Welease Bwian (IRE)**[15] 703 7-8-7 **68**........(v) MillyNaseb(7) 10 77+
(Stuart Williams) *s.i.s: bhd and swtchd lft after 1f: hdwy on inner over 1f out: chsd ldr ins fnl f: r.o strly to ld last strides* **8/1**[3]

10-4 **2** hd **King Crimson**[15] 714 4-9-7 **75**........ CharlesBishop 6 83
(Mick Channon) *led: rdn over 1f out: 2 l clr 1f out: kpt on but worn down fnl 100yds: hdd last strides* **7/1**[2]

41-3 **3** 1 **Summer Isles**[49] 293 6-8-13 **67**........ GrahamLee 3 72
(Paul Midgley) *taken down early: wl in tch in midfield: effrt over 1f out: rdn and hdwy to chse ldrs ins fnl f: kpt on: nvr enough pce to rch ldrs* **14/1**

1003 **4** 3/4 **Jaarih (IRE)**[11] 764 4-9-6 **74**........(p) PaulMulrennan 7 76
(Conor Dore) *taken down early: hld up in tch towards rr: swtchd rt and effrt over 1f out: edging lft but styd on ins fnl f: nt rch ldrs* **9/1**

2622 **5** 1 3/4 **Saved My Bacon (IRE)**[36] 439 5-9-3 **71**........ SilvestreDeSousa 1 67+
(Chris Dwyer) *dwlt: in tch in last trio: effrt over 1f out: trying to cl whn squeezed for room and hmpd 1f out: kpt on fnl 100yds: nvr trbld ldrs* **11/8**[1]

5432 **6** 1 1/4 **Ask The Guru**[10] 775 6-8-10 **64**........(v) RobertHavlin 5 55
(Michael Attwater) *chsd ldrs: rdn over 1f out: losing pl whn hmpd 1f out: wknd ins fnl f* **7/1**[2]

-602 **7** hd **Temple Road (IRE)**[15] 714 8-9-4 **72**........(bt) FrannyNorton 4 62
(Milton Bradley) *s.i.s: hld up in last pair: swtchd lft and effrt over 1f out: kpt on ins fnl f: nvr trbld ldrs* **11/1**

50-0 **8** shd **Pucon**[15] 714 7-9-3 **71**........(p) AdamKirby 2 61
(Roger Teal) *chsd ldr: rdn wl over 1f out: lost 2nd ins fnl f: no ex: wknd fnl 100yds* **25/1**

2600 **9** nk **Desert Strike**[9] 782 10-9-7 **75**........(p) LiamKeniry 9 64
(Conor Dore) *taken down early: in tch in midfield: lost pl whn nt clr run and swtchd rt over 1f out: no imp fnl f* **18/1**

1022 **10** nk **Fujin**[15] 703 5-8-13 **67**........(b) AndrewMullen 8 55
(Shaun Harris) *sn rdn along: chsd ldrs after 1f: no ex u.p over 1f out: wknd ins fnl f* **9/1**

58.44s (-1.76) **Going Correction** -0.275s/f (Stan) **10** Ran SP% **122.3**
Speed ratings (Par 103): **103,102,101,99,97 95,94,94,94,93**
CSF £66.16 CT £806.20 TOTE £12.90: £4.20, £3.80, £4.30; EX 71.60 Trifecta £862.30.
Owner W E Enticknap **Bred** Nils Koop **Trained** Newmarket, Suffolk

FOCUS
This was run at a good pace. The winner is rated back to his best.

904 TOTEPOOL BETTING ON ALL UK RACING H'CAP 7f (P)
8:45 (8:49) (Class 6) (0-60,60) 4-Y-0+ **£3,234** (£962; £481; £240) **Stalls** Low

Form RPR

60-4 **1** **Powerfulstorm**[10] 776 4-9-2 **55** AdamKirby 3 62
(Michael Appleby) *mde all: rdn over 1f out: drvn ins fnl f: a holding on* **11/4**[2]

1315 **2** *nk* **Cookie Ring (IRE)**[8] 792 5-8-10 **56** (v) PaulaMuir(7) 7 62
(Patrick Holmes) *s.i.s: hld up in last pair: c wd and effrt over 1f out: hdwy to chse ldrs 1f out: str chal towards fin: nvr quite getting to wnr* **9/4**[1]

-120 **3** *1* **De Lesseps (USA)**[18] 670 8-8-13 **59** VitorSantos(7) 1 62
(John David Riches) *dwlt and pushed along briefly: sn t.k.h and chsd ldrs: effrt over 1f out: pressed wnr u.p 1f out: lost 2nd and no ex wl ins fnl f* **5/1**[3]

0-02 **4** *½* **Mambo Spirit (IRE)**[28] 542 12-9-4 **60** EoinWalsh(3) 5 62
(Tony Newcombe) *hld up in tch in last pair: effrt to chse ldrs 1f out: kpt on same pce ins fnl f* **5/1**[3]

2222 **5** *2¼* **Anjuna Beach (USA)**[47] 326 6-8-11 **55** ow2 AnnStokell(5) 2 51
(Ann Stokell) *t.k.h: stdd bk into midfield after 1f: effrt whn hmpd and swtchd rt over 1f out: rallied and styd on wl ins fnl f: no threat to ldrs* **8/1**

61-1 **6** *3¾* **Honiton Lace**[43] 356 5-8-12 **56** (tp) JosephineGordon(5) 4 42
(Phil McEntee) *in tch in midfield: effrt to chse ldrs 2f out: no ex over 1f out: wknd ins fnl f* **12/1**

6332 **7** *4½* **Star Pursuits**[15] 707 4-8-11 **50** (b) KieranO'Neill 6 24
(Jimmy Fox) *t.k.h: chsd wnr tl over 1f out: sn edgd rt and lost pl: wknd fnl f* **6/1**

1m 25.82s (-1.38) **Going Correction** -0.275s/f (Stan) **7** Ran SP% **123.9**
Speed ratings (Par 101): **96,95,94,93,91 87,81**
CSF £10.51 TOTE £3.50: £1.50, £2.00; EX 13.20 Trifecta £51.00.
Owner Houghton Bloodstock **Bred** G T Lucas **Trained** Oakham, Rutland

FOCUS
A moderate event in which the winner dictated a fairly steady gallop. Straightforward form.
T/Jkpt: Not won. T/Plt: £610.00 to a £1 stake. Pool: £85,904.01 - 102.79 winning tickets T/Qpdt: £106.60 to a £1 stake. Pool: £9,937.71 - 68.94 winning tickets **Steve Payne**

905 - 918a (Foreign Racing) - See Raceform Interactive

856 WOLVERHAMPTON (A.W) (L-H)
Saturday, March 12

OFFICIAL GOING: Tapeta: standard
Wind: Light behind Weather: Overcast

919 UNIBET OFFER DAILY JOCKEY/TRAINER SPECIALS CLASSIFIED CLAIMING STKS 5f 20y (Tp)
1:40 (1:42) (Class 5) 4-Y-0+ **£3,234** (£962; £481; £240) **Stalls** Low

Form RPR

5131 **1** **Elusivity (IRE)**[4] 868 8-9-3 67 (p) PaulMulrennan 5 78
(Conor Dore) *mde all: shkn up over 1f out: r.o wl: eased nr fin* **9/4**[1]

0162 **2** *2¼* **Summerinthecity (IRE)**[19] 671 9-8-11 70 (p) TonyHamilton 1 64
(Richard Fahey) *chsd wnr: rdn over 1f out: styd on same pce ins fnl f* **11/4**[2]

-540 **3** *nk* **Thataboy (IRE)**[10] 784 5-8-11 67 RichardKingscote 2 63
(Tom Dascombe) *a.p: rdn ins fnl f: styd on same pce* **10/3**[3]

426 **4** *4* **Seraphima**[15] 732 6-8-6 45 (p) JosephineGordon(5) 3 48
(Lisa Williamson) *chsd ldrs: rdn over 1f out: wknd ins fnl f* **125/1**

20-0 **5** *½* **Noverre To Go (IRE)**[3] 872 10-8-9 65 (p) OisinMurphy 6 45
(Ronald Harris) *s.i.s: sn pushed along in rr: rdn and hung lft over 1f out: sn wknd* **12/1**

0043 **6** *2* **Agerzam**[5] 857 6-8-11 67 (b) LukeMorris 7 39
(Ronald Harris) *s.i.s: pushed along in rr: hung lft fr over 1f out: wknd fnl f* **9/2**

5026 **7** *¾* **Jolly Red Jeanz (IRE)**[7] 837 5-8-9 53 (be) AndrewMullen 4 35
(Daniel Mark Loughnane) *s.i.s: sn pushed along in rr: rdn over 1f out: wknd fnl f* **25/1**

1m 0.55s (-1.35) **Going Correction** -0.20s/f (Stan) **7** Ran SP% **111.0**
Speed ratings (Par 103): **102,98,97,91,90 87,86**
CSF £8.15 TOTE £3.00: £1.40, £2.00; EX 9.80 Trifecta £29.90.
Owner Mrs Louise Marsh **Bred** J Costello **Trained** Hubbert's Bridge, Lincs

FOCUS
An ordinary classified claimer and not many got into it. The winner is rated in line with his recent form.

920 LADBROKES LINCOLN TRIAL H'CAP 1m 141y (Tp)
2:15 (2:15) (Class 2) (0-105,104) 4-Y-0+
£31,125 (£9,320; £4,660; £2,330; £1,165; £585) **Stalls** Low

Form RPR

110- **1** **Keystroke**[175] 6542 4-8-12 **92** JimCrowley 2 101+
(Jeremy Noseda) *s.i.s: hld up: hdwy over 1f out: rdn to ld wl ins fnl f: r.o* **4/1**[1]

-113 **2** *nse* **Supersta**[23] 620 5-8-10 **90** (p) AndrewMullen 4 99+
(Michael Appleby) *hld up in tch: plld hrd: hmpd over 7f out: nt clr run wl over 1f out: sn swtchd lft: rdn and ev ch ins fnl f: r.o* **5/1**[2]

-661 **3** *¾* **Intrude**[26] 594 4-8-12 **92** JamieSpencer 7 99
(David Simcock) *hld up: hdwy over 1f out: sn rdn: r.o* **11/2**[3]

-121 **4** *½* **Bold Prediction (IRE)**[14] 749 6-8-9 **89** LukeMorris 10 95
(Ed Walker) *chsd ldrs: rdn to ld ins fnl f: sn hdd and unable qck* **9/1**

-156 **5** *½* **Forceful Appeal (USA)**[7] 833 8-8-9 **89** AndreaAtzeni 9 94
(Simon Dow) *s.i.s: hld up: rdn and r.o ins fnl f: nt rch ldrs* **12/1**

3144 **6** *nk* **Solar Deity (IRE)**[17] 692 7-9-10 **104** (b) OisinMurphy 6 108
(Marco Botti) *hld up: hdwy over 1f out: rdn and nt clr run ins fnl f: r.o* **10/1**

-122 **7** *1¾* **Si Senor (IRE)**[14] 749 5-9-0 **94** AdamKirby 12 94
(Ed Vaughan) *chsd ldrs: rdn over 1f out: no ex wl ins fnl f* **6/1**

110- **8** *1¼* **Sound Advice**[175] 6517 7-9-2 **103** PhilDennis(7) 8 100
(Keith Dalgleish) *prom: led 5f out: rdn over 1f out: hdd and no ex ins fnl f* **33/1**

216- **9** *nk* **Father Bertie**[141] 7426 4-8-8 **88** (p) JasonHart 1 84
(Tim Easterby) *sn led: hdd 5f out: chsd ldr: rdn and ev ch over 1f out: no ex ins fnl f* **16/1**

360- **10** *1½* **Snoano**[245] 4148 4-8-12 **92** GrahamLee 5 85
(Tim Easterby) *hld up: rdn over 2f out: wknd over 1f out* **25/1**

003- **11** *1¼* **Energia Flavio (BRZ)**[216] 5183 5-8-9 **89** TonyHamilton 11 79
(Richard Fahey) *hld up: rdn over 2f out: wknd fnl f* **12/1**

000- **12** *11* **Intense Style (IRE)**[183] 6273 4-8-13 **93** (b[1]) JimmyQuinn 3 58
(Les Eyre) *prom: rdn over 3f out: wknd over 2f out* **50/1**

1m 46.31s (-3.79) **Going Correction** -0.20s/f (Stan) **12** Ran SP% **115.4**
Speed ratings (Par 109): **108,107,107,106,106 106,104,103,103,101 100,90**
CSF £22.20 CT £111.37 TOTE £4.20: £1.40, £1.90, £2.50; EX 25.70 Trifecta £150.90.
Owner Mrs Susan Roy **Bred** Cheveley Park Stud Ltd **Trained** Newmarket, Suffolk
■ Stewards' Enquiry : Luke Morris two-day ban; careless riding (27th-28th Mar)

FOCUS
A typically competitive renewal of this valuable handicap with eight of these holding Lincoln entries, though the race has had little impact on the big event at Doncaster in recent years. Half the field were returning from absences of five months or more, including the winner. A disputed lead between \bSound Advice\p and \bFather Bertie\p made sure there was no hanging about. The unexposed winner is on the upgrade and can do better and the second confirmed his fine recent run.

921 LADBROKES LADY WULFRUNA STKS (ALL-WEATHER CHAMPIONSHIP FAST-TRACK QUALIFIER) (LISTED RACE) 7f 32y (Tp)
2:50 (2:51) (Class 1) 4-Y-**£28,355** (£10,750; £5,380; £2,680; £1,345; £675) **Stalls** High

60-1 **1** **Mister Universe**[7] 833 4-9-3 106 JoeFanning 4 110
(Mark Johnston) *chsd ldr: rdn over 2f out: led ins fnl f: sn hdd: rallied to ld nr fin* **7/2**[3]

142- **2** *nse* **Sovereign Debt (IRE)**[91] 8212 7-9-8 113 AdrianNicholls 7 115
(David Nicholls) *hld up in tch: rdn over 2f out: hung lft over 1f out: led wl ins fnl f: hdd nr fin* **3/1**[1]

2-11 **3** *1¾* **Realize**[35] 486 6-9-3 103 (t) SeanLevey 6 105+
(Stuart Williams) *hld up: hdwy and swtchd rt wl over 1f out: nt clr run and swtchd lft sn after: nt clr run ins fnl f: r.o* **9/2**

310- **4** *shd* **Kelinni (IRE)**[161] 6952 8-9-3 111 ShaneGray 1 105
(Kevin Ryan) *led: rdn over 1f out: hdd and unable qck ins fnl f* **7/1**

63-0 **5** *¾* **Seanie (IRE)**[44] 370 7-9-3 97 (t) AdamKirby 2 103
(David Marnane, Ire) *s.i.s: hld up: hrd rdn and hung lft fr over 1f out: nt rch ldrs* **25/1**

000- **6** *3¾* **Glen Moss (IRE)**[259] 3655 7-9-3 100 PaulMulrennan 5 93
(Michael Dods) *hld up: rdn over 1f out: nvr on terms* **25/1**

1-10 **7** *hd* **Chookie Royale**[35] 483 8-9-3 109 (p) TomEaves 3 92
(Keith Dalgleish) *s.i.s: sn pushed along to chse ldrs: rdn over 2f out: wknd ins fnl f* **10/3**[2]

61-0 **8** *11* **Angelic Lord (IRE)**[35] 483 4-9-3 103 RichardKingscote 8 62
(Tom Dascombe) *prom: rdn over 2f out: sn wknd* **20/1**

1m 25.35s (-3.45) **Going Correction** -0.20s/f (Stan) course record **8** Ran SP% **113.4**
Speed ratings (Par 111): **111,110,108,108,107 103,103,90**
CSF £13.89 TOTE £4.10: £1.30, £1.20, £2.10; EX 14.30 Trifecta £52.30.
Owner Abdulla Al Mansoori **Bred** Car Colston Hall Stud **Trained** Middleham Moor, N Yorks
■ Stewards' Enquiry : Adrian Nicholls two-day ban; used the whip down the shoulder in the forehand position (27th-28th Mar). one-day ban; careless riding (26th Mar). two-day ban; not correcting horse (29th-30th Mar)

FOCUS
The last Fast-Track Qualifier for the All-Weather Mile Championship on Good Friday and a decent Listed event in its own right, containing the last two winners of the race who also finished 1-2 last year. It was quite a rough race, but it produced a thrilling finish and they set a new best time for the 7f trip here since the Tapeta was laid. Mister Universe confirmed the form of his recent Lingfield win.

922 32RED CASINO H'CAP 1m 5f 194y (Tp)
3:25 (3:25) (Class 4) (0-85,82) 4-Y-0+ **£5,175** (£1,540; £769; £384) **Stalls** Low

Form RPR

-421 **1** **Midtech Star (IRE)**[7] 832 4-9-3 **78** (b) AdamKirby 8 88
(Ian Williams) *chsd ldrs: rdn to ld over 2f out: edgd lft ins fnl f: styd on u.p* **13/8**[1]

3-33 **2** *½* **Scarlet Minstrel**[37] 440 4-9-3 **78** OisinMurphy 10 87
(Andrew Balding) *hld up: hdwy over 2f out: rdn to chse wnr over 1f out: hung rt ins fnl f: styd on* **2/1**[2]

56-5 **3** *6* **Singular Quest**[28] 567 4-8-11 **72** RyanPowell 3 73
(Kevin Frost) *hld up: rdn over 2f out: nt clr run wl over 1f out: styd on to go 3rd nr fin* **50/1**

310/ **4** *nk* **Harry Hunt**[30] 7566 9-9-9 **80** LiamKeniry 5 81
(Graeme McPherson) *prom: chsd ldr 11f out tl rdn over 2f out: edgd lft and styd on same pce fr over 1f out* **28/1**

-141 **5** *hd* **Dakota City**[28] 566 5-9-6 **77** (v) AdamBeschizza 1 77
(Julia Feilden) *chsd ldrs: nt clr run over 2f out: rdn over 1f out: wknd ins fnl f* **5/1**[3]

/0-4 **6** *½* **Dovils Date**[47] 329 7-9-3 **74** DavidProbert 2 74
(Tim Vaughan) *led: rdn and hdd over 2f out: wknd fnl f* **14/1**

-500 **7** *1* **Gabrial The Terror (IRE)**[29] 545 6-8-13 **70** (p) TonyHamilton 9 68
(Richard Fahey) *hld up: rdn over 1f out: nvr on terms* **18/1**

3-03 **8** *2* **All The Winds (GER)**[47] 330 11-9-5 **76** (t) LukeMorris 7 71
(Shaun Lycett) *s.s: hld up: rdn over 2f out: wknd fnl f* **12/1**

2m 59.38s (-5.42) **Going Correction** -0.20s/f (Stan)
WFA 4 from 5yo+ 4lb **8** Ran SP% **113.1**
Speed ratings (Par 105): **107,106,103,103,103 102,102,101**
CSF £4.90 CT £98.17 TOTE £3.00: £1.30, £1.10, £8.20; EX 6.10 Trifecta £112.20.
Owner Midtech **Bred** Denis McDonnell **Trained** Portway, Worcs

FOCUS
A fair staying handicap, but there were doubts over the current form of a few. The pace was ordinary and the two market leaders pulled a long way clear of the rest. The first two continue on the run.

923 DOWNLOAD THE NEW UNIBET RACING APP H'CAP 5f 216y (Tp)
4:00 (4:01) (Class 2) (0-105,101) 4-Y-0+
£15,562 (£4,660; £2,330; £1,165; £582; £292) **Stalls** Low

Form RPR

6-65 **1** **Zac Brown (IRE)**[19] 677 5-8-5 **90** AaronJones(5) 6 100
(Charlie Wallis) *mde all: shkn up over 1f out: r.o* **11/1**

3-50 **2** *nk* **Steelriver (IRE)**[19] 677 6-8-12 **92** GrahamGibbons 4 101
(David Barron) *hld up: plld hrd: hdwy over 1f out: rdn to chse wnr and hung lft ins fnl f: r.o* **4/1**[1]

14-3 **3** *1½* **Patrick (IRE)**[11] 771 4-8-9 **89** TonyHamilton 2 93
(Richard Fahey) *w wnr tl rdn over 1f out: styd on same pce ins fnl f* **9/2**[2]

2524 **4** *½* **Boomerang Bob (IRE)**[8] 816 7-9-3 **97** WilliamCarson 10 100
(Jamie Osborne) *s.i.s: hld up: hdwy over 1f out: sn rdn: r.o* **7/1**[3]

1-32 **5** *½* **Barracuda Boy (IRE)**[21] 657 6-9-0 **101** PatrickVaughan(7) 5 102
(Tom Dascombe) *hld up: hdwy over 1f out: r.o* **7/1**[3]

02-4 **6** *nk* **Mappin Time (IRE)**[46] 338 8-8-11 **91** (be) AndrewMullen 1 91
(Tim Easterby) *chsd ldrs: rdn over 1f out: styd on* **18/1**

-240 **7** 1 ½ **Basil Berry**[7] 833 5-9-5 **99** .... SilvestreDeSousa 9 94+
(Chris Dwyer) *free to post: hld up: hmpd 4f out: hdwy over 1f out: nt trble ldrs* **9/2**[2]

2000 **8** ¾ **Anonymous John (IRE)**[14] 749 4-8-10 **90** .... CathyGannon 3 83
(David Evans) *sn pushed along and prom: rdn over 1f out: wknd ins fnl f* **28/1**

0-00 **9** 1 ¾ **Intibaah**[44] 370 6-9-3 **97** .... PatCosgrave 11 84
(George Baker) *hld up: shkn up over 1f out: nvr on terms* **25/1**

-000 **10** nse **Air Of York (IRE)**[17] 694 4-8-0 **85** ow2 .... JosephineGordon(5) 8 72
(David Evans) *prom: lost pl wl over 3f out: n.d after* **33/1**

42-6 **11** ½ **Plucky Dip**[17] 694 5-8-3 **83** .... RyanPowell 7 68
(John Ryan) *chsd ldrs: rdn over 1f out: wknd fnl f* **16/1**

315- **12** 1 **Another Wise Kid (IRE)**[166] 6817 8-9-6 **100** .... GrahamLee 13 82
(Paul Midgley) *prom tl rdn and wknd over 1f out* **40/1**

1m 12.48s (-2.02) **Going Correction** -0.20s/f (Stan) course record **12** Ran SP% **113.5**
Speed ratings (Par 109): **105,104,102,101,101 100,98,97,95,95 94,93**
CSF £50.40 CT £229.28 TOTE £13.40: £3.90, £1.70, £1.50; EX 68.10 Trifecta £400.70.

Owner Dab Hand Racing **Bred** Tally-Ho Stud **Trained** Ardleigh, Essex

FOCUS
A red-hot sprint handicap and a decent pace with the winner and third disputing the lead from the start. Solid form. The winner was on a good mark on last winter's form.

924 32RED.COM H'CAP 7f 32y (Tp)
4:35 (4:36) (Class 4) (0-80,78) 3-Y-O **£5,175** (£1,540; £769; £384) **Stalls** High

Form RPR

2-53 **1** **Ilzam (IRE)**[28] 557 3-9-1 **72** .... (t) AndreaAtzeni 4 79
(Marco Botti) *hld up in tch: shkn up over 1f out: r.o to ld wl ins fnl f: comf* **12/1**

24-1 **2** ½ **Ikerrin Road (IRE)**[22] 639 3-9-7 **78** .... DougieCostello 2 84
(John Quinn) *led: hdd over 4f out: chsd ldr tl led again over 2f out: rdn and hdd wl ins fnl f* **5/1**[3]

31 **3** 1 ¼ **Rocket Power**[27] 582 3-9-7 **78** .... LukeMorris 5 80
(James Tate) *hld up: plld hrd: hdwy over 2f out: rdn over 1f out: styd on same pce ins fnl f* **9/2**[2]

0-10 **4** nk **Secret Insider (USA)**[31] 519 3-9-3 **74** .... MartinHarley 7 75
(Hugo Palmer) *hld up: hdwy over 2f out: rdn over 1f out: styd on same pce ins fnl f* **4/1**[1]

00-1 **5** 2 ¾ **Willsy**[31] 519 3-9-1 **72** .... JFEgan 9 66
(Mick Channon) *hld up: hmpd 3f out: hdwy over 1f out: rdn and hung lft ins fnl f: no ex* **16/1**

00-1 **6** nk **Papou Tony**[17] 691 3-9-6 **77** .... TedDurcan 1 70
(George Baker) *prom: lost pl wl over 2f out: hdwy over 1f out: no ex ins fnl f* **13/2**

4-63 **7** 1 ¾ **Lucymai**[31] 519 3-9-3 **74** .... RobertWinston 8 63
(Dean Ivory) *s.i.s: hdwy over 5f out: nt clr run and lost pl 1/2-way: sme hdwy over 1f out: wknd ins fnl f* **9/2**[2]

4-21 **8** hd **Broughtons Fancy**[28] 565 3-8-6 **68** .... JosephineGordon(5) 10 56
(David Evans) *hld up: rdn over 1f out: nvr on terms* **16/1**

134- **9** 2 **Billy Roberts (IRE)**[133] 7630 3-9-0 **71** .... JasonHart 12 54
(Richard Guest) *s.i.s: hld up: rdn over 2f out: n.d* **33/1**

541- **10** ½ **Vroom (IRE)**[88] 8230 3-9-6 **77** .... (p) DavidProbert 6 58
(Gay Kelleway) *plld hrd and prom: wnt 2nd over 5f out: led over 4f out: rdn and hdd over 2f out: wknd fnl f* **40/1**

40-5 **11** 3 ¼ **Mostashreqah**[50] 296 3-9-1 **72** .... FrannyNorton 3 44
(Milton Bradley) *chsd ldrs: rdn over 2f out: wknd over 1f out* **80/1**

1116 **12** ½ **Englishwoman**[15] 726 3-9-4 **75** .... AdamKirby 11 46
(David Evans) *s.i.s: hld up: rdn over 1f out: wknd fnl f* **20/1**

1m 27.32s (-1.48) **Going Correction** -0.20s/f (Stan) **12** Ran SP% **117.2**
Speed ratings (Par 100): **100,99,98,97,94 94,92,91,89,89 85,84**
CSF £68.23 CT £317.15 TOTE £11.70: £3.20, £2.00, £1.80; EX 98.40 Trifecta £421.10.

Owner Khalid Bin Ali Al Khalifa **Bred** Denis McDonnell **Trained** Newmarket, Suffolk

FOCUS
A competitive and truly run 3yo handicap with half the field having won their most recent starts, but ironically the race went to the only maiden in the field. Nonetheless the form looks solid moving forward, and it has been rated positively.

925 32RED CASINO MAIDEN FILLIES' STKS 1m 141y (Tp)
5:10 (5:12) (Class 5) 3-Y-O+ **£3,234** (£962; £481; £240) **Stalls** Low

Form RPR

02- **1** **Sagely (IRE)**[165] 6838 3-8-7 0 .... SilvestreDeSousa 3 79
(Ed Dunlop) *chsd ldr tl over 6f out: wnt 2nd again over 2f out: rdn over 1f out: wandered ins fnl f: f: r.o to ld towards fin* **9/2**[2]

22- **2** 1 **Intermittent**[135] 7584 3-8-4 0 .... TomMarquand(3) 2 76
(Roger Charlton) *sn led: rdn over 1f out: hdd towards fin* **8/11**[1]

320- **3** 6 **Lady Canford (IRE)**[88] 8234 3-8-7 65 .... PJMcDonald 4 62
(James Bethell) *chsd ldrs: rdn over 2f out: wknd fnl f* **9/2**[2]

4 6 **Yours Forever** 3-8-7 0 .... ShaneGray 1 48
(Kevin Ryan) *s.i.s: hld up: wnt 4th nr fin: nvr on terms* **28/1**

6 **5** nk **Margoesque**[43] 384 3-8-7 0 .... MartinDwyer 7 48
(William Muir) *prom: chsd ldr over 6f out tl rdn over 2f out: wknd over 1f out* **9/1**[3]

0- **6** 1 ¼ **Chestnut Storm (IRE)**[144] 7362 3-8-7 0 .... JoeFanning 8 45
(Ed Dunlop) *s.i.s: hld up: hdwy over 2f out: wknd wl over 1f out* **25/1**

00 **7** 7 **Always Endeavour**[19] 679 3-8-7 0 .... KieranO'Neill 5 29
(Daniel Mark Loughnane) *s.i.s: hld up: rdn and wknd over 2f out* **100/1**

1m 47.97s (-2.13) **Going Correction** -0.20s/f (Stan) **7** Ran SP% **112.6**
Speed ratings (Par 100): **101,100,94,89,89 88,81**
CSF £7.94 TOTE £5.20: £1.90, £1.20; EX 9.00 Trifecta £21.50.

Owner The Sages **Bred** Keatly Overseas Ltd **Trained** Newmarket, Suffolk

FOCUS
An uncompetitive fillies' maiden in which they finished well spread out. The runner-up set the standard.

T/Jkpt: Not won. T/Plt: £16.10 to a £1 stake. Pool: £92,972.57 - 4201.75 winning units. T/Qpdt: £5.90 to a £1 stake. Pool: £7,465.60 - 928.01 winning units. **Colin Roberts**

926 - 934a (Foreign Racing) - See Raceform Interactive

[890] SOUTHWELL (L-H)
Tuesday, March 15

OFFICIAL GOING: Fibresand: standard
Wind: Moderate across Weather: Grey cloud

935 UNIBET OFFER DAILY JOCKEY/TRAINER SPECIALS MAIDEN STKS 5f (F)
1:55 (1:56) (Class 5) 3-Y-O **£3,234** (£962; £481; £240) **Stalls** Centre

Form RPR

323- **1** **September Issue**[140] 7531 3-9-5 0 .... LukeMorris 8 76
(Gay Kelleway) *racd towards stands' rail: trckd ldrs: hdwy 1/2-way and sn cl up: rdn to ld wl over 1f out: edgd rt ent fnl f: styd on* **7/4**[1]

3 **2** 2 ½ **Spice Mill (IRE)**[12] 798 3-9-5 0 .... SilvestreDeSousa 9 67
(Robert Cowell) *dwlt and towards rr stands' rail: pushed along and hdwy 3f out: rdn to chse ldrs 2f out: styng on whn forced to swtchd lft ent fnl f: sn drvn and kpt on* **9/2**[3]

3 1 ½ **Semana Santa** 3-9-0 0 .... GrahamGibbons 4 62+
(David Barron) *racd centre: hld up towards rr: hdwy 1/2-way: rdn to chse ldrs over 1f out: sn sltly hmpd and drvn: kpt on same pce* **9/1**

4 2 ¼ **Chez Vegas** 3-9-5 0 .... BenCurtis 3 54
(Scott Dixon) *dwlt: green and rdn along in rr towards far rail: hdwy 2f out: kpt on u.p appr fnl f: nrst fin* **33/1**

436- **5** nse **Just That Lord**[176] 6586 3-9-5 70 .... KierenFox 6 53
(Bill Turner) *racd centre: slt ld tl hdd 3f out: cl up and led again over 2f out: sn rdn: hdd wl over 1f out: sn drvn and edgd lft: grad wknd* **16/1**

2222 **6** 3 ¼ **Phantom Flipper**[12] 798 3-9-5 70 .... (p) AdrianNicholls 2 42
(David Nicholls) *chsd ldrs: rdn along over 2f out: sn edgd lft and wknd* **2/1**[2]

4 **7** ¾ **Aegean Boy**[12] 798 3-9-5 0 .... AndrewMullen 7 39
(Michael Appleby) *prom: slt ld 3f out: rdn and hdd over 2f out: sn wknd* **25/1**

05- **8** 3 ¼ **Hadley**[174] 6655 3-9-5 0 .... BarryMcHugh 1 27
(Tracy Waggott) *racd towards far side: chsd ldrs: rdn along over 2f out: grad wknd* **40/1**

006- **9** 1 ¾ **Vocalise**[181] 6427 3-8-7 28 .... RPWalsh(7) 5 16
(Charles Smith) *prom: rdn along bef 1/2-way: sn outpcd* **150/1**

59.92s (0.22) **Going Correction** +0.025s/f (Slow) **9** Ran SP% **113.6**
Speed ratings (Par 98): **99,95,92,89,88 83,82,77,74**
CSF £9.64 TOTE £2.30: £1.10, £1.40, £2.10; EX 10.40 Trifecta £45.70.

Owner Short, Moore, Buy & Kerr **Bred** Bearstone Stud Ltd **Trained** Exning, Suffolk

FOCUS
This sprint maiden was won last year by Tommy Docc who went on to be beaten just half a length in the Queen's Vase! Three of these met over C&D 12 days earlier and the 2-3-4 from that race finished 6-2-7 here.

936 LADBROKES H'CAP 7f (F)
2:35 (2:35) (Class 6) (0-60,60) 4-Y-O+ **£2,587** (£770; £384; £192) **Stalls** Low

Form RPR

2222 **1** **Basingstoke (IRE)**[14] 776 7-9-3 **56** .... (b) LukeMorris 5 62
(Daniel Mark Loughnane) *trckd ldrs towards outer: hdwy and wd st: chal over 2f out: rdn to ld 1 1/2f out: edgd lft ins fnl f: drvn out* **9/4**[1]

1-65 **2** ½ **Grey Destiny**[42] 430 6-8-12 **58** .... MathewStill(7) 8 63
(Antony Brittain) *in tch on outer: hdwy 1/2-way and wd st: chsd ldrs 2f out: sn rdn: chal ent fnl f and ev ch: kpt on wl towards fin* **10/1**

460- **3** 2 **I'm Super Too (IRE)**[166] 6878 9-9-2 **60** .... GemmaTutty(5) 3 60
(Karen Tutty) *trckd ldrs: hdwy over 2f out: rdn wl over 1f out: kpt on fnl f* **18/1**

5545 **4** ¾ **Cadeaux Pearl**[21] 681 8-9-0 **53** .... BenCurtis 9 51
(Scott Dixon) *clsd up: rdn along 2f out: drvn over 1f out: kpt on same pce fnl f* **14/1**

-061 **5** 1 ½ **Emblaze**[34] 525 4-8-12 **58** .... PhilDennis(7) 6 52
(Bryan Smart) *led: rdn along over 2f out: hdd 1 1/2f out: sn drvn and grad wknd* **11/1**

-323 **6** ½ **Roger Thorpe**[49] 336 7-9-2 **60** .... PaddyPilley(5) 1 52
(Deborah Sanderson) *towards rr: pushed along and outpcd after 2f: rdn along and hdwy 2f out: kpt on fnl f* **8/1**

6-01 **7** hd **First Excel**[28] 596 4-9-0 **58** .... AaronJones(5) 4 50
(Roy Bowring) *trckd ldrs on inner: hdwy wl over 2f out: rdn and cl up wl over 1f out: sn drvn and grad wknd* **9/2**[3]

/5-5 **8** 5 **Grandad Chunk (IRE)**[61] 177 5-9-5 **58** .... DougieCostello 2 36
(Tracy Waggott) *t.k.h: trckd ldrs: pushed along 3f out: rdn over 2f out: sn wknd* **25/1**

0032 **9** 18 **Tasaaboq**[7] 867 5-8-10 **49** .... (vt) SilvestreDeSousa 7
(Phil McEntee) *s.i.s and lost several l s: a bhd* **7/2**[2]

1m 27.96s (-2.34) **Going Correction** -0.10s/f (Stan) **9** Ran SP% **115.5**
Speed ratings (Par 101): **109,108,106,105,103 103,102,97,76**
CSF £26.16 CT £328.64 TOTE £2.90: £1.20, £2.50, £5.90; EX 24.70 Trifecta £398.20.

Owner The Batham Boys **Bred** Mrs M Togher **Trained** Baldwin's Gate, Staffs

FOCUS
A moderate handicap.

937 UNIBET.CO.UK DAILY ENHANCED PLACE TERMS H'CAP 5f (F)
3:15 (3:15) (Class 6) (0-60,60) 4-Y-O+ **£2,587** (£770; £384; £192) **Stalls** Centre

Form RPR

5356 **1** **Monsieur Jamie**[7] 869 8-9-7 **60** .... (v) FrederikTylicki 1 71
(J R Jenkins) *in tch towards far side: hdwy over 2f out: rdn over 1f out: led jst ins fnl f: kpt on strly* **8/1**

222 **2** 1 ¼ **Imjin River (IRE)**[30] 579 9-8-9 **48** .... (tp) BenCurtis 5 54
(William Stone) *racd centre: cl up: led 2f out: rdn over 1f out: hdd jst ins fnl f: sn drvn and kpt on* **11/2**

0633 **3** 2 ½ **Extreme Supreme**[7] 868 5-9-7 **60** .... (v) TonyHamilton 3 57
(Derek Shaw) *racd towards far side: towards rr: effrt and hdwy 2f out: sn rdn: kpt on fnl f* **9/4**[1]

2213 **4** ¾ **Blue Bounty**[14] 775 5-9-7 **60** .... (p) SaleemGolam 8 54
(Mark H Tompkins) *racd nr stands' rail: cl up: rdn along 2f out: drvn over 1f out: kpt on same pce fnl f* **4/1**[3]

13-2 **5** ¾ **Hit The Lights (IRE)**[7] 868 6-8-12 **58** .... (v) DanielleMooney(7) 4 50
(David Nicholls) *racd centre: chsd ldrs: rdn along wl over 1f out: grad wknd* **7/2**[2]

0-60 **6** 2 ¼ **Coiste Bodhar (IRE)**[49] 340 5-9-5 **58** .... (b) KieranO'Neill 6 42
(Scott Dixon) *racd towards stands' rail: led: rdn along and hdd 2f out: sn drvn and wknd* **14/1**

06-0 **7** *3* **Abonos (IRE)**[65] 136 4-8-11 **50**..............................(e) JoeyHaynes 7 23
(Simon West) *dwlt: racd towards stands' rail: a in rr* **33/1**

234- **8** *3* **Diminutive (IRE)**[147] 7354 4-8-11 **50**..............................(p) MartinDwyer 10 12
(Grace Harris) *s.i.s: racd nr stands' rail: a bhd* **33/1**

59.87s (0.17) **Going Correction** +0.025s/f (Slow) **8** Ran SP% **112.0**
Speed ratings (Par 101): **99,97,93,91,90 87,82,77**
CSF £49.12 CT £130.70 TOTE £9.20: £1.90, £2.30, £1.50; EX 59.70 Trifecta £225.10.
Owner Mark Goldstein **Bred** Greg Parsons **Trained** Royston, Herts

FOCUS
A moderate sprint handicap. It was probably no coincidence that the first three raced straight up the middle of the track, while the others raced more towards the nearside.

938 DAILY PRICE BOOSTS AT UNIBET H'CAP 6f (F)
3:55 (3:55) (Class 4) (0-85,84) 4-Y-O+ **£5,175** (£1,540; £769; £384) **Stalls** Low

Form RPR

-410 **1** **Razin' Hell**[34] 520 5-9-1 **78**..............................(v) BenCurtis 2 86
(John Balding) *qckly away: mde all: rdn wl over 1f out: drvn ins fnl f: kpt on strly* **12/1**

4156 **2** *1 3/4* **Borough Boy (IRE)**[4] 901 6-9-2 **79**..............................(v) TonyHamilton 4 82
(Derek Shaw) *hld up in tch: hdwy over 2f out: rdn to chse ldrs over 1f out: edgd lft and kpt on wl fnl f: tk 2nd nr line* **6/1**[3]

00-2 **3** *nk* **Addictive Dream (IRE)**[35] 508 9-9-2 **79**..............................(be) DavidAllan 8 81
(Garry Moss) *trckd ldrs: hdwy wl over 2f out: chsd wnr 2f out: swtchd lft and rdn over 1f out: chal and ev ch jst ins fnl f: sn drvn and wknd last 100yds* **13/2**

3123 **4** *1 1/2* **Jacob's Pillow**[19] 703 5-8-11 **74**.............................. PaulMulrennan 6 71
(Rebecca Bastiman) *cl up: rdn along over 2f out: drvn wl over 1f out: kpt on same pce* **7/1**

-213 **5** *1/2* **Greyfriarschorista**[20] 694 9-9-0 **80**..............................(vt) SladeO'Hara(3) 9 76
(Giles Bravery) *in rr: hdwy over 2f out: rdn wl over 1f out: kpt on fnl f: nrst fin* **9/2**[1]

-210 **6** *2 1/2* **Clubland (IRE)**[20] 694 7-9-3 **83**.............................. AlistairRawlinson(3) 5 71
(Roy Bowring) *towards rr on outer: wd st: rdn along over 2f out: no hdwy* **8/1**

-235 **7** *2 1/4* **Sir Billy Wright (IRE)**[5] 894 5-9-7 **84**.............................. JFEgan 1 66
(David Evans) *chsd ldrs on inner: rdn along and losing pl whn n.m.r over 3f out: sn btn* **5/1**[2]

60-0 **8** *10* **Dark Side Dream**[60] 198 4-9-2 **79**.............................. SilvestreDeSousa 3 31
(Chris Dwyer) *chsd ldrs: rdn along and edgd lft over 3f out: drvn wl over 2f out and sn wknd* **7/1**

4000 **9** *1/2* **Captain Lars (SAF)**[20] 694 6-8-13 **81**.............................. CallumShepherd(5) 7 31
(Derek Shaw) *dwlt: a in rr* **16/1**

1m 14.46s (-2.04) **Going Correction** -0.10s/f (Stan) **9** Ran SP% **112.2**
Speed ratings (Par 105): **109,106,106,104,103 100,97,83,83**
CSF £79.05 CT £513.27 TOTE £15.70: £3.90, £2.50, £2.10; EX 104.00 Trifecta £704.00.
Owner Timms, Timms & McCabe **Bred** Alan J McCabe **Trained** Scrooby, S Yorks

FOCUS
A fair handicap and four of these met in a similar event over C&D last month. The 1-2-3-8 from that race finished 6-3-7-9 here and very few ever got into this. The winner looks better than ever.

939 LADBROKES CLASSIFIED CLAIMING STKS 1m (F)
4:35 (4:35) (Class 6) 4-Y-O+ **£2,587** (£770; £384; £192) **Stalls** Low

Form RPR

563- **1** **Breathless**[112] 7963 4-8-8 62..............................(t) OisinMurphy 6 67
(Andrew Balding) *hld up: hdwy on outer wl over 2f out: rdn to chse ldrs over 1f out: led ins fnl f: styd on wl* **9/2**[3]

-406 **2** *2* **Limerick Lord (IRE)**[26] 621 4-8-7 61..............................(p) ShelleyBirkett(3) 7 64
(Julia Feilden) *trckd ldrs: hdwy 3f out: rdn to ld wl over 1f out: drvn ent fnl f: sn hdd and kpt on same pce* **7/1**

0-05 **3** *3/4* **Foie Gras**[27] 608 6-8-8 62.............................. SilvestreDeSousa 3 60
(Chris Dwyer) *trckd ldrs on inner: swtchd rt and pushed along 3f out: hdwy to chse ldrs over 2f out: swtchd rt to outer and rdn wl over 1f out: drvn and kpt on same pce fnl f* **9/4**[1]

0-00 **4** *1 1/4* **Solarmaite**[12] 802 7-8-3 65..............................(b) AaronJones(5) 9 57
(Roy Bowring) *led: rdn along wl over 2f out: hdd wl over 1f out: sn drvn and cl up tl wknd ent fnl f* **12/1**

200- **5** *3 1/2* **Steel Stockholder**[178] 6528 10-8-8 62.............................. DavidAllan 2 49
(Antony Brittain) *prom: rdn along over 2f out: grad wknd* **20/1**

1-00 **6** *1/2* **Outlaw Torn (IRE)**[8] 862 7-8-12 65..............................(e) JFEgan 4 52
(Richard Guest) *chsd ldrs: rdn along and outpcd 3f out: plugged on fnl 2f* **10/1**

00-6 **7** *1/2* **Response**[42] 429 6-8-8 62.............................. AndrewMullen 5 46
(Michael Appleby) *chsd ldrs: rdn along over 2f out: sn drvn and wknd* **4/1**[2]

0-30 **8** *21* **Shearian**[42] 429 6-8-8 60..............................(p) FrannyNorton 1
(Tracy Waggott) *cl up on inner: rdn along 3f out: sn wknd* **10/1**

00-0 **9** *3/4* **Honey Required**[50] 334 4-7-13 50.............................. SophieKilloran(7) 8
(Alan Bailey) *dwlt: a bhd* **16/1**

1m 42.6s (-1.10) **Going Correction** -0.10s/f (Stan) **9** Ran SP% **114.5**
Speed ratings (Par 101): **101,99,98,97,93 93,92,71,70**
CSF £35.61 TOTE £4.40: £1.50, £2.30, £1.60; EX 38.20 Trifecta £131.80.Breathless was claimed by C Chapman for £6000.
Owner I A Balding **Bred** Equine Breeding Limited **Trained** Kingsclere, Hants

FOCUS
A moderate classified claimer with few of these coming into the race in much form. The leaders went off hard and the first three all came from off the pace. The race has been rated on the negative side.

940 CORAL.CO.UK H'CAP 1m 4f (F)
5:10 (5:12) (Class 5) (0-75,79) 4-Y-O+ **£3,234** (£962; £481; £240) **Stalls** Low

Form RPR

02-1 **1** **Blades Lad**[16] 446 7-9-4 **70**..............................(p) TomEaves 3 79
(Peter Niven) *trckd ldr: cl up 1/2-way: led 3f out: pushed clr over 2f out: rdn wl over 1f out: drvn ent fnl f: kpt on strly* **5/1**[2]

5-65 **2** *6* **Art Scholar (IRE)**[40] 446 9-9-7 **73**.............................. SilvestreDeSousa 1 74
(Michael Appleby) *hld up in rr: hdwy 4f out: effrt to chse wnr 2f out and sn rdn: swtchd lft and drvn ent fnl f: kpt on same pce* **8/1**[3]

-110 **3** *9* **Edgar (GER)**[13] 786 6-9-5 **71**..............................(v[1]) OisinMurphy 5 66
(David Bridgwater) *half-rrd s: sn chsng ldr: led after 1 1/2f: jnd and rdn over 3f out: sn hdd: drvn 2f out: sn hld and eased fnl f* **9/4**[1]

0-00 **4** *9* **Hydrant**[11] 566 10-9-1 **67**.............................. JFEgan 4 38
(Richard Guest) *led 1 1/2f: trckd ldng pair: pushed along over 4f out: rdn over 3f out: sn outpcd and bhd* **33/1**

2m 39.92s (-1.08) **Going Correction** -0.10s/f (Stan) **4** Ran SP% **61.5**
Speed ratings (Par 103): **99,95,89,83**
CSF £10.53 TOTE £3.10; EX 7.90 Trifecta £10.10.
Owner Crown Select **Bred** David Holgate **Trained** Barton-le-Street, N Yorks

■ Tatting was withdrawn. Price at time of withdrawal 11/10F. Rule 4 applies to all bets - deduction 45p in the pound.

FOCUS
An ordinary middle-distance handicap in which the red-hot favourite Tatting was withdrawn after ending up in the car park and refusing to come out on to the track.

941 DOWNLOAD THE CORAL APP APPRENTICE H'CAP 1m 4f (F)
5:40 (5:40) (Class 6) (0-60,60) 4-Y-O+ **£2,587** (£770; £384; £192) **Stalls** Low

Form RPR

3-23 **1** **Henry Smith**[11] 819 4-8-2 **50**..............................(be) GeorgeWood(7) 6 58
(Garry Moss) *sn trcking ldr: hdwy and cl up 4f out: effrt over 2f out: rdn to ld 1 1/2f out and sn edgd rt: jnd and drvn appr fnl f: styd on strly last 150yds* **11/4**[2]

5213 **2** *2 1/2* **Toboggan's Gift**[22] 674 4-8-7 **51**.............................. JoshDoyle(3) 3 55
(Ann Duffield) *trckd ldrs: pushed along over 4f out: rdn along to chse ldng pair 3f out and wd st: chal over 1f out: sn drvn and ev ch tl no ex last 150yds* **13/8**[1]

2050 **3** *1 1/4* **Annakrista (GER)**[26] 622 8-8-10 **52**..............................(bt) MeganNicholls(3) 2 54
(Zoe Davison) *chsd ldrs: rdn along over 3f out: drvn over 2f out: kpt on fnl f* **25/1**

242- **4** *1* **Hartford Starts (IRE)**[115] 7950 6-8-10 **49**.............................. CallumShepherd 8 49
(Brian Ellison) *hld up in rr: pushed along and hdwy wl over 3f out: rdn to chse ldrs fnl 2f: plugged on one pce* **7/1**

216- **5** *3/4* **El Massivo (IRE)**[41] 5140 6-9-2 **60**.............................. SophieKilloran(5) 5 59
(Harriet Bethell) *in rr: sme hdwy over 3f out: rdn along wl over 2f out: plugged on one pce* **10/1**

-650 **6** *2 1/2* **Luv U Lucky**[33] 527 4-9-0 **55**..............................(tp) JosephineGordon 7 50
(Michael Appleby) *led: rdn along over 3f out: drvn 2f out: hdd 1 1/2f out: sn hung lft to inner and wknd* **5/1**[3]

000- **7** *55* **Synoptic Dream (USA)**[187] 6226 4-8-5 **46** oh1.............................. NoelGarbutt 4
(Derek Shaw) *chsd ldrs on outer: pushed along over 5f out: rdn over 4f out: sn outpcd and bhd* **40/1**

600- **8** *5* **Imperialista**[199] 5863 4-8-2 **46** oh1..............................(p) NathanEvans(3) 1
(Tracy Waggott) *chsd ldrs: rdn along 1/2-way: sn lost pl and bhd* **50/1**

2m 41.33s (0.33) **Going Correction** -0.10s/f (Stan)
WFA 4 from 6yo+ 2lb **8** Ran SP% **111.3**
Speed ratings (Par 101): **94,92,91,90,90 88,52,48**
CSF £7.12 CT £79.73 TOTE £4.10: £1.60, £1.10, £5.50; EX 9.90 Trifecta £107.50.
Owner Pinnacle Duo Partnership **Bred** M Pennell **Trained** Wynyard, Stockton-On-Tees
■ George Wood's first winner.

FOCUS
A moderate apprentice handicap with the winning time 1.41sec slower than the preceding four-runner handicap.
T/Plt: £152.40 to a £1 stake. Pool: £48,341.88 - 231.44 winning tickets. T/Qpdt: £29.20 to a £1 stake. Pool: £5,237.75 - 132.30 winning tickets. **Joe Rowntree**

919 WOLVERHAMPTON (A.W) (L-H)
Tuesday, March 15

OFFICIAL GOING: Tapeta: standard
Wind: Fresh against Weather: Overcast

942 DOWNLOAD THE NEW UNIBET RACING APP H'CAP 5f 216y (Tp)
6:05 (6:06) (Class 5) (0-70,71) 4-Y-O+ **£3,234** (£962; £481; £240) **Stalls** Low

Form RPR

160- **1** **Diatomic (IRE)**[147] 7365 4-8-8 **57**..............................(p) RichardKingscote 2 65
(Tom Dascombe) *hld up: hdwy over 1f out: r.o to ld wl ins fnl f* **12/1**

0-01 **2** *1 1/4* **City Of Angkor Wat (IRE)**[8] 856 6-9-8 **71** 6ex..............................(p) LiamKeniry 1 75
(Conor Dore) *chsd ldrs: wnt 2nd over 1f out: rdn and ev ch ins fnl f: styd on same pce* **5/2**[1]

2602 **3** *nk* **Spowarticus**[12] 799 7-9-2 **65**..............................(b) KieranO'Neill 4 68
(Scott Dixon) *sn led: rdn: hung rt and hdd wl ins fnl f: styd on same pce* **8/1**

1241 **4** *1 1/4* **National Service (USA)**[21] 685 5-9-5 **68**..............................(tp) TimmyMurphy 3 68
(Rebecca Menzies) *s.i.s: hld up: plld hrd: hdwy over 1f out: rdn ins fnl f: no imp* **11/2**[3]

3106 **5** *1* **Al's Memory (IRE)**[27] 616 7-9-3 **66**.............................. AdamBeschizza 8 63
(David Evans) *hld up: rdn over 2f out: swtchd lft and r.o ins fnl f: nvr nrr* **5/1**[2]

4-30 **6** *3/4* **Top Cop**[32] 543 7-8-7 **56**..............................(p) LukeMorris 6 50
(Ronald Harris) *hld up: rdn over 2f out: hdwy over 1f out: no ex ins fnl f* **7/1**

05-5 **7** *1 1/2* **Mutafaakir (IRE)**[15] 764 7-9-7 **70**.............................. JamesSullivan 9 60
(Ruth Carr) *led early: chsd ldr tl rdn over 1f out: edgd lft and wknd ins fnl f* **7/1**

044- **8** *nse* **Groundworker (IRE)**[149] 7312 5-9-7 **70**.............................. GrahamLee 5 60
(Paul Midgley) *plld hrd and prom: hung rt over 3f out: shkn up over 1f out: wknd ins fnl f* **14/1**

1m 13.74s (-0.76) **Going Correction** -0.15s/f (Stan) **8** Ran SP% **111.1**
Speed ratings (Par 103): **99,97,96,95,93 92,90,90**
CSF £39.88 CT £250.34 TOTE £13.90: £3.80, £1.60, £3.00; EX 50.20 Trifecta £339.30.
Owner John Brown **Bred** Tally-Ho Stud **Trained** Malpas, Cheshire

FOCUS
A modest sprint, though the winner ran up to his best form. The first four raced on the rail into the straight.

943 BET NOW WITH THE LADBROKES APP H'CAP 7f 32y (Tp)
6:40 (6:40) (Class 6) (0-65,71) 4-Y-O+ **£2,587** (£770; £384; £192) **Stalls** High

Form RPR

22-2 **1** **Misu Pete**[51] 321 4-8-13 **57**.............................. DarryllHolland 3 64
(Mark Usher) *chsd ldrs: swtchd rt over 4f out: rdn over 1f out: r.o to ld post* **5/1**[1]

05-0 **2** *shd* **Lucky Lodge**[71] 36 6-9-5 **63**.............................. PJMcDonald 6 70
(Antony Brittain) *wnt rt s: plld hrd and sn prom: wnt 2nd over 5f out: rdn to ld 1f out: hdd post* **13/2**[3]

20-4 **3** *hd* **Veeraya**[38] 482 6-9-6 **64**..............................(bt) AdamBeschizza 9 70
(Julia Feilden) *hmpd s: hld up: hdwy on outer over 2f out: rdn over 1f out: r.o* **17/2**

0502 **4** *1 1/4* **Kodiac Lady (IRE)**[8] 859 4-8-5 **56**..............................(be) HollieDoyle(7) 12 61
(Simon West) *hmpd s: hld up: hdwy over 4f out: nt clr run over 1f out: rdn ins fnl f: r.o* **18/1**

0-50 **5** *hd* **Golden Spun (USA)**[42] 426 4-8-11 **62**..............................(p) PhilDennis(7) 11 65
(Michael Dods) *sn led: rdn and hdd 1f out: styd on same pce ins fnl f* **25/1**

1221 **6** *hd* **Binky Blue (IRE)**[8] 859 4-9-13 **71** 6ex................................ LukeMorris 1 74
(Daniel Mark Loughnane) *hld up in tch: nt clr run and swtchd rt over 1f out: sn rdn: styd on* **5/1**[1]

6300 **7** *1 ½* **Orlando Rogue (IRE)**[8] 857 4-9-7 **65**...........................(p) LiamKeniry 5 64
(Conor Dore) *chsd ldrs: rdn over 1f out: no ex ins fnl f* **8/1**

-520 **8** *½* **Black Truffle (FR)**[27] 608 6-9-0 **63**......................(v) RachealKneller(5) 8 60+
(Mark Usher) *hmpd s: hld up: nt clr run over 1f out: r.o ins fnl f: nvr nrr* **10/1**

0050 **9** *1 ¾* **Admirable Art (IRE)**[29] 590 6-8-13 **57**..........................(p) GrahamLee 4 50
(Tony Carroll) *prom: hmpd and lost pl over 4f out: rdn over 1f out: wknd ins fnl f* **8/1**

00-0 **10** *2* **Showtime Blues**[27] 607 4-9-4 **62**..................................(b) AdamKirby 10 50+
(Jim Boyle) *s.i.s and hmpd s: sn pushed along in rr: hdwy u.p over 1f out: wknd and eased fnl f* **11/2**[2]

030- **11** *3 ¼* **Teetotal (IRE)**[174] 6658 6-9-4 **62**.. JasonHart 2 48+
(Nigel Tinkler) *hld up: plld hrd: rdn and wknd over 1f out* **33/1**

1m 28.69s (-0.11) **Going Correction** -0.15s/f (Stan) **11** Ran SP% **115.9**
Speed ratings (Par 101): **94,93,93,92,92 91,90,89,87,85 81**
CSF £36.59 CT £275.93 TOTE £5.60: £2.30, £3.10, £3.30; EX 41.60 Trifecta £279.20.
Owner Saxon House Racing **Bred** A C M Spalding **Trained** Upper Lambourn, Berks

FOCUS
A steadily run race which turned into a bit of a dash from the final bend.

944 LADBROKES H'CAP 7f 32y (Tp)
7:10 (7:11) (Class 4) (0-85,86) 4-Y-O+ **£5,175** (£1,540; £769; £384) **Stalls** High

Form

1144 **1** **Jammy Guest (IRE)**[38] 486 6-9-3 **80**................................ AdamKirby 9 89+
(George Margarson) *hld up: gd hdwy over 1f out: qcknd to ld wl ins fnl f: r.o* **5/4**[1]

6-45 **2** *¾* **Among Angels**[35] 508 4-9-3 **80**...............................(p) StevieDonohoe 2 85
(Kevin Frost) *led 1f: chsd ldr: rdn over 2f out: ev ch wl ins fnl f: styd on* **22/1**

0/4- **3** *1 ¼* **Invincible Diamond (IRE)**[340] 1312 4-9-3 **80**................ MartinDwyer 6 82
(J S Moore) *racd keenly: led 6f out: clr 1/2-way tl shkn up over 1f out: rdn and hdd wl ins fnl f* **40/1**

030- **4** *nse* **Mississippi**[151] 7245 7-9-7 **84**.. GrahamLee 1 86
(Paul Midgley) *plld hrd and prom: nt clr run over 2f out: rdn over 1f out: styd on* **12/1**

1634 **5** *¾* **Depth Charge (IRE)**[13] 788 4-8-8 **71**........................(vt) RobertHavlin 7 71
(Kristin Stubbs) *hld up: hdwy over 1f out: r.o* **6/1**[3]

-441 **6** *hd* **Corporal Maddox**[6] 878 9-9-9 **86** 6ex.......................(p) LiamKeniry 5 85
(Ronald Harris) *hld up: pushed along and hdwy on outer over 2f out: rdn over 1f out: no ex ins fnl f* **11/1**

0-51 **7** *nk* **Logans Lad (IRE)**[43] 424 6-9-2 **79**...............................(vt) LukeMorris 4 78
(Daniel Mark Loughnane) *hld up: hdwy u.p over 1f out: styd on same pce ins fnl f* **5/1**[2]

000- **8** *¾* **Gurkha Friend**[151] 7245 4-9-3 **80**..................................... PJMcDonald 3 77
(Karen McLintock) *trckd ldrs: racd keenly: rdn over 2f out: no ex fnl f* **9/1**

22-0 **9** *¾* **Johnny B Goode (IRE)**[22] 670 4-8-6 **72**.................. SammyJoBell(3) 8 67
(Richard Fahey) *chsd ldrs: rdn over 1f out: wknd ins fnl f* **10/1**

1m 27.94s (-0.86) **Going Correction** -0.15s/f (Stan) **9** Ran SP% **117.3**
Speed ratings (Par 105): **98,97,95,95,94 94,94,93,92**
CSF £35.37 CT £771.66 TOTE £2.40: £1.10, £5.60, £5.10; EX 36.00 Trifecta £673.40.
Owner John Guest Racing **Bred** Robert Power Bloodstock Ltd **Trained** Newmarket, Suffolk

FOCUS
The pace steadied down the back but then the two leaders kicked on plenty soon enough and the winner came from behind.

945 LADBROKES MAIDEN STKS 1m 141y (Tp)
7:40 (7:40) (Class 5) 3-Y-O+ **£3,234** (£962; £481; £240) **Stalls** Low

Form RPR

00- **1** **Vivre Pour Vivre (IRE)**[144] 7431 3-8-8 0................. SilvestreDeSousa 5 77
(Ed Dunlop) *sn pushed along to chse ldrs: nt clr run over 2f out: shkn up: nt clr run and swtchd rt 1f out: rdn to ld wl ins fnl f: r.o* **4/1**[3]

2 *1* **New Agenda**[230] 4772 4-10-0 0.. TedDurcan 6 81
(Paul Webber) *chsd ldrs: rdn over 1f out: ev ch ins fnl f: styd on* **12/1**

4- **3** *½* **Frenchman (FR)**[160] 7032 3-8-8 0.................................. DarryllHolland 4 74
(Charles Hills) *led: rdn over 2f out: hdd and unable qck wl ins fnl f* **5/4**[1]

4 *2 ¼* **Knights Table** 3-8-8 0.. LukeMorris 1 69
(James Tate) *chsd ldrs: pushed along and rn green at times: drvn over 2f out: styd on same pce fnl f* **9/4**[2]

43 **5** *2 ½* **Dor's Law**[20] 691 3-8-3 0.. JimmyQuinn 9 59
(Dean Ivory) *hld up in tch: rdn over 2f out: edgd lft and no ex fnl f* **20/1**

346- **6** *¾* **Ronnie Baird**[146] 7389 3-8-8 76....................................(p) RobertHavlin 7 62
(Kristin Stubbs) *chsd ldr: rdn over 2f out: wknd ins fnl f* **10/1**

7 *16* **Time To Tango (IRE)**[372] 5-10-0 0................................ OisinMurphy 10 35
(Joseph Tuite) *s.i.s: hld up: rdn and wknd over 2f out* **33/1**

5 **8** *1 ¼* **Ksenia (IRE)**[11] 824 3-7-12 0 ow2.......................... KieranSchofield(7) 3 23
(Nigel Tinkler) *s.i.s: hld up: rdn over 3f out: wknd over 2f out* **100/1**

0-4 **9** *6* **Tred Softly (IRE)**[8] 863 3-8-8 0... IanBrennan 2 14
(John Quinn) *hld up: rdn and wknd over 2f out* **40/1**

10 *2* **Dwynant** 3-8-3 0.. RyanPowell 8
(Kevin Frost) *dwlt: hld up: hung rt over 4f out: rdn and wknd over 2f out* **150/1**

1m 47.18s (-2.92) **Going Correction** -0.15s/f (Stan)
WFA 3 from 4yo+ 20lb **10** Ran SP% **123.8**
Speed ratings (Par 103): **106,105,104,102,100 99,85,84,79,77**
CSF £50.43 TOTE £5.20: £1.90, £3.10, £1.30; EX 60.80 Trifecta £190.50.
Owner Mrs Susan Roy **Bred** J Kenny **Trained** Newmarket, Suffolk

FOCUS
A fair maiden and more to come from the winner.

946 32RED H'CAP 2m 119y (Tp)
8:10 (8:11) (Class 6) (0-60,60) 4-Y-O+ **£2,587** (£770; £384; £192) **Stalls** Low

Form RPR

650- **1** **Desktop**[154] 7192 4-9-1 **56**.. PJMcDonald 9 64
(Antony Brittain) *a.p: chsd ldr over 2f out: rdn to ld wl ins fnl f: styd on* **25/1**

0- **2** *1* **Scenic Star (IRE)**[11] 831 6-9-6 **56**.................................... AdamKirby 4 63
(Gavin Cromwell, Ire) *chsd ldr tl led over 2f out: rdn over 1f out: hdd and unable qck wl ins fnl f* **11/10**[1]

42-3 **3** *2 ¼* **Helmsman (IRE)**[60] 195 4-8-12 **58**.................... JosephineGordon(5) 10 62
(J S Moore) *mid-div: hdwy over 3f out: rdn over 2f out: styd on: nt rch ldrs* **10/1**[3]

-000 **4** *6* **Cosette (IRE)**[20] 693 5-9-3 **60** ow1.......................(p) JordanWilliams(7) 8 57
(Bernard Llewellyn) *prom: rdn over 2f out: wknd fnl f* **25/1**

4015 **5** *1 ¾* **Missandei**[18] 731 4-8-6 **54** ow2......................................(t) JoshQuinn(7) 7 49
(Steph Hollinshead) *hld up: rdn over 1f out: nvr trbld ldrs* **20/1**

430- **6** *¾* **Dukes Den**[33] 4023 5-9-8 **58**... LiamKeniry 12 52
(Mark Usher) *hld up: rdn over 4f out: nt clr run over 1f out: nvr nrr* **16/1**

000- **7** *shd* **Roc De Prince**[55] 6067 7-9-9 **59**.. PhillipMakin 3 53
(Keith Dalgleish) *prom: rdn over 2f out: wknd over 1f out* **10/1**[3]

45-3 **8** *¾* **Iguacu**[29] 592 12-8-10 **46**.. SilvestreDeSousa 1 39
(Richard Price) *prom: pushed along over 3f out: sn lost pl: rdn and hld over 1f out* **12/1**

-320 **9** *nse* **Medieval Bishop (IRE)**[29] 592 7-9-7 **60**.................(p) RobHornby(3) 13 53
(Tony Forbes) *hld up: hdwy on outer over 2f out: rdn: edgd lft and wknd over 1f out* **25/1**

0-54 **10** *nk* **Yorkshireman (IRE)**[29] 592 6-8-13 **49**.........................(v) JackGarritty 6 41
(Lynn Siddall) *sn led: rdn and hdd over 2f out: wknd over 1f out* **9/2**[2]

0-40 **11** *1* **Sail With Sultana**[20] 695 5-9-1 **51**...................................... GrahamLee 5 42
(Mark Rimell) *hld up: effrt over 2f out: no ch whn nt clr run over 1f out* **40/1**

30-6 **12** *2 ¾* **Toretto (IRE)**[20] 695 8-9-3 **53**.......................................(b) JimmyQuinn 11 41
(Bernard Llewellyn) *hld up: rdn over 2f out: wknd over 1f out* **33/1**

/0-0 **13** *1* **Storm Hawk (IRE)**[13] 786 9-9-4 **57**.....................(be) DanielMuscutt(3) 2 44
(Emma Owen) *s.s: hld up: rdn over 2f out: sn wknd* **33/1**

3m 38.63s (-5.07) **Going Correction** -0.15s/f (Stan)
WFA 4 from 5yo+ 5lb **13** Ran SP% **122.2**
Speed ratings (Par 101): **105,104,103,100,99 99,99,99,99,98 98,97,96**
CSF £51.07 CT £336.32 TOTE £29.70: £6.50, £1.20, £2.40; EX 98.70 Trifecta £890.60.
Owner Antony Brittain **Bred** Northgate Lodge Stud Ltd **Trained** Warthill, N Yorks

FOCUS
Few got into this staying handicap in which the pace held up well.

947 32RED.COM H'CAP (DIV I) 7f 32y (Tp)
8:40 (8:40) (Class 6) (0-60,60) 3-Y-O **£2,587** (£770; £384; £192) **Stalls** High

Form RPR

536- **1** **Palpitation (IRE)**[151] 7249 3-9-4 **57**......................... RichardKingscote 8 72
(David Brown) *chsd ldr tl led over 2f out: rdn over 1f out: styd on* **9/1**

4-11 **2** *1 ¼* **Nouvelli Dancer (IRE)**[48] 345 3-9-7 **60**......................... OisinMurphy 4 72
(Ivan Furtado) *chsd ldrs: wnt 2nd over 1f out: sn rdn and edgd rt: rdr dropped rein ins fnl f: kpt on* **11/8**[1]

2123 **3** *9* **Israfel**[11] 820 3-9-1 **54**.. CathyGannon 5 44
(Jamie Osborne) *prom: lost pl over 5f out: rdn 1/2-way: nt clr run over 1f out: styd on to go 3rd wl ins fnl f: nt trble ldrs* **7/1**

-534 **4** *1 ½* **Tombe Girl**[13] 785 3-9-4 **57**...(p) GrahamLee 1 43
(Keith Dalgleish) *chsd ldrs: rdn over 2f out: wknd over 1f out* **11/2**[3]

4-60 **5** *2 ¼* **Stone Quercus (IRE)**[18] 725 3-9-7 **60**......................... FrannyNorton 10 41
(James Given) *s.i.s: in rr: rdn over 1f out: nvr nrr* **7/2**[2]

0-41 **6** *1 ¼* **Bertie Buoy**[11] 820 3-9-7 **60**...(v) JasonHart 2 38
(Richard Guest) *led: rdn and hdd over 2f out: wknd fnl f* **9/1**

00-0 **7** *2 ½* **Selena Rose**[18] 735 3-8-7 **46** oh1...............................(b[1]) KieranO'Neill 7 18
(Ronald Harris) *s.i.s: sn pushed along and a in rr* **80/1**

0-03 **8** *½* **Kimbelle**[31] 562 3-8-10 **49**.. SteveDrowne 6 19
(Mark Usher) *hld up: hdwy over 2f out: rdn and wknd over 1f out* **33/1**

20-0 **9** *11* **Tahiti One**[13] 783 3-9-7 **60**.. WilliamCarson 12
(Tony Carroll) *chsd ldrs: hung lft over 4f out: rdn 1/2-way: wknd over 2f out* **40/1**

1m 26.95s (-1.85) **Going Correction** -0.15s/f (Stan) **9** Ran SP% **118.8**
Speed ratings (Par 96): **104,102,92,90,88 86,83,83,70**
CSF £22.39 CT £98.02 TOTE £10.80: £3.10, £1.10, £2.40; EX 27.10 Trifecta £177.40.
Owner D A West **Bred** R M Jennings **Trained** Averham Park, Notts

FOCUS
This was run at a good gallop, the time was quick (0.99sec faster than the 0-85 earlier on the card and 1.28sec faster than the second division of this race) and the first two pulled well clear, suggesting they are both well handicapped.

948 32RED.COM H'CAP (DIV II) 7f 32y (Tp)
9:10 (9:11) (Class 6) (0-60,60) 3-Y-O **£2,587** (£770; £384; £192) **Stalls** High

Form RPR

500- **1** **Blushes (FR)**[173] 6666 3-9-7 **60**.. PatCosgrave 9 67
(Ed Dunlop) *hld up: rdn 1/2-way: hdwy over 1f out: n.m.r: edgd rt and r.o to ld wl ins fnl f* **7/1**[3]

00-2 **2** *1 ¼* **Dream Revival**[60] 202 3-9-4 **57**....................................... LiamKeniry 7 61
(James Unett) *hld up: hdwy over 1f out: sn rdn: styd on* **10/1**

6052 **3** *1 ¼* **Daydream (IRE)**[12] 794 3-9-1 **59**...........................(t) LucyKBarry(5) 2 60
(Jamie Osborne) *led: rdn over 1f out: hdd wl ins fnl f* **4/1**[2]

0-00 **4** *nk* **Rip Van Suzy (IRE)**[13] 785 3-9-4 **57**............................(v[1]) AdamKirby 4 57
(David Evans) *prom: chsd ldr 3f out: rdn over 1f out: ev ch ins fnl f: nt clr run and no ex sn after* **5/2**[1]

0435 **5** *2* **Ashford Island**[13] 785 3-8-8 **47**....................................(p) LukeMorris 5 45
(Mike Murphy) *hmpd s: pushed along and hdwy over 5f out: rdn over 2f out: nt clr run and no ex ins fnl f* **5/2**[1]

0-56 **6** *7* **Pursuit Of Time**[5] 896 3-9-1 **54**................................(p) AndrewMullen 6 32
(Michael Appleby) *prom: rdn over 2f out: wknd over 1f out* **10/1**

550- **7** *3* **Zeebee (IRE)**[175] 6622 3-8-11 **53**.................................. DanielMuscutt(3) 8 24
(Conrad Allen) *hld up: rdn and hung lft over 1f out: a in rr* **25/1**

000- **8** *1 ¼* **Lady Bacchus**[141] 7507 3-8-7 **46** oh1.................................[1] JasonHart 3 14
(Richard Guest) *chsd ldr tl rdn 3f out: wknd over 1f out* **10/1**

1m 28.23s (-0.57) **Going Correction** -0.15s/f (Stan) **8** Ran SP% **120.8**
Speed ratings (Par 96): **97,95,94,93,91 83,80,78**
CSF £77.29 CT £326.08 TOTE £7.90: £1.80, £2.10, £1.50; EX 44.60 Trifecta £154.20.
Owner The Sagacious Lot **Bred** E A R L Ecurie Villebadin **Trained** Newmarket, Suffolk

FOCUS
A moderate handicap, and the slower of the two divisions by 1.28sec. The winner only needed minor improvement to win this race.

T/Plt: £25.50 to a £1 stake. Pool: £112,234.42 - 3,212.68 winning tickets. T/Qpdt: £3.50 to a £1 stake. Pool: £10,222.84 - 2,117.98 winning tickets. **Colin Roberts**

870 KEMPTON (A.W) (R-H)

Wednesday, March 16

OFFICIAL GOING: Polytrack: standard

Weather: cloudy, cold breeze

949 GETTING OUT STKS AT CHELTENHAM H'CAP (DIV I) 1m 4f (P)

6:05 (6:05) (Class 6) (0-65,65) 4-Y-O+ **£2,264** (£673; £336; £168) **Stalls** Centre

Form RPR

0-25 **1** **Sandy Cove**[16] 766 5-9-4 **65** RyanTate(3) 4 72
(James Eustace) *chsd ldrs: pushed along 2f out to take clsr order: rdn 1f out and led ins fnl f: pushed out* **3/1**[2]

/20- **2** ¾ **Tingo In The Tale (IRE)**[124] 7830 7-8-13 **57** SilvestreDeSousa 10 63
(David Arbuthnot) *led after 1f: set stdy pce: rdn 2f out: hdd ins fnl f: no ex* **15/2**

11-2 **3** 1 ½ **Lions Charge (USA)**[54] 295 9-9-6 **64** (tp) LiamKeniry 2 67
(Neil Mulholland) *led for 1f: chsd ldrs: rdn on inner over 1f out: kpt on ins fnl f to snatch 3rd cl home* **9/4**[1]

2632 **4** nk **Peeps**[15] 772 4-9-0 **60** (b) SaleemGolam 8 63
(Mark H Tompkins) *chsd ldrs: rdn over 2f out: ev ch over 1f out: rdn and wknd ins fnl f: lost 3rd cl home* **9/1**

-000 **5** 1 ¾ **Star Anise (FR)**[22] 684 5-8-3 **52** JosephineGordon(5) 1 52
(Paddy Butler) *sluggish away: settled in mid-div: rdn over 2f out: kpt on ins fnl f* **33/1**

0-66 **6** nk **Hiorne Tower (FR)**[40] 461 5-8-12 **56** KierenFox 11 56
(John Best) *dropped in fr wd draw and settled in rr: pushed along over 2f out: rdn ins 2f: no ex* **11/1**

4350 **7** ¾ **Shirataki (IRE)**[14] 781 8-8-7 **56** ow2 CiaranMckee(5) 3 54
(Peter Hiatt) *in rr: tk clsr order over 4f out: rdn 3f out: sn no ex* **20/1**

44-5 **8** 1 ¼ **Yourholidayisover (IRE)**[13] 796 9-8-0 **51** oh3 PaulaMuir(7) 6 47
(Patrick Holmes) *settled in mid-div: lost pl and in rr turning into st: sn btn* **25/1**

-054 **9** nk **Thane Of Cawdor (IRE)**[23] 676 7-8-12 **61** (b) PatrickO'Donnell(5) 7 57
(Joseph Tuite) *in rr on outer: t.k.h: rdn 3f out: outpcd and wknd ins fnl f* **5/1**[3]

-546 **10** 2 ¼ **Munsarim (IRE)**[42] 435 9-9-0 **58** (b) CathyGannon 5 50
(Lee Carter) *missed break and lost several l: latched onto rr gp after 3f: niggled along over 2f out: racd awkwardly and nvr got gng* **20/1**

2m 37.61s (3.11) **Going Correction** +0.025s/f (Slow)
WFA 4 from 5yo+ 2lb **10** Ran SP% **118.8**
Speed ratings (Par 101): **90,89,88,88,87 86,86,85,85,83**
CSF £24.77 CT £60.25 TOTE £3.70: £1.30, £2.30, £1.40; EX 25.30 Trifecta £72.90.
Owner Blue Peter Racing 12 **Bred** D J And Mrs Deer **Trained** Newmarket, Suffolk

FOCUS
Pleasant, dry conditions and standard going for this evening Polytrack fixture. Not many got into this first division of a moderate 1m4f handicap, in which the early pace steadied as soon as the runner-up had secured the lead.

950 GETTING OUT STKS AT CHELTENHAM H'CAP (DIV II) 1m 4f (P)

6:40 (6:41) (Class 6) (0-65,64) 4-Y-O+ **£2,264** (£673; £336; £168) **Stalls** Centre

Form RPR

430- **1** **Avenue Des Champs**[229] 4830 4-8-8 **56** DannyBrock(3) 5 62
(Jane Chapple-Hyam) *led for 1f: chsd ldrs on inner: gng wl over 1f out: rdn between horses 1f out and sn led: kpt on wl* **2/1**[1]

1-26 **2** ½ **Golly Miss Molly**[39] 488 5-9-7 **64** (b) GeorgeBaker 3 69
(Jeremy Gask) *settled in mid-div on inner: swtchd to outer over 2f out: rdn and hdwy 1f out: kpt on wl wout matching wnr* **5/2**[2]

046/ **3** 1 ¼ **Prince Of Islay (IRE)**[574] 5556 5-8-7 **50** (b[1]) JoeFanning 10 53
(Amanda Perrett) *c across fr wdst draw to ld after 1f: set stdy gallop: rdn over 2f out: hdd over 1f out: kpt on* **10/1**

3-50 **4** nk **Bennelong**[28] 606 10-8-7 **57** (v) RhiainIngram(7) 9 60
(Lee Carter) *settled in mid-div: tk clsr order over 2f out: rdn over 1f out: kpt on wl past btn horses ins fnl f* **12/1**

5-60 **5** 2 ½ **Comedy House**[26] 634 8-9-2 **59** (p) LiamKeniry 6 58
(Michael Madgwick) *chsd ldr: pressed ld 4f out: rdn over 2f out: wknd ins fnl f* **20/1**

4-05 **6** 1 ¼ **Abertillery**[20] 709 4-8-12 **57** RobertHavlin 2 54
(Michael Blanshard) *in rr: rdn over 1f out: sn no ex* **12/1**

-060 **7** 2 **Occult**[12] 815 4-9-1 **60** JimCrowley 4 54
(Simon Dow) *in rr: t.k.h: pushed along 3f out: sn rdn and no imp* **12/1**

204- **8** 2 ½ **Voice From Above (IRE)**[151] 7285 7-8-7 **57** PaulaMuir(7) 8 47
(Patrick Holmes) *chsd ldrs on outer: niggled along over 3f out: rdn 3f out: no ex and wknd* **16/1**

010- **9** ¾ **Irondale Express**[48] 2183 5-8-11 **61** CharlieBennett(7) 7 49+
(Barry Brennan) *reluctant to load: stood in stalls and lost several l: a in rr* **33/1**

5-65 **10** shd **Maison Brillet (IRE)**[11] 832 9-9-6 **63** (p) JackMitchell 1 51
(Clive Drew) *in rr: rdn over 2f out: sn struggling in rr* **8/1**[3]

2m 38.22s (3.72) **Going Correction** +0.025s/f (Slow)
WFA 4 from 5yo+ 2lb **10** Ran SP% **118.8**
Speed ratings (Par 101): **88,87,86,86,84 84,82,81,80,80**
CSF £7.12 CT £39.78 TOTE £2.80: £1.40, £1.30, £2.30; EX 7.90 Trifecta £54.30.
Owner The Tuesday Club **Bred** Grovewood Stud **Trained** Dalham, Suffolk

FOCUS
The slower division by 0.61 seconds, and again few got involved.

951 32RED ON THE APP STORE H'CAP 1m (P)

7:10 (7:10) (Class 6) (0-65,65) 4-Y-O+ **£2,264** (£673; £336; £168) **Stalls** Low

Form RPR

111 **1** **Giovanni Di Bicci**[7] 875 4-9-0 **65** (t) RhiainIngram(7) 7 75+
(Jim Boyle) *chsd ldrs on outer: racd keenly: clsd up to press ldrs over 1f out: rdn and led ins fnl f: in control and pushed out nr fin* **5/4**[1]

0-02 **2** 1 **Pike Corner Cross (IRE)**[14] 777 4-9-4 **62** GeorgeBaker 4 67
(Gary Moore) *in rr: outpcd ent st: swtchd to outer and pushed along over 1f out: rdn ins fnl f: kpt on wl to take 2nd cl home: nvr nrr* **7/2**[2]

/3-0 **3** ½ **Nubar Boy**[61] 190 9-9-6 **64** (p) LiamKeniry 8 68
(Ronald Thompson) *led after 2f: rdn 2f out: hdd ins fnl f: lost 2nd cl home* **33/1**

-111 **4** ½ **Celtic Ava (IRE)**[23] 672 4-9-3 **61** LiamJones 2 64
(Pat Phelan) *chsd ldrs: rdn 3f out: kpt on ins fnl f* **8/1**

-331 **5** hd **Gavarnie Encore**[14] 777 4-8-13 **57** DavidProbert 12 59
(Michael Blanshard) *in rr: rdn over 2f out: kpt on ins fnl f* **7/1**[3]

030 **6** 3 ¼ **Dandys Perier (IRE)**[24] 663 5-9-3 **61** OisinMurphy 3 55
(Ronald Harris) *led for 2f: chsd ldr after: rdn and wknd fr 2f out* **33/1**

-064 **7** 1 ½ **Embankment**[14] 777 7-9-7 **65** RobertHavlin 9 56
(Michael Attwater) *s.i.s: in rr: nudged along to get into contention 3f out: nvr picked up* **8/1**

2540 **8** 1 **Blackthorn Stick (IRE)**[14] 777 7-9-0 **58** (p) JimmyQuinn 11 46
(Paul Burgoyne) *in rr: rdn on inner 3f out: short-lived effrt over 2f out: wknd ins fnl f* **20/1**

5305 **9** 2 **Scot Daddy (USA)**[22] 682 4-8-13 **57** SilvestreDeSousa 1 45
(David Dennis) *chsd ldrs on inner: wknd qckly over 1f out* **12/1**

1m 38.87s (-0.93) **Going Correction** +0.025s/f (Slow) **9** Ran SP% **119.7**
Speed ratings (Par 101): **105,104,103,103,102 99,98,97,95**
CSF £5.71 CT £91.49 TOTE £2.20: £1.10, £1.80, £7.40; EX 7.60 Trifecta £126.10.
Owner Epsom Equine Spa Partnership **Bred** Vimal And Gillian Khosla **Trained** Epsom, Surrey

FOCUS
A good contest by 0-65 standards, and further success for one of the pair of runners chasing a four-timer. The early pace was decent.

952 32RED MAIDEN STKS 6f (P)

7:40 (7:42) (Class 4) 3-Y-O+ **£4,690** (£1,395; £697; £348) **Stalls** Low

Form RPR

3 **1** **Rosenborg Rider (IRE)**[26] 639 3-9-1 0 RichardKingscote 11 79
(Ralph Beckett) *sn pressed ldr fr wd draw: stl handy 2f out: rdn over 1f out: kpt on wl to ld 110yds out* **3/1**[2]

4- **2** 1 ¾ **Very Honest (IRE)**[295] 2575 3-8-10 0 MartinDwyer 3 69
(Brett Johnson) *led and t.k.h: increased pce over 4f out: stdd pce fr 3f out to 2f out: rdn clr over 1f out: ld dwindled ins fnl f and hdd 110yds out* **25/1**

05- **3** 1 ½ **Viscount Barfield**[257] 3860 3-9-1 0 [1] OisinMurphy 2 69+
(Andrew Balding) *in rr: stl plenty to do over 2f out: rdn and kpt on wl ins fnl f* **5/1**

3-42 **4** 3 ¼ **Dangerous Thought (USA)**[11] 834 3-9-1 71 (b[1]) RobertHavlin 10 60
(John Gosden) *chsd ldrs: pushed along 2f out and sn no ex* **9/2**[3]

5 2 **Heiba (IRE)** 4-10-0 0 StevieDonohoe 1 58
(Charlie Fellowes) *in rr: pushed along 3f out: rdn and kpt on one pce over 1f out* **7/1**

300- **6** hd **O Dee**[91] 8250 4-10-0 65 (v) RenatoSouza 7 57
(Dean Ivory) *reluctant to load: in rr and t.k.h: sme prog fr over 1f out* **25/1**

235- **7** ¾ **Twisting Hay**[304] 2298 3-9-1 72 JoeFanning 8 51
(Mark Johnston) *chsd ldrs: rdn 2f out: sn no ex and wknd over 1f out* **11/4**[1]

8 6 **Cainhoe Star** 3-9-1 0 WilliamCarson 4 33
(Anthony Carson) *missed break and in rr: rdn 3f out: nvr involved* **16/1**

040- **9** nk **Bit Of A Lad (IRE)**[109] 8033 3-9-1 68 MartinHarley 6 32
(David Brown) *in rr: rdn 2f out: sn hld* **20/1**

0-3 **10** ¾ **Heathfield Park (IRE)**[28] 611 3-8-5 0 JosephineGordon(5) 9 25
(William Stone) *chsd ldrs on inner: lost pl and rdn 2f out: sn no ex* **50/1**

1m 12.11s (-0.99) **Going Correction** +0.025s/f (Slow)
WFA 3 from 4yo 13lb **10** Ran SP% **119.3**
Speed ratings (Par 105): **107,104,102,98,95 95,94,86,86,85**
CSF £81.86 TOTE £4.70: £2.00, £5.00, £2.30; EX 104.40 Trifecta £956.60.
Owner Wing Kwong Ng **Bred** Mrs Claire Doyle **Trained** Kimpton, Hants

FOCUS
A routine sprint maiden, but the performances of the first two look worth marking up.

953 £10 FREE BET AT 32REDSPORT.COM H'CAP 7f (P)

8:10 (8:12) (Class 5) (0-75,75) 4-Y-O+ **£2,911** (£866; £432; £216) **Stalls** Low

Form RPR

5-35 **1** **Burning Blaze**[41] 449 6-9-5 **73** SilvestreDeSousa 5 80
(Brian Ellison) *chsd ldr: rdn and pressed ldr over 2f out: led 2f out: kpt on wl u.str drive to hold off runner-up ins fnl f* **5/1**[3]

6-15 **2** hd **Light From Mars**[65] 142 11-9-7 **75** (p) LukeMorris 8 81
(Ronald Harris) *settled in mid-div on inner: rdn 2f out: jnd ldr and fought on wl ins fnl f: hld nr fin* **8/1**

130/ **3** ½ **Barnmore**[455] 8188 8-9-7 **75** CharlesBishop 7 80
(Peter Hedger) *in rr: rdn over 2f out: gd hdwy over 1f out: nrst fin* **25/1**

3434 **4** ¾ **Be Royale**[14] 780 6-9-5 **73** RobertWinston 11 76
(Michael Appleby) *in rr: rdn ovr 2f out: kpt on ins fnl f: nrst fin* **10/1**

0-06 **5** 1 ¾ **Multitask**[32] 561 6-9-4 **72** LiamKeniry 4 70
(Michael Madgwick) *settled in mid-div: ev ch 2f out: rdn over 1f out: one pce* **3/1**[1]

2333 **6** 1 ¼ **Chelwood Gate (IRE)**[14] 782 6-9-6 **74** (v) GeorgeBaker 9 69
(Patrick Chamings) *led: hdd & wknd fr 2f out* **4/1**[2]

100- **7** 8 **Swot**[155] 7197 4-9-4 **72** JimCrowley 3 45
(Simon Dow) *chsd ldrs: wknd qckly 2f out: sn btn* **14/1**

6U56 **8** ½ **Wink Oliver**[13] 795 4-9-3 **71** TimmyMurphy 10 43
(David Dennis) *in rr: stl plenty to do 3f out: rdn out hands and heels* **20/1**

5-30 **9** 10 **Polar Kite (IRE)**[28] 607 8-8-6 **63** RobHornby(3) 6 8
(Michael Attwater) *stood stl in stalls and missed break: a in rr: t.o* **20/1**

1m 25.54s (-0.46) **Going Correction** +0.025s/f (Slow) **9** Ran SP% **101.9**
Speed ratings (Par 103): **103,102,102,101,99 97,88,88,76**
CSF £30.47 CT £471.49 TOTE £6.10: £1.90, £1.90, £3.70; EX 41.80 Trifecta £783.70.
Owner Mere Civilians **Bred** Redland Bs, Baroness Bs & D Redvers **Trained** Norton, N Yorks

■ Athletic was withdrawn. Price at time of withdrawal 7-2. Rule 4 applies to all bets - deduction 20p in the pound.

■ Stewards' Enquiry : Silvestre De Sousa two-day ban: use of whip (3-31 Mar)

FOCUS
A fairly tight 0-75 with only 5lb covering pretty much all of them on adjusted ratings.

954 32RED CASINO H'CAP 6f (P)

8:40 (8:40) (Class 4) (0-85,85) 3-Y-O **£4,690** (£1,395; £697; £348) **Stalls** Low

Form RPR

100- **1** **A Momentofmadness**[209] 5565 3-9-1 **79** DarryllHolland 4 84
(Charles Hills) *sn led: set brisk tempo and clr 1/2-way: rdn over 2f out: ld reduced nr fin: hld on* **4/1**[3]

1133 **2** ½ **Gorokai (IRE)**[22] 686 3-8-12 **76** (p) JamieSpencer 3 80
(David Simcock) *hmpd s: in rr: stl in last turning into st: rdn on wd outside jst over 1f out: str run ins fnl f to take 2nd nr fin* **13/2**

536- **3** ¾ **Heraldic (USA)**[174] 6667 3-9-7 **85** JoeFanning 5 86
(Mark Johnston) *chsd clr ldr: rdn 2f out: kpt on one pce ins fnl f: lost 2nd nr fin* **5/1**

0-1 **4** 2 ¾ **Big Amigo (IRE)**[33] 544 3-8-11 **75** [1] RichardKingscote 2 68+
(Tom Dascombe) *hmpd s: mid-div on inner: rdn over 2f out: no ex fnl f* **7/2**[2]

110- **5** 3 ¼ **Tikthebox (IRE)**[163] 6978 3-9-1 **79** MartinHarley 1 62
(David Brown) *chsd ldrs on inner: rdn 2f out and sn one pce* **20/1**

400- **6** *1 ¾* **Jazz Legend (USA)**[181] 6462 3-9-4 **82**.............................. TomEaves 7 60
(James Given) *awkward s and hmpd rivals: chsd ldrs: rdn over 2f out: wknd* **25/1**

-125 **7** *nk* **Dark Side Princess**[22] 686 3-8-13 **77**..................(p) SilvestreDeSousa 6 54
(Chris Dwyer) *in rr: rdn over 2f out: nvr involved* **10/1**

6-11 **8** *nse* **Princess Cookie**[35] 515 3-8-9 **76**.............................. DannyBrock(3) 8 53
(Philip McBride) *in rr: rdn and briefly looked like getting involved 2f out: wknd qckly over 1f out* **11/4**[1]

1m 11.45s (-1.65) **Going Correction** +0.025s/f (Slow) **8** Ran SP% **116.6**
Speed ratings (Par 100): **112,111,110,106,102 100,99,99**
CSF £30.68 CT £133.05 TOTE £5.30: £1.40, £2.00, £2.30; EX 42.30 Trifecta £170.60.
Owner Tony Wechsler & Ann Plummer **Bred** D R Tucker **Trained** Lambourn, Berks

FOCUS
The evening's feature, and a race pinched from the front.

955 32RED.COM H'CAP 6f (P)
9:10 (9:10) (Class 5) (0-75,75) 4-Y-O+ **£2,911** (£866; £432; £216) **Stalls** Low

Form RPR

0-5 **1** **Bouclier (IRE)**[44] 416 6-9-2 **70**.............................. WilliamCarson 3 76
(Tony Carroll) *chsd ldrs on inner: t.k.h: pushed along 2f out: rdn 1f out: kpt on wl to ld 100yds out: pushed out* **3/1**[1]

1304 **2** *nk* **Nasri**[7] 872 10-8-11 **65**.............................. JamieSpencer 6 70
(Emma Owen) *racd in mid-div: rdn and effrt 2f out: picked up ins fnl f and kpt on wl for 2nd* **9/1**

2326 **3** *shd* **Gold Beau (FR)**[20] 703 6-8-9 **66**.....................(p) NataliaGemelova(3) 5 71
(Kristin Stubbs) *settled in mid-div on outer: niggled along to go pce 3f out: rdn over 1f out and kpt on wl on outer to take 3rd* **10/1**

-011 **4** *nk* **Rigolleto (IRE)**[7] 873 8-9-3 **71** 6ex..............................(p) GeorgeBaker 8 75
(Anabel K Murphy) *led: rdn over 1f out: hdd 100yds out: wknd and lost two pls nr fin* **9/2**[2]

21-5 **5** *1* **Picket Line**[32] 561 4-9-4 **72**.............................. OisinMurphy 9 73
(Geoffrey Deacon) *hld up in rr: rdn over 1f out: one pce* **14/1**

-121 **6** *shd* **Chetan**[28] 607 4-9-1 **69**..............................(tp) LukeMorris 7 70
(Charlie Wallis) *racd in mid-div: niggled along and rn in snatches fr 3f out: kpt on ins fnl f* **5/1**[3]

43-5 **7** *nk* **Major Valentine**[14] 782 4-8-12 **71**.............................. CiaranMckee(5) 1 71
(John O'Shea) *hld up in rr: taken to inner and rdn over 1f out: kpt on one pce* **7/1**

3302 **8** *½* **Pyroclastic (IRE)**[21] 696 4-8-7 **61**..............................(p) JoeFanning 10 59
(Jim Boyle) *t.k.h on outside in rr: rdn 2f out: one pce* **14/1**

155- **9** *nse* **Quickaswecan**[184] 6382 5-9-7 **75**..............................(t) FrannyNorton 2 73
(Milton Bradley) *chsd ldr: rdn 2f out and upsides: wknd ins fnl f* **25/1**

0525 **10** *1 ¾* **Diamond Charlie (IRE)**[20] 714 8-9-7 **75**.............................. JimCrowley 4 68
(Simon Dow) *mid-div: rdn 2f out: sn hld and wknd fr 1f out* **8/1**

1m 12.13s (-0.97) **Going Correction** +0.025s/f (Slow) **10** Ran SP% **119.7**
Speed ratings (Par 103): **107,106,106,106,104 104,104,103,103,101**
CSF £31.95 CT £246.13 TOTE £4.60: £1.90, £3.00, £2.90; EX 44.00 Trifecta £323.10.
Owner M Chung **Bred** Dayton Investments Ltd **Trained** Cropthorne, Worcs

FOCUS
A modest but tight sprint handicap to finish, and marginally the slowest of the three races over 6f on the night.
T/Plt: £80.20 to a £1 stake. Pool: £92,694.35. 843.43 winning tickets. T/Qpdt: £48.80 to a £1 stake. Pool: £7,444.01. 112.80 winning tickets. **Cathal Gahan**

[935] SOUTHWELL (L-H)
Wednesday, March 16

OFFICIAL GOING: Fibresand: standard
Wind: Moderate, half against changing to fresh, half against after 2.35 race
Weather: Fine & dry

956 LADBROKES H'CAP 1m (F)
1:20 (1:20) (Class 5) (0-70,74) 4-Y-O+ **£3,234** (£962; £481; £240) **Stalls** Low

Form RPR

3-41 **1** **Red Touch (USA)**[6] 893 4-9-10 **74** 6ex.............. AlistairRawlinson(3) 5 85
(Michael Appleby) *prom: pushed along and sltly outpcd 1/2-way: hdwy over 3f out: chal over 2f out: rdn to ld over 1f out: sn edgd lft: kpt on* **4/7**[1]

2-31 **2** *2 ¼* **Eium Mac**[35] 526 7-8-8 **55**..............................(b) RaulDaSilva 6 60
(Neville Bycroft) *dwlt and towards rr: hdwy after 2f: cl up over 3f out: led 3f out: rdn 2f out: hdd 1 1/2f out and sn drvn: kpt on same pce* **6/1**[2]

5110 **3** *shd* **The Firm (IRE)**[29] 598 7-9-2 **66**..............................(be) RobHornby(3) 2 71
(Daniel Mark Loughnane) *hld up: hdwy over 2f out: chsd ldng pair over 1f out: sn rdn: kpt on fnl f* **16/1**

1326 **4** *1 ¾* **Stun Gun**[29] 598 6-8-13 **60**..............................(p) TonyHamilton 4 61
(Derek Shaw) *in rr: pushed along 1/2-way: rdn and hdwy 2f out: kpt on fnl f* **16/1**

60-2 **5** *1* **Sooqaan**[41] 448 5-9-5 **66**.............................. DavidAllan 3 65
(Antony Brittain) *cl up: rdn along 3f out: sn wknd* **8/1**[3]

4326 **6** *6* **Best Tamayuz**[8] 866 5-9-5 **66**..............................(p) LukeMorris 1 50
(Scott Dixon) *slt ld: pushed along and hdd 3f out: rdn over 2f out: sn wknd* **12/1**

1m 42.31s (-1.39) **Going Correction** -0.125s/f (Stan) **6** Ran SP% **108.5**
Speed ratings (Par 103): **101,98,98,96,95 89**
CSF £4.00 TOTE £1.40: £1.10, £2.60; EX 4.40 Trifecta £22.70.
Owner Racing Daily **Bred** Dark Hollow Farm, Dorsey Brown Et Al **Trained** Oakham, Rutland

FOCUS
A modest handicap, though all six of these had previously won here at least once.

957 32RED H'CAP 1m 6f (F)
1:55 (1:55) (Class 5) (0-70,75) 4-Y-O+ **£3,234** (£962; £481; £240) **Stalls** Low

Form RPR

4/ **1** **Down Time (USA)**[15] 4741 6-9-1 **58**..............................(b) BenCurtis 4 71
(Brian Ellison) *hld up in tch: hdwy 4f out: cl up 3f out: led wl over 2f out and sn rdn: clr appr fnl f: kpt on strly* **10/1**[3]

430 **2** *3 ¼* **Moonshine Ridge (IRE)**[43] 428 5-8-10 **53**.............................. NeilFarley 7 62
(Alan Swinbank) *dwlt: sn trcking ldrs: cl up 1/2-way: effrt 3f out: sn rdn: chsd wnr 2f out: sn drvn and kpt on same pce* **25/1**

12 **3** *5* **Lifting Me Higher (IRE)**[8] 865 4-8-13 **60**..............................(p) JFEgan 5 62
(W P Browne, Ire) *sn led: pushed along over 3f out: rdn and hdd wl over 2f out: sn drvn and kpt on one pce* **11/8**[2]

5-31 **4** *5* **Be My Sea (IRE)**[8] 864 5-10-4 **75** 6ex.............................. WilliamCarson 1 71
(Tony Carroll) *trckd ldrs: pushed along on inner over 4f out: rdn over 3f out: sn drvn and outpcd* **5/4**[1]

0366 **5** *½* **Thou Swell (IRE)**[13] 801 4-9-1 **62**.............................. LukeMorris 2 57
(Shaun Harris) *trckd ldrs: pushed along 4f out: rdn 3f out: sn drvn and wknd fnl 2f* **16/1**

000- **6** *62* **Aristocracy**[11] 7192 5-9-5 **62**.............................. JohnFahy 6
(Sally Randell) *chsd ldrs: lost pl and rdn along 1/2-way: sn outpcd and bhd* **100/1**

36-6 **P** **Mr Snoozy**[12] 132 7-9-11 **68**..............................(p) JasonHart 3
(Mark Walford) *rdn along immediately after s: sn 10 l adrift and nvr gng: wl bhd whn p.u 1/2-way* **33/1**

3m 7.6s (-0.70) **Going Correction** -0.125s/f (Stan)
WFA 4 from 5yo+ 4lb **7** Ran SP% **109.3**
Speed ratings (Par 103): **97,95,92,89,89 53,**
CSF £167.78 TOTE £10.70: £3.50, £10.10; EX 67.50 Trifecta £167.60.
Owner Brian Ellison **Bred** Brookdale & Ted Folkerth **Trained** Norton, N Yorks

FOCUS
A modest staying handicap and the betting had a very lopsided look to it, but the market got it wrong.

958 LADBROKES MAIDEN STKS (DIV I) 7f (F)
2:35 (2:39) (Class 5) 3-Y-O+ **£3,234** (£962; £481; £240) **Stalls** Low

Form RPR

222- **1** **Street Duel (USA)**[203] 5747 3-8-13 75.............................. JoeFanning 9 83
(Mark Johnston) *sn led: rdn clr wl over 1f out: kpt on strly* **4/5**[1]

666- **2** *4 ½* **Ocean Ready (USA)**[203] 5747 3-8-13 0.............................. LukeMorris 4 72
(Sir Mark Prescott Bt) *trckd ldrs: hdwy 3f out: rdn to chse wnr wl over 1f out: sn drvn and no imp* **5/1**[3]

0- **3** *2 ¼* **Moueenn**[98] 8152 3-8-13 0.............................. JackMitchell 5 67+
(Roger Varian) *prom on inner tl pushed along and lost pl after 2f: swtchd rt to outer and wd st: rdn on wd outside to chse ldng pair over 1f out: kpt on same pce* **10/3**[2]

0-6 **4** *9* **Chookie Valentine**[9] 863 3-8-13 0.............................. JasonHart 10 39
(Keith Dalgleish) *cl up: rdn along 3f out: drvn over 2f out and sn wknd* **28/1**

5 *1* **Another Go (IRE)** 3-8-13 0.............................. BenCurtis 2 37
(Alan Swinbank) *in tch: hdwy to chse ldrs over 3f out: rdn along over 2f out: grad wknd* **20/1**

6 *4 ½* **La Barata** 3-8-8 0.............................. ShaneGray 6 20+
(Kevin Ryan) *s.i.s and in rr: rdn along and wd st: nvr a factor* **12/1**

7 *8* **Kylie's Kenny**[47] 6-10-0 0.............................. AdamBeschizza 7 8
(Derek Shaw) *dwlt: sn rdn along on inner: a bhd* **100/1**

8 *17* **Katalan (GER)** 3-8-13 0.............................. TomQueally 3
(John Butler) *a in rr: wd st and bhd* **25/1**

1m 28.63s (-1.67) **Going Correction** -0.125s/f (Stan)
WFA 3 from 4yo+ 15lb **8** Ran SP% **116.0**
Speed ratings (Par 103): **104,98,96,86,84 79,70,51**
CSF £5.11 TOTE £1.90: £1.10, £1.90, £1.10; EX 6.20 Trifecta £12.80.
Owner Sultan Ali **Bred** Iadora Farm & Darley **Trained** Middleham Moor, N Yorks

FOCUS
An uncompetitive maiden and they finished well spread out.

959 LADBROKES MAIDEN STKS (DIV II) 7f (F)
3:15 (3:15) (Class 5) 3-Y-O+ **£3,234** (£962; £481; £240) **Stalls** Low

Form RPR

0- **1** **Remarkable**[177] 6596 3-8-13 0..............................(b¹) RobertHavlin 5 82
(John Gosden) *dwlt and pushed along: t.k.h and hdwy to trck ldrs after 1 1/2f: effrt to chal over 2f out: rdn over 1f out: led appr fnl f: sn edgd lft: kpt on* **6/5**[1]

0-46 **2** *2 ¼* **Highwayman**[19] 725 3-8-8 64.............................. CallumShepherd(5) 4 73
(William Jarvis) *slt ld: rdn over 2f out: drvn over 1f out: hdd appr fnl f: kpt on* **7/1**[3]

040- **3** *2* **Bingo George (IRE)**[230] 4791 3-8-13 74.............................. OisinMurphy 1 68
(Andrew Balding) *trckd ldrs on inner: hdwy 3f out: cl up 2f out: sn rdn and ev ch tl drvn and one pce ent fnl f* **15/8**[2]

5- **4** *7* **Real Art**[295] 2575 3-8-8 0.............................. RaulDaSilva 3 44+
(Kevin Ryan) *s.i.s and bhd: sn swtchd rt to outer and wd st: sme hdwy fnl 2f: nvr a factor* **8/1**

30-0 **5** *4* **Illusive Force (IRE)**[8] 866 4-10-0 70.............................. TonyHamilton 8 43
(Derek Shaw) *chsd ldrs: rdn along over 3f out: sn wknd* **20/1**

0/-6 **6** *9* **Muhtadim (IRE)**[31] 582 4-9-7 0.............................. RPWalsh(7) 6 19
(Charles Smith) *in tch: rdn along over 3f out: sn wknd* **50/1**

00 **7** *3* **Monpazier (IRE)**[9] 858 3-8-6 0.............................. CliffordLee(7) 9
(K R Burke) *dwlt: a in rr* **25/1**

0 **8** *6* **Sunshine Quest**[12] 824 4-9-4 0.............................. RachelRichardson(5) 2
(Lucinda Egerton) *cl up: rdn along 1/2-way: sn wknd* **66/1**

1m 28.77s (-1.53) **Going Correction** -0.125s/f (Stan)
WFA 3 from 4yo 15lb **8** Ran SP% **115.9**
Speed ratings (Par 103): **103,100,98,90,85 75,71,65**
CSF £10.26 TOTE £2.20: £1.10, £2.10, £1.30; EX 10.40 Trifecta £26.40.
Owner Cheveley Park Stud **Bred** Cheveley Park Stud Ltd **Trained** Newmarket, Suffolk

FOCUS
The winning time was 0.14sec slower than the first division. The winner looked value for further.

960 DOWNLOAD THE LADBROKES APP H'CAP 7f (F)
3:55 (3:55) (Class 3) (0-95,95) 4-Y-O+ **£7,439** (£2,213; £1,106; £553) **Stalls** Low

Form RPR

-101 **1** **Moon River (IRE)**[31] 581 4-8-11 **85**.............................. BenCurtis 7 94
(Michael Appleby) *mde most: rdn wl over 1f out: drvn and edgd lft ins fnl f: kpt on gamely* **5/1**[3]

-601 **2** *¾* **Trojan Rocket (IRE)**[21] 694 8-8-9 **88**..............................(p) AaronJones(5) 8 95
(Michael Wigham) *disp ld: rdn along over 2f out: drvn over 1f out: kpt on wl u.p fnl f* **16/1**

4-43 **3** *nk* **Showboating (IRE)**[66] 134 8-9-1 **89**.............................. DanielTudhope 11 95
(John Balding) *dwlt and towards rr: hdwy on outer and wd st: rdn 2f out: chsd ldrs over 1f out: drvn and edgd lft ins fnl f: kpt on wl towards fin* **9/1**

-121 **4** *¾* **Philba**[29] 599 4-9-1 **92**..............................(tp) AlistairRawlinson(3) 9 96
(Michael Appleby) *prom: effrt over 2f out and sn cl up: rdn wl over 1f out: drvn and kpt on same pce fnl f* **7/2**[2]

-125 **5** *½* **Nuno Tristan (USA)**[25] 657 4-8-9 **90**.............................. AdamMcNamara(7) 2 93
(Richard Fahey) *chsd ldrs: rdn over 2f out: drvn over 1f out: kpt on same pce fnl f* **7/1**

01-2 **6** *3 ¾* **Ian's Memory (USA)**[29] 599 5-9-7 **95**..............................(b) LukeMorris 12 88
(Jeremy Noseda) *in tch: hdwy and wd st: rdn to chse ldrs 2f out: sn drvn and no imp* **3/1**[1]

2135 **7** *4* **Greyfriarschorista**[1] 938 9-8-2 **81** oh1..............................(vt) NoelGarbutt(5) 3 63
(Giles Bravery) *in tch: rdn along wl over 2f out: sn drvn and wknd* **20/1**

-504 **8** 9 **Westwood Hoe**[29] 599 5-9-2 **90**....(p) TomQueally 5 48
(Tony Coyle) *towards rr: hdwy over 3f out: rdn along wl over 2f out: drvn wl over 1f out: sn wknd* **10/1**
050- **9** 3/4 **Dubai Dynamo**[160] 7060 11-9-2 **90**.... PJMcDonald 4 46
(Ruth Carr) *a towards rr* **66/1**
200- **10** 7 **My Dad Syd (USA)**[156] 7170 4-8-7 **81** oh2.... RyanPowell 6 18+
(Ian Williams) *dwlt: a bhd* **14/1**
1m 27.44s (-2.86) **Going Correction** -0.125s/f (Stan) **10** Ran SP% **114.3**
Speed ratings (Par 107): **111,110,109,108,108 104,99,89,88,80**
CSF £79.56 CT £697.35 TOTE £4.10: £1.10, £5.60, £3.20; EX 78.50 Trifecta £668.10.
Owner Craig Buckingham **Bred** Rockhart Trading Ltd **Trained** Oakham, Rutland
FOCUS
A decent handicap featuring several with good form around here this winter. The first two home disputed the lead from the start.

961 BET&WATCH EVERY RACE AT UNIBET (S) STKS 5f (F)
4:35 (4:35) (Class 6) 3-Y-O+ **£2,587** (£770; £384; £192) **Stalls** Centre

Form RPR
34-2 **1** **Sadie Babes (IRE)**[25] 659 3-7-11 60.... SammyJoBell(3) 1 65
(Richard Fahey) *cl up: led after 1f: rdn clr 1 1/2f out: kpt on strly* **8/13**[1]
1505 **2** 7 **Very First Blade**[8] 868 7-9-7 56....(be) MrLewisStones(7) 2 57
(Michael Mullineaux) *led 1f: chsd wnr: rdn along 2f out: kpt on one pce* **15/2**
423- **3** 1 1/2 **Hello Beautiful (IRE)**[265] 3543 5-8-11 51.... CallumShepherd(5) 3 39
(Brian Ellison) *prom: chsd wnr 1/2-way: rdn 2f out: sn drvn and one pce* **4/1**[2]
-606 **4** 3 1/2 **Coiste Bodhar (IRE)**[1] 937 5-10-0 58....(b) KieranO'Neill 5 39
(Scott Dixon) *chsd ldrs: rdn along 1/2-way: sn drvn and outpcd* **6/1**[3]
1m 0.55s (0.85) **Going Correction** +0.15s/f (Slow)
WFA 3 from 5yo+ 12lb **4** Ran SP% **108.0**
Speed ratings (Par 101): **99,87,85,79**
CSF £5.57 TOTE £1.70; EX 5.50 Trifecta £13.00.
Owner Paul Hyland **Bred** Paul Hyland **Trained** Musley Bank, N Yorks
FOCUS
A moderate seller and very straightforward for the hot favourite.

962 DAILY PRICE BOOSTS AT UNIBET H'CAP 5f (F)
5:15 (5:15) (Class 6) (0-65,65) 3-Y-O **£2,587** (£770; £384; £192) **Stalls** Centre

Form RPR
060- **1** **Ticking Away**[142] 7507 3-9-7 **65**.... SeanLevey 1 83+
(David Brown) *cl up on outer: led over 3f out: eased clr over 1f out: v easily* **6/4**[1]
544- **2** 2 3/4 **Fumbo Jumbo (IRE)**[142] 7517 3-9-5 **63**.... DavidAllan 3 61
(Garry Moss) *slt ld: pushed along and hdd over 3f out: rdn 2f out: sn drvn and kpt on same pce* **5/2**[2]
0-45 **3** 7 **Kiringa**[42] 436 3-8-4 **48**.... KieranO'Neill 7 21
(Robert Cowell) *racd towards stands' rail: chsd ldrs: rdn along and edgd lft wl over 1f out: sn one pce* **20/1**
410- **4** 3 1/2 **Roaring Rory**[171] 6782 3-9-6 **64**.... PJMcDonald 4 24
(Ollie Pears) *prom: rdn along 1/2-way: drvn 2f out and sn wknd* **10/1**
51-6 **5** 2 **Name That Toon**[16] 763 3-8-0 **49**....(v) NoelGarbutt(5) 5 2
(Derek Shaw) *prom: rdn along 1/2-way: sn drvn and wknd* **33/1**
3241 **U** **Rampers (IRE)**[18] 750 3-9-1 **64**.... LucyKBarry(5) 6
(Jamie Osborne) *s.s: rel to r and uns rdr s* **11/4**[3]
1m 0.65s (0.95) **Going Correction** +0.15s/f (Slow) **6** Ran SP% **112.0**
Speed ratings (Par 96): **98,93,82,76,73**
CSF £5.49 TOTE £2.90: £1.80, £1.90; EX 6.30 Trifecta £60.20.
Owner J C Fretwell **Bred** Mrs Fiona Denniff **Trained** Averham Park, Notts
FOCUS
A modest 3yo sprint handicap weakened further when the fancied Rampers was out of the race soon after the start. The first two raced up the centre and the winner bolted up.

963 DAILY UNIBET EARLY PRICES FROM 9AM H'CAP 6f (F)
5:50 (5:50) (Class 6) (0-60,66) 4-Y-O+ **£2,587** (£770; £384; £192) **Stalls** Low

Form RPR
4034 **1** **Sir Geoffrey (IRE)**[8] 869 10-9-2 **56**....(b) KieranO'Neill 8 65
(Scott Dixon) *qckly away and sn led: rdn clr 2f out: drvn and edgd lft to inner rail ins fnl f: kpt on wl towards fin* **10/1**
3-26 **2** 1 **Spitfire**[13] 799 11-9-6 **60**....(t) FrederikTylicki 7 66
(J R Jenkins) *trckd ldrs: hdwy 3f out: effrt 2f out: sn rdn: drvn to chse wnr ent fnl f: kpt on* **11/2**[3]
50-6 **3** 1 3/4 **Secret Look**[72] 36 6-9-6 **60**.... SeanLevey 5 61
(Ed McMahon) *trckd ldng pair: hdwy 3f out: sn chsng wnr: rdn wl over 1f out: drvn ent fnl f and kpt on same pce* **4/1**[2]
-441 **4** 3/4 **Harwoods Star (IRE)**[8] 869 6-9-12 66 6ex....(be) JFEgan 1 65
(John Butler) *dwlt and towards rr: effrt on inner wl over 2f out and sn rdn: drvn to chse ldrs over 1f out: kpt on* **1/1**[1]
5633 **5** 1 **Lucky Mark (IRE)**[8] 869 7-9-4 **58**....(p) DanielTudhope 6 54
(John Balding) *dwlt and towards rr: sme hdwy on outer over 2f out: sn rdn and no imp fnl f* **7/1**
0-40 **6** 4 **Captain Scooby**[8] 869 10-9-3 **57**....(v) JasonHart 3 41
(Richard Guest) *chsd wnr on inner: rdn along 3f out: sn wknd* **28/1**
1m 15.82s (-0.68) **Going Correction** -0.125s/f (Stan) **6** Ran SP% **110.4**
Speed ratings (Par 101): **99,97,95,94,93 87**
CSF £59.48 CT £244.52 TOTE £9.10: £3.10, £3.20; EX 64.10 Trifecta £382.60.
Owner General Sir Geoffrey Howlett **Bred** P Rabbitte **Trained** Babworth, Notts
FOCUS
A moderate handicap in which a 10yo beat an 11yo. Four of these met over C&D the previous week and the 1-3-4-7 from that race finished 4-5-1-6 here.
T/Plt: £106.50 to a £1 stake. Pool: £58,405.11. 400.21 winning tickets. T/Qpdt: £8.10 to a £1 stake. Pool: £6,367.15. 580.37 winning tickets. **Joe Rowntree**

898 CHELMSFORD (A.W) (L-H)
Thursday, March 17

OFFICIAL GOING: Polytrack: standard
Wind: virtually nil Weather: dry

964 TOTEPLACEPOT MASSIVE CHELTENHAM POOL TODAY H'CAP 1m (P)
5:50 (5:51) (Class 6) (0-60,60) 4-Y-O+ **£3,234** (£962; £481; £240) **Stalls** Low

Form RPR
123- **1** **Choral Clan (IRE)**[108] 8046 5-9-5 58.... JackMitchell 8 66
(Philip Mitchell) *off the pce in midfield: clsd 3f out: rdn to chse ldr over 1f out: led 1f out: kpt on and a doing enough fnl 100yds* **5/1**[3]
00-0 **2** 1/2 **Ellaal**[23] 683 7-9-4 57.... PaulMulrennan 1 64
(Ruth Carr) *led: rdn over 1f out: hdd 1f out: kpt on u.p but a hld fnl 100yds* **7/2**[2]
040- **3** 1/2 **Head Coach**[222] 5150 4-9-2 58....(p) DannyBrock(3) 6 64
(Jane Chapple-Hyam) *wl off the pce in last pair: rdn 1/2-way: wnt 3rd jst over 1f out: styd on wl ins fnl f: nvr quite getting to ldrs* **8/1**
-640 **4** 1 1/4 **Wild Flower (IRE)**[34] 547 4-8-11 50.... KieranO'Neill 3 53
(Jimmy Fox) *off the pce in midfield: clsd 3f and sn u.p: wnt 4th jst over 1f out: kpt on same pce ins fnl f* **14/1**
40-0 **5** 11 **Precast**[41] 456 4-9-0 60.... SophieKilloran(7) 5 36
(David Simcock) *wl off the pce in rr: rdn 3f out: no ch fnl 2f* **16/1**
635- **6** 3/4 **Valentine Mist (IRE)**[126] 7820 4-9-4 60.... DanielMuscutt(3) 4 34
(Seamus Mullins) *chsd ldng pair and clr of field: rdn over 3f out: lost pl u.p over 1f out: wknd fnl f* **16/1**
05-0 **7** 6 **Grandest**[73] 36 5-9-7 60.... BenCurtis 2 20
(Brian Ellison) *w ldr tl over 2f out: sn drvn and struggling: lost pl over 1f out: wknd and bhd fnl f* **1/1**[1]
1m 38.94s (-0.96) **Going Correction** -0.20s/f (Stan) **7** Ran SP% **118.4**
Speed ratings (Par 101): **96,95,95,93,82 82,76**
CSF £23.99 CT £140.17 TOTE £4.10: £1.70, £1.80; EX 23.00 Trifecta £126.20.
Owner Bob Harris & Patricia Mitchell **Bred** L Queally **Trained** Kingston Lisle, Oxfordshire
FOCUS
The top two in the market took each other on in front and this was rather set up for something to close from off the pace.

965 TOTEJACKPOT WIN BIG AT CHELTENHAM THIS WEEK H'CAP 1m (P)
6:20 (6:20) (Class 4) (0-85,84) 4-Y-O+ **£8,086** (£2,406; £1,202; £601) **Stalls** Low

Form RPR
32-3 **1** **Mystical Spirit (FR)**[36] 518 4-9-3 **80**.... PaulMulrennan 6 88
(Martyn Meade) *hld up wl in tch in midfield: effrt to chse ldr over 1f out: styd on wl fnl 100yds to ld towards fin* **9/4**[1]
5135 **2** nk **Loyalty**[7] 886 9-9-7 **84**....(v) TonyHamilton 5 91
(Derek Shaw) *chsd ldr tl rdn to ld over 1f out: edgd lft and u.p ins fnl f: hdd and no ex towards fin* **7/2**[2]
-321 **3** 2 1/2 **Franco's Secret**[21] 712 5-9-5 **82**....(v) CharlesBishop 2 83
(Peter Hedger) *stdd s: hld up in tch: effrt on inner wl over 1f out: chsd ldng pair jst ins fnl f: kpt on same pce after* **6/1**
30-2 **4** 1 1/2 **Smokethatthunders (IRE)**[14] 795 6-9-1 **78**.... PatCosgrave 8 76
(James Unett) *stdd s: hld up in tch: effrt jst over 2f out: kpt on ins fnl f but no threat to ldrs* **16/1**
1-12 **5** 3 1/4 **Slovak (IRE)**[27] 632 4-9-0 **77**.... AdamKirby 1 67
(James Tate) *led: rdn ent fnl 2f: hdd and drvn over 1f out: sn outpcd: wknd ins fnl f* **5/1**
-211 **6** 2 **Gracious George (IRE)**[14] 792 6-8-8 **71**.... KieranO'Neill 7 56
(Jimmy Fox) *stdd and dropped in bhd after s: sn niggled along and nvr really travelling in rr: rdn over 2f out: no imp and wl hld over 1f out* **12/1**
-211 **7** 5 **Dutch Garden**[14] 795 4-8-8 **78**....(v) AdamMcNamara(7) 3 51
(David Brown) *taken down early: t.k.h: chsd ldrs tl lost pl u.p over 2f out: bhd 1f out: fin lame* **9/2**[3]
1m 36.63s (-3.27) **Going Correction** -0.20s/f (Stan) **7** Ran SP% **115.7**
Speed ratings (Par 105): **108,107,105,103,100 98,93**
CSF £10.57 CT £40.73 TOTE £3.30: £1.70, £2.50; EX 11.10 Trifecta £42.50.
Owner McPeake Investments(NI) Ltd **Bred** Eric Becq **Trained** Newmarket, Suffolk
■ Stewards' Enquiry : Charles Bishop two-day ban: use of whip (31 Mar and 1 Apr)
FOCUS
They went an ordinary gallop in this fair handicap.

966 TOTETRIFECTA PICK THE WORLD HURDLE 1,2,3 H'CAP 5f (P)
6:50 (6:52) (Class 3) (0-95,94) 4-Y-O+ **£9,703** (£2,887; £1,443; £721) **Stalls** Low

Form RPR
1163 **1** **Bosham**[12] 835 6-9-0 **94**....(bt) NathanEvans(7) 6 104
(Michael Easterby) *mde all and sn clr: pushed along over 1f out: styd on wl: nvr seriously chal* **11/4**[1]
-361 **2** 1 1/2 **Brother Tiger**[39] 492 7-9-6 **93**.... JFEgan 7 98
(David C Griffiths) *disp 2nd bhd clr wnr: swtchd rt and rdn to chse wnr over 1f out: kpt on for clr 2nd but no imp on wnr* **5/1**[3]
6543 **3** 1 **Come On Dave (IRE)**[26] 655 7-8-7 **83**....(b) DanielMuscutt(3) 4 84
(John Butler) *dropped his hd as stalls opened and slowly away: t.k.h in last pair: hdwy into midfield over 1f out: styd on wl u.p ins fnl f: wnt 3rd last strides: nvr threatened wnr* **9/2**[2]
-315 **4** nk **Jebediah Shine**[49] 359 4-8-11 **89**.... JoshDoyle(5) 5 89
(David O'Meara) *disp 2nd bhd clr wnr tl over 1f out: styd on same pce u.p ins fnl f* **8/1**
3131 **5** 1/2 **Crosse Fire**[7] 894 4-9-4 **91** 6ex....(p) KieranO'Neill 2 90
(Scott Dixon) *in tch in midfield: effrt u.p over 1f out: styd on same pce ins fnl f* **8/1**
42-5 **6** 1/2 **Waseem Faris (IRE)**[51] 338 7-9-4 **91**.... RyanMoore 8 88
(Joseph Tuite) *in tch in midfield: effrt and sltly outpcd over 1f out: kpt on ins fnl f: no threat to wnr* **10/1**
0405 **7** hd **Dynamo Walt (IRE)**[12] 835 5-9-1 **88**....(v) TonyHamilton 3 84
(Derek Shaw) *in tch in midfield: rdn over 1f out: kpt on same pce and no imp ins fnl f* **5/1**[3]
5002 **8** 1 **Vimy Ridge**[26] 655 4-8-9 **82**....(p) SaleemGolam 10 74
(Alan Bailey) *dwlt: racd wd: in tch towards rr: effrt and shifting lft over 1f out: no imp ins fnl f* **12/1**
060- **9** 1 **Ticks The Boxes (IRE)**[169] 6861 4-8-10 **83**.... SilvestreDeSousa 11 72
(Michael Herrington) *sn outpcd and detached in last: sme hdwy u.p ins fnl f: n.d* **20/1**
58.33s (-1.87) **Going Correction** -0.20s/f (Stan) **9** Ran SP% **121.9**
Speed ratings (Par 107): **106,103,102,101,100 99,99,98,96**
CSF £17.67 CT £62.32 TOTE £3.80: £1.30, £2.90, £1.80; EX 19.90 Trifecta £101.50.
Owner Peter Easterby **Bred** Rabbah Bloodstock Limited **Trained** Sheriff Hutton, N Yorks
FOCUS
A good sprint handicap.

967 TOTEEXACTA THE EXTRA VALUE FESTIVAL FORECAST H'CAP 1m 2f (P)
7:20 (7:21) (Class 4) (0-85,83) 4-Y-O+ **£8,086** (£2,406; £1,202; £601) **Stalls** Low

Form RPR
452- **1** **Whoopsy Daisy**[187] 6324 4-8-8 **70**.... MartinDwyer 6 77+
(Jane Chapple-Hyam) *stdd s: hld up in tch in last pair: clsd and nt clr run over 1f out: swtchd lft and squeezed between horses ent fnl f: sn chalng and rdn to ld fnl 100yds out: r.o wl* **9/1**
0-56 **2** 1/2 **Lady Marl**[45] 422 5-9-7 **83**.... RyanMoore 4 89
(Gary Moore) *in tch in midfield: effrt over 1f out: drvn and chsd ldrs 1f out: kpt on wl u.p: snatched 2nd last stride* **8/1**

1104 **3** *hd* **Freud (FR)**[7] 888 6-9-3 **79** AdamKirby 3 85
(Ian Williams) *dwlt: sn rcvrd and chsd ldng pair: effrt and drvn to chal over 1f out: led ent fnl f: hdd and one pce fnl 100yds: lost 2nd last stride* **7/4**[1]

1124 **4** *2 1/4* **India's Song**[16] 774 6-8-13 **82** (t) SophieKilloran(7) 5 83
(David Simcock) *hld up in tch in midfield: rdn and hdwy on inner over 1f out: pressing ldrs u.p 1f out: no ex ins fnl f: wknd towards fin* **7/1**[3]

250- **5** *1* **Taper Tantrum (IRE)**[150] 7348 4-9-2 **81** LouisSteward(3) 2 80
(Michael Bell) *chsd ldr: rdn and ev ch 2f out: sn drvn: unable qck and lost pl: wknd ins fnl f* **9/4**[2]

5535 **6** *2* **Stosur (IRE)**[16] 774 5-9-0 **76** (b) SilvestreDeSousa 1 72
(Gay Kelleway) *t.k.h: led: rdn and hdd over 1f out: losing pl whn nudged lft ent fnl f: wknd fnl 150yds* **7/1**[3]

-424 **7** *2 1/2* **Bognor (USA)**[9] 866 5-9-4 **80** LiamJones 7 71
(Michael Appleby) *stdd s: hld up in tch in last pair: effrt over 2f out: drvn and no imp over 1f out: edgd lft and wknd 1f out* **16/1**

2m 5.31s (-3.29) **Going Correction** -0.20s/f (Stan) **7** Ran SP% **119.1**
Speed ratings (Par 105): **105,104,104,102,101 100,98**
CSF £80.10 TOTE £9.20: £4.20, £3.10; EX 106.40 Trifecta £266.70.
Owner Mrs Charles Cyzer **Bred** C A Cyzer **Trained** Dalham, Suffolk

FOCUS
They were well bunched a furlong out in this handicap, but the winner was always going best.

968 TOTEPOOLLIVEINFO.COM MAIDEN STKS 1m 2f (P)
7:50 (7:54) (Class 5) 3-Y-O+ **£5,175** (£1,540; £769; £384) **Stalls** Low

Form RPR

1 **Erhaaf (USA)** 4-10-0 0 RyanMoore 7 84+
(Owen Burrows) *niggled along early: in tch in midfield: effrt in 4th 2f out: swtchd rt over 1f out: hdwy ins fnl f: styd on strly fnl 100yds: led last stride* **4/1**[3]

022- **2** *shd* **Hepplewhite**[148] 7397 3-8-8 83 JackMitchell 8 80
(Robert Eddery) *chsd ldr tl rdn to ld over 1f out: 2 l clr ins fnl f: kpt on same pce u.p and hdd last stride* **13/8**[1]

3P-4 **3** *1 3/4* **Air Of Astana (IRE)**[29] 603 4-10-0 0 MartinHarley 3 81
(Hugo Palmer) *chsd ldrs: effrt in 3rd 2f out: kpt on u.p: chsd ldr briefly ins fnl f: 3rd and kpt on same pce wl ins fnl f* **10/1**

2-33 **4** *3 1/4* **Rivers Of Asia**[28] 618 3-8-8 78 (t) SilvestreDeSousa 5 71
(Philip McBride) *led: rdn over 2f out: hdd and unable qck u.p 1f out: lost 2nd ins fnl f: wknd qckly fnl 100yds* **10/1**

2 **5** *1 3/4* **Angelical Dancer (FR)**[29] 603 3-8-8 0 AndreaAtzeni 4 67
(Marco Botti) *in tch in midfield: 5th and struggling u.p 2f out: sn outpcd: wl hld and one pce fnl f* **9/4**[2]

6 *1* **Edge Of Reason** 3-8-5 0 ow2 [1] AntonioFresu 6 62
(Ed Walker) *s.i.s: clsd and in tch in midfield after 2f: rdn over 2f out: sn outpcd and hung lft over 1f out: swtchd lft and no imp ent fnl f* **33/1**

7 *2* **Alcanar (USA)** 3-8-8 0 WilliamCarson 2 61+
(Michael Bell) *s.i.s: off the pce in last pair: clsd on to rr of field 4f out: sn u.p and struggling: wl btn fnl 2f* **33/1**

8 *2* **Loose Ends** 3-7-10 0 SophieKilloran(7) 1 53
(David Simcock) *s.i.s: off the pce in last pair: clsd on to rr of field 4f out: sn rdn and struggling: wl btn over 2f out* **50/1**

2m 4.82s (-3.78) **Going Correction** -0.20s/f (Stan)
WFA 3 from 4yo 20lb **8** Ran SP% **114.9**
Speed ratings (Par 103): **107,106,105,102,101 100,99,97**
CSF £10.87 TOTE £4.80: £1.50, £1.20, £2.10; EX 14.70 Trifecta £73.80.
Owner Hamdan Al Maktoum **Bred** Shadwell Estate Co Ltd **Trained** Lambourn, Berks
■ A first training success for Owen Burrows, who has taken over the licence from Barry Hills.

FOCUS
A fair maiden and sound form.

969 COLLECT TOTEPOOL WINNINGS AT BETFRED SHOPS FILLIES' H'CAP 6f (P)
8:20 (8:20) (Class 5) (0-75,74) 4-Y-O+ **£5,175** (£1,154; £1,154; £384) **Stalls** Centre

Form RPR

1642 **1** **Invade (IRE)**[21] 713 4-8-12 **65** (t) AndreaAtzeni 1 71
(Stuart Williams) *chsd ldrs: effrt u.p over 1f out: ev ch 1f out: r.o wl to ld wl ins fnl f* **4/1**[2]

6225 **2** *nk* **Saved My Bacon (IRE)**[6] 903 5-9-4 **71** SilvestreDeSousa 4 76
(Chris Dwyer) *taken down early: chsd ldrs: effrt to chal over 1f out: drvn 1f out: kpt on: unable qck wl ins fnl f* **9/4**[1]

40-0 **2** *dht* **Penny Dreadful**[6] 901 4-9-6 **73** (p) KieranO'Neill 2 78
(Scott Dixon) *led: rdn over 1f out: kpt on wl u.p: hdd and one pce wl ins fnl f* **7/1**

1124 **4** *1 1/4* **Camdora (IRE)**[10] 859 4-8-8 **61** WilliamCarson 6 62+
(Jamie Osborne) *rrd as stalls opened: swtchd lft and t.k.h in rr: rdn over 2f out: hdwy u.p 1f out: kpt on u.p: nvr quite getting to ldrs* **9/2**[3]

4-05 **5** *1/2* **Fever Few**[21] 703 7-9-5 **72** MartinHarley 7 71+
(Chris Wall) *awkward leaving stalls: hld up in tch: effrt over 1f out: edgd lft u.p 1f out: styd on same pce ins fnl f* **9/2**[3]

00-1 **6** *1* **Heartsong (IRE)**[21] 713 7-9-0 **72** PatrickO'Donnell(5) 5 68+
(John Gallagher) *stdd s: hld up in tch in rr: effrt over 1f out: kpt on u.p ins fnl f: nvr enough pce to rch ldrs* **12/1**

3-40 **7** *2 1/4* **Alhella**[50] 349 4-9-7 **74** PatCosgrave 3 63
(Mick Quinn) *midfield: effrt and unable qck over 1f out: wknd ins fnl f* **16/1**

1m 12.06s (-1.64) **Going Correction** -0.20s/f (Stan) **7** Ran SP% **113.2**
Speed ratings (Par 100): **102,101,101,99,99 97,94**
PL: 1.60 Penny Dreadful, 0.80 Saved My Bacon, 2.00 Invade; EX: 14.80, 8.50; CSF: 15.39, 6.58; TC: ; TF: 73.90, 42.20; TOTE £5.40.
Owner Happy Valley Racing & Breeding Limited **Bred** Ballylinch Stud **Trained** Newmarket, Suffolk

FOCUS
They went quite steady early on and the pace held up.

970 SIMPLY RED HERE ON 1ST JULY H'CAP 5f (P)
8:50 (8:50) (Class 6) (0-55,54) 3-Y-O+ **£3,234** (£962; £481; £240) **Stalls** Low

Form RPR

5142 **1** **Kuanyao (IRE)**[12] 837 10-8-12 **50** (be) AnnStokell(5) 2 57
(Ann Stokell) *led for 1f: chsd ldr tl rdn to ld over 1f out: styd on wl: rdn out* **9/2**[2]

5335 **2** *1* **Fearbuster (IRE)**[13] 820 3-8-9 **54** JackMitchell 6 52
(Hugo Palmer) *dwlt: hld up in tch in last trio: hdwy over 1f out: styd on wl u.p ins fnl f: wnt 2nd towards fin: nvr getting to wnr* **5/2**[1]

-615 **3** *1/2* **Red Flute**[36] 513 4-8-13 **49** (v) TimClark(3) 5 51
(Denis Quinn) *chsd ldrs tl stdd and swtchd lft after 100yds: in tch in midfield: effrt u.p over 1f out: ev ch ins fnl f: styd on same pce fnl 100yds: lost 2nd towards fin* **9/2**[2]

140 **4** *nse* **Yisty**[27] 635 3-7-12 **48** (v) NoelGarbutt(5) 4 44
(Derek Shaw) *chsd ldrs: rdn over 1f out: drvn and unable over 1f out: styd on same pce ins fnl f* **14/1**

0645 **5** *3/4* **Glenbuck Lass (IRE)**[30] 596 4-8-12 **45** [1] SaleemGolam 9 44
(Alan Bailey) *in tch in midfield: effrt u.p over 1f out: no imp tl styd on fnl 100yds: no threat to ldrs* **12/1**

06-4 **6** *1/2* **Frank Sandatra**[19] 750 3-8-6 **51** KieranO'Neill 1 43
(Peter Crate) *chsd ldr tl led after 1f: rdn and hdd over 1f out: no ex ins fnl f: wknd towards fin* **6/1**

-000 **7** *nk* **Blackasyourhat (IRE)**[12] 837 4-8-13 **46** (t) KierenFox 8 42
(Michael Attwater) *in tch in midfield: effrt and n.m.r over 1f out: kpt on u.p ins fnl f: nvr enough pce to rch ldrs* **9/1**

0-06 **8** *nk* **Barnsdale**[8] 883 3-7-7 **45** MeganEllingworth(7) 3 35
(John Holt) *in tch in rr: effrt over 1f out: kpt on ins fnl f: no threat to ldrs* **33/1**

4264 **9** *1 1/2* **Seraphima**[5] 919 6-8-7 **45** (p) JosephineGordon(5) 7 34
(Lisa Williamson) *taken down early: dwlt: in tch in last trio: effrt over 1f out: no imp u.p 1f out: nvr trbld ldrs* **5/1**[3]

1m 0.17s (-0.03) **Going Correction** -0.20s/f (Stan)
WFA 3 from 4yo+ 12lb **9** Ran SP% **123.2**
Speed ratings (Par 101): **92,90,89,89,88 87,87,86,84**
CSF £17.40 CT £56.37 TOTE £4.80: £1.10, £2.00, £2.60; EX 22.00 Trifecta £87.60.
Owner Geoff Pacey **Bred** Newlands House Stud **Trained** Lincoln, Lincolnshire

FOCUS
A moderate affair.
T/Plt: £133.50 to a £1 stake. Pool: £91,672.97 - 501.18 winning tickets. T/Qpdt: £26.30 to a £1 stake. Pool: £10,969.07 - 307.72 winning tickets. **Stev E Payne**

971 - (Foreign Racing) - See Raceform Interactive

[897]CHANTILLY (R-H)
Thursday, March 17

OFFICIAL GOING: Polytrack: standard

972a PRIX MONTENICA (LISTED RACE) (3YO COLTS & GELDINGS) (POLYTRACK) 6f 110y
2:25 (12:00) 3-Y-O **£20,220** (£8,088; £6,066; £4,044; £2,022)

RPR

1 **Toliman**[22] 3-9-2 0 (p) Pierre-CharlesBoudot 3 102
(G Botti, France) **59/10**[2]

2 *hd* **Hurricane (FR)**[32] 584 3-9-2 0 ChristopheSoumillon 6 101
(J-C Rouget, France) **30/100**[1]

3 *2 1/2* **Bear Faced**[13] 828 3-9-2 0 LukeMorris 2 94
(Sir Mark Prescott Bt) *led: rdn 2f out: hdd and dropped to 3rd fnl f: no ex* **121/10**

4 *3/4* **Post Var (FR)**[114] 7970 3-9-2 0 TheoBachelot 1 92
(S Wattel, France) **92/10**

5 *nk* **Dhevanafushi**[97] 8188 3-9-2 0 FabriceVeron 5 91
(H-A Pantall, France) **83/10**[3]

6 *4 1/2* **See Your Starr (FR)**[13] 3-9-2 0 SebastienMaillot 4 78
(Y Gourraud, France) **25/1**

Owner Robert Ng **Bred** Ecurie Peregrine SAS **Trained** France
WIN (incl. 1 euro stake): 6.90. PLACES: 1.30, 1.10. SF: 16.00

973a- (Foreign Racing) - See Raceform Interactive

[877]LINGFIELD (L-H)
Friday, March 18

OFFICIAL GOING: Polytrack: standard
Wind: Light; half against Weather: Overcast

974 DAILY UNIBET EARLY PRICES FROM 9AM CLAIMING STKS 6f 1y(P)
1:15 (1:15) (Class 6) 4-Y-O+ **£2,264** (£673; £336; £168) **Stalls** Low

Form RPR

1503 **1** **Doctor Parkes**[7] 901 10-9-5 79 AaronJones(5) 3 87
(Stuart Williams) *broke wl: sn stdd bk to trck ldng pair: effrt to chse ldr 1f out: qcknd to ld ins fnl f: sn in command: readily* **7/4**[2]

-442 **2** *2 1/2* **Ballista (IRE)**[9] 878 8-9-7 85 AnnaHesketh(5) 2 81
(Tom Dascombe) *chsd ldr tl led on inner 2f out: rdn over 1f out: hdd ins fnl f: sn outpcd and btn* **5/4**[1]

4010 **3** *1 1/2* **Moonlight Venture**[24] 683 5-9-6 77 (b) LiamKeniry 1 70
(Conor Dore) *dropped to rr and rdn over 4f out: detached and drvn 1/2-way: hdwy 1f out: wnt 3rd ins fnl f: styd on wl fnl 100yds: no threat to wnr* **4/1**[3]

0605 **4** *3 1/4* **Mighty Zip (USA)**[9] 879 4-9-5 75 (p) PhilDennis(7) 6 66
(Kevin Ryan) *taken down early: sn bustled up to ld: rdn and hdd 2f out: 3rd and btn 1f out: wknd ins fnl f* **16/1**

0/0- **5** *2 1/2* **Misleading**[310] 2193 4-8-11 81 CallumShepherd(5) 5 48
(Lee Carter) *in tch in 4th: rdn over 2f out: outpcd and btn wl over 1f out: sn wknd and bhd ins fnl f* **14/1**

1m 11.66s (-0.24) **Going Correction** -0.075s/f (Stan) **5** Ran SP% **113.4**
Speed ratings (Par 101): **98,94,92,88,85**
CSF £4.49 TOTE £2.80: £1.10, £1.40; EX 4.30 Trifecta £11.80.Ballista was the subject of a friendly claim, £10,000.
Owner The Doctor Parkes Partnership **Bred** Joseph Heler **Trained** Newmarket, Suffolk

FOCUS
An ordinary claimer and the two market leaders dominated.

975 CORAL H'CAP 1m 4f (P)
1:45 (1:45) (Class 3) (0-95,90) 4-Y-O **£7,246** (£2,168; £1,084; £542; £270) **Stalls** Low

Form RPR

313- **1** **Silver Quay (IRE)**[100] 8159 4-9-2 **85** KieranO'Neill 5 98+
(Richard Hannon) *stdd s: hld up in rr: clsd 4f out: rdn and hdwy to chse ldrs and carried rt bnd 2f out: led over 1f out: wnt lft but drew wl clr ins fnl f: easily* **7/2**[2]

1612 **2** *5* **Royal Marskell**[20] 747 7-9-9 **90** JimCrowley 4 95
(Gay Kelleway) *bustled along early: chsd ldrs: wnt 2nd over 2f out and pressing ldr whn carried rt bnd 2f out: chsd clr wnr and styd on same pce fnl f* **9/2**[3]

520- **3** *1 1/4* **Le Rock (IRE)**[122] 7885 4-8-5 **74** LiamJones 6 77
(J S Moore) *chsd ldr tl pushed along to ld 3f out: rdn and drifted rt bnd 2f out: hdd over 1f out: no ch w wnr and styd on same pce fnl f* **20/1**

4/32 **4** *1/2* **Music Man (IRE)**[16] 779 6-8-13 **80** SeanLevey 7 82
(Jo Crowley) *hld up in midfield: clsd 4f out: chsd ldrs 2f out: drvn and unable qck over 1f out: no ch w wnr and styd on same pce fnl f* **7/4**[1]

26-0 **5** 1 ¼ **Brandon Castle**[52] 337 4-8-13 **82**................................ DavidProbert 1 82
(Andrew Balding) *t.k.h: hld up in last: clsd 4f out: n.m.r briefly jst over 2f out: no ch w wnr and one pce fnl f* **8/1**

5053 **6** 3 **Masterpaver**[11] 861 5-9-7 **88**......................................(v) FrannyNorton 2 83
(Alan Bailey) *dwlt and rdn along early: sn in midfield: clsd 4f out: lost pl and rdn over 2f out: no ch 1f out* **7/1**

-012 **7** 14 **Spes Nostra**[11] 861 8-9-7 **88**..(b) TomEaves 3 61
(Iain Jardine) *led tl hdd and rdn 3f out: sn lost pl and wl bhd 1f out* **10/1**

2m 29.87s (-3.13) **Going Correction** -0.075s/f (Stan)
WFA 4 from 5yo+ 2lb **7** Ran SP% **114.2**
Speed ratings (Par 107): **107,103,102,102,101 99,90**
CSF £19.50 TOTE £3.60: £1.50, £2.20; EX 17.10 Trifecta £193.40.
Owner H Robin Heffer **Bred** Michael Joyce **Trained** East Everleigh, Wilts

FOCUS
A decent handicap. The early pace was strong with the two leaders going clear, but their riders realised they may have gone too far ahead and steadied things passing the 7f pole. The pace didn't increase again until approaching the home bend.

976 32RED CASINO MAIDEN STKS 1m 1y(P)
2:25 (2:26) (Class 5) 3-Y-O **£2,911** (£866; £432; £216) **Stalls** High

Form RPR

2 **1** **Abareeq**[17] 770 3-9-5 0.. JoeFanning 3 85+
(Mark Johnston) *mde all: rdn and qcknd over 1f out: sn clr and r.o strly: easily* **1/1**[1]

2 6 **Mishwaar** 3-9-5 0.. DarryllHolland 1 68+
(Charles Hills) *dwlt: sn rcvrd and t.k.h in 4th: pushed along and wnt 3rd 2f out: outpcd and no ch w wnr over 1f out: wnt 2nd and kpt on same pce ins fnl f* **7/2**[3]

04- **3** shd **School Fete (IRE)**[154] 7246 3-9-5 0.............................. WilliamCarson 5 68
(Michael Bell) *dwlt: t.k.h in 5th: pushed along over 1f out: no ch w wnr but kpt on ins fnl f and almost snatched 2nd* **16/1**

02- **4** ¾ **Best Of Oregon (USA)**[193] 6164 3-9-5 0......................(t) GeorgeBaker 4 66
(Ed Walker) *chsd wnr: rdn over 1f out: immediately outpcd and hung lft: wl btn 1f out: lost 2 pls ins fnl f* **9/4**[2]

0-5 **5** 3 ½ **Mulled Wine**[48] 400 3-9-5 0... KierenFox 6 58
(John Best) *sn dropped to rr: pushed along over 1f out: no imp: n.d* **50/1**

50- **6** 13 **Shipshape Myfoot**[156] 7212 3-9-0 0.................................. JFEgan 2 22
(Andrew Reid) *chsd ldrs: rdn and lost pl over 2f out: dropping out whn hmpd bnd wl over 1f out: sn bhd* **100/1**

1m 37.33s (-0.87) **Going Correction** -0.075s/f (Stan) **6** Ran SP% **111.8**
Speed ratings (Par 98): **101,95,94,94,90 77**
CSF £4.92 TOTE £1.90: £1.10, £2.50; EX 5.90 Trifecta £24.50.
Owner Hamdan Al Maktoum **Bred** Shadwell Estate Company Limited **Trained** Middleham Moor, N Yorks

FOCUS
An uncompetitive maiden and one-way traffic.

977 32RED.COM FILLIES' H'CAP 1m 1y(P)
3:05 (3:05) (Class 5) (0-70,68) 4-Y-O+ **£2,911** (£866; £432; £216) **Stalls** High

Form RPR

62-1 **1** **Esteemable**[22] 710 4-9-4 **68**.................................... DanielMuscutt(3) 4 80+
(James Fanshawe) *broke wl and led briefly: sn stdd bk and trckd ldrs: wnt 2nd over 3f out: pushed along to ld over 1f out: r.o wl: comf* **5/6**[1]

2-23 **2** 2 **Clary (IRE)**[54] 324 6-9-4 **65**... PatCosgrave 1 71
(James Unett) *sn led: hdd over 5f out: chsd ldr tl over 3f out: effrt on inner wl over 1f out: chsd wnr jst ins fnl f: r.o same pce: eased towards fin* **7/2**[2]

-413 **3** 1 ¼ **Tommys Geal**[16] 777 4-8-13 **60**...................................... AndreaAtzeni 6 63
(Michael Madgwick) *chsd ldr after 1f tl led over 5f out: rdn ent fnl 2f: hdd over 1f out: 3rd and styd on same pce ins fnl f* **6/1**[3]

6064 **4** ½ **Venus Grace**[14] 813 5-8-9 **56**....................................... AndrewMullen 2 58
(Michael Appleby) *hld up in tch: effrt jst over 2f out: kpt on same pce ins fnl f* **10/1**

3022 **5** 1 **Ixelles Diamond (IRE)**[14] 813 5-9-4 **68**........................ DannyBrock(3) 3 68
(Andrew Reid) *t.k.h: hld up in tch: effrt jst over 2f out: drvn and styd on same pce fr over 1f out* **12/1**

0420 **6** 4 ½ **Ajig**[16] 777 5-9-4 **65**..(tp) JohnFahy 5 54
(Eve Johnson Houghton) *stdd bk to rr sn after s: hld up in rr: rdn and outpcd over 2f out: wl btn over 1f out* **16/1**

1m 39.37s (1.17) **Going Correction** -0.075s/f (Stan) **6** Ran SP% **113.7**
Speed ratings (Par 100): **91,89,87,87,86 81**
CSF £4.11 TOTE £2.00: £1.30, £2.30; EX 4.00 Trifecta £12.10.
Owner Mrs C R Philipson **Bred** Mrs M L Parry & P M Steele-Mortimer **Trained** Newmarket, Suffolk

FOCUS
A modest fillies' handicap. The market only wanted to know about one horse and she didn't disappoint.

978 32REDSPORT.COM H'CAP (DIV I) 7f 1y(P)
3:45 (3:48) (Class 5) (0-70,69) 3-Y-O **£2,911** (£866; £432; £216) **Stalls** Low

Form RPR

5-22 **1** **Ruby Wednesday**[22] 706 3-9-5 **67**................................... KierenFox 8 71+
(John Best) *stdd s: hld up in rr: nt clr run over 2f out: swtchd rt and hdwy over 1f out: str run u.p ins fnl f to ld towards fin* **4/1**[2]

-322 **2** ½ **Silver Springs (IRE)**[30] 610 3-9-5 **67**.......................... PatCosgrave 5 69
(David Evans) *bmpd s: chsd ldr: rdn and ev ch 2f out: led 1f out: forged ahd ins fnl f: hdd and no ex towards fin* **4/1**[2]

61-3 **3** ¾ **Ginger Joe**[14] 817 3-9-5 **67**...................................... RichardKingscote 4 67
(David Brown) *bmpd s: sn led: rdn 2f out: hdd 1f out: stl ev ch tl no ex fnl 50yds* **11/2**[3]

630- **4** nse **Zabdi**[106] 8090 3-9-7 **69**... SeanLevey 2 69
(Richard Hannon) *chsd ldrs: effrt over 1f out: drvn 1f out: kpt on wl ins fnl f* **7/2**[1]

-021 **5** 1 ½ **Mossy's Lodge**[30] 611 3-9-3 **65**.................................... WilliamCarson 6 61
(Anthony Carson) *in tch in midfield: effrt on inner over 1f out: styd on same pce ins fnl f* **7/1**

-401 **6** nse **Sunbaked (IRE)**[16] 785 3-9-1 **63**..............................(p) RobertWinston 7 59
(Eve Johnson Houghton) *s.i.s: hld up in last pair: effrt on outer ent fnl 2f: kpt on ins fnl f: nvr threatened ldrs* **7/1**

6435 **7** ½ **Khismet**[14] 817 3-9-7 **69**...(p) JimCrowley 10 63
(Rae Guest) *hld up in tch in midfield: effrt over 1f out: pushed along and styd on same pce ins fnl f* **10/1**

000- **8** 14 **No Body's Fool**[122] 7877 3-8-7 **55** oh10............................ KieranO'Neill 3 12
(Michael Madgwick) *in tch in midfield: rdn and lost pl over 1f out: bhd and wknd 1f out* **100/1**

1m 25.17s (0.37) **Going Correction** -0.075s/f (Stan) **8** Ran SP% **112.7**
Speed ratings (Par 98): **94,93,92,92,90 90,90,74**
CSF £19.75 CT £86.19 TOTE £4.20: £1.50, £1.20, £2.10; EX 12.80 Trifecta £59.20.
Owner Harris, Beckett & Millen **Bred** Best Breeding **Trained** Oad Street, Kent

■ Tamara Love was withdrawn. Price at time of withdrawal 16-1. Rule 4 does not apply.

FOCUS
The first division of an ordinary 3yo handicap.

979 32REDSPORT.COM H'CAP (DIV II) 7f 1y(P)
4:25 (4:26) (Class 5) (0-70,69) 3-Y-O **£2,911** (£866; £432; £216) **Stalls** Low

Form RPR

051- **1** **North Creek**[78] 8409 3-9-6 **68**...................................... TedDurcan 2 81+
(Chris Wall) *hld up in midfield: clsd to chse ldrs 2f out: rdn and qcknd to ld jst over 1f out: r.o strly: eased towards fin: easily* **11/8**[1]

040- **2** 3 ¼ **Mithqaal (USA)**[135] 7701 3-9-3 **65**................................. PatCosgrave 8 67
(Owen Burrows) *dwlt: hld up in tch in last trio: clsd over 1f out: swtchd rt and hdwy over 1f out: chsd clr wnr ins fnl f: kpt on but no ch w wnr* **9/2**[2]

4-10 **3** hd **World's Greatest (USA)**[25] 678 3-9-4 **66**..................... AndreaAtzeni 5 69
(Stuart Williams) *s.i.s: swtchd lft after s: hld up in last trio: hdwy on inner and nt clr run over 1f out: swtchd rt 1f out: battling for 2nd and kpt on ins fnl f: no ch w wnr* **9/2**[2]

2323 **4** 3 ¼ **Guapo Bay**[22] 711 3-8-0 **55**.......................................(p) TinaSmith(7) 3 49
(Richard Hannon) *chsd ldr: rdn ent fnl 2f: led over 1f out: sn hdd and outpcd: lost 2nd and wknd ins fnl f* **20/1**

0-50 **5** 1 **Red Ruffian (IRE)**[56] 291 3-9-0 **62**............................. RobertWinston 1 53
(Dean Ivory) *in tch in midfield: effrt jst over 2f out: outpcd over 1f out: wl hld and plugged on same pce fnl f* **14/1**

-601 **6** 2 **Evening Starlight**[22] 711 3-9-1 **63**............................. RichardKingscote 9 49
(Ron Hodges) *chsd ldr: effrt in cl 3rd ent fnl 2f: no ex and btn jst over 1f out: wknd ins fnl f* **5/1**[3]

66-0 **7** nk **Ron's Ballad**[30] 610 3-8-7 **55** oh10................................ KieranO'Neill 4 41
(Michael Madgwick) *midfield tl dropped to last trio 5f out: rdn over 2f out: no hdwy and wl hld over 1f out* **66/1**

3424 **8** ½ **Zebedee's Girl (IRE)**[11] 858 3-9-1 **63**......................... DavidProbert 7 47
(David Evans) *a in rr: rdn 4f out: drvn and no imp over 1f out: swtchd rt and kpt on same pce ins fnl f* **14/1**

0-60 **9** 7 **Silver Wings (IRE)**[37] 515 3-9-0 **69**.......................(p) RhiainIngram(7) 6 36
(Roger Ingram) *led: rdn ent fnl 2f: hdd over 1f out: sn btn: fdd ins fnl f* **33/1**

1m 24.21s (-0.59) **Going Correction** -0.075s/f (Stan) **9** Ran SP% **117.7**
Speed ratings (Par 98): **100,96,96,92,91 88,88,88,80**
CSF £7.77 CT £22.57 TOTE £1.90: £1.10, £3.00, £1.50; EX 9.30 Trifecta £34.60.
Owner Sheikh Rashid Dalmook Al Maktoum **Bred** Alexis Chetioui **Trained** Newmarket, Suffolk

FOCUS
No hanging about here which suited those coming from off the pace. The winning time was nearly a second quicker than the first division.

980 £10 FREE AT 32RED.COM MAIDEN STKS 1m 4f (P)
5:05 (5:06) (Class 5) 3-Y-O **£2,911** (£866; £432; £216) **Stalls** Low

Form RPR

52 **1** **Shoofly (IRE)**[9] 880 3-9-0 0... DavidProbert 4 77
(Martyn Meade) *chsd ldr tl led jst over 2f out: rdn wl over 1f out: kpt on and a doing enough fnl f: rdn out* **11/8**[1]

2 1 ½ **Harbour Law** 3-9-5 0.. SeanLevey 2 80
(Jo Crowley) *hld up in 4th: rdn 4f out: clsd to chse ldrs 3f out: chsd wnr wl over 1f out: kpt on but hung lft and a hld fnl f* **20/1**

52 **3** 20 **The New Master**[20] 746 3-9-5 0..................................... TomQueally 3 48
(David Elsworth) *stdd s: hld up in 5th: clsd over 5f out: wnt 2nd jst over 2f out: wd bnd and lost pl 2f out: sn btn: wknd over 1f out* **11/4**[2]

52-3 **4** 1 **Templier (IRE)**[9] 880 3-9-5 79...................................(b[1]) JoeFanning 6 46
(Mark Johnston) *racd keenly: led tl rdn and hdd over 2f out: lost pl 2f out: wl btn and hung lft over 1f out: wknd* **3/1**[3]

0-2 **5** 18 **My Isla**[24] 687 3-9-0 0.. AndreaAtzeni 1 12
(James Tate) *chsd ldng pair: rdn 4f out: lost pl over 2f out: sn wknd and wl btn over 1f out: t.o* **7/1**

0 **P** **Super Seer**[25] 675 3-9-5 0... GeorgeBaker 5
(Philip Hide) *s.i.s: nvr on terms: detached last after 2f: t.o whn p.u and dismntd over 2f out* **40/1**

2m 32.0s (-1.00) **Going Correction** -0.075s/f (Stan) **6** Ran SP% **113.5**
Speed ratings (Par 98): **100,99,85,85,73**
CSF £30.14 TOTE £2.20: £1.30, £6.00; EX 22.00 Trifecta £62.60.
Owner Richard Barnes **Bred** M Al-Qatami & K M Al-Mudhaf **Trained** Newmarket, Suffolk

FOCUS
A modest 3yo maiden and the front pair pulled miles clear. The pace was fair.
T/Plt: £9.50 to a £1 stake. Pool: £55,662.87 - 4,262.33 winning units T/Qpdt: £2.90 to a £1 stake. Pool: £3,777.74 - 945.59 winning units **Steve Payne**

942 WOLVERHAMPTON (A.W) (L-H)
Friday, March 18

OFFICIAL GOING: Tapeta: standard
Wind: Light; against Weather: Overcast

981 CORAL CONNECT H'CAP 1m 4f 50y (Tp)
6:10 (6:10) (Class 7) (0-50,50) 4-Y-O+ **£2,587** (£770; £384; £192) **Stalls** Low

Form RPR

4253 **1** **Happy Jack (IRE)**[22] 702 5-9-5 **49**................................(b) AdamKirby 4 55
(Michael Wigham) *a.p: nt clr run over 1f out: rdn to ld and hung lft wl ins fnl f: r.o* **4/1**[2]

4-51 **2** nk **Storytale**[25] 674 4-9-4 **50**.....................................(p) CharlesBishop 9 56
(Dave Roberts) *hld up: hdwy over 2f out: rdn and ev ch ins fnl f: r.o* **5/2**[1]

0435 **3** ¾ **Delagoa Bay (IRE)**[23] 695 8-8-9 **46**........................... BenSanderson(7) 5 50
(Sylvester Kirk) *hld up: hdwy over 3f out: rdn over 2f out: hung lft ins fnl f: r.o to go 3rd nr fin* **16/1**

-630 **4** 1 **Little Choosey**[37] 514 6-9-1 **48**........................(tp) AlistairRawlinson(3) 2 51
(Roy Bowring) *led 1f: chsd ldrs: rdn to ld over 1f out: hdd wl ins fnl f: styd on same pce* **18/1**

1-33 **5** ½ **Mrs Burbidge**[51] 348 6-9-5 **49**.................................(tp) LiamKeniry 12 53
(Neil Mulholland) *chsd ldr after 1f tl led 5f out: rdn and hdd over 1f out: styng on same pce whn hmpd wl ins fnl f* **9/2**[3]

2000 **6** 2 ¼ **Little Flo**[15] 796 5-9-6 **50**.. BenCurtis 6 48
(William Stone) *hld up: hdwy over 1f out: rdr dropped whip sn after: nt clr run and swtchd rt ent fnl f: r.o* **14/1**

06-3 **7** 1 ¼ **Goldmadchen (GER)**[25] 673 8-9-6 **50**............................ TomEaves 7 46
(James Given) *mid-div: hdwy over 5f out: ev ch over 2f out: sn rdn: wknd ins fnl f* **16/1**

-050 **8** 3 **Teide Peak (IRE)**[25] 674 7-9-5 **49**............................(tp) MartinDwyer 3 41
(Grace Harris) *hld up: hdwy u.p over 1f out: wknd ins fnl f* **16/1**

/00- 9 shd **Racing Spirit**[250] 2591 4-9-2 **48** .... RyanPowell 10 39
(Kevin Frost) *s.i.s: sn pushed along in rr: rdn over 1f out: wknd fnl f* **14/1**

3343 10 4 1/2 **Music Hall (FR)**[14] 822 6-9-3 **47** .... DougieCostello 8 31
(Shaun Harris) *trckd ldrs: plld hrd: chsd ldr 4f out: ev ch over 2f out: sn rdn: wknd fnl f* **9/1**

4/06 11 4 1/2 **Witch From Rome**[25] 673 5-8-9 **46** .... GeorgiaCox(7) 1 23
(Nick Lampard) *mid-div: rdn and lost pl over 4f out: wknd 3f out* **28/1**

00-0 12 45 **Strictly Glitz (IRE)**[14] 822 5-9-5 **49** .... (v1) CathyGannon 11
(Clare Ellam) *led after 1f: hdd 5f out: rdn and wknd over 3f out* **80/1**

2m 37.61s (-3.19) **Going Correction** -0.125s/f (Stan)
WFA 4 from 5yo+ 2lb 12 Ran SP% **117.7**
Speed ratings (Par 97): **105,104,104,103,103 101,100,98,98,95 92,62**
CSF £14.21 CT £144.95 TOTE £5.00: £2.40, £2.00, £4.80; EX 16.50 Trifecta £175.00.
Owner G D J Linder **Bred** Rangefield Bloodstock Ltd **Trained** Newmarket, Suffolk

FOCUS
A moderate handicap and straightforward form.

982 BET IN PLAY AT CORAL H'CAP 1m 1f 103y (Tp)
6:40 (6:40) (Class 6) (0-60,60) 4-Y-O+ £2,587 (£770; £384; £192) **Stalls** Low

Form RPR

-413 1 **La Havrese (FR)**[18] 769 5-9-2 **60** .... JoshDoyle(5) 6 67
(Lynn Siddall) *a.p: chsd ldr over 1f out: rdn to ld wl ins fnl f* **5/2**1

1452 2 nk **Cartographic (USA)**[21] 724 4-9-5 **58** .... AdamKirby 9 64
(David Evans) *mid-div: hdwy over 2f out: rdn over 1f out: hung lft ins fnl f: r.o* **7/2**2

0-64 3 1 1/2 **The Dukkerer (IRE)**[7] 898 5-9-7 **60** .... TomEaves 8 64
(James Given) *chsd ldrs: wnt 2nd over 6f out: rdn to ld over 1f out: hdd and no ex wl ins fnl f* **16/1**

26-4 4 3/4 **Ted's Brother (IRE)**[24] 682 8-9-6 **59** .... (e) JasonHart 2 61
(Richard Guest) *hld up: rdn over 2f out: r.o ins fnl f: nt rch ldrs* **12/1**

5112 5 3/4 **On A Whim**[14] 822 4-9-4 **57** .... StevieDonohoe 11 58
(Daniel Mark Loughnane) *chsd ldrs: rdn over 2f out: styd on same pce ins fnl f* **8/1**3

0-62 6 1 **Lynngale**[53] 334 5-9-4 **57** .... ShaneGray 4 56
(Kristin Stubbs) *chsd ldr 3f: remained handy: rdn and nt clr run over 1f out: no ex ins fnl f* **14/1**

-650 7 1/2 **Ali Bin Nayef**[18] 769 4-9-0 **53** .... RobertHavlin 3 51
(Michael Wigham) *hld up: rdn over 1f out: nt clr run ins fnl f: nt trble ldrs* **33/1**

4241 8 1 1/2 **Ferryview Place**[14] 822 7-8-11 **53** .... (p) GeorgeDowning(3) 1 48
(Ian Williams) *hld up: rdn over 1f out: hmpd ins fnl f: n.d* **9/1**

5023 9 1 1/4 **Debit**[23] 701 5-9-3 **59** .... RobHornby(3) 7 52
(Simon Hodgson) *hld up: rdn over 3f out: effrt on outer over 2f out: nvr trbld ldrs* **16/1**

2314 10 1/2 **Celtic Artisan (IRE)**[22] 702 5-9-2 **55** .... (b) OisinMurphy 5 47
(Rebecca Menzies) *led: rdn over 2f out: hdd over 1f out: wknd ins fnl f* **8/1**3

-600 11 6 **Ifan (IRE)**[18] 766 8-9-7 **60** .... DougieCostello 10 40
(Tim Vaughan) *mid-div: hdwy over 4f out: wknd 2f out* **25/1**

1m 59.63s (-1.17) **Going Correction** -0.125s/f (Stan) 11 Ran SP% **115.9**
Speed ratings (Par 101): **100,99,98,97,97 96,95,94,93,92 87**
CSF £10.58 CT £113.32 TOTE £3.50: £1.70, £1.50, £4.40; EX 13.80 Trifecta £97.80.
Owner Jimmy Kay **Bred** S C A Elevage De La Croix De Place **Trained** Colton, N Yorks

FOCUS
The two at the head of the market came to the fore here. Straightforward form.

983 32RED.COM H'CAP 2m 119y (Tp)
7:10 (7:14) (Class 4) (0-85,84) 4-Y-O+ £5,498 (£1,636; £817; £408) **Stalls** Low

Form RPR

120- 1 **Stonecutter (IRE)**[80] 7425 5-9-6 **82** .... AdamKirby 5 89
(James Unett) *chsd ldr: rdn over 2f out: led 1f out: styd on u.p* **3/1**2

0-44 2 1 1/4 **Excellent Puck (IRE)**[29] 619 6-8-11 **78** .... CallumShepherd(5) 4 83
(Shaun Lycett) *led at stdy pce tl qcknd over 3f out: rdn over 2f out: hdd 1f out: styd on same pce towards fin* **8/1**

-651 3 hd **Spiritoftomintoul**[35] 545 7-9-2 **81** .... (t) GeorgeDowning(3) 6 86
(Tony Carroll) *dwlt: hld up: hdwy over 3f out: rdn over 2f out: r.o towards fin* **7/4**1

0-36 4 1 **Communicator**[34] 556 8-9-8 **84** .... (p) OisinMurphy 2 88
(Andrew Balding) *hld up: rdn over 1f out: r.o towards fin: nt rch ldrs* **7/2**3

6155 5 1/2 **Alshan Fajer**[16] 779 6-9-2 **78** .... FrederikTylicki 3 81
(J R Jenkins) *trckd ldrs: plld hrd: rdn over 2f out: no ex ins fnl f* **11/2**

3m 40.76s (-2.94) **Going Correction** -0.125s/f (Stan) 5 Ran SP% **110.1**
Speed ratings (Par 105): **101,100,100,99,99**
CSF £24.25 TOTE £3.50: £1.40, £3.40; EX 20.30 Trifecta £47.70.
Owner Northern Line Racing Ltd **Bred** Gigginstown House Stud **Trained** Wolverhampton, West Midlands

FOCUS
A steadily run race which turned into a bit of a dash from the turn out of the back straight. The first two were always best placed.

984 32RED CASINO MAIDEN FILLIES' STKS 7f 32y (Tp)
7:40 (7:43) (Class 5) 3-Y-O+ £3,557 (£1,058; £529; £264) **Stalls** High

Form RPR

2 1 **Magical Path (IRE)**[14] 824 3-8-10 0 .... MartinHarley 9 74
(Hugo Palmer) *mde virtually all: rdn over 1f out: styd on* **7/4**2

2 1/2 **Battlement** 3-8-10 0 .... WilliamTwiston-Davies 1 73+
(Roger Charlton) *wnt prom over 5f out: chsd wnr over 2f out: shkn up over 1f out: r.o* **10/11**1

3 1 1/4 **Dreaming Lady (IRE)** 3-8-10 0 .... RobertHavlin 4 70+
(James Tate) *plld hrd and prom: rdn over 1f out: styd on same pce ins fnl f* **20/1**

4 1 **Normandie Lady** 3-8-10 0 .... JackGarritty 2 67+
(Richard Fahey) *s.i.s: hdwy over 2f out: rdn over 1f out: styd on same pce ins fnl f* **16/1**

5 7 **Phoenix Beat** 3-8-10 0 .... AdamBeschizza 3 50+
(Gay Kelleway) *mid-div: pushed along 1/2-way: hdwy over 1f out: wknd fnl f* **6/1**3

6 2 1/4 **Raven Banner (IRE)** 3-8-10 0 .... TomEaves 10 45
(Ronald Thompson) *chsd ldrs: wnt 2nd 1/2-way tl rdn over 2f out: wknd over 1f out* **50/1**

7 1 1/4 **Pacohontas** 3-8-7 0 .... JackDuern(3) 8 42
(Dean Ivory) *chsd ldrs tl rdn and wknd over 2f out* **40/1**

0 8 nk **Somepink (IRE)**[56] 298 3-8-10 0 .... FrannyNorton 6 41
(Daniel Mark Loughnane) *s.i.s: hld up: rdn over 2f out: n.d* **66/1**

9 3 3/4 **Summertime Lucy (IRE)** 3-8-10 0 .... JackMitchell 5 32
(Giles Bravery) *sn pushed along in rr: lost tch over 2f out* **50/1**

10 6 **Bravadora (IRE)** 3-8-10 0 .... BenCurtis 12 17
(Scott Dixon) *hld up: plld hrd: hdwy over 4f out: wknd over 2f out* **80/1**

- 11 33 **Aspens Shadow** 4-9-11 0 .... MartinDwyer 7
(Grace Harris) *plld hrd: jnd wnr 6f out tl rdn 1/2-way: hung rt and wknd over 2f out* **66/1**

1m 28.04s (-0.76) **Going Correction** -0.125s/f (Stan)
WFA 3 from 4yo 15lb 11 Ran SP% **124.3**
Speed ratings (Par 100): **99,98,97,95,87 85,83,83,79,72 34**
CSF £3.77 TOTE £2.20: £1.10, £1.10, £4.60; EX 4.10 Trifecta £20.00.
Owner Anglia Bloodstock Syndicate VI **Bred** Miss Annmarie Burke **Trained** Newmarket, Suffolk

FOCUS
A fair maiden.

985 DOWNLOAD THE LADBROKES APP H'CAP 7f 32y (Tp)
8:10 (8:12) (Class 6) (0-55,61) 4-Y-O+ £2,587 (£770; £384; £192) **Stalls** High

Form RPR

6-54 1 **Smalljohn**[24] 681 10-8-13 **54** .... (v) PhilDennis(7) 9 61
(Bryan Smart) *chsd ldr 6f out: led 4f out: rdn and hdd 2f out: rallied to ld ins fnl f: styd on* **6/1**3

-066 2 1/2 **Pipers Piping (IRE)**[32] 590 10-9-0 **51** .... RobHornby(3) 11 57
(Mandy Rowland) *s.i.s: hld up: hdwy over 1f out: rdn and hung lft ins fnl f: r.o* **14/1**

3213 3 nk **Little Indian**[23] 696 6-9-5 **53** .... FrederikTylicki 3 58
(J R Jenkins) *hld up: hdwy 1/2-way: rdn over 1f out: r.o* **3/1**1

0-41 4 1 1/4 **Powerfulstorm**[7] 904 4-9-13 **61** 6ex .... AdamKirby 6 63
(Michael Appleby) *led 3f: rdn to ld again 2f out: hdd ins fnl f: styd on same pce* **9/2**2

-430 5 1 1/4 **Evident (IRE)**[30] 609 6-9-7 **55** .... (p) JFEgan 10 54
(Tony Carroll) *prom: rdn over 2f out: styd on same pce ins fnl f* **8/1**

3210 6 1 1/4 **Lutine Charlie (IRE)**[16] 787 9-9-5 **53** .... (p) MartinHarley 4 49
(Emma Owen) *prom: rdn over 1f out: no ex fnl f* **17/2**

00-5 7 nk **Krazy Paving**[35] 542 4-9-7 **55** .... JackGarritty 5 50
(Anabel K Murphy) *chsd ldrs: rdn over 1f out: no ex fnl f* **11/1**

0214 8 1 **Little Big Man**[30] 609 5-9-5 **53** .... CathyGannon 2 46
(Clare Ellam) *s.i.s hld up: rdn over 2f out: nt trble ldrs* **6/1**3

0-00 9 2 3/4 **Steel Rain**[21] 732 8-9-0 **48** .... OisinMurphy 1 34
(Nikki Evans) *hld up: hdwy u.p over 1f out: wknd ins fnl f* **125/1**

-030 10 3/4 **As A Dream (IRE)**[9] 876 4-8-9 **48** .... EdwardGreatrex(5) 7 32
(Nikki Evans) *hld up: rdn 1/2-way: hung lft over 1f out: a in rr* **20/1**

0/0- 11 2 1/4 **Purana**[92] 8264 5-8-13 **47** .... LemosdeSouza 8 26
(Ms N M Hugo) *hld up: hdwy 1/2-way: rdn and wknd 2f out* **40/1**

1m 27.67s (-1.13) **Going Correction** -0.125s/f (Stan) 11 Ran SP% **116.4**
Speed ratings (Par 101): **101,100,100,98,97 95,95,94,91,90 87**
CSF £84.07 CT £307.04 TOTE £6.90: £2.30, £3.30, £1.60; EX 95.50 Trifecta £336.80.
Owner B Smart **Bred** W H R John And Partners **Trained** Hambleton, N Yorks

FOCUS
An ordinary heat.

986 LADBROKES H'CAP 1m 141y (Tp)
8:40 (8:42) (Class 6) (0-55,55) 4-Y-O+ £2,587 (£770; £384; £192) **Stalls** Low

Form RPR

0-65 1 **Hazel Blue (IRE)**[14] 822 5-9-3 **51** .... DougieCostello 1 58
(David Loughnane) *hld up: hdwy over 2f out: rdn over 1f out: r.o to ld last strides* **16/1**

0254 2 hd **Toymaker**[18] 769 9-9-7 **55** .... (t) AdamKirby 4 62
(Phil McEntee) *led: hdd 7f out: chsd ldrs: rdn to ld ins fnl f: hdd last strides* **9/2**2

30-6 3 2 3/4 **Natalia**[21] 730 7-8-9 **46** oh1 .... (v) RobHornby(3) 12 47
(Sarah Hollinshead) *a.p: chsd ldr over 3f out: led 2f out: rdn and hdd ins fnl f: styd on same pce* **50/1**

3052 4 1 3/4 **Foylesideview (IRE)**[16] 787 4-9-2 **50** .... CathyGannon 10 47
(Harry Chisman) *hld up: hdwy u.p over 1f out: nt rch ldrs* **10/3**1

000- 5 5 **Cheeco**[154] 7264 4-8-12 **46** oh1 .... JamesSullivan 3 33
(Ruth Carr) *hld up: hdwy over 1f out: nvr trbld ldrs* **80/1**

200- 6 1/2 **Mount Cheiron (USA)**[108] 8068 5-8-9 **50** .... CallumRodriguez(7) 11 36
(Richard Ford) *hld up: rdn over 1f out: nvr trbld ldrs* **12/1**

00-4 7 nse **Anneani (IRE)**[16] 787 4-9-2 **50** .... JFEgan 5 37
(Paul Green) *plld hrd and prom: led 4f out: rdn and hdd 2f out: wknd ins fnl f* **10/1**

6360 8 2 1/4 **Malvesi**[22] 707 7-8-13 **47** .... FrannyNorton 7 28
(Mark Johnston) *led 7f out: hdd 4f out: rdn over 2f out: wknd fnl f* **10/1**

2-00 9 1 **Malih**[27] 653 7-9-3 **51** .... JoeyHaynes 9 30
(Eric Wheeler) *hld up: rdn over 2f out: nvr on terms* **25/1**

0-21 10 12 **Overrider**[49] 388 6-8-12 **51** .... (bt) CallumShepherd(5) 2 4
(Shaun Lycett) *prom: rdn over 2f out: sn wknd* **7/1**3

4165 11 13 **Star Links (USA)**[9] 870 10-8-13 **52** .... (bt) EdwardGreatrex(5) 8
(Sylvester Kirk) *sn pushed along and prom: rdn and wknd over 2f out* **7/1**3

2230 U **Bionic Indian**[7] 898 4-9-0 **48** .... (b) MartinHarley 6
(Michael Easterby) *c out of stalls wout rdr* **7/1**3

1m 47.76s (-2.34) **Going Correction** -0.125s/f (Stan) 12 Ran SP% **117.6**
Speed ratings (Par 101): **105,104,102,100,96 95,95,93,93,82 70,**
CSF £85.18 CT £3595.12 TOTE £16.40: £4.30, £1.80, £13.70; EX 125.40 Trifecta £1753.80 Part won..
Owner R G Fell **Bred** Rory O'Brien **Trained** Market Drayton, Shropshire

FOCUS
Another low-grade handicap.
T/Plt: £114.50 to a £1 stake. Pool: £104,656.73 - 666.94 winning units T/Qpdt: £26.90 to a £1 stake. Pool: £8,451.71 - 231.84 winning units **Colin Roberts**

987 - 999a (Foreign Racing) - See Raceform Interactive

981 WOLVERHAMPTON (A.W) (L-H)
Saturday, March 19

OFFICIAL GOING: Tapeta: standard
Wind: Fresh against Weather: Overcast

1000 32REDSPORT.COM MEDIAN AUCTION MAIDEN STKS 1m 141y (Tp)
6:15 (6:16) (Class 5) 3-Y-O £3,881 (£1,155; £577; £288) **Stalls** Low

Form RPR

322- 1 **Tawakkol**[250] 4193 3-9-5 80 .... JoeFanning 4 88+
(Mark Johnston) *chsd ldr tl led 2f out: shkn up over 1f out: rdn ins fnl f: styd on strly* **6/4**1

05- 2 5 **Pushaq (IRE)**[150] 7387 3-9-5 0 .... AdamKirby 1 78
(Marco Botti) *chsd ldrs: rdn to chse wnr over 1f out: edgd lft and no ex ins fnl f* **5/1**3

The Form Book, Raceform Ltd, Newbury, RG14 5SJ

20-2 **3** ¾ **California Lad**[17] 778 3-9-5 78 .... JimCrowley 8 76
(Harry Dunlop) *led: hung rt and hdd 2f out: no ex ins fnl f* **15/8**[2]

0- **4** *shd* **Stetchworth Park**[157] 7218 3-9-5 0 .... JamieSpencer 3 76
(Michael Bell) *hld up: hdwy over 5f out: rdn over 2f out: styd on same pce fr over 1f out* **8/1**

5 *9* **Motivate** 3-9-5 0 .... LukeMorris 5 57
(Sir Mark Prescott Bt) *s.i.s: hld up: shkn up over 2f out: wknd wl over 1f out* **16/1**

6 ¾ **Whacking Bullock (IRE)** 3-9-5 0 .... LiamKeniry 6 55
(Daniel Mark Loughnane) *s.i.s: a in rr: wknd over 2f out* **66/1**

4 **7** *nk* **Star Of Kheleyf**[9] 892 3-9-5 0 .... AndrewMullen 7 55
(Michael Appleby) *s.i.s: in rr: rdn over 4f out: wknd over 2f out* **50/1**

0 **8** *2* **Amazing Moon**[15] 814 3-8-7 0 .... StephenCummins(7) 2 45
(Richard Hughes) *prom: pushed along over 3f out: wknd over 2f out* **100/1**

1m 48.38s (-1.72) **Going Correction** -0.275s/f (Stan) **8** Ran SP% **112.9**
Speed ratings (Par 98): **96,91,90,90,82 82,81,80**
CSF £9.34 TOTE £2.30: £1.02, £2.20, £1.90; EX 8.70 Trifecta £17.40.
Owner Hamdan Al Maktoum **Bred** Bearstone Stud Ltd **Trained** Middleham Moor, N Yorks

FOCUS
A routine maiden with an easy winner and several reasonable handicap prospects behind. The first four were always prominent.

1001 CORAL.CO.UK H'CAP 1m 1f 103y (Tp)
6:45 (6:45) (Class 3) (0-95,94) 4-Y-O+ **£7,439** (£2,213; £1,106; £553) **Stalls** Low

Form RPR

-122 **1** **Perfect Cracker**[19] 767 8-8-13 **89** .... RyanTate(3) 6 97
(Clive Cox) *hld up in tch: racd keenly: nt clr run over 1f out: hmpd ins fnl f: r.o to ld towards fin: comf* **11/4**[1]

2-36 **2** ½ **Mont Ras (IRE)**[19] 767 9-9-7 **94** .... DavidNolan 2 99
(David Loughnane) *led early: chsd ldrs: rdn to ld 1f out: sn hung lft: hdd towards fin* **12/1**

2-21 **3** *nse* **Sheila's Buddy**[28] 656 7-8-11 **84** .... LiamKeniry 3 89
(J S Moore) *hld up: hdwy over 2f out: rdn and edgd rt ins fnl f: sn ev ch: r.o* **15/2**

00-4 **4** *nk* **Viewpoint (IRE)**[12] 860 7-8-12 **85** .... AndrewMullen 10 89
(Michael Appleby) *hld up: hdwy over 1f out: rdn and edgd lft ins fnl f: r.o wl towards fin* **18/1**

12-3 **5** *nk* **Ready (IRE)**[78] 7 6-9-1 **88** .... (p) AdamKirby 7 92
(Ivan Furtado) *chsd ldrs: rdn over 1f out: styd on* **7/2**[2]

5-46 **6** *1* **Capo Rosso (IRE)**[35] 560 6-9-6 **93** .... RichardKingscote 1 96
(Tom Dascombe) *s.i.s: sn rcvrd to ld: rdn and hdd 1f out: hmpd sn after: no ex wl ins fnl f* **6/1**[3]

-061 **7** ¾ **Jack Of Diamonds (IRE)**[17] 788 7-8-10 **88** .... CallumShepherd(5) 4 88
(Roger Teal) *hld up: effrt on outer over 2f out: styd on: nt trble ldrs* **12/1**

052- **8** *nk* **Kapstadt (FR)**[114] 5849 6-8-8 **81** .... StevieDonohoe 9 81
(Ian Williams) *swtchd lft sn after s: hld up: shkn up over 1f out: nvr trbld ldrs* **9/1**

3015 **9** 4½ **Idol Deputy (FR)**[17] 788 10-8-0 **78** .... (p) JosephineGordon(5) 8 69
(James Bennett) *hld up: rdn over 1f out: no ex fnl f* **25/1**

0-50 **10** *8* **Stencive**[17] 779 7-8-9 **82** .... (t) LukeMorris 5 58
(Charlie Wallis) *s.i.s: rcvrd to chse ldr 7f out: rdn over 2f out: sn lost 2nd: wknd fnl f* **25/1**

1m 56.64s (-4.16) **Going Correction** -0.275s/f (Stan) course record **10** Ran SP% **113.3**
Speed ratings (Par 107): **107,106,106,106,105 105,104,104,100,93**
CSF £35.91 CT £218.70 TOTE £2.90: £1.40, £3.60, £2.40; EX 37.20 Trifecta £196.70.
Owner Mildmay Racing **Bred** Mildmay Bloodstock Ltd **Trained** Lambourn, Berks
■ Stewards' Enquiry : Ryan Tate five-day ban; careless riding (2nd-6th Apr)

FOCUS
In a good-quality race, there was a dash to the first bend but the pace soon steadied. The second is the best guide.

1002 DOWNLOAD THE CORAL APP H'CAP 1m 4f 50y (Tp)
7:15 (7:15) (Class 5) (0-70,71) 4-Y-O+ **£3,881** (£1,155; £577; £288) **Stalls** Low

Form RPR

-534 **1** **Indira**[39] 506 5-9-1 **69** .... JosephineGordon(5) 6 77
(John Berry) *chsd ldrs: led over 1f out: sn rdn: styd on wl* **8/1**

3-00 **2** 2¼ **My Lord**[12] 862 8-9-1 **64** .... AdamKirby 7 68
(David Evans) *a.p: rdn to chse wnr over 1f out: styd on same pce ins fnl f* **25/1**

0-13 **3** *nk* **Yasir (USA)**[8] 898 8-8-2 **58** .... SophieKilloran(7) 5 62
(Sophie Leech) *hld up: hdwy over 1f out: sn rdn: styd on* **7/1**

660- **4** *nk* **Able Dash**[171] 6871 6-9-7 **70** .... RichardKingscote 3 73
(Michael Blake) *chsd ldrs: rdn over 3f out: outpcd over 2f out: styd on ins fnl f* **3/1**[2]

-633 **5** 1¾ **Dove Mountain (IRE)**[15] 830 5-8-13 **62** .... (tp) JamieSpencer 10 63
(Gordon Elliott, Ire) *hld up: hdwy over 1f out: rdn ins fnl f: edgd lft and styd on same pce* **2/1**[1]

652 **6** 1¾ **Force Of Destiny (GER)**[22] 728 4-9-2 **67** .... SteveDrowne 1 65
(Mrs Ilka Gansera-Leveque) *chsd ldr tl led over 2f out: rdn and hdd over 1f out: wknd ins fnl f* **12/1**

3546 **7** *5* **Percys Princess**[19] 766 5-9-2 **68** .... (p) AlistairRawlinson(3) 4 58
(Michael Appleby) *sn pushed along in mid-div: rdn over 3f out: wknd over 2f out* **20/1**

06-5 **8** *1* **Moojaned (IRE)**[9] 890 5-8-13 **65** .... PhilipPrince(3) 8 53
(David Evans) *hld up: hdwy over 2f out: wknd over 1f out* **16/1**

-045 **9** 3½ **Ninepointsixthree**[14] 838 6-8-12 **66** .... (v[1]) CiaranMckee(5) 9 49
(John O'Shea) *s.s: hld up: hdwy over 3f out: rdn over 2f out: wknd wl over 1f out* **40/1**

41-2 **10** *3* **My Mo (FR)**[8] 899 4-9-6 **71** .... MartinLane 2 49
(David Dennis) *sn led: rdn and hdd over 2f out: wknd fnl f* **6/1**[3]

2m 35.41s (-5.39) **Going Correction** -0.275s/f (Stan)
WFA 4 from 5yo+ 2lb **10** Ran SP% **120.9**
Speed ratings (Par 103): **106,104,104,104,102 101,98,97,95,93**
CSF £193.96 CT £1479.21 TOTE £9.00: £2.30, £3.30, £2.20; EX 164.90 Trifecta £1183.60.
Owner Severn Crossing Partnership **Bred** Mrs M L Parry & P M Steele-Mortimer **Trained** Newmarket, Suffolk

FOCUS
Not many of these were in top form and the pace was moderate. Straightforward form.

1003 EBF 32RED.COM FILLIES' H'CAP 7f 32y (Tp)
7:45 (7:46) (Class 3) (0-90,87) 4-Y-O+ **£10,396** (£3,111; £1,555; £778; £387) **Stalls** High

Form RPR

3250 **1** **Apache Storm**[18] 771 4-9-2 **82** .... AndrewMullen 6 89
(Michael Appleby) *chsd ldrs: rdn to ld wl ins fnl f: r.o* **10/1**

250- **2** ¾ **Childesplay**[180] 6591 5-9-5 **85** .... OisinMurphy 7 90
(Heather Main) *chsd ldr: rdn over 1f out: led ins fnl f: sn edgd lft and hdd: styd on* **16/1**

-303 **3** *nk* **Elis Eliz (IRE)**[17] 780 4-9-7 **87** .... GeorgeBaker 3 91
(Michael Wigham) *led: rdn over 1f out: hdd ins fnl f: kpt on* **10/3**[2]

1-25 **4** 1¼ **Russian Radiance**[17] 780 4-9-2 **82** .... RichardKingscote 5 83
(Jonathan Portman) *sn prom: rdn and hung lft fr over 1f out: styd on same pce ins fnl f* **4/1**[3]

-600 **5** ¾ **Pretty Bubbles**[34] 581 7-8-10 **76** .... (v[1]) FrederikTylicki 1 76
(J R Jenkins) *hld up: hdwy over 1f out: styd on same pce ins fnl f* **16/1**

36-1 **6** *nk* **Three Gracez**[17] 780 4-9-0 **85** .... PaddyPilley(5) 4 84
(Philip McBride) *hld up: nt clr run over 1f out: rdn ins fnl f: nt trble ldrs* **5/2**[1]

4156 **7** ¾ **Subtle Knife**[17] 780 7-9-1 **81** .... WilliamCarson 2 78
(Giles Bravery) *hld up: rdn over 1f out: nvr trbld ldrs* **25/1**

31-3 **8** 4½ **Mallymkun**[12] 859 4-8-2 **68** .... FrannyNorton 8 54
(K R Burke) *s.i.s: hdwy over 5f out: rdn over 2f out: wknd over 1f out* **4/1**[3]

1m 26.53s (-2.27) **Going Correction** -0.275s/f (Stan) **8** Ran SP% **116.4**
Speed ratings (Par 104): **101,100,99,98,97 97,96,91**
CSF £153.02 CT £656.52 TOTE £11.80: £3.30, £4.00, £1.50; EX 215.90 Trifecta £644.30.
Owner Ferrybank Properties Limited **Bred** Northmore Stud **Trained** Oakham, Rutland

FOCUS
In an above-average field, the pace was medium until quickening off the bend. The winner pretty much repeated November's 7f form

1004 32RED CASINO H'CAP 1m 5f 194y (Tp)
8:15 (8:21) (Class 6) (0-60,60) 4-Y-O+ **£2,587** (£770; £384; £192) **Stalls** Low

Form RPR

051- **1** **Captain George (IRE)**[155] 7262 5-9-4 **54** .... (p) SteveDrowne 12 60
(Michael Blake) *chsd ldrs: rdn over 2f out: styd on to ld wl ins fnl f* **16/1**

500- **2** *nk* **City Dreams (IRE)**[109] 8069 6-9-0 **50** .... DougieCostello 1 56
(Philip Kirby) *chsd ldr tl led over 2f out: rdn over 1f out: hdd wl ins fnl f: styd on* **20/1**

-532 **3** *nk* **Robben**[22] 731 4-9-5 **59** .... (v) JoeFanning 5 64
(John Mackie) *s.i.s: hld up: hdwy on outer over 1f out: rdn and hung lft ins fnl f: styd on* **15/8**[1]

0-64 **4** *nk* **Ring Eye (IRE)**[15] 819 8-8-12 **53** .... CiaranMckee(5) 7 58
(John O'Shea) *s.i.s: hld up: hdwy over 1f out: rdn and carried lft ins fnl f: styd on* **25/1**

0155 **5** 3¾ **Missandei**[4] 946 4-8-12 **52** .... (t) AdamBeschizza 4 51
(Steph Hollinshead) *hld up: racd keenly: hdwy over 2f out: rdn over 1f out: styd on same pce ins fnl f* **10/1**

55-6 **6** ½ **Chauvelin**[32] 601 5-9-5 **55** .... (v) JasonHart 13 54
(Richard Guest) *hld up: hdwy over 6f out: rdn over 3f out: edgd lft and no ex fnl f* **25/1**

30-0 **7** 2¼ **Ballyfarsoon (IRE)**[68] 150 5-8-13 **52** .... (p) GeorgeDowning(3) 11 47
(Ian Williams) *prom: rdn over 3f out: hung lft fr over 1f out: wknd ins fnl f* **12/1**

3365 **8** *7* **Smugglers Lane (IRE)**[11] 865 4-8-8 **51** .... PhilipPrince(3) 8 36
(David Evans) *prom: rdn over 2f out: wknd fnl f* **25/1**

-624 **9** 2¼ **Galuppi**[29] 634 5-9-9 **59** .... (b) FrederikTylicki 3 41
(J R Jenkins) *mid-div: lost pl over 3f out: wknd wl over 1f out* **8/1**[3]

3240 **10** *5* **Astra Hall**[16] 801 7-9-10 **60** .... AdamKirby 9 35
(Michael Appleby) *led at stdy pce tl qcknd over 3f out: rdn and hdd over 2f out: wknd and eased fnl f* **5/1**[2]

3m 1.12s (-3.68) **Going Correction** -0.275s/f (Stan)
WFA 4 from 5yo+ 4lb **10** Ran SP% **101.5**
Speed ratings (Par 101): **99,98,98,98,96 96,94,90,89,86**
CSF £219.37 CT £568.09 TOTE £11.10: £3.10, £5.40, £1.10; EX 92.60 Trifecta £2332.30.
Owner Staverton Owners Group **Bred** Equine Associates Fr **Trained** Trowbridge, Wilts
■ Moulin Rouge was withdrawn. Price at time of withdrawal 5-1. Rule 4 applies to all bets - deduction 15p in the pound.

FOCUS
The pace was moderate until quickening 4f out. A compressed finish to an ordinary race.

1005 UNIBET OFFER DAILY JOCKEY/TRAINER SPECIALS H'CAP 5f 216y (Tp)
8:45 (8:48) (Class 6) (0-52,54) 4-Y-O+ **£2,587** (£770; £384; £192) **Stalls** Low

Form RPR

006- **1** **Ballroom Angel**[227] 5004 4-9-1 **46** .... WilliamTwiston-Davies 6 52
(Philip Hide) *hld up in tch: nt clr run and swtchd rt over 1f out: r.o to ld nr fin* **33/1**

4521 **2** ½ **Multi Quest**[16] 790 4-9-2 **47** .... (b) FrannyNorton 7 51
(John E Long) *chsd ldrs: rdn over 2f out: ev ch ins fnl f: r.o* **15/2**

0-42 **3** *hd* **Wedgewood Estates**[16] 790 5-9-7 **52** .... LukeMorris 8 55
(Tony Carroll) *chsd ldrs: rdn to ld ins fnl f: hdd nr fin* **11/2**[2]

2442 **4** ¾ **First Rebellion**[9] 895 7-9-6 **54** .... (v) GeorgeDowning(3) 10 55
(Tony Carroll) *disp ld tl wnt on over 2f out: rdn and hdd ins fnl f: styd on same pce* **9/1**

-204 **5** ½ **Presto Boy**[16] 790 4-8-12 **50** .... (t) StephanieJoannides(7) 5 50
(Richard Hughes) *s.i.s: hld up: hdwy over 2f out: ev ch ins fnl f: no ex nr fin* **9/1**

0-53 **6** ½ **Diamond Vine (IRE)**[22] 730 8-9-1 **46** oh1 .... (p) OisinMurphy 11 44
(Ronald Harris) *hld up: rdn over 2f out: hdwy u.p over 1f out: styd on* **16/1**

4333 **7** *nk* **Hab Reeh**[9] 895 8-9-7 **52** .... JamesSullivan 1 49
(Ruth Carr) *prom: nt clr run 2f out: shkn up over 1f out: styd on same pce ins fnl f* **11/2**[2]

-001 **8** ½ **Stamp Of Approval (IRE)**[22] 730 4-8-12 **50** .... SamuelClarke(7) 9 46
(Chris Wall) *s.i.s: hld up: pushed along over 2f out: r.o ins fnl f: nvr nrr* **13/2**[3]

3505 **9** ½ **Little**[9] 895 4-8-8 **46** oh1 .... (b) JoshQuinn(7) 4 40
(Steph Hollinshead) *hld up: effrt over 1f out: nt trble ldrs* **14/1**

-665 **10** *1* **Dream Ally (IRE)**[37] 528 6-9-5 **50** .... DougieCostello 3 41
(John Weymes) *hld up: nt clr run over 1f out: swtchd lft and sn rdn: r.o wl ins fnl f* **10/3**[1]

0-00 **11** *6* **Farrah's Choice**[10] 876 4-9-1 **46** oh1 .... TimmyMurphy 2 19
(James Grassick) *disp ld over 3f: wknd fnl f* **33/1**

1m 13.29s (-1.21) **Going Correction** -0.275s/f (Stan) **11** Ran SP% **117.4**
Speed ratings (Par 101): **97,96,96,95,94 93,93,92,92,90 82**
CSF £263.66 CT £1584.36 TOTE £43.80: £7.20, £2.00, £2.20; EX 226.80 Trifecta £2838.60.
Owner P Hide **Bred** David Jamison Bloodstock **Trained** Findon, W Sussex

FOCUS
A low-grade but tight handicap producing a close finish between the first nine. The third and fourth help with the level.
T/Plt: £123.40 to a £1 stake. Pool: £111,878.48 - 661.53 winning units. T/Qpdt: £56.00 to a £1 stake. Pool: £9,241.55 - 121.91 winning units. **Colin Roberts**

1006 - 1013a (Foreign Racing) - See Raceform Interactive

CURRAGH (R-H)

Sunday, March 20

OFFICIAL GOING: Yielding to soft

1014a ELUSIVE PIMPERNEL MAIDEN (PLUS 10 RACE) 6f
2:40 (2:42) 3-Y-O+ **£5,878** (£1,816; £860; £382; £143)

RPR

1 **Stenographer (USA)** 3-9-5 0 KevinManning 16 87+
(J S Bolger, Ire) *w ldrs: disp cl 2nd at 1/2-way: rdn in 3rd 1 1/2f out and r.o wl nr side wl ins fnl f to ld fnl strides* **3/1**[2]

2 ½ **Paddy Power (IRE)**[223] 5205 3-9-5 90 TonyHamilton 12 85
(Richard Fahey) *w ldrs: disp cl 2nd at 1/2-way: pushed along under 2f out: sn rdn and kpt on wl u.p to ld narrowly fnl 50yds: hdd fnl strides* **9/2**[3]

3 hd **Sufoof (IRE)**[144] 7571 3-9-0 78 ChrisHayes 7 79
(Kevin Prendergast, Ire) *led narrowly down centre of trck: stl gng wl w narrow advantage 1 1/2f out: rdn and strly pressed ent fnl f: hdd fnl 50yds and sn dropped to 3rd* **8/1**

4 4 ¼ **The Moore Factor (IRE)**[237] 4710 3-9-5 0 PatSmullen 1 71
(D K Weld, Ire) *chsd far side ldrs early: sn tacked over and 5th 1/2-way: rdn in 4th over 1f out and no imp on ldrs: kpt on one pce ins fnl f* **5/2**[1]

5 hd **Doc Sportello (IRE)** 4-9-11 0 (t) OisinOrr(7) 18 74+
(Edward Lynam, Ire) *s.i.s and towards rr: swtchd rt and hdwy fr 2f out to chse ldrs in mod 7th over 1f out: kpt on ins fnl f: nvr trbld ldrs* **33/1**

6 1 **Youceeyouceecee (IRE)**[147] 7495 4-9-11 0 KillianLeonard(7) 5 71
(Miss Susan A Finn, Ire) *in tch: 7th 1/2-way: rdn into 5th over 1f out and no imp on clr ldrs: one pce fnl f* **33/1**

7 nk **Ardmore (IRE)**[511] 7478 5-10-4 0 RonanWhelan 14 70
(J S Bolger, Ire) *s.i.s and towards rr: sme hdwy on outer fr 2f out into mod 8th on outer over 1f out: kpt on ins fnl f* **16/1**

8 ¾ **Patience A Plenty (IRE)** 3-8-9 0 GaryHalpin(5) 11 59
(Adrian Paul Keatley, Ire) *mid-div: pushed along in mod 6th 1 1/2f out and no imp on clr ldrs ent fnl f: one pce ins fnl f* **33/1**

9 9 **Cassis Sunset (IRE)**[144] 7569 3-9-0 0 SeamieHeffernan 9 30
(Miss Evanna McCutcheon, Ire) *hld up in mid-div: 8th 1/2-way: edgd lft 1 1/2f out and hmpd rival: no imp after: kpt on one pce ins fnl f* **66/1**

10 ½ **Enchanted Dawn (USA)**[161] 7147 3-9-0 0 WayneLordan 8 28
(David Wachman, Ire) *hld up in mid-div: 9th 1/2-way: hmpd 1 1/2f out and no imp after: kpt on one pce ins fnl f* **14/1**

11 1 **Lostforwords (IRE)**[147] 7495 5-9-13 0 GaryCarroll 13 29
(Michael McCullagh, Ire) *s.i.s and towards rr: rdn in 12th over 1f out and no imp: one pce fnl f* **66/1**

12 1 ¼ **Bonfire Bank (IRE)**[261] 3864 3-9-0 0 RossCoakley(5) 10 26
(John C McConnell, Ire) *towards rr: pushed along and struggling bef 1/2-way: no imp over 2f out* **66/1**

13 2 **Periwig (IRE)**[227] 5077 3-8-11 69 RobbieDowney(3) 6 15
(Edward Lynam, Ire) *in rr of mid-div for most: rdn and no imp over 1f out* **33/1**

14 4 ¾ **Hunters Point (IRE)**[207] 5766 3-9-5 0 (t) ShaneFoley 15 4
(John C McConnell, Ire) *s.i.s and towards rr thrght: no imp fr 1/2-way* **66/1**

15 5 **Town Ranger (IRE)** 4-9-6 0 KarenKenny(7) 2
(Peter Casey, Ire) *chsd ldrs far side: 6th 1/2-way: rdn and wknd fr over 2f out* **66/1**

16 1 **Frankwithouthel (IRE)**[51] 392 5-10-4 0 ConnorKing 3
(Patrick Martin, Ire) *chsd ldrs far side early: sn settled in mid-div: 11th 1/2-way: wknd 2f out* **100/1**

17 12 **Brief Angel (IRE)**[9] 908 3-8-7 0 GearoidBrouder(7) 4
(Thomas Cooper, Ire) *s.i.s and towards rr thrght: pushed along fr 1/2-way and no imp 2f out* **100/1**

18 16 **Strada Di Carsoli**[156] 7267 3-9-5 0 ColinKeane 17
(G M Lyons, Ire) *chsd ldrs: 4th 1/2-way: rdn over 2f out and sn wknd* **8/1**

1m 18.31s (2.81) **Going Correction** +0.50s/f (Yiel)
WFA 3 from 4yo+ 13lb **18** Ran SP% **127.7**
Speed ratings: **101,100,100,94,94 92,92,91,79,78 77,75,73,66,60 58,42,21**
CSF £16.67 TOTE £3.70: £1.60, £1.90, £2.80; DF 18.20 Trifecta £107.50.
Owner Godolphin **Bred** WinStar Farm LLC **Trained** Coolcullen, Co Carlow
■ Stewards' Enquiry : Shane Foley 350euro fine: passport irregularity
Ross Coakley 350euro fine: passport irregularity

FOCUS
A keenly contested race, a winner that should progress and a fair few showing promise of one sort or another.

1015a ST PATRICKS FESTIVAL H'CAP 6f
3:15 (3:17) 3-Y-O+ **£10,852** (£3,352; £1,588; £705; £264)

RPR

1 **Bubbly Bellini (IRE)**[23] 741 9-9-11 **88** (p) DeclanMcDonogh 13 92
(Adrian McGuinness, Ire) *disp early and sn settled bhd ldrs: 3rd 1/2-way: rdn to chal 1 1/2f out and led narrowly ins fnl f: all out clsng stages to hold on* **13/2**[3]

2 nk **Club Wexford (IRE)**[148] 7480 5-8-13 **76** KevinManning 2 79
(J S Bolger, Ire) *w.w in rr: last at 1/2-way: prog fr 2f out between horses to chse ldrs ins fnl f: rdn into 2nd wl ins fnl f and kpt on wl to press wnr clsng stages: jst hld* **12/1**

3 hd **Rattling Jewel**[9] 907 4-8-10 **73** WayneLordan 5 75
(Miss Nicole McKenna, Ire) *w ldrs: 4th 1/2-way: rdn 2f out and impr to chal on outer over 1f out: no ex wl ins fnl f where dropped to 3rd* **25/1**

4 ½ **An Saighdiur (IRE)**[30] 642 9-9-9 **86** BillyLee 10 87
(Andrew Slattery, Ire) *disp early and sn led narrowly: 1 l clr at 1/2-way: rdn 2f out and sn jnd tl hdd narrowly ins fnl f: sn no imp on wnr and one pce in 4th clsng stages* **8/1**

5 ½ **Penny Pepper (IRE)**[149] 7447 4-8-12 **75** ChrisHayes 3 74
(Kevin Prendergast, Ire) *hld up towards rr: 10th 1/2-way: hdwy on outer 2f out to chse ldrs far side over 1f out: no ex wl ins fnl f and one pce clsng stages* **9/1**

6 shd **Master Speaker (IRE)**[155] 7298 6-9-9 **86** (t) ConnorKing 9 85
(Martin Hassett, Ire) *hld up: 9th 1/2-way: short of room on inner under 2f out and swtchd rt over 1f out: kpt on ins fnl f where nt clr run: nrst fin* **6/1**[2]

7 ½ **St Brelades Bay (IRE)**[155] 7298 4-9-3 **80** ColmO'Donoghue 7 77
(Mrs John Harrington, Ire) *in tch: 8th 1/2-way: rdn 2f out and sme hdwy u.p whn sltly hmpd and nt clr run ins fnl f: kpt on one pce* **16/1**

8 3 **Laganore (IRE)**[148] 7480 4-9-10 **87** SeamieHeffernan 1 75
(A J Martin, Ire) *hooded to load: dwlt and settled towards rr: 12th 1/2-way: pushed along and tk clsr order far side over 1f out: no imp on ldrs under hands and heels and one pce in 8th wl ins fnl f* **12/1**

9 1 **Shanghai Beauty (IRE)**[178] 6691 4-8-8 **71** ow1 (tp) ShaneFoley 14 55
(K J Condon, Ire) *dwlt sltly and towards rr early tl impr into 6th at 1/2-way: rdn over 1f out and sn no ex: wknd ins fnl f* **8/1**

10 nk **Patrick (IRE)**[8] 923 4-9-5 **89** AdamMcNamara(7) 12 72
(Richard Fahey) *chsd ldrs: 5th 1/2-way: rdn and wknd 2f out: no imp in 11th whn swtchd rt ins fnl f* **4/1**[1]

11 nk **Geological (IRE)**[30] 642 4-9-3 **87** DonaghO'Connor(7) 11 70
(Damian Joseph English, Ire) *cl up: t.k.h: 2nd 1/2-way: rdn on terms briefly 1 1/2f out: sn no ex in 2nd and wknd fnl f* **25/1**

12 4 ¾ **Katimavik (IRE)**[159] 7200 5-9-9 **86** (b) PatSmullen 4 53
(D K Weld, Ire) *in tch: 7th 1/2-way: rdn and wknd over 1f out* **10/1**

13 6 **Deeds Not Words (IRE)**[51] 389 5-8-8 **71** LeighRoche 6 19
(J F Levins, Ire) *w.w towards rr: 11th 1/2-way: pushed along far side fr over 2f out and no imp over 1f out: eased in rr ins fnl f* **14/1**

1m 17.44s (1.94) **Going Correction** +0.50s/f (Yiel) **13** Ran SP% **124.6**
Speed ratings: **107,106,106,105,105 104,104,100,98,98 98,91,83**
CSF £86.04 CT £1901.23 TOTE £6.10: £2.50, £3.10, £11.40; DF 96.30 Trifecta £5471.60.
Owner Gary Devlin & Ms Hazel McGuinness **Bred** J P Hand **Trained** Lusk, Co Dublin

FOCUS
The handicapper had given the winner a chance by dropping him to the same mark as when winning this race a year ago and advantage was taken.

1016a LODGE PARK STUD EUROPEAN BREEDERS FUND PARK EXPRESS STKS (GROUP 3) (F&M) 1m
3:50 (3:51) 3-Y-O+

£33,621 (£10,827; £5,128; £2,279; £1,139; £569)

RPR

1 **Queen Blossom (IRE)**[147] 7492 3-8-10 93 ow1 FMBerry 7 106
(P J Prendergast, Ire) *dwlt sltly and settled in rr: last at 1/2-way: hdwy 2f out: sn swtchd rt and impr between horses to chse ldrs: rdn into 2nd ins fnl f and styd on wl u.p to ld cl home* **16/1**

2 1 **Devonshire (IRE)**[154] 7334 4-9-11 107 WilliamBuick 9 107
(W McCreery, Ire) *chsd ldrs and hung early: cl 2nd at 1/2-way: led under 2f out travelling wl: rdn ins fnl f and strly pressed ins fnl 100yds: hdd clsng stages and no ex* **11/4**[1]

3 3 **Joailliere (IRE)**[301] 2531 4-9-11 0 PatSmullen 10 100
(D K Weld, Ire) *chsd ldrs: 5th 1/2-way: tk clsr order bhd ldrs fr 2f out: rdn in 2nd over 1f out and sn no imp on ldr u.p in 3rd: kpt on one pce* **7/1**

4 ¾ **Glamorous Approach (IRE)**[162] 7116 3-8-9 98 KevinManning 5 94
(J S Bolger, Ire) *chsd ldrs: 3rd 1/2-way: rdn in 3rd fr 3f out and no imp on ldrs u.p in 4th ent fnl f: kpt on one pce* **5/1**[3]

5 hd **Fluff (IRE)**[337] 1524 4-9-11 0 SeamieHeffernan 8 98
(A P O'Brien, Ire) *hld up: 8th 1/2-way: impr to chse ldrs 2f out: sn rdn and no imp on ldrs u.p in 5th ins fnl f: kpt on one pce* **9/2**[2]

6 5 ½ **Military Angel (USA)**[190] 6338 4-9-11 103 KierenFallon 11 85
(M D O'Callaghan, Ire) *hld up bhd ldrs: 4th 1/2-way: pushed along in 5th fr 3f out and sn no imp on ldrs: one pce in 6th ins fnl f* **11/1**

7 ½ **Elusive Approach (IRE)** 4-9-11 0 RoryCleary 6 84?
(J S Bolger, Ire) *w.w towards rr: 9th 1/2-way: rdn 2f out and no imp ent fnl f: kpt on one pce in 7th ins fnl f: nvr nrr* **33/1**

8 2 ¼ **Abbey Angel (IRE)**[10] 886 4-9-11 85 (p) TonyHamilton 4 78
(Richard Fahey) *chsd ldrs early: 7th 1/2-way: rdn in rr under 2f out and no imp: kpt on one pce ins fnl f* **33/1**

9 7 **Steip Amach (IRE)**[147] 7491 4-9-11 101 RonanWhelan 1 62
(J S Bolger, Ire) *hld up towards rr: 10th 1/2-way: sme hdwy far side over 2f out: sn rdn and no ex over 1f out: wknd and eased ins fnl f* **20/1**

10 1 ½ **Queen Catrine (IRE)**[154] 7318 5-9-11 105 ColinKeane 3 58
(G M Lyons, Ire) *chsd ldrs: 6th 1/2-way: tk clsr order bhd ldrs over 2f out: sn rdn and wknd 1 1/2f out: eased ins fnl f* **5/1**[3]

11 nk **Corail (IRE)**[155] 7301 4-9-11 95 (p) ChrisHayes 2 58
(P D Deegan, Ire) *led: narrow advantage at 1/2-way: pushed along over 2f out: hdd u.p under 2f out and sn wknd: eased ins fnl f* **16/1**

1m 46.88s (0.88) **Going Correction** +0.35s/f (Good)
WFA 3 from 4yo+ 17lb **11** Ran SP% **121.4**
Speed ratings: **109,108,105,104,104 98,98,95,88,86 86**
CSF £60.78 TOTE £20.90: £3.90, £1.60, £2.80; DF 58.80 Trifecta £1229.60.
Owner Sean Greaney **Bred** Irish National Stud **Trained** Melitta Lodge, Co Kildare

FOCUS
The weight allowance and the stamina test this mile turned out to be played to the strengths of the winner and she appears to be much improved.

1018a TOTE IRISH LINCOLNSHIRE (PREMIER H'CAP) 1m
4:55 (4:57) 4-Y-O+

£43,382 (£13,970; £6,617; £2,941; £1,470; £735)

RPR

1 **Sruthan (IRE)**[148] 7477 6-9-6 **98** ChrisHayes 3 114
(P D Deegan, Ire) *chsd ldrs: 6th 1/2-way: impr travelling wl bhd ldrs fr 2f out: rdn in 4th over 1f out and qcknd to ld ins fnl f: styd on strly and drew clr: comf* **12/1**

2 4 ¼ **Aussie Valentine (IRE)**[9] 910 5-9-0 **92** (p) ConorHoban 1 98
(P D Deegan, Ire) *sn led narrowly: 2 l clr at 1/2-way: rdn under 2f out and reduced advantage: hdd u.p ins fnl f and sn no ch w wnr: kpt on same pce to jst hold 2nd* **8/1**[2]

3 hd **Gabrial's Kaka (IRE)**[163] 7088 6-8-7 **85** BarryMcHugh 10 91+
(Richard Fahey) *in tch: 8th 1/2-way: rdn 2f out and clsd u.p into 6th ins fnl f: styd on wl into 3rd wl ins fnl f: jst hld for 2nd: nt trble wnr* **12/1**

4 2 ½ **Lily's Rainbow (IRE)**[142] 7610 4-8-11 **89** LeighRoche 2 89
(Mrs Denise Foster, Ire) *chsd ldrs: 4th 1/2-way: rdn 1 1/2f out and ev ch almost on terms over 1f out: no imp on wnr in 3rd wl ins fnl f where dropped to 4th: kpt on one pce* **40/1**

5 nk **Wexford Opera (IRE)**[121] 7933 6-8-4 **82** oh4 RoryCleary 6 81
(J S Bolger, Ire) *chsd ldrs: 3rd 1/2-way: rdn to chal ent fnl f: sn no imp on wnr u.p in 4th and dropped to 5th wl ins fnl f* **25/1**

6 hd **Duchess Andorra (IRE)**[28] 665 5-8-4 **82** oh1 (p) DannyGrant 5 81
(J P Murtagh, Ire) *cl up: 2nd 1/2-way: rdn 2f out and no ex u.p in 5th ent fnl f: kpt on one pce* **25/1**

7 3 **Onenightidreamed (IRE)**[315] 2104 5-9-12 **104** (p) WayneLordan 20 96+
(T Stack, Ire) *mid-div: 10th 1/2-way: rdn and sme hdwy u.p fr under 2f out: no imp in 9th ent fnl f: kpt on into mod 7th ins fnl f* **10/1**[3]

8 ¾ **Spring Offensive (IRE)**[162] 7119 4-8-6 **84**................. MichaelHussey 7 74
(Richard Fahey) *chsd ldrs: rdn in 7th fr 1/2-way and no imp on ldrs ent fnl f: kpt on one pce* **16/1**

9 ¾ **Mohaayed**[152] 7381 4-9-6 **103**... GaryHalpin(5) 22 91+
(Kevin Prendergast, Ire) *in tch: 9th 1/2-way: no imp in 11th ent fnl f: kpt on* **16/1**

10 1 ¼ **Ibergman (IRE)**[155] 7303 4-8-4 **82**.................................... CathyGannon 9 67
(Ms Sheila Lavery, Ire) *hld up: rdn in rr of mid-div over 2f out and no imp u.p in 14th over 1f out: kpt on ins fnl f* **25/1**

11 nk **Withernsea (IRE)**[134] 7754 5-8-10 **95**.................. AdamMcNamara(7) 14 80
(Richard Fahey) *mid-div: rdn over 2f out and no imp on ldrs u.p in 10th ent fnl f: one pce ins fnl f* **11/1**

12 3 ½ **Lady Giselle (IRE)**[147] 7494 6-7-11 **82** oh4...........(p) KillianLeonard(7) 18 59
(John J Walsh, Ire) *in rr of mid-div: rdn 3f out and no imp in 16th 1 1/2f out: kpt on one pce ins fnl f* **25/1**

13 nk **Mandamus (IRE)**[152] 7381 4-9-6 **98**............................... RonanWhelan 8 74
(Ms Sheila Lavery, Ire) *hld up in mid-div: tk clsr order under 2f out: no imp u.p in 9th ent fnl f: wknd ins fnl f* **25/1**

14 4 ½ **Reckless Lad (IRE)**[9] 910 6-8-11 **89**..........................(tp) ShaneFoley 12 55
(Patrick Martin, Ire) *mid-div: rdn in 12th 1 1/2f out and no imp: one pce fnl f* **33/1**

15 1 ½ **Bold Thady Quill (IRE)**[162] 7130 9-8-10 **98**......(tp) AndrewBreslin(10) 16 60
(K J Condon, Ire) *dwlt and in rr: no imp at 1/2-way: kpt on one pce fnl 2f: nvr a factor* **25/1**

16 2 ¼ **Vivat Rex (IRE)**[16] 829 5-8-12 **90**................................(bt) GaryCarroll 13 47
(John James Feane, Ire) *in rr of mid-div: rdn and no imp 2f out: one pce* **33/1**

17 2 ½ **Cailin Mor (IRE)**[155] 7303 4-8-6 **91**........................ ConorMcGovern(7) 21 42
(M Halford, Ire) *settled bhd ldrs: rdn in 6th fr 3f out and sn no ex: wknd fnl 2f* **8/1**[2]

18 shd **Romiac (IRE)**[237] 4712 4-8-5 **83** oh1 ow1..........................(b) BenCurtis 4 34
(Ms Sheila Lavery, Ire) *mid-div best: rdn and wknd fr 3f out* **28/1**

19 ½ **Rivers Of Babylon (IRE)**[206] 5794 4-9-1 **93**.....................(b[1]) BillyLee 17 43
(W McCreery, Ire) *towards rr thrght: pushed along fr 1/2-way and no imp* **33/1**

20 1 ¼ **Princess Aloof (IRE)**[148] 7477 5-9-0 **92**.............(p) ColmO'Donoghue 19 39
(Mrs John Harrington, Ire) *towards rr thrght: pushed along fr 1/2-way and no imp* **20/1**

21 4 ¾ **Nebulla**[173] 6846 4-8-9 **87**... DeclanMcDonogh 15 23
(John M Oxx, Ire) *towards rr thrght: pushed along over 2f out and no imp: eased under 2f out* **20/1**

22 9 ½ **Ashraf (IRE)**[148] 7477 4-9-5 **97**... PatSmullen 11 11
(D K Weld, Ire) *mid-div: pushed along in 12th fr 1/2-way and sn wknd: eased 2f out* **11/4**[1]

1m 46.03s (0.03) **Going Correction** +0.35s/f (Good) **22** Ran SP% **140.8**
Speed ratings: **113,108,108,106,105 105,102,101,101,99 99,96,95,91,89 87,84,84,84,83 78,68**
CSF £98.78 CT £1254.43 TOTE £14.60: £4.80, £2.60, £4.30, £10.90; DF 126.00 Trifecta £2053.60.
Owner Robert Ng **Bred** Messrs J , R & J Hyland **Trained** The Curragh, Co Kildare

FOCUS
A one-two for Paul Deegan, won by a horse that had dropped almost a stone in the ratings from last year and showed in some style that he's much better than a handicapper.

1017 - 1020a (Foreign Racing) - See Raceform Interactive

929 SAINT-CLOUD (L-H)
Sunday, March 20

OFFICIAL GOING: Turf: good to soft

1021a PRIX DE LA MARCHE (CLAIMER) (2YO) (TURF) 4f 110y
1:00 (12:00) 2-Y-O **£8,455** (£3,382; £2,536; £1,691; £845)

RPR

1 **Nuee Ardente (FR)** 2-9-1 0................................ Pierre-CharlesBoudot 2 80
(M Boutin, France) **9/5**[2]

2 4 **Secret Lady** 2-8-8 0.. RichardKingscote 1 57
(Tom Dascombe) *led: rdn and hdd over 1f out: no ex w wnr fnl f* **7/4**[1]

3 1 ¼ **Stella Pyla (FR)** 2-8-8 0.. AntoineHamelin 10 52
(C Baillet, France) **67/10**

4 3 **Batura Sar (FR)** 2-9-1 0.. MickaelBarzalona 8 47
(M Boutin, France) **141/10**

5 3 ½ **Evidence Sarthoise (FR)** 2-8-8 0....................(p) LudovicBoisseau(3) 4 29
(C Plisson, France) **28/1**

6 4 **Hello Traou Land (FR)** 2-8-8 0.................................... EddyHardouin 6 10
(C Baillet, France) **13/2**[3]

7 1 **Keltetu** 2-8-11 0.. CristianDemuro 7 9
(J-V Toux, France) **103/10**

8 nk **Sowgay (FR)** 2-9-1 0...(p) TonyPiccone 9 12
(C Plisson, France) **147/10**

9 nk **Kidane Traou Land (FR)** 2-8-11 0..........................(p) RonanThomas 5 7
(C Plisson, France) **31/1**

10 nk **Esculape D'Emra (FR)** 2-9-1 0..................................(p) ClementCadel 3 9
(C Plisson, France) **175/10**

WIN (incl. 1 euro stake): 2.80 (Nuee Ardente coupled with Batura Star).
Owner M Boutin **Bred**, M Boutin & H Boutin **Trained** France

1023a PRIX EXBURY (GROUP 3) (4YO+) (TURF) 1m 2f
3:10 (12:00) 4-Y-O+ **£29,411** (£11,764; £8,823; £5,882; £2,941)

RPR

1 **Garlingari (FR)**[22] 751 5-8-9 0..............................(p) StephanePasquier 5 110
(Mme C Barande-Barbe, France) *led: rdn 2f out: jnd ent fnl f: styd on and battled bk gamely u.p: edgd ahd again towards fin* **7/1**

2 ½ **Sumbal (IRE)**[155] 7281 4-9-2 0................................. Pierre-CharlesBoudot 7 116
(F-H Graffard, France) *trckd wnr: rdn to chal and upsides ent fnl f: styd on but jst hld in 2nd towards fin* **5/4**[1]

3 1 **Affaire Solitaire (IRE)**[35] 585 6-9-0 0.......................... OlivierPeslier 6 112+
(P Khozian, France) *hld up in last: rdn over 1f out: styd on and wnt 3rd fnl strides: nrst fin* **8/1**

4 nk **Free Port Lux**[98] 8219 5-9-2 0..................................... MickaelBarzalona 1 113
(F Head, France) *in tch on inner: rdn over 1f out: styd on same pce against rail fnl f and nt quite able to chal: lost 3rd fnl strides* **10/3**[2]

5 ½ **Tullius (IRE)**[22] 748 8-9-2 0... JimmyFortune 3 112+
(Andrew Balding) *in tch: rdn and effrt 2f out: outpcd and hld fnl f: jst prevailed for 5th* **9/2**[3]

6 nse **Sussudio (FR)**[8] 931 6-8-9 0.. GregoryBenoist 4 105
(Frau Hella Sauer, Germany) *hld up: rdn over 1f out: styd on fnl f but nvr able to chal: jst lost out for 5th* **9/1**

7 2 **Rooke**[154] 7324 6-8-9 0.. ThomasHenderson 2 101
(D Henderson, France) *midfield: rdn over 2f out: outpcd and dropped to last fnl f* **40/1**

2m 9.98s (-6.02) **7** Ran SP% **121.8**
WIN (incl. 1 euro stake): 7.30. PLACES: 3.00, 1.80. SF: 27.70.
Owner Mme Corine Barande-Barbe **Bred** Mme C Barande Barbe & Mme J J Massy **Trained** France

1024a PRIX OMNIUM II (LISTED RACE) (3YO COLTS & GELDINGS) (TURF) 1m
3:40 (12:00) 3-Y-O **£20,220** (£8,088; £6,066; £4,044; £2,022)

RPR

1 **Dicton**[11] 3-9-2 0... OlivierPeslier 5 106
(Gianluca Bietolini, Italy) **4/1**[2]

2 snk **Barwod**[164] 7070 3-9-2 0...................................... Pierre-CharlesBoudot 9 105
(A Fabre, France) **17/10**[1]

3 1 ¼ **Helene Charisma (FR)**[214] 3-9-2 0............................ CristianDemuro 1 103+
(Mme Pia Brandt, France) **9/2**[3]

4 hd **Millfield (FR)**[140] 7666 3-9-2 0...................................... GregoryBenoist 6 102
(D Smaga, France) **23/5**

5 snk **Cheikeljack (FR)**[164] 7071 3-9-2 0.......................... MickaelBarzalona 8 102
(H-A Pantall, France) **16/1**

6 1 ¼ **Snowmaster (FR)**[143] 3-9-2 0.. FabriceVeron 3 99+
(H-A Pantall, France) **109/10**

7 1 ¼ **Fourioso (FR)**[117] 7970 3-9-2 0................................ StephanePasquier 2 96
(K Borgel, France) **183/10**

8 1 **Fanfaron (FR)**[200] 6007 3-9-2 0.. AlexisBadel 4 94
(D Prod'Homme, France) **196/10**

9 4 **No Education**[140] 7665 3-9-2 0.. JoeyHaynes 7 85
(Jo Hughes) *led: rdn and hdd 2f out: sn no ex and btn: wknd: dropped to last fnl f* **196/10**

1m 42.23s (-5.27) **9** Ran SP% **122.3**
WIN (incl. 1 euro stake): 5.00. PLACES: 1.70, 1.50, 1.70. DF: 9.10. SF: 16.20.
Owner Robert Ng **Bred** Wertheimer Et Frere **Trained** Italy

1022 - 1025a (Foreign Racing) - See Raceform Interactive

956 SOUTHWELL (L-H)
Tuesday, March 22

OFFICIAL GOING: Fibresand: standard
Wind: Virtually nil Weather: Grey cloud

1026 UNIBET OFFER DAILY JOCKEY & TRAINER SPECIALS H'CAP 5f (F)
2:20 (2:21) (Class 6) (0-58,63) 4-Y-O+ **£2,587** (£770; £384; £192) **Stalls** Centre

Form RPR

6064 **1** **Coiste Bodhar (IRE)**[6] 961 5-9-7 **58**............................... KieranO'Neill 1 64
(Scott Dixon) *racd centre: cl up: chal 2f out: rdn to ld and edgd rt ent fnl f: drvn out* **14/1**

2222 **2** hd **Imjin River (IRE)**[7] 937 9-8-11 **48**....................................(tp) BenCurtis 5 53
(William Stone) *racd centre: chsd ldrs: rdn along and sltly outpcd over 2f out: hdwy whn n.m.r and swtchd lft ent fnl f: sn drvn and kpt on wl towards fin* **7/2**[1]

6534 **3** shd **Cerulean Silk**[25] 730 6-8-9 **46** oh1..............................(p) WilliamCarson 8 51
(Tony Carroll) *slt ld: rdn along wl over 1f out: hdd and drvn ent fnl f: kpt on wl* **33/1**

5052 **4** 1 ¼ **Very First Blade**[6] 961 7-9-4 **55**................................(be) RobertHavlin 2 55
(Michael Mullineaux) *racd towards far side: hdwy 1/2-way: rdn to chse ldrs over 1f out: drvn and kpt on same pce fnl f* **9/1**[2]

3561 **5** 1 ¼ **Monsieur Jamie**[7] 937 8-9-12 **63** 6ex........................(v) FrederikTylicki 3 59
(J R Jenkins) *racd towards far side: in tch: hdwy on outer 1/2-way: rdn to chse ldrs over 1f out: sn drvn and no imp* **7/2**[1]

6335 **6** 1 ¼ **Lucky Mark (IRE)**[6] 963 7-9-6 **57**........................(b[1]) DanielTudhope 11 48
(John Balding) *racd towards stands' rail: cl up: rdn along over 2f out: grad wknd* **10/1**[3]

560 **7** nk **Fuel Injection**[39] 542 5-9-6 **57**.................................(p) BarryMcHugh 12 47
(Paul Midgley) *racd towards stands' rail: cl up: disp ld after 2f: rdn along 2f out: drvn over 1f out and grad wknd* **16/1**

35-0 **8** 2 ¼ **Under Approval**[14] 869 5-8-8 **50**...........................(b) GemmaTutty(5) 7 32
(Karen Tutty) *dwlt: sn in tch centre: rdn along 2f out: sn no hdwy* **25/1**

2-02 **9** 4 **Perfect Peak**[14] 869 4-9-0 **58**..................................(vt) NathanEvans(7) 6 26
(Michael Easterby) *dwlt and towards rr: swtchd rt and rdn along after 2f: n.d* **7/2**[1]

5050 **10** 1 ¼ **Little**[3] 1005 4-8-9 **46** oh1..(b) AdamBeschizza 4 9
(Steph Hollinshead) *dwlt: racd towards far side: a in rr* **16/1**

302- **11** 4 **George Bailey (IRE)**[101] 8196 4-8-13 **50**.............................. TomEaves 10
(Suzzanne France) *racd towards stands' rail: in tch: pushed along bef 1/2-way: rdn over 2f out and sn outpcd* **20/1**

326- **12** 5 **Robbian**[139] 7711 5-8-6 **50**... RPWalsh(7) 9
(Charles Smith) *dwlt: sn swtchd rt and rdn along: a in rr* **66/1**

59.74s (0.04) **Going Correction** 0.0s/f (Stan) **12** Ran SP% **117.2**
Speed ratings (Par 101): **99,98,98,96,94 92,92,88,82,80 73,65**
CSF £59.77 CT £1645.38 TOTE £17.10: £6.00, £1.60, £6.30; EX 79.40 Trifecta £4585.70.
Owner Ms Y Lowe **Bred** C Amerian **Trained** Babworth, Notts

FOCUS
A run-of-the-mill sprint handicap with the action typically taking place down the middle of the track. Straightforward form.

1027 LADBROKES MEDIAN AUCTION MAIDEN STKS 1m (F)
2:55 (2:55) (Class 5) 3-5-Y-O **£3,234** (£962; £481; £240) **Stalls** Low

Form RPR

5- **1** **Dubai In Bloom (IRE)**[210] 5709 3-8-6 0.................. SilvestreDeSousa 3 73+
(Simon Crisford) *cl up: led wl over 3f out: pushed clr wl over 1f out: kpt on strly* **15/2**

00 **2** 1 ½ **Melendez (USA)**[20] 789 3-8-11 0................................ WilliamCarson 4 74
(Jamie Osborne) *trckd ldrs: effrt and n.m.r wl over 2f out and sn swtchd lft: rdn wl over 1f out: chsd wnr appr fnl f: sn drvn and no imp* **25/1**

53-2 **3** 1 ¼ **Pickapocket (IRE)**[52] 400 3-8-11 68...........................(p) OisinMurphy 1 71
(Andrew Balding) *trckd ldrs on inner: pushed along wl over 3f out: rdn and outpcd 3f out: hdwy on inner over 2f out: kpt on u.p fnl f* **9/4**[2]

545- **4** 6 **Henry The Explorer (CAN)**[181] 6645 3-8-11 77............. JoeyHaynes 6 57
(Jo Hughes) *chsd ldrs on outer: cl up 3f out: rdn along over 2f out: drvn wl over 1f out and sn wknd* **3/1**[3]

42- **5** *4 1/2* **Magical Lasso (IRE)**[177] 6781 3-8-8 0 JoeDoyle(3) 2 46
(Kevin Ryan) *slt ld: hdd wl over 3f out and sn pushed along: rdn wl over 2f out: sn drvn and wknd* **7/4**[1]

6 *8* **Hooks Lane**[143] 4-10-0 0 TomEaves 5 32
(Shaun Harris) *a in rr: outpcd and bhd fnl 3f* **100/1**

7 *37* **Basil Bear** 4-10-0 0 AdamBeschizza 7
(Deborah Sanderson) *s.i.s and wnt bdly rt s: green and bhd: hdwy and in tch 1/2-way: rdn along over 3f out: wknd qckly: sn bhd and eased* **100/1**

1m 42.53s (-1.17) **Going Correction** -0.075s/f (Stan)
WFA 3 from 4yo 17lb **7** Ran SP% **109.7**
Speed ratings (Par 103): **102,100,99,93,88 80,43**
CSF £117.46 TOTE £5.90: £2.70, £6.50; EX 68.50 Trifecta £369.60.
Owner Mohammed Al Shafar **Bred** Rabbah Bloodstock Limited **Trained** Newmarket, Suffolk

FOCUS
A modest maiden but both the winner and runner-up have something to recommend them going forward. The third helps set the opening level, but it's fluid.

1028 CORAL APP DOWNLOAD FROM THE APP STORE H'CAP 1m 4f (F)
3:30 (3:30) (Class 5) (0-75,76) 4-Y-O+ **£3,234** (£962; £481; £240) **Stalls** Low

Form RPR

-023 **1** **Prayer Time**[12] 890 4-8-8 **63** SaleemGolam 1 71
(Mark H Tompkins) *trckd ldng pair on inner: pushed along over 3f out: swtchd rt to outer and effrt over 2f out: rdn to chal wl over 1f out: styd on to ld jst ins fnl f* **5/1**[2]

2244 **2** *nk* **Comanche Chieftain (CAN)**[12] 890 4-8-11 **66**(p) AndrewMullen 4 74
(Michael Appleby) *led: jnd and pushed along 4f out: styd nr inner rail and rdn wl over 2f out: drvn over 1f out: hdd jst ins fnl f: kpt on gamely* **15/8**[1]

2-11 **3** *5* **Blades Lad**[7] 940 7-9-9 **76** 6ex (p) TomEaves 5 76
(Peter Niven) *cl up: chal 4f out: rdn wl over 2f out: drvn and ev ch over 1f out: wknd ins fnl f* **15/8**[1]

406- **4** *4 1/2* **Chorus of Lies**[148] 7520 4-9-0 **69** JoeFanning 7 62
(Tracy Waggott) *trckd ldng pair: hdwy 4f out: cl up and rdn along 3f out: drvn over 2f out and kpt on one pce* **9/1**

60-0 **5** *2 1/4* **Powderonthebonnet (IRE)**[19] 802 8-8-6 **62** JoeDoyle(3) 6 51
(Richard Phillips) *sltly hmpd s and in rr: rdn along 4f out: plugged on fnl 2f: n.d* **66/1**

0-20 **6** *nk* **The Kid**[39] 545 5-9-7 **74** (p) PhillipMakin 2 63
(John Quinn) *chsd ldrs: rdn along over 3f out: drvn wl over 2f out and sn outpcd* **8/1**[3]

0/00 **7** *3 1/2* **Maria's Choice (IRE)**[26] 712 7-9-5 **72** TimmyMurphy 3 55
(Jim Best) *sltly hmpd s: a in rr* **100/1**

2m 39.61s (-1.39) **Going Correction** -0.075s/f (Stan)
WFA 4 from 5yo+ 2lb **7** Ran SP% **109.8**
Speed ratings (Par 103): **101,100,97,94,92 92,90**
CSF £13.61 TOTE £4.60: £2.40, £1.60; EX 12.70 Trifecta £33.90.
Owner Sarabex **Bred** Sarabex **Trained** Newmarket, Suffolk

FOCUS
Uncompetitive fare and the three to come into the race in any sort of form filled the placings. The first two have been rated as improving slightly.

1029 DAILY UNIBET EARLY PRICES FROM 9AM H'CAP 5f (F)
4:00 (4:00) (Class 4) (0-85,85) 3-Y-O **£5,175** (£1,540; £769; £384) **Stalls** Centre

Form RPR

60-1 **1** **Ticking Away**[6] 962 3-8-8 **72** 6ex ow1 SeanLevey 2 90+
(David Brown) *trckd ldrs: hdwy to take slt ld on bit 1/2-way: eased clr appr fnl f: easily* **8/11**[1]

-641 **2** *1 3/4* **Mysterious Look**[19] 797 3-8-3 **67** KieranO'Neill 3 71
(Ed McMahon) *trckd ldrs: hdwy 2f out: rdn to chal over 1f out and ev ch: drvn fnl f: kpt on but no ch w wnr* **5/1**[3]

633- **3** *2 3/4* **Socialites Red**[185] 6523 3-8-7 **71** BenCurtis 4 65
(Scott Dixon) *cl up: rdn along 2f out: sn drvn and kpt on same pce* **16/1**

-346 **4** *1 1/2* **Thatsallimsaying (IRE)**[28] 686 3-9-6 **84** JFEgan 1 73
(David Evans) *slt ld: hdd and pushed along 1/2-way: sn rdn: drvn wl over 1f out and sn wknd* **28/1**

01-2 **5** *1* **Furiant**[13] 881 3-9-7 **85** JoeFanning 6 70
(Mark Johnston) *cl up: rdn along over 2f out: sn outpcd* **10/3**[2]

015- **6** *17* **Caymus**[147] 7523 3-8-7 **71** BarryMcHugh 5
(Tracy Waggott) *sn outpcd and bhd fr 1/2-way* **100/1**

59.45s (-0.25) **Going Correction** 0.0s/f (Stan) **6** Ran SP% **108.0**
Speed ratings (Par 100): **102,99,94,92,90 63**
CSF £4.37 TOTE £1.60: £1.10, £3.20; EX 4.60 Trifecta £18.00.
Owner J C Fretwell **Bred** Mrs Fiona Denniff **Trained** Averham Park, Notts

FOCUS
A visually stunning performance from the winner, who has been a revelation this year, never off the bridle in coasting home. He's been rated up 10lb on his C&D win six days earlier.

1030 DAILY PRICE BOOSTS AT UNIBET H'CAP 6f (F)
4:30 (4:30) (Class 5) (0-75,73) 4-Y-O+ **£3,234** (£962; £481; £240) **Stalls** Low

Form RPR

0341 **1** **Sir Geoffrey (IRE)**[6] 963 10-8-9 **61** 6ex (b) KieranO'Neill 5 66
(Scott Dixon) *qckly away and led: rdn wl over 1f out: drvn and hdd ins fnl f: rallied gamely to ld again nr fin* **11/1**

0-34 **2** *hd* **Viva Verglas (IRE)**[20] 784 5-8-11 **66** RobHornby(3) 4 70
(Daniel Mark Loughnane) *hld up towards rr: hdwy on outer 2f out: rdn over 1f out: styd on strly fnl f* **7/2**[1]

6023 **3** *nk* **Spowarticus**[7] 942 7-8-13 **65** (b) BenCurtis 3 68
(Scott Dixon) *trckd ldrs on inner: hdwy 2f out: rdn to chal over 1f out: drvn to take slt ld ins fnl f: hdd and no ex towards fin* **15/2**

0034 **4** *1 1/4* **Jaarih (IRE)**[11] 903 4-9-7 **73** (p) PaulMulrennan 8 72
(Conor Dore) *prom: hdwy 1/2-way: rdn 2f out and sn ev ch: drvn over 1f out: kpt on same pce fnl f* **9/2**[2]

2633 **5** *2 1/2* **Danish Duke (IRE)**[12] 893 5-8-11 **63** (p) JamesSullivan 9 54
(Ruth Carr) *trckd ldrs: hdwy over 2f out: rdn over 1f out: sn drvn and no imp* **9/2**[2]

02-2 **6** *1 1/4* **Lackaday**[15] 856 4-9-7 **73** (p) JasonHart 1 60
(Mark Walford) *in tch on inner: hdwy over 2f out: rdn wl over 1f out: sn drvn and no imp* **7/1**[3]

1106 **7** *5* **Speightowns Kid (USA)**[41] 520 8-8-11 **67** ow1 (be) AnnStokell(5) 10 39
(Ann Stokell) *a towards rr* **20/1**

306- **8** *4* **Percy's Gal**[161] 7188 5-9-2 **73** GemmaTutty(5) 6 32
(Karen Tutty) *t.k.h: chsd wnr: rdn along 1/2-way: sn wknd* **10/1**

166- **9** *1* **Daylight**[98] 8236 6-8-11 **63** GrahamGibbons 7 18
(Michael Easterby) *dwlt: a in rr* **12/1**

1m 15.66s (-0.84) **Going Correction** -0.075s/f (Stan) **9** Ran SP% **112.7**
Speed ratings (Par 103): **102,101,101,99,96 94,88,82,81**
CSF £48.11 CT £309.52 TOTE £10.30: £2.50, £1.70, £2.00; EX 61.10 Trifecta £369.70.
Owner General Sir Geoffrey Howlett **Bred** P Rabbitte **Trained** Babworth, Notts

FOCUS
Some in-form sprinters on show, none more so than the veteran winner who was gaining an 18th career success.

1031 32RED APPRENTICE H'CAP 1m (F)
5:05 (5:05) (Class 6) (0-60,63) 3-Y-O **£2,587** (£770; £384; £192) **Stalls** Low

Form RPR

36-1 **1** **Palpitation (IRE)**[7] 947 3-9-10 **63** 6ex AaronJones 6 74
(David Brown) *trckd ldng pair: cl up 3f out: led wl over 1f out: sn pushed clr: styd on strly* **11/10**[1]

6341 **2** *1 1/2* **Footlight**[12] 896 3-9-1 **59** AdamMcNamara(5) 8 64
(Richard Fahey) *towards rr: hdwy 3f out: chsd ldrs 2f out: sn rdn: styd on to chse wnr ins fnl f: no imp* **5/2**[2]

450- **3** *1 1/2* **Mr Lucas (IRE)**[140] 7684 3-8-4 **46** oh1 (p) NathanEvans(3) 5 47
(Peter Niven) *slt ld to 1/2-way: cl up: led again 3f out: rdn along over 2f out: hdd wl over 1f out: sn drvn and kpt on same pce* **33/1**

-436 **4** *1/2* **Rubis**[29] 678 3-9-2 **60** NatalieHambling(5) 2 60
(Richard Fahey) *dwlt and towards rr: hdwy 1/2-way: chsd ldrs 3f out: rdn along over 2f out: drvn wl over 1f out and kpt on same pce* **16/1**

2362 **5** *3 3/4* **Never Say (IRE)**[12] 896 3-8-3 **47** (v[1]) KieranSchofield(5) 9 38
(Jason Ward) *dwlt and in rr: wd st: hdwy 2f out: sn rdn and plugged on fnl f* **17/2**[3]

41 **6** *6* **Rupert Boy (IRE)**[42] 509 3-9-7 **60** (b) NoelGarbutt 3 37
(Scott Dixon) *cl up on inner: slt ld 1/2-way: rdn along and hdd 3f out: styd cl to far rail: sn drvn and wknd* **10/1**

620- **7** *13* **Imshi's Little Bro (IRE)**[265] 3783 3-9-6 **59** [1] GemmaTutty 4 5
(Ivan Furtado) *chsd ldrs towards inner: rdn along over 3f out: sn wknd* **16/1**

0466 **8** *27* **Keep The Silence (IRE)**[19] 794 3-9-4 **57** (p) CallumShepherd 7
(James Tate) *chsd ldrs: rdn along over 3f out: sn wknd* **14/1**

1m 43.58s (-0.12) **Going Correction** -0.075s/f (Stan) **8** Ran SP% **117.2**
Speed ratings (Par 96): **97,95,94,93,89 83,70,43**
CSF £4.03 CT £51.89 TOTE £2.10: £1.20, £1.20, £6.30; EX 4.60 Trifecta £82.20.
Owner D A West **Bred** R M Jennings **Trained** Averham Park, Notts

FOCUS
A low-grade finale won in comfortable fashion by an improving and well-handicapped 3yo.
T/Plt: £248.10 to a £1 stake. Pool: £85,715.05 - 252.14 winning units. T/Qpdt: £6.20 to a £1 stake. Pool: £10,180.70 - 1197.26 winning units. **Joe Rowntree**

1032 - 1033a (Foreign Racing) - See Raceform Interactive

[972]CHANTILLY (R-H)
Tuesday, March 22

OFFICIAL GOING: Polytrack: standard

1034a PRIX DU MAHIEU VILAIN (CLAIMER) (5YO+) (POLYTRACK) 1m
2:55 (12:00) 5-Y-O+ **£6,985** (£2,794; £2,095; £1,397; £698)

RPR

1 **Menardais (FR)**[19] 804 7-9-1 0 PierreBazire(7) 2 88
(P Bary, France) **8/5**[1]

2 *3* **See You Soon (FR)**[85] 5-9-4 0 AnthonyCrastus 4 77
(N Caullery, France) **172/10**

3 *hd* **Lykastos (IRE)**[7] 6-9-3 0 (b) EmmanuelEtienne(5) 6 81
(A Amezzane, France) **43/5**

4 *1 3/4* **Orphic (FR)**[7] 7-9-10 0 RonanThomas 10 79
(J Phelippon, France) **6/1**[3]

5 *1/2* **Kingspone (FR)**[213] 5654 5-9-1 0 UmbertoRispoli 1 69
(Mme P Butel, France) **163/10**

6 *shd* **Chopsoave (FR)**[85] 8-8-7 0 AdrienMoreau(8) 3 69
(N Caullery, France) **93/10**

7 *snk* **Stephill (FR)**[12] 5-9-2 0 (b) Pierre-CharlesBoudot 13 69
(J Phelippon, France) **156/10**

8 *2 1/2* **Tree Of Grace (FR)**[7] 5-8-11 0 GlenBraem 8 59
(Andrew Hollinshead, France) **45/1**

9 *1/2* **Tostaky Blue (FR)**[7] 7-8-11 0 (p) JeremieCatineau(4) 11 61
(A Spanu, France) **35/1**

10 *10* **My Approach (IRE)**[7] 6-8-9 0 MathieuPelletan(6) 7 38
(Robert Collet, France) **65/1**

11 *9* **Servantes (FR)**[5] 5-8-8 0 (b) LudovicBoisseau(3) 12 14
(B Legros, France) **67/1**

12 *3/4* **Elusive Guest (FR)**[86] 8369 5-9-10 0 TonyPiccone 9 25
(Harry Dunlop) *slow to stride: pushed along and hdwy to ld after 1f: scrubbed along whn pressed wl over 2f out: hdd ent fnl 2f: wknd fr 1 1/2f out: eased last 150yds* **23/5**[2]

Owner Mme Georges Sandor **Bred** Georges Sandor **Trained** Chantilly, France
WIN (incl. 1 euro stake): 2.60. PLACES: 1.40, 2.50, 2.00. DF: 19.50. SF: 23.80.

[949]KEMPTON (A.W) (R-H)
Wednesday, March 23

OFFICIAL GOING: Polytrack: standard
Wind: Almost nil Weather: Cloudy

1035 RACING UK ANYWHERE H'CAP 1m (P)
5:45 (5:45) (Class 7) (0-50,50) 4-Y-O+ **£1,940** (£577; £288; £144) **Stalls** Low

Form RPR

4/0- **1** **Theydon Thunder**[384] 789 4-8-13 **45** DanielMuscutt(3) 5 57+
(Peter Charalambous) *wl plcd bhd ldrs: smooth prog 2f out: led over 1f out: sn clr: pushed out* **14/1**

4252 **2** *3 1/4* **Dreaming Again**[14] 876 6-9-6 **49** KieranO'Neill 10 54
(Jimmy Fox) *sn in rr: pushed along over 3f out: no prog tl drvn and styd on fr over 1f out to take 2nd last 100yds: no ch w wnr* **5/2**[1]

00-6 **3** *3/4* **Mount Cheiron (USA)**[5] 986 5-9-0 **50** CallumRodriguez(7) 8 55
(Richard Ford) *towards rr: prog jst over 2f out: rdn to chse wnr 1f out to last 100yds: kpt on* **6/1**[2]

0001 **4** *1 1/4* **My Time**[15] 867 7-9-5 **48** (be) AdamKirby 6 49
(Michael Mullineaux) *in tch in midfield: rdn over 2f out: prog over 1f out: kpt on but nvr gng pce to threaten* **16/1**

0505 **5** *1 1/2* **Sixties Queen**[22] 776 6-9-2 **45** (p) RoystonFfrench 3 43
(Lisa Williamson) *broke fast but didn't ld: chsd ldng pair after 1f: rdn and nt qckn 2f out: fdd fnl f* **25/1**

6020 **6** *1 1/4* **Crowning Star (IRE)**[14] 876 7-9-2 **45** (p) WilliamCarson 11 41
(Steve Woodman) *led after 1f: rdn and hdd over 1f out: wknd tamely fnl f* **8/1**

The Form Book, Raceform Ltd, Newbury, RG14 5SJ

0036 **7** *1 1/4* **Tax Reform (IRE)**^{14} 876 6-8-9 **45**................................ HollieDoyle(7) 1 39
(Natalie Lloyd-Beavis) *s.i.s: wl in rr: tried to make prog on inner over 2f out: urged along and wknd over 1f out* **13/2**^{3}

0061 **8** *1/2* **Chandrayaan**^{14} 876 9-9-4 **47**.................................(v) RobertHavlin 4 39
(John E Long) *hld up in last pair: rdn and fnd nil over 2f out: no ch after: kpt on last 100yds* **8/1**

0/ **9** *hd* **Virgil Earp**^{1614} 5574 9-9-4 **50**.................................. GeorgeDowning(3) 9 42
(Ian Williams) *wl plcd bhd ldrs: rdn over 2f out: wknd wl over 1f out* **13/2**^{3}

5-50 **10** *4* **Let It Go**^{56} 346 4-9-2 **45**.. LukeMorris 7 29
(Tony Carroll) *t.k.h: led 1f: chsd ldr to 2f out: wknd qckly* **25/1**

U00/ **11** *3 1/4* **Water For Life**^{49} 7645 5-8-13 **45**................................ RosieJessop(3) 2 23
(Martin Smith) *s.i.s: a wl in rr: bhd fnl 2f* **33/1**

1m 39.14s (-0.66) **Going Correction** -0.05s/f (Stan) **11** Ran SP% **114.9**
Speed ratings (Par 97): **101,97,97,95,94 93,91,91,91,87 83**
CSF £47.00 CT £243.27 TOTE £19.20: £5.00, £1.40, £2.30; EX 77.70 Trifecta £571.80.
Owner pcracing.co.uk **Bred** Mill Farm Stud **Trained** Newmarket, Suffolk

FOCUS
A moderate handicap but won by a relatively unexposed horse. The runner-up is a fair guide to the level.

1036 32RED CASINO MAIDEN STKS 1m (P)
6:15 (6:20) (Class 5) 3-Y-O+ **£2,911** (£866; £432; £216) **Stalls** Low

Form RPR

052- **1** **Al Hamd (IRE)**^{194} 6276 3-8-11 77..................................... LukeMorris 8 80
(Ed Dunlop) *mde all: shkn up and drew clr 2f out: coasted home fr over 1f out* **8/15**^{1}

5 **2** *5* **Haabis (USA)**^{28} 691 3-8-12 0 ow1...........................(t) StevieDonohoe 5 65
(George Peckham) *chsd ldng trio: shkn up over 2f out: prog to go 2nd over 1f out: one pce and no ch w wnr* **7/1**^{3}

3 *3/4* **General Hazard (IRE)** 3-8-11 0................................. WilliamCarson 7 62
(Michael Bell) *difficult to load into stall: disp 2nd pl: rdn over 2f out: no ch w wnr after: lost 2nd over 1f out: one pce* **25/1**

2 **4** *1/2* **I Can't Stop**^{28} 691 3-8-6 0... RyanPowell 1 58+
(Chris Wall) *dwlt: trying to rcvr whn no room and snatched up after 100yds: in last pair after and rdn over 2f out: no prog tl kpt on wl fnl f* **4/1**^{2}

5 *shd* **London Glory** 3-8-11 0... RobertHavlin 9 61
(Chris Wall) *stdd into rr: pushed along over 2f out: rn green but kpt on fnl f* **12/1**

00 **6** *nk* **Attitude Rocks**^{28} 691 3-8-11 0.. JohnFahy 6 60
(Clive Cox) *disp 2nd pl: rdn over 2f out: no ch w wnr after: lost 2nd over 1f out: one pce after: lost pls nr fin* **14/1**

00- **7** *1/2* **Ancient World (USA)**^{162} 7175 3-8-11 0....................... DarryllHolland 4 59+
(Charles Hills) *n.m.r and snatched up after 1f: shkn up in rr over 2f out: kpt on fnl f but no threat* **16/1**

00 **8** *11* **Zac Courageous (IRE)**^{16} 863 4-9-9 0.................. RachealKneller(5) 2 37
(James Bennett) *n.m.r briefly after 1f: sn in last: bhd whn rn wd bnd 3f out: t.o* **100/1**

1m 40.1s (0.30) **Going Correction** -0.05s/f (Stan)
WFA 3 from 4yo+ 17lb **8** Ran SP% **122.8**
Speed ratings (Par 103): **96,91,90,89,89 89,88,77**
CSF £5.94 TOTE £1.40: £1.02, £2.20, £4.30; EX 6.50 Trifecta £68.40.
Owner Hamdan Al Maktoum **Bred** Shadwell Estate Company Limited **Trained** Newmarket, Suffolk

FOCUS
A steadily run maiden dominated from the front by the odds-on winner. The opening level is fluid.

1037 £10 FREE BET AT 32REDSPORT.COM MEDIAN AUCTION MAIDEN STKS 1m 4f (P)
6:45 (6:45) (Class 6) 3-5-Y-O **£2,264** (£673; £336; £168) **Stalls** Centre

Form RPR

6- **1** **October Storm**^{154} 7397 3-8-6 0................................ SilvestreDeSousa 5 76+
(Mick Channon) *chsd ldr after 1f: rdn 3f out: clsd to ld 2f out: drvn out and asserted fnl f* **15/8**^{2}

500- **2** *2 1/2* **Havisham**^{214} 5639 4-9-12 83.. DavidProbert 3 74
(Andrew Balding) *led: gng best 3f out: shkn up and hdd 2f out: nt qckn after and one pce fnl f* **5/6**^{1}

6-64 **3** *2* **Howardian Hills (IRE)**^{14} 880 3-8-3 65.................. TomMarquand(3) 4 69
(Richard Hannon) *chsd ldng pair after 1f: rdn over 3f out: nvr gng pce to chal but kpt on fnl 2f* **6/1**^{3}

0 **4** *25* **Up North (IRE)**^{16} 863 4-9-12 0.. JimCrowley 6 31
(Micky Hammond) *hld up in last: tk 4th 5f out: shkn up 4f out: stl green and wknd over 2f out: t.o* **33/1**

5 *41* **Tilsworth Phyllis**^{33} 4-9-7 0... KierenFox 1
(J R Jenkins) *chsd ldr 1f: rdn and dropped to last 5f out: sn t.o* **100/1**

2m 34.58s (0.08) **Going Correction** -0.05s/f (Stan)
WFA 3 from 4yo 22lb **5** Ran SP% **107.6**
Speed ratings (Par 101): **97,95,94,77,50**
CSF £3.58 TOTE £2.30: £1.20, £1.10; EX 3.50 Trifecta £4.80.
Owner Jon and Julia Aisbitt **Bred** Meon Valley Stud **Trained** West Ilsley, Berks

FOCUS
It's unlikely the runner-up ran to his rating and the third is probably a better guide. The runner-up has been rated close to last year's Polytrack efforts.

1038 32RED ON THE APP STORE H'CAP (DIV I) 2m (P)
7:15 (7:15) (Class 6) (0-65,64) 4-Y-O+ **£2,264** (£673; £336; £168) **Stalls** Low

Form RPR

233- **1** **Wolf Of Windlesham (IRE)**^{53} 6239 4-9-3 **60**............ StevieDonohoe 8 75+
(Stuart Edmunds) *trckd ldrs: pushed along 3f out: prog to ld wl over 1f out: sn clr: v comf* **11/8**^{1}

0-52 **2** *5* **Jezza**^{28} 695 10-9-1 **58**..(bt) CallumShepherd(5) 7 63
(Victor Dartnall) *hld up towards rr: quick prog to join ldrs 7f out but then t.k.h and stdd: prog arnd rivals over 3f out: led over 2f out to wl over 1f out: no ch w wnr after but hld on for 2nd* **6/1**^{3}

03-5 **3** *1/2* **Takeitfromalady (IRE)**^{28} 698 7-9-12 **64**.......................(b) AdamKirby 6 68
(Lee Carter) *s.i.s: hld up in 8th: gng wl 3f out: drvn and prog jst over 2f out: tk 3rd jst over 1f out: kpt on same pce after* **11/2**^{2}

010- **4** *1/2* **Sinbad The Sailor**^{54} 8121 11-9-11 **63**..........................(t) PatCosgrave 1 67
(George Baker) *bustled along early: towards rr: waiting for a gap 3f out: rdn over 2f out: prog u.p to chal for 3rd 1f out: kpt on same pce* **7/1**

0556 **5** *5* **Thimaar (USA)**^{15} 865 8-9-7 **59**....................................(p) KieranO'Neill 4 57
(Sarah Hollinshead) *trckd ldr: rdn and tried to chal 3f out: wknd wl over 1f out* **14/1**

-440 **6** *3 1/2* **Opera Buff**^{28} 698 7-9-5 **62**..................................(p) EdwardGreatrex(5) 2 56
(Jose Santos) *trckd ldrs: drvn and tried to raise an effrt on inner over 2f out: wknd wl over 1f out* **8/1**

-000 **7** *2 3/4* **Ocean Bentley (IRE)**^{20} 796 4-8-2 **45**............................. RyanPowell 3 35
(Tony Carroll) *led to over 2f out: wknd qckly* **40/1**

000- **8** *8* **Major Franko**^{140} 7705 4-8-10 **53** ow1.................................. KierenFox 9 34
(Michael Attwater) *mostly in last: urged along fr 6f out: no ch fnl 3f* **25/1**

2/06 **9** *5* **Deadline Day (IRE)**^{19} 819 5-8-8 **46**..........................(be) RobertHavlin 5 21
(Michael Mullineaux) *trckd ldng pair to wl over 2f out: wknd rapidly* **25/1**

3m 30.99s (0.89) **Going Correction** -0.05s/f (Stan)
WFA 4 from 5yo+ 5lb **9** Ran SP% **112.2**
Speed ratings (Par 101): **95,92,92,92,89 87,86,82,79**
CSF £9.17 CT £33.57 TOTE £2.10: £1.10, £2.30, £2.30; EX 11.40 Trifecta £25.90.
Owner M W Lawrence **Bred** Joe And Edel Banahan **Trained** Newport Pagnell, Bucks

FOCUS
A moderate staying handicap. Straightforward form rated around the runner-up and fourth.

1039 32RED ON THE APP STORE H'CAP (DIV II) 2m (P)
7:45 (7:46) (Class 6) (0-65,64) 4-Y-O+ **£2,264** (£673; £336; £168) **Stalls** Low

Form RPR

100- **1** **Snow Conditions**^{157} 7307 5-9-10 **62**.............. WilliamTwiston-Davies 1 72
(Philip Hide) *hld up: shoved along in 8th whn pce lifted 4f out: prog on outer fr 3f out: drvn to ld wl over 1f out: styd on wl* **11/1**

-262 **2** *3 1/4* **Golly Miss Molly**^{7} 950 5-9-12 **64**................................(b) MartinLane 7 70
(Jeremy Gask) *t.k.h early: led 2f: sn stdd into midfield: prog on outer 3f out: rdn to ld briefly 2f out: chsd wnr after: kpt on but no imp fnl f* **11/4**^{1}

0022 **3** *3 1/4* **Sudden Wish (IRE)**^{20} 796 7-9-0 **52**............................... JimCrowley 3 54
(Michael Attwater) *hld up in rr: pushed along whn pce lifted 4f out: prog over 2f out and tried to chal: sn outpcd by ldng pair* **10/1**

000- **4** *hd* **Madame Lafite**^{242} 4627 4-9-6 **63**.. TedDurcan 8 65
(Jonathan Portman) *led after 2f to after 4f: styd cl up: rdn over 3f out: outpcd 2f out: one pce after* **13/2**

4353 **5** *2* **Delagoa Bay (IRE)**^{5} 981 8-8-1 **46**......................... BenSanderson(7) 2 46
(Sylvester Kirk) *hld up: urged along over 3f out: nt qckn over 2f out: sn lft bhd by ldrs* **6/1**^{3}

4-53 **6** *nk* **Tidal Way (IRE)**^{21} 786 7-9-11 **63**...................................(p) LukeMorris 5 62
(Shaun Lycett) *led after 4f tl after 7f: pressed ldr after: drvn to chal wl over 2f out: wknd over 1f out* **3/1**^{2}

-503 **7** *hd* **Mighty Thor**^{28} 695 6-9-5 **57**... CharlesBishop 9 56
(Lydia Richards) *trckd ldrs: pushed along over 3f out: rdn and fnd nil over 2f out: sn wknd* **8/1**

-060 **8** *17* **Opus Too (IRE)**^{20} 796 5-8-0 **45**.............................. SophieKilloran(7) 6 24
(John Ryan) *t.k.h: prom: led after 7f: kicked for home 4f out: hdd & wknd over 2f out: eased fnl f* **40/1**

-500 **9** *46* **Citisonsmith (IRE)**^{20} 796 4-8-2 **45**.............................(p) RyanPowell 4
(Tony Carroll) *restless stalls: plld v hrd: fnlly restrained into last after 6f and immediately lost interest: sn t.o* **50/1**

3m 29.96s (-0.14) **Going Correction** -0.05s/f (Stan)
WFA 4 from 5yo+ 5lb **9** Ran SP% **112.2**
Speed ratings (Par 101): **98,96,94,94,93 93,93,84,61**
CSF £39.97 CT £314.98 TOTE £12.00: £4.10, £1.30, £2.50; EX 57.40 Trifecta £388.50.
Owner P Turner, J Davies & The Hides **Bred** Tondoro Srl **Trained** Findon, W Sussex
■ Stewards' Enquiry : Sophie Killoran one-day ban: careless riding (Apr 6)

FOCUS
The faster of the two divisions by 1.03sec. A minor pb from the winner, while the second and third help set the opening level.

1040 32RED.COM H'CAP 6f (P)
8:15 (8:17) (Class 4) (0-85,85) 4-Y-O+ **£4,690** (£1,395; £697; £348) **Stalls** Low

Form RPR

4-61 **1** **Stellarta**^{14} 879 5-9-1 **79**.. DavidProbert 3 85
(Michael Blanshard) *hld up in 7th: prog between rivals fr 2f out: drvn to take narrow ld over 1f out: battled on wl* **6/1**^{3}

342- **2** *hd* **Upstaging**^{242} 4649 4-8-13 **77**... LukeMorris 9 82
(Paul Cole) *wl in tch: clsd fr 2f out to chal over 1f out: w wnr after: kpt on but jst hld nr fin* **14/1**

05-4 **3** *nk* **Dominium (USA)**^{68} 198 9-8-13 **77**............................(b) MartinLane 4 82
(Jeremy Gask) *wl in tch: clsd to chal over 1f out: drvn and kpt on but nt qckn last 100yds* **16/1**

-012 **4** *nk* **Rich Again (IRE)**^{28} 694 7-9-0 **78**.................................(b) TedDurcan 5 83
(James Bethell) *dwlt and n.m.r s: hld up in rr: prog whn nt clr run and swtchd rt over 1f out: rdn and styd on but nvr quite able to chal* **9/2**^{2}

31-2 **5** *3/4* **Under Siege (IRE)**^{12} 901 4-8-8 **79**.......................... SophieKilloran(7) 7 80
(David Simcock) *t.k.h: prom: chal and w ldr 2f out tl nt qckn over 1f out and lost pl sn after: kpt on fnl f* **4/1**^{1}

5001 **6** *1 1/2* **Oriental Relation (IRE)**^{12} 901 5-9-1 **84**..................(v) PhilDennis(5) 11 81
(James Given) *t.k.h: w ldr: led over 2f out to over 1f out: fdd fnl f* **14/1**

-332 **7** *nk* **Quintus Cerialis (IRE)**^{21} 782 4-9-0 **78**........................(p) AdamKirby 8 74
(Clive Cox) *hld up in rr: shkn up 2f out: urged along and kpt on fr over 1f out: nvr really involved* **6/1**^{3}

6-56 **8** *1 1/2* **Varsovian**^{22} 771 6-9-7 **85**.. RenatoSouza 1 76
(Dean Ivory) *t.k.h: pressed ldrs: lost pl 2f out but stl cl up: wknd fnl f* **9/2**^{2}

1-00 **9** *4 1/2* **Secret Glance**^{22} 771 4-8-13 **77**.................................. AdamBeschizza 6 55
(Richard Rowe) *hld up in last: shkn up over 2f out: no prog* **100/1**

-300 **10** *3 3/4* **Luis Vaz De Torres (IRE)**^{22} 771 4-8-9 **80**......(p) AdamMcNamara(7) 2 47
(Richard Fahey) *t.k.h: led to over 2f out: sn wknd* **16/1**

54-6 **11** *6* **Honcho (IRE)**^{21} 782 4-8-7 **71** oh1.................................... RyanPowell 12 20
(John Ryan) *dwlt: nvr gng wl and a in rr: drvn 1/2-way: t.o* **33/1**

1m 10.84s (-2.26) **Going Correction** -0.05s/f (Stan) **11** Ran SP% **114.0**
Speed ratings (Par 105): **113,112,112,111,110 108,108,106,100,95 87**
CSF £83.93 CT £1292.22 TOTE £5.80: £2.10, £3.80, £4.60; EX 67.20 Trifecta £905.60.
Owner Vincent Ward **Bred** Whitsbury Manor Stud & Pigeon House Stud **Trained** Upper Lambourn, Berks

FOCUS
A fair sprint, and a solidly run one too. The runner-up has been rated to his best.

1041 32RED H'CAP 7f (P)
8:45 (8:45) (Class 4) (0-85,85) 4-Y-O+ **£4,690** (£1,395; £697; £348) **Stalls** Low

Form RPR

2-43 **1** **Presumido (IRE)**^{45} 494 6-9-1 **79**.................................... JimCrowley 8 88
(Simon Dow) *stdd s: hld up in rr: gng easily whn eased off rail and prog 2f out: clsd to ld ins fnl f: drvn out* **8/1**^{3}

421 **2** *3/4* **Torreon (IRE)**^{16} 858 5-9-2 **80**.. AdamKirby 4 88+
(John Ryan) *t.k.h: led 1f then restrained bhd ldrs: prog 2f out: hrd rdn to ld briefly jst ins fnl f: styd on but hld last 100yds* **5/2**^{1}

-643 **3** *1 1/2* **Capelita**^{22} 774 5-9-4 **82**... AndrewMullen 11 86
(Michael Appleby) *dropped in fr wd draw and hld up in rr: prog whn nt clr run 2f out: drvn and styd on to take 3rd last 75yds* **8/1**^{3}

2014 **4** *1/2* **Pour La Victoire (IRE)**^{14} 879 6-8-13 **82**...............(b) PaddyPilley(5) 2 84
(Tony Carroll) *stdd s: hld up wl in rr: brought wd and prog fr 2f out: drvn and kpt on fr over 1f out: nvr able to chal* **12/1**

60-0 **5** *hd* **Dutch Art Dealer**[81] 18 5-9-7 **85**.....(p) MartinLane 12 86
(Paul Cole) *dropped in fr wd draw and hld up wl in rr: brought wd and rdn over 2f out: styd on fr over 1f out: nvr able to chal* **11/1**

6142 **6** *hd* **Justice First**[12] 900 4-8-5 **76**..... LukeCarson(7) 6 76
(Ed Dunlop) *wl plcd in chsng gp: prog to ld wl over 1f out: hdd and fdd jst ins fnl f* **8/1**[3]

1130 **7** *½* **Clement (IRE)**[19] 816 6-8-13 **84**.....(v) GeorgiaCox(7) 3 83
(John O'Shea) *hld up in midfield: effrt on inner 2f out: one pce and no hdwy fnl f* **5/1**[2]

0-55 **8** *1 ¾* **Russian Reward (IRE)**[12] 901 4-8-13 **77**.....(tp) LukeMorris 5 71
(Paul Cole) *towards rr: rdn bef 1/2-way: nvr able to threaten ldrs* **8/1**[3]

564- **9** *1* **Mister Musicmaster**[200] 6109 7-9-1 **79**..... DarryllHolland 9 71
(Ron Hodges) *prom: clsd to chal 2f out: wknd qckly fnl f* **33/1**

50-6 **10** *½* **Midnight Rider (IRE)**[14] 879 8-8-13 **80**..... RyanTate(3) 13 70
(Rod Millman) *dropped in fr wd draw and sn in last: nvr a factor: rdn and no prog over 2f out* **33/1**

12-0 **11** *1 ¾* **Pick A Little**[21] 788 8-9-1 **79**..... TimmyMurphy 1 65
(Michael Blake) *chsd ldr after 1f to over 2f out: lost pl qckly and nudged along: nvr involved after* **33/1**

4163 **12** *3 ½* **Majestic Myles (IRE)**[14] 878 8-9-5 **83**.....(v[1]) KierenFox 7 59
(Lee Carter) *led after 1f and shot clr at v str pce: hdd & wknd rapidly wl over 1f out* **33/1**

1m 24.0s (-2.00) **Going Correction** -0.05s/f (Stan) **12** Ran SP% **117.5**
Speed ratings (Par 105): **109,108,106,105,105 105,104,102,101,101 99,95**
CSF £27.11 CT £166.99 TOTE £9.10: £2.90, £1.50, £2.50; EX 27.60 Trifecta £224.80.
Owner Robert Moss **Bred** Lynn Lodge Stud **Trained** Ashtead, Surrey

FOCUS
With the first-time visored Majestic Myles rather taking off in front, this was run at a good gallop and set up for a closer. A small pb from the winner.

1042 WATCH RACING UK IN HD H'CAP 6f (P)
9:15 (9:18) (Class 6) (0-55,55) 4-Y-O+ **£2,264** (£673; £336; £168) **Stalls** Low

Form RPR
2133 **1** **Little Indian**[5] 985 6-9-5 **53**..... FrederikTylicki 2 62
(J R Jenkins) *trckd ldr 2f and again 2f out: rdn to ld over 1f out: styd on wl fnl f* **2/1**[1]

-005 **2** *1* **Not Your Call (IRE)**[34] 617 5-9-1 **49**..... KierenFox 6 55
(Lee Carter) *t.k.h and sn led: rdn and hdd over 1f out: kpt on one pce* **10/1**

5-02 **3** *¾* **Assertive Agent**[14] 872 6-9-6 **54**..... DavidProbert 7 57
(Tony Carroll) *hld up in last trio: waiting for a gap over 2f out on inner: prog over 1f out: tk 3rd fnl f: kpt on* **7/1**

4305 **4** *1* **Evident (IRE)**[5] 985 6-9-7 **55**.....(b) AdamKirby 10 55
(Tony Carroll) *dwlt: hld up in last: drvn and no prog over 2f out: styd on fnl f to take 4th nr fin* **6/1**[3]

3455 **5** *hd* **Hamis Al Bin (IRE)**[13] 889 7-9-6 **54**.....(vt[1]) LukeMorris 8 54
(Milton Bradley) *t.k.h: hld up in last trio: urged along 2f out: kpt on one pce fr over 1f out and nvr able to threaten* **9/1**

4464 **6** *1 ¼* **Burauq**[14] 873 4-9-6 **54**.....(b) FrannyNorton 4 50
(Milton Bradley) *prom: chsd ldr 4f out to 2f out: sn shkn up and nt qckn: fdd* **7/1**

22-2 **7** *1 ¼* **Copper Cavalier**[35] 615 5-9-7 **55**.....(p) RobertHavlin 5 47
(Michael Blanshard) *chsd ldrs: shkn up and fdd fr 2f out* **5/1**[2]

60-0 **8** *nk* **All Or Nothin (IRE)**[39] 563 7-9-5 **53**..... MartinLane 3 44
(Paddy Butler) *hld up in last trio: urged along and tried to make prog 2f out: wknd fnl f* **14/1**

1m 12.59s (-0.51) **Going Correction** -0.05s/f (Stan) **8** Ran SP% **115.0**
Speed ratings (Par 101): **101,99,98,97,97 95,93,93**
CSF £23.67 CT £119.10 TOTE £3.00: £1.10, £3.00, £2.10; EX 22.70 Trifecta £137.80.
Owner Two Little Indians **Bred** D R Tucker **Trained** Royston, Herts

FOCUS
An ordinary sprint handicap in which the pace held up. Straightforward form rated around those close up.
T/Jkpt: Not won. T/Plt: £33.40 to a £1 stake. Pool: £79,729.33 - 1,740.25 winning tickets T/Qpdt: £15.30 to a £1 stake. Pool: £7,909.38 - 382.50 winning tickets **Jonathan Neesom**

[1026]SOUTHWELL (L-H)
Wednesday, March 23

OFFICIAL GOING: Fibresand: standard
Wind: Light across Weather: Grey cloud

1043 32RED AMATEUR RIDERS' CLASSIFIED CLAIMING STKS 1m 6f (F)
2:00 (2:00) (Class 6) 4-Y-O+ **£2,495** (£774; £386; £193) **Stalls** Low

Form RPR
1-53 **1** **Dark Diamond (IRE)**[43] 506 6-10-0 66.....(b) MrRBirkett 5 72
(Julia Feilden) *chsd clr ldr: niggled along after 4f: pushed along and hdwy 5f out: jnd ldr 4f out: led wl over 2f out and sn clr: unchal* **8/13**[1]

1103 **2** *22* **Edgar (GER)**[8] 940 6-10-5 71.....(bt) MissPBridgwater(5) 4 64
(David Bridgwater) *led and sn clr: pushed along and jnd 4f out: rdn along 3f out: sn hdd: wl hld in 2nd whn rdr dropped whip over 1f out: eased fnl f* **2/1**[2]

0-00 **3** *4 ½* **Storm Hawk (IRE)**[8] 946 9-10-3 57.....(b) MrThomasGreatrex(3) 2 44
(Emma Owen) *dwlt and rdn along s: in rr: pushed along and sme hdwy 5f out: rdn wl over 3f out: plugged on* **9/1**[3]

00-0 **4** *77* **Hoonose**[20] 796 7-10-2 35.....(v) BrodieHampson 3
(Emma Owen) *chsd ldng pair: niggled along over 7f out: rdn along wl over 5f out: sn outpcd and wl bhd* **50/1**

3m 9.18s (0.88) **Going Correction** 0.0s/f (Stan) **4** Ran SP% **107.2**
Speed ratings (Par 101): **97,84,81,37**
CSF £2.05 TOTE £1.50; EX 1.90 Trifecta £2.30.Dark Diamond was claimed by Mr M. C. Chapman for £5,000.
Owner R J Creese **Bred** Yeomanstown Stud **Trained** Exning, Suffolk

FOCUS
A moderate amateur riders' classified claimer and what had looked a two-horse race on paper ended up being a one-horse race. It's been rated as straightforward form.

1044 LADBROKES H'CAP 7f (F)
2:30 (2:30) (Class 5) (0-75,71) 4-Y-O+ **£3,234** (£962; £481; £240) **Stalls** Low

Form RPR
00-2 **1** **Azrur (IRE)**[13] 893 6-9-4 **68**..... PhillipMakin 8 78
(Keith Dalgleish) *qckly away: mde all: rdn wl over 1f out: drvn ent fnl f: kpt on wl towards fin* **6/4**[1]

4-50 **2** *½* **Dilgura**[27] 713 6-9-3 **70**..... MatthewCosham(3) 4 79
(Stuart Kittow) *trckd ldrs on inner: hdwy over 2f out: rdn to chse wnr jst over 1f out: drvn and ev ch ins fnl f: no ex towards fin* **16/1**

05-5 **3** *2 ¼* **Surewecan**[14] 877 4-9-1 **65**..... JoeFanning 3 68
(Mark Johnston) *dwlt sltly and in rr: hdwy 1/2-way: chsd ldrs over 2f out: sn chal and rdn: drvn jst over 1f out: kpt on same pce* **5/1**[3]

4062 **4** *3 ½* **Limerick Lord (IRE)**[8] 939 4-8-8 **61**.....(p) ShelleyBirkett(3) 7 54
(Julia Feilden) *prom: rdn along over 2f out: drvn wl over 1f out: sn one pce* **6/1**

4-60 **5** *2 ¼* **Khajaaly (IRE)**[30] 680 9-9-0 **67**.....(vt) RobHornby(3) 2 54
(Daniel Mark Loughnane) *hld up in tch: hdwy on outer wl over 2f out: sn rdn: drvn wl over 1f out: sn no imp* **14/1**

-005 **6** *nk* **Cool Strutter (IRE)**[13] 893 4-8-10 **65**..... EdwardGreatrex(5) 5 51
(Andrew Balding) *t.k.h: trckd ldrs: effrt over 2f out: sn rdn: drvn and edgd lft wl over 1f out: sn btn* **7/2**[2]

0335 **7** *6* **Ocean Legend (IRE)**[14] 875 11-8-13 **66**..... GeorgeDowning(3) 1 36
(Tony Carroll) *trckd ldrs on inner: effrt wl over 2f out and sn rdn along: drvn wl over 1f out: sn wknd* **16/1**

1m 29.22s (-1.08) **Going Correction** 0.0s/f (Stan) **7** Ran SP% **111.6**
Speed ratings (Par 103): **106,105,102,98,96 95,89**
CSF £26.40 CT £95.31 TOTE £2.30: £1.20, £8.70; EX 22.70 Trifecta £101.10.
Owner D Moat **Bred** Kildaragh Stud **Trained** Carluke, S Lanarks

FOCUS
A modest handicap and it paid to be handy. The winner has been rated as building on his latest good run here, and the runner-up fits.

1045 BET&WATCH EVERY RACE AT UNIBET H'CAP 6f (F)
3:05 (3:06) (Class 6) (0-60,60) 3-Y-O **£2,587** (£770; £384; £192) **Stalls** Low

Form RPR
544 **1** **Birrafun (IRE)**[23] 765 3-9-0 **53**..... PJMcDonald 9 56
(Ann Duffield) *trckd ldrs on outer: hdwy 2f out: rdn over 1f out: styd on to ld wl ins fnl f: sn edgd lft: kpt on* **8/1**

5344 **2** *nk* **Tombe Girl**[8] 947 3-9-4 **57**.....(p) PhillipMakin 2 59
(Keith Dalgleish) *towards rr: hdwy on inner over 2f out: rdn along to chse ldrs over 1f out: drvn and ch ins fnl f: kpt on* **3/1**[1]

55-3 **3** *hd* **Cool Crescendo**[75] 104 3-9-4 **57**..... TomEaves 3 58
(Rebecca Menzies) *cl up: chal 2f out: rdn to ld 1f out: sn drvn: hdd wl ins fnl f: no ex towards fin* **5/1**[3]

25 **4** *1 ¾* **Freeze A Crowd (IRE)**[26] 730 3-8-7 **46** oh1.....(t) JoeyHaynes 6 42
(Ben Haslam) *trckd ldrs: hdwy over 2f out: rdn wl over 1f out: drvn ent fnl f: kpt on same pce* **8/1**

1-65 **5** *2 ¾* **Name That Toon**[7] 962 3-8-10 **49**.....(v) TonyHamilton 4 37
(Derek Shaw) *sn led: rdn 2f out: drvn over 1f out: edgd rt and hdd ent fnl f: wknd* **16/1**

000- **6** *3 ¾* **Lucia Sciarra**[179] 6756 3-9-5 **58**..... PaulMulrennan 8 35
(Giles Bravery) *towards rr: swtchd rt to outer and hdwy over 2f out: rdn to chse ldrs wl over 1f out: sn edgd lft and btn* **10/3**[2]

14-0 **7** *6* **Young Windsor (IRE)**[69] 181 3-9-7 **60**.....(v) GrahamLee 7 19
(Ann Duffield) *cl up: rdn along over 2f out: sn drvn and wknd over 1f out* **13/2**

00-0 **8** *nk* **Taroneesh**[23] 763 3-8-7 **46** oh1.....(v) AdamBeschizza 1 4
(Derek Shaw) *a in rr* **25/1**

1m 17.13s (0.63) **Going Correction** 0.0s/f (Stan) **8** Ran SP% **110.0**
Speed ratings (Par 96): **95,94,94,92,88 83,75,74**
CSF £29.80 CT £124.36 TOTE £9.10: £1.70, £1.20, £1.90; EX 31.50 Trifecta £130.20.
Owner Middleham Park Racing CXIX **Bred** Ocal Bloodstock **Trained** Constable Burton, N Yorks
■ Stewards' Enquiry : P J McDonald caution: careless riding

FOCUS
A moderate 3yo handicap. They went a decent pace which suited the hold-up horses this time. Ordinary form.

1046 DAILY PRICE BOOSTS AT UNIBET H'CAP 5f (F)
3:40 (3:43) (Class 4) (0-80,80) 4-Y-O+ **£5,175** (£1,540; £769; £384) **Stalls** Centre

Form RPR
0260 **1** **Sleepy Blue Ocean**[13] 894 10-9-0 **73**.....(p) RobertWinston 1 82
(John Balding) *racd towards far side: chsd ldrs on outer: hdwy wl over 1f out: sn rdn: drvn to chal ins fnl f: kpt on wl to ld last 75yds* **4/1**

1311 **2** *¾* **Elusivity (IRE)**[11] 919 8-8-13 **72**.....(p) PaulMulrennan 6 78
(Conor Dore) *racd towards stands' side: cl up: rdn and ev ch over 1f out: drvn and edgd lft ins fnl f: kpt on* **7/2**[3]

1603 **3** *nk* **Fine 'n Dandy (IRE)**[13] 894 5-8-12 **71**..... FrannyNorton 2 76
(J R Jenkins) *prom centre: led over 2f out: rdn jst over 1f out: drvn ins fnl f: hdd and no ex last 75yds* **2/1**[1]

651- **4** *½* **Casterbridge**[147] 7565 4-9-7 **80**..... NeilFarley 5 83
(Eric Alston) *cl up in centre: rdn along wl over 1f out: drvn and kpt on fnl f* **10/3**[2]

260- **5** *1 ¾* **Henley**[254] 4195 4-8-7 **66**.....(t) BarryMcHugh 4 63
(Tracy Waggott) *slt ld in centre: pushed along 1/2-way and sn hdd rdn wl over 1f out: wknd ent fnl f* **40/1**

200- **6** *2* **Cosmic Chatter**[161] 7223 6-9-7 **80**..... JamesSullivan 7 70
(Ruth Carr) *dwlt and sn outpcd: detached at 1/2-way: pushed along wl over 1f out: styd on strly fnl f: nt rch ldrs* **14/1**

400- **7** *7* **Windforpower (IRE)**[182] 6653 6-8-7 **66**.....(p) JoeFanning 3 31
(Tracy Waggott) *towards rr and sn outpcd: rdn along 2f out: swtchd lft and drvn over 1f out: n.d* **25/1**

59.37s (-0.33) **Going Correction** +0.075s/f (Slow) **7** Ran SP% **111.6**
Speed ratings (Par 105): **105,103,103,102,99 96,85**
CSF £17.42 TOTE £6.50: £2.50, £2.00; EX 17.90 Trifecta £42.20.
Owner Billy Herring **Bred** Exors Of The Late N Ahamad & P C Scott **Trained** Scrooby, S Yorks

FOCUS
A good sprint handicap with a disputed lead and little covering the principals at the line. The winner has been rated to the best of this year's form.

1047 DOWNLOAD THE LADBROKES APP H'CAP 1m (F)
4:10 (4:12) (Class 6) (0-65,65) 4-Y-O+ **£2,587** (£770; £384; £192) **Stalls** Low

Form RPR
00-4 **1** **Star Of The Stage**[13] 893 4-9-4 **62**.....(p) AdamBeschizza 4 69
(Julia Feilden) *mde most: rdn wl over 1f out: drvn ins fnl f: kpt on strly* **15/2**[2]

3264 **2** *1 ¼* **Stun Gun**[7] 956 6-9-2 **60**.....(p) TonyHamilton 14 64
(Derek Shaw) *cl up: chal over 2f out: rdn wl over 1f out: drvn and kpt on same pce fnl f* **15/2**[2]

2221 **3** *¾* **Basingstoke (IRE)**[8] 936 7-9-1 **62** 6ex.....(b) RobHornby(3) 11 64
(Daniel Mark Loughnane) *trckd ldrs: hdwy over 2f out: rdn to chse ldng pair over 1f out: drvn and kpt on same pce fnl f* **7/2**[1]

242- **4** ½ **Im Dapper Too**[183] 6618 5-8-13 **57** PhillipMakin 1 60
(John Davies) *in tch on inner: n.m.r and lost pl wl over 3f out: rdn over 2f out: kpt on u.p fnl f* **14/1**

-652 **5** 1¾ **Grey Destiny**[8] 936 6-8-7 **58** MathewStill(7) 5 55
(Antony Brittain) *t.k.h: towards rr and swtchd lft to inner after 1f: hdwy nr inner rail 2f out: sn rdn and kpt on fnl f: nrst fin* **8/1**[3]

-023 **6** 1 **Princess Peaches**[29] 682 4-9-1 **59** PJMcDonald 9 53
(James Bethell) *chsd ldrs on outer: wd st: rdn over 2f out: drvn wl over 1f out and no imp* **12/1**

-136 **7** 1½ **Falcon's Reign (FR)**[50] 430 7-8-4 **55** (p) RPWalsh(7) 2 46
(Michael Appleby) *towards rr and swtchd markedly rt to outer after 1f: wd st: effrt and rdn over 2f out: sme late hdwy* **20/1**

062- **8** nk **Illustrious Prince (IRE)**[149] 7513 9-8-13 **60** JoeDoyle(3) 12 50
(Julie Camacho) *chsd ldrs on outer: rdn along 2f out: grad wknd* **11/1**

5454 **9** 2½ **Cadeaux Pearl**[8] 936 8-8-9 **53** BenCurtis 6 37
(Scott Dixon) *chsd ldrs: rdn along over 2f out: sn drvn and wknd* **20/1**

256- **10** 3¾ **Invincible Wish (IRE)**[147] 7552 4-9-3 **61** GrahamLee 13 36
(Trevor Wall) *towards rr: wd st: rdn along over 2f out: n.d* **25/1**

01-0 **11** hd **Indomitable Spirit**[82] 2 4-8-11 **58** TimClark(3) 10 33+
(Martin Smith) *dwlt: a in rr* **11/1**

000- **12** nk **Adventureman**[159] 7255 4-9-7 **65** JamesSullivan 3 39
(Ruth Carr) *chsd ldrs on inner: rdn along 3f out: sn wknd* **25/1**

3033 **13** nk **Sylvette**[14] 877 4-8-13 **57** (vt) JackMitchell 7 30
(Roger Varian) *chsd ldrs: rdn along over 3f out: sn wknd* **9/1**

233- **P** **Duc De Seville (IRE)**[10] 6810 4-8-5 **56** (p) RhiainIngram(7) 8
(Michael Chapman) *sn outpcd and bhd: t.o whn virtually p.u over 2f out: dismntd over 1f out* **66/1**

1m 43.47s (-0.23) **Going Correction** 0.0s/f (Stan) **14** Ran SP% **116.6**
Speed ratings (Par 101): **101,99,99,98,96 95,94,93,91,87 87,87,86,**
CSF £56.19 CT £238.71 TOTE £8.80: £2.70, £3.00, £1.70; EX 65.20 Trifecta £454.50.
Owner Mr & Mrs George Bhatti & Partners 2 **Bred** Cheveley Park Stud Ltd **Trained** Exning, Suffolk

FOCUS
A moderate handicap and several of these had a question mark against them at the trip. Very few got into it, with the front pair disputing the lead from the start. The runner-up has been rated pretty much to his mile form in this grade earlier in the year, and the third fits.

1048 CORAL H'CAP (DIV I) 1m 3f (F)
4:40 (4:40) (Class 6) (0-55,55) 4-Y-O+ **£2,587** (£770; £384; £192) **Stalls** Low

Form RPR

40-3 **1** **Frosty The Snowman (IRE)**[20] 801 5-9-1 **49** JamesSullivan 2 57
(Ruth Carr) *towards rr: rdn along and bhd 1/2-way: hdwy 3f out: chsd ldrs over 1f out: drvn ent fnl f: styd on wl to ld last 100yds* **7/2**[2]

/034 **2** 1 **Mcvicar**[15] 601 7-9-4 **52** (p) PhillipMakin 10 58
(John Davies) *trckd ldrs: hdwy over 3f out: rdn to ld wl over 1f out: drvn ent fnl f: hdd and no ex last 100yds* **10/1**

-231 **3** ¾ **Henry Smith**[8] 941 4-8-8 **50** (be) GeorgeWood(7) 8 55
(Garry Moss) *a.p: hdwy 3f out: rdn 2f out: drvn jst over 1f out: kpt on same pce* **2/1**[1]

34-0 **4** nk **Sofias Number One (USA)**[55] 368 8-9-3 **51** (b) JFEgan 7 56
(Roy Bowring) *hld up in rr: stdy hdwy on outer 5f out: chsd ldrs wl over 2f out: rdn wl over 1f out: sn drvn and kpt on* **7/1**[3]

-202 **5** 1¾ **Celestial Dancer (FR)**[30] 674 4-8-7 **47** JosephineGordon(5) 4 49
(Michael Appleby) *trckd ldrs on inner: hdwy over 3f out: rdn to chal 2f out: drvn over 1f out: kpt on one pce* **9/1**

6/0- **6** 1¾ **Sirpertan**[107] 13 5-9-3 **51** DanielTudhope 6 50
(Marjorie Fife) *led: rdn along 3f out: drvn 2f out: sn hdd and grad wknd* **10/1**

04-6 **7** 10 **Zip Wire (IRE)**[70] 157 7-9-4 **52** (v[1]) AndrewMullen 11 35
(Donald McCain) *prom: cl up after 4f: rdn along 3f out: drvn over 2f out: sn wknd* **8/1**

634- **8** 14 **Monopoli**[147] 7567 7-9-7 **55** (p) DavidNolan 1 16
(Ivan Furtado) *chsd ldrs: rdn along over 3f out: sn wknd* **16/1**

660- **9** 2½ **Tricky Issue (IRE)**[233] 4947 4-9-6 **55** JoeFanning 9 12
(Seamus Mullins) *awkward and n.m.r s: in rr: hdwy into midfield 1/2-way: in tch over 3f out: sn rdn and wknd* **33/1**

00-0 **10** 27 **Synoptic Dream (USA)**[8] 941 4-8-11 **46** oh1 (v[1]) AdamBeschizza 5
(Derek Shaw) *towards rr: hdwy to chse ldrs on inner 1/2-way: rdn along over 4f out: sn wknd* **66/1**

2m 27.27s (-0.73) **Going Correction** 0.0s/f (Stan)
WFA 4 from 5yo+ 1lb **10** Ran SP% **117.7**
Speed ratings (Par 101): **102,101,100,100,99 97,90,80,78,59**
CSF £38.94 CT £88.38 TOTE £4.90: £1.80, £2.30, £1.20; EX 52.50 Trifecta £185.40.
Owner Bruce Jamieson, Barbara Dean, Ruth Carr **Bred** Gigginstown House Stud **Trained** Huby, N Yorks

FOCUS
A moderate middle-distance handicap won by a longstanding maiden. Straightforward form.

1049 CORAL H'CAP (DIV II) 1m 3f (F)
5:10 (5:11) (Class 6) (0-55,55) 4-Y-O+ **£2,587** (£770; £384; £192) **Stalls** Low

Form RPR

4302 **1** **Moonshine Ridge (IRE)**[7] 957 5-9-5 **53** NeilFarley 7 65
(Alan Swinbank) *awkward s and bhd: hdwy over 4f out: chsd ldrs 3f out: chal 2f out: rdn to ld 1 1/2f out: kpt on strly* **9/4**[2]

0-50 **2** 5 **Almutamarred (USA)**[38] 582 4-9-4 **53** TimmyMurphy 8 57+
(Kevin Morgan) *dwlt and bhd: swtchd wd after 3f: hdwy 4f out: rdn along 3f out: kpt on u.p fnl 2f* **2/1**[1]

6506 **3** 6 **Luv U Lucky**[8] 941 4-9-6 **55** (tp) AndrewMullen 3 49+
(Michael Appleby) *cl up: rdn to ld 3f out: hdd 1 1/2f out and sn drvn: kpt on one pce* **7/1**

0065 **4** shd **My Tringaling (IRE)**[34] 622 4-9-2 **51** SaleemGolam 1 45
(Stuart Williams) *trckd ldrs: hdwy over 4f out: chsd ldng pair 3f out and sn rdn: drvn 2f out and kpt on one pce* **11/1**

-056 **5** 3¾ **Cool Beans**[19] 822 4-9-0 **52** (p) AlistairRawlinson(3) 2 40+
(Roy Bowring) *slt ld: rdn along and hdd 3f out: drvn over 2f out and sn wknd* **5/1**[3]

0503 **6** 1½ **Annakrista (GER)**[8] 941 8-9-4 **52** (bt) LiamJones 6 37
(Zoe Davison) *chsd ldrs: rdn along 4f out: drvn over 3f out and sn outpcd* **16/1**

536- **7** 22 **Approaching Star (FR)**[192] 6354 5-9-1 **49** GrahamGibbons 9
(Dai Burchell) *midfield: hdwy at 1/2-way: chsd ldrs and rdn along over 4f out: sn wknd* **25/1**

50-0 **8** 16 **Notts So Blue**[19] 822 5-8-12 **46** oh1 JasonHart 10
(Shaun Harris) *midfield: rdn along 5f out: sn wknd and bhd fnl 3f* **33/1**

4-66 **9** 2½ **Aru Cha Cha**[28] 690 5-8-5 **46** oh1 RhiainIngram(7) 5
(Roger Ingram) *t.k.h: chsd ldng pair: pushed along over 5f out: rdn along and lost pl over 4f out: sn bhd* **33/1**

/400 **10** 19 **Royal Roman**[29] 681 4-9-3 **52** DougieCostello 4
(Kevin Frost) *a in rr: bhd fr 1/2-way: t.o fnl 3f* **66/1**

2m 27.65s (-0.35) **Going Correction** 0.0s/f (Stan)
WFA 4 from 5yo+ 1lb **10** Ran SP% **118.7**
Speed ratings (Par 101): **101,97,93,92,90 89,73,61,59,45**
CSF £7.08 CT £26.58 TOTE £3.10: £1.20, £1.50, £2.20; EX 9.10 Trifecta £49.00.
Owner Elm Row Racing Syndicate **Bred** Maddenstown Equine Enterprise Ltd **Trained** Melsonby, N Yorks

FOCUS
They went a good pace and the front pair in the market filled the first two places, but not before both had blown the start, and they took very different routes to reach their final positions. The winning time was 0.38sec slower than the first division. This could easily rate a good few lengths higher but the nature of the race dissuades that for now.
T/Plt: £26.00 to a £1 stake. Pool: £60,698.26 - 1,702.02 winning tickets T/Qpdt: £7.30 to a £1 stake. Pool: £6,431.91 - 648.35 winning tickets **Joe Rowntree**

1050 - 1056a (Foreign Racing) - See Raceform Interactive

1000 WOLVERHAMPTON (A.W) (L-H)
Thursday, March 24

OFFICIAL GOING: Tapeta: standard
Wind: Fresh behind Weather: Overcast

1057 CORAL CASINO H'CAP 1m 4f 50y (Tp)
2:15 (2:15) (Class 6) (0-65,65) 4-Y-O+ **£2,587** (£770; £384; £192) **Stalls** Low

Form RPR

-002 **1** **My Lord**[5] 1002 8-9-6 **64** AdamKirby 7 70
(David Evans) *a.p: shkn up to ld over 2f out: rdn over 1f out: edgd lft ins fnl f: jst hld on* **9/2**[2]

05-0 **2** hd **Senor George (IRE)**[17] 862 9-9-3 **64** RobHornby(3) 6 70
(Simon Hodgson) *hld up: hdwy on outer over 2f out: sn chsng wnr: rdn over 1f out: edgd lft: styd on* **25/1**

3523 **3** 2¾ **Innoko (FR)**[22] 781 6-9-3 **61** WilliamCarson 10 63
(Tony Carroll) *hld up: hdwy over 1f out: hung lft and r.o ins fnl f: wnt 3rd nr fin* **10/1**

-554 **4** ½ **Evervescent (IRE)**[17] 862 7-9-3 **61** PatCosgrave 4 63
(Graeme McPherson) *chsd ldrs: rdn over 1f out: styd on same pce ins fnl f* **7/1**

1-23 **5** 2 **Lions Charge (USA)**[8] 949 9-9-6 **64** (tp) LiamKeniry 8 61
(Neil Mulholland) *hld up: hdwy over 3f out: rdn and hung lft fr over 1f out: no ex fnl f* **6/1**[3]

503- **6** ¾ **Splash Of Verve (IRE)**[173] 6943 4-9-2 **62** JoeyHaynes 11 58+
(Philip Kirby) *s.s: hld up: hdwy on outer 2f out: sn rdn: edgd lft and no ex fnl f* **12/1**

524- **7** 1¾ **Beausant**[166] 7110 4-9-4 **64** (p) SteveDrowne 5 57
(George Baker) *chsd ldr tl led 10f out: rdn and hdd over 2f out: wknd fnl f* **4/1**[1]

-042 **8** 1½ **Golden Thread**[22] 781 6-9-3 **61** CharlesBishop 9 52
(Neil King) *mid-div: hdwy over 3f out: rdn and wknd over 1f out* **10/1**

-364 **9** ½ **Kay Sera**[24] 766 8-9-4 **65** EoinWalsh(3) 3 55
(Tony Newcombe) *s.i.s: sn rcvrd into mid-div: nt clr run and lost pl over 3f out: n.d after* **8/1**

000- **10** 3½ **Moccasin (FR)**[93] 8353 7-9-6 **64** (p) FrannyNorton 2 48
(Geoffrey Harker) *chsd ldrs: nt clr run over 3f out: wknd over 2f out* **20/1**

006- **11** 5 **Lineman**[325] 1465 6-9-2 **65** (p) PaddyPilley(5) 12 41
(Sarah Hollinshead) *swtchd lft sn after s: hld up: rdn over 3f out: a in rr* **33/1**

066- **12** 3¼ **Saint Thomas (IRE)**[213] 5703 9-9-4 **62** GrahamGibbons 1 33
(John Mackie) *led 2f: chsd ldr tl wnt upsides over 6f out: ev ch over 2f out: hmpd and wknd sn after* **22/1**

2m 39.73s (-1.07) **Going Correction** -0.15s/f (Stan)
WFA 4 from 6yo+ 2lb **12** Ran SP% **117.8**
Speed ratings (Par 101): **97,96,95,94,93 92,91,90,90,88 84,82**
CSF £118.11 CT £1076.61 TOTE £4.00: £2.10, £8.00, £2.60; EX 152.50 Trifecta £1330.90.
Owner Mrs I M Folkes **Bred** Mrs Monica Teversham **Trained** Pandy, Monmouths

FOCUS
A moderate handicap and the pace looked ordinary despite a disputed lead.

1058 BET IN PLAY AT CORAL (S) STKS 1m 1f 103y (Tp)
2:50 (2:52) (Class 6) 4-Y-O+ **£2,587** (£770; £384; £192) **Stalls** Low

Form RPR

4/30 **1** **Anton Chigurh**[37] 598 7-8-12 67 SilvestreDeSousa 4 65
(Philip McBride) *w ldr tl led over 7f out: rdn over 1f out: styd on* **9/4**[2]

1003 **2** 1 **Les Gar Gan (IRE)**[17] 862 5-8-13 59 (be) StevieDonohoe 8 64
(Daniel Mark Loughnane) *hld up: hdwy over 1f out: rdn to chse wnr and hung lft ins fnl f: styd on* **9/1**

-510 **3** 1¼ **Vastly (USA)**[31] 676 7-9-4 62 (bt) AdamBeschizza 1 67
(Julia Feilden) *s.i.s: hld up: hdwy and nt clr run over 1f out: r.o to go 3rd post: nt rch ldrs* **10/1**

0511 **4** hd **Tatting**[16] 865 7-9-10 79 PaulMulrennan 7 72
(Conor Dore) *hld up: hdwy over 4f out: rdn and hung lft fr over 1f out: styd on same pce ins fnl f* **11/8**[1]

0450 **5** 1¾ **Arsenale (GER)**[15] 876 5-8-7 45 (p) AndrewMullen 6 52
(Michael Appleby) *s.i.s: hdwy over 6f out: rdn over 2f out: styd on same pce fnl f* **50/1**

6201 **6** 1 **Matraash (USA)**[20] 815 10-9-4 64 (be) AdamKirby 9 61
(Daniel Mark Loughnane) *chsd ldrs: wnt 2nd over 6f out: rdn and ev ch over 2f out: wknd wl ins fnl f* **7/1**[3]

-006 **7** 3 **Evacusafe Lady**[20] 815 5-8-7 56 (t) RyanPowell 2 44
(John Ryan) *prom: lost pl over 5f out: rdn over 1f out: wknd fnl f* **25/1**

0-00 **8** 4½ **Samsonite (IRE)**[20] 823 4-8-12 70 (p) JasonHart 3 41
(Tony Coyle) *led 1f: chsd ldrs: rdn over 3f out: wknd fnl f* **14/1**

2m 0.08s (-0.72) **Going Correction** -0.15s/f (Stan) **8** Ran SP% **116.9**
Speed ratings (Par 101): **97,96,95,94,93 92,89,85**
CSF £23.52 TOTE £3.30: £1.20, £3.00, £3.10; EX 21.90 Trifecta £134.10.The winner was bought by T Dascombe for 6,000gns.
Owner Black Star Racing **Bred** Mr & Mrs G Middlebrook **Trained** Newmarket, Suffolk

FOCUS
An ordinary seller. The winner didn't need to be at his best to win, and the fifth limits the form.

1059 DOWNLOAD THE NEW UNIBET RACING APP H'CAP 5f 20y (Tp)
3:25 (3:25) (Class 6) (0-65,65) 4-Y-O+ **£2,587** (£770; £384; £192) **Stalls** Low

Form RPR

466- **1** **China Excels**[103] 8207 9-8-13 **60** RobHornby(3) 3 68
(Mandy Rowland) *chsd ldr tl rdn to ld over 1f out: r.o* **9/1**

300- **2** 1 3/4 **Lucky Clover**[178] 6813 5-9-0 **58** CathyGannon 1 60
(Malcolm Saunders) *led: rdn and hdd over 1f out: edgd lft ins fnl f: styd on same pce* **12/1**

2-51 **3** 1/2 **Prominna**[31] 669 6-9-1 **62** GeorgeDowning(3) 7 62
(Tony Carroll) *hld up: hdwy over 1f out: rdn: nt clr run and swtchd lft ins fnl f: styd on* **5/1**[3]

5300 **4** 1/2 **Quality Art (USA)**[17] 856 8-9-7 **65** SteveDrowne 5 63
(Simon Hodgson) *hld up: racd keenly: hdwy over 1f out: sn rdn: styd on* **9/2**[2]

435- **5** nk **See Vermont**[208] 5839 8-9-7 **65** (p) PaulMulrennan 2 62
(Rebecca Bastiman) *chsd ldrs: rdn over 1f out: styd on same pce ins fnl f* **7/1**

5155 **6** 3/4 **Your Gifted (IRE)**[27] 733 9-9-6 **64** (v) RaulDaSilva 11 58
(Lisa Williamson) *s.i.s: swtchd lft sn after s: hld up: hdwy over 1f out: rdn and no imp ins fnl f* **12/1**

3621 **7** 2 1/4 **Charlie Lad**[19] 837 4-9-1 **59** LukeMorris 9 45
(Daniel Mark Loughnane) *chsd ldrs: rdn 1/2-way: wknd ins fnl f* **3/1**[1]

0-00 **8** 5 **Dusty Blue**[33] 658 4-9-2 **60** WilliamCarson 8 28
(Tony Carroll) *s.i.s: sme hdwy 3f out: sn rdn: wknd over 1f out* **22/1**

0510 **9** 9 **Give Us A Belle (IRE)**[14] 889 7-8-10 **59** (bt) PaddyPilley(5) 4
(Christine Dunnett) *sn pushed along and prom: lost pl over 3f out: wknd 1/2-way* **17/2**

1m 0.67s (-1.23) **Going Correction** -0.15s/f (Stan) **9** Ran SP% **112.6**
Speed ratings (Par 101): **103,100,99,98,98 96,93,85,70**
CSF £106.98 CT £601.93 TOTE £14.20: £3.30, £4.30, £2.20; EX 126.00 Trifecta £790.20.
Owner Miss M E Rowland **Bred** Brook Stud Bloodstock Ltd **Trained** Lower Blidworth, Notts

FOCUS
A moderate sprint handicap in which the first two were always up there. The winner has been rated as running to his best.

1060 32RED.COM H'CAP (DIV I) 5f 216y (Tp)
4:00 (4:01) (Class 5) (0-75,75) 3-Y-O **£3,881** (£1,155; £577; £288) **Stalls** Low

Form RPR

5-21 **1** **Kyllukey**[31] 668 3-9-3 **71** DarryllHolland 5 76
(Charles Hills) *chsd ldrs: led over 4f out: rdn out* **11/4**[1]

4020 **2** 1/2 **Sir Dudley (IRE)**[20] 821 3-9-2 **75** PhilDennis(5) 3 79
(James Given) *trckd ldrs: racd keenly: rdn to chse wnr and edgd lft over 1f out: styd on* **10/3**[2]

421- **3** 3/4 **Showmethewayavrilo**[148] 7553 3-8-9 **63** CathyGannon 4 64
(Malcolm Saunders) *hld up: hdwy over 1f out: sn rdn and edgd lft: styd on* **7/1**

0-15 **4** 1 1/4 **Wishsong**[56] 365 3-8-9 **68** AnnaHesketh(5) 7 68
(David Nicholls) *s.i.s: hld up: nt clr run over 1f out: r.o ins fnl f: nt rch ldrs* **17/2**

315- **5** shd **Le Manege Enchante (IRE)**[95] 8316 3-9-0 **68** TonyHamilton 9 65
(Derek Shaw) *s.i.s: hld up: rdn over 2f out: nt clr run over 1f out: hung lft and r.o ins fnl f: nvr nrr* **16/1**

5-11 **6** shd **Powerful Dream (IRE)**[15] 883 3-9-2 **70** LukeMorris 8 67
(Ronald Harris) *hld up: hdwy over 1f out: sn rdn: styd on same pce ins fnl f* **5/1**[3]

41-0 **7** 2 1/4 **Vroom (IRE)**[12] 924 3-9-7 **75** (p) AdamKirby 1 65
(Gay Kelleway) *chsd ldrs: rdn over 1f out: wandered and wknd ins fnl f* **12/1**

1-52 **8** 6 **Miss Phillyjinks (IRE)**[27] 726 3-8-12 **66** (b) ShaneKelly 6 38
(Paul D'Arcy) *prom: chsd wnr over 3f out: ev ch over 2f out: sn rdn: wknd over 1f out* **8/1**

1m 14.34s (-0.16) **Going Correction** -0.15s/f (Stan) **8** Ran SP% **114.1**
Speed ratings (Par 98): **95,94,93,91,91 91,88,80**
CSF £11.93 CT £56.19 TOTE £3.60: £1.10, £2.50, £2.30; EX 16.40 Trifecta £75.70.
Owner R J Tufft **Bred** Whatton Manor Stud **Trained** Lambourn, Berks

FOCUS
An ordinary 3yo sprint handicap. The winner has been rated to last year's better 2yo form.

1061 32RED.COM H'CAP (DIV II) 5f 216y (Tp)
4:35 (4:37) (Class 5) (0-75,75) 3-Y-O **£3,881** (£1,155; £577; £288) **Stalls** Low

Form RPR

-342 **1** **Rosealee (IRE)**[43] 515 3-9-3 **71** MartinLane 3 76
(Jeremy Gask) *hld up in tch: racd keenly: shkn up to ld over 1f out: rdn out* **9/2**[2]

30-3 **2** hd **Naziba (IRE)**[22] 783 3-8-8 **62** DavidProbert 1 66
(David Menuisier) *hld up: hdwy over 1f out: rdn and ev ch wl ins fnl f: r.o* **14/1**

-516 **3** 1 1/2 **Kestrel Call (IRE)**[21] 797 3-9-7 **75** (t) RobertHavlin 4 75
(Simon Crisford) *trckd ldrs: plld hrd: shkn up over 1f out: edgd lft and styd on same pce ins fnl f* **5/2**[1]

-011 **4** 1 1/2 **Teversham**[22] 783 3-8-12 **66** IrineuGoncalves 6 61
(Chris Dwyer) *s.i.s: hld up: rdn and r.o ins fnl f: nt trble ldrs* **7/1**

154- **5** 3 1/2 **King Of Swing**[131] 7859 3-9-4 **72** TomEaves 9 57
(James Given) *racd on outer: prom: racd keenly: rdn over 1f out: styd on same pce* **9/2**[2]

3222 **6** nk **Silver Springs (IRE)**[6] 978 3-8-10 **67** PhilipPrince(3) 2 51
(David Evans) *disp ld tl wnt on over 2f out: rdn and hdd over 1f out: wknd wl ins fnl f* **11/2**[3]

65-1 **7** 3 **Alyaa (IRE)**[31] 679 3-9-7 **75** MartinDwyer 8 50
(Conrad Allen) *trckd ldrs: plld hrd: wnt 2nd over 2f out tl shkn up over 1f out: hung lft and wknd ins fnl f* **8/1**

0-50 **8** 2 1/2 **Mostashreqah**[12] 924 3-9-2 **70** FrannyNorton 5 38
(Milton Bradley) *disp ld over 3f: wknd over 1f out* **50/1**

1m 14.14s (-0.36) **Going Correction** -0.15s/f (Stan) **8** Ran SP% **112.6**
Speed ratings (Par 98): **96,95,93,91,87 86,82,79**
CSF £61.40 CT £188.55 TOTE £5.50: £2.00, £3.50, £1.10; EX 63.80 Trifecta £226.30.
Owner The Sutton Veny Syndicate **Bred** Mrs Sandra McCarthy **Trained** Stockbridge, Hants

FOCUS
All eight runners were still within a couple of lengths of each other in a line across the track starting up the home straight. The winning time was 0.2sec quicker than the first division. The winner has been rated as taking a minor step forward.

1062 32REDSPORT.COM H'CAP 1m 4f 50y (Tp)
5:10 (5:10) (Class 6) (0-65,62) 3-Y-O **£2,911** (£866; £432; £216) **Stalls** Low

Form RPR

5330 **1** 1/2 **Frivolous Prince (IRE)**[14] 896 3-8-5 **46** (t) CathyGannon 9 52
(David Evans) *hld up: edgd lft over 2f out: hdwy over 1f out: nt clr run and swtchd lft ins fnl f: r.o* **25/1**

-066 **2** 1 1/4 **Rainbow Lad (IRE)**[20] 818 3-8-10 **51** AndrewMullen 3 55
(Michael Appleby) *chsd ldrs: rdn and edgd lft over 1f out: styd on* **22/1**

3-13 **3** 1 1/4 **Whitecliff Park (IRE)**[43] 517 3-9-2 **62** CallumShepherd(5) 5 64
(Brian Ellison) *hld up: hdwy over 2f out: rdn over 1f out: hung lft ins fnl f: styd on* **11/2**[3]

3520 **4** 1 **Schoolboy Error (IRE)**[27] 729 3-9-4 **59** (b) AdamKirby 1 60
(Jamie Osborne) *chsd ldrs: rdn to ld over 2f out: hdd 1f out: wknd wl ins fnl f* **15/2**

543- **5** 1 1/2 **Nietzsche**[129] 7869 3-9-7 **62** [1] BenCurtis 7 60
(Brian Ellison) *chsd ldr tl wnt upsides 10f out: led over 8f out: rdn and hdd over 2f out: wknd ins fnl f* **5/1**[2]

3155 **6** 6 **Skylark Lady (IRE)**[27] 729 3-9-6 **61** SilvestreDeSousa 6 58+
(Rae Guest) *hmpd after s: pushed along early in rr: effrt whn hmpd over 2f out: n.d after* **13/8**[1]

0-02 **7** 11 **Rockliffe**[42] 533 3-9-4 **59** TomEaves 10 30
(Mick Channon) *chsd ldrs: rdn over 2f out: wknd over 1f out* **22/1**

0-4 **8** 3/4 **Rajapur**[78] 69 3-9-5 **60** DougieCostello 11 30
(Philip Kirby) *hld up: rdn whn nt clr run and swtchd rt over 2f out: sn wknd* **33/1**

00-0 **9** 10 **Packing Empire (IRE)**[21] 794 3-8-9 **50** WilliamCarson 12 4
(Jamie Osborne) *s.s: rdn over 3f out: sn wknd* **20/1**

-503 **10** 7 **Lady Fontenail**[29] 700 3-8-11 **52** FrederikTylicki 2
(Rod Millman) *led: hdd over 8f out: chsd ldr tl rdn over 3f out: wknd over 2f out* **33/1**

045- **D** **Recognition (IRE)**[119] 7999 3-9-4 **59** JackMitchell 4 66
(Roger Varian) *hld up: hdwy over 2f out: shkn up to ld 1f out: rdn out* **17/2**

2m 38.5s (-2.30) **Going Correction** -0.15s/f (Stan) **11** Ran SP% **115.6**
Speed ratings (Par 96): **100,99,99,98,97 93,86,85,78,74 101**
CSF £201.62 CT £4400.50 TOTE £13.60: £3.90, £4.50, £4.80; EX 184.30 Trifecta £2016.90.
Owner Wayne Clifford **Bred** Seamus Fox **Trained** Pandy, Monmouths

FOCUS
A moderate middle-distance 3yo handicap and the pace looked ordinary. It's been rated as straightforward form around the likes of the fourth and fifth.

1063 32RED CASINO MAIDEN FILLIES' STKS 1m 141y (Tp)
5:40 (5:44) (Class 5) 3-Y-O+ **£3,557** (£1,058; £529; £264) **Stalls** Low

Form RPR

22-2 **1** **Intermittent**[12] 925 3-8-4 79 TomMarquand(3) 9 74+
(Roger Charlton) *jnd ldr after 1f: led over 2f out: rdn clr over 1f out: readily* **10/11**[1]

0-2 **2** 3 1/4 **Divine Joy**[38] 591 3-8-7 0 LiamJones 3 67
(Marco Botti) *a.p: rdn to chse wnr over 1f out: styng on same pce whn edgd lft ins fnl f* **7/1**

3 1/2 **Cape Peninsular** 3-8-7 0 LukeMorris 8 66+
(James Tate) *hld up: rdn over 3f out: hdwy and hung lft over 1f out: hung rt and lft ins fnl f: styd on* **25/1**

0- **4** 2 1/4 **Cassie**[36] 7340 6-9-12 0 (t) PatCosgrave 4 66
(Ben Pauling) *sn pushed along and prom: rdn over 3f out: styd on same pce fr over 1f out* **50/1**

5 3/4 **Ramblow** 3-8-4 0 NathanAlison(3) 12 60+
(William Haggas) *wnt lft and rdr lost iron leaving stalls: hld up: r.o ins fnl f: nvr nrr* **40/1**

0- **6** 1/2 **Lady Blanco (USA)**[170] 7013 3-8-7 0 DavidProbert 1 59
(Andrew Balding) *trckd ldrs: racd keenly: rdn over 2f out: wknd fnl f* **16/1**

7 4 1/2 **Mary Beale (IRE)** 3-8-7 0 JoeFanning 2 49
(Mark Johnston) *sn led: hung lft and hdd over 2f out: wknd fnl f* **7/2**[2]

3 **8** 1 1/2 **Flinty Fell (IRE)**[20] 814 3-8-7 0 SilvestreDeSousa 10 46
(Ed Dunlop) *hld up in tch: shkn up over 2f out: wknd over 1f out* **9/2**[3]

9 1 3/4 **Gabrielle** 3-8-7 0 [1] MartinLane 5 43
(Ed Dunlop) *prom: hmpd and lost pl after 1f: rdn and wknd over 1f out* **33/1**

10 12 **Chapess** 3-8-2 0 JosephineGordon(5) 7 17
(Philip McBride) *s.i.s: outpcd* **80/1**

11 2 1/2 **Sonnentanz (IRE)** 3-8-7 0 CathyGannon 11 12
(Daniel Kubler) *s.s: outpcd* **80/1**

1m 47.78s (-2.32) **Going Correction** -0.15s/f (Stan)
WFA 3 from 4yo+ 19lb **11** Ran SP% **124.8**
Speed ratings (Par 100): **104,101,100,98,98 97,93,92,90,80 77**
CSF £8.73 TOTE £2.00: £1.10, £1.90, £4.40; EX 9.40 Trifecta £64.40.
Owner K Abdullah **Bred** Juddmonte Farms Ltd **Trained** Beckhampton, Wilts

FOCUS
An interesting fillies' maiden with a few having already shown ability plus a couple of nicely bred newcomers. The winner has been rated positively and a bit above average for a race of this type around here.

1064 LADBROKES H'CAP 1m 141y (Tp)
6:10 (6:12) (Class 6) (0-65,65) 4-Y-O+ **£2,587** (£770; £384; £192) **Stalls** Low

Form RPR

0-02 **1** **Ellaal**[7] 964 7-8-13 **57** PaulMulrennan 8 65
(Ruth Carr) *mde all: shkn up and edgd rt over 1f out: rdn and hung lft ins fnl f: styd on* **10/3**[2]

-053 **2** 1 **Foie Gras**[9] 939 6-9-4 **62** (p) SilvestreDeSousa 4 68
(Chris Dwyer) *a.p: rdn over 1f out: chsd wnr ins fnl f: r.o* **8/1**

36-1 **3** 3/4 **Lord Of The Storm**[24] 769 8-9-5 **63** KierenFox 9 67
(Michael Attwater) *chsd ldrs: rdn over 1f out: r.o* **7/1**[3]

/300 **4** 1 **Mr Shekells**[31] 680 4-9-5 **63** DanielTudhope 11 65
(Philip McBride) *sn chsng wnr: rdn over 2f out: styd on same pce ins fnl f* **25/1**

2534 **5** 1 3/4 **Hawk Moth (IRE)**[15] 877 8-8-13 **57** (v[1]) LukeMorris 7 56
(John Spearing) *hld up in tch: lost pl over 3f out: hdwy over 1f out: rdn and hung lft ins fnl f: styd on* **16/1**

-325 **6** 1/2 **Red Unico (IRE)**[17] 862 4-9-7 **65** BenCurtis 6 63
(Michael Appleby) *chsd ldrs: rdn over 2f out: no ex ins fnl f* **3/1**[1]

4021 **7** 1 1/4 **Zed Candy Girl**[36] 609 6-9-1 **59** (p) AdamKirby 3 54
(Daniel Mark Loughnane) *hld up: rdn and swtchd rt over 1f out: hung lft ins fnl f: nt trble ldrs* **8/1**

6532 **8** 1/2 **West Leake (IRE)**[15] 877 10-8-13 **57** LiamKeniry 1 51
(Paul Burgoyne) *hld up: rdn over 1f out: nvr on terms* **22/1**

-633 **9** 1/2 **Spirit Of Gondree (IRE)**[21] 792 8-9-4 **62** (b) FrannyNorton 5 55
(Milton Bradley) *hld up: rdn over 1f out: nt trble ldrs* **17/2**

0-03 **10** 1 1/4 **Quadriga (IRE)**[16] 867 6-8-9 **53** ow1 DougieCostello 2 43
(Philip Kirby) *mid-div: hdwy over 3f out: rdn and wknd over 1f out* **18/1**

0000 **11** 1 3/4 **Satchville Flyer**[17] 857 5-8-13 **60** PhilipPrince(3) 10 46
(David Evans) *s.i.s: hld up: rdn over 1f out: hung lft ins fnl f: n.d* **66/1**

1m 48.45s (-1.65) **Going Correction** -0.15s/f (Stan) **11** Ran SP% **114.2**
Speed ratings (Par 101): **101,100,99,98,97 96,95,95,94,93 91**
CSF £28.64 CT £177.80 TOTE £4.30: £1.60, £2.60, £2.80; EX 35.70 Trifecta £241.80.
Owner The Bottom Liners & Paul Saxton **Bred** W And R Barnett Ltd **Trained** Huby, N Yorks

FOCUS
Another moderate handicap in which the pace held up. The runner-up, third and fourth help set the opening level.
T/Jkpt: £49411.00 to a £1 stake. Pool of £139186.08 - 2.00 winning units. T/Plt: £988.60 to a £1 stake. Pool of £93366.46 - 68.94 winning tickets. T/Qpdt: £69.30 to a £1 stake. Pool of £9073.99 - 96.80 winning tickets. **Colin Roberts**

974 LINGFIELD (L-H)
Friday, March 25

OFFICIAL GOING: Polytrack: standard
Wind: nil Weather: bright and sunny

1065 32RED ALL-WEATHER FILLIES' AND MARES' CHAMPIONSHIPS CONDITIONS STKS 7f 1y(P)
1:40 (1:43) (Class 2) 4-Y-0+

£93,375 (£27,960; £13,980; £6,990; £3,495; £1,755) **Stalls** Low

Form RPR
4-11 **1** **Volunteer Point (IRE)**[24] 774 4-9-0 102 GrahamGibbons 3 103
(Mick Channon) *chsd ldng pair: effrt whn carried lft and sltly hmpd wl over 1f out: squeezed through to chal 1f out: led ins fnl f: r.o wl: rdn out* **4/1**[2]
64-2 **2** 2¼ **Bint Dandy (IRE)**[24] 774 5-9-0 88 (b[1]) SilvestreDeSousa 5 97
(Chris Dwyer) *dwlt: sn in tch in midfield and t.k.h: wnt rt 4f out: drvn over 1f out: styd on wl u.p ins fnl f: wnt 2nd towards fin: no threat to wnr* **20/1**
635- **3** ½ **Alfajer**[89] 8374 4-9-0 97 (b[1]) AndreaAtzeni 1 96
(Marco Botti) *t.k.h: hld up in tch in midfield: effrt u.p wl over 1f out: styd on ins fnl f: wnt 3rd towards fin: no threat to wnr* **7/1**[3]
40-1 **4** 1 **Saucy Minx (IRE)**[35] 632 6-9-0 94 JimCrowley 8 93
(Amanda Perrett) *hld up in last pair: effrt wl over 1f out: styd on strly ins fnl f: snatched 4th last stride: nvr trbld ldrs* **10/1**
41-3 **5** shd **Cold As Ice (SAF)**[48] 483 4-9-0 107 PatCosgrave 10 93+
(William Haggas) *chsd ldrs: effrt over 1f out: rdn to ld ent fnl f: hdd ins fnl f: lost action and btn 100yds out: lost 2nd towards fin and eased cl home: dismntd after fin* **4/6**[1]
1560 **6** 1½ **Subtle Knife**[6] 1003 7-9-0 81 WilliamCarson 7 89
(Giles Bravery) *stdd s: hld up in tch in rr: effrt and swtchd rt wl over 1f out: styd on ins fnl f: nvr trbld ldrs* **50/1**
-060 **7** ½ **Primrose Valley**[23] 780 4-9-0 92 (b[1]) LukeMorris 4 87
(Ed Vaughan) *racd keenly: led: rdn and qcknd ent fnl 2f: edgd lft u.p wl over 1f out: hdd ent fnl f: sn outpcd: wknd fnl 100yds* **25/1**
53-4 **8** 1¾ **Secret Hint**[69] 214 5-9-0 90 OisinMurphy 9 83
(Andrew Balding) *chsd ldng trio: effrt and unable qck over 2f out: lost pl over 1f out: wl hld fnl f* **20/1**
13-2 **9** ½ **Diamond Lady**[32] 670 5-9-0 80 FrederikTylicki 6 81
(William Stone) *in tch in midfield: effrt wl over 1f out: sn outpcd and btn: wl hld fnl f* **50/1**
2311 **10** 1½ **Skidby Mill (IRE)**[21] 813 6-9-0 72 JoeFanning 2 77
(Laura Mongan) *stdd after s and t.k.h early: hld up in last trio: effrt 2f out: no imp and bhd 1f out* **66/1**

1m 23.53s (-1.27) **Going Correction** -0.125s/f (Stan) **10** Ran SP% **120.4**
Speed ratings (Par 96): **102,99,98,97,97 95,95,93,92,91**
CSF £81.55 CT £555.07 TOTE £5.10: £1.60, £4.60, £2.60; EX 83.20 Trifecta £316.80.
Owner Box 41 **Bred** G Strawbridge & London Thoroughbred Services Ltd **Trained** West Ilsley, Berks

FOCUS
The third running of this All-Weather Championship meeting. This was the strongest renewal of the Fillies´ and Mares´ and was run at a strong pace. The progressive winner did it nicely. The runner-up, sixth and to some extent the tenth limit the form. The winner has been rated to form.

1066 UNIBET ALL-WEATHER SPRINT CHAMPIONSHIPS CONDITIONS STKS 6f 1y(P)
2:10 (2:14) (Class 2) 4-Y-0+

£93,375 (£27,960; £13,980; £6,990; £3,495; £1,755) **Stalls** Low

Form RPR
-300 **1** **Alben Star (IRE)**[27] 745 8-9-5 103 DavidNolan 5 114
(Richard Fahey) *taken down early: hld up in midfield: effrt and switching rt over 1f out: qcknd u.p ins fnl f to ld 75yds out: sn clr: readily* **7/1**
31-1 **2** 2¼ **Lancelot Du Lac (ITY)**[83] 17 6-9-5 109 RobertWinston 13 107
(Dean Ivory) *chsd ldrs: wnt 2nd 4f out: upsides ldr and travelling wl 2f out: pushed into ld over 1f out: drvn 1f out: hdd 75yds out: sn outpcd* **4/1**[2]
001- **3** ¾ **Goken (FR)**[132] 7856 4-9-5 109 GrahamLee 1 105
(Kevin Ryan) *wl in tch in midfield: effrt and drifting rt over 1f out: chsd ldr ins fnl f: no imp and one pce 3rd fnl 100yds* **5/2**[1]
-416 **4** shd **Boom The Groom (IRE)**[27] 745 5-9-5 101 WilliamCarson 9 105
(Tony Carroll) *taken down early: broke wl to ld: sn stdd and chsd ldr for 2f: styd prom: effrt 2f out: styd on same pce u.p ins fnl f* **16/1**
-113 **5** nk **Realize**[13] 921 6-9-5 103 (t) AndreaAtzeni 7 104
(Stuart Williams) *hld up in tch towards rr: swtchd lft and hdwy u.p over 1f out: kpt on same pce ins fnl f* **5/1**[3]
06-0 **6** nk **Russian Soul (IRE)**[14] 907 8-9-5 103 (b) ShaneFoley 8 105
(M Halford, Ire) *taken down early: stdd s: hld up towards rr: nt clr run wl over 1f out: swtchd lft over 1f out: styd on ins fnl f: nvr threatened ldrs* **25/1**
5-20 **7** ½ **Intransigent**[48] 483 7-9-5 104 OisinMurphy 6 101
(Andrew Balding) *s.i.s: short of room and swtchd lft sn after s: hld up in rr: swtchd lft and hdwy over 1f out: styd on same pce ins fnl f* **16/1**
-341 **8** 2½ **Lightscameraction (IRE)**[27] 745 4-9-5 109 (b) LukeMorris 14 94
(Gay Kelleway) *midfield: hdwy to chse ldr over 4f out: unable qck u.p over 1f out: wknd ins fnl f* **16/1**
5-16 **9** 1 **Rivellino**[27] 755 6-9-5 104 DougieCostello 11 91
(K R Burke) *midfield: unable qck u.p over 2f out: styd on same pce and wl hld fr over 1f out* **11/1**
-100 **10** 1¼ **Chookie Royale**[13] 921 8-9-5 109 (p) TomEaves 12 87
(Keith Dalgleish) *taken down early: s.i.s: a towards rr: rdn over 2f out: no imp: wl hld over 1f out* **16/1**
1631 **11** hd **Bosham**[8] 966 6-9-5 94 (bt) AdamKirby 10 87
(Michael Easterby) *sn led: rdn 2f out: hdd and no ex over 1f out: wknd ins fnl f: eased towards fin* **20/1**
-220 **12** 2¼ **Gamgoom**[27] 745 5-9-5 107 (p) MartinHarley 4 80
(Mario Hofer, Germany) *hld up in tch in midfield: effrt and no rspnse over 1f out: sn btn and bhd whn swtchd rt ins fnl f: eased* **12/1**

1m 9.77s (-2.13) **Going Correction** -0.125s/f (Stan) **12** Ran SP% **125.9**
Speed ratings (Par 109): **109,106,105,104,104 104,103,100,98,97 96,93**
CSF £37.41 CT £94.54 TOTE £10.20: £3.30, £1.90, £1.30; EX 43.00 Trifecta £210.00.
Owner J K Shannon & M A Scaife **Bred** Rathasker Stud **Trained** Musley Bank, N Yorks
■ Stewards' Enquiry : William Carson one-day ban; not to keep straight from the stalls (8th Apr)

FOCUS
A competitive sprint final with the three highest rated in the field drawn widest. It was run at a strong gallop with the winner quickening best. A minor pb from the winner, with the fourth helping to guide.

1067 32RED ALL-WEATHER MARATHON CHAMPIONSHIPS CONDITIONS STKS 1m 7f 169y(P)
2:40 (2:42) (Class 2) 4-Y-0+

£93,375 (£27,960; £13,980; £6,990; £3,495; £1,755) **Stalls** Low

Form RPR
111- **1** **Moonrise Landing (IRE)**[104] 8210 5-9-0 103 JimCrowley 2 106+
(Ralph Beckett) *hld up towards rr: clsd and nt clr run over 2f out: swtchd rt and effrt wl over 1f out: chsd clr ldng pair 1f out: styd on strly u.p to ld cl home* **6/5**[1]
22-1 **2** ½ **Anglophile**[62] 317 5-9-5 102 JamesDoyle 4 105
(Charlie Appleby) *hld up in midfield: rdn and gd hdwy on inner to ld jst over 2f out: clr w rival 1f out: kpt on wl u.p ins fnl f tl hdd and no ex cl home* **5/1**[2]
2-62 **3** ½ **Ballynanty (IRE)**[62] 317 4-9-0 100 (t) OisinMurphy 1 104
(Andrew Balding) *hld up towards rr: short of room: hmpd and stmbld after 1f: clsd 3f out: swtchd lft and gd hdwy on inner jst over 2f out: rdn and chal and clr w rival 1f out: kpt on but unable qck towards fin* **8/1**
-526 **4** 3½ **First Mohican**[18] 861 8-9-5 102 JimmyFortune 5 102
(Alan King) *stdd s: hld up towards rr: clsd and nt clr run over 2f out: swtchd rt and hdwy jst over 1f out: r.o wl to go 4th ins fnl f: no ch w ldrs* **16/1**
-343 **5** 2½ **Blue Surf**[46] 499 7-9-5 99 AdamKirby 8 97
(Amanda Perrett) *in tch in midfield: effrt u.p to press ldrs on outer 2f out: 3rd and outpcd over 1f out: lost 3rd 1f out: wknd fnl f* **20/1**
3-53 **6** ½ **Pearl Castle (IRE)**[22] 793 6-9-5 95 (p) DougieCostello 12 98
(K R Burke) *wl in tch in midfield: clsd to chse ldrs and short of room ent fnl 2f: drvn to go 4th over 1f out: sn no imp and wknd fnl f* **40/1**
6122 **7** ¾ **Royal Marskell**[7] 975 7-9-5 90 LukeMorris 13 96
(Gay Kelleway) *swtchd lft after s: hld up in midfield: effrt over 2f out: outpcd u.p over 1f out: wl hld and plugged on same pce fnl f* **66/1**
14-4 **8** 5 **Shalaman (IRE)**[21] 829 7-9-5 99 (bt[1]) PatSmullen 6 90
(David Marnane, Ire) *hld up in last pair: clsd and nt clr run over 2f out: effrt on inner over 1f out: no real imp: wknd ins fnl f* **33/1**
-223 **9** ¾ **John Reel (FR)**[16] 871 7-9-5 99 JFEgan 9 89
(David Evans) *chsd ldr tl pushed into ld after 3f: rdn 3f out and sn hdd pressed: hdd jst over 2f out: lost pl and btn over 1f out: wknd fnl f* **12/1**
3-31 **10** ½ **Notarised**[22] 793 5-9-5 102 JoeFanning 7 88
(Mark Johnston) *chsd ldrs: rdn and effrt 3f out: sn ev ch tl unable qck jst over 2f out: lost pl over 1f out: wknd fnl f* **6/1**[3]
-111 **11** 12 **Sunblazer (IRE)**[27] 747 6-9-5 97 (t) WilliamTwiston-Davies 10 74
(Kim Bailey) *chsd ldrs: effrt to join ldr 3f out: rdn over 2f out: lost pl u.p over 1f out: wl btn and eased ins fnl f* **14/1**
5-22 **12** 22 **Handsome Dan (IRE)**[41] 567 10-9-5 71 DanielTudhope 3 47
(Sarah Hollinshead) *hld up in last pair: rdn and struggling 3f out: sn bhd: t.o and eased ins fnl f* **100/1**
55-4 **13** 15 **Monaleen (IRE)**[37] 614 5-9-0 91 SilvestreDeSousa 11 24
(Ian Williams) *led for 3f: chsd ldr: rdn 4f out: dropped out rapidly over 3f out: bhd and eased fnl 2f: t.o* **25/1**

3m 18.65s (-7.05) **Going Correction** -0.125s/f (Stan)
WFA 4 from 5yo+ 5lb **13** Ran SP% **124.2**
Speed ratings (Par 109): **112,111,111,109,108 108,107,105,105,104 98,87,80**
CSF £6.89 CT £37.66 TOTE £2.30: £1.40, £1.70, £2.30; EX 8.10 Trifecta £32.00.
Owner P D Savill **Bred** Oak Hill Stud **Trained** Kimpton, Hants
■ Stewards' Enquiry : Jim Crowley three-day ban; careless riding (8th,9th,11th Apr)

FOCUS
A smart staying contest run at an honest pace with the front three finishing clear. The runner-up, sixth and seventh help set the level.

1068 LADBROKES ALL-WEATHER MILE CHAMPIONSHIPS CONDITIONS STKS 1m 1y(P)
3:15 (3:16) (Class 2) 4-Y-0+

£93,375 (£27,960; £13,980; £6,990; £3,495; £877) **Stalls** High

Form RPR
232- **1** **Captain Joy (IRE)**[42] 553 7-9-5 102 PatSmullen 8 110
(Tracey Collins, Ire) *chsd ldrs: wnt 2nd after 2f: rdn over 2f out: styd on to ld 1f out: hld on wl u.p towards fin: gamely* **11/1**
42-2 **2** ½ **Sovereign Debt (IRE)**[13] 921 7-9-5 113 AndreaAtzeni 1 110
(David Nicholls) *hld up in tch in midfield: swtchd lft and hdwy over 1f out: chsd ldrs 1f out: styd on to press ldr wl ins fnl f: kpt on wl but hld towards fin* **11/4**[2]
13-1 **3** 1 **Mindurownbusiness (IRE)**[46] 501 5-9-5 111 JimCrowley 5 107
(Roger Varian) *hld up wl in tch in midfield: swtchd lft and hdwy u.p over 1f out: chsd wnr jst ins fnl f: lost 2nd and jst outpcd wl ins fnl f* **2/1**[1]
-206 **4** 2¾ **Big Baz (IRE)**[29] 720 6-9-5 0 MartinDwyer 2 103
(William Muir) *in tch in midfield: effrt whn hmpd over 1f out: rallied u.p ins fnl f: r.o to snatch 4th last strides: no ch w ldrs* **7/1**
-241 **5** nk **Captain Cat (IRE)**[30] 692 7-9-5 107 GeorgeBaker 7 100
(Roger Charlton) *nt best away but sn rcvrd to ld: rdn 2f out: drifted rt over 1f out: hdd 1f out: sn btn and wknd ins fnl f* **5/1**[3]
0-11 **6** hd **Mister Universe**[13] 921 4-9-5 108 JoeFanning 12 99
(Mark Johnston) *chsd ldng trio: unable qck over 1f out: hld and kpt on same pce ins fnl f* **7/1**
1220 **6** dht **Si Senor (IRE)**[13] 920 5-9-5 94 AdamKirby 11 99
(Ed Vaughan) *stdd and dropped in bhd after s: hld up in rr: effrt over 1f out: styd on ins fnl f: nvr trbld ldrs* **33/1**
1565 **8** 1¼ **Forceful Appeal (USA)**[13] 920 8-9-5 89 LukeMorris 3 96
(Simon Dow) *hld up in tch: swtchd lft and effrt over 1f out: no imp: wl hld and styd on same pce ins fnl f* **66/1**
3-05 **9** 1 **Seanie (IRE)**[13] 921 7-9-5 101 (t) GrahamLee 9 94
(David Marnane, Ire) *hld up in tch towards rr: effrt but stl plenty to do whn hmpd over 1f out: n.d and kpt on same pce after* **33/1**

-304 **10** ½ **Arnold Lane (IRE)**[28] 727 7-9-5 89 SilvestreDeSousa 4 93
(Mick Channon) *led: sn hdd and chsd ldng pair after 2f: effrt 2f out: unable qck and btn over 1f out: wknd ins fnl f* **50/1**

1441 **11** ½ **Jammy Guest (IRE)**[10] 944 6-9-5 80 RyanPowell 6 95+
(George Margarson) *stdd after s: hld up in last pair: effrt on inner over 1f out: nvr enough room and no prog: n.d* **66/1**

0013 **12** 5 **Lunar Deity**[20] 833 7-9-5 99 PatCosgrave 10 80
(Stuart Williams) *dwlt and bustled along early: in tch towards rr but a stuck wd: rdn over 2f out: bhd 1f out* **25/1**

1m 35.2s (-3.00) **Going Correction** -0.125s/f (Stan) **12** Ran SP% **124.7**
Speed ratings (Par 109): **110,109,108,105,105 105,105,104,103,102 102,97**
CSF £42.13 CT £91.52 TOTE £13.50: £3.10, £1.10, £1.50; EX 56.60 Trifecta £177.70.

Owner Herb M Stanley **Bred** Scuderia San Pancrazio Sas **Trained** The Curragh, Co Kildare

FOCUS
A strong renewal of the Mile Championship which was run at a sound pace. The front three pulled clear. The second, third, fourth and fifth have all been rated below their best and this is not form to totally trust.

1069 CORAL EASTER CLASSIC ALL-WEATHER MIDDLE DISTANCE CHAMPIONSHIPS CONDITIONS STKS 1m 2f (P)
3:45 (3:46) (Class 2) 4-Y-O+

£124,500 (£37,280; £18,640; £9,320; £4,660; £2,340) **Stalls** Low

Form RPR

2-11 **1** **Grendisar (IRE)**[27] 748 6-9-5 112 (p) AdamKirby 2 111
(Marco Botti) *broke wl but sn stdd bk into midfield: clsd 4f out: shkn up and effrt over 1f out: chsd ldr ins fnl f: qcknd u.p to ld fnl 75yds: sn in command* **4/6**[1]

01-6 **2** 1 **Fire Fighting (IRE)**[27] 748 5-9-5 108 (b) FMBerry 3 109
(Mark Johnston) *dwlt and bustled along early: hld up in last pair: clsd 4f out: hdwy u.p over 1f out: chsd ldrs ins fnl f: r.o strly to snatch 2nd last stride* **7/1**[3]

435- **3** *shd* **Metropol (IRE)**[40] 585 5-9-5 107 TheoBachelot 7 109
(Mme Pia Brandt, France) *chsd ldr: jnd ldr and travelling bttr over 2f out: rdn to ld wl over 1f out: hdd and no ex fnl 75yds: lost 2nd last stride* **16/1**

10-4 **4** 2¼ **Man Of Harlech**[60] 333 5-9-5 100 [1] OisinMurphy 4 105
(Andrew Balding) *hld up in midfield: clsd 4f out: rdn and hdwy on inner over 1f out: swtchd rt 1f out: kpt on same pce ins fnl f* **16/1**

6-24 **5** 1 **Maverick Wave (USA)**[16] 871 5-9-5 110 JamesDoyle 5 103
(John Gosden) *chsd ldrs: rdn over 2f out: drvn and no imp over 1f out: hld and kpt on same pce fnl f* **4/1**[2]

/3-2 **6** 1¼ **Political Policy (IRE)**[21] 829 5-9-5 98 (tp) RonanWhelan 1 100
(Gavin Cromwell, Ire) *chsd ldrs: unable qck u.p and btn over 1f out: wknd ins fnl f* **33/1**

-360 **7** 1¼ **Complicit (IRE)**[27] 748 5-9-5 99 (t) LukeMorris 10 98
(Paul Cole) *hld up in last pair: clsd 4f out: effrt but stl plenty to do whn sltly hmpd over 1f out: no imp after: nvr trbld ldrs* **33/1**

2151 **8** ½ **Winterlude (IRE)**[18] 861 6-9-5 98 GeorgeBaker 8 97
(Jennie Candlish) *stdd and dropped in bhd after s: hld up in rr: clsd 4f out: swtchd rt and effrt wl over 1f out: no imp* **14/1**

4-51 **9** ½ **Watersmeet**[21] 829 5-9-5 103 JoeFanning 9 96
(Mark Johnston) *led after 1f: jnd and rdn over 2f out: hdd wl over 1f out: sn btn: wknd fnl f* **16/1**

2m 2.94s (-3.66) **Going Correction** -0.125s/f (Stan) **9** Ran SP% **122.7**
Speed ratings (Par 109): **109,108,108,106,105 104,103,103,102**
CSF £6.83 TOTE £1.40: £1.02, £2.60, £4.80; EX 7.40 Trifecta £63.30.

Owner Mohamed Albousi Alghufli **Bred** Old Carhue & Graeng Bloodstock **Trained** Newmarket, Suffolk

FOCUS
A smart renewal of the Middle Distance Championship. It was run at a solid tempo and the well-backed favourite did it well. It's been rated around the runner-up to the better view of his AW form.

1070 UNIBET 3 YEAR OLD SPRINT ALL-WEATHER CHAMPIONSHIPS CONDITIONS STKS 5f 6y(P)
4:15 (4:16) (Class 2) 3-Y-O

£93,375 (£27,960; £13,980; £6,990; £3,495; £1,755) **Stalls** High

Form RPR

1-11 **1** **Wolowitz (IRE)**[21] 821 3-9-5 97 GrahamGibbons 8 97
(David Barron) *chsd ldrs: effrt over 1f out: styd on strly u.p ins fnl f to ld last strides* **4/1**[2]

122- **2** *nk* **Sign Of The Kodiac (IRE)**[111] 8120 3-9-5 91 TomEaves 6 96
(James Given) *chsd ldr: rdn and sltly outpcd over 1f out: rallied u.p ins fnl f: led fnl 50yds: hdd last strides* **25/1**

-112 **3** *nk* **Kadrizzi (FR)**[21] 821 3-9-5 104 RobertWinston 5 95
(Dean Ivory) *dwlt: in tch in rr: effrt and wd bnd 2f out: hdwy ins fnl f: styd on strly fnl 100yds: nt quite rch ldrs* **9/2**[3]

111- **4** *nk* **Quatrieme Ami**[111] 8120 3-9-5 92 DanielTudhope 7 94
(Philip McBride) *in tch in midfield: carried rt over 3f out: effrt over 1f out: kpt on wl fnl 100yds: nvr quite getting to ldrs* **6/1**

-224 **5** *nk* **Krystallite**[21] 821 3-9-0 74 LukeMorris 1 88
(Scott Dixon) *led: rdn and wnt 2 l clr over 1f out: drvn 1f out: hdd fnl 50yds: wknd cl home* **66/1**

-113 **6** ½ **Gracious John (IRE)**[47] 493 3-9-5 109 JFEgan 2 97
(David Evans) *stmbld bdly leaving stalls: sn midfield and plld hrd: swtchd rt over 3f out and then bk lft over 2f out: rdn over 1f out: styng on to chse ldrs whn nt clr run wl ins fnl f: forced to eased towards fin* **5/4**[1]

-225 **7** *hd* **Field Of Vision (IRE)**[21] 821 3-9-5 102 GeorgeBaker 4 90
(Joseph Tuite) *chsd ldrs: rdn ent 2f out: unable qck over 1f out: rallied ins fnl f: styd on same pce towards fin* **14/1**

2311 **8** *hd* **Aguerooo (IRE)**[16] 881 3-9-5 94 (p) KieranO'Neill 3 93
(Richard Hannon) *hld up in last trio: bmpd over 2f out: hdwy on inner over 1f out: kpt on u.p ins fnl f: nt rch ldrs* **10/1**

-554 **9** *nk* **Illegally Blonde (IRE)**[16] 881 3-9-0 88 WilliamCarson 9 83
(Jamie Osborne) *s.i.s: hld up in rr: effrt wl over 1f out: kpt on ins fnl f: nvr trbld ldrs* **50/1**

58.19s (-0.61) **Going Correction** -0.125s/f (Stan) **9** Ran SP% **120.0**
Speed ratings (Par 104): **99,98,98,97,97 96,95,95,95**
CSF £96.60 CT £476.49 TOTE £5.20: £1.50, £6.40, £1.40; EX 129.10 Trifecta £457.30.

Owner Mrs Christine Barron **Bred** Jerry O'Sullivan **Trained** Maunby, N Yorks

FOCUS
The second running of this 3yo sprint. It was run at a sound pace and the field finished in a bunch. It's been rated cautiously for now.

1071 32RED ALL-WEATHER 3 YEAR OLD MILE CHAMPIONSHIPS CONDITIONS STKS 1m 1y(P)
4:45 (4:46) (Class 2) 3-Y-O

£93,375 (£27,960; £13,980; £6,990; £3,495; £1,755) **Stalls** High

Form RPR

-110 **1** **Sea Of Flames**[20] 836 3-9-5 91 SilvestreDeSousa 4 105
(David Elsworth) *taken down early: chsd ldrs: wnt 2nd over 1f out: clsng u.p and swtchd lft over 1f out: styd on u.p to ld fnl 75yds* **10/1**

11-4 **2** 1 **Race Day (IRE)**[20] 836 3-9-5 98 (v[1]) JamesDoyle 8 102
(Saeed bin Suroor) *racd freely: led after 1f and sn clr: rdn and drifted rt over 1f out: drvn 1f out: hdd and no ex fnl 75yds* **9/2**[3]

26-1 **3** *nk* **Haalick (IRE)**[20] 836 3-9-5 101 AndreaAtzeni 1 103+
(Roger Varian) *dwlt: hld up in rr: nt clr run over 2f out: trying to cl whn hmpd on inner ent fnl 2f: hdwy to chse clr ldng pair jst over 1f out: switching rt and r.o wl ins fnl f: nvr gng to rch wnr* **6/4**[1]

-221 **4** 3½ **Yeah Baby Yeah (IRE)**[45] 511 3-9-0 78 DavidProbert 9 83
(Gay Kelleway) *stdd and dropped in after s: hld up in rr: effrt on outer bnd 2f out: styd on to go 4th wl ins fnl f: nvr trbld ldrs* **50/1**

21-3 **5** 2¼ **Special Season**[73] 154 3-9-5 100 (p) PatCosgrave 7 80
(William Haggas) *racd in midfield: 4th and rdn over 2f out: no imp and wl hld over 1f out: wknd ins fnl f* **5/1**

2-21 **6** 2 **Bernie's Boy**[16] 874 3-9-5 80 (p) OisinMurphy 6 73
(Andrew Balding) *led for 1f: chsd ldr tl over 2f out: sn u.p and unable qck: wl btn 1f out: wknd ins fnl f* **50/1**

1313 **7** 1¼ **Bear Faced**[8] 972 3-9-5 90 (p) LukeMorris 5 68
(Sir Mark Prescott Bt) *hld up towards rr: effrt into midfield jst over 2f out: sn outpcd and btn: wknd over 1f out* **20/1**

-1R1 **8** 2½ **Beleave**[21] 817 3-9-0 70 KieranO'Neill 2 54
(Luke Dace) *taken down early and led to post: midfield: hung rt over 2f out: sn edgd bk rt and outpcd: wknd over 1f out* **66/1**

1-11 **9** 24 **Cape Speed (FR)**[51] 434 3-9-5 96 JoeFanning 3
(Mark Johnston) *dwlt and bustled along leaving stalls: a towards rr: rdn and btn 3f out: bhd 2f out: sn eased: t.o* **3/1**[2]

1m 35.54s (-2.66) **Going Correction** -0.125s/f (Stan) **9** Ran SP% **119.1**
Speed ratings (Par 104): **108,107,106,103,100 98,97,95,71**
CSF £54.74 CT £108.03 TOTE £12.60: £2.70, £1.40, £1.40; EX 67.70 Trifecta £213.70.
Owner J C Smith **Bred** Littleton Stud **Trained** Newmarket, Suffolk

FOCUS
With plenty of prominent runners in the field this contest was always likely to be run at a sound pace. Solid form.
T/Plt: £29.90 to a £1 stake. Pool: 217,412.08 - 5,303.18 winning units T/Qpdt: £5.10 to a £1 stake. Pool: 18,611.15 - 2,654.76 winning units **Steve Payne**

MUSSELBURGH (R-H)
Friday, March 25
1072 Meeting Abandoned - Turf problems

1057 WOLVERHAMPTON (A.W) (L-H)
Friday, March 25
OFFICIAL GOING: Tapeta: standard
Wind: Moderate, half behind Weather: Cloudy, bright

1079 BET365 EBF STALLIONS MAIDEN STKS 7f 32y (Tp)
1:55 (1:58) (Class 4) 3-Y-O+ **£5,175** (£1,540; £769; £384) **Stalls** High

Form RPR

226- **1** **Tang Fleming**[167] 7123 3-8-8 78 EdwardGreatrex(5) 1 78+
(Andrew Balding) *in tch on ins: effrt and rdn wl over 1f out: kpt on wl fnl f: led cl home* **11/4**[1]

\- **2** *nse* **Sweet Dragon Fly** 3-8-8 0 MartinLane 7 73
(Paul Cole) *trckd ldrs: effrt over 1f out: drvn to ld ins fnl f: kpt on wl: hdd cl home* **20/1**

02 **3** 1 **Little Miss Kodi (IRE)**[32] 679 3-8-8 0 FrannyNorton 12 70
(Daniel Mark Loughnane) *trckd ldr: effrt and ev ch 2f out: edgd lft ins fnl f: kpt on: hld nr fin* **14/1**

362- **4** 1 **Jordan Sport**[185] 6612 3-8-13 76 TonyHamilton 10 72
(Richard Fahey) *plld hrd early: led: rdn wl over 1f out: hdd ins fnl f: sn no ex* **4/1**[2]

563- **5** 3¼ **Take Charge**[184] 6652 3-8-13 79 DarryllHolland 11 63
(David Brown) *t.k.h: trckd ldrs: effrt and rdn 2f out: outpcd fnl f* **13/2**[3]

6 *nk* **Silver Bid (USA)** 4-10-0 0 SaleemGolam 4 68+
(Alan Bailey) *green bef s: s.i.s: t.k.h in rr: rdn over 2f out: kpt on fnl f: nvr able to chal* **50/1**

7 ½ **Corroyer (IRE)** 3-8-13 0 IanBrennan 8 61
(John Quinn) *hld up in midfield on outside: rdn and outpcd 3f out: edgd lft and no imp wl over 1f out* **7/1**

50 **8** *nk* **Win Lose Draw (IRE)**[40] 582 4-10-0 0 AndrewMullen 5 65
(Michael Appleby) *t.k.h early: in tch: nt clr run briefly 3f out: pushed along and outpcd fr 2f out* **100/1**

5 **9** 2 **Dalavand (IRE)**[24] 770 3-8-13 0 TimmyMurphy 3 55
(Jamie Osborne) *hld up ins: drvn and outpcd wl over 2f out: sn btn* **33/1**

10 *nk* **Rising Sunshine (IRE)** 3-8-10 0 TomMarquand(3) 2 54
(Richard Hannon) *s.i.s: hld up: outpcd and green after 3f: nvr on terms* **8/1**

4- **11** 4½ **St Andrews (IRE)**[207] 5942 3-8-10 0 GeorgeDowning(3) 9 42
(Ian Williams) *dwlt: sn pushed along in rr on outside: struggling 1/2-way: nvr on terms* **7/1**

0 **12** 27 **Katalan (GER)**[9] 958 3-8-13 0 TomQueally 6
(John Butler) *hld up towards rr: struggling bef 1/2-way: btn and eased over 1f out* **100/1**

1m 27.72s (-1.08) **Going Correction** -0.225s/f (Stan)
WFA 3 from 4yo 15lb **12** Ran SP% **114.4**
Speed ratings (Par 105): **97,96,95,94,90 90,90,89,87,87 81,51**
CSF £63.08 TOTE £3.50: £1.20, £11.00, £3.40; EX 66.40 Trifecta £728.40.
Owner Chelsea Thoroughbreds - Cagnes Sur Mer **Bred** J Green & Sons, W Fox & R Frisby **Trained** Kingsclere, Hants

FOCUS
The stalls were on the inside for all races barring this open 7f maiden. Clerk of the course Fergus Cameron said: "We worked it down to two and a half or three inches to ensure the top of the pad does not get too quick. We are finishing it with the gallop master as normal and I wouldn't anticipate any change from racing the previous day." Little got into this with it very much an advantage to race prominently. The third has been rated similar to her second run.

1080 BET365 H'CAP 1m 141y (Tp)
2:25 (2:27) (Class 2) (0-100,97) 3-Y-O **£32,345** (£9,625; £4,810; £2,405) **Stalls** Low

Form RPR
421- **1** **Royal Performer**[207] 5944 3-8-13 89 SeanLevey 4 97
(David Brown) *trckd ldrs gng wl: effrt and rdn over 1f out: led ins fnl f: kpt on strly* **9/2**[1]
210- **2** ½ **Montsarrat (IRE)**[195] 6317 3-8-12 88 PaulMulrennan 1 95
(Mark Johnston) *t.k.h early: led 2f: pressed ldr: rdn to ld 2f out: hdd ins fnl f: kpt on: hld nr fin* **5/1**[2]
605- **3** ¾ **Beaverbrook**[195] 6311 3-9-7 97 FrannyNorton 13 102
(Mark Johnston) *hld up: pushed along after 3f: hdwy 3f out: kpt on fnl f: tk 3rd last stride* **8/1**
-134 **4** nse **Theydon Grey**[15] 887 3-8-9 85 MartinLane 8 90
(Peter Charalambous) *hld up in tch: hdwy to trck ldrs over 2f out: rdn and edgd lft over 1f out: kpt on same pce ins fnl f* **13/2**
163- **5** 3¼ **London Protocol (FR)**[191] 6437 3-8-12 88 (p) BenCurtis 5 87
(K R Burke) *hld up in midfield: effrt and rdn over 2f out: no imp over 1f out* **18/1**
-315 **6** 2 **Theos Lolly (IRE)**[15] 887 3-8-0 76 oh2 CathyGannon 11 70
(Richard Fahey) *t.k.h early: w ldr: led after 2f out 2f out: sn rdn: outpcd fnl f* **40/1**
115- **7** nse **Bathos (IRE)**[170] 7042 3-8-11 87 AdrianNicholls 6 81+
(Mark Johnston) *rrd and lost several l s: gd hdwy on wd outside 3f out: rdn and outpcd fr over 1f out* **10/1**
4-21 **8** ¾ **Sabaani**[36] 618 3-8-6 82 AndrewMullen 9 75
(James Tate) *t.k.h: hld up bhd ldng gp: n.m.r over 4f out to over 2f out: sn rdn and outpcd* **18/1**
312- **9** ½ **Southern Gailes (IRE)**[132] 7852 3-8-4 80 JoeyHaynes 2 71
(K R Burke) *trckd ldrs: rdn over 2f out: wknd over 1f out* **6/1**[3]
312- **10** 1 **Dolphin Vista (IRE)**[154] 7421 3-8-7 83 BarryMcHugh 10 72
(Richard Fahey) *hld up in midfield on outside: struggling 3f out: sn wknd* **8/1**
126- **11** 3¾ **Essenaitch (IRE)**[181] 6731 3-8-12 88 TomQueally 7 69
(David Evans) *stdd s: t.k.h in rr: pushed along and outpcd over 3f out: btn fnl 2f* **40/1**
23-1 **12** 8 **Hutton (IRE)**[38] 600 3-8-0 76 oh1 JamesSullivan 12 40
(Richard Fahey) *in tch on outside: drvn along over 3f out: wknd over 2f out* **20/1**

1m 46.68s (-3.42) **Going Correction** -0.225s/f (Stan) **12** Ran SP% **113.9**
Speed ratings (Par 104): **106,105,104,104,101 100,100,99,99,98 94,87**
CSF £24.78 CT £173.47 TOTE £5.10: £2.00, £2.00, £1.80; EX 27.40 Trifecta £135.20.
Owner J C Fretwell **Bred** Lady Legard **Trained** Averham Park, Notts
■ Stewards' Enquiry : Andrew Mullen one-day ban; careless riding (8th Apr)

FOCUS
A good-quality and valuable handicap and the form looks rock-solid, with the right horses coming to the fore. The pace slowed a little at halfway and again it paid to race handily. The form has been rated on the positive side and should work out well.

1081 BET365.COM H'CAP 1m 5f 194y (Tp)
2:55 (2:58) (Class 2) (0-105,104) 4-Y-O+ **£32,345** (£9,625; £4,810; £2,405) **Stalls** Low

Form RPR
11-1 **1** **Gang Warfare**[59] 337 5-9-1 95 RobertHavlin 1 108+
(Simon Crisford) *hld up in tch: stdy hdwy over 2f out: shkn up to ld 1f out: drvn and kpt on strly fnl f* **3/1**[1]
13-1 **2** 2 **Silver Quay (IRE)**[7] 975 4-8-4 91 6ex TomMarquand(3) 12 101+
(Richard Hannon) *hld up in rr: stdy hdwy over 3f out: rdn and chsd wnr ins fnl f: kpt on wl towards fin: nt pce to chal* **4/1**[2]
214- **3** 6 **Agent Gibbs**[168] 7090 4-8-3 87 (p) JoeyHaynes 10 89
(Ali Stronge) *sn trcking ldr: led over 5f out: rdn over 2f out: hdd 1f out: sn outpcd* **12/1**
61-1 **4** ½ **Two Jabs**[23] 779 6-8-5 85 MartinLane 9 86
(Michael Appleby) *chsd ldng trio: drvn along over 3f out: kpt on same pce fr 2f out* **5/1**[3]
-431 **5** shd **Gabrial The Duke (IRE)**[20] 838 6-8-4 84 (b) BarryMcHugh 11 85
(Richard Fahey) *hld up: pushed along over 3f out: kpt on fr 2f out: nvr able to chal* **33/1**
1556 **6** nse **Luv U Whatever**[37] 614 6-9-2 96 AndrewMullen 2 97
(Michael Appleby) *trckd ldrs: wnt 2nd over 3f out: rdn and ev ch 2f out: outpcd fnl f* **18/1**
10-0 **7** ½ **Wordiness**[18] 861 8-8-7 87 CathyGannon 4 87
(David Evans) *hld up: pushed along over 3f out: hdwy wl over 1f out: sn no imp* **25/1**
1630 **8** nse **Paddys Motorbike (IRE)**[18] 861 4-8-7 91 FrannyNorton 5 91
(David Evans) *midfield: rdn and outpcd wl over 2f out: sn btn* **12/1**
060- **9** 1 **Totalize**[43] 6749 7-9-3 97 BenCurtis 13 96
(Brian Ellison) *s.i.s: hld up: drvn over 3f out: edgd lft and sme late hdwy: nvr on terms* **16/1**
20-6 **10** 19 **Be Perfect (USA)**[27] 747 7-8-7 87 (p) JamesSullivan 6 59
(Ruth Carr) *led to over 5f out: lost pl wl over 2f out: sn struggling* **16/1**
104- **11** 15 **Lycidas (GER)**[46] 4163 7-8-13 93 (t[1]) PaulMulrennan 3 44
(James Ewart) *midfield: drvn and struggling over 4f out: btn over 2f out: t.o* **12/1**
520- **12** 23 **Angel Gabrial (IRE)**[167] 7115 7-9-10 104 TonyHamilton 7 23
(Richard Fahey) *hld up: struggling over 4f out: sn btn: eased whn no ch fnl 2f: t.o* **11/1**

2m 57.95s (-6.85) **Going Correction** -0.225s/f (Stan) course record
WFA 4 from 5yo+ 4lb **12** Ran SP% **116.9**
Speed ratings (Par 109): **110,108,105,105,105 105,104,104,104,93 84,71**
CSF £14.05 CT £125.66 TOTE £3.30: £1.10, £1.40, £4.70; EX 13.30 Trifecta £129.80.
Owner The Hassiakos & Manasseh Partnership **Bred** West Stow Stud Ltd **Trained** Newmarket, Suffolk
■ Stewards' Enquiry : Joey Haynes three-day ban; carelss riding (8th,10th-11th Apr)

FOCUS
They were soon strung out in this useful middle-distance handicap and the front pair, who headed up the betting, came nicely clear. The winner should rate higher again.

1082 EBFSTALLIONS BET365 CONDITIONS STKS (PLUS 10 RACE) 5f 20y (Tp)
3:30 (3:31) (Class 3) 2-Y-O **£9,703** (£2,887; £1,443; £721) **Stalls** Low

Form RPR
1 **Sutter County** 2-9-3 0 FrannyNorton 10 94+
(Mark Johnston) *sn crossed over fr wd draw to press ldr: shkn up to ld 2f out: qcknd clr fnl f: eased nr fin: promising* **3/1**[2]
2 9 **Stringybark Creek** 2-9-3 0 CharlesBishop 11 62
(Mick Channon) *sn in tch on outside: effrt and pushed along over 2f out: hung lft and chsd (clr) wnr ins fnl f: kpt on: no imp* **25/1**
3 2¼ **Decadent Times (IRE)** 2-9-3 0 RichardKingscote 2 54
(Tom Dascombe) *led: rdn and hdd 2f out: no ex and lost 2nd pl ins fnl f* **8/1**
4 1 **Merry Banter** 2-8-12 0 PaulMulrennan 4 45
(Paul Midgley) *dwlt: t.k.h bhd ldng gp: effrt and drifted edgd rt over 1f out: kpt on fnl f: nvr able to chal* **25/1**
5 1 **Khelly's Edge** 2-8-12 0 BenCurtis 7 52+
(Scott Dixon) *s.i.s: rn green in rr: effrt and rdn whn n.m.r briefly wl over 1f out: sn no imp* **17/2**
6 1¾ **Red Mohican** 2-8-7 0 JosephineGordon(5) 9 35
(Phil McEntee) *dwlt: bhd: drvn along over 2f out: hung lft and no imp over 1f out* **50/1**
7 nk **Patrouille De Nuit (IRE)** 2-9-3 0 LiamJones 3 39
(J S Moore) *trckd ldrs: rdn over 2f out: wknd fnl f* **33/1**
8 1 **Davarde (IRE)** 2-9-3 0 TomQueally 6 35+
(David Evans) *dwlt: blkd sn after s: towards rr: drvn along over 2f out: btn over 1f out* **5/2**[1]
9 ½ **Who Told Jo Jo (IRE)** 2-8-12 0 RyanWhile(5) 8 34
(Bill Turner) *towards rr: effrt on wd outside over 2f out: sn wknd* **22/1**
10 nk **Cullingworth (IRE)** 2-9-3 0 TonyHamilton 5 32+
(Richard Fahey) *trckd ldrs tl rdn and wknd fr 2f out* **4/1**[3]
11 7 **Letmestopyouthere (IRE)** 2-9-3 0 CathyGannon 1 7
(David Evans) *missed break: rn green and sn wl bhd: nvr on terms* **16/1**

1m 0.78s (-1.12) **Going Correction** -0.225s/f (Stan) 2y crse rec **11** Ran SP% **118.0**
Speed ratings (Par 96): **99,84,81,79,77 75,74,72,72,71 60**
CSF £83.27 TOTE £3.20: £1.80, £6.90, £2.50; EX 69.60 Trifecta £673.40.
Owner Sheikh Hamdan bin Mohammed Al Maktoum **Bred** Darley **Trained** Middleham Moor, N Yorks

FOCUS
The first British 2yo race of 2016 and it was won in impressive fashion by the Mark Johnston-trained runner. It's hard to gauge the level of the form, the winner could be worth a three-figure rating, but he has plenty of time to show us what he's made of.

1083 BET365 CONDITIONS STKS 5f 20y (Tp)
4:00 (4:00) (Class 2) 3-Y-O+ **£12,938** (£3,850; £1,924; £962) **Stalls** Low

Form RPR
044- **1** **Rah Rah**[244] 4616 3-8-5 102 FrannyNorton 3 100
(Mark Johnston) *chsd ldrs: drvn and outpcd over 3f out: gd hdwy over 1f out: led ins fnl f: sn clr: eased nr fin* **9/4**[2]
002- **2** 2¼ **Red Baron (IRE)**[180] 6784 7-9-3 100 NeilFarley 1 97
(Eric Alston) *led at decent gallop: drvn over 1f out: hdd ins fnl f: no ch w wnr* **11/2**
304- **3** ¾ **Silvanus (IRE)**[185] 6614 11-9-6 95 PJMcDonald 6 97
(Paul Midgley) *w ldr: drvn along over 1f out: edgd lft ins fnl f: kpt on same pce* **50/1**
05-4 **4** nse **Line Of Reason (IRE)**[27] 745 6-9-10 110 PaulMulrennan 4 101
(Paul Midgley) *dwlt: sn in tch: effrt and pushed along 2f out: kpt on same pce fnl f* **2/1**[1]
-325 **5** ¾ **Barracuda Boy (IRE)**[13] 923 6-9-6 100 RichardKingscote 5 94
(Tom Dascombe) *hld up in tch on outside: drvn and outpcd over 2f out: kpt on fnl f: nvr able to chal* **4/1**[3]
014/ **6** shd **Shamshon (IRE)**[664] 2767 5-9-3 100 TimmyMurphy 2 91
(Jamie Osborne) *in tch on ins: stdy hdwy 1/2-way: effrt and shkn up over 1f out: outpcd fnl f: bttr for r* **10/1**

1m 0.06s (-1.84) **Going Correction** -0.225s/f (Stan)
WFA 3 from 5yo+ 12lb **6** Ran SP% **110.5**
Speed ratings (Par 109): **105,101,100,100,98 98**
CSF £14.30 TOTE £2.80: £1.60, £3.50; EX 16.10 Trifecta £156.40.
Owner Godolphin **Bred** Darley **Trained** Middleham Moor, N Yorks

FOCUS
A smart little sprint that was won by the only 3yo in the field, although that didn't look at all likely after 2f. On the face of it the third has run near his best.

1084 CASINO AT BET365.COM H'CAP 5f 20y (Tp)
4:30 (4:30) (Class 4) (0-85,85) 4-Y-O+ **£5,175** (£1,540; £769; £384) **Stalls** Low

Form RPR
0-42 **1** **King Crimson**[14] 903 4-9-0 78 CharlesBishop 7 86
(Mick Channon) *mde all: pushed along 2f out: hrd pressed fnl f: hld on gamely towards fin* **11/2**[3]
-331 **2** ½ **Secret Asset (IRE)**[29] 714 11-8-10 77 (p) RobHornby(3) 2 83
(Lisa Williamson) *trckd ldrs: effrt and wnt 2nd wl over 1f out: rdn and ev ch ins fnl f: kpt on: hld nr fin* **12/1**
000/ **3** 1½ **Pushkin Museum (IRE)**[545] 6736 5-8-8 72 BarryMcHugh 9 73
(Richard Fahey) *prom: drvn over 2f out: rallied over 1f out: kpt on u.p ins fnl f: nt rch first two* **16/1**
300- **4** shd **Top Boy**[162] 7239 6-9-1 79 (v) TonyHamilton 1 79
(Derek Shaw) *in tch on ins: effrt and rdn over 2f out: kpt on same pce ins fnl f* **6/1**
4422 **5** ½ **Ballista (IRE)**[7] 974 8-9-2 85 AnnaHesketh(5) 8 83
(Tom Dascombe) *pressed wnr to wl over 1f out: rallied: no ex ins fnl f* **13/2**
00-1 **6** ¾ **Something Lucky (IRE)**[25] 764 4-9-1 79 ShaneGray 3 75
(Kristin Stubbs) *hld up: rdn and hdwy 2f out: kpt on ins fnl f: nvr able to chal* **3/1**[1]
0020 **7** 2½ **Vimy Ridge**[8] 966 4-9-4 82 (p) SaleemGolam 5 69
(Alan Bailey) *dwlt: bhd: outpcd and hung rt bnd over 2f out: sn n.d* **9/2**[2]
00-2 **8** ¾ **Rusty Rocket (IRE)**[15] 894 7-9-4 82 TomQueally 4 66
(Paul Green) *hld up in tch: struggling over 2f out: btn over 1f out* **11/1**
60-0 **9** 3½ **Scarborough (IRE)**[84] 4 5-9-2 80 PaulMulrennan 6 51
(Paul Midgley) *dwlt: t.k.h: in tch on outside: struggling over 2f out: sn btn* **25/1**

1m 0.29s (-1.61) **Going Correction** -0.225s/f (Stan) **9** Ran SP% **111.9**
Speed ratings (Par 105): **103,102,99,99,98 97,93,92,86**
CSF £65.84 CT £983.14 TOTE £4.90: £1.20, £4.20, £3.50; EX 38.20 Trifecta £297.90.

Owner Billy Parish **Bred** Mickley Stud **Trained** West Ilsley, Berks
FOCUS
Little got into this fair sprint. The runner-up has been rated to his latest.

1085 POKER AT BET365.COM H'CAP — 1m 4f 50y (Tp)
5:00 (5:00) (Class 5) (0-70,69) 4-Y-0+ **£3,234** (£962; £481; £240) **Stalls** Low

Form RPR
5000 **1** **Gabrial The Terror (IRE)**[13] 922 6-9-8 68 TonyHamilton 9 76
(Richard Fahey) *hld up: effrt whn nt clr run briefly 3f out: shkn up and hdwy on outside over 1f out: led and edgd lft ins fnl f: pushed out* **10/3**[2]
05-0 **2** 2 ¾ **Rainford Glory (IRE)**[69] 222 6-8-12 58 BarryMcHugh 7 62
(Tim Fitzgerald) *prom: effrt and pushed along over 2f out: rdn and ev ch ins fnl f: edgd lft: one pce last 50yds* **20/1**
6-32 **3** nk **Competent**[23] 789 4-9-6 68 CathyGannon 6 71
(Kristin Stubbs) *trckd ldr: rdn to ld 2f out: edgd lft and hdd ins fnl f: kpt on same pce* **11/4**[1]
6-44 **4** 3 ¼ **Nolecce**[28] 731 9-8-9 58 RobHornby(3) 2 58
(Tony Forbes) *prom: effrt and rdn 2f out: wknd last 100yds* **6/1**
420- **5** 3 **Yorkindred Spirit**[130] 7876 4-9-7 69 (v) FrannyNorton 4 62
(Mark Johnston) *dwlt: hld up on ins: nt clr run briefly 3f out: effrt on ins 2f out: sn rdn and no imp appr fnl f* **9/2**[3]
5460 **6** ½ **Percys Princess**[6] 1002 5-9-8 68 (b[1]) AndrewMullen 5 60
(Michael Appleby) *led: rdn and hdd 2f out: wknd fnl f* **8/1**
4/00 **7** 2 ¼ **Stand Guard**[17] 864 12-8-13 62 DanielMuscutt(3) 8 51
(John Butler) *hld up: pushed along 3f out: sme hdwy over 1f out: kpt on: nvr able to chal* **50/1**
42-4 **8** 3 **Hartford Starts (IRE)**[10] 941 6-8-5 51 oh2 ShaneGray 3 35
(Brian Ellison) *hld up: drvn and outpcd on outside wl over 2f out: sn wknd* **8/1**
30/6 **9** 2 ¾ **Castlemorris King**[23] 781 8-8-7 58 EdwardGreatrex(5) 1 38
(Brian Barr) *trckd ldrs: drvn along 3f out: wknd 2f out* **33/1**

2m 37.51s (-3.29) **Going Correction** -0.225s/f (Stan)
WFA 4 from 5yo+ 2lb 9 Ran SP% **114.1**
Speed ratings (Par 103): **101,99,98,96,94 94,92,90,89**
CSF £66.73 CT £205.68 TOTE £3.50: £2.10, £4.60, £2.50; EX 67.40 Trifecta £263.60.
Owner Dr Marwan Koukash **Bred** Mrs Joan Murphy **Trained** Musley Bank, N Yorks
FOCUS
Modest handicap form. The second and third help set the opening level.
T/Jkpt: Not won. T/Plt: £112.70 to a £1 stake. Pool: £142,680.01 - 923.50 winning tickets T/Qpdt: £17.50 to a £1 stake. Pool: £9,714.92 - 409.78 winning tickets **Richard Young**

1035 KEMPTON (A.W) (R-H)
Saturday, March 26

OFFICIAL GOING: Polytrack: standard
Wind: Fresh, across (away from stands) Weather: Overcast, drizzly

1086 WATCH RACING UK IN HD MAIDEN FILLIES' STKS (DIV I) (PLUS 10 RACE) — 5f (P)
1:10 (1:10) (Class 4) 2-Y-O **£3,946** (£1,174; £586; £293) **Stalls** Low

Form RPR
1 **Boater (IRE)** 2-9-0 0 JoeFanning 5 83+
(Mark Johnston) *wl away: mde all: stretched clr fr over 1f out: v readily* **8/13**[1]
2 7 **Playful Trickster (IRE)** 2-9-0 0 RichardKingscote 7 58
(Tom Dascombe) *chsd wnr: readily lft bhd over 1f out but kpt on wl fr clr 2nd* **7/1**[2]
3 6 **Madam Prancealot (IRE)** 2-9-0 0 CathyGannon 9 36
(David Evans) *dwlt: racd in 4th but long way off ldng trio: kpt on to take v modest 3rd last 100yds* **25/1**
4 1 **Hot N Sassy (IRE)** 2-9-0 0 LiamJones 10 33
(J S Moore) *dwlt: outpcd in midfield and shoved along: nvr on terms but kpt on fnl f* **33/1**
5 shd **Little Nosegay (IRE)** 2-9-0 0 JFEgan 2 32
(David Evans) *s.i.s and v green early: tried to make prog fr rr arnd rivals 1/2-way: kpt on but nvr remotely on terms* **16/1**
6 nk **Lavender Skye (IRE)** 2-9-0 0 DougieCostello 8 31
(K R Burke) *dwlt: racd in 5th but outpcd and long way off ldng trio: kpt on one pce fr over 1f out* **16/1**
7 ½ **Bills Delight** 2-8-9 0 RyanWhile(5) 6 30
(Bill Turner) *chsd ldng pair and clr of rest: lft bhd wl over 1f out: wknd and lost pls last 100yds* **25/1**
8 1 ¾ **Fastnet Spin (IRE)** 2-9-0 0 AndrewMullen 4 23
(David Evans) *rn green early: dropped to last pair after 2f: nvr a factor* **12/1**
9 1 ¼ **Jenji (IRE)** 2-9-0 0 PatCosgrave 1 19
(David Evans) *s.i.s and v green early: a bhd* **8/1**[3]
10 2 ¼ **Bara Brith** 2-8-11 0 PhilipPrince(3) 3 11
(David Evans) *outpcd and a wl bhd in last pair* **50/1**

1m 0.58s (0.08) **Going Correction** -0.10s/f (Stan) 10 Ran SP% **117.6**
Speed ratings (Par 91): **95,83,74,72,72 71,71,68,66,62**
CSF £5.08 TOTE £1.40: £1.02, £2.50, £4.90; EX 4.60 Trifecta £59.80.
Owner Sheikh Hamdan bin Mohammed Al Maktoum **Bred** Darley **Trained** Middleham Moor, N Yorks
FOCUS
The first division of a juvenile fillies' maiden won by Richard Hannon's very smart Tiggy Wiggy in 2014. They went a decent gallop on standard Polytrack. Just nine 2yo fillies have posted 86 or better winning RPRs in March or April in the past decade, and Johnston saddled a pair of such horses at this meeting.

1087 WATCH RACING UK IN HD MAIDEN FILLIES' STKS (DIV II) (PLUS 10 RACE) — 5f (P)
1:40 (1:41) (Class 4) 2-Y-O **£3,946** (£1,174; £586; £293) **Stalls** Low

Form RPR
1 **Chupalla** 2-9-0 0 JoeFanning 9 92+
(Mark Johnston) *fast away fr wd draw: mde all: pushed along and stretched clr over 1f out: v readily* **6/5**[1]
2 6 **Stormy Clouds (IRE)** 2-9-0 0 SeanLevey 5 70
(Richard Hannon) *trckd ldng pair: chsd wnr wl over 1f out: sn shkn up and readily lft bhd* **5/2**[2]
3 3 ¼ **Rapacity Alexander (IRE)** 2-9-0 0 CathyGannon 8 59
(David Evans) *chsd wnr to wl over 1f out: no ch after and wl btn in 3rd fnl f* **5/1**[3]
4 1 **Mesmeric Moment** 2-9-0 0 PatCosgrave 7 55
(David Evans) *dwlt: jst in tch in 6th: rdn 1/2-way: tk 4th wl over 1f out: kpt on but no ch* **12/1**
5 5 **To Have A Dream (IRE)** 2-9-0 0 MartinDwyer 1 37
(J S Moore) *chsd ldrs disputing 4th: pushed along 1/2-way: wknd over 1f out* **33/1**
6 2 **Princess Way (IRE)** 2-8-11 0 PhilipPrince(3) 4 30
(David Evans) *bucked leaving stalls and sn virtually t.o in 7th: nvr a factor* **25/1**
7 nk **Eid Rose** 2-9-0 0 ShaneGray 2 29
(Kevin Ryan) *chsd ldrs disputing 4th: wknd rapidly wl over 1f out* **10/1**
8 1 ¼ **Thora Barber** 2-9-0 0 AndrewMullen 3 24
(David Evans) *slowly away: rn green and sn t.o in last* **33/1**

1m 0.09s (-0.41) **Going Correction** -0.10s/f (Stan) 8 Ran SP% **117.2**
Speed ratings (Par 91): **99,89,84,82,74 71,70,68**
CSF £4.36 TOTE £2.60: £1.10, £1.10, £1.60; EX 5.30 Trifecta £13.70.
Owner Sheikh Hamdan bin Mohammed Al Maktoum **Bred** Darley **Trained** Middleham Moor, N Yorks
FOCUS
The second division of the juvenile fillies' maiden. They went another decent gallop and the winner clocked a time half-a-second faster than the wide-margin winner of the first race. Just nine 2yo fillies have posted 86 or better winning RPRs in March or April in past decade, and Johnston saddled a pair of such horses at this meeting.

1088 APOLLOBET CASHBACK IF YOU FINISH 2ND MAGNOLIA STKS (LISTED RACE) — 1m 2f (P)
2:15 (2:17) (Class 1) 4-Y-O+
£20,982 (£7,955; £3,981; £1,983; £995; £499) **Stalls** Low

Form RPR
-131 **1** **Our Channel (USA)**[17] 871 5-9-0 103 (p) PatCosgrave 6 105
(William Haggas) *trckd ldr: chal fr 2f out: upsides over 1f out but hanging rt: edgd rt and led last 100yds: kpt on wl* **11/4**[1]
301- **2** nk **Noble Gift**[152] 7511 6-9-0 98 CallumShepherd 5 104
(William Knight) *pushed up to ld: drvn and jnd over 1f out whn briefly edgd lft: hdd last 100yds and sltly impeded by wnr: battled on wl but jst hld* **8/1**
020- **3** 2 ¼ **Maybelater**[169] 7078 4-8-9 89 RichardKingscote 4 95
(Jonathan Portman) *hld up in tch: dropped to rr but stl gng wl 3f out: prog to chse clr ldng pair over 1f out: styd on but no imp* **20/1**
6/1- **4** 1 ½ **Restorer**[147] 7633 4-9-3 106 MartinDwyer 3 100+
(William Muir) *tk v t.k.h: hld up and last after 4f: stl last 2f out: prog over 1f out: tk 4th fnl f but no ch to be involved* **9/2**[3]
-342 **5** 2 ¾ **Truth Or Dare**[17] 871 5-9-0 92 FMBerry 1 92
(William Muir) *t.k.h: chsd ldng pair: rdn and no imp over 2f out: lost 3rd and wknd over 1f out* **9/2**[3]
200- **6** nk **Windshear**[175] 6917 5-9-0 106 SeanLevey 7 92
(Richard Hannon) *chsd ldrs: rdn 3f out: outpcd fr 2f out and no ch after* **7/2**[2]
/00- **7** 8 **What Say You (IRE)**[231] 5145 4-8-9 88 DougieCostello 8 71
(K R Burke) *t.k.h: hld up in last: prog on outer 1/2-way: wknd and wd bnd 2f out: sn bhd* **25/1**
441- **8** 11 **Passover**[154] 7470 5-9-0 97 (t) DavidProbert 2 55
(Andrew Balding) *in tch: rdn and wknd qckly wl over 2f out: t.o* **7/1**

2m 5.08s (-2.92) **Going Correction** -0.10s/f (Stan) 8 Ran SP% **117.5**
Speed ratings (Par 111): **107,106,104,103,101 101,94,86**
CSF £26.37 TOTE £3.10: £1.10, £2.60, £5.40; EX 26.00 Trifecta £362.60.
Owner Abdulla Al Mansoori **Bred** Bluegrass Hall Llc **Trained** Newmarket, Suffolk
■ Stewards' Enquiry : Pat Cosgrave jockey found in breach of Rule (B)54.1 and guilty of careless riding in that he allowed his mount to drift slightly right without taking sufficient corrective action. They cautioned him as to his future conduct in races.
FOCUS
A good quality Listed race. They went a decent gallop. The winner has been rated just below his recent efforts.

1089 APOLLOBET BEST ODDS GUARANTEED ROSEBERY H'CAP (LONDON MIDDLE DISTANCE SERIES QUALIFIER) — 1m 3f (P)
2:50 (2:52) (Class 2) (0-105,102) 4-Y-O+
£28,012 (£8,388; £4,194; £2,097; £1,048; £526) **Stalls** Low

Form RPR
23-1 **1** **Barsanti (IRE)**[30] 708 4-8-6 **85** JackMitchell 1 100+
(Roger Varian) *trckd ldng pair: clsd gng easily to ld jst over 2f out: rdn and clr over 1f out: styd on strly* **7/2**[1]
403- **2** 4 **Dutch Uncle**[253] 4345 4-8-3 **82** FrannyNorton 10 89+
(Ed Dunlop) *trckd ldng quartet: prog 2f out: rdn to chse wnr over 1f out: one pce and no imp* **5/1**[2]
4454 **3** ¾ **Castilo Del Diablo (IRE)**[19] 861 7-8-7 **92** (p) SophieKilloran(7) 9 97
(David Simcock) *s.i.s: mostly in last pair: rdn over 2f out: prog on outer after: styd on wl to take 3rd last 75yds* **12/1**
4 ½ **Cayirli (FR)**[136] 4-8-13 **92** TimmyMurphy 2 96
(Seamus Durack) *trckd ldng trio: shkn up over 2f out: effrt to chse ldng pair ins fnl f: kpt on but lost 3rd last 75yds* **16/1**
2251 **5** 2 ¾ **Pactolus (IRE)**[16] 888 5-8-10 **88** (t) OisinMurphy 4 88
(Stuart Williams) *hld up towards rr: shkn up over 2f out: swtchd lft wl over 1f out: kpt on after and tk 5th nr fin: no ch* **8/1**[3]
-123 **6** hd **Giantstepsahead (IRE)**[35] 656 7-8-6 **87** DanielMuscutt(3) 8 86
(Brian McMath) *led at gd pce: rdn and hdd jst over 2f out: lost 2nd over 1f out: wknd fnl f* **9/1**
2330 **7** 1 ½ **Afonso De Sousa (USA)**[28] 757 6-9-10 **102** DanielTudhope 5 99
(David O'Meara) *nvr bttr than midfield on inner: rdn over 2f out: no prog and btn over 1f out: fdd* **12/1**
3260 **8** 1 ¾ **Whispering Warrior (IRE)**[40] 594 7-9-0 **92** PatCosgrave 3 86
(David Simcock) *settled in rr: urged along 2f out: no significant prog* **10/1**
0-44 **9** ½ **Viewpoint (IRE)**[7] 1001 7-8-7 **85** AndrewMullen 11 78
(Michael Appleby) *t.k.h: wl in tch: hrd rdn and no prog over 2f out: wknd fnl f* **9/1**
446- **10** 6 **Saoi (USA)**[260] 4088 9-8-11 **89** JimCrowley 7 73
(William Knight) *a wl in rr: drvn in last over 2f out: sn bhd* **20/1**
065- **11** ¾ **Master Of Finance (IRE)**[184] 6686 5-9-3 **95** JoeFanning 6 77
(Mark Johnston) *chsd ldr to over 2f out: wknd rapidly wl over 1f out* **9/1**
1043 **12** 20 **Freud (FR)**[9] 967 6-8-3 **81** 1ex MartinDwyer 12 31
(Ian Williams) *unruly to post: slowly away: prog on outer into midfield 1/2-way: wknd rapidly over 2f out: t.o and eased* **25/1**

2m 16.17s (-5.73) **Going Correction** -0.10s/f (Stan)
WFA 4 from 5yo+ 1lb 12 Ran SP% **119.0**
Speed ratings (Par 109): **116,113,112,112,110 110,108,107,107,102 102,87**
CSF £20.02 CT £192.00 TOTE £4.10: £1.70, £2.60, £4.10; EX 17.30 Trifecta £210.90.

Owner Sheikh Mohammed Obaid Al Maktoum **Bred** Glenvale Stud **Trained** Newmarket, Suffolk

FOCUS

A good quality middle-distance handicap. They went an even gallop. Solid form, with those in behind the first two helping set a straightforward level.

1090 APOLLOBET CASINO FREE £10 H'CAP 6f (P)

3:25 (3:25) (Class 2) (0-105,97) 4-Y-O+

£11,827 (£3,541; £1,770; £885; £442; £222) **Stalls** Low

Form RPR

1-11 **1** **Spring Loaded (IRE)**^{35} [657] 4-9-5 **95** ShaneKelly 6 105+
(Paul D'Arcy) *hld up in 6th: pushed along and clsd 2f out: shkn up to ld jst ins fnl f: rdn out and won decisively* **13/8**^{1}

2-60 **2** 1 1/4 **Plucky Dip**^{14} [923] 5-8-1 **80** DannyBrock$^{(3)}$ 2 86
(John Ryan) *hld up in last trio: prog jst over 2f out: drvn to chal 1f out: chsd wnr after: kpt on wl but no imp* **8/1**

-013 **3** 3/4 **Yeeoow (IRE)**^{54} [416] 7-8-7 **83** JoeyHaynes 4 87
(K R Burke) *trckd ldng pair: pushed along bef 1/2-way: clsd to ld over 2f out: drvn and hdd jst ins fnl f: one pce* **14/1**

440- **4** 1 1/4 **Related**^{238} [4858] 6-9-7 **97** (b) MartinLane 8 97
(Paul Midgley) *chsd ldng trio: rdn and nt qckn over 2f out and lost pl sn after: kpt on fnl f to take 4th again nr fin* **15/2**^{3}

005- **5** 1/2 **Mishaal (IRE)**^{253} [4357] 6-9-2 **92** PaulMulrennan 7 91
(Michael Herrington) *led to over 2f out: kpt on and stl rt on terms jst over 1f out: wknd fnl f* **22/1**

-502 **6** hd **Steelriver (IRE)**^{14} [923] 6-9-5 **95** GrahamGibbons 3 93
(David Barron) *hld up in 5th: pushed along 2f out: shkn up and cl enough jst over 1f out: fdd* **3/1**^{2}

1602 **7** 1 3/4 **Searchlight**^{25} [771] 5-8-11 **87** PatCosgrave 5 80
(Jim Boyle) *hld up in last pair: shkn up over 2f out: no prog* **11/1**

/4-3 **8** hd **Invincible Diamond (IRE)**^{11} [944] 4-8-4 **80** MartinDwyer 1 72
(J S Moore) *hld up in last pair: shkn up and no prog over 2f out* **12/1**

016- **9** 3/4 **Secret Missile**^{124} [7958] 6-8-12 **93** (p) HectorCrouch$^{(5)}$ 9 83
(Gary Moore) *chsd ldr to over 2f out: wknd over 1f out* **25/1**

1m 10.48s (-2.62) **Going Correction** -0.10s/f (Stan) **9** Ran SP% **116.9**

Speed ratings (Par 109): **113,111,110,108,108 107,105,105,104**

CSF £15.87 CT £139.27 TOTE £2.30: £1.30, £2.50, £2.60; EX 13.80 Trifecta £185.20.

Owner Rowley Racing **Bred** Swordlestown Little **Trained** Newmarket, Suffolk

FOCUS

A good sprint handicap. They went a decent gallop. Straightforward form rated around the second and third.

1091 APOLLOBET CASHBACK SPECIALS MAIDEN STKS 7f (P)

4:00 (4:00) (Class 4) 3-Y-O+ **£4,690** (£1,395; £697; £348) **Stalls** Low

Form RPR

02- **1** **Ice Age (IRE)**^{248} [4517] 3-8-13 0 RobertWinston 2 77
(Eve Johnson Houghton) *t.k.h: trckd ldng pair: clsd fr 2f out to ld jst over 1f out: drvn out* **25/1**

4 **2** 3/4 **Justice Grace (IRE)**^{36} [639] 3-8-13 0 JohnFahy 8 75
(Ralph Beckett) *chsd ldr: drvn over 2f out: hd quite high and nt qckn: rallied to chse wnr jst ins fnl f: kpt on but a hld* **12/1**

0- **3** 1/2 **Colonel Bossington (IRE)**^{210} [5854] 3-8-13 0 JimCrowley 3 74
(William Knight) *wl in tch: shkn up over 2f out: styd on fr over 1f out to take 3rd last stride* **11/1**^{3}

00- **4** shd **Suqoor**^{222} [5447] 3-8-13 0 IrineuGoncalves 4 73
(Chris Dwyer) *t.k.h: hld up towards rr: prog on inner 2f out: disp 2nd 1f out and cl enough: reminders and one pce after* **66/1**

3-2 **5** nk **Hermitage Bay (USA)**^{53} [428] 3-8-13 0 RobertHavlin 5 73
(John Gosden) *trckd ldng trio: hanging lft whn asked to cl fr over 2f out: nt qckn after but kpt on ins fnl f* **10/11**^{1}

22- **6** 1 3/4 **Cape Banjo (USA)**^{108} [8153] 3-8-13 0 FMBerry 6 68
(Ralph Beckett) *t.k.h: hld up in 6th on outer: rdn over 2f out: no real prog whn carried lft over 1f out: nvr able to threaten* **7/4**^{2}

6- **7** 2 1/2 **Tiz Herself (IRE)**^{320} [2135] 3-8-8 0 RichardKingscote 1 56
(Jonathan Portman) *led: rdn 2f out: hdd & wknd jst over 1f out* **25/1**

50- **8** nse **Michael's Mount**^{201} [6164] 3-8-13 0 PatCosgrave 7 61
(Ed Dunlop) *hld up in last pair: pushed along 2f out: no real prog: nvr involved* **14/1**

0 **9** 1 3/4 **Cainhoe Star**^{10} [952] 3-8-13 0 WilliamCarson 9 56
(Anthony Carson) *hld up: a in last pair: shkn up and no prog over 2f out* **66/1**

1m 26.54s (0.54) **Going Correction** -0.10s/f (Stan) **9** Ran SP% **122.1**

Speed ratings (Par 105): **92,91,90,90,90 88,85,85,83**

CSF £294.76 TOTE £28.90: £5.50, £3.10, £3.60; EX 159.40 Trifecta £5733.40 Part won..

Owner Eden Racing III **Bred** Piercetown Stud **Trained** Blewbury, Oxon

■ Stewards' Enquiry : John Fahy two-day ban: used whip above permitted level (9th & 11th April)

FOCUS

A decent maiden. They went an ordinary gallop. This has a messy feel about it and it's been rated towards the bottom end of the race average.

1092 RACING UK WINTER SEASON TICKET H'CAP 2m (P)

4:35 (4:35) (Class 4) (0-85,83) 4-Y-O+ **£4,690** (£1,395; £697; £348) **Stalls** Low

Form RPR

1/2- **1** **Seaside Sizzler**^{140} [7747] 9-9-11 **82** GeorgeBaker 3 91
(William Knight) *trckd ldrs: prog to go 2nd over 3f out: rdn to ld 2f out: drvn out and kpt on wl* **4/1**^{3}

244- **2** 3/4 **Injun Sands**^{193} [6424] 5-9-5 **79** DannyBrock$^{(3)}$ 5 87
(Jane Chapple-Hyam) *trckd ldrs: shuffled bk on inner fr 5f out and in rr 3f out: prog again over 2f out: drvn to chse wnr over 1f out: styd on but a hld* **7/1**

1-24 **3** 1/2 **Duchess Of Marmite (IRE)**^{51} [440] 4-9-7 **83** ShaneKelly 8 92
(Richard Hughes) *t.k.h: hld up in last: stl on bridle in last whn rn into trble 2f out: prog and nt clr run over 1f out: cajoled along and r.o to take 3rd nr fin: too much to do* **7/2**^{2}

4211 **4** 1 1/4 **Midtech Star (IRE)**^{14} [922] 4-9-6 **82** (v) StevieDonohoe 1 88
(Ian Williams) *trckd ldng pair to 4f out: drvn to chse ldng pair again over 1f out: no imp fnl f and lost 3rd nr fin* **3/1**^{1}

-162 **5** 1 1/2 **Oratorio's Joy (IRE)**^{51} [440] 6-9-6 **77** WilliamCarson 9 81
(Jamie Osborne) *hld up disputing 6th: drvn and nt qckn wl over 2f out: plugged on one pce after: n.d* **20/1**

-445 **6** 2 1/2 **Precision Five**^{51} [440] 7-9-7 **83** (p) JosephineGordon$^{(5)}$ 2 84
(Alan King) *hld up disputing 6th: prog on outer 5f out: disp 3rd over 3f out: rdn over 2f out: steadily fdd* **12/1**

2362 **7** 3/4 **Todd**^{21} [838] 6-9-2 **73** (p) KieranO'Neill 4 73
(Anabel K Murphy) *hld up in last pair: drvn and no rspnse over 2f out: no ch after* **25/1**

560- **8** 8 **Apollo Eleven (IRE)**^{127} [7920] 7-8-12 **69** AndrewMullen 6 60
(Michael Appleby) *led to over 7f out: chsd ldr to over 3f out: wknd qckly wl over 1f out* **50/1**

3311 **9** 6 **Rose Above**^{17} [882] 4-8-10 **72** JimCrowley 7 56
(Andrew Balding) *t.k.h: trckd ldr: led over 7f out: hdd & wknd rapidly 2f out: eased* **5/1**

3m 32.26s (2.16) **Going Correction** -0.10s/f (Stan)

WFA 4 from 5yo+ 5lb **9** Ran SP% **113.6**

Speed ratings (Par 105): **90,89,89,88,88 86,86,82,79**

CSF £30.60 CT £105.86 TOTE £4.10: £1.80, £1.90, £1.70; EX 35.80 Trifecta £178.80.

Owner I J Heseltine **Bred** Redmyre Bloodstock And S Hillen **Trained** Patching, W Sussex

FOCUS

A decent staying handicap. They went a steady gallop until the tempo increased down the back straight the final time. The winner has been rated 3lb off his peak, and the second as running a minor pb.

1093 HIGH DEFINITION RACING UK H'CAP (LONDON MIDDLE DISTANCE SERIES QUALIFIER) 1m 3f (P)

5:10 (5:14) (Class 4) (0-85,85) 4-Y-O+ **£4,690** (£1,395; £697; £348) **Stalls** Low

Form RPR

264- **1** **Captain Navarre**^{148} [7593] 4-8-9 **77** SimonPearce$^{(3)}$ 7 84
(Lydia Pearce) *trckd ldrs: shkn up to chse ldr wl over 2f out: edgd lft after: rdn to ld 1f out: kpt on* **8/1**

/641 **2** 1 1/4 **Elysian Prince**^{38} [616] 5-9-1 **79** (t) LiamJones 9 84
(Neil King) *trckd ldr: led 4f out and sn sent for home: edgd lft fr over 2f out: hdd 1f out: one pce* **7/1**^{3}

1434 **3** hd **Charlies Mate**^{24} [779] 5-9-0 **78** KierenFox 6 83
(John Best) *wl in tch: rdn and prog to chse ldng pair 2f out: tried to chal over 1f out: kpt on but nt qckn* **8/1**

421- **4** 3/4 **Prendergast Hill (IRE)**^{181} [6779] 4-9-6 **85** JimCrowley 1 88
(Ed de Giles) *in tch: rdn over 2f out: tried to cl over 1f out: kpt on but unable to chal* **5/2**^{1}

-116 **5** 1/2 **Buckland Beau**^{24} [779] 5-9-3 **81** StevieDonohoe 10 84
(Charlie Fellowes) *hld up in rr: rdn and prog over 2f out: tried to cl on ldrs over 1f out: kpt on same pce* **10/1**

54-2 **6** 4 **Jolievitesse (FR)**^{80} [66] 4-8-11 **76** JoeyHaynes 3 72
(K R Burke) *prom: rdn and hanging fr over 2f out: steadily wknd* **3/1**^{2}

-562 **7** nk **Lady Marl**^{9} [967] 5-9-6 **84** GeorgeBaker 4 80
(Gary Moore) *hld up towards rr: stl only 8th 2f out: rdn over 1f out: no great prog after* **14/1**

040- **8** 3 **Jacob Cats**^{143} [7704] 7-9-4 **82** (v) FrederikTylicki 8 73
(William Knight) *stdd s: hld up in rr: rdn and no prog over 2f out* **9/1**

230- **9** 3 3/4 **Zambeasy**^{171} [7035] 5-9-1 **79** WilliamTwiston-Davies 5 64
(Philip Hide) *led to 4f out: wknd over 2f out* **20/1**

-060 **10** 24 **Dana's Present**^{24} [788] 7-8-8 **72** LiamKeniry 2 19
(Tom Dascombe) *walked to post and mounted at s: t.k.h: hld up in last: nvr any prog: t.o* **50/1**

2m 18.46s (-3.44) **Going Correction** -0.10s/f (Stan)

WFA 4 from 5yo+ 1lb **10** Ran SP% **120.8**

Speed ratings (Par 105): **108,107,106,106,106 103,102,100,98,80**

CSF £65.29 CT £472.39 TOTE £9.90: £3.10, £2.40, £2.10; EX 85.60 Trifecta £596.30.

Owner Lydia Pearce Racing Partnership 1 **Bred** Shortgrove Manor Stud **Trained** Newmarket, Suffolk

FOCUS

A decent middle-distance handicap. A good initial tempo decreased slightly entering the back straight. The third is among those who help set a straightforward level.

T/Plt: £309.70 to a £1 stake. Pool: £103,062.26 - 242.86 winning tickets T/Qpdt: £257.20 to a £1 stake. Pool: £9,179.32 - 26.40 winning tickets **Jonathan Neesom**

1094 - 1100a (Foreign Racing) - See Raceform Interactive

912 MEYDAN (L-H)

Saturday, March 26

OFFICIAL GOING: Turf: good; dirt: fast

1101a GODOLPHIN MILE SPONSORED BY MEYDAN SOBHA (GROUP 2) (DIRT) 1m (D)

12:20 (12:20) 3-Y-O+

£408,163 (£136,054; £68,027; £34,013; £20,408; £13,605)

RPR

1 **One Man Band (IRE)**^{30} [717] 5-9-0 112 SamHitchcott 1 117
(Doug Watson, UAE) *sn led: rdn clr 2f out: r.o wl* **11/2**^{3}

2 4 3/4 **Faulkner**^{21} [844] 6-9-0 110 DaneO'Neill 4 106+
(Doug Watson, UAE) *mid-div: r.o wl fnl 2f but no ch w wnr* **14/1**

3 nse **Cool Cowboy (USA)**^{21} [842] 5-9-0 112 PatDobbs 8 106
(Doug Watson, UAE) *trckd ldr: ev ch 2 1/2f out: one pce fnl 1 1/2f: lost 2nd cl home* **8/1**

4 4 1/2 **Marking (USA)**^{30} [719] 4-9-0 113 JamesDoyle 2 96
(Kiaran McLaughlin, U.S.A) *s.i.s: trckd ldr: rdn 4f out: r.o same pce fnl 2 1/2f* **5/4**^{1}

5 1 **Sloane Avenue (USA)**^{31} [692] 5-9-0 112 FrankieDettori 9 93
(Jeremy Noseda) *s.i.s: settled in rr: nvr able to chal but r.o same pce fnl 2f* **9/2**^{2}

6 2 1/4 **Prayer For Relief (USA)**^{21} [845] 8-9-0 109 (b) WayneSmith 10 88
(M F De Kock, South Africa) *trckd ldng pair tl outpcd 3f out* **33/1**

7 4 1/4 **Maftool (USA)**^{37} [624] 4-9-0 112 PaulHanagan 5 78
(M Al Mheiri, UAE) *nvr bttr than mid-div* **15/2**

8 1/2 **Gold City (IRE)**^{21} [844] 7-9-0 109 (bt) RichardMullen 6 77
(S Seemar, UAE) *nvr bttr than mid-div* **50/1**

9 3/4 **God's Speed (IRE)**^{7} 5-9-0 110 LJurado 7 75
(H Al Shuwaib, Saudi Arabia) *nvr nr to chal* **66/1**

1m 35.21s (-2.29) **Going Correction** +0.15s/f (Slow) **9** Ran SP% **113.9**

Speed ratings: **117,112,112,107,106 104,100,99,98**

CSF: 75.13; TRICAST: 610.93.

Owner Sheikh Saeed Bin Mohammed Al Maktoum **Bred** Richard A Pegum **Trained** United Arab Emirates

FOCUS
TRAKUS (metres travelled compared to winner): 2nd 0, 3rd +3, 4th +3, 5th +7, 6th +8, 7th +4, 8th +3, 9th +7. On a rapid track, the winner made all through these splits: 25.04 (allow about two seconds for standing start), 22.33, 23.46, 24.38. A fantastic one-two-three for trainer Doug Watson.

1102a DUBAI GOLD CUP SPONSORED BY AL TAYER MOTORS (GROUP 2) (TURF) — 2m

12:55 (12:55) 3-Y-O+

£408,163 (£136,054; £68,027; £34,013; £20,408; £13,605)

RPR

1 **Vazirabad (FR)**[153] 7502 4-8-10 120 ow2............ ChristopheSoumillon 1 118+
(A De Royer-Dupre, France) *broke awkwardly: settled in rr: smooth prog 3f out: led 110yds out: r.o wl* **5/4**[1]

2 *nk* **Big Orange**[144] 7697 5-9-0 116....................................(p) JamieSpencer 7 117
(Michael Bell) *trckd ldr: led 2 1/2f out: hdd 110yds out but r.o wl* **11/2**[3]

3 *4 3/4* **Haafaguinea**[21] 843 6-9-0 113....................................... JamesDoyle 11 111+
(Saeed bin Suroor) *settled in rr: rdn 4f out: r.o same pce fnl 2 1/2f* **7/1**

4 *nse* **Suegioo (FR)**[161] 7277 7-9-0 107...................................(p) PaulHanagan 3 111
(Richard Fahey) *mid-div: nvr able to chal but r.o fnl 2f* **25/1**

5 *4* **Meadow Creek**[23] 811 5-9-0 105... PatDobbs 9 107
(Doug Watson, UAE) *mid-div: chsd ldrs 3 1/2f out: one pce fnl 2 1/2f* **20/1**

6 *2* **Manatee**[23] 805 5-9-0 117... MickaelBarzalona 8 105
(A Fabre, France) *nvr bttr than mid-div* **5/1**[2]

7 *nse* **Tellina (SAF)**[23] 811 6-9-0 106....................................... RyanMoore 10 105
(M F De Kock, South Africa) *trckd ldng trio: rdn 3 1/2f out: r.o same pce fnl 2 1/2f* **16/1**

8 *1 1/4* **Neo Black Dia (JPN)**[35] 8-9-0 113......................... ShinichiroAkiyama 4 103
(Yuichi Shikato, Japan) *trckd ldng pair tl wknd 3f out* **33/1**

9 *nk* **Star Empire (SAF)**[23] 811 9-9-0 111.............................. WayneSmith 5 103
(M F De Kock, South Africa) *s.i.s: a in rr* **20/1**

10 *1* **Certerach (IRE)**[23] 811 8-9-0 106..................................(b) TadhgO'Shea 6 102
(M Halford, Ire) *sn led: hdd & wknd 2 1/2f out* **33/1**

11 *27* **Paradise (GER)**[16] 4-8-4 104.. MircoDemuro 2 67
(Waldemar Hickst, Germany) *a in rr* **50/1**

3m 19.56s (-4.94) **Going Correction** +0.025s/f (Good)
WFA 4 from 5yo+ 5lb **11** Ran SP% **116.1**
Speed ratings: **113,112,110,110,108 107,107,106,106,106 92**
CSF: 7.04; TRICAST: 34.99.
Owner H H Aga Khan **Bred** S C E A Haras De Son Altesse L'Aga Khan **Trained** Chantilly, France

FOCUS
The first two came nicely clear and the form looks sound for the grade. They went 49.72, 51.78, 50.50, 24.47 and the winner clocked 23.09 for the final 400m. The second, third, fourth and fifth help set the standard. TRAKUS: 2nd -6, 3rd +2, 4th +5, 5th +2, 6th -6, 7th -8, 8th -1, 9th -6, 10th -6, 11th -2

1103a UAE DERBY SPONSORED BY THE SAEED & MOHAMMED AL NABOODAH GROUP (GROUP 2) (DIRT) — 1m 1f 110y(D)

1:35 (1:35) 3-Y-O

£816,326 (£272,108; £136,054; £68,027; £40,816; £27,210)

RPR

1 **Lani (USA)**[34] 3-8-9 99.. YutakaTake 3 107
(Mikio Matsunaga, Japan) *broke awkwardly: chsd ldrs 4f out: led 110yds out: r.o wl* **12/1**

2 *3/4* **Polar River (USA)**[23] 808 3-8-7 112 ow2............................ PatDobbs 2 104+
(Doug Watson, UAE) *mid-div: n.m.r 2f out: r.o fnl 1 1/2f: nrst fin* **8/13**[1]

3 *nk* **Yu Change (JPN)**[69] 3-8-9 106.. JoaoMoreira 4 104
(Hideyuki Mori, Japan) *trckd ldr: led 3f out: r.o but hdd 110yds out* **25/1**

4 *1/2* **Vale Dori (ARG)**[23] 808 3-9-1 108.................... ChristopheSoumillon 5 101
(M F De Kock, South Africa) *sn led: hdd 3f out: one pce fnl 2f* **9/2**[2]

5 *1 1/4* **On The Rocks (JPN)**[48] 3-8-9 99.................................. MircoDemuro 6 101+
(Hideyuki Mori, Japan) *trckd ldr: outpcd 4f out: r.o again fnl 2f* **66/1**

6 *3 1/4* **Lazzam**[21] 839 3-8-9 95...(b) FrankieDettori 7 94
(Marco Botti) *a in rr* **25/1**

7 *3 3/4* **Frank Conversation (USA)**[42] 3-8-9 106................(vt) MarioGutierrez 1 86
(Doug O'Neill, U.S.A) *mid-div: rdn 4f out: sn btn* **6/1**[3]

1m 58.41s (-0.39) **Going Correction** +0.15s/f (Slow) **7** Ran SP% **111.3**
Speed ratings: **107,106,106,105,104 102,99**
CSF: 19.13.
Owner Yoko Maeda **Bred** North Hills Co Ltd **Trained** Japan

FOCUS
TRAKUS: 2nd -10, 3rd +1, 4th -9, 5th +4, 6th -3, 7th 0. This was a messy race, the lead changing a few times and the favourite getting into a bit of trouble. The splits through the first mile here 26.49, 23.95, 23.7, 24.76.

1104a AL QUOZ SPRINT SPONSORED BY MEYDAN HOTELS & HOSPITALITY (GROUP 1) (TURF) — 5f (T)

2:10 (2:10) 3-Y-O+

£408,163 (£136,054; £68,027; £34,013; £20,408; £13,605)

RPR

1 **Buffering (AUS)**[77] 8-9-0 115....................................(b) DamianBrowne 9 120
(Robert Heathcote, Australia) *trckd ldr: led 110yds out: r.o wl: comf* **10/1**

2 *3/4* **Ertijaal (IRE)**[51] 450 5-9-0 116... PaulHanagan 6 117
(A R Al Rayhi, UAE) *trckd ldrs: led 1 1/2f out: hdd 110yds out: r.o wl* **11/4**[1]

3 *nk* **Peniaphobia (IRE)**[55] 5-9-0 119...................................(tp) JoaoMoreira 5 116
(A S Cruz, Hong Kong) *wl away: sn led: hdd 1 1/2f out but r.o* **11/2**[3]

4 *3/4* **Jungle Cat (IRE)**[21] 841 4-9-0 112.................................. WilliamBuick 2 114
(Charlie Appleby) *chsd ldrs: ev ch 1 1/2f out: nt qckn fnl f* **20/1**

5 *nk* **Muthmir (IRE)**[28] 745 6-9-0 115....................................... DaneO'Neill 10 112
(William Haggas) *s.i.s: settled in rr: r.o fnl 2 1/2f: nrst fin* **11/1**

6 *3/4* **Fityaan**[21] 841 8-9-0 110...(v) SilvestreDeSousa 11 110
(M Al Mheiri, UAE) *mid-div: r.o fnl 2f but nvr able to chal* **40/1**

7 *shd* **Lady Shipman (USA)**[49] 4-8-9 110..................................(t) IradOrtizJr 13 104
(Kiaran McLaughlin, U.S.A) *s.i.s: chsd ldrs tl outpcd 2 1/2f out* **12/1**

8 *1/2* **Not Listenin'tome (AUS)**[20] 5-9-0 118..........................(t) RyanMoore 4 108
(John Moore, Hong Kong) *nvr bttr than mid-div* **4/1**[2]

9 *shd* **Goldream**[21] 841 7-9-0 116...(p) MartinHarley 8 107
(Robert Cowell) *nvr bttr than mid-div* **20/1**

10 *hd* **Sole Power**[21] 841 9-9-0 118.. ChrisHayes 7 107
(Edward Lynam, Ire) *nvr nr to chal* **8/1**

11 *1* **Sir Maximilian (IRE)**[21] 841 7-9-0 112............................ PatDobbs 12 103
(Ian Williams) *nvr nr to chal* **33/1**

12 *1 1/2* **Bel Canto (JPN)**[118] 5-8-9 112.. YutakaTake 3 93
(Koichi Tsunoda, Japan) *nvr nr to chal* **25/1**

13 *5 3/4* **Naadirr (IRE)**[30] 723 5-9-0 110..........................(p) ChristopheSoumillon 1 77
(Marco Botti) *a in rr* **33/1**

56.34s (-0.76) **Going Correction** +0.275s/f (Good) **13** Ran SP% **120.0**
Speed ratings: **117,115,115,114,113 112,112,111,111,111 109,107,97**
CSF: 34.63; TRICAST: 173.84.
Owner Mrs V Heathcote, S Krslovic Et Al **Bred** Racetree **Trained** Australia

FOCUS
A competitive sprint and well up to standard. The winner clocked 23.60, 21.09 and then 11.65 for the final 200m. The winner has been rated back to his best, with the third, fourth and sixth supporting. TRAKUS: 2nd 0, 3rd +1, 4th -1, 5th +2, 6th 0, 7th +2, 8th 0, 9th 0, 10th -2, 11th 0, 12th +2, 13th -1

1105a DUBAI GOLDEN SHAHEEN SPONSORED BY GULF NEWS (GROUP 1) (DIRT) — 6f (D)

2:45 (2:45) 3-Y-O+

£816,326 (£272,108; £136,054; £68,027; £40,816; £27,210)

RPR

1 **Muarrab**[21] 840 7-9-0 112.. PaulHanagan 7 118
(M Al Mheiri, UAE) *trckd ldrs: rdn 3f out: r.o wl: led 55yds out* **6/1**

2 *nk* **X Y Jet (USA)**[28] 4-9-0 112..(bt) EmisaelJaramillo 3 117
(Jorge Navarro, U.S.A) *sn led: r.o wl but hdd 55yds out* **7/4**[1]

3 *3 3/4* **Morawij**[22] 852 6-9-0 105.. ChrisHayes 9 105
(D Selvaratnam, UAE) *mid-div: r.o fnl 2 1/2f but no ch w ldng pair* **50/1**

4 *1 3/4* **Reynaldothewizard (USA)**[44] 537 10-9-0 113.....(bt) RichardMullen 10 99
(S Seemar, UAE) *nvr nr to chal but r.o wl fnl 2f* **14/1**

5 *3/4* **Super Jockey (NZ)**[20] 7-9-0 115.. JoaoMoreira 6 97
(A T Millard, Hong Kong) *nvr bttr than mid-div* **5/1**[2]

6 *hd* **Confrontation (USA)**[51] 454 6-9-0 113........................... WilliamBuick 8 96
(Kiaran McLaughlin, U.S.A) *s.i.s: nvr nr to chal but r.o fnl 2 1/2f* **11/2**[3]

7 *2 1/4* **Rich Tapestry (IRE)**[21] 840 8-9-0 112........................(b) GeraldMosse 1 89
(C W Chang, Hong Kong) *trckd ldr tl outpcd 2f out* **8/1**

8 *6 3/4* **Domineer**[31] 6-9-0 112...(b) FrankieDettori 5 68
(C Fownes, Hong Kong) *s.i.s: nvr bttr than mid-div* **20/1**

9 *13* **Master Kochanwong (AUS)**[69] 6-9-0 105..............(tp) DouglasWhyte 2 26
(D J Hall, Hong Kong) *trckd ldr tl outpcd 3f out* **14/1**

P **Kifaah**[21] 840 5-9-0 104...(t) DaneO'Neill 4
(A R Al Rayhi, UAE) *s.i.s: a in rr: p.u* **40/1**

1m 10.59s (-1.01) **Going Correction** +0.15s/f (Slow) **10** Ran SP% **116.3**
Speed ratings: **112,111,106,104,103 103,100,91,73,**
CSF: 16.55; TRICAST: 496.06.
Owner Hamdan Al Maktoum **Bred** Stratford Place Stud **Trained** UAE

FOCUS
TRAKUS: 2nd -5, 3rd +3, 4th -4, 5th +2, 6th +8, 7th -7, 8th -2, 9th -6. The form may not be exceptional by Group 1 standards, but this was just a quite brilliant horse race. The runner-up helped force a furious pace from the off and was joined on the turn by the winner ahead of an epic duel up the length of the straight, with neither horse blinking until Muarrab edged ahead in the final strides. The splits were 23.54, 22.78, 24.27. The runner-up has been rated just off the best of his US form, while the third helps set the standard.

1106a DUBAI TURF SPONSORED BY DP WORLD (GROUP 1) (TURF) — 1m 1f (T)

3:45 (3:45) 3-Y-O+

£2,448,979 (£816,326; £408,163; £204,081; £122,448; £81,632)

RPR

1 **Real Steel (JPN)**[27] 4-9-0 116...(t) RyanMoore 14 120
(Yoshito Yahagi, Japan) *trckd ldr: led 1f out: r.o wl* **8/1**

2 *1/2* **Euro Charline**[23] 809 5-8-9 113.................................. FrankieDettori 10 114+
(Marco Botti) *mid-div: r.o fnl 1 1/2f: nrst fin* **25/1**

3 *2* **Tryster (IRE)**[21] 845 5-9-0 116.......................................(p) WilliamBuick 2 114+
(Charlie Appleby) *settled in rr: r.o fnl 2 1/2f but nvr able to chal* **7/4**[1]

4 *hd* **Ertijaal (AUS)**[21] 845 4-9-0 111.................................... DouglasWhyte 12 114
(M F De Kock, South Africa) *settled in rr: r.o fnl 2 1/2f: nrst fin* **33/1**

5 *shd* **Flamboyant (FR)**[49] 5-9-0 113..(t) BriceBlanc 6 114+
(Patrick Gallagher, U.S.A) *racd in rr: r.o wl fnl 2f: nrst fin* **40/1**

6 *nk* **Very Special (IRE)**[23] 809 4-8-9 113............................... JamesDoyle 11 108
(Saeed bin Suroor) *trckd ldr: led 3f out: hdd 1f out: wknd fnl 110yds* **15/2**[3]

7 *nk* **The Corsican (IRE)**[161] 7281 5-9-0 116....................... JamieSpencer 7 113
(David Simcock) *nvr nr to chal* **14/1**

8 *nk* **Intilaaq (USA)**[231] 5144 4-9-0 117.................................... PaulHanagan 8 112
(Roger Varian) *nvr bttr than mid-div* **11/4**[2]

9 *3* **Forjatt (IRE)**[8] 996 8-9-0 109.. ChrisHayes 3 106
(D Selvaratnam, UAE) *mid-div: ev ch 3f out: one pce fnl 2f* **100/1**

10 *nse* **Basateen (IRE)**[30] 721 4-9-0 107....................................... PatDobbs 13 105
(Doug Watson, UAE) *nvr nr to chal but r.o fnl 2f* **33/1**

11 *nk* **Gabrial (IRE)**[161] 7280 7-9-0 113............................. SilvestreDeSousa 15 105
(Richard Fahey) *nvr nr to chal* **33/1**

12 *1 1/4* **Harry's Son (AUS)**[21] 845 4-9-0 111.......................(t) AnthonyDelpech 9 102
(P V Lafferty, South Africa) *nvr nr to chal* **50/1**

13 *hd* **Farrier (USA)**[21] 845 8-9-0 112....................................(p) RichardMullen 5 102
(S Seemar, UAE) *s.i.s: trckd ldrs tl outpcd fnl 2f* **100/1**

14 *shd* **Forries Waltz (SAF)**[58] 372 4-9-0 113............... ChristopheSoumillon 1 102
(M F De Kock, South Africa) *trckd ldrs: ev ch 3f out: wknd fnl 2f* **10/1**

15 *10 1/2* **Ghaamer (USA)**[30] 720 6-9-0 112.................................(t) TadhgO'Shea 4 80
(A R Al Rayhi, UAE) *slowly away: sn led: hdd 3f out: sn btn* **66/1**

1m 47.13s (-1.97) **Going Correction** +0.025s/f (Good) **15** Ran SP% **122.2**
Speed ratings: **109,108,106,106,106 106,105,105,103,103 102,101,101,101,92**
CSF: 199.14; TRICAST: 522.09.
Owner Sunday Racing Co Ltd **Bred** Northern Farm **Trained** Japan

FOCUS
With last year's winner Solow absent through injury, this took less winning than had looked likely. They went 25.89, 23.05, 23.56, and the winner finished in 22.94 and 11.70. The winner, runner-up and fifth help set the standard. TRAKUS: 2nd -1, 3rd -2, 4th +2, 5th -1, 6th -1, 7th -5, 8th +1, 9th -3, 10th -5, 11th -3, 12th +2, 13th -6, 14th -1, 15th -5

1107a DUBAI SHEEMA CLASSIC PRESENTED BY LONGINES (GROUP 1) (TURF) — 1m 4f 11y(T)

4:20 (4:20) 3-Y-O+

£2,448,979 (£816,326; £408,163; £204,081; £122,448; £81,632)

RPR

1 **Postponed (IRE)**[21] 843 5-9-0 121................................. AndreaAtzeni 7 125
(Roger Varian) *mid-div: smooth prog 3f out: led 1 1/2f out: comf* **4/5**[1]

2 2 **Duramente (JPN)**[27] 4-8-13 121 MircoDemuro 4 122
(Noriyuki Hori, Japan) *settled in rr: smooth prog 3 1/2f out: r.o but no ch w wnr* **4/1**[3]
3 1 ½ **Last Impact (JPN)**[27] 6-9-0 119 JoaoMoreira 1 118
(Katsuhiko Sumii, Japan) *settled in rr: r.o fnl 2f: nrst fin* **40/1**
4 ¾ **Highland Reel (IRE)**[104] 8216 4-8-13 121 RyanMoore 8 118
(A P O'Brien, Ire) *sn led: hdd 1 1/2f out: r.o same pce* **3/1**[2]
5 1 **One And Only (JPN)**[41] 5-9-0 117 YutakaTake 5 115
(Shinsuke Hashiguchi, Japan) *trckd ldr: r.o same pce fnl 2 1/2f* **100/1**
6 nk **Dariyan (FR)**[21] 843 4-8-13 117 ChristopheSoumillon 9 116
(A De Royer-Dupre, France) *nvr nr to chal but r.o fnl 2 1/2f* **16/1**
7 1 ¾ **Gailo Chop (FR)**[23] 805 5-9-0 116 (t) ThierryJarnet 6 112
(A De Watrigant, France) *trckd ldr tl outpcd 2f out* **33/1**
8 nk **Sheikhzayedroad**[23] 811 7-9-0 112 MartinHarley 2 112
(David Simcock) *nvr bttr than mid-div* **25/1**
9 9 ½ **The Blue Eye**[28] 757 4-8-13 113 HarryBentley 3 98
(Jassim Al Ghazali, Qatar) *a in rr* **100/1**

2m 26.97s (-4.83) **Going Correction** +0.025s/f (Good)
WFA 4 from 5yo+ 2lb **9** Ran SP% **117.6**
Speed ratings: **117,115,114,114,113 113,112,111,105**
CSF: 4.38; TRICAST: 68.08.
Owner Sheikh Mohammed Obaid Al Maktoum **Bred** St Albans Bloodstock Llp **Trained** Newmarket, Suffolk

FOCUS
The first three in the betting all came into the race officially rated 121, but all the love was for Postponed, who had dotted up in his trial here three weeks earlier, and he justified strong support, winning in style. Highland Reel took them along in 26.59, 25.10, 24.27, 24.39, 23.23 and the winner finished in 23.39. Rock solid form, with the winner back to the best view of his King George win, and the second, third, fifth, sixth and eighth all rated to their marks. TRAKUS: 2nd 0, 3rd -10, 4th -6, 5th -8, 6th +1, 7th 0, 8th -4, 9th -9

1108a DUBAI WORLD CUP SPONSORED BY EMIRATES AIRLINE (GROUP 1) (DIRT) 1m 2f (D)
5:00 (5:00) 3-Y-O+
£4,081,632 (£1,360,544; £680,272; £340,136; £204,081; £136,054)

RPR
1 **California Chrome (USA)**[30] 722 5-9-0 121 (vt) VictorEspinoza 11 127+
(Art Sherman, U.S.A) *trckd ldr: wd: smooth prog 2 1/2f out: led 1 1/2f out: easily* **15/8**[1]
2 3 ¾ **Mubtaahij (IRE)**[21] 844 4-9-0 119 ChristopheSoumillon 4 117
(M F De Kock, South Africa) *trckd ldr on rail: ev ch 2f out: r.o fnl 1 1/2f but no ch w wnr* **16/1**
3 nk **Hoppertunity (USA)**[49] 5-9-0 116 (bt) FlavienPrat 10 117+
(Bob Baffert, U.S.A) *s.i.s: racd in rr: r.o wl fnl 1 1/2f* **25/1**
4 1 ¼ **Special Fighter (IRE)**[21] 844 5-9-0 117 FernandoJara 5 113
(M Al Mheiri, UAE) *trckd ldr: ev ch 2 1/2f out: r.o same pce fnl 2f* **10/1**[3]
5 nk **Frosted (USA)**[51] 452 4-9-0 120 (b) WilliamBuick 9 116+
(Kiaran McLaughlin, U.S.A) *mid-div: chsd ldrs 3f out: r.o same pce* **15/8**[1]
6 nk **Mshawish (USA)**[49] 490 6-9-0 115 FrankieDettori 2 112
(Todd Pletcher, U.S.A) *sn led: hdd 1 1/2f out: wknd fnl f* **9/1**[2]
7 hd **Candy Boy (USA)**[364] 1098 5-9-0 115 PatDobbs 6 112
(Doug Watson, UAE) *mid-div: r.o fnl 2f but nvr able to chal* **100/1**
8 1 **Keen Ice (USA)**[21] 844 4-9-0 120 (bt) RyanMoore 1 110
(Dale Romans, U.S.A) *nvr nr to chal* **12/1**
9 3 ½ **Hokko Tarumae (JPN)**[59] 7-9-0 116 HidekiMiyuki 8 103
(Katsuichi Nishiura, Japan) *nvr bttr than mid-div* **50/1**
10 18 **Teletext (USA)**[42] 5-9-0 113 (t) SilvestreDeSousa 12 67
(S Al Harabi, Saudi Arabia) *slowly away* **50/1**
11 7 ¾ **Vadamos (FR)**[23] 804 5-9-0 113 VincentCheminaud 7 51
(A Fabre, France) *nvr bttr than mid-div* **25/1**
12 hd **Gun Pit (AUS)**[21] 844 5-9-0 115 (bt) JoaoMoreira 3 51
(C Fownes, Hong Kong) *nvr bttr than mid-div* **40/1**

2m 1.83s (-2.87) **Going Correction** +0.15s/f (Slow) **12** Ran SP% **117.3**
Speed ratings: **117,114,113,112,112 112,112,111,108,94 87,87**
CSF: 36.28; TRICAST: 582.67. Placepot: £16.50 to a £1 stake. Pool of £16351.41 - 719.38 winning units. Quadpot: £6.80 to a £1 stake. Pool of £1076.50 - 116.00 winning units..
Owner California Chrome LLC **Bred** Perry Martin & Steve Coburn **Trained** USA

FOCUS
TRAKUS: 2nd -25, 3rd -5, 4th -9, 5th +2, 6th -17, 7th -25, 8th -29, 9th -9, 10th -19, 11th -15, 12th -13. Not a vintage field but a tremendous performance from the winner, who streaked clear in the straight despite having conceded significant ground out wide and his saddle slipping back in the closing stages. The pace was solid - 25.39, 23.59, 23.59, 24.68, 24.58 - and the track record, set by Special Fighter in a Group 1 three weeks earlier, was lowered by 1.26secs.

1109 - 1130a (Foreign Racing) - See Raceform Interactive

1079 WOLVERHAMPTON (A.W) (L-H)
Sunday, March 27

OFFICIAL GOING: Tapeta: standard
Wind: Fresh behind Weather: Sunshine and showers

1110 RENAULT KADJAR H'CAP 5f 20y (Tp)
2:05 (2:05) (Class 5) (0-75,75) 4-Y-O+ **£3,557** (£1,058; £529; £264) **Stalls** Low

Form RPR
-611 1 **Point North (IRE)**[25] 784 9-9-6 **74** (b) DanielTudhope 6 81
(John Balding) *hld up: rdn and r.o ins fnl f to ld nr fin* **85/40**[1]
0344 2 ¾ **Jaarih (IRE)**[5] 1030 4-9-5 **73** (p) PaulMulrennan 7 77
(Conor Dore) *sn chsng ldr: rdn to ld over 1f out: edgd lft ins fnl f: hdd nr fin* **9/4**[2]
540- 3 ½ **Flicka's Boy**[204] 6103 4-9-7 **75** BarryMcHugh 1 79
(Tony Coyle) *hld up: hdwy and nt clr run over 1f out: sn rdn: styd on* **6/1**[3]
423- 4 hd **Our Lord**[276] 3570 4-8-8 **62** LukeMorris 2 65
(Bill Turner) *chsd ldrs: rdn over 1f out: unable qck towards fin* **16/1**
04-6 5 nk **Orient Class**[25] 784 5-8-13 **67** GrahamLee 3 69
(Paul Midgley) *prom: rdn 1/2-way: nt clr run 1f out: styd on* **15/2**
430- 6 2 ¼ **Perardua**[162] 7292 4-9-2 **70** CathyGannon 4 63
(David Evans) *prom: n.m.r and lost pl 4f out: rdn over 1f out: nt trble ldrs* **16/1**
055- 7 1 **Bahamian Sunrise**[150] 7581 4-9-4 **75** (b) MichaelJMMurphy(3) 5 64
(John Gallagher) *sn led: rdn and hdd over 1f out: wknd ins fnl f* **8/1**

1m 1.07s (-0.83) **Going Correction** -0.025s/f (Stan) **7** Ran SP% **111.7**
Speed ratings (Par 103): **105,103,103,102,102 98,97**
CSF £6.82 TOTE £2.70: £2.00, £1.30; EX 8.40 Trifecta £30.00.
Owner Billy Herring **Bred** Barronstown Stud **Trained** Scrooby, S Yorks

FOCUS
Just a modest sprint handicap, but it might throw up the odd winner in the coming weeks. The winner has been rated back to the best of his form since 2013.

1111 ALL NEW RENAULT KADJAR MAIDEN STKS 5f 216y (Tp)
2:40 (2:41) (Class 5) 3-Y-O+ **£3,234** (£962; £481; £240) **Stalls** Low

Form RPR
503- 1 **Avenue Of Stars**[208] 5982 3-9-0 68 (p) PaulMulrennan 9 74
(Karen McLintock) *led: hdd over 4f out: chsd ldr tl led again over 1f out: rdn and edgd lft ins fnl f: styd on* **5/1**
32- 2 1 ¼ **Mister Mischief**[225] 5392 3-9-0 0 GrahamLee 5 70
(Paul Midgley) *hld up: hdwy over 1f out: rdn and edgd lft ins fnl f: r.o to go 2nd nr fin* **7/2**[1]
5 3 ½ **Bromley Cross (IRE)**[27] 765 3-9-0 0 TonyHamilton 3 68
(Richard Fahey) *trckd ldrs: plld hrd: rdn over 1f out: styd on* **4/1**[2]
2 4 shd **Intense Starlet (IRE)**[20] 858 5-9-8 0 SamJames 1 67
(Marjorie Fife) *hld up: hdwy 2f out: rdn over 1f out: styd on* **9/2**[3]
6 5 ½ **Dutch Archer**[27] 765 3-9-0 0 SteveDrowne 8 66+
(Jeremy Gask) *s.i.s: swtchd lft sn after s: hld up: hdwy over 1f out: styd on same pce wl ins fnl f* **8/1**
4 6 2 ¾ **Polly's Serenade**[22] 834 3-8-9 0 ShaneKelly 4 53
(Richard Hughes) *sn chsng wnr: led over 4f out: rdn and hdd over 1f out: wknd ins fnl f* **16/1**
530- 7 nk **Canny Style**[199] 6241 3-8-9 69 ShaneGray 7 52
(Kevin Ryan) *hld up: pushed along over 2f out: nvr on terms* **9/1**
8 2 **Longroom**[353] 1306 4-9-13 0 DuranFentiman 6 54
(Noel Wilson) *prom: rdn over 2f out: wknd over 1f out* **66/1**
4-00 9 1 ½ **Zephyr Breeze**[23] 821 3-9-0 73 BarryMcHugh 2 46
(Noel Wilson) *prom: rdn over 2f out: wknd fnl f* **8/1**

1m 15.56s (1.06) **Going Correction** -0.025s/f (Stan)
WFA 3 from 4yo+ 13lb **9** Ran SP% **116.7**
Speed ratings (Par 103): **91,89,88,88,87 84,83,81,79**
CSF £23.13 TOTE £6.90: £1.70, £1.90, £1.90; EX 29.50 Trifecta £87.70.
Owner Alan Lamont **Bred** Steve Lock & Redmyre Bloodstock **Trained** Ingoe, Northumberland

FOCUS
A modest sprint maiden. The level is fluid.

1112 "ANOTHER ONE DRIVES THE DACIA DUSTER" H'CAP 5f 20y (Tp)
3:15 (3:18) (Class 4) (0-80,79) 3-Y-O **£6,301** (£1,886; £943; £472; £235) **Stalls** Low

Form RPR
36-5 1 **Just That Lord**[12] 935 3-8-9 **67** LukeMorris 1 80+
(Bill Turner) *edgd rt s: mde virtually all: shkn up and edgd rt over 1f out: rdn clr fnl f* **28/1**
1-24 2 3 **Discreet Hero (IRE)**[43] 559 3-9-6 **78** (t) RobertHavlin 4 79
(Simon Crisford) *hmpd s: hld up: r.o to go 2nd wl ins fnl f: no ch w wnr* **5/2**[1]
204- 3 1 **Case Key**[174] 6978 3-9-6 **78** DarryllHolland 2 77
(Charles Hills) *hmpd s: trckd ldrs: nt clr run and lost pl after 1f: hdwy over 1f out: sn rdn: styd on same pce ins fnl f* **3/1**[2]
404- 4 1 **Ravenhoe (IRE)**[156] 7432 3-9-7 **79** JoeFanning 5 73
(Mark Johnston) *prom: rdn over 1f out: styd on same pce fnl f* **3/1**[2]
2-1 5 nk **Dominance**[16] 902 3-8-12 **70** SilvestreDeSousa 3 63
(Rae Guest) *hmpd s: trckd ldrs: plld hrd: rdn over 1f out: wknd ins fnl f* **10/3**[3]
21-5 6 4 ½ **Twentysvnthlancers**[24] 797 3-8-10 **68** MartinLane 7 45
(Paul Midgley) *hld up: rdn and wknd over 1f out* **18/1**
606- 7 1 ¾ **Dark Confidant (IRE)**[174] 6978 3-8-10 **68** JasonHart 6 38
(Richard Guest) *jnd wnr after 1f tl shkn up over 2f out: rdn and wknd over 1f out* **28/1**

1m 0.23s (-1.67) **Going Correction** -0.025s/f (Stan) **7** Ran SP% **113.8**
Speed ratings (Par 100): **112,107,105,104,103 96,93**
CSF £96.43 TOTE £13.20: £7.10, £1.50; EX 70.60 Trifecta £651.70.
Owner Mrs M S Teversham **Bred** Mrs Monica Teversham **Trained** Sigwells, Somerset

FOCUS
A fair 3yo sprint handicap run 0.84secs faster than the opening older-horse Class 5. The winner is bred to be good and there looked no fluke about this. The fourth has been rated a good few lengths below his 2yo peak.

1113 RENAULT ZOE ALL-ELECTRIC MAIDEN AUCTION STKS 1m 1f 103y (Tp)
3:50 (3:51) (Class 5) 3-Y-O **£3,234** (£962; £481; £240) **Stalls** Low

Form RPR
40- 1 **Muthraab Aldaar (IRE)**[170] 7092 3-9-5 0 SilvestreDeSousa 8 75
(Mick Channon) *a.p: chsd ldr over 7f out tl led 6f out: hdd over 3f out: rdn and hung rt fr over 2f out: hmpd over 1f out: rallied to ld ins fnl f: r.o* **5/1**
3-42 2 ½ **Zio Gianni (USA)**[23] 818 3-9-5 71 GeorgeBaker 4 74
(Jamie Osborne) *chsd ldrs: led over 3f out: hmpd over 1f out: sn rdn and edgd lft: hdd ins fnl f: styd on* **12/1**
5- 3 3 **Second Serve (IRE)**[236] 4958 3-9-5 0 JoeFanning 9 68+
(Mark Johnston) *hld up: hdwy over 2f out: edgd lft and styd on to go 3rd ins fnl f: nt rch ldrs* **12/1**
3 4 1 ¼ **Proven Point (IRE)**[27] 768 3-9-5 0 BarryMcHugh 7 66
(Tony Coyle) *led after 1f: hdd 6f out: chsd ldrs: rdn over 2f out: styd on same pce fnl f* **9/2**[3]
0-62 5 ¾ **Red Hot Chilly (IRE)**[18] 874 3-9-5 69 JFEgan 10 65
(Joseph Tuite) *hld up: hdwy over 1f out: edgd lft and styd on ins fnl f: nt trble ldrs* **25/1**
64- 6 ½ **Marmajuke Bay**[165] 7217 3-9-5 0 LiamKeniry 1 64
(Mark Usher) *plld hrd and prom: rdn over 2f out: styd on same pce fr over 1f out* **22/1**
2 7 1 ¾ **Clayton Hall (IRE)**[27] 768 3-9-5 0 TonyHamilton 6 60
(Richard Fahey) *led 1f: chsd ldrs: rdn over 3f out: nt clr run and wknd ins fnl f* **11/4**[2]
53- 8 ½ **Velvet Revolution**[151] 7545 3-9-5 0 LukeMorris 3 59
(Marco Botti) *s.i.s: hld up: rdn whn nt clr run over 3f out: nvr on terms* **2/1**[1]
0- 9 ½ **Street Outlaw (IRE)**[191] 6491 3-9-5 0 StevieDonohoe 5 58
(Daniel Mark Loughnane) *s.i.s: hld up: nvr on terms* **80/1**
00- 10 2 ½ **Susurro**[190] 6536 3-9-0 0 DougieCostello 12 49
(David Simcock) *s.i.s: hld up: a in rr* **66/1**
04-0 11 15 **Cay Location (IRE)**[20] 863 3-9-5 32 KieranO'Neill 2 25
(Ed de Giles) *plld hrd and prom: stdd and lost pl after 1f: hdwy over 5f out: rdn over 3f out: sn wknd* **125/1**

2m 0.17s (-0.63) **Going Correction** -0.025s/f (Stan) **11** Ran SP% **121.9**
Speed ratings (Par 98): **101,100,97,96,96 95,94,93,93,91 77**
CSF £62.38 TOTE £5.70: £2.30, £3.10, £3.60; EX 56.10 Trifecta £579.20.
Owner Jaber Abdullah **Bred** G Devlin **Trained** West Ilsley, Berks

FOCUS
Just an ordinary maiden and it was hard to make significant ground, the winner, second and fourth always in the first four. The level is fluid.

1114 RENAULT CLIO H'CAP — 1m 1f 103y (Tp)
4:25 (4:25) (Class 5) (0-70,70) 4-Y-O+ — **£3,557** (£1,058; £529; £264) **Stalls** Low

Form / RPR

0-13 **1** **Moonday Sun (USA)**[26] 773 7-9-7 **70**............(p) AdamKirby 3 — 80
(John Butler) *mde all: set stdy pce tl qcknd over 2f out: rdn clr over 1f out* **11/4**[2]

1211 **2** 1 ¾ **Rockwood**[33] 683 5-9-5 **68**............(v) PaulMulrennan 1 — 76+
(Karen McLintock) *s.i.s: hld up: nt clr run over 2f out: r.o to go 2nd ins fnl f: no ch w wnr* **15/8**[1]

4435 **3** ¾ **Lean On Pete (IRE)**[19] 864 7-9-1 **67**............(b[1]) JacobButterfield(3) 5 — 72
(Ollie Pears) *hld up: hdwy 2f out: sn rdn: r.o* **7/1**

2/5- **4** 4 ½ **Rock Song**[242] 4751 7-9-2 **65**............ GrahamGibbons 7 — 62
(John Mackie) *plld hrd: sn w wnr: settled into 2nd over 7f out: rdn over 2f out: wknd ins fnl f* **12/1**

00-3 **5** ½ **Cool Music (IRE)**[83] 39 6-8-8 **57**............ PJMcDonald 8 — 53
(Antony Brittain) *hld up: rdn over 2f out: nvr on terms* **17/2**

0-62 **6** 3 **Almanack**[20] 860 6-9-3 **66**............(t) LukeMorris 6 — 56
(Daniel Mark Loughnane) *chsd ldrs: rdn over 2f out: wknd over 1f out* **13/2**[3]

560- **7** 5 **Silver Alliance**[135] 7837 8-9-3 **69**............(p) ShelleyBirkett(3) 2 — 50
(Julia Feilden) *chsd ldrs: rdn over 1f out: wknd fnl f* **16/1**

1m 59.71s (-1.09) **Going Correction** -0.025s/f (Stan) — **7** Ran SP% **111.4**
Speed ratings (Par 103): **103,101,100,96,96 93,89**
CSF £7.86 CT £28.92 TOTE £3.40: £1.80, £1.70; EX 9.50 Trifecta £33.80.
Owner Power Geneva Ltd **Bred** Juddmonte Farms Inc **Trained** Newmarket, Suffolk

FOCUS
The winner made the most of a really easy lead.

1115 RENAULT WOLVERHAMPTON H'CAP — 7f 32y (Tp)
5:00 (5:01) (Class 3) (0-95,94) 3-Y-O **£9,451** (£2,829; £1,414; £708; £352) **Stalls** High

Form / RPR

4-12 **1** **Ikerrin Road (IRE)**[15] 924 3-8-8 **81**............ SilvestreDeSousa 7 — 87
(John Quinn) *a.p: chsd ldr over 5f out: rdn to ld ins fnl f: jst hld on* **11/8**[1]

11 **2** shd **Buying Trouble (USA)**[39] 612 3-8-10 **83**............ AndrewMullen 2 — 89+
(David Evans) *hld up: racd keenly: nt clr run over 2f out: hdwy over 1f out: sn rdn: edgd lft ins fnl f: r.o* **3/1**[2]

314- **3** shd **Arcanada (IRE)**[203] 6130 3-8-12 **85**............ RichardKingscote 6 — 91
(Tom Dascombe) *led: rdn over 1f out: hdd ins fnl f: styd on* **7/2**[3]

110- **4** 4 ½ **Dawaa**[169] 7112 3-9-7 **94**............ JoeFanning 3 — 88
(Mark Johnston) *chsd ldr tl over 5f out: remained handy: rdn over 1f out: no ex ins fnl f* **15/2**

23-1 **5** 4 ½ **September Issue**[12] 935 3-8-7 **80** oh2............[1] LukeMorris 5 — 63
(Gay Kelleway) *hld up: pushed along 1/2-way: wknd wl over 1f out* **17/2**

1m 27.27s (-1.53) **Going Correction** -0.025s/f (Stan) — **5** Ran SP% **111.6**
Speed ratings (Par 102): **107,106,106,101,96**
CSF £5.86 TOTE £1.90: £1.30, £1.50; EX 6.70 Trifecta £12.40.
Owner Mrs S Quinn **Bred** Gerard Kerin **Trained** Settrington, N Yorks

FOCUS
A decent 3yo handicap, with three little to separate three improvers. The opening level is a bit fluid.

1116 DACIA WOLVERHAMPTON H'CAP (DIV I) — 7f 32y (Tp)
5:35 (5:35) (Class 6) (0-65,66) 4-Y-O+ — **£2,943** (£875; £437; £218) **Stalls** High

Form / RPR

2-21 **1** **Misu Pete**[12] 943 4-9-2 **60**............ DarryllHolland 11 — 66
(Mark Usher) *sn prom: chsd ldr 5f out: rdn to ld wl over 1f out: hung lft ent fnl f: all out* **13/2**[3]

0-43 **2** hd **Veeraya**[12] 943 6-9-5 **66**............(bt) ShelleyBirkett(3) 1 — 72
(Julia Feilden) *mid-div: hdwy over 1f out: nt clr run ins fnl f: r.o* **5/1**[2]

0154 **3** shd **Gulland Rock**[17] 889 5-8-12 **56**............ WilliamCarson 3 — 62
(Anthony Carson) *led: rdn and hdd wl over 1f out: nt clr run ins fnl f: r.o* **7/1**

300- **4** 1 ¼ **Spirit Of Wedza (IRE)**[194] 6395 4-9-5 **63**............ ConnorBeasley 8 — 66
(Julie Camacho) *mid-div: hdwy 3f out: rdn over 1f out: styd on* **11/1**

2-15 **5** 2 ¼ **Kyllach Me (IRE)**[63] 320 4-8-13 **62**............(b) PhilDennis(5) 5 — 59
(Bryan Smart) *chsd ldr 2f: remained handy: rdn over 2f out: no ex ins fnl f* **17/2**

0210 **6** nse **Zed Candy Girl**[3] 1064 6-8-12 **59**............(p) GeorgeDowning(3) 9 — 56
(Daniel Mark Loughnane) *dwlt: hld up: hdwy over 1f out: sn rdn: nt trble ldrs* **10/1**

3423 **7** 1 ½ **Oak Bluffs (IRE)**[24] 795 5-9-4 **62**............ TonyHamilton 4 — 55
(Richard Fahey) *pushed along early then plld hrd and hld up in tch: rdn over 2f out: nvr trbld ldrs* **9/2**[1]

400- **8** shd **Saltarello (IRE)**[166] 7189 4-9-6 **64**............ SamJames 10 — 57
(Marjorie Fife) *chsd ldrs: rdn over 2f out: wknd ins fnl f* **25/1**

5024 **9** 3 **Kodiac Lady (IRE)**[12] 943 4-8-7 **58**............(be) HollieDoyle(7) 7 — 44
(Simon West) *hld up: sme hdwy u.p over 1f out: wknd ins fnl f* **16/1**

5-02 **10** 2 ½ **Lucky Lodge**[12] 943 6-9-7 **65**............ PJMcDonald 6 — 45
(Antony Brittain) *hld up: rdn over 2f out: a in rr* **5/1**[2]

1m 29.68s (0.88) **Going Correction** -0.025s/f (Stan) — **10** Ran SP% **115.0**
Speed ratings (Par 101): **93,92,92,91,88 88,86,86,83,80**
CSF £38.45 CT £240.42 TOTE £4.90: £2.60, £2.00, £2.30; EX 40.70 Trifecta £402.60.
Owner Saxon House Racing **Bred** A C M Spalding **Trained** Upper Lambourn, Berks
■ Stewards' Enquiry : William Carson two-day ban: careless riding (Apr 11-12)

FOCUS
The time was a second slower than the other division. The third has been rated to the best of last year's form.

1117 DACIA WOLVERHAMPTON H'CAP (DIV II) — 7f 32y (Tp)
6:05 (6:06) (Class 6) (0-65,65) 4-Y-O+ — **£2,943** (£875; £437; £218) **Stalls** High

Form / RPR

3300 **1** **Flying Fantasy**[18] 872 4-9-1 **64**............ AaronJones(5) 9 — 74
(Stuart Williams) *a.p: led ins fnl f: r.o wl: comf* **11/4**[1]

0-06 **2** 2 ¾ **Colour My World**[33] 681 6-8-12 **56**............(b) JoeFanning 4 — 57
(Ed McMahon) *chsd ldr: rdn and ev ch ins fnl f: styd on same pce* **9/1**

5200 **3** ¾ **Black Truffle (FR)**[12] 943 6-9-0 **63**............(v) RachealKneller(5) 2 — 62+
(Mark Usher) *hld up: hdwy over 1f out: rdn and edgd lft ins fnl f: styd on same pce* **6/1**[3]

0-62 **4** ½ **Kicking The Can (IRE)**[27] 769 5-9-1 **59**............ BarryMcHugh 6 — 57
(David Thompson) *led: stdd pce over 4f out: pushed along and qcknd over 2f out: rdn: hdd and no ex ins fnl f* **6/1**[3]

3-25 **5** 2 ¼ **Moonbi Creek (IRE)**[65] 297 9-8-8 **59**............(t) CallumRodriguez(7) 3 — 52
(Richard Ford) *s.i.s: hld up: r.o ins fnl f: nvr nrr* **16/1**

60-1 **6** hd **Diatomic (IRE)**[12] 942 4-9-4 **62**............(p) RichardKingscote 5 — 54
(Tom Dascombe) *chsd ldrs: rdn over 2f out: wknd ins fnl f* **3/1**[2]

640- **7** nse **Hardy Black (IRE)**[183] 6760 5-9-2 **65**............ EdwardGreatrex(5) 10 — 57
(Kevin Frost) *hld up: racd keenly: rdn over 2f out: nt trble ldrs* **20/1**

-310 **8** 1 ¼ **The Happy Hammer (IRE)**[45] 532 10-9-0 **65**............ LuluStanford(7) 7 — 54
(Eugene Stanford) *hld up: rdn over 2f out: a in rr* **14/1**

046- **9** nk **City Of Night (IRE)**[151] 7554 4-9-2 **60**............ ConnorBeasley 1 — 48
(Julie Camacho) *hld up: rdn over 2f out: sme hdwy over 1f out: wknd ins fnl f* **9/1**

1m 28.68s (-0.12) **Going Correction** -0.025s/f (Stan) — **9** Ran SP% **117.5**
Speed ratings (Par 101): **99,95,95,94,91 91,91,90,89**
CSF £28.79 CT £140.56 TOTE £3.70: £1.60, £3.30, £2.10; EX 28.10 Trifecta £219.20.
Owner Happy Valley Racing & Breeding Limited **Bred** Hascombe And Valiant Studs **Trained** Newmarket, Suffolk

FOCUS
The second leg of a moderate handicap. The winner has been rated back to his best when trained by William Haggas.
T/Plt: £85.00 to a £1 stake. Pool: £75,444.85 - 647.29 winning tickets T/Qpdt: £33.30 to a £1 stake. Pool: £7,345.27 - 162.78 winning tickets **Colin Roberts**

1021 SAINT-CLOUD (L-H)
Thursday, March 24

OFFICIAL GOING: Turf: good

1118a PRIX DU DEBUT (MAIDEN) (UNRACED 2YO) (TURF) — 4f 110y
11:45 (11:45) 2-Y-O — **£9,191** (£3,676; £2,757; £1,838; £919)

RPR

1 **Cavaprun (FR)** 2-9-2 0............ GregoryBenoist 15 — 77
(C Baillet, France) **96/10**

2 1 ¼ **Morigane Forlonge (FR)** 2-8-13 0............ UmbertoRispoli 1 — 69
(A Giorgi, Italy) **151/10**

3 1 ½ **Soho Universe (FR)** 2-9-2 0............ FabriceVeron 4 — 66
(H-A Pantall, France) **148/10**

4 shd **Maiandra (FR)** 2-8-13 0............ OlivierPeslier 10 — 63
(T Lemer, France) **168/10**

5 ½ **Affoburg (FR)** 2-9-2 0............ AlexandreGavilan 2 — 64
(D Guillemin, France) **81/10**

6 nse **Decapulse (IRE)** 2-8-13 0............ CristianDemuro 8 — 60
(J-V Toux, France) **42/1**

7 1 **King Of Castilla** 2-9-2 0............ Pierre-CharlesBoudot 6 — 59
(Gay Kelleway) *in tch: rdn and hung lft over 1f out: kpt on same pce fnl f: lost 2 pls cl home* **17/2**

8 hd **La Dame En Rouge (FR)** 2-8-13 0............ ThierryThulliez 14 — 56
(C Lerner, France) **35/1**

9 3 ½ **Tawaret (FR)** 2-8-13 0............ AlexisBadel 11 — 42
(M Boutin, France) **68/10**[3]

10 hd **Imdancinwithurwife (IRE)** 2-8-13 0............ RichardKingscote 5 — 41
(Tom Dascombe) *prom: rdn over 2f out: hung lft: no ex and wknd fnl f* **6/1**[2]

11 3 **Countess Allegro (FR)** 2-8-13 0............ AntoineHamelin 3 — 29
(Matthieu Palussiere, France) **242/10**

12 1 **Alsylal Dolois (FR)** 2-8-8 0............ ErwannLebreton(8) 7 — 28
(A Bonin, France) **68/1**

13 snk **Wait And Win (FR)** 2-8-13 0............ ThomasMessina 12 — 24
(Mlle S Delaroche, France) **116/1**

14 15 **Mystery Sky (FR)** 2-8-13 0............ EddyHardouin 13
(J-P Lopez, France) **86/1**

P **Dolokhov** 2-9-2 0............ ChristopheSoumillon 9
(J S Moore) *slow to stride: v green in rr and sn wl bhd: p.u* **11/5**[1]

\n\x\x WIN (incl. 1 euro stake): 10.60. PLACES: 3.40, 5.20, 4.60. DF: 86.70. SF:
Owner Ecurie Jarlan **Bred** Ecurie Jarlan **Trained** France

REDCAR (L-H)
Monday, March 28

OFFICIAL GOING: Heavy (soft in places; 6.4)
Wind: fairly strong across Weather: overcast, shower before 7th

1119 MARKET CROSS JEWELLERS FILLIES' H'CAP — 5f
2:05 (2:05) (Class 5) (0-75,69) 4-Y-O+ — **£2,911** (£866; £432; £216) **Stalls** Centre

Form / RPR

-020 **1** **Perfect Peak**[6] 1026 4-8-3 **58**............(vt) NathanEvans(7) 2 — 66
(Michael Easterby) *mde all: rdn over 1f out: pressed jst ins fnl f: hld on wl* **5/1**[3]

336- **2** ½ **Taffetta**[236] 5024 4-9-3 **65**............ BarryMcHugh 3 — 71
(Tony Coyle) *hld up: rdn over 3f out: hdwy 2f out: pressed ldr jst ins fnl f: kpt on* **6/1**

352- **3** 1 ¾ **Penny Royale**[177] 6936 4-9-7 **69**............(p) DavidAllan 4 — 69
(Tim Easterby) *trckd ldr: rdn wl over 1f out: one pce fnl f* **5/2**[1]

23-3 **4** 11 **Hello Beautiful (IRE)**[12] 961 5-7-12 **53** ow3............ BenRobinson(7) 1 — 13
(Brian Ellison) *chsd ldr: rdn 1/2-way: wknd over 1f out* **17/2**

000- **5** hd **Spring Bird**[244] 4719 7-9-2 **64**............ BenCurtis 5 — 23
(Alan Swinbank) *in tch: rdn 1/2-way: sn wknd* **3/1**[2]

112- **6** 11 **Racing Angel (IRE)**[232] 5178 4-9-1 **63**............ WilliamCarson 6
(Mick Quinn) *in tch: rdn and wknd 1/2-way: eased* **5/1**[3]

1m 4.73s (6.13) **Going Correction** +1.325s/f (Soft) — **6** Ran SP% **111.7**
Speed ratings (Par 100): **103,102,99,81,81 63**
CSF £33.28 TOTE £6.70: £2.80, £3.30; EX 48.10 Trifecta £158.30.
Owner M W Easterby **Bred** D F Spence **Trained** Sheriff Hutton, N Yorks

FOCUS
Owing to persistent rain the meeting had to survive a 10am inspection and the ground was given as heavy, soft in places. A 5f sprint to open, but it was hard enough work and three of the six runners finished detached. Moderate form with the winner rated to her best.

1120 TOTEJACKPOT CLASSIFIED (S) STKS — 7f
2:35 (2:37) (Class 6) 3-Y-O+ — **£2,264** (£673; £336; £168) **Stalls** Centre

Form / RPR

-503 **1** **Affectionate Lady (IRE)**[19] 876 5-9-1 **52**............(b) TomEaves 5 — 59
(Keith Reveley) *dwlt: hld up: rdn over 3f out: hdwy over 2f out: sn chsd ldrs: angled rt ent fnl f: styd on to ld 50yds out* **22/1**

4425 **2** 3/4 **Sea Of Uncertainty**[41] 597 3-8-0 63 AndrewMullen 11 52
(Michael Appleby) *prom: led narrowly 3f out: sn rdn: hdd 50yds out: one pce* **14/1**

425- **3** 1/2 **Mitchum**[174] 7010 7-8-10 47 (p) PhilDennis(5) 3 56
(Ron Barr) *trckd ldrs: chal wl over 2f out: rdn 2f out: kpt on same pce* **33/1**

630- **4** 1 **Secret City (IRE)**[164] 7255 10-9-1 62 (b) PaulMulrennan 1 53
(Rebecca Bastiman) *dwlt: hld up: pushed along 4f out: hdwy over 1f out: kpt on fnl f* **9/1**[3]

2/04 **5** 2 1/2 **Ripon Rose**[20] 867 4-9-1 48 GrahamLee 9 47
(Paul Midgley) *chsd ldrs: rdn and outpcd over 2f out: plugged on fr over 1f out* **25/1**

1-30 **6** 1 **Hold On Magnolia**[47] 519 3-7-11 65 SammyJoBell(3) 4 40
(Richard Fahey) *hld up: rdn and hdwy over 2f out: chsd ldrs over 1f out: one pce fnl f* **9/2**[2]

2213 **7** 1 **Basingstoke (IRE)**[5] 1047 7-9-1 59 (b) SilvestreDeSousa 10 42
(Daniel Mark Loughnane) *chsd ldrs: rdn over 2f out: grad wknd fnl f* **5/2**[1]

500- **8** 5 **Miningrocks (FR)**[188] 6618 4-9-1 54 JamesSullivan 16 34
(Ruth Carr) *slowly away: hld up racd keenly: pushed along and hdwy 2f out: rdn over 1f out: wknd ins fnl f* **33/1**

-605 **9** 1 1/4 **Khajaaly (IRE)**[5] 1044 9-9-1 52 (vt) JoeFanning 8 32
(Daniel Mark Loughnane) *hld up: rdn over 3f out: nvr threatened: eased fnl f* **16/1**

40-4 **10** 3 **New Lease Of Life**[25] 799 7-9-1 65 (p) PhillipMakin 13 24
(Keith Dalgleish) *in tch: rdn 3f out: sn btn: eased ins fnl f* **9/1**[3]

3000 **11** 6 **Orlando Rogue (IRE)**[13] 943 4-9-1 64 (p) LiamKeniry 15 4
(Conor Dore) *hld up: nvr threatened* **18/1**

005- **12** 3 1/4 **Leedora**[175] 6977 3-8-0 40 [1] RaulDaSilva 6
(Karen Tutty) *midfield: rdn over 4f out: sn struggling* **80/1**

-300 **13** 5 **Shearian**[13] 939 6-9-1 57 (p) ConnorBeasley 2
(Tracy Waggott) *midfield: rdn 3f out: sn wknd* **25/1**

4045 **14** 7 **Bailiwick**[28] 769 5-9-1 60 (p) DougieCostello 14
(Daniel Kubler) *midfield: rdn over 3f out: sn wknd: eased* **12/1**

0-00 **15** 1/2 **Strictly Glitz (IRE)**[10] 981 5-9-1 45 (v) TonyHamilton 7
(Clare Ellam) *midfield: pushed along and lost pl qckly 5f out: sn bhd* **100/1**

061- **16** 3 **Atreus**[160] 7375 4-8-8 59 (p) NathanEvans(7) 12
(Michael Easterby) *led: rdn whn hdd 3f out: wknd* **16/1**

1m 35.89s (11.39) **Going Correction** +1.55s/f (Heav)
WFA 3 from 4yo+ 15lb **16** Ran SP% **118.3**
Speed ratings (Par 101): **96,95,94,93,90 89,88,82,81,77 70,67,61,53,52 49**
CSF £281.93 TOTE £28.90: £8.00, £4.10, £9.10; EX 289.80 Trifecta £4398.50 Part won..There was no bid for the winner. Miningrocks was claimed by Mrs Sarah Bryan for £6,000.
Owner Paul Collins **Bred** Glencarrig Stud **Trained** Lingdale, Redcar & Cleveland

FOCUS
A strongly run 0-65 classified seller and the form looks straightforward.

1121 TOTEQUADPOT H'CAP 2m 4y
3:10 (3:11) (Class 6) (0-65,65) 4-Y-O+ **£2,264** (£673; £336; £168) **Stalls** Low

Form RPR

0-44 **1** **Alphabetical Order**[35] 675 8-10-0 **65** DanielTudhope 4 75+
(David O'Meara) *hld up: stdy hdwy fr over 3f out: led over 1f out: pushed out: eased nr fin* **11/8**[1]

4-06 **2** 1/2 **Symbolist (IRE)**[42] 592 4-9-1 **57** (v[1]) GrahamLee 3 63
(John Norton) *led: rdn over 2f out: hdd over 1f out: styd on* **11/1**

623/ **3** 4 1/2 **Summerlea (IRE)**[674] 2550 10-8-11 **48** PJMcDonald 5 49
(Micky Hammond) *midfield: hdwy over 3f out: rdn over 2f out: one pce fr over 1f out* **12/1**

0-23 **4** 10 **Ellerina**[47] 521 4-8-5 **47** JoeyHaynes 6 36
(Chris Fairhurst) *prom: rdn over 3f out: hung bdly rt over 2f out: wknd fnl f* **11/2**[2]

5 17 **Roja Dove (IRE)**[11] 5417 7-9-2 **53** (b) PaulMulrennan 9 21
(David Thompson) *s.i.s: hld up: rdn over 3f out: sn wknd* **7/1**[3]

000- **6** 6 **Nashville (IRE)**[149] 7254 7-10-0 **65** NeilFarley 7 26
(Andrew Crook) *midfield towards outer: rdn over 4f out: sn wknd* **28/1**

000- **7** 2 1/2 **Boldbob (IRE)**[8] 4449 4-8-4 **46** oh1 AndrewMullen 8 4
(Micky Hammond) *trckd ldng pair: rdn 4f out: sn wknd* **7/1**[3]

025- **8** 8 **That Be Grand**[122] 7678 5-8-10 **47** DuranFentiman 2
(Shaun Harris) *midfield: rdn 4f out: sn wknd* **20/1**

003- **9** 12 **Seraffimo**[48] 6402 4-8-2 **49** PhilDennis(5) 1
(Sharon Watt) *trckd ldng pair: rdn 4f out: wknd* **10/1**

4m 0.69s (29.29) **Going Correction** +1.90s/f (Heav)
WFA 4 from 5yo+ 5lb **9** Ran SP% **115.8**
Speed ratings (Par 101): **102,101,99,94,86 83,81,77,71**
CSF £18.24 CT £133.06 TOTE £2.30: £1.10, £3.30, £3.10; EX 15.70 Trifecta £125.80.
Owner Great Northern Partnership **Bred** Barrow Hill **Trained** Upper Helmsley, N Yorks

FOCUS
Moderate stuff and the winner proved better than this level on his handicap debut.

1122 PINNACLE RACING SYNDICATE SHARES NOW AVAILABLE H'CAP (PINNACLE CUP STRAIGHT MILE QUALIFIER) 1m
3:45 (3:46) (Class 4) (0-85,84) 4-Y-O+ **£5,498** (£1,636; £817; £408) **Stalls** Centre

Form RPR

6- **1** **Bahama Moon (IRE)**[211] 5892 4-9-3 **80** GrahamGibbons 11 92
(David Barron) *hld up: pushed along and stdy hdwy fr over 2f out: rdn to chal appr fnl f: kpt on wl: led 75yds out* **16/1**

313- **2** 3/4 **Treasury Notes (IRE)**[161] 7338 4-9-0 **77** DanielTudhope 9 88
(David O'Meara) *midfield: rdn and gd hdwy 2f out: led narrowly ins fnl f: hdd 75yds out: kpt on* **5/1**[2]

100- **3** 3 3/4 **Italian Beauty (IRE)**[157] 7433 4-8-3 **71** CallumShepherd(5) 3 73
(Brian Ellison) *led: rdn over 2f out: hdd ins fnl f: no ex fnl 110yds* **20/1**

400- **4** 1/2 **Top Of The Glas (IRE)**[181] 6826 5-9-5 **82** SilvestreDeSousa 16 83
(Brian Ellison) *hld up: rdn and gd hdwy 2f out: sn chsd ldr: no ex ins fnl f* **9/1**

160- **5** 2 1/4 **Dark Ocean (IRE)**[149] 7632 6-9-7 **84** GrahamLee 8 80
(Jedd O'Keeffe) *trckd ldrs: rdn over 2f out: grad wknd appr fnl f* **9/1**

324- **6** 1 3/4 **Salmon Sushi**[219] 5637 5-9-5 **82** DavidAllan 4 74
(Tim Easterby) *dwlt: hld up: rdn over 2f out: kpt on fr over 1f out* **33/1**

105- **7** 1 3/4 **Abushamah (IRE)**[177] 6933 5-9-3 **80** JamesSullivan 14 68
(Ruth Carr) *midfield: rdn over 2f out: no imp* **25/1**

8 4 1/2 **Dawn Mirage**[203] 6173 4-8-13 **76** TonyHamilton 12 53
(Richard Fahey) *trckd ldrs: rdn 3f out: wknd over 1f out* **12/1**

066- **9** 5 **Woody Bay**[142] 7758 6-9-7 **84** JasonHart 10 50
(Mark Walford) *prom: pushed along over 3f out: wknd fnl 2f* **28/1**

6022 **10** nk **Eutropius (IRE)**[20] 866 7-9-5 **82** BenCurtis 15 47
(Alan Swinbank) *midfield: rdn over 3f out: wknd fnl 2f* **12/1**

145/ **11** 3 **Torrid**[563] 6301 5-9-7 **84** DuranFentiman 5 42
(Michael Easterby) *hld up in midfield: rdn 3f out: sn wknd* **66/1**

12 hd **Gulf Of Poets**[260] 4173 4-8-6 **76** NathanEvans(7) 1 34
(Michael Easterby) *prom: rdn 3f out: sn wknd* **33/1**

520- **13** 2 **Kiwi Bay**[142] 7758 11-9-1 **83** PhilDennis(5) 13 36
(Michael Dods) *racd keenly in tch: rdn 3f out: sn wknd* **33/1**

003- **14** 29 **Le Chat D'Or**[152] 7563 8-9-7 **84** (bt) PaulMulrennan 2
(Michael Dods) *dwlt: hld up: rdn along over 4f out: sn btn: eased over 1f out* **10/3**[1]

044- **15** 2 **Tournament**[140] 7778 5-9-3 **80** (t[1]) OisinMurphy 7
(Seamus Durack) *hld up: rdn over 3f out: sn wknd: eased* **11/2**[3]

1m 48.72s (12.12) **Going Correction** +1.55s/f (Heav) **15** Ran SP% **118.8**
Speed ratings (Par 105): **101,100,96,96,93 92,90,85,80,80 77,77,75,46,44**
CSF £85.85 CT £1674.78 TOTE £13.70: £4.10, £2.40, £4.50; EX 107.60 Trifecta £3811.50.
Owner Pryde, Van Der Hoeven & Beaumont **Bred** Ammerland Verwaltung Gmbh & Co Kg **Trained** Maunby, N Yorks

FOCUS
A fair handicap in which a couple of unexposed sorts pulled away.

1123 TOTEPOOL HAPPY EASTER MAIDEN STKS 1m
4:20 (4:21) (Class 5) 3-Y-O+ **£2,911** (£866; £432; £216) **Stalls** Centre

Form RPR

5 **1** **Another Go (IRE)**[12] 958 3-8-11 0 BenCurtis 11 80
(Alan Swinbank) *prom: rdn to ld over 2f out: wandered appr fnl f: kpt on wl* **12/1**

2 4 **Kings Gold (IRE)** 3-8-11 0 PaulMulrennan 10 71
(Michael Dods) *in tch: pushed along over 2f out: rdn and edgd lft over 1f out: wnt 2nd ins fnl f: kpt on but no threat wnr* **9/5**[1]

3 3/4 **Steccando (IRE)** 3-8-11 0 NeilFarley 6 69
(Alan Swinbank) *s.i.s: hld up in midfield: rdn along and rn green over 2f out: hdwy over 1f out: kpt on fnl f* **4/1**[2]

6- **4** 3 1/4 **Bradleysintown (IRE)**[253] 4418 3-8-11 0 ConnorBeasley 8 62
(Michael Dods) *led: rdn whn hdd over 2f out: wknd ins fnl f* **17/2**[3]

5 3 1/4 **High On Light** 3-8-6 0 [1] PJMcDonald 12 50
(Tim Easterby) *dwlt: hld up: rdn and rn green over 2f out: kpt on fnl f* **12/1**

55 **6** 3 3/4 **Peggy Joyce**[18] 892 3-8-6 0 SamJames 2 41
(David Barron) *hld up in rr: drvn over 2f out: minor late hdwy* **16/1**

7 1 **Gateshead (USA)** 4-9-9 0 PhilDennis(5) 9 49
(Bryan Smart) *trckd ldrs: rdn 3f out: wknd over 1f out* **11/1**

60 **8** 2 **Thiepval**[21] 863 4-9-9 0 RobJFitzpatrick(5) 7 44
(Jason Ward) *prom: rdn over 3f out: sn wknd* **50/1**

020- **9** 2 1/4 **Balmusette**[46] 2295 7-9-9 0 TomEaves 5 34
(Keith Reveley) *a towards rr* **12/1**

10 7 **My Lucille (IRE)** 3-8-6 0 AndrewMullen 4 13
(Tim Easterby) *midfield: rdn over 3f out: sn wknd* **16/1**

11 26 **Ginger Charlie** 3-8-11 0 JamesSullivan 3
(Ruth Carr) *in tch: rdn over 4f out: sn wknd* **14/1**

1m 49.32s (12.72) **Going Correction** +1.55s/f (Heav)
WFA 3 from 4yo+ 17lb **11** Ran SP% **118.0**
Speed ratings (Par 103): **98,94,93,90,86 83,82,80,77,70 44**
CSF £33.95 TOTE £13.00: £2.60, £2.10, £1.40; EX 51.70 Trifecta £322.50.
Owner Brian Valentine **Bred** Lutz Oertel **Trained** Melsonby, N Yorks

FOCUS
Just a modest maiden with little previous form to go on.

1124 LILY JO BEEL DESIGNED TODAY'S RACECARD COVER H'CAP (DIV I) 7f
4:55 (4:55) (Class 5) (0-75,74) 4-Y-O+ **£2,911** (£866; £432; £216) **Stalls** Centre

Form RPR

13-3 **1** **Royal Holiday (IRE)**[47] 523 9-9-0 **67** (p) RobertWinston 6 76
(Marjorie Fife) *mde all: rdn and strly pressed fr over 2f out: hld on wl fnl f* **9/2**[1]

256- **2** 3/4 **Mustaqbal (IRE)**[183] 6783 4-8-12 **70** PhilDennis(5) 12 77
(Michael Dods) *in tch: hdwy to chal over 2f out: sn rdn: kpt on but a hld* **20/1**

633- **3** 1 **Final Venture**[276] 3599 4-9-2 **69** BenCurtis 5 73
(Alan Swinbank) *racd keenly in tch: rdn and hdwy to chal 2f out: one pce fnl 110yds* **8/1**

02-0 **4** 1 3/4 **Cliff (IRE)**[18] 893 6-8-13 **66** JoeFanning 3 66
(Nigel Tinkler) *hld up in midfield: rdn over 2f out: hdwy over 1f out: one pce ins fnl f* **9/2**[1]

3256 **5** 8 **Red Unico (IRE)**[4] 1064 4-8-12 **65** (b[1]) AndrewMullen 2 44
(Michael Appleby) *prom: rdn over 2f out: wknd over 1f out* **6/1**[3]

344- **6** 4 1/2 **Shamaheart (IRE)**[150] 7598 6-9-3 **70** DavidAllan 11 37
(Geoffrey Harker) *midfield: rdn 3f out: wknd over 1f out* **11/1**

004- **7** 1 3/4 **Flyball**[233] 5167 4-8-7 **60** JamesSullivan 13 23
(Kenneth Slack) *midfield: rdn over 2f out: wknd fnl 2f* **10/1**

343- **8** hd **Talent Scout (IRE)**[175] 6981 10-8-13 **71** (p) GemmaTutty(5) 9 33
(Karen Tutty) *chsd ldrs: rdn over 3f out: wknd over 2f out* **25/1**

330- **9** 15 **Danot (IRE)**[193] 6457 4-9-4 **71** GrahamLee 4
(Jedd O'Keeffe) *prom: rdn over 3f out: wknd* **11/1**

500- **10** 28 **Slingsby**[163] 7289 5-9-7 **74** (b) GrahamGibbons 7
(Michael Easterby) *dwlt: a in rr: t.o fnl 2f* **25/1**

50-0 **11** 6 **All You (IRE)**[24] 823 4-9-6 **73** [1] DanielTudhope 1
(David O'Meara) *sn pushed along in rr: t.o fnl 2f* **11/2**[2]

005- **12** 1 1/2 **Timoneer (USA)**[105] 8227 6-8-9 **62** JasonHart 8
(Tim Easterby) *a in rr: t.o fnl 2f* **50/1**

1m 34.64s (10.14) **Going Correction** +1.55s/f (Heav) **12** Ran SP% **117.3**
Speed ratings (Par 103): **104,103,102,100,90 85,83,83,66,34 27,25**
CSF £98.99 CT £713.74 TOTE £5.50: £2.10, £3.40, £2.80; EX 106.40 Trifecta £461.70.
Owner Mrs Marion Turner **Bred** E Tynan **Trained** Stillington, N Yorks

FOCUS
The winner, who has been rated to his turf best, made all and few were seriously involved.

1125 LILY JO BEEL DESIGNED TODAY'S RACECARD COVER H'CAP (DIV II) 7f
5:30 (5:31) (Class 5) (0-75,73) 4-Y-O+ **£2,911** (£866; £432; £216) **Stalls** Centre

Form RPR

500- **1** **Sugar Lump**[156] 7464 4-9-3 **69** NeilFarley 12 80
(Eric Alston) *chsd ldrs: rdn over 2f out: led jst ins fnl f: kpt on* **9/1**

051- **2** 1 1/2 **Lavetta**[146] 7675 4-9-7 **73** BenCurtis 5 80
(Alan Swinbank) *dwlt: sn chsd ldrs: rdn over 2f out: kpt on: wnt 2nd nr fin* **9/4**[1]

-505 **3** shd **Golden Spun (USA)**[13] 943 4-8-10 **62** (p) PaulMulrennan 6 69
(Michael Dods) *chsd ldrs: rdn to ld over 2f out: hdd jst ins fnl f: no ex and lost 2nd nr fin* **15/2**

005- **4** *16* **Coolcalmcollected (IRE)**[104] 8237 4-8-13 **65**................ JoeFanning 10 30
(Andrew Crook) *w ldr: rdn over 3f out: wknd fnl 2f* **40/1**

66-0 **5** *1* **Daylight**[6] 1030 6-8-8 **67**..(t) NathanEvans(7) 9 30
(Michael Easterby) *hld up: rdn 3f out: sn wknd* **20/1**

343- **6** *5* **Mr Cool Cash**[164] 7256 4-9-2 **68**... JasonHart 4 18
(Richard Guest) *hld up: pushed along over 3f out: wknd fnl 2f* **4/1**[2]

560- **7** *2½* **Favourite Treat (USA)**[224] 5456 6-9-5 **71**.................(e) JamesSullivan 3 14
(Ruth Carr) *led narrowly: rdn whn hdd over 2f out: wknd* **10/1**

201- **8** *4½* **Uncle Dermot (IRE)**[154] 7513 8-9-7 **73**....................... ConnorBeasley 13 4
(Brendan Powell) *hld up: rdn over 3f out: wknd* **11/2**[3]

166- **9** *46* **Cabal**[136] 7837 9-9-5 **71**... DavidAllan 11
(Geoffrey Harker) *a in rr: eased and t.o fnl 2f* **17/2**

1m 35.88s (11.38) **Going Correction** +1.55s/f (Heav) **9** Ran SP% **114.7**
Speed ratings (Par 103): **96,94,94,75,74 69,66,61,8**
CSF £29.40 CT £163.02 TOTE £11.80: £3.50, £1.70, £2.10; EX 36.20 Trifecta £273.80.
Owner Paul Buist & John Thompson **Bred** T J Cooper **Trained** Longton, Lancs

FOCUS
The front three finished a long way clear, but the time was slower than the first division.

1126 REDCAR RACECOURSE CHEAPEST ADMISSION IN GREAT BRITAIN H'CAP 6f

6:00 (6:01) (Class 6) (0-65,65) 3-Y-O **£2,264** (£673; £336; £168) **Stalls** Centre

Form RPR

000- **1** **Tricky Dicky**[194] 6429 3-8-8 **52**...................................... DuranFentiman 5 60
(Olly Williams) *chsd ldrs: rdn over 2f out: led ins fnl f: edgd lft: kpt on* **33/1**

5242 **2** *2* **Bahamian Sunshine**[26] 783 3-8-13 **64**............(p) AdamMcNamara(7) 9 66
(Richard Fahey) *prom: rdn to ld over 1f out: hdd ins fnl f: edgd lft and one pce* **7/1**

456- **3** *¾* **Mr Orange (IRE)**[142] 7751 3-9-0 **58**............................ DougieCostello 10 58
(Paul Midgley) *chsd ldrs: rdn over 2f out: kpt on* **14/1**

063- **4** *¾* **Dark Command**[187] 6651 3-8-13 **57**............................. PaulMulrennan 1 55+
(Michael Dods) *dwlt: hld up: pushed along and hdwy over 1f out: kpt on fnl f* **10/3**[1]

406- **5** *2¾* **Mustn't Grumble (IRE)**[112] 8136 3-9-1 **64**............(p) JustinNewman(5) 4 54
(Ivan Furtado) *led narrowly: rdn whn hdd over 1f out: wknd ins fnl f* **8/1**

604- **6** *3* **Mecca's Missus (IRE)**[164] 7252 3-9-7 **65**................. ConnorBeasley 12 45
(Michael Dods) *prom: rdn over 2f out: wknd over 1f out* **12/1**

060- **7** *2* **Citadel**[214] 5775 3-8-7 **51** oh2.......................................(p) BarryMcHugh 6 25
(John Wainwright) *hld up: pushed along 1/2-way: nvr threatened* **66/1**

152- **8** *6* **Canford Kilbey (IRE)**[164] 7252 3-8-3 **54**.................. NathanEvans(7) 11 10
(Michael Easterby) *hld up: sn pushed along: nvr threatened* **12/1**

040- **9** *½* **Silver Sands (IRE)**[154] 7516 3-9-7 **65**.............................. DavidAllan 14 20
(Tim Easterby) *midfield: rdn over 2f out: wknd over 1f out* **18/1**

020- **10** *1* **Emerald Asset (IRE)**[187] 6651 3-9-4 **62**........................... GrahamLee 3 14
(Paul Midgley) *midfield: rdn over 2f out: wknd over 1f out* **20/1**

443- **11** *½* **Black Grass**[154] 7517 3-9-0 **58**................................... GrahamGibbons 2 8
(Michael Easterby) *prom: rdn over 2f out: wknd over 1f out* **6/1**[3]

266- **12** *1¼* **Mr Potter**[153] 7540 3-9-6 **64**..(e) JasonHart 7 11
(Richard Guest) *a towards rr* **20/1**

250- **13** *3¾* **Kenstone (FR)**[144] 7715 3-9-4 **62**............................ SilvestreDeSousa 8
(David Dennis) *dwlt: a towards rr* **5/1**[2]

1m 20.45s (8.65) **Going Correction** +1.55s/f (Heav) **13** Ran SP% **118.9**
Speed ratings (Par 96): **104,101,100,99,95 91,89,81,80,79 78,76,71**
CSF £242.09 CT £3405.32 TOTE £37.80: £9.60, £2.40, £4.10; EX 334.80 Trifecta £2024.30.
Owner Eight Gents and a Lady **Bred** Onslow, Stratton & Parry **Trained** Market Rasen, Lincs
■ Stewards' Enquiry : Adam McNamara two-day ban: used whip above permitted level (Apr 11-12)

FOCUS
A moderate yet competitive sprint handicap.
T/Jkpt: Not won. T/Plt: £1,827.90 to a £1 stake. Pool: £81,883.21 - 32.7 winning units T/Qpdt: £23.80 to a £1 stake. Pool: £7,955.55 - 247.06 winning units **Andrew Sheret**

1094 CORK (R-H)
Monday, March 28

OFFICIAL GOING: Heavy

1127a CORK STKS (LISTED RACE) 6f

1:55 (1:57) 3-Y-O+

£19,522 (£6,286; £2,977; £1,323; £661; £330)

RPR

1 **Bobby's Kitten (USA)**[149] 7650 5-9-7 111........................ PatSmullen 3 117
(D K Weld, Ire) *chsd ldrs in 3rd: travelled wl to cl under 2f out: led over 1f out: readily qcknd clr ins fnl f: comf* **5/1**[3]

2 *8½* **Flight Risk (IRE)**[155] 7491 5-9-12 106........................... KevinManning 4 95
(J S Bolger, Ire) *chsd ldr in 2nd: clsr to press ldr 2f out: nt qckn w wnr ent fnl f: kpt on same pce* **7/2**[2]

3 *¾* **An Saighdiur (IRE)**[8] 1015 9-9-7 86......................(b) DeclanMcDonogh 5 87
(Andrew Slattery, Ire) *broke wl and led stands' side: rdn over 2f out: hdd over 1f out and dropped to 3rd: kpt on same pce* **7/1**

4 *4½* **Bold Thady Quill (IRE)**[8] 1018 9-9-7 97............................(tp) BillyLee 2 73
(K J Condon, Ire) *slowly away and sn detached in rr: kpt on for press fr under 2f out: nvr on terms* **8/1**

5 *4½* **Great Minds (IRE)**[163] 7278 6-9-10 105......................... WayneLordan 1 62
(T Stack, Ire) *hld up in 5th towards outer: rdn 2f out and sn no imp: wknd: lame* **5/4**[1]

6 *4¾* **Corail (IRE)**[8] 1016 4-9-2 94..(b) ChrisHayes 7 38
(P D Deegan, Ire) *chsd ldrs on stands' side in 4th: rdn and nt qckn under 2f out: sn no ex* **12/1**

1m 18.54s (5.94) **6** Ran SP% **114.6**
CSF £23.25 TOTE £4.00: £2.40, £1.02; DF 11.50 Trifecta £115.90.
Owner Kenneth L Ramsey **Bred** Kenneth L Ramsey & Sarah K Ramsey **Trained** Curragh, Co Kildare

FOCUS
A very impressive performance from a top-class American import, any question of him not handling the very tacky ground was answered very comprehensively.

1128 - 1130a (Foreign Racing) - See Raceform Interactive

1110 WOLVERHAMPTON (A.W) (L-H)
Tuesday, March 29

OFFICIAL GOING: Tapeta: standard
Wind: Fresh behind Weather: Showers

1131 HOTEL & RACING PACKAGES AVAILABLE APPRENTICE H'CAP 1m 141y (Tp)

2:10 (2:10) (Class 6) (0-60,60) 4-Y-O+ **£2,587** (£770; £384; £192) **Stalls** Low

Form RPR

2542 **1** **Toymaker**[11] 986 9-9-5 **58**..(t) PhilDennis 7 66
(Phil McEntee) *chsd ldr tl led over 2f out: rdn clr over 1f out: styd on* **4/1**[2]

-651 **2** *1* **Hazel Blue (IRE)**[11] 986 5-9-2 **55**................................... JoshDoyle 1 61
(David Loughnane) *a.p: rdn to chse wnr over 1f out: r.o* **3/1**[1]

6525 **3** *¾* **Grey Destiny**[6] 1047 6-9-2 **60**.. MathewStill(5) 6 64
(Antony Brittain) *s.i.s: hld up: plld hrd: hdwy on outer over 3f out: rdn over 1f out: r.o* **5/1**[3]

1-50 **4** *½* **Storm Runner (IRE)**[20] 877 8-9-1 **59**............................. JaneElliott(5) 5 62
(George Margarson) *hld up: hdwy 1/2-way: rdn over 1f out: styd on* **5/1**[3]

0060 **5** *¾* **Evacusafe Lady**[5] 1058 5-8-10 **56**......................(tp) JonathanFisher(7) 3 58
(John Ryan) *prom: lost pl over 3f out: rdn over 1f out: r.o wl ins fnl f* **10/1**

3152 **6** *½* **Cookie Ring (IRE)**[18] 904 5-9-1 **59**.............................(v) PaulaMuir(5) 8 60
(Patrick Holmes) *s.i.s: hld up: styd on u.p ins fnl f: nt rch ldrs* **11/2**

500/ **7** *1* **Poetic Lord**[7] 2795 7-9-4 **60**....................................... DanielleMooney(3) 4 59
(Rebecca Menzies) *sn led at stdy pce: pushed along and hdd over 2f out: no ex ins fnl f* **22/1**

540- **8** *hd* **Last Wish (IRE)**[168] 7185 5-9-7 **60**............................(t[1]) RobJFitzpatrick 9 58
(Richard Guest) *prom: rdn over 1f out: no ex ins fnl f* **16/1**

000- **9** *1¼* **Rebel Yell**[32] 5484 4-8-10 **52**...................................(t) HollieDoyle(3) 2 48
(Richard Price) *hld up: rdn over 1f out: no ex fnl f* **40/1**

1m 54.39s (4.29) **Going Correction** -0.025s/f (Stan) **9** Ran SP% **115.5**
Speed ratings (Par 101): **79,78,77,77,76 75,75,74,73**
CSF £16.43 CT £60.89 TOTE £5.80: £1.50, £1.80, £2.00; EX 13.10 Trifecta £88.30.
Owner Eventmaker Racehorses **Bred** A G Antoniades **Trained** Newmarket, Suffolk

FOCUS
This was steadily run and it paid to race handily with the winner enjoying a good trip and ride.

1132 FOLLOW US ON TWITTER @WOLVESRACES MEDIAN AUCTION MAIDEN STKS 1m 141y (Tp)

2:40 (2:42) (Class 6) 3-5-Y-O **£2,587** (£770; £384; £192) **Stalls** Low

Form RPR

05-2 **1** **Pushaq (IRE)**[10] 1000 3-8-8 78....................................... AndreaAtzeni 6 79
(Marco Botti) *chsd ldrs: rdn over 1f out: styd on to ld towards fin* **11/8**[1]

4 **2** *nse* **Knights Table**[14] 945 3-8-8 0... LukeMorris 1 78
(James Tate) *led at stdy pce tl rdn and qcknd over 2f out: styd on: hdd towards fin* **7/4**[2]

402- **3** *5* **Chicago School (IRE)**[151] 7605 3-8-8 72......................... JoeFanning 2 67
(Mark Johnston) *chsd ldr: shkn up and ev ch over 1f out: no ex ins fnl f* **3/1**[3]

0 **4** *2½* **Lemon Thyme**[25] 814 3-8-3 0... KieranO'Neill 7 57
(Mike Murphy) *mid-div: rdn over 2f out: edgd lft over 1f out: styd on ins fnl f: nt trble ldrs* **40/1**

0 **5** *1* **Dwynant**[14] 945 3-8-3 0... RyanPowell 3 55
(Kevin Frost) *chsd ldrs: rdn over 2f out: wknd fnl f* **100/1**

0 **6** *6* **Allen's Folly**[66] 314 3-7-10 0.. HollieDoyle(7) 8 42+
(Peter Hiatt) *hld up: shkn up over 2f out: nvr on terms* **66/1**

7 *1¾* **King Of Arts (IRE)** 3-8-8 0... TomEaves 5 44+
(David Simcock) *hld up: rdn over 2f out: a in rr* **12/1**

8 *4* **Lord Murphy (IRE)** 3-8-5 0... RobHornby(3) 4 36+
(Daniel Mark Loughnane) *s.s: rdn over 2f out: a bhd* **22/1**

9 *2¾* **Away In May**[103] 5-9-8 0... CathyGannon 9 30+
(John Spearing) *hld up in tch: rdn over 3f out: wknd over 2f out* **100/1**

1m 48.92s (-1.18) **Going Correction** -0.025s/f (Stan)
WFA 3 from 5yo 19lb **9** Ran SP% **121.4**
Speed ratings (Par 101): **104,103,99,97,96 91,89,85,83**
CSF £4.26 TOTE £2.40: £1.10, £1.30, £1.20; EX 5.50 Trifecta £8.30.
Owner El Catorce **Bred** Premier Bloodstock **Trained** Newmarket, Suffolk

FOCUS
An ordinary and lopsided maiden.

1133 ENJOY THE HOTEL PARADE RESTAURANT H'CAP 5f 20y (Tp)

3:15 (3:15) (Class 6) (0-60,60) 4-Y-O+ **£2,587** (£770; £384; £192) **Stalls** Low

Form RPR

-004 **1** **Eland Ally**[22] 857 8-9-5 **58**..(p) OisinMurphy 9 65
(Anabel K Murphy) *hld up: hdwy over 1f out: r.o to ld wl ins fnl f* **11/1**

600 **2** *¾* **Fuel Injection**[7] 1026 5-9-4 **57**.. BarryMcHugh 4 61
(Paul Midgley) *led to 1/2-way: rdn over 1f out: r.o* **8/1**

5100 **3** *hd* **Give Us A Belle (IRE)**[5] 1059 7-9-6 **59**....................(vt) AdamBeschizza 8 63
(Christine Dunnett) *sn w ldr: led 1/2-way: rdn and edgd rt over 1f out: hdd and unable qck wl ins fnl f* **25/1**

2134 **4** *nk* **Blue Bounty**[14] 937 5-9-7 **60**......................................(p) SaleemGolam 1 63
(Mark H Tompkins) *chsd ldrs: rdn over 1f out: r.o* **3/1**[1]

3-30 **5** *¾* **Frangarry (IRE)**[32] 733 4-9-7 **60**............................ GrahamGibbons 10 60
(Alan Bailey) *s.i.s: hld up: rdn and r.o ins fnl f: nt rch ldrs* **15/2**

-106 **6** *nk* **Quantum Dot (IRE)**[19] 889 5-9-4 **57**...........................(b) KieranO'Neill 7 56
(Ed de Giles) *sn pushed along to chse ldrs: rdn 1/2-way: styd on same pce ins fnl f* **14/1**

6210 **7** *½* **Charlie Lad**[5] 1059 4-9-6 **59**... LukeMorris 2 56
(Daniel Mark Loughnane) *prom: rdn 1/2-way: styd on same pce ins fnl f* **5/1**[2]

0501 **8** *1* **Harpers Ruby**[32] 732 6-8-13 **52**....................................... JackGarritty 3 45
(Lynn Siddall) *prom: rdn over 1f out: edgd rt and styd on same pce fnl f* **7/1**

6333 **9** *4½* **Extreme Supreme**[14] 937 5-9-6 **59**..........................(v) TonyHamilton 5 39
(Derek Shaw) *hld up: rdn over 1f out: sn wknd* **11/2**[3]

606- **10** *4½* **Simply Black (IRE)**[350] 1394 5-9-2 **60**......................(p) AnnStokell(5) 6 21
(Ann Stokell) *a in rr: bhd fr 1/2-way* **100/1**

1m 1.3s (-0.60) **Going Correction** -0.025s/f (Stan) **10** Ran SP% **112.3**
Speed ratings (Par 101): **103,101,101,101,99 99,98,96,89,82**
CSF £92.28 CT £2175.02 TOTE £14.30: £3.60, £4.20, £6.70; EX 92.40 Trifecta £2372.80.
Owner Mrs Anabel K Murphy **Bred** Peter Webb **Trained** Wilmcote, Warwicks

FOCUS
This sprint was run at a good pace and everything fell right for the winner.

1134 STAY AT THE WOLVERHAMPTON HOLIDAY INN MAIDEN STKS 1m 4f 50y (Tp)
3:50 (3:50) (Class 5) 3-Y-O **£3,234** (£962; £481; £240) **Stalls** Low

Form RPR

5- **1** **Gambit**[235] 5094 3-9-5 0 RichardKingscote 4 85+
(Tom Dascombe) *a.p: chsd ldr over 2f out: led wl over 1f out: edgd rt and pushed clr fnl f* **4/7**[1]

233 **2** *8* **Ragner**[31] 746 3-9-5 75 JamieSpencer 3 70
(David Simcock) *hld up: plld hrd: hdwy 2f out: rdn to chse ldr fnl f: styd on same pce* **3/1**[2]

3 **3** *2¼* **Hongkong Adventure**[25] 818 3-9-5 0 LukeMorris 1 66
(Rae Guest) *led: rdn over 2f out: hdd wl over 1f out: sn edgd lft: wknd ins fnl f* **11/2**[3]

0- **4** *2¼* **Sogno D'Amore (USA)**[167] 7217 3-9-5 0 JoeFanning 2 62
(Mark Johnston) *chsd ldr: pushed along over 3f out: lost 2nd over 2f out: wknd over 1f out* **12/1**

4556 **5** *2½* **Ready Steady (USA)**[42] 597 3-9-0 52 DougieCostello 5 53
(David Loughnane) *hld up: rdn and wknd over 2f out* **125/1**

2m 40.31s (-0.49) **Going Correction** -0.025s/f (Stan) **5** Ran SP% **112.5**
Speed ratings (Par 98): **100,94,93,91,90**
CSF £2.71 TOTE £1.50: £1.10, £1.80; EX 2.90 Trifecta £5.60.
Owner Laurence Bellman & Caroline Ingram **Bred** S A R L Srl **Trained** Malpas, Cheshire

FOCUS
A nice performance from the winner, who was in a different league to the rest.

1135 WOLVERHAMPTON-RACECOURSE.CO.UK H'CAP 1m 5f 194y (Tp)
4:25 (4:27) (Class 4) (0-85,84) 4-Y-O+ **£5,175** (£1,540; £769; £384) **Stalls** Low

Form RPR

304- **1** **Shrewd**[25] 8175 6-9-12 **84** MartinDwyer 6 93
(Iain Jardine) *chsd ldrs: wnt 2nd over 3f out: shkn up to ld over 1f out: styd on wl* **3/1**[2]

-041 **2** *2½* **Heart Locket**[28] 772 4-8-10 **72** ow2 GrahamGibbons 2 77
(Michael Easterby) *led at stdy pce tl qcknd over 2f out: rdn and hdd over 1f out: styd on same pce ins fnl f: eased whn hld nr fin* **9/1**

-332 **3** *3* **Scarlet Minstrel**[17] 922 4-8-13 **80** EdwardGreatrex(5) 4 81
(Andrew Balding) *chsd ldr tl over 3f out: sn rdn: edgd lft over 1f out: styd on same pce fnl f* **6/4**[1]

2132 **4** *¾* **Zakatal**[40] 619 10-9-5 **77** PJMcDonald 5 77
(Rebecca Menzies) *hld up: rdn over 2f out: hdwy over 1f out: no imp fnl f* **7/1**

4-42 **5** *2¼* **Grand Meister**[33] 704 5-9-9 **81** (b[1]) PhillipMakin 3 78
(John Quinn) *hld up: hdwy over 5f out: rdn over 2f out: wknd over 1f out* **10/3**[3]

/000 **6** *15* **Maria's Choice (IRE)**[7] 1028 7-9-0 **72** TimmyMurphy 1 48
(Jim Best) *prom: lost pl over 3f out: wknd over 2f out* **125/1**

3m 5.66s (0.86) **Going Correction** -0.025s/f (Stan)
WFA 4 from 5yo+ 4lb **6** Ran SP% **111.4**
Speed ratings (Par 105): **96,94,92,92,91 82**
CSF £27.84 TOTE £4.30: £2.10, £2.70; EX 26.90 Trifecta £76.50.
Owner Tapas Partnership **Bred** Darley **Trained** Carrutherstown, D'fries & G'way

FOCUS
A fair handicap though the form is muddling.

1136 BUSINESS VENUE 365 DAYS A YEAR H'CAP 2m 119y (Tp)
5:00 (5:00) (Class 6) (0-65,65) 4-Y-O+ **£2,587** (£770; £384; £192) **Stalls** Low

Form RPR

6060 **1** **Topaling**[20] 882 5-9-7 **60** SaleemGolam 7 70
(Mark H Tompkins) *hld up: nt clr run: swtchd rt and hdwy over 3f out: led over 1f out: sn rdn and edgd lft: styd on u.p* **14/1**

00-2 **2** *½* **City Dreams (IRE)**[10] 1004 6-8-12 **51** DougieCostello 4 60
(Philip Kirby) *hld up: hdwy over 3f out: chsd wnr over 1f out: sn rdn: styd on* **9/2**[2]

-020 **3** *11* **Unex Modigliani (IRE)**[23] 695 7-9-4 **57** (tp) TonyHamilton 8 53
(Derek Shaw) *hld up: hdwy over 3f out: rdn and hung lft fr over 2f out: wknd ins fnl f* **7/1**[3]

3/0- **4** *2¼* **Impeccability**[92] 97 6-8-7 **46** (p) LukeMorris 3 39
(John Mackie) *hung lft almost thrght: chsd ldrs: wnt 2nd over 4f out: led over 2f out: rdn and hdd over 1f out: wknd fnl f* **33/1**

-540 **5** *½* **Yorkshireman (IRE)**[14] 946 6-8-9 **48** (b) JackGarritty 5 41
(Lynn Siddall) *pushed along in rr: hdwy to chse ldr 14f out: rdn over 6f out: lost 2nd over 4f out: sn outpcd: wknd 2f out* **9/1**

50-1 **6** *¾* **Desktop**[14] 946 4-9-1 **59** PJMcDonald 1 51
(Antony Brittain) *led: rdn and hdd over 2f out: wknd over 1f out* **6/5**[1]

00-4 **7** *41* **Hyperlink (IRE)**[27] 786 7-9-11 **64** CharlesBishop 2 6
(Heather Dalton) *chsd ldrs: rdn over 3f out: wknd over 2f out* **16/1**

605- **8** *54* **Burneston**[238] 4978 4-9-7 **65** TedDurcan 6
(James Bethell) *prom: rdn over 6f out: wknd 4f out* **8/1**

3m 37.52s (-6.18) **Going Correction** -0.025s/f (Stan)
WFA 4 from 5yo+ 5lb **8** Ran SP% **112.7**
Speed ratings (Par 101): **113,112,107,106,106 105,86,61**
CSF £73.52 CT £483.22 TOTE £15.10: £3.40, £2.00, £1.80; EX 86.80 Trifecta £422.60.
Owner David Tompkins **Bred** Dullingham Park Stud & M P Bowring **Trained** Newmarket, Suffolk
■ Stewards' Enquiry : Saleem Golam four-day ban: used whip in incorrect place (Apr 12-15)

FOCUS
The first two drew right away from the rest in this moderate staying handicap, though they went a decent gallop.

1137 SPONSOR A RACE BY CALLING 01902 390000 H'CAP 7f 32y (Tp)
5:30 (5:30) (Class 5) (0-75,73) 3-Y-O **£3,234** (£962; £481; £240) **Stalls** High

Form RPR

-112 **1** **Nouvelli Dancer (IRE)**[14] 947 3-9-4 **70** OisinMurphy 2 77
(Ivan Furtado) *prom: lost pl 4f out: hdwy over 1f out: rdn to ld and hung rt ins fnl f: r.o* **15/2**

034- **2** *¾* **Darksiteofthemoon (IRE)**[215] 5785 3-9-7 **73** LukeMorris 3 77
(Marco Botti) *hld up: plld hrd: hdwy 1/2-way: rdn over 1f out: nt clr run ins fnl f: r.o* **7/2**[3]

1512 **3** *1¼* **Inaam (IRE)**[25] 817 3-9-6 **72** DavidNolan 5 73
(Richard Fahey) *hld up: plld hrd: nt clr run wl over 1f out: r.o ins fnl f: nt rch ldrs* **9/1**

6-11 **4** *hd* **Palpitation (IRE)**[7] 1031 3-8-13 **70** AaronJones(5) 6 70
(David Brown) *prom: chsd ldr over 5f out: rdn over 1f out: styd on same pce ins fnl f* **9/4**[1]

-210 **5** *½* **Broughtons Fancy**[17] 924 3-8-11 **66** PhilipPrince(3) 8 65
(David Evans) *led 6f out: rdn over 1f out: hdd ins fnl f: styd on same pce* **25/1**

2431 **6** *½* **Clive Clifton (IRE)**[32] 725 3-9-1 **67** (v) StevieDonohoe 1 65
(David Evans) *sn pushed along to ld: hdd 6f out: chsd ldrs: rdn over 1f out: no ex ins fnl f* **14/1**

4-21 **7** *hd* **Custard The Dragon**[60] 380 3-9-5 **71** GrahamGibbons 7 68
(John Mackie) *sn prom: rdn over 2f out: no ex fnl f* **22/1**

31 **8** *nse* **Bint Arcano (FR)**[25] 824 3-9-6 **72** ConnorBeasley 4 69
(Julie Camacho) *hld up: rdn and nt clr run over 1f out: nvr on terms* **3/1**[2]

1m 28.94s (0.14) **Going Correction** -0.025s/f (Stan) **8** Ran SP% **114.6**
Speed ratings (Par 98): **98,97,95,95,94 94,94,94**
CSF £34.02 CT £241.25 TOTE £8.10: £2.20, £1.70, £2.50; EX 39.30 Trifecta £262.10.
Owner S Laffan **Bred** Colin Kennedy **Trained** Wiseton, Nottinghamshire

FOCUS
This was a bit messy. There was a bit of a battle for the early lead, the pace slackened down the back and then they quickened. The principals came from off the pace.
T/Plt: £95.60 to a £1 stake. Pool: £72,536.79 - 553.66 winning units. T/Qpdt: £69.90 to a £1 stake. Pool: £5,520.65 - 58.40 winning units. **Colin Roberts**

1086 KEMPTON (A.W) (R-H)
Wednesday, March 30

OFFICIAL GOING: Polytrack: standard
Wind: Moderate, across away from stands Weather: Clear

1138 £10 FREE BET AT 32REDSPORT.COM APPRENTICE H'CAP 6f (P)
5:55 (5:55) (Class 6) (0-55,55) 4-Y-O+ **£2,264** (£673; £336; £168) **Stalls** Low

Form RPR

0-00 **1** **Insolenceofoffice (IRE)**[64] 340 8-9-3 **54** (v) CallumRodriguez(3) 2 60
(Richard Ford) *prom: rdn 2f out: led briefly ins fnl f: rallied to get bk up nr fin* **12/1**

0-50 **2** *hd* **Krazy Paving**[12] 985 4-9-5 **53** (b[1]) HollieDoyle 8 58
(Anabel K Murphy) *in tch: effrt 2f out: squeezed through to ld wl ins fnl f: jst ct* **9/1**

-406 **3** *1* **Captain Scooby**[14] 963 10-9-7 **55** (b) SophieKilloran 7 59
(Richard Guest) *hld up towards rr: hdwy 2f out: styng on whn nt clr run ins fnl f: jst snatched 3rd* **25/1**

0000 **4** *shd* **Blackasyourhat (IRE)**[13] 970 4-8-12 **46** oh1 (t) RhiainIngram 1 48
(Michael Attwater) *mid-div: hdwy on inner 2f out: kpt on fnl f* **33/1**

2532 **5** *hd* **Blistering Dancer (IRE)**[33] 730 6-8-9 **46** MitchGodwin(3) 4 47
(Tony Carroll) *led tl jst ins fnl f: one pce* **13/8**[1]

-536 **6** *hd* **Diamond Vine (IRE)**[11] 1005 8-8-7 **46** oh1 (p) CameronNoble(5) 5 47
(Ronald Harris) *bhd tl r.o fr over 1f out* **20/1**

-306 **7** *1¼* **Top Cop**[15] 942 7-9-1 **54** (p) GeorgeWood(5) 3 51
(Ronald Harris) *prom: hrd rdn over 1f out: wknd fnl f* **8/1**

4646 **8** *1½* **Burauq**[7] 1042 4-9-6 **54** (b) LuluStanford 6 46
(Milton Bradley) *in tch tl outpcd fnl 2f* **6/1**[2]

06-1 **9** *1* **Ballroom Angel**[11] 1005 4-9-2 **50** HarryBurns 9 39
(Philip Hide) *stdd in rr s: rdn 3f out: nvr trbld ldrs* **7/1**[3]

0010 **10** *½* **Stamp Of Approval (IRE)**[11] 1005 4-8-13 **50** SamuelClarke(3) 11 37
(Chris Wall) *racd wd: a towards rr* **16/1**

0640 **11** *2* **Black Vale (IRE)**[20] 895 5-8-12 **46** oh1 (t) PatrickVaughan 10 27
(Phil McEntee) *prom on outer tl wknd 2f out* **50/1**

1m 12.66s (-0.44) **Going Correction** -0.05s/f (Stan) **11** Ran SP% **113.1**
Speed ratings (Par 101): **100,99,98,98,98 97,96,94,92,92 89**
CSF £105.86 CT £2667.78 TOTE £16.00: £3.70, £2.70, £6.00; EX 144.60 Trifecta £1320.80.
Owner CCCNLP **Bred** G Kennedy **Trained** Garstang, Lancs

FOCUS
They finished in a bit of a heap in this moderate sprint.

1139 32RED CASINO FILLIES' H'CAP 7f (P)
6:25 (6:25) (Class 5) (0-70,68) 4-Y-O+ **£2,911** (£866; £432; £216) **Stalls** Low

Form RPR

3- **1** *4½* **Baileys Mirage (FR)**[93] 5-9-0 **61** (p) SilvestreDeSousa 3 68
(Chris Dwyer) *disp ld: led after 2f tl over 1f out: one pce* **3/1**[2]

5-40 **2** *5* **Perfect Bounty**[21] 872 4-8-11 **58** LukeMorris 1 52
(Patrick Chamings) *chsd ldrs tl outpcd fnl 2f* **9/1**

3541 **3** *nk* **Rialto Magic**[20] 889 4-8-9 **61** (p) LucyKBarry(5) 6 54
(Jamie Osborne) *s.i.s: bhd: rdn 3f out: nvr rchd ldrs* **7/1**[3]

05-4 **4** *1¼* **Light Rose (IRE)**[58] 414 6-9-4 **65** MartinLane 4 55
(Jeremy Gask) *disp ld for 2f: pressed ldr tl hrd rdn and wknd 2f out* **3/1**[2]

50-0 **6** *5* **Lucky Leyf**[28] 777 4-8-11 **58** WilliamTwiston-Davies 7 35
(Philip Hide) *in tch: hrd rdn over 2f out: sn wknd* **16/1**

0-00 **7** *2¼* **Synoptic Dream (USA)**[7] 1048 4-7-11 **49** oh4 (v) NoelGarbutt(5) 2 20
(Derek Shaw) *s.i.s: drvn along in rr most of way: n.d fnl 3f* **100/1**

663- **D** **Lucy The Painter (IRE)**[162] 7363 4-9-7 **68** HarryBentley 5 87
(Ed de Giles) *hld up: hdwy 2f out: led over 1f out: rdn clr fnl f* **2/1**[1]

1m 24.9s (-1.10) **Going Correction** -0.05s/f (Stan) **7** Ran SP% **112.7**
Speed ratings (Par 100): **98,93,92,91,85 83,104**
CSF £7.96 TOTE £3.10: £1.80, £2.30; EX 9.60 Trifecta £55.70.
Owner G R Bailey Ltd (Baileys Horse Feeds) **Bred** Gr Baileys Ltd **Trained** Newmarket, Suffolk
■ Stewards' Enquiry : Lucy K Barry two-day ban: used whip above permitted level (Apr 13-14)

FOCUS
The first two in this fillies' handicap were having their first outing for new yards. The race has been rated around the runner-up.

1140 32RED ON THE APP STORE MAIDEN STKS 1m 3f (P)
6:55 (6:55) (Class 5) 3-Y-O+ **£2,911** (£866; £432; £216) **Stalls** Low

Form RPR

5- **1** **Biodynamic (IRE)**[147] 7708 3-8-7 0 JoeyHaynes 6 68+
(K R Burke) *mid-div: drvn along 3f out: styd on to ld ins fnl f: rdn out* **6/4**[1]

00- **2** *1¼* **Sky Of Stars (IRE)**[229] 5349 3-8-7 0 LukeMorris 11 66
(William Knight) *sn chsng ldr on outer: rdn to chal ins fnl f: kpt on* **6/1**

3 *½* **Hold Hands**[48] 5-9-9 0 RichardKingscote 5 63
(Brendan Powell) *s.s: sn chsng ldrs: effrt 2f out: rdn to chal ins fnl f: kpt on* **66/1**

0- **4** *1½* **Emperor Napoleon**[126] 7981 3-8-4 0 RobHornby(3) 7 64+
(Andrew Balding) *plld hrd in midfield: lost pl 4f out: rallied and n.m.r on rail 1f out: one pce ins fnl f* **10/1**

5 *nk* **Princess Roania (IRE)**[250] 5-9-9 0 SamJames 12 60+
(Peter Bowen) *s.v.s: t.k.h in rr: rdn over 2f out: styd on wl fr over 1f out* **14/1**

5 **6** *nk* **Earthwindorfire**[33] 728 5-10-0 0 GeorgeBaker 2 64
(Geoffrey Deacon) *led at modest pce: qcknd 3f out: hdd & wknd ins fnl f* **16/1**

60 **7** *½* **Antonio Joli (IRE)**[46] 567 4-9-13 0 FrannyNorton 10 63
(Jo Hughes) *t.k.h towards rr: shkn up over 2f out: nvr rchd chalng position* **100/1**

25 **8** *1¼* **Angelical Dancer (FR)**[13] 968 3-8-7 0 LiamJones 3 58
(Marco Botti) *chsd ldrs tl wknd over 1f out* **7/2**[2]

9 *2½* **Owners Day**[26] 6-9-9 0 LiamKeniry 9 52
(Neil Mulholland) *s.s: a bhd* **100/1**

33 **10** *1¼* **Sarmadee (IRE)**[34] 710 4-9-13 0 CharlesBishop 8 54
(Mick Channon) *plld hrd towards rr: rdn 3f out: nvr nr ldrs* **9/2**[3]

11 *4½* **Icons Image** 3-8-4 0 DanielMuscutt[(3)] 4 43
(Brian McMath) *dwlt: hmpd after 1f: a towards rr: no ch fnl 3f* **33/1**

12 *1¾* **Nightswift**[123] 4-9-13 0 TimmyMurphy 1 43
(James Evans) *prom tl wknd qckly 2f out* **100/1**

2m 23.04s (1.14) **Going Correction** -0.05s/f (Stan)
WFA 3 from 4yo 21lb 4 from 5yo+ 1lb **12** Ran SP% **123.7**
Speed ratings (Par 103): **93,92,91,90,90 90,89,88,87,86 82,81**
CSF £11.75 TOTE £2.60: £1.40, £2.70, £11.10; EX 11.90 Trifecta £438.00.
Owner Hubert John Strecker **Bred** Lodge Park Stud **Trained** Middleham Moor, N Yorks

FOCUS
A fair maiden, but the form looks shaky.

1141 RACING UK IN GLORIOUS HD H'CAP 1m (P)
7:25 (7:25) (Class 6) (0-60,60) 3-Y-O **£2,264** (£673; £336; £168) **Stalls** Low

Form RPR

440- **1** **Here's Two**[169] 7196 3-9-7 **60** GeorgeBaker 3 73+
(Ron Hodges) *t.k.h: prom: led ins fnl f: rdn out* **8/1**

506- **2** *nk* **Kafoo**[239] 4967 3-9-5 **58** PaulHanagan 7 71+
(Ed Dunlop) *prom: led 2f out tl ins fnl f: kpt on* **11/8**[1]

0-05 **3** *4* **Multigifted**[33] 725 3-9-6 **59** LiamKeniry 1 62
(Michael Madgwick) *mid-div on inner: n.m.r 3f out: hrd rdn and hdwy 2f out: wnt 3rd and no imp over 1f out* **16/1**

-545 **4** *½* **Frap**[27] 794 3-9-0 **60** AdamMcNamara[(7)] 10 62
(Richard Fahey) *s.i.s: t.k.h in rr: rdn and r.o fnl 2f* **13/2**[3]

0-14 **5** *2¾* **Big Shoes (IRE)**[20] 896 3-9-1 **54** DarryllHolland 8 50
(Charles Hills) *in tch: rdn and lost pl over 2f out: styd on fnl f* **4/1**[2]

0523 **6** *1* **Daydream (IRE)**[15] 948 3-9-1 **59** LucyKBarry[(5)] 4 52
(Jamie Osborne) *dwlt: prom on outer after 3f: wknd wl over 1f out* **10/1**

3045 **7** *1* **Boom Junior**[20] 896 3-8-7 **46** oh1 (t) WilliamCarson 6 36
(Tony Carroll) *led tl 2f out: sn wknd* **33/1**

056 **8** *4* **Haunted (IRE)**[29] 770 3-8-12 **51** (b[1]) FrannyNorton 2 34
(Milton Bradley) *t.k.h: in tch: squeezed for room 3f out: sn wknd* **25/1**

350- **9** *5* **Commanding Role**[162] 7361 3-8-12 **51** DavidProbert 11 20
(Michael Blanshard) *a bhd* **66/1**

0-00 **10** *2¾* **Taroneesh**[7] 1045 3-8-7 **46** oh1 AdamBeschizza 9 8
(Derek Shaw) *a bhd* **100/1**

0-00 **11** *1½* **Selena Rose**[15] 947 3-8-7 **46** oh1 (p) LukeMorris 5 5
(Ronald Harris) *sn towards rr: rdn and n.d fnl 3f* **100/1**

1m 39.67s (-0.13) **Going Correction** -0.05s/f (Stan) **11** Ran SP% **111.8**
Speed ratings (Par 96): **98,97,93,93,90 89,88,84,79,76 75**
CSF £18.01 CT £174.11 TOTE £8.00: £2.20, £1.60, £3.20; EX 22.70 Trifecta £178.70.
Owner K J Corcoran **Bred** D R Tucker **Trained** Charlton Mackrell, Somerset

FOCUS
This was steadily run and it was an advantage to race handily. The front pair looked well treated.

1142 32RED H'CAP (LONDON MILE SERIES QUALIFIER) 1m (P)
7:55 (7:55) (Class 4) (0-85,83) 4-Y-O+ **£4,690** (£1,395; £697; £348) **Stalls** Low

Form RPR

01 **1** **Harry Holland**[32] 746 4-9-3 **79** MartinDwyer 3 86
(William Muir) *mde all: rdn over 2f out: hld on wl fnl f* **15/2**

326- **2** *1* **Squire**[163] 7348 5-9-0 **76** RobertHavlin 4 81
(Michael Attwater) *dwlt: sn chsng ldrs: effrt 2f out: kpt on u.p fnl f* **9/2**[3]

203- **3** *½* **Red Paladin (IRE)**[161] 7388 6-8-10 **72** (p) TonyHamilton 1 76
(Kristin Stubbs) *dwlt: bhd: hdwy on inner 2f out: kpt on u.p fnl f* **8/1**

143- **4** *nk* **Chevallier**[201] 6286 4-9-0 **81** JordanVaughan[(5)] 6 84
(K R Burke) *prom: outpcd 2f out: styd on fnl f* **7/1**

02-1 **5** *nk* **Bank Of Gibraltar**[84] 74 4-9-4 **80** ShaneKelly 2 82
(Richard Hughes) *prom: chsd wnr after 2f: rdn to chal over 1f out: one pce fnl f* **2/1**[1]

4416 **6** *3* **Corporal Maddox**[15] 944 9-9-7 **83** (p) LukeMorris 8 79
(Ronald Harris) *t.k.h in 5th: hrd rdn and btn 2f out* **25/1**

6-1U **7** *nk* **Isis Blue**[49] 518 6-8-6 **73** AliceMills[(5)] 5 68
(Rod Millman) *dwlt: a in rr* **7/2**[2]

1m 38.91s (-0.89) **Going Correction** -0.05s/f (Stan) **7** Ran SP% **113.0**
Speed ratings (Par 105): **102,101,100,100,99 96,96**
CSF £39.74 CT £276.73 TOTE £8.90: £3.60, £2.70; EX 47.00 Trifecta £233.00.
Owner Muir Racing Partnership - Windsor **Bred** Mrs F M Gordon **Trained** Lambourn, Berks

FOCUS
A fair handicap, dominated from the front by the unexposed winner.

1143 32RED.COM H'CAP 6f (P)
8:25 (8:25) (Class 4) (0-85,84) 4-Y-O+ **£4,690** (£1,395; £697; £348) **Stalls** Low

Form RPR

-115 **1** **Gentlemen**[52] 494 5-9-1 **83** JosephineGordon[(5)] 1 96
(Phil McEntee) *dwlt: sn in midfield: hdwy on inner 2f out: drvn to ld nr fin* **8/1**

4212 **2** *¾* **Torreon (IRE)**[7] 1041 5-9-3 **80** AdamKirby 10 91
(John Ryan) *led fr wd stall: kpt on u.p fnl f: hdd nr fin* **11/10**[1]

-351 **3** *1½* **Burning Blaze**[14] 953 6-8-13 **76** SilvestreDeSousa 4 82
(Brian Ellison) *plld hrd: trckd ldrs: effrt 2f out: kpt on fnl f* **5/1**[2]

/04- **4** *1¼* **Dinneratmidnight**[308] 2609 5-9-3 **80** (e[1]) JasonHart 3 82
(Richard Guest) *prom: drvn along 2f out: no ex fnl f* **33/1**

264- **5** *nse* **Lightning Charlie**[176] 7017 4-8-13 **76** JimCrowley 5 78
(Amanda Perrett) *chsd ldr tl outpcd appr fnl f* **11/2**[3]

-224 **6** *¾* **Head Space (IRE)**[28] 782 8-8-10 **73** LukeMorris 6 72
(Brian Barr) *mid-div: rdn over 2f out: styd on same pce* **12/1**

-065 **7** *1½* **Multitask**[14] 953 6-8-7 **70** KieranO'Neill 2 65
(Michael Madgwick) *towards rr: rdn over 2f out: nvr able to chal* **12/1**

100- **8** *1½* **Rio Ronaldo (IRE)**[154] 7547 4-9-7 **84** PatDobbs 7 74
(Mike Murphy) *t.k.h: prom on outer tl wknd 2f out* **7/1**

00-0 **9** *1¼* **My Dad Syd (USA)**[14] 960 4-9-1 **78** RyanPowell 9 64
(Ian Williams) *a towards rr* **50/1**

000- **10** *7* **Boy In The Bar**[109] 8205 5-9-2 **82** GeorgeDowning[(3)] 8 45
(Ian Williams) *dwlt: rdn along most of way: a bhd* **40/1**

1m 11.49s (-1.61) **Going Correction** -0.05s/f (Stan) **10** Ran SP% **126.0**
Speed ratings (Par 105): **108,107,105,103,103 102,100,98,96,87**
CSF £18.52 CT £56.29 TOTE £10.80: £3.10, £1.02, £2.10; EX 28.70 Trifecta £97.80.
Owner Eventmaker Racehorses **Bred** Mrs Eleanor Kent **Trained** Newmarket, Suffolk

FOCUS
Not a bad handicap and another personal best from the winner.
T/Plt: £166.20 to a £1 stake. Pool: £87,715.80 - 385.23 winning tickets. T/Qpdt: £11.30 to a £1 stake. Pool: £1,4190.06 - 924.94 winning tickets. **Lee McKenzie**

1065 LINGFIELD (L-H)
Wednesday, March 30

OFFICIAL GOING: Polytrack: standard
Wind: light, half behind Weather: overcast, shower races 3 and 7

1144 BESTBETTINGSITES.CO.UK UK'S TOP BETTING SITE OFFERS H'CAP 1m 4f (P)
2:10 (2:11) (Class 5) (0-75,75) 4-Y-O+ **£3,881** (£1,155; £577; £288) **Stalls** Low

Form RPR

110- **1** **Knight Music**[203] 6218 4-9-6 **75** RobertHavlin 3 87
(Michael Attwater) *wl in tch in midfield: hdwy and rdn to press ldr jst over 2f out: led ent fnl f: styd on: rdn out* **10/1**

23-3 **2** *½* **Quality Song (USA)**[28] 779 4-9-6 **75** PatDobbs 7 86
(Richard Hughes) *chsd ldr tl led over 2f out: drvn and hdd ent fnl f: kpt on but a hld ins fnl f* **3/1**[2]

1135 **3** *5* **San Quentin (IRE)**[47] 545 5-9-5 **72** RobertWinston 9 75
(Dean Ivory) *stdd s: hld up in rr: hdwy to press ldrs 2f out: sn drvn and outpcd: plugged on same pce fnl f: eased cl home* **20/1**

451- **4** *½* **Atwix**[162] 7359 4-9-6 **75** (p) JimCrowley 5 77
(Lucy Wadham) *bustled along early: racd in last trio: clsd and nt clr run over 2f out: swtchd rt and rallied over 1f out: wnt 4th 1f out: styd on wl but no threat to ldng pair* **8/1**

-242 **5** *4* **Kelly's Finest (IRE)**[20] 884 4-8-3 **63** (p) JosephineGordon[(5)] 4 59
(Michael Appleby) *chsd ldrs: rdn and losing pl whn swtchd rt and squeezed for room 2f out: wl hld and plugged on same pce after* **25/1**

-213 **6** *½* **Karnage (IRE)**[19] 899 4-9-4 **73** (b) LukeMorris 10 68
(Daniel Kubler) *in tch in midfield: effrt in 4th and edgd lft u.p 2f out: outpcd and wl btn 1f out: wknd* **5/1**[3]

02- **7** *6* **Le Notre**[112] 8159 4-9-6 **75** AdamKirby 1 60
(Jeremy Noseda) *wl in tch in midfield: pushed along at times fr 8f out: reminder and nt clr run 3f out tl 2f out wl btn over 1f out* **2/1**[1]

523- **8** *4* **Bohemian Rhapsody (IRE)**[136] 7474 7-9-8 **75** StevieDonohoe 8 54
(Brendan Powell) *dropped in bhd after s: in rr: rdn over 3f out: sn struggling: no ch fnl 2f* **33/1**

500- **9** *3* **Bazooka (IRE)**[110] 8175 5-9-7 **74** (b[1]) SilvestreDeSousa 2 48
(David Flood) *t.k.h: led tl jst over 2f out: sn btn: wknd qckly over 1f out: bhd and eased ins fnl f* **33/1**

6333 **10** *11* **Berrahri (IRE)**[19] 900 5-9-7 **74** KierenFox 6 31
(John Best) *in tch in midfield: n.m.r over 2f out: sn btn: bhd and eased fr wl over 1f out* **14/1**

2m 29.83s (-3.17) **Going Correction** +0.025s/f (Slow)
WFA 4 from 5yo+ 2lb **10** Ran SP% **116.4**
Speed ratings (Par 103): **111,110,107,107,104 104,100,97,95,88**
CSF £38.46 CT £593.15 TOTE £12.90: £2.70, £1.60, £3.90; EX 54.60 Trifecta £894.60.
Owner The Attwater Partnership **Bred** Mr & Mrs A E Pakenham **Trained** Epsom, Surrey

FOCUS
Not a bad handicap. They went a fair pace and the first pair came clear from the furlong marker.

1145 RACING WELFARE H'CAP 1m 1y(P)
2:40 (2:42) (Class 6) (0-55,55) 4-Y-O+ **£2,587** (£770; £384; £192) **Stalls** High

Form RPR

0644 **1** **Venus Grace**[12] 977 5-9-7 **55** LukeMorris 4 62
(Michael Appleby) *hld up in tch in midfield: effrt to chse ldrs and n.m.r 2f out: drvn and chal ins fnl f: led 75yds out: kpt on* **6/1**

/0-1 **2** *nk* **Theydon Thunder**[7] 1035 4-9-0 **51** 6ex DanielMuscutt[(3)] 3 57
(Peter Charalambous) *chsd ldrs: wd and lost pl bnd wl over 1f out: rallied 1f out: rdn and ev ch ins fnl f: kpt on but hld cl home* **6/4**[1]

-040 **3** *¾* **Togetherwecan (IRE)**[23] 859 4-9-6 **54** SilvestreDeSousa 1 58
(Mark Johnston) *led tl over 5f out: styd w ldr: rdn and ev ch over 2f out: drvn to ld over 1f out: hdd and no ex fnl 75yds* **9/2**[3]

0100 **4** *1½* **Fairy Mist (IRE)**[21] 870 9-9-3 **51** (b) WilliamCarson 2 52
(John Bridger) *trckd ldng trio: effrt on inner u.p over 1f out: pressing ldrs and hrd drvn 1f out: no ex 100yds: wknd towards fin* **16/1**

40-4 **5** *¾* **Play The Blues (IRE)**[21] 876 9-8-13 **50** (t) EoinWalsh[(3)] 7 49
(Henry Tett) *taken down early: stdd s: hld up in tch in rr: clsd on inner and nt clr run 2f out: effrt u.p to chse ldrs 1f out: keeping on same pce and hld whn short of room and swtchd rt towards fin* **14/1**

000- **6** *1½* **Mishrif (USA)**[94] 8370 10-9-7 **55** (b) FrederikTylicki 8 50
(J R Jenkins) *dwlt: sn rcvrd and chsd ldr: led over 5f out: rdn over 2f out: hdd over 1f out: wknd ins fnl f* **16/1**

0524 **7** *2¾* **Foylesideview (IRE)**[12] 986 4-9-2 **50** CathyGannon 6 39
(Harry Chisman) *t.k.h: hld up in tch in midfield: rdn 3f out: sn lost pl: one pce and wl hld fr over 1f out* **4/1**[2]

0-00 **8** *2* **Honey Required**[15] 939 4-8-12 **46** SaleemGolam 5 30
(Alan Bailey) *dwlt: in tch in last pair: pushed along 4f out: outpcd over 2f out: bhd and no imp over 1f out* **66/1**

1m 39.46s (1.26) **Going Correction** +0.025s/f (Slow) **8** Ran SP% **112.4**
Speed ratings (Par 101): **94,93,92,91,90 89,86,84**
CSF £14.88 CT £43.43 TOTE £7.80: £2.40, £1.10, £2.80; EX 18.80 Trifecta £60.20.
Owner Richard and Nicola Hunt **Bred** Rachel Countess Of Coventry **Trained** Oakham, Rutland

FOCUS
A weak handicap thiugh not a bad race of its type, run at an ordinary pace, and it saw a messy finish.

1146 CANTERING CUISINE MAIDEN AUCTION STKS 7f 1y(P)
3:15 (3:16) (Class 5) 3-Y-O **£3,881** (£1,155; £577; £288) **Stalls** Low

Form RPR

1 **Bargain Buy** 3-9-0 0 PatCosgrave 5 73+
(William Haggas) *awkward leaving stalls: hld up in tch towards rr: hdwy to chse ldrs 2f out: rdn to ld 1f out: r.o wl* **3/1**[2]

5- **2** *1* **Lajatico**[252] 4517 3-9-0 0 FrederikTylicki 1 67
(Ed Vaughan) *trckd ldrs: effrt on inner to chal over 1f out: chsd wnr and kpt on same pce ins fnl f: lost 2nd towards fin* **25/1**

04- **3** 1 1/4 **Aldair**[241] 4898 3-9-5 0.......................... SeanLevey 3 69
(Richard Hannon) *led: rdn and hrd pressed over 1f out: hdd 1f out: sn no ex and wknd fnl 100yds* **7/4**[1]

0-35 **4** 2 3/4 **Heads You Win**[40] 633 3-9-0 62.......................... TimmyMurphy 7 57
(Jamie Osborne) *chsd ldrs: wnt 2nd 5f out: rdn and unable qck 2f out: 4th and outpcd over 1f out: kpt on same pce ins fnl f* **16/1**[3]

00- **6** 9 **Concur (IRE)**[295] 3016 3-9-5 0.......................... RobertHavlin 6 37
(Rod Millman) *t.k.h: chsd ldrs tl stdd into midfield over 5f out: hung rt and outpcd bnd 2f out: wknd over 1f out* **66/1**

36 **7** 2 1/4 **Red Rose Riot (IRE)**[20] 885 3-9-0 0.......................... JimCrowley 8 26
(David Menuisier) *s.i.s: hld up in rr: effrt 2f out: sn outpcd and wknd over 1f out* **33/1**

006- **8** 17 **Jersey Roy**[131] 7922 3-9-5 69.......................... TonyHamilton 9
(Richard Fahey) *t.k.h: chsd ldr tl 5f out: chsd ldrs tl rdn and lost pl over 2f out: wl bhd fnl f* **16/1**[3]

00- **9** 1 1/2 **Montague Way (IRE)**[241] 4898 3-9-2 0.......................... RobHornby[(3)] 4
(Andrew Balding) *taken down early: rn green and t.k.h in rr: hdwy on outer 1/2-way: hung rt and dropped to rr over 2f out: wl bhd over 1f out* **25/1**

505- **D** 1 1/4 **Auntie Barber (IRE)**[151] 7629 3-9-0 64.......................... HarryBentley 2 70
(Stuart Williams) *hld up in tch towards rr: effrt in 5th 2f out swtchd rt over 1f out: hdwy u.p 1f out: styd on wl to go 2nd towards fin: no threat to wnr* **3/1**[2]

1m 24.61s (-0.19) **Going Correction** +0.025s/f (Slow) **9** Ran SP% **110.3**
Speed ratings (Par 98): **102,99,98,94,84 82,62,60,100**
CSF £11.29 TOTE £4.00: £1.40, £1.50, £4.70; EX 12.30 Trifecta £147.80.
Owner Sheikh Rashid Dalmook Al Maktoum **Bred** Shane & Nicola O'Neill & R Kent **Trained** Newmarket, Suffolk
■ Dream Voice (16-1) was withdrawn. Rule 4 does not apply.

FOCUS
A modest 3yo maiden. There was a routine pace on and the runner-up sets the level.

1147 CRYSTAL PALACE H'CAP 7f 1y(P)
3:50 (3:50) (Class 6) (0-60,60) 4-Y-O+ **£2,587** (£770; £384; £192) **Stalls** Low

Form RPR

0052 **1** **Not Your Call (IRE)**[7] 1042 5-8-5 **49**.......................... CallumShepherd[(5)] 9 56
(Lee Carter) *taken down early: chsd ldr tl led 2f out: rdn over 1f out: drvn and hld on wl ins fnl f: all out* **8/1**

5400 **2** 1/2 **Blackthorn Stick (IRE)**[14] 951 7-9-3 **56**..........................(p) LiamKeniry 2 62
(Paul Burgoyne) *taken down early: stdd s: hld up in tch in rr: nt clr run over 2f out: hdwy on inner over 1f out: chsd ldrs and drvn ins fnl f: wnt 2nd wl ins fnl f: kpt on but hld cl home* **8/1**

-503 **3** 1/2 **Secret Witness**[21] 873 10-9-7 **60**..........................(b) LukeMorris 5 65
(Ronald Harris) *in tch in midfield: effrt and sltly outpcd wl over 1f out: sn drvn and rallied 1f out: wnt 3rd 50yds: kpt on* **6/1**[3]

3123 **4** 3/4 **Bridge Builder**[70] 257 6-9-3 **59**..........................(p) RobHornby[(3)] 3 62
(Peter Hedger) *chsd ldrs: swtchd rt and effrt over 1f out: drvn to chse wnr ins fnl f: unable qck and lost 2 pls wl ins fnl f* **6/4**[1]

5345 **5** 2 1/2 **Hawk Moth (IRE)**[6] 1064 8-9-4 **57**..........................(p) JimCrowley 1 53
(John Spearing) *in tch in midfield: effrt 2f out: kpt on same pce and no imp ins fnl f* **5/1**[2]

3/4- **6** 2 **Sunshine Always (IRE)**[357] 1271 10-9-7 **60**.......................... KierenFox 4 50
(Michael Attwater) *hld up in tch in last trio: effrt 2f out: no imp u.p fnl f* **14/1**

0-00 **7** 3/4 **Kakapuka**[38] 663 9-9-0 **53**..........................(p) SilvestreDeSousa 8 41
(Anabel K Murphy) *led: hdd 2f out: sn rdn and unable qck: lost 2nd and wknd ins fnl f: eased towards fin* **12/1**

200- **8** 2 1/4 **Mendacious Harpy (IRE)**[169] 7176 5-9-7 **60**.......................... SteveDrowne 7 42
(George Baker) *hld up in tch in last trio: rdn over 2f out: sn outpcd: wl hld and plugged on same pce fr over 1f out* **33/1**

51-6 **9** 24 **Captain Kendall (IRE)**[42] 607 7-8-12 **51**..........................(p) CathyGannon 6
(Harry Chisman) *in tch in midfield: rdn and lost pl over 2f out: wl bhd fnl f* **14/1**

1m 24.82s (0.02) **Going Correction** +0.025s/f (Slow) **9** Ran SP% **117.1**
Speed ratings (Par 101): **100,99,98,98,95 92,92,89,62**
CSF £71.03 CT £417.31 TOTE £10.10: £3.30, £2.10, £2.80; EX 94.00 Trifecta £471.10.
Owner Clear Racing **Bred** Castleton Lyons & Kilboy Estate **Trained** Epsom, Surrey
■ Stewards' Enquiry : Silvestre De Sousa caution: failed to take all reasonable and permissable measures to obtain best possible placing

FOCUS
A moderate handicap, rated around the runner-up.

1148 ORPHEUS CENTRE H'CAP 7f 1y(P)
4:20 (4:20) (Class 6) (0-60,60) 3-Y-O **£2,587** (£770; £384; £192) **Stalls** Low

Form RPR

642 **1** **Music Major**[34] 711 3-8-7 **46** oh1.......................... AdamBeschizza 9 53+
(Michael Attwater) *hld up in tch in last trio: effrt 2f out: swtchd rt and racd v awkwardly over 1f out: str burst ins fnl f to ld fnl 75yds: sn clr* **8/1**

6626 **2** 2 1/4 **Intimately**[34] 711 3-9-1 **54**.......................... RyanClark 4 55
(Jonathan Portman) *t.k.h: chsd ldr: rdn to ld over 1f out: hdd 75yds out: immediately outpcd but kpt on to hold 2nd* **7/1**[3]

-456 **3** 1/2 **Serendib's Glory (IRE)**[26] 817 3-9-0 **60**.......................... MillyNaseb[(7)] 3 60
(Julia Feilden) *chsd ldrs: swtchd rt and effrt over 1f out: rdn and ev ch ins fnl f tl outpcd by wnr 75yds out: kpt on same pce after* **5/1**[2]

05-6 **4** 4 **Aksum**[70] 258 3-9-2 **55**..........................[1] JamieSpencer 6 44
(Michael Bell) *short of room sn after s and dropped to rr: effrt and sltly hmpd wl over 1f out: wnt bdly lft u.p over 1f out: no threat to ldrs and kpt on same pce fnl f* **5/1**[2]

-004 **5** 1 1/2 **Katie Canford**[26] 814 3-9-7 **60**.......................... WilliamCarson 8 45
(John Bridger) *t.k.h: led: rdn and hdd over 1f out: no ex 1f out: wknd ins fnl f* **8/1**

460- **6** shd **Tessellate (IRE)**[154] 7553 3-8-12 **54**.......................... TomMarquand[(3)] 2 39
(Sylvester Kirk) *in tch in midfield: faltered bnd 2f out: swtchd rt and tried to rally over 1f out: no imp and wl hld fnl f* **16/1**

3234 **7** hd **Guapo Bay**[12] 979 3-8-8 **54**..........................(p) TinaSmith[(7)] 7 38
(Richard Hannon) *chsd ldrs 1/2-way: rdn and no ex over 1f out: wknd qckly ins fnl f* **8/1**

-300 **8** 14 **Opera Buffa (IRE)**[55] 443 3-9-5 **58**..........................(b[1]) SilvestreDeSousa 1 5
(Mark Johnston) *hld up in last pair: effrt 2f out: sn btn: wl bhd and eased ins fnl f* **7/1**[3]

4-04 **9** 2 1/2 **Straduff (IRE)**[29] 770 3-9-2 **60**.......................... JosephineGordon[(5)] 5 +
(J S Moore) *wl in tch in midfield: effrt 2f out: sn eased and virtually p.u ins fnl f* **9/2**[1]

1m 25.26s (0.46) **Going Correction** +0.025s/f (Slow) **9** Ran SP% **115.7**
Speed ratings (Par 96): **98,95,94,90,88 88,88,72,69**
CSF £62.81 CT £312.66 TOTE £8.10: £2.50, £2.70, £1.80; EX 59.90 Trifecta £423.60.
Owner Miss K Squance **Bred** Kevin Daniel Crabb **Trained** Epsom, Surrey

FOCUS
This weak 0-60 looked wide open. It was run at a sound pace and the principals were clear at the finish.

1149 RYAN VEHICLES MEDIAN AUCTION MAIDEN FILLIES' STKS 1m 4f (P)
4:55 (4:57) (Class 6) 3-Y-O **£2,587** (£770; £384; £192) **Stalls** Low

Form RPR

00-6 **1** **Spinning Pearl (IRE)**[35] 699 3-9-0 63.......................... JohnFahy 5 63+
(Eve Johnson Houghton) *chsd ldr tl led over 3f out: rdn 2f out and clr over 1f out: kpt on and a doing enough fnl f: eased towards fin* **7/2**[2]

2- **2** 1 1/2 **Siri**[202] 6233 3-9-0 0.......................... SilvestreDeSousa 6 59+
(Mick Channon) *hld up in tch in 5th: swtchd rt and hdwy over 2f out: drvn over 1f out: wnt 3 l 2nd 1f out: styd on but nvr threatened wnr* **30/100**[1]

00-5 **3** 2 1/2 **Regal Galaxy**[69] 274 3-9-0 42.......................... SaleemGolam 1 55
(Mark H Tompkins) *chsd ldrs: effrt on inner over 2f out: chsd wnr 2f out tl 1f out: 3rd and styd on same pce fnl f* **25/1**

4 1 1/2 **Happy Girl** 3-9-0 0.......................... WilliamCarson 7 52
(Dr Jon Scargill) *stdd and swtchd lft after s: hld up in tch in rr: hdwy on outer 3f out: outpcd 2f out: kpt on ins fnl f to go 4th fnl 75yds: no threat to wnr* **20/1**[3]

00- **5** 1 1/2 **Little Orchid**[140] 7793 3-9-0 0.......................... AdamBeschizza 4 50
(Julia Feilden) *in tch in 4th: rdn to chse ldr wl over 2f out tl 2f out: outpcd and btn over 1f out: kpt on same pce fnl f* **50/1**

0-0 **6** 3 1/4 **Perusal (IRE)**[85] 44 3-8-7 0.......................... CharlieBennett[(7)] 3 45
(Jonathan Portman) *led tl over 3f out: lost pl u.p over 1f out: bhd over 1f out* **25/1**

2m 38.16s (5.16) **Going Correction** +0.025s/f (Slow) **6** Ran SP% **113.6**
Speed ratings (Par 93): **83,82,80,79,78 76**
CSF £5.01 TOTE £4.30: £1.90, £1.02; EX 5.60 Trifecta £23.40.
Owner Miss E Johnson Houghton **Bred** T Cahalan & D Cahalan **Trained** Blewbury, Oxon

FOCUS
This very weak maiden was run at an uneven pace, which proved the undoing of the hot favourite.

1150 CENTREPOINT H'CAP 5f 6y(P)
5:25 (5:27) (Class 5) (0-70,70) 4-Y-O+ **£3,881** (£1,155; £577; £288) **Stalls** High

Form RPR

-500 **1** **Picansort**[29] 775 9-9-0 **63**..........................(b) ShaneKelly 1 73
(Peter Crate) *hld up in tch: clsd to trck ldrs and travelling strly 2f out: rdn to ld 1f out: sn qcknd clr: readily* **5/1**

0-00 **2** 3 3/4 **Pucon**[19] 903 7-9-6 **69**..........................(p) LiamKeniry 5 66
(Roger Teal) *racd freely: led: rdn over 1f out: hdd 1f out: sn outpcd by wnr but hld on to 2nd wl ins fnl f* **14/1**

-446 **3** nk **Zipedeedodah (IRE)**[54] 462 4-8-11 **65**..........................(t) EdwardGreatrex[(5)] 8 60
(Joseph Tuite) *midfield: clsd over 1f out: swtchd lft and drvn 1f out: styd on wl ins fnl f: no ch w wnr* **7/1**

0436 **4** nk **Agerzam**[18] 919 6-9-4 **67**..........................(b) RoystonFfrench 3 61
(Ronald Harris) *stdd s: hld up in rr: clsd and swtchd lft over 1f out: styd on strly ins fnl f: no ch w wnr* **14/1**

-235 **5** nk **Pharoh Jake**[21] 873 8-8-8 **57**.......................... WilliamCarson 2 50
(John Bridger) *chsd ldr: drvn to press ldr but unable qck over 1f out: no ch w wnr and styd on same pce ins fnl f* **9/2**[3]

4-60 **6** hd **Honcho (IRE)**[7] 1040 4-9-7 **70**..........................(v) AdamKirby 6 63
(John Ryan) *dwlt: sn in midfield: effrt over 1f out: styd on ins fnl f: no threat to wnr* **3/1**[1]

505- **7** 1/2 **Perfect Pastime**[163] 7349 8-9-5 **68**..........................(p) PatCosgrave 4 59
(Jim Boyle) *sn outpcd in last pair: rdn and hdwy on inner over 1f out: styd on same pce and no imp ins fnl f* **8/1**

4326 **8** 3/4 **Ask The Guru**[19] 903 6-9-1 **64**..........................(v) KierenFox 7 52
(Michael Attwater) *chsd ldrs: rdn 2f out: lost pl over 1f out: wknd ins fnl f* **4/1**[2]

0-50 **9** 7 **Bubbly Bailey**[21] 872 6-8-11 **60**..........................(v) FrederikTylicki 9 23
(J R Jenkins) *midfield but stuck wd: lost pl bnd 2f out: bhd fnl f* **20/1**

58.31s (-0.49) **Going Correction** +0.025s/f (Slow) **9** Ran SP% **121.6**
Speed ratings (Par 103): **104,98,97,97,96 96,95,94,83**
CSF £75.46 CT £503.74 TOTE £6.50: £2.50, £2.60, £3.30; EX 80.20 Trifecta £906.60.
Owner Peter Crate **Bred** Miss Brooke Sanders **Trained** Newdigate, Surrey

FOCUS
Predictably there was no hanging about in this moderate sprint handicap.
T/Plt: £55.30 to a £1 stake. Pool: £70,966.38 - 936.45 winning tickets. T/Qpdt: £14.10 to a £1 stake. Pool: £5,907.12 - 309.61 winning tickets. **Steve Payne**

1043 SOUTHWELL (L-H)
Wednesday, March 30

OFFICIAL GOING: Fibresand: standard
Wind: Moderate half behind Weather: Fine and dry

1151 SOUTHWELLGOLFGLUB.COM MAIDEN STKS 6f (F)
2:20 (2:23) (Class 5) 3-Y-O+ **£3,881** (£1,155; £577; £288) **Stalls** Low

Form RPR

1 **African Blessing** 3-9-1 0.......................... GrahamGibbons 6 72
(David Barron) *trckd ldrs: hdwy over 2f out: chal wl over 1f out: rdn and slt ld ent fnl f: kpt on wl towards fin* **13/2**

6 **2** nk **Silver Bid (USA)**[5] 1079 4-10-0 0.......................... FrannyNorton 5 75
(Alan Bailey) *trckd ldrs on inner: hdwy over 2f out: rdn to chal over 1f out: drvn and ev ch ins fnl f: no ex towards fin* **7/2**[2]

32 **3** 2 1/2 **Spice Mill (IRE)**[15] 935 3-9-1 0.......................... OisinMurphy 9 63
(Robert Cowell) *prom: wd st: led jst over 2f out: sn rdn and edgd lft: hdd and drvn ent fnl f: kpt on same pce* **11/4**[1]

30-3 **4** 2 1/4 **Iconic Figure (IRE)**[76] 177 3-9-1 70.......................... SamJames 11 56
(Steve Gollings) *chsd ldrs: wd st: rdn along and outpcd over 2f out: kpt on u.p fnl f* **16/1**

246- **5** hd **Avalanche Express**[215] 5807 4-10-0 72.......................... MartinDwyer 1 59
(William Muir) *cl up: rdn along over 2f out: n.m.r wl over 1f out: sn drvn and kpt on one pce* **6/1**[3]

40 **6** nk **Aegean Boy**[15] 935 3-9-1 0.......................... AndrewMullen 7 54
(Michael Appleby) *chsd ldrs: rdn along over 2f out: no imp fr over 1f out* **66/1**

00- **7** 1 1/2 **Ordinal**[156] 7516 3-9-1 0.......................... JoeFanning 8 49
(Mark Johnston) *chsd ldrs on outer: wd st: rdn wl over 1f out: no imp fnl f* **7/1**

4 **8** 1 **Chez Vegas**[15] 935 3-9-1 0.......................... BenCurtis 12 46
(Scott Dixon) *in tch on outer: wd st: rdn along over 2f out: sn no imp* **16/1**

4-0 **9** 3 **St Andrews (IRE)**[5] 1079 3-8-12 0.......................... GeorgeDowning[(3)] 3 37
(Ian Williams) *a towards rr* **25/1**

10 *nk* **Kestrel Dot Com** 4-10-0 0 IrineuGoncalves 4 40
(Chris Dwyer) *a towards rr* **66/1**

0 **11** *15* **Eddy Mercs**[43] 600 4-10-0 0 RaulDaSilva 2
(Ivan Furtado) *dwlt: sn outpcd in rr* **50/1**

12 *3/4* **Ay Up Audrey** 5-9-9 0 PaulMulrennan 10
(Rebecca Bastiman) *dwlt and towards rr: rdn along and sme hdwy 1/2-way: sn wknd* **100/1**

0 **13** *2 3/4* **Desafinado (IRE)**[60] 402 4-9-9 0 GeorgeBaker 13
(Miss Joey Ellis) *sn led: rdn along 3f out: hdd jst over 2f out: sn drvn and edgd rt over 1f out: wknd qckly and eased* **33/1**

1m 15.13s (-1.37) **Going Correction** -0.275s/f (Stan)
WFA 3 from 4yo+ 13lb **13** Ran SP% **113.5**
Speed ratings (Par 103): **98,97,94,91,91 90,88,87,83,82 62,61,58**
CSF £26.86 TOTE £8.50: £2.40, £2.30, £1.10; EX 35.40 Trifecta £118.60.
Owner M Rozenbroek **Bred** Michael Turner **Trained** Maunby, N Yorks

FOCUS
A modest maiden, but an open one and it resulted in a thrilling finish between two horses that are entitled to improve further. The race has been rated around the third.

1152 HAPPY WEDDING ANNIVERSARY DENNIS AND MARY H'CAP 1m (F)
2:50 (2:51) (Class 4) (0-80,80) 4-Y-O+ **£5,175** (£1,540; £769; £384) **Stalls** Low

Form RPR

0-36 **1** **Pearl Spectre (USA)**[74] 215 5-9-4 **77** OisinMurphy 7 87
(Andrew Balding) *cl up: led 1 1/2f out and sn rdn: drvn and edgd lft ins fnl f: kpt on wl towards fin* **5/2**[2]

-411 **2** *3/4* **Red Touch (USA)**[14] 956 4-9-4 **80** AlistairRawlinson(3) 5 88
(Michael Appleby) *in rr and sn pushed along: hdwy wl over 2f out: rdn and edgd lft wl over 1f out: sn drvn along on inner to chse ldng pair: kpt on wl u.p: tk 2nd nr fin* **2/1**[1]

265- **3** *1/2* **Sophisticated Heir (IRE)**[155] 7526 6-9-3 **76** DavidNolan 4 83
(David Loughnane) *led: rdn along wl over 2f out: hdd 1 1/2f out: sn drvn: kpt on same pce fnl f* **20/1**

13-3 **4** *2 1/4* **Beautiful Stranger (IRE)**[28] 788 5-8-12 **71** (p) PhillipMakin 6 73
(Keith Dalgleish) *trckd ldrs: effrt wl over 2f out and sn rdn: drvn over 1f out: no imp fnl f* **6/1**[3]

560- **5** *3/4* **Freewheel (IRE)**[316] 2371 6-9-5 **78** DavidAllan 1 78
(Garry Moss) *chsd ldrs on inner: rdn along wl over 2f out: drvn over 1f out: kpt on same pce* **20/1**

1303 **6** *nk* **Patriotic (IRE)**[22] 866 8-9-6 **79** (p) ConnorBeasley 9 79
(Chris Dwyer) *awkward s and towards rr: hdwy on outer and wd st: rdn to chse ldrs over 2f out: sn drvn and no imp* **13/2**

1103 **7** *2 1/2* **The Firm (IRE)**[14] 956 7-8-7 **66** (be) AndrewMullen 8 60
(Daniel Mark Loughnane) *in tch: wd st: rdn over 2f out: sn drvn and one pce* **20/1**

-555 **8** *3 1/2* **Lawyer (IRE)**[27] 802 5-8-12 **71** GrahamGibbons 2 57
(David Barron) *cl up on inner: rdn along wl over 2f out: sn drvn and wknd* **12/1**

0-05 **9** *8* **Illusive Force (IRE)**[14] 959 4-8-2 **66** AaronJones(5) 3 33
(Derek Shaw) *chsd ldrs: rdn along 3f out: sn drvn and wknd* **80/1**

1m 40.82s (-2.88) **Going Correction** -0.275s/f (Stan) **9** Ran SP% **112.7**
Speed ratings (Par 105): **103,102,101,99,98 98,95,92,84**
CSF £7.21 CT £74.21 TOTE £2.90: £1.60, £1.10, £6.60; EX 7.20 Trifecta £110.80.
Owner Qatar Racing Limited **Bred** Estate Of Edward P Evans **Trained** Kingsclere, Hants

FOCUS
A fair handicap in which it paid to be handy. A personal best from the winner.

1153 VISIT ATTHERACES.COM H'CAP 7f (F)
3:25 (3:25) (Class 2) (0-105,103) 4-Y-O+
£12,450 (£3,728; £1,864; £932; £466; £234) **Stalls** Low

Form RPR

1011 **1** **Moon River (IRE)**[14] 960 4-8-6 **88** BenCurtis 8 99
(Michael Appleby) *cl up: led over 2f out: rdn over 1f out: drvn out* **11/4**[1]

035- **2** *1 1/4* **Claim The Roses (USA)**[154] 7547 5-8-8 **90** ow1 OisinMurphy 4 98
(Ed Vaughan) *trckd ldrs: effrt and hdwy 2f out: rdn over 1f out: drvn to chse wnr ins fnl f: kpt on* **17/2**

50-5 **3** *3 1/4* **Lexington Times (IRE)**[26] 816 4-9-0 **96** KieranO'Neill 10 96
(Richard Hannon) *dwlt: sn chsng ldrs: hdwy over 3f out: rdn to chal 2f out: drvn to chse wnr over 1f out: kpt on same pce* **9/1**

062- **4** *1 1/2* **Highland Colori (IRE)**[109] 8199 8-9-3 **99** DavidProbert 6 95
(Andrew Balding) *towards rr: rdn along wl over 2f out: swtchd lft towards inner wl over 1f out: styd on appr fnl f* **5/1**[2]

5-00 **5** *shd* **Pearl Nation (USA)**[41] 624 7-9-6 **102** AndrewMullen 2 97
(Michael Appleby) *towards rr: rdn along over 2f out: drvn wl over 1f out: kpt on fnl f* **12/1**

1214 **6** *1* **Philba**[14] 960 4-8-7 **92** (tp) AlistairRawlinson(3) 5 85
(Michael Appleby) *sn slt ld: hdd wl over 2f out and sn rdn along: drvn wl over 1f out: grad wknd* **11/2**[3]

5065 **7** *nk* **Bertiewhittle**[25] 833 8-8-5 **87** SamJames 1 79
(David Barron) *stdd and swtchd rt sn after s: hld up: a towards rr* **33/1**

-433 **8** *1 1/2* **Showboating (IRE)**[14] 960 8-8-8 **90** (p) ShaneGray 7 78
(John Balding) *hld up towards rr on outer: wd st: rdn over 2f out: n.d* **11/1**

10-0 **9** *3/4* **Sound Advice**[18] 920 7-9-7 **103** PhillipMakin 3 89
(Keith Dalgleish) *chsd ldrs on inner: rdn along 3f out: sn wknd* **25/1**

6012 **10** *3/4* **Trojan Rocket (IRE)**[14] 960 8-8-2 **89** (p) AaronJones(5) 9 73
(Michael Wigham) *dwlt: sn chsng ldrs: rdn along and wd st: sn wknd* **15/2**

1m 26.38s (-3.92) **Going Correction** -0.275s/f (Stan) course record **10** Ran SP% **113.8**
Speed ratings (Par 109): **111,109,105,104,104 102,102,100,99,99**
CSF £26.02 CT £188.38 TOTE £3.00: £1.20, £2.70, £2.90; EX 28.60 Trifecta £278.30.
Owner Craig Buckingham **Bred** Rockhart Trading Ltd **Trained** Oakham, Rutland

FOCUS
A red-hot Fibresand handicap. Four of these met in a 0-95 over C&D two weeks earlier and the 1-2-3-4 from that race finished 1-10-8-6 here. The pace was solid with two of the Mick Appleby trio forcing the tempo, but still very few ever got into it. They took 0.22sec off of Philba's previous course record.

1154 DENNIS WHEATLEY 60TH BIRTHDAY H'CAP 6f (F)
4:00 (4:01) (Class 5) (0-70,69) 4-Y-O+ **£3,881** (£1,155; £577; £288) **Stalls** Low

Form RPR

4414 **1** **Harwoods Star (IRE)**[14] 963 6-9-7 **69** (be) JFEgan 2 79
(John Butler) *chsd ldrs on inner: hdwy wl over 2f out: rdn to chse ldr wl over 1f out: drvn ent fnl f: styd on wl to ld nr fin* **8/1**[3]

0220 **2** *nk* **Fujin**[19] 903 5-9-5 **67** (b) TomEaves 6 76
(Shaun Harris) *led: pushed clr over 2f out: rdn over 1f out: drvn ins fnl f: hdd and no ex towards fin* **8/1**[3]

6200 **3** *4 1/2* **Alpha Tauri (USA)**[20] 893 10-9-4 **66** DavidNolan 7 61
(Charles Smith) *chsd ldrs: wd st: rdn over 2f out: drvn and kpt on same pce fnl f* **12/1**

30-0 **4** *1/2* **Teetotal (IRE)**[15] 943 6-8-6 **61** KieranSchofield(7) 1 54
(Nigel Tinkler) *dwlt and towards rr: hdwy on inner 3f out: rdn to chse ldrs wl over 1f out: drvn and kpt on same pce fnl f* **50/1**

043- **5** *hd* **Giant Spark**[148] 7680 4-9-0 **62** PaulMulrennan 5 54
(Paul Midgley) *dwlt: sn in tch: hdwy 3f out: rdn to chse ldrs whn rdr dropped whip 2f out: kpt on same pce after* **17/2**

0641 **6** *1/2* **Coiste Bodhar (IRE)**[8] 1026 5-8-13 **61** 6ex KieranO'Neill 3 52
(Scott Dixon) *cl up: rdn along wl over 2f out: drvn wl over 1f out: sn wknd* **16/1**

0233 **7** *3 1/4* **Spowarticus**[8] 1030 7-9-3 **65** (b) BenCurtis 4 45
(Scott Dixon) *prom: rdn wl over 2f out: drvn wl over 1f out: sn wknd* **10/3**[2]

646- **8** *nk* **Commanche**[163] 7345 7-9-0 **62** (b) IrineuGoncalves 8 41
(Chris Dwyer) *a towards rr* **10/1**

540- **9** *1/2* **Exotic Guest**[183] 6830 6-9-7 **69** (e[1]) JamesSullivan 11 47
(Ruth Carr) *a towards rr* **33/1**

3351 **10** *1/2* **Monsieur Jimmy**[27] 799 4-9-6 **68** (b) DanielTudhope 9 44
(Declan Carroll) *dwlt: bhd and wd st: nvr a factor* **2/1**[1]

1m 14.24s (-2.26) **Going Correction** -0.275s/f (Stan) **10** Ran SP% **116.7**
Speed ratings (Par 103): **104,103,97,96,96 96,91,91,90,89**
CSF £70.47 CT £785.65 TOTE £8.20: £1.60, £4.30, £3.40; EX 61.10 Trifecta £406.70.
Owner Jameson Racing Ltd **Bred** Barronstown Stud **Trained** Newmarket, Suffolk

FOCUS
An ordinary sprint handicap, but fast and furious stuff and another contest that suited the prominent racers.

1155 VISITSOUTHWELL.COM H'CAP 1m (F)
4:30 (4:30) (Class 5) (0-75,75) 3-Y-O **£3,881** (£1,155; £577; £288) **Stalls** Low

Form RPR

-311 **1** **Pirate's Treasure**[37] 678 3-9-6 **74** DavidAllan 4 86+
(James Tate) *t.k.h: trckd ldrs: hdwy 3f out: chal over 2f out: rdn to ld 1 1/2f out: styd on strly* **9/4**[1]

-104 **2** *1 3/4* **Secret Insider (USA)**[18] 924 3-9-6 **74** GrahamGibbons 1 81
(Hugo Palmer) *cl up: led over 3f out: rdn and jnd over 2f out: hdd 1 1/2f out: drvn and kpt on same pce fnl f* **8/1**

532- **3** *1 1/4* **Planetaria (IRE)**[113] 8143 3-8-12 **66** JamesSullivan 8 70
(Garry Moss) *cl up on outer: pushed along 1/2-way: sn lost pl and towards rr: rdn wl over 2f out: drvn wl over 1f out: styd on fnl f* **11/1**

-012 **4** *1/2* **Daisy Bere (FR)**[49] 522 3-8-10 **71** CliffordLee(7) 6 74
(K R Burke) *chsd ldrs on outer: wd st: rdn 2f out: kpt on fnl f* **3/1**[2]

3110 **5** *3/4* **Kemsing (IRE)**[33] 725 3-8-10 **67** (p) ShelleyBirkett(3) 3 68
(Julia Feilden) *towards rr: hdwy on inner 3f out: rdn to chse ldrs 2f out: drvn over 1f out: kpt on same pce* **9/1**

01- **6** *6* **Davey Boy**[139] 7816 3-9-4 **75** LouisSteward(3) 7 62
(Michael Bell) *slt ld to 1/2-way: cl up: rdn along wl over 2f out: sn wknd* **16/1**

452- **7** *nse* **Hollywood Ken (IRE)**[239] 4958 3-9-0 **68** PhillipMakin 5 55
(Keith Dalgleish) *t.k.h: trckd ldrs: hdwy and cl up over 3f out: rdn over 2f out: sn drvn and grad wknd* **5/1**[3]

00-6 **8** *5* **Esspeegee**[37] 675 3-8-4 **58** KieranO'Neill 2 34
(Alan Bailey) *sn rdn along and outpcd: bhd fr 1/2-way* **100/1**

1m 41.05s (-2.65) **Going Correction** -0.275s/f (Stan) **8** Ran SP% **108.8**
Speed ratings (Par 98): **102,100,99,98,97 91,91,86**
CSF £18.77 CT £143.42 TOTE £3.80: £1.80, £1.80, £2.60; EX 21.50 Trifecta £156.70.
Owner Saif Ali **Bred** Meon Valley Stud **Trained** Newmarket, Suffolk

FOCUS
An ordinary 3yo handicap, but the winner continues to progress.

1156 SOUTHWELL GOLF MEMBERSHIP AMATEUR RIDERS' H'CAP 1m 6f (F)
5:05 (5:06) (Class 6) (0-65,65) 4-Y-O+ **£3,119** (£967; £483; £242) **Stalls** Low

Form RPR

3021 **1** **Moonshine Ridge (IRE)**[7] 1049 5-10-10 **61** 6ex MrSWalker 3 67
(Alan Swinbank) *trckd ldrs: hdwy over 3f out: chsd ldr wl over 2f out: rdn wl over 1f out: slt ld ent fnl f: sn drvn and kpt on wl towards fin* **7/4**[2]

-030 **2** *1 1/4* **Quadriga (IRE)**[6] 1064 6-9-8 **52** MissJAHeneghan(7) 1 56
(Philip Kirby) *awkward and rdr lost iron s: sn rcvrd and trckd ldng pair on inner: effrt 3f out: cl up over 2f out: sn rdn and ev ch tl drvn and no ex ins fnl f* **25/1**

4/1 **3** *2* **Down Time (USA)**[14] 957 6-10-9 **65** (b) MissLWilson(5) 7 67
(Brian Ellison) *trckd ldrs: hdwy to trck ldng pair over 5f out: led 4f out: rdn over 2f out: drvn over 1f out: edgd lft to inner rail and hdd ent fnl f: kpt on same pce* **8/11**[1]

0-54 **4** *8* **Monzino (USA)**[12] 891 8-9-13 **50** MissSBrotherton 8 41
(Michael Chapman) *in tch: pushed along over 4f out: rdn along over 3f out: drvn and plugged on fnl 2f* **33/1**

606- **5** *4* **Weybridge Light**[89] 8198 11-9-6 **48** (b) MrMEnnis(5) 5 34
(David Thompson) *cl up: pushed along 4f out: rdn 3f out: wknd fnl 2f* **28/1**

231- **6** *27* **The Ducking Stool**[159] 7436 9-10-13 **64** MrRBirkett 2 15
(Julia Feilden) *set stdy pce: pushed along 5f out: hdd 4f out: rdn along over 3f out: sn wknd and bhd* **16/1**[3]

/060 **7** *92* **Deadline Day (IRE)**[7] 1038 5-9-9 **46** (bt) MissMMullineaux 6
(Michael Mullineaux) *a in rr: pushed along after 4f: rdn along 1/2-way: sn lost tch and wl bhd fnl 3f* **50/1**

3m 6.78s (-1.52) **Going Correction** -0.275s/f (Stan) **7** Ran SP% **112.3**
Speed ratings (Par 101): **93,92,91,86,84 68,16**
CSF £40.57 CT £53.62 TOTE £2.40: £1.10, £7.10; EX 36.20 Trifecta £53.00.
Owner Elm Row Racing Syndicate **Bred** Maddenstown Equine Enterprise Ltd **Trained** Melsonby, N Yorks

FOCUS
A moderate staying handicap for amateur riders.

T/Plt: £74.80 to a £1 stake. Pool: £85,174.00 - 831.07 winning tickets T/Qpdt: £40.40 to a £1 stake. Pool: £6,512.66 - 119.10 winning tickets **Joe Rowntree**

AMIENS (R-H)
Wednesday, March 30

OFFICIAL GOING: Turf: heavy

1157a PRIX D'ABBEVILLE (CLAIMER) (4YO+) (TURF) 1m 3f
6:40 (12:00) 4-Y-O+ **£4,779** (£1,911; £1,433; £955; £477)

RPR

1 **Demoiselledavignon (FR)**[33] 5-8-7 0........................(p) PierreBazire(6) 4 62
(P Adda, France) **73/10**

2 *shd* **Funky Mary (GER)**[94] 7-9-3 0........................ RonanThomas 7 66
(J Phelippon, France) **19/5**[2]

3 *5* **Murillo (FR)**[100] 6-9-2 0........................ AnthonyCrastus 10 56
(M Boutin, France) **5/1**[3]

4 *1 1/4* **Grand Akbar (FR)**[18] 9-9-6 0........................ Pierre-CharlesBoudot 6 58
(J Phelippon, France) **6/4**[1]

5 *1* **Endio (FR)**[27] 6-8-13 0........................(p) TheoBachelot 5 49
(T Castanheira, France) **63/10**

6 *1 1/2* **Yankee Mail (FR)**[169] 7208 4-8-13 0........................ DougieCostello 8 47
(K R Burke) *cl up on outer: sltly outpcd and shkn up 3f out: rdn and no imp appr 1 1/2f out: wknd fnl f* **18/1**

7 *10* **Norberina (FR)**[236] 4-8-9 0........................ LudovicBoisseau(4) 2 29
(G Cherel, France) **17/1**

8 *6* **No Contest (FR)**[94] 5-8-6 0........................ EmmanuelEtienne(5) 1 15
(G Doleuze, France) **57/1**

9 *15* **La Messalina (FR)**[213] 6-8-8 0........................ DavidBreux 9
(M Aubry, France) **30/1**

2m 44.49s (164.49)
WFA 4 from 5yo+ 1lb **9** Ran SP% **119.0**
WIN (incl. 1 euro stake): 8.30 PLACES: 2.40, 1.70, 2.10. . DF: 20.30. SF: 44.10.
Owner Ecurie Mansonnienne **Bred** Razza Della Sila Srl **Trained** France

964 CHELMSFORD (A.W) (L-H)
Thursday, March 31

OFFICIAL GOING: Polytrack: standard
Wind: light, half against Weather: heavy rain until race 2, dry after

1158 BET TOTEEXACTA FILLIES' H'CAP 1m (P)
6:05 (6:06) (Class 5) (0-75,75) 4-Y-O+ **£5,175** (£1,540; £769; £384) **Stalls** Low

Form RPR

506- 1 **Clotilde**[267] 4033 4-9-4 **72**........................ RichardKingscote 5 82+
(William Knight) *pressed ldrs: gng best 2f out: pushed along and qckdn to ld over 1f out: sn in command: pushed out: comf* **15/8**[1]

06-0 2 *2 1/4* **Deep Blue Sea**[47] 564 4-9-4 **72**........................(t) WilliamCarson 6 77
(Anthony Carson) *stdd and dropped in bhd after s: hld up in tch in rr: effrt over 2f out: hung lft but hdwy over 1f out: stl hanging but styd on to go 2nd wl ins fnl f: no threat to wnr* **7/2**[2]

300- 3 *1 1/4* **Maureb (IRE)**[196] 6473 4-9-2 **70**........................ BarryMcHugh 4 72
(Tony Coyle) *t.k.h: stdd bk towards rr after 1f out: effrt over 1f out: hdwy ins fnl f: styd on to snatch 3rd last strides: no ch w wnr* **12/1**

6005 4 *hd* **Pretty Bubbles**[12] 1003 7-9-7 **75**........................(v) FrederikTylicki 2 77
(J R Jenkins) *chsd ldrs: effrt u.p over 1f out: wnt 2nd but no threat to wnr 1f out: plugged on same pce after: lost 2 pls wl ins fnl f* **7/2**[2]

1-16 5 *2 1/4* **Honiton Lace**[20] 904 5-8-2 **56**........................(tp) KieranO'Neill 1 52
(Phil McEntee) *awkward leaving stalls: t.k.h: hld up in tch towards rr: hdwy on inner over 1f out: drvn and no imp 1f out: wknd ins fnl f* **14/1**

-420 6 *2 3/4* **Primrose Brown**[49] 532 5-8-9 **66**........................ DanielMuscutt(3) 7 56
(Conrad Allen) *sn led: rdn 2f out: hdd over 1f out and sn btn: wknd ins fnl f* **8/1**[3]

430- 7 *3 1/4* **Fidelma Moon (IRE)**[204] 6211 4-9-5 **73**........................ DougieCostello 3 56
(K R Burke) *t.k.h: in tch in midfield: rdn and unable qck over 1f out: sn lost pl and bhd ins fnl f* **8/1**[3]

1m 37.92s (-1.98) **Going Correction** -0.225s/f (Stan) **7** Ran SP% **115.8**
Speed ratings (Par 100): **100,97,96,96,94 91,88**
CSF £8.86 TOTE £2.80: £1.80, £2.50; EX 9.80 Trifecta £62.60.
Owner Chasemore Farm **Bred** Chasemore Farm **Trained** Patching, W Sussex

FOCUS
A modest fillies' handicap, but the winner took it with ease.

1159 BET TOTETRIFECTA H'CAP 6f (P)
6:40 (6:41) (Class 5) (0-70,70) 4-Y-O+ **£5,175** (£1,540; £769; £384) **Stalls** Centre

Form RPR

6000 1 **Colourbearer (IRE)**[28] 799 9-8-13 **62**........................(t) BenCurtis 3 73
(Charlie Wallis) *mde all: rdn clr over 1f out: styd on wl fnl f: rdn out* **20/1**

3042 2 *1 1/2* **Nasri**[15] 955 10-9-3 **66**........................ TomQueally 2 72
(Emma Owen) *chsd ldng pair: effrt over 1f out: drvn and chsd clr wnr ins fnl f: styd on but nvr enough pce to chal* **14/1**

2414 3 *3/4* **National Service (USA)**[16] 942 5-9-4 **67**........................(tp) PaulMulrennan 1 71
(Rebecca Menzies) *hld up in tch in midfield: nt clrest of runs and swtchd rt ent fnl f: rdn and styd on to go 3rd wl ins fnl f: no ch w wnr* **9/1**[3]

5644 4 *1* **Malaysian Boleh**[20] 901 6-9-2 **70**........................(b) CallumShepherd(5) 10 70
(Shaun Lycett) *hld up in tch in rr of main gp: effrt over 1f out: clsng whn sltly hmpd and switching lft 1f out: styd on u.p ins fnl f: wnt 4th cl home: nvr trbld ldrs* **6/1**[2]

3-23 5 *nk* **Ghost Train (IRE)**[43] 615 7-9-0 **63**........................(p) LukeMorris 4 62
(Tim McCarthy) *in tch in midfield: effrt over 1f out: chsd wnr briefly 1f out: sn lost 2nd and btn: outpcd fnl 100yds* **10/1**

506- 6 *2 3/4* **Refuse Colette (IRE)**[152] 7635 7-9-5 **68**........................ WilliamCarson 5 59
(Mick Quinn) *chsd wnr: rdn over 2f out: unable qck over 1f out: lost 2nd 1f out: wknd ins fnl f* **25/1**

-512 7 *nk* **New Rich**[22] 873 6-9-2 **65**........................(b) JohnFahy 8 55
(Eve Johnson Houghton) *in rr: rdn over 2f out: swtchd lft over 1f out: kpt on ins fnl f: nvr trbld ldrs* **11/1**

0211 8 *1 1/4* **Eljaddaaf (IRE)**[22] 872 5-9-3 **66**........................ RobertWinston 6 52
(Dean Ivory) *chsd ldrs: effrt over 1f out: fnd little and btn 1f out: wknd ins fnl f* **5/6**[1]

5-50 9 *1/2* **Mutafaakir (IRE)**[16] 942 7-9-4 **67**........................ JamesSullivan 11 51
(Ruth Carr) *in tch in midfield: lost pl and hrd drvn wl over 1f out: no imp and wl hld 1f out* **50/1**

2-50 P **Spinning Cobblers**[29] 782 5-8-11 **67**........................(v) MillyNaseb(7) 7
(Stuart Williams) *stdd and wnt lft s: detached in rr: lost action over 4f out: sn eased p.u and dismntd (fatally injured)* **10/1**

1m 11.39s (-2.31) **Going Correction** -0.225s/f (Stan) **10** Ran SP% **122.6**
Speed ratings (Par 103): **106,104,103,101,101 97,97,95,94,**
CSF £278.82 CT £1767.78 TOTE £22.80: £4.10, £1.80, £2.90; EX 144.90 Trifecta £5150.40.
Owner Roalco Limited **Bred** Corduff Stud & J Corcorcan **Trained** Ardleigh, Essex

FOCUS
A modest sprint dominated from the front.

1160 ROGER EVANS 70TH CLASSIC MEDIAN AUCTION MAIDEN STKS 1m (P)
7:10 (7:11) (Class 5) 3-5-Y-O **£5,175** (£1,540; £769; £384) **Stalls** Low

Form RPR

622- 1 **Havre De Paix (FR)**[167] 7257 4-9-9 89........................ JimCrowley 4 84
(David Menuisier) *mde all: rdn clr over 1f out: r.o wl and in command fnl f: readily* **3/1**[2]

56- 2 *2* **Both Sides**[242] 4905 3-8-11 0........................ DavidProbert 1 79
(Andrew Balding) *chsd wnr tl 4f out and again 2f out: rdn over 1f out: clr 2nd but no imp on wnr ins fnl f: kpt on* **8/1**[3]

5 3 *6* **Dangerous Secret**[27] 814 3-8-6 0........................ WilliamCarson 5 60
(Dr Jon Scargill) *stdd s: hld up in last pair: rdn over 2f out: swtchd rt and outpcd over 1f out: no ch w ldng pair fnl f: wnt 3rd cl home* **20/1**

03- 4 *3/4* **Timeless Art (IRE)**[173] 7123 3-8-11 0........................ DougieCostello 2 63
(K R Burke) *t.k.h: chsd ldng pair tl wnt 2nd 4f out tl 2f out: sn rdn and no rspnse: 3rd and wl btn 1f out: lost 3rd cl home* **1/2**[1]

5 5 *11* **Motivate**[12] 1000 3-8-11 0........................ LukeMorris 3 38
(Sir Mark Prescott Bt) *in tch in last pair: rdn over 3f out: sn drifted rt and outpcd: wl bhd fnl f* **25/1**

1m 37.77s (-2.13) **Going Correction** -0.225s/f (Stan)
WFA 3 from 4yo 17lb **5** Ran SP% **111.4**
Speed ratings (Par 103): **101,99,93,92,81**
CSF £24.56 TOTE £3.20: £1.70, £3.00; EX 19.30 Trifecta £71.00.
Owner Clive Washbourn **Bred** Mme Elisabeth Erbeya **Trained** Pulborough, W Sussex

FOCUS
A steadily run maiden.

1161 TOTEPOOL BETTING ON ALL UK RACING H'CAP 1m 2f (P)
7:40 (7:42) (Class 4) (0-85,85) 4-Y-O+ **£8,086** (£2,406; £1,202; £601) **Stalls** Low

Form RPR

233- 1 **Dark Red (IRE)**[289] 3256 4-8-11 **75**........................ RyanMoore 1 85
(Ed Dunlop) *trckd ldng pair: effrt over 1f out: rdn to ld 150yds out: r.o wl* **6/4**[1]

P-43 2 *1 1/2* **Air Of Astana (IRE)**[14] 968 4-9-1 **79**........................ MartinHarley 6 86
(Hugo Palmer) *chsd ldr: upsides and rdn 2f out: drvn to ld 1f out: sn hdd and styd on same pce ins fnl f* **9/1**

52-1 3 *1 1/4* **Whoopsy Daisy**[14] 967 4-8-9 **73**........................ MartinDwyer 7 77
(Jane Chapple-Hyam) *stdd s: hld up in tch in rr: clsd and nt clrest of runs over 1f out: sn swtchd rt and hdwy w bandage flapping: drvn and chsd ldng pair ins fnl f: kpt on* **7/2**[3]

2-31 4 *3/4* **Mystical Spirit (FR)**[14] 965 4-9-7 **85**........................ PaulMulrennan 2 88
(Martyn Meade) *in tch in midfield: effrt 2f out: drvn over 1f out: styd on same pce ins fnl f* **9/4**[2]

510- 5 *2* **Freight Train (IRE)**[171] 7172 4-8-12 **76**........................ FrannyNorton 5 75
(Mark Johnston) *led and set stdy gallop: pushed along and qckdn jst over 2f out: drvn and hdd 1f out: sn outpcd: wknd ins fnl f* **12/1**

-652 6 *2 1/4* **Art Scholar (IRE)**[16] 940 9-8-8 **72**........................ AndrewMullen 4 66
(Michael Appleby) *stdd s: hld up in tch in last pair: effrt on inner over 1f out: sn drvn and no imp 1f out: wknd ins fnl f* **33/1**

2m 5.86s (-2.74) **Going Correction** -0.225s/f (Stan) **6** Ran SP% **113.6**
Speed ratings (Par 105): **101,99,98,98,96 94**
CSF £16.15 TOTE £2.60: £1.80, £4.20; EX 16.20 Trifecta £47.40.
Owner The Hon R J Arculli **Bred** T Jones **Trained** Newmarket, Suffolk

FOCUS
A fair handicap.

1162 TOTEPOOLLIVEINFO.COM FOLLOW YOUR TOTE BETS DAILY H'CAP 7f (P)
8:10 (8:12) (Class 6) (0-52,52) 3-Y-O+ **£3,234** (£962; £481; £240) **Stalls** Low

Form RPR

4355 1 **Ashford Island**[16] 948 3-8-3 **46**........................(p) RoystonFfrench 3 50
(Mike Murphy) *chsd ldr for 1f: stdd bk and in tch in midfield: clsd and nt clr run over 1f out: hdwy to chse ldr ins fnl f: r.o wl u.p to ld fnl 50yds* **5/1**[2]

0320 2 *1 1/4* **Tasaaboq**[16] 936 5-9-4 **51**........................(vt) JosephineGordon(5) 5 57
(Phil McEntee) *s.i.s: t.k.h: hld up in last pair: gd hdwy on outer 3f out: chsd ldrs 2f out: rdn to ld 1f out: hung lft ins fnl f: hdd and no ex fnl 50yds* **8/1**

6404 3 *nse* **Wild Flower (IRE)**[14] 964 4-9-7 **49**........................ KieranO'Neill 1 55
(Jimmy Fox) *hld up in tch in midfield: clsd and nt clr run on inner over 1f out: swtchd rt and hdwy ent fnl f: r.o wl u.p fnl 100yds* **7/2**[1]

000- 4 *3/4* **Jack The Laird (IRE)**[156] 7531 3-8-9 **52**........................(p) RenatoSouza 10 50
(Dean Ivory) *chsd ldr after 1f tl 5f out: styd chsng ldrs: edgd lft u.p ent fnl f: r.o same pce fnl 150yds* **8/1**

2004 5 *1 1/4* **Loud**[42] 617 6-9-2 **47**........................(p) SimonPearce(3) 6 48
(Lydia Pearce) *s.i.s: bhd: hdwy over 1f out: styng on whn nt clr run and swtchd rt ins fnl f: kpt on wl towards fin: nvr trbld ldrs* **10/1**

0060 6 *1/2* **Compromise**[27] 824 3-8-3 **46** oh1........................ RyanPowell 7 40
(Conor Dore) *led tl 1/2-way: styd w ldr: rdn over 1f out: no ex 1f out: wknd ins fnl f* **40/1**

/0-0 7 *2* **Purana**[13] 985 5-9-4 **46** oh1........................ LemosdeSouza 11 39
(Mrs Ilka Gansera-Leveque) *t.k.h in midfield tl hdwy to chse ldr 5f out: led 1/2-way: rdn over 1f out: hdd 1f out: wknd ins fnl f* **50/1**

-034 8 *1/2* **Ormanumps (IRE)**[27] 820 3-8-3 **46** oh1........................ AndrewMullen 9 34
(Daniel Mark Loughnane) *in tch in midfield: rdn effrt wl over 1f out: outpcd whn sltly hmpd: racd awkwardly and wnt lft ent fnl f: plugged on same pce fnl f* **6/1**[3]

005- 9 *hd* **Sakhastic**[112] 8166 3-7-10 **46**........................(v) GeorgeWood(7) 13 32
(Christine Dunnett) *stdd and swtchd lft after s: hld up in last trio: rdn 3f out: swtchd rt wl over 1f out: kpt on ins fnl f: nvr trbld ldrs* **16/1**

6-00 10 *3/4* **Toffee Apple (IRE)**[51] 509 3-8-7 **50**........................ LukeMorris 2 34
(Ed Dunlop) *in tch in midfield: unable qck u.p and lost pl over 1f out: wknd ins fnl f* **8/1**

/00- 11 *6* **Major Attitude**[261] 4239 4-9-7 **49**........................ DavidProbert 12 22
(Patrick Chamings) *t.k.h: in tch in midfield: lost pl and rdn wl over 1f out: sn wknd* **12/1**

-000 **12** 1/2 **Cappy Brown**[66] 327 3-8-0 **48** ow1............................[1] PaddyPilley(5) 4 15
(Alan Bailey) *hld up in last quartet: effrt and no hdwy wl over 1f out: bhd fnl f* **9/1**

1m 25.85s (-1.35) **Going Correction** -0.225s/f (Stan)
WFA 3 from 4yo+ 15lb **12** Ran SP% **123.6**
Speed ratings (Par 101): **98,96,96,95,94 93,91,90,90,89 82,82**
CSF £46.98 CT £162.87 TOTE £6.60: £2.60, £2.80, £1.30; EX 62.40 Trifecta £235.40.
Owner MK Horseracing & Lee Bearman 2 **Bred** Kirtlington Stud & Mr C Budgett **Trained** Westoning, Beds

FOCUS
A moderate contest.

1163 @TOTEPOOL JOIN THE POOL PARTY H'CAP 1m 2f (P)
8:40 (8:43) (Class 6) (0-65,65) 3-Y-O **£3,234** (£962; £481; £240) **Stalls** Low

Form RPR
0663 **1** **Rainbow Lad (IRE)**[7] 1062 3-8-7 **51**.............................. AndrewMullen 8 58
(Michael Appleby) *chsd ldrs: rdn 2f out: swtchd lft and hdwy u.p 1f out: styd on to ld fnl 50yds* **11/4**[2]

0-03 **2** 1/2 **Simply Clever**[28] 794 3-8-2 **51** oh5.............................. AaronJones(5) 10 57
(David Brown) *led: rdn and almost 2 l clr over 1f out: hdd and no ex fnl 50yds* **12/1**

0-36 **3** 1/2 **Rock 'n Red (IRE)**[33] 746 3-9-6 **64**.............................. JimCrowley 7 69
(Ed Dunlop) *bhd in early dash: clsd and hld up in last trio after 2f: hdwy whn carried rt and hmpd wl over 1f out: styd on to go 3rd ins fnl f: clsng at fin but nvr quite gng to rch ldrs* **8/1**

101- **4** 4 1/2 **Harlequin Rock**[114] 8143 3-9-7 **65**.............................. WilliamCarson 1 62
(Mick Quinn) *broke wl but under restraint: sddd bk into midfield after 2f out: effrt over 2f out: drifted rt and no imp wl over 1f out: plugged on ins fnl f: wnt 4th cl home* **7/1**

461- **5** 1/2 **Judicial Enquiry**[111] 8177 3-9-4 **62**..............................(p) LukeMorris 6 58
(Ed Walker) *chsd ldrs: effrt in 3rd over 2f out: unable qck and no imp over 1f out: plugged on same pce fnl f* **9/4**[1]

32-6 **6** 1 **Ede's The Mover**[41] 633 3-9-6 **64**.............................. JFEgan 5 58
(Pat Phelan) *hld up in last trio: rdn and effrt over 2f out: stl plenty to do whn carried rt wl over 1f out: no threat to ldrs but plugged on steadily ins fnl f* **20/1**

543 **7** 6 **Blue Vision (FR)**[21] 892 3-9-1 **59**.............................. BenCurtis 4 43
(Alan Swinbank) *short of room after s: sn swtchd lft and hld up in last trio: effrt but stl plenty to do whn carried rt and hmpd wl over 1f out: no prog and wl btn 1f out* **5/1**[3]

005- **8** 5 **Trident Tested**[199] 6376 3-9-6 **64**.............................. KierenFox 3 40
(John Best) *in tch in midfield: rdn and struggling over 2f out: wl btn over 1f out: eased ins fnl f* **10/1**

00-0 **9** 6 **Orangecherie (IRE)**[67] 325 3-8-8 **52**.............................. KieranO'Neill 2 16
(Mike Murphy) *chsd ldrs: rdn over 2f out: sn struggling and wl btn over 1f out: wl bhd and eased ins fnl f* **25/1**

2m 6.3s (-2.30) **Going Correction** -0.225s/f (Stan) **9** Ran SP% **123.1**
Speed ratings (Par 96): **100,99,99,95,95 94,89,85,80**
CSF £38.50 CT £247.54 TOTE £5.40: £2.90, £4.00, £3.60; EX 30.60 Trifecta £272.00.
Owner Craig Buckingham **Bred** Rathbarry Stud **Trained** Oakham, Rutland

FOCUS
The first three finished clear in this modest affair and the winner was on a fair mark.
T/Jkpt: Not won. T/Plt: £544.10 to a £1 stake. Pool of £95236.62 - 127.77 winning tickets.
T/Qpdt: £42.90 to a £1 stake. Pool of £13543.46 - 233.21 winning units. **Steve Payne**

1131 WOLVERHAMPTON (A.W) (L-H)
Thursday, March 31

OFFICIAL GOING: Tapeta: standard
Wind: Light across Weather: Cloudy with sunny spells

1164 THE BLACK COUNTRY'S ONLY RACECOURSE H'CAP 5f 20y (Tp)
2:00 (2:00) (Class 7) (0-50,50) 3-Y-O+ **£2,587** (£770; £384; £192) **Stalls** Low

Form RPR
-203 **1** **Spray Tan**[34] 732 6-9-4 **50**..............................(b) GeorgeDowning(3) 10 55
(Tony Carroll) *a.p: rdn over 1f out: r.o to ld wl ins fnl f* **10/1**

2045 **2** nk **Presto Boy**[12] 1005 4-8-13 **49**.............................. StephanieJoannides(7) 9 53
(Richard Hughes) *mid-div: hdwy: nt clr run and edgd lft over 1f out: r.o* **4/1**[2]

6650 **3** shd **Dream Ally (IRE)**[12] 1005 6-9-5 **48**.............................. LukeMorris 8 52
(John Weymes) *sn led: rdn over 1f out: hdd wl ins fnl f* **3/1**[1]

60-0 **4** 1 3/4 **Bilash**[45] 589 9-9-5 **48**.............................. PaulQuinn 6 45
(Sarah Hollinshead) *pushed along in rr early: rdn over 1f out: r.o ins fnl f: nt trble ldrs* **20/1**

56-6 **5** nse **Joaldo**[21] 892 4-9-2 **45**.............................. PJMcDonald 7 42
(Antony Brittain) *s.i.s: in rr: rdn and hung lft fr over 1f out: nt clr run and swtchd rt ins fnl f: r.o* **10/1**

-554 **6** hd **Salvado (IRE)**[38] 669 6-9-2 **45**.............................. WilliamCarson 1 41
(Tony Carroll) *trckd ldrs: plld hrd: rdn over 1f out: styd on same pce ins fnl f* **8/1**[3]

0-04 **7** 1/2 **Camanche Grey (IRE)**[34] 732 5-9-7 **50**.............................. JoeyHaynes 4 45
(Ben Haslam) *s.i.s: hld up: nt clr run wl over 1f out: sn rdn: styd on same pce ins fnl f* **3/1**[1]

2640 **8** 1 1/2 **Seraphima**[14] 970 6-8-11 **45**..............................(p) JosephineGordon(5) 3 34
(Lisa Williamson) *mid-div: hdwy over 1f out: no ex ins fnl f* **11/1**

0004 **9** 2 1/4 **Justice (IRE)**[20] 902 3-8-1 **45**.............................. JackDuern(3) 11 21
(Dean Ivory) *chsd ldr: rdn over 1f out: wknd ins fnl f* **22/1**

1m 1.68s (-0.22) **Going Correction** -0.075s/f (Stan)
WFA 3 from 4yo+ 12lb **9** Ran SP% **116.7**
Speed ratings (Par 97): **98,97,97,94,94 94,93,90,87**
CSF £50.37 CT £152.24 TOTE £7.80: £3.00, £2.20, £1.10; EX 33.40 Trifecta £139.30.
Owner Silks Racing Partnership **Bred** Lady Whent **Trained** Cropthorne, Worcs

FOCUS
A poor sprint handicap full of horses that find it hard to win and they finished in a heap.

1165 HOLIDAY INN WOLVERHAMPTON H'CAP 1m 141y (Tp)
2:30 (2:30) (Class 6) (0-52,52) 4-Y-O+ **£2,587** (£770; £384; £192) **Stalls** Low

Form RPR
-062 **1** **Engai (GER)**[36] 701 10-9-2 **50**.............................. GeorgeDowning(3) 10 57
(David Bridgwater) *s.i.s: sn pushed along in rr: hdwy over 1f out: r.o to ld nr fin* **13/2**[2]

0-63 **2** 3/4 **Mount Cheiron (USA)**[8] 1035 5-8-10 **48**..........(v[1]) CallumRodriguez(7) 9 53
(Richard Ford) *hld up: rdn over 2f out: hdwy over 1f out: hung lft ins fnl f: r.o* **15/2**[3]

400- **3** hd **Ferdy (IRE)**[198] 6397 7-9-1 **46** oh1.............................. JFEgan 6 51
(Paul Green) *hld up in tch: plld hrd: chsd ldr over 1f out: rdn to ld ins fnl f: hdd nr fin* **10/1**

00-0 **4** nk **Gilmer (IRE)**[76] 197 5-9-2 **52**..............................(t) NoelGarbutt(5) 7 56
(Laura Young) *led after 1f: rdn over 1f out: hdd ins fnl f: styd on same pce* **8/1**

0-63 **5** 2 1/4 **Natalia**[13] 986 7-8-12 **46** oh1..............................(v) RobHornby(3) 2 46
(Sarah Hollinshead) *led 1f: chsd ldr tl rdn over 1f out: no ex ins fnl f* **8/1**

0-12 **6** 3 1/2 **Theydon Thunder**[1] 1145 4-9-3 **51** 6ex.............................. RosieJessop(3) 1 43
(Peter Charalambous) *trckd ldrs: plld hrd: rdn over 1f out: wknd ins fnl f* **15/8**[1]

500- **7** 1 3/4 **Just Five (IRE)**[223] 5590 10-9-2 **47**..............................(v) LukeMorris 4 36
(John Weymes) *mid-div: rdn over 3f out: hdwy u.p over 1f out: wknd ins fnl f* **20/1**

360 **8** 3/4 **Rutterkin (USA)**[29] 787 8-8-8 **46** oh1.............................. VitorSantos(7) 13 33
(John David Riches) *s.s: in rr: rdn over 1f out: nvr on terms* **33/1**

330- **9** 5 **Look Here's Al**[148] 7713 5-9-0 **50**.............................. GemmaTutty(5) 11 27
(Karen Tutty) *mid-div: hung lft and lost pl 1/2-way: wknd over 2f out* **25/1**

-661 **10** 1/2 **Miss Buckaroo (IRE)**[29] 787 4-9-5 **50**.............................. TomEaves 5 26
(James Given) *chsd ldrs: rdn over 2f out: wknd over 1f out* **13/2**[2]

1m 49.62s (-0.48) **Going Correction** -0.075s/f (Stan) **10** Ran SP% **116.1**
Speed ratings (Par 101): **99,98,98,97,95 92,91,90,86,85**
CSF £52.74 CT £485.52 TOTE £5.10: £2.90, £2.40, £3.40; EX 32.40 Trifecta £404.00.
Owner D G Bridgwater **Bred** Gestut Park Wiedingen **Trained** Icomb, Gloucs

FOCUS
Another moderate handicap, but a good pace suited those held up. There was little covering the first four at the line.

1166 WOLVERHAMPTON HOLIDAY INN H'CAP 1m 4f 50y (Tp)
3:00 (3:00) (Class 4) (0-85,90) 4-Y-O+ **£4,851** (£1,443; £721; £360) **Stalls** Low

Form RPR
0616 **1** **Bayan Kasirga (IRE)**[21] 890 6-8-6 **72**.............................. SammyJoBell(3) 3 78
(Richard Fahey) *chsd ldrs: rdn over 3f out: r.o to ld nr fin* **8/1**

2-65 **2** hd **Sbraase**[24] 861 5-9-6 **83**.............................. LukeMorris 4 88
(James Tate) *sn chsng ldrs: rdn to ld and edgd lft ins fnl f: hdd nr fin* **10/11**[1]

635- **3** shd **Full Day**[173] 7124 5-9-2 **79**.............................. BenCurtis 1 84
(Brian Ellison) *sn pushed along to ld: hdd over 5f out: led again over 3f out: sn rdn: hdd ins fnl f: r.o* **9/1**

6-05 **4** 8 **Brandon Castle**[13] 975 4-9-1 **80**.............................. CathyGannon 2 72
(Andrew Balding) *trckd ldr: plld hrd: led over 5f out: hdd over 3f out: sn rdn: wknd over 1f out* **9/2**[2]

1000 **5** 1 1/4 **Yul Finegold (IRE)**[21] 888 6-9-4 **81**.............................. PaulMulrennan 5 71
(Conor Dore) *hld up: rdn over 3f out: wknd wl over 1f out* **6/1**[3]

0150 **6** 8 **Idol Deputy (FR)**[12] 1001 10-8-9 **77**..............................(p) RachealKneller(5) 6 54
(James Bennett) *hld up: rdn over 5f out: wknd wl over 1f out* **16/1**

2m 36.82s (-3.98) **Going Correction** -0.075s/f (Stan)
WFA 4 from 5yo+ 2lb **6** Ran SP% **111.8**
Speed ratings (Par 105): **110,109,109,104,103 98**
CSF £15.80 TOTE £5.10: £2.40, £1.40; EX 11.70 Trifecta £53.10.
Owner Stephen Humphreys **Bred** Lynn Lodge Stud **Trained** Musley Bank, N Yorks
■ Stewards' Enquiry : Sammy Jo Bell two-day ban: used whip above permitted level (Apr 14-15)

FOCUS
Not a bad handicap and a thrilling finish between the front three.

1167 FOLLOW US ON TWITTER @WOLVESRACES MAIDEN STKS 5f 20y (Tp)
3:35 (3:36) (Class 5) 3-Y-O+ **£3,234** (£962; £481; £240) **Stalls** Low

Form RPR
1 **Lapilli** 3-9-1 0.............................. PatCosgrave 1 81+
(William Haggas) *s.i.s: sn prom: led over 1f out: r.o wl: comf* **1/2**[1]

422 **2** 2 1/2 **Hot Stuff**[22] 883 3-8-12 63.............................. GeorgeDowning(3) 3 65
(Tony Carroll) *chsd ldr: shkn up 1/2-way: rdn and ev ch over 1f out: styd on same pce fnl f* **8/1**[3]

6-35 **3** 1 3/4 **One Big Surprise**[28] 791 4-9-8 0.............................. ShaneKelly 4 59
(Richard Hughes) *hld up in tch: rdn over 1f out: styd on same pce* **12/1**

324- **4** 1 1/4 **Shine Likeadiamond**[101] 8330 3-8-10 67.............................. JFEgan 2 49
(Mick Channon) *led: rdn: hung rt and hdd over 1f out: wknd ins fnl f* **6/1**[2]

526- **5** 2 1/2 **Wilde Extravagance (IRE)**[163] 7373 3-9-1 70.............................. ConnorBeasley 6 45
(Julie Camacho) *chsd ldrs: rdn 1/2-way: wknd over 1f out* **8/1**[3]

000 **6** 20 **Bethellie Pride**[38] 679 6-9-8 21.............................. JackGarritty 7
(Lynn Siddall) *s.i.s and wnt rt s: a in rr: lost tch fnl 3f* **66/1**

1m 2.02s (0.12) **Going Correction** -0.075s/f (Stan)
WFA 3 from 4yo+ 12lb **6** Ran SP% **112.4**
Speed ratings (Par 103): **96,92,89,87,83 51**
CSF £5.37 TOTE £1.40: £1.10, £2.40; EX 5.00 Trifecta £16.20.
Owner Sheikh Ahmed Al Maktoum **Bred** Whitsbury Manor Stud **Trained** Newmarket, Suffolk

FOCUS
An uncompetitive sprint maiden.

1168 WOLVERHAMPTON-RACECOURSE.CO.UK H'CAP 5f 216y (Tp)
4:05 (4:05) (Class 3) (0-95,94) 3-Y-O **£7,246** (£2,168; £1,084; £542) **Stalls** Low

Form RPR
151- **1** **Florencio**[168] 7235 3-8-8 **81**.............................. MartinDwyer 3 89
(William Muir) *a.p: shkn up to ld and hung rt fr over 1f out: r.o: comf* **3/1**[3]

4212 **2** 1 3/4 **Kingsley Klarion (IRE)**[47] 559 3-9-4 **91**.............................. JoeFanning 2 93
(Mark Johnston) *chsd ldr: shkn up to ld and carried rt wl over 1f out: sn hdd: edgd lft and styd on same pce ins fnl f* **13/8**[1]

3110 **3** 1 1/4 **Aguerooo (IRE)**[6] 1070 3-9-0 **94**..............................(p) HollieDoyle(7) 4 92
(Richard Hannon) *chsd ldrs: effrt and n.m.r over 1f out: hmpd sn after: edgd lft and styd on same pce ins fnl f* **2/1**[2]

26-1 **4** 1 3/4 **He's A Dreamer (IRE)**[64] 352 3-8-9 **82**.............................. SamJames 1 74
(David O'Meara) *led: hung rt over 2f out: rdn and hdd wl over 1f out: hmpd jst over 1f out: no ex ins fnl f* **5/1**

1m 13.68s (-0.82) **Going Correction** -0.075s/f (Stan) **4** Ran SP% **113.1**
Speed ratings (Par 102): **102,99,98,95**
CSF £8.63 TOTE £4.50; EX 8.50 Trifecta £15.00.
Owner Excel Racing **Bred** Newsells Park Stud **Trained** Lambourn, Berks

The Form Book, Raceform Ltd, Newbury, RG14 5SJ

FOCUS
A decent 3yo sprint handicap, but a rough old race despite the small field. There was a nasty incident involving the winner and third over a furlong from home, but the Stewards deemed that any interference was accidental.

1169 FIND US ON FACEBOOK WOLVERHAMPTON RACECOURSE H'CAP (DIV I) 1m 4f 50y (Tp)
4:40 (4:40) (Class 6) (0-60,60) 4-Y-O+ **£2,587** (£770; £384; £192) **Stalls** Low

Form RPR
000- **1** **Hurricane Volta (IRE)**[93] 8385 5-9-2 **55**....................(p) CharlesBishop 1 61
(Peter Hedger) *chsd ldrs: nt clr run wl over 1f out: rdn to ld ins fnl f: styd on* **22/1**
6500 **2** *shd* **Ali Bin Nayef**[13] 982 4-8-10 **51**.................................... RobertHavlin 10 57
(Michael Wigham) *mid-div: hdwy over 1f out: rdn: edgd lft and ev ch ins fnl f: styd on* **6/1**[3]
-644 **3** *3/4* **Ring Eye (IRE)**[12] 1004 8-8-9 **53**.................................. CiaranMckee[(5)] 7 58
(John O'Shea) *hld up: hdwy over 1f out: rdn and edgd lft ins fnl f: r.o* **5/1**[2]
650- **4** *nk* **Bollihope**[127] 7830 4-9-5 **60**.. JasonHart 5 64
(Richard Guest) *prom: nt clr run fr over 2f out: styd on: nvr able to chal* **6/1**[3]
0-00 **5** *1* **Surround Sound**[41] 640 6-9-7 **60**....................................(t) DavidAllan 3 63
(Tim Easterby) *dwlt: hld up: hdwy u.p over 1f out: r.o: nt rch ldrs* **7/2**[1]
5-10 **6** *nk* **Whisky Marmalade (IRE)**[37] 684 4-9-2 **57**.................... RaulDaSilva 6 59
(Ben Haslam) *chsd ldrs: wnt 2nd over 2f out: rdn to ld over 1f out: hdd and unable qck ins fnl f* **10/1**
00-0 **7** *3* **Mac Tiernan (IRE)**[72] 247 9-8-12 **51**............................ TonyHamilton 2 48
(Philip Kirby) *led 1f: chsd ldr tl over 3f out: rdn over 2f out: wknd ins fnl f* **20/1**
05-3 **8** *nk* **Cantankerous**[34] 731 5-8-8 **47** oh1 ow1....................(p) StevieDonohoe 4 44
(Daniel Mark Loughnane) *hld up: pushed along over 3f out: sme hdwy u.p over 1f out: wknd ins fnl f* **6/1**[3]
463- **9** *shd* **Mister Marcasite**[267] 4028 6-9-6 **59**................................ PJMcDonald 9 56
(Antony Brittain) *led after 1f: rdn and hdd over 1f out: wknd ins fnl f* **6/1**[3]
500- **10** *72* **Ruggero**[131] 7948 6-8-8 **47** oh1 ow1................................... TomEaves 8
(Roy Brotherton) *hld up: rdn and wknd over 4f out* **150/1**

2m 39.88s (-0.92) **Going Correction** -0.075s/f (Stan)
WFA 4 from 5yo+ 2lb **10** Ran SP% **114.9**
Speed ratings (Par 101): **100,99,99,99,98 98,96,96,96,48**
CSF £144.52 CT £776.30 TOTE £20.90: £5.10, £2.60, £1.90; EX 169.60 Trifecta £1729.10.
Owner T Hirschfeld & S Piper **Bred** Lynn Lodge Stud **Trained** Hook, Hampshire

FOCUS
The first division of a moderate middle-distance handicap and the pace was steady resulting in a compressed finish.

1170 FIND US ON FACEBOOK WOLVERHAMPTON RACECOURSE H'CAP (DIV II) 1m 4f 50y (Tp)
5:10 (5:10) (Class 6) (0-60,60) 4-Y-O+ **£2,587** (£770; £384; £192) **Stalls** Low

Form RPR
1125 **1** **On A Whim**[13] 982 4-9-2 **57**..(p) JoeFanning 5 65
(Daniel Mark Loughnane) *hld up: hdwy on outer over 2f out: rdn over 1f out: styd on to ld nr fin* **9/2**[2]
2531 **2** *1/2* **Happy Jack (IRE)**[13] 981 5-8-12 **51**...............................(b) PatDobbs 6 58
(Michael Wigham) *chsd ldrs: wnt 2nd over 2f out: rdn to ld over 1f out: hdd nr fin* **2/1**[1]
/0-5 **3** *1 1/2* **Stynes (IRE)**[38] 674 6-8-8 **47** oh1 ow1......................(t) StevieDonohoe 4 52
(Ali Stronge) *a.p: rdn over 1f out: styd on same pce wl ins fnl f* **16/1**
-100 **4** *2 1/4* **Jethou Island**[56] 438 5-9-4 **57**...(t) ShaneKelly 3 58
(David Menuisier) *led 1f: chsd ldr tl led again over 3f out: rdn and hdd over 1f out: no ex ins fnl f* **40/1**
5-66 **5** *1 3/4* **Chauvelin**[12] 1004 5-9-0 **53**..(v) JasonHart 2 51
(Richard Guest) *hld up: hdwy u.p over 1f out: nt trble ldrs* **11/2**[3]
5-52 **6** *3/4* **Well Owd Mon**[27] 819 6-8-11 **53**...............................(p) RobHornby[(3)] 7 50
(Sarah Hollinshead) *s.s: hld up: rdn over 1f out: nt trble ldrs* **9/1**
00-0 **7** *9* **Renewing**[80] 150 5-8-9 **48** ow2... TomEaves 1 31
(Paul Henderson) *sn pushed along in rr: rdn over 5f out: wknd over 3f out* **9/1**
3200 **8** *1/2* **Medieval Bishop (IRE)**[16] 946 7-9-7 **60**......................(p) JackGarritty 8 42
(Tony Forbes) *led after 1f: hdd over 3f out: rdn and wknd over 2f out* **12/1**
6324 **9** *shd* **Peeps**[15] 949 4-9-5 **60**...(p) SaleemGolam 9 42
(Mark H Tompkins) *s.i.s: sn prom: rdn over 2f out: wknd over 1f out* **7/1**

2m 37.56s (-3.24) **Going Correction** -0.075s/f (Stan)
WFA 4 from 5yo+ 2lb **9** Ran SP% **115.4**
Speed ratings (Par 101): **107,106,105,104,103 102,96,96,96**
CSF £13.88 CT £130.78 TOTE £5.00: £1.80, £1.80, £4.40; EX 15.30 Trifecta £180.20.
Owner R M Brilley **Bred** Minster Stud **Trained** Baldwin's Gate, Staffs

FOCUS
They went a more solid pace in this division and the winning time was 2.32sec quicker than the first leg. The winner found a bit more for the longer trip.

1171 HOTEL & CONFERENCING AT WOLVERHAMPTON FILLIES' H'CAP 1m 103y (Tp)
5:40 (5:40) (Class 5) (0-75,75) 4-Y-O+ **£3,234** (£962; £481; £240) **Stalls** Low

Form RPR
-316 **1** **Southern Storm (IRE)**[29] 788 4-9-7 **75**.............................. FMBerry 4 82+
(Ralph Beckett) *chsd ldr tl rdn over 1f out: r.o to ld wl ins fnl f* **6/5**[1]
0240 **2** *1/2* **Kodiac Lady (IRE)**[4] 1116 4-8-0 **61** oh3......................(e) HollieDoyle[(7)] 3 67
(Simon West) *s.i.s: hld up: hdwy over 1f out: rdn and ev ch ins fnl f: styd on* **16/1**
-232 **3** *1 1/4* **Clary (IRE)**[13] 977 6-8-11 **65**... PatCosgrave 2 68
(James Unett) *s.i.s: sn chsng ldrs: led over 1f out: rdn and hdd wl ins fnl f* **7/2**[3]
0225 **4** *3/4* **Ixelles Diamond (IRE)**[13] 977 5-8-9 **66**..................... DannyBrock[(3)] 5 68
(Andrew Reid) *prom: rdn over 2f out: styd on* **12/1**
3065 **5** *4 1/2* **Boonga Roogeta**[20] 900 7-8-13 **70**............................ RosieJessop[(3)] 1 62
(Peter Charalambous) *led: shkn up over 2f out: rdn and hdd over 1f out: wknd ins fnl f* **5/2**[2]

1m 59.53s (-1.27) **Going Correction** -0.075s/f (Stan) **5** Ran SP% **109.8**
Speed ratings (Par 100): **102,101,100,99,95**
CSF £19.48 TOTE £2.10: £1.20, £5.10; EX 17.90 Trifecta £55.40.
Owner Christopher McHale **Bred** Chris & James McHale **Trained** Kimpton, Hants

FOCUS
An ordinary fillies' handicap and all five were in a line across the track turning in.
T/Plt: £148.90 to a £1 stake. Pool of £77244.15 - 378.47 winning tickets. T/Qpdt: £18.60 to a £1 stake. Pool of £4854.16 -192.76 winning tickets. **Colin Roberts**

FONTAINEBLEAU
Thursday, March 31
OFFICIAL GOING: Turf: very soft

1172a PRIX COR DE CHASSE (LISTED RACE) (3YO+) (TURF) 5f 110y
2:20 (12:00) 3-Y-O+ **£19,117** (£7,647; £5,735; £3,823; £1,911)

RPR
1 **Signs Of Blessing (IRE)**[28] 806 5-9-6 0.............. StephanePasquier 2 117
(F Rohaut, France) **12/5**[1]
2 *6* **Finsbury Square (IRE)**[133] 7910 4-9-6 0........... ChristopheSoumillon 5 97
(F Chappet, France) **19/5**[3]
3 *1 1/4* **Catcall (FR)**[152] 7662 7-9-6 0.. OlivierPeslier 3 93
(P Sogorb, France) **9/1**
4 *snk* **El Suizo (FR)**[178] 6993 4-9-6 0... FabriceVeron 7 93
(H-A Pantall, France) **17/1**
5 *1/2* **Love Spirit**[20] 6-9-6 0... Pierre-CharlesBoudot 9 91
(J Baudron, France) **5/2**[2]
6 *3 1/2* **Gengis (FR)**[133] 7910 6-9-10 0....................................(b) MaximeGuyon 6 83
(G Doleuze, France) **63/10**
7 *4* **Mirza**[26] 841 9-9-10 0..(p) IoritzMendizabal 1 70
(Rae Guest) *chsd wnr: rdn over 1f out: no ex fnl f: wknd* **10/1**
8 *9* **Leading Actress (IRE)**[153] 7610 4-9-3 0............... VincentCheminaud 4 33
(M Delcher Sanchez, France) **34/1**
9 *8* **Indian Sly (FR)**[233] 11-9-6 0................................ MlleLauraPoggionovo 8 10
(P Capelle, France) **86/1**

WIN (incl. 1 euro stake): 3.40. PLACES: 1.70, 1.60, 2.40. DF: 8.50. SF: 16.20
Owner Ecurie Pandora Racing **Bred** S Boucheron **Trained** Sauvagnon, France

1144 LINGFIELD (L-H)
Friday, April 1
OFFICIAL GOING: Polytrack: standard
Wind: Moderate, behind Weather: Fine but cloudy

1173 HENRY SEMMENCE 60TH BIRTHDAY TOUR H'CAP 1m 1y(P)
2:00 (2:02) (Class 5) (0-75,75) 4-Y-O+ **£3,234** (£962; £481; £240) **Stalls** High

Form RPR
240- **1** **Berkeley Vale**[203] 6288 5-9-4 **72**................................(v) RobertWinston 8 80
(Roger Teal) *trckd ldr: rdn 2f out: led 1f out: drvn out and kpt on* **7/1**
3336 **2** *nk* **Chelwood Gate (IRE)**[16] 953 6-9-5 **73**......................(v) DavidProbert 4 80
(Patrick Chamings) *hld up in tch: smooth prog on inner to trck ldng pair over 2f out: shkn up to chal jst over 1f out and upsides: fnd little and jst hld fnl f* **9/2**[2]
-302 **3** *1/2* **Freddy With A Y (IRE)**[28] 815 6-9-4 **72**..................(v) GeorgeBaker 10 78
(Gary Moore) *led: rdn over 2f out: hdd 1f out: kpt on but nt qckn after* **8/1**
-424 **4** *1 1/2* **Van Huysen (IRE)**[29] 795 4-9-4 **75**..........................(p) DannyBrock[(3)] 2 77
(Dominic Ffrench Davis) *trckd ldrs: rdn over 2f out: no imp over 1f out: kpt on same pce after* **4/1**[1]
650- **5** *2* **Wind In My Sails**[213] 5967 4-9-7 **75**................................... KieranO'Neill 6 72
(Ed de Giles) *trckd ldrs: rdn on outer over 2f out: one pce and btn over 1f out* **7/1**
030- **6** *2 1/2* **Good Luck Charm**[130] 7959 7-8-13 **72**..................... HectorCrouch[(5)] 7 63
(Gary Moore) *racd wd in midfield: rdn over 2f out: hanging and outpcd over 1f out: no ch after* **25/1**
030- **7** *nk* **Shifting Star (IRE)**[123] 8049 11-9-4 **72**....................(vt) WilliamCarson 1 63
(John Bridger) *t.k.h: trckd ldng pair to over 2f out: pushed along and steadily lost pl* **33/1**
124- **8** *hd* **Tommy's Secret**[102] 8325 6-9-0 **75**............................... MillyNaseb[(7)] 11 65
(Jane Chapple-Hyam) *dropped in fr wd draw and hld up in last trio: pushed along 3f out: no real prog* **5/1**[3]
5210 **9** *1 1/4* **The Tichborne (IRE)**[23] 879 8-9-0 **68**..........................(b) JackMitchell 5 55
(Roger Teal) *hld up towards rr: gng wl enough over 2f out: rdn and wknd wl over 1f out* **8/1**
-036 **10** *3 1/4* **Mossgo (IRE)**[36] 714 6-9-3 **71**..(t) KierenFox 3 50
(John Best) *dwlt: plld hrd and hld up in last trio: brief effrt over 2f out: wknd over 1f out* **20/1**
-000 **11** *9* **Rail Dancer**[30] 788 4-8-13 **67**....................................... AdamBeschizza 12 25
(Richard Rowe) *dropped in fr wd draw and hld up in last trio: wknd over 2f out: t.o* **66/1**

1m 37.92s (-0.28) **Going Correction** 0.0s/f (Stan) **11** Ran SP% **115.1**
Speed ratings (Par 103): **101,100,100,98,96 94,93,93,92,89 80**
CSF £36.20 CT £263.01 TOTE £8.30: £2.50, £1.60, £2.40; EX 43.60 Trifecta £338.80.
Owner Mrs Muriel Forward & Dr G C Forward **Bred** Edward Hyde **Trained** Great Shefford, Berks

FOCUS
A routine handicap and the gallop was ordinary, which suited those ridden handily.

1174 RETRAINING OF RACEHORSES CLAIMING STKS 1m 5f (P)
2:35 (2:35) (Class 6) 4-Y-O+ **£2,587** (£770; £384; £192) **Stalls** Low

Form RPR
-014 **1** **Jamhoori**[48] 556 8-9-6 77... MartinLane 2 69+
(Jeremy Gask) *stdd s: hld up in last tl quick move to trck ldng pair 7f out: clsd fr 3f out to ld 2f out: pushed along and drew clr over 1f out* **1/4**[1]
-233 **2** *4* **What A Party (IRE)**[28] 815 4-8-12 57.............................(v) DavidProbert 4 53
(Gay Kelleway) *led 2f: led again wl over 3f out: drvn and hdd 2f out: kpt on but no ch w wnr* **4/1**[2]
065- **3** *2 1/4* **Crashing Thew Life**[109] 2776 6-8-11 55....................... HarryPoulton[(5)] 1 52
(Sheena West) *chsd ldng pair to 7f out: rdn wl over 2f out and sn outpcd: modest 3rd again fr over 1f out* **25/1**
-006 **4** *1 3/4* **Investissement**[41] 653 10-8-12 50.....................(b) JosephineGordon[(5)] 3 50
(Paddy Butler) *in tch: rdn 5f out: outpcd over 2f out: plugged on* **20/1**[3]
-300 **5** *nse* **Boston Blue**[21] 634 9-9-4 51..(p) JimCrowley 5 51
(Tony Carroll) *in tch: urged along over 4f out: outpcd over 2f out: plugged on* **33/1**
00-0 **6** *1* **Major Franko**[9] 1038 4-9-0 52...(v[1]) KierenFox 6 47
(Michael Attwater) *t.k.h: led after 2f to wl over 3f out: sn drvn: wl btn over 2f out: wknd fnl f* **50/1**

2m 46.29s (0.29) **Going Correction** 0.0s/f (Stan)
WFA 4 from 6yo+ 2lb **6** Ran SP% **113.5**
Speed ratings (Par 101): **99,96,95,94,94 93**
CSF £1.50 TOTE £1.20: £1.10, £1.20; EX 1.70 Trifecta £6.50.Jamhoori was claimed by Mr Jim Best for £8,000.

Owner Guy Carstairs & Horses First Racing **Bred** Minster Enterprises Ltd **Trained** Stockbridge, Hants

FOCUS

This moderate claimer was all about one horse and he didn't disappoint.

1175 JIGSAW H'CAP 5f 6y(P)

3:10 (3:12) (Class 4) (0-85,84) 4-Y-O+ **£4,916** (£1,463; £731; £365) **Stalls** High

Form RPR

014- **1** **Equally Fast**[181] 6921 4-9-1 **81**..........(b) RobHornby(3) 6 89
(William Muir) *prog to dispute 2nd after 2f: shkn up over 1f out and nudged by rival: led jst ins fnl f: rdn out and a finding enough* **4/1**[2]

00-2 **2** ½ **Bertie Blu Boy**[23] 879 8-9-6 **83**..........(v) GeorgeBaker 2 89
(Lisa Williamson) *led and had field stretched: rdn and hung rt fr over 1f out: hdd jst ins fnl f: styd on* **9/4**[1]

5250 **3** *nk* **Diamond Charlie (IRE)**[16] 955 8-8-10 **73**.......... JimCrowley 3 78
(Simon Dow) *dwlt: off the pce in 5th: effrt over 2f out: drvn and r.o to take 3rd last 100yds: clsng on ldng pair at fin* **8/1**

-426 **4** *2* **Burning Thread (IRE)**[41] 655 9-9-7 **84**..........(b) OisinMurphy 4 82
(David Elsworth) *chsd ldr: rdn and nudged by rival over 1f out: lost 2nd and sn wknd* **5/1**[3]

55-0 **5** *1 ½* **Bahamian Sunrise**[5] 1110 4-8-9 **75**.......... MichaelJMMurphy(3) 1 67
(John Gallagher) *chsd ldng pair early: outpcd and rdn 1/2-way: effrt on inner over 1f out: sn no prog* **16/1**

400- **6** *shd* **Smoothtalkinrascal (IRE)**[175] 7082 6-9-1 **78**.......... ShaneKelly 5 70
(Peter Crate) *restless stalls and slowly away: wl off the pce in last pair: rdn over 1f out: no ch but kpt on* **8/1**

0-00 **7** *4* **Dark Side Dream**[17] 938 4-9-0 **77**..........(p) SilvestreDeSousa 7 55
(Chris Dwyer) *a in last pair and wl off the pce* **5/1**[3]

57.91s (-0.89) **Going Correction** 0.0s/f (Stan) **7** Ran SP% **112.2**
Speed ratings (Par 105): **107,106,105,102,100 99,93**
CSF £12.91 TOTE £4.90: £2.10, £1.80; EX 16.20 Trifecta £89.50.
Owner Muir Racing Partnership - Haydock **Bred** Newsells Park Stud **Trained** Lambourn, Berks

FOCUS

A fair sprint handicap which was always likely to be fast and furious.

1176 HEART FM H'CAP 6f 1y(P)

3:45 (3:46) (Class 5) (0-75,75) 3-Y-O **£3,234** (£962; £481; £240) **Stalls** Low

Form RPR

0202 **1** **Sir Dudley (IRE)**[8] 1060 3-9-7 **75**..........(b1) TomEaves 6 80
(James Given) *pressed ldr: rdn to ld wl over 1f out: edgd rt but kpt on wl* **5/1**[3]

330- **2** ¾ **Black Bess**[158] 7512 3-8-13 **67**.......... WilliamCarson 7 69+
(Jim Boyle) *stdd s: hld up in rr: prog 2f out: rdn and r.o to take 2nd last 50yds: nvr quite able to chal* **25/1**

210- **3** *1* **Shadow Game**[196] 6492 3-9-5 **73**.......... JamesDoyle 8 72
(Mark Johnston) *chsd ldrs: pushed along fr 1/2-way: no imp 2f out: rdn and kpt on fnl f to take 3rd last strides* **7/2**[2]

2226 **4** *nk* **Silver Springs (IRE)**[8] 1061 3-9-1 **69**.......... SilvestreDeSousa 4 67
(David Evans) *led: clr w wnr jst over 2f out: hdd wl over 1f out: fdd and lost 2 pls last 50yds* **14/1**

36-2 **5** *1 ¼* **Strictly Carter**[50] 531 3-8-11 **65**.......... SaleemGolam 9 59
(Alan Bailey) *t.k.h: dropped in fr wd draw and hld up in last pair: sme prog over 1f out: rdn and kpt on fnl f: nvr nrr* **33/1**

6016 **6** ½ **Evening Starlight**[14] 979 3-8-9 **63**.......... DarryllHolland 1 55
(Ron Hodges) *edgd rt s: chsd ldrs: rdn and nt qckn over 2f out: no imp after* **10/1**

220- **7** *nse* **Swanton Blue (IRE)**[176] 7055 3-9-7 **75**.......... JimCrowley 5 67
(Ed de Giles) *chsd ldrs on outer: rdn and nt qckn over 2f out: fdd fnl f* **8/1**

333- **8** *nk* **Another Boy**[164] 7361 3-9-5 **73**..........(p) FMBerry 2 64+
(Ralph Beckett) *n.m.r early stages and dropped towards rr: rdn over 2f out: no prog* **2/1**[1]

4-05 **9** ¾ **Boycie**[39] 678 3-9-3 **71**..........(p) KieranO'Neill 3 60
(Richard Hannon) *t.k.h: n.m.r early stages and dropped to last pair: rdn over 2f out: struggling after: plugged on nr fin* **8/1**

1m 12.16s (0.26) **Going Correction** 0.0s/f (Stan) **9** Ran SP% **117.0**
Speed ratings (Par 98): **98,97,95,95,93 92,92,92,91**
CSF £117.89 CT £495.52 TOTE £4.20: £1.40, £6.80, £1.70; EX 111.70 Trifecta £725.30.
Owner The Cool Silk Partnership **Bred** Mrs Eleanor Kent **Trained** Willoughton, Lincs

FOCUS

A modest 3yo sprint handicap and things got a little tight in the opening furlong.

1177 LINGFIELD PARK H'CAP 1m 7f 169y(P)

4:20 (4:20) (Class 4) (0-85,79) 4-Y-O+ **£4,916** (£1,463; £731; £365) **Stalls** Low

Form RPR

2/0- **1** **Planetoid (IRE)**[32] 1788 8-9-8 **76**..........(b) TimmyMurphy 2 86+
(Jim Best) *trckd ldng pair and a gng wl: clsd to ld on inner over 1f out: easily* **7/2**[2]

6-21 **2** *2* **Shalambar (IRE)**[14] 289 10-9-2 **70**..........(b) JimCrowley 3 73
(Tony Carroll) *pushed up to ld: urged along fr 4f out: edgd rt and hdd over 1f out: kpt on but no ch w wnr* **10/1**

110- **3** *8* **Donna Graciosa (GER)**[154] 7596 4-9-7 **79**.......... SilvestreDeSousa 1 72
(Mark Johnston) *trckd ldr: rdn over 2f out: sn lost 2nd: hmpd over 1f out: wknd tamely* **4/5**[1]

33-3 **4** *9* **Karam Albaari (IRE)**[29] 800 8-9-9 **77**.......... FrederikTylicki 4 60
(J R Jenkins) *hld up in last: shkn up and in tch over 2f out: rdn and wknd qckly wl over 1f out* **4/1**[3]

3m 23.51s (-2.19) **Going Correction** 0.0s/f (Stan)
WFA 4 from 8yo+ 4lb **4** Ran SP% **106.9**
Speed ratings (Par 105): **105,104,100,95**
CSF £26.66 TOTE £4.10; EX 15.70 Trifecta £29.90.
Owner Planetoid Partnership **Bred** Bjorn Nielsen **Trained** Lewes, E Sussex

FOCUS

A fair staying handicap, but this was always likely to be tactical.

1178 CENTREPOINT H'CAP 6f 1y(P)

4:55 (4:55) (Class 5) (0-75,74) 4-Y-O+ **£3,234** (£962; £481; £240) **Stalls** Low

Form RPR

51 **1** **Bouclier (IRE)**[16] 955 6-9-4 **72**.......... WilliamCarson 6 85
(Tony Carroll) *trckd ldng pair: clsd to go 2nd over 1f out: rdn to ld 1f out: drvn clr and r.o strly* **3/1**[2]

1200 **2** *3 ¼* **Seamster**[21] 901 9-9-4 **72**..........(vt) DanielTudhope 3 75
(David O'Meara) *led at gd pce: rdn 2f out: hdd 1f out: no ex and jst hld on for 2nd* **8/1**

023- **3** *shd* **Ripinto (IRE)**[121] 8084 4-9-4 **72**..........(b) GeorgeBaker 2 74
(Jim Boyle) *dwlt sltly: hld up in rr: prog into midfield over 2f out: more hdwy over 1f out but racd awkwardly: tk 3rd fnl f: styd on wl and nrly snatched 2nd* **9/4**[1]

2012 **4** *3* **Bush Warrior (IRE)**[30] 784 5-9-6 **74**..........(v) MartinHarley 7 67
(Anabel K Murphy) *gd spd to press ldr: lost 2nd wl over 1f out: fdd* **8/1**

0-16 **5** ¾ **Heartsong (IRE)**[15] 969 7-9-1 **72**.......... MichaelJMMurphy(3) 1 62
(John Gallagher) *hld up in last trio: effrt on inner 2f out and sme prog into midfield: no hdwy fnl f* **33/1**

00-0 **6** *1* **Swot**[16] 953 4-9-2 **70**.......... JimCrowley 4 57
(Simon Dow) *wl plcd on inner: gng strly 1/2-way: rdn and nt qckn 2f out: sn wl btn* **25/1**

040- **7** ½ **Langley Vale**[203] 6284 7-9-0 **71**..........(p) TomMarquand(3) 9 56
(Roger Teal) *taken down early: racd on outer: prog to chse ldrs 1/2-way: rdn and no rspnse 2f out: sn btn* **25/1**

-110 **8** *1 ¼* **Noble Deed**[21] 901 6-9-6 **74**.......... KierenFox 8 55+
(Michael Attwater) *taken down early: rrd and propped s and nrly uns rdr: detached in last and nvr able to rcvr* **6/1**[3]

60-5 **9** ¾ **Straits Of Malacca**[56] 457 5-9-2 **70**.......... HarryBentley 10 49
(Simon Dow) *a in last trio: shkn up and no prog over 2f out* **33/1**

2-00 **10** *1 ½* **Johnny B Goode (IRE)**[17] 944 4-9-2 **70**..........(v1) JackGarritty 5 44
(Richard Fahey) *taken down early: chsd ldrs: rdn 2f out: wknd qckly* **12/1**

1m 10.84s (-1.06) **Going Correction** 0.0s/f (Stan) **10** Ran SP% **113.5**
Speed ratings (Par 103): **107,102,102,98,97 96,95,93,92,90**
CSF £25.03 CT £61.57 TOTE £2.30: £1.10, £2.30, £1.70; EX 24.90 Trifecta £85.20.
Owner M Chung **Bred** Dayton Investments Ltd **Trained** Cropthorne, Worcs

FOCUS

An ordinary sprint handicap and a tight one with only 4lb covering the ten runners. Few ever got into it.

1179 TTS NETWORKS MAIDEN FILLIES' STKS 1m 2f (P)

5:30 (5:33) (Class 5) 3-Y-O+ **£3,234** (£962; £481; £240) **Stalls** Low

Form RPR

3 **1** **Capricious Cantor (IRE)**[86] 59 3-8-7 0.......... SilvestreDeSousa 2 79+
(Ed Dunlop) *trckd ldng pair: nipped through on inner 2f out: led jst over 1f out: rn green in front: hung rt then veered lft but rdn out and a holding runner-up* **7/4**[2]

544- **2** ½ **Pursuitofthestars (IRE)**[181] 6923 3-8-7 84.......... RobertHavlin 4 78
(John Gosden) *led: shkn up and hdd jst over 1f out: tried to rally and kpt on but a hld* **5/4**[1]

6 **3** *5* **Summer Collection (IRE)**[86] 59 3-8-4 0.......... TomMarquand(3) 7 68
(Charles Hills) *trckd ldr: pushed along 3f out: lost 2nd wl over 1f out and outpcd after: hld on for 3rd* **12/1**

2 **4** ½ **Celestra**[37] 699 3-8-7 0.......... AdamBeschizza 5 67
(Alan King) *dwlt: sn in 5th: urged along fr 1/2-way: drvn over 2f out: nvr on terms but kpt on u.p fnl f* **4/1**[3]

0 **5** *6* **Chapess**[8] 1063 3-8-7 0.......... DavidProbert 6 55
(Philip McBride) *reluctant to enter stall: chsd ldng trio: rdn 3f out: wknd fr 2f out* **200/1**

6 *1 ¼* **Astrosecret** 3-8-7 0.......... SaleemGolam 8 53
(Mark H Tompkins) *hld up in last pair: pushed along jst over 2f out: kpt on steadily after: nt disgracd* **50/1**

7 *2* **Midnight Mood** 3-8-7 0.......... JFEgan 9 49
(Dominic Ffrench Davis) *slowly away: nvr bttr than midfield: rdn and no prog wl over 2f out* **33/1**

0-6 **8** *3 ¼* **Chestnut Storm (IRE)**[20] 925 3-8-7 0.......... MartinLane 3 42
(Ed Dunlop) *hld up in last trio: pushed along and no prog 3f out: fdd fnl 2f* **50/1**

9 *58* **Emerald Petrina (IRE)** 4-9-9 0.......... RyanTate(3) 1
(Heather Main) *hld up: a last: wknd over 3f out: t.o* **100/1**

2m 6.04s (-0.56) **Going Correction** 0.0s/f (Stan)
WFA 3 from 4yo 19lb **9** Ran SP% **116.9**
Speed ratings (Par 100): **102,101,97,97,92 91,89,87,40**
CSF £4.32 TOTE £2.90: £1.60, £1.10, £2.40; EX 5.00 Trifecta £24.10.
Owner Alec Leopold & Ms Leanne Norman **Bred** Mrs S M Rogers & Miss K Rausing **Trained** Newmarket, Suffolk

FOCUS

An uncompetitive fillies' maiden in which only those at the head of the market featured.
T/Plt: £59.30 to a £1 stake. Pool: £66,115.75 - 812.90 winning tickets T/Qpdt: £25.50 to a £1 stake. Pool: £5,876.62 - 170.16 winning tickets **Jonathan Neesom**

1164 WOLVERHAMPTON (A.W) (L-H)

Friday, April 1

OFFICIAL GOING: Tapeta: standard

Wind: Fresh behind Weather: Overcast

1180 NAME A RACE TO ENHANCE YOUR BRAND H'CAP 5f 216y (Tp)

5:45 (5:45) (Class 6) (0-60,60) 4-Y-O+ **£2,587** (£770; £384; £192) **Stalls** Low

Form RPR

0-0 **1** **Spellmaker**[62] 398 7-9-4 **60**.......... EoinWalsh(3) 5 72
(Tony Newcombe) *a.p: chsd ldr over 2f out: rdn to ld and edgd lft fr over 1f out: r.o wl* **6/1**[3]

0066 **2** *3* **Generalyse**[23] 872 7-9-7 **60**..........(p) LukeMorris 1 63
(Anabel K Murphy) *sn pushed along towards rr: rdn over 2f out: hdwy u.p over 1f out: r.o to go 2nd post* **6/1**[3]

40-3 **3** *shd* **Swendab (IRE)**[22] 889 8-9-2 **60**..........(b) CiaranMckee(5) 4 63
(John O'Shea) *sn chsng ldr: led over 4f out: rdn and hdd over 1f out: styd on same pce ins fnl f* **12/1**

50-4 **4** *nk* **Makhfar (IRE)**[23] 875 5-9-6 **59**..........(v) PatCosgrave 3 61
(Kevin Morgan) *s.i.s: pushed along in rr: nt clr run over 1f out: r.o ins fnl f: nt rch ldrs* **5/4**[1]

3065 **5** *2* **Bogsnog (IRE)**[25] 857 6-9-4 **60**.......... JacobButterfield(3) 2 56
(Kristin Stubbs) *chsd ldrs: pushed along and lost pl over 3f out: nt clr run over 2f out: n.d after* **5/1**[2]

465 **6** ½ **Louis Vee (IRE)**[25] 856 8-9-2 **60**.......... EdwardGreatrex(5) 9 55
(John O'Shea) *chsd ldrs: wnt 2nd over 3f out tl rdn over 2f out: wknd fnl f* **12/1**

34-0 **7** *2 ¾* **Diminutive (IRE)**[17] 937 4-8-10 **49**..........(p) StevieDonohoe 6 35
(Grace Harris) *s.i.s: rdn over 2f out: a in rr* **66/1**

424 **8** *1 ¾* **First Rebellion**[13] 1005 7-8-12 **54**..........(v) GeorgeDowning(3) 8 35
(Tony Carroll) *led: hdd over 4f out: rdn over 2f out: wknd over 1f out* **14/1**

1m 14.01s (-0.49) **Going Correction** -0.05s/f (Stan) **8** Ran SP% **113.2**
Speed ratings (Par 101): **101,97,96,96,93 93,89,87**
CSF £40.69 CT £419.45 TOTE £7.60: £1.80, £1.70, £3.00; EX 46.00 Trifecta £413.40.
Owner Joli Racing **Bred** Dxb Bloodstock Ltd **Trained** Yarnscombe, Devon

The Form Book, Raceform Ltd, Newbury, RG14 5SJ

■ Stewards' Enquiry : George Downing one-day ban: failed to keep straight out of the stalls (15 Apr)

FOCUS
The track was cultivated to a depth of three inches and reinstated with a gallop master finish. This was quite competitive for a 46-60 handicap, with a handful holding claims on recent form and several others dangerously well treated at the weights.

1181 LIKE US ON FACEBOOK WOLVERHAMPTON RACECOURSE MEDIAN AUCTION MAIDEN STKS — 5f 216y (Tp)
6:15 (6:15) (Class 6) 3-5-Y-O — **£2,587** (£770; £384; £192) **Stalls** Low

Form — RPR
3 **1** **Semana Santa**[17] 935 3-8-9 0 GrahamGibbons 4 — 72
(David Barron) *chsd ldrs: shkn up over 1f out: sn hung rt: rdn and r.o to ld wl ins fnl f* **11/8**[2]
250- **2** *hd* **Destroyer**[190] 6667 3-9-0 76 MartinDwyer 2 — 76
(William Muir) *chsd ldr tl led wl over 1f out: rdn: hung rt and hdd wl ins fnl f: r.o* **1/1**[1]
526- **3** *10* **John Joiner**[170] 7210 4-9-12 54 SteveDrowne 3 — 49
(Peter Hedger) *led: rdn and hdd wl over 1f out: wknd ins fnl f* **20/1**
4 *9* **Royal Blossom (IRE)** 3-8-9 0 LiamJones 1 — 14
(Michael Wigham) *s.i.s: in rr: shkn up over 2f out: wknd wl over 1f out* **28/1**
5 **5** *10* **Secret Sonnet**[27] 834 3-8-4 0 AaronJones(5) 5
(Stuart Williams) *s.s: outpcd* **12/1**[3]

1m 14.52s (0.02) **Going Correction** -0.05s/f (Stan)
WFA 3 from 4yo 12lb — **5** Ran SP% **108.0**
Speed ratings (Par 101): **97,96,83,71,58**
CSF £2.92 TOTE £2.30: £1.10, £1.10; EX 3.40 Trifecta £10.10.
Owner J G Brown **Bred** J G Brown **Trained** Maunby, N Yorks

FOCUS
Only one of the two experienced runners had shown better than modest form and this presented a good opportunity for an unexposed contender.

1182 HOTEL & CONFERENCING AT WOLVERHAMPTON RACECOURSE H'CAP — 1m 5f 194y (Tp)
6:45 (6:45) (Class 6) (0-60,60) 4-Y-O+ — **£2,587** (£770; £384; £192) **Stalls** Low

Form — RPR
05-1 **1** **Eurato (FR)**[29] 796 6-9-2 **55** (p) LukeMorris 8 — 60+
(Steve Gollings) *chsd ldr over 8f: remained handy: wnt 2nd again over 2f out: rdn over 1f out: styd on u.p to ld wl ins fnl f* **6/4**[1]
2025 **2** *shd* **Celestial Dancer (FR)**[9] 1048 4-8-5 **47** AndrewMullen 6 — 52
(Michael Appleby) *chsd ldrs: wnt 2nd over 5f out: led over 4f out: rdn over 1f out: hdd wl ins fnl f* **10/1**
5323 **3** *½* **Robben**[13] 1004 4-9-3 **59** (v) JoeFanning 4 — 63
(John Mackie) *s.s: hld up: nt clr run over 2f out: hdwy over 1f out: nt clr run and swtchd rt ins fnl f: r.o* **3/1**[2]
5-30 **4** *¾* **Cantankerous**[1] 1169 5-8-3 **47** oh1 ow1 (p) CallumShepherd(5) 7 — 50
(Daniel Mark Loughnane) *hld up in tch: plld hrd: lost pl over 10f out: hdwy u.p over 1f out: styd on* **12/1**
51-1 **5** *shd* **Captain George (IRE)**[13] 1004 5-9-3 **56** (p) SteveDrowne 3 — 60
(Michael Blake) *chsd ldrs: rdn over 3f out: nt clr run fr over 2f out tl over 1f out: styd on* **4/1**[3]
0106 **6** *3 ½* **Easydoesit (IRE)**[35] 731 8-8-9 **55** (p) GeorgiaCox(7) 2 — 53
(Tony Carroll) *hld up: rdn over 2f out: wknd over 1f out* **22/1**
1555 **7** *2 ½* **Missandei**[13] 1004 4-8-9 **51** (t) RoystonFfrench 5 — 47
(Steph Hollinshead) *hld up: hdwy over 4f out: rdn 3f out: nt clr run wl over 1f out: sn wknd* **22/1**
-000 **8** *½* **Several (USA)**[25] 862 4-9-1 **57** [1] DougieCostello 9 — 52
(Kevin Frost) *led at stdy pce tl hdd over 4f out: remained handy: hmpd over 2f out: rdn and hung lft over 1f out: wknd fnl f* **28/1**

3m 8.12s (3.32) **Going Correction** -0.05s/f (Stan)
WFA 4 from 5yo+ 3lb — **8** Ran SP% **113.9**
Speed ratings (Par 101): **88,87,87,87,87 85,83,83**
CSF £17.31 CT £40.62 TOTE £2.40: £1.30, £2.30, £1.10; EX 16.90 Trifecta £61.00.
Owner Northern Bloodstock Racing **Bred** Wertheimer & Frere **Trained** Scamblesby, Lincs

FOCUS
Only a handful of these had proven themselves in form of late and there was no strength in depth to this handicap, though they finished in something of a heap because they went only a steady tempo. The pace did not increase until the final half-mile and there was still only 4l covering the whole field turning in. That made for more than one hard-luck story and finishing positions do not necessarily reflect the horses' relative merits at the weights.

1183 STAY AT THE WOLVERHAMPTON HOLIDAY INN CLASSIFIED STKS — 5f 216y (Tp)
7:15 (7:15) (Class 5) 3-Y-O — **£3,234** (£962; £481; £240) **Stalls** Low

Form — RPR
350- **1** **Thee And Me (IRE)**[160] 7460 3-8-7 68 KevinLundie(7) 1 — 71
(Mike Murphy) *chsd ldrs: hmpd over 2f out: rdn to ld over 1f out: jst hld on* **10/1**
03-0 **2** *hd* **King Of Spin**[65] 352 3-9-0 66 MartinDwyer 2 — 70
(William Muir) *s.i.s: hld up: nt clr run over 2f out: hdwy over 1f out: shkn up to chse wnr fnl f: r.o* **3/1**[1]
6-53 **3** *3* **Fashionata (IRE)**[44] 612 3-9-0 70 GrahamGibbons 5 — 60
(Kristin Stubbs) *hld up: rdn over 1f out: styd on to go 3rd ins fnl f: nt trble ldrs* **3/1**[1]
15-5 **4** *hd* **Le Manege Enchante (IRE)**[8] 1060 3-9-0 68 TonyHamilton 3 — 60
(Derek Shaw) *hld up: hdwy over 2f out: nt clr run over 1f out: swtchd lft ins fnl f: styd on* **4/1**[2]
1-00 **5** *1 ¾* **Feelin Dicky**[29] 797 3-9-0 67 PaulMulrennan 6 — 54
(James Given) *led: racd keenly: rdn and hdd over 1f out: wknd ins fnl f* **17/2**
0-36 **6** *1* **Deben**[28] 824 3-9-0 69 KeaganLatham 4 — 51
(Kevin Ryan) *prom: chsd ldr over 4f out: rdn and ev ch over 1f out: wknd ins fnl f* **11/2**[3]
0-34 **7** *2 ¼* **Emily Goldfinch**[29] 791 3-8-11 68 TimClark(3) 7 — 44
(Phil McEntee) *plld hrd and prom: rdn and wknd over 1f out* **14/1**

1m 14.32s (-0.18) **Going Correction** -0.05s/f (Stan) — **7** Ran SP% **111.7**
Speed ratings (Par 98): **99,98,94,94,92 90,87**
CSF £38.17 TOTE £10.60: £5.20, £1.70; EX 46.30 Trifecta £205.20.
Owner MK Horse Racing & Lee Bearman **Bred** Pat Fullam **Trained** Westoning, Beds

FOCUS
Only 4lb between the entire field for this classified stakes on BHA ratings and, in a contest not run at a breakneck gallop, they were all pretty much in contention at the top of the straight.

1184 NAME A RACE BY CALLING 01902 390000 MAIDEN STKS — 1m 1f 103y (Tp)
7:45 (7:46) (Class 5) 3-Y-O+ — **£3,234** (£962; £481; £240) **Stalls** Low

Form — RPR
00- **1** **Ban Shoof**[150] 7673 3-8-11 0 TomQueally 8 — 75
(Ismail Mohammed) *hld up: hdwy over 2f out: r.o u.p to ld nr fin* **16/1**
030- **2** *nk* **De Aguilar (USA)**[114] 8153 3-8-11 75 WilliamTwiston-Davies 5 — 74
(Roger Charlton) *chsd ldrs: rdn to ld over 1f out: edgd lft ins fnl f: hdd nr fin* **11/2**[3]
3- **3** *hd* **Rasasee (IRE)**[139] 7863 3-8-11 0 AndreaAtzeni 4 — 74
(Marco Botti) *hld up in tch: shkn up over 2f out: swtchd lft over 1f out: rdn and ev ch wl ins fnl f: r.o* **4/7**[1]
4 **4** *6* **Russian Ranger (IRE)**[23] 874 3-8-11 0 RyanClark 1 — 61
(Jonathan Portman) *chsd ldrs: led over 2f out: rdn and hdd over 1f out: wknd ins fnl f* **50/1**
5 *4* **Louvencourt (FR)** 3-8-11 0 JoeFanning 9 — 58+
(Mark Johnston) *s.i.s: sn chsng ldrs: shkn up over 2f out: wknd over 1f out* **11/2**[3]
6 *1 ½* **Broadsword (IRE)** 4-9-9 0 DougieCostello 3 — 48
(Kevin Frost) *s.s: a in rr* **66/1**
0-4 **7** *1 ½* **Cassie**[8] 1063 6-9-9 0 (t) PatCosgrave 2 — 45
(Ben Pauling) *led: rdn and hdd over 2f out: wknd fnl f* **5/1**[2]
0 **8** *18* **Nordenfelt (IRE)**[39] 675 3-8-11 0 OisinMurphy 7 — 8
(Ed Dunlop) *mid-div: pushed along and lost pl over 7f out: rdn 5f out: wknd over 2f out* **40/1**
9 *2* **Bertie Bishop** 4-9-11 0 DanielMuscutt(3) 6 — 8
(Brian McMath) *s.s: hdwy to chse ldr 6f out tl rdn over 3f out: wknd over 2f out* **33/1**

2m 0.19s (-0.61) **Going Correction** -0.05s/f (Stan)
WFA 3 from 4yo+ 17lb — **9** Ran SP% **125.8**
Speed ratings (Par 103): **100,99,99,94,90 89,88,72,70**
CSF £107.01 TOTE £18.90: £3.30, £1.90, £1.10; EX 176.90 Trifecta £1161.60.
Owner Sultan Ali **Bred** Lady Legard **Trained** Newmarket, Suffolk

FOCUS
None of these had shown much better than modest form and though several were unexposed, the chances are that this may not have been a strong maiden. They did not go a great pace either, and that may well have counted against the favourite.

1185 WOLVERHAMPTON-RACECOURSE.CO.UK H'CAP — 1m 1f 103y (Tp)
8:15 (8:16) (Class 5) (0-75,75) 3-Y-O — **£3,234** (£962; £481; £240) **Stalls** Low

Form — RPR
6-21 **1** **Manjaam (IRE)**[22] 887 3-9-8 **74** PatCosgrave 4 — 85+
(Ed Dunlop) *chsd ldrs: led over 1f out: rdn and r.o wl* **9/4**[1]
-214 **2** *2 ½* **Jarir**[35] 729 3-9-7 **73** SeanLevey 6 — 78
(Richard Hannon) *led over 8f out: rdn and hdd over 1f out: styd on same pce ins fnl f* **11/4**[2]
653- **3** *1* **Hairdryer**[168] 7248 3-9-5 **71** OisinMurphy 5 — 74
(Andrew Balding) *plld hrd: trckd ldr over 7f out: rdn and ev ch whn edgd rt over 1f out: hung lft and styd on same pce ins fnl f* **11/2**
635- **4** *1* **Possible Future**[181] 6930 3-9-0 **69** [1] ThomasBrown(3) 3 — 70
(Ismail Mohammed) *hld up: hdwy over 1f out: styd on same pce ins fnl f* **22/1**
3-15 **5** *1 ¾* **Artful Mind**[54] 495 3-9-7 **73** RichardKingscote 7 — 70
(James Unett) *hld up: rdn over 1f out: nvr nrr* **16/1**
6-21 **6** *½* **Cat Royale (IRE)**[44] 603 3-9-5 **74** (p) DannyBrock(3) 1 — 70
(Jane Chapple-Hyam) *led 1f: chsd ldrs: rdn over 2f out: wknd fnl f* **14/1**
1 **7** *6* **Pivotal Flame (IRE)**[25] 863 3-9-2 **68** LukeMorris 8 — 51
(James Tate) *s.i.s: hld up: rdn over 2f out: wknd over 1f out* **9/2**[3]
0-14 **8** *shd* **Zainat (IRE)**[60] 421 3-9-9 **75** DougieCostello 2 — 58
(K R Burke) *prom: rdn over 2f out: wknd over 1f out* **16/1**

1m 58.54s (-2.26) **Going Correction** -0.05s/f (Stan) — **8** Ran SP% **113.8**
Speed ratings (Par 98): **108,105,104,104,102 102,96,96**
CSF £8.47 CT £28.62 TOTE £3.30: £1.20, £1.10, £2.10; EX 8.60 Trifecta £31.70.
Owner Mohammed Jaber **Bred** Ballylinch Stud **Trained** Newmarket, Suffolk

FOCUS
As good a 56-75 3yo handicap as you could hope to see, with each of the six to have run this year already successful in 2016 and the entire field still open to improvement. They went a good pace too and this is decent form for the grade.

1186 FOLLOW US ON TWITTER @WOLVESRACES H'CAP — 7f 32y (Tp)
8:45 (8:46) (Class 5) (0-75,73) 4-Y-O+ — **£3,234** (£962; £481; £240) **Stalls** High

Form — RPR
4-00 **1** **Shamlan (IRE)**[38] 683 4-9-2 **68** (p) StevieDonohoe 4 — 75
(Kevin Frost) *chsd ldrs: rdn over 1f out: r.o to ld post* **7/2**[2]
-315 **2** *hd* **Mr Christopher (IRE)**[30] 777 4-9-0 **66** (p) RichardKingscote 3 — 72
(Tom Dascombe) *led: rdn over 1f out: hdd post* **9/4**[1]
/55- **3** *½* **Inexes**[132] 7949 4-9-7 **73** PhillipMakin 5 — 78
(Marjorie Fife) *hmpd s: sn mid-div: swtchd rt and hdwy over 1f out: r.o* **9/2**[3]
060- **4** *1 ¼* **Available (IRE)**[123] 8054 7-9-3 **69** (tp) JoeFanning 9 — 70
(John Mackie) *chsd ldr: rdn and ev ch over 1f out: styd on same pce ins fnl f* **16/1**
0531 **5** *1 ¼* **Indian Affair**[25] 857 6-9-4 **70** (bt) FrannyNorton 2 — 68
(Milton Bradley) *chsd ldrs: rdn over 1f out: styd on same pce ins fnl f* **8/1**
6345 **6** *hd* **Depth Charge (IRE)**[17] 944 4-9-1 **70** (vt) JacobButterfield(3) 6 — 67
(Kristin Stubbs) *hld up: hdwy over 1f out: styd on same pce ins fnl f* **5/1**
400- **7** *1 ½* **Diamonds A Dancing**[155] 7591 6-8-7 **64** EdwardGreatrex(5) 1 — 57
(John O'Shea) *hld up: rdn 1/2-way: styd on ins fnl f: nvr on terms* **28/1**
-240 **8** *shd* **Swiss Cross**[29] 795 9-9-2 **68** (bt) LukeMorris 7 — 61
(Phil McEntee) *mid-div: rdn over 2f out: styd on same pce fr over 1f out* **11/1**
06-0 **9** *2 ¼* **Ambitious Boy**[58] 433 7-9-1 **72** (p) CiaranMckee(5) 8 — 59
(John O'Shea) *dwlt hld up: a in rr* **16/1**

1m 27.5s (-1.30) **Going Correction** -0.05s/f (Stan) — **9** Ran SP% **122.5**
Speed ratings (Par 103): **105,104,104,102,101 101,99,99,96**
CSF £12.65 CT £37.36 TOTE £6.30: £2.40, £1.50, £2.20; EX 25.50 Trifecta £87.90.
Owner Kevin Frost **Bred** Darley **Trained** Market Drayton, Shropshire

FOCUS
Plenty with questions to answer in a less-than-competitive 61-75 handicap and though they went a good pace few got into it.
T/Jkpt: Not won. T/Plt: £24.20 to a £1 stake. Pool: £94,465.32 - 2,848.73 winning tickets T/Qpdt: £6.50 to a £1 stake. Pool: £12,281.55 - 1,385.62 winning tickets **Colin Roberts**

1187 - 1194a (Foreign Racing) - See Raceform Interactive

DONCASTER (L-H)

Saturday, April 2

OFFICIAL GOING: Soft changing to soft (heavy in places) after race 1 (2.15)

Wind: Moderate against Weather: Cloudy

1195 BETWAY SPRING MILE (H'CAP) 1m (S)

2:15 (2:17) (Class 2) 4-Y-0+

£28,012 (£8,388; £4,194; £2,097; £1,048; £526) **Stalls** High

Form RPR

210- **1** **Lord Of The Rock (IRE)**[231] 5367 4-9-1 **88** PaulMulrennan 4 98+
(Michael Dods) *sn led: rdn wl over 1f out: drvn and hld on wl towards fin* **20/1**

004- **2** *nk* **Donncha (IRE)**[168] 7282 5-9-7 **97** TomMarquand[(3)] 19 106
(Robert Eddery) *hld up towards rr: gd hdwy over 2f out: chsd ldrs over 1f out: rdn to chal ins fnl f and ev ch: drvn and kpt on towards fin* **14/1**

200- **3** *1 ¼* **Instant Attraction (IRE)**[147] 7754 5-9-8 **95** JackGarritty 20 101
(Jedd O'Keeffe) *prom: hdwy and cl up over 1f out: sn rdn and ev ch: drvn and kpt on same pce fnl f* **33/1**

45-2 **4** *1 ½* **Solo Hunter**[63] 401 5-9-2 **89** (b) DavidProbert 18 92
(Martyn Meade) *trckd ldrs: hdwy over 2f out: rdn wl over 1f out: kpt on same pce fnl f* **40/1**

053- **5** *1 ¼* **Finn Class (IRE)**[169] 7247 5-8-10 **88** PhilDennis[(5)] 14 88
(Michael Dods) *in tch: hdwy 3f out: chsd ldrs 2f out: sn rdn and no imp fnl f* **50/1**

343- **6** *1* **Wilde Inspiration (IRE)**[176] 7088 5-9-2 **89** ConnorBeasley 2 86
(Julie Camacho) *chsd ldrs: rdn along over 2f out: grad wknd fr over 1f out* **20/1**

511- **7** *1 ¼* **Right Touch**[196] 6519 6-9-3 **97** AdamMcNamara[(7)] 6 92+
(Richard Fahey) *in tch whn hmpd and lost pl 3f out: rdn along 2f out: styd on fnl f: nrst fin* **12/1**

151- **8** *nk* **Emerald (ITY)**[154] 7632 4-9-0 **87** WilliamBuick 3 81
(Marco Botti) *hld up in rr: hdwy over 2f out: shkn up wl over 1f out: styd on fnl f: nrst fin* **12/1**

16-0 **9** *1* **Father Bertie**[21] 920 4-9-1 **88** (p) DavidAllan 17 80
(Tim Easterby) *cl up: chal 3f out: rdn over 2f out: drvn wl over 1f out: wknd appr fnl f* **25/1**

124- **10** *1 ½* **Predominance (IRE)**[147] 7754 4-9-3 **90** PatCosgrave 15 78+
(William Haggas) *hld up in rr: hdwy wl over 2f out: rdn wl over 1f out: kpt on fnl f* **7/2**[1]

212- **11** *¾* **Edgar Balthazar**[177] 7060 4-9-1 **88** (p) PhillipMakin 21 74
(Keith Dalgleish) *dwlt: sn in midfield: effrt 3f out: rdn over 2f out: sn no imp* **50/1**

10-1 **12** *3 ¾* **Keystroke**[21] 920 4-9-10 **97** 5ex JimCrowley 13 75
(Jeremy Noseda) *midfield: hdwy and swtchd lft 3f out: rdn to chse ldrs 2f out: sn drvn and btn over 1f out* **7/1**[2]

50-0 **13** *1 ¼* **Dubai Dynamo**[17] 960 11-9-3 **90** PJMcDonald 16 65
(Ruth Carr) *nvr bttr than midfield* **100/1**

216- **14** *1* **Master Of Irony (IRE)**[225] 5602 4-8-13 **86** OisinMurphy 1 59
(Ralph Beckett) *towards rr: hdwy on outer and in tch 1/2-way: rdn along wl over 2f out: sn wknd* **15/2**[3]

536- **15** *1 ¼* **Examiner (IRE)**[161] 7470 5-9-4 **91** JamieSpencer 10 61
(Stuart Williams) *in rr and swtchd lft to outer after 1f: hdwy and in tch 3f out: rdn over 2f out: sn wknd* **20/1**

1434 **16** *1* **Big Time (IRE)**[35] 749 5-8-13 **86** (p) FrannyNorton 11 53
(David Nicholls) *chsd ldng pair: rdn along wl over 2f out: drvn and wknd wl over 1f out* **40/1**

464- **17** *1 ¾* **Azraff (IRE)**[157] 7548 4-9-9 **96** (b) RyanMoore 5 59
(Marco Botti) *towards rr: hdwy 1/2-way: in tch 3f out: sn rdn and btn* **9/1**

161- **18** *hd* **Maraakib (IRE)**[151] 7676 4-9-4 **91** DanielTudhope 9 54
(David O'Meara) *chsd ldrs: n.m.r and hmpd 3f out: sn lost pl and bhd* **20/1**

164- **19** *5* **Carnival King (IRE)**[248] 4748 4-8-13 **86** JimmyFortune 8 37
(Brian Meehan) *chsd ldrs: rdn along whn n.m.r and hmpd 3f out: sn wknd* **25/1**

2206 **20** *10* **Si Senor (IRE)**[8] 1068 5-9-2 **89** AdamKirby 22 17
(Ed Vaughan) *a towards rr* **25/1**

04-1 **21** *hd* **Craftsmanship (FR)**[22] 900 5-9-2 **89** 5ex WilliamCarson 12 17
(Robert Eddery) *a in rr* **40/1**

1m 45.8s (6.50) **Going Correction** +1.025s/f (Soft) **21** Ran SP% **124.3**

Speed ratings (Par 109): **108,107,106,104,103 102,101,101,100,98 97,94,92,91,90 89,87,87,82,72 72**

CSF £236.56 CT £9044.54 TOTE £22.60: £5.20, £3.30, £6.40, £8.60; EX 395.70 Trifecta £3885.60.

Owner Geoff & Sandra Turnbull **Bred** Geoff & Sandra Turnbull **Trained** Denton, Co Durham

FOCUS

Paul Mulrennan said after winning the opener: "It's very soft, tough conditions. Only the fittest will survive." A competitive big-field consolation race, effectively an 86-97. The field raced in one group down the centre, with the winner making all from stall 4 and the next three all drawn on the stands' flank. The winner looks on a fair mark, but is entitled to progress again.

1196 BETWAY LINCOLN (HERITAGE H'CAP) 1m (S)

2:45 (2:49) (Class 2) 4-Y-0+

£62,250 (£18,640; £9,320; £4,660; £2,330; £1,170) **Stalls** High

Form RPR

3-03 **1** **Secret Brief (IRE)**[44] 628 4-9-4 **100** WilliamBuick 22 109
(Charlie Appleby) *hld up towards stands' side: smooth hdwy over 3f out: rdn wl over 1f out: edgd persistently lft tl jnd ldr ins fnl f: drvn and kpt on: led towards fin* **12/1**

2-31 **2** *nk* **Bravo Zolo (IRE)**[33] 767 4-9-5 **101** 5ex RyanMoore 2 109+
(Jeremy Noseda) *prom towards far side: rdn to ld over 2f out: jnd ins fnl f: kpt on but hdd towards fin* **12/1**

0500 **3** *½* **Battle Of Marathon (USA)**[26] 740 4-9-6 **102** (p) AdamKirby 18 109
(John Ryan) *hld up: hdwy over 2f out: rdn wl over 1f out: stl only 9th appr fnl f: r.o wl: edgd rt ins fnl f: wnt 3rd towards fin* **50/1**

300- **4** *¾* **Birdman (IRE)**[172] 7177 6-9-3 **104** JoshDoyle[(5)] 21 109
(David O'Meara) *hld up towards stands' side: rdn and hdwy over 2f out: kpt on fnl f* **14/1**

0-44 **5** *3 ¾* **Man Of Harlech**[8] 1069 5-9-4 **100** OisinMurphy 3 97
(Andrew Balding) *hld up towards far side: rdn and sme hdwy over 2f out: plugged on: nvr threatened ldrs* **10/1**

44-0 **6** *hd* **Emell**[28] 833 6-9-9 **105** (b) KieranO'Neill 20 101
(Richard Hannon) *hld up: rdn and hdwy 2f out: edgd lft over 1f out: no ex ins fnl f* **66/1**

301- **7** *2* **Express Himself (IRE)**[169] 7247 5-9-5 **101** JimCrowley 7 93+
(Ed McMahon) *slowly away: hld up: racd keenly: stdy hdwy on bit fr over 4f out: rdn to chal 2f out: wknd fnl f* **12/1**

003- **8** *2* **Farlow (IRE)**[147] 7754 8-9-3 **102** SammyJoBell[(3)] 8 89
(Richard Fahey) *prom: rdn to ld briefly over 2f out: wknd fnl f* **18/1**

120- **9** *shd* **Storm Rock**[126] 8034 4-9-4 **100** DavidProbert 13 87
(Harry Dunlop) *midfield: rdn over 3f out: no imp* **10/1**

110- **10** *shd* **You're Fired (IRE)**[130] 7971 5-9-6 **102** DougieCostello 19 89
(K R Burke) *in tch towards stands' side: rdn 3f out: wknd fnl f* **16/1**

110- **11** *2 ¾* **Mutarakez (IRE)**[289] 3304 4-9-5 **101** PaulHanagan 15 81
(Brian Meehan) *trckd ldrs towards stands' side: racd keenly: rdn over 2f out: hung lft over 1f out: wknd* **7/1**[3]

5462 **12** *4* **Beach Bar (IRE)**[30] 812 5-9-3 **99** PatDobbs 9 70
(Brendan Powell) *led towards centre: hdd over 2f out: wknd* **25/1**

355- **13** *1 ½* **Fire Ship**[87] 7709 7-9-2 **98** GrahamLee 16 66
(William Knight) *prom towards stands' side: rdn over 3f out: wknd over 1f out* **25/1**

00- **14** *1 ¾* **Ocean Tempest**[246] 4817 7-9-3 **99** FrankieDettori 11 63
(John Ryan) *dwlt: sn chsd ldrs towards centre: rdn over 3f out: wknd over 1f out* **16/1**

000- **15** *4* **Rene Mathis (GER)**[168] 7282 6-9-8 **104** DavidNolan 17 58
(Richard Fahey) *in tch: rdn 3f out: sn wknd* **25/1**

000- **16** *9* **Heaven's Guest (IRE)**[168] 7278 6-9-3 **106** AdamMcNamara[(7)] 4 40
(Richard Fahey) *hld up towards far side: rdn over 3f out: sn btn* **25/1**

200/ **17** *15* **Stipulate**[329] 7-9-6 **102** BenCurtis 1
(Brian Ellison) *a towards rr* **50/1**

2-12 **18** *4 ½* **Udododontu (IRE)**[44] 628 4-9-6 **102** JamesDoyle 10 +
(Saeed bin Suroor) *midfield: rdn over 3f out: sn btn: eased fnl 2f* **11/2**[1]

0/ **19** *8* **Lord Of The Land (IRE)**[211] 5-9-6 **102** DanielTudhope 6
(David O'Meara) *in tch: rdn over 3f out: sn wknd* **6/1**[2]

601- **20** *1 ½* **Ingleby Angel (IRE)**[206] 6205 7-9-2 **98** PhillipMakin 14
(Colin Teague) *in tch: rdn and lost pl over 4f out: sn bhd* **66/1**

0-30 **21** *9* **Lat Hawill (IRE)**[33] 767 5-9-2 **101** (p) DanielMuscutt[(3)] 5
(Marco Botti) *chsd ldrs: rdn over 4f out: sn wknd* **66/1**

-423 **22** *1* **Sirius Prospect (USA)**[38] 692 8-9-5 **101** RobertWinston 12
(Dean Ivory) *chsd ldrs: rdn over 3f out: wknd and eased* **33/1**

1m 46.25s (6.95) **Going Correction** +1.025s/f (Soft) **22** Ran SP% **133.8**

Speed ratings (Par 109): **106,105,105,104,100 100,98,96,96,96 93,89,88,86,82 73,58,53,45,44 35,34**

CSF £145.89 CT £6978.32 TOTE £17.80: £4.10, £4.10, £12.80, £4.60; EX 283.80 Trifecta £25424.90.

Owner Godolphin **Bred** Airlie Stud **Trained** Newmarket, Suffolk

FOCUS

After the opening race the ground was changed to soft, heavy in places. The winning time was 0.45sec slower than the Spring Mile, though the ground looked to have been opened up by the runners in the earlier race. With the two bottomweights running off a mark of 98, this was a classy Lincoln, but the conditions certainly seemed to take their toll with a couple of the fancied horses running shockers and the field finished pretty well spread out. They looked like they might split into two early, with the main group staying centre-to-far side while a smaller group of eight started off more towards the nearside, but it wasn't long before the two groups moved closer together. The result suggested there was no great track bias. The winner recorded a length personal best, while it was also an improvement from the runner-up on his recent AW form.

1197 BETWAY CAMMIDGE TROPHY (LISTED RACE) 6f

3:20 (3:21) (Class 1) 3-Y-0+

£20,982 (£7,955; £3,981; £1,983; £995; £499) **Stalls** High

Form RPR

410- **1** **Mobsta (IRE)**[147] 7755 4-9-5 100 SilvestreDeSousa 14 111
(Mick Channon) *racd towards stands' rail: in rr: gd hdwy over 2f out: rdn to ld appr fnl f: kpt on strly* **8/1**

010- **2** *1* **Suedois (FR)**[181] 6972 5-9-5 111 DanielTudhope 12 108
(David O'Meara) *hld up in tch: hdwy over 2f out: swtchd lft and rdn over 1f out: chsd wnr ins fnl f: sn drvn and no imp towards fin* **5/1**[2]

000- **3** *1 ¼* **Maarek**[135] 7910 9-9-5 108 JamieSpencer 2 104
(Miss Evanna McCutcheon, Ire) *towards rr: hdwy over 2f out: chsd ldrs whn n.m.r and swtchd lft jst over 1f out: rdn and edgd rt ins fnl f: kpt on* **13/2**[3]

00-6 **4** *hd* **Glen Moss (IRE)**[21] 921 7-9-5 98 PaulMulrennan 11 103
(Michael Dods) *trckd ldrs: smooth hdwy 2f out: rdn jst over 1f out: drvn and kpt on same pce ins fnl f* **33/1**

010- **5** *1* **Shared Equity**[147] 7755 5-9-5 105 GrahamLee 7 100
(Jedd O'Keeffe) *led: rdn along 2f out: hdd and drvn appr fnl f: grad wknd* **7/1**

15-0 **6** *1* **Another Wise Kid (IRE)**[21] 923 8-9-5 99 RobertWinston 10 97
(Paul Midgley) *racd towards stands' rail: chsd ldrs: cl up 2f out: sn rdn and wknd ent fnl f* **33/1**

15-5 **7** *½* **Move In Time**[35] 745 8-9-10 110 SamJames 13 100
(David O'Meara) *racd towards stands' rail: trckd ldrs: hdwy over 2f out: rdn over 1f out: sn wknd* **16/1**

3001 **8** *1* **Alben Star (IRE)**[8] 1066 8-9-5 109 DavidNolan 5 92
(Richard Fahey) *hld up towards rr: hdwy over 2f out: rdn over 1f out: sn btn* **10/1**

1136 **9** *½* **Gracious John (IRE)**[8] 1070 3-8-10 106 JFEgan 8 91
(David Evans) *prom: rdn along 2f out: sn wknd* **13/2**[3]

605- **10** *1 ¼* **Marsh Hawk**[197] 6502 4-9-0 100 PatDobbs 4 82
(Richard Hannon) *cl up on outer: chal over 2f out: sn rdn and wknd over 1f out* **12/1**

000- **11** *8* **Duke Of Firenze**[215] 5936 7-9-5 95 DavidAllan 1 61
(David C Griffiths) *dwlt: a in rr* **66/1**

001- **12** *1 ½* **Jack Dexter**[147] 7755 7-9-8 106 RyanMoore 9 59
(Jim Goldie) *hld up towards rr: hdwy over 2f out: rdn wl over 1f out: sn btn* **4/1**[1]

300- **13** *7* **Robin Park**[254] 4541 4-9-0 77 TonyHamilton 6 29
(Richard Fahey) *dwlt: t.k.h: a in rr* **100/1**

1m 18.03s (4.43) **Going Correction** +1.025s/f (Soft)

WFA 3 from 4yo+ 12lb **13** Ran SP% **118.0**

Speed ratings (Par 111): **111,109,108,107,106 105,104,103,102,100 90,88,78**

CSF £46.36 TOTE £8.60: £2.60, £2.50, £2.60; EX 64.50 Trifecta £435.40.

Owner Billy Parish **Bred** P J Gleeson **Trained** West Ilsley, Berks

FOCUS
A fair renewal of this Listed event, which was run at a generous pace considering the conditions. The first three came from the rear and this was a sizeable personal best from the winner, though it needs confirming.

1198 BETWAY DONCASTER MILE STKS (LISTED RACE) 1m (R)
3:55 (3:55) (Class 1) 4-Y-O+ **£20,982** (£7,955; £3,981; £1,983) **Stalls** Low

Form RPR
032- **1** **Belardo (IRE)**[168] 7280 4-9-0 117 JamesDoyle 2 114+
(Roger Varian) *trckd ldng pair on inner: effrt and n.m.r wl over 1f out: squeezed through and qcknd to ld ent fnl f: sn clr: readily* **8/13**[1]
1-00 **2** 2 1/4 **Calling Out (FR)**[44] 628 5-9-0 100 JamieSpencer 4 107
(David Simcock) *trckd ldr: cl up over 3f out: effrt to chal over 2f out: ev ch tl rdn and appr fnl f and kpt on same pce* **9/1**
120- **3** 1 3/4 **Custom Cut (IRE)**[181] 6972 7-9-7 117 DanielTudhope 3 110
(David O'Meara) *led: qcknd wl over 1f out: rdn wl over 1f out: hdd ent fnl f: kpt on one pce* **3/1**[2]
050- **4** 2 **Master Carpenter (IRE)**[189] 6755 5-9-0 108 PhillipMakin 6 98
(Rod Millman) *trckd ldng pair: hdwy on outer and cl up over 2f out: rdn over 1f out: sn wknd* **8/1**[3]
1m 46.48s (6.78) **Going Correction** +1.025s/f (Soft) 4 Ran SP% **108.0**
Speed ratings (Par 111): **107,104,103,101**
CSF £6.50 TOTE £1.50; EX 6.10 Trifecta £11.20.
Owner Godolphin & Prince A A Faisal **Bred** Ballylinch Stud **Trained** Newmarket, Suffolk

FOCUS
This Listed event was hit hard by four non-runners, but was still an interesting race because of the warm favourite. The pace was only steady, but it still proved very straightforward for the market leader even though he probably didn't need to match his best in order to win.

1199 BETWAY BROCKLESBY CONDITIONS STKS (PLUS 10 RACE) 5f
4:30 (4:32) (Class 4) 2-Y-O **£6,469** (£1,925; £962; £481) **Stalls** High

Form RPR
1 **The Last Lion (IRE)** 2-9-3 0 FrannyNorton 3 86+
(Mark Johnston) *w ldr: led 3f out: pushed clr appr fnl f: eased towards fin* **4/5**[1]
2 1 3/4 **Simmy's Temple** 2-8-12 0 PhillipMakin 8 73
(Keith Dalgleish) *in tch: pushed along and outpcd 1/2-way: edgd lft to outer appr fnl f: kpt on wl: wnt 2nd 75yds out* **33/1**
3 3 1/4 **Monte Cinq (IRE)** 2-9-3 0 AndrewMullen 4 66
(Jason Ward) *midfield: rdn 2f out: hdwy to go 2nd ins fnl f: lost 2nd 75yds out* **40/1**
4 1/2 **Jollydee (IRE)** 2-8-12 0 PaulMulrennan 9 59
(Paul Midgley) *s.i.s: hld up: pushed along and rn green 2f out: rdn and kpt on wl fnl f* **33/1**
5 2 1/2 **Absolutely Awesome** 2-9-3 0 JFEgan 1 55
(Deborah Sanderson) *chsd ldng pair: rdn 2f out: wknd ins fnl f* **12/1**
6 1 1/4 **Springwood (IRE)** 2-9-3 0 TonyHamilton 5 51
(Richard Fahey) *chsd ldng pair: rdn 1/2-way: wknd fnl f* **8/1**
7 5 **Tallinski (IRE)** 2-9-3 0 BenCurtis 12 33+
(Brian Ellison) *led narrowly: hdd 3f out: remained cl up tl wknd appr fnl f* **13/2**[3]
8 4 1/2 **Crucial Moment** 2-8-12 0 RyanWhile[(5)] 10 17
(Bill Turner) *hld up: pushed along 3f out: wknd over 1f out* **5/1**[2]
9 2 1/2 **Heavenly Cry** 2-8-12 0 NoelGarbutt[(5)] 13 8
(Denis Quinn) *s.i.s: sn pushed along in rr: a bhd* **50/1**
10 3/4 **Paisley Abbey** 2-9-3 0 GrahamLee 11 5
(Paul Midgley) *hld up: sn pushed along: a towards rr* **20/1**
1m 4.9s (4.40) **Going Correction** +1.025s/f (Soft) 10 Ran SP% **119.4**
Speed ratings (Par 94): **105,102,97,96,92 90,82,75,71,69**
CSF £45.71 TOTE £1.80: £1.10, £6.90, £11.10; EX 37.60 Trifecta £988.30.
Owner John Brown & Megan Dennis **Bred** Barronstown Stud And Mrs T Stack **Trained** Middleham Moor, N Yorks

FOCUS
Several non-runners, including the Wesley Ward-trained Create A Dream, took some of the shine off this event, but it still threw up a very promising winner who has a fine pedigree and surely has more to offer.

1200 PARK HILL PRIVATE HOSPITAL MAIDEN STKS 1m 2f 60y
5:05 (5:06) (Class 5) 3-Y-O **£3,881** (£1,155; £577; £288) **Stalls** Low

Form RPR
25- **1** **Hereawi**[171] 7219 3-9-0 0 RichardKingscote 1 75+
(Ralph Beckett) *mde all: rdn along over 2f out: drvn ent fnl f: kpt on wl* **4/1**[2]
40- **2** 2 1/4 **Injam (IRE)**[191] 6687 3-9-5 0 GrahamLee 9 76
(Jedd O'Keeffe) *in tch: hdwy over 3f out and sn rdn along: green and drvn wl over 1f out: styd on wl fnl f* **33/1**
3 hd **Hermann** 3-9-5 0 PatDobbs 7 75+
(Richard Hannon) *trckd ldng pair: pushed along 3f out: rdn wl over 1f out: chsd wnr ent fnl f: sn drvn and kpt on same pce* **12/1**
0-33 **4** 3 1/4 **Albert Boy (IRE)**[31] 785 3-9-5 65 BenCurtis 11 69
(Scott Dixon) *cl up: rdn along 3f out: drvn wl over 1f out: grad wknd* **25/1**
5 3 1/4 **Mahfooz (IRE)** 3-9-5 0 PaulHanagan 8 63+
(Charles Hills) *dwlt and towards rr: hdwy 1/2-way: rdn along to chse ldrs 3f out: drvn and green 2f out: sn one pce* **5/1**[3]
6 3 3/4 **High Command (IRE)** 3-9-5 0 JackMitchell 6 56
(Roger Varian) *trckd ldng pair: effrt over 3f out: green and rdn along over 2f out: sn drvn and one pce* **13/8**[1]
7 14 **Fastnet Blast (IRE)** 3-9-5 0 FrankieDettori 2 29
(John Gosden) *dwlt: a bhd* **7/1**
8 3/4 **Lexington Law (IRE)** 3-9-5 0 KieranO'Neill 10 28
(Richard Hannon) *dwlt: a bhd* **20/1**
9 10 **Dream Factory (IRE)** 3-9-2 0 DanielMuscutt[(3)] 5 9
(Marco Botti) *midfield: effrt and sme hdwy 4f out: rdn along 3f out: sn wknd* **18/1**
10 11 **Neoclassical** 3-9-5 0 RobertHavlin 3
(John Gosden) *dwlt: green: sn rdn along and outpcd in rr: wl bhd fr 1/2-way* **9/1**
2m 19.24s (9.84) **Going Correction** +1.025s/f (Soft) 10 Ran SP% **121.8**
Speed ratings (Par 98): **101,99,99,96,93 90,79,79,71,62**
CSF £136.27 TOTE £4.80: £1.80, £8.00, £3.10; EX 106.80 Trifecta £1291.50.
Owner J H Richmond-Watson **Bred** Lawn Stud **Trained** Kimpton, Hants

FOCUS
Nine of the last ten winners of this maiden (at Doncaster) had run before, but although only three of these had previous experience they finished 1-2-4 and some of the newcomers proved very green and/or were all at sea in the conditions. Not many ever got into it and the winner has been rated to her 2yo debut form.

1201 HARRIET DE-VERE POWELL APPRENTICE H'CAP (R1 GO RACING IN YORKSHIRE FUTURE STAR SERIES) (DIV I) 1m 2f 60y
5:40 (5:40) (Class 5) (0-70,69) 4-Y-O+ **£3,881** (£1,155; £577; £288) **Stalls** Low

Form RPR
00-0 **1** **Bertie Moon**[25] 164 6-8-11 64 CliffordLee[(5)] 13 82
(Keith Dalgleish) *prom towards outer: led over 3f out: pushed clr over 2f out: rdn over 1f out: styd on wl: easily* **6/1**[3]
0021 **2** 10 **My Lord**[9] 1057 8-8-13 66 AledBeech[(5)] 11 65
(David Evans) *hld up: hdwy over 3f out: rdn over 2f out: styd on to go remote 2nd ins fnl f* **9/1**
200- **3** 1 1/4 **Honey Badger**[65] 8044 5-8-8 56 (p[1]) AaronJones 12 53
(Eugene Stanford) *midfield: rdn and hdwy 3f out: wnt 2nd over 1f out: one pce: lost 2nd ins fnl f* **20/1**
0154 **4** 1 **Time Square (FR)**[24] 870 9-8-2 55 oh2 (t) MitchGodwin[(5)] 2 50
(Tony Carroll) *trckd ldrs: rdn over 3f out: plugged on* **20/1**
04-4 **5** 2 1/4 **Shaw Ting**[30] 802 4-9-0 62 (p[1]) GeorgeBuckell 3 52
(Michael Appleby) *in tch: rdn and hdwy to chse clr ldr over 2f out: wknd ins fnl f* **5/1**[2]
6240 **6** 3 1/4 **Galuppi**[14] 1004 5-8-9 62 (b) CameronNoble[(5)] 16 46
(J R Jenkins) *hld up: rdn over 3f out: plugged on fnl 2f: nvr threatened* **25/1**
236- **7** 1 1/2 **Teenage Dream (IRE)**[95] 8385 8-8-0 55 oh5 BenRobinson[(7)] 17 36
(Brian Ellison) *hld up in rr: rdn over 4f out: plugged on fnl 2f: nvr threatened* **20/1**
600- **8** nk **Cape Hideaway**[151] 7675 4-9-0 65 JoshDoyle[(3)] 9 46
(Mark Walford) *hld up in midfield: rdn over 3f out: no imp* **20/1**
000- **9** 2 1/4 **Rioja Day (IRE)**[22] 7190 6-8-7 60 (b) PatrickVaughan[(5)] 8 37
(Jim Goldie) *trckd ldrs: rdn over 3f out: wknd fnl 2f* **25/1**
421- **10** 6 **Hit List (IRE)**[173] 7164 4-9-7 69 EdwardGreatrex 14 34
(Andrew Balding) *midfield towards outer: swtchd lft towards inner over 2f out: sn rdn and wknd* **9/4**[1]
600- **11** nse **Beaumont's Party (IRE)**[92] 7287 9-9-2 67 NathanEvans[(3)] 1 32
(Chris Grant) *midfield: rdn over 3f out: sn wknd* **16/1**
530- **12** nk **San Cassiano (IRE)**[190] 6699 9-9-2 67 PhilDennis[(3)] 4 32
(Ruth Carr) *led narrowly: rdn whn hdd over 3f out: wknd* **20/1**
-004 **13** 1/2 **Hydrant**[18] 940 10-9-0 65 RobJFitzpatrick[(3)] 7 29
(Richard Guest) *pressed ldr: rdn over 3f out: wknd over 2f out* **16/1**
606- **14** 13 **Morocco**[162] 7427 7-8-10 58 [1] GemmaTutty 15
(Karen Tutty) *dwlt: hld up: a towards rr* **16/1**
060- **15** 7 **Thecornishbarron (IRE)**[151] 7694 4-8-13 68 JonathanFisher[(7)] 10
(John Ryan) *hld up: rdn over 3f out: sn wknd* **50/1**
200- **16** 10 **Whitchurch**[113] 8176 4-8-12 60 RachelRichardson 6
(Philip Kirby) *a towards rr* **18/1**
2m 18.9s (9.50) **Going Correction** +1.025s/f (Soft) 16 Ran SP% **128.1**
Speed ratings (Par 103): **103,95,94,93,91 88,87,87,85,80 80,80,80,69,64 56**
CSF £53.89 CT £1052.92 TOTE £6.70: £1.90, £1.70, £5.60, £4.60; EX 68.00 Trifecta £1594.40.
Owner Equus Racing Club **Bred** M E Wates **Trained** Carluke, S Lanarks

FOCUS
A big-field apprentice handicap, but just one horse in it through the last quarter of a mile and he has been rated back to something like his best. It was the quicker division by two seconds.

1202 HARRIET DE-VERE POWELL APPRENTICE H'CAP (R1 GO RACING IN YORKSHIRE FUTURE STAR SERIES) (DIV II) 1m 2f 60y
6:10 (6:13) (Class 5) (0-70,69) 4-Y-O+ **£3,881** (£1,155; £577; £288) **Stalls** Low

Form RPR
454- **1** **Chilworth Bells**[296] 3069 4-9-2 64 JosephineGordon 6 77
(David Barron) *cl up: led over 3f out: hdd over 2f out: cl up and sn rdn along: drvn over 1f out: styd on to ld ins fnl f: sn clr* **7/1**
301- **2** 5 **I Am Not Here (IRE)**[282] 3545 5-9-3 65 CallumShepherd 4 69
(Brian Ellison) *in tch: hdwy 3f out: rdn to chse ldrs 2f out: kpt on u.p fnl f: tk 2nd towards fin* **9/2**[1]
0605 **3** nk **Evacusafe Lady**[4] 1131 5-8-2 55 oh2 (t) RhiainIngram[(5)] 13 58
(John Ryan) *trckd ldrs: hdwy over 4f out: led over 2f out: rdn wl over 1f out: hdd ins fnl f: sn wknd and lost 2nd towards fin* **20/1**
304- **4** 1/2 **Burner (IRE)**[64] 7966 4-9-5 67 [1] RachelRichardson 11 69
(Olly Williams) *hld up: hdwy over 4f out: rdn along to chse ldrs 2f out: styd on same pce fnl f* **16/1**
003- **5** 2 3/4 **Henpecked**[169] 7258 6-8-7 60 AdamMcNamara[(5)] 2 57
(Alistair Whillans) *chsd ldrs: pushed along 4f out: rdn wl over 2f out: kpt on one pce u.p fr over 1f out* **11/2**[3]
4304 **6** 3 1/4 **Rising Breeze (FR)**[28] 832 5-9-3 65 PaddyPilley 5 56
(Tony Carroll) *towards rr: hdwy 3f out: rdn 2f out: styd on appr fnl f: nrst fin* **10/1**
34-0 **7** nk **Monopoli**[10] 1048 7-8-2 55 oh2 (p) GeorgeWood[(5)] 16 45
(Ivan Furtado) *midfield: hdwy 3f out: in tch over 2f out: sn rdn along and kpt on one pce* **14/1**
3266 **8** 10 **Best Tamayuz**[17] 956 5-8-13 61 NoelGarbutt 10 32
(Scott Dixon) *chsd ldng pair: pushed along over 3f out: rdn over 2f out: grad wknd* **20/1**
-006 **9** 1 3/4 **Outlaw Torn (IRE)**[18] 939 7-8-11 62 (e) RobJFitzpatrick[(3)] 1 30
(Richard Guest) *led: rdn along and hdd over 3f out: sn wknd* **20/1**
100- **10** 3/4 **Cassandane (IRE)**[161] 7458 4-8-7 58 CharlieBennett[(3)] 9 24
(Shaun Harris) *chsd ldng pair: rdn along over 3f out: sn wknd* **25/1**
326- **11** 1 1/4 **Aneedh**[150] 7713 6-8-13 64 (b) PhilDennis[(3)] 12 28
(Clive Mulhall) *a towards rr* **5/1**[2]
600- **12** 6 **Lightning Spree (IRE)**[187] 6818 4-9-5 67 GaryHalpin 14 20
(Kevin Ryan) *awkward s and towards rr: hdwy over 3f out: effrt on inner and in tch over 2f out: sn rdn and btn* **14/1**
100- **13** 39 **Dalmarella Dancer (IRE)**[185] 6860 5-9-4 66 JordanVaughan 7
(K R Burke) *midfield: rdn along 4f out: sn wknd* **10/1**
000- **14** 18 **Regal Missile (IRE)**[200] 6398 4-8-7 58 JoshDoyle[(3)] 15
(Mark Walford) *midfield: rdn along 4f out: sn wknd* **25/1**
0-06 **15** 4 1/2 **Munaawib**[58] 449 8-8-5 60 (bt) BenSanderson[(7)] 17
(Deborah Sanderson) *a towards rr* **50/1**
5464 **16** 9 **General Tufto**[52] 526 11-8-7 55 oh10 (b) GeorgeBuckell 8
(Charles Smith) *a towards rr* **50/1**
2m 20.9s (11.50) **Going Correction** +1.025s/f (Soft) 16 Ran SP% **126.0**
Speed ratings (Par 103): **95,91,90,90,88 85,85,77,75,75 74,69,38,23,20 13**
CSF £36.19 CT £623.70 TOTE £6.20: £2.50, £2.00, £6.20, £3.80; EX 37.20 Trifecta £1273.70.
Owner Harrowgate Bloodstock Ltd **Bred** Norman Court Stud **Trained** Maunby, N Yorks

FOCUS
The winning time was two seconds slower than the first division. An ordinary race though the winner is overall progressive.
T/Jkpt: Not won. T/Plt: £556.30 to a £1 stake. Pool: £254,707.67 - 334.18 winning units. T/Qpdt: £10.50 to a £1 stake. Pool: £13,664.32 - 954.98 winning units. **Joe Rowntree & Andrew Sheret**

1138 KEMPTON (A.W) (R-H)

Saturday, April 2

OFFICIAL GOING: Polytrack: standard
Wind: Moderate, across Weather: Sunny becoming cloudy

1203 BETFRED TV/BRITISH STALLION STUDS EBF NOVICE STKS (PLUS 10 RACE) 5f (P)
1:55 (1:55) (Class 4) 2-Y-O **£4,269** (£1,270; £634; £317) **Stalls** Low

Form RPR
2 **1** **Stringybark Creek**[8] 1082 2-9-2 0................................ CharlesBishop 8 78
(Mick Channon) *mde all: rdn over 1f out: kpt on wl fnl f* **9/1**
2 *1 1/4* **Tomily (IRE)** 2-9-2 0.. SeanLevey 5 74+
(Richard Hannon) *hung bdly lft on bnd over 3f out and v wd arnd it: dropped in after: prog on inner to go 3rd over 1f out: shkn up and styd on to take 2nd last 75yds* **5/2**[1]
3 *3/4* **Makman (IRE)** 2-9-2 0.. AndreaAtzeni 2 71+
(Ed Dunlop) *sltly impeded s: chsd ldng pair to over 1f out: shkn up and kpt on wl fnl f to take 3rd again last strides* **5/1**[3]
4 *hd* **Dusker (USA)** 2-9-2 0.. JoeFanning 9 70
(Mark Johnston) *chsd wnr: shkn up and no imp over 1f out: kpt on but lost 2 pls last 75yds* **11/4**[2]
5 *1* **Lucata (IRE)** 2-9-2 0.. LiamJones 3 66
(Tom Dascombe) *sltly impeded s: in rr: rdn and v wd bnd 2f out: kpt on fr over 1f out* **33/1**
P **6** *2 1/2* **Dolokhov**[9] 1118 2-9-2 0.. MartinDwyer 7 57
(J S Moore) *dwlt: outpcd in last of main gp after 2f: kpt on fnl f: no ch* **33/1**
7 *3 1/4* **Rebel Heart** 2-8-11 0.. LukeMorris 6 41
(Bill Turner) *chsd ldrs tl wknd wl over 1f out* **33/1**
8 *5* **New Trier (IRE)** 2-8-11 0..........................(b[1]) JoseValdiviaJr 4 23
(Wesley A Ward, U.S.A) *chsd ldrs: quite wd bnd 2f out and wknd qckly* **5/1**[3]
P **Spin Top** 2-9-2 0.. GeorgeBaker 1
(Joseph Tuite) *rring and wouldn't r properly: immediately t.o: p.u after hanging off crse over 3f out* **12/1**

1m 0.19s (-0.31) **Going Correction** -0.05s/f (Stan) **9** Ran SP% **115.1**
Speed ratings (Par 94): **100,98,96,96,94 90,85,77,**
CSF £31.30 TOTE £8.40: £2.90, £1.40, £2.20; EX 35.90 Trifecta £212.10.
Owner M Channon **Bred** Whatton Manor Stud **Trained** West Ilsley, Berks

FOCUS
Only two of these had experience, and just one of them had previously completed, and that was the winner who had the run of things in front. The form is hard to pin down with confidence, though.

1204 BETFRED "HOME OF GOALS GALORE" H'CAP 7f (P)
2:30 (2:30) (Class 2) (0-105,102) 4-Y-O+
£11,827 (£3,541; £1,770; £885; £442; £222) **Stalls** Low

Form RPR
55-2 **1** **Crazy Chic (IRE)**[54] 503 5-8-12 **93**.......................... AndreaAtzeni 2 102
(Marco Botti) *trckd ldrs: prog to go 2nd over 1f out: drvn and sustained chal fnl f to ld last strides* **4/1**[1]
110- **2** *hd* **Solar Flair**[245] 4860 4-8-9 **90**.......................... LukeMorris 8 98
(William Knight) *trckd ldr: led jst over 2f out but then hanging lft: drvn and hrd pressed fnl f: hanging again nr fin and hdd last strides* **9/2**[2]
524- **3** *1 1/2* **Georgian Bay (IRE)**[103] 8326 6-9-3 **98**..........................(v) JoeyHaynes 7 102
(K R Burke) *hld up towards rr: shkn up on outer over 2f out: prog over 1f out: styd on wl to take 3rd ins fnl f* **10/1**
040- **4** *nk* **Archie (IRE)**[252] 4637 4-8-7 **88**.......................... JohnFahy 1 92
(Clive Cox) *trckd ldrs: rdn 2f out: disp 3rd fr over 1f out: kpt on but nvr able to chal* **12/1**
-221 **5** *1 1/4* **Shyron**[29] 816 5-8-12 **93**.......................... RyanPowell 4 93
(George Margarson) *settled towards rr: shkn up 2f out: nvr a threat but kpt on to take 5th nr fin and then eased* **11/2**[3]
-P40 **6** *3/4* **Mr Bossy Boots (IRE)**[46] 599 5-8-2 **88**..............(t) PatrickO'Donnell[(5)] 5 86
(Ralph Beckett) *dwlt: hld up in last pair: shkn up over 2f out: kpt on same pce fr over 1f out: no threat* **8/1**
0/0- **7** *nse* **Burn The Boats (IRE)**[280] 3670 7-8-11 **92**.......................... MartinLane 6 90
(Mike Murphy) *led: shkn up and hdd jst over 2f out: lost 2nd over 1f out: wknd* **33/1**
0-32 **8** *hd* **Brigliadoro (IRE)**[23] 886 5-8-11 **92**.......................... GrahamGibbons 10 90
(Philip McBride) *hld up on outer: shkn up over 2f out: no prog over 1f out: wl btn after* **8/1**
-556 **9** *2 1/2* **Grey Mirage**[29] 816 7-9-1 **96**..........................(p) LiamJones 3 87
(Marco Botti) *dwlt: stmbld after 1f: a in last pair: rdn and no prog 2f out* **11/1**
-200 **10** *hd* **Intransigent**[8] 1066 7-9-4 **102**.......................... RobHornby[(3)] 9 92
(Andrew Balding) *t.k.h: trckd ldng trio to over 2f out: sn wknd* **10/1**

1m 24.34s (-1.66) **Going Correction** -0.05s/f (Stan) **10** Ran SP% **112.9**
Speed ratings (Par 109): **107,106,105,104,103 102,102,102,99,99**
CSF £20.97 CT £168.08 TOTE £3.60: £1.30, £2.30, £2.80; EX 20.90 Trifecta £104.00.
Owner Scuderia Vittadini Srl **Bred** Scuderia Vittadini Srl **Trained** Newmarket, Suffolk
■ Stewards' Enquiry : Ryan Powell four-day ban: careless riding (Apr 16,18-20)

FOCUS
A decent handicap that should produce winners in the coming months. The winner recorded a small personal best off a fair mark.

1205 BETFRED LOTTO H'CAP 6f (P)
3:00 (3:01) (Class 2) (0-105,96) 4-Y-O+
£11,827 (£3,541; £1,770; £885; £442; £222) **Stalls** Low

Form RPR
21-2 **1** **Dougan**[50] 546 4-8-10 **85**.......................... AndreaAtzeni 2 100+
(David Evans) *hld up in last trio: prog jst over 2f out: trckd ldr jst over 1f out: led 150yds out: shkn up and styd on wl: readily* **2/1**[1]
041- **2** *1 3/4* **Mukaynis (IRE)**[169] 7245 5-8-13 **88**..........................(b) ShaneGray 8 97
(Kevin Ryan) *dwlt: rapid rcvry to ld after 1f: drvn over 1f out: hdd last 150yds: no ch w wnr but kpt on wl* **10/1**
0133 **3** *1 1/2* **Yeeoow (IRE)**[7] 1090 7-8-8 **83**.......................... JoeyHaynes 4 87
(K R Burke) *led 1f: chsd ldr: rdn over 2f out: no imp and lost 2nd jst over 1f out: hld on for 3rd* **13/2**
002- **4** *hd* **Harry Hurricane**[203] 6312 4-9-7 **96**.......................... SteveDrowne 5 98
(George Baker) *restless in stalls: dwlt: hld up in last trio: shkn up over 2f out: one pce and n.d after* **8/1**
0144 **5** *nk* **Hoofalong**[32] 771 6-9-4 **93**..........................(b) TomEaves 6 94
(Michael Easterby) *trckd ldng pair: urged along and no rspnse 2f out: rdn and lost pls fnl f* **7/1**
005- **6** *shd* **Lucky Beggar (IRE)**[161] 7461 6-9-1 **93**..............[1] MichaelJMMurphy[(3)] 7 94
(Charles Hills) *t.k.h: hld up in last: rdn and no prog over 2f out: kpt on fnl f: no ch* **6/1**[3]
60-0 **7** *2* **Ticks The Boxes (IRE)**[16] 966 4-8-6 **81**.......................... LukeMorris 3 75
(Michael Herrington) *t.k.h: hld up in midfield: rdn over 2f out: wknd fnl f* **20/1**
-602 **D** *1/2* **Plucky Dip**[7] 1090 5-8-7 **82**.......................... RyanPowell 1 85
(John Ryan) *a abt same pl: rdn and nt qckn 2f out: one pce after* **7/2**[2]

1m 11.28s (-1.82) **Going Correction** -0.05s/f (Stan) **8** Ran SP% **120.6**
Speed ratings (Par 109): **110,107,105,104,104 104,101,105**
CSF £25.15 CT £116.68 TOTE £2.60: £1.50, £3.90, £2.00; EX 23.10 Trifecta £161.50.
Owner Shropshire Wolves **Bred** Glebe Stud, J F Dean & Lady Trenchard **Trained** Pandy, Monmouths

FOCUS
A decent handicap, albeit lacking progressive runners outside the favourite, in which the winner was the only horse to make up significant ground.

1206 BETFRED "SUPPORTS JACK BERRY HOUSE" FILLIES' CONDITIONS STKS (PLUS 10 RACE) 1m (P)
3:35 (3:36) (Class 2) 3-Y-O **£11,827** (£3,541; £1,770; £885) **Stalls** Low

Form RPR
220- **1** **Marenko**[176] 7075 3-9-0 105.......................... SeanLevey 3 99
(Richard Hannon) *mde all: gng best fr 2f out: hung lft after: rdn and styd on wl fnl f* **7/2**
44-2 **2** *1 1/2* **Tutu Nguru (USA)**[28] 836 3-9-0 96.......................... AndreaAtzeni 1 95
(William Haggas) *hld up in 3rd: chsd wnr over 2f out: sn shkn up: trying to cl whn intimidated fr over 1f out and nvr able to chal seriously: wl hld whn checked last 75yds* **2/1**[1]
1- **3** *nk* **Quality Time (IRE)**[128] 7996 3-9-0 89.......................... HarryBentley 4 94
(Saeed bin Suroor) *t.k.h: chsd wnr to over 2f out: sn shkn up: kpt on again fnl f* **5/2**[2]
21- **4** *3 1/4* **Zest (IRE)**[162] 7422 3-9-0 84.......................... FrederikTylicki 2 86
(James Fanshawe) *t.k.h: hld up in last: shkn up over 2f out: nt qckn and sn btn* **11/4**[3]

1m 37.75s (-2.05) **Going Correction** -0.05s/f (Stan) **4** Ran SP% **110.8**
Speed ratings (Par 101): **108,106,106,102**
CSF £10.91 TOTE £3.30; EX 9.30 Trifecta £18.60.
Owner Cheveley Park Stud **Bred** Cheveley Park Stud Ltd **Trained** East Everleigh, Wilts
■ Stewards' Enquiry : Sean Levey two-day ban: careless riding (Apr 16,18)

FOCUS
The winner, who was a smart juvenile and had upwards of 8lb in hand on RPRs, was bizarrely sent off the outsider of the field. She probably didn't need to improve to win this and the race has been rated around the runner-up.

1207 BETFRED MOBILE SNOWDROP FILLIES' STKS (LISTED RACE) 1m (P)
4:10 (4:10) (Class 1) 4-Y-O+
£20,982 (£7,955; £3,981; £1,983; £995; £499) **Stalls** Low

Form RPR
042- **1** **Kyllachy Queen (IRE)**[127] 8015 4-9-0 100.......................... AndreaAtzeni 5 97+
(Marco Botti) *trckd ldrs: shkn up over 2f out: keeping on at one pce and little imp tl qcknd u.p fnl f: clsd qckly to ld last stride* **3/1**[2]
-111 **2** *hd* **Volunteer Point (IRE)**[8] 1065 4-9-0 102.......................... GrahamGibbons 4 96
(Mick Channon) *hld up in last trio: prog 2f out: led over 1f out and sn looked in command: drvn and r.o fnl f but hdd last strides* **5/2**[1]
100- **3** *1 1/2* **Light And Shade**[154] 7632 4-9-0 91.......................... LukeMorris 2 92
(James Tate) *t.k.h: hld up bhd ldrs: rdn to cl fr 2f out: outpcd over 1f out: styd on after* **14/1**
-230 **4** *1/2* **Lady Lydia (IRE)**[43] 632 5-9-0 75.......................... LiamJones 7 91?
(Conrad Allen) *t.k.h: hld up in last pair: shkn up over 2f out: prog over 1f out: styd on but nvr pce to threaten* **100/1**
0-14 **5** *3/4* **Saucy Minx (IRE)**[8] 1065 6-9-0 94.......................... JoeFanning 9 89
(Amanda Perrett) *stdd s: hld up in last pair: trying to creep clsr whn hmpd over 1f out and dropped to rr: styd on again last 150yds but no ch* **16/1**
026- **6** *hd* **Edge Of Heaven**[182] 6939 4-9-0 85.......................... FrederikTylicki 6 89
(Jonathan Portman) *fast away: stdd and hdd after 100yds: rdn over 2f out: sn lost 2nd and nt qckn: one pce over 1f out* **50/1**
220- **7** *hd* **Merry Me (IRE)**[168] 7282 5-9-0 98.......................... LiamKeniry 3 89
(Andrew Balding) *led after 100yds and maintained stdy pce: kicked for home over 2f out: hdd over 1f out: fdd* **8/1**
1-20 **8** *1/2* **My Call**[56] 483 4-9-0 100.......................... HarryBentley 8 87
(Saeed bin Suroor) *racd on outer in midfield: nt qckn and dropped to last pair fr 2f out: kpt on again nr fin* **5/1**
/10- **9** *1/2* **Redstart**[335] 1909 4-9-0 104.......................... FMBerry 1 86
(Ralph Beckett) *trckd ldng pair: wnt 2nd jst over 2f out: upsides ldr over 1f out but sn outpcd: wknd fnl f* **9/2**[3]

1m 38.62s (-1.18) **Going Correction** -0.05s/f (Stan) **9** Ran SP% **115.0**
Speed ratings (Par 108): **103,102,101,100,100 99,99,99,98**
CSF £10.88 TOTE £4.00: £1.20, £1.70, £3.80; EX 12.50 Trifecta £82.00.
Owner Scuderia Blueberry SRL **Bred** Sc Blueberry S R L **Trained** Newmarket, Suffolk
■ Stewards' Enquiry : Harry Bentley four-day ban: used whip above permitted level (Apr 16,18-20)

FOCUS
A muddling contest. Hand times had the leader reaching the 3f pole over a second slower than the winner of the preceding contest, and also slower to the same point than the pacesetter in the following contest, and there were some relatively lowly rated runners not beaten far, most notably the fourth.

1208 BETFRED "TREBLE ODDS ON LUCKY15'S" CONDITIONS STKS (PLUS 10 RACE) 1m (P)
4:45 (4:46) (Class 2) 3-Y-O
£11,827 (£3,541; £1,770; £885; £442; £222) **Stalls** Low

Form RPR
21-1 **1** **Ennaadd**[37] 705 3-9-0 98.......................... AndreaAtzeni 1 105+
(Roger Varian) *fractious bef ent stalls: hld up in last: smooth prog 2f out: pushed along to chse ldr jst over 1f out: more than a l down and drvn fnl f: r.o wl to ld last stride* **4/6**[1]

35-0 **2** *hd* **Adventurous (IRE)**[28] 836 3-9-0 107 .... JoeFanning 2 104
(Mark Johnston) *fast away: led and dictated average pce: rdn 2f out: styd on wl fnl f but hdd last stride* **10/1**

14- **3** *2* **Knife Edge (IRE)**[164] 7396 3-9-0 0 .... LukeMorris 3 100
(Marco Botti) *t.k.h: cl up: chsd ldr 2f out to jst over 1f out: one pce* **4/1**[2]

424- **4** *nk* **Humphrey Bogart (IRE)**[189] 6752 3-9-0 101 .... SeanLevey 5 99
(Richard Hannon) *t.k.h early: hld up: shkn up over 2f out: tried to cl on ldrs over 1f out: styd on but nt pce to threaten* **6/1**[3]

646- **5** *9* **Kentuckyconnection (USA)**[175] 7116 3-9-0 90 .... FMBerry 6 78
(Bryan Smart) *racd on outer: in tch to over 2f out: sn wknd* **33/1**

6 *3* **Drive Faster**[136] 3-9-3 0 .... MartinHarley 4 74
(Hugo Palmer) *tk fierce hold early: mostly chsd ldr to 2f out: wknd rapidly* **12/1**

1m 37.61s (-2.19) **Going Correction** -0.05s/f (Stan) **6** Ran SP% **114.0**
Speed ratings (Par 104): **108,107,105,105,96 93**
CSF £8.91 TOTE £1.50: £1.30, £3.00; EX 8.00 Trifecta £29.60.
Owner Sheikh Ahmed Al Maktoum **Bred** Darley **Trained** Newmarket, Suffolk

FOCUS
The early leader, who finished runner-up, got to the 3f pole around half a second slower than the front-running winner of the earlier fillies' conditions event, judged on hand times. The form looks strong, with the second and fourth having Group form to their names as 2yos and there is still more to come from the winner.

1209 BETFRED "LIKE US ON FACEBOOK" QUEEN'S PRIZE (H'CAP) 2m (P)
5:20 (5:23) (Class 2) (0-105,102) 4-Y-0+
£11,827 (£3,541; £1,770; £885; £442; £222) **Stalls** Low

Form RPR

4-12 **1** **Haines**[54] 499 5-8-5 84 .... RobHornby(3) 3 92
(Andrew Balding) *trckd ldng pair: wnt 2nd over 2f out: clsd on ldr over 1f out: led jst ins fnl f: rdn clr* **9/2**[3]

140- **2** *1¾* **Gavlar**[175] 7115 5-9-1 91 .... AndreaAtzeni 6 97+
(William Knight) *hld up in 6th: shkn up wl over 2f out and lot to do: prog on outer over 1f out: r.o to take 2nd nr fin: unable to chal* **11/4**[1]

22-6 **3** *½* **Hamelin (IRE)**[70] 317 6-9-12 102 .... (v[1]) GeorgeBaker 1 107
(George Scott) *t.k.h: led at mod pce: kicked on over 3f out: hdd jst ins fnl f: no ex and lost 2nd nr fin* **3/1**[2]

4543 **4** *1* **Castilo Del Diablo (IRE)**[7] 1089 7-8-9 92 .... (p) SophieKilloran(7) 4 96
(David Simcock) *hld up in 5th: rdn wl over 2f out: kpt on fr over 1f out: nvr able to chal* **3/1**[2]

2-41 **5** *nk* **Cotton Club (IRE)**[58] 440 5-8-10 86 .... FrederikTylicki 2 90
(Rod Millman) *hld up in 7th: rdn 3f out: kpt on fr 2f out and nrst fin but no threat* **9/1**

320- **6** *2¾* **Handiwork**[15] 8379 6-8-8 84 .... (p) JoeFanning 8 85
(Steve Gollings) *trckd ldng trio: rdn wl over 2f out: fnd nil and sn btn* **25/1**

2-10 **7** *1½* **Flashman**[14] 317 7-8-8 89 .... (b) HectorCrouch(5) 7 88
(Gary Moore) *chsd ldr to over 2f out: wknd* **33/1**

450- **8** *4* **Highland Castle**[227] 5532 8-8-9 92 .... AdamMcLean(7) 5 86
(David Elsworth) *dwlt: t.k.h: hld up in last: sddle slipped after half a m: nvr able to figure* **16/1**

3m 31.48s (1.38) **Going Correction** -0.05s/f (Stan) **8** Ran SP% **117.5**
Speed ratings (Par 109): **94,93,92,92,92 90,90,88**
CSF £17.86 CT £43.12 TOTE £4.10: £1.90, £1.20, £1.50; EX 12.40 Trifecta £67.60.
Owner Bow River Racing **Bred** Spring Bloodstock Ltd **Trained** Kingsclere, Hants

FOCUS
A steadily run race and few got involved. The winner enjoyed a good trip and continues to progress.
T/Plt: £53.90 to a £1 stake. Pool: £68,545.57 - 927.01 winning units. T/Qpdt: £13.10 to a £1 stake. Pool: £4,028.02 - 226.50 winning units. **Jonathan Neesom**

1210 - 1214a (Foreign Racing) - See Raceform Interactive

1195 DONCASTER (L-H)
Sunday, April 3

OFFICIAL GOING: Soft (heavy in places; 5.9)
Wind: moderate half against Weather: Fine and dry

1215 CROWNHOTEL-BAWTRY.COM H'CAP 7f
1:50 (1:51) (Class 4) (0-85,85) 4-Y-0+ **£5,175** (£1,540; £769; £384) **Stalls** High

Form RPR

000- **1** **Muntadab (IRE)**[165] 7390 4-9-1 79 .... SilvestreDeSousa 1 89
(David Loughnane) *racd centre: prom: led 3f out: rdn over 1f out: drvn ins fnl f: kpt on wl towards fin* **10/1**[3]

024- **2** *nk* **Jan Van Hoof (IRE)**[139] 7874 5-9-7 85 .... DavidNolan 17 94
(Richard Fahey) *racd towards stands' rail: trckd ldrs: hdwy over 2f out: rdn to chse wnr over 1f out: drvn to chal ins fnl f: ev ch tl no ex towards fin* **5/1**[1]

0000 **3** *2¼* **Captain Lars (SAF)**[19] 938 6-9-0 78 .... (p) TonyHamilton 19 81
(Derek Shaw) *racd towards stands' rail: hld up in rr: hdwy over 2f out: rdn wl over 1f out: styd on wl fnl f: nrst fin* **33/1**

00-6 **4** *1* **Moonlightnavigator (USA)**[36] 749 4-9-6 84 .... PhillipMakin 3 84
(John Quinn) *chsd ldrs nr stands' rail: rdn along 2f out: kpt on same pce u.p appr fnl f* **5/1**[1]

220- **5** *3¼* **Fullon Clarets**[177] 7093 4-9-0 85 .... AdamMcNamara(7) 18 77
(Richard Fahey) *prom nr stands' rail: cl up 1/2-way: disp ld 3f out: rdn 2f out: sn drvn and grad wknd* **12/1**

016- **6** *2¼* **Johnny Cavagin**[180] 7016 7-9-4 82 .... (t) TomEaves 20 68
(Ronald Thompson) *trckd ldrs nr stands' rail: pushed along and outpcd over 2f out: sn rdn and kpt on fnl f* **8/1**[2]

000- **7** *1¾* **Properus (IRE)**[159] 7526 4-9-4 82 .... TomQueally 8 64
(Keith Dalgleish) *dwlt: racd centre and hld up towards rr: hdwy over 2f out: sn rdn and kpt on fnl f: collapsed after r and fatally injured* **14/1**

-315 **8** *1¼* **Boots And Spurs**[26] 866 7-9-4 82 .... (v) KieranO'Neill 12 60
(Scott Dixon) *prom centre: rdn along 3f out: sn one pce* **12/1**

056- **9** *nk* **Intisaab**[288] 3412 5-9-2 80 .... SamJames 15 58
(David O'Meara) *racd towards stands' rail: a towards rr* **16/1**

200- **10** *2½* **Purple Rock (IRE)**[163] 7434 4-8-11 82 .... (t) NathanEvans(7) 21 53
(Michael Easterby) *prom nr stands' rail: pushed along over 3f out: rdn over 2f out: sn wknd* **25/1**

014- **11** *½* **Musaaid (IRE)**[261] 4349 4-9-5 83 .... DuranFentiman 16 53
(Michael Easterby) *racd towards stands' rail: dwlt and in rr tl sme late hdwy* **33/1**

120- **12** *2½* **Harlequin Striker (IRE)**[184] 6895 4-9-6 84 ....[1] RobertWinston 4 47
(Dean Ivory) *racd towards centre: cl up: rdn along over 3f: wknd fnl 2f* **11/1**

026- **13** *2½* **Red Tycoon (IRE)**[139] 7874 4-9-6 84 .... GrahamGibbons 5 41
(David Barron) *racd towards centre: in tch: hdwy 3f out: rdn along over 2f out: sn wknd* **11/1**

450- **14** *2½* **Alexandrakollontai (IRE)**[148] 7758 6-9-5 83 .... (b) JamesSullivan 2 33
(Alistair Whillans) *racd centre: a towards rr* **40/1**

500- **15** *1* **Crew Cut (IRE)**[148] 7758 8-9-2 80 .... SaleemGolam 3 28
(Stuart Williams) *racd centre: chsd ldrs: rdn along 3f out: sn wknd* **50/1**

000- **16** *8* **Barkston Ash**[190] 6746 8-9-2 80 .... (p) JasonHart 14 7
(Eric Alston) *racd nr stands' rail: led: rdn along and hdd 3f out: sn wknd* **33/1**

200- **P** **Provident Spirit**[148] 7758 5-9-7 85 .... DanielTudhope 22
(David O'Meara) *racd nr stands' rail: chsd ldrs: pushed along and lost pl over 3f out: bhd whn p.u over 1f out: collapsed and fatally injured* **11/1**

1m 33.41s (7.11) **Going Correction** +1.00s/f (Soft) **17** Ran SP% **123.5**
Speed ratings (Par 105): **99,98,96,94,91 88,86,85,84,82 81,78,75,72,71 62,**
CSF £56.09 CT £1685.03 TOTE £14.00: £3.20, £1.50, £8.50, £1.70; EX 69.80 Trifecta £1884.30.
Owner Fell & High Hopes Partnership **Bred** Mrs James Wigan **Trained** Market Drayton, Shropshire
■ Stewards' Enquiry : Jason Hart one-day ban: failed to ride to draw (Apr 18)
David Nolan four-day ban: used whip above permitted level (Apr 18-21)

FOCUS
A dry night and, due to the testing surface, there were a total of 24 non-runners at the meeting prior to the opener. It certainly looked tacky underfoot. This competitive-looking handicap favoured those drawn high and the runner-up sets the level.

1216 BETFRED "HOME OF GOALS GALORE" MAIDEN STKS (DIV I) 7f
2:20 (2:23) (Class 5) 3-Y-O **£3,881** (£1,155; £577; £288) **Stalls** High

Form RPR

1 **Fisher Green (IRE)** 3-9-5 0 .... PaulMulrennan 2 79
(Michael Dods) *trckd ldrs: edgd rt and led over 1f out: edgd lft fnl f: hld on wl nr fin* **10/1**[3]

3- **2** *½* **Flyboy (IRE)**[173] 7183 3-9-5 0 .... DanielTudhope 10 78
(David O'Meara) *trckd ldrs: effrt 3f out: hung lft: chsd wnr over 1f out: nt qckn clsng stages* **4/9**[1]

3 *2¾* **Sophie P** 3-9-0 0 .... PJMcDonald 8 66
(R Mike Smith) *s.i.s: sn mid-div: effrt over 3f out: swtchd lft over 1f out: kpt on one pce* **33/1**

053- **4** *4* **Siege Of Boston (IRE)**[188] 6814 3-9-5 73 .... JFEgan 9 60
(Deborah Sanderson) *trckd ldr: t.k.h: led over 2f out: hdd over 1f out: wknd last 150yds* **5/1**[2]

5 *10* **Ryedale Rio (IRE)** 3-9-5 0 .... DavidAllan 7 34
(Tim Easterby) *led: hdd over 2f out: swtchd lft over 1f out: sn wknd* **14/1**

6 *2½* **Bit Of A Quirke** 3-9-5 0 .... JasonHart 3 28
(Mark Walford) *s.i.s: in rr: sn pushed along: hung lft and lost pl over 2f out: sn bhd* **25/1**

7 *4* **Brendan (IRE)** 3-9-5 0 .... JackGarritty 6 18
(Jim Goldie) *t.k.h in rr: lost pl over 2f out: sn bhd* **25/1**

06- **8** *19* **Jordan James (IRE)**[216] 5942 3-9-5 0 .... TomEaves 1
(Brian Ellison) *stdd s: mid-div: pushed along over 4f out: lost pl 3f out: sn bhd: t.o* **10/1**[3]

1m 34.1s (7.80) **Going Correction** +1.00s/f (Soft) **8** Ran SP% **121.4**
Speed ratings (Par 98): **95,94,91,86,75 72,67,46**
CSF £15.73 TOTE £10.70: £2.10, £1.10, £7.60; EX 22.20 Trifecta £424.80.
Owner Ritchie Fiddes **Bred** Sandro Garavelli **Trained** Denton, Co Durham

FOCUS
This modest maiden is rated around the fourth.

1217 BETFRED "HOME OF GOALS GALORE" MAIDEN STKS (DIV II) 7f
2:55 (2:56) (Class 5) 3-Y-O **£3,881** (£1,155; £577; £288) **Stalls** High

Form RPR

3-4 **1** **Philadelphia (IRE)**[30] 824 3-9-5 0 .... AndreaAtzeni 9 79
(Roger Varian) *trckd ldrs: t.k.h: effrt over 2f out: chsd clr ldr over 1f out: styd on to ld last 50yds* **13/8**[2]

002- **2** *1¼* **General Alexander (IRE)**[162] 7465 3-9-0 78 .... CallumShepherd(5) 2 76
(Brian Ellison) *led: drvn over 2f out: abt 4 l clr over 1f out: hung lft and hdd last 50yds* **6/4**[1]

3 *½* **Tommy G** 3-9-5 0 .... JackGarritty 8 75+
(Jim Goldie) *hld up towards rr: effrt 3f out: styd on to take 3rd last 100yds: gng on at fin: will improve* **14/1**

3- **4** *8* **Maddys Dream**[265] 4204 3-9-2 0 .... SimonPearce(3) 3 54
(Lydia Pearce) *w ldr: effrt over 2f out: wknd fnl 150yds* **4/1**[3]

5 *1½* **Just Hiss** 3-9-5 0 .... DavidAllan 4 50
(Tim Easterby) *chsd ldr: drvn over 2f out: wknd appr fnl f* **11/1**

5- **6** *9* **Druid's Diamond**[288] 3410 3-9-5 0 .... DougieCostello 7 27
(Mark Walford) *dwlt: sn chsng ldrs: drvn over 4f out: lost pl 3f out: sn bhd* **28/1**

000- **7** *19* **Jon H The Lawman (IRE)**[180] 7011 3-9-5 41 .... TomEaves 5
(Ronald Thompson) *hld up in rr: drvn 3f out: sn bhd: t.o* **50/1**

0 **8** *16* **Temujins Quest (IRE)**[31] 798 3-9-5 0 .... AdamBeschizza 6
(Derek Shaw) *dwlt: in rr: drvn over 4f out: sn bhd: t.o* **50/1**

1m 33.22s (6.92) **Going Correction** +1.00s/f (Soft) **8** Ran SP% **120.5**
Speed ratings (Par 98): **100,98,98,88,87 76,55,36**
CSF £4.71 TOTE £2.20: £1.10, £1.10, £2.80; EX 5.30 Trifecta £30.30.
Owner The Philadelphia Partnership **Bred** John Hutchinson **Trained** Newmarket, Suffolk

FOCUS
This second division of the 7f maiden looked stronger than the preceding event.

1218 BETFRED RACING "FOLLOW US ON TWITTER" H'CAP 6f
3:30 (3:31) (Class 3) (0-95,95) 4-Y-O+ **£7,762** (£2,310; £1,154; £577) **Stalls** High

Form RPR

030- **1** **Roudee**[177] 7091 4-9-0 88 .... RichardKingscote 21 98
(Tom Dascombe) *in tch on outer: hdwy wl over 1f out: rdn ent fnl f: styd on wl to ld nr line* **14/1**

330- **2** *shd* **New Bidder**[175] 7143 5-8-13 87 .... GrahamGibbons 1 97
(David Barron) *cl up: led wl over 2f out: rdn over 1f out: drvn ins fnl f: hdd nr line* **5/1**[1]

030- **3** *1¼* **Ocean Sheridan (IRE)**[148] 7758 4-8-10 84 .... ConnorBeasley 5 90
(Michael Dods) *towards rr: hdwy to trck ldrs over 3f out: effrt 2f out: rdn over 1f out: drvn ins fnl f: kpt on same pce* **16/1**

500- **4** *1¼* **My Name Is Rio (IRE)**[177] 7091 6-9-0 88 .... PaulMulrennan 18 90
(Michael Dods) *trckd ldrs: hdwy and cl up 2f out: rdn to chse ldr jst over 1f out: drvn and edgd lft ins fnl f: kpt on same pce* **6/1**[2]

050- **5** *½* **Hoof It**[148] 7754 9-9-7 95 .... PhillipMakin 7 95+
(Michael Easterby) *hld up towards rr: hdwy wl over 1f out: swtchd lft and rdn ent fnl f: kpt on: nrst fin* **16/1**

300- 6 nk **Navigate (IRE)**[205] 6273 4-9-1 **89** DavidProbert 6 88+
(Martyn Meade) *dwlt and hld up towards rr: hdwy over 2f out: swtchd lft to outer and rdn* **8/1**

400- 7 1/2 **Englishman**[219] 5832 6-8-11 **85** FrannyNorton 4 83
(Milton Bradley) *cl up: rdn along 2f out: drvn appr fnl f: grad wknd* **20/1**

034- 8 nk **Ballymore Castle (IRE)**[173] 7177 4-9-7 **95** TonyHamilton 16 92
(Richard Fahey) *chsd ldrs: hdwy over 2f out: rdn wl over 1f out: grad wknd* **7/1**[3]

305- 9 nse **Joey's Destiny (IRE)**[148] 7754 6-9-7 **95** PatCosgrave 22 91
(George Baker) *hld up: hdwy over 2f out: rdn to chse ldrs over 1f out: drvn and hld whn rdr dropped whip wl ins fnl f* **12/1**

420- 10 1 3/4 **Mass Rally (IRE)**[148] 7758 9-8-7 **86** (b) PhilDennis(5) 8 77
(Michael Dods) *in tch: effrt to chse ldrs 2f out and sn rdn: drvn and no imp appr fnl f* **9/1**

000- 11 3/4 **Tiger Jim**[148] 7754 6-8-10 **84** JackGarritty 11 72
(Jim Goldie) *dwlt and in rr tl sme late hdwy* **12/1**

000- 12 1 1/4 **Kinglami**[125] 8050 7-8-13 **87** (p) JoeFanning 19 71
(John O'Shea) *a towards rr* **25/1**

1315 13 4 **Crosse Fire**[17] 966 4-9-1 **89** (p) KieranO'Neill 3 61
(Scott Dixon) *slt ld: pushed along 1/2-way: sn hdd and rdn: wknd 2f out* **33/1**

340- 14 3/4 **Perfect Pasture**[132] 7958 6-9-4 **92** (v) JamesSullivan 2 61
(Michael Easterby) *dwlt: a towards rr* **22/1**

260- 15 1 3/4 **Adam's Ale**[148] 7754 7-9-2 **90** DougieCostello 20 54
(Mark Walford) *chsd ldrs: rdn along over 2f out: sn wknd* **25/1**

U30- 16 2 **Deauville Prince (FR)**[170] 7245 6-8-10 **89** AnnaHesketh(5) 9 46
(Tom Dascombe) *cl up: disp ld 1/2-way: rdn along over 2f out: sn drvn and wknd* **25/1**

1m 18.26s (4.66) **Going Correction** +1.00s/f (Soft) **16** Ran SP% **122.0**
Speed ratings (Par 107): **108,107,106,104,103 103,102,102,102,100 99,97,92,91,88 86**
CSF £74.60 CT £1207.62 TOTE £20.10: £4.40, £1.90, £4.20, £2.40; EX 146.00 Trifecta £1808.10.
Owner Edwards Hughes Jenkins Roberts & Partner **Bred** Miss D Fleming **Trained** Malpas, Cheshire

FOCUS
A very competitive sprint handicap in which the field merged down the centre from halfway.

1219 BETFRED TV DONCASTER SHIELD (CONDITIONS STKS) 1m 4f
4:05 (4:05) (Class 2) 4-Y-O+ **£12,938** (£3,850; £1,924; £962) **Stalls** Low

Form RPR

1 **Sandro Botticelli (IRE)**[311] 2654 4-8-13 0 (p) FrankieDettori 4 106
(John Ryan) *hld up in last: hdwy over 3f out: chsng ldrs 2f out: led 1f out: wnt clr: v readily* **12/1**

016- 2 4 **Chancery (USA)**[155] 7633 8-9-0 102 DanielTudhope 3 100
(David O'Meara) *hld up in rr: smooth hdwy over 3f out: 2nd 2f out: shkn up to ld briefly over 1f out: styd on same pce* **11/4**[3]

600- 3 6 **Old Town Boy**[218] 5852 5-9-0 89 GrahamGibbons 2 90
(Philip McBride) *chsd ldr: led 3f out: hdd over 1f out: fdd fnl f* **12/1**

004- 4 2 1/2 **Encore L'Amour**[177] 7078 4-8-8 95 RichardKingscote 1 81
(Ralph Beckett) *chsd ldrs: drvn over 3f out: wknd over 1f out* **9/4**[2]

00-6 5 10 **Windshear**[8] 1088 5-9-4 106 PatDobbs 5 74
(Richard Hannon) *led: drvn and hdd 3f out: lost pl over 1f out: eased whn bhd clsng stages* **13/8**[1]

2m 43.0s (8.10) **Going Correction** +0.90s/f (Soft)
WFA 4 from 5yo+ 1lb **5** Ran SP% **110.9**
Speed ratings (Par 109): **109,106,102,100,94**
CSF £44.36 TOTE £7.30: £3.60, £2.20; EX 18.80 Trifecta £73.90.
Owner Graham Smith-Bernal & Alan Dee **Bred** Ask For The Moon Syndicate **Trained** Newmarket, Suffolk

FOCUS
A tactical conditions event, rated around the runner-up.

1220 BETFRED "BE PART OF THE ACTION" H'CAP 1m 2f 60y
4:40 (4:40) (Class 3) (0-95,90) 3-Y-O **£7,762** (£2,310; £1,154; £577) **Stalls** Low

Form RPR

216- 1 **Soldier In Action (FR)**[132] 7955 3-8-11 **80** JoeFanning 7 91+
(Mark Johnston) *trckd ldr: led over 2f out: clr over 1f out: pushed out* **7/2**[3]

41- 2 2 1/4 **Juste Pour Nous**[215] 5977 3-8-12 **81** WilliamBuick 2 87
(Mark Johnston) *chsd ldrs: pushed along over 4f out: kpt on to chse wnr over 1f out: keeping on at fin* **11/4**[2]

512- 3 3 1/2 **Robinnielly (IRE)**[197] 6513 3-8-13 **82** PhillipMakin 5 81
(Keith Dalgleish) *t.k.h: in rr after 1f: hdwy on outside to chse ldrs over 5f out: 2nd over 2f out: fdd fnl f* **12/1**

213- 4 23 **Shahbar**[216] 5944 3-9-1 **84** FrankieDettori 8 39
(Marco Botti) *hld up in last: hdwy on ins over 3f out: effrt over 2f out: drvn and wknd over 1f out: bhd whn heavily eased last 100yds: t.o* **15/8**[1]

231 5 15 **Byres Road**[66] 361 3-8-11 **80** FrannyNorton 6 7
(Mark Johnston) *led: pushed along and hdd 3f out: sn lost pl and bhd: eased clsng stages: t.o* **9/2**

2m 18.75s (9.35) **Going Correction** +0.90s/f (Soft) **5** Ran SP% **109.5**
Speed ratings (Par 102): **98,96,93,75,63**
CSF £13.21 TOTE £5.00: £2.80, £1.30; EX 17.60 Trifecta £63.50.
Owner A D Spence **Bred** Randolf Peters **Trained** Middleham Moor, N Yorks

FOCUS
A fair little 3yo handicap. The bad ground played its part.

1221 BETFRED LOTTO H'CAP 1m 2f 60y
5:15 (5:15) (Class 4) (0-85,85) 4-Y-O+ **£5,175** (£1,540; £769; £384) **Stalls** Low

Form RPR

022- 1 **More Mischief**[156] 7596 4-9-7 **85** GrahamLee 14 98
(Jedd O'Keeffe) *racd wd early: sn trcking ldrs: led over 1f out: styd on wl* **5/1**[2]

060- 2 1 **Burano (IRE)**[167] 7348 7-9-2 **83** ShelleyBirkett(3) 16 94
(David O'Meara) *mid-div: hdwy to trck ldrs over 4f out: chsd wnr fnl f: kpt on wl* **8/1**

515- 3 2 **All My Love (IRE)**[156] 7596 4-8-9 **76** RobHornby(3) 20 83+
(Pam Sly) *in rr: hdwy 3f out: styd on to take 3rd last 100yds* **25/1**

140- 4 2 3/4 **Felix De Vega (IRE)**[176] 7125 4-9-4 **82** GrahamGibbons 11 84
(Michael Easterby) *trckd ldrs: led over 2f out: hdd over 1f out: wknd fnl 150yds* **16/1**

00-4 5 3/4 **Top Of The Glas (IRE)**[6] 1122 5-9-4 **82** BenCurtis 13 83
(Brian Ellison) *chsd ldrs: pushed along 4f out: one pce fnl 2f* **13/2**[3]

13-2 6 1 1/4 **Treasury Notes (IRE)**[6] 1122 4-8-13 **77** DanielTudhope 18 75
(David O'Meara) *rr-div: hdwy into mid-div 4f out: effrt over 2f out: one pce* **9/4**[1]

/06- 7 6 **Woodacre**[167] 7338 9-8-9 **76** JacobButterfield(3) 12 63
(Richard Whitaker) *hld up in rr: hdwy to chse ldrs over 2f out: wknd over 1f out* **33/1**

000- 8 8 **Arcano Gold (IRE)**[216] 5939 4-9-3 **81** TonyHamilton 10 53
(Richard Fahey) *led 2f: chsd ldrs: led briefly 3f out: wknd over 1f out* **8/1**

06- 9 2 1/4 **Homeland (IRE)**[274] 3892 4-9-4 **82** (t) JamesSullivan 7 49
(Brian Rothwell) *wore ear plugs: awkward s: in rr: sme hdwy over 2f out: nvr a factor* **50/1**

146- 10 hd **Plane Song (IRE)**[221] 5743 4-9-3 **81** NeilFarley 5 48
(Alan Swinbank) *trckd ldrs: effrt 3f out: lost pl over 1f out* **25/1**

6412 11 nk **Elysian Prince**[8] 1093 5-9-1 **79** (t) LiamJones 6 45
(Neil King) *mid-div: drvn over 4f out: chsng ldrs 3f out: sn wknd* **16/1**

520- 12 2 1/2 **Gworn**[176] 7125 6-9-6 **84** PJMcDonald 9 46
(R Mike Smith) *mid-div: hdwy on ins and n.m.r over 3f out: wknd 2f out* **16/1**

200- 13 3 **The Character (IRE)**[169] 7295 5-8-9 **80** PatrickVaughan(7) 15 36
(Tom Dascombe) *racd wd early: led after 2f: hdd 3f out: sn lost pl: eased whn bhd clsng stages* **20/1**

26-6 14 4 **Peak Storm**[30] 823 7-8-9 **78** (p) CiaranMckee(5) 8 26
(John O'Shea) *a towards rr: nvr on terms* **33/1**

401- 15 24 **Scrutiny**[14] 7255 5-8-12 **76** ShaneGray 4
(Barry Murtagh) *in rr: bhd 3f out: eased: t.o* **16/1**

2m 16.84s (7.44) **Going Correction** +0.90s/f (Soft) **15** Ran SP% **126.8**
Speed ratings (Par 105): **106,105,103,101,100 99,95,88,86,86 86,84,82,78,59**
CSF £43.31 CT £948.08 TOTE £6.20: £2.10, £4.30, £4.70; EX 50.80 Trifecta £1090.30.
Owner Caron & Paul Chapman **Bred** Cliveden Stud **Trained** Middleham Moor, N Yorks
■ Stewards' Enquiry : Shelley Birkett two-day ban: used whip above permitted level (Apr 18-19)

FOCUS
This modest handicap was a competitive affair. It paid to be handy and the fifth rates the benchmark.

1222 BETFRED MOBILE GENTLEMAN AMATEUR RIDERS' H'CAP 1m 4f
5:45 (5:45) (Class 5) (0-70,71) 4-Y-O+ **£3,743** (£1,161; £580; £290) **Stalls** Low

Form RPR

-441 1 **Alphabetical Order**[6] 1121 8-11-5 **71** 6ex MrThomasGreatrex(3) 15 80+
(David O'Meara) *swtchd lft after s: hld up in rr: effrt and swtchd rt over 2f out: 2nd over 1f out: styd on to ld post* **9/2**[3]

0-01 2 nse **Bertie Moon**[1] 1201 6-10-10 **64** MrJoeWright(5) 6 73
(Keith Dalgleish) *trckd ldrs: led over 2f out: rdn and edgd rt fnl f: hdd post* **9/4**[1]

513- 3 2 **Rock On Bollinski**[28] 7527 6-11-4 **70** (p) KaineWood(3) 9 76
(Brian Ellison) *mid-div: drvn and outpcd over 2f out: hung lft: kpt on to take 3rd clsng stages* **16/1**

6246 4 1 **Deep Resolve (IRE)**[31] 802 5-11-2 **65** MrSWalker 13 69
(Alan Swinbank) *hld up in mid-div: t.k.h: hdwy to chse ldrs over 2f out: kpt on one pce* **9/2**[3]

06-3 5 nk **Dalaki (IRE)**[50] 566 5-11-1 **67** (b) MrRyanBird(3) 3 71
(Des Donovan, Ire) *dwlt: hdwy 8f out: chsng ldrs over 2f out: kpt on one pce fnl f* **25/1**

3/0- 6 1 3/4 **Nam Hai (IRE)**[64] 7250 5-11-1 **69** MrJMorris(5) 11 70
(Kim Bailey) *hld up in last: swtchd outside over 3f out: chsng ldrs over 2f out: wknd fnl 150yds* **14/1**

1/16 7 4 1/2 **Kalahari (IRE)**[39] 693 7-11-7 **70** (p) MrPWMullins 14 64
(Henry Spiller) *hld up in rr: smooth hdwy over 4f out: trcking ldrs over 2f out: rdn and edgd lft over 1f out: wknd fnl f* **3/1**[2]

4-23 8 1 3/4 **Scrafton**[33] 772 5-11-0 **68** MrMEnnis(5) 12 59
(Tony Carroll) *trckd ldrs: t.k.h: effrt over 2f out: wknd over 1f out* **16/1**

00-0 9 10 **Rockweiller**[54] 505 9-10-2 **56** oh11 (b) AidenBlakemore(5) 2 31
(Shaun Harris) *led: hdd over 2f out: sn wknd: eased whn bhd clsng stages* **66/1**

004/ 10 2 **It's A Mans World**[16] 5639 10-10-6 **62** MrMWBrown(7) 5 34
(Brian Ellison) *chsd ldrs: wknd 2f out: eased whn bhd clsng stages* **50/1**

2m 55.57s (20.67) **Going Correction** +0.90s/f (Soft)
WFA 4 from 5yo+ 1lb **10** Ran SP% **117.9**
Speed ratings (Par 103): **67,66,65,64,64 63,60,59,52,51**
CSF £15.05 CT £150.19 TOTE £4.70: £2.00, £2.00, £2.90; EX 20.60 Trifecta £217.60.
Owner Great Northern Partnership **Bred** Barrow Hill **Trained** Upper Helmsley, N Yorks
■ Stewards' Enquiry : Mr Joe Wright two-day ban: used whip above permitted level (tbn)

FOCUS
A moderate handicap, confined to amateur riders, fought out by the two in-form market leaders.
T/Jkpt: Not won. T/Plt: £51.40 to a £1 stake. Pool: £159,401.31 - 2,262.87 winning tickets.
T/Qpdt: £17.50 to a £1 stake. Pool: £9,085.07 - 383.46 winning tickets.
Walter Glynn & Joe Rowntree

1223 - 1225a (Foreign Racing) - See Raceform Interactive

1013 CURRAGH (R-H)
Sunday, April 3

OFFICIAL GOING: Heavy

1226a BIG BAD BOB GLADNESS STKS (GROUP 3) 7f
3:50 (3:55) 3-Y-O+
£27,113 (£8,731; £4,136; £1,838; £919; £459)

RPR

1 **Onenightidreamed (IRE)**[14] 1018 5-9-10 103 (p) WayneLordan 2 114
(T Stack, Ire) *cl up: 3rd 1/2-way: gng wl under 2f out: rdn in cl 2nd ent fnl f and kpt on wl u.p ins fnl f to ld fnl 50yds* **9/1**

2 1/2 **Flight Risk (IRE)**[6] 1127 5-9-7 106 KevinManning 3 110
(J S Bolger, Ire) *chsd ldrs early: racd keenly and led narrowly at 1/2-way: rdn over 1f out and strly pressed: all out ins fnl f and hdd fnl 50yds: kpt on wl wout matching wnr* **12/1**

3 1 **Joailliere (IRE)**[14] 1016 4-9-4 99 PatSmullen 1 104
(D K Weld, Ire) *trckd ldrs tl sn led: hdd narrowly at 1/2-way: rdn in cl 4th over 1f out and clsd u.p into 3rd ins fnl f: kpt on same pce clsng stages to hold 3rd: a hld by ldng pair* **9/1**

4 nk **Sruthan (IRE)**[14] 1018 6-9-7 109 ChrisHayes 4 106
(P D Deegan, Ire) *w.w: 6th 1/2-way: rdn 2f out and clsd u.p in 5th ent fnl f: swtchd rt ins fnl f and kpt on same pce into 4th: hld for 3rd: nvr trbld ldrs* **2/1**[1]

5 1 1/2 **The Happy Prince (IRE)**[161] 7491 4-9-7 108 (t) SeamieHeffernan 8 102
(A P O'Brien, Ire) *w.w in rr: 7th 1/2-way: hdwy 2f out: rdn between horses in 3rd over 1f out: no ex wl ins fnl f where dropped to 5th* **8/1**

6 4 3/4 **Dick Whittington (IRE)**[351] 1492 4-9-7 100 RyanMoore 7 89
(A P O'Brien, Ire) *hld up towards rr: last at 1/2-way: rdn nr side under 2f out and no imp in mod 6th wl ins fnl f: kpt on one pce* **11/4**[2]

7 1 1/4 **Cougar Mountain (IRE)**[228] 5531 5-9-10 114.......(t) ColmO'Donoghue 5 89
(A P O'Brien, Ire) *led narrowly tl sn hdd and settled bhd ldr: dropped to 5th at 1/2-way: rdn 2f out and sn no ex: wknd 1f out* **20/1**

8 8 1/2 **Gordon Lord Byron (IRE)**[137] 7891 8-9-10 110............... ShaneFoley 9 66
(T Hogan, Ire) *settled bhd ldrs: 4th 1/2-way: rdn over 2f out and sn no ex towards rr: eased in rr ins fnl f: scoped wrong* **7/1**[3]

1m 37.5s (6.70) **Going Correction** +1.375s/f (Soft) **8** Ran SP% **116.1**
Speed ratings: **116,115,114,113,112 106,105,95**
CSF £109.63 TOTE £10.80: £2.30, £2.10, £2.70; DF 105.10 Trifecta £322.90.
Owner New Pension Fund Syndicate **Bred** Brian O'Neill **Trained** Golden, Co Tipperary

FOCUS
The absence of Endless Drama due to heavy ground was disappointing and it meant that any potential star in the line-up was missing. The gallop was quite generous given the conditions and plenty of these finished very tired. The winner has been rated to his best.

1227a CORAL.IE ALLEGED STKS (LISTED RACE) 1m 2f
4:25 (4:26) 4-Y-O+ **£20,389** (£6,566; £3,110; £1,382; £691)

RPR

1 **Zhukova (IRE)**[209] 6174 4-9-3 100.. PatSmullen 3 114+
(D K Weld, Ire) *settled bhd ldr in 2nd: tk clsr order fr under 3f out and disp 1 1/2f out where sltly impeded: led narrowly 1f out: drvn clr ins fnl f where edgd sltly rt and styd on wl: comf* **6/1**

2 4 3/4 **Success Days (IRE)**[154] 7664 4-9-10 113........................... ShaneFoley 2 112+
(K J Condon, Ire) *led: 2 l clr at 1/2-way: rdn and wandered sltly over 2f out where pressed clly: jnd 1 1/2f out where hung lft and hdd u.p 1f out: no imp on wnr whn sltly hmpd and hung lft ins fnl f* **9/2**[3]

3 3 **Found (IRE)**[155] 7656 4-9-7 120.. RyanMoore 1 103
(A P O'Brien, Ire) *chsd ldrs: 3rd 1/2-way: dropped to 4th briefly under 3f out: pushed along in 3rd 1 1/2f out and sn no imp on clr ldrs: one pce under hands and heels ins fnl f* **9/10**[1]

4 3 **Bocca Baciata (IRE)**[169] 7279 4-9-5 112.................. ColmO'Donoghue 7 95
(Mrs John Harrington, Ire) *s.i.s and settled in rr: last at 1/2-way: rdn into mod 4th over 1f out and no imp on clr ldrs: one pce fnl f* **3/1**[2]

5 5 **Dragon Fei (IRE)**[103] 6755 6-9-0 90.................................... LeighRoche 5 80
(Dermot Anthony McLoughlin, Ire) *chsd ldrs: 4th 1/2-way: wnt 3rd briefly under 3f out: sn rdn and no imp on clr ldrs u.p in 4th 1 1/2f out: wknd* **33/1**

2m 23.89s (14.59) **Going Correction** +1.90s/f (Heav) **5** Ran SP% **113.0**
Speed ratings: **117,113,110,108,104**
CSF £31.97 TOTE £7.70: £3.00, £2.10; DF 27.00 Trifecta £65.90.
Owner Mrs C C Regalado-Gonzalez **Bred** Mrs C L Weld **Trained** Curragh, Co Kildare

FOCUS
A fascinating affair, but somewhat spoiled by the testing conditions. There was nothing wrong with the gallop, despite the small field, and the winner made an explosive start to her 4yo career, recording a personal best.

1228 - 1229a (Foreign Racing) - See Raceform Interactive

1130 SAINT-CLOUD (L-H)
Sunday, April 3

OFFICIAL GOING: Turf: heavy

1230a PRIX LA FORCE - FIGAROSCOPE (GROUP 3) (3YO) (TURF) 1m 2f
2:40 (12:00) 3-Y-O **£29,411** (£11,764; £8,823; £5,882)

RPR

1 **Cloth Of Stars (IRE)**[154] 7666 3-9-2 0....................... MickaelBarzalona 4 106+
(A Fabre, France) *t.k.h: hld up in rr: gd hdwy 2f out: 2 l 2nd and scrubbed along 1 1/2f out: styd on to ld ent fnl f: asserted fnl 100yds* **7/10**[1]

2 1 1/4 **Viserano (FR)**[49] 584 3-9-2 0.............................. Pierre-CharlesBoudot 2 101
(D Prod'Homme, France) *led: sn wl clr: 8 l ld over 3f out: grad led field towards stands' side st: rdn over 1 1/2f out: hdd ent fnl f: no ex* **49/10**[3]

3 1 1/4 **Ghaaly**[29] 3-9-2 0... ChristopheSoumillon 1 98
(J-C Rouget, France) *w.w in fnl pair: rdn and nt qckn under 2f out: styd on fnl f: nt pce to get on terms* **2/1**[2]

4 dist **Magari (FR)**[22] 930 3-9-2 0.. CristianDemuro 3
(H-A Pantall, France) *chsd clr ldr: rdn and no imp over 2f out: wknd appr fnl f* **69/10**

2m 17.91s (1.91) **4** Ran SP% **121.8**
WIN (incl. 1 euro stake): 1.70. PLACES: 1.20, 1.80. SF: 6.20.
Owner Godolphin SNC **Bred** Peter Anastasiou **Trained** Chantilly, France

1231a PRIX EDMOND BLANC (GROUP 3) (4YO+) (TURF) 1m
3:10 (12:00) 4-Y-O+ **£29,411** (£11,764; £8,823; £5,882; £2,941)

RPR

1 **Maimara (FR)**[183] 6925 4-8-10 0.............................. GregoryBenoist 5 112
(M Delzangles, France) *t.k.h bhd ldrs: rdn to chal appr 1 1/2f out: led wl over 1f out: drvn out fnl f: readily* **7/5**[1]

2 1 3/4 **Stillman (FR)**[22] 931 5-8-11 0..............................(b) OlivierPeslier 6 109
(P Khozian, France) *led after 1f: rdn whn chal over 1 1/2f out: rallied and hdd appr 1f out: kpt on at same pce* **22/5**[2]

3 2 1/2 **Diego Valor (FR)**[133] 5-8-11 0............................ JoseLuisMartinez 1 103
(A Carrasco Sanchez, Spain) *cl up early: dropped towards rr after 2f: nudged along fr 3f out: styd on to chal under 2f out: sn rdn and no further imp appr 1f out: kpt on at one pce* **9/1**

4 1 1/2 **Ross (IRE)**[29] 842 4-8-11 0.................................... IoritzMendizabal 7 100
(P Schiergen, Germany) *w.w in fnl pair on inner: hrd drvn and clsd 2f out: plugged on at one pce fnl f* **69/10**

5 1 1/2 **Incahoots**[43] 660 4-8-8 0.. MaximeGuyon 8 93
(F Head, France) *w.w in fnl pair on outer: rdn and no imp tl styd on 1f out: run petered out last 120yds* **54/10**[3]

6 8 **Palace Prince (GER)**[169] 7281 4-9-0 0............................ EddyHardouin 3 81
(Andreas Lowe, Germany) *led: sn hdd and remained cl up: rdn to hold pl wl over 2f out: wknd appr fnl f* **31/5**

7 12 **Buscavidas (IRE)**[42] 5-8-11 0............................ Pierre-CharlesBoudot 9 50
(A Carrasco Sanchez, Spain) *chsd ldng trio: cl up and rdn 2f out: sn outpcd by ldrs and lost pl: wl hld whn eased ins fnl f* **10/1**

1m 46.12s (-1.38) **7** Ran SP% **121.4**
WIN (incl. 1 euro stake): 2.40. PLACES: 1.20, 1.40, 1.70. DF: 4.20. SF: 11.30.
Owner Alain Louis-Dreyfus **Bred** Le Thenney S.A. & Edy S.R.L. **Trained** France

1232a PRIX ZARKAVA - FONDS EUROPEEN DE L'ELEVAGE (LISTED RACE) (4YO+ FILLIES & MARES) (TURF) 1m 2f 110y
4:15 (12:00) 4-Y-O+ **£17,647** (£7,058; £5,294; £3,529; £1,764)

RPR

1 **Marypop (FR)**[183] 6954 4-8-11 0.................................... MaximeGuyon 6 106+
(Mme Pia Brandt, France) **2/1**[1]

2 3 **Brandybend (IRE)**[148] 7756 4-8-11 0.................................. LukeMorris 7 98
(Marco Botti) *t.k.h: led sn after 1f under a tight hold: rdn whn pressed wl over 1 1/2f out: hdd 1f out: rallied u.p to hold 2nd but no match for wnr* **83/10**

3 hd **Havana Moon (USA)**[123] 8088 4-8-11 0............................ AlexisBadel 4 98+
(M Delzangles, France) **14/1**

4 1 **Pacific Angel (IRE)**[165] 7408 4-8-11 0................. ChristopheSoumillon 3 96
(M Delzangles, France) **9/1**

5 1 1/4 **Ame Bleue**[202] 6392 4-8-11 0...................................... MickaelBarzalona 1 93
(A Fabre, France) **73/10**

6 1 **Rosie Cotton (IRE)**[176] 4-8-11 0................................. IoritzMendizabal 5 91
(Mme Pia Brandt, France) **14/1**

7 3 **Bella Donna Borget (FR)**[132] 5730 4-8-11 0.......... StephanePasquier 8 85
(J Bertran De Balanda, France) **5/1**[3]

8 4 **Mambomiss (FR)**[256] 4537 5-9-2 0.................................... OlivierPeslier 2 82
(D De Watrigant, France) **3/1**[2]

2m 23.75s (4.15) **8** Ran SP% **121.1**
WIN (incl. 1 euro stake): 3.00. PLACES: 1.60, 2.40, 3.00. DF: 12.80. SF: 19.90.
Owner Wood Hall Stud Limited **Bred** A Haddad **Trained** France

1173 LINGFIELD (L-H)
Monday, April 4

OFFICIAL GOING: Polytrack: standard
Wind: light to medium, half behind Weather: overcast, showers from race 5

1233 CANTERING CUISINE NOVICE MEDIAN AUCTION STKS 5f 6y(P)
2:20 (2:24) (Class 5) 2-Y-O **£2,911** (£866; £432; £216) **Stalls** High

Form RPR

2 1 **Stormy Clouds (IRE)**[9] 1087 2-8-11 0.................................. SeanLevey 1 73+
(Richard Hannon) *sn pressing ldr: pushed along and ev ch over 1f out: kpt on under mainly hands and heels to ld wl ins fnl f: pushed out* **4/9**[1]

3 2 1/2 **Decadent Times (IRE)**[10] 1082 2-9-2 0................. RichardKingscote 10 74
(Tom Dascombe) *sn led: rdn over 1f out: kpt on u.p tl hdd and styd on same pce wl ins fnl f* **7/1**[3]

0 3 5 **King Of Castilla**[11] 1118 2-9-2 0.. LukeMorris 6 56
(Gay Kelleway) *broke wl: sn chsng ldng pair and clr of field: effrt 2f out: sn drvn and outpcd by ldng pair: kpt on same pce fnl f* **12/1**

4 3 **Snoozy Sioux (IRE)** 2-8-8 0... TimClark[(3)] 2 40
(Martin Smith) *short of room sn after s: t.k.h: hld up off the pce in 6th: swtchd rt and effrt 2f out: hdwy and wnt modest 4th ins fnl f: kpt on but no ch w ldrs* **66/1**

5 1/2 **Rusumaat (IRE)** 2-9-2 0... PaulHanagan 5 43
(Mark Johnston) *sn rdn and outpcd in last pair: hdwy 1f out and styd on wl ins fnl f: nvr trbld ldrs* **3/1**[2]

4 6 3 1/2 **Hot N Sassy (IRE)**[9] 1086 2-8-11 0..................................... LiamJones 3 26
(J S Moore) *sn rdn and outpcd in rr: plugged on to pass btn horses ins fnl f: n.d* **33/1**

3 7 2 3/4 **Madam Prancealot (IRE)**[9] 1086 2-8-11 0...................... CathyGannon 7 16
(David Evans) *midfield but nvr on terms w ldrs: rdn to go 4th but no imp 2f out: lost 4th ins fnl f: sn fdd* **25/1**

8 5 **Jumping Jack (IRE)** 2-9-2 0... ShaneKelly 4 3
(Richard Hughes) *chsd ldng clr ldng trio tl 2f out: 5th and wl btn whn rn green and hung lft over 1f out: bhd and eased ins fnl f* **12/1**

58.93s (0.13) **Going Correction** 0.0s/f (Stan) **8** Ran SP% **130.4**
Speed ratings (Par 92): **98,97,89,84,83 78,73,65**
CSF £5.94 TOTE £1.50: £1.02, £2.00, £2.60; EX 6.40 Trifecta £27.20.
Owner Chris Giles **Bred** Tally-Ho Stud **Trained** East Everleigh, Wilts

FOCUS
The favourite was well supported and landed the odds in cosy fashion.

1234 RYAN ASSET MANAGEMENT (S) STKS 1m 2f (P)
2:50 (2:52) (Class 6) 3-Y-O **£2,264** (£673; £336; £168) **Stalls** Low

Form RPR

4350 1 **Khismet**[17] 978 3-8-10 68.......................................(p) CharlesEddery[(5)] 3 70
(Rae Guest) *mde all: travelling best 3f out: shkn up and wnt clr wl over 1f out: styd on: eased towards fin: easily* **7/4**[1]

60-6 2 7 **Tessellate (IRE)**[5] 1148 3-8-7 54... LukeMorris 2 47
(Sylvester Kirk) *s.i.s: hld up in tch in rr: rdn over 3f out: nt clr run fr over 2f out: swtchd rt and squeezed between rivals ins fnl f: styd on to go 2nd wl ins fnl f: no ch w wnr* **4/1**[3]

540 3 nk **Il Sassicaia**[33] 789 3-8-9 68.. DanielMuscutt[(3)] 4 51
(Marco Botti) *s.i.s: in tch in 4th: rdn over 4f out: outpcd and wl btn over 1f out: plugged on into modest 3rd towards fin* **9/4**[2]

-434 4 3/4 **Nidnod**[38] 725 3-8-11 56.. WilliamCarson 1 49
(John Bridger) *chsd ldng pair: rdn over 3f out: outpcd and wl btn over 1f out: wnt modest 2nd fnl 100yds: lost 2 pls wl ins fnl f* **4/1**[3]

00-0 5 1 3/4 **Wicked Woo**[39] 711 3-8-7 52... JoeyHaynes 5 41
(Jo Hughes) *chsd wnr: rdn 3f out: outpcd 2f out and wl btn over 1f out: lost 2nd 100yds out: wknd towards fin* **20/1**

2m 7.34s (0.74) **Going Correction** 0.0s/f (Stan) **5** Ran SP% **111.9**
Speed ratings (Par 96): **97,91,91,90,89**
CSF £9.26 TOTE £2.60: £1.50, £2.00; EX 9.10 Trifecta £20.80.Khismet was bought by John Flint for 6,400gns.
Owner Rae Guest **Bred** D J Weston **Trained** Newmarket, Suffolk

FOCUS
A modest affair dominated from the front by the winner.

1235 TTS NETWORKS MAIDEN STKS 1m 1y(P)
3:20 (3:24) (Class 5) 3-Y-O **£2,911** (£866; £432; £216) **Stalls** High

Form RPR

2 1 **Battlement**[17] 984 3-9-0 0... RyanMoore 7 77+
(Roger Charlton) *chsd ldr: upsides whn drifted rt bnd 2f out: rdn to ld over 1f out: r.o wl and holding chalr ins fnl f* **4/11**[1]

2 nk **Taraabut (IRE)** 3-9-5 0 .... PaulHanagan 3 81+
(Richard Hannon) *dwlt: pushed along and sn rcvrd to r in midfield: rdn and hdwy 3f out: chal 1f out: styd on wl ins fnl f but a hld* **4/1**[2]

00- 3 5 **Master Of Heaven**[117] 8152 3-9-5 0 .... PatCosgrave 8 69
(Jim Boyle) *t.k.h: chsd ldng trio: wnt 3rd over 2f out: effrt over 1f out: stl cl enough but unable qck 1f out: outpcd ins fnl f* **50/1**

56- 4 ¾ **Scarlet Pimpernel**[187] 6857 3-9-0 0 .... JimmyFortune 5 62+
(Hughie Morrison) *stdd after s: hld up off the pce in midfield: pushed along 2f out: hdwy over 1f out: styd on steadily ins fnl f: nvr trbld ldrs* **20/1**

60- 5 2½ **Prospectus**[130] 8006 3-9-5 0 .... LiamKeniry 6 61+
(Hughie Morrison) *stdd s: hld up off the pce in rr: shkn up over 2f out: hdwy and swtchd lft jst over 1f out: kpt on steadily ins fnl f: nvr trbld ldrs* **10/1**

0 6 3¼ **Mary Beale (IRE)**[11] 1063 3-9-0 0 .... JamesDoyle 2 48
(Mark Johnston) *led: rdn and hdd over 1f out: sn btn: fdd ins fnl f* **5/1**[3]

55 7 1 **Topalova**[26] 880 3-9-0 0 .... SaleemGolam 1 46
(Mark H Tompkins) *t.k.h: chsd ldng pair tl over 2f out: sn struggling in 5th: wknd over 1f out* **20/1**

00 8 21 **Katalan (GER)**[10] 1079 3-9-5 0 .... TomQueally 4
(John Butler) *a off the pce in last trio: lost tch over 1f out* **66/1**

1m 38.77s (0.57) **Going Correction** 0.0s/f (Stan) 8 Ran SP% **132.0**
Speed ratings (Par 98): **97,96,91,90,88 85,84,63**
CSF £3.00 TOTE £1.30: £1.02, £1.40, £6.20; EX 3.20 Trifecta £54.40.
Owner K Abdullah **Bred** Juddmonte Farms Ltd **Trained** Beckhampton, Wilts

FOCUS
The first two pulled nicely clear in this maiden. The well-placed third is the key to the form.

1236 AVENSYS H'CAP — 1m 7f 169y(P)
3:50 (3:51) (Class 5) (0-70,67) 4-Y-O+ **£2,911** (£866; £432; £216) **Stalls** Low

Form RPR
6526 1 **Force Of Destiny (GER)**[16] 1002 4-9-6 66 .... LukeMorris 1 75+
(Mrs Ilka Gansera-Leveque) *chsd ldr tl led over 3f out: rdn clr wl over 1f out: in n.d fnl f: eased towards fin: dismntd after fin: lame* **3/1**[1]

-666 2 4 **Hiorne Tower (FR)**[19] 949 5-8-13 55 .... KierenFox 2 58
(John Best) *in tch: chsd wnr 3f out: rdn and unable qck 2f out: kpt on same pce fr over 1f out* **8/1**

0-1 3 1¼ **Kawartha**[38] 728 4-9-7 67 .... TomQueally 3 72+
(Robert Stephens) *hld up in last pair: clsd and wl in tch 5f out: nt clr run over 2f out tl swtchd rt bnd wl over 1f out: styd on to go 3rd 75yds out: no ch w wnr* **5/1**[2]

5-02 4 7 **Senor George (IRE)**[11] 1057 9-9-6 65 .... RobHornby(3) 4 58
(Simon Hodgson) *stdd s: hld up in rr: clsd and in tch 5f out: rdn over 2f out: outpcd and wl hld over 1f out: wknd fnl f* **7/1**[3]

300- 5 1½ **Fitzwilliam**[100] 7858 4-8-10 56 .... SilvestreDeSousa 5 47
(Mick Channon) *chsd ldrs: effrt in 3rd 3f out: outpcd and btn over 1f out: lost 3rd and fdd ins fnl f* **5/1**[2]

2-01 6 1½ **Flighty Filia (IRE)**[40] 698 4-9-7 67 .... JimCrowley 7 57
(Amanda Perrett) *hld up in midfield: clsd and in tch 5f out: nt clr run over 2f out: effrt 2f out: sn btn* **3/1**[1]

6-50 7 20 **Moojaned (IRE)**[16] 1002 5-9-6 62 .... JFEgan 6 28
(David Evans) *led: hdd and rdn over 3f out: dropped out qckly over 2f out: t.o ins fnl f* **10/1**

3m 23.65s (-2.05) **Going Correction** 0.0s/f (Stan)
WFA 4 from 5yo+ 4lb 7 Ran SP% **116.0**
Speed ratings (Par 103): **105,103,102,98,98 97,87**
CSF £28.54 TOTE £4.20: £2.10, £3.40; EX 31.60 Trifecta £165.70.
Owner Graf Stauffenberg **Bred** Graf U Grafin V Stauffenberg **Trained** Newmarket, Suffolk

FOCUS
A modest staying contest. The runner-up has been rated close to his winter form.

1237 JEC FILLIES' H'CAP — 6f 1y(P)
4:20 (4:22) (Class 4) (0-80,80) 4-Y-O+ **£4,690** (£1,395; £697; £348) **Stalls** Low

Form RPR
03-1 1 **Elusive Ellen (IRE)**[72] 319 6-8-13 72 .... RyanMoore 5 79+
(Brendan Powell) *in tch: swtchd lft and effrt over 1f out: ev ch 1f out: led wl ins fnl f: r.o wl: rdn out* **2/1**[1]

3-20 2 hd **Diamond Lady**[10] 1065 5-9-7 80 .... FrederikTylicki 2 86
(William Stone) *chsd ldr tl drvn to ld over 1f out: kpt on u.p tl hdd and styd on same pce wl ins fnl f* **5/1**[3]

6421 3 1 **Invade (IRE)**[18] 969 4-8-1 67 .... (t) MillyNaseb(7) 3 70
(Stuart Williams) *in tch in midfield: trckd ldng pair over 3f out: effrt over 1f out: kpt on same pce ins fnl f* **7/2**[2]

-350 4 nk **Glastonberry**[45] 632 8-9-5 78 .... GeorgeBaker 7 80+
(Geoffrey Deacon) *stdd and dropped in bhd sn after s: hld up in rr: clsd and swtchd rt wl over 1f out: hdwy ins fnl f: styd on but nvr gng to rch ldrs* **7/1**

343- 5 nse **Pixeleen**[187] 6870 4-9-3 76 .... CathyGannon 4 78
(Malcolm Saunders) *taken down early: chsd ldrs tl over 3f out: styd in tch in midfield: effrt over 1f out: kpt on u.p fnl 100yds: nvr enough pce to rch ldrs* **7/1**

2252 6 3 **Saved My Bacon (IRE)**[18] 969 5-8-13 72 .... SilvestreDeSousa 6 64
(Chris Dwyer) *stdd bk to last pair after 1f: effrt on outer bnd 2f out: no imp and btn 1f out* **6/1**

-400 7 1¼ **Alhella**[18] 969 4-8-13 72 .... (v[1]) WilliamCarson 1 60
(Mick Quinn) *led: drvn and hdd over 1f out: wknd ins fnl f* **33/1**

1m 11.86s (-0.04) **Going Correction** 0.0s/f (Stan) 7 Ran SP% **114.4**
Speed ratings (Par 102): **100,99,98,98,97 93,92**
CSF £12.43 TOTE £2.80: £1.70, £2.40; EX 10.50 Trifecta £38.80.
Owner Con Harrington **Bred** Mrs Chris Harrington **Trained** Upper Lambourn, Berks

FOCUS
A competitive little sprint. It's been rated around the second and third.

1238 RYAN VEHICLES H'CAP — 1m 1y(P)
4:50 (4:51) (Class 5) (0-75,75) 3-Y-O **£2,911** (£866; £432; £216) **Stalls** High

Form RPR
036- 1 **Beauty Night**[131] 7980 3-9-0 68 .... JohnFahy 4 76
(Clive Cox) *dwlt and rdn along leaving stalls: rcvrd to ld after 1f: rdn clr over 1f out: kpt on and a holding on ins fnl f: rdn out* **8/1**

31-5 2 1 **Frozen Force (IRE)**[75] 253 3-9-1 69 .... JimCrowley 8 74
(Amanda Perrett) *hld up in last trio: effrt wl over 1f out: hdwy u.p 1f out: chsd wnr 100yds: styd in but nvr gng to rch wnr* **6/1**[3]

02- 3 ¾ **Paling**[180] 7033 3-9-5 73 .... RyanMoore 7 77+
(Roger Charlton) *hld up in last trio: effrt on inner 2f out: hdwy over 1f out: styd on u.p ins fnl f: wnt 3rd towards fin: nvr gng to rch wnr* **1/1**[1]

030- 4 nk **Aleko**[199] 6492 3-9-7 75 .... JamesDoyle 5 78
(Mark Johnston) *chsd ldrs: wnt 2nd 5f out: rdn over 2f out: outpcd by wnr over 1f out: kpt on same pce fnl f: lost 2 pls fnl 100yds* **5/1**[2]

4316 5 4 **Clive Clifton (IRE)**[6] 1137 3-8-13 67 .... (v) JFEgan 1 61
(David Evans) *led for 1f: chsd ldrs fr 2f out tl no ex u.p over 1f out: wknd ins fnl f* **12/1**

5-10 6 1 **Timia**[57] 495 3-8-12 66 .... PatCosgrave 3 58
(Ed Dunlop) *in tch in midfield: effrt ent fnl 2f: outpcd and drifted lft 1f out: wknd ins fnl f* **20/1**

2-60 7 10 **Home Again**[47] 610 3-8-9 63 .... CathyGannon 2 32
(Lee Carter) *hld up in tch in midfield: effrt whn drifted rt and lost pl bnd 2f out: wknd over 1f out* **66/1**

0-44 8 9 **Daring Knight**[33] 778 3-9-2 70 .... (b[1]) SilvestreDeSousa 6 18
(Martin Smith) *s.i.s: t.k.h: hld up in rr: rdn and struggling over 2f out: sn bhd* **8/1**

1m 38.27s (0.07) **Going Correction** 0.0s/f (Stan) 8 Ran SP% **117.1**
Speed ratings (Par 98): **99,98,97,96,92 91,81,72**
CSF £56.29 CT £90.18 TOTE £8.60: £2.30, £1.60, £1.20; EX 63.00 Trifecta £159.30.
Owner One Carat Partnership **Bred** R J & S A Carter **Trained** Lambourn, Berks

FOCUS
A fair handicap, but it was a bit of a tactical affair. A small pb from the runner-up.

1239 CENTREPOINT APPRENTICE H'CAP — 1m 4f (P)
5:20 (5:20) (Class 6) (0-60,58) 4-Y-O+ **£2,264** (£673; £336; £168) **Stalls** Low

Form RPR
1-30 1 **Turnbury**[38] 731 5-9-10 58 .... (p) EdwardGreatrex 4 66
(Nikki Evans) *t.k.h early: mde all: rdn and fnd ex over 1f out: clr ins fnl f: eased towards fin* **12/1**

00-0 2 2¾ **Salient**[87] 101 12-9-6 54 .... CallumShepherd 8 57
(Michael Attwater) *chsd wnr: rdn over 2f out: unable qck w wnr over 1f out: styd on same pce ins fnl f* **6/1**[3]

10 3 ¾ **Claude Greenwood**[32] 801 6-9-4 52 .... (b) HectorCrouch 2 53
(Linda Jewell) *chsd ldrs: effrt u.p over 2f out: unable qck over 1f out: styd on same pce ins fnl f* **8/1**

12-0 4 nk **Street Art (IRE)**[88] 84 4-8-12 53 .... KevinLundie(6) 6 54
(Mike Murphy) *hld up in midfield: effrt and hung lft over 1f out: kpt on same pce ins fnl f* **9/2**[1]

6000 5 ½ **Athenian Garden (USA)**[26] 870 9-8-12 46 .... JosephineGordon 3 46
(Paddy Butler) *hld up in last trio: effrt and nt clr run whn swtchd rt over 1f out: kpt on ins fnl f: no threat to wnr* **6/1**[3]

0006 6 nk **Little Flo**[17] 981 5-9-1 49 .... PaddyPilley 7 49
(William Stone) *hld up in last trio: effrt 2f out: sn swtchd rt: kpt on ins fnl f: no threat to wnr* **6/1**[3]

3650 7 ½ **Smugglers Lane (IRE)**[16] 1004 4-8-5 50 .... (v) AledBeech(10) 5 49
(David Evans) *t.k.h: hld up in midfield: effrt and unable qck over 1f out: plugged on same pce ins fnl f* **5/1**[2]

-253 8 1¾ **Awesome Rock (IRE)**[44] 653 7-8-5 47 .... RhiainIngram(8) 1 43
(Roger Ingram) *stdd s: hld up in rr: c wd and effrt wl over 1f out: no imp and wl hld fnl f* **9/2**[1]

2m 34.35s (1.35) **Going Correction** 0.0s/f (Stan)
WFA 4 from 5yo+ 1lb 8 Ran SP% **114.7**
Speed ratings (Par 101): **95,93,92,92,92 91,91,90**
CSF £81.73 CT £616.10 TOTE £9.50: £3.00, £2.60, £2.80; EX 81.90 Trifecta £423.30.
Owner Dragon Racing **Bred** Tarworth Bloodstock & Genesis Green Stud **Trained** Pandy, Monmouths

FOCUS
The positions barely changed in this ordinary handicap, the winner dominating throughout.
T/Jkpt: Not won. T/Plt: £28.10 to a £1 stake. Pool: £81,248.50 - 2104.58 winning units. T/Qpdt: £8.90 to a £1 stake. Pool: £6,899.92 - 573.12 winning units. **Steve Payne**

1032 CHANTILLY (R-H)
Monday, April 4

OFFICIAL GOING: Polytrack: standard

1240a PRIX DE LA VICTOIRE (CONDITIONS) (3YO) (POLYTRACK) — 1m 1f 110y
1:20 (12:00) 3-Y-O **£10,661** (£4,264; £3,198; £2,132; £1,066)

RPR
1 **Heshem (IRE)**[23] 3-8-9 0 .... GregoryBenoist 7 94
(C Ferland, France) **31/10**[2]

2 3½ **Saunter (FR)**[187] 3-8-9 0 .... ThierryJarnet 5 87
(David Menuisier) *t.k.h: hld up bhd ldrs: cl 5th and n.m.r 2f out: rdn to chse ldr over 1f out: lost 2nd fnl 125yds out: rallied to regain 2nd cl home: no ch w wnr* **13/1**

3 ½ **Barhanpour (FR)**[158] 3-8-9 0 .... AlexisBadel 3 86
(A De Royer-Dupre, France) **11/2**

4 1¼ **Candy Real (USA)**[55] 3-9-0 0 .... CristianDemuro 6 88
(Gianluca Bietolini, Italy) **22/5**[3]

5 1¾ **Never Caught (USA)**[158] 3-8-9 0 .... MaximeGuyon 1 80
(A Fabre, France) **21/10**[1]

6 1¾ **Halawate (FR)** 3-8-4 0 .... LouisBeuzelin 2 71
(H-F Devin, France) **41/1**

7 1½ **Et Toi Et Moi (FR)**[31] 3-8-3 0 .... HugoJourniac(7) 8 74
(J-C Rouget, France) **59/10**

8 15 **Top Sensation (FR)**[15] 1022 3-8-10 0 .... AnthonyCrastus 4 43
(T Castanheira, France) **15/1**

2m 1.71s (121.71) 8 Ran SP% **120.8**
WIN (incl. 1 euro stake): 4.10. PLACES: 1.60, 2.90, 1.90. DF: 29.70. SF: 43.70.
Owner Al Shaqab Racing **Bred** Yeguada De Milagro Sa **Trained** France

PONTEFRACT (L-H)
Tuesday, April 5

OFFICIAL GOING: Heavy (5.6)
Wind: fresh 1/2 behind Weather: overcast, breezy, very cool

1241 80S NIGHT ON FRIDAY EVENING 27TH MAY H'CAP (DIV I) — 1m 4y
2:00 (2:01) (Class 5) (0-75,75) 4-Y-O+ **£3,234** (£962; £481; £240) **Stalls** Low

Form RPR
0-24 1 **Sands Chorus**[32] 823 4-9-4 72 .... TomEaves 8 83
(James Given) *sn led: edgd rt fnl f: drvn rt out* **6/1**[3]

The Form Book, Raceform Ltd, Newbury, RG14 5SJ

425- **2** 1 1/4 **Lopes Dancer (IRE)**[283] 3651 4-9-4 **72**................................ BenCurtis 5 80
(Alan Swinbank) *trckd ldrs: 2nd over 2f out: styd on same pce fnl 150yds* **5/1**[2]

00-3 **3** 1 1/4 **Sakhalin Star (IRE)**[32] 823 5-9-0 **68**..............................(e) JoeFanning 3 73
(Richard Guest) *hld up towards rr: t.k.h: effrt and n.m.r over 2f out: 3rd 2f out: kpt on same pce fnl f* **9/2**[1]

660- **4** 5 **Ice Slice (IRE)**[160] 7563 5-9-6 **74**.................................... GrahamLee 10 68
(James Eustace) *hld up in rr: t.k.h: hdwy on outside over 5f out: kpt on one pce over 1f out: tk modest 4th last 100yds* **5/1**[2]

-005 **5** 4 1/2 **Mops Angel**[29] 859 5-8-7 **61** oh1..............................(p) AndrewMullen 2 44
(Michael Appleby) *dwlt: sn mid-div: hdwy to chse ldrs 4f out: wknd fnl 150yds* **10/1**

353- **6** 5 **Cornborough**[121] 7045 5-9-2 **70**.................................... JasonHart 7 42
(Mark Walford) *chsd ldrs: lost pl over 1f out* **9/2**[1]

416- **7** 1 **Tafahom (IRE)**[284] 3589 4-9-7 **75**................................ GrahamGibbons 9 44
(Michael Easterby) *hld up in rr-div: drvn and sme hdwy over 3f out: lost pl over 1f out* **33/1**

00-0 **8** shd **Adventureman**[13] 1047 4-8-9 **63**.................................... JamesSullivan 1 32
(Ruth Carr) *led early: trckd ldrs: t.k.h: effrt over 2f out: wknd over 1f out* **12/1**

0/6- **9** 9 **Handheld**[332] 2084 9-9-4 **75**......................................(p) ShelleyBirkett(3) 6 23
(Julia Feilden) *hld up in rr: hdwy over 2f out: lost pl over 1f out* **28/1**

63-1 **10** 46 **Breathless**[21] 939 4-8-12 **66**......................................(t) BarryMcHugh 4
(Clive Mulhall) *trckd ldrs: t.k.h: drvn over 3f out: sn lost pl and bhd: t.o whn eased over 1f out: virtually p.u clsng stages* **16/1**

1m 55.63s (9.73) **Going Correction** +1.325s/f (Soft) **10** Ran SP% **113.0**
Speed ratings (Par 103): **104,102,101,96,92 87,86,85,76,30**
CSF £34.89 CT £149.79 TOTE £7.20: £2.00, £1.90, £1.90; EX 37.00 Trifecta £164.90.
Owner The Cool Silk Partnership **Bred** Worksop Manor Stud **Trained** Willoughton, Lincs

FOCUS
The going was given as heavy (GoingStick: 5.6). An ordinary handicap dominated from the front. A pb from the winner back on turf, with the third rated to his AW latest.

1242 BREEDERS BACKING RACING "HIGH-RISE" EBF MAIDEN STKS (PLUS 10 RACE) 1m 2f 6y
2:35 (2:37) (Class 4) 3-Y-O **£6,469** (£1,925; £962; £481) **Stalls** Low

Form RPR

64- **1** **Du Moto (IRE)**[231] 5479 3-9-5 .... TedDurcan 6 88+
(Sir Michael Stoute) *hld up in rr: swtchd outside over 1f out: 2nd last 100yds: styd on to ld nr fin* **7/2**[2]

00- **2** 1/2 **Lord Yeats**[162] 7518 3-9-5 .... PJMcDonald 3 80
(Jedd O'Keeffe) *chsd ldr: drvn over 3f out: led over 1f out: hdd and no ex nr fin* **14/1**

323 **3** 3 **Four Mile Beach**[29] 863 3-9-5 74............................ SilvestreDeSousa 2 74
(Mark Johnston) *drvn early to ld: hdd over 1f out: kpt on one pce* **9/2**[3]

3- **4** 1 1/4 **Folly Bergere (IRE)**[157] 7629 3-9-0 .... GrahamLee 5 67
(James Eustace) *sn chsng ldrs: drvn over 3f out: one pce over 1f out* **7/1**

5-6 **5** 3 3/4 **Mr Grumpy**[36] 768 3-9-5 .... PhillipMakin 4 64
(Keith Dalgleish) *t.k.h in rr: hdwy over 4f out: lost pl over 1f out* **33/1**

604- **6** 8 **Brorocco**[181] 7041 3-9-5 79.. DavidProbert 1 48
(Andrew Balding) *edgy befhand: sn trcking ldrs: effrt over 2f out: fnd little and lost pl over 1f out: eased* **11/10**[1]

2m 30.07s (16.37) **Going Correction** +1.35s/f (Soft) **6** Ran SP% **110.1**
Speed ratings (Par 100): **88,87,85,84,81 74**
CSF £43.89 TOTE £3.90: £1.50, £7.30; EX 47.30 Trifecta £190.70.
Owner Mrs Doreen Tabor **Bred** R Scarborough **Trained** Newmarket, Suffolk

FOCUS
Not a strong maiden, but the winner won a shade cosily and has more to offer. It's been rated around the third and fourth for now.

1243 RACING UK ANYWHERE AVAILABLE NOW H'CAP 6f
3:10 (3:11) (Class 3) (0-95,95) 3-Y-O **£7,762** (£2,310; £1,154; £577) **Stalls** Low

Form RPR

021- **1** **Stamp Hill (IRE)**[206] 6304 3-8-8 **82**.............................. TonyHamilton 5 88
(Richard Fahey) *trckd ldrs: effrt and rdn over 1f out: led ins fnl f: hld on wl cl home* **7/2**[1]

125- **2** hd **Candelisa (IRE)**[208] 6244 3-9-7 **95**.................................. GrahamLee 4 100
(Jedd O'Keeffe) *hld up on ins: effrt and hdwy over 1f out: rdn and disp ld ins fnl f: kpt on: jst hld* **5/1**[3]

661- **3** 1 1/4 **Reflektor (IRE)**[162] 7510 3-8-10 **84**.......................... RichardKingscote 3 85
(Tom Dascombe) *led: rdn over 1f out: hdd ins fnl f: hld whn hung rt nr fin* **13/2**

10- **4** 2 3/4 **Ancient Astronaut**[185] 6924 3-8-10 **84**........................ GrahamGibbons 2 77
(John Quinn) *dwlt: t.k.h in rr: stdy hdwy and in tch whn nt clr run briefly over 1f out: sn rdn: kpt on same pce fnl f* **9/2**[2]

110- **5** 5 **Haley Bop (IRE)**[185] 6931 3-9-0 **88**............................ SilvestreDeSousa 6 66
(Mark Johnston) *t.k.h: trckd ldrs: rdn over 2f out: swtchd lft over 1f out: edgd lft and sn wknd* **8/1**

540- **6** 3 1/2 **Dodgy Bob**[200] 6492 3-8-3 **80**.. JoeDoyle(3) 8 47
(Kevin Ryan) *pressed ldr: rdn over 2f out: edgd rt and wknd over 1f out* **28/1**

315- **7** 2 **Explosive Power (IRE)**[164] 7460 3-9-3 **91**.................. DougieCostello 9 52
(K R Burke) *hld up on outside: rdn over 2f out: wknd wl over 1f out* **10/1**

115- **8** 16 **Desert Ruler**[164] 7465 3-8-11 **85**.. TomEaves 10
(Jedd O'Keeffe) *chsd ldrs on outside: drvn over 2f out: wknd wl over 1f out* **14/1**

014- **9** 2 1/2 **Baltic Raider (IRE)**[213] 6085 3-8-5 **79**........................ AndrewMullen 11
(Michael Dods) *hld up: rdn over 2f out: sn wknd* **7/1**

1m 24.16s (7.26) **Going Correction** +1.375s/f (Soft) **9** Ran SP% **113.2**
Speed ratings (Par 102): **106,105,104,100,93 89,86,65,61**
CSF £20.43 CT £106.82 TOTE £4.40: £1.40, £2.10, £3.00; EX 22.50 Trifecta £85.10.
Owner Merchants and Missionaries **Bred** Ms Ellen O'Neill **Trained** Musley Bank, N Yorks

FOCUS
The three who raced on the rail into the straight filled the first three places in this sprint. The front-running third has been rated to his standout Leicester win.

1244 JAMAICAN FLIGHT H'CAP (ROUND 1 OF THE PONTEFRACT STAYERS CHAMPIONSHIP 2016) 2m 1f 216y
3:45 (3:45) (Class 5) (0-75,75) 4-Y-O+ **£3,234** (£962; £481; £240) **Stalls** Low

Form RPR

543/ **1** **Almost Gemini (IRE)**[17] 7506 7-9-3 **66**......................(p) JamesSullivan 8 77+
(Kenneth Slack) *t.k.h: hld up: smooth hdwy to press ldrs over 2f out: rdn to ld appr fnl f: edgd lft: flashed tail and idled ins fnl f: drvn out* **7/2**[2]

006- **2** 1 3/4 **Tuscan Gold**[169] 7341 9-9-8 **71**.. PJMcDonald 5 77
(Micky Hammond) *missed break: t.k.h: hld up in tch: smooth hdwy to ld over 2f out: rdn and hdd appr fnl f: kpt on towards fin* **12/1**

430- **3** 4 1/2 **Madam Lilibet (IRE)**[88] 7597 7-9-2 **65**............................ JoeyHaynes 1 66
(Sharon Watt) *trckd ldrs: effrt and ev ch over 2f out: edgd lft and outpcd appr fnl f* **7/1**

4 4 **American Life (FR)**[25] 9-8-4 **56** oh3.....................(vt) SammyJoBell(3) 10 53
(Sophie Leech) *hld up: pushed along wl over 2f out: hdwy wl over 1f out: kpt on fnl f: nvr able to chal* **11/2**[3]

434- **5** 17 **Riptide**[169] 7341 10-9-6 **69**..(v) DougieCostello 9 47
(Michael Scudamore) *dwlt: hld up: niggled along after 4f: drvn over 4f out: sn outpcd: plugged on fnl f: nvr on terms* **16/1**

205- **6** 9 **Sinakar (IRE)**[35] 8367 5-9-12 **75**...................................... DanielTudhope 6 43
(David O'Meara) *chsd ldr: smooth hdwy and ev ch briefly over 2f out: sn rdn: wknd over 1f out* **9/1**

1-11 **7** 2 **Little Stampy (IRE)**[50] 592 5-9-3 **66**.............................(p) ShaneGray 11 32
(D Broad, Ire) *hld up: drvn over 2f out: sn no imp: btn over 1f out* **12/1**

103- **8** 52 **Suprise Vendor (IRE)**[19] 2128 10-9-0 **63**............................ JasonHart 3
(Stuart Coltherd) *led to over 2f out: sn rdn and wknd qckly: eased whn no ch ins fnl f: t.o* **3/1**[1]

21-2 **9** 9 **Danglydontask**[27] 882 5-8-10 **59**.............................. SilvestreDeSousa 7
(David Arbuthnot) *prom: drvn and hung rt wl over 2f out: sn btn and eased: t.o* **6/1**

4m 32.44s (36.24) **Going Correction** +1.40s/f (Soft) **9** Ran SP% **120.7**
Speed ratings (Par 103): **75,74,72,70,62 58,58,34,30**
CSF £47.01 CT £286.83 TOTE £4.80: £1.80, £4.00, £2.20; EX 59.40 Trifecta £447.00.
Owner E G Tunstall **Bred** Rockhart Trading Ltd **Trained** Hilton, Cumbria

■ Ken Slack's first Flat winner.

■ Roc De Prince was withdrawn. Price at time of withdrawal 12/1. Rule 4 applies to bets struck prior to withdrawal but not to SP bets - deduction 5p in the pound. New market formed.

FOCUS
This was run at a good gallop given the conditions and they finished pretty well strung out. A pb from the winner back on the Flat, with the runner-up rated to his form in this race last year.

1245 WATCH RACING UK ON 3 DEVICES H'CAP 1m 2f 6y
4:20 (4:20) (Class 2) (0-105,98) 4-Y-O+ **£12,450** (£3,728; £1,864; £932; £466; £234) **Stalls** Low

Form RPR

65-0 **1** **Master Of Finance (IRE)**[10] 1089 5-9-3 **94**............ SilvestreDeSousa 2 102
(Mark Johnston) *mde all at modest gallop: shkn up and qcknd clr over 1f out: hld on wl ins fnl f* **11/4**[2]

2 1 1/2 **Invictus (GER)**[40] 4-8-8 **85**.. PJMcDonald 3 90
(Micky Hammond) *t.k.h: hld up in tch: hdwy over 2f out: effrt and chsd (clr) wnr appr fnl f: kpt on fin* **18/1**

526- **3** 1 **Silvery Moon (IRE)**[154] 7676 9-9-1 **92**................................ DavidAllan 4 95
(Tim Easterby) *stdd s: hld up: shkn up and hdwy over 2f out: kpt on fnl f: nrst fin* **5/1**[3]

60-0 **4** 4 1/2 **Snoano**[24] 920 4-8-13 **90**.. GrahamLee 6 84
(Tim Easterby) *hld up: effrt whn nt clr run briefly over 2f out: hdwy and swtchd rt 1f out: kpt on: nt pce to chal* **50/1**

452- **5** 1 3/4 **Lord Ben Stack (IRE)**[276] 3888 4-9-4 **95**...................... DougieCostello 1 86
(K R Burke) *t.k.h: prom: effrt and rdn 2f out: wknd ins fnl f* **5/2**[1]

365- **6** 5 **Hit The Jackpot (IRE)**[206] 6315 7-9-2 **96**.................. ShelleyBirkett(3) 5 77
(David O'Meara) *w ldr to 2f out: sn rdn: lost 2nd and wknd appr fnl f* **16/1**

/30- **7** 13 **Awake My Soul (IRE)**[150] 7757 7-9-7 **98**........................ DanielTudhope 7 53
(David O'Meara) *t.k.h: hld up in tch: rdn whn n.m.r briefly over 2f out: sn wknd* **10/1**

41-0 **8** 13 **Passover**[10] 1088 5-9-6 **97**..(t) DavidProbert 9 26
(Andrew Balding) *trckd ldrs tl rdn and wknd qckly over 2f out* **9/1**

03-0 **9** 4 **Energia Flavio (BRZ)**[24] 920 5-8-1 **81**...................... SammyJoBell(3) 8 2
(Richard Fahey) *t.k.h: hld up on outside: stdy hdwy 1/2-way: rdn and wknd fr 3f out* **11/1**

2m 26.64s (12.94) **Going Correction** +1.425s/f (Soft) **9** Ran SP% **112.4**
Speed ratings (Par 109): **105,103,103,99,98 94,83,73,70**
CSF £48.85 CT £233.32 TOTE £3.90: £1.50, £3.40, £1.70; EX 45.40 Trifecta £206.10.
Owner J David Abell **Bred** Maddenstown Equine Enterprise Ltd **Trained** Middleham Moor, N Yorks

FOCUS
The pace was a modest one and once again racing on the rail appeared to be an advantage. The winner has been rated to his best.

1246 RON AND JOAN SENIOR MAIDEN FILLIES' STKS (PLUS 10 RACE) 6f
4:55 (4:58) (Class 5) 3-Y-O **£3,234** (£962; £481; £240) **Stalls** Low

Form RPR

54- **1** **Wowcha (IRE)**[171] 7284 3-9-0 0................................ RichardKingscote 2 78
(John Quinn) *mde virtually all: rdn over 1f out: kpt on strly fnl f* **15/8**[2]

0- **2** 2 **Bad Girl Caoimhe (IRE)**[162] 7515 3-9-0 0............................ BenCurtis 7 71
(Brian Ellison) *trckd ldrs on outside: rdn and chsd wnr over 1f out: edgd lft: kpt on ins fnl f: nt rch wnr* **14/1**

3 4 1/2 **Excellent World (IRE)** 3-9-0 0... BarryMcHugh 9 57
(Tony Coyle) *s.i.s: rn green in rr: hdwy over 1f out: kpt on fnl f: nvr able to chal* **40/1**

4 2 3/4 **Sciarra** 3-9-0 0.. OisinMurphy 4 48
(Michael Bell) *prom: pushed along over 2f out: outpcd fr over 1f out* **12/1**

223- **5** 1 3/4 **Make Music**[131] 7996 3-9-0 73... DavidProbert 6 42
(Andrew Balding) *t.k.h: disp ld to 2f out: rdn and wknd fnl f* **7/4**[1]

5-4 **6** 4 1/2 **Real Art**[20] 959 3-9-0 0.. GrahamLee 8 28
(Kevin Ryan) *prom: rdn over 2f out: wknd over 1f out* **20/1**

7 27 **My Brown Eyed Girl** 3-8-9 0...................................... GarryWhillans(5) 5
(Susan Corbett) *sn outpcd and bhd: lost tch 1/2-way: t.o* **50/1**

235- **8** 5 **Canford Lilli (IRE)**[177] 7141 3-9-0 74.............................. RobertWinston 10
(Eve Johnson Houghton) *hld up: pushed along and shortlived effrt over 2f out: wknd wl over 1f out: eased whn no ch: t.o* **4/1**[3]

1m 24.79s (7.89) **Going Correction** +1.45s/f (Soft) **8** Ran SP% **114.7**
Speed ratings (Par 95): **105,102,96,92,90 84,48,41**
CSF £27.00 TOTE £3.40: £2.30, £3.30, £5.80; EX 31.00 Trifecta £801.10.
Owner Chasemore Farm **Bred** Desert Star Phoenix Jvc **Trained** Settrington, N Yorks

FOCUS
An ordinary maiden. The opening level is a bit fluid with the form pair (fifth and eighth) below form.

1247 80S NIGHT ON FRIDAY EVENING 27TH MAY H'CAP (DIV II) 1m 4y
5:25 (5:25) (Class 5) (0-75,75) 4-Y-O+ **£3,234** (£962; £481; £240) **Stalls** Low

Form RPR

00-1 **1** **Sugar Lump**[8] 1125 4-9-7 **75** 6ex.. NeilFarley 4 81
(Eric Alston) *trckd ldrs: rdn over 2f out: rallied over 1f out: led ins fnl f: kpt on gamely* **9/4**[1]

330- **2** 3/4 **Pivotman**[209] 6211 8-8-9 **70**..(t) NathanEvans(7) 5 74
(Michael Easterby) *trckd ldrs: smooth hdwy over 2f out: led and rdn over 1f out: hdd ins fnl f: rallied: hld cl home* **8/1**

510- **3** *1* **Cadmium**[130] 5022 5-9-1 **69** PJMcDonald 3 71
(Micky Hammond) *s.i.s: hld up: stdy hdwy over 2f out: effrt and rdn over 1f out: chsng ldrs whn hung lft ins fnl f: kpt on fin* **9/1**

215- **4** *6* **Gone With The Wind (GER)**[181] 7045 5-8-12 **66**.....(t) PaulMulrennan 2 54
(Rebecca Bastiman) *hld up in tch on ins: hdwy and shkn up over 2f out: effrt over 1f out: outpcd fnl f* **6/1**[3]

411- **5** *6* **World Record (IRE)**[168] 7367 6-8-11 **65** WilliamCarson 6 39
(Mick Quinn) *led: rdn over 2f out: hdd over 1f out: wknd ins fnl f* **13/2**

054- **6** *1 1/2* **Storm Check**[243] 5061 4-8-8 **62** JoeyHaynes 8 33
(Andrew Crook) *sn pushed along towards rr: drvn and outpcd 3f out: n.d after* **33/1**

000- **7** *13* **Chosen Character (IRE)**[172] 7247 8-9-2 **75**...........(vt) AnnaHesketh(5) 7 16
(Tom Dascombe) *trckd ldrs tl rdn and wknd over 2f out: eased whn btn ins fnl f* **5/1**[2]

065- **8** *4* **Janaab (IRE)**[160] 7563 6-8-13 **72**.....(t) RachelRichardson(5) 9 4
(Tim Easterby) *s.i.s: hld up on outside: struggling wl over 2f out: sn btn: eased whn no ch ins fnl f* **13/2**

1m 56.13s (10.23) **Going Correction** +1.475s/f (Soft) **8** Ran SP% **112.4**
Speed ratings (Par 103): **107,106,105,99,93 91,78,74**
CSF £20.30 CT £133.27 TOTE £3.20: £1.60, £1.90, £2.90; EX 24.90 Trifecta £146.20.
Owner Paul Buist & John Thompson **Bred** T J Cooper **Trained** Longton, Lancs

FOCUS
This looked a sounder run race than the first division and the time was 0.5sec slower (five races had taken place on the ground since the first division was run). Once again racing on the inside rail was an advantage. The runner-up has been rated close to his best for his current yard.

1248 RACING ON MONDAY 18TH APRIL APPRENTICE H'CAP 1m 2f 6y
5:55 (5:55) (Class 5) (0-75,75) 4-Y-0+ **£3,234** (£962; £481; £240) **Stalls** Low

Form RPR

2400 **1** **Astra Hall**[17] 1004 7-8-4 **61** oh2 GeorgeBuckell(3) 1 74
(Michael Appleby) *pressed ldr: led over 2f out: sn hrd pressed: pushed along and styd on wl fnl f* **3/1**[1]

246- **2** *3 3/4* **Tamayuz Magic (IRE)**[212] 6131 5-9-0 **73**.........(b) NathanEvans(5) 5 79
(Michael Easterby) *dwlt: t.k.h and sn trcking ldrs: smooth hdwy to chal over 1f out: sn rdn: kpt on same pce ins fnl f* **3/1**[1]

/30- **3** *6* **Russian Royale**[108] 6407 6-8-12 **71** RobJFitzpatrick(5) 4 64
(Micky Hammond) *hld up in tch: drvn and outpcd over 3f out: rallied to chse clr ldng pair over 1f out: sn no imp* **7/1**

060- **4** *1 1/2* **Shalamzar (FR)**[42] 8221 7-9-0 **75** LaurenSteade(7) 7 65
(Micky Hammond) *bhd and detached: hdwy to join pack after 3f: drvn and outpcd over 3f out: rallied over 1f out: nvr able to chal* **40/1**

0040 **5** *5* **Hydrant**[3] 1201 10-8-6 **65** AnnaHesketh(5) 3 45
(Richard Guest) *led to over 2f out: rdn and wknd over 1f out* **9/1**

620/ **6** *18* **Champagne Rules**[628] 4359 5-9-1 **74** PhilDennis(5) 6 18
(Sharon Watt) *t.k.h: hld up on outside: hdwy and cl up 1/2-way: outpcd whn hung bdly rt ent st: sn struggling: t.o* **7/2**[2]

-253 **7** *28* **Final**[33] 802 4-9-3 **74** CallumShepherd(3) 8
(Mark Johnston) *prom: pushed along over 4f out: wknd over 2f out: eased whn no ch fr over 1f out: t.o* **5/1**[3]

2m 29.14s (15.44) **Going Correction** +1.50s/f (Heav) **7** Ran SP% **113.8**
Speed ratings (Par 103): **98,95,90,89,85 70,48**
CSF £12.10 CT £56.00 TOTE £3.50: £1.60, £2.40; EX 14.30 Trifecta £54.60.
Owner From The Front Racing **Bred** Miss B Swire **Trained** Oakham, Rutland

FOCUS
A competitive race on paper but the first two had it between them up the straight. It's been rated a bit cautiously.
T/Plt: £505.90 to a £1 stake. Pool: £80,170.30 - 115.68 winning tickets. T/Qpdt: £46.90 to a £1 stake. Pool: £8,755.82 - 137.9 winning tickets. **Walter Glynn & Richard Young**

CATTERICK (L-H)
Wednesday, April 6

OFFICIAL GOING: Soft (5.4)
Wind: strong half against Weather: sunshine and showers

1249 CATTERICKBRIDGE.CO.UK H'CAP 5f
2:00 (2:00) (Class 6) (0-60,60) 3-Y-0 **£2,264** (£673; £336; £168) **Stalls** Low

Form RPR

065- **1** **Baron Bolt**[112] 8244 3-9-7 **60** PJMcDonald 7 73
(Paul Cole) *prom: led 3f out: pushed clr over 1f out: rdn and kpt on fnl f: easily* **11/4**[2]

43-0 **2** *6* **Black Grass**[9] 1126 3-8-12 **58** NathanEvans(7) 6 49
(Michael Easterby) *led narrowly: hdd 3f out: remained cl up tl outpcd by wnr over 1f out: plugged on: edgd rt ins fnl f* **7/2**[3]

4-21 **3** *4* **Sadie Babes (IRE)**[21] 961 3-9-4 **60** SammyJoBell(3) 3 37
(Richard Fahey) *prom: rdn 2f out: wknd fnl f* **6/4**[1]

06-0 **4** *4* **Vocalise**[22] 935 3-8-0 **46** oh1 RPWalsh(7) 5 8
(Charles Smith) *hld up: rdn 1/2-way: nvr threatened* **150/1**

3352 **5** *1 1/2* **Fearbuster (IRE)**[20] 970 3-8-11 **55** NoelGarbutt(5) 4 12
(Hugo Palmer) *dwlt: hld up: rdn 3f out: sn struggling* **6/1**

-060 **6** *2* **Barnsdale**[20] 970 3-8-0 **46** oh1 MeganEllingworth(7) 1
(John Holt) *dwlt: a towards rr* **66/1**

0420 **7** *4* **Rojina (IRE)**[47] 635 3-8-9 **53** JosephineGordon(5) 2
(Lisa Williamson) *w ldr: rdn and outpcd 1/2-way: sn wknd* **28/1**

1m 5.22s (5.42) **Going Correction** +1.00s/f (Soft) **7** Ran SP% **108.8**
Speed ratings (Par 96): **96,86,80,73,71 68,61**
CSF £11.39 TOTE £3.50: £1.60, £2.40; EX 13.40 Trifecta £26.10.
Owner Asprey Wright Meyrick PJL Racing Wilcock **Bred** J A And M A Knox **Trained** Whatcombe, Oxon

FOCUS
All distances as advertised. The going was officially soft and the winning rider in the opener described it as "genuine soft ground". A moderate 3yo sprint handicap to open the card, with the field running into a strong headwind, so given the conditions it wasn't surprising that the winning time was 6.92sec outside standard. They raced up the centre and few were ever in it.

1250 2016 CATTERICK TWELVE FURLONG SERIES H'CAP (QUALIFIER) 1m 3f 214y
2:30 (2:30) (Class 4) (0-85,85) 4-Y-0+ **£6,469** (£1,925; £962; £481) **Stalls** Low

Form RPR

0-21 **1** **Faiseur De Miracle**[44] 675 4-9-4 **83** JoeFanning 6 101
(Micky Hammond) *trckd ldr: led over 2f out: rdn over 1f out: styd on to go clr ins fnl f* **9/2**[2]

404- **2** *6* **Hubertas**[166] 7425 4-9-0 **79**.....(b) PhillipMakin 13 87
(John Quinn) *dwlt: sn midfield: hdwy 4f out: rdn to chse wnr 2f out: one pce fnl f* **5/1**[3]

3401 **3** *12* **Swift Cedar (IRE)**[27] 890 6-8-13 **80** PhilipPrince(3) 3 69
(David Evans) *hld up: rdn over 3f out: plugged on fnl 2f: wnt poor 3rd nr fin* **11/1**

06-0 **4** *1/2* **Dark Ruler (IRE)**[71] 337 7-9-3 **81** BenCurtis 5 69
(Alan Swinbank) *chsd ldr: rdn over 3f out: wknd fnl 2f: lost 3rd nr fin* **4/1**[1]

3554 **5** *nk* **The Lock Master (IRE)**[34] 800 9-8-2 **71**.......(p) JosephineGordon(5) 10 59
(Michael Appleby) *midfield: rdn over 3f out: sn no imp* **22/1**

210- **6** *2 1/2* **Card High (IRE)**[154] 7713 6-8-7 **78**.....(t) HollieDoyle(7) 11 62
(Wilf Storey) *midfield: rdn 3f out: sn no imp* **9/1**

026- **7** *hd* **Longshadow**[116] 8210 6-9-1 **84** CallumShepherd(5) 4 67
(Brian Ellison) *hld up in rr: rdn over 3f out: nvr threatened* **9/1**

230- **8** *13* **Mysterial**[179] 7124 6-8-9 **73** NeilFarley 9 35
(Declan Carroll) *led: rdn whn hdd over 2f out: wknd* **33/1**

340- **9** *17* **Indian Chief (IRE)**[134] 7967 6-8-10 **74** JamesSullivan 1 9
(Rebecca Bastiman) *hld up: sme hdwy into midfield 4f out: wknd over 2f out* **20/1**

000- **10** *1* **Briardale (IRE)**[155] 7676 4-8-10 **75**.....(p) PJMcDonald 7 9
(James Bethell) *midfield: rdn over 3f out: sn wknd* **25/1**

1211 **11** *11* **Play Nicely**[34] 800 4-9-6 **85** GrahamGibbons 8
(David Barron) *in tch: pushed along and outpcd over 4f out: wknd over 2f out* **11/2**

12 *10* **Live Miracle (USA)**[23] 4-9-3 **82** DavidNolan 12
(Venetia Williams) *chsd ldr: pushed along and lost pl over 8f out: wknd 4f out: bhd fnl 3f* **100/1**

2m 50.42s (11.52) **Going Correction** +1.225s/f (Soft)
WFA 4 from 6yo+ 1lb **12** Ran SP% **115.5**
Speed ratings (Par 105): **110,106,98,97,97 95,95,87,75,75 67,61**
CSF £24.68 CT £232.74 TOTE £6.00: £4.20, £1.60, £2.80; EX 33.90 Trifecta £228.80.
Owner The Faiseur De Miracle Partnership **Bred** Newsells Park Stud **Trained** Middleham, N Yorks

FOCUS
Not a bad handicap, but this was attritional in the conditions, with four having got right away starting the turn for home and the field finishing well spread out. The runner-up has been rated to form.

1251 RACING UK IN GLORIOUS HD CLAIMING STKS 7f
3:00 (3:00) (Class 6) 3-Y-0+ **£2,264** (£673; £336; £168) **Stalls** Low

Form RPR

005- **1** **Evanescent (IRE)**[139] 7897 7-9-12 80 PhillipMakin 6 83
(John Quinn) *chsd ldng pair: rdn over 2f out: chal over 1f out: kpt on: led 50yds out* **7/2**[2]

0103 **2** *1/2* **Moonlight Venture**[19] 974 5-9-9 77.....(b) DavidNolan 7 79
(Conor Dore) *chsd ldng pair: rdn over 2f out: led narrowly over 1f out: hdd 50yds out: one pce* **13/2**

400- **3** *3 1/4* **Our Boy Jack (IRE)**[145] 7827 7-9-7 84 AdamMcNamara(7) 4 76+
(Richard Fahey) *midfield: rdn and outpcd 4f out: styd on fnl 2f: wnt 3rd ins fnl f* **4/1**[3]

045- **4** *7* **Tim The Taxi**[323] 2360 3-8-5 60 PhilipPrince(3) 2 46
(Natalie Lloyd-Beavis) *hld up: rdn over 3f out: edgd rt over 2f out: plugged on fnl f: nvr threatened* **80/1**

6145 **5** *2 1/4* **Llewellyn**[50] 598 8-9-9 72.....(b) DanielTudhope 3 47
(Declan Carroll) *led narrowly: rdn over 2f out: hdd over 1f out: wknd* **3/1**[1]

446- **6** *9* **Layla's Hero (IRE)**[119] 8160 9-9-8 78.....(v) JoeFanning 8 26
(David Nicholls) *dwlt: sn midfield: rdn 3f out: wknd fnl 2f* **8/1**

50-0 **7** *4 1/2* **Sunraider (IRE)**[26] 901 9-9-10 79 GrahamGibbons 5 12
(Paul Midgley) *midfield: rdn over 3f out: sn wknd* **11/2**

6054 **8** *7* **Mighty Zip (USA)**[19] 974 4-9-9 67.....(b) JoeDoyle(3) 9
(Kevin Ryan) *pressed ldr: rdn over 3f out: wknd over 2f out* **28/1**

000- **9** *2 1/2* **Hashtag Frenzy**[173] 7252 3-8-1 38.....(p) DanielleMooney(7) 1
(Rebecca Menzies) *a towards rr* **250/1**

1m 34.53s (7.53) **Going Correction** +1.25s/f (Soft)
WFA 3 from 4yo+ 14lb **9** Ran SP% **112.1**
Speed ratings (Par 101): **106,105,101,93,91 80,75,67,64**
CSF £25.26 TOTE £4.20: £1.40, £2.60, £1.70; EX 24.00 Trifecta £138.30.Tim The Taxi was claimed by Mr P D Evans for £6000
Owner Mrs S Quinn **Bred** Oliver Donlon **Trained** Settrington, N Yorks

FOCUS
A fair claimer and they went a scorching pace in the conditions thanks to a disputed lead.

1252 EASTER FAMILY DAY H'CAP 7f
3:30 (3:32) (Class 5) (0-75,73) 4-Y-0+ **£2,911** (£866; £432; £216) **Stalls** Low

Form RPR

103- **1** **Rocco's Delight**[155] 7675 4-9-7 **73** BenCurtis 4 83+
(Brian Ellison) *midfield: rdn over 3f out: gd hdwy over 1f out: led 110yds out: styd on wl* **11/4**[1]

006- **2** *2 1/2* **Dr Red Eye**[209] 6251 8-9-0 **66**.....(p) DanielTudhope 7 69
(Scott Dixon) *chsd ldrs: rdn over 2f out: led appr fnl f: hdd 110yds out: one pce* **8/1**

3-31 **3** *1 1/4* **Royal Holiday (IRE)**[9] 1124 9-9-4 **73** 6ex.........(p) JacobButterfield(3) 10 73
(Marjorie Fife) *dwlt: led over 5f out: rdn whn hdd over 2f out: plugged on* **7/1**[3]

-430 **4** *3 1/2* **Make On Madam (IRE)**[30] 859 4-8-11 **63** DavidAllan 3 54
(Les Eyre) *in tch: rdn and outpcd 3f out: plugged on fnl 2f* **14/1**

22-5 **5** *4 1/2* **Tango Sky (IRE)**[44] 680 7-9-2 **68** DavidNolan 2 47
(Paul Midgley) *midfield: rdn 3f out: no imp* **9/1**

4344 **6** *2 1/4* **Be Royale**[21] 953 6-9-4 **73** AlistairRawlinson(3) 6 46
(Michael Appleby) *hld up: rdn 3f out: minor hdwy over 1f out: nvr threatened* **11/1**

210- **7** *2 1/2* **Orion's Bow**[172] 7289 5-9-0 **73** DanielleMooney(7) 13 40
(David Nicholls) *prom towards outer: rdn to ld over 2f out: hdd appr fnl f: wknd* **28/1**

000- **8** *3* **Red Charmer (IRE)**[161] 7563 6-9-4 **70** PJMcDonald 5 29
(Ann Duffield) *dwlt: hld up: nvr threatened* **20/1**

000- **9** *3/4* **Space War**[138] 7925 9-8-11 **63** JamesSullivan 1 20
(Michael Easterby) *hld up: nvr threatened* **66/1**

05-4 **10** *2 3/4* **Coolcalmcollected (IRE)**[9] 1125 4-8-13 **65** NeilFarley 8 15
(Andrew Crook) *led: hdd over 5f out: remained prom tl wknd over 2f out* **66/1**

132- **11** *1* **Mr Sundowner (USA)**[155] 7675 4-8-10 **62**.....(t) IanBrennan 12 9
(Wilf Storey) *a towards rr* **8/1**

0-21 **12** *7* **Azrur (IRE)**[14] 1044 6-9-7 **73** PhillipMakin 9 2
(Keith Dalgleish) *in tch: rdn over 2f out: sn wknd* **13/2**[2]

040- **13** *10* **Solar Spirit (IRE)**[155] 7683 11-9-2 **68** JoeFanning 11
(Tracy Waggott) *midfield towards outer: rdn over 3f out: sn wknd* **18/1**

1m 35.1s (8.10) **Going Correction** +1.275s/f (Soft) **13** Ran SP% **116.2**
Speed ratings (Par 103): **104,101,99,95,90 88,85,81,80,77 76,68,57**
CSF £22.75 CT £143.18 TOTE £3.20: £1.40, £3.20, £2.40; EX 28.00 Trifecta £195.80.
Owner Mrs J A Martin **Bred** Philip Graham Harvey **Trained** Norton, N Yorks

FOCUS
An ordinary handicap, though quite competitive and a few of these like to force it so a strong pace was always likely. In view of that, the placed horses deserve plenty of credit as they were always up there. The third has been rated close to his turf best.

1253 RACINGUK.COM H'CAP 1m 5f 175y
4:05 (4:05) (Class 5) (0-75,75) 4-Y-O+ **£2,911** (£866; £432; £216) **Stalls** Low

Form RPR
0-30 **1** **Mirsaale**[27] 890 6-9-8 **73**................(p) PhillipMakin 14 95+
(Keith Dalgleish) *mde all: 5 l up 1/2-way: drew further clr on bit fr 3f out: 20 l up tl heavily eased towards fin* **7/1**[3]
6501 **2** *11* **Next Edition (IRE)**[35] 786 8-8-12 **68**................ PhilDennis(5) 12 64
(Philip Kirby) *hld up: hdwy 4f out: rdn to go 2nd 3f out: plugged on but sn no ch w wnr* **25/1**
000- **3** *3/4* **Sherman McCoy**[183] 7008 10-9-3 **68**................ SamJames 5 63
(Marjorie Fife) *chsd ldrs: rdn over 3f out: plugged on* **9/2**[1]
320- **4** *1 1/4* **Stanarley Pic**[179] 7124 5-9-7 **72**................ NeilFarley 4 65
(Alan Swinbank) *midfield: hdwy over 4f out: rdn 3f out: plugged on* **8/1**
04 **5** *2 3/4* **Mr Caffrey**[15] 728 4-9-1 **72**................(p) DanielMuscutt(3) 7 62
(John Flint) *in tch: rdn over 3f out: sn no imp* **8/1**
555- **6** *2* **Stormin Tom (IRE)**[153] 6877 4-8-13 **67**................ DavidAllan 2 54
(Tim Easterby) *midfield: pushed along over 4f out: outpcd over 3f out: plugged on fnl 2f* **14/1**
000/ **7** *1/2* **Hartside (GER)**[15] 5723 7-9-6 **71**................(v) JoeFanning 13 58
(Peter Winks) *midfield: rdn over 3f out: nvr threatened* **11/2**[2]
03-6 **8** *4* **Splash Of Verve (IRE)**[13] 1057 4-8-7 **61**................ ConnorBeasley 8 42
(Philip Kirby) *hld up: nvr threatened* **16/1**
100- **9** *21* **Triple Eight (IRE)**[121] 5555 8-8-9 **67**................ SophieKilloran(7) 11 21
(Philip Kirby) *hld up: bhd fnl 4f* **28/1**
622- **10** *2 3/4* **Jan Smuts (IRE)**[162] 7528 8-8-10 **68**................(t) HollieDoyle(7) 3 19
(Wilf Storey) *a towards rr* **14/1**
000- **11** *5* **Rosairlie (IRE)**[179] 7124 8-9-10 **75**................ PJMcDonald 9 19
(Micky Hammond) *a bhd* **28/1**
526- **12** *4 1/2* **Smile That Smile**[145] 7830 4-8-9 **63**................ SaleemGolam 1 1
(Mark H Tompkins) *chsd ldrs: rdn 4f out: wknd* **10/1**
0- **13** *17* **Columbanus (IRE)**[18] 2952 5-8-6 **57**................(p) JamesSullivan 6
(Kenneth Slack) *chsd ldr: rdn over 3f out: wknd* **11/1**

3m 25.16s (21.56) **Going Correction** +1.30s/f (Soft)
WFA 4 from 5yo+ 3lb **13** Ran SP% **115.7**
Speed ratings (Par 103): **90,83,83,82,81 79,79,77,65,63 60,58,48**
CSF £170.43 CT £865.58 TOTE £8.50: £2.60, £5.80, £2.80; EX 166.00 Trifecta £3836.60.
Owner Equus I **Bred** Mr & Mrs A E Pakenham **Trained** Carluke, S Lanarks
■ Stewards' Enquiry : Sam James seven-day ban: used whip above permitted level (Apr 20-26)

FOCUS
A modest staying handicap and an extraordinary performance from the winner, who totally destroyed this field. The winner has been rated close to his 2014 handicap form.

1254 RACING UK H'CAP 5f 212y
4:35 (4:35) (Class 6) (0-65,65) 4-Y-O+ **£2,587** (£770; £384; £192) **Stalls** Low

Form RPR
2-26 **1** **Lackaday**[15] 1030 4-9-2 65................(p) CallumShepherd(5) 8 76
(Mark Walford) *chsd ldr: rdn over 2f out: led 110yds out: kpt on* **13/2**[3]
244- **2** *2 3/4* **Adiator**[155] 7680 8-8-12 59................(p) JoeDoyle(3) 1 62
(Neville Bycroft) *dwlt: midfield on inner: rdn and hdwy over 2f out: kpt on: wnt 2nd post* **6/1**[2]
6335 **3** *nk* **Danish Duke (IRE)**[15] 1030 5-9-4 62................(p) JamesSullivan 9 64
(Ruth Carr) *led: rdn over 2f out: hdd 110yds out: wknd: lost 2nd post* **16/1**
564- **4** *nk* **Legal Art**[179] 7111 4-8-12 56................ BenCurtis 7 57
(Brian Ellison) *in tch: sn pushed along: rdn 3f out: kpt on same pce* **4/1**[1]
0-04 **5** *hd* **Teetotal (IRE)**[7] 1154 6-8-10 61................ KieranSchofield(7) 5 61
(Nigel Tinkler) *s.i.s: hld up: rdn and hdwy over 2f out: kpt on* **14/1**
020- **6** *1/2* **Armelle (FR)**[155] 7680 5-9-4 62................ DavidAllan 6 61
(Scott Dixon) *chsd ldr: rdn over 2f out: no ex fnl 110yds* **17/2**
340- **7** *2* **Munjally**[196] 6658 5-9-3 61................(v) JackGarritty 3 54
(Patrick Holmes) *hld up: rdn over 3f out: plugged on fnl f: nvr threatened* **11/1**
130- **8** *4* **Reflation**[175] 7224 4-8-13 62................ PhilDennis(5) 11 43
(Michael Dods) *in tch: outpcd and lost pl over 3f out: no threat after* **14/1**
024- **9** *3/4* **Mrs Biggs**[188] 6876 4-9-7 65................ DanielTudhope 10 44
(Declan Carroll) *hld up: nvr threatened* **12/1**
060- **10** *1* **Tancred (IRE)**[145] 7833 5-9-6 64................(p) DavidNolan 2 40
(Conor Dore) *dwlt: a towards rr* **22/1**
3510 **11** *6* **Monsieur Jimmy**[7] 1154 4-8-7 51 oh4................(b) NeilFarley 12 9
(Declan Carroll) *midfield on outside: rdn 3f out: wknd over 2f out* **10/1**
03-0 **12** *10* **Show Boat**[87] 130 4-8-13 57................(p) PJMcDonald 4
(Ann Duffield) *in tch: rdn 3f out: wknd and eased* **10/1**

1m 21.16s (7.56) **Going Correction** +1.325s/f (Soft) **12** Ran SP% **115.9**
Speed ratings (Par 101): **102,98,97,97,97 96,93,88,87,86 78,64**
CSF £44.20 CT £609.69 TOTE £7.10: £2.10, £1.50, £3.40; EX 45.30 Trifecta £492.60.
Owner Champagne Charlies Club **Bred** Andrew Parrish **Trained** Sherriff Hutton, N Yorks

FOCUS
A moderate sprint handicap packed with infrequent winners. This was a race where the pace held up and there was little covering those in behind the winner at the line.

1255 RACING AGAIN 20TH APRIL APPRENTICE H'CAP 5f
5:05 (5:06) (Class 6) (0-65,65) 4-Y-O+ **£2,264** (£673; £336; £168) **Stalls** Low

Form RPR
3-25 **1** **Hit The Lights (IRE)**[22] 937 6-8-10 **59**................(v) DanielleMooney(8) 4 67
(David Nicholls) *prom: rdn to ld over 1f out: kpt on* **9/1**[3]
4063 **2** *1* **Captain Scooby**[7] 1138 10-9-2 **62**................(b) SophieKilloran(5) 10 66
(Richard Guest) *hld up in rr: sn pushed along: stl last appr fnl f: r.o wl* **11/1**
0201 **3** *2* **Perfect Peak**[9] 1119 4-9-3 **64** 6ex................(vt) NathanEvans(6) 1 61
(Michael Easterby) *dwlt: sn chsd ldr: rdn 1/2-way: kpt on same pce* **9/2**[1]
4235 **4** *nse* **Pancake Day**[40] 732 4-8-11 **55**................(tp) RobJFitzpatrick(3) 8 52
(Jason Ward) *hld up: sn pushed along: kpt on fnl f: nrst fin* **9/1**[3]
000- **5** *1/2* **Compton River**[132] 8009 4-9-1 **59**................ PhilDennis(3) 3 54
(Bryan Smart) *led: rdn whn hdd over 1f out: wknd ins fnl f* **9/1**[3]
3411 **6** *1/2* **Sir Geoffrey (IRE)**[15] 1030 10-8-12 **58**................(b) AdamMcNamara(5) 6 51
(Scott Dixon) *dwlt: sn pushed along in rr: minor late hdwy: nvr threatened* **9/2**[1]
03-0 **7** *nk* **Lydiate Lady**[35] 784 4-9-4 **59**................ CallumShepherd 7 51
(Paul Green) *midfield: rdn 1/2-way: one pce and nvr threatened* **9/1**[3]
00-0 **8** *1/2* **Windforpower (IRE)**[14] 1046 6-9-6 **64**................(p) JoshDoyle(3) 2 54
(Tracy Waggott) *midfield: rdn 1/2-way: one pce and nvr threatened* **12/1**
01-2 **9** *1 1/2* **Bahango (IRE)**[37] 764 4-9-6 **64**................(p) AnnaHesketh(3) 5 49
(Patrick Morris) *prom: towards outer: rdn 1/2-way: wknd ins fnl f* **9/1**[3]
2110 **10** *1 3/4* **Boxing Shadows**[40] 733 6-9-5 **65**................ HarryBurns(5) 9 43
(Les Eyre) *dwlt: sn in tch: rdn 1/2-way: wknd fnl f* **7/1**[2]

1m 6.69s (6.89) **Going Correction** +1.45s/f (Soft) **10** Ran SP% **114.9**
Speed ratings (Par 101): **102,100,97,97,96 95,95,94,91,89**
CSF £101.77 CT £517.90 TOTE £11.10: £2.70, £3.80, £1.20; EX 157.70 Trifecta £1191.10.
Owner D Nicholls **Bred** Carrigbeg Stud **Trained** Sessay, N Yorks

FOCUS
A moderate apprentice sprint handicap to end and, as in the opener, they raced up the centre.
T/Plt: £201.20 to a £1 stake. Pool: £76,395.67 - 277.13 winning units T/Qpdt: £23.60 to a £1 stake. Pool: £6,631.74 - 207.4 winning units **Andrew Sheret**

1203 KEMPTON (A.W) (R-H)
Wednesday, April 6

OFFICIAL GOING: Polytrack: standard
Wind: fresh half-against Weather: Bright

1256 WATCH RACING UK IN HD MEDIAN AUCTION MAIDEN STKS 7f (P)
5:45 (5:47) (Class 6) 3-5-Y-O **£2,264** (£673; £336; £168) **Stalls** Low

Form RPR
1 **Toriano** 3-8-11 0................ TomMarquand(3) 3 75
(James Eustace) *chsd ldr: pushed along 2f out: rdn over 1f out and sn led: kpt on wl ins fnl f* **10/3**[3]
3- **2** *nk* **Quebee**[160] 7585 3-8-9 0................ LukeMorris 6 69
(Clive Cox) *settled in 4th: swtchd wdst over 1f out: rdn 1f out: kpt on wl ins fnl f wout matching wnr* **2/1**[2]
6- **3** *1* **King Of Naples**[268] 4208 3-8-7 0................ GeorgeWood(7) 8 71
(James Fanshawe) *in rr of main gp: swtchd to inner and rdn over 1f out: rn green and kpt on wl ins fnl f: improver* **12/1**
224- **4** *1 3/4* **Jayjinski (IRE)**[256] 4646 3-9-0 78................ SeanLevey 2 67
(Richard Hannon) *sn led: rdn 2f out: hdd over 1f out: one pce and dropped out of contention ins fnl f* **6/5**[1]
5 *14* **Forecast**[246] 4-10-0 0................ WilliamTwiston-Davies 1 34
(Martin Keighley) *settled in mid-div: rdn over 2f out: wknd fr over 1f out: t.o* **20/1**
0 **6** *6* **Just Over**[34] 791 3-8-9 0................ AdamBeschizza 5 8
(Robert Cowell) *in rr: pushed along over 3f out: rdn and wknd fr 2f out: t.o* **66/1**
7 *9* **Roman Urn** 3-9-0 0................ TomQueally 7
(Brett Johnson) *missed break and detached fr main gp: clsr 3f out: sn bhd fr 2f out: t.o* **33/1**
8 *14* **Plain Ambition** 5-9-9 0................ SteveDrowne 4
(Dr Jeremy Naylor) *s.i.s: sn struggling: detached in rr fr over 3f out: t.o* **100/1**

1m 26.56s (0.56) **Going Correction** -0.075s/f (Stan)
WFA 3 from 4yo+ 14lb **8** Ran SP% **119.7**
Speed ratings (Par 101): **93,92,91,89,73 66,56,40**
CSF £10.82 TOTE £4.50: £1.70, £1.10, £4.20; EX 12.10 Trifecta £68.40.
Owner Chesneaux, Hassiakos & Littmoden **Bred** Southill Stud **Trained** Newmarket, Suffolk
■ Stewards' Enquiry : George Wood caution: careless riding

FOCUS
The market moves proved a reliable guide in this maiden.

1257 £10 FREE BET AT 32REDSPORT.COM H'CAP 7f (P)
6:15 (6:15) (Class 5) (0-70,70) 3-Y-O **£2,911** (£866; £432; £216) **Stalls** Low

Form RPR
05-3 **1** **Viscount Barfield**[21] 952 3-9-6 **69**................ DavidProbert 9 78
(Andrew Balding) *hld up in rr: prog over 2f out: rdn over 1f out where swtchd to inner: kpt on wl to ld ins fnl f* **4/1**[2]
300- **2** *nk* **Zain Emperor (IRE)**[166] 7430 3-9-6 **69**................ StevieDonohoe 12 77
(Charlie Fellowes) *settled in mid-div: pushed along 2f out: rdn and led over 1f out: hdd ins fnl f: kpt on again nr fin* **7/1**
064- **3** *1 3/4* **Kokoni (IRE)**[160] 7590 3-9-3 **66**................ TedDurcan 5 69
(Sir Michael Stoute) *mid-div: rdn over 2f out: kpt on ins fnl f* **5/2**[1]
353- **4** *3 1/4* **Angie's Girl**[198] 6594 3-9-5 **68**................ AdamKirby 6 62
(Clive Cox) *pressed ldr: rdn 2f out: one pce ins fnl f* **9/2**[3]
040- **5** *hd* **Carlovian**[170] 7337 3-8-13 **62**................ KieranO'Neill 4 56
(Christopher Kellett) *in rr: t.k.h: rdn 2f out: kpt on nicely ins fnl f* **66/1**
4016 **6** *1/2* **Sunbaked (IRE)**[19] 978 3-9-0 **63**................(p) RobertWinston 8 55
(Eve Johnson Houghton) *in rr: mod prog ins fnl f* **16/1**
0114 **7** *nk* **Teversham**[13] 1061 3-9-3 **66**................ IrineuGoncalves 3 58
(Chris Dwyer) *settled in mid-div: nt clr run and swtchd to outer 2f out: hands and heels ins fnl f* **8/1**
003- **8** *1 3/4* **Remember Me**[189] 6851 3-9-7 **70**................ JimCrowley 2 57
(Hughie Morrison) *chsd ldrs on inner: upsides ldrs 2f out: rdn and wknd fr 1f out* **14/1**
014- **9** *5* **Pinch A Kiss**[183] 6997 3-9-4 **67**................ RyanClark 7 40
(Jonathan Portman) *in rr: nt handled bnd where pushed along to hold position: wknd fr 2f out* **33/1**
035- **10** *2 1/4* **Atrayu (IRE)**[197] 6629 3-9-0 **63**................ LukeMorris 11 30
(Paul D'Arcy) *in rr: rdn 2f out: sn wknd* **20/1**
51-6 **11** *18* **Foxinthehenhouse**[61] 459 3-9-7 **70**................ JFEgan 1
(J R Jenkins) *led and set gd pce: rdn and hdd over 1f out: wknd qckly ins fnl f: t.o* **25/1**

1m 25.26s (-0.74) **Going Correction** -0.075s/f (Stan) **11** Ran SP% **116.0**
Speed ratings (Par 98): **101,100,98,94,94 94,93,91,86,83 62**
CSF £30.28 CT £85.17 TOTE £4.90: £1.90, £2.70, £1.60; EX 34.00 Trifecta £133.80.
Owner David Brownlow **Bred** Rockwell Bloodstock **Trained** Kingsclere, Hants

FOCUS
A modest handicap but quite an interesting one. A clear pb from the winner, and a fair pb from the third in line with the better view of his latest maiden run.

1258 32RED CASINO CLASSIFIED STKS 7f (P)
6:45 (6:45) (Class 5) 3-Y-O **£2,911** (£866; £432; £216) **Stalls** Low

Form RPR
00-4 **1** **Suqoor**[11] 1091 3-9-0 75................ IrineuGoncalves 5 84+
(Chris Dwyer) *cl up on outer: t.k.h: led gng wl 2f out: sn clr on bit: nt extended* **8/1**
120- **2** *2* **Stylistik**[179] 7112 3-9-0 72................ KieranO'Neill 3 73
(Luke Dace) *in rr on inner: t.k.h: rdn over 1f out and kpt on ins fnl f: hld on for 2nd* **5/1**[3]

225- **3** *nse* **Zauffaly (FR)**[107] 8323 3-9-0 75 JamesDoyle 4 73
(Ed Dunlop) *in rr: swtchd to outer and rdn 2f out: flashed tail and carried hd awkwardly over 1f out: prog under hands and heels ins fnl f: jst hld for 2nd* **9/2**[2]

01-6 **4** *2 ½* **Silk Gem (IRE)**[88] 123 3-9-0 75 LukeMorris 1 66
(James Tate) *led after 1f: rdn and hdd 2f out: sn wknd* **6/1**

005- **5** *2* **Highly Sprung (IRE)**[218] 5982 3-9-0 75 SilvestreDeSousa 2 61
(Mark Johnston) *wnt lft s: led for 1f: chsd ldr after: rdn and wknd over 1f out* **6/4**[1]

431- **6** *8* **Musical Taste**[169] 7371 3-9-0 75 (t) JFEgan 6 39
(Pat Phelan) *in rr: rdn turning in to st: sn bhd and wknd* **8/1**

1m 25.89s (-0.11) **Going Correction** -0.075s/f (Stan) 6 Ran SP% **111.4**
Speed ratings (Par 98): **97,94,94,91,89 80**
CSF £45.38 TOTE £11.80: £4.80, £2.10; EX 63.60 Trifecta £172.20.
Owner P Venner **Bred** P And Mrs A G Venner **Trained** Newmarket, Suffolk

FOCUS
A tight race on paper but the winner made a mockery of that. It's been rated around the second and third to form for now.

1259 RACING UK IN GLORIOUS HD H'CAP 1m 3f (P)
7:15 (7:15) (Class 6) (0-60,57) 3-Y-O **£2,264** (£673; £336; £168) **Stalls** Low

Form RPR

000- **1** **Captain Peacock**[175] 7218 3-9-7 57 JimCrowley 10 66+
(William Knight) *chsd ldrs on outer: niggled along over 2f out: led gng wl 2f out: rdn and sn clr ins fnl f: easily* **9/4**[1]

6003 **2** *2 ¾* **Betsalottie**[28] 874 3-9-4 54 WilliamTwiston-Davies 1 57
(John Bridger) *settled in mid-div: swtchd off rail and rdn 2f out: kpt on ins fnl f: no ch w wnr* **10/1**

000- **3** *1 ¾* **Smiley Bagel (IRE)**[161] 7560 3-8-12 48 LukeMorris 9 48+
(Ed Walker) *hld up in rr: stl plenty to do turning into st: gd prog under hands and heels on outer ins fnl f: nrst fin* **7/2**[2]

3302 **4** *¾* **Frivolous Prince (IRE)**[13] 1062 3-8-13 49 JFEgan 8 48
(David Evans) *in rr: rdn 2f out: kpt on one pce ins fnl f* **11/2**[3]

006- **5** *½* **Northman (IRE)**[132] 7999 3-8-9 45 (p) SamHitchcott 4 43
(Jim Boyle) *chsd ldrs: rdn 2f out and upsides: one pce and wknd ins fnl f* **33/1**

0-46 **6** *1 ¾* **Harry's Endeavour**[67] 400 3-9-7 57 CathyGannon 2 52
(Daniel Kubler) *in rr: pushed along to hold position thrght: rdn 3f out: one pce* **10/1**

000- **7** *1* **French Legend**[149] 7777 3-9-6 56 [1] DavidProbert 3 49
(Andrew Balding) *squeezed up s: in rr: rdn 3f out: one pce* **9/1**

0-04 **8** *6* **Mikro Polemistis (IRE)**[71] 335 3-8-12 48 SilvestreDeSousa 6 31
(Brian Ellison) *racd in mid-div: rdn and wknd over 2f out* **20/1**

504- **9** *2* **Desert Tango**[155] 7692 3-9-4 54 RyanClark 5 34
(Jonathan Portman) *led for 1f: sn restrained to chse ldrs: t.k.h: one pce and wknd fr over 1f out* **14/1**

200- **10** *8* **Zebedee's Son (IRE)**[167] 7412 3-8-12 55 (p) RhiainIngram(7) 7 21
(Roger Ingram) *led after 1f: rdn and hdd 2f out: wknd qckly fr over 1f out* **40/1**

600- **11** *13* **Charlie Parker (IRE)**[141] 7878 3-8-9 48 (p) DannyBrock(3) 11
(Dominic Ffrench Davis) *rousted along fr wd draw to press ldr after 1f: nudged along to hold pl 3f out: rdn and wknd qckly* **33/1**

2m 20.83s (-1.07) **Going Correction** -0.075s/f (Stan) 11 Ran SP% **116.3**
Speed ratings (Par 96): **100,98,96,96,95 94,93,89,88,82 72**
CSF £24.58 CT £77.75 TOTE £4.20: £1.90, £3.10, £1.70; EX 25.60 Trifecta £87.70.
Owner Chasemore Farm **Bred** Chasemore Farm **Trained** Patching, W Sussex

FOCUS
An ordinary race won by one of the handicap debutants.

1260 32RED H'CAP 1m 3f (P)
7:45 (7:45) (Class 3) (0-90,81) 3-Y-O
£7,158 (£2,143; £1,071; £535; £267; £134) **Stalls** Low

Form RPR

221- **1** **Prince Of Arran**[147] 7793 3-9-5 80 (v) TomQueally 2 88
(Charlie Fellowes) *settled on rail bhd ldrs: t.k.h early: rdn to ld under 2f out: kpt on wl* **7/1**

31- **2** *1 ½* **Lord George (IRE)**[187] 6902 3-9-6 81 JamesDoyle 1 86
(James Fanshawe) *in rr on inner: rdn over 2f out: little prog tl kpt on wl ins fnl f: tk 2nd last strides* **6/4**[1]

403- **3** *hd* **Real Dominion (USA)**[208] 6285 3-9-4 79 [1] DavidProbert 5 83
(Andrew Balding) *in rr: rdn over 2f out: kpt on ins fnl f to take 3rd nr fin* **13/2**[3]

22-1 **4** *hd* **Street Duel (USA)**[21] 958 3-9-5 80 SilvestreDeSousa 3 84
(Mark Johnston) *led: hdd after 3f and settled bhd ldr: rdn over 2f out: wknd ins fnl f and lost two pls nr fin* **5/2**[2]

6-11 **5** *3 ¼* **Jazzy (IRE)**[77] 253 3-9-2 77 CathyGannon 6 75
(Martin Keighley) *s.i.s: t.k.h: rapid prog under restraint to press ldr after 1f: led after 3f: hdd under 2f out: wknd qckly* **12/1**

233- **6** *6* **Knight Commander**[183] 6998 3-9-2 77 JimCrowley 4 64
(William Knight) *racd in 4th and t.k.h early: rdn and wknd over 2f out* **20/1**

2m 20.36s (-1.54) **Going Correction** -0.075s/f (Stan) 6 Ran SP% **106.9**
Speed ratings (Par 102): **102,100,100,100,98 93**
CSF £16.31 TOTE £8.90: £3.30, £1.60; EX 20.00 Trifecta £77.30.
Owner Saeed bel Obaida **Bred** Rabbah Bloodstock Limited **Trained** Newmarket, Suffolk

FOCUS
There was a stop-start gallop and this was a bit of a messy affair. The top weight was rated 9lb below the ceiling for the race. Muddling form.

1261 32RED.COM H'CAP 6f (P)
8:15 (8:20) (Class 6) (0-65,65) 4-Y-O+ **£2,264** (£673; £336; £168) **Stalls** Low

Form RPR

1234 **1** **Bridge Builder**[7] 1147 6-9-1 59 (p) CharlesBishop 6 67
(Peter Hedger) *sn led: rdn over 2f out and clr over 1f out: ld reduced ins fnl f: hld on* **15/8**[1]

5446 **2** *nk* **Only Ten Per Cent (IRE)**[28] 873 8-9-0 61 AlistairRawlinson(3) 5 68
(J R Jenkins) *in rr: rdn 2f out: gd prog ins fnl f: tk 2nd 100yds out: gaining on wnr cl home: jst hld* **16/1**

-254 **3** *1* **For Ayman**[68] 387 5-8-12 63 (t) SeanMooney(7) 2 67
(Joseph Tuite) *in rr: swtchd to rail and rdn over 2f out: tk 2nd fnl f: one pce cl home and lost 2nd last 100yds* **5/1**[3]

5033 **4** *1* **Secret Witness**[7] 1147 10-9-2 60 (b) LukeMorris 4 61
(Ronald Harris) *chsd ldrs: rdn 2f out to chse ldr: one pce ins fnl f and lost two pls* **4/1**[2]

3350 **5** *1* **Ocean Legend (IRE)**[14] 1044 11-9-4 65 GeorgeDowning(3) 8 63
(Tony Carroll) *chsd ldrs on outer: rdn over 2f out: kpt on one pce* **10/1**

00-5 **6** *2 ½* **Catalinas Diamond (IRE)**[28] 872 8-8-13 57 (t) SteveDrowne 1 48
(Pat Murphy) *in rr: rdn and wknd fr 2f out* **20/1**

140- **7** *1 ¼* **The Wee Chief (IRE)**[319] 2513 10-8-10 57 TomMarquand(3) 3 44
(Jimmy Fox) *racd in mid-div: rdn 2f out: sme prog: tl wknd ins fnl f* **20/1**

0-05 **8** *1 ¾* **Noverre To Go (IRE)**[25] 919 10-9-5 63 (p) DavidProbert 7 45
(Ronald Harris) *reluctant to go to post: hld up in mid-div: rdn 2f out and sn wknd* **25/1**

3020 **9** *hd* **Pyroclastic (IRE)**[21] 955 4-9-3 61 (p) AdamKirby 9 42
(Jim Boyle) *rousted along fr wd draw to press ldr: rdn over 2f out: wknd qckly fr over 1f out* **6/1**

1m 12.3s (-0.80) **Going Correction** -0.075s/f (Stan) 9 Ran SP% **114.1**
Speed ratings (Par 101): **102,101,100,98,97 94,92,90,90**
CSF £33.45 CT £132.31 TOTE £2.70: £1.10, £3.50, £3.00; EX 31.90 Trifecta £99.20.
Owner P C F Racing Ltd **Bred** D J And Mrs Deer **Trained** Hook, Hampshire

FOCUS
A modest sprint, dominated by the winner.

1262 32RED ON THE APP STORE H'CAP 1m (P)
8:45 (8:46) (Class 6) (0-65,65) 4-Y-O+ **£1,468** (£1,468; £336; £168) **Stalls** Low

Form RPR

-344 **1** **Golden Wedding (IRE)**[34] 801 4-9-7 65 (p) RobertWinston 6 74
(Eve Johnson Houghton) *chsd ldrs: rdn 2f out: qcknd and led jst over 1f out: kpt on ins fnl f: jnd on post* **7/2**[1]

026- **1** *dht* **Roxie Lot**[155] 7694 4-9-0 61 RobHornby(3) 13 70
(Pam Sly) *in rr: rdn and gd prog fr over 1f out on outer: kpt on wl ins fnl f to dead-heat on line* **12/1**

460- **3** *3* **Henry Grace (IRE)**[210] 6221 5-8-9 53 (b) KieranO'Neill 3 55
(Jimmy Fox) *broke wl and led for 1f: restrained bhd ldrs and t.k.h: rdn 2f out: styd on to take 3rd nr fin: nt gng pce of ldng pair* **16/1**

1010 **4** *hd* **Bookmaker**[35] 777 6-9-6 64 (b) LukeMorris 7 66
(John Bridger) *led after 1f: hdd after 3f: chsd ldrs after: rdn 2f out: one pce ins fnl f* **8/1**[2]

0532 **5** *¾* **Foie Gras**[13] 1064 6-9-5 63 (p) SilvestreDeSousa 1 63
(Chris Dwyer) *chsd ldrs: rdn on inner 2f out: ev ch over 1f out: sn one pce* **7/2**[1]

044- **6** *shd* **Sheikh The Reins (IRE)**[235] 5377 7-8-12 56 KierenFox 8 56
(John Best) *led after 3f: rdn 3f out: hdd over 1f out: wknd and one pce ins fnl f* **8/1**[2]

1526 **7** *hd* **Cookie Ring (IRE)**[8] 1131 5-8-8 59 (v) PaulaMuir(7) 12 58
(Patrick Holmes) *s.i.s and in rr: rdn and sme prog fr over 1f out* **9/1**[3]

54U1 **8** *nk* **Palace Moon**[28] 877 11-9-0 58 (t) JimCrowley 5 57
(Michael Attwater) *racd in mid-div: rdn 2f out: no ex ins fnl f* **12/1**

-504 **9** *½* **Bennelong**[21] 950 10-8-13 57 (v) CathyGannon 10 54
(Lee Carter) *settled in rr: nt clr run turning into st: n.m.r on inner and pushed out under hands and heel fr 1f out* **10/1**

4030 **10** *nk* **Whaleweigh Station**[28] 877 5-9-6 64 LemosdeSouza 14 61
(J R Jenkins) *in rr: rdn 2f out: wandered u.p over 1f out: one pce and wknd under hands and heels after* **25/1**

2106 **10** *dht* **Lutine Charlie (IRE)**[19] 985 9-8-6 53 (p) TomMarquand(3) 9 50
(Emma Owen) *pressed ldr: rdn 2f out: wknd qckly over 1f out* **25/1**

304- **12** *1 ¾* **Mrs Warren**[170] 7345 6-9-3 61 SteveDrowne 2 54
(George Baker) *settled in mid-div on outer: rdn 2f out: one pce* **25/1**

500- **13** *5* **Glorious Dancer**[226] 5693 4-9-5 63 AmirQuinn 11 44
(Lee Carter) *in rr: rdn 2f out and sn no ex: wknd fnl f* **40/1**

1m 40.04s (0.24) **Going Correction** -0.075s/f (Stan) 13 Ran SP% **121.0**
Speed ratings (Par 101): **95,95,92,91,91 90,90,90,89,89 89,87,82**
WIN: Golden Wedding £2.30, Roxie Lot £8.30; PL: Golden Wedding £1.70, Henry Grace £6.10, Roxie Lot £3.60; EX: GW/RL £27.60, RL/GW £45.30; CSF: GW/RL/HG £23.83, RL/GW/HG £26.17..
Owner G A Libson **Bred** Miss A Ward **Trained** Thorney, Cambs
Owner Mrs R F Johnson Houghton **Bred** Mrs R F Johnson Houghton **Trained** Blewbury, Oxon

FOCUS
An ordinary affair and the judge couldn't split the first two at the line.
T/Plt: £82.20 to a £1 stake. Pool of £81053.42 - 719.74 winning tickets. T/Qpdt: £20.20 to a £1 stake. Pool of £10082.89 - 368.03 winning tickets. **Cathal Gahan**

1233 LINGFIELD (L-H)
Wednesday, April 6

OFFICIAL GOING: Polytrack: standard
Wind: strong, across Weather: shower race 1, bright spells after

1263 HAPPY BIRTHDAY CAROLINE WIDGER H'CAP 1m 1y(P)
2:10 (2:10) (Class 6) (0-55,55) 4-Y-O+ **£2,264** (£673; £336; £168) **Stalls** High

Form RPR

225 **1** **Anjuna Beach (USA)**[26] 904 6-9-0 53 AnnStokell(5) 4 60
(Ann Stokell) *stdd s: t.k.h: hld up in rr: effrt u.p over 1f out: str run to ld wl ins fnl f: r.o wl* **8/1**

606- **2** *½* **Jackpot**[133] 7982 6-8-12 46 oh1 (p) LukeMorris 6 52
(Brendan Powell) *chsd ldrs: wnt 2nd 5f out: ev ch and rdn over 1f out: drvn and kpt on ins fnl f* **20/1**

0403 **3** *¾* **Togetherwecan (IRE)**[7] 1145 4-9-6 54 SilvestreDeSousa 1 58
(Mark Johnston) *led: rdn wl over 1f out: drvn and hrd pressed 1f out: hdd and styd on same pce wl ins fnl f* **7/4**[1]

00-5 **4** *¾* **Fairy Pools**[30] 863 5-9-4 52 (b) JimCrowley 2 54
(Les Eyre) *t.k.h: hld up in tch: trckd ldng pair over 4f out: effrt to chal over 1f out: drvn and styd on same pce ins fnl f* **7/1**

64-3 **5** *¾* **Comadoir (IRE)**[90] 87 10-9-0 48 (p) DavidProbert 5 48
(Paul Burgoyne) *wl in tch in midfield: effrt 2f out: drvn and sltly outpcd over 1f out: rallied and styd on again wl ins fnl f* **6/1**[3]

-626 **6** *hd* **Lynngale**[19] 982 5-9-7 55 CathyGannon 7 55
(Kristin Stubbs) *dwlt: in tch in last trio: rdn over 4f out: outpcd wl over 1f out: rallied and kpt on ins fnl f* **4/1**[2]

0-45 **7** *½* **Play The Blues (IRE)**[7] 1145 9-8-13 50 (t) EoinWalsh(3) 8 49
(Henry Tett) *taken down early: stdd s: hld up in last pair: hdwy on outer over 2f out: rdn and outpcd over 1f out: kpt on same pce ins fnl f* **8/1**

000 **8** *8* **Zac Courageous (IRE)**[14] 1036 4-8-12 46 oh1 (v[1]) RyanPowell 3 26
(James Bennett) *chsd ldr tl 5f out: sn rdn and steadily lost pl: bhd over 2f out: wknd over 1f out* **33/1**

1m 39.66s (1.46) **Going Correction** +0.05s/f (Slow) 8 Ran SP% **113.1**
Speed ratings (Par 101): **94,93,92,92,91 91,90,82**
CSF £142.53 CT £405.19 TOTE £6.80: £1.70, £2.80, £1.20; EX 118.10 Trifecta £590.50.
Owner Geoff Pacey **Bred** Daniel J Yates **Trained** Lincoln, Lincolnshire

FOCUS
Extremely moderate form.

1264 MARY HICKEY BISHOPSTOWN BELATED BIRTHDAY BONANZA CLASSIFIED CLAIMING STKS — 6f 1y(P)
2:40 (2:40) (Class 6) 3-Y-O+ — **£2,264** (£673; £336; £168) **Stalls** Low

Form — RPR

46 **1** **Seek The Fair Land**[30] 857 10-9-6 67 ....(b) AdamKirby 5 — 72
(Lee Carter) *chsd ldng pair: swtchd rt and effrt wl over 1f out: rdn to ld jst ins fnl f: in command and r.o wl fnl 100yds* **13/8**[2]

4364 **2** 1 ½ **Agerzam**[7] 1150 6-9-6 67 ....(b) RoystonFfrench 6 — 67
(Ronald Harris) *dwlt: hld up in 4th: hung lft over 2f out: swtchd lft and effrt over 1f out: chsd wnr ins fnl f: styd on but a hld: sddle slipped* **8/1**

5414 **3** 1 ¾ **Rialto Magic**[7] 1139 4-9-0 61 ....(p) LucyKBarry(5) 2 — 61
(Jamie Osborne) *s.i.s: bhd: pushed along ent fnl 2f: hdwy 1f out: rdn and swtchd lft ins fnl f: r.o to go 3rd wl ins fnl f: no threat to wnr* **7/1**[3]

1421 **4** 1 **Kuanyao (IRE)**[20] 970 10-9-2 55 ....(be) AnnStokell(5) 1 — 59
(Ann Stokell) *sn led: rdn over 1f out: hdd jst ins fnl f: no ex and wknd fnl 100yds* **16/1**

-342 **5** hd **Viva Verglas (IRE)**[15] 1030 5-9-10 67 .... LukeMorris 4 — 62
(Daniel Mark Loughnane) *chsd ldr: rdn 2f out: fnd little for press and wknd ins fnl f* **5/4**[1]

1m 11.36s (-0.54) **Going Correction** +0.05s/f (Slow) — **5** Ran SP% **112.0**
Speed ratings (Par 101): **105,103,100,99,99**
CSF £14.32 TOTE £2.20: £1.20, £3.90; EX 14.60 Trifecta £40.00.
Owner John Joseph Smith **Bred** Raimon Bloodstock **Trained** Epsom, Surrey

FOCUS
A typical claimer and not form to dwell on.

1265 RACING WELFARE MAIDEN STKS — 1m 4f (P)
3:10 (3:10) (Class 5) 3-Y-O — **£2,911** (£866; £432; £216) **Stalls** Low

Form — RPR

22- **1** **Across The Stars (IRE)**[145] 7836 3-9-5 0 .... RyanMoore 4 — 84
(Sir Michael Stoute) *t.k.h: hld up in 3rd tl hdwy to press ldr over 8f out: led 7f out: pressed and rdn 2f out: asserted under hands and heels riding 1f out: styd on* **1/5**[1]

5-3 **2** 2 **Second Serve (IRE)**[10] 1113 3-9-5 0 .... SilvestreDeSousa 3 — 81
(Mark Johnston) *s.i.s: t.k.h: hld up in rr tl hdwy to ld 9f out: hdd 7f out: rdn and ev ch over 2f out: no ex 1f out: styd on same pce after* **7/2**[2]

3 26 **Belle Of Seville** 3-8-7 0 .... SeanMooney(7) 1 — 34
(Dominic Ffrench Davis) *chsd ldr tl dropped to rr 9f out: niggled along after: rdn over 4f out: lost tch w ldng pair 3f out: battling for modest 3rd fnl 2f: wnt 3rd cl home* **150/1**

300- **4** nk **Trust The Man (IRE)**[140] 7887 3-9-5 62 ....[1] JimCrowley 2 — 39
(Simon Dow) *stmbld leaving stalls: led tl 9f out: sn dropped to 3rd: rdn over 4f out: lost tch w ldng pair 3f out: lost modest 3rd cl home* **66/1**[3]

2m 34.1s (1.10) **Going Correction** +0.05s/f (Slow) — **4** Ran SP% **107.7**
Speed ratings (Par 98): **98,96,79,79**
CSF £1.21 TOTE £1.30; EX 1.30 Trifecta £4.20.
Owner Saeed Suhail **Bred** Hascombe And Valiant Studs **Trained** Newmarket, Suffolk

FOCUS
A maiden that was taken in 2015 by subsequent St Leger winner Simple Verse. With only the four runners it proved a muddling sort of race, but the class of the winner shone through. The winner has been rated to his 2yo debut form, but the level is fluid.

1266 RYAN VEHICLES FILLIES' H'CAP — 1m 2f (P)
3:40 (3:40) (Class 5) (0-75,81) 4-Y-O+ — **£2,911** (£866; £432; £216) **Stalls** Low

Form — RPR

3161 **1** **Southern Storm (IRE)**[6] 1171 4-9-8 81 6ex ....(v[1]) PatrickO'Donnell(5) 2 — 89+
(Ralph Beckett) *trckd ldng pair: effrt and drifted rt bnd wl over 1f out: stl 3rd and swtchd rt jst over 1f out: str run to ld wl ins fnl f: r.o wl* **5/4**[1]

244- **2** 1 ¼ **Ayr Of Elegance**[225] 5711 4-8-12 66 .... WilliamTwiston-Davies 4 — 71
(Philip Hide) *in tch: effrt to press ldr over 2f out: rdn to ld over 1f out: wandered u.p 1f out: hdd and no ex wl ins fnl f* **8/1**

5224 **3** 3 **Cosmic Halo**[36] 773 7-8-13 67 .... FrederikTylicki 6 — 66
(Richard Fahey) *hld up in tch in last pair: effrt u.p over 1f out: styd on ins fnl f: wnt 3rd towards fin: no threat to wnr* **7/2**[2]

2254 **4** ¾ **Ixelles Diamond (IRE)**[6] 1171 5-8-12 66 .... JFEgan 5 — 64
(Andrew Reid) *t.k.h: hld up in tch in last pair: nt clr run over 2f out: effrt u.p over 1f out: no imp and kpt on same pce fnl f* **10/1**

5215 **5** ¾ **Miss Lillie**[33] 813 5-8-5 62 ....(p) TomMarquand(3) 1 — 58
(Roger Teal) *taken down early: led: rdn and hdd over 1f out: 3rd and no ex ins fnl f: wknd and lost 2 pls towards fin* **8/1**

100- **6** 46 **Toxaris (IRE)**[237] 5312 4-9-1 69 .... RyanMoore 3
(Gary Moore) *chsd ldr: rdn over 2f out: lost pl and dropped to rr over 2f out: eased fr 2f out: t.o* **6/1**[3]

2m 5.92s (-0.68) **Going Correction** +0.05s/f (Slow) — **6** Ran SP% **112.3**
Speed ratings (Par 100): **104,103,100,100,99 62**
CSF £12.08 TOTE £2.10: £1.10, £4.60; EX 11.80 Trifecta £34.10.
Owner Christopher McHale **Bred** Chris & James McHale **Trained** Kimpton, Hants

FOCUS
A modest fillies' handicap, but another good performance from the progressive winner. Muddling form.

1267 BRIAN YORKE 50 YEARS OF SERVICE H'CAP — 7f 1y(P)
4:15 (4:15) (Class 4) (0-85,82) 3-Y-O — **£4,690** (£1,395; £697; £348) **Stalls** Low

Form — RPR

221- **1** **Replenish (FR)**[168] 7389 3-9-7 82 .... FrederikTylicki 2 — 88
(James Fanshawe) *trckd ldng pair: effrt on inner over 1f out: wnt 2nd jst over 1f out: drvn and ev ch ins fnl f: r.o u.p to ld last strides* **4/1**[3]

51-1 **2** shd **North Creek**[19] 979 3-9-2 77 .... TedDurcan 5 — 82
(Chris Wall) *dwlt: in tch in midfield: effrt over 1f out: rdn and hdwy to chse ldng pair ins fnl f: ev ch towards fin: r.o to snatch 2nd on post: jst failed* **5/2**[1]

416- **3** nse **Inland Sea (USA)**[234] 5429 3-9-6 81 .... SeanLevey 3 — 86
(Richard Hannon) *taken down early: t.k.h: led after 1f: rdn ins fnl f: drvn 100yds out: hdd and lost 2 pls last strides* **3/1**[2]

-531 **4** 1 ¼ **Ilzam (IRE)**[25] 924 3-9-2 77 ....(t) RyanMoore 6 — 78
(Marco Botti) *taken down early: hld up in tch: swtchd rt and effrt over 1f out: hdwy ins fnl f: wnt 4th towards fin: nvr enough pce to rch ldrs* **3/1**[2]

-221 **5** ¾ **Ruby Wednesday**[19] 978 3-8-10 71 .... KierenFox 1 — 70
(John Best) *dwlt: hld up in tch: effrt over 1f out: drvn and chsd ldrs ins fnl f: no ex 100yds: outpcd towards fin* **7/1**

-123 **6** 2 ¾ **Winged Dancer**[63] 434 3-9-3 78 .... LukeMorris 4 — 70
(Sylvester Kirk) *led for 1f: chsd ldr tl jst over 1f out: wknd u.p ins fnl f* **20/1**

1m 24.74s (-0.06) **Going Correction** +0.05s/f (Slow) — **6** Ran SP% **115.8**
Speed ratings (Par 100): **102,101,101,100,99 96**
CSF £15.03 TOTE £4.40: £2.00, £1.40; EX 14.00 Trifecta £49.60.
Owner Mac & Friends **Bred** S A Franklin Finance **Trained** Newmarket, Suffolk

FOCUS
Despite the blanket finish, a fair race of unexposed sorts, four of which were coming here off a last-time-out AW success.

1268 HAPPY BIRTHDAY MARY SMITH FILLIES' H'CAP — 1m 1y(P)
4:45 (4:45) (Class 5) (0-75,78) 4-Y-O+ — **£2,911** (£866; £432; £216) **Stalls** High

Form — RPR

06-1 **1** **Clotilde**[6] 1158 4-9-13 78 6ex .... RyanMoore 2 — 85+
(William Knight) *trckd ldrs: wnt 2nd 5f out: effrt 2f out: ev ch and drvn ins fnl f: kpt on u.p to ld cl home* **4/9**[1]

3110 **2** nk **Skidby Mill (IRE)**[12] 1065 6-9-6 71 .... JimCrowley 4 — 77
(Laura Mongan) *led over 6f out and crossed to inner: rdn over 1f out: hrd pressed and drvn ins fnl f: kpt on gamely tl hdd and no ex cl home* **5/1**[2]

2216 **3** ¾ **Binky Blue (IRE)**[22] 943 4-8-10 68 .... GeorgiaCox(7) 1 — 72
(Daniel Mark Loughnane) *t.k.h: led tl over 6f out: trckd ldrs 5f out tl effrt on inner and rdn to chal 1f out: no ex towards fin* **8/1**[3]

425- **4** 1 **Miss Inga Sock (IRE)**[225] 5726 4-9-1 66 .... JohnFahy 3 — 68
(Eve Johnson Houghton) *hld up wl in tch in midfield: swtchd rt and effrt wl over 1f out: styd on but nvr enough pce to rch ldrs ins fnl f* **10/1**

1m 38.25s (0.05) **Going Correction** +0.05s/f (Slow) — **4** Ran SP% **106.1**
Speed ratings (Par 100): **101,100,99,98**
CSF £2.84 TOTE £1.30; EX 2.90 Trifecta £4.60.
Owner Chasemore Farm **Bred** Chasemore Farm **Trained** Patching, W Sussex

FOCUS
A disappointing turnout, with the odds-on winner being made to work hard to get home. Muddling and far from solid form.

1269 HEART FM H'CAP — 7f 1y(P)
5:15 (5:15) (Class 5) (0-70,70) 4-Y-O+ — **£2,911** (£866; £432; £216) **Stalls** Low

Form — RPR

-300 **1** **Polar Kite (IRE)**[21] 953 8-8-10 62 .... RobHornby(3) 11 — 68
(Michael Attwater) *stdd and dropped in bhd after s: hld up in rr: rdn and gd hdwy on inner over 1f out: chal ins fnl f: r.o to ld towards fin* **20/1**

5-53 **2** hd **Surewecan**[14] 1044 4-9-1 64 .... SilvestreDeSousa 5 — 69
(Mark Johnston) *chsd ldr tl rdn to ld over 1f out: hrd pressed and drvn ins fnl f: hdd and unable qck towards fin* **9/4**[1]

0126 **3** nk **Caledonia Laird**[26] 900 5-9-4 67 .... RobertHavlin 6 — 71
(Jo Hughes) *hld up wl in tch in midfield: effrt u.p over 1f out: chsd ldrs ins fnl f: kpt on wl towards fin* **7/1**[2]

-600 **4** ½ **Johnny Splash (IRE)**[36] 775 7-8-13 62 ....(v) JackMitchell 8 — 65
(Roger Teal) *hld up in tch towards rr: effrt and swtchd lft ent fnl f: styd on wl fnl 100yds: nt quite rch ldrs* **25/1**

324- **5** hd **Keene's Pointe**[163] 7513 6-9-1 64 .... CathyGannon 2 — 66
(Kristin Stubbs) *hld up in tch: effrt over 1f out: hdwy ent fnl f: kpt on ins fnl f* **12/1**

3001 **6** nk **Flying Fantasy**[10] 1117 4-9-0 70 6ex .... MillyNaseb(7) 7 — 71+
(Stuart Williams) *chsd ldrs: effrt whn hung rt and v wd bnd 2f out: dropped to rr and looked wl hld over 1f out: rallied u.p 1f out: styd on wl fnl 100yds: nt rch ldrs* **9/4**[1]

2-66 **7** 1 ¼ **Angel Way (IRE)**[84] 162 7-9-4 70 .... MichaelJMMurphy(3) 9 — 68
(John Gallagher) *led: rdn and hdd over 1f out: no ex and styd on same pce ins fnl f* **50/1**

0-00 **8** ½ **For Shia And Lula (IRE)**[44] 680 7-9-2 68 .... GeorgeDowning(3) 3 — 65
(Daniel Mark Loughnane) *hld up in tch: effrt over 1f out: styd on same pce u.p ins fnl f* **8/1**[3]

030- **9** nk **Hipz (IRE)**[183] 7023 5-8-13 69 .... MeganNicholls(7) 1 — 65
(Laura Mongan) *trckd ldrs on inner: effrt and unable qck 1f out: wknd ins fnl f* **33/1**

400- **10** 10 **Living Leader**[176] 7198 7-9-0 68 ....(tp) JennyPowell(5) 10 — 37
(Grace Harris) *in tch in midfield: rdn over 2f out: struggling whn wd and lost pl 2f out: bhd fnl f* **16/1**

1m 24.71s (-0.09) **Going Correction** +0.05s/f (Slow) — **10** Ran SP% **112.2**
Speed ratings (Par 103): **102,101,101,100,100 100,98,98,97,86**
CSF £60.94 CT £367.87 TOTE £18.70: £2.30, £2.30, £1.90; EX 61.00 Trifecta £499.70.
Owner Christian Main **Bred** Holborn Trust Co **Trained** Epsom, Surrey

FOCUS
A run-of-the-mill modest handicap. The winner has been rated to his winter form, with the second and third setting the level.
T/Plt: £26.20 to a £1 stake. Pool of £51816.33 -1438.70 winning tickets. T/Qpdt: £6.70 to a £1 stake. Pool of £3864.39 - 424.36 winning tickets. **Steve Payne**

NOTTINGHAM (L-H)
Wednesday, April 6

OFFICIAL GOING: Heavy (5.3)
Wind: Fresh against Weather: Cloudy with showers

1270 BET TOTEPLACEPOT RACES 1 TO 6 MAIDEN STKS — 1m 75y
2:20 (2:20) (Class 5) 3-Y-O — **£2,911** (£866; £432; £216) **Stalls** Centre

Form — RPR

46- **1** **Angel Grace (IRE)**[146] 7810 3-9-0 0 .... ShaneKelly 3 — 77
(David Menuisier) *trckd ldng pair: swtchd rt and effrt over 2f out: rdn over 1f out: drvn ins fnl f: styd on wl to ld nr line* **14/1**

0- **2** hd **Stratum**[159] 7592 3-9-5 0 .... FrankieDettori 10 — 81
(John Gosden) *sn trcking ldr: hdwy 3f out: rdn to chal over 1f out: drvn to take slt ld ins fnl f: hdd and no ex nr fin* **7/4**[1]

3- **3** 2 ¼ **Finelcity (GER)**[177] 7158 3-9-5 0 ....(b) PatCosgrave 4 — 76
(Harry Dunlop) *led: pushed along wl over 2f out: jnd and rdn over 1f out: hdd jst ins fnl f: sn drvn and rallied: wknd last 75yds* **9/2**[3]

4 ½ **High Draw (FR)** 3-9-5 0 .... DougieCostello 1 — 75+
(K R Burke) *towards rr: green and pushed along on inner 1/2-way: hdwy 3f out: swtchd rt and rdn wl over 1f out: sn chsng ldrs: kpt on wl fnl f* **16/1**

00- **5** 4 ½ **The Graduate (IRE)**[154] 7708 3-9-5 0 .... LiamKeniry 7 — 65+
(Andrew Balding) *dwlt and in rr: hdwy over 2f out: sn rdn and kpt on same pce* **14/1**

04- **6** 1 ½ **Swansway**[182] 7038 3-9-5 0 .... RichardKingscote 8 — 61
(Tom Dascombe) *hld up towards rr: hdwy 5f out: pushed along 3f out: rdn over 2f out: sn no imp* **20/1**

40- **7** *7* **Arithmetic (IRE)**[221] 5851 3-9-5 0 DarryllHolland 6 45
(Charles Hills) *sn chsng ldrs: rdn along 3f out: wknd fnl 2f* **9/1**
0- **8** *5* **Pure Soul**[163] 7516 3-9-2 0 (p) ThomasBrown[(3)] 2 33
(Ismail Mohammed) *trckd ldrs on inner: effrt 4f out: rdn along 3f out: sn wknd* **33/1**
420- **9** *1 1/2* **Able Jack**[186] 6924 3-9-5 79 OisinMurphy 5 30
(Andrew Balding) *dwlt: hdwy to chse ldrs after 2f: pushed along 4f out: rdn over 3f out: sn wknd* **7/2**[2]
1m 57.1s (8.10) **Going Correction** +0.85s/f (Soft) **9** Ran SP% **113.7**
Speed ratings (Par 98): **93,92,90,90,85 84,77,72,70**
CSF £38.30 TOTE £17.30: £3.70, £1.10, £1.60; EX 58.20 Trifecta £314.80.
Owner Clive Washbourn **Bred** Paul McEnery **Trained** Pulborough, W Sussex
FOCUS
Morning rain saw a going change to heavy from heavy, soft in places. There was a strong headwind in the home straight, and all of the races were on the inner track. Distances as advertised. Not the strongest of maidens to open the card but still some positives to take from each of the first four home. The runner-up has been rated as progressing from his debut, as well as the front-running third.

1271 BET TOTEEXACTA H'CAP 5f 13y
2:50 (2:50) (Class 4) (0-85,85) 3-Y-O **£4,851** (£1,443; £721; £360) **Stalls** High

Form RPR
100- **1** **Willytheconqueror (IRE)**[180] 7072 3-9-7 **85** MartinDwyer 3 91
(William Muir) *cl up: pushed along 2f out: rdn over 1f out: carried sltly lft jst ins fnl f: drvn and kpt on to ld last 10yds* **3/1**[2]
6412 **2** *3/4* **Mysterious Look**[15] 1029 3-8-7 **71** oh2 KieranO'Neill 4 74
(Ed McMahon) *cl up: led wl over 1f out: rdn and edgd lft jst ins fnl f: sn drvn hdd and no ex last 100yds* **4/1**[3]
00-1 **3** *4* **A Momentofmadness**[21] 954 3-9-5 **83** DarryllHolland 1 72
(Charles Hills) *carried sltly lft s: racd wd and sn led: pushed along over 2f out: rdn and hdd wl over 1f out: wknd appr fnl f* **13/8**[1]
103- **4** *1 1/4* **Total Power**[248] 4909 3-8-7 **71** MartinLane 2 55
(Brian Ellison) *wnt lft s: trckd ldrs: pushed along after 1 1/2f: rdn along and outpcd 1/2-way: drvn and plugged on fr over 1f out* **8/1**
00-6 **5** *11* **Jazz Legend (USA)**[21] 954 3-9-1 **79** TomEaves 5 24
(James Given) *racd cl to stands' rail: in tch: hdwy 1/2-way: chsd ldrs 2f out: sn rdn and wknd qckly over 1f out* **6/1**
1m 7.63s (6.13) **Going Correction** +1.275s/f (Soft) **5** Ran SP% **108.5**
Speed ratings (Par 100): **101,99,93,91,73**
CSF £14.42 TOTE £4.00: £2.00, £1.50; EX 13.60 Trifecta £31.70.
Owner Perspicacious Punters Racing Club **Bred** Old Carhue & Graeng Bloodstock **Trained** Lambourn, Berks
FOCUS
The stalls were against the stands' rails but the action took place more towards the centre of the track. A length pb from the winner.

1272 BET TOTEQUADPOT RACES 3 TO 6 CONDITIONS STKS 5f 13y
3:20 (3:20) (Class 3) 3-Y-O+ **£7,470** (£2,236; £1,118; £559; £279) **Stalls** High

Form RPR
200- **1** **Lexington Abbey**[179] 7122 5-9-1 95 JamieSpencer 4 98
(Kevin Ryan) *trckd ldng pair: hdwy over 2f out: rdn to ld ent fnl f: sn edgd lft: drvn and kpt on wl towards fin* **11/4**[2]
-000 **2** *1* **Intibaah**[25] 923 6-9-9 94 PatCosgrave 3 102
(George Baker) *hld up in rr: hdwy over 1f out: swtchd lft and rdn ent fnl f: sn chsng wnr: drvn and no imp towards fin* **7/1**
520- **3** *5* **Poyle Vinnie**[179] 7122 6-9-1 105 AndrewMullen 2 76
(Michael Appleby) *trckd ldr: cl up 2f out: rdn to chal wl over 1f out: drvn and ev ch ent fnl f: sn one pce* **13/8**[1]
04-3 **4** *1 1/2* **Silvanus (IRE)**[12] 1083 11-9-9 95 GrahamLee 1 79
(Paul Midgley) *trckd ldrs on outer: shkn up over 2f out: sn rdn btn* **14/1**
300- **5** *1* **Blithe Spirit**[180] 7091 5-8-10 91 JasonHart 6 62
(Eric Alston) *led: pushed along 2f out: jnd and rdn wl over 1f out: drvn and hdd ent fnl f: sn wknd* **10/3**[3]
1m 6.85s (5.35) **Going Correction** +1.275s/f (Soft) **5** Ran SP% **107.0**
Speed ratings (Par 107): **108,106,98,96,94**
CSF £19.22 TOTE £3.20: £1.50, £4.10; EX 18.00 Trifecta £41.30.
Owner Middleham Park Racing Xix **Bred** D R Tucker **Trained** Hambleton, N Yorks
FOCUS
Some useful sprinters on show and the winner was enhancing a fine record at the track. The winner has been rated close to his best.

1273 TOTEPOOL EBF STALLIONS BARRY HILLS FURTHER FLIGHT STKS (LISTED RACE) 1m 6f 15y
3:50 (3:50) (Class 1) 4-Y-O+
£22,684 (£8,600; £4,304; £2,144; £1,076; £540) **Stalls** Low

Form RPR
11-0 **1** **Frosty Berry**[49] 614 7-8-10 82 ShaneGray 5 105
(Ed de Giles) *hld up towards rr: hdwy over 4f out: trckd ldrs over 2f out: effrt and nt clr run over 1f out: swtchd lft and rdn to chal 1f out: carried sltly lft and led ins fnl f: drvn out* **50/1**
542- **2** *nk* **Clever Cookie**[172] 7277 8-9-1 113 GrahamLee 7 110
(Peter Niven) *trckd ldng pair: smooth hdwy over 4f out: cl up over 3f out: slt ld 1 1/2f out: shkn up and edgd lft ent fnl f: sn rdn and hdd ins fnl f: edgd lft and kpt on same pce* **4/6**[1]
0/0- **3** *5* **Seismos (IRE)**[343] 1799 8-9-1 110 AndreaAtzeni 6 103
(Marco Botti) *trckd ldng pair: hdwy 3f out: rdn to chal over 1f out: ev ch and drvn ent fnl f: kpt on same pce* **7/1**[3]
5264 **4** *9* **First Mohican**[12] 1067 8-9-1 102 JimmyFortune 1 90
(Alan King) *trckd ldrs: hdwy and cl up 3f out: rdn to chal 2f out: ev ch tl drvn and wknd appr fnl f* **7/1**[3]
051- **5** *1 3/4* **Nearly Caught (IRE)**[170] 7341 6-9-1 105 GeorgeBaker 3 88
(Hughie Morrison) *led: pushed along 4f out: jnd and rdn 3f out: drvn and hdd 1 1/2f out: sn wknd* **9/2**[2]
-243 **6** *1* **Duchess Of Marmite (IRE)**[11] 1092 4-8-7 85 ShaneKelly 2 82
(Richard Hughes) *hld up in tch: sme hdwy on inner over 4f out: rdn along 3f out: sn outpcd* **25/1**
2- **7** *4 1/2* **Amber Flush**[18] 7341 7-8-10 0 TimClark 8 75
(Martin Smith) *dwlt: a in rr* **100/1**
8 *3 1/4* **Giant Redwood (IRE)**[182] 7048 4-8-12 0 JamieSpencer 4 76
(Michael Bell) *hld up: a towards rr* **20/1**
106- **9** *6* **Eye Of The Storm (IRE)**[195] 6678 6-9-1 105 PatDobbs 9 67
(Amanda Perrett) *chsd ldr: rdn along 4f out: wknd 3f out* **12/1**
3m 21.53s (14.53) **Going Correction** +0.85s/f (Soft)
WFA 4 from 6yo+ 3lb **9** Ran SP% **122.4**
Speed ratings (Par 111): **92,91,88,83,82 82,79,77,74**
CSF £88.72 TOTE £23.30: £7.00, £1.02, £2.20; EX 130.30 Trifecta £515.80.
Owner Ms Julie French **Bred** J H Widdows **Trained** Ledbury, H'fords
FOCUS
This looked an up-to-scratch renewal of this Listed event but there was a turn up with an 82-rated 7yo mare landing the prize. The level is a bit fluid, with the second and third rated below their best.

1274 BET TOTETRIFECTA H'CAP 1m 75y
4:25 (4:26) (Class 3) (0-95,94) 4-Y-O+ **£7,762** (£2,310; £1,154; £577) **Stalls** Centre

Form RPR
240- **1** **Sinfonietta (FR)**[171] 7327 4-8-3 **76** FrannyNorton 4 94
(David Menuisier) *prom: trckd ldr over 5f out: led 3f out: rdn clr 1 1/2f out: eased towards fin: v readily* **9/1**
300- **2** *6* **Spa's Dancer (IRE)**[19] 7470 9-9-0 **87** GrahamLee 1 91
(James Eustace) *s.i.s and bhd: stdy hdwy 3f out: rdn to chse ldrs over 1f out: kpt on wl fnl f: no ch w wnr* **16/1**
31/- **3** *3 1/2* **Hail Clodius (IRE)**[600] 5391 4-9-0 **87** PatDobbs 6 83
(Richard Hannon) *in tch: hdwy 3f out: chsd ldrs whn nt clr run and swtchd rt wl over 1f out: sn rdn and styd on fnl f* **20/1**
/10- **4** *3 1/2* **Greenside**[139] 7899 5-9-1 **88** OisinMurphy 7 76
(Henry Candy) *hld up towards rr: hdwy on wd outside 3f out: chsd ldrs 2f out: sn rdn and one pce* **7/4**[1]
556- **5** *3* **Simply Shining (IRE)**[193] 6750 6-8-9 **82** TonyHamilton 5 63
(Richard Fahey) *trckd ldrs: hdwy 4f out: rdn over 2f out: drvn wl over 1f out: sn wknd* **25/1**
420- **6** *hd* **Jack's Revenge (IRE)**[151] 7758 8-9-3 **90** (bt) PatCosgrave 9 71
(George Baker) *dwlt and in rr: hdwy 3f out: rdn along 2f out: kpt on fnl f* **14/1**
036- **7** *4* **Little Lady Katie (IRE)**[166] 7434 4-8-3 **83** ow3 CliffordLee[(7)] 2 55
(K R Burke) *chsd ldrs: rdn along over 3f out: sn wknd* **8/1**[3]
20-5 **8** *nk* **Taysh (USA)**[96] 7 4-8-9 **82** AndrewMullen 8 53
(Michael Appleby) *in tch: hdwy to chse ldrs over 3f out: rdn over 2f out: sn drvn and wknd* **50/1**
64-4 **9** *1 1/4* **Hillbilly Boy (IRE)**[58] 503 6-9-0 **94** PatrickVaughan[(7)] 10 62
(Tom Dascombe) *prom on outer: chsd wnr 3f out and sn rdn along: drvn 2f out and sn wknd* **16/1**
2311 **10** *18* **Captain Revelation**[29] 866 4-8-9 **82** RichardKingscote 3 9
(Tom Dascombe) *led: rdn along over 3f out: sn hdd & wknd* **7/1**[2]
306- **11** *1* **Get Knotted (IRE)**[184] 6979 4-9-0 **87** (p) PaulMulrennan 12 11
(Michael Dods) *a towards rr* **7/1**[2]
0-50 **12** *3 1/2* **Starboard**[53] 560 7-9-5 **92** JamieSpencer 11 8
(David Simcock) *a towards rr* **12/1**
1m 53.09s (4.09) **Going Correction** +0.85s/f (Soft) **12** Ran SP% **119.2**
Speed ratings (Par 107): **113,107,103,100,97 96,92,92,91,73 72,68**
CSF £141.35 CT £2836.70 TOTE £12.20: £4.20, £5.60, £4.20; EX 195.20 Trifecta £4607.30.
Owner Clive Washbourn **Bred** E A R L Elevage Des Loges Et Al **Trained** Pulborough, W Sussex
FOCUS
A good-quality handicap, but won in emphatic fashion by a horse who looks one to follow. The runner-up has been rated close to last year's form.

1275 TOTEPOOL FLETCH AND LANEY H'CAP 1m 75y
4:55 (4:55) (Class 5) (0-75,75) 3-Y-O **£3,067** (£905; £453) **Stalls** Centre

Form RPR
430- **1** **Motdaw**[168] 7393 3-9-1 **69** GeorgeBaker 7 82
(Mick Channon) *hld up in rr: gd hdwy on outer 3f out: rdn to ld over 1f out: sn clr: kpt on strly* **9/2**[2]
030- **2** *6* **Nutbourne Lad (IRE)**[179] 7105 3-8-11 **65** (b[1]) PatDobbs 1 64
(Amanda Perrett) *trckd ldng pair on inner: hdwy 3f out: cl up 2f out: rdn 1 1/2f out and ev ch: sn drvn and kpt on: no ch w wnr* **10/1**
665- **3** *6* **Hijran (IRE)**[146] 7811 3-8-13 **67** AndreaAtzeni 8 52
(Charlie Fellowes) *t.k.h: trckd ldr: hdwy and cl up over 2f out: sn disp ld: rdn wl over 1f out: one pce* **11/4**[1]
4364 **4** *1/2* **Rubis**[15] 1031 3-8-7 **61** oh2 BarryMcHugh 5 45
(Richard Fahey) *dwlt and in rr: hdwy on inner over 4f out: chsd ldrs over 2f out: sn rdn along and plugged on one pce* **6/1**
360- **5** *1 3/4* **Stars N Angels (IRE)**[247] 4930 3-8-9 **63** AndrewMullen 9 43
(Michael Appleby) *trckd ldng pair: hdwy on outer 3f out: rdn to ld over 2f out: sn drvn and hdd over 1f: sn wknd* **10/1**
600- **6** *1 1/4* **Be Bop Tango (FR)**[201] 6492 3-9-7 **75** DougieCostello 2 52
(K R Burke) *t.k.h: chsd ldrs: rdn along 3f out: sn wknd* **16/1**
120- **7** *8* **Boutan**[195] 6684 3-9-4 **72** LiamKeniry 4 31
(George Baker) *led: rdn along over 3f out: hdd over 2f out and sn wknd* **15/2**
000- **8** *8* **Monsieur Glory**[193] 6745 3-8-8 **62** RichardKingscote 3 2
(Tom Dascombe) *a towards rr* **5/1**[3]
1m 57.14s (8.14) **Going Correction** +0.85s/f (Soft) **8** Ran SP% **111.6**
Speed ratings (Par 98): **93,87,81,80,78 77,69,61**
CSF £45.59 CT £143.10 TOTE £4.40: £1.30, £3.30, £1.60; EX 44.00 Trifecta £160.80.
Owner Derek And Jean Clee **Bred** D D & Mrs J P Clee **Trained** West Ilsley, Berks
FOCUS
A modest 3yo handicap, but run at a strong gallop and producing an impressive winner, albeit suited by being held up. The runner-up has been rated to form.

1276 TOTEWIN BEAT SP 2016 GRAND NATIONAL H'CAP 1m 2f 50y
5:25 (5:25) (Class 5) (0-70,70) 3-Y-O **£2,911** (£866; £432; £216) **Stalls** Low

Form RPR
200- **1** **Walsingham Grange (USA)**[168] 7398 3-9-6 **69** PatCosgrave 8 79
(Pam Sly) *hld up towards rr: hdwy over 3f out: trckd ldrs whn n.m.r over 2f out: led wl over 1f out: sn rdn and kpt on strly* **40/1**
013- **2** *2 3/4* **Gawdawpalin (IRE)**[160] 7577 3-9-6 **69** PatDobbs 4 74
(Sylvester Kirk) *in tch: hdwy over 3f out: chsd ldrs 2f out: sn rdn: drvn to chse wnr and edgd lft ins fnl f: kpt on* **9/2**[2]
466- **3** *1 1/2* **Purple Raven**[158] 7629 3-9-6 **69** JamieSpencer 5 71+
(Michael Bell) *hld up towards rr: hdwy over 3f out: nt clr run and swtchd lft wl over 1f out: sn rdn and kpt on same pce* **4/1**[1]
044- **4** *1 1/4* **Match My Fire (IRE)**[154] 7708 3-9-5 **68** (p) FMBerry 11 68+
(Ralph Beckett) *chsd ldrs: hdwy and cl up over 3f out: led over 2f out and sn rdn: drvn and hdd wl over 1f out: grad wknd* **4/1**[1]
060- **5** *3 3/4* **Visage Blanc**[165] 7472 3-9-5 **68** GeorgeBaker 10 61
(Mick Channon) *hld up towards rr: hdwy 4f out: chsd ldrs over 2f out: sn rdn and ev ch tl drvn and wknd over 1f out* **10/1**
561- **6** *15* **Little Pippin**[161] 7562 3-8-7 **56** oh4 BarryMcHugh 6 20
(Tony Coyle) *hld up in rr: hdwy over 4f out: cl up 3f out: rdn along over 2f out: drvn and wknd wl over 1f out* **20/1**
646- **7** *16* **Bluff Crag**[180] 7092 3-9-6 **69** OisinMurphy 12 3
(Andrew Balding) *chsd ldr: led 3f out: sn rdn and hdd over 2f out: sn wknd* **7/1**[3]

353- **8** *19* **Capital Gearing**[160] 7671 3-8-11 **63**..........................(p) LouisSteward(3) 7
(Henry Spiller) *in tch: hdwy 4f out: cl up over 3f out: sn rdn and wknd qckly over 2f out* **20/1**

34-0 **9** *7* **Billy Roberts (IRE)**[25] 924 3-9-7 **70**.................................... JasonHart 3
(Richard Guest) *dwlt: a in rr* **16/1**

555- **10** *1 3/4* **Top Of The Rocks (FR)**[208] 6262 3-9-2 **65**............. RichardKingscote 2
(Tom Dascombe) *chsd ldrs: rdn along over 4f out: wknd over 3f out* **16/1**

060- **11** *1 1/2* **File Of Facts (IRE)**[216] 6018 3-8-9 **65**...................... PatrickVaughan(7) 9
(Tom Dascombe) *chsd ldrs on inner: rdn along 4f out: wknd 3f out* **50/1**

430- **12** *1 3/4* **Palmerston**[107] 8323 3-9-6 **69**.. AndrewMullen 1
(Michael Appleby) *led: rdn along 4f out: hdd 3f out and sn wknd* **8/1**

2m 26.58s (12.28) **Going Correction** +0.85s/f (Soft) **12** Ran SP% **116.6**
Speed ratings (Par 98): **84,81,80,79,76 64,51,36,31,29 28,27**
CSF £203.60 CT £905.51 TOTE £18.60: £7.60, £1.90, £1.80; EX 129.40 Trifecta £533.10.
Owner Pam's People **Bred** Edward A Seltzer Et Al **Trained** Thorney, Cambs

FOCUS
Another race dominated by those held up - the complexion changing dramatically at the 3f marker. A step up on his 2yo form from the winner, with the usual race standard supporting this level.
T/Jkpt: Not won. T/Plt: £301.70 to a £1 stake. Pool of £60136.38 - 145.50 winning tickets. T/Qpdt: £103.90 to a £1 stake. Pool of £4930.92 - 35.10 winning tickets. **Joe Rowntree**

1277 - 1278a (Foreign Racing) - See Raceform Interactive

LEOPARDSTOWN (L-H)
Wednesday, April 6

OFFICIAL GOING: Soft to heavy changing to heavy after race 1 (3.25)

1279a IRISH STALLION FARMS EUROPEAN BREEDERS FUND NOBLESSE STKS (LISTED RACE) 1m 4f
4:30 (4:30) 4-Y-O+
£23,860 (£7,683; £3,639; £1,617; £808; £404)

RPR

1 **Altesse**[246] 4992 5-9-1 101.. KevinManning 2 102+
(J S Bolger, Ire) *chsd ldrs: edgd sltly rt after 1f: 3rd 1/2-way: rdn in 3rd 1 1/2f out and clsd u.p on outer to chal in 2nd ins fnl f: kpt on best to ld narrowly cl home* **11/4**[2]

2 *1/2* **Ballybacka Queen (IRE)**[171] 7321 5-9-1 100........... DonnachaO'Brien 1 101
(P A Fahy, Ire) *prom tl sn settled bhd ldr in 2nd: tk clsr order bhd ldr under 2f out and rdn to ld 1f out: strly pressed u.p ins fnl f and hdd cl home* **10/1**

3 *4* **Island Remede**[165] 7469 5-9-1 90..................................... ColinKeane 11 95
(Henry De Bromhead, Ire) *attempted to make all: 2 l clr and stl gng wl appr st: rdn and reduced advantage 1 1/2f out: hdd fr 1f out and sn no ex in 3rd* **66/1**

4 *1/2* **Zannda (IRE)**[165] 7477 4-9-5 102......................................(b) PatSmullen 9 99+
(D K Weld, Ire) *chsd ldrs: sltly impeded after 1f: 4th 1/2-way: pushed along in 5th appr st and no imp on ldrs in 4th ent fnl f: kpt on one pce* **7/4**[1]

5 *1 3/4* **Fact Or Folklore (IRE)**[171] 7321 4-9-0 89......................... LeighRoche 8 91+
(W McCreery, Ire) *chsd ldrs early: racd keenly: rdn in 8th 3f out and clsd u.p into mod 6th over 1f out: kpt on ins fnl f: nvr trbld ldrs* **16/1**

6 *2* **Avenante**[171] 7321 4-9-0 91.......................................[1] DeclanMcDonogh 10 88+
(John M Oxx, Ire) *hld up: last 4f out: pushed along in 9th fr 3f out and no imp in mod 9th over 1f out: kpt on ins fnl f: nvr trbld ldrs* **16/1**

7 *1 1/2* **Fluff (IRE)**[17] 1016 4-9-0 0..................................... SeamieHeffernan 5 86+
(A P O'Brien, Ire) *dwlt and towards rr early: clsr in 5th bef 1/2-way: pushed along in 4th appr st and no imp on ldrs u.p in 5th ent fnl f: one pce after* **10/3**[3]

8 *1 3/4* **Princess Aloof (IRE)**[17] 1018 5-9-1 91.................(p) ColmO'Donoghue 7 83+
(Mrs John Harrington, Ire) *hld up in tch: rdn in 6th into st and no imp on ldrs: wknd in 7th over 1f out* **20/1**

9 *6 1/2* **Rock On Rosie (IRE)**[14] 1053 7-9-1 63............................. ChrisHayes 6 72?
(Adrian Brendan Joyce, Ire) *dwlt and in rr early: rdn in 7th 2f out and no ex: wknd over 1f out* **100/1**

10 *8* **Diamond Rio (IRE)**[262] 4432 4-9-0 76............................ RonanWhelan 3 60+
(Anthony Mullins, Ire) *dwlt and towards rr early: 6th 1/2-way: rdn and wknd fr over 3f out* **33/1**

2m 56.79s (21.49) **Going Correction** +2.00s/f (Heav)
WFA 4 from 5yo+ 1lb **10** Ran SP% **117.2**
Speed ratings: **108,107,105,104,103 102,101,100,95,90**
CSF £29.50 TOTE £3.60: £1.40, £2.90, £13.90; DF 28.00 Trifecta £981.20.
Owner Miss K Rausing **Bred** Miss K Rausing **Trained** Coolcullen, Co Carlow

FOCUS
This was the first running of this Listed contest at Leopardstown, having been transferred from Cork. With three runners rated 100 or higher, it was well worthy of Listed status. Colin Keane dictated the fractions on rank outsider \bIsland Remede\p and looked for a brief moment like he might have stolen it. The winner was brave, though, and deserved a success at this level.

1280 - 1283a (Foreign Racing) - See Raceform Interactive

1240 CHANTILLY (R-H)
Wednesday, April 6

OFFICIAL GOING: Turf: heavy; polytrack: standard

1284a PRIX DES CLOSEAUX (MAIDEN) (UNRACED 2YO) (TURF) 5f
3:40 (3:40) 2-Y-O **£9,191** (£3,676; £2,757; £1,838; £919)

RPR

1 **Notre Sage (FR)** 2-8-13 0.................................. ChristopheSoumillon 3 77
(P Decouz, France) **51/10**[3]

2 *1 3/4* **Vega Sicilia (FR)** 2-8-13 0... TheoBachelot 5 71
(Y Barberot, France) **89/10**

3 *3/4* **Elusiva (FR)** 2-8-13 0....................................(b[1]) Pierre-CharlesBoudot 8 68
(P Sogorb, France) **61/10**

4 *snk* **So Hoity Toity** 2-8-13 0.. UmbertoRispoli 4 67
(E J O'Neill, France) **84/10**

5 *1* **Masina City (FR)** 2-8-13 0.. FabriceVeron 9 64
(H-A Pantall, France) **39/10**[2]

6 *8* **Freeze Fly (IRE)** 2-8-13 0.. CristianDemuro 7 35
(J-V Toux, France) **36/1**

7 *2* **Stratton Street (USA)** 2-9-2 0................................ MickaelBarzalona 2 31
(A Fabre, France) *dwlt: in rr: clsd to go 7th 1/2-way: rdn and no further imp over 1 1/2f out: sn lost tch* **19/10**[1]

8 *5* **Fast Kar (IRE)** 2-8-13 0.. AntoineHamelin 6
(Matthieu Palussiere, France) **19/1**

U **Baie D'Amour (FR)** 2-8-13 0.. JoeyHaynes 1
(K R Burke) *settled towards rr: clsd on inner after 2f: abt 2 1/2 l 6th: rowed along and keeping on whn hit rail and uns rdr 2f out* **15/1**

1m 3.86s (5.56) **9** Ran SP% **120.1**
WIN (incl. 1 euro stake): 6.10. PLACES: 2.00, 2.40, 2.30. DF: 30.00. SF: 44.50.
Owner Nunzio Ricignuolo, Mlle Alix Choppin De Janvry Et **Bred** Dream With Me Stable Inc **Trained** France

1286a PRIX DU BOIS ROSIERE (CLAIMER) (3YO) (POLYTRACK) 1m 1f
6:40 (12:00) 3-Y-O **£9,926** (£3,970; £2,977; £1,985; £992)

RPR

1 **Little Ghetto Boy**[22] 3-8-4 0...................................... HugoJourniac(7) 5 70
(J-C Rouget, France) **27/10**[1]

2 *1 1/2* **Super Mac (FR)**[42] 3-9-1 0................................. ChristopheSoumillon 8 71
(Cedric Rossi, France) **6/1**

3 *nk* **Stereo (FR)**[29] 3-8-4 0.. ClementLecoeuvre(7) 3 66
(E Lellouche, France) **42/10**[3]

4 *shd* **Threebagsue (IRE)**[44] 678 3-9-3 0........................(b) IoritzMendizabal 7 72
(J S Moore) **87/10**

5 *1* **Zip Code (FR)**[88] 3-8-11 0.. OlivierPeslier 9 64
(Robert Collet, France) **19/5**[2]

6 *1/2* **Kadooment Day (IRE)**[65] 423 3-8-11 0.......................(p) TonyPiccone 4 63
(K R Burke) **20/1**

7 *3 1/2* **More Than This (FR)**[140] 3-8-11 0................................ UmbertoRispoli 1 56
(T Castanheira, France) **58/1**

8 *2 1/2* **My Man Charlie (FR)**[29] 3-8-4 0................................ AdrienMoreau(7) 6 50
(N Caullery, France) **14/1**

9 *8* **Going Viral (IRE)**[49] 3-9-4 0......................................(b) AntoineHamelin 2 41
(Matthieu Palussiere, France) **57/10**

WIN (incl. 1 euro stake): 3.70. Places: 1.40, 1.90, 1.70. DF: 16.50. SF: 28.50
Owner Ecurie Michel Sardou **Bred** Litex Commerce **Trained** Pau, France

1285 - 1286a (Foreign Racing) - See Raceform Interactive

1158 CHELMSFORD (A.W) (L-H)
Thursday, April 7

OFFICIAL GOING: Polytrack: standard
Wind: virtually nil Weather: mainly dry, shower race 2

1287 TOTEWIN BEAT SP 2015 NATIONAL MAIDEN STKS 1m (P)
5:50 (5:52) (Class 5) 3-Y-O+ **£5,175** (£1,540; £769; £384) **Stalls** Low

Form RPR

3- **1** **Murad Khan (FR)**[169] 7386 3-8-13 0................................ WilliamBuick 6 86+
(Hugo Palmer) *chsd ldrs: clsd and trckd ldng pair 1/2-way: swtchd rt and effrt to chal over 1f out: led ins fnl f: edging lft but drew clr: readily* **4/1**[3]

46- **2** *3* **Under Attack (IRE)**[260] 4526 3-8-13 0........................ StevieDonohoe 2 79+
(Sir Michael Stoute) *restless in stalls: niggled along in midfield: clsd and travelling bttr 1/2-way: rdn 2f out: 5th whn rn green and wandered 1f out: styd on wl ins fnl f to snatch 2nd last strides: no threat to wnr* **10/1**

22- **3** *hd* **Hakam (USA)**[358] 1417 4-10-0 0...................................... PaulHanagan 1 83+
(Charles Hills) *chsd ldr tl led wl over 1f out: sn rdn and pressed: hdd and sltly hmpd ins fnl f: sn outpcd: lost 2nd last strides* **10/11**[1]

500- **4** *1* **Warofindependence (USA)**[233] 5473 4-10-0 0..................... FMBerry 4 80
(Alan Bailey) *hld up in last trio: clsd and in tch 1/2-way: hdwy on inner over 2f out: rdn to chse ldrs 1f out: no ex and outpcd fnl 150yds* **100/1**

06- **5** *3 1/4* **Banham (USA)**[168] 7411 3-8-13 0.......................... WilliamTwiston-Davies 8 69
(Roger Charlton) *hld up in midfield: clsd 1/2-way: rdn and lost pl over 2f out: rallied 1f out and styd on steadily ins fnl f: no threat to ldrs* **20/1**

3-25 **6** *4* **Hermitage Bay (USA)**[12] 1091 3-8-13 88.....................(b[1]) RyanMoore 9 60
(John Gosden) *dwlt: sn rousted along to ld: set str gallop tl 1/2-way: hdd and rdn wl over 1f out: sn hung lft and btn: stl hanging and fdd ins fnl f* **7/2**[2]

3 **7** *1 3/4* **General Hazard (IRE)**[15] 1036 3-8-13 0........................ JamieSpencer 7 56
(Michael Bell) *stdd and wnt rt sn after s: hld up in rr: clsd and in tch 1/2-way: rdn over 1f out: sn btn and bhd fnl f* **40/1**

0 **8** *1 1/2* **Rising Sunshine (IRE)**[13] 1079 3-8-13 0........................ CamHardie 5 52
(Richard Hannon) *pushed rt after s: hld up in last trio: clsd and in tch 1/2-way: rdn 2f out: sn outpcd: bhd fnl f* **50/1**

52 **9** *nk* **Haabis (USA)**[15] 1036 3-8-13 0.............................(t) SilvestreDeSousa 3 58
(George Peckham) *chsd ldrs: rdn ent fnl 2f: no ex and wknd over 1f out: wl btn and eased ins fnl f* **16/1**

1m 41.1s (1.20) **Going Correction** +0.125s/f (Slow)
WFA 3 from 4yo 15lb **9** Ran SP% **119.7**
Speed ratings (Par 103): **99,96,95,94,91 87,85,84,84**
CSF £42.69 TOTE £6.60: £2.30, £2.60, £1.02; EX 46.30 Trifecta £116.10.
Owner V I Araci **Bred** S C E A Haras De Manneville **Trained** Newmarket, Suffolk

FOCUS
A decent maiden. The leader was lit up early and went an overly-strong gallop on standard Polytrack. It's been rated at face value around the runner-up and fifth.

1288 TOTEWIN BEAT SP LAST 4 NATIONALS H'CAP 1m (P)
6:20 (6:21) (Class 4) (0-85,85) 3-Y-O **£8,086** (£2,406; £1,202; £601) **Stalls** Low

Form RPR

023- **1** **Galvanize (USA)**[168] 7411 3-9-0 **78**.................................. RyanMoore 5 80
(Sir Michael Stoute) *chsd ldrs tl wnt 2nd 3f out: rdn and effrt over 2f out: led ent fnl f: styd on wl: rdn out* **3/1**[2]

3156 **2** *1/2* **Theos Lolly (IRE)**[13] 1080 3-8-7 **74**............................ SammyJoBell(3) 4 75
(Richard Fahey) *trckd ldr tl 3f out: styd handy: effrt wl over 1f out: ev ch 1f out: kpt on wl but hld fnl 100yds* **12/1**

331- **3** *shd* **Altarsheed (IRE)**[198] 6628 3-9-7 **85**............................ PaulHanagan 3 86
(Richard Hannon) *in tch in midfield: rdn over 2f out: struggling to qckn and edgd lft over 1f out: no imp tl styd on u.p fnl 100yds* **1/1**[1]

444- **4** *1 1/4* **Berghoff (IRE)**[226] 5709 3-8-9 **73**................................ JimCrowley 6 71
(Philip Hide) *stdd s: hld up in tch: effrt to chse ldrs over 1f out: styd on same pce ins fnl f* **14/1**

031- **5** *3/4* **Danecase**[265] 4354 3-9-7 **85**.. MartinLane 1 81
(David Dennis) *stdd s: hld up in tch in rr: swtchd rt and effrt over 1f out: styd on same pce ins fnl f* **16/1**

215- **6** *2 3/4* **Powderhorn (IRE)**[201] 6522 3-9-7 **85**............................ WilliamBuick 2 75
(Mark Johnston) *led: rdn 2f out: hdd jst over 1f out: no ex u.p and wknd fnl 100yds* **5/1**[3]

1m 41.24s (1.34) **Going Correction** +0.125s/f (Slow) **6** Ran SP% **111.9**
Speed ratings (Par 100): **98,97,97,96,95 92**
CSF £35.06 TOTE £4.10: £1.80, £4.10; EX 31.70 Trifecta £82.60.

Owner Flaxman Stables Ireland Ltd **Bred** Flaxman Holdings Limited **Trained** Newmarket, Suffolk
FOCUS
A decent 3yo handicap. They went a proper gallop. It's been rated around the runner-up.

1289 TOTEQUADPOT YOUR FOUR LEGGED FRIEND MAIDEN FILLIES' STKS 1m 2f (P)
6:50 (6:52) (Class 5) 3-5-Y-O £5,175 (£1,540; £769; £384) **Stalls** Low

Form				RPR
022-	1		**Secret Sense (USA)**155 7700 3-8-9 77 FMBerry 1 (Ralph Beckett) *t.k.h: mde all and set stdy gallop: rdn and wnt clr over 1f out: in command fnl f: comf* **1/2**1	77+
0-	2	3	**Pernickety**223 5822 3-8-9 0 JimCrowley 3 (Lucy Wadham) *in tch in midfield: effrt and swtchd rt over 1f out: sn chsng wnr: clr 2nd but no imp on wnr fnl f: kpt on* **14/1**	71
	3	3 ¾	**Rationality (USA)** 3-8-9 0 (t) WilliamBuick 4 (John Gosden) *in tch in last pair: effrt in 5th over 2f out: styng on whn bmpd 1f out: kpt on steadily ins fnl f: wnt 3rd last strides: no ch w ldng pair* **4/1**2	64+
0-6	4	hd	**Lady Blanco (USA)**14 1063 3-8-9 0 DavidProbert 5 (Andrew Balding) *t.k.h: chsd ldng pair: effrt to chse wnr wl over 1f out: sn dropped to 3rd and outpcd: plugged on: lost 3rd last strides* **20/1**	63
0	5	shd	**Loose Ends**21 968 3-8-4 0 GeorgeBuckell(5) 6 (David Simcock) *s.i.s: hld up in rr: effrt and stl plenty to do over 1f out: styd on ins fnl f and pressing for 3rd cl home: nvr trbld ldrs* **50/1**	63
64-	6	6	**Duchy**170 7362 3-8-9 0 JamieSpencer 7 (Michael Bell) *chsd wnr tl wl over 1f out: sn hung rt and btn: wknd fnl f* **7/1**3	51
	7	13	**Fearless Poppy** 3-8-9 0 RoystonFfrench 2 (Henry Spiller) *s.i.s: hld up in tch: rdn and struggling over 3f out: bhd over 1f out* **50/1**	25

2m 11.03s (2.43) **Going Correction** +0.125s/f (Slow) 7 Ran SP% **114.5**
Speed ratings (Par 100): **95,92,89,89,89 84,74**
CSF £9.43 TOTE £1.60: £1.10, £4.20; EX 10.20 Trifecta £21.50.
Owner Newsells Park Stud **Bred** Newsells Park Stud Limited **Trained** Kimpton, Hants
FOCUS
A fair fillies' maiden won the previous year by subsequent Listed Galtres Stakes winner Martlet. They went a steady gallop. The winner has been rated close to form.

1290 TOTEEXACTA PICK THE 1ST AND 2ND H'CAP 1m 2f (P)
7:20 (7:21) (Class 4) (0-85,85) 4-Y-O+ £8,086 (£2,406; £1,202; £601) **Stalls** Low

Form				RPR
130-	1		**Haalan**194 6739 4-9-7 85 LukeMorris 3 (James Tate) *mde all: rdn and qcknd 2f out: hrd pressed 1f out: hld on gamely u.p ins fnl f: all out* **5/1**	93
020-	2	hd	**Life Less Ordinary (IRE)**230 5589 4-9-0 78 JamieSpencer 1 (Jamie Osborne) *stdd and dropped in bhd after s: hld up in rr: rdn and rapid hdwy to chse wnr and edgd lft wl over 1f out: sn lost 2nd and drvn: styd on strly towards fin* **3/1**2	85
2-13	3	hd	**Whoopsy Daisy**7 1161 4-8-9 73 MartinDwyer 7 (Jane Chapple-Hyam) *hld up in tch: effrt on inner wl over 1f out: drvn and ev ch 1f out: kpt on wl: lost 2nd last strides* **9/2**3	79
36-2	4	3 ¼	**Farham (USA)**31 863 4-8-4 71 SammyJoBell(3) 6 (Richard Fahey) *wl in tch: nt clr run and shuffled bk to rr wl over 1f out: swtchd rt ent fnl f: styd on but no ch w ldrs* **6/1**	71
003-	5	1 ¾	**Victoria Pollard**247 4984 4-9-6 84 DavidProbert 4 (Andrew Balding) *trckd ldrs: effrt 2f out: unable qck in 4th and edgd rt over 1f out: wknd ins fnl f* **8/1**	80
-562	6	8	**Stetchworth (IRE)**28 888 5-9-4 82 SilvestreDeSousa 5 (Mark Johnston) *chsd wnr: rdn and pressing wnr over 2f out: lost 2nd and squeezed for room wl over 1f out: sn dropped to rr and btn over 1f out* **11/4**1	62

2m 8.21s (-0.39) **Going Correction** +0.125s/f (Slow) 6 Ran SP% **111.9**
Speed ratings (Par 105): **106,105,105,103,101 95**
CSF £20.11 TOTE £4.00: £1.90, £1.80; EX 18.40 Trifecta £98.10.
Owner Saeed Manana **Bred** Kirtlington Stud Ltd **Trained** Newmarket, Suffolk
FOCUS
A decent handicap. They went a respectable gallop at best. A small pb from the winner, with the runner-up to form.

1291 TOTETRIFECTA PICK THE 1,2,3 H'CAP 6f (P)
7:50 (7:50) (Class 4) (0-80,80) 4-Y-O+ £8,086 (£2,406; £1,202; £601) **Stalls** Centre

Form				RPR
-021	1		**Merhoob (IRE)**33 834 4-9-4 77 AdamKirby 3 (John Ryan) *chsd ldrs: effrt to chal over 1f out: drvn to ld jst ins fnl f: r.o wl* **7/2**2	86
204-	2	½	**Gold Club**194 6738 5-9-4 77 MartinLane 6 (Ed McMahon) *hld up in tch in last trio: rdn and hdwy over 1f out: chsd wnr wl ins fnl f: r.o wl but nvr quite getting to wnr* **10/1**3	84
6444	3	1	**Malaysian Boleh**7 1159 6-8-6 70 (b) CallumShepherd(5) 9 (Shaun Lycett) *dwlt: sn niggled along in rr: hdwy u.p on inner jst over 1f out: styd on wl to snatch 3rd nr fin: nt rch ldrs* **10/1**3	74
-211	4	½	**Eleuthera**42 703 4-9-2 80 PatrickO'Donnell(5) 4 (Kevin Ryan) *chsd ldr: rdn to chal over 1f out: led 1f out: sn hdd and no ex u.p: lost 2nd and wknd wl ins fnl f* **5/4**1	82
04-4	5	4	**Vallarta (IRE)**28 894 6-9-5 78 JamesSullivan 7 (Ruth Carr) *hld up in tch in last trio: rdn over 2f out: outpcd and btn over 1f out: no ch wl ins fnl f but plugged on to pass btn horses ins fnl f* **12/1**	67
0-02	6	¾	**Penny Dreadful**21 969 4-9-1 74 (p) KieranO'Neill 5 (Scott Dixon) *sn bustled up to ld: rdn and hrd pressed over 1f out: hdd 1f out: sn btn and wknd ins fnl f* **16/1**	61
3000	7	hd	**Luis Vaz De Torres (IRE)**15 1040 4-9-3 79 (p) SammyJoBell(3) 2 (Richard Fahey) *hld up in tch in midfield: short of room after 1f out: effrt over 2f out: drvn and unable qck over 1f out: wknd ins fnl f* **10/1**3	65
1350	8	1 ¾	**Greyfriarschorista**22 960 9-9-7 80 (bt) JimCrowley 1 (Giles Bravery) *in tch in midfield: effrt over 1f out: no imp and btn 1f out: wknd ins fnl f* **10/1**3	61

1m 12.91s (-0.79) **Going Correction** +0.125s/f (Slow) 8 Ran SP% **116.6**
Speed ratings (Par 105): **110,109,108,107,102 101,100,98**
CSF £38.64 CT £325.70 TOTE £4.10: £1.30, £2.10, £3.20; EX 30.50 Trifecta £248.20.
Owner Gerry McGladery **Bred** Airlie Stud **Trained** Newmarket, Suffolk
FOCUS
A fairly decent sprint handicap. They went a proper gallop. A length pb from the winner, with the third helping to set the standard.

1292 COLLECT TOTEPOOL WINNINGS AT BETFRED SHOPS H'CAP 6f (P)
8:20 (8:22) (Class 6) (0-60,60) 3-Y-O £3,234 (£962; £481; £240) **Stalls** Centre

Form				RPR
666-	1		**Tigserin (IRE)**180 7106 3-9-5 58 SaleemGolam 2 (Giles Bravery) *t.k.h: in tch: clsd to trck ldrs over 2f out: rdn to ld over 1f out: r.o wl fnl f* **7/2**1	70+
5-33	2	1 ¼	**Cool Crescendo**15 1045 3-9-4 57 (p) PJMcDonald 5 (Rebecca Menzies) *s.i.s: in tch in rr: hdwy to chse ldrs and swtchd lft over 1f out: chsd wnr jst ins fnl f: kpt on wl but a hld* **4/1**2	65
-665	3	5	**Matilda Gleam**29 883 3-9-4 57 KieranO'Neill 4 (Lisa Williamson) *taken down early: racd keenly: led: rdn and hdd over 1f out: 3rd and btn whn flashed tail u.p ins fnl f: wknd fnl 100yds* **10/1**	50
0606	4	3	**Compromise**7 1162 3-8-7 46 oh1 SilvestreDeSousa 6 (Conor Dore) *sn chsng ldr: rdn and ev ch briefly over 1f out: 4th and btn whn edgd lft 1f out: wknd ins fnl f* **5/1**3	30
0-56	5	8	**Porcupine Creek (IRE)**36 785 3-9-1 54 LukeMorris 7 (Daniel Mark Loughnane) *hld up in tch: effrt over 1f out: sn drvn and little rspnse: wknd fnl f* **7/2**1	14
50-6	6	3 ¼	**Shipshape Myfoot**20 976 3-9-0 53 JFEgan 3 (Andrew Reid) *sn bustled along towards rr: wknd u.p over 1f out: wl bhd fnl f* **20/1**	
333	7	2 ¾	**Lady Lloyd**28 885 3-9-2 60 (v) JosephineGordon(5) 1 (Phil McEntee) *chsd ldrs tl lost pl u.p over 2f out: wknd over 1f out: wl bhd fnl f* **7/2**1	

1m 13.73s (0.03) **Going Correction** +0.125s/f (Slow) 7 Ran SP% **117.2**
Speed ratings (Par 96): **104,102,95,91,81 76,73**
CSF £18.51 TOTE £5.10: £2.60, £2.50; EX 21.80 Trifecta £154.00.
Owner S P Long **Bred** Philip Hore Jnr **Trained** Newmarket, Suffolk
FOCUS
A modest 3yo sprint handicap. They went a decent gallop. The runner-up has been rated close to last year's best effort.
T/Plt: £169.20 to a £1 stake. Pool: £71,350.93 - 307.71 winning units T/Qpdt: £27.80 to a £1 stake. Pool: £9,156.77 - 243.27 winning units. **Steve Payne**

1151 SOUTHWELL (L-H)
Thursday, April 7

OFFICIAL GOING: Fibresand: standard
Wind: Light behind Weather: Overcast

1293 TOTEPOOL BRITISH STALLION STUDS EBF NOVICE STKS 5f (F)
1:50 (1:50) (Class 5) 2-Y-O £3,881 (£1,155; £577; £288) **Stalls** Centre

Form				RPR
	1		**Wick Powell** 2-9-2 0 GrahamGibbons 9 (David Barron) *w ldrs: led 2f out: shkn up and edgd lft ins fnl f: r.o wl* **2/1**2	80+
	2	2 ½	**Mailshot (USA)** 2-9-2 0 JoeFanning 7 (Mark Johnston) *sn led: hdd 2f out: rdn and edgd lft fr over 1f out: styd on same pce ins fnl f* **5/4**1	71
	3	2 ¼	**Percy Toplis** 2-9-2 0 ShaneGray 8 (Kevin Ryan) *s.i.s: hdwy and hung lft fr over 1f out: nt rch ldrs* **20/1**	63+
6	4	1 ½	**Red Mohican**13 1082 2-8-11 0 LukeMorris 4 (Phil McEntee) *chsd ldrs: rdn 1/2-way: wknd fnl f* **18/1**	53
0	5	1 ¼	**Who Told Jo Jo (IRE)**13 1082 2-9-2 0 (p) JFEgan 1 (Bill Turner) *chsd ldrs: hung lft almost thrght: rdn and wknd over 1f out* **20/1**	53
	6	7	**The Fossil** 2-9-2 0 RichardKingscote 2 (Tom Dascombe) *sn outpcd* **12/1**3	28
	7	1 ¼	**Poppy Pivot (IRE)** 2-8-11 0 PJMcDonald 5 (Ann Duffield) *sn pushed along in rr: bhd fr 1/2-way* **16/1**	18
	8	½	**Graton** 2-9-2 0 DougieCostello 6 (K R Burke) *prom: pushed along and lost pl after 1f: bhd fr 1/2-way* **25/1**	22
	9	1 ¾	**Vona (IRE)** 2-8-11 0 TonyHamilton 3 (Richard Fahey) *s.i.s: hdwy over 3f out: rdn and wknd over 1f out* **20/1**	10

59.19s (-0.51) **Going Correction** -0.30s/f (Stan) 9 Ran SP% **114.7**
Speed ratings (Par 92): **92,88,84,82,80 68,66,66,63**
CSF £4.42 TOTE £3.40: £1.30, £1.10, £4.30; EX 7.30 Trifecta £40.50.
Owner Miss N J Barron **Bred** Usk Valley Stud, Martin Graham **Trained** Maunby, N Yorks
FOCUS
Only two of these had run previously. The market got in right for the first two favourites finished first and second. Just fair form.

1294 TOTEEXACTA PICK THE 1ST AND 2ND MAIDEN AUCTION STKS 7f (F)
2:25 (2:26) (Class 5) 3-Y-O £3,881 (£1,155; £577; £288) **Stalls** Low

Form				RPR
62-	1		**White Shaheen**178 7158 3-8-11 0 MartinDwyer 2 (William Muir) *chsd ldrs: shkn up to ld over 2f out: pushed out* **8/13**1	83
002	2	1	**Melendez (USA)**16 1027 3-8-9 72 WilliamCarson 5 (Jamie Osborne) *chsd ldr tl led 3f out: rdn: hung lft and hdd over 2f out: styd on same pce ins fnl f* **5/2**2	78
653-	3	5	**Last Star Falling (IRE)**184 6995 3-8-6 67 JoeFanning 4 (Henry Spiller) *led: rdn and hdd 3f out: wknd fnl f* **20/1**	62
	4	6	**Touchdown Banwell (USA)** 3-8-11 0 1 DavidProbert 3 (Andrew Balding) *s.i.s: in rr: pushed along 1/2-way: wknd over 2f out* **8/1**3	50
6	5	7	**Shulammite Man (IRE)**57 524 3-8-13 0 BenCurtis 1 (Alan Swinbank) *sn outpcd* **50/1**	33

1m 29.5s (-0.80) **Going Correction** -0.025s/f (Stan) 5 Ran SP% **108.3**
Speed ratings (Par 98): **103,101,96,89,81**
CSF £2.26 TOTE £1.50: £1.30, £1.30; EX 2.60 Trifecta £5.50.
Owner Syed Pervez Hussain **Bred** Meon Valley Stud **Trained** Lambourn, Berks
FOCUS
An uncompetitive maiden which went the way the market predicted. The runner-up has been rated to form.

1295 TOTEQUADPOT FOUR PLACES IN FOUR RACES H'CAP 7f (F)
3:00 (3:01) (Class 6) (0-55,55) 4-Y-O+ £3,234 (£962; £481; £240) **Stalls** Low

Form				RPR
0302	1		**Quadriga (IRE)**8 1156 6-9-4 52 DougieCostello 9 (Philip Kirby) *a.p: rdn over 1f out: edgd lft and styd on to ld wl ins fnl f* **3/1**1	59
6304	2	¾	**Little Choosey**20 981 6-9-0 48 (b) KieranO'Neill 3 (Roy Bowring) *led 1f: chsd ldrs: rdn to ld over 1f out: hdd wl ins fnl f* **16/1**	53

0565 **3** 2 ½ **Cool Beans**[15] 1049 4-9-3 **51**....................(b) JFEgan 4 49
(Roy Bowring) *led 6f out: rdn and hdd over 1f out: styd on same pce ins fnl f* **11/2**

5063 **4** 1 ¼ **Luv U Lucky**[15] 1049 4-9-3 **51**....................(tp) AndrewMullen 10 46
(Michael Appleby) *mid-div: sn pushed along: rdn and hung lft over 2f out: hdwy over 1f out: no imp ins fnl f* **7/2**[2]

4640 **5** 4 ½ **General Tufto**[5] 1202 11-8-12 **46** oh1....................(b) BenCurtis 1 29
(Charles Smith) *sn outpcd: r.o ins fnl f: nvr nrr* **14/1**

0500 **6** nk **Admirable Art (IRE)**[23] 943 6-9-7 **55**....................(p) WilliamCarson 2 37
(Tony Carroll) *prom: lost pl after 1f: n.d after* **12/1**

00-5 **7** 2 ¼ **Cheeco**[20] 986 4-8-12 **46** oh1.................... JamesSullivan 6 22
(Ruth Carr) *s.i.s: outpcd* **25/1**

0014 **8** 1 ¼ **My Time**[15] 1035 7-9-0 **48**....................(be) RobertHavlin 7 20
(Michael Mullineaux) *in rr: swtchd lft and sme hdwy 5f out: wknd 3f out* **10/1**

563- **9** nk **Angels Above (IRE)**[230] 5590 4-9-5 **53**....................(be) TomQueally 8 25
(John Butler) *chsd ldrs: rdn over 2f out: sn hung lft and wknd* **5/1**[3]

0- **10** 7 **Insight (IRE)**[241] 5211 5-9-7 **55**....................(p) LukeMorris 5 24
(Steve Gollings) *sn outpcd* **33/1**

1m 30.96s (0.66) **Going Correction** -0.025s/f (Stan) **10** Ran SP% **115.4**
Speed ratings (Par 101): **95,94,91,89,84 84,81,80,80,78**
CSF £52.11 CT £257.86 TOTE £4.80: £1.40, £3.30, £2.20; EX 44.20 Trifecta £381.10.
Owner P Kirby **Bred** Anima Negra Gmbh & Co Kg **Trained** East Appleton, N Yorks
■ Stewards' Enquiry : Dougie Costello four-day ban: used whip above permitted level (Apr 21-24)

FOCUS
A low-grade handicap run at a decent gallop. The winner was fully entitled to win this.

1296 TOTETRIFECTA PICK THE 1, 2, 3 H'CAP 2m (F)
3:35 (3:35) (Class 4) (0-85,84) 4-Y-0+ **£5,175** (£1,540; £769; £384) **Stalls** Low

Form RPR

0211 **1** **Moonshine Ridge (IRE)**[8] 1156 5-8-9 **67** 6ex.................... NeilFarley 6 76
(Alan Swinbank) *s.i.s: hld up: hdwy 4f out: rdn over 2f out: styd on u.p to ld wl ins fnl f* **5/1**

-314 **2** shd **Be My Sea (IRE)**[22] 957 5-9-2 **74**.................... WilliamCarson 2 83
(Tony Carroll) *led 3f: chsd ldr tl led again over 4f out: rdn over 2f out: hdd wl ins fnl f* **6/1**

4/13 **3** 1 ¾ **Down Time (USA)**[8] 1156 6-8-11 **69**....................(b) BenCurtis 3 76
(Brian Ellison) *s.i.s: hld up: rdn over 3f out: styd on u.p fr over 1f out: nt rch ldrs* **4/1**[3]

4315 **4** 6 **Gabrial The Duke (IRE)**[13] 1081 6-9-5 **84**.........(b) AdamMcNamara[(7)] 4 86
(Richard Fahey) *hld up in tch: rdn to chse ldr over 3f out: lost 2nd wl over 1f out: no ex ins fnl f: eased towards fin* **8/1**

-214 **5** 7 **Ruler Of The Nile**[43] 698 4-9-1 **77**.................... LukeMorris 1 68
(Robert Stephens) *prom: rdn over 6f out: nt clr run over 3f out: sn wknd* **7/2**[2]

4001 **6** 6 **Brassbound (USA)**[28] 891 8-9-7 **79**.................... AndrewMullen 7 63
(Michael Appleby) *chsd ldrs: rdn over 3f out: wknd wl over 1f out* **10/3**[1]

-531 **7** 11 **Dark Diamond (IRE)**[15] 1043 6-8-1 **66**....................(b) RhiainIngram[(7)] 5 37
(Michael Chapman) *w ldr tl led after 3f: hdd over 4f out: sn rdn: wknd 3f out* **16/1**

3m 41.73s (-3.77) **Going Correction** -0.025s/f (Stan)
WFA 4 from 5yo+ 4lb **7** Ran SP% **113.2**
Speed ratings (Par 105): **108,107,107,104,100 97,92**
CSF £33.73 TOTE £4.50: £2.40, £2.10; EX 47.90 Trifecta £142.20.
Owner Elm Row Racing Syndicate **Bred** Maddenstown Equine Enterprise Ltd **Trained** Melsonby, N Yorks

FOCUS
Quite a competitive handicap for the grade, and it was run at a medium gallop. The fourth has been rated a bit off his best.

1297 TOTESWINGER THREE WAYS TO WIN H'CAP 1m 4f (F)
4:15 (4:17) (Class 5) (0-70,69) 3-Y-O **£3,881** (£1,155; £577; £288) **Stalls** Low

Form RPR

1105 **1** **Kemsing (IRE)**[8] 1155 3-9-5 **67**.................... RichardKingscote 1 73
(Julia Feilden) *hld up: hdwy over 4f out: chsd ldr over 3f out: rdn to ld ins fnl f: r.o* **7/2**[2]

1550 **2** 3 ½ **Skylark Lady (IRE)**[14] 1062 3-8-13 **61**.................... LukeMorris 5 61
(Rae Guest) *chsd ldrs: rdn over 4f out: sn outpcd: rallied over 1f out: styd on to go 2nd wl ins fnl f* **9/4**[1]

5-44 **3** nse **Asafoetida (IRE)**[43] 699 3-8-13 **64**.................... LouisSteward[(3)] 4 65
(Peter Chapple-Hyam) *led: rdn and hung rt over 1f out: hdd ins fnl f: styd on same pce* **7/1**

6631 **4** 1 ¼ **Rainbow Lad (IRE)**[7] 1163 3-8-10 **58** 6ex.................... AndrewMullen 3 56
(Michael Appleby) *chsd ldr tl rdn over 3f out: styd on same pce fr over 1f out* **4/1**[3]

0-24 **5** 7 **Tartan Bute**[80] 245 3-9-7 **69**....................(b) JoeFanning 2 56
(Mark Johnston) *s.i.s: hdwy to chse ldrs over 10f out: rdn over 3f out: wknd fnl f* **7/2**[2]

2m 42.89s (1.89) **Going Correction** -0.025s/f (Stan) **5** Ran SP% **107.7**
Speed ratings (Par 98): **92,89,89,88,84**
CSF £11.20 TOTE £3.60: £2.10, £1.60; EX 11.50 Trifecta £40.90.
Owner The Fourth Sector Pathfinders **Bred** D Dwan **Trained** Exning, Suffolk

FOCUS
A handicap for 3yos in which the pace was fair, but but it is unlikely to be strong form. A length pb from the winner.

1298 TOTEPOOLLIVEINFO.COM CLAIMING STKS 6f (F)
4:50 (4:52) (Class 6) 3-Y-O+ **£3,234** (£962; £481; £240) **Stalls** Low

Form RPR

5100 **1** **Monsieur Jimmy**[1] 1254 4-9-7 68....................(b) DanielTudhope 1 73+
(Declan Carroll) *prom: hmpd and lost pl over 4f out: hdwy over 2f out: styd on u.p to ld wl ins fnl f* **4/1**[3]

5530 **2** nk **Abi Scarlet (IRE)**[28] 893 7-9-1 67....................(b) BenCurtis 6 66
(Scott Dixon) *sn chsng ldr: led 2f out: rdn over 1f out: hdd wl ins fnl f* **3/1**[1]

6416 **3** 5 **Coiste Bodhar (IRE)**[8] 1154 5-9-5 60....................(p) KieranO'Neill 8 55
(Scott Dixon) *sn led: rdn and hdd over 2f out: no ex fnl f* **10/1**

000- **4** 2 ¼ **Mon Brav**[166] 7461 9-9-3 78.................... BenRobinson[(7)] 9 53
(Brian Ellison) *sn outpcd: r.o ins fnl f: nvr nrr* **6/1**

1060 **5** 1 ¾ **Speightowns Kid (USA)**[16] 1030 8-9-4 65................(be) AnnStokell[(5)] 3 47
(Ann Stokell) *prom: hmpd and lost pl sn after s: effrt over 2f out: wknd over 1f out* **16/1**

0-14 **6** 1 ½ **Sartori**[57] 520 5-9-6 67....................(p) RobertWinston 5 40
(Marjorie Fife) *chsd ldrs: rdn over 2f out: wknd over 1f out* **7/2**[2]

5615 **7** ¾ **Monsieur Jamie**[16] 1026 8-9-8 65....................(v) FrederikTylicki 4 39
(J R Jenkins) *prom: hmpd and lost pl sn after s: n.d after* **12/1**

405- **8** 11 **Star Glimmer (IRE)**[147] 7807 3-8-0 65....................(p) SophieKilloran[(7)] 2
(Henry Spiller) *chsd ldrs: rdn over 2f out: wknd over 1f out* **8/1**

1m 15.7s (-0.80) **Going Correction** -0.025s/f (Stan)
WFA 3 from 4yo+ 12lb **8** Ran SP% **115.3**
Speed ratings (Par 101): **104,103,96,93,91 89,88,73**
CSF £16.60 TOTE £4.30: £1.90, £1.20, £2.60; EX 19.20 Trifecta £118.50.
Owner Ray Flegg & John Bousfield **Bred** J P Repard **Trained** Malton, N Yorks

FOCUS
Exposed sorts in this sprint claimer which was run at a sound gallop. The winner has been rated to his previous best here.

1299 TOTEWIN BEAT SP 2015 GRAND NATIONAL H'CAP 6f (F)
5:25 (5:25) (Class 6) (0-60,60) 4-Y-O+ **£3,234** (£962; £481; £240) **Stalls** Low

Form RPR

2434 **1** **Oscars Journey**[30] 868 6-9-7 **60**....................(v) FrederikTylicki 4 71
(J R Jenkins) *chsd ldrs: hung rt over 3f out: led over 2f out: sn rdn: styd on wl* **5/1**[3]

2205 **2** 2 **Fortinbrass (IRE)**[35] 799 6-9-4 **57**.................... RobertWinston 1 62
(John Balding) *chsd ldrs: rdn over 1f out: styd on same pce ins fnl f* **10/3**[2]

120- **3** 1 **Gaelic Wizard (IRE)**[164] 7522 8-9-0 **58**....................(v) GemmaTutty[(5)] 6 60
(Karen Tutty) *s.i.s: hld up: hdwy 1/2-way: rdn over 1f out: styd on same pce ins fnl f* **25/1**

0524 **4** 2 ½ **Very First Blade**[16] 1026 7-9-2 **55**....................(be) RobertHavlin 5 50
(Michael Mullineaux) *sn led: rdn and hdd over 2f out: no ex fnl f* **9/1**

3356 **5** hd **Lucky Mark (IRE)**[16] 1026 7-9-2 **55**....................(p) BenCurtis 8 49
(John Balding) *hld up: hdwy over 2f out: rdn over 1f out: no ex* **6/1**

0-63 **6** 2 **Secret Look**[22] 963 6-9-3 **59**.................... RobHornby[(3)] 3 47
(Ed McMahon) *prom: rdn over 2f out: wknd over 1f out* **7/4**[1]

-116 **7** 10 **Lizzy's Dream**[52] 589 8-9-1 **54**.................... DanielTudhope 7 12
(Rebecca Bastiman) *prom over 3f: wknd 2f out* **12/1**

1m 16.29s (-0.21) **Going Correction** -0.025s/f (Stan) **7** Ran SP% **111.9**
Speed ratings (Par 101): **100,97,96,92,92 89,76**
CSF £21.01 CT £369.91 TOTE £7.00: £2.90, £2.00; EX 25.80 Trifecta £283.10.
Owner Mrs Theresa McCoubrey **Bred** R B Hill **Trained** Royston, Herts

FOCUS
A low-grade sprint handicap in which all the runners were pretty exposed. The pace wasn't that strong and it paid to race handily. The winner has been rated to the best of this year's form.
T/Plt: £41.70 to a £1 stake. Pool: £49,905.31 - 873.25 winning units T/Qpdt: £36.90 to a £1 stake. Pool: £3,377.52 - 67.7 winning units **Colin Roberts**

1300 - 1307a (Foreign Racing) - See Raceform Interactive

1194 MAISONS-LAFFITTE (R-H)
Thursday, April 7

OFFICIAL GOING: Turf: heavy

1308a PRIX DJEBEL (GROUP 3) (3YO COLTS & GELDINGS) (STRAIGHT) (TURF) 7f (S)
12:10 (12:00) 3-Y-O **£29,411** (£11,764; £8,823; £5,882; £2,941)

RPR

1 **Cheikeljack (FR)**[18] 1024 3-9-2 0.................... VincentCheminaud 7 112
(H-A Pantall, France) *cl up on outer: led after 1f: rdn whn pressed 1 1/2f out and edgd lft wl over 1f out: rdn and styd on wl ins fnl f: wl on top at fin* **18/1**

2 ¾ **Attendu (FR)**[158] 7665 3-9-2 0.................... MaximeGuyon 4 110
(C Laffon-Parias, France) *t.k.h: hld up in tch on inner: drvn and responding whn propped as ldr edgd across him wl over 1f out: styng on u.p whn bmpd ent fnl f: nt able to chal: fin 3rd: plcd 2nd* **13/2**

3 nk **Moon Trouble (IRE)**[171] 7352 3-9-2 0.................... MickaelBarzalona 3 109
(F Head, France) *w.w in fnl trio: shkn up and prog 1 1/2f out: styd on ins fnl f: nvr on terms: fin 4th: plcd 3rd* **4/1**[3]

4 3 **Vedevani (FR)**[211] 6223 3-9-2 0.................... ChristopheSoumillon 6 107+
(A De Royer-Dupre, France) *in rr early: sn chsng ldrs: shkn up to chal between horses 1 1/2f out: styng on whn bdly hmpd by Ribchester and cannoned into Attendu ent fnl f: nt rcvr: fin 5th: plcd 4th* **13/8**[1]

5 1 ¼ **Ribchester (IRE)**[201] 6531 3-9-2 0.................... JamesDoyle 2 110+
(Richard Fahey) *hld up in fnl trio: shkn up and hdwy on outer 2f out: chalng for 2nd whn rdn and veered lft and bdly hmpd rival ent fnl f: styd on u.p but no imp on wnr: fin 2nd disqualified and plcd 5th* **15/8**[2]

6 6 **The Turning Point (FR)**[182] 7071 3-9-2 0.................... IoritzMendizabal 1 82
(J-C Rouget, France) *hld up in fnl trio: last and outpcd whn drvn 3f out: wl hld fnl 1 1/2f* **28/1**

7 1 ¼ **Signs Of Success (IRE)**[41] 3-9-2 0.................... StephanePasquier 5 78
(M Delcher Sanchez, France) *led early: hdd after 1f and trckd ldr: drvn to chal wl over 1 1/2f out: sn rdn and no futher imp: wknd fnl f* **16/1**

1m 28.1s (0.10) **7** Ran SP% **120.8**
WIN (incl. 1 euro stake): 12.50. PLACES: 4.50, 3.00. SF: 70.70.
Owner Mme Jacques Cygler **Bred** Ecurie Des Monceaux **Trained** France

FOCUS
This long-standing Group 3 is often used as a springboard to Guineas success. However, it was a very tactical affair on tough going this year, with the winner dictating, and is unlikely to have a significant bearing on any Classic.

1309a PRIX IMPRUDENCE (GROUP 3) (3YO FILLIES) (STRAIGHT) (TURF) 7f (S)
1:20 (12:00) 3-Y-O **£29,411** (£11,764; £8,823; £5,882; £2,941)

RPR

1 **Spectre (FR)**[182] 7070 3-9-0 0.................... Pierre-CharlesBoudot 10 110
(M Munch, Germany) *w.w bhd front frnk: shkn up to chal 1 1/2f out: styd on gamely to ld wl ins fnl f: drvn out* **22/1**

2 ¾ **Midweek**[203] 3-9-0 0.................... VincentCheminaud 9 108+
(Mme C Head-Maarek, France) *led: rdn whn chal 1 1/2f out: hdd wl ins fnl f: kpt on gamely u.p* **15/2**

3 2 ½ **Rosay (IRE)**[148] 3-9-0 0.................... CristianDemuro 12 101
(J-C Rouget, France) *w.w towards rr: hdwy on outer 2f out: rdn to chse ldng pair wl over 1f out: kpt on ins fnl f but no match for front two* **17/2**

4 1 **Venecia Style (FR)**[21] 973 3-9-0 0.................... ChristopheSoumillon 7 99
(P Sogorb, France) *chsd ldrs: rdn and nt qckn 1 1/2f out: kpt on at one pce fnl f* **13/2**[3]

5 snk **Aim To Please (FR)**[21] 973 3-9-0 0.................... AlexisBadel 4 98+
(F Doumen, France) *w.w in midfield: rowed along fr 2f out: styd on u.p fr ins fnl 1 1/2f: nt pce to get on terms* **17/2**

6 snk **Damila (FR)**[21] 973 3-9-0 0.................... FabriceVeron 1 98
(H-A Pantall, France) *trckd ldr on inner: rdn to hold pl wl over 1 1/2f out: kpt on at one pce fnl f* **18/1**

7 2½ **Villebaudon (FR)**^{288} 3-9-0 0 GregoryBenoist 6 91
(C Ferland, France) *settled in midfield: scrubbed along sn after 1/2-way and no real imp: wl hld fnl f* **7/2**^{2}
8 2½ **Okana**^{21} [973] 3-9-0 0 MaximeGuyon 8 84
(C Laffon-Parias, France) *w.w in rr: rdn and short-lived effrt over 1 1/2f out: sn btn: nvr in contention* **2/1**^{1}
9 1 **Dressed In Fur (IRE)**^{159} [7660] 3-9-0 0 MickaelBarzalona 11 82
(Mme Pia Brandt, France) *trckd ldr on outer: rdn and nt qckn over 1 1/2f out: wknd ins fnl f* **14/1**
10 15 **Nomadic (FR)**^{159} [7660] 3-9-0 0 StephanePasquier 13 41
(P Bary, France) *w.w in fnl pair: rdn and btn over 1 1/2f out: bhd whn eased fnl f* **11/1**
11 2 **Aktoria (FR)**^{169} [7407] 3-9-0 0 OlivierPeslier 5 36
(C Laffon-Parias, France) *settled towards rr: drvn and no imp 2f out: wl adrift fr wl over 1 1/2f out* **22/1**

1m 27.6s (-0.40) **11** Ran SP% **130.7**
WIN (incl. 1 euro stake): 24.00. PLACES: 6.60, 3.50, 3.90. DF: 127.80. SF: 282.70.
Owner MM Racing **Bred** M Munch **Trained** Germany

FOCUS
This is usually a strong pointer for the 3yo fillies division. Again the field shunned the stands' rail and there's every chance it'll work out to be a decent affair.

1310a (Foreign Racing) - See Raceform Interactive

1311a PRIX IDLE BOY (MAIDEN) (3YO COLTS & GELDINGS) (TURF) 6f (S)
2:25 (12:00) 3-Y-O **£9,191** (£3,676; £2,757; £1,838; £919)

RPR
1 **Never Compromise (FR)**^{41} 3-9-2 0 RafaelSchistl 12 86
(Henk Grewe, Germany) **76/10**
2 1¼ **Verbal Link (FR)**^{146} 3-9-2 0 AlexisBadel 10 82
(M Delzangles, France) **11/2**^{2}
3 1¼ **Al Mutanabi (IRE)** 3-9-2 0 AurelienLemaitre 9 78
(G E Mikhalides, France) **9/1**
4 ¾ **Lefortovo (FR)**^{215} [6097] 3-9-2 0 AntoineHamelin 4 76
(Jo Hughes) *t.k.h: hld up towards rr: scrubbed along and swtchd ins 2f out: rdn and styd on to chse ldrs 1f out: kpt on but no imp fnl 150yds* **9/1**
5 1 **Pradesh (IRE)**^{35} [803] 3-9-2 0 MickaelBarzalona 5 73
(A Fabre, France) *w.w in rr: hdwy and nt clr run sn after 1/2-way: styd on u.p fnl f: nvr on terms* **12/5**^{1}
6 nse **Moonwalk Step (FR)** 3-8-13 0 TonyPiccone 3 70
(T Castanheira, France) **68/1**
7 hd **Akohol (IRE)**^{229} 3-9-2 0 (b¹) MaximeGuyon 13 72
(F Head, France) **19/1**
8 2 **Range Of Knowledge (IRE)**^{58} [511] 3-9-2 0 UmbertoRispoli 7 66
(E J O'Neill, France) **57/10**^{3}
9 2½ **Material**^{16} 3-9-2 0 VincentCheminaud 8 58
(Mme C Head-Maarek, France) **18/1**
10 2½ **Daring Lion (GER)**^{249} 3-9-2 0 AlexanderPietsch 1 50
(J Hirschberger, Germany) **9/1**
11 4 **Cracker'Star (FR)**^{6} 3-9-2 0 RichardJuteau 11 37
(C Plisson, France) **99/1**
12 1¼ **Les Pradeaux (FR)**^{118} 3-9-2 0 (p) FabriceVeron 2 33
(H-A Pantall, France) **26/1**
13 dist **Dildiko (FR)** 3-9-2 0 OlivierPeslier 6
(T Lemer, France) **36/1**

1m 15.83s (2.43) **13** Ran SP% **120.5**
WIN (incl. 1 euro stake): 8.60. PLACES: 2.80, 2.30, 3.00. DF: 27.90. SF: 56.70.
Owner Christoph Michael Holschbach **Bred** Scea Haras De Manneville **Trained** Germany

LEICESTER (R-H)
Friday, April 8

OFFICIAL GOING: Heavy (soft in places)
Wind: Light across Weather: Light rain

1312 BARKBY MAIDEN FILLIES' STKS (PLUS 10 RACE) 7f
1:55 (1:56) (Class 5) 3-Y-O **£3,234** (£962; £481; £240) **Stalls** High

Form RPR
032- **1** **Kylla Instinct**^{160} [7637] 3-9-0 77 DanielTudhope 6 76+
(Philip McBride) *chsd ldr tl led over 1f out: edgd rt towards fin: comf* **10/3**^{2}
2 ½ **Emerald Loch** 3-9-0 0 FMBerry 1 71
(Ralph Beckett) *chsd ldrs: outpcd over 1f out: r.o to go 2nd wl ins fnl f* **10/1**^{3}
622- **3** 4½ **Norse Magic**^{167} [7472] 3-9-0 76 RyanMoore 2 59
(Sylvester Kirk) *led at stdy pce tl qcknd over 2f out: rdn and hdd over 1f out: wknd wl ins fnl f* **4/9**^{1}
4 18 **Dutch Treaty** 3-9-0 0 JoeFanning 4 13
(Richard Hannon) *s.i.s: hdwy 1/2-way: shkn up over 2f out: wknd over 1f out* **16/1**

1m 36.31s (10.11) **Going Correction** +1.10s/f (Soft) **4** Ran SP% **107.3**
Speed ratings (Par 95): **86,85,80,59**
CSF £25.69 TOTE £3.70; EX 17.40 Trifecta £32.00.
Owner PMRacing **Bred** Whatton Manor Stud **Trained** Newmarket, Suffolk

FOCUS
There was 0.5mm of rain overnight onto already demanding ground. An uncompetitive fillies' maiden to start.

1313 BURTON OVERY (S) STKS 6f
2:30 (2:30) (Class 6) 3-Y-O **£2,587** (£770; £384; £192) **Stalls** High

Form RPR
2422 **1** **Bahamian Sunshine**^{11} [1126] 3-9-1 64 (p) AdamMcNamara(7) 1 68
(Richard Fahey) *disp ld tl wnt on over 3f out: rdn and hdd over 1f out: led again 1f out: sn hung lft: styd on wl* **15/8**^{2}
2105 **2** 3½ **Broughtons Fancy**^{10} [1137] 3-8-13 70 SilvestreDeSousa 3 57
(David Evans) *disp ld tl over 3f out: sn pushed along: rdn to ld again and edgd rt over 1f out: sn hdd: ev ch whn bdly hmpd ins fnl f: nt rcvr* **4/6**^{1}
-366 **3** 7 **Deben**^{7} [1183] 3-9-0 69 (b¹) TomEaves 2 29
(Kevin Ryan) *s.i.s: sn chsng ldrs: rdn over 2f out: wknd over 1f out* **10/1**^{3}
4 20 **Connie O'Meara (IRE)** 3-8-9 0 JackMitchell 4
(Robert Eddery) *prom tl pushed along and lost pl over 4f out: wknd 1/2-way* **25/1**

1m 19.91s (6.91) **Going Correction** +1.10s/f (Soft) **4** Ran SP% **107.7**
Speed ratings (Par 96): **97,92,83,56**
CSF £3.49 TOTE £2.90; EX 4.10 Trifecta £4.60.There was no bid for the winner.
Owner The Fairweather Foursome **Bred** Mel Roberts & Ms Nicola Meese **Trained** Musley Bank, N Yorks

■ Stewards' Enquiry : Adam McNamara two-day ban: careless riding (22nd-23rd April)

FOCUS
Modest form and there was trouble late on, so the margin between the first two should not be taken literally. The winner has been rated to his best.

1314 KIBWORTH H'CAP 1m 1f 218y
3:05 (3:05) (Class 4) (0-85,84) 3-Y-O **£4,851** (£1,443; £721) **Stalls** Low

Form RPR
00-1 **1** **Vivre Pour Vivre (IRE)**^{24} [945] 3-9-1 78 RyanMoore 1 90+
(Ed Dunlop) *hld up: swtchd lft over 2f out: hdwy to ld over 1f out: pushed clr fnl f* **8/11**^{1}
324- **2** 7 **Skeaping**^{188} [6922] 3-9-7 84 PatDobbs 3 80
(Richard Hannon) *chsd ldr: rdn over 2f out: wknd fnl f* **9/4**^{2}
150- **3** shd **Lido Lady (IRE)**^{253} [4791] 3-8-11 74 JoeFanning 4 70
(Mark Johnston) *sn led: clr 8f out tl shkn up over 2f out: hdd over 1f out: edgd lft and wknd ins fnl f* **5/1**^{3}

2m 21.29s (13.39) **Going Correction** +1.10s/f (Soft) **3** Ran SP% **105.3**
Speed ratings (Par 100): **94,88,88**
CSF £2.52 TOTE £1.50; EX 2.30 Trifecta £2.50.
Owner Mrs Susan Roy **Bred** J Kenny **Trained** Newmarket, Suffolk

FOCUS
There was a false rail from the top from the hill on the back straight all the way to the winning line, increasing the distance by approximately 17 yards. The runner-up has been rated to his form on soft last year. The level is a bit fluid though.

1315 LODDINGTON CONDITIONS STKS (PLUS 10 RACE) 6f
3:40 (3:40) (Class 3) 3-Y-O **£8,821** (£2,640; £1,320; £660) **Stalls** High

Form RPR
3- **1** **C Note (IRE)**^{196} [6711] 3-9-2 0 RyanMoore 3 102+
(Martyn Meade) *hld up in tch: shkn up and nt clr run over 1f out: r.o to ld wl ins fnl f: comf* **4/5**^{1}
122- **2** 1¾ **Lil's Joy (IRE)**^{182} [7102] 3-8-13 106 PatDobbs 4 94
(Giles Bravery) *led: hdd over 4f out: led again over 1f out: rdn: hung rt and hdd wl ins fnl f* **4/1**^{3}
044- **3** 4 **Sixties Sue**^{161} [7594] 3-8-11 88 SilvestreDeSousa 2 80
(Mick Channon) *trckd ldrs: racd keenly: rdn over 1f out: wknd wl ins fnl f* **5/2**^{2}
3464 **4** 17 **Thatsallimsaying (IRE)**^{17} [1029] 3-8-11 80 JFEgan 1 29
(David Evans) *w ldr tl led over 4f out: rdn and hdd over 1f out: sn wknd* **20/1**

1m 16.92s (3.92) **Going Correction** +1.10s/f (Soft) **4** Ran SP% **108.9**
Speed ratings (Par 102): **102,99,94,71**
CSF £4.39 TOTE £1.80; EX 3.60 Trifecta £5.00.
Owner Richard Barnes **Bred** Mountarmstrong Stud **Trained** Newmarket, Suffolk

FOCUS
A decent conditions race and the winner is a horse to follow. The level is fluid given the testing ground.

1316 VIS-A-VIS SYMPOSIUMS NOVICE STKS 5f
4:15 (4:16) (Class 5) 2-Y-O **£2,911** (£866; £432; £216) **Stalls** High

Form RPR
1 **Sterling Silva (IRE)** 2-8-13 0 TomMarquand(3) 5 72+
(Richard Hannon) *chsd ldrs: pushed along over 3f out: rdn over 1f out: sn hung rt and chsng ldr: r.o to ld wl ins fnl f* **7/4**^{2}
5 **2** 1¼ **Lucata (IRE)**^{6} [1203] 2-9-2 0 RichardKingscote 2 67
(Tom Dascombe) *led: shkn up and edgd rt over 1f out: hdd and unable qck wl ins fnl f* **5/4**^{1}
3 2¼ **Sheila's Lad (IRE)** 2-9-2 0 MartinDwyer 3 62
(J S Moore) *s.i.s: sn pushed along in rr: swtchd rt and hdwy over 1f out: hmpd ins fnl f: no ex* **25/1**
4 8 **Sayesse** 2-9-2 0 SilvestreDeSousa 4 30
(Mick Channon) *chsd ldr: rdn 1/2-way: lost 2nd over 1f out: sn wknd* **7/2**^{3}
5 3¼ **Rinky Dink Dawn (IRE)** 2-9-2 0 LiamJones 1 18
(J S Moore) *s.s: hdwy over 3f out: rdn and wknd over 1f out* **40/1**

1m 6.75s (6.75) **Going Correction** +1.10s/f (Soft) **5** Ran SP% **109.3**
Speed ratings (Par 92): **90,88,84,71,66**
CSF £4.24 TOTE £2.30: £1.10, £1.90; EX 4.40 Trifecta £21.40.
Owner Middleham Park Racing XVII **Bred** Kildaragh Stud **Trained** East Everleigh, Wilts

FOCUS
The runner-up was the only one with experience and had shown a reasonable amount of ability, and the winner looked above average in putting him away. It's hard to pin down the level.

1317 BOB SPENCE 70TH BIRTHDAY CELEBRATION H'CAP 1m 60y
4:50 (4:50) (Class 5) (0-75,74) 4-Y-O+ **£2,911** (£866; £432; £216) **Stalls** Low

Form RPR
330- **1** **Bakht A Rawan (IRE)**^{172} [7347] 4-9-2 69 OisinMurphy 4 76
(Stuart Kittow) *chsd ldrs: led over 2f out: rdn over 1f out: edgd lft ins fnl f: styd on* **5/2**^{2}
135- **2** 1¼ **Gannicus**^{161} [7599] 5-9-6 73 (t) MartinDwyer 1 77
(Brendan Powell) *s.i.s: hld up: hdwy to chse wnr over 1f out: sn rdn: edgd rt ins fnl f: kpt on* **11/2**
62-0 **3** 3¾ **Illustrious Prince (IRE)**^{16} [1047] 9-8-12 65 ConnorBeasley 6 60
(Julie Camacho) *hld up: hdwy 2f out: sn rdn: hung rt and no ex ins fnl f* **14/1**
334- **4** 3¼ **Stoneboat Bill**^{185} [7024] 4-9-3 70 DanielTudhope 2 58
(Declan Carroll) *hld up: hdwy over 3f out: rdn over 2f out: wknd fnl f* **4/1**^{3}
356- **5** 5 **Save The Bees**^{118} [6860] 8-9-0 74 LeeByrne(7) 5 50
(Declan Carroll) *led: rdn and hdd over 2f out: wknd over 1f out* **14/1**
305- **6** 8 **Call Out Loud**^{148} [7821] 4-8-10 63 (t) SilvestreDeSousa 3 21
(Michael Appleby) *trckd ldr: plld hrd early: rdn and ev ch over 2f out: wknd over 1f out: eased ins fnl f* **15/8**^{1}

1m 57.24s (12.14) **Going Correction** +1.10s/f (Soft) **6** Ran SP% **112.1**
Speed ratings (Par 103): **87,85,82,78,73 65**
CSF £16.27 TOTE £4.00: £2.00, £2.50; EX 18.80 Trifecta £104.60.
Owner Chris & David Stam **Bred** B V Sangster **Trained** Blackborough, Devon

FOCUS
There was a false rail from the top from the hill on the back straight all the way to the winning line, increasing the distance by approximately 17 yards. A modest handicap. The runner-up has been rated to form.

1318 H.A.C. PIPELINE SUPPLIES H'CAP 7f
5:25 (5:25) (Class 4) (0-85,85) 4-Y-O+ **£4,851** (£1,443; £721; £360) **Stalls** High

Form RPR
-502 **1** **Dilgura**^{16} [1044] 6-8-6 73 MatthewCosham(3) 4 83
(Stuart Kittow) *chsd ldr tl led over 2f out: rdn out* **9/2**

 The Form Book, Raceform Ltd, Newbury, RG14 5SJ

5606 **2** 2¼ **Subtle Knife**[14] 1065 7-8-13 **82** .... PaddyPilley(5) 9 86
(Giles Bravery) *trckd ldrs: rdn over 1f out: styd on same pce ins fnl f* **9/1**

053- **3** 2 **Cincuenta Pasos (IRE)**[153] 7758 5-9-6 **84** .... OisinMurphy 7 83
(Joseph Tuite) *stdd s: hld up: racd keenly: hdwy over 4f out: rdn over 1f out: no ex ins fnl f* **7/2**[2]

0-60 **4** 2¼ **Midnight Rider (IRE)**[16] 1041 8-8-13 **82** .... JordanVaughan(5) 10 75
(Rod Millman) *chsd ldrs: rdn over 1f out: no ex fnl f* **16/1**

540- **5** 1½ **Captain Bob (IRE)**[195] 6758 5-9-7 **85** .... AdamBeschizza 2 74
(Robert Cowell) *hld up: plld hrd: rdn over 1f out: nt trble ldrs* **9/1**

2501 **6** 4½ **Apache Storm**[20] 1003 4-9-7 **85** .... SilvestreDeSousa 3 63
(Michael Appleby) *hld up: plld hrd: rdn and wknd over 1f out* **3/1**[1]

605- **7** 7 **Mister Music**[180] 7146 7-9-3 **81** ....(b) AndreaAtzeni 1 40
(Robert Eddery) *hld up: rdn over 2f out: sn wknd* **4/1**[3]

1400 **8** ½ **Black Dave (IRE)**[31] 866 6-8-6 **77** .... AledBeech(7) 8 35
(David Evans) *plld hrd: led over 4f: wknd over 1f out* **25/1**

1m 32.85s (6.65) **Going Correction** +1.10s/f (Soft) **8** Ran SP% **115.1**
Speed ratings (Par 105): **98,95,93,90,88 83,75,75**
CSF £44.26 CT £157.32 TOTE £5.50: £1.60, £2.70, £1.40; EX 50.60 Trifecta £166.40.
Owner Russell Ingham and Stuart Kittow **Bred** Hopkins, Kittow & Mrs Perry **Trained** Blackborough, Devon

FOCUS
A fair handicap, but the pace was steady and a few of these were keen. It's been rated around the first two.
T/Plt: £112.60 to a £1 stake. Pool: £39,851.88 - 258.22 winning tickets T/Qpdt: £11.70 to a £1 stake. Pool: £2,384.27 - 150.45 winning tickets **Colin Roberts**

1180 WOLVERHAMPTON (A.W) (L-H)

Friday, April 8

OFFICIAL GOING: Tapeta: standard
Wind: light, behind Weather: dry

1319 ROA/RACING POST OWNERS JACKPOT H'CAP (DIV I) 5f 216y (Tp)
5:50 (5:50) (Class 6) (0-55,55) 3-Y-O+ **£2,587** (£770; £384; £192) **Stalls** Low

Form RPR

6503 **1** **Dream Ally (IRE)**[8] 1164 6-9-3 **48** ....(be) LukeMorris 9 56
(John Weymes) *dwlt: in tch in rr: clsd and nt clrest of runs 2f out: swtchd rt and effrt 1f out: rdn and str run to ld wl ins fnl f: sn in command* **9/1**

030- **2** 1 **Iceaxe**[191] 6850 3-8-12 **55** .... RoystonFfrench 4 58
(John Holt) *wl in tch in midfield: swtchd rt and effrt jst over 1f out: hdwy to chal and sltly hmpd ins fnl f: styd on to go 2nd cl home* **16/1**

324- **3** hd **Little Belter (IRE)**[201] 6563 4-9-9 **54** ....(p) PhillipMakin 2 58
(Keith Dalgleish) *taken down early: chsd ldrs: wnt 2nd 4f out: rdn and ev ch over 1f out: led 1f out: hdd and one pce wl ins fnl f: lost 2nd cl home* **2/1**[1]

5325 **4** 1½ **Blistering Dancer (IRE)**[9] 1138 6-8-12 **46** ....(p) GeorgeDowning(3) 1 46
(Tony Carroll) *pushed along leaving stalls: chsd ldr tl 4f out: styd prom: rdn and ev ch over 1f out: no ex ins fnl f: short of room whn sltly hmpd wl ins fnl f* **6/1**[2]

2050 **5** ½ **Rat Catcher (IRE)**[42] 732 6-9-5 **53** ....(p) RobHornby(3) 3 51
(Lisa Williamson) *in tch towards rr: rdn and hdwy over 1f out: swtchd lft and squeezing between rivals to chal ins fnl f: sn jostled and unable qck: kpt on same pce after* **25/1**

3060 **6** ½ **Top Cop**[9] 1138 7-9-9 **54** ....(p) DavidProbert 8 51
(Ronald Harris) *towards rr: effrt on outer 2f out: styd on ins fnl f: nvr trbld ldrs* **12/1**

3054 **7** nk **Evident (IRE)**[16] 1042 6-9-9 **54** ....(p) AdamKirby 10 50
(Tony Carroll) *in tch in midfield but stuck wd: rdn 2f out: outpcd and lost pl over 1f out: rallied and kpt on again ins fnl f: nvr enough pce to chal* **7/1**[3]

002 **8** shd **Fuel Injection**[10] 1133 5-9-10 **55** .... BarryMcHugh 6 51
(Paul Midgley) *taken down early: led: rdn wl over 1f out: hdd 1f out: stl ev ch whn edgd lft ins fnl f: no ex and outpcd whn short of room 75yds out: wknd* **8/1**

006- **9** 2 **Titus Secret**[246] 5069 4-9-1 **46** oh1 .... CathyGannon 5 48+
(Malcolm Saunders) *s.i.s: bhd: gd hdwy u.p on inner over 1f out: chsng ldrs whn nt clr run and hmpd ins fnl f: nt rcvr and nt pushed after* **25/1**

5212 **10** 2½ **Multi Quest**[20] 1005 4-9-4 **49** ....(b) FrannyNorton 7 31
(John E Long) *chsd ldrs: lost pl u.p over 1f out: bhd fnl f* **9/1**

1m 14.46s (-0.04) **Going Correction** 0.0s/f (Stan)
WFA 3 from 4yo+ 12lb **10** Ran SP% **112.5**
Speed ratings (Par 101): **100,98,98,96,95 95,94,94,91,88**
CSF £137.15 CT £406.49 TOTE £6.70: £2.00, £5.60, £1.20; EX 140.80 Trifecta £748.80.
Owner High Moor Racing 4 **Bred** Noel & Roger O'Callaghan **Trained** Middleham Moor, N Yorks

FOCUS
The track had been power harrowed to a depth of 4 inches and reinstated with a gallop master finish. A moderate sprint in which the leaders seemed to go off a little bit too quick. It's rated around the first four.

1320 ROA/RACING POST OWNERS JACKPOT H'CAP (DIV II) 5f 216y (Tp)
6:20 (6:20) (Class 6) (0-55,55) 3-Y-O+ **£2,587** (£770; £384; £192) **Stalls** Low

Form RPR

5366 **1** **Diamond Vine (IRE)**[9] 1138 8-9-1 **46** oh1 ....(p) DavidProbert 7 52
(Ronald Harris) *niggled along in last pair: swtchd rt and effrt over 1f out: hdwy u.p 1f out: led wl ins fnl f: r.o strly* **9/1**

-502 **2** 1 **Krazy Paving**[9] 1138 4-9-8 **53** ....(b) GeorgeBaker 1 56
(Anabel K Murphy) *trckd ldrs on inner: swtchd lft and effrt over 1f out: ev ch and drvn ins fnl f: styd on to go 2nd cl home* **7/4**[1]

230U **3** nk **Bionic Indian**[21] 986 4-8-10 **48** ....(b) NathanEvans(7) 8 50+
(Michael Easterby) *chsd ldrs: clsd to join ldr and travelling strly 2f out: rdn to ld over 1f out: hdd and no ex wl ins fnl f: lost 2nd cl home* **11/4**[2]

-001 **4** 1½ **Insolenceofoffice (IRE)**[9] 1138 8-9-2 **54** ....(v) CallumRodriguez(7) 10 52
(Richard Ford) *in tch in midfield: effrt u.p over 1f out: chsd ldrs 1f out: styd on same pce ins fnl f* **7/1**[3]

4240 **5** 2 **First Rebellion**[7] 1180 7-9-6 **54** ....(v) GeorgeDowning(3) 4 46
(Tony Carroll) *broke fast: led: rdn 2f out: hdd over 1f out: lost 2nd and wknd ins fnl f* **8/1**

3600 **6** 1½ **Rutterkin (USA)**[8] 1165 8-8-8 **46** oh1 ....(b) VitorSantos(7) 3 33+
(John David Riches) *s.i.s: sn rcvrd and in tch in last pair: effrt on inner over 1f out: styd on same pce ins fnl f* **16/1**

500- **7** 3 **Spirit In Time (IRE)**[240] 5255 4-9-1 **46** .... CathyGannon 2 24
(Malcolm Saunders) *t.k.h: hld up in tch in midfield: rdn 2f out: unable qck over 1f out: wknd fnl f* **16/1**

-030 **8** 5 **Kimbelle**[24] 947 3-8-6 **49** .... RyanPowell 5 9
(Mark Usher) *sn dashed up to chse ldr: rdn and lost pl 2f out: sn wknd: bhd ins fnl f* **20/1**

1m 14.75s (0.25) **Going Correction** 0.0s/f (Stan)
WFA 3 from 4yo+ 12lb **8** Ran SP% **113.2**
Speed ratings (Par 101): **98,96,96,94,91 89,85,78**
CSF £24.68 CT £55.76 TOTE £8.50: £2.20, £1.40, £1.60; EX 27.80 Trifecta £88.40.
Owner Ridge House Stables Ltd **Bred** Michael O'Mahony **Trained** Earlswood, Monmouths

FOCUS
The slower of the two divisions by 0.29sec. The first two came from the back off a strong pace.

1321 WOLVERHAMPTON HOLIDAY INN H'CAP 5f 20y (Tp)
6:50 (6:51) (Class 4) (0-80,80) 4-Y-O+ **£5,175** (£1,540; £769; £384) **Stalls** Low

Form RPR

562- **1** **Bowson Fred**[172] 7342 4-8-12 **78** .... NathanEvans(7) 9 92
(Michael Easterby) *chsd ldr: pushed into ld wl over 1f out: clr and r.o wl ins fnl f: comf* **8/1**

-521 **2** 2 **Miracle Garden**[51] 604 4-9-6 **79** ....(p) AdamKirby 1 86
(Roy Brotherton) *chsd ldrs: effrt over 1f out: styd on u.p ins fnl f: wnt 2nd fnl 50yds: no threat to wnr* **7/2**[2]

6000 **3** 1 **Desert Strike**[28] 903 10-8-13 **72** ....(p) LiamKeniry 4 75
(Conor Dore) *taken down early: led and set fast gallop: hdd and rdn wl over 1f out: styd on same pce ins fnl f: lost 2nd 50yds out* **25/1**

00-4 **4** hd **Top Boy**[14] 1084 6-9-5 **78** ....(v) TonyHamilton 2 81
(Derek Shaw) *hld up in tch in midfield: effrt u.p over 1f out: styd on same pce u.p ins fnl f* **5/1**[3]

0124 **5** nk **Rich Again (IRE)**[16] 1040 7-9-5 **78** ....(b) TedDurcan 11 80+
(James Bethell) *off the pce in last pair: hdwy 1f out: styd on strly ins fnl f: nvr trbld ldrs* **3/1**[1]

3312 **6** ½ **Secret Asset (IRE)**[14] 1084 11-9-6 **79** ....(v) GeorgeBaker 3 79
(Lisa Williamson) *stdd s: hld up towards rr: effrt and swtchd rt over 1f out: styd on wl ins fnl f: nvr trbld ldrs* **9/1**

020- **7** ¾ **Ginzan**[179] 7170 8-8-11 **77** .... GeorgiaCox(7) 8 74
(Malcolm Saunders) *in tch in midfield: effrt to chse ldrs and rdn over 1f out: no ex 1f out and styd on same pce ins fnl f* **20/1**

51-4 **8** ¾ **Casterbridge**[16] 1046 4-9-7 **80** .... NeilFarley 5 74
(Eric Alston) *chsd ldrs tl unable qck and hung lft u.p over 1f out: wknd ins fnl f* **6/1**

00-6 **9** 1 **Cosmic Chatter**[16] 1046 6-9-6 **79** .... JamesSullivan 6 70
(Ruth Carr) *dwlt and short of room after s: off the pce in rr: drvn over 1f out: kpt on ins fnl f: nvr trbld ldrs* **33/1**

40-3 **10** 1¾ **Flicka's Boy**[12] 1110 4-9-2 **75** .... BarryMcHugh 10 60
(Tony Coyle) *a towards rr: rdn over 2f out: no imp whn sltly hmpd over 1f out: n.d* **22/1**

520- **11** 1½ **Tom Sawyer**[195] 6765 8-9-3 **76** ....(p) ConnorBeasley 7 55
(Julie Camacho) *midfield: rdn over 2f out: sn struggling: lost pl over 1f out: bhd fnl f* **33/1**

1m 0.64s (-1.26) **Going Correction** 0.0s/f (Stan) **11** Ran SP% **118.1**
Speed ratings (Par 105): **110,106,105,104,104 103,102,101,99,96 94**
CSF £33.84 CT £684.01 TOTE £11.10: £2.80, £1.50, £5.30; EX 44.00 Trifecta £929.40.
Owner Mrs A Jarvis **Bred** Mrs A Jarvis **Trained** Sheriff Hutton, N Yorks
■ Stewards' Enquiry : Barry McHugh one-day ban; careless riding (22nd Apr)

FOCUS
It paid to race handily in this sprint. Improvement from the winner.

1322 SPONSOR A RACE BY CALLING 01902 390000 H'CAP 2m 119y (Tp)
7:20 (7:20) (Class 6) (0-60,56) 4-Y-O+ **£2,587** (£770; £384; £192) **Stalls** Low

Form RPR

22-3 **1** **Lorelei**[36] 796 4-9-1 **51** .... MartinDwyer 9 63+
(William Muir) *hld up off the pce in midfield: clsd and in tch in midfield 1/2-way: smooth prog to join ldrs over 2f out: led 2f out and sn qcknd clr: drifting rt but in command fnl f: comf* **5/1**[2]

-335 **2** 5 **Mrs Burbidge**[21] 981 6-9-3 **49** ....(tp) LiamKeniry 2 53
(Neil Mulholland) *hld up in tch in midfield: swtchd rt and effrt over 2f out: chsd clr wnr 1f out: styd on but no imp* **5/1**[2]

/045 **3** nk **Vedani (IRE)**[21] 634 7-9-7 **53** .... WilliamCarson 1 57
(Tony Carroll) *chsd ldr for 2f: styd chsng ldrs: rdn 3f out: swtchd rt over 2f out: kpt on u.p: no ch w wnr* **18/1**

3535 **4** 1¼ **Delagoa Bay (IRE)**[16] 1039 8-8-7 **46** .... BenSanderson(7) 4 49
(Sylvester Kirk) *rdn along leaving stalls: hld up in midfield: nt clr run over 2f out: hmpd over 1f out: hdwy u.p 1f out: styd on wl ins fnl f: no ch w wnr* **16/1**

30-6 **5** hd **Dukes Den**[24] 946 5-9-5 **56** .... RachealKneller(5) 7 58
(Mark Usher) *pushed along leaving stalls: hld up in rr: clsd and in tch 1/2-way: nt clr run over 2f out: hdwy u.p over 1f out: styd on: no ch w wnr* **13/2**[3]

0-00 **6** shd **Renewing**[8] 1170 5-9-0 **46** ....(p) FrannyNorton 3 48
(Paul Henderson) *wl off the pce in rr and niggled along at times: clsd and in tch 1/2-way: swtchd lft and hdwy over 1f out: styd on ins fnl f: no ch w wnr* **20/1**

-304 **7** 1¾ **Cantankerous**[7] 1182 5-8-13 **45** ....(p) LukeMorris 11 45
(Daniel Mark Loughnane) *hld up off the pce in rr: clsd and in tch 1/2-way: rdn over 3f out: sme hdwy on outer over 2f out: wknd over 1f out* **9/1**

0-22 **8** nk **City Dreams (IRE)**[10] 1136 6-9-5 **51** .... DougieCostello 10 50
(Philip Kirby) *t.k.h: chsd ldr after 2f tl rdn to ld over 2f out: hdd 2f out and outpcd by wnr: lost 2nd 1f out: wknd* **9/4**[1]

0-06 **9** 3 **Kirkman (IRE)**[58] 521 5-9-9 **55** .... PhillipMakin 8 51
(Peter Hiatt) *chsd ldrs: rdn and struggling whn short of room over 2f out: losing pl and edgd rt over 1f out: sn wknd* **20/1**

0600 **10** 16 **Opus Too (IRE)**[16] 1039 5-8-10 **45** .... DannyBrock(3) 6 22
(John Ryan) *led tl rdn and hdd over 2f out: lost pl over 1f out: fdd fnl f* **66/1**

00-0 **11** 21 **Racing Spirit**[21] 981 4-8-10 **46** .... RyanPowell 5
(Kevin Frost) *s.i.s: off the pce in rr: hdwy and in tch in midfield 10f out: rdn and lost pl 5f out: lost tch over 1f out: t.o* **20/1**

3m 38.66s (-5.04) **Going Correction** 0.0s/f (Stan)
WFA 4 from 5yo+ 4lb **11** Ran SP% **114.4**
Speed ratings (Par 101): **111,108,108,107,107 107,106,106,105,97 87**
CSF £27.66 CT £413.35 TOTE £5.40: £1.50, £1.80, £6.00; EX 20.00 Trifecta £699.10.
Owner John O'Mulloy **Bred** Clarendon Farm **Trained** Lambourn, Berks
■ Stewards' Enquiry : William Carson two-day ban; careless riding (22nd-23rd Apr)

FOCUS
A moderate staying handicap but the winner took it easily. The likes of the fourth help with the level.

1323 BLACK COUNTRY'S ONLY RACECOURSE H'CAP 1m 141y (Tp)
7:50 (7:50) (Class 6) (0-60,60) 4-Y-O+ **£2,587** (£770; £384; £192) **Stalls** Low

Form RPR
443- **1** **John Caesar (IRE)**[164] 7538 5-9-7 **60**........................(tp) DanielTudhope 7 69
(Rebecca Bastiman) *hld up off the pce in midfield: clsd to chse ldrs 2f out: swtchd rt and effrt over 1f out: str run to ld wl ins fnl f* **15/2**[3]
5421 **2** ¾ **Toymaker**[10] 1131 9-9-0 **58**.................................(t) PhilDennis(5) 6 65
(Phil McEntee) *in tch in midfield: clsd 4f out: rdn to chal over 1f out: drvn to ld ins fnl f: hdd and one pce wl ins fnl f* **4/1**[1]
0032 **3** ¾ **Les Gar Gan (IRE)**[15] 1058 5-9-6 **59**........................(be) StevieDonohoe 2 64
(Daniel Mark Loughnane) *s.i.s and rdn along leaving stalls: off the pce in rr: clsd and in tch over 3f out: hdwy and swtchd lft 1f out: styd on strly to snatch 3rd last stride: nt rch ldrs* **15/2**[3]
-624 **4** shd **Kicking The Can (IRE)**[12] 1117 5-9-6 **59**...................... BarryMcHugh 8 64
(David Thompson) *t.k.h: chsd clr ldng pair: clsd and wnt 2nd over 3f out: rdn to ld wl over 1f out: hdd ins fnl f: no ex* **10/1**
-406 **5** nk **First Summer**[30] 870 4-9-2 **55**... LukeMorris 4 60
(Shaun Harris) *off the pce in midfield: clsd and in tch over 3f out: rdn over 2f out: hdwy u.p ins fnl f: styd on wl fnl 100yds: nt rch ldrs* **7/1**[2]
61-0 **6** 1 **Atreus**[11] 1120 4-8-13 **59**...(p) NathanEvans(7) 5 61+
(Michael Easterby) *led for 1f: chsd ldr and clr of field tl over 3f out: rdn over 1f out: no ex 1f out: outpcd fnl 75yds* **10/1**
-210 **7** ¾ **Overrider**[21] 986 6-8-7 **51**....................................(bt) CallumShepherd(5) 1 52
(Shaun Lycett) *in tch in midfield: effrt u.p on inner to chse ldrs 1f out: styd on same pce ins fnl f* **16/1**
6-44 **8** 1 ¾ **Ted's Brother (IRE)**[21] 982 8-9-6 **59**..............................(e) JasonHart 11 56
(Richard Guest) *t.k.h: hld up off the pce in rr: clsd and in tch over 3f out: effrt u.p over 1f out: no imp 1f out: wknd ins fnl f* **12/1**
-54U **9** 2 **Patron Of Explores (USA)**[43] 707 5-8-7 **46** oh1................ NeilFarley 9 39
(Patrick Holmes) *v.s.a: t.k.h: hld up wl off the pce in rr: clsd and in tch over 3f out: effrt over 1f out: sn btn: wknd ins fnl f* **20/1**
0-60 **10** ½ **Poppet Rocket (IRE)**[78] 277 4-8-13 **59**............ LamornaBardwell(7) 10 51
(Seamus Mullins) *s.i.s and pushed along early: off the pce in rr: clsd and in tch over 3f out: rdn and no hdwy over 1f out: wknd ins fnl f* **66/1**
-021 **11** nk **Ellaal**[15] 1064 7-9-7 **60**... PaulMulrennan 12 51+
(Ruth Carr) *chsd ldr tl led after 1f and clr w rival: hdd and rdn over 1f out: no ex and wknd fnl f* **4/1**[1]
-000 **12** 66 **Strictly Glitz (IRE)**[11] 1120 5-8-7 **46** oh1...................(v) ConnorBeasley 3
(Clare Ellam) *off the pce in midfield: rdn and lost pl 4f out: t.o fnl 2f* **80/1**

1m 48.29s (-1.81) **Going Correction** 0.0s/f (Stan) **12** Ran SP% **115.3**
Speed ratings (Par 101): **108,107,106,106,106 105,104,103,101,100 100,42**
CSF £35.99 CT £238.53 TOTE £7.90: £2.80, £1.50, £2.60; EX 48.10 Trifecta £198.90.
Owner Mrs K Hall **Bred** Polish Belle Partnership **Trained** Cowthorpe, N Yorks

FOCUS
This was run at a good early gallop but then steadied down the back, before picking up again turning for home. The winner was still below his best form for Jeremy Noseda.

1324 #FOLLOWUS ON TWITTER @WOLVESRACES MAIDEN STKS 7f 32y (Tp)
8:20 (8:21) (Class 5) 3-Y-O+ **£3,557** (£1,058; £529; £264) **Stalls** High

Form RPR
356- **1** **George William**[230] 5635 3-8-12 **76**.. SeanLevey 4 74
(Richard Hannon) *t.k.h: chsd ldr: pushed along to chal over 1f out: rdn and led ins fnl f: r.o wl* **4/6**[1]
0-3 **2** nk **Moueenn**[23] 958 3-8-12 **0**.. JackMitchell 7 73
(Roger Varian) *led: rdn and pressed over 1f out: drvn and hdd ins fnl f: r.o but a hld* **7/4**[2]
0- **3** 4 ½ **Oscar Hughes (IRE)**[188] 6929 3-8-12 **0**....................... ConnorBeasley 2 61
(Julie Camacho) *chsd ldr: rdn over 1f out: sn outpcd by ldng pair: clr 3rd and kpt on same pce fnl f* **66/1**
4 3 ½ **Critical Speed (IRE)** 4-9-7 **0**.. LukeMorris 5 52
(Sylvester Kirk) *s.i.s and v green leaving stalls: rcvrd and in tch in rr over 5f out: effrt in 4th over 2f out: no imp over 1f out: wl hld fnl f* **10/1**[3]
0 **5** 4 ½ **Owners Day**[9] 1140 6-9-7 **0**.. LiamKeniry 1 39
(Neil Mulholland) *hld up in tch: pushed along and n.m.r on inner 3f out: swtchd rt: rdn and outpcd over 1f out: sn btn* **66/1**
00 **6** nse **Somepink (IRE)**[21] 984 3-8-7 **0**.. FrannyNorton 3 34
(Daniel Mark Loughnane) *in tch in midfield: hung lft 3f out: pushed along 2f out: sn outpcd and wl btn 1f out* **100/1**

1m 30.14s (1.34) **Going Correction** 0.0s/f (Stan)
WFA 3 from 4yo+ 14lb **6** Ran SP% **109.4**
Speed ratings (Par 103): **92,91,86,82,77 77**
CSF £1.92 TOTE £1.60: £1.10, £1.10; EX 2.00 Trifecta £15.90.
Owner Lady Coventry & Partners **Bred** Rachel Countess Of Coventry **Trained** East Everleigh, Wilts

FOCUS
A steadily run affair. Muddling form, with the winner rated close to form.

1325 LADIES EVENING FRIDAY 19TH AUGUST H'CAP 7f 32y (Tp)
8:50 (8:50) (Class 6) (0-60,59) 3-Y-O **£2,587** (£770; £384; £192) **Stalls** High

Form RPR
600- **1** **Free To Roam (IRE)**[134] 8005 3-8-12 **50**......................... DavidProbert 7 56
(Philip McBride) *wl in tch in midfield: swtchd rt and effrt over 1f out: hdwy u.p to ld 100yds: r.o wl and gng away at fin* **8/1**
4-40 **2** 1 ¾ **Espoir**[64] 443 3-8-12 **53**..(b[1]) PhilipPrince(3) 1 55
(David Evans) *chsd ldrs: effrt on inner and ev ch over 1f out: kpt on same pce ins fnl f: wnt 2nd last strides* **4/1**[2]
0-00 **3** hd **Tahiti One**[24] 947 3-9-4 **56**.. WilliamCarson 3 57
(Tony Carroll) *t.k.h: led: rdn over 1f out: hdd 100yds out: styd on same pce ins fnl f: lost 2nd last strides* **25/1**
340 **4** 1 ½ **Ventura Falcon (IRE)**[46] 679 3-9-0 **59**......................... HollieDoyle(7) 6 58+
(Richard Hannon) *stdd after s: hld up in tch in last pair: effrt over 1f out: edging lft u.p 1f out: kpt on ins fnl f: nt rch ldrs* **15/2**
0-22 **5** 1 **Dream Revival**[24] 948 3-9-7 **59**.. LiamKeniry 2 54
(James Unett) *t.k.h: chsd ldr: effrt to chal 2f out: no ex 1f out: wknd ins fnl f* **11/4**[1]
0340 **6** ½ **Ormanumps (IRE)**[8] 1162 3-8-7 **45**.................................... LukeMorris 4 39
(Daniel Mark Loughnane) *in tch in midfield: rdn 3f out: drvn and no imp over 1f out: wl hld and kpt on same pce ins fnl f* **11/4**[1]
52-0 **7** ½ **Canford Kilbey (IRE)**[11] 1126 3-8-9 **54**....................... NathanEvans(7) 5 47
(Michael Easterby) *dwlt: hld up in tch in rr: nt clr run over 2f out: effrt u.p over 1f out: sltly hmpd 1f out: kpt on same pce ins fnl f* **5/1**[3]

1m 29.61s (0.81) **Going Correction** 0.0s/f (Stan) **7** Ran SP% **116.7**
Speed ratings (Par 96): **95,93,92,91,89 89,88**
CSF £41.09 TOTE £9.30: £6.10, £2.90; EX 52.70 Trifecta £701.20.
Owner P J McBride **Bred** Tally-Ho Stud **Trained** Newmarket, Suffolk

FOCUS
A moderate heat with improvement from the winner.

1326 MEETING & EVENTS AT WOLVERHAMPTON RACECOURSE H'CAP 7f 32y (Tp)
9:20 (9:21) (Class 5) (0-75,74) 4-Y-O+ **£3,557** (£1,058; £529; £264) **Stalls** High

Form RPR
63-1 **1** **Lucy The Painter (IRE)**[9] 1139 4-9-8 **74** 6ex.................. HarryBentley 3 86+
(Ed de Giles) *trckd ldng pair: effrt on inner over 1f out: rdn to ld jst ins fnl f: r.o strly: readily* **4/5**[1]
-114 **2** 2 ½ **Eastern Dragon (IRE)**[35] 822 6-9-3 **69**........................... MartinHarley 5 74
(Seamus Durack) *t.k.h: chsd ldr: rdn to chal over 1f out: outpcd by wnr ins fnl f: kpt on to go 2nd fnl 50yds* **3/1**[2]
1065 **3** ¾ **Al's Memory (IRE)**[24] 942 7-8-10 **65**............................. PhilipPrince(3) 1 68
(David Evans) *led: rdn and qckná 2f out: drvn and hdd jst ins fnl f: sn outpcd and lost 2nd fnl 50yds* **12/1**
4230 **4** nk **Oak Bluffs (IRE)**[12] 1116 5-8-10 **62**............................ GeorgeChaloner 4 64
(Richard Fahey) *hld up in tch: effrt over 1f out: drvn and styd on same pce ins fnl f* **8/1**[3]
2003 **5** 1 ½ **Black Truffle (FR)**[12] 1117 6-8-11 **63**................................ LiamKeniry 6 61
(Mark Usher) *stdd after s: hld up in tch in rr: effrt on inner over 1f out: rdn and no imp 1f out: wl hld fnl f* **11/1**
/10- **6** 4 ½ **Ershaad (IRE)**[109] 8333 4-9-7 **73**...................................... LukeMorris 7 60
(Shaun Harris) *dwlt: sn rcvrd and wl in tch in midfield: rdn 2f out: no imp: wknd ins fnl f: eased towards fin* **20/1**

1m 30.15s (1.35) **Going Correction** 0.0s/f (Stan) **6** Ran SP% **112.5**
Speed ratings (Par 103): **92,89,88,87,86 81**
CSF £3.40 TOTE £1.70: £1.30, £1.50; EX 4.30 Trifecta £19.80.
Owner J P Carrington **Bred** Bakewell Bloodstock **Trained** Ledbury, H'fords

FOCUS
Another nice performance from the winner, who was well treated but still impressed. The third lends a bit of doubt to the form.
T/Plt: £45.60 to a £1 stake. Pool: £91,874.50 - 1,470.37 winning tickets T/Qpdt: £14.60 to a £1 stake. Pool: £8,496.74 - 429.39 winning tickets **Steve Payne**

1327 - 1333a (Foreign Racing) - See Raceform Interactive

[1263] LINGFIELD (L-H)
Saturday, April 9

OFFICIAL GOING: Polytrack: standard
Wind: mild breeze across Weather: sunny periods

1334 BALLARD AND SHORTALL FILLIES' H'CAP 7f 1y(P)
2:00 (2:00) (Class 5) (0-70,70) 4-Y-O+ **£2,911** (£866; £432; £216) **Stalls** Low

Form RPR
3-2 **1** **Baileys Mirage (FR)**[10] 1139 5-8-12 **61**.......................(b) RyanMoore 8 68
(Chris Dwyer) *trckd ldr: led over 1f out: shkn up and kpt on wl fnl f* **5/2**[1]
446- **2** ¾ **Exoplanet Blue**[115] 8248 4-9-7 **70**...................................... DaneO'Neill 3 75
(Henry Candy) *s.i.s: sn in tch: rdn 2f out: r.o strly fnl f: snatched 2nd fnl strides* **5/2**[1]
00-3 **3** hd **Maureb (IRE)**[9] 1158 4-9-7 **70**.......................................(p) BarryMcHugh 7 74
(Tony Coyle) *chsd ldrs: rdn over 1f out: chsd wnr ent fnl f: a being hld: lost 2nd fnl strides* **8/1**
00-5 **4** 1 ¼ **Two In The Pink (IRE)**[64] 456 6-9-2 **65**.......................... AdamKirby 4 66
(Ralph J Smith) *trckd ldrs: rdn 2f out: kpt on same pce fnl f* **7/1**[3]
306- **5** 2 **Pryers Princess**[197] 6721 4-9-3 **66**................................... OisinMurphy 2 61
(David C Griffiths) *in last pair: effrt on inner 2f out: hld whn swtchd rt jst ins fnl f (b.b.v)* **16/1**
0-46 **6** nk **Potternello (IRE)**[33] 859 4-9-2 **65**........................... SilvestreDeSousa 5 59
(Mick Channon) *led: rdn and hdd over 1f out: kpt on tl fdd fnl 120yds* **6/1**[2]
6441 **7** 1 ½ **Venus Grace**[10] 1145 5-8-3 **52**................................. EdwardGreatrex(5) 1 47
(Michael Appleby) *hld up last: rdn 2f out: little imp* **8/1**
-000 **8** 5 **Dusty Blue**[16] 1059 4-8-8 **57**.. WilliamCarson 6 34
(Tony Carroll) *in tch on outer: effrt 2f out: wknd over 1f out* **50/1**

1m 24.51s (-0.29) **Going Correction** 0.0s/f (Stan) **8** Ran SP% **114.0**
Speed ratings (Par 100): **101,100,99,98,96 95,94,88**
CSF £8.23 CT £41.49 TOTE £3.10: £1.20, £1.30, £2.70; EX 11.60 Trifecta £50.50.
Owner G R Bailey Ltd (Baileys Horse Feeds) **Bred** Gr Baileys Ltd **Trained** Newmarket, Suffolk

FOCUS
A modest fillies' handicap, rated around the third.

1335 EMMA NICHOLSON SOON TO BE MARRIED H'CAP 7f 1y(P)
2:35 (2:35) (Class 3) (0-95,95) 4-Y-O+ **£7,246** (£2,168; £1,084; £542; £270) **Stalls** Low

Form RPR
622- **1** **Exchequer (IRE)**[196] 6746 5-9-2 **90**.................................. SeanLevey 10 101
(David Brown) *mde all: qcknd clr over 1f out: readily* **8/1**[3]
564- **2** 1 ¼ **Easy Tiger**[172] 7364 4-8-4 **81** oh4.................................. RobHornby(3) 9 88
(William Muir) *trckd wnr: rdn over 1f out: kpt on fnl f but readily hld by wnr* **8/1**[3]
-431 **3** 1 **Presumido (IRE)**[17] 1041 6-8-9 **83**................................... HarryBentley 6 87
(Simon Dow) *in tch: rdn to chse ldng pair over 1f out: kpt on same pce fnl f* **10/1**
042- **4** ¾ **Split The Atom (IRE)**[29] 910 4-8-13 **87**......................... SamHitchcott 2 89
(John Patrick Shanahan, Ire) *in tch: rdn to chse ldng pair over 1f out: kpt on same pce fnl f* **14/1**
344- **5** hd **George Cinq**[190] 6892 6-9-0 **88**...................................... FrankieDettori 7 89
(George Scott) *mid-div: rdn 2f out: kpt on ins fnl f* **8/1**[3]
055- **6** nk **Fiftyshadesofgrey (IRE)**[170] 7420 5-9-7 **95**.................... PatCosgrave 4 96
(George Baker) *mid-div: rdn wl over 1f out: kpt on same pce fnl f* **6/1**[1]
300- **7** shd **The Warrior (IRE)**[296] 3338 4-9-7 **95**................................. RyanMoore 8 97+
(Amanda Perrett) *hld up towards rr: nt best of runs briefly whn rdn over 1f out: no imp tl kpt on ins fnl f* **7/1**[2]
3040 **8** ¾ **Arnold Lane (IRE)**[15] 1068 7-9-1 **89**........................... SilvestreDeSousa 3 87
(Mick Channon) *chsd wnr tl rdn over 1f out: fdd ins fnl f* **7/1**[2]
1300 **9** hd **Clement (IRE)**[17] 1041 6-8-3 **82**..............................(v) EdwardGreatrex(5) 1 80
(John O'Shea) *towards rr: hdwy on inner 2f out: effrt over 1f out: fdd fnl f* **14/1**
-002 **10** 1 ¾ **Unforgiving Minute**[35] 833 5-9-3 **91**................................. AdamKirby 13 84
(Gary Moore) *plld hrd: hld up: rdn over 1f out: little imp* **6/1**[1]
5650 **11** ½ **Forceful Appeal (USA)**[15] 1068 8-9-3 **91**........................ OisinMurphy 11 83
(Simon Dow) *a towards rr* **25/1**
6113 **12** ¾ **Fleckerl (IRE)**[31] 879 6-9-3 **91**...(p) LiamKeniry 5 81
(Conor Dore) *s.i.s: a towards rr* **16/1**

225- **13** 2 ½ **Fast Dancer (IRE)**[171] 7390 4-8-10 **84** JFEgan 12 67
(Joseph Tuite) *mid-div: rdn over 2f out: wknd over 1f out* **50/1**
1m 23.3s (-1.50) **Going Correction** 0.0s/f (Stan) **13** Ran SP% **121.0**
Speed ratings (Par 107): **108,106,105,104,104 104,103,103,102,100 100,99,96**
CSF £71.63 CT £658.65 TOTE £9.60: £2.90, £2.70, £3.90; EX 111.30 Trifecta £2690.10.
Owner J C Fretwell **Bred** B Holland, S Hillen & J Cullinan **Trained** Averham Park, Notts

FOCUS
This looked a competitive handicap, but the winner got a totally uncontested lead - he reached the 2f pole in more or less the same time as the winner of the first race, judged on the on-screen timer - and nothing could get near him. The form is rated around the third.

1336 LYNN KELLIER 50TH BIRTHDAY CELEBRATIONS H'CAP 1m 4f (P)
3:10 (3:10) (Class 2) (0-105,100) 4-Y£01,971 (£3,583; £1,791; £896; £446) **Stalls** Low

Form RPR
344- **1** **Top Tug (IRE)**[166] 7511 5-9-3 **95** AdamKirby 4 103
(Alan King) *hld up in tch: gd hdwy over 1f out: led fnl 140yds: r.o: rdn out* **7/1**
044- **2** ¾ **Sagaciously (IRE)**[162] 7596 4-8-9 **88** PaulHanagan 7 95
(Ed Dunlop) *slowly away: sn in tch: rdn and hdwy ent fnl f: drifted lft but r.o strly: clsng on wnr at fin* **20/1**
03-2 **3** 1 ½ **Dutch Uncle**[14] 1089 4-8-5 **84** SilvestreDeSousa 2 89
(Ed Dunlop) *trckd ldrs: led jst over 1f out: rdn and hdd fnl 140yds: no ex: jst hld on for 3rd* **15/8**[1]
1510 **4** shd **Winterlude (IRE)**[15] 1069 6-9-6 **98** GeorgeBaker 1 102
(Jennie Candlish) *hld up: hdwy over 1f out: sn rdn: kpt on whn clr run jst ins fnl f: jst failed to snatch 3rd* **9/2**[3]
5566 **5** 2 ¼ **Luv U Whatever**[15] 1081 6-9-3 **95** AndrewMullen 5 96
(Michael Appleby) *led: rdn whn pressed over 2f out: hdd jst over 1f out: no ex fnl f* **25/1**
60- **6** ¾ **Archangel Raphael (IRE)**[209] 6365 4-9-7 **100** PatDobbs 6 100?
(Amanda Perrett) *trckd ldrs: rdn ent fnl f: no ex fnl 120yds* **33/1**
P15- **7** shd **Hardstone (USA)**[169] 7425 5-9-1 **93** PaulMulrennan 8 92
(Michael Dods) *trckd ldr: rdn to chal over 2f out: wknd fnl f* **10/1**
3-12 **8** 1 ½ **Silver Quay (IRE)**[15] 1081 4-9-4 **97** RyanMoore 9 94
(Richard Hannon) *hld up: hdwy over 3f out: rdn to chse ldrs over 2f out: wknd over 1f out* **5/2**[2]
2m 31.94s (-1.06) **Going Correction** 0.0s/f (Stan)
WFA 4 from 5yo+ 1lb **8** Ran SP% **114.7**
Speed ratings (Par 109): **103,102,101,101,99 99,99,98**
CSF £127.33 CT £365.15 TOTE £9.20: £2.30, £3.80, £1.50; EX 123.20 Trifecta £415.20.
Owner Elite Racing Club **Bred** Wretham Stud **Trained** Barbury Castle, Wilts

FOCUS
The pace seemed modest for much of the way but it clearly picked up in enough time to bring the hold-up horses into it, with the winner, second and fourth filling the last three places on the turn into the home straight. A length pb from the winner.

1337 CHI MURPHY IS TYING THE KNOT MAIDEN STKS 6f 1y(P)
3:45 (3:48) (Class 5) 3-Y-O **£2,911** (£866; £432; £216) **Stalls** Low

Form RPR
- **1** **Dream Dubai** 3-9-5 0 RyanMoore 1 88+
(Sylvester Kirk) *mid-div: str run over 1f out: led ins fnl f: sn hrd pressed: hld on wl: rdn out* **7/2**[2]
2 nk **Maximian (IRE)** 3-9-5 0 WilliamBuick 4 87+
(Charlie Appleby) *mid-div: str run over 1f out to mount str chal ins fnl f: kpt on wl: hld cl home* **7/2**[2]
0- **3** 5 **Al Sailiyah (IRE)**[196] 6756 3-9-0 0 FrankieDettori 6 66
(Richard Hannon) *chsd ldrs: rdn over 1f out: led briefly jst ins fnl f: kpt on but sn outpcd by front pair* **20/1**
-233 **4** 2 ¼ **Cee Jay**[29] 902 3-9-5 70 (v) JamesDoyle 10 64
(Jeremy Noseda) *mid-div: hdwy 2f out: sn rdn: kpt on same pce fnl f* **8/1**
66- **5** 1 ½ **Dnaneer (IRE)**[197] 6701 3-9-0 0 SilvestreDeSousa 2 54+
(William Knight) *led: rdn 2f out: hdd jst ins fnl f: wknd* **16/1**
6 nse **Lilliard (IRE)**[8] 1190 3-9-0 0 SamHitchcott 7 54
(John Patrick Shanahan, Ire) *trckd ldr tl lost pl whn awkward fnl bnd: no ch after* **14/1**
0- **7** 4 ½ **Pacific Salt (IRE)**[180] 7166 3-9-5 0 GeorgeBaker 3 44
(Roger Charlton) *chsd ldrs: rdn over 2f out: wknd jst over 1f out* **6/1**[3]
323- **8** ¾ **Muatadel**[213] 6201 3-9-5 77 PaulHanagan 11 42
(Mark Johnston) *mid-div tl outpcd over 2f out* **11/4**[1]
00 **9** 1 **Cainhoe Star**[14] 1091 3-9-5 0 WilliamCarson 8 39
(Anthony Carson) *s.i.s: a towards rr* **100/1**
10 2 **Cecile Royale** 3-9-0 0 SaleemGolam 5 27
(Stuart Williams) *s.i.s: sn outpcd in rr: nvr on terms* **50/1**
0- **11** 2 ½ **Wild Bloom**[157] 7699 3-9-0 0 HarryBentley 9 19
(Ed Vaughan) *a towards rr* **33/1**
1m 10.7s (-1.20) **Going Correction** 0.0s/f (Stan) **11** Ran SP% **119.7**
Speed ratings (Par 98): **108,107,100,97,95 95,89,88,87,84 81**
CSF £16.08 TOTE £5.20: £2.80, £1.90, £5.00; EX 21.40 Trifecta £261.80.
Owner Malih L Al Basti **Bred** Usk Valley Stud **Trained** Upper Lambourn, Berks
■ Stewards' Enquiry : William Carson one-day ban; careless riding (24th Apr)

FOCUS
Two newcomers pulled nicely clear - they hit the line strongly and were going further away from the pack - and both look comfortably above average with clear potential to do better.

1338 KELLIER FAMILY AND FRIENDS CELEBRATIONS INTERNATIONAL TRIAL STKS (LISTED RACE) 1m 1y(P)
4:15 (4:16) (Class 1) 3-Y-O **£25,519** (£9,675; £4,842; £2,412; £1,210) **Stalls** High

Form RPR
1101 **1** **Sea Of Flames**[15] 1071 3-9-0 100 SilvestreDeSousa 3 103
(David Elsworth) *mde all: drvn whn strly chal fr over 1f out: battled on v gamely: won on nod* **7/4**[1]
150- **2** nse **Ode To Evening**[231] 5640 3-9-0 99 JamesDoyle 1 102
(Mark Johnston) *trckd wnr: rdn for str chal over 1f out: kpt on wl and ev ch thrght fnl f: lost on nod* **8/1**
21- **3** ½ **Predilection (USA)**[143] 7890 3-9-0 0 FrankieDettori 2 101
(John Gosden) *trckd ldng pair: c wdst and rdn ent st: kpt on wl and clsng on ldng pair nring fin* **2/1**[2]
4-22 **4** 2 ¼ **Tutu Nguru (USA)**[7] 1206 3-8-9 96 PatCosgrave 6 91
(William Haggas) *stdd s: last of 5 but wl in tch: rdn over 1f out: kpt on but nt quite pce to get on terms fnl f* **5/1**[3]
313- **5** 1 ½ **Palawan**[210] 6311 3-9-0 100 RyanMoore 4 92
(Richard Hannon) *trckd ldrs: pushed along 3f out: rdn for short-lived effrt over 1f out: eased whn btn fnl f* **7/1**
1m 35.97s (-2.23) **Going Correction** 0.0s/f (Stan) **5** Ran SP% **110.0**
Speed ratings (Par 106): **111,110,110,108,106**
CSF £15.21 TOTE £2.30: £1.40, £4.10; EX 17.10 Trifecta £46.00.
Owner J C Smith **Bred** Littleton Stud **Trained** Newmarket, Suffolk

FOCUS
A competitive Listed race. The winner proved game after setting a sound pace, and is rated to his C&D latest.

1339 MATTHEW URSELL STAG DO CELEBRATIONS MAIDEN STKS 7f 1y(P)
4:50 (4:54) (Class 5) 3-Y-O **£2,911** (£866; £432; £216) **Stalls** Low

Form RPR
0- **1** **Dommersen (IRE)**[171] 7394 3-9-5 0 FrankieDettori 1 79+
(John Gosden) *trckd ldrs: rdn over 1f out: led fnl 140yds: r.o wl to assert towards fin* **5/4**[2]
2 ½ **Banish (USA)** 3-9-5 0 WilliamBuick 8 78+
(Hugo Palmer) *hld up: pushed along over 2f out: rdn and hdwy over 1f out: r.o wl fnl 120yds: wnt 2nd fnl strides* **6/1**[3]
3 nk **Musdam (USA)** 3-9-5 0 RyanMoore 9 77+
(Sir Michael Stoute) *s.i.s: sn mid-div: lost pl and in last trio over 2f out: hdwy over 1f out: chal fnl 100yds: lost 2nd fnl strides* **1/1**[1]
4 2 ¼ **Hidden Gem** 3-9-0 0 AntonioFresu 3 66
(Ed Walker) *mid-div: hdwy ent fnl f: kpt on but nt pce of ldrs* **25/1**
5 1 ½ **Ionization (IRE)** 3-9-0 0 SamHitchcott 4 62
(John Patrick Shanahan, Ire) *disp ld tl rdn into narrow advantage 2f out: no ex whn hdd fnl 140yds* **33/1**
60- **6** nse **The King's Steed**[150] 7792 3-9-5 0 FMBerry 2 67+
(Ralph Beckett) *trckd ldrs: sltly outpcd over 2f out: hdwy ent fnl f: kpt on but nt pce of ldrs* **9/1**
0 **7** 1 ½ **Pacohontas**[22] 984 3-8-9 0 CharlesEddery[(5)] 7 58
(Dean Ivory) *disp ld: rdn 3f out: narrowly hdd 2f out: wknd fnl f* **50/1**
0 **8** 8 **Lord Murphy (IRE)**[11] 1132 3-9-5 0 AdamKirby 6 41
(Daniel Mark Loughnane) *s.i.s: a towards rr* **33/1**
1m 25.85s (1.05) **Going Correction** 0.0s/f (Stan) **8** Ran SP% **130.4**
Speed ratings (Par 98): **94,93,93,90,88 88,87,77**
CSF £10.10 TOTE £2.40: £1.10, £1.80, £1.10; EX 13.40 Trifecta £29.80.
Owner Al Mirqab Racing **Bred** The Lavington Stud **Trained** Newmarket, Suffolk
■ Fashaak (6-1) was withdrawn. Rule 4 applies to bets struck at board prices prior to withdrawal, but not to SP bets. Deduction - 10p in the pound. New market formed.

FOCUS
A fair maiden run at a modest pace but full of likely improvers.

1340 BELATED BIRTHDAY WISHES SARAT KUNWAR H'CAP 1m 2f (P)
5:40 (5:41) (Class 6) (0-65,65) 4-Y-O+ **£2,264** (£673; £336; £168) **Stalls** Low

Form RPR
-613 **1** **Attain**[47] 672 7-9-2 **63** (p) ShelleyBirkett[(3)] 2 72
(Julia Feilden) *in tch: hdwy 2f out: led ent fnl f: r.o wl* **7/1**
40-3 **2** 2 **Head Coach**[23] 964 4-8-11 **58** (p) DannyBrock[(3)] 3 63
(Jane Chapple-Hyam) *in tch: hdwy on inner 2f out: rdn and ev ch ent fnl f: edgd sltly rt: kpt on but no ex* **5/1**[3]
115- **3** hd **Speculator**[184] 7067 4-9-7 **65** ShaneKelly 9 70
(David Menuisier) *hld up towards rr: hdwy on outer fr 4f out: rdn 2f out: r.o fnl f* **5/2**[1]
-022 **4** ½ **Pike Corner Cross (IRE)**[24] 951 4-9-5 **63** RyanMoore 10 67
(Gary Moore) *hld up: nudged along 4f out: rdn 2f out: kpt on ins fnl f: no threat to ldrs* **3/1**[2]
522- **5** nse **Loving Your Work**[173] 7351 5-9-1 **59** PatDobbs 7 63
(Ken Cunningham-Brown) *mid-div: nt clr run on rails 2f out tl 1f out: r.o fnl f but n.d* **20/1**
/430 **6** 1 **Tatawu (IRE)**[50] 640 4-9-7 **65** FMBerry 1 67
(Peter Hiatt) *mid-div tl squeezed up on rails 7f out: last: rdn wl over 1f out: kpt on fnl f* **50/1**
6-13 **7** ½ **Lord Of The Storm**[16] 1064 8-9-5 **63** KierenFox 4 64
(Michael Attwater) *prom: rdn over 2f out: ev ch ent fnl f: fdd* **7/1**
2355 **8** 2 ½ **Runaiocht (IRE)**[29] 898 6-9-0 **58** (b) JimmyQuinn 8 54
(Paul Burgoyne) *s.i.s: plld hrd in rr: hdwy to ld after 7f: rdn over 2f out: hdd ent fnl f: wknd* **12/1**
5-45 **9** 4 ½ **Light Rose (IRE)**[10] 1139 6-9-0 **63** DavidParkes[(5)] 5 51
(Jeremy Gask) *led for 3f: trckd ldr: rdn over 2f out: wknd over 1f out* **25/1**
-0U2 **10** nk **Nouvelle Ere**[29] 898 5-9-0 **61** (t) GeorgeDowning[(3)] 6 48
(Tony Carroll) *in tch: rdn over 4f out: wknd 2f out* **20/1**
2m 6.67s (0.07) **Going Correction** 0.0s/f (Stan) **10** Ran SP% **118.3**
Speed ratings (Par 101): **99,97,97,96,96 96,95,93,90,89**
CSF £40.43 CT £113.15 TOTE £9.50: £2.70, £2.60, £1.30; EX 68.50 Trifecta £303.80.
Owner Newmarket Equine Tours Racing Club **Bred** Millsec Limited **Trained** Exning, Suffolk

FOCUS
A modest handicap.
T/Plt: £48.90 to a £1 stake. Pool: £73,196.15 - 1,091.50 winning tickets. T/Qpdt: £10.90 to a £1 stake. Pool: £4,943.38 - 334.52 winning tickets. **Tim Mitchell**

1319 WOLVERHAMPTON (A.W) (L-H)
Saturday, April 9

OFFICIAL GOING: Tapeta: standard
Wind: Light across Weather: Cloudy

1341 FAMILY FUN DAY MONDAY 8TH AUGUST H'CAP 5f 216y (Tp)
6:20 (6:20) (Class 5) (0-75,74) 4-Y-O+ **£3,234** (£962; £481; £240) **Stalls** Low

Form RPR
60-4 **1** **Available (IRE)**[8] 1186 7-9-0 **67** (tp) JoeFanning 5 76
(John Mackie) *chsd ldr 5f out: rdn to ld over 1f out: r.o* **11/4**[1]
0001 **2** 2 **Colourbearer (IRE)**[9] 1159 9-8-13 **66** (t) BenCurtis 4 69
(Charlie Wallis) *sn led: rdn and hdd over 1f out: styd on same pce ins fnl f* **9/2**[2]
2-40 **3** nk **Ancient Cross**[37] 799 12-8-3 **63** (bt) NathanEvans[(7)] 3 65
(Michael Easterby) *a.p: rdn over 1f out: r.o* **8/1**
-012 **4** nk **City Of Angkor Wat (IRE)**[25] 942 6-9-5 **72** (p) LiamKeniry 9 73+
(Conor Dore) *hld up: hdwy over 1f out: sn rdn: styd on* **6/1**[3]
012- **5** 2 ¼ **Burtonwood**[176] 7259 4-8-12 **65** ConnorBeasley 10 58
(Julie Camacho) *hld up: rdn over 2f out: r.o ins fnl f: nvr nrr* **15/2**
6-00 **6** ¾ **Ambitious Boy**[8] 1186 7-8-12 **70** CiaranMckee[(5)] 8 61
(John O'Shea) *s.i.s: hld up: styd on ins fnl f: nvr nrr* **12/1**
55-0 **7** 3 ¼ **Quickaswecan**[24] 955 5-9-6 **73** (t) RobertWinston 2 54
(Milton Bradley) *chsd ldr 1f: remained handy: rdn over 2f out: wknd ins fnl f* **20/1**
6020 **8** nk **Temple Road (IRE)**[29] 903 8-8-12 **72** (t) LuluStanford[(7)] 7 52
(Milton Bradley) *hld up: rdn over 2f out: wknd fnl f* **16/1**

0-16 **9** *nk* **Diatomic (IRE)**[13] 1117 4-8-9 **62**............................(p) RichardKingscote 1 41
(Tom Dascombe) *prom: rdn over 2f out: wknd over 1f out* **13/2**
1m 12.68s (-1.82) **Going Correction** -0.125s/f (Stan) **9** Ran SP% **113.7**
Speed ratings (Par 103): **107,104,103,103,100 99,95,94,94**
CSF £14.56 CT £86.01 TOTE £3.40: £1.10, £1.80, £3.00; EX 16.50 Trifecta £119.00.
Owner Derbyshire Racing V **Bred** Carrigbeg Stud & David Powell **Trained** Church Broughton , Derbys

FOCUS
Few got into this, with the front two dominating throughout. The winner is rated back to his October C&D win.

1342 BRITISH STALLION STUDS EBF NOVICE FILLIES' STKS (PLUS 10 RACE) 5f 20y (Tp)
6:50 (6:52) (Class 5) 2-Y-O **£3,234** (£962; £481; £240) **Stalls** Low

Form RPR
0 **1** **Imdancinwithurwife (IRE)**[16] 1118 2-9-0 0........... RichardKingscote 3 69
(Tom Dascombe) *mde all: rdn and hung lft ins fnl f: styd on* **16/1**
2 *1* **Rajar** 2-9-0 0... KieranO'Neill 7 65
(Richard Hannon) *hld up: hdwy over 1f out: rdn and nt clr run ins fnl f: r.o* **3/1**[2]
3 *1 ¼* **Kodi Da Capo (IRE)** 2-9-0 0... PhillipMakin 1 61
(Keith Dalgleish) *chsd ldrs: rdn over 1f out: styd on* **4/1**[3]
4 *hd* **Accladora** 2-9-0 0.. JoeFanning 4 60
(Mark Johnston) *chsd ldr: rdn and ev ch over 1f out: no ex ins fnl f* **3/1**[2]
5 *shd* **Hi Milady (IRE)** 2-9-0 0..................................... LiamKeniry 8 60+
(Dominic Ffrench Davis) *s.i.s: sn pushed along in rr: outpcd 2f out: r.o towards fin* **20/1**
4 **6** *¾* **Mesmeric Moment**[14] 1087 2-9-0 0............................ AndrewMullen 2 57
(David Evans) *prom: pushed along 1/2-way: no ex fnl f* **5/2**[1]
7 *½* **Roys Dream** 2-8-13 0 ow2.................................... JacobButterfield[(3)] 5 57
(Kristin Stubbs) *s.i.s: sn pushed along in rr: styd on ins fnl f: nt trble ldrs* **22/1**
1m 2.21s (0.31) **Going Correction** -0.125s/f (Stan) **7** Ran SP% **113.6**
Speed ratings (Par 89): **92,90,88,88,87 86,85**
CSF £62.68 TOTE £11.20: £4.20, £2.30; EX 43.20 Trifecta £141.40.
Owner Hong Kong Crew **Bred** Tally-Ho Stud **Trained** Malpas, Cheshire
■ Log Off (33-1) was withdrawn. Rule 4 does not apply.

FOCUS
Run in driving rain, they finished in a bit of a heap in behind the winner.

1343 #FOLLOWUS ON TWITTER @WOLVESRACES (S) H'CAP 1m 4f 50y (Tp)
7:20 (7:20) (Class 6) (0-60,58) 4-Y-O+ **£2,587** (£770; £384; £192) **Stalls** Low

Form RPR
-133 **1** **Yasir (USA)**[21] 1002 8-9-0 **58**...................................... SophieKilloran[(7)] 9 66
(Sophie Leech) *s.i.s: hld up: hdwy over 1f out: r.o to ld wl ins fnl f* **7/2**[2]
1066 **2** *1 ¼* **Easydoesit (IRE)**[8] 1182 8-8-12 **54**......................(p) EdwardGreatrex[(5)] 6 60
(Tony Carroll) *mid-div: hdwy on outer to ld 2f out: rdn and edgd lft over 1f out: hdd wl ins fnl f* **12/1**
4-50 **3** *hd* **Yourholidayisover (IRE)**[24] 949 9-8-10 **47**.............. DuranFentiman 3 54
(Patrick Holmes) *hld up: hdwy over 4f out: nt clr run and lost pl over 3f out: nt clr run and hmpd wl over 1f out: r.o wl ins fnl f* **22/1**
22 **4** *hd* **Let Me In (IRE)**[33] 862 6-9-7 **58**.....................................(v) MartinLane 5 63
(Bernard Llewellyn) *trckd ldrs: nt clr run over 2f out: rdn over 1f out: unable qck wl ins fnl f* **15/8**[1]
-665 **5** *1 ¼* **Chauvelin**[9] 1170 5-9-0 **51**.......................................(v) ConnorBeasley 10 54
(Richard Guest) *hld up: hdwy and hung lft fr over 1f out: nt rch ldrs* **7/1**[3]
0004 **6** *hd* **Cosette (IRE)**[25] 946 5-9-7 **58**.......................................(p) LiamKeniry 1 62
(Bernard Llewellyn) *mid-div: hdwy and nt clr run over 2f out: rdn over 1f out: styd on same pce ins fnl f* **14/1**
3500 **7** *shd* **Shirataki (IRE)**[24] 949 8-8-11 **53**................................ CiaranMckee[(5)] 2 56
(Peter Hiatt) *hld up: effrt over 1f out: nt trble ldrs* **25/1**
0-00 **8** *2 ¼* **Mac Tiernan (IRE)**[9] 1169 9-8-7 **49**................................. PhilDennis[(5)] 4 49
(Philip Kirby) *chsd ldrs: nt clr run over 2f out: swtchd lft over 1f out: wknd ins fnl f* **25/1**
5-02 **9** *1* **Rainford Glory (IRE)**[15] 1085 6-9-7 **58**......................... BarryMcHugh 7 56
(Tim Fitzgerald) *chsd ldr over 4f: remained handy: ev ch 2f out: sn rdn: wknd ins fnl f* **15/2**
0/0 **10** *9* **Virgil Earp**[17] 1035 9-8-10 **47**.. RyanPowell 11 30
(Ian Williams) *prom: chsd ldr over 7f out tl led over 2f out: sn hdd: wknd fnl f* **28/1**
00-0 **11** *2 ½* **Rebel Yell**[11] 1131 4-8-6 **47**.......................................(t) TomMarquand[(3)] 8 26
(Richard Price) *sn pushed along in rr: hdwy u.p on outer over 2f out: wknd wl over 1f out* **40/1**
/66- **12** *¾* **Red Skipper (IRE)**[281] 1750 11-8-8 **45**......................... CathyGannon 12 23
(John O'Shea) *sn led: hdd over 2f out: wknd over 1f out* **50/1**
2m 39.66s (-1.14) **Going Correction** -0.125s/f (Stan)
WFA 4 from 5yo+ 1lb **12** Ran SP% **115.5**
Speed ratings (Par 101): **98,97,97,96,96 95,95,94,93,87 86,85**
CSF £39.02 CT £802.63 TOTE £4.70: £1.70, £2.60, £5.10; EX 38.00 Trifecta £797.30.No bid for the winner.
Owner Mike Harris Racing Club **Bred** Shadwell Farm LLC **Trained** Elton, Gloucs

FOCUS
A moderate handicap.

1344 WOLVERHAMPTON-RACECOURSE.CO.UK H'CAP 1m 141y (Tp)
7:50 (7:50) (Class 3) (0-95,95) 4-Y-O **£7,246** (£2,168; £1,084; £542; £270) **Stalls** Low

Form RPR
512- **1** **Librisa Breeze**[182] 7119 4-9-4 **92**.. RobertWinston 3 104+
(Dean Ivory) *hld up: swtchd rt and hdwy over 1f out: hung lft and r.o to ld wl ins fnl f* **5/2**[2]
-466 **2** *1* **Capo Rosso (IRE)**[21] 1001 6-9-3 **91**........................ RichardKingscote 2 98
(Tom Dascombe) *led: rdn over 1f out: edgd rt and hdd wl ins fnl f* **11/2**[3]
-362 **3** *1 ¼* **Mont Ras (IRE)**[21] 1001 9-9-6 **94**................................ DougieCostello 5 98
(David Loughnane) *hld up in tch: rdn over 1f out: carried lft ins fnl f: styd on* **12/1**
10-1 **4** *hd* **Revolutionist (IRE)**[30] 886 4-9-7 **95**................................ JoeFanning 4 99
(Mark Johnston) *chsd ldrs: shkn up over 2f out: nt clr run ins fnl f: styd on same pce* **11/8**[1]
601- **5** *¾* **Secret Art (IRE)**[198] 6680 6-9-4 **92**................................... MartinHarley 7 94
(William Knight) *prom: lost pl 6f out: rdn over 2f out: styd on towards fin* **11/1**
530- **6** *½* **Aqua Ardens (GER)**[124] 8132 8-8-13 **87**..........................(t) LiamKeniry 1 88
(George Baker) *hld up: hdwy over 1f out: sn rdn: no ex ins fnl f* **40/1**

2-35 **7** *3 ¾* **Ready (IRE)**[21] 1001 6-9-0 **88**..................................(p) SilvestreDeSousa 6 80
(Ivan Furtado) *chsd ldr: rdn over 2f out: wknd ins fnl f* **6/1**
1m 46.05s (-4.05) **Going Correction** -0.125s/f (Stan) course record **7** Ran SP% **118.8**
Speed ratings (Par 107): **113,112,111,110,110 109,106**
CSF £17.68 TOTE £3.90: £2.90, £2.90; EX 19.30 Trifecta £227.40.
Owner Tony Bloom **Bred** Newsells Park Stud **Trained** Radlett, Herts
■ Stewards' Enquiry : Richard Kingscote caution; careless ridng

FOCUS
A decent handicap won in great style. The form is rated around the second and third.

1345 LIKE WOLVERHAMPTON RACECOURSE ON FACEBOOK H'CAP 7f 32y (Tp)
8:20 (8:21) (Class 5) (0-75,71) 3-Y-O **£3,234** (£962; £481; £240) **Stalls** High

Form RPR
502- **1** **Be Kool (IRE)**[165] 7540 3-9-3 **67**.. BenCurtis 5 70+
(Brian Ellison) *hld up: pushed along over 2f out: rdn and nt clr run ins fnl f: r.o to ld towards fin* **7/2**[2]
21 **2** *½* **Magical Path (IRE)**[22] 984 3-9-7 **71**.............................. MartinHarley 4 72
(Hugo Palmer) *chsd ldr: led over 1f out: sn rdn: edgd rt ins fnl f: hdd towards fin* **5/6**[1]
505- **3** *½* **Kingthistle**[247] 5050 3-8-11 **68**.. NathanEvans[(7)] 2 68
(Michael Easterby) *led: shkn up over 2f out: hdd over 1f out: rdn and ev ch ins fnl f: styd on* **6/1**[3]
405- **4** *nse* **Protest (IRE)**[148] 7823 3-9-1 **65**... LiamKeniry 6 64
(Sylvester Kirk) *a.p: rdn over 1f out: bmpd ins fnl f: styd on* **8/1**
330- **5** *2* **Indie Music**[182] 7112 3-9-0 **67**....................................... TomMarquand[(3)] 1 61
(Sylvester Kirk) *chsd ldrs: rdn over 1f out: no ex ins fnl f* **12/1**
1m 28.32s (-0.48) **Going Correction** -0.125s/f (Stan) **5** Ran SP% **109.9**
Speed ratings (Par 98): **97,96,95,95,93**
CSF £6.87 TOTE £4.00: £1.60, £1.10; EX 8.30 Trifecta £21.00.
Owner Market Avenue Racing & Brian Ellison **Bred** E Lonergan **Trained** Norton, N Yorks

FOCUS
There was a bunched finish to this modest handicap, but the winner looks one to keep on side. The runner-up was close to her maiden form.

1346 AWARD WINNING FINE DINING AT HORIZONS MAIDEN FILLIES' STKS 1m 4f 50y (Tp)
8:50 (8:50) (Class 5) 3-Y-O+ **£3,234** (£962; £481; £240) **Stalls** Low

Form RPR
-363 **1** **Rock 'n Red (IRE)**[9] 1163 3-8-7 65.......................... SilvestreDeSousa 3 69
(Ed Dunlop) *trckd ldrs: rdn to chse ldr over 1f out: edgd lft and styd on u.p to ld nr fin* **7/4**[1]
2 *½* **Introductory (IRE)** 3-8-7 0... JoeFanning 4 68
(Mark Johnston) *chsd ldr after 1f tl shkn up to ld wl over 1f out: edgd lft ins fnl f: hdd nr fin* **13/2**[3]
03 **3** *2 ¾* **Ms Gillard**[44] 706 3-8-7 0... CathyGannon 2 64
(David Simcock) *chsd ldrs: rdn over 2f out: styd on* **12/1**
5 **4** *2 ¼* **Princess Roania (IRE)**[10] 1140 5-10-0 0.......................... SamJames 1 62
(Peter Bowen) *hld up: rdn over 2f out: nvr nrr* **8/1**
5 **5** *½* **Cosmic Tigress**[38] 789 5-10-0 0.. PhillipMakin 6 61
(John Quinn) *led: rdn and hdd over 1f out: wknd ins fnl f* **15/2**
303- **6** *hd* **Forgiving Flower**[157] 7699 3-8-7 67.. BenCurtis 7 59
(K R Burke) *hld up in tch: rdn over 2f out: wkng whn edgd lft fnl f* **3/1**[2]
7 *5* **Cetta's Hill** 3-8-7 0.. CamHardie 5 51
(Stuart Edmunds) *s.i.s: hld up: rdn over 2f out: wknd over 1f out* **25/1**
2m 40.62s (-0.18) **Going Correction** -0.125s/f (Stan)
WFA 3 from 5yo 21lb **7** Ran SP% **109.1**
Speed ratings (Par 100): **95,94,92,91,91 90,87**
CSF £12.29 TOTE £2.70: £1.90, £3.60; EX 12.50 Trifecta £71.80.
Owner The Hon R J Arculli **Bred** The Hon R J Arculli **Trained** Newmarket, Suffolk

FOCUS
Modest and muddling maiden form.

1347 HOTEL & RACING PACKAGES AVAILABLE H'CAP 1m 4f 50y (Tp)
9:20 (9:20) (Class 5) (0-70,68) 4-Y-O+ **£3,234** (£962; £481; £240) **Stalls** Low

Form RPR
250- **1** **Fast Pick (IRE)**[182] 7110 4-8-13 **61**.................................(p) PhillipMakin 3 74+
(Keith Dalgleish) *chsd ldr tl led over 2f out: clr over 1f out: easily* **11/1**
4522 **2** *2 ½* **Cartographic (USA)**[22] 982 4-8-13 **61**.................. SilvestreDeSousa 11 67
(David Evans) *hld up: hdwy u.p over 1f out: styd on to go 2nd wl ins fnl f: no ch w wnr* **9/4**[1]
2442 **3** *1 ¾* **Comanche Chieftain (CAN)**[18] 1028 4-9-6 **68**.........(p) AndrewMullen 9 71
(Michael Appleby) *led: rdn and hdd over 2f out: no ex fnl f* **5/1**[3]
4353 **4** *½* **Lean On Pete (IRE)**[13] 1114 7-9-3 **67**..................(b) JacobButterfield[(3)] 4 69
(Ollie Pears) *hld up: hdwy over 1f out: nt rch ldrs* **11/4**[2]
66-0 **5** *3 ¼* **Saint Thomas (IRE)**[16] 1057 9-8-12 **59**................................ BenCurtis 5 56
(John Mackie) *chsd ldrs: rdn over 1f out: wknd fnl f* **22/1**
02-0 **6** *shd* **Frantical**[99] 2 4-8-9 **57**.. CathyGannon 1 54
(Tony Carroll) *plld hrd and prom: rdn over 1f out: wknd fnl f* **28/1**
-444 **7** *1 ½* **Nolecce**[15] 1085 9-8-7 **57**... RobHornby[(3)] 7 52
(Tony Forbes) *prom: lost pl over 3f out: wknd over 2f out* **14/1**
-602 **8** *shd* **Wildomar**[45] 693 7-9-1 **62**.. ShaneGray 6 56
(Peter Hiatt) *hld up: rdn over 2f out: nvr on terms* **12/1**
0110 **9** *2 ¼* **Pao De Acuca (IRE)**[17] 819 4-9-0 **67**.................(t) EdwardGreatrex[(5)] 2 58
(Jose Santos) *hld up: hdwy over 4f out: hung rt over 3f out: sn wknd* **10/1**
2m 39.57s (-1.23) **Going Correction** -0.125s/f (Stan)
WFA 4 from 6yo+ 1lb **9** Ran SP% **113.7**
Speed ratings (Par 103): **99,97,96,95,93 93,92,92,91**
CSF £35.49 CT £142.20 TOTE £10.90: £3.40, £1.10, £1.60; EX 46.60 Trifecta £166.50.
Owner Ronnie Docherty **Bred** Philip Brady **Trained** Carluke, S Lanarks

FOCUS
A modest affair won by a filly who is nicely ahead of her mark for her new yard.
T/Plt: £197.10 to a £1 stake. Pool: £78,761.99 - 291.64 winning tickets. T/Qpdt: £20.40 to £1 stake. Pool: £8,355.06 - 302.2 winning tickets. **Colin Roberts**

1348 - 1356a (Foreign Racing) - See Raceform Interactive

COMPIEGNE (L-H)
Saturday, April 9

OFFICIAL GOING: Turf: very soft

1357a PRIX DE MERCIERES (MAIDEN) (3YO FILLIES) (TURF) 1m
3:15 (12:00) 3-Y-O **£9,191** (£3,676; £2,757; £1,838; £919)

RPR
1 **Toinette (IRE)**[170] 3-9-0 0................................... Pierre-CharlesBoudot 3
(H-A Pantall, France) **8/5**[1]

2 *1* **Karbayane (FR)**119 3-9-0 0 GregoryBenoist 4
(J-M Beguigne, France) **11/1**
3 *3* **Phoenix Beat**22 984 3-9-0 0 ChristopheSoumillon 11
(Gay Kelleway) *a cl up: shkn up to ld appr 2f out: rdn whn chal under 1 1/2f out: hdd ent fnl f: no ex* **31/5**3
4 *nk* **Flemish Duchesse (FR)** 3-9-0 0 IoritzMendizabal 13
(Andreas Lowe, Germany) **31/10**2
5 *1 1/2* **Reine Gianna (FR)**18 3-9-0 0 CristianDemuro 5
(G Botti, France) **32/5**
6 *3/4* **Ibiza Empress (IRE)** 3-9-0 0 FilipMinarik 12
(C Von Der Recke, Germany) **13/1**
7 *2 1/2* **Meadra (FR)** 3-9-0 0 SebastienMaillot 2
(E Caroux, France) **27/1**
8 *1 1/2* **Nella Di Roma (GER)** 3-8-10 0 AlexanderPietsch 1
(J Hirschberger, Germany) **29/1**
9 *snk* **Amalina (FR)**44 716 3-9-0 0 AnthonyCrastus 9
(N Caullery, France) **20/1**
10 *4* **Valentine Conde (FR)**137 3-9-0 0 MickaelBarzalona 8
(R Chotard, France) **16/1**
11 *6* **Sainte Helene (IRE)**25 3-9-0 0 MarcLerner 10
(C Lerner, France) **42/1**

WIN (incl. 1 euro stake): 2.60. PLACES: 1.50, 2.80, 2.20. DF: 12.60. SF: 15.70.
Owner Rothschild Family **Bred** Famille Rothschild **Trained** France

1358 - 1368a (Foreign Racing) - See Raceform Interactive

1277 LEOPARDSTOWN (L-H)
Sunday, April 10

OFFICIAL GOING: Heavy (soft in places)

1369a LEOPARDSTOWN 1,000 GUINEAS TRIAL STKS (GROUP 3) 7f
3:15 (3:15) 3-Y-O

£26,029 (£8,382; £3,970; £1,764; £882; £441)

RPR
1 **Jet Setting (IRE)**15 1096 3-9-0 97 ShaneFoley 3 112
(Adrian Paul Keatley, Ire) *mde all: 2 l clr at 1/2-way: stl gng wl into st: rdn 1 1/2f out and kpt on wl u.p ins fnl f* **11/2**2
2 *3* **Now Or Never (IRE)**210 6361 3-9-0 104 KierenFallon 5 104
(M D O'Callaghan, Ire) *settled bhd ldr: rdn in 2nd into st and no imp on wnr clr of remainder ins fnl f: kpt on same pce* **7/1**3
3 *2 3/4* **Alice Springs (IRE)**163 7626 3-9-0 112 RyanMoore 1 96+
(A P O'Brien, Ire) *w.w: disp 6th at 1/2-way: plenty to do into st: impr under hands and heels between horses into mod 3rd 1 1/2f out: no imp on wnr ins fnl f: kpt on* **5/4**1
4 *3* **Radiantly**196 6791 3-9-0 103 BillyLee 9 88+
(W McCreery, Ire) *w.w: disp 6th at 1/2-way: rdn into st and no imp on ldrs under 2f out: kpt on one pce in mod 4th ins fnl f* **9/1**
5 *1 3/4* **Red Stars (IRE)**182 7150 3-9-0 93 DeclanMcDonogh 6 84+
(John M Oxx, Ire) *chsd ldrs: 5th 1/2-way: pushed along in 4th into st and no imp on ldrs u.p 1 1/2f out: kpt on one pce in mod 5th ins fnl f* **12/1**
6 *4 3/4* **Miss Elizabeth (IRE)**210 6364 3-9-0 104 WayneLordan 2 71+
(Edward Lynam, Ire) *dwlt and settled in rr: last at 1/2-way: pushed along bef st and no imp in mod 8th under 2f out: kpt on ins fnl f: nvr nrr* **33/1**
7 *3/4* **Ceol An Ghra (IRE)**7 1224 3-9-0 88 RonanWhelan 4 69+
(J S Bolger, Ire) *chsd ldrs: racd keenly early: 4th 1/2-way: rdn and no imp on ldrs over 2f out: wknd over 1f out* **20/1**
8 *4 3/4* **Queen Of Sicily (USA)**267 4411 3-9-0 0 KevinManning 10 56+
(J S Bolger, Ire) *chsd ldrs: racd keenly early: pushed along in 3rd appr st and sn no ex: wknd fr 2f out: eased ins fnl f* **14/1**
9 *19* **Juliette Fair (IRE)**194 6843 3-9-0 103 PatSmullen 8 5+
(D K Weld, Ire) *a bhd: 8th 1/2-way: pushed along in rr under 2f out and no imp: eased fnl f* **7/1**3

1m 34.79s (6.09) **Going Correction** +1.15s/f (Soft) **9** Ran SP% **116.9**
Speed ratings: **111,107,104,101,99 93,92,87,65**
CSF £44.18 TOTE £5.60: £2.00, £2.50, £1.02; DF 41.90 Trifecta £111.60.
Owner Adrian Paul Keatley **Bred** P Kelly **Trained** Friarstown, Co. Kildare

FOCUS
Ability to handle the ground was a key thing here, while the winner has shown both that and was fit from action. Shane Foley has ridden winners from the front in trial races around here before and he was obviously keen to make fitness count. The winner earned a pb.

1370a P.W. MCGRATH MEMORIAL BALLYSAX STKS (GROUP 3) 1m 2f
3:50 (3:50) 3-Y-O

£26,029 (£8,382; £3,970; £1,764; £882; £441)

RPR
1 **Harzand (IRE)**15 1100 3-9-3 0 PatSmullen 4 118+
(D K Weld, Ire) *chsd ldrs: disp 5th at 1/2-way: tk clsr order bhd ldrs on outer over 1f out and rdn into 2nd ins fnl f: styd on wl to ld ins fnl 100yds* **2/1**1
2 *1 1/4* **Idaho (IRE)**161 7666 3-9-3 0 ColmO'Donoghue 1 115+
(A P O'Brien, Ire) *upset in stalls: settled in rr: last at 1/2-way: hdwy on outer appr st and rdn to ld 1 1/2f out: strly pressed u.p wl ins fnl f and hdd ins fnl 100yds: no ex* **8/1**
3 *7 1/2* **Beacon Rock (IRE)**183 7113 3-9-3 110 SeamieHeffernan 7 100
(A P O'Brien, Ire) *chsd ldrs on outer and impr into 2nd after 1f: rdn in 2nd under 3f out and disp briefly into st: sn hdd and no ex whn sltly impeded between horses over 1f out: kpt on one pce in mod 3rd ins fnl f* **8/1**
4 *2 3/4* **Cook Islands (IRE)**186 7050 3-9-3 0 RyanMoore 2 94
(A P O'Brien, Ire) *hld up: disp 5th at 1/2-way: impr into 4th gng wl under 3f out: rdn in cl 3rd under 2f out and no imp on ldrs ent fnl f: kpt on one pce in mod 4th ins fnl f* **5/2**2
5 *3* **Moonlight Magic**168 7492 3-9-3 0 KevinManning 5 88
(J S Bolger, Ire) *hld up bhd ldrs: 4th 1/2-way: clsr in 3rd fr 3f out: disp briefly 2f out tl sn hdd and no ex far side over 1f out: wknd* **3/1**3
6 *13* **Theodorico (IRE)**21 1017 3-9-3 86 RonanWhelan 6 62
(J S Bolger, Ire) *broke wl to ld tl sn jnd briefly: over 1 l clr at 1/2-way: pushed along fr 4f out and jnd u.p into st: hdd far side 2f out and wknd* **25/1**
7 *28* **Play The Game (IRE)**175 7319 3-9-3 100 ShaneFoley 3 6
(John C McConnell, Ire) *disp early briefly tl settled bhd ldrs in 3rd: pushed along and lost pl fr 3f out: sn wknd: eased under 2f out: t.o* **50/1**

2m 19.11s (10.91) **Going Correction** +1.40s/f (Soft) **7** Ran SP% **114.9**
Speed ratings: **112,111,105,102,100 90,67**
CSF £19.08 TOTE £2.80: £1.40, £3.40; DF 14.60 Trifecta £67.90.
Owner H H Aga Khan **Bred** His Highness The Aga Khan's Studs S C **Trained** Curragh, Co Kildare

FOCUS
An intriguing enough Ballysax run on ground nothing like what any of these might face at Epsom. The market was somewhat muddied and the Ballydoyle horses did not perform relative to each other as what the market expected. Two of the rags helped to dicate the pace and the first two finished clear.

1371 - 1373a (Foreign Racing) - See Raceform Interactive

1284 CHANTILLY (R-H)
Sunday, April 10

OFFICIAL GOING: Turf: heavy; polytrack: standard
Meeting switched from Longchamp, which is being redeveloped.

1374a PRIX SIGY (GROUP 3) (3YO) (TURF) 6f
3:15 (12:00) 3-Y-O **£29,411** (£11,764; £8,823; £5,882; £2,941)

RPR
1 **Quiet Reflection**184 7072 3-8-11 0 DougieCostello 10 109
(K R Burke) *t.k.h: hld up bhd ldrs: shkn up and qcknd to ld under 1 1/2f out: drvn clr ent fnl f: hld on gamely u.p* **7/2**2
2 *hd* **Jimmy Two Times (FR)**162 7661 3-8-11 0 VincentCheminaud 11 109+
(A Fabre, France) *w.w in midfield: rdn and hdwy wl over 1f out: styd on strly fnl f: jst failed* **9/1**
3 *1/2* **Post Var (FR)**24 972 3-8-11 0 TheoBachelot 2 107
(S Wattel, France) *hld up towards rr: hdwy into midfield 1/2-way: rdn to chse ldrs over 1f out: styd on u.p: nt pce to chal* **33/1**
4 *2 1/2* **Sangria (SPA)**23 3-8-11 0 IoritzMendizabal 13 99
(F Chappet, France) *front rnk: wnt on bef 1/2-way: rdn appr 1 1/2f out and nt qckn: sn hdd by eventual wnr: kpt on at same pce tl fdd cl home* **16/1**
5 *1 3/4* **Mangusto (FR)**30 3-8-11 0 OlivierPeslier 5 93
(M Delcher Sanchez, France) *tk a t.k.h: hld up towards rr: rdn 2 1/2f out: hdwy on wd outside under 1 1/2f out: styd on ins fnl f: nt pce to get on terms* **25/1**
6 *1 3/4* **Saryshagann (FR)**23 3-8-11 0 ChristopheSoumillon 12 87
(J-C Rouget, France) *w.w towards rr: hdwy into midfield on outer bef 1/2-way: no further prog fr 1 1/2f out: one pce ins fnl f* **9/4**1
7 *snk* **Sasparella (FR)**202 6610 3-8-11 0 MaximeGuyon 6 87
(C Laffon-Parias, France) *cl up: rdn and chsd ldrs 1 1/2f out: no ex u.p ent fnl f and sn dropped away* **9/2**3
8 *1 1/4* **Nordic Dream (IRE)**184 7102 3-8-11 0 Pierre-CharlesBoudot 4 83
(A Fabre, France) *w.w towards rr: hdwy into midfield whn scrubbed along bef 1/2-way: no further imp fr 1 1/2f out: one pce fnl f* **18/1**
9 *1/2* **Risk Major (FR)**9 3-8-11 0 RonanThomas 8 81
(J Phelippon, France) *front rnk: hdd bef 1/2-way: sn rdn and no imp: wknd fnl f* **12/1**
10 *1* **Sao Tome (FR)**30 3-8-8 0 AntoineHamelin 1 75
(C Lerner, France) *broke wl: hld up in midfield on inner: dropped to rr bef 1/2-way: rdn and styd on fr 1 1/2f out: run flattened out fnl 150yds* **50/1**
11 *4* **Noce (FR)**23 3-8-8 0 CristianDemuro 14 62
(C Baillet, France) *cl up on outer: scrubbed along to hold pl 2 1/2f out: grad dropped away fnl 1 1/2f* **16/1**
12 *hd* **Dhevanafushi**24 972 3-8-11 0 FabriceVeron 9 65
(H-A Pantall, France) *w.w in midfield: pushed along sn after 1/2-way: rdn and wknd wl over 1f out* **20/1**
13 *8* **Exceed The Limit**23 3-8-11 0 (b) MickaelBarzalona 7 39
(H-A Pantall, France) *front rnk: rdn and hdd bef 1/2-way: wknd fnl 1 1/2f: wl bhd fnl f* **33/1**
14 *7* **Aboulie (IRE)**162 7660 3-8-11 0 AlexisBadel 3 17
(J-C Rouget, France) *played up in stalls: broke wl and chsd ldrs: rdr lost stirrup and sddle slipped ins first f: lost pl sn after 1/2-way: wl bhd fnl 1 1/2f* **17/2**

1m 13.16s (1.76) **14** Ran SP% **132.9**
PARI-MUTEUL (all including 1 euro stake) WIN 5.40; PLACE 2.20, 3.20, 6.90; DF 26.20; SF 40.20.

Owner Ontoawinner, Strecker & Burke **Bred** Springcombe Park Stud **Trained** Middleham Moor, N Yorks

1375a PRIX D'HARCOURT (GROUP 2) (4YO+) (TURF) 1m 2f
3:45 (12:00) 4-Y-O+ **£54,485** (£21,029; £10,036; £6,691; £3,345)

RPR
1 **Garlingari (FR)**21 1023 5-8-11 0 (p) StephanePasquier 2 117
(Mme C Barande-Barbe, France) *t.k.h: hld up in 3rd: shkn up to press ldr 2f out: rdn to ld 1 1/2f out and jinked rt appr fnl f: drvn clr fnl 150yds: readily* **10/1**
2 *3 1/2* **Sumbal (IRE)**21 1023 4-9-1 0 OisinMurphy 11 114+
(F-H Graffard, France) *w.w in fnl pair: rdn 2 1/2f out: hdwy on outer fr 1 1/2f out: styd on wl u.p fnl f: tk 2nd last 30yds: no ch w wnr* **8/1**
3 *nk* **Affaire Solitaire (IRE)**21 1023 6-8-11 0 OlivierPeslier 8 109
(P Khozian, France) *w.w in midfield on outer: shkn up and gd hdwy 1 1/2f out: rdn to chse ldr ent fnl f: unable to get on terms and grad lft bhd: lost 2nd fnl 30yds* **11/1**
4 *3/4* **Siljan's Saga (FR)**168 7502 6-8-11 0 Pierre-CharlesBoudot 7 108+
(J-P Gauvin, France) *hld up towards rr: rdn and n.m.r wl over 1 1/2f out: nt clr run and impeded 1f out: styd on wl fnl 125yds* **17/2**
5 *1* **Ming Dynasty (FR)**119 8216 4-9-1 0 UmbertoRispoli 10 110+
(M Delzangles, France) *w.w in fnl pair: swtchd outside and hdwy wl over 1 1/2f out: styd on u.p fnl f: nrest at fin* **6/1**3
6 *1/2* **Wild Chief (GER)**190 6956 5-9-1 0 AlexanderPietsch 9 109+
(J Hirschberger, Germany) *w.w towards rr: rdn to make prog on outer 2f out: run flattened out fnl f* **40/1**
7 *3/4* **Silverwave (FR)**189 6970 4-8-11 0 MaximeGuyon 3 103
(P Bary, France) *led: rdn whn pressed 2f out: hdd 1 1/2f out: dropped away fnl f* **11/1**
8 *nk* **Karaktar (IRE)**204 6555 4-8-11 0 ChristopheSoumillon 12 102
(A De Royer-Dupre, France) *t.k.h early: hld up in tch on outer: chsd ldr after 4f: cl 3rd and travelling wl 2f out: sn rdn and fnd little: wknd fnl f* **11/4**1
9 *hd* **Harlem**260 4665 4-8-11 0 VincentCheminaud 6 102
(A Fabre, France) *w.w cl up: rdn and no imp 2f out: n.m.r under 1 1/2f out and shuffled bk: kpt on at same pce* **18/1**
10 *1 3/4* **Beautiful Heroine (IRE)**154 7767 5-8-8 0 GregoryBenoist 1 96
(F-H Graffard, France) *w.w in midfield on inner: rdn to chse ldng gp over 1 1/2f out: n.m.r and hmpd 1f out: effrt and nt clr run sn after: nt rcvr* **28/1**

11 *8* **Free Port Lux**21 1023 5-9-1 0 ThierryJarnet 5 87
(F Head, France) *w.w in midfield: rdn and no imp fr 2f out: wknd 1f out and sn eased* **8/1**
12 *16* **Ampere (FR)**239 5412 4-9-1 0 MickaelBarzalona 4 55
(A Fabre, France) *w.w towards rr: rdn and no hdwy 2f out: sn lost tch and eased* **7/2**2

2m 7.03s (2.23) **12** Ran SP% **132.8**
PARI-MUTUEL (all including 1 euro stake) WIN 10.00; PLACE 3.50, 3.70, 3.50; DF 55.30; SF 115.90.
Owner Mme Corine Barande-Barbe **Bred** Mme C Barande Barbe & Mme J J Massy **Trained** France

FOCUS
It proved hard to make ground.

DUSSELDORF (R-H)
Sunday, April 10

OFFICIAL GOING: Turf: soft

1376a XTIP FRUHJAHRSMEILE (GROUP 3) (4YO+) (TURF) 1m
4:25 (12:00) 4-Y-O+ **£23,529** (£8,823; £4,411; £2,205; £1,470)

RPR
1 **Guiliani (IRE)**154 7767 5-9-6 0 FilipMinarik 6 115+
(Jean-Pierre Carvalho, Germany) *w.w in midfield: shkn up and gd hdwy over 1 1/2f out: rdn and r.o fnl f: led cl home* **5/2**2
2 *3/4* **Lucky Lion**38 804 5-8-11 0 AdriedeVries 2 102
(Andreas Lowe, Germany) *trckd ldr on inner: rdn to ld appr fnl f: r.o u.p: hdd cl home* **11/10**1
3 *1 1/2* **Diplomat (GER)**29 931 5-9-0 0 EduardoPedroza 7 102
(Mario Hofer, Germany) *led: kicked 2 1/2 l clr appr 2f out: styd on u.p: hdd appr fnl f: kpt on gamely u.p* **10/1**
4 *2 3/4* **Nordico (GER)**154 7769 5-9-2 0 (p) AndreasSuborics 5 97
(Mario Hofer, Germany) *hld up in fnl pair: rdn and effrt wl over 1 1/2f out: kpt on u.p fnl f: nt pce to get on terms* **36/5**
5 *2 1/2* **Weltmacht**168 7498 5-8-10 0 MartinSeidl 1 85
(Markus Klug, Germany) *chsd ldrs on inner: rdn and nt qckn wl over 1 1/2f out: sn lft bhd* **91/10**
6 *5* **Drummer (GER)**124 4-9-0 0 AndraschStarke 4 78
(P Schiergen, Germany) *chsd ldrs on outer: rdn and no imp over 1 1/2f out: wknd ins fnl f* **49/10**3
7 *1/2* **Molly Le Clou (GER)**24 4-9-0 0 JackMitchell 3 77
(J Hirschberger, Germany) *w.w in fnl pair: rdn and no imp over 2f out: nvr in contention* **99/10**

1m 44.62s (3.46) **7** Ran SP% **133.5**
TOTE WIN (incl. 10 euro stake) 35; PLACES 15, 12; SF 71.
Owner Stall Ullmann **Bred** G Baron Von Ullmann **Trained** Germany

1119 REDCAR (L-H)
Monday, April 11

OFFICIAL GOING: Heavy (soft in places; 6.5)
Wind: light 1/2 across Weather: fine and sunny

1377 RACING UK DAY PASS JUST £10 NOVICE STKS 5f
2:00 (2:01) (Class 5) 2-Y-O **£2,911** (£866; £432; £216) **Stalls** High

Form RPR
0 1 **Cullingworth (IRE)**17 1082 2-9-2 0 TonyHamilton 2 72
(Richard Fahey) *chsd ldrs: drvn over 1f out: styd on to ld last 50yds* **14/1**
4 2 *1/2* **Merry Banter**17 1082 2-8-11 0 GrahamLee 3 65
(Paul Midgley) *led: drvn over 1f out: hdd and no ex last 50yds* **15/2**
3 *1 3/4* **Another Angel (IRE)** 2-9-2 0 PaulMulrennan 5 64+
(Michael Dods) *dwlt: swtchd lft after s: rn green: hung lft and sn wl outpcd: detached whn hung bdly lft 3f out: hdwy 2f out: styd on to take 3rd last 150yds: will be bttr for experience* **6/4**1
3 4 *11* **Monte Cinq (IRE)**9 1199 2-9-2 0 AndrewMullen 4 24
(Jason Ward) *chsd ldrs: drvn 2f out: lost pl over 1f out* **2/1**2
5 *17* **Mulwith (IRE)** 2-9-2 0 GrahamGibbons 1
(David Barron) *wnt lft s: sn chsng ldrs: wknd 2f out: bhd whn heavily eased last 100yds* **9/2**3

1m 6.86s (8.26) **Going Correction** +1.425s/f (Soft) **5** Ran SP% **109.9**
Speed ratings (Par 92): **90,89,86,68,41**
CSF £98.96 TOTE £9.10: £4.40, £2.90; EX 51.90 Trifecta £248.40.
Owner Tiffin Sandwiches Limited & Partner **Bred** John Foley **Trained** Musley Bank, N Yorks

FOCUS
The going was given as heavy, soft in places (GoingStick: 6.5), and the time of this 2yo contest was almost 10sec above standard. The level is very fluid.

1378 WATCH RACING UK ANYWHERE (S) STKS 5f
2:30 (2:30) (Class 6) 3-Y-O+ **£2,385** (£704; £352) **Stalls** High

Form RPR
25-3 1 **Mitchum**14 1120 7-9-4 52 (p) PhilDennis(5) 3 72
(Ron Barr) *chsd clr ldr: edgd rt over 1f out: led last 150yds: forged clr* **4/1**3
0-40 2 *7* **New Lease Of Life**14 1120 7-9-12 64 (v1) JasonHart 2 50
(Keith Dalgleish) *led: swtchd rt after s: clr over 3f out: hdd last 150yds: rallied to claim modest 2nd nr fin* **6/1**
60-6 3 *1/2* **Mighty Bond**88 177 4-9-9 49 ConnorBeasley 4 45
(Tracy Waggott) *chsd clr ldr: 2nd last 75yds: lost pl nr fin* **25/1**
410- 4 *1 3/4* **Go Go Green (IRE)**181 7188 10-9-12 73 DanielTudhope 6 42
(Jim Goldie) *hld up towards rr: swtchd rt over 1f out: kpt on: nvr a factor* **5/2**1
505- 5 *5* **Rasaman (IRE)**195 6831 12-9-7 73 JoshDoyle(5) 7 24
(Jim Goldie) *chsd ldrs: drvn over 2f out: wknd over 1f out* **9/2**
206- 6 *6* **Rothesay Chancer**265 4483 8-9-12 80 JackGarritty 5
(Jim Goldie) *chsd ldrs: effrt over 2f out: lost pl over 1f out* **3/1**2
505- 7 *11* **Glen Lea (IRE)**209 6398 7-9-4 50 GarryWhillans(5) 1
(Kenny Johnson) *s.i.s: drvn to chse ldrs over 3f out: wknd 2f out: eased whn bhd clsng stages* **33/1**

1m 5.14s (6.54) **Going Correction** +1.425s/f (Soft) **7** Ran SP% **112.8**
Speed ratings (Par 101): **104,92,92,89,81 71,54**
CSF £27.02 TOTE £4.80: £2.30, £3.40; EX 31.90 Trifecta £361.70.No bid for the winner.
Owner P Cartmell **Bred** Conor J C Parsons & Brian M Parsons **Trained** Seamer, N Yorks

FOCUS
With the three highest rated horses all running below their best this took little winning. The winner has been rated up on his form from the recent year, and he could be a good bit better, but this is not totally reliable.

1379 BECOME AN ANNUAL BADGE HOLDER TODAY MEDIAN AUCTION MAIDEN STKS 1m 1f
3:00 (3:01) (Class 5) 3-4-Y-O **£2,911** (£866; £432; £216) **Stalls** Low

Form RPR
-334 1 **Albert Boy (IRE)**9 1200 3-8-11 68 BenCurtis 4 69
(Scott Dixon) *led over 1f: trckd ldr: led 4f out: styd on wl appr fnl f: drvn out* **10/11**1
- 2 *2 1/2* **Phantom Dancer (IRE)** 4-9-9 0 NeilFarley 2 62+
(Alan Swinbank) *trckd ldr: led over 7f out: hdd 4f out: outpcd 2f out: 5th and swtchd outside over 1f out: rallied to take 2nd nr fin* **15/2**
3 *1/2* **Jasper Jay** 3-8-11 0 DuranFentiman 3 61
(Tony Coyle) *hld up in rr: hdwy on ins over 3f out: swtchd outside over 2f out: hung lft and chsd wnr over 1f out: kpt on same pce* **28/1**
536- 4 *3 1/4* **The Excel Queen (IRE)**189 6977 3-8-6 59 BarryMcHugh 5 49
(Tony Coyle) *trckd ldrs: drvn over 4f out: 2nd over 2f out: one pce* **6/1**3
6-4 5 *3/4* **Bradleysintown (IRE)**14 1123 3-8-11 0 ConnorBeasley 1 55
(Michael Dods) *trckd ldrs: t.k.h: drvn over 2f out: one pce* **5/2**2
/04- 6 *29* **Charlie's Approval (IRE)**270 4308 4-9-9 40 DougieCostello 6
(Ben Haslam) *hld up in rr: effrt over 3f out: lost pl over 2f out: sn bhd: heavily eased clsng stages: virtually p.u: t.o* **50/1**

2m 6.41s (13.41) **Going Correction** +1.60s/f (Heav)
WFA 3 from 4yo 17lb **6** Ran SP% **112.4**
Speed ratings (Par 103): **104,101,101,98,97 72**
CSF £8.80 TOTE £1.90: £1.30, £2.90; EX 7.80 Trifecta £88.90.
Owner J Radford **Bred** Clare Castle Farm **Trained** Babworth, Notts

FOCUS
A modest maiden. It's been rated around the winner.

1380 RACING UK PROFITS RETURNED TO RACING H'CAP 1m
3:30 (3:30) (Class 4) (0-85,85) 4-Y-O+ **£6,469** (£1,925; £962; £481) **Stalls** Centre

Form RPR
330- 1 **Imshivalla (IRE)**144 7899 5-9-7 85 GeorgeChaloner 2 93
(Richard Fahey) *trckd ldrs: edgd lft and led over 1f out: drvn out* **4/1**1
05-0 2 *2 1/4* **Abushamah (IRE)**14 1122 5-9-2 80 JamesSullivan 7 83
(Ruth Carr) *hld up in rr: hdwy over 2f out: styd on to take 2nd towards fin* **5/1**2
006- 3 *nk* **Kalk Bay (IRE)**140 7959 9-8-13 77 (t) PaulMulrennan 4 79
(Michael Easterby) *w ldrs: effrt 2f out: kpt on same pce fnl f* **10/1**
422- 4 *2* **Mystic Miraaj**170 7464 4-8-11 75 (p) DavidAllan 10 73+
(Tim Easterby) *w ldrs: t.k.h: led over 2f out: hdd over 1f out: wknd fnl 75yds* **4/1**1
060- 5 *3 1/4* **Osteopathic Remedy (IRE)**207 6455 12-8-13 77 PhillipMakin 9 68
(John Davies) *chsd ldrs: outpcd over 3f out: hdwy over 1f out: one pce* **16/1**
021- 6 *5* **Miss Van Gogh**164 7598 4-8-11 82 HayleyIrvine(7) 8 62
(Richard Fahey) *chsd ldrs: effrt over 2f out: lost pl over 1f out* **7/1**3
142/ 7 *1/2* **Shouranour (IRE)**520 7719 6-9-2 85 (p) JoshDoyle(5) 6 64
(Alan Brown) *led: hdd over 2f out: lost pl over 1f out* **11/1**
150- 8 *19* **Genres**297 3354 4-9-4 82 BenCurtis 5 19
(Alan Swinbank) *hld up towards rr: hdwy over 2f out: wknd qckly over 1f out: t.o* **10/1**
-161 9 *27* **Ziggys Star**70 414 4-8-13 77 AndrewMullen 1
(Michael Appleby) *wnt lft s: sn chsng ldrs: lost pl and eased 2f out: virtually p.u: t.o* **9/1**
306- 10 *3/4* **Gambino (IRE)**196 6817 6-8-12 76 ConnorBeasley 3
(John David Riches) *in rr: lost pl 3f out: sn heavily eased: virtually p.u: t.o* **25/1**

1m 48.73s (12.13) **Going Correction** +1.675s/f (Heav) **10** Ran SP% **115.4**
Speed ratings (Par 105): **106,103,103,101,98 93,92,73,46,45**
CSF £23.39 CT £189.91 TOTE £4.10: £1.40, £2.50, £4.70; EX 28.70 Trifecta £248.90.
Owner Pow Partnership **Bred** M Fahy & Rathbarry Stud **Trained** Musley Bank, N Yorks

FOCUS
A fairly competitive handicap. However, it's been rated a bit cautiously due to the ground.

1381 PINNACLE RACING SYNDICATE SHARES NOW AVAILABLE H'CAP (PINNACLE CUP STRAIGHT MILE SERIES QUAL.) 1m
4:00 (4:00) (Class 5) (0-75,75) 3-Y-O **£2,911** (£866; £432; £216) **Stalls** Centre

Form RPR
020- 1 **Toboggan's Fire**175 7336 3-9-4 72 PJMcDonald 7 75
(Ann Duffield) *hld up in last: effrt over 2f out: styd on to ld last 75yds* **5/1**
666- 2 *1* **Fidra Bay (IRE)**201 6655 3-9-0 68 BenCurtis 5 69
(Alan Swinbank) *sn trcking ldrs: led briefly 150yds out: kpt on same pce* **14/1**
635- 3 *hd* **Picture Painter (IRE)**168 7515 3-9-5 73 JackGarritty 1 73
(Jim Goldie) *trckd ldrs: t.k.h: effrt over 2f out: upsides 1f out: no ex last 75yds* **13/2**
05-1 4 *nk* **Specialv (IRE)**83 248 3-8-6 65 CallumShepherd(5) 2 65
(Brian Ellison) *wnt rt s: led: drvn and wnt rt 2f out: hdd last 150yds: kpt on same pce* **9/2**3
3-10 5 *2 3/4* **Hutton (IRE)**17 1080 3-9-7 75 TonyHamilton 3 68
(Richard Fahey) *bmpd s: sn trcking ldrs: effrt over 2f out: upsides 1f out: wknd fnl 50yds* **7/1**
521- 6 *nk* **Smart Mover (IRE)**168 7507 3-8-11 70 PhilDennis(5) 4 63
(John Quinn) *w ldr: carried rt 2f out: wknd fnl 100yds* **7/2**2
235- 7 *17* **Popsies Joy (IRE)**186 7082 3-8-11 65 DavidAllan 6 18
(Tim Easterby) *in rr: hdwy to trck ldrs over 4f out: effrt over 2f out: lost pl over 1f out: sn eased* **3/1**1

1m 50.96s (14.36) **Going Correction** +1.675s/f (Heav) **7** Ran SP% **114.6**
Speed ratings (Par 98): **95,94,93,93,90 90,73**
CSF £67.77 TOTE £6.60: £3.60, £6.10; EX 79.00 Trifecta £536.50.
Owner Grange Park Racing, T P & D McMahon **Bred** D McMahon **Trained** Constable Burton, N Yorks

■ Stewards' Enquiry : Callum Shepherd caution: careless riding

FOCUS
A modest event. It's been rated as ordinary form.

1382 RACINGUK.COM FILLIES' H'CAP 1m 1f
4:30 (4:31) (Class 5) (0-70,69) 3-Y-0+ **£2,911** (£866; £432; £216) **Stalls** Low

Form RPR
144- **1** **Lady Lekki (IRE)**^{168} 7520 4-10-0 69 .... GrahamLee 4 77
(Ben Haslam) *led: pushed along over 4f out: hdd narrowly last 150yds: styd on to ld post* **6/4**^{1}
5031 **2** *hd* **Affectionate Lady (IRE)**^{14} 1120 5-9-0 55 ....(b) TomEaves 3 62
(Keith Reveley) *dwlt: hld up wl in tch: effrt and n.m.r over 3f out: upsides over 2f out: led narrowly last 150yds: hdd post* **13/8**^{2}
060- **3** *8* **Graceful Act**^{160} 7680 8-8-9 52 oh3 .... PhilDennis$^{(5)}$ 5 46
(Ron Barr) *trckd ldr: effrt 3f out: wknd fnl 2f* **6/1**^{3}
400- **4** *2* **Indian Giver**^{221} 6022 8-8-10 58 .... VitorSantos$^{(7)}$ 1 45
(John David Riches) *s.i.s: sn chsng ldrs: drvn over 3f out: swtchd outside 2f out: wknd over 1f out* **6/1**^{3}

2m 7.37s (14.37) **Going Correction** +1.60s/f (Heav) **4** Ran SP% **106.7**
Speed ratings (Par 100): **100,99,92,90**
CSF £4.15 TOTE £1.90; EX 3.70 Trifecta £8.20.
Owner Go Alfresco Racing **Bred** K Fallon & J Laughton **Trained** Middleham Moor, N Yorks

FOCUS
Not a strong contest. The winner has been rated in line with the better view of her final 3yo start here over 1m6f.

1383 FOLLOW REDCARRACING ON FACEBOOK & TWITTER APPRENTICE MEDIAN AUCTION MAIDEN STKS 7f
5:00 (5:00) (Class 6) 3-4-Y-0 **£2,264** (£673; £336; £168) **Stalls** Centre

Form RPR
340- **1** **Croft Ranger (IRE)**^{178} 7253 3-8-11 64 .... PhilDennis$^{(3)}$ 4 62
(Michael Dods) *trckd ldrs: effrt over 2f out: led over 1f out: jst hld on* **9/4**^{2}
2 *hd* **Irish Optimism (IRE)** 3-9-0 0 .... CallumShepherd 1 62+
(John Quinn) *dwlt: in rr: hdwy to trck ldrs over 3f out: effrt over 2f out: styd on appr fnl f: 2nd last 100yds: jst failed* **4/1**^{3}
5 **3** *3¼* **Ramblow**^{18} 1063 3-8-6 0 .... GeorgiaCox$^{(3)}$ 3 48
(William Haggas) *sn chsng ldrs: pushed along over 3f out: drvn upsides 2f out: one pce fnl 150yds* **11/10**^{1}
0- **4** *3½* **Highway Robber**^{333} 2205 3-8-9 0 .... HollieDoyle$^{(5)}$ 2 45
(Wilf Storey) *trckd ldrs: effrt over 2f out: wknd fnl 150yds* **16/1**
000- **5** *3* **Farang Jai Dee (IRE)**^{209} 6399 4-9-7 47 .... GerO'Neill$^{(7)}$ 6 42
(Declan Carroll) *t.k.h: led: hdd over 1f out: sn wknd* **25/1**
00- **6** *24* **Final Spring (IRE)**^{199} 6701 3-8-6 0 .... JoshDoyle$^{(3)}$ 5
(Jim Goldie) *sn chsng ldrs: rdn over 2f out: wknd over 1f out: bhd whn eased clsng stages: t.o* **25/1**

1m 36.82s (12.32) **Going Correction** +1.675s/f (Heav)
WFA 3 from 4yo 14lb **6** Ran SP% **112.0**
Speed ratings (Par 101): **96,95,92,88,84 57**
CSF £11.56 TOTE £3.20: £1.70, £1.90; EX 11.90 Trifecta £16.40.
Owner Ron Davison & Hugh Linsley **Bred** Mountarmstrong Stud **Trained** Denton, Co Durham

FOCUS
They went quite steady early on in this very modest maiden. The winner probably didn't need to improve.
T/Plt: £2,182.60 to a £1 stake. Pool: £55,582 - 18.59 winning units T/Qpdt: £63.80 to a £1 stake. Pool: £7,131.32 - 82.71 winning units **Walter Glynn**

WINDSOR (R-H)
Monday, April 11

OFFICIAL GOING: Soft (5.5)
Wind: Almost nil Weather: Raining first 6 races

1384 BRITISH STALLION STUDS EBF NOVICE STKS 5f 10y
1:50 (1:50) (Class 5) 2-Y-0 **£3,234** (£962; £481; £240) **Stalls** Low

Form RPR
1 **Awesome Allan (IRE)** 2-9-2 0 .... AdamKirby 3 79
(David Evans) *wl away: led but pressed: rdn wl over 1f out: hdd ins fnl f: rallied gamely to ld last stride* **11/2**^{3}
2 *shd* **Full Intention** 2-9-2 0 .... RichardKingscote 6 79
(Tom Dascombe) *pressed ldr: pushed along 2f out: rdn to ld ins fnl f: kpt on but hdd last stride* **15/8**^{1}
3 *4* **Dontforgettocall** 2-9-2 0 .... OisinMurphy 8 64
(Joseph Tuite) *racd wdst of all: in tch to 1/2-way: sn outpcd: tk 3rd over 1f out: n.d* **28/1**
4 *2* **Mr Scaramanga** 2-9-2 0 .... SeanLevey 5 57+
(Richard Hannon) *dwlt: racd in last and pushed along 1/2-way: prog over 1f out: nvr on terms but kpt on* **11/4**^{2}
5 *6* **Spiritofedinburgh (IRE)** 2-9-2 0 .... FMBerry 1 35
(Brendan Powell) *dwlt: in tch tl wknd 2f out* **16/1**
6 *½* **Iftitah (IRE)** 2-9-2 0 .... LukeMorris 7 34
(George Peckham) *pressed ldng pair: lft bhd fr 1/2-way: lost 3rd and wknd qckly over 1f out* **8/1**
7 *2¼* **Poet's Society** 2-9-2 0 .... JamesDoyle 4 26
(Mark Johnston) *dwlt: in tch to 1/2-way: sn wknd* **7/1**

1m 4.57s (4.27) **Going Correction** +0.80s/f (Soft) **7** Ran SP% **109.8**
Speed ratings (Par 92): **97,96,90,87,77 76,73**
CSF £14.93 TOTE £6.00: £2.90, £1.80; EX 15.40 Trifecta £203.90.
Owner Walters Plant Hire Ltd **Bred** D G Iceton **Trained** Pandy, Monmouths

FOCUS
Luke Morris described the ground as "very soft" and continuous rain throughout the afternoon would have only made it harder work. They came stands' side in this novice event and little got into it, with the first two home in the front pair throughout. The opening level is fluid.

1385 EQUESTRIAN SURFACES LTD H'CAP 6f
2:20 (2:20) (Class 4) (0-85,85) 3-Y-0 **£4,690** (£1,395; £697; £348) **Stalls** Low

Form RPR
306- **1** **Ower Fly**^{278} 4020 3-8-4 75 .... MeganNicholls$^{(7)}$ 4 85
(Richard Hannon) *pressed ldng pair to 1/2-way: lost pl and pushed along in 5th 2f out: swtchd to outer and prog to ld jst over 1f out: qckly drew rt away* **25/1**
460- **2** *6* **Handytalk (IRE)**^{191} 6931 3-9-7 85 .... FrederikTylicki 2 77
(Rod Millman) *hld up in tch: taken to wd outside and pushed along 2f out: prog over 1f out: chsd wnr ins fnl f but no ch* **4/1**^{3}
100- **3** *1¼* **Justice Angel (IRE)**^{163} 7631 3-9-4 82 .... SilvestreDeSousa 3 70+
(David Elsworth) *plld hrd: hld up in tch: prog 1/2-way: rdn to chal jst over 1f out: sn lft bhd by wnr and lost 2nd ins fnl f* **3/1**^{1}

331- **4** *3½* **Wimpole Hall**^{179} 7236 3-9-1 79 .... DavidProbert 6 57
(William Jarvis) *hld up in tch: prog 1/2-way: rdn wl over 1f out: nvr quite able to chal and wknd fnl f* **7/2**^{2}
001- **5** *2* **Stormflower**^{182} 7167 3-8-7 71 .... LiamJones 7 43
(John Bridger) *t.k.h: pressed ldr: led after 2f and sn crossed to nr side rail: drvn 2f out: hdd jst over 1f out: wknd rapidly* **13/2**
1-25 **6** *2¼* **Furiant**^{20} 1029 3-9-6 84 .... JamesDoyle 5 49
(Mark Johnston) *led 2f: chsd ldr to 2f out: wknd qckly over 1f out* **7/1**
203- **7** *10* **Equistar**^{168} 7510 3-9-0 78 .... RichardKingscote 1 13
(Jonathan Portman) *hld up in tch: pushed along on nr side 2f out: wknd and eased: t.o* **6/1**

1m 17.22s (4.22) **Going Correction** +0.875s/f (Soft) **7** Ran SP% **111.2**
Speed ratings (Par 100): **106,98,96,91,89 86,72**
CSF £114.62 TOTE £16.50: £6.60, £2.50; EX 78.10 Trifecta £169.00.
Owner Green Pastures Farm **Bred** Green Pastures Farm **Trained** East Everleigh, Wilts
■ Stewards' Enquiry : Liam Jones one-day ban: careless riding (Apr 25)

FOCUS
A fair handicap. They again came stands' side in the straight but the front two challenged wide, more towards the centre. A bit of a turn up, with the complete outsider a clear-cut winner.

1386 WINDSOR VEHICLE LEASING MAIDEN STKS 1m 2f 7y
2:50 (2:51) (Class 5) 3-Y-0 **£2,911** (£866; £432; £216) **Stalls** Centre

Form RPR
2- **1** **Mountain Bell**^{189} 6986 3-9-0 0 .... OisinMurphy 2 91+
(Ralph Beckett) *led 3f: mostly trckd ldr tl led again 4f out: tk field to far side fr 3f out: shkn up and drew wl clr fr 2f out: eased last 75yds* **6/4**^{1}
03- **2** *10* **Rex Bell (IRE)**^{171} 7435 3-9-5 0 ....(p) FrankieDettori 6 76
(John Gosden) *led after 3f to 4f out: shkn up and lft bhd by wnr fr 2f out: one pce after* **9/2**^{2}
4- **3** *¾* **Apache Song**^{246} 5181 3-9-0 0 .... FrederikTylicki 8 67
(Rod Millman) *hld up: prog after 4f: shkn up to take 3rd jst over 2f out: rdn and kpt on but nvr any threat* **50/1**
60- **4** *3½* **Roderic's Secret (IRE)**^{137} 7998 3-9-5 0 .... DavidNolan 5 65
(David Menuisier) *racd in ldng trio: shkn up 4f out: sn lft bhd by ldng pair: drvn and one pce fnl 2f* **25/1**
52- **5** *nk* **Ballet Concerto**^{201} 6645 3-9-5 0 .... RyanMoore 7 64+
(Sir Michael Stoute) *hld up in last trio: sme prog 3f out but nowhere nr ldrs: disp 3rd 2f out: pushed along and one pce after* **6/4**^{1}
0- **6** *1¾* **Aristocles (IRE)**^{128} 8122 3-9-5 0 .... TedDurcan 1 61+
(Sir Michael Stoute) *hld up in last: pushed along 3f out and already bhd: nvr a factor but plugged on* **20/1**
44 **7** *11* **Russian Ranger (IRE)**^{10} 1184 3-9-5 0 .... RyanClark 3 39
(Jonathan Portman) *chsd ldrs: n.m.r bnd 6f out and dropped to rr: struggling 4f out: t.o* **50/1**
440- **8** *nk* **Glance My Way (IRE)**^{149} 7863 3-9-5 78 .... SeanLevey 9 38
(Richard Hannon) *chsd ldrs: shkn up and outpcd fr 4f out: sn wknd: t.o* **14/1**^{3}

2m 14.14s (5.44) **Going Correction** +0.625s/f (Yiel) **8** Ran SP% **117.4**
Speed ratings (Par 100): **103,95,94,91,91 89,81,80**
CSF £9.05 TOTE £2.30: £1.10, £2.20, £4.00; EX 11.20 Trifecta £135.00.
Owner Qatar Racing Limited **Bred** Theakston Stud **Trained** Kimpton, Hants

FOCUS
Due to rail movement this race was run over 14yds further than advertised. Not a bad little maiden and it was quite an impressive display from the winner. They headed far side in the straight. The runner-up has been rated close to his 2yo form.

1387 ARTHUR J GALLAGHER H'CAP 1m 67y
3:20 (3:21) (Class 5) (0-75,75) 4-Y-0+ **£2,911** (£866; £432; £216) **Stalls** Low

Form RPR
402- **1** **Double Czech (IRE)**^{232} 5661 5-9-0 68 .... DavidProbert 8 77
(Patrick Chamings) *trckd ldr 1f and again 5f out: led field across towards far side 3f out and sn led: drvn over 2f out: hdd briefly over 1f out: kpt on wl fnl f* **6/1**^{1}
-055 **2** *1* **Ravenous**^{38} 815 5-9-3 71 .... KieranO'Neill 11 78
(Luke Dace) *trckd ldrs in 6th: prog over 3f out to chal over 2f out: led briefly over 1f out: drvn and hld fnl f but kpt on* **8/1**
06- **3** *1¾* **Just Be Lucky (IRE)**^{160} 7675 4-9-3 71 .... SilvestreDeSousa 7 74
(Ivan Furtado) *chsd ldrs in 5th: drvn to cl over 2f out: one pce u.p over 1f out* **13/2**^{2}
01-0 **4** *1¼* **Uncle Dermot (IRE)**^{14} 1125 8-9-5 73 .... FMBerry 13 73
(Brendan Powell) *pressed ldrs: rdn over 2f out: kpt on against far rail fr over 1f out but nvr quite able to chal* **10/1**
30-0 **5** *6* **Shifting Star (IRE)**^{10} 1173 11-9-2 70 ....(vt) WilliamCarson 12 56
(John Bridger) *led: styd nr side 3f out: sn hdd then crossed to far side and had lost pl: no threat to ldrs over 1f out* **10/1**
600- **6** *1* **Molten Lava (IRE)**^{126} 8133 4-9-7 75 .... LukeMorris 1 59
(Paul Cole) *stdd s: hld up in 7th: rdn 3f out: no imp on ldrs 2f out: wl btn after* **8/1**
0600 **7** *1* **Dana's Present**^{16} 1093 7-9-1 69 .... LiamJones 3 50
(Tom Dascombe) *sltly awkward s and heavily restrained: hld up wl off the pce in last quartet: drvn over 2f out: plugged on but nvr on terms* **20/1**
406- **8** *1¾* **Marcano (IRE)**^{234} 5577 4-8-11 65 .... FrederikTylicki 5 42
(Rod Millman) *hld up in last quartet and wl off the pce: nudged along on outer of far side gp fr 3f out: v modest late prog: nvr involved* **15/2**^{3}
306- **9** *3¼* **Party Royal**^{119} 8221 6-9-3 71 .... TimmyMurphy 2 41
(Nick Gifford) *hld up wl off the pce in last quartet: bhd over 3f out: nvr involved after* **20/1**
3023 **10** *3¼* **Freddy With A Y (IRE)**^{10} 1173 6-9-5 73 ....(v) GeorgeBaker 14 35
(Gary Moore) *hld up in 8th and off the pce: styd alone nr side fr 3f out and sn no ch* **13/2**^{2}
04-0 **11** *16* **Dark Amber**^{33} 875 6-8-13 72 .... JennyPowell$^{(5)}$ 6
(Brendan Powell) *hld up in last quartet and wl off the pce: rdn over 3f out: no prog: wknd and t.o* **10/1**
10-5 **12** *4½* **Sheer Honesty**^{49} 667 4-8-9 70 .... LuluStanford$^{(7)}$ 9
(Gay Kelleway) *t.k.h: trckd ldr after 1f to 5f out: wknd 3f out: t.o* **20/1**

1m 49.4s (4.70) **Going Correction** +0.70s/f (Yiel) **12** Ran SP% **116.5**
Speed ratings (Par 103): **104,103,101,100,94 93,92,90,87,83 67,63**
CSF £50.38 CT £318.38 TOTE £7.40: £2.20, £3.00, £2.80; EX 66.20 Trifecta £466.60.
Owner P R Chamings **Bred** Henry O'Callaghan **Trained** Baughurst, Hants

FOCUS
Due to rail movement this race was run over 14yds further than advertised. Modest handicap form, it paid to race handily and they headed far side in the straight. The winner has been rated to his best, with the runner-up close to last year's form.

1388 RATHBONE INVESTMENT MANAGEMENT H'CAP (DIV I) 1m 67y
3:50 (3:50) (Class 5) (0-70,70) 3-Y-O **£2,911** (£866; £432; £216) **Stalls** Low

Form RPR
666- **1** **Medburn Dream**[152] 7795 3-8-11 **60**................................ FrannyNorton 8 72+
(Paul Henderson) *mde all: pressed 4f out but stl gng wl: shkn up 2f out and sn hung rt into centre of trck: wandered after but in command: rdn out* **9/1**
043- **2** *2* **Funny Oyster (IRE)**[168] 7507 3-8-4 **56**..................(p) TomMarquand(3) 7 61
(George Baker) *hld up in rr: pushed along over 3f out: prog over 2f out: edgd rt into centre of trck over 1f out: chsd wnr fnl f: styd on but nvr able to chal* **13/2**
504- **3** *2* **Pastoral Star**[201] 6636 3-9-0 **63**.. OisinMurphy 9 63
(Hughie Morrison) *trckd wnr after 2f: tried to chal 4f out but sn pushed along: edgd lft 2f out and already hld: one pce and lost 2nd fnl f* **8/1**
004- **4** *2* **Perfect Quest**[168] 7512 3-9-0 **63**... AdamKirby 10 59
(Clive Cox) *hld up in tch: prog to trck ldrs over 3f out and gng bttr than most: rdn to chal for 2nd 2f out: no ex fnl f* **5/1**[3]
-303 **5** *4 1/2* **Refulgence (FR)**[45] 725 3-8-13 **62**...................................... LiamJones 2 47
(Marco Botti) *trckd ldrs: shkn up 3f out: steadily fdd fnl 2f* **10/1**
0032 **6** *6* **Betsalottie**[5] 1259 3-8-7 **56** oh2.. WilliamCarson 1 28
(John Bridger) *t.k.h: trckd wnr 2f: shkn up over 3f out: wknd 2f out* **4/1**[1]
545- **7** *6* **Elegant Annie**[244] 5241 3-8-12 **68**.............................. CharlieBennett(7) 3 26
(Jonathan Portman) *chsd ldrs: pushed along over 3f out: wknd qckly over 2f out* **25/1**
306- **8** *13* **Silent Dreamer**[165] 7577 3-9-2 **65**............................ SilvestreDeSousa 5
(Mark Johnston) *dwlt: nvr gng wl and a in last pair: t.o* **9/2**[2]
534- **9** *22* **Lee's Hall (IRE)**[144] 7902 3-9-7 **70**.. ShaneKelly 6
(Murty McGrath) *awkward s: a in rr: t.o and eased fnl 2f* **6/1**

1m 51.12s (6.42) **Going Correction** +0.775s/f (Yiel) 9 Ran SP% **116.5**
Speed ratings (Par 98): **98,96,94,92,87 81,75,62,40**
CSF £66.72 CT £492.50 TOTE £14.80: £4.40, £2.00, £2.80; EX 96.40 Trifecta £625.50.
Owner Eddie Evans **Bred** Eddie Evans **Trained** Whitsbury, Hants

FOCUS
Due to rail movement this race was run over 14yds further than advertised. Division one of a pretty moderate handicap, the winner making all and the field coming more towards the far side. It's been rated around the runner-up close to her 2yo form.

1389 RATHBONE INVESTMENT MANAGEMENT H'CAP (DIV II) 1m 67y
4:20 (4:20) (Class 5) (0-70,70) 3-Y-O **£2,911** (£866; £432; £216) **Stalls** Low

Form RPR
455- **1** **Sir Roderic (IRE)**[189] 6990 3-9-4 **67**............................... FrederikTylicki 1 77+
(Rod Millman) *trckd ldrs: poised to chal in centre over 2f out gng easily: led over 1f out and sn rdn: asserted fnl f and won readily* **3/1**[1]
2216 **2** *2 1/2* **Blacklister**[32] 887 3-9-7 **70**.. GeorgeBaker 7 74
(Mick Channon) *trckd ldrs: gng wl whn asked to chal over 2f out: led briefly wl over 1f out: drvn to press wnr after: styd on but readily hld* **3/1**[1]
060- **3** *2 1/2* **Girl With A Pearl (IRE)**[285] 3778 3-9-0 **63**.......................... JamesDoyle 5 61
(Ed Dunlop) *hld up towards rr: in tch 3f out: drvn over 2f out: styd on to take 3rd ins fnl f: unable to threaten* **9/2**[2]
416- **4** *1 1/2* **Beatbybeatbybeat**[188] 6996 3-9-3 **69**......................... ThomasBrown(3) 8 64
(Ismail Mohammed) *nt that wl away but quick prog to chse ldr: rdn to chal over 2f out: btn over 1f out: fdd fnl f* **12/1**
055- **5** *4* **Wharane (FR)**[118] 8234 3-8-12 **61**.................................... JimmyFortune 3 47
(Ian Williams) *trckd ldrs: chal fr 3f out tl wknd wl over 1f out* **8/1**[3]
0-55 **6** *1* **Mulled Wine**[24] 976 3-8-13 **62**.. KierenFox 2 45
(John Best) *led: hung lft bnd over 5f out: hdd wl over 1f out: hanging lft and wknd after* **12/1**
-350 **7** *2 1/2* **Lady McGuffy (IRE)**[40] 783 3-8-2 **56** oh1..................(t) NoelGarbutt(5) 9 34
(Brian Barr) *hld up in rr: effrt and in tch over 2f out: sn rdn and wknd* **20/1**
420- **8** *9* **Chempedak Bay (IRE)**[151] 7807 3-9-2 **65**.......................... LukeMorris 4 22
(Paul Cole) *hld up in rr: shkn up over 3f out: sn struggling: bhd fnl 2f* **9/1**
060- **9** *9* **Gladys Cooper (IRE)**[137] 7996 3-8-11 **60**......................... AntonioFresu 6
(Ed Walker) *a in rr: pushed along and wknd 3f out: t.o* **14/1**

1m 51.27s (6.57) **Going Correction** +0.85s/f (Soft) 9 Ran SP% **116.1**
Speed ratings (Par 98): **101,98,96,94,90 89,87,78,69**
CSF £11.70 CT £39.52 TOTE £4.30: £1.80, £1.50, £1.50; EX 14.90 Trifecta £59.10.
Owner The Links Partnership **Bred** Thomas G Cooke **Trained** Kentisbeare, Devon

FOCUS
Due to rail movement this race was run over 14yds further than advertised. Perhaps the stronger of the two divisions, although the time was 0.15secs slower than the first leg. They again headed centre to far side. It's been rated around the runner-up to his lesser turf mark.

1390 MPM FLOORING LTD H'CAP 1m 2f 7y
4:50 (4:50) (Class 5) (0-75,75) 4-Y-O+ **£2,911** (£866; £432; £216) **Stalls** Centre

Form RPR
00-0 **1** **Bazooka (IRE)**[12] 1144 5-8-13 **72**.......................... EdwardGreatrex(5) 4 82
(David Flood) *t.k.h early: sn hld up in midfield: shkn 3f out: prog in centre gng bttr over 2f out: led over 1f out: drvn and hld on wl* **16/1**
025- **2** *1/2* **Ttainted Love**[181] 7182 4-9-4 **72**....................................(p) TedDurcan 13 81
(Chris Wall) *mostly trckd ldr: led against far rail 2f out: drvn and hdd over 1f out: kpt on wl but jst hld ins fnl f* **7/1**[3]
326- **3** *3 3/4* **Niblawi (IRE)**[214] 6237 4-9-6 **74**.. TomQueally 1 75
(Ismail Mohammed) *wl in tch: rdn and hanging 3f out: prog 2f out: kpt on to take 3rd ins fnl f* **9/1**
6-03 **4** *1/2* **Top Diktat**[54] 605 8-9-7 **75**.. GeorgeBaker 3 75
(Gary Moore) *hld up in last pair: prog over 2f out: drvn to dispute 3rd fnl f: no imp on ldng pair after* **3/1**[1]
23-0 **5** *1 1/4* **Bohemian Rhapsody (IRE)**[12] 1144 7-9-7 **75**..................... FMBerry 12 73
(Brendan Powell) *prog to trck ldrs 1/2-way: drvn over 2f out: steadily fdd against far rail over 1f out* **8/1**
040- **6** *1/2* **Bridey's Lettuce (IRE)**[202] 6626 4-8-13 **67**............ SilvestreDeSousa 9 65
(Ivan Furtado) *dwlt: towards rr: shkn up 3f out: in tch over 2f out: nt clr run over 1f out: kpt on and nrst fin* **7/1**[3]
011- **7** *shd* **Roly Tricks**[179] 7230 5-8-8 **67**.. PaddyPilley(5) 6 63
(Natalie Lloyd-Beavis) *s.i.s and hld up in last pair: shkn up 3f out: no real prog tl kpt on fr over 1f out: nvr a threat* **9/1**
-124 **8** *6* **Saint Honore**[47] 693 4-9-4 **72**.. JFEgan 2 56
(Pat Phelan) *pressed ldrs: rdn over 3f out: wknd qckly over 1f out* **20/1**
6-41 **9** *3/4* **Heezararity**[41] 773 8-9-0 **68**... JimmyFortune 5 51
(Jonathan Geake) *hld up towards rr: effrt 3f out: sn rdn and no prog: wknd over 1f out* **11/2**[2]
0-30 **10** *7* **Rightway (IRE)**[82] 256 5-9-7 **75**....................................... LukeMorris 7 44
(Tony Carroll) *prom: u.p over 3f out: wknd rapidly 2f out* **25/1**
-500 **11** *6* **Altaira**[49] 672 5-8-8 **62**.. WilliamCarson 8 19
(Tony Carroll) *led to 2f out: sn wknd rapidly* **25/1**

2m 17.37s (8.67) **Going Correction** +0.925s/f (Soft) 11 Ran SP% **114.8**
Speed ratings (Par 103): **102,101,98,98,97 96,96,91,91,85 80**
CSF £117.69 CT £1072.25 TOTE £20.80: £5.30, £2.60, £2.50; EX 196.60 Trifecta £4332.10.
Owner Flood Family Racing Limited **Bred** Cyril Kiernan **Trained** Chiseldon, Wiltshire

FOCUS
Due to rail movement this race was run over 14yds further than advertised. A modest handicap. A length pb from the runner-up.

1391 DAVID HASTINGS PHOTOGRAPHER H'CAP 1m 3f 135y
5:20 (5:20) (Class 5) (0-75,75) 4-Y-O+ **£2,911** (£866; £432; £216) **Stalls** Centre

Form RPR
012- **1** **Slunovrat (FR)**[199] 6699 5-9-5 **73**... DavidNolan 7 86
(David Menuisier) *pressed ldr: led after 4f: rdn and jnd 3f out and clr of rest: kpt on wl u.p to assert over 1f out* **7/2**[1]
34- **2** *3 1/2* **Rideonastar (IRE)**[261] 4648 5-9-6 **74**..................................... FMBerry 13 81
(Brendan Powell) *prom: chal and w wnr 3f out and looked to be gng bttr: rdn 2f out: nt qckn over 1f out: one pce fnl f* **7/2**[1]
404- **3** *10* **Deepsand (IRE)**[59] 7527 7-8-11 **65**............................(tp) CharlesBishop 2 56
(Ali Stronge) *s.s: in rr: rdn over 3f out: prog u.p over 2f out: kpt on to take modest 3rd last 100yds* **25/1**
660/ **4** *1 1/2* **Doesyourdogbite (IRE)**[217] 4-9-6 **75**............................... GeorgeBaker 11 64
(Jonjo O'Neill) *hld up in detached last: shkn up and prog fr 3f out: nvr any ch w ldng pair but kpt on to take 4th nr fin* **20/1**
1353 **5** *1 3/4* **San Quentin (IRE)**[12] 1144 5-9-4 **72**............................. RobertWinston 9 58
(Dean Ivory) *hld up wl in rr: pushed along and prog over 3f out: tk 3rd 2f out but no ch w ldng pair: wknd ins fnl f* **20/1**
0005 **6** *1 1/4* **Yul Finegold (IRE)**[11] 1166 6-9-6 **74**.................................. LiamKeniry 6 58
(Conor Dore) *led 4f: chsd wnr to 4f out: sn rdn and lft bhd by ldng pair: hld on to 3rd pl tl 2f out: fdd* **20/1**
01-3 **7** *1 1/4* **Honeymoon Cocktail (FR)**[81] 273 5-9-0 **71**............. RobHornby(3) 16 53
(David Pipe) *trckd ldrs: rdn in 4th over 3f out: lft bhd by ldrs sn after and lost pl: no ch after: plugged on* **6/1**[3]
-465 **8** *6* **Aumerle**[33] 882 4-9-3 **72**.. SilvestreDeSousa 3 44
(Shaun Lycett) *chsd ldrs: rdn over 3f out: sn no prog: wknd 2f out* **9/1**
410/ **9** *2 1/4* **Red Four**[257] 8015 6-9-1 **69**...(p) SteveDrowne 12 38
(George Baker) *wl in tch: rdn over 3f out: lft bhd sn after* **20/1**
356- **10** *hd* **Prairie Town (IRE)**[30] 6505 5-9-5 **73**................................. LukeMorris 1 41
(Tony Carroll) *drvn after 3f: nvr gng wl after and nvr a factor: eased over 1f out* **5/1**[2]
322- **11** *31* **Russian Remarque**[291] 3545 5-9-2 **70**.................................... RyanClark 5
(Jonathan Portman) *trckd ldrs: rdn and lost pl over 3f out: sn wknd and t.o* **12/1**
20/6 **12** *5* **Champagne Rules**[6] 1248 5-9-6 **74**.................................... TomQueally 10
(Sharon Watt) *hld up in rr: pushed along and no prog over 3f out: sn bhd and eased: t.o* **14/1**

2m 39.54s (10.04) **Going Correction** +1.00s/f (Soft)
WFA 4 from 5yo+ 1lb 12 Ran SP% **122.6**
Speed ratings (Par 103): **106,103,97,96,94 94,93,89,87,87 66,63**
CSF £14.11 CT £274.61 TOTE £4.70: £2.00, £1.50, £7.60; EX 19.70 Trifecta £350.30.
Owner Shinco Racing Limited **Bred** Jaques & Marie-Francoise Menuisier **Trained** Pulborough, W Sussex

FOCUS
Due to rail movement this race was run over 14yds further than advertised. The front pair, up there throughout, came a long way clear in this ordinary handicap. The pace was a decent one. Another pb from the winner.
T/Jkpt: Not won. T/Plt: £285.90 to a £1 stake. Pool: £95,630.84 - 244.16 winning units T/Qpdt: £26.70 to a £1 stake. Pool: £9,102.81 - 252.0 winning units **Jonathan Neesom**

NEWMARKET (R-H)
Tuesday, April 12

OFFICIAL GOING: Good to soft changing to soft after race 5 (4.30)
Wind: light, half behind Weather: dry, light cloud until showers race 5 onwards

1392 EBF STALLIONS NEWMARKET COMMUNITY RACEDAY MAIDEN FILLIES' STKS (PLUS 10 RACE) 1m
2:10 (2:12) (Class 4) 3-Y-O **£5,498** (£1,636; £817; £408) **Stalls** High

Form RPR
2- **1** **Swiss Range**[164] 7629 3-9-0 0...[1] FrankieDettori 4 92+
(John Gosden) *lengthy: tall: hld up in tch: clsd to press ldrs 1/2-way: led over 1f out: sn qcknd clr and in n.d fnl f: comf* **7/4**[1]
223- **2** *5* **Golden Stunner (IRE)**[134] 8047 3-9-0 80............................ FMBerry 10 79
(Ralph Beckett) *unf: w ldr: rdn and ev ch 2f out: outpcd by wnr and drifted lft over 1f out: wl hld by wnr but kpt on for clr 2nd fnl f* **11/2**[2]
3 *1 1/2* **Golden Reign (IRE)** 3-9-0 0.. RyanMoore 6 76+
(William Haggas) *tall: s.i.s: hld up towards rr: hdwy in centre over 2f out: styd on to go 3rd ins fnl f: gng on fin but no ch w wnr* **11/1**
03- **4** *3* **My Favourite Thing**[233] 5657 3-9-0 0.............................. AndreaAtzeni 9 69
(Roger Varian) *str: led for 2f: styd pressing ldrs: rdn ent fnl 2f: outpcd wl over 1f out: wl hld 3rd 1f out: lost 3rd and plugged on same pce ins fnl f* **8/1**
00- **5** *1 3/4* **Dora's Field (IRE)**[181] 7212 3-9-0 0.................................. AdamKirby 11 69+
(Ed Dunlop) *stdd s: hld up in tch towards rr: pushed along ent fnl 2f: hdwy but rn green on downhill run over 1f out: swtchd lft and kpt on steadily ins fnl f: no threat to wnr* **100/1**
6 *2 1/2* **Aqualis** 3-9-0 0.. RobertHavlin 8 59
(John Gosden) *tall: t.k.h: wl in tch in midfield: rdn ent fnl 2f: sn outpcd and btn over 1f out: wknd fnl f* **16/1**
7 *2 3/4* **Cliff Face (IRE)** 3-9-0 0... JimCrowley 2 53
(Ed Dunlop) *str: bit bkwd: in tch towards rr: pushed along briefly 1/2-way: rdn and outpcd over 2f out: n.d but plugged on to pass btn horses ins fnl f* **40/1**
3- **8** *3/4* **Dufay (IRE)**[118] 8253 3-9-0 0... WilliamBuick 12 51
(Charlie Appleby) *athletic: t.k.h to post: racd keenly: w ldrs tl led after 2f: rdn and hdd over 1f out: sn outpcd and btn: wknd and eased wl ins fnl f* **13/2**[3]
0-2 **9** *1 1/2* **Performer**[39] 814 3-9-0 0.. SeanLevey 14 47
(Richard Hannon) *str: lw: chsd ldrs: effrt in 5th 3f out: no imp 2f out and btn over 1f out: wknd fnl f* **14/1**

10 1 ¾ **Penny Lane Forever** 3-9-0 0 .... HarryBentley 13 43
(Roger Varian) *w'like: niggled along in midfield: rdn over 2f out: sn struggling and outpcd: wknd over 1f out* **20/1**

11 2 ¼ **Lacey's Lane** 3-9-0 0 .... JamesDoyle 5 38
(Saeed bin Suroor) *lengthy: s.i.s and wnt lft s: in tch towards rr: rdn and struggling over 2f out: sn btn and wknd over 1f out* **16/1**

- **12** ½ **Queen's Code (IRE)** 3-9-0 0 .... PaulHanagan 1 37
(Charles Hills) *cmpt: bit bkwd: t.k.h: hld up in tch in midfield: rdn 3f out: sn struggling and lost pl: wknd wl over 1f out: bhd fnl f* **33/1**

4- **13** 1 ½ **Arcamist**[152] 7809 3-9-0 0 .... DarryllHolland 3 34
(Charles Hills) *w'like: t.k.h: hld up in tch in midfield: rdn over 2f out: sn btn and wknd wl over 1f out: bhd fnl f* **50/1**

14 13 **Theydon Girls** 3-8-11 0 .... RosieJessop(3) 7 4
(Peter Charalambous) *lengthy: v.s.a and wnt lft s: rn green and a in rr: lost tch: 3f out: t.o* **100/1**

1m 42.09s (3.49) **Going Correction** +0.55s/f (Yiel) **14** Ran SP% **117.0**
Speed ratings (Par 97): **104,99,97,94,92 90,87,86,85,83 81,80,79,66**
CSF £9.68 TOTE £2.80: £1.30, £2.10, £2.60; EX 13.00 Trifecta £62.90.
Owner K Abdullah **Bred** Juddmonte Farms Ltd **Trained** Newmarket, Suffolk

FOCUS
Far side course used and stalls on the stands' side .There was 4mm of rain overnight and during the morning, and the going had eased to good to soft (GoingStick: 6.6). Back as a three-day meeting for the first time since 2006, the time of the opener (7.09sec slower than standard) backed up the view of Frankie Dettori, who described the ground as "soft but nice" after riding Galileo Gold in a pre-race gallop. This maiden should produce winners. It's been rated at face value, with the runner-up to form.

1393 EBF STALLIONS NGK SPARK PLUGS CONDITIONS STKS (PLUS 10 RACE) 7f
2:45 (2:45) (Class 3) 3-Y-O **£9,056** (£2,695; £1,346; £673) **Stalls** High

Form RPR

1- **1** **Thikriyaat (IRE)**[173] 7411 3-9-2 0 .... DaneO'Neill 6 102+
(Sir Michael Stoute) *str: racd centre to stands' side: hld up in tch in last pair: hdwy u.p to chal over 1f out: sustained effrt fnl f: to ld towards fin: gamely* **8/1**

212- **2** *nk* **Tabarrak (IRE)**[195] 6869 3-9-2 97 .... PaulHanagan 2 101
(Richard Hannon) *lw: rdn: racd in centre: led: rdn wl 1f out: sn hrd pressed and edgd lft: kpt on gamely u.p tl hdd and no ex towards fin* **2/1**[1]

113- **3** *nk* **Zhui Feng (IRE)**[192] 6924 3-9-6 93 .... PatDobbs 8 104
(Amanda Perrett) *racd nrest stands' rail: chsd ldng pair: effrt to chal over 1f out: kpt on wl u.p ins fnl f: unable qck and hld towards fin* **9/2**

153- **4** *5* **Mohab**[214] 6274 3-9-2 99 .... GrahamLee 4 87
(Kevin Ryan) *racd centre to stands' side: chsd ldr: rdn over 2f out: lost pl and swtchd rt over 1f out: wknd 1f out* **7/2**[3]

1- **5** *5* **Vincent's Forever**[182] 7179 3-9-2 0 .... FrankieDettori 3 73
(John Gosden) *str: swtg: racd in centre: stdd s: t.k.h: hld up in tch in last pair: rdn 3f out: no imp 2f out: wknd jst over 1f out* **3/1**[2]

1m 28.46s (3.06) **Going Correction** +0.55s/f (Yiel) **5** Ran SP% **109.8**
Speed ratings (Par 102): **104,103,103,97,91**
CSF £24.21 TOTE £9.90: £5.00, £1.20; EX 25.60 Trifecta £118.50.
Owner Hamdan Al Maktoum **Bred** Kildaragh Stud **Trained** Newmarket, Suffolk

FOCUS
There wasn't a great deal between the first three at the end of this conditions event. The runner-up has been rated to form.

1394 BEN BURGESS & CO H'CAP 6f
3:20 (3:20) (Class 2) (0-100,99) 4-Y-O+ **£12,938** (£3,850; £1,924; £962) **Stalls** High

Form RPR

100- **1** **Teruntum Star (FR)**[206] 6515 4-9-3 **95** .... JamieSpencer 1 105
(Kevin Ryan) *prom in main gp: rdn and chsd ldr jst over 1f out: led ins fnl f: sn clr: styd on* **16/1**

0650 **2** 1 ½ **Bertiewhittle**[13] 1153 8-8-6 **87** .... RobHornby(3) 3 93+
(David Barron) *stdd after s: in rr: hdwy over 1f out: squeezed through ent fnl f: r.o strly to go 2nd towards fin* **16/1**

1333 **3** ½ **Yeeoow (IRE)**[10] 1205 7-8-7 **85** oh2 .... HarryBentley 10 89
(K R Burke) *lw: broke wl: stdd bk and in tch in midfield: effrt wl over 1f out: chsd clr wnr ins fnl f: kpt on but nvr threatening to chal: lost 2nd towards fin* **14/1**

000- **4** 1 ¾ **Free Code (IRE)**[206] 6519 5-9-0 **92** .... GrahamGibbons 7 90+
(David Barron) *stdd after s: hld up in tch towards rr: pushed along wl over 1f out: hdwy and squeezed through jst over 1f out: styd on to go 4th wl ins fnl f: no threat to wnr* **16/1**

50-2 **5** *1* **Childesplay**[24] 1003 5-8-8 **86** .... OisinMurphy 5 81
(Heather Main) *sn led main gp and chsd overall ldr tl 3f out: styd handy: rdn 2f out: no ex 1f out and plugged on same pce ins fnl f* **14/1**

300- **6** *hd* **Desert Force**[206] 6515 4-9-1 **93** .... PatDobbs 9 88
(Richard Hannon) *in tch: hdwy to ld main gp and chse overall ldr 3f out: rdn and lost 2nd jst over 1f out: no ex and plugged on same pce ins fnl f* **8/1**[2]

000- **7** ½ **Amazour (IRE)**[199] 6758 4-9-1 **93** .... MartinHarley 14 86
(Ismail Mohammed) *hld up in tch towards rr: swtchd rt and hdwy 2f out: hung rt and no imp u.p over 1f out: wknd ins fnl f* **8/1**[2]

-660 **8** *nk* **Justice Good (IRE)**[50] 677 4-9-5 **97** .... (t) SilvestreDeSousa 12 89
(David Elsworth) *hld up in tch in midfield: effrt 2f out: no ex u.p over 1f out: wknd ins fnl f* **12/1**

05-0 **9** 1 ¾ **Lucky Beggar (IRE)**[10] 1205 6-8-13 **91** .... DarryllHolland 4 77
(Charles Hills) *taken down early: sn swtchd rt to r alone on far rail: overall ldr and clr 1/2-way: rdn over 1f out: hdd ins fnl f: sn wknd* **8/1**[2]

006- **10** 1 ¼ **Grandad's World (IRE)**[248] 5134 4-9-4 **96** .... RyanMoore 13 78+
(Richard Fahey) *broke wl: sn stdd bk and hld up in tch towards rr: effrt and no imp wl over 1f out: bhd and eased wl ins fnl f* **3/1**[1]

300- **11** *1* **Gamesome (FR)**[255] 4858 5-9-7 **99** .... TomQueally 2 78
(Paul Midgley) *hld up in tch in midfield: effrt wl over 1f out: sn no imp and btn 1f out: bhd and eased wl ins fnl f* **8/1**[2]

150- **12** ¾ **Golden Amber (IRE)**[157] 7755 5-9-7 **99** .... RobertWinston 8 76
(Dean Ivory) *wl in tch: effrt and hung rt wl over 1f out: continued hanging and no hdwy: lost pl and bhd ins fnl f: eased wl ins fnl f* **9/1**[3]

1m 14.13s (1.93) **Going Correction** +0.55s/f (Yiel) **12** Ran SP% **118.1**
Speed ratings (Par 109): **109,107,106,104,102 102,101,101,99,97 96,95**
CSF £248.19 CT £3687.70 TOTE £22.20: £5.50, £5.60, £3.50; EX 325.10 Trifecta £8260.50.
Owner T A Rahman **Bred** Petra Bloodstock Agency **Trained** Hambleton, N Yorks

FOCUS
A competitive sprint handicap run at a good gallop. The third has been rated close to his winter AW form.

1395 1STSECURITYSOLUTIONS.CO.UK FEILDEN STKS (LISTED RACE) 1m 1f
3:55 (3:56) (Class 1) 3-Y-O **£20,982** (£7,955; £3,981; £1,983) **Stalls** High

Form RPR

110- **1** **Ventura Storm (IRE)**[191] 6968 3-9-0 100 .... RyanMoore 3 102
(Richard Hannon) *trckd ldr: effrt jst over 2f out: rdn to ld wl over 1f out: drvn and kpt finding ex ins fnl f: asserted and styd on strly fnl 75yds: rdn out* **15/8**[1]

41- **2** 1 ¼ **Mustajeer**[201] 6674 3-9-0 0 .... DaneO'Neill 2 99
(Owen Burrows) *athletic: hld up in tch in 3rd: effrt ent fnl 2f: rdn and ev ch over 1f out: kpt on u.p tl no ex wl ins fnl f* **3/1**[3]

1- **3** 1 ¼ **Tathqeef (USA)**[172] 7442 3-9-0 0 .... PaulHanagan 5 97
(John Gosden) *str: lw: hld up in tch in rr: swtchd out and effrt jst over 2f out: cl enough in 3rd and drvn ent fnl f: no ex and outpcd ins fnl f* **7/2**

310- **4** 1 ¼ **Mengli Khan (IRE)**[171] 7463 3-9-0 0 .... MartinHarley 1 94
(Hugo Palmer) *lengthy: led and set stdy gallop: shkn up and hung rt 2f out: sn hdd and continued to hang: btn 4th and plugged on same pce fnl f* **11/4**[2]

1m 56.91s (5.21) **Going Correction** +0.55s/f (Yiel) **4** Ran SP% **108.7**
Speed ratings (Par 106): **98,96,95,94**
CSF £7.60 TOTE £2.70; EX 7.90 Trifecta £12.60.
Owner Middleham Park Racing LXXII **Bred** Laurence Kennedy **Trained** East Everleigh, Wilts

FOCUS
Prior to Intello's victory in 2013 and Golden Horn's success last year this race didn't have much of an impact on the Classics. It's likely this year's won't either, but it was a competitive little race, albeit one run at a steady early gallop, and the second and third, in particular, look capable of doing better. The level is a bit fluid.

1396 LANWADES STUD NELL GWYN STKS (GROUP 3) (FILLIES) 7f
4:30 (4:30) (Class 1) 3-Y-O
£34,026 (£12,900; £6,456; £3,216; £1,614; £810) **Stalls** High

Form RPR

112- **1** **Nathra (IRE)**[186] 7075 3-9-0 110 .... FrankieDettori 11 109+
(John Gosden) *lw: t.k.h early: hld up in tch: clsd to chse ldrs 3f out: led 2f out: rdn over 1f out: asserted under hands and heels riding ins fnl f: r.o wl: comf* **5/4**[1]

62-0 **2** 1 ½ **Squash**[38] 836 3-9-0 102 .... DavidProbert 13 103
(Philip McBride) *chsd ldrs: effrt over 2f out: drvn and ev ch over 1f out: unable qck w wnr ins fnl f: wnt 2nd and kpt on u.p fnl 75yds* **33/1**

13- **3** ¾ **Robanne**[186] 7073 3-9-0 0 .... SilvestreDeSousa 2 101+
(William Knight) *hld up in last trio: stl plenty to do whn swtchd rt and effrt wl over 1f out: sme hdwy ent fnl f: styd on strly fnl 100yds to snatch 3rd last strides: no threat to wnr* **14/1**

311- **4** *hd* **Mix And Mingle (IRE)**[185] 7112 3-9-0 89 .... TedDurcan 12 100
(Chris Wall) *hld up in tch: effrt 2f out: ev ch over 1f out: wnt 2nd and edgd lft ent fnl f: outpcd by wnr and kpt on same pce ins fnl f: lost 2 pls fnl 75yds* **16/1**

14- **5** *nk* **Coolmore (IRE)**[186] 7075 3-9-0 106 .... (p) RyanMoore 7 100
(A P O'Brien, Ire) *led: rdn ent fnl 2f: hdd 2f out but stl ev ch u.p tl unable qck jst ins fnl f: styd on same pce fnl 100yds* **9/2**[3]

11- **6** *nk* **First Victory (IRE)**[186] 7073 3-9-0 0 .... (t) JamesDoyle 9 99
(Saeed bin Suroor) *t.k.h: chsd ldr for over 1f: styd prom: rdn and ev ch wl over 1f out tl unable qck 1f out: styd on same pce ins fnl f* **4/1**[2]

110- **7** ¾ **Epsom Icon**[227] 5844 3-9-0 99 .... CharlesBishop 5 97
(Mick Channon) *stdd s: hld up in tch in last trio: effrt 2f out: nt clr run and swtchd rt jst over 1f out: kpt on ins fnl f: nvr trbld ldrs* **50/1**

213- **8** *1* **Fourth Way (IRE)**[171] 7471 3-9-0 93 .... OisinMurphy 8 94
(Roger Varian) *cmpt: in tch in midfield: effrt to press ldrs and drvn over 1f out: no ex 1f out: wknd ins fnl f* **16/1**

021- **9** ½ **Only Mine (IRE)**[165] 7594 3-9-0 105 .... PatSmullen 14 93
(Joseph G Murphy, Ire) *lw: racd nr stands' rail: chsd ldr over 5f out: ev ch and rdn 2f out: unable qck and beginning to struggle whn short of room and hmpd jst over 1f out: wknd ins fnl f* **10/1**

2214 **10** *10* **Yeah Baby Yeah (IRE)**[18] 1071 3-9-0 84 .... AdamKirby 6 66
(Gay Kelleway) *stdd s: hld up in last trio: rdn 1/2-way: struggling u.p over 2f out: sn wknd: bhd ins fnl f* **100/1**

1m 28.35s (2.95) **Going Correction** +0.55s/f (Yiel) **10** Ran SP% **116.0**
Speed ratings (Par 105): **105,103,102,102,101 101,100,99,98,87**
CSF £55.55 TOTE £2.30: £1.10, £6.90, £3.10; EX 57.60 Trifecta £651.00.
Owner Abdullah Saeed Al Naboodah **Bred** Pier House Stud **Trained** Newmarket, Suffolk

FOCUS
Run in driving rain, they finished in a bit of a heap in behind the winner. Pretty straightforward stuff, with the winner rated to form.

1397 ALEX SCOTT MAIDEN STKS (PLUS 10 RACE) (C&G) 7f
5:05 (5:05) (Class 4) 3-Y-O **£5,175** (£1,540; £769; £384) **Stalls** High

Form RPR

1 **Castle Harbour** 3-9-0 0 .... FrankieDettori 1 86
(John Gosden) *lengthy: racd keenly: sn led and mde rest: rdn wl over 1f out: styd on wl to assert wl ins fnl f: rdn out* **10/3**[2]

402- **2** *1* **Fawaareq (IRE)**[217] 6181 3-9-0 83 .... PaulHanagan 9 84
(Owen Burrows) *lw: hld up in tch in midfield: clsd to chse ldrs 3f out: swtchd lft and effrt to press ldrs over 1f out: kpt on same pce u.p ins fnl f: wnt 2nd last strides* **3/1**[1]

3- **3** *nk* **Archimento**[182] 7179 3-9-0 0 .... SilvestreDeSousa 5 83
(Ed Dunlop) *tall: lengthy: chsd ldr for over 1f: styd chsng ldrs: rdn and ev ch 2f out: sustained chal tl no ex and btn wl ins fnl f: wknd towards fin and lost 2nd last strides* **9/2**[3]

4 *4* **Noble Star (IRE)** 3-9-0 0 .... FrederikTylicki 8 73
(James Fanshawe) *leggy: hld up in tch towards rr: hdwy into midfield 3f out: pushed along and outpcd 2f out: styd on over 1f out: chsd clr trio ins fnl f: kpt on but no imp* **20/1**

5 1 ½ **Raven's Corner (IRE)** 3-9-0 0 .... WilliamBuick 2 69
(John Gosden) *athletic: t.k.h: chsd ldrs: rdn and ev ch 2f out tl no ex over 1f out: wknd ins fnl f* **12/1**

6 ½ **Commodity (IRE)** 3-9-0 0 .... RyanMoore 6 67
(Sir Michael Stoute) *athletic: in tch in last trio: pushed along 1/2-way: sme hdwy into midfield wl over 1f out: outpcd and btn over 1f out: wl hld and kpt on same pce ins fnl f* **15/2**

7 *shd* **Street Poet (IRE)** 3-9-0 0 .... TedDurcan 7 67
(Sir Michael Stoute) *w'like: stdd after s: niggled along in rr: effrt over 2f out: sn outpcd: wl hld and plugged on same pce fr over 1f out* **25/1**

22- **8** *nse* **Menai (IRE)**[309] 2998 3-9-0 0 .... DarryllHolland 4 67
(Charles Hills) *str: swtg: t.k.h: hld up and racd awkwardly in midfield: effrt 2f out: sn btn: wknd fnl f* **10/1**

35- **9** *1 3/4* **Not Touch**[195] 6866 3-9-0 0 .... PatDobbs 11 62
(Richard Hannon) *lengthy: chsd ldrs: wnt 2nd over 5f out tl lost pl wl over 1f out: wknd fnl f* **12/1**

10 *14* **Dream Trader (IRE)** 3-9-0 0 .... AndreaAtzeni 10 26
(Roger Varian) *str: bit bkwd: hld up in tch: rdn over 2f out: sn struggling: bhd over 1f out* **25/1**

1m 30.24s (4.84) **Going Correction** +0.775s/f (Yiel) **10** Ran SP% **115.0**
Speed ratings (Par 100): **103,101,101,96,95 94,94,94,92,76**
CSF £13.13 TOTE £4.40: £1.60, £1.10, £2.50; EX 16.70 Trifecta £44.30.
Owner Bermuda Thoroughbred Racing Limited **Bred** L A C Ashby Newhall Estate Farm **Trained** Newmarket, Suffolk

FOCUS
The going was changed to soft prior to this race. Often a decent maiden, there was plenty to like about the winner's performance, even allowing for his tactical advantage in making the running in what was a fairly steadily run affair. The runner-up sets the standard.

1398 WINNING POST PAVILION EXPERIENCE H'CAP 1m 2f
5:40 (5:41) (Class 3) (0-95,91) 3-Y-O **£9,056** (£2,695; £1,346; £673) **Stalls** High

Form RPR

211- **1** **Speed Company (IRE)**[208] 6454 3-9-5 **89** .... RyanMoore 8 99+
(John Quinn) *str: hld up in tch in rr: swtchd rt and effrt over 1f out: qcknd to chse ldr and wnt lft ins fnl f: led wl ins fnl f: sn in command and eased nr fin* **5/1**[3]

031- **2** *3/4* **Zzoro (IRE)**[182] 7194 3-9-0 **84** .... DarryllHolland 2 87
(Charles Hills) *led: rdn wl over 1f out: drvn 1f out: hdd and no ex wl ins fnl f* **16/1**

421- **3** *1 1/4* **Southdown Lad (IRE)**[174] 7398 3-9-6 **90** .... AndreaAtzeni 4 91
(William Knight) *lw: t.k.h: hld up in tch in last pair: swtchd rt and effrt wl over 1f out: 3rd and kpt on same pce u.p ins fnl f* **7/1**

1- **4** *3 1/4* **Jufn**[152] 7809 3-8-12 **82** .... DaneO'Neill 3 76
(Saeed bin Suroor) *str: swtg: wnt rt s: t.k.h in midfield: chsd ldrs after 2f: wnt 2nd 1/2-way tl jst over 2f out: racd awkwardly on downhill run and outpcd wl over 1f out: wknd ins fnl f* **4/1**[2]

1- **5** *nse* **Mutawaaly (IRE)**[129] 8122 3-9-1 **85** .... PaulHanagan 7 79
(Roger Varian) *str: hld up in tch in midfield: effrt to chal 2f out: unable qck u.p over 1f out: wknd ins fnl f* **11/10**[1]

01- **6** *3* **Zoffanys Pride (IRE)**[167] 7561 3-9-0 **84** .... DavidProbert 6 72
(Andrew Balding) *athletic: chsd ldr tl 1/2-way: lost pl u.p over 1f out: bhd ins fnl f* **10/1**

2m 15.96s (10.16) **Going Correction** +1.00s/f (Soft) **6** Ran SP% **111.8**
Speed ratings (Par 102): **99,98,97,94,94 92**
CSF £69.09 CT £549.49 TOTE £5.50: £2.90, £4.80; EX 53.90 Trifecta £170.80.
Owner Wilson Woo **Bred** Rathasker Stud **Trained** Settrington, N Yorks

FOCUS
Traditionally a strong handicap, with several winners going on to contest Group races. This was perhaps a lesser renewal, withthe unexposed pair disappointing, but the winner showed an impressive turn of foot to come from last. The level is hard to quantify.
T/Jkpt: Not won. T/Plt: £236.60 to a £1 stake. Pool: £115,209.48 - 355.33 winning units. T/Qpdt: £122.50 to a £1 stake. Pool: £6,642.00 - 40.10 winning units. **Steve Payne**

[1293] SOUTHWELL (L-H)
Tuesday, April 12

OFFICIAL GOING: Fibresand: standard
Wind: Moderate half behind Weather: Cloudy

1399 JOIN AT THE RACES ON FACEBOOK H'CAP 1m 3f (F)
2:00 (2:01) (Class 6) (0-65,65) 4-Y-O+ **£3,234** (£962; £481; £240) **Stalls** Low

Form RPR

2464 **1** **Deep Resolve (IRE)**[9] 1222 5-9-7 **65** .... BenCurtis 7 72
(Alan Swinbank) *dwlt and towards rr: stdy hdwy 1/2-way: trckd ldrs 4f out: effrt on outer and wd st: chal 2f out: rdn over 1f out: drvn and edgd lft ins fnl f: styd on to ld nr line* **4/1**[2]

2213 **2** *hd* **Star Ascending (IRE)**[35] 865 4-9-4 **62** .... JoeFanning 8 69
(Jennie Candlish) *trckd ldrs: hdwy and cl up 4f out: led over 2f out: sn jnd and rdn wl over 1f out: drvn and edgd lft ins fnl f: hdd and no ex nr line* **2/1**[1]

-004 **3** *3* **Solarmaite**[28] 939 7-9-4 **62** ....(b) ConnorBeasley 12 64
(Roy Bowring) *trckd ldrs: hdwy over 3f out: cl up over 2f out: rdn wl over 1f out and ev ch: n.m.r and swtchd rt ent fnl f: kpt on same pce* **14/1**

2132 **4** *7* **Toboggan's Gift**[28] 941 4-8-9 **53** .... PJMcDonald 9 43
(Ann Duffield) *midfield: hdwy to trck ldrs 4f out: rdn along wl over 2f out: drvn wl over 1f out and sn no imp* **8/1**

625- **5** *2 3/4* **Ghostly Arc (IRE)**[182] 7185 4-8-12 **56** .... BarryMcHugh 10 42
(Noel Wilson) *slt ld: pushed along 4f out: rdn over 3f out: hdd and drvn over 2f out: grad wknd* **18/1**

00/0 **6** *nse* **Poetic Lord**[14] 1131 7-8-11 **55** ....(vt) PaulMulrennan 6 41
(Rebecca Menzies) *chsd ldrs on inner: pushed along over 4f out: rdn 3f out: plugged on one pce* **50/1**

0-31 **7** *3 1/4* **Frosty The Snowman (IRE)**[20] 1048 5-8-9 **53** .... JamesSullivan 2 33
(Ruth Carr) *in rr: sme hdwy over 3f out: rdn along wl over 2f out: n.d* **5/1**[3]

0-05 **8** *6* **Powderonthebonnet (IRE)**[21] 1028 8-8-12 **59** .... JoeDoyle[(3)] 1 29
(Richard Phillips) *in tch: rdn along 5f out: sn wknd* **80/1**

1-00 **9** *4 1/2* **Hussar Ballad (USA)**[33] 890 7-9-7 **65** .... DavidAllan 4 28
(Antony Brittain) *trckd ldrs: pushed along 4f out: rdn 3f out: wknd fnl 2f* **12/1**

/30- **10** *35* **Ullswater (IRE)**[148] 7876 8-8-13 **62** ....(tp) PhilDennis[(5)] 5
(Philip Kirby) *midfield: rdn along on inner 5f out: sn lost pl and bhd* **33/1**

P64- **P** **Christmas Hamper (IRE)**[234] 5622 4-9-2 **63** .... AlistairRawlinson[(3)] 3
(Michael Appleby) *cl up on inner: pushed along over 6f out: rdn and lost pl over 5f out: bhd whn p.u wl over 3f out: dismntd* **10/1**

2m 25.37s (-2.63) **Going Correction** -0.125s/f (Stan) **11** Ran SP% **116.0**
Speed ratings (Par 101): **104,103,101,96,94 94,92,87,84,59**
CSF £12.06 CT £100.53 TOTE £4.50: £1.70, £1.30, £3.70; EX 13.80 Trifecta £112.50.
Owner Panther Racing Ltd **Bred** Dermot & Catherine Dwan **Trained** Melsonby, N Yorks

FOCUS
They went an even pace in this modest handicap. The winner has been rated to his best, with the runner-up fitting.

1400 AT THE RACES VIRGIN 534 MEDIAN AUCTION MAIDEN STKS 1m (F)
2:35 (2:40) (Class 5) 3-5-Y-O **£3,234** (£962; £481; £240) **Stalls** Low

Form RPR

0022 **1** **Melendez (USA)**[5] 1294 3-8-12 72 .... TimmyMurphy 6 79+
(Jamie Osborne) *t.k.h early: qckly away and crossed to inner rail: mde all: shkn up 2f out and sn clr: readily* **15/8**[1]

444- **2** *5* **Deansgate (IRE)**[194] 6873 3-8-12 72 ....[1] ConnorBeasley 5 65
(Julie Camacho) *t.k.h: trckd ldrs: wd st: hdwy over 2f out: sn rdn: drvn and edgd lft ent fnl f: kpt on but no ch w wnr* **6/1**[2]

3 *1 1/4* **William Hunter**[48] 4-9-13 0 .... WilliamTwiston-Davies 1 66
(Alan King) *trckd ldrs on inner: hdwy 3f out: rdn along over 1f out: kpt on same pce* **10/1**

-462 **4** *2 1/4* **Highwayman**[27] 959 3-8-12 66 ....(b[1]) ShaneKelly 9 57
(William Jarvis) *t.k.h: cl up: rdn along over 2f out: drvn wl over 1f out: sn one pce* **15/8**[1]

530- **5** *1 1/4* **G'Day Aussie**[185] 7105 3-8-12 68 .... TomEaves 3 54
(Brian Ellison) *cl up: rdn along wl over 2f out: drvn wl over 1f out: grad wknd* **8/1**[3]

6 *2 3/4* **Dusky Dawn** 4-9-8 0 .... NeilFarley 4 47
(Alan Swinbank) *s.i.s: hdwy and in tch after 2f: pushed along over 3f out: rdn over 2f out: grad wknd* **25/1**

7 *14* **The Skipper's Cat** 4-9-8 0 .... AndrewMullen 7 15
(Michael Appleby) *dwlt and towards rr: rdn along 1/2-way: sn outpcd and bhd* **33/1**

0 **8** *3 3/4* **Ginger Charlie**[15] 1123 3-8-12 0 .... JamesSullivan 2 7
(Ruth Carr) *chsd ldrs: rdn along over 3f out: sn wknd* **100/1**

5 **9** *25* **Tilsworth Phyllis**[20] 1037 4-9-5 0 .... AlistairRawlinson[(3)] 8
(J R Jenkins) *unruly s: a in rr: bhd fr over 3f out* **100/1**

1m 42.79s (-0.91) **Going Correction** -0.125s/f (Stan)
WFA 3 from 4yo 15lb **9** Ran SP% **112.8**
Speed ratings (Par 103): **99,94,92,90,89 86,72,68,43**
CSF £13.54 TOTE £3.90: £1.70, £1.50, £2.20; EX 12.50 Trifecta £59.50.
Owner Peppe Quintale **Bred** Debby Oxley **Trained** Upper Lambourn, Berks

FOCUS
Not maiden form to dwell on, with the winner out on his own.

1401 VISIT ATTHERACES.COM (S) STKS 6f (F)
3:10 (3:10) (Class 5) 4-Y-O+ **£3,234** (£962; £481; £240) **Stalls** Low

Form RPR

46-6 **1** **Layla's Hero (IRE)**[6] 1251 9-10-4 68 ....(b) PaulMulrennan 3 80
(David Nicholls) *awkward s: chsd ldrs on inner: hdwy over 2f out: rdn over 1f out: chal ent fnl f: kpt on wl to ld last 80yds* **11/1**

2052 **2** *hd* **Fortinbrass (IRE)**[5] 1299 6-8-13 57 .... JoeDoyle[(3)] 7 63
(John Balding) *trckd ldng pair: cl up 1/2-way: rdn to ld 1 1/2f out: drvn and edgd lft ent fnl f: hdd last 80yds: kpt on* **5/1**[3]

-262 **3** *2 1/4* **Spitfire**[27] 963 11-9-2 60 ....(t) ConnorBeasley 6 56
(J R Jenkins) *towards rr: wd st and hdwy over 2f out: rdn wl over 1f out: kpt on fnl f* **6/1**

5302 **4** *3/4* **Abi Scarlet (IRE)**[5] 1298 7-9-9 67 ....(b) BenCurtis 4 60
(Scott Dixon) *cl up: led 3f out and sn rdn: hdd 1 1/2f out: sn drvn and kpt on one pce* **5/2**[1]

2003 **5** *1* **Alpha Tauri (USA)**[13] 1154 10-9-2 65 .... ShaneKelly 5 50
(Charles Smith) *towards rr: wd st: rdn over 2f out: kpt on fnl f: n.d* **6/1**

2002 **6** *2* **Seamster**[11] 1178 9-10-0 72 ....(vt) DanielTudhope 8 56
(David O'Meara) *cl up: effrt on outer 3f out: rdn over 2f out: drvn wl over 1f out: sn wknd* **3/1**[2]

4163 **7** *5* **Coiste Bodhar (IRE)**[5] 1298 5-10-8 60 .... KieranO'Neill 2 48
(Scott Dixon) *slt ld on inner: pushed along and hdd 3f out: sn wknd* **33/1**

1m 16.1s (-0.40) **Going Correction** -0.125s/f (Stan) **7** Ran SP% **110.1**
Speed ratings (Par 103): **97,96,93,92,91 88,82**
CSF £59.44 TOTE £11.70: £4.60, £1.70; EX 71.70 Trifecta £531.30.
Owner D Nicholls **Bred** Epona Bloodstock Ltd **Trained** Sessay, N Yorks

FOCUS
A fair seller run at a sound pace. The winner has been rated back to last year's form.

1402 REMEMBERING DINO - SUPPORT THE RGT FILLIES' H'CAP 5f (F)
3:45 (3:45) (Class 5) (0-75,75) 4-Y-O+ **£3,881** (£1,155; £577; £288) **Stalls** Centre

Form RPR

2526 **1** **Saved My Bacon (IRE)**[8] 1237 5-8-13 **72** .... JosephineGordon[(5)] 7 81
(Chris Dwyer) *in rr and sn pushed along: rdn along 3f out: hdwy 2f out and sn swtchd rt: chsd ldr ins fnl f: sn drvn and styd on wl to ld nr fin* **9/2**[1]

650- **2** *1/2* **Chookie's Lass**[208] 6459 5-8-7 **61** ....(p) JasonHart 8 68
(Keith Dalgleish) *cl up: led 1/2-way: rdn wl over 1f out: drvn ins fnl f: hdd and no ex towards fin* **16/1**

30-6 **3** *3 1/4* **Perardua**[16] 1110 4-8-13 **67** ....(b[1]) CathyGannon 4 62
(David Evans) *slt ld to 1/2-way: cl up and rdn 2f out: drvn over 1f out: kpt on same pce* **6/1**[2]

06-0 **4** *1 1/2* **Percy's Gal**[21] 1030 5-8-13 **72** .... GemmaTutty[(5)] 2 62
(Karen Tutty) *chsd ldrs on outer: rdn along 2f out: sn drvn and kpt on same pce* **10/1**[3]

36-2 **5** *2 3/4* **Taffetta**[15] 1119 4-8-12 **66** .... BarryMcHugh 5 46
(Tony Coyle) *towards rr: rdn along 1/2-way: plugged on fnl f: nvr a threat* **6/1**[2]

510- **6** *1/2* **Margrets Gift**[199] 6765 5-9-7 **75** ....(p) DavidAllan 1 53
(Tim Easterby) *chsd ldng pair: pushed along over 2f out: rdn wl over 1f out: sn wknd* **9/2**[1]

342- **7** *3/4* **Wotnot (IRE)**[214] 6281 4-8-9 **63** .... ConnorBeasley 6 39
(Bryan Smart) *dwlt and towards rr: rdn along 1/2-way: nvr a factor* **9/2**[1]

00-5 **8** *3/4* **Spring Bird**[15] 1119 7-8-8 **62** .... BenCurtis 3 35
(Alan Swinbank) *chsd ldrs: rdn along over 2f out: sn wknd* **6/1**[2]

59.08s (-0.62) **Going Correction** -0.025s/f (Stan) **8** Ran SP% **112.4**
Speed ratings (Par 100): **103,102,97,94,90 89,88,87**
CSF £73.22 CT £433.79 TOTE £5.90: £1.80, £4.20, £1.90; EX 84.00 Trifecta £605.20.
Owner Mrs J Hughes & Mrs C Kemp **Bred** Kenneth Heelan **Trained** Newmarket, Suffolk

FOCUS
A fair, competitive-looking fillies handicap, in which they went a good pace throughout. The runner-up has been rated close to her old best.

1403 AT THE RACES SKY 415 H'CAP 7f (F)
4:20 (4:20) (Class 4) (0-80,79) 4-Y-O+ **£5,175** (£1,540; £769; £384) **Stalls** Low

Form RPR

0564 **1** **Street Force (USA)**[32] 900 5-9-4 **77**................(tp) AlistairRawlinson(3) 3 88
(Michael Appleby) *dwlt and sn swtchd rt to outer: hdwy to chse ldrs after 2f: cl up 3f out: led over 2f out: rdn clr over 1f out: kpt on strly* **5/1**[3]

03-1 **2** 4 ½ **Rocco's Delight**[6] 1252 4-9-4 **79** 6ex...................... CallumShepherd(5) 5 78
(Brian Ellison) *t.k.h: cl up: rdn along and outpcd over 3f out: drvn and edgd lft over 1f out: kpt on fnl f: no ch w wnr* **13/8**[1]

1032 **3** ¾ **Moonlight Venture**[6] 1251 5-9-7 **77**................................(b) LiamKeniry 6 74
(Conor Dore) *cl up: led 1/2-way: hdd over 2f out and sn rdn: drvn and edgd lft ent fnl f: kpt on same pce* **5/2**[2]

4141 **4** 2 ¾ **Harwoods Star (IRE)**[13] 1154 6-9-4 **74**..............................(be) JFEgan 1 64
(John Butler) *trckd ldrs on inner: hdwy wl over 2f out: rdn wl over 1f out: drvn and wknd appr fnl f* **9/1**

00-0 **5** 2 ½ **Paladin (IRE)**[34] 875 7-8-5 **68**..................................[1] MitchGodwin(7) 4 52
(Michael Blake) *a towards rr* **16/1**

510- **6** 6 **In Focus (IRE)**[203] 6616 5-9-7 **77**.. BenCurtis 2 45
(Alan Swinbank) *slt ld to 1/2-way: rdn along 3f out: wknd over 2f out* **15/2**

1m 28.22s (-2.08) **Going Correction** -0.125s/f (Stan) **6** Ran SP% **111.0**
Speed ratings (Par 105): **106,100,100,96,94 87**
CSF £13.30 TOTE £5.90: £2.70, £1.70; EX 14.50 Trifecta £39.40.
Owner Tariq Al Nisf **Bred** Rabbah Bloodstock Llc **Trained** Oakham, Rutland

FOCUS
A fair handicap but the winner was in total command. The winner has been rated back to his best.

1404 FOLLOW AT THE RACES ON TWITTER CLAIMING STKS 1m 3f (F)
4:55 (4:55) (Class 5) 4-Y-O+ **£3,234** (£962; £481; £240) **Stalls** Low

Form RPR

0/0- **1** **Marshgate Lane (USA)**[25] 6532 7-9-10 **99**.....................(p) LiamKeniry 6 89
(Neil Mulholland) *sn led: rdn clr 2f out: styd on str* **11/4**[2]

3036 **2** 6 **Patriotic (IRE)**[13] 1152 8-9-9 **78**..........................(p) JosephineGordon(5) 1 83
(Chris Dwyer) *led early: trckd wnr: effrt 3f out: rdn over 2f out: drvn wl over 1f out: kpt on: no ch w wnr* **7/1**[3]

5114 **3** 7 **Tatting**[19] 1058 7-9-2 **79**.. PaulMulrennan 5 59
(Conor Dore) *t.k.h early: hld up: hdwy on outer over 6f out: chsd ldng pair over 3f out: sn niggled along: rdn over 2f out: sn edgd lft and no imp* **8/11**[1]

00-6 **4** 7 **Lexington Bay (IRE)**[35] 864 8-8-11 **68**.......................(p) PhilDennis(5) 7 47
(Philip Kirby) *dwlt and rdn along s: in rr tl hdwy to chse ldng pair 1/2-way: pushed along over 4f out: rdn over 3f out: sn outpcd* **12/1**

0-00 **5** 13 **Jacobs Son**[43] 766 8-9-2 **67**..(v) DanielTudhope 2 25
(John Balding) *a towards rr* **22/1**

30-0 **6** 24 **Look Here's Al**[12] 1165 5-8-13 **47**..............................(p) GemmaTutty(5) 4
(Karen Tutty) *t.k.h early: chsd ldng pair on inner: lost pl bef 1/2-way: sn swtchd rt to outer and rdn: outpcd and bhd fnl 4f* **100/1**

2m 23.79s (-4.21) **Going Correction** -0.125s/f (Stan) **6** Ran SP% **110.1**
Speed ratings (Par 103): **110,105,100,95,86 68**
CSF £20.62 TOTE £3.40: £1.50, £2.40; EX 14.50 Trifecta £31.00.The winner was bought in for £8,000
Owner The Affordable Partnership **Bred** Edmund A Gann **Trained** Limpley Stoke, Wilts

FOCUS
A fair claimer but the winner proved too classy. The runner-up has been rated to form.

1405 SOUTHWELL GOLF CLUB MEMBERSHIP APPRENTICE H'CAP 1m 6f (F)
5:30 (5:30) (Class 5) (0-70,70) 4-Y-O+ **£3,881** (£1,155; £577; £288) **Stalls** Low

Form RPR

1 **An Fear Ciuin (IRE)**[227] 5873 5-9-10 **70**................(p) CallumRodriguez 4 81+
(Richard Ford) *led: clr after 4f: pushed along 3f out: rdn over 1f out: kpt on wl towards fin* **12/1**

0654 **2** ½ **My Tringaling (IRE)**[20] 1049 4-8-0 **51** oh3..................... MillyNaseb(2) 8 59
(Stuart Williams) *chsd ldng pair: hdwy over 3f out: rdn to chse wnr 2f out: clsd up ent fnl f: ev ch tl no ex towards fin* **15/2**

36-0 **3** 10 **Teenage Dream (IRE)**[10] 1201 8-7-13 **51** oh1........... BenRobinson(6) 5 45
(Brian Ellison) *hld up towards rr: hdwy 4f out: rdn to chse ldng pair 2f out: sn no imp* **7/2**[2]

4222 **4** 5 **Northside Prince (IRE)**[33] 891 10-9-10 **70**................ SophieKilloran 1 57
(Alan Swinbank) *hld up in rr: pushed along over 3f out: rdn wl over 2f out: sme late hdwy* **4/1**[3]

230- **5** 4 **La Fritillaire**[160] 7698 4-8-1 **52**....................................... MitchGodwin(2) 6 33
(James Given) *chsd wnr 4f: prom: rdn along over 4f out: drvn over 3f out and sn wknd* **10/1**

2313 **6** 9 **Henry Smith**[20] 1048 4-8-2 **55**..................................(be) GeorgeWood(4) 2 24
(Garry Moss) *prom: trckd wnr after 4f: clsd up 4f out: rdn along 3f out: drvn over 2f out and sn wknd* **5/2**[1]

1100 **7** 6 **Pao De Acuca (IRE)**[3] 1347 4-8-12 **67**.................(t) RichardCondon(6) 3 27
(Jose Santos) *chsd ldrs on inner: lost pl over 4f out: sn bhd* **10/1**

-544 **8** 7 **Monzino (USA)**[13] 1156 8-8-5 **51** oh3............................. RhiainIngram 7 2
(Michael Chapman) *a in rr: outpcd and bhd fnl 4f* **33/1**

3m 6.49s (-1.81) **Going Correction** -0.125s/f (Stan)
WFA 4 from 5yo+ 3lb **8** Ran SP% **111.4**
Speed ratings (Par 103): **100,99,94,91,88 83,80,76**
CSF £92.44 CT £375.17 TOTE £11.30: £2.70, £2.40, £1.70; EX 81.80 Trifecta £1272.50.
Owner D M Proos **Bred** Miss S A McManus **Trained** Garstang, Lancs

FOCUS
A fair staying handicap and the two principals pulled clear.
T/Plt: £147.20 to a £1 stake. Pool: £69,146.45 - 342.83 winning units. T/Qpdt: £115.90 to a £1 stake. Pool: £4,788.91 - 30.56 winning units. **Joe Rowntree**

BEVERLEY (R-H)
Wednesday, April 13

OFFICIAL GOING: Soft
Wind: Light half against Weather: Cloudy

1406 ACEODDS.COM BET CALCULATOR MAIDEN STKS 1m 1f 207y
2:00 (2:00) (Class 5) 3-Y-O **£3,881** (£1,155; £577; £288) **Stalls** Low

Form RPR

4- **1** **Sightline**[173] 7422 3-9-0 0... GrahamGibbons 7 77
(Ralph Beckett) *trckd ldr: hdwy and cl up 3f out: led wl over 1f out: rdn ent fnl f: drvn and kpt on gamely towards fin* **9/4**[2]

04-3 **2** nk **School Fete (IRE)**[26] 976 3-9-5 0................................. WilliamCarson 1 81
(Michael Bell) *trckd ldng pair: hdwy over 2f out: chsd wnr over 1f out and sn rdn: drvn and ev ch ins fnl f: kpt on* **4/1**[3]

3 4 ½ **Mazaz (IRE)** 3-9-5 0.. NickyMackay 4 72+
(John Gosden) *awkward s and green towards rr: hdwy to trck ldrs over 4f out: effrt 2f out: sn rdn and kpt on same pce fnl f* **2/1**[1]

20 **4** 2 ¾ **Clayton Hall (IRE)**[17] 1113 3-9-5 0................................ TonyHamilton 5 67
(Richard Fahey) *dwlt and towards rr: pushed along 1/2-way: rdn along and hdwy over 2f out: drvn and no imp fnl f* **10/1**

24- **5** shd **Head High (IRE)**[165] 7638 3-9-5 0.. GrahamLee 3 66
(Kevin Ryan) *led: pushed along over 2f out: sn rdn and hdd wl over 1f out: grad wknd* **9/1**

0-4 **6** 20 **Sogno D'Amore (USA)**[15] 1134 3-9-5 0......................... FrannyNorton 6 26
(Mark Johnston) *a in rr: rdn along over 3f out: sn outpcd and bhd* **33/1**

65 **7** 1 ¼ **Shulammite Man (IRE)**[6] 1294 3-9-5 0.............................. BenCurtis 8 24
(Alan Swinbank) *a in rr: rdn along over 3f out: sn outpcd and bhd* **100/1**

5 **8** 98 **Louvencourt (FR)**[12] 1184 3-9-5 0...................................... JoeFanning 2
(Mark Johnston) *chsd ldrs: rdn along 4f out: sn wknd* **14/1**

2m 13.19s (6.19) **Going Correction** +0.575s/f (Yiel) **8** Ran SP% **113.8**
Speed ratings (Par 98): **98,97,94,91,91 75,74,**
CSF £11.65 TOTE £3.40: £1.10, £2.10, £1.30; EX 13.20 Trifecta £46.80.
Owner J H Richmond-Watson **Bred** Lawn Stud **Trained** Kimpton, Hants

FOCUS
Soft ground (GoingStick: 6.3) and temporary safety factors of 12 were in place for all races due to a wet patch of ground on the outside of the track (away from the running line) at the 2f point in the home straight, which was railed off to aid recovery. No more than a fair maiden. The winner has been rated as building on his promising 2yo debut.

1407 WELCOME BACK TO BEVERLEY NOVICE AUCTION STKS 5f
2:35 (2:35) (Class 5) 2-Y-O **£3,780** (£1,131; £565; £283; £141) **Stalls** Low

Form RPR

1 **Orewa (IRE)** 2-9-0 0.. BenCurtis 8 78+
(Brian Ellison) *sltly hmpd s: green and in rr: pushed along 1/2-way: sn swtchd lft to outer: rdn to chse ldrs over 1f out: styd on strly ins fnl f: led last 50yds* **10/1**

32 **2** 3 **Decadent Times (IRE)**[9] 1233 2-8-13 0............................ LiamJones 1 66
(Tom Dascombe) *led: rdn along over 1f out: drvn and edgd lft ent fnl f: hdd & wknd last 50yds* **1/1**[1]

4 **3** ½ **Jollydee (IRE)**[11] 1199 2-8-8 0... PJMcDonald 3 59
(Paul Midgley) *chsd ldng pair: effrt 2f out and sn rdn along: n.m.r and swtchd lft over 1f out: drvn and kpt on same pce fnl f* **3/1**[2]

4 shd **Melesina (IRE)** 2-8-11 0.. TonyHamilton 6 62
(Richard Fahey) *trckd ldr: effrt and cl up 2f out: rdn over 1f out: kpt on same pce ins fnl f* **17/2**

5 2 ¼ **Kroy** 2-8-9 0... JacobButterfield(3) 4 55
(Ollie Pears) *chsd ldrs on inner: hdwy wl over 1f out: rdn and one pce fnl f* **50/1**

6 **6** 4 ½ **Lavender Skye (IRE)**[18] 1086 2-8-8 0............................ FrannyNorton 7 34
(K R Burke) *wnt lft s: in tch: rdn along 1/2-way: sn wknd* **16/1**

7 2 **Our Charlie Brown** 2-9-0 0.. DavidAllan 5 33
(Tim Easterby) *green: a in rr* **7/1**[3]

1m 8.04s (4.54) **Going Correction** +0.875s/f (Soft) **7** Ran SP% **115.0**
Speed ratings (Par 92): **98,93,92,92,88 81,78**
CSF £20.83 TOTE £10.00: £4.10, £1.20; EX 31.40 Trifecta £110.40.
Owner Keith Brown **Bred** Mrs C Regalado-Gonzalez **Trained** Norton, N Yorks

FOCUS
Not a strong maiden but the winner overcame greenness to win comfortably. The runner-up has been rated below his previous form.

1408 N L VAN TRUCK AND CAR HIRE H'CAP 5f
3:10 (3:10) (Class 3) (0-95,92) 4-Y-O+
£7,158 (£2,143; £1,071; £535; £267; £134) **Stalls** Low

Form RPR

410- **1** **Arctic Feeling (IRE)**[172] 7461 8-9-4 **92**....................... SammyJoBell(3) 2 101
(Richard Fahey) *towards rr: hdwy on inner 1/2-way: rdn over 1f out: kpt on to ld last 100yds* **5/1**[3]

00-0 **2** ½ **Intense Style (IRE)**[32] 920 4-9-5 **90**................................ DavidAllan 11 97
(Les Eyre) *in tch: hdwy on outer to chse ldrs 1/2-way: rdn along and edgd rt 2f out: slt ld jst over 1f out: sn drvn and edgd rt ins fnl f: hdd and no ex last 100yds* **25/1**

000- **3** 2 ½ **Kibaar**[215] 6273 4-9-3 **88**... KeaganLatham 6 86
(Kevin Ryan) *cl up: led 1/2-way: rdn along wl over 1f out: hdd appr fnl f: sn drvn and kpt on same pce* **11/1**

450- **4** 1 **Lexington Place**[187] 7091 6-9-3 **88**.............................. JamesSullivan 8 83
(Ruth Carr) *in rr: hdwy 2f out: rdn over 1f out: styd on fnl f: nrst fin* **10/1**

560- **5** nk **Long Awaited (IRE)**[305] 3153 8-9-1 **86**..................(b) GrahamGibbons 3 80
(David Barron) *trckd ldrs: hdwy 2f out: effrt and n.m.r over 1f out: rdn ent fnl f: kpt on same pce* **9/2**[2]

205- **6** ¾ **Singeur (IRE)**[177] 7343 9-8-13 **84**...................................... GrahamLee 5 75
(Rebecca Bastiman) *chsd ldrs: rdn along over 2f out: kpt on same pce* **13/2**

200- **7** 9 **Whozthecat (IRE)**[158] 7758 9-9-0 **85**................................. NeilFarley 7 43
(Declan Carroll) *chsd ldrs: rdn along 2f out: sn wknd* **20/1**

046- **8** 3 ½ **Noble Storm (USA)**[187] 7091 10-9-3 **88**........................... JoeFanning 9 34
(Ed McMahon) *hld up: sme hdwy on outer 1/2-way: sn rdn along and n.d* **12/1**

300- **9** 1 **Masamah (IRE)**[285] 3858 10-9-7 **92**..................................[1] DavidNolan 1 34
(Patrick Morris) *slt ld: rdn along and edgd lft wl over 2f out: sn hdd & wknd* **10/1**

053- **10** 1 ½ **Rural Celebration**[179] 7286 5-8-11 **87**............................ JoshDoyle(5) 4 24
(David O'Meara) *hld up in tch: n.m.r and pushed along 3f out: sn lost pl and bhd* **7/2**[1]

000- **11** 3 ½ **Ballesteros**[179] 7286 7-8-13 **84**.. TomEaves 10 8
(Patrick Morris) *prom: cl up 1/2-way: sn rdn along and wknd wl over 1f out* **25/1**

1m 7.22s (3.72) **Going Correction** +0.95s/f (Soft) **11** Ran SP% **117.1**
Speed ratings (Par 107): **108,107,103,101,101 99,85,79,78,75 70**
CSF £126.13 CT £1320.94 TOTE £4.80: £2.10, £7.40, £4.00; EX 100.90 Trifecta £625.90.
Owner Percy / Green Racing 2 **Bred** John McEnery **Trained** Musley Bank, N Yorks

FOCUS
A competitive sprint handicap. The winner has been rated to form.

1409 BEVERLEY ANNUAL BADGEHOLDERS H'CAP 7f 100y
3:45 (3:45) (Class 4) (0-80,80) 3-Y-O **£5,040** (£1,508; £754; £377; £188) **Stalls** Low

Form RPR
015- **1** **Galesburg (IRE)**[207] 6534 3-9-4 **77** JoeFanning 6 83
(Mark Johnston) *trckd ldr: cl up over 2f out: rdn to chal over 1f out: led appr fnl f: sn drvn and kpt on wl* **5/1**[2]
630- **2** *2* **Zahrat Narjis**[176] 7370 3-8-9 **68** TonyHamilton 2 69
(Richard Fahey) *trckd ldng pair: hdwy on inner 2f out: rdn over 1f out: kpt on u.p fnl f* **12/1**
30-1 **3** *shd* **Motdaw**[7] 1275 3-9-2 **75** 6ex GrahamGibbons 4 76
(Mick Channon) *trckd ldrs: effrt over 2f out and sn pushed along: swtchd lft to outer aNd rdn over 1f out: styd on wl fnl f* **3/1**[1]
31- **4** *hd* **Rebel Lightning (IRE)**[145] 7922 3-9-3 **76** WilliamTwiston-Davies 3 76
(Richard Spencer) *in tch: hdwy over 2f out: rdn to chse ldrs over 1f out: drvn and kpt on fnl f* **6/1**[3]
6-14 **5** *½* **He's A Dreamer (IRE)**[13] 1168 3-9-7 **80** PhillipMakin 1 79
(David O'Meara) *led: pushed along over 2f out: rdn wl over 1f out: hdd and drvn appr fnl f: grad wknd* **5/1**[2]
636- **6** *6* **Silver Streak (IRE)**[173] 7421 3-9-6 **79** PJMcDonald 5 64
(Ann Duffield) *hld up in rr: pushed along 3f out: rdn along over 2f out: sn btn* **14/1**
52-1 **7** *5* **Al Hamd (IRE)**[21] 1036 3-9-7 **80** GrahamLee 7 53+
(Ed Dunlop) *unruly in stalls: s.i.s and lost several l s: a in rr* **3/1**[1]

1m 39.34s (5.54) **Going Correction** +0.80s/f (Soft) 7 Ran SP% **112.0**
Speed ratings (Par 100): **100,97,97,97,96 89,84**
CSF £57.32 TOTE £5.70: £2.30, £7.50; EX 56.50 Trifecta £246.50.
Owner Sheikh Hamdan bin Mohammed Al Maktoum **Bred** Darley **Trained** Middleham Moor, N Yorks

FOCUS
Quite a tight little handicap. It's been rated around the runner-up.

1410 ROA/RACING POST OWNERS JACKPOT H'CAP 1m 4f 16y
4:20 (4:20) (Class 5) (0-75,75) 3-Y-O **£3,780** (£1,131; £565; £283) **Stalls** Low

Form RPR
331 **1** **Project Bluebook (FR)**[42] 789 3-9-4 **72** JasonHart 3 77+
(John Quinn) *trckd ldr: cl up over 2f out: rdn to chal wl over 1f out: drvn ins fnl f: styd on wl to ld towards fin* **15/8**[1]
450- **2** *1* **Matidia**[196] 6859 3-8-9 **63** GrahamGibbons 5 66
(Ralph Beckett) *led: pushed along over 2f out: rdn wl over 1f out: drvn ent fnl f: hdd and no ex towards fin* **4/1**[2]
550- **3** *2* **Sporty Yankee (USA)**[187] 7092 3-8-11 **65** DougieCostello 4 65
(K R Burke) *trckd ldng pair: hdwy over 2f out: rdn wl over 1f out: swtchd lft and drvn appr fnl f: kpt on same pce* **4/1**[2]
445- **4** *3* **Airton**[177] 7336 3-9-2 **70**[1] PJMcDonald 2 65
(James Bethell) *hld up in rr: hdwy over 4f out: chsd ldrs wl over 2f out: rdn wl over 1f out: sn no imp* **15/8**[1]

2m 54.35s (14.55) **Going Correction** +0.875s/f (Soft) 4 Ran SP% **109.6**
Speed ratings (Par 98): **86,85,84,82**
CSF £9.38 TOTE £2.10; EX 6.40 Trifecta £20.60.
Owner Ross Harmon **Bred** S C E A Haras De La Perelle **Trained** Settrington, N Yorks

FOCUS
Just the four runners, but a case could be made for each of them. Muddling form.

1411 FOLLOW US ON TWITTER @BEVERLEY_RACES H'CAP 1m 1f 207y
4:55 (4:55) (Class 4) (0-80,79) 3-Y-O **£5,040** (£1,508; £754; £377; £188) **Stalls** Low

Form RPR
51 **1** **Another Go (IRE)**[16] 1123 3-9-6 **79** BenCurtis 2 87+
(Alan Swinbank) *trckd ldrs: pushed along over 3f out: rdn over 2f out: edgd rt over 1f out: drvn to chse ldr and hung lft ent fnl f: styd on to ld last 110yds* **3/1**[1]
021- **2** *3¾* **Coherent (IRE)**[144] 7946 3-9-4 **77** GrahamGibbons 1 77+
(William Haggas) *sn led: rdn along over 2f out: drvn ent fnl f: hdd & wknd last 110yds* **3/1**[1]
-415 **3** *3¾* **Jintshi**[48] 705 3-9-4 **77** JoeFanning 3 70
(Mark Johnston) *trckd ldr: effrt over 2f out: rdn wl over 1f out: kpt on same pce appr fnl f* **7/2**[2]
030- **4** *1¼* **Icefall (IRE)**[187] 7092 3-9-2 **75** DavidAllan 6 65
(Tim Easterby) *in rr: pushed along over 4f out: rdn wl over 2f out: kpt on u.p fnl f* **9/1**[3]
215- **5** *hd* **Fool To Cry (IRE)**[200] 6761 3-9-4 **77** JackMitchell 5 67
(Roger Varian) *in tch: pushed along over 3f out: rdn over 2f out: sn drvn and plugged on one pce* **3/1**[1]
45-4 **6** *1* **Henry The Explorer (CAN)**[22] 1027 3-9-4 **77** DavidNolan 4 65
(Jo Hughes) *chsd ldng pair: rdn along wl over 2f out: drvn and wknd wl over 1f out* **16/1**

2m 16.4s (9.40) **Going Correction** +0.95s/f (Soft) 6 Ran SP% **113.1**
Speed ratings (Par 100): **100,97,94,93,92 92**
CSF £12.46 TOTE £4.10: £1.40, £2.40; EX 13.20 Trifecta £30.20.
Owner Brian Valentine **Bred** Lutz Oertel **Trained** Melsonby, N Yorks
■ Stewards' Enquiry : Graham Gibbons two-day ban: used whip with excessive force (Apr 27-28)

FOCUS
This proved a real test in the conditions. The runner-up has been rated to form.

1412 NEW SEASON FILLIES' H'CAP 1m 100y
5:30 (5:30) (Class 5) (0-70,70) 4-Y-O+ **£3,780** (£1,131; £565; £283; £141) **Stalls** Low

Form RPR
30-0 **1** **Fidelma Moon (IRE)**[13] 1158 4-9-2 **70** JordanVaughan(5) 7 77
(K R Burke) *t.k.h: cl up: rdn to chal 2f out: led wl over 1f out and sn edgd lft: drvn and edgd lft ins fnl f: kpt on wl towards fin* **8/1**[3]
221- **2** *¾* **Miss Ranger (IRE)**[52] 7067 4-9-1 **64** BenCurtis 5 69
(Brian Ellison) *hld up towards rr: pushed along 1/2-way: rdn over 2f out: drvn and styd on ent fnl f: kpt on* **11/10**[1]
110- **3** *¾* **The Wee Barra (IRE)**[168] 7058 4-8-7 **63** (p) LewisEdmunds(7) 3 67
(Kevin Ryan) *trckd ldng pair: hdwy over 2f out: rdn to chal on outer over 1f out and ev ch: n.m.r ent fnl f: kpt on same pce* **9/1**
4304 **4** *2¼* **Make On Madam (IRE)**[7] 1252 4-9-0 **63** DavidAllan 4 61
(Les Eyre) *awkward s: t.k.h and sn chsng ldrs: rdn along wl over 2f out: drvn over 1f out: kpt on one pce* **11/4**[2]
044- **5** *3* **Big Red**[211] 6397 4-8-7 **56** oh11 BarryMcHugh 9 47
(Rebecca Bastiman) *in rr: hdwy over 2f out: rdn wl over 1f out: swtchd rt ent fnl f: no imp* **22/1**
66-0 **6** *1¾* **Cabal**[16] 1125 9-9-7 **70** (p) FrannyNorton 2 57
(Geoffrey Harker) *chsd ldrs: rdn along wl over 2f out: drvn over 1f out: sn one pce* **9/1**
040- **7** *8* **Bertha Burnett (IRE)**[330] 2374 5-8-7 **56** oh5 JamesSullivan 1 25
(Brian Rothwell) *led: pushed along 3f out: rdn over 2f out: hdd and drvn wl over 1f out: wknd appr fnl f* **22/1**

1m 57.25s (9.65) **Going Correction** +1.025s/f (Soft) 7 Ran SP% **114.1**
Speed ratings (Par 100): **92,91,90,88,85 83,75**
CSF £17.26 CT £80.96 TOTE £10.40: £3.60, £1.40; EX 29.70 Trifecta £173.60.
Owner The Mount Racing Club & Mrs E Burke **Bred** J H Stulen **Trained** Middleham Moor, N Yorks

FOCUS
A modest affair. The winner has been rated close to her old best.
T/Plt: £227.00 to a £1 stake. Pool: £57,835.65 - 185.92 winning units. T/Qpdt: £106.90 to a £1 stake. Pool: £4033.33 - 27.90 winning units. **Joe Rowntree**

1256 KEMPTON (A.W) (R-H)
Wednesday, April 13

OFFICIAL GOING: Polytrack: standard
Wind: light behind Weather: light drizzle race 5

1413 LADIES DAY AT KEMPTON PARK 03.09.16 H'CAP 1m 4f (P)
5:50 (5:50) (Class 6) (0-60,60) 4-Y-O+ **£2,264** (£673; £336; £168) **Stalls** Centre

Form RPR
-321 **1** **Zarliman (IRE)**[28] 255 6-8-12 **51** (p) LiamKeniry 5 59
(Neil Mulholland) *sn chsng ldrs: led 1f out: kpt on: jst hld on* **5/2**[1]
00-1 **2** *shd* **Hurricane Volta (IRE)**[13] 1169 5-9-4 **57** (p) DaneO'Neill 3 65
(Peter Hedger) *mid-div: hdwy over 2f out: chal 1f out: styd on: jst hld* **7/1**[3]
50-4 **3** *2¼* **Bollihope**[13] 1169 4-9-6 **60** ConnorBeasley 10 64
(Richard Guest) *mid-div: hdwy over 2f out: kpt on same pce appr fnl f* **11/2**[2]
4406 **4** *½* **Opera Buff**[9] 1038 7-9-2 **60** (p) EdwardGreatrex(5) 11 63
(Jose Santos) *s.i.s: sn chsng ldrs: upsides 7f out: led briefly over 1f out: kpt on same pce* **25/1**
020- **5** *1¼* **Hatsaway (IRE)**[200] 6736 5-9-7 **60** JFEgan 7 61
(Pat Phelan) *mid-div: hdwy over 2f out: one pce over 1f out* **14/1**
56-0 **6** *½* **Invincible Wish (IRE)**[21] 1047 4-9-2 **59** RobHornby(3) 8 60
(Trevor Wall) *t.k.h in rr: drvn 3f out: styd on wl appr fnl f: fin wl* **14/1**
455- **7** *1¼* **Duke Of Diamonds**[188] 7068 4-9-0 **57** ShelleyBirkett(3) 2 56
(Julia Feilden) *led 1f: chsd ldrs: hmpd after 3f: drvn over 3f out: one pce fnl 2f* **20/1**
0223 **8** *3* **Sudden Wish (IRE)**[21] 1039 7-8-13 **52** TedDurcan 13 46
(Michael Attwater) *led after 1f: hdd over 1f out: sn wknd* **16/1**
652- **9** *nk* **Azure Amour (IRE)**[161] 7705 4-9-3 **57** FrederikTylicki 4 50
(Rod Millman) *prom: hmpd after 3f: hdwy over 2f out: sn chsng ldrs: one pce* **8/1**
0600 **10** *nse* **Occult**[28] 950 4-9-3 **57** HarryBentley 14 50
(Simon Dow) *dwlt: t.k.h in rr: hdwy over 2f out: kpt on one pce over 1f out* **16/1**
44-6 **11** *1* **Sheikh The Reins (IRE)**[7] 1262 7-9-3 **56** KierenFox 12 48
(John Best) *mid-div: effrt over 3f out: lost pl over 2f out* **14/1**
0540 **12** *1¼* **Thane Of Cawdor (IRE)**[28] 949 7-9-2 **60** PatrickO'Donnell(5) 6 50
(Joseph Tuite) *hld up in rr: drvn 3f out: nvr on terms* **8/1**

2m 34.48s (-0.02) **Going Correction** -0.125s/f (Stan)
WFA 4 from 5yo+ 1lb 12 Ran SP% **119.1**
Speed ratings (Par 101): **95,94,93,93,92 91,91,89,88,88 88,87**
CSF £19.48 CT £90.58 TOTE £3.60: £1.50, £2.60, £1.80; EX 22.10 Trifecta £85.60.
Owner M Cahill **Bred** His Highness The Aga Khan's Studs S C **Trained** Limpley Stoke, Wilts
■ Stewards' Enquiry : Ted Durcan two-day ban: careless riding (Apr 27-28)

FOCUS
This moderate handicap was run at a fair enough pace and the form is straightforward.

1414 32RED CASINO MAIDEN AUCTION STKS 6f (P)
6:20 (6:20) (Class 5) 3-Y-O **£2,911** (£866; £432; £216) **Stalls** Low

Form RPR
0-2 **1** **Saeedan (IRE)**[34] 885 3-9-1 0 DanielMuscutt(3) 2 78
(Marco Botti) *chsd ldrs: drvn 3f out: led over 1f out: styd on* **11/2**[3]
335- **2** *1¼* **Jack Nevison**[189] 7039 3-8-13 77 DaneO'Neill 1 69
(Henry Candy) *trckd ldrs: effrt over 2f out: edgd lft: styd on same pce fnl f* **1/1**[1]
0- **3** *nk* **Dream Farr (IRE)**[145] 7921 3-8-13 0 (t) AntonioFresu 5 68+
(Ed Walker) *dwlt: in rr: hdwy over 2f out: kpt on same pce over 1f out* **25/1**
4 *2* **Lightfeet (USA)** 3-9-4 0 RichardKingscote 11 67+
(Jeremy Gask) *swtchd rt s: bhd: hdwy over 1f out: kpt on same pce* **16/1**
3-02 **5** *nk* **King Of Spin**[12] 1183 3-9-1 72 RobHornby(3) 10 66
(William Muir) *rr-div: hdwy over 2f out: kpt on same pce fnl f* **9/2**[2]
0- **6** *nk* **Curious Fox**[167] 7578 3-8-6 0 RobertTart 7 53
(Anthony Carson) *rr-div: hdwy over 2f out: kpt on one pce over 1f out* **100/1**
7 *¾* **Shahaama** 3-8-13 0 MartinHarley 8 59+
(Mick Channon) *hld up in rr: styd on fnl 2f: will improve* **8/1**
0-5 **8** *3¾* **Storming Ambition**[33] 902 3-8-13 0 JimmyQuinn 4 45
(Conrad Allen) *mid-div: drvn over 3f out: fdd over 1f out* **66/1**
23-3 **9** *hd* **Deer Song**[97] 83 3-8-11 64 JFEgan 9 43
(John Bridger) *swtchd rt s: led: hdd over 1f out: hung lft and sn wknd: bhd whn eased clsng stages* **25/1**
06 **10** *½* **Allen's Folly**[15] 1132 3-8-6 0 AdamBeschizza 3 36
(Peter Hiatt) *t.k.h: sn trcking ldr: lost pl over 1f out: bhd whn eased clsng stages* **100/1**
6-0 **11** *2¾* **Tiz Herself (IRE)**[18] 1091 3-8-5 0 DannyBrock(3) 6 29
(Jonathan Portman) *sn trcking ldr: upsides whn hung bdly lft over 2f out: lost pl over 1f out: bhd whn eased clsng stages* **16/1**

1m 12.18s (-0.92) **Going Correction** -0.125s/f (Stan) 11 Ran SP% **117.6**
Speed ratings (Par 98): **101,99,98,96,95 95,94,89,89,88 84**
CSF £11.08 TOTE £5.40: £1.60, £1.10, £7.00; EX 15.70 Trifecta £259.20.
Owner HH Shaikh Ali Zain Alabedeen Al Khalifa **Bred** M O'Donovan **Trained** Newmarket, Suffolk

FOCUS
They didn't hang about in this modest sprint maiden. It should produce its share of future winners. The level is a bit fluid.

1415 £10 FREE BET AT 32REDSPORT.COM H'CAP (DIV I) 7f (P)
6:50 (6:50) (Class 5) (0-70,73) 4-Y-O+ **£2,911** (£866; £432; £216) **Stalls** Low

Form RPR

4002 **1** **Blackthorn Stick (IRE)**[14] 1147 7-8-8 **57**......................(p) JimmyQuinn 2 65
(Paul Burgoyne) *in rr-div: hdwy over 2f out: styd on wl fnl f: led nr fin* **20/1**

515- **2** *nk* **Snappy Guest**[177] 7347 4-9-6 **69**........................ RyanPowell 8 76
(George Margarson) *chsd ldrs: styd on to ld last 50yds: hdd nr fin* **12/1**

4112 **3** *nk* **Exalted (IRE)**[74] 403 5-9-2 **65**................................(t) RichardKingscote 9 71
(William Knight) *swtchd rt after s: led after 150yds: hdd and no ex last 50yds* **9/4**[1]

61 **4** *2 1/4* **Seek The Fair Land**[7] 1264 10-9-10 **73** 6ex....................(b) AdamKirby 6 73
(Lee Carter) *trckd ldrs: t.k.h: one pce appr fnl f* **10/1**

000- **5** *1 1/4* **Victor's Bet (SPA)**[169] 7535 7-9-0 **70**.......................... RhiainIngram(7) 3 67+
(Ralph J Smith) *in rr: styd on wl appr fnl f: nt rch ldrs* **66/1**

-211 **6** *2* **Misu Pete**[17] 1116 4-8-13 **62**.. DarryllHolland 4 53
(Mark Usher) *led 150yds: chsd ldrs: effrt over 2f out: wknd fnl f* **5/1**[3]

0-44 **7** *1 1/4* **Makhfar (IRE)**[12] 1180 5-8-10 **59**......................................(v) ShaneKelly 5 49
(Kevin Morgan) *in rr-div: hdwy over 2f out: one pce whn n.m.r 150yds out* **8/1**

3263 **8** *nse* **Gold Beau (FR)**[28] 955 6-9-4 **67**...............................(p) CathyGannon 10 55
(Kristin Stubbs) *chsd ldrs: wknd appr fnl f* **16/1**

-432 **9** *1 1/2* **Veeraya**[17] 1116 6-9-0 **66**...(bt) ShelleyBirkett(3) 1 50
(Julia Feilden) *trckd ldrs: effrt over 2f out: wknd fnl f* **4/1**[2]

606- **10** *1 1/2* **He's My Boy (IRE)**[207] 6537 5-9-0 **63**............................... TomQueally 11 43
(James Fanshawe) *awkward s: hdwy into mid-div over 3f out: lost pl over 1f out* **15/2**

000/ **11** *8* **Catharina**[609] 5305 4-8-8 **60**.. JackDuern(3) 7 18
(Dean Ivory) *s.i.s: t.k.h in rr: hung lft bnd over 2f out: sn bhd* **33/1**

1m 24.84s (-1.16) **Going Correction** -0.125s/f (Stan) **11** Ran SP% **122.2**
Speed ratings (Par 103): **101,100,100,97,96 94,92,92,90,89 79**
CSF £246.04 CT £774.24 TOTE £26.30: £4.60, £2.60, £2.00; EX 279.70 Trifecta £1710.80.
Owner Knowle Rock Racing **Bred** F Prendergast **Trained** Shepton Montague, Somerset

FOCUS
A competitive affair for the class. There was a sound pace on and the fourth sets the level. The third has been rated to form.

1416 £10 FREE BET AT 32REDSPORT.COM H'CAP (DIV II) 7f (P)
7:20 (7:20) (Class 5) (0-70,70) 4-Y-O+ **£2,911** (£866; £432; £216) **Stalls** Low

Form RPR

400- **1** **Footstepsintherain (IRE)**[202] 6669 6-9-5 **68** ow1.............. AmirQuinn 1 80
(Lee Carter) *stmbld and wnt lft s: mde all: clr over 1f out: drvn out* **8/1**

5-16 **2** *4 1/2* **Etaad (USA)**[67] 482 5-9-1 **69**....................................(b) HectorCrouch(5) 4 69
(Gary Moore) *n.m.r s: chsd ldrs: modest 2nd over 1f out: no ch w wnr* **4/1**[2]

5320 **3** *4 1/2* **West Leake (IRE)**[20] 1064 10-8-9 **58** ow1.......................... LiamKeniry 10 46
(Paul Burgoyne) *hld up in rr: hdwy over 2f out: styd on fnl f: tk modest 3rd nr fin* **16/1**

0640 **4** *1/2* **Embankment**[28] 951 7-9-0 **63**.. KierenFox 7 49
(Michael Attwater) *s.i.s: detached in last: hdwy on outside over 2f out: kpt on fnl f* **13/2**[3]

-532 **5** *3/4* **Surewecan**[7] 1269 4-9-1 **64**.. AdamKirby 2 48
(Mark Johnston) *hmpd s: chsd ldrs: effrt over 2f out: fdd fnl f* **6/4**[1]

400- **6** *nse* **George Baker (IRE)**[217] 6211 9-9-0 **68**........................ DannyBurton(5) 5 52
(George Baker) *mid-div: effrt over 2f out: kpt on over 1f out: nvr a factor* **20/1**

0-00 **7** *1 1/2* **Golden Highway (USA)**[55] 621 4-9-2 **65**................(tp) AndrewMullen 6 45
(Michael Appleby) *in rr: drvn over 2f out: nvr a factor* **33/1**

00-0 **8** *3/4* **Diamonds A Dancing**[12] 1186 6-8-6 **60**............ EdwardGreatrex(5) 3 38
(John O'Shea) *n.m.r s: mid-div: drvn over 2f out: hung lft and one pce* **12/1**

-050 **9** *nse* **Illusive Force (IRE)**[14] 1152 4-8-11 **60**......................... AdamBeschizza 9 38
(Derek Shaw) *mid-div: drvn over 2f out: nvr a factor* **50/1**

U560 **10** *1/2* **Wink Oliver**[28] 953 4-9-7 **70**...(p) MartinLane 8 47
(David Dennis) *in rr: drvn over 2f out: sme hdwy over 1f out: nvr on terms* **14/1**

1m 25.02s (-0.98) **Going Correction** -0.125s/f (Stan) **10** Ran SP% **114.3**
Speed ratings (Par 103): **100,94,89,89,88 88,86,85,85,85**
CSF £38.52 CT £511.88 TOTE £9.70: £2.00, £1.60, £3.70; EX 47.00 Trifecta £532.80.
Owner John Turner **Bred** Ken Carroll **Trained** Epsom, Surrey
■ Stewards' Enquiry : Amir Quinn seven-day ban: used whip above permitted level (Apr 27-May 3)

FOCUS
This second division of the 7f handicap looked weaker than the first and the very well-treated winner dictated. The winner has been rated to his winter 2014/15 C&D form.

1417 32RED H'CAP 2m (P)
7:50 (7:50) (Class 3) (0-95,92) 4-Y-O+
£7,158 (£2,143; £1,071; £535; £267; £134) **Stalls** Low

Form RPR

310- **1** **Steve Rogers (IRE)**[186] 7115 5-9-8 **88**......................... HarryBentley 1 98+
(Roger Varian) *led 2f: trckd ldrs: effrt on ins over 2f out: led 2f out: styd on strly: v readily* **5/6**[1]

112- **2** *3 1/4* **Shades Of Silver**[225] 5974 6-9-8 **88**............................... JimCrowley 6 94
(Ed de Giles) *led after 2f: qckd pce over 4f out: hdd 2f out: kpt on same pce* **11/4**[2]

150- **3** *1/2* **Eton Rambler (USA)**[158] 7757 6-9-8 **88**.......................... PatCosgrave 7 93
(George Baker) *hld up in mid-div: drvn to chse ldrs over 2f out: kpt on same pce* **20/1**

21/1 **4** *1* **Knight's Parade (IRE)**[26] 704 6-8-7 **76**......................(t) DannyBrock(3) 8 80
(Sarah Humphrey) *trckd ldrs: drvn over 2f out: kpt on same pce* **20/1**

0-31 **5** *nk* **Albahar (FR)**[44] 619 5-9-3 **83**...(p) DaneO'Neill 3 87
(Chris Gordon) *chsd ldrs: drvn over 2f out: one pce* **13/2**[3]

50-0 **6** *5* **Highland Castle**[11] 1209 8-9-5 **92**................................ AdamMcLean(7) 5 90
(David Elsworth) *rrd s: t.k.h in rr: hdwy on outside 6f out: edgd rt and lost pl over 2f out* **14/1**

654- **7** *1 1/4* **Saborido (USA)**[231] 5749 10-8-9 **80**.............................. HectorCrouch(5) 4 76
(Amanda Perrett) *chsd ldrs: drvn over 4f out: lost pl over 2f out* **20/1**

-030 **8** *2* **All The Winds (GER)**[32] 922 11-8-8 **79** ow3...........(t) JennyPowell(5) 2 73
(Shaun Lycett) *s.i.s: hld up in rr: sme hdwy 6f out: outpcd over 2f out: wknd over 1f out: eased clsng stages* **33/1**

3m 30.51s (0.41) **Going Correction** -0.125s/f (Stan) **8** Ran SP% **118.4**
Speed ratings (Par 107): **93,91,91,90,90 87,87,86**
CSF £3.15 CT £24.48 TOTE £1.90: £1.10, £1.20, £3.30; EX 4.00 Trifecta £26.30.
Owner Nurlan Bizakov **Bred** Mrs James Wigan **Trained** Newmarket, Suffolk

FOCUS
This fair staying handicap was run at an uneven gallop but the form still looks decent. Another step up from the winner, with the fourth and fifth helping to set the standard.

1418 32RED.COM H'CAP (LONDON MILE SERIES QUALIFIER) 1m (P)
8:20 (8:20) (Class 4) (0-85,85) 4-Y-O+ **£4,690** (£1,395; £697; £348) **Stalls** Low

Form RPR

-343 **1** **Jodies Jem**[34] 886 6-9-2 **83**...................................... TomMarquand(3) 10 91
(William Jarvis) *chsd ldrs: led over 1f out: kpt on wl: drvn out* **14/1**

224- **2** *1* **Commodore (IRE)**[175] 7390 4-9-7 **85**........................... SteveDrowne 12 91
(George Baker) *hld up in rr-div: drvn and hdwy over 3f out: chsng ldrs whn n.m.r and swtchd rt over 1f out: kpt on same pce last 100yds* **7/1**[3]

30/3 **3** *1/2* **Barnmore**[28] 953 8-8-12 **76**... CharlesBishop 7 81
(Peter Hedger) *s.i.s: hld up in rr: hdwy over 2f out: w ldrs over 1f out: kpt on same pce last 100yds* **14/1**

6433 **4** *shd* **Capelita**[21] 1041 5-9-4 **82**.. AndrewMullen 2 87
(Michael Appleby) *led over 1f: trckd ldrs: upsides over 1f out: kpt on same pce last 150yds* **11/1**

4410 **5** *3/4* **Jammy Guest (IRE)**[19] 1068 6-9-7 **85**................................ AdamKirby 9 88+
(George Margarson) *hld up in rr: hdwy over 1f out: n.m.r: kpt on same pce last 150yds* **6/1**[2]

0-05 **6** *3/4* **Dutch Art Dealer**[21] 1041 5-9-5 **83**..................................(p) JimCrowley 8 84
(Paul Cole) *rr-div: hdwy over 2f out: kpt on one pce fnl f* **7/1**[3]

514- **7** *1 1/4* **Cloud Seven**[231] 5750 4-9-4 **82**.. TedDurcan 4 80+
(Chris Wall) *trckd ldrs: n.m.r and swtchd lft over 2f out: hung rt over 1f out: one pce* **5/2**[1]

-514 **8** *1 1/4* **Mezmaar**[49] 694 7-8-11 **75**... ShaneKelly 5 70
(Kevin Morgan) *chsd ldrs: led over 6f out: hdd over 1f out: wkng whn n.m.r fnl 150yds* **6/1**[2]

64-0 **9** *3 1/4* **Mister Musicmaster**[21] 1041 7-8-11 **75**......................... DarryllHolland 6 63
(Ron Hodges) *mid-div: effrt over 2f out: lost pl over 1f out* **25/1**

-1U0 **10** *1 1/4* **Isis Blue**[14] 1142 6-8-3 **72**.. AliceMills(5) 3 57
(Rod Millman) *s.s: detached in last: sme hdwy over 2f out: lost pl over 1f out* **25/1**

10-5 **11** *3* **Freight Train (IRE)**[13] 1161 4-8-11 **75**................... SilvestreDeSousa 11 53
(Mark Johnston) *led over 1f: chsd ldrs: wkng whn hmpd over 1f out* **14/1**

1m 36.8s (-3.00) **Going Correction** -0.125s/f (Stan) **11** Ran SP% **118.2**
Speed ratings (Par 105): **110,109,108,108,107 106,105,104,101,99 96**
CSF £109.26 CT £1423.19 TOTE £14.10: £4.00, £3.70, £4.70; EX 162.60 Trifecta £3003.10.
Owner Mrs M C Banks **Bred** Wickfield Stud And Hartshill Stud **Trained** Newmarket, Suffolk

FOCUS
A decent race for the class, run at a solid pace. The third and fourth help set a solid level.

1419 32RED ON THE APP STORE H'CAP 6f (P)
8:50 (8:51) (Class 5) (0-75,75) 4-Y-O+ **£2,911** (£866; £432; £216) **Stalls** Low

Form RPR

1-55 **1** **Picket Line**[28] 955 4-9-3 **71**... TimmyMurphy 4 80
(Geoffrey Deacon) *chsd ldrs: chal over 1f out: styd on to ld last 100yds: all out* **12/1**

636- **2** *hd* **Darma (IRE)**[296] 3466 4-8-12 **71**.......................... JosephineGordon(5) 8 79
(Martyn Meade) *led: hdd last 100yds: kpt on wl: jst hld* **20/1**

64-5 **3** *3/4* **Lightning Charlie**[14] 1143 4-9-7 **75**.. JimCrowley 1 81+
(Amanda Perrett) *trckd ldrs: n.m.r bnd over 4f out: kpt on wl fnl f* **11/4**[1]

1100 **4** *2 1/4* **Noble Deed**[12] 1178 6-9-6 **74**... KierenFox 2 73
(Michael Attwater) *mid-div: effrt over 2f out: kpt on same pce appr fnl f* **6/1**[3]

602- **5** *nk* **Oat Couture**[214] 6298 4-9-0 **68**... DaneO'Neill 3 66+
(Henry Candy) *in rr: hdwy on inner over 2f out: one pce over 1f out* **25/1**

000- **6** *1/2* **Regal Parade**[149] 7874 12-9-7 **75**..................................(t) DavidProbert 6 71
(Charlie Wallis) *in rr: hdwy on inner over 2f out: one pce over 1f out* **17/2**

0-50 **7** *hd* **Straits Of Malacca**[12] 1178 5-9-0 **68**.............................. HarryBentley 10 64
(Simon Dow) *hld up in rr: sme hdwy on outside 2f out: kpt on: nvr a threat* **40/1**

060- **8** *1 3/4* **Jungle Bay**[128] 8131 9-9-6 **74**..(b) MartinDwyer 5 64
(Jane Chapple-Hyam) *hld up in mid-div: effrt over 2f out: wknd appr fnl f* **16/1**

3-50 **9** *nk* **Major Valentine**[28] 955 4-8-11 **70**................................ CiaranMckee(5) 11 59
(John O'Shea) *dwlt: sn chsng ldrs: wknd over 1f out* **20/1**

23-3 **10** *2 1/4* **Ripinto (IRE)**[12] 1178 4-9-4 **72**...(b) PatCosgrave 7 54
(Jim Boyle) *s.i.s: hdwy to chse ldrs over 4f out: wknd over 1f out* **3/1**[2]

0114 **11** *1 1/4* **Rigolleto (IRE)**[28] 955 8-9-4 **72**.................................(p) GeorgeBaker 9 50
(Anabel K Murphy) *swtchd rt s: w ldr: wknd over 1f out: eased clsng stages* **7/1**

1m 11.4s (-1.70) **Going Correction** -0.125s/f (Stan) **11** Ran SP% **118.4**
Speed ratings (Par 103): **106,105,104,101,101 100,100,98,97,94 93**
CSF £231.21 CT £870.04 TOTE £13.90: £3.30, £3.90, £1.90; EX 210.10 Trifecta £921.90.
Owner Homegrown Partnership **Bred** Mickley Stud **Trained** Compton, Berks
■ Stewards' Enquiry : George Baker one-day ban: failed to ride to draw (Apr27)

FOCUS
It paid to race handily in this modest sprint handicap and the principals were clear at the finish. A pb from the runner-up, with the third rated to form.

1420 RACINGUK.COM H'CAP 6f (P)
9:20 (9:20) (Class 6) (0-65,65) 3-Y-O **£2,264** (£673; £336; £168) **Stalls** Low

Form RPR

21-3 **1** **Showmethewayavrilo**[20] 1060 3-9-5 **63**........................... MartinHarley 4 74
(Malcolm Saunders) *mde all: hld on wl clsng stages* **7/2**[1]

-332 **2** *3/4* **Cool Crescendo**[6] 1292 3-8-6 **57**..................................(p) RowanScott(7) 1 66
(Rebecca Menzies) *chsd ldrs: nt clr run on ins over 2f out: chsd wnr over 1f out: styd on same pce last 75yds* **5/1**[2]

421 **3** *2* **Music Major**[14] 1148 3-8-9 **53**....................................... AdamBeschizza 6 56
(Michael Attwater) *rrd s: in rr: hdwy over 2f out: 3rd 1f out: kpt on same pce* **7/2**[1]

-421 **4** *1 1/4* **Figurante (IRE)**[88] 211 3-9-7 **65**.. CathyGannon 7 64
(Jamie Osborne) *hld up in rr: hdwy over 2f out: kpt on same pce fnl f* **6/1**[3]

030- **5** *2 1/4* **African Showgirl**[293] 3546 3-9-7 **65**............................... SteveDrowne 10 58
(George Baker) *in rr: sme hdwy over 2f out: one pce whn n.m.r over 1f out* **40/1**

640- **6** *3/4* **Lady Nahema (IRE)**[217] 6203 3-9-6 **64**.................. SilvestreDeSousa 11 54
(Ann Duffield) *chsd ldrs: one pce fnl 2f* **12/1**

126- **7** *nk* **Canford Belle**[186] 7107 3-9-5 **63**.. JimCrowley 12 52
(Amanda Perrett) *sn chsng ldrs: one pce over 1f out* **12/1**

50-0 **8** *1 1/4* **Kenstone (FR)**[16] 1126 3-9-1 **59**...................................(p) MartinLane 5 44
(David Dennis) *t.k.h: trckd ldrs: effrt over 2f out: one pce over 1f out* **16/1**

-655 **9** *1 1/4* **Name That Toon**[21] 1045 3-8-2 **51** oh4.......................(p) NoelGarbutt(5) 3 33
(Derek Shaw) *chsd ldrs: drvn over 2f out: wknd over 1f out* **100/1**

0045 **10** ¾ **Katie Canford**[14] 1148 3-9-0 **58**........ WilliamCarson 9 37
(John Bridger) *sn chsng ldrs: wknd appr fnl f* **33/1**

330- **11** 1¾ **Xceleration**[190] 7005 3-9-7 **65**........ FrederikTylicki 2 39
(Ed Vaughan) *mid-div: t.k.h: hdwy to chse ldrs over 2f out: lost pl over 1f out: eased clsng stages* **6/1**[3]

1m 12.67s (-0.43) **Going Correction** -0.125s/f (Stan) **11** Ran SP% **117.3**
Speed ratings (Par 96): **97,96,93,91,88 87,87,85,83,82 80**
CSF £20.58 CT £67.13 TOTE £4.10: £1.10, £3.00, £2.00; EX 25.80 Trifecta £93.70.
Owner Pat Hancock & Eric Jones **Bred** Eric Jones, Pat Hancock **Trained** Green Ore, Somerset

FOCUS
Not a bad sprint handicap for the grade.
T/Plt: £127.20 to a £1 stake. Pool: £62,019.09 - 355.68 winning units. T/Qpdt: £31.50 to a £1 stake. Pool: £10,023.30 - 234.95 winning units. **Walter Glynn**

1392 NEWMARKET (R-H)
Wednesday, April 13

OFFICIAL GOING: Good to soft (6.7)
Wind: light, half behind Weather: bright spells

1421 CELEBRATING 350 YEARS OF MAKING HISTORY WOOD DITTON STKS (PLUS 10 RACE) 1m
2:10 (2:12) (Class 4) 3-Y-O **£6,469** (£1,925; £962; £481) **Stalls** Low

Form RPR

1 **Sky Kingdom (IRE)** 3-9-5 0........ PatSmullen 10 88+
(William Haggas) *str: lengthy: scope: lw: racd keenly: chsd ldr after 2f: upsides and pushed lft over 3f out: pushed into ld over 1f out: styd on wl and in command ins fnl f* **3/1**[1]

2 ¾ **Mulk** 3-9-5 0........ DaneO'Neill 9 86+
(Sir Michael Stoute) *unf: scope: jostled leaving stalls: hld up in tch towards rr: hdwy 3f out: rdn over 1f out: styd on wl to chse wnr wl ins fnl f: gng on at fin but nvr gng to rch wnr* **12/1**

3 1½ **Muntahaa (IRE)** 3-9-5 0........[1] PaulHanagan 11 83
(John Gosden) *lengthy: tall: led: rn green and ducked lft over 3f out: rdn and hdd over 1f out: styd on same pce after: lost 2nd wl ins fnl f* **7/2**[2]

4 2 **Heart Of Lions (USA)** 3-9-5 0........ WilliamBuick 8 80+
(John Gosden) *unf: scope: lw: chsd ldrs: rdn and outpcd over 2f out: rallied and styd on steadily ins fnl f: no threat to wnr* **11/2**[3]

5 ½ **Thundering Blue (USA)** 3-9-5 0........ JimCrowley 4 77
(David Menuisier) *str: in tch in midfield: effrt in 4th 2f out: no imp u.p over 1f out: kpt on same pce ins fnl f* **8/1**

6 1¾ **Shraaoh (IRE)** 3-9-5 0........ FrankieDettori 3 73
(Sir Michael Stoute) *lengthy: tall: scope: in tch towards rr: rdn over 2f out: sme hdwy into midfield wl over 1f out: kpt on steadily ins fnl f: no threat to wnr* **8/1**

7 ¾ **Western Prince** 3-9-5 0........ RobertHavlin 5 71
(John Gosden) *lengthy: str: bit bkwd: in tch in midfield: hdwy to chse ldrs whn pushed lft over 3f out: outpcd whn rn green and hung lft over 1f out: wknd ins fnl f* **9/1**

- **8** 7 **Gatillo** 3-9-5 0........ AdamKirby 7 55
(George Margarson) *leggy: slowly away: short of room and sltly hmpd leaving stalls: in rr: pushed along and sme hdwy into midfield 2f out: nvr on terms w ldrs and plugged on same pce after* **100/1**

9 nse **Swiftee (IRE)** 3-9-5 0........ SilvestreDeSousa 1 55
(Ed Dunlop) *w'like: in tch in midfield: pushed along over 2f out: sn outpcd and wl btn over 1f out* **33/1**

10 4 **Mr Andros** 3-9-5 0........ MartinDwyer 12 46
(Andrew Balding) *str: hld up in tch: hdwy 1/2-way: pushed lft over 3f out: rdn and lost pl over 2f out: wknd wl over 1f out* **66/1**

11 5 **Private Jet** 3-9-5 0........ DarryllHolland 6 34
(Charles Hills) *athletic: str: stdd and jostled s: rn green and a towards rr: bhd and rdn 3f out: lost tch 2f out* **25/1**

12 9 **Spey Secret (IRE)** 3-9-5 0........ RichardKingscote 2 13
(Tom Dascombe) *unf: chsd ldr for 2f: styd prom: rdn and lost pl 3f out: bhd fnl 2f* **28/1**

1m 43.16s (4.56) **Going Correction** +0.475s/f (Yiel) **12** Ran SP% **115.2**
Speed ratings (Par 100): **96,95,93,91,91 89,88,81,81,77 72,63**
CSF £37.12 TOTE £3.80: £1.40, £3.90, £1.80; EX 52.00 Trifecta £265.80.
Owner P Makin **Bred** Paulyn Ltd **Trained** Newmarket, Suffolk

FOCUS
As was the case the previous day racing took place on the Rowley Mile far-side course, but the stalls this time were on the far side of that course. They were racing on fresh ground - GoingStick reading 6.7 - and having ridden in the Godolphin gallop before racing James Doyle described the going as being on the soft side of good. The major yards dominated what looked a good edition of this newcomers' race and there should be plenty of winners to come from it. The race has been rated towards the top of the race standard.

1422 BEN BURGESS & CO EBF NOVICE STKS (PLUS 10 RACE) 5f
2:45 (2:46) (Class 4) 2-Y-O **£4,528** (£1,347; £673; £336) **Stalls** Low

Form RPR

1 **1** **Sutter County**[19] 1082 2-9-8 0........ WilliamBuick 6 92
(Mark Johnston) *tall: str: wnt rt s: chsd ldng pair and niggled along early: clsd and upsides ldrs 2f out: pushed into ld over 1f out: forged ahd ins fnl f: tiring cl home: jst lasted* **4/9**[1]

2 hd **Dream Of Dreams (IRE)** 2-9-2 0........ JamieSpencer 5 85+
(Kevin Ryan) *lengthy: tall: wnt rt s: rn green and outpcd in 6th: swtchd lft and sme prog but stl plenty to do over 1f out: r.o strly ins fnl f: wnt 2nd towards fin: clsng qckly cl home but nvr quite getting to wnr* **10/1**[3]

2 **3** ½ **Tomily (IRE)**[11] 1203 2-8-13 0........ TomMarquand(3) 9 83
(Richard Hannon) *cmpt: in tch in ldng quintet: effrt ent fnl 2f: rdn and ev ch over 1f out: sltly outpcd jst ins fnl f: kpt on again towards fin* **3/1**[2]

4 ¾ **Copper Knight (IRE)** 2-9-2 0........ MartinHarley 3 80
(Hugo Palmer) *str: in tch in ldng quintet: clsd over 2f out: rdn over 1f out: ev ch and rdn 1f out: unable qck ins fnl f: kpt on same pce fnl 100yds* **10/1**[3]

5 8 **Vinnievanbaileys** 2-9-2 0........ SilvestreDeSousa 8 52
(Chris Dwyer) *leggy: sn wl outpcd in last pair: styd on to pass btn horses ins fnl f: n.d* **33/1**

0 **6** 1¾ **Heavenly Cry**[11] 1199 2-8-11 0........ NoelGarbutt(5) 2 45
(Denis Quinn) *leggy: v awkward leaving stalls: sn wl outpcd in last pair: styd on to pass btn horses ins fnl f: n.d* **100/1**

3 **7** 3 **Makman (IRE)**[11] 1203 2-9-2 0........ PaulHanagan 4 34
(Ed Dunlop) *cl-cpld: pushed rt s: racd keenly: led: rdn and hdd over 1f out: sn btn: fdd ins fnl f* **10/1**[3]

8 ½ **Jester Spirit (IRE)** 2-9-2 0........ RichardKingscote 1 33
(Tom Dascombe) *leggy: pressed ldr tl over 2f out: sn u.p: btn over 1f out: fdd fnl f* **33/1**

1m 1.31s (2.21) **Going Correction** +0.475s/f (Yiel) **8** Ran SP% **128.4**
Speed ratings (Par 94): **101,100,99,98,85 83,78,77**
CSF £8.27 TOTE £1.90: £1.10, £2.90, £1.40; EX 6.90 Trifecta £19.40.
Owner Sheikh Hamdan bin Mohammed Al Maktoum **Bred** Darley **Trained** Middleham Moor, N Yorks

FOCUS
A good-quality novice event, in which they went fast, with the first four pulling nicely clear. The favourite made hard work of it on ground he was clearly unhappy on. The level is a bit fluid.

1423 £100,000 TATTERSALLS MILLIONS 3-Y-O SPRINT 6f
3:20 (3:23) (Class 2) 3-Y-O **£54,100** (£24,590; £9,840; £4,910; £2,960) **Stalls** Low

Form RPR

111- **1** **Gifted Master (IRE)**[186] 7113 3-9-5 111........ PatSmullen 4 103
(Hugo Palmer) *mde all: rdn ent fnl f: in command and r.o wl ins fnl f: rdn out: comf* **1/2**[1]

120- **2** 3½ **Waterloo Bridge (IRE)**[165] 7655 3-9-5 109........(t) RyanMoore 2 92
(A P O'Brien, Ire) *t.k.h: chsd wnr: effrt over 1f out: unable qck u.p 1f out: wl hld and styd on same pce ins fnl f* **2/1**[2]

044- **3** 2¼ **Tigerwolf (IRE)**[175] 7394 3-9-5 88........ CharlesBishop 3 85
(Mick Channon) *lw: a 3rd: effrt over 1f out: no imp 1f out: wl hld and styd on same pce after* **12/1**[3]

525- **4** 2½ **Joules**[205] 6586 3-9-5 71........(t) AdamKirby 1 77
(Natalie Lloyd-Beavis) *s.i.s: bhd: rdn and drifted rt over 2f out: wnt 4th ins fnl f: nvr trbld ldrs* **100/1**

202- **5** ¾ **Hillside Dream (IRE)**[170] 7510 3-9-0 74........ JamieSpencer 5 70
(James Tate) *hld up in 4th: pushed along 3f out: no imp and drifted rt u.p 2f out: wl btn and lost 4th ins fnl f* **28/1**

1m 13.21s (1.01) **Going Correction** +0.475s/f (Yiel) **5** Ran SP% **112.1**
Speed ratings (Par 104): **112,107,104,101,100**
CSF £1.81 TOTE £1.40: £1.10, £1.10; EX 1.80 Trifecta £3.00.
Owner Dr Ali Ridha **Bred** Tally-Ho Stud **Trained** Newmarket, Suffolk

FOCUS
A really disappointing turnout for the prize on offer. Only two really mattered and it played out as the market, and previous form, suggested it would. It's been rated around the third, fourth and fifth.

1424 CSP EUROPEAN FREE H'CAP (LISTED RACE) 7f
3:55 (3:58) (Class 1) 3-Y-O
£20,982 (£7,955; £3,981; £1,983; £995; £499) **Stalls** Low

Form RPR

223- **1** **Ibn Malik (IRE)**[186] 7113 3-9-6 **107**........ PaulHanagan 4 112
(Charles Hills) *racd keenly early: mde all: rdn over 1f out: styd on and a doing enough ins fnl f: gng away towards fin* **3/1**[1]

110- **2** 2 **Scrutineer (IRE)**[164] 7665 3-9-2 **103**........ SilvestreDeSousa 5 103
(Mick Channon) *lw: chsd ldng pair tl effrt to chse wnr wl over 1f out: drvn and pressing wnr 1f out: no imp ins fnl f: outpcd fnl 75yds* **7/2**[2]

05-0 **3** 2½ **Great Page (IRE)**[39] 836 3-9-4 **105**........ SeanLevey 3 99
(Richard Hannon) *t.k.h: hld up in tch in last pair: wnt 4th 3f out: effrt 2f out: no imp on wnr: kpt on and wnt 3rd wl ins fnl f* **14/1**

5-02 **4** ¾ **Adventurous (IRE)**[11] 1208 3-9-7 **108**........ WilliamBuick 6 100
(Mark Johnston) *lw: chsd wnr: rdn over 2f out: lost 2nd wl over 1f out and sn outpcd: kpt on same pce after: lost 3rd wl ins fnl f* **11/2**

133- **5** 5 **Raucous**[207] 6531 3-9-5 **106**........ RyanMoore 1 85
(William Haggas) *hld up in tch: effrt in 5th jst over 2f out: no imp: wknd over 1f out* **3/1**[1]

11- **6** 3 **Kachy**[259] 4745 3-9-5 **106**........ RichardKingscote 2 77
(Tom Dascombe) *lw: stdd s: t.k.h: hld up in rr: effrt over 2f out: drifted rt and no hdwy wl over 1f out: sn bhd* **5/1**[3]

1m 26.17s (0.77) **Going Correction** +0.475s/f (Yiel) **6** Ran SP% **110.9**
Speed ratings (Par 106): **114,111,108,108,102 98**
CSF £13.37 TOTE £3.70: £2.10, £2.30; EX 13.00 Trifecta £72.60.
Owner Hamdan Al Maktoum **Bred** Shadwell Estate Company Limited **Trained** Lambourn, Berks

FOCUS
Debatable just how strong a race this was, they went a decent gallop early courtesy of the winner but little got into it and two of the market leaders disappointed. The runner-up has been rated to form.

1425 WEATHERBYS GENERAL STUD BOOK EARL OF SEFTON STKS (GROUP 3) 1m 1f
4:30 (4:32) (Class 1) 4-Y-O+
£34,026 (£12,900; £6,456; £3,216; £1,614; £810) **Stalls** Low

Form RPR

165- **1** **Mahsoob**[235] 5638 5-8-13 110........ PaulHanagan 10 118
(John Gosden) *lw: in tch: hdwy to chse ldr jst over 2f out: sn drvn and str chal wl over 1f out: sustained duel tl forged ahd ins fnl f: styd on strly: rdn out* **10/3**[2]

135- **2** 1¼ **Air Pilot**[179] 7281 7-8-13 116........ FMBerry 2 115
(Ralph Beckett) *led: jnd and rdn wl over 1f out: sustained duel w wnr after tl hdd ins fnl f: no ex fnl 75yds* **15/8**[1]

6-55 **3** 1½ **Tullius (IRE)**[24] 1023 8-8-13 112........ JimmyFortune 9 112
(Andrew Balding) *hld up in tch: swtchd lft and effrt jst over 2f out: no imp tl hdwy 1f out: kpt on wl u.p ins fnl f: wnt 3rd last strides: no threat to ldng pair* **8/1**

20-3 **4** hd **Custom Cut (IRE)**[11] 1198 7-9-4 117........ DanielTudhope 11 117
(David O'Meara) *t.k.h: chsd ldr tl 2f out: 3rd and outpcd u.p over 1f out: styd on same pce after: lost 3rd last strides* **8/1**

5003 **5** ½ **Battle Of Marathon (USA)**[11] 1196 4-9-0 104 ow1........(b) AdamKirby 3 111
(John Ryan) *awkward leaving stalls: hld up in tch: effrt 2f out: hdwy u.p over 1f out: battling for 3rd and kpt on ins fnl f: no threat to ldng pair* **14/1**

2-22 **6** 2½ **Sovereign Debt (IRE)**[19] 1068 7-9-2 112........ ChrisHayes 1 108
(David Nicholls) *t.k.h: in tch: 4th and effrt 2f out: outpcd u.p over 1f out: wknd ins fnl f* **7/1**[3]

-000 **7** nse **Bossy Guest (IRE)**[48] 720 4-8-13 107........ SilvestreDeSousa 8 105
(Mick Channon) *stdd s: t.k.h: hld up in tch in rr: effrt 2f out: kpt on but no real imp: nvr trbld ldrs* **20/1**

100- **8** 6 **Bronze Angel (IRE)**[179] 7282 7-8-13 108........(p) MartinDwyer 5 92
(Marcus Tregoning) *bit bkwd: hld up in tch in last pair: effrt jst over 2f out: sn drvn and no hdwy over 1f out: wknd fnl f* **28/1**

-002 **9** 52 **Calling Out (FR)**[11] 1198 5-8-13 105........ JamieSpencer 6
(David Simcock) *t.k.h: chsd ldrs tl 1/2-way: lost pl 3f out: bhd and rdr looking down jst over 2f out: eased fnl 2f: t.o* **20/1**

1m 53.67s (1.97) **Going Correction** +0.475s/f (Yiel) **9** Ran SP% **112.2**
Speed ratings (Par 113): **110,108,107,107,106 104,104,99,53**
CSF £9.32 TOTE £3.50: £1.60, £1.10, £2.30; EX 11.40 Trifecta £64.60.

Owner Hamdan Al Maktoum **Bred** Shadwell Estate Company Limited **Trained** Newmarket, Suffolk
■ Stewards' Enquiry : Paul Hanagan two-day ban: used whip above the permitted level down the shoulder in the forehand (Apr 27-28)

FOCUS
No great gallop on here, but the big two in the market dominated and the form looks good. The runner-up has been rated close to form.

1426 JULIAN WILSON MEMORIAL EBF STALLIONS MAIDEN STKS (PLUS 10 RACE) 1m 2f
5:05 (5:08) (Class 4) 3-Y-O **£5,498** (£1,636; £817; £408) **Stalls** Low

Form RPR
1 **Winning Story** 3-9-5 0 JamesDoyle 6 93
(Saeed bin Suroor) *tall: str: lw: chsd ldrs: rdn 3f out: hdwy u.p to ld over 1f out: styd on wl fnl f: rdn out* **13/2**[3]
32- **2** 2 **Daqeeq (IRE)**[165] 7638 3-9-5 0 PaulHanagan 3 89
(Simon Crisford) *athletic: lw: chsd ldrs: wnt 2nd 5f out: rdn and ev ch 2f out: chsd wnr jst over 1f out: kpt on same pce fnl f* **11/2**[2]
3 1 **Wings of Desire** 3-9-5 0 RobertHavlin 7 87
(John Gosden) *str: scope: lw: hld up in tch in rr: pushed along 2f out: hdwy into midfield over 1f out: rdn and styd on wl to go 3rd ins fnl f: gng on at fin* **14/1**
4 1 ¾ **Point Of View (IRE)** 3-9-5 0 AndreaAtzeni 2 84
(Roger Varian) *athletic: str: lw: in tch in midfield: effrt 3f out: drvn and unable qck over 1f out: kpt on same pce ins fnl f* **7/1**
42 **5** 3 **Knights Table**[15] 1132 3-9-5 0 JamieSpencer 8 78+
(James Tate) *str: led: rdn over 2f out: hdd over 1f out: 3rd and btn 1f out: wknd ins fnl f* **12/1**
6 1 **Amazing Red (IRE)** 3-9-5 0 SilvestreDeSousa 9 76
(Ed Dunlop) *w'like: hld up in tch in rr: effrt over 2f out: 6th and no imp jst over 1f out: kpt on same pce ins fnl f* **33/1**
7 2 ¼ **Proctor** 3-9-5 0 PatDobbs 10 71
(Stuart Kittow) *str: hld up in tch towards rr: effrt over 2f out: no imp u.p over 1f out: sn wknd* **40/1**
4- **8** 1 ¼ **Satish**[221] 6073 3-9-5 0 (p) FrankieDettori 4 69
(John Gosden) *in tch in midfield: hdwy to chse ldrs 4f out: sn rdn and outpcd 3f out: lost pl and btn 2f out: wknd over 1f out* **6/4**[1]
0- **9** hd **Goldmember**[173] 7431 3-9-5 0 OisinMurphy 11 68
(David Simcock) *cmpt: stdd s: hld up in tch in rr: effrt over 2f out: no imp 2f out: wknd over 1f out* **13/2**[3]
0 **10** 25 **Icons Image**[14] 1140 3-9-5 0 MartinDwyer 1 18
(Brian McMath) *w'like: bit bkwd: chsd ldr tl 5f out: lost pl qckly over 3f out: t.o fnl 2f* **150/1**

2m 11.54s (5.74) **Going Correction** +0.475s/f (Yiel) **10** Ran SP% **115.0**
Speed ratings (Par 100): **96,94,93,92,89 89,87,86,86,66**
CSF £41.16 TOTE £7.10: £2.10, £1.30, £4.10; EX 39.70 Trifecta £299.30.
Owner Godolphin **Bred** Darley **Trained** Newmarket, Suffolk

FOCUS
This looked a good maiden full of interesting types and it's a race that should produce plenty of winners. They raced down the centre and the winner came on the outer more towards the stands' side. It's been rated around the race standard.

1427 TURFTV H'CAP 5f
5:40 (5:40) (Class 3) (0-95,92) 4-Y-O+ **£9,056** (£2,695; £1,346; £673) **Stalls** Low

Form RPR
151- **1** **Brando**[200] 6746 4-9-3 **88** JamieSpencer 7 108+
(Kevin Ryan) *lw: chsd ldr tl rdn to ld 2f out: r.o strly u.p and drew clr fnl f: eased towards fin* **2/1**[1]
110- **2** 3 ¼ **Soie D'Leau**[220] 6135 4-9-1 **86** SilvestreDeSousa 1 94
(Kristin Stubbs) *in tch in midfield: effrt on far rail 2f out: chsd wnr over 1f out: no imp and outpcd ins fnl f: kpt on for clr 2nd* **9/1**
0200 **3** 2 ¾ **Vimy Ridge**[19] 1084 4-8-10 **81** (p) FMBerry 3 79
(Alan Bailey) *sn pushed along in rr: hdwy u.p over 1f out: wnt 3rd 1f out: kpt on: no threat to ldrs* **7/1**
2-56 **4** 1 ¼ **Waseem Faris (IRE)**[27] 966 7-9-4 **89** OisinMurphy 6 83
(Joseph Tuite) *chsd ldrs: rdn 2f out: outpcd u.p over 1f out: battling for wl hld 3rd 1f out: wknd wl ins fnl f* **12/1**
14-1 **5** 1 ¾ **Equally Fast**[12] 1175 4-8-12 **83** (b) MartinDwyer 10 70
(William Muir) *lw: wnt lft s: racd towards centre: in tch: hdwy to chse ldrs 3f out: hung lft and unable qck u.p over 1f out: wknd fnl f* **5/1**[3]
033- **6** nk **Oh So Sassy**[193] 6921 6-9-2 **87** GeorgeBaker 9 73
(Chris Wall) *racd towards centre: in tch: effrt and drifted rt over 1f out: no imp: n.d* **9/2**[2]
5031 **7** ½ **Doctor Parkes**[26] 974 10-8-6 **82** AaronJones(5) 2 66
(Stuart Williams) *a towards rr: rdn 2f out: no imp: n.d* **20/1**
-421 **8** 2 ½ **King Crimson**[19] 1084 4-8-11 **82** CharlesBishop 5 57
(Mick Channon) *led tl rdn and hdd 2f out: sn outpcd and lost 2nd over 1f out: wknd fnl f* **10/1**

1m 0.58s (1.48) **Going Correction** +0.475s/f (Yiel) **8** Ran SP% **112.2**
Speed ratings (Par 107): **107,101,97,95,92 92,91,87**
CSF £20.23 CT £104.27 TOTE £2.80: £1.10, £2.60, £2.40; EX 21.00 Trifecta £129.40.
Owner Mrs Angie Bailey **Bred** Car Colston Hall Stud **Trained** Hambleton, N Yorks

FOCUS
A useful sprint handicap won in good style by a thoroughly progressive sort. The runner-up has been rated to his improved 3yo form for now.
T/Plt: £12.70 to a £1 stake. Pool: £89,228.73 - 5099.71 winning units. T/Qpdt: £6.30 to a £1 stake. Pool: £5793.13 - 673.99 winning units. **Steve Payne**

1428 - (Foreign Racing) - See Raceform Interactive

[1287]CHELMSFORD (A.W) (L-H)
Thursday, April 14

OFFICIAL GOING: Polytrack: standard
Wind: Light across Weather: Cloudy

1429 PLAY SCOOP6SOCCER EVERY WEEK MAIDEN AUCTION STKS 1m 2f (P)
6:10 (6:13) (Class 5) 3-Y-O **£5,175** (£1,540; £769; £384) **Stalls** Low

Form RPR
5-32 **1** **Second Serve (IRE)**[8] 1265 3-9-3 0 SilvestreDeSousa 3 78
(Mark Johnston) *sn led: shkn up over 3f out: rdn and hdd over 1f out: n.m.r sn after: rallied to ld wl ins fnl f* **11/10**[1]
-625 **2** hd **Red Hot Chilly (IRE)**[18] 1113 3-9-0 69 JFEgan 4 74
(Joseph Tuite) *chsd wnr: led over 1f out: sn rdn and edgd lft: hdd wl ins fnl f* **14/1**
3 2 **Niceonecenturion** 3-9-0 0 JimCrowley 2 70
(William Knight) *hld up: swtchd rt over 1f out: rdn and r.o to go 3rd wl ins fnl f: nt trble ldrs* **28/1**
-422 **4** 2 ¾ **Zio Gianni (USA)**[18] 1113 3-9-0 72 WilliamCarson 7 64
(Jamie Osborne) *prom: racd keenly: rdn and hung lft over 1f out: no ex fnl f* **11/4**[2]
0-22 **5** nk **Divine Joy**[21] 1063 3-8-9 72 DanielMuscutt(3) 1 62
(Marco Botti) *chsd ldrs: rdn over 1f out: no ex fnl f* **6/1**[3]
6- **6** hd **Le Tissier**[197] 6865 3-8-10 0 EdwardGreatrex(5) 6 64
(Andrew Balding) *s.i.s: hld up: rdn over 1f out: nvr on terms* **10/1**
046- **7** 8 **Linguist (FR)**[196] 6889 3-9-2 71 (p) FMBerry 5 49
(Harry Dunlop) *hld up: pushed along 4f out: rdn over 2f out: sn wknd* **14/1**

2m 9.77s (1.17) **Going Correction** +0.075s/f (Slow) **7** Ran SP% **114.4**
Speed ratings (Par 98): **98,97,96,94,93 93,87**
CSF £18.94 TOTE £2.20: £1.40, £5.90; EX 19.00 Trifecta £227.80.
Owner S Richards, N Browne & Mrs R Frosell **Bred** Gerrardstown House Stud **Trained** Middleham Moor, N Yorks
■ Stewards' Enquiry : Silvestre De Sousa two-day ban: used whip down the shoulder in the forehand (Apr 28-29)

FOCUS
A fair maiden. The winner has been rated close to his Lingfield latest.

1430 SCOOP6SOCCER THE £1 MILLION FOOTBALL BET H'CAP 1m 2f (P)
6:40 (6:40) (Class 4) (0-80,80) 4-Y-O+ **£8,086** (£2,406; £1,202; £601) **Stalls** Low

Form RPR
2-15 **1** **Daisy Boy (IRE)**[56] 619 5-8-13 **77** (t) AaronJones(5) 7 89
(Stuart Williams) *mde virtually all: rdn over 1f out: styd on* **8/1**[3]
1 **2** nk **Burcan (FR)**[43] 778 4-9-4 **77** JimCrowley 8 88
(Jeremy Noseda) *s.i.s: rcvrd to chse wnr after 1f: rdn and ev ch fr over 1f out: styd on* **3/1**[2]
1 **3** 1 **Appeared**[66] 500 4-9-7 **80** AndreaAtzeni 1 90+
(Roger Varian) *chsd ldrs: nt clr run over 1f out: sn rdn: edgd lft and styd on towards fin* **8/11**[1]
414- **4** 10 **The Third Man**[106] 8405 5-9-4 **77** TomQueally 6 66
(Henry Spiller) *prom: rdn and hung lft fr over 2f out: wknd over 1f out* **33/1**
4343 **5** 2 **Charlies Mate**[19] 1093 5-9-5 **78** KierenFox 4 63
(John Best) *hld up: rdn over 3f out: wknd wl over 1f out* **10/1**
24-0 **6** ½ **Tommy's Secret**[13] 1173 6-9-1 **74** FrederikTylicki 5 58
(Jane Chapple-Hyam) *hld up: rdn over 2f out: n.d* **25/1**
-445 **7** 6 **Dukes Meadow**[35] 888 5-8-12 **71** MartinLane 2 43
(Roger Ingram) *hld up: rdn and wknd over 2f out* **25/1**

2m 7.36s (-1.24) **Going Correction** +0.075s/f (Slow) **7** Ran SP% **113.7**
Speed ratings (Par 105): **107,106,105,97,96 95,91**
CSF £31.61 CT £38.29 TOTE £9.40: £3.60, £1.80; EX 32.60 Trifecta £64.40.
Owner G Johnson **Bred** Shadwell Estate Company Limited **Trained** Newmarket, Suffolk

FOCUS
This was run at a good gallop and the first three finished well clear of the rest. It's been rated slightly positively.

1431 WIN A FOOTBALL FORTUNE WITH SCOOP6SOCCER H'CAP 6f (P)
7:10 (7:10) (Class 5) (0-70,70) 3-Y-O **£5,175** (£1,540; £769; £384) **Stalls** Centre

Form RPR
021- **1** **Irish Eclare (IRE)**[154] 7807 3-9-4 **70** MichaelJMMurphy(3) 6 78
(Charles Hills) *mde virtually all: rdn over 1f out: styd on wl* **6/4**[1]
460- **2** 2 ¼ **Born To Finish (IRE)**[153] 7823 3-9-3 **66** RichardKingscote 3 66+
(Jeremy Gask) *s.i.s: hld up: rdn and r.o to go 2nd wl ins fnl f: nt rch wnr* **7/2**[2]
6-25 **3** ¾ **Strictly Carter**[13] 1176 3-9-2 **65** FMBerry 5 63
(Alan Bailey) *a.p: chsd wnr over 4f out: rdn over 1f out: styd on same pce ins fnl f* **12/1**
046- **4** nk **She's All Mine**[199] 6806 3-9-1 **64** KieranO'Neill 4 61
(Richard Hannon) *prom: racd keenly: n.m.r jst over 5f out: rdn over 21f out: styd on same pce ins fnl f* **20/1**
4-1 **5** ½ **False Id**[35] 885 3-9-6 **69** WilliamCarson 1 64
(Robert Eddery) *hld up: shkn up over 1f out: no imp ins fnl f* **7/2**[2]
040- **6** 2 **In My Place**[159] 7753 3-9-4 **67** GeorgeChaloner 2 56
(Richard Fahey) *chsd ldrs: rdn over 2f out: wknd ins fnl f* **8/1**[3]
00-2 **7** 1 ½ **Basma**[42] 791 3-9-7 **70** DaneO'Neill 7 54
(Owen Burrows) *s.i.s: hdwy over 4f out: rdn over 2f out: wknd fnl f* **10/1**

1m 14.16s (0.46) **Going Correction** +0.075s/f (Slow) **7** Ran SP% **117.1**
Speed ratings (Par 98): **99,96,95,94,93 91,89**
CSF £7.27 CT £45.12 TOTE £3.10: £2.80, £2.20; EX 8.20 Trifecta £47.70.
Owner Mrs Clare Kelvin & Mrs B W Hills **Bred** N Pownall **Trained** Lambourn, Berks

FOCUS
A modest sprint handicap. It's rated around the third.

1432 BET SCOOP6SOCCER AT BETFRED SHOPS FILLIES' H'CAP 6f (P)
7:40 (7:40) (Class 4) (0-85,85) 3-Y-O+ **£8,086** (£2,406; £1,202; £601) **Stalls** Centre

Form RPR
0054 **1** **Pretty Bubbles**[14] 1158 7-9-3 **74** (v) FrederikTylicki 4 84
(J R Jenkins) *a.p: rdn to ld 1f out: styd on* **7/1**
21 **2** ½ **Semra (USA)**[70] 441 3-8-2 **71** PaoloSirigu 2 76+
(Marco Botti) *s.i.s: hld up: nt clr run and swtchd rt over 1f out: r.o to go 2nd wl ins fnl f: nt rch wnr* **2/1**[1]
100- **3** 3 ½ **Rosy Morning (IRE)**[166] 7637 3-8-11 **80** SilvestreDeSousa 1 74
(Mark Johnston) *led: rdn and hdd 1f out: no ex wl ins fnl f* **3/1**[2]
33-3 **4** ½ **Socialites Red**[23] 1029 3-8-2 **71** oh1 KieranO'Neill 3 64
(Scott Dixon) *chsd ldrs: rdn over 1f out: no ex fnl f* **8/1**
313- **5** 1 ¼ **Bournemouth Belle**[292] 3654 3-8-13 **85** TomMarquand(3) 6 74
(Richard Hannon) *hld up: shkn up over 1f out: nvr on terms* **7/2**[3]
000- **6** 4 **Feeling Easy (IRE)**[177] 7363 4-9-3 **74** WilliamCarson 5 53
(Robert Eddery) *chsd ldr: rdn and hung lft over 1f out: wknd fnl f* **10/1**

1m 13.17s (-0.53) **Going Correction** +0.075s/f (Slow)
WFA 3 from 4yo+ 12lb **6** Ran SP% **113.3**
Speed ratings (Par 102): **106,105,100,100,98 93**
CSF £21.82 TOTE £9.30: £4.00, £1.60; EX 24.80 Trifecta £74.80.
Owner Mark Goldstein **Bred** Southill Stud **Trained** Royston, Herts

FOCUS
The leader took them along at a good pace in this fillies' handicap. The winner has been rated to his winter form.

1433 BET SCOOP6SOCCER AT BETFRED.COM H'CAP 5f (P)
8:10 (8:10) (Class 5) (0-75,74) 4-Y-O+ **£5,175** (£1,540; £769; £384) **Stalls** Low

Form RPR
1441 **1** **Welease Bwian (IRE)**[34] 903 7-8-12 **72**.....................(v) MillyNaseb(7) 2 82
(Stuart Williams) *s.i.s: hld up: hdwy and nt clr run over 1f out: n.m.r but r.o to ld wl ins fnl f* **7/2**[2]

-101 **2** ½ **More Spice (IRE)**[44] 775 4-8-12 **65**..........................(b) JamieSpencer 3 73
(Robert Cowell) *prom: swtchd rt over 1f out: rdn and edgd lft ins fnl f: r.o* **5/2**[1]

0360 **3** 1¼ **Mossgo (IRE)**[13] 1173 6-9-3 **70**..(t) KierenFox 1 74
(John Best) *led: rdn over 1f out: hdd ins fnl f: styd on same pce towards fin* **8/1**

00/3 **4** shd **Pushkin Museum (IRE)**[20] 1084 5-9-5 **72**....................... DavidNolan 6 75
(Richard Fahey) *chsd ldrs: rdn to ld ins fnl f: sn hdd: no ex towards fin* **7/2**[2]

1-33 **5** 2¼ **Summer Isles**[34] 903 6-9-0 **67**.................................... PaulMulrennan 4 62
(Paul Midgley) *prom: chsd ldr over 3f out: rdn over 1f out: styd on same pce ins fnl f* **8/1**

4463 **6** nk **Zipedeedodah (IRE)**[15] 1150 4-8-6 **64**.................(t) EdwardGreatrex(5) 8 58
(Joseph Tuite) *s.i.s: sn pushed along in rr: nt trble ldrs* **16/1**

154- **7** 7 **Space Artist (IRE)**[139] 8011 6-9-7 **74**.....................(v) SilvestreDeSousa 7 43
(Nigel Tinkler) *hld up: hdwy over 3f out: rdn 1/2-way: wknd fnl f* **7/1**[3]

1m 0.04s (-0.16) **Going Correction** +0.075s/f (Slow) 7 Ran SP% **113.6**
Speed ratings (Par 103): **104,103,101,101,97 96,85**
CSF £12.53 CT £63.04 TOTE £4.60: £1.60, £2.40; EX 16.90 Trifecta £74.80.
Owner W E Enticknap **Bred** Nils Koop **Trained** Newmarket, Suffolk

FOCUS
A fair little sprint run at a good gallop. The winner has been rated better than ever.

1434 BET SCOOP6SOCCER AT TOTESPORT.COM H'CAP 1m 5f 66y(P)
8:40 (8:40) (Class 5) (0-70,70) 4-Y-O+ **£5,175** (£1,540; £769; £384) **Stalls** Low

Form RPR
30-1 **1** **Avenue Des Champs**[29] 950 4-8-6 **60**....................... DannyBrock(3) 2 70
(Jane Chapple-Hyam) *chsd ldr tl led over 2f out: rdn over 1f out: styd on wl* **5/1**

432- **2** 3¾ **Rock Of Max**[140] 8001 4-9-5 **70**...................................(p) JamieSpencer 8 74
(Michael Bell) *hld up: hdwy over 2f out: sn rdn: edgd lft and chsd wnr ins fnl f: styd on same pce* **9/2**[3]

2111 **3** ½ **Bracken Brae**[35] 884 4-9-2 **67**.. FMBerry 5 70
(Mark H Tompkins) *chsd ldrs: rdn to chse wnr over 2f out: styd on same pce ins fnl f* **4/1**[2]

60-4 **4** ½ **Able Dash**[26] 1002 6-9-7 **70**...................................(v[1]) RichardKingscote 4 73
(Michael Blake) *chsd ldrs: rdn over 2f out: styd on same pce fr over 1f out* **11/4**[1]

-536 **5** 3 **Tidal Way (IRE)**[22] 1039 7-8-8 **62**.......................(p) JosephineGordon(5) 6 60
(Shaun Lycett) *mid-div: rdn over 2f out: styd on same pce appr fnl f* **20/1**

2425 **6** 1 **Kelly's Finest (IRE)**[15] 1144 4-8-12 **63**.......................(p) AndrewMullen 3 60
(Michael Appleby) *led at stdy pce tl qcknd over 3f out: rdn and hdd over 2f out: wknd ins fnl f* **16/1**

20-5 **7** 6 **Yorkindred Spirit**[20] 1085 4-9-3 **68**.......................(v) SilvestreDeSousa 9 59
(Mark Johnston) *mid-div: rdn over 2f out: wknd over 1f out* **16/1**

0006 **8** 13 **Maria's Choice (IRE)**[16] 1135 7-9-4 **67**.......................... TimmyMurphy 7 35
(Jim Best) *hld up: rdn and wknd over 2f out* **50/1**

336- **P** **Front Five (IRE)**[179] 7307 4-9-4 **69**.................................. GeorgeBaker 1
(Martin Bosley) *hld up: rdn over 3f out: sn wknd and eased: p.u over 1f out* **4/1**[2]

2m 55.59s (1.99) **Going Correction** +0.075s/f (Slow)
WFA 4 from 6yo+ 2lb 9 Ran SP% **120.0**
Speed ratings (Par 103): **96,93,93,93,91 90,86,78,**
CSF £28.99 CT £100.79 TOTE £5.10: £1.50, £2.20, £1.70; EX 40.20 Trifecta £121.70.
Owner The Tuesday Club **Bred** Grovewood Stud **Trained** Dalham, Suffolk

FOCUS
This was steadily run. Muddling form, but the third has been rated close to her mark.

1435 SIMPLY RED HERE ON 1ST JULY MAIDEN STKS 5f (P)
9:10 (9:12) (Class 5) 3-Y-O+ **£5,175** (£1,540; £769; £384) **Stalls** Low

Form RPR
23-2 **1** **Paddy Power (IRE)**[25] 1014 3-9-3 85................................ DavidNolan 2 75+
(Richard Fahey) *mde all: shkn up over 1f out: rdn out* **4/6**[1]

62 **2** 2¼ **Silver Bid (USA)**[15] 1151 4-10-0 0... FMBerry 4 72+
(Alan Bailey) *s.i.s and hmpd sn after s: hld up: hdwy over 1f out: r.o to go 2nd wl ins fnl f: no ch w wnr* **7/2**[2]

3432 **3** 1¼ **Justice Rock**[34] 902 3-8-12 62..........................(v) JosephineGordon(5) 1 62
(Phil McEntee) *w wnr tl rdn over 1f out: no ex ins fnl f* **16/1**[3]

64- **4** ¾ **Majestic Girl (IRE)**[168] 7578 3-8-12 0.............................. MartinHarley 3 54
(Robert Cowell) *prom: rdn over 1f out: styd on same pce fnl f* **33/1**

323 **5** 3½ **Spice Mill (IRE)**[15] 1151 3-9-3 67............................. SilvestreDeSousa 5 47
(Robert Cowell) *chsd ldrs: rdn 1/2-way: edgd lft over 1f out: sn wknd* **7/2**[2]

0/ **6** 1½ **Dandy Maid**[1056] 2625 5-9-9 0.. AndrewMullen 6 41
(Michael Appleby) *hld up: rdn and wknd over 1f out* **66/1**

1m 0.46s (0.26) **Going Correction** +0.075s/f (Slow)
WFA 3 from 4yo+ 11lb 6 Ran SP% **114.7**
Speed ratings (Par 103): **100,96,94,93,87 85**
CSF £3.55 TOTE £1.70: £1.10, £1.80; EX 3.90 Trifecta £17.60.
Owner M Scaife & R A Fahey **Bred** Yeguada De Milagro Sa **Trained** Musley Bank, N Yorks

FOCUS
This proved fairly straightforward for the odds-on favourite. The third and fourth set the standard.

T/Plt: £43.50 to a £1 stake. Pool of £75984.78 - 1272.97 winning tickets. T/Qpdt: £7.30 to a £1 stake. Pool of £8802.33 - 884.65 winning tickets. **Colin Roberts**

1421 NEWMARKET (R-H)
Thursday, April 14

OFFICIAL GOING: Good to soft changing to soft after race 5 (4.30)
Wind: light, half behind Weather: bright spells, heavy thundery shower race 4 and 5

1436 NEWMARKET350.CO.UK MAIDEN FILLIES' STKS (PLUS 10 RACE) 7f
2:10 (2:11) (Class 4) 3-Y-O **£5,175** (£1,540; £769; £384) **Stalls** Low

Form RPR
24- **1** **Jadaayil**[223] 6044 3-9-0 0.. PaulHanagan 3 85
(Charles Hills) *t.k.h: chsd ldr tl led 1/2-way: rdn over 2f out: styd on wl: rdn out* **3/1**[1]

326- **2** 1½ **Summer Icon**[173] 7471 3-9-0 79................................ SilvestreDeSousa 8 81+
(Mick Channon) *t.k.h: hld up in last trio: hdwy ent fnl 2f: stl plenty to do in 5th over 1f out: swtchd lft and r.o strly ins fnl f: wnt 2nd fnl 50yds: nvr gng to rch wnr* **9/2**[3]

5- **3** 1½ **Blue Geranium (IRE)**[173] 7472 3-9-0 0......................... FrankieDettori 4 77
(John Gosden) *athletic: lw: t.k.h: chsd ldng trio: effrt to chse ldr over 2f out: kpt on same pce fr over 1f out: lost 2nd fnl 50yds* **3/1**[1]

4 ½ **Clear Water (IRE)** 3-9-0 0.. JamesDoyle 12 76
(Saeed bin Suroor) *str: bit bkwd: hld up in tch in midfield: rdn and outpcd over 2f out: rallied ent fnl f: rn green and drifting lft ins fnl f: styd on but no threat to wnr* **4/1**[2]

0 **5** 1 **Gabrielle**[21] 1063 3-9-0 0.. JimCrowley 1 73
(Ed Dunlop) *led tl 1/2-way: styd trckng ldrs: rdn and outpcd over 2f out: styd on same pce and lost 2 pls ins fnl f* **50/1**

0- **6** 1½ **Lime And Lemon (IRE)**[173] 7472 3-9-0 0........................ OisinMurphy 11 69
(Philip McBride) *unf: lengthy: in tch in midfield: rdn and outpcd over 2f out: 6th and no imp over 1f out: kpt on ins fnl f: no threat to ldrs* **25/1**

344- **7** 2¼ **Natural Wonder**[173] 7472 3-9-0 74....................................... PatDobbs 7 63
(Richard Hannon) *chsd ldng trio tl 3f out: sn outpcd: wknd over 1f out* **9/1**

8 hd **Aspen Again (IRE)** 3-9-0 0.. ShaneKelly 9 62
(David Menuisier) *lengthy: s.i.s and rn green early: a in rr: rdn 3f out: no imp: n.d* **25/1**

9 1 **Glittering** 3-8-11 0... RyanTate(3) 6 60
(James Eustace) *leggy: cl-cpld: in tch in midfield: rdn and outpcd whn rn green over 2f out: wknd over 1f out* **40/1**

10 ¾ **Sante (IRE)** 3-9-0 0... DarryllHolland 10 58
(Charles Hills) *lengthy: bit bkwd: s.i.s and wnt lft sn after s: rn green: clsd and in tch towards rr after 1f: rdn 3f out: sn outpcd: wknd over 1f out* **16/1**

1m 29.38s (3.98) **Going Correction** +0.55s/f (Yiel) 10 Ran SP% **116.2**
Speed ratings (Par 97): **99,97,95,95,93 92,89,89,88,87**
CSF £16.04 TOTE £3.90: £1.50, £1.70, £1.60; EX 18.10 Trifecta £52.00.
Owner Hamdan Al Maktoum **Bred** Shadwell Estate Company Limited **Trained** Lambourn, Berks

FOCUS
With just one small shower in the morning the going remained good to soft. Course configuration was the same as for the previous day - Far-side track in use with the stalls on the far side. Not the deepest maiden ever run at Newmarket, but a nice performance from the winner and a couple of those in behind caught the eye. The winning time was 6.88sec outside standard, suggesting there was still some cut in the ground. Paul Hanagan said: "The ground is better than yesterday, it's dried up a lot" while James Doyle said: "It's dead, tacky." It's been rated around the race standard.

1437 MONTAZ RESTAURANT EBF STALLION FILLIES' MAIDEN STKS (PLUS 10 RACE) 5f
2:45 (2:46) (Class 4) 2-Y-O **£4,528** (£1,347; £673; £336) **Stalls** Low

Form RPR
1 **Fiery Character (IRE)** 2-9-0 0............................... RichardKingscote 6 79
(Tom Dascombe) *unf: scope: mde all: rdn over 1f out: styd on wl to assert ins fnl f: in command and pricking ears towards fin* **33/1**

2 1¼ **Perfect Madge (IRE)** 2-9-0 0....................................... JamieSpencer 5 75
(Kevin Ryan) *lengthy: in tch in midfield: rdn and hdwy 1f out: styd on wl to go 2nd last strides: no real threat to wnr* **8/1**

3 hd **Camargue** 2-9-0 0.. WilliamBuick 1 74
(Mark Johnston) *unf: scope: w ldr: rdn over 1f out: stl ev ch tl no ex and outpcd wl ins fnl f: lost 2nd last strides* **9/2**[2]

4 shd **Lexington Sky (IRE)** 2-9-0 0.. PatDobbs 10 73
(Richard Hannon) *str: in tch in midfield: effrt over 1f out: hdwy 1f out: styd on ins fnl f: nvr enough pce to rch wnr* **7/1**[3]

5 nk **Love Oasis** 2-9-0 0.. JoeFanning 7 72
(Mark Johnston) *str: chsd ldng pair: rdn and unable qck over 1f out: kpt on same pce ins fnl f* **16/1**

6 1¼ **Seafront** 2-9-0 0.. DavidAllan 4 68
(James Tate) *dwlt: in tch towards rr: rdn along over 2f out: hdwy ins fnl f: kpt on but no threat to wnr* **8/1**

7 nk **Zumran** 2-9-0 0.. MartinHarley 2 67
(Hugo Palmer) *leggy: dwlt: hld up in tch towards rr: hdwy to chse ldrs 2f out: rdn and unable qck over 1f out: wknd wl ins fnl f* **15/8**[1]

8 1¼ **Black Redstart** 2-9-0 0... AndreaAtzeni 3 62
(Alan Bailey) *leggy: wl in tch in midfield: effrt over 1f out: no imp u.p 1f out: wknd ins fnl f* **33/1**

9 2¾ **Savannah Slew** 2-9-0 0.. TomEaves 9 52
(James Given) *leggy: unf: s.i.s: pushed along and detached in last: sme hdwy wl over 1f out: wknd 1f out* **25/1**

10 5 **Quantum Field (USA)** 2-9-0 0.. OisinMurphy 11 34
(David Brown) *tall: lengthy: rn green: hld up in tch towards rr: rdn and btn 2f out: bhd fnl f* **7/1**[3]

1m 2.24s (3.14) **Going Correction** +0.55s/f (Yiel) 10 Ran SP% **115.8**
Speed ratings (Par 91): **96,94,93,93,93 91,90,88,84,76**
CSF £271.41 TOTE £28.60: £6.00, £3.00, £1.90; EX 246.30 Trifecta £1312.80.
Owner The Roaring Twenties **Bred** Dermot & John Dwan **Trained** Malpas, Cheshire

FOCUS
An interesting fillies' maiden contested by ten debutantes and the race should produce winners. It paid to be handy with the winner and third disputing the lead from the off. The opening level is a bit guessy.

1438 £200,000 TATTERSALLS MILLIONS 3-Y-O TROPHY 1m 2f
3:20 (3:21) (Class 2) 3-Y-O
£108,220 (£44,280; £19,700; £9,820; £4,920; £1,960) **Stalls** Low

Form RPR
22- **1** **Linguistic (IRE)**[203] 6674 3-9-5 0...................................... WilliamBuick 2 101+
(John Gosden) *str: lw: t.k.h: hld up in tch towards rr: hdwy to press ldr 3f out: rdn to ld wl over 1f out: clr 1f out: styd on: rdn out* **3/1**[2]

The Form Book, Raceform Ltd, Newbury, RG14 5SJ

1- **2** *1 1/4* **Harlequeen**[226] 5970 3-9-0 90 SilvestreDeSousa 8 93
(Mick Channon) *unf: stdd s: t.k.h: hld up in tch towards rr: rdn and hdwy over 2f out: squeezed between rivals and chsd clr wnr 1f out: styd on u.p but nvr getting to wnr* **6/1**[3]

5-1 **3** *1 1/4* **Biodynamic (IRE)**[15] 1140 3-9-5 74 DougieCostello 6 95
(K R Burke) *str: chsd ldrs: rdn 4f out: kpt on wl u.p: wnt 3rd jst ins fnl f: styd on same pce u.p after* **50/1**

22- **4** *2 1/4* **Landofhopeandglory (IRE)**[172] 7492 3-9-5 103 RyanMoore 3 91
(A P O'Brien, Ire) *chsd ldr: rdn and outpcd in 3rd 2f out: no imp after: plugged on same pce ins fnl f* **15/8**[1]

1- **5** *6* **Brave Hero**[141] 7981 3-9-5 90 JamesDoyle 5 79
(Saeed bin Suroor) *gd-bodied: racd keenly: led: hdd and wandered on downhill run wl over 1f out: btn and lost 2nd 1f out: wknd ins fnl f* **3/1**[2]

234- **6** *3* **Ride The Lightning**[179] 7309 3-9-5 75 TomQueally 9 73
(Brian Meehan) *lengthy: in tch: rdn over 2f out: sn outpcd: wl btn in 6th over 1f out* **100/1**

213- **7** *9* **Ninetta (IRE)**[194] 6923 3-9-0 85 PJMcDonald 1 50
(Ann Duffield) *leggy: chsd ldrs tl rdn and lost pl qckly over 2f out: sn bhd* **25/1**

0- **8** *1* **Simply Me**[188] 7077 3-9-0 0 RichardKingscote 4 48
(Tom Dascombe) *str: t.k.h: hld up in tch: rdn 3f out: sn outpcd and btn: bhd over 1f out* **100/1**

-110 **9** *12* **Cape Speed (FR)**[20] 1071 3-9-5 96 JoeFanning 7 29
(Mark Johnston) *cmpt: chsd ldrs: lost pl qckly and rdn 3f out: bhd fnl 2f: eased ins fnl f: t.o* **20/1**

2m 8.93s (3.13) **Going Correction** +0.55s/f (Yiel) **9** Ran SP% **111.6**
Speed ratings (Par 104): **109,108,107,105,100 98,90,90,80**
CSF £19.19 TOTE £3.20: £1.10, £2.20, £11.20; EX 17.20 Trifecta £375.40.
Owner Godolphin **Bred** Ballylinch Stud **Trained** Newmarket, Suffolk

FOCUS
A valuable contest, albeit only a few could be seriously considered. The conditions seemed to take their toll as the field finished well spread out, but the first three all did their reputations no harm at all. The first three have been rated close to the expected standard.

1439 CONNAUGHT ACCESS FLOORING ABERNANT STKS (GROUP 3) 6f
3:55 (3:55) (Class 1) 3-Y-O+
£34,026 (£12,900; £6,456; £3,216; £1,614; £810) **Stalls** Low

Form RPR

113- **1** **Magical Memory (IRE)**[222] 6084 4-9-6 114 FrankieDettori 8 114+
(Charles Hills) *t.k.h: trckd ldrs: effrt and qcknd to ld over 1f out: reduced advantage but a gng to hold on towards fin: rdn out* **3/1**[1]

044- **2** *nk* **Tupi (IRE)**[194] 6932 4-9-6 108 RyanMoore 3 113
(Richard Hannon) *swtg: hld up in tch: effrt over 1f out: hdwy to chse ldng pair ins fnl f: r.o strly u.p fnl 100yds: wnt 2nd last strides: nvr quite getting to wnr* **10/1**

130- **3** *nk* **Mattmu**[222] 6084 4-9-6 113 (p) DavidAllan 1 112
(Tim Easterby) *lw: trckd ldrs: effrt and qcknd to chal wnr over 1f out: kpt on wl u.p ins fnl f: lost 2nd last strides* **7/1**

600- **4** *nse* **Aeolus**[166] 7662 5-9-6 107 GeorgeBaker 4 112
(Ed Walker) *hld up in tch: effrt over 1f out: rdn to chse ldrs 1f out: kpt on wl u.p fnl 100yds: nvr quite getting to wnr* **16/1**

00-3 **5** *hd* **Maarek**[12] 1197 9-9-6 108 JamieSpencer 10 111
(Miss Evanna McCutcheon, Ire) *stdd s: hld up in tch in last pair: hdwy jst over 1f out: swtchd rt and r.o strly ins fnl f: nvr quite getting to ldrs* **9/1**

40/1 **6** *2* **Baccarat (IRE)**[49] 723 7-9-6 111 WilliamBuick 2 105
(Charlie Appleby) *lw: v awkward and throwing hd arnd leaving stalls: hld up in last pair: rdn and hdwy jst over 1f out: kpt on same pce and no imp fnl 100yds* **10/3**[2]

500- **7** *3/4* **Coulsty (IRE)**[180] 7278 5-9-6 109 SeanLevey 12 102
(Richard Hannon) *lw: t.k.h: chsd ldrs: rdn and effrt whn hung lft over 1f out: no ex 1f out: wknd ins fnl f* **12/1**

01-0 **8** *3* **Jack Dexter**[12] 1197 7-9-6 106 JimCrowley 6 93
(Jim Goldie) *swtg: in tch: effrt u.p over 1f out: unable qck and no hdwy 1f out: wknd ins fnl f* **25/1**

10-1 **9** *nk* **Mobsta (IRE)**[12] 1197 4-9-6 106 SilvestreDeSousa 9 92
(Mick Channon) *lw: in tch in midfield: rdn 1/2-way: lost pl u.p over 1f out: wknd ins fnl f* **6/1**[3]

-560 **10** *1 1/2* **Stepper Point**[40] 841 7-9-6 105 (p) MartinDwyer 5 87
(William Muir) *led: rdn and hdd over 1f out: no ex u.p and sn lost pl: wknd ins fnl f* **50/1**

100- **11** *2 1/2* **Son Of Africa**[278] 4128 4-9-6 100 HarryBentley 11 79
(Henry Candy) *t.k.h: w ldr: rdn over 1f out: sn outpcd and lost pl: bhd ins fnl f* **33/1**

1m 14.84s (2.64) **Going Correction** +0.775s/f (Yiel) **11** Ran SP% **116.3**
Speed ratings (Par 113): **113,112,112,112,111 109,108,104,103,101 98**
CSF £32.76 TOTE £3.90: £1.70, £3.10, £2.20; EX 35.40 Trifecta £207.30.
Owner Kennet Valley Thoroughbreds I **Bred** Wardstown Stud Ltd **Trained** Lambourn, Berks

FOCUS
A competitive renewal of the Abernant in which a large blanket would have covered the first five home. The winner has been rated close to his best, and the third close to form.

1440 NOVAE BLOODSTOCK INSURANCE CRAVEN STKS (GROUP 3) (C&G) 1m
4:30 (4:30) (Class 1) 3-Y-O
£34,026 (£12,900; £6,456; £3,216; £1,614; £810) **Stalls** Low

Form RPR

112- **1** **Stormy Antarctic**[165] 7665 3-9-0 112 GeorgeBaker 3 116
(Ed Walker) *str: lw: stdd s: t.k.h: hld up in tch in rr: smooth hdwy over 1f out to ld 1f out: sn clr: pushed out: easily* **9/2**[2]

113- **2** *3 1/2* **Foundation (IRE)**[173] 7463 3-9-0 110 FrankieDettori 5 108
(John Gosden) *trckd ldng pair: effrt jst over 2f out: chsd ldr wl over 1f out: styd on and ev ch briefly ent fnl f: totally outpcd by wnr ins fnl f: wnt 2nd again fnl 75yds* **4/6**[1]

360- **3** *1/2* **Shogun (IRE)**[167] 7624 3-9-0 108 (b) RyanMoore 1 107
(A P O'Brien, Ire) *in tch in 4th: effrt over 2f out: drvn and chsng ldrs over 1f out: no ch w wnr but plugged on u.p to go 3rd towards fin* **12/1**[3]

16-4 **4** *1/2* **Tony Curtis**[47] 756 3-9-0 106 SeanLevey 6 106
(Richard Hannon) *t.k.h: sn led: rdn 2f out: hdd 1f out and immediately outpcd by wnr: lost 2 pls fnl 75yds* **33/1**

12- **5** *10* **Steel Of Madrid (IRE)**[218] 6220 3-9-0 95 PatDobbs 4 83
(Richard Hannon) *str: lw: t.k.h: chsd ldr tl wl over 1f out: sn lost pl u.p: bhd and eased ins fnl f* **25/1**

321- **6** *4* **Very Talented (IRE)**[217] 6247 3-9-0 98 JamesDoyle 2 74
(Saeed bin Suroor) *swtg: t.k.h: hld up in tch in last pair: effrt ent fnl 2f: no imp u.p and btn 1f out: sn eased* **9/2**[2]

1m 44.01s (5.41) **Going Correction** +0.875s/f (Soft) **6** Ran SP% **110.8**
Speed ratings (Par 108): **107,103,103,102,92 88**
CSF £7.73 TOTE £5.30: £1.80, £1.20; EX 9.50 Trifecta £38.10.
Owner P K Siu **Bred** East Bloodstock Ltd **Trained** Upper Lambourn, Berks

FOCUS
It started to rain heavily before this race with plenty of thunder and lightning about for good measure. A fascinating Craven, though the race hasn't been won by a subsequent 2,000 Guineas winner since Haafhd in 2004. For the first time there were no penalties for previous Group winners. The early pace appeared moderate, causing a few to take a hold and not the result many would have expected. It's been rated around the third and fourth.

1441 BEN BURGESS & CO H'CAP 7f
5:05 (5:07) (Class 2) (0-105,105) 4-Y-O+ **£12,938** (£3,850; £1,924; £962) **Stalls** Low

Form RPR

030- **1** **Accession (IRE)**[184] 7177 7-8-7 **91** oh2 MartinLane 13 104
(Charlie Fellowes) *trckd ldrs: hdwy to chse ldr 2f out: rdn to ld over 1f out: styd on strly and drew wl clr fnl f: rdn out* **20/1**

5- **2** *6* **Flaming Spear (IRE)**[189] 7065 4-9-1 **99** RobertWinston 12 96
(Kevin Ryan) *lw: chsd ldrs tl led over 5f out: rdn and hdd over 1f out: wknd ins fnl f* **4/1**[1]

1/6- **3** *hd* **Mutamakkin (USA)**[334] 2284 4-8-8 **92** PaulHanagan 16 89+
(Sir Michael Stoute) *lw: dwlt: bhd: rdn and effrt over 2f out: hdwy to pass btn horses 1f out: styd on strly ins fnl f: no ch w wnr* **11/1**

332- **4** *1 1/2* **Felix Leiter**[159] 7758 4-8-1 **92** oh4 ow1 CliffordLee(7) 2 85
(K R Burke) *led tl over 5f out: chsd ldrs after: rdn over 2f out: outpcd ent fnl f: no ch w wnr and plugged on same pce ins fnl f* **11/1**

-244 **5** *1* **Flash Fire (IRE)**[56] 628 4-9-6 **104** WilliamBuick 4 94
(Charlie Appleby) *chsd ldrs: 3rd and no ex u.p over 1f out: wknd ins fnl f* **10/1**

553- **6** *1 3/4* **Grand Inquisitor**[201] 6758 4-8-12 **96** RyanMoore 6 89+
(Sir Michael Stoute) *hld up in rr: effrt and nt clr run wl over 1f out: swtchd rt and hdwy ins fnl f: styd on: nvr trbld ldrs* **5/1**[2]

03-0 **7** *3/4* **Farlow (IRE)**[12] 1196 8-9-1 **102** SammyJoBell(3) 1 86
(Richard Fahey) *in tch in midfield: effrt over 2f out: 6th and no imp over 1f out: wknd ins fnl f* **9/1**[3]

1132 **8** *3* **Supersta**[33] 920 5-8-9 **93** (p) AndrewMullen 14 69
(Michael Appleby) *hld up in tch: effrt jst over 2f out: no imp u.p over 1f out: wknd ins fnl f* **14/1**

00-0 **9** *1/2* **Heaven's Guest (IRE)**[12] 1196 6-9-7 **105** JackGarritty 10 80
(Richard Fahey) *hld up in tch in midfield: effrt 2f out: 5th and no imp u.p over 1f out: wknd ins fnl f* **9/1**[3]

120- **10** *nk* **Mambo Paradise**[250] 5158 4-8-7 **91** JoeFanning 15 65
(Mark Johnston) *in tch in midfield: hdwy 3f out: rdn and no imp 2f out: wknd fnl f* **25/1**

0-53 **11** *1* **Lexington Times (IRE)**[15] 1153 4-8-11 **95** PatDobbs 7 66
(Richard Hannon) *in tch in midfield: effrt over 2f out: drvn and no imp over 1f out: wknd fnl f* **16/1**

015- **12** *shd* **Dinkum Diamond (IRE)**[173] 7466 8-9-5 **103** CathyGannon 11 74
(Henry Candy) *rdr struggling to remove hood: t.k.h: hld up in rr: effrt over 2f out: nt clrest of runs over 1f out: sn no imp: wknd fnl f* **20/1**

6-16 **13** *2 1/2* **Three Gracez**[26] 1003 4-8-4 **91** oh6 TomMarquand(3) 5 56
(Philip McBride) *in tch in midfield: rdn 3f out: little rspnse and lost pl 2f out: bhd fnl f* **28/1**

101- **14** *1* **Mujassam**[228] 5908 4-9-0 **98** DaneO'Neill 8 60
(Roger Varian) *w ldrs: rdn and lost pl over 2f out: bhd fnl f* **10/1**

/00- **P** **Passing Star**[320] 2719 5-8-9 **93** DarryllHolland 9
(Charles Hills) *in tch in rr: pushed along 3f out: sn lost action and eased: p.u and dismntd wl over 1f out* **66/1**

1m 30.42s (5.02) **Going Correction** +0.975s/f (Soft) **15** Ran SP% **122.4**
Speed ratings (Par 109): **110,103,102,101,100 98,97,93,93,92 91,91,88,87,**
CSF £94.44 CT £703.02 TOTE £19.60: £5.30, £2.40, £4.10; EX 154.20 Trifecta £2697.50.
Owner Lady De Ramsey **Bred** Corduff Stud Ltd **Trained** Newmarket, Suffolk

FOCUS
The going was changed to soft before this race. A hot handicap, but the conditions appeared to sort them out. A pb from the winner.

1442 ROSSDALES H'CAP 6f
5:40 (5:41) (Class 2) (0-100,95) 3-Y-O **£12,938** (£3,850; £1,924; £962) **Stalls** Low

Form RPR

1- **1** **Aclaim (IRE)**[127] 8154 3-8-13 **87** RyanMoore 2 99+
(Martyn Meade) *str: hld up in rr: swtchd rt 2f out: rdn and hdwy over 1f out: led 1f out: in command whn hung lft wl ins fnl f: r.o* **2/1**[1]

1- **2** *1 1/2* **Monteverdi (FR)**[174] 7429 3-8-12 **86** JamieSpencer 12 91
(Jamie Osborne) *str: lw: hld up in rr: rdn and hdwy over 1f out: styd on strly ins fnl f: wnt 2nd last strides: no threat to wnr* **13/2**[3]

132- **3** *nk* **Vibrant Chords**[197] 6853 3-8-13 **87** HarryBentley 5 91
(Henry Candy) *in tch in midfield: effrt wl over 1f out: chal and edgd rt 1f out: styd on same pce ins fnl f: lost 2nd last strides* **4/1**[2]

221- **4** *nk* **Hope Cove**[166] 7637 3-8-8 **82** AntonioFresu 4 85
(Ed Walker) *swtg: broke wl: stdd to chse ldrs and t.k.h: effrt wl over 1f out: ev ch whn squeezed for room 1f out: styd on same pce ins fnl f* **11/1**

2122 **5** *5* **Kingsley Klarion (IRE)**[14] 1168 3-9-3 **91** JoeFanning 3 78
(Mark Johnston) *led for 1f: chsd ldrs tl no ex u.p over 1f out: wknd ins fnl f* **25/1**

0-41 **6** *1 1/2* **Suqoor**[8] 1258 3-8-7 **81** 6ex IrineuGoncalves 7 63
(Chris Dwyer) *t.k.h: chsd ldrs: clsd to join ldr 2f out: rdn to ld over 1f out: hdd 1f out: fdd ins fnl f* **14/1**

51-1 **7** *2 3/4* **Florencio**[14] 1168 3-8-13 **87** MartinDwyer 1 60
(William Muir) *in tch in midfield: effrt over 1f out: sn btn: wknd ins fnl f* **15/2**

144- **8** *nk* **King Robert**[187] 7121 3-9-7 **95** RichardKingscote 10 67
(Bryan Smart) *swtg: t.k.h: chsd ldrs tl led after 1f: rdn and hdd over 1f out: fdd ins fnl f* **8/1**

402- **9** *3 1/4* **Racquet**[247] 5249 3-8-8 **85** TomMarquand(3) 9 47
(Richard Hannon) *dwlt: sn rcvrd and in tch in midfield: effrt over 2f out: sn struggling: wknd and bhd over 1f out* **16/1**

322- **10** *16* **Rial (IRE)**[302] 3286 3-7-11 **76** oh1 NoelGarbutt(5) 11
(Denis Quinn) *chsd ldrs: rdn 1/2-way: lost pl and bhd 2f out: sn lost tch* **50/1**

1m 18.06s (5.86) **Going Correction** +1.075s/f (Soft) **10** Ran SP% **116.2**
Speed ratings (Par 104): **103,101,100,100,93 91,87,87,83,61**
CSF £15.21 CT £49.16 TOTE £3.00: £1.40, £2.30, £1.60; EX 16.80 Trifecta £57.40.
Owner Canning Downs & Partner **Bred** D Farrington And Canning Downs **Trained** Newmarket, Suffolk

■ Stewards' Enquiry : Antonio Fresu two-day ban: careless riding (Apr 28-29)

FOCUS

A competitive 3yo sprint handicap including some completely unexposed types. The first two, who came from last and last-but-one, had won their only previous starts so we should be hearing plenty more from them. A big step up from the winner.

T/Plt: £162.80 to a £1 stake. Pool of £118337.21 - 530.47 winning tickets. T/Qpdt: £34.40 to a £1 stake. Pool of £8210.81 - 176.58 winning tickets. **Steve Payne**

RIPON (R-H)

Thursday, April 14

OFFICIAL GOING: Heavy (soft in places; 4.8)

Wind: light 1/2 against Weather: overcast, cold

1443 EBF/NAGS HEAD PICKHILL NOVICE FILLIES' STKS (PLUS 10 RACE) 5f

2:00 (2:00) (Class 5) 2-Y-O **£3,881** (£1,155; £577; £288) **Stalls** High

Form	Pos	Btn	Horse / Trainer / Comment	RPR
	1		**Coolfitch (IRE)** 2-9-0 0 DanielTudhope 6 (David O'Meara) *trckd ldrs: shkn up to ld over 1f out: edgd lft: drvn out* **11/8**[1]	71+
	2	*2*	**Four Dragons** 2-9-0 0 LiamJones 9 (Tom Dascombe) *led: hdd over 1f out: kpt on same pce* **7/2**[2]	61
	3	*½*	**Born To Boogie** 2-9-0 0 GrahamLee 5 (Chris Grant) *s.i.s: hdwy over 2f out: kpt on to take 3rd towards fin* **25/1**	59
	4	*nk*	**Bonnie Arlene (IRE)** 2-9-0 0 FrannyNorton 3 (Mark Johnston) *chsd ldrs: drvn over 2f out: kpt on one pce over 1f out* **13/2**	58
	5	*1*	**Yes You (IRE)** 2-8-9 0 PhilDennis(5) 2 (James Given) *chsd ldrs: edgd lft and outpcd over 1f out: kpt on towards fin* **12/1**	54
	6	*7*	**Bella Duchess (IRE)** 2-9-0 0 BenCurtis 1 (David C Griffiths) *dwlt: sn chsng ldrs: lost pl over 3f out: sn bhd* **9/1**	29
	7	*21*	**Benidiction (IRE)** 2-9-0 0 GrahamGibbons 4 (Ann Duffield) *half-rrd s: t.k.h: sn w ldrs: lost pl over 1f out: sn wl bhd: eased fnl 100yds: t.o* **6/1**[3]	

1m 9.04s (9.04) **Going Correction** +1.60s/f (Heav) **7** Ran SP% **113.5**

Speed ratings (Par 89): **91,87,87,86,84 73,40**

CSF £6.17 TOTE £2.90: £1.50, £2.60; EX 11.00 Trifecta £97.50.

Owner W Hoffman Racing **Bred** P Kelly **Trained** Upper Helmsley, N Yorks

FOCUS

The rail had been dolled out 6 yards around the bend from the back straight to the home straight adding approximately 12 yards to races 3, 4 and 7 on the round course. This isn't form to get overly excited about due to the ground. The winning rider reported the ground as 'definitely heavy' and 'hard work.'

1444 PPR FOUNDATION H'CAP 6f

2:35 (2:38) (Class 4) (0-85,84) 4-Y-O+ **£4,851** (£1,443; £721; £360) **Stalls** High

Form	Pos	Btn	Horse / Trainer / Comment	RPR
0/	**1**		**Dandyleekie (IRE)**[184] 7200 4-8-10 76 ShelleyBirkett(3) 2 (David O'Meara) *racd far side: in rr: swtchd lft and hdwy over 2f out: r.o to ld in clsng stages: 1st of 7 that gp* **12/1**	86+
600-	**2**	*hd*	**Explain**[236] 5629 4-9-0 77 JamesSullivan 16 (Ruth Carr) *racd stands' side: chsd ldrs: led that gp appr fnl f: edgd rt and kpt on clsng stages: jst hld: 1st of 10 that gp* **28/1**	86
00-0	**3**	*¾*	**Barkston Ash**[11] 1215 8-9-3 80 (p) JasonHart 6 (Eric Alston) *racd far side: chsd ldr: led that side 3f out: hdd and no ex clsng stages: 2nd of 7 that gp* **10/1**	87+
0-50	**4**	*1 ½*	**Classic Seniority**[54] 655 4-9-0 77 PhillipMakin 12 (Marjorie Fife) *led stands' side gp over 1f: chsd ldrs: kpt on same pce fnl f: 2nd of 10 that gp* **25/1**	79
30-4	**5**	*3*	**Mississippi**[30] 944 7-9-7 84 GrahamLee 4 (Paul Midgley) *racd far side: in rr: hdwy 2f out: nvr a threat: 3rd of 7 that gp* **13/2**[1]	77
000-	**6**	*shd*	**Fast Shot**[201] 6746 8-8-11 79 RachelRichardson(5) 10 (Tim Easterby) *racd stands' side: mid-div: hdwy over 2f out: kpt on same pce appr fnl f: 3rd of 10 that gp* **11/1**	72+
000-	**7**	*shd*	**Art Obsession (IRE)**[198] 6831 5-9-3 80 PaulMulrennan 14 (Paul Midgley) *dwlt: sn chsng ldrs stands' side: kpt on same pce over 1f out: 4th of 10 that gp* **9/1**	73
56-0	**8**	*4*	**Intisaab**[11] 1215 5-9-3 80 (v) DanielTudhope 3 (David O'Meara) *racd far side: chsd ldrs: wknd over 1f out: 4th of 7 that gp* **7/1**[2]	61
40-0	**9**	*½*	**Rita's Boy (IRE)**[104] 4 4-9-5 82 (v) BenCurtis 9 (K R Burke) *swtchd lft after s: racd stands' side: led stands' side gp over 4f out: hdd appr fnl f: sn wknd: 5th of 10 that gp* **14/1**	61
450-	**10**	*3*	**Royal Brave (IRE)**[188] 7082 5-9-1 78 BarryMcHugh 13 (Rebecca Bastiman) *racd stands' side: sn bhd: kpt on fnl 2f: nvr a factor: 6th of 10 that gp* **66/1**	48
000-	**11**	*2*	**Ambitious Icarus**[183] 7223 7-9-2 79 (e) ConnorBeasley 15 (Richard Guest) *half- rrd s: racd stands' side: hdwy to chse ldrs over 2f out: wknd over 1f out: 7th of 10 in that gp* **28/1**	43
050-	**12**	*4*	**Piazon**[177] 7363 5-9-6 83 ShaneGray 17 (Kevin Ryan) *racd stands' side: mid-div: drvn over 2f out: nvr a factor: 8th of 10 that gp* **7/1**[2]	35
450-	**13**	*5*	**Eastern Racer (IRE)**[197] 6862 4-8-13 81 (p) CallumShepherd(5) 1 (Brian Ellison) *swvd rt s: racd far side: chsd ldrs: wknd over 2f out: eased over 1f out: 5th of 7 that gp* **8/1**[3]	18+
05-0	**14**	*1 ½*	**Musharrif**[90] 198 4-9-0 77 NeilFarley 11 (Declan Carroll) *racd stands' side: chsd ldrs: wknd 2f out: 9th of 10 that gp* **25/1**	10
2106	**15**	*19*	**Clubland (IRE)**[30] 938 7-9-2 82 RobHornby(3) 7 (Roy Bowring) *racd far side: in rr: eased 2f out: sn wl bhd: 6th of 7 that gp* **16/1**	
540-	**16**	*7*	**Mime Dance**[188] 7093 5-8-13 81 JoshDoyle(5) 8 (David O'Meara) *racd stands' side: in rr: wl bhd fnl 2f: last of 10 that gp* **12/1**	
-160	**17**	*19*	**Uptight (FR)**[34] 901 4-8-12 78 (bt) JoeDoyle(3) 5 (Kevin Ryan) *led far side 3f: sn lost pl and bhd: heavily eased over 1f out: t.o: last of 7 that gp* **33/1**	

1m 22.66s (9.66) **Going Correction** +1.775s/f (Heav) **17** Ran SP% **123.8**

Speed ratings (Par 105): **106,105,104,102,98 98,98,93,92,88 85,80,73,71,46 37,11**

CSF £330.28 CT £3584.24 TOTE £14.20: £3.20, £8.30, £2.90, £6.80; EX 468.00 Trifecta £3200.00 Part won..

Owner Gallop Racing **Bred** Morgan Kavanagh **Trained** Upper Helmsley, N Yorks

FOCUS

This big field spilt into a couple of groups, and there appeared to be no advantage between them. The winner has been rated to last year's form.

1445 RIPONBET SILVER BOWL H'CAP 1m 1f 170y

3:10 (3:10) (Class 3) (0-95,91) 4-Y-O+ **£7,439** (£2,213; £1,106; £553) **Stalls** Low

Form	Pos	Btn	Horse / Trainer / Comment	RPR
40-4	**1**		**Felix De Vega (IRE)**[11] 1221 4-8-5 82 NathanEvans(7) 2 (Michael Easterby) *led over 1f: trckd ldrs: led 2f out: shkn up and wnt clr last 150yds: v readily* **5/2**[1]	97+
364-	**2**	*3 ½*	**Polar Forest**[163] 7676 6-8-12 87 (e) RobJFitzpatrick(5) 4 (Richard Guest) *hld up in mid-div: hdwy over 3f out: swtchd rt 2f out: 3rd over 1f out: kpt on to take 2nd last 50yds: no imp* **8/1**	92
24-6	**3**	*1 ¼*	**Salmon Sushi**[17] 1122 5-8-10 80 JasonHart 6 (Tim Easterby) *dwlt: t.k.h in rr: hdwy 4f out: nt clr run over 2f out: chsd wnr over 1f out: kpt on same pce* **16/1**	82
06-0	**4**	*2 ¾*	**Woodacre**[11] 1221 9-8-6 76 PaulQuinn 5 (Richard Whitaker) *t.k.h in rr: hdwy whn nt clr run 4f out: kpt on same pce to take 4th 1f out* **12/1**	73
0-00	**5**	*7*	**Dubai Dynamo**[12] 1195 11-9-6 90 JamesSullivan 1 (Ruth Carr) *hld up towards rr: hdwy over 3f out: chsng ldrs and nt clr run over 2f out: wknd appr fnl f* **40/1**	72
330-	**6**	*2 ¾*	**Memory Cloth**[145] 7593 9-8-6 76 DuranFentiman 3 (Micky Hammond) *s.i.s: in rr: swtchd outside over 2f out: nvr on terms* **16/1**	53
2225	**7**	*¾*	**Ralphy Lad (IRE)**[42] 800 5-8-7 77 NeilFarley 7 (Alan Swinbank) *trckd ldrs: 2nd over 3f out: wknd over 1f out* **12/1**	52
61-0	**8**	*2 ¼*	**Maraakib (IRE)**[12] 1195 4-9-7 91 DanielTudhope 12 (David O'Meara) *racd wd: sn trcking ldrs: 2nd over 6f out: wknd over 1f out* **6/1**[3]	62
210-	**9**	*1 ½*	**Argaki (IRE)**[196] 6885 6-8-7 82 PhilDennis(5) 8 (Keith Dalgleish) *mid-div: effrt over 3f out: edgd rt and lost pl over 1f out* **33/1**	50
011-	**10**	*1 ¾*	**Swift Emperor (IRE)**[242] 5419 4-9-2 86 GrahamGibbons 11 (David Barron) *trckd ldrs: pushed along over 4f out: lost pl over 1f out* **10/3**[2]	50
0120	**11**	*8*	**Spes Nostra**[27] 975 8-9-5 89 (b) GrahamLee 10 (Iain Jardine) *t.k.h: led over 8f out: hdd 2f out: wknd qckly: bhd whn eased clsng stages* **14/1**	37

2m 19.45s (14.05) **Going Correction** +1.60s/f (Heav) **11** Ran SP% **116.2**

Speed ratings (Par 107): **107,104,103,101,95 93,92,90,89,88 81**

CSF £22.80 CT £265.75 TOTE £4.00: £1.60, £1.60, £4.50; EX 25.30 Trifecta £234.70.

Owner A Simpson, D Fielding & S Hull **Bred** DDE Syndicate **Trained** Sheriff Hutton, N Yorks

FOCUS

The rail had been dolled out 6 yards around the bend from the back straight to the home straight adding approximately 12 yards to this official distance. Quite a decent contest but the easy winner probably won't find ground like this too often in the coming months. The runner-up has been rated close to his best.

1446 RIPON "COCK O' THE NORTH" H'CAP 1m

3:45 (3:45) (Class 3) (0-90,89) 3-Y-O **£7,439** (£2,213; £1,106; £553) **Stalls** Low

Form	Pos	Btn	Horse / Trainer / Comment	RPR
12-0	**1**		**Dolphin Vista (IRE)**[20] 1080 3-9-1 83 TonyHamilton 2 (Richard Fahey) *mde all: over 3 l clr 1f out: rdn out* **3/1**[1]	90
2315	**2**	*¾*	**Byres Road**[11] 1220 3-8-12 80 FrannyNorton 5 (Mark Johnston) *mid-div: sn pushed along: hdwy over 2f out: swtchd rt and 3rd over 1f out: styd on wl to take 2nd in clsng stages* **16/1**	84+
233-	**3**	*1*	**King's Pavilion (IRE)**[174] 7421 3-9-7 89 PaulMulrennan 7 (Mark Johnston) *trckd ldrs: effrt over 3f out: 2nd over 1f out: kpt on same pce* **4/1**[3]	91
215-	**4**	*8*	**Cape Love (USA)**[222] 6086 3-8-12 80 DanielTudhope 4 (David O'Meara) *hld up in rr: effrt 3f out: edgd lft over 1f out: kpt on to take modest 4th last 50yds* **9/1**	64
665-	**5**	*2 ¼*	**Taking Libertys**[208] 6513 3-9-5 87 GrahamLee 9 (Kevin Ryan) *t.k.h: trckd ldr: chal over 3f out: wknd over 1f out* **15/2**	65
205-	**6**	*1 ½*	**Forever A Lady (IRE)**[191] 7006 3-8-13 81 PhillipMakin 3 (Keith Dalgleish) *hld up in mid-div: effrt over 2f out: wknd over 1f out* **14/1**	56
20-1	**7**	*hd*	**Toboggan's Fire**[3] 1381 3-8-3 78 6ex RowanScott(7) 8 (Ann Duffield) *hld up in last: rdn 3f out: nvr on terms* **7/2**[2]	53
130-	**8**	*1*	**Lagenda**[217] 6244 3-9-2 84 KeaganLatham 6 (Kevin Ryan) *chsd ldrs: effrt over 3f out: wknd over 1f out* **10/1**	56

1m 55.44s (14.04) **Going Correction** +1.725s/f (Heav) **8** Ran SP% **110.6**

Speed ratings (Par 102): **98,97,96,88,86 84,84,83**

CSF £47.33 CT £183.66 TOTE £4.10: £1.50, £3.50, £1.70; EX 42.40 Trifecta £186.30.

Owner Y Nasib **Bred** Jim McDonald **Trained** Musley Bank, N Yorks

FOCUS

The rail had been dolled out 6 yards around the bend from the back straight to the home straight adding approximately 12 yards to this official distance. This race's biggest claim to fame is that subsequent Dubai World Cup winner Monterosso won it in 2010. Three pulled well clear. It's been rated around the exposed third.

1447 GO RACING IN YORKSHIRE APPRENTICE H'CAP (PART OF THE GO RACING IN YORKSHIRE FUTURE STARS SERIES) 5f

4:20 (4:20) (Class 4) (0-80,80) 4-Y-O+ **£4,851** (£1,443; £721; £360) **Stalls** High

Form	Pos	Btn	Horse / Trainer / Comment	RPR
024-	**1**		**Ladweb**[182] 7234 6-8-11 72 JordanUys(5) 9 (John Gallagher) *s.s: hdwy over 2f out: nt clr run and swtchd lft over 1f out: edgd rt and led last 50yds: jst hld on* **9/1**	83
066-	**2**	*hd*	**Dominate**[220] 6166 6-9-2 77 (v[1]) AdamMcNamara(5) 13 (George Scott) *mid-div: hdwy to chse ldrs 2f out: styd on to take 2nd last 25yds: jst hld* **5/1**[2]	87
210-	**3**	*2 ½*	**Noodles Blue Boy**[194] 6936 10-8-8 72 RobertDodsworth(8) 12 (Ollie Pears) *w ldr: led over 2f out: edgd rt appr fnl f: hdd and no ex last 50yds* **16/1**	73
220-	**4**	*3 ¼*	**Indian Tinker**[162] 7710 7-9-0 70 DavidParkes 11 (Robert Cowell) *chsd ldrs: wknd fnl f* **17/2**	59
04-4	**5**	*shd*	**Dinneratmidnight**[15] 1143 5-9-9 79 (e) RobJFitzpatrick 1 (Richard Guest) *chsd ldrs: outpcd over 3f out: kpt on fnl f* **16/1**	68+
1-40	**6**	*nk*	**Casterbridge**[6] 1321 4-9-10 80 NathanEvans 8 (Eric Alston) *mid-div: rdn and outpcd over 2f out: kpt on fnl f* **3/1**[1]	68
625-	**7**	*6*	**Eternitys Gate**[241] 5458 5-9-6 79 JoshDoyle(3) 5 (David O'Meara) *mid-div: sme hdwy over 1f out: nvr a factor* **8/1**	45
100-	**8**	*hd*	**Soul Brother (IRE)**[178] 7342 5-9-6 79 (p) HarryBurns(3) 6 (Tim Easterby) *chsd ldrs: wknd over 1f out* **28/1**	45
335-	**9**	*1 ¾*	**Pull The Plug (IRE)**[207] 6559 5-8-12 78 GerO'Neill(10) 3 (Declan Carroll) *s.i.s: nvr a factor* **11/1**	37

302- **10** *nk* **Be Bold**[185] 7170 4-9-9 **79**............ RowanScott 7 37
(Rebecca Bastiman) *dwlt: a in rr* **16/1**

0016 **11** *4 ½* **Oriental Relation (IRE)**[22] 1040 5-9-1 **71**............(v) PhilDennis 4 13
(James Given) *chsd ldrs: lost pl over 1f out* **13/2**[3]

000- **12** *1 ½* **Bronze Beau**[194] 6936 9-8-7 **68**............(t) KieranSchofield(5) 10 5
(Kristin Stubbs) *led: hdd over 2f out: lost pl over 1f out* **28/1**

1m 7.36s (7.36) **Going Correction** +1.60s/f (Heav) **12** Ran SP% **119.5**
Speed ratings (Par 105): **105,104,100,95,95 94,85,84,82,81 74,72**
CSF £54.01 CT £715.81 TOTE £12.70: £4.00, £1.50, £4.90; EX 51.70 Trifecta £227.80.
Owner The Juniper Racing Club & Andrew Bell **Bred** Adweb Ltd **Trained** Chastleton, Oxon

FOCUS
Just a fair sprint in demanding conditions. The field didn't spilt and raced middle to stands' rail. Being drawn high was an advantage considering the draw of the first four. The runner-up has been rated to his form from the latter part of last year.

1448 PETER ROBERTS MEMORIAL H'CAP 6f
4:55 (4:56) (Class 5) (0-75,75) 3-Y-O **£2,911** (£866; £432; £216) **Stalls** High

Form RPR

423- **1** **Bossipop**[294] 3539 3-8-9 **68**............ RachelRichardson(5) 17 77
(Tim Easterby) *racd stands' side: trckd ldrs: edgd rt over 1f out: r.o to ld last 150yds: 1st of 9 that gp* **12/1**

120- **2** *2* **Master Mirasol (IRE)**[159] 7753 3-9-6 **74**............ GrahamLee 4 77
(Kevin Ryan) *racd far side: chsd ldrs: led that gp over 2f out: kpt on same pce last 100yds: 1st of 5 that gp* **9/2**[2]

505- **3** *1 ½* **The Name's Paver**[181] 7253 3-9-1 **69**............ BarryMcHugh 3 68
(Noel Wilson) *racd far side: chsd ldrs: kpt on same pce fnl f: 2nd of 5 that gp* **22/1**

150- **4** *nk* **Sir Theodore (IRE)**[152] 7859 3-9-2 **70**............ WilliamTwiston-Davies 12 68
(Richard Spencer) *led stands' side: hdd and no ex last 150yds: 2nd of 9 that gp* **8/1**

500- **5** *1 ¼* **Mr Chuckles (IRE)**[192] 6978 3-8-10 **69**............ PhilDennis(5) 14 63
(Philip Kirby) *racd stands' side: towards rr: hdwy over 2f out: chsd ldrs over 1f out: kpt on same pce: 3rd of 9 that gp* **20/1**

314- **6** *1 ½* **Indian Pursuit (IRE)**[159] 7753 3-9-6 **74**............ GrahamGibbons 16 63
(John Quinn) *racd stands' side: chsd ldrs: effrt over 2f out: one pce over 1f out: 4th of 9 that gp* **7/2**[1]

30-0 **7** *2 ½* **Canny Style**[18] 1111 3-8-13 **67**............ ShaneGray 13 49
(Kevin Ryan) *racd stands' side: hld up in rr: hdwy to chse ldrs over 2f out: fdd appr fnl f* **22/1**

606- **8** *1* **East Street Revue**[304] 3221 3-8-8 **62**............ DuranFentiman 5 41
(Tim Easterby) *racd far side: chsd ldrs: wknd fnl f: 3rd of 5 that gp* **40/1**

-306 **9** *nse* **Hold On Magnolia**[17] 1120 3-8-11 **65**............(v[1]) TonyHamilton 11 44
(Richard Fahey) *racd stands' side: w ldr: wknd fnl f: 7th of 9 that gp* **16/1**

054- **10** *13* **Tribesman**[190] 7040 3-9-6 **74**............ DanielTudhope 7 14
(Marjorie Fife) *swtchd lft after s: chsd ldrs stands' side: wknd over 1f out: 7th of 9 that gp* **8/1**

5163 **11** *8* **Kestrel Call (IRE)**[21] 1061 3-9-7 **75**............(t) RobertHavlin 1
(Simon Crisford) *led far side: hdd over 2f out: wknd and heavily eased over 1f out: 4th of 5 that gp* **6/1**[3]

103- **12** *13* **Baby Ballerina**[191] 7006 3-8-12 **71**............(p) CallumShepherd(5) 6
(Brian Ellison) *racd far side: chsd ldrs: wknd 2f out: sn heavily eased: last of 5 that gp* **9/1**

66-0 **13** *½* **Mr Potter**[17] 1126 3-8-8 **62**............(e) JasonHart 10
(Richard Guest) *racd stands' side: sn bhd: rdn over 3f out: sn lost tch: 8th of 9 that gp* **33/1**

140- **14** *4* **Anushka Noo Noo**[201] 6761 3-8-10 **67**............ JacobButterfield(3) 9
(Ollie Pears) *racd stands' side: chsd ldrs: lost pl over 3f out: sn wl bhd and lost tch: last of 9 that gp* **25/1**

1m 23.43s (10.43) **Going Correction** +1.775s/f (Heav) **14** Ran SP% **123.2**
Speed ratings (Par 98): **101,98,96,95,94 92,88,87,87,70 59,42,41,36**
CSF £60.99 CT £1238.20 TOTE £18.20: £3.70, £2.50, £5.40; EX 123.50 Trifecta £3352.50 Part won..
Owner Ambrose Turnbull **Bred** Lady Whent **Trained** Great Habton, N Yorks

FOCUS
Unsurprisingly, the field spilt into a couple of groups considering the field size over the straight 6f but, as was the case earlier over the same trip, the advantage wasn't huge. The fourth helps with setting the standard on the stands' side, and the third with those on the far side.

1449 SIS MAIDEN STKS 1m
5:30 (5:31) (Class 5) 3-Y-O **£2,911** (£866; £432; £216) **Stalls** Low

Form RPR

46-6 **1** **Ronnie Baird**[30] 945 3-9-5 74............(p[1]) RobertHavlin 1 78
(Kristin Stubbs) *led: edgd lft appr fnl f: hld on nr fin: all out* **8/1**[3]

3 **2** *hd* **Steccando (IRE)**[17] 1123 3-9-5 0............ NeilFarley 3 77
(Alan Swinbank) *dwlt: sn trcking ldrs: nt clr run on inner 3f out: chal over 1f out: carried lft: no ex nr fin* **10/3**[2]

3-2 **3** *8* **Flyboy (IRE)**[11] 1216 3-9-5 0............ DanielTudhope 4 59
(David O'Meara) *trckd ldrs: t.k.h: effrt over 3f out: upsides over 2f out: edgd rt and wknd fnl 150yds* **10/11**[1]

4 *3* **Agatas Legacy (IRE)** 3-9-0 0............ ConnorBeasley 6 47
(Michael Dods) *dwlt: sn mid-div: drvn to chse ldrs over 3f out: wknd fnl f* **20/1**

5 *8* **Leyburn** 3-9-0 0............ FrannyNorton 12 29
(Mark Johnston) *dwlt: drvn along detached in last: sme hdwy over 2f out: hung rt and sn wknd* **9/1**

0- **6** *3 ½* **Man Of La Mancha (IRE)**[204] 6655 3-9-5 0............ BarryMcHugh 5 26
(Ben Haslam) *chsd ldrs: drvn over 2f out: lost pl over 1f out* **66/1**

055- **7** *12* **Sebastian's Wish (IRE)**[169] 7561 3-9-5 0............ KeaganLatham 9
(Richard Whitaker) *in rr: hdwy over 3f out: rdn over 2f out: sn wknd: bhd whn eased in clsng stages* **25/1**

60- **8** *3 ¾* **Wotabreeze (IRE)**[163] 7673 3-9-5 0............ JasonHart 7
(John Quinn) *mid-div: drvn 4f out: sn chsng ldrs: lost pl over 2f out: bhd whn eased last 100yds* **10/1**

1m 56.33s (14.93) **Going Correction** +1.85s/f (Heav) **8** Ran SP% **115.8**
Speed ratings (Par 98): **99,98,90,87,79 76,64,60**
CSF £34.62 TOTE £8.00: £2.30, £1.10, £1.40; EX 41.60 Trifecta £70.40.
Owner Paramount Racing I **Bred** Stetchworth & Middle Park Studs Ltd **Trained** Norton, N Yorks
■ Stewards' Enquiry : Robert Havlin caution: careless riding

FOCUS
The rail had been dolled out 6 yards around the bend from the back straight to the home straight adding approximately 12 yards to this official distance. A maiden weakened by a couple of well-fancied runners, including the short-priced favourite, coming out during the day. The winner has been rated back to his 2yo form for Hugo Palmer.
T/Plt: £420.10 to a £1 stake. Pool of £69911.93 - 121.46 winning tickets. T/Qpdt: £47.60 to a £1 stake. Pool of £6180.35 - 96.02 winning tickets **Walter Glynn**

BATH (L-H)
Friday, April 15

OFFICIAL GOING: Good to soft (soft in places) changing to soft after race 1 (4.50)
Wind: mild across Weather: overcast

1450 BOB MORETON H'CAP 2m 1f 34y
4:50 (4:50) (Class 6) (0-65,65) 4-Y-O+ **£2,264** (£673; £336; £168) **Stalls** Centre

Form RPR

00-3 **1** **Guards Chapel**[27] 138 8-9-7 **65**............(v) HectorCrouch(5) 12 72
(Gary Moore) *mid-div: rdn over 4f out: hdwy over 2f out: led over 1f out: a holding on: drvn out* **16/1**

10-4 **2** *½* **Sinbad The Sailor**[23] 1038 11-9-8 **61**............(t) SteveDrowne 4 67
(George Baker) *s.i.s: pushed along early: towards rr: midfield 1/2-way: rdn over 4f out: hdwy over 2f out: styd on wl whn chsng wnr fnl f but a being hld* **20/1**

250- **3** *1* **Helium (FR)**[34] 2148 11-8-12 **51**............ CamHardie 11 56
(Alexandra Dunn) *mid-div: hdwy over 3f out: rdn to chse ldrs over 2f out: styd on same pce fr over 1f out* **7/1**

022- **4** *½* **Our Folly**[20] 5548 8-9-12 **65**............(t) OisinMurphy 14 70
(Stuart Kittow) *trckd ldrs: rdn to chal over 2f out ev ch tl ent fnl f: no ex* **3/1**[1]

2-33 **5** *2* **Helmsman (IRE)**[31] 946 4-8-10 **58**............ JosephineGordon(5) 10 60
(J S Moore) *led tl over 4f out: led 3f out: rdn and hdd over 1f out: no ex fnl f* **5/1**[3]

5565 **6** *4 ½* **Thimaar (USA)**[23] 1038 8-9-3 **56**............(p) KieranO'Neill 1 53
(Sarah Hollinshead) *trckd ldr: led over 4f out tl 3f out: sn rdn: wknd jst over 1f out* **20/1**

230- **7** *nse* **Lean Burn (USA)**[13] 7947 10-8-5 **47** ow1............(bt) RobHornby(3) 13 44
(Barry Leavy) *hld up towards rr: styd on fnl 2f: nvr trbld ldrs* **28/1**

61-0 **8** *11* **Bernisdale**[56] 199 8-9-1 **57**............ DanielMuscutt(3) 3 41
(John Flint) *chsd ldrs tl outpcd 3f out* **25/1**

614- **9** *2 ¾* **Agreement (IRE)**[70] 5548 6-9-3 **61**............(b) EdwardGreatrex(5) 7 41
(Nikki Evans) *mid-div: hdwy to trck ldrs over 6f out: rdn over 3f out: wknd over 1f out* **16/1**

0-50 **10** *32* **Noor Al Haya (IRE)**[51] 695 6-8-10 **56**............ MeganNicholls(7) 9
(Laura Mongan) *dwlt: sn mid-div: wknd 2f out* **12/1**

334- **11** *5* **Blue Top**[22] 7313 7-9-1 **54**............ JasonHart 6
(Dai Burchell) *s.i.s: a towards rr* **14/1**

4064 **12** *61* **Opera Buff**[2] 1413 7-9-7 **60**............(p) SilvestreDeSousa 8
(Jose Santos) *chsd ldr tl wknd qckly over 4f out: virtually p.u* **9/2**[2]

0-60 **13** *97* **Toretto (IRE)**[31] 946 8-8-12 **51**............(b) MartinLane 2
(Bernard Llewellyn) *mid-div tl over 7f out: sn bhd: virtually p.u* **25/1**

4m 9.69s (17.79) **Going Correction** +1.075s/f (Soft)
WFA 4 from 5yo+ 4lb **13** Ran SP% **119.1**
Speed ratings (Par 101): **101,100,100,100,99 97,96,91,90,75 73,44,**
CSF £306.47 CT £2443.42 TOTE £13.30: £4.50, £4.70, £3.10; EX 75.90 Trifecta £2271.00 Part won. Pool: £3,028.09 - 0.49 winning units..
Owner Andrew Bradmore **Bred** Mrs J Chandris **Trained** Lower Beeding, W Sussex
■ Stewards' Enquiry : Hector Crouch four-day ban: used whip above permitted level (Apr 29,May 2-4)

FOCUS
Races in which the home turn was used were run over 10 yards further than advertised. They went a fair gallop in this very modest staying handicap, run in softish conditions. The time was around half a minute slower than standard.

1451 RACS GROUP SPECIALISTS MAIDEN STKS 5f 161y
5:20 (5:22) (Class 5) 3-Y-O+ **£3,040** (£904; £452; £226) **Stalls** Centre

Form RPR

55- **1** **Pusey's Secret**[203] 6701 3-8-8 0............ MichaelJMMurphy(3) 10 78
(John Gallagher) *s.i.s: towards rr: hdwy over 2f out: led over 1f out: sn drifted lft: r.o wl to draw clr: readily* **12/1**

46 **2** *6* **Lucky Louie**[56] 639 3-9-2 0............ RobertWinston 7 63
(Roger Teal) *mid-div: hdwy 3f out: effrt to chal over 2f out: kpt on but nt pce of wnr fr over 1f out* **20/1**

3 *shd* **Inclination (IRE)**[147] 7926 3-8-8 0............ RyanTate(3) 9 58
(Clive Cox) *chsd ldrs: rdn to chal over 2f out: kpt on same pce fr over 1f out* **11/4**[2]

4 *7* **African Friend (IRE)** 3-9-2 0............ DaneO'Neill 3 40+
(Henry Candy) *chsd ldrs: rdn to chal over 2f out: one pce fr over 1f out* **4/5**[1]

5 *3* **Dalness Express** 3-8-11 0............ CiaranMckee(5) 1 30
(John O'Shea) *s.i.s: towards rr: hdwy over 2f out: wknd over 1f out* **100/1**

00- **6** *1 ¼* **Tally's Song**[315] 2886 3-8-11 0............ StevieDonohoe 8 21
(Grace Harris) *chsd ldrs: rdn wl over 2f out: wknd over 1f out* **150/1**

0- **7** *1* **Wilspa's Magic (IRE)**[307] 3131 3-8-11 0............ CamHardie 4 17
(Ron Hodges) *mid-div tl wknd over 2f out* **66/1**

20-0 **8** *1 ¼* **Swanton Blue (IRE)**[14] 1176 3-8-13 73............ RobHornby(3) 6 18
(Ed de Giles) *w ldr: rdn wl over 2f out: sn wknd* **13/2**[3]

0/ **9** *1 ¼* **Magical Peak**[525] 7701 4-9-9 0............ CathyGannon 12 12
(John O'Shea) *s.i.s: a towards rr* **100/1**

23-4 **10** *11* **Our Lord**[19] 1110 4-10-0 61............ OisinMurphy 5
(Bill Turner) *led: rdn over 2f out: hdd over 1f out: wknd* **9/1**

1m 17.24s (6.04) **Going Correction** +1.00s/f (Soft)
WFA 3 from 4yo 12lb **10** Ran SP% **122.1**
Speed ratings (Par 103): **99,91,90,81,77 75,74,72,71,56**
CSF £205.52 TOTE £14.20: £3.50, £3.90, £1.50; EX 130.00 Trifecta £950.70.
Owner C R Marks (banbury) **Bred** C R Marks (Banbury) **Trained** Chastleton, Oxon

FOCUS
The official going was changed to Soft before this race. A modest maiden but a taking winner. The time was relatively quick and the winner was a big improver on her 2yo form.

1452 RACS INTERIORS H'CAP 5f 161y
5:50 (5:50) (Class 4) (0-80,81) 3-Y-O **£4,690** (£1,395; £697; £348) **Stalls** Centre

Form RPR

0-15 **1** **Willsy**[34] 924 3-9-0 **72**............ SilvestreDeSousa 8 76
(Mick Channon) *v.s.a: bhd: drvn and hdwy 3f out: r.o strly on far rail fr over 1f out: led fnl 120yds: rdn out* **8/1**

06-1 **2** *nk* **Ower Fly**[4] 1385 3-9-2 **81** 6ex............ MeganNicholls(7) 1 84
(Richard Hannon) *chsd ldrs: rdn to chal over 1f out: led ent fnl f: hdd fnl 120yds: kpt on but no ex* **5/2**[1]

33-0 **3** *nk* **Another Boy**[14] 1176 3-8-10 **73**............(v[1]) PatrickO'Donnell(5) 12 75
(Ralph Beckett) *towards rr on outer: rdn over 3f out: hdwy 2f out: ev ch ins fnl f: kpt on* **17/2**

51 **4** 1/2 **Rhythm And Blues**[46] 765 3-8-11 **72**.............................. RyanTate[(3)] 4 72
(Clive Cox) *chsd ldrs: rdn over 2f out: ev ch ent fnl f: kpt on but no ex towards fin* **11/2**[2]

251- **5** 3 1/4 **Belledesert**[200] 6806 3-8-12 **70**.............................. RoystonFfrench 9 60
(Steph Hollinshead) *led: rdn over 2f out: hdd ent fnl f: wknd* **20/1**

50-1 **6** 2 3/4 **Thee And Me (IRE)**[14] 1183 3-8-8 **73**.............................. KevinLundie[(7)] 6 54
(Mike Murphy) *mid-div: hdwy u.p over 2f out: chsd ldrs over 1f out: kpt on same pce fnl f* **25/1**

21- **7** 3 1/4 **Star Jeanie**[282] 4021 3-9-1 **73**.............................. DaneO'Neill 10 43
(Henry Candy) *sn pushed along: a towards rr* **8/1**

3421 **8** 4 **Rosealee (IRE)**[22] 1061 3-9-3 **75**.............................. MartinLane 5 32
(Jeremy Gask) *mid-div tl wknd over 1f out* **14/1**

04-3 **9** 2 1/4 **Case Key**[19] 1112 3-9-5 **77**.............................. DarryllHolland 13 26
(Charles Hills) *prom: rdn and ev ch over 2f out: wknd over 1f out* **7/1**[3]

0-14 **10** 23 **Big Amigo (IRE)**[30] 954 3-9-3 **75**..............(v[1]) RichardKingscote 3
(Tom Dascombe) *prom tl wknd over 2f out* **7/1**[3]

1m 18.47s (7.27) **Going Correction** +1.00s/f (Soft) **10** Ran SP% **117.0**
Speed ratings (Par 100): **91,90,90,89,85 81,77,71,68,38**
CSF £28.39 CT £182.35 TOTE £7.40: £2.70, £1.40, £3.80; EX 31.70 Trifecta £311.10.
Owner E & R Bastian **Bred** R Bastian **Trained** West Ilsley, Berks
■ Stewards' Enquiry : Darryll Holland two-day ban: used whip without giving colt time to respond (Apr 29,May 2)

FOCUS
A tight finish to this ordinary sprint handicap, with four clear. The winner is rated close to his Windsor figure.

1453 WHITSBURY MANOR STUD & EBF STALLIONS LANSDOWN FILLIES' STKS (LISTED RACE) 5f 11y
6:20 (6:22) (Class 1) 3-Y-O+
£22,684 (£8,600; £4,304; £2,144; £1,076; £540) **Stalls** Centre

Form RPR

-600 **1** **Demora**[57] 626 7-9-0 98.............................. AndrewMullen 14 104
(Michael Appleby) *a.p: led 2f out: rdn and hdd jst over 1f out: rallied gamely to regain ld towards fin* **9/1**

21-0 **2** 1/2 **Iseemist (IRE)**[45] 771 5-9-0 90.............................. ShaneGray 9 102
(John Gallagher) *little slowly away: in last pair: hdwy over 2f out: rdn to ld jst over 1f out: kpt on but no ex whn hdd towards fin* **20/1**

03-3 **3** 3 3/4 **Shadow Hunter (IRE)**[42] 821 3-8-3 95.............................. TomMarquand 13 84
(Paul D'Arcy) *trckd ldrs: rdn and ev ch fr 2f out tl ent fnl f: no ex* **13/2**[2]

05-0 **4** 1 3/4 **Marsh Hawk**[13] 1197 4-9-0 100..............................(b[1]) PatDobbs 2 83
(Richard Hannon) *trckd ldrs: rdn over 2f out: kpt on same pce fnl f* **8/1**

44-3 **5** 1 1/2 **Sixties Sue**[7] 1315 3-8-3 88.............................. SilvestreDeSousa 1 73
(Mick Channon) *towards rr: sn pushed along: rdn whn swtchd rt over 2f out: hdwy over 1f out: kpt on same pce fnl f* **8/1**

132- **6** 2 1/4 **Ridge Ranger (IRE)**[209] 6533 5-9-0 103.............................. JasonHart 5 70
(Eric Alston) *sn mid-div: rdn over 2f out: nvr any imp* **15/8**[1]

/46- **7** 1 1/2 **Spring Fling**[160] 7755 5-9-0 84.............................. DaneO'Neill 7 64
(Henry Candy) *nvr bttr than mid-div* **7/1**[3]

100- **8** 1 **Calypso Choir**[189] 7072 3-8-3 83.............................. SamHitchcott 11 56
(Sylvester Kirk) *mid-div: hdwy over 2f out: sn rdn: wknd over 1f out* **66/1**

165- **9** hd **Rosina**[188] 7121 3-8-3 89.............................. JimmyQuinn 8 55
(Ann Duffield) *sn pushed along: towards rr of midfield: wknd over 1f out* **14/1**

411- **10** 1 1/2 **Thesme**[237] 5644 4-9-0 91.............................. TomEaves 3 55
(Nigel Tinkler) *led tl 2f out: sn wknd* **25/1**

060- **11** 3/4 **Souville**[170] 7547 5-9-0 88.............................. MartinLane 10 52
(Chris Wall) *mid-div: rdn wl over 2f out: wknd over 1f out* **33/1**

201- **12** 1/2 **Iffranesia (FR)**[193] 6993 6-9-4 102.............................. RichardKingscote 12 55
(Robert Cowell) *prom: rdn over 2f out: wknd over 1f out* **8/1**

405- **13** 11 **Lady Clair (IRE)**[29] 973 3-8-3 0.............................. RoystonFfrench 6
(F-H Graffard, France) *chsd ldrs: rdn 3f out: wknd over 1f out* **33/1**

1m 6.25s (3.75) **Going Correction** +1.00s/f (Soft)
WFA 3 from 4yo+ 11lb **13** Ran SP% **126.6**
Speed ratings (Par 108): **110,109,103,100,98 94,92,90,90,87 86,85,68**
CSF £187.17 TOTE £9.80: £3.20, £5.70, £2.40; EX 230.50 Trifecta £1404.20.
Owner A M Wragg **Bred** A M Wragg **Trained** Oakham, Rutland
■ Stewards' Enquiry : Andrew Mullen two-day ban: used whip above permitted level (Apr 29,May 2)

FOCUS
The first two pulled clear in this competitive Listed sprint. Demora is rated close to her best, with the runner-up posting a 7lb pb.

1454 RACS MARKETING / BRITISH STALLION STUDS EBF NOVICE MEDIAN AUCTION STKS 5f 11y
6:50 (6:50) (Class 5) 2-Y-O **£3,557** (£1,058; £529; £264) **Stalls** Centre

Form RPR

1 **Stoneyford Lane (IRE)** 2-9-2 0.............................. RoystonFfrench 6 74
(Steph Hollinshead) *s.i.s: sn pushed along in last pair: hdwy fr over 2f out: str run fnl f: led cl home* **28/1**

2 nk **Kreb's Cycle (IRE)** 2-9-2 0.............................. PatDobbs 1 73+
(Richard Hannon) *trckd ldrs: led wl over 1f out: drifted to far rail: sn rdn: kpt on but no ex whn ct cl home* **7/2**[3]

3 **3** 1 1/4 **Dontforgettocall**[4] 1384 2-9-2 0.............................. OisinMurphy 4 68
(Joseph Tuite) *trckd ldrs: rdn for str chal fr 2f out: drifted lft: no ex ins fnl f* **5/2**[1]

6 **4** 2 1/4 **Princess Way (IRE)**[20] 1087 2-8-11 0.............................. CathyGannon 3 55
(David Evans) *led tl wl over 1f out: sn one pce* **20/1**

5 2 3/4 **Billy's Boots** 2-9-2 0.............................. SilvestreDeSousa 7 50
(Mick Channon) *towards rr but in tch: rdn and hdwy over 2f out: drifted lft over 1f out and no further imp on ldrs* **7/1**

6 12 **Warleggan (FR)** 2-9-2 0.............................. RobertWinston 2 7
(Eve Johnson Houghton) *in tch: rdn over 2f out: wknd over 1f out* **12/1**

6 **7** 4 1/2 **The Fossil**[8] 1293 2-9-2 0..............................(v[1]) RichardKingscote 5
(Tom Dascombe) *prom: rdn wl over 2f out: wknd over 1f out* **8/1**

8 1/2 **Asfaar (IRE)** 2-9-2 0.............................. PaulHanagan 8
(Brian Meehan) *s.i.s: hdwy after 2f to chse ldrs: sn rdn: wknd over 1f out* **11/4**[2]

1m 8.49s (5.99) **Going Correction** +1.00s/f (Soft) **8** Ran SP% **117.0**
Speed ratings (Par 92): **92,91,89,85,81 62,55,54**
CSF £126.52 TOTE £38.30: £5.80, £1.60, £1.30; EX 99.80 Trifecta £1332.60.
Owner Ocean Four **Bred** J C Bloodstock **Trained** Upper Longdon, Staffs

FOCUS
An ordinary race of its type.

1455 RUBY ALICE FILLIES' H'CAP 1m 2f 46y
7:20 (7:20) (Class 4) (0-80,78) 4-Y-O+ **£4,690** (£1,395; £697; £348) **Stalls** Low

Form RPR

450- **1** **Hound Music**[186] 7173 4-8-9 **66**.............................. RichardKingscote 4 76
(Jonathan Portman) *hld up last of the 5: hdwy 2f out: led jst over 1f out: r.o wl: readily* **7/2**[2]

042- **2** 4 **Dizzey Heights (IRE)**[212] 6441 4-8-12 **72**.............................. ShelleyBirkett[(3)] 7 74
(Stuart Kittow) *trckd ldrs: rdn to chal over 2f out: led briefly but hung lft over 1f out: no ex fnl f* **6/4**[1]

4606 **3** 3 1/2 **Percys Princess**[21] 1085 5-8-7 **64** oh1.............................. AndrewMullen 1 59
(Michael Appleby) *led: rdn over 2f out: hdd whn swtchd lft over 1f out: no ex fnl f* **10/1**

310- **4** 1 1/2 **Seebeedee**[221] 6158 4-9-1 **72**.............................. SamHitchcott 2 64
(Harry Dunlop) *trckd ldr: rdn to chal over 2f out: short of room over 1f out: wknd fnl f* **4/1**[3]

6-02 **5** 4 1/2 **Deep Blue Sea**[15] 1158 4-9-1 **72**.............................. WilliamCarson 3 55
(Anthony Carson) *chsd ldrs: rdn over 2f out: wknd over 1f out* **7/2**[2]

2m 21.92s (10.92) **Going Correction** +1.075s/f (Soft) **5** Ran SP% **113.5**
Speed ratings (Par 102): **99,95,93,91,88**
CSF £9.56 TOTE £4.40: £2.10, £1.90; EX 10.70 Trifecta £54.80.
Owner Mrs J Edwards-Heathcote **Bred** The Hon Mrs R Pease **Trained** Upper Lambourn, Berks

FOCUS
Race over 10 yards further than advertised. This fillies' handicap was run at a fairly steady pace. The form is best rated around the runner-up.

1456 CLIFFORD HILLIER H'CAP 1m 3f 144y
7:50 (7:50) (Class 6) (0-65,65) 4-Y-O+ **£2,425** (£721; £360; £180) **Stalls** Low

Form RPR

24-0 **1** **Beausant**[22] 1057 4-9-4 **63**.............................. SteveDrowne 1 70
(George Baker) *mid-div: rdn 3f out: hdwy over 2f out: led ent fnl f: drifted lft: styd on wl to assert fnl 100yds* **17/2**

224- **2** 1 3/4 **Forgiving Glance**[32] 7604 4-8-13 **58**................ WilliamTwiston-Davies 2 63
(Alan King) *trckd ldrs: led 2f out: sn rdn: hdd ent fnl f: hld whn squeezed up on rails fnl 100yds* **5/2**[1]

145- **3** 3 1/2 **Doctor Kehoe**[174] 7458 4-9-1 **60**..............................(v) CathyGannon 11 59
(David Evans) *hld up towards rr: rdn and hdwy over 2f out: ev ch over 1f out: sn edgd lft: kpt on same pce fnl f* **12/1**

154- **4** 3 **Onorina (IRE)**[206] 6626 4-9-3 **62**.............................. SamHitchcott 8 56
(Jim Boyle) *mid-div: hdwy over 2f out: sn rdn: styd on same pce fr over 1f out* **8/1**[3]

0/00 **5** 1/2 **Virgil Earp**[6] 1343 9-8-7 **51** oh4.............................. JimmyQuinn 6 44
(Ian Williams) *mid-div: rdn and hdwy over 2f out: styd on same pce fr over 1f out* **20/1**

-301 **6** nk **Turnbury**[11] 1239 5-8-9 **58**..............................(p) EdwardGreatrex[(5)] 12 51
(Nikki Evans) *trckd ldrs: rdn and ev ch 2f out: sn no ex* **10/1**

000- **7** 3 1/4 **Urban Space**[163] 7713 10-8-10 **57**..............................(t) DanielMuscutt[(3)] 5 44
(John Flint) *chsd ldrs: rdn over 2f out: sn one pce* **16/1**

160- **8** nse **Barista (IRE)**[106] 7367 8-9-4 **62**.............................. CharlesBishop 14 49
(Brian Forsey) *towards rr: rdn over 3f out: little imp* **16/1**

12-1 **9** 3 **The Way You Dance (IRE)**[39] 862 4-9-6 **65**...............(p) LiamKeniry 9 47
(Neil Mulholland) *mid-div: rdn and hdwy to chse ldrs over 2f out: wknd over 1f out* **4/1**[2]

503- **10** 2 1/4 **Port**[282] 4024 4-8-13 **65**.............................. HollieDoyle[(7)] 15 44
(Jimmy Fox) *a towards rr* **20/1**

3640 **11** 1 3/4 **Kay Sera**[22] 1057 8-9-2 **63**.............................. EoinWalsh[(3)] 7 39
(Tony Newcombe) *hld up towards rr: rdn and hdwy over 2f out: wknd over 1f out* **12/1**

5000 **12** 1 **Citisonsmith (IRE)**[23] 1039 4-8-1 **51** oh6.............................. PaddyPilley[(5)] 4 25
(Tony Carroll) *led: rdn and hdd 2f out: sn wknd* **50/1**

0230 **P** **Debit**[28] 982 5-8-6 **57**.............................. RhiainIngram[(7)] 3
(Simon Hodgson) *mid-div whn lost action and p.u after 4f: fatally injured* **20/1**

2m 42.83s (12.23) **Going Correction** +1.075s/f (Soft)
WFA 4 from 5yo+ 1lb **13** Ran SP% **122.7**
Speed ratings (Par 101): **102,100,98,96,96 95,93,93,91,90 89,88,**
CSF £29.25 CT £268.97 TOTE £12.10: £3.70, £1.40, £2.10; EX 43.10 Trifecta £412.90.
Owner Beausant Partnership **Bred** Frank Brady **Trained** Manton, Wilts
■ Stewards' Enquiry : Steve Drowne caution: careless riding

FOCUS
Race over 10 yards further than advertised. A moderate handicap run in the gathering gloom. The first two stuck to the inside in the home straight.
T/Plt: £1,020.10 to a £1 stake. Pool: £73,101.70 - 52.31 winning tickets. T/Qpdt: £35.10 to a £1 stake. Pool: £10,414.67 - 219.20 winning tickets. **Tim Mitchell**

NEWBURY (L-H)
Friday, April 15
1457 Meeting Abandoned - waterlogged

1464 - 1473a (Foreign Racing) - See Raceform Interactive

1429 CHELMSFORD (A.W) (L-H)
Saturday, April 16
OFFICIAL GOING: Polytrack: standard
Wind: Light; half against Weather: Light rain until Race 3; bright spells after

1474 PLAY THE £2.25 MILLION SCOOP6 TODAY MAIDEN STKS (PLUS 10 RACE) 1m (P)
1:35 (1:36) (Class 5) 3-Y-O **£3,881** (£1,155; £577; £288) **Stalls** Low

Form RPR

2- **1** **Taqdeer (IRE)**[134] 8103 3-9-5 0.............................. PaulHanagan 8 96+
(John Gosden) *mde all: rdn and wnt clr over 1f out: in command and r.o wl fnl f: comf* **5/4**[1]

4- **2** 2 1/4 **Mustashry**[178] 7387 3-9-5 0.............................. DaneO'Neill 3 89
(Sir Michael Stoute) *t.k.h: chsd wnr tl over 6f out: rdn and chsd wnr again over 2f out: kpt on but no imp fr over 1f out* **7/1**

4- **3** 2 1/4 **Poet's Word (IRE)**[178] 7395 3-9-5 0.............................. RyanMoore 6 84
(Sir Michael Stoute) *dwlt: in tch in rr: sltly hmpd over 6f out: rdn and effrt in 3rd over 1f out: styd on same pce and no imp after* **3/1**[2]

4 13 **El Hayem (IRE)** 3-9-5 0 FrankieDettori 7 54
(Sir Michael Stoute) *dwlt: in tch in last pair: pushed along and hdwy to press ldr over 4f out: lost 2nd and pushed along over 2f out: sn btn: wknd over 1f out: sn wl bhd* **16/1**

30- 5 1 1/4 **Tiercel**[189] 7113 3-9-5 0 AndreaAtzeni 4 51+
(Roger Varian) *restless in stalls: trckd ldrs: wnt 2nd over 6f out tl over 4f out: rdn 3f out: wknd over 1f out: sn wl bhd* **4/1**[3]

1m 38.21s (-1.69) **Going Correction** -0.025s/f (Stan) 5 Ran SP% **107.8**
Speed ratings (Par 98): **107,104,102,89,88**
CSF £9.91 TOTE £2.00: £1.10, £3.20; EX 8.60 Trifecta £25.50.
Owner Hamdan Al Maktoum **Bred** Maurice Byrne **Trained** Newmarket, Suffolk

FOCUS
This meeting was transferred from Newbury at short notice, and the races were re-opened, after the original venue was declared waterlogged on Friday; tremendous initiative shown by all concerned. A couple of these finished right out the back, so not as competitive a maiden as might have been expected, but still useful form. The time was 0.24sec quicker than the later Spring Cup. The winner is sure to do better still.

1475 FOLLOW BEFTRED ON TWITTER JOHN PORTER STKS (GROUP 3) 1m 5f 66y(P)
2:10 (2:10) (Class 1) 4-Y-O+
£25,519 (£9,675; £4,842; £2,412; £1,210; £607) **Stalls** Low

Form RPR

153- 1 **Dartmouth**[164] 7703 4-8-13 102 RyanMoore 5 114
(Sir Michael Stoute) *chsd ldrs: wnt 2nd 7f out tl led 2f out: rdn over 1f out: responded readily to press and drew clr ins fnl f: comf* **3/1**[2]

1 2 4 1/2 **Sandro Botticelli (IRE)**[13] 1219 4-8-13 107 (p) FrankieDettori 2 107
(John Ryan) *stdd s: hld up in tch in rr: swtchd rt and effrt jst over 2f out: chsd ldrs u.p 1f out: styd on wl to go 2nd wl ins fnl f: no threat to wnr* **5/1**

/1-4 3 1 1/4 **Restorer**[21] 1088 4-8-13 106 MartinDwyer 4 105
(William Muir) *hld up in tch in last pair: rdn over 2f out: hdwy u.p to go 3rd jst over 1f out: styd on same pce ins fnl f* **5/1**

516- 4 hd **Battalion (IRE)**[119] 8310 6-9-0 111 (p) PatCosgrave 1 105
(William Haggas) *stdd s: t.k.h: hld up in tch in 4th: effrt to chse wnr and drifted lft u.p over 1f out: no ex and outpcd jst ins fnl f: kpt on same pce and lost 2 pls wl ins fnl f* **11/4**[1]

3435 5 7 **Blue Surf**[22] 1067 7-9-0 99 PatDobbs 3 94
(Amanda Perrett) *chsd ldr tl 7f out: styd chsng ldrs tl lost pl u.p over 2f out: wknd over 1f out: bhd fnl f* **14/1**

632- 6 nk **Sound Of Freedom (IRE)**[174] 7497 4-8-10 0 AndreaAtzeni 6 91
(Marco Botti) *led tl rdn and hdd 2f out: lost pl u.p over 1f out: wknd ins fnl f* **4/1**[3]

2m 50.43s (-3.17) **Going Correction** -0.025s/f (Stan)
WFA 4 from 6yo+ 1lb 6 Ran SP% **111.7**
Speed ratings (Par 113): **108,105,104,104,100 99**
CSF £17.82 TOTE £3.60: £1.90, £2.10; EX 10.50 Trifecta £61.40.
Owner The Queen **Bred** Darley **Trained** Newmarket, Suffolk

FOCUS
This was originally due to be run over 1m4f5y at Newbury and Dartmouth wasn't declared until the race was switched to Chelmsford. An ordinary Group 3, but the winner is worth keeping onside. He recorded a biggish pb.

1476 BETFRED TV FRED DARLING STKS (GROUP 3) (FILLIES) 7f (P)
2:40 (2:40) (Class 1) 3-Y-O
£25,519 (£9,675; £4,842; £2,412; £1,210; £607) **Stalls** Low

Form RPR

20-1 1 **Marenko**[14] 1206 3-9-0 105 RyanMoore 2 103
(Richard Hannon) *chsd ldr: clsd over 1f out: rdn to ld 1f out: sn in command and kpt on: rdn out* **5/2**[2]

430- 2 1 1/4 **Light Up Our World (IRE)**[190] 7073 3-9-0 100 PatDobbs 4 99
(Richard Hannon) *chsd ldrs: effrt wl over 1f out: styd on u.p to chse wnr 100yds out: kpt on but nvr threatening wnr* **16/1**

113- 3 hd **Besharah (IRE)**[203] 6753 3-9-0 114 PatCosgrave 8 98+
(William Haggas) *hld up in midfield: swtchd rt and stl plenty to do over 1f out: hdwy u.p ins fnl f: wnt 3rd 75yds out: kpt on but nvr threatening wnr* **2/1**[1]

1- 4 1 3/4 **Aljazzi**[168] 7628 3-9-0 0 AndreaAtzeni 7 94+
(Marco Botti) *racd in last pair: pushed along over 3f out: hdwy u.p 1f out: styd on wl fnl 100yds nvr trbld ldrs* **4/1**[3]

135- 5 3/4 **Katie's Diamond (FR)**[195] 6967 3-9-0 108 OisinMurphy 5 92
(K R Burke) *led: jst over 2 l clr and rdn over 2f out: drvn and hdd 1f out: sn outpcd by wnr: lost 2nd 100yds: wknd towards fin* **8/1**

240- 6 nk **Rebel Surge (IRE)**[203] 6753 3-9-0 86 WilliamTwiston-Davies 3 91
(Richard Spencer) *racd in midfield: effrt and stl plenty to do wl over 1f out: sme hdwy and swtchd rt and ins fnl f: styd on: nvr trbld ldrs* **50/1**

61- 7 2 1/2 **Veena (FR)**[185] 7211 3-9-0 80 JamieSpencer 1 84
(David Simcock) *chsd ldrs: rdn and unable qck ent fnl 2f: lost pl over 1f out: wknd ins fnl f* **25/1**

1- P **Nassuvian Pearl**[207] 6621 3-9-0 71 FMBerry 6
(Ralph Beckett) *dwlt: awkward and rdr lost iron leaving stalls: racd v awkwardly in rr: hung bdly rt over 3f out: lost tch and p.u 3f out* **9/1**

1m 25.64s (-1.56) **Going Correction** -0.025s/f (Stan) 8 Ran SP% **114.7**
Speed ratings (Par 105): **107,105,105,103,102 102,99,**
CSF £41.20 TOTE £2.80: £1.10, £4.30, £1.10; EX 49.00 Trifecta £166.90.
Owner Cheveley Park Stud **Bred** Cheveley Park Stud Ltd **Trained** East Everleigh, Wilts

FOCUS
Richard Hannon had the first two home and neither are in the 1,000 Guineas, but the winner is a likeable sort and the fourth can improve. A below-par renewal, rated around the first two.

1477 BETFRED WORLD SNOOKER STARTS TODAY GREENHAM STKS (GROUP 3) (C&G) 7f (P)
3:15 (3:15) (Class 1) 3-Y-O **£25,519** (£9,675; £4,842) **Stalls** Low

Form RPR

212- 1 **Tasleet**[205] 6677 3-9-0 110 PaulHanagan 1 107
(William Haggas) *mde all: drifted rt off bnd 2f out: sn rdn: drvn ins fnl f: kpt on: hrd pressed towards fin: a jst holding on* **4/7**[1]

14-3 2 shd **Knife Edge (IRE)**[14] 1208 3-9-0 100 RyanMoore 3 106
(Marco Botti) *dropped in bhd after s: hld up in cl 3rd: effrt on inner to chse wnr over 1f out: drvn and 1 l down 150yds out: kpt on wl u.p: nt quite get up* **3/1**[2]

215- 3 12 **Log Out Island (IRE)**[183] 7275 3-9-0 110 JamesDoyle 4 85
(Richard Hannon) *t.k.h: pressed wnr: rdn and unable qck jst over 2f out: dropped to 3rd and btn over 1f out: wknd* **9/2**[3]

1m 25.38s (-1.82) **Going Correction** -0.025s/f (Stan) 3 Ran SP% **106.8**
Speed ratings (Par 108): **109,108,95**
CSF £2.51 TOTE £1.40; EX 3.10 Trifecta £3.40.
Owner Hamdan Al Maktoum **Bred** Whitsbury Manor Stud **Trained** Newmarket, Suffolk

■ Stewards' Enquiry : Ryan Moore two-day ban: used whip without giving colt time to respond (May 2-3)

FOCUS
Just a two-horse battle up the straight and neither will be good enough for the 2,000 Guineas (the runner-up isn't even entered), but they are both smart colts. The form hinges on how much the runner-up improved.

1478 BETFRED DOWNLOAD THE MOBILE APP SPRING CUP (H'CAP) 1m (P)
3:50 (3:51) (Class 2) 4-Y-O+
£21,787 (£6,524; £3,262; £1,631; £815; £409) **Stalls** Low

Form RPR

06-3 1 **Gabrial's Kaka (IRE)**[27] 1018 6-8-10 **86** PaulHanagan 1 95
(Richard Fahey) *hld up in tch: clsd to trck ldrs 2f: rdn to chal 1f out: sn led: styd on wl: rdn out* **4/1**[2]

64-0 2 1 3/4 **Azraff (IRE)**[14] 1195 4-9-5 **95** (b) AndreaAtzeni 4 100
(Marco Botti) *dwlt: hld up in tch in rr: swtchd rt and effrt over 1f out: styd on wl u.p ins fnl f: wnt 2nd last stride* **9/2**[3]

606- 3 shd **Earth Drummer (IRE)**[189] 7120 6-9-8 **98** DavidNolan 2 103
(David Loughnane) *led: rdn and forged ahd over 1f out: drvn and hdd jst ins fnl f: styd on same pce after: lost 2nd last stride* **5/1**

11-1 4 1 **Power Game**[104] 31 4-9-3 **93** JamesDoyle 7 95
(Saeed bin Suroor) *chsd ldrs: hdwy to join ldr 6f out: rdn and unable qck over 1f out: hld and styd on same pce ins fnl f* **5/4**[1]

6062 5 shd **Subtle Knife**[8] 1318 7-8-2 **83** PaddyPilley(5) 5 85
(Giles Bravery) *hld up in rr: swtchd rt and nt clr run over 1f out: swtchd bk lft and hdwy jst over 1f out: swtchd lft again ins fnl f: styd on same pce fnl 100yds* **16/1**

3150 6 6 **Boots And Spurs**[13] 1215 7-8-6 **82** (v) KieranO'Neill 3 70
(Scott Dixon) *chsd ldrs early: steadily lost pl: towards rr and no rspnse whn drvn over 2f out: wknd over 1f out* **25/1**

-005 7 16 **Pearl Nation (USA)**[17] 1153 7-9-10 **100** AndrewMullen 6 49
(Michael Appleby) *chsd ldr tl 6f out: rdn over 2f out: lost pl qckly over 1f out: wl bhd ins fnl f* **16/1**

1m 38.45s (-1.45) **Going Correction** -0.025s/f (Stan) 7 Ran SP% **114.9**
Speed ratings (Par 109): **106,104,104,103,103 97,81**
CSF £22.43 TOTE £4.30: £2.00, £2.50; EX 22.30 Trifecta £104.10.
Owner Dr Marwan Koukash **Bred** Dave Orme **Trained** Musley Bank, N Yorks

FOCUS
There were 22 runners over Newbury's straight 1m for this last year and 17 originally declared for this season's race, but just seven took up the Chelmsford option. The form is rated around the second and third.

1479 SIS MAIDEN STKS (PLUS 10 RACE) 1m 2f (P)
4:25 (4:27) (Class 5) 3-Y-O **£3,881** (£1,155; £577; £288) **Stalls** Low

Form RPR

5- 1 **Against The Odds**[129] 8153 3-9-5 0 JimCrowley 6 81+
(Paul Cole) *led for 2f: chsd ldr after tl rdn to ld over 1f out: drvn clr 1f out: styd on wl: rdn out* **2/1**[2]

2 3 **Bullington Bear (FR)** 3-9-5 0 MartinDwyer 3 75
(Jane Chapple-Hyam) *stdd s: hld up in tch in last pair: effrt and swtchd rt over 1f out: drvn to chse ldrs 1f out: wnt 2nd ins fnl f: kpt on but no threat to wnr* **20/1**

3-3 3 1 3/4 **Rasasee (IRE)**[15] 1184 3-9-5 0 AndreaAtzeni 1 71
(Marco Botti) *dwlt and rdn along early: hdwy to ld after 2f: rdn jst over 2f out: drvn and hdd over 1f out: outpcd 1f out: plugged on same pce and lost 2nd ins fnl f* **8/1**

4 1 3/4 **Great Return** 3-9-5 0 JamesDoyle 2 68+
(Saeed bin Suroor) *t.k.h: chsd ldrs: effrt and edgd rt over 1f out: unable qck and swtchd lft 1f out: hld and styd on same pce after* **11/8**[1]

0- 5 nk **Molten Gold**[178] 7397 3-9-5 0 RyanMoore 5 67+
(Andrew Balding) *in tch in midfield: rdn over 2f out: outpcd and btn over 1f out: styd on same pce ins fnl f* **6/1**[3]

6 10 **Dubawi Fifty** 3-9-5 0 PatCosgrave 4 47
(James Tate) *stdd s: hld up in last pair: rdn and no rspnse 3f out: sn struggling: bhd 1f out* **16/1**

2m 7.97s (-0.63) **Going Correction** -0.025s/f (Stan) 6 Ran SP% **111.5**
Speed ratings (Par 98): **101,98,97,95,95 87**
CSF £35.54 TOTE £2.80: £1.40, £9.20; EX 47.50 Trifecta £190.90.
Owner A D Spence **Bred** Mrs P M Ignarski **Trained** Whatcombe, Oxon

FOCUS
Just a fair maiden, but a nice winner. Rather muddling form, but the winner was a big improver.

1480 SIMPLY RED PLAYING AT CCR ON 1ST JULY H'CAP 1m 2f (P)
5:00 (5:01) (Class 3) (0-90,89) 4-Y-O+ **£5,822** (£1,732; £865; £432) **Stalls** Low

Form RPR

250- 1 **Darshini**[185] 7222 4-9-5 **87** RyanMoore 2 97+
(Sir Michael Stoute) *chsd ldrs: rdn jst over 2f out: drvn 1f out: hdwy to ld fnl 75yds: styd on strly: rdn out* **6/4**[1]

51-0 2 1 **Emerald (ITY)**[14] 1195 4-9-5 **87** (p) AndreaAtzeni 1 94+
(Marco Botti) *hld up in tch in midfield: rdn 2f out: drvn and shifting rt 1f out: no hdwy tl styd on strly wl ins fnl f: wnt 2nd last strides* **9/4**[2]

00-1 3 hd **Muntadab (IRE)**[13] 1215 4-9-0 **82** DavidNolan 5 89
(David Loughnane) *chsd ldr: rdn to ld over 1f out: drvn ins fnl f: hdd and styd on same pce fnl 75yds: lost 2nd last strides* **5/1**

062- 4 3/4 **Sarsted**[163] 7717 4-9-1 **83** JimCrowley 4 88
(Hughie Morrison) *led: rdn ent fnl 2f: hdd over 1f out: no ex u.p 1f out: styd on same pce ins fnl f* **9/2**[3]

050- 5 9 **Biotic**[159] 7779 5-9-2 **84** FrederikTylicki 7 71
(Rod Millman) *stdd s and dropped in bhd: hung rt and outpcd 2f out: stl hanging whn pushed along and no hdwy over 1f out: wknd fnl f* **20/1**

100- 6 11 **Fiftyshadesfreed (IRE)**[159] 7779 5-9-7 **89** (p) PatCosgrave 3 54
(George Baker) *in tch in midfield: drvn and unable qck over 2f out: sn btn and wknd over 1f out* **20/1**

231/ 7 7 **New Street (IRE)**[137] 3466 5-9-2 **84** JamieSpencer 8 35
(Jim Best) *a bhd: rdn and no rspnse 3f out: lost tch 2f out* **25/1**

2m 7.51s (-1.09) **Going Correction** -0.025s/f (Stan) 7 Ran SP% **119.0**
Speed ratings (Par 107): **103,102,102,101,94 85,79**
CSF £5.29 CT £13.11 TOTE £2.20: £1.40, £2.30; EX 7.30 Trifecta £24.20.
Owner Robert Ng **Bred** Bluehills Racing Limited **Trained** Newmarket, Suffolk

FOCUS
A fair handicap. The first two are both potentially better than the bare form.
T/Plt: £82.10 to £1 stake. Pool: £78,266.43 - 695.46 winning units T/Qpdt: £27.00 to a £1 stake. Pool: £5,347.03 - 146.20 winning units **Steve Payne**

1270 NOTTINGHAM (L-H)

Saturday, April 16

OFFICIAL GOING: Soft (heavy in places; 5.3)

Wind: virtually nil Weather: sunshine and odd shower

1481 1ST SECURITY APPRENTICE H'CAP 5f 13y

4:50 (4:54) (Class 6) (0-65,65) 4-Y-O+ **£2,264** (£673; £336; £168) **Stalls** High

Form RPR

/0-2 **1** **Lewisham**[64] 543 6-9-5 **60** AlistairRawlinson 3 78
(J R Jenkins) *trckd ldrs: led 2f out: rdn clr fr over 1f out: edgd lft ins fnl f* **9/4**[1]

414- **2** *6* **Tinsill**[157] 7790 5-8-6 **54** (p) KieranSchofield(7) 6 50
(Nigel Tinkler) *hld up in tch: sn pushed along: plugged on fr over 1f out: wnt modest 2nd 110yds out* **9/1**

3000 **3** *1 1/2* **Roy's Legacy**[46] 775 7-8-13 **59** CharlieBennett(5) 4 50
(Shaun Harris) *led narrowly: rdn whn hdd 2f out: one pce and sn no ch w wnr: lost 2nd 110yds out* **11/1**

0632 **4** *nk* **Captain Scooby**[10] 1255 10-9-3 **63** (b) SophieKilloran(5) 8 53
(Richard Guest) *hld up: sn pushed along: plugged on fnl f: nvr threatened* **7/1**

0041 **5** *2 1/4* **Eland Ally**[18] 1133 8-9-6 **61** (p) LouisSteward 9 43
(Anabel K Murphy) *prom: rdn 1/2-way: wknd over 1f out* **9/2**[2]

0040 **6** *2 3/4* **Prigsnov Dancer (IRE)**[50] 730 11-9-3 **65** BenSanderson(7) 10 37
(Deborah Sanderson) *prom: rdn 1/2-way: wknd over 1f out* **10/1**

0-00 **7** *1* **Smart Dj**[68] 504 5-9-0 **55** MichaelJMMurphy 7 23
(Sarah Hollinshead) *s.i.s: hld up: rdn and hdwy to chse ldrs 1/2-way: wknd fnl f* **14/1**

4116 **8** *13* **Sir Geoffrey (IRE)**[10] 1255 10-9-0 **58** (b) PatrickO'Donnell(3) 2
(Scott Dixon) *w ldrs towards outside: rdn 3f out: sn wknd* **5/1**[3]

1m 5.07s (3.57) **Going Correction** +0.775s/f (Yiel) 8 Ran SP% **112.2**
Speed ratings (Par 101): **102,92,90,89,85 81,79,59**
CSF £22.53 CT £180.11 TOTE £3.50: £1.20, £2.70, £3.00; EX 26.10 Trifecta £197.40.
Owner Mrs Theresa McCoubrey **Bred** Whitwell Bloodstock **Trained** Royston, Herts

FOCUS
Inner track used and distances as advertised. A modest apprentice riders' sprint handicap. They went a decent, contested gallop from the stands' rail towards the far side on ground officially described as soft, heavy in places.

1482 1ST SECURITY NOVICE STKS 5f 13y

5:25 (5:26) (Class 5) 2-Y-O **£2,911** (£866; £432; £216) **Stalls** High

Form RPR

0 **1** **Letmestopyouthere (IRE)**[22] 1082 2-9-2 0 CathyGannon 1 79
(David Evans) *wnt lft s: sn prom: pushed along to ld 1/2-way: rdn over 1f out: kpt on to go clr fnl f* **8/1**[3]

2 *3 1/2* **Valentino Boy (IRE)** 2-9-2 0 TomEaves 7 66+
(Brian Ellison) *chsd ldrs: rdn 1/2-way: kpt on same pce* **10/1**

3 *1 3/4* **Champion Harbour (IRE)** 2-9-2 0 TonyHamilton 4 60+
(Richard Fahey) *dwlt: hld up in tch: pushed along and hdwy to chse ldr over 1f out: no ex ins fnl f* **5/2**[1]

4 *5* **Ventura Blues (IRE)** 2-8-11 0 SeanLevey 6 37
(Richard Hannon) *dwlt: hld up: pushed along over 3f out: nvr threatened* **7/2**[2]

52 **5** *2 1/2* **Lucata (IRE)**[8] 1316 2-9-2 0 LiamJones 2 33
(Tom Dascombe) *pressed ldr: rdn 1/2-way: wknd over 1f out* **5/2**[1]

03 **6** *hd* **King Of Castilla**[12] 1233 2-9-2 0 OisinMurphy 3 32
(Gay Kelleway) *led narrowly: hdd 1/2-way: sn rdn: wknd over 1f out* **8/1**[3]

1m 6.0s (4.50) **Going Correction** +0.775s/f (Yiel) 6 Ran SP% **110.7**
Speed ratings (Par 92): **95,89,86,78,74 74**
CSF £75.10 TOTE £9.80: £4.10, £3.30; EX 67.80 Trifecta £859.30.
Owner J Abbey, C Heron & M Nolan **Bred** Mrs J A Dene **Trained** Pandy, Monmouths

FOCUS
An ordinary juvenile novice stakes. They went a decent gallop.

1483 GROSVENOR CASINO NOTTINGHAM MAIDEN STKS 1m 2f 50y

5:55 (5:57) (Class 5) 3-Y-O **£2,911** (£866; £432; £216) **Stalls** Low

Form RPR

1 **Coroberee (IRE)** 3-9-5 0 RobertHavlin 5 90+
(John Gosden) *s.i.s: sn trckd ldr: rdn 3f out: 3 l down over 1f out: styd on: led towards fin* **8/1**[3]

3- **2** *1* **September Stars (IRE)**[176] 7422 3-9-0 0 FMBerry 7 83
(Ralph Beckett) *led: pushed along 3f out: 3 l clr over 1f out: rdn and reduced advantage ins fnl f: wknd and hdd towards fin* **4/7**[1]

3 *7* **Forth Bridge** 3-9-5 0 WilliamCarson 2 75
(Michael Bell) *hld up in tch: rdn over 4f out: sn outpcd: plugged on fr over 1f out* **25/1**

4- **4** *27* **Scottish Summit (IRE)**[147] 7946 3-9-5 0 TedDurcan 1 62
(Sir Michael Stoute) *trckd ldr: rdn over 3f out: wknd 2f out: eased* **5/2**[2]

2m 26.09s (11.79) **Going Correction** +1.05s/f (Soft) 4 Ran SP% **107.2**
Speed ratings (Par 98): **94,93,87,66**
CSF £13.43 TOTE £7.00; EX 14.70 Trifecta £33.10.
Owner R A Scarborough **Bred** Woodnook Farm Pty Ltd **Trained** Newmarket, Suffolk

FOCUS
A fair little 3yo maiden. They went a sensible gallop on the testing surface. The runner-up set a good standard and has been rated to his debut mark.

1484 RACING UK DAY PASS H'CAP 1m 2f 50y

6:25 (6:26) (Class 6) (0-65,65) 3-Y-O **£2,264** (£673; £336; £168) **Stalls** Low

Form RPR

43-6 **1** **Nietzsche**[23] 1062 3-8-13 **62** CallumShepherd(5) 7 81+
(Brian Ellison) *midfield: hdwy to trck ldr gng wl over 2f out: led appr fnl f: pushed along to go clr: eased fnl 110yds* **7/2**[1]

-605 **2** *6* **Stone Quercus (IRE)**[32] 947 3-9-0 **58** (b[1]) TomEaves 10 58
(James Given) *led: racd keenly and sn arnd 5 l clr: rdn and reduced advantage 3f out: hdd appr fnl f: plugged on but no ch w wnr* **10/1**

0-40 **3** *3* **Rajapur**[23] 1062 3-8-11 **55** (p) DougieCostello 13 49
(Philip Kirby) *midfield towards outer: pushed along 3f out: pushed along 3f out: rdn over 1f out: styd on: wnt 3rd towards fin* **25/1**

062- **4** *1/2* **The Juggler**[187] 7159 3-9-7 **65** MartinHarley 8 58
(William Knight) *chsd ldr: rdn over 3f out: plugged on* **5/1**[3]

-020 **5** *2 1/2* **Rockliffe**[23] 1062 3-9-1 **59** CharlesBishop 6 48
(Mick Channon) *chsd clr ldr: rdn over 3f out: wknd ins fnl f* **7/1**

006- **6** *hd* **Ochos Rios**[258] 4898 3-9-0 **58** CathyGannon 11 46
(David Evans) *s.i.s: hld up in rr: rdn over 3f out: plugged on fnl 2f: nvr threatened ldrs* **4/1**[2]

-040 **7** *3 1/4* **Mikro Polemistis (IRE)**[10] 1259 3-8-0 **51** oh5 BenRobinson(7) 5 33
(Brian Ellison) *s.i.s: hld up: rdn and outpcd in rr 4f out: plugged on fnl 2f* **25/1**

005- **8** *1/2* **I'm Ready (IRE)**[121] 8266 3-8-11 **55** TonyHamilton 9 36
(Richard Fahey) *hld up in midfield: rdn over 3f out: wknd over 1f out* **17/2**

000- **9** *21* **Pocket**[136] 8074 3-8-6 **53** RyanTate(3) 4
(James Eustace) *hld up: rdn over 3f out: sn wknd* **33/1**

006- **10** *1 1/4* **Denmead**[206] 6636 3-9-0 **61** DanielMuscutt(3) 2
(John Butler) *hld up in midfield: rdn over 3f out: sn wknd* **8/1**

55-0 **11** *11* **Top Of The Rocks (FR)**[10] 1276 3-9-5 **63** LiamJones 3
(Tom Dascombe) *in tch: sn pushed along: wknd over 3f out* **25/1**

2m 26.45s (12.15) **Going Correction** +1.05s/f (Soft) 11 Ran SP% **116.6**
Speed ratings (Par 96): **93,88,85,85,83 83,80,80,63,62 53**
CSF £36.79 CT £759.59 TOTE £4.60: £1.50, £3.10, £6.40; EX 41.00 Trifecta £798.00.
Owner D Gilbert, M Lawrence, A Bruce, G Wills **Bred** West Stow Stud Ltd **Trained** Norton, N Yorks

FOCUS
A modest 3yo handicap. They went a sensible gallop on the testing ground.

1485 RACINGUK.COM H'CAP 1m 75y

6:55 (6:55) (Class 4) (0-80,77) 3-Y-O **£4,851** (£1,443; £721; £360) **Stalls** Centre

Form RPR

04-4 **1** **Aldair**[17] 1146 3-9-0 **70** SeanLevey 7 71
(Richard Hannon) *racd keenly: trckd ldr: pressed ldr over 3f out: rdn to ld narrowly over 1f out: drvn appr fnl f: hld on gamely* **5/2**[1]

130- **2** *1/2* **Premier Currency (IRE)**[205] 6675 3-9-2 **72** TedDurcan 6 72
(Mike Murphy) *led: jnd over 3f out: rdn over 2f out: hdd narrowly over 1f out: kpt on but a jst hld* **13/2**

2-35 **3** *shd* **Lilbourne Prince (IRE)**[73] 434 3-9-5 **75** CathyGannon 5 75
(David Evans) *midfield: hdwy over 2f out: rdn to chse ldng pair over 1f out: ev ch ins fnl f: kpt on* **3/1**[2]

-210 **4** *4* **Custard The Dragon**[18] 1137 3-9-0 **70** TomEaves 3 61
(John Mackie) *dwlt: hld up: rdn and hdwy over 1f out: wknd ins fnl f* **12/1**

5 *hd* **Clon Rocket (IRE)**[174] 7490 3-9-7 **77** RobertHavlin 4 67
(John Holt) *midfield: rdn 2f out: no imp* **9/2**[3]

320- **6** *11* **Firesnake (IRE)**[172] 7544 3-9-7 **77** DougieCostello 2 42
(K R Burke) *s.i.s: hld up: rdn over 2f out: wknd over 1f out* **16/1**

155- **7** *nk* **Indrapura (IRE)**[218] 6263 3-9-5 **75** (t) MartinHarley 1 39
(Paul Cole) *trckd ldr: rdn over 2f out: wknd over 1f out* **7/1**

1m 57.57s (8.57) **Going Correction** +1.05s/f (Soft) 7 Ran SP% **111.2**
Speed ratings (Par 100): **99,98,98,94,94 83,82**
CSF £17.99 TOTE £3.60: £2.20, £2.70; EX 16.90 Trifecta £65.10.
Owner Khalifa Mohammed Al Attiyah **Bred** Dean, Morrison & Fonthill **Trained** East Everleigh, Wilts

FOCUS
The feature race was a fair 3yo handicap. They went a steady gallop and the first two were always to the fore. The winner improved on his maiden form.

1486 LADIES DAY SATURDAY 7TH MAY INTERACTIVE H'CAP 1m 75y

7:25 (7:25) (Class 6) (0-65,65) 3-Y-O **£2,264** (£673; £336; £168) **Stalls** Centre

Form RPR

00-0 **1** **Zebedee's Son (IRE)**[10] 1259 3-8-1 52 (p) RhiainIngram(7) 11 58
(Roger Ingram) *hld up: rdn and hdwy towards outside over 2f out: chal over 1f out: edgd lft ins fnl f: led narrowly 110yds out: all out* **20/1**

656- **2** *nse* **The Knave (IRE)**[173] 7507 3-8-12 56 KieranO'Neill 5 62
(Scott Dixon) *racd keenly: trckd ldrs: rdn to chal over 2f out: led narrowly appr fnl f: hdd 110yds out: kpt on: jst failed* **5/1**[3]

01-4 **3** *3 1/4* **Harlequin Rock**[16] 1163 3-9-7 65 WilliamCarson 9 63
(Mick Quinn) *hld up: hdwy into midfield over 4f out: rdn over 3f out: outpcd 2f out: styd on fnl f: wnt 3rd 75yds out* **9/2**[2]

6-03 **4** *5* **Ada Misobel (IRE)**[37] 896 3-8-7 51 oh2 (b) JFEgan 3 38
(Roy Bowring) *racd keenly: prom: rdn to ld 2f out: hdd appr fnl f: wknd ins fnl f* **7/1**

4252 **5** *1 3/4* **Sea Of Uncertainty**[19] 1120 3-9-1 62 AlistairRawlinson(3) 8 45
(Michael Appleby) *midfield on outside: hdwy over 3f out: rdn to chal 2f out: wknd ins fnl f* **7/1**

5454 **6** *3 1/2* **Frap**[17] 1141 3-9-1 59 TonyHamilton 7 34
(Richard Fahey) *midfield: rdn over 3f out: sn no imp: hung lft over 1f out: wknd fnl f* **11/4**[1]

16 **7** *1/2* **Rupert Boy (IRE)**[25] 1031 3-9-2 60 (b) TomEaves 1 34
(Scott Dixon) *led: rdn over 3f out: hdd 2f out: wknd* **20/1**

53-0 **8** *1 3/4* **Capital Gearing**[10] 1276 3-9-0 61 LouisSteward(3) 6 31
(Henry Spiller) *hld up: rdn over 3f out: nvr threatened* **15/2**

60-0 **9** *13* **File Of Facts (IRE)**[10] 1276 3-9-4 62 LiamJones 4
(Tom Dascombe) *trckd ldrs: rdn and outpcd over 4f out: sn btn: bhd over 2f out* **25/1**

1m 58.35s (9.35) **Going Correction** +1.05s/f (Soft) 9 Ran SP% **111.6**
Speed ratings (Par 96): **95,94,91,86,84 81,80,79,66**
CSF £110.39 CT £534.63 TOTE £28.30: £4.80, £2.30, £2.20; EX 188.90 Trifecta £1243.80.
Owner Star Contractors Limited **Bred** Jake Patrick Lyons **Trained** Epsom, Surrey

FOCUS
Another modest 3yo handicap. They went quite hard, considering the testing ground, and it turned into a dour scrap for the line.

1487 TODAYS RACING JUST £10 WITH RACINGUK H'CAP 5f 13y

7:55 (7:55) (Class 5) (0-75,72) 3-Y-O **£2,911** (£866; £432; £216) **Stalls** High

Form RPR

031- **1** **Dancing Years (IRE)**[208] 6594 3-9-7 **72** TonyHamilton 3 81
(Richard Fahey) *mde all: pushed along appr fnl f: kpt on: idled towards fin: shade cosily* **4/1**[2]

65-1 **2** *1 1/4* **Baron Bolt**[10] 1249 3-9-6 **71** JimCrowley 5 75
(Paul Cole) *dwlt: sn trckd ldr: rdn over 1f out: kpt on but a hld* **15/8**[1]

233- **3** *2* **Waneen (IRE)**[148] 7921 3-9-7 **72** JFEgan 4 69
(David Evans) *prom: rdn 1/2-way: one pce in 3rd fr over 1f out* **7/1**

03-4 **4** *2 3/4* **Total Power**[10] 1271 3-9-0 **70** CallumShepherd(5) 7 57
(Brian Ellison) *hld up: rdn 3f out: plugged on: nvr threatened* **8/1**

013- **5** *1 1/2* **Searanger (USA)**[209] 6557 3-9-5 **70** PJMcDonald 1 52
(Ann Duffield) *hld up: rdn 1/2-way: nvr threatened* **14/1**

312- **6** *1/2* **Secret Clause**[232] 5815 3-8-10 **64** AlistairRawlinson(3) 6 44
(Michael Appleby) *chsd ldrs: rdn 1/2-way: wknd fnl f* **5/1**[3]

5-54 **7** *5* **Le Manege Enchante (IRE)**[15] 1183 3-9-2 **67** DougieCostello 8 29
(Derek Shaw) *s.i.s: hld up: sn pushed along: hung lft fr 1/2-way: bhd fnl 2f* **10/1**

1m 7.12s (5.62) **Going Correction** +1.10s/f (Soft) 7 Ran SP% **110.8**
Speed ratings (Par 98): **99,97,93,89,87 86,78**
CSF £11.16 CT £46.16 TOTE £3.70: £2.50, £1.10; EX 8.80 Trifecta £37.40.

The Form Book, Raceform Ltd, Newbury, RG14 5SJ

Owner Cheveley Park Stud **Bred** Newberry Stud Company **Trained** Musley Bank, N Yorks

FOCUS

An ordinary 3yo sprint handicap. They went an honest gallop on worsening ground after a heavy storm. Further improvement from the winner.

T/Plt: £8,399.00 to a £1 stake. Pool of £45446.72 - 3.95 winning tickets. T/Qpdt: £189.20 to a £1 stake. Pool of £6113.44 - 23.90 winning tickets. **Andrew Sheret**

THIRSK (L-H)

Saturday, April 16

OFFICIAL GOING: Soft (heavy in places; 5.0)

Wind: Fresh across Weather: Cloudy and showers

1488 BOOK AT THIRSKRACECOURSE.NET FOR DISCOUNTED ENTRY H'CAP (DIV I) 6f

1:45 (1:45) (Class 5) (0-75,75) 4-Y-O+ **£3,234** (£962; £481; £240) **Stalls** High

Form RPR

142- **1** **Off The Scale (IRE)**[255] 5021 4-9-2 **70** DaleSwift 8 77
(Brian Ellison) *trckd ldrs: hdwy and cl up over 2f out: rdn to ld jst over 1f out: drvn out* **9/1**

006- **2** *½* **One Boy (IRE)**[180] 7343 5-9-0 **75** AdamMcNamara(7) 4 80
(Richard Fahey) *trckd ldrs: hdwy over 2f out: effrt over 1f out: rdn to chse wnr ins fnl f: sn drvn and ch tl no ex towards fin* **11/2**[3]

1455 **3** *nk* **Llewellyn**[10] 1251 8-9-2 **70** (b) DanielTudhope 7 74
(Declan Carroll) *led: rdn along 2f out: hdd jst over 1f out: sn drvn and kpt on same pce* **15/2**

43-5 **4** *1 ½* **Giant Spark**[17] 1154 4-8-7 **61** BarryMcHugh 11 60
(Paul Midgley) *hld up towards rr on stands' rail: n.m.r and swtchd lft 2f out: rdn to chse ldrs and n.m.r over 1f out: kpt on* **9/2**[2]

25-0 **5** *¾* **Pennine Warrior**[74] 426 5-9-2 **70** (b) BenCurtis 9 67
(Scott Dixon) *cl up: rdn along 2f out: grad wknd* **8/1**

404- **6** *½* **Sir Domino (FR)**[171] 7565 4-9-3 **71** GrahamLee 12 66
(Kevin Ryan) *hld up in rr: n.m.r on stands' rail 2f out: shkn up over 1f out: styd on: nrst fin* **4/1**[1]

160- **7** *¾* **Jebel Tara**[183] 7256 11-8-13 **67** (bt) PaulMulrennan 10 60
(Alan Brown) *trckd ldr: rdn along over 2f out: grad wknd* **18/1**

43-6 **8** *1 ¼* **Mr Cool Cash**[19] 1125 4-8-12 **66** JasonHart 1 55
(Richard Guest) *in tch: rdn along wl over 2f out: sn btn* **10/1**

40-0 **9** *1* **Exotic Guest**[17] 1154 6-9-0 **68** (p) JamesSullivan 3 54
(Ruth Carr) *dwlt and towards rr: hdwy 1/2-way: rdn to chse ldrs 2f out: sn wknd* **16/1**

44-6 **10** *½* **Shamaheart (IRE)**[19] 1124 6-9-2 **70** (p) DavidAllan 6 54
(Geoffrey Harker) *hld up in midfield: swtchd lft to outer and hdwy over 2f out: rdn wl over 1f out: sn wknd* **16/1**

000- **11** *11* **Dreese (IRE)**[221] 6194 5-9-1 **72** JacobButterfield(3) 5 21
(Marjorie Fife) *dwlt and wnt bdly lft s: bhd: hdwy to chse ldrs on outer 1/2-way: sn rdn along and wknd over 2f out* **20/1**

1m 20.57s (7.87) **Going Correction** +1.30s/f (Soft) **11 Ran SP% 117.3**

Speed ratings (Par 103): **99,98,97,95,94 94,93,91,90,89 74**

CSF £57.76 CT £395.43 TOTE £9.50: £2.80, £2.80, £2.50; EX 72.00 Trifecta £558.70.

Owner John Wade **Bred** Howard Johnson **Trained** Norton, N Yorks

■ Stewards' Enquiry : Barry McHugh two-day ban: careless riding (May 2-3)

FOCUS

Following 8mm of rain overnight the ground had eased to soft, heavy in places and the winning rider in the opener reported conditions to be "heavy, very testing". The home bend was out 7 yards, adding around 20 yards to races over 7f and 1m4f. A modest handicap to start. The pace held out and the form is rated around the third.

1489 BOOK AT THIRSKRACECOURSE.NET FOR DISCOUNTED ENTRY H'CAP (DIV II) 6f

2:20 (2:24) (Class 5) (0-75,74) 4-Y-O+ **£3,234** (£962; £481; £240) **Stalls** High

Form RPR

212- **1** **Pomme De Terre (IRE)**[200] 6830 4-9-7 **74** (b) PaulMulrennan 9 84+
(Michael Dods) *trckd ldrs: hdwy over 2f out: led wl over 1f out: rdn ins fnl f: kpt on strly* **8/1**

2 *1* **Chaplin Bay (IRE)**[186] 7201 4-8-8 **61** JamesSullivan 6 68
(Ruth Carr) *bmpd s: midfield: hdwy over 2f out: rdn over 1f out: chsd wnr ins fnl f: sn drvn and no imp towards fin* **10/1**

6-30 **3** *2 ¾* **Great Expectations**[74] 426 8-9-5 **72** (vt) ConnorBeasley 8 70
(J R Jenkins) *in rr: hdwy over 2f out: n.m.r and swtchd lft over 1f out: rdn and styd on fnl f: nrst fin* **25/1**

000- **4** *shd* **Kenny The Captain (IRE)**[123] 8242 5-9-4 **71** DuranFentiman 2 69
(Tim Easterby) *prom on outer: effrt and cl up 2f out: sn rdn and grad wknd* **10/1**

50- **5** *3 ¼* **Fantasy Justifier (IRE)**[225] 6037 5-9-3 **70** RoystonFfrench 10 57
(Ronald Harris) *in tch: effrt and hdwy 2f out: sn rdn along and one pce fnl f* **14/1**

-261 **6** *nk* **Lackaday**[10] 1254 4-9-0 **72** (p) CallumShepherd(5) 7 59
(Mark Walford) *wnt bdly lft and almost uns rdr s: in rr: hdwy 2f out: kpt on fnl f: n.d* **11/2**[2]

010- **7** *2 ½* **Bold Spirit**[179] 7365 5-8-9 **62** NeilFarley 4 41
(Declan Carroll) *slt ld: rdn along over 2f out: hdd wl over 1f out: sn drvn and wknd* **33/1**

33-3 **8** *4 ½* **Final Venture**[19] 1124 4-9-2 **69** BenCurtis 12 33
(Alan Swinbank) *cl up on stands' rail: effrt over 2f out: sn rdn along and wknd wl over 1f out* **15/8**[1]

2-55 **9** *½* **Tango Sky (IRE)**[10] 1252 7-9-0 **67** GrahamLee 11 30
(Paul Midgley) *trckd ldrs nr stands' rail: rdn along 2f out: sn wknd* **13/2**[3]

6-05 **10** *½* **Daylight**[19] 1125 6-8-7 **67** (t) NathanEvans(7) 5 28
(Michael Easterby) *a towards rr* **25/1**

000- **11** *13* **Harbour Patrol (IRE)**[165] 7675 4-9-3 **70** PJMcDonald 1
(Rebecca Bastiman) *a in rr: rdn along 1/2-way: sn outpcd and bhd* **40/1**

2202 **12** *6* **Fujin**[17] 1154 5-9-3 **70** (v[1]) TomEaves 3
(Shaun Harris) *cl up: rdn along wl over 2f out: sn wknd* **20/1**

1m 19.9s (7.20) **Going Correction** +1.30s/f (Soft) **12 Ran SP% 117.3**

Speed ratings (Par 103): **104,102,99,98,94 94,90,84,84,83 66,58**

CSF £78.21 CT £1911.65 TOTE £7.40: £2.10, £3.20, £5.70; EX 95.80 Trifecta £1428.40.

Owner Dunham Trading Ltd **Bred** Mcmahon Thoroughbreds Ltd **Trained** Denton, Co Durham

FOCUS

The winning time was 0.67sec quicker than the first division. The winner resumed his late 2015 progress.

1490 HAMBLETON SUITE - YOUR PERFECT RECEPTION VENUE (S) STKS 5f

2:55 (2:55) (Class 6) 3-5-Y-O **£2,726** (£805; £402) **Stalls** High

Form RPR

-146 **1** **Sartori**[9] 1298 5-9-13 67 (p) RobertWinston 2 59
(Marjorie Fife) *wnt lft s: sn chsng ldrs: led over 3f out: jnd and rdn 2f out: slt ld and drvn jst over 1f out: kpt on gamely towards fin* **5/2**[1]

0-63 **2** *nk* **Mighty Bond**[5] 1378 4-9-7 49 ConnorBeasley 6 52
(Tracy Waggott) *trckd ldrs: hdwy 1/2-way: chal 2f out and sn rdn: drvn ent fnl f: ev ch tl no ex towards fin* **4/1**[3]

3 *4* **Mary E** 3-8-4 0 ow3 (b[1]) CallumShepherd(5) 3 32
(Brian Ellison) *dwlt: bhd and sn rdn along: hdwy wl over 1f out: styd on fnl f: nrst fin* **7/1**

26-0 **4** *1 ½* **Robbian**[25] 1026 5-9-0 50 RPWalsh(7) 5 32
(Charles Smith) *chsd ldrs: hdwy on outer 1/2-way: rdn to chse ldng pair 2f out: drvn over 1f out: no imp fnl f* **10/1**

0540 **5** *2* **Mighty Zip (USA)**[10] 1251 4-9-13 65 (v[1]) TomEaves 4 31
(Kevin Ryan) *led 2f: sn rdn along: lost pl wl over 2f out: sn in rr* **10/3**[2]

3-34 **6** *3 ½* **Hello Beautiful (IRE)**[19] 1119 5-9-2 49 (b[1]) BenCurtis 7 7
(Brian Ellison) *trckd ldrs: rdn along over 2f out: sn drvn and btn* **5/1**

1m 5.91s (6.31) **Going Correction** +1.30s/f (Soft)

WFA 3 from 4yo+ 10lb **6 Ran SP% 109.9**

Speed ratings (Par 101): **101,100,94,91,88 82**

CSF £12.12 TOTE £3.30: £1.70, £2.10; EX 15.80 Trifecta £100.70.The winner was bought by Johnny Levins Racing for £8,000.

Owner R W Fife **Bred** D R Tucker **Trained** Stillington, N Yorks

■ Stewards' Enquiry : Robert Winston two-day ban: used whip above permitted level (May 2-3)
Connor Beasley two-day ban: used whip above permitted level (May 2-3)

FOCUS

A weak seller with the front pair involved in a dour tussle throughout the last 2f. The form is rated on the nagative side.

1491 EBFSTALLIONS.COM MICHAEL FOSTER EBF CONDITIONS STKS 7f

3:30 (3:31) (Class 3) 4-Y-O+ **£9,337** (£2,796; £1,398; £699; £349) **Stalls** Low

Form RPR

10-4 **1** **Kelinni (IRE)**[35] 921 8-9-10 110 ShaneGray 2 109
(Kevin Ryan) *mde all: rdn and qcknd clr over 2f out: kpt on strly* **6/4**[1]

00-0 **2** *3 ½* **Rene Mathis (GER)**[14] 1196 6-9-3 104 AdamMcNamara(7) 3 100
(Richard Fahey) *trckd ldng pair: hdwy to chse wnr over 2f out: sn rdn: drvn and no imp fnl f* **6/1**[3]

600- **3** *2 ¼* **Balty Boys (IRE)**[168] 7634 7-9-12 112 (b) BenCurtis 4 96
(Brian Ellison) *hld up in rr: pushed along 1/2-way: rdn over 2f out: styd on to chse ldng pair over 1f out: no imp* **7/1**

500- **4** *6* **Toocoolforschool (IRE)**[217] 6313 4-9-0 107 (p) DougieCostello 1 68
(K R Burke) *chsd wnr: rdn along wl over 2f out: sn drvn and wknd* **7/2**[2]

/02- **5** *3 ¾* **Indy (IRE)**[319] 2805 5-9-0 94 GrahamGibbons 5 59
(David Barron) *trckd ldng pair on inner: pushed along wl over 2f out: sn rdn and wknd* **7/2**[2]

1m 35.5s (8.30) **Going Correction** +1.50s/f (Heav) **5 Ran SP% 111.2**

Speed ratings (Par 107): **112,108,105,98,94**

CSF £10.97 TOTE £2.10: £1.30, £2.90; EX 10.50 Trifecta £47.50.

Owner Amplitudo Partnership **Bred** Newberry Stud Farm Ltd **Trained** Hambleton, N Yorks

FOCUS

Rail movement added about 20 yards to the race distance. Formerly run over 6f, this conditions event has been run over 7f since 2012 and has been won by some high-class performers within the past ten years, including the subsequent Group-race winners Utmost Respect, Markab and Breton Rock to name but three. This year's winner very much had his own way, but could do no more than win like he did. He's rated to form.

1492 JW 4X4 NORTHALLERTON H'CAP 5f

4:05 (4:05) (Class 3) (0-95,92) 3-Y-O **£7,439** (£2,213; £1,106; £553) **Stalls** High

Form RPR

61-3 **1** **Reflektor (IRE)**[11] 1243 3-9-0 **85** RichardKingscote 4 93
(Tom Dascombe) *cl up: led wl over 1f out: rdn and edgd rt ent fnl f: kpt on wl* **2/1**[1]

642- **2** *1* **Celebration**[192] 7040 3-8-6 **77** BarryMcHugh 6 81
(Richard Fahey) *trckd ldrs: hdwy on inner 2f out: chsd wnr and swtchd lft jst ins fnl f: sn rdn and kpt on* **7/2**[2]

04-4 **3** *4* **Ravenhoe (IRE)**[20] 1112 3-8-6 **77** JoeFanning 7 67
(Mark Johnston) *hld up: hdwy wl over 1f out: rdn and kpt on fnl f* **11/2**

311- **4** *3 ¼* **El Astronaute (IRE)**[203] 6741 3-9-4 **89** PhillipMakin 5 67
(John Quinn) *led: pushed along 2f out: sn hdd and drvn: wknd over 1f out* **4/1**[3]

500- **5** *½* **Excessable**[211] 6495 3-9-2 **87** (t) DavidAllan 2 64
(Tim Easterby) *hld up in rr: effrt wl over 1f out: sn rdn along and n.d* **11/2**

013- **6** *2* **Midnight Malibu (IRE)**[230] 5895 3-8-3 **79** RachelRichardson(5) 1 48
(Tim Easterby) *chsd ldrs on outer: pushed along over 2f out: sn rdn and wknd* **18/1**

1m 4.45s (4.85) **Going Correction** +1.30s/f (Soft) **6 Ran SP% 111.6**

Speed ratings (Par 102): **113,111,105,99,99 95**

CSF £9.08 TOTE £3.70: £1.90, £2.40; EX 11.90 Trifecta £47.40.

Owner David Lowe **Bred** Hyde Park Stud & Paddy Conney **Trained** Malpas, Cheshire

FOCUS

A decent 3yo sprint handicap in which race-fitness may have proved the key. The winner is rated to a more literal reading of his maiden win.

1493 EILEEN HOUSE 80TH BIRTHDAY H'CAP 1m 4f

4:40 (4:40) (Class 2) (0-100,99) 4-Y-O+ **£12,938** (£3,850; £1,924; £962) **Stalls** High

Form RPR

013- **1** **Cymro (IRE)**[210] 6532 4-9-9 **99** RichardKingscote 7 108+
(Tom Dascombe) *hld up in midfield: smooth hdwy 4f out: trckd ldrs 3f out: led wl over 1f out: sn pushed clr: rdn and edgd lft ent fnl f: kpt on strly* **9/2**[1]

0-04 **2** *1 ¾* **Snoano**[11] 1245 4-8-12 **88** GrahamLee 12 93
(Tim Easterby) *hld up towards rr: stdy hdwy over 3f out: chsd ldrs wl over 1f out: sn rdn: chsd wnr ins fnl f: sn drvn and no imp* **11/1**

100- **3** *1 ¼* **Blue Hussar (IRE)**[161] 7757 5-9-0 **89** PJMcDonald 2 92
(Micky Hammond) *in tch: hdwy over 4f out: chsd ldrs 3f out: rdn 2f out: styd on fnl f* **7/1**

442- **4** *1* **Craggaknock**[176] 7425 5-8-7 **82** JasonHart 16 83
(Mark Walford) *trckd ldrs on outer: hdwy over 3f out: effrt 2f out and sn rdn: drvn and kpt on same pce fnl f* **11/2**[2]

202- **5** 1 ½ **Multellie**[172] 7524 4-8-8 **84** .... DavidAllan 5 83+
(Tim Easterby) *trckd ldr: led over 3f out: rdn along over 2f out: hdd wl over 1f out: sn drvn and grad wknd* **20/1**

341- **6** 2 ½ **Swaheen**[190] 7090 4-9-0 **90** .... ConnorBeasley 15 85+
(Julie Camacho) *hld up in rr: hdwy wl over 2f out: rdn wl over 1f out: styd on fnl f: nrst fin* **11/1**

652- **7** 1 ½ **Buonarroti (IRE)**[161] 7757 5-8-12 **87** .... DanielTudhope 8 80
(Declan Carroll) *hld up in rr: hdwy wl over 2f out: rdn along wl over 1f out: styd on fnl f: nrst fin* **7/1**[3]

0-60 **8** 1 **Be Perfect (USA)**[22] 1081 7-9-3 **92** .... (p) JamesSullivan 11 83
(Ruth Carr) *trckd ldrs: pushed along 4f out: rdn wl over 2f out: sn btn* **66/1**

100- **9** 2 ¾ **Hernandoshideaway**[205] 6679 4-9-6 **96** .... PaulMulrennan 4 83
(Michael Dods) *trckd ldrs: chsd ldng pair 7f out: chsd ldr 3f out: rdn along 2f out: sn drvn and wknd* **10/1**

5-01 **10** 7 **Master Of Finance (IRE)**[11] 1245 5-9-9 **98** .... JoeFanning 9 73
(Mark Johnston) *prom: rdn along over 3f out: wknd over 2f out* **12/1**

000- **11** hd **Aramist (IRE)**[203] 6749 6-9-1 **90** .... NeilFarley 6 65
(Alan Swinbank) *hld up in midfield: hdwy 5f out: chsd ldrs over 3f out: rdn along wl over 2f out and sn wknd* **11/1**

545- **12** ¾ **Only Orsenfoolsies**[80] 7757 7-8-12 **87** .... JackGarritty 10 61
(Micky Hammond) *a towards rr* **33/1**

322- **13** 1 **Kinema (IRE)**[173] 7511 5-9-6 **95** .... BenCurtis 14 67
(Alan Swinbank) *a towards rr* **7/1**[3]

/10- **14** 13 **Chebsey Beau**[168] 6496 6-8-5 **80** .... BarryMcHugh 13 31
(John Quinn) *a bhd* **33/1**

060- **15** 34 **Cyril**[176] 7426 4-8-6 **82** .... ShaneGray 1
(Kevin Ryan) *sn led: rdn along 4f out: hdd over 3f out: sn rdn and wknd* **33/1**

2m 52.96s (16.76) **Going Correction** +1.50s/f (Heav)
WFA 4 from 5yo+ 1lb **15** Ran SP% **119.3**
Speed ratings (Par 109): **104,102,102,101,100 98,97,97,95,90 90,89,89,80,57**
CSF £49.01 CT £1125.43 TOTE £5.90: £2.80, £4.50, £7.60; EX 75.90 Trifecta £1660.80.
Owner D R Passant & Hefin Williams **Bred** Michael McGlynn **Trained** Malpas, Cheshire

FOCUS
Rail movement added about 20 yards to the race distance. A warm middle-distance handicap and the pace was solid without being anything out of the ordinary. Another clear pb from the winner.

1494 RACING UK DAY PASS JUST £10 MEDIAN AUCTION MAIDEN STKS 6f
5:15 (5:15) (Class 5) 3-4-Y-O **£3,234** (£962; £481; £240) **Stalls** High

Form RPR

1 **Oh James** 3-9-3 0 .... JamesSullivan 5 74
(Tim Easterby) *in tch: hdwy on outer over 2f out: chsd ldrs over 1f out: rdn to chal and edgd rt ent fnl f: led last 100yds: r.o wl* **22/1**

256- **2** 2 ¾ **Run Rio Run (IRE)**[254] 5050 3-9-3 68 .... ConnorBeasley 8 65
(Michael Dods) *trckd ldng pair: hdwy to chse ldr 1/2-way: rdn wl over 1f out: drvn ent fnl f: kpt on* **7/1**[3]

02-2 **3** 1 ¼ **General Alexander (IRE)**[13] 1217 3-9-3 78 .... BenCurtis 1 61
(Brian Ellison) *cl up: led after 1f: rdn wl over 1f out: drvn ent fnl f: hdd & wknd last 100yds* **8/15**[1]

53 **4** 3 **Bromley Cross (IRE)**[20] 1111 3-9-3 0 .... JackGarritty 10 51
(Richard Fahey) *in tch: hdwy over 2f out: rdn to chse ldrs over 1f out: n.m.r ent fnl f: one pce* **7/2**[2]

50 **5** 4 ½ **Ksenia (IRE)**[32] 945 3-8-12 0 .... NeilFarley 4 32
(Nigel Tinkler) *chsd ldrs on outer: hdwy 1/2-way: rdn wl over 1f out: sn wknd* **66/1**

6 11 **Another Desperado (IRE)** 3-9-3 0 .... PaulMulrennan 2 2
(Rebecca Bastiman) *slt ld 1f: cl up: rdn along 1/2-way: sn outpcd* **33/1**

7 3 ¼ **Field Officer** 3-9-3 0 .... (e[1]) DavidAllan 11
(Tim Easterby) *a in rr: outpcd and bhd fr 1/2-way* **20/1**

1m 21.26s (8.56) **Going Correction** +1.30s/f (Soft)
WFA 3 from 4yo 11lb **7** Ran SP% **113.5**
Speed ratings (Par 103): **94,90,88,84,78 64,59**
CSF £153.90 TOTE £21.50: £4.70, £2.40; EX 88.20 Trifecta £271.40.
Owner Gremot Racing **Bred** Habton Farms **Trained** Great Habton, N Yorks

FOCUS
This maiden was won by Jack Dexter in 2012, but it looked an uncompetitive event this time around and it went to a newcomer. Fluid form given the worsening ground.

1495 THIRSK RACES SUNDAY FUNDAY 24TH APRIL H'CAP 6f
5:45 (5:45) (Class 6) (0-60,65) 4-Y-O+ **£3,234** (£962; £481; £240) **Stalls** High

Form RPR

5-31 **1** **Mitchum**[5] 1378 7-9-0 **58** 6ex .... (p) PhilDennis(5) 14 72
(Ron Barr) *trckd ldrs: hdwy over 2f out: rdn to ld over 1f out: kpt on strly fnl f* **3/1**[1]

140- **2** 3 **Blue Jacket (USA)**[225] 6071 5-9-3 **56** .... PaulMulrennan 7 61+
(Dianne Sayer) *towards rr: hdwy 1/2-way: chsd ldrs wl over 1f out: drvn to chse wnr ins fnl f: no imp towards fin* **11/1**

00-0 **3** 4 ½ **Saltarello (IRE)**[20] 1116 4-9-7 **60** .... SamJames 4 52
(Marjorie Fife) *wnt rt s: chsd ldrs on outer: pushed along over 2f out: rdn wl over 1f out: kpt on fnl f* **16/1**

-251 **4** ¾ **Hit The Lights (IRE)**[10] 1255 6-9-5 **65** .... (v) DanielleMooney(7) 5 54
(David Nicholls) *sltly hmpd s: sn cl up: led 1/2-way: rdn 2f out: hdd over 1f out: sn drvn and kpt on same pce* **9/1**[3]

/045 **5** 1 ½ **Ripon Rose**[19] 1120 4-8-9 **48** .... (b[1]) BarryMcHugh 11 33
(Paul Midgley) *chsd ldrs on stands' rail: rdn along and sltly outpcd 2f out: kpt on u.p fnl f* **16/1**

0334 **6** hd **Secret Witness**[10] 1261 10-9-7 **60** .... (b) RoystonFfrench 13 44
(Ronald Harris) *chsd ldrs: rdn along over 2f out: drvn over 1f out: one pce* **10/1**

020- **7** 3 ¼ **Betty Boo (IRE)**[269] 4510 6-8-10 **49** .... DuranFentiman 12 23
(Shaun Harris) *towards rr: hdwy over 2f out: sn rdn and plugged on one pce* **33/1**

000- **8** ¾ **White Flag**[173] 7522 5-9-0 **58** .... RachelRichardson(5) 15 30
(Tim Easterby) *bhd tl styd on fnl 2f* **12/1**

350- **9** ¾ **Poolstock**[165] 7680 4-9-2 **55** .... ConnorBeasley 16 25
(Michael Dods) *chsd ldrs: rdn along 1/2-way: sn wknd* **4/1**[2]

00-5 **10** 1 ½ **Farang Jai Dee (IRE)**[5] 1383 4-8-5 **47** .... SammyJoBell(3) 9 12
(Declan Carroll) *chsd ldrs: rdn along over 2f out: sn drvn and wknd* **22/1**

1630 **11** 4 **Coiste Bodhar (IRE)**[4] 1401 5-9-7 **60** .... (p) BenCurtis 3 13
(Scott Dixon) *racd wd: prom: rdn along wl over 2f out: sn drvn and grad wknd* **16/1**

1001 **12** 5 **Monsieur Jimmy**[9] 1298 4-8-8 **47** .... (b) NeilFarley 1
(Declan Carroll) *wnt lft s: in tch on outer: rdn along 1/2-way: sn wknd* **16/1**

2354 **13** 7 **Pancake Day**[10] 1255 4-8-10 **54** .... (p) RobJFitzpatrick(5) 8
(Jason Ward) *slt ld: hdd over 3f out: sn rdn along and wknd over 2f out* **14/1**

5-00 **14** 12 **Under Approval**[25] 1026 5-8-4 **48** .... (b) GemmaTutty(5) 10
(Karen Tutty) *a bhd* **50/1**

6-00 **15** 21 **Abonos (IRE)**[32] 937 4-8-8 **47** .... (be[1]) JasonHart 6
(Simon West) *hmpd s: sn rdn along and a wl bhd* **40/1**

1m 20.81s (8.11) **Going Correction** +1.30s/f (Soft) **15** Ran SP% **122.0**
Speed ratings (Par 101): **97,93,87,86,84 83,79,78,77,75 70,63,54,38,10**
CSF £35.67 CT £479.22 TOTE £3.90: £2.80, £2.50, £4.30; EX 43.80 Trifecta £522.70.
Owner P Cartmell **Bred** Conor J C Parsons & Brian M Parsons **Trained** Seamer, N Yorks

FOCUS
A moderate handicap in which they bet 9-1 bar two. One came up the middle to no avail while the rest raced towards the stands' side.
T/Plt: £186.50 to a £1 stake. Pool of £61090.87 - 239.04 winning tickets. T/Qpdt: £13.10 to a £1 stake. Pool of £4405.23 - 248.75 winning tickets. **Joe Rowntree**

1341 WOLVERHAMPTON (A.W) (L-H)
Saturday, April 16

OFFICIAL GOING: Tapeta: standard
Wind: Fresh across Weather: Fine

1496 AWARD WINNING FINE DINING AT HORIZONS AMATEUR RIDERS' H'CAP 5f 216y (Tp)
6:10 (6:10) (Class 5) (0-70,69) 4-Y-O+ **£2,807** (£870; £435; £217) **Stalls** Low

Form RPR

-020 **1** **Lucky Lodge**[20] 1116 6-10-10 **65** .... (p) MissSBrotherton 2 72
(Antony Brittain) *chsd ldrs: rdn to ld ins fnl f: r.o* **11/1**

5315 **2** nk **Indian Affair**[15] 1186 6-10-7 **69** .... (bt) MrJCJones(7) 7 75
(Milton Bradley) *a.p: rdn over 1f out: edgd lft ins fnl f: r.o* **16/1**

22-0 **3** ¾ **Triple Dream**[101] 68 11-10-0 **62** .... MissPSkipper(7) 1 66
(Milton Bradley) *chsd ldrs: rdn over 1f out: ev ch ins fnl f: unable qck towards fin* **33/1**

4143 **4** 1 **National Service (USA)**[16] 1159 5-10-12 **67** .... (tp) MrPMillman 3 71+
(Rebecca Menzies) *mid-div: hdwy over 2f out: nt clr run and swtchd rt ins fnl f: r.o* **8/1**[3]

0655 **5** ½ **Bogsnog (IRE)**[15] 1180 6-10-1 **59** .... (b[1]) KaineWood(3) 9 58
(Kristin Stubbs) *led: rdn over 1f out: hdd ins fnl f: styd on same pce* **12/1**

-403 **6** ½ **Ancient Cross**[7] 1341 12-10-8 **63** .... (bt) MissJoannaMason 13 61
(Michael Easterby) *mid-div: rdn over 1f out: nt clr run ins fnl f: styd on* **14/1**

3152 **7** ¾ **Mr Christopher (IRE)**[15] 1186 4-10-6 **68** .... (p) MrCJewell(7) 6 64+
(Tom Dascombe) *s.i.s: sn pushed along in rr: racd wd fr 1/2-way: r.o wl ins fnl f: nrst fin* **5/1**[2]

01 **8** nk **Spellmaker**[15] 1180 7-10-12 **67** .... BrodieHampson 8 62
(Tony Newcombe) *hld up: rdn over 1f out: r.o towards fin: nvr nrr* **8/1**[3]

0-22 **9** 1 ¾ **Excellent Aim**[92] 196 9-10-5 **65** .... MissKMargarson(5) 4 54
(George Margarson) *hld up: effrt and edgd lft over 1f out: nt trble ldrs* **14/1**

0422 **10** ½ **Nasri**[16] 1159 10-10-11 **66** .... MrSWalker 12 54
(Emma Owen) *mid-div: lost pl over 4f out: n.d after* **9/1**

24-5 **11** 1 ¾ **Keene's Pointe**[10] 1269 6-10-2 **64** .... MrBenjaminStephens(7) 11 47
(Kristin Stubbs) *s.i.s: hld up: effrt and nt clr run over 1f out: nvr on terms* **22/1**

-155 **12** nk **Kyllach Me (IRE)**[20] 1116 4-10-4 **62** .... (b) MrThomasGreatrex(3) 5 44
(Bryan Smart) *s.i.s: hld up: hdwy whn hmpd over 1f out: nt rcvr* **4/1**[1]

03-0 **13** shd **Red Invader (IRE)**[44] 795 6-10-5 **65** .... MrsRWilson(5) 10 47
(Paul D'Arcy) *chsd ldrs: ev ch 2f out: wknd ins fnl f* **22/1**

1m 14.29s (-0.21) **Going Correction** -0.15s/f (Stan) **13** Ran SP% **115.8**
Speed ratings (Par 103): **95,94,93,92,91 90,89,89,87,86 84,83,83**
CSF £165.40 CT £5683.71 TOTE £12.50: £4.00, £5.70, £8.70; EX 268.30 Trifecta £4253.50 Part won..
Owner Antony Brittain **Bred** Mel Brittain **Trained** Warthill, N Yorks
■ Stewards' Enquiry : Miss K Margarson two-day ban: careless riding (May 6,9)

FOCUS
A wide open sprint handicap run at an even gallop.

1497 MEETINGS & EVENTS AT WOLVERHAMPTON RACECOURSE H'CAP 5f 216y (Tp)
6:40 (6:41) (Class 6) (0-60,60) 3-Y-O **£2,458** (£731; £365; £182) **Stalls** Low

Form RPR

00-0 **1** **Ordinal**[17] 1151 3-9-3 **56** .... SilvestreDeSousa 7 73+
(Mark Johnston) *chsd ldr 5f out: led over 2f out: pushed clr fr over 1f out: easily* **11/8**[1]

030- **2** 7 **Jumeirah Star (USA)**[189] 7107 3-9-2 **55** .... AdamBeschizza 3 49
(Robert Cowell) *chsd ldrs: rdn over 2f out: styd on same pce fr over 1f out* **18/1**

60-6 **3** ½ **Bushwise (IRE)**[43] 820 3-8-7 **46** oh1 .... (p) FrannyNorton 2 39
(Milton Bradley) *chsd ldrs: rdn over 2f out: edgd lft over 1f out: styd on same pce* **33/1**

00-5 **4** nk **Cuban Queen (USA)**[57] 635 3-8-11 **50** .... MartinLane 8 42
(Jeremy Gask) *in rr: rdn over 1f out: r.o ins fnl f: nvr nrr* **18/1**

-225 **5** ¾ **Dream Revival**[8] 1325 3-9-0 **58** .... AnnaHesketh(5) 11 47
(James Unett) *sn outpcd: hdwy over 1f out: nt trble ldrs* **9/1**[3]

0633 **6** ¾ **David's Beauty (IRE)**[47] 763 3-9-3 **56** .... (p) SamHitchcott 5 43
(Brian Baugh) *led: rdn and hdd over 2f out: wknd fnl f* **9/1**[3]

-000 **7** shd **Taroneesh**[17] 1141 3-8-2 **46** oh1 .... (v) AaronJones(5) 4 33
(Derek Shaw) *mid-div: effrt over 1f out: wknd fnl f* **66/1**

-030 **8** nk **Castlerea Tess**[43] 820 3-8-4 **46** oh1 .... RobHornby(3) 10 32
(Sarah Hollinshead) *sn outpcd: nvr nrr* **25/1**

3442 **9** hd **Tombe Girl**[24] 1045 3-9-5 **58** .... (p) PhillipMakin 9 43
(Keith Dalgleish) *hld up: hdwy 2f out: sn rdn: wknd fnl f* **3/1**[2]

-040 **10** 2 ½ **Straduff (IRE)**[17] 1148 3-9-2 **60** .... (p) JosephineGordon(5) 6 38
(J S Moore) *chsd ldrs: rdn over 3f out: wknd wl over 1f out* **12/1**

000- **11** 14 **Soiree**[207] 6623 3-9-2 **55** .... RobertWinston 1
(Eve Johnson Houghton) *mid-div: lost pl 4f out: wknd wl over 1f out* **25/1**

1m 13.37s (-1.13) **Going Correction** -0.15s/f (Stan) **11** Ran SP% **117.4**
Speed ratings (Par 96): **101,91,91,90,89 88,88,88,87,84 65**
CSF £29.35 CT £600.04 TOTE £2.50: £1.20, £4.00, £5.90; EX 26.30 Trifecta £940.40.
Owner Sheikh Hamdan bin Mohammed Al Maktoum **Bred** Darley **Trained** Middleham Moor, N Yorks

FOCUS
A very weak handicap and the market got this spot on as the heavily backed winner absolutely bolted up.

1498 LIKE WOLVERHAMPTON RACECOURSE ON FACEBOOK CLASSIFIED (S) STKS 1m 141y (Tp)

7:10 (7:10) (Class 6) 3-Y-O+ **£2,458** (£731; £365; £182) **Stalls** Low

Form RPR
2335 **1** **Mr Red Clubs (IRE)**[36] 899 7-9-6 69.........................(p[1]) AndrewMullen 2 71
(Michael Appleby) *chsd ldrs: led over 2f out: rdn out* **1/1**[1]
-626 **2** *1¼* **Almanack**[20] 1114 6-9-6 65..(t) DaleSwift 7 67
(Daniel Mark Loughnane) *s.i.s: hld up: rdn over 1f out: r.o to go 2nd wl ins fnl f: nt rch wnr* **11/2**[2]
0-00 **3** *1¼* **Diamonds A Dancing**[3] 1416 6-9-1 60......................(b) CiaranMckee[(5)] 3 64
(John O'Shea) *hld up: hdwy over 1f out: sn rdn: styd on to go 3rd nr fin* **25/1**
6050 **4** *nk* **Khajaaly (IRE)**[19] 1120 9-9-6 65...............................(t) SilvestreDeSousa 4 64
(Daniel Mark Loughnane) *hld up: rdn over 2f out: hdwy over 1f out: kpt on* **9/1**
10-6 **5** *nk* **Rio Falls (IRE)**[71] 464 4-9-3 70.. JoeDoyle[(3)] 6 63
(Jennie Candlish) *prom: chsd ldr over 5f out tl led over 3f out: hdd over 2f out: no ex ins fnl f* **6/1**[3]
/6-0 **6** *4½* **Handheld**[11] 1241 9-9-3 73...(p) ShelleyBirkett[(3)] 1 54
(Julia Feilden) *led: hdd over 6f out: remained handy: rdn over 2f out: wknd fnl f* **12/1**
2130 **7** *9* **Basingstoke (IRE)**[19] 1120 7-9-8 61....................(b) GeorgeDowning[(3)] 5 40
(Daniel Mark Loughnane) *s.i.s: hdwy to join ldr after 1f: led over 6f out: pushed along and hdd over 3f out: wknd over 1f out* **7/1**

1m 49.16s (-0.94) **Going Correction** -0.15s/f (Stan) **7** Ran SP% **113.7**
Speed ratings (Par 101): **98,96,95,95,95 91,83**
CSF £6.82 TOTE £2.40: £1.10, £3.60; EX 8.00 Trifecta £84.20.
Owner Ferrybank Properties Limited **Bred** Tally-Ho Stud **Trained** Oakham, Rutland

FOCUS
A seller in which most had questions to answer and it provided a great opportunity for the reliable Mr Red Clubs to return to winning ways.

1499 VISIT WOLVERHAMPTON-RACECOURSE.CO.UK MAIDEN STKS 1m 4f 50y (Tp)

7:40 (7:41) (Class 5) 3-Y-O+ **£2,975** (£885; £442; £221) **Stalls** Low

Form RPR
3- **1** **Batts Rock (IRE)**[164] 7707 3-8-7 0...................................... JoeFanning 7 79+
(Michael Bell) *chsd ldr after 1f: led over 3f out: shkn up and c clr fr over 1f out: easily* **1/1**[1]
0- **2** *8* **Mawaany (IRE)**[199] 6864 3-8-7 0.............................(v[1]) GrahamGibbons 2 64
(Sir Michael Stoute) *in rr whn swtchd rt after 1f: hdwy to go prom over 9f out: chsd wnr over 2f out: sn rdn: wknd ins fnl f* **2/1**[2]
/ **3** *1¾* **Subordinate (GER)**[26] 7-9-13 0.......................................(t) TimmyMurphy 5 63
(Emma Lavelle) *chsd ldrs: rdn over 2f out: sn outpcd* **33/1**
54 **4** *½* **Princess Roania (IRE)**[7] 1346 5-9-1 0........................ JoshuaBryan[(7)] 1 57
(Peter Bowen) *chsd ldrs: rdn over 2f out: wknd fnl f* **20/1**
5 *1¾* **Cafoo (IRE)** 3-8-7 0.. MartinLane 4 57
(Ed Dunlop) *s.i.s: hld up: rdn and wknd over 2f out* **8/1**[3]
6 *5* **Last Summer**[324] 5-9-10 0.. RobHornby[(3)] 6 51
(Grace Harris) *s.i.s: hld up: rdn and wknd over 2f out* **12/1**
7 *13* **Angel Of Light (IRE)** 4-9-7 0.................................... SilvestreDeSousa 3 25
(Jo Hughes) *led: hdd over 3f out: rdn and wknd wl over 1f out* **20/1**

2m 38.44s (-2.36) **Going Correction** -0.15s/f (Stan)
WFA 3 from 4yo 20lb 4 from 5yo+ 1lb **7** Ran SP% **114.6**
Speed ratings (Par 103): **101,95,94,94,93 89,81**
CSF £3.10 TOTE £1.80: £1.10, £2.80; EX 4.20 Trifecta £50.00.
Owner Lady Bamford **Bred** Lady Bamford **Trained** Newmarket, Suffolk

FOCUS
Probably not a strong maiden but impossible not to be impressed by the winner who looks colt of real potential.

1500 LADIES EVENING FRIDAY 19TH AUGUST H'CAP 1m 4f 50y (Tp)

8:10 (8:10) (Class 6) (0-60,61) 4-Y-O+ **£2,458** (£731; £365; £182) **Stalls** Low

Form RPR
1251 **1** **On A Whim**[16] 1170 4-9-6 60...(p) JoeFanning 6 67
(Daniel Mark Loughnane) *mid-div: hdwy over 1f out: sn rdn: styd on to ld nr fin* **4/1**[2]
6-06 **2** *nk* **Invincible Wish (IRE)**[3] 1413 4-9-2 59.......................... RobHornby[(3)] 9 66
(Trevor Wall) *trckd ldrs: plld hrd: led over 1f out: sn rdn: hdd nr fin* **14/1**
1331 **3** *1¼* **Yasir (USA)**[7] 1343 8-9-1 61.. SophieKilloran[(7)] 3 66
(Sophie Leech) *hld up: hdwy over 1f out: rdn and edgd lft ins fnl f: styd on to go 3rd nr fin* **9/2**[3]
0/6- **4** *nk* **Attenzione (IRE)**[133] 8121 5-9-1 54..............................(b) ShaneKelly 4 58
(S Donohoe, Ire) *mid-div: hdwy over 2f out: rdn over 1f out: styd on same pce ins fnl f* **7/2**[1]
5544 **5** *3* **Evervescent (IRE)**[23] 1057 7-9-7 60................................ LiamKeniry 10 59
(Graeme McPherson) *chsd ldr tl led over 2f out: rdn and hdd over 1f out: no ex ins fnl f* **16/1**
6443 **6** *2½* **Ring Eye (IRE)**[16] 1169 8-8-9 53.................................. CiaranMckee[(5)] 1 48
(John O'Shea) *hld up: hdwy on outer over 2f out: wknd fnl f* **22/1**
-643 **7** *½* **The Dukkerer (IRE)**[29] 982 5-9-7 60............................ AndrewMullen 2 54
(James Given) *hld up: nt clr run 2f out: hdwy over 1f out: wknd ins fnl f* **16/1**
6655 **8** *7* **Chauvelin**[7] 1343 5-8-8 50.......................................(v) JacobButterfield[(3)] 8 33
(Richard Guest) *led: rdn and hdd over 2f out: wknd fnl f* **18/1**
0-43 **9** *shd* **Bollihope**[3] 1413 4-9-6 60.. GrahamGibbons 11 43
(Richard Guest) *prom: shkn up over 2f out: wknd over 1f out* **11/2**
5002 **10** *1¼* **Ali Bin Nayef**[16] 1169 4-8-12 52.. NickyMackay 12 33
(Michael Wigham) *hld up: hdwy over 3f out: rdn over 2f out: wknd over 1f out* **16/1**
0005 **11** *4* **Star Anise (FR)**[31] 949 5-8-6 50........................... JosephineGordon[(5)] 5 25
(Paddy Butler) *in rr: pushed along over 2f out: sn wknd* **28/1**
63-0 **12** *8* **Mister Marcasite**[16] 1169 6-9-5 58............................ SilvestreDeSousa 7 20
(Antony Brittain) *chsd ldrs: rdn over 3f out: wknd over 1f out: eased ins fnl f* **12/1**

2m 36.65s (-4.15) **Going Correction** -0.15s/f (Stan)
WFA 4 from 5yo+ 1lb **12** Ran SP% **120.9**
Speed ratings (Par 101): **107,106,105,105,103 102,101,97,97,96 93,88**
CSF £60.57 CT £268.01 TOTE £4.70: £1.10, £6.20, £1.90; EX 76.40 Trifecta £370.40.
Owner R M Brilley **Bred** Minster Stud **Trained** Baldwin's Gate, Staffs

FOCUS
An open handicap which was run at what looked an even enough gallop and the form looks reasonable for the grade.

1501 HOTEL & RACING PACKAGES AVAILABLE H'CAP 1m 1f 103y (Tp)

8:40 (8:40) (Class 5) (0-70,70) 4-Y-O+ **£3,040** (£904; £452; £226) **Stalls** Low

Form RPR
/5-4 **1** **Rock Song**[20] 1114 7-9-1 64... GrahamGibbons 5 72
(John Mackie) *trckd ldrs: racd keenly: rdn to ld and edgd lft ins fnl f: r.o* **9/1**
2-45 **2** *¾* **Fire And Passion**[45] 778 4-9-3 66..................................(b) MartinLane 9 72
(Jeremy Gask) *led after 1f: hdd over 2f out: rdn and ev ch ins fnl f: styd on* **8/1**
5222 **3** *¾* **Cartographic (USA)**[7] 1347 4-9-0 63....................... SilvestreDeSousa 6 67
(David Evans) *chsd ldrs: rdn to ld over 1f out: hdd ins fnl f: styd on same pce towards fin* **6/4**[1]
-000 **4** *½* **Maverik**[59] 616 8-9-4 67..(t) CharlesBishop 11 70
(Ali Stronge) *stdd s: hld up: hdwy over 1f out: r.o* **20/1**
3534 **5** *1½* **Lean On Pete (IRE)**[7] 1347 7-8-11 67...............(p) RobertDodsworth[(7)] 7 67
(Ollie Pears) *hld up: rdn over 1f out: r.o ins fnl f: nvr nrr* **7/1**[3]
2402 **6** *½* **Kodiac Lady (IRE)**[16] 1171 4-8-6 62.....................(e) HollieDoyle[(7)] 2 61
(Simon West) *hld up: rdn over 1f out: r.o ins fnl f: nt trble ldrs* **22/1**
4131 **7** *hd* **La Havrese (FR)**[29] 982 5-8-10 64................................. JoshDoyle[(5)] 1 63
(Lynn Siddall) *led 1f: remained handy: rdn over 1f out: no ex ins fnl f* **5/1**[2]
535- **8** *1* **Carragold**[117] 8336 10-9-7 70.. DanielTudhope 8 67
(Antony Brittain) *hld up: hdwy 3f out: rdn over 1f out: wknd ins fnl f* **14/1**
440 **9** *¾* **Shining Romeo**[37] 885 4-9-5 68................................. LemosdeSouza 4 63
(Denis Quinn) *hld up: hdwy over 2f out: sn rdn: wknd ins fnl f* **20/1**
6-00 **10** *11* **Mr Frankie**[37] 893 5-9-4 70.. JoeDoyle[(3)] 10 42
(Richard Phillips) *prom: chsd ldr over 7f out: rdn over 2f out: wknd wl over 1f out* **22/1**

1m 59.04s (-1.76) **Going Correction** -0.15s/f (Stan) **10** Ran SP% **115.2**
Speed ratings (Par 103): **101,100,99,99,97 97,97,96,95,85**
CSF £72.30 CT £166.22 TOTE £11.60: £3.70, £2.90, £1.10; EX 100.90 Trifecta £280.20.
Owner Mrs J Mackie **Bred** Shortgrove Manor Stud **Trained** Church Broughton , Derbys

FOCUS
Just ordinary handicap form but there were no excuses for the beaten horses and the favourite was beaten fair and square.

1502 #FOLLOWUS ON TWITTER @WOLVESRACES H'CAP 1m 141y (Tp)

9:10 (9:10) (Class 5) (0-70,70) 4-Y-O+ **£3,040** (£904; £452; £226) **Stalls** Low

Form RPR
204- **1** **Qaffaal (USA)**[173] 7514 5-9-0 63................................... GrahamGibbons 4 75+
(Michael Easterby) *a.p: nt clr run over 1f out: rdn to ld wl ins fnl f: r.o* **6/1**[3]
2 *2* **Pick Your Battle**[64] 552 4-9-2 65.................................(t) RoystonFfrench 7 71
(Iain Jardine) *chsd ldrs: rdn and nt clr run over 1f out: ev ch ins fnl f: styd on same pce* **7/1**
002- **3** *½* **Overlord**[156] 6937 4-8-8 57.. AndrewMullen 11 62
(Mark Rimell) *s.i.s: hld up: rdn over 1f out: r.o ins fnl f: nt rch ldrs* **25/1**
3-11 **4** *1¼* **Jumbo Prado (USA)**[40] 860 7-9-4 67..............................(b) JoeFanning 8 69
(Daniel Mark Loughnane) *sn led: hdd over 7f out: chsd ldrs: rdn to ld ins fnl f: sn hdd: styd on same pce* **5/1**[2]
0-00 **5** *shd* **All You (IRE)**[19] 1124 4-9-7 70...................................(v[1]) DanielTudhope 10 72
(David O'Meara) *chsd ldrs: led over 7f out tl hdd over 4f out: led again over 2f out: rdn and hdd ins fnl f: styd on same pce* **9/1**
0-62 **6** *2½* **Little Lord Nelson**[58] 621 4-9-2 65..............................(t) SaleemGolam 6 61
(Stuart Williams) *chsd ldrs: rdn and ev ch over 1f out: no ex ins fnl f* **9/2**[1]
5253 **7** *½* **Grey Destiny**[18] 1131 6-8-4 60.. MathewStill[(7)] 9 55
(Antony Brittain) *hld up: plld hrd: hdwy to chse ldr over 5f out: led over 4f out: rdn and hdd over 2f out: wknd ins fnl f* **11/1**
6330 **8** *4½* **Spirit Of Gondree (IRE)**[23] 1064 8-8-13 62.........(b) SilvestreDeSousa 2 46
(Milton Bradley) *hld up: rdn over 2f out: hung lft and eased ins fnl f* **12/1**
0000 **9** *nse* **Satchville Flyer**[23] 1064 5-8-6 58.................................. PhilipPrince[(3)] 3 42
(David Evans) *hld up: rdn over 3f out: wknd over 2f out* **40/1**
650- **10** *3½* **Inniscastle Lad**[175] 7464 4-8-11 67.............................. HarryBurns[(7)] 1 43
(Ed Dunlop) *hld up: rdn and wknd over 2f out* **7/1**
-604 **11** *5* **Marmalad (IRE)**[53] 683 4-8-13 67..............................(b) LucyKBarry[(5)] 5 32
(Shaun Lycett) *prom: rdn over 2f out: sn wknd* **17/2**

1m 47.54s (-2.56) **Going Correction** -0.15s/f (Stan) **11** Ran SP% **117.0**
Speed ratings (Par 103): **105,103,102,101,101 99,98,94,94,91 87**
CSF £47.42 CT £1000.48 TOTE £4.80: £1.10, £3.50, £4.80; EX 54.80 Trifecta £1423.00.
Owner Calam & Holdsworth & M Burrows **Bred** Shadwell Farm LLC **Trained** Sheriff Hutton, N Yorks

FOCUS
A wide open handicap.
T/Plt: £158.00 to a £1 stake. Pool of £80792.27 - 373.11 winning tickets. T/Qpdt: £5.80 to a £1 stake. Pool of £10747.21 - 1364.42 winning tickets. **Colin Roberts**

1503 - 1506a (Foreign Racing) - See Raceform Interactive

NAVAN (L-H)

Sunday, April 17

OFFICIAL GOING: Soft to heavy

1507a IRISH STALLION FARMS EUROPEAN BREEDERS FUND SALSABIL STKS (LISTED RACE) (FILLIES) 1m 2f

3:05 (3:05) 3-Y-O

£23,860 (£7,683; £3,639; £1,617; £808; £404)

RPR
1 **Pretty Perfect (IRE)**[175] 7488 3-9-0 95.................... ColmO'Donoghue 2 106+
(A P O'Brien, Ire) *mde all: stl gng wl 3f out: rdn and pressed clly under 2f out: kpt on wl to assert ins fnl f where extended advantage* **9/1**
2 *3½* **Glamorous Approach (IRE)**[28] 1016 3-9-3 98............ KevinManning 6 102
(J S Bolger, Ire) *sn settled in 2nd: niggled along 3f out: sn rdn in cl 2nd and pressed wnr under 2f out: no imp on wnr ins fnl f: kpt on same pce* **7/1**
3 *8½* **Emergent**[193] 7049 3-9-0 0... PatSmullen 1 82+
(D K Weld, Ire) *sn settled bhd ldrs in 3rd: lost pl and pushed along in 4th under 3f out: rdn into 3rd fr 2f out and no imp on ldrs u.p in mod 3rd over 1f out: kpt on one pce ins fnl f* **7/1**
4 *1½* **Best In The World (IRE)**[189] 7150 3-9-3 99................ RyanMoore 4 82+
(A P O'Brien, Ire) *hld up: rdn in 5th over 2f out and no imp on ldrs in mod 4th over 1f out: kpt on one pce ins fnl f* **4/1**[2]

5 *1* **Queen Blossom (IRE)**28 1016 3-9-3 107 FMBerry 3 80+
(P J Prendergast, Ire) *chsd ldrs: clsr in 3rd under 3f out: sn rdn and no imp on ldrs 1 1/2f out where dropped to mod 5th: dropped to rr ins fnl f tl kpt on one pce clsng stages into mod 5th* **6/4**1
6 *3/4* **Kind Of Magic (IRE)**203 6791 3-9-3 100 SeamieHeffernan 5 79+
(A P O'Brien, Ire) *w.w: rdn in rr over 2f out and no imp on ldrs: wnt mod 5th briefly ins fnl f: one pce clsng stages where dropped to rr* **5/1**3
2m 20.47s (4.67) **6** Ran SP% **111.7**
CSF £65.65 TOTE £9.50: £4.30, £2.00; DF 68.20 Trifecta £297.30.
Owner Michael Tabor & Derrick Smith & Mrs John Magnier **Bred** Milanova Syndicate **Trained** Cashel, Co Tipperary

FOCUS
This worked out to be one of the most informative early-season contests last year, as Bocca Baciata beat subsequent Irish 1,000 Guineas winner Pleascach and Diamondsandrubies, who went on to win at Group 1 level too in the Pretty Polly Stakes. This looked a strong line-up beforehand but both \bEmergent\p and \bBest In The World\p were extremely weak in the market, suggesting there were not quite ready for their reappearances. The winner made all, continuing the trend of the afternoon, and won decisively. The runner-up helps with the standard.

1509a HERITAGE STKS (LISTED RACE) 1m
4:15 (4:15) 4-Y-O+
£20,606 (£6,636; £3,143; £1,397; £698; £349)

RPR
1 **Lily's Rainbow (IRE)**28 1018 4-9-0 89 BillyLee 3 103
(Mrs Denise Foster, Ire) *cl up and led after 1f: narrow advantage at 1/2-way: stl travelling wl and extended ld fr 3f out: rdn 1 1/2f out and styd on strly ins fnl f: comf* **16/1**
2 *3 1/4* **Brendan Brackan (IRE)**183 7301 7-9-8 105 ColinKeane 2 104
(G M Lyons, Ire) *led narrowly tl hdd after 1f: 5th 1/2-way: rdn into 2nd under 2f out and sn no imp on easy wnr: kpt on same pce ins fnl f* **8/1**
3 *4 1/2* **Flight Risk (IRE)**14 1226 5-9-5 106 KevinManning 1 91+
(J S Bolger, Ire) *chsd ldrs: 3rd 1/2-way: rdn in 3rd under 2f out and no imp on easy wnr over 1f out: kpt on one pce ins fnl f* **9/2**3
4 *nk* **Onenightidreamed (IRE)**14 1226 5-9-10 108 (p) WayneLordan 4 95+
(T Stack, Ire) *chsd ldrs: short of room between horses after 2f and dropped to 6th: disp 6th at 1/2-way: rdn in 7th under 3f out and clsd u.p into mod 4th ins fnl f: nvr trbld ldrs* **9/4**1
5 *1 3/4* **Mohaayed**28 1018 4-9-5 101 ChrisHayes 8 86+
(Kevin Prendergast, Ire) *hld up in tch: rdn in 6th fr 3f out and no imp on easy wnr u.p in 5th ins fnl f: kpt on one pce* **7/1**
6 *2 1/2* **Ibergman (IRE)**28 1018 4-9-0 81 RonanWhelan 5 75+
(Ms Sheila Lavery, Ire) *hld up: last at 1/2-way: rdn in 8th under 3f out and no imp: n.m.r on inner u.p in 8th ent fnl f: kpt on one pce into mod 6th* **33/1**
7 *3 1/2* **Joailliere (IRE)**14 1226 4-9-0 99 PatSmullen 7 67+
(D K Weld, Ire) *chsd ldrs: 4th 1/2-way: gng wl bhd ldrs under 3f out: rdn under 2f out and sn no ex u.p in 4th: wknd and eased ins fnl f* **11/4**2
8 *4 1/2* **Dragon Fei (IRE)**14 1227 6-9-0 90 LeighRoche 9 57+
(Dermot Anthony McLoughlin, Ire) *chsd ldrs and wnt 2nd after 2f: cl 2nd at 1/2-way: rdn under 3f out and sn no imp on easy wnr: wknd 1 1/2f out: eased ins fnl f* **33/1**
9 *2 1/2* **Jeremys Joy (IRE)**11 1282 4-9-0 80 GaryCarroll 6 51+
(Emmet Michael Butterly, Ire) *sltly awkward s: w.w: disp 6th at 1/2-way: rdn in rr 3f out and no imp: one pce fnl 2f* **14/1**
1m 49.01s (2.71) **9** Ran SP% **117.7**
CSF £139.46 TOTE £15.30: £3.40, £3.10, £2.00; DF 111.50 Trifecta £768.30.
Owner Mrs Ian Fox **Bred** Ardrums House Stud **Trained** Enfield, Co Meath

FOCUS
This was transferred from a waterlogged Cork. It looked a strong renewal beforehand with four of the field boasting three-figure ratings. The winner was a surprise one but he won with real authority. A big pb from her.

1508 - 1512a (Foreign Racing) - See Raceform Interactive

COLOGNE (R-H)
Sunday, April 17

OFFICIAL GOING: Turf: good

1513a KARIN BARONIN VON ULLMANN - SCHWARZGOLD-RENNEN (GROUP 3) (3YO FILLIES) (TURF) 1m
3:40 (12:00) 3-Y-O **£23,529** (£8,823; £4,411; £2,205; £1,470)

RPR
1 **Parvaneh (IRE)**161 7768 3-9-2 0 MarcLerner 10 101+
(Waldemar Hickst, Germany) *w.w in rr: rdn and began to pick up on outer 2f out: stl 9th but styng on over 1f out: r.o u.p fnl f: led cl home* **8/1**
2 *1/2* **La Merced (GER)**176 3-9-2 0 (b) AndraschStarke 5 100
(P Schiergen, Germany) *a in tch: 5th and rdn 3f out: styd on u.p fr wl over 1 1/2f out: led fnl 100yds: hdd cl home: no ex* **36/5**3
3 *1/2* **Dhaba (GER)**182 7323 3-9-2 0 AdriedeVries 8 99+
(Markus Klug, Germany) *t.k.h: hld up in midfield: outpcd and dropped towards rr after 1/2-way: rdn to cl 2f out: styd on u.p fnl f: nvr nrr* **2/1**2
4 *1 1/4* **Tickle Me Blue (GER)**155 3-9-2 0 MartinSeidl 7 96+
(Markus Klug, Germany) *w.w in midfield on outer: rdn and sltly outpcd over 2f out: styd on fnl f: nt pce to get on terms* **176/10**
5 *1/2* **Double Dream (FR)**20 3-9-2 0 EduardoPedroza 2 95
(A Wohler, Germany) *a cl up: rdn to ld 2f out: u.str.p and looked vulnerable ins fnl f: hdd last 100yds and qckly swamped* **9/5**1
6 *2 3/4* **Bastille (GER)**22 3-9-2 0 DanielePorcu 6 89
(P Schiergen, Germany) *w.w towards rr: rdn and effrt 2 1/2f out: kpt on fr over 1f out: nvr on terms* **30/1**
7 *2 1/4* **Whole Lotta Rosie (GER)**204 3-9-2 0 StephenHellyn 9 83
(M Rulec, Germany) *sn led: rdn whn pressed 2 1/2f out: hdd 2f out: sn wknd* **217/10**
8 *2* **Dynamic Lips (IRE)** 3-9-2 0 AndreasHelfenbein 4 79
(Andreas Lowe, Germany) *cl up: rdn and outpcd 2f out: wknd fnl f* **77/10**
9 *1 3/4* **Donna Doria (GER)**175 3-9-2 0 AlexanderPietsch 1 75
(J Hirschberger, Germany) *t.k.h: hld towards rr: tk clsr order 3f out: sn rdn and no further imp: wknd appr fnl f* **206/10**
10 *38* **Quidura** 3-9-2 0 JozefBojko 3
(A Wohler, Germany) *w.w towards rr: rdn and no imp over 2f out: sn wknd and t.o* **106/10**
1m 36.98s (-1.41) **10** Ran SP% **130.1**
WIN (incl. 10 euro stake): 90. PLACES: 23, 20, 17. SF: 1,294.
Owner Darius Racing **Bred** Douglas Taylor **Trained** Germany

1514 - 1515a (Foreign Racing) - See Raceform Interactive

SAN SIRO (R-H)
Sunday, April 17

OFFICIAL GOING: Turf: good

1516a PREMIO AMBROSIANO (GROUP 3) (4YO+) (TURF) 1m 2f
4:05 (12:00) 4-Y-O+ **£21,691** (£9,544; £5,205; £2,602)

RPR
1 **Circus Couture (IRE)**161 7767 4-8-11 0 FabioBranca 2 110
(Stefano Botti, Italy) *settled 4th in indian file field: shkn up to cl fr under 3f out: led 2f out: drvn clr fnl f: won easing down* **5/6**1
2 *5* **Night Wish (GER)**31 6-8-11 0 FrederikTylicki 6 100
(Frau S Steinberg, Germany) *settled next to last: tk cl order 2 1/2f out: rdn to chse eventual wnr 1 1/2f out: kpt on u.p fnl f: no ch w wnr* **42/10**3
3 *hd* **Greg Pass (IRE)**301 4-8-11 0 DarioVargiu 3 100
(Il Cavallo In Testa, Italy) *w.w in 3rd: rdn and chsd ldr wl over 2f out: kpt on at one pce u.p fnl f: jst lost out in sustained dual for 2nd* **51/20**2
4 *1 3/4* **Loritania (IRE)**189 7157 4-8-10 0 SilvanoMulas 4 95
(Il Cavallo In Testa, Italy) *led: rdn and hdd 2f out: kpt on at one pce u.p* **51/20**2
5 *4* **Shocking Blu**28 4-8-11 0 (b) UmbertoRispoli 1 88
(Stefano Botti, Italy) *chsd ldr: rdn and nt qckn 2 1/2f out: sn wknd* **5/6**1
6 *3 1/2* **Cleo Fan (ITY)**14 5-8-11 0 CristianDemuro 5 81
(Stefano Botti, Italy) *w.w in last: rdn and shortlived effrt 2 1/2f out: wl hld ins fnl 2f* **51/20**2
(-6.70) **6** Ran SP% **212.8**
WIN (incl. 1 euro stake): 1.83. PLACES: 1.60, 2.40. DF: 9.61.
Owner Scuderia Effevi SRL **Bred** Azienda Agricola Marriano **Trained** Italy

LES LANDES
Sunday, April 17

OFFICIAL GOING: Turf: good
Wind: Moderate, against Weather: Cloudy early, sunny later

1517a JERSEY BOOKMAKERS H'CAP 5f 100y
3:10 (3:10) (0-65,0) 3-Y-O+ **£1,780** (£640; £380)

RPR
1 **Valmina**235 5733 9-10-12 0 NickSlatter 7 69
(Tony Carroll) *chsd ldrs: led over 1f out: sn clr* **2/1**1
2 *5* **Country Blue (FR)**230 7-10-6 0 (p) MattieBatchelor 1 46
(Mrs A Malzard, Jersey) *prom: led over 2f out tl over 1f out: sn btn* **5/2**2
3 *2* **Chester'slittlegem (IRE)**230 7-8-11 0 (p) NoraLooby 2 16
(Mrs A Corson, Jersey) *off the pce in 6th: hdwy 2f out: styd on* **7/1**
4 *2* **Hawaiian Freeze**245 7-9-10 0 ShaunPayne 6 23
(J Moon, Jersey) *chsd ldrs: led 3f out tl 2f out: sn outpcd* **16/1**
5 *hd* **Chapeau Bleu (IRE)**177 7440 4-10-10 0 EoinWalsh 8 36
(Mrs C Gilbert, Jersey) *s.s: wl bhd tl styd on fnl f* **9/1**
6 *1/2* **Brown Velvet**329 2540 4-10-9 0 MarkQuinlan 5 33
(Mrs A Malzard, Jersey) *in tch tl wknd 2f out* **10/1**
7 *1* **Purley Queen (IRE)**230 7-10-12 0 AliceMills 4 33
(Mrs C Gilbert, Jersey) *s.s: wl bhd tl styng on at fin* **3/1**3
8 *1/2* **Haadeeth**271 4489 9-10-11 0 PhilipPrince 3 31
(K Kukk, Jersey) *led tl over 2f out: sn wknd: bhd whn virtually p.u nr fin: lost both front shoes* **5/1**
Owner Mayden Stud **Bred** Mayden Stud, J A And D S Dewhurst **Trained** Cropthorne, Worcs

1518a DALLAS BURSTON GROUP 2016 JERSEY GUINEAS 1m 100y
3:40 (3:40) 3-Y-O+ **£2,380** (£860; £510)

RPR
1 **Pas D'Action**230 8-10-5 0 JemmaMarshall 5 54
(Mrs A Malzard, Jersey) *in tch: effrt on inner ent st and led wl over 1f out: rdn out* **5/1**3
2 *3* **Tax Reform (IRE)**25 1035 6-9-9 0 EoinWalsh 1 37
(Natalie Lloyd-Beavis) *towards rr: hdwy 2f out: r.o to take 2nd wl ins fnl f* **7/2**2
3 *shd* **First Cat**230 5963 9-10-5 0 PhilipPrince 3 47
(K Kukk, Jersey) *chsd ldrs on outer: led over 2f out: brought wd into st: hdd wl over 1f out: one pce fnl f* **7/2**2
4 *hd* **Benoordenhout (IRE)**329 2543 5-10-5 0 TimClark 4 46
(T Le Brocq, Jersey) *in tch: effrt 2f out: styd on fnl f* **8/1**
5 *12* **Eightfold**266 7-10-5 0 ShaunPayne 6 20
(Mrs A Corson, Jersey) *w ldrs tl wknd 2f out* **11/1**
6 *4* **Spring Dixie (IRE)**106 14 4-9-6 0 MattieBatchelor 7
(Mrs A Malzard, Jersey) *led tl over 2f out: sn wknd* **6/4**1
7 *4* **Engaging Smile**205 6721 4-10-2 0 MissMHooper 2
(J Moon, Jersey) *a in rr: no ch fnl 4f* **6/1**
Owner J Jamouneau **Bred** Jenny Hall Bloodstock Ltd **Trained** St Ouen, Jersey

1519a BLOODSTOCK ADVISORY SERVICES H'CAP 1m 1f
4:50 (4:53) (0-55,12) 3-Y-O+ **£1,780** (£640; £380)

RPR
1 **Grey Panel (FR)**266 4687 8-9-7 0 TimClark 6 45
(T Le Brocq, Jersey) *in tch: effrt 3f out: led over 1f out: rdn clr fnl f* **11/4**1
2 *4* **Captain James (FR)**230 5963 6-10-0 0 EoinWalsh 1 44
(Mrs C Gilbert, Jersey) *chsd ldrs: led 2f out tl over 1f out: one pce* **13/2**
3 *1/2* **Lucifers Shadow (IRE)**230 5963 7-10-4 0 (v) AliceMills 8 47
(Mrs C Gilbert, Jersey) *in tch: rdn to chse ldrs 2f out: one pce fnl f* **9/2**2
4 *2 1/2* **Ocean Crystal**230 5963 4-10-6 0 MarkQuinlan 2 44
(Mrs A Malzard, Jersey) *in tch: wnt prom 4f out: one pce appr fnl f* **15/2**
5 *2* **Fast Freddie**230 5963 12-9-1 0 (p) MissMHooper 5 21
(Mrs A Corson, Jersey) *led tl wknd 2f out* **9/1**
6 *1* **Lady Petrus**230 11-8-5 0 oh4 (p) PhilipPrince 7 8
(K Kukk, Jersey) *prom: lost pl 5f out and sn towards rr: styd on appr fnl f* **12/1**
7 *3* **Carrera**230 6-10-7 0 MattieBatchelor 9 32
(Mrs A Malzard, Jersey) *a mid-div: outpcd fnl 3f* **9/2**2
8 *3* **Wicked Tara**181 7351 6-10-2 12 ow12 ShaunPayne 3 21
(Natalie Lloyd-Beavis) *a towards rr* **11/2**3

9 ¾ **Larch (IRE)**[230] 5963 4-10-12 0 JemmaMarshall 4 29
(Mrs A Malzard, Jersey) *a bhd* **9/2**[2]
10 ½ **Frankki M**[230] 5963 6-8-5 0 oh13 (p) NoraLooby 10
(Mrs A Corson, Jersey) *hld up: rapid hdwy to join ldr 3f out: wknd 2f out* **10/1**

Owner The Le Brocq Boys **Bred** John Berry **Trained** Jersey

[1241] PONTEFRACT (L-H)

Monday, April 18

OFFICIAL GOING: Soft (6.4)
Wind: Strong behind Weather: Heavy cloud

1520 DOUGLAS BARRACLOUGH 80TH BIRTHDAY NOVICE STKS 5f

2:10 (2:11) (Class 5) 2-Y-O **£3,234** (£962; £481; £240) **Stalls** Low

Form RPR
6 **1** **Springwood (IRE)**[16] 1199 2-9-3 0 TonyHamilton 1 72
(Richard Fahey) *trckd ldrs: hdwy on inner 2f out: chsd ldr and swtchd rt over 1f out: rdn to chal jst ins fnl f: styd on wl to ld towards fin* **11/2**[3]
2 nk **Sidewinder (IRE)** 2-9-3 0 RichardKingscote 3 71
(Tom Dascombe) *hld up towards rr: hdwy on inner 2f out: sn trcking ldrs: effrt and n.m.r over 1f out: rdn to chal ins fnl f: led briefly ins last 100yds: hdd and no ex towards fin* **7/2**[2]
3 **3** 2 **Percy Toplis**[11] 1293 2-9-3 0 ShaneGray 6 64+
(Kevin Ryan) *prom: led after 2f: rdn over 1f out: sn jnd: drvn ent fnl f: hdd and no ex last 100yds* **7/2**[2]
5 **4** 1¼ **Absolutely Awesome**[16] 1199 2-9-3 0 JFEgan 5 60
(Deborah Sanderson) *trckd ldrs: pushed along over 2f out: hdwy wl over 1f out: rdn and edgd lft jst over 1f out: n.m.r and drvn ins fnl f: kpt on same pce* **8/1**
5 16 **Trois Bon Amis (IRE)** 2-9-3 0 DavidAllan 8
(Tim Easterby) *cl up: rdn along over 2f out: wknd qckly wl over 1f out* **16/1**
6 1¼ **Queens Parade (IRE)** 2-8-7 0 PhilDennis(5) 2
(Sharon Watt) *sn outpcd and a bhd* **50/1**
7 14 **Sir Viktor (IRE)** 2-9-3 0 DougieCostello 4
(K R Burke) *dwlt: a bhd* **17/2**
4 **8** 20 **Dusker (USA)**[16] 1203 2-9-3 0 WilliamBuick 9 +
(Mark Johnston) *wnt bdly rt s: led: hdd after 2f: cl up on outer and sn pushed along: rdn over 2f out: sn wknd: bhd and eased fr wl over 1f out* **11/4**[1]

1m 9.61s (6.31) **Going Correction** +1.075s/f (Soft) **8** Ran SP% **116.0**
Speed ratings (Par 92): **92,91,88,86,60 58,36,4**
CSF £25.48 TOTE £7.10: £2.30, £1.40, £1.40; EX 28.40 Trifecta £117.80.
Owner Richard Fahey Ebor Racing Club Ltd **Bred** Con Marnane **Trained** Musley Bank, N Yorks

FOCUS
Following a dry night the going remained soft. This opening race was a maiden in all but name, even though it was open to previous winners. The winning time was 7.81sec outside standard and the leaders may have gone off too quick in the conditions, with the front four pulling miles clear of the rest.

1521 RUGBY LEAGUE EVENING ON MONDAY 6TH JUNE H'CAP (DIV I) 1m 4y

2:40 (2:40) (Class 4) (0-85,84) 4-Y-O+ **£5,175** (£1,540; £769; £384) **Stalls** Low

Form RPR
40-0 **1** **Spring Offensive (IRE)**[29] 1018 4-8-13 **83** AdamMcNamara(7) 4 92+
(Richard Fahey) *trckd ldrs: hdwy on outer over 2f out: led 1 1/2f out: rdn and hung bdly rt to stands' rail ins fnl f: styd on wl: uns rdr after line* **7/2**[2]
033- **2** 1½ **Terhaal (IRE)**[171] 7599 4-9-1 **78** DanielTudhope 1 83
(David O'Meara) *hld up in tch: hdwy 3f out: chsd ldrs wl over 1f out: rdn ent fnl f: kpt on* **11/4**[1]
001- **3** nk **Trinity Star (IRE)**[196] 6981 5-9-0 **77** PaulMulrennan 2 81
(Michael Dods) *hld up in rr: hdwy wl over 2f out: rdn over 1f out: kpt on fnl f* **6/1**
30-6 **4** ¾ **Memory Cloth**[4] 1445 9-8-13 **76** (p) JackGarritty 3 79
(Micky Hammond) *hld up: hdwy on inner wl over 2f out: chsd ldrs and n.m.r wl over 1f out: sn swtchd rt and rdn: kpt on fnl f* **16/1**
00-0 **5** hd **Purple Rock (IRE)**[15] 1215 4-9-3 **80** (t) GrahamGibbons 5 82
(Michael Easterby) *trckd ldrs: hdwy over 2f out: sn chsng ldr: rdn wl over 1f out: kpt on same pce fnl f* **25/1**
3-12 **6** 4 **Rocco's Delight**[6] 1403 4-9-2 **79** BenCurtis 6 72
(Brian Ellison) *towards rr: pushed along over 3f out: rdn 2f out: plugged on one pce* **4/1**[3]
134- **7** ¾ **Marsh Pride**[191] 7119 4-9-7 **84** PJMcDonald 10 75
(Ann Duffield) *led: jnd 1/2-way: rdn along over 2f out: hdd 1 1/2f out: sn wknd* **12/1**
000- **8** 10 **Ginger Jack**[133] 8141 9-9-5 **82** AndrewMullen 8 50
(Garry Moss) *chsd ldrs: rdn along 3f out: sn wknd* **20/1**
65-3 **9** 3¾ **Sophisticated Heir (IRE)**[19] 1152 6-9-0 **77** DougieCostello 7 37
(David Loughnane) *trckd ldr: cl up 1/2-way: rdn along over 2f out: sn wknd* **14/1**
005- **10** ¾ **Zeshov (IRE)**[180] 7388 5-8-10 **73** BarryMcHugh 9 31
(Rebecca Bastiman) *chsd ldrs: rdn along over 3f out: sn wknd* **50/1**

1m 52.48s (6.58) **Going Correction** +1.075s/f (Soft) **10** Ran SP% **114.0**
Speed ratings (Par 105): **110,108,108,107,107 103,102,92,88,88**
CSF £12.87 CT £54.30 TOTE £5.40: £1.90, £1.70, £1.60; EX 19.40 Trifecta £110.00.
Owner A Rhodes Haulage And P Timmins **Bred** J Hanly **Trained** Musley Bank, N Yorks

FOCUS
A fair handicap, but another race where the leaders went off too quick. Pbs from the first two.

1522 RIU PALACE MELONERAS H'CAP 6f

3:10 (3:11) (Class 2) (0-100,97) 4-Y-O+
£12,450 (£3,728; £1,864; £932; £466; £117) **Stalls** Low

Form RPR
40-0 **1** **Perfect Pasture**[15] 1218 6-9-2 **92** (v) JamesSullivan 2 105
(Michael Easterby) *hld up: hdwy on inner 3f out: swtchd rt and effrt over 2f out: led wl over 1f out: rdn clr appr fnl f: kpt on strly* **14/1**
30-3 **2** 4 **Ocean Sheridan (IRE)**[15] 1218 4-8-8 **84** ConnorBeasley 10 85
(Michael Dods) *trckd ldrs: hdwy wl over 2f out: rdn to chse wnr over 1f out: sn drvn and no imp* **8/1**
000- **3** 2¼ **The Hooded Claw (IRE)**[198] 6942 5-8-9 **85** DavidAllan 9 79
(Tim Easterby) *trckd ldr: hdwy and cl up over 2f out: led briefly wl over 1f out: sn rdn and hdd: drvn and one pce appr fnl f* **16/1**
551- **4** ½ **Avon Breeze**[182] 7343 7-8-10 **86** GeorgeChaloner 7 79
(Richard Whitaker) *chsd ldrs: rdn along 2f out: drvn and wknd over 1f out* **25/1**
050- **5** 4½ **Redvers (IRE)**[205] 6758 8-8-11 **87** (b) BarryMcHugh 5 66
(Noel Wilson) *hld up: hdwy wl over 2f out: rdn along wl over 1f out: plugged on: n.d* **40/1**
404- **6** 2 **Mukhayyam**[226] 6099 4-8-10 **91** RachelRichardson(5) 6 64
(Tim Easterby) *in rr tl sme late hdwy* **33/1**
045- **6** dht **Beardwood**[163] 7758 4-8-5 **84** SammyJoBell(3) 3 57
(Richard Fahey) *dwlt and bhd: rdn along wl over 2f out: sme late hdwy* **9/4**[1]
40-4 **8** 2 **Related**[23] 1090 6-9-7 **97** (b) MartinLane 1 64
(Paul Midgley) *led: rdn along and hdd 2f out: sn wknd* **6/1**[3]
34-0 **9** 1 **Ballymore Castle (IRE)**[15] 1218 4-9-4 **94** TonyHamilton 4 58
(Richard Fahey) *a towards rr* **5/1**[2]
000- **10** 33 **Red Pike (IRE)**[191] 7122 5-9-5 **95** TomEaves 8
(Bryan Smart) *dwlt: sn chsng ldrs: rdn along 3f out: sn wknd* **12/1**
00-4 **11** 1¼ **My Name Is Rio (IRE)**[15] 1218 6-8-11 **87** PaulMulrennan 11
(Michael Dods) *chsd ldrs: rdn along wl over 2f out: sn wknd* **6/1**[3]
30-0 **12** 4½ **Deauville Prince (FR)**[15] 1218 6-8-11 **87** (p) RichardKingscote 12
(Tom Dascombe) *racd wd: chsd ldrs: rdn along 3f out: sn wknd* **28/1**

1m 21.86s (4.96) **Going Correction** +1.075s/f (Soft) **12** Ran SP% **120.0**
Speed ratings (Par 109): **109,103,100,100,94 91,91,88,87,43 41,35**
CSF £118.81 CT £1847.88 TOTE £18.30: £4.90, £2.20, £4.60; EX 152.10 Trifecta £1967.90.
Owner S Hull, S Hollings & D Swales **Bred** Mrs Jean Turpin **Trained** Sheriff Hutton, N Yorks

FOCUS
A warm sprint handicap which has been won by some smart types in recent years, not least last-year's winner Out Do who has since been successful in Listed company, while the 2013 winner York Glory went on to land that year's Wokingham. With a few of the market leaders disappointing, the form of this year's renewal is hard to gauge, but the winner was impressive. He reproduced his past AW form.

1523 PONTEFRACT MARATHON H'CAP (ROUND 2 OF THE PONTEFRACT STAYERS CHAMPIONSHIP 2016) 2m 5f 122y

3:40 (3:40) (Class 5) (0-75,74) 4-Y-O+ **£3,234** (£962; £481; £240) **Stalls** Low

Form RPR
4 **1** **American Life (FR)**[13] 1244 9-8-4 **55** oh2 (vt) SammyJoBell(3) 2 63
(Sophie Leech) *in tch on inner: hdwy over 4f out: chsd ldr 2f out: rdn to ld over 1f out: drvn out* **9/2**[1]
30-3 **2** 1 **Madam Lilibet (IRE)**[13] 1244 7-8-11 **64** PhilDennis(5) 4 71
(Sharon Watt) *chsd ldrs: niggled along after 5f: pushed along 7f out: hdwy over 3f out: rdn to ld over 2f out: hdd over 1f out: sn drvn and kpt on u.p fnl f* **6/1**[2]
4/0- **3** 5 **Omid**[28] 4632 8-8-7 **55** oh9 (tp) JamesSullivan 10 58
(Kenneth Slack) *led: pushed along 4f out: rdn 3f out: hdd over 2f out: sn drvn and kpt on same pce* **6/1**[2]
00-0 **4** 8 **Roc De Prince**[34] 946 7-8-9 **57** [1] JoeFanning 5 52
(Keith Dalgleish) *trckd ldng pair on inner: chsd ldr 5f out: rdn along 3f out: drvn over 2f out and sn one pce* **14/1**
06-2 **5** 6 **Tuscan Gold**[13] 1244 9-9-11 **73** PJMcDonald 9 63
(Micky Hammond) *dwlt and in rr: hdwy 5f out: rdn along 3f out: plugged on one pce* **9/2**[1]
34-5 **6** 15 **Riptide**[13] 1244 10-9-6 **68** (v) DougieCostello 8 44
(Michael Scudamore) *chsd ldr: rdn along over 4f out: drvn 3f out: sn outpcd* **20/1**
550/ **7** 20 **Sign Manual**[53] 7193 7-9-12 **74** GrahamLee 3 32
(Donald McCain) *hld up in rr: hdwy over 4f out: rdn along to chse ldrs 3f out: sn drvn and wknd: bhd whn eased wl over 1f out* **8/1**[3]
02/- **8** 25 **Filatore (IRE)**[8] 7506 7-9-6 **68** (tp) MartinLane 6 4
(Bernard Llewellyn) *a in rr: rdn along over 7f out: bhd fnl 4f: eased over 2f out* **14/1**
-062 **9** 34 **Symbolist (IRE)**[21] 1121 4-8-7 **61** (v) AndrewMullen 7
(John Norton) *trckd ldrs: t.k.h and n.m.r after 1 1/2f: pushed along over 4f out: rdn over 3f out: sn wknd and bhd whn eased wl over 1f out* **17/2**
6-6P **10** 23 **Mr Snoozy**[17] 957 7-9-8 **70** (p) TomEaves 1
(Mark Walford) *chsd ldrs: rdn along on outer over 5f out: sn lost pl and bhd whn eased 2f out* **8/1**[3]

5m 24.21s (33.21) **Going Correction** +1.075s/f (Soft)
WFA 4 from 7yo+ 6lb **10** Ran SP% **115.8**
Speed ratings (Par 103): **82,81,79,76,74 69,62,52,40,32**
CSF £30.86 CT £163.38 TOTE £5.00: £1.80, £2.80, £2.20; EX 41.50 Trifecta £263.60.
Owner American Life Partnership **Bred** J Y Payet-Descombes **Trained** Elton, Gloucs

FOCUS
This famous marathon event was an even greater test of stamina than usual in the ground and even though they went a sensible pace in the conditions, they still finished well spread out. Four of these met over 2m2f here 13 days earlier and the 2-3-4-5 from there finished 5-2-1-6 here. The form is rated cautiously.

1524 MARY HIBBERT 80TH BIRTHDAY CELEBRATION MAIDEN STKS 6f

4:10 (4:12) (Class 5) 3-Y-O+ **£2,098** (£2,098; £481; £240) **Stalls** Low

Form RPR
1 **Agree (IRE)** 3-9-3 0 BenCurtis 11 82+
(Brian Ellison) *towards rr: gd hdwy on outer over 2f out: sn chal: green and reminders: led and edgd lft over 1f out: rdn clr ent fnl f: jnd on line* **16/1**
6- **1** dht **Brilliant Vanguard (IRE)**[268] 4654 3-9-3 0 PaulMulrennan 4 82+
(Kevin Ryan) *t.k.h: hld up towards rr: gd hdwy over 2f out: chsd ldrs on inner whn nt clr run over 1f out: sn swtchd rt to outer and rdn: styd on strly fnl f to join ldr on line* **7/1**
326- **3** 4 **Dance Alone**[185] 7253 3-9-3 73 GrahamLee 3 69
(Kevin Ryan) *trckd ldrs on inner: hdwy 3f out: chsd ldr 2f out: sn rdn: drvn and kpt on same pce fnl f* **2/1**[1]
000/ **4** ½ **Douglas Bank (IRE)**[640] 4382 4-10-0 0 (b[1]) JFEgan 2 71
(Roy Bowring) *led: rdn along over 2f out: drvn wl over 1f out: hdd over 1f out and kpt on same pce* **100/1**
6 **5** 3½ **Bit Of A Quirke**[15] 1216 3-9-3 0 JasonHart 1 56
(Mark Walford) *dwlt and in rr: hdwy over 2f out: sn rdn and kpt on: n.d* **66/1**
5- **6** 8 **Ss Vega**[175] 7516 3-8-12 0 PJMcDonald 6 26
(James Bethell) *towards rr tl sme late hdwy* **9/1**
332- **7** ¾ **Dacoity**[184] 7283 3-9-3 73 TonyHamilton 10 28
(Richard Fahey) *prom on outer: pushed along 3f out: rdn over 2f out: sn wknd* **4/1**[3]
0- **8** 7 **Bazula (IRE)**[225] 6133 3-9-3 0 DavidAllan 7 6
(Tim Easterby) *in rr: sme hdwy 2f out: sn rdn along and n.d* **33/1**

0 **9** *7* **Longroom**[22] 1111 4-10-0 0 BarryMcHugh 5
(Noel Wilson) *cl up: rdn along wl over 2f out: sn wknd* **100/1**

24 **10** *shd* **Intense Starlet (IRE)**[22] 1111 5-9-9 0 SamJames 9
(Marjorie Fife) *chsd ldrs: rdn along wl over 2f out: sn wknd* **16/1**

52- **11** *22* **Abaco Ridge**[163] 7752 3-8-12 0 FMBerry 8
(Ralph Beckett) *unruly bef s: wnt rt and awkward s: chsd ldrs to 1/2-way: sn wknd and bhd* **3/1**[2]

1m 25.1s (8.20) **Going Correction** +1.075s/f (Soft)
WFA 3 from 4yo+ 11lb **11** Ran SP% **119.0**
Speed ratings (Par 103): **88,88,82,82,77 66,65,56,47,46 17**
WIN: BV £3.90, Z £4.90; PL: BV £1.80, Z £2.90, DA £1.70; Exacta: BV/Z £53.30, Z/BV £48.10; CSF: BV/Z £55.49, Z/BV £62.02; Trifecta: BV/Z/DA £416.80, Z/BV/DA £303.40.
Owner J C G Chua & C K Ong **Bred** Frank Moynihan **Trained** Hambleton, N Yorks
Owner Mrs J A Martin **Bred** Tally-Ho Stud **Trained** Norton, N Yorks

FOCUS
A fair sprint maiden and the first two couldn't be separated by the judge.They should both do better than the bare form.

1525 SIMON BOWETT 70TH BIRTHDAY H'CAP 5f
4:45 (4:46) (Class 5) (0-70,69) 4-Y-O+ **£3,234** (£962; £481; £240) **Stalls** Low

Form RPR

6324 **1** **Captain Scooby**[2] 1481 10-9-1 **63** (b) JasonHart 6 69
(Richard Guest) *dwlt and towards rr: hdwy on inner 1/2-way: in tch whn swtchd rt to outer and rdn over 1f out: styd on strly fnl f: led nr fin* **11/1**

6-25 **2** *nk* **Taffetta**[6] 1402 4-9-4 **66** BarryMcHugh 1 71
(Tony Coyle) *trckd ldrs: hdwy over 2f out: chal over 1f out: rdn to ld ins fnl f: hdd and no ex nr fin* **3/1**[2]

60-5 **3** *3/4* **Henley**[26] 1046 4-9-3 **65** JoeFanning 7 67
(Tracy Waggott) *t.k.h: cl up: rdn to ld wl over 1f out: drvn and hdd ins fnl f: sn edgd lft and kpt on* **16/1**

-000 **4** *3/4* **Johnny B Goode (IRE)**[17] 1178 4-8-13 **68** AdamMcNamara[(7)] 2 68
(Richard Fahey) *in tch: hdwy 2f out: rdn to chse ldrs over 1f out: styng on whn n.m.r wl ins fnl f* **11/4**[1]

3353 **5** *3/4* **Danish Duke (IRE)**[12] 1254 5-9-0 **62** (p) JamesSullivan 3 59
(Ruth Carr) *chsd ldng pair: rdn along wl over 1f out: drvn and kpt on same pce fnl f* **7/2**[3]

44-0 **6** *9* **Groundworker (IRE)**[34] 942 5-9-7 **69** GrahamLee 5 34
(Paul Midgley) *chsd ldrs: rdn along over 2f out: sn wknd* **10/1**

020 **7** *4 1/2* **Fuel Injection**[10] 1319 5-8-7 **55** oh4 PJMcDonald 8 3
(Paul Midgley) *a towards rr* **14/1**

200- **8** *hd* **Henry Morgan**[203] 6815 9-8-8 **56** ow1 TomEaves 4 4
(David Brown) *slt ld: rdn along 2f out: sn hdd & wknd* **16/1**

420- **9** *13* **Poppy In The Wind**[193] 7057 4-9-0 **62** (v) PaulMulrennan 9
(Alan Brown) *a in rr: outpcd and bhd fnl 2f* **20/1**

1m 8.43s (5.13) **Going Correction** +1.075s/f (Soft) **9** Ran SP% **114.5**
Speed ratings (Par 103): **101,100,99,98,96 82,75,75,54**
CSF £43.74 CT £538.37 TOTE £7.10: £1.80, £2.50, £2.50; EX 37.40 Trifecta £220.70.
Owner The Captain Scooby Syndicate **Bred** Hellwood Stud Farm & Paul Davies (h'Gate) **Trained** Ingmanthorpe, W Yorks

FOCUS
A modest sprint handicap with a dramatic finish. Not much depth to it.

1526 RUGBY LEAGUE EVENING ON MONDAY 6TH JUNE H'CAP (DIV II) 1m 4y
5:15 (5:18) (Class 4) (0-85,84) 4-Y-O+ **£5,175** (£1,540; £769; £384) **Stalls** Low

Form RPR

00-0 **1** **Arcano Gold (IRE)**[15] 1221 4-9-2 **79** TonyHamilton 1 89
(Richard Fahey) *trckd ldng pair: hdwy on inner wl over 1f out: rdn to ld ins fnl f: styd on* **7/2**[1]

-241 **2** *1 1/2* **Sands Chorus**[13] 1241 4-8-13 **76** TomEaves 10 83
(James Given) *trckd ldr: hdwy and cl up 2f out: led 1 1/2f out: sn rdn: hdd and drvn ins fnl f: kpt on* **9/2**[2]

45/0 **3** *3 3/4* **Torrid**[21] 1122 5-9-0 **82** NathanEvans[(5)] 3 80+
(Michael Easterby) *hld up in rr: hdwy over 2f out: rdn along wl over 1f out: styd on fnl f* **12/1**

60-5 **4** *2 1/4* **Dark Ocean (IRE)**[21] 1122 6-9-7 **84** GrahamLee 7 77
(Jedd O'Keeffe) *trckd ldrs: hdwy on outer 2f out: sn rdn: drvn and no imp appr fnl f* **7/2**[1]

56-5 **5** *1 1/2* **Save The Bees**[10] 1317 8-8-9 **72** NeilFarley 4 62
(Declan Carroll) *chsd ldrs: rdn along 2f out: sn drvn and one pce* **20/1**

20-0 **6** *3 3/4* **Kiwi Bay**[21] 1122 11-8-13 **81** PhilDennis[(5)] 2 62
(Michael Dods) *t.k.h early: in tch on inner: effrt wl over 2f out: rdn along wl over 1f out: sn btn* **8/1**[3]

412- **7** *4 1/2* **Hickster (IRE)**[119] 8336 5-9-0 **77** (bt[1]) JFEgan 8 48
(Roy Bowring) *led: rdn along over 2f out: hdd 1 1/2f out: sn wknd* **16/1**

8 *2* **Tadaany (IRE)**[191] 7130 4-9-3 **80** DanielTudhope 5 46
(David O'Meara) *hld up: a towards rr* **7/2**[1]

06-0 **9** *13* **Homeland (IRE)**[15] 1221 4-9-2 **79** (t) JamesSullivan 9 15
(Brian Rothwell) *a in rr: outpcd and bhd fnl 2f* **33/1**

1m 52.93s (7.03) **Going Correction** +1.075s/f (Soft) **9** Ran SP% **117.2**
Speed ratings (Par 105): **107,105,101,99,98 94,89,87,74**
CSF £19.70 CT £172.00 TOTE £3.60: £1.40, £2.00, £3.10; EX 19.00 Trifecta £221.20.
Owner Middleham Park Racing XL & Partner **Bred** Trevor Reilly **Trained** Musley Bank, N Yorks

FOCUS
They didn't seem to go much of a pace in this race and the winning time was 0.45sec slower than the first division much earlier on the card. the winner is rated back to his 3yo best.
T/Jkpt: Not won. T/Plt: £454.30 to a £1 stake. Pool: £73,186.77 - 117.60 winning units. T/Qpdt: £117.20 to a £1 stake. Pool: £7,102.40 - 44.82 winning units. **Joe Rowntree**

1384 WINDSOR (R-H)
Monday, April 18

OFFICIAL GOING: Soft (heavy in places) changing to soft after race 2 (5.20)
Wind: virtually nil Weather: light cloud

1527 STARSPORTSBET.CO.UK NOVICE AUCTION FILLIES' STKS (PLUS 10 RACE) 5f 10y
4:50 (4:58) (Class 5) 2-Y-O **£2,911** (£866; £432; £216) **Stalls** Low

Form RPR

0 **1** **Fastnet Spin (IRE)**[23] 1086 2-9-0 0 CathyGannon 2 72
(David Evans) *in tch: sn lost pl and pushed along: drvn to chse ldrs and swtchd rt over 1f out: led ins fnl f: rn green and hung lft in front: kpt on and asserted towards fin* **4/1**[3]

2 *1 1/4* **Zig Zag Girl** 2-8-10 0 CharlesBishop 1 63
(Mick Channon) *in tch in rr: swtchd lft and hdwy to chse ldrs 2f out: rdn and ev ch over 1f out: carried lft and styd on same pce ins fnl f* **2/1**[1]

3 *nk* **Ocean Temptress** 2-8-8 0 DannyBrock[(3)] 6 63
(John Ryan) *uns rdr and galloped off a f bef s: dwlt: sn rcvrd and in tch: chal 2f out: sn rdn to ld: hdd and carried lft ins fnl f: no ex fnl 50yds* **5/1**

4 *6* **Crystal Secret** 2-8-10 0 WilliamCarson 4 40
(John Bridger) *dwlt: in tch: rdn 2f out: outpcd over 1f out: wknd fnl f* **14/1**

5 *1* **She's Rosanna** 2-8-10 0 AdamBeschizza 5 37
(Steph Hollinshead) *dwlt: rn green and hung lft thrght: in tch in midfield: rdn 2f out: wknd fnl f* **15/2**

5 **6** *1/2* **To Have A Dream (IRE)**[23] 1087 2-8-10 0 MartinDwyer 3 35
(J S Moore) *led: rdn and hdd over 1f out: sn btn: wknd fnl f* **5/2**[2]

1m 4.78s (4.48) **Going Correction** +0.525s/f (Yiel) **6** Ran SP% **117.0**
Speed ratings (Par 89): **85,83,82,72,71 70**
CSF £13.15 TOTE £4.80: £1.70, £2.10; EX 14.50 Trifecta £61.70.
Owner Dukes Head Racing **Bred** Rockhart Trading Ltd **Trained** Pandy, Monmouths

FOCUS
The going was given as soft, heavy in places (GoingStick: 5.0). The rail on the inner of the straight was at its normal inner configuration, so the straight was at its maximum width. The top bend was dolled out 4yds from its normal inner configuration, adding 14yds to race distances of 1m plus. Just an ordinary maiden, rated below the usual race average.

1528 ROYAL WINDSOR HORSE SHOW H'CAP 5f 10y
5:20 (5:21) (Class 4) (0-85,85) 4-Y-O+ **£4,690** (£1,395; £697; £348) **Stalls** Low

Form RPR

-060 **1** **Stake Acclaim (IRE)**[54] 694 4-9-7 **85** (p) RobertWinston 1 97
(Dean Ivory) *chsd ldr: rdn and chal over 1f out: led 1f out: in command fnl 100yds: r.o wl* **3/1**[2]

3112 **2** *1 1/4* **Elusivity (IRE)**[26] 1046 8-8-9 **73** (p) LiamKeniry 5 80
(Conor Dore) *led: rdn 2f out: hdd 1f out: no ex u.p and styd on same pce after* **10/1**[3]

000- **3** *1/2* **Majestic Hero (IRE)**[166] 7710 4-8-13 **77** DavidProbert 7 82
(Ronald Harris) *chsd ldrs: rdn 2f out: unable qck u.p over 1f out: kpt on same pce ins fnl f* **10/1**[3]

3442 **4** *1* **Jaarih (IRE)**[22] 1110 4-8-9 **73** (p) OisinMurphy 8 75
(Conor Dore) *in tch in midfield: effrt u.p over 1f out: chsd ldng trio and kpt on same pce ins fnl f* **16/1**

66-2 **5** *nk* **Dominate**[4] 1447 6-8-10 **77** (v) TomMarquand[(3)] 11 78
(George Scott) *in tch in midfield: drvn and unable qck over 1f out: 5th and kpt on same pce ins fnl f* **2/1**[1]

-604 **6** *1/2* **Midnight Rider (IRE)**[10] 1318 8-8-11 **80** JordanVaughan[(5)] 3 79
(Rod Millman) *dwlt: in rr: effrt u.p over 1f out: styd on wl ins fnl f: nvr trbld ldrs* **12/1**

000 **7** *1* **Air Of York (IRE)**[37] 923 4-9-0 **81** PhilipPrince[(3)] 12 76
(David Evans) *awkward leaving stalls: in rr: effrt u.p 2f out: sme hdwy 1f out: styd on same pce ins fnl f* **33/1**

20-0 **8** *nk* **Ginzan**[10] 1321 8-8-12 **76** MartinDwyer 6 70
(Malcolm Saunders) *towards rr: rdn over 2f out: sme prog over 1f out: kpt on ins fnl f: nvr threatened ldrs* **20/1**

1562 **9** *3/4* **Borough Boy (IRE)**[34] 938 6-9-2 **80** (v) AdamBeschizza 4 71
(Derek Shaw) *stdd s: hld up in midfield: drvn 2f out: sme prog 1f out: styd on same pce ins fnl f: nvr trbld ldrs* **20/1**

440- **10** *1 1/2* **Tagula Night (IRE)**[182] 7342 10-9-3 **84** (tp) JackDuern[(3)] 2 70
(Dean Ivory) *in tch in midfield: rdn and unable qck over 1f out: wknd ins fnl f* **25/1**

-000 **11** *2 1/4* **Dark Side Dream**[17] 1175 4-8-2 **71** JosephineGordon[(5)] 9 49
(Chris Dwyer) *in tch in midfield: rdn 2f out: unable qck and btn over 1f out: wknd ins fnl f* **25/1**

10-0 **12** *2 1/4* **Keep It Dark**[108] 4 7-9-2 **80** (t) GeorgeBaker 10 50
(William Knight) *sn bhd: n.d* **10/1**[3]

1m 2.17s (1.87) **Going Correction** +0.525s/f (Yiel) **12** Ran SP% **119.3**
Speed ratings (Par 105): **106,104,103,101,101 100,98,98,97,94 91,87**
CSF £30.37 CT £276.21 TOTE £4.70: £1.90, £2.50, £3.40; EX 36.10 Trifecta £260.40.
Owner M J Yarrow **Bred** G Devlin **Trained** Radlett, Herts

FOCUS
The principals were towards the fore throughout and those held up struggled to land a blow. The winner is progressive on turf.

1529 CALL STAR SPORTS ON 0800 521 321 MAIDEN STKS 1m 2f 7y
5:50 (5:50) (Class 5) 3-Y-O+ **£2,911** (£866; £432; £216) **Stalls** Centre

Form RPR

022- **1** **Baadi**[320] 2837 4-10-0 82 AndreaAtzeni 10 84+
(Charlie Fellowes) *chsd ldrs tl led after 2f: gng best 2f out: sn pushed clr and in command: easily* **2/5**[1]

3 **2** *5* **Hold Hands**[19] 1140 5-9-9 0 JimCrowley 8 67
(Brendan Powell) *led for 2f: chsd wnr after 2f out: rdn over 2f out: unable qck u.p and btn 1f out: wknd ins fnl f* **6/1**[3]

3 *hd* **Ceyhan** 4-10-0 0 OisinMurphy 6 72+
(Joseph Tuite) *s.i.s: hld up in tch towards rr: hdwy to chse ldrs 4f out: rdn and outpcd over 2f out: no ch w wnr but kpt on steadily fnl f* **5/1**[2]

05 **4** *1 3/4* **Owners Day**[10] 1324 6-9-9 0 LiamKeniry 7 63
(Neil Mulholland) *chsd ldrs: rdn and outpcd over 2f out: 4th and kpt on same pce ins fnl f* **33/1**

56 **5** *1/2* **Earthwindorfire**[19] 1140 5-10-0 0 TimmyMurphy 12 67
(Geoffrey Deacon) *hld up in tch in midfield: 7th and pushed along over 2f out: no imp tl styd on steadily ins fnl f: no threat to wnr* **10/1**

6 *3 1/4* **Persaverance** 3-8-11 0 PatDobbs 2 58
(Gary Moore) *in tch in midfield: effrt in 5th over 2f out: no imp: plugged on* **12/1**

0 **7** *3 1/2* **Away In May**[20] 1132 5-9-9 0 CathyGannon 11 49
(John Spearing) *t.k.h: chsd ldrs: grad stdd bk and in last pair 1/2-way: effrt into midfield over 3f out: no threat to wnr and plugged on same pce fnl 2f* **40/1**

00- **8** *26* **Sunny Monday**[195] 7025 4-10-0 0 (p) TomQueally 4
(Emma Owen) *chsd ldrs: rdn 4f out: lost pl 3f out: sn wl btn: t.o over 1f out* **50/1**

0 **9** *1 1/4* **Kestrel Dot Com**[19] 1151 4-10-0 0 IrineuGoncalves 5
(Chris Dwyer) *a towards rr: pushed along 1/2-way: lost tch 3f out: t.o over 1f out* **50/1**

0 **10** *52* **Emerald Petrina (IRE)**[17] 1179 4-9-9 0 DavidProbert 1
(Heather Main) *in tch in midfield: rdn 4f out: sn lost pl: t.o fnl 2f* **66/1**

2m 16.06s (7.36) **Going Correction** +0.725s/f (Yiel)
WFA 3 from 4yo+ 17lb **10** Ran SP% **130.0**
Speed ratings (Par 103): **99,95,94,93,93 90,87,66,65,24**
CSF £4.27 TOTE £1.50: £1.10, £2.20, £1.60; EX 7.20 Trifecta £15.60.
Owner Saleh Al Homaizi & Imad Al Sagar **Bred** Saleh Al Homaizi & Imad Al Sagar **Trained** Newmarket, Suffolk

FOCUS
Race distance increased by 14yds. A pretty weak maiden won fairly comfortably by the odds-on favourite, who is rated to form.

1530 5 STAR GALLOP H'CAP 6f
6:20 (6:21) (Class 3) (0-90,87) 4-Y-O+ **£7,439** (£2,213; £1,106; £553) **Stalls** Low

Form RPR

00-0 **1** **Englishman**^{15} 1218 6-9-2 **82** FrannyNorton 5 92
(Milton Bradley) *trckd ldrs wnt 2nd 2f out: effrt and hung lft over 1f out: sn rdn and ev ch: led ins fnl f: r.o wl* **7/1**

105- **2** *3/4* **Ice Lord (IRE)**^{223} 6185 4-9-6 **86** JohnFahy 1 94+
(Clive Cox) *chsd ldrs: styd towards stands' side over 2f out: drvn and pressing ldrs over 1f out: kpt on fnl 100yds: wnt 2nd towards fin* **7/2**^{2}

605- **3** *1/2* **Links Drive Lady**^{163} 7755 8-9-2 **85** JackDuern$^{(3)}$ 10 91
(Dean Ivory) *s.i.s: hld up in rr: hdwy 1/2-way: rdn to ld over 1f out: hdd ins fnl f: styd on same pce fnl 100yds: lost 2nd towards fin* **16/1**

0003 **4** *2 1/4* **Captain Lars (SAF)**^{15} 1215 6-8-5 **76** (p) CallumShepherd$^{(5)}$ 8 75
(Derek Shaw) *wnt rt s: in tch in midfield: effrt and hdwy over 1f out: kpt on same pce ins fnl f* **16/1**

00-0 **5** *nse* **Kinglami**^{15} 1218 7-9-5 **85** (p) DarryllHolland 9 84
(John O'Shea) *in tch in midfield: rdn 1/2-way: outpcd and drifted rt over 1f out: styd on same pce ins fnl f* **16/1**

-165 **6** *1/2* **Heartsong (IRE)**^{17} 1178 7-8-11 **80** MichaelJMMurphy$^{(3)}$ 11 77
(John Gallagher) *chsd ldr tl led 1/2-way: rdn and hdd over 1f out: no ex u.p and wknd ins fnl f* **16/1**

40-5 **7** *1* **Captain Bob (IRE)**^{10} 1318 5-9-3 **83** AdamBeschizza 3 77
(Robert Cowell) *hld up in tch towards rr: effrt and nt clr run 2f out: swtchd lft and effrt over 1f out: kpt on ins fnl f: nvr threatened ldrs* **14/1**

00-0 **8** *1 1/4* **Crew Cut (IRE)**^{15} 1215 8-8-12 **78** SaleemGolam 2 68
(Stuart Williams) *hld up in tch in midfield: effrt over 1f out: no imp: plugged on same pce ins fnl f* **50/1**

00-6 **9** *nse* **Navigate (IRE)**^{15} 1218 4-9-7 **87** DavidProbert 6 77
(Martyn Meade) *hld up in tch in midfield: effrt 2f out: no imp and sltly hmpd over 1f out: wl btn fnl f* **11/4**^{1}

1-2 **10** *9* **Flowers On Venus (IRE)**^{64} 580 4-9-4 **84** CathyGannon 4 45
(David Evans) *led tl 1/2-way: rdn and little rspnse 2f out: lost pl over 1f out: sn wknd* **4/1**^{3}

3362 **11** *10* **Chelwood Gate (IRE)**^{17} 1173 6-8-8 **74** (v) OisinMurphy 7 3
(Patrick Chamings) *short of room and dropped to rr sn after s: nvr gng wl in rr: lost tch over 1f out* **25/1**

1m 16.14s (3.14) **Going Correction** +0.70s/f (Yiel) **11** Ran SP% **117.4**
Speed ratings (Par 107): **107,106,105,102,102 101,100,98,98,86 73**
CSF £31.61 CT £392.16 TOTE £8.10: £2.30, £1.50, £4.60; EX 38.00 Trifecta £600.20.
Owner E A Hayward **Bred** Peter Winkworth **Trained** Sedbury, Gloucs

FOCUS
The first three came a little way clear in this sprint handicap. The winner built on his latest effort.

1531 FIRSTCO H'CAP 1m 3f 135y
6:50 (6:50) (Class 4) (0-85,85) 4-Y-O+ **£4,690** (£1,395; £697; £348) **Stalls** Centre

Form RPR

-500 **1** **Moojaned (IRE)**^{14} 1236 5-8-7 **74** PhilipPrince$^{(3)}$ 2 84
(David Evans) *mde all: rdn clr 3f out: clsd down ins fnl f but nvr gng to get ct: rdn out* **10/1**

300/ **2** *1 1/2* **Allnecessaryforce (FR)**^{147} 7734 6-8-8 **72** AdamBeschizza 5 79
(Alex Hales) *in tch in last pair: rdn and hdwy over 3f out: chsd clr wnr 2f out: swtchd rt and battled on u.p: clsng on wnr fnl 100yds but nvr a serious threat* **12/1**

-054 **3** *10* **Brandon Castle**^{18} 1166 4-8-13 **78** DavidProbert 3 69
(Andrew Balding) *stdd s: hld up in rr: clsd and nt clr run 3f out: sn swtchd rt and outpcd u.p: no ch w wnr over 1f out: wnt modest 3rd and plugged on same pce fnl f* **11/4**^{1}

245- **4** *1 3/4* **Starwatch**^{196} 6988 9-9-7 **85** (v) WilliamCarson 6 73
(John Bridger) *chsd wnr: rdn 3f out: sn outpcd and wl btn whn lost 2nd 2f out: wknd over 1f out* **10/1**

611- **5** *5* **Goldslinger (FR)**^{145} 6743 4-8-13 **78** RobertWinston 4 57
(Dean Ivory) *chsd ldng pair: rdn 4f out: sn struggling: 5th and wl btn 2f out: wknd* **11/4**^{1}

000- **6** *22* **Pilgrims Rest (IRE)**^{126} 5938 7-9-3 **81** (t) SteveDrowne 7 24
(George Baker) *hld up in tch: rdn over 4f out: sn struggling and wknd 3f out: t.o* **9/1**^{3}

311- **7** *53* **Dolphin Village (IRE)**^{120} 8319 6-8-12 **79** DannyBrock$^{(3)}$ 1
(Jane Chapple-Hyam) *dwlt and bustled along early: hdwy into midfield 8f out: rdn and lost pl over 4f out: lost tch 3f out: t.o eased over 1f out* **7/2**^{2}

2m 36.24s (6.74) **Going Correction** +0.725s/f (Yiel)
WFA 4 from 5yo+ 1lb **7** Ran SP% **111.4**
Speed ratings (Par 105): **106,105,98,97,93 79,43**
CSF £109.91 TOTE £10.20: £5.50, £6.50; EX 90.70 Trifecta £315.80.
Owner Robert Emmanuel **Bred** Shadwell Estate Company Limited **Trained** Pandy, Monmouths

FOCUS
Race distance increased by 14yds. The winner made this a proper test and the first two finished clear.

1532 BROWNS & ALL BAR ONE WINDSOR H'CAP 1m 3f 135y
7:20 (7:21) (Class 5) (0-75,75) 3-Y-O **£2,911** (£866; £432; £216) **Stalls** Centre

Form RPR

-216 **1** **Cat Royale (IRE)**^{17} 1185 3-9-1 **72** (p) DannyBrock$^{(3)}$ 7 78
(Jane Chapple-Hyam) *led tl 7f out: trckd ldrs after: clsd to press ldr over 2f out: rdn to ld over 1f out: urged along and wandered rt ins fnl f: a doing enough: kpt on* **11/2**^{3}

062- **2** *1 1/2* **Argyle (IRE)**^{196} 6977 3-9-0 **68** MartinDwyer 1 71
(William Muir) *chsd ldr tl led 7f out: rdn over 2f out: hdd over 1f out: kpt battling on u.p but a hld ins fnl f* **11/4**^{1}

6-1 **3** *3 1/2* **October Storm**^{26} 1037 3-9-7 **75** GeorgeBaker 2 72+
(Mick Channon) *hld up in tch in rr: shkn up 4f out: sn rdn and outpcd: wl btn 5th over 1f out: styd on 1f out to pass btn horses ins fnl f: wnt 3rd fnl 100yds: no threat to wnr* **11/4**^{1}

3-16 **4** *1 1/4* **Epsom Day (IRE)**^{52} 729 3-9-7 **75** (b) TomQueally 4 70
(John Gosden) *chsd ldrs: wnt 2nd 7f out tl over 2f out: sn drvn and outpcd: 3rd and wl hld over 1f out: plugged on same pce and lost 3rd ins fnl f* **7/2**^{2}

-643 **5** *nse* **Howardian Hills (IRE)**^{26} 1037 3-8-12 **66** PatDobbs 6 61
(Richard Hannon) *in tch: cl 4th and rdn over 2f out: sn outpcd: 4th and wl hld whn drifted lft over 1f out: plugged on* **7/1**

030- **6** *19* **Provoking (USA)**^{171} 7605 3-9-1 **69** CathyGannon 3 32
(David Evans) *stdd s: t.k.h: hld up in tch: rdn over 4f out: sn struggling: lost tch over 2f out: t.o* **10/1**

2m 41.78s (12.28) **Going Correction** +0.725s/f (Yiel) **6** Ran SP% **112.5**
Speed ratings (Par 98): **88,87,84,83,83 71**
CSF £21.02 TOTE £7.20: £3.00, £2.10; EX 20.90 Trifecta £80.50.
Owner Bryan Hirst Ltd & S&G Refurbishments Ltd **Bred** Kellsgrange Stud & Ruskerne Ltd **Trained** Dalham, Suffolk

FOCUS
Race distance increased by 14yds. A modest handicap and muddling form. The winner is rated back to his early 2yo figures.

1533 CLIVEDEN HOUSE HOTEL H'CAP 6f
7:50 (7:52) (Class 6) (0-65,65) 4-Y-O+ **£2,264** (£673; £336; £168) **Stalls** Low

Form RPR

-636 **1** **Secret Look**^{11} 1299 6-8-13 **57** MartinDwyer 7 70
(Ed McMahon) *chsd ldrs tl led over 1f out: edging lft u.p 1f out: a doing enough ins fnl f: pushed out* **9/1**

31-0 **2** *1 1/4* **Posh Bounty**^{40} 873 5-9-3 **61** GeorgeBaker 14 70
(Joseph Tuite) *taken down early: in tch in midfield: effrt over 1f out: chsd wnr ent fnl f: kpt on u.p fnl 100yds but nvr enough pce to chal wnr* **13/2**^{2}

40U- **3** *3 1/2* **Foxford**^{181} 7365 5-8-9 **58** PaddyPilley$^{(5)}$ 10 57+
(Patrick Chamings) *broke wl: w ldr for 2f: styd prom: rdn and racd awkwardly u.p 2f out: outpcd 1f out: no threat to ldng pair and kpt on same pce ins fnl f* **25/1**

2543 **4** *nk* **For Ayman**^{12} 1261 5-8-12 **63** (t) SeanMooney$^{(7)}$ 15 61
(Joseph Tuite) *dwlt: hld up towards rr: hdwy 1/2-way rdn and effrt over 1f out: chsd ldrs and kpt on same pce ins fnl f* **9/1**

656 **5** *1 3/4* **Louis Vee (IRE)**^{17} 1180 8-8-6 **55** (p) CiaranMckee$^{(5)}$ 13 48
(John O'Shea) *nt that wl away: rcvrd and hdwy to chse ldr after 2f: rdn and ev ch 2f out tl outpcd and lost 2nd ent fnl f: wknd ins fnl f* **22/1**

-466 **6** *1/2* **Potternello (IRE)**^{9} 1334 4-9-6 **64** (v) CharlesBishop 4 55
(Mick Channon) *hld up towards rr: effrt and hdwy over 1f out: drvn and kpt on ins fnl f: nvr trbld ldrs* **6/1**^{1}

153- **7** *3/4* **Babyfact**^{183} 7312 5-9-3 **64** TomMarquand$^{(3)}$ 3 53
(Malcolm Saunders) *chsd ldrs: effrt u.p over 1f out: kpt on same pce ins fnl f: nvr trbld ldrs* **14/1**

346- **8** *3/4* **Mad Endeavour**^{255} 5104 5-9-2 **60** OisinMurphy 6 47
(Stuart Kittow) *dwlt: sn in tch in midfield: effrt 2f out swtchd lft and no imp over 1f out: plugged on same pce fnl f* **7/1**^{3}

2355 **9** *1* **Pharoh Jake**^{19} 1150 8-8-11 **55** WilliamCarson 2 39
(John Bridger) *chsd ldrs: led after 2f tl hdd over 1f out: sn lost pl u.p: wknd fnl f* **14/1**

0-56 **10** *6* **Catalinas Diamond (IRE)**^{12} 1261 8-9-4 **62** (t) SteveDrowne 8 28
(Pat Murphy) *bhd: effrt over 1f out: no imp: wknd ins fnl f* **25/1**

46-0 **11** *3/4* **Commanche**^{19} 1154 7-9-2 **65** (b) JosephineGordon$^{(5)}$ 16 28
(Chris Dwyer) *towards rr: rdn 1/2-way: no prog and wl btn over 1f out: wknd* **8/1**

3642 **12** *3 3/4* **Agerzam**^{12} 1264 6-9-7 **65** (b) RoystonFfrench 12 17
(Ronald Harris) *in tch in midfield tl lost pl over 2f out: sn btn and wknd u.p over 1f out* **25/1**

210- **13** *1* **Secret Bird (IRE)**^{195} 7018 4-9-5 **63** RobertWinston 11 12
(Dean Ivory) *stdd s: in tch in midfield: effrt 2f out: sn btn and wknd over 1f out* **13/2**^{2}

-050 **14** *7* **Mac's Power (IRE)**^{63} 590 10-8-13 **57** (t) TomQueally 9
(Willie Musson) *sn niggled along towards rr: effrt u.p 2f out: sn btn: wknd fnl f* **16/1**

2-20 **15** *2* **Copper Cavalier**^{26} 1042 5-8-10 **54** (b^{1}) DavidProbert 5
(Michael Blanshard) *led for 2f: sn rdn and lost pl 1/2-way: bhd over 1f out* **20/1**

00-6 **16** *10* **O Dee**^{33} 952 4-9-4 **62** (b^{1}) RenatoSouza 1
(Dean Ivory) *a towards rr: rdn 2f out: sn lost tch: t.o* **33/1**

1m 17.09s (4.09) **Going Correction** +0.70s/f (Yiel) **16** Ran SP% **127.4**
Speed ratings (Par 101): **100,98,93,93,90 90,89,88,86,78 77,72,71,62,59 46**
CSF £62.93 CT £1508.91 TOTE £12.90: £3.40, £2.30, £8.10, £3.20; EX 95.10 Trifecta £2358.90.

Owner S L Edwards **Bred** S L Edwards **Trained** Lichfield, Staffs

FOCUS
An ordinary but competitive sprint, and straightforward form.
T/Plt: £196.00 to a £1 stake. Pool: £74,623.13 - 277.88 winning units. T/Qpdt: £60.50 to a £1 stake. Pool: £7,881.88 - 96.32 winning units. **Steve Payne**

1534 - 1540a (Foreign Racing) - See Raceform Interactive

1230 SAINT-CLOUD (L-H)
Monday, April 18

OFFICIAL GOING: Turf: very soft

1541a PRIX PENELOPE (GROUP 3) (3YO FILLIES) (TURF) 1m 2f 110y
2:55 (12:00) 3-Y-O **£29,411** (£11,764; £8,823; £5,882; £2,941)

RPR

1 **Camprock (FR)**^{37} 929 3-9-0 0 MaximeGuyon 9 102
(Mme Pia Brandt, France) *midfield early: moved up to trck ldr after 2f: rdn along to ld 1f out: styd on wl u.p fnl f* **16/5**^{2}

2 *1 3/4* **The Juliet Rose (FR)**^{150} 3-9-0 0 StephanePasquier 2 99
(N Clement, France) *settled towards rr: bmpd 2f out: styd on wl u.p: a hld* **63/10**^{3}

3 *snk* **Jadhaba (IRE)**^{167} 3-9-0 0 GregoryBenoist 3 98
(J-C Rouget, France) *sn trcking ldng pair: pushed along fr 3f out: kpt on but nvr cl enough to chal* **23/10**^{1}

4 *hd* **Impressionist (IRE)**^{191} 3-9-0 0 Pierre-CharlesBoudot 5 98
(A Fabre, France) *settled in midfield: rdn along fr 2f out: kpt on u.p but a hld* **9/1**

5 *1 1/4* **Tierra Del Fuego (FR)**^{29} 1022 3-9-0 0 AurelienLemaitre 8 96
(G E Mikhalides, France) *hld up towards rr: chsd ldr fr 2f out but nt pce to chal* **10/1**

6 *1* **Indecence Choisie (FR)**^{12} 1285 3-9-0 0 OlivierPeslier 1 94
(C Ferland, France) *midfield: unable to find gap 2f out: styd on u.p but unable to cl on ldrs* **25/1**

7 *7* **Valenka (GER)**^{21} 3-9-0 0 VincentCheminaud 7 80
(M Munch, Germany) *led: set stdy pce: rdn along 2 1/2f out: kpt on wl tl hdd 1f out: wknd fnl f: eased* **11/1**

8 *2* **Sweet Electra (FR)**^{183} 3-9-0 0 ChristopheSoumillon 6 76
(P Bary, France) *towards rr early: moved up to midfield 3f out: rdn along 2f out but unable qck: eased* **10/1**

9 hd **Coif (IRE)**^{157} 3-9-0 0 MickaelBarzalona 4 76
(A Fabre, France) *hld up towards rr: rdn along fr 2 1/2f out: shortlived effrt: wknd and eased fnl f* **32/5**

2m 23.01s (3.41) **9** Ran SP% **121.7**
WIN (incl. 1 euro stake): 4.20. PLACES: 1.40, 2.10, 1.50. DF:16.10. SF: 30.90.
Owner Ecurie Du Grand Chene **Bred** Mlle M Sundstrom **Trained** France

1542a PRIX HILDEGARDE (MAIDEN) (3YO FILLIES) (TURF) 1m 4f

3:25 (12:00) 3-Y-O **£9,191** (£3,676; £2,757; £1,838; £919)

RPR

1 **En Souplesse (FR)** 3-8-3 0 ClementLecoeuvre(7) 5 80
(E Lellouche, France) **57/1**

2 4 **Felicita (FR)** 3-9-0 0 (p) FabienLefebvre 4 77
(P De Chevigny, France) **41/1**

3 nk **Venerable (FR)**^{29} 3-9-0 0 FabriceVeron 2 77
(H-A Pantall, France) **9/2**^{2}

4 1 1/4 **Dimaniya (FR)**^{27} [1032] 3-9-0 0 ChristopheSoumillon 7 75
(A De Royer-Dupre, France) **1/2**^{1}

5 1 1/2 **Enki Girl (FR)**^{37} 3-8-8 0 NathanKasztelan(6) 8 73
(P Leblanc, France) **11/1**

6 3 1/2 **Natsume (FR)** 3-8-10 0 PierreBazire(4) 1 67
(S Kobayashi, France) **24/1**

7 8 **Evidence (FR)**^{53} [716] 3-9-0 0 TonyPiccone 6 54
(Harry Dunlop) *wnt rt s: led early: hdd after 1f and settled in cl 2nd: rdn along 2f out but unable qck: sn btn: eased fnl f* **7/1**^{3}

8 1/2 **Rainbow Majesty (FR)** 3-8-10 0 OlivierPeslier 9 49
(J-M Beguigne, France) **13/1**

9 20 **Fun Chief (FR)** 3-9-0 0 (p) StephaneLaurent 3 21
(Caroline Auvray, France) **67/1**

2m 48.22s (7.82) **9** Ran SP% **122.4**
WIN (incl. 1 euro stake): 58.40. PLACES: 12.60, 10.00, 2.60. DF: 264.10. SF: 626.50.
Owner Mlle Sarah Lellouche **Bred** E Lellouche & Mlle S Lellouche **Trained** Lamorlaye, France

BRIGHTON (L-H)

Tuesday, April 19

OFFICIAL GOING: Good to soft (soft in places)
Wind: Moderate, half against Weather: Fine

1543 VEOLIA - OFFICIAL RECYCLING PARTNER MAIDEN STKS 5f 59y

4:50 (4:50) (Class 5) 2-Y-O **£2,911** (£866; £432; £216) **Stalls** Low

Form RPR

1 **Visionary (IRE)** 2-9-5 0 JamieSpencer 4 75+
(Robert Cowell) *dwlt: green and sltly outpcd in rr: gd hdwy in centre over 1f out: led ins fnl f: edgd lft: eased nr fin* **3/1**^{2}

3 2 1/2 **Sheila's Lad (IRE)**^{11} [1316] 2-9-5 0 MartinDwyer 6 71
(J S Moore) *t.k.h: prom: led 1f out: hdd and outpcd ins fnl f* **8/1**

3 hd **Raffle King (IRE)** 2-9-5 0 CharlesBishop 2 71
(Mick Channon) *towards rr: hdwy 2f out: hung lft: chal over 1f out: one pce fnl f* **9/4**^{1}

4 4 **Charlie Beer Punt (IRE)** 2-9-5 0 RichardKingscote 7 57
(Tom Dascombe) *pressed ldr: chal 2f out: no ex fnl f* **20/1**

5 1 1/4 **Swell Hill** 2-9-0 0 SeanLevey 3 47
(Richard Hannon) *chsd ldrs tl outpcd fnl 2f* **7/2**^{3}

P 6 2 3/4 **Spin Top**^{17} [1203] 2-9-5 0 OisinMurphy 5 43
(Joseph Tuite) *hld up in 5th: hdwy in centre to ld 2f out: hdd & wknd qckly 1f out* **13/2**

0 7 17 **Bills Delight**^{24} [1086] 2-8-11 0 PhilipPrince(3) 1
(Bill Turner) *led tl 2f out: sn wknd* **33/1**

1m 4.23s (1.93) **Going Correction** +0.225s/f (Good) **7** Ran SP% **110.1**
Speed ratings (Par 92): **93,92,91,85,83 79,51**
CSF £24.59 TOTE £4.60: £2.60, £2.40; EX 28.80 Trifecta £93.10.
Owner Khalifa Dasmal **Bred** K A Dasmal **Trained** Six Mile Bottom, Cambs

FOCUS
The going was good to soft, soft in places (GoingStick: 6.6). The leaders set a decent gallop in this maiden and the winner and third came from the back of the field. Ordinary form.

1544 BRIGHTON&HOVE BUSES - OFFICIAL TRANSPORT PARTNER H'CAP 6f 209y

5:20 (5:21) (Class 6) (0-60,60) 4-Y-O+ **£2,264** (£673; £336; £168) **Stalls** Low

Form RPR

500- 1 **Black Caesar (IRE)**^{132} [8160] 5-9-7 **60** WilliamTwiston-Davies 13 73
(Philip Hide) *chsd ldr: led over 2f out: edgd lft: clr fnl f: rdn out* **6/1**^{1}

4043 2 3 1/2 **Wild Flower (IRE)**^{19} [1162] 4-8-10 **49** KieranO'Neill 1 53
(Jimmy Fox) *prom: chsd wnr wl over 1f out: hung lft: no imp* **10/1**

0000 3 2 3/4 **Duke Of North (IRE)**^{31} [671] 4-9-7 **60** PatCosgrave 7 57
(Jim Boyle) *towards rr: rdn and hdwy 2f out: styd on* **20/1**

5006 4 1 **Admirable Art (IRE)**^{12} [1295] 6-9-0 **53** JFEgan 6 47
(Tony Carroll) *outpcd and sn bhd: styd on fnl 2f* **16/1**

1004 5 3/4 **Fairy Mist (IRE)**^{20} [1145] 9-8-9 **51** (b) DannyBrock(3) 12 43
(John Bridger) *towards rr: rdn 3f out: styd on wl fr over 1f out* **12/1**

1543 6 1 **Gulland Rock**^{23} [1116] 5-9-3 **56** (v^{1}) WilliamCarson 3 46
(Anthony Carson) *w ldr: led after 2f tl over 2f out: wknd over 1f out* **8/1**

-600 7 3 **Soaring Spirits (IRE)**^{61} [621] 6-9-4 **57** (b) RobertWinston 10 39
(Dean Ivory) *mid-div: effrt in centre 2f out: no imp* **7/1**^{3}

-056 8 3 3/4 **Emperors Warrior (IRE)**^{62} [608] 4-8-13 **57** (b) HectorCrouch(5) 5 29
(Gary Moore) *led 2f: prom tl wknd wl over 1f out* **25/1**

0-00 9 2 3/4 **All Or Nothin (IRE)**^{27} [1042] 7-8-13 **57** PatrickO'Donnell(5) 4 22
(Paddy Butler) *chsd ldrs tl wknd 2f out* **33/1**

0306 10 1 1/2 **Dandys Perier (IRE)**^{34} [951] 5-9-7 **60** OisinMurphy 15 21
(Ronald Harris) *prom tl wknd 2f out* **12/1**

0-16 11 1 **Trust Me Boy**^{40} [893] 8-8-12 **51** RobertHavlin 8 9
(John E Long) *sn rdn along in midfield: n.d* **9/1**

0650 12 1 1/4 **Multitask**^{20} [1143] 6-9-2 **55** (p) LiamKeniry 14 10
(Michael Madgwick) *plld hrd: in tch tl wknd 2f out* **13/2**^{2}

-165 13 1 1/4 **Honiton Lace**^{19} [1158] 5-9-0 **56** (tp) GeorgeDowning(3) 2 8
(Phil McEntee) *reluctant to enter stalls: s.s: a bhd* **16/1**

3315 14 2 1/4 **Gavarnie Encore**^{34} [951] 4-9-4 **57** DavidProbert 9
(Michael Blanshard) *a bhd* **8/1**

1m 23.92s (0.82) **Going Correction** +0.225s/f (Good) **14** Ran SP% **120.1**
Speed ratings (Par 101): **104,100,96,95,94 93,90,86,82,81 80,78,77,74**
CSF £63.21 CT £1169.82 TOTE £8.70: £3.10, £2.10, £8.90; EX 67.60 Trifecta £1184.60.
Owner The Long Furlong **Bred** Miss Hilary Mullen **Trained** Findon, W Sussex

FOCUS
An open handicap on paper but the winner came right away in the closing stages to win comfortably. He's rated just above last year's winning course form.

1545 L&S PRINTING - OFFICIAL PRINT PARTNER H'CAP 6f 209y

5:50 (5:51) (Class 4) (0-85,85) 4-Y-O+ **£4,690** (£1,395; £697; £348) **Stalls** Low

Form RPR

-415 1 **Fingal's Cave (IRE)**^{47} [795] 4-8-12 **76** CharlesBishop 9 84
(Mick Channon) *dwlt: t.k.h in rr: hdwy 2f out: led 1f out: rdn out* **5/1**^{3}

440- 2 1 1/4 **Outback Ruler (IRE)**^{200} [6891] 4-9-1 **82** RyanTate(3) 4 87
(Clive Cox) *chsd ldrs: effrt over 2f out: chal 1f out: unable qck ins fnl f* **7/2**^{1}

30-6 3 nk **Good Luck Charm**^{18} [1173] 7-8-7 **71** (b) KierenFox 10 75
(Gary Moore) *dwlt: towards rr: hdwy in centre 1/2-way: jnd ldrs over 2f out: hung lft: one pce fnl f* **14/1**

40-6 4 nk **Cordite (IRE)**^{100} [134] 5-9-7 **85** ^{1} PatCosgrave 8 88
(Jim Boyle) *prom: chal over 2f out: one pce fnl f* **7/1**

20-0 5 2 3/4 **Harlequin Striker (IRE)**^{16} [1215] 4-9-3 **81** RobertWinston 5 79
(Dean Ivory) *mde most tl 1f out: no ex fnl f* **7/1**

0035 6 shd **Baddilini**^{49} [771] 6-9-2 **80** (p) DavidProbert 2 76
(Alan Bailey) *chsd ldrs: hrd rdn over 1f out: one pce* **9/2**^{2}

2-00 7 2 1/4 **Pick A Little**^{27} [1041] 8-9-1 **79** TimmyMurphy 6 69
(Michael Blake) *w ldrs tl wknd over 1f out* **20/1**

40-0 8 2 1/4 **Maymyo (IRE)**^{66} [561] 5-8-7 **71** oh5 (t) SamHitchcott 7 55
(Sylvester Kirk) *a abt same pl* **25/1**

-344 9 2 3/4 **Jimmy's Hall**^{57} [670] 4-8-2 **73** (b) HollieDoyle(7) 1 49
(J S Moore) *s.i.s: in rr: rdn and outpcd 4f out: n.d after* **12/1**

-211 10 12 **Perfect Alchemy (IRE)**^{66} [558] 5-8-12 **76** OisinMurphy 3 20
(Patrick Chamings) *t.k.h: sn towards rr: promising hdwy whn nt clr run over 1f out: nowhere to go: eased fnl f* **17/2**

1m 23.6s (0.50) **Going Correction** +0.225s/f (Good) **10** Ran SP% **115.6**
Speed ratings (Par 105): **106,104,104,103,100 100,98,95,92,78**
CSF £22.63 CT £234.56 TOTE £3.70: £2.60, £1.80, £4.70; EX 29.10 Trifecta £492.30.
Owner The Motley Cru I **Bred** Rathasker Stud **Trained** West Ilsley, Berks

FOCUS
A competitive affair but the time was relatively modest.

1546 HARRINGTONS LETTINGS - OFFICIAL GRANDSTAND SPONSOR H'CAP 7f 214y

6:20 (6:20) (Class 5) (0-75,73) 4-Y-O+ **£2,911** (£866; £432; £216) **Stalls** Low

Form RPR

60-4 1 **Ice Slice (IRE)**^{14} [1241] 5-9-3 **72** RyanTate(3) 7 82+
(James Eustace) *bhd: hdwy over 1f out: str run to ld on line* **9/2**^{1}

1142 2 hd **Eastern Dragon (IRE)**^{11} [1326] 6-9-3 **69** TimmyMurphy 14 78
(Seamus Durack) *chsd ldrs: led wl over 1f out: hrd rdn fnl f: ct on line* **7/1**^{3}

3441 3 1 1/4 **Golden Wedding (IRE)**^{13} [1262] 4-9-4 **70** (p) RobertWinston 9 76
(Eve Johnson Houghton) *in tch: n.m.r 2f out: chsd ldr over 1f out: kpt on* **9/1**

0-40 4 1/2 **Bloodsweatandtears**^{41} [877] 8-8-3 **60** EdwardGreatrex(5) 8 65
(William Knight) *dwlt: bhd: gd hdwy in centre 2f out: hung lft: kpt on fnl f* **12/1**

012- 5 1 1/2 **Knight Of The Air**^{187} [7231] 4-8-4 **61** PaddyPilley(5) 2 63
(Mick Channon) *bhd: rdn 3f out: styd on wl fr over 1f out* **12/1**

0552 6 1 **Ravenous**^{8} [1387] 5-9-5 **71** KieranO'Neill 6 70
(Luke Dace) *prom: chal 2f out: no ex fnl f* **5/1**^{2}

1102 7 1 1/2 **Skidby Mill (IRE)**^{13} [1268] 6-8-13 **72** MeganNicholls(7) 11 68
(Laura Mongan) *mid-div: effrt and hung lft 2f out: no imp* **25/1**

0230 8 1 **Freddy With A Y (IRE)**^{8} [1387] 6-9-2 **73** (b^{1}) HectorCrouch(5) 13 66
(Gary Moore) *chsd ldrs: rdn and outpcd 3f out: wknd wl over 1f out* **16/1**

1-04 9 2 1/2 **Uncle Dermot (IRE)**^{8} [1387] 8-9-7 **73** RichardKingscote 12 61
(Brendan Powell) *led tl wl over 1f out: sn wknd* **7/1**^{3}

450- 10 1/2 **Port Lairge**^{172} [7599] 6-8-13 **68** (v) MichaelJMMurphy(3) 1 55
(John Gallagher) *in tch tl wknd 2f out* **8/1**

360- 11 2 1/4 **Live Dangerously**^{181} [7388] 6-9-7 **73** WilliamCarson 10 54
(John Bridger) *t.k.h early: a bhd* **20/1**

0-60 12 3 1/4 **Response**^{35} [939] 6-8-7 **59** (p) AndrewMullen 4 33
(Michael Appleby) *prom tl wknd 2f out* **12/1**

60-0 13 3 **Tee It Up Tommo (IRE)**^{4} [73] 7-9-5 **71** (tp) PatCosgrave 3 38
(Daniel Steele) *dwlt: bhd: sme hdwy over 2f out: btn whn n.m.r over 1f out* **50/1**

1m 37.01s (1.01) **Going Correction** +0.225s/f (Good) **13** Ran SP% **120.5**
Speed ratings (Par 103): **103,102,101,101,99 98,97,96,93,93 90,87,84**
CSF £35.10 CT £287.59 TOTE £5.60: £2.40, £3.00, £3.50; EX 43.10 Trifecta £423.80.
Owner The MacDougall Two **Bred** Kilfrush Stud **Trained** Newmarket, Suffolk
■ Stewards' Enquiry : Timmy Murphy two-day ban: used whip above permitted level (May 3-4)

FOCUS
Another open handicap, and sound form.

1547 STREAMLINE TAXIS - OFFICIAL TRANSPORT PARTNER H'CAP 1m 1f 209y

6:50 (6:51) (Class 6) (0-60,60) 4-Y-O+ **£2,264** (£673; £336; £168) **Stalls** High

Form RPR

4133 1 **Tommys Geal**^{32} [977] 4-9-4 **60** DanielMuscutt(3) 11 67
(Michael Madgwick) *mid-div: hdwy over 2f out: led in centre over 1f out: jst hld on* **17/2**

233 2 hd **Innoko (FR)**^{26} [1057] 6-9-1 **57** GeorgeDowning(3) 5 64
(Tony Carroll) *chsd ldrs: rdn over 2f out: clsd on wnr fnl f: jst failed* **6/1**^{3}

5-65 3 1 3/4 **Vivo Per Lei (IRE)**^{48} [781] 4-8-11 **50** WilliamCarson 8 53
(Dr Jon Scargill) *mid-div: hdwy and hrd rdn 2f out: styd on fnl f* **20/1**

10-0 4 1 1/4 **Rosie Royale (IRE)**^{47} [801] 4-9-4 **60** TomMarquand(3) 1 61
(Roger Teal) *in tch: rdn over 2f out: styd on fnl f* **11/2**^{2}

314- 5 3/4 **Megalala (IRE)**^{187} [7230] 15-9-1 **54** WilliamTwiston-Davies 9 53
(John Bridger) *led tl over 1f out: no ex ins fnl f* **10/1**

00-3 6 3/4 **Honey Badger**^{17} [1201] 5-8-13 **55** (p) RyanTate(3) 6 53
(Eugene Stanford) *sn rdn along in rr: styd on fnl 2f: nvr nrr* **10/3**^{1}

1045 7 1/2 **Goodwood Moonlight**^{54} [702] 4-8-10 **54** EdwardGreatrex(5) 2 51
(Ian Williams) *prom tl outpcd fnl 2f* **10/1**

5040 8 1 1/4 **Bennelong**^{13} [1262] 10-8-12 **56** (b) CallumShepherd(5) 7 51
(Lee Carter) *chsd ldrs: chal in centre 2f out: btn over 1f out* **8/1**

0-00 9 2 1/4 **Rockweiller**^{16} [1222] 9-8-7 **46** oh1 (b) JFEgan 4 36
(Shaun Harris) *chsd ldr tl hrd rdn and wknd 2f out: eased whn btn ins fnl f* **25/1**

0005 10 5 **Athenian Garden (USA)**^{15} [1239] 9-8-2 **46** PatrickO'Donnell(5) 3 27
(Paddy Butler) *a towards rr* **25/1**

3/5- 11 1/2 **Cappielow Park**^{17} [8077] 7-8-12 **51** (tp) CharlesBishop 10 31
(Ali Stronge) *s.s: a bhd* **10/1**

-000 **12** 2¼ **Rectitude**[48] 787 5-8-7 **46** oh1 SamHitchcott 12 22
(Henry Tett) *in tch tl wknd over 2f out* **100/1**
4-00 **13** 3½ **Strawberryfields**[41] 870 4-8-7 **46** oh1 (p) DavidProbert 13 15
(Des Donovan, Ire) *towards rr: rdn 4f out: n.d fnl 3f* **33/1**
2m 6.73s (3.13) **Going Correction** +0.225s/f (Good) **13** Ran SP% **118.0**
Speed ratings (Par 101): **96,95,94,93,92 92,91,90,89,85 84,82,80**
CSF £54.71 CT £1000.16 TOTE £10.20: £3.00, £3.10, £4.90; EX 27.20 Trifecta £1370.90.
Owner Recycled Products Limited **Bred** Recycled Products Limited **Trained** Denmead, Hants

FOCUS
A moderate handicap. The action developed towards the centre of the track and the winner is rated to her recent AW form..

1548 SUSSEX CLEANING&CARE - OFFICIAL CLEANING PARTNER CLASSIFIED STKS 7f 214y

7:20 (7:20) (Class 6) 3-Y-O+ **£2,264** (£673; £336; £168) **Stalls** Low

Form RPR
00-1 **1** **Free To Roam (IRE)**[11] 1325 3-8-6 55 DavidProbert 9 56
(Philip McBride) *mde all: hld on gamely fnl 2f* **7/4**[1]
00-5 **2** *1* **Fitzwilliam**[15] 1236 4-9-1 55 PaddyPilley(5) 4 58
(Mick Channon) *prom: chal 2f out: kpt on u.p: hld fnl 50yds* **3/1**[2]
6-00 **3** *2* **Ron's Ballad**[32] 979 3-8-6 38 KieranO'Neill 10 49
(Michael Madgwick) *bhd: hdwy over 1f out: fin wl* **66/1**
-000 **4** *nk* **Toffee Apple (IRE)**[19] 1162 3-8-1 47 (b[1]) EdwardGreatrex(5) 8 48
(Ed Dunlop) *in tch on outer: effrt and hrd rdn 2f out: styd on* **20/1**
600- **5** *1½* **Bond Mystery**[216] 6434 4-9-3 44 PhilipPrince(3) 6 49
(Natalie Lloyd-Beavis) *rdn along and bhd: hdwy wd of others in centre 3f out: styd on same pce fnl 2f* **50/1**
63-0 **6** *½* **Angels Above (IRE)**[12] 1295 4-9-6 51 JFEgan 3 48
(John Butler) *towards rr: hdwy on inner 2f out: one pce fnl f* **7/1**
-566 **7** *¾* **Pursuit Of Time**[35] 948 3-8-6 50 AndrewMullen 11 42
(Michael Appleby) *mid-div: effrt and hrd rdn over 1f out: no imp* **20/1**
4344 **8** *¾* **Nidnod**[15] 1234 3-8-6 55 WilliamCarson 12 40
(John Bridger) *mid-div: effrt over 2f out: no ex fnl f* **5/1**[3]
0-00 **9** *2¼* **Notts So Blue**[18] 1049 5-9-6 43 (b) OisinMurphy 2 39
(Shaun Harris) *mid-div tl outpcd fnl 2f* **33/1**
0000 **10** *17* **Cappy Brown**[19] 1162 3-7-13 43 LuluStanford(7) 7
(Alan Bailey) *chsd ldrs tl hanging and wknd 2f out* **20/1**
1-40 **11** *5* **Coup De Vent**[66] 569 5-9-1 53 CiaranMckee(5) 1
(John O'Shea) *chsd ldrs tl wknd over 2f out* **14/1**
0-00 **12** *8* **Soliana**[78] 412 4-8-13 35 (p) GeorgiaCox(7) 5
(John O'Shea) *prom to 1/2-way* **66/1**
1m 38.92s (2.92) **Going Correction** +0.225s/f (Good)
WFA 3 from 4yo+ 14lb **12** Ran SP% **119.4**
Speed ratings (Par 101): **94,93,91,90,89 88,87,87,84,67 62,54**
CSF £6.25 TOTE £2.80: £1.80, £1.60, £14.20; EX 7.70 Trifecta £325.50.
Owner P J McBride **Bred** Tally-Ho Stud **Trained** Newmarket, Suffolk

FOCUS
A low-grade contest. It's hard to be positive about the form and the winner didn't need to improve much to follow up.

1549 FROSTS CARS - OFFICIAL LADIES DAY PARTNER H'CAP 5f 213y

7:50 (7:50) (Class 5) (0-70,69) 4-Y-O+ **£2,911** (£866; £432; £216) **Stalls** Low

Form RPR
1340 **1** **Secret Millionaire (IRE)**[41] 872 9-8-10 **61** (p) TomMarquand(3) 4 66
(Shaun Harris) *t.k.h: sn chsng ldr: led 1f out: drvn out* **4/1**[2]
05-0 **2** *¾* **Perfect Pastime**[20] 1150 8-9-6 **68** (p) PatCosgrave 6 71
(Jim Boyle) *chsd ldrs: nt clr run wl over 1f out: swtchd rt: r.o wl fnl f: clsng at fin* **3/1**[1]
30-0 **3** *1½* **Hipz (IRE)**[13] 1269 5-9-0 **69** MeganNicholls(7) 1 67
(Laura Mongan) *broke wl: sn outpcd in 4th: hdwy 2f out: kpt on fnl f* **4/1**[2]
-050 **4** *1¼* **Noverre To Go (IRE)**[13] 1261 10-9-5 **67** (p) OisinMurphy 5 61
(Ronald Harris) *led at gd pce tl 1f out: no ex* **4/1**[2]
-160 **5** *3¼* **Diatomic (IRE)**[10] 1341 4-9-0 **62** (p) RichardKingscote 3 46
(Tom Dascombe) *hmpd sn after s: a same pl: btn over 1f out* **4/1**[2]
00- **6** *7* **Piazza San Pietro**[138] 8096 10-9-3 **65** (p) TimmyMurphy 2 26
(Zoe Davison) *stdd s: a in rr* **12/1**[3]
1m 12.84s (2.64) **Going Correction** +0.225s/f (Good) **6** Ran SP% **112.7**
Speed ratings (Par 103): **91,90,88,86,82 72**
CSF £16.46 TOTE £4.90: £3.10, £1.10; EX 16.40 Trifecta £39.00.
Owner Wilf Hobson **Bred** James Delaney **Trained** Carburton, Notts

FOCUS
A modest sprint.
T/Plt: £233.00 to a £1 stake. Pool: £64,739.49 - 202.79 winning tickets. T/Qpdt: £19.00 to a £1 stake. Pool: £8,382.86 - 325.16 winning tickets. **Lee McKenzie**

1496 WOLVERHAMPTON (A.W) (L-H)

Tuesday, April 19

OFFICIAL GOING: Tapeta: standard
Wind: Light across Weather: Fine

1550 AJA GENTLEMAN AMATEUR RIDERS' H'CAP 2m 119y (Tp)

2:20 (2:20) (Class 5) (0-75,75) 4-Y-O+ **£2,994** (£928; £464; £232) **Stalls** Low

Form RPR
040/ **1** **Argent Knight**[443] 7107 6-11-7 **75** (p) MrSWalker 2 77+
(Keith Dalgleish) *chsd ldrs: wnt 2nd over 3f out: led over 2f out: shkn up over 1f out: styd on: comf* **6/5**[1]
5354 **2** *1¼* **Delagoa Bay (IRE)**[11] 1322 8-10-2 **56** oh10 MrPMillman 4 53
(Sylvester Kirk) *hld up: pushed along over 7f out: hdwy over 3f out: rdn over 1f out: styd on to go 2nd wl ins fnl f: nt trble wnr* **22/1**
6-53 **3** *1* **Singular Quest**[38] 922 4-10-12 **70** MrAlexEdwards 7 66
(Kevin Frost) *a.p: rdn over 2f out: styd on* **9/2**[3]
0-46 **4** *1* **Dovils Date**[38] 922 7-11-0 **73** MrEDavid(5) 3 68
(Tim Vaughan) *chsd ldr after 1f tl led over 4f out: rdn and hdd over 2f out: styd on same pce fr over 1f out* **4/1**[2]
0-65 **5** *9* **Dukes Den**[11] 1322 5-9-11 **56** oh1 MrHHunt(5) 1 40
(Mark Usher) *hld up: pushed along over 5f out: sme hdwy over 3f out: rdn and wknd over 2f out* **5/1**
-060 **6** *65* **Kirkman (IRE)**[11] 1322 5-10-2 **56** oh4 MrPCollington 5
(Peter Hiatt) *led: hdd over 4f out: rdn whn hmpd and wknd wl over 2f out* **22/1**
000- **7** *27* **Sarafina**[144] 8014 4-9-7 **56** oh11 MrJPearce(5) 6
(David Thompson) *s.i.s: hdwy over 13f out: pushed along over 7f out: sn wknd* **100/1**
3m 40.86s (-2.84) **Going Correction** -0.125s/f (Stan)
WFA 4 from 5yo+ 4lb **7** Ran SP% **110.0**
Speed ratings (Par 103): **101,100,99,99,95 64,51**
CSF £29.61 CT £84.61 TOTE £2.30: £1.40, £3.40; EX 15.70 Trifecta £46.60.
Owner Straightline Construction Ltd **Bred** Mr & Mrs A E Pakenham **Trained** Carluke, S Lanarks

FOCUS
A weak amateur riders' staying handicap, especially with more than half the field out of the weights. They went an even gallop. The form is rated cautiously.

1551 ARC LONG SERVICE AWARDS H'CAP 1m 1f 103y (Tp)

2:50 (2:50) (Class 6) (0-60,60) 3-Y-O **£2,458** (£731; £365; £182) **Stalls** Low

Form RPR
000- **1** **Therthaar**[176] 7510 3-8-7 **46** oh1 ShaneGray 6 63+
(Ismail Mohammed) *chsd ldr tl led 3f out: pushed clr fr over 1f out: easily* **7/1**
006- **2** *7* **Go On Gal (IRE)**[296] 3685 3-8-10 **49** AdamBeschizza 7 50
(Julia Feilden) *a.p: rdn to chse wnr over 1f out: styd on same pce* **33/1**
5205 **3** *nk* **Schoolboy Error (IRE)**[26] 1062 3-9-5 **58** (b) GeorgeBaker 11 58
(Jamie Osborne) *s.i.s: swtchd lft sn after s: hld up: hdwy 2f out: rdn and hung lft fr over 1f out: no imp fnl f* **3/1**[1]
004 **4** *4½* **Fun Money**[78] 413 3-9-2 **55** MartinLane 3 47
(Ed Dunlop) *hld up in tch: nt clr run 3f out: rdn over 2f out: styd on same pce fr over 1f out* **16/1**
-420 **5** *¾* **Granita (USA)**[47] 794 3-9-2 **60** JosephineGordon(5) 12 50
(George Scott) *hld up: stmbld 7f out: rdn over 2f out: styd on ins fnl f: nvr nrr* **16/1**
20-0 **6** *½* **Imshi's Little Bro (IRE)**[28] 1031 3-8-11 **57** JaneElliott(7) 4 47
(Ivan Furtado) *mid-div: rdn over 3f out: sn outpcd: styd on ins fnl f* **33/1**
00-0 **7** *½* **Jon H The Lawman (IRE)**[16] 1217 3-8-7 **46** oh1 JimmyQuinn 9 35
(Ronald Thompson) *hld up: rdn over 3f out: n.d* **66/1**
22-6 **8** *1¼* **Pivotal Dream (IRE)**[89] 274 3-8-6 **52** CharlieBennett(7) 13 38
(Mark Brisbourne) *hld up: rdn over 2f out: sn wknd* **16/1**
3024 **9** *3* **Frivolous Prince (IRE)**[13] 1259 3-8-10 **49** (vt) CathyGannon 10 31
(David Evans) *in rr: drvn along 1/2-way: no ch whn nt clr run over 1f out* **13/2**[3]
0024 **10** *1¾* **Dark Illustrator**[47] 794 3-9-0 **53** DanielTudhope 2 30
(David O'Meara) *chsd ldrs: rdn over 3f out: wknd over 1f out* **8/1**
3000 **11** *6* **Opera Buffa (IRE)**[20] 1148 3-9-2 **55** JoeFanning 5 21
(Mark Johnston) *led: hdd 3f out: sn rdn: wknd over 1f out* **28/1**
600- **12** *8* **Artisandra (FR)**[264] 4790 3-9-2 **55** MartinHarley 8 6
(William Knight) *prom: rdn over 2f out: sn wknd* **9/2**[2]
0550 **13** *99* **Falcon's Fire (IRE)**[47] 794 3-9-0 **53** (p) PhillipMakin 1
(Keith Dalgleish) *rrd s: a bhd* **10/1**
1m 59.39s (-1.41) **Going Correction** -0.125s/f (Stan) **13** Ran SP% **117.7**
Speed ratings (Par 96): **101,94,94,90,89 89,88,87,85,83 78,71,**
CSF £225.64 CT £842.10 TOTE £10.50: £3.10, £9.50, £1.70; EX 436.90 Trifecta £1773.20.
Owner Sultan Ali **Bred** Cheveley Park Stud Ltd **Trained** Newmarket, Suffolk

FOCUS
A moderate 3yo handicap contested entirely by maidens, but it was turned into a procession. There's better to come from the winner.

1552 DOWNLOAD THE AT THE RACES APP FILLIES' H'CAP 1m 4f 50y (Tp)

3:20 (3:20) (Class 5) (0-75,75) 4-Y-O+ **£3,234** (£962; £481; £240) **Stalls** Low

Form RPR
50-1 **1** **Fast Pick (IRE)**[10] 1347 4-9-1 **70** (p) PhillipMakin 5 78+
(Keith Dalgleish) *chsd ldr tl over 8f out: remained handy: pushed along over 3f out: wnt 2nd again over 2f out: led wl over 1f out: sn rdn and edgd lft: styd on* **9/4**[1]
5341 **2** *½* **Indira**[31] 1002 5-9-1 **74** JosephineGordon(5) 1 81
(John Berry) *chsd ldrs: lost pl over 7f out: hdwy over 2f out: rdn to chse wnr ins fnl f: styd on* **4/1**
0412 **3** *3¾* **Heart Locket**[21] 1135 4-8-13 **73** NathanEvans(5) 6 74
(Michael Easterby) *sn led at stdy pce: qcknd 3f out: rdn and hdd wl over 1f out: no ex ins fnl f* **11/4**[2]
51-4 **4** *5* **Atwix**[20] 1144 4-9-6 **75** (p) DanielTudhope 2 68
(Lucy Wadham) *prom: chsd ldr over 8f out tl rdn over 2f out: wknd over 1f out* **3/1**[3]
1153 **5** *3½* **Percella**[40] 884 4-8-13 **68** StevieDonohoe 4 55
(Ian Williams) *s.i.s: hld up: hdwy over 7f out: rdn and wknd over 2f out* **14/1**
2m 38.32s (-2.48) **Going Correction** -0.125s/f (Stan)
WFA 4 from 5yo+ 1lb **5** Ran SP% **109.1**
Speed ratings (Par 100): **103,102,100,96,94**
CSF £11.18 TOTE £2.70: £2.00, £1.50; EX 7.20 Trifecta £17.40.
Owner Ronnie Docherty **Bred** Philip Brady **Trained** Carluke, S Lanarks

FOCUS
A modest fillies' handicap though all five had fairly recent winning form to their name. They didn't go much of a pace until the tempo quickened exiting the back straight. The winner has more to offer.

1553 JOIN THE BLACK COUNTRY CHAMBER OF COMMERCE MAIDEN AUCTION FILLIES' STKS 1m 4f 50y (Tp)

3:50 (3:50) (Class 6) 3-Y-O **£2,458** (£731; £365; £182) **Stalls** Low

Form RPR
6230 **1** **Kelvin Hall**[46] 814 3-9-0 65 FrannyNorton 2 73+
(Mark Johnston) *hld up: hdwy over 3f out: chsd ldr over 2f out: led 1f out: r.o wl: comf* **5/2**[2]
2 **2** *5* **Introductory (IRE)**[10] 1346 3-9-0 0 JoeFanning 3 65
(Mark Johnston) *led: rdn and hdd 1f out: styd on same pce* **4/7**[1]
0-53 **3** *6* **Regal Galaxy**[20] 1149 3-9-0 50 SaleemGolam 5 55
(Mark H Tompkins) *chsd ldr after 1f tl rdn over 2f out: wknd over 1f out* **25/1**
45-0 **4** *4* **Elegant Annie**[8] 1388 3-8-7 68 CharlieBennett(7) 1 49
(Jonathan Portman) *hld up: rdn over 2f out: wknd wl over 1f out* **16/1**[3]
0- **5** *3¾* **Peppy Miller**[320] 2869 3-8-11 0 EoinWalsh(3) 6 43
(George Margarson) *s.i.s: pushed along over 7f out: drvn over 3f out: wknd over 2f out* **25/1**
044- **6** *14* **Long Island**[150] 7936 3-9-0 60 MartinHarley 4 21
(Mark Brisbourne) *chsd ldrs: rdn over 3f out: wknd over 2f out* **25/1**
2m 39.51s (-1.29) **Going Correction** -0.125s/f (Stan) **6** Ran SP% **109.6**
Speed ratings (Par 93): **99,95,91,89,86 77**
CSF £4.05 TOTE £3.30: £1.30, £1.10; EX 5.00 Trifecta £24.40.
Owner Kingsley Park 4 - Ready To Run **Bred** Clive Dennett **Trained** Middleham Moor, N Yorks

FOCUS

A very uncompetitive 3yo fillies' maiden, totally dominated by the Mark Johnston pair and a 1-2 for the trainer, but not in the order most would have anticipated. The time was 1.19sec slower than the handicap for older fillies. It's very possible the winner can improve further.

1554 VISIT ATTHERACES.COM H'CAP — 5f 20y (Tp)

4:20 (4:21) (Class 6) (0-60,56) 3-Y-O — **£2,458** (£731; £365; £182) **Stalls** Low

Form — RPR

3525 **1** **Fearbuster (IRE)**[13] 1249 3-9-1 **55**....................(p) JosephineGordon[(5)] 5 — 60
(Hugo Palmer) *hld up: hdwy 1/2-way: rdn to ld ins fnl f: r.o* **7/1**[3]

66-5 **2** *1/2* **Dnaneer (IRE)**[10] 1337 3-9-6 **55**....................[1] MartinHarley 9 — 58+
(William Knight) *hld up: hdwy over 1f out: sn rdn: r.o* **6/4**[1]

-453 **3** *nk* **Kiringa**[34] 962 3-8-11 **46**.................... JoeFanning 3 — 48
(Robert Cowell) *led: rdn and edgd rt over 1f out: hdd ins fnl f: kpt on* **12/1**

6653 **4** *3/4* **Matilda Gleam**[12] 1292 3-9-3 **55**.................... TimClark[(3)] 8 — 54
(Lisa Williamson) *chsd ldrs: rdn over 1f out: hung lft ins fnl f: styd on* **9/1**

6336 **5** *1 1/2* **David's Beauty (IRE)**[3] 1497 3-9-7 **56**....................(p) DougieCostello 7 — 50
(Brian Baugh) *prom: lost pl 1/2-way: rallied over 1f out: styd on same pce ins fnl f* **8/1**

0606 **6** *2* **Barnsdale**[13] 1249 3-8-3 **45**.................... MeganEllingworth[(7)] 1 — 32
(John Holt) *chsd ldrs: rdn over 1f out: wknd ins fnl f* **100/1**

000- **7** *3/4* **Sirius Move**[141] 8053 3-9-5 **54**.................... DanielTudhope 6 — 38
(David O'Meara) *chsd ldr tl rdn 1/2-way: wknd fnl f* **7/2**[2]

0- **8** *1* **Love Is All Around (IRE)**[60] 641 3-8-13 **55**.................... PJO'Hanlon[(7)] 4 — 35
(Dermot Anthony McLoughlin, Ire) *s.i.s: in rr: rdn over 1f out: wknd fnl f* **12/1**

1m 1.99s (0.09) **Going Correction** -0.125s/f (Stan) — **8** Ran SP% **112.2**

Speed ratings (Par 96): **94,93,92,91,89 85,84,83**

CSF £17.25 CT £124.05 TOTE £4.80: £1.10, £1.50, £2.70; EX 18.30 Trifecta £76.60.

Owner M V Magnier & Partners/ T Hyde **Bred** Denis Brosnan **Trained** Newmarket, Suffolk

FOCUS

A moderate 3yo sprint handicap in which only one had tasted success before. They spread out all over the track after turning for home and the action unfolded under the stands' rail.

1555 FOLLOW @ATTHERACES ON TWITTER H'CAP — 7f 32y (Tp)

4:55 (4:56) (Class 5) (0-75,75) 4-Y-O+ — **£3,234** (£962; £481; £240) **Stalls** High

Form — RPR

0016 **1** **Flying Fantasy**[13] 1269 4-8-12 **71**.................... AaronJones[(5)] 6 — 80+
(Stuart Williams) *a.p: rdn over 1f out: edgd lft and r.o to ld wl ins fnl f* **7/2**[2]

5325 **2** *3/4* **Surewecan**[6] 1416 4-8-12 **66**.................... JoeFanning 5 — 73
(Mark Johnston) *a.p: chsd ldr 5f out: led over 1f out: rdn and hdd wl ins fnl f* **14/1**

-000 **3** *1* **For Shia And Lula (IRE)**[13] 1269 7-8-12 **66**....................(p) FMBerry 4 — 70
(Daniel Mark Loughnane) *led 1f: chsd ldrs: rdn over 1f out: edgd lft and styd on same pce ins fnl f* **14/1**

40-0 **4** *1/2* **Hardy Black (IRE)**[23] 1117 5-8-9 **63**.................... JohnFahy 1 — 66
(Kevin Frost) *a.p: rdn over 1f out: styd on same pce ins fnl f* **50/1**

124 **5** *1 1/4* **Top Offer**[43] 856 7-9-0 **68**.................... ShaneKelly 9 — 68
(Patrick Morris) *hld up: rdn over 2f out: hdwy over 1f out: hung lft ins fnl f: nt rch ldrs* **16/1**

00-4 **6** *1/2* **Spirit Of Wedza (IRE)**[23] 1116 4-8-8 **62**.................... ConnorBeasley 8 — 60
(Julie Camacho) *hld up: racd keenly: rdn over 2f out: styd on ins fnl f: nt trble ldrs* **14/1**

00-0 **7** *nse* **Slingsby**[22] 1124 5-8-13 **72**....................(b) NathanEvans[(5)] 3 — 70
(Michael Easterby) *hld up: rdn over 1f out: styd on ins fnl f: nvr nrr* **5/1**[3]

55-3 **8** *hd* **Inexes**[18] 1186 4-9-7 **75**....................(p) DanielTudhope 7 — 73
(Marjorie Fife) *led 6f out: rdn and hdd over 1f out: no ex ins fnl f* **9/4**[1]

266- **9** *1 1/2* **So It's War (FR)**[215] 6458 5-9-5 **73**....................(p) PhillipMakin 2 — 67
(Keith Dalgleish) *hld up: rdn over 1f out: nvr on terms* **7/1**

0035 **10** *1* **Black Truffle (FR)**[11] 1326 6-8-3 **62**....................(p) JosephineGordon[(5)] 10 — 53
(Mark Usher) *stdd s: hld up: rdn over 1f out: n.d* **33/1**

1m 27.84s (-0.96) **Going Correction** -0.125s/f (Stan) — **10** Ran SP% **112.9**

Speed ratings (Par 103): **100,99,98,97,96 95,95,95,93,92**

CSF £49.80 CT £603.84 TOTE £4.00: £2.10, £4.10, £4.00; EX 34.20 Trifecta £304.60.

Owner Happy Valley Racing & Breeding Limited **Bred** Hascombe And Valiant Studs **Trained** Newmarket, Suffolk

FOCUS

An ordinary handicap, but they went a decent gallop and pace held out. The winner again created a good impression.

1556 AWARD WINNING FINE DINING AT HORIZONS H'CAP — 7f 32y (Tp)

5:25 (5:26) (Class 6) (0-55,53) 4-Y-O+ — **£2,458** (£731; £365; £182) **Stalls** High

Form — RPR

30U3 **1** **Bionic Indian**[11] 1320 4-8-11 **48**....................(b) NathanEvans[(5)] 6 — 55
(Michael Easterby) *chsd ldr tl led 5f out: rdn out* **5/1**[2]

3202 **2** *1* **Tasaaboq**[19] 1162 5-9-0 **51**....................(t) JosephineGordon[(5)] 2 — 56
(Phil McEntee) *chsd ldrs: rdn to chse wnr fnl f: unable qck towards fin* **8/1**

0-04 **3** *3/4* **Gilmer (IRE)**[19] 1165 5-9-6 **52**....................(t) FMBerry 10 — 55
(Laura Young) *a.p: chsd wnr 1/2-way: rdn over 1f out: styd on same pce ins fnl f* **6/1**[3]

1060 **4** *1 1/4* **Lutine Charlie (IRE)**[13] 1262 9-9-5 **51**....................(p) DougieCostello 1 — 52
(Emma Owen) *prom: nt clr run over 2f out: rdn over 1f out: styd on* **25/1**

6-65 **5** *3/4* **Joaldo**[19] 1164 4-8-13 **45**.................... PJMcDonald 11 — 43
(Antony Brittain) *dwlt: hld up: rdn over 1f out: r.o ins fnl f: nvr nrr* **14/1**

0662 **6** *1/2* **Pipers Piping (IRE)**[32] 985 10-9-4 **53**.................... RobHornby[(3)] 8 — 50
(Mandy Rowland) *hld up in tch: rdn over 2f out: no ex fnl f* **6/1**[3]

6-10 **7** *3 1/4* **Ballroom Angel**[20] 1138 4-9-4 **50**.................... GeorgeBaker 7 — 39
(Philip Hide) *hld up: rdn and hung lft over 1f out: nvr on terms* **9/2**[1]

54U0 **8** *1 1/2* **Patron Of Explores (USA)**[11] 1323 5-8-13 **45**....................(v[1]) JackGarritty 5 — 30
(Patrick Holmes) *dwlt: hld up: rdn over 1f out: a in rr* **8/1**

2100 **9** *6* **Overrider**[11] 1323 6-9-4 **50**....................(bt) JoeFanning 4 — 20
(Shaun Lycett) *led 2f: rdn over 2f out: wknd over 1f out* **8/1**

406/ **10** *6* **Captain Devious**[929] 6981 5-8-13 **45**....................[1] StevieDonohoe 3 — 1
(Grace Harris) *hld up: rdn and wknd over 2f out* **100/1**

-000 **P** **Kakapuka**[20] 1147 9-9-6 **52**....................(p) MartinHarley 9
(Anabel K Murphy) *s.v.s: wl bhd whn hung rt 6f out: sn p.u* **16/1**

1m 28.41s (-0.39) **Going Correction** -0.125s/f (Stan) — **11** Ran SP% **114.1**

Speed ratings (Par 101): **97,95,95,93,92 92,88,86,79,73**

CSF £43.35 CT £249.23 TOTE £5.80: £1.80, £2.10, £2.30; EX 38.70 Trifecta £236.90.

Owner A Saha **Bred** Mrs Julie Routledge-Martin **Trained** Sheriff Hutton, N Yorks

FOCUS

A weak handicap, with the top weight rated just 53, and a couple of these seemed very reluctant to exit the stalls. Despite a solid pace, not many ever got into it.

T/Jkpt: Not won. T/Plt: £38.40 to a £1 stake. Pool: £57,681.99 - 1,082.98 winning tickets. T/Qpdt: £7.80 to a £1 stake. Pool: £4,715.94 - 442.77 winning tickets. **Colin Roberts**

1557 - (Foreign Racing) - See Raceform Interactive

[1249]CATTERICK (L-H)

Wednesday, April 20

OFFICIAL GOING: Good to soft (soft in places; 6.2)

Wind: light 1/2 behind Weather: fine and sunny

1558 RACING UK DAY PASS JUST £10 H'CAP — 5f

1:50 (1:50) (Class 6) (0-65,65) 3-Y-O — **£2,264** (£673; £336; £168) **Stalls** Low

Form — RPR

3-02 **1** **Black Grass**[14] 1249 3-8-9 **58**.................... NathanEvans[(5)] 6 — 65
(Michael Easterby) *trckd ldrs: upsides over 2f out: kpt on to ld last 75yds: drvn out* **3/1**[1]

44-2 **2** *1* **Fumbo Jumbo (IRE)**[35] 962 3-9-5 **63**.................... DavidAllan 4 — 66
(Garry Moss) *led: hdd and no ex last 75yds* **9/2**[2]

06-5 **3** *2* **Mustn't Grumble (IRE)**[23] 1126 3-9-4 **62**....................(p) GrahamGibbons 5 — 60
(Ivan Furtado) *trckd ldrs: upsides over 2f out: kpt on same pce fnl f: eased nr fin* **3/1**[1]

003- **4** *6* **Lady Wootton**[195] 7055 3-9-4 **62**.................... PhillipMakin 1 — 37
(Keith Dalgleish) *sn outpcd and in rr: modest 4th over 1f out: nvr on terms* **3/1**[1]

25-0 **5** *6* **The Lillster**[93] 242 3-9-2 **63**.................... GeorgeDowning[(3)] 2 — 16
(Tony Carroll) *sn outpcd and in rr: bhd fnl 3f* **10/1**[3]

-005 **6** *8* **Feelin Dicky**[19] 1183 3-9-7 **65**....................(b[1]) TomEaves 3
(James Given) *trckd ldrs: drvn over 2f out: sn lost pl and bhd* **20/1**

1m 2.23s (2.43) **Going Correction** +0.475s/f (Yiel) — **6** Ran SP% **107.0**

Speed ratings (Par 96): **99,97,94,84,75 62**

CSF £15.06 TOTE £3.70: £1.80, £1.60; EX 18.40 Trifecta £56.10.

Owner T Dewhirst, L Folwell, S Hull & D Swales **Bred** M W Easterby **Trained** Sheriff Hutton, N Yorks

FOCUS

All race distances as advertised. With no rain since Sunday morning the ground continued to dry out and was now officially good to soft, soft in places. The winning time for the opener was 3.93sec outside standard, suggesting there was still some juice in the ground. Phillip Makin said: "The ground is soft, a bit dead", while Tom Eaves said: "It is tacky." A modest 3yo sprint handicap to start and the first three were the only ones ever in it. The winner built on his recent course run.

1559 FOLLOW ON TWITTER @CATTERICKRACES H'CAP — 5f

2:20 (2:20) (Class 5) (0-70,70) 4-Y-O+ — **£2,911** (£866; £432; £216) **Stalls** Low

Form — RPR

2514 **1** **Hit The Lights (IRE)**[4] 1495 6-8-9 **65**....................(v) DanielleMooney[(7)] 1 — 74
(David Nicholls) *awkward s: in rr: drvn and outpcd over 3f out: hdwy 2f out: styd on to ld last 75yds* **2/1**[1]

-402 **2** *1 3/4* **New Lease Of Life**[9] 1378 7-9-1 **64**....................(v) JasonHart 2 — 67
(Keith Dalgleish) *led over 1f: chsd ldrs: kpt on same pce to take 2nd clsng stages* **5/1**

4-65 **3** *nk* **Orient Class**[24] 1110 5-9-2 **65**....................(v) GrahamLee 4 — 67
(Paul Midgley) *w ldr: led over 3f out: hdd and no ex last 75yds* **3/1**[2]

0-00 **4** *3* **Windforpower (IRE)**[14] 1255 6-8-13 **62**....................(p) JoeFanning 3 — 53
(Tracy Waggott) *chsd ldrs: 2nd over 2f out: hung lft: wknd fnl f* **9/1**

422- **5** *2 3/4* **Oriental Splendour (IRE)**[185] 7311 4-9-7 **70**.................... JamesSullivan 7 — 51
(Ruth Carr) *racd wd: hdwy to chse ldrs over 2f out: edgd lft and wknd over 1f out* **4/1**[3]

00-0 **6** *6* **Bronze Beau**[6] 1447 9-9-2 **68**....................(t) JacobButterfield[(3)] 5 — 28
(Kristin Stubbs) *sn chsng ldrs: outpcd over 2f out: sn lost pl* **14/1**

1m 1.93s (2.13) **Going Correction** +0.525s/f (Yiel) — **6** Ran SP% **111.7**

Speed ratings (Par 103): **103,100,99,94,90 80**

CSF £12.22 TOTE £3.90: £2.00, £2.90; EX 11.90 Trifecta £47.50.

Owner Sporting Lives Racing **Bred** Carrigbeg Stud **Trained** Sessay, N Yorks

FOCUS

An ordinary sprint handicap in which the winning time was 0.3sec quicker than the 3yos in the opener. The winner was back to something like his 3yo form.

1560 2016 CATTERICK TWELVE FURLONG SERIES H'CAP (QUALIFIER) (DIV I) — 1m 3f 214y

2:55 (2:55) (Class 5) (0-70,71) 4-Y-O+ — **£3,234** (£962; £481; £240) **Stalls** Low

Form — RPR

4001 **1** **Astra Hall**[15] 1248 7-9-1 **67**.................... GeorgeBuckell[(5)] 7 — 79
(Michael Appleby) *trckd ldr: led over 3f out: drew clr fnl f: pushed out* **8/1**[3]

202- **2** *5* **Applejack Lad**[72] 5229 5-8-11 **58**....................(tp) AndrewMullen 6 — 62
(Michael Smith) *mid-div: hdwy 3f out: 4th over 2f out: styd on to take modest 2nd clsng stages* **16/1**

530- **3** *3/4* **Moon Over Rio (IRE)**[162] 6706 5-9-1 **62**.................... JoeyHaynes 12 — 65
(Ben Haslam) *mid-div: hdwy to chse ldrs over 7f out: drvn 4f out: 2nd 3f out: kpt on same pce* **16/1**

10-4 **4** *1/2* **Frightened Rabbit (USA)**[22] 865 4-9-0 **62**....................(p) PhillipMakin 8 — 64
(Keith Dalgleish) *chsd ldrs: 3rd 3f out: kpt on same pce over 1f out* **7/2**[2]

606- **5** *1 1/4* **Aldreth**[176] 7528 5-9-1 **67**.................... NathanEvans[(5)] 11 — 67+
(Michael Easterby) *in rr: hdwy on outside over 3f out: edgd lft over 2f out: kpt on same pce* **10/1**

5012 **6** *1/2* **Next Edition (IRE)**[14] 1253 8-9-2 **68**.................... PhilDennis[(5)] 4 — 67
(Philip Kirby) *in rr-div: hdwy on ins 3f out: chsng ldrs over 1f out: kpt on one pce* **9/1**

4641 **7** *1* **Deep Resolve (IRE)**[8] 1399 5-9-10 **71** 6ex.................... BenCurtis 10 — 69
(Alan Swinbank) *s.s: hdwy on outer over 2f out: kpt on: nvr nr ldrs* **3/1**[1]

30-0 **8** *3 1/4* **San Cassiano (IRE)**[18] 1201 9-9-4 **65**.................... JamesSullivan 3 — 57
(Ruth Carr) *led 1f: sn mid-div: hdwy over 2f out: wknd fnl f* **12/1**

560- **9** *nk* **Pertuis (IRE)**[209] 6689 10-9-2 **63**.................... GrahamLee 9 — 55
(Micky Hammond) *s.i.s: in rr: sme hdwy over 2f out: nvr on terms* **9/1**

25-0 **10** *18* **That Be Grand**[23] 1121 5-8-7 **54** oh8.................... DuranFentiman 2 — 17
(Shaun Harris) *hld up in mid-div: drvn over 3f out: sn lost pl: bhd fnl 2f: t.o* **50/1**

00-0 **11** *2 1/2* **Whitchurch**[18] 1201 4-8-10 **58**.................... ConnorBeasley 1 — 17
(Philip Kirby) *hld up in rr: bhd fnl 2f: t.o* **20/1**

12 *35* **Qatea (IRE)**[24] 2023 4-9-6 **68**....................(bt) TomEaves 5
(Donald McCain) *led after 1f: hdd over 3f out: sn lost pl and bhd: t.o* **25/1**

2m 45.8s (6.90) **Going Correction** +0.65s/f (Yiel)

WFA 4 from 5yo+ 1lb — **12** Ran SP% **117.5**

Speed ratings (Par 103): **103,99,99,98,98 97,97,94,94,82 80,57**

CSF £124.43 CT £1995.21 TOTE £8.10: £3.20, £3.80, £3.60; EX 101.60 Trifecta £1669.40.

Owner From The Front Racing **Bred** Miss B Swire **Trained** Oakham, Rutland

FOCUS
The first division of an ordinary middle-distance handicap in which they seemed to go a fair pace. The winner still has some mileage in her old form.

1561 2016 CATTERICK TWELVE FURLONG SERIES H'CAP (QUALIFIER) (DIV II) 1m 3f 214y

3:30 (3:32) (Class 5) (0-70,69) 4-Y-O+ **£3,234** (£962; £481; £240) **Stalls** Low

Form RPR

30-3 **1** **Russian Royale**[15] 1248 6-9-7 **69** PJMcDonald 7 79
(Micky Hammond) *mid-div: hdwy over 6f out: led over 1f out: drvn out* **20/1**

01-2 **2** 1 1/4 **I Am Not Here (IRE)**[18] 1202 5-9-3 **65** BenCurtis 10 73
(Brian Ellison) *hld up in rr: hdwy over 3f out: chsng ldrs 2f out: 2nd 1f out: edgd lft: styd on same pce* **9/4**[1]

0/4- **3** 7 **Dry Your Eyes (IRE)**[317] 2993 5-9-6 **68** DanielTudhope 6 65
(David O'Meara) *trckd ldrs: led over 2f out: hdd over 1f out: fdd* **7/1**[3]

00-0 **4** 1/2 **Triple Eight (IRE)**[14] 1253 8-8-12 **65** PhilDennis(5) 4 61
(Philip Kirby) *hld up in mid-div: hung lft bnd 3f out: kpt on fnl 2f: tk modest 4th last 100yds: nvr a threat* **33/1**

00-3 **5** 4 1/2 **Sherman McCoy**[14] 1253 10-9-5 **67** RobertWinston 5 56
(Marjorie Fife) *chsd ldrs: drvn over 4f out: wknd over 1f out* **4/1**[2]

331- **6** 3 1/2 **Nonagon**[175] 7567 5-8-8 **56** (t) IanBrennan 8 39
(Wilf Storey) *bolted 4f gng to s: in rr: hdwy 6f out: chsng ldrs over 2f out: wknd appr fnl f* **16/1**

00-0 **7** 1 1/4 **Moccasin (FR)**[27] 1057 7-9-0 **62** (p) DavidAllan 1 43
(Geoffrey Harker) *in rr: hdwy on inner 2f out: nvr a factor* **16/1**

3-60 **8** 3 **Splash Of Verve (IRE)**[14] 1253 4-8-11 **60** ConnorBeasley 2 36
(Philip Kirby) *led: hdd over 2f out: lost pl over 1f out* **10/1**

6-35 **9** 10 **Dalaki (IRE)**[17] 1222 5-9-5 **67** (b) TonyHamilton 11 27
(Des Donovan, Ire) *s.i.s: sn chsng ldrs: reminders over 3f out: lost pl over 2f out: sn bhd* **7/1**[3]

600- **10** 1/2 **Operateur (IRE)**[224] 4928 8-8-9 **57** RaulDaSilva 3 17
(Ben Haslam) *mid-div: drvn over 6f out: hmpd and lost pl bnd 3f out: sn bhd* **25/1**

600 **11** 29 **Antonio Joli (IRE)**[21] 1140 4-9-1 **64** JoeyHaynes 9
(Jo Hughes) *in rr: sn drvn along: bhd fnl 5f: t.o whn eased over 1f out* **16/1**

2m 45.81s (6.91) **Going Correction** +0.70s/f (Yiel)
WFA 4 from 5yo+ 1lb **11** Ran SP% **114.1**
Speed ratings (Par 103): **104,103,98,98,95 92,92,90,83,83 63**
CSF £61.82 CT £359.79 TOTE £14.80: £3.90, £1.90, £1.50; EX 63.80 Trifecta £346.80.
Owner Raypasha **Bred** Mrs P A & M J Reditt **Trained** Middleham, N Yorks

FOCUS
The winning time was almost identical to the first division and the first two pulled clear. The winner was not an obvious improver.

1562 BREEDERS BACKING RACING EBF MAIDEN FILLIES' STKS (PLUS 10 RACE) 7f

4:00 (4:02) (Class 5) 3-Y-O **£4,204** (£1,251; £625; £312) **Stalls** Low

Form RPR

4 **1** **Normandie Lady**[33] 984 3-9-0 0 TonyHamilton 2 81+
(Richard Fahey) *gave problems loading: chsd ldrs: drvn 3f out: styd on to ld last 150yds: won gng away* **5/1**[3]

0-2 **2** 2 3/4 **Bad Girl Caoimhe (IRE)**[15] 1246 3-9-0 0 BenCurtis 12 73
(Brian Ellison) *chsd ldr: drvn over 2f out: upsides 150yds out: kpt on same pce* **7/4**[1]

34- **3** 2 1/2 **Bonhomie**[146] 7996 3-9-0 0 JoeFanning 10 66
(Michael Bell) *led: drvn 2f out: hdd last 150yds: fdd* **10/3**[2]

45- **4** 4 **Bad Penny (IRE)**[229] 6044 3-9-0 0 DanielTudhope 4 55
(John Quinn) *wore ear plugs: chsd ldrs: one pce fnl 2f* **6/1**

2- **5** 4 1/2 **Ettie Hart (IRE)**[238] 5752 3-9-0 0 GrahamGibbons 5 43
(Mick Channon) *chsd ldrs: drvn over 3f out: wknd over 1f out* **11/1**

6 1 1/2 **Enjoy Life (IRE)** 3-9-0 0 KeaganLatham 11 39
(Kevin Ryan) *mid-div: drvn 3f out: wknd over 1f out* **20/1**

5 **7** 1 **High On Light**[23] 1123 3-9-0 0 DavidAllan 6 36
(Tim Easterby) *rr-div: sme hdwy over 2f out: nvr a factor* **16/1**

0-0 **8** 2 **Don't Tell Nik (IRE)**[51] 768 3-9-0 0 JackGarritty 3 31
(David Loughnane) *mid-div: effrt over 2f out: wknd over 1f out* **200/1**

9 8 **Kyllini** 3-8-11 0 JacobButterfield(3) 1 9
(Marjorie Fife) *s.i.s: in rr: bhd fnl 2f* **33/1**

10 3/4 **Charmed Company (IRE)** 3-9-0 0 JasonHart 8 7
(Keith Dalgleish) *s.i.s: sn detached in rr: nvr on terms* **33/1**

00- **11** 3 1/4 **Annie T**[250] 5341 3-9-0 0 GrahamLee 7
(Paul Midgley) *mid-div: drvn over 3f out: lost pl over 2f out: sn bhd* **100/1**

1m 31.46s (4.46) **Going Correction** +0.75s/f (Yiel) **11** Ran SP% **116.7**
Speed ratings (Par 95): **104,100,98,93,88 86,85,83,74,73 69**
CSF £13.57 TOTE £6.10: £2.00, £1.30, £1.70; EX 18.00 Trifecta £59.40.
Owner A B Phipps **Bred** A B Phipps **Trained** Musley Bank, N Yorks

FOCUS
An ordinary fillies' maiden which was completely dominated by those at the head of the market. The placed horses got racing from some way out, which may have helped the winner. The form is rated around the second and third.

1563 BOOK NOW FOR SATURDAY 28TH MAY H'CAP 7f

4:35 (4:36) (Class 3) (0-90,88) 4-Y-O+ **£7,762** (£2,310; £1,154; £577) **Stalls** Low

Form RPR

51-2 **1** **Lavetta**[23] 1125 4-8-7 **74** oh1 JoeFanning 4 88+
(Alan Swinbank) *chsd ldrs: led 1f out: styd on wl: readily* **9/2**[1]

0-50 **2** 2 1/2 **Taysh (USA)**[14] 1274 4-8-10 **77** BenCurtis 9 85+
(Michael Appleby) *in rr: hdwy on outside over 1f out: hung lft: fin wl to take 2nd clsng stages* **25/1**

000- **3** 1 3/4 **Caprior Bere (FR)**[165] 7754 4-9-5 **86** JoeyHaynes 12 89
(K R Burke) *chsd ldrs on outer: hmpd and pushed lft last 150yds: kpt on same pce* **14/1**

0400 **4** shd **Arnold Lane (IRE)**[11] 1335 7-9-7 **88** TomEaves 1 91
(Mick Channon) *chsd ldrs: drvn over 2f out: kpt on one pce over 1f out: edgd rt 150yds out* **12/1**

20-6 **5** nk **Best Trip (IRE)**[60] 658 9-8-11 **78** JamesSullivan 8 80
(Marjorie Fife) *led: hdd 1f out: fdd* **14/1**

320- **6** 1 1/4 **Breakable**[165] 7758 5-8-10 **82** (p) RachelRichardson(5) 2 81
(Tim Easterby) *chsd ldrs: effrt over 2f out: one pce: eased closinbg stages* **8/1**[3]

20-5 **7** shd **Fullon Clarets**[17] 1215 4-8-9 **83** AdamMcNamara(7) 6 84+
(Richard Fahey) *mid-div: drvn over 3f out: one pce whn hung lft and n.m.r over 1f out* **9/2**[1]

250- **8** 2 3/4 **Green Howard**[221] 6305 8-9-6 **87** (p) GrahamLee 3 78
(Rebecca Bastiman) *in rr: hdwy on inner over 2f out: n.m.r: nvr a threat* **16/1**

043- **9** 2 1/2 **Gerry The Glover (IRE)**[214] 6518 4-9-7 **88** GrahamGibbons 7 72
(Brian Ellison) *s.i.s: in rr: hdwy over 1f out: nvr a factor* **5/1**[2]

240- **10** 11 **Steel Train (FR)**[214] 6519 5-9-6 **87** DanielTudhope 5 41
(David O'Meara) *n rr: sme hdwy over 2f out: hung lft and lost pl over 1f out: eased and bhd clsng stages* **8/1**[3]

600- **11** 1 1/4 **Fuwairt (IRE)**[185] 7326 4-9-2 **83** JackGarritty 13 34
(David Loughnane) *chsd ldrs on outer: effrt over 2f out: lost pl over 1f out: eased and bhd clsng stages* **25/1**

001- **12** 1 1/2 **Comino (IRE)**[176] 7525 5-8-9 **83** (p) LewisEdmunds(7) 11 30
(Kevin Ryan) *chsd ldr towards outside: lost pl over 1f out: bhd whn eased clsng stages* **16/1**

14-0 **U** **Musaaid (IRE)**[17] 1215 4-8-7 **79** NathanEvans(5) 10 77
(Michael Easterby) *mid-div: drvn 4f out: sme hdwy 2f out: edgd lft appr fnl f: wl hld whn hmpd and uns rdr 75yds out* **28/1**

1m 31.26s (4.26) **Going Correction** +0.80s/f (Soft) **13** Ran SP% **119.2**
Speed ratings (Par 107): **107,104,102,102,101 100,100,97,94,81 80,78,**
CSF £122.38 CT £1524.85 TOTE £4.70: £2.00, £6.20, £3.70; EX 98.20 Trifecta £4770.80 Part won..
Owner Guy Reed Racing **Bred** G Reed **Trained** Melsonby, N Yorks

FOCUS
A decent handicap run at a strong pace. Things got a bit tight well inside the last furlong with Musaaid clipping heels and unseating his rider, but the winner was well away by then and was much the best horse on the day. The winner can do better still.

1564 RACINGUK.COM/ANYWHERE 3 DEVICES 1 PRICE H'CAP 7f

5:10 (5:11) (Class 6) (0-60,60) 3-Y-O **£2,264** (£673; £336; £168) **Stalls** Low

Form RPR

3412 **1** **Footlight**[29] 1031 3-9-0 **60** AdamMcNamara(7) 6 72
(Richard Fahey) *w ldr: led over 4f out: forged clr fnl f* **7/2**[2]

61-6 **2** 3 1/2 **Little Pippin**[14] 1276 3-8-12 **51** BarryMcHugh 8 54
(Tony Coyle) *s.i.s: in rr: drvn over 3f out: hdwy on outside over 1f out: styd on to take modest 2nd clsng stages* **16/1**

56-3 **3** 3/4 **Mr Orange (IRE)**[23] 1126 3-9-6 **59** GrahamGibbons 7 60
(Paul Midgley) *hld up in mid-div: hdwy over 2f out: sn chsng ldrs: kpt on same pce over 1f out* **15/8**[1]

053- **4** 3/4 **Fine Example**[209] 6682 3-9-4 **60** JoeDoyle(3) 9 61
(Kevin Ryan) *hld up in rr: hdwy over 2f out: kpt on fnl f* **13/2**

000- **5** 1 1/2 **Moi Aussie**[197] 7011 3-9-2 **55** DaleSwift 5 50
(Ed McMahon) *mid-div: effrt over 2f out: kpt on: nvr a threat* **8/1**

600- **6** 2 1/4 **Wotabond**[153] 7895 3-8-8 **47** GeorgeChaloner 1 36
(Richard Whitaker) *led: hdd over 4f out: sn drvn: outpcd over 2f out: hdwy and swtchd rt 150yds out: kpt on* **16/1**

50-3 **7** 3/4 **Mr Lucas (IRE)**[29] 1031 3-8-12 **46** oh1 (p) NathanEvans(5) 3 33
(Peter Niven) *rr-div: sme hdwy over 2f out: wknd over 1f out* **6/1**[3]

004- **8** 1 1/2 **Blagger**[186] 7283 3-8-7 **46** oh1 (t) JasonHart 10 30
(Richard Guest) *s.i.s: sn chsng ldrs on outside: lost pl 2f out* **20/1**

060- **9** 1 1/2 **Miss Popov**[162] 7783 3-8-8 **47** oh1 ow1 DavidAllan 4 27
(Noel Wilson) *chsd ldrs: 2nd over 2f out: wknd fnl f: eased nr fin* **40/1**

1m 32.91s (5.91) **Going Correction** +0.85s/f (Soft) **9** Ran SP% **114.7**
Speed ratings (Par 96): **100,96,95,94,92 90,89,87,85**
CSF £56.83 CT £133.83 TOTE £3.60: £1.30, £2.40, £1.70; EX 15.00 Trifecta £83.70.
Owner Mrs P B E P Farr **Bred** Worksop Manor Stud **Trained** Musley Bank, N Yorks

FOCUS
A very moderate 3yo handicap but another step up from the winner.

1565 RACING AGAIN 3RD MAY APPRENTICE H'CAP 7f

5:40 (5:41) (Class 6) (0-65,65) 4-Y-O+ **£2,264** (£673; £336; £168) **Stalls** Low

Form RPR

U50- **1** **Bajan Rebel**[211] 6617 5-8-4 **51** oh1 AnnaHesketh(3) 5 57
(Michael Easterby) *chsd ldrs: led appr fnl f: hld on nr fin* **14/1**

60-0 **2** nk **Tancred (IRE)**[14] 1254 5-9-5 **63** (p) PaddyPilley 15 68
(Conor Dore) *in rr: hdwy on outer over 1f out: styd on wl to take 2nd nr fin* **33/1**

222- **3** nk **American Hustle (IRE)**[190] 7190 4-9-4 **65** CallumShepherd(3) 10 69
(Brian Ellison) *chsd ldrs: chsd wnr and kpt on fnl f* **4/1**[2]

006- **4** hd **Iftikaar (IRE)**[152] 7925 6-8-13 **62** CliffordLee(5) 12 66
(Philip Kirby) *mid-div: hdwy on outside over 1f out: styd on to take 4th nr fin* **16/1**

23-0 **5** 3/4 **Tellovoi (IRE)**[97] 178 8-9-4 **65** (v) RobJFitzpatrick(3) 7 67
(Richard Guest) *chsd ldrs: kpt on same pce last 150yds* **16/1**

2106 **6** 1 1/4 **Zed Candy Girl**[24] 1116 6-9-1 **59** (p) NoelGarbutt 3 58
(Daniel Mark Loughnane) *in rr and drvn along: hdwy on outer 2f out: kpt on same pce* **25/1**

04-0 **7** 1 3/4 **Flyball**[23] 1124 4-8-12 **56** (b[1]) JordanVaughan 11 50
(Kenneth Slack) *led: hdd appr fnl f: wknd clsng stages* **7/1**[3]

000- **8** 6 **Grenade**[177] 7521 4-7-13 **51** oh5 PaulaMuir(8) 13 30+
(Patrick Holmes) *half-rrd s: in rr: nvr on terms* **66/1**

/44- **9** nse **Zingiber**[310] 3226 4-8-3 **52** HollieDoyle(5) 2 30
(Wilf Storey) *mid-div: sme hdwy over 1f out: sn wknd* **50/1**

510- **10** 1 **Totally Magic (IRE)**[187] 7255 4-9-1 **62** NathanEvans(3) 4 38
(Richard Whitaker) *in rr: sme hdwy and n.m.r over 1f out: nvr a factor* **8/1**

060- **11** hd **Vecheka (IRE)**[218] 6395 5-8-9 **58** KieranSchofield(5) 8 33
(Micky Hammond) *hmpd s: hdwy into mid-div over 4f out: effrt over 2f out: nvr a factor* **9/1**

24-0 **12** 1 1/2 **Mrs Biggs**[14] 1254 4-8-11 **65** LeeByrne(10) 9 36
(Declan Carroll) *s.i.s: a in rr* **25/1**

10-0 **13** 4 1/2 **Bold Spirit**[4] 1489 5-8-8 **62** (t) GerO'Neill(10) 14 22
(Declan Carroll) *chsd ldrs: lost pl over 1f out: easesd fnl 100yds* **33/1**

30-4 **14** 5 **Secret City (IRE)**[23] 1120 10-9-1 **62** (b) RowanScott(3) 6 9
(Rebecca Bastiman) *mid-div: lost pl bnd 4f out* **20/1**

5053 **15** 22 **Golden Spun (USA)**[23] 1125 4-8-13 **63** (p) PhilDennis(6) 1
(Michael Dods) *trckd ldrs: lost pl bnd 4f out: bhd whn eased 1f out: t.o: b.b.v* **11/4**[1]

1m 32.62s (5.62) **Going Correction** +0.90s/f (Soft) **15** Ran SP% **120.5**
Speed ratings (Par 101): **103,102,102,102,101 99,97,90,90,89 89,87,82,76,51**
CSF £419.69 CT £2242.06 TOTE £12.70: £3.20, £5.80, £1.70; EX 551.90 Trifecta £2338.40.
Owner Julian Rooney **Bred** Aldridge Racing Partnership **Trained** Sheriff Hutton, N Yorks

FOCUS
A modest but competitive apprentice handicap to end the card, and although they went a good pace there was little covering the front five at the line. The winner is rated to the best of last year's form.

T/Jkpt: Not won. T/Plt: £43.60 to a £1 stake. Pool: £44,356.84 - 741.43 winning tickets T/Qpdt: £17.20 to a £1 stake. Pool: £4,378.16 - 187.34 winning tickets **Walter Glynn**

EPSOM (L-H)

Wednesday, April 20

OFFICIAL GOING: Soft (good to soft in places; 5.2)

Wind: Moderate, behind Weather: Sunny

1566 INVESTEC ASSET FINANCE H'CAP 5f

2:00 (2:00) (Class 3) (0-95,92) 4-Y-O+

£12,450 (£3,728; £1,864; £932; £466; £234) **Stalls** High

Form RPR

-545 **1** **Normal Equilibrium**[73] 492 6-8-13 **84** AndreaAtzeni 5 94
(Robert Cowell) *w ldr: led 2f out: hrd pressed fnl f: kpt on wl* **4/1**[2]

30-1 **2** *1* **Roudee**[17] 1218 4-9-7 **92** RichardKingscote 1 98
(Tom Dascombe) *dwlt: racd on outer and rdn in midfield 1/2-way: styd on wl fnl f to take 2nd nr fin* **7/4**[1]

00-0 **3** *½* **Duke Of Firenze**[18] 1197 7-9-5 **90** OisinMurphy 2 94
(David C Griffiths) *chsd ldng pair: rdn to chse wnr over 1f out: chal fnl f: no ex last 100yds and lost 2nd nr fin* **14/1**

511 **4** *1 ½* **Bouclier (IRE)**[19] 1178 6-8-10 **81** WilliamCarson 8 80
(Tony Carroll) *settled in 6th: pushed along 2f out: no prog tl shkn up and r.o wl fnl 100yds: nrst fin* **5/1**[3]

005- **5** *1 ¼* **Monumental Man**[233] 5936 7-8-12 **83** (p) DavidProbert 7 77
(Michael Attwater) *reluctant to go to post: led against rail: hdd 2f out: lost 2nd over 1f out: wknd* **7/1**

3150 **6** *2 ¼* **Crosse Fire**[17] 1218 4-8-9 **80** (p) KieranO'Neill 3 66
(Scott Dixon) *dwlt: a off the pce: rdn and no prog 2f out* **9/1**

00-6 **7** *½* **Smoothtalkinrascal (IRE)**[19] 1175 6-8-7 **78** oh1 ShaneKelly 4 62
(Peter Crate) *a in last and wl off the pce: shkn up briefly and no prog over 1f out* **11/1**

57.74s (2.04) **Going Correction** +0.625s/f (Yiel) **7** Ran SP% **110.5**
Speed ratings (Par 107): **108,106,105,103,101 97,96**
CSF £10.63 CT £79.55 TOTE £4.80: £2.60, £1.50; EX 12.70 Trifecta £75.10.
Owner The Morley Family **Bred** D R Tucker **Trained** Six Mile Bottom, Cambs

FOCUS
The going was given as soft, good to soft in places (GoingStick: 5.2). The rail was dolled out 2yds from 1m2f to 1m, then 8-10yds from 1m to the winning post, adding 35yds to all races bar 5f. Few got into this. The winner is rated close to the balance of his turf form.

1567 INVESTEC DERBY TRIAL (CONDITIONS RACE) (PLUS 10 RACE) 1m 2f 18y

2:30 (2:31) (Class 2) 3-Y-O

£31,125 (£9,320; £4,660; £2,330; £1,165; £585) **Stalls** Low

Form RPR

1- **1** **So Mi Dar**[183] 7362 3-8-9 81 FrankieDettori 3 103+
(John Gosden) *hld up disputing 5th: pushed along 3f out: prog over 2f out: lost whip 1 1/2f out: rdn to ld over 1f out: edgd lft and hrd pressed fnl f: pushed out and a holding on* **3/1**[2]

24-4 **2** *nk* **Humphrey Bogart (IRE)**[18] 1208 3-9-0 99 SeanLevey 1 105
(Richard Hannon) *stdd s: hld up: last tl prog over 2f out: drvn to chse wnr fnl f and sn chalng: styd on wl but a hld* **12/1**

313- **3** *3 ½* **Viren's Army (IRE)**[164] 7765 3-9-0 98 PatDobbs 8 98
(Richard Hannon) *trckd ldng pair: rdn to ld 2f out: hdd over 1f out: outpcd fnl f* **10/1**[3]

4 *3 ½* **Claudio Monteverdi (IRE)**[14] 1277 3-9-0 0 (t) RyanMoore 2 91
(A P O'Brien, Ire) *trckd ldng pair: pushed along 3f out: chal on inner over 2f out tl nt qckn over 1f out: wknd fnl f* **5/6**[1]

513- **5** *¾* **Percy Street**[184] 7339 3-9-0 96 DougieCostello 4 90
(K R Burke) *hld up disputing 5th: rdn 3f out: no real prog after and wl btn over 1f out* **25/1**

05-3 **6** *2 ¾* **Beaverbrook**[26] 1080 3-9-0 98 JamesDoyle 6 84
(Mark Johnston) *led to 3f out: losing pl whn bdly squeezed out over 2f out: wknd* **16/1**

1- **7** *2* **Top Beak (IRE)**[198] 6986 3-9-0 90 JimmyFortune 9 80
(Hughie Morrison) *trckd ldr: led 3f out: sn rdn and hanging lft: hdd 2f out: wknd rapidly fnl f* **10/1**[3]

2m 18.97s (9.27) **Going Correction** +1.10s/f (Soft) **7** Ran SP% **115.2**
Speed ratings (Par 104): **106,105,102,100,99 97,95**
CSF £37.64 TOTE £3.80: £1.80, £4.00; EX 41.40 Trifecta £207.10.
Owner Lord Lloyd-Webber **Bred** Watership Down Stud **Trained** Newmarket, Suffolk

■ Stewards' Enquiry : Jimmy Fortune two-day ban: careless riding (May 4-5)

FOCUS
Race distance increased by 35yds. This looked a deeper race than has often been the case in the past, and the winner, the only filly in the field, put down a marker for the Oaks. They went quicker early on and finished slower than in the handicap later on the card, clocking a final time 0.96sec slower, and it seemed to help the cause of those held up. The form is rated around the third.

1568 INVESTEC CORPORATE BANKING GREAT METROPOLITAN H'CAP 1m 4f 10y

3:05 (3:09) (Class 3) (0-95,93) 4-Y-O+

£12,450 (£3,728; £1,864; £932; £466; £234) **Stalls** Centre

Form RPR

300- **1** **Barwick**[165] 7757 8-8-13 **85** SteveDrowne 7 93
(George Baker) *dwlt: hld up in 10th: gd prog fr 3f out: clsd on ldrs over 1f out: drvn to ld last 150yds: styd on wl* **16/1**

1-12 **2** *1 ½* **Whinging Willie (IRE)**[82] 382 7-8-3 **80** (v) HectorCrouch(5) 8 86
(Gary Moore) *cl up: 4th st: rdn to ld wl over 2f out: kpt on wl whn pressed after: hdd and outpcd last 150yds* **25/1**

21-4 **3** *2 ¼* **Prendergast Hill (IRE)**[25] 1093 4-8-12 **85** JimCrowley 4 87
(Ed de Giles) *dwlt: sn prom: 3rd st: chal gng easily 3f out: chsd new ldr sn after and rdn over 2f out: nt handling trck wl and nt qckn over 1f out: lost 2nd fnl f* **9/2**[2]

110- **4** *½* **Leah Freya (IRE)**[200] 6927 5-9-4 **90** JFEgan 11 92
(Pat Phelan) *hld up in midfield: prog and 7th st: rdn to chse ldng pair over 2f out: kpt on but nvr quite able to chal: lost 3rd fnl f* **14/1**

10-1 **5** *8* **Knight Music**[21] 1144 4-8-8 **81** RobertHavlin 12 70
(Michael Attwater) *broke fast but restrained in 5th: rdn to go 4th briefly over 2f out but no imp on ldrs: wknd over 1f out* **15/2**

000- **6** *5* **Oasis Fantasy (IRE)**[179] 7462 5-9-4 **90** RyanMoore 10 71+
(Ed Dunlop) *hld up in 9th: effrt 3f out: sn rdn and no real prog: wknd fr 2f out* **4/1**[1]

630- **7** *9* **Lungarno Palace (USA)**[214] 6539 5-8-11 **86** MichaelJMMurphy(3) 5 52
(John Gallagher) *in tch in midfield: shkn up sn after 1/2-way: 8th and struggling st: hanging bdly and wl btn over 2f out* **11/1**

14-3 **8** *3 ¼* **Agent Gibbs**[26] 1081 4-9-0 **87** (p) SilvestreDeSousa 6 56
(Ali Stronge) *led 3f: led again 1/2-way: hdd wl over 2f out: sn wknd: eased fnl f* **13/2**[3]

54- **9** *1 ¾* **Steppe Daughter (IRE)**[168] 7704 5-8-8 **80** OisinMurphy 3 38
(Denis Coakley) *dwlt: hld up in 11th: pushed along 5f out: bhd fnl 3f* **25/1**

042- **10** *½* **Wind Place And Sho**[173] 7597 4-9-0 **87** AndreaAtzeni 1 52
(James Eustace) *led after 3f to 1/2-way: cl 2nd but drvn st: wknd wl over 2f out* **7/1**

113- **11** *5* **Scrutinise**[191] 7165 4-9-6 **93** PaulMulrennan 2 43+
(Ed Dunlop) *hld up in 6th: shkn up and lost pl 3f out: sn bhd* **8/1**

46-0 **12** *3 ½* **Saoi (USA)**[25] 1089 9-9-1 **87** WilliamBuick 9 31
(William Knight) *a detached in last: t.o* **20/1**

2m 49.52s (10.62) **Going Correction** +1.10s/f (Soft)
WFA 4 from 5yo+ 1lb **12** Ran SP% **120.2**
Speed ratings (Par 107): **108,107,105,105,99 96,90,88,87,86 83,81**
CSF £371.02 CT £2095.58 TOTE £17.60: £4.60, £5.70, £1.70; EX 666.20 Trifecta £5052.80.
Owner Michael H Watt **Bred** Dullingham Park **Trained** Manton, Wilts

FOCUS
Race distance increased by 35yds. A competitive affair but pretty ordinary form for the grade.

1569 INVESTEC CITY AND SUBURBAN STKS (H'CAP) 1m 2f 18y

3:40 (3:43) (Class 2) (0-105,103) 4-Y-O+

£28,012 (£8,388; £4,194; £2,097; £1,048; £526) **Stalls** Low

Form RPR

33-1 **1** **Dark Red (IRE)**[20] 1161 4-8-2 **84** oh3 FrannyNorton 6 97+
(Ed Dunlop) *t.k.h: trckd ldrs: 3rd st: rdn to ld wl over 1f out: hrd pressed fnl f: hung lft to far side but hld on* **12/1**

452- **2** *¾* **Pacify**[180] 7426 4-8-13 **95** FMBerry 8 106+
(Ralph Beckett) *wl in tch: cl 6th st: prog to press ldrs 2f out: tk 2nd and chal fnl f: carried lft after and nvr able to get past* **4/1**[1]

140- **3** *3* **What About Carlo (FR)**[179] 7470 5-9-4 **100** JimmyFortune 7 105
(Eve Johnson Houghton) *dwlt: hld up in 10th: prog over 2f out: nt on terms w ldng trio whn tk 4th jst over 1f out: styd on wl to snatch 3rd last strides* **7/1**[2]

120/ **4** *nk* **Clayton**[16] 2294 7-9-4 **100** (t) RyanMoore 10 104
(Gary Moore) *pressed ldr: brought field to nr side in st and sn led: drvn and hdd wl over 1f out: lost 2nd fnl f: hanging lft and lost 3rd last strides* **4/1**[1]

523- **5** *3 ¾* **Elbereth**[217] 6444 5-8-13 **95** DavidProbert 9 92
(Andrew Balding) *hld up in 8th: sme prog over 2f out but nt on terms w ldrs fnl 2f: one pce* **7/1**[2]

60-6 **6** *2 ¾* **Archangel Raphael (IRE)**[11] 1336 4-9-2 **98** PatDobbs 11 89
(Amanda Perrett) *trckd ldrs: 4th st: lft bhd over 2f out and sn btn* **25/1**

551- **7** *2* **Interconnection**[190] 7182 5-8-2 **84** (p) WilliamCarson 5 71
(Ed Vaughan) *wl in tch: 5th st: prog to chal on outer over 2f out: wknd qckly over 1f out* **8/1**[3]

500- **8** *3 ¼* **Firestorm (GER)**[179] 7470 5-8-6 **88** [1] KierenFox 1 69
(Michael Attwater) *hld up in 9th: rdn and no real prog 3f out: sn btn* **11/1**

546- **9** *3 ¾* **Tioga Pass**[277] 4395 5-9-2 **98** (b) AndreaAtzeni 3 71
(Paul Cole) *dwlt: mostly in last: struggling over 3f out: sn no ch* **25/1**

040- **10** *6* **Sennockian Star**[193] 7120 6-8-13 **95** (v) SilvestreDeSousa 2 56
(Mark Johnston) *led to over 3f out: sn wknd: eased fnl f* **7/1**[2]

662/ **11** *20* **Slowfoot (GER)**[384] 8-9-7 **103** TimmyMurphy 4 24
(Jim Best) *prom tl 7th and wkng st: t.o* **33/1**

2m 18.01s (8.31) **Going Correction** +1.10s/f (Soft) **11** Ran SP% **115.3**
Speed ratings (Par 109): **110,109,107,106,103 101,99,97,94,89 73**
CSF £57.20 CT £368.20 TOTE £11.20: £2.80, £2.00, £2.70; EX 66.40 Trifecta £569.20.
Owner The Hon R J Arculli **Bred** T Jones **Trained** Newmarket, Suffolk

FOCUS
Race distance increased by 35yds. Another competitive handicap. They went slower early on than in the Derby trial and finished faster, clocking a time 0.96sec quicker. The first two were clear and can do better still.

1570 INVESTEC SPECIALIST CASH PRODUCTS MAIDEN STKS 1m 114y

4:15 (4:15) (Class 5) 3-4-Y-O **£3,881** (£1,155; £577; £288) **Stalls** Low

Form RPR

3-3 **1** **Finelcity (GER)**[14] 1270 3-8-11 0 (b) DaneO'Neill 1 76
(Harry Dunlop) *mde all: rdn 2f out in centre of crse: styd on to draw clr fnl f* **9/1**

2 *3 ½* **Najd** 3-8-11 0 FrankieDettori 2 68+
(Richard Hannon) *trckd ldng pair: c alone to nr side in st: tk 2nd 2f out and clsd on wnr: nrly on terms 1f out: wknd fnl f* **11/1**

5- **3** *7* **Generalship (IRE)**[182] 7397 3-8-11 0 (b[1]) WilliamBuick 5 52
(John Gosden) *trckd wnr: rdn and nt qckn over 2f out: sn lost 2nd and wl btn after* **13/8**[1]

325- **4** *1 ¼* **Yensir**[192] 7144 3-8-11 79 JFEgan 3 49
(Pat Phelan) *hld up in last: tk 4th st: sn shkn up: nvr able to threaten ldrs* **4/1**[3]

2- **5** *30* **Silca Star**[180] 7429 3-8-11 0 SilvestreDeSousa 4
(Mick Channon) *racd in 4th tl dropped to last and wknd st: sn t.o and eased* **15/8**[2]

1m 55.7s (9.60) **Going Correction** +1.10s/f (Soft) **5** Ran SP% **111.2**
Speed ratings (Par 103): **101,97,91,90,63**
CSF £83.95 TOTE £10.90: £4.90, £3.20; EX 73.80 Trifecta £185.20.
Owner The Blue Bar Partnership **Bred** Gestut Hofgut Heymann **Trained** Lambourn, Berks

FOCUS
Race distance increased by 35yds. No more than a fair maiden, 11lb slower than the 3yo handicap. The form is rated around the race averages.

1571 INVESTEC PRIVATE BANKING H'CAP 1m 114y

4:50 (4:50) (Class 4) (0-80,80) 3-Y-O **£5,822** (£1,732; £865; £432) **Stalls** Low

Form RPR

66-1 **1** **Medburn Dream**[9] 1388 3-8-7 **66** 6ex FrannyNorton 7 81+
(Paul Henderson) *mde all: tk field to nr side in st and racd against rail: drvn 2f out: drew clr jst over 1f out: styd on strly* **9/2**[2]

054- **2** *4 ½* **Scarlet Dragon**[180] 7421 3-9-3 **79** TomMarquand(3) 2 83
(Eve Johnson Houghton) *t.k.h: trckd ldrs: 4th st: nt clr run 3f out: effrt to chse wnr jst over 2f out: cl enough u.p over 1f out: kpt on but readily lft bhd fnl f* **7/1**

133- **3** *5* **Machine Learner**[196] 7042 3-9-7 **80** JamieSpencer 8 73+
(Michael Bell) *hld up in last: hanging and gng nowhere 3f out: picked up over 1f out: fin wl to snatch 3rd last stride* **6/1**

3152 **4** *hd* **Byres Road**[6] 1446 3-9-7 **80** SilvestreDeSousa 6 72
(Mark Johnston) *t.k.h: chsd wnr after 2f to 3f out: sn rdn and struggling: lost modest 3rd last stride* **7/2**[1]

41- **5** 2 **Gold Faith (IRE)**[210] 6644 3-9-6 **79** .... FMBerry 4 66
(Ralph Beckett) *chsd wnr 2f and again 3f out to over 2f out: sn floundering and btn* **9/2**[2]

010- **6** 2½ **Blackout (FR)**[215] 6501 3-9-7 **80** .... PatDobbs 5 62
(Richard Hannon) *dwlt: t.k.h: hld up: 7th st: no prog and wl btn over 2f out* **8/1**

31-6 **7** 3¾ **Musical Taste**[14] 1258 3-9-2 **75** .... JFEgan 1 48
(Pat Phelan) *chsd ldrs: 5th and drvn st: wknd 3f out* **28/1**

041- **8** 4½ **Marshal Dan Troop (IRE)**[231] 5992 3-9-6 **79** .... RyanMoore 3 42
(Peter Chapple-Hyam) *hld up: 6th st: no prog 3f out: sn wl btn* **5/1**[3]

1m 54.52s (8.42) **Going Correction** +1.10s/f (Soft) **8** Ran SP% **116.6**
Speed ratings (Par 100): **106,102,97,97,95 93,90,86**
CSF £36.48 CT £192.78 TOTE £5.10: £2.00, £2.60, £1.90; EX 43.80 Trifecta £274.10.
Owner Eddie Evans **Bred** Eddie Evans **Trained** Whitsbury, Hants

FOCUS
Race distance increased by 35yds. Few got into this, with the winner dominating throughout. Not many showed their form behind him.
T/Plt: £688.10 to a £1 stake. Pool: £85,316.28 - 90.51 winning tickets T/Qpdt: £164.80 to a £1 stake. Pool: £6,947.05 - 31.18 winning tickets **Jonathan Neesom**

1334 LINGFIELD (L-H)

Wednesday, April 20

OFFICIAL GOING: Polytrack: standard
Wind: light, half against Weather: sunny

1572 HAPPY 90TH BIRTHDAY HM QUEEN FILLIES' H'CAP 7f 1y(P)
4:45 (4:45) (Class 5) (0-75,75) 3-Y-O **£2,911** (£866; £432; £216) **Stalls** Low

Form RPR

410- **1** **Staintondale Lass (IRE)**[176] 7534 3-9-1 **69** .... OisinMurphy 4 74
(Ed Vaughan) *mde all: rdn and qcknd 2f out: 2 l clr and drvn 1f out: kpt on and a holding on ins fnl f: pushed out fnl 100yds* **16/1**

1 **2** ½ **Bargain Buy**[21] 1146 3-9-7 **75** .... PatCosgrave 5 79+
(William Haggas) *hld up in tch in midfield: swtchd lft and effrt to chse ldrs over 1f out: chsd wnr 150yds out: styd on u.p: nvr quite getting to wnr* **4/6**[1]

66-1 **3** 1¾ **Tigserin (IRE)**[13] 1292 3-8-11 **65** .... SaleemGolam 9 64+
(Giles Bravery) *taken down early: trckd ldrs on outer: effrt and sltly hmpd over 1f out: swtchd rt 1f out: styd on u.p to go 3rd fnl 50yds* **6/1**[2]

654- **4** 1¼ **Himalayan Queen**[160] 7810 3-8-9 **63** .... ShaneKelly 2 59
(William Jarvis) *chsd ldrs: wnt 2nd and rdn wl over 1f out: edgd lft and unable qck ent fnl f: one pce and lost 2 pls fnl 150yds* **20/1**

2215 **5** 1¾ **Ruby Wednesday**[14] 1267 3-9-3 **71** .... KierenFox 7 62
(John Best) *stdd s: hld up in tch in last trio: effrt and wd wl over 1f out: styd on u.p ins fnl f: nvr trbld ldrs* **7/1**[3]

060- **6** hd **Harmony Bay (IRE)**[159] 7823 3-8-9 **68** .... GaryMahon(5) 8 58
(Sylvester Kirk) *hld up in tch in last quartet: swtchd rt and on outer over 2f out: effrt wl over 1f out: styd on ins fnl f: nvr trbld ldrs* **66/1**

535- **7** 1 **Carpe Diem Lady (IRE)**[191] 7161 3-9-1 **69** .... AdamKirby 1 57
(Clive Cox) *dwlt and rdn along early: in tch in last quartet: rdn and no imp 2f out: wl hld and one pce after* **6/1**[2]

30-5 **8** hd **Indie Music**[11] 1345 3-8-11 **65** .... SamHitchcott 3 52
(Sylvester Kirk) *hld up in tch in last quartet: effrt u.p wl over 1f out: no prog: nvr trbld ldrs* **25/1**

20- **9** ¾ **Caitie (IRE)**[223] 6241 3-9-6 **74** .... JimCrowley 6 59
(Paul Cole) *chsd wnr tl wl over 1f out: sn no ex u.p and btn 5th 1f out: wknd ins fnl f* **33/1**

1m 25.3s (0.50) **Going Correction** +0.025s/f (Slow) **9** Ran SP% **120.0**
Speed ratings (Par 95): **98,97,95,94,92 91,90,90,89**
CSF £27.81 CT £85.83 TOTE £20.60: £4.60, £1.10, £1.90; EX 52.30 Trifecta £210.60.
Owner A M Pickering **Bred** Ringfort Stud **Trained** Newmarket, Suffolk

FOCUS
An interesting fillies' handicap on paper but a surprise winner, although there was no fluke about it. Ordinary form.

1573 BELATED HAPPY BIRTHDAY WISHES JON HARRIS CLAIMING STKS 7f 1y(P)
5:15 (5:16) (Class 6) 3-Y-O **£2,264** (£673; £336; £168) **Stalls** Low

Form RPR

6444 **1** **Threebagsue (IRE)**[14] 1286 3-9-0 72 .... (b) JosephineGordon(5) 5 72
(J S Moore) *dwlt: sn pushed along: steadily rcvrd to chse ldr after 2f: upsides 1/2-way: led over 1f out: flashed tail u.p but asserted and hung lft ins fnl f: pushed out fnl 100yds* **15/8**[2]

0- **2** 1½ **Justice Focused (IRE)**[210] 6645 3-9-3 0 .... AdamMcLean(7) 4 72
(David Elsworth) *stdd after s: hld up wl in tch: effrt in 3rd 2f out: no imp and rn green over 1f out: stl green but hdwy ins fnl f: wnt 2nd and styd on wl fnl 50yds: no threat to wnr* **9/2**[3]

1052 **3** 2 **Broughtons Fancy**[12] 1313 3-9-2 64 .... AdamKirby 6 59
(David Evans) *led: rdn 2f out: hdd over 1f out and unable qck u.p: lost btn 2nd and wknd fnl 50yds* **13/8**[1]

2340 **4** 4½ **Guapo Bay**[21] 1148 3-8-5 50 .... (p) TinaSmith(7) 3 42
(Richard Hannon) *dropped to rr but stl in tch after 2f out: effrt in 5th 2f out: sn outpcd and wl hld 1f out: plugged on to go modest 4th towards fin* **20/1**

06-0 **5** hd **Jersey Roy**[21] 1146 3-9-7 68 .... PaulHanagan 7 51
(Richard Fahey) *dwlt: hld up in tch: reminder over 2f out: u.p and outpcd 2f out: wl hld and plugged on same pce ins fnl f* **8/1**

05-0 **6** ½ **Star Glimmer (IRE)**[13] 1298 3-8-13 63 ....[1] RyanWhile(5) 1 47
(Henry Spiller) *taken down early: chsd ldr for 2f: rdn and outpcd in 4th 2f out: wl hld 1f out: wknd and lost 2 pls towards fin* **20/1**

1m 25.78s (0.98) **Going Correction** +0.025s/f (Slow) **6** Ran SP% **111.7**
Speed ratings (Par 96): **95,93,91,85,85 85**
CSF £10.60 TOTE £2.60: £1.80, £2.50; EX 11.80 Trifecta £21.50.Justice Focused was claimed for £10,000 by Claes Bjorling
Owner The Well Fleeced Partnership **Bred** S Couldrige **Trained** Upper Lambourn, Berks

FOCUS
An ordinary claimer run 0.48 secs slower than the opening fillies' handicap and dominated by the market leaders. An improved effort from the second which is the key to the level.

1574 COME RACING ON LADIES DAY MAY 6TH H'CAP 6f 1y(P)
5:45 (5:45) (Class 6) (0-60,62) 3-Y-O **£1,468** (£1,468; £336; £168) **Stalls** Low

Form RPR

0-01 **1** **Ordinal**[4] 1497 3-9-9 **62** 6ex .... JamesDoyle 8 71
(Mark Johnston) *in tch in midfield: wnt 2nd and travelling strly over 2f out: pushed into ld over 1f out: 2 l clr and stl only pushed along ins fnl f: pressed and drvn wl ins fnl f: jnd on post* **2/7**[1]

0166 **1** dht **Evening Starlight**[19] 1176 3-9-7 **60** .... GeorgeBaker 2 68
(Ron Hodges) *hld up in tch towards rr: nt clrest of runs ent fnl 2f: swtchd rt and hdwy over 1f out: wnt 3rd and swtchd lft ins fnl f: wnt 2nd and styd on strly wl ins fnl f: jnd ldr on post* **9/2**[2]

332- **3** 2½ **Cadland Lad (IRE)**[160] 7808 3-8-9 **53** .... (t) JennyPowell(5) 5 53
(John Ryan) *pushed along leaving stalls: sn rcvrd to chse ldrs: rdn over 2f out: chsd ldr 1f out: edgd lft and styd on same pce ins fnl f: lost 2nd wl ins fnl f* **6/1**[3]

6262 **4** 2¼ **Intimately**[21] 1148 3-9-2 **55** .... RyanClark 3 48
(Jonathan Portman) *in tch towards rr: effrt over 1f out: hdwy u.p 1f out: styd on wl ins fnl f: no threat to ldrs* **8/1**

00-0 **5** 4 **No Body's Fool**[33] 978 3-8-7 **46** oh1 .... KieranO'Neill 7 26
(Michael Madgwick) *hld up in tch towards rr: effrt 2f out: no imp u.p 1f out: wknd ins fnl f* **50/1**

-454 **6** 2¼ **Sand By Me**[42] 883 3-8-8 **47** oh1 ow1 .... ShaneKelly 9 20
(Peter Crate) *s.i.s: hld up in tch in rr: effrt and wd wl over 1f out: sn no imp u.p: nvr trbld ldrs* **16/1**

330 **7** 2¾ **Lady Lloyd**[13] 1292 3-9-7 **60** .... (v) AdamKirby 4 24
(Phil McEntee) *chsd ldr tl led over 2f out: rdn and hdd over 1f out: sn btn: wknd ins fnl f* **14/1**

4200 **8** 9 **Rojina (IRE)**[14] 1249 3-8-9 **51** .... RobHornby(3) 1
(Lisa Williamson) *led tl over 1f out: sn lost pl u.p: bhd and eased ins fnl f* **33/1**

1m 13.01s (1.11) **Going Correction** +0.025s/f (Slow) **8** Ran SP% **138.8**
Speed ratings (Par 96): **93,93,89,86,81 78,74,62**
WIN: Ordinal £0.70, ES £3.20; PL: Ordinal £1.02, ES £1.50, CL £2.30; Exacta: O/ES £1.60, ES/O £6.60; CSF: O/ES £1.72, ES/O £3.79; TC: O/ES/CL £3.38, ES/O/CL £6.68; Trifecta: O/ES/CL £5.00, ES/O/CL £22.60.
Owner Miss R Dobson **Bred** Worksop Manor Stud **Trained** Charlton Mackrell, Somerset
Owner Sheikh Hamdan bin Mohammed Al Maktoum **Bred** Darley **Trained** Middleham Moor, N Yorks

FOCUS
A moderate 3yo sprint handicap that produced a dramatic finish. Improved form from Evening Starlight, Ordinally basically confirming his improvement.

1575 RYAN VEHICLES MEDIAN AUCTION MAIDEN STKS 1m 2f (P)
6:15 (6:16) (Class 6) 3-4-Y-O **£2,264** (£673; £336; £168) **Stalls** Low

Form RPR

1 **Combative** 3-8-11 0 .... JimCrowley 7 86
(Amanda Perrett) *hld up in tch in midfield: clsd to press ldng pair ent fnl 2f: rdn to ld 1f out: sn in command: r.o wl* **7/1**

2 1¾ **Regicide (IRE)** 3-8-11 0 .... OisinMurphy 2 83
(James Fanshawe) *dwlt: pushed along early: racd in last trio: clsd and in tch 1/2-way: effrt whn sltly hmpd over 1f out: rn green but hdwy 1f out: chsd wnr ins fnl f: kpt on wl* **8/1**

0-4 **3** 2¼ **Stetchworth Park**[32] 1000 3-8-11 0 .... JamieSpencer 9 78
(Michael Bell) *pushed along early: chsd ldrs: swtchd rt and pushed up to press ldr over 2f out: hung rt u.p and unable qck over 1f out: clr 3rd but plugged on same pce ins fnl f* **5/2**[2]

222- **4** 3 **Van Dyke**[128] 8225 3-8-11 77 .... LiamKeniry 4 73
(Hughie Morrison) *t.k.h: trckd ldrs: nt clr run on inner over 2f out: swtchd lft and effrt u.p to press ldr over 1f out: no ex jst ins fnl f: wknd fnl 100yds* **2/1**[1]

24-2 **5** 1¾ **Skeaping**[12] 1314 3-8-11 84 .... PatDobbs 3 69
(Richard Hannon) *broke wl: led: jnd over 2f out: drvn wl over 1f out: hdd and no ex 1f out: wknd ins fnl f* **11/4**[3]

0- **6** ¾ **Next Train's Gone**[133] 8153 3-8-8 0 .... RyanTate(3) 6 68
(James Eustace) *in tch in midfield: shkn up and outpcd jst over 2f out: no ch but kpt on steadily ins fnl f: swtchd rt towards fin* **66/1**

04-6 **7** 5 **Brorocco**[15] 1242 3-8-11 77 ....[1] DavidProbert 10 58
(Andrew Balding) *t.k.h: sn w ldr: rdn and lost pl ent fnl 2f: sn btn: wknd over 1f out* **14/1**

4 **8** 10 **Happy Girl**[21] 1149 3-8-6 0 .... WilliamCarson 8 34
(Dr Jon Scargill) *dwlt: a same pl and nvr on terms: swtchd rt and flashed tail 3f out: sn lost tch* **50/1**

00/ **9** 22 **Hier Encore (FR)**[578] 6565 4-9-7 0 .... GeorgiaCox(7) 5
(David Menuisier) *s.i.s: nvr travelling wl and a off the pce in last: lost tch over 3f out: t.o* **66/1**

2m 3.39s (-3.21) **Going Correction** +0.025s/f (Slow)
WFA 3 from 4yo 17lb **9** Ran SP% **123.8**
Speed ratings (Par 101): **113,111,109,107,106 105,101,93,75**
CSF £65.31 TOTE £9.40: £2.90, £3.50, £1.10; EX 71.20 Trifecta £470.90.
Owner K Abdullah **Bred** Juddmonte Farms Ltd **Trained** Pulborough, W Sussex

FOCUS
The last two winners of this maiden are now rated in the 100s and there is a fair chance this winner will follow suit. The newcomers dominated and the form is rated around the third and fourth.

1576 RACHEL EDWARDS MEMORIAL RACE H'CAP 1m 1y(P)
6:45 (6:47) (Class 3) (0-95,95) 4-Y-O **£7,246** (£2,168; £1,084; £542; £270) **Stalls** High

Form RPR

100- **1** **Early Morning (IRE)**[207] 6755 5-9-7 **95** .... AdamKirby 1 103
(Harry Dunlop) *led over 6f out: mde rest: rdn and qcknd wl over 1f out: 2 l clr and drvn 1f out: styd on and a doing enough after: rdn out* **3/1**[1]

344- **2** ¾ **Lovely Memory (IRE)**[167] 7718 4-9-0 **88** .... (p) JamesDoyle 5 94
(Saeed bin Suroor) *chsd ldrs: wnt 2nd 5f out: rdn over 2f out: no imp tl kpt on u.p ins fnl f: nvr enough pce to seriously chal wnr* **3/1**[1]

0020 **3** ½ **Unforgiving Minute**[11] 1335 5-9-3 **91** .... WilliamTwiston-Davies 6 96+
(Gary Moore) *stdd s: t.k.h: hld up in last pair: swtchd rt and clsd over 1f out: hdwy 1f out: r.o to go 3rd wl ins fnl f: gng on fin but no threat to wnr* **8/1**[3]

3213 **4** 1 **Franco's Secret**[34] 965 5-8-9 **83** ow1 .... (v) CharlesBishop 8 86
(Peter Hedger) *hld up in tch in midfield: swtchd rt and effrt over 1f out: kpt on ins fnl f: wnt 4th towards fin: nvr enough pce to threaten wnr* **8/1**[3]

4-22 **5** ½ **Bint Dandy (IRE)**[26] 1065 5-9-7 **95** .... (p) SilvestreDeSousa 4 96
(Chris Dwyer) *taken down early: w ldrs: led briefly after 1f: chsd ldng pair 5f out: effrt u.p on inner over 1f out: styd on same pce and lost 2 pls wl ins fnl f* **10/1**

6500 **6** 1¼ **Forceful Appeal (USA)**[11] 1335 8-9-2 **90** .... JimCrowley 7 89
(Simon Dow) *stdd s: hld up in tch in last trio: effrt over 1f out: sme hdwy u.p ins fnl f: nvr trbld ldrs* **16/1**

5560 **7** nk **Grey Mirage**[18] 1204 7-9-4 **95** DanielMuscutt(3) 9 93
(Marco Botti) *trckd ldng trio: nt clrest of runs 2f out: rdn and no rspnse over 1f out: wl hld and kpt on same pce ins fnl f* **8/1**[3]

660- **8** 3/4 **Intiwin (IRE)**[193] 7119 4-8-9 **83** PaulHanagan 2 79
(Richard Fahey) *broke wl and led early: stdd bk into midfield over 6f out: effrt u.p over 1f out: no prog: wknd ins fnl f* **6/1**[2]

10-1 **9** 3 **Silverheels (IRE)**[55] 715 7-8-4 **83** (b) EdwardGreatrex(5) 3 72
(Paul Cole) *s.i.s: in tch but a in rr: rdn 2f out: drvn and no hdwy over 1f out: n.d* **25/1**

1m 36.27s (-1.93) **Going Correction** +0.025s/f (Slow) **9** Ran SP% **116.4**
Speed ratings (Par 107): **110,109,108,107,107 106,105,104,101**
CSF £11.39 CT £64.94 TOTE £3.80: £1.50, £1.30, £3.10; EX 15.10 Trifecta £101.20.
Owner Early Risers **Bred** Lakin Bloodstock/Wardley Bloodstock **Trained** Lambourn, Berks

FOCUS
The feature race and a good handicap from which the last two winners have made up into Group-level performers. The market leaders dominated the closing stages and have the potential to rate higher.

1577 PAUL AND BRADLEY BIGNALL MAIDEN STKS 7f 1y(P)
7:15 (7:18) (Class 5) 3-Y-O **£2,911** (£866; £432; £216) **Stalls** Low

Form RPR

1 **Pure Art** 3-9-0 0 FMBerry 1 77+
(Ralph Beckett) *chsd ldrs: effrt 2f out: no imp tl hdwy u.p ins fnl f: led fnl 50yds: r.o strly* **9/2**[3]

- **2** 3/4 **Dubai Mission (IRE)** 3-9-5 0 PatDobbs 5 80+
(Richard Hannon) *in tch in midfield: hdwy to chse ldrs 2f out: rdn and wnt between rivals to chal over 1f out: led ins fnl f: rn green and drifted rt in front: hdd and no ex fnl 50yds* **4/1**[2]

3 1 3/4 **Sehayli (IRE)** 3-9-5 0 PatCosgrave 12 75+
(William Haggas) *swtchd lft after s: hld up in tch in last trio: gd hdwy on inner 2f out: rdn and chsd ldrs 1f out: sltly impeded and swtchd rt 100yds out: styd on wl to snatch 3rd last stride* **10/1**

42 **4** shd **Justice Grace (IRE)**[25] 1091 3-9-5 0 JohnFahy 11 75
(Ralph Beckett) *led: rdn 2f out: sn hdd but stl ev ch tl no ex ins fnl f: styd on same pce fnl 100yds: lost 3rd last stride* **8/1**

2- **5** nk **Senses Of Dubai**[229] 6057 3-9-5 0 [1] SilvestreDeSousa 9 74+
(Simon Crisford) *hld up in tch in midfield: effrt and hung lft over 1f out: hdwy and sltly impeded ins fnl f: kpt on fnl 100yds: nvr threatened ldrs* **3/1**[1]

0-3 **6** shd **Colonel Bossington (IRE)**[25] 1091 3-9-5 0 JimCrowley 6 74
(William Knight) *pressed ldr: rdn and led wl over 1f out: hdd and no ex whn sltly impeded ins fnl f: styd on same pce after* **9/2**[3]

7 1 1/2 **Atalante** 3-9-0 0 [1] DavidProbert 2 65+
(Andrew Balding) *s.i.s: pushed along and rn green in rr: hdwy 2f out and midfield over 1f out: kpt on same pce ins fnl f* **25/1**

05- **8** 8 **Bruntingthorpe (IRE)**[196] 7038 3-9-2 0 JackDuern(3) 7 48
(Dean Ivory) *wl in tch in midfield: shkn up 2f out: rn green and lost pl wl over 1f out: sn wknd* **66/1**

00 **9** nk **Pacohontas**[11] 1339 3-8-9 0 CharlesEddery(5) 3 42
(Dean Ivory) *in tch in midfield: rdn and lost pl ent fnl 2f: wknd over 1f out* **50/1**

54- **10** 1/2 **Pure Vanity**[204] 6838 3-9-0 0 WilliamTwiston-Davies 10 41
(Roger Charlton) *s.i.s: in tch towards rr: pushed along jst over 2f out: sn outpcd: wknd over 1f out* **14/1**

0 **11** 3 **Roman Urn**[14] 1256 3-9-5 0 TomQueally 8 38
(Brett Johnson) *s.i.s: hld up in last pair: effrt and v wd bnd 2f out: sn btn and bhd* **100/1**

05 **12** 8 **Flashy King (IRE)**[42] 874 3-8-12 0 SeanMooney(7) 4 16
(Joseph Tuite) *t.k.h: chsd ldrs: struggling whn hung rt and lost pl qckly bnd 2f out: wl bhd fnl f* **100/1**

1m 25.66s (0.86) **Going Correction** +0.025s/f (Slow) **12** Ran SP% **117.5**
Speed ratings (Par 98): **96,95,93,93,92 92,90,81,81,80 77,68**
CSF £22.22 TOTE £7.00: £2.20, £2.10, £2.90; EX 26.00 Trifecta £201.90.
Owner R Barnett **Bred** W And R Barnett Ltd **Trained** Kimpton, Hants

FOCUS
An interesting maiden. The time was 0.36 secs slower than fastest of the earlier races over the trip and again newcomers dominated. The form makes sense.

1578 WINIFRED GREENFIELD BIRTHDAY CELEBRATIONS H'CAP 1m 2f (P)
7:45 (7:45) (Class 6) (0-55,55) 4-Y-O+ **£2,264** (£673; £336; £168) **Stalls** Low

Form RPR

-046 **1** **Glasgow Central**[62] 622 5-9-7 **55** AdamKirby 4 63
(Phil McEntee) *in tch in midfield: hdwy to chse ldrs and swtchd rt jst over 2f out: rdn to ld over 1f out: sustained duel w runner-up fnl f: kpt on: rdn out* **4/1**[2]

0-01 **2** 1/2 **Sexy Secret**[87] 326 5-9-3 **54** (p) SimonPearce(3) 6 61
(Lydia Pearce) *chsd ldrs: wnt 2nd 8f out tl led over 2f out: rdn and hdd over 1f out: battled on gamely u.p and sustained duel w wnr after: hld towards fin* **16/1**

0523 **3** 2 1/4 **Top Pocket**[42] 870 4-9-4 **52** GeorgeBaker 1 55
(Michael Madgwick) *chsd ldr for 2f: styd chsng ldrs: swtchd rt and effrt 2f out: cl 3rd and rdn over 1f out: no ex and outpcd ins fnl f* **5/1**

-603 **4** 1 3/4 **Candesta (USA)**[50] 776 6-9-7 **55** (bt) AdamBeschizza 9 54
(Julia Feilden) *in tch in midfield: rdn over 2f out: swtchd rt and hdwy over 1f out: kpt on same pce and no imp ins fnl f* **14/1**

5312 **5** hd **Happy Jack (IRE)**[20] 1170 5-9-5 **53** (b) PatDobbs 2 52
(Michael Wigham) *hld up in tch in midfield: effrt and hdwy 2f out: sn rdn: styd on same pce and no imp ins fnl f* **3/1**[1]

251 **6** 1 1/2 **Anjuna Beach (USA)**[14] 1263 6-9-1 **54** AnnStokell(5) 7 52
(Ann Stokell) *s.i.s: t.k.h: hld up in rr: hdwy 2f out: swtchd rt over 1f out: kpt on same pce ins fnl f: nvr trbld ldrs* **14/1**

0-53 **7** shd **Stynes (IRE)**[20] 1170 6-8-13 **47** (t) SilvestreDeSousa 3 43
(Ali Stronge) *led tl over 2f out: no ex u.p wl over 1f out: wknd fnl f* **9/2**[3]

2522 **8** hd **Dreaming Again**[28] 1035 6-9-1 **49** KieranO'Neill 12 47
(Jimmy Fox) *hld up in last pair: rdn over 3f out: hdwy on inner 2f out: keeping on same pce and no threat to ldrs whn nt clr run and swtchd rt ins fnl f* **16/1**

0420 **9** 6 **Clock On Tom**[42] 870 6-9-4 **52** FMBerry 11 36
(Denis Quinn) *hld up in tch in midfield: hdwy on outer over 2f out: lost pl bnd and rdn wl over 1f out: sn wknd* **14/1**

6-03 **10** hd **Machiavelian Storm (IRE)**[44] 860 4-8-12 **46** oh1 JimCrowley 10 32
(Richard Mitchell) *t.k.h: wl in tch in midfield: nt clr run and shuffled bk jst over 2f out: bhd and rdn wl over 1f out: no rspnse and sn wknd* **33/1**

6053 **11** 9 **Evacusafe Lady**[18] 1202 5-9-0 **55** (t) JonathanFisher(7) 13 22
(John Ryan) *stuck wd: in midfield: hdwy to chse ldrs 7f out tl rdn and lost pl qckly jst over 2f out: bhd fnl f* **10/1**

2m 6.8s (0.20) **Going Correction** +0.025s/f (Slow) **11** Ran SP% **123.6**
Speed ratings (Par 101): **100,99,97,96,96 95,94,94,90,89 82**
CSF £70.21 CT £337.55 TOTE £5.90: £2.70, £5.00, £2.70; EX 97.50 Trifecta £1330.20.
Owner Mrs Rebecca McEntee **Bred** Bolton Grange **Trained** Newmarket, Suffolk

FOCUS
A low-grade but competitive looking handicap run 3.41secs slower than the earlier maiden over the trip. The pace largely held up.
T/Plt: £40.30 to a £1 stake. Pool: £54,170.82 - 979.62 winning units. T/Qpdt: £13.10 to a £1 stake. Pool: £5,589.63 - 313.76 winning units. **Steve Payne**

1374 CHANTILLY (R-H)
Wednesday, April 20
OFFICIAL GOING: Turf: soft; polytrack: standard

1579a PRIX DU PREMIER PAS (MAIDEN) (UNRACED 2YO) (TURF) 5f
3:10 (12:00) 2-Y-O **£9,191** (£3,676; £2,757; £1,838; £919)

RPR

1 **Red Onion** 2-9-2 0 ThierryThulliez 5 80
(C Lerner, France) **12/1**

2 1/2 **Edana (FR)** 2-8-13 0 RafaelSchistl 11 75
(Henk Grewe, Germany) **17/1**

3 2 1/2 **Iyouna (FR)** 2-8-13 0 FabriceVeron 10 66
(H-A Pantall, France) **13/2**[3]

4 1 3/4 **Admiralty Arch** 2-9-2 0 MickaelBarzalona 7 63
(Richard Hannon) *pushed along in midfield: rdn 2f out: kpt on fnl f but nt pce to chal* **2/1**[1]

5 3 **Aiming For Rio (FR)** 2-8-13 0 AntoineHamelin 6 49
(Matthieu Palussiere, France) **9/1**

6 1 3/4 **Almeira (IRE)** 2-8-5 0 AdrienMoreau(8) 8 43
(N Caullery, France) **13/1**

7 2 **Sunday Winner (FR)** 2-9-2 0 StephanePasquier 4 39
(Y Gourraud, France) **13/1**

8 3/4 **Moonlight Dream (FR)** 2-9-2 0 Pierre-CharlesBoudot 2 36
(A Marcialis, Italy) **41/5**

9 3/4 **Highgate (FR)** 2-8-13 0 RaphaelMarchelli 9 30
(F-X De Chevigny, France) **37/1**

10 dist **Assassinate (IRE)** 2-9-2 0 ChristopheSoumillon 1
(Paul Cole) *s.i.s: green in rr: sn t.o* **33/10**[2]

59.43s (1.13) **10** Ran SP% **121.0**
WIN (incl. 1 euro stake): 13.70. Places: 3.90, 4.70, 2.50. DF: 94.30. SF: 204.90..
Owner Ecurie Salabi, N Saltiel & A Anghert **Bred** T De La Heronniere & Mme M-J Goetschy **Trained** France

1580a PRIX DE FONTAINEBLEAU (GROUP 3) (3YO COLTS) (TURF) 1m
3:40 (3:40) 3-Y-O **£29,411** (£11,764; £8,823; £5,882; £2,941)

RPR

1 **Dicton**[31] 1024 3-9-2 0 OlivierPeslier 3 108
(Gianluca Bietolini, Italy) *t.k.h: midfield: rdn to chal between horses whn gap appeared fnl f: led towards fin: shade cosily* **8/1**

2 nk **Taareef (USA)**[142] 8059 3-9-2 0 IoritzMendizabal 4 107+
(J-C Rouget, France) *hld up: rdn and hdwy ent fnl f: wnt 2nd cl home: nt quite pce of wnr* **11/2**[3]

3 1/2 **Almanzor (FR)**[171] 7665 3-9-2 0 Jean-BernardEyquem 8 106
(J-C Rouget, France) *midfield: rdn and effrt over 1f out: styd on fnl f but a jst hld: up for 3rd fnl strides* **12/1**

4 hd **Vedevani (FR)**[13] 1308 3-9-2 0 ChristopheSoumillon 6 106
(A De Royer-Dupre, France) *midfield in tch: chal gng strly and led 2f out: rdn and strly pressed ins fnl f: hdd towards fin: no ex and dropped to 4th* **10/3**[2]

5 snk **Royal Julius (IRE)**[19] 3-9-2 0 ThierryJarnet 9 105+
(A De Watrigant, France) *hld up: rdn over 1f out: nt clrest of runs fnl f but styd on wl enough: nt able to chal* **11/1**

6 3/4 **Helene Charisma (FR)**[31] 1024 3-9-2 0 CristianDemuro 10 104
(Mme Pia Brandt, France) *hld up in last: rdn and hdwy on outer ent fnl f: hung rt: styd on but nt able to chal* **15/2**

7 2 **Estikmaal (IRE)**[194] 3-9-2 0 MickaelBarzalona 7 99
(F Head, France) *trckd ldr: chal gng strly and led early in st: rdn and hdd 2f out: no ex fnl f: wknd* **15/2**

8 3/4 **Millfield (FR)**[31] 1024 3-9-2 0 GregoryBenoist 1 97
(D Smaga, France) *prom on inner: rdn and brief effrt on rail over 1f out: no ex fnl f: wknd* **14/1**

9 10 **Candide (FR)**[195] 7071 3-9-2 0 Pierre-CharlesBoudot 2 74
(A Fabre, France) *midfield on inner: rdn 2f out: no ex and btn over 1f out: wknd* **9/4**[1]

10 dist **Free From Desire (FR)**[28] 3-9-2 0 PierreBazire 5
(G Botti, France) *led: rdn and hdd early in st: no ex and btn: wknd: eased: t.o* **40/1**

1m 38.2s (0.20) **10** Ran SP% **129.0**
WIN (incl. 1 euro stake): 8.20 (Dicton coupled with Free From Desire). PLACES: 2.90, 2.90, 3.50. DF: 27.00. SF: 59.80.
Owner Robert Ng **Bred** Wertheimer Et Frere **Trained** Italy

FOCUS
A key trial for the Poule d'Essai des Poulains next month. There was a sound pace on, but it still saw a bunched finish and the form looks best rated around the fifth.

1581a PRIX DE LA GROTTE (GROUP 3) (3YO FILLIES) (TURF) 1m
4:40 (12:00) 3-Y-O **£29,411** (£11,764; £8,823; £5,882; £2,941)

RPR

1 **Qemah (IRE)**[199] 6967 3-9-0 0 GregoryBenoist 6 113+
(J-C Rouget, France) *t.k.h: hld up in midfield: clsd and rdn to chal fnl f: qcknd to ld and drew clr: pushed out: comf* **4/1**[3]

2 2 1/2 **Kenriya (FR)**[48] 803 3-9-0 0 MaximeGuyon 2 106
(C Ferland, France) *midfield in tch: rdn to chal and led over 1f out: hdd fnl f: no match for wnr but kpt on wl enough for 2nd* **5/1**

3 1 1/4 **Antonoe (USA)**[199] 6967 3-9-0 0 VincentCheminaud 5 103
(P Bary, France) *trckd ldr: led gng wl 2f out: rdn and hdd over 1f out: no ex fnl f: jst hld on for 3rd* **10/3**[2]

4 shd **Trixia (FR)**[182] 7407 3-9-0 0 OlivierPeslier 3 103+
(A De Royer-Dupre, France) *midfield on inner: rdn over 1f out: angled out and kpt on fnl f: jst missed 3rd: nt pce to chal* **7/4**[1]
5 ½ **Chartreuse (IRE)**[182] 7407 3-9-0 0 ThierryJarnet 1 102
(F Head, France) *prom: rdn and effrt over 1f out: outpcd fnl f* **8/1**
6 1¾ **Pleasemetoo (IRE)**[225] 6197 3-9-0 0 MickaelBarzalona 9 98
(A Fabre, France) *hld up in last: rdn 2f out: swtchd to outer and styd on fnl f but n.d* **14/1**
7 2½ **Gherdaiya**[225] 6197 3-9-0 0 Pierre-CharlesBoudot 7 92
(A Fabre, France) *hld up: rdn over 1f out: outpcd fnl f* **11/1**
8 1 **Ella Diva (FR)**[182] 7407 3-9-0 0 CristianDemuro 8 90
(N Caullery, France) *midfield: rdn over 1f out: no ex fnl f: wknd* **33/1**
9 9 **Positive Vibration (IRE)**[24] 3-9-0 0 Jean-BernardEyquem 4 69
(J-C Rouget, France) *led: hdd 2f out: btn and wknd on rail* **40/1**

1m 38.14s (0.14) **9** Ran SP% **127.6**
WIN (incl. 1 euro stake): 3.20 (Qemah combined with Positive Vibration & Gherdaiya). PLACES: 1.50, 1.90, 1.50. DF:18.90. SF: 53.10.
Owner Al Shaqab Racing **Bred** Ecurie Cadran Bissons Sas lei **Trained** Pau, France

FOCUS
A top trial for the Poule d'Essai des Pouliches next month, won by some top-notchers in recent years such as the mighty Zarkava. It had plenty of depth and they went a fair enough pace, so the form ought to prove strong. It's rated at the top end of the race average.

1582a PRIX NOAILLES (GROUP 3) (3YO) (TURF) 1m 2f 110y
5:40 (12:00) 3-Y-O **£29,411** (£11,764; £8,823; £5,882; £2,941)

RPR
1 **Raseed**[173] 7615 3-9-2 0 AurelienLemaitre 4 110+
(F Head, France) *trckd clr ldr: shkn up and clsd rapidly fnl f: led 120yds out: drew clr: pushed out: comf* **5/1**
2 3 **More Than A Dream (IRE)**[32] 3-9-2 0 ChristopheSoumillon 5 104+
(J-C Rouget, France) *midfield on inner: rdn over 1f out: swtchd out fnl f and styd on into 2nd: no match for wnr* **5/2**[2]
3 ¾ **Valkena (FR)**[34] 3-8-13 0 Roberto-CarlosMontenegro 6 100
(C Boutin, France) *led and sn wnt clr: rdn over 1f out: reeled in qckly fnl f: hdd 120yds out: no ex* **25/1**
4 1½ **Cleonte (IRE)**[27] 3-9-2 0 Pierre-CharlesBoudot 2 100+
(A Fabre, France) *midfield: rdn 2f out: nt qckn: plugged on but n.d* **6/5**[1]
5 1½ **Burger And Fries (FR)**[27] 3-9-2 0 Jean-BernardEyquem 3 97
(C Ferland, France) *hld up: rdn 2f out: plugged on same pce and n.d* **9/2**[3]
6 3½ **Chanducoq (FR)**[27] 3-9-2 0 IoritzMendizabal 1 90
(J-P Gallorini, France) *hld up: rdn over 2f out: sn no ex and btn* **20/1**

2m 12.08s (3.28) **6** Ran SP% **117.5**
WIN (incl. 1 euro stake): 4.50. PLACES: 1.80, 1.70. SF: 14.40.
Owner Hamdan Al Maktoum **Bred** Shadwell Estate Company Limited **Trained** France

1406 BEVERLEY (R-H)
Thursday, April 21

OFFICIAL GOING: Good to soft (soft in places in 5f chute; 6.8)
Wind: Moderate behind Weather: Fine & dry

1583 BEVERLEY MINSTER FILLIES' NOVICE AUCTION STKS (PLUS 10 RACE) 5f
1:50 (1:51) (Class 5) 2-Y-O **£2,911** (£866; £432; £216) **Stalls** Low

Form RPR
6 1 **Seafront**[7] 1437 2-9-0 0 RyanMoore 8 80+
(James Tate) *trckd ldrs: hdwy over 2f out: led over 1f out: rdn ins fnl f: kpt on* **1/1**[1]
2 ¾ **Clem Fandango (FR)** 2-9-0 0 PhillipMakin 6 77+
(Keith Dalgleish) *in rr: green and sn pushed along: swtchd lft and rdn along over 2f out: hdwy over 1f out: styd on wl fnl f* **7/2**[2]
4 3 4½ **Accladora**[12] 1342 2-9-0 0 JoeFanning 4 61
(Mark Johnston) *led: rdn along 2f out: hdd over 1f out: sn drvn and kpt on same pce* **8/1**
4 1½ **Whiteandgold** 2-9-0 0 ConnorBeasley 3 56
(Bryan Smart) *hld up in tch: hdwy 2f out: rdn over 1f out: styd on fnl f: nrst fin* **16/1**
5 ½ **Melaniemillie** 2-8-11 0 JacobButterfield(3) 2 54
(Ollie Pears) *trckd ldrs: pushed along over 2f out: rdn along wl over 1f out: kpt on same pce* **66/1**
2 6 1 **Zig Zag Girl**[3] 1527 2-9-0 0 GrahamGibbons 7 50
(Mick Channon) *cl up: chal over 2f out: rdn along and ev ch over 1f out: sn wknd* **6/1**[3]
7 4 **Red Shanghai (IRE)** 2-9-0 0 RichardKingscote 5 36
(Tom Dascombe) *chsd ldrs: rdn along 2f out: grad wknd* **10/1**
8 6 **Kilbaha Lady (IRE)** 2-9-0 0 JasonHart 1 14
(Nigel Tinkler) *dwlt: a in rr* **66/1**
9 ½ **Poet's Time** 2-9-0 0 DavidAllan 9 13
(Tim Easterby) *wnt lft s: a in rr* **25/1**

1m 4.82s (1.32) **Going Correction** +0.075s/f (Good) **9** Ran SP% **119.4**
Speed ratings (Par 89): **92,90,83,81,80 78,72,62,62**
CSF £4.77 TOTE £1.90: £1.10, £2.10, £2.90; EX 6.50 Trifecta £31.60.
Owner Saeed Manana **Bred** Jeremy Green And Sons **Trained** Newmarket, Suffolk

FOCUS
Not easy to know what to make of this form for now, so it's probably wise to presume it's only fair at best. Two pulled clear. After riding in the opener Jason Hart called the ground good to soft and both Philip Makin and Richard Kingscote reckoned it was dead, with Makin saying 'it has dried out a lot'.

1584 SWAN INDUSTRIAL DRIVES H'CAP 7f 100y
2:20 (2:20) (Class 5) (0-70,70) 3-Y-O **£3,780** (£1,131; £565; £283; £141) **Stalls** Low

Form RPR
4-00 1 **Billy Roberts (IRE)**[15] 1276 3-9-4 67 JasonHart 1 76
(Richard Guest) *t.k.h early: mde all: rdn and qcknd clr wl over 1f out: kpt on strly* **13/2**[3]
654- 2 3 **Beverley Bullet**[185] 7336 3-9-0 63 GrahamGibbons 3 65
(Les Eyre) *t.k.h early: trckd ldrs: hdwy over 2f out: rdn to chse wnr wl over 1f out: rdn appr fnl f and kpt on same pce* **9/2**[2]
564- 3 nk **Kirkham**[178] 7510 3-9-4 67 ConnorBeasley 7 68
(Julie Camacho) *in tch: hdwy over 2f out: rdn to chse ldrs over 1f out: kpt on same pce* **12/1**
312- 4 ¾ **Ponty Royale (IRE)**[178] 7517 3-8-13 62 DavidAllan 9 61
(Tim Easterby) *t.k.h: hld up towards rr: hdwy over 2f out: n.m.r and swtchd rt to inner over 1f out: styd on wl fnl f: nrst fin* **9/1**

040- 5 1½ **Carnageo (FR)**[160] 7835 3-9-7 70 TonyHamilton 6 65+
(Richard Fahey) *dwlt and bhd: hdwy wl over 1f out: n.m.r ent fnl f: styd on wl towards fin* **7/1**
2162 6 ½ **Blacklister**[10] 1389 3-9-7 70 RyanMoore 5 64
(Mick Channon) *trckd ldrs on outer: pushed along wl over 2f out: rdn wl over 1f out sn drvn and wknd* **15/8**[1]
1-04 7 ¾ **Autumn Blossom (USA)**[84] 366 3-9-2 65 JoeFanning 8 57
(Mark Johnston) *hld up: effrt wl over 2f out: sn rdn along and n.d* **12/1**
143- 8 2½ **Arcane Dancer (IRE)**[114] 8384 3-8-13 62 TomEaves 4 48
(Lawrence Mullaney) *cl up: pushed along 3f out: rdn over 2f out: drvn 1 1/2f out: wknd* **25/1**
-055 9 12 **Canford Crossing (IRE)**[54] 746 3-9-5 68 PaulQuinn 2 24
(David Nicholls) *a towards rr* **12/1**

1m 35.0s (1.20) **Going Correction** +0.025s/f (Good) **9** Ran SP% **115.7**
Speed ratings (Par 98): **94,90,90,89,87 87,86,83,69**
CSF £35.91 CT £347.38 TOTE £7.10: £2.30, £3.80, £3.50; EX 40.70 Trifecta £448.30.
Owner www.primelawns.co.uk **Bred** Burgage Stud **Trained** Ingmanthorpe, W Yorks

FOCUS
A modest contest for 3yos, won by a horse that pretty much made all. It seemed an advantage to race on the rail.

1585 QUEEN'S OWN YEOMANRY H'CAP 7f 100y
2:50 (2:51) (Class 3) (0-95,89) 3-Y-O **£7,439** (£2,213; £1,106; £553) **Stalls** Low

Form RPR
31- 1 **Garcia**[194] 7123 3-9-1 83 TonyHamilton 3 93+
(Richard Fahey) *trckd ldrs: hdwy 3f out: chal over 1f out and sn rdn: led jst over 1f out: drvn ins fnl f: kpt on strly towards fin* **9/4**[1]
021- 2 1¾ **Arab Poet**[177] 7531 3-9-1 83 RyanMoore 5 88
(Sir Michael Stoute) *t.k.h early: hld up in rr: hdwy 3f out: n.m.r and swtchd lft wl over 1f out: chal ent fnl f: sn rdn and ev ch tl no ex last 100yds* **9/4**[1]
63-5 3 2 **London Protocol (FR)**[27] 1080 3-9-6 88 (p) BenCurtis 2 88
(K R Burke) *t.k.h: slt ld: pushed along 3f out: rdn 2f out: drvn and hdd jst over 1f out: kpt on same pce* **7/1**[2]
15-0 4 2¼ **Desert Ruler**[16] 1243 3-9-2 84 GrahamLee 4 78
(Jedd O'Keeffe) *trckd ldng pair: effrt over 2f out: rdn wl over 1f out: sn drvn and edgd rt: kpt on one pce* **18/1**[3]
33-3 5 5 **King's Pavilion (IRE)**[7] 1446 3-9-7 89 JoeFanning 1 71
(Mark Johnston) *t.k.h: cl up: disp ld 1/2-way: rdn along over 2f out: sn wknd* **9/4**[1]

1m 33.5s (-0.30) **Going Correction** +0.025s/f (Good) **5** Ran SP% **110.1**
Speed ratings (Par 102): **102,100,97,95,89**
CSF £7.49 TOTE £3.30: £3.10, £1.20; EX 8.40 Trifecta £36.20.
Owner Highclere Thoroughbred Racing (Pelham) **Bred** Highclere Stud **Trained** Musley Bank, N Yorks

FOCUS
Only three of these made any great appeal in the betting, and the outsider got loose before the start for a short while. The first two have been rated as improving.

1586 ALAN MCGUINNESS AND ROBIN LUNNESS MEMORIAL H'CAP 1m 4f 16y
3:20 (3:20) (Class 4) (0-85,84) 4-Y-O+ **£5,040** (£1,508; £754; £377; £188) **Stalls** Low

Form RPR
4411 1 **Alphabetical Order**[18] 1222 8-8-13 76 DanielTudhope 5 84+
(David O'Meara) *trckd ldrs: hdwy on outer 3f out: cl up 2f out: chal over 1f out: rdn ent fnl f: drvn and kpt on wl to ld nr fin* **7/2**[2]
1-2 2 nk **Busy Street**[42] 890 4-8-13 77 BenCurtis 8 84+
(Alan Swinbank) *trckd ldr: cl up 4f out: led 2f out: rdn over 1f out: drvn ent fnl f: hdd and no ex nr fin* **9/4**[1]
6-03 3 2 **Dunquin (IRE)**[52] 766 4-8-7 71 PJMcDonald 9 75
(John Mackie) *hld up in rr: hdwy on outer 2f out: rdn over 1f out: styd on wl fnl f: nrst fin* **8/1**
364- 4 hd **Medina Sidonia (IRE)**[215] 6524 4-8-4 73 RachelRichardson(5) 7 77
(Tim Easterby) *trckd ldrs: hdwy over 2f out: rdn over 1f out: drvn ent fnl f: kpt on* **6/1**[3]
10-3 5 ½ **Donna Graciosa (GER)**[20] 1177 4-9-1 79 JoeFanning 3 82+
(Mark Johnston) *trckd ldrs: hdwy over 2f out: effrt and n.m.r over 1f out: ever ch whn nt clr run ins fnl f: kpt on* **7/1**
404- 6 ¾ **Arrowtown**[182] 7417 4-8-7 72 GrahamGibbons 6 74
(Michael Easterby) *hld up towards rr: hdwy over 2f out: nt clr run and swtchd lft over 1f out: rdn and kpt on fnl f* **20/1**
6161 7 ¾ **Bayan Kasirga (IRE)**[21] 1166 6-8-7 73 SammyJoBell(3) 4 73
(Richard Fahey) *trckd ldrs on inner: effrt 2f out and sn n.m.r: swtchd lft: rdn and nt clr run ent fnl f: kpt on same pce* **10/1**
035/ 8 2½ **Kuda Huraa (IRE)**[30] 5379 8-9-3 80 TomEaves 1 76
(Harriet Bethell) *set stdy pce: pushed along 3f out: rdn and hdd 2f out: sn drvn and grad wknd* **33/1**
000- 9 ½ **Swnymor (IRE)**[96] 7165 7-9-7 84 (p) DaleSwift 2 80
(Kevin Frost) *hld up in rr: effrt on inner and nt clr run wl over 1f out: n.d* **20/1**

2m 46.02s (6.22) **Going Correction** +0.375s/f (Good)
WFA 4 from 6yo+ 1lb **9** Ran SP% **112.4**
Speed ratings (Par 105): **94,93,92,92,92 91,91,89,89**
CSF £11.08 CT £55.83 TOTE £2.80: £1.10, £1.60, £3.00; EX 12.10 Trifecta £89.70.
Owner Great Northern Partnership **Bred** Barrow Hill **Trained** Upper Helmsley, N Yorks

FOCUS
The gallop was slow in the early stages, which meant it resulted in a bit of a dash to the line. Being to the fore certainly helped. The first two are probably better than the bare form.

1587 TOUR DE YORKSHIRE STARTS HERE NEXT FRIDAY H'CAP 1m 1f 207y
3:50 (3:50) (Class 5) (0-70,69) 3-Y-O **£3,780** (£1,131; £565; £283) **Stalls** Low

Form RPR
3-61 1 **Nietzsche**[5] 1484 3-9-1 68 6ex CallumShepherd(5) 5 74+
(Brian Ellison) *plld hrd in rr: effrt 3f out and sn pushed along: hdwy 2f out: rdn to chal ent fnl f: sn edgd lft: led last 100yds: styd on* **4/9**[1]
344- 2 1¼ **The Major**[260] 5019 3-9-4 69 LouisSteward(3) 3 72
(Michael Bell) *trckd ldng pair: hdwy on outer over 2f out: led wl over 1f out and sn rdn: edgd rt ent fnl f: sn drvn: hdd and kpt on same pce last 100yds* **5/1**[2]
30-0 3 1¾ **Palmerston**[15] 1276 3-9-6 68 BenCurtis 1 68
(Michael Appleby) *led: pushed along 3f out: rdn and hdd wl over 1f out: sn drvn and kpt on same pce* **9/1**[3]
000- 4 ¾ **Adherence**[185] 7336 3-8-10 58 BarryMcHugh 2 56
(Tony Coyle) *trckd ldr: hdwy and cl up 3f out: rdn along 2f out: sn drvn and kpt on same pce appr fnl f* **9/1**[3]

2m 10.38s (3.38) **Going Correction** +0.375s/f (Good) **4** Ran SP% **105.9**
Speed ratings (Par 98): **101,100,98,98**
CSF £2.82 TOTE £1.30; EX 2.30 Trifecta £5.40.
Owner D Gilbert, M Lawrence, A Bruce, G Wills **Bred** West Stow Stud Ltd **Trained** Norton, N Yorks

FOCUS
It may have made little difference considering they were the market leaders, but the first two came towards the stands' side late on. The proximity of the fourth could be used as a reason to hold the value of this form down, and the winner was below his Nottingham figure.

1588 RAPID LAD H'CAP 1m 1f 207y
4:20 (4:21) (Class 5) (0-75,74) 4-Y-O+ **£3,780** (£1,131; £565; £283; £141) **Stalls** Low

Form RPR
0 **1** **Gulf Of Poets**[24] 1122 4-9-6 **73**.......... DuranFentiman 2 81
(Michael Easterby) *hld up in tch: hdwy on inner 2f out: rdn ent fnl f: styd on to ld last 75yds: drvn out* **33/1**
505- **2** ½ **Jacbequick**[270] 4672 5-9-4 **71**.......... DanielTudhope 3 78+
(David O'Meara) *trckd ldrs: hdwy 2f out: swtchd lft and effrt whn nt clr run jst over 1f out: swtchd rt and rdn ins fnl f: n.m.r: squeezed through and ev ch last 100yds: kpt on* **5/2**[1]
54-1 **3** nk **Chilworth Bells**[19] 1202 4-9-0 **72**.......... JosephineGordon(5) 6 78
(David Barron) *led: rdn along and hdd over 2f out: cl up: drvn to ld again ent fnl f: sn edgd lft: hdd and no ex last 75yds* **5/2**[1]
00-0 **4** ½ **Briardale (IRE)**[15] 1250 4-9-3 **70**.......... PJMcDonald 7 75
(James Bethell) *t.k.h: trckd ldrs: hdwy on outer: hdwy over 2f out: rdn over 1f out: drvn and edgd lft ins fnl f: kpt on towards fin* **16/1**
200- **5** ½ **Age Of Elegance (IRE)**[141] 8081 4-9-6 **73**.......... PhillipMakin 10 77
(David Loughnane) *trckd ldr: cl up over 3f out: slt ld over 2f out and sn rdn: drvn and hdd ent fnl f: kpt on same pce* **11/1**[3]
6526 **6** 3¾ **Art Scholar (IRE)**[21] 1161 9-9-3 **70**.......... AndrewMullen 5 67
(Michael Appleby) *hld up in rr: hdwy 2f out: sn rdn and plugged on fnl f* **10/1**[2]
240- **7** 2½ **Almuhalab**[219] 6395 5-8-13 **66**.......... JamesSullivan 8 58
(Ruth Carr) *t.k.h: chsd ldrs: rdn along wl over 2f out: wknd wl over 1f out* **12/1**
006- **8** ½ **Tiger Twenty Two**[208] 5692 5-8-12 **65**.......... GrahamLee 12 56
(Brian Rothwell) *a towards rr* **50/1**
40-0 **9** hd **Indian Chief (IRE)**[15] 1250 6-9-5 **72**.......... PaulMulrennan 11 62
(Rebecca Bastiman) *stdd and swtchd rt s: hld up and bhd: stdy hdwy on outer over 3f out: chsd ldrs 2f out: sn rdn and wknd* **16/1**
00-0 **10** nk **First Sargeant**[70] 212 6-8-10 **68**..........(p) RachelRichardson(5) 9 58
(Lawrence Mullaney) *dwlt and towards rr: sme hdwy 3f out: rdn along over 2f out: sn wknd* **10/1**[2]
16-0 **11** 1½ **Tafahom (IRE)**[16] 1241 4-9-2 **74**.......... NathanEvans(5) 4 61
(Michael Easterby) *a towards rr* **16/1**

2m 9.64s (2.64) **Going Correction** +0.375s/f (Good) 11 Ran SP% **113.9**
Speed ratings (Par 103): **104,103,103,102,102 99,97,97,97,96 95**
CSF £111.36 CT £293.26 TOTE £36.80: £7.40, £1.60, £1.10; EX 162.90 Trifecta £642.90.
Owner L Westwood, A Chandler & L Hall **Bred** Juddmonte Farms Ltd **Trained** Sheriff Hutton, N Yorks
■ Stewards' Enquiry : Duran Fentiman two-day ban: used whip over permitted level (May 5-6)

FOCUS
A fair handicap that got messy in the final stages for the runner-up. The form is taken at face value.

1589 BEVERLEY FOLK FESTIVAL HERE IN JUNE MAIDEN AUCTION STKS 1m 100y
4:50 (4:53) (Class 5) 3-Y-O **£3,780** (£1,131; £565; £283; £141) **Stalls** Low

Form RPR
22- **1** **Carenot (IRE)**[195] 7092 3-9-0 0.......... RyanMoore 2 68+
(William Haggas) *trckd ldng pair: hdwy over 2f out: nt clr run over 1f out: sn swtchd lft and rdn: drvn ins fnl f: led nr fin* **4/6**[1]
55- **2** ¾ **Dominannie (IRE)**[166] 7752 3-9-0 0.......... BenCurtis 4 65
(Alan Swinbank) *dwlt and t.k.h in rr: hdwy 3f out: chal on outer wl over 1f out: sn rdn and led jst over 1f out: drvn ins fnl f: hdd and no ex towards fin* **22/1**
5 **3** 1 **Just Hiss**[18] 1217 3-9-5 0.......... DavidAllan 3 67+
(Tim Easterby) *hld up: hdwy over 2f out: effrt and n.m.r and hmpd over 1f out: sn rdn and kpt on fnl f* **25/1**
50- **4** 1½ **Fondie (IRE)**[187] 7284 3-9-0 0.......... JoeFanning 5 59
(Mark Johnston) *cl up: rdn to ld over 2f out: drvn and hdd jst over 1f out: wknd ins fnl f* **13/2**[3]
2 **5** 23 **Kings Gold (IRE)**[24] 1123 3-9-5 0.......... PaulMulrennan 1 11
(Michael Dods) *led: rdn along and hdd over 2f out: drvn and wkng whn n.m.r and hmpd over 1f out* **5/2**[2]

1m 49.75s (2.15) **Going Correction** +0.375s/f (Good) 5 Ran SP% **110.1**
Speed ratings (Par 98): **104,103,102,100,77**
CSF £16.55 TOTE £1.60: £1.10, £7.60; EX 12.60 Trifecta £68.20.
Owner P Makin **Bred** Swordlestown Stud **Trained** Newmarket, Suffolk

FOCUS
The betting suggested this would be a two-horse affair but it proved far more competitive than it looked on paper. The runner-up, who collected RPRs of just 49 as a juvenile, is the marker. It was slowly run.
T/Plt: £19.20 to a £1 stake. Pool of £51771.12 - 1964.73 winning tickets. T/Qpdt: £2.70 to a £1 stake. Pool of £3838.55 - 1040.39 winning tickets. **Joe Rowntree**

1590 - 1594a (Foreign Racing) - See Raceform Interactive

1215 DONCASTER (L-H)
Friday, April 22

OFFICIAL GOING: Good to soft (good in places; 7.6)
Wind: Moderate half behind Weather: Cloudy

1595 PREMIER QUALITY FOODS H'CAP (DIV I) 7f
1:40 (1:41) (Class 5) (0-70,70) 4-Y-O+ **£3,881** (£1,155; £577; £288) **Stalls** High

Form RPR
60-0 **1** **Favourite Treat (USA)**[25] 1125 6-9-7 **70**..........(e) JamesSullivan 7 79
(Ruth Carr) *hld up in midfield: hdwy over 2f out and sn trcking ldrs: effrt and nt clr run whn swtchd lft over 1f out: rdn to chal and edgd rt ins fnl f: led last 100yds: kpt on* **20/1**
2-04 **2** nk **Cliff (IRE)**[25] 1124 6-8-9 **65**..........(p) KieranSchofield(7) 12 73
(Nigel Tinkler) *trckd ldr: hdwy 2f out: rdn over 1f out: styd on to ld briefly ins fnl f: hdd: drvn and no ex last 100yds* **9/2**[1]
3-00 **3** 2½ **Picks Pinta**[60] 680 5-9-5 **68**.......... ConnorBeasley 6 69
(John David Riches) *trckd ldrs: hdwy 2f out: rdn over 1f out: drvn and kpt on same pce fnl f* **33/1**
0055 **4** hd **Mops Angel**[17] 1241 5-8-6 **60**..........(p) GeorgeBuckell(5) 9 61
(Michael Appleby) *towards rr: swtchd lft and hdwy on outer after 2f: chsd ldrs wl over 2f out: sn rdn and kpt on fnl f* **12/1**
-062 **5** ¾ **Colour My World**[26] 1117 6-8-7 **56**..........(b) FrannyNorton 8 55
(Ed McMahon) *led: pushed along over 2f out: rdn over 1f out: hdd and hld whn sltly hmpd ins fnl f: wknd* **11/2**[2]
04-4 **6** ½ **Burner (IRE)**[20] 1202 4-9-4 **67**.......... DuranFentiman 2 65
(Olly Williams) *trckd ldrs: rdn along 2f out: drvn jst over 1f out: grad wknd* **12/1**
0-02 **7** 2 **Tancred (IRE)**[2] 1565 5-9-0 **63**..........(p) LiamKeniry 11 55
(Conor Dore) *in rr tl sme late hdwy* **7/1**[3]
156- **8** 1¼ **British Embassy (IRE)**[177] 7559 4-9-4 **67**.......... DavidNolan 4 56
(David Loughnane) *chsd ldrs: rdn along over 3f out: sn drvn and wknd* **8/1**
-466 **9** 3½ **Cascading Stars (IRE)**[77] 456 4-9-5 **68**.......... DaleSwift 13 47
(Daniel Mark Loughnane) *a in rr* **16/1**
-440 **10** 1½ **Ted's Brother (IRE)**[14] 1323 8-8-8 **57**..........(e) JasonHart 1 32
(Richard Guest) *dwlt: sn in midfield: pushed along 1/2-way: rdn wl over 2f out: sn wknd* **15/2**
43-0 **11** 1½ **Talent Scout (IRE)**[25] 1124 10-9-1 **69**..........(p) GemmaTutty(5) 10 40
(Karen Tutty) *a in rr* **20/1**
240- **12** 2¼ **Bonjour Steve**[199] 7023 5-9-1 **67**..........(p) TomMarquand(3) 3 32
(Richard Price) *chsd ldrs: rdn along wl over 2f out: sn wknd* **9/1**
0-00 **13** 9 **Marmarus**[72] 520 5-8-13 **62**.......... PaulMulrennan 5 3
(David Nicholls) *dwlt: a in rr* **25/1**

1m 26.84s (0.54) **Going Correction** -0.10s/f (Good) 13 Ran SP% **116.5**
Speed ratings (Par 103): **92,91,88,88,87 87,84,83,79,77 76,73,63**
CSF £101.12 CT £3077.41 TOTE £26.70: £6.10, £1.40, £8.70; EX 173.70 Trifecta £2852.60 Part won..
Owner Paul Saxton & The Bottom Liners **Bred** Fares Farm Inc **Trained** Huby, N Yorks

FOCUS
The official going was good to soft, good in places. After riding in the opener Liam Keniry said: "The ground is loose but it is not that soft." The front two pulled a little way clear of the rest in the first division of this modest handicap. The winner is rated to last year's form.

1596 PREMIER QUALITY FOODS H'CAP (DIV II) 7f
2:10 (2:10) (Class 5) (0-70,69) 4-Y-O+ **£3,881** (£1,155; £577; £288) **Stalls** High

Form RPR
05-6 **1** **Call Out Loud**[14] 1317 4-8-10 **61**..........(t) AlistairRawlinson(3) 12 72
(Michael Appleby) *trckd ldr: cl up 1/2-way: led wl over 1f out: rdn clr appr fnl f: readily* **11/2**[2]
2304 **2** 1¾ **Oak Bluffs (IRE)**[14] 1326 5-9-2 **64**.......... JackGarritty 8 70
(Richard Fahey) *towards rr: hdwy wl over 2f out: rdn to chse ldrs over 1f out: kpt on fnl f: nrst fin* **6/1**[3]
30-0 **3** 1 **Danot (IRE)**[25] 1124 4-9-7 **69**.......... GrahamLee 7 72
(Jedd O'Keeffe) *trckd ldrs: effrt over 2f out and sn pushed along: rdn wl over 1f out: kpt on u.p fnl f* **15/2**
3456 **4** ¾ **Depth Charge (IRE)**[21] 1186 4-9-7 **69**..........(vt) RobertHavlin 4 70
(Kristin Stubbs) *dwlt: sn in tch: hdwy over 3f out: pushed along over 2f out: rdn to chse ldrs over 1f out: sn drvn and kpt on same pce* **9/1**
0-33 **5** nse **Sakhalin Star (IRE)**[17] 1241 5-9-6 **68**..........(e) JasonHart 2 69
(Richard Guest) *in tch: hdwy 3f out: rdn to chse ldrs over 1f out: drvn ent fnl f: kpt on same pce* **3/1**[1]
000- **6** nse **Niqnaaqpaadiwaaq**[171] 7675 4-9-5 **67**.......... NeilFarley 5 68
(Eric Alston) *led: pushed along and jnd over 2f out: hdd and rdn wl over 1f out: sn drvn and grad wknd* **10/1**
600- **7** 6 **Firgrove Bridge (IRE)**[186] 7345 4-9-5 **67**..........[1] AdamBeschizza 6 52
(Steph Hollinshead) *dwlt: a towards rr* **25/1**
60-3 **8** 1 **I'm Super Too (IRE)**[38] 936 9-8-7 **60**.......... GemmaTutty(5) 3 42
(Karen Tutty) *hld up: a towards rr* **14/1**
00-0 **9** 1¼ **Red Charmer (IRE)**[16] 1252 6-9-6 **68**.......... PJMcDonald 10 47
(Ann Duffield) *a in rr* **11/1**
230- **10** 1¼ **Etienne Gerard**[203] 6903 4-8-12 **67**.......... KieranSchofield(7) 9 42
(Nigel Tinkler) *trckd ldrs: pushed along 3f out: rdn wl over 2f out: sn wknd* **16/1**
1-00 **11** 1 **Indomitable Spirit**[30] 1047 4-8-6 **57**.......... TimClark(3) 1 30
(Martin Smith) *a in rr* **20/1**

1m 25.6s (-0.70) **Going Correction** -0.10s/f (Good) 11 Ran SP% **115.0**
Speed ratings (Par 103): **100,98,96,96,95 95,89,87,86,85 83**
CSF £37.60 CT £248.37 TOTE £5.40: £2.00, £3.10, £2.90; EX 32.80 Trifecta £231.10.
Owner Kings Head Duffield Racing Partnership **Bred** Rabbah Bloodstock Limited **Trained** Oakham, Rutland

FOCUS
The second division of this modest handicap was run 1.24secs quicker than the opening leg. Straightforward form.

1597 SIG MAIDEN FILLIES' STKS 6f
2:45 (2:47) (Class 5) 3-Y-O+ **£3,881** (£1,155; £577; £288) **Stalls** High

Form RPR
2/ **1** **Time Check (USA)**[506] 8007 4-9-7 0.......... KevinStott(3) 8 84+
(Saeed bin Suroor) *trckd ldrs: hdwy over 2f out: led wl over 1f out and sn rdn clr: kpt on* **13/2**
2 nk **Thankyou Stars** 3-8-13 0.......... JoeyHaynes 13 77
(K R Burke) *trckd ldrs: hdwy on outer and cl up over 2f out: rdn to chse wnr over 1f out: kpt on wl fnl f* **6/1**[3]
0 **3** 2½ **My Lucille (IRE)**[25] 1123 3-8-13 0.......... DavidAllan 12 69
(Tim Easterby) *hld up in midfield: hdwy and in tch over 2f out: rdn wl over 1f out: chsd ldng pair ent fnl f: kpt on* **33/1**
4 ¾ **Bella's Venture** 3-8-10 0.......... MichaelJMMurphy(3) 16 67
(John Gallagher) *towards rr: hdwy wl over 2f out: rdn wl over 1f out: kpt on fnl f* **33/1**
5 3 **Any Joy (IRE)** 3-8-13 0.......... GrahamLee 6 57
(Ben Haslam) *prom: cl up 1/2-way: rdn along over 2f out: grad wknd* **20/1**
6 hd **Fly True** 3-8-13 0.......... LukeMorris 9 56
(Jeremy Gask) *towards rr: hdwy over 2f out: rdn wl over 1f out: kpt on: nrst fin* **12/1**
0- **7** 2¾ **Clever Divya**[340] 2341 3-8-13 0.......... LemosdeSouza 2 48
(J R Jenkins) *cl up: led 1/2-way: rdn and hdd wl over 1f out: sn drvn and wknd* **200/1**
02- **8** 2 **Cancan Katy**[231] 6043 3-8-13 0.......... FrannyNorton 3 41
(Tom Dascombe) *chsd ldrs: cl up 1/2-way: rdn along over 2f out: sn drvn and wknd* **4/1**[2]
9 ½ **Scamper** 3-8-13 0.......... WilliamTwiston-Davies 17 40
(Roger Charlton) *racd wd: hld up towards rr: hdwy wl over 2f out: rdn wl over 1f out: sn no imp* **11/4**[1]
10 hd **Archipentura** 4-9-7 0.......... AlistairRawlinson(3) 5 42
(J R Jenkins) *dwlt and bhd: sme hdwy 1/2-way: rdn along wl over 2f out: n.d* **50/1**
11 shd **Zabeel Princess** 3-8-13 0.......... HarryBentley 4 39
(Roger Varian) *dwlt and towards rr: hdwy and in tch 1/2-way: rdn along over 2f out: sn wknd* **4/1**[2]

The Form Book, Raceform Ltd, Newbury, RG14 5SJ

55 **12** *1 1/4* **Secret Sonnet**[21] 1181 3-8-13 0 .... SaleemGolam 14 35
(Stuart Williams) *towards rr: effrt and sme hdwy 3f out: sn rdn along and n.d* **100/1**

60- **13** *5* **Kylla**[258] 5163 3-8-13 0 .... DuranFentiman 15 19
(Shaun Harris) *midfield: hdwy to chse ldrs 3f out: rdn along over 2f out: sn wknd* **200/1**

0 **14** *2 1/2* **The Skipper's Cat**[10] 1400 4-9-10 0 .... AndrewMullen 11 14
(Michael Appleby) *a towards rr* **100/1**

00 **15** *1* **Sunshine Quest**[37] 959 4-9-5 0 .... RachelRichardson[(5)] 1 10
(Lucinda Egerton) *led: hdd 1/2-way: sn rdn along and wknd wl over 2f out* **300/1**

16 *6* **Frenchie** 4-9-10 0 .... DaleSwift 10
(Shaun Harris) *dwlt: a in rr* **100/1**

17 *7* **Striking Nigella**[32] 6-9-3 0 .... RhiainIngram[(7)] 7
(Michael Chapman) *s.i.s: a bhd* **250/1**

1m 13.75s (0.15) **Going Correction** -0.10s/f (Good)
WFA 3 from 4yo+ 11lb **17** Ran SP% **119.3**
Speed ratings (Par 100): **95,94,91,90,86 86,82,79,79,78 78,76,70,66,65 57,48**
CSF £42.58 TOTE £5.60: £1.50, £2.80, £7.90; EX 55.90 Trifecta £1167.20.
Owner Godolphin **Bred** Darley **Trained** Newmarket, Suffolk

FOCUS
A fair maiden and the form is worth noting, although the time was modest. The winner was value for extra.

1598 EQUESTRIAN SURFACES LTD H'CAP 2m 110y
3:20 (3:20) (Class 4) (0-85,85) 4-Y-O+ **£5,175** (£1,540; £769; £384) **Stalls** Low

Form RPR

220- **1** **Hidden Justice (IRE)**[112] 7597 7-9-11 **84** .... PhillipMakin 9 92+
(John Quinn) *trckd ldrs: upsides over 2f out: led over 1f out: styd on wl: eased clsng stages* **10/1**

135- **2** *1 1/4* **Perceus**[34] 7145 4-9-8 **85** .... GrahamLee 8 89
(James Eustace) *hld up in mid-div: pushed along over 4f out: chsng ldrs over 2f out: swtchd rt 1f out: kpt on to take 2nd last 150yds: no imp* **9/2**[2]

0- **3** *1 1/4* **Golden Doyen (GER)**[31] 6749 5-9-7 **80** .... WilliamTwiston-Davies 6 83
(Philip Hobbs) *trckd ldrs: drvn to ld over 3f out: hdd over 2f out: outpcd over 1f out: styd on to take 3rd last 100yds* **7/4**[1]

140- **4** *2 1/2* **Champagne Champ**[193] 7165 4-8-13 **76** .... LiamKeniry 2 76
(Rod Millman) *hld up in mid-div: kpt on fnl 2f: nvr a threat* **9/1**

6- **5** *1 1/4* **Vilman (IRE)**[139] 8124 4-9-5 **82** .... LukeMorris 3 80
(Simon West) *trckd ldrs: led over 2f out: hdd over 1f out: wknd last 150yds* **14/1**

116/ **6** *nk* **Lexi's Boy (IRE)**[38] 3857 8-9-10 **83** ....(tp) DavidNolan 11 81
(Donald McCain) *in rr: pushed along over 5f out: kpt on fnl 2f: nvr a factor* **25/1**

6513 **7** *2* **Spiritoftomintoul**[35] 983 7-9-5 **81** ....(t) GeorgeDowning[(3)] 7 76
(Tony Carroll) *hld up in rr: effrt over 3f out: kpt on fnl 2f: nvr on terms* **5/1**[3]

0-35 **8** *1 3/4* **Hallstatt (IRE)**[51] 786 10-8-9 **68** ....(t) PaulMulrennan 10 61
(John Mackie) *hld up in rr: effrt over 3f out: n.m.r over 2f out: nvr on terms* **16/1**

60-0 **P** **Apollo Eleven (IRE)**[27] 1092 7-8-7 **66** .... AndrewMullen 4
(Michael Appleby) *led: hdd over 3f out: sn lost pl: bhd whn heavily eased over 1f out: sn p.u* **16/1**

3m 45.23s (4.83) **Going Correction** +0.45s/f (Yiel)
WFA 4 from 5yo+ 4lb **9** Ran SP% **112.6**
Speed ratings (Par 105): **106,105,104,103,103 102,101,101,**
CSF £52.98 CT £115.86 TOTE £11.30: £3.30, £2.20, £1.10; EX 79.70 Trifecta £218.40.
Owner Highfield Racing 2 **Bred** Ballylinch Stud **Trained** Settrington, N Yorks

FOCUS
A fair staying handicap and they went a good pace, but the form is rated cautiously. Race distance increased by 6 yards.

1599 I'M BACKING LEWIS ASHLEY MODULAR BUILDINGS H'CAP 6f
3:55 (3:55) (Class 3) (0-90,89) 3-Y-O **£7,762** (£2,310; £1,154; £577) **Stalls** High

Form RPR

0-1 **1** **Remarkable**[37] 959 3-8-8 **76** ....(b) RobertHavlin 14 90+
(John Gosden) *dwlt and hmpd s: in rr: swtchd rt jst over 2f out: gd hdwy over 1f out: rdn and str run ent fnl f: sn hung lft: led last 100yds: styd on strly* **4/1**[1]

312- **2** *1 3/4* **Alqubbah (IRE)**[217] 6503 3-9-6 **88** .... GrahamLee 2 96
(Ed Dunlop) *hld up towards rr: smooth hdwy 3f out: sn trcking ldrs: effrt to ld wl over 1f out: rdn ent fnl f: hdd and no ex last 75yds* **10/1**

14- **3** *3/4* **My Amigo**[267] 4791 3-8-9 **77** .... PJMcDonald 12 83
(Ann Duffield) *cl up: led 1/2-way: rdn along and hdd wl over 1f out: drvn and rallied ent fnl f: kpt on same pce* **8/1**

00-6 **4** *2 3/4* **Glenrowan Rose (IRE)**[49] 821 3-9-7 **89** .... PhillipMakin 7 86
(Keith Dalgleish) *trckd ldrs: hdwy over 2f out: rdn over 1f out: drvn and one pce fnl f* **25/1**

300- **5** *1 3/4* **Quick N Quirky (IRE)**[202] 6931 3-8-8 **76** ....(t) DavidAllan 5 67
(Tim Easterby) *in rr: hdwy over 2f out: rdn over 1f out: styd on fnl f: nrst fin* **25/1**

10-4 **6** *1 1/2* **Ancient Astronaut**[17] 1243 3-9-0 **82** .... GrahamGibbons 16 69
(John Quinn) *hld up: hdwy over 2f out: rdn over 1f out: kpt on fnl f: nrst fin* **13/2**[2]

14- **7** *nk* **Gallipoli (IRE)**[335] 2485 3-9-6 **88** .... TonyHamilton 8 74+
(Richard Fahey) *in rr: pushed along wl over 2f out: rdn and hdwy wl over 1f out: kpt on fnl f: nrst fin* **14/1**

565- **8** *hd* **Dutch Mist**[181] 7471 3-9-3 **88** .... JoeDoyle[(3)] 11 73
(Kevin Ryan) *towards rr tl sme late hdwy* **7/1**[3]

020- **9** *3/4* **Mon Beau Visage (IRE)**[216] 6522 3-8-12 **80** ow1 ...... DanielTudhope 13 63
(David O'Meara) *trckd ldrs: hdwy to chse ldng pair at 1/2-way: rdn along over 2f out: sn wknd* **40/1**

610- **10** *3/4* **Garden World (IRE)**[242] 5704 3-8-12 **80** .... JasonHart 10 60
(Nigel Tinkler) *dwlt and in rr: swtchd rt and rdn along over 2f out: sme hdwy fnl f* **66/1**

104- **11** *nk* **Roll On Rory**[178] 7523 3-8-8 **76** .... AndrewMullen 15 55
(Jason Ward) *a towards rr* **33/1**

453- **12** *shd* **Fatherly Friend (USA)**[217] 6490 3-8-9 **77** ....(t) JoeyHaynes 1 56
(K R Burke) *prom: rdn along wl over 2f out: sn wknd* **9/1**

063- **13** *3/4* **Unilit (IRE)**[181] 7460 3-9-7 **89** .... CathyGannon 9 66
(David Evans) *chsd ldrs: effrt over 2f out: rdn along wl over 1f out: sn wknd* **33/1**

1- **14** *nk* **Gowanless**[179] 7515 3-8-11 **79** .... PaulMulrennan 3 55
(Michael Dods) *chsd ldrs: pushed along bef 1/2-way: sn lost pl and towards rr* **14/1**

63-5 **15** *nse* **Take Charge**[28] 1079 3-8-9 **77** .... LukeMorris 17 52
(David Brown) *midfield: rdn along over 2f out: sn wknd* **16/1**

031- **16** *1 1/4* **Quick March**[228] 6162 3-9-0 **82** ....[1] WilliamTwiston-Davies 4 53
(Roger Charlton) *midfield: pushed along 1/2-way: sn rdn and wknd over 2f out* **10/1**

051- **17** *3* **Dheban (IRE)**[195] 7106 3-8-13 **84** .... TomMarquand[(3)] 6 46
(Richard Hannon) *led to 1/2-way: sn rdn along and wknd qckly 2f out* **20/1**

1m 12.18s (-1.42) **Going Correction** -0.10s/f (Good) **17** Ran SP% **126.6**
Speed ratings (Par 102): **105,102,101,98,95 93,93,93,92,91 90,90,89,89,89 87,83**
CSF £41.79 CT £330.08 TOTE £5.40: £1.20, £2.60, £2.30, £6.60; EX 53.30 Trifecta £490.90.
Owner Cheveley Park Stud **Bred** Cheveley Park Stud Ltd **Trained** Newmarket, Suffolk

FOCUS
A competitive 3yo handicap, in which they went an even gallop, and it was hard not to be impressed by the winner. The form looks sound.

1600 ASHLEIGH SIGNS - ANDY FIRTH - FILLIES' H'CAP 6f
4:25 (4:25) (Class 5) (0-70,68) 4-Y-O+ **£3,881** (£1,155; £577; £288) **Stalls** High

Form RPR

1-02 **1** **Posh Bounty**[4] 1533 5-9-0 **61** .... JFEgan 6 71
(Joseph Tuite) *wore ear plugs: mid-div: effrt over 2f out: led over 1f out: drvn out* **11/4**[1]

21- **2** *2 1/4* **Dream Bounty**[189] 7257 4-9-1 **62** .... RoystonFfrench 1 65
(John Holt) *in tch: hdwy over 2f out: kpt on same pce fnl f* **5/1**[3]

0-00 **3** *nk* **Spirit Of Rosanna**[108] 54 4-8-7 **54** oh2 ....(tp) AdamBeschizza 7 56
(Steph Hollinshead) *led: hdd over 2f out: kpt on same pce appr fnl f* **25/1**

555- **4** *1 1/4* **Goadby**[171] 7680 5-8-12 **59** .... RobertHavlin 5 57
(John Holt) *in rr: hdwy over 2f out: hung lft and kpt on same pce appr fnl f* **9/1**

030- **5** *nk* **Celtic Sixpence (IRE)**[154] 7925 8-9-2 **68** .... DavidParkes[(5)] 9 65
(Nick Kent) *chsd ldrs: kpt on one pce over 1f out* **7/1**

000- **6** *1/2* **Fleurtille**[220] 6408 7-9-7 **68** .... ConnorBeasley 8 63
(Ray Craggs) *mid-div: effrt over 2f out: kpt on fnl f: nvr a threat* **14/1**

600- **7** *1 1/4* **Beau Mistral (IRE)**[191] 7224 7-8-10 **60** .... GeorgeDowning[(3)] 3 51
(Tony Carroll) *chsd ldrs: wknd fnl f* **25/1**

20-6 **8** *hd* **Armelle (FR)**[16] 1254 5-9-0 **61** .... KieranO'Neill 2 52
(Scott Dixon) *w ldr: led over 2f out: hdd over 1f out: wknd last 150yds* **9/1**

64-4 **9** *4 1/2* **Legal Art**[16] 1254 4-8-4 **56** ....(b[1]) CallumShepherd[(5)] 4 32
(Brian Ellison) *s.i.s: in rr: sme hdwy stands' side over 2f out: lost pl over 1f out* **10/3**[2]

1m 12.51s (-1.09) **Going Correction** -0.10s/f (Good) **9** Ran SP% **113.3**
Speed ratings (Par 100): **103,100,99,97,97 96,95,94,88**
CSF £16.32 CT £275.48 TOTE £2.90: £1.10, £1.70, £5.70; EX 10.40 Trifecta £232.80.
Owner The Lamb Inn - Pethy **Bred** Mascalls Stud **Trained** Lambourn, Berks

FOCUS
A competitive fillies' handicap but not the strongest for the grade. It was the best of the C&D times and the form seems sound.

1601 POLYPIPE H'CAP 5f
4:55 (4:56) (Class 4) (0-85,84) 4-Y-O+ **£5,175** (£1,540; £769; £384) **Stalls** High

Form RPR

24-1 **1** **Ladweb**[8] 1447 6-8-4 **72** .... PatrickO'Donnell[(5)] 3 83
(John Gallagher) *trckd ldng pair: cl up 1/2-way: led over 1f out: rdn and edgd rt ins fnl f: kpt on* **15/8**[1]

3-10 **2** *1* **Pensax Lad (IRE)**[75] 492 5-8-8 **74** .... GeorgeDowning[(3)] 5 81
(Ronald Harris) *led: jnd 1/2-way: rdn along 2f out: hdd over 1f out: drvn and kpt on fnl f* **12/1**

1245 **3** *3/4* **Rich Again (IRE)**[14] 1321 7-9-1 **78** ....(b) TedDurcan 9 82+
(James Bethell) *towards rr: hdwy 1/2-way: chsd ldrs on outer wl over 1f out: sn rdn and kpt on fnl f* **9/1**

644- **4** *3/4* **Fredricka**[188] 7286 5-9-7 **84** .... GrahamGibbons 14 86
(David Barron) *broke wl: stdd and dropped in to trck ldrs: effrt and n.m.r over 1f out: sn rdn and hdwy ent fnl f: sn drvn and no imp towards fin* **13/2**[2]

0-44 **5** *1 1/4* **Top Boy**[14] 1321 6-9-0 **77** ....(p) TonyHamilton 4 74
(Derek Shaw) *trckd ldrs on outer: hdwy 2f out: rdn to chse ldng pair over 1f out: sn drvn and kpt on same pce* **7/1**[3]

210- **6** *3/4* **Pea Shooter**[167] 7746 7-9-1 **78** .... DaleSwift 11 72
(Brian Ellison) *trckd ldrs: rdn along wl over 1f out: drvn and one pce ent fnl f* **12/1**

026- **7** *3/4* **Stanghow**[191] 7223 4-9-3 **80** .... DavidAllan 8 72
(Antony Brittain) *hld up towards rr: hdwy wl over 1f out: rdn and kpt on fnl f* **17/2**

335- **8** *1 1/4* **Flash City (ITY)**[192] 7188 8-8-12 **75** ....(p) JamesSullivan 6 62
(Ruth Carr) *t.k.h: trckd ldrs: effrt wl over 1f out: sn rdn and wknd appr fnl f* **20/1**

20-0 **9** *2* **Tom Sawyer**[14] 1321 8-8-12 **75** ....(p) ConnorBeasley 2 55
(Julie Camacho) *a in rr* **33/1**

210- **10** *1/2* **Emjayem**[196] 7082 6-9-3 **80** .... RoystonFfrench 12 58
(Ed McMahon) *plld hrd early: chsd ldng pair: rdn along over 2f out: grad wknd* **18/1**

613- **11** *1* **Bashiba (IRE)**[209] 6765 5-9-3 **80** ....(t) JasonHart 13 55
(Nigel Tinkler) *a in rr* **14/1**

59.25s (-1.25) **Going Correction** -0.10s/f (Good) **11** Ran SP% **116.2**
Speed ratings (Par 105): **106,104,103,102,100 98,97,95,92,91 90**
CSF £25.77 CT £168.67 TOTE £3.10: £1.70, £4.20, £2.40; EX 31.70 Trifecta £344.70.
Owner The Juniper Racing Club & Andrew Bell **Bred** Adweb Ltd **Trained** Chastleton, Oxon

FOCUS
A decent sprint handicap in which nothing got into it from off the pace. The winner was similar to his Ripon form.

1602 PEGLER YORKSHIRE H'CAP 1m 2f 60y
5:25 (5:28) (Class 4) (0-80,80) 3-Y-O **£5,175** (£1,540; £769; £384) **Stalls** Low

Form RPR

-450 **1** **Sark (IRE)**[56] 729 3-8-11 **70** .... CathyGannon 11 77
(David Evans) *hld up in rr: stdy hdwy on outer 3f out: chsd ldrs over 1f out: rdn ent fnl f: styd on strly to ld last 120yds: jst hld on* **25/1**

21- **2** *shd* **Red Verdon (USA)**[139] 8123 3-9-3 **76** .... GrahamLee 7 84+
(Ed Dunlop) *trckd ldrs: pushed along and sltly outpcd 3f out: rdn over 2f out: hdwy over 1f out: n.m.r ent fnl f: styng on whn hmpd last 100yds: fin strly: jst failed* **13/2**

500- **3** *3/4* **Grapevine (IRE)**[175] 7592 3-8-12 **74** .... MichaelJMMurphy[(3)] 6 79
(Charles Hills) *trckd ldrs: hdwy over 4f out: cl up over 2f out: rdn to ld wl over 1f out: drvn ent fnl f: hdd: edgd rt and no ex last 100yds* **11/1**

02-3 **4** *1 1/2* **Paling**[18] 1238 3-9-0 **73** ....[1] WilliamTwiston-Davies 10 75
(Roger Charlton) *hld up towards rr: stdy hdwy on outer 1/2-way: trckd ldrs 3f out: rdn to chal wl over 1f out: ev ch tl drvn ent fnl f and kpt on same pce* **9/2**[2]

12-0 **5** ¾ **Southern Gailes (IRE)**[28] 1080 3-9-5 **78** JoeyHaynes 2 79
(K R Burke) *prom: trckd ldr after 3f: cl up over 3f out: led over 2f out: rdn and hdd wl over 1f out: sn drvn and kpt on one pce* **14/1**

00-1 **6** nk **Walsingham Grange (USA)**[16] 1276 3-9-0 **76** RobHornby(3) 3 76+
(Pam Sly) *in rr: bhd 1/2-way: hdwy 3f out: rdn over 2f out: kpt on appr fnl f: nrst fin* **17/2**

00-1 **7** 2 **Ban Shoof**[21] 1184 3-9-4 **77** TomQueally 5 74
(Ismail Mohammed) *trckd ldng pair: hdwy over 3f out: rdn along over 2f out: sn drvn and wknd over 1f out* **14/1**

055- **8** 3½ **Impediment (IRE)**[161] 7835 3-8-7 **66** oh1 TedDurcan 4 56
(Sir Michael Stoute) *led: pushed along over 3f out: rdn and hdd wl over 2f out: sn drvn and wknd* **4/1**[1]

31- **9** 9 **Nessita**[199] 7013 3-9-4 **77** MartinHarley 1 50
(Hugo Palmer) *chsd ldr 3f: prom tl rdn along over 3f out and sn wknd* **5/1**[3]

3111 **10** 18 **Pirate's Treasure**[23] 1155 3-9-7 **80** LukeMorris 8 19
(James Tate) *t.k.h early: hld up: a towards rr* **7/1**

2m 13.76s (4.36) **Going Correction** +0.45s/f (Yiel) **10** Ran SP% **116.7**
Speed ratings (Par 100): **100,99,99,98,97 97,95,92,85,71**
CSF £179.69 CT £1912.99 TOTE £32.60: £6.80, £3.10, £3.00; EX 174.30 Trifecta £1112.80.
Owner Trevor Gallienne **Bred** Andrew Rosen **Trained** Pandy, Monmouths

FOCUS
Race distance increaded by 6 yards. A competitive 3yo handicap run at a good pace, but a bunch finish and a surprise improver in the winner.
T/Jkpt: Not won. T/Plt: £131.00 to a £1 stake. Pool: £87,332.62 - 486.50 winning tickets T/Qpdt: £15.80 to a £1 stake. Pool: £7,663.00 - 356.82 winning tickets **Joe Rowntree & Walter Glynn**

SANDOWN (R-H)
Friday, April 22

OFFICIAL GOING: Good to soft (good in places, soft patches on home turn on round course)
Wind: Moderate, behind Weather: Overcast, raining race 8

1603 BET365 ESHER CUP (H'CAP) 1m 14y
1:20 (1:20) (Class 2) (0-100,96) 3-Y-O

£15,562 (£4,660; £2,330; £1,165; £582; £292) **Stalls** Low

Form RPR

01- **1** **Czabo**[251] 5378 3-8-10 **85** SilvestreDeSousa 7 97
(Mick Channon) *hld up in rr: prog on wd outside over 2f out: led wl over 1f out: rdn and styd on wl after* **11/1**

152- **2** 2¼ **Midhmaar**[209] 6761 3-8-9 **84** AndreaAtzeni 2 91
(Owen Burrows) *hld up in rr: prog on outer over 2f out to chal wl over 1f out: chsd wnr after: styd on but readily hld* **16/1**

1- **3** 3¼ **California Whip (USA)**[268] 4765 3-8-11 **86** RyanMoore 5 86
(Richard Hannon) *q str: settled in midfield: prog to chal 2f out: rdn to chse ldng pair after and sn lft bhd by them: kpt on* **4/1**[2]

621- **4** 1½ **Von Blucher (IRE)**[178] 7532 3-8-11 **86** (t) FrankieDettori 1 82
(John Gosden) *pushed along early to rch midfield: shkn up and no prog over 2f out: racd sltly awkwardly but kpt on fnl f* **5/2**[1]

411- **5** nk **Ebtihaal (IRE)**[182] 7421 3-9-4 **93** PaulHanagan 4 88
(Saeed bin Suroor) *str: will improve for run: hld up in last: detached over 3f out: shkn up and hanging rt over 2f out: nvr any ch but kpt on fnl f* **5/1**[3]

010- **6** ¾ **Mikmak**[181] 7468 3-9-1 **90** MartinDwyer 6 84
(William Muir) *tk fierce hold early: prom tl wknd wl over 1f out* **20/1**

212- **7** ¾ **Justice Law (IRE)**[232] 6023 3-9-7 **96** JamesDoyle 8 88
(David Elsworth) *sn trckd ldr: led over 3f out: hdd & wknd wl over 1f out* **7/1**

21 **8** 11 **Abareeq**[35] 976 3-8-12 **87** DaneO'Neill 3 54
(Mark Johnston) *lengthy: sltly on toes: prom tl wknd qckly over 2f out: t.o* **15/2**

513- **9** hd **Bobby Wheeler (IRE)**[234] 5973 3-9-0 **89** JohnFahy 9 55
(Clive Cox) *led: hanging on bnd 1/2-way: hdd over 3f out: wknd rapidly 2f out: t.o* **25/1**

1m 45.19s (1.89) **Going Correction** +0.325s/f (Good) **9** Ran SP% **112.3**
Speed ratings (Par 104): **103,100,97,96,95 94,94,83,83**
CSF £163.87 CT £827.63 TOTE £10.40: £2.20, £3.30, £1.70; EX 55.80 Trifecta £477.90.
Owner Norman Court Stud **Bred** Norman Court Stud **Trained** West Ilsley, Berks
■ Stewards' Enquiry : Andrea Atzeni one-day ban; careless riding (6th May)

FOCUS
The round course was at its outermost configuration down back straight and on the home bend, then on the inner up home straight, adding 29 yards to all race distances on the round track. Drying ground but it looked hard work. This was a typically competitive running of the Esher Cup but the pace seemed too strong, with the first five positioned 8th, 7th, 6th, 5th and 9th turning into the straight. The first two challenged widest. A step up from the unexposed winner.

1604 BET365 GORDON RICHARDS STKS (GROUP 3) 1m 2f 7y
1:50 (1:50) (Class 1) 4-Y-O+

£36,861 (£13,975; £6,994; £3,484; £1,748; £877) **Stalls** Low

Form RPR

011- **1** **My Dream Boat (IRE)**[173] 7668 4-9-3 111 AdamKirby 1 120
(Clive Cox) *sltly on toes: hld up in last: cajoled along and clsd fr 2f out: squeezed through rivals fnl f and wl-timed effrt to ld last 100yds: styd on wl* **8/1**[3]

133- **2** 1¼ **Western Hymn**[293] 3913 5-9-0 117 FrankieDettori 4 115
(John Gosden) *trckd ldr: led jst over 2f out: hrd pressed and hd high but fought off rivals fr over 1f out: hdd and outpcd last 100yds* **4/5**[1]

45- **3** 1¼ **Ayrad (IRE)**[251] 5380 5-9-0 112 AndreaAtzeni 5 112
(Roger Charlton) *trckd ldng trio: rdn over 2f out: pressed ldr wl over 1f out: kpt on but hld and lost 2nd ins fnl f* **12/1**

50-4 **4** ¾ **Master Carpenter (IRE)**[20] 1198 5-9-0 108 FrederikTylicki 7 111
(Rod Millman) *hld up in 6th: prog over 2f out: tried to chal over 1f out: kpt on same pce fnl f* **16/1**

-553 **5** nse **Tullius (IRE)**[9] 1425 8-9-0 112 JimmyFortune 3 110
(Andrew Balding) *trckd ldng pair: rdn wl over 2f out: clsd and tried to chal fr over 1f out: kpt on one pce fnl f* **13/2**[2]

303- **6** 5 **Top Notch Tonto (IRE)**[174] 7633 6-9-0 110 (p) BenCurtis 2 100
(Brian Ellison) *hld up in 5th: rdn wl over 2f out: no prog and wl btn over 1f out* **11/1**

1311 **7** 9 **Our Channel (USA)**[27] 1088 5-9-0 103 (p) PatCosgrave 6 82
(William Haggas) *racd freely: led: clr 1/2-way: hdd jst over 2f out: sn wknd: t.o* **10/1**

2m 13.14s (2.64) **Going Correction** +0.325s/f (Good) **7** Ran SP% **111.0**
Speed ratings (Par 113): **102,101,100,99,99 95,88**
CSF £14.03 TOTE £8.40: £3.30, £1.20; EX 16.00 Trifecta £150.80.
Owner Paul & Clare Rooney **Bred** Patrick Monahan **Trained** Lambourn, Berks

FOCUS
This was run over 29 yards further than advertised. Again the main action unfolded wide of the inside rail in the straight. The favourite ran below form and the time was slow, but a smart performance from the winner under his penalty. The form is rated around the third and fourth.

1605 BET365 CLASSIC TRIAL (GROUP 3) 1m 2f 7y
2:20 (2:25) (Class 1) 3-Y-O

£36,861 (£13,975; £6,994; £3,484; £1,748; £877) **Stalls** Low

Form RPR

1- **1** **Midterm**[182] 7431 3-9-1 0 RyanMoore 5 112+
(Sir Michael Stoute) *medium-sized: q str: hld up in 5th: clsd over 2f out: shkn up to ld wl over 1f out: stl pressed fnl f: drvn and asserted last 100yds* **8/11**[1]

41- **2** 1½ **Algometer**[182] 7435 3-9-1 86 JimCrowley 2 109
(David Simcock) *trckd ldng pair: rdn to ld over 2f out: hdd wl over 1f out: kpt on wl and stl pressing ins fnl f: no ex last 100yds* **12/1**

1 **3** 8 **High Grounds (IRE)**[84] 377 3-9-1 89 DarryllHolland 7 93
(Charles Hills) *hld up in last: rdn and nt qckn over 2f out: lft bhd by ldng pair sn after: tk modest 3rd ins fnl f* **4/1**[2]

13-5 **4** ½ **Palawan**[13] 1338 3-9-1 98 PatDobbs 4 92
(Richard Hannon) *hld up in 4th: nt clr run briefly jst over 2f out: sn lft bhd by ldng pair: lost modest 3rd ins fnl f* **20/1**

62-1 **5** 4½ **Dwight D**[98] 202 3-9-1 84 JamieSpencer 6 83
(William Haggas) *str: lw: mde most to over 2f out: sn btn* **14/1**

50-2 **6** 4 **Ode To Evening**[13] 1338 3-9-1 100 JamesDoyle 1 75
(Mark Johnston) *trckd ldr to wl over 2f out: sn wknd* **8/1**[3]

2m 11.11s (0.61) **Going Correction** +0.325s/f (Good) **6** Ran SP% **108.1**
Speed ratings (Par 108): **110,108,102,102,98 95**
CSF £9.72 TOTE £1.80: £1.20, £4.30; EX 8.40 Trifecta £33.60.
Owner K Abdullah **Bred** Juddmonte Farms Ltd **Trained** Newmarket, Suffolk

FOCUS
This was run over 29 yards further than advertised. Unsurprisingly given the way the first two races unfolded, all runners shunned the inside rail, not just in the straight but most of the way round, although the first two did drift towards the fence late on. The first two, who won separate divisions of the same Newbury maiden last year, pulled a long way clear and the time was much the quickest of five good races at the trip. Midterm rates among the better winners of this race, with Algometer a similar improver too.

1606 BET365 MILE (GROUP 2) 1m 14y
2:55 (2:58) (Class 1) 4-Y-O+

£53,874 (£20,425; £10,222; £5,092; £2,555; £1,282) **Stalls** Low

Form RPR

130- **1** **Toormore (IRE)**[131] 8218 5-9-4 114 WilliamBuick 7 120
(Richard Hannon) *sltly on toes: trckd ldr in wl stretched field: led over 2f out to 2f out: drvn and rallied to ld again ins fnl f: hld on wl* **7/2**[2]

225- **2** nk **Dutch Connection**[202] 6952 4-9-1 116 JimCrowley 1 116
(Charles Hills) *lw: t.k.h: trckd ldng pair and clr of rest: led 2f out gng strly: sn rdn: kpt on but hdd ins fnl f: jst hld after* **5/1**[3]

332- **3** 1½ **Breton Rock (IRE)**[196] 7074 6-9-1 113 JamieSpencer 6 113
(David Simcock) *chsd clr ldng trio: rdn over 2f out: kpt on u.p fr over 1f out: nrst fin but unable to threaten* **7/1**

32-1 **4** nk **Belardo (IRE)**[20] 1198 4-9-1 117 JamesDoyle 5 112
(Roger Varian) *hld up bhd in last trio: shkn up over 2f out: limited prog and drvn over 1f out: kpt on and nrst fin but n.d* **13/8**[1]

23-0 **5** 2¼ **Gabrial (IRE)**[27] 1106 7-9-1 114 RyanMoore 4 107
(Richard Fahey) *hld up bhd in last trio: pushed along over 2f out: swtchd rt over 1f out: nvr on terms and nvr involved* **8/1**

106- **6** 3¾ **Adaay (IRE)**[188] 7278 4-9-1 113 PaulHanagan 2 98
(William Haggas) *hld up bhd: in last fr 1/2-way and detached over 3f out: nudged along over 2f out: reminders over 1f out: styd on but no ch and nvr involved* **13/2**

/13- **7** 13 **Barchan (USA)**[433] 560 4-9-1 80 AndreaAtzeni 3 68
(Roger Varian) *lw: led at str pce and stretched field: hdd & wknd over 2f out: t.o* **150/1**

1m 43.06s (-0.24) **Going Correction** +0.325s/f (Good) **7** Ran SP% **114.6**
Speed ratings (Par 115): **114,113,112,111,109 105,92**
CSF £21.30 TOTE £4.30: £2.00, £3.00; EX 20.70 Trifecta £106.00.
Owner Godolphin **Bred** BEC Bloodstock **Trained** East Everleigh, Wilts

FOCUS
This was run over 29 yards further than advertised. Again they didn't want to know the inside rail. The pacemaker Barchan can't have gone that fast as the first three home raced 2nd, 3rd and 4th. Toormore is rated pretty much to his best.

1607 BET365.COM H'CAP 5f 6y
3:30 (3:30) (Class 2) (0-100,99) 3-Y-O

£12,450 (£3,728; £1,864; £932; £466; £234) **Stalls** Low

Form RPR

00-1 **1** **Willytheconqueror (IRE)**[16] 1271 3-8-12 **90** MartinDwyer 2 97+
(William Muir) *chsd clr ldng pair: rdn to go 2nd over 1f out: led jst ins fnl f: drvn and styd on wl* **4/1**[1]

136- **2** 1¼ **Lady Macapa**[153] 7938 3-9-1 **93** JimCrowley 8 96
(William Knight) *pressed ldr and clr of rest: led after 2f: drvn and hdd jst ins fnl f: hld on wl for 2nd* **12/1**

4-35 **3** hd **Sixties Sue**[7] 1453 3-8-10 **88** SilvestreDeSousa 4 90
(Mick Channon) *chsd ldng trio: rdn to go 3rd over 1f out: cl enough jst ins fnl f: nt qckn after* **15/2**

60-2 **4** 2¾ **Handytalk (IRE)**[11] 1385 3-8-7 **85** AndreaAtzeni 5 77
(Rod Millman) *off the pce towards rr: rdn on outer 2f out: tk 4th and edgd rt fnl f: no imp on ldng trio* **9/2**[2]

22-2 **5** 3 **Sign Of The Kodiac (IRE)**[28] 1070 3-9-4 **96** TomEaves 1 77
(James Given) *lw: led against rail: hdd after 2f: lost 2nd over 1f out and sn wknd* **7/1**

0-11 **6** ½ **Ticking Away**[31] 1029 3-8-8 **86** SeanLevey 6 66
(David Brown) *lw: awkward s: a in rr: rdn and no prog 2f out: no ch after* **6/1**[3]

124- **7** 1¼ **Alizoom (IRE)**[254] 5271 3-8-2 **80** [1] JoeFanning 9 55
(Roger Varian) *s.s: mostly in last and off the pce: rdn and no prog 2f out* **7/1**

665- **8** 26 **Riflescope (IRE)**[209] 6741 3-9-7 **99** JamesDoyle 3
(Mark Johnston) *lw: nvr bttr than midfield: rdn 1/2-way: wknd wl over 1f out: virtually p.u fnl f* **6/1**[3]

1m 1.25s (-0.35) **Going Correction** +0.05s/f (Good) **8** Ran SP% **111.2**
Speed ratings (Par 104): **104,102,101,97,92 91,89,48**
CSF £48.38 CT £335.53 TOTE £4.60: £1.90, £2.90, £2.10; EX 61.80 Trifecta £505.80.

Owner Perspicacious Punters Racing Club **Bred** Old Carhue & Graeng Bloodstock **Trained** Lambourn, Berks

FOCUS

A decent 3yo sprint handicap. The runner-up looks the key to the form longer term.

1608 NORDOFF ROBBINS SIR GEORGE MARTIN MEMORIAL MAIDEN FILLIES' STKS (PLUS 10 RACE) (DIV I) 1m 2f 7y

4:05 (4:05) (Class 4) 3-Y-O **£6,469** (£1,925; £962; £481) **Stalls** Low

Form RPR

5- **1** **Southern Stars**[182] 7422 3-9-0 0 FrankieDettori 2 84+
(John Gosden) *q tall: lengthy: mde all: shkn up and decent ld 2f out: kpt on wl and a looked in command* **9/2[3]**

2 *1 ¼* **Ajman Princess (IRE)** 3-9-0 0 AndreaAtzeni 8 81+
(Roger Varian) *athletic: attractive: t.k.h: trckd ldng pair: shkn up whn nt clr run briefly over 1f out: styd on to take 2nd ins fnl f: unable to chal* **4/1[2]**

3 *1* **Hestina (FR)** 3-9-0 0 JimmyFortune 1 79+
(Peter Chapple-Hyam) *q str: v much on toes & green in preliminaries: wl in tch disputing 5th: prog over 2f out: shkn up to chse wnr over 1f out: kpt on but no real imp: lost 2nd ins fnl f* **25/1**

3-4 **4** *1 ¼* **Folly Bergere (IRE)**[17] 1242 3-8-11 0 RyanTate(3) 6 76
(James Eustace) *lw: chsd wnr: shkn up over 2f out: lost 2nd over 1f out: one pce* **14/1**

03- **5** *3 ½* **Taqdees (IRE)**[170] 7708 3-9-0 0 PaulHanagan 5 69
(John Gosden) *athletic: trckd ldng pair: shkn up over 2f out: lost pl and fdd over 1f out* **9/2[3]**

6 *1* **Gloryette** 3-9-0 0 WilliamBuick 3 67
(Ed Dunlop) *w'like: hld up disputing 7th: pushed along and outpcd fr 2f out: n.d after* **20/1**

7 *1 ¼* **Eastern Lady (IND)** 3-9-0 0 RichardKingscote 9 65
(William Knight) *tall: lengthy: dwlt: hld up in last trio: one reminder over 1f out: no threat but nt disgracd* **33/1**

8 *2* **Adalene** 3-9-0 0 OisinMurphy 10 61
(David Simcock) *lengthy: on toes: restrained after s and hld up in last: nudged along and kpt on one pce fnl 2f: nt disgracd* **10/1**

4- **9** *1 ½* **Iona Island**[174] 7629 3-9-0 0 DarryllHolland 7 58
(Charles Hills) *hld up disputing 7th: effrt on outer 3f out: wknd wl over 1f out* **11/1**

5- **10** *4* **Onehelluvatouch**[219] 6436 3-9-0 0 TomEaves 4 50
(Philip Hide) *sltly on toes: wl in tch disputing 5th: reminders and steadily wknd fr jst over 2f out* **33/1**

11 *9* **Atone** 3-9-0 0 RyanMoore 11 32
(Sir Michael Stoute) *athletic: rn v green: a in last trio: shoved along in last 1/2-way: t.o* **3/1[1]**

2m 14.81s (4.31) **Going Correction** +0.325s/f (Good) **11 Ran SP% 119.9**
Speed ratings (Par 97): **95,94,93,92,89 88,87,86,84,81 74**
CSF £22.32 TOTE £5.10: £1.30, £1.90, £7.50; EX 28.00 Trifecta £609.10.
Owner Teruya Yoshida **Bred** Teruya Yoshida **Trained** Newmarket, Suffolk

FOCUS

This was run over 29 yards further than advertised and they again avoided the inside rail in the straight. The first division of a good-looking fillies' maiden. The fourth looks the key to the form.

1609 NORDOFF ROBBINS SIR GEORGE MARTIN MEMORIAL MAIDEN FILLIES' STKS (PLUS 10 RACE) (DIV II) 1m 2f 7y

4:35 (4:38) (Class 4) 3-Y-O **£6,469** (£1,925; £962; £481) **Stalls** Low

Form RPR

0- **1** **Rocaverde (IRE)**[205] 6864 3-9-0 0 FMBerry 4 85
(Ralph Beckett) *q str: mde all: shkn up and 2 l clr over 1f out: rdn out and hld on nr fin* **11/1**

2- **2** *½* **Shall We (IRE)**[162] 7811 3-9-0 0 RyanMoore 3 84
(Sir Michael Stoute) *q tall: lw: trckd ldng trio: shkn up to chse wnr over 1f out: rdn and clsd fnl f: a jst hld* **9/2[2]**

3 *2 ½* **Taffeta Lady** 3-9-0 0 DavidProbert 1 79+
(Lucy Wadham) *leggy: dwlt: hld up in last trio: pushed along fr 3f out: stdy prog after: kpt on wl fnl f to take 3rd last strides* **25/1**

2- **4** *nk* **High Hopes**[181] 7467 3-9-0 0 JamieSpencer 11 78
(David Simcock) *q tall: lw: trckd wnr 3f and again 2f out to over 1f out: one pce after: lost 3rd last strides* **4/1[1]**

5 *¾* **Taqaareed (IRE)** 3-9-0 0 PaulHanagan 8 77+
(John Gosden) *q str: gd walker: green: slowly away: plld hrd early: hld up in last trio: pushed along and prog over 2f out: disp 4th over 1f out: shkn up and one pce after* **4/1[1]**

4- **6** *5* **Pleasure Dome**[162] 7811 3-9-0 0 JimmyFortune 5 67
(Peter Chapple-Hyam) *q tall: unf: hld up in 7th: pushed along on outer over 2f out: no prog over 1f out: wknd fnl f* **10/1**

7 *nk* **Final Stage** 3-9-0 0 JamesDoyle 6 66
(Saeed bin Suroor) *athletic: hld up in 6th: pushed along 3f out: no imp on ldrs 2f out: wknd fnl f* **8/1[3]**

8 *nk* **Disquotational** 3-9-0 0 JimCrowley 2 66
(David Simcock) *str: sltly on toes: hld up in 8th: pushed along over 2f out: no prog over 1f out: wknd fnl f* **40/1**

- **9** *¾* **Eyeshine** 3-9-0 0 FrankieDettori 9 64
(John Gosden) *str: attractive: chsd wnr after 3f to 2f out: wknd* **9/2[2]**

10 *16* **Imaginary** 3-9-0 0 OisinMurphy 10 32
(Heather Main) *w'like: q str: bit bkwd: chsd ldrs in 5th: shkn up wl over 2f out: sn wknd qckly: t.o* **100/1**

11 *2 ¾* **Bonchard** 3-9-0 0 SilvestreDeSousa 7 27
(Emma Owen) *q tall: sltly on toes: dwlt: t.k.h early: hld up in last: wknd over 3f out: t.o* **20/1**

2m 14.69s (4.19) **Going Correction** +0.325s/f (Good) **11 Ran SP% 116.9**
Speed ratings (Par 97): **96,95,93,93,92 88,88,88,87,74 72**
CSF £57.78 TOTE £14.00: £3.90, £1.80, £5.20; EX 70.80 Trifecta £1056.70.
Owner Nigel & Carolyn Elwes **Bred** Aylesfield Farms Stud **Trained** Kimpton, Hants

FOCUS

This was run over 29 yards further than advertised. Like the first leg there was an all-the-way winner and again the runners avoided the inside rail in the straight. The time was 0.12sec faster than the first division. The first two produced big steps up on their debut efforts.

1610 BET365 H'CAP 1m 2f 7y

5:05 (5:13) (Class 3) (0-95,93) 3-Y-O
£9,337 (£2,796; £1,398; £699; £349; £175) **Stalls** Low

Form RPR

432- **1** **Stargazer (IRE)**[205] 6864 3-9-1 87 RyanMoore 1 99+
(Sir Michael Stoute) *lengthy: hld up in midfield: stdy prog over 3f out: led wl over 1f out gng strly: sn pressed: urged along firmly and styd on wl* **8/1**

021- **2** *½* **Lovell**[230] 6097 3-8-13 85 WilliamBuick 2 96+
(Charlie Appleby) *hld up in midfield: prog 3f out: chal 2f out gng strly: chsd wnr sn after: styd on wl but a hld* **8/1**

51- **3** *2 ¼* **Harrison**[194] 7144 3-9-4 90 SilvestreDeSousa 12 97
(Mick Channon) *lw: prog on outer to press ldng pair after 3f: rdn to chal 2f out: chsd ldng pair over 1f out: kpt on but no imp* **5/1[2]**

16-1 **4** *1 ½* **Soldier In Action (FR)**[19] 1220 3-9-1 87 JoeFanning 6 91
(Mark Johnston) *led: rdn over 2f out: hdd and hung lft wl over 1f out: one pce after* **6/1[3]**

321- **5** *1* **Paris Protocol**[205] 6864 3-9-7 93 PatDobbs 4 95
(Richard Hannon) *wl in tch: shkn up over 2f out: outpcd sn after: kpt on fr over 1f out* **8/1**

061- **6** *1 ½* **Gershwin**[189] 7246 3-8-11 83 FrankieDettori 8 82+
(David Lanigan) *hld up in midfield: pushed along and effrt whn nt clr run 2f out: pushed along again and kpt on one pce fr over 1f out* **9/2[1]**

212- **7** *2* **Celebration Day (IRE)**[174] 7630 3-8-9 81 JimCrowley 11 76
(Simon Crisford) *chsd ldr to over 2f out: steadily wknd over 1f out* **12/1**

51- **8** *3 ¼* **Rainbow Dreamer**[177] 7560 3-8-13 85 FergusSweeney 9 73
(Alan King) *hld up in last trio: pushed along over 2f out: edgd rt whn reminder over 1f out: no ch but kpt on* **14/1**

31-3 **9** *10* **Altarsheed (IRE)**[15] 1288 3-9-0 86 PaulHanagan 7 54
(Richard Hannon) *cmpt: chsd ldrs: shoved along 4f out: struggling after: wknd qckly over 1f out: t.o* **25/1**

26-0 **10** *1 ¾* **Essenaitch (IRE)**[28] 1080 3-9-2 88 AdamKirby 5 53
(David Evans) *plld hrd: hld up in last trio: wandered and wknd 3f out: t.o* **66/1**

212- **11** *7* **Dal Harraild**[198] 7042 3-9-1 87 PatCosgrave 10 38
(William Haggas) *hld up in last trio: shkn up 3f out: no prog and wknd 2f out: t.o* **11/1**

5-1 **12** *5* **Gambit**[24] 1134 3-9-2 88 RichardKingscote 3 29
(Tom Dascombe) *q str: pressed ldrs to over 2f out: wknd qckly: t.o* **8/1**

2m 12.89s (2.39) **Going Correction** +0.325s/f (Good) **12 Ran SP% 121.6**
Speed ratings (Par 102): **103,102,100,99,98 97,96,93,85,84 78,74**
CSF £72.56 CT £360.36 TOTE £8.70: £2.90, £3.50, £2.40; EX 87.00 Trifecta £337.30.
Owner Michael Tabor **Bred** Chelston Ireland **Trained** Newmarket, Suffolk

FOCUS

This was run over 29 yards further than advertised. It's usually a hot handicap - subsequent Irish Derby winner Jack Hobbs won last year's race by 12l off a mark of just 85 - and there were loads of interesting types in this latest edition. The form is rated on the positive side. Once more the inside rail was given a wide berth in the straight.

T/Plt: £123.90 to a £1 stake. Pool: £89,591.25 - 527.82 winning tickets T/Qpdt: £29.50 to a £1 stake. Pool: £7,467.53 - 187.00 winning tickets **Jonathan Neesom**

1611 - 1617a (Foreign Racing) - See Raceform Interactive

1172 FONTAINEBLEAU

Friday, April 22

OFFICIAL GOING: Turf: soft

1618a PRIX DE LA CHAPELLE-LA-REINE (CONDITIONS) (4YO+) (TURF) 5f 110y

2:45 (12:00) 4-Y-O+ **£10,294** (£4,117; £3,088; £2,058; £1,029)

RPR

1 **The Right Man**[236] 5921 4-8-11 0 Francois-XavierBertras 6 77
(D Guillemin, France) **13/5[2]**

2 *½* **Blue Soave (FR)**[232] 8-9-6 0 TonyPiccone 7 84
(F Chappet, France) **73/10**

3 *1 ½* **Catcall (FR)**[22] 1172 7-9-4 0 OlivierPeslier 4 77
(P Sogorb, France) **23/10[1]**

4 *¾* **El Suizo (FR)**[22] 1172 4-9-0 0 FabriceVeron 1 71
(H-A Pantall, France) **16/5[3]**

5 *1 ¾* **Intibaah**[16] 1272 6-8-11 0 UmbertoRispoli 3 62
(George Baker) *hld up: rdn over 1f out: kpt on same pce and nt able to chal* **36/5**

6 *1 ¾* **Aviator (FR)**[3] 7-8-11 0 (b) RichardJuteau 9 56
(T Poche, France) **28/1**

7 *2 ½* **Lord Shuffle (GER)**[127] 8-9-4 0 (p) KoenClijmans 2 55
(Stal Gastarui, Belgium) **10/1**

8 *9* **Sunny Sahara**[49] 8-8-11 0 ow3 GerardGuillermo 8 18
(G Guillermo, France) **90/1**

WIN (incl. 1 euro stake): 3.60. PLACES: 1.70, 1.90, 1.40. DF: 14.00. SF: 24.20
Owner Pegase Bloodstock **Bred** Mme D Wigan **Trained** France

1595 DONCASTER (L-H)

Saturday, April 23

OFFICIAL GOING: Good (good to soft in places; 7.8)

Wind: Moderate half against Weather: Cloudy

1619 YORKSHIRE WATER H'CAP 1m 4f

5:00 (5:01) (Class 5) (0-70,69) 3-Y-O **£3,881** (£1,155; £577; £288) **Stalls** Low

Form RPR

600- **1** **Opposition**[183] 7435 3-9-7 69 JamesDoyle 8 81+
(Ed Dunlop) *trckd ldr: led 4f out: rdn wl over 1f out: kpt on strly* **11/4[1]**

446- **2** *2 ½* **Regal Monarch**[131] 8225 3-9-1 63 RichardKingscote 1 68
(Mark Johnston) *trckd ldrs on inner: effrt over 3f out: rdn along 2f out: chsd wnr and drvn over 1f out: no imp* **8/1**

235- **3** *5* **Press Gang**[188] 7309 3-9-4 69 TomMarquand(3) 4 68
(James Eustace) *hld up: hdwy over 3f out: chsd ldrs over 2f out: sn rdn: drvn and one pce fr over 1f out* **12/1**

000- **4** *5* **Dusky Raider (IRE)**[231] 6097 3-9-0 62 PaulMulrennan 2 51
(Michael Dods) *hld up: hdwy over 4f out: rdn wl over 2f out: sn one pce* **14/1**

300- **5** *4 ½* **Livella Fella (IRE)**[190] 7252 3-9-5 67 PhillipMakin 5 49
(Keith Dalgleish) *a in rr* **20/1**

553- **6** *18* **Free Bounty**[165] 7785 3-9-4 66 DavidProbert 3 19
(Philip McBride) *led: pushed along 5f out: hdd 4f out and sn wknd* **5/1[3]**

66-3 **7** *2 ¼* **Purple Raven**[17] 1276 3-9-7 69 JamieSpencer 6 18
(Michael Bell) *trckd ldrs: hdwy over 4f out: effrt and ch 3f out: rdn over 2f out: wknd qckly wl over 1f out and sn eased* **3/1[2]**

-134 **8** *99* **Whitecliff Park (IRE)**[30] 1062 3-9-0 62 RobertWinston 7
(Brian Ellison) *in tch on outer: pushed along over 5f out: rdn 4f out: sn outpcd and bhd* **6/1**

2m 37.19s (2.29) **Going Correction** +0.15s/f (Good) **8 Ran SP% 112.9**
Speed ratings (Par 98): **98,96,93,89,86 74,73,7**
CSF £24.48 CT £222.74 TOTE £3.40: £1.50, £2.20, £3.90; EX 29.00 Trifecta £412.30.

Owner Highclere Thoroughbred Racing(Melbourne) **Bred** Cheveley Park Stud Ltd **Trained** Newmarket, Suffolk

FOCUS

An interesting 3yo handicap featuring a few unexposed horses with the potential to much better this season. They finished quite well strung out for a race of this nature and the winner looks a horse to follow.

1620 MOTT MACDONALD BENTLEY H'CAP — 1m 2f 60y

5:35 (5:37) (Class 3) (0-95,95) 4-Y-O+ **£7,762** (£2,310; £1,154; £577) **Stalls** Low

Form — RPR

65-6 **1** **Hit The Jackpot (IRE)**[18] 1245 7-9-4 **95**.................... ShelleyBirkett(3) 7 — 102
(David O'Meara) *hld up: stdy hdwy 3f out: chsd ldrs over 1f out: rdn to chal ins fnl f: kpt on to ld nr fin* **14/1**

213- **2** shd **American Artist (IRE)**[211] 6713 4-9-2 **90**...................... HarryBentley 5 — 96
(Roger Varian) *trckd ldrs: hdwy to ld wl over 2f out: rdn wl over 1f out: drvn ent fnl f: hdd and no ex towards fin* **4/1**[2]

620- **3** 3/4 **Off Art**[168] 7757 6-9-7 **95**..(p) RobertWinston 12 — 99
(Tim Easterby) *hld up in tch: hdwy over 3f out: chsd ldrs 2f out: sn rdn and cl up: ev ch over 1f out: drvn ins fnl f and kpt on same pce* **16/1**

025- **4** 1 **Croquembouche (IRE)**[170] 7718 7-9-2 **90**.......................... JamieSpencer 10 — 92
(Ed de Giles) *sn led: pushed along 3f out: sn hdd and rdn: drvn wl over 1f out: kpt on same pce* **20/1**

60-2 **5** nk **Burano (IRE)**[20] 1221 7-8-13 **87**.................................. DanielTudhope 1 — 89
(David O'Meara) *hld up in tch on inner: hdwy over 3f out: trckd ldrs over 2f out: effrt wl over 1f out and sn rdn: drvn appr fnl f and kpt on same pce* **9/4**[1]

436- **6** 1/2 **Darrington**[196] 7125 4-8-8 **82**.. TonyHamilton 4 — 83
(Richard Fahey) *in tch: hdwy over 2f out: rdn wl over 1f out: drvn appr fnl f and kpt on same pce* **9/1**

013- **7** 2 **First Sitting**[199] 7044 5-9-7 **95**.. JamesDoyle 6 — 92
(Chris Wall) *hld up towards rr: hdwy wl over 2f out: sn rdn and kpt on fnl f: nrst fin* **13/2**[3]

024- **8** shd **Mistiroc**[168] 7757 5-9-3 **91**.. PhillipMakin 13 — 88+
(John Quinn) *hld up in rr: sme hdwy on wd outside over 2f out: swtchd lft over 1f out: kpt on wl fnl f: nrst fin* **15/2**

530- **9** nk **Newera**[183] 7426 4-8-8 **82**.......................................(p) RichardKingscote 14 — 78
(Tom Dascombe) *dwlt and in rr: hdwy wl over 2f out: rdn wl over 1f out: kpt on fnl f: nrst fin* **16/1**

40/ **10** 3 3/4 **Novelty Seeker (USA)**[1171] 555 7-9-0 **88**.................. PaulMulrennan 2 — 77
(Michael Easterby) *prom: rdn along wl over 3f out: sn wknd* **50/1**

300- **11** 1 3/4 **War Singer (USA)**[81] 7704 9-8-9 **83** ow2......................(bt) TomEaves 15 — 69
(Johnny Farrelly) *prom: hdwy and cl up- over 3f out: rdn along wl over 2f out: sn wknd* **50/1**

0426 **12** 1 1/2 **U S Navy Seal (USA)**[65] 619 4-8-10 **84**.................. ConnorBeasley 11 — 67
(J R Jenkins) *t.k.h early: a in rr* **28/1**

502- **13** 44 **Final Countdown**[189] 6472 5-8-11 **85**................................ RaulDaSilva 9
(John Quinn) *hld up in rr: pushed along over 3f out: rdn over 2f out: sn wknd and eased over 1f out* **25/1**

2m 11.62s (2.22) **Going Correction** +0.425s/f (Yiel) **13** Ran SP% **120.3**
Speed ratings (Par 107): **108,107,107,106,106 105,104,104,103,100 99,98,63**
CSF £66.34 CT £928.27 TOTE £13.40: £3.80, £1.80, £4.70; EX 114.80 Trifecta £252.50.
Owner Hambleton Racing Ltd XXV **Bred** Moyglare Stud Farm Ltd **Trained** Upper Helmsley, N Yorks

FOCUS

A competitive event run at what looked quite a generous gallop and no reason why this form shouldn't stand up.

1621 MORRISON UTILITY SERVICES CHAMPION CUP NEWCOMERS' MAIDEN STKS — 5f

6:05 (6:11) (Class 5) 2-Y-O **£3,881** (£1,155; £577; £288) **Stalls** High

Form — RPR

1 **Hoyamy** 2-9-0 0... DanielTudhope 8 — 74+
(David O'Meara) *cl up: led 3f out: rdn and edgd rt ins fnl f: kpt on wl towards fin* **9/2**[2]

2 hd **Reach High** 2-9-5 0.. JamesDoyle 1 — 78+
(Saeed bin Suroor) *trckd ldrs: hdwy on outer and cl up 1/2-way: rdn to chal: green and edgd rt appr fnl f: sn drvn and ev ch tl no ex towards fin* **11/8**[1]

3 3 **In First Place** 2-9-5 0.. TonyHamilton 7 — 67
(Richard Fahey) *slt ld 2f: cl up: rdn along 2f out: ev ch: kpt on same pce ent fnl f* **6/1**[3]

4 1/2 **Cosmic Beau (IRE)** 2-9-5 0.................................(v1) RichardKingscote 5 — 66
(Tom Dascombe) *dwlt: hld up: hdwy 2f out: rdn to chse ldrs over 1f out: kpt on same pce fnl f* **20/1**

5 nk **Morning Suit (USA)** 2-9-5 0.................................... SilvestreDeSousa 6 — 65
(Mark Johnston) *cl up: pushed along 2f out: rdn and hld whn sltly hmpd and swtchd lft jst over 1f out: one pce after* **8/1**

6 1 1/4 **Sheila's Return** 2-9-0 0... ConnorBeasley 3 — 55
(Bryan Smart) *in tch: green: rdn along and outpcd 1/2-way: kpt on u.p fnl f* **33/1**

7 3/4 **Tawny Port** 2-9-5 0.. TomEaves 9 — 57
(James Given) *dwlt and in rr: hdwy 1/2-way: chsd ldrs 2f out: sn rdn and wknd over 1f out* **25/1**

8 4 1/2 **Kazanan (IRE)** 2-9-0 0... PaulMulrennan 2 — 36
(Michael Dods) *chsd ldrs: rdn along 1/2-way: sn wknd* **8/1**

9 3 3/4 **Dark Hero (IRE)** 2-9-5 0.. DarryllHolland 4 — 28
(Charles Hills) *dwlt: t.k.h: a towards rr* **9/2**[2]

1m 1.05s (0.55) **Going Correction** -0.10s/f (Good) **9** Ran SP% **126.5**
Speed ratings (Par 92): **91,90,85,85,84 82,81,74,68**
CSF £12.04 TOTE £6.70: £2.30, £1.10, £2.10; EX 17.70 Trifecta £112.00.
Owner Salem Rashid **Bred** Barton Stud Partnership **Trained** Upper Helmsley, N Yorks

FOCUS

Some nice pedigrees on show here and the front two pulled clear to give the form a strong feel. This could be a maiden that throws up a few winners.

1622 YORKSHIRE WATER CHARITY MAIDEN STKS — 7f

6:35 (6:44) (Class 4) 3-Y-O+ **£5,175** (£1,540; £769; £384) **Stalls** High

Form — RPR

0- **1** **Forge**[239] 5824 3-9-1 0... RichardKingscote 8 — 96+
(Sir Michael Stoute) *trckd ldr: cl up 1/2-way: led jst over 2f out: shkn up and qcknd clr appr fnl f: readily* **5/6**[1]

522- **2** 5 **Heir To A Throne (FR)**[213] 6652 3-9-1 83......................... ShaneGray 9 — 79
(Kevin Ryan) *led: jnd 1/2-way: hdd and rdn jst over 2f out: drvn over 1f out: no ch w wnr* **12/1**

3 **3** 1 1/4 **Tommy G**[20] 1217 3-9-1 0... DanielTudhope 4 — 76
(Jim Goldie) *hld up towards rr: gd hdwy 1/2-way: chsd ldrs 2f out: sn rdn and kpt on fnl f* **8/1**

4 shd **Horrah** 3-9-1 0.. WilliamTwiston-Davies 1 — 75
(Roger Charlton) *dwlt and in rr: hdwy over 2f out: sn rdn and kpt on fnl f: nrst fin* **33/1**

3- **5** 2 3/4 **Gunmetal (IRE)**[185] 7394 3-9-1 0...................................... DarryllHolland 6 — 68
(Charles Hills) *trckd ldrs: hdwy over 2f out: rdn wl over 1f out: sn one pce* **4/1**[2]

56- **6** 3 1/4 **Pina**[130] 8233 3-8-7 0.. TomMarquand(3) 12 — 54
(Roger Charlton) *chsd ldrs: rdn along over 2f out: grad wknd* **33/1**

330- **7** 5 **Back To Bond**[197] 7092 3-9-1 76.................................. GeorgeChaloner 3 — 46
(Richard Fahey) *chsd ldrs: rdn over 2f out: sn drvn and wknd* **25/1**

8 1/2 **Azizaan** 3-9-1 0... HarryBentley 11 — 44
(Roger Varian) *towards rr: sme hdwy wl over 2f out: sn rdn and n.d* **7/1**[3]

5- **9** 4 **Causey Arch (IRE)**[320] 2977 3-9-1 0.......................... PaulMulrennan 10 — 34
(Michael Dods) *t.k.h: in tch: rdn along 1/2-way: sn outpcd* **50/1**

10 4 **One For Jodie (IRE)** 5-9-11 0.............................. AlistairRawlinson(3) 7 — 28
(Michael Appleby) *dwlt: a in rr* **50/1**

6 **11** 1/2 **Hooks Lane**[32] 1027 4-10-0 0... TomEaves 2 — 26
(Shaun Harris) *dwlt: a in rr* **200/1**

12 15 **Declined** 4-10-0 0.. DavidProbert 5
(David C Griffiths) *walked to s: swtchd lft s and t.k.h: sn chsng ldrs on outer: rdn along 3f out and sn wknd* **66/1**

1m 25.28s (-1.02) **Going Correction** -0.10s/f (Good)
WFA 3 from 4yo+ 13lb **12** Ran SP% **121.5**
Speed ratings (Par 105): **101,96,95,94,91 88,82,81,77,72 72,54**
CSF £12.94 TOTE £2.00: £1.20, £2.20, £2.10; EX 13.70 Trifecta £43.80.
Owner K Abdullah **Bred** Juddmonte Farms Ltd **Trained** Newmarket, Suffolk

FOCUS

Another reasonable maiden and the winner looks quite an exciting colt.

1623 BLACK AND VEATCH H'CAP — 1m (S)

7:05 (7:10) (Class 3) (0-90,90) 3-Y-O **£7,762** (£2,310; £1,154; £577) **Stalls** High

Form — RPR

14-3 **1** **Arcanada (IRE)**[27] 1115 3-9-3 **86**........................ RichardKingscote 4 — 100
(Tom Dascombe) *mde all: rdn wl over 1f out: drvn and edgd lft ins fnl f: kpt on gamely* **9/1**

1- **2** 3/4 **Chelsea Lad (IRE)**[176] 7592 3-9-1 **84**......................... FergusSweeney 2 — 96
(Martyn Meade) *trckd ldrs: hdwy over 2f out: rdn to chse wnr over 1f out: swtchd rt and drvn ins fnl f: kpt on* **8/1**[3]

401- **3** 4 **Bedrock**[183] 7430 3-8-10 **79**.. PatCosgrave 5 — 82
(William Haggas) *hld up: hdwy wl over 2f out: rdn wl over 1f out: kpt on fnl f* **11/2**[2]

12-3 **4** nk **Robinnielly (IRE)**[20] 1220 3-8-13 **82**.............................. PhillipMakin 10 — 84
(Keith Dalgleish) *prom: rdn along jst over 2f out: kpt on same pce* **9/1**

61- **5** 1 1/4 **Column**[205] 6874 3-9-7 **90**.. FrederikTylicki 7 — 89
(James Fanshawe) *towards rr: hdwy 3f out: chsd ldrs wl over 1f out: sn rdn and no imp* **3/1**[1]

62-1 **6** 1 **White Shaheen**[16] 1294 3-8-7 **76**....................................... MartinDwyer 3 — 73
(William Muir) *prom: chsd wnr after 3f: rdn along wl over 2f out: drvn wl over 1f out and sn wknd* **9/1**

32-1 **7** 1 **Kylla Instinct**[15] 1312 3-8-8 **77**.. DavidProbert 6 — 72
(Philip McBride) *hld up towards rr: sme hdwy over 2f out: sn rdn along and n.d* **20/1**

316- **8** 1/2 **Invermere**[196] 7112 3-8-8 **77**.. TonyHamilton 1 — 70
(Richard Fahey) *chsd ldrs: rdn along wl over 2f out: sn wknd* **16/1**

1 **9** hd **Fisher Green (IRE)**[20] 1216 3-8-12 **81**.......................... PaulMulrennan 8 — 74
(Michael Dods) *hld up: a in rr* **12/1**

112 **10** 4 **Buying Trouble (USA)**[27] 1115 3-9-1 **84**........................ CathyGannon 11 — 68
(David Evans) *hld up: a in rr* **11/2**[2]

310- **11** 9 **Show Legend**[209] 6774 3-8-10 **79**...................................... JamieSpencer 9 — 42
(Michael Bell) *hld up in rr: pushed along over 3f out: rdn and outpcd fr owl over 2f out* **25/1**

1m 37.99s (-1.31) **Going Correction** -0.10s/f (Good) **11** Ran SP% **119.1**
Speed ratings (Par 102): **102,101,97,96,95 94,93,93,93,89 80**
CSF £80.13 CT £440.05 TOTE £13.10: £3.90, £3.00, £2.40; EX 120.20 Trifecta £1030.60.
Owner The Arcanada Partnership **Bred** C J Foy **Trained** Malpas, Cheshire

FOCUS

Plenty of potential improvers in tis 3yo handicap but it was dominated by one horse who dictated on his own terms and put all of his rivals in trouble when kicking from the front around two out.

1624 YORKSHIRE WATER CHARITY FILLIES' H'CAP — 1m (S)

7:35 (7:37) (Class 4) (0-80,80) 4-Y-O+ **£5,175** (£1,540; £769; £384) **Stalls** High

Form — RPR

3-11 **1** **Lucy The Painter (IRE)**[15] 1326 4-9-5 **78**........................ HarryBentley 9 — 91+
(Ed de Giles) *trckd ldrs: hdwy over 2f out: rdn to ld jst ins fnl f: kpt on strly* **2/1**[1]

050- **2** 2 1/4 **Azagal (IRE)**[179] 7526 5-9-5 **78**.. DavidAllan 1 — 83
(Tim Easterby) *trckd ldng pair: cl up over 2f out: rdn to take slt ld jst over 1f out: hdd and drvn ins fnl f: kpt on same pce* **9/2**

56-5 **3** 1/2 **Simply Shining (IRE)**[17] 1274 6-9-0 **80**................ AdamMcNamara(7) 5 — 84
(Richard Fahey) *led: pushed along and jnd 2f out: sn rdn: hdd and drvn jst over 1f out: kpt on same pce* **4/1**[3]

2-11 **4** 2 3/4 **Esteemable**[36] 977 4-8-12 **74**...................................... DanielMuscutt(3) 2 — 72
(James Fanshawe) *trckd ldr: cl up 2f out: sn rdn and ev ch tl drvn and wknd ent fnl f* **7/2**[2]

056- **5** 6 **Fray**[219] 6455 5-9-5 **78**.. DanielTudhope 6 — 62
(Jim Goldie) *dwlt: in tch: effrt over 2f out: sn rdn and wknd* **17/2**

133- **6** 1 1/4 **Sahara (IRE)**[220] 6439 4-9-4 **77**.. TedDurcan 8 — 58
(Chris Wall) *hld up: a in rr* **11/2**

1m 40.21s (0.91) **Going Correction** -0.10s/f (Good) **6** Ran SP% **111.5**
Speed ratings (Par 102): **91,88,88,85,79 78**
CSF £20.08 CT £63.34 TOTE £2.70: £1.90, £3.40; EX 14.70 Trifecta £66.20.
Owner J P Carrington **Bred** Bakewell Bloodstock **Trained** Ledbury, H'fords

FOCUS

A couple of in-form contenders in this fillies' handicap, one of which was the winner who is a progressive filly.

1625 WATERAID AMATEUR JOCKEYS ASSOCIATION LADY RIDERS' H'CAP (LADY AMATEUR RIDERS) — 7f

8:05 (8:07) (Class 4) (0-80,80) 4-Y-O+ **£4,991** (£1,548; £773; £387) **Stalls** High

Form — RPR

06-3 **1** **Kalk Bay (IRE)**[12] 1380 9-10-4 **77**......................(t) MissJoannaMason 2 — 88+
(Michael Easterby) *in tch: hdwy to chse ldr 2f out: rdn to ld wl over 1f out: sn clr: styd on* **5/1**[2]

3513 **2** 2 1/4 **Burning Blaze**[24] 1143 6-10-3 **76**............................ MissSBrotherton 10 — 76
(Brian Ellison) *chsd ldrs: rdn along wl over 2f out: kpt on u.p fnl f* **7/1**

0323 **3** ½ **Moonlight Venture**[11] 1403 5-10-4 **77**......................(b) MissGAndrews 15 76
(Conor Dore) *hld up towards rr: hdwy 3f out: rdn 2f out: styd on appr fnl f* **12/1**

22-4 **4** 1 **Mystic Miraaj**[12] 1380 4-9-9 **75**..............................(p) MissEEasterby(7) 9 71+
(Tim Easterby) *hld up towards rr: hdwy wl over 2f out: rdn wl over 1f out: kpt on fnl f* **4/1**[1]

0-24 **5** 1 **Smokethatthunders (IRE)**[37] 965 6-10-2 **75**......... MissMMullineaux 4 68
(James Unett) *in tch: pushed along over 3f out: rdn over 2f out: kpt on appr fnl f* **16/1**

05-5 **6** 1 **Rasaman (IRE)**[12] 1378 12-9-8 **72**.............................. MissAMcCain(5) 3 65+
(Jim Goldie) *towards rr: hdwy over 2f out: rdn wl over 1f out: kpt on same pce* **33/1**

032- **7** 2½ **Trail Blaze (IRE)**[179] 7526 7-9-13 **79**..........................(p) MissHTLees(7) 6 63
(Kevin Ryan) *led 1f: prom tl rdn along over 2f out and grad wknd* **16/1**

341- **8** hd **Buccaneers Vault (IRE)**[228] 6190 4-9-13 **79**............ MissCADods(7) 17 62
(Michael Dods) *midfield: hdwy over 2f out: sn rdn and n.d* **16/1**

600- **9** ½ **Character Onesie (IRE)**[193] 7193 4-9-11 **77**....... MissEmilyBullock(7) 8 59
(Richard Fahey) *prom: chsd ldr 4f out: rdn along over 2f out: wknd over 1f out* **12/1**

56-2 **10** ¾ **Mustaqbal (IRE)**[26] 1124 4-9-6 **72**.............................. MissSEDods(7) 12 52+
(Michael Dods) *a towards rr* **6/1**

10-0 **11** 1¾ **Orion's Bow**[17] 1252 5-9-13 **72**..................................(b) MissCWalton 16 47
(David Nicholls) *plld hrd: cl up: led after 1f: clr 3f out: rdn along 2f out: hdd wl over 1f out: sn wknd* **11/2**[3]

10-6 **12** 3¼ **Ershaad (IRE)**[15] 1326 4-9-8 **70**.............................. MissBeckySmith(3) 5 36
(Shaun Harris) *a towards rr* **50/1**

0056 **13** 3½ **Cool Strutter (IRE)**[31] 1044 4-9-6 **70** ow1........... MissPBridgwater(5) 14 27
(Andrew Balding) *a towards rr* **25/1**

4000 **14** 2¼ **Black Dave (IRE)**[15] 1318 6-9-9 **73**........................ MissEMacKenzie(5) 1 24
(David Evans) *in tch: effrt and sme hdwy wl over 2f out: sn rdn and wknd wl over 1f out* **22/1**

100- **15** nk **Meandmyshadow**[179] 7525 8-10-3 **76**.......................... MissADeniel 11 26
(Alan Brown) *cl up: rdn along 1/2-way: sn wknd* **33/1**

1m 27.58s (1.28) **Going Correction** -0.10s/f (Good) **15** Ran SP% **127.9**
Speed ratings (Par 105): **88,85,84,83,82 81,78,78,77,76 74,71,67,64,64**
CSF £40.15 CT £426.95 TOTE £6.10: £2.30, £2.60, £3.40; EX 39.10 Trifecta £283.20.
Owner Linda Folwell, Steve Hull & David Swales **Bred** Wentworth Racing **Trained** Sheriff Hutton, N Yorks

FOCUS
They seemed to go fairly hard from the outset here but the winner was utterly dominant and is clearly right at the top if his game right now.
T/Plt: £160.40 to a £1 stake. Pool of £55262.57 - 251.46 winning tickets. T/Qpdt: £11.60 to a £1 stake. Pool of £7509.23 - 475.40 winning tickets. **Joe Rowntree**

HAYDOCK (L-H)
Saturday, April 23

OFFICIAL GOING: Good (good to firm in places; 7.6)
Wind: moderate 1/2 against Weather: fine and sunny but cold

1626 APOLLOBET HOME OF CASHBACK OFFERS MAIDEN STKS 1m 3f 200y
1:40 (1:42) (Class 5) 3-Y-0+ **£3,881** (£1,155; £577; £288) **Stalls** Centre

Form RPR

4- **1** **Gunnery (FR)**[183] 7435 3-8-8 0...................................... JamieSpencer 2 84+
(Peter Chapple-Hyam) *hld up in rr-div: hdwy on outer 3f out: 2nd over 1f out: edgd lft: styd on to ld nr fin* **7/4**[1]

0- **2** nk **Superyacht (IRE)**[225] 6285 3-8-8 0............................. StevieDonohoe 7 83
(Sir Michael Stoute) *w ldr: t.k.h: led after 2f: pushed clr over 3f out: rdn over 1f out: hdd and no ex nr fin* **12/1**

6- **3** ¾ **Daphne**[182] 7472 3-8-3 0.. LukeMorris 3 76+
(William Haggas) *trckd ldrs: drvn over 3f out: swtchd rt 2f out: styd on fnl f to take 3rd last 100yds: gng on at fin* **9/2**[3]

4 1½ **Withhold** 3-8-8 0.. GrahamGibbons 6 79
(Charles Hills) *chsd ldrs: pushed along over 5f out: kpt on one pce fnl 2f* **14/1**

0- **5** ½ **Kaatskill Nap (FR)**[242] 5721 3-8-8 0............................ ShaneKelly 4 78
(David Menuisier) *in rr-div: drvn over 4f out: chsng ldrs 3f out: one pce fnl 2f: sltly hmpd 1f out* **20/1**

6 6 **Henry Croft** 3-8-8 0.. NickyMackay 8 72
(John Gosden) *s.i.s: sn chsng ldrs: pushed along over 5f out: 2nd over 3f out: wkng whn sltly hmpd appr fnl f* **11/4**[2]

7 ¾ **Lord Napier (IRE)** 3-8-8 0.................................... RobertTart 1 67
(John Gosden) *s.i.s: brief effrt over 3f out: sn lost pl* **7/1**

8 8 **Question Of Faith**[43] 5-9-9 0................................ PaulMulrennan 9 52
(Martin Todhunter) *s.s: in rr: bhd fnl 3f* **66/1**

005- **9** 28 **District Attorney (IRE)**[194] 5051 7-9-9 47........................ PhilDennis(5) 5 12
(Chris Fairhurst) *led 2f: lost pl over 4f out: bhd fnl 3f: t.o whn virtually p.u clsng stages* **200/1**

2m 35.04s (1.24) **Going Correction** +0.10s/f (Good)
WFA 3 from 5yo+ 20lb **9** Ran SP% **114.8**
Speed ratings (Par 103): **99,98,98,97,96 92,92,87,68**
CSF £24.40 TOTE £2.70: £1.30, £3.20, £1.40; EX 23.50 Trifecta £113.00.
Owner Mrs Fitri Hay **Bred** Laurent Nadot & Herve Nadot **Trained** Newmarket, Suffolk

FOCUS
Race run up the stands' side straight adding 57yds to race distance. An interesting middle-distance maiden with some major stables represented. The early pace was modest. Improved form from the winner but the first few finished bunched.

1627 APOLLOBET DAILY RACING REFUNDS H'CAP 7f
2:10 (2:12) (Class 2) (0-105,103) 4-Y-0+
£28,012 (£8,388; £4,194; £2,097; £1,048; £526) **Stalls** Low

Form RPR

24-0 **1** **Predominance (IRE)**[21] 1195 4-8-11 **90**......................(p) PatCosgrave 1 101+
(William Haggas) *drvn into mid-div sn after s: drvn over 3f out: nt clr run and swtchd rt 1f out: styd on wl to ld last 75yds* **4/1**[1]

01-0 **2** 1 **Withernsea (IRE)**[34] 1018 5-8-13 **95**.......................... SammyJoBell(3) 13 103
(Richard Fahey) *swtchd lft s: t.k.h in mid-div: hdwy over 2f out: nt clr run and swtchd rt over 1f out: styd on to take 2nd last 50yds* **14/1**

24-3 **3** 1¼ **Georgian Bay (IRE)**[21] 1204 6-8-4 **88**.................(v) JordanVaughan(5) 3 93
(K R Burke) *mid-div: hdwy over 2f out: led briefly 100yds out: no ex* **8/1**

6502 **4** ½ **Bertiewhittle**[11] 1394 8-8-7 **89**.............................. RobHornby(3) 4 93
(David Barron) *in rr: hdwy and swtchd rt over 1f out: styd on wl clsng stages* **20/1**

0/0 **5** ½ **Lord Of The Land (IRE)**[21] 1196 5-9-9 **102**................. DanielTudhope 7 104+
(David O'Meara) *trckd ldrs: pushed along over 2f out: keeping on same pce whn n.m.r over 1f out* **11/1**

556- **6** 1 **One Word More (IRE)**[217] 6518 6-9-2 **100**........ RachelRichardson(5) 14 100
(Tim Easterby) *swtchd lft s: hld up in rr: hdwy over 2f out: kpt on fnl f* **25/1**

040- **7** ½ **Outback Traveller (IRE)**[203] 6919 5-9-9 **102**................ JamieSpencer 2 103+
(Robert Cowell) *wnt rt s: sn mid-div: hdwy 3f out: nt clr run 2f out: one pce appr fnl f* **20/1**

10-5 **8** ¾ **Shared Equity**[21] 1197 5-9-9 **102**.................................. GrahamLee 8 98
(Jedd O'Keeffe) *trckd ldrs: upsides over 2f out: wknd last 100yds* **6/1**[2]

12-0 **9** nse **Edgar Balthazar**[21] 1195 4-8-9 **88**.................................(p) JasonHart 9 84
(Keith Dalgleish) *mid-div: reminders 3f out: one pce fnl 2f* **20/1**

11-0 **10** nk **Right Touch**[21] 1195 6-9-4 **97**................................. JackGarritty 10 92
(Richard Fahey) *trckd ldrs: led over 1f out: hdd last 100yds: fdd* **8/1**

000- **11** ¾ **Lincoln (IRE)**[217] 6542 5-8-11 **95**.............................. PaddyPilley(5) 5 88+
(Mick Channon) *swtchd lft s: hld up in rr: hdwy on ins over 3f out: nt clr run fr 2f out: swtchd rt 150yds out: nt rcvr* **7/1**[3]

300- **12** nk **Above The Rest (IRE)**[197] 7088 5-8-13 **92**.............. GrahamGibbons 12 84
(David Barron) *chsd ldrs: upsides over 2f out: wknd last 150yds* **7/1**[3]

00-2 **13** nk **Majestic Moon (IRE)**[50] 816 6-9-7 **103**........... MichaelJMMurphy(3) 11 95
(John Gallagher) *led: drvn over 2f out: hdd & wknd over 1f out* **16/1**

1m 29.6s (-1.10) **Going Correction** +0.10s/f (Good) **13** Ran SP% **120.5**
Speed ratings (Par 109): **110,108,107,106,106 105,104,103,103,103 102,102,101**
CSF £59.05 CT £451.37 TOTE £6.00: £3.20, £4.90, £3.00; EX 73.90 Trifecta £682.30.
Owner HighclereThoroughbredRacing(Queen Anne) **Bred** Lynchbages Edgeridge Ltd & Glenvale Stud **Trained** Newmarket, Suffolk

FOCUS
Race run up the stands' side straight adding 57yds to race distance. A good-class 7f handicap with a few hard-luck stories, but ultimately a decisive winner. The form looks sound enough.

1628 BREEDERS BACKING RACING EBF MAIDEN FILLIES' STKS 1m
2:45 (2:46) (Class 5) 3-Y-0+ **£4,204** (£1,251; £625; £312) **Stalls** Low

Form RPR

1 **Fadillah** 3-9-0 0.. PatCosgrave 11 72+
(William Haggas) *s.i.s: sn hld up in mid-div: trcking ldrs over 4f out: drvn over 2f out: styd on wl fnl 150yds: led nr fin* **6/4**[1]

0 **2** ¾ **Malhama**[59] 699 3-9-0 0.. DaneO'Neill 9 70
(Roger Varian) *trckd ldrs: 2nd over 2f out: led briefly last 50yds: no ex* **7/1**[3]

- **3** 1¼ **Golden Glimmer (IRE)** 3-9-0 0.............................. GrahamGibbons 12 67
(Tom Dascombe) *drvn to ld: hdd and no ex last 50yds* **7/1**[3]

4 shd **Angelic Guest (IRE)** 3-9-0 0.................................... CharlesBishop 2 67+
(Mick Channon) *mid-div: effrt over 3f out: styd on clsng stages* **9/1**

0 **5** hd **Penny Lane Forever**[11] 1392 3-9-0 0.............................. JackMitchell 6 67+
(Roger Varian) *trckd ldrs: nt clr run over 2f out: swtchd rt 1f out: keeping on same pce whn n.m.r clsng stages* **12/1**

00- **6** hd **Tiga Tuan (FR)**[210] 6737 3-9-0 0................................ KeaganLatham 3 66
(Kevin Ryan) *s.i.s: hdwy whn nt clr run over 2f out: kpt on fnl f* **66/1**

04- **7** ½ **Sister Dude**[218] 6491 3-9-0 0...................................... DanielTudhope 10 65
(K R Burke) *chsd ldrs: drvn over 2f out: one pce appr fnl f* **9/2**[2]

8 ½ **Rock Palm (IRE)** 3-8-9 0.. JennyPowell(5) 1 64
(Brendan Powell) *dwlt: hdwy on inner over 2f out: n.m.r: kpt on fnl f* **40/1**

30 **9** ¾ **Flinty Fell (IRE)**[30] 1063 3-9-0 0...................................[1] GrahamLee 5 62
(Ed Dunlop) *mid-div: hdwy to chse ldrs over 4f out: one pce fnl 2f* **16/1**

0/ **10** 8 **No Not Yet**[547] 7407 4-9-9 0...................................... PhilDennis(5) 7 47
(Michael Dods) *t.k.h towards rr: hdwy over 3f out: wnt lft and lost pl over 1f out* **33/1**

43- **11** ¾ **Florenza**[302] 3586 3-9-0 0...................................... PaulMulrennan 13 41
(Chris Fairhurst) *t.k.h in rr: hdwy on outside over 3f out: hung lft and lost pl over 1f out* **16/1**

0- **12** hd **Ocean Gale**[180] 7512 3-8-11 0................................ DanielMuscutt(3) 8 40
(Richard Price) *in rr: drvn over 3f out: bhd fnl 2f* **100/1**

1m 46.23s (2.53) **Going Correction** +0.10s/f (Good)
WFA 3 from 4yo 14lb **12** Ran SP% **120.5**
Speed ratings (Par 100): **91,90,89,88,88 88,88,87,86,78 78,77**
CSF £12.45 TOTE £2.30: £1.10, £2.10, £2.30; EX 10.80 Trifecta £48.70.
Owner Saleh Al Homaizi & Imad Al Sagar **Bred** Ecurie Des Monceaux & Haras De St Pair **Trained** Newmarket, Suffolk

FOCUS
Race run up the stands' side straight adding 57yds to race distance. Those with form set only a modest standard in this fillies' maiden and a newcomer prevailed in a bunch finish. It;s hard to rate the form too highly.

1629 APOLLOBET BET THROUGH YOUR MOBILE H'CAP 1m
3:20 (3:21) (Class 2) (0-105,105) 4-Y-0+
£28,012 (£8,388; £4,194; £2,097; £1,048; £526) **Stalls** Low

Form RPR

10-0 **1** **You're Fired (IRE)**[21] 1196 5-9-2 **102**..................... JordanVaughan(5) 6 111
(K R Burke) *hld up in rr: hdwy on ins over 2f out: upsides over 1f out: styd on to ld last 50yds* **11/1**

111- **2** nk **Erik The Red (FR)**[210] 6739 4-8-10 **91**.............................. ShaneGray 7 100+
(Kevin Ryan) *hld up in rr: hdwy whn nt clr run over 2f out: styd on wl fnl f: tk cl 2nd nr fin* **8/1**

43-6 **3** nk **Wilde Inspiration (IRE)**[21] 1195 5-8-8 **89**................. ConnorBeasley 4 97
(Julie Camacho) *wore ear plugs: mid-div: hdwy over 3f out: led 2f out: hdd and no ex last 50yds* **8/1**

01-0 **4** 2¼ **Express Himself (IRE)**[21] 1196 5-9-6 **101**................... GrahamLee 17 104
(Ed McMahon) *s.i.s: swtchd lft after s: hdwy on ins whn nt clr run over 2f out tl over 1f out: kpt on* **6/1**[1]

206- **5** 1 **Alfred Hutchinson**[157] 7891 8-9-2 **100**..................... ShelleyBirkett(3) 13 100
(David O'Meara) *hld up in rr: stdy hdwy 2f out: effrt and edgd lft appr fnl f: kpt on same pce* **25/1**

214- **6** 3 **Mustaaqeem (USA)**[315] 3158 4-8-8 **89** ow1..................... DaneO'Neill 14 82
(Sir Michael Stoute) *towards rr: effrt on outer 3f out: hmpd 1f out: kpt on: nvr a threat* **13/2**[2]

0-00 **7** 2¾ **Sound Advice**[24] 1153 7-9-8 **103**.................................... JasonHart 9 89+
(Keith Dalgleish) *led early: trckd ldrs: kpt on same pce over 1f out* **40/1**

00-3 **8** ¾ **Instant Attraction (IRE)**[21] 1195 5-9-2 **97**.................. JackGarritty 3 82
(Jedd O'Keeffe) *chsd ldrs: one pce whn hung lft over 1f out* **12/1**

0-14 **9** shd **Revolutionist (IRE)**[14] 1344 4-9-0 **95**.......................... LiamJones 15 79
(Mark Johnston) *mid-div: drvn to chse ldrs 3f out: one pce whn hmpd 1f out* **25/1**

3600 **10** nk **Complicit (IRE)**[29] 1069 5-9-3 **98**..............................(b) LukeMorris 5 82+
(Paul Cole) *mid-div: hdwy over 3f out: one pce whn bdly hmpd over 1f out* **20/1**

000- **11** 3 1/4 **Yourartisonfire**210 6750 6-8-11 **92**....(v) BenCurtis 11 68
(K R Burke) *drvn early to chse ldrs: wknd appr fnl f* **25/1**

6-31 **12** 1 **Gabrial's Kaka (IRE)**7 1478 6-8-9 **90**.... TomQueally 2 63+
(Richard Fahey) *sn chsng ldrs: one pce whn bdly hmpd over 1f out: sn eased* **6/1**1

00-4 **13** 3/4 **Birdman (IRE)**21 1196 6-9-10 **105**.... DanielTudhope 8 77+
(David O'Meara) *in rr: hdwy over 2f out: bdly hmpd over 1f out: sn heavily eased* **10/1**

3300 **14** 2 3/4 **Afonso De Sousa (USA)**28 1089 6-9-6 **101**....(v1) GrahamGibbons 1 66+
(David O'Meara) *sn led: hdd 2f out: sn bdly hmpd and eased* **25/1**

/21- **15** 30 **Classic Collection**183 7426 4-9-3 **98**.... JamesDoyle 12
(Saeed bin Suroor) *sn chsng ldrs: drvn over 3f out: lost pl over 2f out: heavily eased over 1f out: t.o* **15/2**3

1m 42.43s (-1.27) **Going Correction** +0.10s/f (Good) **15** Ran SP% **123.6**
Speed ratings (Par 109): **110,109,109,107,106 103,100,99,99,99 96,95,94,91,61**
CSF £89.42 CT £761.15 TOTE £11.60: £4.80, £3.20, £3.70; EX 122.90 Trifecta £2403.00.

Owner Market Avenue Racing Club & Tim Dykes **Bred** Shefford Valley Stud **Trained** Middleham Moor, N Yorks

■ Stewards' Enquiry : Connor Beasley two-day ban: used whip above permitted level (May 9-10)

FOCUS
Race run up the stands' side straight adding 57yds to race distance. A good-class mile handicap this time, with the two previous winners returning and the time was much quicker than the maidens before after it. The pace collapsed and the first two came from the rear.

1630 APOLLOBET WEEKLY GOLF REFUNDS H'CAP 1m
3:55 (3:57) (Class 5) (0-75,75) 3-Y-O **£4,851** (£1,443; £721; £360) **Stalls** Low

Form RPR

55-1 **1** **Sir Roderic (IRE)**12 1389 3-9-6 **74**.... FrederikTylicki 3 80
(Rod Millman) *trckd ldrs: upsides over 1f out: led last 75yds: drvn out* **3/1**1

045- **2** 1/2 **Shafafya**171 7700 3-9-5 **73**.... DaneO'Neill 7 78
(Ed Dunlop) *t.k.h: trckd ldrs: upsides over 1f out: led briefly last 150yds: no ex clsng stages* **11/1**

410- **3** 1 **Midnight Macchiato (IRE)**210 6761 3-9-5 **73**.... TomQueally 2 76+
(David Brown) *stdd s: hld up towards rr: hdwy and rdn over 1f out: styd on wl to take 3rd last 50yds* **17/2**

0-32 **4** 1 3/4 **Moueenn**15 1324 3-9-7 **75**.... JackMitchell 9 73
(Roger Varian) *chsd ldrs: drvn over 5f out: edgd lft 1f out: kpt on same pce* **8/1**

31- **5** hd **Izmir (IRE)**165 7787 3-9-5 **73**.... PatCosgrave 8 71
(William Haggas) *led early: trckd ldr: led 2f out: hdd last 150yds: fdd* **7/2**2

034- **6** nk **Torremar (FR)**178 7560 3-9-5 **73**.... GrahamLee 5 70
(Kevin Ryan) *s.i.s: in rr-div: drvn over 2f out: kpt on one pce* **9/2**3

05-3 **7** 1 3/4 **Kingthistle**14 1345 3-9-0 **68**.... GrahamGibbons 6 61
(Michael Easterby) *sn led: hdd 2f out: wknd last 150yds: eased clsng stages* **14/1**

14- **8** 4 **Black Magic (IRE)**346 2194 3-9-2 **70**.... JackGarritty 4 53
(Richard Fahey) *hld up in rr: hung rt bnd over 5f out: effrt 4f out: wknd over 1f out* **12/1**

41- **9** 3 1/2 **Pop Culture**289 4065 3-8-8 **67**.... EdwardGreatrex(5) 1 42
(Jonathan Portman) *sn trcking ldrs: drvn over 2f out: lost pl over 1f out* **25/1**

1m 46.15s (2.45) **Going Correction** +0.10s/f (Good) **9** Ran SP% **113.6**
Speed ratings (Par 98): **91,90,89,87,87 87,85,81,78**
CSF £36.11 CT £252.36 TOTE £3.50: £1.20, £3.50, £2.80; EX 39.50 Trifecta £271.80.

Owner The Links Partnership **Bred** Thomas G Cooke **Trained** Kentisbeare, Devon

FOCUS
Race run up the stands' side straight adding 57yds to race distance. A competitive handicap for 3yos run 3.88 secs slower than the preceding older horse contest. The winner built on his Windsor win.

1631 APOLLOBET ONLINE CASINO AND GAMES H'CAP (DIV I) 1m
4:30 (4:32) (Class 5) (0-70,72) 4-Y-O+ **£4,851** (£1,443; £541; £541) **Stalls** Low

Form RPR

00-0 **1** **Chosen Character (IRE)**18 1247 8-9-7 **70**....(vt) LiamJones 11 80
(Tom Dascombe) *chsd ldr: led over 2f out: fnd ex nr fin* **10/1**

53-6 **2** nk **Cornborough**18 1241 5-9-6 **69**.... JasonHart 3 78
(Mark Walford) *hld up towards rr: hdwy whn nt clr run over 2f out: 2nd 1f out: styd on and upsides last 100yds: no ex clsng stages* **5/1**2

000- **3** 2 1/4 **Cymraeg Bounty**219 6471 4-9-6 **69**.... RoystonFfrench 6 73
(Iain Jardine) *hld up in mid-div: hdwy and hung lft over 2f out: styd on same pce fnl f* **5/1**2

42-4 **3** dht **Im Dapper Too**31 1047 5-8-8 **57**.... GrahamGibbons 5 61
(John Davies) *chsd ldrs: kpt on same pce fnl f* **6/1**3

65-0 **5** 2 1/4 **Janaab (IRE)**18 1247 6-9-2 **70**....(t) RachelRichardson(5) 10 68
(Tim Easterby) *mid-div: effrt 3f out: one pce fnl 2f* **8/1**

356- **6** 1/2 **Bush Beauty (IRE)**123 8354 5-8-5 **61**.... SophieKilloran(7) 2 58
(Eric Alston) *hld up in rr: swtchd rt over 2f out: kpt on fnl f* **25/1**

22-3 **7** 3 **American Hustle (IRE)**3 1565 4-9-2 **65**.... BenCurtis 1 55
(Brian Ellison) *t.k.h in rr: hdwy on inner over 2f out: chsng ldrs over 1f out: sn wknd* **10/3**1

54-6 **8** 2 **Storm Check**18 1247 4-8-10 **59**.... NeilFarley 8 44
(Andrew Crook) *mid-div: drvn 4f out: sn outpcd: kpt on fnl f* **50/1**

0-01 **9** 1 **Fidelma Moon (IRE)**10 1412 4-9-4 **72**.... JordanVaughan(5) 9 55
(K R Burke) *chsd ldrs: wknd wl over 1f out* **7/1**

421- **10** 8 **Outlaw Kate (IRE)**254 5296 4-8-0 **56** oh7.... GeorgeWood(7) 4 19
(Michael Mullineaux) *mid-div: drvn over 3f out: lost pl 2f out* **33/1**

3-10 **11** 6 **Breathless**18 1241 4-9-3 **66**....(t) GrahamLee 13 15
(Clive Mulhall) *sn chsng ldrs: drvn over 3f out: lost pl over 2f out: sn bhd* **50/1**

014- **12** 1 **Baltic Prince (IRE)**187 7347 6-9-5 **68**.... LukeMorris 12 15
(Tony Carroll) *led: hdd 2f out: wkng whn heavily eased fnl f* **16/1**

1m 44.09s (0.39) **Going Correction** +0.10s/f (Good) **12** Ran SP% **120.0**
Speed ratings (Par 103): **102,101,99,99,97 96,93,91,90,82 76,75**
WIN: 11.30 Chosen Character; PL: 3.60 Chosen Character, 1.90 Cornborough; EX: 84.50; CSF: 58.67; TC: 144.76, 168.85; TF: 263.00, 213.30;.

Owner Aykroyd And Sons Ltd **Bred** Moyglare Stud Farm Ltd **Trained** Malpas, Cheshire

FOCUS
Race run up the stands' side straight adding 57yds to race distance. The first division of this modest handicap was run 1.66 secs slower than the quickest of the earlier races over the trip. The winner took advantage of a career-low mark.

1632 APOLLOBET ONLINE CASINO AND GAMES H'CAP (DIV II) 1m
5:05 (5:07) (Class 5) (0-70,70) 4-Y-O+ **£4,851** (£1,443; £721; £360) **Stalls** Low

Form RPR

6-24 **1** **Farham (USA)**16 1290 4-9-4 **70**.... SammyJoBell(3) 3 75+
(Richard Fahey) *trckd ldrs: squeezed through 2f out: led last 75yds: all out* **11/4**1

554- **2** shd **Zaria**200 7001 5-8-4 **58**....(p) PatrickO'Donnell(5) 9 62
(Richard Price) *trckd ldrs: led 2f out: hdd last 75yds: kpt on: jst failed* **10/1**

1030 **3** nse **The Firm (IRE)**24 1152 7-9-3 **66**....(be) DaleSwift 1 70
(Daniel Mark Loughnane) *chsd ldrs: effrt over 3f out: upsides last 150yds: jst hld* **16/1**

00-3 **4** 2 **Ferdy (IRE)**23 1165 7-8-7 **56** oh1.... JFEgan 11 55
(Paul Green) *s.s: hdwy 5f out: chsng ldrs 1f out: edgd lft and kpt on same pce* **12/1**

553- **5** nk **The Salmon Man**194 7168 4-9-4 **67**.... GrahamLee 2 68+
(Brendan Powell) *dwlt: hdwy 4f out: nt clr run over 2f out: kpt on one pce over 1f out* **4/1**2

010- **6** 3 1/2 **Day Of The Eagle (IRE)**214 6616 10-9-7 **70**.... GrahamGibbons 4 60
(Michael Easterby) *s.i.s: in rr: drvn over 4f out: nt clr run on inner over 2f out: wknd fnl f* **9/1**

34-4 **7** 1 **Stoneboat Bill**15 1317 4-9-6 **69**.... NeilFarley 8 57
(Declan Carroll) *mid-div: hdwy over 3f out: outpcd over 2f out: kpt on fnl f* **6/1**3

1203 **8** nk **De Lesseps (USA)**43 904 8-8-11 **60**.... LukeMorris 6 47
(John David Riches) *mid-div: drvn over 3f out: chsng ldrs over 2f out: wknd fnl f* **20/1**

2650 **9** 1 1/2 **Saint Pois (FR)**52 782 5-9-4 **70**....(t) GeorgeDowning(3) 12 53
(Tony Carroll) *led early: t.k.h: trckd ldr: led over 3f out: hdd 2f out: wknd fnl f* **8/1**

100- **10** 2 3/4 **Framley Garth (IRE)**203 6933 4-9-6 **69**.... JackGarritty 10 46
(Patrick Holmes) *sn led: hdd over 3f out: wkng whn hmpd over 1f out* **16/1**

1m 45.29s (1.59) **Going Correction** +0.10s/f (Good) **10** Ran SP% **115.4**
Speed ratings (Par 103): **96,95,95,93,93 90,89,88,87,84**
CSF £30.94 CT £379.54 TOTE £3.20: £1.10, £3.50, £4.70; EX 33.50 Trifecta £318.10.

Owner The Matthewman One Partnership **Bred** SF Bloodstock LLC **Trained** Musley Bank, N Yorks

■ Stewards' Enquiry : Patrick O'Donnell two-day ban: use of whip (7-9 May)

FOCUS
Race run up the stands' side straight adding 57yds to race distance. The second leg of this modest handicap was run 1.2 secs slower than the first division and produced a blanket finish. The winner is only rated to form.

1633 APOLLOBET BET ON LOTTERIES H'CAP 1m 2f 95y
5:40 (5:40) (Class 4) (0-80,80) 4-Y-O+ **£8,086** (£2,406; £1,202; £601) **Stalls** Centre

Form RPR

5-41 **1** **Rock Song**7 1501 7-8-5 **67**.... JoeDoyle(3) 11 79
(John Mackie) *led early: trckd ldrs: led wl over 1f out: pushed clr fnl f: v readily* **10/1**

/62- **2** 2 1/4 **Higher Power**303 3567 4-9-7 **80**.... TomQueally 3 88+
(James Fanshawe) *s.i.s: sn pushed along in rr: hdwy over 2f out: chsd ldr fnl 150yds: edgd lft: no imp* **9/4**1

223- **3** 2 1/4 **Muhaafiz (IRE)**219 6476 4-9-4 **77**.... SeanLevey 1 80
(David Brown) *chsd ldrs: effrt over 2f out: kpt on to take modest 3rd clsng stages* **5/1**2

26-2 **4** 3/4 **Squire**24 1142 5-9-7 **80**.... GrahamLee 5 82
(Michael Attwater) *hld up in rr: effrt over 3f out: chsng ldrs over 2f out: kpt on same pce appr fnl f* **7/1**3

/0-0 **5** 1 **Weapon Of Choice (IRE)**32 864 8-8-13 **72**....(t) JackGarritty 2 72
(Dianne Sayer) *in tch: effrt and nt clr run over 2f out: kpt on one pce* **40/1**

3-00 **6** 1 1/2 **Peterhouse (USA)**52 779 4-9-7 **80**.... JFEgan 13 77
(Jason Ward) *s.i.s: in rr: hdwy over 4f out: chsng ldrs and edgd lft over 1f out: one pce* **16/1**

000- **7** hd **Artful Prince**186 7369 6-9-2 **80**....(b) PhilDennis(5) 6 77
(James Given) *in rr: kpt on fnl 2f: nvr a factor* **40/1**

1- **8** 1 **Queen's Novel**199 7031 4-9-6 **79**.... LukeMorris 15 74
(James Tate) *mid-div: effrt over 2f out: one pce whn nt clr run appr fnl f* **9/1**

2110 **9** 5 **Play Nicely**17 1250 4-9-6 **79**.... GrahamGibbons 4 64
(David Barron) *mid-div: reminders over 3f out: wknd 2f out* **20/1**

05-6 **10** 1/2 **Lostock Hall (IRE)**108 73 4-8-6 **72**.... CliffordLee(7) 9 59
(K R Burke) *w ldrs: led over 2f out: hdd wl over 1f out: wkng whn hmpd appr fnl f* **16/1**

644- **11** 1 **Oriental Tiger**198 7058 5-8-9 **68**.... RoystonFfrench 7 51
(Iain Jardine) *in rr: drvn over 3f out: nvr a factor* **14/1**

410- **12** nse **Lord Franklin**196 7125 7-9-7 **80**.... JasonHart 12 63
(Eric Alston) *chsd ldrs: lost pl over 1f out* **25/1**

650- **13** 1 1/2 **King Of Paradise (IRE)**193 7181 7-8-6 **70**.... RachelRichardson(5) 14 50
(Eric Alston) *led: hdd over 2f out: wknd over 1f out* **25/1**

30-0 **14** nse **Mysterial**17 1250 6-8-12 **71**.... NeilFarley 8 51
(Declan Carroll) *mid-div: effrt over 2f out: lost pl over 1f out* **25/1**

614- **15** 3 3/4 **We'll Shake Hands (FR)**294 3906 5-8-12 **74**.... MichaelJMMurphy(3) 10 46
(K R Burke) *mid-div: drvn over 3f out: lost pl 2f out: eased clsng stages* **20/1**

2m 13.51s (-1.99) **Going Correction** +0.10s/f (Good) **15** Ran SP% **123.4**
Speed ratings (Par 105): **111,109,107,106,106 104,104,103,99,99 98,98,97,97,94**
CSF £30.31 CT £132.95 TOTE £12.40: £3.40, £1.70, £2.30; EX 38.00 Trifecta £695.70.

Owner Mrs J Mackie **Bred** Shortgrove Manor Stud **Trained** Church Broughton , Derbys

FOCUS
Race run up the stands' side straight adding 57yds to race distance. A fair and competitive handicap to end with but an easy winner. The winner was still on a good mark on his 2013 form.

T/Plt: £118.90 to a £1 stake. Pool: £102,495.98 - 629.19 winning tickets T/Qpdt: £26.20 to a £1 stake. Pool: £6,781.78 - 191.35 winning tickets **Walter Glynn**

[1312]LEICESTER (R-H)

Saturday, April 23

OFFICIAL GOING: Good to soft

Wind: Light against Weather: Cloudy

1634 TOTESCOOP6 THE MILLIONAIRE MAKER H'CAP — 6f

2:15 (2:15) (Class 4) (0-85,85) 4-Y-O+ **£4,851** (£1,443; £721; £360) **Stalls** High

Form				RPR
U60-	**1**		**Munfallet (IRE)**[231] 6080 5-9-7 **85** SeanLevey 3 (David Brown) *racd keenly: mde virtually all: shkn up over 1f out: rdn and edgd lft ins fnl f: styd on* **11/1**	92
0034	**2**	*nk*	**Captain Lars (SAF)**[5] 1530 6-8-12 **76** (p) JoeFanning 2 (Derek Shaw) *hld up in tch: rdn to chse wnr and hung lft ins fnl f: sn ev ch: styd on* **6/1**[1]	82
00-0	**3**	*¾*	**Ambitious Icarus**[9] 1444 7-9-0 **78** (e) LiamKeniry 11 (Richard Guest) *hld up: hdwy over 1f out: r.o* **25/1**	82
5620	**4**	*nk*	**Borough Boy (IRE)**[5] 1528 6-9-2 **80** (v) MartinLane 8 (Derek Shaw) *hld up: plld hrd: rdn over 2f out: hdwy over 1f out: styd on* **20/1**	83
4166	**5**	*nk*	**Corporal Maddox**[24] 1142 9-9-5 **83** (p) GeorgeBaker 9 (Ronald Harris) *hld up: hdwy over 1f out: r.o* **25/1**	85
2350	**6**	*¾*	**Sir Billy Wright (IRE)**[39] 938 5-9-4 **82** AdamKirby 15 (David Evans) *hld up: rdn over 2f out: hdwy and nt clr run over 1f out: swtchd rt ins fnl f: nt rch ldrs* **13/2**[2]	81
-560	**7**	*2½*	**Varsovian**[31] 1040 6-9-5 **83** RenatoSouza 10 (Dean Ivory) *prom: rdn over 1f out: no ex ins fnl f* **20/1**	74
042-	**8**	*¾*	**Syrian Pearl**[206] 6862 5-9-4 **82** TedDurcan 6 (Chris Wall) *s.i.s: hld up: hdwy over 2f out: shkn up over 1f out: no ex ins fnl f* **7/1**[3]	71+
320-	**9**	*¾*	**Evening Attire**[158] 7880 5-8-11 **75** RyanPowell 4 (William Stone) *chsd ldrs: rdn over 2f out: edgd lft over 1f out: wknd fnl f* **12/1**	61
00-0	**10**	*½*	**Rio Ronaldo (IRE)**[24] 1143 4-9-5 **83** JimCrowley 12 (Mike Murphy) *hld up: plld hrd: hdwy over 1f out: sn rdn: wknd ins fnl f* **8/1**	68
0310	**11**	*¾*	**Doctor Parkes**[10] 1427 10-9-2 **80** SaleemGolam 13 (Stuart Williams) *mid-div: rdn and lost pl over 2f out: nt clr run over 1f out: n.d after* **33/1**	62
020-	**12**	*nk*	**Flexible Flyer**[206] 6862 7-9-5 **83** IrineuGoncalves 1 (Chris Dwyer) *s.i.s: hdwy over 4f out: rdn over 2f out: wknd fnl f* **8/1**	65
000	**13**	*1½*	**Air Of York (IRE)**[5] 1528 4-9-0 **81** PhilipPrince(3) 5 (David Evans) *chsd ldrs: rdn over 2f out: wknd fnl f* **16/1**	58
-452	**14**	*6*	**Among Angels**[39] 944 4-9-4 **82** (p) SilvestreDeSousa 14 (Kevin Frost) *hld up: rdn over 2f out: sn wknd* **6/1**[1]	40

1m 14.12s (1.12) **Going Correction** +0.125s/f (Good) **14** Ran SP% **118.7**

Speed ratings (Par 105): **97,96,95,95,94 93,90,89,88,87 86,86,84,76**

CSF £68.84 CT £1670.26 TOTE £15.80: £6.00, £3.20, £8.50; EX 90.40 Trifecta £637.20 Part won..

Owner J C Fretwell **Bred** Miss Joann Lyons **Trained** Averham Park, Notts

FOCUS

A false fail from the top of the hill on the back straight all the way to the winning line increased all the distances on the round course by approx 17yds. A wide-open sprint handicap. Initially they raced down the centre before spreading across the track, and it paid to race handily.

1635 TOTESCOOP6 PLAY FOR BIG MONEY TODAY NOVICE MEDIAN AUCTION STKS — 5f

2:50 (2:50) (Class 5) 2-Y-O **£3,234** (£962; £481; £240) **Stalls** High

Form				RPR
	1		**Hyperfocus (IRE)** 2-9-2 0 WilliamBuick 5 (Hugo Palmer) *hld up in tch: shkn up to ld and edgd lft 1f out: r.o wl* **9/4**[1]	86+
5	**2**	*5*	**Billy's Boots**[8] 1454 2-9-2 0 SilvestreDeSousa 4 (Mick Channon) *chsd ldrs: rdn over 1f out: styd on same pce fnl f* **11/2**[2]	66
	3	*hd*	**Rapid Rise (IRE)** 2-9-2 0 SeanLevey 8 (David Brown) *chsd ldrs: shkn up over 1f out: styd on same pce fnl f* **6/1**[3]	65
	4	*½*	**Primrose Place** 2-8-11 0 KieranO'Neill 1 (Richard Hannon) *wnt rt s: hld up: hdwy over 1f out: styd on same pce fnl f* **10/1**	58
	5	*shd*	**Arc Royal** 2-9-2 0 LiamKeniry 6 (Tom Dascombe) *sn pushed along in rr: hdwy 1/2-way: rdn over 1f out: styd on same pce* **12/1**	64
	6	*2*	**Il Sicario (IRE)** 2-9-2 0 JoeFanning 7 (Mark Johnston) *sn pushed along in rr: swtchd rt over 1f out: nvr on terms* **6/1**[3]	56
	7	*shd*	**Fethiye Boy** 2-9-2 0 RobertHavlin 3 (Ronald Harris) *led: rdn and hdd 1f out: wknd ins fnl f* **6/1**[3]	56
	8	*17*	**Silver Asset (IRE)** 2-9-2 0 GeorgeBaker 9 (Michael Wigham) *chsd ldr to 1/2-way: wknd over 1f out* **14/1**

1m 2.35s (2.35) **Going Correction** +0.125s/f (Good) **8** Ran SP% **112.5**

Speed ratings (Par 92): **86,78,77,76,76 73,73,46**

CSF £14.07 TOTE £4.00: £1.60, £1.70, £2.00; EX 13.60 Trifecta £55.50.

Owner MPH Racing - II **Bred** Stephanie Von Schilcher & Gavan Kinch **Trained** Newmarket, Suffolk

FOCUS

Probably a modest novice contest, but the winner looks very useful.

1636 TOTEQUADPOT FOUR PLACES IN FOUR RACES H'CAP — 1m 3f 183y

3:25 (3:27) (Class 3) (0-95,84) 3-Y-O **£9,451** (£2,829; £1,414; £708; £352) **Stalls** Low

Form				RPR
64-1	**1**		**Du Moto (IRE)**[18] 1242 3-9-2 **79** TedDurcan 5 (Sir Michael Stoute) *hld up: hdwy over 2f out: rdn to ld over 1f out: styd on wl* **7/2**[3]	88+
22-2	**2**	*3½*	**Hepplewhite**[37] 968 3-9-6 **83** AndreaAtzeni 2 (Robert Eddery) *hld up in tch: shkn up over 2f out: rdn to ld over 1f out: sn hdd: no ex ins fnl f* **10/1**	85
40-2	**3**	*¾*	**Injam (IRE)**[21] 1200 3-8-13 **76** PaulHanagan 4 (Jedd O'Keeffe) *prom: rdn and lost pl over 2f out: hdwy over 1f out: edgd rt: styd on* **10/1**	77
41-2	**4**	*1¼*	**Juste Pour Nous**[20] 1220 3-9-6 **83** JoeFanning 3 (Mark Johnston) *led 2f: chsd ldrs: rdn over 2f out: styd on same pce fnl f* **3/1**[2]	82
25-1	**5**	*1½*	**Hereawi**[21] 1200 3-8-13 **76** FMBerry 7 (Ralph Beckett) *chsd ldr tl led over 2f out: rdn and hdd over 1f out: wknd ins fnl f* **11/4**[1]	73
410-	**6**	*11*	**East Indies**[203] 6924 3-9-7 **84**[1] WilliamBuick 8 (John Gosden) *hld up: plld hrd: racd wd and hdwy to ld 10f out: shkn up and hdd over 2f out: wknd and eased over 1f out* **6/1**	63
40-1	**7**	*12*	**Muthraab Aldaar (IRE)**[27] 1113 3-8-12 **75** SilvestreDeSousa 6 (Mick Channon) *hld up: hdwy over 3f out: rdn and hung rt over 2f out: wknd and eased over 1f out* **10/1**	35

2m 36.05s (2.15) **Going Correction** +0.225s/f (Good) **7** Ran SP% **115.4**

Speed ratings (Par 102): **101,98,98,97,96 89,81**

CSF £37.68 CT £320.05 TOTE £5.00: £2.60, £4.60; EX 37.60 Trifecta £225.10.

Owner Mrs Doreen Tabor **Bred** R Scarborough **Trained** Newmarket, Suffolk

FOCUS

Race distance increaded by 17 yards. This fair 3yo handicap was run at a sound pace and is rated around the consistent runner-up.

1637 TOTESCOOP6 EBF STALLIONS KING RICHARD III STKS (FORMERLY THE LEICESTERSHIRE STAKES) (LISTED RACE) — 7f

4:00 (4:01) (Class 1) 4-Y-O+

£28,355 (£10,750; £5,380; £2,680; £1,345; £675) **Stalls** High

Form				RPR
610-	**1**		**Home Of The Brave (IRE)**[224] 6313 4-9-3 109 (t) WilliamBuick 2 (Hugo Palmer) *sn w ldr: led over 5f out: shkn up over 1f out: r.o wl* **11/4**[1]	118
00-0	**2**	*2½*	**Coulsty (IRE)**[9] 1439 5-9-3 107 SeanLevey 5 (Richard Hannon) *chsd ldrs: rdn over 2f out: styd on same pce ins fnl f* **12/1**	111
026-	**3**	*nse*	**Here Comes When (IRE)**[197] 7074 6-9-3 111 JimCrowley 8 (Andrew Balding) *plld hrd and prom: rdn over 1f out: styd on same pce ins fnl f* **9/1**	111
150-	**4**	*¾*	**Johnny Barnes (IRE)**[174] 7668 4-9-3 110 RobertHavlin 9 (John Gosden) *dwlt: hld up: hdwy over 1f out: sn rdn: styd on same pce ins fnl f* **18/1**	109+
625-	**5**	*½*	**Markaz (IRE)**[197] 7074 4-9-3 111 PaulHanagan 7 (Owen Burrows) *s.i.s: plld hrd and sn trcking ldrs: rdn and ev ch over 1f out: no ex ins fnl f* **11/2**[3]	108
035-	**6**	*1¾*	**White Lake**[289] 4076 4-9-3 103[1] AndreaAtzeni 1 (Roger Varian) *hld up: rdn over 1f out: nt trble ldrs* **8/1**	103
/40-	**7**	*1¼*	**Convey**[245] 5638 4-9-3 106 TedDurcan 10 (Sir Michael Stoute) *hld up: hung rt fr over 2f out: nvr on terms* **12/1**	100
4-06	**8**	*1½*	**Emell**[21] 1196 6-9-3 103 (b) KieranO'Neill 11 (Richard Hannon) *prom: rdn over 2f out: wknd over 1f out* **40/1**	96
122-	**9**	*hd*	**Mitchum Swagger**[175] 7634 4-9-3 108 GeorgeBaker 3 (David Lanigan) *hld up: shkn up over 2f out: wknd over 1f out* **7/2**[2]	95
440-	**10**	*1*	**Code Red**[224] 6313 4-9-3 110 MartinDwyer 6 (William Muir) *led: hdd over 5f out: remained handy tl rdn: edgd lft and wknd over 1f out* **9/1**	92

1m 24.6s (-1.60) **Going Correction** +0.125s/f (Good) **10** Ran SP% **118.5**

Speed ratings (Par 111): **114,111,111,110,109 107,106,104,104,103**

CSF £38.08 TOTE £3.10: £1.10, £4.60, £2.80; EX 40.40 Trifecta £302.60.

Owner Flemington Bloodstock Partnership **Bred** Earl Ecurie Du Grand Chene **Trained** Newmarket, Suffolk

FOCUS

A tight-looking Listed event on paper. The form is straightforward, the winner in keeping with a more positive view of last season's Curragh win.

1638 TOTEPOOLLIVEINFO.COM H'CAP — 7f

4:35 (4:37) (Class 5) (0-75,75) 3-Y-O **£3,234** (£962; £481; £240) **Stalls** High

Form				RPR
025-	**1**		**Poet's Beauty (IRE)**[190] 7249 3-9-1 **72** (p) ThomasBrown(3) 6 (Ismail Mohammed) *led to 1/2-way: led again 2f out: rdn out* **6/1**[2]	79
60-5	**2**	*1½*	**Stars N Angels (IRE)**[17] 1275 3-8-7 **61** (p) AndrewMullen 5 (Michael Appleby) *chsd ldrs: rdn to chse wnr over 1f out: edgd lft: styd on same pce ins fnl f* **14/1**	64
25-3	**3**	*½*	**Zauffaly (FR)**[17] 1258 3-9-7 **75** (b[1]) JimCrowley 2 (Ed Dunlop) *hld up: hdwy 2f out: rdn over 1f out: styd on same pce ins fnl f* **10/1**	77
54-1	**4**	*2¼*	**Wowcha (IRE)**[18] 1246 3-9-7 **75** WilliamBuick 11 (John Quinn) *hld up: hdwy u.p over 1f out: edgd rt and styd on same pce ins fnl f* **7/4**[1]	71
16-6	**5**	*2¼*	**Zeeoneandonly (IRE)**[82] 419 3-9-1 **72** (v) PhilipPrince(3) 4 (David Evans) *racd keenly: prom: jnd wnr over 5f out: led 1/2-way: hdd 2f out: no ex ins fnl f* **20/1**	61
323-	**6**	*½*	**Just Fab (IRE)**[156] 7904 3-9-2 **70** AndreaAtzeni 7 (Marco Botti) *prom: pushed along and lost pl 3f out: n.d after* **8/1**[3]	58
2104	**7**	*nk*	**Custard The Dragon**[7] 1485 3-9-1 **69** PaulHanagan 12 (John Mackie) *s.i.s: hld up: hdwy u.p over 1f out: no ex ins fnl f* **9/1**	56
21-5	**8**	*2*	**Shypen**[105] 123 3-9-4 **72** JoeFanning 10 (George Margarson) *prom: rdn over 2f out: wknd fnl f* **16/1**	54
40-3	**9**	*½*	**Bingo George (IRE)**[38] 959 3-9-3 **71** LiamKeniry 1 (Andrew Balding) *hld up: plld hrd: hdwy over 2f out: rdn over 1f out: wknd fnl f* **14/1**	52
320-	**10**	*3¾*	**Touch Of Color**[187] 7346 3-9-1 **69** AdamKirby 9 (Clive Cox) *mid-div: pushed along 1/2-way: wknd over 2f out* **20/1**	39
1140	**11**	*½*	**Teversham**[17] 1257 3-8-6 **65** JosephineGordon(5) 8 (Chris Dwyer) *chsd ldrs: rdn over 2f out: wknd over 1f out* **16/1**	34
450-	**12**	*shd*	**Caponova (IRE)**[186] 7371 3-8-11 **65**[1] WilliamCarson 13 (Tom Dascombe) *prom tl rdn and wknd over 2f out* **50/1**	34
430-	**13**	*3¼*	**Kodimoor (IRE)**[224] 6328 3-9-1 **69**[1] JohnFahy 3 (Christopher Kellett) *prom: rdn 1/2-way: wknd over 2f out* **50/1**	29

1m 26.82s (0.62) **Going Correction** +0.125s/f (Good) **13** Ran SP% **119.4**

Speed ratings (Par 98): **101,99,98,96,93 93,92,90,89,85 84,84,81**

CSF £83.25 CT £830.47 TOTE £8.70: £2.50, £4.70, £5.20; EX 153.70 Trifecta £1593.90.

Owner Dr Ali Ridha **Bred** Rabbah Bloodstock Limited **Trained** Newmarket, Suffolk

FOCUS

A modest handicap. Again the riders shunned either rail and the form is best rated around the third.

1639 TOTEPOOL BETTING ON ALL UK RACING MAIDEN STKS — 1m 1f 218y

5:10 (5:13) (Class 5) 3-Y-O+ **£2,911** (£866; £432; £216) **Stalls** Low

Form				RPR
223-	**1**		**Imperial Aviator**[124] 8323 3-8-10 83 FMBerry 8 (Roger Charlton) *a.p: chsd wnr over 2f out: rdn to ld and edgd rt ins fnl f: r.o* **10/1**	94
6-	**2**	*½*	**Ulysses (IRE)**[183] 7435 3-8-10 0 TedDurcan 1 (Sir Michael Stoute) *led at stdy pce tl qcknd 3f out: rdn and hdd ins fnl f: r.o* **9/4**[2]	93

3 6 **Uae Prince (IRE)** 3-8-10 0 AndreaAtzeni 9 81
(Roger Varian) *hld up in tch: shkn up over 1f out: sn edgd rt: no ex fnl f* **4/5**[1]
5- 4 1 3/4 **Autocratic**[185] 7394 3-8-10 0 WilliamBuick 10 78
(Sir Michael Stoute) *hld up: hdwy over 2f out: sn rdn: styd on same pce fr over 1f out* **5/1**[3]
44- 5 shd **Yangtze**[212] 6687 3-8-10 0 JoeFanning 5 77
(Sir Michael Stoute) *hld up: hdwy over 1f out: nt trble ldrs* **25/1**
0- 6 6 **Pennerley**[183] 7422 3-8-2 0 RyanTate(3) 6 60
(James Eustace) *hld up: rdn over 2f out: nvr on terms* **100/1**
7 3 1/2 **Wishpoint (USA)** 3-8-10 0 WilliamCarson 3 58
(Michael Bell) *hld up: hdwy 1/2-way: rdn over 3f out: wknd wl over 1f out* **40/1**
0 8 8 **Nightswift**[24] 1140 4-9-13 0 TimmyMurphy 4 45
(James Evans) *chsd ldrs tl wknd over 2f out* **150/1**
9 3/4 **Placedela Concorde** 3-8-10 0 RobertTart 2 41
(Anthony Carson) *s.i.s: hld up: rdn and wknd over 2f out* **50/1**
0- 10 1 1/2 **Lake Placid**[201] 6986 3-8-10 0 JimCrowley 7 38
(Charles Hills) *prom: racd keenly: jnd ldr over 8f out tl rdn over 2f out: wknd over 1f out* **22/1**

2m 12.47s (4.57) **Going Correction** +0.225s/f (Good)
WFA 3 from 4yo 17lb **10** Ran SP% **126.3**
Speed ratings (Par 103): **90,89,84,83,83 78,75,69,68,67**
CSF £34.73 TOTE £8.10: £2.60, £1.80, £1.02; EX 41.10 Trifecta £107.10.
Owner Daniel Hunt & Mrs Eileen Markham **Bred** Daniel Hunt **Trained** Beckhampton, Wilts

FOCUS
Race distance increased by 17 yards. Usually a decent maiden. They went a routine pace and two came well clear inside the final furlong.

1640 COLLECT TOTEPOOL WINNINGS AT BETFRED SHOPS H'CAP 1m 1f 218y
5:45 (5:45) (Class 5) (0-70,69) 4-Y-O+ **£3,234** (£962; £481; £240) **Stalls** Low

Form RPR
4400 1 **Shining Romeo**[7] 1501 4-9-3 **65** FMBerry 8 71
(Denis Quinn) *mde all: rdn over 1f out: jst hld on* **16/1**
550- 2 hd **Al Fatih (IRE)**[51] 7925 5-9-2 **64** TimmyMurphy 2 70+
(Steve Flook) *hld up: hdwy 2f out: sn rdn: nt clr run ins fnl f: r.o wl towards fin* **12/1**
4306 3 1/2 **Tatawu (IRE)**[14] 1340 4-9-1 **63** WilliamCarson 7 67
(Peter Hiatt) *a.p: chsd wnr over 2f out: rdn over 1f out: styd on* **18/1**
465- 4 hd **Inflexiball**[211] 6715 4-8-9 **57** JoeFanning 6 61
(John Mackie) *trckd ldrs: racd keenly: rdn over 1f out: styd on* **8/1**
-540 5 3/4 **Viserion**[66] 616 4-9-1 **68** GeorgeBuckell(5) 10 70
(David Simcock) *hld up: hdwy over 2f out: rdn over 1f out: edgd rt and styd on ins fnl f* **4/1**[2]
620- 6 5 **Collodi (GER)**[131] 8221 7-9-7 **69** JimmyQuinn 3 61
(David Bridgwater) *s.s: hld up: rdn over 1f out: nt trble ldrs* **20/1**
0/3- 7 nk **Mollasses**[22] 6324 5-9-7 **69** GeorgeBaker 9 61
(Harry Whittington) *chsd ldr tl rdn over 2f out: wknd ins fnl f* **2/1**[1]
5545 8 shd **The Lock Master (IRE)**[17] 1250 9-9-7 **69** (p) AndrewMullen 1 60
(Michael Appleby) *pushed along in rr early: rdn and outpcd over 2f out: nvr on terms after* **7/1**
220- 9 nse **Scent Of Power**[190] 7265 4-8-4 **55** oh2 TimClark(3) 5 46
(Barry Leavy) *hld up: rdn over 2f out: nt trble ldrs* **25/1**
/301 10 1 1/2 **Anton Chigurh**[30] 1058 7-8-12 **67** PatrickVaughan(7) 4 55
(Tom Dascombe) *hld up: hdwy over 2f out: sn rdn: wknd over 1f out* **5/1**[3]

2m 12.74s (4.84) **Going Correction** +0.225s/f (Good) **10** Ran SP% **121.1**
Speed ratings (Par 103): **89,88,88,88,87 83,83,83,83,82**
CSF £199.93 CT £3483.83 TOTE £19.40: £5.70, £5.00, £7.00; EX 331.20 Trifecta £1660.70 Part won..
Owner John Mangan **Bred** Newsells Park Stud **Trained** Newmarket, Suffolk

FOCUS
Race distance increased by 17 yards. This moderate handicap was run at an ordinary pace and, resulting in a tight finish, the winner dictated.
T/Plt: £247.30 to a £1 stake. Pool of £45108.58 - 133.11 winning tickets. T/Qpdt: £32.00 to a £1 stake. Pool of £4737.72 - 109.40 winning tickets. **Colin Roberts**

1443 RIPON (R-H)
Saturday, April 23

OFFICIAL GOING: Good to soft (7.0)
Wind: Breezy, half against Weather: Cloudy, bright

1641 CLARO BAR NOVICE AUCTION STKS (PLUS 10 RACE) 5f
2:05 (2:05) (Class 4) 2-Y-O **£5,175** (£1,540; £769; £384) **Stalls** High

Form RPR
05 1 **Who Told Jo Jo (IRE)**[16] 1293 2-8-5 0 NathanEvans(5) 6 76
(Bill Turner) *mde all: rdn over 1f out: drew clr ins fnl f* **10/1**
2 3 1/4 **Mama Africa (IRE)** 2-8-7 0 PJMcDonald 8 61
(David Barron) *prom: rdn along over 1f out: chsd wnr ins fnl f: kpt on: no imp* **5/2**[1]
3 2 1/2 **Boundsy (IRE)** 2-9-0 0 TonyHamilton 1 59
(Richard Fahey) *trckd ldrs on outside: effrt and pushed along over 1f out: outpcd ins fnl f* **11/2**[3]
4 4 2 3/4 **Bonnie Arlene (IRE)**[9] 1443 2-8-11 0 FrannyNorton 4 48
(Mark Johnston) *sn pushed along and outpcd: hdwy over 1f out: kpt on fnl f: nt pce to chal* **7/2**[2]
5 1/2 **Shadow Wing (IRE)** 2-8-11 0 RichardKingscote 3 44
(Tom Dascombe) *t.k.h early: pressed ldr: drvn over 1f out: wknd ins fnl f* **5/2**[1]
6 2 **Powerless (IRE)** 2-8-10 0 DavidAllan 7 36+
(Tim Easterby) *dwlt: hld up: pushed along over 2f out: no imp fr over 1f out* **18/1**
7 1 1/4 **Mr Enthusiastic** 2-8-10 0 BarryMcHugh 5 32
(Noel Wilson) *dwlt: hld up in tch: rdn and green wl over 1f out: sn btn* **33/1**
8 5 **Nobility (IRE)** 2-8-10 0 DuranFentiman 2 14
(Tim Easterby) *hld up on outside: rdn over 2f out: wknd over 1f out* **25/1**

1m 3.65s (3.65) **Going Correction** +0.60s/f (Yiel) **8** Ran SP% **115.9**
Speed ratings (Par 94): **94,88,84,80,79 76,74,66**
CSF £35.85 TOTE £12.00: £2.90, £1.50, £1.30; EX 37.20 Trifecta £245.50.
Owner The Harefield Racing Club **Bred** James And Joe Brannigan **Trained** Sigwells, Somerset

FOCUS
After a dry morning the official going remained good to soft. The opener was an ordinary novice auction stakes.

1642 DOWNLOAD THE FREE ATTHERACES APP H'CAP 2m
2:40 (2:40) (Class 2) (0-105,93) 4-Y-O+ **£22,641** (£6,737; £3,367; £1,683) **Stalls** Low

Form RPR
301 1 **Mirsaale**[17] 1253 6-9-8 **89** (p) PhillipMakin 6 100
(Keith Dalgleish) *pressed ldr: clr of rest over 5f out: led 4f out: rdn and clr over 1f out: kpt on wl fnl f: unchal* **8/1**[3]
500- 2 2 1/4 **My Reward**[189] 7295 4-9-5 **90** DavidAllan 7 97
(Tim Easterby) *t.k.h: hld up in midfield: pushed along over 3f out: hdwy to chse (clr) wnr over 1f out: edgd rt: kpt on: nt pce to chal* **18/1**
100- 3 3 1/4 **Gabrial's King (IRE)**[196] 7115 7-9-11 **92** GeorgeChaloner 5 95
(Richard Fahey) *hld up in tch: effrt and hdwy wl over 2f out: rdn and kpt on same pce fr over 1f out* **10/1**
060- 4 nk **Saved By The Bell (IRE)**[196] 7115 6-9-11 **92** DavidNolan 8 95
(David O'Meara) *hld up: pushed along over 3f out: hdwy over 1f out: no imp fnl f* **12/1**
40-2 5 1 **Gavlar**[21] 1209 5-9-7 **93** CallumShepherd(5) 4 95+
(William Knight) *dwlt: hld up in midfield on ins: effrt and swtchd to outside wl over 2f out: rdn and no imp fr over 1f out* **6/1**[1]
-364 6 2 1/4 **Communicator**[36] 983 8-9-2 **83** (p) DavidProbert 3 82
(Andrew Balding) *in tch: rdn over 2f out: hung rt and outpcd over 1f out* **11/1**
061- 7 nk **Grumeti**[55] 7115 8-9-7 **88** AdamBeschizza 10 86
(Alan King) *hld up: drvn over 3f out: hdwy over 1f out: no imp fnl f* **8/1**[3]
520- 8 1 1/2 **Saigon City**[266] 4887 6-9-7 **88** TomEaves 14 85
(Declan Carroll) *hld up: rdn over 4f out: sme hdwy over 1f out: nt pce to chal* **25/1**
20P- 9 nse **Gabrial's Star**[218] 6496 7-9-11 **92** (b) TonyHamilton 9 89
(Richard Fahey) *hld up: rdn over 3f out: no imp whn nt clr run over 1f out* **14/1**
300- 10 2 **Min Alemarat (IRE)**[301] 3649 5-9-11 **92** PJMcDonald 13 86
(Tim Easterby) *hld up: drvn along over 4f out: nvr on terms* **40/1**
-600 11 2 1/2 **Be Perfect (USA)**[7] 1493 7-9-9 **90** (p) JamesSullivan 2 81
(Ruth Carr) *led: clr w one other over 5f out: hdd 4f out: wknd over 1f out* **22/1**
20-1 12 1 1/4 **Stonecutter (IRE)**[36] 983 5-9-3 **84** OisinMurphy 12 74
(James Unett) *prom: rdn 4f out: wknd over 2f out* **10/1**
254- 13 18 **Rhythmical**[212] 6679 4-8-12 **83** RichardKingscote 11 51
(Mark Johnston) *in tch: lost pl over 3f out: sn struggling: eased whn no ch over 1f out* **15/2**[2]
426- P **Yorkidding**[197] 7090 4-8-13 **84** FrannyNorton 1
(Mark Johnston) *trckd ldrs: lost pl qckly over 4f out: p.u over 2f out* **6/1**[1]

3m 38.14s (6.34) **Going Correction** +0.60s/f (Yiel)
WFA 4 from 5yo+ 4lb **14** Ran SP% **119.3**
Speed ratings (Par 109): **108,106,105,105,104 103,103,102,102,101 100,99,90,**
CSF £139.38 CT £1461.68 TOTE £5.90: £1.60, £7.40, £4.40; EX 162.90 Trifecta £2087.40 Part won..
Owner Equus I **Bred** Mr & Mrs A E Pakenham **Trained** Carluke, S Lanarks

FOCUS
Not the strongest staying handicap for the grade, with the topweight 12lb below the ceiling, but it was competitive and they went an uneven pace. Race distance 12 yards further than advertised.

1643 RIPONBET PLACE6 LUCKY DIP H'CAP 1m
3:15 (3:15) (Class 3) (0-90,89) 4-Y-O+ **£10,997** (£3,272; £1,635; £817) **Stalls** Low

Form RPR
3-26 1 **Treasury Notes (IRE)**[20] 1221 4-9-0 **82** ow1 DavidNolan 9 92+
(David O'Meara) *hld up: stdy hdwy whn nt clr run over 2f out: effrt over 1f out: led and hrd pressed wl ins fnl f: jst hld on* **6/1**
11-0 2 shd **Swift Emperor (IRE)**[9] 1445 4-9-4 **86** PhillipMakin 10 95
(David Barron) *pressed ldr: drvn and sltly outpcd over 1f out: rallied and disp ld wl ins fnl f: kpt on: jst hld* **14/1**
6-00 3 1 1/2 **Father Bertie**[21] 1195 4-9-6 **88** (p) DavidAllan 6 94
(Tim Easterby) *led: rdn and qcknd 2 l clr over 1f out: hdd wl ins fnl f: sn no ex* **9/1**
6-1 4 3/4 **Bahama Moon (IRE)**[26] 1122 4-9-4 **86** FrannyNorton 2 90+
(David Barron) *t.k.h: hld up on ins: effrt whn nt clr run over 3f out to over 2f out: effrt and rdn over 1f out: kpt on same pce ins fnl f* **7/2**[1]
42/0 5 nk **Shouranour (IRE)**[12] 1380 6-9-0 **82** (p) RobertWinston 12 86
(Alan Brown) *hld up on outside: effrt and hdwy over 2f out: sn rdn: kpt on same pce ins fnl f* **40/1**
16-0 6 1/2 **Master Of Irony (IRE)**[21] 1195 4-9-3 **85** (v[1]) OisinMurphy 7 87
(Ralph Beckett) *s.i.s: hld up: hdwy over 3f out: rdn over 2f out: edgd rt: kpt on same pce ins fnl f* **9/2**[2]
06-0 7 4 **Auspicion**[52] 788 4-8-9 **77** JamesSullivan 3 70
(Tom Tate) *t.k.h: trckd ldrs: rdn over 2f out: n.m.r briefly over 1f out: sn wknd* **16/1**
30-1 8 4 **Imshivalla (IRE)**[12] 1380 5-9-0 **89** AdamMcNamara(7) 4 73
(Richard Fahey) *t.k.h early: in tch on outside: rdn wl over 2f out: wknd over 1f out* **11/2**[3]
00-3 9 1 **Our Boy Jack (IRE)**[17] 1251 7-8-7 **82** NatalieHambling(7) 1 64
(Richard Fahey) *t.k.h in midfield: drvn and outpcd 3f out: n.d after* **14/1**
-005 10 1/2 **Dubai Dynamo**[9] 1445 11-9-6 **88** PJMcDonald 11 69
(Ruth Carr) *hld up: rdn and outpcd over 3f out: nvr on terms* **16/1**
64-2 11 1 1/4 **Polar Forest**[9] 1445 6-9-0 **87** (e) RobJFitzpatrick(5) 8 65
(Richard Guest) *hld up in tch: rdn over 3f out: wknd over 2f out* **15/2**
66-0 12 3 **Woody Bay**[26] 1122 6-9-2 **84** TomEaves 5 55
(Mark Walford) *t.k.h: trckd ldrs: rdn over 3f out: wknd over 2f out* **40/1**

1m 45.54s (4.14) **Going Correction** +0.60s/f (Yiel) **12** Ran SP% **121.8**
Speed ratings (Par 107): **103,102,101,100,100 99,95,91,90,90 89,86**
CSF £89.70 CT £759.55 TOTE £7.10: £1.70, £3.90, £4.50; EX 113.30 Trifecta £871.90.
Owner T Proctor **Bred** Ammerland Verwaltung Gmbh & Co Kg **Trained** Upper Helmsley, N Yorks
■ Stewards' Enquiry : David Nolan two-day ban: use of whip (7 & 9 May)

FOCUS
Race distance 12 yards further than advertised. A useful, well-contested handicap.

1644 VISIT ATTHERACES.COM H'CAP 6f
3:50 (3:50) (Class 2) (0-105,105) 4-Y-O+ **£16,172** (£4,812; £2,405; £1,202) **Stalls** High

Form RPR
51-4 1 **Avon Breeze**[5] 1522 7-8-2 **86** PaulQuinn 8 95
(Richard Whitaker) *prom: effrt and plld out over 1f out: led ins fnl f: hld on wl u.p* **16/1**

614- 2 nk **George Dryden (IRE)**[224] 6312 4-9-2 **100** .... PJMcDonald 14 108+
(Ann Duffield) *hld up: nt clr run over 2f out: effrt and hdwy against stands' rail over 1f out: chsd wnr ins fnl f: kpt on wl: jst hld* **8/1**

310- 3 1 3/4 **Nameitwhatyoulike**[168] 7755 7-9-1 **99** .... TomEaves 9 101
(Bryan Smart) *pressed ldr: rdn and led over 1f out to ins fnl f: edgd rt and sn no ex* **7/1**[3]

050- 4 nk **Growl**[203] 6942 4-8-5 **89** .... BarryMcHugh 12 90
(Richard Fahey) *s.i.s: hld up: stdy hdwy over 1f out: pushed along and kpt on fnl f: nrst fin* **10/1**

660- 5 2 **Kimberella**[182] 7461 6-8-4 **88** .... FrannyNorton 2 83+
(David Nicholls) *swtchd to r alone far rail: gd spd tl rdn and no ex fnl f* **10/1**

60-0 6 1/2 **Adam's Ale**[20] 1218 7-8-4 **88** .... DuranFentiman 4 81
(Mark Walford) *trckd ldrs: rdn along over 2f out: outpcd fnl f* **16/1**

104- 7 hd **Tatlisu (IRE)**[196] 7122 6-8-11 **102** .... AdamMcNamara[(7)] 6 94
(Richard Fahey) *in tch on outside: rdn over 2f out: no ex fr over 1f out* **6/1**[2]

0010 8 1 **Alben Star (IRE)**[21] 1197 8-9-7 **105** .... DavidNolan 1 94
(Richard Fahey) *hld up on outside of stands' side gp: pushed along over 2f out: no imp fr over 1f out* **12/1**

600- 9 3/4 **Eccleston**[196] 7122 5-8-10 **94** ....(v) TonyHamilton 13 81
(Richard Fahey) *dwlt and hmpd s: bhd: pushed along over 2f out: nvr rchd ldrs* **4/1**[1]

0400 10 3/4 **Green Door (IRE)**[65] 626 5-9-2 **100** .... OisinMurphy 3 84
(Robert Cowell) *led tl rdn and hdd over 1f out: wknd ins fnl f* **22/1**

000- 11 1/2 **Gran Canaria Queen**[183] 7424 7-8-4 **88** .... JamesSullivan 11 71
(Tim Easterby) *midfield against stands' rail: rdn whn nt clr run over 1f out: sn wknd* **33/1**

240- 12 16 **Pipers Note**[196] 7122 6-9-2 **100** .... GeorgeChaloner 10 32
(Richard Whitaker) *dwlt: sn midfield: rdn over 2f out: wknd over 1f out: eased whn no ch fnl f* **9/1**

430- 13 4 1/2 **Handsome Dude**[230] 6135 4-8-1 **90** .... NoelGarbutt[(5)] 5 7
(David Barron) *midfield: struggling 1/2-way: sn lost tch* **12/1**

1m 15.05s (2.05) **Going Correction** +0.60s/f (Yiel) **13** Ran SP% **120.5**
Speed ratings (Par 109): **110,109,107,106,104 103,103,101,100,99 99,77,71**
CSF £139.89 CT £1028.37 TOTE £21.00: £6.60, £2.70, £1.50; EX 223.70 Trifecta £2488.10 Part won..
Owner Grange Park Racing II & Partner **Bred** Hellwood Stud Farm **Trained** Scarcroft, W Yorks
■ Stewards' Enquiry : Tom Eaves £290 fine: required to attend a course but left the course within 5 mins of weighed-in

FOCUS
An ultra-competitive sprint and smart form.

1645 RIPONBET OUR PROFITS STAY IN RACING H'CAP 1m 4f 10y
4:25 (4:26) (Class 2) (0-110,102) 4-Y-O+ **£16,172** (£4,812; £2,405; £1,202) **Stalls** Low

Form RPR

01-2 1 **Noble Gift**[28] 1088 6-8-12 **98** .... CallumShepherd[(5)] 6 102+
(William Knight) *mde all: drvn and pricked ears fr 2f out: hld on wl towards fin* **7/4**[1]

04-0 2 nk **Lycidas (GER)**[29] 1081 7-9-1 **96** .... StevieDonohoe 3 98
(James Ewart) *prom: drvn and outpcd over 2f out: rallied fnl f: squeezed through and chsd wnr last 75yds: kpt on* **20/1**

-536 3 3/4 **Pearl Castle (IRE)**[29] 1067 6-9-1 **96** .... JoeyHaynes 2 97
(K R Burke) *trckd ldrs: effrt and rdn 3f out: edgd rt over 1f out: kpt on ins fnl f* **5/1**

16-2 4 3/4 **Chancery (USA)**[20] 1219 8-9-7 **102** .... DavidNolan 4 102
(David O'Meara) *hld up in last pl: hdwy on outside 3f out: rdn and edgd rt over 1f out: kpt on same pce ins fnl f* **5/2**[2]

-310 5 3/4 **Notarised**[29] 1067 5-9-7 **102** .... FrannyNorton 5 102
(Mark Johnston) *pressed ldr: drvn over 3f out: rallied: one pce whn hmpd and lost two pls last 75yds* **7/2**[3]

2m 42.91s (6.21) **Going Correction** +0.60s/f (Yiel) **5** Ran SP% **108.6**
Speed ratings (Par 109): **103,102,102,101,101**
CSF £29.29 TOTE £1.90: £1.30, £4.10; EX 23.40 Trifecta £83.60.
Owner Canisbay Bloodstock **Bred** Theakston Stud **Trained** Patching, W Sussex

FOCUS
Race distance 12 yards further than advertised. A smart handicap and a game winner, but they finished in a heap.

1646 LADIES DAY 16TH JUNE MAIDEN STKS (PLUS 10 RACE) 1m 1f 170y
4:55 (4:56) (Class 4) 3-Y-O **£5,175** (£1,540; £769; £384) **Stalls** Low

Form RPR

2- 1 **Victory Bond**[183] 7435 3-9-5 0 .... OisinMurphy 2 95+
(William Haggas) *mde all: shkn up and qcknd clr wl over 1f out: promising* **2/5**[1]

46-2 2 7 **Under Attack (IRE)**[16] 1287 3-9-5 80 .... StevieDonohoe 1 83+
(Sir Michael Stoute) *chsd wnr: effrt over 2f out: outpcd wl over 1f out: eased whn hld ins fnl f* **10/3**[2]

55- 3 10 **On Fire**[196] 7123 3-9-5 0 .... PJMcDonald 6 61
(James Bethell) *hld up: hdwy over 3f out: pushed along and outpcd fr 2f out* **20/1**

4 1 3/4 **Zorlu (IRE)** 3-9-5 0 ....(b[1]) SteveDrowne 4 57
(Hugo Palmer) *trckd ldrs: rdn over 3f out: wknd fr 2f out* **12/1**[3]

5 20 **Rich Pursuit** 3-9-5 0 .... JoeyHaynes 5 16
(James Bethell) *s.i.s: hld up: effrt on outside over 3f out: wknd over 2f out* **33/1**

0-44 6 1/2 **Young Christian**[89] 331 3-9-5 72 .... JamesSullivan 3 15
(Tom Tate) *trckd ldrs: rdn over 3f out: wknd over 2f out* **25/1**

2m 10.73s (5.33) **Going Correction** +0.60s/f (Yiel) **6** Ran SP% **113.7**
Speed ratings (Par 100): **102,96,88,87,71 70**
CSF £2.00 TOTE £1.40: £1.10, £2.30; EX 2.60 Trifecta £12.50.
Owner Bloomsbury Stud **Bred** Bloomsbury Stud **Trained** Newmarket, Suffolk

FOCUS
Race distance 12 yards further than advertised. An uncompetitive maiden and the short-priced favourite made no mistake.

1647 TRADITIONAL FAMILY FUNDAY SUNDAY 15TH MAY H'CAP 5f
5:30 (5:32) (Class 4) (0-85,82) 3-Y-O **£7,762** (£2,310; £1,154; £577) **Stalls** High

Form RPR

431- 1 **Gwendolyn (GER)**[133] 8204 3-9-0 **75** .... OisinMurphy 1 85+
(Robert Cowell) *hld up on outside: hdwy to ld wl over 1f out: rdn and sn edgd lft: kpt on wl fnl f* **10/3**[1]

16- 2 1 1/2 **Flowing Clarets**[161] 7859 3-9-0 **75** .... DavidNolan 8 78+
(Richard Fahey) *walked to s: s.i.s: bhd and outpcd: gd hdwy on outside over 1f out: chsd wnr ins fnl f: kpt on* **7/2**[2]

2021 3 3 1/4 **Sir Dudley (IRE)**[22] 1176 3-9-5 **80** ....(b) PJMcDonald 2 71
(James Given) *w ldrs: rdn over 2f out: kpt on same pce fnl f* **6/1**

0U0- 4 1 1/2 **New Road Side**[211] 6703 3-9-6 **81** .... BarryMcHugh 3 67
(Tony Coyle) *prom: rdn over 2f out: outpcd whn n.m.r briefly ins fnl f* **16/1**

144- 5 3/4 **Misu Moneypenny**[156] 7896 3-8-8 **69** .... IanBrennan 5 52
(Scott Dixon) *in tch: rdn and outpcd whn n.m.r briefly appr 2f out: sn no imp* **16/1**

500- 6 shd **Crombay (IRE)**[203] 6931 3-8-11 **72** .... DavidAllan 7 55
(Tim Easterby) *mde most tl rdn and hdd wl over 1f out: sn wknd* **6/1**

421- 7 5 **Early Bird (IRE)**[200] 7003 3-8-13 **74** .... JamesSullivan 6 39
(Richard Fahey) *t.k.h: prom: rdn and outpcd over 1f out: sn btn* **4/1**[3]

-256 8 9 **Furiant**[12] 1385 3-9-7 **82** .... FrannyNorton 4 14
(Mark Johnston) *w ldrs to 1/2-way: sn lost pl: btn over 1f out* **10/1**

1m 2.2s (2.20) **Going Correction** +0.60s/f (Yiel) **8** Ran SP% **114.7**
Speed ratings (Par 100): **106,103,98,96,94 94,86,72**
CSF £15.32 CT £66.26 TOTE £5.50: £1.20, £1.80, £2.10; EX 18.10 Trifecta £94.90.
Owner Sheikh Khalifa, Sheikh Suhaim, QRL **Bred** Graf U Grafin V Stauffenberg **Trained** Six Mile Bottom, Cambs

FOCUS
A decent, open-looking sprint for 3yos and a progressive winner.
T/Plt: £504.70 to a £1 stake. Pool of £66272.29 - 95.84 winning tickets. T/Qpdt: £30.10 to a £1 stake. Pool of £4878.32 - 119.92 winning tickets. **Richard Young**

1550 WOLVERHAMPTON (A.W) (L-H)
Saturday, April 23

OFFICIAL GOING: Tapeta: standard
Wind: fine Weather: virtually nil

1648 WOLVERHAMPTON HOLIDAY INN APPRENTICE H'CAP 5f 216y (Tp)
6:20 (6:22) (Class 5) (0-75,75) 4-Y-O+ **£3,234** (£962; £481; £240) **Stalls** Low

Form RPR

1520 1 **Mr Christopher (IRE)**[7] 1496 4-8-11 **68** ....(p) AnnaHesketh[(3)] 5 78
(Tom Dascombe) *midfield on inner: nudged along and hdwy 2f out: swtchd rt off rail appr fnl f: led jst ins fnl f: rdn and kpt on wl* **5/1**[3]

-551 2 2 **Picket Line**[10] 1419 4-9-6 **74** .... JosephineGordon 1 77
(Geoffrey Deacon) *chsd ldng pair: rdn over 2f out: ev ch over 1f out: one pce fnl f* **11/4**[2]

4036 3 shd **Ancient Cross**[7] 1496 12-8-5 **62** ....(bt) NathanEvans[(3)] 6 65
(Michael Easterby) *chsd ldng pair: rdn over 2f out: kpt on same pce* **7/1**

330- 4 1 **Surety (IRE)**[260] 5091 5-9-7 **75** .... EdwardGreatrex 3 75+
(James Tate) *slowly away: hld up in rr: rdn and hdwy on outside 2f out: kpt on same pce* **5/2**[1]

326- 5 1/2 **Rafaaf (IRE)**[265] 4910 8-8-4 **61** oh4 .... MeganNicholls[(3)] 4 59
(Richard Phillips) *hld up: rdn over 2f out: kpt on ins fnl f: nvr threatened ldrs* **40/1**

0124 6 1 1/4 **City Of Angkor Wat (IRE)**[14] 1341 6-9-4 **72** ....(p) PaddyPilley 8 66
(Conor Dore) *prom: rdn over 2f out: wknd ins fnl f* **13/2**

520- 7 shd **Tavener**[206] 6863 4-9-0 **71** .... JoshDoyle[(3)] 9 65
(David O'Meara) *s.i.s: hld up: rdn 2f out: nvr threatened* **14/1**

662- 8 2 1/2 **Toni's A Star**[192] 7224 4-8-7 **64** .... GeorgiaCox[(3)] 2 50
(Tony Carroll) *led: rdn 2f out: hdd jst ins fnl f: wknd* **28/1**

025- 9 1 1/2 **Essaka (IRE)**[165] 7789 4-8-3 **62** .... MitchGodwin[(5)] 7 43
(Tony Carroll) *chsd ldng pair towards outer: rdn over 2f out: wknd over 1f out* **66/1**

1m 13.39s (-1.11) **Going Correction** -0.15s/f (Stan) **9** Ran SP% **111.8**
Speed ratings (Par 103): **101,98,98,96,96 94,94,91,89**
CSF £18.21 CT £93.73 TOTE £5.80: £1.70, £1.40, £2.70; EX 20.80 Trifecta £89.30.
Owner Mrs M C Antrobus **Bred** Denis McDonnell **Trained** Malpas, Cheshire

FOCUS
A fair sprint which was soundly run, the winner steadily progressive on AW since joining this yard.

1649 AWARD WINNING FINE DINING AT HORIZONS H'CAP 1m 5f 194y (Tp)
6:50 (6:51) (Class 6) (0-65,61) 4-Y-O+ **£2,587** (£770; £384; £192) **Stalls** Low

Form RPR

253/ 1 **Minstrels Gallery (IRE)**[26] 2046 7-9-10 **61** .... JimCrowley 1 72+
(Lucy Wadham) *mde all: pushed clr 2f out: rdn and kpt on fnl f: easily* **11/8**[1]

2000 2 4 1/2 **Medieval Bishop (IRE)**[23] 1170 7-9-4 **58** ....(p) RobHornby[(3)] 2 62
(Tony Forbes) *trckd ldr: rdn 3f out: plugged on but no ch w wnr fnl 2f* **25/1**

16-5 3 1 1/4 **El Massivo (IRE)**[22] 941 6-9-8 **59** .... DaleSwift 6 61
(Harriet Bethell) *slowly away: sn midfield: rdn over 3f out: plugged on* **8/1**[3]

3040 4 1/2 **Cantankerous**[15] 1322 5-8-9 **46** ....(be[1]) JackMitchell 8 47
(Daniel Mark Loughnane) *slowly away: hld up: pushed along and hdwy over 2f out: rdn over 1f out: one pce fnl f* **12/1**

3233 5 5 **Robben**[22] 1182 4-9-6 **59** ....(v) PaulHanagan 3 53
(John Mackie) *hld up in rr: rdn over 3f out: nvr threatened* **2/1**[2]

214- 6 6 **Lacey**[159] 7871 7-9-10 **61** ....(b) AdamKirby 7 47
(Sarah Hollinshead) *in tch: rdn to briefly chse ldr over 3f out: wknd over 1f out* **17/2**

000- 7 5 **Blythe Star (IRE)**[165] 7782 4-7-13 **45** .... MitchGodwin[(7)] 4 24
(Christopher Kellett) *midfield: pushed along over 5f out: wknd over 2f out* **22/1**

3m 4.77s (-0.03) **Going Correction** -0.15s/f (Stan)
WFA 4 from 5yo+ 2lb **7** Ran SP% **113.0**
Speed ratings (Par 101): **94,91,90,90,87 84,81**
CSF £36.01 CT £206.68 TOTE £2.20: £1.80, £5.30; EX 29.10 Trifecta £89.40.
Owner G Pascoe & S Brewer **Bred** Morecool Stud **Trained** Newmarket, Suffolk

FOCUS
A very one-sided handicap. The winner was well treated on his hurdles form this winter and never looked in any danger having been allowed to control things from the front. This was feasible on the winner's hurdles form.

1650 COMBINE BUSINESS WITH RACING AT WOLVERHAMPTON H'CAP 5f 20y (Tp)
7:20 (7:21) (Class 3) (0-90,90) 3-Y-O **£7,246** (£2,168; £1,084; £542; £270) **Stalls** Low

Form RPR

060- 1 **Encore D'Or**[273] 4653 4-9-12 **89** .... MartinHarley 7 104+
(Robert Cowell) *trckd ldng pair: rdn to chal over 1f out: led 110yds out: drvn and kpt on* **7/4**[1]

62-1 2 3/4 **Bowson Fred**[15] 1321 4-9-2 **84** .... NathanEvans[(5)] 11 96
(Michael Easterby) *led narrowly: rdn over 1f out: hdd 110yds out: kpt on* **7/2**[2]

2-46 **3** 2½ **Mappin Time (IRE)**[42] 923 8-9-13 **90**......(be) AndrewMullen 4 93
(Tim Easterby) *hld up in midfield: rdn 3f out: r.o fr appr fnl f: wnt 3rd post* **8/1**[3]
5212 **4** nse **Miracle Garden**[15] 1321 4-9-2 **79**......(p) AdamKirby 10 82
(Roy Brotherton) *midfield: rdn 2f out: kpt on* **10/1**
006- **5** ½ **Snap Shots (IRE)**[203] 6942 4-9-6 **88**......(t) AnnaHesketh(5) 8 89
(Tom Dascombe) *s.i.s: hld up: rdn 1/2-way: kpt on fnl f* **12/1**
3154 **6** ¾ **Jebediah Shine**[37] 966 4-9-6 **88**...... JoshDoyle(5) 6 86
(David O'Meara) *pressed ldr: rdn over 2f out: wknd ins fnl f* **18/1**
4050 **7** nk **Dynamo Walt (IRE)**[37] 966 5-9-9 **86**......(v) AdamBeschizza 1 83
(Derek Shaw) *midfield: rdn 3f out: one pce and nvr threatened* **22/1**
0160 **8** ¾ **Oriental Relation (IRE)**[9] 1447 5-9-2 **84**......(v) PhilDennis(5) 3 79
(James Given) *in tch: rdn 1/2-way: wknd over 1f out* **18/1**
53-6 **9** 2½ **Stocking**[106] 106 4-9-7 **84**...... JackMitchell 5 70
(Roger Varian) *hld up: rdn 1/2-way: nvr threatened* **10/1**
1130 **10** 7 **Fleckerl (IRE)**[14] 1335 6-9-13 **90**......(p) JimCrowley 2 50
(Conor Dore) *v.s.a: a bhd* **16/1**
59.96s (-1.94) **Going Correction** -0.15s/f (Stan) **10** Ran SP% **116.3**
Speed ratings (Par 107): **109,107,103,103,102 101,101,100,96,84**
CSF £7.46 CT £38.80 TOTE £3.10: £1.50, £1.70, £3.00; EX 12.10 Trifecta £85.90.
Owner Newsells Park Stud **Bred** Newsells Park Stud **Trained** Six Mile Bottom, Cambs
FOCUS
A useful contest, the promising winner showing why he was heavily backed on his first start for Robert Cowell. The pace was sound, few ever threatening a serious blow.

1651 LADIES EVENING ON FRIDAY 19TH AUGUST MAIDEN STKS 1m 4f 50y (Tp)
7:50 (7:50) (Class 5) 3-Y-O+ **£3,234** (£962; £481; £240) **Stalls** Low

Form RPR
3 **1** **Wings of Desire**[10] 1426 3-8-7 0...... RobertHavlin 6 79+
(John Gosden) *midfield: pushed along and hdwy over 2f out: rdn to ld 1f out: styd on wl to go clr* **8/15**[1]
5 **2** 4½ **Mahfooz (IRE)**[21] 1200 3-8-7 0...... PaulHanagan 4 72+
(Charles Hills) *led: rdn 2f out: edgd rt and hdd 1f out: no ex* **6/1**[3]
3 ½ **Pumblechook** 3-8-7 0...... MartinLane 1 71+
(Lucy Wadham) *hld up: rdn over 2f out: styd on fr over 1f out: wnt 3rd ins fnl f* **20/1**
0- **4** 7 **Blenheim Warrior**[266] 4849 4-9-12 0...... ShaneKelly 3 62
(Richard Hughes) *dwlt: hld up: pushed along over 2f out: sme late hdwy: nvr threatened* **50/1**
0-0 **5** nk **Street Outlaw (IRE)**[27] 1113 3-8-7 0...... LukeMorris 2 60
(Daniel Mark Loughnane) *in tch: rdn 3f out: wknd over 1f out* **200/1**
-432 **6** shd **Air Of Astana (IRE)**[23] 1161 4-9-12 81...... MartinHarley 7 61
(Hugo Palmer) *trckd ldr: rdn over 2f out: wknd fnl f* **7/2**[2]
02- **7** 27 **The Coffee Hunter (FR)**[51] 1373 4-9-12 0......(t) AdamKirby 5 18
(Nick Williams) *in tch on outer: rdn over 3f out: sn wknd and bhd* **28/1**
2m 36.89s (-3.91) **Going Correction** -0.15s/f (Stan)
WFA 3 from 4yo 20lb **7** Ran SP% **112.4**
Speed ratings (Par 103): **107,104,103,99,98 98,80**
CSF £4.06 TOTE £1.60: £1.20, £2.00; EX 3.50 Trifecta £14.60.
Owner Lady Bamford **Bred** Lady Bamford **Trained** Newmarket, Suffolk
FOCUS
Not a maiden with a great deal of depth but the winner could be anything. The third also made an encouraging debut.

1652 BUSINESS VENUE 365 DAYS A YEAR H'CAP 1m 1f 103y (Tp)
8:20 (8:22) (Class 5) (0-75,75) 4-Y-O+ **£3,234** (£962; £481; £240) **Stalls** Low

Form RPR
2342 **1** **Off The Pulse**[50] 823 6-9-7 **75**......(p) JoeFanning 8 83
(John Mackie) *racd keenly: hld up: rdn and hdwy 2f out: styd on wl: led towards fin* **5/1**[3]
-131 **2** 1 **Moonday Sun (USA)**[27] 1114 7-9-7 **75**......(p) AdamKirby 1 81
(John Butler) *led: rdn and strly pressed 2f out: kpt on: hdd towards fin* **9/2**[2]
04-1 **3** ¾ **Qaffaal (USA)**[7] 1502 5-9-0 **68**...... GrahamGibbons 7 72
(Michael Easterby) *trckd ldr: rdn to chal strly 2f out: no ex towards fin* **6/5**[1]
4-02 **4** 2 **Qasser (IRE)**[18] 708 7-9-4 **72**...... LukeMorris 2 72
(Harry Whittington) *trckd ldr: rdn over 2f out: no ex fnl 110yds* **9/1**
26-3 **5** 3¾ **Niblawi (IRE)**[12] 1390 4-9-6 **74**...... TomQueally 3 66
(Ismail Mohammed) *s.i.s: hld up in rr: rdn over 3f out: minor late hdwy: nvr threatened* **8/1**
1-20 **6** 3½ **My Mo (FR)**[35] 1002 4-9-3 **71**......(p[1]) MartinLane 5 56
(David Dennis) *midfield: rdn 3f out: wknd over 1f out* **20/1**
-000 **7** 12 **Mr Frankie**[7] 1501 5-8-10 **67**...... JoeDoyle(3) 9 27
(Richard Phillips) *midfield on outer: rdn over 3f out: sn wknd* **66/1**
-001 **8** 3¼ **Shamlan (IRE)**[22] 1186 4-9-3 **71**......(p) StevieDonohoe 6 24
(Kevin Frost) *in tch: rdn over 3f out: wknd over 2f out* **14/1**
1m 59.79s (-1.01) **Going Correction** -0.15s/f (Stan) **8** Ran SP% **114.3**
Speed ratings (Par 103): **98,97,96,94,91 88,77,74**
CSF £27.69 CT £43.11 TOTE £6.50: £2.40, £2.50, £1.02; EX 29.80 Trifecta £56.10.
Owner G B Maher **Bred** Mrs V E Hughes **Trained** Church Broughton , Derbys
FOCUS
This appeals as pretty solid form for the level. The leaders started racing a fair way out, setting it up for the closing winner.

1653 LIKE WOLVERHAMPTON RACECOURSE ON FACEBOOK MAIDEN STKS 1m 141y (Tp)
8:50 (8:51) (Class 5) 3-Y-O+ **£3,234** (£962; £481; £240) **Stalls** Low

Form RPR
42- **1** **Muzdawaj**[190] 7251 3-8-13 0...... PaulHanagan 9 86+
(William Haggas) *in tch: pushed along over 2f out: hdwy over 1f out: rdn ins fnl f: kpt on wl: led towards fin* **5/2**[2]
0- **2** ½ **Divisionist**[253] 5333 3-8-13 0...... GrahamGibbons 13 85
(Sir Michael Stoute) *trckd ldr: rdn to chal over 1f out: led narrowly jst ins fnl f: kpt on but hdd towards fin* **16/1**
32- **3** ¾ **Sacred Trust**[129] 8251 3-8-13 0...... MartinHarley 7 83
(Hugo Palmer) *led: rdn and pressed over 1f out: hdd jst ins fnl f: one pce* **3/1**[3]
4 **4** 1½ **Heart Of Lions (USA)**[10] 1421 3-8-13 0...... WilliamBuick 5 80
(John Gosden) *trckd ldr: rdn over 2f out: kpt on same pce* **11/10**[1]
5 6 **Hayward Field (IRE)** 3-8-13 0...... JackMitchell 11 66+
(Roger Varian) *hld up in midfield: pushed along and sme hdwy 3f out: kpt on fr over 1f out: nvr threatened ldrs* **25/1**
5- **6** 2 **Sixties Groove (IRE)**[164] 7793 3-8-13 0...... JimCrowley 1 61+
(Jeremy Noseda) *hld up: pushed along and sme hdwy 3f out: kpt on fr over 1f out* **16/1**
55 **7** 5 **Motivate**[23] 1160 3-8-13 0...... LukeMorris 6 50
(Sir Mark Prescott Bt) *in tch: rdn 3f out: grad wknd* **80/1**
6 **8** 8 **Whacking Bullock (IRE)**[35] 1000 3-8-10 0...... JacobButterfield(3) 4 31
(Daniel Mark Loughnane) *slowly away: hld up: nvr threatened* **100/1**
000 **9** 1 **Katalan (GER)**[19] 1235 3-8-13 0...... TomQueally 2 29
(John Butler) *midfield: rdn over 3f out: sn wknd* **100/1**
0/0 **10** 11 **Dutch Barney**[47] 863 6-9-7 0...... BeckyBrisbourne(7) 3 7
(Mark Brisbourne) *a towards rr* **150/1**
6 **11** 4½ **Broadsword (IRE)**[22] 1184 4-9-9 0...... StevieDonohoe 12
(Kevin Frost) *midfield: pushed along over 5f out: sn struggling* **100/1**
12 12 **Mondrian Jones** 3-8-10 0...... MichaelJMMurphy(3) 8
(Charles Hills) *slowly away: a in rr* **40/1**
1m 47.93s (-2.17) **Going Correction** -0.15s/f (Stan)
WFA 3 from 4yo+ 15lb **12** Ran SP% **124.1**
Speed ratings (Par 103): **103,102,101,100,95 93,89,81,81,71 67,56**
CSF £42.80 TOTE £3.60: £1.40, £4.40, £1.10; EX 39.20 Trifecta £133.60.
Owner Hamdan Al Maktoum **Bred** Shadwell Estate Company Limited **Trained** Newmarket, Suffolk
FOCUS
A good maiden for the course, the winner potentially very useful and the next three home all look capable of winning a similar event. The pace was sound, the field well strung out.

1654 #FOLLOWUS ON TWITTER @WOLVESRACES H'CAP 1m 141y (Tp)
9:20 (9:21) (Class 6) (0-60,60) 4-Y-O+ **£2,587** (£770; £384; £192) **Stalls** Low

Form RPR
334- **1** **Diamond Runner (IRE)**[180] 7508 4-8-3 **49** ow1..(p) BenSanderson(7) 12 57
(Deborah Sanderson) *midfield: smooth hdwy 2f out: rdn over 1f out: led 110yds out: kpt on wl* **33/1**
1-06 **2** 1¾ **Atreus**[15] 1323 4-9-5 **58**......(p) GrahamGibbons 7 62
(Michael Easterby) *racd keenly: trckd ldrs: rdn 2f out: led 1f out: sn hung lft: hdd 110yds out: one pce* **10/3**[2]
0323 **3** 1¼ **Les Gar Gan (IRE)**[15] 1323 5-9-6 **59**......(be) StevieDonohoe 5 61
(Daniel Mark Loughnane) *s.i.s: hld up in rr: rdn over 2f out: r.o towards outside fr over 1f out: nrst fin* **9/2**[3]
0060 **4** ¾ **Outlaw Torn (IRE)**[21] 1202 7-9-7 **60**......(e) JasonHart 6 62
(Richard Guest) *prom: rdn over 2f out: keeping on in cl 3rd whn hmpd ins fnl f: nt rcvr* **9/1**
0500 **5** 1 **Illusive Force (IRE)**[10] 1416 4-9-4 **57**......(p) AdamBeschizza 2 55
(Derek Shaw) *midfield: rdn over 2f out: kpt on same pce* **28/1**
-045 **6** nk **John Potts**[52] 787 11-8-7 **46** oh1......(p) LukeMorris 8 43
(Brian Baugh) *midfield: rdn over 2f out: kpt on same pce* **16/1**
3236 **7** 1 **Roger Thorpe**[39] 936 7-9-3 **59**...... JackDuern(3) 4 54
(Deborah Sanderson) *led: 4 l clr over 3f out: rdn and reduced advantage over 1f out: hdd 1f out: wknd* **12/1**
4505 **8** nk **Arsenale (GER)**[30] 1058 5-8-7 **46** oh1......(p) AndrewMullen 10 41
(Michael Appleby) *hld up: rdn over 3f out: minor late hdwy: nvr threatened* **20/1**
4033 **9** 3¼ **Togetherwecan (IRE)**[17] 1263 4-9-0 **53**...... JoeFanning 11 41
(Mark Johnston) *midfield: rdn over 2f out: sn no imp* **12/1**
2-06 **10** ½ **Frantical**[14] 1347 4-9-1 **57**...... GeorgeDowning(3) 9 44
(Tony Carroll) *hld up: rdn over 3f out: sn struggling* **11/1**
00/0 **11** 1 **Catharina**[10] 1415 4-8-6 **50**...... CharlesEddery(5) 3 35
(Dean Ivory) *dwlt: hld up: nvr threatened* **66/1**
4212 **12** hd **Toymaker**[15] 1323 9-9-2 **60**......(t) PhilDennis(5) 1 44
(Phil McEntee) *trckd ldrs: rdn over 2f out: wknd over 1f out* **3/1**[1]
1m 47.85s (-2.25) **Going Correction** -0.15s/f (Stan) **12** Ran SP% **118.5**
Speed ratings (Par 101): **104,102,101,100,99 99,98,98,95,95 94,93**
CSF £137.30 CT £625.50 TOTE £33.90: £8.00, £1.90, £2.30; EX 223.40 Trifecta £2821.00 Part won..
Owner Bawtry Racing Club **Bred** Edmond Kent **Trained** Sturton-le-Steeple, Notts
FOCUS
A modest contest which was soundly run. Straightforward form.
T/Plt: £14.60 to a £1 stake. Pool of £75180.68 - 3740.87 winning tickets. T/Qpdt: £3.90 to a £1 stake. Pool of £6719.76 - 1272.45 winning tickets. **Andrew Sheret**

1655 - 1661a (Foreign Racing) - See Raceform Interactive

MUSSELBURGH (R-H)
Sunday, April 24

OFFICIAL GOING: Good to firm (good in places; 8.0)
Wind: Light, behind Weather: Fine, dry

1662 TOTEPLACEPOT MAIDEN STKS 1m 2y
2:00 (2:01) (Class 5) 3-Y-O+ **£3,234** (£962; £481; £240) **Stalls** Low

Form RPR
6- **1** **Huntlaw**[199] 7056 3-9-0 0...... JoeFanning 3 79
(Mark Johnston) *led: rdn and hdd over 2f out: rdn and rallied fnl f: regained ld nr fin* **6/1**
0-2 **2** nk **Amazement (GER)**[97] 245 3-9-0 0...... KierenFallon 6 78
(James Tate) *chsd ldr: shkn up to ld over 2f out: kpt on fnl f: hdd nr fin* **11/4**[3]
/23- **3** 4 **Tawdeea**[254] 5356 4-9-9 87...... JoshDoyle(5) 7 73
(David O'Meara) *hld up in tch: effrt on outside over 2f out: chsd clr ldng pair over 1f out: kpt on fnl f: nvr able to chal* **5/2**[2]
4- **4** 4½ **Sayedaati Saadati (IRE)**[248] 5551 3-9-0 0...... JamieSpencer 1 59
(Kevin Ryan) *chsd ldrs: effrt and drvn along 3f out: wknd over 1f out* **2/1**[1]
5 6 **Jethro (IRE)**[37] 5-9-9 0...... CallumShepherd(5) 5 49
(Brian Ellison) *unruly bef s: bhd: drvn and outpcd over 3f out: n.d after* **22/1**
6 2¼ **Miss Macchiato (IRE)** 3-8-3 0 ow1...... RowanScott(7) 4 36
(Ann Duffield) *t.k.h early: dwlt: hld up in tch: rdn over 3f out: sn struggling* **25/1**
1m 40.61s (-0.59) **Going Correction** -0.125s/f (Firm)
WFA 3 from 4yo+ 14lb **6** Ran SP% **111.1**
Speed ratings (Par 103): **97,96,92,88,82 79**
CSF £22.25 TOTE £7.40: £2.70, £1.90; EX 23.80 Trifecta £73.70.
Owner Duke Of Roxburghe **Bred** Floors Farming **Trained** Middleham Moor, N Yorks
FOCUS
All distances as advertised. The official going was good to firm, good in places. The opener was an interesting little maiden and there was a dramatic finish.

1663 TOTEJACKPOT H'CAP 7f 33y
2:30 (2:30) (Class 5) (0-75,73) 4-Y-O+ **£3,234** (£962; £481; £240) **Stalls** Low

Form RPR
3252 **1** **Surewecan**[5] 1555 4-8-13 **65**...... JoeFanning 5 72
(Mark Johnston) *early ldr: trckd ldr: shkn up to ld over 2f out: rdn and hld on wl ins fnl f* **85/40**[1]

000- **2** 1/2 **Gold Flash**^{256} 5272 4-9-7 **73**..(p) PhillipMakin 4 78
(Keith Dalgleish) *trckd ldng pair: effrt and pushed along over 2f out: chsd wnr wl ins fnl f: kpt on* **7/1**

241- **3** nse **Opt Out**^{194} 7190 6-8-11 **63**..(p) ConnorBeasley 6 68
(Alistair Whillans) *hld up: rdn and hdwy over 1f out: kpt on ins fnl f* **13/2**

0-33 **4** 2 **Maureb (IRE)**^{15} 1334 4-9-5 **71**..(v^{1}) BarryMcHugh 1 71
(Tony Coyle) *sn led: rdn and hdd over 2f out: rallied: no ex and lost two pls wl ins fnl f* **11/2**^{2}

250- **5** 3/4 **Royal Duchess**^{208} 6831 6-9-2 **71**.............................. SammyJoBell$^{(3)}$ 3 69
(Lucy Normile) *hld up: effrt on outside over 2f out: kpt on ins fnl f: nt pce to chal* **9/1**

242- **6** 1 1/4 **Salvatore Fury (IRE)**^{201} 7017 6-9-6 **72**..........................(p) JasonHart 7 66
(Keith Dalgleish) *stdd s: t.k.h in rr: pushed along and hdwy over 1f out: no imp fnl f* **11/1**

423- **7** 1 **Star Of Spring (IRE)**^{189} 7314 4-9-3 **69**.......................... AndrewMullen 9 61
(Iain Jardine) *hld up: pushed along on outside over 2f out: sn no imp* **6/1**^{3}

420- **8** 1/2 **Dark Crystal**^{216} 6585 5-9-1 **67**.............................. JackGarritty 8 57
(Linda Perratt) *in tch: rdn over 2f out: wknd over 1f out* **16/1**

553- **9** 6 **Takahiro**^{361} 1803 4-8-2 **57** ow3.............................. JoeDoyle$^{(3)}$ 2 31
(Linda Perratt) *prom: drvn and outpcd over 2f out: wknd wl over 1f out* **40/1**

1m 27.25s (-1.75) **Going Correction** -0.125s/f (Firm) **9** Ran SP% **114.2**
Speed ratings (Par 103): **105,104,104,102,101 99,98,98,91**
CSF £17.13 CT £82.32 TOTE £2.50: £1.10, £2.60, £2.10; EX 20.40 Trifecta £120.10.
Owner Douglas Livingston **Bred** Christopher & Annabelle Mason **Trained** Middleham Moor, N Yorks

FOCUS
A fair handicap and they went an even pace.

1664 TOTEQUADPOT H'CAP 1m 208y
3:00 (3:01) (Class 4) (0-80,80) 4-Y-O+ **£5,175** (£1,540; £769; £384) **Stalls** Low

Form RPR

341- **1** **Bright Flash**^{199} 7058 4-9-6 **79**.............................. SeanLevey 9 91+
(David Brown) *pressed ldr: led over 1f out: rdn clr fnl f* **9/2**^{2}

210- **2** 2 1/4 **Hidden Rebel**^{210} 6785 4-9-7 **80**.............................. ConnorBeasley 8 85
(Alistair Whillans) *t.k.h early: hld up in midfield: effrt and rdn over 2f out: kpt on to take 2nd towards fin: nt rch wnr* **7/1**

-210 **3** 3/4 **Azrur (IRE)**^{18} 1252 6-8-11 **70**.............................. PhillipMakin 2 73
(Keith Dalgleish) *led: rdn over 2f out: hdd over 1f out: one pce and lost 2nd towards fin* **9/1**

450- **4** 3/4 **Nonchalant**^{231} 6136 5-8-12 **76**..........................(v) JoshDoyle$^{(5)}$ 3 77
(David O'Meara) *prom: effrt and rdn 2f out: kpt on same pce fnl f* **11/1**

2112 **5** shd **Rockwood**^{28} 1114 5-8-10 **69**..........................(v) BarryMcHugh 4 70
(Karen McLintock) *hld up: hdwy on outside over 2f out: kpt on fnl f: nvr able to chal* **6/1**^{3}

334- **6** 1 1/4 **Bahamian C**^{145} 8062 5-9-1 **77**.............................. SammyJoBell$^{(3)}$ 7 75
(Richard Fahey) *s.i.s: hld up: rdn over 2f out: kpt on fnl f: nvr rchd ldrs* **8/1**

0-50 **7** 3/4 **Freight Train (IRE)**^{11} 1418 4-9-1 **74**.............................. JoeFanning 1 71
(Mark Johnston) *trckd ldrs: rdn over 2f out: edgd lft over 1f out: wknd ins fnl f* **9/1**

/06- **8** 1 3/4 **Royal Regent**^{321} 2982 4-8-11 **75**.............................. AnnaHesketh$^{(5)}$ 5 68
(Lucy Normile) *s.i.s: hld up: effrt on ins 3f out: outpcd fr 2f out* **50/1**

25-2 **9** 3 3/4 **Lopes Dancer (IRE)**^{19} 1241 4-9-1 **74**.............................. KierenFallon 6 59
(Alan Swinbank) *midfield: pushed along thrght: drvn over 3f out: wknd fr 2f out* **5/2**^{1}

1m 50.67s (-3.23) **Going Correction** -0.125s/f (Firm) **9** Ran SP% **114.9**
Speed ratings (Par 105): **105,103,102,101,101 100,99,98,94**
CSF £35.76 CT £273.09 TOTE £5.60: £2.10, £2.30, £2.80; EX 37.00 Trifecta £457.90.
Owner J C Fretwell **Bred** Lady Legard **Trained** Averham Park, Notts

FOCUS
A fair handicap taken by an improving filly.

1665 TOTETRIFECTA H'CAP 1m 7f 165y
3:30 (3:30) (Class 5) (0-75,81) 4-Y-O+ **£3,881** (£1,155; £577; £288) **Stalls** High

Form RPR

220- **1** **Sisyphus**^{211} 6763 4-9-5 **72**.............................. AndrewMullen 3 81
(Ollie Pears) *plld hrd early: trckd ldrs: led after 4f: mde rest: pushed clr fr over 1f out: comf* **12/1**

40/1 **2** 4 **Argent Knight**^{5} 1550 6-10-4 **81** 6ex..........................(p) PhillipMakin 4 86+
(Keith Dalgleish) *prom: effrt and plld out over 2f out: chsd (clr) wnr over 1f out: kpt on: nt pce to chal* **13/8**^{1}

05-6 **3** 1 1/4 **Sinakar (IRE)**^{19} 1244 5-9-6 **74**.............................. JoshDoyle$^{(5)}$ 9 77
(David O'Meara) *prom: effrt and chsd wnr over 2f out to over 1f out: kpt on same pce fnl f* **5/1**^{3}

002- **4** hd **Pass Muster**^{14} 4484 9-9-6 **74**.............................. PhilDennis$^{(5)}$ 1 77
(Philip Kirby) *t.k.h early: trckd ldrs: rdn over 2f out: one pce fnl f* **14/1**

22-0 **5** 3/4 **Jan Smuts (IRE)**^{18} 1253 8-9-5 **68**..........................(tp) IanBrennan 11 70
(Wilf Storey) *hld up: pushed along over 2f out: hdwy on outside over 1f out: kpt on fnl f: nvr able to chal* **22/1**

406- **6** 3/4 **Rockthe runway (IRE)**^{191} 7254 7-9-9 **72**.............................. ConnorBeasley 5 73
(Michael Dods) *awkward s: hld up: rdn over 2f out: kpt on fnl f: nvr on terms* **4/1**^{2}

343- **7** nse **Love Marmalade (IRE)**^{160} 7875 6-9-5 **75**.............................. RowanScott$^{(7)}$ 8 76
(Alistair Whillans) *hld up: rdn and effrt 2f out: sn no imp* **16/1**

541- **8** 1 **La Bacouetteuse (FR)**^{208} 6827 11-9-4 **70**..........................(b) JoeDoyle$^{(3)}$ 2 70
(Iain Jardine) *midfield on ins: drvn over 3f out: outpcd fr 2f out* **12/1**

004- **9** 6 **Aleksandar**^{165} 7187 7-9-3 **66**.............................. JackGarritty 7 59
(Jim Goldie) *hld up in midfield: rdn and outpcd over 2f out: btn over 1f out* **22/1**

-234 **10** 1/2 **Ellerina**^{27} 1121 4-8-3 **56** oh9..........................(v^{1}) JoeFanning 6 48
(Chris Fairhurst) *t.k.h: led 4f: chsd wnr tl rdn and wknd over 2f out* **33/1**

3m 31.54s (211.54) **Going Correction** -0.125s/f (Firm)
WFA 4 from 5yo+ 4lb **10** Ran SP% **114.3**
Speed ratings (Par 103): **99,97,96,96,95 95,95,95,92,91**
CSF £30.55 CT £114.46 TOTE £15.20: £2.90, £1.50, £1.80; EX 52.00 Trifecta £278.30.
Owner Charles Wentworth **Bred** Charles Wentworth **Trained** Norton, N Yorks

FOCUS
A fair staying handicap, in which the pace was steady, and not many got into it.

1666 TOTESWINGER H'CAP 5f 1y
4:00 (4:00) (Class 4) (0-80,80) 4-Y-O+ **£5,175** (£1,540; £769; £384) **Stalls** High

Form RPR

515- **1** **Alpha Delphini**^{188} 7342 5-9-6 **79**.............................. ConnorBeasley 2 88
(Bryan Smart) *cl up: effrt and ev ch over 1f out: led ins fnl f: rdn out* **3/1**^{2}

10-3 **2** 1 1/4 **Noodles Blue Boy**^{10} 1447 10-8-6 **72**.............................. RobertDodsworth$^{(7)}$ 7 77
(Ollie Pears) *led: rdn and edgd rt over 1f out: hdd ins fnl f: kpt on same pce nr fin* **5/2**^{1}

0-30 **3** 1/2 **Flicka's Boy**^{16} 1321 4-9-1 **74**.............................. BarryMcHugh 6 77
(Tony Coyle) *cl up: effrt and rdn over 1f out: kpt on same pce ins fnl f* **9/2**^{3}

0-16 **4** nk **Something Lucky (IRE)**^{30} 1084 4-9-6 **79**.............................. ShaneGray 4 81
(Kristin Stubbs) *chsd ldng gp: rdn over 2f out: kpt on fnl f: nvr able to chal* **6/1**

600- **5** 2 1/4 **Classy Anne**^{219} 6494 6-9-3 **76**.............................. JackGarritty 1 70
(Jim Goldie) *wnt rt s: t.k.h in rr: drvn along 1/2-way: kpt on fnl f: nvr rchd ldrs* **8/1**

300- **6** 1/2 **Bunce (IRE)**^{208} 6830 8-8-8 **67**.............................. JoeFanning 3 59
(Linda Perratt) *prom: rdn along over 2f out: wknd fnl f* **12/1**

06-6 **7** 15 **Rothesay Chancer**^{13} 1378 8-9-7 **80**.............................. JasonHart 5 18
(Jim Goldie) *bhd: struggling 1/2-way: lost tch over 1f out: eased whn btn* **10/1**

59.11s (-1.29) **Going Correction** -0.125s/f (Firm) **7** Ran SP% **113.9**
Speed ratings (Par 105): **105,103,102,101,98 97,73**
CSF £10.87 CT £31.84 TOTE £4.10: £1.70, £2.00; EX 10.00 Trifecta £38.80.
Owner The Alpha Delphini Partnership **Bred** Mrs B A Matthews **Trained** Hambleton, N Yorks
■ Connor Beasley's first winner since suffering serious injuries in a fall last July.

FOCUS
A fair sprint, in which it paid to race prominently, with the first three home having travelled up with the pace throughout.

1667 TOTEEXACTA H'CAP 7f 33y
4:30 (4:31) (Class 6) (0-60,60) 3-Y-O **£2,587** (£770; £384; £192) **Stalls** Low

Form RPR

00-5 **1** **Arizona Sunrise**^{53} 783 3-9-7 **60**.............................. SeanLevey 5 67
(David Brown) *t.k.h early: trckd ldr: led over 1f out: rdn and hrd pressed ins fnl f: hld on gamely* **11/4**^{1}

63-4 **2** nse **Dark Command**^{27} 1126 3-9-4 **57**..........................(p) ConnorBeasley 1 64
(Michael Dods) *trckd ldrs: effrt and plld out over 1f out: disp ld ins fnl f: kpt on: jst hld* **11/4**^{1}

00-0 **3** 3 **Monsieur Glory**^{18} 1275 3-9-7 **60**..........................(v^{1}) RichardKingscote 4 59
(Tom Dascombe) *trckd ldrs: effrt and rdn over 2f out: kpt on same pce fnl f* **10/1**

4420 **4** 1/2 **Tombe Girl**^{8} 1497 3-9-5 **58**..........................(p) PhillipMakin 7 56
(Keith Dalgleish) *led: rdn and hdd over 1f out: kpt on same pce fnl f* **17/2**

3644 **5** 2 1/2 **Rubis**^{18} 1275 3-9-6 **59**..........................(v^{1}) JackGarritty 3 50
(Richard Fahey) *s.i.s: t.k.h in rr: effrt and rdn over 2f out: hung rt over 1f out: no imp* **9/2**^{2}

006- **6** 11 **Granite City Doc**^{237} 5941 3-9-2 **55**.............................. KeaganLatham 8 16
(Lucy Normile) *bhd: drvn and short-lived effrt over 2f out: sn wknd* **18/1**

604- **7** 12 **Trikingdom**^{218} 6546 3-9-4 **57**.............................. KierenFallon 2
(Alan Swinbank) *t.k.h: hld up in tch: hmpd and lost grnd after 1f: drvn along and hung rt over 2f out: sn wknd* **8/1**^{3}

003- **8** 1 1/4 **Alba Dawn (IRE)**^{199} 7054 3-9-7 **60**..........................(p) JasonHart 6
(Keith Dalgleish) *s.i.s: hld up on outside: rdn along over 3f out: wknd over 2f out* **12/1**

1m 28.22s (-0.78) **Going Correction** -0.125s/f (Firm) **8** Ran SP% **115.2**
Speed ratings (Par 96): **99,98,95,94,92 79,65,64**
CSF £10.17 CT £64.39 TOTE £4.20: £1.90, £1.10, £2.30; EX 12.20 Trifecta £87.20.
Owner Miss C A Carr **Bred** Mr & Mrs J Davis & Trickledown Stud **Trained** Averham Park, Notts

FOCUS
Only a modest handicap, in which all the runners were maidens, but it was competitive.

1668 TOTEPLACE APPRENTICE RIDERS H'CAP 5f 1y
5:00 (5:03) (Class 6) (0-60,60) 4-Y-O+ **£2,587** (£770; £384; £192) **Stalls** High

Form RPR

000- **1** **Lady Poppy**^{210} 6788 6-8-11 **57**.............................. KieranSchofield$^{(7)}$ 3 64
(Jedd O'Keeffe) *trckd ldrs: effrt and rdn on outside over 1f out: led ins fnl f: drvn and hld on wl cl home* **7/2**^{2}

1160 **2** nk **Lizzy's Dream**^{17} 1299 8-8-9 **53**.............................. RowanScott$^{(5)}$ 5 59
(Rebecca Bastiman) *in tch: gng wl whn nt clr run over 1f out to ins fnl f: kpt on wl cl home: jst hld* **14/1**

0003 **3** 2 1/2 **Roy's Legacy**^{8} 1481 7-9-0 **58**.............................. CharlieBennett$^{(5)}$ 1 55
(Shaun Harris) *led: rdn over 2f out: hdd ins fnl f: kpt on same pce* **10/1**

00-5 **4** 3/4 **Compton River**^{18} 1255 4-8-13 **57**.............................. PhilDennis$^{(5)}$ 6 51
(Bryan Smart) *w ldrs: rdn over 1f out: outpcd ins fnl f* **5/1**^{3}

0026 **5** 1/2 **Seamster**^{12} 1401 9-9-2 **60**..........................(vt) JoshDoyle$^{(5)}$ 7 52
(David O'Meara) *w ldrs: drvn along over 1f out: no ex ins fnl f* **5/2**^{1}

000- **6** 7 **Lady Cordie**^{248} 5552 4-8-7 **46** oh1.............................. JoeDoyle 4 13
(Jim Goldie) *bhd and sn outpcd: no ch fr 1/2-way* **28/1**

553- **7** 3 1/4 **Mystical King**^{209} 6815 6-8-7 **46** oh1.............................. SammyJoBell 8 2+
(Linda Perratt) *reluctant to enter stalls: s.i.s: sn wl bhd: no ch fr 1/2-way* **14/1**

59.78s (-0.62) **Going Correction** -0.125s/f (Firm) **7** Ran SP% **93.3**
Speed ratings (Par 101): **99,98,94,93,92 81,76**
CSF £31.12 CT £216.48 TOTE £3.50: £2.40, £3.40; EX 31.10 Trifecta £136.40.
Owner Ingham Racing Syndicate **Bred** Whatton Manor Stud **Trained** Middleham Moor, N Yorks
■ Hurricane Alert and Little Belter were withdrawn. Prices at time of withdrawal 25/1 & 7/2 respectively. Rule 4 applies to all bets - deduction 20p in the pound.

FOCUS
The finale was another modest handicap. There was drama at the start and Hurricane Alert was withdrawn after unshipping his rider on the way to post and crashing through the rails. Little Belter was also a late withdrawal after getting upset in the stalls.
T/Plt: £44.90 to a £1 stake. Pool: £92,332.00 - 1,500.01 winning tickets T/Qpdt: £7.70 to a £1 stake. Pool: £8,732.73 - 838.23 winning tickets **Richard Young**

1488 THIRSK (L-H)
Sunday, April 24

OFFICIAL GOING: Good (good to soft in places; 7.9)
Wind: light 1/2 behind Weather: fine and sunny

1669 RACING UK ANYWHERE AVAILABLE NOW MAIDEN STKS 5f
1:50 (1:54) (Class 5) 3-Y-O **£3,881** (£1,155; £577; £288) **Stalls** High

Form RPR

52- **1** **Sanaadh**^{200} 7038 3-9-5 0.............................. DavidNolan 3 78+
(Richard Fahey) *chsd ldrs: drvn and hung lft over 1f out: kpt on to ld last 50yds* **4/1**^{2}

540- **2** nk **Corridor Kid (IRE)**^{319} 3056 3-9-5 72.............................. TonyHamilton 2 74
(Derek Shaw) *w ldrs: led appr fnl f: hdd and no ex last 50yds* **25/1**

3 2¼ **Alsvinder** 3-9-5 0 DanielTudhope 6 66+
(David O'Meara) *w ldr: t.k.h: led wl over 1f out: hdd appr fnl f: kpt on same pce* **1/2**[1]

052- 4 1¼ **Never In Doubt**[181] 7516 3-9-5 75 GeorgeChaloner 7 61
(Richard Whitaker) *wnt lft s: chsd ldrs: edgd lft and one pce fnl 150yds* **6/1**[3]

66- 5 1½ **King's Currency**[188] 7337 3-9-5 0 GrahamLee 1 56
(Jedd O'Keeffe) *wnt lft s: hdwy over 2f out: sn chsng ldrs: wknd fnl f* **40/1**

6 1 **Wishing Tree** 3-9-0 0 BenCurtis 4 47
(Brian Ellison) *sn outpcd and in rr: sme hdwy over 2f out: nvr a factor* **33/1**

7 7 **Noah Amor (IRE)** 3-9-5 0 PaulMulrennan 9 27
(David Nicholls) *led: t.k.h: hdd wl over 1f out: sn wknd* **16/1**

00 8 1¼ **Temujins Quest (IRE)**[21] 1217 3-9-5 0 AdamBeschizza 5 22
(Derek Shaw) *s.i.s: sn outpcd and in rr: sme hdwy over 2f out: sn lost pl and bhd* **200/1**

9 2 **Andys Girl (IRE)** 3-9-0 0 DaleSwift 8 10
(Brian Ellison) *s.i.s: sn wl outpcd and detached in last* **25/1**

1m 1.0s (1.40) **Going Correction** +0.55s/f (Yiel) **9** Ran SP% **120.4**
Speed ratings (Par 98): **110,109,105,103,101 99,88,86,83**
CSF £95.14 TOTE £5.00: £1.10, £5.80, £1.10; EX 114.80 Trifecta £226.90.
Owner Jaber Abdullah **Bred** Rabbah Bloodstock Limited **Trained** Musley Bank, N Yorks

FOCUS
Drying ground. This was just a fair sprint maiden.

1670 BET WITH YOUR RACING UK APP H'CAP 6f
2:20 (2:24) (Class 6) (0-60,60) 3-Y-O **£3,234** (£962; £481; £240) **Stalls** High

Form RPR

30-2 1 **Iceaxe**[16] 1319 3-9-5 58 RoystonFfrench 2 69
(John Holt) *mde all on far side: kpt on wl fnl f: 1st of 6 that gp* **12/1**

050- 2 1½ **Seaperle**[229] 6188 3-8-13 52 DavidAllan 16 61+
(Tim Easterby) *racd stands' side: chsd ldrs: led that gp over 1f out: hung lft: styd on wl: nt rch wnr: 1st of 9 that gp* **9/1**

505- 3 3 **Whispering Wolf**[221] 6427 3-8-9 51 JacobButterfield(3) 4 48
(Suzzanne France) *racd far side: chsd ldrs: kpt on fnl f: 2nd of 6 that gp* **50/1**

00-1 4 shd **Tricky Dicky**[27] 1126 3-9-6 59 DuranFentiman 18 59
(Olly Williams) *dwlt: racd stands' side: hld up in mid-div: kpt on fnl f: 2nd of 9 that gp* **3/1**[1]

-213 5 ½ **Sadie Babes (IRE)**[18] 1249 3-8-12 58 AdamMcNamara(7) 5 54
(Richard Fahey) *racd far side: chsd wnr: upsides over 1f out: edgd rt and grad wknd: 3rd of 6 that gp: b.b.v* **7/1**[2]

0-62 6 1 **Comparinka**[51] 820 3-9-3 56 (p) BenCurtis 6 49
(Scott Dixon) *racd far side: in tch: sn drvn along: kpt on appr fnl f: 4th of 6 that gp* **20/1**

004- 7 nk **Pilgrims Path**[131] 8239 3-9-7 60 (p) DaleSwift 17 55
(Scott Dixon) *led stands' side gp after 2f: kpt on one pce over 1f out: 3rd of 9 that gp* **20/1**

60-0 8 1¼ **Dalalah**[107] 105 3-9-2 55 GeorgeChaloner 8 46
(Richard Guest) *swtchd rt s: racd stands' side: mid-div: hdwy over 2f out: nvr rchd ldrs: 4th of 9 that gp* **25/1**

4563 9 3¼ **Serendib's Glory (IRE)**[25] 1148 3-9-4 60 ShelleyBirkett(3) 3 38
(Julia Feilden) *racd far side: sn outpcd: nvr a factor: 5th of 6 that gp* **20/1**

05-0 10 shd **Sakhastic**[24] 1162 3-8-7 46 oh1 (b[1]) AdamBeschizza 15 27
(Christine Dunnett) *racd stands' side: chsd ldrs: lost pl over 1f out: 5th of 9 that gp* **25/1**

030- 11 3¼ **Laila Honiwillow**[213] 6666 3-9-6 59 GrahamLee 12 30
(Jedd O'Keeffe) *racd stands' side: in rr: bhd fnl 2f: 6th of 9 that gp* **8/1**[3]

266- 12 1½ **Spirit Of Zebedee (IRE)**[139] 8130 3-9-2 55 (p) TomEaves 9 22
(John Quinn) *racd stands' side: rr-div: nvr a factor: 7th of 9 that gp* **11/1**

6-04 13 ¾ **Vocalise**[18] 1249 3-8-0 46 oh1 RPWalsh(7) 10 10
(Charles Smith) *racd stands' side: chsd ldrs: edgd lft and lost pl over 1f out: 8th of 9 that gp* **100/1**

060- 14 5 **Mission Mars**[254] 5353 3-9-4 57 DavidNolan 1 3
(Patrick Holmes) *racd far side: chsd ldrs: drvn 3f out: lost pl over 1f out: bhd whn eased clsng stages: last of 6 that gp* **33/1**

-003 15 1 **Tahiti One**[16] 1325 3-9-3 56 RobertWinston 14
(Tony Carroll) *racd stands' side: led that grioup 2f: chsd ldrs: hung lft and lost pl over 1f out: bhd whn eased clsng stages: last of 9 that gp* **10/1**

1m 16.15s (3.45) **Going Correction** +0.55s/f (Yiel) **15** Ran SP% **111.6**
Speed ratings (Par 96): **99,97,93,92,92 90,90,88,84,84 80,78,77,70,69**
CSF £84.95 CT £3864.74 TOTE £13.20: £4.30, £2.80, £9.50; EX 164.20 Trifecta £2591.60 Part won..
Owner J R Holt **Bred** Llety Farms **Trained** Peckleton, Leics
■ Reinforced and Hadley were withdrawn. Prices at time of withdrawal 7/1 and 40/1 respectively. Rule 4 applies to all bets - deduction 10p in the pound.

FOCUS
A moderate sprint handicap. The majority raced near side, but six went far side including the 1st, 3rd, 5th and 6th.

1671 HAPPY 4TH BIRTHDAY ELLIOTT ROBINSON H'CAP 1m
2:50 (2:53) (Class 5) (0-70,70) 3-Y-O **£3,881** (£1,155; £577; £288) **Stalls** Low

Form RPR

505- 1 **Island Flame (IRE)**[191] 7248 3-9-2 65 RobertWinston 1 70+
(Richard Fahey) *hld up in rr-div: hdwy 3f out: r.o to ld last 100yds* **8/1**

66-2 2 1¼ **Fidra Bay (IRE)**[13] 1381 3-9-5 68 BenCurtis 2 70
(Alan Swinbank) *trckd ldrs: 2nd 2f out: styd on same pce last 100yds* **8/1**

663- 3 1½ **Mango Chutney**[173] 7684 3-8-10 59 GrahamGibbons 4 60+
(John Davies) *wnt rt s: mid-div: hdwy 6f out: effrt over 2f out: hmpd and swtchd rt last 100yds: tk 3rd nr fin* **18/1**

006- 4 ½ **Miramonte Dancer (IRE)**[256] 5263 3-8-11 60 DavidAllan 3 57
(David C Griffiths) *led: hdd and no ex last 100yds* **66/1**

240- 5 2½ **Allfredandnobell (IRE)**[202] 6978 3-8-13 62 GrahamLee 6 54
(Micky Hammond) *mid-div: outpcd over 5f out: kpt on one pce fnl 2f* **8/1**

32-3 6 3 **Planetaria (IRE)**[25] 1155 3-9-3 66 ShaneKelly 10 51
(Garry Moss) *trckd ldrs: 2nd 3f out: wknd over 1f out* **9/2**[2]

502- 7 9 **Strathearn (IRE)**[153] 7955 3-8-12 68 LuluStanford(7) 5 32
(Michael Bell) *hmpd s: in rr-div: brief effrt 3f out: lost pl over 1f out: bhd whn eased clsng stages* **5/1**[3]

20-3 8 1¼ **Lady Canford (IRE)**[43] 925 3-9-2 65 (p) PJMcDonald 9 26
(James Bethell) *in rr: drvn over 3f out: bhd fnl 2f: eased clsng stages* **8/1**

440- 9 ¾ **Mr Globetrotter (USA)**[184] 7423 3-9-4 67 PaulMulrennan 7 26
(Michael Dods) *in rr and sn drvn along: bhd fnl 3f: eased clsng stages* **4/1**[1]

42-5 10 11 **Magical Lasso (IRE)**[33] 1027 3-9-7 70 (p) TomEaves 8 4
(Kevin Ryan) *trckd ldrs: drvn over 3f out: bhd whn heavily eased clsng stages* **14/1**

1m 45.29s (5.19) **Going Correction** +0.675s/f (Yiel) **10** Ran SP% **112.7**
Speed ratings (Par 98): **101,99,98,97,95 92,83,82,81,70**
CSF £67.95 CT £784.13 TOTE £7.80: £2.40, £2.30, £5.00; EX 56.90 Trifecta £747.90.
Owner Northumbria Leisure Ltd **Bred** Christopher Maye **Trained** Musley Bank, N Yorks

FOCUS
The home bend was dolled out circa seven yards from the inside line, adding about 20 yards to the race distance.

1672 WATCH RACING UK IN HD H'CAP 5f
3:20 (3:21) (Class 4) (0-85,85) 4-Y-O+ **£5,175** (£1,540; £769; £384) **Stalls** High

Form RPR

334- 1 **Tumblewind**[292] 3987 6-9-4 82 GeorgeChaloner 7 91
(Richard Whitaker) *chsd ldrs: led over 1f out: kpt on wl* **12/1**

0-00 2 1 **Rita's Boy (IRE)**[10] 1444 4-9-3 81 (v) BenCurtis 9 87
(K R Burke) *towards rr: sn drvn along: hdwy over 1f out: chsd wnr last 100yds: kpt on* **8/1**[3]

511- 3 2½ **Bapak Asmara (IRE)**[295] 3891 4-9-4 82 GrahamLee 10 78
(Kevin Ryan) *mid-div: effrt over 2f out: hung lft and chsd wnr over 1f out: kpt on same pce* **9/4**[1]

00-0 4 ¾ **Whozthecat (IRE)**[11] 1408 9-9-6 84 NeilFarley 6 77
(Declan Carroll) *chsd ldrs: outpcd over 1f out: kpt on fnl 100yds* **33/1**

0-20 5 hd **Rusty Rocket (IRE)**[30] 1084 7-9-3 81 JFEgan 5 74
(Paul Green) *chsd ldrs: kpt on same pce over 1f out* **20/1**

-326 6 1½ **Pearl Acclaim (IRE)**[87] 359 6-9-4 82 PaulQuinn 4 69
(David Nicholls) *chsd ldrs: one pce over 1f out* **8/1**[3]

05-5 7 1¼ **Mishaal (IRE)**[29] 1090 6-9-6 84 TomEaves 3 67
(Michael Herrington) *chsd ldrs: n.m.r appr fnl f: one pce* **20/1**

000- 8 1¾ **Desert Ace (IRE)**[183] 7461 5-9-7 85 (p) PaulMulrennan 2 61+
(Michael Dods) *swtchd rt after 1f: in rr: hdwy over 2f out: nt clr run over 1f out: nt rcvr* **8/1**[3]

204- 9 hd **Free Zone**[188] 7343 7-9-3 81 (p) DanielTudhope 8 57
(David O'Meara) *chsd ldrs: lost pl over 1f out* **4/1**[2]

000- 10 nk **Captain Dunne (IRE)**[190] 7286 11-9-1 84 RachelRichardson(5) 1 59
(Tim Easterby) *led: hdd over 1f out: wknd* **20/1**

400- 11 2 **Apricot Sky**[193] 7223 6-8-13 77 TonyHamilton 11 44
(David Nicholls) *dwlt: in rr: nvr on terms* **16/1**

1m 1.53s (1.93) **Going Correction** +0.55s/f (Yiel) **11** Ran SP% **114.9**
Speed ratings (Par 105): **106,104,100,99,98 96,94,91,91,90 87**
CSF £95.92 CT £296.45 TOTE £14.60: £4.20, £2.20, £1.20; EX 130.50 Trifecta £657.20.
Owner Nice Day Out Partnership **Bred** Hellwood Stud Farm **Trained** Scarcroft, W Yorks

FOCUS
A fair sprint handicap. They all stayed near side this time.

1673 100% RACINGUK PROFITS RETURNED TO RACING MAIDEN AUCTION STKS 6f
3:50 (3:52) (Class 6) 3-Y-O **£3,234** (£962; £481; £240) **Stalls** High

Form RPR

204- 1 **Top Of The Bank**[231] 6133 3-9-2 80 (p) GrahamLee 1 73
(Kevin Ryan) *wnt lft s: swtchd rt after s: w ldr: led over 3f out: drvn out* **6/4**[1]

4 2 ½ **Sciarra**[19] 1246 3-8-10 0 OisinMurphy 3 66
(Michael Bell) *swtchd rt after s: led tl over 3f out: upsides 1f out: no ex clsng stages* **9/2**[3]

3 1½ **Olympic Duel (IRE)** 3-8-11 0 AdamBeschizza 2 62
(Peter Hiatt) *in rr: hdwy over 2f out: kpt on to take 3rd last 50yds* **40/1**

00- 4 2½ **Round The Island**[165] 7795 3-9-3 0 GeorgeChaloner 6 61
(Richard Whitaker) *chsd ldrs: hung lft and one pce over 1f out* **14/1**

0-4 5 1½ **Highway Robber**[13] 1383 3-8-7 0 HollieDoyle(7) 4 53
(Wilf Storey) *chsd ldrs: edgd lft over 2f out: n.m.r and fdd over 1f out* **50/1**

6 nk **Diamond Avalanche (IRE)**[197] 7128 3-9-1 71 DavidNolan 9 53
(Patrick Holmes) *chsd ldrs: lost pl over 1f out* **7/2**[2]

7 1 **Big Time Dancer (IRE)** 3-9-0 0 JamesSullivan 10 49
(Dianne Sayer) *s.i.s: in rr: nvr a factor* **20/1**

0- 8 ½ **Fool's Dream**[184] 7422 3-8-9 0 TomEaves 5 43
(Bryan Smart) *dwlt: in rr: sme hdwy 2f out: nvr on terms* **40/1**

22-0 9 1½ **Rial (IRE)**[10] 1442 3-8-2 72 NoelGarbutt(5) 8 36
(Denis Quinn) *chsd ldrs: drvn 3f out: lost pl over 1f out* **9/1**

40- 10 4 **Cape Crusader (IRE)**[229] 6189 3-8-13 0 PaulMulrennan 7 30
(Michael Dods) *mid-div: effrt over 2f out: lost pl over 1f out: eased clsng stages* **14/1**

1m 16.78s (4.08) **Going Correction** +0.55s/f (Yiel) **10** Ran SP% **115.3**
Speed ratings (Par 96): **94,93,91,88,86 85,84,83,81,76**
CSF £7.88 TOTE £2.40: £1.20, £1.70, £5.40; EX 8.60 Trifecta £142.90.
Owner J Hanson **Bred** D Carroll **Trained** Hambleton, N Yorks

FOCUS
Just an ordinary sprint maiden.

1674 RACING UK DAY PASS JUST £10 H'CAP (DIV I) 1m 4f
4:20 (4:20) (Class 6) (0-65,65) 4-Y-O+ **£3,234** (£962; £481; £240) **Stalls** High

Form RPR

00-0 1 **Solid Justice (IRE)**[96] 247 5-8-7 51 oh4 JoeyHaynes 4 59
(Kenny Johnson) *chsd ldrs: led over 1f out: hld on nr fin* **40/1**

3 2 nk **Wishing Well**[53] 789 4-9-5 64 PJMcDonald 6 72
(Micky Hammond) *hld up in mid-div: hdwy to chse ldrs over 3f out: hung lft and 3rd over 1f out: styd on to take 2nd nr fin* **5/2**[1]

130- 3 ¾ **Tourtiere**[222] 6410 8-9-7 65 BenCurtis 11 71
(Andrew Crook) *swtchd lft after s: sn led: hdd over 1f out: kpt on same pce* **12/1**

04-0 4 1¾ **Voice From Above (IRE)**[39] 950 7-8-4 55 PaulaMuir(7) 3 59
(Patrick Holmes) *hld up in rr: hdwy 3f out: nt clr run and swtchd rt wl over 1f out: styd on to take 4th last 50yds* **14/1**

266- 5 1 **Rockabilly Riot (IRE)**[9] 6410 6-9-4 62 GrahamLee 2 64
(Martin Todhunter) *hld up in mid-div: hdwy to chse ldrs 3f out: wknd over 1f out* **9/1**

-005 6 5 **Surround Sound**[24] 1169 6-9-2 60 (bt) DavidAllan 5 54
(Tim Easterby) *dwlt: hld up in rr: hdwy over 2f out: nvr a factor* **4/1**[2]

400- 7 5 **Midnight Warrior**[190] 7290 6-8-13 57 DaleSwift 7 43
(Ron Barr) *hld up in rr: t.k.h: hdwy 7f out: effrt 3f out: edgd lft and lost pl over 1f out* **10/1**

004- 8 1¼ **Intensified (IRE)**[191] 7265 5-8-8 52 JamesSullivan 1 36
(Ruth Carr) *chsd ldrs: wknd over 1f out* **17/2**

604- 9 shd **Lightning Steps**[222] 6402 4-8-6 52 oh2 NeilFarley 9 35
(Declan Carroll) *led early: chsd ldrs: drvn 3f out: wknd over 1f out* **20/1**

6512 **10** 3 3/4 **Hazel Blue (IRE)**[26] 1131 5-8-11 **55** .... GrahamGibbons 10 33+
(David Loughnane) *t.k.h: hdwy to trck ldrs after 4f: chsng ldrs over 3f out: wknd over 1f out: eased* **6/1**[3]

006/ **11** 10 **Tayarat (IRE)**[294] 811 11-8-2 **51** oh6 .... NoelGarbutt(5) 8 13
(Michael Chapman) *s.s: in rr: bhd fnl 3f* **100/1**

2m 48.24s (12.04) **Going Correction** +0.675s/f (Yiel)
WFA 4 from 5yo+ 1lb **11** Ran SP% **115.0**
Speed ratings (Par 101): **86,85,85,84,83 80,76,75,75,73 66**
CSF £134.76 CT £1326.92 TOTE £43.00: £10.10, £1.80, £2.60; EX 223.00 Trifecta £3686.60.
Owner R Naylor **Bred** John O'Connor **Trained** Newburn, Tyne & Wear

FOCUS
This was run over 20 yards further than advertised. A moderate handicap run 4.61sec slower than the second division. The winner was very well in on last season's best form.

1675 RACING UK DAY PASS JUST £10 H'CAP (DIV II) 1m 4f
4:50 (4:50) (Class 6) (0-65,65) 4-Y-0+ **£3,234** (£962; £481; £240) **Stalls** High

Form RPR

0342 **1** **Mcvicar**[5] 1048 7-8-11 **55** .... (p) DanielTudhope 8 63
(John Davies) *hld up towards rr: hdwy and swtchd rt 2f out: str run to ld last 150yds: forged clr* **5/1**[2]

/0-6 **2** 3 3/4 **Sirpertan**[32] 1048 5-8-7 **51** oh1 .... JamesSullivan 7 53
(Marjorie Fife) *hld up towards rr: hdwy 6f out: led 2f out: hdd and no ex last 150yds* **12/1**

0203 **3** 1 3/4 **Unex Modigliani (IRE)**[26] 1136 7-8-12 **56** .... (vt[1]) TonyHamilton 6 55
(Derek Shaw) *hld up in rr: hdwy on outer whn sltly hmpd 2f out: edgd lft over 1f out: kpt on to take modest 3rd clsng stages* **11/1**

55-6 **4** 1 1/4 **Stormin Tom (IRE)**[18] 1253 4-9-1 **65** .... RachelRichardson(5) 5 62
(Tim Easterby) *chsd ldr: drvn over 3f out: one pce fnl 2f* **7/2**[1]

00-0 **5** nk **Cape Hideaway**[22] 1201 4-9-3 **62** .... GrahamGibbons 9 59
(Mark Walford) *mid-div: drvn 7f out: outpcd over 3f out: kpt on fnl 2f* **11/1**

64-P **6** hd **Christmas Hamper (IRE)**[12] 1399 4-8-12 **60** .... AlistairRawlinson(3) 1 56
(Michael Appleby) *led: hdd 2f out: one pce* **9/1**

0-0 **7** 1 **Insight (IRE)**[17] 1295 5-8-7 **51** oh3 .... (p) PJMcDonald 3 46
(Steve Gollings) *hmpd s: hld up in rr: effrt 3f out: kpt on: nvr a factor* **50/1**

0231 **8** 16 **Prayer Time**[33] 1028 4-9-5 **64** .... (b[1]) SaleemGolam 10 33
(Mark H Tompkins) *t.k.h: sn trcking ldrs: lost pl 2f out: eased whn bhd clsng stages* **6/1**[3]

-502 **9** 4 **Almutamarred (USA)**[32] 1049 4-8-10 **55** .... ShaneKelly 2 18
(Kevin Morgan) *dwlt: sn chsng ldrs: wknd wl over 1f out: eased whn bhd clsng stages* **7/2**[1]

056- **10** 1 3/4 **Al Furat (USA)**[280] 4421 8-8-2 **51** oh6 .... (p) NoelGarbutt(5) 4 25+
(Ron Barr) *wnt lft s: t.k.h: sn trcking ldrs: sddle slipped after 2f: lost pl over 2f out: sn eased and bhd* **33/1**

2m 43.63s (7.43) **Going Correction** +0.675s/f (Yiel)
WFA 4 from 5yo+ 1lb **10** Ran SP% **114.7**
Speed ratings (Par 101): **102,99,98,97,97 97,96,85,83,82**
CSF £62.20 CT £628.37 TOTE £6.10: £2.10, £3.20, £2.90; EX 60.10 Trifecta £515.20.
Owner Ms D Nicholson **Bred** J Breslin **Trained** Piercebridge, Durham

FOCUS
This was run over 20 yards further than advertised. The time was much faster than the first division and it paid to be held up. It;s unlikey the winner was any better than rated.

1676 TOTEPOOL THIRSK HUNT CUP THIS SATURDAY H'CAP 6f
5:20 (5:23) (Class 6) (0-60,60) 4-Y-0+ **£3,234** (£962; £481; £240) **Stalls** High

Form RPR

3254 **1** **Blistering Dancer (IRE)**[16] 1319 6-8-7 **46** .... JoeyHaynes 5 53
(Tony Carroll) *led far side gp: clr that side over 1f out: jst hld on: 1st of 8 that gp* **20/1**

2-00 **2** hd **Artbeat (IRE)**[74] 525 4-8-12 **51** .... AdamBeschizza 2 57
(Julia Feilden) *racd far side: chsd ldrs: 2nd that gp over 1f out: styd on last 150yds: jst hld: 2nd of 8 that gp* **33/1**

506 **3** 3 1/4 **Humour (IRE)**[54] 775 5-9-3 **59** .... DannyBrock(3) 15 59
(Christine Dunnett) *racd stands' side: chsd ldrs: led that gp 2f out: kpt on same pce: 1st of 10 that gp* **12/1**[3]

40-0 **4** 1 **Munjally**[18] 1254 5-9-7 **60** .... (v) DavidNolan 17 57
(Patrick Holmes) *racd stands' side: chsd ldrs: tk 2nd that side last 100yds* **8/1**[2]

516- **5** 2 1/4 **Consistant**[225] 6297 8-9-4 **60** .... EoinWalsh(3) 20 50
(Brian Baugh) *racd stands;' side: chsd ldrs: 2nd that gp over 1f out: one pce: 3rd of 10 that gp* **25/1**

20-3 **6** nse **Gaelic Wizard (IRE)**[17] 1299 8-9-0 **58** .... (v) GemmaTutty(5) 13 48
(Karen Tutty) *racd stands' side: chsd ldrs: effrt 2f out: kpt on same pce: 4th of 10 that gp* **14/1**

-045 **7** hd **Teetotal (IRE)**[18] 1254 6-9-2 **60** .... RachelRichardson(5) 8 46
(Nigel Tinkler) *racd far side: mid-div: hdwy over 2f out: kpt on one pce: 3rd of 8 that gp* **7/1**[1]

44-2 **8** 1/2 **Adiator**[18] 1254 8-9-6 **59** .... (p) TomEaves 1 44
(Neville Bycroft) *racd far side: w ldr: one pce fnl 2f: 4th of 8 that gp* **12/1**[3]

3-00 **9** 2 1/4 **Lydiate Lady**[18] 1255 4-9-4 **57** .... JFEgan 6 35
(Paul Green) *racd far side: chsd ldrs: drvn over 2f out: wknd over 1f out: 5th of 8 that gp* **14/1**

5-40 **10** 1/2 **Galvanize**[52] 799 5-9-4 **57** .... PaulMulrennan 16 36
(Noel Wilson) *racd stands' side: in rr: kpt on fnl 2f: nvr a factor: 5th of 10 that gp* **12/1**[3]

60-3 **11** 1/2 **Graceful Act**[13] 1382 8-8-10 **49** .... DavidAllan 12 27
(Ron Barr) *racd stands' side: in rr and sn drvn along: sme hdwy 2f out: nvr on terms: 6th of 10 that gp* **16/1**

3330 **12** 4 1/2 **Hab Reeh**[36] 1005 8-8-13 **52** .... (p) JamesSullivan 9 13
(Ruth Carr) *racd far side: chsd ldrs: lost pl over 2f out: 6th of 8 that gp* **16/1**

650- **13** 3/4 **Indego Blues**[181] 7522 7-9-7 **60** .... PaulQuinn 10 19
(David Nicholls) *racd far side: in rr: nvr on terms: 7th of 8 that gp* **7/1**[1]

/-66 **14** 2 1/2 **Muhtadim (IRE)**[39] 959 4-8-7 **53** .... RPWalsh(7) 11 8
(Charles Smith) *racd stands' side: chsd ldrs: drvn over 2f out: lost pl over 1f out: 7th of 10 that gp* **40/1**

000 **15** 3 1/2 **Abonos (IRE)**[8] 1495 4-8-1 **47** ow1 .... EvaMoscrop(7) 19
(Simon West) *racd stands' side: chsd ldrs: lost pl 2f out: 8th of 10 that gp* **50/1**

0-16 **16** 2 3/4 **Invectus Hero**[95] 257 4-9-5 **58** .... (p) TonyHamilton 4
(Derek Shaw) *racd far side: chsd ldrs: hung bdly rt over 2f out: sn eased: last of 8 that gp* **14/1**

-000 **17** 1/2 **Under Approval**[8] 1495 5-8-7 **46** .... (b) NeilFarley 14
(Karen Tutty) *led stands' side gp: hdd 2f out: sn wknd: 9th of 10 that gp* **50/1**

0-06 **18** 11 **Look Here's Al**[12] 1404 5-8-8 **47** .... (bp[1]) RaulDaSilva 18
(Karen Tutty) *racd stands' side: chsd ldrs: rdn over 2f out: sn lost pl: bhd whn eased clsng stages: last of 10 that gp* **25/1**

1m 15.33s (2.63) **Going Correction** +0.55s/f (Yiel) **18** Ran SP% **112.7**
Speed ratings (Par 101): **104,103,99,98,95 95,94,94,91,90 89,83,82,79,74 71,70,55**
Mighty Bond was withdrawn. Price at time of withdrawal 8/1. Rule 4 applies to all bets - deduction 10p in the pound. CSF £453.31 CT £6093.09 TOTE £20.30: £4.20, £6.10, £3.20, £2.40; EX 305.20 Trifecta £3392.50 Part won..
Owner Mrs Evelyn Madden **Bred** Springmount Stud **Trained** Cropthorne, Worcs

FOCUS
Like in the earlier race in which the field split, the far side proved the place to be - the first two raced on that part of the track. Very ordinary form.
T/Jkpt: Not won. T/Plt: £326.20 to a £1 stake. Pool: £94,669.45 - 211.81 winning tickets T/Qpdt: £17.30 to a £1 stake. Pool: £8,301.72 - 353.57 winning tickets **Walter Glynn**

1677 - 1684a (Foreign Racing) - See Raceform Interactive

CAPANNELLE (R-H)
Sunday, April 24

OFFICIAL GOING: Turf: good

1685a PREMIO REGINA ELENA - ITALIAN 1000 GUINEAS (GROUP 3) (3YO FILLIES) (TURF) 1m
3:35 (12:00) 3-Y-0 **£47,794** (£21,029; £11,470; £5,735)

RPR

1 **Conselice**[21] 3-8-11 0 .... SilvanoMulas 11 98
(Stefano Botti, Italy) *a cl up: qcknd to ld wl over 2 1/2f out: r.o u.p fnl f: a holding runner-up* **7/1**

2 1 **La Trinacria (USA)** 3-8-11 0 .... CarloFiocchi 10 96
(Agostino Affe', Italy) *hld up in midfield: hdwy 2 1/2f out: rdn to chse ldr fr under 2f out: r.o u.p fnl f: a hld by wnr* **183/10**

3 1 **Eternity Star (IRE)**[138] 3-8-11 0 .... GiuseppeCannarella 5 93
(Giuseppe Cannarella, Italy) *settled in midfield: rdn whn outpcd appr 2f out: sn edgd rt u.p: styd on wl fnl f: wnt 3rd cl home* **46/1**

4 hd **Endless Summer (ITY)**[168] 7764 3-8-11 0 .... MarcoMonteriso 4 93
(M Guarnieri, Italy) *w.w in midfield: rdn and hdwy 2 1/2f out: chal between horses over 2f out: kpt on at same pce fnl f: lost 3rd cl home* **197/10**

5 nk **Valuta Pregiata**[21] 3-8-11 0 .... AndreaAtzeni 9 92
(Stefano Botti, Italy) *chsd ldr: rdn and nt qckn wl over 2f out: styd on at same pce u.p appr fnl f* **79/10**

6 5 **Aquila Solitaria (IRE)**[182] 3-8-11 0 .... DarioVargiu 1 81
(Il Cavallo In Testa, Italy) *cl up: drvn to join ldrs 2f out: sn no further imp: wknd ins fnl f* **66/10**[3]

7 snk **Roderic Queen (IRE)**[168] 7764 3-8-11 0 .... AntonioFresu 2 80
(G Di Chio, Italy) *towards rr: lost pl and last wl bef 1/2-way: sme late hdwy but nvr in contention* **28/1**

8 2 **Al Hayyah (IRE)**[37] 3-8-11 0 .... FrankieDettori 7 76
(F Rohaut, France) *w.w in midfield: hdwy and rdn to press ldrs over 2f out: sn struggling: wknd ins fnl f* **51/20**[2]

9 8 **Leader Queen**[21] 3-8-11 0 .... GermanoMarcelli 6 57
(Francesco Pisano, Italy) *w.w in rr: rdn and no imp wl over 2f out: sn wl btn* **90/1**

10 3/4 **Naldina (IRE)**[217] 3-8-11 0 .... MarioEsposito 8 56
(Riccardo Santini, Italy) *w.w towards rr: rdn and no imp 2 1/2f out: wl hld fnl 1 1/2f* **39/1**

11 4 **Victim Of Love (ITY)**[168] 7764 3-8-11 0 .... FabioBranca 3 46
(Stefano Botti, Italy) *led: hdd wl over 2 1/2f out: wknd fnl 2f: wl hld whn heavily eased* **76/100**[1]

1m 36.4s (-3.40) **11** Ran SP% **141.1**
WIN (incl. 1 euro stake): 8.02. PLACES: 3.18, 4.23, 10.05. DF: 140.14.
Owner Stefano Botti **Bred** Miss Jackie Penny **Trained** Italy

1686a PREMIO PARIOLI - ITALIAN 2000 GUINEAS (GROUP 3) (3YO COLTS) (TURF) 1m
4:50 (12:00) 3-Y-0 **£47,794** (£21,029; £11,470; £5,735)

RPR

1 **Poeta Diletto**[21] 3-9-2 0 .... AndreaAtzeni 10 102
(Stefano Botti, Italy) *pressed ldr: drvn to ld over 2f out: r.o u.p fnl f: a jst holding runner-up* **87/20**[3]

2 hd **Qatar Dream (IRE)**[35] 3-9-2 0 .... FrankieDettori 11 102
(F Rohaut, France) *w.w in tch: 5th and styng on whn rdn 2f out: chsd ldr appr 1f out: sustained chal u.p fnl f: a jst hld* **95/40**[1]

3 2 1/2 **Super Chic (IRE)**[21] 3-9-2 0 .... DarioVargiu 3 96
(Il Cavallo In Testa, Italy) *w.w in midfield: tk clsr order 1/2-way: rdn and pressed ldrs 2f out: nt pce of front two ins fnl f: jst hld 3rd* **79/20**[2]

4 shd **Lucan Sweet (ITY)**[210] 3-9-2 0 .... SilvanoMulas 6 96
(Il Cavallo In Testa, Italy) *settled in midfield: hdwy under 2f out: styd on wl fnl f: jst missed 3rd* **79/20**[2]

5 1 1/4 **Michele Strogoff**[35] 3-9-2 0 .... Francois-XavierBertras 2 93
(Simone Brogi, France) *w.w in midfield: rdn and hdwy 3f out: chsd ldrs wl over 2f out: kpt on u.p but grad lft bhd fnl f* **129/10**

6 6 **Nice Name (IRE)**[35] 3-9-2 0 .... LucaManiezzi 12 79
(Marco Gasparini, Italy) *racd in fnl 3rd: tk clsr order on outer 3f out: styd on u.p over 1f out: nvr on terms* **79/10**

7 2 **Basileus (IRE)**[189] 7329 3-9-2 0 .... (b) WilliamBuick 5 74
(Stefano Botti, Italy) *w.w in midfield: rdn and no imp fnl 2f* **79/10**

8 2 **Voice Of Love (IRE)**[35] 3-9-2 0 .... FabioBranca 14 70
(Stefano Botti, Italy) *prom on outer: rdn and btn appr 2f out* **81/10**

9 1 1/4 **Giogiobbo**[301] 3704 3-9-2 0 .... SilvestreDeSousa 16 67
(Francesco Santella, Italy) *tk v str hold: sn restrained towards rr: sme hdwy over 1 1/2f out: nvr in contention* **235/10**

10 nk **Irishman Mark (IRE)**[138] 3-9-2 0 .... SalvatoreBasile 4 66
(Agostino Affe', Italy) *towards rr: sme mod prog 2 1/2f out: nvr trbld ldng gp* **41/1**

11 1/2 **Dylan Dancing (IRE)**[21] 3-9-2 0 .... FedericoBossa 7 65
(A Marcialis, Italy) *led: rdn and hdd over 2f out: sn wknd* **49/1**

12 1 **Neruda (IRE)** 3-9-2 0 .... MartinHarley 9 63
(Waldemar Hickst, Germany) *cl up: nt qckn whn rdn over 2f out: sn dropped away* **136/10**

13 2 **Gagner Sa Vie (ITY)** 3-9-2 0 .... CarloFiocchi 15 58
(Endo Botti, Italy) *hld up in fnl 3rd: sme hdwy 3f out: sn rdn and wl btn fr 1 1/2f out* **40/1**

14 *2* **Exclusive Potion (FR)**[35] 3-9-2 0 NicolaPinna 13 53
(Stefano Botti, Italy) *hld up in tch: rdn and wknd fr 2f out* **269/10**
15 *2* **Don Aurelio (IRE)** 3-9-2 0 GabrieleBietolini 8 49
(G Di Chio, Italy) *a among bkmarkers: nvr in contention* **99/10**
16 *nse* **Staisenzapenzieri (IRE)**[133] 3-9-2 0 MarioEsposito 1 49
(Francesco Santella, Italy) *a in rr: nvr involved* **95/1**
1m 35.8s (-4.00) **16** Ran SP% **160.9**
WIN (incl. 1 euro stake): 5.33. PLACES: 1.71, 1.65, 1.90. DF: 18.73.
Owner Scuderia Blueberry SRL **Bred** Scuderia Blueberry SRL **Trained** Italy

1687 - (Foreign Racing) - See Raceform Interactive

[1579]CHANTILLY (R-H)
Sunday, April 24

OFFICIAL GOING: Turf: good to soft; polytrack: standard

1688a PRIX DE BARBEVILLE (GROUP 3) (4YO+) (TURF) 1m 7f
3:45 (12:00) 4-Y-O+ **£29,411** (£11,764; £8,823; £5,882; £2,941)

RPR
1 **Fly With Me (FR)**[23] 1194 6-8-13 0 (p) MaximeGuyon 8 111+
(E Libaud, France) *w.w in midfield: shkn up and hdwy on outer over 1 1/2f out: sustained run fnl f: led cl home* **11/4**[2]
2 *nk* **Candarliya (FR)**[190] 7279 4-9-0 0 ChristopheSoumillon 3 115
(A De Royer-Dupre, France) *led early: sn hdd and w.w in tch: shkn up to chal fr 2f out: led ent fnl f: hdd cl home: no ex* **15/8**[1]
3 *1 3/4* **Trip To Rhodos (FR)**[203] 6973 7-8-13 0 CristianDemuro 9 109
(Pavel Tuma, Czech Republic) *hld up towards rr: rdn and styd on to chse ldng gp over 1 1/2f out: nt clr run and swtchd ins 1f out: kpt on u.p but nt pce to rch first two* **25/1**
4 *1/2* **Kicky Blue (GER)**[27] 1130 6-8-9 0 AlexisBadel 6 104
(T Clout, France) *sn led: rdn whn pressed over 2f out and rallied: hdd ent fnl f: no ex* **18/1**
5 *1/2* **Walzertakt (GER)**[182] 7502 7-9-3 0 IoritzMendizabal 12 111
(Jean-Pierre Carvalho, Germany) *prom on outer: rdn to hold pl over 2 1/2f out: styd on u.p: nt pce to mount a chal* **33/1**
6 *snk* **Hale Soriano**[23] 1194 5-8-9 0 ThierryJarnet 7 103
(P Bary, France) *w.w cl up: rdn and nt qckn 1 1/2f out: styd on at same pce fnl f* **7/1**
7 *1 1/2* **Kloud Gate (FR)**[23] 1194 4-8-9 0 UmbertoRispoli 1 104
(Gianluca Bietolini, Italy) *w.w in midfield: rdn and kpt on appr fnl f: nvr in contention* **18/1**
8 *1 3/4* **Alex My Boy (IRE)**[182] 7502 5-9-3 0 OlivierPeslier 13 107
(A Wohler, Germany) *settled towards rr: rdn and effrt wl over 1 1/2f out: sn btn* **17/2**
9 *nk* **Prince Nomad (FR)**[23] 1194 5-8-9 0 StephanePasquier 11 99
(Y Gourraud, France) *w.w toward rr: no real imp fnl 2f* **14/1**
10 *snk* **Mille Et Mille**[182] 7502 6-9-5 0 ThierryThulliez 4 108
(C Lerner, France) *hld up in midfield: rdn and nt qckn over 2f out: sn wknd* **5/1**[3]
11 *1* **Keen Glance (IRE)**[33] 6-8-6 0 VincentCheminaud 10 94
(Y Gourraud, France) *w.w in rr: rdn and no imp fr 2f out: nvr a factor* **25/1**
12 *5* **Shimrano (GER)**[294] 3944 4-9-3 0 FabriceVeron 2 102
(M Delzangles, France) *chsd ldng gp: rdn and wknd 2f out* **33/1**
3m 18.13s (2.03)
WFA 4 from 5yo+ 3lb **12** Ran SP% **131.9**
WIN (incl. 1 euro stake): 4.90. PLACES: 1.70, 2.20, 3.90. DF: 8.40. SF: 19.70.
Owner Ecurie Luck **Bred** Sca La Barbotiere **Trained** France

FOCUS
It proved hard to make up ground in the straight.

KREFELD (R-H)
Sunday, April 24

OFFICIAL GOING: Turf: good

1689a PREIS DER SWK STADTWERKE KREFELD - DR BUSCH-MEMORIAL (GROUP 3) (3YO) (TURF) 1m 110y
3:30 (12:00) 3-Y-O **£23,529** (£8,823; £4,411; £2,205; £1,470)

RPR
1 **Millowitsch (GER)**[235] 6007 3-9-2 0 AndreasHelfenbein 2 103+
(Markus Klug, Germany) *settled in midfield: shkn up and hdwy to chal ldrs on inner 2f out: rdn and swtchd outside as wnr edgd rt 1 1/2f out: styd on u.p appr fnl f: inched clsr and got up on line* **33/10**[2]
2 *nse* **El Loco (GER)**[168] 7768 3-9-2 0 AdrieDeVries 7 103
(Markus Klug, Germany) *led: rdn and edgd rt 1 1/2f out: styd on gamely u.p fnl f: hdd fnl stride* **33/10**[2]
3 *2 1/4* **Noor Al Hawa (FR)**[225] 6341 3-9-2 0 EduardoPedroza 1 98
(A Wohler, Germany) *w.w in midfield: scrubbed along 3f out and no real imp: styd on u.p to go 3rd 1f out: kpt on fnl f: nt pce to chal first two* **21/10**[1]
4 *1 3/4* **Capitano (GER)** 3-9-2 0 AlexanderPietsch 3 94
(J Hirschberger, Germany) *w.w in fnl pair: shkn up and hdwy on inner fr 2f out: kpt on ins fnl f: nvr trbld ldrs* **123/10**
5 *1* **Parthenius (GER)**[168] 7768 3-9-2 0 AndreasSuborics 6 92
(Mario Hofer, Germany) *chsd ldr: rdn to chal wl over 1 1/2f out: sn struggling and dropped away ins fnl f* **11/2**[3]
6 *1 1/4* **Molly King (GER)** 3-9-2 0 IanFerguson 5 89
(J Hirschberger, Germany) *t.k.h: hld up in rr: hrd rdn and effrt 1 1/2f out: no real imp appr fnl f: sn btn and eased* **212/10**
7 *hd* **Jarahi (IRE)** 3-9-2 0 MichaelCadeddu 4 89
(Andreas Lowe, Germany) *w.w in midfield on outer: rdn and no imp ins fnl 1 1/2f: sn btn* **81/10**
8 *1 1/2* **Volcancito (SWI)** 3-9-2 0 AndraschStarke 8 86
(A Wohler, Germany) *hld up towards rr: rdn and short-lived effrt on outer wl over 1 1/2f out: wknd ins fnl f* **6/1**
1m 43.36s (-3.24) **8** Ran SP% **131.5**
WIN (incl. 10 euro stake): 43. PLACES: 17, 17, 15. SF: 147.
Owner Dr Alexandra Margarete Renz **Bred** Frau Dr Alexandra Margarete Renz **Trained** Germany

[1025]SHA TIN (R-H)
Sunday, April 24

OFFICIAL GOING: Turf: good to yielding changing to yielding after race 1 (8.00)

1690a AUDEMARS PIGUET QEII CUP (GROUP 1) (3YO+) (TURF) 1m 2f
9:35 (12:00) 3-Y-O+
£998,248 (£385,288; £175,131; £99,824; £57,793; £35,026)

RPR
1 **Werther (NZ)**[35] 1025 4-9-0 0 (b) HughBowman 5 123
(John Moore, Hong Kong) **91/20**[2]
2 *4 1/2* **Military Attack (IRE)**[56] 761 8-9-0 0 NashRawiller 9 114
(C Fownes, Hong Kong) **70/1**
3 *1 1/4* **Blazing Speed**[21] 7-9-0 0 (t) NeilCallan 3 112
(A S Cruz, Hong Kong) **24/1**
4 *nk* **Lovely Day (JPN)**[21] 6-9-0 0 JoaoMoreira 1 111
(Yasutoshi Ikee, Japan) **19/10**[1]
5 *nk* **Designs On Rome (IRE)**[21] 6-9-0 0 TommyBerry 2 110
(John Moore, Hong Kong) **13/2**
6 *1 1/4* **Nuovo Record (JPN)**[21] 5-8-10 0 YutakaTake 7 104
(Makoto Saito, Japan) **11/1**
7 *1* **Helene Happy Star (IRE)**[32] 5-9-0 0 BlakeShinn 12 106
(John Moore, Hong Kong) **29/1**
8 *2* **Highland Reel (IRE)**[29] 1107 4-9-0 0 RyanMoore 6 102
(A P O'Brien, Ire) *pushed along early to chse ldng gp: sn shuffled bk into midfield: rdn and lost pl 2 1/2f out: sme prog u.p but nt in contention whn nt clr run more than 1f out: no further imp* **48/10**[3]
9 *1 1/4* **Ertijaal (AUS)**[29] 1106 4-9-0 0 DouglasWhyte 11 99
(M F De Kock, South Africa) **56/1**
10 *4 3/4* **Rising Romance (NZ)**[15] 1364 5-8-10 0 (p) DamianLane 4 86
(David A Hayes & Tom Dabernig, Australia) **62/1**
11 *2 1/2* **Horse Of Fortune (SAF)**[32] 5-9-0 0 KarisTeetan 10 85
(A T Millard, Hong Kong) **16/1**
12 *nk* **Satono Crown (JPN)**[70] 4-9-0 0 ZacPurton 8 84
(Noriyuki Hori, Japan) **7/1**
13 *3* **Helene Super Star (USA)**[32] 6-9-0 0 (tp) BrettPrebble 13 78
(A S Cruz, Hong Kong) **121/1**
2m 1.32s (-0.08) **13** Ran SP% **122.7**
PARI-MUTUEL (all including 10 hkd stake): WIN 55.50; PLACE 19.50, 101.00, 55.50; DF 1946.50.

Owner Johnson Chen **Bred** C D Allison, C V & J A Barnao et al **Trained** Hong Kong

FOCUS
The first two came from the rear.

AYR (L-H)
Monday, April 25

OFFICIAL GOING: Good to firm (good in places; 7.4)
Wind: Almost nil Weather: Overcast

1691 RACING UK 1 PRICE 3 DEVICES MAIDEN STKS 6f
2:20 (2:26) (Class 5) 3-Y-O+ **£3,234** (£962; £481; £240) **Stalls** Low

Form RPR
2 **1** **Irish Optimism (IRE)**[14] 1383 3-9-3 0 PhillipMakin 6 77
(John Quinn) *cl up: ev ch over 2f out: rdn and edgd lft over 1f out: led ins fnl f: drvn out* **5/1**[3]
220- **2** *1* **Geno (IRE)**[205] 6931 3-9-3 74 (p) GrahamLee 8 74
(Kevin Ryan) *trckd ldrs: led over 2f out: sn hrd pressed: rdn and hdd ins fnl f: kpt on same pce towards fin* **5/2**[1]
3 *1 1/4* **Insurplus (IRE)** 3-9-3 0 DanielTudhope 9 70+
(Jim Goldie) *slowly away: t.k.h in rr: hdwy 1/2-way: effrt and chsng ldrs whn bmpd ins fnl f: kpt on: improve* **40/1**
3 **4** *nk* **Sophie P**[22] 1216 3-8-12 0 PJMcDonald 5 64
(R Mike Smith) *prom: rdn along over 2f out: hung lft u.p and bmpd rival ins fnl f: kpt on same pce* **13/2**
0 **5** *6* **Patience A Plenty (IRE)**[36] 1014 3-8-12 0 KierenFallon 10 45
(Adrian Paul Keatley, Ire) *hld up on outside: hdwy and prom over 2f out: rdn and outpcd over 1f out* **5/1**[3]
403- **6** *1 3/4* **Overhaugh Street**[182] 7515 3-9-3 74 JasonHart 2 44
(Keith Dalgleish) *led: rdn and hdd over 2f out: wknd over 1f out* **9/1**
7 *1* **Sabrina Brazzo** 3-8-12 0 ConnorBeasley 7 36
(Michael Dods) *t.k.h: hld up in tch: outpcd and edgd lft over 2f out: sn btn* **16/1**
8 *3 1/4* **Portland Street (IRE)** 3-9-3 0 PaulMulrennan 3 31
(Bryan Smart) *slowly away: rn green in rr: detached over 3f out: sme late hdwy: nvr on terms* **9/2**[2]
000- **9** *2* **Sneakin'Pete**[200] 7056 3-9-3 0 JamesSullivan 1 24
(Linda Perratt) *hld up: rdn and outpcd over 2f out: sn wknd* **200/1**
00-6 **10** *2 1/2* **Final Spring (IRE)**[14] 1383 3-8-12 0 BarryMcHugh 4 11
(Jim Goldie) *t.k.h: prom tl rdn and wknd fr 2f out* **100/1**
1m 13.93s (1.53) **Going Correction** +0.10s/f (Good) **10** Ran SP% **113.2**
Speed ratings (Par 103): **93,91,90,89,81 79,77,73,70,67**
CSF £17.31 TOTE £5.40: £1.80, £1.40, £5.80; EX 17.80 Trifecta £335.00.
Owner Harlen Ltd **Bred** Cathal Ennis **Trained** Settrington, N Yorks

FOCUS
Track at full width and all distances as advertised. The ground had dried out appreciably on a cold day. ORDinary maiden form, set around the runner-up and the fourth. THe winner was up a stone or so on his debut.

1692 WATCH ON THE RACING UK APP H'CAP 6f
2:50 (2:57) (Class 5) (0-70,70) 4-Y-O+ **£3,234** (£962; £481; £240) **Stalls** Low

Form RPR
450- **1** **Mo Henry**[24] 1191 4-8-8 57 (p) KierenFallon 7 67
(Adrian Paul Keatley, Ire) *t.k.h: trckd ldrs: nt clr run briefly over 2f out: rdn to ld over 1f out: edgd lft: drvn out* **9/2**[2]
50-2 **2** *1 1/4* **Chookie's Lass**[13] 1402 5-9-0 63 JasonHart 11 68
(Keith Dalgleish) *t.k.h: led to over 1f out: rallied: kpt on ins fnl f: hld towards fin* **17/2**
4-50 **3** *1 1/2* **Keene's Pointe**[9] 1496 6-9-0 63 TonyHamilton 1 63+
(Kristin Stubbs) *hld up: nt clr run over 2f out: hdwy over 1f out: kpt on fnl f: nrst fin* **9/1**

0-00 **4** *shd* **Exotic Guest**[9] 1488 6-9-3 **66**........................(p) JamesSullivan 3 66
(Ruth Carr) *t.k.h: hld up: rdn and hdwy over 1f out: kpt on same pce ins fnl f* **7/1**

200- **5** *1½* **Jinky**[195] 7188 8-9-7 **70**........................ GeorgeChaloner 6 65
(Linda Perratt) *awkward s: sn midfield: effrt and pushed along over 1f out: kpt on same pce ins fnl f* **11/1**

3-54 **6** *½* **Giant Spark**[9] 1488 4-8-11 **60**........................ PaulMulrennan 2 53+
(Paul Midgley) *in tch: rdn over 2f out: rallied over 1f out: kpt on ins fnl f: no imp* **4/1**[1]

400- **7** *¾* **Goninodaethat**[200] 7057 8-8-10 **59**........................ GrahamLee 8 50
(Jim Goldie) *prom: drvn along 2f out: outpcd fnl f* **16/1**

60-0 **8** *1* **Jebel Tara**[9] 1488 11-9-2 **65**........................(bt) ShaneGray 5 53
(Alan Brown) *cl up: rdn over 2f out: wknd ins fnl f* **16/1**

530- **9** *1* **Star Cracker (IRE)**[192] 7255 4-9-4 **67**........................ DanielTudhope 4 52
(Jim Goldie) *hld up: pushed along over 2f out: nvr rchd ldrs* **5/1**[3]

30-0 **10** *hd* **Reflation**[19] 1254 4-8-7 **61**........................ PhilDennis(5) 9 45
(Michael Dods) *dwlt: hld up on outside: rdn over 2f out: wknd over 1f out* **20/1**

402- **11** *4* **Amber Crystal**[271] 4750 4-8-13 **62**........................ PJMcDonald 10 33
(Linda Perratt) *trckd ldrs tl rdn and wknd over 1f out* **25/1**

1m 12.45s (0.05) **Going Correction** +0.10s/f (Good) **11** Ran SP% **116.6**
Speed ratings (Par 103): **103,101,99,99,97 96,95,94,92,92 87**
CSF £42.26 CT £337.82 TOTE £7.10: £2.30, £2.90, £2.70; EX 58.00 Trifecta £417.50.
Owner Shevlin Whelan Syndicate **Bred** Shevlin-Whelan Syndicate **Trained** Friarstown, Co. Kildare

FOCUS
A moderate handicap. The winner is rated close to last year's turf best.

1693 RACING UK H'CAP 5f
3:20 (3:23) (Class 5) (0-75,73) 3-Y-O+ **£3,234** (£962; £481; £240) **Stalls** Low

Form RPR

3- **1** **Anonymous Lady (IRE)**[17] 1328 4-9-11 **70**........................(t) KierenFallon 5 78+
(Adrian Paul Keatley, Ire) *trckd ldrs: shkn up to ld over 1f out: kpt on wl fnl f* **5/4**[1]

044- **2** *1¼* **Koptoon**[247] 5629 4-9-12 **71**........................(t) AndrewMullen 3 74
(Michael Appleby) *pressed ldr: rdn and ev ch over 1f out: kpt on same pce ins fnl f* **6/4**[2]

10-4 **3** *¾* **Go Go Green (IRE)**[14] 1378 10-10-0 **73**........................ DanielTudhope 1 73
(Jim Goldie) *dwlt: in tch: effrt and rdn over 1f out: kpt on ins fnl f: no imp* **5/1**[3]

000- **4** *4* **Blue Sonic**[195] 7188 6-9-10 **69**........................ PJMcDonald 2 55
(Linda Perratt) *led: rdn and hdd over 1f out: sn wknd* **16/1**

1m 1.32s (1.92) **Going Correction** +0.10s/f (Good) **4** Ran SP% **107.0**
Speed ratings (Par 103): **88,86,84,78**
CSF £3.36 TOTE £2.30; EX 3.80 Trifecta £6.00.
Owner A P Keatley & Miss S Shiels **Bred** Aidan Sexton **Trained** Friarstown, Co. Kildare

FOCUS
A depleted field but a convincing winner, who didn't need to match last year's C&D form.

1694 WEDDINGS AT WESTERN HOUSE HOTEL H'CAP 7f 50y
3:50 (3:53) (Class 4) (0-85,85) 4-Y-O+ **£5,175** (£1,540; £769; £384) **Stalls** High

Form RPR

102- **1** **Funding Deficit (IRE)**[212] 6738 6-9-1 **79**........................ DanielTudhope 5 87
(Jim Goldie) *hld up: stdy hdwy over 2f out: effrt and rdn over 1f out: led ins fnl f: kpt on wl* **7/1**

514- **2** *hd* **Sea Wolf (IRE)**[170] 7758 4-9-4 **82**........................ PaulMulrennan 7 89
(Michael Dods) *hld up in tch: hdwy to ld over 1f out: rdn and hdd ins fnl f: kpt on: hld nr fin* **10/3**[2]

00-0 **3** *¾* **Gurkha Friend**[41] 944 4-9-0 **78**........................ GrahamLee 3 84+
(Karen McLintock) *chsd ldrs: rdn over 2f out: rallied over 1f out: kpt on ins fnl f* **9/1**

20-0 **4** *3* **Gworn**[22] 1221 6-9-5 **83**........................ PJMcDonald 1 80
(R Mike Smith) *sn trcking ldr: rdn and ev ch over 1f out: wknd ins fnl f* **5/1**[3]

003- **5** *3* **Mount Tahan (IRE)**[206] 6895 4-9-7 **85**........................ KeaganLatham 6 74
(Kevin Ryan) *led at decent gallop: rdn and hdd over 1f out: wknd fnl f* **9/4**[1]

50-0 **6** *1¾* **Alexandrakollontai (IRE)**[22] 1215 6-9-3 **81**........................(b) JamesSullivan 4 65
(Alistair Whillans) *bhd and outpcd: rdn along 1/2-way: kpt on fnl f: nvr able to chal* **20/1**

00-3 **7** *7* **Townsville**[111] 50 4-9-4 **82**........................ PhillipMakin 2 47
(Keith Dalgleish) *t.k.h: trckd ldrs: rdn over 2f out: wknd over 1f out* **15/2**

1m 30.93s (-2.47) **Going Correction** -0.20s/f (Firm) **7** Ran SP% **109.5**
Speed ratings (Par 105): **106,105,104,101,98 96,88**
CSF £27.89 TOTE £7.60: £2.60, £2.30; EX 18.30 Trifecta £52.50.
Owner D G Pryde **Bred** Rancho San Peasea S A **Trained** Uplawmoor, E Renfrews

FOCUS
A 78-85 handicap run at a sound gallop and the first three home came from off the pace. The form is rated at face value, but there are doubts.

1695 CONFERENCE AND EVENTS AT AYR RACECOURSE H'CAP (DIV I) 1m
4:20 (4:23) (Class 6) (0-65,65) 4-Y-O+ **£2,264** (£673; £336; £168) **Stalls** Low

Form RPR

140- **1** **Haidees Reflection**[217] 6585 6-9-2 **60**........................ DanielTudhope 2 67
(Jim Goldie) *trckd ldrs: smooth hdwy over 1f out: rdn to ld ins fnl f: kpt on wl* **9/2**[3]

3-05 **2** *¾* **Tellovoi (IRE)**[5] 1565 8-9-2 **65**........................(v) RobJFitzpatrick(5) 3 70
(Richard Guest) *s.v.s: hld up: hdwy over 2f out: effrt and rdn on outside over 1f out: kpt on wl to take 2nd nr fin* **7/2**[1]

0236 **3** *shd* **Princess Peaches**[33] 1047 4-9-0 **58**........................ PJMcDonald 9 63
(James Bethell) *trckd ldr: led over 2f out: rdn and hdd ins fnl f: kpt on same pce: lost 2nd nr fin* **8/1**

00-0 **4** *2¼* **Lightning Spree (IRE)**[23] 1202 4-9-7 **65**........................ ShaneGray 1 65
(Kevin Ryan) *s.i.s: plld hrd: hld up in tch on ins: effrt and rdn 2f out: no imp fnl f* **8/1**

020- **5** *1¾* **Let Right Be Done**[195] 7189 4-9-6 **64**........................ GeorgeChaloner 4 59
(Linda Perratt) *t.k.h: trckd ldrs: rdn and ev ch over 1f out: wknd ins fnl f* **12/1**

-404 **6** *2½* **Incurs Four Faults**[88] 368 5-8-10 **54**........................ JasonHart 8 43
(Keith Dalgleish) *t.k.h: led: rdn and hdd over 2f out: wknd over 1f out* **4/1**[2]

220- **7** *2* **Call Me Crockett (IRE)**[129] 8292 4-9-0 **63**........................(p) PhilDennis(5) 7 48
(Iain Jardine) *t.k.h: hld up: rdn and outpcd over 2f out: sn btn* **11/2**

2510 **8** *17* **Schottische**[56] 769 6-8-12 **56**........................(p) KierenFallon 10
(Alan Bailey) *hld up in tch on outside: struggling over 2f out: sn wknd: t.o* **14/1**

1m 42.49s (-1.31) **Going Correction** -0.20s/f (Firm) **8** Ran SP% **112.4**
Speed ratings (Par 101): **98,97,97,94,93 90,88,71**
CSF £19.88 CT £120.32 TOTE £4.90: £1.50, £2.30, £2.70; EX 24.50 Trifecta £71.90.
Owner Johnnie Delta Racing **Bred** Mrs J Way **Trained** Uplawmoor, E Renfrews

FOCUS
The leader dropped anchor and it paid to race close to the pace. Very ordinary form, the third helping with the level.

1696 CONFERENCE AND EVENTS AT AYR RACECOURSE H'CAP (DIV II) 1m
4:50 (4:53) (Class 6) (0-65,65) 4-Y-O+ **£2,264** (£673; £336; £168) **Stalls** Low

Form RPR

2 **1** **Pick Your Battle**[9] 1502 4-9-7 **65**........................(t) RoystonFfrench 1 72
(Iain Jardine) *trckd ldrs: rdn to ld over 1f out: kpt on wl fnl f* **5/2**[1]

4400 **2** *1¾* **Ted's Brother (IRE)**[3] 1595 8-8-13 **57**........................(e) JasonHart 10 59
(Richard Guest) *s.i.s: hld up: hdwy 2f out: sn rdn: chsd wnr wl ins fnl f: kpt on* **10/1**

15-4 **3** *shd* **Gone With The Wind (GER)**[20] 1247 5-9-7 **65**........(t) PaulMulrennan 6 67
(Rebecca Bastiman) *hld up: hdwy to trck ldrs wl over 1f out: sn pushed along: kpt on ins fnl f* **8/1**

4- **4** *3½* **Rock Montjeu (IRE)**[33] 1053 4-8-9 **53**........................ KierenFallon 3 46+
(Adrian Paul Keatley, Ire) *dwlt: hld up: drvn over 2f out: swtchd rt and hdwy over 1f out: kpt on fnl f: nt pce to chal* **3/1**[2]

540- **5** *1* **Alans Pride (IRE)**[220] 6497 4-9-4 **62**........................ ConnorBeasley 4 53
(Michael Dods) *trckd ldr: led over 2f out to over 1f out: wknd ins fnl f* **11/2**[3]

0455 **6** *3¼* **Ripon Rose**[9] 1495 4-8-7 **51** oh4........................ BarryMcHugh 7 34
(Paul Midgley) *t.k.h: prom: drvn along over 2f out: wknd fnl f* **20/1**

600- **7** *4½* **Elle Dorado**[190] 7314 4-8-11 **55**........................ DougieCostello 5 27
(David Loughnane) *t.k.h: hld up in tch: rdn and outpcd over 2f out: n.d after* **33/1**

205- **8** *½* **Kopassus (IRE)**[216] 6617 4-8-10 **59**........................ JordanNason(5) 9 30
(Lawrence Mullaney) *led to over 2f out: wknd over 1f out* **8/1**

600- **9** *2½* **Galilee Chapel (IRE)**[182] 7513 7-8-7 **51** oh1........(b) JamesSullivan 8 16
(Alistair Whillans) *t.k.h: hld up on outside: struggling over 2f out: sn wknd* **16/1**

1m 43.8s **Going Correction** -0.20s/f (Firm) **9** Ran SP% **113.9**
Speed ratings (Par 101): **92,90,90,86,85 82,77,77,74**
CSF £28.02 CT £174.39 TOTE £4.00: £1.80, £3.10, £1.70; EX 28.70 Trifecta £142.30.
Owner S Middleton **Bred** Horizon Bloodstock Limited **Trained** Carrutherstown, D'fries & G'way

FOCUS
Division two, and the pace was much steadier. A ready and relatively unexposed winner, and straightforward form in behind.

1697 SPRING PROMOTION AT WESTERN HOUSE HOTEL H'CAP 1m 2f
5:25 (5:25) (Class 5) (0-70,70) 4-Y-O+ **£3,234** (£962; £481; £240) **Stalls** Low

Form RPR

1 **Nice Vintage (IRE)**[121] 2731 4-8-0 **56** oh1........(v) RobbieDolan(7) 6 66+
(Adrian Paul Keatley, Ire) *s.i.s: hld up: hdwy on outside to ld over 2f out: rdn and edgd lft over 1f out: kpt on wl fnl f* **8/1**

345- **2** *2½* **Testa Rossa (IRE)**[157] 7923 6-8-9 **58**........................(p) KierenFallon 2 63
(Jim Goldie) *hld up: rdn over 2f out: hdwy to chse wnr over 1f out: kpt on fnl f: nt rch wnr* **13/2**[3]

130- **3** *¾* **Hero's Story**[157] 7920 6-8-7 **56** oh1........................ JamesSullivan 1 59
(Jim Goldie) *prom: effrt and rdn 2f out: kpt on ins fnl f* **10/1**

030- **4** *½* **Remember Rocky**[249] 5554 7-9-1 **67**........................(p) SammyJoBell(3) 9 69
(Lucy Normile) *hld up in tch: rdn over 2f out: kpt on fnl f: no imp* **13/2**[3]

5/35 **5** *½* **Thankyou Very Much**[16] 801 6-8-12 **61**........................(p) PJMcDonald 8 62
(James Bethell) *hld up bhd ldng gp: rdn along over 2f out: kpt on fnl f: n.d* **13/2**[3]

0405 **6** *½* **Hydrant**[20] 1248 10-8-11 **60**........................ ConnorBeasley 11 60
(Richard Guest) *trckd ldr: effrt and rdn over 2f out: no ex over 1f out* **5/1**[2]

405- **7** *6* **Haymarket**[200] 7058 7-9-0 **70**........................ AdamMcNamara(7) 7 58
(R Mike Smith) *s.i.s: sn chsng ldrs: led over 4f out to over 2f out: wknd fnl f* **9/2**[1]

00-6 **8** *15* **Moon Arc (IRE)**[76] 506 4-8-11 **60**........................(p) JasonHart 5 18
(Keith Dalgleish) *s.i.s: hld up: rdn over 3f out: hung lft and wknd over 2f out* **11/1**

10-3 **9** *2¼* **The Wee Barra (IRE)**[12] 1412 4-8-7 **63**........................(p) LewisEdmunds(7) 4 17
(Kevin Ryan) *hld up: rdn along over 3f out: sn n.d: btn fnl 2f* **8/1**

060- **10** *28* **Troy Boy**[320] 3042 6-8-2 **56** oh11........................(v[1]) PhilDennis(5) 3
(Rebecca Bastiman) *led to over 4f out: wknd quicky 3f out: t.o* **33/1**

2m 8.82s (-3.18) **Going Correction** -0.20s/f (Firm) **10** Ran SP% **117.4**
Speed ratings (Par 103): **104,102,101,101,100 100,95,83,81,59**
CSF £59.63 CT £531.13 TOTE £19.60: £2.80, £2.90, £3.20; EX 75.10 Trifecta £546.80.
Owner Lillies And Dubs Syndicate **Bred** Colman O'Flynn Jnr **Trained** Friarstown, Co. Kildare

FOCUS
An open looking 56-70 handicap run at just a steady pace and five still in with a big shout entering the final furlong. The form is set around the second to fourth.

1698 RACING UK'S PROFITS RETURNED TO RACING H'CAP 1m 2f
5:55 (5:57) (Class 6) (0-65,62) 3-Y-O **£2,264** (£673; £336; £168) **Stalls** Low

Form RPR

463- **1** **Sattelac**[242] 5775 3-9-7 **62**........................ PhillipMakin 9 66
(Keith Dalgleish) *prom: effrt over 2f out: led ins fnl f: rdn out* **7/2**[2]

06-1 **2** *1¾* **New Abbey Angel (IRE)**[61] 700 3-9-7 **62**........................ GrahamLee 4 63
(Gay Kelleway) *t.k.h: led: rdn and carried hd high over 1f out: hdd ins fnl f: sn no ex* **9/4**[1]

000- **3** *2* **Kazoey**[254] 5392 3-8-7 **48** oh3........................ DuranFentiman 5 45
(Chris Fairhurst) *trckd ldr: rdn over 2f out: kpt on same pce ins fnl f* **50/1**

060- **4** *3¾* **Wayside Magic**[215] 6655 3-9-4 **59**........................ PaulMulrennan 2 49
(Michael Dods) *prom: drvn along over 2f out: edgd lft: kpt on same pce fr over 1f out* **6/1**

04-0 **5** *7* **Blagger**[5] 1564 3-8-7 **48** oh3........................(t) ConnorBeasley 10 25
(Richard Guest) *s.i.s: hld up: rdn and outpcd over 4f out: sme late hdwy: nvr on terms* **14/1**

600- **6** *6* **Hazely**[132] 8232 3-8-9 **50**........................ PJMcDonald 1 15
(James Bethell) *trckd ldrs: rdn over 2f out: wknd over 1f out* **9/2**[3]

5565 **7** *10* **Ready Steady (USA)**[27] 1134 3-8-11 **52**........................ DougieCostello 3
(David Loughnane) *s.i.s: hld up: struggling over 2f out: sn btn* **14/1**

0-60 **8** *18* **Esspeegee**[26] 1155 3-8-11 **52**........................ KierenFallon 7
(Alan Bailey) *hld up: rdn and struggling 3f out: sn btn: t.o* **15/2**

2m 11.87s (-0.13) **Going Correction** -0.20s/f (Firm) **8** Ran SP% **112.5**
Speed ratings (Par 96): **92,90,89,86,80 75,67,53**
CSF £11.39 CT £316.38 TOTE £4.00: £1.40, £1.70, £5.30; EX 11.70 Trifecta £264.50.
Owner Tom Young **Bred** Jenny Hall Bloodstock & Sideways Bloodstock **Trained** Carluke, S Lanarks

FOCUS
A steadily-run low grade handicap but nothing got into it from the rear. The winner is rated a minor improver.

T/Jkpt: Not won. T/Plt: £44.90 to a £1 stake. Pool: £71,365.15 - 1,158.68 winning tickets T/Qpdt: £13.50 to a £1 stake. Pool: £5,029.28 - 275.4 winning tickets **Richard Young**

[1474]CHELMSFORD (A.W) (L-H)

Monday, April 25

OFFICIAL GOING: Polytrack: standard

Wind: light, half against Weather: showers

1699 TOTEPOOL FOLLOW US ON TWITTER H'CAP 1m 2f (P)

2:00 (2:01) (Class 5) (0-75,75) 4-Y-O+ **£5,175** (£1,540; £769; £384) **Stalls** Low

Form RPR

21-0 **1** **Hit List (IRE)**[23] 1201 4-9-1 **69** OisinMurphy 5 76+
(Andrew Balding) *mde all: rdn and qcknd wl over 1f out: hld on gamely ins fnl f: rdn out* **3/1**[2]

4244 **2** 1 **Van Huysen (IRE)**[24] 1173 4-9-7 **75** (p) JamesDoyle 4 80
(Dominic Ffrench Davis) *t.k.h: chsd wnr thrght: rdn wl over 1f out: kpt on same pce ins fnl f* **3/1**[2]

111 **3** ¾ **Giovanni Di Bicci**[40] 951 4-9-4 **72** (t) FrankieDettori 3 76+
(Jim Boyle) *t.k.h: chsd ldng pair: swtchd rt and effrt over 1f out: kpt on same pce u.p ins fnl f* **11/8**[1]

66-0 **4** 3 ¾ **Theydon Bois**[81] 437 4-8-9 **63** (v) MartinLane 1 59
(Peter Charalambous) *stdd s: hld up in rr: effrt wl over 1f out: no imp and sn outpcd: kpt on same pce ins fnl f* **14/1**

0004 **5** shd **Maverik**[9] 1501 8-8-12 **66** (t) CharlesBishop 2 62
(Ali Stronge) *t.k.h: hld up in tch in 4th: clsd 3f out: rdn and unable qck over 1f out: outpcd and btn 1f out: lost 4th last stride* **8/1**[3]

2m 10.79s (2.19) **Going Correction** +0.10s/f (Slow) **5** Ran SP% **109.9**
Speed ratings (Par 103): **95,94,93,90,90**
CSF £12.17 TOTE £2.80: £1.70, £1.50; EX 12.70 Trifecta £18.70.
Owner Another Bottle Racing 2 **Bred** G A E & J Smith Bloodstock Ltd **Trained** Kingsclere, Hants

FOCUS
A meeting originally scheduled for Yarmouth. The pace was steady and first three home raced 1-2-3 for the majority of the contest. The form is rated around the second.

1700 TOTEPOOL LIKE US ON FACEBOOK H'CAP 7f (P)

2:30 (2:30) (Class 5) (0-70,70) 4-Y-O+ **£5,175** (£1,540; £769; £384) **Stalls** Low

Form RPR

3100 **1** **The Happy Hammer (IRE)**[29] 1117 10-8-8 **64** LuluStanford(7) 5 71
(Eugene Stanford) *hld up in midfield: effrt wl over 1f out: swtchd rt jst over 1f out: styd on to chal and edgd lft 100yds out: led towards fin* **12/1**

4220 **2** nk **Nasri**[9] 1496 10-9-3 **66** JamieSpencer 2 72
(Emma Owen) *chsd ldrs: rdn ent fnl 2f: ev ch and drvn over 1f out: led fnl 100yds: hdd and no ex towards fin* **5/1**

4443 **3** ¾ **Malaysian Boleh**[18] 1291 6-9-1 **69** (b) CallumShepherd(5) 7 73
(Shaun Lycett) *in tch in midfield: effrt over 1f out: hdwy u.p to ld 1f out: edgd rt and hdd 100yds out: styd on same pce towards fin* **3/1**[1]

5260 **4** nk **Cookie Ring (IRE)**[19] 1262 5-8-3 **59** (v) PaulaMuir(7) 3 66+
(Patrick Holmes) *stdd s: t.k.h: hld up in tch in rr: clsd and swtchd rt jst over 1f out: n.m.r ins fnl f: gng for gap whn squeezed out and hmpd wl ins fnl f: kpt on same pce after* **4/1**[3]

4000 **5** ½ **Alhella**[21] 1237 4-9-7 **70** WilliamCarson 4 72
(Mick Quinn) *led: rdn ent fnl 2f: hrd pressed and drvn over 1f out: hdd 1f out: no ex and one pce fnl 100yds* **20/1**

2116 **6** 1 **Misu Pete**[12] 1415 4-8-13 **62** OisinMurphy 6 61+
(Mark Usher) *chsd ldng pair: nt clr run fr over 1f out: trying to switch rt and get out after: gap nvr c and rdr gave up and eased towards fin* **10/3**[2]

5600 **7** 4 ½ **Wink Oliver**[12] 1416 4-9-6 **69** (p) MartinLane 1 56
(David Dennis) *stdd s: t.k.h: hld up in last pair: effrt on outer 2f out: no imp over 1f out: wknd fnl f* **5/1**

1m 28.07s (0.87) **Going Correction** +0.10s/f (Slow) **7** Ran SP% **113.9**
Speed ratings (Par 103): **99,98,97,97,96 95,90**
CSF £69.18 TOTE £12.00: £7.00, £2.60; EX 78.80 Trifecta £365.60.
Owner newmarketracingclub.co.uk **Bred** Rathbarry Stud **Trained** Newmarket, Suffolk

FOCUS
A couple of these met significant trouble in the straight and it looked like the best two horses on the day finished 4th and 6th. The winner was seemingly back to his 2014 form.

1701 MYTOTEPOOL.COM EBF MAIDEN STKS 7f (P)

3:00 (3:01) (Class 5) 3-Y-O **£5,175** (£1,540; £769; £384) **Stalls** Low

Form RPR

2- **1** **War Story (IRE)**[159] 7888 3-9-5 0 AdamKirby 6 88
(Luca Cumani) *chsd ldr tl led after 1f: mde rest: rdn and qcknd ent fnl 2f: styd on wl: rdn out* **7/2**[3]

5 **2** 1 ½ **Raven's Corner (IRE)**[13] 1397 3-9-5 0 WilliamBuick 9 84
(John Gosden) *chsd ldng pair: effrt and swtchd rt 2f out: kpt on u.p but nvr enough pce to chal wnr: wnt 2nd wl ins fnl f* **6/1**

33- **3** nk **Aristocratic**[212] 6751 3-9-0 0 RyanMoore 10 78
(Sir Michael Stoute) *t.k.h early: led for 1f: chsd wnr after: rdn 2f out: drvn and kpt on same pce fr over 1f out: lost 2nd wl ins fnl f* **5/4**[1]

44-3 **4** 2 ½ **Tigerwolf (IRE)**[12] 1423 3-9-5 88 CharlesBishop 4 76
(Mick Channon) *hld up in midfield: hdwy 1/2-way: 4th and no imp whn hung lft over 1f out: kpt on but no threat to ldrs ins fnl f* **5/2**[2]

0- **5** 3 **City By The Bay**[217] 6596 3-9-0 0 GaryMahon(5) 5 68
(Richard Hannon) *in tch in midfield: pushed along over 2f out: sme hdwy 1f out: kpt on ins fnl f: no threat to ldrs* **33/1**

0-0 **6** hd **Pure Soul**[19] 1270 3-9-2 0 (p) ThomasBrown(3) 3 68
(Ismail Mohammed) *chsd ldng trio: rdn and outpcd in 5th over 1f out: wl hld and plugged on same pce fnl f* **66/1**

7 2 ½ **Diamond Geyser (IRE)** 3-9-5 0 LemosdeSouza 2 61
(Luca Cumani) *dwlt: hld up in last trio: pushed along over 1f out: sme hdwy and swtchd lft 1f out: kpt on but no threat to ldrs* **33/1**

3-4 **8** 3 ¾ **Maddys Dream**[22] 1217 3-9-2 0 SimonPearce(3) 1 51
(Lydia Pearce) *in tch in midfield: rdn and no imp over 1f out: sn wknd* **33/1**

50 **9** 3 ¾ **Dalavand (IRE)**[31] 1079 3-9-5 0 TimmyMurphy 8 41
(Jamie Osborne) *stdd s: hld up in last trio: pushed along and no hdwy over 1f out: sn wknd* **100/1**

10 1 ½ **Missed The Cut** 3-9-5 0 JimCrowley 7 37
(Michael Wigham) *stdd s: hld up in rr: pushed along and no hdwy over 1f out: sn wknd* **50/1**

1m 26.87s (-0.33) **Going Correction** +0.10s/f (Slow) **10** Ran SP% **122.8**
Speed ratings (Par 98): **105,103,102,100,96 96,93,89,85,83**
CSF £24.68 TOTE £4.10: £1.10, £2.00, £1.80; EX 19.00 Trifecta £50.70.
Owner Geoff Grimish **Bred** SF Bloodstock LLC **Trained** Newmarket, Suffolk

FOCUS
The form is useful, although few were involved. The third and fourth set a good standard.

1702 TOTEPOOL BETTING ON ALL UK RACING H'CAP 1m (P)

3:30 (3:32) (Class 4) (0-80,80) 4-Y-O+ **£8,086** (£2,406; £1,202; £601) **Stalls** Low

Form RPR

2210 **1** **Welliesinthewater (IRE)**[74] 532 6-9-2 **75** (v) MartinLane 2 82
(Derek Shaw) *restless in stalls: mde all: rdn wl over 1f out: drvn 1f out: kpt on and a holding on towards fin* **6/1**

301- **2** ¾ **Mezzotint (IRE)**[126] 8325 7-9-7 **80** AdamKirby 5 85+
(Lee Carter) *stdd s: hld up in tch in last pair: hdwy over 1f out: drvn to chse wnr 150yds out: styd on u.p: nvr getting to wnr* **9/2**

50-5 **3** ½ **Taper Tantrum (IRE)**[39] 967 4-9-6 **79** JamieSpencer 4 83
(Michael Bell) *sn pushed up to chse wnr: rdn wl over 1f out: drvn and styd on same pce fnl f* **10/3**[1]

113- **4** 1 ¼ **Classical Rose**[219] 6537 4-8-12 **71** FrederikTylicki 7 72+
(Charlie Fellowes) *stdd s: hld up in tch in last pair: effrt and c wd wl over 1f out: sn hung rt but hdwy to chse ldrs 1f out: kpt on ins fnl f* **4/1**[3]

14-4 **5** ½ **The Third Man**[11] 1430 5-9-4 **77** DaneO'Neill 3 77
(Henry Spiller) *in tch in midfield: swtchd rt and effrt 2f out: unable qck u.p over 1f out: styd on same pce ins fnl f* **8/1**

00-3 **6** 2 ½ **Italian Beauty (IRE)**[28] 1122 4-8-7 **71** CallumShepherd(5) 1 65
(Brian Ellison) *pushed along thrght: sn chsng ldrs: rdn 3f out: lost pl over 1f out: wknd ins fnl f* **7/2**[2]

4240 **7** 9 **Bognor (USA)**[39] 967 5-9-6 **79** JimCrowley 6 51
(Michael Attwater) *in tch in midfield: rdn and lost pl over 1f out: bhd and eased ins fnl f* **14/1**

1m 40.01s (0.11) **Going Correction** +0.10s/f (Slow) **7** Ran SP% **115.5**
Speed ratings (Par 105): **103,102,101,100,100 97,88**
CSF £33.52 TOTE £6.50: £3.10, £2.10; EX 35.40 Trifecta £136.90.
Owner The Whiteman Partnership **Bred** Brendan Ryan **Trained** Sproxton, Leics

FOCUS
A fair handicap but the winner got his own way in front. He built on his winter form.

1703 TOTEPOOLLIVEINFO.COM H'CAP 1m (P)

4:00 (4:02) (Class 5) (0-70,70) 3-Y-O **£5,175** (£1,540; £769; £384) **Stalls** Low

Form RPR

1- **1** **We Are Ninety (IRE)**[181] 7544 3-9-7 **70** JimCrowley 4 85+
(Hugo Palmer) *chsd ldrs: swtchd lft 4f out and sn led: wnt clr and rdn over 1f out: in n.d and r.o wl fnl f: eased nr fin: easily* **5/4**[1]

031- **2** 4 **Cryptic (IRE)**[138] 8155 3-9-7 **70** AndreaAtzeni 3 76
(Luca Cumani) *chsd ldng trio: effrt to chse clr wnr over 1f out: no imp on wnr but kpt on for clr 2nd* **4/1**[3]

64-3 **3** 7 **Kokoni (IRE)**[19] 1257 3-9-4 **67** RyanMoore 2 57+
(Sir Michael Stoute) *dwlt: hld up in rr of main gp: rdn over 2f out: sme hdwy over 1f out: wnt modest 3rd 1f out: plugged on: no ch w ldng pair* **2/1**[2]

221- **4** 3 ½ **Marcle (IRE)**[195] 7196 3-9-2 **65** DaneO'Neill 7 47
(Ed de Giles) *chsd ldr: carried rt 4f out: 3rd and outpcd over 1f out: wl btn whn lost 3rd 1f out: wknd ins fnl f* **12/1**

-424 **5** 2 ¾ **Dangerous Thought (USA)**[40] 952 3-9-7 **70** (b) JamesDoyle 9 45
(John Gosden) *hld up in tch in midfield: rdn ent fnl 2f: no prog and hung lft over 1f out: sn wknd and wl btn fnl f* **16/1**

540- **6** 1 **Compton Lady (IRE)**[208] 6859 3-8-12 **64** [1] ThomasBrown(3) 8 37
(Ismail Mohammed) *hld up in rr of main gp: rdn over 2f out: no imp and outpcd wl over 1f out: wl btn fnl f* **50/1**

0-05 **7** 2 ¼ **Tamara Love (IRE)**[60] 706 3-8-13 **62** (t) JackMitchell 1 30
(Stuart Williams) *rrd as stalls opened and lost many l s: t.k.h: clsd and in tch 5f out: rdn wl over 1f out: sn btn* **33/1**

35- **8** 10 **Arize (IRE)**[157] 7922 3-9-4 **67** FrankieDettori 6 12
(David Brown) *hung rt thrght: led: hung rt 4f out and hdd over 3f out: lost pl over 2f out: wl bhd and eased ins fnl f: t.o* **20/1**

1m 39.65s (-0.25) **Going Correction** +0.10s/f (Slow) **8** Ran SP% **121.0**
Speed ratings (Par 98): **105,101,94,90,87 86,84,74**
CSF £7.21 CT £9.98 TOTE £2.40: £1.10, £1.40, £1.70; EX 8.30 Trifecta £14.90.
Owner Lady Mimi Manton **Bred** Minch Bloodstock & Brittas Stud **Trained** Newmarket, Suffolk

FOCUS
A well above-average 0-70 in which the winner had them strung out in a time 0.36sec quicker than preceding older-horse 0-80. The first two were clear and the form is rated on the positive side.

1704 COLLECT TOTEPOOL WINNINGS AT BETFRED SHOPS MAIDEN FILLIES' STKS 1m 2f (P)

4:30 (4:34) (Class 5) 3-4-Y-O **£5,175** (£1,540; £769; £384) **Stalls** Low

Form RPR

44-2 **1** **Pursuitofthestars (IRE)**[24] 1179 3-8-11 84 WilliamBuick 4 81
(John Gosden) *mde all: rdn and wnt 2 l clr 2f out: kpt on ins fnl f: rdn out* **9/4**[1]

2 1 ¼ **Rasmiya (IRE)** 3-8-11 0 FrankieDettori 2 78+
(William Haggas) *s.i.s: rn green early and reminder after 1f: in tch in midfield: effrt in 5th whn hung rt bnd over 2f out: hdwy to chse clr wnr over 1f out: kpt on ins fnl f: nvr threatening wnr* **9/4**[1]

3 2 ½ **Sherdat (IRE)** 3-8-11 0 JackMitchell 1 73
(Roger Varian) *chsd ldrs: effrt over 2f out: wnt 3rd over 1f out: kpt on same pce ins fnl f* **5/1**[3]

4 8 **Sugar Strand (USA)** 3-8-11 0 JamesDoyle 3 57+
(Saeed bin Suroor) *chsd ldng trio: hdwy to press ldr 1/2-way: rdn and unable qck 2f out: dropped to 4th and wl btn over 1f out: wknd fnl f* **3/1**[2]

5 2 ¾ **Sisania (IRE)** 3-8-11 0 LiamJones 8 51
(Marco Botti) *s.i.s: rn green and pushed along in rr: rdn and outpcd 3f out: wl hld but plugged on fr over 1f out* **25/1**

6 nk **Heavensfield** 3-8-11 0 ow3 ThomasBrown(3) 7 53
(Mark H Tompkins) *hld up in tch in last trio: rdn over 3f out: struggling and outpcd over 2f out: wl hld and plugged on fr over 1f out* **50/1**

0 **7** 3 ¾ **Theydon Girls**[13] 1392 3-8-8 0 RosieJessop(3) 6 43
(Peter Charalambous) *t.k.h: chsd ldr tl 1/2-way: rdn and outpcd over 2f out: wknd over 1f out* **100/1**

8 1 ½ **Wassail** 3-8-12 0 ow1 OisinMurphy 5 41
(Ed de Giles) *s.i.s: rn green thrght: sn in tch in midfield: rdn and outpcd over 3f out: bhd over 1f out* **10/1**

2m 8.55s (-0.05) **Going Correction** +0.10s/f (Slow) **8** Ran SP% **119.1**
Speed ratings (Par 100): **104,103,101,94,92 92,89,87**
CSF £7.84 TOTE £3.20: £1.20, £1.10, £1.80; EX 8.40 Trifecta £23.00.
Owner Al Mirqab Racing **Bred** Grundy Bloodstock Srl **Trained** Newmarket, Suffolk

The Form Book, Raceform Ltd, Newbury, RG14 5SJ

FOCUS
A fair fillies' maiden and the second looks one to follow. The winner was another to make all and is rated to form.

1705 BOOK TICKETS AT CHELMSFORDCITYRACECOURSE.COM H'CAP 1m 2f (P)
5:00 (5:05) (Class 6) (0-60,58) 3-Y-O **£3,234** (£962; £481; £240) **Stalls** Low

Form RPR
2053 **1** **Schoolboy Error (IRE)**[6] 1551 3-9-7 **58**........................ WilliamCarson 6 64+
(Jamie Osborne) *in tch in midfield: pushed along 4f out: clsd and gng wl whn nt clr run over 2f out: rdn and hdwy to chse ldr over 1f out: drvn to ld ins fnl f: styd on* **5/2**[1]

-032 **2** 1 1/4 **Simply Clever**[25] 1163 3-9-3 **54**........................ FrankieDettori 4 58
(David Brown) *led: rdn 2f out: hrd pressed 1f out: hdd and styd on same pce ins fnl f* **3/1**[2]

06-2 **3** 1 1/2 **Go On Gal (IRE)**[6] 1551 3-8-12 **49**........................ AdamBeschizza 8 50
(Julia Feilden) *hld up in tch in midfield: effrt and bmpd jst over 2f out: swtchd rt and hdwy over 1f out: kpt on u.p to go 3rd wl ins fnl f* **10/1**

5-64 **4** 2 **Aksum**[26] 1148 3-8-10 **54**........................ LuluStanford(7) 1 51
(Michael Bell) *hld up wl in tch in midfield: nt clr run over 2f out: hdwy over 1f out: cl 3rd and swtchd rt jst ins fnl f: sn rdn and fnd little: lost 3rd and wknd wl ins fnl f* **12/1**

-145 **5** 4 1/2 **Big Shoes (IRE)**[26] 1141 3-9-2 **53**........................ DarryllHolland 7 42
(Charles Hills) *lost front shoe on way to s: rdn along leaving stalls: hdwy to chse ldr after 2f: rdn over 2f out: lost 2nd and no ex over 1f out: wknd fnl f* **7/1**

055- **6** 7 **Nutzma**[137] 8167 3-8-12 **49**........................ OisinMurphy 9 25
(Mike Murphy) *chsd ldrs: rdn 3f out: lost pl and btn 2f out: wknd over 1f out* **20/1**

0-20 **7** 2 3/4 **Divine Touch**[53] 794 3-8-12 **49**........................(p) JackMitchell 2 19
(Robert Eddery) *chsd ldrs: travelling wl over 2f out: rdn and no rspnse over 1f out: sn btn: fdd fnl f* **11/1**

00-0 **8** 14 **Pocket**[9] 1484 3-8-11 **51**........................(b[1]) RyanTate(3) 5
(James Eustace) *s.i.s: nvr travelling wl in rr: rdn and struggling whn hmpd and wnt sharply rt over 2f out: sn wl bhd* **33/1**

550 **U** **Topalova**[21] 1235 3-9-3 **57**........................ ThomasBrown(3) 3 +
(Mark H Tompkins) *rdn along leaving stalls: hld up in tch in last trio: clsd on inner whn nt clr run: clipped heels: stmbld and uns rdr over 2f out* **4/1**[3]

2m 11.22s (2.62) **Going Correction** +0.10s/f (Slow) **9** Ran SP% **118.9**
Speed ratings (Par 96): **93,92,90,89,85 80,77,66,**
CSF £10.45 CT £64.26 TOTE £3.20: £1.50, £1.30, £2.70; EX 11.80 Trifecta £64.90.
Owner Appletree Stud, M Gumienny & A Signy **Bred** Paul Monaghan & T J Monaghan **Trained** Upper Lambourn, Berks

FOCUS
The field bunched up on the final turn and this was a muddling race. The winner built on his recent improved effort.
T/Plt: £42.50 to a £1 stake. Pool: £59,435.07 - 1,019.01 winning tickets T/Qpdt: £4.30 to a £1 stake. Pool: £5,611.85 - 956.58 winning tickets **Steve Payne**

1399 SOUTHWELL (L-H)
Monday, April 25

OFFICIAL GOING: Fibresand: standard
Wind: Fresh behind Weather: Cloudy

1706 IRISH STALLION FARMS EBF NOVICE MEDIAN AUCTION STKS 5f (F)
2:10 (2:10) (Class 5) 2-Y-O **£3,881** (£1,155; £577; £288) **Stalls** Centre

Form RPR
1 **Sumner Beach** 2-9-2 0........................ BenCurtis 4 72
(Brian Ellison) *dwlt: trckd ldrs: hdwy on outer over 2f out: rdn to chal ent fnl f: sn led and edgd lft: kpt on strly* **2/1**[2]

2 2 1/4 **Danielsflyer (IRE)** 2-9-2 0........................ GrahamGibbons 1 64
(David Barron) *trckd ldr: cl up whn stmbld sltly 3f out: sn rcvrd and chal 2f out: rdn to ld over 1f out: hdd ent fnl f: no ex last 120yds* **6/5**[1]

3 1 1/2 **Princess Holly** 2-8-11 0........................ AdamBeschizza 2 54
(Robert Cowell) *slt ld: rdn along 2f out: hdd over 1f out: grad wknd* **5/1**[3]

4 2 1/2 **Vaux (IRE)** 2-9-2 0........................ JoeyHaynes 3 50
(Ben Haslam) *cl up: rdn along over 2f out: wknd over 1f out* **8/1**

1m 0.96s (1.26) **Going Correction** +0.075s/f (Slow) **4** Ran SP% **106.6**
Speed ratings (Par 92): **92,88,86,82**
CSF £4.68 TOTE £3.30; EX 5.10 Trifecta £8.90.
Owner Keith Brown **Bred** Hellwood Stud Farm **Trained** Norton, N Yorks

FOCUS
An ordinary juvenile novice contest with a small field of newcomers. They went a decent gallop on standard Fibresand. THe time was poor and this is fair form at best.

1707 DOWNLOAD THE AT THE RACES APP H'CAP 1m (F)
2:40 (2:40) (Class 5) (0-75,74) 4-Y-O+ **£3,881** (£1,155; £577; £288) **Stalls** Low

Form RPR
3010 **1** **Anton Chigurh**[2] 1640 7-8-7 **67**........................ PatrickVaughan(7) 2 78
(Tom Dascombe) *trckd ldrs: hdwy over 2f out: led 1 1/2f out: sn edgd lft: styd on strly* **11/1**

124- **2** 2 3/4 **Mutamid**[216] 6634 4-9-7 **74**........................ TomQueally 1 79
(Ismail Mohammed) *trckd ldrs on inner: hdwy 3f out: chsd ldrs 2f out: sn rdn to chal and ev ch tl drvn ent fnl f and kpt on same pce* **10/3**[1]

-313 **3** 2 1/4 **Royal Holiday (IRE)**[19] 1252 9-9-7 **74**........................(p) RobertWinston 6 74
(Marjorie Fife) *led: hdd 3f out: cl up and sn rdn: drvn wl over 1f out and sn one pce* **7/2**[2]

0303 **4** 3/4 **The Firm (IRE)**[2] 1632 7-8-10 **66**........................(be) RobHornby(3) 4 64
(Daniel Mark Loughnane) *trckd ldr: hdwy to ld 3f out: rdn along over 2f out: hdd 1 1/2f out: sn n.m.r: swtchd rt: drvn and one pce* **7/2**[2]

0624 **5** 3 **Limerick Lord (IRE)**[33] 1044 4-8-5 **63**........................(p) JosephineGordon(5) 3 54
(Julia Feilden) *cl up: effrt on outer 3f out: rdn along over 2f out: sn drvn and wknd* **7/1**

6405 **6** 14 **General Tufto**[18] 1295 11-8-7 **60** oh15........................(b) JoeyHaynes 5 19
(Charles Smith) *chsd ldrs: rdn along after over 5f: sn lost pl and bhd* **66/1**

2530 **7** 4 1/2 **Final**[20] 1248 4-9-5 **72**........................(b[1]) FrannyNorton 7 21
(Mark Johnston) *rdn along on outer sn after s: sn outpcd and drvn along 6f out: sn bhd* **4/1**[3]

1m 42.86s (-0.84) **Going Correction** 0.0s/f (Stan) **7** Ran SP% **109.8**
Speed ratings (Par 103): **104,101,99,98,95 81,76**
CSF £43.72 TOTE £11.10: £4.20, £2.40; EX 63.30 Trifecta £123.80.
Owner Panarea Racing & Partner **Bred** Mr & Mrs G Middlebrook **Trained** Malpas, Cheshire

FOCUS
A fair handicap run at a decent gallop. The winner is rated close to his best since 2013.

1708 VISIT ATTHERACES.COM MAIDEN FILLIES' STKS 1m (F)
3:10 (3:11) (Class 5) 3-Y-O+ **£3,881** (£1,155; £577; £288) **Stalls** Low

Form RPR
6 **1** **Dusky Dawn**[13] 1400 4-9-11 0........................ BenCurtis 7 78
(Alan Swinbank) *trckd ldng pair: hdwy on outer to ld 3 1/2f out: rdn along 2f out: drvn and edgd rt ent fnl f: kpt on wl last 100yds* **7/1**[3]

2 1 1/2 **Catalan (IRE)** 3-8-11 0........................ RobertWinston 3 71
(Hughie Morrison) *trckd ldrs: hdwy over 3f out and sn chsng wnr: effrt to chal 2f out: sn rdn and ev ch tl drvn ent fnl f: kpt on same pce* **2/1**[2]

-2 **3** 19 **Phantom Dancer (IRE)**[14] 1379 4-9-11 0........................ NeilFarley 2 31
(Alan Swinbank) *led: hdd 3 1/2f out: sn rdn along and outpcd: drvn over 2f out: plugged on u.p appr fnl f* **7/1**[3]

322- **4** hd **Combe Hay (FR)**[207] 6889 3-8-11 77........................ TomQueally 1 26
(Henry Spiller) *trckd ldrs: hdwy over 3f out: rdn to chse ldng pair over 2f out: sn drvn and plugged on same pce: lost remote 3rd ins fnl f* **6/5**[1]

0-60 **5** 10 **Riverlynx (IRE)**[70] 590 4-9-11 40........................ JoeyHaynes 4 7
(Ben Haslam) *prom: rdn along on inner over 3f out: sn drvn and wknd wl over 2f out* **66/1**

6 16 **Ogwen Valley Girl**[61] 5-9-4 0........................ MrLewisStones(7) 5
(Michael Mullineaux) *sn rdn along and outpcd in rr: bhd fr over 3f out* **200/1**

0- **7** shd **Sparks (IRE)**[367] 1637 4-9-6 0........................ AaronJones(5) 6
(Sarah-Jayne Davies) *chsd ldrs: pushed along 1/2-way: sn outpcd and bhd whn eased over 1f out* **20/1**

1m 43.3s (-0.40) **Going Correction** 0.0s/f (Stan)
WFA 3 from 4yo+ 14lb **7** Ran SP% **110.5**
Speed ratings (Par 100): **102,100,81,81,71 55,55**
CSF £20.01 TOTE £8.10: £2.40, £1.60; EX 23.00 Trifecta £85.20.
Owner Countrywide Classics Limited **Bred** Countrywide Classics Ltd **Trained** Melsonby, N Yorks

FOCUS
A fair fillies' maiden. They went a respectable gallop and the winner was a big improver..

1709 AT THE RACES VIRGIN 534 H'CAP 5f (F)
3:40 (3:41) (Class 6) (0-55,53) 4-Y-O+ **£3,234** (£962; £481; £240) **Stalls** Centre

Form RPR
3540 **1** **Pancake Day**[9] 1495 4-9-6 **52**........................(v) JFEgan 1 60
(Jason Ward) *cl up centre: led 1 1/2f out: sn rdn: drvn out towards fin* **11/4**[1]

43-5 **2** 1 1/4 **Wattaboutsteve**[106] 136 5-8-7 **46**........................ RhiainIngram(7) 8 50
(Ralph J Smith) *racd towards stands' rail: in rr: swtchd lft to centre and hdwy over 2f out: rdn wl over 1f out: styd on wl fnl f* **12/1**

6153 **3** shd **Red Flute**[39] 970 4-9-0 **49**........................(v) TimClark(3) 4 52
(Denis Quinn) *slt ld: pushed along 2f out: rdn and hdd 1 1/2f out: sn drvn and kpt on same pce* **11/1**

2222 **4** 3 3/4 **Imjin River (IRE)**[34] 1026 9-9-3 **49**........................(tp) BenCurtis 9 39
(William Stone) *racd nr stands' rail: chsd ldrs: rdn along 2f out: hdwy and drvn over 1f out: sn edgd lft and no imp* **3/1**[2]

5244 **5** 1 **Very First Blade**[18] 1299 7-9-0 **53**........................(be) MrLewisStones(7) 6 39
(Michael Mullineaux) *chsd ldrs: rdn along over 2f out: sn drvn and one pce* **7/1**

/6 **6** 3 3/4 **Dandy Maid**[11] 1435 5-9-4 **53**........................ AlistairRawlinson(3) 2 26
(Michael Appleby) *dwlt: sn swtchd lft to outer: in rr and rdn along 1/2-way: nvr a factor* **11/1**

6-00 **7** nk **Willow Spring**[75] 513 4-8-13 **45**........................ MartinDwyer 5 16
(Conrad Allen) *dwlt: racd in centre: sn chsng ldng pair: rdn 2f out: drvn and edgd lft wl over 1f out: sn wknd* **33/1**

40 **8** 1/2 **Camanche Grey (IRE)**[25] 1164 5-9-2 **48**........................(b[1]) RaulDaSilva 3 18
(Ben Haslam) *dwlt hdwy to chse ldrs on outer after 1f: rdn along over 2f out: sn wknd* **5/1**[3]

02-0 **9** 2 1/4 **George Bailey (IRE)**[34] 1026 4-9-1 **50**........................ JacobButterfield(3) 7 12
(Suzzanne France) *racd towards stands' rail: in tch: rdn along over 2f out: sn wknd* **25/1**

59.83s (0.13) **Going Correction** +0.075s/f (Slow) **9** Ran SP% **112.0**
Speed ratings (Par 101): **101,99,98,92,91 85,84,83,80**
CSF £34.86 CT £309.77 TOTE £3.20: £1.50, £3.20, £2.70; EX 36.60 Trifecta £276.50.
Owner Trojan Racing **Bred** Stuart Matheson **Trained** Middleham, N Yorks

FOCUS
A moderate sprint handicap. They went a strong gallop. The winner repwated his February form.

1710 FOLLOW AT THE RACES ON TWITTER H'CAP 7f (F)
4:10 (4:10) (Class 6) (0-60,60) 3-Y-O **£3,234** (£962; £481; £240) **Stalls** Low

Form RPR
-034 **1** **Ada Misobel (IRE)**[9] 1486 3-8-10 **49**........................(p) JFEgan 5 55
(Roy Bowring) *mde all: rdn and edgd rt wl over 1f out: drvn clr ent fnl and edgd rt again: kpt on wl towards fin* **5/1**[3]

35-0 **2** 1 1/2 **Atrayu (IRE)**[19] 1257 3-9-7 **60**........................ GrahamGibbons 1 62
(Paul D'Arcy) *trckd ldrs: effrt over 2f out: sn rdn and carried hd high: chsd wnr ent fnl f: sn drvn and no imp towards fin* **2/1**[1]

54 **3** 2 1/4 **Freeze A Crowd (IRE)**[33] 1045 3-8-7 **46** oh1........................(t) JoeyHaynes 4 42
(Ben Haslam) *trckd wnr: hdwy and cl up wl over 2f out: sn rdn and ev ch tl drvn appr fnl f and kpt on same pce* **11/2**

434- **4** 1 1/2 **Cranberry Park (IRE)**[226] 6329 3-9-2 **55**........................ BenCurtis 2 47
(Brian Ellison) *chsd ldrs: rdn along over 2f out: drvn wl over 1f out and sn one pce* **13/2**

000- **5** hd **Pericles (IRE)**[178] 7592 3-9-4 **60**........................ LouisSteward(3) 3 51
(Peter Chapple-Hyam) *swtchd to inner s: hld up in rr: hdwy 3f out: styd nr far rail and rdn over 2f out: drvn wl over 1f out: n.d* **5/2**[2]

1m 30.68s (0.38) **Going Correction** 0.0s/f (Stan) **5** Ran SP% **107.3**
Speed ratings (Par 96): **97,95,92,91,90**
CSF £14.59 TOTE £3.20: £1.60, £1.40; EX 13.70 Trifecta £27.70.
Owner L P Keane **Bred** Leinster Syndicate **Trained** Edwinstowe, Notts

FOCUS
A moderate 3yo handicap run at a decent gallop. The winner is rated near her best 2yo form.

1711 JOIN AT THE RACES ON FACEBOOK FILLIES' H'CAP 1m 4f (F)
4:40 (4:40) (Class 5) (0-70,70) 4-Y-O+ **£3,881** (£1,155; £577; £288) **Stalls** Low

Form RPR
0043 **1** **Solarmaite**[13] 1399 7-8-13 **62**........................(p) JFEgan 2 70
(Roy Bowring) *set stdy pce: qcknd 4f out: rdn along 2f out: drvn appr fnl f and kpt on strly* **7/2**[3]

3-44 **2** 1 1/4 **Favorite Girl (GER)**[28] 420 8-8-9 **63**........................ GeorgeBuckell(5) 3 68
(Michael Appleby) *trckd wnr: pushed along wl over 3f out: rdn over 2f out: drvn over 1f out: kpt on same pce fnl f* **9/4**[2]

2111 **3** *10* **Moonshine Ridge (IRE)**[18] 1296 5-9-7 **70**.......................... BenCurtis 1 59
(Alan Swinbank) *dwlt: sn trcking ldng pair: pushed along 4f out: rdn wl over 3f out: drvn over 1f out: sn one pce* **11/10**[1]
600- **4** *14* **Sant'Elia**[268] 4849 4-9-0 **64**.. TomQueally 4 31
(Mark H Tompkins) *hld up in rr: effrt and sme hdwy over 5f out: rdn along 4f out: drvn 3f out and sn outpcd* **14/1**

2m 40.61s (-0.39) **Going Correction** 0.0s/f (Stan)
WFA 4 from 5yo+ 1lb **4** Ran SP% **107.3**
Speed ratings (Par 100): **101,100,93,84**
CSF £11.27 TOTE £3.60; EX 8.90 Trifecta £17.10.
Owner S R Bowring **Bred** S R Bowring **Trained** Edwinstowe, Notts

FOCUS
A modest little fillies' handicap. They went a respectable gallop at best, the winner having the run of things up front.

1712 SOUTHWELL GOLF CLUB PAY & PLAY H'CAP 6f (F)
5:15 (5:15) (Class 5) (0-70,68) 4-Y-O+ **£3,881** (£1,155; £577; £288) **Stalls** Low

Form RPR
0522 **1** **Fortinbrass (IRE)**[13] 1401 6-8-7 **57**...................................... JoeDoyle(3) 5 66
(John Balding) *cl up: chal 2f out: rdn over 1f out: drvn ins fnl f: kpt on gamely to ld nr line* **3/1**[1]
0012 **2** *nk* **Colourbearer (IRE)**[16] 1341 9-9-6 **67**.................................(t) BenCurtis 2 75
(Charlie Wallis) *slt ld: rdn 2f out: drvn ent fnl f: hdd and no ex nr line* **4/1**[2]
0010 **3** *1* **Monsieur Jimmy**[9] 1495 4-9-7 **68**.......................................(b) DavidAllan 1 73
(Declan Carroll) *dwlt and sn pushed along in rr: rdn along in rr bef 1/2-way: hdwy over 2f out: chsd ldrs and n.m.r ent fnl f: sn drvn and kpt on* **3/1**[1]
2330 **4** *1 ¾* **Spowarticus**[26] 1154 7-9-1 **65**..(b) TimClark(3) 3 64
(Scott Dixon) *cl up: wd st: rdn 2f out and sltly outpcd: drvn over 1f out: kpt on fnl f* **6/1**[3]
-050 **5** *nk* **Daylight**[9] 1489 6-8-8 **60**...(t) NathanEvans(5) 4 58
(Michael Easterby) *trckd ldrs: hdwy on inner wl over 2f out: rdn wl over 1f out: ev ch appr fnl f: sn drvn and one pce* **11/1**
0035 **6** *1 ¾* **Alpha Tauri (USA)**[13] 1401 10-9-2 **63**.............................. TomQueally 6 56
(Charles Smith) *cl up: effrt on outer over 2f out: sn rdn and ev ch: drvn over 1f out and grad wknd* **8/1**
0605 **7** *4 ½* **Speightowns Kid (USA)**[18] 1298 8-8-13 **65**.............(be) AnnStokell(5) 7 43
(Ann Stokell) *chsd ldrs: rdn along wl over 2f out: sn wknd* **14/1**

1m 16.53s (0.03) **Going Correction** 0.0s/f (Stan) **7** Ran SP% **110.4**
Speed ratings (Par 103): **99,98,97,94,94 92,86**
CSF £14.02 TOTE £2.80: £2.50, £2.90; EX 13.80 Trifecta £34.50.
Owner Billy Herring **Bred** Tom Wallace **Trained** Scrooby, S Yorks
■ Stewards' Enquiry : Joe Doyle two-day ban: used whip above permitted level (May 9-10)

FOCUS
Another modest handicap. They went a decent gallop. The runner-up is rated to his Chelmsford win.
T/Plt: £971.90 to a £1 stake. Pool: £42,990.9 - 32.29 winning tickets T/Qpdt: £83.70 to a £1 stake. Pool: £4,240.49 - 37.47 winning tickets **Joe Rowntree**

1527 WINDSOR (R-H)
Monday, April 25

OFFICIAL GOING: Good to soft (6.3)
Wind: Fresh, behind Weather: Changeable but stayed dry

1713 BRITISH STALLION STUDS EBF NOVICE STKS (PLUS 10 RACE) 5f 10y
5:30 (5:30) (Class 4) 2-Y-O **£4,269** (£1,270; £634; £317) **Stalls** Low

Form RPR
1 **Legendary Lunch (IRE)** 2-9-2 0.. PatDobbs 1 84
(Richard Hannon) *trckd ldr: chal over 1f out and rn green: chsd new ldr fnl f: styd on fnl f to ld last strides* **2/1**[2]
4 **2** *nk* **Copper Knight (IRE)**[12] 1422 2-9-2 0.............................. SteveDrowne 2 83
(Hugo Palmer) *nt that wl away: t.k.h and sn trckd ldng pair: swtchd to outer 2f out: rdn to ld jst ins fnl f: hung lft after: hdd last strides* **5/4**[1]
1 **3** *2 ½* **Awesome Allan (IRE)**[14] 1384 2-9-8 0.............................. AdamKirby 5 80
(David Evans) *led: rdn over 1f out: hdd jst ins fnl f: no ex* **5/1**[3]
4 *3* **Dr Julius No** 2-9-2 0.. FMBerry 9 63
(Ralph Beckett) *s.i.s: hld up in 6th: outpcd whn tk 4th over 1f out: shkn up and kpt on steadily after* **16/1**
5 *7* **Son Castello (IRE)** 2-9-2 0.. JimmyFortune 8 38
(Brian Meehan) *trckd ldrs: rn green after 2f: outpcd sn after: wknd over 1f out* **33/1**
6 *shd* **Jet Setter (IRE)** 2-9-2 0.. JamieSpencer 7 38
(Brian Meehan) *wl in tch: pushed along and wknd wl over 1f out* **16/1**
7 *10* **Hawridge Glory (IRE)** 2-9-2 0...................................... FrederikTylicki 4
(Rod Millman) *slowly away: rn green in last and sn wl bhd* **50/1**

1m 1.52s (1.22) **Going Correction** +0.10s/f (Good) **7** Ran SP% **111.1**
Speed ratings (Par 94): **94,93,89,84,73 73,57**
CSF £4.53 TOTE £3.70: £1.60, £1.30; EX 7.30 Trifecta £15.90.
Owner The Rat Pack Partnership 2016 **Bred** Johnston King **Trained** East Everleigh, Wilts

FOCUS
Inner of straight dolled out 6yds at 6f down to the intersection, then inner configuration thereafter to the winning line. Top bend dolled out 8yds from normal inner configuration, adding 30yds to race distances of 1m-plus. This will probably work out to be an above-average affair, with the average ratings for this race over the years a help in assessing the form.

1714 WORLDPAY TOTAL PAYMENTS FOR BUSINESS MAIDEN STKS 1m 67y
6:00 (6:05) (Class 5) 3-Y-O **£2,911** (£866; £432; £216) **Stalls** Low

Form RPR
3- **1** **Limitless (IRE)**[139] 8144 3-9-5 0.......................................[1] JamieSpencer 7 87+
(Jamie Osborne) *in tch in midfield: pushed along 1/2-way: clsd on ldrs 2f out: swtchd to nr side rail and rdn to ld ins fnl f: styd on wl* **10/1**
52- **2** *1 ¼* **Wave Reviews**[187] 7394 3-9-5 0...................................... PatCosgrave 9 84
(William Haggas) *pressed ldr: led over 2f out: sn pressed and rdn: hdd and nt qckn ins fnl f* **10/11**[1]
03- **3** *1 ½* **Desert Haze**[184] 7472 3-9-0 0.. FMBerry 4 76
(Ralph Beckett) *trckd ldng pair: wnt 2nd and chal 2f out: stl upsides 1f out: one pce* **8/1**[3]
4 *3* **Morando (FR)** 3-9-5 0.. HarryBentley 14 74+
(Roger Varian) *s.s: in rr: pushed along and prog into midfield 1/2-way: rdn and kpt on fr over 2f out: n.d but nrst fin* **33/1**
5 *2 ¾* **Warrior Prince** 3-9-5 0.. FrederikTylicki 11 67
(Ed Dunlop) *trckd ldng trio: effrt on outer to chal 2f out: wknd jst over 1f out* **100/1**
6 *2* **Patent** 3-9-5 0.. PatDobbs 8 63
(Richard Hannon) *s.i.s: towards rr: pushed along 3f out: n.d but kpt on steadily* **33/1**
2- **7** *2 ¼* **Kuantan**[194] 7218 3-9-5 0...................................... WilliamTwiston-Davies 10 58
(Roger Charlton) *chsd ldng quartet: shkn up wl over 2f out: nvr able to cl: wknd fnl f* **9/1**
8 *nse* **Star Blaze** 3-9-5 0.. SilvestreDeSousa 1 57
(Mick Channon) *nvr bttr than midfield: rdn wl over 2f out: no imp after: wknd fnl f* **16/1**
43- **9** *½* **Jimenez (IRE)**[303] 3633 3-9-5 0.................................... JimmyFortune 5 56
(Brian Meehan) *led: gng wl over 3f out: hdd over 2f out: sn wknd* **20/1**
10 *2 ¼* **Makzeem** 3-9-5 0.. GeorgeBaker 3 51+
(Roger Charlton) *s.s: detached in last pair: urged along and modest prog 1/2-way: no hdwy after* **7/1**[2]
11 *3* **Magnificent Madiba** 3-9-5 0.. SteveDrowne 12 44
(George Baker) *a towards rr: struggling fr 1/2-way* **66/1**
64- **12** *3 ¼* **Fandango (GER)**[166] 7793 3-9-5 0...................................... MartinLane 6 37
(Jeremy Gask) *chsd ldrs in 6th: shkn up and wknd wl over 2f out* **66/1**
0 **13** *2 ½* **Private Jet**[12] 1421 3-9-2 0................................ MichaelJMMurphy(3) 2 31
(Charles Hills) *s.i.s: a in rr: struggling fr 1/2-way* **66/1**
14 *nk* **The Detainee** 3-9-0 0.. DavidParkes(5) 13 30
(Jeremy Gask) *s.s: a struggling in last pair* **100/1**

1m 45.46s (0.76) **Going Correction** +0.25s/f (Good) **14** Ran SP% **118.1**
Speed ratings (Par 98): **106,104,103,100,97 95,93,93,92,90 87,84,81,81**
CSF £18.29 TOTE £16.00: £3.50, £1.10, £2.50; EX 31.40 Trifecta £210.30.
Owner Michael Buckley & Michael Watt **Bred** Ballylinch Stud **Trained** Upper Lambourn, Berks

FOCUS
Race distance increased by 30yds. A fair 3yo maiden run at a decent pace. The runner-up rates a solid benchmark and the winner is useful.

1715 MCR SYSTEMS SYMPHONY MAIDEN STKS 1m 2f 7y
6:30 (6:30) (Class 5) 3-Y-O+ **£2,911** (£866; £432; £216) **Stalls** Centre

Form RPR
1 **Choreographer (IRE)** 3-8-11 0...................................... AndreaAtzeni 4 85+
(Roger Varian) *fractious preliminaries: t.k.h: trckd ldng pair: wnt 2nd wl over 2f out: pushed into ld jst over 1f out: readily* **9/2**[3]
03-2 **2** *2* **Rex Bell (IRE)**[14] 1386 3-8-11 80....................................(p) RobertHavlin 2 81
(John Gosden) *led: shkn up over 2f out: hdd jst over 1f out: kpt on same pce* **3/1**[2]
3 *2 ¼* **Pointel (FR)** 3-8-11 0.. FrederikTylicki 6 77+
(James Fanshawe) *sn hld up in rr: pushed along 3f out: kpt on steadily fnl 2f to take 3rd last strides* **33/1**
0 **4** *½* **Bunbury**[61] 691 4-10-0 0.. ShaneKelly 1 79+
(Richard Hughes) *hld up in last: gng easily whn nt clr run over 2f out: prog over 1f out: pushed along and kpt on promisingly to take 4th fnl stride* **33/1**
32- **5** *nse* **Magnum (IRE)**[185] 7431 3-8-11 0.................................... JimmyFortune 7 75
(Brian Meehan) *trckd ldng trio: urged along over 3f out: nvr gng pce to rch ldrs: disp 3rd over 1f out: one pce* **11/10**[1]
6 *1 ¾* **Sir George Somers (USA)** 3-8-11 0.................................. TedDurcan 3 72
(Sir Michael Stoute) *dwlt: hld up in tch: pushed along to dispute 3rd wl over 1f out: fdd* **17/2**
7 *3 ½* **Glorious Legend (IRE)** 3-8-11 0...................................... AntonioFresu 5 65
(Ed Walker) *slowly away: mostly in rr: fdd fr over 2f out* **33/1**
8 *2 ¾* **King Julien (IRE)** 3-8-11 0.. JimCrowley 8 59
(Jeremy Noseda) *trckd ldr to wl over 2f out: sn shoved along and lost pl: wknd* **20/1**
00 **9** *14* **Away In May**[7] 1529 5-9-9 0.............................. WilliamTwiston-Davies 9 29
(John Spearing) *hld up in rr: prog 1/2-way: cl up 3f out tl wknd rapidly 2f out* **100/1**

2m 14.25s (5.55) **Going Correction** +0.25s/f (Good)
WFA 3 from 4yo+ 17lb **9** Ran SP% **115.9**
Speed ratings (Par 103): **87,85,83,83,83 81,78,76,65**
CSF £17.58 TOTE £6.40: £1.70, £1.40, £4.70; EX 17.10 Trifecta £298.70.
Owner China Horse Club **Bred** Roundhill Stud **Trained** Newmarket, Suffolk

FOCUS
Race distance increased by 30yds. A good maiden in which paid to race handily, but the form may not prove too solid. The runner-up looks the best guide.

1716 PHIL RENDELL FORTY TENTH BIRTHDAY H'CAP 1m 2f 7y
7:00 (7:00) (Class 4) (0-85,85) 4-Y-O+ **£4,690** (£1,395; £697; £348) **Stalls** Centre

Form RPR
412- **1** **Weetles**[178] 7593 4-9-3 **81**.. AdamKirby 11 90+
(Clive Cox) *trckd ldng trio: clsd to ld wl over 1f out: drvn out and in command fnl f* **3/1**[1]
3-23 **2** *1 ½* **Dutch Uncle**[16] 1336 4-9-6 **84**................................ SilvestreDeSousa 5 90
(Ed Dunlop) *t.k.h: trckd ldr to 1/2-way: styd cl up: effrt 2f out: rdn to chse wnr ins fnl f: kpt on but no imp* **7/2**[2]
13- **3** *¾* **Alcatraz (IRE)**[308] 3461 4-9-5 **83**...................................... PatCosgrave 2 88
(George Baker) *t.k.h: trckd ldrs: rdn and nt qckn 2f out: kpt on fnl f to take 3rd nr fin* **17/2**
411- **4** *½* **Nayel (IRE)**[283] 4359 4-9-5 **83**.. PatDobbs 8 87
(Richard Hannon) *prom: trckd ldr 1/2-way: rdn to chal 2f out: chsd wnr tl ins fnl f: one pce* **5/1**[3]
-034 **5** *shd* **Top Diktat**[14] 1390 8-8-10 **74**...................................... FergusSweeney 9 77
(Gary Moore) *hld up in last trio but wl in tch: effrt on outer over 2f out: drvn and kpt on same pce fr over 1f out: nvr able to chal* **20/1**
1165 **6** *½* **Buckland Beau**[30] 1093 5-9-2 **80**...................................... JamieSpencer 7 82+
(Charlie Fellowes) *stdd s: t.k.h and hld up in last: pushed along over 2f out: prog jst over 1f out: styd on but too late to threaten* **16/1**
45-4 **7** *¾* **Starwatch**[7] 1531 9-9-7 **85**...(v) WilliamCarson 6 86
(John Bridger) *led: rdn 2f out: sn hdd: steadily wknd fnl f* **20/1**
305- **8** *nk* **Plymouth Sound**[196] 7172 4-9-6 **84**................................ RobertWinston 10 84+
(Eve Johnson Houghton) *awkward to post: hld up in 7th: lost pl over 4f out and in last trio: pushed along 2f out: nt clr run over 1f out and swtchd lft: stl pushed along and kpt on: nvr involved* **13/2**
-213 **9** *¾* **Sheila's Buddy**[37] 1001 7-9-6 **84**...................................... MartinDwyer 1 83
(J S Moore) *t.k.h: hld up towards rr: rdn 2f out and in tch: nt qckn over 1f out: no prog after* **12/1**
-230 **10** *½* **Gaelic Silver (FR)**[54] 779 10-8-6 **75**.......................(p) HectorCrouch(5) 3 73
(Gary Moore) *wl in tch: effrt on outer over 2f out: stl cl up over 1f out: wknd fnl f* **25/1**
500- **11** *9* **Silver Mountain**[292] 4017 5-8-7 **74**............................ TomMarquand(3) 4 54
(J R Jenkins) *hld up in rr but in tch: wknd over 2f out: sn bhd* **50/1**

2m 12.44s (3.74) **Going Correction** +0.25s/f (Good) **11** Ran SP% **116.7**
Speed ratings (Par 105): **95,93,93,92,92 92,91,91,90,90 83**
CSF £12.51 CT £79.95 TOTE £4.20: £2.50, £1.60, £1.80; EX 13.60 Trifecta £102.10.

Owner D B Clark, A R Bentall, Mrs M V Penfold **Bred** Bugley Stud (millestan) Partnership **Trained** Lambourn, Berks

FOCUS

Race distance increased by 30yds. This fair handicap was run at an average pace and it suited the prominent racers. Improvement from the first four.

1717 MICHAEL LONSDALE LTD H'CAP 1m 3f 135y

7:30 (7:31) (Class 4) (0-80,80) 4-Y-O+ **£4,690** (£1,395; £697; £348) **Stalls** Centre

Form RPR

30-0 **1** **Zambeasy**[30] 1093 5-9-4 **77** JamieSpencer 3 88
(Philip Hide) *led after 3f to 5f out: taken to far side 3f out and sn led again: rdn and hdd over 1f out: rallied u.p fnl f: led last strides* **18/1**

103- **2** *shd* **Stockhill Diva**[185] 7433 6-9-5 **78** FMBerry 10 88
(Brendan Powell) *t.k.h: hld up in midfield: followed wnr to far side over 2f out and sn clsd: rdn to ld over 1f out: kpt on but hdd last strides* **7/1**[2]

15-3 **3** *3 ½* **All My Love (IRE)**[22] 1221 4-9-2 **76** PatCosgrave 5 80+
(Pam Sly) *hld up: styd nr side st: prog over 2f out: drvn to ld gp jst ins fnl f: no ch w ldng pair far side* **2/1**[1]

240- **4** *1* **Forced Family Fun**[192] 7250 6-9-6 **79** SteveDrowne 9 82+
(George Baker) *dwlt: hld up in last pair: styd nr side in st: prog 2f out: rdn to chse gp ldr wl ins fnl f: no ch* **8/1**[3]

351- **5** *1 ½* **Instant Karma (IRE)**[21] 7366 5-9-7 **80** WilliamTwiston-Davies 7 80+
(Michael Bell) *prom: lft chsng ldr nr side 3f out to 2f out: fdd* **8/1**[3]

5001 **6** *¾* **Moojaned (IRE)**[7] 1531 5-9-4 **80** 6ex PhilipPrince(3) 8 79+
(David Evans) *racd freely: led 3f and again 5f out: styd nr side 3f out and sn lost overall ld: hdd & wknd in gp jst ins fnl f* **8/1**[3]

-121 **7** *hd* **Fern Owl**[61] 693 4-9-0 **74** JimCrowley 1 73+
(Hughie Morrison) *hld up in tch: gng strly over 3f out: styd nr side after: rdn 2f out: steadily wknd* **11/1**

40-0 **8** *11* **Jacob Cats**[30] 1093 7-9-7 **80** (v) FrederikTylicki 2 60+
(William Knight) *dwlt: shoved along in last early: t.k.h after 4f and sn in midfield: styd nr side 3f out: sn wknd* **12/1**

1555 **9** *1 ¾* **Alshan Fajer**[38] 983 6-9-2 **78** TomMarquand(3) 4 55+
(J R Jenkins) *hld up: no prog nr side 3f out: sn wknd* **33/1**

02-0 **10** *16* **Le Notre**[26] 1144 4-8-12 **75** (vt[1]) DanielMuscutt(3) 11 26+
(Jeremy Noseda) *prom: wknd qckly 3f out: t.o* **20/1**

346- **11** *1 ½* **Magical Thomas**[168] 7779 4-9-4 **78** AdamKirby 6 27
(Neil Mulholland) *wl in tch: taken to far side over 2f out but already struggling: t.o* **12/1**

2m 30.91s (1.41) **Going Correction** +0.25s/f (Good)
WFA 4 from 5yo+ 1lb **11** Ran SP% **115.9**
Speed ratings (Par 105): **105,104,102,101,100 100,100,92,91,81 80**
CSF £136.88 CT £368.10 TOTE £19.80: £3.90, £3.00, £1.50; EX 184.00 Trifecta £889.10.
Owner Heart Of The South Racing **Bred** Frank Brady **Trained** Findon, W Sussex

FOCUS

Race distance increased by 30yds. They were strung out early in this modest handicap, but the pace steadied around 5f out. The first pair came clear on the far side and the second is the best guide.

1718 BELL EVENTS H'CAP 1m 3f 135y

8:00 (8:02) (Class 5) (0-70,70) 3-Y-O **£2,911** (£866; £432; £216) **Stalls** Centre

Form RPR

50-0 **1** **Michael's Mount**[30] 1091 3-9-6 **69** PatCosgrave 4 74+
(Ed Dunlop) *cl up in 4th: rdn to ld 2f out: drvn and styd on fr over 1f out* **15/8**[1]

64-6 **2** *1 ½* **Marmajuke Bay**[29] 1113 3-9-6 **69** (p) SteveDrowne 1 71
(Mark Usher) *mde most: set mod pce but pushed along fr 5f out: rdn and hdd 2f out: kpt on but a hld fnl f* **11/2**

006- **3** *1 ¼* **Hearty (IRE)**[138] 8153 3-8-10 **59** JimCrowley 2 59
(Jeremy Noseda) *cl up in last: moved up to chal 2f out: drvn and kpt on one pce in 3rd fr jst over 1f out* **5/1**[3]

000- **4** *4* **Coarse Cut (IRE)**[203] 6986 3-9-2 **65** RobertWinston 3 58
(Eve Johnson Houghton) *trckd ldng pair: sltly outpcd over 2f out: no imp after* **8/1**

035- **5** *1 ½* **Duck A L'Orange (IRE)**[193] 7229 3-9-7 **70** JamieSpencer 5 61
(Michael Bell) *mostly trckd ldr to jst over 2f out: steadily fdd over 1f out* **2/1**[2]

2m 37.55s (8.05) **Going Correction** +0.25s/f (Good) **5** Ran SP% **111.3**
Speed ratings (Par 98): **83,82,81,78,77**
CSF £12.34 TOTE £2.60: £1.90, £1.20; EX 6.70 Trifecta £55.40.
Owner Miltil Consortium **Bred** Southill Stud **Trained** Newmarket, Suffolk

FOCUS

Race distance increased by 30yds. All five of these were handicap debutants and stepping up in distance. They went an uneven pace and came down the centre in the home straight. Hard form to read, the winner another improver.

T/Plt: £13.50 to a £1 stake. Pool: £78,454.36 - 4,229.22 winning tickets T/Qpdt: £10.80 to a £1 stake. Pool: £7,500.47 - 513.10 winning tickets **Jonathan Neesom**

1648 WOLVERHAMPTON (A.W) (L-H)

Monday, April 25

OFFICIAL GOING: Tapeta: standard

Wind: Fresh across Weather: Overcast

1719 AWARD WINNING FINE DINING AT HORIZONS NOVICE STKS 5f 216y (Tp)

5:20 (5:20) (Class 5) 2-Y-O **£2,911** (£866; £432; £216) **Stalls** Low

Form RPR

0 **1** **Thora Barber**[30] 1087 2-8-11 0 CathyGannon 3 78
(David Evans) *sn pushed along and prom: drvn 1/2-way: chsd ldr over 1f out: r.o to ld post* **25/1**

3 **2** *hd* **Camargue**[11] 1437 2-8-11 0 JoeFanning 7 77
(Mark Johnston) *chsd ldrs: wnt 2nd over 4f out: led over 2f out: rdn clr over 1f out: hdd post* **5/4**[1]

3 *8* **Roseland (USA)** 2-8-11 0 MartinHarley 5 53+
(Hugo Palmer) *hld up: hdwy wl over 1f out: wknd ins fnl f* **9/4**[2]

5 **4** *2 ¼* **Vinnievanbaileys**[12] 1422 2-9-2 0 LukeMorris 2 51
(Chris Dwyer) *sn pushed along and prom: rdn and lost pl over 2f out: nvr on terms after* **11/1**

5 *4 ½* **Suetonius** 2-9-2 0 DaleSwift 1 38
(Ed McMahon) *led 1f: chsd ldrs tl rdn and wknd 2f out* **33/1**

6 *1 ¼* **Erica Bing** 2-8-6 0 JosephineGordon(5) 6 29
(Jo Hughes) *s.i.s: sn pushed along in rr: swtchd lft 4f out: bhd fr 1/2-way* **80/1**

2 **7** *4 ½* **Playful Trickster (IRE)**[30] 1086 2-8-11 0 RichardKingscote 4 16
(Tom Dascombe) *led 5f out: rdn and hdd over 2f out: wknd over 1f out* **7/2**[3]

1m 14.52s (0.02) **Going Correction** -0.125s/f (Stan) **7** Ran SP% **113.8**
Speed ratings (Par 92): **94,93,83,80,74 72,66**
CSF £56.72 TOTE £18.50: £10.20, £1.10; EX 84.70 Trifecta £338.70.
Owner E R Griffiths **Bred** Whatton Manor Stud & Robert Cornelius **Trained** Pandy, Monmouths

FOCUS

The first 6f race of the year for 2yos. Conditions were quite blustery at Dunstall Park and that would have made life a bit more difficult for these inexperienced juveniles. The first two finished a long way clear.

1720 #FOLLOWUS ON TWITTER @WOLVESRACES H'CAP 5f 216y (Tp)

5:50 (5:50) (Class 6) (0-60,60) 4-Y-O+ **£2,264** (£673; £336; £168) **Stalls** Low

Form RPR

2022 **1** **Tasaaboq**[6] 1556 5-8-7 **51** (t) JosephineGordon(5) 2 59
(Phil McEntee) *hld up: hdwy over 1f out: rdn to ld wl ins fnl f: r.o* **4/1**[2]

0662 **2** *1 ½* **Generalyse**[24] 1180 7-9-6 **59** (p) MartinHarley 4 62
(Anabel K Murphy) *chsd ldrs: rdn to ld over 1f out: hdd and unable qck wl ins fnl f* **6/1**[3]

5031 **3** *hd* **Dream Ally (IRE)**[17] 1319 6-9-1 **54** (be) LukeMorris 3 56
(John Weymes) *mid-div: rdn over 2f out: hdwy over 1f out: hung lft and r.o ins fnl f: wnt 3rd nr fin* **4/1**[2]

-305 **4** *½* **Frangarry (IRE)**[27] 1133 4-9-5 **58** RobertTart 6 59
(Alan Bailey) *mid-div: pushed along and hdwy over 2f out: rdn and ev ch over 1f out: styd on same pce ins fnl f* **10/3**[1]

600- **5** *¾* **Fossa**[143] 8104 6-9-4 **57** JoeFanning 9 56
(Mark Brisbourne) *prom: chsd ldr over 2f out: rdn and ev ch over 1f out: styd on same pce ins fnl f* **20/1**

0000 **6** *1 ¾* **Satchville Flyer**[9] 1502 5-9-3 **56** CathyGannon 10 49+
(David Evans) *dwlt: hld up: rdn over 1f out: r.o ins fnl f: nvr nrr* **14/1**

0-33 **7** *½* **Swendab (IRE)**[24] 1180 8-9-1 **59** (b) CiaranMckee(5) 7 51+
(John O'Shea) *rrd s: in rr: rdn 1/2-way: r.o ins fnl f: nrst fin* **12/1**

0504 **8** *2* **Noverre To Go (IRE)**[6] 1549 10-9-7 **60** (p) DavidProbert 8 46
(Ronald Harris) *chsd ldr tl led over 3f out: rdn and hdd over 1f out: wknd ins fnl f* **8/1**

0505 **9** *1 ¼* **Rat Catcher (IRE)**[17] 1319 6-8-9 **51** (p) RobHornby(3) 1 33+
(Lisa Williamson) *rrd s: hld up: rdn over 3f out: nvr on terms* **14/1**

5010 **10** *½* **Harpers Ruby**[27] 1133 6-8-13 **52** JackGarritty 5 33
(Lynn Siddall) *led: hdd over 3f out: rdn over 1f out: wknd fnl f* **16/1**

1m 13.79s (-0.71) **Going Correction** -0.125s/f (Stan) **10** Ran SP% **120.1**
Speed ratings (Par 101): **99,97,96,96,95 92,92,89,87,87**
CSF £29.33 CT £98.85 TOTE £4.30: £1.80, £2.60, £1.30; EX 36.90 Trifecta £100.10.
Owner Mrs Rita Baker **Bred** Tim Bostwick **Trained** Newmarket, Suffolk

FOCUS

Quite a competitive little heat for the grade and the pace looked reasonably generous from the outset.

1721 LADIES EVENING FRIDAY 19TH AUGUST H'CAP 5f 20y (Tp)

6:20 (6:20) (Class 6) (0-65,64) 3-Y-O+ **£2,264** (£673; £336; £168) **Stalls** Low

Form RPR

1556 **1** **Your Gifted (IRE)**[32] 1059 9-9-13 **63** (v) RaulDaSilva 8 72
(Lisa Williamson) *a.p: racd keenly: rdn to ld 1f out: edgd lft: r.o* **14/1**

3004 **2** *1 ¼* **Quality Art (USA)**[32] 1059 8-10-0 **64** JoeFanning 6 68
(Simon Hodgson) *hld up in tch: shkn up to chse wnr ins fnl f: styd on same pce* **13/2**[3]

35-5 **3** *1 ¼* **See Vermont**[32] 1059 8-10-0 **64** (p) TomEaves 7 64
(Rebecca Bastiman) *s.i.s: hld up: hdwy over 1f out: sn rdn: styd on same pce ins fnl f* **12/1**

040- **4** *½* **Hamish McGonagain**[125] 8348 3-9-2 **62** RichardKingscote 4 56
(Jeremy Gask) *hld up: rdn over 1f out: r.o ins fnl f: nt rch ldrs* **3/1**[1]

6-53 **5** *1* **Mustn't Grumble (IRE)**[5] 1558 3-8-11 **62** (p) JosephineGordon(5) 1 52
(Ivan Furtado) *disp ld 4f: no ex ins fnl f* **10/3**[2]

6565 **6** *hd* **Louis Vee (IRE)**[7] 1533 8-9-3 **58** (p) CiaranMckee(5) 3 51
(John O'Shea) *chsd ldrs: rdn over 1f out: no ex ins fnl f* **10/1**

2100 **7** *1* **Charlie Lad**[27] 1133 4-9-8 **58** LukeMorris 5 48
(Daniel Mark Loughnane) *disp ld 4f: wknd ins fnl f* **8/1**

241U **8** *nk* **Rampers (IRE)**[40] 962 3-9-4 **64** CathyGannon 2 49
(Jamie Osborne) *s.i.s: hld up: rdn over 1f out: nt trble ldrs* **7/1**

2031 **9** *hd* **Spray Tan**[25] 1164 6-8-13 **52** (b) GeorgeDowning(3) 9 40
(Tony Carroll) *s.i.s: hld up: rdn over 1f out: nvr on terms* **16/1**

1m 0.9s (-1.00) **Going Correction** -0.125s/f (Stan)
WFA 3 from 4yo+ 10lb **9** Ran SP% **114.4**
Speed ratings (Par 101): **103,101,99,98,96 96,94,94,93**
CSF £100.68 CT £1130.80 TOTE £14.80: £5.00, £3.20, £1.20; EX 139.00 Trifecta £411.50.
Owner Anthony Thomas Sykes **Bred** Rathasker Stud **Trained** Saighton, Cheshire

FOCUS

Several course regulars on show in what looked an open heat on paper. This rates a step up from the winner.

1722 COMBINE BUSINESS WITH RACING AT WOLVERHAMPTON CLAIMING STKS 1m 4f 50y (Tp)

6:50 (6:50) (Class 6) 4-Y-O+ **£2,264** (£673; £336; £168) **Stalls** Low

Form RPR

-440 **1** **Viewpoint (IRE)**[30] 1089 7-9-11 85 LukeMorris 3 91+
(Michael Appleby) *chsd ldr tl shkn up to ld over 1f out: rdn clr fnl f: eased towards fin* **9/4**[2]

0362 **2** *6* **Patriotic (IRE)**[13] 1404 8-9-3 78 (p) JosephineGordon(5) 5 76
(Chris Dwyer) *chsd ldrs: rdn over 1f out: chsd wnr ins fnl f: no imp* **8/1**[3]

/0-1 **3** *5* **Marshgate Lane (USA)**[13] 1404 7-9-11 99 (p) LiamKeniry 4 71
(Neil Mulholland) *led: racd keenly: rdn and hdd over 1f out: wknd fnl f* **4/5**[1]

0-65 **4** *12* **Rio Falls (IRE)**[9] 1498 4-9-4 65 JoeFanning 6 46
(Jennie Candlish) *hld up: rdn and wknd over 2f out* **20/1**

6 **5** *½* **Last Summer**[9] 1499 5-9-3 0 CiaranMckee(5) 1 48
(Grace Harris) *s.i.s: hld up: rdn over 4f out: sn wknd* **66/1**

250- **6** *26* **Certification (IRE)**[214] 6689 6-9-8 72 TomEaves 7 7
(Andrew Crook) *hld up: rdn over 5f out: wknd 4f out* **66/1**

2m 37.29s (-3.51) **Going Correction** -0.125s/f (Stan)
WFA 4 from 5yo+ 1lb **6** Ran SP% **105.2**
Speed ratings (Par 101): **106,102,98,90,90 73**
CSF £16.24 TOTE £3.10: £1.40, £2.70; EX 15.10 Trifecta £27.90.
Owner Richard and Nicola Hunt **Bred** F Dunne **Trained** Oakham, Rutland

FOCUS
Only three mattered in this claimer and they finished clear of the rest. Th result, however, didn't go the way the market expected as odds-on favourite Marshgate Lane didn't reproduce the level of form he showed on Fibresand last time. The winner is rated to this winter's form.

1723 LIKE WOLVERHAMPTON RACECOURSE ON FACEBOOK MAIDEN FILLIES' STKS 7f 32y (Tp)
7:20 (7:24) (Class 5) 3-Y-O+ **£2,911** (£866; £432; £216) **Stalls** High

Form RPR
5- **1** **Malmostosa**187 7392 3-9-0 0 MartinHarley 10 81+
(Marco Botti) *hld up: hdwy over 1f out: shkn up to ld ins fnl f: r.o: comf* **6/1**3
2 1 1/4 **Coronation Day** 3-9-0 0 LukeMorris 5 75
(James Tate) *a.p: rdn over 2f out: styd on same pce ins fnl f* **7/2**2
2- **3** *hd* **Alyday**177 7628 3-9-0 0 GrahamGibbons 7 74
(Sir Michael Stoute) *chsd ldrs: led over 1f out: sn rdn: edgd lft and hdd ins fnl f: styd on same pce* **4/6**1
4 4 1/2 **Check 'Em Tuesday (IRE)** 3-9-0 0 DaleSwift 9 62
(Daniel Mark Loughnane) *s.i.s: hld up: hdwy over 1f out: no ex fnl f* **80/1**
4 **5** 1 1/4 **Hidden Gem**16 1339 3-9-0 0 LiamKeniry 4 58
(Ed Walker) *chsd ldr tl led over 2f out: rdn and hdd over 1f out: wknd ins fnl f* **10/1**
6 1 3/4 **Cliffhanger** 3-9-0 0 JoeFanning 2 54
(Paul Cole) *led: shkn up and hdd over 2f out: wknd fnl f* **20/1**
4 **7** 3/4 **Dutch Treaty**17 1312 3-9-0 0 SeanLevey 1 52
(Richard Hannon) *chsd ldrs: rdn over 2f out: wknd over 1f out* **25/1**
003- **8** 1/2 **Caledonia Duchess**224 6385 3-9-0 72 JoeyHaynes 6 50
(Jo Hughes) *hld up: shkn up over 2f out: sn wknd* **20/1**
9 1/2 **Ray Of Light (IRE)** 3-9-0 0 KieranO'Neill 3 49
(Richard Hannon) *s.i.s: hld up: rdn over 2f out: sn wknd* **20/1**

1m 28.26s (-0.54) **Going Correction** -0.125s/f (Stan) **9** Ran SP% **125.0**
Speed ratings (Par 100): **98,96,96,91,89 87,86,86,85**
CSF £27.53 TOTE £9.50: £2.50, £1.60, £1.20; EX 42.30 Trifecta £75.00.
Owner Promenade Bloodstock Limited **Bred** Brook Stud Bloodstock Ltd **Trained** Newmarket, Suffolk

FOCUS
A potentially decent fillies' maiden in which the front three finished nicely clear, and this could throw up a few future winners. The form is rated around the third.

1724 WOLVERHAMPTON-RACECOURSE.CO.UK H'CAP 7f 32y (Tp)
7:50 (7:50) (Class 4) (0-80,80) 4-Y-O+ **£4,690** (£1,395; £697; £348) **Stalls** High

Form RPR
1426 **1** **Justice First**33 1041 4-9-3 **76** MartinHarley 4 84
(Ed Dunlop) *mid-div: hdwy over 1f out: shkn up to ld ins fnl f: edgd lft: r.o* **11/2**3
4-00 **2** 3/4 **Mister Musicmaster**12 1418 7-8-13 **72** RichardKingscote 3 78
(Ron Hodges) *chsd ldrs: nt clr run over 1f out: sn rdn: r.o* **8/1**
42-2 **3** 3/4 **Upstaging**33 1040 4-9-5 **78** LukeMorris 6 82
(Paul Cole) *chsd ldrs: rdn to ld over 1f out: hdd and edgd lft ins fnl f: kpt on* **6/4**1
215- **4** *nse* **Arlecchino's Leap**140 8131 4-9-5 **78** (p) LiamKeniry 2 82
(Mark Usher) *mid-div: hdwy over 1f out: sn rdn: styd on* **8/1**
6-60 **5** 3 1/2 **Peak Storm**22 1221 7-8-7 **71** ow2 CiaranMckee(5) 5 65
(John O'Shea) *s.i.s: hld up: effrt over 1f out: no ex ins fnl f* **25/1**
-006 **6** 1 **Ambitious Boy**16 1341 7-8-9 **68** CathyGannon 1 60
(John O'Shea) *s.i.s: hld up: rdn over 2f out: n.d* **20/1**
200- **7** 3 **Spryt (IRE)**199 7093 4-9-2 **80** JoshDoyle(5) 8 64
(David O'Meara) *led: rdn and hdd over 1f out: wknd ins fnl f* **9/2**2
4-30 **8** 3 1/4 **Invincible Diamond (IRE)**30 1090 4-9-2 **80** JosephineGordon(5) 7 55
(J S Moore) *pushed along to join ldr 6f out: rdn and ev ch over 1f out: wknd fnl f* **9/1**

1m 26.94s (-1.86) **Going Correction** -0.125s/f (Stan) **8** Ran SP% **114.4**
Speed ratings (Par 105): **105,104,103,103,99 98,94,90**
CSF £48.32 CT £97.24 TOTE £4.90: £1.80, £3.80, £1.10; EX 50.20 Trifecta £110.50.
Owner Robert Ng **Bred** Whitsbury Manor Stud & Rangefield Bld **Trained** Newmarket, Suffolk

FOCUS
A mixed bag in terms of the recent form of these runners and it looked a good opportunity for Upstaging to add to his sole previous success, but he was beaten fair and square. The winner is capable of rating a bit higher.

1725 HOTEL & RACING PACKAGES AVAILABLE FILLIES' H'CAP 7f 32y (Tp)
8:20 (8:22) (Class 6) (0-65,65) 3-Y-O+ **£2,264** (£673; £336; £168) **Stalls** High

Form RPR
4214 **1** **Figurante (IRE)**12 1420 3-9-1 **65** CathyGannon 8 68
(Jamie Osborne) *chsd ldr: rdn over 2f out: edgd lft ins fnl f: styd on to ld last strides* **11/2**2
53-3 **2** *nk* **Last Star Falling (IRE)**18 1294 3-9-1 **65** JoeFanning 11 67
(Henry Spiller) *a.p: rdn over 2f out: styd on to ld wl ins fnl f: hdd last strides* **33/1**
4424 **3** *nk* **Colourfilly**63 667 4-9-12 **63** (p) RichardKingscote 7 70
(Tom Dascombe) *led: rdn over 1f out: hdd wl ins fnl f* **11/2**2
0-00 **4** 2 1/4 **Canny Style**11 1448 3-9-1 **65** TomEaves 2 61
(Kevin Ryan) *chsd ldrs: rdn over 2f out: no ex wl ins fnl f* **16/1**
504 **5** 2 **Smirnova (IRE)**60 706 3-9-0 **64** PaoloSirigu 1 55
(Marco Botti) *prom: rdn over 2f out: styd on same pce fnl f* **12/1**
-246 **6** 1/2 **Pyla (IRE)**54 777 4-10-0 **65**1 LemosdeSouza 12 60+
(Denis Quinn) *s.i.s: hld up: plld hrd: r.o ins fnl f: nvr nrr* **12/1**
00-1 **7** *nk* **Blushes (FR)**41 948 3-9-0 **64** LukeMorris 3 53+
(Ed Dunlop) *mid-div: rdn 1/2-way: nvr trbld ldrs* **5/2**1
4026 **8** 1 **Kodiac Lady (IRE)**9 1501 4-9-3 **61** (be) RowanScott(7) 9 53+
(Simon West) *s.i.s: hld up: rdn over 1f out: nvr on terms* **12/1**
340- **9** 1 **Fairy Duchess (IRE)**233 6101 4-9-11 **62** LiamKeniry 6 51+
(John Butler) *hld up: rdn over 1f out: n.d* **22/1**
63-0 **10** 2 3/4 **Daybreak Lady**112 40 3-8-12 **62** JoeyHaynes 10 40+
(Jo Hughes) *mid-div: rdn over 2f out: wknd over 1f out* **28/1**
065- **11** 2 1/2 **Smile Of Approval (IRE)**171 7730 3-8-12 **62** RyanClark 4 33+
(Jonathan Portman) *s.i.s: hld up: plld hrd: a in rr* **16/1**
650- **12** 6 **Zophilly (IRE)**145 8073 3-8-12 **62** MartinHarley 5 19
(Jeremy Gask) *mid-div: racd keenly: rdn over 2f out: sn wknd* **10/1**3

1m 28.46s (-0.34) **Going Correction** -0.125s/f (Stan)
WFA 3 from 4yo 13lb **12** Ran SP% **114.0**
Speed ratings (Par 98): **96,95,95,92,90 89,89,88,87,84 81,74**
CSF £174.37 CT £1038.57 TOTE £6.30: £2.40, £7.80, £2.90; EX 163.30 Trifecta £346.40.
Owner The Hon A Blyth **Bred** Mount Coote Stud **Trained** Upper Lambourn, Berks

FOCUS
An open 3yo fillies' handicap on paper but nothing could get into it from off the pace and the first four home filled those places throughout. Ordinary form, the winner essentially to her 2yo best.

T/Plt: £60.50 to a £1 stake. Pool: £57,630.83 - 694.88 winning tickets T/Qpdt: £20.30 to a £1 stake. Pool: £6,364.39 - 230.98 winning tickets **Colin Roberts**

1726 - 1729a (Foreign Racing) - See Raceform Interactive

NAAS (L-H)
Monday, April 25

OFFICIAL GOING: Good (good to yielding in places)

1730a WOODLANDS STKS (LISTED RACE) 5f
6:40 (6:42) 3-Y-O+
£19,522 (£6,286; £2,977; £1,323; £661; £330)

RPR
1 **Fort Del Oro (IRE)**197 7149 4-9-7 107 BillyLee 4 108+
(Edward Lynam, Ire) *hld up on far side: prog to chse ldrs in 3rd 1f out: styd on wl to ld fnl 100yds: kpt on wl* **13/8**1
2 1 **Monsieur Joe (IRE)**204 6971 9-9-12 108 PatSmullen 3 109
(Paul Midgley) *broke wl to ld far side gp: 2nd overall: disp ins fnl f tl hdd fnl 100yds: kpt on wl: no ex w wnr cl home* **14/1**
3 1/2 **Abstraction (IRE)**58 745 6-9-9 97 ShaneFoley 8 105
(Miss Natalia Lupini, Ire) *racd alone stands' side and sn clr ldr: advantage reduced ent fnl f and hdd fnl 100yds: dropped to 3rd* **33/1**
4 1 3/4 **Flight Risk (IRE)**8 1509 5-9-9 104 KevinManning 6 98+
(J S Bolger, Ire) *hld up: pushed along 1/2-way: rdn in 7th 1f out: kpt on wl clsng stages into 4th: nvr nrr* **9/1**
5 *shd* **Shrill**233 6115 3-8-8 92 DeclanMcDonogh 5 89
(W McCreery, Ire) *t.k.h early to trck ldrs on far side: wnt 3rd 2f out: no ex ins fnl f and dropped to 5th cl home* **20/1**
6 3/4 **The Happy Prince (IRE)**22 1226 4-9-9 108 (t) SeamieHeffernan 1 95
(A P O'Brien, Ire) *trckd ldr of far side gp: 4th at 1/2-way: no imp ins fnl f: wknd* **9/2**3
7 1/2 **Maarek**11 1439 9-9-12 108 ColinKeane 9 96
(Miss Evanna McCutcheon, Ire) *sn pushed along in rr: 9th 1f out: kpt on wl clsng stages: nvr nrr* **7/2**2
8 1 **Moviesta (USA)**225 6360 6-9-12 110 ChrisHayes 10 93
(Edward Lynam, Ire) *hld up: pushed along and no imp over 1f out: kpt on wout threatening* **9/1**
9 1/2 **Independence Day (IRE)**227 6269 3-8-13 100 WayneLordan 2 84
(David Wachman, Ire) *chsd ldrs on far side: rdn and nt qckn over 1f out: sn one pce* **14/1**
10 11 **Madame Thunder (IRE)**24 1190 3-8-8 81 (t1) LeighRoche 7 39
(D J Bunyan, Ire) *a towards rr: nvr a factor: detached under 2f out* **66/1**

57.94s (-4.06)
WFA 3 from 4yo+ 10lb **10** Ran SP% **121.0**
CSF £28.74 TOTE £2.50: £1.30, £3.40, £7.40; DF 31.30 Trifecta £387.10.
Owner Ballylinch Stud **Bred** Ballylinch Stud **Trained** Dunshaughlin, Co Meath

FOCUS
This looked reasonably open but the winner put these to the sword readily and looks as though there's a top sprint in her.

1731 - 1733a (Foreign Racing) - See Raceform Interactive

1450 BATH (L-H)
Tuesday, April 26

OFFICIAL GOING: Good (good to firm in places; 8.3)
Wind: quite strong across Weather: sunny periods with snow showers

1734 WYVERN ICES H'CAP 1m 5y
1:40 (1:40) (Class 6) (0-60,60) 3-Y-O **£2,911** (£866; £432; £216) **Stalls** Low

Form RPR
000- **1** **Ebbisham (IRE)**182 7531 3-9-5 **58** PatCosgrave 13 69+
(Jim Boyle) *a.p: led over 2f out: pushed 4 l clr fnl f: eased towards fin* **5/1**2
43-2 **2** 1 1/2 **Funny Oyster (IRE)**15 1388 3-9-6 **59** (p) SteveDrowne 5 62
(George Baker) *trckd ldrs: rdn over 2f out: chsd wnr over 1f out: kpt on but wl hld fnl f* **4/1**1
600- **3** 1 1/2 **Becca Campbell (IRE)**226 6364 3-9-3 **56** JohnFahy 11 56
(Eve Johnson Houghton) *drvn along leaving stalls: sn led: rdn and hdd over 2f out: kpt on ins fnl f* **16/1**
-402 **4** 1/2 **Espoir**18 1325 3-8-11 **53** (b) PhilipPrince(3) 6 52
(David Evans) *mid-div: rdn and hdwy whn swtchd rt over 2f out: hung lft fr over 1f out: styd on fnl f* **9/1**
630- **5** *nk* **Monday Club**137 8177 3-9-6 **59** JFEgan 9 57
(Dominic Ffrench Davis) *mid-div: swtchd rt over 2f out: sn rdn: styd on fnl f* **8/1**3
406- **6** 1 **Patanjali (IRE)**216 6643 3-9-5 **58** RobertWinston 1 56+
(Eve Johnson Houghton) *hld up towards rr: rdn over 2f out: nt clrest of runs ent fnl f: styd on but n.d after* **17/2**
004- **7** *nk* **Outback Princess**257 5303 3-9-0 **53** SamHitchcott 2 48
(Gary Moore) *towards rr of mid-div: rdn and hdwy over 2f out: nvr threatened: kpt on same pce fnl f* **25/1**
000- **8** *nk* **Rosie's Vision**180 7584 3-8-12 **56** RachealKneller(5) 7 50
(Mark Usher) *racd keenly: in tch: hdwy over 3f out: outpcd over 2f out* **33/1**
00-6 **9** *nk* **Concur (IRE)**27 1146 3-8-13 **52** FrederikTylicki 4 45
(Rod Millman) *nvr bttr than mid-div* **12/1**
250- **10** 1/2 **Lady Rocka**182 7534 3-9-7 **60** FMBerry 12 52
(Amanda Perrett) *trckd ldrs: rdn and ev ch 2f out: wkng whn squeezed up jst ins fnl f* **9/1**
5030 **11** 3/4 **Lady Fontenail**33 1062 3-8-5 **49** AliceMills(5) 10 39
(Rod Millman) *mid-div: rdn over 2f out: no imp: wknd fnl f* **16/1**
0004 **12** 4 1/2 **Toffee Apple (IRE)**7 1548 3-8-8 **47** (b) MartinLane 8 27
(Ed Dunlop) *hld up towards rr: rdn over 2f out: little imp: wknd fnl f* **17/2**
000- **13** 8 **Britannia Boy**208 6884 3-8-7 **46** oh1 (p) DavidProbert 3 6
(Mark Usher) *racd keenly: stdd towards rr: rdn over 2f out: nvr threatened* **66/1**

1m 44.26s (3.46) **Going Correction** +0.175s/f (Good) **13** Ran SP% **116.6**
Speed ratings (Par 96): **89,87,86,85,85 84,83,83,83,82 82,77,69**
CSF £24.18 CT £308.67 TOTE £7.90: £2.80, £1.60, £4.60; EX 26.50 Trifecta £691.20.
Owner The 'In Recovery' Partnership **Bred** John Quigley **Trained** Epsom, Surrey
■ Stewards' Enquiry : Frederik Tylicki one-day ban: careless riding (May 10)
Philip Prince two-day ban: careless riding (May 10-11)

FOCUS
Rail was moved out around the bottom bend up to the 3f marker, resulting in 10yds being added to all race distances that travel around the bottom bend. Steve Drowne described the ground as being "just on the fast side of good". A moderate handicap, but the form doesn't look bad for the level and the winner was really well backed. It did pay to race prominently, though.

1735 ROA/RACING POST OWNERS JACKPOT H'CAP — 1m 5y
2:10 (2:10) (Class 6) (0-65,65) 4-Y-O+ **£3,040** (£904; £452; £226) **Stalls** Low

Form — RPR

00-0 **1** **Saint Helena (IRE)**[90] 348 8-9-0 **61**..........(b) PhilipPrince(3) 8 — 67
(Mark Gillard) *dwlt: bhd: hdwy on outer fr over 2f out: led ent fnl f: kpt on* **66/1**

12-5 **2** ½ **Knight Of The Air**[7] 1546 4-9-3 **61**.......... GeorgeBaker 4 — 66
(Mick Channon) *mid-div: hdwy to ld jst over 2f out: sn rdn: hdd ent fnl f: kpt on* **11/2**[1]

0-00 **3** 1¼ **Dovil's Duel (IRE)**[57] 769 5-8-11 **58**.......... EoinWalsh(3) 12 — 62
(Tony Newcombe) *hld up bhd: hdwy but nvr clrest of runs fr over 2f out tl jst over 1f out: wnt 3rd ins fnl f: kpt on same pce fnl 120yds* **12/1**

06-0 **4** ½ **Marcano (IRE)**[15] 1387 4-9-7 **65**..........[1] FrederikTylicki 6 — 66
(Rod Millman) *trckd ldrs: rdn and ev ch over 1f out: kpt on but no ex fnl f* **7/1**[2]

25-4 **5** 6 **Miss Inga Sock (IRE)**[20] 1268 4-9-7 **65**.......... RobertWinston 5 — 51
(Eve Johnson Houghton) *trckd ldrs: rdn over 2f out: kpt on tl no ex fnl f* **8/1**[3]

0003 **6** ½ **Duke Of North (IRE)**[7] 1544 4-9-2 **60**.......... PatCosgrave 1 — 46
(Jim Boyle) *racd keenly in midfield: hdwy over 2f out: styng on at same pce whn hmpd jst over 1f out* **12/1**

-000 **7** 1¼ **Vivre La Reve**[73] 563 4-9-0 **58**.......... DavidProbert 14 — 40
(James Unett) *in tch: effrt over 2f out: wknd fnl f* **50/1**

560- **8** nk **Harry Bosch**[211] 6811 6-8-4 **51** oh2.......... ShelleyBirkett(3) 15 — 32
(Julia Feilden) *trckd ldr: rdn to ld briefly over 2f out: wknd fnl f* **11/1**

-420 **9** ¾ **McDelta**[57] 769 6-8-13 **57**.......... TimmyMurphy 9 — 36
(Geoffrey Deacon) *mid-div: lost pl whn nt clr run over 1f out: nvr any threat* **11/1**

000- **10** ¾ **Wordismybond**[190] 7347 7-8-13 **64**.......... ChrisKelly(7) 16 — 42
(Richard Hughes) *mid-div: rdn over 2f out: nvr any imp* **16/1**

0-41 **11** hd **Star Of The Stage**[34] 1047 4-9-7 **65**..........(p) AdamBeschizza 13 — 42
(Julia Feilden) *nvr bttr than mid-div* **11/2**[1]

0021 **12** hd **Blackthorn Stick (IRE)**[13] 1415 7-9-2 **60**..........(p) JimmyQuinn 11 — 40
(Paul Burgoyne) *towards rr of mid-div: pushed along whn nt best of runs of runs over 1f out: nvr any imp* **12/1**

530- **13** 1 **Cape Spirit (IRE)**[223] 6441 4-8-7 **58**.......... JoshuaBryan(7) 2 — 32
(Andrew Balding) *towards rr of mid-div: rdn over 2f out: no imp* **25/1**

2155 **14** hd **Miss Lillie**[20] 1266 5-9-3 **61**..........(p) JamieSpencer 10 — 45
(Roger Teal) *led: rdn and hdd over 2f out: hld whn hmpd over 1f out: eased fnl f* **14/1**

255- **15** 2¾ **Lady Bayside**[191] 7314 8-9-5 **63**.......... FMBerry 3 — 32
(Malcolm Saunders) *in tch: rdn over 2f out: hld whn short of room over 1f out* **14/1**

1m 41.52s (0.72) **Going Correction** +0.175s/f (Good) **15** Ran SP% **120.6**
Speed ratings (Par 101): **103,102,101,100,94 94,93,92,91,91 91,90,89,89,86**
CSF £401.20 CT £4795.50 TOTE £33.30: £5.60, £1.30, £5.70; EX 251.60 Trifecta £2266.70 Part won..
Owner Adrian Hosie **Bred** Frank O'Malley **Trained** Holwell, Dorset

FOCUS
Race distance increased by 10yds. There was a right old turn up here, the complete outsider coming from behind for the upset. The winner was back to last spring's form.

1736 MJ CHURCH NOVICE MEDIAN AUCTION STKS — 5f 11y
2:45 (2:45) (Class 6) 2-Y-O **£2,587** (£770; £384; £192) **Stalls** Centre

Form — RPR

2 **1** **Kreb's Cycle (IRE)**[11] 1454 2-9-2 0.......... PatDobbs 8 — 82
(Richard Hannon) *trckd ldrs: chal 2f out: rdn to ld ent fnl f: kpt on wl towards fin* **1/2**[1]

2 1 **Havelock (IRE)** 2-9-2 0.......... WilliamBuick 9 — 78
(Mark Johnston) *trckd ldr: led over 2f out: sn rdn whn strly chal: hdd ent fnl f: kpt on but no ex* **11/2**[2]

3 3¾ **El Torito (IRE)** 2-9-2 0.......... PatCosgrave 5 — 65+
(Jim Boyle) *slowly away: bhd: stdy prog fr 2f out: kpt on fnl f: wnt 3rd nring fin* **20/1**

4 nk **Nazik** 2-9-2 0.......... JFEgan 3 — 64
(David Evans) *outpcd early in last trio: hdwy over 2f out: chsd front pair over 1f out: nt pce to get on terms: lost 3rd nring fin* **16/1**

0 **5** 3¾ **New Trier (IRE)**[24] 1203 2-8-11 0..........(b) JoseValdiviaJr 1 — 45
(Wesley A Ward, U.S.A) *led: rdn and hdd over 2f out: wknd fnl f* **8/1**[3]

6 ½ **Dandy Roll (IRE)** 2-9-2 0.......... FMBerry 6 — 49
(Ralph Beckett) *in last pair: rdn 2f out: sme hdwy whn nt best of runs jst over 1f out: wknd fnl f* **12/1**

7 2 **Dravid** 2-9-2 0.......... FrederikTylicki 2 — 41
(Rod Millman) *chsd ldrs: rdn over 2f out: wknd ent fnl f* **10/1**

8 6 **Waves (IRE)** 2-8-11 0.......... RobertWinston 4 — 15
(Eve Johnson Houghton) *in tch: effrt over 2f out: wknd over 1f out* **33/1**

1m 4.14s (1.64) **Going Correction** +0.175s/f (Good) **8** Ran SP% **123.5**
Speed ratings (Par 90): **92,90,84,83,77 77,73,64**
CSF £4.41 TOTE £1.70: £1.02, £1.80, £5.20; EX 5.40 Trifecta £44.90.
Owner Middleham Park Racing CIV **Bred** Michael Fennessy **Trained** East Everleigh, Wilts

FOCUS
The two at the head of the market dominated and both look useful. The winner is rated as having improved by a few lengths.

1737 DRIBUILD H'CAP — 1m 2f 46y
3:20 (3:20) (Class 4) (0-80,79) 4-Y-O+ **£5,175** (£1,540; £769; £384) **Stalls** Low

Form — RPR

624- **1** **Iftiraaq (IRE)**[111] 5384 5-9-5 **77**..........(p) GeorgeBaker 1 — 85
(Seamus Durack) *trckd ldr: led jst over 2f out: kpt on wl fnl f: readily* **3/1**[2]

0224 **2** 1¼ **Icebuster**[46] 899 8-9-3 **75**.......... FrederikTylicki 3 — 80
(Rod Millman) *trckd ldrs: rdn over 2f out: kpt on fnl f but a being hld by wnr* **7/1**

20-2 **3** ½ **Mountain Rescue (IRE)**[96] 267 4-9-6 **78**.......... WilliamBuick 4 — 82
(Chris Wall) *racd keenly early: trckd ldrs: rdn over 2f out: kpt on ins fnl f* **4/1**[3]

20-2 **4** 1 **Life Less Ordinary (IRE)**[19] 1290 4-9-7 **79**.......... JamieSpencer 6 — 81
(Jamie Osborne) *stdd s: last: did nt appear to be travelling early: pushed along and stdy prog over 2f out: wnt 4th ent fnl f: kpt on but nt pce to threaten* **2/1**[1]

3-33 **5** ¾ **Bushel (USA)**[58] 266 6-8-13 **74**.......... EoinWalsh(3) 2 — 75
(Tony Newcombe) *in tch: rdn over 2f out: kpt on but nt pce to get involved fnl f* **33/1**

520- **6** shd **Sunday Royal (FR)**[151] 8014 4-9-3 **75**.......... SamHitchcott 5 — 75
(Harry Dunlop) *in tch: rdn over 2f out: kpt on but nt pce to get on terms fnl f* **16/1**

-452 **7** 1 **Fire And Passion**[10] 1501 4-8-9 **67**..........(b) MartinLane 7 — 65
(Jeremy Gask) *led tl rdn jst over 2f out: no ex fnl f* **8/1**

2m 11.39s (0.39) **Going Correction** +0.175s/f (Good) **7** Ran SP% **110.8**
Speed ratings (Par 105): **105,104,103,102,102 102,101**
CSF £22.34 TOTE £3.80: £1.80, £2.80; EX 20.30 Trifecta £92.50.
Owner The Acorn Partnership **Bred** Shadwell Estate Company Limited **Trained** Upper Lambourn, Berkshire

■ Stewards' Enquiry : William Buick caution: careless riding

FOCUS
Race distance increased by 10yds. Fair form, although there wasn't much of a gallop on. It's been rated around the runner-up.

1738 ROYAL AIR FORCES ASSOCIATION H'CAP — 1m 2f 46y
3:55 (3:55) (Class 5) (0-75,75) 3-Y-O **£3,040** (£904; £452; £226) **Stalls** Low

Form — RPR

060- **1** **Shabbah (IRE)**[169] 7777 3-8-10 **64**.......... TedDurcan 8 — 82+
(Sir Michael Stoute) *slowly away: sn trcking ldr: led 5f out: shkn up to go clr over 1f out: comf* **11/4**[1]

13-2 **2** 2¾ **Gawdawpalin (IRE)**[20] 1276 3-9-3 **71**.......... FMBerry 9 — 81
(Sylvester Kirk) *trckd ldrs: rdn to chse wnr over 2f out: styd on but a being comf hld by wnr fnl f* **8/1**

001- **3** 4 **City Of Ideas**[164] 7863 3-9-7 **75**.......... RobertHavlin 6 — 77+
(John Gosden) *mid-div: pushed along over 3f out: rdn and drifted lft fr 2f out: wnt hld 3rd over 1f out: styd on same pce* **9/2**[3]

2142 **4** 2¾ **Jarir**[25] 1185 3-9-6 **74**.......... PatDobbs 11 — 71
(Richard Hannon) *hld up towards rr: rdn over 2f out: hdwy over 1f out: styd on fnl f: wnt 4th nring fin* **8/1**

06-5 **5** shd **Banham (USA)**[19] 1287 3-9-5 **73**.......... GeorgeBaker 1 — 69
(Roger Charlton) *broke wl: led for 1f: settled in tch: rdn and hung lft fr 2f out: styd on but nt pce to get involved* **16/1**

000- **6** shd **Pack It In (IRE)**[186] 7435 3-8-11 **65**.......... JimmyFortune 12 — 61
(Brian Meehan) *hld up bhd: hdwy on outer 2f out: sn rdn: styd on same pce fnl f* **33/1**

01- **7** ½ **Disobedience (USA)**[118] 8404 3-9-7 **75**.......... WilliamBuick 2 — 70
(Charlie Appleby) *s.i.s: led after 1f tl 5f out: rdn wl over 2f out: sn btn* **3/1**[2]

00-2 **8** 8 **Sky Of Stars (IRE)**[27] 1140 3-9-4 **72**.......... JamieSpencer 10 — 51
(William Knight) *mid-div: pushed along to hold pl over 5f out: nvr threatened: wknd over 1f out* **33/1**

515- **9** 1¾ **Kismet Hardy**[155] 7955 3-9-2 **75**.......... GaryMahon(5) 13 — 51
(Richard Hannon) *little slowly away: sn trcking ldr: rdn over 2f out: wknd over 1f out* **25/1**

433- **10** 1¼ **Hygrove Percy**[191] 7309 3-9-6 **74**.......... LiamKeniry 4 — 47
(Neil Mulholland) *s.i.s: sn trcking ldrs: snatched up after 1f: rdn over 2f out: sn wknd* **16/1**

02-4 **11** 14 **Best Of Oregon (USA)**[39] 976 3-9-3 **71**..........(t) AntonioFresu 5 — 16
(Ed Walker) *little slowly away: sn cl up: rdn over 2f out: sn wknd: eased fnl f* **25/1**

2m 12.72s (1.72) **Going Correction** +0.175s/f (Good) **11** Ran SP% **117.4**
Speed ratings (Par 98): **100,97,94,92,92 92,91,85,84,83 71**
CSF £24.17 CT £95.37 TOTE £5.00: £2.20, £3.00, £1.80; EX 34.50 Trifecta £131.90.
Owner Abdullah Saeed Al Naboodah **Bred** Sunderland Holdings Inc **Trained** Newmarket, Suffolk

FOCUS
Race distance increased by 10yds. Not a bad race for the level, with many of the top yards represented, and the favourite won with plenty in hand. The form is rated on the positive side.

1739 BLOOR HOMES MAIDEN STKS — 1m 3f 144y
4:30 (4:30) (Class 5) 3-Y-O+ **£3,749** (£1,107; £553) **Stalls** Low

Form — RPR

22- **1** **Red Cardinal (IRE)**[178] 7640 4-9-13 0.......... JamieSpencer 3 — 82
(David Simcock) *mid-div: hdwy over 2f out: rdn to ld over 1f out: edgd lft: hrd drvn towards fin: hld on* **5/2**[2]

0-2 **2** nk **Mawaany (IRE)**[10] 1499 3-8-8 0..........(v) TedDurcan 2 — 79
(Sir Michael Stoute) *s.i.s: sn mid-div: rdn and hdwy over 2f out: wnt 2nd ins fnl f: kpt on wl cl home: jst failed* **12/1**

0-4 **3** 1¾ **Emperor Napoleon**[27] 1140 3-8-8 0.......... DavidProbert 11 — 76
(Andrew Balding) *racd keenly: trckd ldrs: chal over 2f out tl ent fnl f: kpt on same pce* **14/1**

3 **4** 1¼ **Mazaz (IRE)**[13] 1406 3-8-8 0.......... RobertHavlin 5 — 74
(John Gosden) *slowly away: sn cl up: rdn to ld over 2f out tl over 1f out: kpt on same pce fnl f* **6/5**[1]

63 **5** 2½ **Summer Collection (IRE)**[25] 1179 3-8-3 0.......... NickyMackay 7 — 65
(Charles Hills) *in tch: rdn to chse ldrs over 2f out: sn one pce* **25/1**

30-2 **6** 7 **De Aguilar (USA)**[25] 1184 3-8-8 75.......... MartinLane 6 — 58
(Roger Charlton) *trckd ldrs: rdn over 2f out: wknd fnl f* **16/1**

/3 **7** 2¼ **Subordinate (GER)**[10] 1499 7-10-0 0..........(t) TimmyMurphy 12 — 56
(Emma Lavelle) *hld up: sme prog 2f out: nvr trbld ldrs* **66/1**

4-3 **8** 3 **Apache Song**[15] 1386 3-8-3 0.......... JimmyQuinn 8 — 44
(Rod Millman) *trckd ldr: led over 3f out tl rdn over 2f out: wknd jst over 1f out* **16/1**

9 1¼ **Ma Peek (USA)** 3-8-9 0 ow1.......... LiamKeniry 4 — 48
(Brian Meehan) *dwlt: a towards rr* **10/1**[3]

0- **10** nk **Chelsea's Boy (IRE)**[188] 7397 3-8-8 0.......... SamHitchcott 9 — 47
(Clive Cox) *s.i.s: a towards rr* **22/1**

00- **11** 23 **Spring Overture**[303] 3683 4-9-8 0.......... FMBerry 10 — 4
(Brendan Powell) *led tl over 3f out: sn rdn: wknd 2f out* **100/1**

0 **12** 1¾ **Angel Of Light (IRE)**[10] 1499 4-9-8 0.......... JFEgan 1 — 1
(Jo Hughes) *a towards rr* **100/1**

2m 31.31s (0.71) **Going Correction** +0.175s/f (Good)
WFA 3 from 4yo 20lb 4 from 7yo 1lb **12** Ran SP% **120.9**
Speed ratings (Par 103): **104,103,102,101,100 95,93,91,91,90 75,74**
CSF £32.26 TOTE £3.10: £1.20, £2.60, £5.20; EX 22.00 Trifecta £308.70.
Owner Walters Plant Hire Ltd **Bred** Lynch Bages Ltd **Trained** Newmarket, Suffolk

FOCUS
Race distance increased by 10yds. This looked a reasonable maiden and it should produce winners. It was soundly run.

1740 PARKER TRANSPORT H'CAP — 1m 3f 144y
5:05 (5:06) (Class 6) (0-60,59) 3-Y-O — **£2,726** (£805; £402) **Stalls** Low

Form — RPR

-466 **1** **Harry's Endeavour**[20] 1259 3-9-3 **55**........................(p) TimmyMurphy 11 — 64
(Daniel Kubler) *mid-div: hdwy over 2f out: sn rdn: led jst over 1f out: styd on wl: drvn out* **14/1**

000- **2** ½ **Scarpeta (FR)**[137] 8177 3-8-9 **47**.................................... FrederikTylicki 2 — 55
(Mark Johnston) *prom: drvn to ld over 2f out tl over 1f out: kpt on wl to regain 2nd fnl 120yds: rallying towards fin* **11/2**[2]

00-3 **3** ¾ **Smiley Bagel (IRE)**[20] 1259 3-8-10 **48**............................ AntonioFresu 1 — 55
(Ed Walker) *s.i.s: sn mid-div: trckd ldrs 5f out: rdn to chal over 2f out: led over 1f out: sn hdd: no ex fnl 120yds* **10/3**[1]

55-5 **4** 3 ½ **Wharane (FR)**[15] 1389 3-9-7 **59**.................................... JimmyFortune 13 — 60
(Ian Williams) *stdd s: rdn and stdy prog fr over 2f out: styd on fnl f: wnt 4th cl home* **7/1**

00-0 **5** nk **French Legend**[20] 1259 3-9-2 **54**.................................... DavidProbert 9 — 55
(Andrew Balding) *mid-div: hdwy over 2f out: sn rdn: kpt on same pce fnl f* **10/1**

0205 **6** ¾ **Rockliffe**[10] 1484 3-9-5 **57**.. JFEgan 6 — 57
(Mick Channon) *prom: led 5f out: rdn wl over 2f out: sn hdd: no ex fnl f* **13/2**[3]

0-60 **7** hd **Chestnut Storm (IRE)**[25] 1179 3-9-3 **55**............................ MartinLane 3 — 54+
(Ed Dunlop) *hld up towards rr: struggling 3f out: styd on fr over 1f out but nvr any threat* **16/1**

002- **8** 2 ¾ **Nanny Makfi**[183] 7507 3-8-8 **49**................................ MatthewCosham(3) 4 — 44
(Stuart Kittow) *racd keenly early: mid-div: struggling 3f out: nvr a danger* **10/1**

00-0 **9** 1 **Charlie Parker (IRE)**[20] 1259 3-8-2 **47** ow1.............(p) SeanMooney(7) 7 — 40
(Dominic Ffrench Davis) *towards rr: hdwy after 2f: in tch: effrt over 2f out: sn wknd* **40/1**

06-5 **10** 4 ½ **Northman (IRE)**[20] 1259 3-8-7 **45**................................(p) SamHitchcott 5 — 31
(Jim Boyle) *led tl 5f out: rdn to chse ldrs wl over 2f out: wknd over 1f out* **20/1**

04-0 **11** 7 **Desert Tango**[20] 1259 3-9-0 **52**.. RyanClark 12 — 27
(Jonathan Portman) *w ldrs: rdn over 2f out: wknd wl over 1f out* **16/1**

304- **12** 13 **Bulge Bracket**[253] 5448 3-9-6 **58**.. LiamKeniry 8 — 12
(Tom Dascombe) *mid-div tl over 3f out: sn wknd* **18/1**

060- **13** 7 **Compton Sky (USA)**[183] 7507 3-9-3 **55**......................(b) RobertHavlin 14
(Jo Hughes) *stdd s: a towards rr* **14/1**

2m 34.49s (3.89) **Going Correction** +0.175s/f (Good) — **13** Ran SP% **120.0**
Speed ratings (Par 96): **94,93,93,90,90 90,90,88,87,84 79,71,66**
CSF £89.60 CT £325.34 TOTE £16.20: £5.30, £3.00, £1.50; EX 163.50 Trifecta £668.30.
Owner Andrew Stonehill **Bred** Mrs B E Moore **Trained** Lambourn, Berks

FOCUS
Race distance increased by 10yds. A lowly 3yo handicap, but plenty of potential improvers and the first three came a few lengths clear.
T/Jkpt: Not won. T/Plt: £96.70 to a £1 stake. Pool: £65,911.67 - 497.17 winning units. T/Qpdt: £14.20 to a £1 stake. Pool: £5,393.46 - 279.32 winning units. **Tim Mitchell**

1543 BRIGHTON (L-H)
Tuesday, April 26

OFFICIAL GOING: Good to firm (9.4)
Wind: Fresh, across away from stand Weather: Sunny spells, cold

1741 VEOLIA - OFFICIAL RECYCLING PARTNER NOVICE AUCTION STKS — 5f 213y
1:50 (1:50) (Class 5) 2-Y-O — **£2,911** (£866; £432; £216) **Stalls** Centre

Form — RPR

4 **1** **Sayesse**[18] 1316 2-8-12 0... CharlesBishop 5 — 77
(Mick Channon) *hld up in 5th: hdwy to ld 2f out: rdn clr fnl f* **8/1**

2 3 ¾ **Masquerade Bling (IRE)** 2-8-6 0.. CamHardie 3 — 60
(Simon Hodgson) *dwlt: in tch: rdn over 2f out: effrt on inner over 1f out: styd on to take 2nd ins fnl f* **50/1**

32 **3** ¾ **Sheila's Lad (IRE)**[7] 1543 2-8-11 0.................................. MartinDwyer 1 — 63
(J S Moore) *disp ld for 4f: one pce ent fnl f* **5/2**[2]

64 **4** 1 ¼ **Princess Way (IRE)**[11] 1454 2-8-7 0.................................. CathyGannon 2 — 55
(David Evans) *disp ld for 4f: no ex over 1f out* **5/1**[3]

5 1 ¼ **Areyoutheway (IRE)** 2-9-0 0..............................(v[1]) RichardKingscote 4 — 58
(Tom Dascombe) *pressed ldrs: rdn over 2f out: sn outpcd* **5/1**[3]

6 1 **Nile Empress** 2-8-10 0.. MartinHarley 6 — 51
(Hugo Palmer) *s.s: hdwy and prom in centre 2f out: wknd over 1f out* **2/1**[1]

1m 10.62s (0.42) **Going Correction** -0.075s/f (Good) — **6** Ran SP% **108.3**
Speed ratings (Par 92): **94,89,88,86,84 83**
CSF £199.46 TOTE £10.00: £4.00, £4.60; EX 177.80 Trifecta £506.00.
Owner Lord Ilsley Racing (Steele Syndicate) **Bred** Llety Farms **Trained** West Ilsley, Berks

FOCUS
Rail movements meant that all races were run over 5yds further than advertised. Charles Bishop, who rode the opening winner, said: "It is good to firm and is drying out and going to get quicker through the day." A moderate auction event in which the winner and second came from off the pace. The form is tentatively rated around the time and the fourth.

1742 BRIGHTON&HOVE BUSES - OFFICIAL TRANSPORT PARTNER H'CAP — 7f 214y
2:20 (2:20) (Class 6) (0-55,55) 4-Y-O+ — **£2,264** (£673; £336; £168) **Stalls** Centre

Form — RPR

0045 **1** **Fairy Mist (IRE)**[7] 1544 9-9-3 **51**..............................(b) WilliamCarson 5 — 57
(John Bridger) *hld up towards rr: nt clr run over 2f out: hdwy to ld over 1f out: edgd lft and narrowly hdd ins fnl f: rallied to ld on line* **13/2**[3]

3006 **2** hd **Stanlow**[73] 563 6-8-7 **48**.. GeorgeWood(7) 7 — 54
(Michael Mullineaux) *bhd: hdwy on inner 2f out: slt ld ins fnl f: kpt on wl: hdd on line* **12/1**

0604 **3** 1 ½ **Lutine Charlie (IRE)**[7] 1556 9-9-3 **51**..................(p) RichardKingscote 8 — 53
(Emma Owen) *chsd ldrs: led 2f out tl over 1f out: n.m.r ins fnl f: kpt on* **8/1**

06-2 **4** 5 **Jackpot**[20] 1263 6-8-12 **46**..(p) CathyGannon 1 — 36
(Brendan Powell) *in tch: rdn 3f out: jnd ldrs 2f out: n.m.r and no ex 1f out* **12/1**

0-52 **5** 2 ½ **Fitzwilliam**[7] 1548 4-9-2 **55**.. PaddyPilley(5) 2 — 39
(Mick Channon) *towards rr: rdn and sme hdwy 2f out: btn over 1f out* **2/1**[1]

-000 **6** 1 ¾ **Malih**[39] 986 7-9-4 **52**.. MartinHarley 6 — 32
(Eric Wheeler) *bhd: effrt in centre 2f out: no imp* **10/1**

0504 **7** ½ **Khajaaly (IRE)**[10] 1498 9-9-4 **52**......................................(vt) AdamKirby 9 — 31
(Daniel Mark Loughnane) *hld up in midfield: effrt and hung lft over 1f out: unable to chal* **6/1**[2]

/0-0 **8** ½ **Norphin**[100] 233 6-8-5 **46** oh1..................................... RhiainIngram(7) 10 — 23
(Simon Hodgson) *prom: lost pl 3f out: sn struggling* **66/1**

56-0 **9** 1 ¾ **Nifty Kier**[110] 79 7-8-7 **46**.. JosephineGordon(5) 3 — 19
(Phil McEntee) *prom tl wknd over 1f out* **9/1**

0-00 **10** 5 **Just Marion (IRE)**[83] 431 4-8-7 **46** oh1................. EdwardGreatrex(5) 4 — 7
(James Grassick) *led tl 2f out: wknd over 1f out* **50/1**

0206 **11** 2 ¾ **Crowning Star (IRE)**[34] 1035 7-8-12 **46** oh1.............(tp) JackMitchell 11 — 1
(Steve Woodman) *prom tl wknd wl over 1f out* **16/1**

1m 36.09s (0.09) **Going Correction** -0.075s/f (Good) — **11** Ran SP% **115.9**
Speed ratings (Par 101): **96,95,94,89,86 85,84,84,82,77 74**
CSF £80.62 CT £633.94 TOTE £6.80: £2.10, £4.50, £2.50; EX 113.00 Trifecta £639.50.
Owner J J Bridger **Bred** Sandro Garavelli **Trained** Liphook, Hants
■ Stewards' Enquiry : Paddy Pilley caution: careless riding

FOCUS
Race distance increased by 5yds. The principals in this poor handicap raced up the inside rail. Straightforward form.

1743 EBF STALLIONS BREEDING WINNERS FILLIES' H'CAP — 1m 1f 209y
2:55 (2:56) (Class 3) (0-90,89) 4-Y-O+ — **£8,821** (£2,640; £1,320; £660) **Stalls** High

Form — RPR

655- **1** **Tears Of The Sun**[169] 7779 5-9-12 **89**................................ AdamKirby 4 — 97
(Clive Cox) *hld up: rdn to ld over 2f out: edgd lft: clr fnl f: pushed out* **5/4**[1]

03-5 **2** 3 **Victoria Pollard**[19] 1290 4-9-1 **83**............................ EdwardGreatrex(5) 2 — 85
(Andrew Balding) *trckd ldr: led briefly 3f out: outpcd fnl 2f* **9/2**[3]

1611 **3** nk **Southern Storm (IRE)**[20] 1266 4-9-3 **85**.............(v) PatrickO'Donnell(5) 1 — 86
(Ralph Beckett) *hld up in tch: effrt over 2f out: one pce* **5/2**[2]

11-0 **4** 17 **Roly Tricks**[15] 1390 5-8-2 **70** oh3.................................... PaddyPilley(5) 3 — 55
(Natalie Lloyd-Beavis) *led tl wknd over 2f out* **5/1**

2m 5.38s (1.78) **Going Correction** -0.075s/f (Good) — **4** Ran SP% **107.9**
Speed ratings (Par 104): **89,86,86,72**
CSF £6.91 TOTE £2.00; EX 8.90 Trifecta £10.20.
Owner Dr Bridget Drew & Partners **Bred** Dr Bridget Drew & John Burke **Trained** Lambourn, Berks

FOCUS
Race distance increased by 5yds. They didn't go a bad pace in this decent little fillies' handicap. It wasn't a strong race for the grade but the winner has been given a bit of credit.

1744 HARRINGTONS LETTINGS - OFFICIAL GRANDSTAND SPONSOR H'CAP — 5f 59y
3:30 (3:30) (Class 4) (0-85,85) 4-Y-O+ — **£4,690** (£1,395; £697; £348) **Stalls** Centre

Form — RPR

4210 **1** **King Crimson**[13] 1427 4-9-1 **79**...................................... CharlesBishop 4 — 89+
(Mick Channon) *broke wl: mde all at str pce: a in control: rdn and hld on wl fnl 2f* **5/1**

646- **2** 1 ½ **Major Pusey**[224] 6423 4-8-9 **76**............................ MichaelJMMurphy(3) 2 — 79
(John Gallagher) *chsd ldrs: rdn 3f out: wnt 2nd over 1f out: kpt on fnl f* **3/1**[1]

320- **3** 1 ¾ **Lady Kyllar**[277] 4578 4-9-7 **85**.. AdamKirby 1 — 82
(George Margarson) *outpcd in rr tl styd on fr over 1f out* **3/1**[1]

4246 **4** 4 ½ **Desert Command**[47] 894 6-9-0 **78**..............................(p) MartinHarley 3 — 59
(Robert Cowell) *in tch tl hrd rdn and btn over 1f out* **4/1**[3]

4225 **5** 7 **Ballista (IRE)**[32] 1084 8-9-5 **83**...............................(p) RichardKingscote 5 — 38
(Tom Dascombe) *chsd wnr tl wknd over 1f out* **7/2**[2]

1m 1.08s (-1.22) **Going Correction** -0.075s/f (Good) — **5** Ran SP% **108.9**
Speed ratings (Par 105): **106,103,100,93,82**
CSF £19.46 TOTE £4.60: £2.10, £2.00; EX 19.60 Trifecta £48.90.
Owner Billy Parish **Bred** Mickley Stud **Trained** West Ilsley, Berks

FOCUS
Race distance increased by 5yds. An ordinary sprint handicap in which nothing got in a blow at the winner, who posted a good time. The form is rated around the second.

1745 STREAMLINE TAXIS - OFFICIAL TRANSPORT PARTNER H'CAP — 5f 213y
4:05 (4:05) (Class 5) (0-70,69) 3-Y-O — **£2,911** (£866; £432; £216) **Stalls** Centre

Form — RPR

001- **1** **Nag's Wag (IRE)**[202] 7030 3-9-5 **67**.................................... MartinHarley 2 — 72
(George Baker) *s.s: hld up in 5th: hdwy 2f out: led 1f out: rdn out* **4/1**[1]

-253 **2** 1 ¼ **Strictly Carter**[12] 1431 3-9-2 **64**.. RobertTart 1 — 65
(Alan Bailey) *prom: n.m.r 3f out: disp ld 2f out tl led briefly over 1f out: kpt on same pce* **5/1**[3]

60-2 **3** ½ **Born To Finish (IRE)**[12] 1431 3-9-0 **67**.......................... DavidParkes(5) 5 — 66
(Jeremy Gask) *s.s: towards rr: hdwy 2f out: r.o fnl f* **4/1**[1]

-106 **4** 3 ¼ **Timia**[22] 1238 3-9-4 **66**.. AdamKirby 7 — 55
(Ed Dunlop) *chsd ldrs tl outpcd appr fnl f* **11/2**

26-0 **5** nk **Canford Belle**[13] 1420 3-8-9 **62**.................................... HectorCrouch(5) 8 — 50
(Amanda Perrett) *chsd ldr: disp ld 2f out tl over 1f out: sn wknd* **8/1**

4323 **6** 2 ¼ **Justice Rock**[12] 1435 3-8-9 **62**..............................(v) JosephineGordon(5) 3 — 43
(Phil McEntee) *led tl 2f out: wknd over 1f out* **8/1**

260- **7** 9 **Addicted To Luck**[185] 7471 3-9-7 **69**................................ CathyGannon 4 — 21
(David Evans) *outpcd: sn bhd: eased whn no ch fnl f* **9/2**[2]

1m 10.37s (0.17) **Going Correction** -0.075s/f (Good) — **7** Ran SP% **112.5**
Speed ratings (Par 98): **95,93,92,88,87 84,72**
CSF £23.19 CT £83.09 TOTE £5.10: £2.70, £2.90; EX 25.80 Trifecta £124.10.
Owner George Baker **Bred** Mrs Ann Foley & Mr William Neville **Trained** Manton, Wilts

FOCUS
Race distance increased by 5yds. They went a good gallop in this moderate handicap. Sound if limited form.

1746 FROSTS CARS - OFFICIAL LADIES DAY PARTNER H'CAP — 6f 209y
4:40 (4:40) (Class 5) (0-75,73) 4-Y-O+ — **£2,911** (£866; £432; £216) **Stalls** Centre

Form — RPR

0-63 **1** **Good Luck Charm**[7] 1545 7-9-0 **71**.........................(b) HectorCrouch(5) 4 — 79
(Gary Moore) *t.k.h in 6th: hdwy to dispute ld over 1f out: led ins fnl f: drvn out* **7/2**[1]

330 **2** ¾ **Sarmadee (IRE)**[27] 1140 4-9-0 **73**............................ KillianHennessy(7) 2 — 79+
(Mick Channon) *stdd s: bhd: hdwy and hrd rdn over 1f out: fin wl* **8/1**[3]

15-2 **3** ½ **Snappy Guest**[13] 1415 4-9-5 **71**...................................... RyanPowell 3 — 76
(George Margarson) *hld up in 5th: hdwy 2f out: disp ld over 1f out tl ins fnl f: kpt on* **7/2**[1]

50-0 **4** 3 **Port Lairge**[7] 1546 6-8-13 **68**..............................(v) MichaelJMMurphy(3) 6 — 65
(John Gallagher) *sn prom: jnd ldrs 3f out tl hung lft over 1f out: one pce* **9/2**[2]

3440 **5** 1 ¼ **Jimmy's Hall**[7] 1545 4-9-7 **73**..(b) LiamJones 7 — 66
(J S Moore) *in tch: jnd ldrs 3f out tl wl over 1f out: sn wknd* **16/1**

06-2 **6** 2 3/4 **Dr Red Eye**[20] 1252 8-9-1 **67**...........(p) CathyGannon 1 53
(Scott Dixon) *mde most tl wknd over 1f out* **7/2**[1]

2400 **7** 6 **Swiss Cross**[25] 1186 9-8-9 **66**...........(t) JosephineGordon(5) 5 36
(Phil McEntee) *prom tl wknd wl over 1f out* **10/1**

1m 22.43s (-0.67) **Going Correction** -0.075s/f (Good) **7** Ran SP% **110.9**
Speed ratings (Par 103): **100,99,98,95,93 90,83**
CSF £29.67 TOTE £3.80: £3.10, £2.70; EX 25.80 Trifecta £96.00.
Owner Heart Of The South Racing **Bred** John And Caroline Penny **Trained** Lower Beeding, W Sussex

FOCUS
Race distance increased by 5yds. A modest handicap in which the first three came from the rear. The winner is rated similar to last year's form.

1747 L&S PRINTING - OFFICIAL PRINT PARTNER APPRENTICE H'CAP 1m 1f 209y
5:15 (5:18) (Class 6) (0-65,65) 4-Y-O+ **£2,264** (£673; £336; £168) **Stalls** High

Form RPR

6000 **1** **Ifan (IRE)**[39] 982 8-8-6 **55**...........(p) MitchGodwin(5) 8 62
(Tim Vaughan) *chsd ldr: led over 2f out: drvn out* **10/3**[1]

-130 **2** 1 1/4 **Lord Of The Storm**[17] 1340 8-9-5 **63**........... CharlesEddery 2 68
(Michael Attwater) *chsd ldrs: wnt 2nd 2f out: jnd wnr over 1f out tl ins fnl f: kpt on same pce* **7/1**

3233 **3** 1 3/4 **Les Gar Gan (IRE)**[3] 1654 5-8-12 **59**...........(be) JoshQuinn(3) 3 61
(Daniel Mark Loughnane) *dwlt: towards rr: rdn over 2f out: hdwy over 1f out: styd on wl fnl f* **4/1**[3]

335- **4** 1 3/4 **Roy Rocket (FR)**[247] 5659 6-9-2 **60**........... AdamMcLean 6 58+
(John Berry) *rring in stalls: stdd s: hld up and bhd: rdn and hdwy over 1f out: styd on* **7/2**[2]

3016 **5** 3 3/4 **Turnbury**[11] 1456 5-9-0 **63**...........(p) CliffordLee(5) 5 54
(Nikki Evans) *prom tl wknd 1f out* **14/1**

14-5 **6** 3 3/4 **Megalala (IRE)**[7] 1547 15-8-10 **54**........... DavidParkes 7 38
(John Bridger) *led tl over 2f out: wknd wl over 1f out* **8/1**

-200 **7** 3 1/2 **Ruzeiz (USA)**[60] 724 7-9-2 **60**...........(p) AnnaHesketh 1 37
(Peter Hedger) *hld up in 6th: hrd rdn and wknd 2f out* **12/1**

-024 **8** 1 **Senor George (IRE)**[22] 1236 9-9-7 **65**........... RhiainIngram 4 41
(Simon Hodgson) *hld up in 5th: rdn 3f out: wknd 2f out* **9/1**

2m 2.47s (-1.13) **Going Correction** -0.075s/f (Good) **8** Ran SP% **113.3**
Speed ratings (Par 101): **101,100,98,97,94 91,88,87**
CSF £26.35 CT £94.64 TOTE £3.80: £1.40, £2.50, £1.50; EX 26.70 Trifecta £187.00.
Owner WRB Racing 61 and Derek & Jean Clee **Bred** Dr John Waldron **Trained** Aberthin, Vale of Glamorgan

■ Stewards' Enquiry : Mitch Godwin two-day ban: used whip above permitted level (May 10-11)

FOCUS
Race distance increased by 5yds. Nothing really got into this from the rear. The well backed winner was entitled to win this.
T/Plt: £2342.50 to a £1 stake. Pool: £44,765.90 - 13.95 winning units. T/Qpdt: £66.60 to a £1 stake. Pool: £5,191.57 - 57.65 winning units. **Lee McKenzie**

1572 LINGFIELD (L-H)
Tuesday, April 26

OFFICIAL GOING: Polytrack: standard
Wind: medium, half against Weather: bright spells and sleet showers

1748 COME RACING ON LADIES DAY MAY 6TH H'CAP 1m 4f (P)
4:35 (4:36) (Class 6) (0-55,55) 4-Y-O+ **£2,264** (£673; £336; £168) **Stalls** Low

Form RPR

-643 **1** **Bamako Du Chatelet (FR)**[60] 724 5-9-7 **55**........... JamesDoyle 7 61
(Ian Williams) *chsd ldrs: effrt to chse clr ldr over 2f out: clsd u.p over 1f out: led ins fnl f: styd on* **11/10**[1]

2230 **2** 3/4 **Sudden Wish (IRE)**[13] 1413 7-9-4 **52**........... JimCrowley 1 57
(Michael Attwater) *hld up towards rr: hdwy into midfield 7f out: effrt in 5th 2f out: wnt 3rd and clsng over 1f out: drvn and pressing wnr 100yds: kpt on* **12/1**

0044 **3** 1 1/4 **Dynamo (IRE)**[54] 796 5-8-5 **46** oh1...........(t) StephanieJoannides(7) 2 49
(Richard Hughes) *t.k.h: hld up towards rr: clipped heels and stmbld bnd 9f out: hdwy in 8th 2f out: swtchd rt and pushed along over 1f out: r.o strly ins fnl f: nt rch ldrs* **10/1**

6550 **4** 3 **Chauvelin**[10] 1500 5-9-0 **48**...........(v) ConnorBeasley 8 46
(Richard Guest) *mde most: rdn and kicked clr 3f out: 5 l clr 2f: reduced advantage 1f out: hdd ins fnl f: sn btn and wknd towards fin* **8/1**[3]

0064 **5** nk **Investissement**[25] 1174 10-8-11 **50**...........(tp) CallumShepherd(5) 6 48
(Paddy Butler) *awkward leaving stalls and slowly away: hld up in rr: hdwy on inner over 2f out: 7th 2f out: styd on ins fnl f: nvr threatened ldrs* **25/1**

46/3 **6** nk **Prince Of Islay (IRE)**[41] 950 5-9-2 **50**...........(b) FrannyNorton 9 47
(Amanda Perrett) *chsd ldr after 2f: rdn and outpcd 3f out: kpt on same pce u.p fnl 2f* **7/1**[2]

500- **7** 7 **Willshebetrying**[85] 594 5-8-13 **47**...........(v) SeanLevey 3 33
(Jim Best) *in tch in midfield: rdn and outpcd 3f out: wknd 2f out* **33/1**

0005 **8** 3 **Ron Waverly (IRE)**[64] 673 6-8-12 **46** oh1...........(tp) WilliamCarson 4 27
(Paddy Butler) *chsd ldr for 2f: styd chsng ldrs: drvn and outpcd over 2f out: wknd over 1f out* **50/1**

0662 **9** 1/2 **Easydoesit (IRE)**[17] 1343 8-9-0 **55**...........(p) GeorgiaCox(7) 14 35
(Tony Carroll) *s.i.s: hld up in rr* **14/1**

006- **10** 1 1/4 **Caerleon Kate**[327] 2867 4-8-11 **46** oh1........... JackMitchell 11 24
(Rod Millman) *in tch in midfield: lost pl and in last pair 5f out: rdn over 3f out: sn btn* **25/1**

0066 **11** 1 1/2 **Little Flo**[22] 1239 5-8-9 **48**........... AaronJones(5) 10 24
(William Stone) *chsd ldrs tl lost pl u.p over 2f out: wl bhd fnl f* **16/1**

6-01 **12** 3 **Fleetwood Poppy**[66] 653 4-9-0 **49**........... KierenFox 12 20
(Michael Attwater) *in tch in midfield: rdn and effrt on outer bnd 4f out: sn btn: bhd fnl f* **16/1**

0/00 **13** 7 **Pandora's Pyx**[62] 697 4-8-11 **46** oh1...........(p) JohnFahy 5 6
(Gary Moore) *t.k.h early: hld up in tch: rdn 4f out: lost pl 3f out: wl bhd fnl f* **33/1**

0000 **14** 79 **Zac Courageous (IRE)**[20] 1263 4-8-11 **46** oh1...........(p) MartinDwyer 13
(James Bennett) *rdn along leaving stalls: midfield but stuck wd: reminder 9f out and again 6f out: rdn and lost tch over 3f out: eased over 2f out: t.o* **66/1**

2m 31.47s (-1.53) **Going Correction** 0.0s/f (Stan)
WFA 4 from 5yo+ 1lb **14** Ran SP% **123.5**
Speed ratings (Par 101): **105,104,103,101,101 101,96,94,94,93 92,90,85,33**
CSF £14.98 CT £101.81 TOTE £2.60: £1.50, £2.30, £3.40; EX 20.30 Trifecta £91.90.
Owner Macable Partnership **Bred** S N C Ecurie Jouenne Gerard **Trained** Portway, Worcs

FOCUS
A moderate heat. The winner was entitled to win this on his better figures.

1749 HAPPY BIRTHDAY ANDREW PERKINS EBF MAIDEN STKS 5f 6y(P)
5:10 (5:11) (Class 5) 2-Y-O **£3,234** (£962; £481; £240) **Stalls** High

Form RPR

1 **Kananee (USA)** 2-9-5 0........... JamesDoyle 6 82
(Saeed bin Suroor) *chsd ldr: effrt 2f out: pushed into ld over 1f out: fnd ex whn pressed ins fnl f: r.o wl* **13/8**[1]

2 1 1/2 **Monks Stand (USA)** 2-9-5 0........... JimCrowley 4 77
(Jeremy Noseda) *dwlt: pushed along in 5th early: hdwy over 2f out: rdn and swtchd lft over 1f out: pressed wnr ins fnl f: r.o same pce fnl 100yds* **8/1**

322 **3** 3 **Decadent Times (IRE)**[13] 1407 2-9-5 0........... RichardKingscote 1 66
(Tom Dascombe) *wnt rt s: led: rdn and hdd over 1f out: no ex u.p: 3rd and outpcd ins fnl f* **9/4**[2]

4 2 3/4 **Tiggaliscious (IRE)** 2-9-0 0........... SeanLevey 2 51
(Richard Hannon) *s.i.s: sn rcvrd and chsd ldrs: rdn and unable qck over 1f out: wknd ins fnl f* **7/2**[3]

5 1 **Glenys The Menace (FR)** 2-9-0 0........... KierenFox 5 47
(John Best) *s.i.s: detached in last: rdn wl over 1f out: no imp and hung rt ins fnl f: nvr trbld ldrs* **33/1**

6 3 **Ortano (USA)** 2-9-5 0........... FrannyNorton 3 42
(Mark Johnston) *rn green: chsd ldrs tl lost pl over 2f out: rn green and hung rt bnd 2f out: bhd fnl f* **10/1**

58.83s (0.03) **Going Correction** 0.0s/f (Stan) **6** Ran SP% **114.2**
Speed ratings (Par 92): **99,96,91,87,85 81**
CSF £15.73 TOTE £2.50: £1.30, £5.00; EX 15.10 Trifecta £45.60.
Owner Godolphin **Bred** Darley **Trained** Newmarket, Suffolk

FOCUS
A maiden that should throw up a winner or two. A nice start from Kananee.

1750 HAPPY 21ST BIRTHDAY OLIVER BOYD H'CAP 1m 1y(P)
5:40 (5:41) (Class 4) (0-85,78) 3-Y-O **£5,175** (£1,540; £769; £384) **Stalls** High

Form RPR

410- **1** **Royal Reserve**[185] 7468 3-9-4 **75**........... MartinDwyer 2 87+
(William Muir) *pushed along leaving stalls: hld up in tch in midfield: effrt on inner 2f out: led over 1f out: clr and in command fnl f: r.o wl: readily* **6/1**[3]

5314 **2** 3 3/4 **Ilzam (IRE)**[20] 1267 3-9-7 **78**...........(t) JamesDoyle 8 80
(Marco Botti) *taken down early: dropped in bhd after s: hdwy on inner 2f out: chsd ldng pair over 1f out: styd u.p to go 2nd wl ins fnl f: no ch w wnr* **5/1**[2]

51- **3** nk **D'Niro (IRE)**[167] 7792 3-9-7 **78**........... AdamKirby 7 79
(Harry Dunlop) *taken down early: nt that wl away: hdwy to ld over 6f out: rdn and drifted rt bnd 2f out: sn hdd and outpcd: wl hld and styd on same pce ins fnl f: lost 2nd wl ins fnl f* **9/4**[1]

20-2 **4** 1 1/2 **Stylistik**[20] 1258 3-8-13 **75**........... CallumShepherd(5) 3 72
(Luke Dace) *hld up in tch in last pair: effrt and wd bnd 2f out: hdwy 1f out: styd on u.p ins fnl f: no threat to ldrs* **14/1**

550- **5** nk **Fashaak (IRE)**[206] 6924 3-9-7 **78**........... SeanLevey 4 75
(Richard Hannon) *t.k.h: chsd ldrs tl stdd bk into midfield over 6f out: nt clr run over 2f out tl rdn and hdwy over 1f out: kpt on same pce ins fnl f* **5/1**[2]

022- **6** 2 1/2 **Percy's Romance**[203] 7013 3-9-2 **73**........... JimCrowley 5 64
(Sir Michael Stoute) *chsd ldrs: rdn 2f out: unable qck and lost pl over 1f out: wknd ins fnl f* **7/1**

44-4 **7** nk **Bergholt (IRE)**[19] 1288 3-9-2 **73**........... RichardKingscote 6 63
(Philip Hide) *in tch in midfield: effrt and wd bnd 2f out: sn drvn and no hdwy: plugged on same pce fnl f* **8/1**

516- **8** 8 **Daleelak (IRE)**[185] 7465 3-9-6 **77**........... DaneO'Neill 1 48
(Mark Johnston) *led tl over 6f out: rdn and no ex 2f out: lost pl and btn over 1f out: fdd 1f out: eased wl ins fnl f* **16/1**

1m 37.0s (-1.20) **Going Correction** 0.0s/f (Stan) **8** Ran SP% **114.5**
Speed ratings (Par 100): **106,102,102,100,100 98,97,89**
CSF £35.99 CT £87.82 TOTE £7.10: £2.00, £1.30, £1.60; EX 42.10 Trifecta £153.90.
Owner Muir Racing Partnership - Chester **Bred** New England, Myriad & Watership Down **Trained** Lambourn, Berks

FOCUS
An interesting little handicap and a good performance from the winner, who looks a good few pounds ahead of his mark. The second is the best guide.

1751 RYAN VEHICLES H'CAP 1m 2f (P)
6:15 (6:15) (Class 5) (0-70,70) 4-Y-O+ **£2,911** (£866; £432; £216) **Stalls** Low

Form RPR

21-1 **1** **Bridge Of Sighs**[68] 621 4-9-2 **65**........... AdamKirby 4 74+
(Martin Smith) *hld up in tch in 3rd: swtchd lft and effrt over 1f out: qcknd u.p to ld jst ins fnl f: sn edgd rt but r.o wl: rdn out* **9/4**[2]

3022 **2** 1 1/2 **I'm Harry**[52] 832 7-9-6 **69**...........(vt) JamesDoyle 1 75
(George Baker) *chsd ldr: effrt 2f out: drvn and ev ch briefly 1f out: kpt on same pce ins fnl f: chsd wnr fnl 75yds* **2/1**[1]

-410 **3** 3/4 **Heezararity**[15] 1390 8-9-5 **68**........... RichardKingscote 5 73
(Jonathan Geake) *sn bustled along to ld: rdn over 2f out: drvn 2f out: hdd jst ins fnl f: unable qck and sltly hmpd sn after: one pce fnl 100yds* **5/1**

6131 **4** 2 1/2 **Attain**[17] 1340 7-9-1 **67**...........(p) ShelleyBirkett(3) 6 67
(Julia Feilden) *hld up in 4th: effrt 2f out: styd on same pce and no imp fnl f* **3/1**[3]

0060 **5** 2 1/2 **Maria's Choice (IRE)**[12] 1434 7-9-1 **64**........... MartinDwyer 3 59?
(Jim Best) *hld up in last: rdn over 2f out: no imp: nvr trbld ldrs* **25/1**

2m 6.62s (0.02) **Going Correction** 0.0s/f (Stan) **5** Ran SP% **109.6**
Speed ratings (Par 103): **99,97,97,95,93**
CSF £7.09 TOTE £3.00: £1.70, £1.10; EX 6.60 Trifecta £17.70.
Owner SN Racing VI **Bred** S Nunn **Trained** Newmarket, Suffolk

FOCUS
A modest affair in which they went round in more or less single file to the turn in. The form is rated around the second, with the fifth a slight doubt.

1752 INJURED JOCKEYS FUND H'CAP 7f 1y(P)
6:50 (6:51) (Class 3) (0-95,93) 4-Y-O **£7,246** (£2,168; £1,084; £542; £270) **Stalls** Low

Form RPR

P406 **1** **Mr Bossy Boots (IRE)**[24] 1204 5-8-11 **88**...........(t) PatrickO'Donnell(5) 2 95+
(Ralph Beckett) *hld up wl in tch in midfield: nt clr run over 1f out: swtchd rt ent fnl f: qcknd and str run u.p ins fnl f: led towards fin* **6/1**[3]

144- **2** 1 **Goring (GER)**[186] 7434 4-8-13 **85**........... JohnFahy 4 88
(Eve Johnson Houghton) *chsd ldrs: hdwy to ld over 2f out: rdn 2f out: battled on wl u.p tl hdd and no ex towards fin* **8/1**

2215 **3** ½ **Shyron**[24] 1204 5-9-7 **93** AdamKirby 6 95
(George Margarson) *hld up in tch in rr: hdwy and rdn to press ldrs 2f out: ev ch and drvn over 1f out: kpt on wl tl no ex towards fin* **7/4**[1]

4313 **4** ½ **Presumido (IRE)**[17] 1335 6-8-12 **84** JimCrowley 3 84
(Simon Dow) *stdd after s and t.k.h early: hld up in tch in last pair: effrt over 1f out: kpt on u.p ins fnl f* **7/1**

64-2 **5** hd **Easy Tiger**[17] 1335 4-8-13 **85** MartinDwyer 1 85
(William Muir) *chsd ldr: upsides over 2f out: rdn and ev ch 2f out: drvn and stl ev ch 1f out tl no ex and btn wl ins fnl f: wknd towards fin* **11/4**[2]

6 ¾ **Charlie Bear**[438] 551 4-9-4 **90** WilliamCarson 5 88
(Jamie Osborne) *sn led and crossed to inner: hdd over 2f out: rdn and outpcd 2f out: styd on same pce fnl f* **8/1**

1m 25.31s (0.51) **Going Correction** 0.0s/f (Stan) **6** Ran SP% **112.0**
Speed ratings (Par 107): **97,95,95,94,94 93**
CSF £49.49 TOTE £6.80: £2.70, £5.60; EX 54.20 Trifecta £176.90.
Owner P J Scargill & Partner **Bred** Kilfrush Stud **Trained** Kimpton, Hants

FOCUS
They went fairly steady early on here, before winding things up heading into the straight. There was a bunch finish and the winner is better than the bare form.

1753 RACING WELFARE MEDIAN AUCTION MAIDEN STKS 5f 6y(P)
7:25 (7:27) (Class 6) 3-4-Y-O **£2,264** (£673; £336; £168) **Stalls** High

Form RPR

062- **1** **Aragon Knight**[269] 4873 3-8-12 78 HectorCrouch(5) 7 76
(Heather Main) *chsd ldrs: effrt and clsd to ld 2f out: styd on wl ins fnl f: rdn out* **6/1**

00- **2** nk **Verne Castle**[209] 6856 3-9-0 0 RobHornby(3) 3 75
(Andrew Balding) *in tch in midfield: effrt on inner to chal over 1f out: styd on u.p but a jst hld ins fnl f* **3/1**[1]

30- **3** 2½ **Teajan (IRE)**[191] 7310 3-9-3 0 AdamKirby 6 66
(James Tate) *in tch in midfield: effrt 2f out: rdn to chse ldng pair 1f out: styd on same pce and no imp ins fnl f* **3/1**[1]

643- **4** 2 **Westbourne Grove (USA)**[193] 7260 3-9-3 56 JimCrowley 2 59
(Robert Cowell) *hung rt: led for over 1f: pressed ldr tl rdn and outpcd over 1f out: wl hld 4th and kpt on same pce fnl f* **5/1**[3]

600- **5** 1¼ **Fabulous Flyer**[252] 5491 3-8-12 0 RichardKingscote 5 49
(Jeremy Gask) *stdd after s: bhd: pushed along and hdwy over 1f out: kpt on ins fnl f: nvr trbld ldrs* **33/1**

0-6 **6** ¾ **Curious Fox**[13] 1414 3-8-12 0 WilliamCarson 1 47
(Anthony Carson) *outpcd in last trio: pushed along over 1f out: kpt on ins fnl f: nvr trbld ldrs* **25/1**

023- **7** 2½ **Entertaining Ben**[136] 8204 3-9-3 70 (p) MartinDwyer 4 43
(William Muir) *w ldr tl led over 3f out: hdd and rdn 2f out: sn no ex and btn: fdd ins fnl f* **7/2**[2]

0 **8** 1½ **Cecile Royale**[17] 1337 3-8-12 0 JackMitchell 8 32
(Stuart Williams) *stdd after s: hld up off the pce in last trio: n.d* **16/1**

58.79s (-0.01) **Going Correction** 0.0s/f (Stan) **8** Ran SP% **115.8**
Speed ratings (Par 101): **100,99,95,92,90 89,85,82**
CSF £24.72 TOTE £6.60: £1.60, £1.50, £1.60; EX 28.20 Trifecta £154.50.
Owner Mr & Mrs D R Guest **Bred** Executive Bloodlines **Trained** Kingston Lisle, Oxon

FOCUS
No more than a fair maiden. It's been rated cautiously.

1754 CHRIS HARRIS BIRTHDAY CELEBRATIONS FILLIES' H'CAP 7f 1y(P)
7:55 (7:55) (Class 5) (0-70,68) 4-Y-O+ **£2,911** (£866; £432; £216) **Stalls** Low

Form RPR

3-21 **1** **Baileys Mirage (FR)**[17] 1334 5-9-4 **65** (b) SilvestreDeSousa 4 71+
(Chris Dwyer) *mde all: pressed over 2f out: pushed along over 1f out: rdn jst ins fnl f: fnd enough to assert wl ins fnl f: eased nr fin* **8/11**[1]

-004 **2** ½ **First Experience**[73] 558 5-9-2 **68** CallumShepherd(5) 1 73
(Lee Carter) *in tch in 3rd: pushed along over 2f out: hdwy to press ldr over 1f out: ev ch 1f out: no ex and one pce fnl 75yds* **4/1**[2]

2163 **3** 1½ **Binky Blue (IRE)**[20] 1268 4-9-7 **68** AdamKirby 2 69
(Daniel Mark Loughnane) *stdd s: hld up in tch in 4th: effrt ent fnl 2f: chsd ldng pair 1f out: styd on same pce ins fnl f* **4/1**[2]

330- **4** 4 **Isntshesomething**[146] 8078 4-8-9 **56** ConnorBeasley 5 46
(Richard Guest) *awkward leaving stalls: sn rcvrd and chsd wnr: pushed along to press ldr over 2f out: no ex u.p and lost pl over 1f out: wknd ins fnl f* **10/1**[3]

1m 25.01s (0.21) **Going Correction** 0.0s/f (Stan) **4** Ran SP% **107.0**
Speed ratings (Par 100): **98,97,95,91**
CSF £3.83 TOTE £1.80; EX 3.80 Trifecta £4.60.
Owner G R Bailey Ltd (Baileys Horse Feeds) **Bred** Gr Baileys Ltd **Trained** Newmarket, Suffolk

FOCUS
A modest fillies' handicap and hardly solid form with the winner getting an easy lead.
T/Plt: £42.00 to a £1 stake. Pool: £44,173.63 - 766.99 winning units. T/Qpdt: £26.00 to a £1 stake. Pool: £5,432.53 - 154.36 winning units. **Steve Payne**

1481 NOTTINGHAM (L-H)
Tuesday, April 26

OFFICIAL GOING: Good to soft (good in places; 7.4)
Wind: Moderate across Weather: Sunshine and wintry showers

1755 32RED £10 FREE MEDIAN AUCTION MAIDEN STKS 1m 75y
2:00 (2:04) (Class 5) 3-Y-O **£3,408** (£1,006; £503) **Stalls** Centre

Form RPR

2-2 **1** **Siri**[27] 1149 3-9-0 0 SilvestreDeSousa 6 74
(Mick Channon) *cl up: led 1/2-way: pushed along over 2f out: jnd and rdn over 1f out: drvn ins fnl f: hld on gamely towards fin* **9/1**

4 **2** nse **High Draw (FR)**[20] 1270 3-9-5 0 DougieCostello 7 79
(K R Burke) *trckd ldrs: hdwy on outer over 3f out: effrt wl over 1f out and sn chal: rdn and ev ch ent fnl f: sn drvn and kpt on: jst failed* **2/1**[2]

3-3 **3** 3¼ **Archimento**[14] 1397 3-9-5 0 PaulMulrennan 3 73
(Ed Dunlop) *t.k.h early: trckd ldrs: hdwy 3f out: chsd wnr 2f out: rdn over 1f out: n.m.r appr fnl f: kpt on same pce* **11/8**[1]

0- **4** 1¼ **Corpus Chorister (FR)**[195] 7219 3-9-0 0 ShaneKelly 4 67
(David Menuisier) *led: hdd 1/2-way and sn pushed along: rdn and outpcd over 2f out: kpt on fnl f* **14/1**

5 1 **Compas Scoobie** 3-9-5 0 AndreaAtzeni 2 66
(Roger Varian) *t.k.h: trckd ldrs: hdwy over 3f out: rdn to chse ldrs over 2f out: drvn wl over 1f out: sn one pce* **12/1**

6 1½ **Naqdy** 3-9-5 0 PaulHanagan 8 63
(William Haggas) *dwlt and bhd: hdwy on inner 3f out: swtchd rt 2f out: sn rdn and no imp* **8/1**[3]

05- **7** 1 **Moon Over Mobay**[160] 7890 3-9-0 0 OisinMurphy 1 56
(Andrew Balding) *chsd ldng pair: pushed along 4f out: rdn 3f out: sn wknd* **33/1**

04 **8** 4½ **Lemon Thyme**[28] 1132 3-8-7 0 KevinLundie(7) 5 45
(Mike Murphy) *a towards rr: rdn along 3f out: sn outpcd* **100/1**

1m 48.4s (-0.60) **Going Correction** -0.05s/f (Good) **8** Ran SP% **114.8**
Speed ratings (Par 98): **101,100,97,96,95 93,92,88**
CSF £27.58 TOTE £5.90: £1.90, £1.20, £1.20; EX 33.00 Trifecta £82.20.
Owner Dave and Gill Hedley **Bred** G Hedley & Mike Channon Bloodstock Limited **Trained** West Ilsley, Berks

FOCUS
Inner track in operation. The ground had eased slightly and was now good, good to soft in places. The rail was out 2yds on the back straight and home bend, adding 6yds to race distances on the round course. An ordinary maiden to start and they didn't go a great pace, but a thrilling finish. The winning time suggested the ground was indeed on the easy side with Dougie Costello describing it as "good, good to soft in places" while Paul Mulrennan said it was "tacky and quite hard work". The winner was up a length or so on her best.

1756 32RED ON THE APP STORE H'CAP 1m 75y
2:35 (2:36) (Class 5) (0-75,75) 4-Y-O+ **£3,408** (£1,006; £503) **Stalls** Centre

Form RPR

40-1 **1** **Berkeley Vale**[25] 1173 5-9-7 **75** (v) OisinMurphy 3 83
(Roger Teal) *trckd ldrs: hdwy 3f out and sn chsng ldrs: led 1 1/2f out and sn rdn: drvn ins fnl f: kpt on wl* **6/1**[3]

540- **2** ¾ **Mr Pickwick**[180] 7586 4-9-4 **72** [1] TomQueally 9 78
(James Fanshawe) *trckd ldr: cl up 1/2-way: led 3f out: jnd and rdn 2f out: hdd 1 1/2f out: drvn and rallied ins fnl f: no ex last 120yds* **7/2**[2]

06- **3** hd **Lulani (IRE)**[241] 5866 4-9-6 **74** SilvestreDeSousa 4 79
(Harry Dunlop) *led: pushed along and hdd 3f out: rdn over 2f out: n.m.r on inner and swtchd rt ins fnl f: kpt on wl towards fin* **7/2**[2]

226- **4** 1¼ **Belle Travers**[201] 7058 4-9-7 **75** PaulHanagan 1 78
(Richard Fahey) *trckd ldrs: hdwy 3f out: effrt on outer 2f out and sn rdn: drvn ent fnl f and no imp* **15/8**[1]

000- **5** 6 **Ganymede**[181] 7555 5-9-2 **73** (b) TomMarquand(3) 5 62
(Eve Johnson Houghton) *in tch: hdwy 3f out: rdn along over 2f out: sn drvn and one pce* **8/1**

330- **6** 4 **Arms Around Me (IRE)**[143] 8118 4-8-11 **70** PhilDennis(5) 2 50
(James Given) *dwlt and in rr: pushed along on inner over 3f out: sn rdn and nvr a factor* **22/1**

3/6- **7** 12 **Lewis Valentine (IRE)**[359] 1904 4-9-7 **75** TomEaves 7 27
(James Given) *dwlt and towards rr: hdwy to chse ldrs after 3f: rdn along over 3f out: sn drvn and wknd* **25/1**

1m 48.61s (-0.39) **Going Correction** -0.05s/f (Good) **7** Ran SP% **112.8**
Speed ratings (Par 103): **99,98,98,96,90 86,74**
CSF £26.43 CT £83.72 TOTE £5.80: £2.40, £1.90; EX 24.40 Trifecta £92.10.
Owner Mrs Muriel Forward & Dr G C Forward **Bred** Edward Hyde **Trained** Great Shefford, Berks

FOCUS
Rail movement added 6yds to race distance. An ordinary handicap in which they went a modest early pace and the time was fractionally slower than the opening maiden. The first four came clear and the frist two look to be improving.

1757 32RED EBF FILLIES' H'CAP 1m 75y
3:05 (3:05) (Class 3) (0-90,90) 4-Y-O+ **£9,703** (£2,887; £1,443; £721) **Stalls** Centre

Form RPR

21-6 **1** **Miss Van Gogh**[15] 1380 4-8-13 **82** PaulHanagan 9 94
(Richard Fahey) *hld up in rr: hdwy over 3f out: str run on outer fr over 2f out: rdn to ld ent fnl f: kpt on strly* **12/1**

213- **2** 3¼ **Ghinia (IRE)**[178] 7632 5-8-12 **84** RobHornby(3) 2 89
(Pam Sly) *led: qcknd clr over 2f out: rdn over 1f out: hdd and drvn ent fnl f: kpt on same pce* **5/1**[3]

00-0 **3** 2¼ **What Say You (IRE)**[31] 1088 4-9-3 **86** DougieCostello 1 86
(K R Burke) *trckd ldng pair on inner: pushed along over 3f out: rdn and sltly outpcd over 2f out: sn drvn and kpt on fnl f* **16/1**

400- **4** ½ **Loaves And Fishes**[180] 7587 4-9-7 **90** DanielTudhope 6 89
(David O'Meara) *chsd ldr: rdn along over 2f out: drvn wl over 1f out: kpt on one pce* **10/1**

0111 **5** ½ **Moon River (IRE)**[27] 1153 4-9-2 **85** BenCurtis 7 83
(Michael Appleby) *trckd ldng pair: hdwy on outer to chse ldr wl over 2f out: rdn wl over 1f out: sn drvn and kpt on one pce* **8/1**

1-21 **6** 3 **Lavetta**[6] 1563 4-8-10 **79** 6ex JoeFanning 8 70
(Alan Swinbank) *t.k.h: in tch on outer: hdwy 3f out: rdn along 2f out: sn drvn and btn* **3/1**[1]

112- **7** 7 **La Superba (IRE)**[209] 6861 4-9-0 **86** (p) TomMarquand(3) 4 61
(David Elsworth) *dwlt and in rr: sme hdwy on inner 3f out: rdn along over 2f out: sn btn* **8/1**

26-6 **8** 1½ **Edge Of Heaven**[24] 1207 4-9-2 **85** OisinMurphy 3 56
(Jonathan Portman) *trckd ldrs on inner: effrt over 3f out: sn rdn along and wknd* **14/1**

024- **9** 13 **Teosroyal (IRE)**[234] 6079 4-8-13 **82** [1] SilvestreDeSousa 5 23
(Simon Crisford) *in tch: rdn along over 4f out: wknd over 3f out* **4/1**[2]

1m 46.57s (-2.43) **Going Correction** -0.05s/f (Good) **9** Ran SP% **113.2**
Speed ratings (Par 104): **110,106,104,104,103 100,93,92,79**
CSF £69.48 CT £972.27 TOTE £10.00: £4.00, £1.50, £5.90; EX 94.60 Trifecta £1200.50.
Owner Dyson Racing & D Powell **Bred** Mrs D O Joly **Trained** Musley Bank, N Yorks

FOCUS
Rail movement added 6yds to race distance. This was a decent fillies' handicap, run at a solid pace, and the winner was most impressive. The first two came from the rear.

1758 32REDSPORT.COM FILLIES' H'CAP (DIV I) 1m 2f 50y
3:35 (3:35) (Class 5) (0-75,75) 3-Y-O **£3,408** (£1,006; £503) **Stalls** Low

Form RPR

214- **1** **Mirsaalah**[249] 5579 3-9-2 **70** AndreaAtzeni 5 84
(James Tate) *mde most: rdn clr wl over 1f out: drvn ins fnl f: jst hld on* **6/1**[2]

1- **2** nse **The Black Princess (FR)**[174] 7699 3-9-6 **74** FrankieDettori 2 88
(John Gosden) *hld up in rr: hdwy on inner 4f out: pushed along 3f out: swtchd rt to outer and rdn over 2f out: chsd wnr wl over 1f out: drvn ent fnl f: styd on wl towards fin: jst failed* **4/9**[1]

22-3 **3** 14 **Norse Magic**[18] 1312 3-9-7 **75** SilvestreDeSousa 7 62
(Sylvester Kirk) *hld up and bhd: hdwy 3f out: rdn 2f out: styd on to take modest 3rd ins fnl f* **12/1**

45-1 **4** ½ **Bocking End (IRE)**[61] 706 3-9-1 **72** LouisSteward(3) 1 58
(Michael Bell) *trckd ldrs on inner: hdwy over 3f out: rdn along over 2f out: sn drvn and kpt on one pce* **20/1**

03-6 **5** ¾ **Forgiving Flower**[17] 1346 3-8-13 **67** DougieCostello 6 52
(K R Burke) *trckd ldrs: pushed along over 3f out: rdn wl over 2f out: sn drvn and one pce* **25/1**
435 **6** 1 **Dor's Law**[42] 945 3-8-6 **63** JackDuern(3) 10 46
(Dean Ivory) *hld up towards rr: sme hdwy 3f out: sn rdn and n.d* **20/1**
460- **7** 7 **Mistymoistymorning (IRE)**[199] 7105 3-8-11 **68**(t) DannyBrock(3) 9 38
(John Ryan) *chsd ldrs on outer: rdn along over 3f out: sn wknd* **40/1**
035- **8** 7 **La Celebs Ville (IRE)**[213] 6744 3-9-4 **72** GrahamGibbons 4 28
(Tom Dascombe) *cl up on inner: rdn along over 3f out: sn wknd* **14/1**
054- **9** 5 **Poster Girl**[215] 6684 3-9-5 **73** OisinMurphy 8 20
(Jonathan Portman) *trckd ldrs: hdwy to chse ldng pair over 4f out: rdn along 3f out: sn wknd* **10/1**[3]

2m 14.0s (-0.30) **Going Correction** -0.05s/f (Good) **9** Ran SP% **122.8**
Speed ratings (Par 95): **99,98,87,87,86 85,80,74,70**
CSF £9.27 CT £37.14 TOTE £7.60: £2.10, £1.10, £1.80; EX 17.50 Trifecta £96.10.
Owner Saif Ali **Bred** Mr & Mrs A E Pakenham **Trained** Newmarket, Suffolk

FOCUS
Rail movement added 6yds to race distance. An ordinary 3yo fillies' handicap in which the majority were stepping up in trip and a very lopsided betting market. The first two produced a stirring finish and pulled miles clear of the rest, showing useful form. This looked the stronger division visually and that was backed up by the much faster winning time.

1759 32REDSPORT.COM FILLIES' H'CAP (DIV II) 1m 2f 50y
4:10 (4:10) (Class 5) (0-75,74) 3-Y-O **£3,408** (£1,006; £503) **Stalls** Low

Form RPR
0124 **1** **Daisy Bere (FR)**[27] 1155 3-9-4 **71** JoeyHaynes 1 81
(K R Burke) *trckd ldng pair on inner: hdwy 3f out: led over 2f out: rdn over 1f out: kpt on wl fnl f* **7/1**
5-32 **2** 1¾ **Zeehan**[92] 331 3-9-0 **70** RyanTate(3) 8 76+
(Clive Cox) *hld up in tch: hdwy 3f out: pushed along and sltly outpcd 2f out: sn rdn and kpt on wl fnl f* **7/2**[2]
0-31 **3** 1 **Genuine Approval (IRE)**[81] 458 3-9-2 **72** DannyBrock(3) 2 76
(Jonathan Portman) *led: pushed along and jnd 3f out: rdn and hdd over 2f out: drvn over 1f out: kpt on*
46-1 **4** 2 **Angel Grace (IRE)**[20] 1270 3-9-7 **74** ShaneKelly 7 74
(David Menuisier) *trckd ldrs: hdwy on outer and cl up 3f out: rdn over 2f out: drvn wl over 1f out: kpt on same pce* **9/4**[1]
65-3 **5** 10 **Hijran (IRE)**[20] 1275 3-9-0 **67** AndreaAtzeni 4 48
(Charlie Fellowes) *hld up in rr: sme hdwy over 3f out: sn rdn and n.d* **6/1**
62-0 **6** 9 **Mollie's Girl (IRE)**[103] 171 3-8-13 **66** AndrewMullen 3 30
(Michael Appleby) *in tch: effrt over 3f out: sn rdn along and n.d* **25/1**
220- **7** 2¼ **Little Lotte (IRE)**[196] 7207 3-8-12 **65** DougieCostello 5 25
(Tom Gretton) *dwlt: a in rr* **50/1**
606- **8** 1¾ **La Mortola**[186] 7422 3-9-5 **72**(b[1]) FrankieDettori 9 29
(John Gosden) *towards rr: hdwy to join ldrs after 3f: sn chsng ldr: rdn along wl over 3f out: sn wknd* **5/1**[3]

2m 15.7s (1.40) **Going Correction** -0.025s/f (Good) **8** Ran SP% **111.3**
Speed ratings (Par 95): **93,91,90,89,81 74,72,70**
CSF £30.00 CT £237.48 TOTE £6.50: £1.80, £1.10, £3.40; EX 22.10 Trifecta £210.70.
Owner Mrs Elaine M Burke **Bred** S N C Regnier & San Gabriel Inv Inc **Trained** Middleham Moor, N Yorks

FOCUS
Rail movement added 6yds to race distance. They also finished well spread out in this division, with the first four pulling clear, and the winning time was 1.7sec slower than the first leg. The form is rated around the third.

1760 32RED.COM H'CAP 1m 6f 15y
4:45 (4:45) (Class 4) (0-80,79) 4-Y-O+ **£6,469** (£1,925; £962; £481) **Stalls** Low

Form RPR
401- **1** **Maoi Chinn Tire (IRE)**[182] 7528 9-9-1 **70** TomQueally 4 78
(Jennie Candlish) *hld up in rr: stdy hdwy on wd outside over 3f out: chal 2f out: rdn to ld and edgd lft over 1f out: drvn ins fnl f: kpt on gamely* **16/1**
166- **2** ½ **Desdichado**[198] 7145 4-9-7 **78** AndreaAtzeni 12 85
(Ralph Beckett) *hld up in midfield: hdwy 3f out: chsd ldrs 2f out: rdn and ev ch jst over 1f out: drvn ins fnl f: no ex towards fin* **9/2**[2]
446- **3** ¾ **Hurry Home Poppa (IRE)**[134] 8223 6-8-10 **65** JoeFanning 2 71
(John Mackie) *hld up towards rr: hdwy over 3f out: chsd ldrs 2f out: rdn over 1f out: kpt on* **7/1**[3]
0-11 **4** ½ **Avenue Des Champs**[12] 1434 4-8-6 **66** DannyBrock(3) 6 71+
(Jane Chapple-Hyam) *led: rdn clr over 2f out: hdd over 1f out: sn drvn and kpt on* **9/2**[2]
213- **5** 2 **All For The Best (IRE)**[158] 7920 4-9-3 **74**(p) ShaneKelly 10 76
(Robert Stephens) *trckd ldrs: smooth hdwy over 4f out: rdn over 2f out: drvn over 1f out and kpt on same pce* **16/1**
260- **6** ¾ **Perfect Summer (IRE)**[35] 8064 6-9-6 **78**(p) GeorgeDowning(3) 11 79
(Ian Williams) *hld up and bhd: hdwy over 4f out: rdn along wl over 2f out: kpt on appr fnl f: nrst fin* **25/1**
132- **7** ¾ **Caged Lightning (IRE)**[44] 7564 6-9-9 **78**(p) PaulHanagan 9 78
(Steve Gollings) *cl up: rdn along 3f out: drvn 2f out and grad wknd* **7/1**[3]
54-5 **8** shd **Paddys Runner**[41] 566 4-8-13 **73** TomMarquand(3) 7 73
(Alan King) *trckd ldrs: hdwy 3f out: rdn along 2f out: sn drvn and one pce* **3/1**[1]
150- **9** 6 **The Quarterjack**[119] 8383 7-9-1 **70** BenCurtis 5 62
(Charlie Wallis) *prom: rdn along on inner over 3f out: sn drvn and wknd* **25/1**
140- **10** 11 **Kodicil (IRE)**[172] 7140 8-9-0 **69**(p) DougieCostello 1 45
(Mark Walford) *chsd ldrs: rdn along over 4f out: sn wknd* **25/1**
0016 **11** 11 **Brassbound (USA)**[19] 1296 8-9-10 **79**(p) AndrewMullen 3 40
(Michael Appleby) *chsd ldrs: pushed along over 5f out: rdn 4f out: sn drvn and wknd* **25/1**

3m 11.58s (4.58) **Going Correction** -0.05s/f (Good)
WFA 4 from 5yo+ 2lb **11** Ran SP% **113.5**
Speed ratings (Par 105): **84,83,83,83,81 81,81,80,77,71 64**
CSF £79.74 CT £555.28 TOTE £16.10: £4.50, £1.80, £1.60; EX 128.00 Trifecta £1649.70.
Owner Ms Jennie Candlish **Bred** Mrs E Thompson **Trained** Basford Green, Staffs

FOCUS
Rail movement added 6yds to race distance. A fair staying handicap and they didn't go mad up front but the first three came from the rear. This was close to the winner's old best.

1761 32RED CASINO H'CAP 5f 13y
5:20 (5:23) (Class 5) (0-70,70) 3-Y-O **£3,234** (£962; £481; £240) **Stalls** Centre

Form RPR
244- **1** **Evangelical**[189] 7360 3-8-13 **69** AdamMcNamara(7) 5 78+
(Richard Fahey) *dwlt and bmpd s: in rr: hdwy 1/2-way: rdn to chal over 1f out: led jst ins fnl f: kpt on strly* **11/10**[1]
442- **2** 2¼ **First Bombardment**[174] 7706 3-9-7 **70** AndreaAtzeni 2 71
(David O'Meara) *t.k.h: trckd ldr towards stands' rail: hdwy to chal 2f out: sn rdn and ev ch tl drvn and kpt on same pce fnl f* **10/3**[2]
4222 **3** nk **Hot Stuff**[26] 1167 3-8-11 **63** GeorgeDowning(3) 4 63
(Tony Carroll) *trckd ldrs towards stands' rail: hdwy 2f out: rdn to ld wl over 1f out: drvn: edgd lft and hdd jst ins fnl f: kpt on same pce* **8/1**
-520 **4** shd **Miss Phillyjinks (IRE)**[33] 1060 3-9-2 **65**(p) ShaneKelly 3 65
(Paul D'Arcy) *racd on stands' rail: led: rdn along 2f out: hdd wl over 1f out: sn drvn and kpt on same pce* **8/1**
060 **5** 1¾ **Allen's Folly**[13] 1414 3-8-4 **56** oh8 DannyBrock(3) 1 49
(Peter Hiatt) *racd wd: prom: rdn along 2f out: sn drvn and one pce* **25/1**
540- **6** 6 **Kingstreet Lady**[183] 7507 3-8-10 **59** JoeFanning 6 31
(Richard Price) *wnt lft s: sn pushed along: a in rr* **6/1**[3]

1m 2.14s (0.64) **Going Correction** +0.20s/f (Good) **6** Ran SP% **111.1**
Speed ratings (Par 98): **102,98,97,97,94 85**
CSF £4.80 TOTE £1.80: £1.10, £2.50; EX 3.50 Trifecta £9.70.
Owner Cheveley Park Stud **Bred** Cheveley Park Stud Ltd **Trained** Musley Bank, N Yorks

FOCUS
A modest 3yo sprint handicap in which all bar the complete outsider raced centre-to-nearside throughout. The winner looked a standout on potential.
T/Plt: £144.20 to a £1 stake. Pool: £59,192.93 - 299.61 winning units. T/Qpdt: £34.20 to a £1 stake. Pool: £4,157.96 - 89.82 winning units. **Joe Rowntree**

1719 WOLVERHAMPTON (A.W) (L-H)
Tuesday, April 26

OFFICIAL GOING: Tapeta: standard
Wind: Fresh across Weather: Sunshine and showers

1762 QUILTER CHEVIOT SUPPORTING PERRY RDA APPRENTICE H'CAP 1m 1f 103y (Tp)
5:55 (5:55) (Class 5) (0-75,70) 4-Y-O+ **£2,911** (£866; £432; £216) **Stalls** Low

Form RPR
3351 **1** **Mr Red Clubs (IRE)**[10] 1498 7-9-3 **69**(p) GeorgeBuckell(3) 7 76
(Michael Appleby) *a.p: chsd ldr over 6f out: rdn to ld 1f out: r.o* **2/1**[1]
611- **2** nk **Omotesando**[202] 7045 6-9-2 **70** CharlieBennett(5) 5 76
(Mark Brisbourne) *chsd ldrs: rdn over 1f out: chsd wnr ins fnl f: r.o* **7/1**
005 **3** 4 **All You (IRE)**[10] 1502 4-9-1 **69**(v) JoshDoyle(5) 2 67
(David O'Meara) *led: rdn and hdd 1f out: no ex ins fnl f* **5/2**[2]
5345 **4** ½ **Lean On Pete (IRE)**[10] 1501 7-9-3 **66**(p) JacobButterfield 1 63
(Ollie Pears) *chsd ldr tl over 6f out: remained handy: rdn over 2f out: styd on same pce fnl f* **5/1**[3]
0530 **5** 4 **Evacusafe Lady**[6] 1578 5-8-2 **56** oh1(t) LuluStanford(5) 3 45
(John Ryan) *hld up: rdn over 2f out: nvr trbld ldrs* **12/1**
0260 **6** 1¼ **Kodiac Lady (IRE)**[1] 1725 4-8-7 **61**(e) RowanScott(5) 4 47
(Simon West) *hld up in tch: shkn up over 2f out: wknd over 1f out* **12/1**
065- **7** 2½ **Moment To Dream**[182] 7542 4-8-2 **58** MillyNaseb(7) 8 39
(Julia Feilden) *hld up: pushed along 3f out: wknd over 1f out* **18/1**
060- **8** 40 **Darkening Night**[60] 3614 4-8-8 **60** CiaranMckee(3) 6
(Sarah-Jayne Davies) *s.i.s: hld up: racd keenly: rdn and wknd over 3f out* **25/1**

1m 59.11s (-1.69) **Going Correction** -0.20s/f (Stan) **8** Ran SP% **115.6**
Speed ratings (Par 103): **99,98,95,94,91 90,87,52**
CSF £17.00 CT £36.06 TOTE £2.70: £1.40, £1.80, £1.60; EX 11.00 Trifecta £31.80.
Owner Ferrybank Properties Limited **Bred** Tally-Ho Stud **Trained** Oakham, Rutland

FOCUS
A modest handicap in which the gallop was on the steady side. The winner came down the centre in the straight and the form is rated around him.

1763 PERSIMMON HOMES COMMUNITY CHAMPIONS H'CAP 5f 216y (Tp)
6:30 (6:31) (Class 4) (0-85,84) 3-Y-O **£4,568** (£1,367; £683; £342; £170) **Stalls** Low

Form RPR
106- **1** **Red Artist**[291] 4087 3-9-2 **79** RoystonFfrench 6 87
(Simon Crisford) *pushed along early in rr: hdwy over 3f out: shkn up to ld ins fnl f: rdn out* **12/1**
1- **2** nk **King Cole (USA)**[185] 7454 3-9-0 **77** OisinMurphy 4 84+
(Robert Cowell) *s.i.s: pushed along in rr early: swtchd rt over 2f out: sn hung rt: hdwy over 1f out: rdn to chse wnr ins fnl f: r.o wl* **2/1**[2]
601- **3** 2 **Curtain Call**[193] 7243 3-9-1 **78** TonyHamilton 8 78
(Richard Fahey) *led 1f: chsd ldr tl shkn up to ld over 1f out: rdn: edgd lft and hdd ins fnl f: styd on same pce* **25/1**
0-16 **4** ¾ **Thee And Me (IRE)**[11] 1452 3-8-8 **71** KieranO'Neill 7 69
(Mike Murphy) *trckd ldrs: rdn over 1f out: styd on same pce ins fnl f* **28/1**
011- **5** nk **Parkour (IRE)**[164] 7859 3-9-6 **83** LukeMorris 5 80
(Marco Botti) *hld up: rdn over 2f out: styd on ins fnl f: nt rch ldrs* **13/8**[1]
-211 **6** 2 **Kyllukey**[33] 1060 3-8-13 **76** DarryllHolland 2 67
(Charles Hills) *led 5f out: rdn and hdd over 1f out: wknd ins fnl f* **14/1**
3-31 **7** 3 **The Commendatore**[108] 126 3-8-9 **72** GrahamGibbons 1 53
(David Barron) *chsd ldrs: n.m.r wl over 3f out: rdn over 2f out: wknd fnl f* **8/1**[3]
400- **8** 2 **Farkle Minkus**[206] 6931 3-9-7 **84**(p) JasonHart 3 59
(Keith Dalgleish) *sn pushed along to chse ldrs: nt clr run and lost pl over 3f out: rdn and wknd over 1f out* **9/1**

1m 12.9s (-1.60) **Going Correction** -0.20s/f (Stan) **8** Ran SP% **114.2**
Speed ratings (Par 100): **102,101,98,97,97 94,90,88**
CSF £36.35 CT £614.71 TOTE £13.90: £2.80, £1.90, £2.80; EX 47.00 Trifecta £628.00.
Owner Sir Alex Ferguson & Peter Done **Bred** Clive Dennett **Trained** Newmarket, Suffolk

FOCUS
A useful handicap run at no more than a reasonable gallop. The winner came down the centre in the straight and the first two did well to pull a couple of lengths clear in the closing stages. A sound effort from the winner.

1764 GRAINLINK (S) STKS 7f 32y (Tp)
7:05 (7:05) (Class 6) 3-Y-O **£2,264** (£673; £336; £168) **Stalls** High

Form RPR
0523 **1** **Broughtons Fancy**[6] 1573 3-8-9 64 NoelGarbutt(5) 2 61
(David Evans) *hld up: rdn over 2f out: hdwy over 1f out: r.o to ld towards fin* **10/3**[2]
2525 **2** shd **Sea Of Uncertainty**[10] 1486 3-9-0 62 BenCurtis 4 61
(Michael Appleby) *led: rdn over 1f out: sn edgd rt: hdd towards fin* **9/2**[3]
0166 **3** 2¼ **Sunbaked (IRE)**[20] 1257 3-9-0 62(p) RobertWinston 5 55
(Eve Johnson Houghton) *chsd ldrs: wnt 2nd over 1f out: shkn up and edgd lft ins fnl f: styd on same pce* **9/4**[1]

-536 **4** *1 3/4* **Kadooment Day (IRE)**[20] 1286 3-9-0 67 .... JoeyHaynes 3 51
(K R Burke) *chsd ldr: rdn over 2f out: lost 2nd over 1f out: no ex ins fnl f*
9/4[1]

-500 **5** *3 3/4* **Thief Of Hearts**[63] 688 3-8-9 49 .... LukeMorris 1 37
(Bill Turner) *chsd ldrs: rdn over 2f out: wknd fnl f* **25/1**

00-0 **6** *1 3/4* **Sirius Move**[7] 1554 3-8-9 54 ....[1] JoshDoyle(5) 6 37
(David O'Meara) *hld up: rdn over 2f out: wknd over 1f out* **25/1**

1m 28.41s (-0.39) **Going Correction** -0.20s/f (Stan) **6** Ran SP% **110.5**
Speed ratings (Par 96): **94,93,91,89,85 83**
CSF £17.78 TOTE £3.00: £1.70, £2.80; EX 15.50 Trifecta £45.50.
Owner Lynn Cullimore & Mrs E Evans **Bred** Michael E Broughton **Trained** Pandy, Monmouths

FOCUS
A modest seller in which the gallop was an ordinary one. The winner raced centre to far side in the straight and the form is best rated around the second.

1765 NFU MUTUAL BRIDGNORTH MAIDEN STKS 7f 32y (Tp)
7:40 (7:41) (Class 5) 4-Y-O+ **£2,911** (£866; £432; £216) **Stalls** High

Form RPR

22-3 **1** **Hakam (USA)**[19] 1287 4-9-5 80 .... PaulHanagan 6 80+
(Charles Hills) *hld up: hdwy over 2f out: shkn up to ld and edgd lft wl ins fnl f: r.o* **4/9**[1]

22- **2** *1/2* **Madame Butterfly (IRE)**[305] 3593 4-9-0 0 .... DanielTudhope 1 74+
(David O'Meara) *led: hdd over 5f out: chsd ldr tl 4f out: remained handy: led wl over 1f out: rdn and hdd whn carried lft wl ins fnl f: kpt on* **7/2**[2]

/32- **3** *1 3/4* **Mickey Haller (IRE)**[265] 5007 4-9-5 73 .... JoeFanning 2 74
(Brian Meehan) *a.p: rdn over 1f out: styd on same pce ins fnl f* **5/1**[3]

4 **4** *1/2* **Critical Speed (IRE)**[18] 1324 4-9-0 0 .... LukeMorris 7 68
(Sylvester Kirk) *hld up: hdwy over 1f out: styd on u.p* **20/1**

00 **5** *nk* **Kestrel Dot Com**[8] 1529 4-9-5 0 .... IrineuGoncalves 3 72
(Chris Dwyer) *prom: chsd ldr 4f: led wl over 1f out: sn rdn and hdd: no ex ins fnl f* **100/1**

0 **6** *11* **Bertie Bishop**[25] 1184 4-9-2 0 .... DanielMuscutt(3) 4 42
(Brian McMath) *hld up: rdn and wknd over 1f out* **100/1**

0- **7** *20* **Hazel's Song**[354] 2051 4-9-0 0 .... RoystonFfrench 5
(Steph Hollinshead) *chsd ldr: led over 5f out: rdn and hdd wl over 1f out: sn wknd* **125/1**

1m 27.62s (-1.18) **Going Correction** -0.20s/f (Stan) **7** Ran SP% **115.7**
Speed ratings (Par 103): **98,97,95,94,94 81,59**
CSF £2.46 TOTE £1.60: £1.10, £1.70; EX 3.00 Trifecta £5.10.
Owner Hamdan Al Maktoum **Bred** Jay W Bligh **Trained** Lambourn, Berks

FOCUS
Fair form from the principals but the gallop was an ordinary one and is held down by the proximity of the fifth. The winner edged towards the far side in the closing stages.

1766 BERRYS H'CAP 2m 119y (Tp)
8:10 (8:10) (Class 4) (0-85,82) 4-Y-O+ **£4,690** (£1,395; £697) **Stalls** Low

Form RPR

1324 **1** **Zakatal**[28] 1135 10-9-7 77 .... PJMcDonald 1 86
(Rebecca Menzies) *chsd ldr who wnt clr 12f out: tk clsr order over 6f out: led over 2f out: sn rdn clr* **11/8**[1]

0-50 **2** *17* **Yorkindred Spirit**[12] 1434 4-8-6 66 ....(v) JoeFanning 5 66
(Mark Johnston) *hld up: hdwy to chse wnr over 2f out: outpcd wl over 1f out: eased fnl f* **3/1**[2]

0601 **3** *33* **Topaling**[28] 1136 5-8-10 66 .... LukeMorris 4 15
(Mark H Tompkins) *plld hrd: led: wnt clr 12f out: c bk to the field over 6f out: hdd: wknd and eased over 2f out* **11/8**[1]

3m 38.28s (-5.42) **Going Correction** -0.20s/f (Stan)
WFA 4 from 5yo+ 4lb **3** Ran SP% **109.2**
Speed ratings (Par 105): **104,96,80**
CSF £5.33 TOTE £2.20; EX 6.70 Trifecta £8.50.
Owner David Furman & John Sugarman **Bred** H H The Aga Khan's Studs Sc **Trained** Mordon, Co. Durham

FOCUS
A disappointing turnout for the money and a race that didn't take anything in the way of winning given one of the joint favourites pulled too hard and the outsider remains below her best. The gallop was an ordinary one and the winner raced just off the inside rail in the straight. He is rated to form.

1767 JEWSON TIMBER & BUILDING SUPPLIES MEDIAN AUCTION MAIDEN STKS 1m 141y (Tp)
8:40 (8:40) (Class 6) 3-5-Y-O **£2,264** (£673; £336; £168) **Stalls** Low

Form RPR

44- **1** **White Poppy (IRE)**[188] 7392 3-8-7 0 .... OisinMurphy 7 77
(Andrew Balding) *chsd ldr: led over 2f out: sn edgd lft: edgd rt ins fnl f: drvn out* **4/1**[3]

2 *1 1/4* **Rebel Cause (IRE)** 3-8-12 0 .... WilliamTwiston-Davies 6 79
(Richard Spencer) *s.i.s: sn prom: rdn over 2f out: chsd wnr over 1f out: styd on* **20/1**

425 **3** *4* **Knights Table**[13] 1426 3-8-12 80 .... LukeMorris 4 72
(James Tate) *sn pushed along to ld: rdn and hdd over 2f out: hmpd wl over 1f out: no ex ins fnl f* **10/11**[1]

4 *hd* **Zanjabeel** 3-8-12 0 ....(t) PaulHanagan 1 71+
(Simon Crisford) *chsd ldrs: rdn over 2f out: hmpd wl over 1f out: styd on same pce* **5/2**[2]

0 **5** *12* **Time To Tango (IRE)**[42] 945 5-9-6 0 .... SeanMooney(7) 5 48
(Joseph Tuite) *hld up: rdn over 2f out: a in rr: no ch whn hung rt fnl f* **66/1**

6 *3/4* **Outback Guy (IRE)** 3-8-12 0 .... DougieCostello 3 43
(Kevin Frost) *s.i.s: in rr and pushed along over 5f out: wknd over 2f out* **100/1**

0- **7** *1 1/2* **Three Brothers (FR)**[174] 7707 3-8-12 0 .... CamHardie 2 40
(Harry Dunlop) *chsd ldrs: hmpd 7f out: rdn over 3f out: wknd over 2f out* **28/1**

1m 47.66s (-2.44) **Going Correction** -0.20s/f (Stan)
WFA 3 from 5yo 15lb **7** Ran SP% **111.6**
Speed ratings (Par 101): **102,100,97,97,86 85,84**
CSF £59.34 TOTE £5.80: £2.30, £5.40; EX 81.00 Trifecta £162.50.
Owner Qatar Racing Limited **Bred** John Malone **Trained** Kingsclere, Hants
■ Stewards' Enquiry : Oisin Murphy two-day ban: careless riding (May 10-11)

FOCUS
Little strength in depth but fair form from the principals in a race in which the two market leaders failed to live up to expectations. The gallop was an ordinary one and the winner came down the centre. The form is rated around the race average.

1768 EMERYS BUILDERS MERCHANTS STOKE & TELFORD H'CAP 1m 141y (Tp)
9:10 (9:10) (Class 6) (0-55,55) 3-Y-O+ **£2,264** (£673; £336; £168) **Stalls** Low

Form RPR

00-1 **1** **Therthaar**[7] 1551 3-8-5 51 6ex .... ShaneGray 10 59+
(Ismail Mohammed) *a.p: led over 1f out: rdn out* **2/5**[1]

0000 **2** *1 1/2* **Citisonsmith (IRE)**[11] 1456 4-8-12 46 oh1 ....(b) GeorgeDowning(3) 6 51
(Tony Carroll) *chsd ldrs: rdn over 1f out: chsd wnr ins fnl f: r.o* **66/1**

3042 **3** *1 3/4* **Little Choosey**[19] 1295 6-9-5 50 ....(tp) KieranO'Neill 7 51
(Roy Bowring) *mid-div: hdwy over 1f out: sn rdn: r.o* **12/1**[3]

-043 **4** *2* **Gilmer (IRE)**[7] 1556 5-9-7 52 ....(t) OisinMurphy 1 49
(Laura Young) *led over 7f out: rdn and hdd over 1f out: no ex ins fnl f* **10/1**[2]

-635 **5** *hd* **Natalia**[26] 1165 7-8-12 46 oh1 ....(v) JackDuern(3) 2 42
(Sarah Hollinshead) *mid-div: hdwy over 1f out: styd on same pce fnl f* **25/1**

0634 **6** *hd* **Luv U Lucky**[19] 1295 4-9-4 49 ....(p) LukeMorris 3 45
(Michael Appleby) *chsd ldrs: rdn over 1f out: no ex ins fnl f* **12/1**[3]

5240 **7** *3/4* **Foylesideview (IRE)**[27] 1145 4-9-4 49 .... CathyGannon 9 43
(Harry Chisman) *hld up: rdn over 2f out: styd on ins fnl f: nvr nrr* **20/1**

033- **8** *2 1/2* **Captain Gerald**[187] 7412 3-8-1 54 ....(p) LuluStanford(7) 5 40
(John Ryan) *hld up: rdn over 1f out: nt trble ldrs* **18/1**

00-0 **9** *6* **Hashtag Frenzy**[20] 1251 3-8-0 46 oh1 ....(p) RaulDaSilva 11 20
(Rebecca Menzies) *sn pushed along to ld: hdd over 7f out: chsd ldr tl rdn and wknd over 1f out* **80/1**

0-40 **10** *9* **Anniversarie**[73] 568 4-9-8 53 .... DougieCostello 4 11
(John Norton) *s.s: hld up: rdn and wknd over 2f out* **66/1**

055- **11** *24* **Carcharias (IRE)**[203] 7011 3-8-9 55 ....(p) LiamKeniry 8
(Ed de Giles) *s.i.s: hld up: plld hrd: rdn over 3f out: wknd over 2f out* **12/1**[3]

1m 47.69s (-2.41) **Going Correction** -0.20s/f (Stan)
WFA 3 from 4yo+ 15lb **11** Ran SP% **121.7**
Speed ratings (Par 101): **102,100,99,97,97 96,96,94,88,80 59**
CSF £68.64 CT £201.75 TOTE £1.50: £1.10, £17.60, £2.70; EX 66.20 Trifecta £472.80.
Owner Sultan Ali **Bred** Cheveley Park Stud Ltd **Trained** Newmarket, Suffolk

FOCUS
A moderate handicap which went to the short-priced market leader. The gallop was a modest one and the winner raced towards the inside rail in the straight. He did not need to hit the heights of his previous win.
T/Plt: £63.60 to a £1 stake. Pool: £65,049.96 - 746.07 winning units. T/Qpdt: £20.50 to a £1 stake. Pool: £6,475.04 - 232.79 winning units. **Colin Roberts**

1769 - (Foreign Racing) - See Raceform Interactive

ASCOT (R-H)
Wednesday, April 27

OFFICIAL GOING: Good to soft (good in places; str 7.5; rnd 6.5)
Wind: virtually nil Weather: bright spells

1770 SODEXO CONDITIONS STKS (PLUS 10 RACE) 5f
2:10 (2:12) (Class 2) 2-Y-O
£8,715 (£2,609; £1,304; £652; £326; £163) **Stalls** High

Form RPR

1 **Create A Dream (USA)** 2-8-6 0 ....(b[1]) JoseValdiviaJr 2 87
(Wesley A Ward, U.S.A) *mde all: pushed along over 1f out: hld on gamely towards fin: all out* **5/1**[3]

2 *shd* **Deningy** 2-8-11 0 .... SilvestreDeSousa 6 94+
(David Evans) *chsd ldng trio and wl in tch: effrt to chse ldng pair whn squeezed for room and snatched up over 1f out: swtchd rt ins fnl f: r.o strly towards fin: fin 3rd: awrdd 2nd*

1 **3** *nk* **The Last Lion (IRE)**[25] 1199 2-8-11 0 .... FrannyNorton 4 90
(Mark Johnston) *chsd wnr: effrt and edgd lft u.p over 1f out: steadily clsd ins fnl f: nvr quite getting to wnr: fin 2nd: disqualified and plcd 3rd* **8/15**[1]

1 **4** *2* **Sterling Silva (IRE)**[19] 1316 2-8-11 0 .... PatDobbs 3 83
(Richard Hannon) *chsd ldrs: effrt 2f out: unable qck u.p 1f out: styd on same pce after* **9/2**[2]

5 *2 3/4* **Captain Hawk** 2-8-11 0 .... DarryllHolland 7 73+
(Charles Hills) *slowly away and rn green early: rcvrd and in tch in 5th after 2f: rdn 2f out: sn outpcd: wl hld and styd on same pce fr over 1f out* **25/1**

6 *11* **Inner Circle (IRE)** 2-8-11 0 .... JimCrowley 5 34
(Richard Hannon) *wnt rt s and s.i.s: a outpcd in last pair: rdn 1/2-way: lost tch 2f out* **25/1**

7 *1/2* **Compton Lane** 2-8-11 0 .... FrederikTylicki 1 32
(Rod Millman) *wnt rt s and s.i.s: a outpcd in last pair: rdn and lost tch ent fnl 2f* **40/1**

1m 2.28s (1.78) **Going Correction** +0.375s/f (Good) **7** Ran SP% **115.0**
Speed ratings (Par 98): **100,99,99,96,91 74,73**
CSF £81.85 TOTE £6.30: £2.10, £5.50; EX 92.10 Trifecta £167.10.
Owner St Elias Stables LLC **Bred** St Elias Stables LLC **Trained** North America
■ Jose Valdivia's first winner in Britain.
■ Stewards' Enquiry : Franny Norton four-day ban: careless riding (May 11-13,15)

FOCUS
This is often a pointer towards Royal Ascot. It was eventful, but there was a decent pace on and the fourth gives it a solid look. The form is rated as ordinary for the grade.

1771 SPINAL INJURIES ASSOCIATION EBF STALLIONS STKS (CONDITIONS RACE) (PLUS 10 RACE) (ROUND COURSE) 1m (R)
2:45 (2:48) (Class 3) 3-Y-O **£9,703** (£2,887; £1,443; £721) **Stalls** Low

Form RPR

316- **1** **Dawn Of Hope (IRE)**[201] 7075 3-8-12 90 .... AndreaAtzeni 4 96+
(Roger Varian) *pressed ldr tl pushed into ld 2f: sn rdn and qcknd: forged ahd u.p 1f out: r.o strly: rdn out* **15/8**[1]

130- **2** *1 1/4* **Raaqy (IRE)**[229] 6272 3-8-12 94 .... PaulHanagan 1 93
(Owen Burrows) *t.k.h: trckd ldng pair: shkn up 2f out: sn rdn: drvn and r.o ins fnl f: rdn fnl 50yds: nt enough pce to chal wnr* **7/1**

30-2 **3** *1/2* **Light Up Our World (IRE)**[11] 1476 3-8-12 102 .... PatDobbs 2 92
(Richard Hannon) *led and set stdy gallop: hdd 2f out: sn rdn and qcknd w wnr: jst outpcd 1f out: styd on same pce u.p ins fnl f: lost 2nd fnl 50yds* **5/2**[2]

26-2 **4** *shd* **Summer Icon**[13] 1436 3-8-12 80 SilvestreDeSousa 3 91
(Mick Channon) *stdd s: t.k.h: hld up in tch in 4th: effrt 2f out: hdwy u.p and battling for 2nd ins fnl f: no ex towards fin* **9/2**[3]

216- **5** *3 ¾* **Doubly Motivated (IRE)**[215] 6709 3-8-12 88 DarryllHolland 5 83
(Charles Hills) *stdd and dropped in bhd after s: t.k.h: hld up in rr: effrt 2f out: sn rdn and outpcd: wl hld fnl f* **5/1**

1m 45.33s (4.63) **Going Correction** +0.375s/f (Good) **5** Ran SP% **110.7**
Speed ratings (Par 102): **91,89,89,89,85**
CSF £14.86 TOTE £2.50: £1.40, £3.80; EX 15.00 Trifecta £36.70.

Owner Saleh Al Homaizi & Imad Al Sagar **Bred** Gerrardstown House Stud **Trained** Newmarket, Suffolk

FOCUS
Race distance increased by 4yds. It's a long time since this threw up a top-notch filly and, throwing up a bunched finish, it's no more than fair form this year. The 1-2 fit the recent race standard.

1772 LONGINES SAGARO STKS (GROUP 3) 2m
3:20 (3:20) (Class 1) 4-Y-0+

£34,026 (£12,900; £6,456; £3,216; £1,614; £810) **Stalls** Low

Form RPR

102- **1** **Mizzou (IRE)**[250] 5598 5-9-2 111 AndreaAtzeni 6 114
(Luca Cumani) *led for 2f: styd chsng ldrs: effrt to press ldrs and rdn over 2f out: drvn and chalng over 1f out: styd on u.p to ld wl ins fnl f: hld on gamely: all out* **11/4**[3]

42-2 **2** *nk* **Clever Cookie**[21] 1273 8-9-2 113 RyanMoore 10 113
(Peter Niven) *swtchd rt after 1f: hld up in tch in midfield: effrt 3f out: hdwy to go 3rd 2f out and sn swtchd lft: hdwy u.p and ev ch ins fnl f: styd on but hld cl home* **9/4**[1]

111- **3** *½* **Flying Officer (USA)**[193] 7277 6-9-7 115 FrankieDettori 8 117
(John Gosden) *hdwy to ld after 2f: rdn 2f out: drvn ent fnl f: battled on wl tl hdd and no ex wl ins fnl f* **5/2**[2]

36-4 **4** *1 ½* **Suegioo (FR)**[32] 1102 7-9-2 109 (p) PaulHanagan 2 110
(Richard Fahey) *hld up off the pce in last trio: clsd 4f out: effrt ent fnl 2f: hdwy u.p to go 4th ent fnl f: styd on but nvr getting to ldng trio* **12/1**

111- **5** *hd* **Burmese**[208] 6896 4-8-12 96 PatSmullen 7 111+
(Marcus Tregoning) *in tch in midfield: effrt over 2f out: chsng ldrs but struggling to qckn whn nt clr run: hmpd and swtchd lft over 1f out: kpt on u.p ins fnl f* **12/1**

12 **6** *1 ½* **Sandro Botticelli (IRE)**[11] 1475 4-8-12 107 (p) ShaneKelly 3 108
(John Ryan) *stdd s: hld up off the pce in rr: clsd 4f out: effrt jst over 2f out: no imp tl hdwy 1f out: kpt on u.p ins fnl f: nvr threatened ldrs* **25/1**

240- **7** *3 ¾* **Glaring**[262] 5194 5-9-2 108 JimCrowley 1 104
(Amanda Perrett) *chsd ldrs: effrt over 2f out: unable qck and edgd lft over 1f out: wknd ins fnl f* **33/1**

/0-3 **8** *6* **Seismos (IRE)**[21] 1273 8-9-2 107 (b¹) SilvestreDeSousa 4 99
(Marco Botti) *s.i.s: steadily rcvrd and hdwy to chse ldr after 3f: rdn and ev ch 3f out tl lost pl jst over 2f out: wknd over 1f out* **25/1**

2-0 **9** *22* **Amber Flush**[21] 1273 7-8-13 0 TimClark 5 67
(Martin Smith) *a last trio: rdn over 5f out: dropped to last over 4f out: lost tch 3f out* **150/1**

3m 30.4s (1.40) **Going Correction** +0.375s/f (Good)
WFA 4 from 5yo+ 4lb **9** Ran SP% **112.7**
Speed ratings (Par 113): **111,110,110,109,109 109,107,104,93**
CSF £8.78 TOTE £3.60: £1.60, £1.20, £1.30; EX 11.20 Trifecta £25.90.

Owner Jon S Kelly **Bred** Matrix Bloodstock **Trained** Newmarket, Suffolk

FOCUS
Race distance increased by about 15yds. A leading trial for the Gold Cup. The gallop suited those racing handily, but the form looks rock-solid by Group 3 standards. Mizzou is rated up 2lb on his form in this last year.

1773 MERRIEBELLE STABLE PAVILION STKS (GROUP 3) 6f
3:55 (3:58) (Class 1) 3-Y-O

£45,368 (£17,200; £8,608; £4,288; £2,152; £1,080) **Stalls** High

Form RPR

11-1 **1** **Gifted Master (IRE)**[14] 1423 3-9-4 111 PatSmullen 5 114+
(Hugo Palmer) *wnt sharply rt and bmpd rival leaving stalls: mde all: rdn over 1f out: readily asserted and wnt clr 1f out: r.o strly: comf* **3/1**[2]

-1 **2** *2 ¼* **Dream Dubai**[18] 1337 3-9-1 86 SilvestreDeSousa 9 103+
(Sylvester Kirk) *hld up in tch in last pair: effrt 2f out: hdwy u.p 1f out: styd on wl ins fnl f: wnt 2nd fnl 50yds: no threat to wnr* **16/1**

1360 **3** *1 ½* **Gracious John (IRE)**[25] 1197 3-9-1 102 AdamKirby 7 98
(David Evans) *t.k.h: chsd ldrs: rdn to chse wnr ent fnl 2f: no ex and outpcd 1f out: kpt on same pce after: lost 2nd fnl 50yds* **25/1**

121- **4** *¾* **Dhahmaan (IRE)**[186] 7460 3-9-1 102 FrankieDettori 3 96
(Marco Botti) *dwlt and squeezed for room leaving stalls: hld up in last pair: effrt 2f out: hdwy u.p 1f out: kpt on ins fnl f: no threat to wnr* **8/1**

3-1 **5** *nk* **C Note (IRE)**[19] 1315 3-9-1 99 FergusSweeney 1 95
(Martyn Meade) *hld up in tch: effrt 2f out: drvn and no imp over 1f out tl styd on steadily ins fnl f: no threat to wnr* **13/2**[3]

510- **6** *1 ¼* **Orvar (IRE)**[207] 6931 3-9-1 100 AndreaAtzeni 8 91
(Richard Hannon) *chsd wnr: rdn over 2f out: sn lost 2nd and struggling: lost pl jst over 1f out: wknd ins fnl f* **33/1**

212- **7** *1* **Washington DC (IRE)**[26] 1190 3-9-1 113 (t) RyanMoore 2 87
(A P O'Brien, Ire) *hld up in tch: hdwy 2f out: 3rd and drvn over 1f out: little rspnse and sn outpcd: wknd ins fnl f* **1/1**[1]

430- **8** *3* **Zebstar (IRE)**[201] 7072 3-9-1 95 JFEgan 6 78
(James Unett) *in tch in midfield: rdn over 2f out: sn struggling and lost pl: wknd over 1f out* **66/1**

135- **9** *19* **Priceless**[180] 7594 3-8-12 99 PaulHanagan 4 14
(Clive Cox) *taken down early: bmpd leaving stalls: plld hrd and sn chsing ldrs: rdn and lost pl ent fnl 2f: sn dropped out: wl bhd and eased ins fnl f* **25/1**

1m 14.54s (0.04) **Going Correction** +0.375s/f (Good) **9** Ran SP% **117.5**
Speed ratings (Par 108): **114,111,109,108,107 105,104,100,75**
CSF £46.18 TOTE £3.50: £1.80, £3.90, £5.70; EX 40.60 Trifecta £409.20.

Owner Dr Ali Ridha **Bred** Tally-Ho Stud **Trained** Newmarket, Suffolk

FOCUS
A Group 3 sprint for the Classic generation with a cracking effort from Gifted Master to defy a penalty. Big improvement from Dubai Dream.

1774 STRATFORD PLACE STUD PARADISE STKS (LISTED RACE) (STRAIGHT) 1m (S)
4:30 (4:34) (Class 1) 4-Y-0+

£20,982 (£7,955; £3,981; £1,983; £995; £499) **Stalls** High

Form RPR

624- **1** **Gm Hopkins**[179] 7634 5-9-0 112 RyanMoore 3 116+
(John Gosden) *hld up in tch in midfield: pushed along and effrt jst over 1f out: hdwy and swtchd lft ins fnl f: qcknd readily under hands and heels to ld 100yds out: r.o wl* **5/2**[2]

0035 **2** *¾* **Battle Of Marathon (USA)**[14] 1425 4-9-0 107 (p) AdamKirby 2 114
(John Ryan) *hld up in tch in last pair: effrt and swtchd rt over 2f out: hdwy u.p and swtchd rt again ins fnl f: styd on wl to go 2nd 50yds* **14/1**

200- **3** *1 ¼* **Arod (IRE)**[172] 7761 5-9-0 118 OisinMurphy 1 111
(Peter Chapple-Hyam) *w ldr tl led over 2f out: rdn wl over 1f out: drvn 1f out: hdd and one pce fnl 100yds* **13/8**[1]

134- **4** *1 ¼* **Decorated Knight**[200] 7118 4-9-0 107 AndreaAtzeni 7 109
(Roger Charlton) *chsd ldrs: rdn and pressing ldr wl over 1f out: drvn and unable qck jst ins fnl f: kpt on same pce after* **7/1**[3]

436- **5** *½* **Hors De Combat**[200] 7118 5-9-0 106 PatSmullen 4 107
(James Fanshawe) *t.k.h: chsd ldrs: wnt 2nd over 2f out: sn rdn and pressing ldr tl no ex jst ins fnl f: wknd fnl 100yds* **8/1**

2415 **6** *½* **Captain Cat (IRE)**[33] 1068 7-9-0 107 (p) JamieSpencer 6 106
(Roger Charlton) *stdd s: hld up in rr: clsd over 1f out: nt clrest of runs and swtchd lft 1f out: kpt on same pce ins fnl f* **14/1**

00-3 **7** *5* **Balty Boys (IRE)**[11] 1491 7-9-5 110 (b) SilvestreDeSousa 8 100
(Brian Ellison) *racd alone towards stands' rail: led tl over 2f out: sn rdn and lost pl over 1f out: wknd fnl f* **22/1**

06-3 **8** *12* **Moheet (IRE)**[61] 744 4-9-0 104 FrankieDettori 5 67
(Richard Hannon) *in tch in midfield: effrt ent fnl 2f: drvn and btn over 1f out: sn wknd: fin lame* **16/1**

1m 41.96s (1.16) **Going Correction** +0.375s/f (Good) **8** Ran SP% **113.8**
Speed ratings (Par 111): **109,108,107,105,105 104,99,87**
CSF £36.29 TOTE £3.30: £1.30, £4.00, £1.10; EX 38.90 Trifecta £94.30.
Owner R J H Geffen **Bred** Cadran-Earl Blot-Scea Des Bissons **Trained** Newmarket, Suffolk

FOCUS
A solid Listed event. All bar \bBalty Boys\p kept away from the stands' rail and the form is straightforward enough. GM Hopkins is rstaed to his C&D handiap form.

1775 REDCENTRIC APPRENTICE H'CAP (STRAIGHT) 1m (S)
5:00 (5:02) (Class 4) (0-85,85) 4-Y-0+ **£6,469** (£1,925; £962; £481) **Stalls** High

Form RPR

105- **1** **Balmoral Castle**[191] 7348 7-9-7 **85** RyanTate 9 98
(Jonathan Portman) *towards rr: hdwy 3f out: swtchd rt and barged through gap over 2f out: led 2f out: hung lft but drew clr 1f out: r.o strly* **16/1**

550- **2** *5* **Dutch Law**[200] 7119 4-8-13 **82** CharlieBennett(5) 7 83
(Hughie Morrison) *hld up towards rr: hdwy 3f out: gng for gap w wnr whn squeezed out and hmpd over 2f out: hdwy to chse wnr and drvn whn hung lft over 1f out: outpcd by wnr fnl f: kpt on* **7/1**[2]

412- **3** *1 ½* **Bastille Day**[180] 7598 4-8-10 **79** AdamMcLean(5) 5 77
(David Elsworth) *in tch in midfield: effrt 2f out: rdn to chse ldrs over 1f out: wnt 3rd and styd on same pce fnl f* **8/1**[3]

1-42 **4** *½* **Steal The Scene (IRE)**[98] 260 4-9-4 **85** GaryMahon(3) 10 83
(Richard Hannon) *hld up in tch in midfield: shuffled bk towards rr over 2f out: swtchd rt and hdwy over 1f out: kpt on u.p fnl f: no threat to wnr* **14/1**

331- **5** *¾* **Oasis Spear**[244] 5787 4-8-12 **83** SamuelClarke(7) 17 78
(Chris Wall) *chsd ldrs: effrt 2f out: sn hung rt and unable qck over 1f out: kpt on same pce fnl f* **10/1**

4-00 **6** *2* **Dark Amber**[16] 1387 6-8-0 **71** oh1 SeanMooney(7) 3 61
(Brendan Powell) *hld up in rr: swtchd rt and hdwy 2f out: kpt on: nvr trbld ldrs* **33/1**

35-2 **7** *3* **Gannicus**[19] 1317 5-8-7 **74** (tp) JennyPowell(3) 16 57
(Brendan Powell) *chsd ldrs: rdn and ev ch over 2f out tl unable qck wl over 1f out: wknd fnl f* **10/1**

43-4 **8** *3 ¾* **Chevallier**[28] 1142 4-9-0 **81** JordanVaughan(3) 14 56
(K R Burke) *t.k.h: rdn and effrt ent fnl 2f: sn outpcd: edgd lft and wknd over 1f out* **7/1**[2]

450- **9** *½* **Suitor**[234] 6131 4-8-8 **75** CallumShepherd(3) 15 48
(Brian Ellison) *s.i.s: hld up in rr: pushed along and hdwy 3f out: rdn and no hdwy 2f out: wknd over 1f out* **20/1**

221- **10** *½* **Pensax Boy**[148] 8067 4-8-13 **77** GeorgeDowning 13 49
(Ian Williams) *chsd ldr: rdn to ld over 2f out: sn hdd and no ex: wknd over 1f out* **10/1**

2555 **11** *4 ½* **Robert The Painter (IRE)**[51] 860 8-9-2 **80** (v) DannyBrock 12 42
(Lee Carter) *led tl over 2f out: sn u.p and struggling: wkng whn hmpd over 1f out* **13/2**[1]

4450 **12** *2 ½* **Dukes Meadow**[13] 1430 5-8-2 **71** oh3 (p) RhiainIngram(5) 11 27
(Roger Ingram) *wl in tch in midfield: effrt and pushed rt over 2f out: sn drvn and btn: wknd over 1f out* **40/1**

-361 **13** *2 ¼* **Pearl Spectre (USA)**[28] 1152 5-9-3 **81** RobHornby 4 32
(Andrew Balding) *in tch in midfield: rdn over 2f out: no imp and sn struggling: wknd over 1f out* **9/1**

6110 **14** *2 ¾* **St Patrick's Day (IRE)**[73] 581 4-9-6 **84** KevinStott 8 29
(J R Jenkins) *sn bhd and nvr travelling wl: n.d* **20/1**

111- **15** *1 ¼* **Sabre Rock**[420] 775 6-9-1 **79** (t) ShelleyBirkett 2 21
(Julia Feilden) *in tch in midfield: rdn and lost pl wl over 2f out: sn wl btn: bhd and eased wl ins fnl f* **16/1**

400- **16** *3 ½* **Cricklewood Green (USA)**[160] 7898 5-8-8 **79** BenSanderson(7) 1 13
(Sylvester Kirk) *hld up towards rr: hdwy 3f out: rdn jst over 2f out: sn btn and wknd: wl bhd and eased towards fin* **12/1**

66-6 **17** *4 ½* **Woofie (IRE)**[111] 82 4-8-5 **74** (p) MeganNicholls(5) 6
(Laura Mongan) *in tch in midfield: rdn and lost pl over 2f out: sn wl btn: wl bhd and eased ins fnl f* **25/1**

1m 42.49s (1.69) **Going Correction** +0.375s/f (Good) **17** Ran SP% **131.6**
Speed ratings (Par 105): **106,101,99,99,98 96,93,89,89,88 84,81,79,76,75 71,67**
CSF £124.86 CT £1000.80 TOTE £21.70: £4.40, £2.30, £2.50, £3.00; EX 199.50 Trifecta £2066.90.
Owner J G B Portman **Bred** Springcombe Park Stud **Trained** Upper Lambourn, Berks
■ Stewards' Enquiry : Ryan Tate three-day ban: careless riding (May 11-13)

FOCUS
This apprentice riders' handicap was wide open and, after a decent early pace, they finished pretty well strung out. A clear pb from the winner and the form could be rated even higher.

T/Plt: £138.50 to a £1 stake. Pool: £102,985.18 - 542.62 winning tickets T/Qpdt: £9.60 to a £1 stake. Pool: £10,662.45 - 818.27 winning tickets **Steve Payne**

1741 BRIGHTON (L-H)
Wednesday, April 27

OFFICIAL GOING: Good to firm (firm in places; 9.6)
Wind: Fresh, against Weather: Sunny

1776 TOTEPLACEPOT RACING'S FAVOURITE BET/ EBF STALLIONS NOVICE MEDIAN AUCTION STKS 5f 59y
4:35 (4:35) (Class 5) 2-Y-O **£3,234** (£962; £481) **Stalls** Centre

Form RPR
0 **1** **Assassinate (IRE)**7 1579 2-9-2 0 (b1) LukeMorris 5 74
(Paul Cole) *chsd ldr: led wl over 1f out: hung lft: clr fnl f: comf* **11/4**3
2 4 1/2 **Tap Tap Boom** 2-9-2 0 SteveDrowne 6 58
(George Baker) *dwlt: outpcd in 3rd: kpt on to take 2nd ins fnl f* **5/2**2
525 **3** 2 1/2 **Lucata (IRE)**11 1482 2-9-2 0 (v1) GeorgeBaker 4 49
(Tom Dascombe) *racd freely: led tl wl over 1f out: sn btn* **1/1**1
1m 3.26s (0.96) **Going Correction** -0.05s/f (Good) 3 Ran SP% **105.2**
Speed ratings (Par 92): **90,82,78**
CSF £8.33 TOTE £3.50; EX 6.00 Trifecta £6.10.
Owner P F I Cole Ltd **Bred** Ms Marie Higgins **Trained** Whatcombe, Oxon
FOCUS
After a dry, breezy night and a windswept day, the ground had dried out accordingly with firm in places added to the previous day's forecast of good to firm. The rail was dolled out from the 4.5f pole to the 2f marker, adding 5yds to each race distance. This is unlikely to represent strong form, with the favourite far too free.

1777 TOTEJACKPOT WIN BIG TODAY H'CAP 7f 214y
5:05 (5:05) (Class 5) (0-75,75) 3-Y-O **£2,911** (£866; £432; £216) **Stalls** Centre

Form RPR
1-52 **1** **Frozen Force (IRE)**23 1238 3-9-3 **71** PatDobbs 2 78
(Amanda Perrett) *travelled wl in 5th: shkn up and chsd ldr 1f out: drvn to ld fnl stride* **9/2**3
30-4 **2** shd **Aleko**23 1238 3-9-7 **75** FrannyNorton 5 81
(Mark Johnston) *pressed ldr: led jst over 1f out: kpt on u.p fnl f: hdd fnl stride* **7/2**2
032- **3** 4 **Vizier**144 8123 3-9-7 **75** (p) HarryBentley 1 72
(Roger Varian) *dwlt: chsd ldrs: rdn over 2f out: one pce appr fnl f* **5/2**1
4-13 **4** 1/2 **Fable Of Arachne**89 376 3-8-2 **61** (t) AaronJones(5) 6 57
(Stuart Williams) *dwlt: chsd ldrs on outer: brought v wd into st: one pce appr fnl f* **14/1**
010- **5** 2 **Executor**216 6675 3-9-4 **72** GeorgeBaker 4 63
(Roger Charlton) *led tl jst over 1f out: no ex fnl f* **5/2**1
55-0 **6** 2 **Indrapura (IRE)**11 1485 3-9-5 **73** (t) LukeMorris 3 59
(Paul Cole) *in rr: pushed along 1/2-way: wknd 2f out* **14/1**
1m 36.49s (0.49) **Going Correction** -0.05s/f (Good) 6 Ran SP% **110.9**
Speed ratings (Par 98): **95,94,90,90,88 86**
CSF £19.87 TOTE £6.10: £3.00, £2.70; EX 16.20 Trifecta £82.70.
Owner A D Spence **Bred** J Kenny **Trained** Pulborough, W Sussex
FOCUS
The rail was dolled out from the 4.5f pole to the 2f marker, adding 5yds to each race distance. Quite a competitive handicap for 3yos, in which two pulled clear. The first two franked the form of their Lingfield meeting.

1778 TOTEQUADPOT FOUR PLACES IN FOUR RACES H'CAP 1m 3f 196y
5:40 (5:40) (Class 6) (0-60,60) 4-Y-O+ **£2,587** (£770; £384; £192) **Stalls** Centre

Form RPR
0-12 **1** **Hurricane Volta (IRE)**14 1413 5-9-7 **60** (p) CharlesBishop 5 67
(Peter Hedger) *t.k.h in 5th: effrt in centre 2f out: narrow ld fnl f: all out* **11/4**2
603- **2** hd **Longside**130 8312 4-9-6 **60** LukeMorris 1 67
(James Eustace) *trckd ldrs: led briefly over 1f out: w wnr fnl f: r.o wl* **4/1**3
332 **3** 1 3/4 **Innoko (FR)**8 1547 6-9-4 **57** (t) GeorgeBaker 3 61
(Tony Carroll) *t.k.h in 4th: led 2f out tl over 1f out: kpt on same pce* **6/4**1
0050 **4** 7 **Star Anise (FR)**11 1500 5-8-2 **46** oh1 JosephineGordon(5) 2 39
(Paddy Butler) *dwlt: hld up in rr: rdn and wknd 2f out* **16/1**
103 **5** 1/2 **Claude Greenwood**23 1239 6-8-5 **49** (b) HectorCrouch(5) 8 41
(Linda Jewell) *sn led: hdd & wknd 2f out* **14/1**
-030 **6** 12 **Silver Lining (IRE)**47 898 4-9-3 **57** (t) WilliamTwiston-Davies 6 30
(Mark Hoad) *trckd ldr: rdn over 2f out: sn wknd* **10/1**
2m 37.85s (5.15) **Going Correction** -0.05s/f (Good)
WFA 4 from 5yo+ 1lb 6 Ran SP% **108.3**
Speed ratings (Par 101): **80,79,78,74,73 65**
CSF £12.97 CT £18.18 TOTE £2.60: £2.20, £2.40; EX 12.60 Trifecta £20.20.
Owner T Hirschfeld & S Piper **Bred** Lynn Lodge Stud **Trained** Hook, Hampshire
FOCUS
The rail was dolled out from the 4.5f pole to the 2f marker, adding 5yds to each race distance. An ordinary race of its type for the level, with the three that headed the market coming away. A bit more improvement from the winner.

1779 TOTEEXACTA MAIDEN AUCTION STKS 1m 1f 209y
6:15 (6:15) (Class 6) 3-Y-O **£2,587** (£770; £384; £192) **Stalls** High

Form RPR
05-2 **1** **Auntie Barber (IRE)**28 1146 3-8-12 70 HarryBentley 1 73+
(Stuart Williams) *hld up in 3rd: led 2f out: clr fnl f: comf* **5/4**1
6-6 **2** 5 **Le Tissier**13 1429 3-8-10 0 EdwardGreatrex(5) 5 64
(Andrew Balding) *led: unbalanced and hanging fr 4f out: hdd 2f out: sn outpcd* **9/2**3
0-6 **3** 3 3/4 **Mischief Maisy (IRE)**102 219 3-8-12 0 PatDobbs 6 53
(Amanda Perrett) *plld hrd: trckd ldr tl wknd 2f out* **8/1**
050- **4** 1/2 **Four Poets**182 7561 3-9-3 67 JimCrowley 4 57
(David Simcock) *hld up in 4th: effrt over 2f out: wknd over 1f out* **2/1**2
2m 4.76s (1.16) **Going Correction** -0.05s/f (Good) 4 Ran SP% **107.1**
Speed ratings (Par 96): **93,89,86,85**
CSF £6.84 TOTE £1.80; EX 6.80 Trifecta £13.60.
Owner J W Parry **Bred** Mrs Martin Armstrong **Trained** Newmarket, Suffolk
FOCUS
The rail was dolled out from the 4.5f pole to the 2f marker, adding 5yds to each race distance. Probably weak maiden form.

1780 TOTETRIFECTA PICK THE 1, 2, 3 H'CAP 7f 214y
6:50 (6:50) (Class 5) (0-70,70) 4-Y-O+ **£2,911** (£866; £432; £216) **Stalls** Centre

Form RPR
-423 **1** **Stormbound (IRE)**49 875 7-8-12 **61** (b) LukeMorris 6 71
(Paul Cole) *hld up in 5th: plld wd to centre and rdn 2f out: hdwy over 1f out: led ins fnl f: styd on wl* **3/1**2
00-1 **2** 3 3/4 **Black Caesar (IRE)**8 1544 5-9-3 **66** 6ex WilliamTwiston-Davies 3 67
(Philip Hide) *chsd ldrs: led over 1f out tl ins fnl f: one pce* **15/8**1
11-5 **3** 3 1/4 **World Record (IRE)**22 1247 6-9-2 **65** FrannyNorton 4 59
(Mick Quinn) *chsd ldr: led over 2f out tl over 1f out: sn wknd* **4/1**3
0-05 **4** 6 **Shifting Star (IRE)**16 1387 11-9-7 **70** (vt) WilliamCarson 2 50
(John Bridger) *led tl over 2f out: wknd wl over 1f out* **6/1**
0003 **5** 8 **For Shia And Lula (IRE)**8 1555 7-9-3 **66** (p) FMBerry 1 28
(Daniel Mark Loughnane) *hld up in 4th: rdn and wknd 2f out* **11/2**
1m 34.83s (-1.17) **Going Correction** -0.05s/f (Good) 5 Ran SP% **109.5**
Speed ratings (Par 103): **103,99,96,90,82**
CSF £8.94 TOTE £4.30: £2.20, £1.10; EX 8.80 Trifecta £21.90.
Owner P F I Cole Ltd **Bred** A Footstep Away Syndicate **Trained** Whatcombe, Oxon
FOCUS
The rail was dolled out from the 4.5f pole to the 2f marker, adding 5yds to each race distance. Nothing more than a modest handicap, but it was run at a decent gallop. the winner is rated to his turf best.

1781 TOTESWINGER 3 WAYS TO WIN H'CAP 6f 209y
7:25 (7:25) (Class 6) (0-55,55) 4-Y-O+ **£2,587** (£770; £384; £192) **Stalls** Centre

Form RPR
4433 **1** **Malaysian Boleh**2 1700 6-9-1 **49** (b) JimCrowley 3 61
(Shaun Lycett) *dwlt: bhd: hdwy over 1f out: r.o to ld fnl 75yds: hld on wl nr fin* **7/4**1
-353 **2** hd **One Big Surprise**27 1167 4-9-6 **54** ShaneKelly 2 65
(Richard Hughes) *t.k.h: chsd ldrs: led ins fnl f tl fnl 75yds: r.o* **11/4**2
3455 **3** 2 3/4 **Hawk Moth (IRE)**28 1147 8-9-7 **55** (b) LukeMorris 6 59
(John Spearing) *dwlt: towards rr: hdwy on inner over 2f out: led over 1f out tl ins fnl f: one pce* **9/2**3
4-35 **4** 3 1/4 **Comadoir (IRE)**21 1263 10-8-13 **47** (p) JimmyQuinn 4 42
(Paul Burgoyne) *w ldrs tl wknd 1f out* **12/1**
-000 **5** 1 3/4 **Just Marion (IRE)**1 1742 4-8-7 **46** oh1 PaddyPilley(5) 5 37
(James Grassick) *in tch: pushed along 4f out: wknd over 1f out* **50/1**
6504 **6** nk **Jonnie Skull (IRE)**62 707 10-8-9 **48** (vt) JosephineGordon(5) 1 38
(Phil McEntee) *led tl wknd over 1f out* **10/1**
0045 **7** 2 **Loud**27 1162 6-8-10 **47** (p) SimonPearce(3) 7 31
(Lydia Pearce) *dwlt: sn prom: outpcd 3f out: sn btn* **8/1**
1m 22.75s (-0.35) **Going Correction** -0.05s/f (Good) 7 Ran SP% **111.1**
Speed ratings (Par 101): **100,99,96,92,90 90,88**
CSF £6.26 CT £16.09 TOTE £3.80: £1.50, £2.90; EX 8.10 Trifecta £22.00.
Owner D Gilbert, M Lawrence, A Bruce, G Wills **Bred** John & Sue Davis **Trained** Clapton-on-the-Hill, Gloucs
FOCUS
The rail was dolled out from the 4.5f pole to the 2f marker, adding 5yds to each race distance. A race which contained horses that have done most of their recent racing on the AW. Not bad form for the grade.

1782 TOTEPOOL BETTING ON ALL UK RACING H'CAP 5f 59y
7:55 (7:55) (Class 5) (0-70,70) 4-Y-O+ **£2,911** (£866; £432; £216) **Stalls** Centre

Form RPR
3260 **1** **Ask The Guru**28 1150 6-9-0 **63** (p) JimmyQuinn 3 69
(Michael Attwater) *chsd ldr: chal over 1f out: drvn to ld wl ins fnl f* **9/2**2
00-0 **2** hd **Royal Bajan (USA)**117 4 8-9-7 **70** (p) PatDobbs 1 75
(Robert Cowell) *led: hrd rdn and hdd wl ins fnl f: r.o* **3/1**1
2503 **3** 1 **Diamond Charlie (IRE)**26 1175 8-8-11 **60** JimCrowley 2 62
(Simon Dow) *dwlt: plld hrd in 4th: chal over 1f out: one pce ins fnl f* **3/1**1
5U6- **4** hd **Whitecrest**195 7234 8-9-6 **69** LukeMorris 4 70
(John Spearing) *chsd ldrs: outpcd and hrd rdn over 1f out: rallied and r.o wl nr fin* **3/1**1
-344 **5** nk **Time Medicean**72 589 10-8-10 **62** GeorgeDowning(3) 6 62
(Tony Carroll) *dwlt: in tch: outpcd and drvn along over 1f out: rallied and r.o wl nr fin* **5/1**3
1m 2.55s (0.25) **Going Correction** -0.05s/f (Good) 5 Ran SP% **109.8**
Speed ratings (Par 103): **96,95,94,93,93**
CSF £17.90 TOTE £5.80: £2.30, £2.30; EX 19.10 Trifecta £61.20.
Owner Canisbay Bloodstock **Bred** Redmyre Bloodstock & Tweenhills Stud **Trained** Epsom, Surrey
FOCUS
The rail was dolled out from the 4.5f pole to the 2f marker, adding 5yds to each race distance. A modest sprint, in which the outsider was sent off at only 5-1. More doubts than positives over the form.
T/Plt: £188.10 to a £1 stake. Pool: £37,312.27 - 144.78 winning units. T/Qpdt: £8.00 to a £1 stake. Pool: £4,781.56 - 440.08 winning units. **Lee McKenzie**

1520 PONTEFRACT (L-H)
Wednesday, April 27

OFFICIAL GOING: Good changing to good to soft after race 2 (2.35)
Wind: moderate 1/2 behind Weather: changeable, mostly overcast and cold, wintry showers

1783 WILLIAM HILL SUPPORTS NRC/BRITISH STALLION STUDS EBF NOVICE STKS (PLUS 10 RACE) 5f
2:00 (2:03) (Class 4) 2-Y-O **£4,528** (£1,347; £673; £336) **Stalls** Low

Form RPR
2 **1** **Mailshot (USA)**20 1293 2-9-2 0 JamesDoyle 6 80
(Mark Johnston) *w ldr: styd on fnl f: led last 50yds* **4/1**3
2 **2** nk **Valentino Boy (IRE)**11 1482 2-9-2 0 TomEaves 4 79
(Brian Ellison) *led: drvn over 1f out: hdd and no ex last 50yds* **7/2**2
3 8 **Springforth** 2-9-2 0 JackGarritty 8 50
(Richard Fahey) *s.i.s: in rr and sn drvn along: hdwy on outside 2f out: kpt on to take modest 3rd clsng stages* **7/1**
4 nk **White Royale (USA)** 2-8-11 0 GrahamLee 2 44
(Kevin Ryan) *trckd ldrs: drvn over 2f out: fdd appr fnl f* **12/1**
5 5 **Double Dutch** 2-9-2 0 PhillipMakin 3 31
(John Quinn) *chsd ldrs: drvn over 2f out: outpcd over 1f out: sn wknd* **7/1**

6 1 3/4 **Coverham (IRE)** 2-9-2 0 PJMcDonald 5 25
(James Bethell) *dwlt: in rr: and drvn along: brief effrt over 2f out: sn wknd* **12/1**

0 7 7 **Zumran**[13] 1437 2-8-11 0 MartinHarley 7
(Hugo Palmer) *trckd ldrs: drvn over 2f out: lost pl wl over 1f out: bhd whn eased clsng stages* **5/2**[1]

1m 4.55s (1.25) **Going Correction** +0.025s/f (Good) **7** Ran SP% **111.2**
Speed ratings (Par 94): **91,90,77,77,69 66,55**
CSF £17.29 TOTE £4.10: £2.20, £2.00; EX 19.30 Trifecta £44.40.
Owner Sheikh Hamdan bin Mohammed Al Maktoum **Bred** Darley **Trained** Middleham Moor, N Yorks
■ Seminole Dream was withdrawn. Price at time of withdrawal 22-1. Rule 4 does not apply.

FOCUS
Jack Garritty described the ground as "tacky". The front pair, both boasting previous experience, drew clear in this novice event. The form could easily be rated 4-6lb better.

1784 TOTEPOOL SUPPORTS THE NRC/BREEDERS BACKING RACING EBF MAIDEN STKS 1m 2f 6y
2:35 (2:35) (Class 5) 3-Y-O **£3,881** (£1,155; £577; £288) **Stalls** Low

Form RPR
6 1 **Amazing Red (IRE)**[14] 1426 3-9-5 0 PaulMulrennan 8 89+
(Ed Dunlop) *swtchd lft after s: hld up in rr: hdwy to trck ldrs over 2f out: sn n.m.r: led last 150yds: drvn out* **7/2**[2]

2 2 3/4 **Timekeeping (IRE)** 3-9-5 0[1] JamesDoyle 2 83
(Saeed bin Suroor) *trckd ldrs: pushed along over 3f out: upsides over 2f out: led over 1f out: edgd lft and hdd last 150yds: no ex* **9/4**[1]

5- 3 4 1/2 **Ice Galley (IRE)**[182] 7561 3-9-5 0 GrahamLee 3 74
(Kevin Ryan) *mid-div: hdwy to chse ldrs over 3f out: drvn over 2f out: kpt on same pce appr fnl f* **8/1**

02- 4 1/2 **Hammer Gun (USA)**[196] 7217 3-9-5 0 TedDurcan 5 73
(Sir Michael Stoute) *mid-div: effrt and chsng ldrs over 3f out: kpt on same pce appr fnl f* **11/2**

00-2 5 2 1/4 **Lord Yeats**[22] 1242 3-9-5 77 PJMcDonald 6 69
(Jedd O'Keeffe) *led: drvn over 3f out: hdd over 1f out: wknd last 150yds* **5/1**[3]

0-6 6 1 3/4 **Aristocles (IRE)**[16] 1386 3-9-5 0 StevieDonohoe 7 65+
(Sir Michael Stoute) *in rr: drvn and sme hdwy over 2f out: nvr a factor* **25/1**

5- 7 1 1/2 **Alquffaal**[196] 7217 3-9-5 0 DaneO'Neill 9 62+
(Roger Varian) *swtchd lft after s: t.k.h in rr: hdwy 5f out: pushed along over 3f out: nvr a threat* **8/1**

00- 8 24 **Mr Turner**[189] 7397 3-9-5 0 PhillipMakin 1 14
(Mark H Tompkins) *chsd ldrs: upsides over 2f out: lost pl over 1f out: bhd and eased clsng stages* **50/1**

2m 13.31s (-0.39) **Going Correction** +0.075s/f (Good) **8** Ran SP% **113.1**
Speed ratings (Par 98): **104,101,98,97,96 94,93,74**
CSF £11.52 TOTE £4.90: £1.40, £1.40, £2.20; EX 14.00 Trifecta £93.90.
Owner The Hon R J Arculli **Bred** Foursome Thoroughbreds, Muir & Waldron **Trained** Newmarket, Suffolk

FOCUS
The ground was changed to good to soft following this contest. Quite an interesting maiden, run at a good pace, and a really taking winner with a bright future. The form is rated at the top end of the race average.

1785 BETFRED SUPPORTS THE NRC H'CAP 1m 4y
3:10 (3:10) (Class 5) (0-75,75) 4-Y-O+ **£3,234** (£962; £481; £240) **Stalls** Low

Form RPR
60-5 1 **Freewheel (IRE)**[28] 1152 6-9-6 74 DavidAllan 12 83
(Garry Moss) *prom: drvn 3f out: n.m.r and edgd lft appr fnl f: led last 100yds: all out* **9/1**

034- 2 shd **Newmarket Warrior (IRE)**[194] 7255 5-8-12 66 (p) RoystonFfrench 6 74
(Iain Jardine) *mid-div: drvn over 2f out: upsides fnl f: jst hld* **9/1**

06-3 3 2 1/2 **Just Be Lucky (IRE)**[16] 1387 4-9-2 70 MartinHarley 9 72
(Ivan Furtado) *chsd ldrs: effrt over 2f out: upsides over 1f out: kpt on same pce last 150yds* **13/2**[3]

420- 4 nk **Le Laitier (FR)**[167] 7813 5-8-9 63 KieranO'Neill 1 65
(Scott Dixon) *chsd ldrs: drvn over 2f out: led narrowly over 1f: hdd and no ex last 100yds* **25/1**

-000 5 1/2 **Samsonite (IRE)**[34] 1058 4-8-11 65 BarryMcHugh 2 65+
(Tony Coyle) *in rr: drvn over 3f out: styd on over 1f out: nrst fin* **14/1**

43-1 6 1 1/2 **John Caesar (IRE)**[19] 1323 5-8-10 64 (tp) PaulMulrennan 11 61
(Rebecca Bastiman) *s.i.s: in rr: drvn 3f out: edgd rt over 1f out: kpt on* **16/1**

0-64 7 1 **Memory Cloth**[9] 1521 9-9-6 74 (p) PJMcDonald 10 69
(Micky Hammond) *in rr: sn pushed along: hdwy over 1f out: styng on at fin* **8/1**

30-2 8 1 1/4 **Pivotman**[22] 1247 8-9-3 71 (bt) GrahamGibbons 5 63
(Michael Easterby) *mid-div: hdwy on inner over 2f out: n.m.r over 1f out: wknd last 100yds: eased nr fin* **5/2**[1]

020- 9 3/4 **Normandy Knight**[237] 6019 4-8-11 72 HayleyIrvine[(7)] 8 62+
(Richard Fahey) *chsd ldr: upsides over 5f out: led briefly over 1f out: wknd fnl 150yds* **12/1**

122- 10 2 1/2 **Know Your Name**[159] 7925 5-9-7 75 NeilFarley 4 59+
(Eric Alston) *led: hung rt and hdd over 1f out: wknd fnl 150yds* **6/1**[2]

110- 11 1 **Tanawar (IRE)**[205] 6981 6-9-0 68 JamesSullivan 3 50
(Ruth Carr) *hld up in rr: hdwy over 2f out: chsng ldrs over 1f out: wknd fnl f* **16/1**

1m 46.08s (0.18) **Going Correction** +0.125s/f (Good) **11** Ran SP% **117.3**
Speed ratings (Par 103): **104,103,101,101,100 99,98,96,96,93 92**
CSF £87.20 CT £579.41 TOTE £14.30: £4.10, £3.40, £2.30; EX 109.50 Trifecta £946.10.
Owner Pinnacle Four Partnership **Bred** La Chunga Syndicate **Trained** Wynyard, Stockton-On-Tees

FOCUS
Modest handicap form, although they did go a really good gallop. The winner is rated close to his best since he was a 3yo.

1786 LADBROKES MOBILE FILLIES' H'CAP 1m 2f 6y
3:45 (3:47) (Class 3) (0-90,90) 3-Y-O **£9,337** (£2,796; £1,398; £699; £349) **Stalls** Low

Form RPR
111- 1 **Maleficent Queen**[223] 6456 4-10-0 90 PhillipMakin 1 99+
(Keith Dalgleish) *w ldr: led after 2f: qcknd 3 l clr over 2f out: reminder 1f out: drvn and edgd rt: eased nr fin* **11/8**[1]

15- 2 1 1/2 **Engage (IRE)**[207] 6923 3-8-4 83 LiamJones 4 84
(Sir Michael Stoute) *hld up in last: hdwy over 4f out: 3rd over 1f out: kpt on to take 2nd last 50yds* **9/4**[2]

120- 3 1 **Empress Ali (IRE)**[172] 7756 5-9-12 88 JamesSullivan 6 90
(Tom Tate) *led 2f: drvn to chse wnr over 2f out: kpt on same pce over 1f out* **10/1**

412- 4 10 **Deodoro (USA)**[191] 7346 3-8-2 81 RoystonFfrench 5 60
(Mark Johnston) *chsd ldrs: pushed along over 4f out: outpcd 3f out: lost pl over 1f out: tk poor 4th last 150yds: bhd whn eased clsng stages* **4/1**[3]

2243 5 3 1/2 **Cosmic Halo**[21] 1266 7-8-6 71 oh5 SammyJoBell[(3)] 2 46
(Richard Fahey) *trckd ldrs: pushed along 3f out: wknd over 1f out: bhd whn eased nr fin* **11/1**

2m 14.35s (0.65) **Going Correction** +0.175s/f (Good)
WFA 3 from 4yo+ 17lb **5** Ran SP% **110.3**
Speed ratings (Par 104): **104,102,102,94,91**
CSF £4.73 TOTE £2.40: £1.50, £1.90; EX 5.50 Trifecta £13.10.
Owner Weldspec Glasgow Limited **Bred** Kassala Limited **Trained** Carluke, S Lanarks

FOCUS
A useful fillies' handicap on paper, but the favourite was very much gifted the race, being allowed to dictate at a slow gallop and never looking in any danger. The form is rated at face value.

1787 NORTHERN RACING COLLEGE H'CAP 6f
4:15 (4:16) (Class 4) (0-80,80) 4-Y-O+ **£5,175** (£1,540; £769; £384) **Stalls** Low

Form RPR
4-45 1 **Dinneratmidnight**[13] 1447 5-9-4 77 (e) ConnorBeasley 12 88+
(Richard Guest) *swtchd lft after s: led early: chsd wnr: led appr fnl f: drvn out* **12/1**

0-03 2 1 1/2 **Barkston Ash**[13] 1444 8-9-7 80 (p) JasonHart 8 85
(Eric Alston) *sn led: hdd appr fnl f: kpt on same pce* **9/2**[2]

122- 3 1 1/2 **Normandy Barriere (IRE)**[324] 2987 4-9-7 80 TomEaves 5 80
(Nigel Tinkler) *chsd ldrs: 3rd 1f out: kpt on same pce* **6/1**[3]

350- 4 nse **Manatee Bay**[183] 7525 6-9-4 77 (v) BarryMcHugh 10 77+
(David Nicholls) *dwlt: swtchd lft after s: in rr: hdwy 2f out: kpt on fnl f: tk 4th last 50yds* **33/1**

0-00 5 2 3/4 **Sunraider (IRE)**[21] 1251 9-9-4 77 GrahamLee 6 68
(Paul Midgley) *mid-div: drvn over 2f out: kpt on appr fnl f: no threat* **11/1**

40-0 6 nk **Mime Dance**[13] 1444 5-9-6 79 SamJames 3 69
(David O'Meara) *chsd ldrs: wknd fnl 75yds* **10/1**

00-6 7 3 1/4 **Fast Shot**[13] 1444 8-9-0 78 (p) RachelRichardson[(5)] 2 58
(Tim Easterby) *mid-div: drvn over 2f out: nvr a threat* **5/2**[1]

00-4 8 2 1/2 **Mon Brav**[20] 1298 9-8-11 77 BenRobinson[(7)] 7 49
(Brian Ellison) *chsd ldrs: hmpd: stmbld and lost pl after 100yds: nvr a factor after* **33/1**

004- 9 3/4 **York Glory (USA)**[245] 5755 8-9-3 76 JamesSullivan 11 46
(Ruth Carr) *awkward s: sn chsng ldrs: lost pl over 1f out: bhd whn eased clsng stages* **16/1**

5-05 10 4 1/2 **Pennine Warrior**[11] 1488 5-8-9 68 (p) KieranO'Neill 4 23
(Scott Dixon) *in rr: drvn over 3f out: bhd whn eased last 100yds* **10/1**

0-00 11 47 **Ticks The Boxes (IRE)**[25] 1205 4-9-6 79 PaulMulrennan 1
(Michael Herrington) *s.s: t.k.h in rr: wl bhd whn heavily eased over 1f out: virtually p.u: t.o: lame* **9/1**

1m 17.24s (0.34) **Going Correction** +0.225s/f (Good) **11** Ran SP% **117.0**
Speed ratings (Par 105): **106,104,102,101,98 97,93,90,89,83 20**
CSF £64.99 CT £366.13 TOTE £18.10: £5.40, £2.20, £1.60; EX 101.70 Trifecta £628.50.
Owner J Toes & J O'Loan **Bred** Bumble Bloodstock Ltd **Trained** Ingmanthorpe, W Yorks
■ Stewards' Enquiry : Connor Beasley one-day ban: failed to ride to draw (May 11); three-day ban: careless riding (May 12,13,15)

FOCUS
Little got into this fair sprint. The winner is arted back to his old level.

1788 CORAL - PROUD SUPPORTERS OF THE NRC H'CAP (DIV I) 6f
4:50 (4:53) (Class 5) (0-75,75) 3-Y-O **£3,234** (£962; £481; £240) **Stalls** Low

Form RPR
03-1 1 **Avenue Of Stars**[31] 1111 3-9-4 72 (p) GrahamLee 1 80
(Karen McLintock) *trckd ldrs on inner: led over 2f out: drvn out* **9/2**[2]

221- 2 2 1/2 **Extortion**[212] 6814 3-9-7 75 PaulMulrennan 9 75
(Bryan Smart) *chsd ldrs: kpt on to take 2nd clsng stages* **8/1**[3]

26-5 3 3/4 **Wilde Extravagance (IRE)**[27] 1167 3-9-0 68 ConnorBeasley 8 66
(Julie Camacho) *w ldrs: kpt on same pce fnl f* **25/1**

05-3 4 2 1/4 **The Name's Paver**[13] 1448 3-9-1 69 (p) BarryMcHugh 3 59
(Noel Wilson) *hld up in mid-div: hdwy over 2f out: kpt on same pce over 1f out* **10/1**

245- 5 nse **The Lynch Man**[194] 7251 3-9-3 71 PhillipMakin 10 61
(John Quinn) *wnt rt s: in rr: hdwy over 2f out: kpt on fnl f* **9/1**

00-2 6 1 3/4 **Zain Emperor (IRE)**[21] 1257 3-9-6 74 StevieDonohoe 2 59
(Charlie Fellowes) *s.i.s: hdwy over 2f out: chsng ldrs over 1f out: wknd fnl 75yds* **7/4**[1]

1-33 7 8 **Ginger Joe**[40] 978 3-8-13 67 GrahamGibbons 6 26
(David Brown) *led: hdd over 2f out: wknd fnl f: eased clsng stages* **17/2**

03-0 8 1 **Baby Ballerina**[13] 1448 3-9-1 69 (p) TomEaves 7 25
(Brian Ellison) *chsd ldrs: drvn and outpcd over 2f out: wknd fnl f* **20/1**

514- 9 12 **Athollblair Boy (IRE)**[243] 5808 3-9-7 75 JasonHart 4
(Nigel Tinkler) *s.i.s: t.k.h: sn trcking ldrs: lost pl over 2f out: eased fnl f* **16/1**

226 10 14 **Phantom Flipper**[43] 935 3-9-2 70 (p) TonyHamilton 5
(David Nicholls) *chsd ldrs: lost pl over 2f out: bhd whn eased over 1f out* **14/1**

1m 20.0s (3.10) **Going Correction** +0.275s/f (Good) **10** Ran SP% **116.4**
Speed ratings (Par 98): **90,86,85,82,82 80,69,68,52,33**
CSF £40.35 CT £827.03 TOTE £5.60: £1.70, £1.70, £7.00; EX 42.60 Trifecta £1148.70.
Owner Alan Lamont **Bred** Steve Lock & Redmyre Bloodstock **Trained** Ingoe, Northumberland

FOCUS
Again little got into this and the time was fractionally faster than division two. The winner built on his Wolverhampton win.

1789 CORAL - PROUD SUPPORTERS OF THE NRC H'CAP (DIV II) 6f
5:25 (5:25) (Class 5) (0-75,75) 3-Y-O **£3,234** (£962; £481; £240) **Stalls** Low

Form RPR
21-6 1 **Smart Mover (IRE)**[16] 1381 3-8-9 70 AdamMcNamara[(7)] 10 76+
(John Quinn) *swtchd lft s: in rr: hdwy and nt clr run over 1f out: styd on strly fnl 150yds: led nr fin* **8/1**[3]

41- 2 nk **Captain Dion**[184] 7516 3-9-7 75 GrahamLee 6 77
(Kevin Ryan) *chsd ldrs: kpt on wl fnl f: tk cl 2nd post* **2/1**[1]

-154 3 shd **Wishsong**[34] 1060 3-8-9 68 AnnaHesketh[(5)] 1 70
(David Nicholls) *t.k.h: led after 100yds: pushed over 2 l clr over 1f out: hdd nr fin* **7/1**[2]

601- 4 1 3/4 **Danzeb (IRE)**[220] 6557 3-9-3 71 PJMcDonald 8 67
(Ann Duffield) *trckd ldrs: t.k.h: effrt over 2f out: kpt on fnl f* **16/1**

1630 **5** *1* **Kestrel Call (IRE)**[13] 1448 3-9-6 **74**................................(t) RobertHavlin 4 67
(Simon Crisford) *trckd ldrs: t.k.h: n.m.r over 1f out tl ins last 150yds: kpt on* **7/1**[2]

00-6 **6** *1 ¼* **Be Bop Tango (FR)**[21] 1275 3-9-5 **73**.......................... DougieCostello 3 62
(K R Burke) *mid-div: effrt over 2f out: kpt on same pce* **10/1**

00-5 **7** *hd* **Mr Chuckles (IRE)**[13] 1448 3-9-0 **68**.......................... JoeyHaynes 5 57
(Philip Kirby) *in rr: drvn over 2f out: kpt on appr fnl f* **7/1**[2]

050- **8** *¾* **Piccardo**[168] 7795 3-8-11 **65**.. TonyHamilton 2 51
(Richard Fahey) *led 100yds: chsd ldrs: wandered and wknd last 150yds* **9/1**

015- **9** *1 ¾* **Miningggold**[194] 7243 3-9-1 **69**.. DavidAllan 7 50
(Tim Easterby) *hld up towards rr: nvrr a factor* **10/1**

1m 20.04s (3.14) **Going Correction** +0.325s/f (Good) **9** Ran SP% **116.0**
Speed ratings (Par 98): **92,91,91,89,87 86,85,84,82**
CSF £24.50 CT £121.46 TOTE £7.10: £1.70, £1.10, £2.80; EX 29.60 Trifecta £206.30.
Owner Racing Ventures 2014 1 **Bred** L K I Bloodstock Ltd **Trained** Settrington, N Yorks
■ Stewards' Enquiry : Anna Hesketh two-day ban: used whip in incorrect place (May 11-12)

FOCUS
This was run in only a fractionally slower time than the first division and the winner did well to pick up from off the pace. The winner looks a bit better than the bare form.

1790 GO RACING IN YORKSHIRE FUTURE STARS APPRENTICE H'CAP (ROUND 3) 5f
6:00 (6:00) (Class 5) (0-70,70) 4-Y-O+ **£3,234** (£962; £481; £240) **Stalls** Low

Form RPR

6300 **1** **Coiste Bodhar (IRE)**[11] 1495 5-8-10 **58**................. NatalieHambling(3) 7 68
(Scott Dixon) *mde all: edgd rt wl over 1f out: drvn rt out* **16/1**

12-5 **2** *2 ¼* **Burtonwood**[18] 1341 4-9-5 **64**... RowanScott 1 66
(Julie Camacho) *chsd wnr: kpt on same pce fnl f* **9/2**[3]

-252 **3** *1 ½* **Taffetta**[9] 1525 4-9-4 **66**.. AdamMcNamara(3) 2 63
(Tony Coyle) *sn chsng ldrs: effrt over 2f out: kpt on same pce over 1f out* **15/8**[1]

5141 **4** *½* **Hit The Lights (IRE)**[7] 1559 6-9-8 **70** 6ex.............(v) DanielleMooney(3) 3 65
(David Nicholls) *trckd ldrs: effrt over 2f out: one pce over 1f out* **3/1**[2]

14-2 **5** *1 ¾* **Tinsill**[11] 1481 5-8-4 **54**...(p) KieranSchofield(5) 4 42
(Nigel Tinkler) *chsd ldrs: one pce over 1f out* **8/1**

-400 **6** *3 ¼* **Galvanize**[3] 1676 5-8-5 **57**... BenRobinson(7) 6 34
(Noel Wilson) *hood removed v late: slowly away: sme hdwy over 1f out: nvr on terms* **9/1**

000- **7** *12* **Pabusar**[134] 8240 8-8-8 **60**... LaurenSteade(7) 5
(Micky Hammond) *s.s: racd wd: bhd: lost tch over 1f out* **12/1**

1m 4.58s (1.28) **Going Correction** +0.375s/f (Good) **7** Ran SP% **112.7**
Speed ratings (Par 103): **104,100,98,97,94 89,70**
CSF £82.86 TOTE £12.80: £4.70, £2.20; EX 88.70 Trifecta £232.80.
Owner Ms Y Lowe **Bred** C Amerian **Trained** Babworth, Notts

FOCUS
Modest sprinting form and another all-the-way winner. He's rated in line with his better form of the past year.
T/Jkpt: Not won. T/Plt: £131.00 to a £1 stake. Pool: £60,521.85 - 337.22 winning tickets T/Qpdt: £30.50 to a £1 stake. Pool: £3,842.48 - 93.10 winning tickets **Walter Glynn**

1762 WOLVERHAMPTON (A.W) (L-H)
Wednesday, April 27

OFFICIAL GOING: Tapeta: standard
Wind: Fresh across Weather: Sunshine and showers

1791 HS BUTYL APPRENTICE H'CAP 1m 141y (Tp)
1:50 (1:51) (Class 6) (0-55,54) 4-Y-O+ **£2,264** (£673; £336; £168) **Stalls** Low

Form RPR

-632 **1** **Mount Cheiron (USA)**[27] 1165 5-9-2 **49**................(p) CallumRodriguez 7 55
(Richard Ford) *s.i.s: plld hrd and sn prom: trckd ldr over 6f out: rdn over 2f out: styd on to ld wl ins fnl f* **3/1**[2]

6266 **2** *¾* **Lynngale**[21] 1263 5-9-4 **54**.....................................(p[1]) KieranSchofield(3) 3 58
(Kristin Stubbs) *led: rdn over 1f out: hdd and unable qck wl ins fnl f* **6/1**[3]

00-0 **3** *1* **Just Five (IRE)**[27] 1165 10-8-13 **46**............................... PatrickVaughan 1 48
(John Weymes) *chsd ldrs: rdn over 1f out: sn edgd lft: styd on* **25/1**

34-1 **4** *4 ½* **Diamond Runner (IRE)**[4] 1654 4-9-2 **54** 6ex........(p) CameronNoble(5) 4 47
(Deborah Sanderson) *prom: pushed along over 3f out: rdn over 2f out: edgd lft and no ex fnl f* **1/1**[1]

6610 **5** *2 ¾* **Miss Buckaroo (IRE)**[27] 1165 4-9-2 **49**............................. HarryBurns 6 36
(James Given) *chsd ldrs: lost pl 7f out: rdn over 2f out: wknd over 1f out* **10/1**

320- **6** *1 ¼* **Zeteah**[198] 7162 6-9-2 **52**...(t) MitchGodwin(3) 5 36
(Tony Carroll) *hld up: rdn over 2f out: wknd over 1f out* **10/1**

1m 49.91s (-0.19) **Going Correction** -0.15s/f (Stan) **6** Ran SP% **111.3**
Speed ratings (Par 101): **94,93,92,88,86 84**
CSF £20.34 TOTE £3.10: £1.40, £2.60; EX 18.60 Trifecta £89.40.
Owner The Style Council **Bred** Swettenham Stud **Trained** Garstang, Lancs

FOCUS
A weak apprentice handicap. It paid to be handy and the order didn't change that much. Not much to take from this going forward.

1792 POLYROOF PRODUCTS LTD H'CAP 7f 32y (Tp)
2:20 (2:21) (Class 6) (0-60,60) 3-Y-O **£2,264** (£673; £336; £168) **Stalls** High

Form RPR

0-64 **1** **Packing (IRE)**[70] 610 3-9-7 **60**....................................... WilliamCarson 5 67
(Jamie Osborne) *mid-div: hdwy over 2f out: rdn to ld and hung lft ins fnl f: styd on* **3/1**[1]

4213 **2** *nk* **Music Major**[14] 1420 3-9-0 **53**....................................... AdamBeschizza 2 59
(Michael Attwater) *hld up: hdwy 1/2-way: nt clr run over 2f out: rdn and swtchd rt ins fnl f: r.o wl* **3/1**[1]

5-02 **3** *2* **Atrayu (IRE)**[2] 1710 3-9-4 **60**...................................... TomMarquand(3) 7 61+
(Paul D'Arcy) *led: rdn clr 2f out: hdd and unable qck ins fnl f* **13/2**[3]

40-5 **4** *1 ½* **Carlovian**[21] 1257 3-9-5 **58**.. JoeFanning 9 56
(Christopher Kellett) *hld up: hdwy over 1f out: hung lft and r.o ins fnl f: nvr nrr* **10/1**

360 **5** *1 ¼* **Red Rose Riot (IRE)**[28] 1146 3-9-6 **59**............................... DavidNolan 6 54
(David Menuisier) *s.i.s: hld up: r.o ins fnl f: nrst fin* **22/1**

0-00 **6** *1 ½* **Kenstone (FR)**[14] 1420 3-9-4 **57**......................................(p) MartinLane 3 48
(David Dennis) *chsd ldr: rdn to chse ldr over 2f out: wknd ins fnl f* **16/1**

000- **7** *nk* **Broughtons Mystery**[167] 7808 3-9-2 **55**............................ TomQueally 1 49
(Willie Musson) *stdd s: hld up: nt clr run ins fnl f: nvr nr to chal* **50/1**

000- **8** *2* **Gold Eliza (IRE)**[221] 6536 3-9-3 **56**................................... SeanLevey 8 41
(Richard Hannon) *chsd ldrs: rdn over 2f out: wknd fnl f* **13/2**[3]

3551 **9** *1 ½* **Ashford Island**[27] 1162 3-8-11 **50**................................(p) PatCosgrave 4 32
(Mike Murphy) *prom: rdn over 2f out: wknd fnl f* **11/2**[2]

1m 28.02s (-0.78) **Going Correction** -0.15s/f (Stan) **9** Ran SP% **113.3**
Speed ratings (Par 96): **98,97,95,93,92 90,90,87,86**
CSF £11.18 CT £52.62 TOTE £3.60: £1.20, £1.20, £2.70; EX 12.40 Trifecta £86.00.
Owner Mr & Mrs I Barratt **Bred** Century Bloodstock **Trained** Upper Lambourn, Berks

FOCUS
A moderate 3yo handicap, but they went a decent pace with the joint-favourites fighting out the finish. Improvement from the winner.

1793 EBF STALLIONS ROOF CARE (NORTH STAFFS) LTD NOVICE FILLIES' STKS (PLUS 10 RACE) 5f 216y (Tp)
2:55 (2:57) (Class 5) 2-Y-O **£3,234** (£962; £481; £240) **Stalls** Low

Form RPR

1 **Wedding Dress** 2-9-0 0... PatCosgrave 3 75
(David Brown) *s.i.s: sn rcvrd to chse ldr: rdn over 2f out: styd on to ld wl ins fnl f* **8/1**[3]

3 **2** *1* **Kodi Da Capo (IRE)**[18] 1342 2-9-0 0................................. TomQueally 2 72
(Keith Dalgleish) *disp ld tl over 3f out: chsd ldr tl led wl over 1f out: rdn: edgd lft and hdd wl ins fnl f* **8/1**[3]

5 **3** *4* **Hi Milady (IRE)**[18] 1342 2-9-0 0... LiamKeniry 4 60
(Dominic Ffrench Davis) *prom: pushed along over 3f out: sn outpcd: rallied u.p and hung lft over 1f out: styd on to go 3rd wl ins fnl f* **11/1**

4 *1 ¼* **Pacofilha** 2-9-0 0.. SamHitchcott 5 56
(Paul Cole) *sn pushed along in rr: hdwy u.p over 2f out: swtchd rt ins fnl f: styd on* **33/1**

5 **5** *¾* **Love Oasis**[13] 1437 2-9-0 0... JoeFanning 1 54
(Mark Johnston) *disp ld tl wnt on over 3f out: hdd wl over 1f out: hung lft and wknd ins fnl f* **8/11**[1]

6 *3 ¼* **Hazell Berry (IRE)** 2-9-0 0... CathyGannon 10 43
(David Evans) *sn chsng ldrs: lost pl 4f out: n.d after* **33/1**

7 *¾* **Josiane (IRE)** 2-9-0 0.. SeanLevey 9 41
(Richard Hannon) *prom: lost pl after 1f: rdn and wknd over 2f out* **14/1**

8 *2 ¼* **Tennessee Rose (IRE)** 2-9-0 0............................... RichardKingscote 8 34
(Tom Dascombe) *chsd ldrs: pushed along and lost pl over 3f out: wknd over 2f out* **4/1**[2]

1m 13.65s (-0.85) **Going Correction** -0.15s/f (Stan) **8** Ran SP% **121.0**
Speed ratings (Par 89): **99,97,92,90,89 84,83,80**
CSF £73.36 TOTE £8.30: £1.80, £1.60, £2.90; EX 64.00 Trifecta £412.30.
Owner J C Fretwell **Bred** Newsells Park Stud **Trained** Averham Park, Notts

FOCUS
An interesting novice fillies' event despite the lack of any previous winners. The first two pulled clear and the form could be rated higher.

1794 RECTICEL INSULATION PERFECT H'CAP (DIV I) 5f 216y (Tp)
3:30 (3:31) (Class 6) (0-55,54) 3-Y-O+ **£2,264** (£673; £336; £168) **Stalls** Low

Form RPR

0-54 **1** **Cuban Queen (USA)**[11] 1497 3-8-8 **49**............................. MartinLane 3 55
(Jeremy Gask) *a.p: shkn up over 1f out: r.o u.p to ld nr fin* **10/1**

00-4 **2** *shd* **Jack The Laird (IRE)**[27] 1162 3-8-11 **52**...................(p) RobertWinston 6 58
(Dean Ivory) *chsd ldr: rdn to ld over 1f out: hdd nr fin* **6/4**[1]

-000 **3** *2 ¼* **Smart Dj**[11] 1481 5-9-5 **52**.................................. MichaelJMMurphy(3) 2 54
(Sarah Hollinshead) *chsd ldrs: swtchd rt over 1f out: sn rdn: styd on same pce ins fnl f* **25/1**

3661 **4** *nk* **Diamond Vine (IRE)**[19] 1320 8-9-6 **50**...........................(p) DavidProbert 8 51
(Ronald Harris) *sn pushed along in rr: rdn over 2f out: r.o ins fnl f: nrst fin* **10/1**

-023 **5** *nk* **Assertive Agent**[35] 1042 6-9-7 **54**............................... TomMarquand(3) 7 54
(Tony Carroll) *hld up: hdwy and nt clr run over 1f out: nt trble ldrs* **8/1**[3]

0313 **6** *1* **Dream Ally (IRE)**[2] 1720 6-9-3 **54**........................(be) PatrickVaughan(7) 9 51
(John Weymes) *chsd ldrs: rdn over 2f out: no ex ins fnl f* **4/1**[2]

06-0 **7** *1* **Titus Secret**[19] 1319 4-9-1 **45**... CathyGannon 5 44+
(Malcolm Saunders) *s.s: sn pushed along in rr: nt clr run ins fnl f: n.d: sddle slipped* **12/1**

2120 **8** *½* **Multi Quest**[19] 1319 4-9-5 **49**...(b) SamHitchcott 1 42
(John E Long) *led: rdn and hdd over 1f out: wknd ins fnl f* **18/1**

1m 13.43s (-1.07) **Going Correction** -0.15s/f (Stan)
WFA 3 from 4yo+ 11lb **8** Ran SP% **106.1**
Speed ratings (Par 101): **101,100,97,97,97 95,94,93**
CSF £21.88 CT £297.42 TOTE £10.20: £2.20, £1.60, £4.50; EX 29.40 Trifecta £697.00.
Owner M Moss & P Bamford **Bred** Phyllis M Wyeth **Trained** Stockbridge, Hants

FOCUS
The first division of a very moderate handicap with only two fancied according to the market. The finish was fought out between a couple of unexposed 3yos with straightforward form in behind.

1795 RECTICEL INSULATION PERFECT H'CAP (DIV II) 5f 216y (Tp)
4:05 (4:05) (Class 6) (0-55,54) 3-Y-O+ **£2,264** (£673; £336; £168) **Stalls** Low

Form RPR

1 **Its Only Mossy (IRE)**[166] 7840 3-8-13 **54**........................ TomQueally 9 64+
(Jennie Candlish) *sn chsng ldrs: led 5f out: edgd rt over 3f out: pushed clr fr over 1f out: comf* **5/2**[2]

-423 **2** *3* **Wedgewood Estates**[39] 1005 5-9-10 **54**........................... DavidProbert 5 56
(Tony Carroll) *hld up: hdwy over 2f out: rdn to chse wnr ins fnl f: edgd rt: styd on same pce* **11/2**[3]

0452 **3** *hd* **Presto Boy**[27] 1164 4-8-13 **50**................................. StephenCummins(7) 4 51
(Richard Hughes) *broke wl: sn lost pl: hdwy and hung lft over 1f out: kpt on* **6/1**

0U31 **4** *1 ½* **Bionic Indian**[8] 1556 4-9-5 **54** 6ex..............................(b) NathanEvans(5) 6 51
(Michael Easterby) *s.i.s: hdwy to chse wnr 4f out: hmpd over 3f out: rdn over 1f out: no ex ins fnl f* **13/8**[1]

600- **5** *4 ½* **Lady Zodiac (IRE)**[209] 6888 4-9-1 **48**........................ MarcMonaghan(3) 1 31
(Philip McBride) *led 1f: chsd ldrs: rdn over 2f out: wknd over 1f out* **14/1**

3404 **6** *¾* **Guapo Bay**[7] 1573 3-8-2 **50**..(p) TinaSmith(7) 3 28
(Richard Hannon) *s.i.s: in rr: pushed along over 2f out: sn wknd* **14/1**

00-6 **7** *3 ¼* **Tally's Song**[12] 1451 3-8-4 **45**... MartinDwyer 7 13
(Grace Harris) *chsd ldrs: hmpd over 3f out: sn rdn: wknd over 1f out* **50/1**

1m 13.44s (-1.06) **Going Correction** -0.15s/f (Stan)
WFA 3 from 4yo+ 11lb **7** Ran SP% **111.6**
Speed ratings (Par 101): **101,97,96,94,88 87,83**
CSF £15.76 CT £71.11 TOTE £3.10: £1.90, £3.10; EX 18.10 Trifecta £53.80.
Owner Mrs G Hennessy **Bred** James And Sarah Mulcahy **Trained** Basford Green, Staffs

FOCUS
A dominant display from the winner and like the first division it went to a 3yo. The winning time was almost identical to the first leg. Straightforward form.

1796 JOHN BRASH JB RED H'CAP — 1m 4f 50y (Tp)
4:40 (4:41) (Class 6) (0-65,65) 4-Y-O+ **£2,264** (£673; £336; £168) **Stalls** Low

Form RPR
2511 **1** **On A Whim**[11] [1500] 4-9-4 **63**........(p) JoeFanning 12 72
(Daniel Mark Loughnane) *hld up in tch: shkn up over 1f out: rdn ins fnl f: styd on to ld nr fin* **11/4**[2]
314 **2** *hd* **Obboorr**[68] [640] 7-9-7 **65**........ DavidNolan 1 73
(Tim Fitzgerald) *chsd ldrs: rdn over 2f out: led ins fnl f: hdd nr fin* **9/4**[1]
-235 **3** *2 1/2* **Lions Charge (USA)**[34] [1057] 9-9-5 **63**........(tp) LiamKeniry 11 67
(Neil Mulholland) *a.p: chsd ldr 10f out: rdn to ld over 1f out: hdd ins fnl f: styd on same pce* **9/1**
02-3 **4** *2* **Overlord**[11] [1502] 4-8-12 **57**........ AndrewMullen 10 57
(Mark Rimell) *hld up: hdwy over 1f out: nt rch ldrs* **11/2**[3]
6-05 **5** *3 3/4* **Saint Thomas (IRE)**[18] [1347] 9-8-13 **57**........ DavidProbert 6 51
(John Mackie) *hld up: hdwy over 5f out: lost pl 4f out: effrt over 1f out: wknd fnl f* **16/1**
0U20 **6** *nk* **Nouvelle Ere**[18] [1340] 5-9-0 **61**........(t) TomMarquand(3) 5 55
(Tony Carroll) *led: rdn over 2f out: hdd over 1f out: wknd ins fnl f* **22/1**
024- **7** *2 3/4* **Racing Knight (IRE)**[303] [3717] 4-9-6 **65**........ JohnFahy 9 55
(Kevin Frost) *chsd ldrs: rdn over 2f out: wknd over 1f out* **16/1**
00- **8** *1 1/2* **Druot**[282] [4452] 4-8-13 **65**........[1] StephenCummins(7) 3 52
(Richard Hughes) *hld up: nvr on terms* **14/1**
4256 **9** *1* **Kelly's Finest (IRE)**[13] [1434] 4-8-12 **62**........(p) GeorgeBuckell(5) 8 48
(Michael Appleby) *hld up: hdwy u.p over 2f out: wknd over 1f out* **10/1**
/000 **10** *8* **Stand Guard**[33] [1085] 12-8-10 **57**........ DanielMuscutt(3) 7 30
(John Butler) *hld up: pushed along over 3f out: sn wknd* **33/1**

2m 39.32s (-1.48) **Going Correction** -0.15s/f (Stan)
WFA 4 from 5yo+ 1lb **10** Ran SP% **117.6**
Speed ratings (Par 101): **98,97,96,94,92 92,90,89,88,83**
CSF £9.45 CT £48.22 TOTE £3.80: £1.70, £1.40, £1.90; EX 11.20 Trifecta £44.50.
Owner R M Brilley **Bred** Minster Stud **Trained** Baldwin's Gate, Staffs

FOCUS
A modest middle-distance handicap in which they went an ordinary gallop until things quickened up turning for home. The field was reduced by one when Lexington Bay was withdrawn after arriving at the start minus the declared cheekpieces. Straightforward form.

1797 UP ON THE ROOF H'CAP — 1m 141y (Tp)
5:10 (5:10) (Class 3) (0-95,93) 4-Y-O+ **£7,246** (£2,168; £1,084; £542; £270) **Stalls** Low

Form RPR
0610 **1** **Jack Of Diamonds (IRE)**[39] [1001] 7-9-2 **88**........ RobertWinston 5 95
(Roger Teal) *hld up in tch: rdn to ld ins fnl f: r.o* **8/1**
4662 **2** *3/4* **Capo Rosso (IRE)**[18] [1344] 6-9-7 **93**........ RichardKingscote 4 98
(Tom Dascombe) *chsd ldr: hmpd and swtchd rt over 7f out: shkn up over 3f out: led over 1f out: rdn and hdd ins fnl f: styd on* **3/1**[1]
333- **3** *nk* **Outer Space**[128] [8326] 5-9-0 **91**........ LucyKBarry(5) 1 95
(Jamie Osborne) *hld up: hdwy and nt clr run over 1f out: swtchd rt: r.o* **9/1**
110- **4** *shd* **Oracolo (IRE)**[291] [4148] 4-8-12 **91**........ SophieKilloran(7) 6 96+
(David Simcock) *hld up: hdwy and nt clr run over 1f out: r.o* **15/2**
00-6 **5** *1* **Fiftyshadesfreed (IRE)**[11] [1480] 5-9-1 **87**........(p) LiamKeniry 9 89
(George Baker) *hld up: hdwy: nt clr run and swtchd lft over 1f out: r.o* **25/1**
4112 **6** *2 1/4* **Red Touch (USA)**[28] [1152] 4-8-8 **83** ow1........ AlistairRawlinson(3) 7 80
(Michael Appleby) *chsd ldrs: hmpd over 7f out: rdn over 2f out: styd on same pce fr over 1f out* **5/1**[3]
0-05 **7** *1/2* **Purple Rock (IRE)**[9] [1521] 4-8-3 **80**........(t) NathanEvans(5) 2 75
(Michael Easterby) *chsd ldrs: rdn over 1f out: no ex ins fnl f* **13/2**
011 **8** *hd* **Harry Holland**[28] [1142] 4-8-10 **82**........ MartinDwyer 8 77
(William Muir) *led: edgd lft over 7f out: rdn over 2f out: hdd over 1f out: no ex ins fnl f* **9/2**[2]
340- **9** *nse* **Santefisio**[181] [7588] 10-9-2 **88**........(b) TomQueally 10 83
(Keith Dalgleish) *hld up: effrt over 1f out: no ex fnl f* **16/1**

1m 47.84s (-2.26) **Going Correction** -0.15s/f (Stan) **9** Ran SP% **115.8**
Speed ratings (Par 107): **104,103,103,102,102 100,99,99,99**
CSF £32.36 CT £223.78 TOTE £9.00: £2.90, £1.50, £2.60; EX 29.20 Trifecta £316.00.
Owner Inside Track Racing Club **Bred** Gigginstown House Stud **Trained** Great Shefford, Berks

FOCUS
A decent handicap, if lacking improvers, and they went a good pace. There was a bit of trouble involving the leaders starting the bend away from the stands. The form is taken at face value.

1798 NFRC (MIDLANDS) MAIDEN FILLIES' STKS (PLUS 10 RACE) — 1m 141y (Tp)
5:45 (5:50) (Class 5) 3-Y-O **£2,911** (£866; £432; £216) **Stalls** Low

Form RPR
02- **1** **Bombilate (USA)**[175] [7699] 3-9-0 0........ WilliamBuick 7 73
(Charlie Appleby) *mde all: rdn over 1f out: edgd lft ins fnl f: all out* **5/4**[1]
6- **2** *hd* **Corked (IRE)**[149] [8047] 3-8-11 0........ MarcMonaghan(3) 4 72
(Hugo Palmer) *chsd ldrs: rdn and ev ch ins fnl f: r.o* **7/2**[2]
0- **3** *2 3/4* **Loveisreckless (IRE)**[190] [7360] 3-9-0 0........(b[1]) MartinDwyer 6 66+
(William Muir) *uns rdr and got loose prior to the s: s.i.s: hld up: rdn and r.o wl ins fnl f: nt rch ldrs* **50/1**
002- **4** *1 3/4* **Chelabella**[160] [7904] 3-8-11 71........ LouisSteward(3) 5 62
(Michael Bell) *prom: rdn over 2f out: styd on same pce fnl f* **12/1**
05 **5** *1/2* **Dwynant**[29] [1132] 3-9-0 0........ RyanPowell 8 61
(Kevin Frost) *chsd wnr over 7f out tl rdn over 1f out: no ex ins fnl f* **80/1**
0-6 **6** *3/4* **Lime And Lemon (IRE)**[13] [1436] 3-9-0 0........ DavidProbert 9 59
(Philip McBride) *hld up: hdwy over 2f out: rdn over 1f out: styd on same pce* **6/1**[3]
6 **7** *1/2* **Raven Banner (IRE)**[40] [984] 3-9-0 0........ LiamKeniry 13 58
(Daniel Mark Loughnane) *s.i.s: hld up: styd on fr over 1f out: nvr nrr* **100/1**
4 **8** *hd* **Yours Forever**[46] [925] 3-9-0 0........ KeaganLatham 1 58
(Kevin Ryan) *prom: rdn over 2f out: wknd ins fnl f* **50/1**
9 *2* **Best Laid Plans** 3-9-0 0........ RichardKingscote 2 53
(James Tate) *mid-div: rdn over 2f out: nvr trbld ldrs* **33/1**
00-5 **10** *1 3/4* **Dora's Field (IRE)**[15] [1392] 3-9-0 0........ MartinLane 12 49+
(Ed Dunlop) *s.i.s: hld up: nvr on terms* **8/1**
11 *hd* **Al Haffanah (IRE)** 3-9-0 0........ SeanLevey 10 48
(Richard Hannon) *mid-div: rdn over 2f out: wkng whn hung lft fnl f* **16/1**
0 **12** *1* **Cliff Face (IRE)**[15] [1392] 3-8-7 0........ LukeCarson(7) 11 46+
(Ed Dunlop) *s.s: a in rr* **20/1**
13 *6* **Jessica Jo (IRE)** 3-9-0 0........ JoeFanning 3 32
(Mark Johnston) *mid-div: pushed along and lost pl after 1f: rdn over 3f out: wknd over 2f out* **25/1**

1m 49.0s (-1.10) **Going Correction** -0.15s/f (Stan) **13** Ran SP% **123.3**
Speed ratings (Par 95): **98,97,95,93,93 92,92,92,90,88 88,87,82**
CSF £5.21 TOTE £2.70: £1.90, £1.50, £5.10; EX 8.70 Trifecta £362.70.
Owner Godolphin **Bred** Gallagher's Stud **Trained** Newmarket, Suffolk

FOCUS
Quite an interesting 3yo fillies' maiden with some big stables represented. It paid to be handy and not many got into it. Rather a muddling race, rated cautiously.
T/Plt: £105.00 to a £1 stake. Pool: £52,287.67 - 363.33 winning tickets T/Qpdt: £49.20 to a £1 stake. Pool: £4,708.55 - 70.74 winning tickets **Colin Roberts**

1699 CHELMSFORD (A.W) (L-H)
Thursday, April 28

OFFICIAL GOING: Polytrack: standard
Wind: light, half behind Weather: overcast

1799 ANDERSON FOUNDATION CHARITY FILLIES' NOVICE AUCTION STKS (PLUS 10 RACE) — 5f (P)
5:55 (5:56) (Class 5) 2-Y-O **£4,528** (£1,347; £673; £336) **Stalls** Low

Form RPR
1 **Gerrard's Fur Coat** 2-8-9 0........ RichardKingscote 2 59
(Tom Dascombe) *mde all: rdn over 1f out: hld on wl ins fnl f: rdn out* **5/1**[3]
0 **2** *3/4* **Black Redstart**[14] [1437] 2-8-10 0........ AndreaAtzeni 4 57
(Alan Bailey) *trckd ldrs: nt clr run jst over 2f out tl swtchd rt and effrt over 1f out: styd on u.p to chse wnr wl ins fnl f: kpt on* **5/2**[2]
3 *1/2* **Luv U Always** 2-8-10 0........ JimmyQuinn 5 55
(Jo Hughes) *chsd ldrs on outer: effrt and rdn to chse wnr over 1f out: kpt on same pce u.p ins fnl f: lost 2nd wl ins fnl f* **12/1**
4 *hd* **Mightaswellsmile** 2-8-11 0........ JimCrowley 8 55+
(James Given) *wnt rt s and s.i.s: rn green and detached in last tl rapid hdwy fnl f: fin v strly: nt quite rch ldrs* **8/1**
5 *nk* **Secret Ballerina** 2-8-10 0........ AdamBeschizza 6 53
(Julia Feilden) *swtchd lft after s: in tch: effrt over 1f out: kpt on ins fnl f: nvr quite enough pce to chal* **12/1**
6 *nk* **Baby Gal** 2-8-10 0........ JackMitchell 7 52
(Giles Bravery) *bmpd s: in tch: effrt over 2f out: styd on ins fnl f: nvr quite enough pce to chal* **20/1**
7 *1/2* **Chotto (IRE)** 2-8-12 0........ HarryBentley 1 53
(George Scott) *trckd ldrs: effrt u.p but unable qck over 1f out: kpt on same pce ins fnl f* **2/1**[1]
6 **8** *3 3/4* **Bella Duchess (IRE)**[14] [1443] 2-8-11 0........ BenCurtis 3 38
(David C Griffiths) *chsd wnr: rdn jst over 2f out: lost 2nd and btn over 1f out: wknd ins fnl f* **12/1**

1m 1.86s (1.66) **Going Correction** +0.075s/f (Slow) **8** Ran SP% **117.5**
Speed ratings (Par 89): **89,87,87,86,86 85,84,78**
CSF £18.50 TOTE £5.10: £1.30, £1.80, £1.30; EX 17.40 Trifecta £87.90.
Owner Paul & Clare Rooney **Bred** Clare Lloyd & Nell Kent **Trained** Malpas, Cheshire

FOCUS
Not a strong contest but it was run at a fair pace.

1800 ANDERSON GROUP MAIDEN STKS — 1m (P)
6:30 (6:32) (Class 5) 3-Y-O+ **£5,175** (£1,540; £769; £384) **Stalls** Low

Form RPR
2- **1** **Symbolic**[190] [7395] 3-9-0 0........ FrankieDettori 5 87+
(John Gosden) *mde all: pushed along and readily qcknd clr over 1f out: in n.d fnl f: easily* **4/6**[1]
54- **2** *6* **Wafi Star (IRE)**[261] [5242] 3-9-0 0........ JimCrowley 3 69
(Simon Crisford) *chsd ldng pair: wnt 2nd wl over 1f out: sn rdn and outpcd by wnr: kpt on same pce fnl f* **8/1**
53 **3** *1 1/4* **Dangerous Secret**[28] [1160] 3-8-9 0........ JimmyQuinn 8 61
(Dr Jon Scargill) *t.k.h early and dropped in bhd: nt clr run over 2f out: pushed along and sme hdwy over 1f out: kpt on ins fnl f: wnt 3rd last strides: no ch w wnr* **50/1**
4 *hd* **Istanbul Bey** 3-9-0 0........ PatCosgrave 1 66
(William Haggas) *dwlt: sn in tch in midfield: effrt in 3rd but outpcd by wnr over 1f out: kpt on same pce fnl f: lost 3rd last strides* **5/1**[3]
6- **5** *2* **Royal Mahogany (IRE)**[163] [7879] 3-8-11 0........ KevinStott(3) 7 61
(Luca Cumani) *dwlt: sn in tch in midfield: pushed along over 3f out: rdn over 2f out: outpcd and no ch w wnr over 1f out: kpt on same pce fnl f* **12/1**
0 **6** *4 1/2* **Street Poet (IRE)**[16] [1397] 3-9-0 0........ RyanMoore 6 56
(Sir Michael Stoute) *chsd wnr: clipped heels and stmbld after 1f: rdn ent fnl 2f: lost 2nd and no ex over 1f out: lost wl hld 3rd 1f out and sn eased* **7/2**[2]
0 **7** *2* **Dream Trader (IRE)**[16] [1397] 3-9-0 0........ AndreaAtzeni 4 51
(Roger Varian) *t.k.h: hld up in tch in midfield: swtchd rt and effrt wl over 1f out: sn btn and wknd over 1f out* **25/1**
0 **8** *3 1/4* **One For Jodie (IRE)**[5] [1622] 5-9-11 0........ AlistairRawlinson(3) 2 41
(Michael Appleby) *hld up in tch in last pair: pushed along briefly 4f out: rdn and rn green over 2f out: sn btn and bhd over 1f out* **100/1**

1m 41.41s (1.51) **Going Correction** +0.075s/f (Slow)
WFA 3 from 5yo 14lb **8** Ran SP% **124.5**
Speed ratings (Par 103): **95,89,87,87,85 81,79,75**
CSF £8.38 TOTE £1.70: £1.10, £3.30, £6.00; EX 7.10 Trifecta £40.50.
Owner Cheveley Park Stud **Bred** Cheveley Park Stud Ltd **Trained** Newmarket, Suffolk

FOCUS
A fair maiden but lacking depth, run at an even tempo. The winner is useful.

1801 MAYOR OF CHELMSFORD H'CAP — 6f (P)
7:00 (7:01) (Class 3) (0-95,92) 4-Y-O+ **£9,730** (£3,368) **Stalls** Centre

Form RPR
1446 **1** **Hoofalong**[26] [1205] 6-9-6 **92**........(b) HarryBentley 2 98
(Michael Easterby) *trckd ldr: effrt and upsides over 1f out: sn drvn: led 150yds out: r.o and asserted fnl 100yds* **4/5**[1]
1506 **2** *1 1/2* **Crosse Fire**[8] [1566] 4-9-3 **89**........(p) BenCurtis 1 90
(Scott Dixon) *led and set stdy gallop: rdn and qcknd 2f out: jnd over 1f out: hdd 150yds out: outpcd fnl 100yds* **5/1**[3]
1151 **R** **Gentlemen**[29] [1143] 5-8-11 **88**........ JosephineGordon(5) 4
(Phil McEntee) *ref to r* **6/4**[2]

1m 15.28s (1.58) **Going Correction** +0.075s/f (Slow) **3** Ran SP% **112.2**
Speed ratings (Par 107): **92,90,**
CSF £4.77 TOTE £1.60; EX 4.10 Trifecta £6.10.
Owner A Chandler, L Westwood, D & Y Blunt **Bred** D F Spence **Trained** Sheriff Hutton, N Yorks

FOCUS
Much of the interest was taken out of this contest at the start as the in-form Gentlemen refused to race. The winner didn't need to improve.

1802 YMCA PRESIDENT, LADY RUGGLES-BRISE'S H'CAP — 1m 5f 66y(P)
7:30 (7:31) (Class 3) (0-95,93) 4-Y-O+

£8,715 (£2,609; £1,304; £652; £326; £163) **Stalls** Low

Form — RPR

120- **1** **Dannyday**[250] 5639 4-9-1 **85** .... RyanMoore 8 101+
(Sir Michael Stoute) *hld up off the pce in last pair: clsd 4f out: rdn to ld over 1f out: sn clr: styd on strly: easily* **7/4**[1]

260- **2** 3 ¾ **Graceland (FR)**[222] 6541 4-8-10 **83** .... LouisSteward(3) 5 90
(Michael Bell) *stdd s: hld up off the pce in rr: clsd and in tch 4f out: trckd wnr through over 2f out: rdn to chse wnr over 1f out: no threat to wnr but kpt on for clr 2nd fnl f* **11/1**

0536 **3** 7 **Masterpaver**[41] 975 5-9-2 **88** .... SammyJoBell(3) 4 85
(Richard Fahey) *hld up off the pce in midfield: clsd 4f out: effrt and pushed rt over 1f out: hdwy u.p to go modest 3rd 1f out: kpt on same pce after* **6/1**

-121 **4** 4 ½ **Haines**[26] 1209 5-9-3 **89** .... RobHornby(3) 6 79
(Andrew Balding) *midfield: clsd and in tch 4f out: effrt jst over 2f out: battling for 3rd but outpcd over 1f out: wknd fnl f* **7/2**[3]

-151 **5** 2 ¼ **Daisy Boy (IRE)**[14] 1430 5-8-8 **82** ....(t) AaronJones(5) 7 68
(Stuart Williams) *led and sn clr w rival: rdn over 2f out: hdd over 1f out: sn btn and wknd* **11/4**[2]

000- **6** 16 **Ayahuasca (USA)**[216] 6728 6-9-6 **89** ....(p) OisinMurphy 2 51
(Takashi Kodama, Ire) *chsd ldr and sn clr of field: rdn and ev ch 3f out: lost pl qckly and wnt rt over 1f out: bhd and eased ins fnl f* **25/1**

7 2 ¼ **Shingwedzi (SAF)**[312] 5-9-10 **93** .... JamesDoyle 3 52
(Ed Dunlop) *dwlt: sn rcvrd to chse clr ldng pair: rdn 3f out: sn struggling and dropped to last 2f out: sn bhd: eased ins fnl f* **14/1**

2m 48.53s (-5.07) **Going Correction** +0.075s/f (Slow)
WFA 4 from 5yo+ 1lb — 7 Ran SP% **118.4**
Speed ratings (Par 107): **118,115,111,108,107 97,96**
CSF £23.75 CT £99.59 TOTE £2.00: £1.20, £6.40; EX 20.30 Trifecta £82.80.
Owner Sir Evelyn De Rothschild **Bred** Southcourt Stud **Trained** Newmarket, Suffolk

FOCUS
A competitive handicap run at a sound pace. The first three were in rear turning for home and the first two came clear. The smart winner can do better.

1803 TONI & GUY CHELMSFORD H'CAP — 5f (P)
8:00 (8:00) (Class 5) (0-75,75) 4-Y-O+ **£5,175** (£1,540; £769; £384) **Stalls** Low

Form — RPR

5261 **1** **Saved My Bacon (IRE)**[16] 1402 5-9-6 **75** .... SilvestreDeSousa 1 83
(Chris Dwyer) *s.i.s: hld up in rr: hdwy over 2f out: rdn to chal over 1f out: led and edgd lft jst ins fnl f: r.o wl* **2/1**[1]

255- **2** 1 **Shackled N Drawn (USA)**[250] 5620 4-9-6 **75** .... CharlesBishop 2 79
(Peter Hedger) *stdd s: t.k.h: chsd ldng pair: clsd to join ldrs and rdn over 1f out: styd on same pce ins fnl f* **5/2**[2]

6033 **3** 1 ¼ **Fine 'n Dandy (IRE)**[36] 1046 5-9-2 **71** .... OisinMurphy 3 71
(J R Jenkins) *racd freely: led: rdn and hrd pressed over 1f out: hdd jst ins fnl f: no ex and outpcd wl ins fnl f* **3/1**[3]

-303 **4** nk **Flicka's Boy**[4] 1666 4-9-5 **74** .... DuranFentiman 4 73
(Tony Coyle) *chsd ldr: rdn and ev ch over 1f out: sltly outpcd whn short of room and swtchd rt jst ins fnl f: kpt on same pce after* **6/1**

1246 **5** 1 **City Of Angkor Wat (IRE)**[5] 1648 6-9-3 **72** ....(p) LiamKeniry 5 67
(Conor Dore) *in tch in last pair: outpcd and rdn over 1f out: drifted and kpt on ins fnl f* **6/1**

59.61s (-0.59) **Going Correction** +0.075s/f (Slow) — 5 Ran SP% **115.5**
Speed ratings (Par 103): **107,105,103,102,101**
CSF £7.76 TOTE £2.30: £1.90, £1.80; EX 7.50 Trifecta £10.50.
Owner Mrs J Hughes & Mrs C Kemp **Bred** Kenneth Heelan **Trained** Newmarket, Suffolk

FOCUS
This looked competitive enough for the grade despite the small field. The winner rates a small pb.

1804 BOOK SIMPLY RED TICKETS AT CHELMSFORDCITYRACECOURSE.COM H'CAP — 1m (P)
8:30 (8:32) (Class 5) (0-70,76) 3-Y-O **£5,175** (£1,540; £769; £384) **Stalls** Low

Form — RPR

003- **1** **Oh This Is Us (IRE)**[120] 8404 3-9-7 **70** .... PatDobbs 7 79+
(Richard Hannon) *stdd s: hld up in tch in rr: smooth hdwy on inner to join ldrs over 1f out: sn rdn to ld and qcknd clr: r.o: eased cl home* **8/1**[3]

534- **2** 1 ¼ **Thaqaffa (IRE)**[319] 3201 3-9-4 **67** .... DaneO'Neill 5 73+
(Marcus Tregoning) *in tch in midfield: swtchd rt and hdwy over 1f out: 3rd and wandered rt 1f out: wnt 2nd ins fnl f: styd on wl* **12/1**

1-1 **3** 2 ½ **We Are Ninety (IRE)**[3] 1703 3-9-13 **76** 6ex .... JimCrowley 10 76
(Hugo Palmer) *chsd ldr: upsides 2f out: rdn to ld over 1f out: sn drvn: hdd and outpcd by wnr: lost 2nd and kpt on same pce ins fnl f* **4/9**[1]

04-3 **4** nk **Jassur**[99] 253 3-8-11 **63** ....(p) DanielMuscutt(3) 9 63
(Marco Botti) *hld up in tch in last trio: rdn and hdwy over 1f out: kpt on and pressing for 3rd towards fin: no threat to wnr* **14/1**

506- **5** 1 ¾ **Cliffs Of Dover**[230] 6276 3-9-4 **67** .... DarryllHolland 6 63
(Charles Hills) *bustled along leaving stalls: sn chsng ldrs and t.k.h: hdwy to ld 5f out: rdn and hdd over 1f out: no ex: wknd ins fnl f* **12/1**

02-1 **6** ¾ **Be Kool (IRE)**[19] 1345 3-9-7 **70** .... BenCurtis 1 64
(Brian Ellison) *t.k.h: hld up in tch in midfield: effrt over 1f out: sn unable qck u.p and btn 1f out: wknd ins fnl f* **6/1**[2]

16-4 **7** 5 **Beatbybeatbybeat**[17] 1389 3-9-1 **67** .... ThomasBrown(3) 4 49
(Ismail Mohammed) *sn led: hdd 5f out: sn lost pl and btn: wknd fnl f* **25/1**

-154 **8** 4 ½ **Trodero**[55] 817 3-9-6 **69** .... JimmyQuinn 2 41
(Dr Jon Scargill) *in tch in midfield: rdn and lost pl over 1f out: bhd and wknd 1f out* **25/1**

1m 40.0s (0.10) **Going Correction** +0.075s/f (Slow) — 8 Ran SP% **124.4**
Speed ratings (Par 98): **102,100,98,97,96 95,90,85**
CSF £104.71 CT £130.52 TOTE £8.60: £2.10, £2.40, £1.10; EX 56.90 Trifecta £224.20.
Owner Team Wallop **Bred** Herbertstown House Stud **Trained** East Everleigh, Wilts

FOCUS
The pace was honest for this uncompetitive handicap. Clear pbs from the unexposed 1-2.

1805 LADIES DAY 16TH JUNE H'CAP — 1m (P)
9:00 (9:02) (Class 6) (0-65,71) 4-Y-O+ **£3,234** (£962; £481; £240) **Stalls** Low

Form — RPR

5325 **1** **Foie Gras**[22] 1262 6-9-4 **62** ....(p) SilvestreDeSousa 2 68
(Chris Dwyer) *hld up in tch in midfield: effrt u.p in 5th over 2f out: drvn and hdwy over 1f out: str chal ins fnl f: styd on wl to ld towards fin* **6/1**[3]

60-0 **2** nk **Thecornishbarron (IRE)**[26] 1201 4-9-7 **65** .... JackMitchell 3 70
(John Ryan) *chsd ldrs: wnt 3rd 3f out: rdn to chal over 1f out: led and edgd lft jst ins fnl f: hdd and no ex towards fin* **33/1**

2120 **3** 3 ½ **Toymaker**[5] 1654 9-8-11 **60** ....(tp) JosephineGordon(5) 5 57
(Phil McEntee) *chsd ldrs: wnt 2nd over 4f out: rdn and ev ch 2f out: led over 1f out: hdd jst ins fnl f: wknd fnl 100yds* **10/1**

-626 **4** 1 ¾ **Little Lord Nelson**[12] 1502 4-9-0 **65** ....(t) MillyNaseb(7) 7 58
(Stuart Williams) *in tch in midfield: effrt in 4th jst over 2f out: unable qck u.p over 1f out: edgd lft and styd on same pce ins fnl f* **9/2**[2]

234- **5** ½ **Titan Goddess**[150] 8044 4-9-2 **60** .... ShaneKelly 8 51
(Mike Murphy) *stdd s and dropped in bhd: hld up in last pair: effrt over 2f out: kpt on ins fnl f: no threat to ldrs* **16/1**

52- **6** 1 ¾ **County Wexford (IRE)**[255] 5444 5-9-7 **65** .... JimCrowley 4 52
(Miss Joey Ellis) *w ldrs tl led 5f out: rdn and hdd over 1f out: sn outpcd: wknd fnl f* **9/2**[2]

21 **7** 8 **Pick Your Battle**[3] 1696 4-9-13 **71** 6ex ....(t) RoystonFfrench 6 39
(Iain Jardine) *dwlt: nvr travelling wl in last pair: rdn over 2f out: wknd over 1f out* **6/4**[1]

-000 **8** 13 **Golden Highway (USA)**[15] 1416 4-8-11 **58** ....(tp) AlistairRawlinson(3) 1
(Michael Appleby) *led tl 5f out: u.p 3f out and sn lost pl: bhd over 1f out: eased ins fnl f* **16/1**

1m 40.17s (0.27) **Going Correction** +0.075s/f (Slow) — 8 Ran SP% **114.4**
Speed ratings (Par 101): **101,100,97,95,94 93,85,72**
CSF £163.84 CT £1929.78 TOTE £4.90: £1.70, £4.70, £4.00; EX 90.10 Trifecta £801.00.
Owner Mrs Shelley Dwyer **Bred** Sir Eric Parker **Trained** Newmarket, Suffolk

FOCUS
A modest handicap run at a steady pace.
T/Plt: £22.00 to a £1 stake. Pool: £56,231.05 - 1,858.44 winning tickets. T/Qpdt: £9.70 to a £1 stake. Pool: £5,354.22 - 408.24 winning tickets. **Steve Payne**

1748 LINGFIELD (L-H)
Thursday, April 28

OFFICIAL GOING: Polytrack: standard
Wind: Fresh, behind Weather: Fine but cloudy

1806 RUDRIDGE LTD MEDIAN AUCTION MAIDEN STKS — 1m 1y(P)
1:50 (1:50) (Class 6) 3-Y-O **£2,264** (£673; £336; £168) **Stalls** High

Form — RPR

5 **1** **London Glory**[36] 1036 3-9-5 0 .... GeorgeBaker 5 73+
(Chris Wall) *sn chsd ldng pair: pushed along 3f out: rdn to cl over 1f out: tk 2nd on inner fnl f: styd on to ld last 100yds* **5/2**[2]

334- **2** 1 ½ **Invigorate**[184] 7544 3-9-5 67 .... AdamKirby 2 69
(Harry Dunlop) *led: sent for home over 2f out: sltly wd bnd sn after: drvn and hdd last 100yds: nt qckn* **9/4**[1]

3 1 ¼ **Wasseem (IRE)** 3-9-5 0 ....(t) SilvestreDeSousa 3 66
(Simon Crisford) *pressed ldr: rdn over 2f out: one pce and lost 2nd fnl f* **3/1**[3]

004- **4** 4 ½ **Rebel Raiser**[239] 5992 3-9-5 72 ....(p) WilliamTwiston-Davies 1 55
(Richard Spencer) *in tch: rdn over 2f out: fnd little and btn over 1f out* **10/1**

5 1 **Isaak (FR)** 3-9-5 0 .... DavidProbert 6 53
(Andrew Balding) *s.i.s and pushed along in last pair early: shkn up over 2f out: wknd over 1f out* **8/1**

2-5 **6** 2 ½ **Ettie Hart (IRE)**[8] 1562 3-9-0 0 .... CharlesBishop 4 42
(Mick Channon) *t.k.h: hld up in last pair: shkn up over 2f out: sn lft bhd* **12/1**

1m 37.9s (-0.30) **Going Correction** -0.075s/f (Stan) — 6 Ran SP% **112.2**
Speed ratings (Par 96): **98,96,95,90,89 87**
CSF £8.56 TOTE £3.80: £2.10, £1.20; EX 9.80 Trifecta £24.60.
Owner Fung Lok Li **Bred** F L Li **Trained** Newmarket, Suffolk

FOCUS
Modest maiden form.

1807 RSM H'CAP — 1m 7f 169y(P)
2:20 (2:21) (Class 6) (0-60,60) 4-Y-O+ **£2,264** (£673; £336; £168) **Stalls** Low

Form — RPR

0443 **1** **Dynamo (IRE)**[2] 1748 5-8-0 **46** oh1 ....(t) StephanieJoannides(7) 11 54+
(Richard Hughes) *t.k.h: trckd ldng quartet after 5f: smooth prog over 2f out: pushed into ld 1f out: comf* **11/4**[2]

2-31 **2** 3 ¼ **Lorelei**[20] 1322 4-9-3 **60** .... MartinDwyer 4 64
(William Muir) *hld up in midfield: prog 3f out: rdn to press ldrs 2f out: styd on fnl f to take 2nd last stride* **9/4**[1]

3-60 **3** shd **Broughtons Berry (IRE)**[64] 695 5-8-8 **47** .... SilvestreDeSousa 10 51
(Willie Musson) *sn trckd ldng pair: wnt 2nd over 2f out: drvn to ld over 1f out: hdd 1f out: one pce and lost 2nd last stride* **8/1**[3]

2332 **4** 2 ¾ **What A Party (IRE)**[27] 1174 4-9-0 **57** ....(v) DavidProbert 3 58
(Gay Kelleway) *pressed ldr: led 3f out: drvn and hdd over 1f out: fdd ins fnl f* **10/1**

3240 **5** 6 **Peeps**[28] 1170 4-9-2 **59** ....(b) DarryllHolland 5 52
(Mark H Tompkins) *s.s: t.k.h: hld up in last pair: plenty to do 3f out: pushed along and prog over 2f out: rdn to take 5th fnl f: nvr on terms* **10/1**

/64- **6** 2 ¼ **Warrant Officer**[21] 5000 6-8-7 **46** oh1 .... LemosdeSouza 7 37
(Sheena West) *hld up in rr: rdn and struggling over 3f out: last 2f out: passed a few late on* **16/1**

450/ **7** nse **Double Dealites**[604] 6007 6-8-10 **49** .... JFEgan 6 40
(Jamie Poulton) *a in rr: rdn and struggling 5f out: n.d after* **16/1**

6000 **8** 1 ¼ **Opus Too (IRE)**[20] 1322 5-8-0 **46** oh1 ....(t) RhiainIngram(7) 2 35
(John Ryan) *led to 3f out: sn wknd* **66/1**

65-3 **9** 1 ½ **Crashing Thew Life**[27] 1174 6-8-11 **55** .... HarryPoulton(5) 8 42
(Sheena West) *wl in tch: rdn 3f out: steadily wknd after* **16/1**

0/0- **10** 2 ¼ **Kent Ragstone (USA)**[13] 8198 7-8-8 **52** ....(t[1]) EdwardGreatrex(5) 9 37
(Daniel Steele) *prog to chse ldrs after 6f: rdn 5f out: wknd over 3f out* **12/1**

006- **11** 1 ½ **Let's Confer**[184] 7537 7-8-7 **46** oh1 ....(p) JoeFanning 1 29
(Michael Attwater) *s.s: sn in tch in midfield: rdn 3f out: sn wknd* **33/1**

3m 26.03s (0.33) **Going Correction** -0.075s/f (Stan)
WFA 4 from 5yo+ 4lb — 11 Ran SP% **116.5**
Speed ratings (Par 101): **96,94,94,92,89 88,88,88,87,86 85**
CSF £9.21 CT £42.88 TOTE £3.40: £1.50, £1.20, £2.40; EX 8.80 Trifecta £51.30.
Owner Foxtrot NH Racing Partnership X **Bred** Colm McEvoy **Trained** Upper Lambourn, Berkshire

FOCUS
A moderate staying handicap.

1808 PREMIER SHOWFREIGHT H'CAP — 1m 2f (P)
2:50 (2:50) (Class 5) (0-75,75) 4-Y-O+ — **£2,911** (£866; £432) **Stalls** Low

Form — RPR

50-0 **1** **Inniscastle Lad**[12] 1502 4-8-11 **65**.........................(b) SilvestreDeSousa 2 — 71
(Ed Dunlop) *mde all: first one of the trio to be off the bridle 3f out: drvn and pressed 2f out: edgd rt over 1f out but kpt on wl* **5/1**[3]

2-52 **2** 2 ½ **Robins Pearl (FR)**[94] 332 4-9-7 **75**.................................... AdamKirby 3 — 76
(Harry Dunlop) *trckd wnr: moved up to chal over 2f out gng strly: hanging rt bnd sn after: rdn and fnd little after* **4/5**[1]

234- **3** ½ **China Girl (IND)**[161] 7906 4-9-0 **68**..........................[1] RichardKingscote 4 — 68
(William Knight) *awkward s: t.k.h: hld up in last: shkn up wl over 2f out and sn outpcd: tried to cl on inner over 1f out: hung rt fnl f and no rspnse* **15/8**[2]

2m 8.84s (2.24) **Going Correction** -0.075s/f (Stan) — **3** Ran SP% **107.0**
Speed ratings (Par 103): **88,86,85**
CSF £9.40 TOTE £3.80; EX 8.10 Trifecta £6.50.
Owner E A L Dunlop **Bred** G Doyle & Lord Margadale **Trained** Newmarket, Suffolk

FOCUS
There was an upset here, with the outsider of three dictating throughout in a slowly run race. It's hard to be positive about this.

1809 HASLEMERE BUILDING COMPANY H'CAP — 7f 1y(P)
3:20 (3:22) (Class 4) (0-85,85) 3-Y-O — **£4,690** (£1,395; £697; £348) **Stalls** Low

Form — RPR

-416 **1** **Suqoor**[14] 1442 3-9-5 **83**.. SilvestreDeSousa 8 — 93+
(Chris Dwyer) *t.k.h early: mde all: rdn clr over 1f out: in n.d fnl f* **7/2**[1]

15- **2** 2 **Shaiyem (IRE)**[236] 6090 3-9-0 **78**.................................... FrankieDettori 3 — 80+
(Richard Hannon) *hld up in midfield: shkn up on inner 2f out: prog over 1f out: tk 2nd ins fnl f: no ch to threaten wnr* **5/1**[2]

210- **3** ½ **Barleysugar (IRE)**[201] 7112 3-9-7 **85**.................................... PatDobbs 2 — 86+
(Sir Michael Stoute) *hld up towards rr: effrt on outer 2f out: rdn over 1f out: r.o to take 3rd nr fin: nvr nr to chal* **7/2**[1]

02-1 **4** ¾ **Ice Age (IRE)**[33] 1091 3-9-1 **79**.................................... RobertWinston 4 — 78
(Eve Johnson Houghton) *trckd ldrs: rdn 2f out: tk 2nd briefly jst ins fnl f: fdd nr fin* **7/1**[3]

5123 **5** 1 ¼ **Inaam (IRE)**[30] 1137 3-8-9 **73**.................................... GeorgeChaloner 5 — 69
(Richard Fahey) *t.k.h: trckd ldng pair 1/2-way: rdn 2f out: chal for a pl over 1f out: wknd fnl f* **12/1**

10- **6** shd **Experto Crede (IRE)**[294] 4071 3-9-7 **85**.......................... GeorgeBaker 9 — 80+
(Ed Walker) *stdd s: hld up in last: hanging sltly lft whn rdn over 1f out: r.o fnl f: no ch to be involved* **5/1**[2]

02-3 **7** 6 **Chicago School (IRE)**[30] 1132 3-8-8 **72**......................(b) JoeFanning 10 — 51
(Mark Johnston) *t.k.h: chsd wnr: outpcd wl over 1f out: lost 2nd jst ins fnl f: wknd rapidly* **20/1**

010- **8** 2 **English Hero**[187] 7460 3-8-13 **77**.............................. RichardKingscote 7 — 51
(William Knight) *hld up in last pair: rdn and no prog 2f out: sn bhd* **25/1**

203- **9** 4 ½ **Cautious Optimism**[180] 7637 3-8-12 **76**......................(p) MartinDwyer 6 — 38
(William Muir) *t.k.h: trckd ldng pair to 1/2-way: wknd over 2f out* **12/1**

1m 23.49s (-1.31) **Going Correction** -0.075s/f (Stan) — **9** Ran SP% **114.3**
Speed ratings (Par 100): **104,101,101,100,98 98,91,89,84**
CSF £20.71 CT £64.77 TOTE £4.10: £1.60, £2.10, £1.90; EX 25.10 Trifecta £58.10.
Owner P Venner **Bred** P And Mrs A G Venner **Trained** Newmarket, Suffolk

FOCUS
This looked an interesting handicap and it should throw up a winner or two. It has been rated on the positive side.

1810 OYSTER PARTNERSHIP H'CAP — 1m 4f (P)
3:55 (3:55) (Class 5) (0-70,67) 4-Y-O+ — **£2,911** (£866; £432; £216) **Stalls** Low

Form — RPR

15-3 **1** **Speculator**[19] 1340 4-9-4 **65**.. ShaneKelly 3 — 74+
(David Menuisier) *trckd ldrs: pushed along 2f out: produced to ld jst ins fnl f: pushed clr* **7/4**[1]

02-5 **2** 1 ¼ **Harlestone Hopes**[99] 261 4-8-11 **65**..........................(p) HarryBurns(7) 6 — 70
(Ed Dunlop) *trckd ldr 3f: styd cl up: waiting for a gap 2f out: swtchd to inner and rdn over 1f out: styd on to take 2nd ins fnl f: nt pce to threaten* **5/1**[3]

44-2 **3** nk **Ayr Of Elegance**[22] 1266 4-9-6 **67**.................... WilliamTwiston-Davies 4 — 71
(Philip Hide) *led 1f: slt stumble over 9f out: urged along over 4f out: nt gng as wl as those in front over 2f out: drvn and styd on wl fnl f to take 3rd last strides* **5/1**[3]

-251 **4** hd **Sandy Cove**[43] 949 5-9-4 **67**.. RyanTate(3) 5 — 71
(James Eustace) *trckd ldr after 3f: chal 3f out: sn rdn: tk narrow ld over 1f out: hdd and nt qckn jst ins fnl f* **3/1**[2]

525- **5** 3 ¾ **Glens Wobbly**[141] 8159 8-8-12 **58**.................................... DarryllHolland 8 — 56
(Jonathan Geake) *pushed up to ld after 1f: jnd and rdn 3f out: kpt on tl hdd over 1f out: wknd fnl f* **12/1**

000- **6** 2 ¼ **Mercy Me**[193] 7308 4-9-4 **65**.. RyanPowell 7 — 59
(John Ryan) *hld up in last pair: rdn and no prog over 2f out: wl btn over 1f out* **12/1**

0605 **7** hd **Maria's Choice (IRE)**[2] 1751 7-9-4 **64**.......................... TimmyMurphy 2 — 58
(Jim Best) *hld up in last pair: detached in last over 2f out and nudged along: reminder fnl f: nvr involved* **33/1**

2m 31.43s (-1.57) **Going Correction** -0.075s/f (Stan)
WFA 4 from 5yo+ 1lb — **7** Ran SP% **113.0**
Speed ratings (Par 103): **102,101,100,100,98 96,96**
CSF £10.69 CT £35.64 TOTE £2.40: £1.50, £3.00; EX 11.50 Trifecta £47.10.
Owner Gail Brown Racing (VI) **Bred** Old Mill Stud **Trained** Pulborough, W Sussex

FOCUS
A comfortable success for the favourite in this modest handicap. The form is set around the second and third.

1811 CRYSTAL PALACE FOOTBALL CLUB FILLIES' H'CAP — 6f 1y(P)
4:30 (4:30) (Class 5) (0-70,71) 4-Y-O+ — **£2,911** (£866; £432; £216) **Stalls** Low

Form — RPR

-211 **1** **Baileys Mirage (FR)**[2] 1754 5-9-10 **71** 6ex...........(b) SilvestreDeSousa 2 — 82
(Chris Dwyer) *pressed ldr: led wl over 1f out: drvn and styd on wl fnl f* **5/4**[1]

4213 **2** 1 ¼ **Invade (IRE)**[24] 1237 4-9-1 **67**......................................(t) AaronJones(5) 4 — 73
(Stuart Williams) *hld up disputing 4th: shkn up over 2f out: drvn and prog to go 2nd fnl f: r.o but nvr able to chal* **9/4**[2]

06-6 **3** 2 **Refuse Colette (IRE)**[28] 1159 7-9-4 **65**......................(v) WilliamCarson 1 — 65
(Mick Quinn) *pushed up to chse ldng pair: drvn over 2f out: n.m.r on inner over 1f out: disp 2nd briefly sn after: one pce* **7/1**[3]

-450 **4** 3 ¾ **Light Rose (IRE)**[19] 1340 6-8-10 **62**.............................. DavidParkes(5) 6 — 50
(Jeremy Gask) *hld up in last: wl off the pce over 2f out: no ch whn drvn over 1f out: kpt on to take 4th nr fin: nvr involved* **14/1**

-002 **5** ½ **Pucon**[29] 1150 7-9-7 **68**..(p) LiamKeniry 3 — 54
(Roger Teal) *racd freely: led: rdn and hdd wl over 1f out: lost 2nd and wknd fnl f* **10/1**

500- **6** 1 **Angel Flores (IRE)**[225] 6435 5-9-1 **62**.............................. OisinMurphy 5 — 45
(Lee Carter) *hld up disputing 4th: shkn up over 2f out: no prog and wl btn after* **12/1**

1m 10.52s (-1.38) **Going Correction** -0.075s/f (Stan) — **6** Ran SP% **111.2**
Speed ratings (Par 100): **106,104,101,96,96 94**
CSF £4.13 TOTE £2.10: £1.10, £2.10; EX 4.10 Trifecta £12.60.
Owner G R Bailey Ltd (Baileys Horse Feeds) **Bred** Gr Baileys Ltd **Trained** Newmarket, Suffolk

FOCUS
An ordinary fillies' contest run at a sound pace.Doubts over the field bar the 1-2.

1812 DAVE SACKETT INTERACTIVE 3-Y-O FILLIES' H'CAP — 6f 1y(P)
5:05 (5:05) (Class 4) (0-80,80) 3-Y-O — **£4,690** (£1,395; £697; £348) **Stalls** Low

Form — RPR

31- **1** **Exist**[191] 7360 3-9-5 78.. RobertHavlin 4 — 94+
(John Gosden) *mde all: shkn up and drew clr over 1f out: readily* **11/8**[1]

100- **2** 4 **Hawatif (IRE)**[271] 4877 3-9-7 80.. JoeFanning 7 — 81+
(Mark Johnston) *hld up in last pair: pushed along over 2f out: stl last 1f out and rdn: styd on to take 2nd last strides* **12/1**

520- **3** nk **Cherry Kool**[208] 6922 3-9-2 75.. SeanLevey 1 — 75
(Stuart Williams) *trckd ldng pair: rdn to chse wnr wl over 1f out: sn lft bhd: lost 2nd last strides* **7/2**[2]

2264 **4** ½ **Silver Springs (IRE)**[27] 1176 3-8-7 69.......................... PhilipPrince(3) 6 — 67
(David Evans) *chsd wnr: tried to chal over 2f out: lost 2nd wl over 1f out: outpcd after* **16/1**

55-1 **5** nse **Pusey's Secret**[13] 1451 3-9-2 78.......................... MichaelJMMurphy(3) 2 — 76
(John Gallagher) *hld up in last pair: pushed along over 2f out: rdn and no ch w wnr over 1f out but kpt on fnl f* **7/2**[2]

10- **6** shd **Serradura (IRE)**[220] 6594 3-9-0 73.................................... DarryllHolland 5 — 71
(Charles Hills) *t.k.h early: hld up in tch: shkn up and outpcd wl over 1f out: kpt on same pce fnl f* **8/1**[3]

1m 11.67s (-0.23) **Going Correction** -0.075s/f (Stan) — **6** Ran SP% **111.2**
Speed ratings (Par 97): **98,92,92,91,91 91**
CSF £18.74 CT £46.72 TOTE £1.90: £1.30, £4.20; EX 9.30 Trifecta £42.10.
Owner Cheveley Park Stud **Bred** Whitsbury Manor Stud **Trained** Newmarket, Suffolk

FOCUS
They finished in a heap behind the easy winner in this fillies' sprint handicap. She impressed, but the time was relatively slow.
T/Plt: £37.90 to a £1 stake. Pool: £57,635.03 - 1,108.81 winning tickets. T/Qpdt: £21.70 to a £1 stake. Pool: £4,068.35- 138.10 winning tickets. **Jonathan Neesom**

1377 REDCAR (L-H)
Thursday, April 28

OFFICIAL GOING: Soft (good to soft in places; 6.8)
Wind: fresh 1/2 behind Weather: overcast, cold, rain last 2

1813 RACING UK ANYWHERE (S) STKS — 5f
2:05 (2:06) (Class 6) 2-Y-O — **£2,385** (£704; £352) **Stalls** Centre

Form — RPR

1 **Baltic Beau** 2-8-12 0.. TonyHamilton 2 — 55+
(Richard Fahey) *dwlt: drvn to sn chse ldrs: outpcd over 2f out: styd on to ld 1f out: drvn out* **8/11**[1]

2 ¾ **Trust The Indian** 2-8-7 0.. NathanEvans(5) 3 — 48
(Bill Turner) *wnt rt s: chsd ldrs: rdn 2f out: kpt on same pce last 150yds* **9/2**[2]

0 **3** shd **Eid Rose**[33] 1087 2-8-7 0.. ShaneGray 5 — 43+
(Kevin Ryan) *chsd ldrs: drvn and outpcd over 2f out: styd on fnl f: gng on at fin* **8/1**[3]

60 **4** 2 ¼ **The Fossil**[13] 1454 2-8-12 0..(v) LiamJones 6 — 40
(Tom Dascombe) *led: edgd lft and hdd 1f out: wknd last 100yds* **16/1**

56 **5** 1 ¾ **To Have A Dream (IRE)**[10] 1527 2-8-7 0....................(b[1]) JoeyHaynes 1 — 29
(J S Moore) *swvd bdly lft s and sn reminders: hdwy 2f out: sn chsng ldrs: wknd fnl f* **14/1**

0 **6** 6 **Paisley Abbey**[26] 1199 2-8-12 0..(p) GrahamLee 4 — 12
(Paul Midgley) *hmpd s: in rr: sme hdwy 2f out: lost pl appr fnl f* **9/1**

1m 2.85s (4.25) **Going Correction** +0.475s/f (Yiel) — **6** Ran SP% **109.7**
Speed ratings (Par 90): **85,83,83,80,77 67**
CSF £4.02 TOTE £1.60: £1.50, £1.60; EX 3.80 Trifecta £15.10.There was no bid for the winner. Trust The Indian was the subject of a friendly claim.
Owner Nick Bradley Racing 11 **Bred** Mrs K J Stephens **Trained** Musley Bank, N Yorks

FOCUS
Joey Haynes said of the ground: "It's on the easy side, they are getting their toe in", while Shane Gray and Tony Hamilton said: "It is a bit dead." Ordinary selling form, the well-backed newcomer just doing enough.

1814 ALLAN BROWN MEMORIAL MAIDEN FILLIES' STKS — 6f
2:35 (2:36) (Class 5) 3-Y-O+ — **£2,911** (£866; £432; £216) **Stalls** Centre

Form — RPR

025- **1** **Cersei**[180] 7628 3-9-0 77.. JamieSpencer 10 — 71+
(David Simcock) *trckd ldrs: led appr fnl f: pushed out: readily* **15/8**[1]

2 3 ½ **Brockholes** 3-9-0 0.. TonyHamilton 11 — 60
(Richard Fahey) *sn chsng ldrs: kpt on fnl f: tk modest 2nd nr fin* **9/1**[3]

3 ½ **Anna Barkova (IRE)** 3-9-0 0.. JoeyHaynes 4 — 59
(K R Burke) *w ldrs: drvn over 2f out: hung lft over 1f out: kpt on same pce* **14/1**

4 1 ¾ **Table Manners** 4-9-8 0.. MissEmmaSayer(3) 1 — 56
(Wilf Storey) *dwlt: hdwy into midfield over 3f out: outpcd over 1f out: kpt on wl last 150yds* **66/1**

606- **5** nk **Tweetheart**[255] 5438 3-8-9 60......................................(p) PhilDennis(5) 6 — 52
(Ron Barr) *w ldrs: t.k.h: kpt on one pce fnl f* **66/1**

0-3 **6** 1 **Al Sailiyah (IRE)**[19] 1337 3-9-0 0.. KieranO'Neill 8 — 49
(Richard Hannon) *led: hdd appr fnl f: wknd last 150yds* **4/1**[2]

0 **7** ¾ **Shahaama**[15] 1414 3-9-0 0.. GrahamLee 12 — 46
(Mick Channon) *hld up in rr: effrt over 2f out: chsng ldrs over 1f out: one pce* **4/1**[2]

3 **8** 1 **Mary E**[12] 1490 3-8-9 0..(b) CallumShepherd(5) 9 — 43
(Brian Ellison) *dwlt: sn drvn along in rr: kpt on over 1f out: nvr a factor* **20/1**

0 **9** *nk* **Kyllini**[8] 1562 3-8-11 0.. JacobButterfield(3) 2 42
(Marjorie Fife) *chsd ldrs: one pce fnl 2f* **100/1**

50 **10** *3 ¾* **High On Light**[8] 1562 3-9-0 0.. DavidAllan 3 30
(Tim Easterby) *s.i.s: in rr: drvn over 2f out: sn bhd* **25/1**

11 *½* **Eisha Baby** 3-8-7 0.. HollieDoyle(7) 7 29
(Richard Hannon) *s.v.s: sn drvn along in rr: bhd fnl 2f* **9/1**[3]

1m 14.72s (2.92) **Going Correction** +0.475s/f (Yiel)
WFA 3 from 4yo+ 11lb **11** Ran SP% **114.0**
Speed ratings (Par 100): **99,94,93,91,90 89,88,87,86,81 81**
CSF £18.53 TOTE £2.70: £1.10, £2.50, £5.00; EX 17.70 Trifecta £109.60.
Owner Al Asayl Bloodstock Ltd **Bred** Al Asayl Bloodstock Ltd **Trained** Newmarket, Suffolk

FOCUS
Ordinary fillies' maiden form, the 77-rated favourite winning with plenty in hand. She's rated to form, but the race lacked depth.

1815 RACING UK PROFITS RETURNED TO RACING MAIDEN AUCTION STKS 7f
3:05 (3:05) (Class 6) 3-Y-O **£2,385** (£704; £352) **Stalls** Centre

Form RPR
6-3 **1** **King Of Naples**[22] 1256 3-8-12 0.............................. GeorgeWood(7) 2 91+
(James Fanshawe) *trckd ldrs: shkn up to ld over 1f out: drew rt away fnl 150yds* **5/2**[2]

0 **2** *9* **Corroyer (IRE)**[34] 1079 3-9-5 0.. PhillipMakin 6 68
(John Quinn) *dwlt: sn trcking ldrs: drvn over 2f out: edgd lft over 1f out: kpt on to take modest 2nd last 100yds* **6/1**

5-3 **3** *2 ¾* **Lajatico**[29] 1146 3-9-0 0.. FrederikTylicki 1 56
(Ed Vaughan) *w ldr: effrt 2f out: kpt on same pce appr fnl f* **2/1**[1]

04- **4** *1 ½* **Muroor**[198] 7179 3-9-5 0.. DanielTudhope 5 57
(David O'Meara) *led: qcknd pce over 2f out: hdd appr fnl f: fdd clsng stages* **11/4**[3]

0-3 **5** *9* **Oscar Hughes (IRE)**[20] 1324 3-9-5 0.......................... ConnorBeasley 4 35
(Julie Camacho) *trckd ldrs: t.k.h: drvn 3f out: sn lost pl and bhd* **20/1**

6 *1 ½* **Connemera Queen** 3-9-0 0.. RoystonFfrench 9 26
(Tracy Waggott) *dwlt: sn trcking ldrs: drvn over 2f out: sn lost pl and bhd* **50/1**

1m 29.49s (4.99) **Going Correction** +0.475s/f (Yiel) **6** Ran SP% **109.6**
Speed ratings (Par 96): **90,79,76,74,64 62**
CSF £16.56 TOTE £3.40: £2.10, £4.80; EX 15.70 Trifecta £37.20.
Owner P S Ryan **Bred** Meon Valley Stud **Trained** Newmarket, Suffolk

FOCUS
Modest maiden form but quite a taking effort by the winner, although there are suspicions this fell apart and doubts over the reliability of the form.

1816 RACINGUK.COM/ANYWHERE: 3 DEVICES, 1 PRICE H'CAP 1m 1f
3:35 (3:35) (Class 5) (0-70,70) 3-Y-O **£2,911** (£866; £432; £216) **Stalls** Low

Form RPR
20- **1** **Maulesden May (IRE)**[192] 7336 3-9-5 **68**.......................... PhillipMakin 2 72
(Keith Dalgleish) *sn chsng ldr: drvn upsides over 2f out: styd on to ld clsng stages* **9/1**

3341 **2** *nk* **Albert Boy (IRE)**[17] 1379 3-9-7 **70**.............................. DanielTudhope 6 73
(Scott Dixon) *led: drvn over 2f out: hdd and no ex clsng stages* **11/4**[1]

5-14 **3** *1 ¼* **Specialv (IRE)**[17] 1381 3-9-2 **65**.. DaleSwift 3 65
(Brian Ellison) *hld up towards rr: t.k.h: hdwy on ins to chse ldrs over 2f out: upsides 150yds out: kpt on same pce* **5/1**[3]

4546 **4** *nk* **Frap**[12] 1486 3-8-9 **58**.. TonyHamilton 8 59+
(Richard Fahey) *hld up in last: hdwy over 3f out: trcking ldrs and nt clr run fr 2 out: swtchd rt last 75yds: gng on at fin* **10/1**

00-6 **5** *5* **Ice Alert (IRE)**[115] 40 3-9-4 **67**..(t) LiamJones 4 55
(Marco Botti) *mid-div: sn pushed along: hdwy over 2f out: sn chsng ldrs: wknd fnl 150yds* **11/1**

60-3 **6** *1* **Girl With A Pearl (IRE)**[17] 1389 3-8-13 **62**.......................... GrahamLee 1 48
(Ed Dunlop) *dwlt: sn trcking ldrs: drvn over 4f out: wknd fnl 150yds* **7/2**[2]

30-2 **7** *1 ¾* **Zahrat Narjis**[15] 1409 3-8-13 **69**.............................. AdamMcNamara(7) 5 51
(Richard Fahey) *hld up towards rr: effrt over 3f out: hdwy to chse ldrs over 2f out: wknd fnl f* **7/2**[2]

2m 1.32s (8.32) **Going Correction** +0.875s/f (Soft) **7** Ran SP% **115.2**
Speed ratings (Par 98): **98,97,96,96,91 91,89**
CSF £34.49 CT £140.01 TOTE £11.80: £4.80, £2.60; EX 57.20 Trifecta £176.30.
Owner The County Set (Two) **Bred** Yeomanstown Stud **Trained** Carluke, S Lanarks

FOCUS
This looked an open 3yo handicap and so it proved, several having their chance late on and it going to one of the outsiders. The frist two were always prominent off a modest pace.

1817 RACING UK PROFITS RETURNED TO RACING H'CAP 7f
4:10 (4:10) (Class 4) (0-85,81) 3-Y-O+ **£6,469** (£1,925; £962; £481) **Stalls** Centre

Form RPR
62-4 **1** **Jordan Sport**[34] 1079 3-8-9 **75**.. JamieSpencer 8 84+
(Richard Fahey) *stdd and swtchd lft s: t.k.h in rr: nt clr run and swtchd lft over 1f out: led on bit 1f out: edgd rt: pushed out: v comf* **3/1**[2]

414- **2** *1 ¼* **Slemy (IRE)**[264] 5165 5-9-7 **74**.. JamesSullivan 1 80
(Ruth Carr) *t.k.h in rr: stdy hdwy 2f out: chsd wnr last 150yds: no imp* **10/1**[3]

0/1 **3** *nk* **Dandyleekie (IRE)**[14] 1444 4-9-12 **79**.......................... DanielTudhope 7 84
(David O'Meara) *trckd ldrs: effrt over 2f out: kpt on to take 3rd last 100yds* **5/2**[1]

15-1 **4** *2 ¼* **Galesburg (IRE)**[15] 1409 3-9-1 **81**.. FrannyNorton 5 75
(Mark Johnston) *led 1f: w ldrs: one pce fnl f* **3/1**[2]

0220 **5** *nk* **Eutropius (IRE)**[31] 1122 7-10-0 **81**.. NeilFarley 2 80
(Alan Swinbank) *chsd ldrs: one pce fnl f* **12/1**

5 **6** *¾* **Clon Rocket (IRE)**[12] 1485 3-8-9 **75**.............................. RoystonFfrench 4 67
(John Holt) *w ldrs: drvn to ld over 2f out: hdd 1f out: one pce* **14/1**

160- **7** *10* **Muqarred (USA)**[295] 4015 4-9-11 **78**.......................... DougieCostello 3 49
(David Loughnane) *trckd ldrs: drvn over 2f out: lost pl over 1f out: bhd whn eased clsng stages* **33/1**

301- **8** *17* **Dutch Breeze**[194] 7288 5-9-11 **78**..(p) DavidAllan 6 4
(Tim Easterby) *restless in stalls: t.k.h: hdwy to ld after 1f: hdd over 2f out: sn lost pl: bhd whn heavily eased fnl f* **12/1**

1m 28.4s (3.90) **Going Correction** +0.475s/f (Yiel)
WFA 3 from 4yo+ 13lb **8** Ran SP% **112.7**
Speed ratings (Par 105): **96,94,94,91,91 90,79,59**
CSF £31.62 CT £84.27 TOTE £4.10: £1.60, £1.90, £1.40; EX 31.90 Trifecta £95.70.
Owner Jaber Abdullah **Bred** Rabbah Bloodstock Limited **Trained** Musley Bank, N Yorks

FOCUS
A fair handicap and no surprise to see it go to one of the 3yos. The winner has the potential to rate higher.

1818 WIN A VIP DAY @ REDCARRACING.CO.UK CLAIMING STKS 6f
4:45 (4:45) (Class 6) 3-Y-O+ **£2,385** (£704; £352) **Stalls** Centre

Form RPR
05-1 **1** **Evanescent (IRE)**[22] 1251 7-9-9 82.. PhillipMakin 7 83
(John Quinn) *led 1f: chsd ldrs: styd on fnl f: led nr fin* **5/2**[1]

6-61 **2** *nk* **Layla's Hero (IRE)**[16] 1401 9-9-7 78..........................(v) PaulMulrennan 2 80
(David Nicholls) *trckd ldrs: led over 1f out: hdd and no ex nr fin* **15/2**

004- **3** *3 ¾* **Red Refraction (IRE)**[299] 3898 6-9-11 82.......................... KieranO'Neill 6 73
(Richard Hannon) *chsd ldrs: effrt over 2f out: one pce appr fnl f* **4/1**[3]

4553 **4** *nse* **Llewellyn**[12] 1488 8-9-6 71..(b) DanielTudhope 3 68
(Declan Carroll) *t.k.h: led after 1f: hdd over 1f out: kpt on one pce* **6/1**

203- **5** *1 ¾* **Victoire De Lyphar (IRE)**[218] 6656 9-9-5 75.............(e) JamesSullivan 5 61
(Ruth Carr) *chsd ldrs: drvn and hung lft over 2f out: sn racing alone far side: wknd fnl f* **13/2**

3233 **6** *¾* **Moonlight Venture**[5] 1625 5-9-7 77..(b) DavidNolan 4 61
(Conor Dore) *chsd ldrs: drvn over 2f out: one pce* **7/2**[2]

1m 13.7s (1.90) **Going Correction** +0.475s/f (Yiel) **6** Ran SP% **110.2**
Speed ratings (Par 101): **106,105,100,100,98 97**
CSF £20.42 TOTE £3.40: £1.70, £4.50; EX 16.90 Trifecta £65.10.Evanescent was claimed by Mr A. Carroll for £10,000.
Owner Mrs S Quinn **Bred** Oliver Donlon **Trained** Settrington, N Yorks

FOCUS
The front pair came away late on in what was a reasonable little claimer.

1819 DOWNLOAD YOUR RACING UK IPAD APP H'CAP 1m
5:20 (5:24) (Class 6) (0-60,66) 3-Y-O **£2,385** (£704; £352) **Stalls** Centre

Form RPR
666- **1** **Intalza (IRE)**[177] 7684 3-8-5 **47**..(p) JoeDoyle(3) 2 55
(Michael Herrington) *trckd ldrs: 2nd over 1f out: styd on to ld last 100yds: drvn out* **16/1**

0400 **2** *2* **Mikro Polemistis (IRE)**[12] 1484 3-8-3 **47** ow1.... CallumShepherd(5) 11 51
(Brian Ellison) *w ldrs: drvn to ld over 2f out: hdd and no ex last 100yds* **20/1**

055- **3** *6* **Saxon Gold (IRE)**[218] 6654 3-9-7 **60**.. PhillipMakin 8 50+
(John Davies) *wnt lft s: t.k.h in rr: hdwy over 2f out: kpt on to take modest 3rd towards fin* **15/2**[3]

36-4 **4** *¾* **The Excel Queen (IRE)**[17] 1379 3-9-5 **58**.......................... BarryMcHugh 4 47
(Tony Coyle) *led 1f: chsd ldrs: one pce appr fnl f* **12/1**

60-0 **5** *2 ½* **Citadel**[31] 1126 3-8-2 **46** oh1..(p) NathanEvans(5) 6 29
(John Wainwright) *chsd ldrs: drvn over 2f out: fdd over 1f out* **25/1**

0-30 **6** *hd* **Mr Lucas (IRE)**[8] 1564 3-8-7 **46** oh1..........................(b[1]) ConnorBeasley 10 29
(Peter Niven) *t.k.h: led after 1f: hdd over 2f out: hung rt and wknd fnl f* **20/1**

4121 **7** *¾* **Footlight**[8] 1564 3-9-6 **66** 6ex.. AdamMcNamara(7) 9 47
(Richard Fahey) *trckd ldrs: drvn over 2f out: edgd lft and wknd over 1f out* **7/4**[1]

6052 **8** *19* **Stone Quercus (IRE)**[12] 1484 3-9-5 **58**..........................(b) TomEaves 7
(James Given) *dwlt: t.k.h: hdwy to trck ldrs after 2f: drvn over 2f out: sn wknd: bhd whn heavily eased clsng stages* **7/2**[2]

000- **9** *9* **Rokerby Hall**[185] 7515 3-9-4 **57**..(p) DavidAllan 3
(Tim Easterby) *chsd ldrs: drvn over 3f out: lost pl 2f out: bhd whn heavily eased clsng stages* **10/1**

1m 45.7s (9.10) **Going Correction** +0.475s/f (Yiel) **9** Ran SP% **106.4**
Speed ratings (Par 96): **73,71,65,64,61 61,60,41,32**
CSF £256.57 CT £2157.10 TOTE £16.20: £3.60, £6.00, £1.60; EX 274.70 Trifecta £2099.30.
Owner K Fitzsimons **Bred** Patrick Ryan **Trained** Cold Kirby, N Yorks
■ Great Colaci was withdrawn. Price at time of withdrawal 10/1. Rule 4 applies to all bets - deduction 5p in the pound.

FOCUS
Two of the outsiders came clear in this moderate handicap.
T/Jkpt: Not won. T/Plt: £57.10 to a £1 stake. Pool: £61,075.01 -780.54 winning tickets. T/Qpdt: £24.50 to a £1 stake. Pool: £4,331.74 - 130.50 winning tickets. **Walter Glynn**

1820- 1821a (Foreign Racing) - See Raceform Interactive

1687 CHANTILLY (R-H)
Thursday, April 28

OFFICIAL GOING: Turf: soft; polytrack: standard

1822a PRIX ALLEZ FRANCE (GROUP 3) (4YO+ FILLIES & MARES) (TURF) 1m 2f
2:20 (12:00) 4-Y-O+ **£29,411** (£11,764; £8,823; £5,882; £2,941)

RPR
1 **Marypop (FR)**[25] 1232 4-8-8 0.. MaximeGuyon 2 103
(Mme Pia Brandt, France) *hld up in midfield: rowed along and hdwy whn bmpd wkng rival gng between horses 2f out: styd on to chse ldrs over 1f out: rdn and qcknd to ld fnl 1/2f: readily* **18/5**[2]

2 *¾* **Nymeria (GER)**[32] 4-8-10 0.. AndreasSuborics 12 103
(Waldemar Hickst, Germany) *w.w in rr: rdn and hdwy whn nt clr run 2f out and again appr 1f out: r.o u.p fnl f: nvr quite on terms w wnr* **11/1**

3 *shd* **Contribution**[17] 4-8-8 0.. VincentCheminaud 3 101
(A Fabre, France) *w.w in midfield on inner: hdwy on rail under 2f out: chsd ldng pair over 1f out: rdn to mount chal 150yds out: sn no ex: lost 2nd cl home* **12/1**

4 *1 ¼* **Beautiful Heroine (IRE)**[18] 1375 5-9-1 0............ ChristopheSoumillon 7 106
(F-H Graffard, France) *dwlt: w.w in fnl pair: tk clsr order sn after 1/2-way: rdn and styd on fnl f: nt pce to get on terms* **23/5**[3]

5 *nk* **Thank You Bye Bye (FR)**[13] 4-8-8 0.............................. MlleIsisMagnin 6 98
(J-P Gauvin, France) *a cl up: rdn to chse ldr 2f out: styd on to ld 1 1/2f out: hdd fnl half-f: no ex* **35/1**

6 *¾* **Ame Bleue**[25] 1232 4-8-10 0.. Pierre-CharlesBoudot 4 98
(A Fabre, France) *settled towards rr: clsd fr 2 1/2f out: rdn and n.m.r over 1f out: styd on at same pce: nvr in contention* **20/1**

7 *½* **Amazona (GER)**[31] 4-8-8 0.. CristianDemuro 11 95
(Jean-Pierre Carvalho, Germany) *led: rdn and hdd 1 1/2f out: one pce u.p fnl f* **14/1**

8 *2* **Sassella (IRE)**[160] 7935 4-8-8 0.. MickaelBarzalona 10 91
(A Fabre, France) *chsd ldng trio: hrd rdn and nt qckn wl over 1 1/2f out: sn btn* **23/1**

9 ½ **Sainte Amarante (FR)**[222] 6555 4-8-10 0.................... GregoryBenoist 8 92
(Yves de Nicolay, France) *hld up towards rr: last and rdn 2f out: short-lived effrt under 1 1/2f out: nvr in contention* **24/1**

10 ½ **We Are (IRE)**[207] 6969 5-8-10 0.. ThierryJarnet 1 91
(F Head, France) *trckd ldr on inner: rdn and nt qckn 2f out: sn wknd* **19/10**[1]

11 1 **Si Luna (GER)**[32] 7-9-1 0... OlivierPeslier 9 94
(W Mongil, Germany) *settled towards rr: moved into midfield bef 1/2-way: shkn up and no imp whn bmpd under 2f out: sn btn* **14/1**

12 ½ **Weltmacht**[18] 1376 5-8-8 0.................................... IoritzMendizabal 5 86
(Markus Klug, Germany) *t.k.h: hld up in midfield on outer: rdn and no hdwy wl over 2f out: wkng whn bmpd 2f out and cannoned into anther rival* **75/1**

2m 4.27s (-0.53) 12 Ran SP% **120.5**
WIN (incl. 1 euro stake): 4.60. PLACES: 1.80, 3.60, 3.40. DF: 24.80. SF: 46.20.
Owner Wood Hall Stud Limited **Bred** A Haddad **Trained** France

1823 - (Foreign Racing) - See Raceform Interactive

CHEPSTOW (L-H)

Friday, April 29

OFFICIAL GOING: Good to soft (7.8)
Wind: moderate half behind Weather: sunny, shower race 1

1824 COUNTY MARQUEES H'CAP 1m 4f 23y
1:45 (1:46) (Class 5) (0-75,75) 4-Y-O+ **£4,851** (£1,443; £721; £360) **Stalls** Low

Form RPR

0056 **1** **Yul Finegold (IRE)**[18] 1391 6-9-2 **70**................................ OisinMurphy 7 79
(Conor Dore) *mde all: clr after 3f: 12 l up 1/2-way: only 4 l ahd and shkn up 3f out: drvn and styd on wl fnl 2f* **8/1**

055- **2** 1 ¾ **Opera Lad (IRE)**[230] 6310 4-9-4 **73**................................... DavidProbert 4 79
(Andrew Balding) *chsd ldrs: rdn to chse wnr 2f out: styd on u.p but a being hld* **7/2**[2]

5 **3** 2 **Forecast**[23] 1256 4-8-3 **61** oh1...................................... TomMarquand[(3)] 8 64
(Martin Keighley) *hld up in 4th: rdn over 3f out: wnt 3rd 1f out: kpt on same pce* **20/1**

2132 **4** 2 ½ **Star Ascending (IRE)**[17] 1399 4-8-11 **66**.......................... TomQueally 1 65
(Jennie Candlish) *hld up: hmpd after 1f: rdn 4f out: one pce fnl 2f* **3/1**[1]

0-13 **5** shd **Kawartha**[25] 1236 4-8-12 **67**.............................. WilliamTwiston-Davies 2 66
(Robert Stephens) *chsd wnr: 12 l down in 2nd 1/2-way: rdn 3f out: unable qck: lost 2nd 2f out: grad wknd* **5/1**[3]

3-34 **6** 32 **Karam Albaari (IRE)**[28] 1177 8-9-7 **75**................................... FMBerry 6 60
(J R Jenkins) *dwlt: sltly hmpd after 1f: sn clsd and in tch w main bunch: rdn 4f out: no further imp: wknd over 1f out: eased: t.o* **11/1**

354- **F** **May Be Some Time**[46] 6300 8-8-12 **66**..............................(t) PatDobbs 3
(Stuart Kittow) *hld up: fell fatally after 1f* **3/1**[1]

2m 41.69s (2.69) **Going Correction** +0.15s/f (Good)
WFA 4 from 6yo+ 1lb 7 Ran SP% **113.1**
Speed ratings (Par 103): **97,95,94,92,92 71,**
CSF £35.17 CT £539.80 TOTE £10.00: £5.70, £2.30; EX 53.10 Trifecta £545.60.
Owner Mrs Louise Marsh **Bred** Mascara Partnership **Trained** Hubbert's Bridge, Lincs

FOCUS
Following 3mm of rain on Wednesday and another 4mm on Thursday the going was given as good to soft (GoingStick: 7.8). A modest handicap marred by a fatal injury to May Be Some Time. A good ride on the winner with the runner-up rating a small pb.

1825 EQUESTRIAN SURFACES LTD FILLIES' H'CAP 1m 2f 36y
2:15 (2:15) (Class 5) (0-75,75) 4-Y-O+ **£4,851** (£1,443; £721; £360) **Stalls** Low

Form RPR

300- **1** **Distant High**[194] 7308 5-8-4 **61** oh1..........................(p) TomMarquand[(3)] 4 68
(Richard Price) *chsd ldrs: relegated to 5th 1/2-way: rdn 4f out: hdwy over 2f out: kpt on to ld narrowly jst ins fnl f: r.o: won on nod* **15/2**

21-2 **2** shd **Miss Ranger (IRE)**[16] 1412 4-8-5 **64**.......................... CallumShepherd[(5)] 2 71
(Brian Ellison) *s.i.s: hld up in last: rdn and swtchd rt over 3f out: hdwy on outer over 1f out: disp ld jst ins fnl f: r.o: lost on nod* **2/1**[1]

112- **3** 3 **Ickymasho**[134] 8261 4-9-7 **75**..................................... OisinMurphy 3 76
(Jonathan Portman) *t.k.h: chsd ldrs: led 2f out: sn rdn: hdd jst ins fnl f: no ex* **4/1**[3]

030- **4** ¾ **Phantom River**[161] 7925 4-8-13 **67**.................. WilliamTwiston-Davies 1 66
(Alan King) *hld up: clsd 1/2-way: sltly outpcd by ldrs 3f out: styd on fnl f* **8/1**

241- **5** 2 ¼ **Perceived**[229] 6354 4-9-5 **73**... FergusSweeney 5 68
(Henry Candy) *led early: chsd ldr after: rdn to ld over 2f out: sn hdd: lost 2nd over 1f out: sn wknd* **3/1**[2]

662- **6** 2 ¼ **Jersey Jewel (FR)**[244] 5870 4-9-5 **73**.................................. LiamJones 6 63
(Tom Dascombe) *s.i.s: sn rcvrd to ld: rdn and hdd over 2f out: wknd wl over 1f out* **7/1**

2m 10.93s (0.33) **Going Correction** +0.15s/f (Good) 6 Ran SP% **113.7**
Speed ratings (Par 100): **104,103,101,100,99 97**
CSF £23.44 TOTE £9.70: £4.70, £1.70; EX 28.50 Trifecta £103.00.
Owner My Left Foot Racing Syndicate **Bred** Claydons Bloodstock & Rae Guest Racing **Trained** Ullingswick, H'fords

FOCUS
A modest fillies' handicap. It was sound run but the form is pretty ordinary.

1826 FRASER LAWSON ENTERTAINMENTS LTD MAIDEN STKS 1m 2f 36y
2:50 (2:50) (Class 5) 3-Y-O+ **£4,851** (£1,443; £721; £360) **Stalls** Low

Form RPR

04- **1** **Snan (IRE)**[191] 7397 3-8-10 0.. SeanLevey 3 75+
(Richard Hannon) *led to 5f out: styd in 2nd tl led again over 3f out: rdn 2f out: jnd ins fnl f: r.o gamely: won on nod* **7/2**[2]

2- **2** shd **Girling (IRE)**[200] 7161 3-8-5 0.. JohnFahy 10 69+
(Ralph Beckett) *trckd ldrs: wnt 3rd 6f out: chsd wnr 2f out: chal and ev ch ins fnl f: r.o: lost on nod* **5/6**[1]

45/ **3** ¾ **Touch The Sky**[919] 7469 5-9-13 0.................................... OisinMurphy 2 75+
(David Elsworth) *chsd ldrs: rdn 3f out: kpt on u.p: jst hld by ldng pair fnl f* **11/2**[3]

000- **4** 2 ¼ **Panko (IRE)**[183] 7590 3-8-10 38.. KieranO'Neill 5 68+
(Ed de Giles) *chsd ldng gp: shkn up 3f out: outpcd by ldrs 2f out: r.o wl fnl f: improve* **66/1**

5 ¾ **Hills Of Rome (IRE)** 3-8-10 0.. PatDobbs 1 66+
(Richard Hannon) *s.i.s: hld up towards rr: shkn up and clsd 4f out: pushed along fnl 2f: kpt on* **8/1**

0-4 **6** 2 ¾ **Blenheim Warrior**[6] 1651 4-9-13 0.................................. TimmyMurphy 7 64+
(Richard Hughes) *hld up in mid-div: shkn up 3f out: swtchd rt 2f out: kpt on steadily: improve* **14/1**

00- **7** 2 ¾ **Kenobe Star (IRE)**[116] 2359 4-9-13 0.............................. MartinLane 11 58
(David Dennis) *chsd ldrs: rdn over 3f out: wknd fnl f* **66/1**

50- **8** 3 ¼ **Fix Up Look Sharp**[218] 6672 5-9-8 0.......................... HarryPoulton[(5)] 4 52
(Jamie Poulton) *t.k.h: chsd ldrs: rdn over 2f out: one pce* **66/1**

00- **9** 1 ½ **Pongo Twistleton**[189] 7431 3-8-10 0.. FMBerry 9 46
(Jonjo O'Neill) *mid-div: rdn 4f out: no real imp: wknd over 1f out* **50/1**

00- **10** 2 **Author's Dream**[164] 7879 3-8-10 0.................................. JimCrowley 8 42
(William Knight) *a in rr: last and rdn 2f out: passed a few rivals fnl f* **25/1**

00- **11** 1 ½ **Russian Rascal**[186] 7510 3-8-10 0................................... TomQueally 13 39
(Stuart Kittow) *rrd s: in rr and t.k.h: sme hdwy after 4f: rdn 4f out: wknd 2f out* **66/1**

12 ¾ **Gaelic Master (IRE)** 3-8-10 0........................... WilliamTwiston-Davies 6 37
(Michael Scudamore) *s.s: rdn along 6f out: a in rr* **50/1**

06- **13** 5 **New Revive**[249] 5695 4-9-13 0.. DavidProbert 12 30
(Patrick Chamings) *t.k.h: prom: led 5f out tl over 3f out: rdn over 2f out: sn wknd* **50/1**

2m 13.07s (2.47) **Going Correction** +0.15s/f (Good)
WFA 3 from 4yo+ 17lb 13 Ran SP% **125.6**
Speed ratings (Par 103): **96,95,95,93,92 90,88,85,84,83 81,81,77**
CSF £6.91 TOTE £4.00: £1.20, £1.30, £2.10; EX 8.40 Trifecta £51.40.
Owner Al Shaqab Racing **Bred** Slow Sand Syndicate **Trained** East Everleigh, Wilts

FOCUS
The market leaders came to the fore in this maiden. There are doubts over several of these but positives to be taken from the front six.

1827 DRIBUILD DASH VETERANS' H'CAP (ROUND 1 OF THE CHEPSTOW SPRINT SERIES) 5f 16y
3:25 (3:26) (Class 5) (0-75,73) 6-Y-O+ **£4,851** (£1,443; £721; £360) **Stalls** Centre

Form RPR

546- **1** **Edged Out**[194] 7311 6-9-6 **72**.. DavidProbert 2 80
(Christopher Mason) *trckd ldrs: led over 2f out: rdn over 1f out: r.o* **8/1**

1122 **2** nk **Elusivity (IRE)**[11] 1528 8-9-7 **73**....................................(p) OisinMurphy 3 80
(Conor Dore) *cl up: led over 3f out tl over 2f out: sn rdn: hung lft over 1f out: kpt on: jst hld* **2/1**[2]

0-21 **3** ¾ **Lewisham**[13] 1481 6-9-1 **70**.. TomMarquand[(3)] 6 74+
(J R Jenkins) *hld up bhd ldrs: pushed along 1/2-way: wnt 3rd 1f out: hung lft: r.o* **7/4**[1]

2246 **4** 2 ¼ **Head Space (IRE)**[30] 1143 8-9-6 **72**................................ FrannyNorton 1 68
(Brian Barr) *walked to s: s.i.s: sn rcvrd to chse ldrs: rdn 2f out: one pce and lost 3rd 1f out* **7/1**[3]

-330 **5** 1 ½ **Swendab (IRE)**[4] 1720 8-9-2 **73**..............................(v) CiaranMckee[(5)] 8 64
(John O'Shea) *sn rdn along: chsd ldrs: one pce and no hdwy fnl f* **12/1**

5656 **6** ¾ **Louis Vee (IRE)**[4] 1721 8-8-0 **59** oh4.........................(p) LuluStanford[(7)] 5 47
(John O'Shea) *s.i.s: sn rdn along towards rr: no imp on ldrs whn swtchd rt 1f out* **12/1**

500- **7** nk **Steel City Boy (IRE)**[386] 1292 13-8-0 **59** oh14................. RPWalsh[(7)] 7 46
(Shaun Harris) *wnt to post early: led over 1f: chsd ldrs: rdn 2f out: wknd over 1f out* **66/1**

-000 **8** 3 ½ **Steel Rain**[42] 985 8-8-2 **59** oh10............................... EdwardGreatrex[(5)] 4 33
(Nikki Evans) *chsd ldrs: rdn after 2f: wknd over 1f out* **25/1**

58.82s (-0.48) **Going Correction** -0.15s/f (Firm) 8 Ran SP% **114.0**
Speed ratings: **97,96,95,91,89 88,87,82**
CSF £24.30 CT £41.05 TOTE £10.60: £2.60, £1.40, £1.10; EX 25.70 Trifecta £65.10.
Owner Christopher & Annabelle Mason **Bred** Christopher & Annabelle Mason **Trained** Caewent, Monmouthshire

FOCUS
Few got into this, the first two dominating from the start.

1828 TRADETEAM H'CAP 1m 14y
4:00 (4:00) (Class 4) (0-80,80) 3-Y-O **£6,469** (£1,925; £962; £481) **Stalls** Centre

Form RPR

6-11 **1** **Medburn Dream**[9] 1571 3-9-0 **73** 6ex.............................. FrannyNorton 8 85+
(Paul Henderson) *mde all: edgd rt fr 2f out: pushed along and r.o: comf* **7/4**[1]

2441 **2** 2 ½ **Lord Huntingdon**[50] 892 3-9-4 **77**..................................... OisinMurphy 5 81
(Andrew Balding) *trckd ldrs: rdn over 2f out: wnt 2nd 1f out: kpt on but a being hld by comfortable wnr* **10/1**

-115 **3** 1 ¼ **Jazzy (IRE)**[23] 1260 3-9-4 **77**.. TomQueally 7 78
(Martin Keighley) *wnt to post early: trckd wnr: rdn 3f out: lost 2nd 1f out: no ex* **8/1**[3]

414- **4** 3 ½ **Bukle (IRE)**[229] 6353 3-8-8 **70**... RyanTate[(3)] 10 63
(Rod Millman) *mid-div: several l adrift of ldng gp 1/2-way: rdn over 2f out: hdwy over 1f out: styd on* **25/1**

0-13 **5** 2 ¾ **Motdaw**[16] 1409 3-9-2 **80**.. PaddyPilley[(5)] 2 71
(Mick Channon) *mid-div: several l adrift of ldng gp 1/2-way: sn rdn and no imp* **9/1**

60-6 **6** 3 ¾ **The King's Steed**[20] 1339 3-8-10 **69**.. FMBerry 1 55
(Ralph Beckett) *hld up towards rr: pushed along over 5f out: no real imp on ldrs: wknd 1f out* **7/1**[2]

33-6 **7** ¾ **Knight Commander**[23] 1260 3-9-2 **75**................................ JimCrowley 9 51
(William Knight) *s.s and sn pushed along: a towards rr* **9/1**

40-0 **8** ¾ **Glance My Way (IRE)**[18] 1386 3-9-3 **76**............................ SeanLevey 3 51
(Richard Hannon) *rdn 1/2-way: a in rr* **25/1**

22-6 **9** 6 **Cape Banjo (USA)**[34] 1091 3-9-2 **80**....................[1] PatrickO'Donnell[(5)] 13 41
(Ralph Beckett) *hld up: pushed along 1/2-way: a in rr* **7/1**[2]

015- **10** 7 **Art Echo**[191] 7389 3-9-4 **77**... RyanClark 4 22
(Jonathan Portman) *chsd ldrs: rdn 3f out: wknd 1f out* **16/1**

1m 33.81s (-2.39) **Going Correction** -0.15s/f (Firm) 10 Ran SP% **115.1**
Speed ratings (Par 100): **105,102,101,97,95 91,90,89,83,76**
CSF £20.02 CT £109.21 TOTE £2.40: £1.30, £2.80, £2.90; EX 20.00 Trifecta £108.30.
Owner Eddie Evans **Bred** Eddie Evans **Trained** Whitsbury, Hants

FOCUS
This was run at a good pace and the in-form winner dominated throughout. Not many got involved and the form is rated around the third.

1829 A QUALITY SERVICE LTD (AQS) H'CAP 6f 16y
4:30 (4:31) (Class 6) (0-65,65) 3-Y-O **£2,587** (£770; £384; £192) **Stalls** Centre

Form RPR

0-63 **1** **Bushwise (IRE)**[13] 1497 3-8-7 **51** oh6...........................(p) FrannyNorton 2 60
(Milton Bradley) *mid-div: hdwy to chse ldrs 1/2-way: led narrowly 1f out: edgd rt u.p: rdn out* **14/1**

400- **2** *nk* **Greenfyre (IRE)**[221] 6594 3-9-4 **65**........................... TomMarquand(3) 12 73
(Richard Hannon) *towards rr: hdwy 2f out: rdn and ev ch 1f out: no ex towards fin* **11/2**

0-34 **3** *4* **Iconic Figure (IRE)**[30] 1151 3-9-7 **65**................................ JimCrowley 5 61
(Steve Gollings) *led to 1/2-way: styd cl up: rdn 2f out: kpt on fnl f but no ch w ldng pair* **5/1**[3]

044- **4** *nk* **Sabato (IRE)**[129] 8348 3-9-4 **62**......................... WilliamTwiston-Davies 3 57
(Fergal O'Brien) *chsd ldrs: chal 1/2-way: led briefly appr fnl f: unable qck* **7/1**

45-4 **5** *3/4* **Tim The Taxi**[23] 1251 3-8-13 **60**...................................... PhilipPrince(3) 7 53
(David Evans) *wnt to post early: awkward s: in rr: rdn over 2f out: hdwy over 1f out: swtchd lft ins fnl f: r.o* **9/2**[2]

500- **6** *nse* **Baz's Boy**[207] 6985 3-8-2 **51** oh5............................. EdwardGreatrex(5) 10 44
(John Flint) *chsd ldrs: rdn over 2f out: kpt on same pce* **6/1**

506- **7** *2 1/4* **Blackdown Warrior**[277] 4698 3-8-4 **51** oh1........................ RyanTate(3) 1 37
(Rod Millman) *cl up: led narrowly 3f out tl appr fnl f: no ex* **20/1**

30-5 **8** *1 1/4* **African Showgirl**[16] 1420 3-9-7 **65**................................. SteveDrowne 6 47
(George Baker) *mid-div: rdn 1/2-way: hld fnl 2f* **13/2**

550- **9** *2* **Macho Mac**[189] 7430 3-9-7 **65**.. OisinMurphy 4 41
(Hughie Morrison) *t.k.h: trckd ldrs: rdn over 2f out: wknd over 1f out* **7/2**[1]

0560 **10** *2 1/4* **Haunted (IRE)**[30] 1141 3-8-7 **51** oh1 ow1...................(b) DavidProbert 11 20
(Milton Bradley) *half-rrd s: towards rr: rdn over 2f out: btn whn eased appr fnl f* **33/1**

00-0 **11** *2 1/4* **Montague Way (IRE)**[30] 1146 3-8-8 **55**......................... RobHornby(3) 9 18
(Andrew Balding) *sn towards rr: no ch fr 1/2-way* **16/1**

1m 11.54s (-0.46) **Going Correction** -0.15s/f (Firm) **11** Ran SP% **132.8**
Speed ratings (Par 96): **97,96,91,90,89 89,86,85,82,79 76**
CSF £100.76 CT £470.47 TOTE £17.50: £4.30, £1.90, £1.90; EX 150.90 Trifecta £1012.90.
Owner E A Hayward **Bred** B Kennedy & Mrs Ann Marie Kennedy **Trained** Sedbury, Gloucs

FOCUS
An ordinary heat, but the first two came nicely clear. A surprise winner but the form could be rated higher.

1830 WESTERN MEDICAL SUPPLIES H'CAP (DIV I) 2m 49y
5:05 (5:05) (Class 6) (0-65,65) 4-Y-O+ **£2,587** (£770; £384; £192) **Stalls** Low

Form RPR
0046 **1** **Cosette (IRE)**[20] 1343 5-9-4 **57**......................(p) WilliamTwiston-Davies 8 66
(Bernard Llewellyn) *sn led: mde rest: rdn 3f out: styd on strly and in command fnl 2f: eased nr fin* **7/1**

5656 **2** *3 3/4* **Thimaar (USA)**[14] 1450 8-9-1 **54**..................................(b) KieranO'Neill 10 58
(Sarah Hollinshead) *trckd ldrs: wnt 2nd after 4f: rdn 3f out: kpt on but outpcd by wnr fnl 2f* **10/1**

3 *1 1/4* **Pillard (FR)**[27] 4-9-8 **65**.. FMBerry 7 67
(Jonjo O'Neill) *mid-div: rdn 4f out: wnt 3rd over 2f out: one pce and no further imp* **6/4**[1]

14-0 **4** *1 3/4* **Agreement (IRE)**[14] 1450 6-9-2 **60**.......................(b) EdwardGreatrex(5) 6 60
(Nikki Evans) *chsd ldrs: rdn 3f out: lost 3rd over 2f out: one pce* **7/1**

000- **5** *1* **Aaman (IRE)**[13] 5990 10-8-8 **47**.......................................(t) DavidProbert 9 46
(Bernard Llewellyn) *towards rr: clsd 4f out: rdn over 2f out: one pce* **16/1**

150- **6** *2 1/4* **Taste The Wine (IRE)**[162] 5548 10-9-2 **62**............(t) JordanWilliams(7) 5 58
(Bernard Llewellyn) *s.i.s: towards rr: rdn 3f out: no real imp* **9/2**[2]

-006 **7** *1 1/2* **Renewing**[21] 1322 5-8-7 **46** oh1.................................(p) FrannyNorton 4 40
(Paul Henderson) *led early: trckd wnr tl relegated to 3rd after 4f: rdn 4f out: wknd over 2f out* **6/1**[3]

550- **8** *18* **River Du Nord (FR)**[242] 5962 9-8-2 **46** oh1....................... AliceMills(5) 2 19
(Sue Gardner) *alwayds in rr: rdn 4f out: no ch fnl 2f: t.o* **25/1**

400- **9** *6* **Poetic License (IRE)**[155] 8003 4-8-1 **46** oh1 ow3.......... PaddyPilley(5) 3 14
(James Grassick) *towards rr: rdn 5f out: lost tch 2f out: t.o* **33/1**

3m 40.56s (1.66) **Going Correction** +0.15s/f (Good)
WFA 4 from 5yo+ 4lb **9** Ran SP% **119.2**
Speed ratings (Par 101): **101,99,98,97,97 96,95,86,83**
CSF £76.64 CT £161.20 TOTE £7.60: £1.70, £3.10, £1.20; EX 49.90 Trifecta £169.60.
Owner Smerdon Tree Services Ltd **Bred** R N Auld **Trained** Fochriw, Caerphilly

FOCUS
Moderate handicap form. The pace held up and the winner will remain well treated after a rise for this.

1831 WESTERN MEDICAL SUPPLIES H'CAP (DIV II) 2m 49y
5:40 (5:40) (Class 6) (0-65,63) 4-Y-O+ **£2,587** (£770; £384; £192) **Stalls** Low

Form RPR
-522 **1** **Jezza**[37] 1038 10-9-2 **59**...(bt) CallumShepherd(5) 8 67
(Victor Dartnall) *s.i.s: last tl shkn up to improve into 6th 6f out: drvn 3f out: stl 4th 1f out: styd on wl to ld nr fin* **9/4**[1]

643- **2** *1/2* **Fuzzy Logic (IRE)**[19] 5548 7-8-8 **46**...............................(b) DavidProbert 1 53
(Bernard Llewellyn) *rdn along early: towards rr: hdwy after 6f: rdn 4f out: wnt 3rd 3f out: led narrowly fnl 100yds tl hdd nr fin* **4/1**[3]

-106 **3** *1 1/4* **Tarakkom (FR)**[81] 498 4-8-8 **55**............................... CiaranMckee(5) 7 61
(Peter Hiatt) *a.p: rdn to chal 3f out: led wl over 1f out: hdd fnl 100yds: no ex* **8/1**

00-4 **4** *2 3/4* **Madame Lafite**[37] 1039 4-9-7 **63**.. JimCrowley 2 66
(Jonathan Portman) *a;ways prom: led narrowly 7f out: rdn 3f out: hdd wl over 1f out: no ex ins fnl f* **3/1**[2]

30-0 **5** *1 3/4* **Lean Burn (USA)**[14] 1450 10-8-2 **45**............................... NoelGarbutt(5) 3 46
(Barry Leavy) *mid-div tl lost pl and dropped to last 6f out: rdn andd struggling 4f out: styd on fnl 2f: nt threaten ldrs* **20/1**

6 *1/2* **Arthur's Queen (FR)**[134] 5-9-2 **61**.................................. WilliamCox(7) 6 61
(Carroll Gray) *hld up towards rr: rdn and struggling 5f out: styd on fnl 2f: nt threaten ldrs* **16/1**

/005 **7** *5* **Virgil Earp**[14] 1456 9-8-7 **45**.. MartinLane 5 39
(Ian Williams) *mid-div: rdn 4f out: wknd 2f out* **13/2**

34-0 **8** *3/4* **Blue Top**[14] 1450 7-8-9 **50**.. PhilipPrince(3) 4 43
(Dai Burchell) *led tl hdd 7f out: styd prom: rdn 4f out: wknd 2f out* **10/1**

3m 40.66s (1.76) **Going Correction** +0.15s/f (Good)
WFA 4 from 5yo+ 4lb **8** Ran SP% **119.9**
Speed ratings (Par 101): **101,100,100,98,97 97,95,94**
CSF £12.26 CT £62.70 TOTE £2.70: £1.60, £1.30, £2.70; EX 11.90 Trifecta £57.20.
Owner Mrs J Scrivens **Bred** C P Ranson **Trained** Brayford, Devon

FOCUS
This was run in a similar time to the first division. Straightforward form.
T/Jkpt: Part won. T/Plt: £30.70 to a £1 stake. Pool: £72,694.51 - 1728.01 winning tickets T/Qpdt: £3.80 to a £1 stake. Pool: £7,783.68 - 1,478.32 winning tickets **Richard Lowther**

1806 LINGFIELD (L-H)
Friday, April 29

OFFICIAL GOING: Polytrack: standard
Wind: Fresh, half behind Weather: Fine but cloudy

1832 BERRINGERS CHARTERED ACCOUNTANTS (S) STKS 1m 1y(P)
2:05 (2:06) (Class 6) 3-Y-O+ **£2,264** (£673; £336; £168) **Stalls** High

Form RPR
202- **1** **Faintly (USA)**[162] 7908 5-9-2 **77**............................... GeorgeDowning(3) 1 56+
(Tony Carroll) *trckd ldng pair: wnt 2nd 2f out: rdn to ld over 1f out and hung fire sltly: drvn to assert last 100yds* **15/8**[1]

2100 **2** *1 1/4* **The Tichborne (IRE)**[28] 1173 8-9-10 **68**.......................(b) JackMitchell 4 58
(Roger Teal) *led 1f: trckd ldr: led again over 2f out: hdd over 1f out: pressed wnr tl fnl 100yds: no ex and jst hld on for 2nd* **3/1**[2]

30-6 **3** *shd* **El Duque**[117] 32 5-9-5 **53**.. KieranShoemark(5) 3 58
(Bill Turner) *in tch in 4th: rdn over 2f out: styd on fnl f on outer: nrly snatched 2nd* **25/1**

-304 **4** *shd* **Ubla (IRE)**[81] 502 3-8-5 **67**.. LukeMorris 2 49
(Gay Kelleway) *hld up in 5th: effrt 2f out: rdn and hanging over 1f out: styd on fnl f: nrly grabbed a pl* **4/1**

14 **5** *2* **Seek The Fair Land**[16] 1415 10-10-1 **68**.....................(v) CharlesBishop 6 58
(Lee Carter) *t.k.h early: hld up in last: effrt 2f out: one pce and nvr able to threaten* **7/2**[3]

/0-5 **6** *7* **Misleading**[42] 974 4-8-12 **76**.. RhiainIngram(7) 7 31
(Lee Carter) *nt that wl away but pushed up to ld after 1f: rdn and hdd over 2f out: wknd over 1f out* **16/1**

1m 37.51s (-0.69) **Going Correction** -0.075s/f (Stan)
WFA 3 from 4yo+ 14lb **6** Ran SP% **111.7**
Speed ratings (Par 101): **100,98,98,98,96 89**
CSF £7.68 TOTE £2.30: £1.50, £2.60; EX 8.10 Trifecta £62.50.There was no bid for the winner
Owner J Babb **Bred** Juddmonte Farms Inc **Trained** Cropthorne, Worcs

FOCUS
A moderate seller which the market got right. Typical form for the grade. The principals were probably all below form.

1833 CHRISTOPHER PIERPOINT CLASSIC H'CAP 5f 6y(P)
2:40 (2:41) (Class 6) (0-60,60) 4-Y-O+ **£2,264** (£673; £336; £168) **Stalls** High

Form RPR
3550 **1** **Pharoh Jake**[11] 1533 8-9-2 **55**.. WilliamCarson 1 63
(John Bridger) *chsd ldng pair: rdn over 2f out: wnt 2nd over 1f out: drvn to ld last 75yds: styd on* **4/1**[2]

1533 **2** *1* **Red Flute**[4] 1709 4-8-7 **49**...(v) TimClark(3) 7 53
(Denis Quinn) *led and stretched field: drvn over 1f out: hdd and no ex last 75yds* **5/1**[3]

3-40 **3** *1/2* **Our Lord**[14] 1451 4-9-7 **60**.. LukeMorris 5 63
(Bill Turner) *dwlt: sn chsd ldng trio but nvr on terms: drvn 1/2-way: kpt on fr over 1f out to take 3rd ins fnl f* **7/2**[1]

-200 **4** *3/4* **Copper Cavalier**[11] 1533 5-9-1 **54**................................(b) RobertHavlin 2 54
(Michael Blanshard) *chsd ldr to over 1f out: one pce fnl f* **6/1**

6400 **5** *hd* **Black Vale (IRE)**[30] 1138 5-8-2 **46** oh1..................(t) JosephineGordon(5) 8 45
(Phil McEntee) *dwlt: outpcd and pushed along in 5th: tried to cl on inner over 1f out: kpt on one pce and n.d* **20/1**

5050 **6** *1 3/4* **Rocket Rob (IRE)**[51] 873 10-9-7 **60**............................. StevieDonohoe 9 53
(Willie Musson) *hld up: stmbld sltly sn after s: outpcd and wl off the pce bef 1/2-way: urged along and kpt on fr over 1f out: no ch* **8/1**

1003 **7** *6* **Give Us A Belle (IRE)**[31] 1133 7-9-7 **60**.................(bt) AdamBeschizza 3 31
(Christine Dunnett) *slowly away: outpcd in last pair: wknd 2f out: t.o* **12/1**

-500 **8** *24* **Bubbly Bailey**[30] 1150 6-9-4 **57**..................................(v) FrederikTylicki 4 +
(J R Jenkins) *s.v.s: a t.o and fin in own time* **8/1**

58.22s (-0.58) **Going Correction** -0.075s/f (Stan) **8** Ran SP% **107.9**
Speed ratings (Par 101): **101,99,98,97,97 94,84,46**
CSF £21.45 CT £64.83 TOTE £5.90: £2.00, £1.50, £1.20; EX 21.90 Trifecta £57.80.
Owner J J Bridger Mrs J Stamp **Bred** J J Bridger **Trained** Liphook, Hants
■ Kuanyao was withdrawn. Price at time of withdrawal 10-1. Rule 4 applies to all bets - deduction 5p in the pound.

FOCUS
A moderate sprint handicap, but the pace was strong. The form looks straightforward.

1834 RAY AND RENEE UPTON H'CAP 1m 1y(P)
3:15 (3:15) (Class 6) (0-60,59) 4-Y-O+ **£2,264** (£673; £336; £168) **Stalls** High

Form RPR
3550 **1** **Runaiocht (IRE)**[20] 1340 6-9-5 **57**................................(b) JimmyQuinn 4 64
(Paul Burgoyne) *hld up in midfield: gng easily over 2f out: prog to chse ldr over 1f out: drvn ahd ins fnl f: styd on* **4/1**[2]

-003 **2** *1 1/4* **Diamonds A Dancing**[13] 1498 6-9-0 **59**.....................(b) GeorgiaCox(7) 2 63
(John O'Shea) *hld up in rr: waiting for room over 2f out: prog on inner over 1f out: tried to chal fnl f: kpt on same pce* **8/1**

0521 **3** *3/4* **Not Your Call (IRE)**[30] 1147 5-8-11 **52**......................... DannyBrock(3) 5 54
(Lee Carter) *led: 2 l clr 2f out: hdd and one pce ins fnl f* **3/1**[1]

22-5 **4** *nk* **Loving Your Work**[20] 1340 5-9-7 **59**................................. PatCosgrave 10 60
(Ken Cunningham-Brown) *hld up in rr: waiting for room 2f out: prog over 1f out: drvn and kpt on but nvr gng pce to threaten* **5/1**[3]

3203 **5** *1 1/2* **West Leake (IRE)**[16] 1416 10-9-5 **57**.................................... LiamKeniry 1 55
(Paul Burgoyne) *t.k.h: trckd ldrs: wnt 2nd jst over 2f out to over 1f out: fdd* **8/1**

4U10 **6** *7* **Palace Moon**[23] 1262 11-9-6 **58**.......................................(t) GeorgeBaker 9 39
(Michael Attwater) *chsd ldr 1f: styd prom: rdn to dispute 2nd jst over 2f out: stl cl up jst over 1f out: wknd and heavily eased* **8/1**

/4-6 **7** *1/2* **Sunshine Always (IRE)**[30] 1147 10-9-6 **58**........................ LukeMorris 8 38
(Michael Attwater) *in tch: rdn over 2f out: wknd wl over 1f out* **12/1**

0610 **8** *4* **Chandrayaan**[37] 1035 9-8-9 **47**.....................................(v) RobertHavlin 7 17
(John E Long) *a in rr: wknd 2f out: sn bhd* **33/1**

0-54 **9** *1 1/2* **Fairy Pools**[23] 1263 5-8-13 **51**.. JimmyFortune 6 18
(Les Eyre) *chsd ldr after 1f to jst over 2f out: wknd rapidly* **14/1**

460 **10** *2* **Munsarim (IRE)**[44] 949 9-9-5 **57**..................................(p) CathyGannon 3 19
(Lee Carter) *s.s: a last and mostly detached fr rest* **16/1**

1m 37.64s (-0.56) **Going Correction** -0.075s/f (Stan) **10** Ran SP% **118.2**
Speed ratings (Par 101): **99,97,97,96,95 88,87,83,82,80**
CSF £36.67 CT £110.14 TOTE £4.80: £2.00, £3.50, £1.20; EX 43.40 Trifecta £208.30.
Owner Knowle Rock Racing **Bred** J S Bolger **Trained** Shepton Montague, Somerset

FOCUS
Another moderate handicap. The winner was rated to his best form of last year.

1835 6TH BARRY GURR MEMORIAL H'CAP — 1m 4f (P)
3:45 (3:47) (Class 6) (0-65,65) 3-Y-O — **£2,264** (£673; £336; £168) **Stalls** Low

Form | RPR

45-1 **1** **Recognition (IRE)**[36] 1062 3-9-6 **64** ... JackMitchell 8 — 74+
(Roger Varian) *hld up in last: prog on outer to chse ldr over 2f out: clsd to ld jst over 1f out: sn clr: comf* **5/4**[1]

060- **2** *1 1/2* **Gimlet**[146] 8123 3-9-7 **65** ... WilliamBuick 2 — 70+
(Hugo Palmer) *led to over 9f out: disp 2nd pl tl drvn and no rspnse over 3f out and sn wl outpcd: fnlly picked up over 1f out: r.o to take 2nd last 75yds: too late to threaten* **5/1**[3]

0-61 **3** *2 1/2* **Spinning Pearl (IRE)**[30] 1149 3-9-5 **63** ... CharlesBishop 3 — 64
(Eve Johnson Houghton) *hld up in tch: outpcd 3f out and waiting for room sn after: rdn over 1f out and kpt on to take 3rd nr fin: no ch* **7/1**

61-5 **4** *1 1/4* **Judicial Enquiry**[29] 1163 3-9-4 **62** ... (p) GeorgeBaker 7 — 61
(Ed Walker) *hld up in tch: quick move to ld over 3f out and sn had several in trble: rdn and hdd jst over 1f out: folded tamely and lost 2 pls last 75yds* **9/2**[2]

62-4 **5** *7* **The Juggler**[13] 1484 3-9-6 **64** ... MartinHarley 5 — 51
(William Knight) *pushed up to ld over 9f out: hdd over 3f out and sn drvn: wknd wl over 1f out* **5/1**[3]

000- **6** *5* **Sir Renos Santi**[211] 6873 3-8-7 **51** oh6 ... MartinDwyer 4 — 30
(Ian Williams) *s.i.s: pushed up to dispute 2nd: rdn over 4f out: dropped to last 3f out and sn bhd* **25/1**

2m 32.51s (-0.49) **Going Correction** -0.075s/f (Stan) — **6** Ran SP% **112.3**
Speed ratings (Par 96): **98,97,95,94,89 86**
CSF £7.93 CT £29.75 TOTE £2.40: £1.70, £2.20; EX 9.20 Trifecta £35.60.
Owner A D Spence **Bred** J Yeomans, B McGarvey & A Everard **Trained** Newmarket, Suffolk

FOCUS
A modest middle-distance handicap, but the winner looks progressive.

1836 MR & MRS O'DONOGHUE H'CAP — 5f 6y(P)
4:15 (4:18) (Class 4) (0-85,85) 4-Y-O+ — **£4,690** (£1,395; £697; £348) **Stalls** High

Form | RPR

4-15 **1** **Equally Fast**[16] 1427 4-9-5 **83** ... (b) MartinDwyer 2 — 88
(William Muir) *chsd ldr: drvn to chal 1f out: gd battle after: led last strides* **2/1**[2]

0-22 **2** *shd* **Bertie Blu Boy**[28] 1175 8-9-5 **83** ... (v) GeorgeBaker 3 — 88
(Lisa Williamson) *led: drvn over 1f out: jnd fnl f: kpt on but hdd last strides* **7/4**[1]

3126 **3** *nk* **Secret Asset (IRE)**[21] 1321 11-9-1 **79** ... (v) LukeMorris 1 — 83
(Lisa Williamson) *chsd ldng pair: rdn over 2f out: clsd u.p to chal ins fnl f: upsides nr fin: no ex last strides* **5/1**[3]

/16- **4** *1* **Just Us Two (IRE)**[314] 3407 4-9-7 **85** ... FrederikTylicki 4 — 87+
(Robert Cowell) *racd on outer: in tch in last: rdn over 2f out: trying to cl whn nt clr run jst ins fnl f: one pce after* **2/1**[2]

57.76s (-1.04) **Going Correction** -0.075s/f (Stan) — **4** Ran SP% **119.7**
Speed ratings (Par 105): **105,104,104,102**
CSF £6.61 TOTE £2.70; EX 6.20 Trifecta £12.90.
Owner Muir Racing Partnership - Haydock **Bred** Newsells Park Stud **Trained** Lambourn, Berks
■ Stewards' Enquiry : Martin Dwyer caution: careless riding

FOCUS
Not a bad little sprint handicap despite the small field, and a cracking finish. The first two reproducing their recent C&D form.

1837 HAPPY BIRTHDAY ELAINE COOK MAIDEN STKS — 7f 1y(P)
4:45 (4:45) (Class 5) 3-Y-O+ — **£2,911** (£866; £432; £216) **Stalls** Low

Form | RPR

324- **1** **Noble Peace**[170] 7795 3-9-0 85 ... DaneO'Neill 1 — 81
(Henry Candy) *t.k.h: hld up in last: prog on inner jst over 2f out: rdn to ld jst over 1f out: styd on wl* **2/1**[2]

2 **2** *3/4* **Banish (USA)**[20] 1339 3-9-0 0 ... WilliamBuick 2 — 79
(Hugo Palmer) *trckd ldng pair: pushed along to chse ldr wl over 2f out: rdn to chal over 1f out: nt qckn as wnr wnt past: tk 2nd nr fin* **1/1**[1]

22-0 **3** *nk* **Menai (IRE)**[17] 1397 3-8-11 75 ... MichaelJMMurphy(3) 3 — 78
(Charles Hills) *led: rdn: hdd and nt qckn jst over 1f out: kpt on same pce and lost 2nd nr fin* **7/2**[3]

60- **4** *11* **Semille Obon**[121] 8394 4-9-13 0 ... (p) CharlesBishop 4 — 53
(Jamie Poulton) *chsd ldr to wl over 2f out: sn wknd and bhd* **100/1**

5 *nse* **Excel Quest** 3-9-0 0 ... LukeMorris 5 — 48
(Ed Walker) *in tch in 4th: rdn and wknd over 2f out: sn bhd* **10/1**

1m 25.38s (0.58) **Going Correction** -0.075s/f (Stan)
WFA 3 from 4yo 13lb — **5** Ran SP% **115.6**
Speed ratings (Par 103): **93,92,91,79,79**
CSF £4.68 TOTE £3.10: £1.30, £1.40; EX 5.80 Trifecta £12.60.
Owner One Too Many & Candy **Bred** The Pocock Family **Trained** Kingston Warren, Oxon

FOCUS
An uncompetitive maiden and rather muddling form. The winner is rated a length off his 2yo best.

1838 HAPPY BIRTHDAY AOIFE HEARNE H'CAP — 6f 1y(P)
5:20 (5:21) (Class 5) (0-75,75) 4-Y-O+ — **£2,911** (£866; £432; £216) **Stalls** Low

Form | RPR

4-53 **1** **Lightning Charlie**[16] 1419 4-9-2 **75** ... KieranShoemark(5) 1 — 84+
(Amanda Perrett) *trckd ldng pair: wnt 2nd 2f out: chal over 1f out: led ins fnl f: drvn to assert nr fin* **13/8**[1]

0003 **2** *1* **Desert Strike**[21] 1321 10-9-3 **71** ... (p) LiamKeniry 6 — 77
(Conor Dore) *led: drvn and jnd over 1f out: narrowly hdd ins fnl f: kpt on but hld last 75yds* **4/1**[2]

46-2 **3** *3/4* **Exoplanet Blue**[20] 1334 4-9-4 **72** ... DaneO'Neill 7 — 76+
(Henry Candy) *chsd ldng trio: taken wd bnd 2f out and drvn: r.o to take 3rd fnl f: clsd on ldng pair fin but nvr able to chal* **4/1**[2]

-606 **4** *2 1/4* **Honcho (IRE)**[30] 1150 4-9-0 **68** ... StevieDonohoe 4 — 64
(John Ryan) *chsd ldr to 2f out: steadily fdd fnl f* **5/1**[3]

-500 **5** *1 1/2* **Straits Of Malacca**[16] 1419 5-8-7 **66** ... JosephineGordon(5) 3 — 58
(Simon Dow) *chsd ldrs in 5th: rdn and effrt wl over 1f out: sn no hdwy* **10/1**

6-00 **6** *3/4* **Renounce (IRE)**[86] 433 4-9-5 **73** ... LukeMorris 8 — 62
(Charlie Wallis) *hld up in 6th: rdn 2f out: no hdwy and btn over 1f out* **12/1**

513- **7** *1* **Red Cossack (CAN)**[184] 7559 5-9-2 **70** ... (t) WilliamCarson 5 — 56
(Paul Webber) *restless stalls: blindfold stl on whn they opened and slowly away: nvr rcvrd and a in last pair* **12/1**

415- **8** *nk* **Monna Valley**[223] 6550 4-8-11 **65** ... (t) AdamBeschizza 2 — 50
(Stuart Williams) *a in last pair: rdn and no prog 2f out* **8/1**

1m 10.53s (-1.37) **Going Correction** -0.075s/f (Stan) — **8** Ran SP% **130.3**
Speed ratings (Par 103): **106,104,103,100,98 97,96,95**
CSF £9.94 CT £25.82 TOTE £3.80: £1.10, £2.20, £1.80; EX 15.00 Trifecta £47.30.
Owner Lightning Charlie Partnership **Bred** J A E Hobby **Trained** Pulborough, W Sussex

FOCUS
An ordinary sprint handicap and not many got into it. The winner built on his latest form.
T/Plt: £18.30 to a £1 stake. Pool: £59,267.79 - 2,357.43 winning tickets T/Qpdt: £9.40 to a £1 stake. Pool: £3,751.13 - 292.60 winning tickets **Jonathan Neesom**

1662 MUSSELBURGH (R-H)
Friday, April 29

OFFICIAL GOING: Good to soft (soft in places) changing to soft after race 3 (3.05)
Wind: Fairly strong, across Weather: Overcast, showers

1839 TURCAN CONNELL H'CAP — 5f 1y
1:55 (1:55) (Class 6) (0-65,65) 3-Y-O — **£2,587** (£770; £384; £192) **Stalls** High

Form | RPR

4-22 **1** **Fumbo Jumbo (IRE)**[9] 1558 3-9-5 **63** ... DavidAllan 2 — 72
(Garry Moss) *wnt rt s: cl up on outside: effrt and rdn over 1f out: led ins fnl f: pushed out* **11/8**[1]

20-0 **2** *2* **Emerald Asset (IRE)**[32] 1126 3-9-2 **60** ... (p) GrahamLee 5 — 62
(Paul Midgley) *prom: rdn along over 2f out: hdwy to chse wnr ins fnl f: kpt on: nt pce to chal* **12/1**

553- **3** *1* **Bond Bombshell**[215] 6782 3-9-4 **62** ... DanielTudhope 3 — 60
(David O'Meara) *led: drvn along over 1f out: hdd ins fnl f: sn outpcd* **4/1**[3]

604- **4** *1* **Whispering Soul (IRE)**[215] 6782 3-8-7 **51** ... (b) PJMcDonald 6 — 46
(Ann Duffield) *chsd ldrs: drvn along over 2f out: kpt on same pce fnl f* **15/2**

000- **5** *1/2* **Dutch Dream**[204] 7056 3-9-1 **59** ... GeorgeChaloner 1 — 52
(Linda Perratt) *dwlt: bhd and outpcd: rallied fnl f: nvr able to chal* **20/1**

4-22 **6** *1/2* **La Asomada**[60] 763 3-9-4 **62** ... GrahamGibbons 7 — 53
(David Barron) *cl up: rdn over 2f out: outpcd ins fnl f* **3/1**[2]

1m 2.7s (2.30) **Going Correction** +0.40s/f (Good) — **6** Ran SP% **111.3**
Speed ratings (Par 96): **97,93,92,90,89 89**
CSF £18.62 CT £52.09 TOTE £2.30: £1.80, £3.50; EX 14.60 Trifecta £61.50.
Owner Pinnacle Four Partnership **Bred** Tally-Ho Stud **Trained** Wynyard, Stockton-On-Tees

FOCUS
The ground was good to firm after being watered (7mm) two days prior to racing, but there was subsequently more rain than was forecast - 7mm overnight into race day and another 5mm in the morning, with further showers around - and conditions deteriorated to good to soft, soft in places. Racing was on the temporary Flat track, using the sand bend, and distances were as advertised.

1840 WEATHERBYS PRIVATE BANK BRITISH STALLION STUDS EBF NOVICE STKS (PLUS 10 RACE) — 5f 1y
2:30 (2:30) (Class 4) 2-Y-O — **£4,204** (£1,251; £625; £312) **Stalls** High

Form | RPR

1 **Lomu (IRE)** 2-9-2 0 ... JasonHart 6 — 78
(Keith Dalgleish) *dwlt: t.k.h in rr: hdwy on outside over 1f out: rdn and led ins fnl f: kpt on wl* **11/1**

0 **2** *1/2* **Tallinski (IRE)**[27] 1199 2-9-2 0 ... TomEaves 2 — 76
(Brian Ellison) *led: rdn over 1f out: hdd ins fnl f: kpt on: hld nr fin* **9/2**[3]

3 *3 3/4* **The Nazca Lines (IRE)** 2-9-2 0 ... PhillipMakin 3 — 66+
(John Quinn) *noisy in paddock: w ldrs: rdn over 1f out: kpt on same pce fnl f* **4/1**[2]

4 *2* **Kahrab (IRE)** 2-9-2 0 ... JoeFanning 7 — 56
(Mark Johnston) *colty and noisy in paddock: prom: rdn 2f out: wknd fnl f* **13/2**

5 *7* **Scuzeme** 2-9-2 0 ... GrahamGibbons 1 — 30
(David Barron) *dwlt: sn cl up: rdn over 1f out: wknd fnl f* **10/11**[1]

1m 3.59s (3.19) **Going Correction** +0.425s/f (Yiel) — **5** Ran SP% **112.2**
Speed ratings (Par 94): **91,90,84,81,69**
CSF £56.90 TOTE £14.90: £5.20, £3.40; EX 54.40 Trifecta £206.70.
Owner Steve Macdonald **Bred** Michael G Daly **Trained** Carluke, S Lanarks

FOCUS
The first two home in the opening race challenged widest and so did the winner of this. A nice start from the winner on softening ground.

1841 BAM CONSTRUCTION H'CAP — 1m 2y
3:05 (3:05) (Class 5) (0-70,70) 4-Y-O+ — **£3,234** (£962; £481; £240) **Stalls** Low

Form | RPR

0210 **1** **Ellaal**[21] 1323 7-8-11 **60** ... PaulMulrennan 9 — 71
(Ruth Carr) *w ldr: led 1/2-way: rdn and clr over 1f out: hld on wl fnl f* **5/1**[3]

403- **2** *1 3/4* **Silver Duke (IRE)**[9] 7186 5-8-12 **61** ow1 ... (b[1]) DanielTudhope 7 — 67
(Jim Goldie) *t.k.h: hld up in rr: rdn over 2f out: hdwy on outside to chse (clr) wnr over 1f out: kpt on: nt pce to chal* **10/1**

5550 **3** *2 1/2* **Lawyer (IRE)**[30] 1152 5-9-5 **68** ... GrahamGibbons 8 — 68
(David Barron) *trckd ldrs: effrt and rdn over 2f out: kpt on same pce fr over 1f out* **11/4**[2]

253- **4** *nse* **Ingleby Spring (IRE)**[197] 7231 4-8-11 **60** ... TonyHamilton 5 — 60
(Richard Fahey) *hld up in tch: drvn and outpcd over 2f out: rallied fnl f: nvr able to chal* **6/1**

0-00 **5** *5* **Adventureman**[24] 1241 4-8-11 **60** ... JamesSullivan 2 — 49
(Ruth Carr) *t.k.h: trckd ldrs: rdn over 2f out: wknd wl over 1f out* **12/1**

40-0 **6** *3 1/2* **Last Wish (IRE)**[31] 1131 5-8-8 **57** ... JasonHart 6 — 38
(Richard Guest) *s.i.s: bhd: rdn along over 3f out: nvr on terms* **25/1**

2103 **7** *4* **Azrur (IRE)**[5] 1664 6-9-7 **70** ... PhillipMakin 4 — 41
(Keith Dalgleish) *led to 1/2-way: pressed wnr: rdn over 2f out: wknd over 1f out: eased whn btn ins fnl f* **2/1**[1]

1m 44.65s (3.45) **Going Correction** +0.55s/f (Yiel) — **7** Ran SP% **111.6**
Speed ratings (Par 103): **104,102,99,99,94 91,87**
CSF £49.19 CT £160.05 TOTE £6.10: £3.10, £5.40; EX 47.80 Trifecta £202.60.
Owner The Bottom Liners & Paul Saxton **Bred** W And R Barnett Ltd **Trained** Huby, N Yorks

FOCUS
The rain continued and the ground was changed to soft all over following this race. The winner is better on turf.

1842 HBJ CLAIMS SOLUTIONS SOLICITORS H'CAP — 1m 5f 164y
3:35 (3:35) (Class 5) (0-70,69) 4-Y-O+ **£3,234** (£962; £481; £240) **Stalls** Low

Form RPR
-310 **1** **Frosty The Snowman (IRE)**[17] 1399 5-8-8 **53** JamesSullivan 2 59
(Ruth Carr) *in tch: drvn along over 3f out: rallied to chse ldr over 1f out: led ins fnl f: kpt on wl* **5/1**
/4-3 **2** *1* **Dry Your Eyes (IRE)**[9] 1561 5-9-9 **68** DanielTudhope 4 73+
(David O'Meara) *t.k.h: cl up: led gng wl over 2f out: sn rdn: hdd ins fnl f: kpt on same pce towards fin* **6/4**[1]
00-0 **3** *4* **Boldbob (IRE)**[12] 1121 4-8-3 **50** oh5 (p) DuranFentiman 1 49
(Micky Hammond) *t.k.h: w ldr 2f: stdd and prom on ins: effrt whn nt clr run briefly over 2f out: sn rdn: kpt on fnl f: no imp* **25/1**
234- **4** *1 1/4* **Merchant Of Dubai**[140] 6331 11-9-10 **69** GrahamLee 7 67
(Jim Goldie) *led 2f: chsd ldrs: pushed along and effrt over 2f out: outpcd fr over 1f out* **4/1**[3]
060- **5** *8* **Jammy Moment**[185] 7524 5-9-9 **68** [1] PhillipMakin 5 54
(Keith Dalgleish) *s.i.s: hdwy to ld after 2f: rdn and hdd over 2f out: wknd over 1f out: eased whn btn ins fnl f* **9/4**[2]

3m 12.7s (10.80) **Going Correction** +0.575s/f (Yiel)
WFA 4 from 5yo+ 2lb **5 Ran SP% 111.3**
Speed ratings (Par 103): **92,91,89,88,83**
CSF £13.19 TOTE £5.40: £2.30, £1.50; EX 9.80 Trifecta £68.80.
Owner Bruce Jamieson, Barbara Dean, Ruth Carr **Bred** Gigginstown House Stud **Trained** Huby, N Yorks
■ Stewards' Enquiry : James Sullivan two-day ban: used whip above permitted level (May 13,15)

FOCUS
A moderate staying handicap. The winner is rated to last winners' form.

1843 WEATHERBYS PRIVATE BANK H'CAP — 5f 1y
4:10 (4:10) (Class 4) (0-80,73) 4-Y-O+ **£6,469** (£1,925; £962; £481) **Stalls** High

Form RPR
0-53 **1** **Henley**[11] 1525 4-8-13 **65** JoeFanning 1 73
(Tracy Waggott) *mde virtually all: pushed along 1f out: edgd lft and kpt on wl last 100yds* **6/4**[1]
0-43 **2** *2* **Go Go Green (IRE)**[4] 1693 10-9-7 **73** DanielTudhope 4 74
(Jim Goldie) *s.s: bhd: rdn and hdwy on outside over 1f out: chsd wnr ins fnl f: kpt on: nt gng pce to chal* **10/3**[3]
0/34 **3** *1/2* **Pushkin Museum (IRE)**[15] 1433 5-9-6 **72** DavidNolan 2 71
(Richard Fahey) *trckd ldrs: effrt and rdn over 1f out: kpt on same pce ins fnl f* **11/4**[2]
00-6 **4** *3 1/4* **Bunce (IRE)**[5] 1666 8-9-1 **67** PJMcDonald 5 55
(Linda Perratt) *prom: rdn over 2f out: wknd ins fnl f* **7/1**
1-20 **5** *3 3/4* **Bahango (IRE)**[23] 1255 4-8-11 **63** (v) ShaneGray 3 37
(Patrick Morris) *disp ld to over 1f out: wknd ent fnl f* **10/1**

1m 3.05s (2.65) **Going Correction** +0.45s/f (Yiel) **5 Ran SP% 111.3**
Speed ratings (Par 105): **96,92,92,86,80**
CSF £6.90 TOTE £2.50: £1.50, £1.90; EX 9.00 Trifecta £18.30.
Owner David Tate **Bred** Dandy's Farm **Trained** Spennymoor, Co Durham

FOCUS
Like in the other two 5f races on the card, the winner raced wide of the near rail for the most part. The winner is rated back to his best, with the next close to form.

1844 CORE OIL AND GAS 10TH ANNIVERSARY H'CAP — 7f 33y
4:40 (4:40) (Class 4) (0-80,80) 4-Y-O+ **£5,175** (£1,540; £769; £384) **Stalls** Low

Form RPR
633- **1** **Swift Approval (IRE)**[215] 6783 4-9-7 **80** (p) TomEaves 4 96+
(Kevin Ryan) *pressed ldr: led gng wl 3f out: shkn up and qcknd clr wl over 1f out: drvn and kpt on wl fnl f: eased cl home* **4/1**[3]
00-2 **2** *3 1/2* **Gold Flash**[5] 1663 4-9-0 **73** (p) PhillipMakin 6 78
(Keith Dalgleish) *dwlt: hld up in last pl: rdn over 2f out: hdwy to chse (clr) wnr over 1f out: kpt on fnl f: no imp* **9/4**[1]
150- **3** *4* **Sovereign Bounty**[290] 4247 4-9-0 **73** GrahamLee 2 68
(Jedd O'Keeffe) *prom on ins: effrt whn nt clr run over 2f out to wl over 1f out: swtchd lft and kpt on fnl f: nvr able to chal* **5/1**
0000 **4** *3/4* **Luis Vaz De Torres (IRE)**[22] 1291 4-9-5 **78** DavidNolan 3 71
(Richard Fahey) *plld hrd early: trckd ldrs: rdn over 2f out: outpcd fr over 1f out: btn fnl f* **15/2**
00-0 **5** *6* **Art Obsession (IRE)**[15] 1444 5-9-6 **79** PaulMulrennan 1 56
(Paul Midgley) *led tl rdn and hdd 3f out: rallied: wknd wl over 1f out* **10/3**[2]
030- **6** *3 3/4* **Ralphy Boy (IRE)**[195] 7289 7-9-5 **78** PJMcDonald 5 45
(Alistair Whillans) *trckd ldrs on outside: effrt over 2f out: wknd over 1f out* **6/1**

1m 32.22s (3.22) **Going Correction** +0.60s/f (Yiel) **6 Ran SP% 116.6**
Speed ratings (Par 105): **105,101,96,95,88 84**
CSF £14.12 TOTE £3.70: £1.70, £1.70; EX 15.90 Trifecta £44.40.
Owner Middleham Park Racing XLIX **Bred** Mrs Jean Brennan **Trained** Hambleton, N Yorks

FOCUS
The first two both looked ahead of their marks but there are doubts over the winner's improvement.

1845 BRUCE STEVENSON INSURANCE BROKERS H'CAP — 7f 33y
5:15 (5:15) (Class 6) (0-60,60) 4-Y-O+ **£2,587** (£770; £384; £192) **Stalls** Low

Form RPR
50-1 **1** **Bajan Rebel**[9] 1565 5-8-6 **50** NathanEvans(5) 2 61
(Michael Easterby) *hld up: stdy hdwy gng wl over 2f out: effrt and led ins fnl f: pushed clr last 75yds* **9/4**[1]
0615 **2** *2 3/4* **Emblaze**[45] 936 4-9-0 **58** PhilDennis(5) 3 62
(Bryan Smart) *t.k.h early: led: rdn 2f out: hung lft and hdd ins fnl f: kpt on same pce* **9/1**
0-30 **3** *3 1/4* **Lendal Bridge**[60] 769 5-9-2 **55** BenCurtis 9 50
(Tony Coyle) *hld up in tch: rdn along over 2f out: hdwy over 1f out: kpt on fnl f: no imp* **4/1**[2]
60-0 **4** *1/2* **Vecheka (IRE)**[9] 1565 5-9-5 **58** PJMcDonald 7 52
(Micky Hammond) *hld up: rdn over 2f out: plugged on fnl f: nvr able to chal* **17/2**
245 **5** *hd* **Top Offer**[10] 1555 7-9-7 **60** GrahamLee 8 54
(Patrick Morris) *hld up: drvn over 2f out: effrt on outside over 1f out: sn no imp* **9/2**[3]
563- **6** *nk* **Yair Hill (IRE)**[227] 6398 8-8-11 **53** (p) SammyJoBell(3) 1 46
(Thomas Cuthbert) *trckd ldrs: stdy hdwy over 2f out: rdn over 1f out: sn outpcd* **14/1**
00-5 **7** *5* **Great Demeanor (USA)**[8] 867 6-8-4 **46** oh1 (vt) JoeDoyle(3) 5 26
(Dianne Sayer) *midfield on ins: drvn and outpcd 1/2-way: btn fnl 2f* **10/1**
660- **8** *1 1/2* **Bushtiger (IRE)**[343] 2469 4-8-7 **46** JamesSullivan 4 22
(Ruth Carr) *cl up: rdn over 2f out: sn wknd* **9/1**
3000 **9** *1/2* **Shearian**[32] 1120 6-9-1 **54** (p) ConnorBeasley 6 29
(Tracy Waggott) *chsd ldrs: rdn over 2f out: wknd wl over 1f out* **14/1**

1m 33.2s (4.20) **Going Correction** +0.625s/f (Yiel) **9 Ran SP% 121.9**
Speed ratings (Par 101): **101,97,94,93,93 93,87,85,85**
CSF £25.44 CT £81.10 TOTE £2.70: £1.70, £2.00, £2.30; EX 20.20 Trifecta £101.10.
Owner Julian Rooney **Bred** Aldridge Racing Partnership **Trained** Sheriff Hutton, N Yorks

FOCUS
A moderate contest, but a well-handicapped winner who looks as good as ever.
T/Plt: £285.80 to a £1 stake. Pool: £48,463.46 - 123.78 winning tickets T/Qpdt: £16.20 to a £1 stake. Pool: £4,522.12 - 206.08 winning tickets **Richard Young**

1618 FONTAINEBLEAU
Friday, April 29

OFFICIAL GOING: Turf: very soft

1846a PRIX COLONEL BRUNO DE GALBERT (CLAIMER) (4YO+) (GENTLEMEN RIDERS) (TURF) — 1m 7f
1:45 (1:45) 4-Y-O+ **£5,882** (£2,352; £1,764; £1,176; £588)

RPR
1 **Solmen (FR)**[70] 8-10-8 0 MrJean-PhilippeBoisgontier 3 59
(K Demme, Germany) **13/10**[1]
2 *1* **Helmsman (IRE)**[14] 1450 4-10-4 0 MrFTett(5) 8 62
(J S Moore) *broke wl fr wd draw and trckd ldr (pair clr): rdn to chal 2f out: styd on to ld ent fnl 1 1/2f: hdd 110yds out: no ex* **59/10**[3]
3 *1 1/4* **Roskilly (IRE)**[16] 5-11-1 0 (p) MrEMonfort 7 64
(P Monfort, France) **33/10**[2]
4 *1 3/4* **Praticks (IRE)**[425] 5-10-12 0 MrThibaudMace 5 58
(J-F Doucet, France) **9/1**
5 *6* **Glamorous Dream (FR)**[102] 7-10-0 0 MrAdrienDesespringalle(4) 4 43
(Mme M-C Chaalon, France) **100/1**
6 *hd* **Demoiselledavignon (FR)**[16] 5-10-4 0 MrGuilainBertrand 6 43
(P Adda, France) **29/1**
7 *2* **Ataman Ermak (IRE)**[25] 5-10-7 0 (b) MrJulienL'Hostis(4) 1 48
(S Gouyette, France)
8 *4 1/2* **A Coeur Ouvert (FR)**[663] 10-10-11 0 (p) MrFlorentGuy 2 42
(H-A Pantall, France)

WIN (incl. 1 euro stake): 2.30. Places: 1.20, 1.70, 1.50. DF: 6.40. SF: 10.40.
Owner Hans Bartl \n **Bred** Mme Ursula Roder & Haras De Preaux **Trained** Germany

1619 DONCASTER (L-H)
Saturday, April 30

OFFICIAL GOING: Good to soft changing to soft after race 1 (5.15)
Wind: Virtually nil Weather: Cloudy with wintry showers

1847 WILLIAM TRUEMAN H'CAP — 6f 110y
5:15 (5:16) (Class 5) (0-75,75) 3-Y-O **£3,881** (£1,155; £577; £288) **Stalls** High

Form RPR
51- **1** **Mywayistheonlyway (IRE)**[157] 7975 3-9-5 **73** FergusSweeney 4 78+
(Martyn Meade) *dwlt and towards rr: sn swtchd lft to outer and hdwy over 2f out: rdn to chse ldrs over 1f out: styd on to chal ins fnl f: led last 50yds* **3/1**[1]
-151 **2** *1/2* **Willsy**[15] 1452 3-9-7 **75** PaulMulrennan 6 78
(Mick Channon) *prom: pushed along wl over 2f out: sn rdn along and sltly outpcd: drvn and hdwy ent fnl f: kpt on wl towards fin* **11/2**
541- **3** *1/2* **Swirral Edge**[205] 7055 3-9-1 **69** SeanLevey 1 71+
(David Brown) *dwlt: midfield: hdwy over 2f out: rdn to chal over 1f out: drvn and slt ld ins fnl f: hdd and no ex last 50yds* **9/2**[2]
140- **4** *hd* **Wiley Post**[193] 7361 3-9-1 **69** DaneO'Neill 9 70+
(Richard Hannon) *cl up: led wl over 1f out: jnd and rdn ent fnl f: sn hdd: drvn and no ex last 100yds* **10/1**
3-44 **5** *hd* **Total Power**[14] 1487 3-8-10 **69** CallumShepherd(5) 7 69
(Brian Ellison) *t.k.h: hld up in rr: hdwy over 2f out: swtchd lft and rdn over 1f out: styd on wl fnl f* **16/1**
40-6 **6** *1* **In My Place**[16] 1431 3-8-8 **65** SammyJoBell(3) 5 63
(Richard Fahey) *chsd ldrs: rdn along 2f out: drvn over 1f out: kpt on same pce* **16/1**
514 **7** *1/2* **Rhythm And Blues**[15] 1452 3-9-4 **72** (p) JohnFahy 8 68
(Clive Cox) *prom: cl up over 2f out: rdn over 1f out: wknd appr fnl f* **5/1**[3]
-025 **8** *2 1/2* **King Of Spin**[17] 1414 3-8-13 **70** LouisSteward(3) 12 59
(William Muir) *a in rr* **11/1**
214- **9** *3 1/2* **Lady Nayef**[197] 7261 3-9-6 **74** JFEgan 10 53
(John Butler) *led: pushed along over 2f out: sn rdn: hdd wl over 1f out: sn wknd* **16/1**
06-0 **10** *8* **East Street Revue**[16] 1448 3-8-2 **61** oh1 RachelRichardson(5) 13 18
(Tim Easterby) *chsd ldrs: rdn along 1/2-way: wknd over 2f out* **20/1**

1m 24.16s (4.26) **Going Correction** +0.525s/f (Yiel) **10 Ran SP% 115.1**
Speed ratings (Par 98): **96,95,94,94,94 93,92,89,85,76**
CSF £19.02 CT £71.69 TOTE £3.80: £1.50, £2.10, £1.90; EX 15.30 Trifecta £61.00.
Owner Richard Morecombe **Bred** M Duffy **Trained** Newmarket, Suffolk

FOCUS
The going was given as good to soft (GoingStick: 7.4) but was changed to soft after the first race had been run. The rail on the round course was out from 1m2f to where the round course meets the straight, adding about 6yds to the race distances of the last two races on the card. They finished in a bit of a heap here but there were one or two noteworthy performances. The bare form is pretty ordinary.

1848 TRUEMAN FAMILY H'CAP — 6f
5:45 (5:49) (Class 3) (0-90,89) 4-Y-O+ **£7,762** (£2,310; £1,154; £577) **Stalls** High

Form RPR
000- **1** **See The Sun**[217] 6762 5-9-0 **82** DaneO'Neill 7 94
(Tim Easterby) *qckly away and mde all: clr 1/2-way: rdn over 1f out: kpt on wl towards fin* **16/1**
10-2 **2** *1 1/2* **Soie D'Leau**[17] 1427 4-9-4 **86** TonyHamilton 16 93
(Kristin Stubbs) *prom: chsd wnr over 2f out: rdn wl over 1f out: drvn and kpt on fnl f* **10/1**[3]
505- **3** *1/2* **God Willing**[217] 6750 5-9-6 **88** (t) FrederikTylicki 8 94
(Declan Carroll) *chsd ldrs: hdwy over 2f out: rdn along wl over 1f out: kpt on fnl f* **12/1**

00-0 **4** ½ **Tiger Jim**[27] 1218 6-8-11 **82** RyanTate(3) 17 86+
(Jim Goldie) *bhd: hdwy over 2f out: rdn wl over 1f out: styd on wl fnl f: nrst fin* **15/2**[2]
50-0 **5** hd **Eastern Racer (IRE)**[16] 1444 4-8-7 **80** (p) CallumShepherd(5) 15 83
(Brian Ellison) *in tch: hdwy on wd outside over 2f out: sn rdn and kpt on fnl f* **25/1**
30-0 **6** nk **Handsome Dude**[7] 1644 4-9-6 **88** JohnFahy 18 90
(David Barron) *towards rr: hdwy on wd outside 3f out: rdn along over 2f out: kpt on fnl f* **20/1**
002- **7** 1 ¼ **Personal Touch**[246] 5798 7-9-0 **82** AndrewMullen 5 80
(Michael Appleby) *prom: sn chsng wnr: rdn along 2f out: sn drvn and grad wknd* **10/1**[3]
003- **8** ½ **Canyari (IRE)**[190] 7424 5-9-2 **87** (p) SammyJoBell(3) 11 84
(Richard Fahey) *towards rr: hdwy over 2f out: sn rdn: kpt on fnl f* **11/2**[1]
20-0 **9** 2 **Mass Rally (IRE)**[27] 1218 9-9-1 **83** (b) PaulMulrennan 10 73+
(Michael Dods) *hld up in tch: gd hdwy over 2f out: chsd ldrs wl over 1f out: sn rdn and wknd appr fnl f* **11/2**[1]
0-45 **10** 1 ¼ **Mississippi**[16] 1444 7-9-1 **83** GrahamLee 12 69
(Paul Midgley) *in tch in midfield: pushed along 1/2-way: sn rdn and lost pl over 2f out* **10/1**[3]
200- **11** 3 ½ **Master Bond**[222] 6598 7-8-13 **86** JoshDoyle(5) 6 61
(David O'Meara) *chsd ldrs: rdn along over 2f out: sn drvn and wknd* **33/1**
00-0 **12** 3 ¼ **Gran Canaria Queen**[7] 1644 7-8-13 **86** RachelRichardson(5) 3 51
(Tim Easterby) *s.i.s: a in rr* **25/1**
200- **13** ½ **Regal Dan (IRE)**[217] 6762 6-9-7 **89** DanielTudhope 14 52
(David O'Meara) *chsd ldrs: rdn along 1/2-way: sn wknd* **10/1**[3]
00-3 **14** 13 **Kibaar**[17] 1408 4-9-6 **88** KeaganLatham 2 10
(Kevin Ryan) *dwlt: hdwy 4f out: chsd ldrs 1/2-way: rdn over 2f out and sn wknd* **14/1**
53-0 **15** 6 **Rural Celebration**[17] 1408 5-9-5 **87** (p) ShaneGray 9
(David O'Meara) *prom: rdn along over 3f out: sn lost pl and bhd* **25/1**

1m 15.38s (1.78) **Going Correction** +0.525s/f (Yiel) **15** Ran SP% **118.4**
Speed ratings (Par 107): **109,107,106,105,105 105,103,102,100,98 93,89,88,71,63**
CSF £144.98 CT £1774.41 TOTE £23.80: £6.80, £2.30, £5.10; EX 292.80 Trifecta £1586.40 Part won..
Owner C H Stevens **Bred** R C Dollar **Trained** Great Habton, N Yorks
■ Harwoods Volante (14-1) was withdrawn not under orders. Rule 4 applies to all bets. Deduction - 5p in the £.
FOCUS
This looked competitive but the well-handicapped winner took the race apart. It will be interseting to see if he can build on this.

1849 DONCASTER RACECOURSE WELCOMES TOUR DE YORKSHIRE MAIDEN STKS 6f
6:15 (6:19) (Class 5) 3-4-Y-O **£3,234** (£962; £481; £240) **Stalls** High

Form RPR
2 **1** **Maximian (IRE)**[21] 1337 3-9-2 0 MartinLane 1 84+
(Charlie Appleby) *prom: cl up 1/2-way: led wl over 2f out: rdn over 1f out: jnd ent fnl f and sn drvn: hld on gamely* **11/10**[1]
3- **2** shd **Foresight (FR)**[175] 7752 3-9-2 0 PatCosgrave 8 83+
(David Simcock) *trckd ldrs: hdwy and cl up over 2f out: rdn to chal ent fnl f: sn drvn and ev ch tl no ex nr line* **9/2**[3]
2- **3** 5 **Mazzini**[149] 8090 3-9-2 0 FrederikTylicki 6 67
(James Fanshawe) *trckd ldrs: hdwy wl over 2f out: sn chsng ldng pair: rdn over 1f out: kpt on same pce fnl f* **7/4**[2]
06- **4** 1 ½ **The Armed Man**[187] 7515 3-9-2 0 AndrewElliott 3 62
(Chris Fairhurst) *led: rdn along 1/2-way: hdd wl over 2f out: sn drvn and kpt on one pce* **66/1**
60- **5** 1 ¼ **Stormy Art (IRE)**[194] 7337 3-9-2 0 PaulMulrennan 11 58+
(Michael Dods) *hld up towards rr: hdwy over 2f out: rdn wl over 1f out: sn no imp* **40/1**
45- **6** 2 ½ **L'Apogee**[311] 3510 3-9-2 0 TonyHamilton 2 50+
(Richard Fahey) *a towards rr* **16/1**
0 **7** ¾ **Brendan (IRE)**[27] 1216 3-9-2 0 DanielTudhope 5 48
(Jim Goldie) *hld up: a in rr* **50/1**
6- **8** ½ **Frozon**[206] 7039 3-9-2 0 DaleSwift 4 46
(Brian Ellison) *a in rr* **33/1**
65 **9** 21 **Dutch Archer**[34] 1111 3-9-2 0 NickyMackay 7
(Jeremy Gask) *prom: cl up after 2f: rdn along 1/2-way: sn wknd* **33/1**

1m 16.64s (3.04) **Going Correction** +0.525s/f (Yiel) **9** Ran SP% **119.8**
Speed ratings (Par 103): **102,101,95,93,91 88,87,86,58**
CSF £6.84 TOTE £2.10: £1.40, £1.60, £1.10; EX 8.60 Trifecta £11.50.
Owner Godolphin **Bred** Scea Haras De Saint Pair **Trained** Newmarket, Suffolk
FOCUS
An interesting maiden, the first three all bringing good form to the race, and a real battle between the first two inside the last. They can probably both do better.

1850 WALTER CROOKS NO LONGER A NOVICE STKS 5f
6:45 (6:47) (Class 5) 2-Y-O **£3,881** (£1,155; £577; £288) **Stalls** High

Form RPR
1 **Afandem (IRE)** 2-8-13 0 MarcMonaghan(3) 10 89+
(Hugo Palmer) *cl up: led wl over 1f out: rdn ent fnl f: styd on strly* **6/1**
5 **2** 3 ¼ **Rusumaat (IRE)**[26] 1233 2-9-2 0 DaneO'Neill 9 74
(Mark Johnston) *trckd ldrs: effrt 2f out and sn rdn: styd on to chse wnr ins fnl f: no imp towards fin* **10/1**
3 1 ¾ **Northern Thunder (IRE)** 2-9-2 0 SeanLevey 11 68+
(Richard Hannon) *trckd ldrs: hdwy 2f out: swtchd lft and rdn jst over 1f out: kpt on fnl f* **7/1**
3 **4** 1 **Another Angel (IRE)**[19] 1377 2-9-2 0 PaulMulrennan 7 64
(Michael Dods) *slt ld: pushed along over 2f out: hdd and rdn wl over 1f out: drvn ent fnl f and sn one pce* **5/2**[1]
5 2 ½ **Breaking Free** 2-9-2 0 PatCosgrave 6 55
(John Quinn) *dwlt and in rr tl sme late hdwy* **20/1**
6 1 **Norwegian Highness (FR)** 2-8-11 0 ShaneGray 3 47
(Kevin Ryan) *dwlt and in rr tl sme late hdwy* **5/1**[3]
3 **7** 1 ¼ **Champion Harbour (IRE)**[14] 1482 2-9-2 0 TonyHamilton 5 50
(Richard Fahey) *cl up on outer: rdn and edging lft over 1f out: wandered and lost action ent fnl f: sn eased* **7/2**[2]
8 5 **Sliceoflife** 2-9-2 0 LukeMorris 1 29
(Marco Botti) *chsd ldrs: rdn along over 2f out: sn wknd* **18/1**
5 **9** ¾ **Mulwith (IRE)**[19] 1377 2-9-2 0 DanielTudhope 4 27
(David Barron) *chsd ldrs on outer: rdn along 3f out: sn lost pl and bhd* **20/1**

1m 2.35s (1.85) **Going Correction** +0.525s/f (Yiel) **9** Ran SP% **118.1**
Speed ratings (Par 92): **106,100,98,96,92 90,88,80,79**
CSF £65.49 TOTE £7.40: £2.10, £3.60, £2.00; EX 82.00 Trifecta £585.20.
Owner Hamad Rashed Bin Ghedayer **Bred** Rabbah Bloodstock Limited **Trained** Newmarket, Suffolk
FOCUS
Previous experience often pays off in these novice races, so it was a good performance from the Hugo Palmer-trainer newcomer to take this by a clear margin. He looks pretty useful.

1851 WHEATLEY PALLETS H'CAP 7f
7:15 (7:16) (Class 2) (0-105,98) 3-Y-O
£12,450 (£3,728; £1,864; £932; £466; £234) **Stalls** High

Form RPR
134- **1** **Carrington (FR)**[213] 6853 3-8-10 **87** MartinLane 3 91+
(Charlie Appleby) *dwlt and in rr: hdwy and in tch on outer after 3f: cl up over 2f out: rdn to ld over 1f out: drvn ins fnl f: kpt on wl towards fin* **3/1**[1]
201- **2** ½ **Another Touch**[224] 6513 3-9-1 **92** TonyHamilton 2 94+
(Richard Fahey) *hld up and bhd: stdy hdwy wl over 1f out: chsd ldrs ent fnl f: sn rdn and kpt on wl towards fin* **5/1**[3]
0-21 **3** ½ **Dream Mover (IRE)**[71] 638 3-8-9 **86** LukeMorris 6 87
(Marco Botti) *t.k.h early: trckd ldr: effrt wl over 1f out: sn rdn: chsd wnr ins fnl f: sn drvn and kpt on* **7/2**[2]
10-4 **4** ¾ **Dawaa**[34] 1115 3-9-0 **91** DaneO'Neill 7 90
(Mark Johnston) *led: pushed along 2f out: rdn and hdd over 1f out: drvn and kpt on fnl f* **9/1**
540- **5** hd **Young John (IRE)**[169] 7834 3-8-3 **83** SammyJoBell(3) 4 81
(Richard Fahey) *trckd ldrs: effrt 2f out: rdn over 1f out: drvn and kpt on fnl f* **12/1**
15-0 **6** nk **Explosive Power (IRE)**[25] 1243 3-8-8 **90** JordanVaughan(5) 5 87
(K R Burke) *trckd ldrs: pushed along 2f out: rdn over 1f out: kpt on same pce fnl f* **9/1**
25-2 **7** ½ **Candelisa (IRE)**[25] 1243 3-9-7 **98** GrahamLee 9 94
(Jedd O'Keeffe) *hld up in tch: effrt and sme hdwy on outer wl over 1f out: sn rdn: drvn and no imp fnl f* **3/1**[1]

1m 30.58s (4.28) **Going Correction** +0.525s/f (Yiel) **7** Ran SP% **116.6**
Speed ratings (Par 104): **96,95,94,94,93 93,92**
CSF £19.01 CT £54.51 TOTE £4.10: £2.60, £2.30; EX 17.70 Trifecta £72.60.
Owner Godolphin **Bred** Haras S A R L Haras D'Etreham Et Al **Trained** Newmarket, Suffolk
FOCUS
The early pace wasn't strong and the result was a bunched finish. The winner is a potential improver.

1852 1STSECURITYSOLUTIONS.CO.UK H'CAP 1m 6f 132y
7:45 (7:45) (Class 4) (0-85,81) 4-Y-O+ **£5,175** (£1,540; £769; £384) **Stalls** Low

Form RPR
330- **1** **Braes Of Lochalsh**[197] 7250 5-9-2 **73** DanielTudhope 5 80+
(Jim Goldie) *hld up towards rr: hdwy 4f out: chsd ldrs over 2f out: rdn to ld over 1f out: drvn out* **12/1**
13-3 **2** hd **Rock On Bollinski**[27] 1222 6-9-0 **71** (p) SeanLevey 7 77+
(Brian Ellison) *dwlt and hld up in rr: niggled along over 4f out: hdwy wl over 2f out: rdn to chse ldrs over 1f out: drvn and styd on wl fnl f* **7/1**
3142 **3** 1 ¼ **Be My Sea (IRE)**[23] 1296 5-9-5 **76** WilliamCarson 9 80
(Tony Carroll) *trckd ldrs: hdwy 5f out and sn cl up: led wl over 2f out and sn rdn: hdd over 1f out and sn drvn: kpt on same pce ins fnl f* **7/2**[2]
6-5 **4** ½ **Vilman (IRE)**[8] 1598 4-9-6 **80** LukeMorris 2 84
(Simon West) *hld up in rr: stdy hdwy over 3f out: chal on outer 2f out: sn rdn and edgd lft appr fnl f: sn drvn and kpt on same pce* **12/1**
04-2 **5** ¾ **Hubertas**[24] 1250 4-9-2 **81** (b) CallumShepherd(5) 3 84
(John Quinn) *hld up in tch: hdwy over 3f out: chsd ldrs over 2f out: rdn and ev ch over 1f out: drvn ent fnl f and kpt on same pce* **11/4**[1]
64-4 **6** 2 ½ **Medina Sidonia (IRE)**[9] 1586 4-8-8 **73** RachelRichardson(5) 8 73
(Tim Easterby) *trckd ldng pair: effrt on inner 3f out and sn cl up: rdn 2f out and ev ch: drvn and wknd appr fnl f* **11/2**[3]
20-4 **7** 10 **Stanarley Pic**[24] 1253 5-9-0 **71** BenCurtis 6 58
(Alan Swinbank) *cl up: led 7f out: rdn along 3f out: sn hdd & wknd wl over 1f out* **13/2**
00-0 **8** 26 **Swnymor (IRE)**[9] 1586 7-9-9 **80** (p) DaleSwift 1 33
(Kevin Frost) *dwlt: a in rr* **25/1**
20-3 **9** 51 **Le Rock (IRE)**[43] 975 4-8-8 **73** JosephineGordon(5) 4
(J S Moore) *led: hdd 7f out: chsd ldr: pushed along over 5f out: rdn over 4f out: sn lost pl and bhd* **10/1**

3m 19.19s (11.79) **Going Correction** +0.925s/f (Soft)
WFA 4 from 5yo+ 3lb **9** Ran SP% **118.4**
Speed ratings (Par 105): **105,104,104,103,103 102,96,83,55**
CSF £95.27 CT £362.49 TOTE £15.10: £5.10, £2.10, £1.90; EX 64.70 Trifecta £441.80.
Owner Johnnie Delta Racing **Bred** Jim Goldie **Trained** Uplawmoor, E Renfrews
■ Stewards' Enquiry : Sean Levey two-day ban; used whip over the permitted level (15th, 16th May)
FOCUS
Race distance increased by about 6yds. This was quite a test in the ground but the field finished well bunched. The winner progressed last year.

1853 SIS APPRENTICE H'CAP 1m 4f
8:15 (8:15) (Class 4) (0-85,82) 4-Y-O+ **£5,175** (£1,540; £769; £384) **Stalls** Low

Form RPR
/31- **1** **Desert Encounter (IRE)**[200] 7186 4-9-3 **82** GeorgeBuckell(3) 1 95+
(David Simcock) *trckd ldrs: smooth hdwy on outer and cl up 3f out: led on bit jst over 2f out: shkn up ent fnl f: kpt on strly* **5/2**[3]
42-4 **2** 2 ¼ **Craggaknock**[14] 1493 5-9-4 **82** CallumShepherd(3) 5 88
(Mark Walford) *sn led and set stdy pce: jnd and pushed along 3f out: hdd and rdn jst over 2f out: drvn over 1f out: kpt on* **6/4**[1]
051- **3** 1 ½ **Parnell's Dream**[218] 6699 4-8-8 **73** PatrickO'Donnell(3) 2 77
(Ralph Beckett) *trckd ldr: effrt on inner 4f out: cl up 3f out: rdn along over 2f out: drvn over 1f out: kpt on same pce fnl f* **9/4**[2]
150- **4** 2 ¾ **Arabian Oasis**[20] 1792 4-8-13 **80** PhilDennis(5) 3 79
(Philip Kirby) *t.k.h: trckd ldng pair: hdwy on outer and cl up over 4f out: effrt 3f out and ev ch: rdn over 2f out: sn drvn and one pce* **20/1**
100- **5** 6 **Ronald Gee (IRE)**[214] 6826 9-8-11 **72** RyanTate 4 62
(Jim Goldie) *hld up in rr: effrt 4f out: rdn along 3f out: sn btn* **14/1**

2m 47.79s (12.89) **Going Correction** +0.925s/f (Soft)
WFA 4 from 5yo+ 1lb **5** Ran SP% **110.8**
Speed ratings (Par 105): **94,92,91,89,85**
CSF £6.73 TOTE £3.50: £2.00, £1.20; EX 7.00 Trifecta £11.40.
Owner Abdulla Al Mansoori **Bred** Tally-Ho Stud **Trained** Newmarket, Suffolk
FOCUS
Race distance increased by about 6yds. They went no pace early and this turned into a relative test of speed. The form is a bit muddling but the winner has been given a bit of a chance.
T/Plt: £296.10 to a £1 stake. Pool: £50,692.36 - 124.94 winning tickets. T/Qpdt: £27.40 to a £1 stake. Pool: £6,510.44 - 175.40 winning tickets. **Joe Rowntree**

GOODWOOD (R-H)

Saturday, April 30

OFFICIAL GOING: Straight course - good to soft (good in places); round course - good

Wind: Moderate, half against Weather: Fine but cloudy

1854 BETFRED "FOLLOW US ON TWITTER" (H'CAP) 1m 6f

1:45 (1:45) (Class 5) (0-75,72) 4-Y-O+ **£3,234** (£962; £481; £240) **Stalls** Low

Form RPR

000/ **1** **Rayvin Black**[49] 7353 7-9-3 **70**............................... EdwardGreatrex(5) 14 84
(Oliver Sherwood) *led after 100yds: mde rest at decent pce: rdn 3f out: clr whn edgd rt fr 2f out: styd on strly* **11/8**[1]

54-4 **2** *5* **Onorina (IRE)**[15] 1456 4-8-12 **62**.................................... CathyGannon 7 69
(Jim Boyle) *hld up in midfield: prog 1/2-way: chsd wnr over 3f out: clr of rest 2f out but no imp: one pce after* **14/1**

/0-6 **3** *1/2* **Nam Hai (IRE)**[27] 1222 5-9-5 **67**...................... WilliamTwiston-Davies 6 73
(Kim Bailey) *hld up in rr: pushed along and prog over 3f out: rdn to go 3rd over 1f out but no ch: styd on to cl on runner-up nr fin* **10/1**

001- **4** *3 1/4* **Sweet Selection**[156] 8001 4-9-6 **70**................................ RobertHavlin 9 72
(Hughie Morrison) *hld up in last quartet: shkn up and prog over 3f out: no imp on ldrs 2f out: kpt on* **5/1**[2]

435- **5** *1/2* **Medburn Cutler**[159] 7960 6-9-7 **69**..........................(p) JamieSpencer 12 70
(Paul Henderson) *prom: disp 2nd briefly over 3f out: wknd over 1f out* **8/1**[3]

10-4 **6** *6* **Starcrossed**[116] 43 4-9-5 **69**..(b[1]) PatDobbs 2 62
(Eve Johnson Houghton) *prom: chsd ldng pair after 6f to over 3f out: sn wknd* **14/1**

-230 **7** *1 1/4* **Scrafton**[27] 1222 5-9-2 **67**... GeorgeDowning(3) 3 58
(Tony Carroll) *towards rr: hrd rdn over 3f out: no real prog* **33/1**

/44- **8** *1 1/2* **Royal Battalion**[29] 242 5-9-8 **70**..................................(p) LiamKeniry 5 59
(Gary Moore) *chsd ldrs to over 3f out: wknd* **25/1**

3-53 **9** *1 3/4* **Takeitfromalady (IRE)**[38] 1038 7-9-2 **64**.......................(v) KierenFox 13 50
(Lee Carter) *nvr bttr than midfield: shkn up and no prog over 3f out: sn wknd* **25/1**

3535 **10** *3 3/4* **San Quentin (IRE)**[19] 1391 5-9-6 **68**........................... DarryllHolland 11 49
(Dean Ivory) *hld up in rr: stdy prog on outer over 3f out and looked to be gng wl enough: shkn up and wknd 2f out* **33/1**

-212 **11** *33* **Shalambar (IRE)**[29] 1177 10-9-2 **64**...............................(v) KierenFallon 8
(Tony Carroll) *sn shoved along in last and nvr gng wl: t.o* **20/1**

650 **12** *nk* **Executive Order**[68] 675 7-8-3 **54** oh8 ow1........................ TimClark(3) 4
(Martin Smith) *nvr bttr than midfield: wknd 4f out: t.o over 2f out* **100/1**

65- **13** *2 1/4* **Shareni (IRE)**[56] 1293 7-9-10 **72**....................................... JoeyHaynes 1
(Zoe Davison) *chsd ldrs to 1/2-way: sn struggling: wknd 5f out: t.o* **100/1**

0-02 **14** *18* **Salient**[26] 1239 12-8-6 **54**.. JimmyQuinn 10
(Michael Attwater) *led 100yds: chsd wnr to over 3f out: wknd rapidly: t.o and eased over 1f out* **20/1**

3m 7.72s (4.12) **Going Correction** +0.225s/f (Good)
WFA 4 from 5yo+ 2lb **14** Ran SP% **117.4**
Speed ratings (Par 103): **97,94,93,92,91 88,87,86,85,83 64,64,63,52**
CSF £19.43 CT £145.25 TOTE £2.30: £1.40, £3.90, £3.20; EX 25.80 Trifecta £235.10.
Owner R White & V J Walsh **Bred** Mystic Meg Limited **Trained** Upper Lambourn, Berks
■ Stewards' Enquiry : Kieren Fallon two-day ban; used whip above permitted level (15th,16th May)

FOCUS
The first 2f of the Mile course were dolled out 6yds. The distance of this race was as advertised. 'Good, lovely ground' was the general view from jockeys on the going. No hanging around here, with the winning favourite ensuring it was a thorough test at the distance. The winner is rated back to his old Flat level.

1855 BETFRED TV EBF STALLIONS DAISY WARWICK STKS (LISTED RACE) 1m 4f

2:15 (2:17) (Class 1) 4-Y-O+ **£23,680** (£8,956; £4,476; £2,236) **Stalls** High

Form RPR

211- **1** **Carnachy (IRE)**[202] 7145 4-9-0 95....................................... SeanLevey 4 105
(David Simcock) *trckd ldrs: clsd to ld 2f out: rdn and styd on wl fr over 1f out* **10/1**

111- **2** *1 1/2* **Bateel (IRE)**[224] 6541 4-9-0 97... JamieSpencer 3 103+
(David Simcock) *stdd s: hld up in last pair: tried to make prog on inner over 2f out: nt clr run and swtchd lft wl over 1f out: hdwy to chse wnr ins fnl f: styd on but no imp* **15/8**[1]

263- **3** *2* **Twitch (IRE)**[162] 7935 4-9-0 92.....................................(p) DarryllHolland 2 99
(Hugo Palmer) *led: rdn and hdd 2f out: one pce and lost 2nd ins fnl f* **22/1**

22-1 **4** *hd* **More Mischief**[27] 1221 4-9-0 91...................................... JoeyHaynes 10 99
(Jedd O'Keeffe) *wl in tch: effrt on outer over 2f out: styd on but nvr quite pce to chal: nrly snatched 3rd* **12/1**

44-2 **5** *3 3/4* **Sagaciously (IRE)**[21] 1336 4-9-0 90...................... RichardKingscote 12 93
(Ed Dunlop) *towards rr: effrt over 2f out: one pce and no imp on ldrs whn edgd rt over 1f out* **33/1**

135- **6** *1 1/2* **Miss Marjurie (IRE)**[254] 5568 6-9-1 110............................ ShaneKelly 6 91
(Denis Coakley) *t.k.h: hld up towards rr: prog on inner 3f out: cl enough whn rdn wl over 1f out: sn wknd* **9/2**[2]

102- **7** *1 1/2* **California (IRE)**[184] 7587 4-9-0 94.................................... RobertHavlin 5 88
(John Gosden) *prom: stl wl there over 2f out: wknd qckly wl over 1f out* **8/1**[3]

5-40 **8** *1/2* **Monaleen (IRE)**[36] 1067 5-9-1 91..................................... SteveDrowne 9 87
(Ian Williams) *a towards rr: shkn up and no real prog wl over 2f out* **100/1**

513- **9** *5* **Moderah**[189] 7469 4-9-0 104... KierenFallon 1 79
(James Fanshawe) *t.k.h: hld up in midfield: rdn and cl up bhd ldrs 2f out: wknd over 1f out: eased* **12/1**

1P0- **10** *1 1/2* **Yarrow (IRE)**[254] 5569 4-9-0 92.. TedDurcan 13 77
(Sir Michael Stoute) *trckd ldr to 3f out: sn wknd* **25/1**

46-0 **11** *3/4* **Tioga Pass**[10] 1569 5-9-1 95... PatDobbs 11 76
(Paul Cole) *hld up in last pair: effrt on outer 3f out: sn no prog and btn* **50/1**

04-4 **12** *3/4* **Encore L'Amour**[27] 1219 4-9-0 94... FMBerry 8 75
(Ralph Beckett) *hld up in midfield: effrt u.p over 2f out: wknd wl over 1f out* **40/1**

020- **13** *nse* **Pamona (IRE)**[161] 7952 4-9-0 100.................................... HarryBentley 7 75
(Luca Cumani) *in tch in midfield: rdn and no prog 3f out: sn wknd* **10/1**

2m 40.58s (2.18) **Going Correction** +0.225s/f (Good)
WFA 4 from 5yo+ 1lb **13** Ran SP% **114.2**
Speed ratings (Par 111): **101,100,98,98,96 95,94,93,90,89 88,88,88**
CSF £26.12 TOTE £10.50: £3.10, £1.30, £6.50; EX 38.50 Trifecta £700.20.
Owner St Albans Bloodstock Limited **Bred** Summerhill & J Osborne **Trained** Newmarket, Suffolk

FOCUS
Race distance as advertised. Two really progressive fillies from the David Simcock yard came to the fore in this Listed contest, although they didn't finish in the order the market anticipated, with the winner enduring a more favourable trip. The third has been rated as improving.

1856 BETFRED "TREBLE ODDS ON LUCKY 15'S" H'CAP 7f

2:50 (2:51) (Class 2) (0-100,100) 4-Y-O+**£32,345** (£9,625; £4,810; £2,405) **Stalls** Low

Form RPR

0046 **1** **Russian Realm**[52] 871 6-8-12 **91**....................................... ShaneKelly 5 99
(Richard Hughes) *hld up in midfield: prog 2f out gng wl: rdn to ld 150yds out: styd on wl* **14/1**

40-1 **2** *nk* **Sinfonietta (FR)**[24] 1274 4-8-10 **89**................................... KierenFallon 4 96
(David Menuisier) *trckd ldrs: rdn over 2f out: chsd ldr over 1f out: tried to chal fnl f: styd on but nt pce of wnr last 100yds* **6/1**[2]

00-0 **3** *nk* **Lincoln (IRE)**[7] 1627 5-9-0 **93**.. CharlesBishop 15 99+
(Mick Channon) *hld up in midfield: stdy prog on outer over 2f out: rdn to chal fnl f: nt qckn last 100yds* **9/1**

1-00 **4** *1/2* **Right Touch**[7] 1627 6-8-9 **95**.................................. AdamMcNamara(7) 9 100+
(Richard Fahey) *hld up in last trio: shkn up and no prog over 2f out: stl wl in rr jst over 1f out: r.o fnl f: fin best* **10/1**

10-2 **5** *nk* **Solar Flair**[28] 1204 4-9-0 **93**....................................... RichardKingscote 2 97
(William Knight) *led: drvn over 1f out: hdd and no ex fnl 150yds* **11/2**[1]

4230 **6** *shd* **Sirius Prospect (USA)**[28] 1196 8-9-2 **98**.....................(p) JackDuern(3) 1 102
(Dean Ivory) *dwlt: sn chsd ldrs on inner: rdn 2f out: lost pl over 1f out: styd on again ins fnl f* **25/1**

0-01 **7** *nk* **Perfect Pasture**[12] 1522 6-9-7 **100**..............................(v) TedDurcan 7 103
(Michael Easterby) *hld up in rr: reminder wl over 2f out: rdn over 1f out: styd on fnl f: nrst fin but no real threat* **22/1**

660- **8** *hd* **Czech It Out (IRE)**[175] 7754 6-8-11 **90**................................... FMBerry 6 92
(Amanda Perrett) *wl in tch: rdn and nt qckn over 1f out: styd on ins fnl f: nvr able to chal* **10/1**

05-0 **8** *dht* **Joey's Destiny (IRE)**[27] 1218 6-8-13 **92**........................... LiamKeniry 12 94
(George Baker) *hld up towards rr: shkn up on outer over 2f out: styd on fnl f but nvr able to chal* **25/1**

560- **10** *hd* **Room Key**[217] 6739 4-9-4 **97**.. JamieSpencer 11 99
(Eve Johnson Houghton) *stdd s and swtchd across fr wd draw: hld up in last trio: tried to creep clsr fr 2f out: shkn up and clsd on ldrs 1f out: edgd rt and one pce after* **14/1**

55-6 **11** *2 1/4* **Fiftyshadesofgrey (IRE)**[21] 1335 5-9-2 **95**..................(t) SteveDrowne 8 93+
(George Baker) *slowly away: sn in tch: rdn and effrt on inner over 2f out: keeping on one pce and hld whn squeezed for room 100yds out: eased* **9/1**

22-1 **12** *1 1/4* **Exchequer (IRE)**[21] 1335 5-8-13 **92**................................... SeanLevey 14 84
(David Brown) *trckd ldrs on outer: rdn to dispute 2nd briefly over 1f out: wknd qckly ins fnl f* **8/1**[3]

00-6 **13** *1/2* **Desert Force**[18] 1394 4-8-13 **92**... PatDobbs 16 83
(Richard Hannon) *hld up in last trio: shkn up over 2f out: no real prog over 1f out* **20/1**

01-0 **14** *3/4* **Mujassam**[16] 1441 4-9-5 **98**... HarryBentley 3 87
(Roger Varian) *chsd ldr to over 1f out: wknd* **12/1**

62-4 **15** *3 1/2* **Highland Colori (IRE)**[31] 1153 8-9-6 **99**........................ DavidProbert 10 79
(Andrew Balding) *chsd ldng pair to 2f out: wknd* **20/1**

1m 27.92s (0.92) **Going Correction** +0.225s/f (Good) **15** Ran SP% **121.6**
Speed ratings (Par 109): **103,102,102,101,101 101,100,100,100,100 97,96,95,95,91**
CSF £88.29 CT £827.68 TOTE £17.20: £4.40, £2.50, £3.50; EX 132.60 Trifecta £790.30.
Owner The Queens & R Hughes **Bred** Cheveley Park Stud Ltd **Trained** Upper Lambourn, Berkshire

FOCUS
Race run over 12yds further than advertised. These 7f handicaps here are always ultra-competitive and they finished in a bit of a heap. The winner was close to last year's handicap form.

1857 BETFRED "SUPPORTS JACK BERRY HOUSE" H'CAP 5f

3:25 (3:25) (Class 3) (0-95,95) 4-Y-O+ **£9,703** (£2,887; £1,443; £721) **Stalls** High

Form RPR

600- **1** **Marmalady (IRE)**[193] 7363 6-8-8 **82**..................................... TedDurcan 6 92
(Robert Cowell) *stdd s: hld up in last: prog over 1f out: coaxed along and hanging but chsd ldr ins fnl f: shkn up and r.o towards nr side to ld last 75yds* **16/1**

02-5 **2** *1* **Harry Hurricane**[28] 1205 4-9-7 **95**................................... SteveDrowne 9 102
(George Baker) *hld up bhd ldrs gng wl: shkn up and prog to ld over 1f out: rdn fnl f: hdd and outpcd last 75yds* **8/1**

-564 **3** *1 3/4* **Waseem Faris (IRE)**[17] 1427 7-8-11 **88**................... TomMarquand(3) 2 89
(Joseph Tuite) *racd on outer: cl up: prog to ld 2f out: hdd over 1f out: one pce fnl f* **14/1**

0-02 **4** *3/4* **Intense Style (IRE)**[17] 1408 4-9-5 **93**...................................... FMBerry 8 92
(Les Eyre) *chsd ldrs: rdn 2f out and no prog: styd on again ins fnl f towards nr side* **7/1**[3]

100- **5** *3/4* **Sydney Ruffdiamond**[238] 6080 4-8-11 **85**........................... ShaneKelly 3 82
(Richard Hughes) *stdd s: hld up in last pair: prog to cl on ldrs on outer over 1f out: nt qckn fnl f: one pce* **10/1**

0601 **6** *nk* **Stake Acclaim (IRE)**[12] 1528 4-8-12 **89**...................(p) JackDuern(3) 1 85
(Dean Ivory) *racd on outer: in tch: prog to press new ldr wl over 1f out: fdd fnl f* **2/1**[1]

5451 **7** *2 3/4* **Normal Equilibrium**[10] 1566 6-9-1 **89**............................. JamieSpencer 7 76
(Robert Cowell) *led and tk field down centre: hdd 2f out: sn btn* **9/2**[2]

-651 **8** *shd* **Zac Brown (IRE)**[49] 923 5-8-13 **92**................................ AaronJones(5) 4 79
(Charlie Wallis) *pressed ldng pair to 2f out: wknd over 1f out* **10/1**

05-5 **9** *1* **Monumental Man**[10] 1566 7-8-8 **82**...........................(p) DavidProbert 5 65
(Michael Attwater) *pressed ldr to 2f out: wknd over 1f out* **16/1**

58.85s (-1.35) **Going Correction** -0.05s/f (Good) **9** Ran SP% **111.7**
Speed ratings (Par 107): **108,106,103,102,101 100,96,96,94**
CSF £131.29 CT £1823.18 TOTE £14.20: £3.00, £2.30, £3.20; EX 102.20 Trifecta £1548.40.
Owner Heart Of The South Racing **Bred** Tribes Man Syndicate **Trained** Six Mile Bottom, Cambs

FOCUS
Race distance as advertised. They went off fast and the closers were favoured. The winner looks back to her best.

1858 BETFRED "1400 SHOPS NATIONWIDE" EBF CONQUEROR STKS (LISTED RACE) (F&M) 1m

4:00 (4:00) (Class 1) 3-Y-O+

£22,684 (£8,600; £4,304; £2,144; £1,076; £540) **Stalls** Low

Form RPR

226- **1** **Blond Me (IRE)**[203] 7138 4-9-7 103.................................... DavidProbert 5 109
(Andrew Balding) *hld up in 5th: shkn up on outer 2f out: clsd qckly to ld jst ins fnl f: r.o wl and sn clr* **4/1**[3]

-123 **2** *3 ½* **Oakley Girl**[89] 422 4-9-7 84 .... FMBerry 7 101
(Stuart Williams) *hld up in last: rdn whn nt clr run over 1f out: r.o fnl f to take 2nd last strides* **14/1**

532- **3** *nk* **Black Cherry**[218] 6707 4-9-7 102 .... PatDobbs 1 100
(Richard Hannon) *led: 5 l clr after 3f: c bk to field 3f out: rdn 2f out: hdd 1f out and sn outpcd: kpt on* **11/4**[1]

1112 **4** *nk* **Volunteer Point (IRE)**[28] 1207 4-9-7 102 .... CharlesBishop 4 100
(Mick Channon) *sltly awkward s: hld up in 6th: nt clr run fr 2f out tl swtchd rt over 1f out: styd on fnl f to take 4th last strides: no ch* **6/1**

-321 **5** *½* **Pure Diamond**[58] 807 3-8-10 103 .... HarryBentley 3 97
(Saeed bin Suroor) *trckd ldng trio: waiting for room over 2f out: prog to go 2nd over 1f out: led briefly 1f out: sn outpcd: lost pls last strides* **3/1**[2]

20-6 **6** *4* **Military Angel (USA)**[41] 1016 4-9-7 102 .... KierenFallon 6 89
(M D O'Callaghan, Ire) *chsd ldng pair: rdn over 2f out: wknd over 1f out* **8/1**

055- **7** *1* **Mothers Finest (IRE)**[218] 6707 4-9-7 95 .... JoeyHaynes 2 87
(K R Burke) *chsd ldr: rdn over 2f out: lost 2nd and wknd over 1f out* **9/1**

1m 39.34s (-0.56) **Going Correction** +0.225s/f (Good)
WFA 3 from 4yo 14lb **7** Ran SP% **113.7**
Speed ratings (Par 111): **111,107,107,106,106 102,101**
CSF £54.21 TOTE £5.10: £2.30, £6.00; EX 69.90 Trifecta £165.80 Part won..
Owner Mrs Barbara M Keller **Bred** Wardstown Stud Ltd **Trained** Kingsclere, Hants

FOCUS
Race run over 12yds further than advertised. This had looked quite a tight Listed event but it produced a clear-cut winner. This rates a pb.

1859 BETFRED MOBILE MEDIAN AUCTION MAIDEN STKS 7f
4:35 (4:37) (Class 5) 3-Y-O **£3,234** (£962; £481; £240) **Stalls** Low

Form RPR

0- **1** **Showing Off (IRE)**[218] 6711 3-9-5 0 .... HarryBentley 2 79+
(Henry Candy) *hld up bhd ldng trio: waiting for a gap over 2f out tl over 1f out: drvn through to ld 1f out: styd on wl* **11/8**[1]

50-2 **2** *1* **Destroyer**[29] 1181 3-9-2 76 .... (p) RobHornby(3) 8 76
(William Muir) *t.k.h: w ldng pair: chal and upsides wl over 1f out: chsd wnr fnl f: styd on but a safely hld* **8/1**

0- **3** *1* **Torch**[199] 7217 3-9-5 0 .... PatDobbs 4 73+
(Richard Hannon) *settled in last trio: pushed along wl over 2f out: rdn and prog jst over 1f out: r.o to take 3rd nr fin* **8/1**

4 *shd* **Hilltop Ranger (IRE)** 3-9-0 0 .... RichardKingscote 7 68+
(Daniel Kubler) *settled in last trio: pushed along over 2f out: prog jst over 1f out: styd on encouragingly to take 4th nr fin* **25/1**

0 **5** *1* **Mr Andros**[17] 1421 3-9-5 0 .... DavidProbert 5 70
(Andrew Balding) *t.k.h: hld up bhd ldrs: tried to mount a chal over 1f out: one pce after* **33/1**

53 **6** *nk* **Phoenix Beat**[21] 1357 3-9-0 0 .... FMBerry 3 65
(Gay Kelleway) *t.k.h: pressed ldr: chal and upsides fr 2f out to 1f out: fdd* **16/1**

230- **7** *¾* **Ejayteekay**[148] 8103 3-9-0 72 .... RobertHavlin 9 62
(Hughie Morrison) *hld up in tch: cl enough on outer jst over 2f out: sn rdn and fnd nil: wl btn over 1f out* **7/1**[3]

2- **8** *1 ¼* **Langham**[136] 8243 3-9-0 0 .... TedDurcan 1 59
(Martyn Meade) *led: jnd 2f out: hdd & wknd 1f out* **11/4**[2]

00- **9** *4 ½* **Mr Standfast**[130] 8349 3-9-5 0 .... KierenFox 6 52
(Alan Phillips) *t.k.h: hld up in last pair: rdn over 2f out: no prog and sn btn* **100/1**

1m 29.19s (2.19) **Going Correction** +0.225s/f (Good) **9** Ran SP% **117.2**
Speed ratings (Par 98): **96,94,93,93,92 92,91,89,84**
CSF £13.64 TOTE £2.30: £1.50, £2.20, £2.70; EX 14.70 Trifecta £73.10.
Owner Bloomsbury Stud **Bred** Bloomsbury Stud **Trained** Kingston Warren, Oxon

FOCUS
Race run over 12yds further than advertised. Average maiden form, with little depth.

1860 BETFRED "BET ON THE EUROVISION SONG CONTEST" STKS (H'CAP) 1m 1f 192y
5:10 (5:10) (Class 5) (0-70,70) 3-Y-O **£3,234** (£962; £481; £240) **Stalls** Low

Form RPR

022- **1** **Goldenfield (IRE)**[156] 7999 3-9-4 67 .... (p) LiamKeniry 4 82
(Gary Moore) *mde all: drew clr over 2f out: rdn over 1f out: styd on wl: unchal* **12/1**

030- **2** *2 ½* **Peloponnese (FR)**[199] 7219 3-9-4 67 .... TedDurcan 3 77
(Sir Michael Stoute) *in tch in midfield: rdn and prog over 3f out: tk 2nd over 1f out: styd on but no imp on wnr* **7/1**[2]

006- **3** *hd* **Blakeney Point**[171] 7793 3-8-11 65 .... KieranShoemark(5) 10 75
(Roger Charlton) *in tch: rdn and prog on outer fr 3f out: styd on to dispute 2nd fnl f: no imp on wnr* **10/1**

0326 **4** *2 ½* **Betsalottie**[19] 1388 3-8-7 56 .... CathyGannon 14 61
(John Bridger) *hld up in last: rdn and prog fr wl over 3f out: kpt on fr over 1f out: nrst fin* **25/1**

-220 **5** *4* **Gabster (IRE)**[64] 729 3-8-12 66 .... HectorCrouch(5) 13 63
(Amanda Perrett) *racd on outer in midfield: u.p towards rr over 3f out: kpt on fr over 1f out on wd outside: n.d* **20/1**

124- **6** *1 ½* **Ripoll (IRE)**[152] 8055 3-8-6 62 .... (t) BenSanderson(7) 5 56
(Sylvester Kirk) *chsd ldrs: rdn to dispute 2nd over 3f out to 2f out: wknd* **18/1**

00-1 **7** *nk* **Captain Peacock**[24] 1259 3-9-3 66 .... RichardKingscote 11 59
(William Knight) *hld up in midfield: dropped to last and struggling bdly 4f out: passed wkng rivals fr over 2f out* **9/4**[1]

035- **8** *¾* **Pourquoi Non (IRE)**[165] 7878 3-9-4 67 .... DavidProbert 7 59
(Denis Coakley) *hld up towards rr: rdn and no prog 3f out: wl btn fnl 2f* **10/1**

-440 **9** *2 ¾* **Daring Knight**[26] 1238 3-9-4 70 .... TimClark(3) 2 56
(Martin Smith) *chsd wnr but sn chivvied along: lost 2nd over 3f out: steadily wknd u.p* **33/1**

3631 **10** *1* **Rock 'n Red (IRE)**[21] 1346 3-9-4 70 .... RobHornby(3) 1 54
(Ed Dunlop) *prom: trckd wnr over 3f out gng wl enough: rdn and no rspnse over 2f out: wknd qckly over 1f out* **10/1**

20-0 **11** *1* **Boutan**[24] 1275 3-9-4 70 .... TomMarquand(3) 8 52
(George Baker) *hld up in rr: sme prog fr 3f out: nt rch ldrs u.p wl over 1f out: sn wknd* **28/1**

30-2 **12** *1 ½* **Nutbourne Lad (IRE)**[24] 1275 3-9-2 65 .... (b) FMBerry 9 44
(Amanda Perrett) *chsd ldrs: u.p by 1/2-way: wknd fr 3f out* **9/1**[3]

34-0 **13** *6* **Lee's Hall (IRE)**[19] 1388 3-9-4 67 .... [1] ShaneKelly 12 34
(Murty McGrath) *hld up wl in rr: gng bttr than many over 3f out: rdn and no prog wl over 2f out: wknd* **20/1**

340- **14** *17* **Bay Of St Malo (IRE)**[189] 7467 3-9-7 70 .... PatDobbs 6
(Richard Hannon) *hld up: effrt over 3f out: sltly checked over 2f out and wknd rapidly: t.o* **14/1**

2m 9.46s (1.36) **Going Correction** +0.225s/f (Good) **14** Ran SP% **119.9**
Speed ratings (Par 98): **103,101,100,98,95 94,94,93,91,90 89,88,83,70**
CSF £86.47 CT £886.77 TOTE £13.40: £4.10, £2.30, £3.90; EX 111.00 Trifecta £1350.70.
Owner Mr & Mrs W W Fleming **Bred** Gigginstown House Stud **Trained** Lower Beeding, W Sussex

FOCUS
Race distance as advertised. A modest handicap and the winner got first run, but the race should produce winners at a similar level. It was the pick of the times on the round course.
T/Plt: £416.80 to a £1 stake. Pool: £101,860.03 - 178.37 winning units. T/Qpdt: £117.10 to a £1 stake. Pool: £6,236.99 - 39.40 winning units. **Jonathan Neesom**

1436 NEWMARKET (R-H)
Saturday, April 30

OFFICIAL GOING: Good to soft (good in places; far side 7.0, centre 7.1, stands' side 7.2)
Wind: light, behind Weather: light cloud, bright spells

1861 CHAMPIONSOFRACING.CO.UK SUFFOLK STKS (H'CAP) 1m 1f
2:00 (2:01) (Class 2) 3-Y-O+
£28,012 (£8,388; £4,194; £2,097; £1,048; £526) **Stalls** High

Form RPR

631- **1** **Knight Owl**[173] 7776 6-8-1 88 .... GeorgeWood(7) 4 97
(James Fanshawe) *trckd ldrs tl led on bit wl over 1f out: sn rdn: styd on wl fnl f: rdn out* **20/1**

36-0 **2** *½* **Examiner (IRE)**[28] 1195 5-8-10 90 .... OisinMurphy 11 98+
(Stuart Williams) *lw: hld up in tch towards rr: clsd and nt clr run over 1f out: swtchd lft and hdwy jst over 1f out: styd on wl u.p ins fnl f: wnt 2nd cl home* **16/1**

-140 **3** *½* **Revolutionist (IRE)**[7] 1629 4-9-1 95 .... JamesDoyle 5 102
(Mark Johnston) *lw: led: rdn over 2f out: hrd drvn and hdd wl over 1f out: battled on wl u.p and stl ev ch: styd on same pce fnl 100yds: lost 2nd cl home* **14/1**

450- **4** *hd* **Strong Steps**[197] 7247 4-8-8 88 .... (p) LukeMorris 7 95
(Hugo Palmer) *chsd ldrs: wnt 2nd 3f out tl over 2f out: drvn and unable qck over 1f out: rallied ins fnl f: kpt on fnl 100yds* **16/1**

035- **5** *½* **Master The World (IRE)**[182] 7634 5-9-10 104 .... (p) SilvestreDeSousa 2 109
(David Elsworth) *t.k.h: hld up in tch in midfield: effrt and hdwy 2f out: drvn and chsd ldrs over 1f out: kpt on same pce ins fnl f* **8/1**[3]

111- **6** *½* **Arthenus**[203] 7119 4-9-6 100 .... FrederikTylicki 10 104+
(James Fanshawe) *in tch in midfield: shkn up briefly 1/2-way: edging rt wl over 1f out: stl cl enough and wandered 1f out: nt clrest of runs and swtchd lft and rt ins fnl f: kpt on same pce fnl 100yds* **5/1**[2]

/11- **7** *¾* **Intimation**[301] 3897 4-8-10 90 .... PatSmullen 14 93+
(Sir Michael Stoute) *lw: hld up in tch in midfield: nt clr run 2f out: swtchd lft and effrt u.p over 1f out: hdwy 1f out: kpt on ins fnl f* **9/2**[1]

/6-3 **8** *1 ¼* **Mutamakkin (USA)**[16] 1441 4-8-12 92 .... PaulHanagan 16 92
(Sir Michael Stoute) *lw: t.k.h: in tch in midfield: rdn 3f out: unable qck over 1f out: drvn and styd on same pce fnl f* **9/2**[1]

1-02 **9** *nk* **Emerald (ITY)**[14] 1480 4-8-8 88 .... (p) AndreaAtzeni 1 87
(Marco Botti) *hld up in rr: swtchd lft after 1f: effrt whn nt clr run and swtchd rt over 1f out: kpt on but no real imp fnl f* **14/1**

000- **10** *½* **Niceofyoutotellme**[168] 7857 7-9-9 103 .... JimCrowley 3 101
(Ralph Beckett) *taken down early: t.k.h: hld up in tch: effrt 2f out: drvn over 1f out: styd on same pce and no imp fnl f* **12/1**

0-01 **11** *1 ¾* **Spring Offensive (IRE)**[12] 1521 4-8-7 87 .... PatrickMathers 6 81
(Richard Fahey) *in tch in midfield: rdn ent fnl 2f: unable qck over 1f out: wknd ins fnl f* **12/1**

4-10 **12** *nk* **Craftsmanship (FR)**[28] 1195 5-8-6 86 .... (p) WilliamCarson 9 80
(Robert Eddery) *in tch towards rr: niggled along 1/2-way: sme hdwy u.p over 1f out: swtchd rt 1f out: no imp ins fnl f* **50/1**

-000 **13** *13* **El Tren (IRE)**[65] 722 5-9-1 95 .... AdamBeschizza 13 60
(Michael Attwater) *in tch in midfield: lost pl and rdn 3f out: bhd over 1f out* **80/1**

113- **14** *2* **Demonstration (IRE)**[140] 8208 4-8-3 83 .... (p) JoeFanning 12 44
(William Jarvis) *dwlt: sn rcvrd and chsd ldr tl 3f out: lost pl 2f out: wkng whn pushed lft over 1f out: bhd ins fnl f* **25/1**

1m 50.93s (-0.77) **Going Correction** +0.10s/f (Good) **14** Ran SP% **116.4**
Speed ratings (Par 109): **107,106,106,105,105 105,104,103,103,102 101,100,89,87**
CSF £292.99 CT £4678.56 TOTE £25.50: £6.20, £6.40, £4.20; EX 515.90 Trifecta £5040.30 Part won.
Owner Miss Annabelle Condon **Bred** Car Colston Hall Stud **Trained** Newmarket, Suffolk

FOCUS
Stands' Side course used. Stalls Stand Side except 1m4f: Centre Cut off. The going was given as good to soft, good in places prior to the opener after Head of Racing Michael Prosser walked the track at lunchtime. He said 'It's definitely on the slow side of good right now, but it's very even and consistent around the whole course. There is a fair tailwind which will definitely assist the runners, it's coming from slightly across but is mostly from behind.' This looked a really strong handicap to open the two-day meeting, and some decent types have landed it in the past like Confront, Green Destiny and Tullius. The first and third raced raced away from the main bunch in a smaller group. A pb from the winner, the rider's claim helping.

1862 PEARL BLOODSTOCK PALACE HOUSE STKS (GROUP 3) 5f
2:30 (2:33) (Class 1) 3-Y-O+
£34,026 (£12,900; £6,456; £3,216; £1,614; £810) **Stalls** High

Form RPR

505- **1** **Profitable (IRE)**[230] 6367 4-9-3 107 .... AdamKirby 20 116
(Clive Cox) *racd nr side: midfield overall: rdn and hdwy over 1f out: drvn and ev ch ins fnl f: styd on wl u.p to ld towards fin: 1st of 5 in gp* **20/1**

-124 **2** *½* **Jungle Cat (IRE)**[35] 1104 4-9-3 113 .... WilliamBuick 18 114
(Charlie Appleby) *lw: racd along in centre: in tch: effrt over 1f out: hdwy and pressing ldrs 1f out: kpt on wl u.p ins fnl f: wnt 2nd towards fin* **6/1**[2]

110- **3** *nk* **Waady (IRE)**[238] 6084 4-9-3 112 .... PaulHanagan 22 113+
(John Gosden) *on toes: racd nr side: chsd nr side ldr and prom overall: effrt 2f out: drvn and pressing ldrs 1f out: kpt on wl fnl 100yds: 2nd of 5 in gp* **9/2**[1]

036- **4** *nk* **Spirit Quartz (IRE)**[275] 4805 8-9-3 108 .... (p) MartinHarley 4 112
(Robert Cowell) *on toes: swtg: racd far side: hld up in tch and travelled strly: hdwy over 1f out: rdn to chal 1f out: led ins fnl f: hdd and no ex towards fin: 1st of 15 in gp* **20/1**

01-2 **5** nk **Take Cover**[63] 745 9-9-3 111 OisinMurphy 14 111
(David C Griffiths) *taken down early: led to s: racd far side: led: rdn ent fnl f: hdd ins fnl f: no ex and one pce fnl 75yds: 2nd of 15 in gp* **11/1**

00-4 **6** hd **Aeolus**[16] 1439 5-9-3 108 LukeMorris 6 110
(Ed Walker) *racd far side: in tch towards rr: rdn over 2f out: hdwy u.p ent fnl f: kpt on wl ins fnl f: 3rd of 15 in gp* **16/1**

200- **7** 3/4 **Kingsgate Native (IRE)**[210] 6916 11-9-3 107 JamesDoyle 1 107
(Robert Cowell) *racd far side: in tch towards rr: effrt 2f out: hdwy u.p and swtchd rt 1f out: kpt on ins fnl f: 4th of 15 in gp* **33/1**

000/ **8** 3/4 **Hay Chewed (IRE)**[588] 6549 5-9-0 95 MartinDwyer 19 102
(Conrad Allen) *lw: racd nr side: led gp and chsd ldr overall: rdn over 1f out: no ex jst ins fnl f: wknd fnl 75yds: 3rd of 5 in gp* **100/1**

160- **9** nk **Justineo**[253] 5600 7-9-3 105 JimCrowley 3 104
(Robert Cowell) *racd far side: chsd ldrs: effrt 2f out: drvn over 1f out: styd on same pce ins fnl f: 5th of 15 in gp* **33/1**

5-50 **10** 1/2 **Move In Time**[28] 1197 8-9-6 110 DanielTudhope 11 105
(David O'Meara) *racd far side: in tch towards rr: effrt over 1f out: drvn ins fnl f: kpt on: 6th of 15 in gp* **16/1**

0-30 **11** nk **Sole Power**[35] 1104 9-9-9 114 RyanMoore 9 107
(Edward Lynam, Ire) *racd far side: hld up in tch in midfield: effrt and swtchd rt ent fnl f: kpt on same pce and no imp ins fnl f: 7th of 15 in gp* **6/1**[2]

501- **12** nk **Cotai Glory**[234] 6210 4-9-3 108 GeorgeBaker 10 100
(Charles Hills) *sltly on toes: taken down early: racd far side: racd keenly: chsd ldr tl no ex u.p over 1f out: wknd ins fnl f: 8th of 15 in gp* **10/1**[3]

5-44 **13** nk **Line Of Reason (IRE)**[36] 1083 6-9-3 108 PatSmullen 12 99
(Paul Midgley) *racd far side: t.k.h: hld up in tch towards rr: effrt over 1f out: styd on same pce and no imp ins fnl f: 9th of 15 in gp* **25/1**

40-0 **14** 2 1/4 **Desert Law (IRE)**[56] 835 8-9-3 104 MartinLane 7 90
(Paul Midgley) *racd far side: broke wl: stdd and chsd ldrs: effrt to chse wnr over 1f out tl ent fnl f: wknd ins fnl f: 10th of 15 in gp* **50/1**

01-3 **15** 1/2 **Goken (FR)**[36] 1066 4-9-3 108 GrahamLee 13 89
(Kevin Ryan) *racd far side: t.k.h: chsd ldrs: rdn and no ex over 1f out: wknd ins fnl f: 11th of 15 in gp* **14/1**

516- **16** 1/2 **Dutch Masterpiece**[206] 7036 6-9-3 107 (v) JimmyFortune 17 87
(Gary Moore) *taken down early: racd nr side: s.i.s: hld up in rr: effrt u.p over 1f out: no prog: n.d: 4th of 5 in gp* **28/1**

U10- **17** shd **Humidor (IRE)**[209] 6971 9-9-3 104 PatCosgrave 21 86
(George Baker) *taken down early: racd nr side: in tch in midfield: no ex u.p over 1f out: wknd ins fnl f: 5th of 5 in gp* **66/1**

100- **18** 1/2 **Steps (IRE)**[189] 7461 8-9-6 113 (v) AndreaAtzeni 8 88
(Roger Varian) *racd far side: a towards rr sn pushed along: drvn and no hdwy 1/2-way: n.d: 12th of 15 in gp* **16/1**

-000 **19** 2 1/2 **Mirza**[30] 1172 9-9-3 105 (p) FrankieDettori 2 76
(Rae Guest) *racd far side: chsd ldrs: no ex u.p over 1f out: wknd fnl f: 13th of 15 in gp* **33/1**

01-0 **20** nk **Iffranesia (FR)**[15] 1453 6-9-0 101 AdamBeschizza 15 72
(Robert Cowell) *swtchd rt sn after s and racd far side: in tch in midfield: rdn 1/2-way: lost pl and wknd over 1f out: 14th of 15 in gp* **40/1**

1-12 **21** 1 3/4 **Lancelot Du Lac (ITY)**[36] 1066 6-9-3 108 RobertWinston 5 68
(Dean Ivory) *racd far side: a towards rr: rdn 2f out: sn struggling: bhd ins fnl f: 15th of 15 in gp* **10/1**[3]

58.59s (-0.51) **Going Correction** +0.10s/f (Good) **21** Ran SP% **130.1**
Speed ratings (Par 113): **108,107,106,106,105 105,104,103,102,101 101,100,100,96,95 95,94,94,90,89 86**
CSF £129.40 TOTE £26.30: £5.90, £2.30, £2.70; EX 217.10 Trifecta £1921.00.
Owner A D Spence **Bred** Con Harrington **Trained** Lambourn, Berks

FOCUS
It doesn't come more open than this edition of the Palace House. With the biggest field since Dandy Man won in 2006, there was unsurprisingly a scorching pace on, and there was no bias in the draw. There was little between the form principals on their respective bests and Waady is a good benchmark.

1863 DUNADEN AT OVERBURY JOCKEY CLUB STKS (GROUP 2) 1m 4f
3:05 (3:05) (Class 1) 4-Y-O+ **£56,980** (£21,770; £11,030; £5,630; £2,960) **Stalls** Centre

Form RPR

413- **1** **Exosphere**[224] 6516 4-9-0 110 RyanMoore 5 120
(Sir Michael Stoute) *hld up in tch in midfield: clsd and travelling strly 3f out: effrt 2f out: led ent fnl f: styd on strly and drew clr: readily* **17/2**[3]

111- **2** 4 **Simple Verse (IRE)**[196] 7279 4-9-2 116 OisinMurphy 6 115
(Ralph Beckett) *lw: mostly chsd ldr: pushed along to press ldr over 2f out: rdn to ld 2f out: drvn and hdd ent fnl f: outpcd by wnr and kpt on same pce for clr 2nd fnl f* **7/1**[2]

05-2 **3** 5 **Big Orange**[35] 1102 5-9-1 116 (p) FrankieDettori 7 105
(Michael Bell) *lw: led: rdn over 3f out: drvn and hdd 2f out: 3rd and outpcd over 1f out: wl hld and plugged on same pce fnl f* **7/1**[2]

1-43 **4** 2 **Restorer**[14] 1475 4-9-0 106 MartinDwyer 3 102
(William Muir) *chsd ldrs: effrt and ev ch over 2f out: no ex and btn over 1f out: drifted rt and wknd ins fnl f* **40/1**

111- **5** 5 **Star Storm (IRE)**[210] 6917 4-9-0 107 TomQueally 1 94
(James Fanshawe) *lw: hld up in tch in last pair: clsd and pressing ldrs over 2f out: rdn 2f out: sn outpcd and btn: fdd ins fnl f* **14/1**

113- **P** **Jack Hobbs**[196] 7281 4-9-0 123 WilliamBuick 2
(John Gosden) *stdd s: hld up in tch in last pair: effrt over 2f out: sn btn and eased wl over 1f out: p.u and dismntd 1f out* **8/15**[1]

2m 30.92s (-1.08) **Going Correction** +0.10s/f (Good)
WFA 4 from 5yo 1lb **6** Ran SP% **109.9**
Speed ratings (Par 115): **107,104,101,99,96**
CSF £60.19 TOTE £10.30: £3.40, £2.60; EX 66.20 Trifecta £199.50.
Owner K Abdullah **Bred** Juddmonte Farms Ltd **Trained** Newmarket, Suffolk

FOCUS
The re-positioning of the bend into the home straight increased the distance of this race by 9yds. Two of the 4yos in this quality field stood out on what they had done last season but the race saw another one of that age group take a big step forward in form, and owns a deeply impressive winner. The race was weakened by Jack Hobbs pulling up but Exosphere is given full credit in the ratings.

1864 QIPCO 2000 GUINEAS STKS (BRITISH CHAMPIONS SERIES) (GROUP 1) (ENTIRE COLTS & FILLIES) 1m
3:45 (3:46) (Class 1) 3-Y-O
£283,550 (£107,500; £53,800; £26,800; £13,450; £6,750) **Stalls** High

Form RPR

113- **1** **Galileo Gold**[209] 6968 3-9-0 110 FrankieDettori 1 121
(Hugo Palmer) *lw: racd keenly: chsd ldrs: rdn and ev ch ent fnl 2f: led and hung lft u.p over 1f out: racing against stands' rail and styd on wl ins fnl f: rdn out* **14/1**

212- **2** 1 1/2 **Massaat (IRE)**[203] 7114 3-9-0 116 PaulHanagan 8 117
(Owen Burrows) *h.d.w: t.k.h: chsd ldrs: rdn to ld jst over 2f out: drvn and hdd over 1f out: kpt on same pce ins fnl f* **9/1**

21-2 **3** 2 **Ribchester (IRE)**[23] 1308 3-9-0 113 WilliamBuick 3 112
(Richard Fahey) *in tch in midfield: clsd to chse ldrs and rdn jst over 2f out: unable qck and swtchd sltly rt over 1f out: 3rd and styd on same pce ins fnl f* **33/1**

2- **4** 1/2 **Air Vice Marshal (USA)**[294] 4149 3-9-0 107 SeamieHeffernan 13 111
(A P O'Brien, Ire) *lw: chsd ldrs: effrt jst over 2f out: unable qck u.p over 1f out: 4th and hld whn swtchd rt ins fnl f: styd on same pce after* **20/1**

46-5 **5** 1 1/4 **Kentuckyconnection (USA)**[28] 1208 3-9-0 90 (b[1]) ConnorBeasley 4 108
(Bryan Smart) *in tch towards rr: effrt u.p and pushed rt wl over 1f out: hdwy to pass btn horses 1f out: kpt on but no threat to ldrs ins fnl f* **100/1**

145- **6** 1/2 **Zonderland**[189] 7468 3-9-0 106 AdamKirby 12 107
(Clive Cox) *lw: hld up in tch towards rr: effrt 2f out: 5th and no imp whn nt clr run and swtchd rt ent fnl f: pushed rt jst ins fnl f: styd on same pce after* **33/1**

15-6 **7** 2 3/4 **First Selection (SPA)**[58] 807 3-9-0 109 [1] JimCrowley 10 101
(Simon Crisford) *led tl hdd and rdn jst over 2f out: lost pl over 1f out: wknd ins fnl f* **66/1**

120- **8** nk **Herald The Dawn (IRE)**[209] 6968 3-9-0 113 KevinManning 11 100
(J S Bolger, Ire) *str: q lengthy: lw: stdd s: t.k.h: hld up in tch in rr: effrt over 2f out: drvn and no imp wl over 1f out: kpt on to pass btn horses ins fnl f: nvr threatened ldrs* **25/1**

132- **9** hd **Buratino (IRE)**[217] 6754 3-9-0 117 JamesDoyle 2 100
(Mark Johnston) *hld up in tch in midfield: effrt 2f out: drvn and no imp over 1f out: wknd ins fnl f* **14/1**

13-3 **10** 3/4 **Zhui Feng (IRE)**[18] 1393 3-9-0 100 TomQueally 6 98
(Amanda Perrett) *t.k.h: chsd ldrs: rdn and ev ch briefly ent fnl 2f: sn outpcd and lost pl over 1f out: wknd fnl f* **80/1**

12-1 **11** 4 **Stormy Antarctic**[16] 1440 3-9-0 114 GeorgeBaker 9 89
(Ed Walker) *on toes: edgy: stdd s: t.k.h: hld up in tch in rr: effrt and hdwy over 2f out: swtchd rt wl over 1f out: sn drvn and no hdwy: wknd 1f out: bhd and eased wl ins fnl f* **7/1**[2]

111- **12** 1 1/4 **Air Force Blue (USA)**[203] 7114 3-9-0 124 (t) RyanMoore 5 86
(A P O'Brien, Ire) *stdd s: t.k.h early: hld up in tch towards rr: clsd 3f out: rdn and effrt over 2f out: no rspnse and btn wl over 1f out: bhd and eased ins fnl f* **4/5**[1]

511- **13** 1 **Marcel (IRE)**[189] 7463 3-9-0 116 PatSmullen 7 84
(Peter Chapple-Hyam) *lw: in tch in midfield: rdn and lost pl over 2f out: bhd 1f out* **8/1**[3]

1m 35.91s (-2.69) **Going Correction** +0.10s/f (Good) **13** Ran SP% **120.7**
Speed ratings (Par 112): **117,115,113,111,111 108,108,108,107 103,102,101**
CSF £128.28 CT £4194.25 TOTE £11.10: £2.70, £3.50, £6.90; EX 152.60 Trifecta £3541.20.
Owner Al Shaqab Racing **Bred** Brian O'Rourke **Trained** Newmarket, Suffolk

FOCUS
This year's 2000 Guineas had eight individual Group winners in attendance. However, with Air Force Blue flopping, and those racing handily being at an advantage, it was a muddling affair. The proximity of the 90-rated fifth further complicates the form. Galileo Gold is rated up nearly a stone on his 2yo form, but a shade off the Guineas standard.

1865 HARBOUR WATCH CHAMPION TWO-YEAR-OLD H'CAP 6f
4:20 (4:24) (Class 2) (0-100,97) 3-Y-O **£12,938** (£3,850; £1,924; £962) **Stalls** High

Form RPR

-121 **1** **Ikerrin Road (IRE)**[34] 1115 3-8-7 **83** ShaneFoley 3 93
(John Quinn) *q str: travelled strly: chsd ldr tl pushed into ld over 1f out: rdn ins fnl f: styd on wl and a doing enough ins fnl f* **8/1**

1- **2** 1 **Yattwee (USA)**[144] 8144 3-9-4 **94** JamesDoyle 10 101
(Saeed bin Suroor) *athletic: chsd ldr: rdn and ev ch wl over 1f out: edging rt and unable qck w wnr ent fnl f: stl edging rt but kpt on ins fnl f: a hld* **5/2**[1]

116- **3** 1 **Venturous (IRE)**[217] 6754 3-9-7 **97** WilliamBuick 7 101
(Charlie Appleby) *lw: t.k.h: chsd ldng trio: nt clr run 2f out tl hdwy and carried rt ent fnl f: kpt on u.p: nvr enough pce to threaten wnr* **4/1**[2]

21-4 **4** shd **Hope Cove**[16] 1442 3-8-7 **83** AndreaAtzeni 4 86
(Ed Walker) *in tch in midfield: effrt to chse ldrs and drvn over 1f out: styd on same pce ins fnl f* **5/1**[3]

21-1 **5** 1 **Stamp Hill (IRE)**[25] 1243 3-8-10 **86** PaulHanagan 1 86
(Richard Fahey) *stdd after s: hld up in tch in last trio: effrt over 1f out: hdwy and drvn 1f out: kpt on same pce ins fnl f* **5/1**[3]

00-0 **6** 1 **Calypso Choir**[15] 1453 3-8-7 **83** SamHitchcott 8 80
(Sylvester Kirk) *dwlt: sn rcvrd and t.k.h in midfield: effrt u.p to press ldrs over 1f out: no ex 1f out: wknd ins fnl f* **50/1**

-225 **7** 1/2 **Take The Helm**[56] 836 3-9-3 **93** JimmyFortune 2 88
(Brian Meehan) *stdd after s: t.k.h: hld up in last trio: effrt and swtchd rt over 1f out: kpt on but no threat to ldrs ins fnl f* **25/1**

1103 **8** 3 1/4 **Aguerooo (IRE)**[30] 1168 3-8-11 **94** (p) HollieDoyle(7) 6 79
(Richard Hannon) *in tch in midfield: rdn and lost pl 2f out: sn btn: wknd fnl f* **22/1**

335- **9** 1/2 **Plagiarism (USA)**[252] 5625 3-8-12 **88** JoeFanning 9 71
(Mark Johnston) *t.k.h: led tl over 1f out: sn btn: wknd ins fnl f* **25/1**

315- **10** 20 **Whitman**[224] 6531 3-9-7 **97** SilvestreDeSousa 5 16
(Mark Johnston) *hld up in tch in rr: effrt over 2f out: no hdwy and wknd over 1f out: sn bhd and eased ins fnl f* **10/1**

1m 12.03s (-0.17) **Going Correction** +0.10s/f (Good) **10** Ran SP% **116.1**
Speed ratings (Par 104): **105,103,102,102,100 99,98,94,93,67**
CSF £27.12 CT £95.54 TOTE £8.90: £2.60, £2.00, £1.70; EX 33.90 Trifecta £196.00.
Owner Mrs S Quinn **Bred** Gerard Kerin **Trained** Settrington, N Yorks

FOCUS
Twilight Son is the massive standout recent winner of this, as plenty of the remainder struggled to build on success in this. The early gallop didn't look overly strong and it paid to be prominent, maybe also because of the tailwind. Interseting handicap form, rated around the fourth.

1866 HAVANA GOLD NEWMARKET STKS (LISTED RACE) (C&G) 1m 2f
4:55 (4:57) (Class 1) 3-Y-O
£22,684 (£8,600; £4,304; £2,144; £1,076; £540) **Stalls** High

Form RPR

111- **1** **Hawkbill (USA)**[234] 6220 3-9-0 98 WilliamBuick 1 107
(Charlie Appleby) *lw: t.k.h: chsd ldrs: wnt 2nd 1/2-way: rdn to ld and hung rt over 1f out: kpt on wl ins fnl f: rdn out* **14/1**

1- **2** 1 1/4 **Abdon**[249] 5721 3-9-0 0 FrankieDettori 3 104+
(Sir Michael Stoute) *leggy: athletic: stdd s: t.k.h early: hld up in tch towards rr: effrt 2f out: hdwy to chse wnr and swtchd lft over 1f out: kpt on same pce ins fnl f* **9/2**[3]

1 **3** *1* **Sky Kingdom (IRE)**[17] 1421 3-9-0 0................................ PatSmullen 5 102+
(William Haggas) *hld up in tch in last trio: effrt 2f out: hdwy u.p 1f out: wnt 3rd ins fnl f: kpt on but nvr enough pce to chal* **11/4**[1]

11-1 **4** *1 1/2* **Speed Company (IRE)**[18] 1398 3-9-0 96........................ RyanMoore 4 99
(John Quinn) *stdd s: hld up in tch in rr: effrt and swtchd lft over 1f out: hdwy to pass btn horses and styd on steadily ins fnl f: nvr trbld ldrs* **9/2**[3]

5-36 **5** *hd* **Beaverbrook**[10] 1567 3-9-0 98.. JoeFanning 8 99
(Mark Johnston) *chsd ldrs tl hdwy to ld after 2f: rdn 2f out: drvn and hdd over 1f out: 3rd and no ex 1f out: wknd ins fnl f* **22/1**

1-3 **6** *1* **Tathqeef (USA)**[18] 1395 3-9-0 95................................. PaulHanagan 2 97
(John Gosden) *lw: hld up in tch in midfield: effrt 2f out unable qck and no imp over 1f out: styd on same pce ins fnl f* **5/1**

13-5 **7** *hd* **Percy Street**[10] 1567 3-9-0 96........................(v[1]) DougieCostello 7 96
(K R Burke) *t.k.h: hld up in tch in midfield: swtchd rt 4f out: rdn 2f out: sn outpcd: kpt on same pce fnl f* **33/1**

120- **8** *10* **Cymric (USA)**[183] 7624 3-9-0 112.............................(p) JamesDoyle 6 76
(John Gosden) *edgy: t.k.h: led for 2f: chsd ldr tl 1/2-way: styd chsng ldrs tl lost pl u.p over 1f out: wl btn and eased ins fnl f* **7/2**[2]

2m 4.82s (-0.98) **Going Correction** +0.10s/f (Good) **8** Ran SP% **115.9**
Speed ratings (Par 106): **107,106,105,104,103 103,102,94**
CSF £76.66 TOTE £13.90: £3.00, £1.80, £1.60; EX 63.30 Trifecta £304.80.
Owner Godolphin **Bred** Helen K Groves Revokable Trust **Trained** Newmarket, Suffolk

FOCUS
This 3yo Listed race turned into something of a sprint from the cutaway. The winner improved on his AW form and the next two stepped forward too.

1867 QIPCO SUPPORTS RACING WELFARE H'CAP — 1m
5:30 (5:34) (Class 2) (0-105,93) 3-Y-O **£12,938** (£3,850; £1,924; £962) **Stalls** High

Form RPR

31- **1** **Folkswood**[273] 4859 3-9-3 **89**................................ WilliamBuick 7 101+
(Charlie Appleby) *lw: trckd ldrs: effrt 2f out: hdwy u.p to ld jst ins fnl f: styd on strly and gng away at fin* **7/4**[1]

2-01 **2** *2 3/4* **Dolphin Vista (IRE)**[16] 1446 3-9-1 **87**........................ FrankieDettori 6 93
(Richard Fahey) *chsd ldrs: effrt 2f out: hdwy over 1f out: drvn and pressing wnr jst ins fnl f: no ex and btn ins fnl f: wknd towards fin* **7/1**

162- **3** *3/4* **Zodiakos (IRE)**[213] 6852 3-9-3 **89**.............................. AndreaAtzeni 4 93
(Hugo Palmer) *lw: stdd s: hld up in tch in rr: effrt and hdwy over 1f out: kpt on ins fnl f: wnt 3rd 75yds out: kpt on but no threat to wnr* **9/1**

5-10 **4** *1* **Alyaa (IRE)**[37] 1061 3-7-11 **74** oh1............................... NoelGarbutt(5) 8 76
(Conrad Allen) *swtg: racd along towards stands' side: led: clr and rdn ent fnl 2f: drvn and hdd jst ins fnl f: sn btn and kpt on same pce after* **40/1**

22-1 **5** *4 1/2* **Tawakkol**[42] 1000 3-9-2 **88**... PaulHanagan 1 80
(Mark Johnston) *chsd ldrs: effrt 2f out: drvn and unable qck over 1f out: wknd fnl f* **12/1**

10-2 **6** *2 1/4* **Montsarrat (IRE)**[36] 1080 3-9-5 **91**...................... SilvestreDeSousa 2 77
(Mark Johnston) *stdd s: t.k.h: hld up in tch: effrt 2f out: rdn and btn over 1f out: wknd fnl f* **9/2**[2]

115- **7** *8* **Bahaarah (IRE)**[240] 6027 3-9-7 **93**................................ RyanMoore 5 61
(Richard Hannon) *hld up in tch in last pair: shkn up briefly 2f out: sn btn and hld together on downhill run wl over 1f out: bhd and eased ins fnl f* **10/1**

1-5 **8** *15* **Brave Hero**[16] 1438 3-9-4 **90**.. JamesDoyle 9 24
(Saeed bin Suroor) *stdd s: hld up in rr: effrt jst over 2f out: sn btn: bhd and eased ins fnl f* **5/1**[3]

1m 37.15s (-1.45) **Going Correction** +0.10s/f (Good) **8** Ran SP% **112.9**
Speed ratings (Par 104): **111,108,107,106,102 99,91,76**
CSF £14.22 CT £84.60 TOTE £2.80: £1.30, £1.70, £2.70; EX 16.40 Trifecta £118.90.
Owner Godolphin **Bred** Hascombe And Valiant Studs **Trained** Newmarket, Suffolk

FOCUS
An interesting handicap to finish the card with, which contained some unexposed types. The early pace was nothing more than ordinary, and all but one of the field (the outsider) raced in the centre of the track. The time was only a stone slower than the Guineas and the form is rated on the positive side.
T/Jkpt: Not won. T/Plt: £16,246.30 to a £1 stake. Pool: £20,6035.77 - 9.27 winning tickets. T/Qpdt: £151.50 to a £1 stake. Pool: £12,617.11 - 61.62 winning tickets. **Steve Payne**

1669 THIRSK (L-H)
Saturday, April 30

OFFICIAL GOING: Soft changing to soft (heavy in places) after race 5 (4.30)
Wind: light half behind Weather: sunny, rain between races 3 and 5

1868 TOTESCOOP6 PLAY TODAY NOVICE AUCTION STKS — 5f
2:10 (2:10) (Class 5) 2-Y-O **£3,234** (£962; £481; £240) **Stalls** High

Form RPR

1 **Rainbow Mist (IRE)** 2-9-2 0.. PJMcDonald 2 78
(Ann Duffield) *mde all: rdn over 1f out: edgd lft: kpt on wl to draw clr ins fnl f* **13/2**[3]

2 *4* **Wheneverwecan (IRE)** 2-8-11 0............................... FrannyNorton 1 59
(Mark Johnston) *pressed ldr: rdn 2f out: sn one pce* **2/1**[2]

3 *3/4* **Harome (IRE)** 2-9-2 0.. SamJames 4 61
(David Loughnane) *hld up in tch: rdn 2f out: kpt on ins fnl f* **12/1**

4 *1 1/2* **Tranquil Tracy** 2-8-8 0.. JacobButterfield(3) 3 51
(John Norton) *dwlt: sn pushed along in rr: kpt on ins fnl f* **40/1**

5 *1/2* **Lawless Louis** 2-9-2 0.. PhillipMakin 5 54
(David O'Meara) *chsd ldng pair: rdn 1/2-way: wknd ins fnl f* **10/11**[1]

1m 4.12s (4.52) **Going Correction** +0.825s/f (Soft) **5** Ran SP% **109.2**
Speed ratings (Par 92): **96,89,88,86,85**
CSF £19.53 TOTE £5.90: £1.90, £1.40; EX 17.90 Trifecta £62.40.
Owner Craig Buckingham **Bred** Skymarc Farm **Trained** Constable Burton, N Yorks

FOCUS
The going was officially soft. Home bend out about 7yds from inside line and stables bend out about 2yds, adding around 20yds to the 1m race and around 24yds to the 1m4f race. Straight dolled out around 4yds from the stands' rail, but sprint race distances were not affected. This opening novice event was contested by five newcomers and the market couldn't have got it more wrong. Phillip Makin said of the conditions: "It very gluey and holding ground, not nice at all", while P J McDonald said: "It's bordering on heavy."

1869 TOTESCOOP6 THE MILLIONAIRE MAKER H'CAP — 6f
2:45 (2:45) (Class 4) (0-80,83) 4-Y-O+ **£6,469** (£1,925; £962; £481) **Stalls** High

Form RPR

000- **1** **Kommander Kirkup**[239] 6045 5-8-13 **77**........................ PhilDennis(5) 1 87
(John Davies) *in tch far side: rdn and hdwy over 1f out: led 110yds out: kpt on* **40/1**

0-65 **2** *1 1/4* **Best Trip (IRE)**[10] 1563 9-9-3 **76**.................................. SamJames 3 82
(Marjorie Fife) *led far side gp and overall ldr: rdn over 2f out: hdd 110yds out: one pce* **8/1**[3]

-406 **3** *3/4* **Casterbridge**[16] 1447 4-9-6 **79**....................................... NeilFarley 18 83
(Eric Alston) *led stands' side gp: rdn over 2f out: kpt on: 1st 8 in gp* **20/1**

000- **4** *2* **Duke Cosimo**[224] 6540 6-9-4 **77**.................................. PhillipMakin 17 74+
(Michael Herrington) *dwlt: hld up stands' side: pushed along over 1f out: swtchd lft ins fnl f: kpt on wl: nrst fin: 2nd of 8 in gp* **33/1**

00-4 **5** *nk* **Kenny The Captain (IRE)**[14] 1489 5-8-11 **70**............ DuranFentiman 8 66
(Tim Easterby) *dwlt: sn chsd ldr far side: rdn over 2f out: one pce: 3rd of 9 in gp* **8/1**[3]

0-60 **6** *1 1/4* **Cosmic Chatter**[22] 1321 6-9-4 **77**........................(p) JamesSullivan 14 69
(Ruth Carr) *midfield: rdn over 2f out: plugged on: 3rd of 8 in gp* **28/1**

06-2 **7** *1 1/2* **One Boy (IRE)**[14] 1488 5-9-4 **77**................................ JackGarritty 19 64
(Richard Fahey) *prom stands' side: rdn over 2f out: wknd ins fnl f: 4th of 8 in gp* **8/1**[3]

0-00 **8** *1 3/4* **Orion's Bow**[7] 1625 5-8-12 **71**................................(b) RoystonFfrench 5 53
(David Nicholls) *chsd ldr far side: rdn over 2f out: wknd fnl f: 4th of 9 in gp* **8/1**[3]

354- **9** *1* **Royal Connoisseur (IRE)**[155] 8013 5-8-10 **69**........ GeorgeChaloner 16 48
(Richard Fahey) *prom stands' side: rdn over 2f out: wknd over 1f out: 5th of 8 in gp* **16/1**

0342 **10** *hd* **Captain Lars (SAF)**[7] 1634 6-9-5 **78**........................(p) TonyHamilton 9 56
(Derek Shaw) *hld up far side: rdn 3f out: nvr threatened: 5th of 9 in gp* **14/1**

610- **11** *1 3/4* **Mercers Row**[178] 7710 9-9-7 **80**..................................... DavidNolan 2 52
(Michael Herrington) *hld up far side: rdn over 2f out: nvr threatened: 6th of 9 in gp* **33/1**

00-0 **12** *3/4* **Apricot Sky**[6] 1672 6-9-4 **77**..................................... FrannyNorton 4 47
(David Nicholls) *trckd ldr far side: rdn over 2f out: wknd over 1f out: 7th of 9 in gp* **50/1**

12-1 **13** *nse* **Pomme De Terre (IRE)**[14] 1489 4-9-6 **79**...............(b) PaulMulrennan 15 49
(Michael Dods) *hld up stands' side: rdn over 2f out: nvr threatened: 6th of 8 in gp* **6/1**[2]

2616 **14** *3 1/4* **Lackaday**[14] 1489 4-8-8 **72**...................................(p) CallumShepherd(5) 6 31
(Mark Walford) *hld up far side: rdn 3f out: wknd over 1f out: 8th of 9 in gp* **20/1**

-451 **15** *2 1/4* **Dinneratmidnight**[3] 1787 5-9-10 **83** 6ex......................(e) JasonHart 12 35
(Richard Guest) *chsd ldrs stands' side: rdn 3f out: wknd over 1f out: 7th of 8 in gp* **4/1**[1]

42-1 **16** *2 1/2* **Off The Scale (IRE)**[14] 1488 4-9-0 **73**.............................. DaleSwift 13 17
(Brian Ellison) *hld up stands' side: rdn over 2f out: wknd over 1f out: last of 8 in gp* **11/1**

204- **17** *12* **See The Storm**[220] 6641 8-9-1 **74**................................. PJMcDonald 7
(Ann Duffield) *prom far side: lost pl qckly 3f out: sn bhd: eased* **33/1**

1m 16.72s (4.02) **Going Correction** +0.825s/f (Soft) **17** Ran SP% **125.8**
Speed ratings (Par 105): **106,104,103,100,100 98,96,94,92,92 90,89,89,84,81 78,62**
CSF £321.85 CT £6766.31 TOTE £52.60: £12.20, £1.80, £5.00, £5.90; EX 577.10 Trifecta £2007.20 Part won..
Owner Kevin Kirkup **Bred** W M Lidsey **Trained** Piercebridge, Durham
■ Stewards' Enquiry : Paul Mulrennan caution; careless riding

FOCUS
A competitive sprint handicap. The field predictably split into two with the front pair coming from the far-side group, but the third horse, who raced nearside, wasn't beaten that far which suggests there was no great bias. THe surprise winner is rated close to his best.

1870 TOTEPOOLLIVEINFO.COM MAIDEN STKS — 5f
3:20 (3:21) (Class 4) 3-Y-O+ **£5,175** (£1,540; £769; £384) **Stalls** High

Form RPR

032- **1** **Udontdodou**[175] 7751 3-9-4 79.. JasonHart 6 78+
(Richard Guest) *prom: led over 1f out: pushed clr: easily* **8/11**[1]

2 *7* **Evenlode (IRE)** 3-9-4 0.. GrahamGibbons 5 52
(David Barron) *dwlt: hld up in tch: rdn over 1f out: kpt on to go 2nd 50yds out: no ch w wnr* **9/1**[3]

544- **3** *1 1/2* **Springtime Winnie**[207] 7010 4-9-9 44.............................. NeilFarley 4 46
(Eric Alston) *led: rdn 2f out: hdd over 1f out: wknd ins fnl f: lost 2nd 50yds out* **25/1**

622- **4** *5* **Sunnyside Bob (IRE)**[183] 7601 3-9-4 77......................... PhillipMakin 1 29
(David O'Meara) *dwlt: hld up: pushed along 3f out: rdn and hdwy to chse ldrs over 1f out: wknd ins fnl f* **2/1**[2]

6 **5** *5* **Another Desperado (IRE)**[14] 1494 3-9-4 0..................... BarryMcHugh 2 11
(Rebecca Bastiman) *prom: pushed along and lost pl over 3f out: wknd over 1f out* **50/1**

0-0 **6** *5* **Bazula (IRE)**[12] 1524 3-9-4 0... DavidAllan 3
(Tim Easterby) *chsd ldrs: rdn 1/2-way: sn wknd* **50/1**

1m 3.42s (3.82) **Going Correction** +0.825s/f (Soft)
WFA 3 from 4yo 10lb **6** Ran SP% **109.0**
Speed ratings (Par 105): **102,90,88,80,72 64**
CSF £7.64 TOTE £1.60: £1.10, £3.80; EX 5.60 Trifecta £34.60.
Owner Mrs Alison Guest **Bred** Times Of Wigan Ltd **Trained** Ingmanthorpe, W Yorks

FOCUS
Not a particularly competitive sprint maiden and they finished well spread out. The easy winner is rated to form.

1871 TOTEPOOL THIRSK HUNT CUP H'CAP — 1m
3:55 (3:57) (Class 2) (0-100,100) 4-Y-O+ **£16,172** (£4,812; £2,405; £1,202) **Stalls** Low

Form RPR

53-5 **1** **Finn Class (IRE)**[28] 1195 5-8-9 **88**................................. TomEaves 2 96
(Michael Dods) *trckd ldng pair: angled rt to outer 2f out: sn rdn: chal fnl f: kpt on: led nr fin* **16/1**

0-30 **2** *shd* **Instant Attraction (IRE)**[7] 1629 5-9-4 **97**.................. JackGarritty 5 104
(Jedd O'Keeffe) *led: hdd 5f out: remained cl up: rdn over 2f out: led again over 1f out: strly pressed fnl f: kpt on: hdd nr fin* **13/2**[2]

560- **3** *hd* **Fort Bastion (IRE)**[175] 7754 7-9-2 **95**........................ PhillipMakin 9 101
(David O'Meara) *midfield: pushed along and hdwy 3f out: rdn to chse ldr over 1f out: ev ch ins fnl f: kpt on* **9/1**[3]

26-3 **4** *5* **Silvery Moon (IRE)**[25] 1245 9-8-13 **92**........................... DavidAllan 17 87
(Tim Easterby) *hld up: rdn 3f out: kpt on fr over 1f out* **11/1**

3-63 **5** *2* **Wilde Inspiration (IRE)**[7] 1629 5-8-8 **90**.................. JoeDoyle(3) 13 80
(Julie Camacho) *midfield towards outer: rdn over 3f out: no imp* **4/1**[1]

100- **6** *shd* **Two For Two (IRE)**[254] 5567 8-9-7 **100**......................... PJMcDonald 1 90
(David Loughnane) *dwlt: sn prom: led 5f out: rdn over 2f out: hdd over 1f out: wknd ins fnl f* **50/1**

200- **7** *3/4* **King To Be (IRE)**[253] 5602 4-8-7 **89**...................... ShelleyBirkett(3) 15 77+
(David O'Meara) *hld up in rr: pushed along and sme hdwy over 1f out: kpt on ins fnl f* **9/1**[3]

-600 **8** 2 3/4 **Al Khan (IRE)**84 486 7-8-8 **87**....(p) BarryMcHugh 7 69
(Kevin Ryan) *in tch on inner: rdn over 2f out: wknd over 1f out* **33/1**
050- **9** 2 **Glenalmond (IRE)**175 7754 4-8-11 **90**....(p) BenCurtis 10 67
(K R Burke) *midfield: rdn over 3f out: wknd over 2f out* **25/1**
2-5 **10** 1 1/4 **Indy (IRE)**14 1491 5-8-13 **92**.... GrahamGibbons 18 66
(David Barron) *chsd ldng pair towards outer: rdn over 3f out: wknd fnl 2f* **18/1**
20-0 **11** nk **Storm Rock**28 1196 4-9-6 **99**.... FrannyNorton 6 73
(Harry Dunlop) *chsd ldng pair: rdn over 3f out: wknd fnl 2f* **4/1**1
156- **12** shd **Home Cummins (IRE)**124 8380 4-8-10 **89**.... GeorgeChaloner 14 63
(Richard Fahey) *hld up: rdn over 3f out: nvr threatened* **12/1**
04-6 **13** 4 **Mukhayyam**12 1522 4-8-10 **89**.... JasonHart 16 53
(Tim Easterby) *hld up: rdn over 3f out: sn wknd* **33/1**
01-0 **14** 1/2 **Ingleby Angel (IRE)**28 1196 7-9-5 **98**.... RoystonFfrench 12 61
(Colin Teague) *dwlt: midfield: rdn over 3f out: sn wknd* **50/1**
06-3 **15** 2 1/2 **Earth Drummer (IRE)**14 1478 6-9-5 **98**.... DavidNolan 11 55
(David Loughnane) *hld up in midfield: rdn 3f out: sn wknd* **12/1**

1m 47.67s (7.57) **Going Correction** +1.175s/f (Soft) **15** Ran SP% **121.8**
Speed ratings (Par 109): **109,108,108,103,101 101,100,98,96,94 94,94,90,89,87**
CSF £112.82 CT £1013.43 TOTE £16.80: £5.20, £2.30, £4.40; EX 152.60 Trifecta £1127.40.
Owner M D Pearson **Bred** Rabbah Bloodstock Limited **Trained** Denton, Co Durham

FOCUS
Rail movement added about 20yds to the race distance. It started to rain heavily before this race, a typically competitive renewal of the Thirsk Hunt Cup. The first three produced a thrilling finish and pulled clear of the rest. Small pbs from the first two.

1872 TOTEEXACTA PICK THE 1ST & 2ND FILLIES' H'CAP 5f
4:30 (4:31) (Class 4) (0-85,88) 3-Y-O+ **£6,469** (£1,925; £962; £481) **Stalls** High

Form RPR
35-0 **1** **Pull The Plug (IRE)**16 1447 5-9-2 **77**.... GerO'Neill(7) 7 84
(Declan Carroll) *dwlt: hld up: tk str hold: short of room and hmpd on rail 2f out: pushed along and gd hdwy jst ins fnl f: squeezed through gap 75yds out: led nr fin* **9/1**
44-5 **2** nk **Misu Moneypenny**7 1647 3-8-4 **68**....(p) NickyMackay 8 70
(Scott Dixon) *chsd ldng pair: rdn 2f out: led 110yds out: edgd rt: hdd nr fin* **8/1**2
31-1 **3** 3 3/4 **Gwendolyn (GER)**7 1647 3-9-4 **82**.... PhillipMakin 4 73+
(Robert Cowell) *trckd ldng pair: led 2f out: sn rdn: hdd 110yds out: wknd* **4/6**1
10-6 **4** shd **Margrets Gift**18 1402 5-9-6 **74**....(p) DavidAllan 1 66
(Tim Easterby) *hld up: pushed along over 3f out: kpt on ins fnl f: nvr threatened* **10/1**
-335 **5** 1 1/2 **Summer Isles**16 1433 6-8-13 **67**.... BarryMcHugh 3 54
(Paul Midgley) *led narrowly: rdn whn hdd 2f out: wknd ins fnl f* **9/1**
00-3 **6** 10 **Rosy Morning (IRE)**16 1432 3-9-0 **78**.... FrannyNorton 2 25
(Mark Johnston) *prom: rdn 2f out: wknd* **17/2**3

1m 6.09s (6.49) **Going Correction** +1.00s/f (Soft)
WFA 3 from 5yo+ 10lb **6** Ran SP% **110.7**
Speed ratings (Par 102): **88,87,81,81,78 62**
CSF £71.34 CT £106.70 TOTE £11.90: £4.40, £2.50; EX 79.10 Trifecta £238.20.
Owner C Harding **Bred** Peter Molony **Trained** Malton, N Yorks
■ Ger O'Neill's first winner.

FOCUS
The rain continued to lash down. A fair fillies' sprint handicap, but a rather messy race and the conditions appeared to take their toll on a couple. The first two are rated to form.

1873 TOTETRIFECTA PICK THE 1, 2, 3 MAIDEN STKS 1m 4f
5:05 (5:08) (Class 5) 3-Y-O+ **£3,234** (£962; £481; £240) **Stalls** High

Form RPR
1 **The Tartan Spartan (IRE)** 3-8-8 0.... GrahamGibbons 10 83
(John Patrick Shanahan, Ire) *led: hdd 10f out: trckd ldrs: rdn over 4f out: chal 3f out: led over 1f out: styd on* **6/1**3
2 2 3/4 **High Bridge**45 5-10-0 0.... PhillipMakin 5 81
(Charlie Appleby) *s.i.s: sn trckd ldrs: led over 4f out: jnd 3f out: sn rdn: hdd over 1f out: one pce* **4/6**1
00- **3** 11 **Transpennine Star**187 7518 3-8-8 0.... TomEaves 3 61
(Michael Dods) *hld up: rdn and hdwy into modest 3rd over 2f out: plugged on* **25/1**
6 **4** 2 1/4 **Rosette**116 51 4-9-8 0.... NeilFarley 2 54
(Alan Swinbank) *trckd ldrs: rdn and outpcd over 3f out: plugged on fnl 2f* **16/1**
55 **5** 1 1/4 **Cosmic Tigress**21 1346 5-9-9 0.... JasonHart 8 52+
(John Quinn) *hld up: pushed along over 3f out: plugged on: nvr threatened* **10/1**
56-0 **6** hd **Prairie Town (IRE)**19 1391 5-10-0 71....(p) JackGarritty 7 57
(Tony Carroll) *hld up: rdn and outpcd over 5f out: plugged on fnl 2f* **11/2**2
0 **7** 1/2 **Question Of Faith**7 1626 5-9-9 0.... DavidNolan 11 51
(Martin Todhunter) *midfield: pushed along over 4f out: nvr threatened* **25/1**
0/ **8** 10 **Not Another Bill**724 2081 5-9-7 0....1 SamuelClarke(7) 4 40
(Chris Wall) *prom: led 10f out: hdd over 4f out: sn wknd* **25/1**
9 29 **Desert Sensation (IRE)**11 4-9-13 0....(t) RoystonFfrench 1
(Tracy Waggott) *hld up in rr: pushed along and struggling over 7f out: t.o fnl 3f* **20/1**
10 72 **Life Story** 4-9-13 0.... PJMcDonald 6
(John Davies) *slowly away: hdwy on outside to press ldr over 9f out: lost pl qckly 4f out: sn bhd: eased* **28/1**

2m 52.88s (16.68) **Going Correction** +1.35s/f (Soft)
WFA 3 from 4yo 20lb 4 from 5yo 1lb **10** Ran SP% **124.4**
Speed ratings (Par 103): **98,96,88,87,86 86,86,79,60,12**
CSF £10.44 TOTE £7.40: £1.50, £1.10, £5.20; EX 15.60 Trifecta £207.70.
Owner Thistle Bloodstock Limited **Bred** Thistle Bloodstock Ltd **Trained** Kells, Co Kilkenny

FOCUS
The going was changed to soft, heavy in places before this race. Rail movement added about 24yds to the race distance. A modest middle-distance maiden, but made more interesting by the presence of a decent bumper performer plus a few winning hurdlers. It developed into a bit of a slog and the first two pulled a long way clear. There wasn't much depth to this.

1874 TOTESWINGER THREE WAYS TO WIN H'CAP 5f
5:40 (5:43) (Class 4) (0-85,85) 4-Y-O+ **£6,469** (£1,925; £962; £481) **Stalls** High

Form RPR
00-0 **1** **Soul Brother (IRE)**16 1447 5-8-13 **77**....(b1) DavidAllan 10 89
(Tim Easterby) *in tch far side: rdn and hdwy over 1f out: led 1f out: kpt on* **11/1**
35-0 **2** 2 1/2 **Flash City (ITY)**8 1601 8-8-9 **73**....(p) JamesSullivan 6 76
(Ruth Carr) *in tch far side: rdn and hdwy to chal appr fnl f: kpt on* **12/1**
3266 **3** 1 1/4 **Pearl Acclaim (IRE)**6 1672 6-9-4 **82**.... FrannyNorton 4 81
(David Nicholls) *racd far side: led: rdn 2f out: hdd 1f out: one pce* **9/1**
21/- **4** 1/2 **Clergyman**561 7254 4-9-2 **80**.... BarryMcHugh 1 77+
(Rebecca Bastiman) *slowly away: hld up far side: rdn 1/2-way: kpt on fnl f: nrst fin* **25/1**
4424 **5** 1 1/2 **Jaarih (IRE)**12 1528 4-8-4 **73**....(p) JosephineGordon(5) 2 64
(Conor Dore) *in tch far side: rdn 2f out: plugged on* **6/1**2
26-0 **6** 2 **Stanghow**8 1601 4-9-1 **79**.... PhillipMakin 7 63
(Antony Brittain) *prom far side: rdn 2f out: wknd ins fnl f* **9/1**
00-0 **7** nk **Ballesteros**17 1408 7-9-4 **82**.... GeorgeChaloner 3 65
(Patrick Morris) *chsd ldrs far side: rdn 1/2-way: wknd ins fnl f* **20/1**
04-0 **8** 4 1/2 **Free Zone**6 1672 7-9-3 **81**....(v) DavidNolan 5 48
(David O'Meara) *prom far side: rdn 1/2-way: wknd 2f out* **9/1**
05-6 **9** 2 **Singeur (IRE)**17 1408 9-9-4 **82**.... TomEaves 13 42
(Rebecca Bastiman) *led trio stands' side: rdn and clrly bhd main gp fr 1/2-way* **14/1**
-002 **10** 1 1/2 **Rita's Boy (IRE)**6 1672 4-9-3 **81**....(v) BenCurtis 11 35
(K R Burke) *dwlt: chsd ldr in trio stands' side: rdn 3f out: sn struggling* **11/4**1
60-5 **11** 1 3/4 **Long Awaited (IRE)**17 1408 8-9-7 **85**....(b) GrahamGibbons 12 33
(David Barron) *hld up in trio stands' side: a towards rr* **13/2**3
54-0 **12** 5 **Space Artist (IRE)**16 1433 6-8-2 **73**....(v) KieranSchofield(7) 8 3
(Nigel Tinkler) *s.i.s: hld up far side: bhd fr 1/2-way* **40/1**

1m 3.83s (4.23) **Going Correction** +1.00s/f (Soft) **12** Ran SP% **118.0**
Speed ratings (Par 105): **106,102,100,99,96 93,93,85,82,80 77,69**
CSF £132.31 CT £1260.89 TOTE £18.60: £3.80, £4.50, £3.40; EX 200.70 Trifecta £2105.20 Part won..
Owner C H Stevens **Bred** Michael Downey & Roalso Ltd **Trained** Great Habton, N Yorks

FOCUS
A fair sprint handicap to end, but a major track bias with the larger group who went far side enjoying a huge advantage, while the trio who stayed nearside, including the first two favourites, had no chance. Blinkers sparked the winner into form.
T/Plt: £880.70 to a £1 stake. Pool: £53,378.20 - 44.24 winning units. T/Qpdt: £235.50 to a £1 stake. Pool: £3,023.80 - 9.50 winning units. **Andrew Sheret**

1875 - 1877a (Foreign Racing) - See Raceform Interactive

HAMILTON (R-H)
Sunday, May 1

OFFICIAL GOING: Soft (good to soft in places; 7.1)
Wind: Fresh, across Weather: Overcast

1878 TOTEEXACTA H'CAP 5f 7y
1:40 (1:40) (Class 5) (0-70,67) 4-Y-O+ **£4,528** (£1,347; £673; £336) **Stalls** Centre

Form RPR
-311 **1** **Mitchum**15 1495 7-8-13 **64**....(p) PhilDennis(5) 8 74
(Ron Barr) *cl up: rdn along over 1f out: led ins fnl f: kpt on wl* **2/1**1
0-06 **2** 1/2 **Bronze Beau**11 1559 9-9-3 **63**....(tp) ShaneGray 6 71
(Kristin Stubbs) *led and sn crossed to stands' rail: rdn along over 1f out: hdd ins fnl f: kpt on same pce cl home* **10/1**
4022 **3** 1 1/2 **New Lease Of Life**11 1559 7-9-4 **64**....(v) PhillipMakin 9 67
(Keith Dalgleish) *trckd ldrs: rdn along 2f out: kpt on same pce ins fnl f* **4/1**3
0004 **4** 2 **Johnny B Goode (IRE)**13 1525 4-9-0 **67**.... AdamMcNamara(7) 2 63
(Richard Fahey) *in tch: rdn and outpcd over 2f out: kpt on ins fnl f: nt pce to chal* **7/2**2
53-0 **5** 2 **Mystical King**7 1668 6-8-7 **53** oh8....(p) JamesSullivan 4 42
(Linda Perratt) *cl up on outside: rdn along 2f out: wknd ins fnl f* **33/1**
260- **6** 2 1/4 **A Lovable Rogue**177 7061 4-8-13 **59**....(p) GrahamLee 3 40
(R Mike Smith) *bhd and sn rdn along: hung rt over 2f out: nvr on terms* **8/1**
3241 **7** 1 1/4 **Captain Scooby**13 1525 10-9-4 **64**....(b) JasonHart 1 40
(Richard Guest) *dwlt: bhd and outpcd: nvr on terms* **9/1**
606- **8** 3/4 **It's Time For Bed**217 6788 4-8-7 **53** oh4.... PJMcDonald 7 26
(Linda Perratt) *in tch on outside: rdn over 2f out: wknd over 1f out* **25/1**

1m 2.0s (2.00) **Going Correction** +0.40s/f (Good) **8** Ran SP% **112.5**
Speed ratings (Par 103): **100,99,96,93,90 86,84,83**
CSF £22.65 CT £72.34 TOTE £2.30: £1.10, £3.20, £1.50; EX 24.80 Trifecta £82.80.
Owner P Cartmell **Bred** Conor J C Parsons & Brian M Parsons **Trained** Seamer, N Yorks

FOCUS
A modest sprint in which few ever threatened to get competitive.The winner's best form since he was a 2yo.

1879 TOTETRIFECTA H'CAP 6f 6y
2:10 (2:11) (Class 4) (0-80,80) 4-Y-O+ **£6,469** (£1,925; £962; £481) **Stalls** Centre

Form RPR
04-6 **1** **Sir Domino (FR)**15 1488 4-8-11 **70**.... GrahamLee 3 80+
(Kevin Ryan) *hld up in tch on outside: pushed along and hdwy to ld over 1f out: edgd lft: kpt on wl fnl f* **13/2**3
3-30 **2** 1 1/4 **Final Venture**15 1489 4-8-10 **69**.... BenCurtis 1 75
(Alan Swinbank) *led to over 1f out: rdn and kpt on fnl f* **11/2**2
-032 **3** nk **Barkston Ash**4 1787 8-9-7 **80**....(p) JasonHart 7 85+
(Eric Alston) *chsd ldrs: drvn and outpcd over 2f out: rallied ins fnl f: nt pce to chal* **15/8**1
4-45 **4** 1 3/4 **Vallarta (IRE)**24 1291 6-9-4 **77**.... JamesSullivan 4 76
(Ruth Carr) *hld up in tch: effrt and pushed along over 2f out: edgd rt and no imp fnl f* **8/1**
1234 **5** 2 1/4 **Jacob's Pillow**47 938 5-9-1 **74**.... TomEaves 8 66
(Rebecca Bastiman) *cl up: rdn over 2f out: wknd ins fnl f* **12/1**
0-03 **6** 5 **Ambitious Icarus**8 1634 7-9-6 **79**....(e) ConnorBeasley 5 55
(Richard Guest) *dwlt: bhd and sn pushed along: outpcd fr over 2f out* **8/1**
02-0 **7** 10 **Be Bold**17 1447 4-9-6 **79**.... BarryMcHugh 6 23
(Rebecca Bastiman) *bhd: struggling over 2f out: sn btn* **20/1**
000- **8** 1/2 **Aprovado (IRE)**190 7464 4-9-4 **77**....(p) PaulMulrennan 2 20
(Michael Dods) *chsd ldrs: rdn and lost pl over 2f out: sn struggling* **10/1**

1m 13.74s (1.54) **Going Correction** +0.40s/f (Good) **8** Ran SP% **107.3**
Speed ratings (Par 105): **105,103,102,100,97 90,77,76**
CSF £36.48 CT £79.65 TOTE £7.80: £2.30, £1.90, £1.10; EX 28.80 Trifecta £292.00.
Owner Hambleton Racing Ltd XXXV **Bred** J Payet-Descombes & J Payet-Descombes **Trained** Hambleton, N Yorks
■ Something Lucky was withdrawn. Price at time of withdrawal 14/1. Rule 4 applies to all bets - deduction 5p in the pound.

FOCUS
A fair handicap which was soundly run, the leading pair both relatively unexposed for races of this nature. The winner is rated back close to his early form.

1880 TOTEPOOLLIVEINFO.COM BUTTONHOOK H'CAP 1m 5f 14y
2:45 (2:46) (Class 3) (0-95,96) 4-Y-O+ **£12,938** (£3,850; £1,924; £962) **Stalls** Low

Form				RPR
515-	**1**		**Sir Chauvelin**[22] 7090 4-8-2 **76** oh1 JamesSullivan 8	86
			(Jim Goldie) *bhd and sn pushed along: plenty to do 3f out: gd hdwy over 1f out: kpt on wl fnl f to ld towards fin* **10/1**	
6-04	**2**	½	**Dark Ruler (IRE)**[25] 1250 7-8-5 **79** NeilFarley 3	88
			(Alan Swinbank) *prom: stdy hdwy and chsd ldr over 1f out: sn rdn: led briefly wl ins fnl f: hld cl home* **10/1**	
011	**3**	1¼	**Mirsaale**[8] 1642 6-9-8 **96** (p) PhillipMakin 10	103
			(Keith Dalgleish) *pressed ldr: led gng wl over 3f out: rdn over 1f out: hdd and no ex wl ins fnl f* **5/2**[1]	
	4	2	**Time Of My Life (GER)**[196] 5-8-10 **84** JackGarritty 2	88
			(Patrick Holmes) *hld up: hdwy whn nt clr run briefly over 2f out: effrt and rdn over 1f out: one pce fnl f* **28/1**	
41-6	**5**	3¼	**Swaheen**[15] 1493 4-9-2 **90** ConnorBeasley 6	89
			(Julie Camacho) *dwlt: hld up: hdwy over 2f out: rdn: edgd rt and no imp fr over 1f out* **13/2**[3]	
030-	**6**	1	**Innocent Touch (IRE)**[156] 6520 5-8-12 **86** TonyHamilton 4	84
			(Richard Fahey) *trckd ldrs: wnt 2nd over 2f out to over 1f out: sn rdn and wknd* **7/1**	
0-35	**7**	4½	**Donna Graciosa (GER)**[10] 1586 4-8-4 **78** FrannyNorton 11	69
			(Mark Johnston) *prom: drvn along over 3f out: wknd fr 2f out* **12/1**	
00-0	**8**	shd	**Aramist (IRE)**[15] 1493 6-9-0 **88** BenCurtis 1	79
			(Alan Swinbank) *midfield: rdn 1/2-way: outpcd over 3f out: n.d after* **6/1**[2]	
4-02	**9**	16	**Lycidas (GER)**[8] 1645 7-9-8 **96** PaulMulrennan 9	63
			(James Ewart) *led to over 3f out: sn rdn and wknd: eased whn no ch* **10/1**	
46-6	**10**	22	**Maid Of The Glens (IRE)**[28] 1228 5-8-13 **87** SamHitchcott 7	21
			(John Patrick Shanahan, Ire) *in tch on outside: effrt over 3f out: wknd over 2f out: t.o* **11/1**	

2m 56.68s (2.78) **Going Correction** +0.40s/f (Good) **10** Ran SP% **115.4**
Speed ratings (Par 107): **107,106,105,104,102 102,99,99,89,75**
CSF £104.41 CT £328.33 TOTE £12.60: £3.20, £4.20, £1.10; EX 144.30 Trifecta £611.50.
Owner J Fyffe **Bred** W M Johnstone **Trained** Uplawmoor, E Renfrews

FOCUS
A pretty useful handicap. The gallop looked sound enough given the conditions and the form should prove solid. After rail movements the actual race distance was 1m5f38yds.

1881 CAROLYN MURRAY 40TH BIRTHDAY CELEBRATIONS H'CAP 1m 3f 14y
3:20 (3:21) (Class 5) (0-70,70) 4-Y-O+ **£4,528** (£1,347; £673; £336) **Stalls** Low

Form				RPR
31-6	**1**		**Nonagon**[11] 1561 5-8-7 **56** (t) ShaneGray 9	65
			(Wilf Storey) *hld up in rr: plenty to do over 3f out: gd hdwy over 1f out: sn rdn: led wl ins fnl f: kpt on wl* **10/1**	
03-5	**2**	¾	**Henpecked**[29] 1202 6-8-3 **59** RowanScott(7) 2	67+
			(Alistair Whillans) *trckd ldrs: shkn up 3f out: led over 1f out to wl ins fnl f: nt qckn* **4/1**[2]	
660-	**3**	6	**Schmooze (IRE)**[201] 7185 7-8-11 **60** JackGarritty 5	58
			(Linda Perratt) *hld up: pushed along over 3f out: hdwy on outside over 2f out: rdn and outpcd ins fnl f* **16/1**	
0-44	**4**	1	**Frightened Rabbit (USA)**[11] 1560 4-8-13 **62** (p) PhillipMakin 10	58
			(Keith Dalgleish) *trckd ldr: rdn over 2f out: edgd lft over 1f out: sn outpcd* **11/4**[1]	
061-	**5**	2	**Celtic Power**[223] 6581 4-9-5 **68** DanielTudhope 11	61
			(Jim Goldie) *chsd clr ldng trio: rdn over 4f out: rallied over 2f out: outpcd fr over 1f out* **13/2**	
50-0	**6**	1¼	**King Of Paradise (IRE)**[8] 1633 7-9-5 **68** JasonHart 4	59
			(Eric Alston) *led: rdn over 2f out: hdd over 1f out: sn wknd* **9/2**[3]	
4-04	**7**	½	**Voice From Above (IRE)**[7] 1674 7-7-13 **55** PaulaMuir(7) 1	45
			(Patrick Holmes) *hld up: rdn over 4f out: rallied over 2f out: wknd wl over 1f out* **7/1**	
604-	**8**	5	**Sthenic (FR)**[108] 3319 4-9-7 **70** PJMcDonald 7	51
			(Micky Hammond) *hld up towards rr: drvn and outpcd over 4f out: sn btn* **18/1**	
040-	**9**	3½	**New Colours**[188] 7519 5-8-5 **54** JamesSullivan 8	29
			(Linda Perratt) *hld up: pushed along over 5f out: short-lived effrt on outside 3f out: sn wknd* **33/1**	

2m 30.65s (5.05) **Going Correction** +0.40s/f (Good) **9** Ran SP% **113.9**
Speed ratings (Par 103): **97,96,92,91,89 89,88,85,82**
CSF £49.09 CT £638.92 TOTE £10.80: £2.60, £1.80, £3.80; EX 67.10 Trifecta £733.80.
Owner Geegeez.co.uk 1 **Bred** Raymond Clive Tooth **Trained** Muggleswick, Co Durham

FOCUS
A fair handicap. After rail movements the actual race distance was 1m3f38yds. The leaders seemed to go off pretty hard, the winner coming from last to first. The first two finished clear.

1882 BRITISH STALLION STUDS "TANGERINE TREES" EBF CONDITIONS STKS (PLUS 10 RACE) 5f 7y
3:55 (3:55) (Class 2) 3-Y-O **£17,430** (£5,219; £2,609; £1,304; £652) **Stalls** Centre

Form				RPR
0-64	**1**		**Glenrowan Rose (IRE)**[9] 1599 3-8-9 88 PhillipMakin 2	93
			(Keith Dalgleish) *mde all: rdn over 1f out: kpt on strly fnl f* **7/2**[3]	
5-03	**2**	¾	**Taexali (IRE)**[59] 807 3-9-0 92 SamHitchcott 6	94
			(John Patrick Shanahan, Ire) *pressed wnr: rdn over 1f out: edgd lft ins fnl f: kpt on* **13/2**	
012-	**3**	2¾	**Mr Lupton (IRE)**[211] 6931 3-9-5 102 TonyHamilton 5	89
			(Richard Fahey) *t.k.h: trckd ldrs: rdn along over 1f out: kpt on same pce fnl f* **13/8**[1]	
-353	**4**	2¼	**Sixties Sue**[9] 1607 3-8-9 89 GrahamLee 1	71
			(Mick Channon) *cl up: rdn over 1f out: outpcd ins fnl f* **11/4**[2]	
340-	**5**	½	**Holy Grail (IRE)**[234] 6244 3-8-9 87 [1] AndrewElliott 3	70
			(Simon West) *s.i.s: outpcd after 2f: no imp whn hung lft wl over 1f out* **12/1**	

1m 0.19s (0.19) **Going Correction** +0.40s/f (Good) **5** Ran SP% **108.0**
Speed ratings (Par 105): **114,112,108,104,104**
CSF £23.26 TOTE £3.50: £1.90, £3.10; EX 11.80 Trifecta £60.40.
Owner Weldspec Glasgow Limited **Bred** Tipper House Stud **Trained** Carluke, S Lanarks

FOCUS
A good prize and it attracted a useful field, though a few of them may not prove the easiest to place to advantage in the near future. The form is rated around the winner and not entirely solid.

1883 SODEXO MAIDEN STKS 1m 67y
4:30 (4:31) (Class 5) 3-5-Y-O **£4,528** (£1,347; £673; £336) **Stalls** Low

Form				RPR
23-3	**1**		**Tawdeea**[7] 1662 4-10-0 87 DanielTudhope 7	84
			(David O'Meara) *hld up: rdn and hdwy over 2f out: led ins fnl f: pushed out cl home* **5/1**	
	2	1¼	**Warp Factor (IRE)**[22] 1352 3-9-1 0 SamHitchcott 3	78
			(John Patrick Shanahan, Ire) *pressed ldr: drvn over 2f out: ev ch over 1f out to ins fnl f: kpt on: hld towards fin* **4/1**[3]	
32	**3**	1	**Steccando (IRE)**[17] 1449 3-9-1 0 BenCurtis 1	76
			(Alan Swinbank) *trckd ldrs: rdn over 2f out: kpt on ins fnl f* **5/2**[1]	
620-	**4**	nk	**Weekend Offender (FR)**[204] 7123 3-9-1 77 GrahamLee 4	75
			(Kevin Ryan) *t.k.h: led: rdn over 2f out: hdd ins fnl f: sn outpcd* **7/2**[2]	
2-	**5**	2	**Euchen Glen**[227] 6454 3-9-1 0 PaulMulrennan 6	71
			(Jim Goldie) *hld up: rn green and outpcd over 3f out: styd on steadily fr 2f out: nvr nr ldrs* **7/2**[2]	
00-	**6**	29	**Macmidnight**[280] 4670 4-9-4 0 GarryWhillans(5) 5	2
			(Donald Whillans) *hld up: drvn along over 3f out: wknd fr over 2f out: t.o* **66/1**	

1m 52.99s (4.59) **Going Correction** +0.40s/f (Good)
WFA 3 from 4yo 13lb **6** Ran SP% **111.2**
Speed ratings (Par 103): **93,91,90,90,88 59**
CSF £24.36 TOTE £4.60: £2.00, £3.00; EX 25.40 Trifecta £37.10.
Owner Middleham Park Racing LXVI **Bred** Shadwell Estate Company Limited **Trained** Upper Helmsley, N Yorks

FOCUS
After rail movements the actual race distance was 1m91yds. A fairly useful maiden. The leaders probably pressed for home a fair way out under the conditions, setting it up nicely for the winner. The form makes sense at face value.

1884 JORDAN ELECTRICS H'CAP 1m 67y
5:05 (5:05) (Class 5) (0-75,74) 4-Y-O+ **£4,528** (£1,347; £673; £336) **Stalls** Low

Form				RPR
-626	**1**		**Archie's Advice**[66] 708 5-9-1 **68** JasonHart 4	80
			(Keith Dalgleish) *hld up: smooth hdwy to ld over 1f out: sn rdn and edgd rt: kpt on wl fnl f* **7/2**[1]	
0-04	**2**	2¼	**Lightning Spree (IRE)**[6] 1695 4-8-12 **65** [1] ShaneGray 10	72
			(Kevin Ryan) *s.i.s: hld up in rr: stdy hdwy over 2f out: plld out and effrt over 1f out: kpt on to take 2nd cl home: nt rch wnr* **9/1**	
13-	**3**	hd	**Lara Carbonara (IRE)**[25] 1282 4-8-10 **63** SamHitchcott 1	69
			(John Patrick Shanahan, Ire) *in tch: hdwy and cl up over 2f out: sn rdn: wnt 2nd briefly ins fnl f tl no ex nr fin* **9/1**	
11-	**4**	1¼	**Dolphin Rock**[242] 5991 9-8-3 **63** (b) CallumRodriguez(7) 11	66
			(Richard Ford) *t.k.h: led: rdn and hdd over 1f out: outpcd ins fnl f* **13/2**	
/54-	**5**	1½	**Grand Canyon (IRE)**[329] 2960 4-9-6 **73** DanielTudhope 3	73
			(David O'Meara) *t.k.h: cl up: effrt and rdn over 2f out: no ex appr fnl f* **4/1**[2]	
0-03	**6**	shd	**Danot (IRE)**[9] 1596 4-9-2 **69** GrahamLee 7	69
			(Jedd O'Keeffe) *trckd ldrs: drvn over 2f out: kpt on same pce fr over 1f out* **9/1**	
03-3	**7**	7	**Red Paladin (IRE)**[32] 1142 6-9-5 **72** (p) TonyHamilton 9	56
			(Kristin Stubbs) *slowly away: bhd: rdn over 3f out: no imp fr 2f out* **8/1**	
10-3	**8**	½	**Cadmium**[26] 1247 5-9-2 **69** PJMcDonald 5	52
			(Micky Hammond) *prom: drvn along 3f out: wknd 2f out* **5/1**[3]	
260-	**9**	2¼	**Gun Case**[223] 6593 4-9-7 **74** ConnorBeasley 2	51
			(Alistair Whillans) *hld up: rdn along over 3f out: wknd over 2f out* **14/1**	

1m 53.24s (4.84) **Going Correction** +0.40s/f (Good) **9** Ran SP% **120.0**
Speed ratings (Par 103): **91,88,88,87,85 85,78,78,75**
CSF £37.09 CT £269.70 TOTE £4.90: £1.80, £3.10, £4.60; EX 36.80 Trifecta £255.20.
Owner A R M Galbraith **Bred** G L S Partnership **Trained** Carluke, S Lanarks

FOCUS
A fair handicap. After rail movements the actual race distance was 1m91yds. The winner is rated close to form.
T/Plt: £191.90 to a £1 stake. Pool: £70,580.67 - 268.37 winning tickets. T/Qpdt: £86.80 to a £1 stake. Pool: £5,139.30 - 43.80 winning tickets. **Richard Young**

1861 NEWMARKET (R-H)
Sunday, May 1

OFFICIAL GOING: Good (overall 7.7, far side 7.5, centre 7.8, stands' side 8.0)
Wind: light, half behind Weather: mainly sunny, light cloud

1885 QIPCO SUPPORTING BRITISH RACING STKS (H'CAP) 1m 4f
1:50 (1:50) (Class 2) (0-105,103) 4-Y-O+
£28,012 (£8,388; £4,194; £2,097; £1,048; £526) **Stalls** Centre

Form				RPR
00-6	**1**		**Oasis Fantasy (IRE)**[11] 1568 5-8-10 **89** (b[1]) SilvestreDeSousa 10	96+
			(Ed Dunlop) *stdd after s: t.k.h: hld up in rr: clsd and in tch 7f out: pushed along and hdwy 2f out: swtchd rt and rdn to chal 1f out: led ins fnl f: r.o strly* **7/1**	
6300	**2**	1½	**Paddys Motorbike (IRE)**[37] 1081 4-8-11 **90** AndreaAtzeni 9	95
			(David Evans) *midfield: clsd and in tch 7f out: effrt over 2f out: hdwy to chal wl over 1f out: led 1f out: hdd and styd on same pce ins fnl f* **14/1**	
000-	**3**	1½	**Goodwood Mirage (IRE)**[44] 4345 6-8-6 **85** WilliamCarson 1	88
			(Michael Bell) *chsd ldr and clr in ldng quartet tl 7f out: rdn to ld over 2f out: hdd 2f out but stl ev ch tl no ex jst ins fnl f: 3rd and styd on same pce fnl 150yds* **20/1**	
611-	**4**	2	**Oceanographer**[150] 8093 4-9-10 **103** (p) WilliamBuick 4	102
			(Charlie Appleby) *lw: t.k.h: chsd ldng pair and clr in ldng quartet tl 7f out: pushed along to chal over 2f out: led 2f out: sn drvn: hdd 1f out: no ex: wknd fnl 100yds* **5/2**[1]	
200-	**5**	2¾	**Forgotten Hero (IRE)**[142] 7469 7-9-3 **96** (t) JimCrowley 6	91
			(Kim Bailey) *stdd s: t.k.h: hld up off the pce in last trio: clsd and in tch 7f out: hdwy over 2f out: chsng ldrs but unable qck u.p over 1f out: wknd ins fnl f* **14/1**	
-042	**6**	6	**Snoano**[15] 1493 4-8-11 **90** PaulHanagan 7	75
			(Tim Easterby) *off the pce in midfield: clsd and in tch 7f out: rdn and effrt to chse ldrs 2f out: no ex u.p jst over 1f out: wknd fnl f* **7/1**	
-120	**7**	6	**Silver Quay (IRE)**[22] 1336 4-9-4 **97** RyanMoore 8	73
			(Richard Hannon) *stdd s: hld up off the pce in last pair: clsd and in tch 7f out: rdn over 2f out: sn outpcd and btn: no ch over 1f out* **10/1**	

-510 **8** 2 1/2 **Watersmeet**[37] 1069 5-9-8 **101** .... JoeFanning 2 73
(Mark Johnston) *lw: led: rdn and hdd over 2f out: sn struggling and lost pl over 1f out: wknd jst over 1f out* **13/2**[3]

0-01 **9** 1/2 **Bazooka (IRE)**[20] 1390 5-8-0 **79** oh2 .... JoeyHaynes 5 50
(David Flood) *taken down early: off the pce in midfield: clsd and in tch 7f out: rdn over 2f out: sn outpcd and btn: bhd over 1f out* **20/1**

12-1 **10** 6 **Slunovrat (FR)**[20] 1391 5-8-0 **79** .... JimmyQuinn 3 40
(David Menuisier) *t.k.h: chsd ldrs and clr in ldng quartet tl 7f out: rdn 3f out: sn struggling and lost pl: bhd over 1f out* **6/1**[2]

2m 32.46s (0.46) **Going Correction** +0.125s/f (Good) **10** Ran SP% **113.1**
Speed ratings (Par 109): **103,102,101,99,97 93,89,88,87,83**
CSF £96.73 CT £1840.59 TOTE £7.50: £2.40, £3.20, £4.90; EX 91.10 Trifecta £1159.20.
Owner Windflower Overseas & J L Dunlop OBE **Bred** Windflower Overseas **Trained** Newmarket, Suffolk

FOCUS

Stands' Side course used. Stalls Stands' side except 1m4f: Centre. No rain overnight and a drying day saw the ground upgraded to good all over, and there was a strong crosswind. This race was run over 9 yards further than advertised. It wasn't the most competitive edition of this good-quality handicap and few landed a blow at the business end. It suited the closers. The form is rated a bit cautiously.

1886 CHARM SPIRIT AT TWEENHILLS IN 2017 DAHLIA STKS (GROUP 2) (F&M) 1m 1f

2:25 (2:26) (Class 1) 4-Y-0+

£51,039 (£19,350; £9,684; £4,824; £2,421; £1,215) **Stalls** High

Form RPR

0- **1** **Usherette (IRE)**[27] 4-9-0 109 .... MickaelBarzalona 4 117
(A Fabre, France) *w'like: sltly on the leg: stdd bk after s: hld up in midfield: shkn up and hdwy over 1f out: wnt 2nd and swtchd rt jst over 1f out: sn rdn and chalng: led 100yds out: styd on wl: drvn out* **5/1**[3]

166- **2** 1 **Arabian Queen (IRE)**[197] 7279 4-9-0 116 .... SilvestreDeSousa 9 116
(David Elsworth) *sltly on toes: led: rdn over 1f out: edging lft but keeping on wl over 1f out: hrd pressed 1f out: hdd 100yds out: no ex and one pce after* **7/1**

110- **3** 4 1/2 **Amazing Maria (IRE)**[232] 6338 5-9-0 117 .... JamesDoyle 3 106
(David O'Meara) *lw: chsd ldng trio: rdn and hdwy over 2f out: cl 3rd and drvn over 1f out: unable qck 1f out: wknd ins fnl f* **6/1**

203- **4** 1/2 **Irish Rookie (IRE)**[211] 6925 4-9-0 111 .... FergusSweeney 1 105
(Martyn Meade) *stdd after s: hld up in last pair: rdn and hdwy over 2f out: chsng ldrs but unable qck u.p over 1f out: kpt on same pce ins fnl f* **9/1**

3 **5** nk **Furia Cruzada (CHI)**[64] 748 4-9-0 110 .... WilliamBuick 6 104+
(John Gosden) *stdd and short of room leaving stalls: hld up in last trio: nt clr run 2f out: swtchd lft and no hdwy on downhill run over 1f out: swtchd rt and hdwy 1f out: hanging rt but styd on ins fnl f: nvr threatened ldrs* **16/1**

42-1 **6** 2 3/4 **Kyllachy Queen (IRE)**[29] 1207 4-9-0 102 .... AndreaAtzeni 2 98
(Marco Botti) *hld up in tch in midfield: effrt u.p over 1f out: unable qck and btn 1f out: wknd ins fnl f* **33/1**

512- **7** hd **Jazzi Top**[210] 6969 4-9-0 115 .... FrankieDettori 8 98
(John Gosden) *t.k.h: mostly chsd ldr: rdn 2f out: sn lost 2nd and btn: wknd fnl f* **5/2**[1]

013- **8** 6 **Persona Grata**[182] 7667 5-9-0 103 .... JimCrowley 5 85
(Ed Walker) *stdd s: hld up in rr: swtchd rt and effrt 2f out: sn rdn and btn: bhd fnl f* **33/1**

202- **9** 12 **Crystal Zvezda**[205] 7078 4-9-0 106 .... RyanMoore 7 58
(Sir Michael Stoute) *plld hrd and ref to settle: chsd ldrs tl 2f out: sn lost pl and sltly hmpd: bhd and eased jst over 1f out* **9/2**[2]

1m 51.06s (-0.64) **Going Correction** +0.125s/f (Good) **9** Ran SP% **112.0**
Speed ratings (Par 115): **107,106,102,101,101 98,98,93,82**
CSF £38.10 TOTE £6.00: £1.90, £2.50, £2.50; EX 37.70 Trifecta £221.70.
Owner Godolphin SNC **Bred** Darley **Trained** Chantilly, France

FOCUS

A strong Dahlia Stakes. There was a solid pace set on the stands' side and the first pair were clear at the finish. The placed horses set the level and Usherette posted a biggish pb.

1887 LONGHOLES.COM REHAB AND PRE-TRAINING H'CAP 6f

3:00 (3:01) (Class 2) 4-Y-0+

£28,012 (£8,388; £4,194; £2,097; £1,048; £526) **Stalls** High

Form RPR

0-01 **1** **Englishman**[13] 1530 6-8-4 **85** .... JoeFanning 15 96
(Milton Bradley) *wl in tch in midfield and travelled strly: shkn up and clsd to chal ent fnl f: pushed along and led ins fnl f: r.o wl: quite comf* **12/1**

233- **2** 1/2 **Seeking Magic**[135] 8288 8-8-8 **92** ....(t) RyanTate(3) 12 101
(Clive Cox) *racd keenly: led: rdn over 1f out: hrd drvn and hrd pressed 1f out: hdd ins fnl f: kpt on but a hld* **20/1**

1-21 **3** 2 3/4 **Dougan**[29] 1205 4-8-12 **93** .... AndreaAtzeni 8 94+
(David Evans) *lw: stdd bk after s: hld up in rr and swtchd to stands' rail after 2f: effrt and swtchd lft over 1f out: swtchd rt and hdwy 1f out: wnt 3rd ins fnl f: r.o strly: nvr got to rch ldrs* **6/1**[2]

3333 **4** 2 3/4 **Yeeoow (IRE)**[19] 1394 7-8-4 **85** .... JoeyHaynes 1 77
(K R Burke) *chsd ldrs: rdn over 1f out: drvn and no ex 1f out: wknd ins fnl f* **14/1**

20-3 **5** 1 **Poyle Vinnie**[25] 1272 6-9-10 **105** .... AndrewMullen 10 94
(Michael Appleby) *chsd ldrs: rdn and pressing ldr over 1f out: drvn and no ex 1f out: wknd ins fnl f* **20/1**

0-03 **6** 1 1/4 **Golden Steps (FR)**[64] 755 5-9-5 **100** .... FrankieDettori 16 85
(Marco Botti) *swtg: taken down early: hld up in tch towards rr: rdn and hdwy 2f out: edging rt and no imp 1f out: kpt on same pce fnl f* **9/2**[1]

630- **7** 1/2 **Field Game**[212] 6893 4-8-6 **87** ....(t) NickyMackay 17 70
(Hughie Morrison) *taken down early: chsd ldr: rdn and pressing ldr briefly over 1f out: sn outpcd and btn 1f out: wknd ins fnl f* **20/1**

00-1 **8** 3/4 **Teruntum Star (FR)**[19] 1394 4-9-6 **101** .... RyanMoore 4 82
(Kevin Ryan) *midfield: sme hdwy u.p over 1f out: no imp and kpt on same pce fnl f* **6/1**[2]

30-2 **9** 1 1/2 **New Bidder**[28] 1218 5-8-9 **90** .... GrahamGibbons 5 66
(David Barron) *lw: taken down early: wl in tch in midfield: rdn and effrt jst over 2f out: no imp over 1f out and btn whn carried rt 1f out: wknd ins fnl f* **6/1**[2]

020- **10** nk **Clear Spring (IRE)**[191] 7424 8-9-2 **97** .... JimCrowley 11 72
(John Spearing) *in tch in midfield: rdn and no hdwy over 1f out: wknd ins fnl f* **33/1**

160- **11** 1/2 **Huntsmans Close**[256] 5528 6-9-7 **102** .... JamesDoyle 7 75
(Roger Charlton) *taken down early and led rdrless to s: hld up in tch in last quartet: effrt 2f out: sme hdwy over 1f out: sn no imp: wknd ins fnl f* **10/1**[3]

4-00 **12** 3/4 **Ballymore Castle (IRE)**[13] 1522 4-8-10 **91** .... PaulHanagan 2 62
(Richard Fahey) *on toes: a in rr: rdn 2f out: no hdwy: plugged on to pass btn horses ins fnl f: n.d* **10/1**[3]

6600 **13** hd **Justice Good (IRE)**[19] 1394 4-9-0 **95** ....(t) SilvestreDeSousa 14 65
(David Elsworth) *restless in stalls: in tch in last quartet: rdn and no hdwy over 1f out: wl btn 1f out: wknd ins fnl f* **20/1**

0-50 **14** 3/4 **Captain Bob (IRE)**[13] 1530 5-8-0 **81** .... JimmyQuinn 9 49
(Robert Cowell) *in tch in midfield: shuffled bk and nt clrest of runs wl over 1f out: rdn and no hdwy over 1f out: wknd ins fnl f* **14/1**

105- **15** 4 1/2 **Bold**[323] 3162 4-8-0 **81** oh1 .... RyanPowell 13 34
(Stuart Williams) *chsd ldrs: rdn and losing pl over 2f out: bhd 1f out: wknd* **50/1**

601- **16** 2 1/4 **Pharmaceutical (IRE)**[201] 7198 4-8-3 **84** .... KieranO'Neill 6 30
(Stuart Williams) *hld up in tch towards rr: rdn and no hdwy over 1f out: sn losing pl: bhd 1f out: wknd* **25/1**

1m 11.48s (-0.72) **Going Correction** +0.125s/f (Good) **16** Ran SP% **128.0**
Speed ratings (Par 109): **109,108,104,101,99 98,97,96,94,93 93,92,92,91,85 82**
CSF £241.65 CT £1667.42 TOTE £15.20: £3.50, £3.80, £1.90, £3.20; EX 303.10 Trifecta £3704.90.
Owner E A Hayward **Bred** Peter Winkworth **Trained** Sedbury, Gloucs

FOCUS

This looked hugely competitive, but a high draw was a massive advantage and the first pair dominated the finish. Pace held out.

1888 QIPCO 1000 GUINEAS STKS (BRITISH CHAMPIONS SERIES) (GROUP 1) (FILLIES) 1m

3:40 (3:43) (Class 1) 3-Y-0

£297,018 (£112,606; £56,355; £28,073; £14,088; £7,070) **Stalls** High

Form RPR

211- **1** **Minding (IRE)**[205] 7075 3-9-0 120 .... RyanMoore 8 121+
(A P O'Brien, Ire) *v relaxed: lw: pressed ldrs: clsd and pushed into ld over 2f out: rdn and gng clr whn drifted rt over 1f out: in command and styd on strly fnl f: readily* **11/10**[1]

121- **2** 3 1/2 **Ballydoyle (IRE)**[210] 6967 3-9-0 113 ....(t) SeamieHeffernan 15 115+
(A P O'Brien, Ire) *lengthy: a bit warm: hld up in rr: nt clr run on stands' rail over 2f out: rdn and hdwy between rivals over 1f out: styd on wl ins fnl f: wnt 2nd towards fin: no threat to wnr* **15/2**[3]

12-3 **3** 1/2 **Alice Springs (IRE)**[21] 1369 3-9-0 111 .... ColmO'Donoghue 3 111
(A P O'Brien, Ire) *hld up in tch in midfield: clsd 2f out: rdn to chse wnr and edgd lft ent fnl f: kpt on but no imp: lost 2nd towards fin* **16/1**

241- **4** nk **Fireglow**[183] 7631 3-9-0 105 .... JamesDoyle 16 110
(Mark Johnston) *chsd ldrs: rdn 2f out: outpcd by wnr and edgd rt ent fnl f: kpt on same pce u.p after* **40/1**

12-1 **5** 2 **Nathra (IRE)**[19] 1396 3-9-0 110 .... FrankieDettori 4 106
(John Gosden) *lw: stdd s: hld up in midfield: effrt over 2f out: hdwy u.p over 1f out: kpt on same pce and no threat to wnr fnl f* **8/1**

412- **6** nk **Turret Rocks (IRE)**[210] 6967 3-9-0 110 .... KevinManning 13 105
(J S Bolger, Ire) *bustled along leaving stalls: hmpd sn after s: sn chsng ldr: drvn and chsd wnr over 2f out: outpcd and bmpd jst over 1f out: wknd jst ins fnl f* **20/1**

11-4 **7** 1 **Mix And Mingle (IRE)**[19] 1396 3-9-0 100 .... TedDurcan 12 106+
(Chris Wall) *stdd s: hld up in tch in rr: hdwy over 1f out: keeping on but no threat to wnr whn squeezed for room and hmpd jst over 1f out: kpt on same pce after* **50/1**

2 **8** hd **Midweek**[24] 1309 3-9-0 107 .... VincentCheminaud 14 102+
(Mme C Head-Maarek, France) *unf: scope: q tall: bit edgy: stdd s: hmpd and dropped to last quartet sn after s: nt clr run on stands' rail over 2f out: swtchd lft and sltly hmpd 2f out: hdwy u.p over 1f out: no imp 1f out: wknd ins fnl f* **12/1**

20-1 **9** 1 **Jet Setting (IRE)**[21] 1369 3-9-0 106 .... ShaneFoley 5 100
(Adrian Paul Keatley, Ire) *pressed ldrs: rdn over 2f out: outpcd by wnr over 1f out: carried lft and hmpd ent fnl f: wknd ins fnl f* **33/1**

1-4 **10** 3 1/4 **Aljazzi**[15] 1476 3-9-0 98 .... JimCrowley 2 92
(Marco Botti) *stdd s: hld up in tch in last quartet: sme hdwy u.p over 1f out: no imp 1f out: wknd ins fnl f* **100/1**

10-0 **11** 1/2 **Epsom Icon**[19] 1396 3-9-0 97 .... CharlesBishop 11 91
(Mick Channon) *hld up wl in tch in midfield: effrt and no hdwy over 1f out: wknd ins fnl f* **100/1**

13-3 **12** 4 **Robanne**[19] 1396 3-9-0 100 .... SilvestreDeSousa 1 82
(William Knight) *hld up in tch in midfield: effrt 2f out: drvn and no hdwy over 1f out: wknd ins fnl f* **50/1**

315- **13** 2 1/4 **Blue Bayou**[231] 6361 3-9-0 107 .... JimmyFortune 6 77
(Brian Meehan) *stdd s: hld up in tch in midfield: lost pl and rdn over 2f out: no hdwy u.p and swtchd rt over 1f out: wknd fnl f* **50/1**

126- **14** 5 **Illuminate (IRE)**[184] 7626 3-9-0 115 .... PatSmullen 9 65
(Richard Hannon) *stdd s: hld up in tch in midfield: rdn and no rspnse on downhill run over 1f out: sn btn: wknd fnl f* **25/1**

21- **15** 6 **Sharja Queen**[256] 5515 3-9-0 0 .... AndreaAtzeni 7 52
(Roger Varian) *t.k.h: chsd ldrs: rdn and lost pl over 2f out: towards rr whn hmpd wl over 1f out: wl bhd fnl f* **66/1**

121- **16** 2 **Lumiere**[218] 6753 3-9-0 116 .... WilliamBuick 10 47
(Mark Johnston) *led and sn crossed to r against stands' rail: hdd and rdn over 2f out: sn dropped out: bhd over 1f out* **13/2**[2]

1m 36.53s (-2.07) **Going Correction** +0.125s/f (Good) **16** Ran SP% **120.7**
Speed ratings (Par 110): **115,111,111,110,108 108,107,107,106,102 102,98,96,91,85 83**
CSF £8.36 CT £96.60 TOTE £2.10: £1.10, £3.00, £5.10; EX 12.30 Trifecta £57.70.
Owner Derrick Smith & Mrs John Magnier & Michael Tabor **Bred** Orpendale, Chelston & Wynatt **Trained** Cashel, Co Tipperary

■ Aidan O'Brien's 250th Group/Grade 1 success. A 1-2-3 for daughters of Galileo.
■ Stewards' Enquiry : William Buick one-day ban: failed to ride to draw (May 15); two-day ban: careless riding (May 16-17)

FOCUS

A deep 1000 Guineas. They went a sound pace against the stands' side and the top 2yo form came to the fore. It was a 1-2-3 for the Aidan O'Brien stable - the first time a trainer has achieved this feat in a British Classic since 1918 - and the form looks very solid. Minding rates along Finsceal Beo as the best 1000 Guineas winners this century. She extended her Moyglare superiority over Ballydoyle and Alice Springs.

1889 HOT STREAK FUTURE STARS MAIDEN STKS (PLUS 10 RACE) 5f

4:15 (4:20) (Class 4) 2-Y-0 **£6,469** (£1,925; £962; £481) **Stalls** High

Form RPR

1 **Global Applause** 2-9-5 0 .... RyanMoore 2 93
(Ed Dunlop) *lengthy: trckd ldng pair: clsd and upsides 2f out: pushed into ld over 1f out: readily wnt clr and drifted lft jst ins fnl f: r.o wl: easily* **7/4**[1]

2 3 3/4 **Hakeem (FR)** 2-9-5 0 HarryBentley 5 80
(Richard Hannon) *unf: scope: hld up in tch in last quartet: hdwy and swtchd rt over 1f out: chsd clr wnr and edgd lft ins fnl f: kpt on but no imp* **9/2**[3]

3 2 **Top Score** 2-9-5 0 JamesDoyle 4 72
(Saeed bin Suroor) *athletic: free to post: w ldr: rdn over 1f out: outpcd by wnr in 2nd 1f out: 3rd and wknd ins fnl f* **13/2**

4 2 **Gulliver** 2-9-5 0 AndreaAtzeni 7 65+
(Hugo Palmer) *q str: v green: s.i.s: t.k.h: in tch in last quartet: rdn and sme hdwy over 1f out: swtchd lft and kpt on wl ins fnl f: no ch w wnr* **11/2**

5 1 **Await The Storm (IRE)** 2-9-5 0 JimmyFortune 10 62
(Brian Meehan) *cmpt: in tch in midfield: swtchd lft and effrt jst over 2f out: outpcd and rn green over 1f out: wknd ins fnl f* **33/1**

6 3/4 **Toy Theatre** 2-9-0 0 WilliamBuick 1 54
(Mark Johnston) *q str: rn green in rr: shkn up and rn green over 1f out: sn btn: wl hld and kpt on same pce fnl f* **12/1**

7 nse **Rose Berry** 2-9-0 0 IrineuGoncalves 3 54
(Chris Dwyer) *leggy: racd keenly: led: rdn and hdd over 1f out: no ex and btn 1f out: wknd ins fnl f* **50/1**

8 5 **Charlie Chaplin (GER)** 2-9-5 0 WilliamCarson 6 41
(Robert Eddery) *athletic: dwlt: rn green in last quartet: rdn and btn over 1f out: wknd fnl f* **4/1**[2]

9 3 1/2 **Walter Raleigh (IRE)** 2-9-5 0 AdamKirby 9 28
(John Ryan) *unf: q tall: hld up in tch towards rr: pushed along over 1f out: sn btn: bhd fnl f* **33/1**

1m 0.04s (0.94) **Going Correction** +0.125s/f (Good) 9 Ran SP% **118.8**
Speed ratings (Par 95): **97,91,87,84,83 81,81,73,68**
CSF £10.06 TOTE £2.80: £1.30, £1.90, £2.10; EX 11.60 Trifecta £64.10.
Owner Dr Johnny Hon **Bred** R F And S D Knipe **Trained** Newmarket, Suffolk

FOCUS
This is usually a fair 2yo maiden and the impressive winner is rated towards the top end of the race averages.

1890 TWEENHILLS PRETTY POLLY STKS (LISTED RACE) (FILLIES) 1m 2f
4:50 (4:53) (Class 1) 3-Y-O
£22,684 (£8,600; £4,304; £2,144; £1,076; £540) **Stalls** High

Form RPR

2-1 1 **Swiss Range**[19] 1392 3-9-0 92 FrankieDettori 8 104+
(John Gosden) *stdd s: hld up in tch in last pair: swtchd lft and effrt 2f out: rdn and qcknd smartly to ld jst over 1f out: drew clr and pushed out ins fnl f: impressive* **6/4**[1]

521- 2 3 **Chicadoro**[218] 6744 3-9-0 84 AndreaAtzeni 3 98
(Ralph Beckett) *athletic: t.k.h: pressed ldr: rdn to ld and wandered lft over 1f out: sn hdd: outpcd by wnr but kpt on for clr 2nd ins fnl f* **16/1**

3 2 3/4 **Even Song (IRE)**[190] 7475 3-9-0 0 RyanMoore 6 96+
(A P O'Brien, Ire) *q lengthy: lw: hld up in tch towards rr: nt clr run and swtchd lft and rt over 1f out: swtchd lft ins fnl f: pushed along and styd on wl to go 3rd towards fin: no ch w wnr* **3/1**[2]

11-6 4 3/4 **First Victory (IRE)**[19] 1396 3-9-5 102 (t) JamesDoyle 9 96
(Saeed bin Suroor) *chsd ldrs: effrt 2f out: edgd rt and no ex u.p 1f out: wknd ins fnl f: lost 3rd towards fin* **6/1**[3]

01- 5 2 3/4 **Tiptree (IRE)**[183] 7629 3-9-0 93 AdamKirby 4 86
(Luca Cumani) *q tall: green in prelims: t.k.h: wl in tch in midfield: effrt 2f out: rdn and unable qck over 1f out: wknd ins fnl f* **13/2**

120- 6 1 1/4 **Peru**[183] 7631 3-9-0 81 PatSmullen 7 83
(Hugo Palmer) *led and set stdy gallop: drvn and hdd over 1f out: struggling to qckn and sltly hmpd jst over 1f out: wknd ins fnl f* **14/1**

13- 7 2 3/4 **Turning The Table (IRE)**[226] 6503 3-9-0 82 JimCrowley 1 78
(David Simcock) *w'like: chsd ldng pair: rdn 2f out: unable qck u.p and btn 1f out: wknd ins fnl f* **16/1**

5-21 8 1 **Australian Queen**[71] 654 3-9-0 80 SilvestreDeSousa 5 76
(David Elsworth) *lengthy: str: lw: stdd s: hld up in last pair: swtchd rt and effrt 2f out: sn no imp: wknd over 1f out* **25/1**

10- 9 7 **Rayaa**[260] 5385 3-9-0 71 JFEgan 2 62
(John Butler) *sltly on toes: stdd s: t.k.h: hld up in tch: rdn over 2f out: sn struggling: bhd over 1f out* **100/1**

2m 5.4s (-0.40) **Going Correction** +0.125s/f (Good) 9 Ran SP% **115.9**
Speed ratings (Par 104): **106,103,101,100,98 97,95,94,89**
CSF £29.42 TOTE £2.40: £1.10, £4.00, £1.60; EX 27.90 Trifecta £122.60.
Owner K Abdullah **Bred** Juddmonte Farms Ltd **Trained** Newmarket, Suffolk
■ Stewards' Enquiry : Andrea Atzeni caution: careless riding

FOCUS
This Listed event has come back into fashion of late and it ought to work out to be a fair race. The time was low but the winner impressed and the 2-3 fit the race standard.

1891 QATAR RACING H'CAP 1m 2f
5:25 (5:28) (Class 3) (0-95,95) 3-Y-O **£9,703** (£2,887; £1,443; £721) **Stalls** High

Form RPR

2-1 1 **Taqdeer (IRE)**[15] 1474 3-8-13 **87** PaulHanagan 5 98+
(John Gosden) *wl made: stdd and squeezed for room leaving stalls: hld up in last pair: effrt 2f out: hdwy and swtchd rt jst over 1f out: rdn to chal ins fnl f: led fnl 100yds: r.o wl* **15/8**[1]

1- 2 1/2 **Prize Money**[193] 7397 3-9-7 **95** JamesDoyle 6 105+
(Saeed bin Suroor) *lw: wl in tch in midfield: rdn and effrt 2f out: chal over 1f out: drvn to ld 1f out: sn hrd pressed: hdd and styd on same pce fnl 100yds* **9/4**[2]

220- 3 2 **New Caledonia (IRE)**[208] 7006 3-8-11 **85** WilliamBuick 2 91
(Mark Johnston) *racd in centre tl 5f out: chsd ldr: rdn over 1f out: stl cl enough in 3rd 1f out: no ex and outpcd fnl 100yds* **33/1**

01- 4 5 **Chester Street**[207] 7032 3-8-4 **78** SilvestreDeSousa 7 74
(Roger Charlton) *athletic: led: rdn 2f out: drvn and hdd 1f out: sn btn and wknd ins fnl f* **9/1**

1 5 2 1/4 **Sam Missile (IRE)**[116] 65 3-8-7 **84** DanielMuscutt[(3)] 3 76
(James Fanshawe) *w'like: hld up in tch: effrt 2f out: 5th and no ex whn wandered 1f out: wknd ins fnl f* **8/1**

33-3 6 6 **Machine Learner**[11] 1571 3-8-6 **80** WilliamCarson 4 60
(Michael Bell) *chsd ldrs: rdn 3f out: sn struggling and lost pl 2f out: bhd and wl btn over 1f out* **33/1**

23-1 7 4 **Galvanize (USA)**[24] 1288 3-8-7 **81** AndreaAtzeni 1 53
(Sir Michael Stoute) *lw: racd in centre tl 5f out: in tch in midfield: effrt wl over 1f out: outpcd and btn 6th 1f out: fdd ins fnl f* **16/1**

10-4 8 1 3/4 **Mengli Khan (IRE)**[19] 1395 3-9-3 **91** FrankieDettori 8 59
(Hugo Palmer) *lw: t.k.h: chsd ldrs: rdn 3f out: lost pl and btn over 1f out: fdd ins fnl f* **11/2**[3]

2m 3.54s (-2.26) **Going Correction** +0.125s/f (Good) 8 Ran SP% **113.8**
Speed ratings (Par 103): **114,113,112,108,106 101,98,96**
CSF £6.18 CT £90.82 TOTE £2.90: £1.40, £1.40, £4.40; EX 7.20 Trifecta £133.30.
Owner Hamdan Al Maktoum **Bred** Maurice Byrne **Trained** Newmarket, Suffolk

FOCUS
This was a strong 3yo handicap and the time was quick, 19lb faster than the Pretty Polly. The first two are likely to be running in Group races before long.
T/Jkpt: £11,772.60 to a £1 stake. Pool: £49,743.73 - 3 winning tickets. T/Plt: £190.20 to a £1 stake. Pool: £203,052.16 - 779.30 winning tickets. T/Qpdt: £11.30 to a £1 stake. Pool: £18,260.63 - 1,189.24 winning tickets. **Steve Payne**

SALISBURY (R-H)
Sunday, May 1

OFFICIAL GOING: Good to soft (7.9)
Wind: mild breeze against Weather: sunny periods

1892 BETFRED "LIKE US ON FACEBOOK" MAIDEN STKS (DIV I) 6f
1:35 (1:36) (Class 5) 3-Y-O+ **£3,557** (£1,058; £529; £264) **Stalls** Low

Form RPR

- 1 **Ebony N Ivory** 3-9-4 0 FrederikTylicki 8 78+
(Roger Varian) *mde all: rdn whn strly chal fr 2f out: kpt on v gamely fnl f: drvn out* **11/2**

24-4 2 nk **Jayjinski (IRE)**[25] 1256 3-9-4 75 [1] SeanLevey 4 77
(Richard Hannon) *trckd ldrs: rdn for str chal fr 2f out: ev ch thrght fnl f: kpt on* **3/1**[2]

6- 3 1 1/4 **He's My Cracker**[191] 7423 3-9-4 0 JohnFahy 10 73
(Clive Cox) *trckd ldrs: rdn to chse ldng pair fr 2f out: kpt on but nt quite pce to get on terms ins fnl f* **9/2**[3]

52-0 4 5 **Abaco Ridge**[13] 1524 3-8-13 0 RichardKingscote 1 52
(Ralph Beckett) *w wnr tl rdn wl over 2f out: sn one pce* **12/1**

5 1 **Harlech** 3-8-10 0 KevinStott[(3)] 7 49+
(Saeed bin Suroor) *unsettled stalls: trckd ldrs: effrt 3f out: sn one pce* **9/4**[1]

6 3 1/2 **Sir Compton** 3-9-4 0 DaneO'Neill 5 43
(Stuart Kittow) *s.i.s: in last pair: rdn over 2f out: nt pce to get on terms: wknd fnl f* **14/1**

6- 7 1 1/2 **Pushy Lady**[281] 4646 3-8-8 0 AliceMills[(5)] 2 33
(Rod Millman) *in tch tl outpcd over 3f out: no threat after* **16/1**

0/0 8 nk **Magical Peak**[16] 1451 4-9-4 0 CiaranMckee[(5)] 3 35
(John O'Shea) *s.i.s: a in last pair* **100/1**

00- 9 1/2 **Captain Joey (IRE)**[219] 6711 3-9-4 0 TomQueally 9 39+
(Charles Hills) *racd keenly: hld up: rdn over 2f out: wknd fnl f* **25/1**

1m 15.73s (0.93) **Going Correction** +0.20s/f (Good)
WFA 3 from 4yo 10lb 9 Ran SP% **114.4**
Speed ratings (Par 103): **101,100,98,92,90 86,84,83,83**
CSF £22.14 TOTE £5.60: £2.10, £1.60, £1.40; EX 17.60 Trifecta £70.90.
Owner Newsells Park Stud **Bred** Newsells Park Stud **Trained** Newmarket, Suffolk

FOCUS
The first division of a fair maiden. They went a respectable gallop on good to soft ground. The form is set around the second.

1893 BETFRED "CITY BOWL" H'CAP 1m 6f 21y
2:05 (2:06) (Class 3) (0-95,94) 4-Y-O+
£13,695 (£4,100; £2,050; £1,025; £512; £257)

Form RPR

34-2 1 **Rideonastar (IRE)**[20] 1391 5-8-5 **75** MartinDwyer 6 86
(Brendan Powell) *led for 1f: trckd ldr: shkn up to ld jst over 3f out: 3 l clr and in command ent fnl f: comf* **6/1**[3]

111- 2 1 1/2 **Magic Circle (IRE)**[191] 7425 4-9-1 **86** RichardKingscote 12 95+
(Ralph Beckett) *mid-div: pushed along whn swtchd to centre over 3f out: rdn wl over 2f out: hdwy fr wl over 1f out: wnt 3 l 2nd ent fnl f: styd on but nvr threatening to rch wnr* **2/1**[1]

50-3 3 3 3/4 **Eton Rambler (USA)**[18] 1417 6-9-4 **88** PatCosgrave 13 92
(George Baker) *trckd ldrs: rdn to chse wnr over 2f out tl ent fnl f: styd on same pce* **14/1**

400- 4 2 1/4 **Resiliency (IRE)**[256] 5532 5-8-12 **87** GeorgeBuckell[(5)] 4 88
(Michael Appleby) *in tch: rdn in 4th fr 3f out: styd on same pce fnl 2f* **9/1**

3323 5 3 3/4 **Scarlet Minstrel**[33] 1135 4-8-9 **80** DavidProbert 11 76
(Andrew Balding) *racd keenly: trckd ldrs: rdn 3f out: sn one pce: no ex fnl f* **14/1**

-415 6 2 1/2 **Cotton Club (IRE)**[29] 1209 5-9-2 **86** FrederikTylicki 3 78
(Rod Millman) *mid-div: rdn over 2f out: nvr any imp* **25/1**

364- 7 2 **King Calypso**[165] 7892 5-8-3 **78** EdwardGreatrex[(5)] 10 67
(Denis Coakley) *nudged along towards rr: struggling 4f out: styd on past btn horses fnl f: nvr trbld ldrs* **20/1**

5104 8 nk **Winterlude (IRE)**[22] 1336 6-9-10 **94** TimmyMurphy 7 83
(Jennie Candlish) *hld up towards rr: rdn over 2f out: little imp* **16/1**

/60- 9 1 1/2 **Continuum**[317] 3345 7-9-7 **94** RobHornby[(3)] 8 81
(Peter Hedger) *dwlt: last most of way: nvr any danger* **20/1**

212- 10 1 **Mark Hopkins**[202] 7165 4-9-4 **89** TomQueally 1 74
(David Elsworth) *racd freely: led after 1f: rdn and hdd 3f out: sn hld: wknd over 1f out* **7/2**[2]

2436 11 3 1/4 **Duchess Of Marmite (IRE)**[25] 1273 4-9-0 **85** (b) ShaneKelly 9 66
(Richard Hughes) *racd keenly: in tch: rdn 4f out: nvr threatened: wknd wl over 1f out* **16/1**

565- 12 7 **Mystery Drama**[115] 5312 6-8-7 **77** CamHardie 2 48
(Alexandra Dunn) *mid-div: rdn 3f out: wknd 2f out* **80/1**

3m 4.8s (-2.60) **Going Correction** +0.025s/f (Good)
WFA 4 from 5yo+ 1lb 12 Ran SP% **119.5**
Speed ratings (Par 107): **108,107,105,103,101 100,99,98,97,97 95,91**
CSF £17.65 CT £166.78 TOTE £7.20: £2.20, £1.10, £3.70; EX 24.70 Trifecta £168.10.
Owner D & J Newell **Bred** Derek & Judith Newell **Trained** Upper Lambourn, Berks

FOCUS
The feature contest was a good staying handicap. They went a respectable gallop at best. This rates a pb from the winner.

1894 BETFRED "LIKE US ON FACEBOOK" MAIDEN STKS (DIV II) 6f
2:35 (2:38) (Class 5) 3-Y-O+ **£3,557** (£1,058; £529; £264) **Stalls** Low

Form RPR

402- 1 **Short Work**[193] 7393 3-9-4 79 (p) RichardKingscote 10 84
(Ralph Beckett) *wnt rt s: trckd ldrs: rdn to chal jst over 1f out: led fnl 120yds: kpt on* **9/2**[3]

325- 2 nk **Dark Shot**[164] 7903 3-9-4 81 DavidProbert 3 83
(Andrew Balding) *led tl 3f out: rallied to regain ld jst over 1f out: hdd fnl 120yds: kpt on* **5/1**

3 2 1/4 **Nightingale Valley** 3-8-13 0 MartinDwyer 5 71
(Stuart Kittow) *outpcd in last pair and detached over 3f out: hdwy over 1f out: r.o wl fnl f: wnt 3rd fnl towards fin* **66/1**
04- 4 shd **Topology**[191] 7429 3-9-4 0 ShaneKelly 6 75
(Joseph Tuite) *mid-div: outpcd 3f out: r.o wl fnl f: wnt 4th towards fin* **14/1**
02- 5 3/4 **Mutarajjil (IRE)**[172] 7795 3-9-4 0 DaneO'Neill 4 73+
(Roger Varian) *racd keenly: prom: led 3f out: rdn and hdd jst over 1f out: no ex ins fnl f* **2/1**[1]
0-3 6 2 **Dream Farr (IRE)**[18] 1414 3-9-4 0 (t) GeorgeBaker 7 67
(Ed Walker) *racd keenly: in tch: rdn over 2f out: sn one pce* **14/1**
7 3 1/4 **Staffa (IRE)** 3-8-13 0 TomQueally 2 51
(Denis Coakley) *trckd ldrs: rdn over 2f out: wknd ins fnl f* **40/1**
022- 8 4 1/2 **Operative**[226] 6498 3-9-4 81 (p) PatCosgrave 9 55
(Ed de Giles) *hmpd bdly s: mid-div: rdn over 2f out: wknd ent fnl f* **5/2**[2]
9 1 **Frosty De Winter** 3-9-4 0 LiamKeniry 1 39
(Chris Gordon) *s.i.s: outpcd over 3f out: a in rr* **66/1**

1m 15.49s (0.69) **Going Correction** +0.20s/f (Good) **9** Ran SP% **115.5**
Speed ratings (Par 103): **103,102,99,99,98 95,91,85,84**
CSF £27.08 TOTE £6.60: £2.00, £2.20, £8.30; EX 29.40 Trifecta £2419.30.
Owner The Pickford Hill Partnership **Bred** Downfield Cottage Stud **Trained** Kimpton, Hants

FOCUS
The second division of the maiden was a stronger contest in terms of prior form and the winning time was marginally quicker. The form is rated around the runner-up.

1895 BETFRED "HOME OF GOALS GALORE" FILLIES' CONDITIONS STKS (PLUS 10 RACE) 5f
3:10 (3:11) (Class 3) 2-Y-O **£7,115** (£2,117; £1,058; £529) **Stalls** Low

Form RPR
21 1 **Stormy Clouds (IRE)**[27] 1233 2-9-0 0 SeanLevey 5 85+
(Richard Hannon) *travelled wl: led after 1f: in command fr 2f out: comf* **1/3**[1]
01 2 2 1/4 **Fastnet Spin (IRE)**[13] 1527 2-9-0 0 CathyGannon 1 72
(David Evans) *disp for over 1f: trckd ldrs: swtchd lft over 2f out: sn rdn to chse wnr: kpt on but nt pce to get on terms fnl f* **9/2**[2]
3 2 **Fair Selene** 2-8-6 0 HectorCrouch(5) 2 62
(Heather Main) *prom whn squeezed up ins 1st f: last but in tch: hdwy 3f out: rdn to chal for 2nd wl over 1f out tl no ex ins fnl f* **20/1**
4 6 **Limelight Lady** 2-8-11 0 RichardKingscote 3 40
(Harry Dunlop) *pushed along to press ldrs for over 1f: chsd ldrs tl wknd over 1f out* **14/1**
5 3 3/4 **Daffodil Mulligan** 2-8-11 0 MartinDwyer 4 27
(J S Moore) *disp ld for over 1f: pressed wnr: drvn 3f out: wknd over 1f out* **10/1**[3]

1m 3.07s (2.07) **Going Correction** +0.20s/f (Good) **5** Ran SP% **113.7**
Speed ratings (Par 94): **91,87,84,74,68**
CSF £2.44 TOTE £1.20: £1.10, £1.70; EX 2.20 Trifecta £11.70.
Owner Chris Giles & Richard Webb **Bred** Tally-Ho Stud **Trained** East Everleigh, Wilts

FOCUS
A fair juvenile fillies' conditions contest in terms of prior form which proved a stepping stone to much greater things for Illuminate and Tiggy Wiggy in the last two years. A good step forward from the winner. They went a decent gallop.

1896 BETFRED "SUPPORTS JACK BERRY HOUSE" H'CAP 1m 1f 198y
3:50 (3:51) (Class 4) (0-85,84) 3-Y-O **£5,175** (£1,540; £769; £384) **Stalls** Low

Form RPR
41- 1 **Mainstream**[200] 7218 3-9-4 81 StevieDonohoe 1 88+
(Sir Michael Stoute) *s.i.s: last but wl in tch: tk clsr order over 4f out: swtchd lft 2f out: qcknd up wl to ld fnl 120yds: readily* **9/4**[1]
-231 2 1 1/4 **Carry Me Home**[53] 880 3-9-1 78 DarryllHolland 3 82
(Charles Hills) *led: rdn whn strly chal 2f out: sn drifted lft: hdd fnl 120yds: kpt on but nt pce of wnr* **6/1**[3]
5-11 3 1/2 **Sir Roderic (IRE)**[8] 1630 3-9-1 78 FrederikTylicki 2 81+
(Rod Millman) *trckd ldr: chal 3f out: rdn and ev ch fr wl over 1f out tl no ex fnl 100yds* **11/4**[2]
215- 4 7 **Loading (IRE)**[135] 8286 3-9-2 79 SeanLevey 6 68
(Richard Hannon) *racd in 4th: effrt 2f out: wknd fnl f* **10/1**
01-6 5 3 **Zoffanys Pride (IRE)**[19] 1398 3-9-7 84 DavidProbert 4 67
(Andrew Balding) *trckd ldrs: rdn whn briefly short of room 2f out: wknd jst over 1f out* **8/1**

2m 12.86s (2.96) **Going Correction** +0.025s/f (Good) **5** Ran SP% **91.9**
Speed ratings (Par 101): **89,88,87,82,79**
CSF £10.34 TOTE £2.50: £1.10, £2.10; EX 7.10 Trifecta £24.10.
Owner The Queen **Bred** The Queen **Trained** Newmarket, Suffolk
■ Jufn was withdrawn. Price at time of withdrawal 4/1. Rule 4 applies to all bets - deduction 20p in the pound.
■ Stewards' Enquiry : Stevie Donohoe one-day ban: careless riding (May 15)

FOCUS
A decent 3yo handicap. They went an ordinary gallop and there could be more to come from the winner.

1897 BETFRED "GOALS GALORE EXTRA" EBF STALLIONS MAIDEN STKS 1m 4f
4:25 (4:25) (Class 5) 3-Y-O **£4,204** (£1,251; £625; £312) **Stalls** Low

Form RPR
2 1 **Harbour Law**[44] 980 3-9-5 0 GeorgeBaker 1 91+
(Laura Mongan) *trckd ldr: chal over 3f out: led over 2f out: rdn clr over 1f out: r.o wl* **4/1**[2]
3 2 2 3/4 **Forth Bridge**[15] 1483 3-9-5 0 WilliamTwiston-Davies 6 85
(Michael Bell) *led: rdn and hdd over 2f out: styd on same pce fnl f* **7/1**
03-3 3 4 1/2 **Real Dominion (USA)**[25] 1260 3-9-5 80 DavidProbert 3 78
(Andrew Balding) *trckd ldrs: rdn to chse ldng pair in cl 3rd over 2f out: no ex ent fnl f* **5/4**[1]
0- 4 10 **Afnaan**[166] 7878 3-9-5 0 FrederikTylicki 4 62
(Saeed bin Suroor) *in tch: hdwy over 3f out: sn rdn in cl 4th: wknd over 1f out* **7/1**
- 5 1/2 **Kesselring** 3-9-5 0 SeanLevey 7 61
(Richard Hannon) *trckd ldrs tl outpcd over 3f out: nvr bk on terms* **9/2**[3]
6 11 **Mister Showman** 3-9-5 0 RyanClark 2 43
(Jonathan Portman) *s.i.s: racd keenly and sn trcking ldrs: rdn 3f out: sn wknd* **28/1**
7 73 **Pause For Applause** 3-9-5 0 [1] RichardKingscote 5
(Jonathan Portman) *s.i.s: racd green: sn rdn along and detached: lost tch over 4f out: eased fnl 3f* **25/1**

2m 37.94s (-0.06) **Going Correction** +0.025s/f (Good) **7** Ran SP% **114.9**
Speed ratings (Par 99): **101,99,96,89,89 81,33**
CSF £31.76 TOTE £4.30: £2.00, £2.60; EX 31.50 Trifecta £67.70.
Owner Mrs Jackie Cornwell **Bred** Hascombe And Valiant Studs **Trained** Epsom, Surrey

FOCUS
A fairly decent middle-distance 3yo maiden won by the Queen's Gold Cup winner Estimate in 2012. They went a respectable gallop but the first two were always prominent. The winner built on his debut form.

1898 BETFRED TV FILLIES' H'CAP 6f 212y
5:00 (5:01) (Class 3) (0-90,88) 3-Y-O+ **£7,762** (£2,310; £1,154; £577) **Stalls** Low

Form RPR
5021 1 **Dilgura**[23] 1318 6-9-2 79 MatthewCosham(3) 2 88
(Stuart Kittow) *trckd ldrs: nt clr run over 2f out tl over 1f out: led ins fnl f: kpt on wl: rdn out* **7/2**[1]
065- 2 1 1/4 **Blossomtime**[243] 5972 3-9-2 88 MartinLane 1 90
(Charlie Appleby) *s.i.s: in tch: hdwy 3f out: sn rdn: kpt on to go 2nd fnl f but a being hld* **7/2**[1]
004- 3 1 1/2 **Justice Lass (IRE)**[193] 7389 3-8-7 79 DavidProbert 5 77
(David Elsworth) *prom: led 2f out: sn rdn: hdd ins fnl f: no ex* **4/1**[2]
23-5 4 2 **Make Music**[26] 1246 3-8-1 73 CathyGannon 8 65
(Andrew Balding) *trckd ldrs: rdn over 2f out: kpt on tl no ex fnl 120yds* **9/1**
13-5 5 1 1/4 **Bournemouth Belle**[17] 1432 3-8-8 83 TomMarquand(3) 6 72
(Richard Hannon) *trckd ldrs: rdn over 2f out: nt pce to chal: no ex fnl 120yds* **10/1**
10- 6 2 **Welsh Gem**[361] 1997 4-9-4 78 JohnFahy 4 65
(Clive Cox) *sn pushed along in last pair: rdn 3f out: nvr gng pce to get involved* **10/1**
-660 7 4 1/2 **Angel Way (IRE)**[25] 1269 7-8-10 70 ShaneKelly 3 45
(John Gallagher) *led tl 2f out: sn wknd* **20/1**
4334 8 18 **Capelita**[18] 1418 5-9-5 82 AlistairRawlinson(3) 7 9+
(Michael Appleby) *v awkwardly away: nvr rcvrd: a bhd* **9/2**[3]

1m 28.66s (0.06) **Going Correction** +0.20s/f (Good)
WFA 3 from 4yo+ 12lb **8** Ran SP% **115.6**
Speed ratings (Par 104): **107,105,103,101,100 97,92,72**
CSF £16.06 CT £50.69 TOTE £4.10: £1.90, £1.30, £2.20; EX 17.20 Trifecta £98.90.
Owner Russell Ingham and Stuart Kittow **Bred** Hopkins, Kittow & Mrs Perry **Trained** Blackborough, Devon

FOCUS
A fair fillies' handicap run at a decent gallop. This rates a small pb from the winner.

1899 BETFRED MOBILE SPORTS LADY RIDERS' H'CAP (FOR LADY AMATEUR RIDERS) 6f 212y
5:35 (5:35) (Class 6) (0-65,67) 4-Y-O+ **£2,807** (£870; £435; £217) **Stalls** Low

Form RPR
00-5 1 **Victor's Bet (SPA)**[18] 1415 7-10-2 65 MissEllaSmith(5) 7 77
(Ralph J Smith) *s.i.s: towards rr: swtchd to centre over 3f out: pushed along and stdy prog fr wl over 2f out: kpt on wl to ld towards fin* **3/1**[2]
3532 2 3/4 **One Big Surprise**[4] 1781 4-9-5 54 MissPBridgwater(5) 10 64
(Richard Hughes) *trckd ldr: led 2f out: sn hung rt: kpt on but no ex whn hdd towards fin* **3/1**[2]
23-1 3 1/2 **Choral Clan (IRE)**[45] 964 5-9-12 61 MissCRobinson(5) 8 70
(Philip Mitchell) *hld up bhd ldrs: hdwy 2f out: styd on w wnr ins fnl f: no ex cl home* **9/1**[3]
0032 4 2 **Diamonds A Dancing**[2] 1834 6-10-1 59 (b) BrodieHampson 1 63
(John O'Shea) *trckd ldrs: rdn and ev ch 2f out: kpt on same pce ins fnl f* **12/1**
200- 5 1 1/2 **Byrd In Hand (IRE)**[169] 7858 9-9-1 52 (v) MissTannyaBagoban(7) 6 52
(John Bridger) *led tl 2f out: kpt on same pce fnl f* **20/1**
5-61 6 7 **Call Out Loud**[9] 1596 4-10-9 67 (t) MissSBrotherton 4 48
(Michael Appleby) *trckd ldrs: effrt 2f out: nt pce to chal: wknd fnl f* **9/4**[1]
650/ 7 1 1/2 **Zafraaj**[613] 5820 5-9-4 51 [1] MissPFuller(3) 3 29
(Pat Murphy) *hld up bhd ldrs: outpcd over 3f out: styd on again fnl f but no ch* **66/1**
5434 8 6 **For Ayman**[13] 1533 5-9-11 62 (t) MrsCPownall(7) 5 24
(Joseph Tuite) *trckd ldrs: effrt over 2f out: wknd over 1f out* **9/1**[3]
5-06 9 33 **Amenable (IRE)**[52] 895 9-9-13 57 (be) MissJoannaMason 9
(Ann Stokell) *a towards rr: lost tch 3f out* **33/1**

1m 30.31s (1.71) **Going Correction** +0.20s/f (Good) **9** Ran SP% **117.7**
Speed ratings (Par 101): **98,97,96,94,92 84,82,76,38**
CSF £12.53 CT £72.44 TOTE £3.90: £1.40, £1.60, £2.60; EX 12.50 Trifecta £81.20.
Owner Homecroft Wealth & Clear Racing **Bred** Jose Simo Vazquez **Trained** Epsom, Surrey

FOCUS
A modest handicap for lady amateur riders. They went a respectable gallop and this sin't bad form for the grade.
T/Plt: £40.10 to a £1 stake. Pool: £60,365.09 - 1,097.72 winning tickets. T/Qpdt: £10.80 to a £1 stake. Pool: £3,865.25 - 264.10 winning tickets. **Tim Mitchell**

1900 - 1906a (Foreign Racing) - See Raceform Interactive

HANOVER (L-H)
Sunday, May 1

OFFICIAL GOING: Turf: good to soft

1907a GROSSER PREIS VON ROSSMANN (LISTED RACE) (4YO+ FILLIES & MARES) (TURF) 1m 2f
4:05 (12:00) 4-Y-O+ **£10,294** (£4,779; £2,205; £1,102)

RPR
1 **Royal Solitaire (IRE)**[35] 4-9-2 0 DanielePorcu 3 102+
(P Schiergen, Germany) **27/10**[1]
2 2 1/4 **Bravo Girl (FR)**[175] 7769 4-9-2 0 StephenHellyn 11 97
(Waldemar Hickst, Germany) **114/10**
3 1 1/4 **Arles (FR)**[35] 4-9-2 0 JozefBojko 10 95
(A Wohler, Germany) **26/5**[3]
4 1 3/4 **Icecapada (IRE)**[59] 809 4-9-4 0 ElioneChaves 4 93
(Niels Petersen, Norway) **146/10**
5 4 1/4 **Haalan**[24] 1290 4-9-0 0 LukeMorris 7 81
(James Tate) *pushed along to join ldrs after 1f: sn led: 1 l clr whn cocked jaw and tried to run out fnl bnd (over 2 1/2f out) dropping into midfield: rdn and chsd ldng gp fr 1 1/2f out: wknd ins fnl f* **126/10**
6 1 **Rose Rized (GER)**[183] 4-9-2 0 AndreasHelfenbein 1 81
(P Schiergen, Germany) **157/10**
7 1/2 **Techno Queen (IRE)**[189] 7498 5-9-4 0 FranciscoDaSilva 8 82
(T Potters, Germany) **13/2**
8 hd **Anna Mia (GER)** 4-9-0 0 FilipMinarik 6 77
(Melanie Sauer, Germany) **129/10**
9 15 **Wild Motion (GER)** 4-9-0 0 MartinSeidl 5 47
(Markus Klug, Germany) **3/1**[2]

The Form Book, Raceform Ltd, Newbury, RG14 5SJ

10 *2 1/4* **Salve Estelle (GER)**[174] 7781 4-9-0 0........................ AndreasSuborics 9 43
(Waldemar Hickst, Germany) **66/10**
11 *9* **Simplon**[238] 7-9-0 0.. PatrickGibson 2 25
(P Vovcenko, Germany) **33/1**
WIN (incl. 10 euro stake): 37. PLACES: 19, 31, 21. SF: 358
Owner Gestut Ammerland **Bred** Janus Bloodstock Inc & Stilvi Compania Financiera **Trained** Germany

MUNICH (L-H)

Sunday, May 1

OFFICIAL GOING: Turf: good

1908a PFERDEWETTEN.DE - BAVARIAN CLASSIC (GROUP 3) (3YO) (TURF) 1m 2f

3:45 (12:00) 3-Y-O **£23,529** (£8,823; £4,411; £2,205; £1,470)

RPR

1 **Isfahan (GER)**[182] 7666 3-9-2 0.................................. EduardoPedroza 3 103+
(A Wohler, Germany) *w.w in midfield on outer: drvn to chse ldr over 2f out: upsides ldr fr 1 1/2f out: r.o gamely u.p: led fnl 120yds and asserted* **11/5**[1]

2 *2* **Nacar (GER)**[34] 3-9-2 0.. KoenClijmans 5 99
(Mario Hofer, Germany) *led: kicked clr 2 1/2f out: jnd by eventual wnr 1 1/2f out: rallied gamely u.p: hdd fnl 120yds: no ex* **231/10**

3 *1 3/4* **Karajol (GER)** 3-9-2 0... RafaelSchistl 8 96
(Jean-Pierre Carvalho, Germany) *w.w towards rr: hdwy u.p wl over 2f out: chsd ldng pair fr 1 1/2f out: styd on fnl f but no imp on ldrs* **104/10**

4 *1/2* **Pagino (GER)**[203] 7155 3-9-2 0.. MarcLerner 7 95
(Waldemar Hickst, Germany) *t.k.h: hld up in fnl pair: rdn and hdwy 2 1/2f out: sn chsng ldrs: styd on u.p: run flattened out ins fnl f* **53/10**[3]

5 *2* **Izzo (GER)** 3-9-2 0...(p) EddyHardouin 1 91
(Mario Hofer, Germany) *w.w in midfield on outer: rdn and effrt over 2f out: kpt on at same pce fr wl over 1f out* **104/10**

6 *hd* **Berghain (IRE)**[147] 3-9-2 0... AlexanderPietsch 2 90
(J Hirschberger, Germany) *cl up on inner: rdn and outpcd 2f out: sn btn* **14/5**[2]

7 *nse* **Licinius (GER)**[27] 3-9-2 0.. IanFerguson 6 90
(Yasmin Almenrader, Germany) *w.w in fnl pair: rdn and effrt 2f out: kpt on at one pce: nvr in contention* **98/10**

8 *3* **Weltmeister (GER)** 3-9-2 0.. AndraschStarke 4 84
(P Schiergen, Germany) *chsd ldr on outer: rdn and unable qck fr 2 1/2f out: grad dropped away fnl 1 1/2f*

2m 11.21s (2.24) **8** Ran SP% **104.4**
WIN (incl. 10 euro stake): 32. PLACES: 16, 26, 26. SF: 428.
Owner Darius Racing **Bred** Rennstall Wohler **Trained** Germany

1541 SAINT-CLOUD (L-H)

Sunday, May 1

OFFICIAL GOING: Turf: good

1909a PRIX GANAY (GROUP 1) (4YO+) (TURF) 1m 2f 110y

2:45 (12:00) 4-Y-O+ **£126,044** (£50,426; £25,213; £12,595; £6,308)

RPR

1 **Dariyan (FR)**[36] 1107 4-9-2 0.............................. ChristopheSoumillon 11 118+
(A De Royer-Dupre, France) *w.w in rr: hdwy on inner over 2 1/2f out: nt clr run and angled out appr fnl 2f: rdn and bmpd whn chalng between horses 1 1/2f out: qcknd to ld wl over 1f out: r.o fnl f: a holding: runner-up* **6/4**[1]

2 *1 1/4* **Silverwave (FR)**[21] 1375 4-9-2 0................................... MaximeGuyon 8 116
(P Bary, France) *settled towards rr: hdwy on outer over 2f out: sn rdn and chal ldrs 1 1/2f out: chsd eventual wnr fr wl over 1f out: nt pce to get on terms* **25/1**

3 *3* **Garlingari (FR)**[21] 1375 5-9-2 0............................(p) StephanePasquier 1 110
(Mme C Barande-Barbe, France) *t.k.h early: a cl up: rdn to chal ldrs 1 1/2f out: kpt on u.p fr 1 1/2f out: nt pce to match front two* **7/2**[2]

4 *1 1/4* **Wild Chief (GER)**[21] 1375 5-9-2 0.............................. FabienLefebvre 3 107
(J Hirschberger, Germany) *cl up: rdn to chse ldng pair under 2f out: nt qckn u.p fr 1 1/2f out: one pce fnl f* **33/1**

5 *snk* **The Corsican (IRE)**[36] 1106 5-9-2 0.......................... JamieSpencer 10 107
(David Simcock) *w.w in midfield: rdn and nt qckn 2f out: styd on u.p fnl f: nt pce to get on terms* **11/2**[3]

6 *snk* **Sumbal (IRE)**[21] 1375 4-9-2 0.. OisinMurphy 7 107
(F-H Graffard, France) *trckd ldr: pressed ldr fr 3f out: led 2f out: hdd wl over 1f out: one pce u.p fnl f* **9/1**

7 *3/4* **Air Pilot**[18] 1425 7-9-2 0.. FMBerry 2 107+
(Ralph Beckett) *w.w in midfield on inner: rdn and no real imp whn n.m.r 2f out: styng on u.p whn nt clr run ins fnl f: nvr plcd to chal* **13/2**

8 *nk* **Siljan's Saga (FR)**[21] 1375 6-8-13 0....................... Pierre-CharlesBoudot 5 102
(J-P Gauvin, France) *w.w in fnl pair on inner: nt clr run and snatched up under 2f out and lost all momentum: keeping on again but n.m.r wl ins fnl f: nvr in contention* **8/1**

9 *5 1/2* **Norse King (FR)**[34] 1130 7-9-2 0.. AlexisBadel 6 94
(Mme M Bollack-Badel, France) *t.k.h: hld up towards rr: last and outpcd 2f out: nvr figured* **18/1**

10 *6* **Ming Dynasty (FR)**[21] 1375 4-9-2 0................................ UmbertoRispoli 9 82
(M Delzangles, France) *sn led: pressed fr 3f out: sn hrd rdn: hdd 2f out: wknd ins fnl 1 1/2f* **14/1**

2m 7.72s (-11.88) **10** Ran SP% **130.8**
WIN (incl. 1 euro stake): 3.00. PLACES: 1.60, 3.60, 2.00. DF: 30.60. SF: 35.70.
Owner H H Aga Khan **Bred** H H The Aga Khans Stud **Trained** Chantilly, France

FOCUS
This didn't look a vintage renewal of a well-established Group 1 moved this year to Saint-Cloud from Longchamp, especially when Gailo Chop came out the previous day due to sustaining a tendon injury that will require an extensive break. The pace appeared to be decent enough and two pulled away.

1910a PRIX DU MUGUET (GROUP 2) (4YO+) (TURF) 1m

3:55 (12:00) 4-Y-O+ **£54,485** (£21,029; £10,036; £6,691; £3,345)

RPR

1 **Vadamos (FR)**[36] 1108 5-9-1 0............................ Pierre-CharlesBoudot 2 118
(A Fabre, France) *chsd ldr on inner: angled out to chal 2 1/2f out: rdn to ld ent fnl 2f: qcknd clr appr 1f out: comf* **13/2**[3]

2 *3 1/2* **Ervedya (FR)**[231] 6370 4-9-1 0.............................. ChristopheSoumillon 9 115+
(J-C Rouget, France) *w.w towards rr: gd hdwy on outer fr 2f out: wnt 2nd ent fnl f: kpt on under hands and heels: no ch w wnr* **8/11**[1]

3 *1 1/4* **Mr Owen (USA)**[231] 6375 4-8-11 0................................ UmbertoRispoli 6 108+
(F Rohaut, France) *settled in fnl trio: nt clr run 2 1/2f out: hdwy u.p wl over 1 1/2f out: styd on fnl f to go 3rd cl home: nvr on terms* **17/2**

4 *hd* **Siyoushake (IRE)**[164] 7911 4-8-8 0.......................... StephanePasquier 11 104
(F Head, France) *w.w in rr: rdn over 2f out: prog wl over 1 1/2f out: styd on fnl f: tk 4th cl home: nvr nrr* **33/1**

5 *3/4* **Sovereign Debt (IRE)**[18] 1425 7-8-11 0.............................. ChrisHayes 5 105
(David Nicholls) *t.k.h: chsd ldng trio on outer: 3rd and rdn fr 2 1/2f out: rallied gamely u.p: lost two pls cl home* **12/1**

6 *3/4* **Leader Writer (FR)**[50] 931 4-8-11 0................................ FabriceVeron 1 104
(H-A Pantall, France) *w.w in midfield: clsd on ldrs appr 2f out: sn rdn and btn* **40/1**

7 *3* **Incahoots**[28] 1231 4-8-8 0... MaximeGuyon 3 94
(F Head, France) *chsd ldng trio on inner: rdn and nt qckn 2f out: wknd ins fnl f* **33/1**

8 *1 3/4* **Menardais (FR)**[10] 7-8-11 0... NicolasPerret 10 93
(T Castanheira, France) *settled in fnl trio: last and rdn 2f out: sme mod late prog but nvr a factor* **33/1**

9 *2* **Maimara (FR)**[28] 1231 4-8-8 0.. GregoryBenoist 8 85
(M Delzangles, France) *t.k.h: hld up in midfield: rdn and nt qckn over 2f out: sn btn and dropped away* **4/1**[2]

10 *nk* **Stillman (FR)**[28] 1231 5-8-11 0.....................................(b) CristianDemuro 7 88
(P Khozian, France) *led: hdd ent fnl 2f: wknd u.p fr wl over 1f out* **20/1**

11 *10* **Epicuris**[24] 1307 4-8-11 0.. ThierryThulliez 4 65
(Mme C Head-Maarek, France) *nvr settled: impeded after 1f and restrained in 3rd: bmpd and squeezed out turning for home over 2 1/2f out: sn rdn and no rspnse: wknd ins fnl 2f* **16/1**

1m 36.93s (-10.57) **11** Ran SP% **131.4**
WIN (incl. 1 euro stake): 8.50. PLACES: 2.20, 1.30, 2.20. DF: 5.70. SF: 22.70.
Owner Scea Haras De Saint Pair **Bred** Scea Haras De Saint Pair **Trained** Chantilly, France

FOCUS
The form is rated around the fourth and sixth.

1690 SHA TIN (R-H)

Sunday, May 1

OFFICIAL GOING: Turf: good

1911a CHAIRMAN'S SPRINT PRIZE (GROUP 1) (3YO+) (TURF) 6f

8:30 (12:00) 3-Y-O+

£499,124 (£192,644; £87,565; £49,912; £28,896; £17,513)

RPR

1 **Chautauqua (AUS)**[29] 1213 5-9-0 0.................................... TommyBerry 6 120
(Michael, Wayne & John Hawkes, Australia) **9/5**[1]

2 *nk* **Lucky Bubbles (AUS)**[28] 4-9-0 0...................................... BrettPrebble 1 119
(K W Lui, Hong Kong) **33/10**[2]

3 *1 1/4* **Strathmore (AUS)**[42] 4-9-0 0...(bt) NeilCallan 11 115
(A T Millard, Hong Kong) **217/1**

4 *3/4* **Gold-Fun (IRE)**[63] 762 7-9-0 0...(v) OlivierPeslier 5 113
(Richard Gibson, Hong Kong) **84/10**

5 *nk* **Amazing Kids (NZ)**[28] 4-9-0 0... NashRawiller 4 112
(J Size, Hong Kong) **21/1**

6 *1 3/4* **Not Listenin'tome (AUS)**[36] 1104 5-9-0 0............(t) JamesMcDonald 12 106
(John Moore, Hong Kong) **71/1**

7 *shd* **Divine Boy (AUS)**[28] 4-9-0 0...(b) KCLeung 10 106
(Y S Tsui, Hong Kong) **379/1**

8 *1/2* **Aerovelocity (NZ)**[91] 7-9-0 0..(vt) ZacPurton 14 104+
(P O'Sullivan, Hong Kong) **10/1**

9 *nk* **Mongolian Saturday (USA)**[140] 8217 6-9-0 0............... DouglasWhyte 2 103+
(Enebish Ganbat, U.S.A) **30/1**

10 *shd* **Thewizardofoz (AUS)**[81] 4-9-0 0.....................................(b) JoaoMoreira 9 103
(J Size, Hong Kong) **43/10**[3]

11 *3/4* **Charles The Great (IRE)**[28] 7-9-0 0.............................(t) GeraldMosse 7 100
(John Moore, Hong Kong) **61/1**

12 *1 1/4* **Super Jockey (NZ)**[36] 1105 7-9-0 0.................................... KarisTeetan 13 96+
(A T Millard, Hong Kong) **274/1**

13 *nk* **Peniaphobia (IRE)**[36] 1104 5-9-0 0......................(tp) MatthewChadwick 8 95+
(A S Cruz, Hong Kong) **19/1**

14 *5 1/4* **Buffering (AUS)**[36] 1104 8-9-0 0.................................(b) DamianBrowne 3 79+
(Robert Heathcote, Australia) **12/1**

1m 8.69s (68.69) **14** Ran SP% **122.1**
PARI-MUTUEL (all including 10 hkd stake): WIN 28.00; PLACE 14.00, 15.50, 317.50; DF 64.00.
Owner R & C Legh Racing, G P I Racing Et Al **Bred** Woodbury Pty Ltd **Trained** Australia

1912a CHAMPIONS MILE (GROUP 1) (3YO+) (TURF) 1m

9:10 (12:00) 3-Y-O+

£698,774 (£269,702; £122,591; £69,877; £40,455; £24,518)

RPR

1 **Maurice (JPN)**[140] 8218 5-9-0 0.......................................(t) JoaoMoreira 6 122+
(Noriyuki Hori, Japan) **23/20**[1]

2 *2* **Contentment (AUS)**[28] 5-9-0 0..(e) BrettPrebble 2 117
(J Size, Hong Kong) **39/10**[2]

3 *3/4* **Packing Pins (NZ)**[28] 5-9-0 0... GeraldMosse 1 115+
(P F Yiu, Hong Kong) **10/1**

4 *1/2* **Beauty Only (IRE)**[28] 5-9-0 0...(t) NeilCallan 10 114+
(A S Cruz, Hong Kong) **83/10**

5 *½* **Safety Check (IRE)**[66] 720 5-9-0 0 .... JamesMcDonald 4 113
(Charlie Appleby) *w.w in midfield: rdn and n.m.r 2f out: styd on fr over 1f out: nt pce to get on terms* **27/1**

6 *1* **Beauty Flame (IRE)**[63] 762 6-9-0 0 .... (t) MatthewChadwick 3 111
(A S Cruz, Hong Kong) **24/1**

7 *¾* **Gun Pit (AUS)**[36] 1108 5-9-0 0 .... (t) CYHo 5 109
(C Fownes, Hong Kong) **168/1**

8 *shd* **Giant Treasure (USA)**[63] 761 5-9-0 0 .... (b) OlivierPeslier 9 109
(Richard Gibson, Hong Kong) **54/10**[3]

9 *shd* **Rewarding Hero**[28] 7-9-0 0 .... TommyBerry 7 108
(John Moore, Hong Kong) **28/1**

10 *½* **Dundonnell (USA)**[28] 6-9-0 0 .... (t) NashRawiller 12 107
(C Fownes, Hong Kong) **178/1**

11 *shd* **Secret Weapon**[28] 6-9-0 0 .... (b¹) TyeAngland 8 107
(C H Yip, Hong Kong) **19/1**

12 *11* **Bow Creek (IRE)**[29] 1214 5-9-0 0 .... (t) ZacPurton 11 82
(J O'Shea, Australia) *rousted along early to switch ins fr wd draw and take pitch on rail towards rr: rdn and no imp 2f out: sn wknd: wl btn whn eased ins fnl f* **57/1**

1m 34.08s (-0.62) **12** Ran SP% **121.3**
PARI-MUTUEL (all including 10 hkd stake): WIN 21.50; PLACE 13.00, 19.50, 29.50; DF 68.50.
Owner Kazumi Yoshida **Bred** Togawa Bokujo **Trained** Japan

1734 BATH (L-H)

Monday, May 2

OFFICIAL GOING: Good to firm (firm in places) chaning to good after race 2 (2.30)
Wind: quite strong across Weather: heavy rain at times clearing mid-afternoon

1913 GREGOR HEATING H'CAP 5f 11y

1:55 (1:55) (Class 6) (0-60,60) 4-Y-O+ **£3,234** (£962; £481; £240) **Stalls** Centre

Form RPR

00-2 **1** **Lucky Clover**[39] 1059 5-9-5 **58** .... MartinHarley 11 68
(Malcolm Saunders) *drifted lft s: trckd ldr: led wl over 1f out: kpt on wl: rdn out* **7/2**[1]

26-3 **2** *1¼* **John Joiner**[31] 1181 4-8-9 **53** .... JosephineGordon(5) 7 59
(Peter Hedger) *sltly hmpd s: trckd ldrs: rdn 2f out: chsd wnr ent fnl f: edgd lft: kpt on but a being hld* **11/2**[3]

5022 **3** *1¾* **Krazy Paving**[24] 1320 4-9-2 **55** .... (p) OisinMurphy 9 54
(Anabel K Murphy) *mid-div: rdn over 2f out: no real imp tl r.o ent fnl f: wnt 3rd nring fin* **5/1**[2]

1066 **4** *½* **Quantum Dot (IRE)**[34] 1133 5-9-2 **55** .... (b) KieranO'Neill 5 52
(Ed de Giles) *led: rdn and hdd wl over 1f out: no ex ins fnl f: lost 3rd nring fin* **12/1**

-560 **5** *2¼* **Catalinas Diamond (IRE)**[14] 1533 8-9-7 **60** .... (t) SteveDrowne 10 49
(Pat Murphy) *hld up: swtchd rt and stdy prog fr 2f out: kpt on same pce fnl f* **7/1**

06-0 **6** *3¾* **Simply Black (IRE)**[34] 1133 5-8-13 **57** .... (p) AnnStokell(5) 6 34
(Ann Stokell) *sltly hmpd s: in tch: rdn over 2f out: wknd fnl f* **50/1**

0310 **7** *½* **Spray Tan**[7] 1721 6-8-10 **52** .... (b) GeorgeDowning(3) 1 26
(Tony Carroll) *wnt lft s: midfield: rdn over 2f out: nvr threatened: fdd fnl f* **12/1**

324- **8** *4½* **Mc Diamond (IRE)**[152] 8075 4-9-6 **59** .... SilvestreDeSousa 3 23
(Michael Mullineaux) *chsd ldrs: rdn wl over 2f out: sn wknd* **7/2**[1]

50-0 **9** *2½* **Zebs Lad (IRE)**[108] 197 4-9-0 **58** .... (p) EdwardGreatrex(5) 2 7
(Nikki Evans) *s.i.s: a towards rr* **18/1**

334- **10** *5* **Hurricane Alert**[293] 4243 4-9-2 **60** .... DavidParkes(5) 4
(Natalie Lloyd-Beavis) *chsd ldrs tl wknd 2f out* **25/1**

1m 2.96s (0.46) **Going Correction** +0.125s/f (Good) **10** Ran SP% **115.5**
Speed ratings (Par 101): **101,99,96,95,91 85,85,77,73,65**
CSF £22.46 CT £90.60 TOTE £5.40: £1.60, £1.90, £1.80; EX 26.00 Trifecta £128.30.
Owner M S Saunders **Bred** Cobhall Court Stud **Trained** Green Ore, Somerset
■ Stewards' Enquiry : Martin Harley three-day ban: careless riding (May 16-18)

FOCUS
Rail moved out around the bottom bend to the 3f pole, adding 10yds to races on the round course. The ground had continued to dry out running up to the meeting and was officially good to firm, firm in places, though it started to rain before the opener. The rain had got in, but by how much wasn't clear with the jockeys describing the conditions as between "good" and "soft". A moderate sprint handicap to start and few got into it. A slight pb from the runner-up.

1914 GREGOR RENEWABLE HEATING H'CAP 2m 1f 34y

2:30 (2:30) (Class 4) (0-85,85) 4-Y-O+ **£5,498** (£1,636; £817; £408) **Stalls** Centre

Form RPR

00-2 **1** **Havisham**[40] 1037 4-9-2 **80** .... (p) OisinMurphy 2 86
(Andrew Balding) *led: swtchd rt to avoid 2 people wl over 2f out and hdd: rallied gamely u.p: styd on wl to regain ld wl ins fnl f: drvn out* **7/2**[2]

050- **2** *½* **Snowy Dawn**[234] 6266 6-8-9 **70** .... RoystonFfrench 6 75
(Steph Hollinshead) *mid-div: hdwy over 6f out: rdn to ld wl over 2f out where carried sltly rt: styd on but no ex whn hdd wl ins fnl f* **20/1**

315- **3** *shd* **Fitzwilly**[156] 7140 6-9-1 **76** .... SilvestreDeSousa 7 81+
(Mick Channon) *slowly away: in last pair: hdwy wl over 2f out: sn rdn: wnt 3rd wl over 1f out: 5 l down ent fnl f: styd on wl fnl 120yds* **15/8**[1]

2114 **4** *14* **Midtech Star (IRE)**[37] 1092 4-8-2 **66** oh1 .... (p) FrannyNorton 4 55
(Ian Williams) *mid-div: rdn over 3f out: chal for hld 4th fr 2f out: nvr trbld ldrs* **6/1**

6/0- **5** *6* **Linguine (FR)**[105] 8379 6-9-10 **85** .... (p) MartinHarley 5 68
(Seamus Durack) *trckd ldrs: rdn to chse ldng pair 3f out: wknd over 1f out* **12/1**

642- **6** *19* **Sunny Future (IRE)**[233] 6300 10-9-2 **77** .... WilliamTwiston-Davies 8 39
(Malcolm Saunders) *mid-div: in last pair 7f out: rdn into 4th briefly 3f out: wknd over 2f out* **14/1**

54-0 **7** *11* **Saborido (USA)**[19] 1417 10-8-12 **78** .... KieranShoemark(5) 3 28
(Amanda Perrett) *trckd ldrs: rdn over 3f out: wknd over 2f out* **16/1**

8 *17* **Notnowsam**[17] 7266 6-8-1 **67** oh4 ow1 .... (p) EdwardGreatrex(5) 9
(Dan Skelton) *sn struggling in last: nvr threatened to get on terms: eased whn wl btn fnl 2f* **5/1**[3]

6/ **9** *8* **East India**[135] 1182 4-9-7 **85** .... SteveDrowne 1 7
(Rebecca Curtis) *trckd ldr tl rdn over 3f out: wknd over 2f out* **25/1**

3m 55.92s (4.02) **Going Correction** +0.40s/f (Good)
WFA 4 from 5yo+ 3lb **9** Ran SP% **116.8**
Speed ratings (Par 105): **106,105,105,99,96 87,82,74,70**
CSF £70.18 CT £169.10 TOTE £4.10: £1.20, £6.10, £1.30; EX 94.00 Trifecta £241.90.
Owner David Brownlow **Bred** Newsells Park Stud **Trained** Kingsclere, Hants

FOCUS
Rail movement added 10yds to race distance. A fair staying handicap and the easing conditions made this a real test. There was drama when two members of the groundstaff were stood on the track as the runners started to make their way up the home straight on the final circuit, but they moved swiftly out of the way when they realised what was happening. The winner has been rated close to form.

1915 SHIRLEY FLASKETT 80TH BIRTHDAY NOVICE MEDIAN AUCTION STKS 5f 11y

3:05 (3:06) (Class 6) 2-Y-O **£3,234** (£962; £481; £240) **Stalls** Centre

Form RPR

1 **Berkshire Boy (IRE)** 2-9-2 0 .... OisinMurphy 5 78+
(Andrew Balding) *dwlt bdly: bhd: hdwy over 1f out: str run ins fnl f: led fnl 75yds: won gng away: readily* **20/1**

2 *1¼* **Mister Sunshine (IRE)** 2-9-2 0 .... JohnFahy 6 72
(Clive Cox) *in tch: hung rt over 2f out where drifted to centre: sn rdn: r.o ins fnl f: wnt 2nd cl home* **12/1**

53 **3** *nk* **Hi Milady (IRE)**[5] 1793 2-8-11 0 .... LiamKeniry 1 65
(Dominic Ffrench Davis) *mid-div: rdn and hdwy over 1f out: sn hung lft: ev ch briefly fnl 75yds: lost 2nd cl home* **14/1**

4 *1* **Zebspear (IRE)** 2-9-2 0 .... JFEgan 10 67
(Joseph Tuite) *chsd ldr: rdn to ld over 1f out: no ex whn hdd fnl 75yds* **28/1**

5 *½* **Secret Coin (IRE)** 2-8-11 0 .... WilliamCarson 8 60
(Jamie Osborne) *mid-div: rdn and hdwy to chse ldrs over 1f out: kpt on same pce fnl f* **20/1**

6 *1¼* **Mutahaady (IRE)** 2-9-2 0 .... PaulHanagan 2 64+
(Richard Hannon) *s.i.s: sn outpcd and detached: r.o wl fnl f: nvr trbld ldrs* **5/4**[1]

4 **7** *2* **Cosmic Beau (IRE)**[9] 1621 2-9-2 0 .... (v) RichardKingscote 7 53
(Tom Dascombe) *led: set decent pce: rdn and hdd over 1f out: fdd fnl 120yds* **7/2**[2]

0 **8** *nk* **Fethiye Boy**[9] 1635 2-9-2 0 .... MartinHarley 3 52
(Ronald Harris) *trckd ldrs: rdn and ev ch over 1f out: fdd fnl 120yds* **8/1**

52 **9** *3½* **Billy's Boots**[9] 1635 2-9-2 0 .... SilvestreDeSousa 4 46
(Mick Channon) *chsd ldrs: rdn over 2f out: wknd over 1f out* **5/1**[3]

10 *7* **Lilly Ballerina (IRE)** 2-8-8 0 .... GeorgeDowning(3) 9 9
(Tony Carroll) *s.i.s: sn outpcd: a in rr* **33/1**

1m 6.12s (3.62) **Going Correction** +0.40s/f (Good) **10** Ran SP% **124.7**
Speed ratings (Par 91): **87,85,84,82,82 80,76,76,70,59**
CSF £241.69 TOTE £14.70: £4.00, £2.60, £4.00; EX 190.40 Trifecta £580.20.
Owner Berkshire Parts & Panels Ltd **Bred** Ms Vanessa Teehan **Trained** Kingsclere, Hants

FOCUS
The going was changed to good before this race. An ordinary novice event, but several had a chance passing the furlong pole and this was very much a race of changing fortunes. The level is very fluid.

1916 ONECOM H'CAP 1m 5y

3:40 (3:40) (Class 4) (0-80,77) 4-Y-O+ **£5,498** (£1,636; £817; £408) **Stalls** Low

Form RPR

30-1 **1** **Bakht A Rawan (IRE)**[24] 1317 4-9-3 **73** .... SilvestreDeSousa 7 78
(Stuart Kittow) *trckd ldrs: chal 2f out: led ent fnl f: kpt on wl: rdn out* **6/4**[1]

00-6 **2** *1* **Molten Lava (IRE)**[21] 1387 4-9-5 **75** .... (b¹) MartinHarley 1 78
(Paul Cole) *mid-div: rdn over 2f out: hdwy over 1f out: kpt on ins fnl f: wnt 2nd cl home* **10/1**

6500 **3** *nse* **Saint Pois (FR)**[9] 1632 5-8-9 **68** .... GeorgeDowning(3) 8 71
(Tony Carroll) *hld up: rdn and hdwy over 2f out: kpt on ins fnl f: wnt 3rd cl home* **10/1**

250- **4** *¾* **Hot Mustard**[187] 7563 6-9-6 **76** .... MartinDwyer 2 77
(William Muir) *trckd ldr: chal over 1f out: rdn and ev ch ent fnl f: no ex whn losing 2 pls cl home* **4/1**[2]

6000 **5** *¾* **Dana's Present**[21] 1387 7-8-11 **67** .... LiamKeniry 6 66+
(Tom Dascombe) *hld up: hdwy whn hmpd over 1f out: kpt on fnl f but nvr any threat* **14/1**

0/33 **6** *1½* **Barnmore**[19] 1418 8-9-7 **77** .... CharlesBishop 9 73
(Peter Hedger) *stdd s: in last pair: rdn over 1f out: kpt on but nt pce to get on terms fnl f* **6/1**[3]

-040 **7** *hd* **Uncle Dermot (IRE)**[13] 1546 8-9-1 **71** .... RichardKingscote 4 67
(Brendan Powell) *trckd ldr: rdn over 2f out: ev ch over 1f out: fdd ins fnl f* **10/1**

-000 **8** *nk* **Pick A Little**[13] 1545 8-9-7 **77** .... TimmyMurphy 3 72
(Michael Blake) *led: rdn 2f out: hdd ent fnl f: no ex* **16/1**

404- **9** *1¼* **Silver Dixie (USA)**[178] 7731 6-9-7 **77** .... (p) SteveDrowne 5 69
(Peter Hedger) *hld up in last pair: rdn 2f out: short of room briefly 1f out: kpt on fnl f but nt pce to get involved* **16/1**

1m 43.78s (2.98) **Going Correction** +0.40s/f (Good) **9** Ran SP% **120.0**
Speed ratings (Par 105): **101,100,99,99,98 96,96,96,95**
CSF £19.10 CT £119.51 TOTE £2.40: £1.10, £3.50, £3.30; EX 15.80 Trifecta £127.80.
Owner Chris & David Stam **Bred** B V Sangster **Trained** Blackborough, Devon

FOCUS
Rail movement added 10yds to race distance. A fair handicap, but not run at a great pace and they finished in a bit of a heap. The runner-up helps the standard.

1917 PTS PLUMBING CLASSIFIED STKS 1m 5y

4:15 (4:15) (Class 6) 3-Y-O **£3,408** (£1,006; £503) **Stalls** Low

Form RPR

000- **1** **Gunman**[219] 6730 3-8-11 64 .... TomMarquand(3) 5 70
(Richard Hannon) *pressed ldr: led 2f out: hung rt u.p over 1f out: drifted lft ins fnl f: idling and kpt up to work fnl f* **12/1**

46-4 **2** *1¼* **She's All Mine**[18] 1431 3-9-0 63 .... KieranO'Neill 4 67
(Richard Hannon) *hld up: hdwy 2f out: rdn whn hmpd over 1f out: kpt on to chse wnr ins fnl f but a being hld* **8/1**

000- **3** *1* **Rebel State (IRE)**[172] 7809 3-9-0 64 .... (t) WilliamTwiston-Davies 3 65
(Richard Spencer) *hld up: rdn and hdwy on far rails fr 2f out: ev ch ent fnl f: no ex fnl 120yds* **7/1**[3]

440 **4** *2½* **Russian Ranger (IRE)**[21] 1386 3-9-0 64 .... RyanClark 7 59
(Jonathan Portman) *trckd ldrs: rdn over 2f out: nt pce to chal: no ex fnl f* **20/1**

05-4 **5** *2¼* **Protest (IRE)**[23] 1345 3-9-0 65 .... LiamKeniry 6 53
(Sylvester Kirk) *led: rdn and hdd 2f out: wknd ent fnl f* **7/2**[2]

06-2 **6** *2¾* **Kafoo**[33] 1141 3-9-0 63 .... (b¹) PaulHanagan 1 47
(Ed Dunlop) *trckd ldrs: rdn over 2f out: wknd ent fnl f* **10/11**[1]

1m 45.45s (4.65) **Going Correction** +0.40s/f (Good) **6** Ran SP% **110.7**
Speed ratings (Par 97): **92,90,89,87,85 82**
CSF £94.00 TOTE £16.70: £4.80, £2.10; EX 58.80 Trifecta £219.70.
Owner Mrs J K Powell **Bred** Miss A V Hill **Trained** East Everleigh, Wilts

The Form Book, Raceform Ltd, Newbury, RG14 5SJ

FOCUS
Rail movement added 10yds to race distance. A tight classified event with just 3lb covering the six runners, all maidens coming into it, and not form to get too excited about. It provided a 1-2 for trainer Richard Hannon. The level is fluid. A minor pb from the winner.

1918 GREGOR HEATING WORCESTER BOSCH ACCREDITED H'CAP 1m 2f 46y
4:50 (4:53) (Class 6) (0-60,59) 3-Y-O **£3,408** (£1,006; £503) **Stalls** Low

Form RPR
000- **1** **Elocution**[242] 6025 3-8-10 **48**.................... OisinMurphy 4 64
(Denis Coakley) *trckd ldrs: rdn over 2f out: led over 1f out: sn clr: comf* **5/2**[2]
06-0 **2** *8* **Denmead**[16] 1484 3-9-4 **59**.................... DanielMuscutt(3) 5 59
(John Butler) *led for 1f: trckd ldr: rdn to ld jst over 1f out: edgd lft and bmpd whn hdd over 1f out: kpt on same pce fnl f* **10/1**[3]
5-54 **3** *½* **Wharane (FR)**[6] 1740 3-9-7 **59**.................... (v[1]) SilvestreDeSousa 7 58
(Ian Williams) *trckd ldrs: rdn over 2f out: chalng whn edgd rt and bmpd over 1f out: sn hld: kpt on same pce fnl f* **8/11**[1]
0-62 **4** *6* **Tessellate (IRE)**[28] 1234 3-9-0 **52**.................... SamHitchcott 3 39
(Sylvester Kirk) *led after 1f: rdn and hdd jst over 2f out: stl jst upsides whn squeezed out over 1f out: hld after: fdd fnl f* **12/1**
0300 **5** *51* **Kimbelle**[24] 1320 3-8-4 **47**....................[1] JosephineGordon(5) 1
(Mark Usher) *last but in tch: struggling 7f out: wknd over 2f out* **25/1**

2m 13.43s (2.43) **Going Correction** +0.40s/f (Good) **5 Ran SP% 107.1**
Speed ratings (Par 97): **106,99,99,94,53**
CSF £22.25 TOTE £3.20: £1.40, £3.20; EX 22.70 Trifecta £28.70.
Owner Sue Huntingdon & Partners **Bred** N C Appleton **Trained** West Ilsley, Berks

FOCUS
Rail movement added 10yds to race distance. A modest 3yo handicap and another race contested entirely by maidens. The market only wanted to know about two horses and one of them bolted up. The form has been taken at face value.

1919 PLUMB AND PARTS CENTER FILLIES' H'CAP 1m 3f 144y
5:25 (5:25) (Class 4) (0-80,80) 4-Y-O+ **£6,145** (£1,828; £913; £456) **Stalls** Low

Form RPR
3412 **1** **Indira**[13] 1552 5-8-13 **77**.................... JosephineGordon(5) 3 89
(John Berry) *trckd ldr: led gng best over 2f out: clr over 1f out: eased towards fin* **7/1**
103- **2** *3¼* **Saumur**[209] 7024 4-8-12 **71**.................... PaulHanagan 1 76
(Denis Coakley) *slowly away: in last pair: rdn and hdwy over 2f out: wnt 2nd over 1f out: styd on but no ch w easy wnr* **9/2**[3]
50-1 **3** *¾* **Hound Music**[17] 1455 4-9-2 **75**.................... RichardKingscote 8 79
(Jonathan Portman) *slowly away: trckd ldrs: rdn over 2f out: wnt hld 3rd over 1f out: styd on same pce* **9/2**[3]
522- **4** *4* **Eager Beaver**[171] 7825 4-9-4 **77**.................... MartinDwyer 5 74
(William Muir) *led: rdn and hdd over 2f out: wknd fnl f* **11/2**
03-1 **5** *nk* **Kuriosa (IRE)**[121] 26 4-9-3 **79**.................... (p) DanielMuscutt(3) 2 76
(Marco Botti) *slowly away: trckd ldrs: rdn 3f out: one pce fnl 2f* **4/1**[2]
013- **6** *6* **Heartless**[261] 5383 4-9-5 **78**.................... OisinMurphy 7 65
(Andrew Balding) *dwlt: a in last: struggling 3f out: nvr any imp* **11/4**[1]

2m 33.62s (3.02) **Going Correction** +0.40s/f (Good) **6 Ran SP% 110.9**
Speed ratings (Par 102): **105,102,102,99,99 95**
CSF £36.60 CT £150.79 TOTE £9.00: £3.70, £2.40; EX 44.60 Trifecta £87.10.
Owner Severn Crossing Partnership **Bred** Mrs M L Parry & P M Steele-Mortimer **Trained** Newmarket, Suffolk

FOCUS
Rail movement added 10yds to race distance. A fair middle-distance fillies' handicap to end, but the pace was ordinary and the winner bolted up. The runners came centre-to-nearside up the home straight. The second and third have been rated close to their marks.
T/Plt: £2,037.80 to a £1 stake. Pool: £68,838.66 - 24.66 winning tickets T/Qpdt: £323.90 to a £1 stake. Pool: £4,334.38 - 9.90 winning tickets **Tim Mitchell**

1583 BEVERLEY (R-H)
Monday, May 2

OFFICIAL GOING: Good (7.6)
Wind: Fresh against Weather: Heavy cloud and showers

1920 MAYPOLE DANCERS MAIDEN FILLIES' STKS (PLUS 10 RACE) 1m 4f 16y
1:45 (1:45) (Class 5) 3-Y-O **£3,780** (£1,131; £565; £283) **Stalls** Low

Form RPR
3 **1** **Hestina (FR)**[10] 1608 3-9-0 0.................... PaulMulrennan 2 79
(Peter Chapple-Hyam) *hld up: hdwy over 3f out: sn trcking ldr: cl up 2 1/2f out: shkn up to ld over 1f out: clr fnl f* **8/13**[1]
0 **2** *5* **Lacey's Lane**[20] 1392 3-9-0 0.................... JamesDoyle 3 71
(Saeed bin Suroor) *trckd ldr: hdwy to ld after 2f: set stdy pce: pushed along and qcknd 3f out: sn jnd: rdn and hdd over 1f out: sn one pce* **15/8**[2]
0- **3** *28* **Ballycoyle Girl (IRE)**[212] 6929 3-9-0 0.................... DuranFentiman 4 26
(Tony Coyle) *led 1 1/2f: trckd ldng pair: hdwy over 3f out: rdn and hung bdly lft over 2f out: sn drvn and outpcd* **33/1**
0- **4** *½* **Cool Silk Girl**[212] 6923 3-9-0 0.................... TomEaves 1 25
(James Given) *chsd ldng pair whn edgd lft bnd after 1 1/2f: sn trcking ldr: pushed along and hung lft bnd 4f out: sn rdn and wl outpcd in rr wl over 2f out: plodded on* **12/1**[3]

2m 43.56s (3.76) **Going Correction** +0.075s/f (Good) **4 Ran SP% 107.3**
Speed ratings (Par 96): **90,86,68,67**
CSF £1.97 TOTE £1.60; EX 1.60 Trifecta £6.70.
Owner Paul Hancock **Bred** Mlle Camille Collet & Mlle Louise Collet **Trained** Newmarket, Suffolk

FOCUS
The going was given as good (GoingStick: 7.6) but it was raining as the meeting got under way. A safety factor limit of 12 runners for all races was again in place due to the wet patch at the 2f mark, which was dolled off. The favourite overcame market weakness to take this maiden. It's been rated around the winner's debut run.

1921 MAYDAY RACEDAY NOVICE MEDIAN AUCTION STKS 5f
2:20 (2:21) (Class 6) 2-Y-O **£2,587** (£770; £384; £192) **Stalls** Low

Form RPR
1 **Twizzell** 2-8-11 0.................... PJMcDonald 9 78
(Ann Duffield) *sn led: rdn clr appr fnl f: kpt on strly* **4/1**[1]
2 *4½* **Chevalier Du Lac (IRE)** 2-9-2 0.................... JasonHart 2 67
(John Quinn) *trckd ldrs: hdwy 2f out: rdn over 1f out: kpt on fnl f* **8/1**
3 *¾* **Alwalaa (IRE)** 2-8-11 0.................... JoeFanning 1 59
(Mark Johnston) *trckd ldrs: hdwy 1/2-way: chsd wnr wl over 1f out: kpt on same pce fnl f* **4/1**[1]
4 *½* **Tagur (IRE)** 2-9-2 0.................... TomEaves 11 62+
(Kevin Ryan) *towards rr: hdwy over 2f out: rdn to chse ldrs over 1f out: sn no imp* **9/1**
5 *1½* **Tough To Bear** 2-8-13 0.................... JacobButterfield(3) 4 57
(Ollie Pears) *cl up on inner: rdn along over 2f out: edgd lft and drvn over 1f out: kpt on same pce* **14/1**
6 *¾* **Volta Do Mar (IRE)** 2-8-11 0.................... TonyHamilton 10 49+
(Richard Fahey) *s.i.s: green and bhd: hdwy over 2f out: rdn jst over 1f out: styd on wl fnl f: nrst fin* **15/2**
0 **7** *shd* **Kilbaha Lady (IRE)**[11] 1583 2-8-11 0.................... AndrewMullen 8 49+
(Nigel Tinkler) *towards rr: pushed along 1/2-way: rdn 2f out: kpt on fnl f* **50/1**
8 *¾* **Hollywood Harry (IRE)** 2-9-2 0.................... PhillipMakin 3 51
(Keith Dalgleish) *dwlt and towards rr: effrt and sme hdwy on inner 1/2-way: sn rdn along and n.d* **5/1**[2]
9 *3¾* **Bellamay** 2-8-11 0.................... DuranFentiman 6 33
(John Weymes) *a towards rr* **40/1**
3 **10** *¾* **Born To Boogie**[18] 1443 2-8-11 0.................... GrahamLee 7 30
(Chris Grant) *chsd ldng pair: effrt on outer 2f out and sn rdn: wknd qckly appr fnl f* **6/1**[3]
11 *13* **Mystic Maeve (IRE)** 2-8-11 0.................... DougieCostello 5
(David Loughnane) *a towards rr: rdn along and outpcd fr 1/2-way* **25/1**

1m 5.59s (2.09) **Going Correction** +0.15s/f (Good) **11 Ran SP% 118.7**
Speed ratings (Par 91): **89,81,80,79,77 76,76,74,68,67 46**
CSF £36.37 TOTE £4.90: £1.70, £2.90, £1.70; EX 43.90 Trifecta £171.50.
Owner John Dance **Bred** Whitsbury Manor Stud **Trained** Constable Burton, N Yorks

FOCUS
The winner knew her job in this novice. The winner has been rated near the best winners of this race.

1922 BEVERLEY FOLK FESTIVAL HERE IN JUNE H'CAP 5f
2:55 (2:56) (Class 5) (0-75,75) 3-Y-O **£3,780** (£1,131; £565; £283; £141) **Stalls** Low

Form RPR
42-2 **1** **First Bombardment**[6] 1761 3-9-2 **70**.................... DanielTudhope 6 78
(David O'Meara) *trckd ldrs: hdwy to chse ldr 3f out: rdn over 1f out: drvn ins fnl f: styd on wl to ld nr line* **11/2**[3]
3-34 **2** *hd* **Socialites Red**[18] 1432 3-9-0 **68**.................... BenCurtis 3 75
(Scott Dixon) *qckly away and set solid pce: pushed clr 2f out: rdn over 1f out: drvn ionside fnl f: hdd and no ex nr line* **6/1**
365- **3** *6* **Penny Pot Lane**[177] 7753 3-9-0 **68**.................... GeorgeChaloner 2 53
(Richard Whitaker) *in tch on inner: n.m.r and swtchd lft 2f out: effrt and rdn over 1f out: swtchd lft and drvn ent fnl f: kpt on towards fin* **17/2**
045- **4** *1¾* **Van Gerwen**[228] 6470 3-9-0 **68**.................... DavidAllan 7 47
(Les Eyre) *chsd ldrs: rdn along wl over 1f out: kpt on same pce* **9/1**
13-5 **5** *nse* **Searanger (USA)**[16] 1487 3-9-0 **68**.................... PJMcDonald 5 47
(Ann Duffield) *cl up 2f: trckd ldrs: rdn along over 2f out: grad wknd* **20/1**
04-0 **6** *¾* **Roll On Rory**[10] 1599 3-9-6 **74**.................... AndrewMullen 9 50
(Jason Ward) *towards rr: effrt over 2f out and sn rdn: kpt on u.p fnl f* **16/1**
551- **7** *¾* **Laughton**[218] 6782 3-9-3 **71**.................... GrahamLee 10 45+
(Kevin Ryan) *towards rr: effrt on outer 2f out: sn rdn and kpt on fnl f* **4/1**[1]
-533 **8** *1½* **Fashionata (IRE)**[31] 1183 3-9-2 **70**.................... (p) GrahamGibbons 1 38
(Kristin Stubbs) *dwlt and sn outpcd: rdn along and wl detached 1/2-way: hdwy wl over 1f out: kpt on fnl f* **13/2**
4-43 **9** *nk* **Ravenhoe (IRE)**[16] 1492 3-9-7 **75**.................... JoeFanning 8 42
(Mark Johnston) *trckd ldrs: rdn wl over 1f out: wknd appr fnl f* **5/1**[2]
0-65 **10** *8* **Jazz Legend (USA)**[26] 1271 3-9-6 **74**.................... TomEaves 11 12
(James Given) *in tch: rdn along 2f out: sn drvn and wknd over 1f out* **25/1**
54-0 **11** *3½* **Tribesman**[18] 1448 3-9-4 **72**.................... SamJames 12
(Marjorie Fife) *chsd ldrs on outer: rdn along over 2f out: sn wknd* **33/1**
15-6 **12** *14* **Caymus**[41] 1029 3-8-13 **67**.................... TonyHamilton 4
(Tracy Waggott) *chsd ldrs on inner: rdn along 2f out: sn wknd* **33/1**

1m 4.18s (0.68) **Going Correction** +0.15s/f (Good) **12 Ran SP% 120.6**
Speed ratings (Par 99): **100,99,90,87,87 86,84,82,81,69 63,41**
CSF £37.45 CT £280.64 TOTE £7.10: £2.60, £1.90, £3.60; EX 48.10 Trifecta £375.90.
Owner Northern Hart Racing & Partner **Bred** Habton Farms **Trained** Upper Helmsley, N Yorks

FOCUS
Few got into this. The winner has been rated to his best form since his debut.

1923 MADDY PRIOR AT BEVERLEY FOLK FESTIVAL H'CAP 1m 1f 207y
3:30 (3:30) (Class 4) (0-80,79) 4-Y-O+ **£5,040** (£1,508; £754; £377; £188) **Stalls** Low

Form RPR
1100 **1** **Play Nicely**[9] 1633 4-9-0 **72**.................... GrahamGibbons 4 80
(David Barron) *trckd ldrs on inner: hdwy 2f out: n.m.r over 1f out: rdn and squeezed through wl ins fnl f to ld nr fin* **14/1**
05-2 **2** *nk* **Jacbequick**[11] 1588 5-9-1 **73**.................... DanielTudhope 3 80
(David O'Meara) *trckd ldrs on inner: swtchd lft and effrt jst over 1f out: sn chal and rdn: drvn to take slt ld last 100yds: hdd and no ex nr fin* **9/4**[1]
60-0 **3** *shd* **Cyril**[16] 1493 4-9-7 **79**.................... (p) ShaneGray 2 86
(Kevin Ryan) *trckd ldr: hdwy over 2f out: rdn wl over 1f out: drvn ent fnl f: sn ev ch: no ex towards fin* **8/1**
-500 **4** *2¾* **Freight Train (IRE)**[8] 1664 4-9-2 **74**.................... JoeFanning 1 75
(Mark Johnston) *led: pushed along 2f out: rdn appr fnl f: drvn and hdd last 100yds: wknd towards fin* **7/1**[3]
-300 **5** *shd* **Warfare**[72] 656 7-9-7 **79**.................... BarryMcHugh 5 80
(Tim Fitzgerald) *hld up in rr: stdy hdwy 3f out: chsd ldrs over 1f out: sn rdn and kpt on fnl f* **16/1**
600- **6** *1¼* **King Of The Celts (IRE)**[192] 7427 8-8-5 **68**........ RachelRichardson(5) 6 67
(Tim Easterby) *trckd ldng pair: effrt on outer over 2f out: rdn wl over 1f out: drvn and kpt on same pce fnl f* **11/1**
0-04 **7** *1¾* **Briardale (IRE)**[11] 1588 4-8-12 **70**.................... PJMcDonald 8 65
(James Bethell) *hld up towards rr: effrt wl over 2f out: rdn wl over 1f out: n.d* **8/1**
314- **8** *3* **Skiddaw Valleys**[219] 6743 4-9-2 **74**.................... BenCurtis 10 63
(Alan Swinbank) *chsd ldrs on outer: rdn along wl over 2f out: sn drvn and wknd* **11/1**
-006 **9** *3* **Peterhouse (USA)**[9] 1633 4-9-6 **78**.................... GrahamLee 9 61
(Jason Ward) *hld up: a towards rr* **4/1**[2]
06-4 **10** *5* **Chorus of Lies**[41] 1028 4-8-10 **68**.................... TonyHamilton 7 41
(Tracy Waggott) *chsd ldrs: rdn along wl over 2f out: sn wknd* **28/1**

2m 6.35s (-0.65) **Going Correction** +0.075s/f (Good) **10 Ran SP% 118.2**
Speed ratings (Par 105): **105,104,104,102,102 101,100,97,95,91**
CSF £46.33 CT £282.55 TOTE £16.70: £4.20, £1.60, £2.70; EX 65.10 Trifecta £700.30.
Owner Lets Be Lucky Racing 5 **Bred** Susanna Ballinger **Trained** Maunby, N Yorks

FOCUS
A competitive handicap in which each of the first four went odds-on in running at one stage or another. It's been rated around the runner-up.

1924 BEVERLEY ANNUAL BADGEHOLDERS H'CAP 1m 100y
4:05 (4:05) (Class 4) (0-85,85) 4-Y-O+ **£6,301** (£1,886; £943; £472; £235) **Stalls** Low

Form RPR
403- **1** **Rousayan (IRE)**202 7193 5-9-0 **78** DanielTudhope 9 93
(David O'Meara) *trckd ldrs: hdwy 2f out: rdn to chse ldr over 1f out: led ins fnl f: kpt on strly* **6/1**3
0 **2** 3 **Dawn Mirage**35 1122 4-8-11 **75** (p) TonyHamilton 4 83
(Richard Fahey) *led 3f: chsd ldr: rdn along 2f out: drvn over 1f out: kpt on u.p fnl f* **12/1**
0-13 **3** 1 **Muntadab (IRE)**16 1480 4-9-5 **83** DavidNolan 2 89
(David Loughnane) *trckd ldng pair: effrt on inner 2f out: rdn over 1f out: styng on whn n.m.r and swtchd lft ins fnl f: styd on towards fin* **4/1**1
050- **4** hd **Hulcolt (IRE)**226 6537 5-8-12 **76** GrahamGibbons 7 81
(Ivan Furtado) *trckd ldrs: hdwy to ld after 3f: clr 2f out: rdn over 1f out: drvn and hdd ins fnl f: wknd towards fin* **20/1**
2412 **5** 2 **Sands Chorus**14 1526 4-9-0 **78** TomEaves 6 79
(James Given) *prom: rdn along over 2f out: swtchd lft and drvn over 1f out: kpt on one pce* **7/1**
0-06 **6** 3/4 **Kiwi Bay**14 1526 11-8-10 **79** PhilDennis(5) 8 78
(Michael Dods) *hld up: hdwy over 2f out: rdn along wl over 1f out: kpt on fnl f* **33/1**
0050 **7** hd **Dubai Dynamo**9 1643 11-9-7 **85** PJMcDonald 12 84
(Ruth Carr) *hld up towards rr: hdwy wl over 1f out: sn rdn and kpt on fnl f* **20/1**
310- **8** 3/4 **Echo Of Lightning**185 7599 6-9-0 **78** (p) BenCurtis 10 75
(Brian Ellison) *stdd and swtchd rt s: hld up and bhd: hdwy on outer wl over 2f out: rdn along wl over 1f out: no imp fnl f* **22/1**
5-02 **9** nk **Abushamah (IRE)**21 1380 5-9-2 **80** JamesSullivan 3 76
(Ruth Carr) *hld up in rr: sme hdwy on inner wl over 1f out: sn rdn and no imp* **4/1**1
002- **10** 3/4 **Border Bandit (USA)**222 6656 8-8-12 **76** (p) JoeFanning 11 70
(Tracy Waggott) *a towards rr* **25/1**
32-0 **11** 10 **Trail Blaze (IRE)**9 1625 7-8-12 **79** (p) JoeDoyle(3) 1 50
(Kevin Ryan) *chsd ldrs on inner: rdn along wl over 2f out: sn wknd* **20/1**
0-64 **12** 2 3/4 **Moonlightnavigator (USA)**29 1215 4-9-5 **83** PhillipMakin 5 48
(John Quinn) *chsd ldrs: rdn along 3f out: sn wknd* **9/2**2
1m 45.63s (-1.97) **Going Correction** +0.075s/f (Good) **12** Ran SP% **118.1**
Speed ratings (Par 105): **112,109,108,107,105 105,104,104,103,103 93,90**
CSF £65.10 CT £329.49 TOTE £7.30: £1.90, £3.20, £1.90; EX 75.40 Trifecta £385.80.
Owner The Roses Partnership **Bred** Haras De Son Altesse L'Aga Khan Scea **Trained** Upper Helmsley, N Yorks

FOCUS
A good performance from the winner in a race otherwise dominated by the four up front. A length pb from the winner.

1925 RACING AGAIN ON TUESDAY 10 MAY H'CAP (DIV I) 7f 100y
4:40 (4:41) (Class 5) (0-70,69) 4-Y-O+ **£3,780** (£1,131; £565; £283; £141) **Stalls** Low

Form RPR
053 **1** **All You (IRE)**6 1762 4-9-7 **69** (v) DanielTudhope 10 76
(David O'Meara) *in tch: hdwy on outer wl over 2f out: chsd ldr over 1f out: rdn to chal ent fnl f: sn drvn: kpt on to ld on line* **5/1**2
-052 **2** nse **Tellovoi (IRE)**7 1695 8-8-12 **65** (v) RobJFitzpatrick(5) 9 72
(Richard Guest) *dwlt and in rr: t.k.h and sn chsng ldrs: hdwy 4f out: led 3f out: rdn wl over 1f out: jnd and drvn ent fnl f: kpt on gamely: hdd on line* **6/1**3
2360 **3** 1 1/4 **Roger Thorpe**9 1654 7-8-5 **58** PaddyPilley(5) 11 62
(Deborah Sanderson) *trckd ldrs: hdwy 3f out: chsd ldr 2f out: rdn over 1f out: drvn and cl up whn edging rt and n.m.r ins fnl f: kpt on same pce towards fin* **14/1**
3042 **4** 1/2 **Oak Bluffs (IRE)**10 1596 5-8-10 **65** AdamMcNamara(7) 4 68+
(Richard Fahey) *in rr: gd hdwy on wd outside over 2f out: rdn over 1f out: styd on to chse ldrs ent fnl f: sn drvn and no imp* **3/1**1
0-30 **5** 1 **I'm Super Too (IRE)**10 1596 9-8-5 **58** GemmaTutty(5) 2 58
(Karen Tutty) *hld up towards rr: hdwy over 2f out: rdn wl over 1f out: kpt on fnl f: nrst fin* **14/1**
065- **6** 1 **Relight My Fire**223 6616 6-9-1 **68** (p) RachelRichardson(5) 7 66
(Tim Easterby) *in tch: hdwy to chse ldrs 2f out: rdn over 1f out: kpt on same pce fnl f* **8/1**
1434 **7** 4 1/2 **National Service (USA)**16 1496 5-9-5 **67** (tp) PaulMulrennan 1 53
(Rebecca Menzies) *midfield: hdwy over 2f out: rdn along wl over 1f out: n.d* **9/1**
2-03 **8** 2 1/4 **Illustrious Prince (IRE)**24 1317 9-8-13 **64** 1 JoeDoyle(3) 8 45
(Julie Camacho) *s.i.s and wl bhd tl kpt on fnl 2f* **8/1**
040- **9** 1/2 **Midlight**146 8147 4-8-12 **60** KeaganLatham 5 39
(Richard Whitaker) *chsd ldr: rdn along wl over 2f out: sn wknd* **16/1**
240 **10** 2 1/4 **Intense Starlet (IRE)**14 1524 5-9-5 **67** SamJames 3 41
(Marjorie Fife) *chsd ldrs: rdn along over 3f out: sn wknd* **20/1**
4-46 **11** 2 1/4 **Burner (IRE)**10 1595 4-9-4 **66** (b1) DuranFentiman 6 34
(Olly Williams) *set str pce: pushed along and hdd 3f out: sn rdn and wknd over 2f out* **14/1**
1m 34.15s (0.35) **Going Correction** +0.075s/f (Good) **11** Ran SP% **118.8**
Speed ratings (Par 103): **101,100,99,98,97 96,91,88,88,85 83**
CSF £35.55 CT £317.55 TOTE £5.00: £1.90, £2.00, £5.10; EX 31.50 Trifecta £702.50.
Owner A Turton, J Blackburn, L Bond & J Kay **Bred** Stowell Hill Ltd **Trained** Upper Helmsley, N Yorks
■ Stewards' Enquiry : Paddy Pilley two-day ban: used whip down the shoulder in the forehand (May 16-17)

FOCUS
An open handicap. Ordinary form rated around the runner-up to form.

1926 RACING AGAIN ON TUESDAY 10 MAY H'CAP (DIV II) 7f 100y
5:15 (5:16) (Class 5) (0-70,68) 4-Y-O+ **£3,780** (£1,131; £565; £283; £141) **Stalls** Low

Form RPR
3044 **1** **Make On Madam (IRE)**19 1412 4-9-1 **62** GrahamGibbons 12 70
(Les Eyre) *trckd ldng pair on inner: swtchd lft and hdwy over 1f out: rdn to ld ins fnl f: styd on wl* **9/1**
0312 **2** 1 1/4 **Affectionate Lady (IRE)**21 1382 5-8-10 **57** (b) TomEaves 3 62
(Keith Reveley) *dwlt and in rr whn hmpd after 1f: hdwy on outer over 3f out: chsd ldrs 2f out: rdn over 1f out: kpt on fnl f* **13/2**3
1350 **3** 1 3/4 **Mercury**77 590 4-8-11 **58** (b) ShaneGray 7 59
(Kevin Ryan) *trckd ldr: hdwy and cl up 3f out: rdn to ld over 1f out: drvn and hdd ins fnl f: kpt on same pce* **12/1**
3-00 **4** nk **Talent Scout (IRE)**10 1595 10-9-1 **67** (p) GemmaTutty(5) 8 67
(Karen Tutty) *t.k.h: set sound pce: jnd wl over 2f out and sn rdn: hdd over 1f out: sn drvn and wknd fnl f* **20/1**
-042 **5** 1/2 **Cliff (IRE)**10 1595 6-9-0 **68** KieranSchofield(7) 11 67
(Nigel Tinkler) *trckd ldrs: hdwy over 2f out: rdn and n.m.r over 1f out and again ins fnl f: kpt on* **4/1**1
6-06 **6** 1/2 **Cabal**19 1412 9-9-7 **68** (v) DavidAllan 1 65
(Geoffrey Harker) *hld up towards rr: gd hdwy on outer wl over 2f out: rdn to chse ldrs over 1f out: drvn ent fnl f: kpt on same pce* **12/1**
2466 **7** nk **Pyla (IRE)**7 1725 4-9-4 **65** LemosdeSouza 6 66+
(Denis Quinn) *hld up in tch on inner: hdwy 2f out: effrt whn nt clr run and hmpd over 1f out: keeping on whn nt clr run again ins fnl f: nt rcvr* **13/2**3
400- **8** nk **Just Paul (IRE)**199 7256 6-9-0 **61** JackGarritty 2 59+
(Micky Hammond) *trckd ldrs: effrt on inner 2f out and sn n.m.r: rdn over 1f out: n.m.r ins fnl f: kpt on* **11/2**2
05-0 **9** nse **Kopassus (IRE)**7 1696 4-8-12 **59** PaulMulrennan 9 55
(Lawrence Mullaney) *trckd ldrs: hdwy over 2f out: rdn over 1f out: drvn and one pce fnl f* **10/1**
0-00 **10** 2 **Red Charmer (IRE)**10 1596 6-9-4 **65** PJMcDonald 4 56
(Ann Duffield) *a towards rr* **7/1**
0-60 **11** 9 **Ershaad (IRE)**9 1625 4-9-6 **67** DougieCostello 10 35
(Shaun Harris) *a towards rr* **40/1**
5/0- **12** 1 1/2 **Prince Of Time**366 1871 4-8-11 **65** CallumRodriguez(7) 5 29
(Richard Ford) *a towards rr* **20/1**
1m 34.93s (1.13) **Going Correction** +0.075s/f (Good) **12** Ran SP% **121.0**
Speed ratings (Par 103): **96,94,92,92,91 91,90,90,90,88 77,76**
CSF £66.24 CT £727.99 TOTE £11.50: £2.90, £2.20, £3.70; EX 85.30 Trifecta £1133.30.
Owner G Parkinson & Baz Gibson **Bred** Mrs T Brudenell **Trained** Catwick, N Yorks
■ Stewards' Enquiry : Lemos de Souza three-day ban: careless riding (May 16-18)

FOCUS
The slower of the two divisions by 0.78sec. A bit of a messy affair, with the leaders tiring in the closing stages and blocking the path of one or two of the closers. The winner has been rated back to last year's C&D win.

1927 WHITE RABBIT APPRENTICE H'CAP 7f 100y
5:50 (5:50) (Class 6) (0-65,65) 3-Y-O **£2,587** (£770; £384; £192) **Stalls** Low

Form RPR
43-0 **1** **Arcane Dancer (IRE)**11 1584 3-9-1 **59** (p) JoshDoyle(3) 9 63
(Lawrence Mullaney) *chsd ldng pair: effrt wl over 1f out: rdn appr fnl f: styd on to ld last 100yds: kpt on wl* **33/1**
60-0 **2** 1/2 **Wotabreeze (IRE)**18 1449 3-9-0 **62** GeorgeWood(7) 4 65
(John Quinn) *midfield: hdwy over 2f out: swtchd lft and rdn jst over 1f out: styd on strly fnl f* **11/1**
0-52 **3** nse **Stars N Angels (IRE)**9 1638 3-9-7 **62** (p) GeorgeBuckell 5 65
(Michael Appleby) *chsd ldrs: hdwy on outer over 2f out: rdn to chal ent fnl f: ev ch tl nt qckn towards fin* **11/2**3
404- **4** 1/2 **Perceysvivace**206 7092 3-9-5 **65** AdamMcNamara(5) 8 66+
(Richard Fahey) *bhd: pushed along 1/2-way: rdn over 2f out: hdwy over 1f out: sn swtchd lft and rdn: styd on wl fnl f: nrst fin* **9/2**2
53-4 **5** 3/4 **Fine Example**12 1564 3-9-5 **60** PatrickO'Donnell 11 60+
(Kevin Ryan) *hld up and bhd: hdwy on outer over 2f out: rdn wl over 1f out: styd on fnl f: nrst fin* **10/1**
6-00 **6** 1 1/4 **Mr Potter**18 1448 3-9-1 **59** (e) RobJFitzpatrick(3) 3 55
(Richard Guest) *chsd ldr: cl up 3f out: led 2f out and sn rdn: hdd and drvn over 1f out: rallied to take slt ld ins fnl f: hdd & wknd last 100yds* **25/1**
40-1 **7** 3/4 **Croft Ranger (IRE)**21 1383 3-9-6 **64** PhilDennis(3) 10 59
(Michael Dods) *chsd ldrs: effrt 2f out: sn rdn and sltly outpcd: kpt on fnl f* **16/1**
54-2 **8** hd **Beverley Bullet**11 1584 3-9-4 **64** HarryBurns(5) 7 58
(Les Eyre) *dwlt and towards rr: rapid hdwy on outer and rn wd bnd over 4f out: cl up 3f out: rdn to ld wl over 1f out: drvn and hdd jst ins fnl f: wknd* **9/2**2
50-2 **9** 1/2 **Seaperle**8 1670 3-8-11 **52** RachelRichardson 6 45
(Tim Easterby) *a towards rr* **4/1**1
0-11 **10** 1 **Free To Roam (IRE)**13 1548 3-9-0 **55** CallumShepherd 2 45
(Philip McBride) *led: rdn along 3f out: hdd 2f out: sn drvn and wknd over 1f out* **8/1**
1-62 **11** 6 **Little Pippin**12 1564 3-8-12 **53** JordanVaughan 1 28
(Tony Coyle) *chsd ldrs: rdn along over 2f out: sn drvn and wknd* **16/1**
1m 35.87s (2.07) **Going Correction** +0.075s/f (Good) **11** Ran SP% **118.8**
Speed ratings (Par 97): **91,90,90,89,88 87,86,86,85,84 77**
CSF £362.81 CT £2366.88 TOTE £24.80: £8.30, £4.90, £3.40; EX 433.10 Trifecta £1674.30 Part won..
Owner S Rimmer **Bred** Eimear Mulhern & Abbeville Stud **Trained** Great Habton, N Yorks

FOCUS
A moderate handicap. The third has been rated to his latest form.
T/Jkpt: Not won. T/Plt: £85.30 to a £1 stake. Pool: £47,833.53 - 409.32 winning tickets T/Qpdt: £33.10 to a £1 stake. Pool: £4,966.44 - 110.90 winning tickets **Joe Rowntree**

1713 WINDSOR (R-H)
Monday, May 2

OFFICIAL GOING: Good (7.7)
Wind: Moderate, behind Weather: Bright becoming overcast, light rain from race 5

1928 TOTEPLACEPOT RACING'S FAVOURITE BET APPRENTICE TRAINING SERIES H'CAP 6f
1:40 (1:41) (Class 5) (0-70,70) 4-Y-O+ **£2,911** (£866; £432; £216) **Stalls** Low

Form RPR
1/00 **1** **Summersault (IRE)**91 424 5-8-13 **62** SophieKilloran 15 73+
(Jamie Osborne) *in tch: prog on outer to chse ldr over 1f out: shkn up to ld jst ins fnl f: styd on wl* **16/1**
330- **2** 2 **Darrell Rivers**203 7171 4-8-9 **63** MillyNaseb(5) 6 68
(Giles Bravery) *led: hung lft fr 2f out: hdd and nt qckn jst ins fnl f: eased whn btn nr fin* **8/1**
3152 **3** 1 **Indian Affair**16 1496 6-9-4 **70** (bt) LuluStanford(3) 11 72
(Milton Bradley) *chsd ldrs: rdn over 2f out: kpt on one pce fr over 1f out* **6/1**1
200- **4** 1 1/2 **Pettochside**154 8051 7-8-13 **67** MitchGodwin(5) 8 64+
(John Bridger) *wl in rr: gd prog on outer over 2f out: to press ldrs over 1f out: one pce fnl f* **12/1**
3505 **5** 3/4 **Ocean Legend (IRE)**26 1261 11-9-1 **64** GeorgiaCox 10 59
(Tony Carroll) *chsd ldrs: rdn over 2f out: in tch over 1f out: one pce* **14/1**

-021 **6** *1* **Posh Bounty**[10] 1600 5-8-12 **68** SeanMooney(7) 3 59
(Joseph Tuite) *mostly in midfield: rdn 2f out: kpt on fnl f but nvr able to threaten* **13/2**[2]

4350 **7** *1/2* **Encapsulated**[54] 873 6-8-13 **62** RhiainIngram 4 52
(Roger Ingram) *towards rr: rdn over 2f out: sme prog over 1f out: no imp after* **33/1**

00-0 **8** *1 3/4* **Living Leader**[26] 1269 7-9-0 **67** ow3 (p) RossTurner(7) 14 54
(Grace Harris) *s.i.s: struggling in rr bef 1/2-way: modest late hdwy* **25/1**

0-06 **9** *1/2* **Swot**[31] 1178 4-9-4 **67** KevinLundie 7 50
(Roger Teal) *outpcd and a off the pce* **22/1**

2110 **10** *1 1/4* **Eljaddaaf (IRE)**[32] 1159 5-8-12 **66** PaulBooth(5) 12 45
(Dean Ivory) *v s.i.s: wl bhd tl r.o u.p ins fnl f* **9/1**

201- **11** *1/2* **Harrison Stickle**[217] 6807 4-8-12 **66** JordanUys(5) 13 43
(John Gallagher) *prom: chsd ldr 1/2-way to over 1f out: wknd qckly* **7/1**[3]

1123 **12** *2 3/4* **Exalted (IRE)**[19] 1415 5-9-3 **66** (t) PaddyBradley 1 34
(William Knight) *chsd ldrs to 1/2-way: lost pl u.p* **6/1**[1]

0-0 **13** *3/4* **Cloak And Degas (IRE)**[120] 28 4-9-3 **66** (v) CharlieBennett 9 32
(Tim McCarthy) *chsd ldr to 1/2-way: sn wknd* **33/1**

5-02 **14** *1* **Perfect Pastime**[13] 1549 8-9-2 **68** (p) HollieDoyle(3) 5 31
(Jim Boyle) *rrd s and lost many l: a wl bhd* **14/1**

0-03 **15** *1/2* **Hipz (IRE)**[13] 1549 5-9-5 **68** MeganNicholls 2 29
(Laura Mongan) *a towards rr: rdn and no prog over 2f out* **14/1**

1m 11.64s (-1.36) **Going Correction** -0.10s/f (Good) **15** Ran SP% **123.2**
Speed ratings (Par 103): **105,102,101,99,98 96,96,93,93,91 90,87,86,84,84**
CSF £135.58 CT £887.84 TOTE £20.30: £5.60, £3.50, £2.60; EX 226.70 Trifecta £2113.60 Part won..
Owner Mrs F Walwyn A Taylor D Christian **Bred** Dr Dean Harron & Kemal Kurt **Trained** Upper Lambourn, Berks

FOCUS
Race distance as advertised. A modest sprint and they came centre-field in the straight. The third has been rated close to his recent effort.

1929 TOTEJACKPOT PICK 6 WINNERS TODAY H'CAP 6f
2:15 (2:17) (Class 4) (0-85,85) 4-Y-0+ **£4,690** (£1,395; £697; £348) **Stalls** Low

Form RPR

0-00 **1** **Crew Cut (IRE)**[14] 1530 8-8-12 **76** SaleemGolam 9 86
(Stuart Williams) *t.k.h: hld up in rr: last 2f out: rapid prog on wd outside over 1f out: drvn and r.o to ld last strides* **16/1**

3-11 **2** *1/2* **Elusive Ellen (IRE)**[28] 1237 6-8-12 **76** JimmyQuinn 8 84+
(Brendan Powell) *prom on outer: pressed ldr 2f: led 1f out: styd on but hdd nr fin* **16/1**

53-3 **3** *nk* **Cincuenta Pasos (IRE)**[24] 1318 5-9-6 **84** (t) FMBerry 7 91
(Joseph Tuite) *hld up in rr: prog on outer fr 2f out: clsd to chal fnl f: styd on same pce after* **8/1**[3]

-611 **4** *2* **Stellarta**[40] 1040 5-9-3 **81** DavidProbert 13 82
(Michael Blanshard) *pressed ldrs on outer: nt qckn over 1f out: one pce after* **8/1**[3]

6024 **5** *1/2* **Plucky Dip**[30] 1205 5-9-2 **80** ShaneKelly 5 79
(John Ryan) *chsd ldrs: rdn and no imp 2f out: styd on ins fnl f* **14/1**

2122 **6** *1 3/4* **Torreon (IRE)**[33] 1143 5-9-5 **83** AdamKirby 12 76
(John Ryan) *pressed ldr to 2f out: steadily wknd* **9/4**[1]

0-63 **7** *1 1/4* **Perardua**[20] 1402 4-8-8 **72** CathyGannon 14 61
(David Evans) *towards rr: rdn 2f out: one pce after and n.d* **25/1**

001- **8** *3/4* **Popeswood (IRE)**[184] 7635 4-9-4 **82** FergusSweeney 11 69
(Ron Hodges) *hld up in rr: pushed along in last pair 2f out: modest late prog: nvr involved* **20/1**

20-3 **9** *nse* **Lady Kyllar**[6] 1744 4-9-7 **85** JamieSpencer 10 72
(George Margarson) *hld up in rr: sme prog into midfield 2f out: no hdwy after: reminder fnl f then eased nr fin* **8/1**[3]

0-00 **10** *1 1/4* **Keep It Dark**[14] 1528 7-9-1 **79** JimCrowley 4 62
(William Knight) *led against nr side rail: carried hd high and racd awkwardly fr 2f out: hdd & wknd 1f out* **28/1**

6020 **11** *nk* **Searchlight**[37] 1090 5-8-13 **77** PatCosgrave 2 59
(Jim Boyle) *chsd ldrs: drvn 2f out: wknd jst over 1f out* **16/1**

0-05 **12** *1* **Kinglami**[14] 1530 7-9-5 **83** (p) DarryllHolland 3 62
(John O'Shea) *chsd ldrs: lost pl after 2f and in midfield after: rn into trble fr over 1f out: eased whn no ch fnl f* **8/1**[3]

05-3 **13** *2* **Links Drive Lady**[14] 1530 8-9-4 **85** JackDuern(3) 1 72
(Dean Ivory) *missed break bdly: mostly in last trio: effrt 2f out: no ch whn short of room ins fnl f* **7/1**[2]

1m 11.43s (-1.57) **Going Correction** -0.10s/f (Good) **13** Ran SP% **124.1**
Speed ratings (Par 105): **106,105,104,102,101 99,97,96,96,94 94,93,90**
CSF £252.61 CT £2217.61 TOTE £29.20: £10.60, £2.30, £4.80; EX 431.40 Trifecta £1316.00 Part won..
Owner Paul W Stevens **Bred** Rathbarry Stud **Trained** Newmarket, Suffolk
■ Stewards' Enquiry : Cathy Gannon caution: careless riding
Darryll Holland

FOCUS
Race distance as advertised. They stayed stands' side this time but the winner came down the outer. A small pb from the third.

1930 TOTEQUADPOT FOUR PLACES IN FOUR RACES MAIDEN STKS (DIV I) 1m 67y
2:50 (2:52) (Class 5) 3-4-Y-0 **£2,911** (£866; £432; £216) **Stalls** Low

Form RPR

4 **1** **Morando (FR)**[7] 1714 3-9-1 0 HarryBentley 7 88+
(Roger Varian) *reluctant to enter stalls: prom in chsng gp: in 2nd pl 3f out: led over 2f out: rdn clr over 1f out* **7/2**[2]

2 *5* **Aflame** 3-8-10 0 TedDurcan 8 71+
(Sir Michael Stoute) *hld up early: prog over 4f out: chsd ldng pair 2f out: styd on to take 2nd ins fnl f: no ch w wnr* **6/1**[3]

0 **3** *2 3/4* **Swiftee (IRE)**[19] 1421 3-9-1 0 FrederikTylicki 5 70
(Ed Dunlop) *prom in chsng gp: lft in ld 3f out: rdn and hdd over 2f out: one pce and lost 2nd ins fnl f* **33/1**

4 *1 3/4* **Sund City (FR)** 3-8-10 0 DavidProbert 2 61
(Harry Dunlop) *chsd ldrs: shkn up and no imp on ldng pair over 2f out: one pce after* **50/1**

3 **5** *2 1/2* **Niceonecenturion**[18] 1429 3-9-1 0 JimCrowley 6 60
(William Knight) *wl off the pce in last quartet early: clsr but stl in rr 3f out: shkn up over 1f out: plugged on* **12/1**

6 *2 1/4* **Shrubland** 3-9-1 0 AntonioFresu 10 55
(Ed Walker) *off the pce in rr early: rdn 3f out: hung lft and no real prog fr 2f out* **50/1**

00- **7** *1/2* **Bigger And Better**[212] 6924 3-9-1 0 SeanLevey 13 54
(Richard Hannon) *chsd ldrs: rdn 3f out: sn struggling and btn* **16/1**

8 *1/2* **Perpetual Change (IRE)** 3-9-1 0 AdamKirby 11 53
(Clive Cox) *prom in chsng gp: urged along bef 1/2-way: struggling fr 3f out* **33/1**

9 *1 3/4* **Catskill Mountains (IRE)** 3-9-1 0 AndreaAtzeni 4 49
(Roger Varian) *s.s: wl bhd early: jst in tch in rr 3f out: sn wknd* **10/1**

10 *1 1/2* **Ravens Heart (IRE)** 4-10-0 0 RenatoSouza 12 48
(Dean Ivory) *off the pce in rr early: jst in tch 3f out: sn shkn up: wknd 2f out* **40/1**

11 *6* **Spring In Kentucky**[214] 4-9-2 0 KimberleyVanderVegt(7) 1 29
(Daniel Kubler) *chsd ldr and sn wl clr of rest: lft in ld over 4f out: hung lft after: hdd 3f out: sn wknd* **40/1**

0 **12** *7* **Western Prince**[19] 1421 3-9-1 0 FrankieDettori 9 15+
(John Gosden) *led: clr w one rival whn hung bdly lft bnd over 4f out and hdd: continued to hang lft after and dropped away fr 2f out* **11/4**[1]

0- **13** *23* **Iballisticvin**[293] 4234 3-9-1 0 FergusSweeney 14
(Gary Moore) *s.i.s: sn t.o* **66/1**

1m 42.66s (-2.04) **Going Correction** -0.05s/f (Good)
WFA 3 from 4yo 13lb **13** Ran SP% **102.0**
Speed ratings (Par 103): **108,103,100,98,96 93,93,92,91,89 83,76,53**
CSF £16.87 TOTE £3.50: £1.20, £1.80, £8.60; EX 19.30 Trifecta £368.40.
Owner H H Sheikh Mohammed Bin Khalifa Al Thani **Bred** Guy Pariente Holding Sprl **Trained** Newmarket, Suffolk
■ Eljeemi (9-2) was withdrawn. Rule 4 applies to all bets. Deduction - 15p in the pound.

FOCUS
Race run over 30yds further than advertised. This had looked a decent maiden, but with Eljeemi withdrawn at the start and the favourite running off the course, the winner may ultimately have faced a pretty simple task. The time was still 0.91secs quicker than division two and the form looks above average.

1931 TOTEQUADPOT FOUR PLACES IN FOUR RACES MAIDEN STKS (DIV II) 1m 67y
3:25 (3:25) (Class 5) 3-4-Y-0 **£2,911** (£866; £432; £216) **Stalls** Low

Form RPR

23- **1** **Wild Hacked (USA)**[175] 7777 3-9-1 0 LukeMorris 14 87
(Marco Botti) *pressed ldr: rdn to chal 2f out: racd sltly awkwardly but drvn to ld ins fnl f* **5/2**[1]

5- **2** *1/2* **Silk Cravat**[237] 6181 3-9-1 0 RobertHavlin 3 86
(Simon Crisford) *led: rdn and pressed 2f out: kpt on wl but hdd and hld ins fnl f* **5/2**[1]

0 **3** *4* **Lexington Law (IRE)**[30] 1200 3-9-1 0 SeanLevey 6 77
(Richard Hannon) *mostly chsd ldng pair: lft bhd by them fr 2f out and pushed along: one pce after: eased whn secure in 3rd pl last 75yds* **25/1**

4 *3/4* **On The Bill (IRE)** 3-9-1 0 FrederikTylicki 5 75
(Ed Dunlop) *chsd ldrs: pushed along firmly to dispute 3rd over 2f out: outpcd sn after: kpt on one pce* **33/1**

04 **5** *shd* **Bunbury**[7] 1715 4-10-0 0 ShaneKelly 9 78+
(Richard Hughes) *hld up in last trio: appeared to run into trble over 3f out: pushed along and styd on steadily fr over 2f out: nrly snatched a pl: likely to improve* **15/2**[3]

3 **6** *4* **Major Assault**[62] 770 3-9-1 0 AdamKirby 11 66
(Clive Cox) *chsd ldrs: urged along over 3f out: wknd 2f out* **7/1**[2]

7 *1* **Idyllic (IRE)** 3-8-10 0 TedDurcan 12 58+
(Sir Michael Stoute) *slowly away: mostly in last pair: pushed along over 2f out: no prog tl styd on steadily fnl f* **16/1**

8 *3/4* **Cliff Edge (IRE)** 3-9-1 0 AndreaAtzeni 4 62
(Roger Varian) *in tch in midfield: urged along over 3f out: sn lft bhd: kpt on fnl f* **10/1**

6 **9** *nk* **Persaverance**[14] 1529 3-9-1 0 FergusSweeney 13 61
(Gary Moore) *towards rr: pushed along and outpcd over 2f out: one pce and n.d after* **40/1**

0- **10** *1* **Khor Al Udaid**[145] 8153 3-9-1 0 (b[1]) FrankieDettori 10 59
(John Gosden) *free to post: hld up in rr: pushed along and no prog over 2f out* **7/1**[2]

11 *3/4* **So Much Water (FR)** 4-9-9 0 SaleemGolam 7 55
(John Berry) *prom: chsd ldr 3f out: wknd over 2f out* **50/1**

00- **12** *5* **Buzz Lightyere**[147] 8138 3-8-12 0 RobHornby(3) 2 45
(Michael Attwater) *a towards rr: shoved along and no prog over 3f out: bhd fnl 2f* **25/1**

13 *2 3/4* **Poppy Time** 3-8-7 0 RyanTate(3) 8 34
(James Eustace) *slowly away: mostly in last: bhd fnl 2f* **33/1**

1m 43.57s (-1.13) **Going Correction** -0.05s/f (Good)
WFA 3 from 4yo 13lb **13** Ran SP% **126.9**
Speed ratings (Par 103): **103,102,98,97,97 93,92,91,91,90 89,84,82**
CSF £7.74 TOTE £3.30: £1.50, £2.00, £7.30; EX 11.50 Trifecta £169.00.
Owner Khalid Bin Ali Al Khalifa **Bred** Moyglare Stud **Trained** Newmarket, Suffolk

FOCUS
Race run over 30yds further than advertised. The joint market leaders came clear, although this looked the lesser of the two divisions and the time was 0.91secs slower. The race has been rated as up to scratch.

1932 TOTETRIFECTA PICK THE 1,2,3 FILLIES' H'CAP 1m 67y
4:00 (4:00) (Class 3) (0-95,85) 4-Y-0+ **£7,439** (£2,213; £1,106; £553) **Stalls** Low

Form RPR

6-11 **1** **Clotilde**[26] 1268 4-9-2 **80** JimCrowley 2 89+
(William Knight) *pressed ldr: rdn to ld wl over 1f out: styd on wl: readily* **3/1**[2]

636- **2** *2 1/4* **Gleaming Girl**[191] 7464 4-8-1 **72** SophieKilloran(7) 4 76
(David Simcock) *plld hrd early: hld up in tch: outpcd 3f out: rdn over 1f out on outer: styd on to take 2nd ins fnl f: no ch w wnr* **6/1**[3]

163- **3** *1/2* **Hala Madrid**[255] 5588 4-8-10 **74** DavidProbert 1 77
(Andrew Balding) *t.k.h: led: rdn and hdd wl over 1f out: fdd and lost 2nd ins fnl f* **3/1**[2]

1- **4** *2 1/4* **Somethingthrilling**[210] 6983 4-9-7 **85** JamieSpencer 3 83
(David Elsworth) *s.i.s: t.k.h: hld up bhd ldng pair: outpcd and rdn 3f out: nvr able to cl after* **6/4**[1]

2304 **5** *1 1/4* **Lady Lydia (IRE)**[30] 1207 5-9-4 **82** LiamJones 5 77
(Conrad Allen) *hld up in last: outpcd 3f out: rdn and sme prog to dispute 3rd over 1f out: n.d and fdd ins fnl f* **12/1**

1m 42.98s (-1.72) **Going Correction** -0.05s/f (Good) **5** Ran SP% **112.0**
Speed ratings (Par 104): **106,103,103,101,99**
CSF £20.17 TOTE £3.60: £2.00, £1.90; EX 13.40 Trifecta £44.50.
Owner Chasemore Farm **Bred** Chasemore Farm **Trained** Patching, W Sussex

FOCUS
Race run over 30yds further than advertised. The favourite didn't come up to expectations but this was still a fair fillies' handicap, with the winner continuing at the top of her game. The second and third have been rated to form.

1933 TOTEEXACTA PICK THE 1ST AND 2ND H'CAP 1m 2f 7y
4:35 (4:35) (Class 4) (0-85,84) 4-Y-O+ **£4,690** (£1,395; £697; £348) **Stalls** Centre

Form RPR
1 **Cape Discovery**[239] 6143 4-9-3 **80** ShaneKelly 2 84+
(Richard Hughes) *hld up in tch: prog wl over 2f out: rdn wl over 1f out: styd on to ld ins fnl f: drvn out* **20/1**
4120 2 ½ **Elysian Prince**[29] 1221 5-8-12 **75** (t) LiamJones 7 78
(Neil King) *pressed ldr: rdn to chal fr 3f out: upsides ins fnl f: jst hld by wnr nr fin* **8/1**
002 3 ½ **Mister Musicmaster**[7] 1724 7-9-4 **81** DarryllHolland 10 83
(Ron Hodges) *trckd ldrs: clsd over 2f out: rdn to chal over 1f out: nt qckn fnl f but kpt on to take 3rd nr fin* **16/1**
50-5 4 ½ **Biotic**[16] 1480 5-9-5 **82** FrederikTylicki 4 83
(Rod Millman) *hld up towards rr but in tch: rdn 3f out: nt qckn and no imp 2f out: styd on ins fnl f to take 4th last strides* **12/1**
031- 5 ½ **Trimoulet**[145] 8157 7-9-7 **84** TomQueally 3 84
(Daniel Kubler) *led: hrd pressed and rdn fr 3f out: hdd and no ex ins fnl f: lost pls last strides* **7/1**[3]
231- 6 2½ **Mediation**[177] 7748 4-9-5 **82** AndreaAtzeni 5 77
(Roger Varian) *chsd ldrs but wd bnd after 4f: rdn 3f out: nt qckn and hld 2f out: fdd* **5/2**[2]
0-04 7 hd **Barren Brook**[59] 815 9-8-10 **73** LukeMorris 1 68
(Laura Mongan) *hld up in last trio: rdn 4f out: no prog and wl hld after: styd on fnl f* **33/1**
331- 8 1 **Harold Lloyd**[292] 4276 4-9-2 **79** FergusSweeney 6 72
(Henry Candy) *wl in tch: clsd on ldrs 3f out: nt qckn u.p 2f out: wl hld over 1f out: fdd* **9/4**[1]
3-05 9 3½ **Bohemian Rhapsody (IRE)**[21] 1390 7-8-11 **74** FMBerry 8 60
(Brendan Powell) *hld up in rr: pushed along and no prog over 3f out: no ch fnl 2f* **10/1**
010- 10 2 **The Gay Cavalier**[153] 8062 5-8-4 **74** (t) JonathanFisher(7) 9 56
(John Ryan) *s.v.s: and detached early: in tch after 4f: wknd over 2f out* **25/1**

2m 6.49s (-2.21) **Going Correction** -0.05s/f (Good) **10** Ran SP% **117.2**
Speed ratings (Par 105): **106,105,105,104,104 102,102,101,98,97**
CSF £168.69 CT £2631.38 TOTE £25.80: £5.30, £2.40, £3.50; EX 257.60 Trifecta £4741.00 Part won..
Owner Thames Boys **Bred** Hascombe And Valiant Studs **Trained** Upper Lambourn, Berkshire

FOCUS
Race run over 30yds further than advertised. The two who dominated the market both flopped and several had their chance, with it going to one of the outsiders. A turf pb from the runner-up.

1934 TOTESWINGER THREE WAYS TO WIN H'CAP 1m 3f 135y
5:10 (5:13) (Class 4) (0-85,85) 4-Y-O+ **£4,690** (£1,395; £697; £348) **Stalls** Centre

Form RPR
-1 1 **Walpole (IRE)**[79] 567 4-8-13 **77** JamieSpencer 5 85+
(Hugo Palmer) *hld up in last: rdn whn pce lifted 3f out: clsd to ld wl over 1f out: stl looked green but styd on wl u.p fnl f* **1/1**[1]
500- 2 ¾ **Priors Brook**[166] 7893 5-8-13 **77** DavidProbert 7 81
(Andrew Balding) *cl up: trckd ldr 5f out: rdn to chal 2f out: pressed wnr sn after: styd on u.p but a hld ins fnl f* **10/1**
4-30 3 2 **Agent Gibbs**[12] 1568 4-9-7 **85** AdamKirby 2 86
(Ali Stronge) *led after 1f: awkward briefly bnd 5f out: kicked on for home 3f out: hdd wl over 1f out: one pce* **4/1**[2]
/324 4 ½ **Music Man (IRE)**[45] 975 6-9-2 **80** JimCrowley 4 80
(Laura Mongan) *hld up: effrt wl over 2f out: nt qckn wl over 1f out: one pce after* **9/1**
200- 5 hd **Prince Of Paris**[353] 2240 4-8-12 **76** RobertHavlin 6 76?
(Roger Ingram) *trckd ldrs: rdn 3f out: on terms 2f out: nt qckn u.p sn after: wl hld fnl f* **33/1**
00- 6 7 **Azilian**[134] 8319 4-8-11 **75** LukeMorris 1 63
(Paul Cole) *led 1f: chsd ldr to 5f out: wknd 2f out* **7/1**[3]

2m 29.74s (0.24) **Going Correction** -0.05s/f (Good) **6** Ran SP% **104.5**
Speed ratings (Par 105): **97,96,95,94,94 90**
CSF £10.02 TOTE £1.60: £1.20, £4.20; EX 12.90 Trifecta £27.70.
Owner Roldvale Limited **Bred** Roundhill Stud **Trained** Newmarket, Suffolk
■ Tangramm was withdrawn. Price at time of withdrawal 12-1. Rule 4 applies to all bets - deduction 5p in the pound.

FOCUS
Race run over 30yds further than advertised. Not a terribly strong handicap, with Tangramm withdrawn at the start, but the favourite got it done. Muddling form. It's been taken at face value for now, with the runner-up rated to last year's C&D reappearance figure.

1935 COLLECT TOTEPOOL WINNINGS AT BETFRED SHOPS H'CAP 5f 10y
5:45 (5:46) (Class 5) (0-75,75) 3-Y-O **£2,911** (£866; £432; £216) **Stalls** Low

Form RPR
6-51 1 **Just That Lord**[36] 1112 3-9-7 **75** RobertWinston 9 90+
(Bill Turner) *racd towards outer: pressed ldr: shkn up to ld over 1f out: drew clr fnl f: eased nr fin* **12/1**
14 2 3½ **Justice Lady (IRE)**[61] 783 3-8-9 **63** MartinLane 8 64
(David Elsworth) *mde most and racd towards outer: hdd over 1f out: no ch w wnr fnl f: hld on for 2nd* **9/2**[2]
4122 3 ½ **Mysterious Look**[26] 1271 3-9-2 **73** RobHornby(3) 2 72
(Ed McMahon) *hld up in rr: prog wl over 1f out: rdn and styd on to take 3rd ins fnl f* **16/1**
01-5 4 ¾ **Stormflower**[21] 1385 3-9-2 **70** LiamJones 7 67
(John Bridger) *chsd ldrs: rdn after 2f: effrt to dispute 3rd 1f out: kpt on* **28/1**
401- 5 ¾ **Pine Ridge**[197] 7310 3-9-7 **75** AdamKirby 1 69
(Clive Cox) *chsd ldrs: rdn 1/2-way: disp 3rd u.p over 1f out: fdd* **7/1**[3]
5-12 6 ¾ **Baron Bolt**[16] 1487 3-9-4 **72** LukeMorris 3 63
(Paul Cole) *towards rr: shuffled along fr 1/2-way: no great prog over 1f out: nvr involved* **9/1**
633- 7 ½ **Storm Melody**[208] 7040 3-9-7 **75** FMBerry 11 65
(Jonjo O'Neill) *hld up in rr: pushed along 2f out: sme prog on outer over 1f out: nvr on terms and nvr involved* **25/1**
1 8 2 **Lapilli**[32] 1167 3-9-7 **75** PatCosgrave 4 57
(William Haggas) *pressed ldrs: racd against nr side fr 3f out: shkn up wl over 1f out: sn wknd* **6/5**[1]
3-30 9 1¾ **Deer Song**[19] 1414 3-8-7 **61** oh1 WilliamCarson 5 37
(John Bridger) *racd against nr side: w ldrs to 1/2-way: wknd over 1f out* **33/1**
4-30 10 2¼ **Case Key**[17] 1452 3-9-7 **75** DarryllHolland 6 43
(Charles Hills) *lost pl after 1f: sn in last pair: bhd over 1f out* **16/1**
050- 11 14 **Lady Kheleyf**[157] 8010 3-8-8 **62** HarryBentley 10
(George Margarson) *free to post: in tch to 1/2-way: sn wknd: t.o* **40/1**

58.44s (-1.86) **Going Correction** -0.10s/f (Good) **11** Ran SP% **118.3**
Speed ratings (Par 99): **110,104,103,102,101 100,99,96,93,89 67**
CSF £63.53 CT £896.40 TOTE £14.70: £3.90, £1.50, £2.80; EX 111.90 Trifecta £1141.00.
Owner Mrs M S Teversham **Bred** Mrs Monica Teversham **Trained** Sigwells, Somerset

FOCUS
Race distance as advertised. An ordinary sprint that produced a clear-cut winner. The third has been rated to his recent form.
T/Plt: £4,124.10 to a £1 stake. Pool: £81,636.54 - 14.45 winning tickets T/Qpdt: £68.80 to a £1 stake. Pool: £6,773.9 - 72.80 winning tickets **Jonathan Neesom**

1936 - 1937a (Foreign Racing) - See Raceform Interactive

1223 CURRAGH (R-H)
Monday, May 2

OFFICIAL GOING: Straight course - soft; round course - yielding

1938a POWER EUROPEAN BREEDERS FUND TETRARCH STKS (LISTED RACE) 7f
3:00 (3:00) 3-Y-O
£23,860 (£7,683; £3,639; £1,617; £808; £404)

RPR
1 **Awtaad (IRE)**[43] 1017 3-9-3 106 ChrisHayes 4 103+
(Kevin Prendergast, Ire) *chsd ldrs: 3rd 1/2-way: impr into 2nd under 2f out and sn disp: rdn to ld ins fnl f and styd on wl to assert clsng stages: comf* **13/8**[2]
2 2 **Blue De Vega (GER)**[191] 7478 3-9-6 110 ColinKeane 2 100+
(M D O'Callaghan, Ire) *w.w: hdwy in 6th fr 1/2-way to chse ldrs far side in 4th: sn rdn and wnt 3rd u.p ent fnl f: kpt on into 2nd clsng stages: nt trble easy wnr* **6/4**[1]
3 ¾ **Embiran (IRE)**[43] 1019 3-9-3 0 PatSmullen 5 94+
(D K Weld, Ire) *cl up in 2nd: led narrowly gng wl 2f out: rdn and strly pressed 1f out: sn hdd and no imp on wnr: dropped to 3rd clsng stages: jst hld on for 3rd* **5/1**[3]
4 nk **Pacodali (IRE)**[23] 1349 3-9-3 85 (p) ConnorKing 1 93+
(J P Murtagh, Ire) *hld up: last at 1/2-way: tk clsr order in 6th over 2f out: rdn in 5th over 1f out and kpt on wl into nvr nrr 4th clsng stages: jst failed for 3rd: nrst fin* **33/1**
5 ½ **Collision Course (IRE)**[14] 1538 3-9-3 0 ShaneFoley 3 92
(A Oliver, Ire) *led: narrow advantage at 1/2-way: rdn and hdd 2f out: no ex u.p ent fnl f and dropped to 4th: kpt on same pce and dropped to 5th clsng stages* **66/1**
6 4¾ **Round Two (IRE)**[321] 3249 3-9-3 106 KevinManning 8 79
(J S Bolger, Ire) *chsd ldrs: 4th 1/2-way: sn pushed along and no ex u.p fr 2f out: dropped to 6th over 1f out and one pce after* **7/1**
7 10 **Roibeard (IRE)**[259] 5466 3-9-3 0 EmmetMcNamara 6 52
(G M Lyons, Ire) *w.w: 5th 1/2-way: rdn and wknd to rr over 2f out* **40/1**

1m 28.82s (-1.98) **Going Correction** +0.05s/f (Good) **7** Ran SP% **114.1**
Speed ratings: **113,110,109,109,108 103,92**
CSF £4.41 TOTE £2.80: £1.50, £1.40; DF 4.90 Trifecta £12.20.
Owner Hamdan Al Maktoum **Bred** Shadwell Estate Company Limited **Trained** Friarstown, Co Kildare

FOCUS
No Ballydoyle runner but a smart race. They went steady and the fifth limits the form.

1939a CANFORD CLIFFS EUROPEAN BREEDERS FUND ATHASI STKS (GROUP 3) (F&M) 7f
3:35 (3:35) 3-Y-O+
£32,536 (£10,477; £4,963; £2,205; £1,102; £551)

RPR
1 **Dolce Strega (IRE)**[17] 1467 3-8-11 97 BillyLee 4 103+
(W McCreery, Ire) *chsd ldrs: 5th 1/2-way: impr bhd ldrs gng wl in 4th fr 2f out: sn swtchd rt and rdn in 3rd ent fnl f: clsd u.p on outer to ld narrowly clsng stages: kpt on wl* **9/2**[2]
2 nk **Steip Amach (IRE)**[8] 1680 4-9-9 99 KevinManning 7 106
(J S Bolger, Ire) *cl up in 2nd tl sn disp and led narrowly: rdn and jnd briefly under 2f out: narrow advantage and strly pressed ent fnl f: all out wl ins fnl f and hdd clsng stages* **6/1**[3]
3 1¼ **Ainippe (IRE)**[233] 6338 4-9-12 106 ColinKeane 3 106+
(G M Lyons, Ire) *broke wl to ld tl sn jnd and hdd narrowly: cl 2nd at 1/2-way: disp gng wl under 2f out: rdn in cl 2nd ent fnl f and no ex wl ins fnl f where dropped to 3rd* **8/11**[1]
4 2¾ **Miss Elizabeth (IRE)**[22] 1369 3-8-11 103 ChrisHayes 1 91
(Edward Lynam, Ire) *chsd ldrs: 4th 1/2-way: effrt in 3rd fr 2f out: sn rdn and no ex u.p in 4th ent fnl f: kpt on same pce* **12/1**
5 4½ **Molly Dolly (IRE)**[218] 6797 4-9-9 95 KierenFallon 2 83
(W T Farrell, Ire) *on toes befhand and rrd in stalls: chsd ldrs early tl sn settled towards rr: pushed along in rr after 1/2-way and no imp on ldrs in 5th over 1f out: one pce fnl f* **20/1**
6 ¾ **Gussy Goose (IRE)**[277] 4801 4-9-9 95 (p) WayneLordan 5 81
(David Wachman, Ire) *s.i.s and pushed along in rr early: clsr in 6th at 1/2-way: rdn over 2f out in rr and no imp u.p in 6th 1f out: one pce fnl f* **16/1**
7 8 **Waitaki (IRE)**[8] 1677 3-8-11 82 (b[1]) PatSmullen 6 55
(D K Weld, Ire) *chsd ldrs: 3rd 1/2-way: rdn over 2f out and sn lost pl: no imp in 6th 1 1/2f out where eased* **10/1**

1m 29.23s (-1.57) **Going Correction** +0.05s/f (Good)
WFA 3 from 4yo 12lb **7** Ran SP% **117.8**
Speed ratings: **110,109,108,105,99 99,89**
CSF £32.55 TOTE £5.00: £1.70, £3.30; DF 30.80 Trifecta £46.90.
Owner Renzo Forni **Bred** Renzo Forni **Trained** Rathbride, Co Kildare

FOCUS
Not an especially strong renewal and the favourite was not at her best. A small pb from the winner.

1940a CAMELOT EUROPEAN BREEDERS FUND MOORESBRIDGE STKS (GROUP 3) 1m 2f
4:10 (4:10) 4-Y-O+ **£32,536** (£10,477; £4,963; £2,205; £1,102)

RPR

1 **Found (IRE)**[29] 1227 4-9-7 119 RyanMoore 3 119+
(A P O'Brien, Ire) *w.w in rr: tk clsr order bhd ldrs over 2f out: n.m.r bhd ldrs travelling wl in 3rd over 1f out: pushed along and prog through narrow gap between horses to ld fnl 100yds: sn in command: comf* **11/8**[2]

2 1 1/4 **Success Days (IRE)**[29] 1227 4-9-3 113 ShaneFoley 2 112
(K J Condon, Ire) *trckd ldrs early tl sn wnt 2nd: racd keenly early and led after 2f: rdn 2f out and strly pressed over 1f out: hdd u.p fnl 100yds and no ch w wnr: kpt on wl* **6/1**[3]

3 2 1/2 **Fascinating Rock (IRE)**[198] 7281 5-9-10 123 PatSmullen 6 114
(D K Weld, Ire) *w.w towards rr: 4th 1/2-way: impr into 2nd gng wl over 2f out: sn pushed along and no ex ins fnl f where dropped to 3rd: kpt on same pce under hands and heels clsng stages* **11/10**[1]

4 8 **Hot Sauce (IRE)**[199] 7272 4-9-0 97 [1] KierenFallon 1 88
(John Joseph Murphy, Ire) *trckd ldr early tl sn dropped to 3rd: pushed along 2f out and no imp on ldrs under hands and heels in 4th over 1f out: eased wl ins fnl f* **40/1**

5 41 **The Steward (USA)**[94] 385 5-9-3 96 (v[1]) LeighRoche 5 9
(D K Weld, Ire) *broke wl to ld tl hdd after 2f: rdn into st and sn no imp on ldr: wknd to rr over 2f out and sn eased: t.o* **50/1**

2m 11.17s (1.87) **Going Correction** +0.525s/f (Yiel) **5 Ran SP% 108.4**
Speed ratings: **113,112,110,103,70**
CSF £9.41 TOTE £2.70: £1.30, £2.30; DF 9.30 Trifecta £14.10.
Owner Michael Tabor & Derrick Smith & Mrs John Magnier **Bred** Roncon, Wynatt & Chelston **Trained** Cashel, Co Tipperary

FOCUS
Pretty much a Group 1 on ratings, though Fascinating Rock was seemingly undercooked. Found is rated to his mark.

1941 - 1943a (Foreign Racing) - See Raceform Interactive

[1776]BRIGHTON (L-H)
Tuesday, May 3

OFFICIAL GOING: Good (good to soft in places) changing to good after race 1 (2.20)
Wind: Fresh, against Weather: Sunny

1944 VEOLIA - OFFICIAL RECYCLING PARTNER NOVICE STKS 5f 59y
2:20 (2:21) (Class 5) 2-Y-O **£2,911** (£866; £432) **Stalls** Centre

Form RPR

23 1 **Tomily (IRE)**[20] 1422 2-8-13 0 TomMarquand(3) 2 90
(Richard Hannon) *mde all: shkn up 2f out: sn clr: easily* **4/11**[1]

01 2 6 **Assassinate (IRE)**[6] 1776 2-9-6 0 LukeMorris 4 74
(Paul Cole) *chsd wnr: chal 2f out: hung lft: sn outpcd* **5/1**[2]

0 3 15 **Jumping Jack (IRE)**[29] 1233 2-9-2 0 ShaneKelly 1 11
(Richard Hughes) *dwlt: hld up in 3rd: outpcd 2f out: btn whn swvd bdly rt over 1f out* **16/1**[3]

1m 4.27s (1.97) **Going Correction** +0.325s/f (Good) **3 Ran SP% 95.9**
Speed ratings (Par 93): **97,87,63**
CSF £1.63 TOTE £1.10; EX 1.60 Trifecta £1.80.
Owner Des Anderson **Bred** D J Anderson **Trained** East Everleigh, Wilts

FOCUS
Following 7mm of rain the previous day the going was given as good, good to soft in places (GoingStick: 8.1), but that was swiftly changed to good all round after the first race. The rail was dolled out from the 6f marker to the 2f pole, adding 9yds to each race distance. This proved a straightforward task for the favourite.

1945 L&S PRINTING - OFFICIAL PRINT PARTNER H'CAP 5f 213y
2:50 (2:50) (Class 5) (0-75,75) 4-Y-O+ **£2,911** (£866; £432; £216) **Stalls** Centre

Form RPR

560- 1 **Fear Or Favour (IRE)**[195] 7390 5-9-7 75 AdamKirby 5 85
(Clive Cox) *chsd ldr: drvn to ld wl over 1f out: rdn out fnl 50yds* **5/2**[1]

1/ 2 nk **Jaywalker (IRE)**[769] 1106 5-9-4 72 CharlesBishop 3 81
(Mick Channon) *led: hung lft and hdd wl over 1f out: ev ch fnl f: unable qck fnl 50yds* **6/1**

0-00 3 3 1/4 **Ginzan**[15] 1528 8-9-7 75 CathyGannon 8 74
(Malcolm Saunders) *in tch: rdn over 2f out: styd on same pce* **11/2**

6-00 4 1/2 **Commanche**[15] 1533 7-8-8 62 (b) SilvestreDeSousa 9 59
(Chris Dwyer) *outpcd in 6th: hung lft and styd on fr over 1f out: nvr nrr* **5/1**[3]

20-4 5 nse **Indian Tinker**[19] 1447 7-8-11 68 LouisSteward(3) 1 65
(Robert Cowell) *rrd s: prom: chal 2f out: one pce ent fnl f* **7/2**[2]

60-0 6 3 3/4 **Jungle Bay**[20] 1419 9-9-4 72 (b) MartinDwyer 2 57
(Jane Chapple-Hyam) *dwlt: in rr: effrt 2f out: wknd over 1f out* **14/1**

00-6 7 3 1/2 **Piazza San Pietro**[14] 1549 10-8-7 61 oh1 WilliamCarson 6 35
(Zoe Davison) *chsd ldrs tl wknd over 1f out* **50/1**

3001 8 3/4 **Polar Kite (IRE)**[27] 1269 8-8-7 64 RobHornby(3) 4 35
(Michael Attwater) *missed break and lost 10 l: a bhd* **16/1**

1m 11.42s (1.22) **Going Correction** +0.325s/f (Good) **8 Ran SP% 111.6**
Speed ratings (Par 103): **104,103,99,98,98 93,88,87**
CSF £17.03 CT £72.96 TOTE £3.10: £1.50, £1.90, £1.80; EX 18.30 Trifecta £93.80.
Owner Alan G Craddock **Bred** Shadwell Estate Company Limited **Trained** Lambourn, Berks

FOCUS
Race distance increased by 9yds. The first two finished nicely clear in this sprint handicap and this could possibly prove a bit above average.

1946 STREAMLINE TAXIS - OFFICIAL TRANSPORT PARTNER H'CAP 7f 214y
3:20 (3:20) (Class 4) (0-80,80) 3-Y-O+ **£4,690** (£1,395; £697; £348) **Stalls** Centre

Form RPR

0-41 1 **Ice Slice (IRE)**[14] 1546 5-9-7 76 RyanTate(3) 4 87
(James Eustace) *mde virtually all: kicked clr 2f out: comf* **5/2**[1]

113 2 4 **Mariee**[86] 495 3-9-1 80 FrannyNorton 5 79+
(Mark Johnston) *towards rr: hrd rdn and hdwy over 1f out: r.o to take 2nd ins fnl f* **3/1**[2]

01-2 3 2 **Mezzotint (IRE)**[8] 1702 7-10-0 80 OisinMurphy 6 77
(Lee Carter) *in tch: effrt in centre over 2f out: wnt 5 l 2nd over 1f out tl ins fnl f: one pce* **7/1**

15-0 4 3 3/4 **Kismet Hardy**[7] 1738 3-8-7 75 TomMarquand(3) 1 61
(Richard Hannon) *outpcd in rr: nvr rchd ldrs* **8/1**

0144 5 2 1/2 **Pour La Victoire (IRE)**[41] 1041 6-9-6 72 (b) LukeMorris 2 55
(Tony Carroll) *hld up in 5th: rdn to chse ldrs 2f out: wknd over 1f out* **11/2**[3]

60-0 6 3 1/2 **Live Dangerously**[14] 1546 6-9-6 72 WilliamCarson 7 47
(John Bridger) *prom: rdn 3f out: wknd 2f out* **16/1**

5- 7 1 1/4 **Henshaw**[199] 7302 3-8-13 78 DarryllHolland 3 47
(Charles Hills) *pressed wnr tl wknd 3f out* **8/1**

1m 36.0s **Going Correction** +0.325s/f (Good)
WFA 3 from 5yo+ 13lb **7 Ran SP% 109.6**
Speed ratings (Par 105): **113,109,107,103,100 97,96**
CSF £9.23 TOTE £2.80: £1.20, £2.00; EX 9.60 Trifecta £35.90.
Owner The MacDougall Two **Bred** Kilfrush Stud **Trained** Newmarket, Suffolk

FOCUS
Race distance increased by 9yds. A fair handicap. The winner has been rated back to his best.

1947 SUSSEX CLEANING & CARE - OFFICIAL CLEANING PARTNER H'CAP 1m 3f 196y
3:55 (3:55) (Class 5) (0-70,70) 4-Y-O+ **£2,911** (£866; £432; £216) **Stalls** High

Form RPR

20-5 1 **Hatsaway (IRE)**[20] 1413 5-9-0 63 JFEgan 2 72
(Pat Phelan) *chsd ldrs: squeezed through and led wl over 1f out: drvn out* **9/2**[3]

314- 2 hd **Flutterbee**[210] 7000 4-8-13 62 (p) SteveDrowne 1 70
(George Baker) *dwlt: hld up in rr: gd hdwy in centre to ld briefly 2f out: styd w wnr: r.o wl* **8/1**

133- 3 2 1/2 **Safira Menina**[210] 7000 4-8-11 63 TimClark(3) 4 67
(Martin Smith) *dwlt: hld up in 5th: hdwy to press ldrs 2f out: one pce fnl f* **8/1**

2-13 4 1 1/2 **Tempuran**[96] 358 7-9-7 70 OisinMurphy 5 72
(David Bridgwater) *chsd ldrs: led briefly over 2f out: one pce appr fnl f* **7/2**[1]

200- 5 4 **Highlife Dancer**[181] 7713 8-8-6 62 KillianHennessy(7) 6 58
(Mick Channon) *w ldr: led over 3f out tl over 2f out: wknd over 1f out* **13/2**

52-5 6 4 **Pink Ribbon (IRE)**[108] 212 4-9-1 64 (p) LukeMorris 3 53
(Sylvester Kirk) *led tl over 3f out: prom whn squeezed for room wl over 1f out: qckly lost pl* **5/1**

34-3 7 13 **China Girl (IND)**[5] 1808 4-9-5 68 RichardKingscote 8 36
(William Knight) *plld hrd in rr: rdn and lost tch 3f out* **4/1**[2]

2m 36.34s (3.64) **Going Correction** +0.325s/f (Good) **7 Ran SP% 112.6**
Speed ratings (Par 103): **100,99,98,97,94 91,83**
CSF £37.91 CT £276.14 TOTE £5.80: £3.30, £2.70; EX 44.10 Trifecta £242.10.
Owner P Wheatley **Bred** Grangecon Stud **Trained** Epsom, Surrey
■ Stewards' Enquiry : J F Egan one-day ban; careless riding (17th May)

FOCUS
Race distance increased by 9yds. They went fairly steady early on here. The fourth has been rated close to his turf form.

1948 LETSDOBUSINESS.ORG BRIGHTON 12 MAY CLASSIFIED STKS 1m 1f 209y
4:25 (4:25) (Class 6) 3-Y-O+ **£2,264** (£673; £336; £168) **Stalls** High

Form RPR

000- 1 **Hint Of Grey (IRE)**[195] 7397 3-7-12 32 GeorgeWood(7) 8 57
(Don Cantillon) *dwlt: towards rr: hrd rdn over 2f out: hdwy over 1f out: styd on to ld ins fnl f* **10/1**

25-4 2 2 **Tamujin (IRE)**[102] 294 8-9-1 49 (b) DavidParkes(5) 2 54
(Ken Cunningham-Brown) *dwlt: t.k.h in rr: hdwy in centre over 1f out: styd on to take 2nd ins fnl f* **28/1**

544- 3 1 **Edge (IRE)**[218] 6808 5-9-6 50 WilliamTwiston-Davies 3 52
(Bernard Llewellyn) *towards rr: hdwy over 2f out: led wl over 1f out: hung lft: hdd and no ex ins fnl f* **14/1**

000- 4 1/2 **Tyrannical**[224] 6628 3-8-5 53 LukeMorris 7 50
(Sir Mark Prescott Bt) *chsd ldrs: rdn and lost pl 5f out: rallied to press ldrs 2f out: one pce* **9/4**[1]

-060 5 1 1/4 **Frantical**[10] 1654 4-9-3 55 GeorgeDowning(3) 1 49
(Tony Carroll) *hld up in 6th: n.m.r and hdwy on inner over 2f out: cl 2nd whn hmpd on rail jst over 1f out: sn btn* **7/1**[3]

4361 6 3/4 **Solveig's Song**[55] 870 4-9-6 50 (p) WilliamCarson 5 47
(Steve Woodman) *in tch: rdn 4f out: pressed ldrs in centre over 2f out: sn outpcd* **17/2**

0330 7 6 **Togetherwecan (IRE)**[10] 1654 4-9-6 52 FrannyNorton 4 36
(Mark Johnston) *led tl 3f out: w ldrs tl wknd wl over 1f out* **8/1**

04-0 8 1 1/2 **Outback Princess**[7] 1734 3-8-5 53 KierenFox 10 32
(Gary Moore) *chsd ldr tl wknd 3f out* **12/1**

525 9 7 **Fitzwilliam**[7] 1742 4-9-6 53 SilvestreDeSousa 6 20
(Mick Channon) *prom: led 3f out tl hrd rdn and wknd wl over 1f out: eased whn btn fnl f* **3/1**[2]

2m 6.52s (2.92) **Going Correction** +0.325s/f (Good)
WFA 3 from 4yo+ 15lb **9 Ran SP% 116.8**
Speed ratings (Par 101): **101,99,98,98,97 96,91,90,85**
CSF £244.71 TOTE £12.90: £2.40, £5.20, £4.10; EX 358.70 Trifecta £1154.80.
Owner Mrs Catherine Reed **Bred** Kildaragh Stud **Trained** Newmarket, Suffolk
■ Stewards' Enquiry : George Downing one-day ban; careless riding (17th May)
George Wood two-day ban; used whip above permitted level (17th-18th May)

FOCUS
Race distance increased by 9yds. A weak race. The third has been rated to his end-of-2015 level.

1949 ACTIONCHALLENGE.COM LONDON2BRIGHTON 16 MAY H'CAP 6f 209y
4:55 (4:55) (Class 6) (0-60,60) 4-Y-O+ **£2,264** (£673; £336; £168) **Stalls** Centre

Form RPR

4553 1 **Hawk Moth (IRE)**[6] 1781 8-9-2 55 (p) LukeMorris 6 63
(John Spearing) *towards rr on outer: hdwy over 1f out: r.o to ld nr fin* **5/1**[2]

5-06 2 1/2 **Deluxe**[63] 773 4-9-0 60 PaddyBradley(7) 7 67
(Pat Phelan) *prom: drvn to chal ins fnl f: r.o* **6/1**[3]

0432 3 nk **Wild Flower (IRE)**[14] 1544 4-8-11 50 KieranO'Neill 11 56
(Jimmy Fox) *led: hrd rdn 2f out: kpt on fnl f: hdd nr fin* **7/2**[1]

04-0 4 1/2 **Mrs Warren**[27] 1262 6-9-6 59 SteveDrowne 10 64
(George Baker) *dwlt: bhd: rdn 3f out: gd hdwy fnl f* **17/2**

0005 5 3/4 **Just Marion (IRE)**[6] 1781 4-8-2 46 oh1 PaddyPilley(5) 5 49
(James Grassick) *chsd ldrs: wnt 2nd wl over 1f out tl ins fnl f: kpt on* **66/1**

6 hd **Zephyros (GER)**[185] 5-9-7 60 JimmyQuinn 2 64+
(David Bridgwater) *chsd ldrs: lost pl and n.m.r 2f out: styd on fnl f* **16/1**

04-0 7 1/2 **Indus Valley (IRE)**[116] 97 9-9-1 54 (b) OisinMurphy 8 55
(Lee Carter) *towards rr: rdn and hdwy over 1f out: no imp fnl f* **14/1**

334 8 1 1/2 **Bold Max**[54] 895 5-8-10 49 (p) SilvestreDeSousa 9 46
(Zoe Davison) *w ldr: hrd rdn over 1f out: wknd ins fnl f* **22/1**

1331 9 1 1/4 **Little Indian**[41] 1042 6-9-5 58 FrederikTylicki 3 52
(J R Jenkins) *mid-div on outer: rdn over 2f out: no ex fnl f* **15/2**

6-00 **10** ¾ **Titus Secret**[6] [1794] 4-8-7 **46** oh1 .... CathyGannon 4 40
(Malcolm Saunders) *plld hrd in rr: rdn 2f out: nvr trbld ldrs* **14/1**

5436 **11** 5 **Gulland Rock**[14] [1544] 5-9-3 **56** .... WilliamCarson 1 34+
(Anthony Carson) *rring in stalls: mid-div: rdn 3f out: wknd over 1f out* **13/2**

1m 24.86s (1.76) **Going Correction** +0.325s/f (Good) **11** Ran SP% **113.9**
Speed ratings (Par 101): **102,101,101,100,99 99,98,97,95,94 89**
CSF £33.89 CT £119.57 TOTE £6.10: £2.50, £2.40, £1.50; EX 38.20 Trifecta £162.20.
Owner Kinnersley Partnership **Bred** Dr D Harron **Trained** Kinnersley, Worcs

FOCUS
Race distance increased by 9yds. A moderate handicap. The third limits the form.

1950 BHF.ORG.UK LONDON TO BRIGHTON 19 JUNE H'CAP 5f 59y
5:25 (5:27) (Class 5) (0-70,70) 4-Y-O+ **£2,911** (£866; £432; £216) **Stalls** Centre

Form RPR

U6-4 **1** **Whitecrest**[6] [1782] 8-9-6 **69** .... LukeMorris 6 76
(John Spearing) *chsd ldrs: outpcd wl over 1f out: str run to ld fnl 50yds* **7/1**

3401 **2** 1 **Secret Millionaire (IRE)**[14] [1549] 9-8-11 **63** .... (p) TomMarquand(3) 3 66
(Shaun Harris) *bhd: hdwy on inner to ld wl over 1f out: hdd and outpcd by wnr fnl 50yds* **5/1**[3]

240- **3** nk **Ada Lovelace**[134] [8331] 6-9-2 **70** .... PatrickO'Donnell(5) 1 72
(John Gallagher) *prom: rdn 2f out: kpt on fnl f* **4/1**[2]

4636 **4** ¾ **Zipedeedodah (IRE)**[19] [1433] 4-8-13 **62** .... (t) OisinMurphy 2 61
(Joseph Tuite) *in tch: effrt and hrd rdn over 1f out: kpt on fnl f* **11/2**

5001 **5** nk **Picansort**[34] [1150] 9-8-9 **58** .... (b) ShaneKelly 5 56
(Peter Crate) *towards rr: rdn over 2f out: styng on wl at fin* **11/2**

0-02 **6** 12 **Royal Bajan (USA)**[6] [1782] 8-9-7 **70** .... (p) SilvestreDeSousa 4 26
(Robert Cowell) *led at str pce tl wl over 1f out: wknd ent fnl f: eased whn btn* **15/8**[1]

1m 3.52s (1.22) **Going Correction** +0.325s/f (Good) **6** Ran SP% **114.7**
Speed ratings (Par 103): **103,101,100,99,99 80**
CSF £41.69 TOTE £8.60: £2.70, £2.40; EX 45.00 Trifecta £130.00.
Owner G M Eales **Bred** J Spearing And Kate Ive **Trained** Kinnersley, Worcs

FOCUS
Race distance increased by 9yds. A modest sprint run at a good gallop. The runner-up has been rated close to his latest 6f form.
T/Jkpt: Not won. T/Plt: £752.20 to a £1 stake. Pool: £69,285.50 - 67.24 winning tickets. T/Qpdt: £163.70 to a £1 stake. Pool: £5,406.18 - 24.43 winning tickets. **Lee McKenzie**

1558 CATTERICK (L-H)
Tuesday, May 3

OFFICIAL GOING: Good to soft (good in places; 7.5)
Wind: Moderate half against Weather: Cloudy with sunny periods

1951 CATTERICK BADGEHOLDERS' GUEST EVENING FILLIES' NOVICE AUCTION STKS (PLUS 10 RACE) 5f
5:55 (5:56) (Class 5) 2-Y-O **£2,911** (£866; £432; £216) **Stalls** Low

Form RPR

2 **1** **Clem Fandango (FR)**[12] [1583] 2-9-0 0 .... PhillipMakin 8 82+
(Keith Dalgleish) *trckd ldr: cl up 1/2-way: led 1 1/2f out: pushed clr fnl f: readily* **4/6**[1]

0 **2** 4½ **Poppy Pivot (IRE)**[26] [1293] 2-9-0 0 .... PJMcDonald 6 63
(Ann Duffield) *trckd ldrs: hdwy 2f out: sn rdn: styd on fnl f* **16/1**

42 **3** 2¾ **Merry Banter**[22] [1377] 2-9-0 0 .... GrahamLee 1 53
(Paul Midgley) *led: jnd 1/2-way and sn pushed along: rdn and hdd 1 1/2f out: grad wknd* **9/2**[2]

4 1½ **Best Bid (IRE)** 2-9-0 0 .... JasonHart 4 48
(John Quinn) *dwlt and in rr: pushed along and hdwy 1/2-way: rdn wl over 1f out: kpt on fnl f* **20/1**

5 ¾ **Limbrick** 2-9-0 0 .... TonyHamilton 7 45
(Richard Fahey) *chsd ldng pair: rdn along 2f out: sn wknd* **15/2**[3]

6 6 **Miss Monro (IRE)** 2-9-0 0 .... BenCurtis 3 23
(Brian Ellison) *in rr and sn rdn along: outpcd and bhd fr 1/2-way* **22/1**

0 **7** 9 **Red Shanghai (IRE)**[12] [1583] 2-9-0 0 .... GrahamGibbons 2
(Tom Dascombe) *chsd ldrs: rdn along 1/2-way: sn wknd and bhd* **33/1**

1m 1.69s (1.89) **Going Correction** +0.225s/f (Good) **7** Ran SP% **107.9**
Speed ratings (Par 90): **93,85,81,79,77 68,53**
CSF £10.91 TOTE £1.70: £1.50, £4.10; EX 11.10 Trifecta £33.40.
Owner Middleham Park Racing LXXV **Bred** John Raw **Trained** Carluke, S Lanarks

FOCUS
Race distance as advertised. Not a particularly strong juvenile event and the favourite was much too good. It's not easy to pin the level of the form.

1952 RACING UK DAY PASS JUST £10 CLAIMING STKS 1m 3f 214y
6:25 (6:25) (Class 6) 4-Y-O+ **£2,264** (£673; £336; £168) **Stalls** Centre

Form RPR

4-13 **1** **Chilworth Bells**[12] [1588] 4-9-8 73 .... JosephineGordon(5) 8 79
(David Barron) *cl up: led over 4f out: pushed along 2f out: jnd and rdn jst over 1f out: kpt on gamely towards fin* **2/1**[1]

1143 **2** nk **Tatting**[21] [1404] 7-8-11 77 .... PaulMulrennan 7 63
(Conor Dore) *hld up towards rr: hdwy and in tch over 4f out: effrt 2f out: swtchd lft and rdn to chal over 1f out: drvn and ev ch ins fnl f: no ex nr fin* **11/4**[3]

560- **3** 5 **Itlaaq**[356] [2195] 10-8-10 79 .... (t) NathanEvans(5) 5 59
(Michael Easterby) *hld up in rr: hdwy over 3f out: effrt to chse ldrs wl over 1f out: rdn ent fnl f and kpt on same pce* **5/2**[2]

56-0 **4** 10 **Al Furat (USA)**[9] [1675] 8-9-0 45 .... (p) PhilDennis(5) 4 47
(Ron Barr) *t.k.h early: trckd ldrs: hdwy over 3f out: chsd wnr 2f out: sn rdn and one pce fr over 1f out* **100/1**

510- **5** 1½ **Fillydelphia (IRE)**[179] [6820] 5-9-0 56 .... JackGarritty 9 39
(Patrick Holmes) *cl up: chsd wnr over 4f out: rdn along over 2f out: drvn wl over 1f out: sn wknd* **16/1**

35-0 **6** 9 **Carragold**[17] [1501] 10-9-5 69 .... PJMcDonald 1 30
(Antony Brittain) *trckd ldrs on inner: pushed along over 4f out: rdn along over 3f out: wknd over 2f out* **9/1**

400- **7** 13 **Testing (FR)**[168] [7543] 5-8-8 49 .... JamesSullivan 3
(David Thompson) *in tch: pushed along 1/2-way: rdn along over 4f out: outpcd and bhd fnl 3f* **100/1**

5440 **8** hd **Monzino (USA)**[21] [1405] 8-8-10 40 .... NoelGarbutt(5) 6 5
(Michael Chapman) *a in rr: rdn along and bhd fr over 4f out* **100/1**

000/ **9** dist **Rising Rainbow**[561] [7332] 5-8-13 15 .... (b) RaulDaSilva 2
(Ivan Furtado) *slt ld: racd wd bk st: hdd over 4f out: sn rdn along and lost pl: rn v wd home turn to stands' rails: t.o and eased over 1f out* **28/1**

2m 43.82s (4.92) **Going Correction** +0.325s/f (Good) **9** Ran SP% **110.9**
Speed ratings (Par 101): **96,95,92,85,84 78,70,70,4**
CSF £7.17 TOTE £4.10: £2.50, £1.10, £1.20; EX 11.50 Trifecta £20.70.
Owner Harrowgate Bloodstock Ltd **Bred** Norman Court Stud **Trained** Maunby, N Yorks

FOCUS
Race run over 12yds further than advertised. The market leaders dominated this claimer. The winner did not need to improve to score.

1953 BOOK NOW FOR 20TH MAY MAIDEN STKS 7f
6:55 (6:57) (Class 5) 3-Y-O+ **£2,911** (£866; £432; £216) **Stalls** Low

Form RPR

1 **Dutch Artist (IRE)**[583] [6797] 4-10-0 0 .... DanielTudhope 4 83+
(David O'Meara) *trckd ldr: hdwy and cl up over 2f out: rdn wl over 1f out: drvn ins fnl f: styd on to ld nr line* **11/4**[2]

3 **2** nk **Musdam (USA)**[24] [1339] 3-9-2 0 .... GrahamGibbons 3 79
(Sir Michael Stoute) *trckd ldng pair: hdwy over 2f out: chal over 1f out: rdn to ld ent fnl f: green and sn edgd lft: hung lft ins last 50yds: awkward and hdd nr line* **5/4**[1]

53 **3** ¾ **Just Hiss**[12] [1589] 3-9-2 0 .... DavidAllan 2 76
(Tim Easterby) *led: rdn along wl over 1f out: hdd ent fnl f and sn drvn: keeping on wl on inner whn n.m.r last 100yds and again nr line* **11/4**[2]

0- **4** 11 **Tallulah Fleur**[190] [7515] 3-8-11 0 .... PJMcDonald 5 41
(Ann Duffield) *chsd ldrs: rdn along over 2f out: sn one pce* **16/1**

00-0 **5** 6 **Grenade**[13] [1565] 4-10-0 44 .... DavidNolan 1 34
(Patrick Holmes) *chsd ldrs: rdn along wl over 2f out: sn outpcd* **100/1**

6 1¼ **Oyster Card** 3-9-2 0 .... AndrewMullen 7 27
(Michael Appleby) *in tch: rdn along wl over 2f out: sn outpcd* **14/1**[3]

420- **7** 7 **Playboy Bay**[182] [7675] 4-9-9 59 .... (p) PhilDennis(5) 9 12
(Ron Barr) *a in rr* **33/1**

0 **8** 24 **Striking Nigella**[11] [1597] 6-9-4 0 .... NoelGarbutt(5) 6
(Michael Chapman) *dwlt: a bhd* **200/1**

1m 28.51s (1.51) **Going Correction** +0.325s/f (Good)
WFA 3 from 4yo+ 12lb **8** Ran SP% **114.8**
Speed ratings (Par 103): **104,103,102,90,83 81,73,46**
CSF £6.59 TOTE £3.80: £1.20, £1.10, £2.00; EX 6.80 Trifecta £14.20.
Owner N D Crummack & D Lumley **Bred** Limestone & Tara Studs **Trained** Upper Helmsley, N Yorks

■ The Cheese Gang (100-1) was withdrawn. Rule 4 does not apply.
■ Stewards' Enquiry : Graham Gibbons one-day ban; careless riding (17th May)

FOCUS
Race run over 12yds further than advertised. Only three looked to matter here and there was little between them at the line. A Stewards' inquiry was called after the runner-up edged across the third close home, and in doing so losing momentum as his rider had to correct him. It probably didn't make a difference to the result, although the margins were narrow. The runner-up set a good standard and it's been rated around him.

1954 CATTERICKBRIDGE.CO.UK H'CAP 7f
7:25 (7:26) (Class 4) (0-80,80) 4-Y-O+ **£6,469** (£1,925; £962; £481) **Stalls** Low

Form RPR

-502 **1** **Taysh (USA)**[13] [1563] 4-9-6 **79** .... BenCurtis 10 89
(Michael Appleby) *trckd ldr: led wl over 2f out: rdn wl over 1f out: drvn out* **3/1**[2]

6-26 **2** 3 **Dr Red Eye**[7] [1746] 8-8-8 **67** .... (p) PJMcDonald 7 69
(Scott Dixon) *led: jnd over 3f out: rdn and hdd wl over 2f out: sn drvn: kpt on wl u.p fnl f* **15/2**[3]

0-03 **3** hd **Gurkha Friend**[8] [1694] 4-9-5 **78** .... GrahamLee 9 79
(Karen McLintock) *hld up: effrt 3f out and sn pushed along: rdn and hdwy wl over 1f out: styd on fnl f: nrst fin* **11/4**[1]

516- **4** ¾ **Ski Blast**[238] [6195] 5-9-1 **74** .... DavidNolan 5 73
(Ivan Furtado) *towards rr: hdwy over 2f out: sn rdn: styd on appr fnl f: nrst fin* **12/1**

010- **5** 1 **Nonno Giulio (IRE)**[241] [6109] 5-8-10 **74** .... JoshDoyle(5) 1 71
(David Loughnane) *chsd ldrs: rdn along wl over 2f out: drvn wl over 1f out: kpt on same pce* **22/1**

00-0 **6** ½ **Dreese (IRE)**[17] [1488] 5-8-8 **70** .... JacobButterfield(3) 11 65
(Marjorie Fife) *s.i.s and bhd: rdn along 1/2-way: hdwy 2f out: styd on fnl f: nrst fin* **33/1**

120- **7** 2 **Jay Kay**[199] [7288] 7-9-4 **77** .... JoeyHaynes 3 67
(K R Burke) *chsd ldrs on inner: rdn along over 2f out: drvn wl over 1f out: sn one pce* **9/1**

4-0U **8** 1 **Musaaid (IRE)**[13] [1563] 4-8-13 **77** .... NathanEvans(5) 2 64
(Michael Easterby) *hld up towards rr: sme hdwy on outer 1/2-way: rdn along over 2f out: n.d* **8/1**

0-01 **9** 10 **Favourite Treat (USA)**[11] [1595] 6-9-1 **74** .... (e) JamesSullivan 8 34
(Ruth Carr) *chsd ldrs: rdn along wl over 2f out: sn drvn and wknd* **15/2**[3]

1m 28.38s (1.38) **Going Correction** +0.325s/f (Good) **9** Ran SP% **111.3**
Speed ratings (Par 105): **105,101,101,100,99 98,96,95,83**
CSF £24.36 CT £64.94 TOTE £4.10: £1.80, £2.50, £1.50; EX 24.50 Trifecta £74.90.
Owner Craig Buckingham **Bred** Normandy Farm Llc **Trained** Oakham, Rutland

FOCUS
Race run over 12yds further than advertised. Little got into this, the first two home being in the front pair throughout, and the winner did it nicely. The form has been taken at face value, with the runner-up rated to his penultimate C&D form.

1955 GO RACING IN YORKSHIRE H'CAP 1m 7f 177y
7:55 (7:59) (Class 6) (0-65,65) 4-Y-O+ **£2,587** (£770; £384; £192) **Stalls** Low

Form RPR

23/3 **1** **Summerlea (IRE)**[36] [1121] 10-8-9 **48** .... JackGarritty 4 61
(Micky Hammond) *trckd ldrs: hdwy 5f out and sn cl up: led 3f out: sn jnd and rdn wl over 1f out: slt ld and drvn ins fnl f: hld on gamely towards fin* **7/1**[3]

11 **2** shd **Eurato (FR)**[32] [1182] 6-9-4 **57** .... (p) PaulMulrennan 3 70
(Steve Gollings) *trckd ldrs: hdwy over 4f out: chsd wnr wl over 2f out and sn cl up: chal wl over 1f out and sn rdn: drvn and ev ch ins fnl f: jst failed* **11/4**[1]

0-04 **3** 6 **Triple Eight (IRE)**[13] [1561] 8-9-12 **65** .... JoeFanning 6 71
(Philip Kirby) *hld up: stdy hdwy over 3f out: rdn along to chse ldrs wl over 1f out: styd on fnl f* **16/1**

55-0 **4** ¾ **Duke Of Diamonds**[20] [1413] 4-8-10 **55** .... ShelleyBirkett(3) 11 60
(Julia Feilden) *prom: effrt 3f out and sn cl up: rdn along 2f out: drvn and kpt on same pce appr fnl f* **10/1**

20-0 **5** *1 3/4* **Balmusette**[36] 1123 7-9-2 **55** .... JamesSullivan 10 58+
(Keith Reveley) *hld up towards rr: hdwy on outer 3f out: rdn wl over 1f out: styd on fnl f* **4/1**[2]

60-0 **6** *1/2* **Pertuis (IRE)**[13] 1560 10-9-9 **62** .... GrahamLee 7 64
(Micky Hammond) *hld up towards rr: hdwy over 3f out: chsd ldrs 2f out: sn rdn and kpt on same pce* **20/1**

0-16 **7** *2* **Desktop**[35] 1136 4-9-3 **59** .... PJMcDonald 12 59
(Antony Brittain) *t.k.h: trckd ldrs: led after 7f: pushed along and hdd 3f out: sn drvn and wknd* **8/1**

323- **8** *3/4* **Silver Shuffle (IRE)**[37] 7187 9-9-6 **62** .... MissEmmaSayer(3) 14 61
(Dianne Sayer) *hld up in rr: hdwy wl over 2f out: sn rdn and plugged on fr over 1f out* **12/1**

00-6 **9** *9* **Nashville (IRE)**[36] 1121 7-9-7 **60** .... NeilFarley 1 48
(Andrew Crook) *a towards rr* **33/1**

565/ **10** *11* **Sory**[88] 7078 9-8-11 **50** .... DougieCostello 2 25
(Tina Jackson) *nvr bttr than midfield* **80/1**

5405 **11** *8* **Yorkshireman (IRE)**[35] 1136 6-8-8 **47** .... JoeyHaynes 15 12
(Lynn Siddall) *prom: rdn along over 5f out: sn wknd* **25/1**

0-32 **12** *6* **Madam Lilibet (IRE)**[15] 1523 7-9-7 **65** .... PhilDennis(5) 13 23
(Sharon Watt) *in tch on outer: pushed along after 5f: rdn and lost pl qckly 1/2-way: sn bhd* **12/1**

30-0 **13** *61* **Ullswater (IRE)**[21] 1399 8-9-4 **57** ....(tp) TonyHamilton 5
(Philip Kirby) *led 7f: chsd ldr tl rdn along and lost pl over 4f out: sn bhd* **50/1**

3m 38.29s (6.29) **Going Correction** +0.325s/f (Good)
WFA 4 from 5yo+ 3lb **13** Ran SP% **115.4**
Speed ratings (Par 101): **97,96,93,93,92 92,91,91,86,81 77,74,43**
CSF £24.21 CT £300.06 TOTE £8.70: £3.20, £1.50, £3.50; EX 36.80 Trifecta £567.10.
Owner Oakwood Minions **Bred** Mrs Clodagh McStay **Trained** Middleham, N Yorks
■ Fair Trade (25-1) was withdrawn. Rule 4 does not apply.
■ Stewards' Enquiry : Paul Mulrennan four-day ban; used whip above permitted level (17th-20th May)

FOCUS
Race run over 24yds further than advertised. No great gallop on here and the front pair came clear. Moderate form. The winner has been rated to his 2014 level.

1956 DON'T MISS SATURDAY 28TH MAY H'CAP 5f
8:25 (8:25) (Class 5) (0-75,74) 4-Y-O+ **£2,911** (£866; £432; £216) **Stalls** Low

Form RPR

1222 **1** **Elusivity (IRE)**[4] 1827 8-9-7 **74** ....(p) PaulMulrennan 1 82
(Conor Dore) *qckly away: mde all: rdn over 1f out and kpt on strly* **7/4**[1]

-531 **2** *3* **Henley**[4] 1843 4-9-4 **71** 6ex .... JoeFanning 6 68
(Tracy Waggott) *chsd wnr: rdn wl over 1f out: drvn ins fnl f: no imp towards fin* **5/2**[2]

1414 **3** *2* **Hit The Lights (IRE)**[6] 1790 6-8-10 **70** ....(v) DanielleMooney(7) 7 60
(David Nicholls) *chsd ldrs on outer: hdwy 2f out: sn rdn: drvn and kpt on same pce fnl f* **9/2**[3]

0406 **4** *3 1/4* **Prigsnov Dancer (IRE)**[17] 1481 11-8-5 **63** .... NoelGarbutt(5) 3 41
(Deborah Sanderson) *towards rr: rdn along 1/2-way: kpt on u.p fnl f* **25/1**

4-06 **5** *1/2* **Groundworker (IRE)**[15] 1525 5-9-0 **67** .... GrahamLee 5 44
(Paul Midgley) *prom: rdn along over 2f out: sn drvn and wknd* **16/1**

233- **6** *1 3/4* **Imperial Legend (IRE)**[188] 7565 7-9-6 **73** .... PaulQuinn 2 43
(David Nicholls) *a towards rr* **8/1**

220- **7** *5* **Majestic Manannan (IRE)**[213] 6936 7-8-9 **62** .... AndrewMullen 4 14
(David Nicholls) *in tch on inner: rdn along 2f out: sn wknd* **12/1**

1m 0.31s (0.51) **Going Correction** +0.225s/f (Good) **7** Ran SP% **111.6**
Speed ratings (Par 103): **104,99,96,90,90 87,79**
CSF £5.94 CT £14.79 TOTE £2.90: £1.90, £1.80; EX 6.20 Trifecta £15.70.
Owner Mrs Louise Marsh **Bred** J Costello **Trained** Hubbert's Bridge, Lincs

FOCUS
Race distance as advertised. They headed centre-field in the straight and little got into it, the front pair holding their positions. The winner has been rated to his best form for this yard.
T/Plt: £6.80 to a £1 stake. Pool: £62,742.00 - 6,647.64 winning tickets. T/Qpdt: £4.50 to a £1 stake. Pool: £5,333.00 - 871.95 winning tickets. **Joe Rowntree**

JAGERSRO (R-H)
Tuesday, May 3

OFFICIAL GOING: Dirt: standard

1957a PRAMMS MEMORIAL (LISTED RACE) (4YO+) (DIRT) 1m 143y(D)
7:55 (12:00) 4-Y-O+ **£56,270** (£20,096; £10,450; £4,823; £4,823)

RPR

1 **Hurricane Red (IRE)**[173] 6-9-4 0 .... JacobJohansen 4 99
(Lennart Reuterskiold Jr, Sweden) **13/4**[2]

2 *hd* **Silver Ocean (USA)**[75] 628 8-9-4 0 .... ElioneChaves 11 99
(Niels Petersen, Norway) **69/10**

3 *1 1/4* **Famous Mark (MOR)**[183] 4-9-4 0 .... AbderrahimFaddoul 10 96
(P Bary, France) **16/1**

4 *1 1/2* **Avon Pearl**[61] 812 7-9-4 0 ....(b) CarlosLopez 3 93
(Rune Haugen) **19/2**

4 *dht* **Giftorm (USA)**[68] 717 6-9-4 0 .... OliverWilson 8 93
(Fredrik Reuterskiold, Sweden) **9/2**[3]

6 *8* **Brownie (FR)**[202] 4-9-4 0 .... RafaelSchistl 12 75
(Bent Olsen, Denmark) **47/1**

7 *1 1/4* **Nordico (GER)**[23] 1376 5-9-4 0 ....(p) AndreasSuborics 5 73
(Mario Hofer, Germany) **12/1**

8 *2 1/2* **Captain Joy (IRE)**[39] 1068 7-9-4 0 .... ChrisHayes 1 67
(Tracey Collins, Ire) *trckd ldr: rdn to ld 3f out: hdd appr st: no ex and btn: wknd* **19/10**[1]

9 *1/2* **Energia Colonial (BRZ)**[75] 624 8-9-4 0 .... Per-AndersGraberg 2 66
(Niels Petersen, Norway) **21/1**

10 *3/4* **Giovanni Boldini (USA)**[226] 5-9-4 0 .... NikolajStott 9 64
(Flemming Velin, Denmark) **39/1**

11 *1* **Coprah**[13] 8-9-4 0 .... NelsonDeSouza 6 62
(Cathrine Erichsen, Norway) **62/1**

12 *dist* **Dickie Dickens (NOR)**[170] 6-9-4 0 ....(b) MarcosRobaldo 7
(Are Hyldmo, Norway) **37/1**

1m 46.0s (106.00) **12** Ran SP% **125.3**

Owner Stall Zada **Bred** Grangemore Stud **Trained** Sweden

1799 CHELMSFORD (A.W) (L-H)
Wednesday, May 4

OFFICIAL GOING: Polytrack: standard
Wind: light, half behind Weather: sunny

1958 SCOOP6SOCCER THE £1 MILLION FOOTBALL BET H'CAP 6f (P)
5:45 (5:45) (Class 3) (0-90,89) 4-Y-O+ **£8,894** (£2,646; £1,322; £661) **Stalls** Centre

Form RPR

151R **1** **Gentlemen**[6] 1801 5-9-1 **88** .... JosephineGordon(5) 4 97
(Phil McEntee) *taken down early and led to post: s.i.s: swtchd lft and hdwy u.p over 1f out: styd on wl to ld fnl 100yds: a doing enough after: rdn out* **7/1**

-330 **2** *1/2* **Patrick (IRE)**[45] 1015 4-9-7 **89** .... TonyHamilton 9 96
(Richard Fahey) *taken down early: hld up in tch in last trio: hdwy towards inner over 1f out: rdn to ld jst ins fnl f: drvn and hdd 100yds out: kpt on but a hld after* **5/1**[3]

6204 **3** *1 1/2* **Borough Boy (IRE)**[11] 1634 6-8-12 **80** ....(v) MartinLane 1 82
(Derek Shaw) *broke wl: stdd bk and t.k.h in midfield: clsd and nt clr run over 1f out: gap opened and drvn 1f out: outpcd fnl 100yds* **8/1**

0211 **4** *nk* **Merhoob (IRE)**[27] 1291 4-8-12 **80** .... ShaneKelly 5 81
(John Ryan) *dwlt and pushed along early: rcvrd and hdwy to trck ldrs after 1f: shkn up to ld over 1f out: drvn and hrd pressed 1f out: sn hdd and no ex: outpcd fnl 100yds* **9/2**[2]

5132 **5** *1 1/4* **Burning Blaze**[11] 1625 6-8-2 **77** .... GeorgeWood(7) 7 74
(Brian Ellison) *in tch in midfield: effrt over 1f out: edgd lft and styd on same pce ins fnl f* **6/1**

1-25 **6** *4* **Under Siege (IRE)**[42] 1040 4-8-10 **78** .... MartinHarley 8 62
(David Simcock) *hld up in tch: effrt u.p over 1f out: no imp 1f out: btn whn sltly hmpd ins fnl f: wknd fnl 100yds* **10/3**[1]

-026 **7** *3/4* **Penny Dreadful**[27] 1291 4-8-7 **75** oh1 ....(p) LukeMorris 2 57
(Scott Dixon) *led: rdn and hdd over 1f out: no ex and u.p 1f out: sn wknd* **20/1**

60-1 **8** *2 1/4* **Munfallet (IRE)**[11] 1634 5-9-6 **88** .... SeanLevey 6 63
(David Brown) *chsd ldng pair: rdn over 2f out: lost pl and btn over 1f out: bhd ins fnl f* **8/1**

5062 **9** *shd* **Crosse Fire**[6] 1801 4-9-7 **89** ....(p) DaleSwift 3 64
(Scott Dixon) *racd keenly: chsd ldr: rdn over 2f out: lost pl over 1f out: bhd ins fnl f* **16/1**

1m 13.06s (-0.64) **Going Correction** +0.15s/f (Slow) **9** Ran SP% **117.6**
Speed ratings (Par 107): **110,109,107,106,105 99,98,95,95**
CSF £42.68 CT £291.71 TOTE £4.80: £2.60, £2.30, £2.90; EX 34.60 Trifecta £211.90.
Owner Eventmaker Racehorses **Bred** Mrs Eleanor Kent **Trained** Newmarket, Suffolk

FOCUS
Those ridden with a bit of patience came to the fore in this sprint handicap. Another pb from the winner, a small pb from the runner-up, with the third rated close to form.

1959 BET SCOOP6SOCCER AT BETFRED SHOPS H'CAP 1m (P)
6:15 (6:15) (Class 2) (0-100,93) 4-Y-O+ **£12,938** (£3,850; £1,924; £962) **Stalls** Low

Form RPR

1320 **1** **Supersta**[20] 1441 5-9-7 **93** ....(p) AndrewMullen 7 100
(Michael Appleby) *t.k.h: hld up in tch in midfield: effrt over 1f out: hdwy to chal and edging lft ins fnl f: led fnl 50yds: sn in command and r.o wl* **6/1**[3]

0203 **2** *3/4* **Unforgiving Minute**[14] 1576 5-9-5 **91** .... WilliamTwiston-Davies 4 96
(Gary Moore) *t.k.h: chsd ldng pair: rdn to ld over 1f out: sn drvn: kpt on wl tl hdd and one pce fnl 50yds* **7/2**[2]

3425 **3** *1 1/4* **Truth Or Dare**[39] 1088 5-9-6 **92** .... MartinDwyer 2 95
(William Muir) *hld up in tch in midfield: effrt in 4th 2f out: swtchd rt and rdn to press ldrs jst over 1f out: stl pressing ldrs whn squeezed for room wl ins fnl f* **2/1**[1]

3431 **4** *1 1/2* **Jodies Jem**[21] 1418 6-8-11 **86** .... TomMarquand(3) 1 85
(William Jarvis) *chsd ldr: rdn and ev ch over 1f out: drvn and no ex jst ins fnl f: outpcd fnl 100yds* **7/2**[2]

/0-0 **5** *1* **Burn The Boats (IRE)**[32] 1204 7-9-4 **90** .... TedDurcan 3 86
(Mike Murphy) *stdd s: t.k.h: hld up in tch in rr: effrt u.p over 1f out: styd on same pce ins fnl f* **14/1**

3033 **6** *1/2* **Elis Eliz (IRE)**[46] 1003 4-8-8 **87** .... GeorgeWood(7) 5 82
(Michael Wigham) *in tch in midfield: effrt over 1f out: struggling to qckn whn sltly impeded jst over 1f out: styd on same pce ins fnl f* **11/1**

140/ **7** *4* **Storm King**[572] 7081 7-9-0 **86** ....(p) LukeMorris 9 72
(David C Griffiths) *led: c centre st: sn rdn and hdd: wknd 1f out* **25/1**

300- **8** *1/2* **Pastoral Player**[204] 7177 9-8-10 **89** .... CharlieBennett(7) 10 74
(Hughie Morrison) *taken down early: stdd and dropped in bhd after s: hld up in tch in rr: effrt over 1f out: no prog* **20/1**

1m 39.82s (-0.08) **Going Correction** +0.15s/f (Slow) **8** Ran SP% **115.7**
Speed ratings (Par 109): **106,105,104,102,101 101,97,96**
CSF £27.64 CT £57.13 TOTE £6.50: £1.60, £1.50, £1.20; EX 16.20 Trifecta £62.90.
Owner Rod In Pickle Partnership **Bred** Cheveley Park Stud Ltd **Trained** Oakham, Rutland

FOCUS
The early gallop wasn't particularly strong but the winner still got there from off the pace. The third has been rated to his winter 1m form.

1960 BET SCOOP6SOCCER AT BETFRED.COM FILLIES' H'CAP 1m (P)
6:45 (6:45) (Class 3) (0-90,84) 3-Y-O **£8,894** (£2,646; £1,322; £661) **Stalls** Low

Form RPR

134- **1** **Mise En Rose (USA)**[207] 7112 3-9-7 **84** .... WilliamBuick 5 94
(Charlie Appleby) *chsd ldrs: effrt in 4th jst over 2f out: rdn to ld over 1f out: asserted and edgd lft jst ins fnl f: styd on wl: readily* **9/4**[2]

2-1 **2** *2 3/4* **Shaan (IRE)**[112] 163 3-9-6 **83** .... FrankieDettori 4 86
(Richard Hannon) *chsd ldr: rdn to ld wl over 1f out: sn hdd: styd on same pce ins fnl f* **7/4**[1]

012- **3** *2* **Indigo**[188] 7577 3-8-1 **69** .... JosephineGordon(5) 2 67
(Mark Usher) *chsd ldrs: effrt jst over 2f out: 3rd and styd on same pce fnl f* **25/1**

615- **4** *3* **Sepal (USA)**[223] 6684 3-8-10 **76** .... TomMarquand(3) 7 67
(Charles Hills) *bustled along leaving stalls: hdwy u.p but stl plenty to do over 1f out: kpt on fnl f: no ch w ldrs* **11/1**

U21- **5** *2 1/4* **Lilly Vega (IRE)**[160] 7998 3-8-9 **72** .... JoeyHaynes 1 58
(K R Burke) *led: rdn ent fnl 2f: hdd wl over 1f out: sn outpcd: wknd fnl f* **5/1**[3]

61- **6** *4* **Auntinet**[140] 8253 3-9-1 **78** .... NickyMackay 8 54
(John Gosden) *hld up in tch: hdwy on outer to chse ldrs 4f out: rdn and lost pl over 2f out: wl btn over 1f out* **7/1**

1-6 **7** *1* **Sweet Temptation (IRE)**[103] 296 3-8-13 **76**................ SaleemGolam 3 50
(Stuart Williams) *hld up in tch in last trio: rdn over 2f out: no hdwy: bhd over 1f out* **25/1**

623- **8** *1* **Hidden Treasures**[138] 8280 3-8-12 **75**............................ TonyHamilton 6 46
(Richard Fahey) *hld up in tch in last trio: effrt over 2f out: sn struggling: bhd over 1f out* **20/1**

1m 39.83s (-0.07) **Going Correction** +0.15s/f (Slow) **8** Ran SP% **117.1**
Speed ratings (Par 100): **106,103,101,98,96 92,91,90**
CSF £6.59 CT £68.90 TOTE £3.80: £1.70, £1.10, £3.90; EX 9.50 Trifecta £69.60.

Owner Godolphin **Bred** Hinkle Farms **Trained** Newmarket, Suffolk

FOCUS
Not a bad fillies' handicap. It's been rated around the third.

1961 PLAY SCOOP6SOCCER EVERY WEEK MEDIAN AUCTION MAIDEN STKS 1m 2f (P)
7:15 (7:18) (Class 5) 3-5-Y-O **£5,175** (£1,540; £769; £384) **Stalls** Low

Form RPR
56-2 **1** **Both Sides**[34] 1160 3-8-13 79.. DavidProbert 2 79
(Andrew Balding) *trckd ldrs: clsd and shkn up to chal over 1f out: rdn to ld 1f out: styd on wl and drew clr fnl 100yds* **5/4**[1]

6252 **2** *2 1/2* **Red Hot Chilly (IRE)**[20] 1429 3-8-13 74.................................. JFEgan 3 74
(Joseph Tuite) *led: rdn and hrd pressed over 1f out: hdd and no ex ins fnl f* **9/4**[2]

0 **3** *3 3/4* **Dream Factory (IRE)**[32] 1200 3-8-13 0............................. LukeMorris 6 67
(Marco Botti) *wl in tch in 4th: rdn and outpcd 4f out: no imp but kpt on after: swtchd rt over 1f out: wnt 3rd 1f out: no threat to ldng pair* **16/1**

22 **4** *6* **Introductory (IRE)**[15] 1553 3-8-8 0............................... PaulMulrennan 5 50
(Mark Johnston) *w ldrs: rdn over 2f out: dropped to 3rd and btn over 1f out: 4th and wknd fnl f* **7/1**

5 **5** *15* **Cafoo (IRE)**[18] 1499 3-8-13 0.. PatCosgrave 1 25
(Ed Dunlop) *sn niggled along: in tch in last pair: rdn 5f out and immediately outpcd: lost tch over 2f out* **6/1**[3]

05 **6** *3 3/4* **Chapess**[33] 1179 3-8-5 0.. TomMarquand(3) 4 12
(Philip McBride) *t.k.h early: hld up in tch in last pair: rdn and outpcd over 5f out: lost tch over 2f out* **33/1**

2m 8.8s (0.20) **Going Correction** +0.15s/f (Slow) **6** Ran SP% **110.8**
Speed ratings (Par 103): **105,103,100,95,83 80**
CSF £4.12 TOTE £2.10: £1.50, £1.60; EX 5.00 Trifecta £34.70.

Owner George Strawbridge **Bred** George Strawbridge **Trained** Kingsclere, Hants

FOCUS
A fair maiden. Straightforward form, with the first two rated to their pre-race marks.

1962 SIMPLY RED HERE ON 1ST JULY MAIDEN FILLIES' STKS 1m 5f 66y(P)
7:45 (7:47) (Class 5) 3-Y-O+ **£5,175** (£1,540; £769; £384) **Stalls** Low

Form RPR
03-5 **1** **Taqdees (IRE)**[12] 1608 3-8-8 69....................................... NickyMackay 1 69
(John Gosden) *mde all: dictated stdy gallop tl rdn and qcknd 2f out: hrd pressed whn wnt rt and bmpd chalr 150yds out: hld on wl after: drvn out* **6/5**[1]

6- **2** *1/2* **Admiral's Sunset**[236] 6277 3-8-8 0...................................... SeanLevey 5 68
(Hughie Morrison) *hld up wl in tch in midfield: effrt to chse wnr over 1f out: chalng whn bmpd and pushed rt 150yds: kpt on u.p but a hld after* **15/8**[2]

0- **3** *5* **Shine**[217] 6866 3-8-8 0.. LukeMorris 4 61
(Jonathan Portman) *chsd ldng pair: rdn 2f out: drvn and outpcd over 1f out: 3rd and wl hld whn drifted rt ins fnl f* **14/1**

05 **4** *nse* **Loose Ends**[27] 1289 3-8-3 0....................................... GeorgeBuckell(5) 3 61
(David Simcock) *stdd s: hld up in tch in rr: rdn outpcd over 1f out: kpt on ins fnl f: pressing for 3rd cl home: no ch w ldng pair* **8/1**[3]

00-5 **5** *4 1/2* **Little Orchid**[35] 1149 3-8-5 48...................................... ShelleyBirkett(3) 2 54?
(Julia Feilden) *t.k.h: hld up wl in tch in midfield: nt clr run on inner over 2f out: effrt over 1f out: sn btn: wknd fnl f* **50/1**

003- **6** *1/2* **Grey's Angel**[182] 7698 4-10-0 62...................................... DavidProbert 6 54
(Philip McBride) *chsd wnr: rdn jst over 2f out: lost pl and btn over 1f out: bhd fnl f* **8/1**[3]

0 **7** *5* **Cetta's Hill**[25] 1346 3-8-8 0.. CamHardie 7 46
(Stuart Edmunds) *hld up in tch in last pair: shortlived effrt on outer over 2f out: lost pl wl over 1f out: sn bhd* **50/1**

3m 1.21s (7.61) **Going Correction** +0.15s/f (Slow)
WFA 3 from 4yo 20lb **7** Ran SP% **113.0**
Speed ratings (Par 100): **82,81,78,78,75 75,72**
CSF £3.53 TOTE £1.90: £1.10, £1.40; EX 4.20 Trifecta £18.80.

Owner Hamdan Al Maktoum **Bred** Sunderland Holdings Inc **Trained** Newmarket, Suffolk

FOCUS
A modest maiden in which the winner enjoyed the run of things. The form looks a bit shaky.

1963 WIN A FOOTBALL FORTUNE WITH SCOOP6SOCCER CONDITIONS STKS 1m 6f (P)
8:15 (8:15) (Class 2) 4-Y-O+ **£12,938** (£3,850; £1,924; £962) **Stalls** Low

Form RPR
110- **1** **Amour De Nuit (IRE)**[200] 7277 4-9-3 106.......................... LukeMorris 2 107
(Sir Mark Prescott Bt) *mde all: rdn jst over 2f out: edging rt fr over 1f out: hrd pressed 1f out: hld on wl: drvn out* **15/8**[2]

51-5 **2** *nk* **Nearly Caught (IRE)**[28] 1273 6-9-4 102........................... GeorgeBaker 4 106
(Hughie Morrison) *chsd wnr: effrt jst over 2f out: hung rt bnd wl over 1f out: drifting rt but ev ch ins fnl f: styd on* **5/4**[1]

2644 **3** *nk* **First Mohican**[28] 1273 8-9-4 101..................................... JimmyFortune 3 105
(Alan King) *stdd s: hld up in 4th: clsd and in tch 4f out: effrt 2f out: cl 3rd and drvn 1f out: ev ch ins fnl f: styd on* **4/1**[3]

100- **4** *14* **Mymatechris (IRE)**[320] 3345 5-9-4 103..........................(t) DavidProbert 1 89
(Andrew Balding) *stdd and awk* **8/1**

3m 4.63s (1.43) **Going Correction** +0.15s/f (Slow)
WFA 4 from 5yo+ 1lb **4** Ran SP% **110.3**
Speed ratings (Par 109): **101,100,100,92**
CSF £4.73 TOTE £3.40; EX 4.70 Trifecta £6.70.

Owner L A Larratt - Osborne House **Bred** Wardley Bloodstock **Trained** Newmarket, Suffolk

FOCUS
Just the four runners but a good race and a close finish. The runner-up has been rated close to his best.

1964 BET SCOOP6SOCCER AT TOTESPORT.COM H'CAP 5f (P)
8:45 (8:45) (Class 4) (0-85,85) 4-Y-O+ **£8,086** (£2,406; £1,202; £601) **Stalls** Low

Form RPR
-445 **1** **Top Boy**[12] 1601 6-8-11 **75**...(v) MartinLane 5 85
(Derek Shaw) *stdd s: hld up in tch in last pair: clsd and nt clr run over 1f out: edgd lft 1f out: gap opened and qcknd through to ld 75yds out: r.o strly* **5/1**[3]

4411 **2** *1* **Welease Bwian (IRE)**[20] 1433 7-8-5 **76**.......................(v) MillyNaseb(7) 1 82
(Stuart Williams) *s.i.s: hld up in tch in rr: rdn and hdwy on inner over 1f out: wnt 2nd wl ins fnl f: kpt on* **9/2**[2]

110- **3** *1* **Grand Beauty (IRE)**[214] 6916 4-9-3 **84**...................... TomMarquand(3) 6 86+
(Robert Cowell) *led for 1f: chsd ldr after: rdn and ev ch over 1f out: led ins fnl f: hdd and no ex fnl 75yds* **12/1**

2-12 **4** *3/4* **Bowson Fred**[11] 1650 4-9-2 **85**...................................... NathanEvans(5) 7 85+
(Michael Easterby) *chsd ldrs: rdn and effrt over 1f out: drvn and unable qck 1f out: styd on same pce after* **11/10**[1]

0333 **5** *2 1/4* **Fine 'n Dandy (IRE)**[6] 1803 5-8-2 **71**...................... JosephineGordon(5) 4 63
(J R Jenkins) *led after 1f: rdn over 1f out: drvn and hdd ins fnl f: sn btn: wknd fnl 100yds* **7/1**

340- **6** *3/4* **Noble Asset**[229] 6494 5-9-4 **82**.. LukeMorris 2 71
(Milton Bradley) *chsd ldrs: rdn and effrt over 1f out: struggling to qckn whn bmpd 1f out: sn wknd* **12/1**

10-0 **7** *4 1/2* **Emjayem**[12] 1601 6-9-1 **79**.. MartinDwyer 8 52
(Ed McMahon) *in tch in midfield: effrt wl over 1f out: sn lost pl: wknd fnl f* **25/1**

59.22s (-0.98) **Going Correction** +0.15s/f (Slow) **7** Ran SP% **114.2**
Speed ratings (Par 105): **113,111,109,108,105 103,96**
CSF £27.44 CT £254.35 TOTE £5.90: £2.10, £2.10; EX 24.00 Trifecta £122.10.
Owner Brian Johnson (Northamptonshire) **Bred** Mrs C R Philipson & Mrs H G Lascelles **Trained** Sproxton, Leics

FOCUS
The first two came from the back of the field in this sprint handicap. The winner has been rated to last autumn's turf form.
T/Plt: £25.80 to a £1 stake. Pool of £65632.37 - 1852.79 winning tickets. T/Qpdt: £5.60 to a £1 stake. Pool of £6766.16 - 880.95 winning tickets. **Steve Payne**

CHESTER (L-H)
Wednesday, May 4

OFFICIAL GOING: Good to soft changing to good (good to soft in places) after race 1 (2.10)
Wind: Moderate, half behind Weather: Fine

1965 STELLAR GROUP LILY AGNES CONDITIONS STKS (PLUS 10 RACE) 5f 16y
2:10 (2:12) (Class 2) 2-Y-O
£12,450 (£3,728; £1,864; £932; £466; £234) **Stalls** Low

Form RPR
42 **1** **Copper Knight (IRE)**[9] 1713 2-8-12 0............................... JamesDoyle 5 89
(Hugo Palmer) *lw: trckd ldrs: led over 1f out: sn hung lft: r.o wl fnl f and a in command* **11/4**[2]

1 **2** *2* **Stoneyford Lane (IRE)**[19] 1454 2-8-12 0.................... RoystonFfrench 4 81
(Steph Hollinshead) *str: racd off the pce: pushed along 3f out: hdwy over 1f out: wnt 2nd ins fnl f: styd on but no imp on wnr* **12/1**

3 *1 1/2* **Our Greta (IRE)** 2-8-7 0... OisinMurphy 3 70
(Michael Appleby) *leggy: missed break: bhd: nt clr run and swtchd rt over 1f out: hdwy to chse ldrs after: kpt on same pce fnl 100yds* **33/1**

1 **4** *2 1/2* **Fiery Character (IRE)**[20] 1437 2-8-7 0.................... RichardKingscote 2 61
(Tom Dascombe) *rrd in stalls bef s: w ldr: led over 2f out: hdd over 1f out: no ex ins fnl f* **10/11**[1]

13 **5** *1 3/4* **Awesome Allan (IRE)**[9] 1713 2-8-12 0................... SilvestreDeSousa 8 60
(David Evans) *w'like: lengthy: chsd ldrs: rdn whn bmpd over 1f out: wknd ins fnl f* **12/1**

01 **6** *2 1/4* **Letmestopyouthere (IRE)**[18] 1482 2-8-12 0................. CathyGannon 6 52
(David Evans) *leggy: coltish in paddock: s.i.s: in rr: outpcd 3f out: nvr a threat* **9/1**[3]

0 **7** *3 1/2* **Patrouille De Nuit (IRE)**[40] 1082 2-8-12 0.................... DarryllHolland 1 39
(J S Moore) *cmpt: led: hdd over 2f out: sn short of room on inner briefly: wknd over 1f out* **40/1**

1m 2.58s (1.58) **Going Correction** +0.35s/f (Good) **7** Ran SP% **109.8**
Speed ratings (Par 99): **101,97,95,91,88 85,79**
CSF £31.37 TOTE £3.70: £1.70, £4.30; EX 26.60 Trifecta £303.00.
Owner Anglia Bloodstock Syndicate VIII **Bred** Wardstown Stud Ltd **Trained** Newmarket, Suffolk

FOCUS
After a dry night the ground was officially good to soft, but it was changed to good, good to soft in places after the first. Running rail on very inside, so all distances as advertised. An interesting Lily Agnes, as it usually is, but the market only wanted to know about two of the seven runners and one of them won in decent style. The winning time was 3.38sec outside standard, suggesting there was still some juice in the ground. After riding in the opener both Royston ffrench and Oisin Murphy said the going was "on the soft side", while Richard Kingscote said it was "nearly good". The winner has been rated as building on his latest.

1966 ARKLE FINANCE CHESHIRE OAKS (FOR THE ROBERT SANGSTER MEMORIAL CUP) (LISTED RACE) (FILLIES) 1m 3f 79y
2:40 (2:41) (Class 1) 3-Y-O
£34,026 (£12,900; £6,456; £3,216; £1,614; £810) **Stalls** Low

Form RPR
1 **Somehow (IRE)**[28] 1280 3-9-0 0.. RyanMoore 6 94+
(A P O'Brien, Ire) *str: hld up: pushed along over 4f out: on inner w work to do over 2f out: swtchd rt and hdwy over 1f out: r.o to ld fnl 150yds: in control cl home* **8/15**[1]

33- **2** *1/2* **Moorside**[182] 7700 3-9-0 0... DarryllHolland 3 93
(Charles Hills) *tall: hld up: pushed along and hdwy on inner 3f out: wnt 2nd and rdn over 1f out: chalng wl ins fnl f: hld nr fin* **10/1**

1- **3** *1/2* **Diamonds Pour Moi**[156] 8048 3-9-0 76............................ OisinMurphy 4 92
(Ralph Beckett) *athletic: chsd ldrs: rdn over 2f out: chalng ins fnl f but unable qck: styd on but hld nr fin* **6/1**[2]

210- **4** 2 ¼ **Dessertoflife (IRE)**208 7075 3-9-5 101 JoeFanning 5 94
(Mark Johnston) *dwlt: in rr: pushed along whn nt clr run and snatched up over 1f out: styd on ins fnl f: nt trble ldrs* **16/1**

01- **5** nk **Play Gal**191 7518 3-9-0 76 AdamKirby 2 87
(David Evans) *unf: lw: led: pushed along over 2f out: rdn over 1f out: hdd fnl 150yds: fdd* **25/1**

4-21 **6** 4 **Pursuitofthestars (IRE)**9 1704 3-9-0 84 AndreaAtzeni 1 80
(John Gosden) *lw: chsd ldrs: effrt and wnt 2nd 3f out: lost 2nd over 1f out: wknd fnl f* **8/1**3

16-5 **7** 11 **Doubly Motivated (IRE)**7 1771 3-9-0 88 FrannyNorton 7 60
(Charles Hills) *racd keenly: w ldr: lost 2nd 3f out: wknd 2f out* **20/1**

14-1 **8** 53 **Mirsaalah**8 1758 3-9-0 70 PatSmullen 8
(James Tate) *chsd ldrs: rdn over 3f out: sn wknd: t.o over 2f out* **11/1**

2m 29.05s (4.25) **Going Correction** +0.35s/f (Good) **8** Ran SP% **122.5**
Speed ratings (Par 104): **98,97,97,95,95 92,84,45**
CSF £8.25 TOTE £1.50: £1.10, £3.00, £2.20; EX 8.20 Trifecta £38.40.
Owner Michael Tabor & Derrick Smith & Mrs John Magnier **Bred** Orpendale, Chelston & Wynatt **Trained** Cashel, Co Tipperary
■ Stewards' Enquiry : Ryan Moore two-day ban: careless riding (May 18-19)

FOCUS
Race distance as advertised. A race revolving around the favourite, they initially went a fair gallop before the pace slowed and the form doesn't look terribly strong. It's been rated among the lesser renewals.

1967 BETWAY CHESTER CUP (HERITAGE H'CAP) 2m 2f 147y
3:10 (3:15) (Class 2) 4-Y-O+
£73,908 (£22,248; £11,124; £5,544; £2,784; £1,404) **Stalls** High

Form RPR
656/ **1** **No Heretic**32 6144 8-8-13 **93** JamieSpencer 4 101
(Nicky Henderson) *ref to settle in tch: impr 2f out: r.o to ld narrowly ins fnl f: kpt finding for press nr fin* **11/1**

211- **2** shd **Nakeeta**221 6749 5-8-13 **93** RoystonFfrench 15 100
(Iain Jardine) *lw: midfield: rdn and hdwy 2f out: upsides chalng strly ins fnl f: r.o u.p: jst hld nr fin* **20/1**

1- **3** 1 ¼ **Silver Concorde**50 7493 8-9-3 **97** PatSmullen 9 102
(D K Weld, Ire) *lw: midfield: rdn and hdwy over 1f out: r.o ins fnl f: edgd lft and clsng towards fin* **5/1**2

211- **4** 1 ¼ **Gabrial The Hero (USA)**128 8379 7-9-0 **94**(p) PaulHanagan 12 98
(Richard Fahey) *midfield: rdn and hdwy over 1f out: styd on to chse ldrs ins fnl f: kpt on same pce fnl 100yds* **12/1**

00-3 **5** ½ **Gabrial's King (IRE)**11 1642 7-8-12 **92** GeorgeChaloner 17 96
(Richard Fahey) *hld up in rr: hdwy on outer 6f out: chsd ldrs over 3f out: led over 1f out: hdd ins fnl f: no ex fnl 100yds* **22/1**

203- **6** hd **Quick Jack (IRE)**39 1099 7-9-9 **103** RyanMoore 16 106+
(A J Martin, Ire) *hld up: rdn and forced wd over 1f out: hdwy sn after: styd on ins fnl f: nt trble ldrs* **8/1**3

60-0 **7** shd **Totalize**17 1081 7-8-10 **95** CallumShepherd(5) 10 98+
(Brian Ellison) *hld up: rdn on inner over 1f out: hdwy after: r.o ins fnl f: nt rch ldrs* **20/1**

20-0 **8** 1 ¼ **Angel Gabrial (IRE)**40 1081 7-9-10 **104** JamesDoyle 18 106+
(Richard Fahey) *in rr: rdn 2f out: nt clr run over 1f out: rdn ins fnl f: styd on: nt trble ldrs* **33/1**

1-11 **9** nk **Gang Warfare**40 1081 5-9-10 **104** RobertHavlin 2 106
(Simon Crisford) *in tch: effrt whn nt clr run over 1f out: sn rdn to chse ldrs: one pce fnl 100yds* **8/1**3

066- **10** 2 ¼ **Le Maitre Chat (USA)**168 7892 5-8-13 **93**(p) FrannyNorton 7 92
(Ian Williams) *midfield: nt clr run over 1f out: kpt on u.p ins fnl f: no real imp* **12/1**

111/ **11** 3 ¼ **Venue**15 6128 6-8-12 **92** TomEaves 1 88
(Donald McCain) *midfield: rdn over 2f out: one pce fnl f and no ipression* **33/1**

10-1 **12** ½ **Steve Rogers (IRE)**21 1417 5-9-0 **94** AndreaAtzeni 3 90
(Roger Varian) *chsd ldrs: rdn over 1f out: wknd fnl f* **7/2**1

2230 **13** 1 ½ **John Reel (FR)**40 1067 7-9-5 **99** AdamKirby 5 93
(David Evans) *lw: led: rdn and hdd 2f out: wknd fnl f* **10/1**

/05- **14** 3 ¾ **Duke Of Clarence (IRE)**355 2251 7-9-6 **100** DavidNolan 8 90
(Richard Fahey) *chsd ldr: pushed along 3f out: led 2f out: hdd over 1f out: wknd ins fnl f* **33/1**

00-0 **15** 1 ¼ **Min Alemarat (IRE)**11 1642 5-8-12 **92** DavidAllan 11 81
(Tim Easterby) *hld up: rdn over 2f out on outer: no bttr than midfield: bhd fr 2f out* **66/1**

100- **16** 7 **Heartbreak City (FR)**39 1099 6-9-4 **103**(t) DonnachaO'Brien(5) 6 85
(A J Martin, Ire) *racd keenly: midfield: tk clsr order 1 m out: rdn and wknd 2f out: eased wl ins fnl f* **14/1**

003- **17** 38 **William Of Orange**38 7425 5-9-2 **96** GrahamLee 14 40
(Donald McCain) *lw: chsd ldrs: wknd qckly over 2f out: eased whn wl btn fnl f: t.o* **20/1**

4m 10.48s (5.68) **Going Correction** +0.35s/f (Good) **17** Ran SP% **129.5**
Speed ratings (Par 109): **102,101,101,100,100 100,100,100,99,98 97,97,96,95,94 91,75**
CSF £225.21 CT £1263.69 TOTE £12.90: £3.70, £4.80, £1.80, £2.70; EX 302.40 Trifecta £3477.50.
Owner Mrs Fitri Hay **Bred** Belgrave Bloodstock Ltd **Trained** Upper Lambourn, Berks

FOCUS
An ultra-competitive Chester Cup as usual and although the pace was an even one, they didn't go mad. There seemed no real bias with regard to position in the field, as the winner was never too far away while the placed horses came from further back. It provided a thrilling finish. The level is a bit fluid and probably not the most literal piece of form.

1968 BOODLES DIAMOND H'CAP 5f 16y
3:45 (3:48) (Class 2) (0-105,98) 4-Y-O+
£18,675 (£5,592; £2,796; £1,398; £699; £351) **Stalls** Low

Form RPR
60-5 **1** **Kimberella**11 1644 6-8-10 **87** FrannyNorton 3 96
(David Nicholls) *chsd ldrs: nt clr run over 1f out: r.o ins fnl f to ld fnl 150yds: in control nr fin* **5/1**3

0-12 **2** ¾ **Roudee**14 1566 4-9-3 **94** RichardKingscote 1 100
(Tom Dascombe) *led: rdn over 1f out: hdd fnl 150yds: hld nr fin* **7/2**1

1-41 **3** ½ **Avon Breeze**11 1644 7-9-0 **91** PaulQuinn 6 95
(Richard Whitaker) *midfield: hdwy on inner 2f out: r.o to chal wl ins fnl f: hld nr fin* **14/1**

50-4 **4** 1 **Growl**11 1644 4-8-12 **89** PaulHanagan 4 89
(Richard Fahey) *lw: chsd ldrs: rdn over 1f out: ev ch ins fnl f: nt qckn: edgd lft and kpt on towards fin* **7/2**1

41-2 **5** 1 **Mukaynis (IRE)**32 1205 5-8-13 **90**(b) ShaneGray 2 91+
(Kevin Ryan) *midfield: hdwy 2f out: nt clr run over 1f out: denied a run ins fnl f: kpt on same pce fnl 75yds* **9/2**2

250- **6** ½ **Confessional**193 7461 9-8-10 **87**(e) DavidAllan 15 82+
(Tim Easterby) *hld up: hdwy 2f out: rdn over 1f out: styd on ins fnl f: nt trble ldrs* **50/1**

00-5 **7** 1 ½ **Blithe Spirit**28 1272 5-9-0 **91** JasonHart 8 81
(Eric Alston) *w ldr: rdn over 1f out: stl ev ch ins fnl f: edgd rt: wknd fnl 75yds* **18/1**

000- **8** ½ **Lexi's Hero (IRE)**208 7091 8-8-3 **83**(v) SammyJoBell(3) 9 71
(Richard Fahey) *midfield: rdn over 1f out: one pce and no imp ins fnl f* **16/1**

50-4 **9** 2 ¼ **Lexington Place**21 1408 6-8-11 **88** JamesSullivan 7 68
(Ruth Carr) *hld up: rdn on inner over 1f out: kpt on: nvr able to chal* **16/1**

4000 **10** 1 ¼ **Green Door (IRE)**11 1644 5-9-7 **98** JamieSpencer 13 73
(Robert Cowell) *stdd s: hld up: rdn over 1f out: no imp* **25/1**

1-00 **11** 3 ½ **Seve**72 677 4-8-13 **90** LiamJones 5 53
(Tom Dascombe) *sed awkwardly: chsd ldrs: pushed along 3f out: sn wknd* **20/1**

46-0 **12** shd **Noble Storm (USA)**21 1408 10-8-10 **87** KieranO'Neill 10 49
(Ed McMahon) *midfield tl rdn and wknd 2f out* **80/1**

00-0 **13** hd **Masamah (IRE)**21 1408 10-8-13 **90**(p) GrahamLee 12 52
(Patrick Morris) *chsd ldrs tl rdn and wknd 2f out* **66/1**

06-5 **14** 1 ½ **Snap Shots (IRE)**11 1650 4-8-10 **87**(tp) SilvestreDeSousa 11 43
(Tom Dascombe) *in rr: nvr a threat: eased whn wl btn ins fnl f* **16/1**

1m 1.62s (0.62) **Going Correction** +0.35s/f (Good) **14** Ran SP% **122.2**
Speed ratings (Par 109): **109,107,107,105,103 103,100,99,96,94 88,88,88,85**
CSF £22.21 CT £238.20 TOTE £6.90: £2.50, £2.50, £2.80; EX 26.70 Trifecta £328.00.
Owner C Titcomb **Bred** P And Mrs A G Venner **Trained** Sessay, N Yorks

FOCUS
Race distance as advertised. A few of these wanted to make it and they predictably went fast. The low-drawn runners came to the fore. The runner-up helps with the standard, with the third confirming her Ripon latest.

1969 HOMESERVE CONDITIONS STKS 5f 16y
4:20 (4:21) (Class 3) 3-Y-O+
£9,960 (£2,982; £1,491; £745; £372; £187) **Stalls** Low

Form RPR
6140 **1** **Sir Maximilian (IRE)**39 1104 7-9-4 112(p) KierenFallon 3 114
(Ian Williams) *midfield: hdwy 2f out: big effrt and bmpd ent st: led 1f out: r.o wl to draw clr fnl 100yds* **5/2**1

112- **2** 4 **Maljaa**204 7178 4-9-4 107(b) PaulHanagan 5 100
(Roger Varian) *lw: chsd ldrs: rdn whn bmpd ent st: nt qckn over 1f out: styd on to take 2nd fnl 150yds: nt pce of wnr* **5/2**1

203- **3** ½ **Canny Kool**220 6784 4-9-4 103 BenCurtis 1 98
(Brian Ellison) *chsd ldrs: pushed along over 2f out: wnt 2nd briefly over 1f out: styd on same pce fnl 150yds* **6/1**2

16-0 **4** 1 ¾ **Dutch Masterpiece**4 1862 6-9-11 107(v) RyanMoore 2 99
(Gary Moore) *hld up: hung rt most of way: rdn over 1f out: kpt on ins fnl f: nvr a threat* **13/2**3

0-02 **5** 1 **Rene Mathis (GER)**18 1491 6-9-4 103 DavidNolan 7 88
(Richard Fahey) *bhd: styd on fnl f: nvr nrr* **12/1**

02-2 **6** 2 **Red Baron (IRE)**40 1083 7-9-4 100 NeilFarley 4 81
(Eric Alston) *led: rdn over 1f out: sn hdd: wknd ins fnl f* **6/1**2

220/ **7** ½ **Jane's Memory (IRE)**593 6513 4-8-13 95 AndreaAtzeni 6 74
(Rae Guest) *midfield: lost pl after 1f: n.d after* **40/1**

2255 **8** 1 ½ **Ballista (IRE)**8 1744 8-9-4 83 RichardKingscote 8 74
(Tom Dascombe) *chsd ldr tl over 1f out: wknd ins fnl f* **50/1**

1m 1.06s (0.06) **Going Correction** +0.35s/f (Good) **8** Ran SP% **111.1**
Speed ratings (Par 107): **113,106,105,103,101 98,97,95**
CSF £7.81 TOTE £3.20: £1.10, £1.60, £2.10; EX 9.20 Trifecta £40.20.
Owner Paul Wildes **Bred** Holborn Trust Co **Trained** Portway, Worcs

FOCUS
A decent conditions sprint and a strong pace was always likely with a few in here that like to force it. The leaders probably went off too quick, but they still finished very much as official ratings suggested they should. The winner has been rated in line with the better view of his Dubai form for now.

1970 STELLAR GROUP MAIDEN STKS (PLUS 10 RACE) 1m 2f 75y
4:55 (4:55) (Class 3) 3-Y-O **£8,715** (£2,609; £1,304; £652; £326) **Stalls** High

Form RPR
2 **1** **Mulk**21 1421 3-9-5 0 PaulHanagan 4 81+
(Sir Michael Stoute) *racd keenly: hld up bhd ldrs: hdwy 2f out: led over 1f out: r.o wl to draw clr ins fnl f* **30/100**1

4- **2** 2 ¾ **Exoteric**126 8404 3-9-5 0 DarryllHolland 2 75+
(Charles Hills) *str: racd keenly: hld up bhd ldrs: rn green: rdn and nt qckn 2f out: wnt 2nd 1f out: kpt on ins fnl f: no ch w wnr* **3/1**2

03- **3** 1 ¾ **Monaco Rose**202 7229 3-9-0 0 GeorgeChaloner 3 66+
(Richard Fahey) *cl-cpld: hld up: niggled along 4f out: outpcd 2f out: kpt on ins fnl f: nvr a threat* **11/1**3

4 8 **Gamesters Boy** 3-9-5 0 LiamJones 6 55
(Mark Brisbourne) *w'like: str: w ldr: led 3f out: sn rdn: hdd over 1f out: wknd ins fnl f* **50/1**

0-05 **5** 13 **Wicked Woo**30 1234 3-9-0 50 DougieCostello 1 24
(Jo Hughes) *led: hdd 3f out: wknd over 1f out* **66/1**

2m 15.61s (4.41) **Going Correction** +0.35s/f (Good) **5** Ran SP% **113.7**
Speed ratings (Par 103): **96,93,92,86,75**
CSF £1.67 TOTE £1.30: £1.10, £1.40; EX 1.50 Trifecta £2.70.
Owner Hamdan Al Maktoum **Bred** Cheveley Park Stud Ltd **Trained** Newmarket, Suffolk

FOCUS
Race distance as advertised. Little depth to this maiden and they went steady. The short-price favourite was much the best. Muddling form, with the winner not needing to match his debut form.

1971 DEEPBRIDGE CAPITAL H'CAP 1m 4f 66y
5:25 (5:28) (Class 3) (0-90,87) 3-Y-O
£9,960 (£2,982; £1,491; £745; £372; £187) **Stalls** Low

Form RPR
21-2 **1** **Red Verdon (USA)**12 1602 3-9-0 **80** RyanMoore 7 91+
(Ed Dunlop) *str: hld up: hdwy over 2f out: wnt 2nd over 1f out: r.o to ld fnl 110yds: in command nr fin* **5/2**2

6-14 **2** 1 ¼ **Soldier In Action (FR)**12 1610 3-9-7 **87** FrannyNorton 2 96
(Mark Johnston) *led: kicked on over 2f out: rdn over 1f out: hdd fnl 110yds: hld nr fin* **2/1**1

31-2 **3** 12 **Zzoro (IRE)**[22] 1398 3-9-7 **87**.. DarryllHolland 4 77
(Charles Hills) *chsd ldr for 4f: remained handy: rdn over 1f out: one pce fnl f* **9/2**[3]

622- **4** 3 1/4 **So Celebre (GER)**[189] 7561 3-8-9 **75**......................... SilvestreDeSousa 1 60
(Ian Williams) *lengthy: chsd ldrs: wnt 2nd after 4f: rdn and lost 2nd over 1f out: sn wknd* **9/1**

6-61 **5** 7 **Ronnie Baird**[20] 1449 3-8-12 **78**......................................(p) RobertHavlin 6 51
(Kristin Stubbs) *midfield: rdn over 3f out: wknd 2f out* **33/1**

3-11 **6** 46 **Cape Of Glory (IRE)**[111] 182 3-9-7 **87**............................ AndreaAtzeni 5
(James Tate) *lw: in rr: rdn over 7f out: eased 2f out: t.o* **14/1**

525- **P** **Antioco (IRE)**[210] 7041 3-8-7 **73**.. PaulHanagan 3
(Richard Fahey) *leggy: hld up: rdn over 2f out: wnt wrong whn n.d over 1f out: p.u ins fnl f: dismntd* **6/1**

2m 41.06s (2.56) **Going Correction** +0.35s/f (Good) **7** Ran SP% **114.0**
Speed ratings (Par 103): **105,104,96,94,89 58,**
CSF £7.88 TOTE £2.80: £1.40, £2.10; EX 8.40 Trifecta £26.00.
Owner The Hon R J Arculli **Bred** Liberty Road Stables **Trained** Newmarket, Suffolk

FOCUS
Race distance as advertised. No gallop on here and the runner-up had everything go his way, so the fact the winner was able to quite readily run him down, the pair clear, was impressive. It's tricky to pin down the level, although it fits with the better recent renewals of this race.
T/Jkpt: £4260.00 to a £1 stake. Pool of £15000.00 - 2.50 winning units. T/Plt: £31.30 to a £1 stake. Pool of £146041.78 - 3403.20 winning tickets. T/Qpdt: £8.50 to a £1 stake. Pool of £11315.96 - 980.84 winning tickets. **Darren Owen**

1965 CHESTER (L-H)
Thursday, May 5

OFFICIAL GOING: Good (7.9)
Wind: Almost Nil Weather: Sunny

1972 GATELEY PLC ORIGINAL LEGAL THINKING H'CAP 1m 2f 75y
2:10 (2:13) (Class 2) (0-105,100) 4-Y-O+

£18,675 (£5,592; £2,796; £1,398; £699; £351) **Stalls** High

Form RPR

3-11 **1** **Dark Red (IRE)**[15] 1569 4-8-11 **90**............................ SilvestreDeSousa 10 102+
(Ed Dunlop) *chsd ldrs: effrt over 1f out: r.o to ld fnl 110yds: in control cl home* **11/2**[2]

0-41 **2** nk **Felix De Vega (IRE)**[21] 1445 4-8-6 **90**.......................... NathanEvans(5) 1 98
(Michael Easterby) *led: rdn over 1f out: hdd fnl 110yds: r.o u.p but hld nr fin* **13/2**

1221 **3** 1 **Perfect Cracker**[47] 1001 8-8-5 **87**...................................... RyanTate(3) 2 93
(Clive Cox) *racd keenly: trckd ldrs: rdn and ch over 1f out: nt qckn ins fnl f: kpt on but hld nr fin* **10/1**

101- **4** 1 1/2 **English Summer**[201] 7285 9-8-13 **92**.........................(t) GeorgeChaloner 7 95
(Richard Fahey) *in tch: rdn and swtchd lft over 1f out: styd on ins fnl f: no imp fnl 75yds* **25/1**

13-2 **5** nk **American Artist (IRE)**[12] 1620 4-8-13 **92**........................ AndreaAtzeni 9 95+
(Roger Varian) *lw: hld up: pushed along and hdwy ent fnl f: styd on: nt rch ldrs* **7/1**

40-0 **6** nk **Sennockian Star**[15] 1569 6-9-0 **93**....................................(v) JoeFanning 8 95
(Mark Johnston) *midfield: rdn over 1f out: styd on ins fnl f: no imp on ldrs* **8/1**

40/0 **7** 1/2 **Novelty Seeker (USA)**[12] 1620 7-8-6 **85**........................ JamesSullivan 4 86
(Michael Easterby) *midfield: rdn over 1f out: kpt on ins fnl f: one pce towards fin* **80/1**

40-3 **8** 3/4 **What About Carlo (FR)**[15] 1569 5-9-7 **100**...................... GeorgeBaker 3 100+
(Eve Johnson Houghton) *lw: missed break: in rr: rdn over 1f out: kpt on: nvr able to chal* **6/1**[3]

-010 **9** 1 **Master Of Finance (IRE)**[19] 1493 5-9-5 **98**.................... FrannyNorton 6 96
(Mark Johnston) *s.i.s: n.m.r and hmpd jst after s: in rr: rdn over 1f out: one pce ins fnl f* **14/1**

50-1 **10** 4 **Darshini**[19] 1480 4-8-12 **91**..(p) RyanMoore 5 81+
(Sir Michael Stoute) *lw: chsd ldr: pushed along over 2f out: u.p whn n.m.r and hmpd over 1f out: sn dropped away: eased fnl 150yds* **4/1**[1]

360- **11** 3/4 **Perrault (IRE)**[224] 6679 4-8-5 **84**..................................... PaulHanagan 11 73+
(Richard Fahey) *chsd ldrs: dropped to midfield over 6f out: pushed along and outpcd over 2f out: bhd over 1f out* **10/1**

2m 14.25s (3.05) **Going Correction** +0.45s/f (Yiel) **11** Ran SP% **116.5**
Speed ratings (Par 109): **105,104,103,102,102 102,101,101,100,97 96**
CSF £40.79 CT £350.28 TOTE £5.90: £1.90, £3.60, £3.30; EX 45.40 Trifecta £474.60.
Owner The Hon R J Arculli **Bred** T Jones **Trained** Newmarket, Suffolk

FOCUS
Following a dry night the going was given as good (GoingStick: 7.9). The running rail had been moved out by 3yds between the 6f and 1 1/2f point after racing on Wednesday. Race distance increased by 14yds. A decent handicap to start, but they crawled for much of the way with several taking a grip as a result, and the race didn't really start until inside the last 3f. The winning time was 6.55sec outside standard and it was crucial to be near the pace. Paul Hanagan said the ground was "a bit quicker than yesterday", while Nathan Evans described it as "perfect good ground". The form is rated around the runner-up with the form on the upgrade.

1973 BETWAY HUXLEY STKS (FOR THE TRADESMAN'S CUP) (GROUP 3) 1m 2f 75y
2:40 (2:40) (Class 1) 4-Y-O+

£42,532 (£16,125; £8,070; £4,020; £2,017; £1,012) **Stalls** High

Form RPR

110- **1** **Cannock Chase (USA)**[144] 8216 5-9-7 116........................ RyanMoore 5 120
(Sir Michael Stoute) *lw: chsd ldrs: effrt appr fnl f: led 1f out: r.o wl: rdn out towards fin* **11/4**[2]

33-2 **2** 1 **Western Hymn**[13] 1604 5-9-0 117.................................... FrankieDettori 6 111
(John Gosden) *hld up towards rr: effrt and hdwy over 1f out: styd on ins fnl f: wnt 2nd fnl 110yds: nt pce to trble wnr* **6/4**[1]

0-44 **3** shd **Master Carpenter (IRE)**[13] 1604 5-9-0 108.................. FrederikTylicki 4 111
(Rod Millman) *hld up in midfield: pushed along 2f out: rdn and hdwy over 1f out: styd on ins fnl f: nt pce to trble wnr* **14/1**

3-05 **4** 2 **Gabrial (IRE)**[13] 1606 7-9-0 114.. PaulHanagan 3 107
(Richard Fahey) *hld up in rr: effrt over 1f out: kpt on ins fnl f: nvr able to chal* **7/1**[3]

16-4 **5** 1 1/2 **Battalion (IRE)**[19] 1475 6-9-0 111................................(p) PatCosgrave 7 104
(William Haggas) *racd keenly: chsd ldr: rdn to ld appr fnl f: hung lft and hdd 1f out: wknd fnl 100yds* **10/1**

03-6 **6** 2 3/4 **Top Notch Tonto (IRE)**[13] 1604 6-9-0 110.........................(p) BenCurtis 1 99
(Brian Ellison) *led: rdn and hdd over 1f out: sn wknd* **20/1**

1-62 **7** 3/4 **Fire Fighting (IRE)**[41] 1069 5-9-0 108..................................(b) AdamKirby 2 98
(Mark Johnston) *chsd ldrs: pushed along over 3f out: outpcd and btn over 1f out* **8/1**

2m 11.65s (0.45) **Going Correction** +0.45s/f (Yiel) **7** Ran SP% **110.8**
Speed ratings (Par 113): **116,115,115,113,112 110,109**
CSF £6.77 TOTE £3.00: £2.20, £1.20; EX 7.70 Trifecta £57.50.
Owner Saeed Suhail **Bred** Hascombe Stud **Trained** Newmarket, Suffolk

FOCUS
Race distance increased by 14yds. This Group 3 was run at a good gallop, the front three for most of the way dropping out to finish in the last three places. A smart effort from Cannock Chase, even if the runner-up wasn't at his best.

1974 MBNA CHESTER VASE (GROUP 3) (C&G) 1m 4f 66y
3:10 (3:10) (Class 1) 3-Y-O

£42,532 (£16,125; £8,070; £4,020; £2,017; £1,012) **Stalls** Low

Form RPR

1 **US Army Ranger (IRE)**[32] 1229 3-9-0 0............................ RyanMoore 3 109+
(A P O'Brien, Ire) *str: cl-cpld: mainly chsd ldr: effrt on inner to ld narrowly jst over 1f out: r.o gamely whn hrd pressed ins fnl f: kpt finding for press* **4/11**[1]

14- **2** shd **Port Douglas (IRE)**[194] 7463 3-9-4 105.................(tp) SeamieHeffernan 1 112
(A P O'Brien, Ire) *str: lw: led: rdn and lugged lft over 1f out: sn hdd narrowly: r.o for press and continued to press wnr ins fnl f: jst hld under hand ride cl home* **11/2**[2]

140- **3** 7 **Ormito (GER)**[186] 7666 3-9-0 94.. DavidProbert 6 97
(Andrew Balding) *hld up in rr: rdn to go pce over 2f out: kpt on to take 3rd ins fnl f: unable to trble front pair* **20/1**

5-13 **4** 2 **Biodynamic (IRE)**[21] 1438 3-9-0 94.............................. DougieCostello 5 94
(K R Burke) *s.i.s: chsd ldrs: pushed along over 3f out: rdn 2f out: no imp on front pair over 1f out: one pce after* **12/1**[3]

13 **5** 10 **High Grounds (IRE)**[13] 1605 3-9-0 96............................ DarryllHolland 4 78
(Charles Hills) *lw: broke wl: ref to settle: hld up: hdwy over 4f out: sn prom: rdn and outpcd 2f out: wknd over 1f out* **14/1**

2-15 **6** 2 1/4 **Dwight D**[13] 1605 3-9-0 84.. JamieSpencer 2 74
(William Haggas) *lw: racd keenly: in tch: lost pl 4f out: u.p whn checked jst over 2f out: hung lft whn bhd over 1f out* **33/1**

2m 41.07s (2.57) **Going Correction** +0.45s/f (Yiel) **6** Ran SP% **110.8**
Speed ratings (Par 109): **109,108,104,102,96 94**
CSF £2.70 TOTE £1.30: £1.10, £2.30; EX 3.30 Trifecta £15.80.
Owner Mrs John Magnier & Michael Tabor & Derrick Smith **Bred** Orpendale, Chelston & Wynatt **Trained** Cashel, Co Tipperary

FOCUS
Race distance increased by 20yds. The Chester Vase has been a good pointer to the Derby in its long history, though Ruler Of The World in 2013 was the only horse to win this and then triumph at Epsom since Shergar in 1981. All bar Ormito in this field held a Derby entry. They only went an ordinary pace, with a few pulling as a result, and although it ended up as a 1-2 for trainer Aidan O'Brien as many would have predicted, the result didn't really make things any clearer with regards to Epsom. The first two progressed with the third and fourth close to their marks.

1975 BOODLES DIAMOND H'CAP 7f 122y
3:45 (3:47) (Class 2) (0-100,100) 3-Y-O

£18,675 (£5,592; £2,796; £1,398; £699; £351) **Stalls** Low

Form RPR

26-1 **1** **Tang Fleming**[41] 1079 3-8-2 **86** oh7......................... EdwardGreatrex(5) 7 92
(Andrew Balding) *chsd ldrs: effrt to take 2nd over 1f out: r.o to ld narrowly fnl 150yds: gamely did enough* **9/1**

23-6 **2** nse **Above N Beyond**[61] 836 3-9-2 **95**..........................(t) RichardKingscote 1 100
(Tom Dascombe) *lw: led: rdn over 1f out: hdd narrowly fnl 150yds: r.o for press: jst hld* **9/2**[2]

221- **3** 2 1/2 **Dark Devil (IRE)**[225] 6652 3-8-7 **86** oh2.......................... PaulHanagan 8 85+
(Richard Fahey) *swtchd lft s: in rr: hdwy over 1f out: r.o ins fnl f: nt rch front pair* **7/1**[3]

3-35 **4** 3/4 **King's Pavilion (IRE)**[14] 1585 3-8-9 **88**.......................... WilliamBuick 6 85+
(Mark Johnston) *bmpd sn after s: in rr: pushed along 4f out: hdwy 2f out: styd on ins fnl f: nt rch ldrs* **16/1**

0-26 **5** 1/2 **Ode To Evening**[13] 1605 3-9-7 **100**.................................... JamesDoyle 2 96
(Mark Johnston) *chsd ldrs: pushed along to take 2nd 2f out: lost 2nd and nt qckn over 1f out: styd on same pce ins fnl f* **8/1**

115- **6** 1/2 **Storm Rising (IRE)**[197] 7396 3-8-11 **90**............................ RyanMoore 3 84+
(Richard Hannon) *hld up: pushed along 2f out: hdwy over 1f out: kpt on ins fnl f: nvr able to trble ldrs* **7/2**[1]

344- **7** 3 1/4 **Still On Top**[199] 7339 3-9-3 **96**... DavidAllan 4 82
(Tim Easterby) *midfield: niggled along over 3f out: one pce whn nt clr run ins fnl f: no imp after* **10/1**

4-31 **8** 4 1/2 **Arcanada (IRE)**[12] 1623 3-9-0 **93**................................ SilvestreDeSousa 9 68
(Tom Dascombe) *lw: chsd ldr tl rdn 2f out: wknd jst over 1f out: eased whn wl btn ins fnl f* **7/2**[1]

65-5 **9** 5 **Taking Libertys**[21] 1446 3-8-7 **86** oh1..................................(p) TomEaves 5 49
(Kevin Ryan) *restless in stalls: midfield: pushed along 4f out: rdn and wknd 2f out* **25/1**

1m 34.96s (1.16) **Going Correction** +0.45s/f (Yiel) **9** Ran SP% **115.1**
Speed ratings (Par 105): **112,111,109,108,108 107,104,99,94**
CSF £49.04 CT £303.99 TOTE £12.60: £3.20, £2.00, £2.00; EX 72.20 Trifecta £346.10.
Owner Chelsea Thoroughbreds - Cagnes Sur Mer **Bred** J Green & Sons, W Fox & R Frisby **Trained** Kingsclere, Hants

FOCUS
Race distance increased by 13yds. A competitive handicap in which the first two finished nicely clear. The winner was 7lb out of the handicap, but this wasn't a fluke.

1976 BETWAY EBF STALLIONS MAIDEN STKS (PLUS 10 RACE) 5f 16y
4:20 (4:21) (Class 3) 2-Y-O

£8,715 (£2,609; £1,304; £652; £326; £163) **Stalls** Low

Form RPR

1 **Mehmas (IRE)** 2-9-5 0.. FrankieDettori 9 83+
(Richard Hannon) *athletic: str: lw: hld up: hdwy 2f out: swtchd rt over 1f out: r.o ins fnl f to ld towards fin: won a shade cosily* **5/1**[3]

2 3/4 **Madam Dancealot (IRE)** 2-9-0 0.. JFEgan 3 75
(Joseph Tuite) *leggy: led: rdn over 1f out: hdd towards fin: nt pce of wnr fnl strides* **22/1**

2 **3** 1 1/4 **Full Intention**[24] 1384 2-9-5 0.................................. RichardKingscote 12 76
(Tom Dascombe) *str: w ldr: rdn and lugged lft 1f out: stl ev ch ins fnl f: no ex towards fin* **5/2**[1]

0 **4** 1 **Vona (IRE)**[28] 1293 2-9-0 0... JackGarritty 2 67
(Richard Fahey) *leggy: chsd ldrs: rdn and nt qckn over 1f out: sltly disorganised ins fnl f: styd on same pce fnl 100yds* **20/1**

2 **5** 3 **Four Dragons**[21] 1443 2-9-0 0 LiamJones 6 56
(Tom Dascombe) *leggy: chsd ldrs: pushed along 2f out: rdn over 1f out: kpt on same pce ins fnl f* **13/2**

6 3/4 **Lostock** 2-9-5 0 TonyHamilton 7 59+
(Richard Fahey) *leggy: str: missed break: racd keenly: hld up: pushed along 3f out: rdn and hdwy 1f out: edgd lft ins fnl f: styd on: nt trble ldrs* **8/1**

4 **7** 3/4 **Melesina (IRE)**[22] 1407 2-9-0 0 PaulHanagan 8 51+
(Richard Fahey) *cl-cpld: in rr: sn pushed along: outpcd 3f out: styd on ins fnl f: nt pce to get competitive* **12/1**

5 **8** 1 1/4 **She's Rosanna**[17] 1527 2-9-0 0 AdamBeschizza 4 47
(Steph Hollinshead) *w'like: dwlt: in tch: n.m.r sn after s: rdn over 2f out: outpcd over 1f out: wknd ins fnl f* **25/1**

9 3/4 **Redrosezorro** 2-9-5 0 JasonHart 1 49
(Eric Alston) *w'like: bit bkwd: swtg: s.i.s: rn green: sn pushed along and outpcd: nvr a threat* **14/1**

33 **10** 1 3/4 **Percy Toplis**[17] 1520 2-9-5 0 ShaneGray 5 43
(Kevin Ryan) *unf: midfield: rdn over 2f out: wknd over 1f out* **9/2**[2]

1m 2.73s (1.73) **Going Correction** +0.45s/f (Yiel) **10** Ran SP% **115.2**
Speed ratings (Par 97): **104,102,100,99,94 93,92,90,88,86**
CSF £109.82 TOTE £5.40: £1.90, £6.50, £1.70; EX 120.40 Trifecta £423.60.
Owner Al Shaqab Racing **Bred** Epona Bloodstock Ltd **Trained** East Everleigh, Wilts

FOCUS
Race distance increased by 10yds. Seven of the last ten winners of this maiden had been placed on their debut, but this time the first two home were newcomers, suggesting they are above-average, especially the winner. Another good edition of this event, and rated as such.

1977 PERFECTION SECRETS H'CAP 6f 18y
4:55 (4:56) (Class 3) (0-90,89) 3-Y-O
£9,960 (£2,982; £1,491; £745; £372; £187) **Stalls** Low

Form RPR

00-3 **1** **Justice Angel (IRE)**[24] 1385 3-8-12 **80** SilvestreDeSousa 5 88+
(David Elsworth) *lw: chsd ldrs: effrt to ld 1f out: r.o ins fnl f: pushed out and in control nr fin* **11/2**[2]

1-31 **2** nk **Reflektor (IRE)**[19] 1492 3-9-7 **89** RichardKingscote 6 96
(Tom Dascombe) *led: rdn over 1f out: sn hdd: continued to chal ins fnl f: hld nr fin* **4/1**[1]

42-2 **3** nk **Celebration**[19] 1492 3-8-9 **77** TonyHamilton 7 83
(Richard Fahey) *chsd ldr: rdn 2f out: chalng ins fnl f: nt qckn nr fin* **6/1**[3]

140 **4** 2 1/2 **Big Amigo (IRE)**[20] 1452 3-8-7 **75** oh3 LukeMorris 2 73
(Tom Dascombe) *lw: midfield: rdn and hdwy over 1f out: kpt on ins fnl f: no imp on ldrs* **18/1**

120- **5** 1 3/4 **Alsaaden**[278] 4877 3-9-5 **87** PaulHanagan 3 79+
(Richard Hannon) *hld up in midfield: rdn over 2f out: edgd rt ins fnl f: styd on: nt pce to trble ldrs* **11/2**[2]

1225 **6** 1 1/2 **Kingsley Klarion (IRE)**[21] 1442 3-9-5 **87** FrannyNorton 1 75
(Mark Johnston) *chsd ldrs: rdn 2f out: one pce u.p ins fnl f* **4/1**[1]

1-10 **7** 1 3/4 **Florencio**[21] 1442 3-9-4 **86** JamesDoyle 11 68
(William Muir) *lw: midfield: rdn over 2f out: outpcd fnl f* **10/1**

6-35 **8** 3/4 **Outback Blue**[76] 638 3-8-3 **76** NoelGarbutt(5) 4 56
(David Evans) *hld up: pushed along over 2f out: plugged on but n.d fnl f* **25/1**

300- **9** 3 3/4 **Wayward Hoof**[215] 6931 3-8-11 **79** DougieCostello 14 47
(K R Burke) *missed break: in rr: u.p over 1f out: nvr a threat* **33/1**

4644 **10** 1 1/4 **Thatsallimsaying (IRE)**[27] 1315 3-8-9 **77** CathyGannon 10 41
(David Evans) *lw: dwlt: in rr: pushed along over 2f out: nvr a threat* **25/1**

36-3 **11** 13 **Heraldic (USA)**[50] 954 3-9-3 **85** WilliamBuick 8 7
(Mark Johnston) *chsd ldrs tl rdn and wknd over 2f out* **14/1**

1m 15.98s (2.18) **Going Correction** +0.45s/f (Yiel) **11** Ran SP% **116.7**
Speed ratings (Par 103): **103,102,102,98,96 94,92,91,86,84 67**
CSF £26.93 CT £137.56 TOTE £6.20: £1.80, £1.80, £1.50; EX 26.80 Trifecta £132.40.
Owner Robert Ng **Bred** Robert Ng & Dermot Farrington **Trained** Newmarket, Suffolk

FOCUS
Race distance increased by 13yds. The early pace wasn't hectic and it proved hard to make up ground from off the pace. The second and third ran similar races to their recent meeting at Thirsk.

1978 T&L LEASING H'CAP 1m 2f 75y
5:25 (5:26) (Class 3) (0-90,89) 4-Y-O+
£9,960 (£2,982; £1,491; £745; £372; £187) **Stalls** High

Form RPR

30-0 **1** **Newera**[12] 1620 4-9-0 **82** (p) RichardKingscote 2 90+
(Tom Dascombe) *midfield: hdwy over 1f out: r.o ins fnl f: led fnl 75yds* **5/1**[2]

0-25 **2** nk **Burano (IRE)**[12] 1620 7-9-2 **87** ShelleyBirkett(3) 9 94
(David O'Meara) *hmpd s: hld up: nt clr run and hdwy over 1f out: r.o to chal ins fnl f: hld nr fin* **8/1**

3155 **3** shd **Dance Of Fire**[57] 871 4-9-4 **86** (p) DavidProbert 3 93
(Andrew Balding) *chsd ldrs: wnt 2nd over 2f out: led jst bef over 1f out: hdd fnl 75yds: hld nr fin* **10/1**

10-0 **4** 2 1/2 **Lord Franklin**[12] 1633 7-8-11 **79** JasonHart 1 81
(Eric Alston) *disp ld: led over 2f out: rdn and hdd jst over 1f out: no ex fnl 100yds* **20/1**

3-00 **5** 1 1/4 **Energia Flavio (BRZ)**[30] 1245 5-8-11 **79** GeorgeChaloner 6 79
(Richard Fahey) *midfield: rdn and nt clr run over 1f out: styd on to chse ldrs ins fnl f: no imp fnl 75yds* **33/1**

00-2 **6** 1 **Spa's Dancer (IRE)**[29] 1274 9-9-5 **87** (p) GrahamLee 7 85
(James Eustace) *dwlt: in rr: pushed along wl over 7f out: hdwy over 1f out: styd on u.p ins fnl f: nt pce to trble ldrs* **12/1**

0-45 **7** 2 1/4 **Top Of The Glas (IRE)**[15] 1221 5-8-12 **80** BenCurtis 11 73
(Brian Ellison) *hld up: pushed along over 2f out: rdn over 1f out: kpt on ins fnl f: nvr able to chal* **8/1**

00-0 **8** nse **The Character (IRE)**[32] 1221 5-8-11 **79** (p) LiamJones 5 72
(Tom Dascombe) *pushed along and wnt rt jst after s: chsd ldrs: rdn over 2f out: one pce over 1f out* **16/1**

62-4 **9** 2 1/4 **Sarsted**[19] 1480 4-8-12 **80** RyanMoore 8 69
(Hughie Morrison) *lw: bdly hmpd s: racd keenly: hld up: swtchd rt over 1f out: nvr a threat* **7/1**[3]

31-4 **10** 7 **Modernism**[117] 121 7-9-2 **84** PaulHanagan 13 60
(Richard Fahey) *midfield: rdn 2f out: wknd fnl f* **20/1**

604- **11** 6 **Emirates Airline**[187] 7632 4-9-7 **89** JamesDoyle 4 53
(Saeed bin Suroor) *lw: racd keenly: disp ld: rdn and hdd over 2f out: wknd over 1f out* **4/1**[1]

152- **12** 16 **Mustaqqil (IRE)**[244] 6050 4-8-12 **80** DanielTudhope 10 14
(David O'Meara) *hmpd s: racd keenly: hld up in midfield: rdn and wknd 2f out* **16/1**

5-24 **13** 27 **Solo Hunter**[33] 1195 5-9-7 **89** (b) FergusSweeney 14
(Martyn Meade) *dwlt: chsd ldrs after 2f: rdn and wknd over 3f out: eased whn wl btn over 1f out: t.o* **16/1**

2m 13.78s (2.58) **Going Correction** +0.45s/f (Yiel) **13** Ran SP% **118.3**
Speed ratings (Par 107): **107,106,106,104,103 102,101,101,99,93 88,76,54**
CSF £43.07 CT £389.84 TOTE £5.80: £2.40, £4.90, £1.10; EX 42.00 Trifecta £286.50.
Owner D R Passant **Bred** Kirtlington Stud Ltd **Trained** Malpas, Cheshire

FOCUS
Race distance increased by 14yds. A competitive 0-90 handicap and run at a much truer pace than the opening 0-105 handicap. It produced a thrilling three-way finish. The winner carried last year's progression over, with the second to form.
T/Jkpt: Not won. T/Plt: £30.40 to a £1 stake. Pool: £149,052.38 - 3578.86 winning units. T/Qpdt: £7.80 to a £1 stake. Pool: £8,196.71 - 773.81 winning units. **Darren Owen**

1979 - 1986a (Foreign Racing) - See Raceform Interactive

1770 ASCOT (R-H)
Friday, May 6

OFFICIAL GOING: Good to firm (str 8.6, rnd 8.5)
Wind: virtually nil Weather: sunny

1987 TIMES+ APPRENTICE H'CAP 2m
5:30 (5:30) (Class 3) (0-90,90) 4-Y-O+ **£7,762** (£2,310; £1,154; £577) **Stalls** Low

Form RPR

0/12 **1** **Argent Knight**[12] 1665 6-8-10 **76** (p) JoeDoyle 5 84
(Keith Dalgleish) *hld up in tch: hdwy on inner over 2f out: rdn to chal and edgd lft over 1f out: sustained duel w rival after: r.o wl: won on the nod* **3/1**[1]

/2-1 **2** nse **Seaside Sizzler**[41] 1092 9-9-2 **85** CallumShepherd(3) 2 92
(William Knight) *trckd ldrs: shkn up over 4f out: swtchd lft and effrt 3f out: rdn to ld but hrd pressed over 1f out: sustained duel w wnr after: r.o wl: lost on the nod* **13/2**

0-00 **3** 2 3/4 **Wordiness**[42] 1081 8-9-3 **86** NoelGarbutt(3) 12 90
(David Evans) *hld up in tch towards rr: hdwy into midfield 3f out: effrt and unable qck 2f out: rallied u.p over 1f out: styd on to go 3rd fnl 50yds* **25/1**

-315 **4** 1/2 **Albahar (FR)**[23] 1417 5-8-12 **83** (p) MeganNicholls(5) 1 86
(Chris Gordon) *swtg: v.s.a: clsd and in tch in rr after 2f: hdwy but v wd bnd over 2f out: hdwy to chse ldrs over 1f out: no ex 1f out: kpt on same pce and lost 3rd fnl 50yds* **18/1**

/00- **5** 2 **Tindaro (FR)**[264] 2502 9-8-13 **82** (t) EdwardGreatrex(3) 10 83
(Paul Webber) *t.k.h: hld up in tch: effrt and edgd rt over 2f out: hdwy u.p over 1f out: styd on same pce ins fnl f* **33/1**

246- **6** nk **Lady Of Yue**[189] 7597 6-8-2 **71** oh4 AaronJones(3) 8 71
(Eugene Stanford) *hld up in tch in rr: hdwy on inner over 1f out: styd on ins fnl f: no threat to ldrs* **20/1**

100- **7** 3/4 **See And Be Seen**[189] 7597 6-8-9 **78** (p) PatrickO'Donnell(3) 6 77
(Sylvester Kirk) *chsd ldr tl led over 2f out: rdn and hdd over 1f out: sn outpcd and btn: wknd ins fnl f* **20/1**

032- **8** nk **Nigel**[211] 7068 4-8-9 **78** TomMarquand 13 77
(Richard Hughes) *lw: t.k.h: hld up in tch in midfield: effrt and swtchd lft wl over 1f out: no imp and styd on same pce after* **5/1**[2]

340- **9** 3/4 **Arty Campbell (IRE)**[186] 6896 6-9-3 **83** AlistairRawlinson 14 81
(Bernard Llewellyn) *lw: t.k.h: stdd s: hdwy to chse ldrs after 2f: rdn and unable qck 2f out: lost pl over 1f out: wknd ins fnl f* **14/1**

33-5 **10** 1/2 **Percy Veer**[125] 19 4-8-12 **88** BenSanderson(7) 3 86
(Sylvester Kirk) *swtg: t.k.h: chsd ldrs: rdn ent fnl 2f: lost pl and btn over 1f out: wknd ins fnl f* **12/1**

12-2 **11** shd **Shades Of Silver**[23] 1417 6-9-9 **89** MarcMonaghan 11 86
(Ed de Giles) *lw: led: rdn and hdd over 2f out: sn struggling and lost pl 2f out: bhd ins fnl f* **7/1**

424- **12** 1 1/2 **Daghash**[217] 6896 7-8-11 **80** KieranShoemark(3) 4 76
(Stuart Kittow) *t.k.h: hld up in tch in midfield: rdn 3f out: unable qck and lost pl 2f out: bhd ins fnl f* **11/2**[3]

3m 34.45s (5.45) **Going Correction** 0.0s/f (Good)
WFA 4 from 5yo+ 3lb **12** Ran SP% **118.8**
Speed ratings (Par 107): **86,85,84,84,83 83,82,82,82,82 82,81**
CSF £21.00 CT £416.52 TOTE £3.60: £1.70, £2.00, £6.60; EX 24.60 Trifecta £366.70.
Owner Straightline Construction Ltd **Bred** Mr & Mrs A E Pakenham **Trained** Carluke, S Lanarks

FOCUS
Race distance increased by 15yds. A good quality staying handicap but several of these were keen in the early stages, off what looked to the naked eye a pretty sedate gallop through the first half mile. Quie a compressed finish, and the form is rated around the 1-2.

1988 BRITISH STALLIONS STUDS EBF MAIDEN FILLIES' STKS (PLUS 10 RACE) 5f
6:00 (6:02) (Class 4) 2-Y-O **£5,175** (£1,540; £769; £384) **Stalls** Centre

Form RPR

32 **1** **Camargue**[11] 1719 2-9-0 0 JoeFanning 3 83
(Mark Johnston) *mde all: shkn up and fnd ex over 1f out: styd on wl fnl f: readily* **11/4**[1]

2 2 1/4 **Romantic View** 2-9-0 0 WilliamBuick 6 75+
(Charlie Appleby) *lengthy: str: lw: t.k.h: chsd ldrs: wnt 2nd after 2f: effrt over 1f out: drifted rt and kpt on same pce ins fnl f* **16/1**

3 1 1/2 **Tropical Rock** 2-9-0 0 FMBerry 7 70+
(Ralph Beckett) *tall: str: s.i.s and rn green early: in tch in rr of main gp: swtchd rt and clsd into midfield 1/2-way: rdn over 1f out: hdwy to go 3rd ins fnl f: styd on steadily but no threat to wnr* **10/1**

4 hd **Amlak** 2-9-0 0 FrankieDettori 11 69+
(Richard Hannon) *str: racd keenly: chsd wnr for 2f: styd chsng ldrs: pushed along and rn green over 1f out: hdwy ins fnl f: styd on steadily fnl 100yds: pressing for 3rd cl home: no threat to wnr* **9/2**[3]

5 1 1/2 **Reeh (IRE)** 2-9-0 0 NickyMackay 8 63+
(John Gosden) *athletic: racd keenly: chsd ldrs: rdn and unable qck over 1f out: no ex 1f out: wknd ins fnl f* **9/2**[3]

6 shd **Jule In The Crown** 2-9-0 0 CharlesBishop 9 63+
(Mick Channon) *tall: plld hrd early: chsd ldrs tl stdd bk to rr of main gp after 2f: effrt jst over 1f out: kpt on steadily fnl 100yds: no threat to wnr* **3/1**[2]

7 1 1/2 **Her Terms** 2-9-0 0 PatCosgrave 2 58
(William Haggas) *leggy: athletic: chsd ldrs: rdn 2f out: no ex u.p jst over 1f out: wknd ins fnl f* **8/1**

8 1 3/4 **Kodiac Moment (IRE)** 2-9-0 0 JimmyFortune 1 51
(Brian Meehan) *cmpt: s.i.s: sn rcvrd and hld up in tch in midfield: rdn over 1f out: unable qck and wknd ins fnl f* **33/1**

9 8 **Royal Melody** 2-8-9 0 EdwardGreatrex(5) 5 23
(Heather Main) *w'like: v.s.a: rn green and a detached in rr* **66/1**

10 *7* **The Night Is Ours (IRE)** 2-9-0 0 .... LiamJones 4 19
(J S Moore) *neat: s.i.s: rn green: in tch in rr of main gp: wnt lft after 1f: rdn 1/2-way: sn struggling: bhd fnl f* **66/1**

1m 0.17s (-0.33) **Going Correction** -0.175s/f (Firm) **10** Ran SP% **120.0**
Speed ratings (Par 92): **95,91,89,88,86 86,83,80,68,66**
CSF £49.16 TOTE £3.70: £1.60, £3.20, £3.50; EX 37.70 Trifecta £291.10.
Owner Sheikh Hamdan bin Mohammed Al Maktoum **Bred** Darley **Trained** Middleham Moor, N Yorks

FOCUS
This looked a potentially informative fillies' maiden featuring a host of well-bred newcomers, but experience told as the only filly in the race to have seen the track before proved much the best on the day.

1989 PERFECT TEN MAIDEN FILLIES' STKS 1m 2f
6:30 (6:34) (Class 4) 3-Y-O+ **£5,175** (£1,540; £769; £384) **Stalls** Low

Form RPR

4- **1** **Abingdon (USA)**[158] 8048 3-8-12 0 .... TedDurcan 10 89+
(Sir Michael Stoute) *tall: lengthy: chsd ldrs: effrt to chse clr ldr 2f out: rdn and styd on strly ins fnl f: led fnl 50yds: rdn out* **9/2**[3]

2 **2** *1/2* **Ajman Princess (IRE)**[14] 1608 3-8-12 0 .... AndreaAtzeni 13 88
(Roger Varian) *lw: w ldr tl led over 5f out: rdn clr 2f out: drvn ins fnl f: worn down and hdd fnl 50yds: one pce* **5/4**[1]

3 *3* **Skiffle** 3-8-12 0 .... WilliamBuick 1 82+
(Charlie Appleby) *athletic: stood and half-rrd as stalls opened and v.s.a: in rr: clsd on to bk of field 7f out: effrt but stl plenty to do over 2f out: hdwy to chse ldng pair 1f out: kpt on: nvr threatened ldrs* **4/1**[2]

20- **4** *1/2* **Dot Green (IRE)**[200] 7339 3-8-12 0 .... SaleemGolam 6 81
(Mark H Tompkins) *w'like: in tch in midfield: n.m.r ent fnl 2f: rdn and hdwy over 1f out: wnt 3rd briefly jst over 1f out: 4th and kpt on ins fnl f: no threat to ldrs* **25/1**

5 *1* **Desert Way (IRE)** 3-8-12 0 .... FMBerry 7 79+
(Ralph Beckett) *str: stdd after s: hld up in last trio: plenty to do and hdwy towards inner over 1f out: no threat to ldrs but kpt on steadily ins fnl f* **20/1**

6 *1/2* **Haddajah (IRE)** 3-8-12 0 .... FrankieDettori 12 78+
(Sir Michael Stoute) *str: stdd s: hld up in last quartet: stl towards rr whn nt clr run and swtchd lft over 1f out: styd on wl ins fnl f: no threat to ldrs* **8/1**

7 *1 1/4* **Straw Hat (IRE)** 3-8-12 0 .... PatCosgrave 3 76
(William Haggas) *str: in tch in midfield: effrt jst over 2f out: 4th and unable qck wl over 1f out: styd on same pce after* **16/1**

0-6 **8** *3 1/4* **Pennerley**[13] 1639 3-8-9 0 .... TomMarquand(3) 5 69
(James Eustace) *athletic: bustled along leaving stalls: in tch in midfield: rdn and unable qck over 2f out: wknd over 1f out* **100/1**

0 **9** *3/4* **Aspen Again (IRE)**[22] 1436 3-8-12 0 .... ShaneKelly 8 68
(David Menuisier) *led tl over 5f out: styd w ldr tl 3rd and outpcd u.p 2f out: wknd over 1f out* **50/1**

3 **10** *1 1/2* **Cape Peninsular**[43] 1063 3-8-12 0 .... LukeMorris 9 65
(James Tate) *athletic: t.k.h: hld up on midfield: dropped towards rr 6f out: rdn 3f out: no hdwy: wl btn whn hung lft ins fnl f* **25/1**

55- **11** *2* **Sunlit Waters**[158] 8048 3-8-12 0 .... JamieSpencer 2 61
(Eve Johnson Houghton) *str: in tch in midfield: struggling to qckn whn sltly short of room wl over 1f out: sn wknd* **66/1**

3 **12** *13* **Rationality (USA)**[29] 1289 3-8-12 0 .... (t) NickyMackay 4 35
(John Gosden) *tall: t.k.h: chsd ldrs tl lost pl and bhd 2f out: no ch and eased ins fnl f* **20/1**

2m 6.82s (-0.58) **Going Correction** 0.0s/f (Good) **12** Ran SP% **121.3**
Speed ratings (Par 102): **102,101,99,98,98 97,96,94,93,92 90,80**
CSF £10.01 TOTE £5.90: £2.00, £1.30, £1.50; EX 16.10 Trifecta £64.90.
Owner Ballymacoll Stud **Bred** Ballymacoll Stud **Trained** Newmarket, Suffolk

FOCUS
Race distance increased by 9yds. A quality maiden featuring a stack of smartly-bred fillies and a host of these ran with promise, so although the early gallop wasn't strong, this looks a race that will throw up plenty of future winners. The second and fourth set a good standard.

1990 MONTFORT H'CAP 6f
7:05 (7:07) (Class 3) (0-95,93) 4-Y-O+ **£7,762** (£2,310; £1,154; £577) **Stalls** Centre

Form RPR

402- **1** **Muir Lodge**[203] 7245 5-9-3 **89** .... (t) PatCosgrave 7 97
(George Baker) *hld up in tch: effrt and rdn to chse ldrs jst over 1f out: drvn to ld ins fnl f: styd on wl: drvn out* **14/1**

1-20 **2** *1/2* **Flowers On Venus (IRE)**[18] 1530 4-8-12 **84** .... AndreaAtzeni 12 90+
(David Evans) *stdd s: hld up in rr: effrt over 1f out: str run u.p ins fnl f: wnt 2nd wl ins fnl f: r.o* **10/1**

605- **3** *3/4* **Shipyard (USA)**[146] 8200 7-9-0 **89** .... AlistairRawlinson(3) 8 93
(Michael Appleby) *hld up in tch: rdn and hdwy over 1f out: edging rt and ev ch ins fnl f: styd on same pce and lost 2nd wl ins fnl f* **16/1**

463- **4** *shd* **Shore Step (IRE)**[238] 6273 6-9-7 **93** .... WilliamBuick 2 97
(Mick Channon) *mde most: rdn over 1f out: hdd ins fnl f: no ex and outpcd wl ins fnl f* **6/1**[3]

05-2 **5** *hd* **Ice Lord (IRE)**[18] 1530 4-9-1 **87** .... AdamKirby 9 90
(Clive Cox) *lw: hld up in tch: effrt 2f out: hdwy and drvn to chse ldrs whn edgd rt 1f out: styd on same pce ins fnl f* **5/2**[1]

3334 **6** *2 1/4* **Yeeoow (IRE)**[5] 1887 7-8-13 **85** .... JoeyHaynes 5 81
(K R Burke) *w ldr: rdn and ev ch over 2f out tl unable qck ent fnl f: wknd ins fnl f* **8/1**

216- **7** *1/2* **Cartmell Cleave**[244] 6078 4-9-4 **90** .... TedDurcan 10 84
(Stuart Kittow) *stdd s: hld up in tch: hdwy to chse ldrs whn short of room and swtchd lft jst over 1f out: no imp after* **7/2**[2]

0245 **8** *hd* **Plucky Dip**[4] 1929 5-8-5 **80** .... (p) JoeDoyle(3) 6 74
(John Ryan) *w ldrs tl lost pl u.p wl over 1f out: styd on same pce after* **14/1**

360- **9** *3/4* **Major Crispies**[216] 6942 5-9-1 **87** .... LukeMorris 3 78
(James Eustace) *hld up in tch in midfield: effrt 2f out: sn drvn and unable qck: wknd ins fnl f* **25/1**

0-25 **10** *1/2* **Childesplay**[24] 1394 5-8-11 **86** .... TomMarquand(3) 1 76
(Heather Main) *in tch towards rr: effrt and sme hdwy 2f out: sn no imp: wknd ins fnl f* **9/1**

50-5 **11** *4* **Redvers (IRE)**[18] 1522 8-8-13 **85** .... (b) JoeFanning 11 62
(Noel Wilson) *lw: dwlt: hld up in tch in rr: effrt wl over 1f out: no hdwy: bhd ins fnl f* **28/1**

1m 12.16s (-2.34) **Going Correction** -0.175s/f (Firm) **11** Ran SP% **121.8**
Speed ratings (Par 107): **108,107,106,106,105 102,102,102,101,100 95**
CSF £151.69 CT £2312.42 TOTE £19.90: £4.60, £3.30, £4.90; EX 226.70 Trifecta £2307.20.
Owner Turf Club 2014 **Bred** Langton Stud **Trained** Manton, Wilts

FOCUS
A really competitive handicap and plenty to take from it. Sound form. The runner-up did best of the quartet that raced a bit detached from the rest.

1991 AGV H'CAP 7f
7:40 (7:41) (Class 2) (0-105,105) 3-Y-O **£18,675** (£5,592; £2,796; £1,398; £699; £351) **Stalls** Centre

Form RPR

12-2 **1** **Tabarrak (IRE)**[24] 1393 3-8-13 **97** .... FrankieDettori 7 108
(Richard Hannon) *lw: mde all: rdn over 1f out: edgd rt and bmpd chalr ins fnl f: hld on gamely towards fin* **3/1**[2]

212- **2** *hd* **Atlantic Sun**[198] 7396 3-8-4 **91** .... TomMarquand(3) 6 101
(Richard Hannon) *chsd wnr thrght: rdn 2f out: drvn and ev ch whn bmpd ins fnl f: kpt on wl u.p: jst hld* **4/1**[3]

14-2 **3** *5* **Turbine (IRE)**[77] 644 3-8-5 **89** .... JoeFanning 3 86
(Mark Johnston) *w'like: stdd and wnt rt s: hld up in tch in midfield: rdn 2f out: hdwy to chse ldng pair over 1f out: outpcd fnl f* **9/1**

200- **4** *1/2* **Madrinho (IRE)**[195] 7468 3-8-11 **95** .... SeanLevey 2 90
(Richard Hannon) *stdd and bmpd s: hld up in tch in rr: swtchd rt and effrt wl over 1f out: outpcd 1f out: 4th and kpt on same pce after* **22/1**

336- **5** *7* **Twin Sails**[209] 7114 3-9-7 **105** .... RobertWinston 4 81
(Dean Ivory) *hld up in tch in last pair: effrt over 1f out: sn btn: wknd fnl f* **11/1**

1-12 **6** *nk* **Comicas (USA)**[64] 807 3-9-0 **98** .... (p) WilliamBuick 5 73
(Charlie Appleby) *lw: in tch in midfield: effrt u.p 2f out: no imp and btn over 1f out: wknd ins fnl f* **15/8**[1]

-024 **7** *3 3/4* **Adventurous (IRE)**[23] 1424 3-9-7 **105** .... AdamKirby 1 70
(Mark Johnston) *chsd ldrs: rdn 2f out: lost pl and btn over 1f out: sn wknd* **8/1**

1m 25.11s (-2.49) **Going Correction** -0.175s/f (Firm) **7** Ran SP% **113.6**
Speed ratings (Par 105): **107,106,101,100,92 92,87**
CSF £15.19 CT £94.15 TOTE £3.60: £2.10, £2.60; EX 15.70 Trifecta £80.00.
Owner Hamdan Al Maktoum **Bred** Rathbarry Stud & F & N Woods **Trained** East Everleigh, Wilts

FOCUS
Good 3yo handicap form with the front two pulling clear and coming together in the final furlong, with the winner giving his rival a bump as he carried him across the track. The stewards' enquiry could have gone either way but they deemed the result wasn't effected by the interference. A 1-2-4 for Richard Hannon.

1992 MITIE TOTAL SECURITY H'CAP 1m (S)
8:10 (8:13) (Class 4) (0-85,85) 3-Y-O **£5,175** (£1,540; £769; £384) **Stalls** Centre

Form RPR

415- **1** **Taurean Star (IRE)**[196] 7432 3-9-5 **83** .... JamieSpencer 7 92+
(Michael Bell) *stdd s: hld up in rr: clsd and nt clr run 2f out: hdwy and switching rt over 1f out: qcknd to chal between rivals ins fnl f: led 75yds out: r.o wl* **25/1**

13- **2** *1/2* **Banksea**[188] 7630 3-8-13 **77** .... AndreaAtzeni 4 85+
(Luca Cumani) *str: chsd ldr tl led over 3f out: rdn 2f out: kpt on wl u.p tl hdd and one pce fnl 75yds* **15/2**

0-42 **3** *3/4* **Aleko**[9] 1777 3-8-11 **75** .... WilliamBuick 19 81
(Mark Johnston) *hld up in tch in midfield: effrt wl over 1f out: drvn and hdwy to press ldrs ins fnl f: kpt on towards fin* **16/1**

51- **4** *hd* **Ballard Down (IRE)**[142] 8246 3-9-4 **82** .... GeorgeBaker 1 88
(William Knight) *unf: scope: lw: stdd s: hld up in rr: swtchd rt and hdwy 2f out: rdn to chal 1f out: unable qck and one pce fnl 75yds* **33/1**

21-4 **5** *2* **Zest (IRE)**[34] 1206 3-9-6 **84** .... FrederikTylicki 20 85+
(James Fanshawe) *athletic: stdd and dropped in bhd after s: t.k.h: hld up in rr: nt clr run 2f out: swtchd lft: rdn and hdwy over 1f out: styd on ins fnl f: no threat to ldrs* **11/2**[2]

41- **6** *2 3/4* **Rostova (USA)**[207] 7160 3-9-3 **81** .... TedDurcan 18 76
(Sir Michael Stoute) *hld up in tch in midfield: effrt 2f out: hdwy over 1f out: kpt on same pce and no imp ins fnl f* **12/1**

011- **7** *3/4* **Sheila's Treat (IRE)**[156] 8076 3-8-3 **72** .... EdwardGreatrex(5) 2 65
(Denis Coakley) *hld up in tch: swtchd rt and hdwy u.p 2f out: no imp over 1f out: wl hld and styd on same pce fnl f* **33/1**

21- **8** *3* **Baydar**[171] 7879 3-9-4 **82** .... FrankieDettori 9 68+
(Hugo Palmer) *wl in tch in midfield: clsd to press ldrs over 3f out: rdn and ev ch over 2f out tl no ex over 1f out: wknd fnl f* **7/2**[1]

31-5 **9** *1* **Danecase**[29] 1288 3-9-7 **85** .... MartinLane 17 69
(David Dennis) *chsd ldrs: rdn and ev ch over 2f out: hung rt and btn over 1f out: wknd ins fnl f* **50/1**

61- **10** *1* **Marylebone**[179] 7777 3-9-4 **82** .... JoeFanning 3 64
(Ed Walker) *tall: t.k.h: hld up in tch in midfield: effrt 2f out: no imp u.p whn sltly hmpd over 1f out: wknd fnl f* **8/1**

644- **11** *1* **Pacommand**[137] 8323 3-8-8 **72** .... LukeMorris 14 51
(Marco Botti) *tall: in tch in midfield: shuffled bk towards rr and rdn over 2f out: sme hdwy but no ch w ldrs over 1f out: no imp fnl f* **33/1**

35-3 **12** *hd* **Picture Painter (IRE)**[25] 1381 3-8-9 **73** .... KierenFallon 10 52
(Jim Goldie) *in tch in midfield: lost pl and rdn over 3f out: n.d fnl 2f* **25/1**

01- **13** *4 1/2* **Kummiya**[171] 7878 3-8-12 **76** .... FMBerry 8 45
(Roger Charlton) *cmpt: stdd s: t.k.h early: hld up in tch in midfield: no imp u.p whn sltly impeded over 1f out: sn wknd* **7/1**[3]

0-1 **14** *1 3/4* **Telegram**[111] 219 3-9-4 **85** .... TomMarquand(3) 6 50
(Richard Hannon) *str: in tch in midfield: rdn over 2f out: sn struggling and lost pl over 1f out: wknd fnl f* **25/1**

110- **15** *1* **Goodwood Zodiac (IRE)**[208] 7142 3-9-7 **85** .... AdamKirby 13 47
(William Knight) *in tch in midfield: rdn 3f out: lost pl 2f out: sn wl btn* **33/1**

10-1 **16** *1* **Royal Reserve**[10] 1750 3-9-3 **81** 6ex .... MartinDwyer 16 41
(William Muir) *in tch in midfield: hdwy to press ldrs and rdn over 2f out: sn struggling and lost pl over 1f out: wknd fnl f* **7/1**[3]

6-00 **17** *nk* **Essenaitch (IRE)**[14] 1610 3-9-2 **85** .... NoelGarbutt(5) 12 44
(David Evans) *led tl over 3f out: lost pl and bhd 2f out: sn wknd* **66/1**

1m 38.96s (-1.84) **Going Correction** -0.175s/f (Firm) **17** Ran SP% **125.8**
Speed ratings (Par 101): **102,101,100,100,98 95,95,92,91,90 89,88,84,82,81 80,80**
CSF £194.13 CT £3241.65 TOTE £29.40: £4.30, £2.60, £3.30, £7.70; EX 396.40 Trifecta £2884.90 Part won..
Owner Brian Goodyear **Bred** Denis McDonnell **Trained** Newmarket, Suffolk

FOCUS
Really strong 3yo handicap form and no surprise if one or two of these came back here for the Britannia Stakes at the Royal meeting. The time was good and the form is rated around the third.
T/Plt: £897.00 to a £1 stake. Pool of £79,800.22 - 64.94 winning units. T/Qpdt: £95.00 to a £1 stake. Pool of £7,655.17 - 59.59 winning units. **Steve Payne**

1972 CHESTER (L-H)

Friday, May 6

OFFICIAL GOING: Good (7.7)
Wind: Nil Weather: Sunny

1993 CRABBIE'S EARL GROSVENOR H'CAP 7f 122y

2:10 (2:14) (Class 2) (0-105,103) 4-Y-0+

£18,675 (£5,592; £2,796; £1,398; £699; £351) **Stalls** Low

Form RPR

4-40 **1** **Hillbilly Boy (IRE)**[30] 1274 6-8-10 **92**........................ RichardKingscote 4 102
(Tom Dascombe) *mde all: rdn over 1f out: drvn out and styd on wl fnl f* **13/2**

-310 **2** 2½ **Gabrial's Kaka (IRE)**[13] 1629 6-8-8 **90**........................ GeorgeChaloner 2 94
(Richard Fahey) *midfield: pushed along and hdwy over 1f out: wnt 2nd ins fnl f: styd on: nt rch wnr* **4/1**[1]

4004 **3** 2¼ **Arnold Lane (IRE)**[16] 1563 7-8-4 **86**........................ SilvestreDeSousa 1 84
(Mick Channon) *chsd ldrs: rdn to take 2nd over 1f out: lost 2nd ins fnl f: styd on same pce fnl 150yds* **11/2**[2]

-000 **4** 1½ **Sound Advice**[13] 1629 7-9-5 **101**........................ PhillipMakin 6 95
(Keith Dalgleish) *in tch: effrt 2f out: no imp over 1f out: kpt on same pce ins fnl f* **6/1**[3]

6000 **5** 1 **Al Khan (IRE)**[6] 1871 7-8-5 **87**........................ ShaneGray 10 79+
(Kevin Ryan) *swtchd lft s: hld up in rr: nt clr run wl over 1f out: hdwy sn after: styd on ins fnl f: nvr able to trble ldrs* **16/1**

40-4 **6** nse **Archie (IRE)**[34] 1204 4-8-6 **88**........................ JohnFahy 5 80
(Clive Cox) *chsd wnr: rdn over 2f out: lost 2nd over 1f out: nt qckn u.p: one pce ins fnl f* **6/1**[3]

0-00 **7** nk **Jallota**[78] 623 5-9-7 **103**........................ DarryllHolland 8 95+
(Charles Hills) *hmpd early on: hld up: rdn wl over 1f out: kpt on ins fnl f: no imp: eased whn n.d fnl 75yds* **11/1**

50-0 **8** 1¼ **Glenalmond (IRE)**[6] 1871 4-8-8 **90**........................(p) JoeyHaynes 3 78
(K R Burke) *hld up: rdn over 2f out: kpt on ins fnl f: no imp: eased whn wl hld fnl 100yds* **12/1**

44-2 **9** 3½ **Goring (GER)**[10] 1752 4-8-3 **85**........................ JimmyQuinn 12 64
(Eve Johnson Houghton) *midfield: rdn over 1f out: no imp: wknd ins fnl f* **20/1**

-010 **10** 2¼ **Perfect Pasture**[6] 1856 6-8-13 **100**........................(v) NathanEvans(5) 7 74
(Michael Easterby) *towards rr: rdn over 2f out: nvr a threat* **12/1**

1214 **11** 4½ **Bold Prediction (IRE)**[55] 920 6-8-8 **90**........................ FrannyNorton 9 52
(Ed Walker) *sed awkwardly: chsd ldrs: rdn 3f out: wknd 2f out* **14/1**

1m 34.45s (0.65) **Going Correction** +0.35s/f (Good) **11** Ran SP% **118.3**
Speed ratings (Par 109): **110,107,105,103,102 102,102,101,97,95 90**
CSF £32.88 CT £139.15 TOTE £10.00: £3.00, £1.50, £2.30; EX 43.20 Trifecta £201.30.
Owner Macguire's Bloodstock Ltd **Bred** Tipper House Stud **Trained** Malpas, Cheshire

FOCUS
The rail was moved out a further 3 yards between the 6f and 8.5f points after racing on Thursday. The actual race distance of the opener was 7f 146yds. Jockeys involved in the first agreed that the ground was a little faster than it had been the previous day. This good handicap lacked improvers, but the form seems sound enough. The winner is rated back to his best.

1994 BETDAQ DEE STKS (LISTED RACE) (C&G) 1m 2f 75y

2:40 (2:40) (Class 1) 3-Y-O

£42,532 (£16,125; £8,070; £4,020; £2,017; £1,012) **Stalls** High

Form RPR

13-3 **1** **Viren's Army (IRE)**[16] 1567 3-9-0 98........................ SilvestreDeSousa 4 104
(Richard Hannon) *prom for 2f: in tch: effrt to ld 1f out: hrd pressed ins fnl f: all out* **12/1**

22-1 **2** shd **Linguistic (IRE)**[22] 1438 3-9-0 100........................ WilliamBuick 3 104
(John Gosden) *hld up: effrt on outer over 2f out: rdn and hdwy over 1f out: r.o and chalng ins fnl f: jst failed* **11/10**[1]

3 hd **Housesofparliament (IRE)**[14] 1614 3-9-0 102........(t) SeamieHeffernan 1 103
(A P O'Brien, Ire) *in tch: effrt over 1f out: r.o for press and chalng ins fnl f: jst hld* **11/2**[3]

235- **4** 2½ **Platitude**[223] 6731 3-9-0 97........................ StevieDonohoe 5 98
(Sir Michael Stoute) *in tch: trckd ldrs after 2f: wnt 2nd wl over 2f out: rdn and led wl over 1f out: sn hdd: stl ch u.p ins fnl f: no ex fnl 75yds* **16/1**

4 **5** 2 **Cook Islands (IRE)**[26] 1370 3-9-0 99........................ RyanMoore 8 96
(A P O'Brien, Ire) *in rr: niggled along 4f out: nt clr run over 2f out: effrt and swtchd lft to chse ldrs ins fnl f: one pce fnl 100yds: eased whn hld towards fin* **2/1**[2]

122- **6** 10 **Kingston Kurrajong**[222] 6775 3-9-0 89........................ DavidProbert 6 75
(Andrew Balding) *led after 1f: rdn and hdd wl over 1f out: sn wknd* **25/1**

0-10 **7** 24 **Ban Shoof**[14] 1602 3-9-0 74........................(p) ThomasBrown 2 30
(Ismail Mohammed) *led for 1f: remained w ldr: pushed along 5f out: wknd qckly 2f out: eased whn wl btn ins fnl f* **100/1**

2m 11.48s (0.28) **Going Correction** +0.35s/f (Good) **7** Ran SP% **114.7**
Speed ratings (Par 107): **112,111,111,109,108 100,80**
CSF £26.06 TOTE £12.30: £3.30, £1.30; EX 29.00 Trifecta £118.20.
Owner Middleham Park Racing XXX **Bred** Ruskerne Ltd **Trained** East Everleigh, Wilts

■ Stewards' Enquiry : William Buick four-day ban (20-23 May): used whip above permitted level
Seamie Heffernan two-day ban (20-21 May): used whip above permitted level

FOCUS
Race distance increased by 26yds. They appeared to go a fair gallop early, but the winner sat prominent and there was little between the first three at the line. This won't be having any bearing on the Derby, although it was the best time on the card. It's hard to be overly positive about the form.

1995 BOODLES DIAMOND ORMONDE STKS (GROUP 3) 1m 5f 89y

3:10 (3:10) (Class 1) 4-Y-O+ **£42,532** (£16,125; £8,070; £4,020; £2,017) **Stalls** Low

Form RPR

53-1 **1** **Dartmouth**[20] 1475 4-9-3 114........................ RyanMoore 2 115
(Sir Michael Stoute) *mde all: rdn over 1f out: edgd lft whn pressed ins fnl f: r.o u.p: a doing enough nr fin* **1/1**[1]

233- **2** nk **Wicklow Brave**[160] 7277 7-9-0 112........................[1] WilliamBuick 7 111
(W P Mullins, Ire) *hld up: forced to wait for run wl over 1f out: effrt sn after on inner: rdr lost whip ins fnl f: r.o and clsd nr fin* **4/1**[2]

165- **3** ¾ **Elidor**[283] 4726 6-9-0 106........................ SilvestreDeSousa 5 110
(Mick Channon) *chsd ldr for nrly 2f out: remained prom: effrt to take 2nd over 1f out: r.o and chalng ins fnl f: no ex nr fin* **10/1**

13-1 **4** 1½ **Cymro (IRE)**[20] 1493 4-9-0 105........................ RichardKingscote 6 108
(Tom Dascombe) *chsd wnr after nrly 2f: rdn over 2f out: lost 2nd over 1f out: stl cl up ins fnl f: nt qckn u.p and wanted to lug lft: styd on same pce fnl 75yds* **5/1**[3]

3- **5** 3 **Father Christmas (IRE)**[322] 3342 4-9-0 108........................ SeamieHeffernan 1 103
(A P O'Brien, Ire) *hld up: pushed along 3f out: rdn whn outpcd over 1f out: nvr able to chal* **6/1**

2m 58.7s (6.00) **Going Correction** +0.35s/f (Good) **5** Ran SP% **110.0**
Speed ratings (Par 113): **95,94,94,93,91**
CSF £5.28 TOTE £1.90: £1.10, £2.50; EX 4.10 Trifecta £11.80.
Owner The Queen **Bred** Darley **Trained** Newmarket, Suffolk

FOCUS
Actual race distance 1m 5f 133yds. This didn't look a strong renewal, and the winner was able to dictate a modest pace. He more than confirmed his Lingfield win.

1996 BETWAY EBF STALLIONS H'CAP 5f 16y

3:45 (3:46) (Class 2) (0-105,105) 3-Y-O

£18,675 (£5,592; £2,796; £1,398; £699; £351) **Stalls** Low

Form RPR

11-6 **1** **Kachy**[23] 1424 3-9-7 **105**........................ RichardKingscote 3 111
(Tom Dascombe) *w ldr: led 4f out: rdn over 1f out: r.o wl fnl f* **5/2**[2]

11-4 **2** 1¼ **El Astronaute (IRE)**[20] 1492 3-8-5 **89**........................ SilvestreDeSousa 1 91
(John Quinn) *led for 1f: checked sltly 3f out: lost 2nd over 2f out: rdn to take 2nd over 1f out: tried to chal: nt qckn ins fnl f* **15/8**[1]

140- **3** 1 **Powerallied (IRE)**[216] 6931 3-8-2 **86** oh2........................ PatrickMathers 7 84
(Richard Fahey) *in tch: pushed along over 3f out: rdn to chse ldrs over 1f out: kpt on ins fnl f: nt quite pce of first two* **9/1**

65-0 **4** 2½ **Riflescope (IRE)**[14] 1607 3-9-0 **98**........................ WilliamBuick 4 87+
(Mark Johnston) *bhd: outpcd over 2f out: rdn and over 1f out: styd on ins fnl f: no imp under hand ride fnl 100yds* **10/1**

30-0 **5** 2¾ **Zebstar (IRE)**[9] 1773 3-8-11 **95**........................ JFEgan 6 74
(James Unett) *towards rr: pushed along over 3f out: rdn over 1f out: nvr able to trble ldrs* **11/1**

310- **6** nse **Mont Kiara (FR)**[203] 7275 3-8-8 **92**........................ FrannyNorton 5 71
(Kevin Ryan) *chsd ldrs: racd in 2nd over 2f out tl over 1f out: wknd ins fnl f* **9/2**[3]

2-25 **7** 3¾ **Sign Of The Kodiac (IRE)**[14] 1607 3-8-11 **95**........................ TomEaves 8 60
(James Given) *chsd ldrs: rdn over 2f out: wknd over 1f out* **22/1**

1m 2.12s (1.12) **Going Correction** +0.35s/f (Good) **7** Ran SP% **113.3**
Speed ratings (Par 105): **105,103,101,97,93 92,86**
CSF £7.46 CT £33.17 TOTE £3.30: £1.90, £1.10; EX 9.40 Trifecta £41.90.
Owner Jones Lowe Mound Trowbridge **Bred** Denniff Farms Ltd **Trained** Malpas, Cheshire

FOCUS
Race distance increased by 20yds. A useful sprint, there was no hanging around and the class-dropper proved much too good. He is rated back to oform.

1997 SUSTAINABLE GROUP (UK) LTD H'CAP 7f 2y

4:20 (4:20) (Class 4) (0-85,86) 4-Y-O+

£7,470 (£2,236; £1,118; £559; £279; £140) **Stalls** Low

Form RPR

000- **1** **Khelman (IRE)**[181] 7758 6-8-11 **83**........................ AdamMcNamara(7) 1 91
(Richard Fahey) *sed awkwardly: midfield: hdwy whn nt clr run over 1f out: r.o to ld fnl 110yds: in command after* **11/2**[3]

3110 **2** ¾ **Captain Revelation**[30] 1274 4-8-9 **81**........................ PatrickVaughan(7) 12 87
(Tom Dascombe) *chsd ldrs: rdn to ld over 1f out: hdd fnl 110yds: hld after* **25/1**

4151 **3** nse **Fingal's Cave (IRE)**[17] 1545 4-9-2 **81**........................ SilvestreDeSousa 7 88+
(Mick Channon) *racd keenly: hld up: hdwy whn nt clr run over 1f out: chalng whn tightened up ins fnl f: styd on: fin 4th: promoted to 3rd* **7/2**[1]

25-0 **4** 1 **Fast Dancer (IRE)**[27] 1335 4-9-5 **84**........................ JFEgan 8 87
(Joseph Tuite) *midfield: rdn and hdwy over 1f out: chalng whn edgd lft ins fnl f: kpt on towards fin: fin 3rd: disqualified and plcd 4th* **8/1**

6-31 **5** 1 **Kalk Bay (IRE)**[13] 1625 9-8-13 **83**........................(t) NathanEvans(5) 10 83
(Michael Easterby) *hld up: rdn and hdwy over 1f out: chsd ldrs ins fnl f: kpt on same pce fnl 75yds* **8/1**

0-00 **6** 1½ **Deauville Prince (FR)**[18] 1522 6-9-5 **84**........................(vt) RichardKingscote 2 80
(Tom Dascombe) *led: rdn and hdd over 1f out: fdd fnl 100yds* **4/1**[2]

0-04 **7** 1½ **Whozthecat (IRE)**[12] 1672 9-9-5 **84**........................ SeamieHeffernan 5 76
(Declan Carroll) *chsd ldrs: effrt over 1f out: no ex ins fnl f* **20/1**

000- **8** nk **Meshardal (GER)**[239] 6248 6-9-6 **85**........................ FrannyNorton 11 76
(Ruth Carr) *hld up: pushed along over 1f out: no imp* **12/1**

1665 **9** 2¼ **Corporal Maddox**[13] 1634 9-9-3 **82**........................(p) DavidProbert 4 67
(Ronald Harris) *dwlt: hld up: rdn over 1f out: nvr a threat* **20/1**

00-3 **10** ½ **The Hooded Claw (IRE)**[18] 1522 5-9-6 **85**........................ JackGarritty 6 68
(Tim Easterby) *w ldr tl rdn over 1f out: wknd ins fnl f* **11/2**[3]

1m 29.18s (2.68) **Going Correction** +0.35s/f (Good) **10** Ran SP% **116.3**
Speed ratings (Par 105): **98,97,95,96,94 93,91,91,88,87**
CSF £135.89 CT £564.69 TOTE £6.50: £2.00, £4.50, £1.60; EX 187.30 Trifecta £4184.20.
Owner S & G Clayton **Bred** Oghill House Stud & Jimmy Hyland **Trained** Musley Bank, N Yorks

FOCUS
Actual race distance 7f 26yds. Fair handicap form, but it became rather messy in the home straight. The winner is rated back to his old best.

1998 LDF MAIDEN FILLIES' STKS (PLUS 10 RACE) 7f 2y

4:50 (4:54) (Class 4) 3-Y-O

£7,470 (£2,236; £1,118; £559; £279; £140) **Stalls** Low

Form RPR

-3 **1** **Golden Glimmer (IRE)**[13] 1628 3-9-0 0........................ RichardKingscote 4 85+
(Tom Dascombe) *mde all: rdn over 1f out: sn clr: r.o wl: eased cl home* **5/2**[2]

423- **2** 4½ **Dark Intention (IRE)**[210] 7092 3-9-0 68........................ TomEaves 6 71
(Lawrence Mullaney) *chsd wnr: rdn over 1f out: sn outpcd and no ch* **8/1**

-0 **3** 4½ **Queen's Code (IRE)**[24] 1392 3-9-0 0........................ DarryllHolland 2 59
(Charles Hills) *hld up: rdn over 2f out: hdwy over 1f out: styd on to take 3rd fnl 100yds: nvr able to chal* **14/1**

3-0 **4** 1 **Dufay (IRE)**[24] 1392 3-9-0 0........................ FrannyNorton 7 56
(Charlie Appleby) *racd on outer: chsd ldrs: rdn over 1f out: one pce fnl f* **9/4**[1]

3- **5** 3¼ **Zeb's Fantasy (IRE)**[238] 6291 3-9-0 69........................ DavidProbert 3 47
(Ross O'Sullivan, Ire) *in tch: rdn over 1f out: no imp: wl btn ins fnl f* **11/1**

5 **6** 4 **Any Joy (IRE)**[14] 1597 3-8-7 0........................ GeorgeWood(7) 5 37
(Ben Haslam) *towards rr: rdn over 3f out: rn green: nvr a threat* **18/1**

4 **7** 1½ **Angelic Guest (IRE)**[13] 1628 3-9-0 0........................ SilvestreDeSousa 1 33+
(Mick Channon) *in tch: pushed along 3f out: n.m.r on inner and snatched up 2f out: wknd over 1f out* **3/1**[3]

0- **8** *nse* **Sunshineandbubbles**[230] 6548 3-8-11 0 LouisSteward(3) 8 32
(Daniel Mark Loughnane) *in rr: rdn 2f out: nvr a threat* **40/1**

1m 29.2s (2.70) **Going Correction** +0.35s/f (Good) **8** Ran SP% **118.2**
Speed ratings (Par 98): **98,92,87,86,82 78,76,76**
CSF £23.79 TOTE £2.90: £1.10, £1.90, £3.70; EX 26.10 Trifecta £190.60.
Owner Chasemore Farm **Bred** Lynchbages Edgeridge Ltd & Glenvale Stud **Trained** Malpas, Cheshire
■ Stewards' Enquiry : Franny Norton one-day ban (20 May): careless riding

FOCUS
Race distance increased by 24yds. No great gallop on here and it paid to race up with the pace. The runner-up was rated 68, so the form looks ordinary with a couple of fancied runners disappointing. The first two were always prominent.

1999 TCC 10TH BIRTHDAY APPRENTICE H'CAP 1m 4f 66y
5:20 (5:23) (Class 4) (0-85,88) 4-Y-0+
£9,337 (£2,796; £1,398; £699; £349; £175) **Stalls** Low

Form RPR
4121 **1** **Indira**[4] 1919 5-9-2 **83** 6ex JosephineGordon(3) 9 93
(John Berry) *a handy: led 1f out: flashed tail ins fnl f: r.o wl fnl 75yds* **7/1**

003/ **2** *2 1/4* **Repeater**[26] 1371 7-8-7 **76** (b) KillianLeonard(5) 7 82
(Miss Amanda Mooney, Ire) *racd keenly: hld up: hdwy after 4f: led 2f out: rdn and hdd 1f out: kpt on but outpcd by wnr fnl 75yds* **25/1**

043- **3** *2* **Trendsetter (IRE)**[175] 6520 5-9-0 **85** GeorgeWood(7) 6 88
(John Quinn) *midfield: rdn and hdwy over 1f out: chsd ldrs ins fnl f: kpt on: nt pce of front two* **5/1**[2]

1-56 **4** *1 1/4* **Corton Lad**[57] 888 6-9-0 **85** (tp) CliffordLee(7) 11 86
(Keith Dalgleish) *in tch: hdwy to go 2nd after 4f: led over 2f out: sn hdd: styd on same pce ins fnl f* **25/1**

-133 **5** *shd* **Whoopsy Daisy**[29] 1290 4-8-10 **74** DannyBrock 10 75
(Jane Chapple-Hyam) *chsd ldrs: rdn and nt qckn over 1f out: kpt on one pce ins fnl f* **14/1**

60-2 **6** *1 1/2* **Graceland (FR)**[8] 1802 4-9-5 **83** LouisSteward 3 81+
(Michael Bell) *missed break: hld up: hdwy into midfield over 5f out: effrt 2f out: no imp over 1f out: no ex ins fnl f* **5/2**[1]

3154 **7** *1* **Gabrial The Duke (IRE)**[29] 1296 6-9-0 **83** (b) AdamMcNamara(5) 2 80
(Richard Fahey) *s.s: rdn along early: in rr: u.p 4f out: kpt on ins fnl f: unable to trble ldrs* **5/1**[2]

-442 **8** *1* **Excellent Puck (IRE)**[49] 983 6-9-0 **78** EoinWalsh 8 73
(Shaun Lycett) *chsd ldrs: rdn over 2f out: sn lost pl: n.d after* **25/1**

210- **9** *4* **Onda District (IRE)**[220] 6835 4-8-7 **77** CallumRodriguez(5) 4 66
(Richard Ford) *hld up in rr: struggling 4f out: nvr a threat* **25/1**

0-01 **10** *3 3/4* **Newera**[1] 1978 4-9-5 **88** 6ex (p) AnnaHesketh(5) 5 71+
(Tom Dascombe) *hld up: rdn 3f out: nvr a threat* **8/1**

0-00 **11** *1 1/4* **The Character (IRE)**[1] 1978 5-8-10 **79** (p) PatrickVaughan(5) 1 60+
(Tom Dascombe) *led: hdd over 2f out: wknd over 1f out* **13/2**[3]

2m 42.88s (4.38) **Going Correction** +0.35s/f (Good) **11** Ran SP% **120.9**
Speed ratings (Par 105): **99,97,96,95,95 94,93,92,90,87 86**
CSF £175.79 CT £943.37 TOTE £8.40: £1.90, £7.70, £1.40; EX 137.10 Trifecta £640.70.
Owner Severn Crossing Partnership **Bred** Mrs M L Parry & P M Steele-Mortimer **Trained** Newmarket, Suffolk

FOCUS
Actual race distance 1m4f 104yds. The gallop was pretty sedate in this fair handicap for apprentices. The third looks the best guide.
T/Jkpt: Not won. T/Plt: £22.70 to a £1 stake. Pool: £14,9287.02 - 4791.88 winning tickets T/Qpdt: £7.90 to a £1 stake. Pool: £8,221.25 - 765.02 winning tickets **Darren Owen**

1832 LINGFIELD (L-H)
Friday, May 6

OFFICIAL GOING: Polytrack: standard
Wind: Almost nil Weather: Fine, warm

2000 HEART FM MAIDEN STKS 1m 4f (P)
1:30 (1:32) (Class 5) 3-Y-0
£3,234 (£962; £481; £240) **Stalls** Low

Form RPR
43- **1** **Tetradrachm**[192] 7532 3-9-5 0 GeorgeBaker 3 82+
(David Lanigan) *mde all: rdn whn jnd over 2f out: kpt on wl to assert fnl f* **10/3**[2]

4-32 **2** *3/4* **School Fete (IRE)**[23] 1406 3-9-5 82 JamieSpencer 4 80
(Michael Bell) *trckd wnr: chal and upsides fr over 2f out to 1f out: fnd little and outbattled after* **5/6**[1]

3 *2 1/4* **Torquay** 3-9-0 0 LukeMorris 1 71
(Harry Dunlop) *free to post: t.k.h early: trckd ldng pair: pushed along and outpcd over 2f out: rdn over 1f out: kpt on again fnl f* **33/1**

0 **4** *3 1/2* **Fastnet Blast (IRE)**[34] 1200 3-9-5 0 (b[1]) FrankieDettori 6 70
(John Gosden) *trckd ldrs: rdn 3f out: outpcd whn hung rt and wd bnd 2f out: one pce and nvr on terms after* **9/2**[3]

0-5 **5** *1* **Molten Gold**[20] 1479 3-9-5 0 JimmyFortune 10 69
(Andrew Balding) *hld up in tch: pushed along 3f out and sn outpcd: no imp fnl 2f* **10/1**

0 **6** *1 3/4* **Lord Napier (IRE)**[13] 1626 3-9-5 0 (p) RobertTart 8 66
(John Gosden) *stdd s: hld up and a last of main gp: already detached whn pushed along 3f out: no ch after: kpt on fnl f* **12/1**

6-50 **7** *166* **Northman (IRE)**[10] 1740 3-9-5 44 (p) PatCosgrave 9
(Jim Boyle) *pushed along after 3f: u.str.p by 1/2-way and sn dropped away: t.o whn virtually p.u over 3f out* **66/1**

2m 31.9s (-1.10) **Going Correction** +0.05s/f (Slow) **7** Ran SP% **117.0**
Speed ratings (Par 99): **105,104,103,100,100 98,**
CSF £6.74 TOTE £4.40: £1.90, £1.10; EX 8.20 Trifecta £102.40.
Owner B E Nielsen **Bred** Paramount Bloodstock **Trained** Newmarket, Suffolk

FOCUS
This meeting was moved to the Polytrack in order to protect the turf track for Saturday's Classic trial fixture. Not the deepest of maidens to start with and few got into it. The runner-up's mark of 82 set the benchmark.

2001 STEVE SPARKES MEMORIAL FILLIES' H'CAP 1m 1y(P)
2:00 (2:00) (Class 4) (0-80,77) 4-Y-0+ **£5,175** (£1,540; £769; £384) **Stalls** High

Form RPR
0042 **1** **First Experience**[10] 1754 5-8-7 **68** CallumShepherd(5) 3 75
(Lee Carter) *trckd ldrs: shkn up and c between rivals to ld jst ins fnl f: hrd pressed after: drvn out and hld on wl* **7/1**

2110 **2** *1/2* **Perfect Alchemy (IRE)**[17] 1545 5-9-6 **76** JoeFanning 5 82
(Patrick Chamings) *stdd s: hld up in last: nipped through on inner over 1f out to chal fnl f: w wnr after: jst hld nr fin* **4/1**[3]

220/ **3** *1 3/4* **Mystic Jade**[567] 7237 4-9-4 **74** SeanLevey 1 76
(Richard Hannon) *t.k.h early: trckd ldrs: rdn over 2f out: tried to chal over 1f out: one pce fnl f* **2/1**[1]

1020 **4** *nk* **Skidby Mill (IRE)**[17] 1546 6-9-2 **72** JimCrowley 2 73
(Laura Mongan) *led 1f: trckd ldr and t.k.h after: rdn over 2f out: nt qckn over 1f out: one pce after* **9/2**

-125 **5** *3/4* **Slovak (IRE)**[50] 965 4-9-7 **77** LukeMorris 4 76
(James Tate) *led after 1f: rdn over 2f out: hdd jst ins fnl f: wknd* **11/4**[2]

1m 38.51s (0.31) **Going Correction** +0.05s/f (Slow) **5** Ran SP% **110.7**
Speed ratings (Par 102): **100,99,97,97,96**
CSF £33.55 TOTE £5.20: £2.20, £2.40; EX 20.90 Trifecta £54.20.
Owner Clear Racing with SMD Investments **Bred** Northmore Stud **Trained** Epsom, Surrey

FOCUS
A fair fillies' handicap. They went just an ordinary pace and all five were in a line across the track passing the furlong pole.

2002 VICTORIA HUMBLES & SEAN PACEY MATRIMONIAL H'CAP 6f 1y(P)
2:30 (2:30) (Class 4) (0-80,80) 3-Y-0 **£5,175** (£1,540; £769; £384) **Stalls** Low

Form RPR
221- **1** **Happy Call**[169] 7903 3-9-6 **79** (v) JimCrowley 9 86
(Simon Crisford) *chsd ldr: clr of rest fr 1/2-way: rdn 2f out: no imp tl styd on wl last 150yds to ld fnl stride* **9/2**[2]

0213 **2** *shd* **Sir Dudley (IRE)**[13] 1647 3-9-7 **80** (b) FrankieDettori 1 86
(James Given) *led and sn had field stretched out: stl gng strly 2f out: 2 l up and drvn fnl f: fdd and collared last stride* **5/1**[3]

2-14 **3** *2 3/4* **Ice Age (IRE)**[8] 1809 3-9-6 **79** RobertWinston 4 76
(Eve Johnson Houghton) *chsd ldrs but nt on terms: pushed along and outpcd 1/2-way: rdn and styd on fr over 1f out to take 3rd nr fin* **11/2**

4210 **4** *1* **Rosealee (IRE)**[21] 1452 3-9-1 **74** MartinLane 7 68
(Jeremy Gask) *off the pce in midfield: pushed along and prog to chse clr ldng pair over 2f out: no imp after: lost 3rd nr fin* **16/1**

3-15 **5** *2 1/2* **September Issue**[40] 1115 3-9-4 **77** LukeMorris 3 63
(Gay Kelleway) *sn outpcd and shoved along towards rr: nvr any ch: kpt on fnl f* **11/1**

21-1 **6** *1* **Irish Eclare (IRE)**[22] 1431 3-9-1 **77** MichaelJMMurphy(3) 2 60
(Charles Hills) *tried to press ldng pair but unable to do so and sn pushed along in 3rd: lost pl over 2f out: wl btn after* **3/1**[1]

30-2 **7** *1/2* **Black Bess**[35] 1176 3-8-11 **70** PatCosgrave 8 51
(Jim Boyle) *nvr bttr than midfield and sn pushed along: wl outpcd and n.d fr 1/2-way* **6/1**

8 *3/4* **Medicean El Diablo**[168] 7926 3-8-2 **68** MitchGodwin(7) 5 47
(Jimmy Fox) *settled in last pair and immediately wl bhd: shkn up over 2f out: no prog and nvr in it* **16/1**

31-0 **9** *1/2* **Quick March**[14] 1599 3-9-7 **80** GeorgeBaker 6 57
(Roger Charlton) *stdd s: hld up in last and immediately wl bhd in strly run r: shkn up 2f out: no prog and nvr in it* **9/1**

1m 11.1s (-0.80) **Going Correction** +0.05s/f (Slow) **9** Ran SP% **119.6**
Speed ratings (Par 101): **107,106,103,101,98 97,96,95,94**
CSF £28.39 CT £129.40 TOTE £4.90: £1.60, £2.00, £2.20; EX 23.10 Trifecta £124.40.
Owner Sheikh Daij Al Khalifa **Bred** J A And Mrs Duffy **Trained** Newmarket, Suffolk

FOCUS
A competitive 3yo sprint handicap, but despite a scorching gallop the first two were the only ones ever in it and those held up had no chance.

2003 H G BUCK ONE, TWO, SIXER H'CAP 5f 6y(P)
3:00 (3:00) (Class 3) (0-95,92) 4-Y-0 **£9,451** (£2,829; £1,414; £708; £352) **Stalls** High

Form RPR
60-1 **1** **Encore D'Or**[13] 1650 4-9-7 **92** MartinHarley 1 102+
(Robert Cowell) *cl up: trckd ldr 1/2-way: rdn to chal over 1f out: led jst ins fnl f: styd on and a in command after* **2/5**[1]

0-03 **2** *1/2* **Duke Of Firenze**[16] 1566 7-9-5 **90** FMBerry 5 97
(David C Griffiths) *dwlt: in tch in rr: prog wl over 1f out: drvn and kpt on fnl f to take 2nd last 100yds: nvr quite able to threaten wnr* **11/1**[3]

614 **3** *3/4* **Sandfrankskipsgo**[62] 835 7-9-4 **89** GeorgeBaker 6 93
(Peter Crate) *fast away: led: rdn 2f out: hdd jst ins fnl f: kpt on but lost 2nd last 100yds* **9/1**[2]

0500 **4** *1 3/4* **Dynamo Walt (IRE)**[13] 1650 5-8-13 **84** (v) MartinLane 4 82
(Derek Shaw) *pushed along in last: wd bnd 2f out: rdn and kpt on same pce to take 4th nr fin* **11/1**[3]

1263 **5** *1* **Secret Asset (IRE)**[7] 1836 11-8-8 **79** (v) LukeMorris 3 73
(Lisa Williamson) *chsd ldrs: rdn and no rspnse wl over 1f out: no imp after* **20/1**

-222 **6** *1* **Bertie Blu Boy**[7] 1836 8-8-5 **83** (v) KevinLundie(7) 2 74
(Lisa Williamson) *unable to ld: chsd ldr to 1/2-way: rdn 2f out: wknd fnl f* **9/1**[2]

58.41s (-0.39) **Going Correction** +0.05s/f (Slow) **6** Ran SP% **112.9**
Speed ratings (Par 107): **105,104,103,100,98 97**
CSF £6.08 TOTE £1.40: £1.10, £3.90; EX 7.40 Trifecta £24.20.
Owner Newsells Park Stud **Bred** Newsells Park Stud **Trained** Six Mile Bottom, Cambs

FOCUS
A warm sprint handicap, but a very lopsided betting market. They were always going to go a strong pace and the winner looks as though he will end up much better than this level.

2004 GREATER LONDON PROPERTIES MAIDEN FILLIES' STKS (PLUS 10 RACE) 6f 1y(P)
3:35 (3:35) (Class 5) 3-Y-0 **£3,234** (£962; £481; £240) **Stalls** Low

Form RPR
4-2 **1** **Very Honest (IRE)**[51] 952 3-9-0 0 LukeMorris 9 83
(Brett Johnson) *mde all: dashed for home over 2f out: clr after: rdn out* **6/1**[2]

236- **2** *3* **Cinders (IRE)**[270] 5219 3-9-0 72 JimmyFortune 3 73
(Hughie Morrison) *chsd ldng pair: wnt 2nd jst over 2f out: sn rdn and no imp on wnr: styd on* **16/1**

3 *2 1/4* **Kindly** 3-9-0 0 JimCrowley 4 66+
(Simon Crisford) *in tch in midfield: prog on inner over 2f out: chsd clr ldng pair over 1f out: kpt on same pce* **14/1**

0- **4** *1* **May Rose (IRE)**[155] 8091 3-9-0 0 MartinHarley 7 63+
(Marco Botti) *dwlt: prog fr rr on outer 1/2-way: shkn up to chal for 3rd over 1f out: one pce after* **14/1**

03-0 **5** *1 1/4* **Caledonia Duchess**[11] 1723 3-9-0 72 SamHitchcott 6 59
(Jo Hughes) *chsd ldrs: urged along fr 1/2-way: sn outpcd: no imp after* **33/1**

5-3 **6** *hd* **Blue Geranium (IRE)**[22] 1436 3-9-0 0 FrankieDettori 2 58+
(John Gosden) *dwlt: n.m.r after 1f: tried to make prog over 3f out but nvr much room: rdn 2f out: kpt on fnl f: no ch* **8/13**[1]

	7	2 ½	**Roccor** 3-9-0 0 .... SeanLevey 8	50
			(Richard Hannon) *towards rr on outer: wd bnd 2f out: pushed along and no real prog over 1f out* **20/1**	
40-	8	2 ½	**Meroula (FR)**[207] 7158 3-9-0 0 .... SteveDrowne 10	42
			(Harry Dunlop) *chsd wnr to jst over 2f out: wknd* **66/1**	
0-	9	¾	**Fol O'Yasmine**[210] 7077 3-9-0 0 .... PatCosgrave 12	40
			(William Haggas) *restless stalls: a in rr: shkn up and no prog 2f out* **8/1**[3]	
33-	10	hd	**Ulfah Dream**[190] 7578 3-9-0 0 .... PaoloSirigu 1	39
			(Marco Botti) *plld v hrd: hld up in last pair: no prog 2f out* **20/1**	

1m 12.67s (0.77) **Going Correction** +0.05s/f (Slow) **10** Ran SP% **120.5**
Speed ratings (Par 96): **96,92,89,87,86 85,82,79,78,77**
CSF £92.56 TOTE £5.00: £1.50, £4.60, £2.70; EX 61.10 Trifecta £498.00.
Owner J Daniels, B R Johnson and Omni **Bred** Darley **Trained** Epsom, Surrey

FOCUS
An ordinary 3yo fillies' sprint maiden and another race where the pace held up.

2005 ORPHEUS CENTRE MAIDEN STKS — 7f 1y(P)

4:05 (4:09) (Class 5) 3-Y-O+ **£3,234** (£962; £481; £240) **Stalls** Low

Form				RPR
4-3	1		**Frenchman (FR)**[52] 945 3-8-11 0 .... MichaelJMMurphy(3) 7	74
			(Charles Hills) *mde all: rdn 2f out: looked in command fnl f: ld dwindled nr fin: jst lasted* **3/1**[2]	
-2	2	shd	**Dubai Mission (IRE)**[16] 1577 3-9-0 0 .... SeanLevey 13	73
			(Richard Hannon) *sn chsd wnr: rdn 2f out: nt qckn over 1f out and looked hld after: kpt on fnl f: jst failed* **5/6**[1]	
	3	1	**Red Trooper (FR)** 3-9-0 0 .... SteveDrowne 2	71+
			(George Baker) *chsd clr ldng trio and wl ahd of rest: clsd 1/2-way: rdn over 2f out: styd on to take 3rd ins fnl f: nrst fin* **20/1**	
0-	4	1 ¾	**Sexton Blake (IRE)**[245] 6036 3-8-9 0 .... HectorCrouch(5) 12	66
			(Gary Moore) *chsd ldng pair and clr of rest early: rdn over 2f out: one pce and lost 3rd ins fnl f* **25/1**	
0-5	5	hd	**City By The Bay**[11] 1701 3-8-9 0 .... GaryMahon(5) 6	65+
			(Richard Hannon) *chsd clr ldng quartet: rdn and tried to cl fr 3f out: nvr on terms but kpt on fr over 1f out* **10/1**[3]	
00	6	3 ¾	**Dream Trader (IRE)**[8] 1800 3-9-0 0 .... JackMitchell 9	55+
			(Roger Varian) *wl off the pce early in midfield: gng bttr than many fr 3f out but no ch: pushed along and one pce fnl 2f* **33/1**	
	7	hd	**Tasteofexcellence (IRE)** 3-8-6 0 .... PhilipPrince(3) 4	50
			(Roger Ingram) *racd in midfield but wl off the pce: rdn 3f out: nvr able to make much prog* **66/1**	
	8	½	**Lobster Cocktail (IRE)** 3-9-0 0 .... AntonioFresu 5	53+
			(Ed Walker) *slowly away: wl off the pce towards rr: sme prog over 2f out: shkn up and rn green over 1f out: no hdwy after* **16/1**	
5-6	9	4	**Sixties Groove (IRE)**[13] 1653 3-9-0 0 .... JimCrowley 1	43+
			(Jeremy Noseda) *sn long way off the pce in last quartet: nvr involved* **10/1**[3]	
	10	1 ¾	**Princess Zoffany (IRE)**[209] 7126 3-8-2 0 ....[1] MitchGodwin(7) 8	33
			(Jimmy Fox) *sn long way off the pce in last quartet: nvr a factor* **100/1**	
	11	hd	**Dltripleseven (IRE)** 3-9-0 0 .... ShaneKelly 14	37
			(Richard Hughes) *swvd rt s: t.k.h early and wl in rr: brief effrt 3f out: sn no ch* **33/1**	
00-	12	5	**Cancellara**[256] 5695 4-9-12 0 .... KierenFox 3	28
			(Michael Attwater) *reluctant to enter stalls: slowly away: a long way adrift in last trio* **100/1**	
0-	13	shd	**Dubai Empress (IRE)**[207] 7160 3-8-6 0 .... NathanAlison(3) 10	19
			(William Haggas) *restless stalls: slowly away: a long way adrift in last trio* **20/1**	

1m 24.81s (0.01) **Going Correction** +0.05s/f (Slow)
WFA 3 from 4yo 12lb **13** Ran SP% **126.3**
Speed ratings (Par 103): **101,100,99,97,97 93,93,92,87,85 85,79,79**
CSF £5.71 TOTE £4.10: £1.60, £1.10, £5.10; EX 7.40 Trifecta £70.50.
Owner Kennet Valley Thoroughbreds V **Bred** S C E A Ecurie De Montfort & K Morice **Trained** Lambourn, Berks

FOCUS
An uncompetitive maiden with them betting 10-1 bar two. They got sorted out very early and this was yet another race dominated by those that raced on or near the pace, although admittedly that did include the two market leaders.

2006 TIM FRANKS H'CAP (FOR LADY AMATEUR RIDERS) — 7f 1y(P)

4:40 (4:40) (Class 5) (0-75,74) 4-Y-O+ **£3,119** (£967; £483; £242) **Stalls** Low

Form				RPR
00-0	1		**Space War**[30] 1252 9-9-6 **62** ....(t) MissJoannaMason(3) 8	71
			(Michael Easterby) *trckd ldng pair: wnt 2nd over 2f out: led wl over 1f out but sn jnd: gd battle after tl drvn ahd last 75yds* **5/1**[3]	
00-6	2	¾	**George Baker (IRE)**[23] 1416 9-9-6 **66** .... AmeliaGlass(7) 6	73
			(George Baker) *trckd ldr to over 2f out: styd cl up and disp ld on inner over 1f out: pushed along and gd battle w wnr after: no ex nr fin* **12/1**	
0-54	3	shd	**Two In The Pink (IRE)**[27] 1334 6-9-8 **64** .... BrodieHampson(3) 2	70
			(Ralph J Smith) *chsd ldrs: rdn 3f out: effrt u.p to go 3rd over 1f out: clsd last 100yds: nrly snatched 2nd* **9/2**[2]	
145	4	5	**Seek The Fair Land**[7] 1832 10-9-8 **68** ....(v) MissAWallace(7) 5	61
			(Lee Carter) *hld up in tch: pushed along over 2f out: tk 4th jst over 1f out but nvr on terms w ldrs* **8/1**	
1263	5	1	**Caledonia Laird**[30] 1269 5-10-0 **67** .... MissSBrotherton 1	57
			(Jo Hughes) *hld up in last of main gp: nt clr run on inner 3f out: no ch but stl gng strly whn nt clr run on inner 1f out: swtchd rt and kpt on* **5/2**[1]	
4-00	6	½	**Alketios (GR)**[65] 777 5-9-4 **64** .... MissBeckyButler(7) 3	53
			(Gary Moore) *hld up: pushed along and no imp on ldrs over 2f out: no ch after* **7/1**	
0400	7	4	**Bennelong**[17] 1547 10-9-2 **60** oh4 .... MissPFuller(5) 7	38
			(Lee Carter) *led and clr: 5 l ld at 1/2-way: hdd & wknd qckly wl over 1f out* **20/1**	
3620	8	22	**Chelwood Gate (IRE)**[18] 1530 6-10-0 **74** ....(v) MissEChamings(7) 4	
			(Patrick Chamings) *rel to r and lost at least 20 l: a t.o* **9/2**[2]	

1m 25.09s (0.29) **Going Correction** +0.05s/f (Slow) **8** Ran SP% **117.7**
Speed ratings (Par 103): **100,99,99,93,92 91,87,61**
CSF £63.55 CT £293.67 TOTE £7.80: £2.40, £3.80, £2.10; EX 85.40 Trifecta £525.70.
Owner M W Easterby **Bred** Shutford Stud And O F Waller **Trained** Sheriff Hutton, N Yorks

FOCUS
An ordinary lady amateurs' handicap. The leader went off far too quick, but the front pair were always handy in the chasing group.

T/Plt: £55.60 to a £1 stake. Pool: £49,504.90 - 649.10 winning tickets T/Qpdt: £14.30 to a £1 stake. Pool: £3,877.24 - 199.40 winning tickets **Jonathan Neesom**

1755 NOTTINGHAM (L-H)

Friday, May 6

OFFICIAL GOING: Good to firm (good in places)
Wind: Light behind Weather: Cloudy

2007 RACINGUK.COM FILLIES' NOVICE MEDIAN AUCTION STKS (PLUS 10 RACE) — 5f 13y

5:10 (5:14) (Class 5) 2-Y-O **£3,067** (£905; £453) **Stalls** High

Form				RPR
	1		**Spin Doctor** 2-9-0 0 .... TonyHamilton 4	78+
			(Richard Fahey) *chsd ldrs: shkn up to ld over 1f out: edgd rt: r.o* **11/4**[2]	
3	2	1	**Rapacity Alexander (IRE)**[41] 1087 2-9-0 0 .... CathyGannon 15	74
			(David Evans) *led: hung lft thrght: shkn up and hdd over 1f out: nt clr run ins fnl f: styd on* **6/4**[1]	
	3	½	**Magical Forest (IRE)** 2-9-0 0 .... JamesDoyle 10	75+
			(Marco Botti) *s.i.s: hdwy over 3f out: n.m.r over 1f out: styd on* **12/1**	
4	4	1 ¾	**Primrose Place**[13] 1635 2-9-0 0 .... KieranO'Neill 7	66
			(Richard Hannon) *prom: chsd ldr over 3f out tl rdn over 1f out: no ex wl ins fnl f* **10/1**[3]	
4	5	1 ½	**Snoozy Sioux (IRE)**[32] 1233 2-8-11 0 .... TimClark(3) 12	61
			(Martin Smith) *plld hrd and prom: rdn over 1f out: no ex ins fnl f* **33/1**	
0	6	nk	**Savannah Slew**[22] 1437 2-9-0 0 .... TomQueally 8	60+
			(James Given) *s.i.s and hmpd s: in rr tl styd on ins fnl f: nvr nrr* **25/1**	
5	7	1 ½	**Yes You (IRE)**[22] 1443 2-8-9 0 .... PhilDennis(5) 11	54
			(James Given) *chsd ldr tl over 3f out: remained handy: rdn over 1f out: wknd fnl f* **14/1**	
0	8	2	**Roys Dream**[27] 1342 2-9-0 0 .... RobertHavlin 2	47
			(Kristin Stubbs) *chsd ldrs: rdn 1/2-way: edgd lft and wknd over 1f out* **25/1**	
5	9	1 ¼	**Shadow Wing (IRE)**[13] 1641 2-9-0 0 .... LiamKeniry 6	43
			(Tom Dascombe) *mid-div: rdn and wknd over 1f out* **20/1**	
	10	2 ¾	**Misty Moo** 2-8-9 0 .... GeorgeBuckell(5) 5	33
			(Michael Appleby) *sn outpcd* **40/1**	
02	11	½	**Black Redstart**[8] 1799 2-9-0 0 .... OisinMurphy 9	31
			(Alan Bailey) *sn pushed along towards rr: wknd 2f out* **12/1**	
	12	5	**Clear As A Bell (IRE)** 2-9-0 0 .... DuranFentiman 3	13
			(Tim Easterby) *hdwy on outer to get in tch over 3f out: hung lft 1/2-way: sn wknd* **66/1**	

59.55s (-1.95) **Going Correction** -0.425s/f (Firm) **12** Ran SP% **117.1**
Speed ratings (Par 90): **98,96,95,92,90 89,87,84,82,77 77,69**
CSF £6.47 TOTE £3.30: £1.40, £1.10, £3.10; EX 9.20 Trifecta £83.30.
Owner Cheveley Park Stud **Bred** Cheveley Park Stud Ltd **Trained** Musley Bank, N Yorks

FOCUS
They were on the outer track for the first time this year, distances were as advertised, and the going was good, good to firm in places. The stalls were on the stands' side for sprints, the centre over 1m and on the inside for the remainder. A well-backed newcomer scored with authority from her main market rival in this maiden, and looks a useful prospect.

2008 RACING UK PROFITS RETURNED TO RACING MAIDEN STKS — 1m 2f 50y

5:40 (5:44) (Class 5) 3-Y-O **£3,067** (£905; £453) **Stalls** Low

Form				RPR
4-3	1		**Poet's Word (IRE)**[20] 1474 3-9-5 0 .... RyanMoore 15	88+
			(Sir Michael Stoute) *a.p: shkn up to ld over 1f out: pushed out: comf* **9/4**[1]	
3	2	2 ¼	**Muntahaa (IRE)**[23] 1421 3-9-5 0 .... DaneO'Neill 2	84
			(John Gosden) *racd keenly: led over 8f out: rdn and hdd over 1f out: styd on same pce ins fnl f* **9/4**[1]	
6	3	1 ½	**Shraaoh (IRE)**[23] 1421 3-9-5 0 .... StevieDonohoe 11	80+
			(Sir Michael Stoute) *hld up: pushed along over 2f out: hdwy over 1f out: r.o to go 3rd wl ins fnl f* **9/1**[3]	
	4	1	**Indulged** 3-9-0 0 .... TomQueally 1	73+
			(James Fanshawe) *hld up: hdwy over 1f out: nt rch ldrs* **25/1**	
0	5	nk	**Makzeem**[11] 1714 3-9-5 0 .... WilliamTwiston-Davies 9	78+
			(Roger Charlton) *hld up: hdwy over 3f out: no ex ins fnl f* **14/1**	
5-	6	1	**Alfahad (IRE)**[163] 7981 3-9-5 0 .... GrahamLee 8	76
			(Ed Dunlop) *chsd ldrs: rdn over 1f out: wknd ins fnl f* **20/1**	
40-	7	1 ¼	**Guns Of Leros (USA)**[197] 7411 3-9-5 0 .... LiamKeniry 5	73
			(Gary Moore) *chsd ldrs: rdn over 2f out: wknd fnl f* **100/1**	
	8	1	**Sleeplessinseattle** 3-9-0 0 .... TonyHamilton 13	66
			(James Fanshawe) *mid-div: hdwy 1/2-way: rdn and n.m.r over 1f out: sn wknd* **50/1**	
4	9	4	**Great Return**[20] 1479 3-9-5 0 .... JamesDoyle 7	63
			(Saeed bin Suroor) *sn led: hdd over 8f out: chsd ldr tl rdn over 2f out: wknd over 1f out* **4/1**[2]	
	10	1	**Rowlestonerendezvu** 3-8-11 0 .... GeorgeDowning(3) 10	56
			(Tony Carroll) *s.i.s: sme hdwy over 3f out: sn rdn and wknd* **200/1**	
0	11	1 ¾	**Placedela Concorde**[13] 1639 3-9-5 0 .... WilliamCarson 12	58
			(Anthony Carson) *prom: rdn over 2f out: wknd wl over 1f out* **200/1**	
00	12	9	**Icons Image**[23] 1426 3-9-2 0 .... DanielMuscutt(3) 14	40
			(Brian McMath) *hld up: pushed along over 4f out: wknd over 3f out* **250/1**	
00	13	5	**Lord Murphy (IRE)**[27] 1339 3-9-2 0 .... RobHornby(3) 6	30
			(Daniel Mark Loughnane) *hld up: pushed along 4f out: wknd sn after* **150/1**	
	14	67	**Los Olivos (USA)** 3-9-5 0 .... GrahamGibbons 3	
			(William Haggas) *s.i.s: sn pushed along in rr: wknd over 4f out* **25/1**	

2m 9.27s (-5.03) **Going Correction** -0.575s/f (Hard) course record **14** Ran SP% **115.7**
Speed ratings (Par 99): **97,95,94,93,92 92,91,90,87,86 84,77,73,20**
CSF £6.24 TOTE £3.60: £2.20, £1.30, £3.10; EX 8.60 Trifecta £47.60.
Owner Saeed Suhail **Bred** Woodcote Stud Ltd **Trained** Newmarket, Suffolk

FOCUS
The pace was not very strong but the market leaders filled the first two places in this useful maiden. The runner-up set a good standard and is rated close to form.

2009 RACING UK DAY PASS JUST £10 MAIDEN FILLIES' STKS (PLUS 10 RACE) — 1m 75y

6:10 (6:14) (Class 5) 3-Y-O **£2,911** (£866; £432; £216) **Stalls** Centre

Form				RPR
3-	1		**Snow Moon**[205] 7219 3-9-0 0 .... RobertHavlin 3	89+
			(John Gosden) *trckd ldrs: led over 1f out: sn clr: easily* **1/1**[1]	
	2	2 ½	**Trainnah** 3-8-7 0 .... GeorgiaCox(7) 12	79+
			(William Haggas) *s.i.s: pushed along early in rr: swtchd rt over 2f out: hdwy and edgd lft fr over 1f out: r.o to go 2nd wl ins fnl f: no ch w wnr* **20/1**	

3-2 **3** *2* **Quebee**[30] 1256 3-9-0 0........................ JohnFahy 9 74
(Clive Cox) *chsd ldrs: led over 2f out: rdn and hdd over 1f out: no ex ins fnl f* **10/1**

4- **4** *1 ½* **Pietrafiore (IRE)**[143] 8232 3-9-0 0........................ JamesDoyle 6 70
(Charlie Appleby) *sn led: hdd 6f out: led again over 3f out: rdn and hdd over 2f out: wknd ins fnl f* **5/1**[2]

5 *nk* **Beauty Sleep (IRE)** 3-9-0 0........................ GrahamGibbons 2 70
(William Haggas) *mid-div: hdwy 1/2-way: rdn over 1f out: wknd ins fnl f* **33/1**

4- **6** *1* **Nicarra (IRE)**[207] 7161 3-9-0 0........................ CathyGannon 5 67+
(Henry Candy) *plld hrd and prom: led 6f out: hdd over 3f out: sn rdn: wknd fnl f* **25/1**

7 *2* **Fire Jet (IRE)** 3-9-0 0........................ RoystonFfrench 4 62
(John Mackie) *hld up: hdwy over 2f out: rdn and wknd over 1f out* **125/1**

0- **8** *nse* **Cosmic Storm**[210] 7077 3-9-0 0........................ OisinMurphy 11 62
(Ralph Beckett) *prom tl rdn and wknd over 1f out* **11/2**[3]

00 **9** *3* **Cliff Face (IRE)**[9] 1798 3-9-0 0........................ DaneO'Neill 1 55
(Ed Dunlop) *hld up: hdwy over 3f out: wknd over 1f out* **100/1**

10 *1* **Zain Arion (IRE)** 3-9-0 0........................ StevieDonohoe 14 53
(Charlie Fellowes) *hld up: sme hdwy over 3f out: rdn and wknd wl over 1f out* **100/1**

11 *3* **Jantina** 3-9-0 0........................(v[1]) RyanMoore 17 46
(Sir Michael Stoute) *hld up: slipped bnd over 4f out: nvr on terms* **16/1**

12 *1* **Brief Visit** 3-9-0 0........................ LiamKeniry 16 43
(Andrew Balding) *hld up: sme hdwy over 3f out: wknd over 2f out* **50/1**

13 *2 ¼* **Apache Myth** 3-9-0 0........................ GrahamLee 13 38
(James Eustace) *mid-div: hdwy over 5f out: wknd over 2f out* **40/1**

14 *20* **Purple Party (IRE)** 3-9-0 0........................ TomQueally 15
(George Margarson) *prom: lost pl 6f out: pushed along 1/2-way: wknd 3f out* **100/1**

0 **15** *2 ¼* **Rock Palm (IRE)**[13] 1628 3-8-9 0........................ JennyPowell(5) 10
(Brendan Powell) *prom: hung rt over 5f out: rdn and wknd over 2f out* **50/1**

16 *11* **Queen Elsa (IRE)** 3-9-0 0........................ DougieCostello 7
(K R Burke) *s.i.s: a in rr: wknd over 3f out* **50/1**

1m 44.12s (-4.88) **Going Correction** -0.575s/f (Hard) **16** Ran SP% **120.7**
Speed ratings (Par 96): **101,98,96,95,94 93,91,91,88,87 84,83,81,61,59 48**
CSF £29.28 TOTE £1.70: £1.10, £5.10, £3.00; EX 24.00 Trifecta £139.70.
Owner Lady Bamford **Bred** Lady Bamford **Trained** Newmarket, Suffolk

FOCUS
The leading form contender hammered her rivals in this maiden. The level is set around the third and fourth.

2010 RACING UK IN HD NOW! H'CAP 1m 75y
6:45 (6:46) (Class 4) (0-80,82) 4-Y-O+ **£4,851** (£1,443; £721; £360) **Stalls** Centre

Form RPR

-411 **1** **Ice Slice (IRE)**[3] 1946 5-9-6 **82** 6ex........................ RyanTate(3) 5 93
(James Eustace) *led 1f: chsd ldr: rdn to ld over 1f out: all out* **7/4**[1]

251- **2** *nk* **Winterval**[307] 3905 4-9-6 **79**........................ HarryBentley 9 89+
(Roger Varian) *prom: rdn to chse wnr over 1f out: edgd lft ins fnl f: styd on* **2/1**[2]

356- **3** *1 ½* **Alnashama**[185] 7690 4-9-2 **75**........................ DaneO'Neill 4 82
(Charles Hills) *led after 1f: rdn and hdd over 1f out: no ex towards fin* **12/1**

6-33 **4** *nk* **Just Be Lucky (IRE)**[9] 1785 4-8-11 **70**........................ AndrewMullen 2 76
(Ivan Furtado) *trckd ldrs: racd keenly: rdn over 1f out: styd on* **8/1**

205- **5** *1 ¼* **Stardrifter**[214] 6981 4-9-1 **74**........................ TonyHamilton 11 77
(Richard Fahey) *hld up: hdwy over 1f out: nt rch ldrs* **20/1**

400- **6** *2 ½* **Order Of Service**[151] 8131 6-9-5 **78**........................ GrahamLee 10 76
(Shaun Harris) *s.s: bhd tl styd on towards fin: nvr nrr* **50/1**

3302 **7** *½* **Sarmadee (IRE)**[10] 1746 4-9-0 **73**........................ RyanMoore 12 69
(Mick Channon) *hld up: pushed along over 2f out: nvr trbld ldrs* **7/1**[3]

4-06 **8** *nk* **Tommy's Secret**[22] 1430 6-8-13 **72**........................ AdamBeschizza 8 68
(Jane Chapple-Hyam) *prom: rdn over 3f out: wknd fnl f* **16/1**

1m 43.05s (-5.95) **Going Correction** -0.575s/f (Hard) course record **8** Ran SP% **113.6**
Speed ratings (Par 105): **106,105,104,103,102 100,99,99**
CSF £5.35 CT £28.18 TOTE £2.60: £1.10, £1.60, £3.60; EX 5.90 Trifecta £42.00.
Owner The MacDougall Two **Bred** Kilfrush Stud **Trained** Newmarket, Suffolk

FOCUS
There were several withdrawals in this handicap and the pace was steady, but the in-form favourite beat his main market rival and the pair pulled clear.

2011 RACING UK IN GLORIOUS HD FILLIES' H'CAP 1m 75y
7:20 (7:21) (Class 5) (0-75,74) 3-Y-O **£3,067** (£905; £453) **Stalls** Centre

Form RPR

1- **1** **Little Avon**[206] 7175 3-9-5 **72**........................ OisinMurphy 6 75
(Ralph Beckett) *mde all: rdn over 1f out: edgd lft ins fnl f: styd on* **5/2**[2]

04-4 **2** *hd* **Perfect Quest**[25] 1388 3-8-6 **62**........................ RyanTate(3) 5 65
(Clive Cox) *pushed along in rr early: hdwy over 2f out: nt clr run over 1f out: rdn to chse wnr and edgd rt ins fnl f: r.o wl* **9/2**[3]

1- **3** *1 ¼* **Shufoog**[254] 5753 3-9-4 **71**........................ DaneO'Neill 2 72+
(William Haggas) *chsd ldrs: rdn to chse wnr over 1f out: cl up whn hmpd ins fnl f: styd on same pce: eased whn hld nr fin* **15/8**[1]

45-4 **4** *¾* **Bad Penny (IRE)**[16] 1562 3-9-0 **67**........................ GrahamLee 4 65
(John Quinn) *prom: rdn over 1f out: styd on same pce fnl f* **25/1**

2-1 **5** *¾* **Wings Of Esteem (IRE)**[86] 524 3-9-4 **71**........................ DougieCostello 3 67
(K R Burke) *racd keenly and sn trcking wnr: shkn up and lost 2nd over 1f out: no ex ins fnl f* **7/1**

065- **6** *1 ¼* **Kilim**[162] 7996 3-9-0 **67**........................ LemosdeSouza 8 60
(Luca Cumani) *hld up: shkn up over 2f out: nvr nr to chal* **8/1**

1m 46.49s (-2.51) **Going Correction** -0.575s/f (Hard) **6** Ran SP% **109.0**
Speed ratings (Par 96): **89,88,87,86,86 84**
CSF £13.12 CT £21.49 TOTE £2.50: £1.40, £2.40; EX 15.00 Trifecta £42.40.
Owner Qatar Racing Limited **Bred** Qatar Bloodstock Ltd **Trained** Kimpton, Hants
■ Stewards' Enquiry : Ryan Tate two-day ban (20-21 May): gave filly insufficient time to respond
Oisin Murphy two-day ban (20-21 May): careless riding

FOCUS
An interesting handicap involving several unexposed types and three last-time-out winners.

2012 RACING UK HD ON SKY432 H'CAP 1m 2f 50y
7:50 (7:52) (Class 5) (0-75,75) 3-Y-O **£2,911** (£866; £432; £216) **Stalls** Low

Form RPR

60-1 **1** **Shabbah (IRE)**[10] 1738 3-9-2 **70** 6ex........................ RyanMoore 10 78+
(Sir Michael Stoute) *mde all: shkn up over 1f out: r.o wl: comf* **1/2**[1]

00-4 **2** *1 ½* **Panko (IRE)**[7] 1826 3-8-7 **61** oh16........................ KieranO'Neill 7 65
(Ed de Giles) *chsd wnr after 1f: rdn over 2f out: hung lft fr over 1f out: styd on same pce ins fnl f* **6/1**[2]

-324 **3** *1 ¾* **Moueenn**[13] 1630 3-9-7 **75**........................ HarryBentley 6 76
(Roger Varian) *chsd ldrs: pushed along over 3f out: no ex wl ins fnl f* **9/1**[3]

040- **4** *¾* **Clever Bob (IRE)**[222] 6774 3-9-6 **74**........................ JFEgan 5 73
(Joseph Tuite) *prom: rdn over 2f out: styd on same pce fnl f* **25/1**

204 **5** *nk* **Clayton Hall (IRE)**[23] 1406 3-9-5 **73**........................ TonyHamilton 8 71
(Richard Fahey) *chsd ldrs: rdn over 2f out: no ex fnl f* **20/1**

046- **6** *1 ½* **Pinstripe**[149] 8152 3-8-7 **68**........................ GabrieleMalune(7) 9 63+
(Luca Cumani) *hld up: shkn up and edgd lft over 1f out: nvr nr ldrs* **6/1**[2]

502- **7** *½* **Shadow Spirit**[219] 6858 3-9-6 **74**........................ GrahamLee 1 68
(James Eustace) *hld up: racd keenly: shkn up over 2f out: n.d* **33/1**

53-0 **8** *½* **Velvet Revolution**[40] 1113 3-9-1 **69**........................(p) JamesDoyle 4 62
(Marco Botti) *s.i.s: hld up: rdn over 1f out: nvr on terms* **20/1**

1051 **9** *1 ¾* **Kemsing (IRE)**[29] 1297 3-9-5 **73**........................ AdamBeschizza 2 63
(Julia Feilden) *hld up: rdn 3f out: wknd fnl f* **25/1**

2m 12.05s (-2.25) **Going Correction** -0.575s/f (Hard) **9** Ran SP% **125.4**
Speed ratings (Par 99): **86,84,83,82,82 81,80,80,79**
CSF £4.17 CT £17.43 TOTE £1.50: £1.10, £1.50, £2.30; EX 5.10 Trifecta £25.60.
Owner Abdullah Saeed Al Naboodah **Bred** Sunderland Holdings Inc **Trained** Newmarket, Suffolk
■ Stewards' Enquiry : James Doyle jockey said colt missed break

FOCUS
The hot favourite made all and the hold-up runners couldn't get involved.

2013 WATCH RACING UK TODAY JUST £10 H'CAP 6f 15y
8:20 (8:22) (Class 6) (0-60,59) 4-Y-O+ **£2,264** (£673; £336; £168) **Stalls** High

Form RPR

056- **1** **Pandar**[256] 5679 7-9-2 **57**........................ DanielMuscutt(3) 6 79
(Patrick Chamings) *chsd ldrs: led over 3f out: clr fnl 2f: easily* **9/2**[2]

034- **2** *9* **Minty Jones**[184] 7712 7-8-13 **51**........................(v) HarryBentley 7 43
(Michael Mullineaux) *chsd ldrs: rdn over 2f out: styng on same pce whn hmpd over 1f out* **14/1**

-010 **3** *1* **First Excel**[52] 936 4-9-6 **58**........................(b[1]) JFEgan 3 47
(Roy Bowring) *hld up: hdwy u.p over 2f out: hung rt over 1f out: styd on same pce* **8/1**

6555 **4** *¾* **Bogsnog (IRE)**[20] 1496 6-9-6 **58**........................(b) TonyHamilton 13 45
(Kristin Stubbs) *stmbld s: in rr whn hmpd over 3f out: r.o towards fin: nvr nrr* **6/1**[3]

063 **5** *shd* **Humour (IRE)**[12] 1676 5-9-4 **59**........................ DannyBrock(3) 1 45
(Christine Dunnett) *in rr: hdwy u.p on outer over 1f out: no ex fnl f* **8/1**

55-4 **6** *½* **Goadby**[14] 1600 5-9-7 **59**........................ RoystonFfrench 8 44
(John Holt) *mid-div: rdn 1/2-way: nvr trbld ldrs* **13/2**

-002 **7** *½* **Artbeat (IRE)**[12] 1676 4-8-13 **51**........................ AdamBeschizza 9 34
(Julia Feilden) *sn pushed along in rr: edgd rt over 3f out: rdn and edgd lft over 2f out: n.d* **7/2**[1]

6-04 **8** *nk* **Robbian**[20] 1490 5-8-3 **48**........................ RPWalsh(7) 5 31
(Charles Smith) *s.i.s: sn prom: rdn over 2f out: hmpd and wknd over 1f out* **50/1**

20-0 **9** *nse* **Betty Boo (IRE)**[20] 1495 6-8-10 **48**........................ DuranFentiman 14 30
(Shaun Harris) *led: hdd over 3f out: rdn over 2f out: wknd over 1f out* **33/1**

622- **10** *1* **Man Of Music**[218] 6888 5-8-10 **48**........................ WilliamCarson 11 27
(Tony Carroll) *chsd ldrs: rdn over 2f out: wknd over 1f out* **10/1**

U314 **11** *17* **Bionic Indian**[9] 1795 4-9-0 **52**........................(b) GrahamGibbons 2
(Michael Easterby) *prom: lost pl over 3f out: sn rdn: wknd 2f out* **10/1**

1m 11.91s (-2.79) **Going Correction** -0.425s/f (Firm) **11** Ran SP% **120.0**
Speed ratings (Par 101): **101,89,87,86,86 85,85,84,84,83 60**
CSF £67.46 CT £498.49 TOTE £6.20: £2.50, £2.40, £3.80; EX 84.40 Trifecta £497.20.
Owner O S Harris **Bred** Miss F Vittadini **Trained** Baughurst, Hants

FOCUS
This was all about the well treated winner, who trounced his rivals in this minor sprint handicap.
T/Plt: £6.40 to a £1 stake. Pool: £38,883.82 - 4412.97 winning units. T/Qpdt: £3.60 to a £1 stake. Pool: £3,597.09 - 739.2 winning units. **Colin Roberts**

1641 RIPON (R-H)
Friday, May 6

OFFICIAL GOING: Good (good to soft in places; 7.4)
Wind: Light, half against Weather: Overcast

2014 SIS TRADING SERVICES NOVICE AUCTION STKS 5f
5:50 (5:50) (Class 5) 2-Y-O **£3,881** (£1,155; £577; £288) **Stalls** High

Form RPR

1 **Katrine (IRE)** 2-8-10 0........................ PaulMulrennan 4 72
(Mark Johnston) *mde all: shkn up and edgd lft over 1f out: kpt on strly fnl f* **4/1**[2]

5 **2** *2 ¼* **Kroy**[23] 1407 2-8-7 0........................ JacobButterfield(3) 3 57
(Ollie Pears) *bmpd s: outpcd in rr: hdwy over 1f out: kpt on fnl f: nvr able to chal* **14/1**

3 *1 ¾* **Pulsating (IRE)** 2-8-7 0........................ PJMcDonald 6 47
(Rebecca Menzies) *pressed ldrs: rdn over 2f out: wknd fnl f* **9/2**[3]

6 **4** *1 ½* **Powerless (IRE)**[13] 1641 2-8-11 0........................ DavidAllan 1 46
(Tim Easterby) *in tch: rdn and effrt over 2f out: wknd over 1f out* **14/1**

5 *3* **Allux Boy (IRE)** 2-9-2 0........................ JasonHart 2 40
(Nigel Tinkler) *s.i.s and bmpd s: bhd: shortlived effrt over 2f out: wknd over 1f out* **12/1**

6 *10* **Redarna** 2-8-11 0........................ JamesSullivan 5
(Dianne Sayer) *noisy in paddock: bhd and green: lost tch fr over 3f out: t.o* **33/1**

051 **D** *2* **Who Told Jo Jo (IRE)**[13] 1641 2-8-13 0........................ JordanVaughan(5) 7 73
(Bill Turner) *pressed wnr: rdn over 2f out: effrt and swtchd rt appr fnl f: kpt on same pce last 100yds* **1/1**[1]

1m 1.08s (1.08) **Going Correction** +0.15s/f (Good) **7** Ran SP% **112.1**
Speed ratings (Par 93): **97,90,87,85,80 64,93**
CSF £8.05 TOTE £4.80: £3.10, £1.10; EX 7.00 Trifecta £27.30.
Owner Mark Johnston Racing Ltd **Bred** Rocal Bloodstock Ltd **Trained** Middleham Moor, N Yorks

FOCUS
No more than a fair juvenile novice event with the ground reported to 'good'.

2015 SIS STREAM (S) STKS 1m 1f 170y
6:20 (6:20) (Class 6) 3-4-Y-O **£3,234** (£962; £481; £240) **Stalls** Low

Form RPR

0005 **1** **Samsonite (IRE)**[9] 1785 4-9-10 65........................ BarryMcHugh 3 66+
(Tony Coyle) *hld up: stdy hdwy to chse ldrs over 3f out: rdn to ld over 1f out: kpt on wl fnl f* **10/3**[2]

0520 **2** *2 ¼* **Stone Quercus (IRE)**[8] 1819 3-8-9 58........................(p) PaulMulrennan 7 59
(James Given) *hld up on outside: hdwy to press ldr after 3f: rdn over 3f out: rallied: chsd wnr over 1f out: one pce ins fnl f* **5/1**[3]

3625 **3** *nk* **Never Say (IRE)**[45] 1031 3-8-4 47 .... RaulDaSilva 2 53
(Jason Ward) *hld up in tch: effrt and rdn over 3f out: kpt on ins fnl f: nt pce to chal* **12/1**

20-0 **4** *1* **Scent Of Power**[13] 1640 4-9-5 53 .... DanielTudhope 1 52
(Barry Leavy) *led: rdn over 2f out: hdd over 1f out: outpcd fnl f* **10/1**

0-36 **5** *8* **Italian Beauty (IRE)**[11] 1702 4-9-5 71 .... BenCurtis 8 37
(Brian Ellison) *hld up: drvn and outpcd over 4f out: short-lived effrt over 2f out: sn no imp* **7/5**[1]

400- **6** *7* **Jubilee Song**[261] 5509 4-9-5 52 .... GeorgeChaloner 6 24
(Richard Whitaker) *t.k.h: hld up in tch: drvn and struggling 3f out: sn wknd* **25/1**

0550 **7** *17* **Canford Crossing (IRE)**[15] 1584 3-8-9 65 .... AdrianNicholls 5
(David Nicholls) *plld hrd: prom tl rdn and wknd fr 3f out: t.o* **8/1**

5- **8** *6* **Washington Winkle**[213] 7025 4-9-10 42 .... (t) DavidNolan 4
(Donald McCain) *chsd ldrs tl rdn and wknd over 3f out: t.o* **33/1**

2m 9.01s (3.61) **Going Correction** +0.225s/f (Good)
WFA 3 from 4yo 15lb **8** Ran SP% **116.1**
Speed ratings (Par 101): **94,92,91,91,84 79,65,60**
CSF £20.77 TOTE £5.40: £1.10, £2.80, £3.30; EX 33.20 Trifecta £135.10.There was no bid for the winner. Stone Quercus was claimed by Mr D. McCain Jnr for £6,000.
Owner Course & Distance Racing & Chris Green **Bred** Darley **Trained** Norton, N Yorks

FOCUS
Race distance increased by 12yds. Probably just an ordinary seller run at a stop-start gallop in which the first four finished clear.

2016 SIS HORSES IN-RUNNING H'CAP 6f
6:55 (6:55) (Class 4) (0-85,85) 4-Y-O+ **£7,762** (£2,310; £1,154; £577) **Stalls** High

Form RPR

050- **1** **Straightothepoint**[171] 7880 4-9-1 79 .... PaulMulrennan 2 88
(Bryan Smart) *cl up far side: rdn over 2f out: led and hrd pressed last 50yds: hld on wl: 1st of 9 in gp* **14/1**

0/13 **2** *hd* **Dandyleekie (IRE)**[8] 1817 4-8-12 79 .... ShelleyBirkett(3) 8 87
(David O'Meara) *hld up far side: hdwy on outer of gp over 1f out: kpt on to chal towards fin: jst hld: 2nd of 9 in gp* **13/2**[3]

0323 **3** *nk* **Barkston Ash**[5] 1879 8-9-2 80 .... (p) JasonHart 3 87
(Eric Alston) *led and overall ldr far side: rdn and qcknd 2f out: hdd last 50yds: sn no ex: 3rd of 9 in gp* **4/1**[1]

00-2 **4** *1 ½* **Explain**[22] 1444 4-9-1 79 .... JamesSullivan 5 82
(Ruth Carr) *hld up far side: rdn and hdwy over 1f out: kpt on same pce wl ins fnl f: 4th of 9 in gp* **11/2**[2]

2453 **5** *¾* **Rich Again (IRE)**[14] 1601 7-9-0 78 .... (b) PJMcDonald 1 78
(James Bethell) *wnt rt s: in tch far side: rdn over 2f out: kpt on ins fnl f: 5th of 9 in gp* **16/1**

2/1 **6** *3* **Time Check (USA)**[14] 1597 4-9-1 82 .... KevinStott(3) 16 73+
(Saeed bin Suroor) *prom gng wl stands' side: smooth hdwy to ld that gp over 1f out: sn rdn: kpt on to pull clr of remainder of stands' side bunch fnl f: nt rch far side ldrs: 1st of 7 in gp* **11/2**[2]

6-25 **7** *½* **Dominate**[18] 1528 6-9-2 80 .... (v) ConnorBeasley 7 69
(George Scott) *s.i.s: hld up in tch far side: effrt and rdn over 2f out: outpcd over 1f out: 6th of 9 in gp* **14/1**

-504 **8** *2 ¾* **Classic Seniority**[22] 1444 4-8-13 77 .... PhillipMakin 6 57
(Marjorie Fife) *hld up in tch far side: rdn over 2f out: edgd rt and outpcd over 1f out: 7th of 9 in gp* **10/1**

-036 **9** *½* **Ambitious Icarus**[5] 1879 7-9-1 79 .... (e) PatrickMathers 13 58+
(Richard Guest) *mounted on crse and taken early to post: hld up stands' side: rdn over 2f out: hdwy to chse stands' side ldr ins fnl f: no imp: 2nd of 7 in gp* **28/1**

650- **10** *¾* **Honeysuckle Lil (IRE)**[231] 6494 4-8-6 75 .... RachelRichardson(5) 9 51
(Tim Easterby) *hld up far side: drvn and outpcd over 2f out: n.d after: 8th of 9 in gp* **33/1**

13-0 **11** *shd* **Bashiba (IRE)**[14] 1601 5-8-9 80 .... (t) KieranSchofield(7) 14 56+
(Nigel Tinkler) *led stands' side gp to over 1f out: sn hung rt and outpcd: 3rd of 7 in gp* **50/1**

50-0 **12** *1* **Royal Brave (IRE)**[22] 1444 5-8-12 76 .... BarryMcHugh 10 49+
(Rebecca Bastiman) *hld up in tch stands' side: drvn and outpcd over 2f out: n.d after: 4th of 7 in gp* **50/1**

03/- **13** *1* **Sleeper King (IRE)**[515] 8078 5-9-7 85 .... DanielTudhope 4 54
(David O'Meara) *trckd far side ldrs tl rdn and wknd over 2f out: last of 9 in gp* **11/1**

50-0 **14** *3* **Piazon**[22] 1444 5-9-4 82 .... (p) ShaneGray 11 42+
(Kevin Ryan) *taken early to post: hld up stands' side: rdn along 2f out: sn outpcd: 5th of 7 in gp* **16/1**

0-06 **15** *1 ½* **Alexandrakollontai (IRE)**[11] 1694 6-8-12 81 ....(b) GarryWhillans(5) 12 36+
(Alistair Whillans) *wnt rt s: bhd on outside of stands' side gp: drvn and outpcd fr 1/2-way: 6th of 7 in gp* **33/1**

0-00 **16** *1 ¼* **Slingsby**[17] 1555 5-8-7 71 oh1 .... (b) DavidAllan 15 22+
(Michael Easterby) *cl up stands' side gp tl rdn and wknd fr 2f out: last of 7 in gp* **20/1**

1m 12.99s (-0.01) **Going Correction** +0.15s/f (Good) **16** Ran SP% **124.6**
Speed ratings (Par 105): **106,105,105,103,102 98,97,94,93,92 92,90,89,85,83 81**
CSF £98.26 CT £444.39 TOTE £19.50: £4.80, £2.70, £1.90, £1.40; EX 155.00 Trifecta £1466.80.

Owner Crossfields Racing **Bred** Crossfields Bloodstock Ltd **Trained** Hambleton, N Yorks

FOCUS
A competitive sprint in which the field split into two groups with nine of the 16 racing far side and they filled the first five places.

2017 SIS INFINITE RACING GAMES H'CAP 1m 1f 170y
7:30 (7:32) (Class 3) (0-90,90) 4-Y-O+ **£12,938** (£3,850; £1,924; £962) **Stalls** Low

Form RPR

210- **1** **Dance King**[191] 7548 6-9-2 85 .... (tp) DavidAllan 13 93
(Tim Easterby) *s.i.s: hld up: effrt and plld to outside 2f out: hdwy to ld appr fnl f: edgd rt: rdn and r.o wl* **16/1**

4-63 **2** *¾* **Salmon Sushi**[22] 1445 5-8-11 80 .... JasonHart 3 86
(Tim Easterby) *s.i.s: t.k.h: hld up on ins: nt clr run over 3f out tl swtchd to outside 2f out: hdwy to chse wnr ins fnl f: r.o* **8/1**

420- **3** *1 ¼* **Salieris Mass**[205] 7222 4-9-6 89 .... AdrianNicholls 11 92
(Mark Johnston) *s.i.s: sn pushed along in rr: gd hdwy on outside and ev ch over 1f out: hung rt ins fnl f: r.o* **12/1**

1-00 **4** *¾* **Maraakib (IRE)**[22] 1445 4-9-7 90 .... DanielTudhope 2 94+
(David O'Meara) *t.k.h: in tch on ins: hdwy whn nt clr run over 2f out to over 1f out: squeezed through and bmpd ins fnl f: kpt on* **7/1**[3]

36-6 **5** *nk* **Darrington**[13] 1620 4-8-13 82 .... JackGarritty 7 83
(Richard Fahey) *led: rdn over 2f out: hdd appr fnl f: one pce whn hmpd ins fnl f* **13/2**[2]

13-5 **6** *½* **Illusive (IRE)**[69] 749 5-9-6 89 .... (tp) ConnorBeasley 6 90+
(George Scott) *prom: drvn and outpcd wl over 1f out: kpt on ins fnl f: no imp* **7/1**[3]

13-0 **7** *1 ¾* **New Strategy (IRE)**[113] 172 4-8-13 85 .... (tp) KevinStott(3) 12 82
(Saeed bin Suroor) *hld up in tch: smooth hdwy over 3f out: effrt and ev ch over 1f out: one pce whn hmpd ins fnl f: sn btn* **12/1**

4-20 **8** *1* **Polar Forest**[13] 1643 6-9-1 87 .... (e) JacobButterfield(3) 4 82
(Richard Guest) *hld up in midfield: drvn and outpcd over 2f out: sme late hdwy: nvr rchd ldrs* **20/1**

6-04 **9** *½* **Woodacre**[22] 1445 9-8-7 76 oh2 .... GeorgeChaloner 8 70
(Richard Whitaker) *t.k.h: pressed ldr: drvn and ev ch tl wknd over 1f out* **13/2**[2]

50-0 **10** *6* **Genres**[25] 1380 4-8-9 78 .... BenCurtis 1 59
(Alan Swinbank) *hld up on ins: drvn and outpcd over 2f out: sn btn* **18/1**

435- **11** *1 ¾* **El Beau (IRE)**[41] 7676 5-9-2 85 .... PhillipMakin 5 63
(John Quinn) *prom: lost pl wl over 2f out: eased whn btn ins fnl f* **9/1**

2 **12** *4 ½* **Invictus (GER)**[31] 1245 4-9-2 85 .... PJMcDonald 10 53
(Micky Hammond) *hld up towards rr: drvn and struggling over 2f out: sn btn* **6/1**[1]

2m 5.72s (0.32) **Going Correction** +0.225s/f (Good) **12** Ran SP% **118.4**
Speed ratings (Par 107): **107,106,105,104,104 104,102,101,101,96 95,91**
CSF £138.36 CT £1606.58 TOTE £21.50: £5.80, £3.40, £6.40; EX 249.70 Trifecta £1808.10 Part won..
Owner Ambrose Turnbull **Bred** Meon Valley Stud **Trained** Great Habton, N Yorks

FOCUS
Race distance increased by 12yds. A competitive handicap run at a decent gallop and the first three were the last three turning for home. There were also a few hard-luck stories.

2018 ROA/RACING POST OWNERS JACKPOT H'CAP 2m
8:00 (8:00) (Class 5) (0-75,74) 4-Y-O+ **£3,881** (£1,155; £577; £288) **Stalls** High

Form RPR

2-05 **1** **Jan Smuts (IRE)**[12] 1665 8-8-11 68 .... (tp) HollieDoyle(7) 5 75
(Wilf Storey) *hld up in midfield: stdy hdwy over 2f out: effrt and chsd ldr over 1f out: kpt on to ld towards fin* **14/1**

5-64 **2** *hd* **Stormin Tom (IRE)**[12] 1675 4-8-7 65 .... RachelRichardson(5) 3 72
(Tim Easterby) *cl up: led over 3f out: rdn and edgd rt over 1f out: kpt on fnl f: hdd towards fin* **8/1**

06-5 **3** *2 ½* **Aldreth**[16] 1560 5-8-12 67 .... NathanEvans(5) 4 71
(Michael Easterby) *in tch on ins: rdn over 2f out: swtchd rt over 1f out: kpt on same pce ins fnl f* **4/1**[1]

2224 **4** *¾* **Northside Prince (IRE)**[24] 1405 10-9-5 69 .... NeilFarley 1 72
(Alan Swinbank) *trckd ldrs: drvn along over 2f out: kpt on same pce fnl f* **12/1**

5-63 **5** *2 ½* **Sinakar (IRE)**[12] 1665 5-9-10 74 .... DanielTudhope 9 74
(David O'Meara) *cl: rdn over 2f out: edgd rt and outpcd over 1f out* **9/2**[2]

0126 **6** *1 ¾* **Next Edition (IRE)**[16] 1560 8-9-4 68 .... ConnorBeasley 10 66
(Philip Kirby) *s.i.s: hld up: rdn over 4f out: hdwy on outside over 2f out: edgd rt and outpcd over 1f out* **20/1**

32 **7** *hd* **Wishing Well**[12] 1674 4-8-11 64 .... PJMcDonald 11 62
(Micky Hammond) *t.k.h: in tch: outpcd 3f out: n.d after* **5/1**[3]

6-25 **8** *1 ¾* **Tuscan Gold**[18] 1523 9-9-9 73 .... (p) JackGarritty 12 69
(Micky Hammond) *s.i.s: hld up: rdn and outpcd 3f out: sme late hdwy: nvr on terms* **11/1**

41 **9** *1 ¼* **American Life (FR)**[18] 1523 9-8-4 57 .... (b) SammyJoBell(3) 7 51
(Sophie Leech) *s.i.s: hld up: rdn along over 3f out: sn outpcd: btn fnl 2f* **11/1**

324- **10** *4 ½* **Dew Pond**[185] 7679 4-8-12 65 .... DavidAllan 6 54
(Tim Easterby) *hld up on outside: hdwy and prom over 3f out: rdn and wknd wl over 1f out* **7/1**

0-64 **11** *17* **Lexington Bay (IRE)**[24] 1404 8-9-1 65 .... (p) PhillipMakin 2 33
(Philip Kirby) *led to over 3f out: sn rdn and lost pl: lost tch fnl 2f* **25/1**

3m 36.93s (5.13) **Going Correction** +0.225s/f (Good)
WFA 4 from 5yo+ 3lb **11** Ran SP% **118.1**
Speed ratings (Par 103): **96,95,94,94,93 92,92,91,90,88 79**
CSF £122.03 CT £539.84 TOTE £15.10: £4.00, £2.70, £2.30; EX 109.00 Trifecta £928.00 Part won..
Owner H S Hutchinson & W Storey **Bred** Tipper House Stud **Trained** Muggleswick, Co Durham

FOCUS
Race distance increased by 12yds. Mainly exposed performers in this staying handicap which was run at a fair gallop and they were soon well strung out.

2019 SIS ON-DEMAND RACING GAMES MAIDEN STKS 6f
8:30 (8:30) (Class 5) 3-Y-O **£3,881** (£1,155; £577; £288) **Stalls** High

Form RPR

2-23 **1** **General Alexander (IRE)**[20] 1494 3-8-12 78 .... (p) BenRobinson(7) 7 81
(Brian Ellison) *mde virtually all: rdn clr fr 2f out* **13/8**[2]

36-6 **2** *5* **Silver Streak (IRE)**[23] 1409 3-9-5 75 .... PJMcDonald 5 65
(Ann Duffield) *wnt rt s: sn trcking ldrs: effrt and chsd (clr) wnr over 1f out: no imp fnl f* **4/1**[3]

3 *3 ½* **Line Sport (IRE)** 3-9-5 0 .... DavidNolan 8 54
(Richard Fahey) *dwlt: in tch: rn green and sn pushed along: plugged on fr 2f out: no imp* **6/4**[1]

0 **4** *1 ¾* **Big Time Dancer (IRE)**[12] 1673 3-9-5 0 .... JamesSullivan 2 48
(Dianne Sayer) *bmpd and carried rt sn after s: outpcd and bhd: hdwy and hung rt fnl f: nvr rchd ldrs* **22/1**

00 **5** *4* **Kyllini**[8] 1814 3-8-11 0 .... JacobButterfield(3) 3 30
(Marjorie Fife) *dwlt and carried rt sn after s: sn pushed along in tch: struggling 1/2-way: btn fnl 2f* **25/1**

0 **6** *2* **Noah Amor (IRE)**[12] 1669 3-9-5 0 .... AdrianNicholls 6 29
(David Nicholls) *wnt bdly rt s: plld hrd and disp ld to over 2f out: wknd over 1f out* **12/1**

0-0 **7** *6* **Fool's Dream**[12] 1673 3-9-0 0 .... ConnorBeasley 1 5
(Bryan Smart) *carried rt and bmpd s: in tch tl rdn and wknd over 3f out* **25/1**

1m 13.94s (0.94) **Going Correction** +0.15s/f (Good) **7** Ran SP% **117.8**
Speed ratings (Par 99): **99,92,87,85,80 77,69**
CSF £8.84 TOTE £2.00: £1.50, £1.90; EX 10.20 Trifecta £15.90.
Owner Mrs J A Martin **Bred** Mountarmstrong Stud **Trained** Norton, N Yorks

FOCUS
An uncompetitive sprint maiden with several hampered at the start. The first two were fully exposed.
T/Plt: £915.10 to a £1 stake. Pool of £50,897.85 - 40.60 winning units. T/Qpdt: £174.60 to a £1 stake. Pool of £6,396.62 - 27.10 winning units. **Richard Young**

2020 - 2022a (Foreign Racing) - See Raceform Interactive

1987 ASCOT (R-H)

Saturday, May 7

OFFICIAL GOING: Good to firm (str 8.5; rd 8.1)

Wind: Almost nil Weather: Cloudy, warm

2023 TOTEPOOLLIVEINFO.COM NOVICE STKS (PLUS 10 RACE) 5f

1:55 (1:55) (Class 3) 2-Y-O **£7,762** (£2,310; £1,154; £577) **Stalls** Centre

Form RPR

2 **1** **Reach High**[14] 1621 2-9-2 0 WilliamBuick 7 85
(Saeed bin Suroor) *w ldr: led over 1f out: rdn to hold on narrowly fnl f: jst prevailed* **4/5**[1]

2 *nse* **Harry Angel (IRE)** 2-9-2 0 AdamKirby 6 85+
(Clive Cox) *in tch: effrt over 1f out: pressed wnr fnl f: r.o wl: jst failed* **7/2**[2]

1 **3** *1 3/4* **Visionary (IRE)**[18] 1543 2-9-8 0 MartinHarley 2 85
(Robert Cowell) *slt ld tl over 1f out: one pce ins fnl f* **17/2**

4 *2 1/2* **Super Julius** 2-9-2 0 ShaneKelly 3 70
(Eve Johnson Houghton) *stdd s: hld up in tch: rdn 2f out: sn outpcd* **33/1**

5 *1 1/4* **Prerogative (IRE)** 2-9-2 0 SeanLevey 1 65+
(Richard Hannon) *wnt rt s: plld hrd: chsd ldrs tl wknd over 1f out* **9/1**

3 **6** *3/4* **Raffle King (IRE)**[18] 1543 2-9-2 0 CharlesBishop 5 62
(Mick Channon) *plld hrd: in tch tl wknd over 1f out* **8/1**[3]

1m 0.2s (-0.30) **Going Correction** -0.025s/f (Good) **6** Ran SP% **112.4**
Speed ratings (Par 97): **101,100,98,94,92 90**
CSF £3.85 TOTE £1.70: £1.20, £2.10; EX 4.90 Trifecta £11.80.
Owner Godolphin **Bred** Darley **Trained** Newmarket, Suffolk

FOCUS

They watered overnight, putting 4mm down, but the going was still given as good to firm (GoingStick: Straight: 8.5, Round 8.1). The rail on the Round course was positioned approximately 3yds out from its innermost position from the 1m4f start to the home straight, adding 10yds to the 1m4f races. The odds-on winner set a fair standard, but was all out to get off the mark.

2024 LEO BANCROFT SIGNATURE HAIRCARE H'CAP 1m 4f

2:30 (2:34) (Class 3) (0-95,92) 4-Y-O+ **£9,703** (£2,887; £1,443; £721) **Stalls** Low

Form RPR

440- **1** **King Bolete (IRE)**[259] 5639 4-9-5 **90** AndreaAtzeni 6 98+
(Roger Varian) *mde all: drvn along and hld on wl fnl f* **5/1**[3]

114- **2** *1 1/4* **Duretto**[211] 7076 4-9-7 **92** JimCrowley 11 98
(Andrew Balding) *trckd ldrs: chal over 1f out: hrd rdn: one pce fnl f* **9/2**[2]

-544 **3** *3/4* **Plutocracy (IRE)**[70] 747 6-9-5 **90** AdamKirby 12 95+
(Gary Moore) *stdd s: hld up in rr: pushed along and r.o fnl 2f: nrest at fin* **16/1**

312- **4** *3/4* **Perestroika**[273] 5133 4-8-12 **88** HectorCrouch[(5)] 2 92
(Henry Candy) *prom: hrd rdn 2f out: styd on same pce* **11/1**

1- **5** *1 3/4* **Sign Of A Victory (IRE)**[53] 8125 7-9-3 **88** WilliamBuick 7 89
(Nicky Henderson) *dwlt: hld up towards rr: rdn 3f out: sme hdwy 2f out: nvr able to chal* **2/1**[1]

4 **6** *nk* **Cayirli (FR)**[42] 1089 4-9-7 **92** TimmyMurphy 4 92
(Seamus Durack) *t.k.h in midfield: n.m.r 4f out: no hdwy fnl 2f* **12/1**

215- **7** *1 3/4* **Forever Popular (USA)**[302] 4089 4-8-11 **82** PatCosgrave 1 80
(William Haggas) *in tch on rail: n.m.r over 4f out tl over 3f out: outpcd fnl 2f* **9/1**

113- **8** *3 1/2* **Classic Villager**[209] 7145 4-9-5 **90** AndrewMullen 8 82
(Michael Appleby) *towards rr: rdn over 2f out: n.d* **8/1**

221/ **9** *2 3/4* **Pasaka Boy**[574] 7110 6-9-4 **92** DannyBrock[(3)] 5 80
(Jonathan Portman) *t.k.h: prom tl wknd 2f out* **33/1**

30-0 **10** *2* **Lungarno Palace (USA)**[17] 1568 5-9-0 **85** (p) TomQueally 9 69
(John Gallagher) *a towards rr: lost tch over 2f out* **28/1**

2m 33.2s (0.70) **Going Correction** +0.275s/f (Good) **10** Ran SP% **117.6**
Speed ratings (Par 107): **108,107,106,106,105 104,103,101,99,98**
CSF £28.07 CT £338.36 TOTE £6.30: £1.90, £2.00, £4.60; EX 26.70 Trifecta £317.90.
Owner Sheikh Mohammed Obaid Al Maktoum **Bred** Ship Commodities International **Trained** Newmarket, Suffolk

FOCUS

Race distance increased by 10yds. This was a bit of tactical affair, with the winner dominating from the front. The form is rated around the runner-up.

2025 CAREY GROUP BUCKHOUNDS STKS (LISTED RACE) 1m 4f

3:05 (3:07) (Class 1) 4-Y-O+
£25,519 (£9,675; £4,842; £2,412; £1,210; £607) **Stalls** Low

Form RPR

1/0- **1** **Elite Army**[357] 2276 5-9-0 104 WilliamBuick 2 109
(Saeed bin Suroor) *plld hrd: cl up: fnd gap and effrt 2f out: led over 1f out: hrd rdn fnl f: jst hld on* **3/1**[1]

546- **2** *hd* **Scotland (GER)**[324] 3303 5-9-0 109 JimCrowley 6 108
(Andrew Balding) *stdd s: hld up in rr: swtchd outside and hdwy over 2f out: chal fnl f: r.o wl: jst hld* **9/2**[2]

521- **3** *3* **Missed Call (IRE)**[185] 7703 6-8-12 98 TomQueally 4 101
(James Fanshawe) *in tch: led 2f out tl over 1f out: one pce fnl f* **9/2**[2]

323- **4** *1 3/4* **Oriental Fox (GER)**[196] 7485 8-9-0 109 JoeFanning 7 100
(Mark Johnston) *cl up: led briefly over 2f out: no ex over 1f out* **3/1**[1]

1- **5** *1 3/4* **Torcedor (IRE)**[14] 1659 4-9-0 102 (b) WayneLordan 1 98
(David Wachman, Ire) *chsd ldrs tl rdn and btn 2f out* **3/1**[1]

0 **6** *14* **Giant Redwood (IRE)**[31] 1273 4-9-0 0 WilliamCarson 5 75
(Michael Bell) *led tl wknd over 2f out* **33/1**[3]

2m 32.03s (-0.47) **Going Correction** +0.275s/f (Good) **6** Ran SP% **114.3**
Speed ratings (Par 111): **112,111,109,108,107 98**
CSF £17.29 TOTE £3.40: £1.90, £2.50; EX 11.30 Trifecta £39.60.
Owner Godolphin **Bred** Darley **Trained** Newmarket, Suffolk

FOCUS

Race distance increased by 10yds. A competitive Listed contest that was decided by the winner's ability to quicken against stayers off a steady pace. The third is the best guide.

2026 EBF BREEDERS' SERIES FILLIES' H'CAP 1m (S)

3:40 (3:44) (Class 2) 3-Y-O+
£28,012 (£8,388; £4,194; £2,097; £1,048; £526) **Stalls** Centre

Form RPR

00-3 **1** **Light And Shade**[35] 1207 4-9-3 **91** MartinHarley 9 99
(James Tate) *gng wl towards rr: shkn up and hdwy over 1f out: led towards centre ins fnl f: edgd rt: rdn out* **11/2**[3]

-224 **2** *shd* **Tutu Nguru (USA)**[28] 1338 3-8-6 **93** AndreaAtzeni 7 98
(William Haggas) *dwlt: bhd: swtchd rt and hdwy 2f out: jnd wnr on far rail ins fnl f: r.o wl* **4/1**[2]

000- **3** *3/4* **Margaret's Mission (IRE)**[224] 6755 5-8-11 **85** KierenFallon 4 91
(Jim Goldie) *hld up in 6th: rdn and hdwy over 2f out: pressed ldrs fnl f: r.o* **8/1**

-225 **4** *1 1/2* **Bint Dandy (IRE)**[17] 1576 5-8-11 **90** (b) JosephineGordon[(5)] 5 93
(Chris Dwyer) *chsd ldng pair: wnt 2nd and chal 2f out: kpt on same pce* **10/1**

1115 **5** *1 1/2* **Moon River (IRE)**[11] 1757 4-8-9 **83** AndrewMullen 1 82
(Michael Appleby) *trckd ldr: led 3f out tl ins fnl f: no ex* **10/1**

000- **6** *1 1/4* **Gratzie**[246] 6040 5-9-1 **89** CharlesBishop 6 85
(Mick Channon) *hld up in 5th: rdn 2f out: no imp* **16/1**

300- **7** *3* **Pandora (IRE)**[280] 4876 4-9-10 **98** WilliamBuick 3 87
(David O'Meara) *dwlt: towards rr: rdn 3f out: carried rt 2f out: n.d* **6/1**

0-10 **8** *1/2* **Imshivalla (IRE)**[14] 1643 5-8-8 **89** AdamMcNamara[(7)] 2 77
(Richard Fahey) *chsd ldrs tl hrd rdn and wknd 2f out* **14/1**

22-1 **9** *27* **Havre De Paix (FR)**[37] 1160 4-9-1 **89** JimCrowley 8 15
(David Menuisier) *led tl 3f out: wknd over 2f out: eased* **3/1**[1]

1m 38.56s (-2.24) **Going Correction** -0.025s/f (Good)
WFA 3 from 4yo+ 13lb **9** Ran SP% **116.5**
Speed ratings (Par 96): **110,109,109,107,106 104,101,101,74**
CSF £28.06 CT £177.38 TOTE £6.50: £2.00, £1.60, £2.70; EX 21.30 Trifecta £168.60.
Owner Saeed Manana **Bred** M H And Mrs G Tourle **Trained** Newmarket, Suffolk
■ Stewards' Enquiry : Kieren Fallon two-day ban: use of whip (21-22 May)

FOCUS

A competitive fillies' handicap run at a good gallop, and it suited those held up. A length pb from the winner.

2027 TOTESCOOP6 VICTORIA CUP (HERITAGE H'CAP) 7f

4:15 (4:17) (Class 2) 4-Y-O+
£65,362 (£19,572; £9,786; £4,893; £1,837; £1,837) **Stalls** Centre

Form RPR

2445 **1** **Flash Fire (IRE)**[23] 1441 4-9-6 **104** AdamKirby 29 114
(Charlie Appleby) *chsd ldrs: led over 1f out: rdn out* **20/1**

-253 **2** *3/4* **Mutawathea**[64] 816 5-8-10 **99** (p) EdwardGreatrex[(5)] 6 107
(Simon Crisford) *chsd ldrs: drvn to chal 2f out: hung lft fnl f: kpt on* **25/1**

510- **3** *nk* **Buckstay (IRE)**[203] 7282 6-9-9 **107** (p) JamieSpencer 2 114+
(Peter Chapple-Hyam) *stdd s: hld up in rr: hdwy over 1f out: str run to take 3rd nr fin* **10/1**

15-0 **4** *1 1/2* **Dinkum Diamond (IRE)**[23] 1441 8-9-5 **103** CathyGannon 21 106
(Henry Candy) *in tch: effrt 2f out: one pce fnl f* **33/1**

6-30 **5** *shd* **Earth Drummer (IRE)**[7] 1871 6-9-0 **98** ShaneKelly 4 104+
(David Loughnane) *stdd s: hld up towards rr: effrt and nt clr run over 1f out: fin wl* **50/1**

53-6 **5** *dht* **Grand Inquisitor**[23] 1441 4-8-12 **96** TedDurcan 19 99
(Sir Michael Stoute) *mid-div: rdn 3f out: styd on fnl f* **8/1**[3]

60-3 **7** *hd* **Fort Bastion (IRE)**[7] 1871 7-8-8 **97** (v) JoshDoyle[(5)] 14 99
(David O'Meara) *dwlt: towards rr: hdwy over 1f out: styd on* **16/1**

00-0 **8** *hd* **The Warrior (IRE)**[28] 1335 4-8-11 **95** JimCrowley 12 97+
(Amanda Perrett) *dwlt: in rr tl styd on wl fr over 1f out* **20/1**

0-20 **9** *1 1/4* **Majestic Moon (IRE)**[14] 1627 6-9-0 **101** MichaelJMMurphy[(3)] 25 99
(John Gallagher) *prom tl outpcd fnl 2f* **33/1**

250- **10** *nse* **Miracle Of Medinah**[191] 7588 5-8-13 **97** LiamKeniry 23 95
(Mark Usher) *towards rr tl styd on fr over 1f out* **66/1**

-160 **11** *2 1/4* **Rivellino**[43] 1066 6-9-0 **103** JordanVaughan[(5)] 7 95
(K R Burke) *in tch: chsd ldrs 2f out: wknd fnl f* **33/1**

4-01 **12** *nk* **Predominance (IRE)**[14] 1627 4-8-12 **96** (p) PatCosgrave 11 87+
(William Haggas) *stdd s: hld up towards rr: rdn 2f out: swtchd rt over 1f out: nvr able to chal* **6/1**[1]

40-0 **13** *nse* **Outback Traveller (IRE)**[14] 1627 5-9-2 **100** MartinHarley 8 91+
(Robert Cowell) *trckd ldrs gng wl: led 2f out tl wknd over 1f out* **7/1**[2]

30-1 **14** *1/2* **Accession (IRE)**[23] 1441 7-8-11 **100** KieranShoemark[(5)] 17 90
(Charlie Fellowes) *prom tl wknd over 1f out* **25/1**

4061 **15** *1* **Mr Bossy Boots (IRE)**[11] 1752 5-8-2 **91** (t) PatrickO'Donnell[(5)] 22 78
(Ralph Beckett) *towards rr: rdn 3f out: n.d* **33/1**

5-21 **16** *hd* **Crazy Chic (IRE)**[35] 1204 5-8-13 **97** AndreaAtzeni 28 84
(Stuart Williams) *towards rr: n.m.r over 1f out: nvr able to chal* **16/1**

-025 **17** *3/4* **Rene Mathis (GER)**[3] 1969 6-9-5 **103** JackGarritty 3 88
(Richard Fahey) *mid-div: effrt 2f out: no imp whn hmpd over 1f out* **33/1**

-060 **18** *hd* **Emell**[14] 1637 6-9-4 **107** (b) KierenFallon 18 97
(Richard Hannon) *prom tl wknd over 1f out: eased whn btn* **25/1**

00-4 **19** *1* **Free Code (IRE)**[25] 1394 5-8-5 **92** RobHornby[(3)] 24 73
(David Barron) *bhd: drvn along 3f out: nvr nr ldrs* **14/1**

3201 **20** *nse* **Supersta**[3] 1959 5-8-10 **94** 6ex (p) AndrewMullen 20 75
(Michael Appleby) *chsd ldrs tl wknd 2f out* **20/1**

0-00 **21** *1 1/2* **Heaven's Guest (IRE)**[23] 1441 6-8-12 **103** AdamMcNamara[(7)] 10 80
(Richard Fahey) *a towards rr* **20/1**

0-40 **22** *2 1/2* **Related**[19] 1522 6-8-11 **95** (b) TomQueally 1 65
(Paul Midgley) *racd wd: led tl wknd 2f out* **33/1**

024- **23** *6* **Squats (IRE)**[245] 6078 4-8-7 **98** GeorgiaCox[(7)] 13 52
(William Haggas) *mid-div tl wknd 2f out* **20/1**

/04- **24** *3/4* **Valley Of Fire**[287] 4639 4-8-10 **94** CamHardie 5 46
(William Haggas) *dwlt: mid-div: outpcd 2f out: btn whn hmpd over 1f out* **33/1**

-116 **25** *3* **Mister Universe**[43] 1068 4-9-10 **108** JoeFanning 15 52
(Mark Johnston) *prom tl outpcd 2f out: btn whn hmpd over 1f out* **33/1**

12-1 **26** *11* **Hold Tight**[112] 220 4-8-12 **96** WilliamBuick 9 10
(Saeed bin Suroor) *mid-div tl squeezed for room and wknd over 1f out: eased whn btn* **8/1**[3]

1m 25.35s (-2.25) **Going Correction** -0.025s/f (Good) **26** Ran SP% **138.9**
Speed ratings (Par 109): **111,110,109,108,107 107,107,107,106,106 103,103,103,102,101 101,100,100,98,98 97,94,87,86,83**
CSF £446.54 CT £5313.81 TOTE £13.90: £5.30, £5.90, £3.30, £9.50; EX 772.80 Trifecta £9433.20.
Owner Godolphin **Bred** Darley **Trained** Newmarket, Suffolk

FOCUS

A competitive handicap as one would expect, and they came up the centre of the track. One or two met trouble in running, but the winner was comfortably the best and posted a clear pb.

2028 ROSLING KING H'CAP 6f

4:45 (4:49) (Class 4) (0-80,80) 4-Y-O+ **£6,469** (£1,925; £962; £481) **Stalls** Centre

Form RPR

22-3 **1** **Normandy Barriere (IRE)**[10] 1787 4-9-7 **80** WilliamBuick 2 89+
(Nigel Tinkler) *in tch: clsd on ldrs 2f out: led 1f out: rdn out* **4/1**[2]

6-00 **2** *3/4* **Intisaab**[23] 1444 5-9-2 **78** (p) ShelleyBirkett[(3)] 22 84+
(David O'Meara) *towards rr: hdwy over 1f out: swtchd rt ins fnl f: r.o to take 2nd nr fin* **14/1**

2114 **3** *nk* **Merhoob (IRE)**[3] 1958 4-9-7 **80** AdamKirby 20 85
(John Ryan) *mid-div: angled through and hdwy fr 2f out: styd on fnl f* **10/1**

0-12 **4** *shd* **Until Midnight (IRE)**[71] 727 6-8-6 **72** GeorgiaCox(7) 13 77
(Eugene Stanford) *prom: chal 1f out: kpt on* **12/1**

5512 **5** *1/2* **Picket Line**[14] 1648 4-8-10 **74** JosephineGordon(5) 18 77
(Geoffrey Deacon) *prom: chal ins fnl f: kpt on* **25/1**

3100 **6** *1/2* **Doctor Parkes**[14] 1634 10-9-5 **78** PatCosgrave 1 79
(Stuart Williams) *prom: led 2f out tl 1f out: one pce* **33/1**

04-2 **7** *3/4* **Gold Club**[30] 1291 5-9-5 **78** MartinLane 19 77
(Ed McMahon) *towards rr: rdn 2f out: styd on wl fnl f* **10/1**

5-43 **8** *1/2* **Dominium (USA)**[45] 1040 9-9-4 **77** (b) FrederikTylicki 15 74
(Jeremy Gask) *chsd ldrs tl outpcd fnl 2f* **25/1**

52 **9** *1/2* **Light From Mars**[52] 953 11-9-4 **77** (p) JamieSpencer 10 73
(Ronald Harris) *dwlt: bhd tl sme late hdwy* **25/1**

135- **10** *nse* **Magical Daze**[243] 6155 4-9-1 **74** TedDurcan 4 70
(Sylvester Kirk) *towards rr: drvn along 2f out: styd on fnl f* **33/1**

42-6 **11** *1/2* **Salvatore Fury (IRE)**[13] 1663 6-8-11 **70** (p) JimCrowley 8 64+
(Keith Dalgleish) *a in midfield* **8/1**[3]

1004 **12** *3/4* **Noble Deed**[24] 1419 6-9-0 **73** JoeFanning 12 65
(Michael Attwater) *prom: led after 1f tl 4f out: wknd over 1f out* **33/1**

44-2 **13** *shd* **Koptoon**[12] 1693 4-8-12 **71** (t) AndrewMullen 17 62
(Michael Appleby) *mid-div: hmpd over 1f out: nvr able to chal* **25/1**

00-6 **14** *1* **Regal Parade**[24] 1419 12-8-9 **73** (t) KieranShoemark(5) 9 61
(Charlie Wallis) *chsd ldrs tl wknd over 1f out* **33/1**

5-05 **15** *hd* **Bahamian Sunrise**[36] 1175 4-8-11 **73** MichaelJMMurphy(3) 14 61
(John Gallagher) *plld hrd: led for 1f: prom tl wknd over 1f out* **50/1**

1414 **16** *hd* **Harwoods Star (IRE)**[25] 1403 6-8-8 **74** (v[1]) DavidEgan(7) 3 61
(John Butler) *dwlt: racd wd: sn chsng ldrs: chal 2f out: sn wknd* **50/1**

11-1 **17** *1/2* **The Big Lad**[66] 782 4-9-7 **80** ShaneKelly 5 65
(Richard Hughes) *in tch tl wknd whn btn fnl f* **3/1**[1]

-005 **18** *hd* **Sunraider (IRE)**[10] 1787 9-9-2 **75** TomQueally 7 60
(Paul Midgley) *a towards rr* **25/1**

00-6 **19** *1* **Feeling Easy (IRE)**[23] 1432 4-8-12 **71** AndreaAtzeni 21 52
(Robert Eddery) *a bhd* **16/1**

5201 **20** *2 3/4* **Mr Christopher (IRE)**[14] 1648 4-8-10 **74** (p) AnnaHesketh(5) 6 47
(Tom Dascombe) *prom: led 4f out tl 2f out: wknd over 1f out* **20/1**

430- **21** *12* **Vincentti (IRE)**[172] 7880 6-8-11 **75** JordanNason(5) 16 9
(Ronald Harris) *a bhd: no ch fnl 2f* **50/1**

1m 13.61s (-0.89) **Going Correction** -0.025s/f (Good) **21** Ran SP% **136.2**
Speed ratings (Par 105): **104,103,102,102,101 101,100,99,98,98 98,97,96,95,95 95,94,94,92,89 73**
CSF £55.16 CT £565.38 TOTE £5.40: £1.50, £4.40, £3.30, £3.20; EX 104.30 Trifecta £1023.90.
Owner Eddie Carswell **Bred** Tinnakill Bloodstock & L Cantillon **Trained** Langton, N Yorks

FOCUS
The early pace wasn't hectic and the closers could never quite get there. The form is rated around the third and fourth.
T/Jkpt: Not won. T/Plt: £227.50 to a £1 stake.Pool: £167,498.40 - 537.34 winning units. T/Qpdt: £48.00 to a £1 stake. Pool: £13,446.91 - 207.15 winning units **Lee McKenzie**

1626 HAYDOCK (L-H)
Saturday, May 7

OFFICIAL GOING: Good changing to good (good to firm in places) after race 6 (4.30)
Wind: light 1/2 behind Weather: fine

2029 PERTEMPS NETWORK H'CAP 1m
1:40 (1:41) (Class 3) (0-95,95) 3-Y-O **£8,086** (£2,406; £1,202; £601) **Stalls** Low

Form RPR

15-2 **1** **Shaiyem (IRE)**[9] 1809 3-8-3 **80** TomMarquand(3) 2 88+
(Richard Hannon) *trckd ldrs: t.k.h: hung lft and led 1f out: drvn out* **5/1**[1]

12-5 **2** *1 1/4* **Steel Of Madrid (IRE)**[23] 1440 3-9-7 **95** DarryllHolland 5 100+
(Richard Hannon) *s.i.s: in rr: drvn 4f out: hdwy over 1f out: styd on wl to take 2nd nr fin* **17/2**

54-2 **3** *1 1/4* **Scarlet Dragon**[17] 1571 3-8-5 **79** JohnFahy 13 81
(Eve Johnson Houghton) *racd wd: sn trcking ldrs: pushed wd over 4f out: led over 2f out: hdd 1f out: kpt on same pce* **13/2**[3]

13- **4** *1/2* **Bell Heather (IRE)**[247] 6023 3-8-6 **80** PatrickMathers 10 81
(Richard Fahey) *t.k.h in mid-div: effrt over 2f out: kpt on same pce to take 4th last 100yds* **14/1**

441- **5** *2 1/4* **Zealous (IRE)**[204] 7248 3-8-7 **81** BenCurtis 9 77
(Alan Swinbank) *led early: trckd ldrs: t.k.h: effrt over 2f out: one pce appr fnl f* **14/1**

15-0 **6** *shd* **Bathos (IRE)**[43] 1080 3-8-13 **87** PaulMulrennan 6 82
(Mark Johnston) *w ldr: hmpd and pushed wd bnd over 4f out: upsides 3f out: one pce appr fnl f* **9/1**

641- **7** *2 1/4* **Dollar Reward**[225] 6720 3-8-5 **79** ow1 DavidProbert 3 69
(Sir Michael Stoute) *hld up in rr: nt clr run over 2f out: hdwy to chse ldrs over 1f out: wknd fnl 150yds* **11/2**[2]

53-0 **8** *4 1/2* **Fatherly Friend (USA)**[15] 1599 3-8-2 **76** oh1 (t) JoeyHaynes 8 56
(K R Burke) *in rr-div: drvn over 3f out: lost pl over 1f out* **33/1**

1- **9** *1 1/2* **Bronte Flyer**[241] 6204 3-8-3 **77** JimmyQuinn 7 53
(Ann Duffield) *s.i.s: t.k.h: sn trcking ldrs: n.m.r bnd over 4f out: wknd over 1f out* **9/1**

051- **10** *4* **Easy Code**[226] 6683 3-8-8 **82** RichardKingscote 1 49
(William Haggas) *sn led: hung rt bnd over 4f out: hdd over 2f out: wknd fnl f* **13/2**[3]

210 **11** *nk* **Abareeq**[15] 1603 3-8-13 **87** DaneO'Neill 11 54
(Mark Johnston) *prom racing wd: lost pl over 5f out: drvn over 2f out: nvr a factor* **12/1**

122- **12** *13* **Novinophobia**[214] 7006 3-8-5 **79** BarryMcHugh 4 16
(Richard Fahey) *s.i.s: t.k.h: hdwy whn hmpd over 4f out: lost pl over 1f out: eased whn bhd in clsng stages* **20/1**

1m 41.85s (-1.85) **Going Correction** -0.30s/f (Firm) **12** Ran SP% **118.0**
Speed ratings (Par 103): **97,95,94,94,91 91,89,84,83,79 79,66**
CSF £46.88 CT £285.75 TOTE £6.30: £2.00, £2.70, £2.50; EX 38.40 Trifecta £220.60.
Owner Al Shaqab Racing **Bred** E O'Neill **Trained** East Everleigh, Wilts

FOCUS
The actual race distance was 37yds further than advertised. The official going remained good on both the Flat and jumps courses. Clerk of the course Kirkland Tellwright said: "We're starting on good both courses. We've watered the jumps course and that will be easier". The opener was a very useful 3yo handicap and it was wide-open, providing Richard Hannon with a 1-2. It was a messy race, run at a muddling pace, but the form is worth noting. The 1-2 Hannon pair were unexposed and the form is rated around the third.

2030 PERTEMPS NETWORK SPRING TROPHY STKS (LISTED RACE) 7f
2:45 (2:45) (Class 1) 3-Y-O+
£20,982 (£7,955; £3,981; £1,983; £995; £499) **Stalls** Low

Form RPR

243- **1** **So Beloved**[189] 7634 6-9-7 113 DanielTudhope 1 117+
(David O'Meara) *trckd ldng pair gng wl: smooth hdwy to ld appr fnl f: v readily* **10/3**[1]

0-01 **2** *2* **You're Fired (IRE)**[14] 1629 5-9-7 105 DougieCostello 4 111
(K R Burke) *in rr: hdwy over 4f out: chsng ldrs 3f out: cl 2nd appr fnl f: kpt on same pce: no imp* **8/1**

25-5 **3** *1* **Markaz (IRE)**[14] 1637 4-9-7 111 DaneO'Neill 7 108
(Owen Burrows) *in rr: outpcd and drvn over 3f out: hung lft and kpt on fnl 2f: tk 3rd last 100yds* **4/1**[2]

0-02 **4** *2* **Coulsty (IRE)**[14] 1637 5-9-7 110 RichardKingscote 2 103
(Richard Hannon) *chsd ldrs: drvn 3 out: kpt on one pce over 1f out: tk modest 4th last 150yds* **9/2**[3]

/31- **5** *2 1/4* **Absolutely So (IRE)**[328] 3200 6-9-7 109 DavidProbert 5 97
(Andrew Balding) *hld up in rr: effrt over 2f out: kpt on fnl 150yds: nvr a threat: tk modest 5th in clsng stages* **6/1**

303- **6** *nk* **Salateen**[196] 7466 4-9-7 106 PhillipMakin 6 96
(David O'Meara) *swtchd lft after s: w ldr: wknd fnl 150yds* **16/1**

0-41 **7** *1 1/4* **Kelinni (IRE)**[21] 1491 8-9-7 110 ShaneGray 3 93
(Kevin Ryan) *led: t.k.h: hdd appr fnl f: wknd fnl 150yds* **4/1**[2]

1m 26.46s (-4.24) **Going Correction** -0.30s/f (Firm) **7** Ran SP% **112.5**
Speed ratings (Par 111): **112,109,108,106,103 103,101**
CSF £29.04 TOTE £4.10: £1.80, £3.10; EX 20.50 Trifecta £76.80.
Owner Sprint Thoroughbred Racing **Bred** Juddmonte Farms Ltd **Trained** Upper Helmsley, N Yorks

FOCUS
Race distance 37yds further than advertised. An open-looking Listed event, albeit not the strongest for the grade, but the top-rated winner did it nicely. He looks to have improved again.

2031 PERTEMPS NETWORK CONDITIONS STKS 6f
3:55 (3:56) (Class 2) 3-Y-O+ **£12,450** (£3,728; £1,864; £932; £466) **Stalls** Centre

Form RPR

111- **1** **Don't Touch**[231] 6517 4-9-4 106 TonyHamilton 5 112+
(Richard Fahey) *trckd ldrs: effrt over 2f out: led last 75yds: edgd lft: drvn out* **6/4**[1]

0/16 **2** *1 1/4* **Baccarat (IRE)**[23] 1439 7-9-4 111 PhillipMakin 2 108
(Charlie Appleby) *trckd ldrs: effrt and edgd lft over 1f out: led briefly last 150yds: no ex in clsng stages* **2/1**[2]

400- **3** *1/2* **Watchable**[216] 6971 6-9-4 109 (p) DanielTudhope 1 107
(David O'Meara) *w ldr: drvn 2f out: hung lft and led over 1f out: hdd last 150yds: styd on same pce* **3/1**[3]

3255 **4** *1 3/4* **Barracuda Boy (IRE)**[43] 1083 6-9-7 99 RichardKingscote 3 104
(Tom Dascombe) *led: drvn over 2f out: hdd over 1f out: kpt on same pce* **14/1**

4-33 **5** *2 1/2* **Georgian Bay (IRE)**[14] 1627 6-9-4 88 (v) DougieCostello 4 93
(K R Burke) *s.i.s: sn drvn in last: sme hdwy over 2f out: nvr a threat* **33/1**

1m 10.9s (-2.90) **Going Correction** -0.30s/f (Firm) **5** Ran SP% **107.9**
Speed ratings (Par 109): **107,105,104,102,99**
CSF £4.57 TOTE £2.20: £2.20, £1.10; EX 4.40 Trifecta £5.90.
Owner Nicholas Wrigley & Kevin Hart **Bred** Cheveley Park Stud Ltd **Trained** Musley Bank, N Yorks

FOCUS
Race distance as advertised. An interesting conditions event with the future in mind and smart form. There's more to come from the winner.

2000 LINGFIELD (L-H)
Saturday, May 7

OFFICIAL GOING: Turf course - good (good to firm in places; 7.6); polytrack: standard
Wind: light, behind Weather: sunny and warm

2032 BETFRED "FOLLOW US ON TWITTER" H'CAP 7f 1y(P)
1:45 (1:47) (Class 4) (0-85,85) 4-Y-O+ **£4,916** (£1,463; £731; £365) **Stalls** Low

Form RPR

160- **1** **Acclio (IRE)**[196] 7473 5-8-12 **76** JamieSpencer 5 86
(James Tate) *in tch: effrt to press ldrs 2f out: chsd ldr and drvn over 1f out: kpt on u.p to ld fnl 50yds: gng away at fin* **9/2**

2111 **2** *3/4* **Baileys Mirage (FR)**[9] 1811 5-8-11 **75** (b) SilvestreDeSousa 4 83
(Chris Dwyer) *pressed ldr tl led 2f out: rdn over 1f out: hrd pressed 1f out: hdd and one pce fnl 50yds* **3/1**[2]

540- **3** *1* **Baltic Brave (IRE)**[191] 7588 5-9-7 **85** (t) RyanMoore 2 90
(Hughie Morrison) *trckd ldrs: effrt in 3rd over 1f out: nvr enough room and styd on same pce ins fnl f* **15/8**[1]

4105 **4** *3/4* **Jammy Guest (IRE)**[24] 1418 6-9-6 **84** RyanPowell 3 87
(George Margarson) *stdd s: hld up in tch in rr: swtchd rt and effrt over 1f out: styd on fnl 100yds: nvr enough pce to chal* **4/1**[3]

0-64 **5** *2 1/4* **Cordite (IRE)**[18] 1545 5-9-6 **84** SamHitchcott 1 81
(Jim Boyle) *taken down early: led: rdn over 2f out: hdd over 1f out and immediately outpcd: wknd ins fnl f* **8/1**

1m 24.5s (-0.30) **Going Correction** +0.10s/f (Slow) **5** Ran SP% **109.1**
Speed ratings (Par 105): **105,104,103,102,99**
CSF £17.65 TOTE £6.00: £2.50, £1.70; EX 19.00 Trifecta £32.90.
Owner Saeed Manana **Bred** E Mulryan **Trained** Newmarket, Suffolk

FOCUS
Fair form, with the runner-up at the top of her game at present. The winner is rated to his old best.

2033 BETFRED "RACING'S BIGGEST SUPPORTER" H'CAP 1m 1y(P)
2:20 (2:20) (Class 3) (0-95,95) 4-Y-O+ **£7,309** (£2,187; £1,093; £547; £272) **Stalls** High

Form RPR

121/ **1** **Jailawi (IRE)**[623] 5686 5-8-12 **89** ThomasBrown(3) 5 97+
(Ismail Mohammed) *hld up in tch in 4th: effrt to chse ldr over 1f out: styd on wl ins fnl f to ld cl hone* **13/2**[3]

6622 **2** *nk* **Capo Rosso (IRE)**[10] 1797 6-9-6 **94** .... SilvestreDeSousa 3 101
(Tom Dascombe) *led: rdn 2f out: drvn over 1f out: kpt on u.p: hdd and no ex cl home* **7/1**

112- **3** *1 ¾* **Scottish Glen**[224] 6758 10-9-5 **93** .... FrannyNorton 8 96
(Patrick Chamings) *stdd after s: hld up in tch in midfield: hdwy u.p 1f out: wnt 3rd ins fnl f: kpt on* **14/1**

2032 **4** *hd* **Unforgiving Minute**[3] 1959 5-9-3 **91** .... FergusSweeney 1 94
(Gary Moore) *stdd after s: hld up in 5th: nt clrest of runs over 1f out: swtchd rt and hdwy 1f out: kpt on ins fnl f* **9/2**[2]

33-3 **5** *1 ½* **Outer Space**[10] 1797 5-9-3 **91** .... RyanMoore 9 90+
(Jamie Osborne) *stdd after s: hld up in last trio: nt clr run and swtchd rt over 1f out: kpt on ins fnl f: no threat to ldrs* **7/2**[1]

1630 **6** *2 ¾* **Majestic Myles (IRE)**[45] 1041 8-8-7 **81** .... OisinMurphy 4 74
(Lee Carter) *t.k.h: chsd ldr: rdn ent fnl 2f: lost 2nd and btn over 1f out: wknd ins fnl f* **33/1**

003- **7** *3 ¼* **Bow And Arrow**[280] 4860 4-9-7 **95** ....(p) JamesDoyle 2 80
(Charlie Appleby) *chsd ldng pair: rdn and btn over 1f out: fdd ins fnl f* **7/2**[1]

2153 **8** *1 ¾* **Shyron**[11] 1752 5-9-4 **92** .... JamieSpencer 7 73+
(George Margarson) *stdd s: hld up in last pair: swtchd rt over 1f out: no imp and hung lft: sn wknd and eased wl ins fnl f* **15/2**

-530 **9** *½* **Lexington Times (IRE)**[23] 1441 4-8-13 **94** .... HollieDoyle(7) 6 74+
(Richard Hannon) *v.s.a: bhd: steadily rcvrd and in tch 3f out: rdn wl over 1f out: sn btn: bhd fnl f* **10/1**

1m 36.64s (-1.56) **Going Correction** +0.10s/f (Slow) **9** Ran SP% **118.9**
Speed ratings (Par 107): **111,110,108,108,107 104,101,99,99**
CSF £52.86 CT £626.06 TOTE £12.10: £4.10, £2.90, £3.00; EX 78.70 Trifecta £1613.50.

Owner Saeed H Al Tayer **Bred** Stock Vale Ltd **Trained** Newmarket, Suffolk

FOCUS
Useful handicap form. The winner was progressive at three and is rated closer to his old form.

2034 BETFRED "BE PART OF THE ACTION" CHARTWELL FILLIES' STKS (GROUP 3) (F&M) 7f 1y(P)

2:50 (2:51) (Class 1) 3-Y-O+

£34,026 (£12,900; £6,456; £3,216; £1,614; £810) **Stalls** Low

Form RPR

120- **1** **Ashadihan**[261] 5566 3-8-7 104 ow1 ....(p) JamieSpencer 3 102+
(Kevin Ryan) *stdd after s: hld up in last trio: wd and effrt bnd wl over 1f out: hdwy 1f out: str run u.p to ld towards fin* **10/1**

211- **2** *1* **Light Music**[196] 7471 3-8-6 98 .... OisinMurphy 4 98
(William Haggas) *stdd s: t.k.h: hld up in tch in midfield: nt clr run ent fnl 2f: swtchd rt over 1f out: hdwy 1f out: chsd ldr ins fnl f: styd on: wnt 2nd again last stride* **11/4**[2]

2-02 **3** *shd* **Squash**[25] 1396 3-8-6 102 .... SilvestreDeSousa 8 98
(Philip McBride) *chsd ldr: rdn to ld over 1f out: drvn and kpt on ins fnl f: hdd and no ex towards fin: lost 2nd last stride* **8/1**

1-3 **4** *1 ¾* **Quality Time (IRE)**[35] 1206 3-8-6 92 .... MartinLane 1 93
(Saeed bin Suroor) *chsd ldrs: effrt over 1f out: ev ch whn bmpd and hmpd 1f out: styd on same pce ins fnl f* **8/1**

526- **5** *nse* **Make Fast**[181] 7764 3-8-6 96 .... MartinDwyer 7 93
(Andrew Balding) *dwlt: t.k.h: hld up in tch in last trio: swtchd rt and effrt over 1f out: hdwy 1f out: kpt on wl fnl 100yds* **25/1**

-145 **6** *½* **Saucy Minx (IRE)**[35] 1207 6-9-4 94 .... JamesDoyle 10 98+
(Amanda Perrett) *in tch in midfield but stuck wd: hdwy to chse ldrs 3f out: ev ch and hung lft over 1f out: stl hanging and btn ins fnl f: wknd fnl 100yds* **16/1**

3045 **7** *2 ½* **Lady Lydia (IRE)**[5] 1932 5-9-4 82 .... LiamJones 9 89?
(Conrad Allen) *stdd s and dropped in bhd: hld up in last pair: effrt over 1f out: sltly hmpd and swtchd rt 1f out: no imp ins fnl f* **50/1**

1124 **8** *¾* **Volunteer Point (IRE)**[7] 1858 4-9-4 102 .... RyanMoore 5 87+
(Mick Channon) *t.k.h: hld up wl in tch in midfield: effrt to chse ldrs whn squeezed for room and snatched up 1f out: nt rcvr and eased ins fnl f* **5/2**[1]

44-1 **9** *2 ¼* **Rah Rah**[43] 1083 3-8-6 102 .... FrannyNorton 2 77+
(Mark Johnston) *led: rdn and hdd over 1f out: losing pl whn squeezed for room and snatched up 1f out: nt rcvr: bhd and eased ins fnl f* **9/2**[3]

1m 24.51s (-0.29) **Going Correction** +0.10s/f (Slow)
WFA 3 from 4yo+ 12lb **9** Ran SP% **116.4**
Speed ratings (Par 110): **105,103,103,101,101 101,98,97,94**
CSF £38.06 TOTE £12.40: £3.60, £1.60, £2.40; EX 72.30 Trifecta £292.20.

Owner T A Rahman **Bred** Highbank Stud Llp **Trained** Hambleton, N Yorks

FOCUS
A race usually run on the turf track, the finish was dominated by the 3yos. They didn't go much of a gallop and the winner did really well to come from so far back. She's rated better than the bare form.

2035 BETFRED MOBILE OAKS TRIAL FILLIES' STKS (LISTED RACE) 1m 3f 106y

3:25 (3:25) (Class 1) 3-Y-O **£22,684** (£8,600; £4,304; £2,144; £1,076) **Stalls** High

Form RPR

4- **1** **Seventh Heaven (IRE)**[19] 1537 3-9-0 93 .... RyanMoore 3 100
(A P O'Brien, Ire) *trckd ldr: effrt to chal 2f out: led over 1f out: sustained duel w runner-up after: r.o wl and a jst holding rival ins fnl f: rdn out* **7/4**[1]

31- **2** *nk* **Architecture (IRE)**[206] 7219 3-9-0 82 .... FMBerry 1 99
(Hugo Palmer) *t.k.h early: trckd ldng pair: swtchd rt and chal 2f out: sn rdn: sustained duel w wnr after: r.o but a jst hld ins fnl f* **11/4**[3]

2-1 **3** *5* **Mountain Bell**[26] 1386 3-9-0 95 .... OisinMurphy 6 92
(Ralph Beckett) *racd keenly: sn led but nvr totally settled: jnd and rdn 2f out: hdd over 1f out: no ex and btn jst ins fnl f: outpcd and nt given a hrd time after* **15/8**[2]

31 **4** *2* **Capricious Cantor (IRE)**[36] 1179 3-9-0 85 .... SilvestreDeSousa 5 87
(Ed Dunlop) *t.k.h early: hld up in tch in 4th: effrt whn rn green and hung lft over 2f out: stl hanging: outpcd and wl hld over 1f out* **12/1**

001- **5** *6* **Natural Beauty**[170] 7904 3-9-0 76 ....(t) JamesDoyle 2 77
(John Gosden) *hld up in tch in rr: effrt 3f out: sn struggling: wl btn over 1f out* **25/1**

2m 33.36s (1.86) **Going Correction** +0.10s/f (Good) **5** Ran SP% **109.4**
Speed ratings (Par 104): **97,96,93,91,87**
CSF £6.82 TOTE £2.50: £1.20, £1.90; EX 6.60 Trifecta £15.40.

Owner Derrick Smith & Mrs John Magnier & Michael Tabor **Bred** La Traviata Syndicate **Trained** Cashel, Co Tipperary

FOCUS
Race distance as advertised. Not a terribly strong edition of the race and the favourite got it done despite looking unhappy on the track. The pace was a steady one.

2036 BETFRED DERBY TRIAL STKS (LISTED RACE) (C&G) 1m 3f 106y

4:00 (4:00) (Class 1) 3-Y-O **£56,710** (£21,500; £10,760; £5,360; £2,690) **Stalls** High

Form RPR

4-42 **1** **Humphrey Bogart (IRE)**[17] 1567 3-9-0 104 .... SeanLevey 1 107
(Richard Hannon) *stdd after s: hld up in tch in rr: effrt u.p 2f out: clsd to chse ldrs and edgd lft jst ins fnl f: styd on wl to ld towards fin* **9/2**[3]

31- **2** *½* **Carntop**[217] 6926 3-9-0 98 .... FMBerry 3 106+
(Ralph Beckett) *chsd ldr for 2f: settled in 3rd after: effrt to chse ldr 2f out: rdn to ld over 1f out: drvn ins fnl f: hdd and no ex towards fin* **7/4**[1]

22-1 **3** *1* **Across The Stars (IRE)**[31] 1265 3-9-0 84 .... SilvestreDeSousa 4 106+
(Sir Michael Stoute) *t.k.h: hld up in tch in 4th: effrt 2f out: clsd u.p and chsng ldrs 1f out: trying to switch rt and bmpd jst ins fnl f: hemmed in and styd on same pce after: wnt 3rd towards fin* **6/1**

22-4 **4** *1* **Landofhopeandglory (IRE)**[23] 1438 3-9-0 102 .... RyanMoore 2 103
(A P O'Brien, Ire) *led: rdn over 2f out: hdd over 1f out: unable qck u.p: styd on same pce and lost 2 pls ins fnl f: nt clrest of runs wl ins fnl f* **9/2**[3]

1 **5** *8* **Winning Story**[24] 1426 3-9-0 95 ....(p) JamesDoyle 5 90
(Saeed bin Suroor) *s.i.s: hdwy to join ldr after 2f: rdn and rn green over 2f out: sn lost pl 2f out and btn over 1f out: wknd fnl f* **3/1**[2]

2m 28.29s (-3.21) **Going Correction** +0.10s/f (Good) **5** Ran SP% **112.0**
Speed ratings (Par 107): **115,114,113,113,107**
CSF £13.09 TOTE £5.50: £2.00, £1.70; EX 16.00 Trifecta £72.20.

Owner Chelsea Thoroughbreds - Saint Tropez **Bred** Ringfort Stud **Trained** East Everleigh, Wilts

FOCUS
Race distance as advertised. As in the Oaks trial they went a steady pace and the first four finished on top of each other. It's safe to say this race won't have an impact on the Derby.

2037 BETFRED.COM H'CAP 1m 2f

4:35 (4:35) (Class 2) (0-100,98) 4-Y-O **£11,971** (£3,583; £1,791; £896; £446) **Stalls** Low

Form RPR

-232 **1** **Dutch Uncle**[12] 1716 4-8-7 **84** .... SilvestreDeSousa 6 90
(Ed Dunlop) *mde all: pushed along and wnt clr over 2f out: rdn over 1f out: reduced advantage wl ins fnl f: a doing enough: rdn out* **2/1**[2]

1- **2** *1* **Winter House**[387] 1434 4-8-12 **89** .... JamesDoyle 7 93+
(Saeed bin Suroor) *hld up in midfield: effrt and stl plenty to do 3f out: hdwy and edgd lft over 1f out: styd on to go 2nd wl ins fnl f: nvr gng to rch wnr: eased cl home* **15/8**[1]

1/-3 **3** *½* **Hail Clodius (IRE)**[31] 1274 4-8-10 **87** .... SeanLevey 5 90
(Richard Hannon) *t.k.h: chsd ldrs tl wnt 2nd 7f out: rdn over 2f out: no imp tl kpt on u.p ins fnl f: lost 2nd wl ins fnl f* **6/1**[3]

300- **4** *1 ¾* **Zand (IRE)**[182] 7757 6-9-0 **91** .... FrannyNorton 4 91
(Mark Johnston) *chsd wnr tl 7f out: 3rd and rdn over 2f out: no imp tl kpt on steadily ins fnl f: nvr enough pce to threaten wnr* **15/2**

1-00 **5** *4 ½* **Passover**[32] 1245 5-9-4 **95** ....[1] OisinMurphy 3 86
(Andrew Balding) *stdd s: hld up in last pair: effrt and plenty to do over 2f out: no real prog: nvr trbld ldrs* **10/1**

00-0 **6** *2 ¾* **Firestorm (GER)**[17] 1569 5-8-8 **85** .... RobertTart 1 70
(Michael Attwater) *hld up in midfield: plenty to do and drvn over 2f out: no prog: nvr trbld ldrs* **14/1**

62/0 **7** *166* **Slowfoot (GER)**[8] 1569 8-9-7 **98** .... TimmyMurphy 2
(Jim Best) *stdd s: hld up in last pair: lost tch 3f out: virtually p.u fnl 2f: t.o* **50/1**

2m 9.07s (-1.43) **Going Correction** +0.10s/f (Good) **7** Ran SP% **111.9**
Speed ratings (Par 109): **109,108,107,106,102 100,**
CSF £5.86 TOTE £3.00: £1.60, £1.80; EX 6.20 Trifecta £22.00.

Owner The Hon R J Arculli **Bred** Cheveley Park Stud Ltd **Trained** Newmarket, Suffolk

FOCUS
Race distance as advertised. The market leaders came to the fore in what was a decent handicap, with the runner-up the one to take from the race moving forward. A minor pb from the winner.

2038 BETFRED TV SCOOP6/BRITISH STALLION STUDS EBF NOVICE STKS (PLUS 10 RACE) 5f

5:05 (5:05) (Class 4) 2-Y-O **£4,269** (£1,270; £634; £317) **Stalls** High

Form RPR

1 **Tibr (USA)** 2-9-2 0 .... SilvestreDeSousa 2 89+
(Ed Dunlop) *dwlt: sn rcvrd and chsd ldng pair after 1f: swtchd lft and effrt 1/2-way: led and edgd rt over 1f out: r.o wl fnl f: rdn out* **13/8**[2]

0 **2** *1* **Poet's Society**[26] 1384 2-9-2 0 .... FrannyNorton 1 85
(Mark Johnston) *awkward leaving stalls and rdr unbalanced early: chsd ldr after 1f: rdn and led briefly over 1f out: sn hdd and carried rt: styd on same pce ins fnl f* **11/1**

21 **3** *3* **Kreb's Cycle (IRE)**[11] 1736 2-9-5 0 .... RyanMoore 4 82
(Richard Hannon) *chsd ldr tl hmpd and dropped bk to 4th after 1f: nvr travelling wl enough after: swtchd lft and pushed along over 1f out: wnt 3rd ins fnl f: no threat to ldrs* **5/4**[1]

4 *2* **Reign On** 2-9-2 0 .... FMBerry 5 67
(Ralph Beckett) *s.i.s: in tch in rr: pushed along over 1f out: sn outpcd and btn 1f out: wnt 4th ins fnl f* **16/1**

5 *1 ½* **Sword Exceed (GER)** 2-9-2 0 .... JamesDoyle 3 62
(Charlie Appleby) *led and crossed to stands' rail after 1f: rdn and hdd over 1f out: hmpd sn after and btn 1f out: wknd ins fnl f* **5/1**[3]

57.33s (-0.87) **Going Correction** -0.275s/f (Firm) **5** Ran SP% **113.4**
Speed ratings (Par 95): **95,93,88,85,83**
CSF £18.30 TOTE £2.30: £1.60, £3.40; EX 17.90 Trifecta £51.50.

Owner Abdullah Saeed Al Naboodah **Bred** Don Alberto Corporation **Trained** Newmarket, Suffolk

FOCUS
A good little novice contest, the well-regarded winner doing it nicely.

T/Plt: £90.30 to a £1 stake. Pool: £66,741.41 - 539.37 winning units. T/Qpdt: £9.60 to a £1 stake. Pool: £5,007.15 - 382.36 winning units. **Steve Payne**

2007 NOTTINGHAM (L-H)

Saturday, May 7

OFFICIAL GOING: Good to firm (good in places; 8.4)

Wind: Light half behind Weather: Fine and dry

2039 RACINGUK.COM MAIDEN STKS 6f 15y

2:10 (2:11) (Class 5) 3-Y-O+ **£3,067** (£905; £453) **Stalls** Centre

Form RPR

1 **Mustallib (IRE)** 3-9-2 0 HarryBentley 6 88+
(Charles Hills) *trckd ldrs: hdwy over 2f out and sn cl up: rdn to ld appr fnl f: styd on* **3/1**[3]

-256 2 1 1/4 **Hermitage Bay (USA)**[30] 1287 3-9-2 80 (p) RobertHavlin 3 83
(John Gosden) *led: pushed along and jnd wl over 1f out: rdn: edgd lft and hdd appr fnl f: sn drvn and kpt on same pce* **9/4**[1]

00 3 8 **Shahaama**[9] 1814 3-8-11 0 GrahamLee 2 52
(Mick Channon) *wnt lft s: sn in tch: hdwy 1/2-way: rdn to chse ldng pair wl over 1f out: kpt on same pce* **7/1**

4 3 1/4 **Justice Smart (IRE)** 3-9-2 0 StevieDonohoe 9 47+
(Sir Michael Stoute) *dwlt: green and sn outpcd in rr: pushed along 1/2-way: hdwy wl over 1f out: kpt on fnl f* **5/2**[2]

65 5 nk **Bit Of A Quirke**[19] 1524 3-9-2 0 JasonHart 8 46
(Mark Walford) *cl up: pushed along 1/2-way: sn rdn and grad wknd* **16/1**

40 6 3/4 **Star Of Kheleyf**[49] 1000 3-8-13 0 AlistairRawlinson(3) 7 44
(Michael Appleby) *a towards rr* **33/1**

04 7 5 **Still Kicking (IRE)**[99] 380 3-9-2 0 BillyLee 5 28
(Phil McEntee) *chsd ldrs: rdn along wl over 2f out: sn wknd* **80/1**

06 8 10 **Just Over**[31] 1256 3-8-11 0 AdamBeschizza 4
(Robert Cowell) *a towards rr* **100/1**

9 5 **Ace Rebel** 3-9-2 0 (t) WilliamTwiston-Davies 1
(Richard Spencer) *bmpd s and towards rr: hdwy and in tch after 2f: rdn along: green and wandered over 2f out: sn wknd* **14/1**

1m 11.34s (-3.36) **Going Correction** -0.45s/f (Firm) 9 Ran SP% **114.6**
Speed ratings (Par 103): **104,102,91,87,86 85,79,65,59**
CSF £10.04 TOTE £4.30: £1.10, £1.10, £2.70; EX 9.60 Trifecta £70.10.

Owner Hamdan Al Maktoum **Bred** Wardstown Stud Ltd **Trained** Lambourn, Berks

FOCUS

Outer track used. Distances as advertised. The going remained good to firm, good in places with the bends having been watered during the morning. After the opener Graham Lee said: "It's good ground out there." An uncompetitive sprint maiden to start and they raced up the centre, with the first two eventually pulling clear.

2040 MOST RELIABLE BET DG TAXIS H'CAP (A JOCKEY CLUB GRASSROOTS SPRINT SERIES QUALIFIER) 5f 13y

2:40 (2:42) (Class 5) (0-75,75) 4-Y-O+ **£2,911** (£866; £432; £216) **Stalls** Centre

Form RPR

55-2 1 **Shackled N Drawn (USA)**[9] 1803 4-9-7 **75** HarryBentley 4 84+
(Peter Hedger) *stdd s and t.k.h: trckd ldrs: smooth hdwy 1/2-way: led wl over 1f out: rdn ent fnl f: drvn out towards fin* **4/1**[3]

606- 2 3/4 **Classic Pursuit**[159] 8051 5-8-12 **66** (p) RaulDaSilva 7 73
(Ivan Furtado) *in tch: pushed along 1/2-way: rdn 2f out: sn swtchd rt towards stands' rail: styd on strly fnl f* **3/1**[1]

5-02 3 1 **Flash City (ITY)**[7] 1874 8-9-5 **73** (p) JamesSullivan 2 76
(Ruth Carr) *trckd ldrs: hdwy 2f out: rdn over 1f out: kpt on fnl f* **7/2**[2]

00/4 4 1 **Douglas Bank (IRE)**[19] 1524 4-9-0 **68** (b) JFEgan 5 67
(Roy Bowring) *swtchd rt after 1f to r nr stands' rail: cl up: rdn along 2f out: sn drvn and grad wknd* **8/1**

0030 5 nse **Give Us A Belle (IRE)**[8] 1833 7-8-2 **61** oh10 (bt) PaddyPilley(5) 3 60
(Christine Dunnett) *racd centre: cl up: led 2f out and sn rdn: jnd and drvn over 1f out: sn hdd: wknd ins fnl f* **33/1**

3001 6 3/4 **Coiste Bodhar (IRE)**[10] 1790 5-8-3 **64** ow1 NatalieHambling(7) 8 61
(Scott Dixon) *racd towards centre: led: pushed along and hdd 2f out: sn rdn and wknd over 1f out* **9/1**

00-0 7 3 **Firgrove Bridge (IRE)**[15] 1596 4-8-11 **65** (p[1]) AdamBeschizza 6 51
(Steph Hollinshead) *towards rr: rdn along 1/2-way: nvr a factor* **22/1**

013- 8 4 1/2 **Outrage**[248] 5984 4-9-3 **71** LukeMorris 1 41
(Daniel Kubler) *in tch: sme hdwy on outer wl over 1f out: sn rdn and wknd* **5/1**

58.75s (-2.75) **Going Correction** -0.45s/f (Firm) 8 Ran SP% **112.3**
Speed ratings (Par 103): **104,102,101,99,99 98,93,86**
CSF £15.80 CT £44.69 TOTE £3.80: £1.10, £1.60, £1.70; EX 24.80 Trifecta £111.40.

Owner Ron Smith Recycling Ltd **Bred** Pam & Martin Wygod **Trained** Hook, Hampshire

FOCUS

An ordinary sprint handicap. The majority of the field started off up the centre, while one came straight over to the stands' rail and the main group eventually drifted over to join him as the race progressed.

2041 DG EXECUTIVE SERVICE NOW AVAILABLE H'CAP 1m 6f 15y

3:15 (3:17) (Class 4) (0-85,80) 4-Y-O+ **£4,851** (£1,443; £721) **Stalls** Low

Form RPR

-350 1 **Hallstatt (IRE)**[15] 1598 10-8-6 **66** (t) JoeDoyle(3) 1 71
(John Mackie) *trckd ldr: effrt on inner over 2f out: sn cl up: rdn and qcknd to ld jst over 1f out: edgd rt jst ins fnl f: kpt on strly* **5/1**[3]

41-6 2 1/2 **Cotillion**[76] 440 10-8-12 **69** (p) StevieDonohoe 4 73
(Ian Williams) *trckd ldng pair: hdwy and cl up on outer 4f out: chal over 2f out: rdn over 1f out and ev ch: edgd lft and drvn jst ins fnl f: kpt on* **11/4**[2]

11-5 3 6 **Goldslinger (FR)**[19] 1531 4-9-6 **78** RobertWinston 2 77
(Dean Ivory) *t.k.h: set stdy pce: hung rt bnd after 2f: jnd 4f out: pushed along 3f out: rdn wl over 1f out: hdd jst over 1f out: drvn whn n.m.r and hmpd jst ins fnl f: one pce after* **13/8**[1]

3m 9.96s (2.96) **Going Correction** -0.55s/f (Hard)
WFA 4 from 5yo+ 1lb 3 Ran SP% **81.4**
Speed ratings (Par 105): **69,68,65**
CSF £9.14 TOTE £4.10; EX 8.40 Trifecta £8.40.

Owner NSU Leisure & Mrs Carolyn Seymour **Bred** Darley **Trained** Church Broughton , Derbys

■ Winter Spice was withdrawn. Price at time of withdrawal 5/2. Rule 4 applies to all bets - deduct 25p in the pound.

FOCUS

This fair staying handicap was hit by four non-runners plus the late withdrawal of Winter Spice. Unsurprisingly it became a tactical affair.

2042 EBF STALLIONS WEATHERBYS GENERAL STUD BOOK KILVINGTON FILLIES' STKS (LISTED RACE) 6f 15y

3:50 (3:50) (Class 1) 3-Y-O+

£22,684 (£8,600; £4,304; £2,144; £1,076; £540) **Stalls** Centre

Form RPR

32-6 1 **Ridge Ranger (IRE)**[22] 1453 5-9-3 103 JasonHart 11 105
(Eric Alston) *cl up nr stands' rail: led wl over 1f out: rdn ent fnl f: kpt on strly* **5/1**[1]

5-04 2 1 **Marsh Hawk**[22] 1453 4-9-3 99 (b) JFEgan 12 102
(Richard Hannon) *racd nr stands' rail: led: pushed along 2f out: sn hdd and rdn: drvn and kpt on wl fnl f* **14/1**

12-2 3 1 3/4 **Alqubbah (IRE)**[15] 1599 3-8-7 92 TomEaves 4 93
(Ed Dunlop) *trckd ldrs: hdwy 2f out: swtchd lft to outer and rdn over 1f out: drvn and kpt on fnl f* **13/2**[3]

212- 4 nse **Imtiyaaz (IRE)**[259] 5644 4-9-3 91 HarryBentley 13 96
(Roger Varian) *racd nr stands' rail: trckd ldrs: hdwy 2f out: rdn over 1f out: kpt on fnl f* **8/1**

1-02 5 shd **Iseemist (IRE)**[22] 1453 5-9-3 97 JoeyHaynes 5 96
(John Gallagher) *cl up nr stands' rail: rdn along 2f out: drvn ent fnl f: kpt on same pce* **9/1**

-240 6 shd **Divine (IRE)**[72] 723 5-9-3 100 GrahamLee 7 96+
(Mick Channon) *dwlt and in rr: hdwy nr stands' rail 2f out: rdn over 1f out: swtchd lft and drvn ent fnl f: kpt on: nrst fin* **6/1**[2]

5-03 7 3 3/4 **Great Page (IRE)**[24] 1424 3-8-7 100 KieranO'Neill 6 81
(Richard Hannon) *hld up: swtchd lft to outer and effrt 2f out: sn rdn and no imp fnl f* **8/1**

60-0 8 1/2 **Souville**[22] 1453 5-9-3 88 (p) GeorgeBaker 2 82+
(Chris Wall) *wnt lft s and in rr: sme hdwy on outer 2f out: sn rdn along and n.d* **28/1**

156- 9 2 1/4 **Queen's Pearl (IRE)**[226] 6676 4-9-3 94 JackMitchell 10 75
(Roger Varian) *trckd ldrs: rdn along 2f out: sn drvn and wknd* **10/1**

526- 10 3 **Byzantium**[209] 7149 4-9-3 101 BillyLee 9 65
(Edward Lynam, Ire) *plld hrd: trckd ldrs: n.m.r 1/2-way: sn rdn along and wknd 2f out* **5/1**[1]

63-0 11 2 1/4 **Unilit (IRE)**[15] 1599 3-8-7 87 PhilipPrince 8 55
(David Evans) *prom: rdn along 1/2-way: sn wknd* **100/1**

221- 12 4 **Swiss Affair**[215] 6989 4-9-3 85 RobertHavlin 3 45
(John Gosden) *in tch towards outer: effrt over 2f out: sn rdn along and wknd* **12/1**

1m 10.42s (-4.28) **Going Correction** -0.45s/f (Firm)
WFA 3 from 4yo+ 10lb 12 Ran SP% **121.1**
Speed ratings (Par 108): **110,108,106,106,106 106,101,100,97,93 90,85**
CSF £78.29 TOTE £5.40: £1.30, £3.50, £2.70; EX 80.70 Trifecta £1142.70.

Owner Con Harrington **Bred** Con Harrington **Trained** Longton, Lancs

FOCUS

This fillies' Listed event had gone to a 3yo twice in the past three years (both Irish-trained), but this was one for the older brigade. They raced centre-to-nearside and the pace held up as the trio that disputed the lead for most of the way finished first, second and fifth.

2043 DG EXECUTIVE SERVICE FOR ANY OCCASION H'CAP (A JC GRASSROOTS MIDDLE DISTANCE SERIES QUALIFIER) 1m 2f 50y

4:25 (4:25) (Class 4) (0-80,80) 4-Y-O+ **£4,851** (£1,443; £721; £360) **Stalls** Low

Form RPR

30-4 1 **Aldeburgh**[62] 605 7-9-5 **78** WilliamTwiston-Davies 1 86
(Nigel Twiston-Davies) *trckd ldr: cl up 4f out: chal 2f out: sn rdn: drvn to ld last 100yds: hld on gamely* **14/1**

1-22 2 hd **I Am Not Here (IRE)**[17] 1561 5-8-3 **67** CallumShepherd(5) 3 77+
(Brian Ellison) *hld up in rr: gd hdwy on inner 3f out: rdn to chse ldng pair over 1f out: swtchd rt to outer ent fnl f: fin strly: jst failed* **11/4**[1]

12-0 3 nk **Hickster (IRE)**[19] 1526 5-9-4 **77** (t) JFEgan 5 83
(Roy Bowring) *led: pushed along 3f out: jnd and rdn 2f out: drvn over 1f out: hdd last 100yds: kpt on* **14/1**

5-60 4 3 1/4 **Lostock Hall (IRE)**[14] 1633 4-8-11 **70** JoeyHaynes 6 70
(K R Burke) *in tch: hdwy over 3f out: chsd ldrs 2f out and sn rdn: drvn and no imp fnl f* **14/1**

600- 5 2 1/4 **Eurystheus (IRE)**[182] 7758 7-9-2 **78** (p) AlistairRawlinson(3) 10 73
(Michael Appleby) *trckd ldrs: hdwy on outer over 3f out: rdn along 2f out: sn one pce* **12/1**

232- 6 1/2 **Ataman (IRE)**[201] 7340 4-9-4 **77** GeorgeBaker 2 71
(Chris Wall) *t.k.h and hld up in rr whn stmbld bdly after 1f: hdwy on outer wl over 2f out: rdn wl over 1f out: sn no imp* **7/2**[2]

2435 7 4 **Cosmic Halo**[10] 1786 7-8-4 **66** oh1 SammyJoBell(3) 7 52
(Richard Fahey) *hld up: a in rr* **16/1**

00-0 8 3/4 **Artful Prince**[14] 1633 6-9-5 **78** (b) TomEaves 4 63
(James Given) *trckd ldrs on inner: hdwy over 3f out: rdn along wl over 2f out: sn wknd* **9/1**

-411 9 6 **Rock Song**[14] 1633 7-8-13 **75** JoeDoyle(3) 8 48
(John Mackie) *chsd ldrs: rdn along over 3f out: sn wknd* **4/1**[3]

31/0 10 3 1/4 **New Street (IRE)**[21] 1480 5-9-7 **80** StevieDonohoe 9 46
(Jim Best) *prom: rdn along over 3f out: sn wknd* **50/1**

2m 10.2s (-4.10) **Going Correction** -0.55s/f (Hard) 10 Ran SP% **114.4**
Speed ratings (Par 105): **94,93,93,91,89 88,85,85,80,77**
CSF £51.53 CT £561.94 TOTE £12.40: £4.00, £1.10, £4.80; EX 84.10 Trifecta £932.00.

Owner W E Sturt **Bred** Juddmonte Farms Ltd **Trained** Naunton, Gloucs

FOCUS

A fair handicap, but they didn't go a great pace which resulted in some taking a keen hold. Very few ever got into it.

2044 NK MOTORS H'CAP 1m 75y

4:55 (4:55) (Class 5) (0-75,75) 3-Y-O **£2,911** (£866; £432; £216) **Stalls** Centre

Form RPR

1- 1 **Cajoled (FR)**[144] 8232 3-9-5 **73** (t) RobertHavlin 8 81+
(George Scott) *hld up towards rr: smooth hdwy on outer 3f out: led wl over 1f out: sn clr: pushed out* **6/1**[3]

36-1 2 1 3/4 **Beauty Night**[33] 1238 3-9-4 **72** JohnFahy 4 75
(Clive Cox) *prom: led after 2f: pushed along 3f out: rdn over 2f out: hdd wl over 1f out: sn drvn and kpt on u.p fnl f* **5/1**[2]

021- 3 nk **Brave Archibald (IRE)**[191] 7577 3-9-3 **71** LukeMorris 7 74+
(Paul Cole) *trckd ldrs: hdwy 3f out: effrt whn n.m.r wl over 1f out and again appr fnl f: sn swtchd rt and kpt on wl towards fin* **16/1**

-140 **4** *nk* **Zainat (IRE)**[36] 1185 3-9-6 **74**............ JoeyHaynes 9 75
(K R Burke) *in tch: hdwy on outer to chse ldrs 4f out: cl up over 2f out: rdn wl over 1f out: kpt on same pce* **20/1**

4-41 **5** *½* **Aldair**[21] 1485 3-9-4 **72**............ KieranO'Neill 1 73+
(Richard Hannon) *in tch on inner: effrt whn n.m.r over 2f out: swtchd rt and rdn wl over 1f out: kpt on fnl f* **5/1**[2]

065- **6** *½* **Third Rock (IRE)**[171] 7889 3-9-0 **68**............ StevieDonohoe 6 70+
(Sir Michael Stoute) *dwlt and bhd: hdwy over 2f out: sn rdn and styd on fnl f: nrst fin* **7/1**

003- **7** *1* **Claymore (IRE)**[199] 7395 3-9-5 **73**............ GeorgeBaker 2 70
(David Lanigan) *led 2f: cl up on inner: pushed along wl over 2f out: rdn wl over 1f out: drvn and one pce appr fnl f* **11/4**[1]

1626 **8** *¾* **Blacklister**[16] 1584 3-9-3 **71**............ JFEgan 3 66
(Mick Channon) *nvr bttr than midfield* **10/1**

006- **9** *1* **Centuro (USA)**[189] 7638 3-8-8 **67**............ CallumShepherd(5) 12 60
(Jonjo O'Neill) *dwlt: a in rr* **50/1**

4-44 **10** *11* **Peak Hill**[72] 705 3-9-2 **75**............ NoelGarbutt(5) 11 42
(David Evans) *in tch: hdwy to chse ldrs 1/2-way: rdn along over 2f out: drvn wl over 1f out: sn wandered and wknd* **14/1**

60-0 **11** *11* **Addicted To Luck**[11] 1745 3-8-10 **67**............ PhilipPrince(3) 10 9
(David Evans) *a in rr* **33/1**

1m 43.97s (-5.03) **Going Correction** -0.55s/f (Hard) **11** Ran SP% **118.1**
Speed ratings (Par 99): **103,101,100,100,100 99,98,97,96,85 74**
CSF £35.58 CT £462.25 TOTE £7.20: £3.00, £4.10, £3.50; EX 44.80 Trifecta £1070.60.

Owner Niarchos Family **Bred** Famille Niarchos **Trained** Newmarket, Suffolk

FOCUS
An ordinary 3yo handicap, but the winner is likely to prove a league or two above this level.

2045 GENTING CASINO NOTTINGHAM APPRENTICE TRAINING SERIES H'CAP (DIV I) 1m 75y

5:30 (5:30) (Class 6) (0-65,66) 4-Y-O+ **£2,264** (£673; £336; £168) **Stalls** Centre

Form RPR

06-0 **1** **He's My Boy (IRE)**[24] 1415 5-9-0 **63**............ GeorgeWood(5) 6 72
(James Fanshawe) *trckd ldrs: hdwy on inner whn n.m.r 3f out: sn swtchd markedly rt to outer and chal 2f out: led and edgd lft wl over 1f out: rdn clr and hung bdly rt ent fnl f: kpt on wl towards fin* **4/1**[2]

3-60 **2** *1 ½* **Mr Cool Cash**[21] 1488 4-9-6 **64**............ GLavery 4 69
(Richard Guest) *hld up towards rr: stdy hdwy 3f out: chsd ldrs 2f out: rdn over 1f out: styd on fnl f* **4/1**[2]

0-11 **3** *1 ¾* **Bajan Rebel**[8] 1845 5-8-10 **57**............ DanielleMooney(3) 5 58
(Michael Easterby) *trckd ldng pair: hdwy 3f out: led 2 1/2f out: sn rdn and hdd wl over 1f out: kpt on u.p fnl f* **4/1**[2]

4-45 **4** *2* **Shaw Ting**[35] 1201 4-8-11 **60**............(p) MitchGodwin(5) 7 56
(Michael Appleby) *prom: cl up after 2f: chal over 3f out: rdn over 2f out: drvn and kpt on one pce appr fnl f* **10/3**[1]

0434 **5** *½* **Gilmer (IRE)**[11] 1768 5-8-8 **52**............(t) MeganNicholls 2 47
(Laura Young) *led: rdn along over 3f out: hdd wl over 2f out: drvn wl over 1f out and one pce* **11/1**

4-14 **6** *1 ¾* **Diamond Runner (IRE)**[10] 1791 4-8-5 **54**............(p) BenSanderson(5) 3 45
(Deborah Sanderson) *trckd ldng pair on inner: hdwy and cl up 3f out: rdn along over 2f out: sn drvn and grad wknd* **7/1**[3]

0-00 **7** *¾* **Whitchurch**[17] 1560 4-8-7 **56**............ CliffordLee(5) 8 45
(Philip Kirby) *towards rr: hdwy on outer 3f out: rdn 2f out: n.d* **20/1**

660- **8** *9* **Imperial Link**[165] 7962 4-8-9 **56** ow1............ PatrickVaughan(3) 1 24
(John O'Shea) *a in rr* **20/1**

1m 44.03s (-4.97) **Going Correction** -0.55s/f (Hard) **8** Ran SP% **113.4**
Speed ratings (Par 101): **102,100,98,96,96 94,93,84**
CSF £20.03 CT £66.00 TOTE £5.20: £2.60, £1.10, £1.80; EX 22.90 Trifecta £54.70.

Owner P S Ryan **Bred** Rossenarra Bloodstock Limited **Trained** Newmarket, Suffolk

FOCUS
A moderate apprentice handicap.

2046 GENTING CASINO NOTTINGHAM APPRENTICE TRAINING SERIES H'CAP (DIV II) 1m 75y

6:00 (6:00) (Class 6) (0-65,65) 4-Y-O+ **£2,264** (£673; £336; £168) **Stalls** Centre

Form RPR

000- **1** **Charles De Mille**[234] 6434 8-8-7 **54**............ HarryBurns(3) 7 62
(Jedd O'Keeffe) *hld up: hdwy on inner over 2f out: rdn over 1f out: led ins fnl f* **4/1**[2]

054- **2** *½* **Lord Reason**[177] 7812 4-9-4 **65**............ LuluStanford(3) 6 72
(John Butler) *hld up: hdwy over 2f out: rdn over 1f out: ev ch ins fnl f: drvn and no ex towards fin* **11/2**[3]

3603 **3** *2 ¼* **Roger Thorpe**[5] 1925 7-8-9 **58**............(p) BenSanderson(5) 4 59
(Deborah Sanderson) *led and sn wl clr (30 l): rdn wl over 1f out: hdd ins fnl f: kpt on same pce* **3/1**[1]

06-4 **4** *nk* **Iftikaar (IRE)**[17] 1565 6-8-13 **62**............ CliffordLee(5) 3 63
(Philip Kirby) *chsd clr ldr: hdwy over 2f out: rdn over 1f out: ev ch ent fnl f: sn drvn and kpt on same pce* **3/1**[1]

4065 **5** *1 ¾* **First Summer**[29] 1323 4-8-10 **54**............(p) CharlieBennett 9 50
(Shaun Harris) *towards rr: sme hdwy over 2f out: rdn wl over 1f out: no imp* **9/1**

4002 **6** *2 ¾* **Ted's Brother (IRE)**[12] 1696 8-8-8 **57**............(e) MillyNaseb(5) 1 47
(Richard Guest) *hld up towards rr: hdwy over 2f out: rdn wl over 1f out: sn drvn and one pce* **4/1**[2]

1m 44.5s (-4.50) **Going Correction** -0.55s/f (Hard) **6** Ran SP% **115.4**
Speed ratings (Par 101): **100,99,97,96,95 92**
CSF £26.39 CT £74.49 TOTE £4.80: £1.60, £3.90; EX 26.30 Trifecta £115.20.

Owner Mrs Liz Ingham **Bred** St Clare Hall Stud **Trained** Middleham Moor, N Yorks

FOCUS
The third horse went tearing off in front in this division, with the rest of the field ignoring him, and it was no surprise that the pace collapsed. The winning time was nearly half a second slower than the first leg.

T/Plt: £337.60 to a £1 stake. Pool of £43889.99 - 94.89 winning tickets. T/Qpdt: £261.90 to a £1 stake. Pool of £2690.45 - 7.6 winning tickets. **Joe Rowntree**

1868 THIRSK (L-H)

Saturday, May 7

OFFICIAL GOING: Good (good to soft in places; 7.8)
Wind: fresh across Weather: mixture of sunshine and cloud

2047 PENNINE BREWING CRAFT BEER & CIDER FESTIVAL (S) STKS 6f

5:35 (5:35) (Class 6) 3-5-Y-O **£2,587** (£770; £384; £192) **Stalls** High

Form RPR

0044 **1** **Johnny B Goode (IRE)**[6] 1878 4-9-6 67............ GeorgeChaloner 5 63
(Richard Fahey) *mde all: rdn over 1f out: kpt on* **13/8**[1]

0 **2** *¾* **Ay Up Audrey**[38] 1151 5-9-1 0............ JamesSullivan 6 56
(Rebecca Bastiman) *hld up: rdn and hdwy over 1f out: wnt 2nd ins fnl f: kpt on* **100/1**

04-6 **3** *1* **Charlie's Approval (IRE)**[26] 1379 4-9-1 38............(b[1]) RaulDaSilva 2 53
(Ben Haslam) *hld up: rdn over 2f out: hdwy over 1f out: kpt on* **40/1**

-020 **4** *3 ¼* **Tancred (IRE)**[15] 1595 5-9-12 65............(p) DavidNolan 3 54
(Conor Dore) *chsd ldng pair: rdn over 2f out: wknd ins fnl f* **9/2**[3]

050 **5** *1* **Pennine Warrior**[10] 1787 5-9-9 66............(b) BenCurtis 7 48
(Scott Dixon) *prom: rdn over 2f out: wknd over 1f out* **11/4**[2]

35-0 **6** *3 ¾* **Brean Splash Susie**[86] 528 5-9-2 48............[1] NathanEvans(5) 1 35
(Bill Turner) *dwlt: sn chsd ldng pair: rdn 1/2-way: sn wknd* **16/1**

500- **7** *13* **Tsarglas**[130] 8385 5-9-12 40............(tp) ConnorBeasley 8 1
(Colin Teague) *chsd ldng pair: rdn 1/2-way: sn wknd and bhd* **100/1**

25R- **8** *34* **Fly With Emirates (IRE)**[336] 2936 4-9-6 0............ SamJames 9
(Marjorie Fife) *virtually ref to r: a t.o* **9/2**[3]

1m 16.53s (3.83) **Going Correction** +0.25s/f (Good) **8** Ran SP% **111.4**
Speed ratings (Par 101): **84,83,81,77,76 71,53,8**
CSF £162.38 TOTE £2.30: £1.10, £9.30, £5.30; EX 52.20 Trifecta £469.00.
Owner Jonathan Gill **Bred** Noel Brosnan **Trained** Musley Bank, N Yorks
■ There was no bid for the winner.

FOCUS
Plenty with questions to answer in a race no stronger than was to be expected for a seller, and with one or two of those with chances at the weights under-performing it probably took little winning.

2048 RACING UK IN GLORIOUS HD MAIDEN STKS 1m

6:05 (6:10) (Class 5) 3-Y-O+ **£3,234** (£962; £481; £240) **Stalls** Low

Form RPR

4-2 **1** **Mustashry**[21] 1474 3-9-1 0............ DaneO'Neill 11 96+
(Sir Michael Stoute) *trckd ldrs: led 2f out: nudged clr: easily* **10/11**[1]

2 *6* **Sunglider (IRE)**[250] 5956 3-9-1 84............ DanielTudhope 13 78
(David O'Meara) *in tch on outer: rdn over 2f out: wnt 2nd over 1f out: kpt on but no ch w wnr* **5/1**[3]

3 *2 ¼* **Throckley**[168] 5-10-0 0............ SamJames 10 75
(John Davies) *hld up: pushed along and hdwy over 2f out: rdn over 1f out: kpt on* **100/1**

05- **4** *1 ¾* **Tap The Honey**[224] 6745 3-9-1 0............ DougieCostello 7 67
(K R Burke) *trckd ldrs: rdn over 2f out: sn one pce* **25/1**

0- **5** *3 ¼* **Sabre Squadron (IRE)**[197] 7431 3-9-1 0............ PaulMulrennan 2 58
(Peter Chapple-Hyam) *in tch: pushed along over 3f out: grad wknd fnl 2f* **3/1**[2]

6 *nk* **Austerity (IRE)** 3-9-1 0............ BenCurtis 3 58+
(Alan Swinbank) *s.i.s: hld up in midfield: pushed along and hdwy over 3f out: no further imp fnl 2f* **20/1**

7 *½* **Wallangarra** 3-9-1 0............ AdamBeschizza 5 56
(Jeremy Gask) *s.i.s: sn midfield: rdn over 3f out: nvr threatened* **50/1**

5 **8** *½* **Hayward Field (IRE)**[14] 1653 3-9-1 0............ ShaneGray 9 55+
(Roger Varian) *midfield: pushed along over 3f out: nvr threatened* **5/1**[3]

-23 **9** *1 ¼* **Phantom Dancer (IRE)**[12] 1708 4-9-9 0............ NeilFarley 8 50+
(Alan Swinbank) *dwlt: racd keenly: hld up in midfield: pushed along over 2f out: nvr threatened* **25/1**

5-0 **10** *2* **Causey Arch (IRE)**[14] 1622 3-9-1 0............ ConnorBeasley 12 46+
(Michael Dods) *hld up: nvr threatened* **100/1**

11 *3* **Truly**[457] 5-9-9 0............ RoystonFfrench 4 36
(Colin Teague) *racd keenly: sn led: rn wd on bnd 4f out: hdd 2f out: wknd* **125/1**

5 **12** *2 ½* **Rich Pursuit**[14] 1646 3-9-1 0............ PJMcDonald 14 31
(James Bethell) *hld up: nvr threatened* **100/1**

13 *1* **Ellerslie Joe**[69] 4-10-0 0............ JamesSullivan 1 32
(Tom Tate) *in tch: rdn over 3f out: sn wknd* **66/1**

0/0 **14** *2* **No Not Yet**[14] 1628 4-9-4 0............ PhilDennis(5) 6 21
(Michael Dods) *midfield: rdn over 3f out: sn wknd* **100/1**

056/ **15** *51* **Private Dancer**[711] 2655 5-10-0 60............ DuranFentiman 15
(Ron Barr) *tk str hold to post: chsd ldr: wknd qckly 4f out* **100/1**

1m 43.92s (3.82) **Going Correction** +0.625s/f (Yiel)
WFA 3 from 4yo+ 13lb **15** Ran SP% **132.4**
Speed ratings (Par 103): **105,99,96,95,91 91,90,90,89,87 84,81,80,78,27**
CSF £6.63 TOTE £2.00: £1.10, £1.60, £19.90; EX 9.50 Trifecta £292.30.
Owner Hamdan Al Maktoum **Bred** Shadwell Estate Company Limited **Trained** Newmarket, Suffolk

FOCUS
Very few of these had shown they were likely maiden winners and this was much less competitive than the size of the field might suggest, with few getting seriously involved. Rail movement added about 25yds to the standard distance.

2049 DICK PEACOCK SPRINT H'CAP 6f

6:35 (6:38) (Class 5) (0-75,75) 3-Y-O **£3,234** (£962; £481; £240) **Stalls** High

Form RPR

45-4 **1** **Van Gerwen**[5] 1922 3-9-0 **68**............[1] DavidAllan 1 77
(Les Eyre) *chsd ldr far side: rdn to chal 2f out: led 75yds out: kpt on* **14/1**

54-5 **2** *½* **King Of Swing**[44] 1061 3-9-2 **70**............ JamesSullivan 5 77
(James Given) *hld up far side: rdn and hdwy over 1f out: kpt on: wnt 2nd nr fin: 2nd of 8 in gp* **11/1**

23-1 **3** *nse* **Bossipop**[23] 1448 3-9-1 **74**............ RachelRichardson(5) 8 81
(Tim Easterby) *midfield far side: rdn and hdwy over 2f out: led narrowly over 1f out: hdd 75yds out: no ex and lost 2nd nr fin: 3rd of 8 in gp* **17/2**[3]

21-0 **4** *3 ¾* **Fruit Salad**[74] 686 3-8-13 **67**............ DanielTudhope 2 62+
(James Bethell) *midfield far side: rdn over 2f out: kpt on ins fnl f: 4th of 8 in gp* **22/1**

0-21 **5** *1 ¼* **Iceaxe**[13] 1670 3-8-11 **65**............ RoystonFfrench 4 56
(John Holt) *led far side and overall ldr: rdn whn hdd over 1f out: wknd fnl f: 5th of 8 in gp* **15/2**[1]

3-50 **6** *7* **Take Charge**[15] 1599 3-9-6 **74**............ GrahamGibbons 7 42
(David Brown) *chsd ldr far side: rdn over 2f out: wknd over 1f out: 6th of 8 in gp* **16/1**

01-4 **7** ½ **Danzeb (IRE)**[10] 1789 3-9-3 **71** .... PJMcDonald 9 38
(Ann Duffield) *midfield: rdn 1/2-way: wknd over 1f out: 7th of 8 in gp* **16/1**
04-6 **8** ¾ **Mecca's Missus (IRE)**[40] 1126 3-8-11 **65** .... ConnorBeasley 3 29
(Michael Dods) *a towards rr far side: last of 8 in gp* **20/1**
100- **9** 4½ **Letbygonesbeicons**[212] 7055 3-8-6 **67** .... RowanScott(7) 17 17
(Ann Duffield) *hld up stands' side: rdn and hdwy over 1f out: kpt on: 1st of 8 in gp* **33/1**
30-0 **10** 2 **Kodimoor (IRE)**[14] 1638 3-8-13 **67** .... NeilFarley 12 11
(Christopher Kellett) *chsd ldrs stands' side: rdn over 2f out: wknd fnl f: 2nd of 8 in gp* **66/1**
201- **11** nk **Cheeky Angel (IRE)**[212] 7056 3-9-4 **72** .... PaulMulrennan 10 15+
(Michael Dods) *dwlt: sn in tch stands' side: rdn over 2f out: wknd fnl f: 3rd of 8 in gp* **8/1**[2]
20-2 **12** 2¾ **Master Mirasol (IRE)**[23] 1448 3-9-7 **75** .... KeaganLatham 13 9
(Kevin Ryan) *prom stands' side: rdn over 2f out: wknd fnl f: 4th of 8 in gp* **8/1**[2]
32-2 **13** 1½ **Mister Mischief**[41] 1111 3-9-2 **70** .... GrahamLee 16
(Paul Midgley) *hld up stands' side: rdn over 2f out: nvr threatened: 5th of 8 in gp* **9/1**
14-6 **14** 1½ **Indian Pursuit (IRE)**[23] 1448 3-9-5 **73** ....(p) PhillipMakin 11
(John Quinn) *hld up stands' side: nvr threatened: 6th of 8 in gp* **10/1**
26-3 **15** 5 **Dance Alone**[19] 1524 3-9-5 **73** .... ShaneGray 15
(Kevin Ryan) *a towards rr stands' side: 7th of 8 in gp* **9/1**
56-2 **16** 3 **Run Rio Run (IRE)**[21] 1494 3-8-9 **68** .... PhilDennis(5) 14
(Michael Dods) *led stands' side gp tl wknd qckly over 2f out* **11/1**

1m 13.46s (0.76) **Going Correction** +0.25s/f (Good) **16** Ran SP% **122.2**
Speed ratings (Par 99): **104,103,103,98,96 87,86,85,79,76 76,72,70,68,62 58**
CSF £154.35 CT £1408.70 TOTE £17.90: £5.30, £3.80, £2.20, £5.40; EX 256.70 Trifecta £2713.10.
Owner Sunpak Potatoes **Bred** Broughton Bloodstock **Trained** Catwick, N Yorks

FOCUS
Potentially a cracking 61-75 handicap, with plenty of these three-year-old sprinters open to improvement, and this contest was vindication for the decision to switch it from a race for older horses.\n\x\x Only downside was that we got two races for the price of one as the field split, with groups racing wide apart on either side of the track in what were effectively separate contests - with all those who raced on the far side beating all those on the other side. None of those who raced on the near side is as bad as the result makes them look, they are probably all worth another chance.

2050 ABF THE SOLDIERS' CHARITY FILLIES' H'CAP 5f

7:05 (7:05) (Class 5) (0-75,74) 3-Y-O+ **£3,234** (£962; £481; £240) **Stalls** High

Form RPR
00-6 **1** **Crombay (IRE)**[14] 1647 3-8-13 **70** .... DavidAllan 5 73
(Tim Easterby) *chsd ldr: rdn 2f out: led 1f out: kpt on* **7/2**[2]
4-00 **2** ¾ **Mrs Biggs**[17] 1565 4-9-3 **65** .... DanielTudhope 6 69
(Declan Carroll) *hld up: rdn 1/2-way: hdwy over 1f out: kpt on: wnt 2nd 110yds out* **10/1**
21-0 **3** ½ **Early Bird (IRE)**[14] 1647 3-9-2 **73** .... TonyHamilton 7 71
(Richard Fahey) *chsd ldrs: rdn 1/2-way: kpt on* **13/2**[3]
00- **4** shd **Ruby's Day**[201] 7342 7-9-9 **71** .... TomEaves 9 73
(David Brown) *hld up: sme hdwy 2f out: rdn and hung lft over 1f out: kpt on ins fnl f* **14/1**
245- **5** 1¼ **Aberlady (USA)**[226] 6667 3-8-12 **69** .... GrahamGibbons 3 62
(Sir Michael Stoute) *trckd ldr: rdn 2f out: wknd ins fnl f* **2/1**[1]
3355 **6** ¾ **Summer Isles**[7] 1872 6-9-4 **66** .... PaulMulrennan 4 61
(Paul Midgley) *led: rdn 2f out: hdd 1f out: wknd* **10/1**
-144 **7** 1½ **Jess**[65] 797 3-8-9 **66** ....(p) ShaneGray 8 51
(Kevin Ryan) *midfield: rdn 3f out: nvr threatened* **13/2**[3]
00-0 **8** ¾ **Meandmyshadow**[14] 1625 8-9-12 **74** ....(b) DaleSwift 1 61
(Alan Brown) *sn pushed along: a towards rr* **16/1**

1m 0.28s (0.68) **Going Correction** +0.25s/f (Good) **8** Ran SP% **113.0**
WFA 3 from 4yo+ 9lb
Speed ratings (Par 100): **104,102,102,101,99 98,96,95**
CSF £36.79 CT £215.38 TOTE £4.60: £2.60, £4.30, £2.40; EX 40.40 Trifecta £260.40.
Owner Richard Taylor & Philip Hebdon **Bred** Knocklong House Stud **Trained** Great Habton, N Yorks

FOCUS
Very few had the recent form to make them solid propositions in a typically less-than-competitive fillies' handicap which was weakened by the withdrawal of likely leading contender \bMisu Moneypenny\p. They finished in something of a heap, which was another sign that this is probably not great form.

2051 ELWICK STUD H'CAP 1m 4f

7:35 (7:35) (Class 4) (0-80,80) 4-Y-O+ **£5,175** (£1,540; £769; £384) **Stalls** High

Form RPR
46-2 **1** **Tamayuz Magic (IRE)**[32] 1248 5-8-10 **74** ....(b) NathanEvans(5) 6 84+
(Michael Easterby) *trckd ldr: chal 3f out: led 2f out: rdn over 1f out: styd on wl* **9/2**[2]
303/ **2** 2¾ **Frederic**[108] 7349 5-8-11 **70** .... PJMcDonald 5 74
(Micky Hammond) *midfield: rdn 3f out: hdwy 2f out: styd on: wnt 2nd 50yds out* **12/1**
020- **3** 1¼ **Poetic Verse**[193] 7524 6-9-2 **80** .... CallumShepherd(5) 2 82
(John Quinn) *in tch: trckd ldr over 3f out: rdn to chal over 2f out: one pce fnl f: lost 2nd 50yds out* **18/1**
1/0- **4** 1½ **Osaruveetil (IRE)**[360] 2195 5-9-7 **80** .... DanielTudhope 7 80
(David O'Meara) *in tch: trckd ldr gng wl 3f out: rdn 2f out: sn one pce* **2/1**[1]
013/ **5** 3 **Another Lincolnday**[630] 5449 5-8-11 **70** .... TomEaves 12 65+
(Michael Herrington) *hld up: gd hdwy on outside over 3f out: rdn over 2f out: wknd appr fnl f* **50/1**
44-1 **6** ¾ **Lady Lekki (IRE)**[26] 1382 4-8-13 **72** .... GrahamLee 11 66
(Ben Haslam) *hld: rdn over 3f out: plugged on ins fnl f: nvr threatened* **12/1**
3133 **7** ½ **Royal Holiday (IRE)**[12] 1707 9-8-10 **72** ....(p) JacobButterfield(3) 3 65
(Marjorie Fife) *led: rdn 3f out: hdd 2f out: sn wknd* **25/1**
-033 **8** ½ **Dunquin (IRE)**[16] 1586 4-8-12 **71** .... GrahamGibbons 10 63
(John Mackie) *hld up: racd keenly: hdwy into midfield 8f out: rdn 3f out: sn wknd* **9/2**[2]
14-0 **9** 4½ **We'll Shake Hands (FR)**[14] 1633 5-8-13 **72** .... DougieCostello 8 57
(K R Burke) *dwlt: hld up: nvr threatened* **33/1**
2250 **10** 10 **Ralphy Lad (IRE)**[23] 1445 5-9-3 **76** .... BenCurtis 13 45
(Alan Swinbank) *in tch: rdn over 3f out: sn wknd* **7/1**[3]
10-0 **11** 4½ **Chebsey Beau**[21] 1493 6-9-4 **77** .... RaulDaSilva 9 39
(John Quinn) *chsd ldr: rdn 4f out: sn wknd* **28/1**

2m 42.16s (5.96) **Going Correction** +0.625s/f (Yiel) **11** Ran SP% **115.0**
Speed ratings (Par 105): **105,103,102,101,99 98,98,98,95,88 85**
CSF £53.41 CT £883.26 TOTE £5.00: £1.80, £3.30, £3.90; EX 59.70 Trifecta £518.20.
Owner W H & Mrs J A Tinning **Bred** Eimear Mulhern **Trained** Sheriff Hutton, N Yorks

FOCUS
Plenty of these had something to prove on the score of recent form, stamina or effectiveness on the ground, in a race run over about 30yds more than the standard distance due to rail movement, but they went a fair pace.

2052 JW 4X4 NORTHALLERTON H'CAP 5f

8:05 (8:06) (Class 6) (0-60,60) 4-Y-O+ **£2,587** (£770; £384; £192) **Stalls** High

Form RPR
210- **1** **Perfect Words (IRE)**[157] 8071 6-9-3 **59** .... JacobButterfield(3) 3 67
(Marjorie Fife) *chsd ldrs: rdn 2f out: kpt on to ld 110yds out* **14/1**
000- **2** 1 **Whipphound**[218] 6897 8-9-2 **55** .... JamesSullivan 8 59
(Ruth Carr) *hld up: pushed along and hdwy over 1f out: rdn and kpt on fnl f* **9/1**
-004 **3** ¾ **Windforpower (IRE)**[17] 1559 6-9-7 **60** ....(p) ConnorBeasley 13 62
(Tracy Waggott) *prom: rdn 1/2-way: kpt on* **9/1**
0033 **4** shd **Roy's Legacy**[13] 1668 7-9-3 **56** .... DaleSwift 11 57
(Shaun Harris) *prom: rdn 1/2-way: kpt on* **16/1**
1602 **5** ½ **Lizzy's Dream**[13] 1668 8-9-2 **55** .... DanielTudhope 7 55
(Rebecca Bastiman) *hld up: rdn 1/2-way: swtchd rt over 1f out: kpt on* **5/1**[1]
0-54 **6** shd **Compton River**[13] 1668 4-9-2 **55** .... PaulMulrennan 5 54
(Bryan Smart) *dwlt: hld up in midfield: bit short of room over 1f out: swtchd lft ent fnl f: kpt on* **8/1**[3]
00-0 **7** 1½ **Pabusar**[10] 1790 8-9-4 **57** ....(v[1]) PJMcDonald 6 51
(Micky Hammond) *hld up: rdn 1/2-way: kpt on ins fnl f* **20/1**
600- **8** ¾ **Sunrise Dance**[214] 7009 7-8-7 **46** oh1 .... JoeyHaynes 2 37
(Kenny Johnson) *led: rdn over 1f out: hdd 110yds out: wknd* **10/1**
0000 **9** ½ **Under Approval**[13] 1676 5-8-7 **46** oh1 ....(e[1]) NeilFarley 10 35
(Karen Tutty) *in tch: rdn 1/2-way: wknd fnl f* **33/1**
2-00 **9** dht **George Bailey (IRE)**[12] 1709 4-8-13 **52** .... TomEaves 1 41
(Suzzanne France) *midfield: rdn 1/2-way: nvr threatened* **25/1**
00-1 **11** ¾ **Lady Poppy**[13] 1668 6-9-0 **60** .... KieranSchofield(7) 4 47
(Jedd O'Keeffe) *midfield: rdn 2f out: nvr threatened* **5/1**[1]
550- **12** 5 **Mini Minstrel**[231] 6526 4-8-7 **46** .... RoystonFfrench 9 15
(Colin Teague) *dwlt: hld up: a towards rr* **66/1**
-000 **13** ½ **Willow Spring**[12] 1709 4-8-2 **46** oh1 ....(b) NoelGarbutt(5) 15 13+
(Conrad Allen) *1 of 3 who racd stands ' side: in tch overall: wknd 1/2-way* **66/1**
5401 **14** 6 **Pancake Day**[12] 1709 4-9-3 **56** ....(b) JFEgan 17 +
(Jason Ward) *1 of 3 who racd stands' side: sn bhd* **15/2**[2]
00-0 **15** 1¼ **Steel City Boy (IRE)**[8] 1827 13-8-7 **46** oh1 .... DuranFentiman 16 +
(Shaun Harris) *1 of 3 who racd stands' side: a bhd* **40/1**
000- **R** **A J Cook (IRE)**[255] 5742 6-8-9 **53** ....(t) PhilDennis(5) 12
(Ron Barr) *rrd s and ref to r* **14/1**

1m 0.87s (1.27) **Going Correction** +0.25s/f (Good) **16** Ran SP% **121.5**
Speed ratings (Par 101): **99,97,96,96,95 95,92,91,90,90 89,81,80,71,69**
CSF £126.44 CT £1260.46 TOTE £13.80: £2.30, £2.50, £3.30, £2.30; EX 228.60 Trifecta £1918.60.
Owner Green Lane **Bred** Rathasker Stud **Trained** Stillington, N Yorks

FOCUS
Nothing like so strong a race as the big field might suggest, with the plentiful question marks to be expected of runners in a 46-60 handicap. With the far side clearly the place to be, only three raced on the stands' side. That trio occupied the final three positions but each is worth another chance.

2053 THIRSK "IRISH DAY" NEXT SATURDAY H'CAP 6f

8:35 (8:35) (Class 6) (0-60,60) 4-Y-O+ **£2,587** (£770; £384; £192) **Stalls** High

Form RPR
0-36 **1** **Gaelic Wizard (IRE)**[13] 1676 8-8-13 **57** ....(v) GemmaTutty(5) 2 65
(Karen Tutty) *dwlt: sn in tch: rdn and hdwy 2f out: led 1f out: kpt on wl* **20/1**
0103 **2** 1¼ **Monsieur Jimmy**[12] 1712 4-8-7 **46** ....(b) DavidAllan 5 50
(Declan Carroll) *hld up: rdn and hdwy over 2f out: kpt on fnl f: wnt 2nd towards fin* **14/1**
501- **3** nk **Anieres Boy**[219] 6880 4-9-6 **59** .... GrahamGibbons 17 62+
(Michael Easterby) *led narrowly: rdn whn hdd 2f out: remained cl up: no ex and lost 2nd towards fin* **10/1**
20-0 **4** ¾ **Poppy In The Wind**[19] 1525 4-9-7 **60** ....(v) DaleSwift 6 61
(Alan Brown) *chsd ldrs: rdn over 2f out: kpt on* **33/1**
-546 **5** ½ **Giant Spark**[12] 1692 4-9-6 **59** ....(p) PaulMulrennan 15 59+
(Paul Midgley) *dwlt: sn chsd ldrs: rdn 1/2-way: kpt on same pce* **11/2**[2]
4-00 **6** 1½ **Flyball**[17] 1565 4-9-3 **56** ....(b) GrahamLee 7 51
(Kenneth Slack) *pressed ldr: rdn to ld 2f out: hdd 1f out: wknd* **3/1**[1]
406- **7** nk **Euxton**[197] 7441 4-9-5 **58** .... DanielTudhope 10 52
(Lawrence Mullaney) *chsd ldrs: rdn over 2f out: wknd ins fnl f* **7/1**[3]
00-0 **8** hd **White Flag**[21] 1495 5-8-13 **57** .... RachelRichardson(5) 14 51+
(Tim Easterby) *outpcd in rr tl kpt on ins fnl f* **14/1**
0-04 **9** 1¼ **Munjally**[13] 1676 5-9-6 **59** ....(v) DavidNolan 4 49
(Patrick Holmes) *midfield: rdn 1/2-way: wknd fnl f* **12/1**
550- **10** shd **Barwah (USA)**[228] 6617 5-8-10 **49** .... JasonHart 12 39
(Peter Niven) *hld up in midfield: rdn 1/2-way: nvr threatened* **20/1**
0-60 **11** ½ **Armelle (FR)**[15] 1600 5-9-6 **59** .... BenCurtis 3 47
(Scott Dixon) *chsd ldrs: rdn over 2f out: wknd over 1f out* **12/1**
3300 **12** 1¾ **Hab Reeh**[13] 1676 8-8-11 **50** ....(p) JamesSullivan 9 33
(Ruth Carr) *a towards rr* **33/1**
50-0 **13** 4 **Indego Blues**[13] 1676 7-9-5 **58** .... PaulQuinn 8 29
(David Nicholls) *midfield: sn pushed along: wknd over 2f out* **16/1**
0450 **14** 4½ **Teetotal (IRE)**[13] 1676 6-9-5 **58** ....(p) TomEaves 16 15
(Nigel Tinkler) *midfield: rdn 1/2-way: sn struggling* **20/1**
144- **15** 30 **Sekuras Girl (IRE)**[228] 6618 4-8-13 **52** ....(p) BarryMcHugh 13
(Clive Mulhall) *s.i.s: a towards rr* **33/1**

1m 14.27s (1.57) **Going Correction** +0.25s/f (Good) **15** Ran SP% **119.7**
Speed ratings (Par 101): **99,97,96,95,95 93,92,92,90,90 90,87,82,76,36**
CSF £254.05 CT £3012.88 TOTE £20.50: £4.80, £3.90, £4.00; EX 304.00 Trifecta £2502.90.
Owner Grange Park Racing **Bred** Mrs Mary Gallagher **Trained** Osmotherley, N Yorks

FOCUS
Even off their lowly marks, there were few runners obviously well treated in this 46-60 handicap
T/Plt: £391.60 to a £1 stake. Pool of £57834.94 - 107.79 winning tickets. T/Qpdt: £274.20 to a £1 stake. Pool of £6875.56 - 18.55 winning tickets. **Andrew Sheret**

2054 - 2062a (Foreign Racing) - See Raceform Interactive

2021 **CHURCHILL DOWNS** (L-H)

Saturday, May 7

OFFICIAL GOING: Dirt: fast; turf: firm

2063a KENTUCKY DERBY PRESENTED BY YUM! BRANDS (GRADE 1) (3YO) (DIRT) 1m 2f (D)

11:34 (12:00) 3-Y-O **£1,109,931** (£272,108; £136,054; £68,027; £40,816)

RPR

1 **Nyquist (USA)**35 1210 3-9-0 0 MarioGutierrez 13 124+
(Doug O'Neill, U.S.A) **23/10**1

2 1 1/4 **Exaggerator (USA)**28 1366 3-9-0 0 KentJDesormeaux 11 121
(J Keith Desormeaux, U.S.A) **51/10**2

3 3 1/4 **Gun Runner (USA)**42 3-9-0 0 FlorentGeroux 5 115
(Steven Asmussen, U.S.A) **103/10**3

4 hd **Mohaymen (USA)**35 1210 3-9-0 0 JuniorAlvarado 14 114
(Kiaran McLaughlin, U.S.A) **118/10**

5 nse **Suddenbreakingnews (USA)**20 1515 3-9-0 0 LuisSQuinonez 2 114+
(Donnie K Von Hemel, U.S.A) **246/10**

6 2 1/4 **Destin (USA)**56 3-9-0 0 (b) JavierCastellano 9 110
(Todd Pletcher, U.S.A) **18/1**

7 2 1/2 **Brody's Cause (USA)**28 1360 3-9-0 0 LuisSaez 19 105
(Dale Romans, U.S.A) **249/10**

8 3/4 **Mo Tom (USA)**42 3-9-0 0 CoreyJLanerie 4 103
(Thomas Amoss, U.S.A) **26/1**

9 1/2 **Lani (USA)**42 1103 3-9-0 0 YutakaTake 8 102
(Mikio Matsunaga, Japan) **29/1**

10 3 3/4 **Mor Spirit (USA)**28 1366 3-9-0 0 (b) GaryStevens 17 95
(Bob Baffert, U.S.A) **128/10**

11 hd **My Man Sam (USA)**28 1360 3-9-0 0 IradOrtizJr 6 94
(Chad C Brown, U.S.A) **195/10**

12 2 1/2 **Tom's Ready (USA)**42 3-9-0 0 (b) BrianJosephHernandezJr 12 89
(Dallas Stewart, U.S.A) **49/1**

13 1 1/4 **Creator (USA)**20 1515 3-9-0 0 (b) RicardoSantanaJr 3 87
(Steven Asmussen, U.S.A) **164/10**

14 nk **Outwork (USA)**28 1355 3-9-0 0 JohnRVelazquez 15 86
(Todd Pletcher, U.S.A) **269/10**

15 1 1/2 **Danzing Candy (USA)**28 1366 3-9-0 0 MikeESmith 20 83
(Clifford Sise Jr, U.S.A) **26/1**

16 6 3/4 **Trojan Nation (USA)**28 1355 3-9-0 0 AaronTGryder 1 70
(Patrick Gallagher, U.S.A) **42/1**

17 5 3/4 **Oscar Nominated (USA)**35 3-9-0 0 (b) JulienRLeparoux 7 58
(Michael J Maker, U.S.A) **42/1**

18 4 1/4 **Majesto (USA)**35 1210 3-9-0 0 EmisaelJaramillo 18 50
(Gustavo Delgado, U.S.A) **57/1**

19 1/2 **Whitmore (USA)**20 1515 3-9-0 0 (b) VictorEspinoza 10 49
(Ronald Moquett, U.S.A) **30/1**

P **Shagaf (USA)**28 1355 3-9-0 0 JoelRosario 16
(Chad C Brown, U.S.A) **56/1**

2m 1.31s (0.12) **20** Ran SP% **121.9**
PARI-MUTUEL (all including 2 usd stake): WIN 6.60; PLACE (1-2) 4.80, 5.40; SHOW (1-2-3) 3.60, 4.20, 6.00; SF 30.60.
Owner Reddam Racing LLC **Bred** Summerhill Farm **Trained** USA

FOCUS
No late withdrawals so the two also-eligibles failed to make the line-up and a full field of 20 went to post. There was a downpour just under two hours before the off, but the track was not sealed. The rain only lasted a few minutes and conditions remained officially fast, although there were patches of standing water on the course. Conditions were really quick, with the winner and third never far away from a scorching pace. The splits were 22.58, 45.72 (23.14), 1:10.40 (24.68), 1:35.61 (25.21) and the clock stopped in 2:01.31 (25.70). It was the quickest time since Funny Cide went 2:01.19 in 2003, but he earned a 109 Beyer speed figure compared to 103 for Nyquist. This did not look a vintage Kentucky Derby - they were a relatively slow bunch through the preps - but the right horses came to the fore and the winner now has quite a CV. It's interesting to note that since the qualifying criteria changed ahead of the 2013 edition, from Graded-stakes earnings to points picked up in prep races, the Derby has been won by four straight favourites and this time the 1-2-3-4 were in market order. That's understandable, with fewer wacky types to get in the way and upset the rhythm. It's also worth considering that since Santa Anita switched back to dirt in late 2010, four of the six runnings have been won by horses trained in California. They had the 1-2-3 last year and the 1-2 this time.

2064 - 2066a (Foreign Racing) - See Raceform Interactive

1367 **LEOPARDSTOWN** (L-H)

Sunday, May 8

OFFICIAL GOING: Good (good to yielding in places)

2067a AMETHYST STKS (GROUP 3) 1m

2:25 (2:28) 3-Y-O+

£26,029 (£8,382; £3,970; £1,764; £882; £441)

RPR

1 **Steip Amach (IRE)**6 1939 4-9-6 99 KevinManning 3 109
(J S Bolger, Ire) *settled bhd ldr: gng wl in 2nd into st: rdn to ld over 1f out: hdd u.p ins fnl 150yds tl rallied far side in clsng stages to regain advantage fnl strides* **14/1**

2 shd **Cougar Mountain (IRE)**35 1226 5-9-12 114 (t) RyanMoore 8 115
(A P O'Brien, Ire) *chsd ldrs early tl dropped to 7th bef 1/2-way: niggled along 3f out and dropped to rr bef st: swtchd to outer and r.o wl fr 1 1/2f out to ld ins fnl 150yds: strly pressed clsng stages and hdd fnl strides* **3/1**2

3 2 **In My Pocket (IRE)**211 7127 4-9-9 99 DeclanMcDonogh 1 107
(John M Oxx, Ire) *dwlt and in rr early tl impr to chse ldrs after 1f: disp 3rd at 1/2-way: rdn in 3rd 1 1/2f out and no imp on ldrs u.p wl ins fnl f: kpt on same pce* **16/1**

4 1 **Brendan Brackan (IRE)**21 1509 7-9-9 105 GaryCarroll 2 105
(G M Lyons, Ire) *dwlt sltly and pushed along bhd ldrs to sn ld: extended advantage and over 2 l clr at 1/2-way: rdn 2f out and reduced ld: hdd over 1f out and sn no imp on ldrs u.p in 4th: kpt on same pce* **8/1**

5 nk **Alphonsus**37 1190 3-8-10 102 ColmO'Donoghue 6 101
(John M Oxx, Ire) *w.w towards rr: wnt 6th bef 1/2-way: rdn 2f out and no imp on ldrs u.p in 5th wl ins fnl f: kpt on same pce* **9/1**

6 nk **Sruthan (IRE)**35 1226 6-9-9 107 ChrisHayes 5 104
(P D Deegan, Ire) *hld up in tch: 5th 1/2-way: rdn 2f out and no imp on ldrs in 6th wl ins fnl f: kpt on same pce* **6/1**3

7 3/4 **Queen Catrine (IRE)**49 1016 5-9-6 105 ColinKeane 7 99
(G M Lyons, Ire) *w.w: last at 1/2-way: rdn towards rr and sme hdwy far side 1f out: n.m.r on inner ins fnl f and one pce clsng stages* **12/1**

8 1/2 **Custom Cut (IRE)**25 1425 7-10-0 116 DanielTudhope 4 106
(David O'Meara) *nodded sltly leaving gate: prom tl sn settled bhd ldrs in 3rd: disp 3rd at 1/2-way: rdn 2f out and sn no imp on ldrs: dropped to rr ins fnl f* **7/4**1

1m 40.32s (-0.88) **Going Correction** +0.025s/f (Good)
WFA 3 from 4yo+ 13lb **8** Ran SP% **117.0**
Speed ratings: **105,104,102,101,101 101,100,100**
CSF £57.28 TOTE £14.70: £2.80, £1.40, £3.50; DF 73.80 Trifecta £968.00.
Owner Mrs J S Bolger **Bred** J S Bolger **Trained** Coolcullen, Co Carlow

FOCUS
An informative race one would think and the winner certainly ran above her mark to land this.

2068a DERRINSTOWN STUD 1,000 GUINEAS TRIAL (GROUP 3) (FILLIES) 1m

3:00 (3:00) 3-Y-O

£26,029 (£8,382; £3,970; £1,764; £882; £441)

RPR

1 **Now Or Never (IRE)**28 1369 3-9-0 104 KierenFallon 1 107+
(M D O'Callaghan, Ire) *chsd ldrs: 3rd 1/2-way: hdwy on outer fr under 3f out to ld fr 2f out: sn clr and in command 1f out: eased wl ins fnl f: easily* **13/8**1

2 1 3/4 **Radiantly**28 1369 3-9-0 102 WayneLordan 4 101+
(W McCreery, Ire) *in rr and pushed along early: 5th 1/2-way: impr bhd ldrs into 4th over 2f out: rdn into mod 2nd 1 1/2f out and no imp on easy wnr: kpt on same pce: a hld by eased down wnr* **7/2**2

3 6 **Emergent**21 1507 3-9-0 0 (b1) PatSmullen 2 87
(D K Weld, Ire) *cl up in 2nd: rdn in 2nd 2f out and hung lft: sn dropped to mod 3rd u.p 1 1/2f out and no imp on easy wnr: kpt on one pce ins fnl f to hold mod 3rd* **7/1**

4 1/2 **Siamsaiocht (IRE)**212 7097 3-9-0 93 KevinManning 5 86
(J S Bolger, Ire) *chsd ldrs: 4th 1/2-way: rdn in 4th fr 3f out and sn lost pl u.p: mod 5th 1 1/2f out: kpt on u.p on outer into mod 4th wl ins fnl f: hld for mod 3rd* **6/1**

5 1 1/2 **Misty Millie (IRE)**21 1510 3-9-0 0 ColinKeane 3 83
(P Cluskey, Ire) *led: 1 l clr at 1/2-way: strly pressed into st and hdd 2f out: short of room on inner in 3rd under 2f out and no ex: wknd fnl f* **8/1**

6 7 **Kind Of Magic (IRE)**21 1507 3-9-0 99 RyanMoore 6 66
(A P O'Brien, Ire) *hld up: in last at 1/2-way: pushed along in rr bef st and no imp u.p 1 1/2f out: one pce* **5/1**3

1m 42.09s (0.89) **Going Correction** +0.025s/f (Good) **6** Ran SP% **114.9**
Speed ratings: **96,94,88,87,86 79**
CSF £7.80 TOTE £2.20: £1.20, £2.40; DF 9.60 Trifecta £37.80.
Owner Now Or Never Partnership **Bred** Tally-Ho Stud **Trained** The Curragh, Co. Kildare

FOCUS
A very smart performance from the winner, catapulting her into a leading contender for the Irish 1000 Guineas despite the likelihood of it being a very hot race.

2069a DERRINSTOWN STUD DERBY TRIAL STKS (GROUP 3) 1m 2f

3:35 (3:35) 3-Y-O

£43,382 (£13,970; £6,617; £2,941; £1,470; £735)

RPR

1 **Moonlight Magic**28 1370 3-9-3 104 KevinManning 5 109
(J S Bolger, Ire) *chsd ldrs: 3rd 1/2-way: rdn in 3rd under 2f out and impr to ld ins fnl f: kpt on wl in clsng stages* **6/1**

2 1 1/4 **Shogun (IRE)**24 1440 3-9-3 108 RyanMoore 2 107+
(A P O'Brien, Ire) *hld up in tch: 5th 1/2-way: pushed along in 5th fr 3f out and impr bhd ldrs fr 2f out: rdn in 4th 1 1/2f out and kpt on wl between horses wl ins fnl f into nvr nrr 2nd fnl strides: nrst fin* **10/3**2

3 1/2 **Idaho (IRE)**28 1370 3-9-3 108 SeamieHeffernan 3 106+
(A P O'Brien, Ire) *hld up: 7th 1/2-way: 6th 3f out: rdn 1 1/2f out and kpt on wl u.p in 5th ent fnl f into nvr nrr 3rd fnl strides: nrst fin* **15/8**1

4 shd **Beacon Rock (IRE)**28 1370 3-9-3 109 ColmO'Donoghue 4 105
(A P O'Brien, Ire) *chsd ldr: 2nd 1/2-way: tk clsr order bhd ldr under 3f out: rdn to ld fr 2f out tl hdd u.p ins fnl f: no ex u.p in 2nd clsng stages and dropped to 4th fnl strides* **8/1**

5 3/4 **Saafarr**21 1511 3-9-3 84 (t) RonanWhelan 1 104?
(J S Bolger, Ire) *led: 3 l clr at 1/2-way: rdn w reduced advantage under 3f out: hdd fr 2f out and no ex u.p in 3rd ins fnl f: one pce and dropped to 5th clsng stages* **66/1**

6 2 1/4 **Lieutenant General (IRE)**14 1683 3-9-3 99 DonnachaO'Brien 8 99+
(A P O'Brien, Ire) *settled in rr: last at 1/2-way: tk clsr order into st and rdn in 6th ent fnl f: kpt on same pce: nvr trbld ldrs* **33/1**

7 2 3/4 **Tirmizi (FR)**197 7476 3-9-3 0 PatSmullen 7 94
(D K Weld, Ire) *hld up in tch: 4th 1/2-way: pushed along in 4th under 3f out and no imp on ldrs fr 2f out: dropped to 6th over 1f out: one pce fnl f* **4/1**3

8 1 3/4 **Ventura Storm (IRE)**26 1395 3-9-3 101 FMBerry 6 90
(Richard Hannon) *hld up towards rr: lost action briefly at pathway after 3f: 6th 1/2-way: rdn in rr over 2f out and no imp: one pce fnl f* **8/1**

2m 7.74s (-0.46) **Going Correction** +0.025s/f (Good) **8** Ran SP% **118.8**
Speed ratings: **102,101,100,100,99 98,95,94**
CSF £27.45 TOTE £8.20: £2.10, £1.60, £1.02; DF 31.90 Trifecta £78.60.
Owner Godolphin **Bred** Darley **Trained** Coolcullen, Co Carlow

FOCUS
The Derby picture became even murkier after this contest, with the winner coming back to form after a disappointing effort on his seasonal bow and the Ballydoyle representatives looking below the required standard.

2070 - 2072a (Foreign Racing) - See Raceform Interactive

1685 CAPANNELLE (R-H)

Sunday, May 8

OFFICIAL GOING: Turf: good

2073a PREMIO PRESIDENTE DELLA REPUBBLICA (GROUP 2) (4YO+) (TURF) 1m 1f

3:40 (12:00) 4-Y-O+ **£64,338** (£28,308; £15,441; £7,720)

RPR

1 **Diplomat (GER)**28 1376 5-9-2 0 DarioVargiu 1 110
(Mario Hofer, Germany) *cl up on inner: outpcd and rdn 3f out: swtchd outside and began to cl 2f out: led appr fnl f: r.o u.p* **107/10**2

2 3 **Circus Couture (IRE)**21 1516 4-9-2 0 FabioBranca 7 104
(Stefano Botti, Italy) *a cl up: chsd ldr 3f out: drvn to ld over 2f out: hdd appr fnl f: no ex* **8/11**1

3 3 3/4 **Saint Bernard**28 7-9-2 0 SalvatoreSulas 2 96
(Simone Langiano, Italy) *w.w towards rr: hdwy over 2f out: styd on fnl f: nvr on terms* **39/1**

4 2 **Porsenna (IRE)**21 6-9-2 0 LucaManiezzi 6 92
(Stefano Botti, Italy) *dwlt: w.w in rr: hdwy wl over 1 1/2f out: styd on fnl f: nrest at fin* **162/10**3

5 1 3/4 **Kaspersky (IRE)**28 5-9-2 0 UmbertoRispoli 4 88
(Endo Botti, Italy) *plld hrd: chsd ldr: rdn and nt qckn 2f out: wknd fnl f* **8/11**1

6 dist **Celticus (IRE)**49 6-9-2 0 SilvanoMulas 3
(Stefano Botti, Italy) *led: hdd over 2f out: sn wknd* **8/11**1

P **Lodovico Il Moro (IRE)**21 6-9-2 0 CarloFiocchi 5
(Endo Botti, Italy) *hld up towards rr: rdn and lost tch fr 3f out: wl bhd whn p.u* **8/11**1

1m 48.3s (-6.40) **7** Ran SP% **248.5**
WIN (incl. 1 euro stake): 11.66. PLACES: 2.20, 1.33. DF: 10.91.
Owner Eckhard Sauren **Bred** Gestut Rottgen **Trained** Germany

1513 COLOGNE (R-H)

Sunday, May 8

OFFICIAL GOING: Turf: good

2074a FRUHJAHRS-MEILE DES CARL JASPERS VERSICHERUNGSKONTORS (LISTED RACE) (4YO+) (TURF) 1m

2:40 (12:00) 4-Y-O+ **£10,294** (£4,779; £2,205; £1,102)

RPR

1 **Wildpark (GER)**238 6373 5-9-0 0 (b) FilipMinarik 6 103+
(Melanie Sauer, Germany) **78/10**

2 3 **Lucky Lion**28 1376 5-9-3 0 AdriedeVries 3 99+
(Andreas Lowe, Germany) **6/5**1

3 1 **Drummer (GER)**28 1376 4-9-0 0 AndraschStarke 1 94+
(P Schiergen, Germany) **26/5**3

4 1 1/2 **Celestial Path (IRE)**172 7891 4-9-0 0 LukeMorris 4 91+
(Sir Mark Prescott Bt) *chsd ldng trio on outer: scrubbed along 3f out and no immediate imp: hrd rdn 2f out and kpt on at same pce: nvr able to match front three* **7/5**2

5 1/2 **Star System (IRE)**34 6-9-0 0 StephenHellyn 7 89+
(M Rulec, Germany) **25/1**

6 1 **Brisanto**203 7328 4-9-3 0 (b) DanielePorcu 8 90+
(M G Mintchev, Germany) **18/1**

7 4 **Felician (GER)**182 7767 8-9-6 0 AndreasSuborics 2 84
(Ferdinand J Leve, Germany) **114/10**

1m 35.51s (-2.88) **7** Ran SP% **131.8**
WIN (incl. 10 euro stake) 88; PLACES 30, 15; SF 268.
Owner Gestut Brummerhof **Bred** Gestut Brummerhof **Trained** Germany

2075a GERLING-PREIS (GROUP 2) (4YO+) (TURF) 1m 4f

4:20 (12:00) 4-Y-O+ **£29,411** (£11,397; £5,882; £2,941; £1,838)

RPR

1 **Ito (GER)**161 8042 5-9-6 0 FilipMinarik 6 117+
(Jean-Pierre Carvalho, Germany) *led after 1f: mde rest: upped tempo fr over 2f out: drvn and edgd lft ent fnl f: rdn: responded and edgd rt: styd on strly* **4/5**1

2 3/4 **Sirius (GER)**41 5-9-0 0 (b) StephenHellyn 8 109
(Andreas Lowe, Germany) *w.w in rr: hdwy fr 2 1/2f out: rdn to chse ldr ent fnl f: styd on u.p: nvr quite on terms* **13/5**2

3 4 **Fair Mountain (GER)**14 4-9-0 0 EduardoPedroza 3 103
(A Wohler, Germany) *led early: hdd after 1f and remained cl up: rdn and nt qckn appr 2f out: styd on same pce appr fnl f: no match for front two* **149/10**

4 2 **Early Morning (GER)**41 7-8-10 0 AdriedeVries 5 96
(Dr A Bolte, Germany) *w.w in fnl trio: tk clsr order u.p 2f out: kpt on same pce fnl f: nt pce to trble first three* **103/10**

5 2 1/2 **Eric (GER)**12 5-9-0 0 AlexanderPietsch 2 96
(C Von Der Recke, Germany) *settled in midfield: rdn and nt qckn 2f out: styd on at same pce fr 1 1/2f out: nvr trbld ldrs* **207/10**

6 nk **Shadow Sadness (GER)**41 4-9-0 0 JozefBojko 1 95
(C Von Der Recke, Germany) *settled in midfield: rdn and no real prog 2 1/2f out: plugged on at one pce* **50/1**

7 1 **Night Wish (GER)**21 1516 6-9-0 0 AndraschStarke 7 94
(Frau S Steinberg, Germany) *a towards rr: rdn and dropped to last under 3f out: plugged on fnl 1 1/2f but nvr in contention* **47/10**3

8 1 **Vif Monsieur (GER)**71 751 6-9-0 0 KoenClijmans 4 92
(Mario Hofer, Germany) *cl up on outer: rdn and no imp over 2 1/2f out: grad dropped away fr wl over 1f out* **26/1**

9 1 **Shivajia (GER)**196 7498 4-9-0 0 DanielePorcu 10 91
(U Stech, Germany) *hld up towards rr: rdn and no imp 4f out: wl hld fnl 1 1/2f* **269/10**

2m 25.33s (-7.57) **9** Ran SP% **129.9**
WIN (incl. 10 euro stake) 18; PLACES 13, 14, 22; SF 47.
Owner Gestut Schlenderhan **Bred** Gestut Schlenderhahn **Trained** Germany

1909 SAINT-CLOUD (L-H)

Sunday, May 8

OFFICIAL GOING: Turf: good

2076a PRIX GREFFULHE (GROUP 2) (3YO COLTS & FILLIES) (TURF) 1m 2f

2:45 (12:00) 3-Y-O **£54,485** (£21,029; £10,036; £6,691; £3,345)

RPR

1 **Cloth Of Stars (IRE)**35 1230 3-9-2 0 MickaelBarzalona 5 113+
(A Fabre, France) *settled in fnl pair: rdn 2f out: clsd fr over 1 1/2f out: fnd stride u.p appr 1f out: r.o to ld 125yds out: drvn clr* **11/8**1

2 2 1/2 **Robin Of Navan (FR)**189 7666 3-9-2 0 TonyPiccone 2 108
(Harry Dunlop) *pressed ldr on inner: shkn up and lened to ld wl over 2f out: styd on fnl f: hdd 125yds out: no ex* **11/8**1

3 1/2 **Kidmenever (IRE)**9 3-9-2 0 AntoineHamelin 3 107
(F Vermeulen, France) *led on outer: rdn and hdd wl over 2f out: rallied u.p: kpt on at one pce fnl f* **40/1**3

4 hd **Apilobar (FR)**57 930 3-9-2 0 CristianDemuro 4 107
(F Vermeulen, France) *t.k.h: hld up in tch: outpcd and drvn more than 3f out: sn dropped to last and u.p: styd on fnl f: nt pce to get on terms* **6/1**2

5 1/2 **Le Juge (IRE)**59 897 3-9-2 0 Pierre-CharlesBoudot 1 106
(A Fabre, France) *w.w in rr: prog fr 2 1/2f out: kpt on at same pce fr wl over 1f out* **6/1**2

2m 3.7s (-12.30) **5** Ran SP% **115.2**
WIN (incl. 1 euro stake): 2.30. PLACES: 1.30, 1.30. SF: 5.80.
Owner Godolphin SNC **Bred** Peter Anastasiou **Trained** Chantilly, France

2077a PRIX D'HEDOUVILLE (GROUP 3) (4YO+) (TURF) 1m 4f

4:00 (12:00) 4-Y-O+ **£29,411** (£11,764; £8,823; £5,882; £2,941)

RPR

1 **One Foot In Heaven (IRE)**19 1557 4-8-10 0 ow1 ChristopheSoumillon 4 110+
(A De Royer-Dupre, France) *w.w in fnl trio: shkn up 2f out: rdn and hdwy wl ins fnl 1 1/2f: r.o u.p fr 1f out: led last 150yds: sn asserted* **11/8**1

2 1 **Harlem**28 1375 4-8-9 0 VincentCheminaud 7 107+
(A Fabre, France) *a cl up on outer: rdn and n.m.r 1 1/2f out: angled out ins fnl f: styd on wl: tk 2nd cl home: nvr on terms w wnr* **7/2**3

3 hd **Grey Lion (IRE)**41 1130 4-8-9 0 MaximeGuyon 1 107
(A Fabre, France) *trckd ldr on inner: angled out to chal fr 1 1/2f out: kpt on at same pce u.p fnl f: lost 2nd cl home* **9/1**

4 3/4 **Tiberian (FR)**19 1557 4-8-11 0 AdrienFouassier 2 107
(Alain Couetil, France) *cl up bhd ldng trio: drvn wl over 1 1/2f out: styd on to press ldrs 1f out: kpt on at one pce fnl f* **11/4**2

5 3/4 **Golden Wood (FR)**26 6-8-9 0 MickaelBarzalona 3 104
(Charley Rossi, France) *led: rdn whn pressed 1 1/2f out: hdd 150yds out: no ex* **18/1**

6 1 1/2 **Lady Of Kyushu (USA)**179 7806 4-8-8 0 StephanePasquier 5 101
(F-H Graffard, France) *w.w in fnl trio: last and rdn wl ins fnl 1 1/2f: styd on fr 1f out: nvr in contention* **8/1**

7 3/4 **Havana Moon (USA)**35 1232 4-8-6 0 AlexisBadel 6 98
(M Delzangles, France) *dwlt: t.k.h and hld up in fnl trio: nvr really settled: rdn and no imp 1 1/2f out: wknd ins fnl f* **16/1**

2m 34.16s (-6.24) **7** Ran SP% **123.3**
WIN (incl. 1 euro stake): 2.90. PLACES: 1.80, 2.00. SF: 10.40.
Owner Fair Salinia Ltd **Bred** Craigavon Agro Ltd **Trained** Chantilly, France

L'ANCRESSE

Monday, May 2

OFFICIAL GOING: Firm (good in places)

Wind: Moderate, behind Weather: Cloudy

2078a BETWAY BAILIWICK CUP H'CAP 1m 6f

2:15 (2:20) 3-Y-O+ **£2,100** (£875; £525)

RPR

1 **My Lord**12 1201 8-10-12 0 PhilipPrince 3 76
(David Evans) *trckd ldr: led 4f out: easily* **2/7**1

2 7 **Fourni (IRE)**15 3682 7-9-3 0 JemmaMarshall 2 43
(Mrs A Malzard, Jersey) *led tl 4f out: sn outpcd by wnr* **6/1**3

3 7 **King Kenny**15 11-9-4 0 (p) NoraLooby 1 34
(Mrs A Corson, Jersey) *hld up: unable to chal fr 4f out* **3/1**2

Owner Mrs I M Folkes **Bred** Mrs Monica Teversham **Trained** Pandy, Monmouths

2079a RAVENSCROFT INVESTMENT MANAGEMENT H'CAP 1m

3:25 (3:30) (0-65,0) 3-Y-O+ **£3,100** (£1,200; £700)

RPR

1 **Al's Memory (IRE)**24 1326 7-10-12 0 PhilipPrince 1 68
(David Evans) *led tl 5f out: rdn to ld again over 3f out: nt looking keen but drvn clr fr over 2f out* **2/7**1

2 4 **Tax Reform (IRE)**15 1518 6-9-5 0 MattieBatchelor 4 38
(Natalie Lloyd-Beavis) *trckd ldrs: rdn and ch fr 3f out: kpt on one pce to take 2nd nr fin* **5/1**3

3 1/2 **Pas D'Action**15 1518 8-9-12 0 (p) JemmaMarshall 2 44
(Mrs A Malzard, Jersey) *trckd ldr: led 5f out tl over 3f out: wknd fnl f: lost 2nd nr fin* **9/4**2

4 12 **Frankki M**15 1519 6-8-5 0 oh24 (p) NoraLooby 3
(Mrs A Corson, Jersey) *a last: outpcd and btn over 3f out* **12/1**

Owner Mrs Rachel Barnes **Bred** Brian Miller **Trained** Pandy, Monmouths

2080a THE LATE MRS RUTH O'RORKE H'CAP 1m 4f

4:00 (4:05) (0-55,0) 3-Y-O+ **£2,400** (£1,000; £600)

RPR

1 **Carrera**15 1519 6-10-7 0 MattieBatchelor 3 48
(Mrs A Malzard, Jersey) *trckd ldr: dropped to last and reluctant after 4f: rdn to chal 3f out: led over 1f out: drvn out* **9/4**2

2 2 1/2 **Wicked Tara**15 1519 6-9-7 0 JemmaMarshall 2 30
(Natalie Lloyd-Beavis) *hld up: rapid hdwy to ld over 3f out: hdd over 1f out: no ex* **5/4**1

3 1 ½ **Toretto (IRE)**[17] 1450 8-10-12 0................................(p) RobertWilliams 4 47
(Jan Coomer, Guernsey) *led tl 3f out: immediately outpcd* **12/1**
4 ¾ **Albecq**[245] 4-10-5 0.. PhilipPrince 1 38
(David Evans) *t.k.h: trckd ldr: drvn and wknd rapidly 2f out* **11/1**[3]
Owner Malzard Racing **Bred** Norman Court Stud **Trained** St Ouen, Jersey

2081a HUNSCOTE STUD H'CAP 6f
4:30 (4:40) 3-Y-O+ **£2,400** (£1,000; £600)

RPR
1 **Satchville Flyer**[7] 1720 5-10-6 0.. PhilipPrince 3 49
(David Evans) *wnt to post early: broke best: mde all: drvn out* **1/2**[1]
2 4 **Chester'slittlegem (IRE)**[15] 1517 7-9-1 0..........................(b) NoraLooby 2 17
(Mrs A Corson, Jersey) *outpcd in rr: kpt on to go 2nd nr fin* **4/1**[3]
3 ¾ **Country Blue (FR)**[15] 1517 7-10-12 0......................(p) MattieBatchelor 4 40
(Mrs A Malzard, Jersey) *trckd ldr: drvn and no ex over 2f out: lost 2nd nr fin* **11/8**[2]
Owner Anthony Cooke **Bred** Newsells Park Stud **Trained** Pandy, Monmouths

1944 BRIGHTON (L-H)
Monday, May 9

OFFICIAL GOING: Good to firm (watered; 8.5)
Wind: light, across Weather: sunny, clouding over from race 3

2082 BRITISH STALLION STUDS EBF NOVICE STKS 5f 213y
1:50 (1:50) (Class 5) 2-Y-O **£3,234** (£962; £481; £240) **Stalls** Low

Form RPR
4 1 **Mr Scaramanga**[28] 1384 2-9-2 0.. SeanLevey 3 73
(Richard Hannon) *dwlt: hld up in tch in rr: swtchd rt and gd hdwy over 1f out: rdn to ld ent fnl f: hld on wl fnl f: rdn out* **7/2**[2]
54 2 nk **Vinnievanbaileys**[14] 1719 2-9-2 0..............................(b[1]) FrederikTylicki 1 72
(Chris Dwyer) *sn roused along to chse ldr: rdn after 2f: edgd rt and led over 1f out: hdd ent fnl f: battled on wl u.p: hld towards fin* **33/1**
2 3 ¾ **Monks Stand (USA)**[13] 1749 2-9-2 0................................ JimCrowley 4 73+
(Jeremy Noseda) *trckd ldrs: hemmed in and nt clr run over 2f out: bmpd and pushed lft over 1f out: swtchd rt and in the clr but plenty to do in 4th jst over 1f out: rdn and styd on wl ins f: nvr quite getting to ldng pair* **4/7**[1]
44 4 5 **Bonnie Arlene (IRE)**[16] 1641 2-8-11 0..................... SilvestreDeSousa 6 49
(Mark Johnston) *led: rdn 2f out: hdd and bmpd over 1f out: 3rd and btn 1f out: wknd ins fnl f* **10/1**[3]
5 5 **Altiko Tommy (IRE)** 2-9-2 0.. LiamKeniry 5 38
(George Baker) *in tch: hdwy on outer to chse ldrs 3f out: rdn and edgd lft over 1f out: sn outpcd: wknd fnl f* **20/1**
6 ¾ **Control Centre (IRE)** 2-9-2 0... KieranO'Neill 2 35
(Richard Hannon) *dwlt: in tch: nt clr run on inner over 2f out: rdn 2f out: outpcd and btn over 1f out: wknd fnl f* **10/1**[3]
1m 9.37s (-0.83) **Going Correction** -0.225s/f (Firm) **6** Ran SP% **111.8**
Speed ratings (Par 93): **96,95,94,87,81 80**
CSF £81.00 TOTE £6.60: £1.70, £7.80; EX 96.80 Trifecta £354.10.
Owner Chelsea Thoroughbreds - Golden Gun **Bred** Lordship Stud **Trained** East Everleigh, Wilts
FOCUS
The watered ground was given as good to firm. An ordinary juvenile novice to start and the odds-on favourite found significant trouble. A lesser renewal of this event.

2083 LETSDOBUSINESS.ORG/BRIGHTON 12 MAY H'CAP 6f 209y
2:20 (2:20) (Class 6) (0-60,58) 3-Y-O **£2,264** (£673; £336; £168) **Stalls** Centre

Form RPR
0-00 1 **Let There Be Light**[102] 361 3-9-4 55................................ AdamKirby 3 63
(Gay Kelleway) *chsd ldr tl led 5f out: rdn and qcknd over 2f out: drvn and asserted 1f out: styd on wl* **5/1**[3]
021- 2 2 **Bahamian Boy**[151] 8166 3-8-12 56.............................. CharlieBennett(7) 6 59
(Hughie Morrison) *stdd s: t.k.h: hld up in tch: stmbld 5f out: swtchd rt and effrt over 2f out: chsd wnr and edgd lft jst over 1f out: styd on same pce ins fnl f* **11/10**[1]
000- 3 2 ¼ **Ormering**[230] 6623 3-8-11 51.. TomMarquand(3) 7 48
(Roger Teal) *led for 2f: chsd wnr after: rdn over 2f out: 3rd and no ex whn sltly impeded ent fnl f: kpt on same pce after* **10/1**
-053 4 ¾ **Multigifted**[40] 1141 3-9-7 58..(v[1]) LiamKeniry 5 53
(Michael Madgwick) *in tch in 4th: pushed along 4f out: outpcd u.p and swtchd rt over 1f out: styd on same pce after* **3/1**[2]
3-66 5 3 ½ **Fiftytintsofsilver (IRE)**[96] 436 3-8-7 49................. CharlesEddery(5) 1 34
(Gay Kelleway) *t.k.h: trckd ldrs: swtchd rt and rdn jst over 2f out: no ex u.p and btn 4th 1f out: sn wknd* **12/1**
50-0 6 15 **Daioni**[119] 140 3-8-6 50.. ChrisKelly(7) 4
(Richard Hughes) *s.i.s: in tch in rr: struggling and pushed along 4f out: wl bhd over 1f out* **16/1**
1m 23.42s (0.32) **Going Correction** -0.225s/f (Firm) **6** Ran SP% **112.0**
Speed ratings (Par 97): **89,86,84,83,79 62**
CSF £10.94 TOTE £5.50: £3.00, £1.10; EX 14.20 Trifecta £60.50.
Owner Kerr, Watt and Newman **Bred** Winterbeck Manor Stud **Trained** Exning, Suffolk
FOCUS
A moderate handicap in which the winner had the run of things. He's rated rate back towards last year's better form.

2084 HARRINGTONSLETTINGS.CO.UK FILLIES' H'CAP 6f 209y
2:50 (2:54) (Class 4) (0-85,83) 4-Y-O+ **£4,690** (£1,395; £697; £348) **Stalls** Centre

Form RPR
000- 1 **Lyfka**[201] 7390 4-9-6 82...(t) JimCrowley 5 88
(Paul Cole) *stdd s: hdwy to chse ldr after 2f: clsd and upsides over 2f out: rdn 2f out: drvn 1f out: led ins fnl f: kpt on wl* **9/2**
36-2 2 ½ **Gleaming Girl**[7] 1932 4-8-3 72..................................... SophieKilloran(7) 3 76
(David Simcock) *sddle slipped gng to s: dismntd and led fnl 3f to post: stdd s: sn led: rdn 2f out: drvn ent fnl f: hdd ins fnl f: kpt on same pce fnl 100yds* **7/4**[1]
0625 3 1 ½ **Subtle Knife**[23] 1478 7-0-7 83.. WilliamCarson 2 83
(Giles Bravery) *w ldr and stdd after s: stdd bk into 4th after 1f: swtchd rt and shkn up over 2f out: outpcd u.p over 1f out: rallied and styd on fnl 100yds: wnt 3rd last strides* **5/2**[2]
0541 4 nk **Pretty Bubbles**[25] 1432 7-9-4 80..................................(v) FrederikTylicki 1 79
(J R Jenkins) *reluctant early: ldr: hdd after 1f and settled in 3rd: effrt on inner to chal over 1f out: sn drvn: no ex 100yds: outpcd towards fin* **11/4**[3]
1m 23.05s (-0.05) **Going Correction** -0.225s/f (Firm) **4** Ran SP% **109.8**
Speed ratings (Par 102): **91,90,89,88**
CSF £12.76 TOTE £6.70; EX 15.20 Trifecta £40.10.
Owner A H Robinson **Bred** A H & C E Robinson **Trained** Whatcombe, Oxon
FOCUS
A poor turnout numerically for this fillies' handicap and there was no pace on through the first half-furlong or so, before it picked up to be a solid gallop. The form is rated around the second.

2085 ACTIONCHALLENGE.COM LONDON2BRIGHTON 16 MAY H'CAP 1m 1f 209y
3:20 (3:20) (Class 5) (0-75,71) 4-Y-O+ **£2,911** (£866; £432; £216) **Stalls** High

Form RPR
0-01 1 **Inniscastle Lad**[11] 1808 4-9-6 70............................(b) SilvestreDeSousa 4 79
(Ed Dunlop) *mde all: rdn 2f out: drvn and asserted ent fnl f: in command 150yds: styd on wl: eased cl home* **3/1**[2]
340/ 2 1 ½ **Officer Drivel (IRE)**[52] 2481 5-9-3 67..........................(v[1]) TimmyMurphy 1 73
(Jim Best) *chsd wnr tl 4f out: effrt in 3rd 2f out: chsd wnr again ins fnl f: styd on but no serious threat to wnr* **10/1**
2442 3 3 **Van Huysen (IRE)**[14] 1699 4-9-7 71...............................(p) JimCrowley 5 71
(Dominic Ffrench Davis) *chsd ldng pair tl wnt 2nd 4f out: effrt 2f out: sn drvn and unable qck: lost 2nd ins fnl f: wknd towards fin* **13/8**[1]
1302 4 4 **Lord Of The Storm**[13] 1747 8-8-13 63.................................. KierenFox 2 55
(Michael Attwater) *stdd s: hld up in tch in rr: effrt u.p over 1f out: no imp 1f out: wknd ins fnl f* **3/1**[2]
60-0 5 13 **Silver Alliance**[43] 1114 8-9-4 68................................(p) AdamBeschizza 3 34
(Julia Feilden) *in tch in last pair: effrt 3f out: sn drvn: dropped to last and btn over 1f out: wknd fnl f* **7/1**[3]
1m 59.42s (-4.18) **Going Correction** -0.225s/f (Firm) **5** Ran SP% **109.7**
Speed ratings (Par 103): **104,102,100,97,86**
CSF £28.11 TOTE £2.90: £2.00, £3.40; EX 18.90 Trifecta £67.70.
Owner E A L Dunlop **Bred** G Doyle & Lord Margadale **Trained** Newmarket, Suffolk
FOCUS
Another small field and an uncompetitive handicap, rated around the runner-up.

2086 BHF.ORG.UK LONDON TO BRIGHTON 19 JUNE H'CAP 1m 1f 209y
3:50 (3:50) (Class 6) (0-60,60) 4-Y-O+ **£2,264** (£673; £336; £168) **Stalls** High

Form RPR
0461 1 **Glasgow Central**[19] 1578 5-9-7 60.. AdamKirby 4 67
(Phil McEntee) *dwlt: hld up in tch: clsd to trck ldrs 4f out: swtchd rt and chsd ldr over 2f out: rdn to chal and clr w ldr over 1f out: edging lft and led ins fnl f: styd on: rdn out* **2/1**[2]
0001 2 ¾ **Ifan (IRE)**[13] 1747 8-8-12 58....................................(p) MitchGodwin(7) 1 64
(Tim Vaughan) *led: rdn and wnt clr w wnr over 1f out: sn drvn: hdd ins fnl f: styd on same pce after* **10/11**[1]
3616 3 6 **Solveig's Song**[6] 1948 4-8-11 50...............................(p) JackMitchell 2 44
(Steve Woodman) *hld up in tch in rr: clsd and nt clr run over 2f out: swtchd rt and effrt 2f: rdn and chsd clr ldng pair over 1f out: no imp* **6/1**[3]
0-00 4 17 **Norphin**[13] 1742 6-8-0 46 oh1.. RhiainIngram(7) 6 8
(Simon Hodgson) *hld up in tch: rdn 3f out: hung lft and unable qck 2f out: sn outpcd and wl btn over 1f out: wknd* **100/1**
-000 5 hd **Farrah's Choice**[51] 1005 4-8-2 46 oh1............................ PaddyPilley(5) 3 7
(James Grassick) *t.k.h: chsd ldr for 1f: styd chsng ldrs: rdn 3f out: unable qck and carried lft 2f out: sn btn: wknd over 1f out* **40/1**
00-0 6 15 **Cassandane (IRE)**[37] 1202 4-9-4 57............................ FergusSweeney 5
(Shaun Harris) *dwlt: rcvrd and hdwy to chse ldr after 1f tl lost pl u.p over 2f out: bhd 2f out: sn lost tch: t.o and eased ins fnl f* **14/1**
2m 0.59s (-3.01) **Going Correction** -0.225s/f (Firm) **6** Ran SP% **110.1**
Speed ratings (Par 101): **100,99,94,81,80 68**
CSF £3.96 TOTE £3.10: £1.20, £1.30; EX 4.50 Trifecta £8.30.
Owner Mrs Rebecca McEntee **Bred** Bolton Grange **Trained** Newmarket, Suffolk
FOCUS
A moderate handicap. The winner built on his recent confidence-boosting win.

2087 DONATELLO RESTAURANT BRIGHTON H'CAP 7f 214y
4:20 (4:20) (Class 6) (0-60,60) 4-Y-O+ **£2,264** (£673; £336; £168) **Stalls** Centre

Form RPR
00-0 1 **Wordismybond**[13] 1735 7-9-7 60.................................... TimmyMurphy 3 71+
(Richard Hughes) *t.k.h: chsd ldr tl 3f out: styd chsng ldrs: swtchd rt to chse ldng again and travelling strly over 1f out: rdn to ld ins fnl f: r.o wl: readily* **5/1**[3]
60-0 2 2 ½ **Harry Bosch**[13] 1735 6-8-9 48.................................(b) AdamBeschizza 1 50
(Julia Feilden) *led: rdn wl over 1f out: jnd and drvn ent fnl f: hdd and one pce ins fnl f* **5/1**[3]
1550 3 1 **Miss Lillie**[13] 1735 5-9-0 60.....................................(p) GeorgeWood(7) 2 60
(Roger Teal) *taken down early: stdd s: t.k.h: chsd ldrs early: sn stdd into midfield: effrt and swtchd out rt 2f out: kpt on same pce ins fnl f: wnt 3rd wl ins fnl f* **9/2**[2]
6043 4 1 **Lutine Charlie (IRE)**[13] 1742 9-8-6 50..............(p) JosephineGordon(5) 4 47
(Emma Owen) *t.k.h: chsd ldrs tl wnt 2nd 5f out: rdn 2f out: lost 2nd and unable qck over 1f out: styd on same pce ins fnl f: lost 3rd fnl 50yds* **7/2**[1]
00-5 5 8 **Lady Zodiac (IRE)**[12] 1795 4-8-6 48............................ DanielMuscutt(3) 7 26
(Philip McBride) *hld up in tch in rr of main gp: effrt 2f out: sn drvn and outpcd: wknd over 1f out* **14/1**
3300 6 3 **Togetherwecan (IRE)**[6] 1948 4-8-13 52............................ JimCrowley 5 23
(Mark Johnston) *in tch in midfield: rdn 3f out: drvn and outpcd 2f out: sn wknd* **9/2**[2]
0300 7 5 **Whaleweigh Station**[33] 1262 5-9-5 58.......................(p) LemosdeSouza 6 17
(J R Jenkins) *t.k.h: hld up in tch: rdn over 2f out: sn struggling: wknd over 1f out* **5/1**[3]
00-0 8 14 **Poetic License (IRE)**[10] 1830 4-8-2 46 oh1.................. PaddyPilley(5) 8
(James Grassick) *s.i.s: a outpcd in rr: t.o and eased ins fnl f* **100/1**
1m 33.67s (-2.33) **Going Correction** -0.225s/f (Firm) **8** Ran SP% **116.2**
Speed ratings (Par 101): **102,99,98,97,89 86,81,67**
CSF £30.66 CT £112.10 TOTE £7.10: £2.10, £2.20, £1.30; EX 39.80 Trifecta £265.30.
Owner T W Wellard & Partners **Bred** Henry And Mrs Rosemary Moszkowicz **Trained** Upper Lambourn, Berkshire
FOCUS
Few got into this lowly handicap. The winner is rated back to form.

2088 JAMESROSSJEWELLERS.COM H'CAP 5f 59y
4:50 (4:50) (Class 5) (0-70,70) 4-Y-O+ **£2,911** (£866; £432; £216) **Stalls** Low

Form RPR
56-1 1 **Pandar**[3] 2013 7-8-11 63 6ex.. DanielMuscutt(3) 3 77+
(Patrick Chamings) *chsd ldrs: rdn 1/2-way: drvn over 1f out: hdwy to chal ins fnl f: led wl ins fnl f: sn in command: eased cl home* **1/2**[1]
1012 2 1 ¼ **More Spice (IRE)**[25] 1433 4-9-4 67...............................(b) AdamBeschizza 5 76
(Robert Cowell) *led: rdn over 1f out: drvn ins fnl f: hdd and no ex wl ins fnl f* **6/1**[2]

2601 **3** 1 1/4 **Ask The Guru**[12] 1782 6-9-1 **64** ... (p) JimmyQuinn 2 69
(Michael Attwater) *t.k.h: chsd ldr: rdn over 1f out: drvn and no ex jst ins fnl f: outpcd fnl 100yds* **9/1**[3]

5033 **4** 1 1/4 **Diamond Charlie (IRE)**[12] 1782 8-8-11 **60** ... JimCrowley 6 60
(Simon Dow) *stdd s: t.k.h: hld up in tch: clsd on outer 1/2-way: rdn over 1f out: sn no imp: wl hld and one pce ins fnl f* **10/1**

4012 **5** 1 **Secret Millionaire (IRE)**[6] 1950 9-9-0 **63** ... (p) FergusSweeney 4 59
(Shaun Harris) *stdd s: t.k.h: hld up in tch: effrt 2f out: no imp u.p over 1f out: wl hld and one pce fnl f* **9/1**[3]

0415 **6** 2 **Eland Ally**[23] 1481 8-8-11 **60** ... (p) KieranO'Neill 1 49
(Anabel K Murphy) *taken down early: t.k.h: hld up in tch: effrt on inner 2f out: no imp over 1f out: bhd ins fnl f* **33/1**

1m 0.75s (-1.55) **Going Correction** -0.225s/f (Firm) 6 Ran SP% **113.0**
Speed ratings (Par 103): **103,101,99,97,95 92**
CSF £4.13 TOTE £1.50: £1.20, £1.90; EX 4.20 Trifecta £12.50.
Owner O S Harris **Bred** Miss F Vittadini **Trained** Baughurst, Hants

FOCUS
The top weight was only rated 67 but this was a fair race for the grade, with the rejuvenated winner nicely in under his penalty, the second still going the right way and the third recently successful under the same conditions.
T/Plt: £650.80 to a £1 stake. Pool: £46,405.74 - 52.05 winning tickets T/Qpdt: £80.80 to a £1 stake. Pool: £4,434.73 - 40.60 winning tickets **Steve Payne**

1839 MUSSELBURGH (R-H)
Monday, May 9

OFFICIAL GOING: Good to firm (8.3)
Wind: Fresh, across Weather: Sunny

2089 RACING UK NOW IN HD! H'CAP (FOR AMATEUR RIDERS) 2m
2:10 (2:10) (Class 6) (0-65,58) 4-Y-O+ **£2,495** (£774; £386; £193) **Stalls** Low

Form RPR

4-P6 **1** **Christmas Hamper (IRE)**[15] 1675 4-10-6 **58** ... HarryReed(5) 5 66
(Michael Appleby) *trckd ldrs: hdwy to ld over 5f out: hrd pressed fr over 2f out: hld on gamely ins fnl f* **4/1**[3]

400- **2** hd **Exclusive Contract (IRE)**[221] 6877 5-11-0 **58** ... MissSBrotherton 4 66
(Ollie Pears) *t.k.h: prom: hdwy to press wnr over 5f out: disp ld fr over 2f out: rdn over 1f out: kpt on fnl f: jst hld* **4/1**[3]

0-04 **3** 7 **Roc De Prince**[21] 1523 7-10-11 **55** ... MrSWalker 8 54
(Keith Dalgleish) *hld up bhd ldng gp: effrt and pushed along whn edgd rt over 2f out: plugged on fnl f: nt gng pce of first two* **11/4**[1]

540- **4** 1 1/2 **Byronegetonefree**[18] 8198 5-9-12 **45** ... MissRMcDonald(3) 1 43
(Stuart Coltherd) *cl up: rdn and effrt over 3f out: drifted lft 2f out: wknd ins fnl f* **11/1**

40-0 **5** 10 **New Colours**[8] 1881 5-10-10 **54** ... (p) MrTHamilton 7 40
(Linda Perratt) *in tch: drvn along over 3f out: wknd fr 2f out* **25/1**

500- **6** 11 **Stradater (IRE)**[244] 6187 7-10-8 **57** ...[1] MrRyanNichol(5) 6 29
(Sandy Thomson) *hld up: drvn along over 3f out: sn no imp: btn fnl 2f: t.o* **12/1**

60-0 **7** 14 **Troy Boy**[14] 1697 6-9-12 **45** ... MissBeckySmith(3) 3 1
(Rebecca Bastiman) *led at modest gallop: hdd over 5f out: cl up tl rdn and wknd fr 3f out: t.o* **50/1**

/0-3 **8** 20 **Omid**[21] 1523 8-10-1 **52** ... (tp) MissAMSlack(7) 2
(Kenneth Slack) *bhd: detached after 3f: lost tch fr 1/2-way: t.o* **3/1**[2]

3m 31.7s (-1.80) **Going Correction** -0.225s/f (Firm)
WFA 4 from 5yo+ 3lb 8 Ran SP% **113.5**
Speed ratings (Par 101): **95,94,91,90,85 80,73,63**
CSF £20.06 CT £50.01 TOTE £4.20: £1.40, £1.80, £1.60; EX 21.30 Trifecta £81.30.
Owner Infinity Racing **Bred** Ballymacoll Stud Farm Ltd **Trained** Oakham, Rutland

FOCUS
Race distance increased by 7yds. They went steadily in this staying handicap, confined to amateur riders. The winner is rated pretty much to his best.

2090 BRITISH STALLION STUDS EBF NOVICE MEDIAN AUCTION STKS 5f
2:40 (2:41) (Class 5) 2-Y-O **£3,234** (£962; £481; £240) **Stalls** High

Form RPR

2 **1** **Wheneverwecan (IRE)**[9] 1868 2-8-11 0 ... JoeFanning 4 73
(Mark Johnston) *pressed ldr: shkn up to ld over 1f out: sn hrd pressed: kpt on wl fnl f* **3/1**[2]

2 nk **Hamidans Girl (IRE)** 2-8-11 0 ... PhillipMakin 3 72
(Keith Dalgleish) *t.k.h early: trckd ldrs: squeezed through and ev ch appr fnl f: kpt on: no ex cl home* **7/1**[3]

22 **3** 4 **Valentino Boy (IRE)**[12] 1783 2-9-2 0 ... TomEaves 6 63
(Brian Ellison) *led: rdn over 2f out: hdd whn n.m.r briefly appr fnl f: outpcd ins fnl f* **10/11**[1]

4 3 1/2 **Smiley Riley (IRE)** 2-9-2 0 ... BarryMcHugh 2 50
(Tony Coyle) *in tch: sn rdn along: no imp fr 2f out* **33/1**

5 3/4 **Galahad** 2-9-2 0 ... TonyHamilton 1 47
(Richard Fahey) *wnt rt s: sn pushed along and rn green in rr: no imp fr 1/2-way* **8/1**

6 7 **Zebedee Cat (IRE)** 2-9-2 0 ... GrahamLee 5 22
(Iain Jardine) *noisy in paddock: slowly away: a bhd and outpcd* **12/1**

59.32s (-1.08) **Going Correction** -0.225s/f (Firm) 6 Ran SP% **111.6**
Speed ratings (Par 93): **99,98,92,86,85 74**
CSF £23.04 TOTE £3.30: £1.40, £3.40; EX 27.10 Trifecta £46.50.
Owner Douglas Livingston **Bred** Michael O'Mahony **Trained** Middleham Moor, N Yorks

FOCUS
Not a bad novice event, the first two pulling clear.

2091 MACBET GUARANTEED ODDS, ALL UK/IRISH RACING H'CAP (DIV I) 1m
3:10 (3:10) (Class 5) (0-70,69) 4-Y-O+ **£3,234** (£962; £481; £240) **Stalls** Low

Form RPR

2101 **1** **Ellaal**[10] 1841 7-9-4 **66** ... PaulMulrennan 8 72
(Ruth Carr) *led 1f: pressed ldr: effrt and disp ld fr over 2f out: edgd lft over 1f out: styd on gamely u.p fnl f to ld nr fin* **9/2**[2]

2521 **2** shd **Surewecan**[15] 1663 4-9-7 **69** ... JoeFanning 3 74
(Mark Johnston) *dwlt: pushed up to ld after 1f: jnd over 2f out: rdn over 1f out: kpt on fnl f: hdd cl nr fin* **7/2**[1]

03-2 **3** nk **Silver Duke (IRE)**[10] 1841 5-9-0 **62** ... (b) DanielTudhope 7 66+
(Jim Goldie) *hld up: pushed along over 3f out: effrt and swtchd to outside over 1f out: kpt on wl fnl f: jst hld* **7/1**

53-4 **4** hd **Ingleby Spring (IRE)**[10] 1841 4-8-12 **60** ... TonyHamilton 4 64
(Richard Fahey) *prom: effrt over 2f out: kpt on ins fnl f* **12/1**

41-3 **5** 2 **Opt Out**[15] 1663 6-9-2 **64** ... (p) PJMcDonald 6 63
(Alistair Whillans) *s.i.s: hld up: effrt on outside over 2f out: sn rdn: kpt on same pce ins fnl f* **6/1**[3]

20-5 **6** nk **Let Right Be Done**[14] 1695 4-9-2 **64** ... GeorgeChaloner 5 62
(Linda Perratt) *in tch: rdn over 3f out: rallied 2f out: no imp fnl f* **33/1**

-335 **7** 1/2 **Sakhalin Star (IRE)**[17] 1596 5-9-6 **68** ... (e) JasonHart 2 65
(Richard Guest) *trckd ldrs: drvn along over 2f out: edgd rt: outpcd over 1f out* **6/1**[3]

5-43 **8** 2 1/2 **Gone With The Wind (GER)**[14] 1696 5-9-3 **65** ... (t) GrahamLee 1 56
(Rebecca Bastiman) *s.i.s: hld up: rdn and outpcd over 2f out: n.d after* **17/2**

00-0 **9** 4 1/2 **Just Paul (IRE)**[7] 1926 6-8-13 **61** ... JackGarritty 9 41
(Micky Hammond) *prom: effrt over 2f out: wknd wl over 1f out* **7/1**

1m 38.52s (-2.68) **Going Correction** -0.225s/f (Firm) 9 Ran SP% **115.1**
Speed ratings (Par 103): **104,103,103,103,101 101,100,98,93**
CSF £20.58 CT £108.62 TOTE £4.40: £1.40, £1.70, £2.20; EX 18.70 Trifecta £97.50.
Owner The Bottom Liners & Paul Saxton **Bred** W And R Barnett Ltd **Trained** Huby, N Yorks

FOCUS
Race distance increased by 7yds. This moderate handicap was run at an average pace and produced a tight finish as a result. It was marginally the slower division. The winner is rated to his best form of last summer.

2092 MACBET GUARANTEED ODDS, ALL UK/IRISH RACING H'CAP (DIV II) 1m
3:40 (3:40) (Class 5) (0-70,68) 4-Y-O+ **£3,234** (£962; £481; £240) **Stalls** Low

Form RPR

0522 **1** **Tellovoi (IRE)**[7] 1925 8-9-5 **66** ... (v) JasonHart 8 77
(Richard Guest) *mde all: rdn over 2f out: kpt on strly fnl f* **5/2**[1]

4-60 **2** 2 1/2 **Shamaheart (IRE)**[23] 1488 6-9-7 **68** ... (p) DavidAllan 5 73
(Geoffrey Harker) *s.i.s: hld up: stdy hdwy over 2f out: rdn to chse wnr over 1f out: kpt on same pce ins fnl f* **5/1**[3]

-003 **3** 2 1/4 **Picks Pinta**[17] 1595 5-9-6 **67** ... PatrickMathers 9 67
(John David Riches) *dwlt: sn prom on outside: rdn and wnt 2nd over 2f out to over 1f out: sn one pce* **8/1**

-005 **4** 3/4 **Adventureman**[10] 1841 4-8-11 **58** ... JamesSullivan 1 56
(Ruth Carr) *t.k.h: trckd ldrs: rdn over 2f out: rallied over 1f out: no imp fnl f* **11/2**

20-0 **5** 1 1/4 **Dark Crystal**[15] 1663 5-9-4 **65** ... JackGarritty 6 60
(Linda Perratt) *in tch: nt clr run over 3f out to over 2f out: rdn and edgd lft over 1f out: sn no imp* **11/1**

400- **6** 2 1/2 **Dancin Alpha**[319] 3555 5-8-13 **60** ... BenCurtis 7 49
(Alan Swinbank) *pressed wnr to over 2f out: sn drvn and outpcd: btn fnl f* **12/1**

20-0 **7** 4 **Call Me Crockett (IRE)**[14] 1695 4-9-1 **62** ... (p) RoystonFfrench 3 41
(Iain Jardine) *hld up: rdn over 2f out: sn wknd* **14/1**

32-0 **8** 1 3/4 **Mr Sundowner (USA)**[33] 1252 4-9-1 **62** ... (t) PaulMulrennan 2 37
(Wilf Storey) *t.k.h: hld up on outside: rdn over 2f out: wknd wl over 1f out* **4/1**[2]

1m 38.23s (-2.97) **Going Correction** -0.225s/f (Firm) 8 Ran SP% **114.4**
Speed ratings (Par 103): **105,102,100,99,98 95,91,90**
CSF £15.17 CT £86.29 TOTE £2.80: £1.60, £1.40, £2.20; EX 17.20 Trifecta £65.80.
Owner Mrs Alison Guest **Bred** Whisperview Trading Ltd **Trained** Ingmanthorpe, W Yorks

FOCUS
Race distance increased by 7yds. They went a fair pace in this second division of the 1m handicap, which was the faster by 0.29sec. Plenty went right for the winner who has a lot of better back form.

2093 CENTRAL TAXIS FASTER, GREENER, SAFER H'CAP 1m 4f 100y
4:10 (4:10) (Class 5) (0-75,75) 4-Y-O+ **£3,234** (£962; £481; £240) **Stalls** Low

Form RPR

1610 **1** **Bayan Kasirga (IRE)**[18] 1586 6-9-0 **71** ... SammyJoBell(3) 11 80
(Richard Fahey) *hld up: pushed along over 4f out: hdwy on outside to ld over 1f out: rdn and r.o wl fnl f* **11/1**

0-00 **2** 1 3/4 **San Cassiano (IRE)**[19] 1560 9-8-9 **63** ... JamesSullivan 6 69
(Ruth Carr) *chsd ldrs: wnt 2nd 5f out: rdn along 3f out: lost 2nd over 1f out: rallied fnl f to regain 2nd pl towards fin* **14/1**

50-4 **3** 1/2 **Nonchalant**[15] 1664 5-9-7 **75** ... (v) DanielTudhope 12 80
(David O'Meara) *cl up: led after 3f: rdn over 2f out: hdd over 1f out: kpt on fnl f tl no ex and lost 2nd towards fin* **5/1**[1]

/355 **4** 1 1/2 **Thankyou Very Much**[14] 1697 6-8-5 **59** ... (p) PJMcDonald 9 62
(James Bethell) *midfield: drvn along over 3f out: rallied over 1f out: kpt on fnl f: nt pce to chal* **14/1**

3421 **5** nse **Mcvicar**[15] 1675 7-8-9 **63** ... (p) GrahamLee 2 66
(John Davies) *prom: drvn along over 3f out: rallied wl over 1f out: kpt on same pce fnl f* **6/1**[2]

-414 **6** 3/4 **Archipeligo**[5] 566 5-8-12 **73** ... (p) AdamMcNamara(7) 7 75
(Iain Jardine) *t.k.h early: hld up on outside: effrt and hdwy over 2f out: edgd rt and outpcd over 1f out* **8/1**

43-0 **7** 1 3/4 **Love Marmalade (IRE)**[15] 1665 6-9-6 **74** ... JoeFanning 5 73
(Alistair Whillans) *prom: drvn along over 3f out: outpcd fr 2f out* **5/1**[1]

45-2 **8** 6 **Testa Rossa (IRE)**[14] 1697 6-8-2 **59** ... (p) JoeDoyle(3) 13 48
(Jim Goldie) *hld up: rdn over 4f out: shortlived effrt on outside over 2f out: btn over 1f out* **7/1**[3]

60-4 **9** 1/2 **Shalamzar (FR)**[34] 1248 7-9-4 **72** ... JackGarritty 14 60
(Micky Hammond) *awkward s: hld up: drvn and struggling over 3f out: nvr on terms* **33/1**

026/ **10** 1 **Norfolk Sound**[18] 7635 5-8-2 **56** ... (t) PatrickMathers 10 43
(Stuart Coltherd) *midfield: drvn along over 3f out: btn fnl 2f* **66/1**

60-5 **11** 3 1/4 **Jammy Moment**[10] 1842 5-8-12 **66** ... PhillipMakin 4 48
(Keith Dalgleish) *slowly away: hld up: drvn and struggling over 3f out: sn btn* **10/1**

0-00 **12** 1/2 **Indian Chief (IRE)**[18] 1588 6-9-1 **69** ... (t) PaulMulrennan 8 50
(Rebecca Bastiman) *hld up: rdn along over 3f out: edgd rt and sn wknd* **22/1**

-323 **13** 4 **Competent**[45] 1085 4-9-0 **68** ... GrahamGibbons 3 42
(Kristin Stubbs) *led 3f: chsd ldr to 5f out: rdn and wknd fr 3f out* **10/1**

2m 40.35s (-1.65) **Going Correction** -0.225s/f (Firm) 13 Ran SP% **119.9**
Speed ratings (Par 103): **96,94,94,93,93 92,91,87,87,86 84,84,81**
CSF £153.92 CT £875.76 TOTE £13.60: £2.90, £4.30, £2.70; EX 177.00 Trifecta £2616.80.
Owner Stephen Humphreys **Bred** Lynn Lodge Stud **Trained** Musley Bank, N Yorks

FOCUS
Race distance increased by 7yds. This looked wide open and it was run at a decent pace yet not that many had a say. Pretty ordinary form.

2094 HIGH DEFINITION RACING UK MAIDEN STKS — 1m 1f
4:40 (4:40) (Class 5) 4-Y-O+ — **£3,234** (£962; £481; £240) **Stalls** Low

Form — RPR

25-5 **1** — **Ghostly Arc (IRE)**[27] 1399 4-9-5 55 — BarryMcHugh 2 — 67
(Noel Wilson) *mde all: rdn over 2f out: edgd lft fr over 1f out: hld on wl cl home* — **8/1**[3]

22-2 **2** *shd* **Madame Butterfly (IRE)**[13] 1765 4-9-0 75 — DanielTudhope 6 — 61
(David O'Meara) *chsd wnr: pushed along over 2f out: drvn and swtchd rt 1f out: sn ev ch: kpt on fnl f: jst hld* — **1/5**[1]

3 *19* **Chiron (IRE)**[766] 7-9-5 0 — JasonHart 3 — 24
(Keith Dalgleish) *chsd ldrs: drvn and outpcd over 3f out: sn no ch w first two* — **6/1**[2]

00 **4** *hd* **Question Of Faith**[9] 1873 5-9-0 0 — PaulMulrennan 1 — 19
(Martin Todhunter) *sn outpcd and pushed along: drvn and sme hdwy over 3f out: sn no imp* — **14/1**

0 **5** *15* **Silva Samourai**[128] 23 7-9-5 0 — JoeyHaynes 5
(Susan Corbett) *in tch: struggling after 3f: n.d after: btn over 3f out* **100/1**

6 *36* **Little Miss Nelly** 6-9-0 0 — GrahamLee 4
(Fred Watson) *s.s: sn t.o* — **33/1**

1m 50.46s (-3.44) **Going Correction** -0.225s/f (Firm) — **6** Ran SP% **119.3**
Speed ratings (Par 103): **106,105,89,88,75 43**
CSF £10.92 TOTE £12.20: £3.50, £1.10; EX 17.60 Trifecta £35.00.
Owner G J Paver **Bred** Troytown Bloodstock **Trained** Middleham, N Yorks

FOCUS
Race distance increased by 7yds. A very weak maiden with no depth, and the winner's profile does not point to obvious improvement.

2095 RACING UK DAY PASS JUST £10 H'CAP — 7f 30y
5:10 (5:11) (Class 5) (0-75,75) 3-Y-O — **£3,234** (£962; £481; £240) **Stalls** Low

Form — RPR

00-5 **1** — **Quick N Quirky (IRE)**[17] 1599 3-9-7 75 — (t) DavidAllan 10 — 79
(Tim Easterby) *hld up on outside: effrt over 2f out: rdn to ld ins fnl f: kpt on wl* — **9/2**[2]

-001 **2** *nk* **Billy Roberts (IRE)**[18] 1584 3-9-6 74 — JasonHart 5 — 77
(Richard Guest) *dwlt: t.k.h: hld up in rr: effrt whn nt clr run over 2f out: edgd rt and hdwy over 1f out: pressed wnr wl ins fnl f: kpt on* — **3/1**[1]

06-4 **3** *1* **Miramonte Dancer (IRE)**[15] 1671 3-8-6 60 — PJMcDonald 9 — 60
(David C Griffiths) *led: rdn over 2f out: edgd lft and hdd ins fnl f: kpt on same pce* — **13/2**

100- **4** *¾* **Penwortham (IRE)**[217] 6978 3-9-7 75 — TonyHamilton 1 — 73
(Richard Fahey) *hld up in tch on ins: effrt and pushed along 2f out: n.m.r briefly and swtchd lft appr fnl f: one pce last 100yds* — **7/1**

5-30 **5** *3½* **Kingthistle**[16] 1630 3-8-13 67 — GrahamGibbons 6 — 56
(Michael Easterby) *trckd ldrs: wnt 2nd over 4f out: rdn: edgd rt and outpcd 2f out: n.d after: eased whn hld ins fnl f* — **7/1**

255- **6** *3* **Strummer (IRE)**[214] 7055 3-9-0 68 — TomEaves 2 — 49
(Kevin Ryan) *t.k.h: trckd ldr to over 4f out: effrt and rdn over 2f out: wknd ins fnl f* — **10/1**

-143 **7** *6* **Specialv (IRE)**[11] 1816 3-8-6 65 — CallumShepherd(5) 8 — 30
(Brian Ellison) *bhd: drvn and struggling over 3f out: btn fnl 2f* — **17/2**

55-2 **8** *½* **Dominannie (IRE)**[18] 1589 3-8-11 65 — BenCurtis 11 — 28
(Alan Swinbank) *t.k.h: prom tl rdn: edgd rt and wknd fr over 2f out* **6/1**[3]

1m 27.62s (-1.38) **Going Correction** -0.225s/f (Firm) — **8** Ran SP% **115.4**
Speed ratings (Par 99): **98,97,96,95,91 88,81,80**
CSF £18.62 CT £87.49 TOTE £4.70: £1.60, £1.40, £2.40; EX 17.20 Trifecta £131.30.
Owner Neil Arton **Bred** John Quigley **Trained** Great Habton, N Yorks

FOCUS
Race distance increased by 7yds. They went a routine pace in this modest handicap and it looks best rated around the runner-up.

2096 WATCH RACING UK IN HD H'CAP — 7f 30y
5:45 (5:46) (Class 6) (0-60,59) 4-Y-O+ — **£2,587** (£770; £384; £192) **Stalls** Low

Form — RPR

40-2 **1** — **Blue Jacket (USA)**[23] 1495 5-9-4 56 — JamesSullivan 11 — 64+
(Dianne Sayer) *hld up in midfield: smooth hdwy and plld out over 1f out: led ins fnl f: edgd rt: pushed out* — **3/1**[1]

2363 **2** *½* **Princess Peaches**[14] 1695 4-9-7 59 — (p) PJMcDonald 1 — 66
(James Bethell) *cl up: ev ch over 1f out to ins fnl f: edgd both ways u.p: hld cl home* — **6/1**[3]

455 **3** *1¾* **Top Offer**[10] 1845 7-8-13 58 — AdamMcNamara(7) 6 — 63
(Patrick Morris) *s.i.s: hld up: stdy hdwy whn nt clr run over 2f out: effrt and swtchd rt over 1f out: cl 3rd and styng on whn bdly hmpd towards fin* — **7/1**

-541 **4** *hd* **Smalljohn**[52] 985 10-9-0 57 — (v) PhilDennis(5) 4 — 58
(Bryan Smart) *led: rdn over 2f out: hdd ins fnl f: sn hmpd and no ex* **6/1**[3]

660- **5** *¾* **Joyful Star**[167] 7968 6-8-12 50 — GrahamLee 12 — 53
(Fred Watson) *hld up: hdwy over 2f out: cl up whn no room and hmpd ins fnl f: nt rcvr* — **25/1**

63-6 **6** *1¼* **Yair Hill (IRE)**[10] 1845 8-9-1 53 — (p) JoeFanning 10 — 49
(Thomas Cuthbert) *hld up: effrt on outside over 2f out: rdn and no imp over 1f out* — **14/1**

-062 **7** *1¼* **Atreus**[16] 1654 4-9-2 59 — (p) NathanEvans(5) 5 — 52
(Michael Easterby) *cl up: effrt and ev ch over 1f out: no ex whn bmpd ins fnl f: sn btn* — **9/2**[2]

2604 **8** *2½* **Cookie Ring (IRE)**[14] 1700 5-9-0 59 — (v) PaulaMuir(7) 3 — 45
(Patrick Holmes) *dwlt: bhd: rdn over 2f out: no imp fr over 1f out* — **14/1**

0026 **9** *5* **Ted's Brother (IRE)**[2] 2046 8-9-5 57 — (e) JasonHart 2 — 29
(Richard Guest) *trckd ldrs: rdn over 2f out: sn wknd* — **13/2**

53-0 **10** *5* **Takahiro**[15] 1663 4-8-9 50 — JoeDoyle(3) 8 — 9
(Linda Perratt) *hld up bhd ldng gp: drvn and outpcd over 2f out: sn btn* — **50/1**

1m 27.04s (-1.10) **Going Correction** -0.225s/f (Firm) — **10** Ran SP% **116.7**
Speed ratings (Par 101): **97,96,94,94,93 91,90,87,81,76**
CSF £21.12 CT £119.65 TOTE £3.90: £1.30, £2.70, £2.70; EX 21.40 Trifecta £139.10.
Owner Andrew Sayer **Bred** Juddmonte Farms Inc **Trained** Hackthorpe, Cumbria

FOCUS
Race distance increased by 7yds. There was a very messy finish to this weak handicap. The winner looks highly likely to do better.
T/Jkpt: Not won. T/Plt: £65.80 to a £1 stake. Pool: £45,629.34 - 505.67 winning tickets T/Qpdt: £9.00 to a £1 stake. Pool: £4,662.30 - 379.42 winning tickets **Richard Young**

1928 WINDSOR (R-H)
Monday, May 9

OFFICIAL GOING: Good (good to firm in places; 8.2) racing abandoned after race 3 (6.20) due to unsafe ground
Wind: Almost nil Weather: Light rain

2097 SKY BET NOVICE FILLIES' STKS (PLUS 10 RACE) — 5f 10y
5:20 (5:24) (Class 4) 2-Y-O — **£3,946** (£1,174; £586; £293) **Stalls** Low

Form — RPR

1 — **Sea Of Snow (USA)** 2-9-0 0 — JamesDoyle 3 — 75+
(Mark Johnston) *trckd ldrs: rn green whn asked for effrt 2f out: prog to ld 1f out but hrd pressed: rdn and styd on wl* — **9/2**[3]

4 **2** *nk* **Tiggaliscious (IRE)**[13] 1749 2-9-0 0 — SeanLevey 6 — 74
(Richard Hannon) *trckd ldrs: prog to chal and w wnr 1f out: styd on but jst hld last 75yds* — **9/4**[1]

3 **3** *3¾* **Princess Holly**[14] 1706 2-9-0 0 — AndreaAtzeni 1 — 60
(Robert Cowell) *led against nr side rail: rdn and hdd 1f out: fdd* — **9/2**[3]

4 *shd* **Whiteley (IRE)** 2-9-0 0 — SilvestreDeSousa 4 — 60
(Mick Channon) *trckd ldrs: plld out and rdn 2f out: no imp over 1f out: kpt on* — **7/2**[2]

5 *¾* **Joshlee (IRE)** 2-9-0 0 — ShaneKelly 5 — 57+
(Richard Hughes) *hld up in last: pushed along over 1f out: kpt on fnl f but short of room nr fin: shaped w promise* — **9/1**

3 **6** *2* **Luv U Always**[11] 1799 2-9-0 0 — JFEgan 8 — 50
(Jo Hughes) *spd fr wd draw and w ldr: hanging lft after 2f: losing pl whn sltly short of room over 1f out: wknd* — **10/1**

0 **7** *2¼* **Josiane (IRE)**[12] 1793 2-8-11 0 — TomMarquand(3) 7 — 42
(Richard Hannon) *a in rr: pushed along on outer 2f out: no prog* — **14/1**

1m 1.73s (1.43) **Going Correction** +0.05s/f (Good) — **7** Ran SP% **115.1**
Speed ratings (Par 92): **90,89,83,83,82 78,75**
CSF £15.29 TOTE £4.20: £1.90, £1.60; EX 14.10 Trifecta £54.30.
Owner Sheikh Hamdan bin Mohammed Al Maktoum **Bred** Darley **Trained** Middleham Moor, N Yorks
■ Stewards' Enquiry : Silvestre De Sousa caution: careless riding

FOCUS
A total of 13mm irrigation had been applied to the whole of the racecourse since Thursday, and the going was given as good, good to firm in places (GoingStick: 8.2). All of the inner running rail had been moved to provide fresh racing lines. The inner of the straight was dolled out 11yds at 6f and 6yds at the winning line. The top bend was dolled out 12yds from its normal inner configuration, adding 45yds to race distances of 1m plus. No more than fair novice form on the face of it.

2098 SKY BET MEDIAN AUCTION MAIDEN STKS — 1m 2f 7y
5:50 (5:52) (Class 5) 3-5-Y-O — **£2,911** (£866; £432; £216) **Stalls** Centre

Form — RPR

24- **1** — **Central Square (IRE)**[226] 6740 4-10-0 0 — AndreaAtzeni 3 — 89+
(Roger Varian) *chsd ldrs: pushed along fr 1/2-way: picked up and prog over 2f out: rdn to ld jst over 1f out: styd on wl: readily* — **11/10**[1]

23- **2** *1½* **Paris Magic**[145] 8246 3-8-13 0 — JamesDoyle 1 — 85+
(Hugo Palmer) *chsd ldr: rdn over 2f out: led briefly over 1f out: styd on fnl f but readily hld* — **9/4**[2]

0-23 **3** *4½* **California Lad**[51] 1000 3-8-13 76 — (v[1]) SilvestreDeSousa 8 — 76
(Harry Dunlop) *led: stretched field and sent for home over 3f out: hdd over 1f out: drvn out to hold on for 3rd* — **10/1**

6 **4** *hd* **Sir George Somers (USA)**[14] 1715 3-8-13 0 — TedDurcan 4 — 76
(Sir Michael Stoute) *trckd ldrs: shkn up 3f out: nvr nr enough to chal but kpt on steadily to press for 3rd ins fnl f* — **6/1**[3]

3 **5** *7* **William Hunter**[27] 1400 4-10-0 0 — WilliamTwiston-Davies 11 — 63
(Alan King) *in tch in midfield: urged along and outpcd in 8th over 3f out: sme prog into 5th over 1f out: nvr on terms* — **25/1**

0 **6** *¾* **Magnificent Madiba**[14] 1714 3-8-13 0 — SteveDrowne 5 — 60
(George Baker) *in tch in midfield: urged along and outpcd in 7th over 3f out: n.d after: kpt on* — **66/1**

7 *1* **Faction** 3-8-13 0 — OisinMurphy 7 — 58
(Andrew Balding) *disp 2nd pl to wl over 2f out: wknd* — **33/1**

00- **8** *1* **Hamilton Terrace**[173] 7890 3-8-9 0 ow1 — SeanLevey 6 — 52
(Henry Candy) *in tch in midfield: urged along and outpcd in 6th over 3f out: pushed along and one pce after* — **66/1**

9 *2* **Pastoral Music** 3-8-13 0 — JimmyFortune 12 — 52+
(Hughie Morrison) *slowly away: wl bhd in last: pushed along and kpt on steadily fr 3f out: nt disgracd* — **20/1**

10 *12* **Charioteer** 3-8-13 0 — FrederikTylicki 9 — 28
(Ed Dunlop) *slowly away: a bhd in last quartet* — **25/1**

0/ **11** *hd* **Intimidator (IRE)**[550] 7682 5-10-0 0 — StevieDonohoe 2 — 29
(Miss Joey Ellis) *restless stalls: a bhd in last quartet* — **100/1**

- **12** *31* **The Black Cygnet** 3-8-8 0 — WilliamCarson 10
(David Menuisier) *dwlt: a bhd in last quartet: t.o* — **66/1**

2m 7.58s (-1.12) **Going Correction** +0.05s/f (Good)
WFA 3 from 4yo+ 15lb — **12** Ran SP% **122.6**
Speed ratings (Par 103): **106,104,101,101,95 94,94,93,91,82 81,57**
CSF £3.45 TOTE £2.80: £1.50, £1.20, £1.20; EX 5.40 Trifecta £20.70.
Owner Clipper Logistics **Bred** Mrs Cherry Faeste **Trained** Newmarket, Suffolk

FOCUS
Race distance increased by 45yds. The market leaders came to the fore here, and with the third rated 76 and a fairly reliable guide, this looks decent maiden form. It makes a fair deal of sense.

2099 SKY BET H'CAP — 1m 2f 7y
6:20 (6:22) (Class 4) (0-80,79) 3-Y-O — **£4,690** (£1,395; £697; £348) **Stalls** Centre

Form — RPR

00-3 **1** — **Grapevine (IRE)**[17] 1602 3-9-1 76 — MichaelJMMurphy(3) 9 — 79
(Charles Hills) *slowly away: rapid prog to ld after 2f: mde rest at mod pce: slipped bnd 5f out: kicked on over 2f out: drvn over 1f out: a had enough of a ld to hold on* — **4/1**[2]

31-4 **2** *¾* **Rebel Lightning (IRE)**[26] 1409 3-9-4 76 — WilliamTwiston-Davies 5 — 77
(Richard Spencer) *hld up in tch: rdn and nt qckn 2f out: styd on to take 2nd wl ins fnl f: a hld* — **8/1**

01-3 **3** *hd* **Bedrock**[16] 1623 3-9-7 79 — PatCosgrave 8 — 80
(William Haggas) *trckd ldrs: rdn and nt qckn 2f out: kpt on to dispute 2nd wl ins fnl f: a hld* — **11/4**[1]

4412 **4** *nk* **Lord Huntingdon**[10] 1828 3-9-6 78 — OisinMurphy 6 — 78
(Andrew Balding) *prog to trck wnr after 3f: rdn and nt qckn over 2f out: lost 2nd and one pce wl ins fnl f* — **5/1**[3]

15-4 **5** *shd* **Loading (IRE)**[8] 1896 3-9-7 **79** SeanLevey 4 79+
(Richard Hannon) *hld up in last: rdn 2f out: swtchd to outer and styd on fnl f: nvr able to rch ldrs* **20/1**

32-1 **6** *½* **King Of Dreams**[118] 153 3-9-7 **79** JamieSpencer 3 78
(David Simcock) *led 2f: sn in 3rd: rdn and nt qckn 2f out: lost pl over 1f out: one pce after* **4/1**[2]

-353 **7** *1 ¼* **Lilbourne Prince (IRE)**[23] 1485 3-9-4 **76** AdamKirby 2 74
(David Evans) *hld up in rr: pushed along over 2f out: gng bttr but nowhere to go fr wl over 1f out: nvr able to make any prog* **11/1**

3142 **8** *½* **Ilzam (IRE)**[13] 1750 3-9-6 **78** (t) JamesDoyle 10 74
(Marco Botti) *hld up: rdn 2f out: tried to make prog over 1f out but nvr a threat* **14/1**

30-2 **9** *19* **Premier Currency (IRE)**[23] 1485 3-9-1 **73** TedDurcan 1 31
(Mike Murphy) *sn hld up in tch: appeared to be gng wl 3f out: sn wknd and eased: t.o* **14/1**

2m 8.86s (0.16) **Going Correction** +0.05s/f (Good) **9** Ran SP% **120.9**
Speed ratings (Par 101): **101,100,100,100,99 99,98,98,82**
CSF £34.59 CT £81.24 TOTE £5.50: £2.00, £3.20, £1.10; EX 44.40 Trifecta £224.90.
Owner Mrs J K Powell **Bred** Colman O'Flynn Jnr **Trained** Lambourn, Berks

FOCUS
Race distance increased by 45yds. A bit of a messy affair pace-wise and they finished in a heap. It's hard to be confident about the form. The rain that had fallen prior to and during this race, and which contributed to the slip of the winner on the bend, resulted in the rest of the meeting being abandoned on safety grounds.

2100 SKY BET ROYAL WINDSOR SPRINT SERIES H'CAP (A QUALIFIER FOR THE WINDSOR SPRINT SERIES) 6f
() (Class 3) (0-90,) 3-Y-O+ £

2101 SKY BET ROYAL WINDSOR STKS (LISTED RACE) (C&G) 1m 67y
() (Class 1) 3-Y-O+ £

2102 SKY BET TOP PRICE EVERY FAVOURITE H'CAP 1m 67y
() (Class 5) (0-70,) 3-Y-O £

2103 SKY BET CASH OUT H'CAP 1m 3f 135y
() (Class 5) (0-75,) 3-Y-O £

T/Plt: £2.50 to a £1 stake. Pool: £86,235.37 - 25,013.19 winning units T/Qpdt: £1.20 to a £1 stake. Pool: £7,884.39 - 4,547.84 winning units **Jonathan Neesom**

1791 WOLVERHAMPTON (A.W) (L-H)
Monday, May 9

OFFICIAL GOING: Tapeta: standard
Wind: Light against Weather: Sunny spells

2104 #FOLLOWUS ON TWITTER @WOLVESRACES NOVICE AUCTION STKS 5f 20y (Tp)
2:00 (2:02) (Class 5) 2-Y-O **£2,911** (£866; £432; £216) **Stalls** Low

Form RPR

036 **1** **King Of Castilla**[23] 1482 2-9-2 0 (t) LukeMorris 7 66
(Gay Kelleway) *pushed along in rr early: hdwy at 1/2-way: rdn to ld ins fnl f: styd on* **5/1**[3]

2 *½* **Affordability** 2-9-3 0 ow1 DaleSwift 2 65
(Daniel Mark Loughnane) *w ldrs: led 4f out: sn hdd: rdn to ld over 1f out: hdd ins fnl f: styd on* **40/1**

3 *1* **Kody Ridge (IRE)** 2-9-2 0 MartinLane 3 61
(David Dennis) *prom: n.m.r over 1f out: edgd lft ins fnl f: styd on* **8/1**

33 **4** *1* **Dontforgettocall**[24] 1454 2-9-2 0 OisinMurphy 6 57
(Joseph Tuite) *led 1f: chsd ldrs: rdn over 1f out: styd on same pce ins fnl f* **11/8**[1]

43 **5** *1 ¼* **Accladora**[18] 1583 2-8-11 0 FrannyNorton 4 48
(Mark Johnston) *prom: pushed along and lost pl 4f out: styd on towards fin* **11/2**

1 **6** *nk* **Gerrard's Fur Coat**[11] 1799 2-8-11 0 PatrickVaughan(7) 1 53
(Tom Dascombe) *pushed along to chse ldrs: led over 3f out: rdn and hdd over 1f out: no ex ins fnl f* **4/1**[2]

5 **7** *11* **Secret Ballerina**[11] 1799 2-8-8 0 ShelleyBirkett(3) 5 7
(Julia Feilden) *s.i.s: hld up: rdn and wknd over 1f out* **12/1**

1m 3.62s (1.72) **Going Correction** +0.025s/f (Slow) **7** Ran SP% **115.4**
Speed ratings (Par 93): **87,86,84,83,81 80,62**
CSF £147.11 TOTE £6.80: £4.00, £10.60; EX 170.30 Trifecta £2047.10.
Owner Rioja Racing **Bred** Llety Farms **Trained** Exning, Suffolk

FOCUS
Not the most demanding event of its type but it was run at a solid pace, the winner coming from well back to get off the mark at the fourth attempt. The form is rated cautiously.

2105 BUSINESS VENUE 365 DAYS A YEAR H'CAP 1m 5f 194y (Tp)
2:30 (2:31) (Class 5) (0-70,70) 4-Y-O+ **£2,911** (£866; £432; £216) **Stalls** Low

Form RPR

53/1 **1** **Minstrels Gallery (IRE)**[16] 1649 7-9-8 **68** GeorgeBaker 5 78+
(Lucy Wadham) *chsd ldrs: rdn to ld over 1f out: styd on* **13/8**[1]

5111 **2** *3 ¼* **On A Whim**[12] 1796 4-9-8 **69** (p) LukeMorris 3 74
(Daniel Mark Loughnane) *hld up: hdwy over 4f out: rdn and ev ch over 1f out: styd on same pce ins fnl f* **7/2**[2]

0-0P **3** *2 ¼* **Apollo Eleven (IRE)**[17] 1598 7-9-4 **64** AndrewMullen 7 66
(Michael Appleby) *sn led: rdn and hdd over 2f out: hung lft over 1f out: styd on same pce* **50/1**

-350 **4** *hd* **Dalaki (IRE)**[19] 1561 5-9-6 **66** (b) DavidProbert 6 68
(Des Donovan, Ire) *hld up: hdwy 5f out: rdn and ev ch over 1f out: wknd ins fnl f* **12/1**

4650 **5** *1* **Aumerle**[28] 1391 4-9-9 **70** OisinMurphy 4 71
(Shaun Lycett) *chsd ldrs: pushed along and lost pl over 3f out: rallied over 1f out: hung lft and wknd ins fnl f* **10/1**

111- **6** *1* **Le Torrent**[212] 7110 4-9-8 **69** HarryBentley 8 68+
(Simon Dow) *chsd ldr tl led over 2f out: rdn and hdd over 1f out: wknd ins fnl f* **13/2**[3]

14-6 **7** *11* **Lacey**[16] 1649 7-8-11 **60** (b) JackDuern(3) 2 44
(Sarah Hollinshead) *s.i.s: hld up: rdn and wknd over 2f out* **20/1**

45-3 **8** *½* **Doctor Kehoe**[24] 1456 4-8-13 **60** (v) CathyGannon 1 43
(David Evans) *prom: rdn over 4f out: sn lost pl: wknd over 2f out* **13/2**[3]

4/2- **9** *16* **Mister Bob (GER)**[472] 270 7-9-10 **70** (p) DaneO'Neill 9 31
(James Bethell) *s.i.s: hld up: rdn and wknd over 2f out* **20/1**

3m 3.03s (-1.77) **Going Correction** +0.025s/f (Slow)
WFA 4 from 5yo+ 1lb **9** Ran SP% **115.3**
Speed ratings (Par 103): **106,104,102,102,102 101,95,95,85**
CSF £6.95 CT £192.14 TOTE £2.10: £1.20, £1.90, £8.50; EX 8.80 Trifecta £204.60.
Owner G Pascoe & S Brewer **Bred** Morecool Stud **Trained** Newmarket, Suffolk

FOCUS
An interesting race for the grade featuring some in-form and well-handicapped rivals, the winner proving he was firmly in both categories. The pace was sound and the winner backed up his latest C&D win.

2106 LIKE WOLVERHAMPTON RACECOURSE ON FACEBOOK H'CAP 5f 216y (Tp)
3:00 (3:01) (Class 5) (0-70,70) 3-Y-O **£3,234** (£962; £481; £240) **Stalls** Low

Form RPR

1 **1** **Its Only Mossy (IRE)**[12] 1795 3-9-0 **63** TomQueally 10 72+
(Jennie Candlish) *a.p: chsd ldr over 4f out: led 1/2-way: rdn and hung lft over 1f out: r.o wl* **7/2**[3]

234- **2** *2 ¼* **Just Glamorous (IRE)**[230] 6629 3-9-6 **69** LukeMorris 6 71
(Ronald Harris) *chsd ldrs: rdn over 2f out: chsd wnr and hung lft over 1f out: styd on same pce ins fnl f* **10/1**

1543 **3** *hd* **Wishsong**[12] 1789 3-9-2 **70** AnnaHesketh(5) 9 71
(David Nicholls) *mid-div: hdwy over 2f out: edgd lft 1f out: styd on same pce* **10/1**

1-31 **4** *1* **Showmethewayavrilo**[26] 1420 3-9-5 **68** MartinHarley 8 66
(Malcolm Saunders) *led 1f: chsd ldrs: rdn over 2f out: styd on same pce fnl f* **3/1**[2]

-540 **5** *2* **Le Manege Enchante (IRE)**[23] 1487 3-9-2 **65** MartinLane 4 56
(Derek Shaw) *s.i.s: styd on fr over 1f out: nt trble ldrs* **12/1**

06-0 **6** *nk* **Dark Confidant (IRE)**[43] 1112 3-9-2 **65** FrannyNorton 1 55
(Richard Guest) *edgd rt s: led 5f out: hdd 1/2-way: n.m.r 1f out: wknd ins fnl f* **12/1**

0-32 **7** *3 ½* **Naziba (IRE)**[46] 1061 3-9-2 **65** GeorgeBaker 5 44
(David Menuisier) *edgd rt s: hld up: rdn over 2f out: edgd lft and wknd over 1f out* **5/2**[1]

000- **8** *17* **R Bar Open (FR)**[211] 7141 3-9-2 **65** SamHitchcott 2
(Dean Ivory) *hmpd s: sn pushed along in rr: wknd over 2f out* **20/1**

1m 14.28s (-0.22) **Going Correction** +0.025s/f (Slow) **8** Ran SP% **114.1**
Speed ratings (Par 99): **102,99,98,97,94 94,89,67**
CSF £37.61 CT £317.79 TOTE £4.10: £1.20, £2.60, £2.60; EX 40.50 Trifecta £328.10.
Owner Mrs G Hennessy **Bred** James And Sarah Mulcahy **Trained** Basford Green, Staffs

FOCUS
Competitive enough despite the non runners and the winner maintained his unbeaten record for Jennie Candlish in good style, improving again. It was well run.

2107 VISIT WOLVERHAMPTON-RACECOURSE.CO.UK H'CAP 7f 32y (Tp)
3:30 (3:30) (Class 6) (0-60,60) 3-Y-O **£2,458** (£731; £365; £182) **Stalls** High

Form RPR

00-5 **1** **Moi Aussie**[19] 1564 3-8-13 **52** MartinDwyer 8 61
(Ed McMahon) *chsd ldrs: led 1/2-way: rdn over 1f out: hdd ins fnl f: rallied to ld post* **14/1**

-023 **2** *nse* **Atrayu (IRE)**[12] 1792 3-9-7 **60** LukeMorris 1 69
(Paul D'Arcy) *chsd ldr: jnd wnr 1/2-way: rdn to ld and hung lft ins fnl f: hdd post* **6/4**[1]

2255 **3** *3 ½* **Dream Revival**[23] 1497 3-9-5 **58** HarryBentley 7 59
(James Unett) *hld up: nt clr run over 2f out: hdwy over 1f out: r.o to go 3rd ins fnl f: nt rch ldrs* **5/1**[2]

3663 **4** *1 ¼* **Deben**[31] 1313 3-9-7 **60** ShaneGray 4 57
(Kevin Ryan) *hld up: hdwy over 2f out: rdn over 1f out: styd on same pce fnl f* **12/1**

05-0 **5** *4 ½* **Bruntingthorpe (IRE)**[19] 1577 3-9-3 **56** SamHitchcott 5 42
(Dean Ivory) *prom: rdn over 2f out: wknd over 1f out* **16/1**

50-0 **6** *3 ½* **Commanding Role**[40] 1141 3-8-9 **48** DavidProbert 6 26
(Michael Blanshard) *sn pushed along in rr: sme hdwy over 1f out: n.d* **66/1**

5236 **7** *9* **Daydream (IRE)**[40] 1141 3-9-0 **58** (t) LucyKBarry(5) 12 14
(Jamie Osborne) *sn chsng ldrs on outer: rdn over 2f out: sn wknd: hung lft over 1f out* **7/1**[3]

5630 **8** *6* **Serendib's Glory (IRE)**[15] 1670 3-9-3 **59** (p) ShelleyBirkett(3) 3
(Julia Feilden) *prom: rdn over 2f out: wknd over 1f out* **8/1**

5660 **9** *1 ¾* **Pursuit Of Time**[20] 1548 3-8-10 **49** AndrewMullen 10
(Michael Appleby) *hld up: effrt on outer over 2f out: sn wknd* **25/1**

5-45 **10** *2 ¾* **Tim The Taxi**[10] 1829 3-9-2 **58** PhilipPrince(3) 9
(David Evans) *s.s: hld up: rdn 3f out: sn wknd* **8/1**

60-0 **11** *8* **Kylla**[17] 1597 3-8-7 **46** oh1 DuranFentiman 2
(Shaun Harris) *led to 1/2-way: wknd over 2f out* **100/1**

1m 29.96s (1.16) **Going Correction** +0.025s/f (Slow) **11** Ran SP% **118.0**
Speed ratings (Par 97): **94,93,89,88,83 79,69,62,60,57 47**
CSF £35.24 CT £130.22 TOTE £21.20: £5.10, £1.10, £1.80; EX 54.50 Trifecta £303.10.
Owner The C H F Partnership **Bred** The C H F Partnership **Trained** Lichfield, Staffs

FOCUS
A competitive event for the grade, although all of them were maidens, and run at a generous pace, the front two leaving the distinct impression they were value for even more than the margin back to the third would suggest.

2108 FAMILY FUN DAY ON FRIDAY 8TH AUGUST FILLIES' H'CAP 1m 141y (Tp)
4:00 (4:00) (Class 5) (0-70,70) 3-Y-O **£3,234** (£962; £481; £240) **Stalls** Low

Form RPR

5-14 **1** **Bocking End (IRE)**[13] 1758 3-9-4 **70** LouisSteward(3) 5 76
(Michael Bell) *mde all: rdn and hung rt over 1f out: styd on wl* **12/1**

3035 **2** *1 ¼* **Refulgence (FR)**[28] 1388 3-8-12 **61** LiamJones 10 64
(Marco Botti) *chsd ldrs: rdn over 2f out: edgd rt ins fnl f: styd on* **25/1**

3-1 **3** *nk* **Singyoursong (IRE)**[121] 122 3-9-1 **69** GeorgeBuckell(5) 11 71+
(David Simcock) *hld up in tch: rdn over 1f out: edgd rt: styd on* **6/5**[1]

40-1 **4** *½* **Here's Two**[40] 1141 3-9-3 **66** GeorgeBaker 2 67
(Ron Hodges) *chsd wnr 2f: remained handy: wnt 2nd again over 2f out: rdn over 1f out: edgd rt and styd on same pce ins fnl f* **7/1**[3]

2141 **5** *1 ¼* **Figurante (IRE)**[14] 1725 3-9-4 **67** CathyGannon 6 65+
(Jamie Osborne) *hld up: hdwy over 1f out: no imp ins fnl f* **6/1**[2]

05-0 **6** *2* **Moon Over Mobay**[13] 1755 3-8-13 **62** DavidProbert 1 56
(Andrew Balding) *prom: rdn over 3f out: no ex ins fnl f* **16/1**

660- **7** *nk* **Cape Crystal (IRE)**[231] 6588 3-8-12 **61** LukeMorris 12 54
(Sir Mark Prescott Bt) *prom: chsd wnr over 6f out tl rdn over 2f out: no ex ins fnl f* **14/1**

00-6 **8** *2* **Tiga Tuan (FR)**[16] 1628 3-9-5 **68** KeaganLatham 3 56
(Kevin Ryan) *dwlt: hld up: hdwy over 1f out: sn rdn: nt clr run: edgd lft and wknd ins fnl f* **6/1**[2]
400- **9** *2* **Always A Dream**[130] 8409 3-9-0 **63** MartinHarley 8 47
(Chris Wall) *hld up: rdn over 1f out: nvr on terms* **11/1**
0-50 **10** *nk* **Indie Music**[19] 1572 3-8-13 **62** SamHitchcott 4 45
(Sylvester Kirk) *mid-div: rdn over 3f out: wknd over 1f out* **33/1**
60-6 **11** *1 1/4* **Harmony Bay (IRE)**[19] 1572 3-8-10 **66** BenSanderson(7) 13 46
(Sylvester Kirk) *wnt rt s: hld up: hdwy on outer over 2f out: sn rdn: wknd wl over 1f out* **80/1**

1m 50.03s (-0.07) **Going Correction** +0.025s/f (Slow) **11** Ran SP% **123.1**
Speed ratings (Par 96): **101,99,99,99,98 96,96,94,92,92 91**
CSF £281.96 CT £630.49 TOTE £13.10: £3.00, £6.50, £1.20; EX 212.40 Trifecta £1201.10.
Owner W J and T C O Gredley **Bred** Howard Barton Stud **Trained** Newmarket, Suffolk

FOCUS
A heavily backed favourite for this fillies' handicap but she couldn't reward the support behind an enterprisingly ridden winner. The form is rated around the second.

2109 AWARD WINNING FINE DINING AT HORIZONS MEDIAN AUCTION MAIDEN STKS 1m 141y (Tp)

4:30 (4:32) (Class 6) 3-5-Y-O **£2,458** (£731; £365; £182) **Stalls** Low

Form RPR
22- **1** **Cambodia (IRE)**[130] 8410 3-8-13 0 LukeMorris 6 76
(Chris Wall) *racd keenly: mde all: qcknd over 2f out: shkn up over 1f out: styd on* **5/6**[1]
5 **2** *1 1/4* **Compas Scoobie**[13] 1755 3-8-13 0 HarryBentley 1 73
(Roger Varian) *chsd wnr to 1/2-way: remained handy: rdn over 1f out: chsd wnr again ins fnl f: styd on* **9/2**[3]
6 **3** *hd* **Naqdy**[13] 1755 3-8-13 0 DaneO'Neill 3 73+
(William Haggas) *s.i.s: sn chsng ldrs: rdn over 1f out: r.o* **5/1**
353- **4** *1/2* **Charmy**[130] 8410 3-8-8 71 DavidProbert 7 67
(Andrew Balding) *a.p: chsd wnr 1/2-way: rdn and edgd lft over 1f out: styd on same pce ins fnl f* **3/1**[2]
6- **5** *16* **Ballyer Rallyer (IRE)**[192] 7605 3-8-13 0[1] ShaneGray 5 38
(Daniel Mark Loughnane) *s.i.s: hld up: plld hrd: nvr on terms* **28/1**
6 *nk* **Sid Sweeney** 3-8-13 0 MartinDwyer 2 38
(Gay Kelleway) *prom: pushed along 1/2-way: wknd over 2f out* **28/1**
60 **7** *1 3/4* **Whacking Bullock (IRE)**[16] 1653 3-8-13 0 AndrewMullen 4 34
(Daniel Mark Loughnane) *a in rr: wknd over 2f out* **100/1**
0 **8** *1 1/2* **King Of Arts (IRE)**[41] 1132 3-8-8 0 GeorgeBuckell(5) 8 31
(David Simcock) *hld up: wknd over 2f out* **40/1**

1m 49.77s (-0.33) **Going Correction** +0.025s/f (Slow) **8** Ran SP% **124.7**
Speed ratings (Par 101): **102,100,100,100,86 85,84,82**
CSF £5.82 TOTE £1.80: £1.10, £1.60, £1.80; EX 5.70 Trifecta £16.30.
Owner Des Thurlby **Bred** James Waldron **Trained** Newmarket, Suffolk

FOCUS
An interesting maiden in which the four at the head of the market dominated proceedings, the winner looking a useful prospect. It's hard to rate this any higher initially.

2110 COMBINE BUSINESS WITH RACING AT WOLVERHAMPTON AMATEUR RIDERS' H'CAP 1m 4f 50y (Tp)

5:00 (5:01) (Class 6) (0-55,55) 4-Y-O+ **£2,370** (£735; £367; £183) **Stalls** Low

Form RPR
3136 **1** **Henry Smith**[27] 1405 4-10-8 **54** (be) MissPBridgwater(5) 4 63
(Garry Moss) *chsd ldrs: rdn over 2f out: led over 1f out: styd on* **8/1**
1/6- **2** *1 1/4* **The Bay Bandit**[179] 763 9-10-3 **51** (p) MissRWaterson(7) 1 58+
(Neil Mulholland) *hld up: hdwy on outer over 3f out: chsd wnr ins fnl f: styd on same pce* **16/1**
6620 **3** *4 1/2* **Easydoesit (IRE)**[13] 1748 8-11-0 **55** (p) MissJoannaMason 11 55
(Tony Carroll) *s.i.s: hld up: hdwy over 1f out: styd on to go 3rd nr fin: nt trble ldrs* **25/1**
0453 **4** *hd* **Vedani (IRE)**[31] 1322 7-10-12 **53** StanSheppard 7 52
(Tony Carroll) *prom: lost pl 4f out: r.o ins fnl f* **11/2**[3]
4440 **5** *1/2* **Nolecce**[30] 1347 9-10-9 **55** TobyEley(5) 2 54
(Tony Forbes) *chsd ldrs: rdn over 1f out: wknd ins fnl f* **12/1**
5000 **6** *1/2* **Shirataki (IRE)**[30] 1343 8-10-6 **52** MissMollyKing(5) 10 50
(Peter Hiatt) *s.i.s: hld up: hdwy over 1f out: edgd lft ins fnl f: styd on same pce* **16/1**
5504 **7** *2 1/4* **Chauvelin**[13] 1748 5-9-13 **47** (b[1]) MrTomFanshawe(7) 5 41
(Richard Guest) *prom: led and edgd lft over 4f out: hdd over 1f out: wknd ins fnl f* **5/1**[2]
450- **8** *hd* **Sakhra**[181] 7782 5-10-5 **46** oh1 MrPCollington 8 40
(Mark Brisbourne) *chsd ldrs: hmpd over 4f out: rdn and lost pl over 2f out: n.d after* **18/1**
0/06 **9** *2* **Poetic Lord**[27] 1399 7-10-12 **53** (tp) MissCWalton 9 44
(Rebecca Menzies) *mid-div: hdwy over 3f out: sn rdn: wknd fnl f* **33/1**
-526 **10** *1* **Well Owd Mon**[39] 1170 6-10-11 **52** (p) MrPMillman 12 41
(Sarah Hollinshead) *s.i.s: hld up: racd keenly: hdwy over 5f out: nt clr run and lost pl over 3f out: n.d after* **11/1**
-512 **11** *7* **Storytale**[52] 981 4-10-10 **51** MrAlexEdwards 6 29
(Dave Roberts) *led at stdy pce tl hdd over 4f out: wknd over 2f out* **2/1**[1]
0-60 **12** *9* **Heat Storm (IRE)**[91] 498 5-10-2 **50** (t) MrADean(7) 3 14
(James Unett) *s.s: a bhd* **80/1**

2m 44.83s (4.03) **Going Correction** +0.025s/f (Slow) **12** Ran SP% **117.6**
Speed ratings (Par 101): **87,86,83,83,82 82,80,80,79,78 74,68**
CSF £125.53 CT £3036.17 TOTE £9.30: £2.10, £2.60, £3.90; EX 114.40 Trifecta £1337.90.
Owner Pinnacle Duo Partnership **Bred** M Pennell **Trained** Wynyard, Stockton-On-Tees

FOCUS
A low-grade amateur rider's event run at a sound pace with one of the few progressive runners in the field emerging on top. An improved effort from the winner.
T/Plt: 168.90 to a £1 stake. Pool: £70,821.73 - 305.99 winning tickets T/Qpdt: £9.20 to a £1 stake. Pool: £6,126.74 - 491.77 winning tickets **Colin Roberts**

2111 - 2113a (Foreign Racing) - See Raceform Interactive

ROSCOMMON (R-H)
Monday, May 9

OFFICIAL GOING: Flat course - yiedling; jumps course - good

2114a KNOCKCROGHERY H'CAP 1m 3f 183y

7:10 (7:11) (50-85,80) 4-Y-O+ **£5,426** (£1,676; £794; £352; £132)

RPR
1 **Synopsis**[211] 7148 4-9-11 **77** GaryCarroll 3 84
(G M Lyons, Ire) *in tch: 8th into st: swtchd lft and rdn on outer under 2f out: clsd u.p to chal in 3rd ins fnl f and styd on wl to ld clsng stages where edgd rt* **6/1**[3]
2 *3/4* **Sweet Cherry (IRE)**[17] 7613 5-8-7 **64** GaryHalpin(5) 13 70
(E D Delany, Ire) *dwlt and in rr early tl impr into mid-div after 2f: clsr bhd ldrs fr 4f out: rdn into 2nd 1 1/2f out and led ins fnl f: all out wl ins fnl f and hdd clsng stages* **11/1**
3 *nk* **Deor (IRE)**[2] 2060 5-9-5 **76** 5ex TomMadden(5) 5 82
(John E Kiely, Ire) *chsd ldrs tl sn led: jnd after 3f and hdd over 5f out: lost pl and pushed along in 5th appr st: swtchd lft and kpt on again u.p into 3rd between horses wl ins fnl f: a hld* **3/1**[1]
4 *3/4* **Sense Of Victory (IRE)**[235] 6488 4-9-8 **74** ColinKeane 10 78
(J P Murtagh, Ire) *led tl sn hdd and settled bhd ldrs: pushed along in 6th appr st and wnt 4th u.p under 2f out: no imp on wnr clsng stages where short of room and edgd sltly lft: kpt on* **9/1**
5 *3/4* **Red House Hill (IRE)**[16] 1661 6-9-2 **68** PatSmullen 9 71
(C Byrnes, Ire) *in rr of mid-div: 12th appr st: sme hdwy 2f out: nt clr run over 1f out and sn swtchd lft: kpt on clsng stages where sltly hmpd: nrst fin* **6/1**[3]
6 *1 1/4* **Rock On Rosie (IRE)**[2] 2056 7-9-1 **67** RonanWhelan 12 68
(Adrian Brendan Joyce, Ire) *chsd ldrs: racd keenly: pushed along in 2nd into st: rdn to ld 2f out: strly pressed and hdd ins fnl f: wknd clsng stages* **14/1**
7 *2* **The Fox Tully (IRE)**[33] 1282 11-9-4 **70** ConnorKing 4 68
(Gerard Keane, Ire) *mid-div: 7th appr st: rdn and no imp on ldrs under 2f out: kpt on one pce* **25/1**
8 *3/4* **Black Benny (IRE)**[198] 4769 11-9-5 **71** (t) BillyLee 8 68
(J P Broderick, Ire) *hld up towards rr: tk clsr order fr 2f out: no imp ent fnl f: kpt on one pce in 8th wl ins fnl f* **33/1**
9 *3* **Dancingwithangels (IRE)**[8] 1904 7-9-3 **69** RoryCleary 2 61
(Thomas Cleary, Ire) *dwlt and towards rr early: pushed along in 9th appr st and no imp over 2f out: kpt on one pce* **16/1**
10 *1 1/4* **Along The Shore (IRE)**[22] 1512 4-8-5 **62** (t) AnaO'Brien(5) 7 52
(A P O'Brien, Ire) *cl up and disp after 3f tl hdd over 5f out: pushed along in 3rd into st and sn no ex u.p: wknd fnl 2f* **9/2**[2]
11 *2* **Commander Won (IRE)**[283] 4845 4-9-3 **69** SeamieHeffernan 6 56
(Dermot Anthony McLoughlin, Ire) *towards rr: pushed along and no imp 2f out* **14/1**
12 *2 1/4* **Bazooka (IRE)**[8] 1885 5-9-11 **77** KierenFallon 16 60
(David Flood) *hld up towards rr: racd keenly rdn in 10th into st and no imp: eased fnl f* **12/1**
13 *2 1/2* **Shamar (FR)**[8] 1904 8-9-8 **79** (t) RossCoakley(5) 15 58
(R K Watson, Ire) *sn chsd ldrs: cl 3rd after 2f: led narrowly over 5f out: rdn and hdd 2f out: wknd: eased ins fnl f* **25/1**
14 *2 3/4* **Redera (IRE)**[176] 7152 10-9-3 **69** WayneLordan 1 44
(A J Martin, Ire) *a bhd: pushed along over 4f out and no imp in rr into st* **40/1**

2m 44.19s (0.89) **14** Ran SP% **130.1**
CSF £73.97 CT £246.83 TOTE £6.80: £2.50, £3.80, £1.70; DF 83.70 Trifecta £276.20.
Owner David Spratt **Bred** Cheveley Park Stud Ltd **Trained** Dunsany, Co Meath

FOCUS
This was a very competitive handicap and the right horses were involved. The form has been rated around the balance of the placed horses.

2020 CHANTILLY (R-H)
Monday, May 9

OFFICIAL GOING: Turf: good; polytrack: standard

2115a PRIX DE LA GRANGE AUX BELLES (CONDITIONS) (3YO FILLIES) (TURF) 1m 2f

1:50 (12:00) 3-Y-O **£10,661** (£4,264; £3,198; £2,132; £1,066)

RPR
1 **Gargotiere (FR)**[15] 3-9-0 0 Pierre-CharlesBoudot 7 84
(H-F Devin, France) **21/10**[1]
2 *shd* **War Flag (USA)**[26] 3-9-0 0 ChristopheSoumillon 3 84
(J-C Rouget, France) **11/5**[2]
3 *1* **Dimaniya (FR)**[21] 1542 3-8-9 0 AlexisBadel 4 77
(A De Royer-Dupre, France) **31/5**
4 *3/4* **Beraymi (IRE)**[171] 3-8-9 0 VincentCheminaud 1 76
(A Fabre, France) *chsd ldr: rdn over 1f out: short of room on rail ins fnl f: kpt on same pce* **54/10**[3]
5 *1 1/4* **Mary Sun (FR)**[218] 3-9-0 0 RafaelSchistl 2 78
(Henk Grewe, Germany) **15/1**
6 *3/4* **Corny (FR)** 3-9-0 0 CristianDemuro 6 77
(C Ferland, France) **71/10**
7 *6* **Yeah Baby Yeah (IRE)**[27] 1396 3-9-0 0 MaximeGuyon 5 65
(Gay Kelleway) *trckd ldrs: rdn and outpcd 2f out: bmpd sn afterwards: hmpd over 1f out: wknd and eased ins fnl f* **11/1**

2m 4.82s (0.02) **7** Ran SP% **120.0**
WIN (incl. 1 euro stake): 3.10. PLACES: 1.80, 1.70. sf: 8.30.
Owner Ctsse Bertrand De Tarragon **Bred** Ecurie Maulepaire **Trained** France

2116 - 2117a (Foreign Racing) - See Raceform Interactive

1920 **BEVERLEY (R-H)**

Tuesday, May 10

OFFICIAL GOING: Good to firm (8.2)

Wind: Light behind Weather: Heavy cloud and rain

2118 VERY BRITISH RACEDAY SATURDAY 28 MAY (S) STKS — 5f

2:00 (2:00) (Class 6) 3-Y-O **£2,587** (£770; £384; £192) **Stalls** Low

Form RPR

10-4 **1** **Roaring Rory**[55] 962 3-8-8 62............................(p) JacobButterfield(3) 3 67
(Ollie Pears) *cl up 1/2-way: rdn clr appr fnl f: kpt on strly* **3/1**[2]

-226 **2** *3* **La Asomada**[11] 1839 3-8-6 62.. SamJames 1 51
(David Barron) *trckd ldng pair: pushed along over 2f out: rdn wl over 1f out: drvn and kpt on fnl f* **6/4**[1]

04-0 **3** *nk* **Pilgrims Path**[16] 1670 3-8-11 58.......................................(p) BenCurtis 2 55
(Scott Dixon) *chsd ldrs on inner: pushed along and sltly outpcd 1/2-way: swtchd lft and rdn along on outer wl over 1f out: drvn and kpt on fnl f* **5/1**[3]

440- **4** *3* **Rise Up Singing**[207] 7252 3-8-6 48............................ RoystonFfrench 6 39
(Colin Teague) *sn slt ld: hdd and pushed along 1/2-way: rdn wl over 1f out: drvn over 1f out and grad wknd* **50/1**

40-0 **5** *7* **Bit Of A Lad (IRE)**[55] 952 3-8-11 62...............................(v) TomEaves 4 19
(David Brown) *chsd ldrs: rdn along on outer 2f out: sn drvn and wknd* **9/1**

505 **6** *3 3/4* **Ksenia (IRE)**[24] 1494 3-8-6 47..................................... SilvestreDeSousa 5
(Nigel Tinkler) *chsd ldrs: rdn along 2f out: sn drvn and btn* **8/1**

-040 **7** *1 3/4* **Vocalise**[16] 1670 3-7-13 28.. RPWalsh(7) 8
(Charles Smith) *chsd ldrs on outer: rdn along bef 1/2-way: sn outpcd and bhd* **100/1**

30 **8** *3* **Mary E**[12] 1814 3-7-13 0..(b) BenRobinson(7) 7
(Brian Ellison) *sn rdn along in rr: outpcd and detached 1/2-way: sme late hdwy* **10/1**

1m 1.55s (-1.95) **Going Correction** -0.15s/f (Firm) **8 Ran SP% 114.8**
Speed ratings (Par 97): **109,104,103,98,87 81,78,74**
CSF £7.92 TOTE £4.10: £1.40, £1.10, £1.60; EX 9.40 Trifecta £38.50.No bid for the winner.
Owner Ownaracehorse Ltd (ownaracehorse.co.uk) **Bred** R S Hoskins & Hermes Services **Trained** Norton, N Yorks

FOCUS
A total of 9mm of watering had taken place between Friday and Monday, and the going was given as good to firm (GoingStick: 8.2). The running rail was at its regular configuration, with safety factors back to normal. All distances as advertised. They finished well strung out in this seller and there weren't many positives to be had.

2119 RACING UK IN GLORIOUS HD NOVICE STKS — 5f

2:30 (2:30) (Class 5) 2-Y-O **£3,780** (£1,131; £565; £283; £141) **Stalls** Low

Form RPR

1 **1** **Orewa (IRE)**[27] 1407 2-9-6 0.. BenCurtis 3 79
(Brian Ellison) *trckd ldrs: pushed along over 2f out: green and rdn over 1f out: hdwy ent fnl f: styd on wl to ld nr fin* **7/4**[1]

2 *hd* **Carson City** 2-9-2 0... TonyHamilton 1 74
(Richard Fahey) *led: pushed along wl over 1f out: rdn ent fnl f: sn jnd and drvn: kpt on: hdd nr line* **7/2**[2]

3 *2* **Book Of Poetry (IRE)** 2-9-2 0.. JoeFanning 5 67+
(Mark Johnston) *in rr towards outer: pushed along wl over 1f out: sn swtchd rt and hdwy appr fnl f: styd on wl towards fin* **9/2**[3]

4 *1* **Major Jumbo** 2-9-2 0... TomEaves 8 63
(Kevin Ryan) *trckd ldrs: hdwy on outer 2f out: rdn: green and edgd rt ent fnl f: kpt on same pce* **16/1**

5 *3/4* **Ventura Secret (IRE)** 2-9-2 0.. DavidAllan 2 61
(Tim Easterby) *in tch on inner: hdwy wl over 1f out: rdn and kpt on fnl f* **17/2**

6 **6** *nk* **Sheila's Return**[17] 1621 2-8-11 0.................................. PaulMulrennan 6 55
(Bryan Smart) *cl up: rdn along 2f out: drvn and edgd lft jst over 1f out: sn wknd* **11/1**

7 *4 1/2* **Ray Donovan (IRE)** 2-9-2 0.. DanielTudhope 7 44
(David O'Meara) *chsd ldng pair: rdn along 2f out: wknd and hld whn n.m.r and hmpd ent fnl f* **8/1**

8 *7* **Commander Blue** 2-9-2 0.. RoystonFfrench 4 18
(Steph Hollinshead) *in rr: rdn along over 2f out: n.d* **40/1**

1m 2.82s (-0.68) **Going Correction** -0.15s/f (Firm) **8 Ran SP% 115.1**
Speed ratings (Par 93): **99,98,95,93,92 92,85,73**
CSF £7.94 TOTE £2.10: £1.40, £1.40, £1.50; EX 9.90 Trifecta £20.70.
Owner Keith Brown **Bred** Mrs C Regalado-Gonzalez **Trained** Norton, N Yorks

FOCUS
The favourite set a fair standard for the newcomers to aim at. The form is rated around the race averages.

2120 ANNIE OXTOBY MEMORIAL H'CAP — 5f

3:00 (3:00) (Class 5) (0-70,70) 4-Y-O+ **£3,780** (£1,131; £565; £283; £141) **Stalls** Low

Form RPR

66-1 **1** **China Excels**[47] 1059 9-8-13 65.. RobHornby(3) 7 74
(Mandy Rowland) *mde all: rdn over 1f out: clr ent fnl f: kpt on wl towards fin* **10/1**

5-53 **2** *3/4* **See Vermont**[15] 1721 8-9-1 64....................................(p) PaulMulrennan 5 70
(Rebecca Bastiman) *trckd ldrs: swtchd lft and effrt over 1f out: sn rdn to chse wnr ent fnl f: drvn and kpt on towards fin* **11/2**[2]

1600 **3** *1 1/2* **Oriental Relation (IRE)**[17] 1650 5-9-7 70.........................(v) TomEaves 6 71
(James Given) *midfield: hdwy wl over 1f out: sn rdn and edgd rt jst over 1f out: styd on wl towards fin* **13/2**

0043 **4** *nk* **Windforpower (IRE)**[3] 2052 6-8-11 60...........................(p) JoeFanning 4 60+
(Tracy Waggott) *t.k.h: chsd ldrs 1f: sn lost pl and in rr: pushed along 2f out: rdn and hdwy over 1f out: n.m.r ent fnl f: kpt on wl towards fin* **9/2**[1]

-000 **5** *2* **Ypres**[64] 856 7-8-11 65.. CallumShepherd(5) 3 57+
(Jason Ward) *in rr: hdwy 2f out: rdn over 1f out: styd on whn n.m.r and swtchd lft ent fnl f: sn rdn and kpt on wl towards fin* **8/1**

22-5 **6** *nk* **Oriental Splendour (IRE)**[20] 1559 4-9-6 69....................... JamesSullivan 8 60
(Ruth Carr) *in rr: hdwy 2f out: rdn to chse ldrs over 1f out: n.m.r ent fnl f and kpt on same pce* **9/1**

2523 **7** *1/2* **Taffetta**[13] 1790 4-9-3 66... BarryMcHugh 12 55
(Tony Coyle) *swtchd rt s and hld up in rr: swtchd lft to outer and hdwy 2f out: in tch and rdn along over 1f out: drvn and hung bdly lft to stands' rail ins fnl f: no imp* **12/1**

52-3 **8** *1 1/4* **Penny Royale**[43] 1119 4-9-6 69.....................................(p) DavidAllan 11 54
(Tim Easterby) *cl up: rdn along wl over 1f out: grad wknd appr fnl f* **6/1**[3]

5405 **9** *shd* **Mighty Zip (USA)**[24] 1490 4-8-7 63......................(p) LewisEdmunds(7) 10 48
(Kevin Ryan) *trckd ldrs on inner: effrt 2f out and sn rdn: drvn and wknd over 1f out* **20/1**

4-25 **10** *3/4* **Tinsill**[13] 1790 5-8-0 56 oh3......................................(p) KieranSchofield(7) 1 38
(Nigel Tinkler) *chsd ldrs on inner: rdn along 2f out: sn drvn and wknd* **12/1**

0-00 **11** *1 1/4* **Incomparable**[96] 444 11-8-7 56 oh9.........................(p) PJMcDonald 9 33
(Scott Dixon) *a towards rr* **50/1**

20-0 **12** *4 1/2* **Majestic Manannan (IRE)**[7] 1956 7-8-13 62.............. AndrewMullen 14 23
(David Nicholls) *cl up on outer: rdn along wl over 1f out: sn drvn and wknd* **25/1**

1m 2.32s (-1.18) **Going Correction** -0.15s/f (Firm) **12 Ran SP% 117.3**
Speed ratings (Par 103): **103,101,99,98,95 95,94,92,92,91 89,81**
CSF £62.19 CT £390.91 TOTE £8.30: £2.30, £2.20, £2.50; EX 70.50 Trifecta £437.90.
Owner Miss M E Rowland **Bred** Brook Stud Bloodstock Ltd **Trained** Lower Blidworth, Notts

FOCUS
A competitive sprint on paper, but it was dominated throughout by the winner. The form is rated around the second.

2121 JAMES "DOUG" NORRIS IS 60 TODAY H'CAP — 1m 100y

3:30 (3:30) (Class 4) (0-85,84) 4-Y-O+ **£6,301** (£1,886; £943; £472; £235) **Stalls** Low

Form RPR

50-4 **1** **Hulcolt (IRE)**[8] 1924 5-8-13 76.................................... GrahamGibbons 6 85
(Ivan Furtado) *cl up: led 1 1/2f out: rdn and kpt on wl fnl f* **9/2**[2]

0-53 **2** *1 1/2* **Taper Tantrum (IRE)**[15] 1702 4-9-1 81............................ LouisSteward(3) 3 87
(Michael Bell) *trckd ldng pair on inner: swtchd lft and effrt over 1f out: sn chsng wnr: rdn ins fnl f: no imp towards fin* **5/1**[3]

525- **3** *1 3/4* **Hard To Handel**[200] 7434 4-9-6 83................................ DanielTudhope 10 85+
(David O'Meara) *trckd ldrs: hdwy over 2f out: rdn over 1f out: kpt on fnl f* **9/1**

001- **4** *hd* **Chiswick Bey (IRE)**[194] 7591 8-8-9 72........................ TonyHamilton 14 73+
(Richard Fahey) *in rr: hdwy on inner over 2f out: rdn to chse ldrs over 1f out: kpt on wl fnl f* **25/1**

253- **5** *1 1/4* **Pumaflor (IRE)**[167] 7598 4-8-12 75............................ GeorgeChaloner 4 73
(Richard Whitaker) *chsd ldrs: rdn along wl over 2f out: drvn wl over 1f out: kpt on same pce* **18/1**

221- **6** *3/4* **Count Montecristo (FR)**[232] 6583 4-9-4 81...................... TomEaves 5 77
(Kevin Ryan) *led: jnd 3f out: rdn along 2f out: sn hdd: drvn and wknd appr fnl f* **4/1**[1]

-241 **7** *nse* **Farham (USA)**[17] 1632 4-8-6 72................................ SammyJoBell(3) 7 68
(Richard Fahey) *hld up: hdwy on outer over 2f out: rdn to chse ldrs over 1f out: drvn: edgd rt and kpt on same pce fnl f* **13/2**

6-00 **8** *2 1/2* **Auspicion**[17] 1643 4-8-12 75.. JamesSullivan 1 66
(Tom Tate) *midfield: sme hdwy on inner 3f out: rdn along 2f out: no imp fnl f* **14/1**

34-0 **9** *1* **Marsh Pride**[22] 1521 4-9-7 84.. PJMcDonald 8 72
(Ann Duffield) *chsd ldrs: effrt wl over 2f out and sn rdn: drvn and wknd wl over 1f out* **9/1**

05-0 **10** *1* **Zeshov (IRE)**[22] 1521 5-8-8 71..................................... BarryMcHugh 12 57
(Rebecca Bastiman) *a towards rr* **80/1**

000- **11** *2 3/4* **Inspector Norse**[316] 3723 5-8-3 71..................... RachelRichardson(5) 9 51
(Tim Easterby) *a towards rr* **33/1**

02-0 **12** *2 1/2* **Border Bandit (USA)**[8] 1924 8-8-13 76.......................(p) JoeFanning 11 50
(Tracy Waggott) *towards rr: swtchd to outer and sme hdwy 3f out: rdn over 2f out and sn wknd* **16/1**

315- **13** *29* **Regal Ways (IRE)**[42] 7287 4-8-6 74.......................... CallumShepherd(5) 2
(Brian Ellison) *towards rr: rdn along 3f out: drvn over 2f out: sn wknd and bhd* **25/1**

1m 44.5s (-3.10) **Going Correction** -0.225s/f (Firm) **13 Ran SP% 117.9**
Speed ratings (Par 105): **106,104,102,102,101 100,100,98,97,96 93,90,61**
CSF £25.91 CT £203.57 TOTE £5.30: £2.00, £2.30, £3.40; EX 26.40 Trifecta £389.10.
Owner Ron Hull **Bred** Kilshannig Stud **Trained** Wiseton, Nottinghamshire

FOCUS
This looked quite open but few got into it. It was sound run and the winner is rated back to form.

2122 HIGH DEFINITION RACING UK MAIDEN STKS — 7f 100y

4:00 (4:01) (Class 5) 3-Y-O **£3,780** (£1,131; £565; £283; £141) **Stalls** Low

Form RPR

02-2 **1** **Fawaareq (IRE)**[28] 1397 3-9-5 83.................................... PaulHanagan 4 82
(Owen Burrows) *trckd ldr: cl up 3f out: chal wl over 1f out: sn rdn and edgd rt: drvn end edgd rt 1f out: slt ld ins fnl f and hanging rt: drvn out* **2/5**[1]

22-2 **2** *nk* **Heir To A Throne (FR)**[17] 1622 3-9-5 83............................ ShaneGray 6 81
(Kevin Ryan) *led: jnd 3f out and sn pushed along: rdn wl over 1f out: drvn: edgd lft and sltly hmpd ent fnl f: sn hdd: kpt on wl* **4/1**[2]

3 *1 1/4* **Haraz (IRE)**[251] 6002 3-9-5 81...................................... DanielTudhope 2 78
(David O'Meara) *trckd ldng pair: effrt wl over 1f out: swtchd lft: drvn and ch ins fnl f: kpt on same pce* **7/1**[3]

00- **4** *9* **Clear Evidence**[201] 7411 3-9-5 0........................... WilliamTwiston-Davies 5 55
(Michael Bell) *trckd ldrs: pushed along wl over 2f out: rdn wl over 1f out: sn no imp* **22/1**

000- **5** *1 1/2* **Whitkirk**[189] 7673 3-9-5 36... TomEaves 7 52
(Jedd O'Keeffe) *wnt lft s: t.k.h and towards rr: pushed along over 3f out: rdn over 2f out: plugged on: nvr a factor* **100/1**

0 **6** *10* **Portland Street (IRE)**[15] 1691 3-9-5 0.......................... PaulMulrennan 3 27
(Bryan Smart) *chsd ldrs on inner: rdn along wl over 2f out: sn drvn and wknd* **50/1**

7 *1/2* **Beadlam (IRE)** 3-9-0 0.. SilvestreDeSousa 1 20
(David Loughnane) *s.i.s and green in rr: a bhd* **50/1**

1m 32.27s (-1.53) **Going Correction** -0.225s/f (Firm) **7 Ran SP% 113.2**
Speed ratings (Par 99): **99,98,97,86,85 73,73**
CSF £2.24 TOTE £1.30: £1.10, £1.60; EX 2.70 Trifecta £4.60.
Owner Hamdan Al Maktoum **Bred** Shadwell Estate Company Limited **Trained** Lambourn, Berks

FOCUS
A fair maiden, with the first three all coming into the race rated in the low 80s. They finished clear and are rated close to their marks.

2123 HAPPY 70TH BIRTHDAY GRAHAM ROBERTS H'CAP — 1m 1f 207y

4:30 (4:33) (Class 5) (0-70,70) 3-Y-O **£3,780** (£1,131; £565; £283; £141) **Stalls** Low

Form RPR

00-5 **1** **Livella Fella (IRE)**[17] 1619 3-9-2 65............................... PhillipMakin 11 72
(Keith Dalgleish) *trckd ldrs: cl up 1/2-way: led 3f out: rdn and hdd 2f out: cl up: drvn and edgd lft ent fnl f: styd on to ld again last 75yds* **12/1**

44-2 **2** 3/4 **The Major**[19] 1587 3-9-4 **70**... LouisSteward(3) 7 76
(Michael Bell) *trckd ldrs: smooth hdwy on outer 3f out: led 2f out: rdn and edgd lft over 1f out: drvn and hung lft to stands' rail ent fnl f: hdd and no ex last 75yds* **7/2**[1]

004- **3** 3 3/4 **Kajaki (IRE)**[178] 7863 3-9-7 **70**... ShaneGray 9 68
(Kevin Ryan) *chsd ldng pair: hdwy 3f out: rdn 2f out: drvn and edgd rt jst over 1f out: kpt on u.p fnl f* **8/1**

0-03 **4** hd **Palmerston**[19] 1587 3-9-4 **67**... BenCurtis 4 65+
(Michael Appleby) *t.k.h: hld up in rr: sddle slipped 6f out to 3f out: hdwy wl over 2f out: rdn wl over 1f out: swtchd rt to inner and drvn ent fnl f: kpt on wl towards fin* **7/1**[3]

550U **5** 1/2 **Topalova**[15] 1705 3-8-8 **57**... SaleemGolam 6 54
(Mark H Tompkins) *hld up towards rr: hdwy over 2f out: effrt whn n.m.r and swtchd lft over 1f out: sn rdn and kpt on fnl f* **9/1**

-114 **6** 4 1/2 **Palpitation (IRE)**[42] 1137 3-9-7 **70**... TomEaves 8 58
(David Brown) *trckd ldrs: effrt on outer: wl over 2f out and sn rdn: wkng and hld whn sltly hmpd over 1f out* **9/1**

652- **7** nk **Like No Other**[148] 8224 3-9-7 **70**... GrahamGibbons 3 57
(Les Eyre) *in tch: effrt and hdwy over 2f out: rdn wl over 1f out: swtchd rt and drvn appr fnl f: sn one pce* **5/1**[2]

144- **8** 1 1/2 **Royal Pearl**[176] 7870 3-9-0 **63**... DougieCostello 5 47
(Tom Gretton) *dwlt and in rr: rdn along and hdwy 2f out: swtchd rt over 1f out: kpt on fnl f* **33/1**

-040 **9** 1 3/4 **Autumn Blossom (USA)**[19] 1584 3-9-0 **63**... JoeFanning 2 44
(Mark Johnston) *chsd ldrs: rdn along over 2f out: drvn wl over 1f out: sn wknd* **7/1**[3]

030- **10** 29 **Lozah**[209] 7212 3-9-3 **66**... SilvestreDeSousa 10
(David Loughnane) *led: rdn along and hdd 3f out: sn drvn and wknd* **20/1**

2m 7.48s (0.48) **Going Correction** -0.225s/f (Firm) **10** Ran SP% **110.4**
Speed ratings (Par 99): **89,88,85,85,84 81,81,79,78,55**
CSF £48.73 CT £312.68 TOTE £13.10: £3.00, £2.10, £2.70; EX 63.80 Trifecta £362.90.
Owner Middleham Park Racing Xxiii **Bred** Manister House Stud **Trained** Carluke, S Lanarks
■ G'day Aussie (11-1). Rule 4 applies to all bets. Deduction - 5p in the pound.

FOCUS
A modest handicap. The winner is rated to her early level.

2124 BEVERLEY MIDDLE DISTANCE SERIES H'CAP 1m 4f 16y
5:00 (5:00) (Class 6) (0-60,60) 3-Y-O **£2,587** (£770; £384; £192) **Stalls** Low

Form RPR

00-2 **1** **Scarpeta (FR)**[14] 1740 3-9-0 **53**... JoeFanning 3 61
(Mark Johnston) *trckd ldr: cl up 5f out: led over 3f out: rdn wl over 1f out: drvn ins fnl f: hld on wl towards fin* **11/8**[1]

00-4 **2** 3/4 **Adherence**[19] 1587 3-9-3 **56**... BarryMcHugh 7 63
(Tony Coyle) *trckd ldrs: hdwy 3f out: rdn over 1f out: chsd wnr ins fnl f: sn drvn and kpt on* **11/1**

4002 **3** 3/4 **Mikro Polemistis (IRE)**[12] 1819 3-8-5 **49**... CallumShepherd(5) 5 55
(Brian Ellison) *hld up in tch: effrt on inner and n.m.r over 2f out: sn rdn along: swtchd lft and hdwy over 1f out: kpt on strly fnl f* **14/1**

5500 **4** 2 3/4 **Falcon's Fire (IRE)**[21] 1551 3-9-0 **53**... PhillipMakin 10 54
(Keith Dalgleish) *dwlt and bhd: hdwy over 3f out: rdn wl over 1f out: styd on wl fnl f: nrst fin* **20/1**

420- **5** 1 **Permera**[204] 7336 3-9-6 **59**... SaleemGolam 8 59
(Mark H Tompkins) *trckd ldrs: hdwy over 3f out: c lose up over 2f out: rdn wl over 1f out: drvn and one pce ent fnl f* **12/1**

6314 **6** 3 **Rainbow Lad (IRE)**[33] 1297 3-9-2 **55**... BenCurtis 1 50
(Michael Appleby) *led: jnd 5f out: rdn along and hdd over 3f out: drvn over 2f out: sn wknd* **6/1**[2]

1455 **7** 1 1/4 **Big Shoes (IRE)**[15] 1705 3-8-12 **51**... DarryllHolland 9 44
(Charles Hills) *hld up: effrt and sme hdwy over 3f out: rdn along over 2f out: sn btn* **10/1**

0-05 **8** 1/2 **Citadel**[12] 1819 3-8-7 **46** oh1...(v) RoystonFfrench 2 38
(John Wainwright) *chsd ldrs on inner: rdn along over 3f out: sn wknd* **100/1**

445- **9** 3/4 **Goodknight Percy (IRE)**[240] 6346 3-9-7 **60**...(p) TomEaves 11 51
(Kevin Ryan) *a towards rr* **14/1**

540- **10** 2 1/4 **Miss Marina Bay**[249] 6042 3-9-2 **55**... RyanPowell 4 42
(Sir Mark Prescott Bt) *towards rr: sme hdwy on outer 4f out: rdn along 3f out and nvr a factor* **15/2**[3]

0-40 **11** 2 **Tred Softly (IRE)**[56] 945 3-9-5 **58**... DougieCostello 6 42
(John Quinn) *hld up: a towards rr* **20/1**

2m 39.58s (-0.22) **Going Correction** -0.225s/f (Firm) **11** Ran SP% **117.1**
Speed ratings (Par 97): **91,90,90,88,87 85,84,84,83,82 81**
CSF £17.26 CT £155.82 TOTE £2.10: £1.10, £4.20, £3.30; EX 19.80 Trifecta £185.40.
Owner Brian Yeardley **Bred** Mme Michele Bliard **Trained** Middleham Moor, N Yorks

FOCUS
Stamina came to the fore in this moderate middle-distance handicap for 3yos. There's more to come from the winner.
T/Jkpt: Not won. T/Plt: £27.20 to a £1 stake. Pool: £63,633.38 - 1,706.30 winning tickets. T/Qpdt: £21.60 to a £1 stake. Pool: £4,265.41 - 145.54 winning tickets. **Joe Rowntree**

1824 CHEPSTOW (L-H)
Tuesday, May 10

OFFICIAL GOING: Soft (7.6)
Wind: slight half against Weather: cloudy, drizzle from race 6

2125 DRIBUILD DASH NOVICE AUCTION STKS 5f 16y
5:25 (5:25) (Class 5) 2-Y-O **£3,234** (£962; £481; £240) **Stalls** Centre

Form RPR

4 **1** **Nazik**[14] 1736 2-9-2 0... JFEgan 9 71
(David Evans) *w ldr: rdn to ld 2f out: jnd 1f out: hld on wl u.p* **3/1**[2]

2 **2** nk **Tap Tap Boom**[13] 1776 2-9-2 0... SteveDrowne 1 70
(George Baker) *chsd ldrs: rdn 2f out: ev ch fnl f: jst hld* **4/1**[3]

3 3 **Just An Idea (IRE)** 2-9-2 0... LukeMorris 4 59
(Harry Dunlop) *narrow ld tl rdn and hdd 2f out: outpcd by ldng pair fnl f* **6/1**

26 **4** 1/2 **Zig Zag Girl**[19] 1583 2-8-11 0... CharlesBishop 10 52
(Mick Channon) *t.k.h: in rr but wl in tch: pushed along over 1f out: kpt on same pce fnl f* **4/1**[3]

5 **5** 2 1/2 **Secret Coin (IRE)**[8] 1915 2-8-11 0... WilliamCarson 5 43
(Jamie Osborne) *bmpd leaving stalls: in rr but wl in tch: clsd 1/2-way: rdn over 1f out: outpcd fnl f* **11/4**[1]

46 **6** shd **Hot N Sassy (IRE)**[36] 1233 2-8-6 0... JosephineGordon(5) 2 43
(J S Moore) *cl up to 1/2-way: last and rdn 2f out: no imp after* **20/1**

1m 1.06s (1.76) **Going Correction** +0.20s/f (Good) **6** Ran SP% **110.7**
Speed ratings (Par 93): **93,92,87,86,82 82**
CSF £14.80 TOTE £3.60: £2.30, £1.90; EX 13.90 Trifecta £67.00.
Owner Naser Buresli **Bred** Abingdon & Witney College **Trained** Pandy, Monmouths

FOCUS
There was 21mm of rain the previous evening and overnight, resulting in the ground softening considerably. John Egan felt it was "soft but not holding - they're getting through it". A couple of key non-runners here and it was left looking quite a modest event. They raced near to the stands' rail. The form is rated around the race average.

2126 EQUESTRIAN SURFACES LTD H'CAP 1m 4f 23y
5:55 (5:56) (Class 6) (0-65,65) 3-Y-O **£2,587** (£770; £384; £192) **Stalls** Low

Form RPR

46-2 **1** **Regal Monarch**[17] 1619 3-9-7 **65**... FrannyNorton 6 76
(Mark Johnston) *chsd ldrs: wnt 2nd 3f out: led over 1f out: drvn and styd on wl* **11/4**[1]

00-1 **2** 1 1/4 **Hint Of Grey (IRE)**[7] 1948 3-8-0 **51** 6ex... GeorgeWood(7) 3 60
(Don Cantillon) *hld up: hdwy over 3f out: sn rdn: styd on to go 2nd 100yds out: a being hld by wnr* **7/1**[3]

0-06 **3** 2 **Stonecoldsoba**[69] 778 3-8-13 **57**... CathyGannon 12 63
(David Evans) *led after 1f: racd wd tl crossed over after 4f: rdn over 2f out: hdd over 1f out: one pce after: lost 2nd 100yds out* **28/1**

316- **4** 3 **Masterson (IRE)**[223] 6859 3-9-5 **63**... GeorgeBaker 11 64
(Mick Channon) *hld up: hdwy 3f out: rdn in 4th 2f out: kpt on same pce* **9/1**

60-5 **5** 7 **Prospectus**[36] 1235 3-9-6 **64**... LiamKeniry 9 54
(Hughie Morrison) *t.k.h in mid-div: sme hdwy 3f out: rdn and no further imp fnl 2f* **5/1**[2]

6435 **6** 6 **Howardian Hills (IRE)**[22] 1532 3-9-3 **64**... TomMarquand(3) 10 44
(Richard Hannon) *led 1f: trckd ldr: rdn 4f out: lost 2nd 3f out: wknd 2f out* **12/1**

2205 **7** 1/2 **Gabster (IRE)**[10] 1860 3-9-2 **65**... HectorCrouch(5) 5 44
(Amanda Perrett) *prom 1f: sn in mid-div: pushed along over 4f out: wknd over 2f out* **16/1**

222- **8** hd **Tenzing Norgay**[201] 7412 3-9-5 **63**... LukeMorris 4 42
(Sir Mark Prescott Bt) *s.i.s: in rr: rdn over 4f out: hdwy to chse ldrs 3f out: wknd 2f out* **5/1**[2]

4661 **9** 1 3/4 **Harry's Endeavour**[14] 1740 3-9-4 **62**...(p) TimmyMurphy 8 38
(Daniel Kubler) *chsd ldrs: rdn 3f out: sn wknd* **14/1**

0-63 **10** 14 **Mischief Maisy (IRE)**[13] 1779 3-8-12 **56**... JimCrowley 1 10
(Amanda Perrett) *mid-div tl rdn and lost pl 5f out: no ch fnl 3f* **25/1**

0-05 **11** nk **French Legend**[14] 1740 3-8-9 **53**... DavidProbert 13 6
(Andrew Balding) *chsd ldrs: rdn over 3f out: wknd over 2f out* **12/1**

2m 43.32s (4.32) **Going Correction** +0.575s/f (Yiel) **11** Ran SP% **117.7**
Speed ratings (Par 97): **108,107,105,103,99 95,94,94,93,84 84**
CSF £22.01 CT £448.30 TOTE £3.10: £1.60, £1.60, £7.90; EX 24.60 Trifecta £591.10.
Owner East Layton Stud Ltd **Bred** A H Bennett **Trained** Middleham Moor, N Yorks

FOCUS
Little got into this 3yo handicap, the first and third being up there throughout, and the runner-up therefore needs her effort upgrading. The winner has improved this year.

2127 PHIL BESSANT LIMITED - CHARTERED MANAGEMENT ACCOUNTANTS FILLIES' H'CAP 1m 2f 36y
6:25 (6:25) (Class 5) (0-70,69) 4-Y-O+ **£3,234** (£962; £481; £240) **Stalls** Low

Form RPR

054 **1** **Owners Day**[22] 1529 6-9-1 **63**... LiamKeniry 7 72
(Neil Mulholland) *t.k.h: chsd ldrs: pushed along over 3f out: bmpd twice arnd 2f out: led and hung lft over 1f out: styd on u.p* **8/1**

-400 **2** 2 1/4 **Coup De Vent**[21] 1548 5-8-7 **55** oh3...(be[1]) LukeMorris 5 59
(John O'Shea) *hld up towards rr: rdn over 3f out: hdwy over 2f out: ev ch over 1f out: outpcd by wnr ins fnl f* **25/1**

00-1 **3** 1 1/2 **Distant High**[11] 1825 5-8-13 **64**...(p) TomMarquand(3) 4 65
(Richard Price) *prom: trckd ldr after 2f: rdn 3f out: ev ch over 2f out tl over 1f out: one pce* **9/4**[2]

2544 **4** 2 **Ixelles Diamond (IRE)**[34] 1266 5-8-13 **64**... DanielMuscutt(3) 2 61
(Andrew Reid) *t.k.h: chsd ldr 2f: styd prom: rdn 4f out: led over 2f out: sn edgd rt: hdd and carried lft over 1f out: one pce* **6/1**[3]

-006 **5** 1 1/4 **Dark Amber**[13] 1775 6-9-7 **69**... FMBerry 3 64
(Brendan Powell) *s.i.s: towards rr: rdn and clsd over 3f out: one pce and no imp fnl 2f* **13/8**[1]

6 3/4 **Balmont Belle (IRE)**[508] 8234 6-8-7 **58**... TimClark(3) 1 51
(Barry Leavy) *half rrd as stalls opened and s.s: bhd: rdn 3f out: styd on fnl f but nvr able to threaten* **25/1**

400- **7** 5 **Suzi Icon**[224] 6840 4-8-9 **57**... JFEgan 6 40
(John Butler) *led: rdn over 3f out: hdd over 2f out: sn hung rt: wknd appr fnl f* **8/1**

2m 15.41s (4.81) **Going Correction** +0.575s/f (Yiel) **7** Ran SP% **113.1**
Speed ratings (Par 100): **103,101,100,98,97 96,92**
CSF £158.28 TOTE £10.20: £4.80, £10.00; EX 117.70 Trifecta £397.10.
Owner The Dickinsons, Clegg, Finch & Lacey **Bred** C And Mrs Wilson **Trained** Limpley Stoke, Wilts

FOCUS
Moderate handicap form, with the front two in the market disappointing, although an unexposed winner. A step up from the winner with the second to her AW form.

2128 STREAMLINE LEISURE SUPPORTS THE NATIONAL EISTEDDFOD AUCTION STKS 1m 14y
6:55 (6:55) (Class 6) 3-Y-O **£2,587** (£770; £384; £192) **Stalls** Centre

Form RPR

0- **1** **Threat Assessed (IRE)**[200] 7435 3-9-5 0... JohnFahy 7 81+
(Clive Cox) *ct on heels jst after leaving stalls: towards rr: hdwy after 2f: qcknd to ld over 2f out: nudged along and easily drew clr fnl f* **5/4**[1]

5-33 **2** 6 **Zauffaly (FR)**[17] 1638 3-9-5 75...(b) JimCrowley 8 66
(Ed Dunlop) *chsd ldrs: rdn and unable qck 3f out: kpt on fnl f to go 2nd nr fin: no ch w wnr* **11/8**[2]

0-0 **3** nk **Wilspa's Magic (IRE)**[25] 1451 3-9-0 0... DavidProbert 9 60
(Ron Hodges) *led narrowly 2f: styd prom: rdn and unable qck over 2f out: disp modest 2nd fnl f* **66/1**

00- **4** nk **Reaver (IRE)**[183] 7777 3-9-5 0... RobertWinston 4 64
(Eve Johnson Houghton) *cl up: led after 2f: pushed along and hdd over 2f out: sn outpcd by wnr: hld modest 2nd tl lost 2 pls nr fin* **10/1**

462- **5** 10 **Arcanista (IRE)**[238] 6413 3-9-0 63... ShaneKelly 2 37
(Richard Hughes) *hld up: rdn and no imp on ldrs 3f out: wknd appr fnl f* **8/1**[3]

4-00 **6** 24 **Cay Location (IRE)**[44] 1113 3-9-5 31............................(p) KieranO'Neill 3
(Ed de Giles) *cl up: rdn and qckly lost pl over 3f out: t.o fnl f* **100/1**
1m 36.26s (0.06) **Going Correction** +0.20s/f (Good) **6** Ran SP% **109.2**
Speed ratings (Par 97): **107,101,100,100,90 66**
CSF £3.02 TOTE £2.50: £1.60, £1.10; EX 2.90 Trifecta £42.40.
Owner Alan G Craddock **Bred** Roundhill Stud **Trained** Lambourn, Berks

FOCUS
Little depth to this modest maiden, with the runner-up not looking to run to his 75 rating, but a taking effort from the winner nonetheless.

2129 STEDMAN BROTHERS EVENTS SUPPORTS THE NATIONAL EISTEDDFOD H'CAP 1m 14y
7:25 (7:25) (Class 5) (0-75,74) 4-Y-O+ **£3,234** (£962; £481; £240) **Stalls** Centre

Form RPR
55-0 **1** **Lady Bayside**[14] 1735 8-8-3 **61**............................ JosephineGordon(5) 1 69
(Malcolm Saunders) *led: drvn 2f out: jnd ins fnl f: asserted fnl 100yds* **8/1**[3]
13-0 **2** 1 1/4 **Red Cossack (CAN)**[11] 1838 5-9-3 **70**....................(t) WilliamCarson 12 75
(Paul Webber) *hld up in 4th: rdn and hdwy 3f out: chal ins fnl f: nt qckn fnl 100yds: jst hld 2nd* **11/1**
02-1 **3** shd **Double Czech (IRE)**[29] 1387 5-9-4 **71**.......................... DavidProbert 11 76
(Patrick Chamings) *cl up: rdn and ev ch 2f out: sn unable qck: kpt on ins fnl f: jst missed 2nd* **4/5**[1]
54-2 **4** 1 **Zaria**[17] 1632 5-8-2 **60**..(p) PatrickO'Donnell(5) 8 64
(Richard Price) *trckd ldng pair: upsides 3f out: rdn 2f out: hit on hd by rival's whip over 1f out and sn lost grnd on ldrs: styd on ins fnl f* **5/2**[2]
0-00 **5** 6 **Yeats Magic (IRE)**[108] 313 4-9-7 **74**............................ GeorgeBaker 9 63
(Ronald Harris) *s.s: bhd: clsd 1/2-way: rdn over 2f out: wknd over 1f out* **16/1**
1m 36.94s (0.74) **Going Correction** +0.20s/f (Good) **5** Ran SP% **109.5**
Speed ratings (Par 103): **104,102,102,101,95**
CSF £73.79 TOTE £9.40: £5.10, £5.10; EX 89.40 Trifecta £180.70.
Owner M S Saunders **Bred** M Saunders & T Bostwick **Trained** Green Ore, Somerset

FOCUS
Only five of the 12 originally declared took part in what was a modest handicap. The winner took advantage of a good mark.

2130 NEPTUNUS STRUCTURES H'CAP 6f 16y
7:55 (7:55) (Class 5) (0-70,70) 4-Y-O+ **£3,234** (£962; £481; £240) **Stalls** Centre

Form RPR
50-5 **1** **Fantasy Justifier (IRE)**[24] 1489 5-9-6 **69**.................... GeorgeBaker 11 77+
(Ronald Harris) *prom: rdn to ld over 1f out: hld on gamely u.p ins fnl f* **6/1**[3]
0216 **2** nk **Posh Bounty**[8] 1928 5-9-5 **68**.. JFEgan 10 75
(Joseph Tuite) *mid-div: swtchd rt after 1f: drvn over 2f out: r.o wl fnl f: tk 2nd post but jst hld by wnr* **6/1**[3]
16-5 **3** shd **Consistant**[16] 1676 8-8-10 **59**.. SamHitchcott 1 66+
(Brian Baugh) *s.i.s: towards rr: pushed along and hdwy 1/2-way: rdn 2f out: ev ch ins fnl f: jst hld: lost 2nd post* **25/1**
5040 **4** 2 **Noverre To Go (IRE)**[15] 1720 10-9-1 **64**...................... SteveDrowne 2 65
(Ronald Harris) *prom: led after 2f: rdn over 2f out: hdd over 1f out: kpt on fnl f* **20/1**
1523 **5** hd **Indian Affair**[8] 1928 6-9-7 **70**......................................(bt) FrannyNorton 9 70
(Milton Bradley) *chsd ldrs: rdn 2f out: sltly outpcd over 1f out: kpt on towards fin* **11/2**[2]
40-0 **6** 1/2 **Bonjour Steve**[18] 1595 5-8-13 **65**..........................(p) TomMarquand(3) 16 63
(Richard Price) *chsd ldrs: rdn over 2f out: styd on same pce fnl f* **6/1**[3]
6361 **7** shd **Secret Look**[22] 1533 6-9-1 **64**..................................... MartinDwyer 3 62
(Ed McMahon) *in tch towards rr: clsd 1/2-way: drvn over 1f out: unable qck fnl f* **9/2**[1]
46-0 **8** 1 1/4 **Mad Endeavour**[22] 1533 5-8-6 **58**........................(t) MatthewCosham(3) 4 52
(Stuart Kittow) *midfield: rdn 1/2-way: edgd rt and rdn 2f out: sn one pce and no real imp* **9/1**
0066 **9** nk **Ambitious Boy**[15] 1724 7-9-2 **65**...................................... CathyGannon 6 58
(John O'Shea) *s.s: bhd: rdn over 3f out: styd on fnl f but nvr any ch* **14/1**
000- **10** 1 1/2 **Orbit The Moon (IRE)**[210] 7197 8-9-1 **64**...............(tp) StevieDonohoe 15 52
(Grace Harris) *chsd ldrs: outpcd over 2f out: no imp after* **33/1**
10-0 **11** 2 1/4 **Secret Bird (IRE)**[22] 1533 4-8-13 **62**......................... RobertWinston 17 43
(Dean Ivory) *led 2f: styd prom: rdn 1/2-way: wknd appr fnl f* **20/1**
200- **12** nse **Jaganory (IRE)**[205] 7312 4-8-8 **62**............................ EdwardGreatrex(5) 7 43
(Christopher Mason) *chsd ldrs: rdn over 2f out: wknd over 1f out* **12/1**
-024 **13** hd **Mambo Spirit (IRE)**[60] 904 12-8-13 **65**........................ EoinWalsh(3) 8 45
(Tony Newcombe) *s.s: bhd: swtchd rt after 1f: rdn 1/2-way: nvr any ch* **25/1**
1m 12.55s (0.55) **Going Correction** +0.20s/f (Good) **13** Ran SP% **120.9**
Speed ratings (Par 103): **104,103,103,100,100 99,99,98,97,95 92,92,92**
CSF £39.06 CT £881.47 TOTE £7.60: £3.00, £2.80, £5.70; EX 48.10 Trifecta £342.70.
Owner RHS Ltd & Farley & Northern Marking Ltd **Bred** Denis And Mrs Teresa Bergin **Trained** Earlswood, Monmouths

FOCUS
They were spread across the track in this sprint. The winner is rated to his best.

2131 NATIONAL EISTEDDFOD OF WALES DAY H'CAP 2m 49y
8:25 (8:25) (Class 6) (0-60,61) 4-Y-O+ **£2,587** (£770; £384; £192) **Stalls** Low

Form RPR
1063 **1** **Tarakkom (FR)**[11] 1831 4-9-0 **56**................................... CathyGannon 3 64
(Peter Hiatt) *racd keenly: mde virtually all: drvn over 2f out: 2 l up 1f out: jnd 100yds out: stuck nk out to assert last strides* **7/2**[1]
43-2 **2** hd **Fuzzy Logic (IRE)**[11] 1831 7-8-10 **49**............................(b) DavidProbert 1 57
(Bernard Llewellyn) *rousted along early: mid-div: rdn to chse wnr over 2f out: 2 l down 1f out: styd on and ev ch fnl 100yds: hld last strides* **4/1**[2]
6/36 **3** 4 **Prince Of Islay (IRE)**[14] 1748 5-8-11 **50**........................(b) FrannyNorton 8 53
(Amanda Perrett) *chsd ldrs: drvn over 3f out: outpcd by ldng pair over 2f out: stuck on same pce to hold 3rd* **9/2**[3]
4-04 **4** 1/2 **Agreement (IRE)**[11] 1830 6-9-1 **59**...................(b) EdwardGreatrex(5) 6 61
(Nikki Evans) *rdn along early: towards rr: drvn 4f out: no real imp tl styd on fnl f* **8/1**
6562 **5** 5 **Thimaar (USA)**[11] 1830 8-9-1 **54**...............................(b) KieranO'Neill 4 50
(Sarah Hollinshead) *trckd wnr tl drvn and lost 2nd over 3f out: one pce after* **5/1**
50-6 **6** 2 3/4 **Taste The Wine (IRE)**[11] 1830 10-9-1 **61** ow1....(t) JordanWilliams(7) 10 54
(Bernard Llewellyn) *a abt same pl: rdn 3f out: one pce and nvr able to chal* **10/1**
6 **7** nk **Arthur's Queen (FR)**[11] 1831 5-8-12 **58**................... MeganNicholls(7) 2 51
(Carroll Gray) *chsd ldrs: rdn and outpcd 3f out: styd on again ins fnl f* **16/1**
3542 **8** 1 1/2 **Delagoa Bay (IRE)**[21] 1550 8-8-4 **50**........................ BenSanderson(7) 12 41
(Sylvester Kirk) *s.i.s: effrt 4f out: a towards rr* **12/1**
0/6- **9** 33 **Proud Times (USA)**[43] 1032 10-9-0 **53**.....................(p) CharlesBishop 11 4
(Ali Stronge) *towards rr: rdn 5f out: eased 3f out: t.o* **33/1**
3m 47.15s (8.25) **Going Correction** +0.575s/f (Yiel)
WFA 4 from 5yo+ 3lb **9** Ran SP% **113.8**
Speed ratings (Par 101): **102,101,99,99,97 95,95,94,78**
CSF £17.21 CT £62.62 TOTE £3.90: £1.80, £1.90, £1.70; EX 15.10 Trifecta £133.80.
Owner Phil Kelly **Bred** Shadwell Farm **Trained** Hook Norton, Oxon

FOCUS
No hanging around in this staying handicap, with duelling leaders early, and the winner, who was one of those, was as brave as they come in the finish. The first two were both up slightly on recent C&D form.
T/Plt: £2,466.00 to a £1 stake. Pool: £64,656.93 - 19.14 winning tickets. T/Qpdt: £366.00 to a £1 stake. Pool: £6,574.20 - 13.29 winning tickets. **Richard Lowther**

2132 - 2139a (Foreign Racing) - See Raceform Interactive

2115 CHANTILLY (R-H)
Tuesday, May 10

OFFICIAL GOING: Turf: good to soft; polytrack: standard

2140a PRIX DE GUICHE (GROUP 3) (3YO COLTS) (TURF) 1m 1f
11:40 (12:00) 3-Y-O **£29,411** (£11,764; £8,823; £5,882)

RPR
1 **Almanzor (FR)**[20] 1580 3-9-2 0.......................... ChristopheSoumillon 2 111+
(J-C Rouget, France) *mde all: travelling strly 2f out: qcknd clr appr fnl f: easily* **10/11**[1]
2 2 **Floodlight (USA)**[47] 3-9-2 0.................................... VincentCheminaud 4 103
(A Fabre, France) *chsd ldr: rdn and nt qckn 2f out: dropped to last appr fnl f: rallied u.p to regain 2nd cl home: no ch w wnr* **6/4**[2]
3 hd **Gardol City (FR)**[16] 3-9-2 0.. CristianDemuro 3 103
(G Botti, France) *w.w in 3rd: clsd to press for 2nd 2f out: styd on to go 2nd over 1f out: sn rdn and kpt on at one pce: lost 2nd cl home* **7/1**[3]
4 nse **Ankle (FR)**[30] 3-9-2 0... MaximeGuyon 1 102
(C Ferland, France) *settled in rr: rdn to stay on and go 3rd wl over 1f out: kpt on at same pce fnl f* **17/2**
1m 53.98s (2.88) **4** Ran SP% **115.4**
WIN (incl. 1 euro stake): 2.00. PLACES: 1.10, 1.10. SF: 2.90.
Owner Ecurie Antonio Caro & Gerard Augustin-Normand **Bred** Haras D'Etreham **Trained** Pau, France

2141a PRIX DU VAL SAINT-GEORGES (CONDITIONS) (3YO) (POLYTRACK) 6f 110y
12:10 (12:00) 3-Y-O **£10,661** (£4,264; £3,198; £2,132; £1,066)

RPR
1 **Basilia**[20] 3-8-10 0..(b) Pierre-CharlesBoudot 10 87
(Mme A Fabre, France) **154/10**
2 snk **Spiritfix**[42] 3-8-6 0.. MaximeGuyon 7 83
(A Fabre, France) **47/10**[2]
3 1 1/4 **House Of Dixie (USA)**[56] 3-8-11 0 ow1............. ChristopheSoumillon 6 84
(J-C Rouget, France) **19/10**[1]
4 1/2 **Pop By (USA)**[189] 3-8-10 0..................................... StephanePasquier 11 82
(F-H Graffard, France) **9/1**
5 hd **Never Compromise (FR)**[33] 1311 3-9-0 0...................... RafaelSchistl 9 85
(Henk Grewe, Germany) **10/1**
6 1 **Octavia (FR)**[39] 3-8-6 0 ow1.. LukasDelozier(5) 1 79
(H-A Pantall, France) **18/1**
7 1 3/4 **Secretjim (FR)**[273] 3-8-4 0.. PierreBazire(5) 2 72
(P Bary, France) **32/1**
8 snk **Laris (FR)**[44] 3-9-0 0... AntoineWerle 5 77
(T Lemer, France) **15/1**
9 2 1/2 **Accurate**[20] 3-9-0 0.. VincentCheminaud 4 70
(A Fabre, France) **9/1**
10 4 1/2 **Signs Of Success (IRE)**[33] 1308 3-9-0 0.................... CristianDemuro 8 57
(M Delcher Sanchez, France) **54/10**[3]
11 15 **Joules**[27] 1423 3-8-9 0.. IoritzMendizabal 3
(Natalie Lloyd-Beavis) *chsd ldrs: rdn and n.m.r appr 2f out: wknd 1 1/2f out: sn wl bhd and eased ins fnl f* **24/1**
\n\x\x WIN (incl. 1 euro stake): 16.40. PLACES: 3.10, 1.80, 1.40. DF: 60.70. SF:
Owner Mme Andre Fabre **Bred** Ecurie Peregrine SAS **Trained** France

2142 - (Foreign Racing) - See Raceform Interactive

1913 BATH (L-H)
Wednesday, May 11

OFFICIAL GOING: Soft (good to soft in places; 6.6)
Wind: almost nil Weather: overcast/humid

2143 WELLSWAY BATH H'CAP 5f 161y
5:30 (5:30) (Class 6) (0-60,60) 3-Y-O **£2,264** (£673; £336; £168) **Stalls** Centre

Form RPR
-631 **1** **Bushwise (IRE)**[12] 1829 3-9-3 56.................................(p) OisinMurphy 1 61
(Milton Bradley) *chsd ldrs: rdn wl over 2f out: led jst ins fnl f: r.o* **10/3**[2]
06-0 **2** 3/4 **Blackdown Warrior**[12] 1829 3-8-0 46........................ GeorgeWood(7) 6 49
(Rod Millman) *chsd ldrs: rdn wl over 2f out: r.o ins fnl f: wnt 2nd cl home* **8/1**
0605 **3** nk **Allen's Folly**[15] 1761 3-8-9 48.. CathyGannon 4 50
(Peter Hiatt) *rdn over 2f out: hdd jst ins fnl f: no ex cl home* **12/1**
44-4 **4** 3/4 **Sabato (IRE)**[12] 1829 3-9-7 60.. TimmyMurphy 3 59
(Fergal O'Brien) *outpcd in last: hdwy over 1f out: styd on to go 4th ins fnl f: nvr gng pce to get involved* **4/1**[3]
005- **5** 2 3/4 **Secretfact**[289] 4704 3-8-12 51.. MartinDwyer 9 41
(Malcolm Saunders) *sn pressed ldr: rdn and ev ch 2f out tl ent fnl f: wknd* **12/1**
6-05 **6** 9 **Canford Belle**[15] 1745 3-9-1 59.............................. KieranShoemark(5) 7 19
(Amanda Perrett) *in tch: rdn 3f out: wknd over 1f out* **9/2**
406 **7** 8 **Aegean Boy**[42] 1151 3-9-3 59................................. AlistairRawlinson(3) 5
(Michael Appleby) *little slowly away and sn pushed along to stay in tch: wknd 2f out* **3/1**[1]
1m 15.2s (4.00) **Going Correction** +0.525s/f (Yiel) **7** Ran SP% **112.8**
Speed ratings (Par 97): **94,93,92,91,87 75,65**
CSF £28.58 CT £280.69 TOTE £2.90: £2.30, £5.70; EX 27.10 Trifecta £205.20.
Owner E A Hayward **Bred** B Kennedy & Mrs Ann Marie Kennedy **Trained** Sedbury, Gloucs

FOCUS
With the ground having changed from firm to soft during the previous 24 hours, there were many non-runners and conditions were vastly different from those expected for those who remained. In this moderate sprint, the field came wide towards the stands' rail. The winner might well rate higher still.

2144 HEROS CHARITY H'CAP 1m 2f 46y
6:00 (6:02) (Class 6) (0-65,64) 4-Y-O+ **£2,385** (£704; £352) **Stalls** Low

Form RPR
-003 **1** **Dovil's Duel (IRE)**[15] 1735 5-8-12 **58** EoinWalsh(3) 7 67
(Tony Newcombe) *t.k.h: hld up in last: smooth hdwy to ld over 2f out: sn drifted rt: styd on wl: pushed out* **3/1**[1]
00-6 **2** 3 ½ **Weardiditallgorong**[125] 84 4-9-5 **62** (b) CathyGannon 8 65
(Des Donovan, Ire) *trckd ldrs: rdn over 2f out: chsd wnr over 1f out: styd on but a being hld fnl f* **20/1**
52-0 **3** 1 **Azure Amour (IRE)**[28] 1413 4-8-7 **57** GeorgeWood(7) 16 58
(Rod Millman) *hld up in last pair: hdwy over 2f out: sn rdn: styd on same pce fr over 1f out* **9/1**
224 **4** 3 ¼ **Let Me In (IRE)**[32] 1343 6-8-12 **55** (v) WilliamTwiston-Davies 12 50
(Bernard Llewellyn) *in tch: hdwy and ev ch briefly over 2f out: sn rdn: wknd jst over 1f out* **5/1**
53-0 **5** 1 ¾ **Castle Talbot (IRE)**[126] 71 4-9-6 **63** OisinMurphy 2 55
(Richard Hughes) *led after 2f: rdn and hdd over 2f out: sn btn* **9/2**[3]
-062 **6** 2 ½ **Invincible Wish (IRE)**[25] 1500 4-9-4 **61** PatCosgrave 4 48
(Trevor Wall) *trckd ldrs: rdn to chal briefly over 2f out: sn short of room and wknd* **11/2**
-21 **7** 19 **Kristal Hart**[61] 898 7-9-1 **58** (p) LiamKeniry 13 11
(Neil Mulholland) *led for 2f: remained upsides ldr: rdn over 2f out: sn wknd* **7/2**[2]

2m 16.97s (5.97) **Going Correction** +0.65s/f (Yiel) **7 Ran SP% 112.2**
Speed ratings (Par 101): **102,99,98,95,94 92,77**
CSF £56.61 CT £478.88 TOTE £4.60: £2.30, £7.40; EX 59.80 Trifecta £708.50.
Owner David Gilbert **Bred** David Allan **Trained** Yarnscombe, Devon

FOCUS
Rail movements added 10yds to the distance of this race. The pace was solid, making it a good test. The form is rated around the runner-up.

2145 WEATHERBYS HAMILTON H'CAP 1m 2f 46y
6:30 (6:30) (Class 5) (0-75,75) 3-Y-O **£2,911** (£866; £432; £216) **Stalls** Low

Form RPR
00-6 **1** **Pack It In (IRE)**[15] 1738 3-8-3 **64** (b[1]) JordanUys(7) 2 72
(Brian Meehan) *racd keenly: disp ld for 2f: remained upsides ldr: led gng best over 3f out: rdn clr over 1f out: readily* **6/1**
00-5 **2** 3 ¾ **The Graduate (IRE)**[35] 1270 3-8-11 **65** OisinMurphy 6 66
(Andrew Balding) *trckd ldrs: sltly outpcd over 3f out: hdwy over 1f out: styd on into 2nd fnl f but no ch w wnr* **7/4**[1]
0-00 **3** 4 ½ **Glance My Way (IRE)**[12] 1828 3-9-3 **71** SeanLevey 4 63
(Richard Hannon) *disp ld for over 2f: trckd ldrs: rdn over 2f out: chsd wnr wl over 1f out tl no ex fnl f* **8/1**
6-1 **4** 6 **Jive Time**[107] 331 3-9-7 **75** MartinHarley 8 56
(James Tate) *trckd ldrs: edgd sltly rt whn rdn to chse wnr over 2f out tl wl over 1f out: wknd ent fnl f* **5/2**[2]
4153 **5** 1 **Jintshi**[28] 1411 3-9-7 **75** DarryllHolland 1 54
(Mark Johnston) *led after 2f: hdd over 3f: sn rdn: fading whn sltly hmpd over 2f out* **4/1**[3]

2m 16.62s (5.62) **Going Correction** +0.65s/f (Yiel) **5 Ran SP% 110.3**
Speed ratings (Par 99): **103,100,96,91,90**
CSF £17.02 TOTE £7.40: £3.40, £1.20; EX 19.70 Trifecta £76.20.
Owner The C3 Partnership **Bred** Lisa Kelly & Skymarc Farm **Trained** Manton, Wilts

FOCUS
Rail movements added 10yds to the distance of this race. The pace was moderate until they quickened up 3f out. The 1-2 were closely matched on Newbury maiden form from October.

2146 G PLAN FILLIES' H'CAP 5f 161y
7:00 (7:00) (Class 5) (0-75,75) 4-Y-O+ **£2,911** (£866; £432; £216) **Stalls** Centre

Form RPR
2162 **1** **Posh Bounty**[1] 2130 5-8-7 **68** SeanMooney(7) 8 75
(Joseph Tuite) *sn pushed along in last: rdn and hdwy over 1f out: drifted rt fnl f: kpt on wl to ld towards fin* **9/4**[1]
-003 **2** ¾ **Ginzan**[8] 1945 8-9-7 **75** MartinHarley 7 80
(Malcolm Saunders) *trckd ldrs: led over 1f out: sn rdn: no ex whn hdd towards fin* **11/4**[2]
3504 **3** 1 ¼ **Glastonberry**[37] 1237 8-8-13 **72** JosephineGordon(5) 3 72
(Geoffrey Deacon) *trckd ldr: str chal fr 2f out: rdn and ev ch ent fnl f: no ex fnl 120yds* **9/2**
53-0 **4** ½ **Babyfact**[23] 1533 5-8-9 **63** OisinMurphy 4 62
(Malcolm Saunders) *led: rdn whn jnd 2f out: hdd over 1f out: kpt on same pce* **7/2**[3]
-630 **5** nk **Perardua**[9] 1929 4-9-4 **72** CathyGannon 6 70
(David Evans) *trckd ldrs: rdn 2f out: keeping on at same pce in cl 4th whn squeezed out fnl 120yds* **8/1**

1m 13.74s (2.54) **Going Correction** +0.525s/f (Yiel) **5 Ran SP% 109.0**
Speed ratings (Par 100): **104,103,101,100,100**
CSF £8.48 TOTE £3.90: £2.40, £2.10; EX 9.50 Trifecta £33.60.
Owner The Lamb Inn - Pethy **Bred** Mascalls Stud **Trained** Lambourn, Berks
■ Stewards' Enquiry : Sean Mooney one-day ban: careless riding (May 25)

FOCUS
The runners went to the middle of the course on the soft ground. The winner is rated to her Chepstow for the previous night.

2147 WEATHERBYS HAMILTON NOVICE MEDIAN AUCTION STKS 5f 161y
7:30 (7:31) (Class 6) 2-Y-O **£2,587** (£770; £384; £192) **Stalls** Centre

Form RPR
6 **1** **Erica Bing**[16] 1719 2-8-11 0 JFEgan 7 70
(Jo Hughes) *led for over 2f: pressed ldr: rdn into narrow advantage jst over 1f out: kpt on gamely to assert fnl 120yds* **25/1**
2 ¾ **Juan Horsepower** 2-9-2 0 SeanLevey 8 73
(Richard Hannon) *chsd ldrs: rdn in cl 3rd over 2f out: kpt on to go 2nd fnl 140yds: a being hld by wnr* **11/8**[1]
3 **3** 2 ¼ **El Torito (IRE)**[15] 1736 2-9-2 0 PatCosgrave 4 65
(Jim Boyle) *prom: led over 3f out: rdn and narrowly hdd jst over 1f out: fdd fnl 140yds* **2/1**[2]
4 8 **Skilful Lord (IRE)** 2-9-2 0 MartinDwyer 3 39
(Stuart Kittow) *s.i.s: rn green: sn pushed along in last: wnt wl hld 4th ent fnl f: nvr trbld ldrs* **8/1**
5 4 ½ **Battle Of Wits (IRE)** 2-8-11 0 JosephineGordon(5) 2 24
(J S Moore) *s.i.s: sn pushed along in last pair: wnt hld 4th over 1f out tl wknd ent fnl f* **20/1**
6 3 ½ **Debonaire David** 2-9-2 0 ShaneKelly 1 12
(Richard Hughes) *chsd ldrs: rdn over 2f out: wknd over 1f out* **4/1**[3]

1m 15.65s (4.45) **Going Correction** +0.525s/f (Yiel) **6 Ran SP% 115.2**
Speed ratings (Par 91): **91,90,87,76,70 65**
CSF £62.42 TOTE £15.20: £4.20, £1.50; EX 75.60 Trifecta £191.00.
Owner Richard Kent & Jo Hughes **Bred** Mickley Stud & Sue Shone **Trained** Lambourn, Berks

FOCUS
The runners stayed middle to far side in the straight, and the race went to the only filly. The pace held up and the form seems only fair.

2148 DAVID BROWN MEMORIAL H'CAP 1m 5y
8:00 (8:02) (Class 6) (0-60,60) 3-Y-O **£2,264** (£673; £336; £168) **Stalls** Low

Form RPR
0- **1** **Sister Blandina (IRE)**[17] 1679 3-8-13 **52** ShaneKelly 5 63+
(J P Murtagh, Ire) *hld up towards rr: hdwy fr 3f out: rdn to ld ent fnl f: styd on wl: readily* **7/4**[1]
00-0 **2** 2 ¼ **Gold Eliza (IRE)**[14] 1792 3-9-0 **53** KieranO'Neill 16 56
(Richard Hannon) *towards rr: rdn and hdwy over 2f out: swtchd lft whn chsng ldng pair ent fnl f: styd on to go 2nd nring fin: no ch w wnr* **12/1**
0-60 **3** nk **Concur (IRE)**[15] 1734 3-8-10 **49** JackMitchell 12 51
(Rod Millman) *led: rdn 3 l clr over 2f out: hdd ent fnl f: sn hld by wnr: no ex cl home* **10/1**
06-6 **4** 2 ¼ **Patanjali (IRE)**[15] 1734 3-9-5 **58** CharlesBishop 1 55
(Eve Johnson Houghton) *mid-div: rdn over 2f out: hdwy wl over 1f out to go 4th: styd on same pce fnl f* **9/1**
000- **5** 3 ¼ **Desert Cross**[217] 7039 3-9-2 **55** LiamKeniry 2 44
(Jonjo O'Neill) *hld up towards rr: rdn over 2f out: hdwy over 1f out: styd on fnl f* **14/1**
50-4 **6** 3 ½ **Fondie (IRE)**[20] 1589 3-9-7 **60** DarryllHolland 14 41
(Mark Johnston) *sn pressing ldr: rdn wl over 2f out: wknd ent fnl f* **3/1**[2]
0030 **7** 2 ¼ **Tahiti One**[17] 1670 3-9-3 **56** WilliamTwiston-Davies 4 32
(Tony Carroll) *trckd ldrs: rdn over 2f out: wknd fnl f* **16/1**
3404 **8** ½ **Ventura Falcon (IRE)**[33] 1325 3-9-4 **57** SeanLevey 8 32
(Richard Hannon) *awkward leaving stalls: mid-div: rdn 3f out: nvr threatened: wknd fnl f* **8/1**[3]
50-0 **9** 8 **Links Bar Marbella (IRE)**[102] 400 3-8-12 **51** JFEgan 13 8
(Eric Wheeler) *trckd ldrs: rdn over 3f out: wknd 2f out* **25/1**
5600 **10** 7 **Haunted (IRE)**[12] 1829 3-8-8 **47** (b) RoystonFfrench 11
(Milton Bradley) *s.i.s: sn mid-div: rdn over 3f out: wknd over 2f out* **33/1**

1m 47.07s (6.27) **Going Correction** +0.65s/f (Yiel) **10 Ran SP% 118.6**
Speed ratings (Par 97): **94,91,91,89,85 82,80,79,71,64**
CSF £25.52 CT £174.49 TOTE £3.10: £2.00, £4.10, £1.80; EX 25.40 Trifecta £232.50.
Owner Bridge Bloodstock Partnership **Bred** Mrs R McKeon **Trained** Coolaghknock Glebe,Co Kildare

FOCUS
Rail movements added 10yds to the distance of this race. The pace was respectable for the conditions, making stamina a significant factor. The winner proved very well treated.

2149 SIS FILLIES' H'CAP 1m 5f 22y
8:30 (8:30) (Class 5) (0-75,72) 4-Y-O+ **£3,067** (£905; £453) **Stalls** High

Form RPR
0461 **1** **Cosette (IRE)**[12] 1830 5-8-11 **62** (p) WilliamTwiston-Davies 4 71+
(Bernard Llewellyn) *mde all: kicked on 3f out: styd on strly to draw clr over 1f out: comf* **9/4**[1]
6063 **2** 3 ¼ **Percys Princess**[26] 1455 5-8-4 **62** GeorgeWood(7) 5 64
(Michael Appleby) *w wnr tl rdn wl over 2f out: hld wl over 1f out but styd on for clr 2nd* **7/2**[3]
625 **3** 5 **Oratorio's Joy (IRE)**[46] 1092 6-9-4 **69** CathyGannon 8 64
(Jamie Osborne) *trckd ldrs: rdn wl over 2f out: wnt hld 3rd ent fnl f: nt pce to get involved* **7/2**[3]
310- **4** ¾ **Ragdollianna**[177] 6325 12-8-6 **57** ow1 JFEgan 2 50
(Mark Hoad) *trckd ldrs: rdn over 2f out: styd on same pce: wnt hld 4th ins fnl f* **12/1**
5423 **5** 1 ¼ **Hope You Dance (FR)**[67] 838 4-9-3 **68** MartinHarley 6 60
(David Simcock) *trckd ldng pair: rdn wl over 2f out: nt pce to get on terms: wknd ent fnl f* **5/2**[2]

3m 0.59s (8.59) **Going Correction** +0.65s/f (Yiel) **5 Ran SP% 111.5**
Speed ratings (Par 100): **99,97,93,93,92**
CSF £10.52 TOTE £3.40: £1.80, £1.70; EX 10.20 Trifecta £38.50.
Owner Smerdon Tree Services Ltd **Bred** R N Auld **Trained** Fochriw, Caerphilly

FOCUS
Rail movements added 10yds to the distance of this race. The winner dictated an ordinary pace until being dashed for home off the bend. She built on her Chepstow form but there are doubts over the others.
T/Plt: £160.60 to a £1 stake. Pool of £57841.59 - 262.80 winning tickets. T/Qpdt: £13.10 to a £1 stake. Pool of £6138.05 - 344.30 winning tickets. **Tim Mitchell**

2032 LINGFIELD (L-H)
Wednesday, May 11

OFFICIAL GOING: Polytrack: standard
Wind: light, behind Weather: dry after morning showers

2150 RACING WELFARE CLAIMING STKS 1m 2f (P)
1:50 (1:50) (Class 6) 3-Y-O+ **£2,587** (£770; £384; £192) **Stalls** Low

Form RPR
0-13 **1** **Marshgate Lane (USA)**[16] 1722 7-10-0 90 (p) LiamKeniry 7 84
(Neil Mulholland) *in tch in midfield: wnt 2nd 2f out: swtchd rt and effrt over 1f out: rdn to ld 1f out: styd on wl: rdn out* **9/4**[1]
1/1- **2** 2 ½ **Street Artist (IRE)**[482] 159 6-10-0 86 PatCosgrave 1 79
(David Nicholls) *led: rdn and hrd pressed over 1f out: hdd 1f out: outpcd by wnr but kpt on for clr 2nd* **4/1**[3]
6-60 **3** 2 ¼ **Woofie (IRE)**[14] 1775 4-9-13 71 (b[1]) LukeMorris 6 74
(Laura Mongan) *chsd ldr tl 7f out: wl in tch after: effrt u.p 2f out: sn drvn and outpcd: kpt on same pce fnl f* **40/1**
6440 **4** nk **Spiritual Star (IRE)**[94] 494 7-9-12 82 (t) WilliamCarson 3 72
(Anthony Carson) *stdd s: hld up in rr: clsd and wl in tch whn nt clr run 2f out: effrt over 1f out: sn outpcd and btn: kpt on same pce after* **7/1**
5550 **5** 9 **Robert The Painter (IRE)**[14] 1775 8-10-0 78 (b[1]) AmirQuinn 4 57
(Lee Carter) *hld up in tch: hdwy to chse ldr 7f out: upsides 5f out tl rdn and lost pl 2f out: sn btn: wl btn and eased ins fnl f* **16/1**

2300 **6** *11* **Gaelic Silver (FR)**^{16} 1716 10-9-7 83........................(p) HectorCrouch$^{(5)}$ 2 34
(Gary Moore) *t.k.h: trckd ldrs: effrt and wd bnd 2f out: sn btn: wl bhd and eased ins fnl f* **5/1**

5626 **7** *36* **Stetchworth (IRE)**^{34} 1290 5-9-12 82.................................. AdamKirby 5
(Mark Johnston) *in tch in rr: rdn over 3f out: sn dropped out: t.o and eased fnl 2f* **7/2^{2}**

2m 4.15s (-2.45) **Going Correction** -0.05s/f (Stan) **7** Ran SP% **110.5**
Speed ratings (Par 101): **107,105,103,102,95 86,58**
CSF £10.63 TOTE £3.60: £1.50, £1.70; EX 12.40 Trifecta £140.20.
Owner The Affordable Partnership **Bred** Edmund A Gann **Trained** Limpley Stoke, Wilts

FOCUS
This fixture was originally due to take place at Yarmouth. Not a bad little claimer to start, with the winner rated 90 and four of the other six rated in the 80s. The pace was ordinary and it favoured those ridden handily, though the first two were the pair most favoured by the weights. The third looks the key to the form.

2151 HEART FM H'CAP 1m 2f (P)
2:20 (2:20) (Class 5) (0-75,73) 4-Y-O+ **£2,911** (£866; £432; £216) **Stalls** Low

Form RPR

-063 **1** **Shimba Hills**^{51} 616 5-9-6 **72**........................(tp) WilliamTwiston-Davies 3 78
(Lawney Hill) *in tch: effrt u.p to chal 2f out: drvn to ld 1f out: hld on u.p fnl f: drvn out* **8/1^{3}**

3330 **2** *nk* **Berrahri (IRE)**^{42} 1144 5-9-6 **72**.. KierenFox 6 77
(John Best) *chsd ldr for 2f: effrt between rivals to chal jst over 1f out: drvn and ev ch thrght fnl f: a jst hld* **7/1^{2}**

-520 **3** *2* **Pearly Prince**^{61} 899 4-9-4 **70**... RobertHavlin 1 71
(Peter Hedger) *stdd s: hld up in rr: clsd and wl in tch over 3f out: effrt 2f out: no imp tl hdwy u.p ins fnl f: wnt 3rd wl ins fnl f: kpt on* **8/1^{3}**

-346 **4** *1/2* **Karam Albaari (IRE)**^{12} 1824 8-9-7 **73**..........................(p) AdamKirby 4 73
(J R Jenkins) *off the pair in last pair: clsd and in tch 1/2-way: effrt u.p 2f out: hdwy ins fnl f: styd on to go 4th towards fin: nvr trbld ldrs* **8/1^{3}**

303- **5** *1 1/4* **Rustique**^{196} 7552 4-8-11 **63**.. AntonioFresu 8 61
(Ed Walker) *sn led: hrd pressed and rdn 2f out: hdd 1f out: no ex: wknd and lost 2 pls wl ins fnl f* **8/1^{3}**

410- **6** *1 1/2* **With Approval (IRE)**^{161} 8084 4-9-2 **68**.............................. LukeMorris 2 63
(Laura Mongan) *broke wl: sn stdd bk and in tch: nt clr run on inner jst over 2f out: drvn and fnd little over 1f out: styd on same pce fnl f* **16/1**

4103 **7** *5* **Heezararity**^{15} 1751 8-9-2 **68**.. LiamKeniry 5 53
(Jonathan Geake) *bustled along early: chsd ldr after 2f out tl drvn and lost pl jst over 2f out: wknd over 1f out* **8/1^{3}**

20/ **R** **Labaik (FR)**^{322} 5-9-4 **70**... DaneO'Neill 7
(Owen Burrows) *ref to r: tk no part* **5/4^{1}**

2m 5.4s (-1.20) **Going Correction** -0.05s/f (Stan) **8** Ran SP% **118.4**
Speed ratings (Par 103): **102,101,100,99,98 97,93,**
CSF £64.41 CT £469.15 TOTE £10.60: £3.00, £1.70, £3.40; EX 72.60 Trifecta £587.60.
Owner Shimba Hills/Fortnum Racing Partnership **Bred** G Hedley & Mike Channon Bloodstock Limited **Trained** Aston Rowant, Oxon

FOCUS
The complexion of this ordinary handicap completely changed when the warm favourite did a "Hamlet" as the stalls opened. The winning time was 1.25sec slower than the claimer. Rather muddling form.

2152 INJURED JOCKEYS FUND CLASSIFIED STKS 1m 1y(P)
2:50 (2:50) (Class 6) 3-Y-O **£2,587** (£770; £384; £192) **Stalls** High

Form RPR

3044 **1** **Ubla (IRE)**^{12} 1832 3-9-0 65... DavidProbert 3 69
(Gay Kelleway) *broke wl: sn stdd bk and hld up in tch in midfield: gd hdwy on inner and swtchd rt over 1f out: drvn and ev ch 1f out: led ins fnl f: r.o wl* **12/1**

-322 **2** *nk* **Santiburi Spring**^{75} 725 3-9-0 65.. KierenFox 6 68
(John Best) *w ldr: rdn and ev ch 2f out: sn led and drvn: hdd ins fnl f: kpt on wl but a jst hld after* **6/1**

430- **3** *1/2* **Matilda's Law**^{240} 6376 3-9-0 65... TedDurcan 10 67
(Chris Wall) *stdd bk after s: hld up in last pair: gd hdwy on inner over 1f out: chsd ldrs and rdn 1f out: kpt on same pce fnl 100yds* **20/1**

450- **4** *hd* **Athlon (IRE)**^{175} 7890 3-9-0 62... ShaneKelly 1 67+
(David Lanigan) *dwlt: hld up in tch: pushed along over 2f out: stuck wd bnd 2f out: hdwy u.p 1f out: edgd lft and kpt on wl ins fnl f* **7/2^{1}**

350- **5** *1* **Pretty Jewel**^{221} 6922 3-9-0 65.. LukeMorris 2 64
(James Tate) *chsd ldrs: edgd out rt and jostling w rival 2f out: drvn over 1f out: keeping on same pce whn bmpd and pushed lft ins fnl f* **8/1**

560- **6** *nse* **Forecaster**^{195} 7585 3-9-0 65... WilliamCarson 5 64
(Michael Bell) *dwlt: in tch in midfield: pushed along and jostled 2f out: rdn and hdwy 1f out: nvr enough room and styd on same pce wl ins fnl f* **9/2^{3}**

004- **7** *1* **Paco Pat**^{147} 8244 3-9-0 62.. DaneO'Neill 9 63
(Richard Hannon) *dwlt: hld up in last pair: stuck bhd a wall of horses jst over 2f out: swtchd rt and effrt over 1f out: kpt on ins fnl f: nvr trbld ldrs* **14/1**

04-3 **8** *nk* **Pastoral Star**^{30} 1388 3-8-7 62................................(p) CharlieBennett$^{(7)}$ 4 61
(Hughie Morrison) *rdn along leaving stalls: hdwy to ld after 1f: rdn ent fnl 2f: hdd wl over 1f out: no ex 1f out: wknd ins fnl f* **8/1**

3165 **9** *2 1/4* **Clive Clifton (IRE)**^{37} 1238 3-9-1 65 ow1.........................(v) AdamKirby 7 63
(David Evans) *chsd ldrs on outer: rdn over 2f out: lost pl u.p over 1f out: btn whn hmpd ins fnl f: bhd fnl 100yds* **4/1^{2}**

1m 37.9s (-0.30) **Going Correction** -0.05s/f (Stan) **9** Ran SP% **116.0**
Speed ratings (Par 97): **99,98,98,98,97 96,95,95,93**
CSF £82.39 TOTE £17.80: £4.10, £2.20, £7.00; EX 108.90 Trifecta £1632.70.
Owner Peter Petrovic **Bred** Tenuta Genzianella **Trained** Exning, Suffolk

FOCUS
A modest 3yo classified event, with eight of the nine remaining runners maidens going into it, and they rather finished in a bunch. Not easy to get with this form.

2153 COME TO COUNTRYSIDE DAY JUNE 4 H'CAP 1m 1y(P)
3:25 (3:25) (Class 6) (0-65,65) 4-Y-O+ **£2,587** (£770; £384; £192) **Stalls** High

Form RPR

-410 **1** **Star Of The Stage**^{15} 1735 4-9-7 **65**........................(p) AdamBeschizza 10 73
(Julia Feilden) *led for 1f: chsd ldr after: rdn to ld over 1f out: sn drvn clr: in command and styd on wl after* **8/1**

0010 **2** *1 3/4* **Polar Kite (IRE)**^{8} 1945 8-9-3 **64**...................................... RobHornby$^{(3)}$ 8 68+
(Michael Attwater) *stdd and swtchd lft after s: hld up wl off the pce in rr: clsd 1/2-way: creeping nr on inner over 2f out: rdn and hdwy over 1f out: chsd clr wnr 100yds out: kpt on but nvr threatened* **16/1**

0035 **3** *1 1/2* **For Shia And Lula (IRE)**^{14} 1780 7-9-6 **64**....................(p) AdamKirby 12 64
(Daniel Mark Loughnane) *chsd ldr tl led after 1f: stdd gallop 1/2-way: drvn and qcknd over 2f out: hdd and outpcd over 1f out: kpt on same pce after: lost 2nd 100yds* **12/1**

0104 **4** *nk* **Bookmaker**^{35} 1262 6-9-5 **63**...(b) WilliamCarson 5 62
(John Bridger) *chsd ldrs: rdn over 2f out: unable qck u.p over 1f out: styd on same pce fnl f* **8/1**

0224 **5** *1 1/4* **Pike Corner Cross (IRE)**^{32} 1340 4-9-5 **63**.......... RichardKingscote 11 59
(Gary Moore) *chsd ldrs: rdn ent fnl 2f: drvn and styd on same pce fr over 1f out* **3/1^{1}**

-504 **6** *1* **Storm Runner (IRE)**^{43} 1131 8-8-7 **58**............................ JaneElliott$^{(7)}$ 6 52
(George Margarson) *hld up in tch in rr of main gp: effrt over 1f out: hdwy u.p 1f out: styd on fnl f: nvr trbld ldrs* **20/1**

0-05 **7** *3/4* **Paladin (IRE)**^{29} 1403 7-9-7 **65**... MartinLane 3 57
(Michael Blake) *hld up in tch in midfield: effrt u.p wl over 1f out: unable qck and styd on same pce after* **20/1**

6404 **8** *2 1/2* **Embankment**^{28} 1416 7-9-4 **62**... RobertHavlin 7 48
(Michael Attwater) *s.i.s: off the pce in last trio: clsd and in tch 1/2-way: effrt and wd bnd 2f out: sn edgd lft and no imp: nvr trbld ldrs* **8/1**

1126 **9** *nk* **Gunner Moyne**^{63} 877 4-9-1 **64**..............................(t) HectorCrouch$^{(5)}$ 9 50
(Gary Moore) *stdd s: hld up off the pce in last trio: clsd and in tch 1/2-way: effrt wl over 1f out: sn carried lft and no imp: nvr trbld ldrs* **7/1^{3}**

3-03 **10** *nse* **Nubar Boy**^{56} 951 9-9-6 **64**...(p) DaleSwift 1 49
(Daniel Mark Loughnane) *in tch in midfield: rdn 2f out: lost pl and btn over 1f out: wknd fnl f* **6/1^{2}**

52-0 **11** *1/2* **Chella Thriller (SPA)**^{123} 127 7-9-4 **62**......................... DavidProbert 2 46
(Ralph J Smith) *in tch in midfield: rdn 2f out: sn lost pl and wknd* **12/1**

0000 **12** *1* **Mr Frankie**^{18} 1652 5-9-0 **63**... CiaranMckee$^{(5)}$ 4 45
(Richard Phillips) *in tch in midfield: lost pl and rdn 2f out: sn wknd: bhd ins fnl f* **50/1**

1m 38.14s (-0.06) **Going Correction** -0.05s/f (Stan) **12** Ran SP% **117.9**
Speed ratings (Par 101): **98,96,94,94,93 92,91,88,88,88 88,87**
CSF £124.55 CT £1530.79 TOTE £11.20: £3.30, £5.10, £2.70; EX 159.80 Trifecta £918.10.
Owner Mr & Mrs George Bhatti & Partners 2 **Bred** Cheveley Park Stud Ltd **Trained** Exning, Suffolk

FOCUS
A moderate handicap which looked to be quite a competitive one, but it was taken apart by the winner. Those that raced up with the pace appeared to be favoured. This was up there with the winner's best 2015 form.

2154 RETRAINING OF RACEHORSES FILLIES' H'CAP 1m 1y(P)
4:00 (4:00) (Class 4) (0-85,85) 4-Y-O+ **£5,175** (£1,540; £769; £384) **Stalls** High

Form RPR

-111 **1** **Lucy The Painter (IRE)**^{18} 1624 4-9-6 **84**........................ HarryBentley 4 93+
(Ed de Giles) *s.i.s: in tch in 4th: effrt in 3rd over 1f out: stl 2 l down 1f out: str run u.p ins fnl f: led towards fin* **8/11^{1}**

-114 **2** *1/2* **Esteemable**^{18} 1624 4-8-7 **74**...................................... DanielMuscutt$^{(3)}$ 1 79+
(James Fanshawe) *hld up in tch in 3rd: hdwy to chse ldr 2f out: rdn and chal 1f out: drvn ins fnl f: r.o wl: jst outpcd by wnr towards fin* **11/4^{2}**

-223 **3** *nse* **Free Running (IRE)**^{68} 813 4-8-4 **73**.................... EdwardGreatrex$^{(5)}$ 2 78
(Simon Crisford) *led: rdn and qcknd over 2f out: drvn over 1f out: hrd pressed ins fnl f: hdd and no ex towards fin* **9/2^{3}**

6-60 **4** *7* **Edge Of Heaven**^{15} 1757 4-9-7 **85**............................ RichardKingscote 3 73
(Jonathan Portman) *chsd ldr tl 2f out: sn u.p and outpcd: 4th and wknd fnl f* **14/1**

1m 37.0s (-1.20) **Going Correction** -0.05s/f (Stan) **4** Ran SP% **109.4**
Speed ratings (Par 102): **104,103,103,96**
CSF £3.05 TOTE £1.50; EX 3.10 Trifecta £3.90.
Owner J P Carrington **Bred** Bakewell Bloodstock **Trained** Ledbury, H'fords

FOCUS
A good fillies' handicap despite the small field and three of them produced a cracking finish. The pace was ordinary and it developed into something of a sprint. The form is rated around the third.

2155 CANTERING CUISINE H'CAP 7f 1y(P)
4:30 (4:30) (Class 6) (0-60,60) 3-Y-O+ **£2,587** (£770; £384; £192) **Stalls** Low

Form RPR

4046 **1** **Guapo Bay**^{14} 1795 3-7-11 **48**..(b^{1}) TinaSmith$^{(7)}$ 9 53
(Richard Hannon) *dwlt: sn rcvrd to chse ldng pair and clr of field tl 1/2-way: carried rt bnd bnd 2f out: rallied and rdr dropped whip over 1f out: chsd clr wnr ins fnl f: r.o wl to ld last strides* **33/1**

5213 **2** *nk* **Not Your Call (IRE)**^{12} 1834 5-9-1 **52**..................... CallumShepherd$^{(5)}$ 4 60
(Lee Carter) *taken down early: led and clr w 2 rivals tl stdd gallop 1/2-way: rdn and kicked 3 l clr 2f out: drvn 1f out: grad worn down and hdd last strides* **3/1^{2}**

3310 **3** *3/4* **Little Indian**^{8} 1949 6-9-12 **58**... AdamKirby 3 64
(J R Jenkins) *pushed along and nt travelling early: off the pce in last trio: clsd and in tch 1/2-way: effrt wd 2f out: hdwy 1f out: styd on strly ins fnl f: nvr quite getting to ldrs* **6/1**

2004 **4** *nk* **Copper Cavalier**^{12} 1833 5-9-7 **53**...............................(b) DavidProbert 11 59
(Michael Blanshard) *stdd and dropped in bhd after s: hld up off the pce in last pair: clsd and in tch 1/2-way: effrt whn nt clr run and swtchd rt over 1f out: r.o wl ins fnl f: nvr quite getting to ldrs* **14/1**

-541 **5** *1/2* **Cuban Queen (USA)**^{14} 1794 3-8-9 **53**................................ MartinLane 2 53
(Jeremy Gask) *stdd s: midfield: clsd and in tch 1/2-way: effrt over 1f out: styd on ins fnl f: nvr enough pce to get on terms* **11/4^{1}**

6000 **6** *hd* **Soaring Spirits (IRE)**^{22} 1544 6-9-11 **57**.........................(v) DaneO'Neill 5 60
(Dean Ivory) *chsd clr ldng trio: clsd and in tch 1/2-way: rdn and lft chsng clr ldr wl over 1f out: lost 2nd and no ex ins fnl f: wknd towards fin* **8/1**

0210 **7** *1* **Blackthorn Stick (IRE)**^{15} 1735 7-10-0 **60**....................(p) JimmyQuinn 7 61
(Paul Burgoyne) *taken down early: s.i.s: hld up off the pce in last trio: clsd and in tch 1/2-way: n.m.r over 1f out: hdwy u.p 1f out: stuck bhd rivals and unable to cl fnl 100yds* **5/1^{3}**

0451 **8** *shd* **Fairy Mist (IRE)**^{15} 1742 9-9-8 **54**..............................(b) WilliamCarson 1 54
(John Bridger) *stdd s: hld up off the pce in last quartet: clsd and in tch 1/2-way: hdwy u.p over 1f out: kpt on same pce ins fnl f* **16/1**

00-6 **9** *12* **Angel Flores (IRE)**^{13} 1811 5-9-13 **59**.................................. AmirQuinn 8 27
(Lee Carter) *racd keenly: chsd ldr and clr in ldng trio: rdn and unable qck whn drifted rt bnd 2f out: losing pl whn hmpd over 1f out: bhd and eased ins fnl f* **33/1**

4-60 **10** *2 1/4* **Sunshine Always (IRE)**^{12} 1834 10-9-9 **55**.................. RobertHavlin 10 17
(Michael Attwater) *midfield: clsd and in tch 1/2-way: rdn 2f out: sn lost pl: bhd and eased ins fnl f* **33/1**

1m 25.14s (0.34) **Going Correction** -0.05s/f (Stan)
WFA 3 from 5yo+ 12lb **10** Ran SP% **115.1**
Speed ratings (Par 101): **96,95,94,94,93 93,92,92,78,76**
CSF £127.45 CT £711.54 TOTE £24.80: £5.40, £1.10, £2.60; EX 162.20 Trifecta £1852.20.
Owner R Hannon **Bred** J R Shannon **Trained** East Everleigh, Wilts

FOCUS
A moderate handicap, but one that will stay with the winning jockey always. The leaders went off very hard, but even so the pace held up with the first and second always in the leading trio. The winner had fallen a fair way in the weights.

2156 JIGSAW MAIDEN STKS 6f 1y(P)
5:00 (5:01) (Class 5) 3-Y-O+ **£2,911** (£866; £432; £216) **Stalls** Low

Form RPR
0- **1** **Aleef (IRE)**347 2723 3-9-0 0 DaneO'Neill 8 84+
(Charles Hills) *t.k.h: chsd ldr after 1f tl led 4f out: mde rest: rdn and wnt clr over 1f out: r.o wl* **4/1**2
6- **2** 1 1/4 **Loaded (IRE)**236 6498 3-9-0 0 DavidProbert 6 77
(Andrew Balding) *off the pce in 5th: clsd and in tch whn n.m.r and edgd rt jst over 2f out: hdwy over 1f out: lft 3rd ins fnl f: styd on to go 2nd fnl 50yds: no threat to wnr* **10/1**
3 1 3/4 **Cold Snap (IRE)** 3-9-0 0 RobertHavlin 5 71
(William Jarvis) *s.i.s: rn green in rr early: clsd and in tch whn nt clr run jst over 2f out: hdwy over 1f out: lft 4th and swtchd rt ins fnl f: kpt on to go 3rd cl hoe: no threat to wnr* **9/2**3
40- **4** nk **Geoff Potts (IRE)**229 6702 3-9-0 0 1 MartinLane 7 70
(Jeremy Gask) *taken down early and ponied to s: stdd s: hld up in last pair: clsd and in tch over 2f out: rdn and hdwy 1f out: swtchd rt and hdwy ins fnl f: styd on strly fnl 100yds: no threat to wnr* **12/1**
53- **5** nk **Hepworth Marble (IRE)**291 4622 3-8-4 0 HectorCrouch(5) 3 64
(Gary Moore) *led for 2f: chsd wnr after: rdn and unable qck over 1f out: no imp after: lost 2nd and wknd fnl 50yds* **16/1**
23-0 **6** 3 3/4 **Muatadel**32 1337 3-9-0 77 RichardKingscote 2 57
(Mark Johnston) *chsd ldr for 1f: rdn over 3f out: lost pl u.p 2f out: wknd 1f out* **5/1**
0-36 **7** 2 1/4 **Colonel Bossington (IRE)**21 1577 3-9-1 75 ow1 AdamKirby 1 51+
(William Knight) *chsd ldrs: rdn and effrt in 3rd over 1f out: stl 3rd but keeping on same pce and hld whn eased ins fnl f* **2/1**1

1m 11.21s (-0.69) **Going Correction** -0.05s/f (Stan) 7 Ran SP% **110.8**
Speed ratings (Par 103): **102,100,98,97,97 92,89**
CSF £39.25 TOTE £3.80: £1.70, £2.90; EX 48.20 Trifecta £216.90.
Owner Hamdan Al Maktoum **Bred** Sarah Fortune **Trained** Lambourn, Berks

FOCUS
A modest 3yo maiden and not the easiest race to assess with the pair rated in the 70s both running poorly for whatever reason, but it's hard not to have been impressed by the winner.
T/Plt: £1,486.10 to a £1 stake. Pool of £50488.79 - 24.80 winning tickets. T/Qpdt: £206.70 to a £1 stake. Pool of £4190.05 - 15.0 winning tickets. **Steve Payne**

YORK (L-H)
Wednesday, May 11
OFFICIAL GOING: Good (good to firm in places; 7.8)
Wind: Moderate half against Weather: Fine & dry

2157 888SPORT STKS (H'CAP) 1m 2f 88y
2:10 (2:12) (Class 2) (0-100,99) 4-Y-O+
£15,562 (£4,660; £2,330; £1,165; £582; £292) **Stalls** Low

Form RPR
11-4 **1** **Nayel (IRE)**16 1716 4-8-4 85 oh2 TomMarquand(3) 4 95
(Richard Hannon) *chsd ldrs: drvn 4f out: styd on to ld over 1f out: hung lft: drvn rt out* **12/1**
52-2 **2** 1/2 **Pacify**21 1569 4-9-7 99 FMBerry 9 108
(Ralph Beckett) *lw: hld up in rr: hdwy over 3f out: swtchd lft over 2f out: upsides over 1f out: no ex clsng stages* **6/1**3
11-2 **3** 1/2 **Erik The Red (FR)**18 1629 4-9-1 93 ShaneGray 2 101
(Kevin Ryan) *hld up in mid-div: t.k.h: smooth hdwy over 2f out: n.m.r and edgd rt over 1f out: styd on wl: tk 3rd last 50yds: gng on at fin* **4/1**2
30-0 **4** 1 **Awake My Soul (IRE)**36 1245 7-9-4 96 SamJames 12 102
(David O'Meara) *swtg: hld up in rr: hdwy over 2f out: styd on fnl f: tk 4th post* **33/1**
1403 **5** hd **Revolutionist (IRE)**11 1861 4-9-4 96 WilliamBuick 6 102
(Mark Johnston) *lw: led: hdd over 1f out: kpt on same pce* **11/1**
5-61 **6** 2 3/4 **Hit The Jackpot (IRE)**18 1620 7-9-6 98 DanielTudhope 10 98
(David O'Meara) *lw: hld up in rr-div: hdwy 3f out: kpt on fnl f* **14/1**
20-3 **7** 1 1/4 **Off Art**18 1620 6-9-3 95 (p) DavidAllan 3 93
(Tim Easterby) *chsd ldrs: one pce over 1f out* **12/1**
420- **8** 1/2 **Spanish Squeeze (IRE)**168 7977 4-9-6 98 RyanMoore 14 95
(Hugo Palmer) *hld up in rr: t.k.h: effrt over 3f out: kpt on: nvr a threat* **7/2**1
20-3 **9** 8 **Empress Ali (IRE)**14 1786 5-8-10 88 JamesSullivan 1 69
(Tom Tate) *chsd ldrs: upsides over 2f out: wknd fnl f* **16/1**
0100 **10** 3 3/4 **Master Of Finance (IRE)**6 1972 5-9-6 98 SilvestreDeSousa 5 71
(Mark Johnston) *s.i.s: sn chsng ldrs: wkng whn n.m.r over 1f out: eased fnl 150yds* **16/1**
52-0 **11** 8 **Buonarroti (IRE)**25 1493 5-8-9 87 FrederikTylicki 11 44
(Declan Carroll) *in rr: bhd fnl 2f* **25/1**
6-34 **12** 1 1/2 **Silvery Moon (IRE)**11 1871 9-9-0 92 JasonHart 13 46
(Tim Easterby) *in rr-div: effrt 4f out: hung lft over 2f out: sn lost pl* **20/1**
00-0 **13** 27 **Hernandoshideaway**25 1493 4-9-2 94 1 PaulMulrennan 7
(Michael Dods) *sltly on toes: trckd ldrs: t.k.h: wknd over 1f out: bhd whn eased clsng stages* **20/1**

2m 8.51s (-3.99) **Going Correction** -0.15s/f (Firm) 13 Ran SP% **115.0**
Speed ratings (Par 109): **109,108,108,107,107 105,104,103,97,94 87,86,65**
CSF £75.02 CT £342.97 TOTE £14.50: £3.80, £2.30, £1.60; EX 70.30 Trifecta £290.20.
Owner Capri M7 **Bred** John Cullinan **Trained** East Everleigh, Wilts

FOCUS
The rail alignment around the home bend resulted in this race being run over 42yds shorter than advertised. There'd been 5.3mm of rain since the previous afternoon, but the going remained pretty decent, with Tom Marquand describing it as "lovely ground, on the good side". GoingStick readings were as follows: Overall 7.8, Far side 7.8, Centre 7.9, Stands' side 7.7. No hanging around here, with the closers seen to best advantage, and the form of this good handicap looks rock-solid. The race is rated around the fourth.

2158 INFINITY TYRES STKS (H'CAP) 6f
2:40 (2:44) (Class 2) (0-105,104) 4-Y-O+
£15,562 (£4,660; £2,330; £1,165; £582; £292) **Stalls** Centre

Form RPR
00-1 **1** **See The Sun**11 1848 5-8-5 88 JamesSullivan 5 97
(Tim Easterby) *slt ld 1 1/2f: cl up: led again wl over 1f out: sn rdn: drvn ins fnl f: kpt on wl towards fin* **9/1**3
2-1U **2** nk **Mythmaker**90 529 4-8-11 94 ConnorBeasley 9 102
(Bryan Smart) *trckd ldrs: effrt 2f out and sn rdn: styd on wl fnl f* **25/1**
00-0 **3** nk **Red Pike (IRE)**23 1522 5-8-9 92 TomEaves 1 99
(Bryan Smart) *sltly on toes: cl up: led after 1 1/2f: rdn and hdd wl over 1f out: drvn and kpt on fnl f* **50/1**
540- **4** 3/4 **Zanetto**221 6918 6-8-12 95 PhillipMakin 4 100
(John Quinn) *lw: trckd ldrs: hdwy on outer over 2f out: rdn and ev ch over 1f out: drvn and kpt on same pce fnl f* **20/1**
0-64 **5** hd **Glen Moss (IRE)**39 1197 7-9-3 100 PaulMulrennan 6 104
(Michael Dods) *chsd ldrs: rdn along wl over 1f out: drvn and kpt on same pce fnl f* **16/1**
50-5 **6** nk **Hoof It**38 1218 9-8-5 93 NathanEvans(5) 12 96
(Michael Easterby) *chsd ldrs: prom 1/2-way: rdn along 2f out: drvn appr fnl f: kpt on same pce* **10/1**
000- **7** 1 **Hawkeyethenoo (IRE)**201 7424 10-8-6 89 AndreaAtzeni 10 89
(Jim Goldie) *in rr: hdwy over 2f out: sn rdn and styd on appr fnl f: nrst fin* **25/1**
03-0 **8** 1 **Canyari (IRE)**11 1848 5-8-0 86 (p) SammyJoBell(3) 7 83
(Richard Fahey) *trckd ldrs: hdwy over 2f out: rdn over 1f out: grad wknd* **20/1**
600- **9** hd **Love Island**201 7424 7-8-7 90 (t) GeorgeChaloner 3 86
(Richard Whitaker) *towards rr: pushed along 1/2-way: hdwy 2f out: sn rdn: kpt on fnl f* **33/1**
126- **10** 1 1/2 **George Bowen (IRE)**214 7122 4-9-2 99 TonyHamilton 14 91
(Richard Fahey) *in tch: rdn along 2f out: sn no imp* **10/1**
-024 **11** nse **Intense Style (IRE)**11 1857 4-8-10 93 DavidAllan 2 84
(Les Eyre) *chsd ldrs: rdn along 2f out: grad wknd* **25/1**
14-2 **12** 1 3/4 **George Dryden (IRE)**18 1644 4-9-7 104 PJMcDonald 11 90
(Ann Duffield) *dwlt and in rr tl sme late hdwy* **8/1**2
00-0 **13** 1 3/4 **Gamesome (FR)**29 1394 5-9-0 97 TomQueally 8 77
(Paul Midgley) *swtg: dwlt: sn pushed along into midfield: rdn 2f out and sn wknd* **20/1**
000- **14** 1 **Bogart**242 6312 7-8-5 88 (p) ShaneGray 15 65
(Kevin Ryan) *in tch: effrt 2f out: sn rdn and btn* **8/1**2
05-3 **15** 1 1/2 **God Willing**11 1848 5-8-5 88 (t) SilvestreDeSousa 17 60
(Declan Carroll) *towards rr: hdwy on outer and in tch 1/2-way: rdn along over 2f out: sn wknd* **12/1**
000- **16** 1 1/2 **Highland Acclaim (IRE)**201 7424 5-8-11 94 DanielTudhope 18 61
(David O'Meara) *a towards rr* **20/1**
04-0 **17** shd **Tatlisu (IRE)**18 1644 6-9-4 101 RyanMoore 13 68
(Richard Fahey) *a towards rr* **10/1**
5-2 **18** 2 3/4 **Flaming Spear (IRE)**27 1441 4-9-2 99 (p) RobertWinston 16 57
(Kevin Ryan) *a towards rr* **4/1**1

1m 11.23s (-0.67) **Going Correction** +0.15s/f (Good) 18 Ran SP% **128.6**
Speed ratings (Par 109): **110,109,109,108,107 107,106,104,104,102 102,100,97,96,94 92,92,88**
CSF £227.35 CT £10542.49 TOTE £10.40: £2.70, £5.10, £10.40, £5.70; EX 241.50 Trifecta £5826.40.
Owner C H Stevens **Bred** R C Dollar **Trained** Great Habton, N Yorks

FOCUS
A competitive event which should have a bearing on some of the major sprint handicaps this season. However there appeared a notable track/pace bias. The main action occurred on the far side of the track, which was where the pace was, and the leaders just didn't come back. Several leading contenders who raced towards the stands' side could never get involved, with the last five home drawn 15-17-18-13-16. Horses who raced on this section of the track probably deserve another chance. See The Sun continued Yorkshire trainers' domination of this race.

2159 DUKE OF YORK CLIPPER LOGISTICS STKS (GROUP 2) 6f
3:15 (3:16) (Class 1) 3-Y-O+
£68,052 (£25,800; £12,912; £6,432; £3,228; £1,620) **Stalls** Centre

Form RPR
13-1 **1** **Magical Memory (IRE)**27 1439 4-9-8 114 FrankieDettori 4 118+
(Charles Hills) *trckd ldrs: drvn over 1f out: led last 150yds: kpt on* **5/2**1
10-2 **2** 1/2 **Suedois (FR)**39 1197 5-9-8 110 DanielTudhope 9 115
(David O'Meara) *chsd ldrs: led over 1f out: hdd last 150yds: kpt on wl in clsng stages* **12/1**
613- **3** 1 **Danzeno**207 7278 5-9-8 113 PaulHanagan 6 112
(Michael Appleby) *lw: w ldrs: swtchd rt after 1f: upsides 3f out: hung lft: kpt on same pce last 100yds* **11/2**3
010- **4** 1 1/4 **Eastern Impact (IRE)**207 7278 5-9-8 112 JackGarritty 2 108
(Richard Fahey) *w ldrs: fdd fnl 75yds* **12/1**
112- **5** 1 3/4 **Twilight Son**207 7278 4-9-13 117 FergusSweeney 11 107+
(Henry Candy) *hld up in rr: hdwy over 2f out: styd on fnl f* **4/1**2
44-2 **6** 1 1/2 **Tupi (IRE)**27 1439 4-9-8 109 PatDobbs 1 97
(Richard Hannon) *chsd ldrs: drvn over 2f out: wknd appr fnl f* **12/1**
/4-6 **7** 1 **Dick Whittington (IRE)**38 1226 4-9-8 113 RyanMoore 7 94
(A P O'Brien, Ire) *dwlt: in rr: effrt over 2f out: kpt on one pce: nvr a factor* **16/1**
30-3 **8** shd **Mattmu**27 1439 4-9-8 113 (p) DavidAllan 10 94
(Tim Easterby) *sltly on toes: chsd ldrs: upsides over 1f out: hld whn sltly hmpd 150yds out: fdd* **8/1**
1-30 **9** 3 1/4 **Goken (FR)**11 1862 4-9-8 107 (t) JamieSpencer 3 83
(Kevin Ryan) *led: hdd over 1f out: sn wknd: eased nr fin* **33/1**
650- **10** 1 **Moonraker**214 7122 4-9-8 101 SilvestreDeSousa 8 80
(Mick Channon) *s.s: a bhd* **33/1**
10-0 **11** 1/2 **Moviesta (USA)**16 1730 6-9-8 110 AndreaAtzeni 5 79
(Edward Lynam, Ire) *half rrd s: in rr: hdwy over 2f out: lost pl over 1f out* **25/1**
1-00 **12** 1 **Jack Dexter**27 1439 7-9-8 105 WilliamBuick 12 75
(Jim Goldie) *outpcd in rr: sme hdwy over 1f out: nvr a factotr: eased in clsng stages* **50/1**

1m 10.52s (-1.38) **Going Correction** +0.15s/f (Good) 12 Ran SP% **115.7**
Speed ratings (Par 115): **115,114,113,111,109 107,105,105,101,99 99,97**
CSF £32.24 TOTE £3.10: £1.40, £3.70, £2.20; EX 34.40 Trifecta £222.40.
Owner Kennet Valley Thoroughbreds I **Bred** Wardstown Stud Ltd **Trained** Lambourn, Berks

FOCUS
The time was only 0.71secs quicker than the handicap over the trip and it's a bit debatable what the form is worth, with there an apparent draw/track bias. Still, the race produced another really likeable effort from Magical Memory, with Suedois helping with the standard.

2160 TATTERSALLS MUSIDORA STKS (GROUP 3) (FILLIES) 1m 2f 88y
3:45 (3:45) (Class 1) 3-Y-O
£56,710 (£21,500; £10,760; £5,360; £2,690; £1,350) **Stalls** Low

Form RPR
1-1 **1** **So Mi Dar**[21] 1567 3-9-0 101 FrankieDettori 6 112+
(John Gosden) *two handlers: sltly on toes: stdd s: hld up in rr: hdwy over 3f out: shkn up to ld 2f out: clr appr fnl f: pushed out: v readily* **4/5**[1]
41-4 **2** *4* **Fireglow**[10] 1888 3-9-0 105 WilliamBuick 2 103
(Mark Johnston) *lw: sn chsng ldrs: drvn 4f out: kpt on same pce fnl 2f* **3/1**[2]
0-22 **3** *hd* **Promising Run (USA)**[90] 534 3-9-4 107 JamesDoyle 3 107
(Saeed bin Suroor) *t.k.h: sn trcking ldrs: effrt over 2f out: kpt on same pce over 1f out* **20/1**
1-2 **4** *hd* **Harlequeen**[27] 1438 3-9-0 91 SilvestreDeSousa 5 103
(Mick Channon) *t.k.h in rr: effrt and outpcd over 3f out: hung lft and kpt on appr fnl f* **7/1**[3]
-210 **5** *4 1/2* **Australian Queen**[10] 1890 3-9-0 80 JamieSpencer 4 94
(David Elsworth) *lw: s.i.s: hdwy to chse ldrs after 3f: wknd fnl 150yds* **66/1**
0-23 **6** *1* **Light Up Our World (IRE)**[14] 1771 3-9-0 102 PatDobbs 1 92
(Richard Hannon) *chsd ldrs: wknd fnl f* **50/1**
1-4 **7** *6* **Best In The World (IRE)**[24] 1507 3-9-0 98 RyanMoore 7 87
(A P O'Brien, Ire) *bit lean: led: hdd 2f out: wknd over 1f out: bhd whn eased in clsng stages* **17/2**

2m 9.07s (-3.43) **Going Correction** -0.15s/f (Firm) **7 Ran SP% 111.8**
Speed ratings (Par 106): **107,103,103,103,99 99,94**
CSF £3.15 TOTE £1.80: £1.10, £1.80; EX 4.10 Trifecta £22.10.
Owner Lord Lloyd-Webber **Bred** Watership Down Stud **Trained** Newmarket, Suffolk

FOCUS
Rail movements meant this was run over 42yds shorter than advertised. They went a pretty steady pace in this traditional Oaks trial and it became a bit of a sprint up the straight, in which they raced up the centre. So Mi Dar was undeniably impressive, strongly suggesting that Minding won't have it easy at Epsom. Fireglow is rated more in line with her 2yo form.

2161 CONUNDRUM HR CONSULTING STKS (H'CAP) 7f
4:20 (4:21) (Class 3) (0-95,94) 3-Y-O **£12,938** (£3,850; £1,924; £962) **Stalls** Low

Form RPR
1 **1** **Castle Harbour**[29] 1397 3-8-13 **86** FrankieDettori 4 102+
(John Gosden) *hld up in rr: gd hdwy on inner 1/2-way: cl up over 2f out: rdn to ld over 1f out: edgd rt ins fnl f: kpt on wl* **9/2**[1]
1-3 **2** *1 1/2* **California Whip (USA)**[19] 1603 3-8-13 **86** RyanMoore 18 97+
(Richard Hannon) *lw: hld up in rr: hdwy 3f out: chsd ldrs over 1f out: sn rdn: styd on to chse wnr ins fnl f: no imp towards fin* **6/1**[3]
1-2 **3** *1 3/4* **Monteverdi (FR)**[27] 1442 3-9-1 **88** JamieSpencer 16 94
(Jamie Osborne) *stdd and swtchd lft s: hld up and bhd: swtchd lft to inner and gd hdwy over 2f out: chsd ldrs and rdn over 1f out: kpt on fnl f* **13/2**
30-0 **4** *1 1/4* **Lagenda**[27] 1446 3-8-8 **84** (p) JoeDoyle[(3)] 3 87
(Kevin Ryan) *slt ld: rdn along over 2f out: drvn and hdd over 1f out: kpt on gamely u.p fnl f* **66/1**
13-0 **5** *nk* **Abe Lincoln (USA)**[67] 836 3-9-6 **93** JimCrowley 8 95+
(Jeremy Noseda) *lw: hld up in midfield: hdwy whn nt clr run and lost pl over 2f out: sn swtchd lft towards inner and rdn: styd on strly appr fnl f: nrst fin* **11/2**[2]
00-2 **6** *1/2* **Hawatif (IRE)**[13] 1812 3-8-7 **80** JoeFanning 1 81
(Mark Johnston) *trckd ldrs: hdwy 1/2-way and sn cl up: chal over 2f out: sn rdn to dispute ld wl over 1f out and ev ch: drvn and kpt on same pce fnl f* **33/1**
133- **7** *1 1/4* **Eqleem**[270] 5396 3-9-2 **89** PaulHanagan 2 86
(Mark Johnston) *lw: hld up towards rr: gd hdwy towards inner 1/2-way: chsd ldrs 2f out: sn rdn and no imp* **25/1**
023- **8** *1/2* **Reputation (IRE)**[235] 6513 3-8-10 **83** PhillipMakin 17 79+
(John Quinn) *towards rr: hdwy on wd outside wl over 2f out: rdn wl over 1f out: kpt on fnl f* **33/1**
01- **9** *hd* **Constantino (IRE)**[236] 6491 3-8-7 **80** TonyHamilton 14 76+
(Richard Fahey) *swtg: chsd ldrs: rdn along wl over 2f out: drvn wl over 1f out: grad wknd* **10/1**
012- **10** *hd* **Albernathy**[320] 3587 3-9-0 **87** WilliamBuick 20 82+
(Charlie Appleby) *hld up in rr: hdwy on wd outside over 2f out: sn rdn and kpt on fnl f* **7/1**
3-53 **11** *1 3/4* **London Protocol (FR)**[20] 1585 3-8-8 **86** (p) JordanVaughan[(5)] 5 76
(K R Burke) *cl up: disp ld 1/2-way: rdn along wl over 2f out: sn drvn and wknd* **33/1**
65-0 **12** *1/2* **Dutch Mist**[19] 1599 3-9-0 **87** TomEaves 11 76
(Kevin Ryan) *midfield: rdn along 3f out: sn wknd* **33/1**
5-04 **13** *3/4* **Desert Ruler**[20] 1585 3-8-9 **82** GrahamLee 15 69
(Jedd O'Keeffe) *midfield: effrt 3f out: rdn along and edgd lft over 2f out: sn wknd* **33/1**
010- **14** *3/4* **Worlds His Oyster**[224] 6853 3-8-11 **84** GrahamGibbons 13 69+
(John Quinn) *hld up towards rr: sme hdwy whn n.m.r and sltly hmpd over 2f out: sn in rr* **33/1**
12-0 **15** *3/4* **Justice Law (IRE)**[19] 1603 3-9-7 **94** SilvestreDeSousa 19 77+
(David Elsworth) *hld up in tch on outer: hdwy over 4f out: chsd ldrs 3f out: rdn along over 2f out: sn wknd* **14/1**
6-1 **16** *1 1/4* **Brilliant Vanguard (IRE)**[23] 1524 3-8-7 **80** PaulMulrennan 9 60+
(Kevin Ryan) *hld up: hdwy 3f out: in tch whn n.m.r and hmpd over 2f out: sn lost pl and bhd* **25/1**
10-6 **17** *hd* **Blackout (FR)**[21] 1571 3-8-2 **78** TomMarquand[(3)] 6 57
(Richard Hannon) *lw: prom: rdn along over 3f out: sn wknd* **50/1**
21-1 **18** *1/2* **Replenish (FR)**[35] 1267 3-8-11 **84** FrederikTylicki 12 62
(James Fanshawe) *chsd ldrs: rdn along over 2f out: sn wknd* **12/1**
10-0 **19** *5* **Garden World (IRE)**[19] 1599 3-8-5 **78** JamesSullivan 7 42
(Nigel Tinkler) *lw: in tch: pushed along 3f out: sn rdn and wknd* **100/1**
15-6 **20** *12* **Powderhorn (IRE)**[34] 1288 3-8-11 **84** FMBerry 10 16
(Mark Johnston) *chsd ldrs: rdn along over 3f out: sn wknd* **50/1**

1m 24.95s (-0.35) **Going Correction** +0.05s/f (Good) **20 Ran SP% 128.9**
Speed ratings (Par 103): **104,102,100,98,98 97,96,95,95,95 93,92,92,91,90 88,88,88,82,68**
CSF £27.88 CT £188.76 TOTE £5.40: £2.00, £1.90, £2.30, £14.90; EX 25.00 Trifecta £114.90.
Owner Bermuda Thoroughbred Racing Limited **Bred** L A C Ashby Newhall Estate Farm **Trained** Newmarket, Suffolk

FOCUS
The right horses came to the fore, helped by making their moves on the faster part of the track on the inside of the field, in what looked a strong 3yo handicap. Plenty of pace on early and it set up for the closers. The winner impressed.

2162 BRITISH STALLION STUDS EBF NOVICE STKS (PLUS 10 RACE) 5f
4:50 (4:53) (Class 3) 2-Y-O **£12,938** (£3,850; £1,924; £962) **Stalls** High

Form RPR
1 **1** **Kananee (USA)**[15] 1749 2-9-8 0 JamesDoyle 3 89
(Saeed bin Suroor) *q str: mde all: drvn and kpt on fnl f* **5/4**[1]
2 *hd* **Medici Banchiere** 2-9-2 0 DougieCostello 9 82+
(K R Burke) *athletic: gd walker: s.s: in rr: hdwy and swtchd lft over 2f out: hung bdly lft over 1f out: kpt on wl: jst hld* **33/1**
3 *1* **Logi (IRE)** 2-9-2 0 RyanMoore 6 79+
(Richard Hannon) *cl-cpld: mid-div: hdwy over 1f out: kpt on same pce* **9/1**
3 **4** *1* **The Nazca Lines (IRE)**[12] 1840 2-9-2 0 PhillipMakin 1 75
(John Quinn) *leggy: sn chsng ldrs: kpt on same pce appr fnl f* **8/1**
3 **5** *2* **In First Place**[18] 1621 2-9-2 0 PaulHanagan 4 68
(Richard Fahey) *athletic: chsd ldrs: one pce over 1f out* **7/1**[3]
6 *nk* **Mistime (IRE)** 2-8-11 0 JoeFanning 5 62
(Mark Johnston) *leggy: sn w wnr: kpt on one pce appr fnl f* **25/1**
7 *1 3/4* **Computable** 2-9-2 0 DavidAllan 8 61+
(Tim Easterby) *str: bit bkwd: swtchd lft after s: hld up: hdwy over 2f out: chsng ldrs over 1f out: fdd last 75yds: will improve* **5/1**[2]
8 *3* **Comedy School (USA)** 2-8-11 0 WilliamBuick 10 50
(Mark Johnston) *unf: mid-div: drvn over 2f out: lost pl over 1f out: eased clsng stages* **14/1**
9 *3 3/4* **La Haule Lady** 2-8-11 0 GrahamLee 2 31
(Paul Midgley) *leggy: dwlt: outpcd and lost pl after 1f: sn bhd* **50/1**

1m 0.32s (1.02) **Going Correction** +0.15s/f (Good) **9 Ran SP% 110.1**
Speed ratings (Par 97): **97,96,95,93,90 89,87,82,76**
CSF £48.50 TOTE £2.10: £1.10, £6.50, £2.20; EX 49.70 Trifecta £290.90.
Owner Godolphin **Bred** Darley **Trained** Newmarket, Suffolk
■ Hemingway was withdrawn. Price at time of withdrawal 9/1. Rule 4 applies to all bets - deduct 10p in the pound.

FOCUS
This didn't look the strongest of contests, with no real market confidence behind any of the newcomers, the most interesting of which was withdrawn at the start. The field came stands' side, although the runner-up ended up far side, really coming home strongly once on that faster part of the track. The winner built on his debut effort and is rated in line with the race average.

2163 CONSTANT SECURITY STKS (H'CAP) 1m 4f
5:20 (5:21) (Class 4) (0-85,85) 4-Y-O+ **£9,703** (£2,887; £1,443; £721) **Stalls** Centre

Form RPR
13 **1** **Appeared**[27] 1430 4-9-5 **83** AndreaAtzeni 12 97+
(Roger Varian) *q str: lw: sn trcking ldr: drvn to ld over 1f out: jinked rt 1f out: fnd ex in clsng stages* **5/1**[2]
0-24 **2** *1 1/2* **Life Less Ordinary (IRE)**[15] 1737 4-9-1 **79** JamieSpencer 4 87
(Jamie Osborne) *hld up in rr: hdwy 4f out: led over 2f out: hdd over 1f out: no ex last 50yds* **14/1**
1-14 **3** *2* **Two Jabs**[47] 1081 6-9-7 **85** AndrewMullen 8 90
(Michael Appleby) *chsd ldrs: drvn and outpcd over 2f out: edgd lft over 1f out: kpt on fnl f* **16/1**
4-26 **4** *shd* **Jolievitesse (FR)**[46] 1093 4-8-12 **76** JoeyHaynes 16 81
(K R Burke) *mid-div: hdwy over 3f out: upsides over 1f out: kpt on same pce* **33/1**
2-42 **5** *nk* **Craggaknock**[11] 1853 5-9-4 **82** JasonHart 15 86
(Mark Walford) *in rr: drvn 4f out: styd on wl over 1f out: gng on at fin* **16/1**
26-P **6** *1 1/2* **Yorkidding**[18] 1642 4-9-6 **84** SilvestreDeSousa 3 86
(Mark Johnston) *chsd ldrs: kpt on same pce over 1f out* **12/1**
1-22 **7** *2* **Busy Street**[20] 1586 4-9-3 **81** BenCurtis 7 80
(Alan Swinbank) *lw: dwlt: hdwy 7f out: drvn 3f out: one pce whn edgd rt over 1f out* **11/1**
0-11 **8** *1/2* **Fast Pick (IRE)**[22] 1552 4-8-12 **76** (p) PhillipMakin 17 74
(Keith Dalgleish) *chsd ldrs: drvn over 4f out: hung lft and one pce fnl 2f* **10/1**
315- **9** *3/4* **Sellingallthetime (IRE)**[197] 7524 5-9-0 **83** (p) GeorgeBuckell[(5)] 18 80
(Michael Appleby) *in rr: hdwy on outer 5f out: outpcd over 3f out: kpt on fnl 2f* **20/1**
000- **10** *1 1/4* **Tapis Libre**[196] 7564 8-8-11 **80** NathanEvans[(5)] 5 75
(Michael Easterby) *hld up towards rr: hdwy over 3f out: one pce fnl 2f* **50/1**
020- **11** *3 1/2* **Cloud Monkey (IRE)**[197] 7524 6-8-13 **77** GrahamLee 11 66
(Martin Todhunter) *in rr-div: sme hdwy over 3f out: wknd fnl 2f* **66/1**
501- **12** *1* **Dominada (IRE)**[188] 6525 4-8-8 **79** BenRobinson[(7)] 10 67
(Brian Ellison) *dwlt: in rr: hdwy 3f out: hung lft 2f out: wknd fnl f* **33/1**
02-5 **13** *3/4* **Multellie**[25] 1493 4-9-6 **84** DavidAllan 14 70
(Tim Easterby) *in rr: hdwy over 3f out: lost pl over 1f out* **10/1**
23-3 **14** *nk* **Muhaafiz (IRE)**[18] 1633 4-8-13 **77** RyanMoore 13 66
(David Brown) *chsd ldrs: wkng whn n.m.r over 1f out: sn eased* **7/1**[3]
3005 **15** *hd* **Warfare**[9] 1923 7-9-1 **79** BarryMcHugh 1 65
(Tim Fitzgerald) *trckd ldrs: lost pl over 1f out* **66/1**
240- **16** *1 1/4* **Endless Credit (IRE)**[210] 6136 6-9-0 **78** PJMcDonald 6 62
(Micky Hammond) *in rr: hdwy over 3f out: wknd fnl 2f* **40/1**
000- **17** *5* **Odeon**[197] 7524 5-9-2 **80** TomEaves 9 56
(James Given) *led: hdd over 2f out: wknd over 1f out: eased clsng stages* **20/1**
11-0 **18** *2 3/4* **Sabre Rock**[14] 1775 6-8-8 **75** (t) ShelleyBirkett[(3)] 19 46
(Julia Feilden) *in rr: bhd whn eased clsng stages* **66/1**
1-43 **19** *1/2* **Prendergast Hill (IRE)**[21] 1568 4-9-7 **85** JimCrowley 2 55
(Ed de Giles) *in rr: hdwy over 3f out: chsng ldrs over 2f out: wknd over 1f out: heavily eased fnl 150yds* **9/2**[1]
000- **20** *14* **Carthage (IRE)**[13] 8038 5-8-11 **75** (b) PaulMulrennan 20 23
(Brian Ellison) *s.v.s: detached in last: sme hdwy 6f out: lost pl over 3f out: bhd whn heavily eased in clsng stages* **20/1**

2m 31.59s (-1.61) **Going Correction** -0.15s/f (Firm) **20 Ran SP% 129.0**
Speed ratings (Par 105): **99,98,96,96,96 95,94,93,93,92 90,89,88,88,88 87,84,82,82,72**
CSF £68.51 CT £1076.28 TOTE £5.60: £1.80, £3.10, £4.00, £9.20; EX 79.60 Trifecta £1356.40.
Owner Sheikh Mohammed Obaid Al Maktoum **Bred** Darley **Trained** Newmarket, Suffolk

FOCUS
Race distance 42yds shorter than advertised. A competitive handicap which didn't feature many unexposed types, but the winner was an obvious exception. He's capable of better. They went a reasonable gallop.
T/Jkpt: Not won. T/Plt: £32.60 to a £1 stake. Pool of £228281.66 - 5102.65 winning tickets.
T/Qpdt: £4.20 to a £1 stake. Pool of £16253.12 - 2798.35 winning tickets.
Walter Glynn & Joe Rowntree

2164 - 2166a (Foreign Racing) - See Raceform Interactive

1726 NAAS (L-H)

Wednesday, May 11

OFFICIAL GOING: Yielding to soft (soft in places)

2167a IRISH NATIONAL STUD EUROPEAN BREEDERS FUND BLUE WIND STKS (GROUP 3) 1m 2f

6:40 (6:40) 3-Y-O+

£34,705 (£11,176; £5,294; £2,352; £1,176; £588)

RPR

1 **Zhukova (IRE)**38 1227 4-9-9 109 PatSmullen 2 117
(D K Weld, Ire) *chsd ldrs in 3rd: rdn to ld over 2f out and sn clr: styd on wl to extend advantage ins fnl f: comf* **11/10**1

2 7 1/2 **Pretty Perfect (IRE)**24 1507 3-8-9 106 SeamieHeffernan 5 102
(A P O'Brien, Ire) *sn led: hdd over 2f out and nt qckn w wnr: kpt on same pce in clr 2nd ins fnl f* **3/1**2

3 5 1/2 **Bocca Baciata (IRE)**17 1680 4-9-12 111 ColmO'Donoghue 1 94
(Mrs John Harrington, Ire) *t.k.h early and sn restrained in 5th: rdn to chse ldrs in 3rd over 2f out: no imp appr fnl f: kpt on one pce* **4/1**3

4 3 1/2 **How High The Moon (IRE)**227 6791 3-8-9 99 MichaelHussey 4 85
(A P O'Brien, Ire) *racd in rr: pushed along in 5th over 2f out: kpt on one pce into 4th appr fnl f: nvr nrr* **20/1**

5 15 **Glamorous Approach (IRE)**24 1507 3-8-9 103 KevinManning 6 56
(J S Bolger, Ire) *sn trckd ldr in 2nd: rdn 3f out: nt qckn in 3rd over 2f out: sn wknd: eased ins fnl f* **8/1**

6 11 **Queen Blossom (IRE)**24 1507 3-8-12 106 ChrisHayes 3 37
(P J Prendergast, Ire) *chsd ldrs in 4th: rdn in 5th over 3f out: sn dropped to rr and no ex: eased ins fnl f* **16/1**

2m 16.62s (1.02)
WFA 3 from 4yo 15lb **6 Ran SP% 114.4**
CSF £4.79 TOTE £1.90: £1.60, £2.50; DF 4.80 Trifecta £9.00.
Owner Mrs C C Regalado-Gonzalez **Bred** Mrs C L Weld **Trained** Curragh, Co Kildare

FOCUS
A really convincing display here from a high class filly. A pb from the winner, with the runner-up rated to her latest form.

2168 - 2171a (Foreign Racing) - See Raceform Interactive

2076 SAINT-CLOUD (L-H)

Wednesday, May 11

OFFICIAL GOING: Turf: good to soft

2172a PRIX DE MAUREPAS (CLAIMER) (3YO) (TURF) 7f

3:55 (12:00) 3-Y-O **£8,455** (£3,382; £2,536; £1,691; £845)

RPR

1 **Bombay Night (FR)**50 3-8-7 0 FlorentGavilan(8) 4 76
(H-A Pantall, France) **39/1**

2 3/4 **Lila Mahyana (FR)**23 3-9-2 0 MickaelBarzalona 5 75
(J Reynier, France) **27/10**1

3 2 **Top Sensation (FR)**37 1240 3-8-11 0 UmbertoRispoli 6 65
(T Castanheira, France) **54/10**

4 3/4 **Rip Van Suzy (IRE)**57 948 3-8-11 0 AurelienLemaitre 8 63
(Jo Hughes) *midfield: rdn over 2f out: kpt on u.p but nt pce to chal* **15/1**

5 1 1/2 **Samarie**21 3-8-11 0 MaximeGuyon 11 59
(Mme Pia Brandt, France) **18/5**2

6 1/2 **Park Square (FR)** 3-9-1 0 (b) VincentCheminaud 9 61
(H-A Pantall, France) **19/1**

7 3/4 **Amisha (FR)**135 3-8-8 0 AntoineHamelin 3 52
(J Parize, France) **18/1**

8 1 1/2 **Koskoroba (FR)**17 3-9-4 0 Pierre-CharlesBoudot 12 58
(M Boutin, France) **42/10**3

8 dht **Monsieur Bernard (FR)**40 3-8-13 0 PierreBazire(5) 10 58
(G Botti, France) **43/5**

10 15 **Dahlia Bere (FR)**136 3-8-8 0 RonanThomas 7 8
(J Phelippon, France) **20/1**

11 20 **Wimple's Lad (IRE)** 3-8-8 0 EddyHardouin 1
(N Milliere, France) **30/1**

1m 30.51s (-1.69) **11 Ran SP% 121.0**
WIN (incl. 1 euro stake): 40.60. PLACES: 6.70, 1.60, 2.00. DF: 71.90. SF: 196.80..
Owner Erich Schmid **Bred** E Schmid **Trained** France

1885 NEWMARKET (R-H)

Thursday, May 12

OFFICIAL GOING: Good to firm (good in places; 7.7)
Wind: light, across Weather: sunny and warm

2173 CELEBRATING 350 YEARS OF MAKING HISTORY NOVICE AUCTION STKS (PLUS 10 RACE) 6f

5:10 (5:13) (Class 4) 2-Y-O **£4,204** (£1,251; £625; £312) **Stalls Low**

Form RPR

41 1 **Sayesse**16 1741 2-9-2 0 GeorgeBaker 3 77
(Mick Channon) *chsd ldrs: clsd to press ldr 2f out: rdn to ld over 1f out: hrd pressed and edgd lft u.p ins fnl f: hld on wl* **7/2**1

2 shd **Mutoondresdashorse** 2-9-0 0 LukeMorris 11 75
(Paul Cole) *wnt lft s: t.k.h early: hld up in tch: rdn and hdwy over 1f out: str chal ins fnl f: rn green and hung lft wl ins fnl f: jst hld* **22/1**

3 2 1/2 **Kings Heart (IRE)** 2-9-2 0 SteveDrowne 2 69
(Mark Usher) *in tch midfield: clsd to chse ldrs over 1f out: nt clr run and swtchd rt ins fnl f: sn chsng ldng pair: kpt on* **33/1**

61 4 1 1/2 **Springwood (IRE)**24 1520 2-9-1 0 AdamMcNamara(7) 10 71
(Richard Fahey) *in tch in midfield: effrt u.p and unable qck over 1f out: styd on same pce ins fnl f* **11/2**

5 nk **Spirit Of Sarwan (IRE)** 2-8-12 0 RichardKingscote 8 60
(Julia Feilden) *chsd ldr tl wl over 1f out: unable qck u.p 1f out: wknd fnl 100yds* **12/1**

6 nse **Golden Guest** 2-9-2 0 TomQueally 5 64+
(George Margarson) *s.i.s: in tch in last trio: rdn over 2f out: hdwy 1f out: styd on wl ins fnl f: nvr trbld ldrs* **33/1**

7 3/4 **Melissa Jane** 2-8-5 0 AntonioFresu 9 50
(Henry Spiller) *in tch in midfield: rdn 2f out: unable qck and outpcd over 1f out: rallied and kpt on ins fnl f: no threat to ldrs* **33/1**

8 nse **Hope Against Hope (IRE)** 2-8-11 0 JoeFanning 6 56
(Mark Johnston) *chsd ldrs: rdn and pressing ldrs over 1f out: no ex 1f out: 5th and btn whn bdly hmpd and snatched up ins fnl f: wknd fnl 100yds* **4/1**2

9 shd **Global Revival (IRE)** 2-9-2 0 AdamKirby 7 61+
(Ed Dunlop) *in tch in last trio: rdn over 1f out: kpt on ins fnl f: nt clr run towards fin: nvr trbld ldrs* **12/1**

10 2 1/2 **At The Beach** 2-9-2 0 PatDobbs 1 53
(Richard Hannon) *in tch in midfield: pushed along 2f out: stmbld sltly wl over 1f out: sn outpcd and wknd ins fnl f* **9/2**3

11 11 **Secret Dragon (IRE)** 2-8-4 0 JosephineGordon(5) 4 13
(Jamie Osborne) *sn dropped to rr and rn green: lost tch 2f out* **6/1**

1m 14.91s (2.71) **Going Correction** +0.30s/f (Good) **11 Ran SP% 118.6**
Speed ratings (Par 95): **93,92,89,87,87 87,86,86,85,82 67**
CSF £86.29 TOTE £4.40: £2.00, £8.40, £13.10; EX 78.20 Trifecta £1248.30.
Owner Lord Ilsley Racing (Steele Syndicate) **Bred** Llety Farms **Trained** West Ilsley, Berks

FOCUS
Probably fairly useful form from the leading pair who pulled clear. The bare form can't be rated any higher but plenty of these are likely to improve next time.

2174 EUINSURE H'CAP 1m 2f

5:45 (5:47) (Class 5) (0-75,75) 4-Y-O+ **£3,881** (£1,155; £577; £288) **Stalls Low**

Form RPR

3063 1 **Tatawu (IRE)**19 1640 4-8-9 63 WilliamCarson 1 70
(Peter Hiatt) *chsd ldr tl led 3f out: drvn over 1f out: styd on gamely u.p fnl f: all out* **16/1**

0-02 2 1/2 **Thecornishbarron (IRE)**14 1805 4-9-0 68 JackMitchell 16 77+
(John Ryan) *s.i.s: niggled along in rr early: clsd and nt clr run 2f out tl swtchd lft ins fnl f: str run fnl 100yds: wnt 2nd towards fin: nvr quite getting to wnr* **33/1**

25-2 3 3/4 **Ttainted Love**31 1390 4-9-7 75 (p) TedDurcan 14 79
(Chris Wall) *hld up in tch in midfield: effrt and hdwy over 1f out: chsd wnr and hung rt 1f out: styd on same pce ins fnl f: lost 2nd towards fin* **8/1**2

0-62 4 3/4 **Molten Lava (IRE)**10 1916 4-9-7 75 (b) LukeMorris 9 78
(Paul Cole) *t.k.h: hld up in tch in midfield: effrt: hdwy to chse ldrs and edgd rt jst ins fnl f: styd on same pce fnl 100yds* **16/1**

1U00 5 hd **Isis Blue**29 1418 6-9-3 71 (p) FrederikTylicki 5 73
(Rod Millman) *hld up wl in tch in midfield: rdn ent fnl 2f: hdwy u.p and chsd ldrs 1f out: styd on same pce u.p fnl 150yds* **16/1**

45/3 6 1 1/4 **Touch The Sky**13 1826 5-9-7 75 RyanMoore 10 76+
(David Elsworth) *t.k.h: hld up wl in tch in midfield: clsd to chse ldrs 2f out: sn unable qck but stl cl enough 1f out: one pce: hld and nt given a hrd time fnl 100yds* **5/4**1

1-11 7 hd **Bridge Of Sighs**16 1751 4-9-2 70 AdamKirby 7 71+
(Martin Smith) *hld up in tch towards rr: clsd and n.m.r 2f out: nt clr run over 1f out tl swtchd lft and rdn jst ins fnl f: styd on but no threat to ldrs* **12/1**3

2-24 8 2 **Sword Of The Lord**81 665 6-9-3 71 (p) TomQueally 3 66
(Nigel Twiston-Davies) *hld up in tch towards rr: hdwy on far rail over 2f out: nt clr run over 1f out tl swtchd lft ins fnl f: rdn and kpt on but nvr any ch w ldrs: eased cl home* **25/1**

001 9 1 1/2 **Shining Romeo**19 1640 4-8-13 67 FMBerry 4 59
(Denis Quinn) *chsd ldrs: wnt 2nd over 2f out: rdn and unable qck over 1f out: lost 2nd 1f out: wknd ins fnl f* **16/1**

6-06 10 2 1/2 **Handheld**26 1498 9-8-10 67 (p) ShelleyBirkett(3) 11 54
(Julia Feilden) *chsd ldrs: rdn and unable qck wl over 1f out: sn lost pl: wknd 1f out* **66/1**

26-4 11 1/2 **Belle Travers**16 1756 4-8-13 74 AdamMcNamara(7) 13 60
(Richard Fahey) *stdd s: hld up in tch in rr: effrt 2f out: no imp and hung bdly rt over 1f out: wl hld fnl f* **8/1**2

10-0 12 2 1/2 **Cornelious (IRE)**130 33 4-9-5 73 DarryllHolland 15 54
(Clifford Lines) *hld up in tch in rr: effrt and no imp whn carried rt and hmpd over 1f out: bhd ins fnl f* **12/1**3

52-6 13 1/2 **County Wexford (IRE)**14 1805 5-8-6 63 DanielMuscutt(3) 6 43
(Miss Joey Ellis) *led tl 3f out: losing pl u.p 2f out: bhd fnl f* **25/1**

2m 7.39s (1.59) **Going Correction** +0.30s/f (Good) **13 Ran SP% 117.7**
Speed ratings (Par 103): **105,104,104,103,103 102,102,100,99,97 96,94,94**
CSF £468.53 CT £4471.63 TOTE £24.50: £7.30, £5.30, £2.40; EX 732.00 Trifecta £5809.50 Part won..
Owner Bob Coles **Bred** Shadwell Estate Company Limited **Trained** Hook Norton, Oxon

FOCUS
A fair handicap, the runner-up very unlucky. The gallop wasn't strong, the race not really beginning in earnest until the final 3f, and the time was 30lb slower than the next. The winner found a bit on his recent form.

2175 CJ MURFITT LTD EBF STALLIONS MAIDEN STKS (PLUS 10 RACE) 1m 2f

6:15 (6:21) (Class 4) 3-Y-O **£5,498** (£1,636; £817; £408) **Stalls Low**

Form RPR

5- 1 **Firnas**258 5824 3-9-5 0 WilliamBuick 9 96+
(Charlie Appleby) *hld up in tch in rr of main gp: hdwy 3f out: rdn to ld and edgd rt wl over 1f out: sn clr: r.o strly: eased towards fin: v easily* **9/2**3

03 2 5 **Lexington Law (IRE)**10 1931 3-9-5 0 PatDobbs 2 81
(Richard Hannon) *hld up in tch in midfield: effrt over 2f out: swtchd rt and n.m.r over 1f out: wnt between rivals 1f out: styd on to go 2nd fnl 50yds: no ch w wnr* **25/1**

03- 3 1 **Perigee**197 7560 3-9-5 0 NickyMackay 4 79
(John Gosden) *hld up in tch in midfield: effrt jst over 2f out: rdn and chalng for placings over 1f out: wnt 2nd 1f out: kpt on same pce and no ch w wnr: lost 2nd fnl 50yds* **25/1**

32-2 4 1/2 **Daqeeq (IRE)**29 1426 3-9-5 90 DaneO'Neill 12 78
(Simon Crisford) *chsd ldr tl pushed into ld over 2f out: rdn and hdd wl over 1f out: sn outpcd: lost wl hld 2nd 1f out: plugged on same pce ins fnl f* **11/4**2

4 5 6 **Point Of View (IRE)**29 1426 3-9-5 0 AndreaAtzeni 6 66
(Roger Varian) *led tl over 2f out: sn pushed along and unable qck: no ch w wnr but stl ch of a pl 1f out: wknd qckly fnl 150yds* **5/4**1

5- 6 5 **Master Gunner (USA)**239 6442 3-9-5 0 RyanMoore 11 56
(Sir Michael Stoute) *hld up in tch: clsd to chse ldrs over 2f out: sn pushed along: nt handle downhill run and lost pl wl over 1f out: wl hld and nt given a hrd time fnl f* **14/1**

7 *9* **Marshall Aid (IRE)** 3-9-5 0 .... JamesDoyle 3 38
(Hugo Palmer) *trckd ldng trio: rdn over 2f out: sn struggling: wknd wl over 1f out: wl btn and eased ins fnl f* **40/1**

0- **8** *4 ½* **Wannabe Friends**[300] 4340 3-9-5 0 .... AdamKirby 7 29
(Luca Cumani) *t.k.h: hld up in tch in midfield: effrt to chse ldrs 3f out: lost pl and btn 2f out: wl btn and eased ins fnl f* **16/1**

9 *1 ¾* **Cadeaux Boxer** 3-9-5 0 .... RichardKingscote 1 26
(Martin Smith) *t.k.h: chsd ldrs tl 3f out: sn lost pl and wl btn 2f out: wl bhd and eased ins fnl f* **100/1**

10 *11* **Askari** 3-9-5 0 .... JackMitchell 5
(Roger Varian) *in tch in rr of main gp: rdn and struggling over 3f out: sn lost tch: t.o and eased ins fnl f* **33/1**

11 *45* **Balancing Time** 3-9-5 0 .... TomQueally 10
(Amanda Perrett) *s.i.s: rn green and sn rdn in detached last trio: t.o fnl 2f: virtually p.u ins fnl f* **66/1**

0- **12** *4 ½* **On Budget (IRE)**[286] 4831 3-9-5 0 .... WilliamCarson 14
(Anthony Carson) *stdd and wnt lft s: a detached in last trio: t.o fnl 2f: virtually p.u fnl f* **100/1**

0 **13** *39* **Missed The Cut**[17] 1701 3-9-5 0 .... GeorgeBaker 13
(Michael Wigham) *stdd s: a wl off the pce in last trio: t.o fnl 2f: virtually p.u fnl f* **100/1**

2m 6.61s (0.81) **Going Correction** +0.30s/f (Good) **13** Ran SP% **119.4**
Speed ratings (Par 101): **108,104,103,102,98 94,86,83,81,73 37,33,2**
CSF £114.74 TOTE £5.30: £1.40, £4.70, £6.20; EX 91.00 Trifecta £1097.30.
Owner Godolphin **Bred** Watership Down Stud **Trained** Newmarket, Suffolk

FOCUS
Probably not quite as strong a race as looked the case beforehand, a couple running below expectations, particularly the favourite, but it's still hard not to be taken with the performance of the winner. The form is rated around the second and third.

2176 JOSEF SEIBEL EUROPEAN COMFORT SHOE H'CAP 1m 4f
6:45 (6:55) (Class 4) (0-85,85) 4-Y-O+ **£7,762** (£2,310; £1,154; £577) **Stalls** Centre

Form RPR

1211 **1** **Indira**[6] 1999 5-9-0 **83** 6ex .... JosephineGordon(5) 8 92+
(John Berry) *hld up in tch in midfield: clsd and travelling wl 3f out: led 2f out: sn rdn: pressed ins fnl f: hld on wl: rdn out* **2/1**[1]

0-15 **2** *½* **Knight Music**[22] 1568 4-9-3 **81** .... RobertHavlin 5 89
(Michael Attwater) *hld up in tch in midfield: nt clr run over 2f out: rdn and hdwy to chse wnr over 1f out: chal ins fnl f: styd on but hld fnl 100yds* **12/1**

11-0 **3** *2* **Dolphin Village (IRE)**[24] 1531 6-9-1 **79** .... LukeMorris 1 84
(Jane Chapple-Hyam) *chsd ldrs: nt clr run and swtchd lft 2f out: swtchd lft again and rdn to chse ldrs over 1f out: kpt on same pce ins fnl f* **20/1**

54-0 **4** *3* **Rhythmical**[19] 1642 4-9-3 **81** .... JoeFanning 6 81
(Mark Johnston) *off the pce in last trio: rdn over 3f out: hdwy and hmpd over 1f out: styd on to go 4th ins fnl f: no threat to ldrs* **4/1**[3]

-303 **5** *2 ¼* **Agent Gibbs**[10] 1934 4-9-7 **85** .... AdamKirby 2 81
(Ali Stronge) *led: rdn over 2f out: hdd and drvn 2f out: outpcd and btn 1f out: wknd ins fnl f* **12/1**

0-00 **6** *2 ½* **Jacob Cats**[17] 1717 7-9-0 **78** .... FrederikTylicki 11 70
(William Knight) *stdd s: hld up off the pce in rr: clsd 6f out: rdn and hdwy 3f out: no imp over 1f out: wknd ins fnl f* **16/1**

6-00 **7** *2 ¼* **Saoi (USA)**[22] 1568 9-9-6 **84** .... GeorgeBaker 9 73
(William Knight) *stdd s: hld up off the pce in last pair: clsd and in tch 6f out: effrt on inner over 1f out: sn rdn and btn: wknd fnl f* **10/1**

00-3 **8** *12* **Goodwood Mirage (IRE)**[11] 1885 6-9-7 **85** .... WilliamCarson 4 55
(Michael Bell) *s.i.s: sn rcvrd to chse ldrs: rdn 3f out: lost pl and btn over 1f out: wl bhd and eased ins fnl f* **3/1**[2]

222- **9** *10* **Deep Blue Diamond**[239] 6431 4-8-2 **71** oh1 .... NoelGarbutt(5) 7 25
(Denis Quinn) *t.k.h: chsd ldr tl 3f out: sn lost pl and btn: wl bhd and eased ins fnl f* **33/1**

2m 33.54s (1.54) **Going Correction** +0.30s/f (Good) **9** Ran SP% **116.4**
Speed ratings (Par 105): **106,105,104,102,100 99,97,89,83**
CSF £28.34 CT £377.94 TOTE £2.50: £1.50, £3.40, £3.20; EX 33.40 Trifecta £322.90.
Owner Severn Crossing Partnership **Bred** Mrs M L Parry & P M Steele-Mortimer **Trained** Newmarket, Suffolk

FOCUS
Race distance increased by 9yds. This looks solid enough form for the level, the winner well-in off the same mark as when successful last week. Her form is similarly rated.

2177 DISCOVERNEWMARKET.CO.UK MAIDEN FILLIES' STKS (PLUS 10 RACE) 7f
7:20 (7:26) (Class 5) 3-Y-O **£3,881** (£1,155; £577; £288) **Stalls** Low

Form RPR

6-24 **1** **Summer Icon**[15] 1771 3-9-0 90 .... SilvestreDeSousa 11 86
(Mick Channon) *chsd ldr: rdn to chal over 1f out: drvn to ld ins fnl f: hld on: all out* **5/4**[1]

0- **2** *hd* **Delve (IRE)**[213] 7161 3-9-0 0 .... RyanMoore 7 85
(Sir Michael Stoute) *led: rdn and wnt clr w wnr over 1f out: drvn and hdd ins fnl f: battled on wl but hld towards fin* **6/1**[3]

3 *6* **Fashion Parade** 3-9-0 0 .... DarryllHolland 5 69
(Charles Hills) *hld up in tch in midfield: effrt and pushed along wl over 1f out: hdwy over 1f out: styd on to go 3rd wl ins fnl f: no threat to ldng pair* **25/1**

4 *nk* **Poole Belle (IRE)** 3-9-0 0 .... FergusSweeney 9 68
(Henry Candy) *hld up in tch towards rr: rdn and hdwy whn nt clr run and swtchd rt over 1f out: styd on to press for 3rd ins fnl f: kpt on but no threat to ldrs* **25/1**

0- **5** *1 ¼* **Heart Of An Angel**[262] 5696 3-8-11 0 .... LouisSteward(3) 13 65
(Philip McBride) *hld up in tch towards rr: rdn and hdwy 2f out: kpt on ins fnl f: no threat to ldrs* **66/1**

2 **6** *½* **Coronation Day**[17] 1723 3-9-0 0 .... LukeMorris 14 64
(James Tate) *t.k.h: hld up in tch in midfield: rdn and hdwy 2f out: 4th and no imp over 1f out: wl hld and plugged on same pce ins fnl f* **9/1**

7 *¾* **Wonderful Life (IRE)** 3-9-0 0 .... WilliamTwiston-Davies 4 62
(Richard Spencer) *hld up wl in tch in midfield: effrt and hdwy 2f out: 3rd and no imp over 1f out: lost 3rd and wknd ins fnl f* **33/1**

6-0 **8** *2 ¼* **Cloud Nine (FR)**[92] 516 3-8-11 0 .... GeorgeDowning(3) 1 56
(Tony Carroll) *hld up in tch towards rr: effrt and n.m.r on far rail wl over 1f out: sn rdn and no imp: wknd ins fnl f* **200/1**

05- **9** *½* **Happy Tidings**[234] 6588 3-9-0 0 .... RichardKingscote 2 54
(Tom Dascombe) *chsd ldrs: rdn and unable qck wl over 1f out: losing pl whn hung lft jst over 1f out: wknd ins fnl f* **3/1**[2]

10 *2 ¼* **Moving Robe (IRE)** 3-8-9 0 .... NoelGarbutt(5) 6 48
(Conrad Allen) *in tch in midfield: rdn 3f out: no hdwy and outpcd 2f out: wknd jst over 1f out* **100/1**

05 **11** *2 ¼* **Gabrielle**[28] 1436 3-9-0 0 .... PatCosgrave 16 42
(Ed Dunlop) *stdd s: t.k.h: hld up in tch towards rr: rdn and hdwy 2f out: no imp and edgd rt over 1f out: wknd ins fnl f* **16/1**

0- **12** *½* **Color Force (IRE)**[194] 7629 3-9-0 0 .... TomQueally 17 41
(Gay Kelleway) *in tch in midfield: rdn 3f out: lost pl and btn wl over 1f out: wknd fnl f* **66/1**

13 *hd* **Baileys Perle (IRE)**[147] 3-9-0 0 .... FrederikTylicki 8 40
(Chris Dwyer) *in tch in midfield: lost pl and rdn 2f out: sn bhd* **50/1**

14 *1 ½* **Dance Band (IRE)** 3-9-0 0 .... AndreaAtzeni 12 36
(Roger Varian) *chsd ldrs: rdn and lost pl 2f out: wknd over 1f out* **9/1**

15 *4* **Infiniti (IRE)** 3-9-0 0 .... SaleemGolam 3 25
(Rae Guest) *hld up in last pair: rdn and rn green over 2f out: sn btn* **100/1**

16 *2 ½* **Isostatic** 3-9-0 0 .... MartinLane 10 19
(Rae Guest) *s.i.s: rn green in rr: rdn over 2f out: sn wknd* **66/1**

1m 26.43s (1.03) **Going Correction** +0.30s/f (Good) **16** Ran SP% **129.2**
Speed ratings (Par 96): **106,105,98,98,97 96,95,93,92,90 87,86,86,84,80 77**
CSF £9.57 TOTE £2.40: £1.20, £2.40, £7.90; EX 11.10 Trifecta £202.90.
Owner Allen, Porter, Voute Partnership 1 **Bred** New Hall Stud **Trained** West Ilsley, Berks

FOCUS
The leading pair pulled well clear in this maiden, the runner-up's performance particularly promising on just her second visit to the racecourse. The winner set a high standard and is rated close to her Ascot form.

2178 NEWMARKETRACECOURSES.CO.UK FILLIES' H'CAP (GRASSROOTS FLAT MIDDLE DISTANCE SERIES QUALIFIER) 1m
7:55 (7:57) (Class 5) (0-75,75) 3-Y-O **£3,881** (£1,155; £577; £288) **Stalls** Low

Form RPR

1 **1** **Mukaabra**[78] 697 3-9-7 **75** .... AndreaAtzeni 2 82+
(James Tate) *in tch in midfield: swtchd lft and effrt to chal between horses over 1f out: led ins fnl f: r.o wl: rdn out* **3/1**[2]

35-0 **2** *¾* **Carpe Diem Lady (IRE)**[22] 1572 3-8-13 **67** .... DaneO'Neill 7 72
(Clive Cox) *chsd ldr: rdn and ev ch 2f out: drvn to ld over 1f out: hdd and styd on same pce ins fnl f* **22/1**

451- **3** *¾* **Little Kipling**[205] 7357 3-8-12 **66** .... HarryBentley 10 69
(Stuart Williams) *stdd s: hld up in tch in rr: rdn and effrt over 1f out: styd on u.p ins fnl f: wnt 3rd cl home* **20/1**

21 **4** *nk* **Battlement**[38] 1235 3-9-6 **74** .... GeorgeBaker 12 76+
(Roger Charlton) *stdd s: t.k.h: hld up in tch in rr: clsd to chse ldrs and travelling wl 3f out: rdn to chal and drifted rt 1f out: no ex fnl 100yds: outpcd and lost 3rd cl home* **7/4**[1]

061- **5** *2* **Crowning Glory (FR)**[168] 7997 3-9-1 **69** .... FMBerry 6 66
(Ralph Beckett) *in tch in midfield: effrt 2f out: effrt u.p to chse ldrs over 1f out: no ex jst ins fnl f: wknd wl ins fnl f* **16/1**

22-4 **6** *3 ½* **Combe Hay (FR)**[17] 1708 3-9-4 **75** .... LouisSteward(3) 1 64
(Henry Spiller) *stdd s: hld up in tch in rr: clsd on far rail 2f out: swtchd lft and rdn over 1f out: sn btn: wknd ins fnl f* **20/1**

00-2 **7** *¾* **Greenfyre (IRE)**[13] 1829 3-9-1 **69** .... PatDobbs 11 56
(Richard Hannon) *chsd ldrs: rdn 2f out: losing pl whn sltly short of room jst over 1f out: wknd ins fnl f* **14/1**

2-21 **8** *¾* **Siri**[16] 1755 3-9-6 **74** .... SilvestreDeSousa 8 59
(Mick Channon) *led: rdn 2f out: hdd and no ex over 1f out: wknd fnl f* **13/2**[3]

22-6 **9** *2 ¾* **Percy's Romance**[16] 1750 3-9-4 **72** .... RyanMoore 5 51
(Sir Michael Stoute) *wl in tch in midfield: rdn and lost pl ent fnl 2f: bhd over 1f out* **8/1**

0-20 **10** *1 ¼* **Zahrat Narjis**[14] 1816 3-9-1 **69** .... DavidNolan 4 45
(Richard Fahey) *in tch in midfield: rdn over 2f out: sn struggling and bhd over 1f out* **33/1**

60-0 **11** *11* **Mistymoistymorning (IRE)**[16] 1758 3-8-4 **65** ....(t) LuluStanford(7) 9 14
(John Ryan) *chsd ldrs: rdn and lost pl 3f out: bhd over 1f out* **50/1**

1m 39.37s (0.77) **Going Correction** +0.30s/f (Good) **11** Ran SP% **117.1**
Speed ratings (Par 96): **108,107,106,106,104 100,99,99,96,95 84**
CSF £73.62 CT £1150.99 TOTE £4.00: £1.60, £6.40, £4.20; EX 70.40 Trifecta £970.10.
Owner Sheikh Juma Dalmook Al Maktoum **Bred** Biddestone Stud Ltd **Trained** Newmarket, Suffolk

FOCUS
This appeals as strong form for the level, the principals all progressive.

2179 HOME OF RACING H'CAP 1m
8:25 (8:29) (Class 4) (0-85,83) 3-Y-O **£6,469** (£1,925; £962; £481) **Stalls** Low

Form RPR

03-1 **1** **Oh This Is Us (IRE)**[14] 1804 3-9-1 **77** .... PatDobbs 10 90+
(Richard Hannon) *hld up in tch: squeezed out and dropped to rr 2f out: smooth hdwy to chse ldrs 1f out: rdn and qcknd to ld ins fnl f: r.o wl: readily* **10/1**

10-3 **2** *2* **Midnight Macchiato (IRE)**[19] 1630 3-8-13 **75** .... TomQueally 3 80
(David Brown) *chsd ldrs: wnt 2nd 1/2-way: rdn and ev ch 2f out: drvn over 1f out: chsd wnr but nt pce of wnr ins fnl f* **6/1**[3]

1132 **3** *¾* **Mariee**[9] 1946 3-9-4 **80** .... JoeFanning 13 83
(Mark Johnston) *chsd ldr tl 1/2-way: styd handy: hdwy to ld over 2f out: sn rdn and sustained duel w runner-up: hdd and outpcd by wnr ins fnl f* **13/2**

313- **4** *¾* **Four On Eight**[204] 7398 3-9-5 **81** .... RyanMoore 4 82
(Luca Cumani) *in tch in midfield: swtchd lft and effrt 2f out: hdwy u.p to chse ldrs 1f out: styd on same pce ins fnl f* **7/2**[1]

150- **5** *1* **Salvo**[245] 6241 3-9-6 **82** .... StevieDonohoe 8 81
(Charlie Fellowes) *bmpd s: hld up in tch in midfield: effrt 2f out: hdwy u.p to chse ldrs 1f out: no imp and one pce ins fnl f* **16/1**

300- **6** *¾* **Cleverconversation (IRE)**[204] 7398 3-8-12 **77** ....[1] DannyBrock(3) 12 74
(Jane Chapple-Hyam) *chsd ldrs: rdn and ev ch 2f out tl no ex ent fnl f: wknd fnl 150yds* **20/1**

316- **7** *1* **Zaina Rizeena**[238] 6454 3-9-4 **80** .... DavidNolan 2 75
(Richard Fahey) *stdd and wnt lft s: t.k.h: hld up in tch in rr: swtchd rt and hdwy on far rail over 1f out: no imp 1f out: wknd wl ins fnl f* **33/1**

1- **8** *¾* **Dutch Gallery**[286] 4831 3-9-4 **80** .... RichardKingscote 11 73
(Tom Dascombe) *in tch in midfield: effrt 2f out: no imp u.p over 1f out: wknd ins fnl f* **12/1**

3-41 **9** *2 ¾* **Philadelphia (IRE)**[39] 1217 3-9-4 **80** ....[1] AndreaAtzeni 7 66
(Roger Varian) *stdd and wnt lft s: t.k.h: hld up in rr: effrt 2f out: sn no imp: wl btn 1f out* **11/2**[2]

012- **10** *3 ¾* **Edification**[240] 6419 3-9-7 **83** .... FergusSweeney 9 60
(Martyn Meade) *stdd s: t.k.h: hld up in tch in rr: effrt 2f out: sn drvn and no hdwy: wknd fnl f* **12/1**

222- **11** *10* **Gold Trade (IRE)**[210] 7237 3-9-5 **81** .... JamesDoyle 6 34
(Hugo Palmer) *t.k.h: led tl over 2f out: sn lost pl: bhd over 1f out: eased ins fnl f* **8/1**

2-10 **12** *7* **Al Hamd (IRE)**[29] 1409 3-9-4 **80** DaneO'Neill 1 16+
(Ed Dunlop) *racd alone towards far rail: in tch in midfield: rdn 2f out: sn lost pl: bhd and eased ins fnl f* **20/1**

1m 39.04s (0.44) **Going Correction** +0.30s/f (Good) **12** Ran SP% **119.2**
Speed ratings (Par 101): **109,107,106,105,104 103,102,102,99,95 85,78**
CSF £67.50 CT £433.85 TOTE £13.20: £4.10, £3.20, £2.20; EX 85.70 Trifecta £1089.70.
Owner Team Wallop **Bred** Herbertstown House Stud **Trained** East Everleigh, Wilts

FOCUS
A few of these look likely to go on to better things in 2016, which makes the performance of the easy winner all the more impressive.
T/Plt: £1,449.10 to a £1 stake. Pool: £59,453.99 - 29.95 winning units. T/Qpdt: £47.10 to a £1 stake. Pool: £7,001.77 - 109.87 winning units. **Steve Payne**

1892 SALISBURY (R-H)
Thursday, May 12

OFFICIAL GOING: Good to soft (soft in places; 7.2)
Wind: almost nil Weather: sunny

2180 GLEBE FARM STUD NOVICE STKS 5f
1:55 (1:55) (Class 5) 2-Y-O **£3,557** (£1,058; £529; £264) **Stalls** Low

Form RPR
1 **Bohemian Flame (IRE)** 2-9-2 0 DavidProbert 1 75+
(Andrew Balding) *s.i.s: in last pair: sn nudged along: hdwy 2f out: led over 1f out: kpt on wl: rdn out* **4/1**[3]

0 **2** *3/4* **Davarde (IRE)**[48] 1082 2-9-2 0 CathyGannon 4 72
(David Evans) *led: rdn and drifted lft bef being hdd 2f out: rallied and ev ch ent fnl f: kpt on* **7/2**[2]

0 **3** *1 1/2* **Compton Lane**[15] 1770 2-9-2 0 HarryBentley 5 67
(Rod Millman) *in tch: hdwy over 2f out: rdn to ld briefly wl over 1f out: kpt on same pce fnl f* **16/1**

4 *1 1/4* **Nibras Bounty (IRE)** 2-9-2 0 SeanLevey 2 62
(Richard Hannon) *trckd ldrs: looking to mount chal whn nt clr run over 2f out: sn rdn: nt pce to get on terms but kpt on to snatch 4th fnl strides* **11/10**[1]

P6 **5** *nk* **Spin Top**[23] 1543 2-9-2 0 (v[1]) OisinMurphy 8 61
(Joseph Tuite) *trckd ldrs: rdn whn edgd sltly rt bef ldng briefly 2f out: no ex fnl f: lost 4th fnl strides* **16/1**

6 *3 3/4* **Rock On Dandy (FR)** 2-9-2 0 MartinHarley 6 48
(Harry Dunlop) *chsd ldrs: rdn whn hmpd over 2f out: hld after: wknd fnl f* **33/1**

7 *2 1/4* **Wentwell Yesterday (IRE)** 2-9-2 0 WilliamCarson 7 40
(Jamie Osborne) *in tch: effrt over 2f out: nvr quite threatened: fdd fnl f* **9/1**

8 *26* **Met By Moonlight** 2-8-4 0 MitchGodwin(7) 3
(Ron Hodges) *rn green: s.i.s: sn outpcd: a in rr* **66/1**

1m 3.08s (2.08) **Going Correction** +0.175s/f (Good) **8** Ran SP% **116.0**
Speed ratings (Par 93): **90,88,86,84,83 77,74,32**
CSF £18.74 TOTE £4.70: £1.30, £1.70, £3.80; EX 22.00 Trifecta £162.30.
Owner Kennet Valley Thoroughbreds II **Bred** John & Anne-Marie O'Connor **Trained** Kingsclere, Hants

FOCUS
The ground was good to soft, soft in places for the opener, a moderate juvenile maiden in which those with experience hadn't shown much form. They raced away from the far rail. It's been rated in line with the race average.

2181 BATHWICK TYRES EBF STALLIONS BREEDING WINNERS FILLIES' H'CAP 1m 1f 198y
2:25 (2:26) (Class 4) (0-85,79) 3-Y-O **£7,762** (£2,310; £1,154; £577) **Stalls** Low

Form RPR
60-5 **1** **Visage Blanc**[36] 1276 3-8-9 **67** JFEgan 4 75
(Mick Channon) *trckd ldr: drvn to chal fr wl over 2f out: led ent fnl f: styd on wl to assert fnl 120yds* **7/1**

-322 **2** *2* **Zeehan**[16] 1759 3-9-0 **72** JohnFahy 5 76
(Clive Cox) *led: rdn whn strly pressed over 2f out: hdd ent fnl f: no ex fnl 120yds* **7/2**[2]

31- **3** *2 1/2* **Purple Magic**[188] 7730 3-9-0 **72** WilliamTwiston-Davies 3 71
(Michael Bell) *cl up: hrd rdn to take hld 3rd over 2f out: styd on same pce fnl f* **11/2**

2-21 **4** *6* **Intermittent**[49] 1063 3-9-2 **79** KieranShoemark(5) 6 66
(Roger Charlton) *hld up: rdn and stdy prog fr wl over 2f out: wnt 4th over 1f out: styd on but nvr any threat* **11/4**[1]

5-21 **5** *3 1/4* **Auntie Barber (IRE)**[15] 1779 3-9-2 **74** OisinMurphy 2 55
(Stuart Williams) *cl up: nt clr run briefly over 3f out: sn rdn: nt pce to get involved* **9/2**[3]

44-0 **6** *3 1/2* **Natural Wonder**[28] 1436 3-9-1 **73** SeanLevey 7 47
(Richard Hannon) *cl up: effrt 3f out: wknd 2f out* **11/1**

40-0 **7** *nse* **Bay Of St Malo (IRE)**[12] 1860 3-8-7 **68** TomMarquand(3) 1 41
(Richard Hannon) *trckd ldr: rdn 3f out: wknd 2f out* **11/1**

2m 11.3s (1.40) **Going Correction** +0.175s/f (Good) **7** Ran SP% **111.6**
Speed ratings (Par 98): **101,99,97,92,90 87,87**
CSF £30.05 CT £141.65 TOTE £9.90: £5.00, £1.50; EX 36.00 Trifecta £164.40.
Owner Norman Court Stud **Bred** Norman Court Stud **Trained** West Ilsley, Berks

FOCUS
A competitive little handicap featuring four last time out winners. They went a slow pace, suiting those ridden prominently. The runner-up has been rated a length up on her Nottingham latest, with the third to her maiden form.

2182 SMITH & WILLIAMSON MAIDEN FILLIES' STKS (DIV I) 1m 1f 198y
3:00 (3:00) (Class 5) 3-Y-O+ **£3,557** (£1,058; £529; £264) **Stalls** Low

Form RPR
1 **Sovereign Parade (IRE)** 3-8-13 0 RobertHavlin 11 90+
(John Gosden) *mid-div: hdwy 3f out: sn rdn: no further imp tl qcknd up wl jst over 1f out: str run to ld towards fin: readily* **5/6**[1]

0- **2** *1* **Julia Dream**[229] 6756 3-8-13 0 MartinHarley 4 81
(William Haggas) *trckd ldrs: str chal 2f out: sn rdn: narrow advantage jst over 1f out: kpt on but no ex whn hdd towards fin* **9/2**[2]

- **3** *1 3/4* **Ecureuil (IRE)** 3-8-10 0 MarcMonaghan(3) 1 77
(Hugo Palmer) *disp ld tl over 5f out: trckd ldr: led over 2f out: sn rdn: hdd jst over 1f out: no ex fnl 120yds* **14/1**

0 **4** *2* **Eastern Lady (IND)**[20] 1608 3-8-8 0 CallumShepherd(5) 2 73
(William Knight) *disp ld tl outrt ldr over 5f out: rdn and hdd over 2f out: kpt on tl no ex ins fnl f* **20/1**

5 *1/2* **Tangba** 3-8-13 0 HarryBentley 3 72
(Roger Varian) *trckd ldrs: rdn over 3f out: nvr threatened to rch ldrs but r.o wl fnl f* **14/1**

6 *nse* **Dubka** 3-8-13 0 TedDurcan 12 72
(Sir Michael Stoute) *wnt lft s: hld up towards rr: hdwy over 2f out: nvr threatened to rch ldrs but r.o wl fnl f* **14/1**

0- **7** *11* **Peppard**[213] 7161 3-8-13 0 DarryllHolland 10 50
(Charles Hills) *taken to s early: hld up towards rr: stmbld over 4f out: sme late prog: nvr trbld ldrs* **12/1**[3]

32 **8** *1* **Hold Hands**[24] 1529 5-10-0 0 FMBerry 5 49
(Brendan Powell) *trckd ldrs: rdn 3f out: wknd over 1f out* **12/1**[3]

0 **9** *1 1/4* **Midnight Mood**[41] 1179 3-8-13 0 LiamKeniry 7 45
(Dominic Ffrench Davis) *mid-div tl wknd 2f out* **100/1**

10 *1/2* **Dancing Rainbow (GR)** 3-8-8 0 HectorCrouch(5) 14 44
(Amanda Perrett) *carried lft s: a towards rr* **66/1**

0 **11** *29* **Imaginary**[20] 1609 3-8-13 0 OisinMurphy 13
(Heather Main) *carried sltly lft s: mid-div tl wknd 4f out: eased fnl 2f* **150/1**

12 *8* **Three Loves (IRE)** 3-8-13 0 DavidProbert 6
(Andrew Balding) *s.i.s: bhd: hmpd over 4f out: sn struggling and btn: eased fnl 2f* **33/1**

2m 10.98s (1.08) **Going Correction** +0.175s/f (Good)
WFA 3 from 5yo 15lb **12** Ran SP% **119.0**
Speed ratings (Par 100): **102,101,99,98,97 97,88,88,87,86 63,57**
CSF £4.32 TOTE £1.80: £1.20, £1.60, £3.30; EX 6.10 Trifecta £52.10.
Owner Isa Salman & Isa Abdulla **Bred** Lynch Bages Ltd & Camas Park Stud **Trained** Newmarket, Suffolk

FOCUS
An intriguing maiden in which the experienced runners couldn't really be considered, and it was the newcomers who dominated. They went a sensible gallop, with the majority racing away from the far rail. It's been rated around the race standard.

2183 SMITH & WILLIAMSON MAIDEN FILLIES' STKS (DIV II) 1m 1f 198y
3:35 (3:36) (Class 5) 3-Y-O+ **£3,557** (£1,058; £529; £264) **Stalls** Low

Form RPR
2-2 **1** **Shall We (IRE)**[20] 1609 3-8-13 0 TedDurcan 8 91+
(Sir Michael Stoute) *mde all: rdn over 1f out: styd on strly fnl f: comf* **1/1**[1]

04- **2** *3* **Malmoosa (IRE)**[201] 7467 3-8-13 0 SeanLevey 10 85
(Brian Meehan) *trckd ldrs: rdn to chse wnr fr wl over 1f out: styd on but nt pce to chal* **9/1**

52- **3** *2 1/4* **Mytimehascome**[164] 8048 3-8-13 0 HarryBentley 7 80
(Roger Varian) *trckd ldrs: rdn over 2f out: kpt on but nt pce to chal* **3/1**[2]

6 **4** *3/4* **Aqualis**[30] 1392 3-8-13 0 RobertHavlin 3 79
(John Gosden) *in tch: rdn 3f out: styd on fnl f but nt pce to get on terms* **8/1**[3]

5 *hd* **Dawn Horizons** 3-8-13 0 MartinHarley 4 79+
(William Haggas) *hld up towards rr: hdwy over 2f out: styd on nicely fnl f wout threatening to get involved* **25/1**

33- **6** *2 1/4* **Denham Sound**[254] 5970 3-8-13 0 CathyGannon 11 74
(Henry Candy) *in tch: rdn 3f out: sn one pce* **18/1**

6-2 **7** *1* **Corked (IRE)**[15] 1798 3-8-10 0 MarcMonaghan(3) 13 72
(Hugo Palmer) *trckd ldr: rdn to chal 3f out tl over 2f out: fdd ins fnl f* **12/1**

8 *2 1/4* **Leaping** 3-8-8 0 [1] KieranShoemark(5) 14 68
(Roger Charlton) *nvr bttr than mid-div* **66/1**

9 *3* **Lily Trotter** 3-8-13 0 FMBerry 2 62
(Ralph Beckett) *hld up towards rr: struggling 4f out: sme late prog: nvr threatened* **33/1**

10 *2 3/4* **Hepburn** 3-8-13 0 CharlesBishop 9 56
(Ali Stronge) *mid-div: rdn wl over 2f out: nvr any imp: fdd fnl f* **100/1**

0- **11** *6* **Princess Raihana**[202] 7422 3-8-10 0 TomMarquand(3) 12 44
(Marco Botti) *s.i.s: a towards rr* **66/1**

3 **12** *2 1/2* **Belle Of Seville**[36] 1265 3-8-6 0 SeanMooney(7) 5 39
(Dominic Ffrench Davis) *struggling 5f out: a bhd* **100/1**

0 **13** *2 1/2* **Wassail**[17] 1704 3-8-13 0 LiamKeniry 1 34
(Ed de Giles) *mid-div: rdn 3f out: wknd 2f out* **100/1**

2m 11.41s (1.51) **Going Correction** +0.175s/f (Good) **13** Ran SP% **121.8**
Speed ratings (Par 100): **100,97,95,95,95 93,92,90,88,86 81,79,77**
CSF £11.61 TOTE £2.00: £1.30, £1.80, £1.70; EX 15.40 Trifecta £40.20.
Owner Niarchos Family **Bred** Niarchos Family **Trained** Newmarket, Suffolk

FOCUS
There was more experience on show for the second division of this maiden, run in a 0.43s slower time than the first division, courtesy of a sedate pace. The third has been rated close to her 2yo form.

2184 GEORGE SMITH HORSEBOXES CLAIMING STKS 6f 212y
4:05 (4:05) (Class 5) 3-Y-O **£3,234** (£962; £481; £240) **Stalls** Low

Form RPR
5231 **1** **Broughtons Fancy**[16] 1764 3-8-4 69 CathyGannon 9 68
(David Evans) *trckd ldr: led 2f out: edgd rt whn rdn clr: comf* **10/11**[1]

3500 **2** *6* **Lady McGuffy (IRE)**[31] 1389 3-7-7 53 (t) SophieKilloran(7) 6 48
(Brian Barr) *hld up in tch: hdwy 3f out: rdn to chse wnr over 1f out: nvr threatened: kpt on same pce* **10/1**

-050 **3** *6* **Boycie**[41] 1176 3-9-2 70 (b[1]) GaryMahon(5) 4 53
(Richard Hannon) *led: rdn and hdd 2f out: no ex fnl f* **3/1**[2]

0300 **4** *3 3/4* **Lady Fontenail**[16] 1734 3-8-4 46 ow1 [1] AliceMills(5) 8 30
(Rod Millman) *bmpd leaving stalls: in last pair: styd on fnl f but nvr any threat* **25/1**

65-0 **5** *2 1/2* **Smile Of Approval (IRE)**[17] 1725 3-8-5 62 DannyBrock(3) 1 23
(Jonathan Portman) *hld up in tch: rdn over 2f out: nvr threatened: fdd fnl f* **12/1**

64- **6** *nk* **Rock Icon**[150] 8224 3-8-13 0 JimmyQuinn 2 27
(Patrick Chamings) *trckd ldr: rdn 3f out: wknd jst over 1f out* **20/1**

350- **7** *24* **Dismantle (IRE)**[157] 8129 3-8-12 69 (p) StevieDonohoe 5
(Grace Harris) *trckd ldr: rdn 3f out: wknd 2f out: eased ins fnl f* **8/1**[3]

00-0 **8** *10* **Britannia Boy**[16] 1734 3-7-12 33 (p[1]) MitchGodwin(7) 7
(Mark Usher) *dwlt: a bhd and nvr rcvrd: eased fnl f* **100/1**

1m 29.35s (0.75) **Going Correction** +0.175s/f (Good) **8** Ran SP% **114.9**
Speed ratings (Par 99): **102,95,88,84,81 80,53,41**
.Broughtons Fancy was claimed by Mr A. S. Reid for £6000;\n\x\x Lady McGuffy was bought by Mr P. D. Evans for £4000
Owner Lynn Cullimore & Mrs E Evans **Bred** Michael E Broughton **Trained** Pandy, Monmouths

FOCUS
A moderate claimer and there was a clear-cut winner. They went a strong gallop. The winner has been rated back to her early winter AW form.

2185 BATHWICK TYRES SALISBURY H'CAP (DIV I) 6f
4:35 (4:35) (Class 5) (0-75,75) 3-Y-O **£3,234** (£962; £481; £240) **Stalls** Low

Form RPR
410- **1** **Dancing Star**[264] 5625 3-9-7 **75** DavidProbert 7 82+
(Andrew Balding) *trckd ldr: led over 3f out: rdn 2f out: hld on: all out* **7/2**[2]

-212 **2** *hd* **Cultured Knight**[70] 797 3-9-5 **73**.............................. TimmyMurphy 14 79+
(Richard Hughes) *hld up: stdy prog fr over 3f out: str chal whn rdn jst ins fnl f: kpt on: jst hld* **17/2**
003- **3** *1 3/4* **Hitman**[202] 7430 3-9-4 **75**.............................. RobHornby(3) 9 75+
(William Muir) *s.i.s: outpcd in last: swtchd to centre and hdwy fr 2f out: disp cl 2nd ent fnl f: sn no ex* **3/1**[1]
35-0 **4** *2 1/2* **Not Touch**[30] 1397 3-9-7 **75**.............................. SeanLevey 8 67
(Richard Hannon) *s.i.s: towards rr: rdn whn swtchd lft and hdwy 2f out: styd on fnl f* **6/1**
33-3 **5** *1 1/4* **Waneen (IRE)**[26] 1487 3-9-4 **72**.............................. JFEgan 5 60
(Joseph Tuite) *led tl over 3f out: rdn and ev ch 2f out: sn hld: no ex fnl f* **11/1**
40-4 **6** *hd* **Wiley Post**[12] 1847 3-8-12 **69**.............................. TomMarquand(3) 6 57
(Richard Hannon) *mid-div: rdn over 2f out: no imp tl styd on fnl f* **5/1**[3]
3-32 **7** *4* **Sandacres**[90] 544 3-9-2 **70**.............................. OisinMurphy 3 45
(Laura Mongan) *prom for over 2f: chsd ldrs: rdn 3f out: wknd fnl f* **25/1**
21-0 **8** *1* **Star Jeanie**[27] 1452 3-9-2 **70**.............................. CathyGannon 11 42
(Henry Candy) *chsd ldrs: rdn over 2f out: wknd ent fnl f* **12/1**
0-00 **9** *8* **Swanton Blue (IRE)**[27] 1451 3-9-4 **72**.............................. KieranO'Neill 1 18
(Ed de Giles) *prom tl lost pl after 2f out: sn in rr* **20/1**
01- **10** *4* **Desirable**[148] 8244 3-8-11 **65**.............................. LiamKeniry 2
(Hughie Morrison) *chsd ldrs tl wknd 2f out* **20/1**

1m 15.75s (0.95) **Going Correction** +0.175s/f (Good) **10** Ran SP% **118.1**
Speed ratings (Par 99): **100,99,97,94,92 92,86,85,74,69**
CSF £32.72 CT £100.30 TOTE £3.30: £1.70, £2.70, £1.30; EX 15.60 Trifecta £90.60.
Owner J C Smith **Bred** Littleton Stud **Trained** Kingsclere, Hants

FOCUS
A fair sprint handicap featuring several unexposed types, including the first two home. The pace was fair. The form is hard to read, with the time a stone slower than the second division.

2186 BATHWICK TYRES SALISBURY H'CAP (DIV II) 6f
5:05 (5:07) (Class 5) (0-75,75) 3-Y-O **£3,234** (£962; £481; £240) **Stalls** Low

Form RPR
6-65 **1** **Zeeoneandonly (IRE)**[19] 1638 3-8-13 **70**..................(v) PhilipPrince(3) 1 78
(David Evans) *a.p: led 3f out: sn drvn: edgd lft over 1f out: kpt finding a little more whn strly pressed fnl f: hld on wl* **10/1**
060- **2** *nk* **Shanghai Glory (IRE)**[204] 7389 3-9-4 **75**......... MichaelJMMurphy(3) 12 82
(Charles Hills) *trckd ldrs: rdn for str chal fr wl over 1f out: ev ch thrght fnl f: hld cl home* **3/1**[1]
024- **3** *2 3/4* **Papa Luigi (IRE)**[242] 6351 3-9-5 **73**.............................. SeanLevey 4 71
(Richard Hannon) *trckd ldrs: rdn over 2f out: kpt on but nt pce to chal* **3/1**[1]
462 **4** *1 3/4* **Lucky Louie**[27] 1451 3-9-0 **68**.............................. RobertWinston 9 61
(Roger Teal) *hmpd s: sn outpcd in last: swtchd to centre and hdwy fr 2f out: r.o into 4th fnl f: nt rch ldrs* **6/1**[2]
03-0 **5** *4 1/2* **Equistar**[31] 1385 3-9-7 **75**.............................. MartinHarley 13 53
(Jonathan Portman) *mid-div: hdwy into 4th whn rdn 2f out: nvr threatened ldrs: fdd fnl f* **12/1**
0-23 **6** *1 1/4* **Born To Finish (IRE)**[16] 1745 3-8-8 **67**.............................. DavidParkes(5) 8 41
(Jeremy Gask) *outpcd towards rr: hdwy 2f out: no further imp fnl f* **10/1**
00-2 **7** *6* **Verne Castle**[16] 1753 3-9-5 **73**.............................. DavidProbert 3 28
(Andrew Balding) *chsd ldrs: rdn over 2f out: wknd ent fnl f* **7/1**[3]
644- **8** *1 1/4* **Mr Marchwood**[191] 7689 3-9-3 **71**.............................. LiamKeniry 10 22
(Sylvester Kirk) *mid-div for 2f: sn outpcd in rr* **20/1**
433- **9** *3 3/4* **Arctic Flower (IRE)**[149] 8230 3-8-0 **71** oh10.............. MitchGodwin(7) 2
(John Bridger) *led for 3f: wknd over 1f out* **100/1**
660- **10** *1 1/2* **Keiba (IRE)**[198] 7531 3-9-2 **70**.............................. TimmyMurphy 11 4
(Gary Moore) *stdd s: a towards rr* **20/1**
-500 **11** *hd* **Mostashreqah**[49] 1061 3-8-13 **67**.............................. CathyGannon 14
(Milton Bradley) *mid-div: hdwy 3f out: wknd and hung rt over 1f out* **50/1**

1m 14.7s (-0.10) **Going Correction** +0.175s/f (Good) **11** Ran SP% **115.1**
Speed ratings (Par 99): **107,106,102,100,94 92,84,83,78,76 76**
CSF £37.96 CT £116.00 TOTE £12.80: £3.70, £2.00, £1.20; EX 51.20 Trifecta £237.70.
Owner E R Griffiths **Bred** Cloneymore Farm Ltd **Trained** Pandy, Monmouths

FOCUS
Not much winning form on offer in this sprint handicap, run in a time 1.05sec faster than the first division. The form has been taken at face value for now, with the first two close to their 2yo bests.

2187 LITTLETON STUD RACING EXCELLENCE APPRENTICE H'CAP (WHIPS SHALL BE CARRIED BUT NOT USED) 6f 212y
5:40 (5:40) (Class 5) (0-70,70) 4-Y-0+ **£3,234** (£962; £481; £240) **Stalls** Low

Form RPR
0036 **1** **Duke Of North (IRE)**[16] 1735 4-8-10 **59**.............................. RhiainIngram 12 68
(Jim Boyle) *mid-div: hdwy over 2f out: tk narrow advantage over 1f out: kpt on wl* **16/1**
650- **2** *nk* **Doctor Bong**[185] 7775 4-9-0 **70**.............................. JoshuaBryan(7) 7 78
(Andrew Balding) *led: narrowly hdd jst over 1f out: kpt on wl w ev ch fnl f: hld cl home* **6/1**[3]
2-52 **3** *3 1/2* **Knight Of The Air**[16] 1735 4-9-0 **63**.............................. AdamMcLean 6 62+
(Mick Channon) *hld up: hdwy fr 2f out: wnt 3rd ent fnl f: styd on but no further imp on front pair* **5/1**[2]
6-04 **4** *2 3/4* **Marcano (IRE)**[16] 1735 4-8-10 **64**.............................. GeorgeWood(5) 8 55
(Rod Millman) *trckd ldr: chal 3f out tl 2f out: no ex fnl f* **5/2**[1]
2400 **5** *2 3/4* **Bognor (USA)**[17] 1702 5-9-1 **67**.............................. HarryBurns(3) 13 51
(Michael Attwater) *mid-div: hdwy 3f out: effrt over 2f out: fdd fnl f* **16/1**
000- **6** *hd* **Aye Aye Skipper (IRE)**[202] 7446 6-8-4 **58**.............................. JordanUys(5) 5 41
(Ken Cunningham-Brown) *trckd ldrs: hmpd ins 1st f: effrt 3f out: wknd fnl f* **8/1**
6614 **7** *1 1/4* **Diamond Vine (IRE)**[15] 1794 8-8-2 **56** oh6............(p) CameronNoble(5) 1 36
(Ronald Harris) *towards rr: sme late prog past btn horses: nvr a factor* **33/1**
00-5 **8** *1/2* **Ganymede**[16] 1756 5-9-7 **70**..............................(b) MeganNicholls 11 48
(Eve Johnson Houghton) *slowly away: nvr bttr than mid-div* **8/1**
40-5 **9** *1 1/4* **Welsh Inlet (IRE)**[118] 191 8-9-1 **69**.............................. MitchGodwin(5) 10 44
(John Bridger) *trckd ldr: rdn 3f out: wknd jst over 1f out* **16/1**
510- **10** *3/4* **Champagne Bob**[191] 7675 4-9-4 **70**.............................. JordanWilliams(3) 9 43
(Richard Price) *mid-div tl wknd 2f out* **9/1**
063- **11** *8* **Super Icon**[280] 5071 4-8-11 **60**.............................. GeorgiaCox 2 11
(Malcolm Saunders) *mid-div: pushed along over 3f out: wknd over 2f out* **16/1**

1m 29.66s (1.06) **Going Correction** +0.175s/f (Good) **11** Ran SP% **118.2**
Speed ratings (Par 103): **100,99,95,92,89 89,87,87,85,84 75**
CSF £109.70 CT £573.76 TOTE £21.00: £5.70, £2.60, £1.80; EX 161.20 Trifecta £2380.70 Part won..
Owner The Paddock Space Partnership **Bred** Kenilworth Partnership **Trained** Epsom, Surrey
■ Stewards' Enquiry : Joshua Bryan three-day ban: careless riding (May 26-28)

FOCUS
The finale was an average handicap where it again proved hard to come from behind. The winner has been rated to his winter best, and the second close to form.
T/Plt: £20.10 to a £1 stake. Pool: £37,031.77 - 1341.87 winning units. T/Qpdt: £2.10 to a £1 stake. Pool: £4,841.23 - 1389.09 winning units. **Tim Mitchell**

2157 YORK (L-H)
Thursday, May 12

OFFICIAL GOING: Good to firm (good in places; 8.0)
Wind: moderate 1/2 against Weather: fine and sunny, warm

2188 BETFRED "SUPPORTS JACK BERRY HOUSE" STKS (H'CAP) 5f
2:10 (2:12) (Class 2) (0-105,103) 4-Y-0+
£15,562 (£4,660; £2,330; £1,165; £582; £292) **Stalls** Centre

Form RPR
-032 **1** **Duke Of Firenze**[6] 2003 7-8-8 **90**.............................. DavidAllan 4 102+
(David C Griffiths) *in tch: hdwy over 2f out: rdn to ld jst over 1f out: clr ins fnl f: kpt on* **10/1**
51-1 **2** *3/4* **Brando**[29] 1427 4-9-1 **97**.............................. JamieSpencer 15 105+
(Kevin Ryan) *dwlt and towards rr: hdwy on outer wl over 1f out: rdn appr fnl f: styd on strly* **11/2**[1]
11-0 **3** *1* **Thesme**[27] 1453 4-8-9 **91**.............................. TomEaves 10 95
(Nigel Tinkler) *lw: racd towards stands' side: w ldr: rdn and ev ch over 1f out: kpt on same pce ins fnl f* **12/1**
2-26 **4** *1* **Red Baron (IRE)**[8] 1969 7-9-4 **100**.............................. NeilFarley 3 101
(Eric Alston) *racd towards far rail: slt ld: rdn wl over 1f out: sn drvn and edgd lft: hdd jst over 1f out: kpt on same pce* **12/1**
331- **5** *1/2* **Doctor Sardonicus**[229] 6732 5-8-10 **92**.............................. WilliamBuick 16 91
(David Simcock) *lw: hld up: hdwy on outer 2f out: rdn over 1f out: styd on fnl f: nrst fin* **16/1**
1331 **6** *3/4* **Royal Birth**[68] 835 5-8-8 **95**..............................(t) AaronJones(5) 6 91
(Stuart Williams) *sltly hmpd s: sn chsng ldrs: rdn and ch over 1f out: sn drvn and kpt on same pce* **8/1**[2]
10-1 **7** *hd* **Arctic Feeling (IRE)**[29] 1408 8-8-12 **97**.............................. SammyJoBell(3) 5 93
(Richard Fahey) *in tch towards far side: pushed along and sltly outpcd over 2f out: sn rdn and kpt on fnl f* **20/1**
5-00 **8** *shd* **Lucky Beggar (IRE)**[30] 1394 6-8-2 **89**.............................. EdwardGreatrex(5) 13 84
(Charles Hills) *towards rr: hdwy 2f out: sn rdn and kpt on fnl f* **12/1**
4510 **9** *1/2* **Normal Equilibrium**[12] 1857 6-8-7 **89**.............................. SilvestreDeSousa 2 82
(Robert Cowell) *trckd ldrs: hdwy 2f out: rdn and ev ch over 1f out: drvn and wknd fnl f* **14/1**
14/6 **10** *3/4* **Shamshon (IRE)**[48] 1083 5-9-4 **100**..............................(t) FrankieDettori 9 91
(Jamie Osborne) *lw: chsd ldrs: rdn along 2f out: grad wknd* **12/1**
624- **11** *3/4* **Toofi (FR)**[236] 6517 5-9-7 **103**.............................. AndreaAtzeni 11 91+
(Robert Cowell) *swtg: bhd tl sme late hdwy* **9/1**[3]
606- **12** *hd* **Distant Past**[229] 6747 5-8-8 **90**.............................. ShaneGray 12 77
(Kevin Ryan) *in rr: effrt over 2f out: sn rdn along and n.d* **25/1**
00-0 **13** *hd* **Son Of Africa**[28] 1439 4-9-1 **97**.............................. JamesDoyle 7 84
(Henry Candy) *swtg: wnt lft s: a towards rr* **11/1**
0-00 **14** *nk* **Desert Law (IRE)**[12] 1862 8-9-7 **103**.............................. MartinLane 1 89
(Paul Midgley) *swtg: racd on far rail: cl up: rdn and n.m.r over 1f out: grad wknd* **20/1**
0-06 **15** *hd* **Adam's Ale**[19] 1644 7-8-4 **86**.............................. DuranFentiman 14 71
(Mark Walford) *towards rr: rdn along on outer 1/2-way: n.d* **33/1**
14-6 **16** *3/4* **Meadway**[131] 17 5-8-10 **92**..............................(p) PaulMulrennan 17 74
(Bryan Smart) *racd towards stands' side: chsd ldrs: rdn over 2f out: sn wknd* **28/1**
0-22 **17** *nk* **Fast Track**[68] 835 5-8-13 **95**.............................. GrahamGibbons 8 76
(David Barron) *racd centre: cl up: rdn 2f out: wknd over 1f out* **11/1**

58.23s (-1.07) **Going Correction** +0.05s/f (Good) **17** Ran SP% **125.3**
Speed ratings (Par 109): **110,108,107,105,104 103,103,103,102,101 99,99,99,98,98 97,96**
CSF £60.60 CT £714.26 TOTE £11.40: £2.70, £2.00, £3.10, £3.10; EX 83.70 Trifecta £1011.60.
Owner Adlam,Damary-Thompson,Wilson,Griffiths **Bred** Cheveley Park Stud Ltd **Trained** Bawtry, S Yorks

FOCUS
Race distance as advertised. Running into a slight headwind in the straight, the ground would have been drying all the time and Andrea Atzeni described it as "fast". There was a big advantage in racing on the far side of the track on the opening day and the winner again came from there in this good-quality sprint, but there was pace across the track and it's doubtful track position was as significant here. The third helps with the initial standard.

2189 BETFRED MIDDLETON STKS (GROUP 2) (F&M) 1m 2f 88y
2:40 (2:42) (Class 1) 4-Y-0+
£68,052 (£25,800; £12,912; £6,432; £3,228; £1,620) **Stalls** Low

Form RPR
153- **1** **Beautiful Romance**[208] 7279 4-9-0 112.............................. JamesDoyle 4 114
(Saeed bin Suroor) *lw: trckd ldrs: hdwy 3f out: cl up 2f out: sn chal: rdn to ld appr fnl f: sn drvn and kpt on wl towards fin* **5/1**[3]
261- **2** *1 1/4* **Koora**[201] 7469 4-9-0 107.............................. JamieSpencer 5 111
(Luca Cumani) *hld up in tch: hdwy wl over 2f out: effrt and nt clr run over 1f out: swtchd rt and rdn ins fnl f: styd on wl: tk 2nd nr line* **8/1**
112- **3** *nk* **Journey**[208] 7279 4-9-0 114.............................. FrankieDettori 8 110
(John Gosden) *lw: trckd ldr: smooth hdwy to ld wl over 2f out: jnd and rdn wl over 1f out: hdd and drvn appr fnl f: kpt on same pce last 150yds: lost 2nd nr line* **5/4**[1]
520- **4** *1/2* **Speedy Boarding**[208] 7279 4-9-0 104.............................. FrederikTylicki 3 109
(James Fanshawe) *trckd ldng pair on inner: hdwy 3f out: rdn along and n.m.r wl over 1f out: drvn along on inner and styng on whn n.m.r ins fnl f: kpt on u.p towards fin* **8/1**
604- **5** *8* **Lady Of Dubai**[242] 6359 4-9-0 109.............................. AndreaAtzeni 7 98
(Roger Varian) *trckd ldrs: hdwy on outer over 2f out: rdn to chal over 1f out: sn disp ld and ev ch tl drvn and wknd ins fnl f* **9/2**[2]
00-2 **6** *2 1/4* **Ballybacka Queen (IRE)**[36] 1279 5-9-0 100.............................. KevinManning 1 89
(P A Fahy, Ire) *led: pushed along wl over 3f out: rdn and hdd wl over 2f out: wknd and hld whn n.m.r on inner over 1f out* **33/1**
02-0 **7** *12* **Crystal Zvezda**[11] 1886 4-9-0 106.............................. RyanMoore 6 65
(Sir Michael Stoute) *awkward s and dwlt: a bhd* **10/1**

2m 8.85s (-3.65) **Going Correction** -0.05s/f (Good) **7** Ran SP% **113.5**
Speed ratings (Par 115): **112,111,110,110,103 102,92**
CSF £42.63 TOTE £5.70: £2.20, £3.80; EX 37.70 Trifecta £77.50.
Owner Godolphin **Bred** Rabbah Bloodstock Limited **Trained** Newmarket, Suffolk

FOCUS

Rail alignment around the home bend resulted in the distance of this race being reduced by 31yds. This fillies' and mares' Group 2 has gone to some genuine Group 1 performers in recent years, with Sariska and Midday to name but two. The early pace looked decent for this year's renewal, but it soon steadied and didn't pick up again until inside the last 3f. There wasn't much covering the principals at the line, but the form still looks strong. The winner has been rated to form, and the fourth helps with the standard.

2190 BETFRED DANTE STKS (GROUP 2) 1m 2f 88y

3:15 (3:15) (Class 1) 3-Y-O

£90,736 (£34,400; £17,216; £8,576; £4,304; £2,160) **Stalls** Low

Form RPR

31 **1** **Wings of Desire**[19] 1651 3-9-0 88 FrankieDettori 9 115+
(John Gosden) *t.k.h early: hld up in rr: stdy hdwy on outer 3f out: trckd ldrs 2f out: effrt to chse ldr ent fnl f: sn rdn to chal: kpt on wl to ld nr fin* **9/1**[3]

125- **2** *nk* **Deauville (IRE)**[201] 7463 3-9-0 110 (t) RyanMoore 12 114
(A P O'Brien, Ire) *swtg: prom: trckd ldr 1/2-way: led over 2f out: rdn ent fnl f: drvn last 100yds: hdd and no ex towards fin* **13/2**[2]

13-2 **3** *1 ½* **Foundation (IRE)**[28] 1440 3-9-0 110 WilliamBuick 5 111+
(John Gosden) *lw: t.k.h: hld up towards rr: hdwy 3f out: n.m.r wl over 1f out: sn rdn: chsd ldng pair ins fnl f: kpt on* **13/2**[2]

513- **4** *2 ¾* **Muntazah**[229] 6752 3-9-0 103 PaulHanagan 1 106+
(Owen Burrows) *lw: t.k.h early: trckd ldrs on inner: n.m.r and sltly outpcd 3f out: pushed along and hdwy 2f out: rdn and n.m.r over 1f out: swtchd lft and drvn ent fnl f: kpt on same pce* **16/1**

1-1 **5** *3 ¼* **Midterm**[20] 1605 3-9-0 112 PatSmullen 3 99
(Sir Michael Stoute) *hld up in rr: hdwy 3f out: rdn along on outer 2f out: drvn over 1f out: kpt on one pce* **5/4**[1]

2-1 **6** *1 ¼* **Victory Bond**[19] 1646 3-9-0 93 PatCosgrave 6 97
(William Haggas) *str: t.k.h early: chsd ldrs: hdwy 3f out: rdn along 2f out: drvn and wandered ent fnl f: sn wknd* **12/1**

1 **7** *nse* **Choreographer (IRE)**[17] 1715 3-9-0 87 AndreaAtzeni 2 96+
(Roger Varian) *t.k.h early: hld up towards rr: effrt on inner and nt clr run over 2f out: rdn and nt clr run again over 1f out: squeezed through on inner ins fnl f: kpt on: nrst fin* **16/1**

51-3 **8** *nk* **Harrison**[20] 1610 3-9-0 93 SilvestreDeSousa 7 96
(Mick Channon) *in tch: hdwy to chse ldrs over 3f out: rdn along and edgd lft over 2f out: sn drvn and wknd wl over 1f out* **16/1**

3- **9** *nk* **Black Sea (IRE)**[32] 1368 3-9-0 103 (t) SeamieHeffernan 8 95
(A P O'Brien, Ire) *swtg: hld up: a towards rr* **20/1**

6-55 **10** *2* **Kentuckyconnection (USA)**[12] 1864 3-9-0 108 (b) PaulMulrennan 11 91
(Bryan Smart) *chsd ldrs on outer: hdwy 4f out: rdn along over 2f out: sn wknd* **33/1**

1011 **11** *4 ½* **Sea Of Flames**[33] 1338 3-9-0 101 JamesDoyle 10 82
(David Elsworth) *set stdy pce: qcknd up 1/2-way: rdn along over 3f out: hdd over 2f out: sn wknd* **50/1**

1-0 **12** *12* **Top Beak (IRE)**[22] 1567 3-9-0 90 (t) JimmyFortune 4 58
(Hughie Morrison) *chsd ldr on inner: pushed along over 3f out: sn rdn and wknd over 2f out* **100/1**

2m 7.37s (-5.13) **Going Correction** -0.05s/f (Good) **12** Ran SP% **117.1**
Speed ratings (Par 111): **118,117,116,114,111 110,110,110,110,108 105,95**
CSF £63.83 TOTE £8.10: £2.40, £2.10, £1.90; EX 57.90 Trifecta £202.60.
Owner Lady Bamford **Bred** Lady Bamford **Trained** Newmarket, Suffolk

FOCUS

Rail alignment around the home bend resulted in the distance of this race being reduced by 31yds. The biggest field for this, the leading Derby trial, since 1984, but having hugged the far rail in the straight there were a few who found trouble and the short-price favourite, who headed up the Derby betting prior to the race, disappointed. They went a steady enough gallop (time still 1.48sec quicker than the Middleton) and doubtful this form would be good enough to win a standard Derby, but the winner is hugely progressive and it's hardly a vintage year. The form makes sense rated around the second, third and fourth.

2191 BETFRED TV HAMBLETON STKS (H'CAP) (LISTED RACE) 1m

3:45 (3:49) (Class 1) (0-110,108) 4-Y-O+

£28,355 (£10,750; £5,380; £2,680; £1,345; £675) **Stalls** Low

Form RPR

112- **1** **Always Smile (IRE)**[330] 3279 4-9-4 **105** JamesDoyle 16 114+
(Saeed bin Suroor) *lw: hld up in tch: hdwy over 2f out: chsd ldrs on outer over 1f out: rdn to ld 1f out: sn edgd lft: drvn out* **8/1**[1]

40-0 **2** *nk* **Convey**[19] 1637 4-9-1 **102** (p) RyanMoore 8 110+
(Sir Michael Stoute) *lw: hld up in tch: hdwy over 2f out: nt clr run over 1f out: swtchd lft and rdn jst ins fnl f: sn chsng wnr: drvn and ch last 100yds: no ex towards fin* **10/1**[2]

56-6 **3** *1 ¼* **One Word More (IRE)**[19] 1627 6-8-11 **98** DavidAllan 5 103
(Tim Easterby) *swtg: hld up in rr: hdwy 3f out: swtchd rt towards outer wl over 1f out: sn rdn and styd on appr fnl f* **14/1**

-005 **4** *½* **Glory Awaits (IRE)**[84] 623 6-8-13 **100** (b) JamieSpencer 11 104
(David Simcock) *trckd ldrs: hdwy over 2f out: rdn to chal over 1f out: ev ch whn hung lft appr fnl f: sn drvn and kpt on same pce* **20/1**

04-2 **5** *½* **Donncha (IRE)**[40] 1195 5-9-0 **101** AndreaAtzeni 4 104+
(Robert Eddery) *hld up towards rr: hdwy over 2f out: effrt whn n.m.r and swtchd lft over 1f out: sn rdn and styd on wl fnl f* **8/1**[1]

10-4 **6** *½* **Oracolo (IRE)**[15] 1797 4-8-7 **94** oh3 MartinDwyer 12 96
(David Simcock) *hld up towards rr: hdwy over 2f out: nt clr run jst over 1f out: sn swtchd lft and rdn: styd on wl towards fin* **16/1**

210- **7** *nse* **Baraweez (IRE)**[243] 6340 6-9-5 **106** DaleSwift 17 107
(Brian Ellison) *swtg: trckd ldr: cl up 3f out: rdn 2f out: sn led: drvn and hdd appr fnl f: kpt on same pce* **66/1**

35-5 **8** *¾* **Master The World (IRE)**[12] 1861 5-9-3 **104** (p) SilvestreDeSousa 9 104
(David Elsworth) *towards rr: hdwy over 2f out: rdn whn n.m.r wl over 1f out: swtchd rt and kpt on u.p fnl f* **8/1**[1]

1-04 **9** *¾* **Express Himself (IRE)**[19] 1629 5-9-0 **101** JimCrowley 14 99
(Ed McMahon) *dwlt and in rr: hdwy wl over 2f out: rdn wl over 1f out: no imp* **8/1**[1]

36-5 **10** *nse* **Hors De Combat**[15] 1774 5-9-5 **106** PatSmullen 10 104
(James Fanshawe) *chsd ldrs: rdn along over 2f out: grad wknd* **12/1**

411- **11** *1* **Third Time Lucky (IRE)**[229] 6755 4-9-1 **102** PaulHanagan 7 98
(Richard Fahey) *plld hrd: chsd ldng pair: rdn along 3f out: wknd 2f out* **8/1**[1]

00-6 **12** *1* **Two For Two (IRE)**[12] 1871 8-8-12 **99** RaulDaSilva 15 92
(David Loughnane) *a towards rr* **80/1**

0-40 **13** *nk* **Birdman (IRE)**[19] 1629 6-9-4 **105** PhillipMakin 1 98
(David O'Meara) *trckd ldrs: pushed along over 3f out: rdn wl over 2f out: sn wknd* **14/1**

55-0 **14** *nk* **Mothers Finest (IRE)**[12] 1858 4-8-8 **95** JoeyHaynes 3 87
(K R Burke) *chsd ldrs: rdn along 3f out: sn wknd* **50/1**

10-1 **15** *2* **Lord Of The Rock (IRE)**[40] 1195 4-8-7 **94** oh1 PaulMulrennan 6 81
(Michael Dods) *swtg: led: rdn along 3f out: drvn and hdd wl over 1f out: grad wknd* **11/1**[3]

0-30 **16** *½* **Balty Boys (IRE)**[15] 1774 7-9-7 **108** BenCurtis 13 94
(Brian Ellison) *hld up in rr: effrt wl over 2f out: sn rdn and nvr a factor* **40/1**

06-5 **17** *4 ½* **Alfred Hutchinson**[19] 1629 8-8-13 **100** (p) DavidNolan 18 76
(David O'Meara) *hld up towards rr: hdwy on outer 3f out: rdn along 2f out: sn wknd* **16/1**

1-00 **18** *½* **Ingleby Angel (IRE)**[12] 1871 7-8-9 **96** RoystonFfrench 2 71
(Colin Teague) *in tch on inner: pushed along 3f out: sn rdn and wknd* **100/1**

0/05 **19** *5* **Lord Of The Land (IRE)**[19] 1627 5-9-1 **102** DanielTudhope 19 65
(David O'Meara) *prom: chsd ldng pair over 3f out and sn prom: rdn along 2f out: hld whn n.m.r and hmpd wl over 1f out: sn wknd* **12/1**

1m 36.34s (-2.66) **Going Correction** -0.05s/f (Good) **19** Ran SP% **126.3**
Speed ratings (Par 111): **111,110,109,108,108 107,107,107,106,106 105,104,104,103,101 101,96,96,91**
CSF £83.30 CT £1157.79 TOTE £7.60: £2.50, £2.50, £3.50, £5.50; EX 94.30 Trifecta £6517.80.
Owner Godolphin **Bred** Darley **Trained** Newmarket, Suffolk

FOCUS

Rail alignment around the home bend resulted in the distance of this race being reduced by 31yds. A red-hot and competitive handicap run at a true pace, but with such a big field and the runners staying against the inside rail, racing room was always going to be tight. The finish was fought out between two horses that had only raced eight times between them previously, so it's worth taking a positive view of the form. It's set around the third.

2192 BRITISH STALLION STUDS EBF WESTOW STKS (LISTED RACE) 5f

4:15 (4:16) (Class 1) 3-Y-O

£25,519 (£9,675; £4,842; £2,412; £1,210; £607) **Stalls** Low

Form RPR

535- **1** **Easton Angel (IRE)**[237] 6495 3-8-11 103 PaulMulrennan 4 101
(Michael Dods) *trckd ldrs: led 2f out: edgd rt fnl f: drvn out* **10/3**[1]

3603 **2** *¾* **Gracious John (IRE)**[15] 1773 3-9-5 102 PatSmullen 10 106
(David Evans) *wnt rt s: racd towards stands' side: hdwy to chse ldrs over 2f out: 2nd 1f out: kpt on same pce last 50yds* **13/2**

610- **3** *1 ¼* **Fine Blend (IRE)**[195] 7594 3-9-0 98 MartinDwyer 1 97
(William Muir) *lw: chsd ldrs: outpcd over 3f out: hdwy over 1f out: 3rd last 150yds: kpt on same pce* **25/1**

3-33 **4** *3* **Shadow Hunter (IRE)**[27] 1453 3-9-0 95 ShaneKelly 8 86
(Paul D'Arcy) *chsd ldrs: effrt 2f out: kpt on one pce* **11/1**

65-0 **5** *½* **Rosina**[27] 1453 3-8-11 89 PJMcDonald 9 81
(Ann Duffield) *trckd ldrs: outpcd over 2f out: kpt on fnl f* **33/1**

10-6 **6** *1 ¼* **Orvar (IRE)**[15] 1773 3-9-5 98 JamesDoyle 6 84
(Richard Hannon) *lw: chsd ldrs: drvn over 2f out: edgd lft over 1f out: one pce* **16/1**

31-1 **7** *¾* **Exist**[14] 1812 3-8-11 90 FrankieDettori 7 74
(John Gosden) *lw: trckd ldrs: led over 3f out: hdd 2f out: wknd fnl f* **7/2**[2]

36-2 **8** *¾* **Lady Macapa**[20] 1607 3-8-11 94 JimCrowley 2 71
(William Knight) *led over 1f: chsd ldrs: wknd fnl f* **11/2**

360- **F** **Areen (IRE)**[244] 6269 3-9-2 106 DanielTudhope 5
(David O'Meara) *w ldrs: fell over 2f out: fatally injured* **9/2**[3]

58.41s (-0.89) **Going Correction** +0.05s/f (Good) **9** Ran SP% **113.2**
Speed ratings (Par 107): **109,107,105,101,100 98,97,95,**
CSF £24.78 TOTE £4.10: £1.50, £2.30, £4.50; EX 24.10 Trifecta £492.10.
Owner Al Shaqab Racing & Ritchie Fiddes **Bred** James Waldron **Trained** Denton, Co Durham

FOCUS

Race distance as advertised. Not a terribly strong Listed event, the runner-up raced solo towards the stands' side and his run seemed to confirm the previous day's track bias had more or less been wiped out. The runner-up has been rated close to his AW best and the better view of his turf form.

2193 STRATFORD PLACE STUD BREEDS GROUP WINNERS EBF STALLIONS MAIDEN STKS (PLUS 10 RACE) 6f

4:45 (4:49) (Class 3) 2-Y-O **£12,938** (£3,850; £1,924; £962) **Stalls** High

Form RPR

4 **1** **Admiralty Arch**[22] 1579 2-9-5 0 JimmyFortune 1 86+
(Richard Hannon) *angular: chsd ldrs: drvn over 2f out: styd on to ld last 75yds* **14/1**

2 *1 ¼* **Masham Star (IRE)** 2-9-5 0 SilvestreDeSousa 3 82+
(Mark Johnston) *str: led: hdd and no ex last 75yds* **11/2**[3]

4 **3** *¾* **Gulliver**[11] 1889 2-9-5 0 PatSmullen 9 80
(Hugo Palmer) *dwlt: in rr: hdwy over 3f out: chsng ldrs over 1f out: edgd lft: kpt on same pce last 150yds* **7/4**[1]

4 *1* **Tafaakhor (IRE)** 2-9-5 0 FrankieDettori 7 77+
(Richard Hannon) *cmpt: hld up in rr: hdwy over 3f out: chsng ldrs over 1f out: edgd lft: kpt on same pce: will improve* **3/1**[2]

5 *5* **Thornton** 2-9-5 0 TonyHamilton 2 62
(Richard Fahey) *unf: scope: chsd ldrs: wknd appr fnl f* **13/2**

3 **6** *3* **Harome (IRE)**[12] 1868 2-9-5 0 SamJames 6 53
(David Loughnane) *w'like: bit on the leg: chsd ldrs: lost pl over 1f out* **33/1**

7 *nk* **My Girl Maisie (IRE)** 2-9-0 0 PatrickMathers 4 47
(Richard Guest) *w'like: s.i.s: drvn over 3f out: chsng ldrs over 2f out: lost pl over 1f out* **50/1**

0 **8** *3* **Charlie Chaplin (GER)**[11] 1889 2-9-5 0 (p) KierenFallon 5 43
(Robert Eddery) *chsd ldrs: drvn 3f out: lost pl over 1f out* **7/1**

9 *½* **Lou's Diamond** 2-9-0 0 GrahamGibbons 8 37
(Michael Easterby) *leggy: s.i.s: sn chsng ldrs: wknd over 1f out* **50/1**

1m 12.97s (1.07) **Going Correction** +0.05s/f (Good) **9** Ran SP% **116.1**
Speed ratings (Par 97): **94,92,91,90,83 79,78,74,74**
CSF £88.27 TOTE £11.00: £2.90, £2.00, £1.20; EX 51.70 Trifecta £190.50.
Owner W H Ponsonby **Bred** G B Partnership **Trained** East Everleigh, Wilts

FOCUS

Race distance as advertised. An interesting maiden, but the first four pulled well clear of the others. The field raced centre-to-nearside and the main action unfolded up the middle. The winner has been rated in line with the race average.

2194 RACING UK NOW IN HD STKS (H'CAP) 2m 88y

5:20 (5:20) (Class 3) (0-90,90) 4-Y-O+ **£12,938** (£3,850; £1,924; £962) **Stalls** Low

Form RPR

20-0 **1** **Saigon City**[19] 1642 6-9-8 **88** TomEaves 14 95
(Declan Carroll) *trckd ldrs: hdwy over 3f out and sn pushed along: swtchd rt and rdn wl over 1f out: led appr fnl f: sn drvn and kpt on strly* **33/1**

216- **2** 1 3/4 **The Cashel Man (IRE)**[223] 6896 4-9-0 **88** GeorgeBuckell(5) 5 93+
(David Simcock) *hld up in rr: hdwy on outer over 3f out: rdn wl over 1f out: styd on strly fnl f: tk 2nd on line* **4/1**[2]

005- **3** nse **Rite To Reign**[195] 7597 5-9-7 **87** GrahamGibbons 3 92
(Philip McBride) *lw: hld up towards rr: hdwy 4f out: effrt and n.m.r 2f out: swtchd lft and rdn to chse ldrs over 1f out: drvn to chse wnr ins fnl f: kpt on: lost 2nd on line* **14/1**

335/ **4** shd **Cardinal Walter (IRE)**[55] 1843 7-9-10 **90** JamieSpencer 4 95
(Nicky Henderson) *lw: hld up in rr: hdwy over 3f out: rdn to chse ldrs 2f out: drvn and kpt on same pce fnl f* **11/4**[1]

61-0 **5** 3/4 **Grumeti**[19] 1642 8-9-8 **88** AdamBeschizza 15 92
(Alan King) *in tch: hdwy over 3f out: led wl over 2f out: drvn and hdd appr fnl f: grad wknd* **12/1**

0/ **6** 1/2 **Matorico (IRE)**[19] 5-9-4 **84** (tp) JimCrowley 7 88+
(Jonjo O'Neill) *hld up towards rr: stdy hdwy over 2f out: chsd ldrs and shkn up over 1f out: sn rdn and kpt on fnl f* **7/1**[3]

104- **7** 1 3/4 **Waterclock (IRE)**[68] 5292 7-8-11 **77** (p) PJMcDonald 10 78
(Micky Hammond) *towards rr: effrt over 3f out and sn rdn along: plugged on u.p fnl 2f* **33/1**

1220 **8** 1/2 **Royal Marskell**[48] 1067 7-9-8 **88** SilvestreDeSousa 16 89
(Gay Kelleway) *trckd ldrs: hdwy over 4f out: rdn along wl over 2f out: drvn over 1f out and one pce* **28/1**

42-0 **9** 3 1/2 **Wind Place And Sho**[22] 1568 4-9-4 **87** (p) GrahamLee 13 84
(James Eustace) *trckd ldr: led 7f out: rdn along over 3f out: hdd wl over 2f out and grad wknd* **16/1**

403/ **10** 1 3/4 **Daliance (IRE)**[20] 652 7-8-8 **74** (b) TonyHamilton 8 68
(Noel Williams) *trckd ldrs on inner: hdwy 4f out: rdn along 3f out: drvn over 2f out and grad wknd* **80/1**

4111 **11** 1/2 **Alphabetical Order**[21] 1586 8-9-3 **83** PhillipMakin 1 77
(David O'Meara) *hld up: hdwy 4f out: rdn along wl over 2f out: sn drvn and one pce* **15/2**

20-1 **12** nse **Sisyphus**[18] 1665 4-8-9 **78** AndrewMullen 12 72
(Ollie Pears) *lw: ed: edgd rt bnd after 4f: sn hung bdly rt and racd v wd: hdd 7f out: edgd lft to join field and cl up 4f out: rdn wl over 2f out: drvn over 1f out: sn wknd* **8/1**

410- **13** 3/4 **Katie Gale**[267] 5526 6-8-13 **79** ShaneKelly 9 72
(Michael Appleby) *prom: rdn along 4f out: drvn 3f out: sn wknd* **40/1**

0001 **14** 1/2 **Gabrial The Terror (IRE)**[48] 1085 6-8-3 **72** (p) SammyJoBell(3) 2 64
(Richard Fahey) *a towards rr* **20/1**

350/ **15** 3 3/4 **Poitin**[34] 1332 6-9-1 **84** RobbieDowney(3) 6 72
(Keith Henry Clarke, Ire) *in tch: hdwy to chse ldrs over 4f out: rdn along 3f out: n.m.r wl over 2f out: sn wknd* **20/1**

3m 32.08s (-2.42) **Going Correction** -0.05s/f (Good)
WFA 4 from 5yo+ 3lb **15** Ran SP% **124.8**
Speed ratings (Par 107): **104,103,103,103,102 102,101,101,99,98 98,98,98,97,95**
CSF £157.78 CT £2012.78 TOTE £39.20: £7.70, £2.20, £5.30; EX 260.60 Trifecta £4916.80 Part won..
Owner C H Stephenson,Tate,Flegg & Bousfield **Bred** Martin Percival **Trained** Malton, N Yorks

FOCUS
Rail alignment around the home bend resulted in the distance of this race being reduced by 31yds. A competitive staying handicap and they went a solid pace. The winner was never too far away, but the second, third and fourth were dropped right out early. The fourth has been rated close to his old Flat form.
T/Jkpt: not won. T/Plt: £349.40 to a £1 stake. Pool: £223,206.88 - 466.24 winning units. T/Qpdt: £37.80 to a £1 stake. Pool: £16,325.98 - 318.93 winning units. **Joe Rowntree & Walter Glynn**

2195 - (Foreign Racing) - See Raceform Interactive

1878 HAMILTON (R-H)
Friday, May 13

OFFICIAL GOING: Good to firm (good in places; 8.0)
Wind: Breezy, half against Weather: Cloudy, bright

2196 IRISH STALLION FARMS EBF NOVICE STKS (PLUS 10 RACE) (£20K HIGHLAND SPRING WATER SERIES QUALIFIER) 5f 7y
5:45 (5:48) (Class 4) 2-Y-O **£4,269** (£1,270; £634; £317) **Stalls** High

Form RPR

1 **1** **Lomu (IRE)**[14] 1840 2-9-9 0 PhillipMakin 5 85
(Keith Dalgleish) *dwlt: t.k.h and sn prom: effrt and plld out over 1f out: rdn to ld ins fnl f: kpt on wl* **11/10**[1]

4 **2** nk **Whiteandgold**[22] 1583 2-8-11 0 PaulMulrennan 3 72
(Bryan Smart) *pressed ldr: led 1/2-way: rdn over 1f out: hdd ins fnl f: kpt on: hld nr fin* **9/1**

3 **3** 3 1/4 **Rapid Rise (IRE)**[20] 1635 2-8-13 0 JoeDoyle(3) 7 65
(David Brown) *prom: drvn and outpcd 2f out: rallied fnl f: tk 3rd cl home: nt rch first two* **4/1**[2]

4 **4** nse **Tagur (IRE)**[11] 1921 2-9-2 0 ShaneGray 2 65
(Kevin Ryan) *trckd ldrs on outside: rdn along 2f out: kpt on same pce ins fnl f* **9/1**

4 **5** nk **Kahrab (IRE)**[14] 1840 2-9-2 0 JoeFanning 6 64
(Mark Johnston) *t.k.h early: led to 1/2-way: styd cl up and sn rdn along: one pce ins fnl f: no ex and lost two pls nr fin* **9/2**[3]

6 4 **Chickenfortea (IRE)** 2-8-13 0 NeilFarley 4 47
(Eric Alston) *t.k.h: hld up: checked and carried lft over 3f out: sn outpcd: n.d after* **25/1**

0 **7** hd **Benidiction (IRE)**[29] 1443 2-8-11 0 GrahamLee 1 44
(Ann Duffield) *wnt rt s: hld up and t.k.h on outside: swtchd lft over 3f out: rdn over 2f out: wknd wl over 1f out* **25/1**

59.48s (-0.52) **Going Correction** -0.20s/f (Firm) **7** Ran SP% **113.5**
Speed ratings (Par 95): **96,95,90,90,89 83,83**
CSF £12.09 TOTE £1.90: £1.40, £3.90; EX 15.80 Trifecta £50.80.
Owner Steve Macdonald **Bred** Michael G Daly **Trained** Carluke, S Lanarks

FOCUS
The rail on the loop was out 6 yards adding approximately 24 yards to races two, three and four. The stalls were on stands' side for races at 5f and 1m4f, the centre for the 6f events and on the inside for the 1m and 1m1f contests. The favourite had to work quite hard in this novice but came out on top to make it 2-2. Those in behind the first two probably dictate the level.

2197 WATCH RACING UK IN HD MAIDEN STKS 1m 1f 34y
6:15 (6:15) (Class 5) 3-Y-O+ **£3,881** (£1,155; £577; £288) **Stalls** Low

Form RPR

1 **Sindarban (IRE)**[222] 5738 5-10-0 85 PhillipMakin 1 87
(Keith Dalgleish) *t.k.h: mde all: rdn over 1f out: hld on wl fnl f* **9/2**[3]

5- **2** hd **Fastnet Tempest (IRE)**[205] 7395 3-9-0 0 GrahamLee 2 84+
(William Haggas) *dwlt: hld up in tch: smooth hdwy over 2f out: edgd rt and chsd wnr over 1f out: sn rdn: kpt on fnl f: jst hld* **11/8**[1]

2 **3** 4 1/2 **Warp Factor (IRE)**[12] 1883 3-9-0 0 TadhgO'Shea 8 74
(John Patrick Shanahan, Ire) *t.k.h: chsd ldrs: drvn along over 3f out: rallied 2f out: outpcd fnl f* **15/8**[2]

0 **4** 15 **Jessica Jo (IRE)**[16] 1798 3-8-9 0 JoeFanning 6 36
(Mark Johnston) *chsd ldr: drvn along over 3f out: wknd fr 2f out* **28/1**

2-5 **5** 7 **Euchen Glen**[12] 1883 3-9-0 0 PaulMulrennan 4 26
(Jim Goldie) *t.k.h: hld up in last pl: struggling over 3f out: sn btn* **7/1**

1m 56.23s (-3.47) **Going Correction** -0.20s/f (Firm)
WFA 3 from 4yo+ 14lb **5** Ran SP% **111.0**
Speed ratings (Par 103): **107,106,102,89,83**
CSF £11.33 TOTE £5.30: £1.70, £1.30; EX 9.90 Trifecta £21.30.
Owner Paul & Clare Rooney **Bred** His Highness The Aga Khan's Studs S C **Trained** Carluke, S Lanarks

FOCUS
Race distance increased by 24yds. They went a good pace and the first two pulled clear in this maiden. The winner has been rated in line with the better view of his 3yo maiden form in Ireland.

2198 RACING TOGETHER H'CAP 1m 67y
6:50 (6:50) (Class 5) (0-75,75) 4-Y-O+ **£3,881** (£1,155; £577; £288) **Stalls** Low

Form RPR

005- **1** **Push Me (IRE)**[185] 7784 9-9-4 **72** RoystonFfrench 1 81
(Iain Jardine) *hld up in midfield: nt clr run over 2f out: effrt and hdwy over 1f out: led wl ins fnl f: kpt on strly* **8/1**[2]

5-22 **2** 3/4 **Jacbequick**[11] 1923 5-9-0 **73** (p) JoshDoyle(5) 2 81
(David O'Meara) *in tch: effrt and rdn 2f out: chal briefly wl ins fnl f: hld nr fin* **2/1**[1]

-042 **3** hd **Lightning Spree (IRE)**[12] 1884 4-8-9 **63** ShaneGray 11 70
(Kevin Ryan) *slowly away: hld up: weaved through fr 2f out: rdn and r.o wl fnl f: hld nr fin* **10/1**

22-0 **4** 1 **Know Your Name**[16] 1785 5-9-7 **75** NeilFarley 8 80
(Eric Alston) *midfield: hdwy over 2f out: rdn: edgd rt and led over 1f out: hdd and no ex wl ins fnl f* **10/1**

44-0 **5** 1 3/4 **Oriental Tiger**[20] 1633 5-8-13 **67** PaulMulrennan 10 68+
(Iain Jardine) *s.i.s: hld up: stdy hdwy whn nt clr run over 2f out: effrt over 1f out: kpt on fnl f: nt pce to chal* **20/1**

20-0 **6** 2 1/2 **Normandy Knight**[16] 1785 4-9-4 **72** TonyHamilton 7 67
(Richard Fahey) *prom: hdwy to ld over 2f out: rdn and hdd over 1f out: wknd ins fnl f* **17/2**[3]

1330 **7** 2 1/4 **Royal Holiday (IRE)**[6] 2051 9-9-4 **72** (p) SamJames 6 62
(Marjorie Fife) *led: drvn and hdd over 3f out: wknd wl over 1f out* **12/1**

10-0 **8** hd **Tanawar (IRE)**[16] 1785 6-9-0 **68** (b) JamesSullivan 3 58
(Ruth Carr) *t.k.h: hld up: rdn along over 2f out: no imp fr over 1f out* **33/1**

66-0 **9** 1 **So It's War (FR)**[24] 1555 5-9-4 **72** (p) PhillipMakin 9 59
(Keith Dalgleish) *pressed ldr: led over 3f out to over 2f out: sn rdn: wknd over 1f out* **9/1**

000- **10** hd **Arantes**[22] 6826 5-9-2 **75** (p) NathanEvans(5) 13 62
(R Mike Smith) *s.i.s: hld up: hdwy on outside over 3f out: hung lft and outpcd fr 2f out* **40/1**

06-0 **11** 4 1/2 **Gambino (IRE)**[32] 1380 6-9-3 **74** JoeDoyle(3) 4 50+
(John David Riches) *hld up: smooth hdwy on outside 3f out: rdn and wknd over 1f out* **22/1**

036- **12** 2 1/2 **Tectonic (IRE)**[235] 6581 7-9-2 **70** (p) JoeFanning 5 41
(Keith Dalgleish) *t.k.h: in tch on ins: pushed along over 2f out: wknd over 1f out* **14/1**

13-3 **13** 1 3/4 **Lara Carbonara (IRE)**[12] 1884 4-8-9 **63** TadhgO'Shea 12 30
(John Patrick Shanahan, Ire) *sn pushed along to chse ldrs: drvn along over 3f out: wknd over 2f out* **12/1**

1m 46.21s (-2.19) **Going Correction** -0.20s/f (Firm) **13** Ran SP% **119.7**
Speed ratings (Par 103): **102,101,101,100,98 95,93,93,92,92 87,85,83**
CSF £23.20 CT £174.64 TOTE £11.80: £4.20, £1.50, £2.20; EX 31.20 Trifecta £241.50.
Owner Alex and Janet Card **Bred** Mrs Dolores Gleeson **Trained** Carrutherstown, D'fries & G'way

FOCUS
Race distance increased by 24yds. The leaders set decent gallop and the first four all came from off the pace. Sound form, with the fourth rated close to form.

2199 ROUTE 74 TRUCKSTOP BRAVEHEART H'CAP 1m 4f 14y
7:25 (7:25) (Class 3) (0-95,95) 4-Y-O+ **£16,172** (£4,812; £2,405; £1,202) **Stalls** High

Form RPR

15-1 **1** **Sir Chauvelin**[12] 1880 4-8-8 **82** 6ex ow1 PaulMulrennan 3 93
(Jim Goldie) *hld up on ins: stdy hdwy whn nt clr run over 2f out to over 1f out: squeezed through to ld ent fnl f: drvn and r.o wl* **7/1**

113- **2** 1 3/4 **Fabricate**[200] 7511 4-9-7 **95** (p) TonyHamilton 10 102
(Michael Bell) *t.k.h early: hld up towards rr: shkn up 1/2-way: bk on bridle and hdwy over 3f out: led over 1f out: edgd rt and hdd ent fnl f: one pce* **11/4**[2]

-564 **3** 3 3/4 **Corton Lad**[7] 1999 6-8-11 **85** (tp) PhillipMakin 8 86
(Keith Dalgleish) *hld up in tch: effrt over 2f out: rdn to chse ldng pair over 1f out: outpcd last 100yds* **5/1**[3]

6000 **4** 1/2 **Be Perfect (USA)**[20] 1642 7-8-13 **87** (p) JamesSullivan 9 87
(Ruth Carr) *led: hrd pressed fr 3f out: rdn and hdd over 1f out: kpt on same pce fnl f* **14/1**

130- **5** 1 1/4 **Sikandar (IRE)**[20] 5643 4-8-8 **82** (tp) BarryMcHugh 5 80
(Brian Ellison) *slowly away and wnt lft s: bhd: struggling over 3f out: styd on fnl f: nvr able to chal* **12/1**

-211 **6** shd **Faiseur De Miracle**[37] 1250 4-9-6 **94** GrahamLee 1 92+
(Micky Hammond) *trckd ldrs: effrt whn nt clr run over 2f out to over 1f out: wknd fnl f* **9/4**[1]

6-60 **7** 2 **Maid Of The Glens (IRE)**[12] 1880 5-8-13 **87** (b) TadhgO'Shea 4 82
(John Patrick Shanahan, Ire) *dwlt: sn rdn to chse ldr: chal and rdn 3f out: wknd 1f out* **22/1**

24-0 **8** 1 3/4 **Mistiroc**[20] 1620 5-9-3 **91** (p) TomEaves 6 83
(John Quinn) *prom: effrt and rdn over 2f out: wknd wl over 1f out* **6/1**

2m 33.57s (-5.03) **Going Correction** -0.20s/f (Firm) **8** Ran SP% **119.6**
Speed ratings (Par 107): **108,106,104,104,103 103,101,100**
CSF £27.94 CT £108.36 TOTE £6.50: £1.30, £1.50, £2.10; EX 28.20 Trifecta £121.10.
Owner J Fyffe **Bred** W M Johnstone **Trained** Uplawmoor, E Renfrews

FOCUS
Race distance increased by 24yds. The pace was fair in this good handicap and the winner scored in decent style from the clear second. It's been rated around the third close to his latest/turf best.

2200 WHEELERS DINER WILLIAM WALLACE H'CAP 6f 6y
7:55 (7:57) (Class 4) (0-85,82) 3-Y-O **£6,469** (£1,925; £962; £481) **Stalls** Centre

Form RPR

40-6 **1** **Dodgy Bob**[38] 1243 3-9-3 **78** (p) ShaneGray 4 82
(Kevin Ryan) *cl up: rdn to ld over 1f out: kpt on wl fnl f* **9/1**

10-5 **2** *hd* **Tikthebox (IRE)**[58] 954 3-9-2 **77** TomEaves 5 80
(David Brown) *led: rdn over 2f out: hdd over 1f out: rallied: kpt on: jst hld* **18/1**

14-3 **3** *3/4* **My Amigo**[21] 1599 3-9-4 **79** PJMcDonald 3 80
(Ann Duffield) *dwlt: sn prom: effrt and rdn 2f out: kpt on ins fnl f* **7/4**[1]

20-6 **4** *1 1/2* **Firesnake (IRE)**[27] 1485 3-8-9 **75** (p) JordanVaughan(5) 8 71
(K R Burke) *hld up: edgd lft and hdwy over 1f out: kpt on fnl f: nt rch ldrs* **40/1**

6 **5** *4 1/2* **Lilliard (IRE)**[34] 1337 3-8-9 **70** TadhgO'Shea 7 52
(John Patrick Shanahan, Ire) *prom: drvn along over 2f out: outpcd over 1f out* **12/1**

513- **6** *1/2* **Ormskirk**[217] 7087 3-9-5 **80** TonyHamilton 2 60
(Richard Fahey) *prom on outside: rdn over 2f out: wknd over 1f out* **7/1**[3]

21-2 **7** *1/2* **Extortion**[16] 1788 3-9-0 **75** PaulMulrennan 10 54
(Bryan Smart) *hld up towards stands' side: outpcd over 2f out: sn btn* **10/3**[2]

00-0 **8** *1* **Farkle Minkus**[17] 1763 3-9-7 **82** (p) PhillipMakin 9 57
(Keith Dalgleish) *in tch towards stands' side: effrt over 2f out: wknd over 1f out* **9/1**

021- **9** *1 3/4* **Wilsons Ruby (IRE)**[190] 7715 3-8-6 **67** BarryMcHugh 1 37
(Brian Ellison) *t.k.h: in tch tl rdn and wknd over 1f out* **20/1**

3-61 **10** *7* **Toledo**[102] 419 3-8-11 **72** SamJames 6 19
(Marjorie Fife) *chsd ldrs tl rdn and wknd wl over 1f out* **20/1**

1m 11.77s (-0.43) **Going Correction** -0.20s/f (Firm) **10** Ran SP% **116.9**
Speed ratings (Par 101): **94,93,92,90,84 84,83,82,79,70**
CSF £151.10 CT £414.82 TOTE £11.50: £2.90, £3.60, £1.50; EX 221.40 Trifecta £593.60.

Owner Jack Berry & John Nixon **Bred** Whatton Manor Stud & Robert Cornelius **Trained** Hambleton, N Yorks

FOCUS
They raced centre to stands' side in this minor handicap and the first four pulled clear. The winner has been rated back to his early 2yo form.

2201 BANNOCKBURN H'CAP 6f 6y
8:30 (8:30) (Class 6) (0-65,69) 3-Y-O+ **£2,911** (£866; £432; £216) **Stalls** Centre

Form RPR

2 **1** **Chaplin Bay (IRE)**[27] 1489 4-9-6 **63** JamesSullivan 9 77
(Ruth Carr) *hld up: hdwy on outside to ld over 1f out: clr whn carried lft by loose horse ins fnl f: kpt on wl* **7/2**[2]

-503 **2** *4 1/2* **Keene's Pointe**[18] 1692 6-9-6 **63** TonyHamilton 5 64
(Kristin Stubbs) *hld up: rdn along over 2f out: hdwy to chse (clr) wnr ins fnl f: kpt on: no imp* **12/1**

11 **3** *1* **Its Only Mossy (IRE)**[4] 2106 3-8-13 **69** 6ex JoeDoyle(3) 7 64+
(Jennie Candlish) *led: carried to stands' rail by loose horse after 2f: rdn and hdd over 1f out: kpt on same pce fnl f* **6/4**[1]

60-6 **4** *nk* **A Lovable Rogue**[12] 1878 4-9-2 **59** (p) PJMcDonald 6 56
(R Mike Smith) *bhd: drvn and outpcd over 3f out: gd hdwy fnl f: kpt on: nt pce to chal* **20/1**

0505 **5** *2 1/2* **Daylight**[18] 1712 6-9-2 **64** (t) NathanEvans(5) 2 53
(Michael Easterby) *bmpd sn after s: t.k.h and sn cl up: effrt and ev ch over 1f out: wknd ins fnl f* **6/1**[3]

100- **6** *1 1/4* **Desire**[210] 7256 4-9-7 **64** (p) GeorgeChaloner 3 49
(Richard Fahey) *prom: rdn and edgd rt over 2f out: wknd over 1f out* **12/1**

-500 **7** *3/4* **Major Valentine**[30] 1419 4-9-2 **64** (p) CiaranMckee(5) 8 47
(John O'Shea) *prom: rdn along over 2f out: wknd over 1f out* **16/1**

42-0 **8** *4* **Wotnot (IRE)**[31] 1402 4-9-5 **62** PaulMulrennan 4 33
(Bryan Smart) *chsd ldrs tl wknd fr 2f out* **25/1**

0223 **U** **New Lease Of Life**[12] 1878 7-9-7 **64** (v) PhillipMakin 1
(Keith Dalgleish) *stmbld and uns rdr leaving stalls* **8/1**

1m 10.93s (-1.27) **Going Correction** -0.20s/f (Firm)
WFA 3 from 4yo+ 10lb **9** Ran SP% **117.5**
Speed ratings (Par 101): **100,94,92,92,88 87,86,80,**
CSF £45.61 CT £88.70 TOTE £4.70: £1.40, £3.10, £1.20; EX 48.90 Trifecta £131.10.

Owner Miss B Houlston,Mrs M Chapman,Mrs R Carr **Bred** Stonethorn Stud Farms Ltd **Trained** Huby, N Yorks

FOCUS
The winner powered clear in this minor handicap and there was drama at the start when \bNew Lease Of Life\p stumbled and unseated his rider. A pb from the winner.

2202 MCGRATTAN PILING & SUPPLIES H'CAP 5f 7y
9:00 (9:00) (Class 5) (0-75,75) 4-Y-O+ **£3,881** (£1,155; £577; £288) **Stalls** High

Form RPR

-302 **1** **Final Venture**[12] 1879 4-9-1 **69** NeilFarley 6 82
(Alan Swinbank) *cl up stands' side: shkn up to ld over 1f out: rdn clr ins fnl f: comf* **85/40**[1]

-3 **2** *3* **Little Belter (IRE)**[35] 1319 4-8-3 **57** (v1) JoeFanning 2 59
(Keith Dalgleish) *chsd centre ldr: effrt and rdn 2f out: edgd lft and chsd wnr ins fnl f: kpt on: nt pce to chal* **7/2**[3]

2-60 **3** *1* **Salvatore Fury (IRE)**[6] 2028 6-9-2 **70** (p) PhillipMakin 5 69
(Keith Dalgleish) *t.k.h: trckd stands' side ldrs: rdn along over 1f out: kpt on same pce ins fnl f* **5/2**[2]

3535 **4** *1* **Danish Duke (IRE)**[25] 1525 5-8-7 **61** (p) JamesSullivan 4 56
(Ruth Carr) *racd wout off-fore shoe: swtchd lft and prom stands' side gp: rdn over 2f out: kpt on same pce fnl f* **15/2**

305 **5** *shd* **Swendab (IRE)**[14] 1827 8-8-11 **70** (b) CiaranMckee(5) 7 65
(John O'Shea) *led stands' side gp: rdn over 2f out: hdd over 1f out: outpcd ins fnl f* **18/1**

-062 **6** *1 1/4* **Bronze Beau**[12] 1878 9-8-9 **63** (tp) ShaneGray 1 53
(Kristin Stubbs) *racd w one other in centre: spd tl rdn and wknd fnl f* **11/2**

58.89s (-1.11) **Going Correction** -0.20s/f (Firm) **6** Ran SP% **115.2**
Speed ratings (Par 103): **100,95,93,92,91 89**
CSF £10.33 TOTE £3.60: £2.00, £1.50; EX 10.40 Trifecta £37.80.

Owner Brian Valentine **Bred** Newsells Park Stud **Trained** Melsonby, N Yorks

FOCUS
The favourite delivered in good style near the stands' rail in this sprint handicap. The runner-up has been rated to his Wolverhampton latest.

T/Plt: £17.20 to a £1 stake. Pool: £57,130.48 - 2413.45 winning units. T/Qpdt: £8.40 to a £1 stake. Pool: £5,847.07 - 509.20 winning units. **Richard Young**

NEWBURY (L-H)
Friday, May 13

OFFICIAL GOING: Soft (good to soft in places; 5.1) changing to good to soft (soft in places) after race 1 (1.30)
Wind: mild breeze across Weather: cloudy with sunny periods Rails: Rail is currently set up on inside line. All race distances as described.

2203 WELCOME TO THE STARLIGHT RACEDAY MAIDEN STKS (PLUS 10 RACE) (DIV I) 6f 8y
1:30 (1:30) (Class 4) 2-Y-O **£6,469** (£1,925; £962; £481) **Stalls** Centre

Form RPR

1 **Medieval (IRE)** 2-9-5 0 JamieSpencer 7 84
(Paul Cole) *trckd ldr: rdn to chal 2f out: led fnl 130yds: kpt on wl* **9/2**[3]

2 *1/2* **Spiritous (USA)** 2-9-5 0 JamesDoyle 3 83
(John Gosden) *led after 1f: rdn over 1f out: hdd fnl 130yds: kpt on* **7/2**[2]

3 *1 3/4* **Our Boy (IRE)** 2-9-5 0 FMBerry 1 77+
(David Evans) *trckd ldrs: rdn 2f out: nt quite pce to chal: kpt on ins fnl f* **12/1**

4 *nk* **Diable D'Or (IRE)** 2-9-5 0 ShaneKelly 5 76+
(Eve Johnson Houghton) *led for 1f: trckd ldrs: rdn 2f out: kpt on same pce fnl f* **25/1**

5 *3 3/4* **Wahash (IRE)** 2-9-5 0 PatDobbs 4 65
(Richard Hannon) *trckd ldrs: ev ch 2f out: sn rdn: wknd fnl f* **3/1**[1]

6 *nk* **Waqaas** 2-9-5 0 DaneO'Neill 9 64
(Charles Hills) *s.i.s: sn cl up: rdn 2f out: wknd ent fnl f* **9/2**[3]

7 *1 1/4* **Challow (IRE)** 2-9-5 0 LiamKeniry 2 60
(Sylvester Kirk) *s.i.s: in last pair: hdwy 3f out: effrt over 2f out: wknd jst over 1f out* **66/1**

8 *3/4* **Brise De Mer (FR)** 2-9-5 0 SteveDrowne 6 58
(George Baker) *chsd ldrs tl 2f out* **33/1**

9 *shd* **War Of Succession** 2-9-5 0 OisinMurphy 8 58
(Andrew Balding) *s.i.s: struggling 1/2-way: a towards rr* **6/1**

1m 16.41s (3.41) **Going Correction** +0.375s/f (Good) **9** Ran SP% **113.8**
Speed ratings (Par 95): **92,91,89,88,83 83,81,80,80**
CSF £20.01 TOTE £5.80: £2.10, £1.40, £4.10; EX 22.80 Trifecta £245.50.

Owner Mrs Fitri Hay **Bred** Patrick Cassidy **Trained** Whatcombe, Oxon

FOCUS
Rail on inside line and all distances as advertised. Following the downpours earlier in the week the ground had started to dry out a little and the going was now officially soft, good to soft in places (from soft). No previous form to go on in the first division of this maiden, which has been won by some decent sorts in recent years, including the likes of Canford Cliffs and Strong Suit. Very few ever got into this, with the first two at the sharp end throughout and the winning time was 5.91sec outside standard, suggesting the ground was still testing. James Doyle described the ground as "dead", while Dane O'Neill described it as "gluey". The level is a bit fluid.

2204 WELCOME TO THE STARLIGHT RACEDAY MAIDEN STKS (PLUS 10 RACE) (DIV II) 6f 8y
2:00 (2:05) (Class 4) 2-Y-O **£6,469** (£1,925; £962; £481) **Stalls** Centre

Form RPR

1 **Cunco (IRE)** 2-9-5 0 RobertHavlin 8 88+
(John Gosden) *trckd ldrs: shkn up over 1f out: qcknd ent fnl f: led fnl 70yds: readily* **7/2**[2]

2 *3/4* **Isomer (USA)** 2-9-5 0 OisinMurphy 4 83
(Andrew Balding) *s.i.s: in last pair but wl in tch: hdwy over 2f out: led over 1f out: kpt on but nt pce of wnr whn hdd fnl 70yds* **9/2**[3]

3 *2 3/4* **Oceanus (IRE)** 2-9-5 0 RyanMoore 5 75
(Ed Dunlop) *trckd ldr: ev ch 2f out: sn rdn: kpt on but nt pce of front pair* **15/8**[1]

4 *hd* **Barrington (IRE)** 2-9-5 0 DarryllHolland 9 74
(Charles Hills) *racd keenly: trckd ldrs: rdn over 1f out: kpt on but nt pce to chal* **5/1**

5 *1* **Latest Quest (IRE)** 2-9-5 0 GeorgeBaker 2 71
(Sylvester Kirk) *trckd ldr: led 2f out: sn rdn and hdd: no ex and lost 2 pls fnl 130yds* **25/1**

6 *15* **Zebulon (IRE)** 2-9-5 0 PatDobbs 6 26
(Richard Hannon) *led: rdn: hung rt and hdd 2f out: sn wknd* **7/1**

7 *4* **Zamadance** 2-9-5 0 FMBerry 3 14
(Sylvester Kirk) *dwlt: a detached in last* **33/1**

1m 16.4s (3.40) **Going Correction** +0.375s/f (Good) **7** Ran SP% **111.1**
Speed ratings (Par 95): **92,91,87,87,85 65,60**
CSF £18.37 TOTE £3.20: £1.60, £2.50; EX 16.20 Trifecta £43.70.

Owner Don Alberto Stable **Bred** Don Alberto Corporation **Trained** Newmarket, Suffolk

FOCUS
The ground was changed to good to soft, soft in places before this race. Again no form to go on in this division, but all eyes were on one horse. The winning time was almost identical to the first leg, but the race will be remembered for some time. Traditionally a strong maiden, but the form will take time to settle.

2205 DARREN BIRD H'CAP 1m 2f 6y
2:35 (2:35) (Class 5) (0-70,69) 4-Y-O+ **£4,528** (£1,347; £673; £336) **Stalls** Centre

Form RPR

2-54 **1** **Loving Your Work**[14] 1834 5-8-11 **59** PatDobbs 5 69
(Ken Cunningham-Brown) *mid-div: smooth hdwy but nt clr run briefly 3f out: sltly outpcd whn front pair kicked on 2f out: r.o strly ent fnl f: led fnl 80yds: comf* **13/2**

4-01 **2** *1 1/4* **Beausant**[28] 1456 4-9-7 **69** SteveDrowne 6 76
(George Baker) *mid-div: smooth hdwy fr 4f out: disputing ld whn pce qcknd 2f out: outrt ldr ent fnl f: no ex whn hdd fnl 80yds* **7/2**[2]

000- **3** *1 3/4* **Choral Festival**[156] 8157 10-9-5 **67** WilliamCarson 15 70
(John Bridger) *mid-div: smooth hdwy over 3f out: disputing ld whn pce qcknd 2f out: hdd ent fnl f: kpt on but no ex* **20/1**

46-3 **4** *1 1/2* **Carolinae**[81] 675 4-9-0 **62** OisinMurphy 12 62
(Charlie Fellowes) *stdd s: hdwy fr over 3f out: rdn and ch 2f out: kpt on same pce fnl f* **9/4**[1]

40/2 **5** *10* **Officer Drivel (IRE)**[4] 2085 5-9-5 **67** (b1) TimmyMurphy 14 47
(Jim Best) *prom: led over 4f out: rdn and hdd 2f out: sn outpcd* **6/1**[3]

000- **6** *3 1/4* **Moncarno**[212] 7213 6-9-0 **62** KierenFox 8 36
(John Best) *trckd ldrs: rdn over 2f out: wknd jst over 1f out* **66/1**

040- **7** *4* **Prince Of Cardamom (IRE)**[11] 6301 4-8-12 **60** (p) DarryllHolland 1 26
(Jonathan Geake) *trckd ldrs: rdn and ev ch over 2f out: wknd over 1f out* **66/1**

1-04 **8** *8* **Roly Tricks**[17] 1743 5-9-0 **67** PaddyPilley(5) 2 17
(Natalie Lloyd-Beavis) *hld up towards rr: hdwy u.p over 3f out: hung lft and wknd 2f out* **14/1**

-206 **9** *22* **My Mo (FR)**[20] 1652 4-9-2 **64** (p) ColinKeane 3
(David Dennis) *led tl over 4f out: wknd over 2f out: eased* **10/1**

0-32 **10** *8* **Head Coach**[34] 1340 4-8-7 **58** (p) DannyBrock(3) 7
(Jane Chapple-Hyam) *rrd leaving stalls: bhd: hdwy 4f out: sn rdn: wknd over 2f out: eased* **8/1**

500- **11** *10* **Gracesome (IRE)**[205] 7384 5-8-7 **55** oh3 CathyGannon 9
(Michael Blanshard) *mid-div for 3f: towards rr: struggling and no threat fr 3f out: eased fr over 1f out* **66/1**

2m 11.6s (2.80) **Going Correction** +0.375s/f (Good) **11** Ran SP% **116.7**
Speed ratings (Par 103): **103,102,100,99,91 88,85,79,61,55 47**
CSF £28.71 CT £429.39 TOTE £6.50: £1.70, £1.60, £4.00; EX 33.10 Trifecta £912.90.
Owner Danebury Racing Stables **Bred** Dukes Stud & Overbury Stallions Ltd **Trained** Danebury, Hants

FOCUS
An ordinary handicap in which the two leaders appeared to go off too quick and set it up for the closers. The front four pulled well clear. The winner has been rated close to his best.

2206 STARLIGHT H'CAP 6f 8y
3:10 (3:10) (Class 2) (0-100,100) 4-Y-O+**£19,407** (£5,775; £2,886; £1,443) **Stalls** Centre

Form RPR

20-0 **1** **Clear Spring (IRE)**[12] 1887 8-9-4 **97** ColinKeane 13 106
(John Spearing) *mid-div: hdwy 2f out: sn rdn: led jst ins fnl f: r.o wl* **25/1**

121- **2** *1 1/4* **Francisco**[336] 3110 4-8-4 **88** ow1 GaryMahon(5) 10 93+
(Richard Hannon) *led: rdn 2f out: sn drifted lft: hdd jst ins fnl f: fin on far side rail: kpt on but no ex fnl 100yds* **14/1**

-213 **3** *nk* **Dougan**[12] 1887 4-9-0 **93** JamieSpencer 4 97
(David Evans) *s.i.s: towards rr: hdwy 2f out: sn rdn: wnt 3rd over 1f out: kpt on ins fnl f* **9/2**[2]

1-50 **4** *1/2* **B Fifty Two (IRE)**[106] 370 7-9-7 **100** DarryllHolland 7 102
(Charles Hills) *sn pushed along towards rr: hdwy over 1f out: r.o ins fnl f but nvr rching ldrs* **33/1**

030- **5** *1 1/4* **Kickboxer (IRE)**[328] 3381 5-9-7 **100** JamesDoyle 12 98
(Saeed bin Suroor) *mid-div: rdn over 1f out: kpt on ins fnl f but no pce to get involved* **12/1**

2-52 **6** *2 3/4* **Harry Hurricane**[13] 1857 4-9-2 **95** SteveDrowne 11 85
(George Baker) *racd keenly: trckd ldrs: rdn wl over 1f out: fdd ins fnl f* **16/1**

-036 **7** *hd* **Golden Steps (FR)**[12] 1887 5-9-7 **100** JimmyFortune 3 89
(Marco Botti) *hld up towards rr: rdn 2f out: kpt on fnl f: nvr any threat* **10/1**

250- **8** *3/4* **Charles Molson**[203] 7424 5-9-4 **97** GeorgeBaker 5 84
(Patrick Chamings) *s.i.s: towards rr: rdn over 1f out: little imp* **12/1**

-011 **9** *2* **Englishman**[12] 1887 6-8-12 **91** 6ex RyanMoore 6 71
(Milton Bradley) *mid-div: rdn 2f out: sn drifted lft: nvr any imp* **7/2**[1]

30-0 **10** *1 1/4* **Field Game**[12] 1887 4-8-1 **87** (t) CharlieBennett(7) 8 63
(Hughie Morrison) *trckd ldrs: rdn wl over 2f out: wknd over 1f out* **25/1**

141- **11** *nk* **Mullionheir**[272] 5381 4-9-1 **94** KierenFox 2 69
(John Best) *mid-div: swtchd lft for effrt over 2f out: nvr threatened: wknd over 1f out* **7/1**[3]

321- **12** *7* **Little Palaver**[226] 6870 4-8-10 **89** GeraldMosse 9 42
(Clive Cox) *trckd ldr: rdn over 2f out: wknd over 1f out* **14/1**

0-60 **13** *7* **Desert Force**[13] 1856 4-8-11 **90** PatDobbs 1 20
(Richard Hannon) *chsd ldrs tl wknd 2f out* **10/1**

1m 13.71s (0.71) **Going Correction** +0.375s/f (Good) **13** Ran SP% **116.3**
Speed ratings (Par 109): **110,108,107,107,105 101,101,100,98,96 95,86,77**
CSF £327.08 CT £1933.12 TOTE £35.70: £9.70, £3.90, £1.50; EX 482.30 Trifecta £7513.70 Part won..
Owner H James **Bred** Rocal Bloodstock **Trained** Kinnersley, Worcs

FOCUS
A warm sprint handicap, but the pace wasn't frantic. The winner has been rated back to form, with the runner-up to a small pb, and the fourth to his best sprint form since his 2yo days (bar standout Chesham win).

2207 COOLMORE STUD MAIDEN STKS (PLUS 10 RACE) 7f (S)
3:45 (3:47) (Class 4) 3-Y-O **£6,469** (£1,925; £962; £481) **Stalls** Centre

Form RPR

0- **1** **Smuggler's Moon**[337] 3074 3-9-5 0 JimmyFortune 13 80
(Brian Meehan) *mid-div: pushed along over 2f out: swtchd rt and hdwy over 1f out: led fnl 100yds: r.o strly* **20/1**

3-5 **2** *1/2* **Gunmetal (IRE)**[20] 1622 3-9-2 0 MichaelJMMurphy(3) 7 78
(Charles Hills) *led: rdn 2f out: drifted rt ent fnl f: kpt on but no ex whn hdd fnl 100yds* **8/1**

3 *1 3/4* **Edward Lewis** 3-9-5 0 RobertHavlin 17 74
(John Gosden) *in tch: rdn and hdwy over 1f out: swtchd lft ent fnl f: kpt on same pce* **9/1**

4 *1* **Predetermined (IRE)** 3-9-5 0[1] OisinMurphy 8 71
(Andrew Balding) *trckd ldrs: rdn 2f out: kpt on same pce fnl f* **25/1**

00- **5** *1/2* **Silhouette (IRE)**[290] 4730 3-9-5 0 TimmyMurphy 14 70
(Daniel Kubler) *wnt rt s: towards rr of midfield: rdn over 2f out: kpt on ins fnl f* **200/1**

0 **6** *3/4* **Lillyput (IRE)**[126] 102 3-8-9 0 PaddyPilley(5) 10 63
(Mick Channon) *trckd ldrs: rdn over 2f out: sn one pce* **100/1**

3- **7** *1 1/4* **Chess Master (IRE)**[248] 6180 3-9-5 0 JamesDoyle 2 64
(Charlie Appleby) *trckd ldrs: swtchd lft and effrt 2f out: sn one pce* **1/1**[1]

2- **8** *1/2* **Mamillius**[291] 4705 3-9-5 0 SteveDrowne 1 63
(George Baker) *s.i.s: towards rr: hdwy into midfield over 2f out: sn rdn: no further imp fnl f* **6/1**[2]

2 **9** *1 1/4* **Emerald Loch**[35] 1312 3-9-0 0 FMBerry 5 55
(Ralph Beckett) *prom: rdn 2f out: wknd fnl f* **15/2**[3]

00 **10** *shd* **Rising Sunshine (IRE)**[36] 1287 3-9-5 0 PatDobbs 15 59
(Richard Hannon) *hmpd s: towards rr: sme late prog: nvr any threat* **50/1**

11 *shd* **Sixties Idol** 3-9-0 0 CharlesBishop 11 54
(Mick Channon) *a towards rr* **33/1**

12 *3 1/2* **Dream Free** 3-9-5 0 GeorgeBaker 16 50
(David Lanigan) *s.i.s: a towards rr* **16/1**

13 *nse* **Royal Hero** 3-9-0 0 HectorCrouch(5) 9 49
(Amanda Perrett) *mid-div: rdn over 2f out: wknd fnl f* **50/1**

0- **14** *2 1/4* **Cockney Boy**[226] 6865 3-9-0 0 PatrickO'Donnell(5) 6 43
(John Gallagher) *trckd ldrs: rdn over 2f out: wknd over 1f out* **80/1**

30 **15** *12* **General Hazard (IRE)**[36] 1287 3-9-5 0 WilliamCarson 3 11
(Michael Bell) *mid-div tl wknd over 2f out* **66/1**

1m 28.71s (3.01) **Going Correction** +0.375s/f (Good) **15** Ran SP% **122.7**
Speed ratings (Par 101): **97,96,94,93,92 91,90,89,88,88 88,84,84,81,67**
CSF £167.99 TOTE £28.00: £5.00, £2.50, £2.80; EX 275.50 Trifecta £1381.30.
Owner Manton Thoroughbreds **Bred** Bugley Stud (alchemilla) Partnership **Trained** Manton, Wilts

FOCUS
Not a particularly competitive maiden despite the size of the field, though a few of these had shown some promise. It's been rated to the lower end of the race standard.

2208 BATHWICK TYRES EBF STALLIONS MAIDEN STKS (PLUS 10 RACE) 1m 2f 6y
4:15 (4:16) (Class 4) 3-Y-O **£6,469** (£1,925; £962; £481) **Stalls** Centre

Form RPR

6-2 **1** **Ulysses (IRE)**[20] 1639 3-9-5 0 RyanMoore 11 99+
(Sir Michael Stoute) *a.p: led 3f out: pushed wl clr over 1f out: v easily* **4/11**[1]

2 *8* **New World Power (JPN)** 3-9-5 0 OisinMurphy 3 78+
(Roger Varian) *mid-div: hdwy 2f out: sn rdn: styd on to go 2nd ins fnl f but no ch w v easy wnr* **5/1**[2]

3 *1 1/2* **Burguillos** 3-9-5 0 JimmyFortune 8 75
(Alan King) *trckd ldrs: outpcd by wnr over 1f out: no ex whn lost 2nd ins fnl f* **20/1**

4 *1/2* **The Begum** 3-9-0 0 FMBerry 5 71+
(Ralph Beckett) *hmpd s: towards rr: hdwy 3f out: rdn 2f out: styng on upsides runner-up whn nt clr run ent fnl f: swtchd rt and styd on fnl 120yds* **25/1**

-5 **5** *3/4* **Kesselring**[12] 1897 3-9-5 0 PatDobbs 9 73
(Richard Hannon) *led tl 3f out: sn rdn: no ex ent fnl f* **25/1**

6 *3/4* **Marmelo** 3-9-5 0 RobertHavlin 12 71
(Hughie Morrison) *s.i.s: towards rr of midfield: rdn and stdy prog fr over 2f out: styd on fnl f but nt pce to get involved* **66/1**

0- **7** *3/4* **Dostoyevsky (IRE)**[135] 8404 3-9-5 0 GeorgeBaker 7 70
(David Lanigan) *wnt lft s: towards rr: hung lft fr over 2f out: styd on fnl f but nvr any threat* **14/1**

3 **8** *1 1/4* **Pointel (FR)**[18] 1715 3-9-5 0 FrederikTylicki 10 67
(James Fanshawe) *trckd ldrs: rdn 2f out: wknd jst over 1f out* **13/2**[3]

9 *11* **Vanishing Point** 3-9-5 0 LiamKeniry 4 45
(Andrew Balding) *hmpd s: a towards rr* **33/1**

0 **10** *1/2* **Glorious Legend (IRE)**[18] 1715 3-9-5 0 AntonioFresu 1 44
(Ed Walker) *mid-div: rdn over 2f out: wknd over 1f out* **66/1**

40- **11** *60* **Easy Easy**[215] 7144 3-9-5 0 AdamBeschizza 2
(Alan King) *s.i.s: a towards rr: wknd over 1f out: eased* **66/1**

2m 11.12s (2.32) **Going Correction** +0.375s/f (Good) **11** Ran SP% **129.9**
Speed ratings (Par 101): **105,98,97,97,96 95,95,94,85,85 37**
CSF £2.96 TOTE £1.40: £1.10, £1.90, £6.70; EX 3.70 Trifecta £47.40.
Owner Flaxman Stables Ireland Ltd **Bred** Flaxman Stables Ireland Ltd **Trained** Newmarket, Suffolk

FOCUS
A particularly uncompetitive maiden in which few could be seriously fancied. The race went to script, but the winner was still hugely impressive. The level is a bit fluid with little to go on.

2209 JOHN SUNLEY MEMORIAL H'CAP 1m 3f 5y
4:50 (4:50) (Class 4) (0-85,85) 3-Y-O **£6,469** (£1,925; £962; £481) **Stalls** Centre

Form RPR

321- **1** **Primitivo**[207] 7346 3-9-3 **81** GeorgeBaker 6 96+
(Alan King) *travelled wl: hld up: smooth prog fr 4f out: led 2f out: drew effrtlessly clr: heavily eased towards fin* **5/1**[2]

0-43 **2** *2 1/2* **Emperor Napoleon**[17] 1739 3-8-9 **73** OisinMurphy 1 80
(Andrew Balding) *ducked lft s: in tch: rdn over 2f out: hdwy over 1f out: chsd wnr but no ch ent fnl f: drifted lft: styd on* **12/1**

51-0 **3** *2 1/2* **Rainbow Dreamer**[21] 1610 3-9-6 **84** JamesDoyle 7 87
(Alan King) *mid-div: hdwy 4f out: rdn 2f out: styd on into 3rd fnl f* **9/1**

5-1 **4** *3/4* **Against The Odds**[27] 1479 3-9-5 **83** JimCrowley 12 84+
(Paul Cole) *trckd ldrs: led 3f out tl rdn 2f out: sn outpcd by wnr: lost 2nd ent fnl f: no ex whn lost 3rd towards fin* **15/2**[3]

4-1 **5** *3/4* **Gunnery (FR)**[20] 1626 3-9-7 **85** JamieSpencer 2 85
(Peter Chapple-Hyam) *hld up towards rr: nt best of runs fr 3f out but steadily nudged clsr: rdn 2f out: styd on but nt pce to get involved* **4/1**[1]

34-6 **6** *1 1/2* **Ride The Lightning**[29] 1438 3-8-11 **75** JimmyFortune 4 72
(Brian Meehan) *in tch: ev ch 3f out: sn rdn: hld 2f out: fdd fnl f* **25/1**

646- **7** *1/2* **Ravens Quest**[144] 8323 3-8-8 **72** RobertHavlin 10 69
(Hughie Morrison) *racd keenly: hld up: rdn whn swtchd rt 2f out: styd on past btn horses fnl f* **20/1**

04-1 **8** *nk* **Snan (IRE)**[14] 1826 3-8-13 **77** PatDobbs 5 73
(Richard Hannon) *led for 2f: trckd ldrs: rdn 3f out: wknd over 1f out* **12/1**

-211 **9** *2 3/4* **Manjaam (IRE)**[42] 1185 3-9-3 **81** RyanMoore 8 72
(Ed Dunlop) *mid-div: sme hdwy over 1f out but nvr threatened: wknd ent fnl f* **4/1**[1]

2312 **10** *2 1/4* **Carry Me Home**[12] 1896 3-9-0 **78** DarryllHolland 11 66
(Charles Hills) *led after 2f: hdd 3f out: wknd over 1f out* **16/1**

2161 **11** *6* **Cat Royale (IRE)**[25] 1532 3-8-10 **77** (p) DannyBrock(3) 9 54
(Jane Chapple-Hyam) *trckd ldrs: rdn 3f out: wknd over 1f out* **14/1**

2m 25.61s (4.41) **Going Correction** +0.375s/f (Good) **11** Ran SP% **115.0**
Speed ratings (Par 101): **98,96,94,93,93 92,91,91,89,87 83**
CSF £62.15 CT £524.52 TOTE £5.00: £2.30, £3.90, £2.60; EX 61.90 Trifecta £546.90.
Owner N Farrell, L Field, T Mellor & B Cognet **Bred** Mrs L H Field **Trained** Barbury Castle, Wilts

FOCUS
A fair 3yo handicap, but they went no pace which makes the winner's performance even more impressive. It's been rated as strong form, with the fourth and fifth rated close to their maiden wins.

2210 FOURTOLD APPRENTICE H'CAP 1m 4f 5y
5:20 (5:20) (Class 5) (0-70,72) 4-Y-O+ **£3,881** (£1,155; £577; £288) **Stalls** Centre

Form RPR

604- **1** **The New Pharaoh (IRE)**[203] 7436 5-8-11 **65** SamuelClarke(5) 14 73+
(Chris Wall) *hld up towards rr: hdwy fr 3f out: hmpd 2f out: str run ent fnl f: led fnl 120yds: styd on wl* **4/1**[2]

2121 **2** *2* **My Lord**[11] 2078 8-9-4 **72** 6ex AledBeech(5) 6 77
(David Evans) *racd keenly: hld up: hdwy over 3f out: led 2f out: edgd rt whn rdn: no ex whn hdd fnl 120yds* **8/1**[3]

0-46 **3** *1 1/4* **Blenheim Warrior**[14] 1826 4-8-9 **65** StephenCummins(7) 1 68+
(Richard Hughes) *slowly away: bhd: hmpd on bnd 6f out: little hdwy in centre whn hmpd 2f out: styd on wl fnl f: snatched 3rd cl home* **5/2**[1]

-530 **4** *nk* **Takeitfromalady (IRE)**[13] 1854 7-8-9 **63** (b) CameronNoble(5) 11 66
(Lee Carter) *mid-div: chsng ldrs whn hmpd 2f out: styd on same pce fnl f: lost 3rd cl home* **25/1**

0-04 **5** *6* **Rosie Royale (IRE)**[24] 1547 4-8-10 **59** KevinLundie 2 52
(Roger Teal) *mid-div tl lost pl 6f out: hdwy 4f out: rdn to chse ldrs over 2f out: nt pce to chal: fdd ins fnl f* **11/1**

50-0 **6** *1 3/4* **The Quarterjack**[17] 1760 7-9-1 **69** (p) MitchGodwin(5) 10 59
(Charlie Wallis) *disp ld tl 3f out: wknd ent fnl f* **20/1**

406- **7** *nk* **Royal Reef (IRE)**^{235} 6599 4-9-4 **67**.................................. PaddyBradley 3 57
(William Knight) *trckd ldrs: rdn over 2f out: wknd ent fnl f* **16/1**
014- **8** *shd* **Merry Dancer (IRE)**^{163} 8077 4-8-10 **59**...................... MeganNicholls 8 48
(Patrick Chamings) *disp ld tl 3f out: wknd over 1f out* **9/1**
22-0 **9** *13* **Russian Remarque**^{32} 1391 5-9-7 **70**.......................... CharlieBennett 13 39
(Jonathan Portman) *trckd ldrs: led 3f out: sn rdn: hdd whn swvd rt 2f out: sn wknd* **20/1**
210- **10** *74* **Rum Swizzle**^{179} 7871 4-9-4 **67**.................................. KillianHennessy 12
(Harry Dunlop) *mid-div: rdn over 3f out: sn wknd* **9/1**
-056 **11** *1* **Abertillery**^{26} 950 4-8-7 **56** oh1.. GeorgiaCox 9
(Michael Blanshard) *trckd ldr tl rdn over 4f out: wknd over 3f out* **20/1**

2m 40.24s (4.74) **Going Correction** +0.375s/f (Good) **11** Ran SP% **112.0**
Speed ratings (Par 103): **99,97,96,96,92 91,91,91,82,33 32**
CSF £31.55 CT £93.43 TOTE £5.40: £1.90, £2.20, £1.50; EX 35.90 Trifecta £119.50.
Owner Ms Aida Fustoq **Bred** Deerfield Farm **Trained** Newmarket, Suffolk
■ Stewards' Enquiry : Cameron Noble ten-day ban; failing to ride out (27th May - 6th June)
Killian Hennessy jockey said filly stopped quickly.

FOCUS
A modest apprentice handicap and the pace was ordinary. There was some argy-bargy coming to the last 2f in which the first four were all compromised, but the result didn't appear to be affected. It's been rated around the runner-up and fourth.
T/Plt: £218.30 to a £1 stake. Pool of £53194.02 - 177.81 winning tickets. T/Qpdt: £70.60 to a £1 stake. Pool of £5816.67 - 60.90 winning tickets. **Tim Mitchell**

2173 NEWMARKET (R-H)

Friday, May 13

OFFICIAL GOING: Good to firm (good in places; 7.7)
Wind: light, half behind Weather: overcast

2211 CHEMTEST EBF NOVICE FILLIES' STKS (PLUS 10 RACE) 6f
2:10 (2:10) (Class 4) 2-Y-O **£4,528** (£1,347; £673; £336) **Stalls** High

Form RPR
1 **Kilmah** 2-9-0 0.. RichardKingscote 1 84+
(Mark Johnston) *dwlt: sn rcvrd and chsd ldr over 4f out: rdn and ev ch over 1f out: led jst ins fnl f: styd on strly* **14/1**
61 **2** *2* **Seafront**^{22} 1583 2-9-3 0.. LukeMorris 8 81
(James Tate) *in tch in midfield: rdn over 2f out: hrd drvn and no hdwy over 1f out tl kpt on ins fnl f: wnt 2nd last strides: no threat to wnr* **7/1**
4 **3** *nk* **Lexington Sky (IRE)**^{29} 1437 2-8-11 0..................... TomMarquand$^{(3)}$ 3 77
(Richard Hannon) *t.k.h early: led: rdn over 1f out: hdd jst ins fnl f: no ex and outpcd fnl 100yds: lost 2nd last strides* **3/1**^{2}
4 *1* **Arabian Hope (USA)** 2-9-0 0... WilliamBuick 2 74
(Saeed bin Suroor) *t.k.h early: chsd ldr tl settled in 3rd over 4f out: pushed along over 1f out: drifted rt and unable qck 1f out: kpt on same pce fnl f* **6/4**^{1}
5 *3/4* **High On Love (IRE)** 2-9-0 0....................................... StevieDonohoe 4 72
(Charlie Fellowes) *in tch towards rr: effrt and rn green over 1f out: no imp and drifting rt 1f out: kpt on same pce ins fnl f* **50/1**
3 **6** *3* **Ocean Temptress**^{25} 1527 2-9-0 0.................................... JackMitchell 6 63
(John Ryan) *s.i.s: in tch in rr: effrt in centre 2f out: no imp over 1f out: wknd ins fnl f* **25/1**
7 *shd* **Al Nafoorah** 2-9-0 0.. PatCosgrave 7 63
(Ed Dunlop) *in tch towards rr: rdn 2f out: no hdwy u.p over 1f out: wknd ins fnl f* **7/2**^{3}

1m 13.84s (1.64) **Going Correction** +0.20s/f (Good) **7** Ran SP% **112.2**
Speed ratings (Par 92): **97,94,93,92,91 87,87**
CSF £101.19 TOTE £16.50: £5.70, £3.00; EX 102.00 Trifecta £302.50.
Owner Abdulla Al Mansoori **Bred** Mildmay Bloodstock Ltd **Trained** Middleham Moor, N Yorks

FOCUS
An informative 2yo maiden, in which the top three in the market attracted good support. It's been rated as just above the race average.

2212 STREETS CHARTERED ACCOUNTANTS H'CAP 1m
2:45 (2:45) (Class 5) (0-70,70) 3-Y-O **£3,234** (£962; £481; £240) **Stalls** High

Form RPR
-103 **1** **World's Greatest (USA)**^{56} 979 3-9-4 **67**....................(t) MartinHarley 1 75+
(Stuart Williams) *hld up wl in tch in midfield: clsd to ld and travelling wl 2f out: rdn over 1f out: drvn ins fnl f: hld on towards fin* **16/1**
000- **2** *nk* **Prosecute (FR)**^{221} 6986 3-9-7 **70**................................ StevieDonohoe 3 77+
(David Simcock) *awkward leaving stalls and slowly away: hld up in rr: hdwy into midfield 1/2-way: hdwy and rdn to chse ldrs whn swtchd lft over 1f out: wnt 2nd and chalng wl ins fnl f: kpt on wl: nvr quite getting to wnr* **11/2**^{2}
46-0 **3** *1 1/4* **Bluff Crag**^{37} 1276 3-8-13 **67**....................................... EdwardGreatrex$^{(5)}$ 5 71
(Andrew Balding) *chsd ldrs: effrt 2f out: rdn and cl enough in 4th over 1f out: kpt on same pce u.p ins fnl f: snatched 3rd last stride* **7/1**^{3}
442- **4** *shd* **Weather Front (USA)**^{206} 7353 3-9-6 **69**......................... LukeMorris 11 73
(James Tate) *t.k.h: hld up in tch in midfield: swtchd rt and effrt over 2f out: drvn and hdwy to press wnr over 1f out: no ex ins fnl f: lost 2 pls wl ins fnl f* **8/1**
04-6 **5** *4 1/2* **Swansway**^{37} 1270 3-8-13 **62**....................................... RichardKingscote 6 55
(Tom Dascombe) *towards rr: rdn 3f out: swtchd rt 2f out: hdwy to pass btn rivals over 1f out: modest 5th 1f out: kpt on but nvr on terms* **10/1**
1-43 **6** *8* **Harlequin Rock**^{27} 1486 3-9-1 **64**...(v^{1}) JFEgan 2 42
(Mick Quinn) *w ldrs: rdn and ev ch briefly 2f out: sn outpcd and lost pl over 1f out: wl btn and eased ins fnl f* **14/1**
4-34 **7** *3* **Jassur**^{15} 1804 3-8-10 **62**...(p) DanielMuscutt$^{(3)}$ 9 30
(Marco Botti) *hld up in tch in midfield: rdn over 2f out: no hdwy: drvn and wknd over 1f out* **11/1**
-66 **8** *hd* **Dilly Daydream (IRE)**^{78} 706 3-8-11 **60**........................ SaleemGolam 8 28
(Giles Bravery) *a towards rr: rdn 1/2-way: sn struggling and no imp: wknd over 1f out* **50/1**
6-42 **9** *hd* **She's All Mine**^{11} 1917 3-8-11 **63**............................ TomMarquand$^{(3)}$ 10 30
(Richard Hannon) *stdd s: t.k.h: hld up in rr: rdn 3f out: no imp and wl btn whn hung rt over 1f out* **9/1**
00-0 **10** *5* **Artisandra (FR)**^{24} 1551 3-8-0 **56** oh4........................ GeorgeWood$^{(7)}$ 12 12
(William Knight) *w ldrs: rdn over 2f out: sn struggling and lost pl: wknd over 1f out: wl bhd fnl f* **25/1**
00-1 **11** *1 3/4* **Ebbisham (IRE)**^{17} 1734 3-9-3 **66**..................................... PatCosgrave 7 18
(Jim Boyle) *t.k.h: led: rdn and hdd 2f out: sn btn and wknd over 1f out: wl btn and eased ins fnl f* **5/1**^{1}

625- **12** *9* **Party Thyme**^{205} 7393 3-9-2 **65**.. WilliamBuick 4
(Chris Wall) *in tch in midfield: rdn 3f out: sn struggling and wl btn 2f out: bhd and eased fnl f* **11/2**^{2}

1m 39.75s (1.15) **Going Correction** +0.20s/f (Good) **12** Ran SP% **116.8**
Speed ratings (Par 99): **102,101,100,100,95 87,84,84,84,79 77,68**
CSF £100.24 CT £684.72 TOTE £15.60: £4.70, £2.60, £3.40; EX 174.10 Trifecta £3884.60.
Owner D A Shekells **Bred** Darley **Trained** Newmarket, Suffolk

FOCUS
This featured a host of potential improvers. It was run a strong pace and rates as solid form for the grade. Four pulled nicely clear. The third has been rated to his maiden form.

2213 BUILDING SERVICES DESIGN H'CAP 7f
3:20 (3:22) (Class 4) (0-80,80) 4-Y-O+ **£5,175** (£1,540; £769; £384) **Stalls** High

Form RPR
-260 **1** **Exceeding Power**^{93} 518 5-8-1 **67**............................. GeorgeWood$^{(7)}$ 8 75
(Martin Bosley) *hld up in tch in midfield: swtchd lft and hdwy over 1f out: rdn to ld jst ins fnl f: r.o wl: rdn out* **17/2**^{3}
31- **2** *1* **Rouge Nuage (IRE)**^{192} 7690 6-9-1 **74**............................ JimmyQuinn 7 79
(Conrad Allen) *chsd ldrs: effrt 2f out: drvn and chal over 1f out: led 1f out: sn hdd and styd on same pce ins fnl f* **16/1**
-052 **3** *shd* **My Target (IRE)**^{78} 712 5-8-13 **75**........................... LouisSteward$^{(3)}$ 10 80
(Michael Wigham) *stdd s: hld up in tch in rr: clsd and nt clr run wl over 1f out: swtchd lft and hdwy over 1f out: styd on wl u.p ins fnl f: nt rch ldrs* **4/1**^{1}
545- **4** *3/4* **Anastazia**^{134} 8414 4-8-13 **72**.. LukeMorris 5 75
(Paul D'Arcy) *hld up in tch in midfield: rdn and effrt 2f out: hdwy to chse ldrs and drvn 1f out: kpt on same pce ins fnl f* **9/1**
123- **5** *1* **Song Of Norway**^{219} 7034 5-9-4 **77**................................. WilliamBuick 3 77
(Chris Wall) *hld up in tch in midfield: nt clr run 2f out: effrt u.p over 1f out: styd on same pce ins fnl f* **4/1**^{1}
6 *2 1/4* **Frozen Lake (USA)**^{210} 7269 4-8-11 **70**................. RichardKingscote 11 64
(Mary Hambro) *led: rdn over 1f out: hdd and no ex 1f out: wknd ins fnl f* **9/2**^{2}
1-53 **7** *1/2* **World Record (IRE)**^{16} 1780 6-8-7 **66** oh3............................... JFEgan 9 59
(Mick Quinn) *w ldr: rdn 2f out: no ex and outpcd jst over 1f out: wknd ins fnl f* **20/1**
-245 **8** *3/4* **Smokethatthunders (IRE)**^{20} 1625 6-9-1 **74**.............. StevieDonohoe 4 65
(James Unett) *hld up in rr: effrt 2f out: sme modest hdwy fnl f: nvr trbld ldrs* **16/1**
00-4 **9** *2 1/4* **Warofindependence (USA)**^{36} 1287 4-9-0 **78**.... JosephineGordon$^{(5)}$ 2 63
(Alan Bailey) *t.k.h: chsd ldrs: rdn ent fnl 2f: drvn and btn over 1f out: wknd ins fnl f* **20/1**
3-30 **10** *13* **Ripinto (IRE)**^{30} 1419 4-8-13 **72**.. PatCosgrave 6 22
(Jim Boyle) *in tch in midfield: effrt and n.m.r wl over 1f out: unbalanced on downhill run over 1f out and sn btn: bhd and eased ins fnl f* **12/1**
5641 **11** *1 1/2* **Street Force (USA)**^{31} 1403 5-9-2 **78**..............(tp) AlistairRawlinson$^{(3)}$ 12 24
(Michael Appleby) *s.i.s: sn rdn along: wknd u.p over 1f out: bhd ins fnl f* **10/1**

1m 25.41s (0.01) **Going Correction** +0.20s/f (Good) **11** Ran SP% **116.8**
Speed ratings (Par 105): **107,105,105,104,103 101,100,99,97,82 80**
CSF £134.87 CT £622.98 TOTE £8.60: £2.50, £4.30, £2.20; EX 101.50 Trifecta £937.70.
Owner The Chalfonts **Bred** Rabbah Bloodstock Limited **Trained** Chalfont St Giles, Bucks

FOCUS
Another hotly contested handicap, though there's a suspicion the majority of these are at their most effective on artificial surfaces. They went hard up front and it suited those ridden with restraint. A small turf pb from the runner-up.

2214 EDMONDSON HALL SOLICITORS & SPORTS LAWYERS H'CAP 1m 2f
3:55 (3:58) (Class 3) (0-90,90) 4-Y-O+ **£7,762** (£2,310; £1,154; £577) **Stalls** High

Form RPR
51-0 **1** **Interconnection**^{23} 1569 5-9-1 **84**....................................(p) LukeMorris 8 94
(Ed Vaughan) *chsd ldr: rdn to ld over 1f out: edgd lft and hld on wl ins fnl f: rdn out* **7/1**
000- **2** *3/4* **Gold Prince (IRE)**^{202} 7470 4-8-12 **86**.................. EdwardGreatrex$^{(5)}$ 10 94
(Sylvester Kirk) *led: rdn 2f out: hdd over 1f out: rallied u.p ins fnl f but a hld* **20/1**
4401 **3** *3 1/2* **Viewpoint (IRE)**^{18} 1722 7-8-2 **78**............................ GeorgeWood$^{(7)}$ 4 79
(Michael Appleby) *stdd and awkward leaving stalls: hld up in last pair: hdwy and hung rt over 1f out: kpt on same pce ins fnl f* **4/1**^{2}
1/2- **4** *hd* **Shakopee**^{393} 1440 4-9-3 **86**... WilliamBuick 12 87
(Luca Cumani) *t.k.h: chsd ldng pair: cl 3rd and rdn 2f out: unable qck on downhill run over 1f out: styd on same pce ins fnl f* **9/4**^{1}
12-3 **5** *1 1/4* **Bastille Day**^{16} 1775 4-8-3 **79**................................ AdamMcLean$^{(7)}$ 6 77
(David Elsworth) *hld up in tch in midfield: effrt 2f out: drvn and no imp over 1f out: wl hld and plugged on same pce fnl f* **9/2**^{3}
05-0 **6** *6* **Plymouth Sound**^{18} 1716 4-9-0 **83**.......................... RichardKingscote 13 69
(Eve Johnson Houghton) *hld up in tch: effrt 2f out: unable qck and uncomfortable on downhill run over 1f out: wl btn fnl f* **7/1**
4260 **7** *3/4* **U S Navy Seal (USA)**^{20} 1620 4-8-13 **82**................................ JFEgan 1 67
(J R Jenkins) *bmpd leaving stalls: stdd and dropped in after s: hld up in last pair: rdn 3f out: no imp u.p 2f out: wknd over 1f out* **40/1**
14-0 **8** *22* **Cloud Seven**^{30} 1418 4-8-13 **82**...................................... MartinHarley 2 23
(Chris Wall) *stdd and wnt rt s: t.k.h: hld up in tch in midfield: hdwy into 4th 3f out: lost pl and rdn 2f out: sn btn: bhd and eased ins fnl f* **15/2**

2m 5.97s (0.17) **Going Correction** +0.20s/f (Good) **8** Ran SP% **112.9**
Speed ratings (Par 107): **107,106,103,103,102 97,97,79**
CSF £125.39 CT £631.30 TOTE £7.70: £2.40, £5.30, £1.40; EX 135.20 Trifecta £676.60.
Owner Salem Rashid **Bred** Newsells Park Stud **Trained** Newmarket, Suffolk

FOCUS
Five non runners meant this was not as strong as originally advertised. They went very steadily early on and it developed into a sprint. The runner-up has been rated close to his standout heavy ground win last year.

2215 NEWMARKETRACECOURSES.CO.UK MAIDEN FILLIES' STKS (PLUS 10 RACE) 1m 4f
4:25 (4:30) (Class 5) 3-Y-O **£3,881** (£1,155; £577; £288) **Stalls** Centre

Form RPR
6-3 **1** **Daphne**^{20} 1626 3-9-0 0.. PatCosgrave 1 80
(William Haggas) *chsd ldr: clsd and rdn to ld 2f out: sn edging lft: stl edging lft but hld on gamely ins fnl f* **9/4**^{2}
0 **2** *shd* **Talent To Amuse (IRE)**^{131} 29 3-9-0 0.......................... JackMitchell 5 79
(Roger Varian) *chsd ldng pair: effrt to press wnr 2f out: ev ch and edgd lft wl over 1f out: stl edging lft but kpt on wl fnl f: jst hld* **25/1**
3 **3** *2 1/2* **Taffeta Lady**^{21} 1609 3-9-0 0....................................... RichardKingscote 7 75
(Lucy Wadham) *chsd ldng trio: effrt 2f out: stl cl enough in 3rd whn sltly impeded and swtchd rt ent fnl f: outpcd ins fnl f* **11/10**^{1}

6 **4** 2 1/4 **Heavensfield**[18] 1704 3-9-0 0 SaleemGolam 6 71
(Mark H Tompkins) *hld up in last pair: effrt over 2f out: 4th and no imp over 1f out: edgd lft and styd on same pce ins fnl f* **100/1**

6 **5** 2 1/2 **Gloryette**[21] 1608 3-9-0 0 WilliamBuick 3 67
(Ed Dunlop) *stdd s: t.k.h early: hld up in tch: effrt 2f out: no imp over 1f out: wl hld and one pce fnl f* **8/1**

5 **6** 3 **Sisania (IRE)**[18] 1704 3-9-0 0 LiamJones 4 63
(Marco Botti) *racd keenly: led tl hdd and rdn 2f out: sn outpcd and lost pl: wknd ins fnl f* **50/1**

7 nk **Queen Of The Stars** 3-9-0 0 MartinHarley 2 62
(William Haggas) *s.i.s: hld up in midfield: effrt 2f out: sn outpcd and bhd over 1f out: wknd ins fnl f* **6/1**[3]

2m 37.63s (5.63) **Going Correction** +0.20s/f (Good) 7 Ran SP% **110.6**
Speed ratings (Par 96): **89,88,87,85,84 82,81**
CSF £45.08 TOTE £2.90: £1.60, £7.90; EX 43.20 Trifecta £111.90.
Owner The Queen **Bred** The Queen **Trained** Newmarket, Suffolk

FOCUS
Race distance increased by 9yds. This lacked the depth generally associated with maiden races at this venue. Not solid form.

2216 LEONARD ORAM RETIREMENT H'CAP 1m
5:00 (5:00) (Class 3) (0-95,92) 4-Y-0+ **£7,762** (£2,310; £1,154; £577) **Stalls** High

Form RPR

020- **1** **Arrowzone**[192] 7676 5-8-10 **86** JosephineGordon(5) 6 94
(Ivan Furtado) *chsd ldr: rdn 2f out: stl 2 l down 1f out: styd on fnl 100yds: led cl home: immediately pricked ears and jst hld on* **7/1**[3]

20-6 **2** shd **Jack's Revenge (IRE)**[37] 1274 8-9-3 **88** (bt) PatCosgrave 7 95
(George Baker) *stdd s: hld up in tch in rr: effrt 2f out: swtchd rt over 1f out and bk lft 1f out: styd on wl u.p ins fnl f: str chal cl home: jst hld* **8/1**

44-5 **3** 1/2 **George Cinq**[34] 1335 6-8-13 **87** TomMarquand(3) 8 93
(George Scott) *racd against stands' rail: led: rdn and drifting rt over 1f out: stl 2 l clr 1f out: grad worn down fnl 100yds: hdd and no ex cl home* **7/1**[3]

050- **4** hd **Rotherwick (IRE)**[146] 8308 4-9-0 **85** (t) LukeMorris 3 90
(Paul Cole) *in tch in midfield: effrt 2f out: no imp over 1f out tl drvn and kpt on wl fnl 100yds: nt quite rch ldrs* **5/2**[1]

-020 **5** nk **Emerald (ITY)**[13] 1861 4-9-3 **88** (p) LiamJones 5 93+
(Marco Botti) *hld up in tch: rdn 2f out: outpcd and looked wl hld over 1f out: rallied ins fnl f: r.o strly fnl 100yds* **7/1**[3]

6-53 **6** 1/2 **Simply Shining (IRE)**[20] 1624 6-8-5 **79** SammyJoBell(3) 4 82
(Richard Fahey) *chsd ldrs: rdn 2f out: no imp tl drvn and kpt on ins fnl f: nvr quite enough pce to rch ldrs* **8/1**

01-5 **7** 7 **Secret Art (IRE)**[34] 1344 6-9-7 **92** WilliamBuick 2 86
(William Knight) *racd in centre: hld up in tch: effrt 2f out: rdn and no hdwy over 1f out: btn and eased ins fnl f* **9/2**[2]

00-0 **8** 31 **Yourartisonfire**[20] 1629 6-9-5 **90** (v) MartinHarley 1 2
(K R Burke) *racd in centre: a in rr: rdn 3f out: lost tch 2f out: t.o* **20/1**

1m 38.66s (0.06) **Going Correction** +0.20s/f (Good) 8 Ran SP% **111.2**
Speed ratings (Par 107): **107,106,106,106,105 105,98,67**
CSF £57.58 CT £313.05 TOTE £9.30: £2.80, £2.10, £1.70; EX 78.20 Trifecta £430.50.
Owner Ron Hull **Bred** J K Beckitt & Son **Trained** Wiseton, Nottinghamshire

FOCUS
Another strongly run affair, in which the first six finished in a heap. The winner has been rated back to his best, with the runner-up close to last year's C&D run.

2217 DIRECTA "HANDS AND HEELS" APPRENTICE SERIES H'CAP 6f
5:30 (5:34) (Class 5) (0-75,75) 4-Y-0+ **£3,234** (£962; £481; £240) **Stalls** High

Form RPR

55-0 **1** **Upavon**[112] 288 6-8-10 **67** (t) MillyNaseb(3) 6 79+
(Stuart Williams) *broke wl: stdd bk and travelled strly in midfield: hdwy to chse ldrs over 1f out: pushed into ld 1f out: r.o strly: readily* **10/3**[1]

12-6 **2** 2 1/2 **Racing Angel (IRE)**[46] 1119 4-8-8 **62** LuluStanford 10 65
(Mick Quinn) *sn led: rdn 2f out: hdd over 1f out: stl ev ch tl outpcd by wnr and battling for 2nd fnl f: kpt on same pce* **16/1**

5-00 **3** shd **Musharrif**[29] 1444 4-9-4 **75** GerO'Neill(3) 8 78
(Declan Carroll) *chsd ldr: rdn and ev ch 2f out: led over 1f out: hdd 1f out: outpcd by wnr and battling for 2nd fnl f: kpt on* **10/1**

5-23 **4** 1/2 **Snappy Guest**[17] 1746 4-9-0 **71** JaneElliott(3) 1 72+
(George Margarson) *in tch in last trio: effrt and swtchd rt 2f out: chsd ldng trio 1f out: kpt on same pce and no ch w wnr ins fnl f* **7/2**[2]

020- **5** 8 **East Coast Lady (IRE)**[206] 7366 4-9-7 **75** AdamMcNamara 5 47
(William Stone) *dwlt: in tch towards rr: rdn and hdwy 2f out: no hdwy u.p over 1f out: wknd fnl f* **11/2**[3]

6064 **6** 2 3/4 **Honcho (IRE)**[14] 1838 4-8-13 **72** JonathanFisher(5) 9 34
(John Ryan) *bhd: rdn 4f out: no imp tl styd on to pass btn rivals ins fnl f: nvr trbld ldrs* **10/1**

1140 **7** 1 1/2 **Rigolleto (IRE)**[30] 1419 8-9-4 **72** (p) PatrickVaughan 4 29
(Anabel K Murphy) *chsd ldrs: rdn 1/2-way: lost pl and btn over 1f out: wknd fnl f* **25/1**

210- **8** 1 **Lolita**[214] 7170 4-9-4 **75** GeorgeWood(3) 3 28
(J R Jenkins) *broke wl: sn stdd to chse ldrs and t.k.h: rdn 2f out: sn outpcd and btn: wknd fnl f* **10/1**

30-0 **9** 2 **Etienne Gerard**[21] 1596 4-8-11 **65** (p) KieranSchofield 7 11
(Nigel Tinkler) *dwlt: in tch in last pair: rdn after 2f out: no imp 2f out: wknd over 1f out* **16/1**

1-26 **10** 8 **Royal Normandy**[117] 236 4-9-0 **73** (v) WilliamCox(5) 2
(Andrew Balding) *in tch in midfield: rdn over 2f out: lost pl and swtchd lft 2f out: sn wknd and bhd* **6/1**

1m 12.85s (0.65) **Going Correction** +0.20s/f (Good) 10 Ran SP% **117.9**
Speed ratings (Par 103): **103,99,99,98,88 84,82,81,78,67**
CSF £57.65 CT £490.57 TOTE £4.10: £1.40, £3.10, £3.80; EX 60.70 Trifecta £615.60.
Owner Morley, Reynolds & Watkins **Bred** Major-Gen Guy Watkins **Trained** Newmarket, Suffolk
■ Stewards' Enquiry : Milly Naseb seven-day ban; used whip down the shoulder in the backhand position (tba)

FOCUS
A typically competitive race of its type. The runner-up has been rated to form, and the third close to form.
T/Plt: £3,103.80 to a £1 stake. Pool of £59696.55 - 14.04 winning tickets. T/Qpdt: £89.60 to a £1 stake. Pool of £6637.86 - 54.80 winning tickets.. **Steve Payne**

[2188] YORK (L-H)
Friday, May 13

OFFICIAL GOING: Good to firm (7.8)
Wind: moderate half against Weather: grey cloud & cool

2218 RALPH RAPER MEMORIAL STKS (H'CAP) 5f
2:20 (2:21) (Class 3) (0-90,90) 3-Y-O **£12,938** (£3,850; £1,924; £962) **Stalls** Centre

Form RPR

-242 **1** **Discreet Hero (IRE)**[47] 1112 3-8-9 **78** (t) AndreaAtzeni 15 87+
(Simon Crisford) *stdd s and sn swtchd lft: hld up in rr: gd hdwy 2f out: chsd ldrs over 1f out: qcknd ent fnl f: led last 120yds: sn rdn and edgd lft: kpt on* **8/1**[3]

1-42 **2** 1 1/2 **El Astronaute (IRE)**[7] 1996 3-9-6 **89** SilvestreDeSousa 9 93
(John Quinn) *prom: hdwy and cl up 2f out: rdn to chal over 1f out: ev ch whn drvn and edgd lft ent fnl f: kpt on* **5/1**[2]

3-21 **3** shd **Paddy Power (IRE)**[29] 1435 3-9-2 **85** DavidNolan 3 89
(Richard Fahey) *cl up: slt ld 2f out: rdn over 1f out: drvn ent fnl f: hdd last 120yds: kpt on same pce* **9/1**

51-0 **4** 1 **Dheban (IRE)**[21] 1599 3-8-12 **81** FrankieDettori 7 81
(Richard Hannon) *sltly hmpd s and hld up in rr: hdwy 2f out: rdn over 1f out: kpt on fnl f* **16/1**

13-6 **5** shd **Midnight Malibu (IRE)**[27] 1492 3-8-4 **78** RachelRichardson(5) 10 78
(Tim Easterby) *chsd ldrs: rdn wl over 1f out: drvn and kpt on same pce fnl f* **33/1**

01-3 **6** nse **Curtain Call**[17] 1763 3-8-9 **78** TonyHamilton 1 77
(Richard Fahey) *trckd ldng pair: cl up 2f out: sn rdn: drvn and edgd lft ent fnl f: kpt on one pce* **8/1**[3]

00-5 **7** 1 3/4 **Excessable**[27] 1492 3-9-2 **85** (t) DavidAllan 8 78
(Tim Easterby) *hld up in tch: hdwy 2f out: rdn along whn n.m.r over 1f out: sn one pce* **11/1**

315- **8** nk **Teresar (IRE)**[217] 7072 3-9-7 **90** AdamKirby 6 82
(Henry Candy) *chsd ldrs: rdn along 2f out: sn drvn and wknd appr fnl f* **9/1**

U0-4 **9** nk **New Road Side**[20] 1647 3-8-10 **79** BarryMcHugh 14 70
(Tony Coyle) *towards rr: rdn along over 2f out: n.d* **66/1**

215- **10** hd **Spike (IRE)**[219] 7040 3-8-7 **76** oh1 PJMcDonald 11 66
(David Barron) *in rr and sn edging lft: pushed along and hung lft over 2f out: swtchd lft and rdn ent fnl f: kpt on towards fin* **33/1**

-511 **11** 1 **Just That Lord**[11] 1935 3-8-12 **81** 6ex RobertWinston 5 79+
(Bill Turner) *cl up: rdn along 2f out: drvn over 1f out: hld whn n.m.r and hmpd jst ins fnl f: eased after* **9/4**[1]

110- **12** 2 1/4 **Lydia's Place**[196] 7601 3-8-11 **87** CliffordLee(7) 2 66
(Richard Guest) *slt ld: rdn along and hdd 2f out: sn drvn and wknd over 1f out* **16/1**

402- **13** nk **Ayresome Angel**[236] 6557 3-8-9 **83** PhilDennis(5) 4 61
(Bryan Smart) *dwlt and wnt bdly lft s: sn chsng ldrs on inner: rdn along 2f out: sn drvn and wknd* **20/1**

1m 0.42s (1.12) **Going Correction** +0.30s/f (Good) 13 Ran SP% **121.9**
Speed ratings (Par 103): **103,100,100,98,98 98,95,95,94,94 92,89,88**
CSF £47.21 CT £389.71 TOTE £9.20: £3.00, £2.30, £3.10; EX 43.10 Trifecta £332.50.
Owner Ms A Quinn & Partners **Bred** Haras De Bernesq **Trained** Newmarket, Suffolk

FOCUS
It was a mainly overcast but dry lead up to racing and, despite 2mm of watering the previous evening, the going was upgraded to good to firm all over prior to the opener. Same rail alignment as Thursday, having the following impact on race distances: Race 3 (1m), race 4 (1m6f) and races 5 & 7 (1m4f) reduced by 31 yards. All others as advertised. This was a good-quality 3yo sprint handicap, in which the main action developed down the centre of the track. It's been rated around the fourth and fifth.

2219 LANGLEYS SOLICITORS EBF MARYGATE FILLIES' STKS (LISTED RACE) 5f
2:55 (2:55) (Class 1) 2-Y-O
£25,519 (£9,675; £4,842; £2,412; £1,210; £607) **Stalls** High

Form RPR

04 **1** **Vona (IRE)**[8] 1976 2-8-12 0 JackGarritty 3 85
(Richard Fahey) *racd centre: trckd ldrs: hdwy wl over 1f out: rdn ent fnl f: styd on wl to ld towards fin* **33/1**

1 **2** 1 **Boater (IRE)**[48] 1086 2-8-12 0 AndreaAtzeni 2 81
(Mark Johnston) *racd centre: slt ld: rdn over 1f out: drvn ins fnl f: hdd and no ex towards fin* **11/8**[1]

2 **3** hd **Perfect Madge (IRE)**[29] 1437 2-8-12 0 KeaganLatham 4 81
(Kevin Ryan) *dwlt and in rr: hdwy 2f out: chsd ldrs ent fnl f: n.m.r and swtchd rt last 100yds: styd on wl towards fin* **12/1**

1 **4** 1/2 **Twizzell**[11] 1921 2-8-12 0 PJMcDonald 10 79+
(Ann Duffield) *hld up towards stands' rail: hdwy 1/2-way and sn trcking ldrs: effrt wl over 1f out: rdn and ev ch ent fnl f: drvn: edgd rt and no ex last 50yds* **12/1**

4 **5** 2 **Amlak**[7] 1988 2-8-12 0 FrankieDettori 7 72+
(Richard Hannon) *racd on stands' tail: cl up: disp ld 1/2-way: rdn over 1f out and ev ch: drvn ins fnl f: wknd last 100yds* **15/2**[3]

55 **6** 1 **Love Oasis**[16] 1793 2-8-12 0 SilvestreDeSousa 8 68
(Mark Johnston) *trckd ldrs towards stands' side: pushed along and lost pl 1/2-way: sn in rr and rdn: styd on u.p appr fnl f* **16/1**

1 **7** 1 3/4 **Coolfitch (IRE)**[29] 1443 2-8-12 0 SamJames 11 62+
(David O'Meara) *trckd ldrs on stands' rail: rdn along wl over 1f out: sn one pce* **12/1**

4 **8** 1/2 **Mightaswellsmile**[15] 1799 2-8-12 0 TomEaves 6 60
(James Given) *chsd ldrs: rdn along over 2f out: sn wknd* **40/1**

9 1 **Carlton Frankie** 2-8-12 0 GrahamGibbons 5 56
(Michael Easterby) *t.k.h early: trckd ldrs: effrt over 2f out: sn rdn: green and grad wknd* **20/1**

211 **10** 2 **Stormy Clouds (IRE)**[12] 1895 2-8-12 0 SeanLevey 9 49
(Richard Hannon) *prom: rdn along over 2f out: sn wknd* **3/1**[2]

5 **11** 4 1/2 **Khelly's Edge**[49] 1082 2-8-12 0 DaleSwift 1 33
(Scott Dixon) *hld rrd s: sn chsng ldrs on outer: rdn along 1/2-way: sn lost pl and bhd* **50/1**

1m 0.51s (1.21) **Going Correction** +0.30s/f (Good) 11 Ran SP% **119.9**
Speed ratings (Par 98): **102,100,100,99,96 94,91,90,89,86 78**
CSF £78.76 TOTE £47.90: £9.00, £1.10, £3.10; EX 138.30 Trifecta £1731.20.
Owner Nick Bradley Racing (Trading Places) **Bred** Colm McEvoy **Trained** Musley Bank, N Yorks

FOCUS
This looked a modest 2yo affair for Listed status. There was a solid pace on and, although this time the stands' side was favoured, the first pair fought it out down the centre. It's been rated as a par renewal.

2220 LONGINES IRISH CHAMPIONS WEEKEND FILLIES' STKS (REGISTERED AS MICHAEL SEELY MEMORIAL) (LISTED) 1m

3:30 (3:31) (Class 1) 3-Y-O

£25,519 (£9,675; £4,842; £2,412; £1,210; £607) **Stalls** Low

Form RPR

123- **1** **Nemoralia (USA)**[196] 7626 3-9-0 112 FrankieDettori 1 113+
(Jeremy Noseda) *hld up: smooth hdwy on outer 3f out: cl up 2f out: led on bit 1 1/2f out: shkn up and pushed clr ent fnl f: styd on strly: readily* **6/5**[1]

10- **2** *6* **Aljuljalah (USA)**[217] 7073 3-9-0 0 AndreaAtzeni 7 99
(Roger Varian) *prom: trckd ldr after 2f: cl up over 3f out: led wl over 2f out: rdn 2f out: sn hdd and drvn: kpt on u.p fnl f: no ch w wnr* **9/1**[3]

312- **3** *1* **Thetis (IRE)**[231] 6709 3-9-0 102 TedDurcan 9 97
(Sir Michael Stoute) *stdd and swtchd lft s: hld up and bhd: hdwy on outer 3f out: rdn to chse wnr over 1f out: drvn ent fnl f: kpt on same pce* **7/2**[2]

01-1 **4** *5* **Czabo**[21] 1603 3-9-0 95 SilvestreDeSousa 2 86
(Mick Channon) *trckd ldrs: effrt wl over 2f out and sn pushed along: rdn and n.m.r wl over 1f out: sn drvn and one pce* **7/2**[2]

40-6 **5** *2* **Rebel Surge (IRE)**[27] 1476 3-9-0 91 WilliamTwiston-Davies 6 81
(Richard Spencer) *t.k.h early: trckd ldrs: hdwy 1/2-way: rdn along over 2f out: drvn wl over 1f out: sn btn* **33/1**

20-6 **6** *1 1/4* **Peru**[12] 1890 3-9-0 81 GrahamGibbons 4 78
(Hugo Palmer) *chsd ldr: pushed along over 4f out: rdn wl over 3f out: sn wknd* **25/1**

531- **7** *6* **Our Joy (IRE)**[197] 7584 3-9-0 80 AdamKirby 5 64
(Clive Cox) *led: pushed along over 3f out: rdn and hdd wl over 2f out: sn drvn and wknd* **20/1**

1m 37.71s (-1.29) **Going Correction** +0.025s/f (Good) **7** Ran SP% **111.4**
Speed ratings (Par 104): **107,101,100,95,93 91,85**
CSF £12.29 TOTE £2.00: £1.30, £3.90; EX 11.80 Trifecta £36.30.
Owner T Allan, J Lovat & C Pigram **Bred** Alberta Davies **Trained** Newmarket, Suffolk

FOCUS
Race distance reduced by 31yds. This fillies' Listed prize featured a mixed bunch and the clear form choice proved a class apart. The winner has been rated as stepping up 4lb on her 2yo form.

2221 BETWAY YORKSHIRE CUP (BRITISH CHAMPIONS SERIES) (GROUP 2) 1m 6f

4:05 (4:10) (Class 1) 4-Y-O+ **£90,736** (£34,400; £17,216; £8,576; £4,304) **Stalls** Low

Form RPR

2-22 **1** **Clever Cookie**[16] 1772 8-9-1 113 (p) PJMcDonald 2 115
(Peter Niven) *trckd ldrs on inner: hdwy over 2f out: chal wl over 1f out: rdn to ld ent fnl f: drvn and kpt on wl towards fin* **5/2**[2]

201- **2** *1/2* **Curbyourenthusiasm (IRE)**[245] 6270 5-9-1 101 FergusSweeney 1 114
(David Simcock) *s.s: hld up and bhd: hdwy on outer over 2f out: chsd ldng pair ent fnl f: sn rdn and ev ch whn edgd lft ins fnl 100yds: kpt on wl towards fin* **15/2**[3]

140- **3** *nk* **Second Step (IRE)**[208] 7335 5-9-1 118 AndreaAtzeni 3 113
(Luca Cumani) *trckd ldr: cl up over 3f out: led wl over 2f out: rdn wl over 1f out: hdd ent fnl f: sn drvn and rallied: no ex towards fin* **10/11**[1]

6-44 **4** *6* **Suegioo (FR)**[16] 1772 7-9-1 109 (p) DavidNolan 4 105
(Richard Fahey) *trckd ldng pair: hdwy on outer 3f out: rdn along over 2f out: sn drvn and one pce* **15/2**[3]

40-0 **5** *8* **Glaring**[16] 1772 5-9-1 107 (t) SilvestreDeSousa 6 94
(Amanda Perrett) *led: rdn along over 3f out: hdd and drvn over 2f out: sn wknd* **10/1**

3m 1.12s (0.92) **Going Correction** +0.025s/f (Good) **5** Ran SP% **113.6**
Speed ratings (Par 115): **98,97,97,94,89**
CSF £20.31 TOTE £2.90: £1.60, £2.50; EX 17.40 Trifecta £22.90.
Owner P D Niven **Bred** Mrs J A Niven **Trained** Barton-le-Street, N Yorks

■ Flying Officer was withdrawn. Price at time of withdrawal 6/4. Rule 4 applies to all bets struck prior to withdrawal but not to SP bets - deduction 40p in the pound. New market formed.

■ Stewards' Enquiry : Andrea Atzeni two-day ban; used whip down the shoulder in the forehand position (27th-28th May)

FOCUS
Race distance reduced by 31yds. A diluted edition of the Yorkshire Cup, with original favourite Flying Officer withdrawn after getting loose beforehand. It was run at a routine pace and turned into a dash around 3f out. The winner has been rated close to his best.

2222 BETWAY JORVIK STKS (H'CAP) 1m 4f

4:40 (4:42) (Class 2) 4-Y-O+

£31,125 (£9,320; £4,660; £2,330; £1,165; £585) **Stalls** Centre

Form RPR

3-11 **1** **Barsanti (IRE)**[48] 1089 4-8-12 96 AndreaAtzeni 6 110+
(Roger Varian) *trckd ldrs: smooth hdwy to ld 2f out: pushed clr 1f out: rdn ins fnl f: kpt on wl* **15/8**[1]

0-61 **2** *2* **Oasis Fantasy (IRE)**[12] 1885 5-8-11 95 6ex (b) SilvestreDeSousa 10 103
(Ed Dunlop) *hld up and bhd: hdwy wl over 2f out: swtchd rt to outer and rdn over 1f out: drvn and styd on wl fnl f* **11/2**[2]

44-1 **3** *2* **Top Tug (IRE)**[34] 1336 5-9-1 99 AdamKirby 8 104
(Alan King) *t.k.h early: trckd ldrs: hdwy over 2f out: rdn over 1f out: drvn and kpt on fnl f* **11/2**[2]

25-4 **4** *1 1/2* **Croquembouche (IRE)**[20] 1620 7-8-6 90 KieranO'Neill 2 93
(Ed de Giles) *led: pushed along over 3f out: rdn along over 2f out: hdd 2f out and sn drvn: grad wknd* **14/1**

-620 **5** *nse* **Fire Fighting (IRE)**[8] 1973 5-9-10 108 (b) FrankieDettori 5 111
(Mark Johnston) *dwlt and towards rr: hdwy 3f out: rdn to chse ldrs over 1f out: drvn and kpt on fnl f* **10/1**[3]

30-6 **6** *1* **Innocent Touch (IRE)**[12] 1880 5-8-2 86 PatrickMathers 3 87
(Richard Fahey) *t.k.h early: trckd ldng pair: effrt 3f out: rdn along over 2f out: drvn wl over 1f out: kpt on same pce* **10/1**[3]

00-3 **7** *5* **Blue Hussar (IRE)**[27] 1493 5-8-5 89 AndrewMullen 9 82
(Micky Hammond) *in tch: hdwy on outer 3f out: rdn along over 2f out: sn outpcd* **12/1**

6-24 **8** *1 1/2* **Chancery (USA)**[20] 1645 8-9-3 101 JackGarritty 4 92
(David O'Meara) *hld up: a towards rr* **14/1**

023- **9** *shd* **Fattsota**[232] 6686 8-9-5 103 DavidNolan 7 93
(David O'Meara) *trckd ldr: effrt 3f out: cl up over 2f out: sn rdn and wknd* **11/1**

5363 **10** *3 1/2* **Pearl Castle (IRE)**[20] 1645 6-8-11 95 DougieCostello 1 80
(K R Burke) *chsd ldrs: rdn along on inner 4f out: wknd over 3f out* **28/1**

2m 29.98s (-3.22) **Going Correction** +0.025s/f (Good) **10** Ran SP% **116.5**
Speed ratings (Par 109): **111,109,108,107,107 106,103,102,102,99**
CSF £11.85 CT £48.53 TOTE £2.80: £1.30, £1.80, £2.10; EX 12.80 Trifecta £48.40.
Owner Sheikh Mohammed Obaid Al Maktoum **Bred** Glenvale Stud **Trained** Newmarket, Suffolk

FOCUS
Race distance reduced by 31yds. Run at a pretty even gallop, the right horses came to the fore and the form looks solid. It's been rated around the front-running fourth.

2223 EBF STALLIONS BREEDING WINNERS FRANK WHITTLE PARTNERSHIP STKS (FILLIES' H'CAP) 7f

5:10 (5:11) (Class 3) (0-90,90) 4-Y-O+ **£12,938** (£3,850; £1,924; £962) **Stalls** Low

Form RPR

010- **1** **Lil Sophella (IRE)**[217] 7093 7-8-9 78 JackGarritty 4 87
(Patrick Holmes) *hld up in rr: hdwy on outer 2f out: rdn to chse ldng pair ins fnl f: drvn and styd on wl to ld nr fin* **16/1**

3-40 **2** *1/2* **Secret Hint**[49] 1065 5-9-5 88 DavidProbert 8 95
(Andrew Balding) *hld up towards rr: stdy hdwy on outer 3f out: cl up on bit 2f out: slt ld over 1f out: rdn jst ins fnl f: drvn and edgd lft last 100yds: hdd and no ex towards fin* **6/1**[3]

20-6 **3** *1/2* **Breakable**[23] 1563 5-8-8 82 (p) RachelRichardson[(5)] 9 88
(Tim Easterby) *hld up: hdwy 3f out: trckd ldrs 2f out: effrt to chal over 1f out: rdn to dispute ld 1f out: sn drvn and ev ch tl no ex towards fin* **6/1**[3]

50-2 **4** *1 1/2* **Azagal (IRE)**[20] 1624 5-8-9 78 DavidAllan 5 80+
(Tim Easterby) *hld up in rr: hdwy wl over 2f out: trckd ldrs whn nt clr run over 1f out: swtchd lft and rdn ent fnl f: sn no imp* **9/2**[1]

-160 **5** *2* **Three Gracez**[29] 1441 4-9-2 85 DougieCostello 6 82
(Philip McBride) *hld up towards rr: hdwy over 2f out: nt clr run over 1f out: rdn ent fnl f: sn drvn and no imp* **12/1**

-334 **6** *5* **Maureb (IRE)**[19] 1663 4-8-2 76 oh5 (p) PhilDennis[(5)] 10 59
(Tony Coyle) *cl up on outer: led after 2f: rdn along over 2f out: drvn and hdd over 1f out: grad wknd* **33/1**

5016 **7** *2 3/4* **Apache Storm**[35] 1318 4-9-2 85 AndrewMullen 11 61
(Michael Appleby) *chsd ldrs: rdn along wl over 2f out: sn drvn and wknd* **16/1**

606- **8** *2* **Invoke (IRE)**[143] 8342 5-9-5 88 TomQueally 7 58
(Keith Dalgleish) *chsd ldrs: rdn along over 2f out: drvn and wknd over 1f out: hld whn hung lft jst ins fnl f* **11/1**

61 **9** *nk* **Dusky Dawn**[18] 1708 4-8-9 78 BenCurtis 1 47
(Alan Swinbank) *led 2f: prom: rdn along wl over 2f out: sn wknd* **12/1**

-216 **10** *1* **Lavetta**[17] 1757 4-8-12 81 AndreaAtzeni 2 48
(Alan Swinbank) *prom: pushed along 3f out: cl up on inner and rdn wl over 1f out: hld whn hmpd jst ins fnl f: eased* **5/1**[2]

20-0 **11** *22* **Mambo Paradise**[29] 1441 4-9-7 90 SilvestreDeSousa 3
(Mark Johnston) *towards rr: sme hdwy on inner 3f out: rdn over 2f out: sn wknd and bhd* **6/1**[3]

1m 25.31s (0.01) **Going Correction** +0.20s/f (Good) **11** Ran SP% **116.1**
Speed ratings (Par 104): **107,106,105,104,101 96,93,90,90,89 64**
CSF £107.79 CT £663.53 TOTE £22.10: £4.80, £2.60, £2.60; EX 188.40 Trifecta £779.60.
Owner Mrs S B Porteous **Bred** Waterford Hall Stud **Trained** Middleham, N Yorks

FOCUS
A fair handicap and the way the race was run it very much set up for the closers. Another step up from the winner, with the third rated to form.

2224 7IM SUPPORTS CYSTIC FIBROSIS CARE STKS (H'CAP) 1m 4f

5:40 (5:40) (Class 4) (0-80,79) 3-Y-O **£9,703** (£2,887; £1,443; £721) **Stalls** Centre

Form RPR

056- **1** **Master Blueyes (IRE)**[221] 6986 3-9-0 72 DougieCostello 2 81+
(Alan King) *hld up towards rr: gd hdwy on inner over 2f out: nt clr run over 1f out: squeezed through to chse ldng pair ent fnl f: sn swtchd rt and rdn: styd on wl to ld last 50yds* **10/1**

-321 **2** *3/4* **Second Serve (IRE)**[29] 1429 3-9-6 78 SilvestreDeSousa 8 86
(Mark Johnston) *led: pushed along over 2f out: rdn wl over 1f out: drvn ins fnl f: hdd and no ex last 50yds* **13/2**[2]

052- **3** *1 1/4* **West Drive (IRE)**[191] 7708 3-9-7 79 AndreaAtzeni 12 85
(Roger Varian) *trckd ldr: effrt over 2f out: rdn over 1f out and ev ch: drvn ins fnl f: kpt on same pce towards fin* **3/1**[1]

3311 **4** *1 1/4* **Project Bluebook (FR)**[30] 1410 3-9-4 76 JasonHart 3 80
(John Quinn) *trckd ldrs on inner: hdwy 3f out: rdn wl over 1f out: sn drvn and sltly outpcd: kpt on u.p fnl f* **11/1**

-611 **5** *shd* **Nietzsche**[22] 1587 3-9-0 77 CallumShepherd[(5)] 10 81
(Brian Ellison) *hld up towards rr: stdy hdwy on outer 3f out: chsd ldrs 2f out: sn rdn and ev ch over 1f out: drvn and kpt on same pce fnl f* **14/1**

0-43 **6** *2 3/4* **Stetchworth Park**[23] 1575 3-9-7 79 WilliamTwiston-Davies 9 78
(Michael Bell) *prom: chsd ldrs over 2f out: rdn wl over 1f out: sn drvn and kpt on one pce* **14/1**

0-16 **7** *3/4* **Walsingham Grange (USA)**[21] 1602 3-9-1 76 RobHornby[(3)] 1 74
(Pam Sly) *in tch: hdwy to chse ldrs 3f out: rdn 2f out: sn drvn and one pce* **7/1**[3]

521 **8** *nk* **Shoofly (IRE)**[56] 980 3-9-5 77 FergusSweeney 14 75
(Martyn Meade) *hld up in rr: hdwy wl over 2f out: rdn wl over 1f out: n.d* **8/1**

01-0 **9** *1 1/2* **Disobedience (USA)**[17] 1738 3-9-3 75 (b[1]) AdamKirby 13 70
(Charlie Appleby) *bhd: sme hdwy on outer wl over 2f out: sn rdn and n.d* **13/2**[2]

50-3 **10** *14* **Sporty Yankee (USA)**[30] 1410 3-8-7 65 JoeyHaynes 4 38
(K R Burke) *towards rr: sme hdwy over 4f out: rdn along over 3f out: n.d* **16/1**

30-4 **11** *2 3/4* **Icefall (IRE)**[30] 1411 3-9-1 73 DavidAllan 11 42
(Tim Easterby) *t.k.h: in tch: hdwy on outer to chse ldrs after 2f: rdn along over 3f out: sn wknd* **25/1**

24-5 **U** **Head High (IRE)**[30] 1406 3-9-2 74 KeaganLatham 6
(Kevin Ryan) *wnt rt and uns rdr s* **33/1**

2m 32.56s (-0.64) **Going Correction** +0.025s/f (Good) **12** Ran SP% **118.7**
Speed ratings (Par 101): **103,102,101,100,100 98,98,98,97,87 86,**
CSF £73.77 CT £246.94 TOTE £12.20: £3.70, £2.30, £1.60; EX 113.80 Trifecta £447.20.
Owner The Barbury Lions **Bred** T Boylan **Trained** Barbury Castle, Wilts

FOCUS
Race distance reduced by 31yds. A useful 3yo handicap, run at an ordinary gallop, and the fact the second, third and fourth were up there throughout, suggests the winners effort can be upgraded considering he came from behind. It's been rated on the positive side.
T/Jkpt: Not won. T/Plt: £217.60 to a £1 stake. Pool of £199103.10 - 667.66 winning tickets.
T/Qpdt: £44.30 to a £1 stake. Pool of £14059.70 - 234.77 winning tickets. **Joe Rowntree**

2225 - 2228a (Foreign Racing) - See Raceform Interactive

[1611]DUNDALK (A.W) (L-H)

Friday, May 13

OFFICIAL GOING: Polytrack: standard

2229a WWW.DUNDALKSTADIUM.COM H'CAP 6f (P)

8:00 (8:03) (45-65,65) 4-Y-0+ **£4,069** (£1,257; £595; £264; £99)

RPR

1 **Cappadocia (IRE)**[98] 469 6-8-8 **45**................................ RonanWhelan 3 62+
(John James Feane, Ire) *cl up and sn settled bhd ldrs: disp 3rd at 1/2-way: impr into 2nd fr 2f out and rdn to ld 1f out: drvn clr and styd on strly: easily* **11/4**[1]

2 4 1/4 **Kiss The Stars (IRE)**[98] 468 6-9-4 **62**....................... KillianLeonard[(7)] 8 65
(T G McCourt, Ire) *sn led narrowly: jnd briefly bef 1/2-way: rdn and 1 l clr under 2f out: sn strly pressed and hdd u.p 1f out: sn no imp on wnr in 2nd: kpt on same pce* **7/1**

3 1 3/4 **Hardy Black (IRE)**[24] 1555 5-9-11 **62**............................(p) PatSmullen 11 60+
(Kevin Frost) *upset in stalls: chsd ldrs: disp 3rd at 1/2-way: rdn under 2f out and no imp on ldrs u.p in 3rd wl ins fnl f: kpt on same pce* **9/2**[3]

4 1/2 **Missile Command (IRE)**[28] 1466 8-8-9 **46**....................(p) LeighRoche 1 42
(Jane M Foley, Ire) *in tch: t.k.h early and short of room on inner in 6th after 1f where lost pl: 8th bef 1/2-way: tk clsr order into st and prog far side 2f out into 4th: no imp on ldrs and kpt on same pce clsng stages* **10/1**

5 nk **Ask Dad**[18] 1727 6-9-8 **64**..(t) DonaghO'Connor[(5)] 4 59
(Damian Joseph English, Ire) *upset in stalls: mid-div: rdn and sme hdwy under 2f out to chse ldrs: kpt on into nvr nrr 5th wl ins fnl f* **3/1**[2]

6 1/2 **Invincible Missile (IRE)**[21] 1616 4-8-8 **45**......................(p) RoryCleary 2 39
(T G McCourt, Ire) *towards rr: rdn into st and clsd u.p into mod 7th ent fnl f: kpt on* **25/1**

7 1 1/2 **Virile (IRE)**[18] 1727 5-9-9 **60**...................................(b) SeamieHeffernan 10 49
(S Donohoe, Ire) *chsd ldrs tl impr to dispute briefly bef 1/2-way: sn rdn in 2nd and lost pl fr 2f out: no ex and wknd ins fnl f* **12/1**

8 1 1/2 **Catwilldo (IRE)**[161] 8110 6-8-8 **48**..........................(b) RobbieDowney[(3)] 6 32
(Garvan Donnelly, Ire) *dwlt: sn settled in mid-div: disp 7th fr 1/2-way: rdn and no imp on ldrs nr side fr 2f out: one pce after* **8/1**

9 2 1/2 **Regal Power**[18] 1732 7-8-8 **45**... DannyGrant 12 21
(Marcus Callaghan, Ire) *towards rr: rdn into st and no imp fr 2f out* **33/1**

10 1 **Royal Avatar (IRE)**[11] 1464 5-7-12 **45**......................... SeanDavis[(10)] 13 18
(Donal Kinsella, Ire) *towards rr: rdn into st and no imp fr 2f out* **33/1**

11 3 3/4 **Caminel (IRE)**[42] 1191 5-9-3 **59**..........................(b) DonnachaO'Brien[(5)] 5 20
(Keith Henry Clarke, Ire) *mid-div: rdn in 9th bef 1/2-way and no imp appr st: swtchd lft 2f out and one pce after* **11/1**

12 4 1/2 **Art World (IRE)**[26] 1505 4-9-6 **57**.. ConnorKing 9
(James Coyle, Ire) *cl up: disp 3rd at 1/2-way: lost pl into st and no ex u.p 2f out: sn wknd* **25/1**

1m 12.36s (72.36) **12** Ran SP% **132.2**
CSF £24.84 CT £92.20 TOTE £3.00: £1.30, £2.50, £2.00; DF 24.40 Trifecta £238.00.
Owner Miss K Hickey **Bred** Rathasker Stud **Trained** Curragh, Co Kildare

FOCUS
Moderate stuff and an easy winner. The fourth helps set the standard.

2230 - 2231a (Foreign Racing) - See Raceform Interactive

[1769]MAISONS-LAFFITTE (R-H)

Friday, May 13

OFFICIAL GOING: Turf: heavy

2232a PRIX TEXANITA (GROUP 3) (3YO) (TURF) 5f 110y

4:00 (12:00) 3-Y-0 **£29,411** (£11,764; £8,823; £5,882; £2,941)

RPR

1 **Ross Castle (IRE)**[23] 3-8-10 0.. TonyPiccone 6 105
(Matthieu Palussiere, France) *in rr: last and rdn 1 1/2f out: r.o u.p and edgd rt ins fnl f: led cl home* **215/10**

2 snk **Sangria (SPA)**[33] 1374 3-8-10 0.................................. IoritzMendizabal 12 105
(F Chappet, France) *hld up in midfield: hdwy on outer sn after 1/2-way: rdn and styd on wl to ld 100yds out: hdd cl home: no ex* **8/1**

3 1 1/4 **Damila (FR)**[36] 1309 3-8-7 0.. FabriceVeron 5 98
(H-A Pantall, France) *chsd ldng pair: drvn to ld ent fnl f: sn hrd rdn and no ex: hdd 100yds out* **16/1**

4 nse **Post Var (FR)**[33] 1374 3-8-10 0...................................... TheoBachelot 1 101
(S Wattel, France) *towards rr: rdn and styd on appr 1/2-way: disp 3rd whn sltly impeded 50yds out* **3/1**[1]

5 nse **Lil's Joy (IRE)**[35] 1315 3-8-7 0.................................. MickaelBarzalona 4 98
(Giles Bravery) *pressed ldr: led sn after 1/2-way: rdn whn pressed wl over 1f out: hdd ent fnl f: no ex* **58/10**[2]

6 1 3/4 **Willytheconqueror (IRE)**[21] 1607 3-8-10 0..................... MartinDwyer 3 95
(William Muir) *chsd ldrs: nt qckn u.p 1 1/2f out: kpt on same pce fnl f* **13/2**[3]

7 1 1/4 **Mangusto (FR)**[33] 1374 3-8-10 0.................................... MaximeGuyon 7 91
(M Delcher Sanchez, France) *dwlt: w.w towards rr: rdn and hdwy wl over 1 1/2f out: struggling whn n.m.r and bmpd 1f out* **11/1**

8 1 **Largent Du Bonheur (FR)**[23] 3-8-10 0.............. VincentCheminaud 10 87
(M Delzangles, France) *w.w in tch: rdn and nt qckn fr wl over 1 1/2f out: sn btn* **15/2**

9 nk **Aboulie (IRE)**[33] 1374 3-8-11 0... AlexisBadel 9 87
(J-C Rouget, France) *w.w in midfield: rdn and no impressed whn bmpd wl over 1f out: wl btn whn eased* **58/10**[2]

10 8 **Shot In The Dark (FR)**[14] 3-8-10 0......................... StephanePasquier 8 60
(F Chappet, France) *led: hdd sn after 1/2-way: wknd qckly ins fnl 1 1/2f: eased ins fnl f* **44/5**

1m 7.69s (0.39) **10** Ran SP% **119.5**
PARI-MUTUEL (all including 1 euro stake): WIN 22.50; PLACE 6.50, 3.30, 4.50; DF 72.50; SF 222.20.
Owner Matthieu Palussiere **Bred** Bluegate Stud **Trained** France

[1847]DONCASTER (L-H)

Saturday, May 14

OFFICIAL GOING: Good (good to firm in places; 8.1)

Wind: Moderate half behind Weather: Dry & cool

2233 CROWNHOTEL-BAWTRY.COM APPRENTICE H'CAP 1m 4f

5:45 (5:45) (Class 5) (0-70,71) 4-Y-0+ **£3,234** (£962; £481; £240) **Stalls** Low

Form RPR

216- 1 **Always Resolute**[28] 7250 5-8-12 **64**....................... CallumShepherd[(3)] 12 77+
(Brian Ellison) *hld up towards rr: hdwy on inner 1/2-way: swtchd rt and effrt over 2f out: chsd ldrs over 1f out: rdn to chal appr fnl f: led last 100yds: kpt on strly* **5/2**[1]

03-2 2 4 **Longside**[17] 1778 4-9-0 **63**.. ThomasBrown 4 70
(James Eustace) *trckd ldrs: hdwy over 3f out: led 1 1/2f out: sn jnd and rdn: drvn ins fnl f: hdd and no ex last 100yds* **12/1**

5450 3 4 **The Lock Master (IRE)**[21] 1640 9-9-4 **67**..............(p) AlistairRawlinson 5 68
(Michael Appleby) *trckd ldrs: hdwy 4f out: led over 3f out: rdn along over 2f out: hdd 1 1/2f out: sn drvn and kpt on same pce* **12/1**

362- 4 3/4 **Kristjano (GER)**[177] 7901 4-8-13 **69**.......................... SamuelClarke[(7)] 3 68+
(Chris Wall) *hld up towards rr: hdwy on inner 3f out: n.m.r over 2f out: rdn wl over 1f out: kpt on appr fnl f* **6/1**[2]

0-05 5 1/2 **Cape Hideaway**[20] 1675 4-8-11 **60**................................(p) RobHornby 2 59
(Mark Walford) *chsd ldng pair: pushed along over 3f out: rdn wl over 2f out: kpt on same pce* **16/1**

555 6 2 1/4 **Cosmic Tigress**[14] 1873 5-8-10 **59**......................... MichaelJMMurphy 16 54
(John Quinn) *hld up in rr: hdwy over 4f out: in tch and rdn 2f out: sn no imp* **20/1**

6-55 7 2 1/2 **Save The Bees**[26] 1526 8-9-3 **71** ow1................................ GLavery[(5)] 15 62
(Declan Carroll) *hld up in rr: hdwy over 3f out: rdn along over 2f out: plugged on one pce* **20/1**

0-30 8 1 1/2 **The Wee Barra (IRE)**[19] 1697 4-8-13 **62**...........................(p) JoeDoyle 18 51
(Kevin Ryan) *chsd clr ldr: tk clsr order 4f out: cl up 3f out: rdn along over 2f out: sn drvn and grad wknd* **20/1**

00-0 9 3/4 **Midnight Warrior**[20] 1674 6-8-4 **56**.................................. PhilDennis[(3)] 14 43
(Ron Barr) *hld up towards rr: hdwy 3f out: rdn along over 2f out: plugged on one pce* **33/1**

2622 10 nk **Golly Miss Molly**[52] 1039 5-8-12 **66**.........................(b) DavidParkes[(5)] 19 53
(Jeremy Gask) *a towards rr* **14/1**

40-6 11 3/4 **Bridey's Lettuce (IRE)**[33] 1390 4-8-10 **66**................... GeorgeWood[(7)] 1 52
(Ivan Furtado) *chsd ldrs: rdn along on inner 3f out: sn wknd* **15/2**[3]

-444 12 4 1/2 **Frightened Rabbit (USA)**[13] 1881 4-8-5 **61**...............(p) CliffordLee[(7)] 7 40
(Keith Dalgleish) *a towards rr* **12/1**

24-0 13 1 3/4 **Racing Knight (IRE)**[17] 1796 4-9-2 **65**......................... DanielMuscutt 10 41
(Kevin Frost) *hld up towards rr: sme hdwy wl over 2f out: sn rdn along and wknd* **16/1**

33-3 14 1 **Safira Menina**[11] 1947 4-9-0 **63**.. TimClark 17 37
(Martin Smith) *trckd ldrs: effrt over 3f out: sn rdn and wknd* **16/1**

0-00 15 1/2 **Mysterial**[21] 1633 6-8-13 **69**...................................... GerO'Neill[(7)] 20 42
(Declan Carroll) *led and sn clr: rdn along 4f out: hdd over 3f out and sn wknd* **20/1**

5-00 16 12 **That Be Grand**[24] 1560 5-8-2 **56** oh10............................ HollieDoyle[(5)] 9 10
(Shaun Harris) *midfield: rdn along over 3f out: sn wknd* **66/1**

33-0 17 nse **Flying Power**[120] 199 8-9-1 **64**..................................... JacobButterfield 11 18
(John Norton) *a in rr* **20/1**

2m 32.36s (-2.54) **Going Correction** -0.10s/f (Good) **17** Ran SP% **130.3**
Speed ratings (Par 103): **104,101,98,98,97 96,94,93,93,92 92,89,88,87,87 79,79**
CSF £31.83 CT £332.72 TOTE £3.70: £1.30, £3.10, £3.00, £2.20; EX 41.30 Trifecta £641.00.
Owner Market Avenue Racing Club Ltd **Bred** Jarvis Associates **Trained** Norton, N Yorks

FOCUS
As advertised the official going description was good, good to firm in places. Race distance increased by 6yds. The opener was a modest handicap but the form looks sound for the grade.

2234 ROBINSONS OF BAWTRY MEDIAN AUCTION MAIDEN STKS 6f

6:15 (6:20) (Class 5) 3-4-Y-0 **£3,234** (£962; £481; £240) **Stalls** High

Form RPR

40 1 **Chez Vegas**[45] 1151 3-9-3 0... DaleSwift 20 77
(Scott Dixon) *chsd ldrs: rdn to ld over 2f out: kpt on wl* **33/1**

2 1 1/4 **Get Up And Dance** 3-8-12 0... GrahamLee 13 68+
(William Haggas) *dwlt: sn in tch: pushed along 2f out: rdn and kpt on fnl f: wnt 2nd towards fin* **7/2**[1]

22-0 3 1 **Operative**[13] 1894 3-9-3 81.. ShaneGray 9 70
(Ed de Giles) *prom: carried hd high and wandered u.p fr appr fnl f: one pce: lost 2nd towards fin* **4/1**[2]

2 4 1 **Najd**[24] 1570 3-9-3 0.. SeanLevey 6 67
(Richard Hannon) *dwlt: sn in tch: rdn 2f out: kpt on same pce* **4/1**[2]

45- 5 1/2 **Sea Of Hope (IRE)**[213] 7211 3-8-12 0.................. RichardKingscote 19 60+
(Jeremy Gask) *hld up: rdn and gd hdwy 2f out: sn chsd ldr: hung persistently lft fr appr fnl f: no ex fnl 110yds* **25/1**

00- 6 nk **Bryght Boy**[159] 8138 3-9-3 0.. AntonioFresu 8 64
(Ed Walker) *hld up: rdn and hdwy over 1f out: kpt on fnl f* **40/1**

3 7 nk **Insurplus (IRE)**[19] 1691 3-9-3 0.................................... PhillipMakin 16 63
(Jim Goldie) *hld up: pushed along over 2f out: r.o ins fnl f: nrst fin* **9/2**[3]

4 8 3/4 **Bella's Venture**[22] 1597 3-8-9 0......................... MichaelJMMurphy[(3)] 10 58+
(John Gallagher) *prom: rdn over 2f out: keeping on in dispute of 3rd whn hmpd ent fnl f: nt rcvr* **12/1**

5-00 9 2 **Kopassus (IRE)**[12] 1926 4-9-8 57................................ JordanNason[(5)] 18 57
(Lawrence Mullaney) *led: rdn whn hdd over 2f out: wknd fnl f* **100/1**

5 10 2 3/4 **Heiba (IRE)**[59] 952 4-9-13 0.. StevieDonohoe 2 48
(Charlie Fellowes) *s.i.s: hld up: nvr threatened* **9/1**

0-0 11 1 **Clever Divya**[22] 1597 3-8-12 0.................................... LemosdeSouza 12 37
(J R Jenkins) *hld up: rdn over 2f out: nvr threatened* **100/1**

0-4 12 1 **Tallulah Fleur**[11] 1953 3-8-12 0.. PJMcDonald 4 34
(Ann Duffield) *prom: rdn over 2f out: wknd over 1f out* **50/1**

13 2 1/4 **Hodgkins Trust (IRE)** 3-8-12 0.......................[1] DavidParkes[(5)] 14 32
(Jeremy Gask) *a towards rr* **25/1**

00- 14 shd **Savannah Star**[220] 7039 3-8-12 0.................................... DougieCostello 5 27
(Nick Kent) *prom: rdn and lost pl 1/2-way: sn wknd* **150/1**

0 15 3/4 **Glittering**[30] 1436 3-8-9 0... ThomasBrown[(3)] 7 24
(James Eustace) *dwlt: a towards rr* **25/1**

1m 12.21s (-1.39) **Going Correction** -0.10s/f (Good)
WFA 3 from 4yo 10lb **15** Ran SP% **119.6**
Speed ratings (Par 103): **105,103,102,100,100 99,99,98,95,91 90,89,86,86,85**
CSF £138.42 TOTE £18.80: £4.20, £1.90, £1.90; EX 162.70 Trifecta £895.10.
Owner Chesterfield Estates **Bred** G A G Equestrian **Trained** Babworth, Notts

FOCUS
A fair maiden and a big-priced winner.

2235 CHINA ROSE OF BAWTRY NOVICE AUCTION STKS 5f
6:45 (6:47) (Class 5) 2-Y-O **£3,881** (£1,155; £577; £288) **Stalls** High

Form RPR

5 **1** **Lawless Louis**[14] 1868 2-9-0 0 .... PhillipMakin 3 73
(David O'Meara) *mde all: jnd and rdn over 1f out: drvn ins fnl f: kpt on wl* **15/8**[1]

2 *nk* **Bourbonisto** 2-8-12 0 .... RaulDaSilva 4 70
(Ben Haslam) *dwlt: green and sn pushed along in rr: hdwy on outer over 2f out: rdn over 1f out: hung lft ent fnl f: sn ev ch: no ex towards fin* **25/1**

3 *nse* **Dubai Knights (IRE)** 2-9-2 0 .... PJMcDonald 5 74
(Ann Duffield) *trckd wnr on stands' rail: hdwy and cl up 2f out: rdn to chal over 1f out: drvn ins fnl f and ev ch tl no ex towards fin* **4/1**[3]

4 *3 ½* **Katebird (IRE)** 2-8-11 0 .... FrannyNorton 2 56
(Mark Johnston) *chsd ldrs: rdn along and outpcd 1/2-way: kpt on fnl f* **7/2**[2]

0 **5** *1 ¼* **Chotto (IRE)**[16] 1799 2-8-2 0 .... GeorgeWood(7) 8 50
(George Scott) *trckd ldrs: effrt and hdwy over 2f out: rdn wl over 1f out: kpt on same pce* **8/1**

6 *2 ¼* **Emerald Secret (IRE)** 2-8-9 0 .... GrahamLee 6 42+
(Paul Midgley) *in tch: green and pushed along over 2f out: sn n.m.r: rdn and hung lft wl over 1f out: sn outpcd* **18/1**

7 *½* **Cappanarty Con** 2-9-2 0 .... RenatoSouza 1 47
(Dean Ivory) *cl up: rdn along 2f out: sn wknd* **14/1**

5 **8** *hd* **Limbrick**[11] 1951 2-8-4 0 .... SammyJoBell(3) 9 37+
(Richard Fahey) *chsd ldrs on inner: rdn along 2f out: sn wknd* **7/1**

1m 0.63s (0.13) **Going Correction** -0.10s/f (Good) 8 Ran SP% **116.4**
Speed ratings (Par 93): **94,93,93,87,85 82,81,81**
CSF £54.22 TOTE £2.70: £1.20, £4.00, £1.50; EX 48.60 Trifecta £211.80.
Owner James Gaffney **Bred** Brendan Boyle & Ashbrittle Stud **Trained** Upper Helmsley, N Yorks
■ Stewards' Enquiry : George Wood one-day ban: careless riding (28 May)

FOCUS
Just an ordinary novice.

2236 EBF BREEDERS' SERIES FILLIES' FINE & COUNTRY H'CAP (A TBA BONUS RACE) 1m 2f 60y
7:15 (7:15) (Class 3) (0-95,90) 3-Y-O+ **£12,938** (£3,850; £1,924; £962) **Stalls** Low

Form RPR

4-25 **1** **Sagaciously (IRE)**[14] 1855 4-10-0 **90** .... RichardKingscote 4 101+
(Ed Dunlop) *sn trcking ldr: cl up 1/2-way: led 3f out: rdn clr over 1f out: kpt on* **5/1**[3]

12-0 **2** *¾* **La Superba (IRE)**[18] 1757 4-9-10 **86** ....(p) GrahamLee 1 93
(David Elsworth) *trckd ldrs: hdwy 3f out: effrt and swtchd rt over 1f out: sn rdn: kpt on fnl f* **20/1**

44-2 **3** *1* **Lovely Memory (IRE)**[24] 1576 4-9-13 **89** ....(p) JamesDoyle 3 94
(Saeed bin Suroor) *trckd ldrs: hdwy 3f out: chsd wnr over 2f out: rdn wl over 1f out: drvn and kpt on fnl f* **3/1**[1]

1-61 **4** *3 ½* **Miss Van Gogh**[18] 1757 4-9-6 **89** .... AdamMcNamara(7) 7 87
(Richard Fahey) *hld up in rr: effrt and hdwy on outer wl over 2f out: rdn wl over 1f out: sn drvn and no imp* **6/1**

12-4 **5** *½* **Deodoro (USA)**[17] 1786 3-8-4 **81** .... FrannyNorton 2 77
(Mark Johnston) *trckd ldr on inner: pushed along over 3f out: n.m.r: swtchd rt and rdn over 2f out: drvn wl over 1f out: sn one pce* **8/1**

10-2 **6** *3* **Hidden Rebel**[20] 1664 4-9-5 **81** .... PJMcDonald 8 72
(Alistair Whillans) *in tch: effrt 3f out: sn rdn along and n.d* **12/1**

521- **7** *4* **All About Time**[273] 5397 4-9-9 **85** .... PhillipMakin 5 68
(David O'Meara) *hld up: a in rr* **6/1**

41-1 **8** *5* **Bright Flash**[20] 1664 4-9-10 **86** .... SeanLevey 6 59+
(David Brown) *plld hrd and sn led: pushed along over 4f out: hdd 3f out and sn rdn: wknd over 2f out* **4/1**[2]

2m 9.14s (-0.26) **Going Correction** -0.10s/f (Good)
WFA 3 from 4yo 15lb 8 Ran SP% **113.8**
Speed ratings (Par 104): **97,96,95,92,92 90,86,82**
CSF £92.88 CT £348.78 TOTE £5.40: £1.70, £4.00, £1.40; EX 97.00 Trifecta £517.90.
Owner The Sagacious Lot **Bred** Keatly Overseas Ltd **Trained** Newmarket, Suffolk

FOCUS
Race distance increased by 6yds. A competitive handicap, albeit not the strongest for the grade, and they went an ordinary pace.

2237 PORTLAND OF BAWTRY USED CARS H'CAP 1m (R)
7:45 (7:46) (Class 3) (0-95,91) 3-Y-O **£7,762** (£2,310; £1,154; £577) **Stalls** Low

Form RPR

3-1 **1** **Murad Khan (FR)**[37] 1287 3-9-3 **87** .... GrahamLee 1 96+
(Hugo Palmer) *t.k.h: trckd ldrs on inner: hdwy 2f out: rdn to chal ent fnl f: led last 75yds: kpt on* **6/1**[2]

145- **2** *nk* **Nimr**[224] 6924 3-9-0 **84** .... TonyHamilton 8 91+
(Richard Fahey) *hld up in tch: hdwy 1/2-way: effrt over 2f out: rdn to ld 1 1/2f out: jnd and drvn ent fnl f: hdd and no ex last 75yds* **8/1**[3]

15-6 **3** *1 ½* **Storm Rising (IRE)**[9] 1975 3-9-6 **90** .... SeanLevey 4 94
(Richard Hannon) *trckd ldrs: hdwy over 2f out: rdn wl over 1f out: drvn and kpt on fnl f* **10/1**

1 **4** *1 ¾* **Ultimate Star**[78] 735 3-8-9 **79** .... OisinMurphy 10 79
(David Simcock) *hld up in rr: hdwy wl over 2f out: rdn wl over 1f out: styd on fnl f* **8/1**[3]

2-1 **5** *2* **Symbolic**[16] 1800 3-9-4 **88** .... RobertHavlin 5 83
(John Gosden) *hld up towards rr: hdwy on outer 3f out: chsd ldrs wl over 1f out: sn rdn and no imp* **11/8**[1]

34-1 **6** *2* **Carrington (FR)**[14] 1851 3-9-7 **91** .... WilliamBuick 6 82+
(Charlie Appleby) *v.s.a and rel to r: sn detached by 15 l: rn wd home turn: sn t.k.h and hdwy to join field: in tch and rdn along 2f out: sn edgd lft and one pce* **6/1**[2]

1524 **7** *4 ½* **Byres Road**[24] 1571 3-8-11 **81** .... FrannyNorton 7 61
(Mark Johnston) *led: pushed along over 3f out: rdn over 2f out: drvn and hdd wl over 1f out: wknd* **33/1**

341- **8** *2 ¾* **Dark Crescent (IRE)**[211] 7249 3-8-7 **80** .... MichaelJMMurphy(3) 9 54
(Charles Hills) *cl up: disp ld over 2f out: rdn wl over 1f out: sn drvn and wknd* **10/1**

610- **9** *22* **Azhar**[330] 3341 3-9-5 **89** .... JamesDoyle 2 13
(Saeed bin Suroor) *trckd ldng pair: hdwy 3f out and sn cl up: shkn up 2f out: wknd qckly and eased over 1f out* **33/1**

1m 38.44s (-1.26) **Going Correction** -0.10s/f (Good) 9 Ran SP% **117.0**
Speed ratings (Par 103): **102,101,100,98,96 94,89,87,65**
CSF £53.73 CT £474.25 TOTE £6.10: £2.40, £2.30, £3.50; EX 47.90 Trifecta £435.60.
Owner V I Araci **Bred** S C E A Haras De Manneville **Trained** Newmarket, Suffolk

FOCUS
A good 3yo handicap, featuring several unexposed types, and the form should work out.

2238 COLEMANS PIZZERIA AND STEAKHOUSE H'CAP 6f
8:15 (8:18) (Class 4) (0-80,80) 4-Y-O+ **£5,175** (£1,540; £769; £384) **Stalls** Low

Form RPR

-652 **1** **Best Trip (IRE)**[14] 1869 9-9-5 **78** .... SamJames 1 87
(Marjorie Fife) *mde all: rdn over 1f out: drvn ins fnl f: hld on wl towards fin* **14/1**

0-41 **2** *nk* **Available (IRE)**[35] 1341 7-9-2 **75** ....(tp) FrannyNorton 13 83
(John Mackie) *chsd ldr: rdn wl over 1f out: drvn ins fnl f: kpt on wl towards fin* **16/1**

0-40 **3** *1 ½* **Mon Brav**[17] 1787 9-9-1 **74** .... BenCurtis 16 77
(Brian Ellison) *in rr: pushed along 1/2-way: rdn and hdwy 2f out: drvn over 1f out: styd on wl fnl f* **20/1**

00-0 **4** *nk* **Fuwairt (IRE)**[24] 1563 4-9-5 **78** ....[1] RaulDaSilva 6 80
(David Loughnane) *in rr: pushed along 1/2-way: hdwy wl over 1f out and sn rdn: drvn and kpt on fnl f: nrst fin* **50/1**

346- **5** *1* **Nezar (IRE)**[140] 8357 5-9-6 **79** ....(v) OisinMurphy 9 78
(John Quinn) *dwlt and bhd: hdwy 2f out: rdn over 1f out: kpt on wl fnl f: nrst fin* **8/1**

610- **6** *1 ¼* **Ace Master**[287] 4885 8-8-12 **76** ....(b) CallumShepherd(5) 19 71
(Roy Bowring) *racd alone nr stands' rail: cl up: edgd across to join field 1/2-way: rdn over 2f out: drvn over 1f out: kpt on same pce* **25/1**

0-05 **7** *½* **Art Obsession (IRE)**[15] 1844 5-9-4 **77** .... GrahamLee 15 70
(Paul Midgley) *towards rr: hdwy over 2f out: rdn over 1f out: kpt on fnl f* **20/1**

304- **8** *¾* **Barney McGrew (IRE)**[299] 4438 13-8-13 **72** .... PaulMulrennan 10 63
(Michael Dods) *chsd ldrs: rdn along 2f out: sn drvn and grad wknd* **25/1**

0-22 **9** *½* **Gold Flash**[15] 1844 4-9-1 **74** ....(p) PhillipMakin 11 63
(Keith Dalgleish) *chsd ldrs: rdn along 2f out: drvn and wknd over 1f out* **7/1**[2]

/132 **10** *½* **Dandyleekie (IRE)**[8] 2016 4-9-4 **80** .... ShelleyBirkett(3) 17 68+
(David O'Meara) *swtchd lft s and hld up in rr: sme hdwy 2f out: effrt and n.m.r wl over 1f out: n.d* **5/1**[1]

25-0 **11** *nk* **Eternitys Gate**[30] 1447 5-9-5 **78** .... DougieCostello 5 65
(David O'Meara) *midfield: rdn along 2f out: no hdwy* **25/1**

364- **12** *½* **Gothic Empire (IRE)**[261] 5784 4-9-0 **76** .... DanielMuscutt(3) 7 61
(James Fanshawe) *nvr bttr than midfield* **15/2**[3]

54-0 **13** *1 ¾* **Royal Connoisseur (IRE)**[14] 1869 5-8-8 **67** .... GeorgeChaloner 3 47
(Richard Fahey) *in tch on outer: rdn along over 2f out: sn wknd* **11/1**

1656 **14** *18* **Heartsong (IRE)**[26] 1530 7-9-2 **78** .... MichaelJMMurphy(3) 14
(John Gallagher) *chsd ldrs: rdn along wl over 2f out: sn wknd and eased fnl f* **25/1**

0-00 **15** *64* **Ballesteros**[14] 1874 7-9-7 **80** .... JamieSpencer 4
(Richard Fahey) *chsd ldrs: pushed along 1/2-way: lost action and wknd qckly jst over 2f out: sn bhd and heavily eased* **12/1**

1m 12.31s (-1.29) **Going Correction** -0.10s/f (Good) 15 Ran SP% **107.5**
Speed ratings (Par 105): **104,103,101,101,99 98,97,96,95,95 94,94,91,67,**
CSF £148.95 CT £2826.71 TOTE £14.40: £4.50, £4.70, £5.50; EX 197.80 Trifecta £2050.90 Not won..
Owner Mrs Jo McHugh **Bred** Limetree Stud **Trained** Stillington, N Yorks
■ Intisaab (11-2) andYork Glory (16-1) were withdrawn. Rule 4 applies to all bets. Deduction - 15p in the pound.

FOCUS
A decent and competitive sprint handicap, in which the first two were up there throughout.

2239 SUN FAVOURITE H'CAP 7f
8:45 (8:51) (Class 4) (0-85,83) 3-Y-O **£5,175** (£1,540; £769; £384) **Stalls** Low

Form RPR

50-5 **1** **Fashaak (IRE)**[18] 1750 3-9-1 **77** .... SeanLevey 12 84
(Richard Hannon) *prom: led over 2f out: rdn over 1f out: kpt on* **10/1**

312- **2** *¾* **Fighting Temeraire (IRE)**[173] 7956 3-9-6 **82** .... RobertWinston 15 87+
(Dean Ivory) *hld up: stl gng wl whn n.m.r wl over 1f out: swtchd lft: sn pushed along and hdwy: r.o wl fnl f: wnt 2nd towards fin* **7/1**[3]

2-41 **3** *½* **Jordan Sport**[16] 1817 3-9-6 **82** .... JamieSpencer 9 86
(Richard Fahey) *stdd s: tk str hold: hld up: pushed along and hdwy 2f out: chsd ldr jst ins fnl f: edgd lft: rdn and one pce: lost 2nd towards fin* **11/4**[1]

43-0 **4** *1 ¾* **Florenza**[21] 1628 3-8-11 **73** .... AndrewElliott 17 72
(Chris Fairhurst) *prom: rdn over 2f out: hung persistently lft fr appr fnl f: one pce* **50/1**

31-4 **5** *hd* **Wimpole Hall**[33] 1385 3-8-11 **78** .... CallumShepherd(5) 7 76
(William Jarvis) *dwlt: hld up: pushed along and hdwy 3f out: rdn 2f out: kpt on same pce fnl f* **25/1**

03-4 **6** *½* **Timeless Art (IRE)**[44] 1160 3-9-2 **78** ....[1] DougieCostello 6 75
(K R Burke) *in tch: rdn over 2f out: sltly hmpd jst ins fnl f: kpt on fnl 110yds* **9/1**

220- **7** *2* **Dark Forest**[233] 6674 3-8-12 **74** .... JasonHart 11 66
(Simon West) *led: rdn whn hdd over 2f out: wknd fnl 110yds* **40/1**

314- **8** *1 ¾* **Rio's Cliffs**[206] 7398 3-9-3 **79** .... FergusSweeney 5 66
(Martyn Meade) *trckd ldrs: rdn over 2f out: wknd ins fnl f* **14/1**

1-50 **9** *6* **Danecase**[8] 1992 3-9-6 **82** .... MartinLane 8 79+
(David Dennis) *hld up: pushed along and hdwy 3f out: sn chsd ldrs: bdly hmpd jst ins fnl f: eased* **25/1**

04-3 **10** *1 ¼* **Justice Lass (IRE)**[13] 1898 3-9-2 **78** .... GrahamLee 16 45
(David Elsworth) *chsd ldrs: rdn over 2f out: wknd over 1f out* **12/1**

02-0 **11** *1 ½* **Racquet**[30] 1442 3-9-4 **83** .... TomMarquand(3) 4 46
(Richard Hannon) *hld up: rdn over 2f out: sn btn* **20/1**

221- **12** *1 ¼* **Always Welcome (USA)**[144] 8349 3-9-7 **83** .... RobertHavlin 18 43
(John Gosden) *in tch: rdn over 2f out: wknd over 1f out* **5/1**[2]

0-21 **13** *1* **Saeedan (IRE)**[31] 1414 3-8-13 **78** .... DanielMuscutt(3) 14 35
(Marco Botti) *chsd ldrs: rdn over 2f out: wknd over 1f out* **20/1**

1562 **14** *2 ¾* **Theos Lolly (IRE)**[37] 1288 3-8-12 **74** .... TonyHamilton 2 24
(Richard Fahey) *trckd ldrs: rdn over 2f out: sn wknd* **22/1**

0-46 **15** *3 ¾* **Ancient Astronaut**[22] 1599 3-9-4 **80** .... PhillipMakin 3 20
(John Quinn) *hld up: rdn 3f out: sn wknd* **16/1**

036- **16** *¾* **Quoteline Direct**[221] 7006 3-9-3 **79** .... PJMcDonald 1 17
(Micky Hammond) *in tch: rdn over 3f out: wknd* **50/1**

1121 **17** *25* **Nouvelli Dancer (IRE)**[46] 1137 3-8-13 **75** .... OisinMurphy 13
(Ivan Furtado) *chsd ldrs: rdn along 4f out: sn lost pl and struggling: eased* **14/1**

1m 25.69s (-0.61) **Going Correction** -0.10s/f (Good) 17 Ran SP% **129.8**
Speed ratings (Par 101): **99,98,97,95,95 94,92,90,83,82 80,79,77,74,70 69,41**
CSF £74.94 CT £254.48 TOTE £12.90: £2.70, £2.30, £1.40, £11.60; EX 99.10 Trifecta £509.20.
Owner Al Shaqab Racing **Bred** Michael Morrissey **Trained** East Everleigh, Wilts

FOCUS
A useful 3yo handicap which could well produce future winners.

T/Plt: 699.90 Pool: 83946.75 T/Qpdt: 122.70 Pool: 8081.17 **Joe Rowntree & Andrew Sheret**

2203 NEWBURY (L-H)

Saturday, May 14

OFFICIAL GOING: Good (good to soft in places; 6.3)
Wind: Fresh, half behind Weather: Fine

2240 OLYMPIC GLORY CONDITIONS STKS (PLUS 10 RACE) 6f 8y
2:10 (2:11) (Class 2) 2-Y-O **£32,345** (£9,625; £4,810; £2,405) **Stalls** Centre

Form RPR

1 **1** **Mehmas (IRE)**[9] 1976 2-9-5 0 FrankieDettori 5 102+
(Richard Hannon) *lw: hld up towards rr: hdwy over 1f out: led jst ins fnl f: pushed clr* **3/1**[2]

1 **2** 3 ¼ **Global Applause**[13] 1889 2-9-5 0 RyanMoore 1 92
(Ed Dunlop) *lw: trckd ldrs: led over 1f out tl jst ins fnl f: one pce* **4/6**[1]

01 **3** 1 ¾ **Thora Barber**[19] 1719 2-9-0 0 CathyGannon 6 82
(David Evans) *unf: dwlt: sn prom: lost pl and hrd rdn 2f out: styd on fnl f* **33/1**

21 **4** *shd* **Mailshot (USA)**[17] 1783 2-9-5 0 JamesDoyle 8 86
(Mark Johnston) *leggy: swtg: pressed ldr: led 3f out tl over 1f out: no ex* **12/1**

01 **5** *nse* **Cullingworth (IRE)**[33] 1377 2-9-5 0 DavidNolan 7 86
(Richard Fahey) *w'like: stdd s: hld up in rr: rdn over 2f out: styd on fnl f* **50/1**

6 1 ½ **Medicine Jack**[6] 2066 2-9-5 0 ColinKeane 2 82
(G M Lyons, Ire) *w'like: t.k.h: trckd ldrs tl outpcd over 1f out: 4th and btn whn hung lft ins fnl f* **7/1**[3]

21 **7** 15 **Stringybark Creek**[42] 1203 2-9-5 0 GeorgeBaker 3 37
(Mick Channon) *unf: scope: led tl 3f out: wknd wl over 1f out* **22/1**

1 **U** **Berkshire Boy (IRE)**[12] 1915 2-9-5 0 OisinMurphy 4
(Andrew Balding) *str: swvd lft and uns rdr sn after s* **12/1**

1m 14.16s (1.16) **Going Correction** +0.15s/f (Good) 8 Ran SP% **122.1**
Speed ratings (Par 99): **98,93,91,91,91 89,69,**
CSF £5.68 TOTE £4.30: £1.50, £1.10, £8.10; EX 6.70 Trifecta £103.00.
Owner Al Shaqab Racing **Bred** Epona Bloodstock Ltd **Trained** East Everleigh, Wilts

FOCUS
No rain overnight and a dry morning saw the going updated to good to soft prior to racing. The rail was moved out around the 5f to 7f points to give fresh ground. With seven of these eight juveniles having won last time out this was obviously a good-quality event. They went steadily, but the winner impressed and the second gives it a decent look. The third and fourth could both have their pre-race form this high.

2241 AL RAYYAN STKS (REGISTERED AS THE ASTON PARK STAKES) (GROUP 3) 1m 4f 5y
2:45 (2:45) (Class 1) 4-Y-O+ **£56,710** (£21,500; £10,760; £5,360; £2,690) **Stalls** Centre

Form RPR

130- **1** **Astronereus (IRE)**[266] 5641 5-9-0 107 PatDobbs 2 114
(Amanda Perrett) *warm: chsd ldng pair: rdn over 2f out: styd on to ld ins fnl f* **14/1**

45-3 **2** 1 ¼ **Ayrad (IRE)**[22] 1604 5-9-0 112 AndreaAtzeni 3 112
(Roger Charlton) *chsd ldr: led 3f out: hung lft and hdd ins fnl f: kpt on* **8/1**[3]

11-1 **3** 1 ½ **Carnachy (IRE)**[14] 1855 4-8-11 101 RyanMoore 4 107
(David Simcock) *sltly on toes: led at modest pce tl 3f out: one pce fnl f* **7/2**[2]

230- **4** 2 ¾ **Eagle Top**[223] 6970 5-9-0 120 FrankieDettori 1 105
(John Gosden) *s.i.s: t.k.h in rr: hdwy in centre 3f out: shkn up 2f out: wknd 1f out* **4/6**[1]

11-5 **5** 4 ½ **Star Storm (IRE)**[14] 1863 4-9-3 107 TomQueally 5 101
(James Fanshawe) *swtg: in tch tl rdn and wknd over 1f out* **10/1**

2m 38.41s (2.91) **Going Correction** +0.15s/f (Good) 5 Ran SP% **109.1**
Speed ratings (Par 113): **96,95,94,92,89**
CSF £101.80 TOTE £15.00: £4.10, £2.60; EX 57.00 Trifecta £184.60.
Owner John Connolly & Odile Griffith **Bred** Team Hogdala Ab **Trained** Pulborough, W Sussex

FOCUS
This had been upgraded from Listed level since last year. It was run at a muddling sort of pace and, with Eagle Top flopping again, the form looks best rated around the runner-up. A minor pb from the winner.

2242 TORONADO CARNARVON STKS (LISTED RACE) 6f 8y
3:20 (3:20) (Class 1) 3-Y-O
£39,697 (£15,050; £7,532; £3,752; £1,883; £945) **Stalls** Centre

Form RPR

15-3 **1** **Log Out Island (IRE)**[28] 1477 3-9-3 109 [1] JamesDoyle 2 112
(Richard Hannon) *mde all: sn 10 l clr: shkn up 2f out: unchal* **7/1**

0-11 **2** 3 ¼ **Remarkable**[22] 1599 3-9-0 87 (b) RobertHavlin 8 99+
(John Gosden) *lengthy: lw: t.k.h towards rr: effrt 2f out: styd on to easy chse wnr fnl f* **9/2**[2]

1120 **3** 3 ¾ **Buying Trouble (USA)**[21] 1623 3-8-9 84 AndreaAtzeni 1 82
(David Evans) *prom in chsng gp: styd on same pce fnl 2f: nvr able to chal* **40/1**

21-4 **4** 1 ½ **Dhahmaan (IRE)**[17] 1773 3-9-3 102 WilliamBuick 5 85
(Marco Botti) *mid-div: rdn and losing pl over 2f out: styd on fnl f* **6/1**[3]

246- **5** ½ **King Of Rooks**[252] 6092 3-9-3 105 FrankieDettori 7 83
(Richard Hannon) *prom in chsng gp: modest 2nd and rdn over 2f out: fdd over 1f out* **9/1**

31- **6** 1 ½ **Taneen (USA)**[259] 5854 3-9-0 90 DaneO'Neill 4 75
(Roger Varian) *stdd s: sn in midfield: hdwy over 2f out: wnt modest 2nd over 1f out: sn wknd* **10/1**

-12 **7** *nk* **Dream Dubai**[17] 1773 3-9-0 106 RyanMoore 6 74
(Sylvester Kirk) *prom in chsng gp: rdn over 2f out: sn btn* **15/8**[1]

240- **8** 4 ½ **Dream Destination (IRE)**[203] 7460 3-9-0 95 PatDobbs 3 60
(Sylvester Kirk) *dwlt: a bhd* **25/1**

36-5 **9** 2 ½ **Twin Sails**[8] 1991 3-9-0 102 RobertWinston 9 52
(Dean Ivory) *prom in chsng gp tl wknd 2f out* **20/1**

16- **10** 2 ¼ **Sunflower**[231] 6753 3-8-9 0 DavidProbert 10 40
(Andrew Balding) *stdd s: t.k.h towards rr: rdn and no ch fnl 2f* **18/1**

1m 12.2s (-0.80) **Going Correction** +0.15s/f (Good) 10 Ran SP% **115.2**
Speed ratings (Par 107): **111,106,101,99,99 97,96,90,87,84**
CSF £37.15 TOTE £8.60: £2.50, £1.70, £5.50; EX 39.50 Trifecta £755.60.
Owner Godolphin **Bred** Yeomanstown Stud **Trained** East Everleigh, Wilts

FOCUS
This interesting 3yo sprint proved something of a non-event with the winner gifted an unassailable early lead. He's been rated as improving, but there's some doubt about him repeating this.

2243 AL SHAQAB LOCKINGE STKS (BRITISH CHAMPIONS SERIES) (GROUP 1) 1m (S)
3:55 (3:58) (Class 1) 4-Y-O+
£198,485 (£75,250; £37,660; £18,760; £9,415; £4,725) **Stalls** Centre

Form RPR

2-14 **1** **Belardo (IRE)**[22] 1606 4-9-0 117 AndreaAtzeni 6 122
(Roger Varian) *lw: wnt lft s: bhd: hdwy and swtchd lft over 1f out: str run to ld wl ins fnl f* **8/1**

5-22 **2** 1 **Euro Charline**[49] 1106 5-8-11 113 RyanMoore 7 116
(Marco Botti) *lw: in tch: effrt 2f out: led over 1f out tl wl ins fnl f: kpt on same pce* **12/1**

222- **3** *nk* **Endless Drama (IRE)**[357] 2521 4-9-0 116 ColinKeane 2 118
(G M Lyons, Ire) *lw: travelled wl towards rr: hdwy and chal 2f out: hrd rdn over 1f out: unable qck* **8/1**

212- **4** 1 ¼ **Limato (IRE)**[223] 6972 4-9-0 119 HarryBentley 4 115+
(Henry Candy) *hld up: hdwy whn nt clr run 2f out: chsng ldrs whn nt clr run and swtchd rt over 1f out: one pce* **3/1**[1]

30-1 **5** 2 ¼ **Toormore (IRE)**[22] 1606 5-9-0 119 JamesDoyle 11 110
(Richard Hannon) *lw: chsd ldr: led 3f out tl over 1f out: wknd ins fnl f* **9/2**[2]

-054 **6** *hd* **Gabrial (IRE)**[9] 1973 7-9-0 110 DavidNolan 5 110
(Richard Fahey) *hmpd s: bhd: rdn over 2f out: sme late hdwy* **50/1**

110- **7** 1 ¼ **Kodi Bear (IRE)**[210] 7280 4-9-0 118 GeraldMosse 3 107
(Clive Cox) *chsd ldrs: rdn over 2f out: wknd over 1f out* **11/2**[3]

24-1 **8** ½ **Gm Hopkins**[17] 1774 5-9-0 114 RobertHavlin 10 105
(John Gosden) *towards rr: sme hdwy and n.m.r over 2f out: no imp over 1f out* **16/1**

25-2 **9** 14 **Dutch Connection**[22] 1606 4-9-0 116 WilliamBuick 9 73
(Charles Hills) *lw: chsd ldrs tl wknd 2f out* **10/1**

50-4 **10** ¾ **Johnny Barnes (IRE)**[21] 1637 4-9-0 109 FrankieDettori 8 72
(John Gosden) *towards rr: effrt over 2f out: sn wknd* **22/1**

65-1 **11** 8 **Mahsoob**[31] 1425 5-9-0 116 DaneO'Neill 13 53
(John Gosden) *chsd ldrs tl wknd over 2f out* **10/1**

13-0 **12** 23 **Barchan (USA)**[22] 1606 4-9-0 80 JackMitchell 12
(Roger Varian) *led at gd pce tl 3f out: wknd qckly* **200/1**

1m 38.18s (-1.52) **Going Correction** +0.15s/f (Good) 12 Ran SP% **119.4**
Speed ratings (Par 117): **113,112,111,110,108 108,106,106,92,91 83,60**
CSF £99.74 CT £811.44 TOTE £9.10: £2.80, £2.80, £2.50; EX 103.10 Trifecta £1166.70.
Owner Godolphin & Prince A A Faisal **Bred** Ballylinch Stud **Trained** Newmarket, Suffolk

FOCUS
For the second year running the Group 1 Lockinge lacked a real star and looked a wide open race. There was a modest pace on down the centre, before a dash for home around 3f out, the form looks best rated around the runner-up. A length pb from Belardo.

2244 AL ZUBARAH LONDON GOLD CUP (OPEN H'CAP) 1m 2f 6y
4:30 (4:30) (Class 2) 3-Y-O
£43,575 (£13,048; £6,524; £3,262; £1,631; £819) **Stalls** Centre

Form RPR

23-1 **1** **Imperial Aviator**[21] 1639 3-8-13 **85** OisinMurphy 3 105+
(Roger Charlton) *trckd ldrs: led 2f out: clr over 1f out: easily* **7/2**[1]

115- **2** 4 ½ **Cartago**[217] 7116 3-9-5 **91** AndreaAtzeni 4 99
(John Gosden) *mid-div: short of room after 2f: hdwy and squeezed through 2f out: chsd easy wnr fnl f* **14/1**

21-3 **3** 1 ¼ **Southdown Lad (IRE)**[32] 1398 3-9-4 **90** MartinHarley 5 95
(William Knight) *mid-div: hdwy to chal 2f out: hrd rdn: sn outpcd* **20/1**

211- **4** 1 ½ **Danehill Kodiac (IRE)**[245] 6317 3-9-1 **87** PatDobbs 6 89+
(Richard Hannon) *chsd ldrs: rdn and sltly outpcd 3f out: styd on same pce fnl 2f* **22/1**

6-21 **5** 2 **Both Sides**[10] 1961 3-8-7 **79** DavidProbert 10 77
(Andrew Balding) *towards rr: rdn 3f out: hdwy over 1f out: nvr rchd ldrs* **25/1**

21-1 **6** 1 ½ **Prince Of Arran**[38] 1260 3-8-12 **84** (v) TomQueally 13 79+
(Charlie Fellowes) *stdd s: t.k.h and sn in midfield: nt clr run 3f out: swtchd rt 2f out: hrd rdn: no imp* **9/1**

0-11 **7** ½ **Vivre Pour Vivre (IRE)**[36] 1314 3-9-2 **88** RyanMoore 2 82+
(Ed Dunlop) *plld hrd: in tch tl outpcd 2f out* **15/2**

11-5 **8** ¾ **Ebtihaal (IRE)**[22] 1603 3-9-7 **93** DaneO'Neill 14 86
(Saeed bin Suroor) *lw: mid-div: struggling to hold pl 3f out: n.d whn sltly hmpd 2f out* **10/1**

1344 **9** 1 ½ **Theydon Grey**[50] 1080 3-8-13 **85** JimmyQuinn 12 75
(Peter Charalambous) *in tch: rdn whn n.m.r 2f out: wknd* **40/1**

3-22 **10** 1 ¾ **Gawdawpalin (IRE)**[18] 1738 3-8-3 **75** SamHitchcott 9 61
(Sylvester Kirk) *on and off the bridle towards rr: mod effrt and drvn along whn carried rt 2f out: n.d* **20/1**

13-4 **11** 2 **Shahbar**[41] 1220 3-8-12 **84** FrankieDettori 11 66
(Marco Botti) *stdd s: pushed along after 4f: a towards rr* **20/1**

-135 **12** *nk* **Motdaw**[15] 1828 3-8-1 **78** PaddyPilley(5) 8 71+
(Mick Channon) *stdd s: t.k.h towards rr: hdwy on inner 3f out: n.m.r over 2f out: sn btn and eased* **50/1**

211- **13** ¾ **Good Run (FR)**[196] 7630 3-9-5 **91** JamesDoyle 15 71
(Saeed bin Suroor) *lw: a bhd* **5/1**[2]

14 2 **Spader (IRE)**[27] 1508 3-9-1 **87** ColinKeane 7 63
(G M Lyons, Ire) *t.k.h: chsd ldr: led 3f out tl wknd 2f out* **11/1**

-142 **15** 8 **Soldier In Action (FR)**[10] 1971 3-9-6 **92** FMBerry 1 52
(Mark Johnston) *led tl 3f out: prom and drvn along whn bdly hmpd on rail 2f out: n.d after* **7/1**[3]

2m 8.13s (-0.67) **Going Correction** +0.15s/f (Good) 15 Ran SP% **124.1**
Speed ratings (Par 105): **108,104,103,102,100 99,99,98,97,95 94,93,93,91,85**
CSF £50.43 CT £889.28 TOTE £4.80: £1.90, £4.50, £6.70; EX 64.70 Trifecta £1567.80.
Owner Qatar Racing, D Hunt & Mrs E Markham **Bred** Daniel Hunt **Trained** Beckhampton, Wilts

■ Stewards' Enquiry : Tom Queally three-day ban: careless riding (May 28,30,31)

FOCUS
Race distance increased by 14yds. Always a red-hot 3yo handicap. The decent early pace steadied around halfway, but it was still a proper test and the form is strong. Another step up from the eased down Imperial Aviator.

2245 HARAS DE BOUQUETOT FILLIES' TRIAL STKS (LISTED RACE) 1m 2f 6y
5:05 (5:06) (Class 1) 3-Y-O
£39,697 (£15,050; £7,532; £3,752; £1,883; £945) **Stalls** Centre

Form RPR
1-13 **1** **We Are Ninety (IRE)**[16] 1804 3-9-0 81 JimCrowley 2 104
(Hugo Palmer) *in tch: effrt and hrd rdn over 1f out: led ins fnl f: drvn out* **12/1**
415- **2** *nk* **Beautiful Morning**[218] 7075 3-9-0 102 JamesDoyle 8 103
(Luca Cumani) *lw: t.k.h: chsd ldr: led 2f out tl ins fnl f: kpt on* **11/4**[1]
11 **3** *1 ¼* **Nezwaah**[103] 421 3-9-0 83 AndreaAtzeni 6 101
(Roger Varian) *str: chsd ldrs: rdn to chal over 1f out: kpt on same pce* **9/2**[2]
15- **4** *nse* **Queen's Trust**[218] 7073 3-9-0 93 RyanMoore 1 102+
(Sir Michael Stoute) *hld up towards rr: hdwy on inner over 2f out: looking for room then hmpd 1f out: r.o fnl f* **5/1**[3]
0-00 **5** *1 ¾* **Epsom Icon**[13] 1888 3-9-3 97 GeorgeBaker 9 100
(Mick Channon) *stdd s: hld up in rr: hdwy to press ldrs in centre over 1f out: no ex fnl f* **16/1**
1- **6** *shd* **Chastushka (IRE)**[203] 7472 3-9-0 0 WilliamBuick 4 97
(John Gosden) *prom tl wknd 1f out* **11/2**
1 **7** *nk* **Beauly**[89] 591 3-9-0 77 FMBerry 10 96
(Charles Hills) *w'like: bit on the leg: hld up in rr: hdwy whn nt best of runs fr 2f out: nvr able to chal* **33/1**
31- **8** *1 ½* **Last Tango Inparis**[203] 7467 3-9-0 0 OisinMurphy 3 93
(Hughie Morrison) *lw: hld up towards rr: rdn and n.d fnl 2f* **11/1**
150- **9** *¾* **Gypsy Eyes (IRE)**[218] 7073 3-9-0 92 DarryllHolland 7 92
(Charles Hills) *t.k.h in midfield: effrt over 2f out: wknd over 1f out* **20/1**
5-1 **10** *4 ½* **Southern Stars**[22] 1608 3-9-0 84 FrankieDettori 5 83+
(John Gosden) *racd freely: sn led: hdd 2f out: n.m.r and wknd over 1f out* **8/1**

2m 9.14s (0.34) **Going Correction** +0.15s/f (Good) **10** Ran SP% **117.6**
Speed ratings (Par 104): **104,103,102,102,101 101,101,99,99,95**
CSF £45.52 TOTE £11.50: £3.00, £1.30, £1.90; EX 45.20 Trifecta £226.80.
Owner Lady Mimi Manton **Bred** Minch Bloodstock & Brittas Stud **Trained** Newmarket, Suffolk

FOCUS
Race distance increased by 14yds. A tight Listed affair for fillies. There was a routine pace on and plenty held a chance from 2f out, but the form still looks decent enough. A big step up from the winner.

2246 PLANTEUR H'CAP 1m (S)
5:35 (5:38) (Class 2) (0-105,104) 4-Y-O+
£24,900 (£7,456; £3,728; £1,864; £932; £468) **Stalls** Centre

Form RPR
4-02 **1** **Azraff (IRE)**[28] 1478 4-8-12 95 AndreaAtzeni 2 104
(Marco Botti) *hld up in midfield: smooth hdwy 2f out: led ent fnl f: rdn out* **16/1**
3102 **2** *1 ¼* **Gabrial's Kaka (IRE)**[8] 1993 6-8-8 91 PatrickMathers 7 97
(Richard Fahey) *t.k.h: chsd ldrs: rdn to chal over 1f out: kpt on same pce* **8/1**
50-4 **3** *¾* **Strong Steps**[14] 1861 4-8-6 89 (p) DavidProbert 11 93+
(Hugo Palmer) *lw: chsd ldr: led 3f out tl wl over 1f out: kpt on ins fnl f* **11/1**
0-12 **4** *nk* **Sinfonietta (FR)**[14] 1856 4-8-8 91 ShaneKelly 4 95
(David Menuisier) *prom: led wl over 1f out tl ent fnl f: one pce* **7/1**
14-6 **5** *1 ¾* **Mustaaqeem (USA)**[21] 1629 4-8-5 88 HarryBentley 5 88
(Sir Michael Stoute) *lw: in tch: effrt over 2f out: one pce appr fnl f* **7/2**[1]
065- **6** *1 ¾* **Spark Plug (IRE)**[210] 7282 5-9-7 104 JimmyFortune 10 100
(Brian Meehan) *bhd tl rdn and styd on fnl 2f* **13/2**[3]
55-0 **7** *1 ¼* **Fire Ship**[42] 1196 7-8-11 94 MartinHarley 1 87
(William Knight) *mid-div: hdwy 2f out: rdn and btn over 1f out* **20/1**
100- **8** *2* **Directorship**[238] 6542 10-8-11 94 LiamKeniry 6 82
(Patrick Chamings) *bhd: rdn and sme hdwy 2f out: no further prog* **50/1**
6000 **9** *shd* **Complicit (IRE)**[21] 1629 5-8-12 95 (bt) JimCrowley 8 83
(Paul Cole) *in tch tl outpcd fnl 2f* **16/1**
40-2 **10** *1 ¼* **Outback Ruler (IRE)**[25] 1545 4-8-2 85 oh1 RyanTate 9 70
(Clive Cox) *hld up in midfield: outpcd and btn 2f out* **25/1**
/-33 **11** *3 ¼* **Hail Clodius (IRE)**[7] 2037 4-8-4 87 KieranO'Neill 13 64
(Richard Hannon) *restrained and rrd s: sn led: hdd 3f out: hrd rdn and wknd 2f out* **16/1**
11-6 **12** *1* **Arthenus**[14] 1861 4-9-3 100 FrederikTylicki 12 75
(James Fanshawe) *towards rr: rdn 3f out: n.d fnl 2f* **9/2**[2]
24-2 **13** *25* **Commodore (IRE)**[31] 1418 4-7-12 86 EdwardGreatrex(5) 3
(George Baker) *hld up towards rr: hdwy 3f out: hrd rdn and wknd over 1f out: bhd whn virtually p.u fnl 100yds* **12/1**

1m 38.35s (-1.35) **Going Correction** +0.15s/f (Good) **13** Ran SP% **121.6**
Speed ratings (Par 109): **112,110,110,109,107 106,104,102,102,101 98,97,72**
CSF £138.39 CT £1534.89 TOTE £16.00: £3.70, £3.10, £3.90; EX 167.50 Trifecta £1690.80.
Owner Saleh Al Homaizi & Imad Al Sagar **Bred** Lodge Park Stud **Trained** Newmarket, Suffolk

FOCUS
A good-quality handicap, rated around the runner-up. The winner is rated back to form.
T/Jkpt: Not won. T/Plt: £403.70 to a £1 stake. Pool: £18,6610.48 - 337.43 winning tickets.
T/Qpdt: £90.80 to a £1 stake. Pool: £14,632.67 - 119.20 winning tickets. **Lee McKenzie**

2211 NEWMARKET (R-H)
Saturday, May 14
OFFICIAL GOING: Good to firm (good in places; 7.9)
Wind: Light behind Weather: Overcast

2247 BETFAIR TAP TAP BOOM H'CAP 7f
1:50 (1:50) (Class 3) (0-95,95) 4-Y-O+ **£7,762** (£2,310; £1,154; £577) **Stalls** High

Form RPR
200- **1** **Fieldsman (USA)**[225] 6895 4-8-13 87 SilvestreDeSousa 1 95
(George Scott) *s.i.s: hld up: hdwy over 2f out: rdn over 1f out: r.o to ld nr fin* **12/1**
010- **2** *hd* **Ghalib (IRE)**[189] 7755 4-9-5 93 LukeMorris 2 100
(Ed Walker) *chsd ldrs: rdn over 1f out: led wl ins fnl f: hdd nr fin* **14/1**
32-4 **3** *¾* **Felix Leiter**[30] 1441 4-8-6 87 CliffordLee(7) 4 92
(K R Burke) *led: hdd over 5f out: remained w ldrs: rdn over 2f out: led over 1f out: hdd wl ins fnl f: kpt on* **11/2**[1]
5024 **4** *½* **Bertiewhittle**[21] 1627 8-8-9 88 JosephineGordon(5) 12 92
(David Barron) *s.i.s: hld up: hdwy over 1f out: rdn and edgd rt ins fnl f: r.o* **8/1**[2]
4-25 **5** *½* **Easy Tiger**[18] 1752 4-8-7 81 oh1 MartinDwyer 14 83
(William Muir) *chsd ldrs: led 4f out: rdn and hdd over 1f out: styd on* **10/1**[3]
065- **6** *¾* **Misterioso (IRE)**[231] 6742 4-8-13 87 WilliamCarson 3 87
(Jamie Osborne) *s.i.s: hld up: hdwy over 2f out: rdn over 1f out: styd on* **16/1**
42-0 **7** *1 ¼* **Syrian Pearl**[21] 1634 5-8-7 81 TedDurcan 8 78
(Chris Wall) *hld up: hdwy: nt clr run and swtchd rt over 1f out: nt rch ldrs* **14/1**
-424 **8** *nk* **Steal The Scene (IRE)**[17] 1775 4-8-4 85 MitchGodwin(7) 6 81
(Richard Hannon) *a.p: rdn over 2f out: styd on same pce fnl f* **8/1**[2]
00-P **9** *1* **Passing Star**[30] 1441 5-9-2 93 MichaelJMMurphy(3) 17 86
(Charles Hills) *hld up: hdwy and edgd rt over 1f out: sn rdn: styd on same pce ins fnl f* **66/1**
64-0 **10** *hd* **Carnival King (IRE)**[42] 1195 4-8-5 86 JordanUys(7) 9 79+
(Brian Meehan) *s.i.s: sn pushed along into mid-div: rdn and lost pl over 2f out: nt clr run over 1f out: r.o towards fin* **8/1**[2]
000- **11** *5* **Smaih (GER)**[257] 5930 4-9-2 90 AdamKirby 11 69
(Jamie Osborne) *hld up: rdn over 2f out: nvr trbld ldrs* **16/1**
02-0 **12** *¾* **Personal Touch**[14] 1848 7-8-7 81 AndrewMullen 15 58
(Michael Appleby) *chsd ldrs: led over 5f out: hdd 4f out: rdn and wknd over 1f out* **14/1**
-005 **13** *2 ¼* **Athletic**[79] 712 7-8-8 85 (v) TomMarquand(3) 16 56
(Andrew Reid) *s.i.s: hld up: rdn: nt clr run and swtchd lft over 1f out: wknd fnl f* **11/1**
006- **14** *3 ¼* **Enlace**[224] 6932 4-9-7 95 JoeFanning 10 57
(Mark Johnston) *prom: rdn over 2f out: wknd over 1f out* **16/1**
000- **15** *1* **Firmdecisions (IRE)**[249] 6185 6-9-6 94 PatCosgrave 7 54
(Dean Ivory) *chsd ldrs: rdn 1/2-way: wknd over 1f out* **12/1**

1m 24.87s (-0.53) **Going Correction** +0.075s/f (Good) **15** Ran SP% **120.7**
Speed ratings (Par 107): **106,105,104,104,103 102,101,101,100,99 94,93,90,86,85**
CSF £169.42 CT £725.71 TOTE £11.70: £4.10, £4.20, £3.00; EX 232.80 Trifecta £458.70.
Owner Chelsea Thoroughbreds - Lazenby **Bred** H Sexton, S Sexton & Silver Fern Farm **Trained** Newmarket, Suffolk

FOCUS
After the first most of the jockeys said the ground was on the fast side of good. The opener was a decent handicap, if lacking in progressive types. The principals raced towards the far side of the track, with the first three home drawn 1-2-4, and there was something of a blanket finish. The winner rates back to a better view of his 2yo form.

2248 BETFAIR "MORE TO PLAY FOR" MAIDEN STKS 1m
2:25 (2:26) (Class 5) 3-Y-O **£3,881** (£1,155; £577; £288) **Stalls** High

Form RPR
0 **1** **Star Blaze**[19] 1714 3-9-5 0 SilvestreDeSousa 6 86
(Mick Channon) *chsd ldrs: outpcd over 2f out: rallied over 1f out: r.o to ld and hung rt wl ins fnl f* **8/1**[3]
0-3 **2** *¾* **Torch**[14] 1859 3-9-5 0 SeanLevey 9 84
(Richard Hannon) *chsd ldrs: rdn over 2f out: ev ch ins fnl f: styd on* **16/1**
2- **3** *½* **Ehtiraas**[232] 6711 3-9-5 0 JoeFanning 10 83
(Owen Burrows) *chsd ldr: shkn up to ld over 1f out: rdn and hdd wl ins fnl f* **11/10**[1]
4 *2* **Huge Future** 3-9-5 0 AdamKirby 4 78+
(Saeed bin Suroor) *s.i.s: sn pushed along in rr: rdn 1/2-way: hung rt and r.o ins fnl f: nvr nrr* **10/3**[2]
5-3 **5** *1 ½* **Generalship (IRE)**[24] 1570 3-9-5 0 (b) NickyMackay 8 74
(John Gosden) *led: rdn and hdd over 1f out: no ex ins fnl f* **11/1**
5 **6** *2 ¼* **Warrior Prince**[19] 1714 3-9-5 0 PatCosgrave 2 69
(Ed Dunlop) *mid-div: hdwy over 3f out: rdn and ev ch over 1f out: wknd ins fnl f* **10/1**
00 **7** *¾* **Western Prince**[12] 1930 3-9-5 0 [1] RobertTart 7 67
(John Gosden) *hld up: pushed along over 4f out: hdwy over 3f out: wknd fnl f* **16/1**
0 **8** *1 ¼* **Diamond Geyser (IRE)**[19] 1701 3-9-5 0 LemosdeSouza 5 64
(Luca Cumani) *hld up: rdn over 1f out: nvr trbld ldrs* **50/1**
6-5 **9** *9* **Royal Mahogany (IRE)**[16] 1800 3-9-2 0 KevinStott(3) 3 43
(Luca Cumani) *hld up: pushed along over 3f out: sn wknd* **100/1**
10 *5* **Justice Lucky (USA)** 3-9-5 0 LiamKeniry 12 31
(David Elsworth) *pushed along in rr early: rdn over 3f out: sn wknd* **33/1**

1m 38.75s (0.15) **Going Correction** +0.075s/f (Good) **10** Ran SP% **116.9**
Speed ratings (Par 99): **102,101,100,98,97 95,94,93,84,79**
CSF £124.74 TOTE £8.60: £2.70, £2.90, £1.10; EX 101.20 Trifecta £381.50.
Owner Jon and Julia Aisbitt **Bred** Jon And Julia Aisbitt **Trained** West Ilsley, Berks

FOCUS
Mukhadram is the best name on this race's recent roll of honour, with Captain Cat another very smart former winner. This was another good edition, rated arobnd the place averages.

2249 BETFAIR ACCA EDGE H'CAP 1m 6f
3:00 (3:00) (Class 2) (0-105,97) 4-Y-O+
£18,675 (£5,592; £2,796; £1,398; £699; £351) **Stalls** Centre

Form RPR
31-1 **1** **Desert Encounter (IRE)**[14] 1853 4-8-12 89 JamieSpencer 6 97+
(David Simcock) *hld up: hdwy over 3f out: swtchd lft over 2f out: shkn up ins fnl f: styd on to ld nr fin* **2/1**[1]
012/ **2** *shd* **Poyle Thomas**[682] 3859 7-8-9 90 PatrickO'Donnell(5) 4 96
(Ralph Beckett) *rrd s: hld up: hdwy over 3f out: rdn over 1f out: r.o* **17/2**
15-0 **3** *nk* **Hardstone (USA)**[35] 1336 5-9-2 92 SeanLevey 3 97
(Michael Dods) *led 1f: chsd ldrs: led over 2f out: rdn over 1f out: hdd nr fin* **12/1**
4 *2 ¼* **Wolfcatcher (IRE)**[59] 4681 4-9-3 94 (p) AdamKirby 7 96
(Charlie Appleby) *a.p: chsd ldr after 3f: rdn and ev ch over 2f out: no ex wl ins fnl f* **4/1**[2]
00-4 **5** *2* **Resiliency (IRE)**[13] 1893 5-8-5 86 GeorgeBuckell(5) 1 85
(Michael Appleby) *prom: nt clr run and lost pl over 3f out: sn rdn: styd on ins fnl f* **5/1**[3]
530- **6** *3 ½* **Vive Ma Fille (GER)**[247] 6243 4-9-6 97 JoeFanning 5 91
(Mark Johnston) *led after 1f: rdn and hdd over 2f out: wknd ins fnl f* **7/1**
5-23 **7** *3 ¼* **Intense Tango**[105] 194 5-8-12 88 DougieCostello 2 78
(K R Burke) *prom: rdn over 2f out: wknd over 1f out* **9/1**

3m 0.36s (3.36) **Going Correction** +0.20s/f (Good)
WFA 4 from 5yo+ 1lb **7** Ran SP% **110.7**
Speed ratings (Par 109): **98,97,97,96,95 93,91**
CSF £18.43 TOTE £2.60: £1.30, £4.40; EX 17.20 Trifecta £145.50.
Owner Abdulla Al Mansoori **Bred** Tally-Ho Stud **Trained** Newmarket, Suffolk

The Form Book, Raceform Ltd, Newbury, RG14 5SJ

FOCUS
Race distance increased by 9yds. Mount Athos landed this event on his way to winning a Group 3 in 2012, and Tiger Cliff won it before taking the Ebor in 2013. With the top weight rated 8lb below the maximum, this wasn't a strong race for the grade. It's been rated around the third.

2250 BETFAIR CASH OUT KING CHARLES II STKS (LISTED RACE) 7f
3:35 (3:35) (Class 1) 3-Y-O **£20,982** (£7,955; £3,981; £1,983; £995) **Stalls** High

Form RPR

1-1 **1** **Thikriyaat (IRE)**[32] 1393 3-9-0 98 TedDurcan 2 107+
(Sir Michael Stoute) *chsd ldrs: shkn up to ld 1f out: edgd rt: rdn out* **13/8**[1]

215- **2** *nk* **Dragon Mall (USA)**[217] 7113 3-9-0 93 [1] JamieSpencer 5 106
(David Simcock) *hld up: hdwy over 1f out: rdn and ev ch ins fnl f: r.o* **7/1**

10-2 **3** *1 ¾* **Scrutineer (IRE)**[31] 1424 3-9-0 103 SilvestreDeSousa 4 101
(Mick Channon) *a.p: rdn over 1f out: styd on* **2/1**[2]

1-42 **4** *½* **Race Day (IRE)**[50] 1071 3-9-0 98 (p) AdamKirby 3 100
(Saeed bin Suroor) *chsd ldr tl rdn to ld over 1f out: sn hdd: styd on same pce ins fnl f* **4/1**[3]

540- **5** *3 ½* **Elronaq**[227] 6869 3-9-0 100 SteveDrowne 1 90
(Charles Hills) *led: rdn and hdd over 1f out: wknd ins fnl f* **14/1**

1m 25.25s (-0.15) **Going Correction** +0.075s/f (Good) 5 Ran SP% **110.6**
Speed ratings (Par 107): **103,102,100,100,96**
CSF £13.05 TOTE £2.10: £1.30, £3.00; EX 10.50 Trifecta £21.80.
Owner Hamdan Al Maktoum **Bred** Kildaragh Stud **Trained** Newmarket, Suffolk

FOCUS
A fair renewal of this Listed event. The form is taken at face value with the runner-up the key.

2251 BETFAIR PRICE RUSH SPRINT TROPHY (H'CAP) 6f
4:10 (4:11) (Class 2) (0-105,102) 3-Y-O
£28,012 (£8,388; £4,194; £2,097; £1,048; £526) **Stalls** High

Form RPR

230- **1** **Show Stealer**[259] 5844 3-8-4 85 MartinDwyer 3 96
(Rae Guest) *hld up: hdwy over 1f out: r.o to ld wl ins fnl f* **22/1**

113- **2** *½* **Marsha (IRE)**[204] 7449 3-9-0 95 LukeMorris 4 104
(Sir Mark Prescott Bt) *hld up: hdwy over 2f out: rdn to ld over 1f out: hdd wl ins fnl f* **8/1**

12-3 **3** *2* **Mr Lupton (IRE)**[13] 1882 3-9-7 102 JamieSpencer 6 105
(Richard Fahey) *s.i.s: hld up: hdwy over 1f out: edgd lft wl ins fnl f: nt rch ldrs* **10/1**

25-2 **4** *1 ¼* **Dark Shot**[13] 1894 3-8-0 81 NickyMackay 10 80+
(Andrew Balding) *chsd ldrs: led 1/2-way: rdn and hdd 2f out: styng on same pce whn nt clr run wl ins fnl f* **14/1**

14-0 **5** *1* **Gallipoli (IRE)**[22] 1599 3-8-6 87 BarryMcHugh 7 83
(Richard Fahey) *prom: hmpd over 4f out: rdn over 2f out: sn outpcd: styd on towards fin* **10/1**

341- **6** *shd* **Nisser**[292] 4704 3-8-1 85 TomMarquand(3) 8 80
(Richard Hannon) *s.i.s: hld up: hdwy 1/2-way: rdn and hung rt fr over 1f out: styd on same pce* **6/1**[2]

640- **7** *shd* **Dark Defender**[224] 6931 3-8-1 82 JoeFanning 12 77
(Keith Dalgleish) *hld up: rdn over 2f out: edgd rt over 1f out: nt trble ldrs* **14/1**

16-3 **8** *nk* **Venturous (IRE)**[14] 1865 3-9-2 97 AdamKirby 2 91
(Charlie Appleby) *led: hdd over 4f out: rdn to ld again 2f out: hdd over 1f out: no ex ins fnl f* **2/1**[1]

4161 **9** *shd* **Suqoor**[16] 1809 3-8-11 92 SilvestreDeSousa 9 86
(Chris Dwyer) *plld hrd and prom: led and edgd rt over 4f out: hdd 1/2-way: rdn over 1f out: wknd ins fnl f* **7/1**[3]

2250 **10** *1 ¼* **Take The Helm**[14] 1865 3-8-3 91 JordanUys(7) 5 81
(Brian Meehan) *prom: rdn over 1f out: wknd fnl f* **16/1**

215- **11** *¾* **Sahreej (IRE)**[239] 6492 3-8-10 91 SteveDrowne 11 78
(Charles Hills) *chsd ldrs: rdn over 2f out: edgd lft over 1f out: wknd fnl f* **16/1**

1m 11.35s (-0.85) **Going Correction** +0.075s/f (Good) 11 Ran SP% **118.9**
Speed ratings (Par 105): **108,107,104,103,101 101,101,101,100,99 98**
CSF £190.24 CT £1891.37 TOTE £23.00: £5.90, £2.50, £3.20; EX 249.60 Trifecta £712.40.
Owner Colin Joseph **Bred** Max Weston **Trained** Newmarket, Suffolk

FOCUS
A valuable sprint handicap, won by the high-class Eastern Impact two years ago. The finish was dominated by the two fillies in the line-up and the first three all came from the rear. The form makes sense and fits the race standard.

2252 BETFAIR EXCHANGE H'CAP 1m 4f
4:45 (4:45) (Class 3) (0-95,87) 3-Y-O **£9,703** (£2,887; £1,443) **Stalls** Centre

Form RPR

00-1 **1** **Opposition**[21] 1619 3-8-13 79 SilvestreDeSousa 2 86+
(Ed Dunlop) *chsd ldr tl rdn to ld over 1f out: r.o wl* **4/6**[1]

1-24 **2** *1 ¾* **Juste Pour Nous**[21] 1636 3-9-3 83 JoeFanning 1 87
(Mark Johnston) *led: rdn over 2f out: hdd over 1f out: styd on same pce wl ins fnl f* **3/1**[2]

3-1 **3** *1* **Batts Rock (IRE)**[28] 1499 3-9-5 85 JamieSpencer 4 87
(Michael Bell) *hld up: hdwy to join ldrs over 2f out: rdn over 1f out: styng on same pce whn hung rt ins fnl f* **10/3**[3]

2m 40.15s (8.15) **Going Correction** +0.20s/f (Good) 3 Ran SP% **108.1**
Speed ratings (Par 103): **80,78,78**
CSF £2.92 TOTE £1.50; EX 3.20 Trifecta £3.20.
Owner Highclere Thoroughbred Racing(Melbourne) **Bred** Cheveley Park Stud Ltd **Trained** Newmarket, Suffolk

FOCUS
Race distance increased by 9yds. A disappointing turnout but an interesting race nonetheless. They didn't go a great gallop, however, and the form is a bit muddling.

2253 READ HUGO PALMER EXCLUSIVELY AT BETFAIR H'CAP 5f
5:15 (5:18) (Class 4) (0-85,85) 4-Y-O+ **£5,175** (£1,540; £769; £384) **Stalls** High

Form RPR

00-3 **1** **Majestic Hero (IRE)**[26] 1528 4-8-13 77 JamieSpencer 3 87
(Ronald Harris) *chsd ldr: rdn over 1f out: led ins fnl f: r.o u.p* **8/1**

2101 **2** *1 ½* **King Crimson**[18] 1744 4-9-5 83 SilvestreDeSousa 5 88
(Mick Channon) *led: rdn and edgd rt over 1f out: edgd lft: hdd and unable qck ins fnl f* **11/2**[1]

-202 **3** *1* **Diamond Lady**[40] 1237 5-9-5 83 RyanPowell 14 84
(William Stone) *a.p: rdn over 1f out: styd on* **25/1**

346- **4** *nk* **Escalating**[271] 5464 4-9-0 78 AndrewMullen 9 78
(Michael Appleby) *s.i.s: sn chsng ldrs: rdn over 1f out: styd on* **6/1**[2]

000- **5** *½* **Royal Mezyan (IRE)**[144] 8347 5-9-2 83 LouisSteward(3) 2 81
(Henry Spiller) *chsd ldrs: rdn and edgd rt over 1f out: styd on same pce ins fnl f* **40/1**

20-0 **6** *¾* **Flexible Flyer**[21] 1634 7-9-3 81 IrineuGoncalves 10 76
(Chris Dwyer) *dwlt: sn pushed along in rr: styd on ins fnl f: nvr nrr* **20/1**

4451 **7** *½* **Top Boy**[10] 1964 6-9-2 80 (v) MartinLane 11 74
(Derek Shaw) *hld up: hdwy u.p over 1f out: no ex ins fnl f* **8/1**

-500 **8** *½* **Captain Bob (IRE)**[13] 1887 5-9-1 79 (p) AdamBeschizza 8 71
(Robert Cowell) *sn pushed along in rr: swtchd rt and hdwy 1f out: no ex ins fnl f* **7/1**[3]

622 **9** *½* **Silver Bid (USA)**[30] 1435 4-8-2 71 JosephineGordon(5) 7 61
(Alan Bailey) *chsd ldrs: rdn over 1f out: no ex fnl f* **9/1**

33-6 **10** *hd* **Oh So Sassy**[31] 1427 6-9-7 85 TedDurcan 12 74
(Chris Wall) *hld up: hung rt over 1f out: n.d* **8/1**

1006 **11** *¾* **Doctor Parkes**[7] 2028 10-8-8 77 AaronJones(5) 6 64
(Stuart Williams) *prom: hung rt and sn lost pl: n.d after* **16/1**

063- **12** *1* **Oeil De Tigre (FR)**[365] 2249 5-8-11 75 WilliamCarson 1 58
(Tony Carroll) *s.i.s: hld up: rdn over 1f out: sn hung rt: nvr on terms* **28/1**

521- **13** *3 ½* **Princess Tansy**[255] 5984 4-8-4 75 SophieKilloran(7) 4 45
(David Simcock) *hld up in tch: pushed along 1/2-way: edgd rt over 1f out: sn wknd* **16/1**

59.72s (0.62) **Going Correction** +0.075s/f (Good) 13 Ran SP% **111.8**
Speed ratings (Par 105): **98,95,94,93,92 91,90,89,89,88 87,86,80**
CSF £43.74 CT £937.37 TOTE £8.20: £2.90, £2.10, £5.30; EX 45.50 Trifecta £914.60.
Owner Mrs Jackie Jarrett & Ridge House Stables **Bred** Mrs Diane Williams **Trained** Earlswood, Monmouths

■ Free To Love was withdrawn. Price at time of withdrawal 10-1. Rule 4 applies to all bets - deduction 5p in the pound.

FOCUS
Few got into this fair sprint handicap, the leaders not coming back. A pb from the winner.
T/Plt: £87.90 to a £1 stake. Pool: £102,724.58 - 852.35 winning tickets T/Qpdt: £27.20 to a £1 stake. Pool: £7,174.52 - 195.15 winning tickets **Colin Roberts**

2047 THIRSK (L-H)
Saturday, May 14

OFFICIAL GOING: Good to firm (good in places, 9.9)
Wind: light 1/2 against Weather: fine

2254 IRISH STALLION FARMS EBF MAIDEN FILLIES' STKS (PLUS 10 RACE) 5f
1:45 (1:47) (Class 4) 2-Y-O **£4,269** (£1,270; £634; £317) **Stalls** High

Form RPR

1 **Kocollada (IRE)** 2-9-0 0 TonyHamilton 9 71+
(Richard Fahey) *in rr: sn drvn along: hdwy over 1f out: swtchd ins: styd on wl to ld clsng stages* **5/2**[1]

2 *¾* **Conistone** 2-9-0 0 GrahamLee 4 68
(James Bethell) *mid-div: nt clr run 2f out: swtchd lft over 1f out: n.m.r 100yds out: kpt on to take 2nd nr fin* **50/1**

32 **3** *½* **Kodi Da Capo (IRE)**[17] 1793 2-9-0 0 PhillipMakin 6 66
(Keith Dalgleish) *w ldrs: led over 1f out: edgd lft and hdd clsng stages* **4/1**[2]

4 *1 ¼* **Indigo Beat** 2-9-0 0 PJMcDonald 10 62+
(Ann Duffield) *sn in rr: hdwy over 1f out: swtchd lft: styd on wl clsng stages* **6/1**[3]

5 *¾* **Lady Cristal (IRE)** 2-9-0 0 JoeyHaynes 2 59+
(K R Burke) *w ldrs: wkng whn hmpd fnl 75yds* **6/1**[3]

6 **6** *1 ¼* **Norwegian Highness (FR)**[14] 1850 2-9-0 0 ShaneGray 7 54
(Kevin Ryan) *w ldrs: led over 2f out: hdd over 1f out: sn wknd* **4/1**[2]

7 *½* **Queen Celeste (IRE)** 2-9-0 0 FrannyNorton 1 53+
(Mark Johnston) *swtchd rt after s: led tl over 2f out: lost pl over 1f out: kpt on clsng stages* **12/1**

8 *shd* **Cosmic Sky** 2-9-0 0 DavidAllan 3 52
(Tim Easterby) *mid-div: wkng whn hmpd over 1f out* **16/1**

9 *nk* **Frozen Kiss** 2-9-0 0 ConnorBeasley 8 51
(Bryan Smart) *in rr and sn drvn along: hdwy over 2f out: sn chsng ldrs: lost pl fnl f* **16/1**

1m 0.17s (0.57) **Going Correction** -0.10s/f (Good) 9 Ran SP% **118.6**
Speed ratings (Par 92): **91,89,89,87,85 83,83,82,82**
CSF £134.07 TOTE £3.90: £1.60, £5.40, £1.60; EX 86.20 Trifecta £361.40.
Owner Sheikh Rashid Dalmook Al Maktoum **Bred** Mrs O M E McKeever **Trained** Musley Bank, N Yorks

■ Stewards' Enquiry : Phillip Makin one-day ban: careless riding (May 28)

FOCUS
A fair juvenile fillies' maiden. They went a decent gallop on ground officially described as good to firm, good in places. The third is used as a tentative guide to the level.

2255 BDS YORKSHIRE H'CAP 6f
2:15 (2:18) (Class 6) (0-65,65) 3-Y-O **£2,587** (£770; £384; £192) **Stalls** High

Form RPR

6-33 **1** **Mr Orange (IRE)**[24] 1564 3-9-0 58 GrahamGibbons 13 64
(Paul Midgley) *hld up in mid-div: hdwy to trck over 2f out: styd on to ld last 150yds* **5/1**[1]

-343 **2** *nk* **Iconic Figure (IRE)**[15] 1829 3-9-5 63 PaulMulrennan 14 69
(Steve Gollings) *hld up towards rr: hdwy over 2f out: upsides ins fnl f: kpt on wl clsng stages* **7/1**[3]

30-0 **3** *½* **Laila Honiwillow**[20] 1670 3-8-13 57 JackGarritty 12 63
(Jedd O'Keeffe) *hld up towards rr: hmpd and swtchd rt 2f out: hung rt and styd on strly fnl f: fin wl* **25/1**

35-0 **4** *shd* **Arize (IRE)**[19] 1703 3-9-7 65 TomEaves 3 69
(David Brown) *led: hung rt and hdd over 1f out: kpt on same pce last 75yds* **25/1**

4221 **5** *½* **Bahamian Sunshine**[36] 1313 3-9-0 65 (p) AdamMcNamara(7) 9 67
(Richard Fahey) *trckd ldrs: led over 1f out: hdd last 150yds: kpt on same pce* **6/1**[2]

0-20 **6** *2* **Seaperle**[12] 1927 3-8-11 55 DavidAllan 8 51
(Tim Easterby) *s.s: hdwy far side to chse ldrs over 2f out: fdd last 150yds* **6/1**[2]

03-4 **7** *2 ¼* **Lady Wootton**[24] 1558 3-9-3 61 PhillipMakin 7 50
(Keith Dalgleish) *s.i.s: in rr: reminders after 1f: hdwy over 2f out: kpt on one pce over 1f out* **9/1**

-460 **8** *1 ½* **Men United (FR)**[72] 797 3-9-1 64 CallumShepherd(5) 2 49
(Roy Bowring) *chsd ldrs: wknd appr fnl f* **10/1**

360- **9** *3 ½* **Miss Uppity**[150] 8244 3-8-13 57 TonyHamilton 15 31
(Ivan Furtado) *s.i.s: racd stands' side 1f: hdwy to chse ldrs over 2f out: wknd fnl f* **16/1**

66-5 **10** *1 ½* **King's Currency**[20] 1669 3-9-1 59 GrahamLee 6 29
(Jedd O'Keeffe) *mid-div: drvn over 2f out: lost pl over 1f out* **7/1**[3]

5-05 **11** *1* **The Lillster**[24] 1558 3-8-13 **60** .... GeorgeDowning(3) 4 27
(Tony Carroll) *prom: lost pl 3f out* **40/1**

3322 **12** *½* **Cool Crescendo**[31] 1420 3-9-2 **60** .... (p) PJMcDonald 10 25
(Rebecca Menzies) *restless in stalls: chsd ldrs: hung rt and wknd fnl 2f* **11/1**

005- **13** *4* **Kingfisher Girl**[293] 4673 3-8-10 **57** .... AlistairRawlinson(3) 1 10
(Michael Appleby) *chsd ldrs: wknd 2f out: bhd whn eased clsng stages* **25/1**

1m 13.25s (0.55) **Going Correction** -0.10s/f (Good) **13** Ran SP% **117.5**
Speed ratings (Par 97): **92,91,90,90,90 87,84,82,77,75 74,73,68**
CSF £36.79 CT £594.57 TOTE £7.00: £2.40, £2.20, £9.00; EX 41.80 Trifecta £833.60.
Owner J Blackburn & A Turton **Bred** Rathbarry Stud **Trained** Westow, N Yorks
■ Comparinka (25-1) was withdrawn. Rule 4 does not apply.

FOCUS
A modest 3yo handicap. They went a strong gallop but it was an odd race in a way as although it was dominated by horses drawn high, they completely shunned the stands' rail to finish central to far side. The opening level is a bit fluid.

2256 MARION GIBSON BROWN MEMORIAL H'CAP (DIV I) 1m
2:50 (2:52) (Class 4) (0-85,85) 4-Y-O+ **£4,851** (£1,443; £721; £360) **Stalls** Low

Form RPR

06-0 **1** **Get Knotted (IRE)**[38] 1274 4-9-7 **85** .... (p) PaulMulrennan 8 93
(Michael Dods) *trckd ldrs on outer: upsides over 2f out: led last 150yds: hld on towards fin* **12/1**

-020 **2** *nk* **Abushamah (IRE)**[12] 1924 5-9-1 **79** .... JamesSullivan 4 86
(Ruth Carr) *hld up towards rr: hdwy on ins over 3f out: swtchd rt appr fnl 2f: upsides 1f out: no ex nr fin* **5/1**[2]

16-4 **3** *½* **Ski Blast**[11] 1954 5-8-10 **74** .... TomEaves 10 80
(Ivan Furtado) *s.i.s: drvn over 3f out: hdwy over 2f out: chsng ldrs over 1f out: kpt on same pce last 100yds* **12/1**

5300 **4** *hd* **Final**[19] 1707 4-8-7 **71** oh2 .... FrannyNorton 6 76
(Mark Johnston) *in rr and sn drvn along: hdwy and swtchd rt appr fnl f: kpt on wl* **33/1**

-005 **5** *nk* **Energia Flavio (BRZ)**[9] 1978 5-8-13 **77** .... GeorgeChaloner 1 82
(Richard Fahey) *sn trcking ldrs: n.m.r over 1f out: kpt on same pce fnl 150yds* **7/1**[3]

5021 **6** *¾* **Taysh (USA)**[11] 1954 4-9-7 **85** .... BenCurtis 5 88
(Michael Appleby) *trckd ldrs: led over 1f out: hdd last 150yds: wknd clsng stages* **3/1**[1]

2205 **7** *½* **Eutropius (IRE)**[16] 1817 7-9-2 **80** .... NeilFarley 9 82
(Alan Swinbank) *in rr: hdwy over 1f out: kpt on one pce over 1f out* **12/1**

5/03 **8** *1 ½* **Torrid**[26] 1526 5-8-13 **82** .... NathanEvans(5) 11 80
(Michael Easterby) *wnt rt s: sn chsng ldrs: drvn over 2f out: wknd fnl f* **5/1**[2]

60-5 **9** *6* **Osteopathic Remedy (IRE)**[33] 1380 12-8-11 **75** .... ConnorBeasley 7 60
(John Davies) *mid-div: effrt 3f out: lost pl over 1f out* **12/1**

01-0 **10** *3 ½* **Comino (IRE)**[24] 1563 5-9-0 **81** .... JoeDoyle(3) 3 58
(Kevin Ryan) *led: hdd over 1f out: wknd last 200yds* **11/1**

520- **11** *8* **Cosmic Ray**[152] 8227 4-8-13 **77** .... DaleSwift 2 35
(Daniel Mark Loughnane) *tooik t.k.h in mid-div: reminders over 3f out: lost pl 2f out: eased whn bhd clsng strages* **25/1**

1m 39.2s (-0.90) **Going Correction** -0.05s/f (Good) **11** Ran SP% **116.7**
Speed ratings (Par 105): **102,101,101,101,100 99,99,97,91,88 80**
CSF £70.50 CT £760.81 TOTE £13.00: £3.80, £1.90, £3.00; EX 84.20 Trifecta £950.50.
Owner D Neale **Bred** Rossenarra Bloodstock Limited **Trained** Denton, Co Durham

FOCUS
Race distance increased by 25yds. The first division of a decent 1m handicap. They went a strong gallop.

2257 MARION GIBSON BROWN MEMORIAL H'CAP (DIV II) 1m
3:25 (3:26) (Class 4) (0-85,85) 4-Y-O+ **£4,851** (£1,443; £721; £360) **Stalls** Low

Form RPR

00-0 **1** **Ginger Jack**[26] 1521 9-9-1 **79** .... DavidAllan 3 89
(Garry Moss) *hld up in mid-div: effrt over 2f out: w ldr over 1f out: kpt on to ld last 50yds* **9/2**[1]

0005 **2** *nk* **Al Khan (IRE)**[8] 1993 7-9-4 **85** .... JoeDoyle(3) 4 94
(Kevin Ryan) *trckd ldrs: smooth hdwy to ld over 1f out whn hit over hd by rival rdr's whip: wandered sltly: hdd and no ex last 50yds* **9/2**[1]

4125 **3** *2* **Sands Chorus**[12] 1924 4-9-0 **78** .... TomEaves 9 82
(James Given) *led: edgd rt and hdd over 1f out: kpt on same pce* **9/2**[1]

01-3 **4** *1* **Trinity Star (IRE)**[26] 1521 5-8-13 **77** .... (p) PaulMulrennan 5 79
(Michael Dods) *s.i.s: in rr: drvn over 3f out: hdwy over 2f out: kpt on same pce fnl f* **9/2**[1]

000- **5** *¾* **Hanseatic**[238] 6520 7-8-11 **75** .... CamHardie 6 75
(Michael Easterby) *hld up in rr: effrt over 3f out: one pce over 1f out* **10/1**[3]

-640 **6** *hd* **Moonlightnavigator (USA)**[12] 1924 4-9-3 **81** .... PhillipMakin 2 80
(John Quinn) *chsd ldrs: one pce whn sltly hmpd over 1f out* **7/1**[2]

00-0 **7** *nk* **Character Onesie (IRE)**[21] 1625 4-8-9 **76** .... SammyJoBell(3) 8 75
(Richard Fahey) *in rr: effrt over 3f out: swtchd rt over 1f out: one pce* **11/1**

6-00 **8** *hd* **Woody Bay**[21] 1643 6-9-4 **82** .... JasonHart 7 82
(Mark Walford) *trckd ldrs: effrt over 2f out: one pce whn sltly hmpd over 1f out* **18/1**

0 **9** *7* **Tadaany (IRE)**[26] 1526 4-9-2 **80** .... (v) SamJames 1 61
(David O'Meara) *sn chsng ldrs: stmbld bnd over 4f out: edgd lft and lost pl over 1f out: sn heavily eased* **12/1**

1m 39.97s (-0.13) **Going Correction** -0.05s/f (Good) **9** Ran SP% **115.6**
Speed ratings (Par 105): **98,97,95,94,93 93,93,93,86**
CSF £24.21 CT £96.73 TOTE £5.80: £1.50, £2.10, £1.70; EX 26.70 Trifecta £128.80.
Owner C H McGhie **Bred** Darley **Trained** Wynyard, Stockton-On-Tees

FOCUS
The second division of a decent 1m handicap. They went an even gallop and the winning time was nearly a second slower.

2258 CONSTANT SECURITY SERVICES H'CAP 5f
4:00 (4:01) (Class 2) (0-100,100) 4-Y-O+ **£12,938** (£3,850; £1,924; £962) **Stalls** High

Form RPR

1-40 **1** **Judicial (IRE)**[82] 677 4-8-13 **92** .... (e) ConnorBeasley 9 101
(Julie Camacho) *led to s: chsd ldr: led 2f out: drvn out* **14/1**

-264 **2** *1 ¾* **Red Baron (IRE)**[2] 2188 7-9-7 **100** .... NeilFarley 5 103
(Eric Alston) *led: hdd 2f out: styd on same pce last 75yds* **9/4**[1]

4-34 **3** *½* **Silvanus (IRE)**[38] 1272 11-9-2 **95** .... GrahamLee 10 96
(Paul Midgley) *trckd ldrs: effrt and hung lft over 1f out: kpt on same pce last 100yds* **25/1**

0-51 **4** *hd* **Kimberella**[10] 1968 6-8-13 **92** .... FrannyNorton 1 92
(David Nicholls) *chsd ldrs: drvn and hung rt over 1f out: kpt on same pce* **11/2**[3]

465- **5** *1* **Barnet Fair**[224] 6921 8-8-10 **89** .... PaulMulrennan 11 86+
(David Nicholls) *hld up in rr: hdwy over 2f out: chsng ldrs over 1f out: kpt on same pce* **8/1**

0000 **6** *½* **Green Door (IRE)**[10] 1968 5-9-5 **98** .... PhillipMakin 4 93
(Robert Cowell) *chsd ldrs: effrt over 2f out: one pce over 1f out* **11/1**

0-40 **7** *3 ¼* **Lexington Place**[10] 1968 6-8-7 **86** .... JamesSullivan 7 69
(Ruth Carr) *stdd s: hld up in rr: sme hdwy 2f out: nvr a factor* **11/1**

000- **8** *2* **Blaine**[204] 7424 6-8-13 **92** .... TomEaves 2 68
(David Nicholls) *sn outpcd and bhd: sme hdwy over 1f out: nvr on terms* **16/1**

06-0 **9** *1 ½* **Grandad's World (IRE)**[32] 1394 4-9-1 **94** .... TonyHamilton 6 65
(Richard Fahey) *chsd ldrs: lost pl over 1f out* **9/1**

/00- **10** *hd* **Fast Act (IRE)**[366] 2223 4-9-7 **100** .... ShaneGray 3 70
(Kevin Ryan) *sn outpcd and in rr: nvr on terms* **25/1**

34-1 **11** *2 ½* **Tumblewind**[20] 1672 6-8-8 **87** .... GeorgeChaloner 12 48
(Richard Whitaker) *chsd ldrs stands' side: drvn 2f out: lost pl over 1f out* **5/1**[2]

57.59s (-2.01) **Going Correction** -0.10s/f (Good) **11** Ran SP% **120.8**
Speed ratings (Par 109): **112,109,108,108,106 105,100,97,94,94 90**
CSF £46.89 CT £810.31 TOTE £19.50: £4.50, £1.70, £4.60; EX 66.30 Trifecta £1068.40.
Owner Elite Racing Club **Bred** Elite Racing Club **Trained** Norton, N Yorks

FOCUS
The feature contest was a good sprint handicap. They went a strong gallop.

2259 WHARTON CONSTRUCTION H'CAP 6f
4:35 (4:35) (Class 3) (0-90,90) 4-Y-O+ **£7,439** (£2,213; £1,106; £553) **Stalls** High

Form RPR

0-24 **1** **Explain**[8] 2016 4-8-10 **79** .... JamesSullivan 13 90
(Ruth Carr) *hld up in rr: hdwy and swtchd stands' side over 2f out: led over 1f out: pushed out* **13/2**

0-06 **2** *¾* **Handsome Dude**[14] 1848 4-9-4 **87** .... (b) GrahamGibbons 10 95+
(David Barron) *hld up in mid-div: hdwy over 2f out: nt clr run and swtchd rt over 1f out: styd on to take 2nd last 50yds* **12/1**

45-6 **3** *1* **Beardwood**[26] 1522 4-8-13 **82** .... TonyHamilton 15 87
(Richard Fahey) *in rr: hdwy and c stands' side over 1f out: styd on to take 3rd clsng stages* **11/1**

0-44 **4** *½* **Growl**[10] 1968 4-8-12 **88** .... AdamMcNamara(7) 3 91
(Richard Fahey) *mid-div: hdwy far side over 2f out: chsng ldrs over 1f out: kpt on same pce fnl 150yds* **4/1**[1]

15-1 **5** *1 ½* **Alpha Delphini**[20] 1666 5-9-0 **83** .... ConnorBeasley 11 82+
(Bryan Smart) *w ldrs: kpt on same pce fnl f* **10/1**

26-0 **6** *½* **Red Tycoon (IRE)**[41] 1215 4-8-13 **82** .... PhillipMakin 7 79
(David Barron) *chsd ldrs: outpcd over 2f out: kpt on fnl f* **25/1**

50-4 **7** *1 ¼* **Manatee Bay**[17] 1787 6-8-8 **77** .... (v) FrannyNorton 5 70
(David Nicholls) *in rr: hdwy 2f out: kpt on fnl f* **16/1**

50-6 **8** *½* **Confessional**[10] 1968 9-9-4 **87** .... (e) DavidAllan 9 78
(Tim Easterby) *led: hdd over 1f out: fdd last 100yds* **16/1**

150- **9** *½* **Dragon King (IRE)**[204] 7424 4-9-7 **90** .... PaulMulrennan 12 80
(Michael Dods) *w ldrs: kpt on same pce over 1f out* **6/1**[3]

400- **10** *hd* **Signore Piccolo**[211] 7245 5-8-10 **84** .... JoshDoyle(5) 6 73
(David O'Meara) *chsd ldrs: wknd over 1f out* **16/1**

-040 **11** *½* **Whozthecat (IRE)**[8] 1997 9-8-11 **80** .... (v) NeilFarley 8 68
(Declan Carroll) *w ldrs: wknd appr fnl f* **16/1**

3233 **12** *½* **Barkston Ash**[8] 2016 8-8-11 **80** .... (p) JasonHart 16 66
(Eric Alston) *chsd ldrs stands' side: lost pl over 1f out* **11/2**[2]

10-0 **13** *5* **Mercers Row**[14] 1869 9-8-10 **79** .... PJMcDonald 4 49
(Michael Herrington) *chsd ldrs: wknd over 1f out* **50/1**

030- **14** *nk* **Fyrecracker (IRE)**[221] 7016 5-8-8 **77** .... TomEaves 14 46
(Grant Tuer) *in rr: bhd and hing rt over 1f out* **33/1**

620- **15** *nk* **Gabrial The Tiger (IRE)**[266] 5629 4-8-9 **78** .... GeorgeChaloner 2 46
(Richard Fahey) *in rr: drvn 3f out: nvr on terms* **33/1**

0-06 **16** *4* **Mime Dance**[17] 1787 5-8-8 **77** .... SamJames 1 32
(David O'Meara) *chsd ldrs: lost pl over 2f out* **25/1**

1m 10.75s (-1.95) **Going Correction** -0.10s/f (Good) **16** Ran SP% **127.2**
Speed ratings (Par 107): **109,108,106,106,104 103,101,101,100,100 99,98,92,91,91 85**
CSF £81.66 CT £870.48 TOTE £8.90: £2.20, £3.60, £3.30, £1.40; EX 119.00 Trifecta £1061.80.
Owner The Beer Stalkers & Ruth Carr **Bred** Tibthorpe Stud **Trained** Huby, N Yorks

FOCUS
Race distance increased by 30yds. Another decent handicap. They went a strong gallop once again.

2260 JUSTGIVING.COM/MARCIA-SANDERSON FOR MACMILLAN MAIDEN STKS 1m 4f
5:10 (5:10) (Class 5) 3-Y-O+ **£3,234** (£962; £481; £240) **Stalls** High

Form RPR

0-0 **1** **Goldmember**[31] 1426 3-8-9 0 .... PaulMulrennan 8 91+
(David Simcock) *hld up towards rr: hdwy 7f out: 3rd over 4f out: led over 1f out: edgd lft: drew clr fnl 150yds: comf* **5/2**[2]

4 **2** *5* **Withhold**[21] 1626 3-8-9 0 .... GrahamGibbons 5 82+
(Charles Hills) *mid-div: hmpd and lost pl bnd after 2f: drvn to chse ldrs over 8f out: 2nd 7f out: drvn to ld over 2f out: hdd over 1f out: keeping on same pce whn hmpd and swtchd rt 150yds out* **5/4**[1]

5-3 **3** *4* **Ice Galley (IRE)**[17] 1784 3-8-9 0 .... TomEaves 7 75
(Kevin Ryan) *led 1f: w ldr: led over 7f out: hdd over 2f out: kpt on same pce* **6/1**[3]

6 **4** *hd* **Edge Of Reason**[58] 968 3-8-4 0 .... JamesSullivan 1 69
(Ed Walker) *s.i.s: hld up in rr: hdwy over 3f out: kpt on same pce fnl 2f* **18/1**

64 **5** *12* **Rosette**[14] 1873 4-9-9 0 .... BenCurtis 4 52
(Alan Swinbank) *s.i.s: detached in last: stmbld bnd over 3f out: kpt on fnl 2f: nvr on terms* **33/1**

33 **6** *4* **Hongkong Adventure**[46] 1134 3-8-9 0 .... DavidAllan 2 49
(Rae Guest) *chsd ldrs: drvn 4f out: lost pl over 2f out* **14/1**

5 **7** *2 ½* **Jethro (IRE)**[20] 1662 5-9-7 0 .... BenRobinson(7) 3 47
(Brian Ellison) *mid-div: drvn and 4th 4f out: lost pl over 2f out* **33/1**

0 **8** *12* **Desert Sensation (IRE)**[14] 1873 4-10-0 0 .... (t) ConnorBeasley 9 27
(Tracy Waggott) *drvn to chse ldr: led after 1f: hdd and reminders over 7f out: lost pl over 3f out: sn bhd: eased clsng stages* **100/1**

9 *4* **Gran Paradiso (IRE)**[206] 7402 4-10-0 0 .... (p) JackGarritty 10 21
(Micky Hammond) *chsd ldrs: reminders and lost pl over 5f out: sn bhd: eased clsng stages* **8/1**

2m 34.74s (-1.46) **Going Correction** -0.05s/f (Good)
WFA 3 from 4yo+ 19lb **9** Ran SP% **117.2**
Speed ratings (Par 103): **102,98,96,95,87 85,83,75,72**
CSF £6.02 TOTE £4.10: £1.30, £1.10, £1.90; EX 8.20 Trifecta £28.50.
Owner Qatar Racing Limited **Bred** Elite Racing Club **Trained** Newmarket, Suffolk

FOCUS
A fair middle-distance maiden. They went just a respectable gallop until the tempo increased down the back straight.

2261 THIRSK RACES NEXT 13TH & 14TH JUNE H'CAP 5f
5:40 (5:41) (Class 4) (0-85,85) 4-Y-O+ **£4,851** (£1,443; £721; £360) **Stalls** High

Form RPR
506- **1** **Bondi Beach Boy**^{231} [6765] 7-9-0 **78**........................ GeorgeChaloner 10 87
(James Turner) *s.i.s: in rr: hdwy over 2f out: chsng ldrs over 1f out: led last 150yds: edgd lft: kpt on* **12/1**
10-6 **2** *1* **Pea Shooter**^{22} [1601] 7-8-13 **77**.. BenCurtis 8 82
(Brian Ellison) *s.i.s: hdwy to chse ldrs over 2f out: kpt on same pce fnl 100yds* **8/1**
16-4 **3** *1* **Just Us Two (IRE)**^{15} [1836] 4-9-7 **85**............................. PaulMulrennan 6 87+
(Robert Cowell) *s.i.s: hdwy over 2f out: nt clr run appr fnl f: swtchd lft: kpt on* **5/1**^{2}
2663 **4** *shd* **Pearl Acclaim (IRE)**^{14} [1874] 6-9-3 **81**................................ TomEaves 9 82
(David Nicholls) *sn chsng ldrs: kpt on same pce fnl 150yds* **7/1**
33-6 **5** *nk* **Imperial Legend (IRE)**^{11} [1956] 7-8-8 **72**.......................... PaulQuinn 11 72
(David Nicholls) *in rr: hdwy 2f out: kpt on fnl f* **14/1**
00-0 **6** *3/4* **Master Bond**^{14} [1848] 7-9-6 **84**...................................... ConnorBeasley 1 82
(David O'Meara) *s.i.s: sn drvn along: hdwy to chse ldrs over 1f out: one pce whn forced rt 150yds out* **9/1**
00-0 **7** *1* **Captain Dunne (IRE)**^{20} [1672] 11-8-13 **82**.......... RachelRichardson$^{(5)}$ 7 76
(Tim Easterby) *led: hdd & wknd fnl 150yds* **9/1**
0-00 **8** *1* **Apricot Sky**^{14} [1869] 6-8-4 **75**.................................... DanielleMooney$^{(7)}$ 3 65
(David Nicholls) *in rr: hdwy over 2f out: sn chsng ldrs: wknd over 1f out* **28/1**
-023 **9** *2 1/2* **Flash City (ITY)**^{7} [2040] 8-8-8 **72**.................................(p) JamesSullivan 4 53
(Ruth Carr) *chsd ldrs: lost pl over 1f out* **13/2**^{3}
44-4 **10** *shd* **Fredricka**^{22} [1601] 5-9-5 **83**... GrahamGibbons 5 64
(David Barron) *sn chsng ldrs: drvn over 2f out: lost pl appr fnl f* **7/2**^{1}
000- **11** *nk* **Landing Night (IRE)**^{239} [6494] 4-8-5 **76**.....................(p) RowanScott$^{(7)}$ 2 56
(Ann Duffield) *chsd ldrs: lost pl over 1f out* **14/1**

58.18s (-1.42) **Going Correction** -0.10s/f (Good) **11** Ran SP% **120.3**
Speed ratings (Par 105): **107,105,103,103,103 101,100,98,94,94 94**
CSF £107.03 CT £553.11 TOTE £16.60: £4.30, £2.70, £1.80; EX 149.20 Trifecta £1079.20.
Owner G R Turner & H Turner **Bred** G R & H Turner **Trained** Norton-le-Clay, N Yorks

FOCUS
A decent sprint handicap. They went an even gallop.
T/Plt: £131.20 to a £1 stake. Pool: £78,744.41 - 437.90 winning tickets. T/Qpdt: £31.10 to a £1 stake. Pool: £5,242.10 - 124.50 winning tickets. **Walter Glynn**

2262 - 2263a (Foreign Racing) - See Raceform Interactive

^{2014}RIPON (R-H)
Sunday, May 15

OFFICIAL GOING: Good to firm (good in places; 8.2)
Wind: Light, half against Weather: Overcast

2264 SPIRIT OF HARROGATE SLINGSBY GIN CHARITY NOVICE STKS (DIV I) 6f
2:00 (2:03) (Class 5) 2-Y-O **£3,234** (£962; £481; £240) **Stalls** High

Form RPR
3 **1** **Top Score**^{14} [1889] 2-9-2 0.. DavidProbert 9 89
(Saeed bin Suroor) *trckd ldrs: swtchd rt and shkn up to ld 1f out: rdn and r.o wl fnl f* **4/6**^{1}
2 *3 3/4* **Montataire (IRE)** 2-9-2 0... JoeFanning 5 78
(Mark Johnston) *dwlt: sn pressing ldr: ev ch and green over 1f out: chsd wnr ins fnl f: one pce: bttr for r* **13/2**^{3}
1 **3** *1 1/2* **Rainbow Mist (IRE)**^{15} [1868] 2-9-6 0................................ PJMcDonald 2 77
(Ann Duffield) *t.k.h: led tl rdn and hdd 1f out: outpcd ins fnl f* **3/1**^{2}
4 *1 3/4* **Gerrard's Return** 2-9-2 0... RichardKingscote 8 68
(Tom Dascombe) *prom: rdn over 2f out: outpcd over 1f out: n.d after* **16/1**
0 **5** *3 3/4* **Our Charlie Brown**^{32} [1407] 2-9-2 0.................................... DavidAllan 1 57+
(Tim Easterby) *dwlt: sn in tch: rdn and outpcd over 2f out: no imp fr over 1f out* **25/1**
6 *3* **Geego** 2-9-2 0.. TonyHamilton 7 48
(Richard Fahey) *hld up: pushed along and outpcd 1/2-way: n.d after* **14/1**
7 *1* **Mr C (IRE)** 2-8-13 0.. JacobButterfield$^{(3)}$ 4 45
(Ollie Pears) *slowly away: rn green in rr: nvr on terms* **40/1**

1m 13.06s (0.06) **Going Correction** -0.075s/f (Good) **7** Ran SP% **117.2**
Speed ratings (Par 93): **96,91,89,86,81 77,76**
CSF £6.23 TOTE £1.70: £1.10, £3.30; EX 6.10 Trifecta £11.60.
Owner Godolphin **Bred** Darley **Trained** Newmarket, Suffolk
■ Sir Viktor was withdrawn. Price at time of withdrawal 20-1. Rule 4 does not apply.

FOCUS
This was run at a sound pace and should prove fair form, rated around the race average.

2265 SPIRIT OF HARROGATE SLINGSBY GIN CHARITY NOVICE STKS (DIV II) 6f
2:30 (2:32) (Class 5) 2-Y-O **£3,234** (£962; £481; £240) **Stalls** High

Form RPR
1 **Cuppacoffee (IRE)** 2-9-2 0.. PJMcDonald 2 77
(Ann Duffield) *pressed ldr: led gng wl over 1f out: sn hrd pressed and rdn: hld on gamely wl ins fnl f* **7/2**^{2}
4 **2** *1/2* **Vaux (IRE)**^{20} [1706] 2-9-2 0... JoeyHaynes 6 75
(Ben Haslam) *fly-jmpd s: hld up in tch on outside: hdwy over 2f out: ev ch over 1f out to ins fnl f: kpt on: hld nr fin* **20/1**
1 **3** *6* **Baltic Beau**^{17} [1813] 2-9-2 0.. JackGarritty 7 57
(Richard Fahey) *sn pushed along to trck ldrs: rdn along 2f out: outpcd fnl f* **11/4**^{1}
6 **4** *nk* **Ortano (USA)**^{19} [1749] 2-9-2 0.. JoeFanning 9 56
(Mark Johnston) *t.k.h led: rdn and hdd over 1f out: edgd rt and outpcd fnl f* **5/1**^{3}
5 *2* **Sheppard's Gift** 2-8-11 0.. DavidAllan 3 45
(Tim Easterby) *s.i.s: bhd and green: sme hdwy over 1f out: nvr able to chal* **25/1**
6 *3/4* **Night Shadow** 2-9-2 0.. DaleSwift 5 48
(Scott Dixon) *dwlt: sn in tch: drvn and outpcd over 2f out: n.d after* **25/1**
4 **7** *hd* **Tranquil Tracy**^{15} [1868] 2-8-8 0.................................. JacobButterfield$^{(3)}$ 8 42
(John Norton) *t.k.h: hld up bhd ldng gp: drvn and outpcd wl over 2f out: sn btn* **16/1**

1m 13.61s (0.61) **Going Correction** -0.075s/f (Good) **7** Ran SP% **83.9**
Speed ratings (Par 93): **92,91,83,82,80 79,79**
CSF £34.85 TOTE £3.70: £2.10, £4.00; EX 30.40 Trifecta £78.30.
Owner A Starkie, C A Gledhill & B Craig **Bred** Mrs Brid Cosgrove **Trained** Constable Burton, N Yorks
■ Ashurst Beacon was withdrawn. Price a time of withdrawal 15/8. Rule 4 applies to all bets - deduction 30p in the pound.

FOCUS
The second division of the novice event, run at a brisk pace. The front pair came clear.

2266 PREMEX SERVICES SUPPORTING WOODEN SPOON CHARITY (S) STKS 6f
3:00 (3:01) (Class 6) 2-Y-O **£3,234** (£962; £481; £240) **Stalls** High

Form RPR
264 **1** **Zig Zag Girl**^{5} [2125] 2-8-9 0.. SilvestreDeSousa 3 74
(Mick Channon) *mde all: clr 1/2-way: shkn up fr 2f out: unchal* **7/4**^{1}
3 **2** *10* **Springforth**^{18} [1783] 2-9-0 0.. TonyHamilton 1 49
(Richard Fahey) *chsd wnr thrght: drvn along over 2f out: sn no imp* **7/4**^{1}
5 **3** *3* **Areyoutheway (IRE)**^{19} [1741] 2-9-0 0....................(p) RichardKingscote 2 40
(Tom Dascombe) *dwlt: bhd: rdn 1/2-way: kpt on fnl f: nvr on terms* **7/2**^{2}
03 **4** *3 3/4* **Eid Rose**^{17} [1813] 2-8-9 0... DavidAllan 5 24
(Scott Dixon) *t.k.h early: trckd ldrs: rdn over 2f out: sn btn* **12/1**^{3}
66 **5** *1 1/2* **Lavender Skye (IRE)**^{32} [1407] 2-8-9 0.................................. BenCurtis 4 19
(K R Burke) *prom: drvn and outpcd 1/2-way: struggling fnl 2f* **16/1**

1m 12.28s (-0.72) **Going Correction** -0.075s/f (Good) **5** Ran SP% **108.5**
Speed ratings (Par 91): **101,87,83,78,76**
CSF £4.83 TOTE £2.80: £1.30, £1.10; EX 4.60 Trifecta £10.90.The winner was bought by Paul Dixon for £16,000.
Owner M Channon **Bred** Steven Fisher **Trained** West Ilsley, Berks

FOCUS
A typically weak 2yo seller but the winner rates well above average for the grade.

2267 M.C.H. HUTCHINSON MEMORIAL EBF "BREEDERS SERIES" FILLIES" H'CAP 6f
3:35 (3:35) (Class 3) (0-95,92) 3-Y-O+ **£12,938** (£3,850; £1,924; £962) **Stalls** High

Form RPR
-641 **1** **Glenrowan Rose (IRE)**^{14} [1882] 3-9-4 **92**.......................... PhillipMakin 6 96
(Keith Dalgleish) *pressed ldr: led over 1f out: drvn and kpt on wl fnl f* **11/4**^{1}
10- **2** *hd* **Giddy**^{240} [6492] 3-8-0 **77**.. SammyJoBell$^{(3)}$ 7 80
(Richard Fahey) *prom: nt clr run briefly over 2f out: effrt and pushed along over 1f out: kpt on wl fnl f: jst hld* **10/3**^{2}
0260 **3** *3/4* **Penny Dreadful**^{11} [1958] 4-8-9 **73**......................................(p) BenCurtis 3 77
(Scott Dixon) *led: rdn and hdd over 1f out: rallied: no ex wl ins fnl f* **25/1**
00-0 **4** *1* **Love Island**^{4} [2158] 7-9-12 **90**....................................(t) GeorgeChaloner 5 91
(Richard Whitaker) *prom: rdn along over 2f out: kpt on same pce ins fnl f* **6/1**^{3}
-413 **5** *nk* **Avon Breeze**^{11} [1968] 7-9-10 **91**................................ JacobButterfield$^{(3)}$ 8 91
(Richard Whitaker) *hld up on ins: drvn and outpcd 1/2-way: rallied and edgd rt over 1f out: kpt on fnl f: no imp* **7/1**
0-00 **6** *hd* **Gran Canaria Queen**^{15} [1848] 7-9-0 **83**.............. RachelRichardson$^{(5)}$ 2 82
(Tim Easterby) *dwlt: hld up on outside: rdn over 2f out: hdwy over 1f out: no imp fnl f* **8/1**
40-5 **7** *4* **Holy Grail (IRE)**^{14} [1882] 3-8-4 **85**..................................... RowanScott$^{(7)}$ 9 68
(Simon West) *hld up: rdn over 2f out: btn over 1f out* **20/1**
3-60 **8** *1 3/4* **Stocking**^{22} [1650] 4-9-5 **83**..(p) JackMitchell 4 64
(Roger Varian) *hld up: rdn over 2f out: edgd rt and wknd over 1f out* **12/1**
35-0 **9** *6* **Plagiarism (USA)**^{15} [1865] 3-8-11 **85**...................................... JoeFanning 1 44
(Mark Johnston) *cl up on outside: drvn along over 2f out: wknd wl over 1f out* **10/1**

1m 11.9s (-1.10) **Going Correction** -0.075s/f (Good)
WFA 3 from 4yo+ 10lb **9** Ran SP% **113.0**
Speed ratings (Par 107): **104,103,102,101,101 100,95,93,85**
CSF £11.55 CT £182.02 TOTE £2.70: £1.10, £2.10, £6.70; EX 10.00 Trifecta £159.50.
Owner Weldspec Glasgow Limited **Bred** Tipper House Stud **Trained** Carluke, S Lanarks

FOCUS
A fair sprint handicap for fillies.

2268 RIPON, YORKSHIRE'S GARDEN RACECOURSE H'CAP 1m
4:10 (4:14) (Class 2) (0-105,93) 4-Y-O+ **£14,231** (£4,235; £2,116; £1,058) **Stalls** Low

Form RPR
-010 **1** **Spring Offensive (IRE)**^{15} [1861] 4-8-9 **88** ow1...... AdamMcNamara$^{(7)}$ 7 96
(Richard Fahey) *early ldr: prom: effrt and rdn 2f out: led and edgd rt ins fnl f: hld on wl* **7/2**^{2}
40-0 **2** *nk* **Steel Train (FR)**^{25} [1563] 5-8-12 **87**................................ ShelleyBirkett$^{(3)}$ 3 94
(David O'Meara) *hld up in tch: effrt and swtchd lft over 1f out: ev ch ins fnl f: edgd rt: kpt on: hld nr fin* **20/1**
1-02 **3** *1 1/2* **Swift Emperor (IRE)**^{22} [1643] 4-9-3 **89**........................ GrahamGibbons 2 92+
(David Barron) *trckd ldrs: ct in pocket against ins rail fr over 2f out: fnlly in clr and rdn last 100yds: kpt on towards fin: unlucky* **7/4**^{1}
4-60 **4** *hd* **Mukhayyam**^{15} [1871] 4-8-8 **85**............................... RachelRichardson$^{(5)}$ 8 88
(Tim Easterby) *t.k.h: pressed ldr: rdn over 2f out: edgd rt and kpt on same pce ins fnl f* **28/1**
2-00 **5** *1 1/4* **Edgar Balthazar**^{22} [1627] 4-9-0 **86**.........................(p) SilvestreDeSousa 6 89+
(Keith Dalgleish) *dwlt: sn led at modest gallop: ridd en over 2f out: hdd ins fnl f: sn hmpd and no ex* **5/1**^{3}
0500 **6** *1/2* **Dubai Dynamo**^{13} [1924] 11-8-11 **83**.................................... PJMcDonald 4 82
(Ruth Carr) *hld up on ins: rdn and swtchd lft over 2f out: hdwy over 1f out: no imp fnl f* **6/1**
00- **7** *14* **He's No Saint**^{204} [7455] 5-9-2 **93**......................................(v) JoshDoyle$^{(5)}$ 9 58
(David O'Meara) *plld hrd: in tch on outside: rdn 3f out: wknd fr 2f out* **8/1**

1m 40.04s (-1.36) **Going Correction** -0.075s/f (Good) **7** Ran SP% **108.9**
Speed ratings (Par 109): **103,102,101,101,99 99,85**
CSF £58.08 CT £142.79 TOTE £4.40: £2.00, £7.30; EX 55.10 Trifecta £173.20.
Owner A Rhodes Haulage And P Timmins **Bred** J Hanly **Trained** Musley Bank, N Yorks
■ Prince Of Johanne was withdrawn. Price at time of withdrawal 16-1. Rule 4 does not apply.
■ Stewards' Enquiry : Adam McNamara caution (reduced from three-day ban on appeal): careless riding

FOCUS
Race distance increased by about 18yds. A fair and competitive handicap.

2269 VW VAN CENTRE (WEST YORKSHIRE) H'CAP 1m 1f 170y
4:45 (4:46) (Class 4) (0-80,80) 3-Y-O **£6,469** (£1,925; £962; £481) **Stalls** Low

Form RPR
02-1 **1** **Sagely (IRE)**^{64} [925] 3-9-7 **80**..................................... SilvestreDeSousa 3 91+
(Ed Dunlop) *hld up in tch: rdn and hdwy to ld 2f out: drifted rt over 1f out: drew clr fnl f: comf* **5/2**^{2}

2-34 **2** 5 **Robinnielly (IRE)**[22] 1623 3-9-7 **80** PhillipMakin 4 81+
(Keith Dalgleish) *t.k.h: cl up: effrt and chsd wnr wl over 1f out: kpt on same pce fnl f* **2/1**[1]

04-4 **3** 1 **Perceysvivace**[13] 1927 3-8-7 **66** oh1 PatrickMathers 1 65
(Richard Fahey) *hld up in last pl: hdwy on outside over 2f out: chsd ldrs and edgd rt over 1f out: kpt on same pce fnl f* **4/1**[3]

155- **4** 4 **Pickett's Charge**[241] 6454 3-8-12 **71** BarryMcHugh 6 62
(Tony Coyle) *dwlt: sn prom: rdn and effrt over 2f out: wknd over 1f out* **12/1**

260- **5** nk **Becky The Thatcher**[211] 7284 3-8-9 **68** PJMcDonald 2 58
(Micky Hammond) *hld up in tch: effrt and drvn along over 2f out: sn no imp* **20/1**

3412 **6** 8 **Albert Boy (IRE)**[17] 1816 3-8-12 **71** BenCurtis 9 45
(Scott Dixon) *led at ordinary gallop for 2f: pressed ldr: drvn over 2f out: wknd wl over 1f out* **8/1**

15-4 **7** 8 **Cape Love (USA)**[31] 1446 3-9-5 **78** DavidNolan 8 35
(David O'Meara) *led after 2f and maintained ordinary gallop: rdn and hdd 2f out: sn wknd* **16/1**

2m 4.61s (-0.79) **Going Correction** -0.075s/f (Good) **7** Ran SP% **111.4**
Speed ratings (Par 101): **100,96,95,92,91 85,78**
CSF £7.53 CT £15.61 TOTE £3.30: £1.60, £2.00; EX 9.10 Trifecta £35.40.
Owner The Sages **Bred** Keatly Overseas Ltd **Trained** Newmarket, Suffolk
■ Lilly Vega was withdrawn. Price at time of withdrawal 14-1. Rule 4 applies to all bets - deduction 5p in the pound.

FOCUS
Race distance increased by about 18yds. A modest handicap, run at a fair pace.

2270 MIDDLEHAM TRAINERS ASSOCIATION APPRENTICE H'CAP 5f
5:15 (5:15) (Class 5) (0-75,73) 4-Y-O+ **£3,557** (£1,058; £529; £264) **Stalls** High

Form RPR

0005 **1** **Pearl Noir**[74] 784 6-8-8 **65** (b) NatalieHambling(5) 5 72
(Scott Dixon) *led at decent gallop: rdn and edgd lft 1f out: edgd rt and kpt on wl towards fin* **13/2**

3034 **2** ½ **Flicka's Boy**[17] 1803 4-9-2 **73** AdamMcNamara(5) 2 78
(Tony Coyle) *sn outpcd: hdwy over 2f out: swtchd rt and chsd wnr ins fnl f: kpt on: hld nr fin* **11/4**[2]

4143 **3** 1 **Hit The Lights (IRE)**[12] 1956 6-8-12 **69** (v) DanielleMooney(5) 4 70
(David Nicholls) *t.k.h: disp ld to over 1f out: kpt on same pce ins fnl f* **11/2**

150- **4** nk **Rainbow Orse**[206] 7416 4-9-1 **70** (p) AaronJones(3) 1 70
(Robert Cowell) *chsd ldng pair: drvn along over 2f out: kpt on same pce over 1f out* **4/1**[3]

0-32 **5** ¾ **Noodles Blue Boy**[21] 1666 10-8-13 **72** RobertDodsworth(7) 3 70
(Ollie Pears) *prom: rdn and outpcd over 2f out: rallied and edgd rt over 1f out: one pce fnl f* **9/4**[1]

0-00 **6** 8 **Pabusar**[8] 2052 8-8-0 **59** oh3 LaurenSteade(7) 6 28
(Micky Hammond) *s.i.s: sn wl bhd: nvr on terms* **16/1**

59.59s (-0.41) **Going Correction** -0.075s/f (Good) **6** Ran SP% **112.0**
Speed ratings (Par 103): **100,99,97,97,95 83**
CSF £24.50 TOTE £7.10: £5.10, £1.80; EX 29.50 Trifecta £148.00.
Owner P J Dixon & Partners **Bred** Mrs Yvette Dixon **Trained** Babworth, Notts
■ Stewards' Enquiry : Natalie Hambling two-day ban: used whip above permitted level (May 30-31)

FOCUS
A modest sprint handicap.

2271 RUTH CARR MACMILLAN CHARITY RACE MAIDEN STKS 1m 1f
5:45 (5:47) (Class 5) 3-Y-O **£3,234** (£962; £481; £240) **Stalls** Low

Form RPR

0-22 **1** **Amazement (GER)**[21] 1662 3-9-5 75 DavidAllan 5 83
(James Tate) *pressed ldr: led gng wl over 2f out: rdn clr over 1f out: kpt on wl: eased nr fin* **5/6**[1]

2 **2** 3½ **Sunglider (IRE)**[8] 2048 3-9-5 82 PhillipMakin 7 75
(David O'Meara) *chsd ldrs on outside: drvn and outpcd over 3f out: rallied to chse (clr) wnr over 1f out: kpt on fnl f: no imp* **7/4**[2]

63-3 **3** 12 **Mango Chutney**[21] 1671 3-9-5 59 GrahamGibbons 2 52
(John Davies) *t.k.h: led at modest gallop: rdn and hdd over 2f out: lost 2nd and wknd over 1f out* **15/2**[3]

50 **4** 4½ **Rich Pursuit**[8] 2048 3-9-5 0 (p) JoeyHaynes 4 39
(James Bethell) *s.i.s: t.k.h: hld up: rdn and outpcd over 3f out: n.d after* **66/1**

06- **5** 2¼ **Calypso Delegator (IRE)**[234] 6687 3-9-5 0 PJMcDonald 1 34
(Micky Hammond) *s.i.s: sn in tch on ins: drvn and outpcd over 3f out: sn n.d* **40/1**

3 **6** 15 **Jasper Jay**[34] 1379 3-9-5 0 DuranFentiman 3 1
(Tony Coyle) *hld up: outpcd and hung lft over 4f out: sn struggling: t.o* **20/1**

0 **7** 16 **Bravadora (IRE)**[58] 984 3-9-0 0 DaleSwift 6
(Scott Dixon) *plld hrd: prom tl wknd 4f out: t.o* **66/1**

1m 54.01s (-0.69) **Going Correction** -0.075s/f (Good) **7** Ran SP% **112.9**
Speed ratings (Par 99): **100,96,86,82,80 66,52**
CSF £2.39 TOTE £2.00: £1.50, £1.40; EX 3.00 Trifecta £5.80.
Owner Sheikh Juma Dalmook Al Maktoum **Bred** Gestut Ammerland **Trained** Newmarket, Suffolk

FOCUS
Race distance increased by about 18yds. An ordinary maiden, rated around the runner-up.
T/Plt: £127.20 to a £1 stake. Pool: £76,627.94 - 439.74 winning tickets T/Qpdt: £18.70 to a £1 stake. Pool: £5,862.05 - 230.87 winning tickets **Richard Young**

1505 NAVAN (L-H)
Sunday, May 15

OFFICIAL GOING: Good to firm (good in places)

2272a COOLMORE STUD POWER STKS (LISTED RACE) 5f 182y
1:45 (1:46) 3-Y-O
£20,606 (£6,636; £3,143; £1,397; £698; £349)

RPR

1 **Washington DC (IRE)**[18] 1773 3-9-3 112 (t) SeamieHeffernan 7 111+
(A P O'Brien, Ire) *chsd ldrs: impr into 2nd under 2f out and qcknd wl to ld over 1f out: kpt on wl to assert ins fnl f: comf* **13/8**[1]

2 2¼ **Diamond Fields (IRE)**[23] 1611 3-8-12 88 WayneLordan 10 99+
(T Stack, Ire) *hld up in tch: pushed along in 5th after 1/2-way and r.o wl u.p ins fnl f into nvr nrr 2nd cl home: nt trble wnr* **16/1**

3 nk **Only Mine (IRE)**[33] 1396 3-8-12 103 GaryCarroll 2 98
(Joseph G Murphy, Ire) *cl up bhd ldrs far side early: rdn under 2f out and swtchd rt disputing 3rd over 1f out: rdn into 2nd briefly ins fnl f and no imp on wnr clsng stages where dropped to 3rd* **9/1**

4 ¾ **Most Beautiful**[44] 1190 3-9-1 106 (p) ConnorKing 4 99
(David Wachman, Ire) *hld up in tch: disp 5th at 1/2-way: lost pl and rdn in 6th ins fnl f: kpt on u.p between horses into nvr threatening 4th in clsng stages* **9/2**[2]

5 1 **Shrill**[20] 1730 3-8-12 93 BillyLee 9 92
(W McCreery, Ire) *disp early and sn settled bhd ldr: disp 2nd at 1/2-way: rdn 1 1/2f out and no imp on wnr ins fnl f: wknd clsng stages* **10/1**

6 ¾ **Blood Moon**[4] 2166 3-9-3 90 (b[1]) ColinKeane 8 95
(G M Lyons, Ire) *disp early and sn led: rdn clr briefly under 2f out: sn strly pressed and hdd over 1f out: no imp on wnr and wknd fnl f* **25/1**

7 ½ **Waterloo Bridge (IRE)**[32] 1423 3-9-8 108 (t) ColmO'Donoghue 3 98
(A P O'Brien, Ire) *late to post: towards rr: pushed along in 9th 2f out and sme hdwy over 1f out: kpt on one pce in 7th ins fnl f* **6/1**[3]

8 1 **Miss Elizabeth (IRE)**[13] 1939 3-8-12 101 ChrisHayes 11 85
(Edward Lynam, Ire) *in tch: rdn in 8th fr under 2f out and no imp on ldrs over 1f out: one pce fnl f* **20/1**

9 nk **Promised Money (IRE)**[219] 7072 3-8-12 92 (t) ShaneFoley 12 84
(Edward Lynam, Ire) *towards rr: n.m.r bhd horses briefly bef 1/2-way: pushed along and no imp in 11th 1 1/2f out: kpt on one pce ins fnl f* **33/1**

10 nk **Taexali (IRE)**[14] 1882 3-9-3 94 DeclanMcDonogh 6 88
(John Patrick Shanahan, Ire) *cl up early: pushed along and dropped to rr fr 1/2-way: no imp in rr over 1f out: kpt on again ins fnl f* **20/1**

11 1¾ **Juliette Fair (IRE)**[35] 1369 3-8-12 103 (b[1]) PatSmullen 5 78
(D K Weld, Ire) *towards rr: pushed along fr 1/2-way and n.m.r bhd horses: rdn in 10th under 2f out and no imp: one pce fnl f* **18/1**

12 2½ **Independence Day (IRE)**[20] 1730 3-9-3 99 (p) KevinManning 1 75
(David Wachman, Ire) *hld up in tch: rdn disputing 7th 2f out and sn no imp on ldrs: wknd fnl f* **33/1**

1m 10.52s (-4.08) **12** Ran SP% **120.1**
CSF £29.50 TOTE £2.30: £1.02, £5.20, £3.20; DF 29.60 Trifecta £217.10.
Owner Mrs John Magnier & Michael Tabor & Derrick Smith **Bred** P Hyland & C & J McHale **Trained** Cashel, Co Tipperary

FOCUS
This Listed contest produced an impressive winner. It's been rated around the balance of the winner, runner-up, fifth and sixth.

2274a (Foreign Racing) - See Raceform Interactive

2275a COOLMORE VINTAGE CROP STKS (GROUP 3) 1m 6f
3:20 (3:20) 4-Y-O+ **£28,198** (£9,080; £4,301)

RPR

1 **Bondi Beach (IRE)**[22] 1659 4-9-6 118 SeamieHeffernan 2 110+
(A P O'Brien, Ire) *w.w in rr of trio: pushed along over 2f out and impr after reminder to ld narrowly ins fnl f where hung sltly: kpt on wl to assert in clsng stages: workmanlike* **1/9**[1]

2 1½ **Toe The Line (IRE)**[22] 1659 7-9-1 101 ColinKeane 1 102
(John E Kiely, Ire) *settled bhd ldr in 2nd: gng wl into st and led fr 2f out: rdn and strly pressed over 1f out: hdd narrowly ins fnl f and kpt on wl wout matching wnr in clsng stages* **8/1**[2]

3 4¼ **Silwana (IRE)**[22] 1659 5-9-1 106 (p) ShaneFoley 4 96
(Takashi Kodama, Ire) *led and sn clr: 2 l clr 5f out: rdn over 2f out and sn hdd: dropped to rr over 1f out and one pce after* **14/1**[3]

3m 5.03s (-9.97)
WFA 4 from 5yo+ 1lb **3** Ran SP% **107.8**
CSF £1.62 TOTE £1.10; DF 1.60 Trifecta £1.40.
Owner L J Williams/Mrs J Magnier/M Tabor/D Smith **Bred** One Moment In Time Syndicate **Trained** Cashel, Co Tipperary

FOCUS
It was a shame that so few turned up here, and little was apparently learned. The runner-up has been rated to par.

2276 - 2279a (Foreign Racing) - See Raceform Interactive

128 DEAUVILLE (R-H)
Sunday, May 15

OFFICIAL GOING: Turf: good; polytrack: standard

2280a PRIX DE SAINT-GERMAIN (CLAIMER) (2YO) (TURF) 5f
12:35 (12:00) 2-Y-O **£9,926** (£3,970; £2,977; £1,985; £992)

RPR

1 **Rainbow Black**[19] 2-9-1 0 UmbertoRispoli 2 68
(A Giorgi, Italy) **66/10**

2 nk **Assassinate (IRE)**[12] 1944 2-9-8 0 (b) ChristopheSoumillon 4 74
(Paul Cole) *disp ld: rdn 2f out: r.o wl: jst denied* **13/5**[2]

3 nse **La Dame En Rouge (FR)**[20] 2-8-11 0 ThierryThulliez 6 63
(C Lerner, France) **48/10**

4 1¼ **Elusiva (FR)**[39] 1284 2-8-11 0 (p) Pierre-CharlesBoudot 5 58
(P Sogorb, France) **12/5**[1]

5 snk **Kitgame (FR)**[17] 1821 2-9-1 0 (p) MickaelBarzalona 7 62
(D Prod'Homme, France) **23/5**[3]

6 1 **Tawaret (FR)**[19] 2-8-11 0 GregoryBenoist 3 54
(M Boutin, France) **15/2**

7 12 **Wait And Win (FR)**[26] 2-8-8 0 EddyHardouin 1 8
(Mlle S Delaroche, France) **46/1**

WIN (incl. 1 euro stake): 7.60. PLACES: 3.10, 2.20. SF: 34.10
Owner Pietro Sinistri **Bred** Fernham Farm Ltd **Trained** Italy

2281a PRIX HOCQUART (GROUP 2) (3YO COLTS & FILLIES) (TURF) 1m 2f
1:35 (12:00) 3-Y-O **£54,485** (£21,029; £10,036; £6,691; £3,345)

RPR

1 **Mekhtaal**[32] 1428 3-9-2 0 GregoryBenoist 3 112+
(J-C Rouget, France) *mde all: rdn clr fr 2f out: comf* **11/4**[2]

2 6 **Thewayyouwish (IRE)**[29] 1504 3-9-2 0 ChristopheSoumillon 1 100
(J-C Rouget, France) *prom: outpcd by clr wnr fr over 1f out but kpt on wl* **14/1**

3 ½ **Royal Julius (IRE)**[25] 1580 3-9-2 0 ThierryJarnet 2 99
(A De Watrigant, France) *t.k.h: towards rr: rdn 2f out: kpt on to take 3rd cl home: no ch w clr wnr* **15/2**

4 ½ **Dalgarno (FR)**[21] 3-9-2 0 StephanePasquier 4 98
(N Clement, France) *midfield: rdn over 2f out: stdy hdwy to press 2nd ins fnl f: no ex and lost 3rd clsng stages* **4/1**[3]

The Form Book, Raceform Ltd, Newbury, RG14 5SJ

5 nk **Barwod**[26] 3-9-2 0 Pierre-CharlesBoudot 7 97
(A Fabre, France) *hld up towards rr: rdn and stdy hdwy fr 2f out: briefly pressed 2nd ins fnl f: no ex clsng stages* **15/8**[1]
6 nk **Ventura Storm (IRE)**[7] 2069 3-9-2 0 RyanMoore 6 85
(Richard Hannon) *hld up in rr: rdn and outpcd 2f out: kpt on wl fnl f but n.d* **7/1**
7 6 **Incitator (FR)**[9] 3-9-2 0 AlexisBadel 5 85
(Mme M Bollack-Badel, France) *chsd ldr: lost pl 2f out: sn wl btn* **20/1**

2m 7.03s (-3.17) **7 Ran SP% 117.1**
WIN (incl. 1 euro stake): 3.30. PLACES: 2.10, 3.50. SF: 30.40.
Owner Al Shaqab Racing **Bred** Haras Du Mezeray And Skymarc Farm **Trained** Pau, France

2282a POULE D'ESSAI DES POULICHES (GROUP 1) (3YO FILLIES) (STRAIGHT) (TURF) 1m (R)
2:15 (12:00) 3-Y-O **£189,066** (£75,639; £37,819; £18,893; £9,463)

RPR

1 **La Cressonniere (FR)**[56] 1022 3-9-0 0 CristianDemuro 1 113
(J-C Rouget, France) *trckd ldrs: led narrowly over 2f out: sn drvn: styd on wl to assert ins fnl f: readily* **15/2**
2 1 **Nathra (IRE)**[14] 1888 3-9-0 0 FrankieDettori 14 111+
(John Gosden) *towards rr of midfield: rdn 2f out: styd on wl to snatch 2nd cl home* **10/1**
3 hd **Qemah (IRE)**[25] 1581 3-9-0 0 GregoryBenoist 7 110+
(J-C Rouget, France) *t.k.h: towards rr of midfield: stmbld 6f out: hdwy fr 2f out: ev ch ins fnl f: no ex clsng stages* **5/2**[1]
4 hd **Besharah (IRE)**[29] 1476 3-9-0 0 ChristopheSoumillon 6 110
(William Haggas) *in tch: rdn 2f out: ev ch ins fnl f: no ex clsng stages* **12/1**
5 ½ **Spectre (FR)**[38] 1309 3-9-0 0 Pierre-CharlesBoudot 2 109
(M Munch, Germany) *hld up towards rr: rdn and stdy hdwy fr 2f out: styd on wl fnl f but nt quite able to chal* **20/1**
6 nk **Sasparella (FR)**[35] 1374 3-9-0 0 MaximeGuyon 9 108
(C Laffon-Parias, France) *hld up in rr: hdwy fr over 2f out: drvn and kpt on fnl f but nt quite able to chal* **33/1**
7 1½ **Alice Springs (IRE)**[14] 1888 3-9-0 0 RyanMoore 11 105
(A P O'Brien, Ire) *in tch: effrt 2f out: fdd ins fnl f* **3/1**[2]
8 hd **Come Alive**[26] 3-9-0 0 MickaelBarzalona 10 104
(A Fabre, France) *chsd ldr: led narrowly under 3f out: sn drvn: hdd over 2f out: wknd ins fnl f* **4/1**[3]
9 ¾ **Syrita (FR)**[26] 3-9-0 0 OlivierPeslier 12 103
(M Nigge, France) *towards rr of midfield: rdn and unable qck 2f out: wknd ins fnl f* **66/1**
10 hd **Aim To Please (FR)**[38] 1309 3-9-0 0 AlexisBadel 4 102
(F Doumen, France) *plld hrd in midfield: rdn and outpcd over 2f out: eased whn short of room ins fnl f* **50/1**
11 3 **Kenriya (FR)**[25] 1581 3-9-0 0 JamieSpencer 3 95
(C Ferland, France) *midfield: rdn and outpcd over 2f out: wknd 1f out* **25/1**
12 8 **Antonoe (USA)**[25] 1581 3-9-0 0 VincentCheminaud 13 77
(P Bary, France) *in tch: rdn and lost pl over 2f out: sn wl btn* **16/1**
13 8 **Huda (FR)**[20] 3-9-0 0 EddyHardouin 8 58
(M Le Forestier, France) *midfield: rdn 3f out: sn struggling* **200/1**
14 nk **Positive Vibration (IRE)**[25] 1581 3-9-0 0 Jean-BernardEyquem 5 58
(J-C Rouget, France) *pushed along to ld: hdd under 3f out: sn wl btn* **200/1**

1m 36.0s (-4.80) **14 Ran SP% 124.0**
WIN (incl. 1 euro stake): 8.40. PLACES: 3.10, 2.90, 1.70. DF: 43.90. SF: 79.10.
Owner Ecurie Antonio Caro & Gerard Augustin-Normand **Bred** Franklin Finance **Trained** Pau, France

FOCUS
This was an open edition of the French 1,000 Guineas. They went a sound pace down the centre and the second and fourth are a decent guide for the form.

2283a POULE D'ESSAI DES POULAINS (GROUP 1) (3YO COLTS) (STRAIGHT) (TURF) 1m (R)
3:20 (12:00) 3-Y-O **£231,080** (£92,448; £46,224; £23,091; £11,566)

RPR

1 **The Gurkha (IRE)**[28] 1511 3-9-2 0 RyanMoore 11 122+
(A P O'Brien, Ire) *in tch: rdn to ld over 1f out: drew clr ins fnl f: impressive* **4/1**[2]
2 5½ **First Selection (SPA)**[15] 1864 3-9-2 0 JimCrowley 13 109
(Simon Crisford) *led: drvn over 2f: hdd and outpcd by clr wnr over 1f out: dropped to 3rd ins fnl f but battled on wl to regain 2nd cl home* **50/1**
3 nse **Dicton**[25] 1580 3-9-2 0 OlivierPeslier 4 109
(Gianluca Bietolini, Italy) *towards rr of midfield: short of room over 1f out: styd on wl fnl f: jst failed to snatch 2nd: no ch w wnr* **18/1**
4 hd **George Patton (USA)**[26] 3-9-2 0 IoritzMendizabal 12 108
(J-C Rouget, France) *hld up towards rr: rdn and hdwy fr 2f out: wnt 2nd ins fnl f but no ch w wnr: kpt on but w awkward hd carriage and lost two pls cl home* **9/1**
5 ¾ **Zarak (FR)**[26] 3-9-2 0 ChristopheSoumillon 1 107
(A De Royer-Dupre, France) *hld up in rr: rdn and hdwy fr 2f out: chal for a pl ins fnl f but nvr any ch w wnr: no ex cl home* **2/1**[1]
6 snk **Crazy Horse**[204] 7468 3-9-2 0 FrankieDettori 8 106
(John Gosden) *t.k.h: towards rr of midfield: drvn 2f out: kpt on steadily fnl f but nvr able to chal* **10/1**
7 hd **Taareef (USA)**[25] 1580 3-9-2 0 Jean-BernardEyquem 10 106
(J-C Rouget, France) *prom: rdn over 2f out: no ex ins fnl f* **20/1**
8 hd **Moon Trouble (IRE)**[38] 1308 3-9-2 0 MickaelBarzalona 6 105
(F Head, France) *hld up in rr: hdwy over 2f out: rdn 2f out: kpt on same pce* **33/1**
9 1¾ **Attendu (FR)**[38] 1308 3-9-2 0 MaximeGuyon 9 101
(C Laffon-Parias, France) *midfield: rdn and unable qck 2f out: short of room whn keeping on steadily ins fnl f* **20/1**
10 1¼ **Jimmy Two Times (FR)**[35] 1374 3-9-2 0 VincentCheminaud 5 99
(A Fabre, France) *towards rr of midfield: rdn and unable qck 2f out: n.d* **20/1**
11 2 **Zelzal (FR)**[39] 1285 3-9-2 0 GregoryBenoist 2 94
(J-C Rouget, France) *prom: rdn over 1f out: wknd tamely 1f out* **5/1**[3]
12 1 **Alignement**[31] 3-9-2 0 Pierre-CharlesBoudot 7 92
(C Laffon-Parias, France) *trckd ldrs: rdn over 2f out: lost pl over 1f out: eased whn btn fnl f* **40/1**
13 4 **Birchwood (IRE)**[198] 7624 3-9-2 0 JamesDoyle 3 82
(Richard Fahey) *trckd ldrs: rdn and lost pl 2f out: sn wl btn* **14/1**

1m 36.97s (-3.83) **13 Ran SP% 122.6**
WIN (incl. 1 euro stake): 8.60. PLACES: 3.30, 11.50, 3.20.. Df: 205.60. SF: 322.10.
Owner Derrick Smith & Mrs John Magnier & Michael Tabor **Bred** Chintz Syndicate **Trained** Cashel, Co Tipperary

FOCUS
This looked a fair edition of the French 2,000 Guineas. They split into two groups early before converging mid-track, and the winner was a class apart. The second down to the seventh have been rated close to their marks.

1517 LES LANDES
Sunday, May 15

OFFICIAL GOING: Turf: good changing to good to firm after race 1
Wind: Fresh, behind Weather: Sunny

2284a BLOODSTOCK ADVISORY SERVICES H'CAP 7f
3:05 (3:09) 3-Y-O+ **£1,780** (£640; £380)

RPR

1 **Pas D'Action**[13] 2079 8-9-7 0 (p) JemmaMarshall 11 53
(Mrs A Malzard, Jersey) *hld up: hdwy 4f out: chal over 1f out: led ins fnl f: drvn out* **4/1**[2]
2 1½ **Tax Reform (IRE)**[13] 2079 6-9-0 0 PhilipPrince 9 42
(Natalie Lloyd-Beavis) *prom: led 2f out tl ins fnl f: one pce* **4/1**[2]
3 2 **Valmina**[28] 1517 9-10-12 0 NickSlatter 3 63
(K Kukk, Jersey) *chsd ldrs: kpt on same pce fnl 2f* **2/1**[1]
4 1½ **Brown Velvet**[28] 1517 4-9-12 0 TimClark 6 45
(Mrs A Malzard, Jersey) *mid-div: hdwy over 1f out: styd on same pce fnl f* **14/1**
5 1½ **Country Blue (FR)**[13] 2081 7-10-0 0 (p) MattieBatchelor 10 43
(Mrs A Malzard, Jersey) *led: sn 4 l clr: hdd 2f out: wknd over 1f out* **9/2**[3]
6 5 **Chester'slittlegem (IRE)**[13] 2081 7-8-5 0 oh2 (b) NoraLooby 4 6
(Mrs A Corson, Jersey) *nvr trbld ldrs* **5/1**
7 shd **Frankki M**[13] 2079 6-8-5 0 oh29 (v) JennyPowell 8 6
(Mrs A Corson, Jersey) *bhd tl styd on fnl 2f* **25/1**
8 1½ **Chapeau Bleu (IRE)**[28] 1517 4-10-1 0 MarkQuinlan 1 26
(Mrs C Gilbert, Jersey) *chsd clr ldr tl over 2f out: wknd over 1f out* **7/1**
9 shd **Purley Queen (IRE)**[28] 1517 7-10-4 0 AliceMills 7 28
(Mrs C Gilbert, Jersey) *in tch tl wknd 2f out* **11/2**
10 12 **Engaging Smile**[28] 1518 4-10-9 0 ShaunPayne 5 1
(J Moon, Jersey) *sn outpcd towards rr* **14/1**
11 12 **Spanish Bounty**[273] 11-9-10 0 MissMHooper 2
(Mrs A Malzard, Jersey) *sn bhd* **5/1**

Owner J Jamouneau **Bred** Jenny Hall Bloodstock Ltd **Trained** St Ouen, Jersey

2285a PLANTAGENOT 1 MILE H'CAP 1m 100y
4:15 (4:18) (0-50,0) 3-Y-O+ **£1,780** (£640; £380)

RPR

1 **Admirable Art (IRE)**[26] 1544 6-10-12 0 (p) NickSlatter 4 64
(Tony Carroll) *trckd ldrs: led over 1f out: sn clr* **7/2**[3]
2 8 **Lucifers Shadow (IRE)**[28] 1519 7-10-7 0 (v) AliceMills 1 41
(Mrs C Gilbert, Jersey) *prom: led over 2f out tl over 1f out: sn outpcd by wnr* **5/2**[2]
3 1 **Fast Freddie**[13] 12-9-3 0 (p) NoraLooby 7 21
(Mrs A Corson, Jersey) *sn led: hdd over 2f out: kpt on u.p* **8/1**
4 ½ **Albecq**[13] 2080 4-10-5 0 JemmaMarshall 6 36
(Mrs A Malzard, Jersey) *bhd tl styd on fnl 2f* **12/1**
5 1½ **First Cat**[28] 1518 9-10-7 0 PhilipPrince 2 34
(K Kukk, Jersey) *in tch: effrt and brought wd into st: one pce* **4/1**
6 1½ **Bond Mystery**[26] 1548 4-10-6 0 RyanClark 8 30
(Natalie Lloyd-Beavis) *a abt same pl: btn 2f out* **7/1**
7 shd **Grey Panel (FR)**[28] 1519 8-10-2 0 TimClark 9 26
(T Le Brocq, Jersey) *hld up in midfield: effrt on inner ent st: btn over 1f out* **9/4**[1]
8 2½ **Carrera**[13] 2080 6-10-9 0 MattieBatchelor 5 27
(Mrs A Malzard, Jersey) *sn towards rr: n.d fnl 3f* **15/2**
9 nk **Captain James (FR)**[28] 1519 6-10-4 0 MarkQuinlan 3 22
(Mrs C Gilbert, Jersey) *first away: prom tl wknd over 1f out* **13/2**
10 15 **Rainbow Charlie**[258] 5-8-8 0 (p) JennyPowell 10
(Mrs A Corson, Jersey) *a bhd: t.o fnl 4f* **25/1**

Owner D Morgan **Bred** Longview Stud & Bloodstock Ltd **Trained** Cropthorne, Worcs

HOPPEGARTEN (R-H)
Sunday, May 15

OFFICIAL GOING: Turf: good

2286a COMER GROUP INTERNATIONAL OLEANDER-RENNEN (GROUP 3) (4YO+) (TURF) 2m
4:20 (12:00) 4-Y-O+ **£23,529** (£8,823; £4,411; £2,205; £1,470)

RPR

1 **Wasir (GER)**[44] 1194 4-8-11 0 RafaelSchistl 6 103
(A Wohler, Germany) *sn led and mde rest: rdn 2f out: styd on wl and a in control* **16/1**
2 2 **Alex My Boy (IRE)**[21] 1688 5-9-4 0 (b) EduardoPedroza 9 105
(A Wohler, Germany) *trckd wnr: rdn over 2f out: styd on but a hld* **6/4**[1]
3 2 **Bebe Cherie (FR)**[36] 7154 4-8-8 0 MartinSeidl 5 96+
(Markus Klug, Germany) *midfield: rdn 2f out: styd on and wnt 3rd cl home: nt able to chal* **25/1**
4 nk **Rock Of Romance (IRE)**[44] 1194 6-8-11 0 JozefBojko 2 95
(A Wohler, Germany) *in tch: rdn over 2f out: styd on same pce and wl hld: lost 3rd cl home* **192/10**
5 ½ **Walzertakt (GER)**[21] 1688 7-9-4 0 RenePiechulek 4 102
(Jean-Pierre Carvalho, Germany) *hld up: rdn into st: plugged on but n.d* **12/5**[2]
6 nk **Lovato (GER)**[28] 4-8-11 0 AndraschStarke 7 97+
(P Schiergen, Germany) *dwlt: hld up: rdn 2f out: plugged on against rail but n.d* **78/10**
7 nse **Iraklion (GER)**[21] 4-9-0 0 FilipMinarik 8 100
(Christian Sprengel, Germany) *dwlt: hld up in last: rdn into st: styd on towards fin but n.d* **179/10**
8 ¾ **The Twisler**[155] 8210 4-9-0 0 AndreasSuborics 1 100
(Jane Chapple-Hyam) *in tch: rdn over 2f out: styd on same pce tl no ex and fdd nring fin* **36/5**

9 *nk* **Space Cowboy (GER)**[19] 4-8-11 0................................ FrederikTylicki 3 96
(Markus Klug, Germany) *midfield: rdn 2f out: outpcd and btn fnl f: dropped to last towards fin* **47/10**[3]

3m 26.1s (206.10)
WFA 4 from 5yo+ 3lb **9** Ran SP% **130.5**
WIN (incl. 10 euro stake): 170. PLACES: 39, 15, 46. SF: 818.
Owner Darius Racing **Bred** Gestut Rottgen **Trained** Germany

GRANVILLE-ST PAIR SUR MER
Sunday, May 15

OFFICIAL GOING: Turf: good

2287a PRIX POZZO IMMOBILIER (MAIDEN) (3YO COLTS & GELDINGS) (TURF) 1m 110y
1:00 (12:00) 3-Y-O **£3,308** (£1,323; £992; £661; £330)

RPR
1 **Lefortovo (FR)**[38] 1311 3-8-10 0.............................. EmmanuelEtienne(6) 3 76
(Jo Hughes)
2 *4* **Northlands**[42] 3-8-10 0..(b[1]) LukasDelozier(6) 5 67
(H-A Pantall, France)
3 *10* **Petit Prince (FR)**[243] 3-8-10 0.................................... LucasGutierrez(6) 1 45
(Charley Rossi, France)
4 *5* **Dominor (FR)** 3-8-10 0..(b) FlavienMasse(6) 4 34
(C Plisson, France)
5 *20* **Dragan Darnoult (FR)** 3-8-11 0.............................. MlleAmelieSimon 2
(P Loth, France)

Owner L Ormsby,H Downs,R Bedford & J Hughes **Bred** Ecurie Haras De Beauvoir **Trained** Lambourn, Berks

2082 BRIGHTON (L-H)
Monday, May 16

OFFICIAL GOING: Good (good to firm in places) changing to good to firm after race 1 (2.10)
Wind: virtually nil Weather: sunny

2288 STREAMLINE TAXIS H'CAP 5f 59y
2:10 (2:10) (Class 5) (0-70,69) 3-Y-O **£2,911** (£866; £432; £216) **Stalls** Centre

Form RPR
0-36 **1** **Al Sailiyah (IRE)**[18] 1814 3-9-4 **66**.. PatDobbs 4 72
(Richard Hannon) *chsd ldr: effrt over 1f out: rdn and ev ch ins fnl f: styd on u.p to ld fnl 50yds: edgd rt towards fin* **6/1**
50-4 **2** *½* **Sir Theodore (IRE)**[32] 1448 3-9-4 **69**......................... LouisSteward(3) 6 73
(Richard Spencer) *wl in tch in midfield: effrt and edgd lft over 1f out: chal ins fnl f: keeping on but hld whn nudged rt towards fin: snatched 2nd last stride* **4/1**[3]
34-2 **3** *shd* **Just Glamorous (IRE)**[7] 2106 3-9-7 **69**............................ LukeMorris 2 73
(Ronald Harris) *dwlt: sn rcvrd to chse ldrs and t.k.h: rdn to chal over 1f out: drvn to ld 1f out: hdd and no ex fnl 50yds: lost 2nd last stride* **9/4**[1]
2-15 **4** *4* **Dominance**[50] 1112 3-9-6 **68**.................................... SilvestreDeSousa 1 58
(Rae Guest) *taken down early: led: rdn over 1f out: hdd 1f out: no ex and wknd fnl 100yds* **3/1**[2]
066- **5** *¾* **The Special One (IRE)**[252] 6163 3-8-13 **61**......................... JohnFahy 3 48
(Clive Cox) *squeezed for room and dropped to rr sn after s: pushed along in detached last: sme hdwy and edging lft over 1f out: kpt on ins fnl f: nvr trbld ldrs* **10/1**
0-05 **6** *6* **No Body's Fool**[26] 1574 3-8-2 **50** oh5............................... KieranO'Neill 7 16
(Michael Madgwick) *sn pushed along and outpcd in 6th: nvr on terms* **100/1**
23-0 **7** *5* **Entertaining Ben**[20] 1753 3-9-3 **68**..............................(p) RobHornby(3) 5 17
(William Muir) *chsd ldrs: sddle slipped after 1f: rdr of no assistance and lost pl 2f out: bhd fnl f* **9/1**

1m 2.04s (-0.26) **Going Correction** 0.0s/f (Good) **7** Ran SP% **110.1**
Speed ratings (Par 99): **102,101,101,94,93 83,75**
CSF £27.76 TOTE £5.30: £3.10, £2.40; EX 33.60 Trifecta £82.80.
Owner Al Shaqab Racing **Bred** Pier House Stud & Martinstown **Trained** East Everleigh, Wilts

FOCUS
Rail dolled-out between the 4.5f and 2.5f markers, adding 4yds to each race distance. There was no hanging around in this tight-looking 3yo sprint handicap. The third is a good benchmark.

2289 FROSTS4CARS.CO.UK NOVICE AUCTION STKS 5f 213y
2:40 (2:41) (Class 5) 2-Y-O **£2,911** (£866; £432) **Stalls** Centre

Form RPR
2 **1** **Mister Sunshine (IRE)**[14] 1915 2-9-2 0.............................. AdamKirby 2 80+
(Clive Cox) *t.k.h early: mde all: shkn up and edgd rt over 2f out: wnt clr under hands and heels over 1f out: styd on: easily* **8/13**[1]
3 **2** *6* **Kody Ridge (IRE)**[7] 2104 2-9-2 0.. MartinLane 3 62
(David Dennis) *chsd wnr: rdn: edgd lft and outpcd over 1f out: wl hld and kpt on same pce ins fnl f* **7/4**[2]
50 **3** *9* **Secret Ballerina**[7] 2104 2-8-11 0................................ AdamBeschizza 1 30
(Julia Feilden) *in tch in 3rd: rdn over 2f out: outpcd u.p and btn over 1f out: wknd fnl f* **10/1**[3]

1m 11.16s (0.96) **Going Correction** 0.0s/f (Good) **3** Ran SP% **107.4**
Speed ratings (Par 93): **93,85,73**
CSF £1.98 TOTE £1.60; EX 2.30 Trifecta £2.00.
Owner Tony Perkins **Bred** Miss Monica McNicholl **Trained** Lambourn, Berks

FOCUS
Rail movement added 4yds to race distance. An ordinary little novice event.

2290 HARRINGTONSLETTINGS.CO.UK H'CAP 5f 213y
3:15 (3:16) (Class 4) (0-80,79) 4-Y-O+ **£5,175** (£1,540; £769; £384) **Stalls** Centre

Form RPR
5-01 **1** **Upavon**[3] 2217 6-8-9 **67**...(t) PatCosgrave 6 73+
(Stuart Williams) *stdd bk into midfield sn after s: hld up in tch: effrt ent fnl 2f: hdwy and hung lft over 1f out: chal 1f out: led ins fnl f: hld on cl home* **11/8**[1]
2-23 **2** *nk* **Upstaging**[21] 1724 4-9-6 **78**...(b) LukeMorris 7 83
(Paul Cole) *dwlt: bustled along in last pair: rdn over 2f out: hdwy u.p 1f out: styd on to press wnr towards fin: hld cl home* **11/2**[3]
5-50 **3** *nk* **Monumental Man**[16] 1857 7-9-7 **79**...........................(p) AdamBeschizza 3 83
(Michael Attwater) *led: clr and rdn over 1f out: hdd ins fnl f: kpt on but a hld after: lost 2nd towards fin* **33/1**
1/2 **4** *1¼* **Jaywalker (IRE)**[13] 1945 5-9-4 **76**.............................. SilvestreDeSousa 1 79+
(Mick Channon) *chsd ldrs: chsd clr ldr 2f out: rdn and clsd over 1f out: cl 3rd and ev ch whn squeezed out and snatched up wl ins fnl f: eased off and one pce after* **3/1**[2]
30-0 **5** *1¾* **Vincentti (IRE)**[9] 2028 6-9-1 **73**.......................................(p) DavidProbert 5 67
(Ronald Harris) *in tch in last trio: effrt 2f out: hdwy u.p over 1f out: no ex ins fnl f: kpt on same pce* **16/1**
46-2 **6** *3½* **Major Pusey**[20] 1744 4-9-1 **76**.............................. MichaelJMMurphy(3) 2 59
(John Gallagher) *chsd ldrs tl lost pl u.p over 1f out: wknd fnl f* **9/1**
3320 **7** *hd* **Quintus Cerialis (IRE)**[54] 1040 4-9-5 **77**..........................(p) AdamKirby 4 60
(Clive Cox) *sn outpcd in rr and rdn along: swtchd rt over 4f out: n.d* **12/1**
300- **8** *hd* **Monarch Maid**[245] 6382 5-8-8 **71**.................................. DavidParkes(5) 8 53
(Peter Hiatt) *chsd ldr 2f out: sn lost pl: hung rt and wknd over 1f out* **25/1**

1m 9.33s (-0.87) **Going Correction** 0.0s/f (Good) **8** Ran SP% **112.9**
Speed ratings (Par 105): **105,104,104,102,100 95,95,95**
CSF £9.11 CT £162.12 TOTE £2.20: £1.30, £1.50, £4.90; EX 9.30 Trifecta £73.90.
Owner Morley, Reynolds & Watkins **Bred** Major-Gen Guy Watkins **Trained** Newmarket, Suffolk
■ Stewards' Enquiry : Adam Beschizza two-day ban: used whip down the shoulder in the forehand (May 30-31)

FOCUS
Rail movement added 4yds to race distance. Not a bad sprint for the class. It was run at a good pace and there was a tight finish. The winner was well in after his Newmarket win.

2291 WINNER GROUP H'CAP 1m 1f 209y
3:45 (3:46) (Class 4) (0-80,80) 3-Y-O **£5,040** (£1,508; £754; £377; £188) **Stalls** High

Form RPR
2-34 **1** **Paling**[24] 1602 3-9-0 **73**.. WilliamTwiston-Davies 5 79
(Roger Charlton) *chsd ldr: effrt to chal 2f out: wandered lft but rdn to ld over 1f out: styd on wl: rdn out* **3/1**[1]
21-3 **2** *1¼* **Brave Archibald (IRE)**[9] 2044 3-8-12 **71**........................... LukeMorris 6 74
(Paul Cole) *stdd after s: hld up in tch in last trio: effrt over 2f out: hdwy u.p ins fnl f: styd on to go 2nd last strides: nvr threatening wnr* **8/1**
32-5 **3** *hd* **Magnum (IRE)**[21] 1715 3-9-7 **80**...................................(b[1]) JimmyFortune 4 82
(Brian Meehan) *chsd ldng pair: effrt over 2f out: hdwy u.p to chse wnr 1f out: kpt on but no imp ins fnl f: lost 2nd last strides* **6/1**[3]
15-5 **4** *hd* **Fool To Cry (IRE)**[33] 1411 3-9-3 **76**................................... HarryBentley 3 78
(Roger Varian) *hld up in tch in midfield: effrt over 2f out: hdwy u.p 1f out: squeezing between rivals 100yds out: styd on but no threat to wnr* **13/2**
550- **5** *1¾* **Nucky Thompson**[175] 7955 3-8-8 **72**.......................[1] EdwardGreatrex(5) 8 71
(Richard Spencer) *stdd after s: hld up in tch in rr: hdwy u.p and drifting lft over 1f out: nt clrest of runs ins fnl f: styd on same pce fnl 100yds* **25/1**
0-01 **6** *¾* **Michael's Mount**[21] 1718 3-9-0 **73**.................................... PatCosgrave 7 70
(Ed Dunlop) *led: rdn 2f out: drvn and hdd over 1f out: no ex ins fnl f: wknd fnl 75yds* **3/1**[1]
5-45 **7** *3¼* **Loading (IRE)**[7] 2099 3-9-4 **77**.. PatDobbs 2 68
(Richard Hannon) *s.i.s: hld up in tch in last pair: effrt over 2f out: drifting lft and no imp over 1f out* **5/1**[2]
006- **8** *½* **Calliope**[217] 7160 3-8-7 **66**... DavidProbert 1 56
(Andrew Balding) *t.k.h: hld up in tch in midfield: rdn over 2f out: lost pl and bhd 1f out: wknd fnl f* **16/1**

2m 5.31s (1.71) **Going Correction** 0.0s/f (Good) **8** Ran SP% **115.1**
Speed ratings (Par 101): **93,92,91,91,90 89,87,86**
CSF £28.24 CT £135.34 TOTE £3.70: £1.60, £1.80, £1.90; EX 21.20 Trifecta £81.30.
Owner K Abdullah **Bred** Juddmonte Farms Ltd **Trained** Beckhampton, Wilts

FOCUS
Rail movement added 4yds to race distance. A fair 3yo handicap. It was run at a steady early pace and racing handily was an advantage. A step up from the winner.

2292 DONATELLO RESTAURANT BRIGHTON FILLIES' H'CAP 1m 1f 209y
4:20 (4:20) (Class 5) (0-70,70) 4-Y-O+ **£3,234** (£962; £481; £240) **Stalls** High

Form RPR
6163 **1** **Solveig's Song**[7] 2086 4-8-0 **51** ow1......................(p) EdwardGreatrex(5) 6 59
(Steve Woodman) *hld up in tch in midfield: effrt over 2f out: hdwy u.p to ld 1f out: styd on wl* **11/2**
3324 **2** *2* **What A Party (IRE)**[18] 1807 4-8-11 **57**..............................(p) LukeMorris 7 61
(Gay Kelleway) *chsd ldr tl led 2f out: sn rdn and edgd lft: hdd 1f out: styd on same pce ins fnl f* **9/2**[3]
1331 **3** *nk* **Tommys Geal**[27] 1547 4-9-0 **63**..................................... DanielMuscutt(3) 4 67
(Michael Madgwick) *stdd s: hld up in tch in rr: rdn and hdwy 2f out: cl enough in 3rd whn nt clrest of runs and swtchd rt 1f out: kpt on same pce after* **7/2**[2]
0541 **4** *2¼* **Owners Day**[6] 2127 6-9-10 **70** 7ex.. LiamKeniry 3 69
(Neil Mulholland) *wl in tch in midfield: effrt ent fnl 2f: chsd ldrs and edgd lft u.p 1f out: styd on same pce ins fnl f* **3/1**[1]
6542 **5** *shd* **My Tringaling (IRE)**[34] 1405 4-8-0 **53**............................. MillyNaseb(7) 2 51
(Stuart Williams) *hld up in tch in last pair: effrt and rdn over 1f out: no imp and swtchd rt 1f out: styd on same pce after* **5/1**
65-0 **6** *6* **Moment To Dream**[20] 1762 4-8-6 **52**.......................... AdamBeschizza 5 38
(Julia Feilden) *led: rdn hdd 2f out: no ex and btn 1f out: wknd ins fnl f* **20/1**
255/ **7** *2* **Aramadyh**[63] 1135 5-9-5 **65**.. TimmyMurphy 1 47
(Jim Best) *chsd ldrs tl 5f out: pushed along 4f out: lost pl and bhd whn short of room over 2f out: wl btn over 1f out* **25/1**
00-6 **8** *13* **Toxaris (IRE)**[40] 1266 4-9-2 **67**.................................... HectorCrouch(5) 9 23
(Gary Moore) *chsd ldrs: rdn 3f out: lost pl and btn 2f out: bhd and virtually p.u ins fnl f* **12/1**

2m 3.8s (0.20) **Going Correction** 0.0s/f (Good) **8** Ran SP% **113.8**
Speed ratings (Par 100): **99,97,97,95,95 90,88,78**
CSF £30.05 CT £98.04 TOTE £6.90: £2.20, £1.50, £1.90; EX 30.20 Trifecta £122.80.
Owner Sally Woodman D Mortimer **Bred** Mrs Sally Woodman & Mr D Mortimer **Trained** East Lavant, W Sussex

FOCUS
Rail movement added 4yds to race distance. A moderate fillies' handicap, rated around the placed horses.

2293 JAMESROSSJEWELLERS.COM H'CAP 7f 214y
4:55 (4:55) (Class 6) (0-65,63) 3-Y-O **£2,264** (£673; £336; £168) **Stalls** Low

Form RPR
-355 **1** **Heads You Win**[47] 1146 3-9-6 **62**...................................... TimmyMurphy 9 67
(Jamie Osborne) *s.i.s: hld up in tch in last pair: hdwy over 2f out: rdn to chal ent fnl f: edgd lft but styd on u.p to ld wl ins fnl f* **6/1**[3]

5510 **2** *hd* **Ashford Island**[19] 1792 3-8-8 **50**....................(p) KieranO'Neill 8 54
(Mike Murphy) *t.k.h: hld up in tch in midfield: effrt to chal over 1f out: rdn to ld 1f out: edgd lft u.p ins fnl f: hdd wl ins fnl f: kpt on but jst hld towards fin* **10/1**

4404 **3** *1* **Russian Ranger (IRE)**[14] 1917 3-9-6 **62**....................(p) RyanClark 3 64
(Jonathan Portman) *hld up in tch in midfield: lost pl and rdn 3f out: hdwy u.p 1f out: edgd lft but styd on to go 3rd wl ins fnl f: nvr gng to rch ldrs* **12/1**

00-0 **4** *½* **Buzz Lightyere**[14] 1931 3-9-3 **62**.................... RobHornby(3) 2 63
(Michael Attwater) *hld up in tch in midfield: chsng ldrs and nt clr run over 1f out: swtchd rt 1f out: styng on whn bmpd ins fnl f: hld in 4th but keeping on whn bmpd again towards fin* **15/2**

2-56 **5** *1½* **Ettie Hart (IRE)**[18] 1806 3-8-13 **55**.................... CharlesBishop 5 52
(Mick Channon) *led: rdn jst over 2f out: drvn and hdd 1f out: no ex: wknd fnl 100yds and lost 2 pls wl ins fnl f* **11/1**

500- **6** *1¾* **Constable Clouds (USA)**[269] 5586 3-8-13 **60**.......(p) HectorCrouch(5) 1 53
(Gary Moore) *chsd ldr tl over 2f out: sn rdn: no ex u.p over 1f out: wknd ins fnl f* **9/2**[2]

-001 **7** *2¼* **Let There Be Light**[7] 2083 3-9-5 **61** 6ex.................... LukeMorris 7 49
(Gay Kelleway) *chsd ldng pair tl wnt 2nd over 2f out: sn rdn: unable qck and lost pl over 1f out: wknd ins fnl f* **9/4**[1]

-006 **8** *72* **Kenstone (FR)**[19] 1792 3-8-13 **55**....................(v[1]) MartinLane 4
(David Dennis) *stdd s: t.k.h: hld up in last pair: hdwy on outer over 3f out: sn btn: virtually p.u ins fnl f: t.o* **7/1**

1m 36.31s (0.31) **Going Correction** 0.0s/f (Good) **8** Ran SP% **112.6**
Speed ratings (Par 97): **98,97,96,96,94 93,90,18**
CSF £61.16 CT £694.84 TOTE £6.80: £2.60, £1.90, £4.50; EX 67.00 Trifecta £369.50.
Owner Heads You Win Partnership **Bred** Park Farm Racing **Trained** Upper Lambourn, Berks
■ Stewards' Enquiry : Ryan Clark one-day ban: careless riding (May 30)

FOCUS
Rail movement added 4yds to race distance. They went a sound pace in this modest 3yo handicap.

2294 BRIGHTON&HOVE COACHES OFFICIAL TRANSPORT PARTNER MAIDEN STKS 6f 209y
5:30 (5:30) (Class 5) 3-Y-O+ **£2,911** (£866; £432; £216) **Stalls** Low

Form RPR

2- **1** **Feed The Goater (FR)**[303] 4381 3-9-3 0.................... KieranO'Neill 5 72
(Richard Hannon) *chsd ldrs: rdn and hdwy over 1f out: sn ev ch: led wl ins fnl f: hld on wl: rdn out* **11/8**[1]

50- **2** *shd* **Dheyaa (IRE)**[220] 7077 3-8-12 0.................... DavidProbert 3 66
(Owen Burrows) *hld up in tch in last pair: effrt 2f out: rdn and hdwy over 1f out: ev ch fnl 100yds: r.o wl: jst hld* **3/1**[2]

3 *½* **Red Box** 3-8-12 0....................[1] LukeMorris 1 65+
(Sir Mark Prescott Bt) *dwlt: t.k.h early: hld up in tch in rr: shkn up 2f out: rdn and gd hdwy over 1f out: led 1f out: rn green in front and hdd wl ins fnl f: kpt on* **3/1**[2]

0-0 **4** *2¼* **Fol O'Yasmine**[10] 2004 3-8-12 0.................... PatCosgrave 4 59
(William Haggas) *t.k.h: hld up in tch in midfield: effrt 2f out: chsng ldrs and nt clrest of runs jst over 1f out: kpt on same pce ins fnl f* **8/1**[3]

00-5 **5** *5* **Nelson's Pride**[72] 837 5-9-2 40....................(t) RhiainIngram(7) 8 49?
(Roger Ingram) *racd freely: sn led: clr after 2f: rdn over 1f out: hdd 1f out: sn wknd* **66/1**

0-0 **6** *2½* **Iballisticvin**[14] 1930 3-9-3 0.................... LiamKeniry 6 43
(Gary Moore) *chsd ldr tl hung lft over 1f out: sn btn: wknd ins fnl f* **66/1**

0- **7** *nk* **Dream Dana (IRE)**[234] 6720 3-8-12 0.................... TimmyMurphy 2 37
(Jamie Osborne) *in tch in midfield: swtchd lft and rdn over 2f out: outpcd and btn over 1f out: : wknd fnl f* **14/1**

1m 22.31s (-0.79) **Going Correction** 0.0s/f (Good)
WFA 3 from 4yo+ 11lb **7** Ran SP% **112.9**
Speed ratings (Par 103): **104,103,103,100,95 92,91**
CSF £5.57 TOTE £2.20: £1.90, £2.40; EX 6.20 Trifecta £11.90.
Owner Middleham Park Racing LXXI **Bred** Haras Du Mezeray **Trained** East Everleigh, Wilts

FOCUS
Rail movement added 4yds to race distance. This modest maiden was run at a brisk pace. The winner has been rated close to last year's debut.
T/Plt: £245.50 to a £1 stake. Pool: £60,329.49 - 179.33 winning tickets T/Qpdt: £52.20 to a £1 stake. Pool: £6,913.21 - 97.84 winning tickets **Steve Payne**

1634 LEICESTER (R-H)
Monday, May 16

OFFICIAL GOING: Good (good to firm in places)
Wind: Light behind Weather: Fine

2295 BRITISH STALLION STUDS EBF NOVICE STKS (PLUS 10 RACE) 5f
6:10 (6:11) (Class 4) 2-Y-O **£4,528** (£1,347; £673; £336) **Stalls** High

Form RPR

4 **1** **Reign On**[9] 2038 2-9-2 0.................... SeanLevey 4 73
(Ralph Beckett) *in tch: sn pushed along: chsd ldr over 1f out: rdn and r.o to ld wl ins fnl f* **3/1**[2]

2 *nk* **Broadhaven Honey (IRE)** 2-8-11 0.................... MartinDwyer 3 67
(Ed McMahon) *chsd ldrs: rdn over 1f out: r.o wl* **14/1**

3 **3** *nk* **Alwalaa (IRE)**[14] 1921 2-8-11 0.................... WilliamBuick 1 66
(Mark Johnston) *led: rdn and edgd lft over 1f out: hdd and unable qck wl ins fnl f* **4/7**[1]

6 **4** *7* **Iftitah (IRE)**[35] 1384 2-9-2 0.................... StevieDonohoe 6 46
(George Peckham) *s.i.s: swtchd rt and hdwy 4f out: rdn 1/2-way: wknd fnl f* **9/1**[3]

5 *9* **Papa Delta** 2-8-13 0.................... GeorgeDowning(3) 2 14
(Tony Carroll) *chsd ldrs: rdn 1/2-way: wknd wl over 1f out* **66/1**

6 *8* **Elemento** 2-8-11 0.................... JosephineGordon(5) 5
(Phil McEntee) *prom: rdn 1/2-way: wknd wl over 1f out* **40/1**

1m 1.27s (1.27) **Going Correction** -0.175s/f (Firm) **6** Ran SP% **109.3**
Speed ratings (Par 95): **82,81,81,69,55 42**
CSF £37.49 TOTE £3.70: £1.30, £4.50; EX 28.50 Trifecta £48.10.
Owner What Asham Partnership **Bred** J A And M A Knox **Trained** Kimpton, Hants

FOCUS
A false rail was in place from the top of the hill on the back straight all the way to the winning line, increasing all distances on the round course by 17 yards. A modest juvenile novice contest and they went a decent gallop on ground officially described as good, good to firm in places.

2296 J.F. HERRING H'CAP 1m 1f 218y
6:40 (6:40) (Class 4) (0-80,79) 4-Y-O+ **£4,690** (£1,395; £697; £348) **Stalls** Low

Form RPR

0-23 **1** **Mountain Rescue (IRE)**[20] 1737 4-9-6 **78**.................... WilliamBuick 12 86
(Chris Wall) *a.p: chsd ldr 1/2-way: shkn up to ld over 1f out: rdn and edgd rt ins fnl f: styd on* **7/2**[1]

41-5 **2** *1½* **Perceived**[17] 1825 4-8-9 **72**.................... JennyPowell(5) 5 77
(Henry Candy) *chsd ldr to 1/2-way: remained handy: rdn over 1f out: chsd wnr ins fnl f: styd on same pce towards fin* **16/1**

1312 **3** *¾* **Moonday Sun (USA)**[23] 1652 7-9-6 **78**....................(p) JamesDoyle 11 81
(John Butler) *trckd ldrs: rdn over 2f out: styd on same pce wl ins fnl f* **17/2**

01 **4** *nk* **Gulf Of Poets**[25] 1588 4-9-0 **77**.................... NathanEvans(5) 10 79
(Michael Easterby) *hld up in tch racd keenly: rdn over 1f out: edgd rt ins fnl f: styd on* **9/1**

420- **5** *¾* **Compton Mill**[202] 7535 4-9-4 **76**....................(t) JimCrowley 6 78
(Hughie Morrison) *led after 1f: rdn and hdd over 1f out: hmpd ins fnl f: styd on same pce* **10/1**

60-0 **6** *hd* **Muqarred (USA)**[18] 1817 4-9-4 **76**.................... RaulDaSilva 1 77
(David Loughnane) *led 1f: chsd ldrs: rdn over 2f out: kpt on ins fnl f* **25/1**

2242 **7** *nk* **Icebuster**[20] 1737 8-9-3 **75**.................... FrederikTylicki 4 75
(Rod Millman) *s.i.s: hld up: racd keenly: hdwy over 2f out: swtchd rt over 1f out: styd on: nt rch ldrs* **6/1**[2]

04-0 **8** *1* **Silver Dixie (USA)**[14] 1916 6-9-1 **76**....................(p) TomMarquand(3) 9 74
(Peter Hedger) *s.i.s: hld up: rdn over 2f out: styd on ins fnl f: nt trble ldrs* **20/1**

210- **9** *1¼* **Captain Swift (IRE)**[182] 7524 5-8-13 **71**.................... TomQueally 8 66
(John Mackie) *hld up: hdwy u.p over 1f out: no imp ins fnl f* **25/1**

34-6 **10** *½* **Bahamian C**[22] 1664 5-8-10 **75**.................... AdamMcNamara(7) 3 69
(Richard Fahey) *hld up: rdn over 1f out: nvr on terms* **11/1**

03U- **11** *nk* **Satanic Beat (IRE)**[163] 7474 7-9-2 **74**.................... StevieDonohoe 14 68
(Phil Middleton) *hld up: rdn over 2f out: n.d* **33/1**

350- **12** *6* **Mystery Code**[73] 7172 4-9-7 **79**.................... FergusSweeney 13 61
(Alan King) *mid-div: rdn over 3f out: wknd wl over 1f out* **15/2**[3]

11-2 **13** *5* **Omotesando**[20] 1762 6-8-10 **75**.................... CharlieBennett(7) 2 47
(Mark Brisbourne) *mid-div: rdn over 2f out: wknd over 1f out* **14/1**

2m 7.55s (-0.35) **Going Correction** +0.10s/f (Good) **13** Ran SP% **114.2**
Speed ratings (Par 105): **105,103,103,102,102 102,101,101,100,99 99,94,90**
CSF £56.54 CT £440.48 TOTE £4.40: £1.80, £5.50, £2.50; EX 81.10 Trifecta £505.10.
Owner ValueRacingClub.co.uk **Bred** Lady Richard Wellesley **Trained** Newmarket, Suffolk
■ Stewards' Enquiry : William Buick one-day ban: careless riding (May 30)

FOCUS
Race distance increased by 17yds. A decent handicap and they went a proper gallop, but the pace held up and the winner can possibly do better now..

2297 JAMES WARD (S) STKS 1m 60y
7:10 (7:10) (Class 6) 3-Y-O+ **£2,264** (£673; £336; £168) **Stalls** Low

Form RPR

03-5 **1** **Victoire De Lyphar (IRE)**[18] 1818 9-9-7 72....................(e) JamesSullivan 7 67
(Ruth Carr) *in rr: hdwy to go 3rd 1/2-way: led 2f out: rdn and hung lft over 1f out: styd on* **7/2**[2]

0-63 **2** *2* **El Duque**[17] 1832 5-9-2 55.................... KieranShoemark(5) 3 62
(Bill Turner) *hld up: hdwy over 3f out: jnd wnr 2f out: sn rdn: styd on same pce ins fnl f* **8/1**[3]

5505 **3** *15* **Robert The Painter (IRE)**[5] 2150 8-9-0 78....................(b) GeorgeWood(7) 1 26+
(Lee Carter) *led at fast pce: rdn and hdd 2f out: wknd over 1f out* **5/6**[1]

00/0 **4** *8* **Rising Rainbow**[13] 1952 5-9-7 12....................(be) PaddyAspell 4 7
(Ivan Furtado) *s.i.s: hld up: hung lft: rdn and wknd wl over 2f out* **100/1**

3/0- **5** *20* **Moxey**[464] 470 5-9-7 43.................... RyanPowell 5
(Christopher Kellett) *w ldrs 6f: remained handy tl rdn over 3f out: wknd wl over 2f out* **150/1**

300- **6** *99* **Balducci**[259] 5953 9-9-7 88.................... RaulDaSilva 6 +
(David Loughnane) *sn pushed along to join ldr: drvn over 3f out: hung lft over 2f out: sn wknd and eased: virtually p.u fnl f* **7/2**[2]

1m 45.05s (-0.05) **Going Correction** +0.10s/f (Good) **6** Ran SP% **111.8**
Speed ratings (Par 101): **104,102,87,79,59**
CSF £29.57 TOTE £4.00: £1.60, £5.20; EX 28.20 Trifecta £74.60.
Owner P Newell & Mrs R Carr **Bred** Mrs Monica Hackett **Trained** Huby, N Yorks

FOCUS
Race distance increased by 17yds. A decent seller, but the two main form horses took each other on at a suicidal gallop.

2298 SARTORIUS MAIDEN STKS 6f
7:40 (7:40) (Class 5) 3-Y-O **£3,067** (£905; £453) **Stalls** High

Form RPR

32 **1** **Musdam (USA)**[13] 1953 3-9-5 0.................... StevieDonohoe 1 87
(Sir Michael Stoute) *a.p: chsd ldr over 1f out: rdn to ld ins fnl f: r.o* **6/1**

0- **2** *½* **Silent Attack**[255] 6052 3-9-5 0.................... JamesDoyle 9 85
(Saeed bin Suroor) *trckd ldrs: rdn over 1f out: chsd wnr ins fnl f: edgd rt: r.o* **13/8**[1]

-22 **3** *2¼* **Dubai Mission (IRE)**[10] 2005 3-9-5 0.................... SeanLevey 2 78
(Richard Hannon) *led: rdn over 1f out: hdd ins fnl f: styd on same pce* **9/2**[3]

0 **4** *5* **Scamper**[24] 1597 3-9-0 0.................... WilliamBuick 3 57
(Roger Charlton) *hld up: shkn up over 2f out: hdwy over 1f out: wknd ins fnl f* **20/1**

5 *½* **Walking Primrose (FR)** 3-9-0 0.................... ShaneGray 4 55
(Kevin Ryan) *hld up in tch: shkn up and edgd rt over 2f out: wknd fnl f* **33/1**

6 *1* **Princess Momoka** 3-9-0 0.................... AndreaAtzeni 5 52
(Roger Varian) *s.i.s: rn green in rr: shkn up over 2f out: n.d* **10/1**

0- **7** *½* **Romantic Angel (USA)**[200] 7585 3-8-11 0.................... ThomasBrown(3) 7 51
(Ismail Mohammed) *chsd ldr tl rdn over 1f out: wknd fnl f* **66/1**

2-3 **8** *½* **Mazzini**[16] 1849 3-9-5 0.................... TomQueally 6 54
(James Fanshawe) *dwlt: hld up: plld hrd: rdn over 1f out: wknd fnl f* **3/1**[2]

1m 11.74s (-1.26) **Going Correction** -0.175s/f (Firm) **8** Ran SP% **113.8**
Speed ratings (Par 99): **101,100,97,90,90 88,87,87**
CSF £15.92 TOTE £4.50: £1.40, £1.30, £1.30; EX 22.30 Trifecta £58.50.
Owner Saeed Suhail **Bred** Timothy S O'Toole **Trained** Newmarket, Suffolk

FOCUS
A fair 3yo maiden and they went a decent gallop. The winner is improving.

2299 JOHN FERNELEY H'CAP — 1m 60y
8:10 (8:12) (Class 4) (0-80,80) 3-Y-O — **£4,690** (£1,395; £697; £348) **Stalls** Low

Form — RPR

143- **1** **Dubai's Secret**[210] 7346 3-9-6 **79** ... SeanLevey 4 — 86
(Richard Hannon) *hld up: hmpd 6f out: hdwy over 2f out: sn rdn: led wl ins fnl f: styd on* **12/1**

-113 **2** 3/4 **Sir Roderic (IRE)**[15] 1896 3-9-5 **78** ... FrederikTylicki 9 — 83
(Rod Millman) *trckd ldrs: wnt 2nd over 3f out: rdn over 2f out: styd on* **10/1**

01-4 **3** *nk* **Chester Street**[15] 1891 3-9-5 **78** ... GeorgeBaker 7 — 83
(Roger Charlton) *a.p: rdn over 1f out: edgd rt ins fnl f: styd on to go 3rd nr fin* **11/10**[1]

000- **4** 3/4 **Miniaturist (FR)**[233] 6761 3-9-4 **77** ... JamesDoyle 6 — 80
(Mark Johnston) *sn led: rdn over 1f out: hdd and unable qck wl ins fnl f* **20/1**

023- **5** *3* **Absolute Zero (IRE)**[228] 6873 3-9-4 **77** ... AndreaAtzeni 3 — 73
(Roger Varian) *hld up: rdn over 2f out: hdwy over 1f out: nt rch ldrs* **11/2**[3]

13-4 **6** *9* **Bell Heather (IRE)**[9] 2029 3-9-0 **80** ... AdamMcNamara(7) 2 — 55
(Richard Fahey) *prom: racd keenly: edgd lft 6f out: rdn over 2f out: wknd and eased fnl f* **5/1**[2]

10-0 **7** *21* **Show Legend**[23] 1623 3-9-3 **76** ... JamieSpencer 10 — 3
(Michael Bell) *chsd ldr 5f: sn rdn: wknd and eased over 1f out* **33/1**

0-16 **8** *2* **Papou Tony**[65] 924 3-9-2 **75** ... TedDurcan 5
(George Baker) *hld up: rdn over 2f out: sn wknd and eased* **12/1**

1m 44.75s (-0.35) **Going Correction** +0.10s/f (Good) — **8** Ran SP% **111.8**
Speed ratings (Par 101): **105,104,103,103,100 91,70,68**
CSF £117.65 CT £237.64 TOTE £12.80: £2.70, £2.60, £1.10; EX 73.60 Trifecta £249.30.
Owner Saeed Manana **Bred** Mrs T A Foreman **Trained** East Everleigh, Wilts

FOCUS
Race distance increased by 17yds. A fair 3yo handicap and they went another decent gallop.

2300 HENRY ALKEN H'CAP — 1m 3f 183y
8:40 (8:40) (Class 5) (0-70,69) 3-Y-O — **£2,911** (£866; £432; £216) **Stalls** Low

Form — RPR

06-3 **1** **Blakeney Point**[16] 1860 3-9-1 **68** ... KieranShoemark(5) 3 — 75+
(Roger Charlton) *a.p: rdn to ld 1f out: r.o* **5/2**[1]

35-5 **2** *1* **Duck A L'Orange (IRE)**[21] 1718 3-9-6 **68** ... JamieSpencer 5 — 73+
(Michael Bell) *hld up: hdwy over 1f out: rdn and edgd rt ins fnl f: r.o to go 2nd nr fin* **12/1**

35-3 **3** *hd* **Press Gang**[23] 1619 3-9-4 **69** ... TomMarquand(3) 10 — 74
(James Eustace) *hld up: rdn over 2f out: hdwy over 1f out: edgd lft ins fnl f: r.o* **5/1**[2]

304- **4** 3/4 **St Michel**[181] 7878 3-9-7 **69** ... RyanPowell 8 — 73+
(Sir Mark Prescott Bt) *a.p: racd keenly: led over 2f out: rdn and hdd 1f out: styd on same pce wl ins fnl f* **6/1**[3]

06-3 **5** *1* **Hearty (IRE)**[21] 1718 3-8-11 **59** ... JimCrowley 6 — 61
(Jeremy Noseda) *chsd ldr: rdn and ev ch over 1f out: styd on same pce ins fnl f* **9/1**

03-3 **6** *shd* **Monaco Rose**[12] 1970 3-8-12 **67** ... AdamMcNamara(7) 7 — 69
(Richard Fahey) *hld up: hdwy over 2f out: rdn over 1f out: edgd rt ins fnl f: styd on* **10/1**

0-66 **7** *7* **Aristocles (IRE)**[19] 1784 3-9-6 **68** ... StevieDonohoe 1 — 59
(Sir Michael Stoute) *chsd ldrs: rdn over 2f out: wknd fnl f* **8/1**

2301 **8** 4 1/2 **Kelvin Hall**[27] 1553 3-9-7 **69** ... JamesDoyle 9 — 52
(Mark Johnston) *hld up: hdwy over 2f out: rdn and wknd over 1f out* **8/1**

20-0 **9** *7* **Little Lotte (IRE)**[20] 1759 3-8-5 **60** ... (p) GeorgeWood(7) 4 — 32
(Tom Gretton) *led: rdn over 3f out: hdd over 2f out: wknd over 1f out* **66/1**

2m 37.23s (3.33) **Going Correction** +0.10s/f (Good) — **9** Ran SP% **110.0**
Speed ratings (Par 99): **92,91,91,90,90 89,85,82,77**
CSF £31.71 CT £128.39 TOTE £3.20: £1.30, £3.40, £2.00; EX 29.50 Trifecta £158.20.
Owner Axom LX **Bred** Mr & Mrs A E Pakenham **Trained** Beckhampton, Wilts

FOCUS
Race distance increased by 17yds. A modest 3yo middle-distance handicap and they went a steady gallop.
T/Plt: £162.50 to a £1 stake. Pool: £63,716.01 - 286.09 winning tickets T/Qpdt: £17.10 to a £1 stake. Pool: £6,760.36 - 292.54 winning tickets **Colin Roberts**

[1813]REDCAR (L-H)
Monday, May 16

OFFICIAL GOING: Good to firm (watered; 9.9)
Wind: light against Weather: sunny

2301 CONGRATULATIONS ON PROMOTION MIDDLESBROUGH FC #UTB NOVICE MEDIAN AUCTION STKS — 6f
1:50 (1:51) (Class 5) 2-Y-O — **£2,911** (£866; £432; £216) **Stalls** Centre

Form — RPR

52 **1** **Rusumaat (IRE)**[16] 1850 2-9-2 0 ... DaneO'Neill 7 — 88+
(Mark Johnston) *mde all: pushed clr over 1f out: edgd lft ins fnl f: eased towards fin* **6/5**[1]

0 **2** *7* **Tawny Port**[23] 1621 2-9-2 0 ... TomEaves 9 — 65
(James Given) *s.i.s: hld up: pushed along and hdwy over 1f out: wnt 2nd ins fnl f: kpt on* **20/1**

3 *1* **Jamacho** 2-9-2 0 ... DaleSwift 11 — 62
(Brian Ellison) *chsd ldr: rdn over 2f out: outpcd over 1f out: kpt on ins fnl f: wnt 3rd towards fin* **5/1**[2]

4 *nk* **Servo (IRE)** 2-9-2 0 ... BenCurtis 5 — 61
(Alan Swinbank) *chsd ldr: pushed along over 2f out: rdn over 1f out: one pce* **7/1**

5 *hd* **Heir Of Excitement (IRE)** 2-9-2 0 ... ShaneGray 6 — 61
(Kevin Ryan) *chsd ldr: rdn over 2f out: one pce* **16/1**

0 **6** *6* **Graton**[39] 1293 2-9-2 0 ... DougieCostello 10 — 43
(K R Burke) *chsd ldr: rdn over 2f out: wknd over 1f out* **50/1**

7 *3* **Parkwarden (IRE)** 2-9-2 0 ... ConnorBeasley 12 — 34
(Chris Grant) *in tch: edgd rt over 2f out: sn pushed along: rdn over 1f out: sn wknd* **100/1**

8 1/2 **Yorkshire Bounty** 2-9-2 0 ... GeorgeChaloner 3 — 32
(Richard Fahey) *midfield: sn pushed along: wknd over 1f out* **12/1**

9 2 1/4 **I Call The Shots** 2-8-13 0 ... JacobButterfield(3) 4 — 25
(Ollie Pears) *dwlt: hld up: bit short of room 2f out: sn pushed along: nvr threatened* **66/1**

5 **10** 3 1/4 **Breaking Free**[16] 1850 2-9-2 0 ... PhillipMakin 1 — 16
(John Quinn) *midfield: rdn over 3f out: wknd over 1f out* **11/2**[3]

11 1 1/4 **Newgate Sioux** 2-8-11 0 ... BarryMcHugh 8 — 7
(Tony Coyle) *hld up: rdn over 2f out: sn wknd* **50/1**

1m 11.14s (-0.66) **Going Correction** +0.05s/f (Good) — **11** Ran SP% **114.7**
Speed ratings (Par 93): **106,96,95,94,94 86,82,82,79,74 73**
CSF £32.70 TOTE £1.90: £1.30, £5.00, £1.90; EX 23.10 Trifecta £128.80.
Owner Hamdan Al Maktoum **Bred** J C Bloodstock **Trained** Middleham Moor, N Yorks

FOCUS
The ground had been watered and the official going description was good to firm. The opener was an ordinary novice and the favourite outclassed his rivals.

2302 WATCH RACING UK IN HD H'CAP — 5f
2:20 (2:25) (Class 6) (0-60,60) 3-Y-O — **£2,264** (£673; £336; £168) **Stalls** Centre

Form — RPR

131- **1** **Show Palace**[203] 7517 3-9-5 **58** ... GrahamLee 9 — 66+
(Jennie Candlish) *mde all: kpt on pushed out fnl f: shade cosily* **7/2**[1]

4533 **2** 3/4 **Kiringa**[27] 1554 3-8-7 **46** ... JamesSullivan 6 — 48
(Robert Cowell) *in tch: rdn 2f out: hdwy and ev ch appr fnl f: kpt on* **12/1**

600- **3** *hd* **Chip Or Pellet**[203] 7516 3-8-7 **46** oh1 ... AndrewMullen 12 — 47
(Nigel Tinkler) *dwlt: sn midfield: sn pushed along: hdwy over 1f out: kpt on* **20/1**

04-0 **4** *nk* **Emerald Bay**[136] 3 3-9-7 **60** ... RobertWinston 8 — 60
(Ivan Furtado) *prom: rdn over 2f out: kpt on* **12/1**

060- **5** *nk* **Lady Joanna Vassa (IRE)**[280] 5205 3-8-10 **49** ... ConnorBeasley 7 — 48
(Richard Guest) *w ldr: rdn 2f out: one pce fnl f* **5/1**[2]

04-4 **6** 3/4 **Whispering Soul (IRE)**[17] 1839 3-8-11 **50** ... (b) PJMcDonald 16 — 46
(Ann Duffield) *hld up: rdn and hdwy over 1f out: kpt on fnl f* **12/1**

40-4 **7** 2 3/4 **Hamish McGonagain**[21] 1721 3-9-7 **60** ... RichardKingscote 5 — 47
(Jeremy Gask) *midfield: rdn 2f out: bit short of room appr fnl f: kpt on* **13/2**[3]

640- **8** *shd* **Emilie Bronte**[213] 7244 3-9-3 **56** ... AndrewElliott 15 — 42+
(Chris Fairhurst) *outpcd in rr tl kpt on fnl f* **25/1**

00-4 **9** *hd* **Round The Island**[22] 1673 3-9-7 **60** ... GeorgeChaloner 10 — 45
(Richard Whitaker) *s.i.s: sn midfield: rdn 2f out: edgd lft appr fnl f: one pce* **15/2**

40-0 **10** 2 1/4 **I T Guru**[129] 105 3-9-1 **54** ... (t) DavidAllan 1 — 31
(Noel Wilson) *midfield: rdn and outpcd 1/2-way: no threat after* **25/1**

40-4 **11** 3/4 **Rise Up Singing**[6] 2118 3-8-9 **48** ... RoystonFfrench 17 — 23
(Colin Teague) *chsd ldrs: rdn 1/2-way: wknd appr fnl f* **40/1**

000- **12** *shd* **Our Place In Loule**[237] 6613 3-9-5 **58** ... (b[1]) BarryMcHugh 3 — 32
(Noel Wilson) *prom: rdn 1/2-way: wknd over 1f out* **33/1**

0-60 **13** *shd* **Final Spring (IRE)**[21] 1691 3-8-4 **46** oh1 ... JoeDoyle(3) 13 — 20
(Jim Goldie) *a towards rr* **50/1**

600- **14** 1/2 **Nefetari**[236] 6651 3-8-7 **46** oh1 ... JimmyQuinn 11 — 18
(Alan Brown) *chsd ldrs: rdn 1/2-way: wknd over 1f out* **66/1**

546- **15** 1/2 **Irish Cailin (IRE)**[232] 6782 3-9-7 **60** ... PaulMulrennan 2 — 30
(Paul Midgley) *hld up: rdn 1/2-way: sn btn* **9/1**

06-5 **16** 3/4 **Tweetheart**[18] 1814 3-9-2 **60** ... (p) PhilDennis(5) 4 — 28
(Ron Barr) *s.i.s: a towards rr* **16/1**

58.71s (0.11) **Going Correction** +0.05s/f (Good) — **16** Ran SP% **124.2**
Speed ratings (Par 97): **101,99,99,99,98 97,92,92,92,88 87,87,87,86,85 84**
CSF £44.28 CT £763.24 TOTE £3.30: £1.50, £2.00, £4.90, £3.80; EX 20.70 Trifecta £397.40.
Owner P and Mrs G A Clarke **Bred** M C Humby **Trained** Basford Green, Staffs
■ Midnight Robbery was withdrawn. Price at time of withdrawal 50-1. Rule 4 does not apply.
■ Stewards' Enquiry : George Chaloner one-day ban: careless riding (May 30)

FOCUS
A modest 3yo sprint handicap, in which they finished in a bit of a heap, and it paid to race handily. The winner can probably win again.

2303 FOLLOW @RACING_UK ON TWITTER MAIDEN FILLIES' STKS (DIV I) — 7f
2:50 (2:53) (Class 5) 3-Y-O+ — **£2,911** (£866; £432; £216) **Stalls** Centre

Form — RPR

1 **Owaseyf (USA)** 3-9-0 0 ... JackMitchell 5 — 73+
(Roger Varian) *in tch: smooth hdwy to ld 2f out: kpt on pushed out: comf* **4/1**

2 **2** 2 1/2 **Brockholes**[18] 1814 3-9-0 0 ... TonyHamilton 10 — 66
(Richard Fahey) *trckd ldrs: wnt 2nd and ev ch wl over 1f out: sn rdn: edgd lft appr fnl f: kpt on same pce* **10/3**[2]

5 **3** *nk* **Sonnet (IRE)**[84] 679 3-9-0 0 ... DarryllHolland 4 — 65
(Charles Hills) *dwlt: hld up: rdn over 2f out: hdwy over 1f out: kpt on fnl f* **3/1**[1]

6 **4** *1* **Fly True**[24] 1597 3-9-0 0 ... DaneO'Neill 7 — 62
(Jeremy Gask) *hld up: hdwy over 2f out: rdn over 1f out: kpt on* **6/1**

0 **5** 3/4 **Indibeau**[104] 428 4-9-11 0 ... AndrewMullen 6 — 64
(Garry Moss) *led: hdd 5f out: remained prom: rdn over 2f out: one pce* **66/1**

02-0 **6** 2 1/4 **Cancan Katy**[24] 1597 3-9-0 82 ... RichardKingscote 3 — 54
(Tom Dascombe) *in tch: rdn over 2f out: wknd fnl f* **7/2**[3]

/50- **7** 1/2 **Euro Mac**[307] 4232 4-9-11 41 ... AndrewElliott 2 — 57?
(Neville Bycroft) *hld up: rdn and outpcd over 3f out: sme hdwy over 1f out: nvr threatened* **66/1**

0- **8** *7* **Tarnend Lass**[374] 2055 3-8-9 0 ... RachelRichardson(5) 1 — 34
(Tim Easterby) *in tch: rdn over 3f out: wknd 2f out* **33/1**

-0 **9** *14* **Lowrie**[94] 544 3-9-0 0 ... [1] PatrickMathers 8
(John David Riches) *tk str hold: led 5f out: hdd 2f out: wknd and eased* **125/1**

1m 24.12s (-0.38) **Going Correction** +0.05s/f (Good)
WFA 3 from 4yo 11lb — **9** Ran SP% **111.3**
Speed ratings (Par 100): **104,101,100,99,98 96,95,87,71**
CSF £16.66 TOTE £4.60: £1.50, £2.00, £1.50; EX 17.10 Trifecta £53.00.
Owner Sheikh Ahmed Al Maktoum **Bred** Darley **Trained** Newmarket, Suffolk

FOCUS
The first division of fair maiden, taken in good style by a well-bred newcomer.

2304 FOLLOW @RACING_UK ON TWITTER MAIDEN FILLIES' STKS (DIV II) — 7f
3:25 (3:25) (Class 5) 3-Y-O+ — **£2,911** (£866; £432; £216) **Stalls** Centre

Form — RPR

6 **1** **Connemera Queen**[18] 1815 3-9-0 0 ... RobertWinston 2 — 65
(Tracy Waggott) *prom: rdn to ld over 2f out: kpt on* **50/1**

03 **2** 1 3/4 **My Lucille (IRE)**[24] 1597 3-9-0 0 ... DavidAllan 6 — 60
(Tim Easterby) *hld up in tch: racd keenly: bit short of room 2f out: hdwy to chse ldr appr fnl f: rdn and one pce* **2/1**[2]

60 **3** 1 3/4 **Raven Banner (IRE)**[19] 1798 3-9-0 0 .... DaleSwift 8 56
(Daniel Mark Loughnane) *in tch: rdn over 2f out: kpt on same pce* **11/1**

650- **4** 1 **Someone Exciting**[180] 7887 3-8-9 48 .... PhilDennis(5) 9 53
(David Thompson) *hld up in tch: rdn and hdwy to chse ldrs over 1f out: one pce* **33/1**

6 **5** 1 3/4 **Enjoy Life (IRE)**[26] 1562 3-9-0 0 .... TomEaves 1 48
(Kevin Ryan) *led: hdd over 2f out: sn rdn: wknd ins fnl f* **5/1**[3]

3 **6** 3/4 **Anna Barkova (IRE)**[18] 1814 3-9-0 0 .... JoeyHaynes 5 46
(K R Burke) *trckd ldng pair: rdn over 1f out: hung lft: wknd ins fnl f* **13/8**[1]

0 **7** 5 **Sabrina Brazzo**[21] 1691 3-9-0 0 .... ConnorBeasley 3 33
(Michael Dods) *chsd ldng pair: rdn over 3f out: sn wknd* **14/1**

02 **8** 3 1/2 **Ay Up Audrey**[9] 2047 5-9-11 0 .... PaulMulrennan 10 27
(Rebecca Bastiman) *dwlt: hld up: nvr threatened* **14/1**

50-0 **9** 7 **Mini Minstrel**[9] 2052 4-9-11 42 .... RoystonFfrench 4 8
(Colin Teague) *chsd ldng pair: rdn over 3f out: wknd* **200/1**

1m 24.2s (-0.30) **Going Correction** +0.05s/f (Good)
WFA 3 from 4yo+ 11lb **9** Ran SP% **115.2**
Speed ratings (Par 100): **103,101,99,97,95 95,89,85,77**
CSF £149.09 TOTE £35.10: £7.20, £1.40, £2.90; EX 140.60 Trifecta £1294.50.
Owner Northumbria Leisure Ltd **Bred** T G Holdcroft **Trained** Spennymoor, Co Durham

FOCUS
The second division of the fillies' maiden looked less competitive than the first leg, but it was run in a similar time.

2305 RACINGUK.COM/DAYPASS H'CAP 5f
3:55 (3:56) (Class 3) (0-90,87) 3-Y-0+ **£7,439** (£2,213; £1,106; £553) **Stalls** Centre

Form RPR

-205 **1** **Rusty Rocket (IRE)**[22] 1672 7-9-5 **80** .... PJMcDonald 7 88
(Paul Green) *chsd ldrs: rdn 2f out: led narrowly ins fnl f: kpt on* **12/1**

1546 **2** nse **Jebediah Shine**[23] 1650 4-9-7 **87** .... JoshDoyle(5) 5 95
(David O'Meara) *w ldr: led 1/2-way: rdn 2f out: hdd narrowly ins fnl f: kpt on: jst failed* **9/1**

3-00 **3** 1 **Bashiba (IRE)**[10] 2016 5-9-3 **78** .... (t) TomEaves 10 82
(Nigel Tinkler) *hld up: sme hdwy 2f out: angled towards outer appr fnl f: rdn and kpt on* **16/1**

0-30 **4** hd **Kibaar**[16] 1848 4-9-7 **85** .... JoeDoyle(3) 6 89
(Kevin Ryan) *trckd ldrs: rdn over 1f out: kpt on* **13/2**

0-50 **5** 1 **Long Awaited (IRE)**[16] 1874 8-9-10 **85** .... (b) PhillipMakin 9 85
(David Barron) *hld up: hdwy on bit over 1f out: rdn appr fnl f: one pce* **12/1**

0-01 **6** hd **Soul Brother (IRE)**[16] 1874 5-9-8 **83** .... (b) DavidAllan 4 82
(Tim Easterby) *hld up: rdn over 1f out: kpt on ins fnl f: nvr threatened* **4/1**[2]

421- **7** nk **Olivia Fallow (IRE)**[280] 5207 4-9-11 **86** .... GrahamLee 1 84
(Paul Midgley) *in tch: rdn 2f out: wknd fnl 110yds* **5/1**[3]

10-3 **8** nse **Grand Beauty (IRE)**[12] 1964 4-9-9 **84** .... RichardKingscote 2 82
(Robert Cowell) *prom: rdn 2f out: wknd fnl 110yds* **7/2**[1]

1/-4 **9** 2 **Clergyman**[16] 1874 4-9-5 **80** .... BarryMcHugh 8 71
(Rebecca Bastiman) *s.i.s: hld up: nvr threatened* **10/1**

0-36 **10** 11 **Rosy Morning (IRE)**[16] 1872 3-8-7 **76** .... PaulMulrennan 3 24
(Mark Johnston) *led narrowly: hdd 1/2-way: wknd and eased* **25/1**

57.9s (-0.70) **Going Correction** +0.05s/f (Good)
WFA 3 from 4yo+ 8lb **10** Ran SP% **116.4**
Speed ratings (Par 107): **107,106,105,105,103 103,102,102,99,81**
CSF £114.93 CT £1775.44 TOTE £14.90: £4.10, £2.20, £5.70; EX 154.10 Trifecta £3508.90.
Owner Seven Stars Racing **Bred** Mike Hyde **Trained** Lydiate, Merseyside

FOCUS
A decent sprint handicap and the pace was strong. The winner has been rated back to last year's best.

2306 PINNACLE RACING SYNDICATE SHARES NOW AVAILABLE H'CAP (PINNACLE CUP MILE SERIES QUALIFIER) 1m
4:30 (4:33) (Class 5) (0-70,69) 3-Y-O **£2,911** (£866; £432; £216) **Stalls** Centre

Form RPR

2-36 **1** **Planetaria (IRE)**[22] 1671 3-9-3 **65** .... AndrewMullen 5 70
(Garry Moss) *mde all: rdn 2f out: kpt on* **11/2**[3]

40-0 **2** nk **Arithmetic (IRE)**[40] 1270 3-9-7 **69** .... DarryllHolland 2 73+
(Charles Hills) *hld up: pushed along and hdwy over 2f out: rdn over 1f out: r.o fnl f* **13/2**

4-60 **3** 1 1/4 **Mecca's Missus (IRE)**[9] 2049 3-8-13 **61** .... (p) BarryMcHugh 11 62
(Michael Dods) *hld up: pushed along and hdwy over 2f out: rdn to chse ldr over 1f out: kpt on same pce* **16/1**

3-42 **4** 1 1/4 **Dark Command**[22] 1667 3-8-12 **60** .... (p) PaulMulrennan 10 58
(Michael Dods) *hld up in midfield: hdwy 3f out: rdn and ev ch over 1f out: drvn ent fnl f: edgd lft and one pce* **3/1**[1]

3-01 **5** 1 **Arcane Dancer (IRE)**[14] 1927 3-9-0 **62** .... (p) TomEaves 1 58
(Lawrence Mullaney) *in tch: hdwy and ev ch 2f out: sn rdn: wknd ins fnl f* **11/1**

55-3 **6** 6 **On Fire**[23] 1646 3-9-1 **63** .... PJMcDonald 7 45
(James Bethell) *midfield: rdn over 2f out: wknd over 1f out* **4/1**[2]

6634 **7** 3 **Deben**[7] 2107 3-8-9 **60** .... (p) JoeDoyle(3) 3 35
(Kevin Ryan) *pressed ldr: rdn over 2f out: wknd over 1f out* **12/1**

3-32 **8** 10 **Last Star Falling (IRE)**[21] 1725 3-9-4 **66** .... TonyHamilton 8 18
(Henry Spiller) *chsd ldng pair: rdn over 2f out: sn wknd* **14/1**

00-0 **9** 3 **Canford Thompson**[116] 275 3-9-3 **65** .... GrahamLee 12 10
(Micky Hammond) *midfield: rdn over 3f out: sn wknd* **16/1**

40-0 **10** 3/4 **Anushka Noo Noo**[32] 1448 3-8-13 **64** .... JacobButterfield(3) 4 8
(Ollie Pears) *chsd ldng pair: rdn 4f out: sn wknd* **33/1**

660- **11** 1/2 **Black Hambleton**[210] 7336 3-9-3 **65** .... SamJames 9 8
(Bryan Smart) *a towards rr* **8/1**

1m 36.43s (-0.17) **Going Correction** +0.05s/f (Good) **11** Ran SP% **122.2**
Speed ratings (Par 99): **102,101,100,99,98 92,89,79,76,75 74**
CSF £39.27 CT £425.92 TOTE £5.20: £1.80, £2.70, £5.80; EX 45.60 Trifecta £975.80.
Owner Pinnacle Four Partnership **Bred** Fastnet Stud Ltd **Trained** Wynyard, Stockton-On-Tees
■ Kirkham was withdrawn. Price at time of withdrawal 6-1. Rule 4 applies to bets placed prior to withdrawal, but no to SP bets - deduction 10p in the pound. New market formed.

FOCUS
A modest but competitive 3yo handicap.

2307 RACING UK PROFITS RETURNED TO RACING MEDIAN AUCTION MAIDEN STKS 1m
5:05 (5:08) (Class 6) 3-5-Y-O **£2,385** (£704; £352) **Stalls** Centre

Form RPR

2 **1** **Catalan (IRE)**[21] 1708 3-8-11 0 .... RobertWinston 5 74
(Hughie Morrison) *trckd ldrs: pushed along to ld 2f out: rdn appr fnl f: kpt on* **3/1**[2]

3-33 **2** 3/4 **Archimento**[20] 1755 3-9-2 82 .... PaulMulrennan 1 77
(Ed Dunlop) *prom: led over 4f out: pushed along whn hdd 2f out: rdn and edgd lft appr fnl f: kpt on same pce* **1/2**[1]

-446 **3** 3 1/4 **Young Christian**[23] 1646 3-9-2 72 .... AndrewElliott 8 70
(Tom Tate) *midfield: pushed along over 3f out: rdn 2f out: styd on fnl f: wnt 3rd towards fin* **16/1**

0 **4** nk **Truly**[9] 2048 5-9-9 0 .... RoystonFfrench 7 67
(Colin Teague) *trckd ldrs: rdn over 2f out: kpt on same pce* **100/1**

6/3- **5** 4 1/2 **Mumford**[382] 1831 4-10-0 72 .... DavidAllan 11 62
(Geoffrey Harker) *hld up: pushed along and hdwy into midfield over 2f out: plugged on fnl f* **14/1**

20-0 **6** 3 1/4 **Playboy Bay**[13] 1953 4-9-9 57 .... (p) PhilDennis(5) 2 54
(Ron Barr) *dwlt: sn midfield: rdn over 2f out: wknd fnl f* **66/1**

000- **7** 2 1/4 **Blue Jay (FR)**[164] 8102 3-9-2 0 .... JimmyQuinn 3 46
(Ronald Thompson) *midfield: rdn over 2f out: sn wknd* **150/1**

325- **8** 2 1/4 **Bay Mirage (IRE)**[254] 6098 3-9-2 76 .... TomEaves 4 41
(Kevin Ryan) *led: hdd over 4f out: rdn over 3f out: wknd over 1f out* **7/1**[3]

60 **9** 4 1/2 **Hooks Lane**[23] 1622 4-10-0 0 .... (e[1]) DougieCostello 12 33
(Shaun Harris) *slowly away: a towards rr* **150/1**

56/0 **10** 3/4 **Private Dancer**[9] 2048 5-10-0 55 .... BarryMcHugh 6 32
(Ron Barr) *early to post: midfield: rdn over 3f out: sn wknd* **100/1**

11 nse **Brother Khee**[443] 5-9-11 0 .... (vt[1]) MissEmmaSayer(3) 9 32
(Wilf Storey) *slowly away: a in rr* **33/1**

1m 37.14s (0.54) **Going Correction** +0.05s/f (Good)
WFA 3 from 4yo+ 12lb **11** Ran SP% **124.5**
Speed ratings (Par 101): **99,98,95,94,90 86,84,82,77,77 77**
CSF £5.17 TOTE £4.70: £1.30, £1.10, £3.40; EX 6.70 Trifecta £37.30.
Owner Sir Thomas Pilkington & Mrs Sonia Rogers **Bred** Gigginstown House Stud **Trained** East Ilsley, Berks

FOCUS
A weak maiden and the form makes sense with a minor personal best from the winner.

2308 RACINGUK.COM H'CAP 1m 2f
5:35 (5:35) (Class 6) (0-60,60) 3-Y-O **£2,385** (£704; £352) **Stalls** Low

Form RPR

0-03 **1** **Monsieur Glory**[22] 1667 3-9-5 **58** .... (v) RichardKingscote 12 65
(Tom Dascombe) *prom: led over 2f out: rdn over 1f out: hung persistently lft but a doing enough* **8/1**

050- **2** 3/4 **Melgate Melody**[261] 5860 3-8-11 **50** .... KeaganLatham 7 55
(Michael Easterby) *trckd ldrs: rdn over 2f out: chsd ldr appr fnl f: styd on* **16/1**

5004 **3** 1 1/4 **Falcon's Fire (IRE)**[6] 2124 3-9-0 **53** .... PhillipMakin 2 56+
(Keith Dalgleish) *midfield: pushed along and hdwy 2f out: angled to outer appr fnl f: rdn and kpt on* **9/2**[1]

0-00 **4** 2 3/4 **Jon H The Lawman (IRE)**[27] 1551 3-8-7 **46** oh1 .... JimmyQuinn 11 44
(Ronald Thompson) *trckd ldrs: rdn 3f out: one pce* **25/1**

-620 **5** 1 **Little Pippin**[14] 1927 3-8-13 **52** .... BarryMcHugh 8 48
(Tony Coyle) *hld up: rdn and hdwy 2f out: kpt on same pce* **25/1**

55-3 **6** 1 **Saxon Gold (IRE)**[18] 1819 3-9-5 **58** .... ConnorBeasley 1 52
(John Davies) *dwlt: sn in tch: rdn 3f out: one pce* **7/1**[3]

-403 **7** 1 1/2 **Rajapur**[30] 1484 3-9-1 **54** .... (p) DougieCostello 13 45
(Philip Kirby) *midfield: rdn over 2f out: no imp* **10/1**

560- **8** hd **Kerry Icon**[146] 8348 3-8-11 **50** .... RoystonFfrench 10 41
(Iain Jardine) *hld up: pushed along over 3f out: kpt on fr appr fnl f: nvr threatened* **25/1**

40-5 **9** nk **Allfredandnobell (IRE)**[22] 1671 3-9-7 **60** .... JoeyHaynes 9 50
(Micky Hammond) *hld up: pushed along and hdwy 2f out: rdn and in tch 2f out: wknd fnl f* **13/2**[2]

200- **10** nk **The Resdev Way**[236] 6654 3-8-13 **52** .... GeorgeChaloner 15 42
(Richard Whitaker) *sn led: rdn whn hdd over 2f out: wknd appr fnl f* **25/1**

05-0 **11** 2 1/4 **I'm Ready (IRE)**[30] 1484 3-9-0 **53** .... TonyHamilton 3 38
(Richard Fahey) *midfield on inner: rdn over 2f out: hung lft: wknd fnl f* **12/1**

000 **12** 2 1/2 **Monpazier (IRE)**[61] 959 3-8-7 **46** oh1 .... AndrewMullen 14 27
(K R Burke) *s.i.s: a towards rr* **10/1**

004- **13** 2 1/2 **Siberian Power (IRE)**[303] 4376 3-8-7 **46** oh1 .... PaulMulrennan 5 22
(Jennie Candlish) *a towards rr* **8/1**

00-3 **14** 6 **Kazoey**[21] 1698 3-8-7 **46** oh1 .... DuranFentiman 6 10
(Chris Fairhurst) *midfield: rdn over 3f out: sn wknd* **14/1**

0-00 **15** 6 **Trulove**[75] 785 3-8-7 **46** oh1 .... [1] PatrickMathers 4
(John David Riches) *hld up: rdn over 3f out: sn btn* **100/1**

2m 6.91s (-0.19) **Going Correction** +0.05s/f (Good) **15** Ran SP% **121.0**
Speed ratings (Par 97): **102,101,100,98,97 96,95,95,95,94 92,90,88,84,79**
CSF £121.63 CT £655.10 TOTE £6.60: £2.80, £3.90, £2.50; EX 64.00 Trifecta £344.80.
Owner Kangyu Int Racing (HK) Ltd & F Ma **Bred** Crossfields Bloodstock Ltd **Trained** Malpas, Cheshire

FOCUS
The finale was only a moderate 3yo handicap.
T/Jkpt: Not won. T/Plt: £346.20 to a £1 stake. Pool: £50,394.40 - 106.24 winning tickets T/Qpdt: £50.50 to a £1 stake. Pool: £4,320.43 - 63.20 winning tickets **Andrew Sheret**

2097 WINDSOR (R-H)
Monday, May 16

OFFICIAL GOING: Good (good to firm in places; 7.7)
Wind: Light, behind Weather: Fine

2309 OFFICEPOD.CO.UK CLAIMING STKS 6f
6:00 (6:00) (Class 5) 3-Y-O+ **£2,911** (£866; £432; £216) **Stalls** Low

Form RPR

60-1 **1** **Fear Or Favour (IRE)**[13] 1945 5-9-10 80 .... AdamKirby 1 77
(Clive Cox) *chsd ldrs: swtchd rt wl over 1f out towards nr side rail and sn in 2nd: drvn to ld jst ins fnl f: styd on wl* **7/4**[1]

324- **2** 1 1/4 **Great Fun**[254] 6094 5-9-10 81 .... JimmyFortune 5 73
(Brian Meehan) *chsd ldrs: drvn 2f out: cl up 1f out: styd on to take 2nd nr fin* **5/2**[2]

-004 **3** nk **Commanche**[13] 1945 7-9-3 60 .... (b) SilvestreDeSousa 7 65
(Chris Dwyer) *nt that wl away but gd spd fr wd draw to ld: sn crossed towards nr side: rdn 2f out: hdd and one pce jst ins fnl f* **9/1**

40-0 **4** 3/4 **Tagula Night (IRE)**[28] 1528 10-9-7 82 .... (vt) JackDuern(3) 4 70
(Dean Ivory) *wl in tch: effrt on outer 2f out: on terms w ldrs over 1f out: kpt on same pce after* **8/1**

-006 **5** 1/2 **Renounce (IRE)**[17] 1838 4-9-2 70 .... (t) DannyBrock(3) 2 63
(Charlie Wallis) *t.k.h: hld up in last but wl in tch: rdn 2f out: nt qckn and no imp on ldrs over 1f out: kpt on* **33/1**

0060 **6** *¾* **Doctor Parkes**[2] 2253 10-9-2 77 .... AaronJones(5) 6 63
(Stuart Williams) *in tch: effrt on wd outside 2f out: in tch over 1f out: one pce fnl f* **5/1**[3]

2465 **7** *2¾* **City Of Angkor Wat (IRE)**[18] 1803 6-9-6 71 ....(p) OisinMurphy 3 53
(Conor Dore) *t.k.h: racd against nr side rail: chsd ldr to wl over 1f out: wknd fnl f* **20/1**

360- **8** *17* **Kaaber (USA)**[138] 8401 5-8-13 50 ....(b) GaryMahon(5) 8
(Roy Brotherton) *in tch: rdn 1/2-way: sn btn: t.o* **125/1**

1m 12.61s (-0.39) **Going Correction** -0.175s/f (Firm) **8** Ran SP% **111.2**
Speed ratings (Par 103): **95,93,92,91,91 90,86,63**
CSF £5.80 TOTE £2.80: £1.40, £1.10, £1.80; EX 7.10 Trifecta £26.20.Fear Or Favour was claimed by Mr G. O. Scott for £12,000. Renounce was subject to a friendly claim of £7,000.
Owner Alan G Craddock **Bred** Shadwell Estate Company Limited **Trained** Lambourn, Berks

FOCUS
Most of theses came into this with questions to answer and they finished in a bit of a heap, so although the form horse won the race, this form wouldn't be anything out of the ordinary.

2310 BRITISH STALLION STUDS EBF NOVICE FILLIES' STKS (PLUS 10 RACE) 5f 10y
6:30 (6:31) (Class 4) 2-Y-O **£4,269** (£1,270; £634; £317) **Stalls** Low

Form RPR

6 **1** **Jule In The Crown**[10] 1988 2-9-0 0 .... SilvestreDeSousa 2 84+
(Mick Channon) *mde virtually all: shkn up over 1f out: in command fnl f: readily* **4/5**[1]

2 *2* **Barroche (IRE)** 2-9-0 0 .... JohnFahy 5 76
(Clive Cox) *rn green in last pair early and pushed along: prog on outer 2f out: shkn up to take 2nd ins fnl f: styd on but no imp on wnr* **14/1**

42 **3** *1¼* **Tiggaliscious (IRE)**[7] 2097 2-9-0 0 .... PatDobbs 1 71
(Richard Hannon) *pressed ldr: shkn up over 1f out: lost 2nd and one pce ins fnl f* **9/4**[2]

4 *nk* **Speed Freak** 2-9-0 0 .... OisinMurphy 8 70
(Ralph Beckett) *slowly away: racd in last pair: pushed along and sme prog fr 2f out: swtchd lft jst over 1f out: kpt on to press for 3rd nr fin: nt disgracd* **16/1**

5 *2½* **Polly's Angels (IRE)** 2-9-0 0 .... ShaneKelly 3 61
(Richard Hughes) *chsd ldng pair and cl up: rdn 2f out: lost 3rd over 1f out: wknd fnl f* **10/1**[3]

6 *¾* **Felstead Queen** 2-9-0 0 .... JFEgan 7 58
(Joseph Tuite) *in tch: urged along 1/2-way: sn outpcd: nvr on terms after* **66/1**

7 *hd* **Miss Rosina (IRE)** 2-9-0 0 .... HarryBentley 4 58
(George Margarson) *in tch: pushed along after 2f: struggling fr 2f out: fdd* **66/1**

1m 0.26s (-0.04) **Going Correction** -0.175s/f (Firm) **7** Ran SP% **110.9**
Speed ratings (Par 92): **93,89,87,87,83 82,81**
CSF £13.51 TOTE £1.90: £1.10, £5.10; EX 12.50 Trifecta £24.10.
Owner M Stewkesbury **Bred** Mervyn Stewkesbury **Trained** West Ilsley, Berks

FOCUS
Probably not the deepest of fillies' maidens - certainly not as strong as the one the winner ran in at Ascot on debut, and she duly obliged this time.

2311 WEATHERBYS PRIVATE BANKING NOVICE STKS (PLUS 10 RACE) 5f 10y
7:00 (7:01) (Class 3) 2-Y-O **£10,350** (£3,080; £1,539; £769) **Stalls** Low

Form RPR

1 **1** **Sea Of Snow (USA)**[7] 2097 2-9-3 0 .... FrannyNorton 2 86
(Mark Johnston) *pressed ldr and racd against nr side rail: shkn up 2f out: led jst ins fnl f: hung lft after but hld on wl* **5/1**[2]

1 **2** *½* **Legendary Lunch (IRE)**[21] 1713 2-9-8 0 .... PatDobbs 3 89
(Richard Hannon) *led: shkn up over 1f out: hdd and nt qckn jst ins fnl f: carried lft after but a hld* **1/5**[1]

4 **3** *3¼* **Zebspear (IRE)**[14] 1915 2-9-2 0 .... JFEgan 4 71
(Joseph Tuite) *wnt lft s: pressed ldng pair: stl wl there jst over 1f out: one pce fnl f* **12/1**[3]

4 *6* **Valley Lodge** 2-9-2 0 .... AdamBeschizza 6 50
(Julia Feilden) *dwlt and sltly impeded s: in tch in last pair: shkn up 2f out: wknd over 1f out* **33/1**

5 *3¾* **George Ravenscar** 2-9-2 0 .... HarryBentley 1 36
(Ed Vaughan) *slowly away: in tch in last pair: rdn 2f out: sn wknd aft* **33/1**

1m 0.55s (0.25) **Going Correction** -0.175s/f (Firm) **5** Ran SP% **113.6**
Speed ratings (Par 97): **91,90,85,75,69**
CSF £6.76 TOTE £5.10: £1.80, £1.10; EX 7.10 Trifecta £14.10.
Owner Sheikh Hamdan bin Mohammed Al Maktoum **Bred** Darley **Trained** Middleham Moor, N Yorks

■ Stewards' Enquiry : Franny Norton one-day ban: careless riding (May 30)

FOCUS
A turn up here as Legendary Lunch was backed as if defeat was out of the question to follow up his maiden win at this course, but he didn't settle early and was toppled by a filly who looks pretty good in her own right.

2312 OAKLEY COURT HOTEL MAIDEN FILLIES' STKS 1m 67y
7:30 (7:31) (Class 5) 3-Y-O+ **£2,911** (£866; £432; £216) **Stalls** Low

Form RPR

1 **Youre Always Right (IRE)** 3-9-0 0 .... JohnFahy 1 82
(Clive Cox) *trckd ldng pair: pushed along and clsd fr 2f out: rdn to ld jst ins fnl f: styd on wl* **12/1**

2 *1½* **Dame Judi (IRE)** 3-9-0 0 .... SilvestreDeSousa 9 79
(Simon Crisford) *led: pushed along and hdd over 3f out: kpt on and rdn to ld again over 1f out: hdd jst ins fnl f: styd* **3/1**[1]

3 *2¼* **Irrevocable (IRE)** 3-9-0 0 .... JimmyFortune 10 73+
(Roger Charlton) *s.s: detached in last to 1/2-way: prog against nr side rail fr 3f out: pushed along to take 3rd ins fnl f: styd on encouragingly* **10/1**

4 *1¾* **Idealist** 3-9-0 0 .... HarryBentley 8 69
(Roger Varian) *hld up in 9th: rdn and prog into midfield over 2f out: kpt on same pce fr over 1f out* **4/1**[2]

5 *1¾* **I Am (IRE)** 3-9-0 0 .... NickyMackay 13 65+
(John Gosden) *rn green in midfield: pushed along on wd outside over 2f out: kpt on steadily fr over 1f out* **9/2**[3]

-4 **6** *1¼* **Harikiri (IRE)**[86] 654 3-8-11 0 .... MichaelJMMurphy(3) 11 62
(Charles Hills) *pressed ldr: led over 3f out gng wl: shkn up and wandered fr 2f out: hdd & wknd over 1f out* **20/1**

7 *¾* **Pixel (IRE)** 3-9-0 0 .... JFEgan 3 60+
(Jeremy Noseda) *mostly in last trio: pushed along over 3f out: swtchd lft twice fr 2f out: nvr involved but kpt on* **10/1**

8 *¾* **Encore Moi** 3-9-0 0 .... FMBerry 4 60
(Marco Botti) *trckd ldng pair: shkn up 3f out: wknd 2f out: eased whn no ch* **14/1**

0 **9** *1* **Archipentura**[24] 1597 4-9-9 0 .... AlistairRawlinson(3) 12 59
(J R Jenkins) *t.k.h early: trckd ldrs: pushed along over 3f out: wknd on outer 2f out* **100/1**

4 **10** *1¾* **Sund City (FR)**[14] 1930 3-9-0 0 .... FrannyNorton 6 52
(Harry Dunlop) *t.k.h early: wl in tch: lost pl 3f out: steadily wknd* **8/1**

11 *7* **Snow Pixie (USA)** 3-9-0 0 .... OisinMurphy 5 35
(Ed Dunlop) *in tch in midfield: shkn up 3f out: wknd 2f out* **14/1**

12 *13* **Martyna** 3-9-0 0 .... CathyGannon 7 4
(John Spearing) *s.i.s: a in rr: struggling 1/2-way: t.o* **40/1**

1m 46.64s (1.94) **Going Correction** +0.45s/f (Yiel)
WFA 3 from 4yo 12lb **12** Ran SP% **121.7**
Speed ratings (Par 100): **108,106,104,102,100 99,98,98,97,95 88,75**
CSF £48.65 TOTE £15.50: £4.20, £2.20, £3.70; EX 66.00 Trifecta £1420.70.
Owner Paul & Clare Rooney **Bred** Fontstown Stud **Trained** Lambourn, Berks

FOCUS
Those that had experience hadn't achieved a great deal so no surprise this went to one of the newcomers. The race distance was 45 yards further than advertised.

2313 EQUESTRIAN SURFACES LTD H'CAP 1m 3f 135y
8:00 (8:00) (Class 3) (0-95,90) 4-Y-O+ **£7,439** (£2,213; £1,106; £553) **Stalls** Centre

Form RPR

1 **1** **Cape Discovery**[14] 1933 4-9-0 **83** .... ShaneKelly 2 89
(Richard Hughes) *trckd clr ldng pair: pushed along over 3f out: rdn to cl fr 2f out: disp ld jst ins fnl f: drvn and hld last 100yds: hld on* **3/1**[2]

430- **2** *nk* **Green Light**[191] 7757 5-9-4 **87** .... FMBerry 3 92
(Ralph Beckett) *t.k.h early: hld up in 5th: rdn 3f out: clsd fr 2f out: disp ld jst ins fnl f: no ex last 75yds* **2/1**[1]

00-1 **3** *hd* **Barwick**[26] 1568 8-9-7 **90** .... SteveDrowne 4 94
(George Baker) *dwlt: hld up in last: rdn over 2f out: prog over 1f out: tk 3rd last 100yds and pressed ldng pair: jst hld* **3/1**[2]

3-30 **4** *2¼* **Safira Menina**[2] 2233 4-8-4 **76** oh13 .... TimClark(3) 7 76?
(Martin Smith) *hld up in last pair: rdn 3f out: tried to cl on outer 2f out: nt qckn wl over 1f out: one pce after* **20/1**

635/ **5** *½* **Nabhan**[23] 7726 4-9-7 **90** .... WilliamTwiston-Davies 1 89
(Bernard Llewellyn) *led and clr w one rival: shkn up and hdd 3f out: kpt on and led again over 1f out: hdd and fdd jst ins fnl f* **16/1**

3-52 **6** *4* **Victoria Pollard**[20] 1743 4-9-0 **83** ....(p) DavidProbert 6 76
(Andrew Balding) *pressed ldr and clr of rest: pushed into narrow ld 3f out: hdd & wknd over 1f out* **5/1**[3]

1100 **7** *6* **St Patrick's Day (IRE)**[19] 1775 4-8-10 **82** .... AlistairRawlinson(3) 5 65
(J R Jenkins) *hld up in 4th: shkn up wl over 2f out: sn wknd and bhd* **20/1**

2m 32.66s (3.16) **Going Correction** +0.45s/f (Yiel) **7** Ran SP% **115.4**
Speed ratings (Par 107): **107,106,106,105,104 102,98**
CSF £9.64 TOTE £3.70: £2.00, £1.80; EX 11.30 Trifecta £29.20.
Owner Thames Boys **Bred** Hascombe And Valiant Studs **Trained** Upper Lambourn, Berkshire

FOCUS
With the top weight rated 5lb below the ceiling rating, this wouldn't be the strongest of races for the grade and nearly all of them still had some sort of chance entering the final furlong. The race distance was 45 yards further than advertised.

2314 CITIPOST MAIL 10TH ANNIVERSARY H'CAP 5f 10y
8:30 (8:30) (Class 4) (0-80,79) 3-Y-O **£4,690** (£1,395; £697; £348) **Stalls** Low

Form RPR

32-1 **1** **Udontdodou**[16] 1870 3-9-7 **79** .... JasonHart 4 94+
(Richard Guest) *hld up bhd ldrs: cl up and swtchd to nr side over 1f out: rdn to ld jst ins fnl f: hung lft but sn clr* **13/8**[1]

310- **2** *2½* **Silken Skies (IRE)**[206] 7432 3-9-5 **77** .... AdamKirby 6 81
(Clive Cox) *pressed ldng pair: chal on outer fr 2f out: led briefly 1f out: sn outpcd by wnr* **11/1**

01-1 **3** *nk* **Nag's Wag (IRE)**[20] 1745 3-8-13 **71** .... SteveDrowne 2 74
(George Baker) *pushed along in last pair after 2f: no prog 2f out: r.o against nr side rail fnl f to take 3rd nr fin* **12/1**

2122 **4** *½* **Cultured Knight**[4] 2185 3-9-1 **73** .... ShaneKelly 1 74
(Richard Hughes) *pressed ldr: upsides fr 2f out to 1f out: one pce fnl f* **5/2**[2]

3-11 **5** *½* **Bring On A Spinner**[123] 181 3-8-10 **73** .... AaronJones(5) 3 72
(Stuart Williams) *hld up in last pair: effrt 2f out: hanging lft and no imp on ldrs fr over 1f out* **13/2**

62-1 **6** *2¼* **Aragon Knight**[20] 1753 3-9-1 **78** .... HectorCrouch(5) 5 69
(Heather Main) *mde most: hrd pressed 2f out: hdd & wknd 1f out* **11/2**[3]

144- **7** *3¾* **The Burnham Mare (IRE)**[167] 8065 3-8-12 **70** .... LiamJones 7 48
(J S Moore) *sn pushed along in 5th: struggling fr 2f out: wl btn over 1f out* **33/1**

59.21s (-1.09) **Going Correction** -0.175s/f (Firm) **7** Ran SP% **114.4**
Speed ratings (Par 101): **101,97,96,95,94 91,85**
CSF £20.81 TOTE £2.30: £1.50, £3.40; EX 21.20 Trifecta £125.70.
Owner Mrs Alison Guest **Bred** Times Of Wigan Ltd **Trained** Ingmanthorpe, W Yorks

FOCUS
This looked a competitive sprint handicap on paper, featuring a host of in-form sprinters, but the winner looks some way ahead of his mark and is clearly ahead of the game at the moment.
T/Plt: £15.30 to a £1 stake. Pool: £67,237.94 - 3,187.63 winning tickets T/Qpdt: £10.70 to a £1 stake. Pool: £5,780.59 - 397.18 winning tickets **Jonathan Neesom**

2074 COLOGNE (R-H)
Monday, May 16

OFFICIAL GOING: Turf: good

2315a MEHL-MULHENS-RENNEN - GERMAN 2000 GUINEAS (GROUP 2) (3YO COLTS & FILLIES) (TURF) 1m
4:05 (12:00) 3-Y-O **£73,529** (£22,058; £9,558; £5,147; £2,205)

RPR

1 **Knife Edge (IRE)**[30] 1477 3-9-2 0 .... RyanMoore 5 108
(Marco Botti) *mde all: set stdy pce: drvn over 1f out: jst hld on: all out* **8/5**[1]

2 *nse* **Degas (GER)**[29] 3-9-2 0 .... AdriedeVries 3 108+
(Markus Klug, Germany) *hld up in rr: smooth hdwy fr 2f out: drvn 1f out: styd on strly: jst failed* **32/5**

3 *2¼* **Noor Al Hawa (FR)**[22] 1689 3-9-2 0 .... EduardoPedroza 4 103
(A Wohler, Germany) *t.k.h: in tch: j. path 5f out: rdn over 2f out: chal over 1f out: no ex ins fnl f* **51/10**[3]

The Form Book, Raceform Ltd, Newbury, RG14 5SJ

4 ¾ **Millowitsch (GER)**[22] 1689 3-9-2 0........................ AndreasHelfenbein 9 101
(Markus Klug, Germany) *t.k.h: midfield on outer: hdwy over 2f out: drvn 2f out: styd on fnl f but nvr able to chal* **23/10**[2]

5 2 ¼ **Parvaneh (IRE)**[29] 1513 3-8-13 0........................ MarcLerner 10 93
(Waldemar Hickst, Germany) *towards rr: pushed along 4f out: rdn over 2f out: kpt on wl on but nvr able to chal* **81/10**

6 2 ½ **Baroncello (GER)**[23] 3-9-2 0........................ AndraschStarke 6 90
(Andreas Lowe, Germany) *t.k.h: chsd ldr: rdn and outpcd 2f out: wknd steadily fnl f* **227/10**

7 ½ **Molly King (GER)**[22] 1689 3-9-2 0........................ AlexanderPietsch 1 89
(J Hirschberger, Germany) *t.k.h: towards rr: rdn over 2f out: kpt on steadily: n.d* **28/1**

8 nk **Omar Bradley (USA)**[23] 3-9-2 0........................ Per-AndersGraberg 8 89
(Flemming Velin, Denmark) *midfield: hdwy on inner over 2f out: effrt 2f out: wknd over 1f out* **129/10**

9 2 **Royal Shaheen (FR)**[23] 3-9-2 0........................(b) JoseLuisSilverio 7 84
(A Wohler, Germany) *s.i.s: plld hrd in midfield: hmpd 5f out: effrt 2f out: wknd over 1f out* **48/1**

10 8 **Veneto (GER)**[36] 3-9-2 0........................ RafaelSchistl 2 66
(Andreas Lowe, Germany) *rousted along in early stages: in tch: effrt over 2f out: wknd and eased 1f out* **233/10**

1m 34.33s (-4.06) **10** Ran SP% **130.7**
WIN (incl. 10 euro stake): 26. PLACES: 16, 19, 20. SF: 161.
Owner Mrs John Magnier & Michael Tabor & Derrick Smith **Bred** Attalea Partnership **Trained** Newmarket, Suffolk

2280 DEAUVILLE (R-H)
Monday, May 16

OFFICIAL GOING: Polytrack: standard, turf: good

2316a POUR MOI COOLMORE PRIX SAINT-ALARY (GROUP 1) (3YO FILLIES) (TURF) 1m 2f
1:50 (12:00) 3-Y-O **£105,036** (£42,022; £21,011; £10,496; £5,257)

RPR

1 **Jemayel (IRE)**[22] 1687 3-9-0 0........................(p) GregoryBenoist 1 106
(J-C Rouget, France) *midfield on inner: rdn to chal over 1f out: led ins fnl f: styd on: jst prevailed* **14/1**

2 hd **Camprock (FR)**[28] 1541 3-9-0 0........................ MickaelBarzalona 5 106
(Mme Pia Brandt, France) *midfield in tch: rdn to chal over 1f out: styd on ev ch fnl f: jst denied* **6/5**[1]

3 1 ½ **Hawksmoor (IRE)**[220] 7075 3-9-0 0........................(b[1]) FrankieDettori 8 103
(Hugo Palmer) *led: rdn and strly pressed 2f out: hung rt 1f out: battled on tl hdd ins fnl f: no ex and jst hld on for 3rd* **5/2**[2]

4 hd **Left Hand**[27] 3-9-0 0........................ MaximeGuyon 2 103+
(C Laffon-Parias, France) *midfield on outer: rdn 2f out: styd on fnl f and wnt 4th cl home: jst missed 3rd but nt pce to chal* **16/1**

5 snk **Magnanime**[22] 1687 3-9-0 0........................ TonyPiccone 9 102
(F Chappet, France) *trckd ldr: rdn to chal 2f out: styd on but outpcd by front pair fnl f and lost 4th cl home* **11/1**

6 1 ¼ **Rosvana (FR)**[14] 3-9-0 0........................ ChristopheSoumillon 6 100+
(A De Royer-Dupre, France) *prom on inner: rdn and effrt over 1f out: stl ch whn hmpd ent fnl f: nt rcvr and fdd* **5/1**[3]

7 1 **Meri Devie (FR)**[30] 1504 3-9-0 0........................ StephanePasquier 7 98
(N Clement, France) *restrained and hld up: rdn 2f out: plugged on but no real imp and n.d* **28/1**

8 1 **Restiana (FR)**[30] 1504 3-9-0 0........................(b) JamieSpencer 4 96
(P Sogorb, France) *dwlt sltly: hld up and a towards rr: rdn 2f out: plugged on but no real imp and n.d* **18/1**

9 3 ½ **Tierra Del Fuego (FR)**[28] 1541 3-9-0 0........................ OlivierPeslier 3 89
(G E Mikhalides, France) *hld up: a towards rr: rdn and dropped to last over 1f out: sn wl btn* **18/1**

2m 7.93s (-2.27) **9** Ran SP% **125.5**
WIN (incl. 1 euro stake): 12.50. PLACES: 2.10, 1.30, 1.60. DF: 13.30. SF: 37.10.
Owner Al Shaqab Racing **Bred** S F Bloodstock LLC **Trained** Pau, France

2317a PRIX DE SAINT-GEORGES (GROUP 3) (3YO+) (TURF) 5f
2:20 (12:00) 3-Y-O+ **£29,411** (£11,764; £8,823; £5,882; £2,941)

RPR

1 **Finsbury Square (IRE)**[20] 1769 4-9-0 0........(b) ChristopheSoumillon 10 109
(F Chappet, France) *midfield: gd hdwy to ld narrowly 1f out: fended off chalr ins fnl f: rdn out* **5/1**[3]

2 hd **Son Cesio (FR)**[20] 1769 5-9-6 0........................ VincentCheminaud 4 114
(H-A Pantall, France) *midfield: rdn 2f out: styd on wl to chal ins fnl f: jst hld* **14/1**

3 1 ½ **Ride Like The Wind (IRE)**[20] 1769 4-9-2 0............ MickaelBarzalona 6 105
(F Head, France) *dwlt: towards rr: drvn under 2f out: kpt on wl fnl f to snatch 3rd cl home* **14/1**

4 nse **Mirza**[16] 1862 9-9-2 0........................(p) FrankieDettori 9 105
(Rae Guest) *midfield: rdn and unable qck over 2f out: kpt on wl ins fnl f: nrst fin* **14/1**

5 nk **Signs Of Blessing (IRE)**[46] 1172 5-9-0 0.............. StephanePasquier 1 102
(F Rohaut, France) *midfield: drvn over 2f out: stdy hdwy to hold ev ch 1f out: wknd clsng stages* **13/8**[1]

6 shd **Sir Maximilian (IRE)**[12] 1969 7-9-0 0........................(p) JamieSpencer 5 101
(Ian Williams) *hld up in rr: rdn and stdy hdwy fr over 1f out: kpt on fnl f: nrst fin* **10/3**[2]

7 2 **Monsieur Joe (IRE)**[21] 1730 9-9-0 0........................ OlivierPeslier 3 94
(Paul Midgley) *prom: rdn over 1f out: fdd ins fnl f* **10/1**

8 1 **Gengis (FR)**[46] 1172 6-9-2 0........................(b) UmbertoRispoli 8 92
(G Doleuze, France) *led: rdn and hdd 1f out: wknd fnl f* **20/1**

9 1 **Spirit Quartz (IRE)**[16] 1862 8-9-2 0........................(p) MartinHarley 2 89
(Robert Cowell) *trckd ldrs: ev ch over 1f out: wknd 1f out* **11/2**

10 nk **Pupa Di Saronno (FR)**[20] 1769 5-8-10 0........................ FabriceVeron 7 82
(H-A Pantall, France) *trckd ldrs: rdn over 2f out: wknd and eased 1f out* **33/1**

57.7s (0.20) **10** Ran SP% **130.0**
WIN (incl. 1 euro stake): 5.90. PLACES: 2.00, 4.20, 3.50. DF: 30.70. SF: 61.10.
Owner Berend Van Dalfsen **Bred** Berend Van Dalfsen **Trained** France

FRAUENFELD (R-H)
Monday, May 16

OFFICIAL GOING: Turf: good

2318a GROSSER PREIS DER THURGAUER KANTONALBANK (CONDITIONS) (4YO+) (TURF) 1m 4f
2:15 (12:00) 4-Y-O+

£6,530 (£2,612; £1,959; £1,306; £653; £544)

RPR

1 **Le Colonel (GER)** 4-9-4 0........................ ClementL'Heureux 7 75
(A Schaerer, Switzerland) **69/10**

2 nk **Zand (IRE)**[9] 2037 6-8-7 0........................ JoeFanning 2 63
(Mark Johnston) *led: hdd after 1/2-way and trckd new ldr: rdn to chal again into st: ev ch fnl f: styd on: jst hld* **13/10**[1]

3 nse **Fabrino (IRE)**[246] 8-9-4 0........................ RobertHavlin 1 74
(M Weiss, Switzerland) **29/10**[2]

4 2 ½ **Sing With Bess (IRE)**[246] 5-9-1 0........................ KierenFox 3 67
(M Weiss, Switzerland) **18/5**[3]

5 nk **Runaway (GER)**[85] 664 9-9-4 0........................(p) VaclavJanacek 8 70
(Frau M Muller, Switzerland) **9/1**

6 1 ½ **Maroosh**[246] 7-9-0 0........................(b) TimBurgin 5 63
(A Schennach, Switzerland) **135/10**

7 ½ **Chaotic Carnival**[267] 5-8-11 0........................(b) NicolasGuilbert 6 59
(Julien Lemee, Switzerland) **89/10**

8 1 **Halling River (IRE)**[246] 9-9-4 0........................(b) MilanZatloukal 4 65
(M Weiss, Switzerland) **58/10**

2m 38.49s (158.49) **8** Ran SP% **145.2**
.
Owner A Krauliger & V Krauliger **Bred** Stiftung Gestut Fahrhof **Trained** Switzerland

2150 LINGFIELD (L-H)
Tuesday, May 17

OFFICIAL GOING: Polytrack: standard
Wind: light, half behind Weather: light cloud

2319 JOCKEY DOOR MAC BARBADOS NOVICE STKS 6f 1y(P)
1:50 (1:50) (Class 5) 2-Y-O **£3,234** (£962; £481; £240) **Stalls** Low

Form RPR

23 1 **Monks Stand (USA)**[8] 2082 2-9-2 0........................ JimCrowley 3 87
(Jeremy Noseda) *chsd ldr: rdn to ld jst over 1f out: asserted u.p ins fnl f: r.o strly: readily* **1/1**[1]

02 2 2 **Poet's Society**[10] 2038 2-9-2 0........................ JamesDoyle 1 81
(Mark Johnston) *led: rdn clr w wnr over 1f out: hdd jst over 1f out: clr 2nd and styd on same pce ins fnl f* **11/4**[2]

3 7 **Zamjar** 2-9-2 0........................ RyanMoore 4 60+
(Ed Dunlop) *in tch: carried wd bnd 2f out: wl hld 3rd and styd on same pce fr wl over 1f out* **9/2**[3]

4 2 ¼ **Restore (IRE)** 2-9-2 0........................ PatDobbs 5 53
(Richard Hannon) *dwlt: hld up in tch in rr: effrt 2f out: sn outpcd and wl hld 4th fr wl over 1f out* **10/1**

5 3 ¼ **Espresso Freddo (IRE)** 2-9-2 0........................ LukeMorris 2 44
(Sir Mark Prescott Bt) *dwlt: sn rcvrd to chse ldng pair: rn green and hung rt bnd 2f out: sn dropped to rr and no ch over 1f out* **25/1**

1m 11.62s (-0.28) **Going Correction** -0.075s/f (Stan) **5** Ran SP% **107.8**
Speed ratings (Par 93): **98,95,86,83,78**
CSF £3.75 TOTE £1.50: £1.20, £1.70; EX 4.80 Trifecta £8.80.
Owner Mrs Susan Roy **Bred** Blackstone Farm Llc **Trained** Newmarket, Suffolk

FOCUS
A fair contest run at a sound pace and dominated by the two runners with experience.

2320 RYAN VEHICLES MAIDEN STKS (DIV I) 1m 1y(P)
2:20 (2:20) (Class 5) 3-Y-O+ **£2,911** (£866; £432; £216) **Stalls** High

Form RPR

22 1 **Banish (USA)**[18] 1837 3-9-2 0........................ RyanMoore 2 86
(Hugo Palmer) *mde all: hung rt bnd 2f out: sustained duel w runner-up after: drvn ins fnl f: hld on: rdn out* **2/1**[2]

52 2 hd **Raven's Corner (IRE)**[22] 1701 3-9-2 0........................ JamesDoyle 5 85
(John Gosden) *chsd wnr: upsides whn carried rt 2f out: drvn and sustained duel w wnr after: kpt on u.p: hld towards fin* **6/5**[1]

0-0 3 4 **Cosmic Storm**[11] 2009 3-8-11 0........................ OscarPereira 9 70
(Ralph Beckett) *chsd ldrs: rdn and outpcd over 1f out: chsd clr ldng pair 1f out: no imp and styd on same pce ins fnl f* **33/1**

4 nk **Egyptian (USA)** 3-9-2 0........................ AdamKirby 6 75+
(Jeremy Noseda) *in tch in midfield: rdn and flashed tail 2f out: hdwy to go 4th 1f out: battling for 3rd and kpt on ins fnl f: no threat to ldrs* **6/1**[3]

5 2 ¼ **Jabbaar** 3-9-2 0........................ RobertHavlin 8 69+
(Owen Burrows) *stdd after s: hld up in rr: effrt on inner and stl plenty to do 2f out: hdwy 1f out: kpt on ins fnl f: nvr trbld ldrs* **14/1**

44 6 1 **Critical Speed (IRE)**[21] 1765 4-9-9 0........................ LukeMorris 7 65
(Sylvester Kirk) *sn dropped to last trio: in tch: shkn up and wd bnd 2f out: modest hdwy fnl f: nvr trbld ldrs* **50/1**

0 7 1 ¼ **Catskill Mountains (IRE)**[15] 1930 3-9-2 0........................ FrederikTylicki 4 64
(Roger Varian) *in tch in midfield: rdn 2f out: sn lost pl and btn: wknd fnl f* **20/1**

8 1 ¾ **Signal Hill (IRE)** 3-9-2 0........................ DavidProbert 1 60
(Andrew Balding) *dwlt: sn rcvrd and chsd ldrs after 2f: rdn and outpcd over 1f out: lost 3rd 1f out: sn wknd* **20/1**

9 6 **Keyman (IRE)** 3-9-2 0........................ OisinMurphy 3 45
(Jeremy Gask) *broke wl: sn stdd and t.k.h in midfield: hung lft and lost pl over 2f out: bhd over 1f out* **33/1**

1m 37.75s (-0.45) **Going Correction** -0.075s/f (Stan)
WFA 3 from 4yo 12lb **9** Ran SP% **117.1**
Speed ratings (Par 103): **99,98,94,94,92 91,90,88,82**
CSF £4.49 TOTE £3.00: £1.10, £1.10, £6.50; EX 6.10 Trifecta £73.70.
Owner HighclereThoroughbredRacing-Smart Strike **Bred** Nicole Gunther **Trained** Newmarket, Suffolk

FOCUS
The pace was solid for this interesting maiden with the market leaders always in control. The race has been rated around the runner-up.

2321 RYAN VEHICLES MAIDEN STKS (DIV II) 1m 1y(P)
2:55 (2:55) (Class 5) 3-Y-O+ **£2,911** (£866; £432; £216) **Stalls** High

Form RPR

44 **1** **Heart Of Lions (USA)**[24] 1653 3-9-2 0 JamesDoyle 2 84
(John Gosden) *hld up wl in tch in midfield: effrt in 3rd jst over 2f out: rdn to chse ldr jst over 1f out: qcknd u.p to ld wl ins fnl f: sn in command* **8/11**[1]

2-60 **2** 1 ½ **Cape Banjo (USA)**[18] 1828 3-8-11 77 PatrickO'Donnell(5) 8 80
(Ralph Beckett) *chsd ldng pair: wnt 2nd 3f out: rdn to ld and edgd lft 2f out: clr over 1f out: drvn ins fnl f: hdd and outpcd wl ins fnl f* **8/1**[3]

20- **3** 1 ½ **Heartstone (IRE)**[221] 7077 3-8-11 0 DarryllHolland 1 71
(Charles Hills) *hld up in tch in last trio: effrt in 4th 2f out: kpt on wl ins fnl f: wnt 3rd fnl 50yds* **20/1**

2-5 **4** 1 ¼ **Senses Of Dubai**[27] 1577 3-9-2 0 RobertHavlin 4 74
(Simon Crisford) *sn led: hdd: sltly impeded and rdn 2f out: unable qck and lost 2nd jst over 1f out: plugged on same pce fnl f* **3/1**[2]

50 **5** 7 **Hayward Field (IRE)**[10] 2048 3-9-2 0 FrederikTylicki 5 57+
(Roger Varian) *hld up in tch towards rr: stuck bhd horses over 2f out: swtchd rt and hdwy 2f out: kpt on but no ch w ldrs* **12/1**

06- **6** 3 ¼ **Alzebarh (IRE)**[244] 6428 3-8-11 0 TomQueally 3 44
(James Fanshawe) *hld up in tch in midfield: 6th and outpcd jst over 2f out: wl btn over 1f out* **50/1**

7 3 ½ **Willyegolassiego** 3-8-11 0 LiamKeniry 9 35
(Neil Mulholland) *s.i.s: rcvrd and in tch after 2f: rdn over 2f out: sn outpcd: wl btn over 1f out* **66/1**

00- **8** 1 ½ **Passing Dream**[160] 8153 3-8-11 0 OisinMurphy 7 32+
(Hughie Morrison) *s.i.s: steadily rcvrd: hdwy into midfield 5f out: rdn over 2f out: sn lost pl and btn: no ch over 1f out* **66/1**

3- **9** 77 **Courtsider**[183] 7872 4-9-9 0 JimCrowley 6
(Lucy Wadham) *w ldr tl 3f out: sn lost pl: bhd and virtually p.u fr over 1f out: t.o* **14/1**

1m 37.55s (-0.65) **Going Correction** -0.075s/f (Stan)
WFA 3 from 4yo 12lb **9** Ran SP% **118.1**
Speed ratings (Par 103): **100,98,97,95,88 85,82,80,3**
CSF £7.73 TOTE £1.60: £1.10, £1.80, £3.50; EX 7.50 Trifecta £70.20.
Owner Godolphin **Bred** Mark Basinger Mueller Thoroughbred **Trained** Newmarket, Suffolk

FOCUS
Another fair maiden which was run at an honest pace. The time was similar to the first division and the winner has been rated close to his Wood Ditton figure.

2322 GOOD LUCK CRYSTAL PALACE H'CAP 7f 1y(P)
3:25 (3:30) (Class 5) (0-75,75) 3-Y-O **£2,911** (£866; £432; £216) **Stalls** Low

Form RPR

1 **1** **Toriano**[41] 1256 3-9-7 75 AdamKirby 6 86+
(James Eustace) *trckd ldng pair: wnt 2nd and swtchd out rt wl over 1f out: sn rdn and chalng: led ins fnl f: asserted u.p 100yds out: r.o wl: readily* **7/2**[2]

315- **2** 1 ¼ **Cote D'Azur**[229] 6881 3-9-1 69 LukeMorris 4 76
(Sir Mark Prescott Bt) *t.k.h: led: rdn and wnt clr w wnr over 1f out: hdd ins fnl f: styd on same pce fnl 100yds* **7/1**

10-1 **3** 2 **Staintondale Lass (IRE)**[27] 1572 3-9-6 74 OisinMurphy 8 76
(Ed Vaughan) *chsd ldrs: effrt wl over 1f out: chsd clr ldng pair 1f out: styd on u.p: nvr enough pce to chal* **14/1**

10-3 **4** 2 ¼ **Shadow Game**[46] 1176 3-9-5 73 JamesDoyle 1 69
(Mark Johnston) *in tch in midfield: effrt on inner over 1f out: kpt on ins fnl f: no threat to ldrs* **16/1**

03-0 **5** 1 **Claymore (IRE)**[10] 2044 3-9-5 73 ShaneKelly 9 66
(David Lanigan) *in tch in midfield: effrt wl over 1f out: kpt on same pce fr over 1f out: nvr threatened ldr* **10/1**

40-2 **6** ½ **Mithqaal (USA)**[60] 979 3-8-12 66 RobertHavlin 5 58+
(Owen Burrows) *stdd after s: hld up in rr: plenty to do and swtchd rt over 1f out: kpt on ins fnl f: nvr trbld ldrs* **5/1**[3]

2644 **7** hd **Silver Springs (IRE)**[19] 1812 3-8-11 68 PhilipPrince(3) 7 59
(David Evans) *t.k.h: chsd ldr tl wl over 1f out: sn outpcd u.p: wknd ins fnl f* **50/1**

31-2 **8** nse **Cryptic (IRE)**[22] 1703 3-9-5 73 RyanMoore 10 64
(Luca Cumani) *dwlt: sn rcvrd and in tch in midfield: effrt 2f out: no imp and nt clrest of runs over 1f out: wl hld and plugged on same pce fnl f* **7/4**[1]

1-60 **9** 1 ½ **Sweet Temptation (IRE)**[13] 1960 3-9-5 73 AdamBeschizza 3 60
(Stuart Williams) *stdd s: hld up in tch in rr: effrt wl over 1f out: no imp and wl hld fnl f* **66/1**

0-30 **10** 1 **Bingo George (IRE)**[24] 1638 3-9-0 68 DavidProbert 2 52
(Andrew Balding) *hld up in last pair: effrt bnd wl over 1f out: no imp: bhd and wl hld fnl f* **25/1**

1m 23.88s (-0.92) **Going Correction** -0.075s/f (Stan) **10** Ran SP% **116.7**
Speed ratings (Par 99): **102,100,98,95,94 94,93,93,92,90**
CSF £27.97 CT £306.73 TOTE £4.90: £2.00, £2.10, £4.00; EX 33.30 Trifecta £208.00.
Owner Chesneaux, Hassiakos & Littmoden **Bred** Southill Stud **Trained** Newmarket, Suffolk

FOCUS
A useful contest for the grade run at a fair pace. The winner is unexposed and progressing.

2323 RETRAINING OF RACEHORSES H'CAP 1m 2f (P)
4:00 (4:02) (Class 6) (0-55,55) 4-Y-O+ **£2,587** (£770; £384; £192) **Stalls** Low

Form RPR

-653 **1** **Vivo Per Lei (IRE)**[28] 1547 4-8-9 50 GeorgeWood(7) 1 58
(Dr Jon Scargill) *hld up towards rr: stdy hdwy fr 1/2-way: chsd ldrs and swtchd rt over 1f out: rdn to chal between horses 1f out: styd on wl to ld towards fin: rdn out* **12/1**

/6-2 **2** nk **The Bay Bandit**[8] 2110 9-9-3 51 (p) LiamKeniry 5 58
(Neil Mulholland) *hld up in tch in midfield: effrt to chse ldrs 2f out: rdn and ev ch on inner jst over 1f out: led ins fnl f: kpt on wl u.p tl hdd and styd on same pce towards fin* **5/1**[1]

0540 **3** 1 ¾ **Understory (USA)**[69] 870 9-9-2 50 RyanTate 6 54
(Tim McCarthy) *chsd ldrs: wnt 2nd 3f out: rdn and ev ch over 1f out: led jst over 1f out: hdd ins fnl f: outpcd fnl 75yds* **12/1**

6034 **4** 1 ½ **Candesta (USA)**[27] 1578 6-9-6 54 (tp) AdamBeschizza 4 55
(Julia Feilden) *hld up in midfield: nt clr run jst over 2f out: swtchd rt and rallied over 1f out: kpt on u.p ins fnl f: nvr threatened ldrs* **8/1**[2]

4-60 **5** 1 ¼ **Sheikh The Reins (IRE)**[34] 1413 7-9-6 54 KierenFox 3 52
(John Best) *hld up in last pair: hdwy on inner and nt clr run jst over 2f out: rdn and prog over 1f out: kpt on ins fnl f: nvr threatened ldrs* **10/1**[3]

0450 **6** nk **Goodwood Moonlight**[28] 1547 4-9-5 53 (v) AdamKirby 12 51
(Ian Williams) *sn bustled up to ld: rdn 2f out: hdd jst over 1f out: no ex and wknd ins fnl f* **8/1**[2]

043/ **7** 1 ½ **Eugenic**[574] 7346 5-9-5 53 FrederikTylicki 9 48
(Rod Millman) *hld up in tch in midfield: pushed along and lost pl 2f out: rallied and kpt on ins fnl f: no threat to ldrs* **25/1**

035 **8** 1 **Claude Greenwood**[20] 1778 6-9-3 51 (b) RobertHavlin 10 44
(Linda Jewell) *chsd ldng trio: rdn 2f out: outpcd and losing pl whn pushed rt over 1f out: wknd ins fnl f* **25/1**

5-42 **9** hd **Tamujin (IRE)**[14] 1948 8-8-11 50 (b) DavidParkes(5) 11 43
(Ken Cunningham-Brown) *s.i.s: hld up in last quartet: rdn and effrt but stl plenty to do wl over 1f out: sme hdwy fnl f: nvr trbld ldrs* **16/1**

006- **10** 2 ¼ **Gypsy Major**[168] 8069 4-9-2 50 (p) LukeMorris 14 38
(Garry Moss) *t.k.h: wl in tch in midfield: rdn 2f out: no ex u.p and lost pl over 1f out: wknd fnl f* **8/1**[2]

0605 **11** ¾ **Frantical**[14] 1948 4-9-5 53 SilvestreDeSousa 7 40
(Tony Carroll) *t.k.h: hld up in last quartet: plenty to do and swtchd lft wl over 1f out: no imp: n.d* **5/1**[1]

0306 **12** 3 **Silver Lining (IRE)**[20] 1778 4-9-2 55 (t) GaryMahon(5) 8 36
(Mark Hoad) *dwlt: a towards rr: short of room over 5f out: rdn ent fnl 2f: no rspnse: wknd over 1f out* **25/1**

00-5 **13** 1 ¾ **Byrd In Hand (IRE)**[16] 1899 9-9-2 50 WilliamCarson 13 28
(John Bridger) *chsd ldr tl over 3f out: sn rdn: lost pl qckly ent fnl 2f: wknd and bhd ins fnl f* **25/1**

0062 **14** 10 **Rezwaan**[69] 870 9-9-4 52 (b) ShaneKelly 2 11
(Murty McGrath) *stdd s: hld up in rr: hdwy on outer into midfield 1/2-way: rdn and lost pl 3f out: bhd fnl 2f* **12/1**

2m 5.29s (-1.31) **Going Correction** -0.075s/f (Stan) **14** Ran SP% **120.1**
Speed ratings (Par 101): **102,101,100,99,98 97,96,95,95,93 93,90,89,81**
CSF £67.54 CT £736.79 TOTE £13.20: £3.60, £2.20, £4.40; EX 92.40 Trifecta £1358.20.
Owner Kingree Bloodstock **Bred** Des Vere Hunt Farm Co Ltd **Trained** Newmarket, Suffolk

FOCUS
The pace was strong for this modest handicap.

2324 CANTERING CUISINE H'CAP 1m 1y(P)
4:30 (4:30) (Class 4) (0-80,80) 4-Y-O+ **£5,175** (£1,540; £769; £384) **Stalls** High

Form RPR

13-4 **1** **Classical Rose**[22] 1702 4-8-12 71 FrederikTylicki 5 80
(Charlie Fellowes) *hld up in tch in midfield: hdwy to chse ldrs over 1f out: rdn to chal 1f out: sustained effrt and r.o wl to ld towards fin* **8/1**[3]

4413 **2** nk **Golden Wedding (IRE)**[28] 1546 4-8-11 70 (p) CharlesBishop 6 78
(Eve Johnson Houghton) *chsd ldrs: cl 4th and travelling wl 2f out: effrt to chal over 1f out: rdn to ld 1f out: sustained duel w wnr after: hdd and no ex towards fin* **8/1**[3]

0204 **3** 2 **Skidby Mill (IRE)**[11] 2001 6-8-12 71 JimCrowley 10 74
(Laura Mongan) *chsd ldr tl over 6f out: styd chsng ldrs tl wnt 2nd again over 3f out: rdn to ld over 1f out: hdd 1f out: no ex and one pce ins fnl f* **20/1**

00-0 **4** hd **Cricklewood Green (USA)**[20] 1775 5-9-4 77 PatDobbs 8 80
(Sylvester Kirk) *stdd s: hld up in rr: stuck bhd horses over 2f out: rdn and hdwy on inner over 1f out: styd on ins fnl f: nt rch ldrs* **10/1**

0-11 **5** ¾ **Berkeley Vale**[21] 1756 5-9-4 77 (v) RobertWinston 4 78
(Roger Teal) *chsd ldrs: effrt and rdn over 1f out: kpt on ins fnl f: nvr enough pce to rch ldrs* **5/1**[2]

2-15 **6** shd **Bank Of Gibraltar**[48] 1142 4-9-7 80 ShaneKelly 1 80
(Richard Hughes) *stdd s: t.k.h: hld up in last trio: hdwy 3f out: rdn and unable qck wl over 1f out: kpt on ins fnl f: nvr enough pce to threaten ldrs* **5/1**[2]

3435 **7** 1 ¾ **Charlies Mate**[33] 1430 5-9-5 78 KierenFox 7 74
(John Best) *stdd after s: hld up in rr: effrt and swtchd rt over 1f out: kpt on ins fnl f: nvr trbld ldrs* **10/1**

0-51 **8** 2 ¼ **Freewheel (IRE)**[20] 1785 6-9-5 78 AdamKirby 2 69
(Garry Moss) *in tch in midfield: rdn and reminder 4f out: rdn over 2f out: lost pl and no hdwy over 1f out: wl hld fnl f* **11/4**[1]

6531 **9** 1 ¾ **Al's Memory (IRE)**[15] 2079 7-8-2 66 oh1 NoelGarbutt(5) 9 53
(David Evans) *led: rdn and hdd over 1f out: no ex u.p: wknd ins fnl f* **25/1**

0-06 **10** 19 **Firestorm (GER)**[10] 2037 5-9-7 80 RobertHavlin 3 21
(Michael Attwater) *sn bustled up to chse ldr over 6f out: lost 2nd and rdn over 3f out: lost pl and bhd 2f out: eased ins fnl f* **8/1**[3]

1m 36.46s (-1.74) **Going Correction** -0.075s/f (Stan) **10** Ran SP% **120.1**
Speed ratings (Par 105): **105,104,102,102,101 101,99,97,95,76**
CSF £72.60 CT £1276.98 TOTE £11.60: £3.30, £1.90, £4.90; EX 56.60 Trifecta £651.20.
Owner F J Perry **Bred** T M Jennings **Trained** Newmarket, Suffolk

FOCUS
They went a strong pace for this open handicap and a personal best from the winner.

2325 PRIESTLEY H'CAP 1m 1y(P)
5:00 (5:05) (Class 6) (0-60,60) 3-Y-O **£2,587** (£770; £384; £192) **Stalls** High

Form RPR

3264 **1** **Betsalottie**[17] 1860 3-9-3 56 WilliamCarson 4 65
(John Bridger) *mde all: rdn and fnd ex 2f out: clr over 1f out: styd on strly: rdn out* **5/1**[2]

60-0 **2** 3 **Gladys Cooper (IRE)**[36] 1389 3-9-4 57 AntonioFresu 5 59
(Ed Walker) *chsd wnr tl over 5f out: styd chsng ldrs: rdn 2f out: bmpd over 1f out: wnt 3rd 1f out: styd on u.p to go 2nd fnl 75yds: no threat to wnr* **14/1**

2132 **3** ½ **Music Major**[20] 1792 3-9-3 56 AdamBeschizza 10 57+
(Michael Attwater) *hld up in tch in last trio: hdwy 2f out: nt clr run and swtchd lft over 1f out: styd on wl u.p ins fnl f: no threat to wnr* **7/2**[1]

00-0 **4** ¾ **Broughtons Mystery**[20] 1792 3-9-2 55 LukeMorris 2 54
(Willie Musson) *hld up in midfield: rdn and effrt 2f out: hdwy over 1f out: styd on u.p ins fnl f: no threat to wnr* **14/1**

500 **5** 1 ¾ **Dalavand (IRE)**[22] 1701 3-9-7 60 TimmyMurphy 9 55+
(Jamie Osborne) *dwlt: in tch in midfield but stuck wd: rdn 2f out: styd on same pce fnl f* **16/1**

0-01 **6** nse **Zebedee's Son (IRE)**[31] 1486 3-8-10 56 (p) RhiainIngram(7) 1 51
(Roger Ingram) *chsd ldrs: effrt to chse clr wnr 2f out: no imp: lost 2nd and wknd fnl 75yds* **14/1**

00-0 **7** 1 ¼ **Rosie's Vision**[21] 1734 3-8-9 53 [1] RachealKneller(5) 6 45
(Mark Usher) *hld up in last pair: rdn and hdwy on inner over 1f out: no imp u.p fnl f: nvr trbld ldrs* **33/1**

060- **8** 1 **Lazizah**[221] 7077 3-9-2 58 LouisSteward(3) 12 47+
(Marcus Tregoning) *stdd s: hld up in rr: stl plenty whn swtchd lft and effrt over 1f out: sn rdn and no hdwy: n.d* **10/1**

4024 **9** ½ **Espoir**[21] 1734 3-9-0 **53**....................(v[1]) CathyGannon 3 44+
(David Evans) *hld up in midfield: short of room and lost pl over 3f out: nvr much room and hmpd again over 2f out: no ch fnl f* **14/1**

30-5 **10** 1¼ **Monday Club**[21] 1734 3-9-5 **58**.................... AdamKirby 8 43
(Dominic Ffrench Davis) *chsd ldrs: effrt u.p to press ldrs 2f out: outpcd and btn over 1f out: wknd fnl f* **8/1**

000- **11** 1¾ **Just Fred (IRE)**[153] 8245 3-9-4 **57**.................... OisinMurphy 7 38
(Denis Coakley) *in tch in midfield: effrt whn short of room and hmpd over 1f out: sn btn and wknd fnl f* **8/1**

0-36 **12** 1½ **Girl With A Pearl (IRE)**[19] 1816 3-9-7 **60**..........(b[1]) SilvestreDeSousa 11 37
(Ed Dunlop) *t.k.h: chsd wnr over 5f out tl 2f out: losing pl whn bmpd over 1f out: sn bhd* **6/1**[3]

1m 38.97s (0.77) **Going Correction** -0.075s/f (Stan) **12** Ran SP% **120.0**
Speed ratings (Par 97): **93,90,89,88,87 86,85,84,84,82 81,79**
CSF £74.21 CT £284.01 TOTE £6.30: £1.90, £5.70, £1.80; EX 87.70 Trifecta £529.20.
Owner Mrs Liz Gardner **Bred** P A & M J Reditt & Catridge Stud **Trained** Liphook, Hants

FOCUS
An open contest.

2326 TTS NETWORKS APPRENTICE H'CAP 1m 4f (P)
5:35 (5:35) (Class 6) (0-60,60) 4-Y-O+ **£2,587** (£770; £384; £192) **Stalls** Low

Form RPR

6431 **1** **Bamako Du Chatelet (FR)**[21] 1748 5-9-10 **60**........(p) MarcMonaghan 6 72
(Ian Williams) *chsd ldrs: effrt and rdn to chal between rivals over 1f out: led jst ins fnl f: r.o strly and drew clr: readily* **2/1**[1]

1361 **2** 3½ **Henry Smith**[8] 2110 4-9-5 **60** 6ex....................(be) GeorgeWood[(5)] 7 66
(Garry Moss) *chsd ldr: rdn to ld 2f out: sddle slipped over 1f out: hdd jst ins fnl f: sn outpcd: kpt on for clr 2nd* **4/1**[3]

4000 **3** 2¼ **Bennelong**[11] 2006 10-9-3 **56**....................(b) RhiainIngram[(3)] 3 58
(Lee Carter) *hld up in tch in midfield: effrt in 5th 2f out: no imp: wnt 3rd wl ins fnl f: kpt on but no threat to ldrs* **33/1**

2302 **4** 1½ **Sudden Wish (IRE)**[21] 1748 7-9-5 **55**.................... KieranShoemark 8 55
(Michael Attwater) *chsd ldrs: effrt ent fnl 2f: unable qck and outpcd over 1f out: wl hld and plugged on same pce fnl f* **12/1**

-010 **5** ¾ **Fleetwood Poppy**[21] 1748 4-8-13 **49**.................... ThomasBrown 12 48
(Michael Attwater) *led: edgd lft 9f out: rdn and hdd 2f out: no ex and btn 3rd 1f out: wknd ins fnl f* **33/1**

-030 **6** *hd* **Machiavelian Storm (IRE)**[27] 1578 4-8-5 **46** oh1....... LuluStanford[(5)] 9 44
(Richard Mitchell) *hld up in tch in midfield: rdn in 6th 2f out: no imp: wl hld whn swtchd lft 1f out: plugged on same pce* **25/1**

-655 **7** ½ **Dukes Den**[28] 1550 5-8-11 **54**.................... JaneElliott[(7)] 1 52
(Mark Usher) *hld up in last quartet: effrt 2f out: no imp and wl hld 1f out* **20/1**

215- **8** ½ **Cabuchon (GER)**[202] 7566 9-8-10 **56**....................(vt) AledBeech[(10)] 5 53
(David Evans) *stdd s: hld up in last quartet: stl lots to do and rdn over 1f out: no prog: n.d* **20/1**

600 **9** 6 **Munsarim (IRE)**[18] 1834 9-9-4 **57**....................(v) PaddyBradley[(3)] 4 44
(Lee Carter) *s.i.s: hld up in rr and nvr on terms: hung rt bnd 2f out: no ch after* **33/1**

0640 **10** *nse* **Opera Buff**[32] 1450 7-8-13 **59**....................(p) CharlotteClayton[(10)] 11 46
(Rae Guest) *racd wd: midfield tl dropped to last pair 5f out: wd and lost tch bnd 2f out* **16/1**

4431 **U** **Dynamo (IRE)**[19] 1807 5-8-7 **53**.................... StephanieJoannides[(10)] 10
(Richard Hughes) *bustled along leaving stalls: pressed ldrs tl squeezed for room: clipped heels: stmbld and uns rdr 9f out* **9/4**[2]

2m 32.38s (-0.62) **Going Correction** -0.075s/f (Stan) **11** Ran SP% **119.9**
Speed ratings (Par 101): **99,96,95,94,93 93,93,92,88,88**
CSF £9.46 CT £191.91 TOTE £2.90: £1.50, £1.90, £9.00; EX 12.70 Trifecta £313.90.
Owner Macable Partnership **Bred** S N C Ecurie Jouenne Gerard **Trained** Portway, Worcs

FOCUS
A competitive race for the grade run at a fair pace.
T/Jkpt: Not won. T/Plt: £61.50 to a £1 stake. Pool: £62,631.87 - 742.76 winning tickets. T/Qpdt: £46.40 to a £1 stake. Pool: £5,126.07 - 81.6 winning tickets. **Steve Payne**

NEWCASTLE (A.W) (L-H)
Tuesday, May 17

OFFICIAL GOING: Tapeta: standard
Wind: Breezy, half against Weather: Overcast, dry

2327 EXTRA PLACE BETTING AT 188BET MAIDEN STKS 1m 2f 42y (Tp)
2:00 (2:00) (Class 5) 3-Y-O **£3,881** (£1,155; £577; £288) **Stalls** High

Form RPR

05-4 **1** **Tap The Honey**[10] 2048 3-9-5 72.................... JoeyHaynes 3 84
(K R Burke) *t.k.h early: trckd ldrs: hdwy to ld 3f out: pushed clr fr over 1f out: unchal* **9/1**

25 **2** 4½ **Kings Gold (IRE)**[26] 1589 3-9-5 0.................... ConnorBeasley 11 75
(Michael Dods) *s.i.s: hld up: stdy hdwy 3f out: effrt and chsd (clr) wnr appr fnl f: hung lft: sn no imp* **13/2**

3 2¼ **Gibbs Hill (GER)** 3-9-5 0.................... AndreaAtzeni 6 71+
(Roger Varian) *rn green in midfield: stdy hdwy over 3f out: effrt and chsd (clr) wnr briefly over 1f out: kpt on same pce fnl f* **9/2**[3]

05- **4** 3¼ **Silva Eclipse**[204] 7518 3-9-5 0.................... GrahamLee 10 64
(Jedd O'Keeffe) *t.k.h: chsd ldrs: drvn and outpcd 2f out: kpt on ins fnl f: nvr rchd ldrs* **16/1**

323 **5** ¾ **Steccando (IRE)**[16] 1883 3-9-5 78.................... BenCurtis 7 63
(Alan Swinbank) *hld up on outside: stdy hdwy and prom over 2f out: sn rdn: wknd ins fnl f* **5/2**[1]

554 **6** 2 **The Magic Pencil (IRE)**[74] 818 3-9-5 69.................... ShaneGray 12 59+
(Kevin Ryan) *racd wd: prom: rdn along over 2f out: wknd over 1f out* **7/1**

7 *nse* **Jetstream Express (IRE)** 3-9-0 0.................... EdwardGreatrex[(5)] 9 58+
(Simon Crisford) *t.k.h: cl up: hung rt bnd over 4f out: rallied and ev ch 3f out: wknd over 1f out* **7/2**[2]

8 24 **Percy's Endeavour** 3-9-0 0.................... JasonHart 8
(Mark Walford) *s.i.s: hld up: outpcd and rn green 3f out: sn btn* **25/1**

0 **9** 4 **My Brown Eyed Girl**[42] 1246 3-8-9 0.................... GarryWhillans[(5)] 4
(Susan Corbett) *midfield: drvn and outpcd over 3f out: btn fnl 2f* **100/1**

0-00 **10** 20 **Don't Tell Nik (IRE)**[27] 1562 3-9-0 40.................... RaulDaSilva 2
(David Loughnane) *led tl rdn and hdd 3f out: sn wknd* **200/1**

060- **11** 15 **Harly Forest**[255] 6096 3-9-0 0....................(b[1]) CallumShepherd[(5)] 5
(Brian Ellison) *bhd: struggling 1/2-way: nvr on terms* **150/1**

2m 10.9s (0.50) **Going Correction** 0.0s/f (Stan) **11** Ran SP% **116.7**
Speed ratings (Par 99): **98,94,92,90,89 87,87,68,65,49 37**
CSF £65.41 TOTE £11.30: £2.50, £2.60, £1.60; EX 85.20 Trifecta £465.70.
Owner Mrs Elaine M Burke **Bred** Laundry Cottage Stud Farm **Trained** Middleham Moor, N Yorks

FOCUS
There will be no speed figures here until there is sufficient data to calculate median times. The first meeting to take place here on the new Tapeta surface. The going was described as standard and likely to ride slightly slower than the Tapeta course at Wolverhampton. A fair maiden, and a winner who has the potential to climb up the ranks.

2328 BEST ODDS GUARANTEED AT 188BET H'CAP 1m 2f 42y (Tp)
2:35 (2:35) (Class 4) (0-85,85) 4-Y-O+ **£6,469** (£1,925; £962; £481) **Stalls** High

Form RPR

3-31 **1** **Tawdeea**[16] 1883 4-9-7 **85**.................... SamJames 7 94+
(David O'Meara) *hld up in midfield: hdwy over 2f out: chsd ldrs over 1f out: edgd lft and led last 150yds: kpt on strly* **9/1**

13-0 **2** 1½ **Demonstration (IRE)**[17] 1861 4-9-5 **83**....................(p) JoeFanning 11 89
(William Jarvis) *led: rdn over 2f out: hdd last 150yds: kpt on: nt pce of wnr* **13/2**[2]

-133 **3** 1¾ **Muntadab (IRE)**[15] 1924 4-9-5 **83**.................... RaulDaSilva 14 86
(David Loughnane) *t.k.h early: trckd ldrs: hdwy and ev ch over 2f out to ins fnl f: no ex nr fin* **8/1**[3]

-450 **4** *nse* **Top Of The Glas (IRE)**[12] 1978 5-8-9 **78**.............. CallumShepherd[(5)] 5 80
(Brian Ellison) *t.k.h: prom: drvn and outpcd over 3f out: rallied over 1f out: kpt on ins fnl f: nt rch ldrs* **13/2**[2]

-131 **5** ¾ **Chilworth Bells**[14] 1952 4-8-8 **77**.................... JosephineGordon[(5)] 6 78
(David Barron) *midfield: rdn and outpcd over 3f out: rallied over 1f out: kpt on fnl f: no imp* **10/1**

0060 **6** 1¼ **Peterhouse (USA)**[15] 1923 4-8-12 **76**....................(p) BenCurtis 4 74
(Jason Ward) *t.k.h: hld up: rdn and effrt on outside over 2f out: kpt on fnl f: no imp* **25/1**

051- **7** 1½ **Optima Petamus**[218] 7169 4-9-2 **80**.................... JackGarritty 9 75
(Patrick Holmes) *hld up: rdn and outpcd 3f out: hdwy over 1f out: kpt on: nvr rchd ldrs* **33/1**

3421 **8** 2¾ **Off The Pulse**[24] 1652 6-9-2 **80**....................(p) GrahamGibbons 2 70
(John Mackie) *hld up on ins: drvn and outpcd wl over 2f out: n.d after* **8/1**[3]

00-0 **9** 2¼ **Monsieur Chevalier (IRE)**[117] 266 9-8-11 **80**(p) RachelRichardson[(5)] 12 65
(Lucinda Egerton) *s.i.s: hld up: effrt on outside 3f out: outpcd fnl 2f* **50/1**

121 **10** 12 **Biff Johnson (IRE)**[78] 766 4-9-4 **82**....................(p) PhillipMakin 10 43
(Keith Dalgleish) *pressed ldr: rdn and ev ch briefly 2f out: wknd wl over 1f out* **7/2**[1]

4326 **11** 5 **Air Of Astana (IRE)**[24] 1651 4-9-3 **81**.................... GrahamLee 1 32
(Hugo Palmer) *prom: pushed along over 2f out: wknd wl over 1f out* **13/2**[2]

50-4 **12** 12 **Arabian Oasis**[17] 1853 4-9-0 **78**.................... PJMcDonald 3 5
(Philip Kirby) *midfield: drvn and outpcd over 3f out: btn fnl 2f* **16/1**

-200 **13** 3¼ **Polar Forest**[11] 2017 6-9-2 **85**....................(e) EdwardGreatrex[(5)] 8 6
(Richard Guest) *hld up: struggling over 3f out: sn btn* **16/1**

2m 8.91s (-1.49) **Going Correction** 0.0s/f (Stan) **13** Ran SP% **124.0**
Speed ratings (Par 105): **105,103,102,102,101 100,99,97,95,85 81,72,69**
CSF £68.14 CT £502.72 TOTE £9.40: £3.10, £1.90, £2.90; EX 73.70 Trifecta £579.80.
Owner Middleham Park Racing LXVI **Bred** Shadwell Estate Company Limited **Trained** Upper Helmsley, N Yorks

FOCUS
A competitive handicap. They appeared to go fairly steady early and the pace held up.

2329 TAPETA FOOTINGS H'CAP (DIV I) 1m 5y (Tp)
3:05 (3:07) (Class 6) (0-60,60) 4-Y-O+ **£3,234** (£962; £481; £240) **Stalls** Centre

Form RPR

50-0 **1** **Barwah (USA)**[10] 2053 5-8-9 **48**.................... JackGarritty 5 62
(Peter Niven) *hld up: smooth hdwy over 2f out: led over 1f out: drvn and hld on wl fnl f* **10/1**

3122 **2** ½ **Affectionate Lady (IRE)**[15] 1926 5-8-10 **49**..................(b) JoeFanning 9 62
(Keith Reveley) *hld up: smooth hdwy to ld briefly over 1f out: sn rdn: kpt on fnl f: hld towards fin* **7/2**[1]

46-0 **3** 2½ **City Of Night (IRE)**[51] 1117 4-9-4 **57**....................(e[1]) ConnorBeasley 4 64
(Julie Camacho) *hld up on far side of gp: hdwy whn nt clr run and swtchd lft over 1f out: kpt on ins fnl f: nt pce to chal* **12/1**

6244 **4** *shd* **Kicking The Can (IRE)**[39] 1323 5-9-6 **59**.................... JamesSullivan 3 66
(David Thompson) *prom on far side of gp: rdn and effrt 2f out: kpt on same pce ins fnl f* **7/1**[2]

060- **5** 2¾ **Nelson's Bay**[207] 7427 7-8-13 **59**.................... HollieDoyle[(7)] 1 60
(Wilf Storey) *hld up: pushed along over 3f out: hdwy over 1f out: edgd lft: kpt on same pce fnl f* **10/1**

0-00 **6** 2¾ **Reflation**[22] 1692 4-9-0 **58**....................(p) PhilDennis[(5)] 14 53
(Michael Dods) *dwlt: t.k.h and sn midfield: drvn over 1f out: outpcd fnl f* **20/1**

00-5 **7** *nk* **Steel Stockholder**[63] 939 10-9-7 **60**.................... DavidAllan 6 54
(Antony Brittain) *cl up: led over 2f out to over 1f out: wknd ins fnl f* **20/1**

1-10 **8** ¾ **Thello**[119] 247 4-8-10 **56**.................... KieranSchofield[(7)] 11 49+
(Nigel Tinkler) *cl up: rdn and ev ch over 2f out: wknd over 1f out* **7/1**[2]

551- **9** 2¼ **Glasgon**[214] 7264 6-9-0 **60**.................... RowanScott[(7)] 10 48
(Ray Craggs) *w ldrs: led 1/2-way to over 2f out: wknd over 1f out* **9/1**

02-2 **10** 4½ **Applejack Lad**[27] 1560 5-9-6 **59**....................(tp) GrahamLee 13 37+
(Michael Smith) *chsd ldrs on nr side of gp: rdn over 2f out: wknd over 1f out* **8/1**[3]

-303 **11** 14 **Lendal Bridge**[18] 1845 5-8-12 **51**.................... DuranFentiman 8
(Tony Coyle) *t.k.h early: prom on nr side of gp: drvn over 3f out: wknd over 2f out* **14/1**

0-06 **12** 1¼ **Last Wish (IRE)**[18] 1841 5-9-2 **55**.................... JasonHart 7
(Richard Guest) *sn rdn along and cl up: lost pl qckly over 3f out: sn btn* **20/1**

06-0 **13** *shd* **Morocco**[45] 1201 7-9-3 **56**....................(b[1]) SamJames 12 +
(Karen Tutty) *led on nr side of gp to 1/2-way: sn lost pl and struggling* **33/1**

05-0 **14** 40 **Glen Lea (IRE)**[36] 1378 7-8-10 **49**.................... JoeyHaynes 2
(Kenny Johnson) *bhd: struggling 1/2-way: sn lost tch: t.o* **66/1**

1m 41.69s (3.09) **Going Correction** +0.175s/f (Slow) **14** Ran SP% **119.6**
Speed ratings (Par 101): **91,90,88,87,85 82,82,81,79,74 60,59,59,19**
CSF £41.51 CT £438.13 TOTE £11.70: £4.10, £1.50, £5.60; EX 57.20 Trifecta £774.90.
Owner Keep The Faith Partnership **Bred** Shadwell Farm LLC **Trained** Barton-le-Street, N Yorks

FOCUS
An ordinary handicap. The first three were held up towards the back early on.

2330 TAPETA FOOTINGS H'CAP (DIV II) 1m 5y (Tp)
3:40 (3:41) (Class 6) (0-60,60) 4-Y-O+ **£3,234** (£962; £481; £240) **Stalls** Centre

Form RPR
4-40 **1** **Legal Art**[25] 1600 4-9-3 **56** BenCurtis 9 63+
(Brian Ellison) *hld up: smooth hdwy on nr side of gp over 2f out: led over 1f out: drvn and hld on wl fnl f* **14/1**
2530 **2** *1 1/4* **Grey Destiny**[31] 1502 6-9-6 **59** PJMcDonald 12 63
(Antony Brittain) *hld up: stdy hdwy gng wl over 2f out: rdn over 1f out: kpt on to take 2nd towards fin: nt rch wnr* **17/2**
5005 **3** *nk* **Illusive Force (IRE)**[24] 1654 4-8-11 **55**(v[1]) CallumShepherd[(5)] 4 59
(Derek Shaw) *prom: led gng wl over 2f out: sn rdn: hdd over 1f out: one pce ins fnl f: no ex and lost 2nd cl home* **11/1**
-030 **4** *1/2* **Illustrious Prince (IRE)**[15] 1925 9-9-5 **58** ConnorBeasley 7 60
(Julie Camacho) *hld up in midfield: effrt and rdn on far side over gp over 2f out: hdwy over 1f out: kpt on ins fnl f* **11/1**
320- **5** *1 1/4* **Life Knowledge (IRE)**[238] 6618 4-9-7 **60** DavidNolan 8 60
(Patrick Holmes) *hld up: hdwy and prom over 2f out: sn rdn: kpt on same pce fnl f* **13/2**[3]
4046 **6** *1/2* **Incurs Four Faults**[22] 1695 5-9-1 **54** GrahamLee 2 53
(Keith Dalgleish) *w ldrs on far side of gp to over 2f out: rdn and wknd fnl f* **8/1**
00-0 **7** *1 1/4* **Galilee Chapel (IRE)**[22] 1696 7-8-9 **48**(b) BarryMcHugh 13 44
(Alistair Whillans) *dwlt: hld up: hdwy and rdn over 2f out: no imp fr over 1f out* **18/1**
056- **8** *1 1/2* **Who's Shirl**[200] 7602 10-9-6 **59** AndrewElliott 5 52
(Chris Fairhurst) *prom 2f: sn lost pl: edgd lft and rallied over 1f out: no imp fnl f* **28/1**
0-30 **9** *1 1/4* **Graceful Act**[23] 1676 8-8-8 **47** RoystonFfrench 10 37
(Ron Barr) *hld up on nr side of gp: drvn and outpcd over 3f out: n.d after* **33/1**
604 **10** *1/2* **Outlaw Torn (IRE)**[24] 1654 7-9-6 **59**(e) JasonHart 3 48
(Richard Guest) *disp ld to over 2f out: drvn and wknd over 1f out* **4/1**[1]
0620 **11** *4 1/2* **Atreus**[8] 2096 4-9-6 **59** GrahamGibbons 1 38
(Michael Easterby) *led towards far side of gp: rdn and hdd over 2f out: wknd over 1f out* **6/1**[2]
040- **12** *13* **Riponian**[271] 5553 6-8-12 **51** JoeyHaynes 14 6
(Susan Corbett) *cl up on nr side of gp to 1/2-way: sn drvn and lost pl: btn over 2f out: eased whn no ch* **25/1**
00-0 **13** *1 1/2* **Regal Missile (IRE)**[45] 1202 4-9-4 **57**(b[1]) PhillipMakin 11 9
(Mark Walford) *prom: rdn along over 3f out: sn outpcd: btn and eased fr 2f out* **16/1**
030/ **14** *nk* **Wild Hill Boy**[621] 6074 6-8-10 **49** DavidAllan 6
(David C Griffiths) *midfield on far side of gp: rdn sn after 1/2-way: wknd over 2f out* **25/1**

1m 41.52s (2.92) **Going Correction** +0.175s/f (Slow) **14** Ran SP% **117.8**
Speed ratings (Par 101): **92,90,90,89,88 88,86,85,84,83 79,66,64,64**
CSF £120.37 CT £1403.99 TOTE £12.80: £3.80, £2.20, £3.10; EX 89.80 Trifecta £2839.10.
Owner Kristian Strangeway **Bred** The Sakal Family **Trained** Norton, N Yorks
■ Stewards' Enquiry : Ben Curtis caution: careless riding

FOCUS
The faster of the two divisions by 0.17sec. Again it paid to be held up.

2331 188BET.CO.UK H'CAP 7f 14y (Tp)
4:10 (4:11) (Class 3) (0-95,95) 3-Y-O+ **£12,938** (£3,850; £1,924; £962) **Stalls** Centre

Form RPR
4-23 **1** **Turbine (IRE)**[11] 1991 3-8-8 **86** JoeFanning 1 93
(Mark Johnston) *cl up on far side of gp: led over 2f out: shkn up over 1f out: kpt on wl fnl f* **4/1**[2]
10-1 **2** *1* **Peril**[99] 503 5-9-9 **95** EdwardGreatrex[(5)] 12 103
(Simon Crisford) *dwlt: sn pushed along in rr: hdwy on nr side of gp to chse wnr over 1f out: kpt on ins fnl f: nt pce to chal* **11/8**[1]
-300 **3** *1 1/4* **Lat Hawill (IRE)**[45] 1196 5-10-0 **95** PhillipMakin 10 100
(Keith Dalgleish) *hld up in tch: stdy hdwy over 2f out: effrt and rdn over 1f out: kpt on same pce ins fnl f* **14/1**
0-50 **4** *1 1/4* **Fullon Clarets**[27] 1563 4-9-0 **81** DavidNolan 9 83
(Richard Fahey) *cl up: rdn over 2f out: edgd lft fr over 1f out: kpt on same pce fnl f* **14/1**
43-0 **5** *nk* **Gerry The Glover (IRE)**[27] 1563 4-9-7 **88** DaleSwift 13 89
(Brian Ellison) *hld up bhd ldng gp towards nr side: drvn and hdwy over 2f out: no imp over 1f out* **16/1**
0-04 **6** *hd* **Tiger Jim**[17] 1848 6-9-1 **82** JackGarritty 7 82
(Jim Goldie) *dwlt: bhd: rdn along over 2f out: hdwy over 1f out: nt pce to chal* **9/1**
15- **7** *1/2* **Wall Of Fire (IRE)**[249] 6274 3-9-0 **92**(b[1]) GrahamLee 11 87
(Hugo Palmer) *hld up: pushed along and outpcd over 3f out: rallied fnl f: no imp* **12/1**
-033 **8** *nse* **Gurkha Friend**[14] 1954 4-8-9 **81** oh2 NathanEvans[(5)] 8 80
(Karen McLintock) *led to over 2f out: rallied: outpcd whn n.m.r ins fnl f* **20/1**
2/05 **9** *hd* **Shouranour (IRE)**[24] 1643 6-9-0 **81** oh1(p) BenCurtis 2 79
(Alan Brown) *prom on far side of gp: drvn along over 2f out: wknd ins fnl f* **40/1**
3-51 **10** *1 1/2* **Finn Class (IRE)**[17] 1871 5-9-10 **91** ConnorBeasley 6 85
(Michael Dods) *trckd ldrs: drvn and outpcd wl over 2f out: n.d after* **8/1**[3]

1m 25.03s (-1.17) **Going Correction** +0.175s/f (Slow)
WFA 3 from 4yo+ 11lb **10** Ran SP% **117.3**
Speed ratings (Par 107): **113,111,110,109,108 108,107,107,107,105**
CSF £9.89 CT £70.80 TOTE £4.80: £1.70, £1.60, £4.60; EX 11.50 Trifecta £163.70.
Owner Sheikh Hamdan bin Mohammed Al Maktoum **Bred** Nanallac Stud **Trained** Middleham Moor, N Yorks

FOCUS
A decent handicap and a good performance by the winner, who recorded a personal best.

2332 MOBILE BETTING AT 188BET H'CAP 6f (Tp)
4:40 (4:43) (Class 5) (0-70,70) 4-Y-O+ **£4,528** (£1,347; £673; £336) **Stalls** Centre

Form RPR
-000 **1** **Orion's Bow**[17] 1869 5-9-6 **69** RoystonFfrench 12 85
(David Nicholls) *t.k.h: in tch: smooth hdwy to ld over 1f out: rdn clr fnl f* **4/1**[1]
0201 **2** *3 3/4* **Lucky Lodge**[31] 1496 6-9-4 **67**(p) DuranFentiman 8 71
(Antony Brittain) *hld up: pushed along over 2f out: hdwy over 1f out: kpt on to take 2nd nr fin: no ch w wnr* **9/1**
2-30 **3** *shd* **American Hustle (IRE)**[24] 1631 4-9-2 **65**(p) BenCurtis 11 69
(Brian Ellison) *led tl rdn and hdd over 1f out: kpt on fnl f: no ex and lost 2nd cl home* **17/2**
-004 **4** *nk* **Exotic Guest**[22] 1692 6-8-13 **62**(p) JackGarritty 5 65
(Ruth Carr) *hld up: rdn and hdwy on nr side of gp over 1f out: kpt on ins fnl f: nrst fin* **8/1**[3]
4340 **5** *3* **National Service (USA)**[15] 1925 5-9-2 **65**(tp) JoeFanning 3 58
(Rebecca Menzies) *hld up in tch towards far side: stdy hdwy over 2f out: effrt over 1f out: outpcd fnl f* **8/1**[3]
2630 **6** *2 1/4* **Gold Beau (FR)**[34] 1415 6-9-4 **67**(p) ShaneGray 14 53
(Kristin Stubbs) *prom on nr side of gp: drvn along 1/2-way: no imp fr over 1f out* **14/1**
30-0 **7** *1 1/2* **Star Cracker (IRE)**[22] 1692 4-9-2 **65**(p) PhillipMakin 7 46
(Jim Goldie) *t.k.h: hld up: effrt and edgd lft wl over 1f out: sn no imp* **18/1**
6-04 **8** *1/2* **Percy's Gal**[35] 1402 5-9-2 **70** GemmaTutty[(5)] 13 50
(Karen Tutty) *t.k.h: prom on nr side of gp: drvn and outpcd wl over 1f out: n.d after* **25/1**
00-6 **9** *1 1/2* **Fleurtille**[25] 1600 7-9-2 **65**(p) ConnorBeasley 6 40
(Ray Craggs) *prom towards far side of gp: drvn along over 2f out: wknd over 1f out* **28/1**
1550 **10** *3/4* **Kyllach Me (IRE)**[31] 1496 4-8-13 **62**(b) SamJames 10 34
(Bryan Smart) *hld up: rdn along over 2f out: nvr rchd ldrs* **20/1**
4331 **11** *hd* **Malaysian Boleh**[20] 1781 6-9-1 **69**(b) CallumShepherd[(5)] 9 41
(Shaun Lycett) *trckd ldrs: drvn along 1/2-way: wknd over 1f out* **7/1**[2]
1032 **12** *hd* **Monsieur Jimmy**[10] 2053 4-9-5 **68**(b) DavidAllan 2 39
(Declan Carroll) *cl up: rdn and ev ch over 2f out: wknd fnl f* **17/2**
06-5 **13** *1* **Pryers Princess**[38] 1334 4-9-3 **66** JasonHart 4 34
(David C Griffiths) *s.i.s: hld up: effrt on nr side of gp over 2f out: sn btn* **22/1**
5534 **14** *11* **Llewellyn**[19] 1818 8-9-0 **70**(b) GerO'Neill[(7)] 1
(Declan Carroll) *racd on far side of gp: t.k.h: cl up tl rdn and wknd fr 2f out* **14/1**

1m 13.01s (0.51) **Going Correction** +0.175s/f (Slow) **14** Ran SP% **120.8**
Speed ratings (Par 103): **103,98,97,97,93 90,88,87,85,84 84,84,82,68**
CSF £37.24 CT £297.54 TOTE £5.60: £2.50, £2.70, £2.40; EX 52.00 Trifecta £414.60.
Owner T J Swiers **Bred** Cheveley Park Stud Ltd **Trained** Sessay, N Yorks

FOCUS
A modest sprint handicap won by the gambled-on favourite, who has been rated back to his early 3yo form.

2333 188BET DAILY HORSE RACING CHARTER MAIDEN STKS 5f (Tp)
5:10 (5:13) (Class 5) 3-Y-O **£3,881** (£1,155; £577; £288) **Stalls** Centre

Form RPR
3 **1** **Alsvinder**[23] 1669 3-9-5 0 DavidNolan 12 85+
(David O'Meara) *trckd ldrs on nr side of gp: rdn to ld over 1f out: kpt on strly fnl f* **13/8**[1]
2 *1 1/2* **Acclaim The Nation (IRE)** 3-9-5 0 JasonHart 7 80
(Eric Alston) *t.k.h: trckd ldrs: effrt and ev ch over 1f out: kpt on same pce last 100yds* **5/1**[3]
5 **3** *3 3/4* **Ryedale Rio (IRE)**[44] 1216 3-9-5 0 DavidAllan 3 67
(Tim Easterby) *t.k.h: cl up on outside of gp: ev ch over 2f out: kpt on same pce fr over 1f out* **25/1**
33 **4** *1* **Tommy G**[24] 1622 3-9-5 0 PhillipMakin 10 63
(Jim Goldie) *hld up bhd ldng gp: pushed along and effrt over 1f out: kpt on fnl f: nvr able to chal* **11/2**
03- **5** *nk* **First Rate**[212] 7310 3-9-5 0 AndreaAtzeni 5 62
(Roger Varian) *led tl rdn and hdd over 1f out: wknd ins fnl f* **9/4**[2]
6 **6** *3/4* **Wishing Tree**[23] 1669 3-9-0 0 DaleSwift 8 54
(Brian Ellison) *in tch: rdn over 2f out: outpcd fnl f* **25/1**
7 *1* **Jabbarockie** 3-9-5 0 RaulDaSilva 6 56
(Paul Green) *s.i.s: hld up: rdn and hung to far side over 2f out: btn over 1f out* **16/1**
0-06 **8** *8* **Bazula (IRE)**[17] 1870 3-9-5 0 DuranFentiman 9 28
(Tim Easterby) *trckd ldrs: drvn along over 2f out: wknd wl over 1f out* **66/1**
000 **9** *6* **Temujins Quest (IRE)**[23] 1669 3-9-5 0(v[1]) JackGarritty 2 7
(Derek Shaw) *s.i.s: sn wl bhd: no ch fr 1/2-way* **125/1**

1m 0.01s (0.51) **Going Correction** +0.175s/f (Slow) **9** Ran SP% **116.8**
Speed ratings (Par 99): **102,99,93,92,91 90,88,75,66**
CSF £10.23 TOTE £2.60: £1.30, £1.80, £3.30; EX 12.10 Trifecta £151.10.
Owner F Gillespie **Bred** Northern Bloodstock Inc **Trained** Upper Helmsley, N Yorks

FOCUS
A fair maiden, and the first two look to have a future.

2334 MOBILE BETTING AT 188BET FILLIES' H'CAP 5f (Tp)
5:45 (5:46) (Class 5) (0-70,70) 3-Y-O+ **£3,881** (£1,155; £577; £288) **Stalls** Centre

Form RPR
651- **1** **Coto (IRE)**[15] 1937 4-9-1 **64** CallumShepherd[(5)] 4 78
(M J Tynan, Ire) *hld up in tch on far side of gp: smooth hdwy over 1f out: led ins fnl f: rdn and r.o wl* **5/1**[3]
0-04 **2** *2* **Poppy In The Wind**[10] 2053 4-9-1 **59**(v) PhillipMakin 2 66
(Alan Brown) *cl up on far side of gp: hdwy to ld appr fnl f: hdd ins fnl f: kpt on same pce* **16/1**
321- **3** *1 1/4* **Rose Marmara**[217] 7184 3-9-4 **70** DavidNolan 5 70
(Richard Fahey) *prom towards far side of gp: smooth hdwy over 2f out: rdn and effrt over 1f out: one pce fnl f* **8/1**
33-0 **4** *1 1/4* **Ulfah Dream**[11] 2004 3-9-2 **68** PaoloSirigu 1 63
(Marco Botti) *led on far side of gp: rdn and hdd appr fnl f: sn outpcd* **20/1**
600- **5** *4* **Mayfield Girl (IRE)**[189] 7789 6-8-13 **57** DuranFentiman 3 41
(Antony Brittain) *cl up on far side of gp: rdn over 2f out: wknd fnl f* **25/1**
15-0 **6** *nk* **Miningg old**[20] 1789 3-9-1 **67** JackGarritty 10 47+
(Tim Easterby) *hmpd s: bhd centre: rdn and hdwy over 1f out: nvr rchd ldrs* **22/1**
5561 **7** *1 1/2* **Your Gifted (IRE)**[22] 1721 9-9-7 **65**(v) RaulDaSilva 12 43+
(Lisa Williamson) *wnt lft and blkd s: hld up centre: rdn over 1f out: nt pce to chal* **10/1**
0-22 **8** *1/2* **Chookie's Lass**[22] 1692 5-9-6 **64** JasonHart 8 40
(Keith Dalgleish) *prom centre: rdn over 2f out: btn over 1f out* **9/2**[2]
-221 **9** *2* **Fumbo Jumbo (IRE)**[18] 1839 3-9-2 **68** DavidAllan 7 34
(Garry Moss) *in tch centre: drvn along 1/2-way: sn wknd* **10/3**[1]
4-52 **10** *1 3/4* **Misu Moneypenny**[17] 1872 3-9-4 **70**(p) DaleSwift 9 30
(Scott Dixon) *wnt rt and bmpd s: bhd on nr side of gp: drvn over 2f out: sn btn* **8/1**
53-3 **11** *nse* **Bond Bombshell**[18] 1839 3-8-10 **62** SamJames 11 22
(David O'Meara) *bmpd s: hld up on nr side of gp: shortlived effrt 1/2-way: btn over 1f out* **14/1**

310- **12** *9* **Bondi Beach Babe**[234] 6760 6-9-0 **65**......................(p) MitchGodwin(7) 6
(James Turner) *prom centre: drvn along 1/2-way: sn lost pl* **16/1**
59.46s (-0.04) **Going Correction** +0.175s/f (Slow)
WFA 3 from 4yo+ 8lb **12** Ran SP% **120.6**
Speed ratings (Par 100): **107,103,101,99,93 92,90,89,86,83 83,69**
CSF £81.16 CT £641.47 TOTE £6.80: £2.20, £4.50, £1.90; EX 108.50 Trifecta £583.50.
Owner M J Tynan **Bred** Centaur Bloodstock Agency **Trained** Moyglass, Co Tipperary
FOCUS
The pace was with the low numbers and the first five home were drawn in the bottom five stalls.
T/Plt: £641.80 to a £1 stake. Pool: £61,571.36 - 70.03 winning tickets. T/Qpdt: £54.20 to a £1 stake. Pool: £5,472.41 - 74.70 winning tickets. **Richard Young**

2039 NOTTINGHAM (L-H)
Tuesday, May 17

OFFICIAL GOING: Good to firm (good in places) changing to good to firm after race 4 (3.50)
Wind: Light against Weather: Fine & dry

2335 BETVICTOR MILLION POUND GOAL EBF NOVICE STKS 6f 15y
2:10 (2:10) (Class 5) 2-Y-O **£3,234** (£962; £481; £240) **Stalls** High

Form RPR
2 **1** **Hakeem (FR)**[16] 1889 2-9-2 0... HarryBentley 2 89+
(Richard Hannon) *cl up: led wl over 2f out: cruised clr on bit over 1f out: unchal* **1/16**[1]
2 *5* **Roar (IRE)** 2-9-2 0.. JamieSpencer 7 65
(Brian Ellison) *trckd ldng pair: pushed along 1/2-way: rdn 2f out: drvn and kpt on same pce fnl f* **7/1**[2]
3 *nk* **Padleyourowncanoe** 2-9-2 0.. SteveDrowne 3 64
(Daniel Mark Loughnane) *dwlt and wnt lft s: sn to inner and trckd ldrs: swtchd lft and hdwy wl over 1f out: sn rdn and kpt on same pce* **20/1**
0 **4** *5* **Misty Moo**[11] 2007 2-8-11 0.. AndrewMullen 6 44
(Michael Appleby) *slt ld on inner: pushed along 1/2-way: sn hdd: cl up and rdn 2f out: drvn over 1f out: wknd* **20/1**
5 *3 1/2* **Nordic Combined (IRE)** 2-9-2 0...................................... TomEaves 4 39
(Brian Ellison) *hld up in rr: sme hdwy 2f out: sn rdn along and n.d* **12/1**[3]
1m 15.32s (0.62) **Going Correction** -0.25s/f (Firm) **5** Ran SP% **123.8**
Speed ratings (Par 93): **85,78,77,71,66**
CSF £2.15 TOTE £1.10: £1.10, £1.90; EX 2.30 Trifecta £10.60.
Owner H H Sheikh Mohammed Bin Khalifa Al Thani **Bred** Sarl De Chambure Haras D'Etreham Et Al **Trained** East Everleigh, Wilts
FOCUS
After the opener winning rider Harry Bentley said: "It's quick out there. There isn't much good in the ground - it's fast enough." A weakly contested event which proved easy pickings for the prohibitively priced favourite.

2336 ROA/RACING POST OWNERS JACKPOT H'CAP (DIV I) (A JOCKEY CLUB GRASSROOTS SPRINT SERIES QUALIFIER) 6f 15y
2:45 (2:45) (Class 5) (0-75,75) 3-Y-O **£2,911** (£866; £432; £216) **Stalls** High

Form RPR
-310 **1** **The Commendatore**[21] 1763 3-9-3 **71**.................................(b) FMBerry 6 83
(David Barron) *wl away and sn in ld nr stands' rail: rdn along wl over 1f out: drvn ent fnl f and kpt on wl towards fin* **8/1**[3]
20-2 **2** *2 3/4* **Geno (IRE)**[22] 1691 3-9-6 **74**.......................................(b[1]) JamieSpencer 9 77
(Kevin Ryan) *trckd ldrs: cl up after 2f: effrt 2f out: sn rdn and ev ch: drvn ins fnl f and kpt on same pce* **9/2**[2]
65-3 **3** *nk* **Penny Pot Lane**[15] 1922 3-8-13 **67**........................... GeorgeChaloner 11 69
(Richard Whitaker) *trckd ldrs on inner: pushed along wl over 2f out: rdn and n.m.r over 1f out: kpt on wl u.p towards fin* **16/1**
0-66 **4** *1* **In My Place**[17] 1847 3-8-7 **64**.. SammyJoBell(3) 8 63
(Richard Fahey) *in tch on inner: effrt over 2f out: swtchd lft and hdwy over 1f out: rdn ent fnl f: kpt on same pce* **8/1**[3]
-164 **5** *1/2* **Thee And Me (IRE)**[21] 1763 3-8-8 **69**........................... KevinLundie(7) 5 66
(Mike Murphy) *chsd ldrs: rdn along 2f out: drvn appr fnl f: kpt on one pce* **16/1**
4-14 **6** *1 1/2* **Wowcha (IRE)**[24] 1638 3-9-7 **75**................................ RichardKingscote 7 67+
(John Quinn) *in tch: pushed along 1/2-way: swtchd lft and hdwy whn hmpd 2f out: sn swtchd lft again and rdn: kpt on fnl f* **11/4**[1]
0-26 **7** *3* **Zain Emperor (IRE)**[20] 1788 3-9-5 **73**.......................... StevieDonohoe 4 56
(Charlie Fellowes) *hld up: hdwy on outer whn hmpd 2f out: sn rdn and n.d after* **9/2**[2]
5433 **8** *2 3/4* **Wishsong**[8] 2106 3-8-11 **70**.. AnnaHesketh(5) 1 44
(David Nicholls) *in tch: chsd ldrs over 3f out: rdn and hung bdly lft 2f out: sn wknd* **14/1**
56 **9** *2 1/2* **Clon Rocket (IRE)**[19] 1817 3-8-11 **72**................... MeganEllingworth(7) 2 38
(John Holt) *dwlt and awkward s: a in rr* **20/1**
14-0 **10** *13* **Black Magic (IRE)**[24] 1630 3-9-0 **68**............................ TonyHamilton 10
(Richard Fahey) *chsd ldrs: pushed along over 3f out: sn rdn and wknd wl over 2f out: bhd and eased over 1f out* **16/1**
1m 13.26s (-1.44) **Going Correction** -0.25s/f (Firm) **10** Ran SP% **114.3**
Speed ratings (Par 99): **99,95,94,93,92 90,86,83,79,62**
CSF £43.01 CT £579.68 TOTE £9.50: £2.50, £2.00, £4.60; EX 55.60 Trifecta £1171.40.
Owner Ron Hull **Bred** J K Beckitt & Son **Trained** Maunby, N Yorks
■ Stewards' Enquiry : Anna Hesketh caution: careless riding
FOCUS
An ordinary sprint handicap. The main action took place close to the stands' rail. It was a second quicker than the other division.

2337 ROA/RACING POST OWNERS JACKPOT H'CAP (DIV II) (A JOCKEY CLUB GRASSROOTS SPRINT SERIES QUALIFIER) 6f 15y
3:15 (3:27) (Class 5) (0-75,74) 3-Y-O **£2,911** (£866; £432; £216) **Stalls** High

Form RPR
12-6 **1** **Secret Clause**[31] 1487 3-8-11 **64**.................................... AndrewMullen 3 68
(Michael Appleby) *trckd ldng pair: swtchd lft to outer and hdwy over 2f out: led wl over 1f out and sn rdn: drvn ins fnl f: kpt on wl towards fin* **25/1**
14-0 **2** *nk* **Atholblair Boy (IRE)**[20] 1788 3-9-6 **73**......................... WilliamBuick 10 76
(Nigel Tinkler) *hld up in rr on inner: hdwy 1/2-way: swtchd lft to outer and rdn wl over 1f out: styd on strly fnl f* **16/1**
51-0 **3** *nk* **Laughton**[15] 1922 3-9-4 **71**.. JamieSpencer 8 73
(Kevin Ryan) *hld up in rr: hdwy over 2f out: rdn and n.m.r over 1f out: styd on fnl f* **11/4**[1]
32-0 **4** *shd* **Dacoity**[29] 1524 3-9-5 **72**.. TonyHamilton 1 74
(Richard Fahey) *trckd ldrs: hdwy over 2f out: rdn to chal over 1f out: drvn and ev ch ins fnl f: wknd last 100yds* **12/1**

4-52 **5** *1 1/2* **King Of Swing**[10] 2049 3-9-7 **74**... TomEaves 5 71
(James Given) *trckd ldrs: effrt over 2f out: rdn along wl over 1f out: sn drvn and no imp* **3/1**[2]
0-20 **6** *1 1/4* **Greenfyre (IRE)**[5] 2178 3-8-13 **69**............................ TomMarquand(3) 7 62
(Richard Hannon) *cl up: rdn along over 2f out: drvn over 1f out: wknd fnl f* **11/2**
2532 **7** *5* **Strictly Carter**[21] 1745 3-8-11 **64**..................................... FrannyNorton 9 41
(Alan Bailey) *racd nr stands' rail: led: hdd wl over 2f out: sn rdn and wknd wl over 1f out* **7/1**
53-4 **8** *shd* **Angie's Girl**[41] 1257 3-9-1 **68**... JohnFahy 4 45
(Clive Cox) *cl up: led wl over 2f out: sn rdn: hdd wl over 1f out and sn wknd* **5/1**[3]
2-00 **9** *2* **Rial (IRE)**[23] 1673 3-9-5 **72**... GeorgeBaker 6 42
(Denis Quinn) *chsd ldrs: rdn along over 2f out: sn wknd* **100/1**
326- **10** *13* **Song Of Paradise**[139] 8402 3-9-2 **69**................................ TedDurcan 2
(Chris Wall) *dwlt: a in rr* **33/1**
1m 14.26s (-0.44) **Going Correction** -0.25s/f (Firm) **10** Ran SP% **117.6**
Speed ratings (Par 99): **92,91,91,91,89 87,80,80,77,60**
CSF £370.87 CT £1495.64 TOTE £20.00: £5.30, £3.40, £1.70; EX 442.40 Trifecta £1066.70.
Owner Almond and Gary Burns **Bred** Orbit Performance **Trained** Oakham, Rutland
■ Mutarajjil (2-1) was withdrawn. Rule 4 applies to bets struck at board prices prior to withdrawal, not to SP bets. Deduction - 30p in the \n\x\x pound. New market formed
FOCUS
This was delayed due to an injury to Dane O'Neill, who was unseated at the start from Mutarajjil, who'd been favourite. A new market was formed. The leaders dropped away and the time was a second slower than the first division. Unlike that race, the principals raced more out in the centre.

2338 BETVICTOR MILLION POUND GOAL H'CAP 2m 9y
3:50 (3:52) (Class 5) (0-75,75) 4-Y-O+ **£2,911** (£866; £432; £216) **Stalls** Low

Form RPR
01-4 **1** **Sweet Selection**[17] 1854 4-9-3 **70**................................. GeorgeBaker 13 83+
(Hughie Morrison) *trckd ldr: led 4f out: rdn clr 2f out: styd on strly* **11/4**[1]
3501 **2** *3 1/4* **Hallstatt (IRE)**[10] 2041 10-8-13 **67**..........................(t) TomMarquand(3) 10 71
(John Mackie) *s.i.s and lost 6 l s: jnd field after 4f: hdwy over 3f out: rdn along on outer over 2f out: styd on appr fnl f: nrst fin* **10/1**
22-4 **3** *hd* **Our Folly**[32] 1450 8-9-0 **65**..(t) MartinLane 9 69
(Stuart Kittow) *in tch on inner: hdwy 3f out: rdn along 2f out: drvn and kpt on fnl f* **7/1**[3]
4-56 **4** *1* **Riptide**[29] 1523 10-9-2 **67**... DougieCostello 7 70
(Michael Scudamore) *hld up in tch: effrt 4f out: rdn along and outpcd wl over 2f out: styd on u.p fnl f* **16/1**
1-20 **5** *nk* **Danglydontask**[42] 1244 5-8-8 **59**....................................... TedDurcan 5 61
(David Arbuthnot) *trckd ldrs: hdwy to chse wnr over 2f out: sn rdn: drvn over 1f out: hld ins fnl f and n.m.r towards fin* **7/1**[3]
206- **6** *2 1/4* **Ivanhoe**[15] 7436 6-9-1 **66**.. SteveDrowne 14 66
(Michael Blanshard) *set stdy pce: pushed along over 4f out: rdn and hdd over 3f out: drvn over 2f out and sn wknd* **16/1**
0-05 **7** *1 1/2* **Balmusette**[14] 1955 7-8-5 **56** oh1...................................... AndrewMullen 15 54
(Keith Reveley) *trckd ldrs: hdwy on outer 1/2-way: cl up over 4f out: rdn along 3f out: drvn 2f out and kpt on same pce* **4/1**[2]
01-1 **8** *9* **Maoi Chinn Tire (IRE)**[21] 1760 9-9-9 **74**..................... JamieSpencer 12 67
(Jennie Candlish) *hld up in rr: hdwy over 3f out: effrt over 2f out: sn rdn and btn* **4/1**[2]
0-40 **9** *36* **Hyperlink (IRE)**[49] 1136 7-8-11 **62**................................ TonyHamilton 3 6
(Heather Dalton) *chsd ldng pair on inner: pushed along 1/2-way: rdn 4f out: sn wknd* **33/1**
3m 32.74s (-1.76) **Going Correction** -0.25s/f (Firm) course record
WFA 4 from 5yo+ 2lb **9** Ran SP% **115.5**
Speed ratings (Par 103): **94,92,92,91,91 90,89,85,67**
CSF £31.60 CT £175.09 TOTE £3.00: £1.70, £2.60, £2.50; EX 28.70 Trifecta £155.60.
Owner Paul Brocklehurst **Bred** S A Douch **Trained** East Ilsley, Berks
FOCUS
The official going was amended to good to firm all round after this event, the first on the round course. Rail movements meant that this was run over 24yds further than advertised. A modest staying handicap run at a steady initial pace.

2339 EBF BETVICTOR MILLION POUND GOAL FILLIES' H'CAP 1m 2f 50y
4:20 (4:22) (Class 4) (0-80,77) 3-Y-O **£6,469** (£1,925; £962; £481) **Stalls** Low

Form RPR
1 **1** **Fadillah**[24] 1628 3-9-6 **76**... PatCosgrave 2 81+
(William Haggas) *trckd ldng pair: hdwy 3f out: effrt to chal 2f out: sn led and rdn: drvn ins fnl f: kpt on wl towards fin* **8/15**[1]
02-1 **2** *nk* **Bombilate (USA)**[20] 1798 3-9-6 **76**................................. WilliamBuick 3 80
(Charlie Appleby) *slt ld: pushed along and hdd 3f out: rdn and led again briefly over 2f out: hdd wl over 1f out: sn drvn and ev ch tl no ex nr fin* **11/2**[2]
02-0 **3** *1/2* **Shadow Spirit**[11] 2012 3-9-0 **73**................................ TomMarquand(3) 7 76
(James Eustace) *cl up: slt ld 3f out: rdn: hung bdly rt and hdd over 2f out: drvn over 1f out and ev ch tl no ex towards fin* **20/1**
041- **4** *2 1/4* **Sunscape (IRE)**[202] 7545 3-9-2 **72**.. FMBerry 4 70
(Hughie Morrison) *trckd ldng pair: effrt 3f out: rdn along over 2f out: sn swtchd lft and drvn over 1f out: kpt on same pce* **10/1**
1 **5** *7* **Mighty Lady**[114] 325 3-9-3 **73**... JimmyQuinn 5 57
(Robyn Brisland) *t.k.h: hld up in rr: sme hdwy 3f out: rdn along over 2f out: sn btn* **6/1**[3]
6 *3/4* **Della Valle (GER)**[180] 3-8-12 **75**................................ KevinLundie(7) 1 58
(Mike Murphy) *dwlt: t.k.h in rr: sme hdwy 3f out: rdn along over 2f out: sn btn* **40/1**
2m 11.84s (-2.46) **Going Correction** -0.25s/f (Firm) **6** Ran SP% **111.2**
Speed ratings (Par 98): **99,98,98,96,90 90**
CSF £3.85 CT £23.28 TOTE £1.50: £1.30, £1.60; EX 4.30 Trifecta £21.40.
Owner Saleh Al Homaizi & Imad Al Sagar **Bred** Ecurie Des Monceaux & Haras De St Pair **Trained** Newmarket, Suffolk
FOCUS
This was run over 12yds further than advertised. A fair fillies' handicap run at an ordinary gallop won by a highly regarded filly.

2340 EBF BETVICTOR MILLION POUND GOAL MAIDEN STKS 1m 75y
4:50 (4:53) (Class 5) 3-Y-O **£3,881** (£1,155; £577; £288) **Stalls** Centre

Form RPR
1 **Blair House (IRE)** 3-9-5 0.. WilliamBuick 4 90+
(Charlie Appleby) *trckd ldrs: hdwy on outer wl over 2f out: chal over 1f out: rdn to ld ins fnl f: sn edgd lft and qckd clr* **14/1**
0 **2** *2 3/4* **Azizaan**[24] 1622 3-9-5 0... HarryBentley 3 81
(Roger Varian) *trckd ldrs: effrt and nt clr run 2f out: squeezed through and rdn to ld jst over 1f out: hdd ins fnl f: kpt on* **6/1**

3 2 1/4 **Daafik** 3-9-5 0 ...... MartinLane 5 76
(Simon Crisford) *trckd ldrs: hdwy 3f out: sn cl up: rdn and ev ch over 1f out: kpt on same pce* **7/1**

2-0 4 2 1/2 **Kuantan**[22] 1714 3-9-5 0 ...... GeorgeBaker 10 70
(Roger Charlton) *cl up: slt ld wl over 2f out: rdn wl over 1f out: sn edgd lft and hdd appr fnl f: sn wknd* **4/1**[3]

6 5 2 **Patent**[22] 1714 3-9-2 0 ...... TomMarquand[(3)] 7 65
(Richard Hannon) *slt ld: hdd and rdn along wl over 2f out: cl up tl drvn and wknd over 1f out* **3/1**[1]

0 6 hd **Cliff Edge (IRE)**[15] 1931 3-9-5 0 ...... PatCosgrave 8 65
(Roger Varian) *a towards rr* **20/1**

7 3/4 **Staunch** 3-9-5 0 ...... JohnFahy 9 63
(Clive Cox) *a towards rr* **10/1**

8 3 **Mokhalad** 3-9-5 0 ...... TedDurcan 6 56
(Sir Michael Stoute) *hld up: sme hdwy on inner 3f out: rdn along over 2f out: sn wknd* **7/2**[2]

9 46 **Jamindeh** 3-9-5 0 ...... RichardKingscote 1
(Ian Williams) *dwlt and bhd: green and outpcd fr over 3f out* **66/1**

1m 45.29s (-3.71) **Going Correction** -0.25s/f (Firm) **9** Ran SP% **116.0**
Speed ratings (Par 99): **108,105,103,100,98 98,97,94,48**
CSF £95.74 TOTE £10.30: £2.60, £2.40, £3.10; EX 50.00 Trifecta £292.30.
Owner Godolphin **Bred** Darley **Trained** Newmarket, Suffolk

FOCUS
An interesting maiden, run over 12yds further than advertised. The fourth, fifth and race standard help with the form.

2341 BETVICTOR MILLION POUND GOAL CLASSIFIED STKS 1m 75y
5:20 (5:20) (Class 5) 3-Y-O **£2,911** (£866; £432; £216) **Stalls** Centre

Form RPR

242- 1 **Pirouette**[187] 7810 3-9-0 70 ...... WilliamBuick 9 78
(Hughie Morrison) *trckd ldrs: hdwy wl over 2f out: rdn to chal over 1f out: led ent fnl f: kpt on strly* **4/1**[2]

6260 2 2 1/4 **Blacklister**[10] 2044 3-9-0 68 ...... JFEgan 4 73
(Mick Channon) *led: pushed along 3f out: rdn clr 2f out: jnd and drvn over 1f out: hdd ent fnl f: kpt on same pce* **7/1**

40-5 3 2 3/4 **Carnageo (FR)**[26] 1584 3-9-0 69 ...... TonyHamilton 8 67
(Richard Fahey) *chsd ldr: rdn along over 2f out: drvn over 1f out: kpt on same pce* **5/1**[3]

4-22 4 2 1/2 **The Major**[7] 2123 3-9-0 70 ...... JamieSpencer 11 61
(Michael Bell) *hld up in rr: hdwy on outer wl over 2f out: rdn to chse ldrs over 1f out: sn no imp* **2/1**[1]

2155 5 1 **Ruby Wednesday**[27] 1572 3-9-0 70 ...... MartinDwyer 6 59
(John Best) *chsd ldrs: rdn along over 2f out: drvn and hld whn n.m.r over 1f out* **12/1**

1-03 6 shd **Strictly Art (IRE)**[97] 522 3-9-0 62 ...... FrannyNorton 10 58
(Alan Bailey) *chsd ldng pair: rdn along 3f out: wknd 2f out* **33/1**

14-4 7 1 **Bukle (IRE)**[18] 1828 3-9-0 69 ...... HarryBentley 3 56
(Rod Millman) *hld up in tch on inner whn clipped heels and stmbld after 1 1/2f: in tch: effrt on inner 3f out: rdn along over 2f out: sn wknd* **8/1**

00-1 8 1/2 **Gunman**[15] 1917 3-8-11 68 ...... TomMarquand[(3)] 12 55
(Richard Hannon) *a towards rr* **8/1**

66-6 9 3/4 **King Oswald (USA)**[81] 735 3-9-0 70 ......(t) PatCosgrave 7 53
(James Unett) *dwlt and in rr: hdwy on inner 4f out: rdn along 3f out: sn wknd* **50/1**

1m 45.25s (-3.75) **Going Correction** -0.25s/f (Firm) **9** Ran SP% **117.3**
Speed ratings (Par 99): **108,105,103,100,99 99,98,97,97**
CSF £32.69 TOTE £4.00: £2.10, £1.90, £2.50; EX 44.70 Trifecta £204.00.
Owner The End-R-Ways Partnership & Partners **Bred** The Lavington Stud **Trained** East Ilsley, Berks

FOCUS
A tightly knit classified stakes, run over 12yds further than advertised. The form looks ordinary with the favourite disappointing.

2342 MILLION REASONS TO BET ON EURO2016 BETVICTOR H'CAP 5f 13y
5:55 (5:55) (Class 5) (0-70,70) 4-Y-O+ **£2,911** (£866; £432; £216) **Stalls** High

Form RPR

0350 1 **Powerful Wind (IRE)**[78] 764 7-9-7 70 ...... RichardKingscote 8 82
(Charlie Wallis) *carried rt s and sn led on stands' rail: sn clr: rdn over 1f out: kpt on strly* **14/1**

3603 2 2 1/4 **Mossgo (IRE)**[33] 1433 6-9-7 70 ......(t) GeorgeBaker 5 74
(John Best) *awkward and wnt rt and lft s: racd centre: prom: effrt 2f out: rdn over 1f out: drvn and kpt on fnl f* **14/1**

0305 3 3/4 **Give Us A Belle (IRE)**[10] 2040 7-8-2 56 oh1......(bt) PaddyPilley[(5)] 12 57
(Christine Dunnett) *stmbld s: racd nr stands' rail: chsd wnr: rdn along 2f out: drvn over 1f out: kpt on u.p towards fin* **20/1**

06-2 4 1/2 **Classic Pursuit**[10] 2040 5-9-4 67 ......(p) MartinDwyer 3 66
(Ivan Furtado) *racd towards centre: hld up in tch: hdwy 2f out and sn rdn: drvn to chse ldrs ins fnl f: no imp towards fin* **5/2**[2]

-403 5 1 1/2 **Our Lord**[18] 1833 4-8-11 60 ...... JFEgan 1 54
(Bill Turner) *racd centre: chsd ldrs: rdn along wl over 1f out: drvn and one pce ent fnl f* **14/1**

-026 6 hd **Royal Bajan (USA)**[14] 1950 8-9-7 70 ......(p) FMBerry 11 63
(Robert Cowell) *racd towards stands' rail: chsd ldrs: rdn and hdwy 2f out: drvn over 1f out: wknd fnl f* **16/1**

340- 7 hd **Aussie Ruler (IRE)**[343] 3019 4-9-5 68 ...... FrannyNorton 14 61
(Daniel Mark Loughnane) *hmpd s and in rr: sme hdwy wl over 1f out: sn rdn and n.d* **13/2**[3]

0204 8 3 3/4 **Tancred (IRE)**[10] 2047 5-9-0 63 ......(b) KieranO'Neill 9 42
(Conor Dore) *hmpd s: a in rr* **20/1**

00-2 9 2 1/2 **Whipphound**[10] 2052 8-8-8 57 ...... TonyHamilton 4 27
(Ruth Carr) *a towards rr* **8/1**

0122 10 nk **More Spice (IRE)**[8] 2088 4-9-4 67 ......(b) JamieSpencer 15 36
(Robert Cowell) *wnt lft s: a in rr* **9/4**[1]

59.17s (-2.33) **Going Correction** -0.25s/f (Firm) **10** Ran SP% **119.2**
Speed ratings (Par 103): **108,104,103,102,100 99,99,93,89,88**
CSF £197.26 CT £3858.18 TOTE £19.60: £3.50, £2.80, £5.80; EX 106.40 Trifecta £1086.50.
Owner Anthony Cooke **Bred** Miss Ciara Doyle **Trained** Ardleigh, Essex

FOCUS
The pace held up in this modest sprint handicap. The winner made all on the rail while the runner-up raced down the middle of the track. The winner has been rated close to last year's best.
T/Plt: £19.00 to a £1 stake. Pool: £51,019.59 - 1955.35 winning tickets. T/Qpdt: £8.10 to a £1 stake. Pool: £4,149.42 - 378.40 winning tickets. **Joe Rowntree**

WETHERBY (L-H)
Tuesday, May 17

OFFICIAL GOING: Good to firm (8.7)
Wind: light 1/2 behind Weather: fine

2343 GO RACING IN YORKSHIRE SUMMER FESTIVAL APPRENTICE H'CAP 1m 2f
5:40 (5:40) (Class 6) (0-65,65) 4-Y-O+ **£2,587** (£770; £384; £192) **Stalls** Centre

Form RPR

003- 1 **Duke Of Yorkshire**[202] 7566 6-9-1 57 ......(p) RachelRichardson[(3)] 2 65
(Tim Easterby) *mde all: shkn up over 1f out: styd on: unchal* **8/1**

6430 2 2 3/4 **The Dukkerer (IRE)**[31] 1500 5-9-7 60 ...... SammyJoBell 12 63
(James Given) *chsd wnr thrght: drvn over 2f out: kpt on same pce over 1f out: no imp* **9/1**

104- 3 2 **Qibtee (FR)**[147] 8345 6-9-6 62 ...... JosephineGordon[(3)] 16 61+
(Les Eyre) *hld up towards rr: effrt over 3f out: nt clr run over 1f out: kpt on to take modest 3rd nr fin* **16/1**

00-0 4 3/4 **Dalmarella Dancer (IRE)**[45] 1202 5-9-9 65 ...... JordanVaughan[(3)] 4 63+
(K R Burke) *s.v.s: in rr: hdwy on ins over 2f out: nt clr run over 1f out: kpt on to take modest 4th nr fin* **7/1**[3]

132- 5 nk **Bold Henmie (IRE)**[19] 6388 5-8-7 53 ...... KieranSchofield[(7)] 3 50
(Philip Kirby) *trckd ldrs: effrt over 2f out: edgd rt 1f out: kpt on one pce* **10/1**

461- 6 3/4 **Sublimation (IRE)**[204] 7519 6-9-11 64 ...... RobHornby 5 60
(Steve Gollings) *trckd ldrs: effrt over 2f out: kpt on one pce* **4/1**[1]

40-5 7 1/2 **Alans Pride (IRE)**[22] 1696 4-9-5 61 ......(p) PhilDennis[(3)] 10 56
(Michael Dods) *t.k.h in mid-div: effrt over 2f out: one pce whn nt clr run 1f out* **5/1**[2]

-460 8 3/4 **Burner (IRE)**[15] 1925 4-9-12 65 ...... ShelleyBirkett 6 60+
(Olly Williams) *mid-div: effrt 3f out: one pce whn nt clr run 1f out* **14/1**

-020 9 hd **Rainford Glory (IRE)**[38] 1343 6-8-12 58 ......(p) AdamMcNamara[(7)] 9 51
(Tim Fitzgerald) *trckd ldrs: drvn over 2f out: one pce* **8/1**

-000 10 3/4 **Hussar Ballad (USA)**[35] 1399 7-9-4 64 ...... MathewStill[(7)] 15 55+
(Antony Brittain) *s.s: t.k.h in rr: effrt over 2f out: swtchd rt ent fnl f: nvr a factor* **12/1**

542- 11 6 **Gabrial's Hope (FR)**[256] 6069 7-9-4 57 ...... JacobButterfield 14 37+
(Tracy Waggott) *s.v.s: t.k.h in rr: effrt over 2f out: wknd over 1f out* **20/1**

2m 9.05s (0.05) **Going Correction** -0.05s/f (Good) **11** Ran SP% **115.5**
Speed ratings (Par 101): **97,94,93,92,92 91,91,90,90,90 85**
CSF £76.57 CT £1124.39 TOTE £9.90: £3.60, £4.80, £4.70; EX 113.90 Trifecta £2461.40.
Owner Habton Farms **Bred** Redhill Bloodstock & Tweenhills Stud **Trained** Great Habton, N Yorks
■ Stewards' Enquiry : Kieran Schofield one-day ban: careless riding (May 31)

FOCUS
There will be no speed figures here until there is sufficient data to calculate median times. All race distances were as advertised. Officially good to firm ground, watered during a dry week leading up to racing. Runners with solid credentials on recent form were thin on the ground in this typically less-than-competitive apprentice handicap and very few got into it.

2344 RACING UK PROFITS RETURNED TO RACING MAIDEN AUCTION STKS 5f 110y
6:10 (6:10) (Class 5) 2-Y-O **£2,911** (£866; £432; £216) **Stalls** High

Form RPR

2 1 **Chevalier Du Lac (IRE)**[15] 1921 2-9-5 0 ...... CamHardie 1 78
(John Quinn) *mde all: shkn up and wnt clr appr fnl f: easily* **15/8**[1]

43 2 6 **Jollydee (IRE)**[34] 1407 2-9-0 0 ...... BarryMcHugh 7 53
(Paul Midgley) *chsd wnr thrght: drvn over 2f out: kpt on: no imp* **13/2**

3 1 1/4 **He's A Toff (IRE)** 2-9-5 0 ...... AndrewMullen 5 54
(Tim Easterby) *in rr: hdwy over 3f out: chsng ldrs over 2f out: kpt on to take modest 3rd last 100yds* **14/1**

4 1 1/4 **A Sure Welcome** 2-9-5 0 ...... GeorgeChaloner 9 50
(John Spearing) *in rr: n.m.r on inner over 2f out: swtchd rt last 150yds: kpt on to take modest 4th nr fin* **22/1**

5 3/4 **Stubytuesday** 2-9-5 0 ...... GrahamGibbons 3 47
(Michael Easterby) *mid-div: hdwy over 3f out: one pce fnl 2f* **28/1**

6 hd **Traveltalk (IRE)** 2-9-5 0 ...... TomEaves 6 47
(Brian Ellison) *chsd ldrs: fdd fnl 150yds* **12/1**

7 3/4 **Belle's Angel (IRE)** 2-9-0 0 ...... PJMcDonald 10 39
(Ann Duffield) *in rr: drvn over 3f out: kpt on fnl 2f: nvr a factor* **9/1**

0 8 3 **Ray Donovan (IRE)**[7] 2119 2-9-0 0 ...... JoshDoyle[(5)] 8 34
(David O'Meara) *hld up in mid-div: effrt 2f out: wknd fnl f* **4/1**[2]

U **Showdance Kid** 2-9-5 0 ...... JoeyHaynes 2
(K R Burke) *rrd s: uns rdr* **5/1**[3]

1m 7.58s (1.58) **Going Correction** -0.05s/f (Good) **9** Ran SP% **116.9**
Speed ratings (Par 93): **87,79,77,75,74 74,73,69,**
CSF £14.81 TOTE £2.50: £1.20, £2.30, £4.10; EX 12.30 Trifecta £144.70.
Owner Bill Hobson **Bred** Vincent Hannon **Trained** Settrington, N Yorks

FOCUS
The trio with experience in this maiden auction were all open to improvement and two of them filled the first two places, though they were always in those positions and this was another race dominated by those up with the pace from the off.

2345 RACING UK HD ON SKY432 H'CAP 7f
6:40 (6:43) (Class 4) (0-80,79) 4-Y-O+ **£4,690** (£1,395; £697; £348) **Stalls** High

Form RPR

14-2 1 **Slemy (IRE)**[19] 1817 5-9-3 75 ...... JamesSullivan 16 84
(Ruth Carr) *hld up towards rr: stdy hdwy over 2f out: n.m.r and plld wd over 1f out: styd on to ld towards fin* **6/1**[1]

50-3 2 1 **Sovereign Bounty**[18] 1844 4-8-13 71 ...... GrahamLee 5 77
(Jedd O'Keeffe) *led 1f: trckd ldrs: led appr fnl f: hdd and no ex towards fin* **6/1**[1]

00-0 3 1 **Spryt (IRE)**[22] 1724 4-9-2 79 ...... JoshDoyle[(5)] 1 82
(David O'Meara) *trckd ldrs: upsides over 1f out: edgd lft and kpt on same pce last 100yds* **15/2**[3]

41-0 4 1/2 **Buccaneers Vault (IRE)**[24] 1625 4-9-7 79 ...... ConnorBeasley 15 81+
(Michael Dods) *hld up in rr: hdwy and nt clr run fr over 2f out tl 1f out: styd on wl clsng stages* **18/1**

200- 5 hd **Gold Hunter (IRE)**[199] 7635 6-9-0 75 ...... JoeDoyle[(3)] 8 76+
(Steve Flook) *hld up towards rr: hdwy on ins over 2f out: nt clr run tl last 100yds: styd on wl at fin* **18/1**

-602 6 1 **Shamaheart (IRE)**[8] 2092 6-8-10 68 ......(p) GrahamGibbons 2 72+
(Geoffrey Harker) *mid-div: hdwy over 2f out: chsng ldrs over 1f out: 4th and keeping on same pce whn bdly hmpd last 75yds* **9/1**

00-6 **7** 2 1/2 **Niqnaaqpaadiwaaq**[25] 1596 4-8-8 **66**.................................. NeilFarley 9 58
(Eric Alston) *swtchd lft after s: led after 1f: hdd over 3f out: fdd appr fnl f* **16/1**

400- **8** 1/2 **Amood (IRE)**[235] 6705 5-9-3 **75**...................................... AndrewElliott 11 66
(Simon West) *trckd ldrs: led over 3f out: hdd appr fnl f: sn wknd* **14/1**

5-30 **9** 1 3/4 **Inexes**[28] 1555 4-9-3 **75**...................................... TomEaves 13 61
(Marjorie Fife) *s.i.s: swtchd lft after s: in rr: hdwy over 2f out: one pce* **16/1**

104- **10** 2 1/4 **Devious Spirit (IRE)**[200] 7599 4-8-12 **70**.................... GeorgeChaloner 4 50
(Richard Fahey) *trckd ldrs: effrt over 2f out: wknd over 1f out* **12/1**

21-0 **11** 2 1/2 **Pensax Boy**[20] 1775 4-9-2 **77**.................................. GeorgeDowning(3) 14 50
(Ian Williams) *mid-div: sn pushed along: wknd over 1f out* **13/2**[2]

000- **12** 1 **Disclosure**[221] 7079 5-8-3 **66**.................................. JosephineGordon(5) 3 36
(Les Eyre) *mid-div: hdwy over 2f out: lost pl over 1f out* **25/1**

01-0 **13** 6 **Dutch Breeze**[19] 1817 5-9-6 **78**...................................... AndrewMullen 6 32
(Tim Easterby) *chsd ldrs: drvn over 3f out: lost pl 2f out* **25/1**

1-30 **14** 4 1/2 **Mallymkun**[59] 1003 4-8-10 **68**...................................... JoeyHaynes 7 10
(K R Burke) *mid-div: drvn over 2f out: sn lost pl* **25/1**

10-6 **15** *shd* **In Focus (IRE)**[35] 1403 5-9-2 **77**............................ JacobButterfield(3) 12 19
(Alan Swinbank) *sn chsng ldrs: wknd 2f out* **20/1**

1m 25.25s (-1.75) **Going Correction** -0.05s/f (Good) **15** Ran SP% **116.6**
Speed ratings (Par 105): **108,106,105,105,104 103,100,100,98,95 92,91,84,79,79**
CSF £36.57 CT £275.54 TOTE £6.00: £2.40, £2.20, £3.00; EX 17.00 Trifecta £396.10.
Owner J A Swinburne **Bred** Derek Veitch **Trained** Huby, N Yorks
■ Stewards' Enquiry : Josh Doyle three-day ban: careless riding (May 31-Jun 2)

FOCUS
Not a single 2016 winner in a less than competitive 61-80 handicap. They went a good pace, which suited the first and the fourth, but there was plenty of trouble on the inside rail.

2346 RACING UK DAY PASS JUST £10 H'CAP 5f 110y
7:10 (7:12) (Class 4) (0-80,80) 4-Y-O+ **£4,690** (£1,395; £697; £348) **Stalls** High

Form RPR

0-62 **1** **Pea Shooter**[3] 2261 7-9-4 **77**...................................... BenCurtis 5 84
(Brian Ellison) *trckd ldng pair: effrt 2f out: styd on to ld last 75yds* **3/1**[1]

6-06 **2** 3/4 **Stanghow**[17] 1874 4-9-5 **78**...................................... GrahamLee 3 83
(Antony Brittain) *t.k.h: led tl over 4f out: w ldr: led 1f out: hdd and no ex last 75yds* **12/1**

5-60 **3** *hd* **Singeur (IRE)**[17] 1874 9-9-7 **80**...................................... BarryMcHugh 2 84
(Rebecca Bastiman) *t.k.h: w ldr: led over 4f out: hdd 1f out: kpt on same pce* **8/1**

6-20 **4** 3/4 **One Boy (IRE)**[17] 1869 5-8-10 **76**............................ AdamMcNamara(7) 7 77
(Richard Fahey) *trckd ldrs: effrt over 1f out: edgd lft and kpt on same pce* **11/2**[3]

4535 **5** 1/2 **Rich Again (IRE)**[11] 2016 7-9-4 **77**..................................(b) PJMcDonald 9 77
(James Bethell) *s.i.s: in rr: drvn over 2f out: kpt on fnl f* **13/2**

0360 **6** *hd* **Ambitious Icarus**[11] 2016 7-9-4 **77**............................(e) ConnorBeasley 1 76
(Richard Guest) *s.i.s: in rr: drvn over 3f out: chsng ldrs over 2f out: one pce* **12/1**

424- **7** 3/4 **Questo**[335] 3298 4-9-0 **73**...................................... RoystonFfrench 8 70
(Tracy Waggott) *s.i.s: in rr: hdwy over 2f out: swtchd ins over 1f out: kpt on one pce* **25/1**

-606 **8** 1/2 **Cosmic Chatter**[17] 1869 6-9-2 **75**..................................(p) JamesSullivan 10 70
(Ruth Carr) *in rr: drvn over 3f out: kpt on over 1f out: nvr a threat* **9/1**

4063 **9** 1 1/2 **Casterbridge**[17] 1869 4-9-6 **79**...................................... NeilFarley 6 69
(Eric Alston) *chsd ldrs: drvn over 2f out: wknd fnl 150yds* **9/2**[2]

1m 5.76s (-0.24) **Going Correction** -0.05s/f (Good) **9** Ran SP% **112.2**
Speed ratings (Par 105): **99,98,97,96,96 95,94,94,92**
CSF £38.93 CT £257.58 TOTE £4.30: £1.80, £3.30, £2.00; EX 40.90 Trifecta £314.20.
Owner Mrs Andrea Mallinson **Bred** R F And S D Knipe **Trained** Norton, N Yorks

FOCUS
There was only 7lb between top and bottom weight in this 66-80 handicap, which was run at a decent tempo though the pace held out.

2347 FOLLOW @RACING_UK ON TWITTER H'CAP 1m
7:40 (7:42) (Class 5) (0-75,78) 4-Y-O+ **£2,911** (£866; £432; £216) **Stalls** High

Form RPR

10-5 **1** **Nonno Giulio (IRE)**[14] 1954 5-9-4 **72**............................ PJMcDonald 4 83
(David Loughnane) *t.k.h in mid-div: hdwy over 2f out: led last 150yds: forged clr* **22/1**

53-5 **2** 3 **Pumaflor (IRE)**[7] 2121 4-9-7 **75**...................................... GeorgeChaloner 16 79
(Richard Whitaker) *chsd ldrs: drvn over 3f out: styd on same pce last 150yds* **12/1**

054- **3** 1/2 **Courier**[185] 7853 4-8-10 **67**...................................... JacobButterfield(3) 6 70
(Marjorie Fife) *led: hdd and no ex last 150yds* **25/1**

65-6 **4** *shd* **Relight My Fire**[15] 1925 6-8-8 **67**........................(p) RachelRichardson(5) 1 70
(Tim Easterby) *trckd ldng pair on inner: nt clr run fr over 2f out: styd on fnl 100yds* **5/1**[1]

531 **5** 3/4 **All You (IRE)**[15] 1925 4-8-13 **72**..................................(v) JoshDoyle(5) 14 73+
(David O'Meara) *s.i.s: swtchd lft after s: in rr: hdwy on inner and nt clr run 2f out: styd on wl fnl 150yds* **5/1**[1]

05-1 **6** *shd* **Push Me (IRE)**[4] 2198 9-9-10 **78** 6ex............................ RoystonFfrench 7 79+
(Iain Jardine) *in rr: nt clr run and swtchd lft over 2f out: several positions: styd on wl fnl f: nt rch ldrs* **5/1**[1]

23-0 **7** 3/4 **Inshaa**[67] 901 4-9-2 **70**...................................... GrahamLee 13 69+
(Michael Herrington) *hld up in rr: nt clr run over 2f out: hdwy on outside over 1f out: styng on wl at fin* **20/1**

0-00 **8** 1 1/4 **Artful Prince**[10] 2043 6-9-7 **75**..................................(b) TomEaves 2 71
(James Given) *mid-div: drvn over 2f out: one pce fnl 2f* **15/2**[2]

10-6 **9** 3/4 **Day Of The Eagle (IRE)**[24] 1632 10-8-11 **70**............ NathanEvans(5) 10 64
(Michael Easterby) *dwlt: towards rr: kpt on fnl 2f: nvr a factor* **20/1**

6-20 **10** *nk* **Mustaqbal (IRE)**[24] 1625 4-8-13 **72**............................ PhilDennis(5) 11 66
(Michael Dods) *w ldr: t.k.h: hung lft and fdd fnl f* **9/1**[3]

00-0 **11** 1 3/4 **Harbour Patrol (IRE)**[31] 1489 4-8-13 **67**...................... BarryMcHugh 5 57
(Rebecca Bastiman) *chsd ldrs: wknd over 1f out* **66/1**

411- **12** 6 **Venutius**[229] 6878 9-9-5 **73**...................................... DaleSwift 15 49
(Ed McMahon) *mid-div: lost pl over 1f out: bhd whn eased clsng stages* **12/1**

56-0 **13** 1 1/4 **British Embassy (IRE)**[25] 1595 4-8-12 **66**.................... SamJames 3 39
(David Loughnane) *chsd ldrs: lost pl over 1f out: bhd whn eased clsng stages* **33/1**

6-00 **14** 14 **Tafahom (IRE)**[26] 1588 4-9-2 **70**...................................... JamesSullivan 12 11
(Michael Easterby) *in rr: bhd whn eased clsng stages* **28/1**

5003 **15** 11 **Saint Pois (FR)**[15] 1916 5-8-11 **68**............................ GeorgeDowning(3) 9
(Tony Carroll) *chsd ldrs: drvn over 3f out: lost pl 2f out: sn heavily eased* **14/1**

1m 39.42s (-1.58) **Going Correction** -0.05s/f (Good) **15** Ran SP% **119.4**
Speed ratings (Par 103): **105,102,101,101,100 100,99,98,97,97 95,89,88,74,63**
CSF £245.20 CT £6647.43 TOTE £25.60: £5.50, £5.00, £8.20; EX 448.40 Trifecta £4233.30 Part won. Pool: £5,644.48 - 0.01 winning units..
Owner Stephen Louch **Bred** Ballygallon Stud Limited **Trained** Market Drayton, Shropshire

FOCUS
Several with claims for this 61-75 handicap on recent form, but again there was trouble in running in this largish field and a couple of notable hard-luck stories.

2348 PRISTINE CARS YORKSHIRE'S LARGEST SUV 4X4 CENTRE H'CAP 1m 6f
8:10 (8:11) (Class 5) (0-70,68) 3-Y-O **£2,911** (£866; £432; £216) **Stalls** Low

Form RPR

-245 **1** **Tartan Bute**[40] 1297 3-9-7 **68**...................................... JoeFanning 4 77
(Mark Johnston) *trckd ldrs: drvn over 3f out: cl 2nd and carried rt over 2f out: edgd lft and styd on to ld last 50yds* **10/1**[3]

0-42 **2** *nk* **Adherence**[7] 2124 3-8-9 **56**...................................... BarryMcHugh 3 64
(Tony Coyle) *trckd ldrs: led after 3f: edgd rt over 2f out: crowded fnl 150yds: hdd and no ex last 50yds* **3/1**[2]

60-2 **3** 2 3/4 **Gimlet**[18] 1835 3-9-6 **67**...................................... GrahamLee 5 71
(Hugo Palmer) *hld up in mid-div: chsd ldrs after 5f: drvn over 3f out: edgd lft over 1f out: kpt on same pce* **3/1**[2]

-112 **4** 1/2 **Kalamata**[81] 729 3-9-6 **67**...................................... AndreaAtzeni 7 70
(Roger Varian) *hld up in rr: effrt 4f out: kpt on same pce over 1f out* **7/4**[1]

650 **5** 3 1/2 **Shulammite Man (IRE)**[34] 1406 3-8-2 **49** oh2................ JimmyQuinn 8 48
(Alan Swinbank) *dwlt: hld up in rr: drvn over 3f out: chsng ldrs over 2f out: wknd appr fnl f* **25/1**

461- **6** 4 **Heaven Scent**[225] 6977 3-8-12 **66**............................ RowanScott(7) 1 59
(Ann Duffield) *led 2f: trckd ldrs: t.k.h: drvn over 3f out: wknd appr fnl f* **10/1**[3]

000- **7** 12 **Bazzat (IRE)**[236] 6674 3-8-2 **49** oh4............................ RyanPowell 2 25
(John Ryan) *w ldrs: led briefly after 2f: reminders over 3f out: lost pl over 1f out: bhd whn eased clsng stages* **33/1**

3m 7.74s (2.74) **Going Correction** -0.05s/f (Good) **7** Ran SP% **111.3**
Speed ratings (Par 99): **90,89,88,87,85 83,76**
CSF £37.93 CT £110.11 TOTE £9.30: £3.50, £2.00; EX 50.20 Trifecta £231.10.
Owner Frank Bird **Bred** Newsells Park Stud **Trained** Middleham Moor, N Yorks

FOCUS
Some apparently progressive young stayers in this 51-70 handicap, which was run at a fair pace. The winner was stepping up on his maiden form.

2349 RACING AGAIN HERE NEXT TUESDAY EVENING MAIDEN AUCTION STKS 7f
8:40 (8:41) (Class 5) 3-Y-O **£2,911** (£866; £432; £216) **Stalls** High

Form RPR

30-0 **1** **Back To Bond**[24] 1622 3-8-12 74.................................. GeorgeChaloner 1 70
(Richard Fahey) *mde all: drvn 3f out: fnd ex clsng stages* **8/1**[3]

3 **2** *nk* **Haraz (IRE)**[7] 2122 3-8-12 81............................ ShelleyBirkett(3) 4 72
(David O'Meara) *trckd ldrs: effrt over 2f out: effrt over 1f out: upsides fnl 100yds: no ectra nr fin* **13/8**[1]

52 **3** *nk* **Compas Scoobie**[8] 2109 3-9-0 0...................................... AndreaAtzeni 6 70
(Roger Varian) *trckd ldrs: effrt 3f out: kpt on same pce last 75yds* **15/8**[2]

4 1 **Bahamian Dollar** 3-8-11 0.. EoinWalsh(3) 8 70+
(James Tate) *in rr: drvn over 3f out: chsng ldrs on inner over 2f out: nt clr run: kpt on same pce last 75yds* **20/1**

3 **5** 1/2 **Excellent World (IRE)**[42] 1246 3-8-7 0.......................... BarryMcHugh 9 59
(Tony Coyle) *in rr: outpcd over 2f out: styd on over 1f out* **8/1**[3]

3 **6** 2 1/4 **Olympic Duel (IRE)**[23] 1673 3-8-12 0............................ GrahamLee 2 58
(Peter Hiatt) *chsd ldrs: one pce fnl 2f* **16/1**

00- **7** *nk* **Fire Diamond**[296] 4666 3-8-12 0...................................... BenCurtis 3 57
(Tom Dascombe) *w wnr: drvn over 2f out: wknd last 100yds* **40/1**

6 **8** 1 **Austerity (IRE)**[10] 2048 3-9-1 0...................................... JoeFanning 7 58
(Alan Swinbank) *stmbld s: swtchd lft after s: in rr: drvn over 3f out: nvr a factor* **16/1**

1m 27.28s (0.28) **Going Correction** -0.05s/f (Good) **8** Ran SP% **114.1**
Speed ratings (Par 99): **96,95,95,94,93 91,90,89**
CSF £21.35 TOTE £9.20: £2.50, £1.10, £1.10; EX 25.60 Trifecta £59.30.
Owner P D Smith Holdings Ltd **Bred** P D Smith Holdings Ltd **Trained** Musley Bank, N Yorks
■ Stewards' Enquiry : Shelley Birkett two-day ban: used whip above permitted level (May 31-Jun 1)

FOCUS
A handful of these had hinted at the ability to win in modest company and this was probably not a strong maiden auction, with the now traditional hard-luck story on the inside.
T/Plt: £1,395.20 to a £1 stake. Pool: £58,296.48 - 30.50 winning tickets. T/Qpdt: £125.50 to a £1 stake.Pool: £6,344.63 - 37.40 winning tickets. **Walter Glynn**

2350 - 2357a (Foreign Racing) - See Raceform Interactive

1691 AYR (L-H)
Wednesday, May 18

OFFICIAL GOING: Good to soft (good in places) changing to good to soft (soft in places) after race 3 (2.35)
Wind: Breezy, half against Weather: Overcast, raining

2358 EBF STALLIONS FAMOUS GROUSE NOVICE STKS (PLUS 10 RACE) 6f
1:30 (1:32) (Class 4) 2-Y-O **£4,269** (£1,270; £634; £317) **Stalls** Centre

Form RPR

2 **1** **Danielsflyer (IRE)**[23] 1706 2-9-2 0...................................... PhillipMakin 2 80
(David Barron) *bmpd s: sn prom: hdwy to ld 1f out: rdn out fnl f* **12/1**

3 **2** 1 1/2 **Northern Thunder (IRE)**[18] 1850 2-9-2 0.......................... KierenFallon 1 76
(Richard Hannon) *wnt rt and bmpd rival s: sn w ldr: pushed along ev ch fr 2f out to 1f out: hung rt and bmpd rival ins fnl f: kpt on: nt pce of wnr* **7/2**[3]

3 3 1/4 **Dalton** 2-9-2 0.. TonyHamilton 4 66
(Richard Fahey) *led: rdn and hdd 1f out: bmpd and outpcd ins fnl f* **5/2**[2]

4 5 **Man About Town (IRE)** 2-9-2 0...................................... DougieCostello 6 51
(K R Burke) *dwlt: in tch: rdn and edgd lft over 1f out: sn outpcd: n.d after* **25/1**

5 **5** 2 1/4 **Captain Hawk**[21] 1770 2-9-2 0...................................... DarrylHolland 3 44+
(Charles Hills) *bmpd s: t.k.h: hld up in tch: nt clr run briefly and outpcd 2f out: sn wknd* **9/4**[1]

3 **6** *10* **Book Of Poetry (IRE)**[8] 2119 2-9-2 0................................ JoeFanning 5 14
(Mark Johnston) *t.k.h: trckd ldrs tl edgd lft and wknd wl over 1f out: eased whn btn ins fnl f* **4/1**

1m 16.58s (4.18) **Going Correction** +0.675s/f (Yiel) **6** Ran SP% **113.1**
Speed ratings (Par 95): **99,97,92,86,83 69**
CSF £53.66 TOTE £11.10: £3.90, £2.30; EX 45.30 Trifecta £249.60.
Owner Elliott Brothers & Peacock & Partner **Bred** Michael McGlynn **Trained** Maunby, N Yorks

FOCUS
Following 15mm of rain over the previous 24hrs the going had eased to good to soft, good in places (GoingStick: 7.2). The track was at its full width and distances were as advertised. One or two of these juveniles failed to run their races and they finished well strung out, but it's a race that should throw up a winner or two.

2359 BRITVIC SOFT DRINKS H'CAP (DIV I) 6f
2:00 (2:03) (Class 6) (0-60,60) 3-Y-O+ **£2,587** (£770; £384; £192) **Stalls** Centre

Form RPR
3000 **1** **Hab Reeh**[11] 2053 8-9-0 **48**..(p) JamesSullivan 7 57
(Ruth Carr) *prom towards stands' side: shkn up and effrt over 1f out: led ins fnl f: nudged out* **9/1**
50-0 **2** *½* **Poolstock**[32] 1495 4-9-6 **54**..(p) ConnorBeasley 5 62
(Michael Dods) *t.k.h: cl up: rdn to ld over 1f out: hdd ins fnl f: kpt on: hld nr fin* **4/1**[1]
30-0 **3** *5* **Spoken Words**[96] 547 7-8-9 **46** oh1..............................(p) JoeDoyle(3) 3 39
(John David Riches) *led: rdn and hdd over 1f out: outpcd ins fnl f* **20/1**
0-00 **4** *nk* **Dalalah**[24] 1670 3-8-9 **52**.. JasonHart 2 42
(Richard Guest) *hld up in tch: effrt and rdn 2f out: no imp fnl f* **10/1**
3-05 **5** *1 ¾* **Mystical King**[17] 1878 6-8-12 **46** oh1........................(p) GeorgeChaloner 1 32
(Linda Perratt) *chsd ldrs: rdn over 2f out: wknd fnl f* **16/1**
60-0 **6** *1* **Miss Popov**[28] 1564 3-8-0 **46** oh1................................ SammyJoBell(3) 6 27
(Noel Wilson) *dwlt: hld up in tch: rdn over 2f out: wknd over 1f out* **33/1**
400- **7** *8* **Sea Of Green**[205] 7522 4-9-9 **57**.................................... DanielTudhope 4 16
(Jim Goldie) *dwlt: hld up: rdn along over 2f out: wknd over 1f out* **4/1**[1]
02-0 **8** *2 ½* **Amber Crystal**[23] 1692 4-9-5 **60**............................. AdamMcNamara(7) 9 12
(Linda Perratt) *racd against stands' rail: bhd: struggling over 2f out: sn btn* **7/1**[3]
03-0 **9** *2* **Alba Dawn (IRE)**[24] 1667 3-9-2 **59**..............................(b[1]) JoeFanning 10 3
(Keith Dalgleish) *missed break: bhd: shortlived effrt 1/2-way: sn wknd* **8/1**
00-0 **10** *25* **Captain Joey (IRE)**[17] 1892 3-8-7 **50**.............................. KierenFallon 8
(Charles Hills) *bhd towards stands' side: struggling 1/2-way: lost tch fnl 2f: eased* **9/2**[2]

1m 16.48s (4.08) **Going Correction** +0.675s/f (Yiel)
WFA 3 from 4yo+ 9lb **10** Ran SP% **114.5**
Speed ratings (Par 101): **99,98,91,91,88 87,76,73,70,37**
CSF £44.08 CT £705.14 TOTE £10.00: £2.50, £1.90, £6.30; EX 50.50 Trifecta £539.20.
Owner Grange Park Racing & Mrs B Taylor **Bred** The Anglo Irish Choral Society **Trained** Huby, N Yorks

FOCUS
An ordinary handicap in which frequent winners were thin on the ground.

2360 BRITVIC SOFT DRINKS H'CAP (DIV II) 6f
2:35 (2:36) (Class 6) (0-60,58) 3-Y-O+ **£2,587** (£770; £384; £192) **Stalls** Centre

Form RPR
00-6 **1** **Lady Cordie**[24] 1668 4-8-10 **45**.. JoeDoyle(3) 2 52
(Jim Goldie) *in tch: effrt and hdwy over 1f out: kpt on wl fnl f: led last stride* **33/1**
0014 **2** *nse* **Insolenceofoffice (IRE)**[40] 1320 8-9-1 **54**........(p) CallumRodriguez(7) 8 61
(Richard Ford) *prom: rdn along 2f out: led ins fnl f: kpt on: hdd last stride* **11/2**[2]
00- **3** *2* **Mo Wonder**[17] 1900 3-8-10 **51**.. KierenFallon 3 50
(Adrian Paul Keatley, Ire) *chsd ldrs: drvn along over 2f out: rallied: kpt on fnl f* **9/2**[1]
00-0 **4** *½* **Goninodaethat**[23] 1692 8-9-12 **58**.................................... GrahamLee 10 57
(Jim Goldie) *trckd ldr: led gng wl over 1f out: rdn and hdd ins fnl f: sn no ex* **9/2**[1]
400- **5** *1 ½* **Duncan Of Scotland (IRE)**[187] 7840 3-8-13 **57**.....(b) SammyJoBell(3) 9 50
(Lee Smyth, Ire) *led tl rdn and hdd over 1f out: kpt on same pce fnl f* **6/1**[3]
34-4 **6** *¾* **Cranberry Park (IRE)**[23] 1710 3-8-13 **54**..........................(p) BenCurtis 4 45
(Brian Ellison) *hld up: rdn along over 2f out: hdwy over 1f out: sn no imp* **6/1**[3]
5554 **7** *7* **Bogsnog (IRE)**[12] 2013 6-9-11 **57**..............................(b) TonyHamilton 6 29
(Kristin Stubbs) *chsd ldrs: drvn along over 2f out: wknd over 1f out* **9/2**[1]
000- **8** *5* **Northern Beau (IRE)**[26] 1614 3-8-4 **45**...................(p[1]) PatrickMathers 1
(Miss Clare Louise Cannon, Ire) *in tch: drvn and outpcd over 2f out: btn over 1f out* **16/1**
06-0 **9** *10* **It's Time For Bed**[17] 1878 4-9-0 **46**............................ GeorgeChaloner 5
(Linda Perratt) *hld up in tch: drvn along over 2f out: wknd* **20/1**
00-0 **10** *shd* **Sneakin'Pete**[23] 1691 3-8-4 **45**.. JamesSullivan 7
(Linda Perratt) *dwlt: bhd and outpcd: struggling fr 1/2-way* **66/1**

1m 17.43s (5.03) **Going Correction** +0.675s/f (Yiel)
WFA 3 from 4yo+ 9lb **10** Ran SP% **113.6**
Speed ratings (Par 101): **93,92,90,89,87 86,77,70,57,57**
CSF £198.38 CT £1012.36 TOTE £34.90: £9.50, £2.30, £1.80; EX 367.90 Trifecta £3152.90.
Owner Stuart & Emma Earley & Valerie Lampard **Bred** Emma Earley & Valerie Lampard **Trained** Uplawmoor, E Renfrews

FOCUS
The ground was changed to good to soft, soft in places after this race. This was the slower of the two divisions by 0.95sec.

2361 CIROC H'CAP 7f 50y
3:10 (3:11) (Class 4) (0-85,85) 4-Y-O+ **£5,498** (£1,636; £817; £408) **Stalls** High

Form RPR
0052 **1** **Al Khan (IRE)**[4] 2257 7-9-4 **85**.. JoeDoyle(3) 7 97+
(Kevin Ryan) *t.k.h early: trckd ldrs: smooth hdwy to ld ins fnl f: shkn up and qcknd clr: readily* **11/4**[1]
550- **2** *2 ½* **Alejandro (IRE)**[235] 6742 7-9-7 **85**.................................... DavidNolan 6 90
(David O'Meara) *led at stdy gallop: rdn along 2f out: hdd ins fnl f: kpt on: no ch w ready wnr* **11/4**[1]
2-31 **3** *1 ½* **Hakam (USA)**[22] 1765 4-9-4 **82**.................................... DarryllHolland 4 83
(Charles Hills) *hld up: effrt and shkn up over 1f out: kpt on fnl f: nt pce to chal* **4/1**[2]
02-1 **4** *1* **Funding Deficit (IRE)**[23] 1694 6-9-4 **82**........................ DanielTudhope 5 80
(Jim Goldie) *t.k.h: trckd ldr: rdn over 2f out: outpcd ins fnl f* **4/1**[2]
-010 **5** *3 ¾* **Favourite Treat (USA)**[15] 1954 6-8-10 **74**..................(e) JamesSullivan 2 62
(Ruth Carr) *hld up: rdn and swtchd rt 2f out: sn no imp: btn fnl f* **14/1**

356 **6** *3 ¾* **Baddilini**[29] 1545 6-9-0 **78**..(p) KierenFallon 3 57
(Alan Bailey) *trckd ldrs: rdn and outpcd over 2f out: sn wknd* **8/1**[3]

1m 36.15s (2.75) **Going Correction** +0.35s/f (Good) **6** Ran SP% **111.1**
Speed ratings (Par 105): **98,95,93,92,88 83**
CSF £10.21 TOTE £3.50: £2.20, £1.60; EX 10.20 Trifecta £30.50.
Owner J C G Chua **Bred** Galadari Sons Stud Company Limited **Trained** Hambleton, N Yorks

FOCUS
This was steadily run and the winner, who has an excellent record here, showed a nice turn of foot to take it.

2362 CCE ENTERPRISES H'CAP 1m 2f
3:45 (3:45) (Class 5) (0-75,75) 4-Y-O+ **£3,234** (£962; £481; £240) **Stalls** Low

Form RPR
1 **1** **Nice Vintage (IRE)**[23] 1697 4-8-8 **62**..............................(v) KierenFallon 7 78+
(Adrian Paul Keatley, Ire) *hld up in last pl on outside: gd hdwy on bit to ld over 2f out: shkn up and clr whn drifted lft over 1f out: kpt on wl: eased nr fin* **3/1**[1]
54-5 **2** *3 ½* **Grand Canyon (IRE)**[17] 1884 4-9-3 **71**........................ DanielTudhope 10 76
(David O'Meara) *t.k.h early: trckd ldrs: effrt and wnt 2nd over 2f out: kpt on fnl f: nt rch eased-down wnr* **9/2**[3]
06-0 **3** *¾* **Royal Regent**[24] 1664 4-9-0 **71**.................................... SammyJoBell(3) 5 77+
(Lucy Normile) *s.i.s: hld up: hdwy whn nt clr run over 2f out: rallied and chsd clr ldng pair over 1f out: kpt on fnl f: nrst fin* **18/1**
-002 **4** *9* **San Cassiano (IRE)**[9] 2093 9-8-9 **63**............................ JamesSullivan 3 48
(Ruth Carr) *chsd ldr: drvn along over 2f out: outpcd wl over 1f out* **4/1**[2]
-066 **5** *hd* **Kiwi Bay**[16] 1924 11-9-2 **75**.. PhilDennis(5) 1 60
(Michael Dods) *t.k.h early: in tch on ins: rdn along over 2f out: no imp fr wl over 1f out* **12/1**
141- **6** *1* **Hillgrove Angel (IRE)**[246] 6415 4-9-2 **70**.................... RoystonFfrench 8 53
(Iain Jardine) *hld up in tch: drvn and effrt over 2f out: no imp and hld over 1f out* **8/1**
3-34 **7** *nk* **Beautiful Stranger (IRE)**[49] 1152 5-9-6 **74**..................(p) PhillipMakin 2 56
(Keith Dalgleish) *t.k.h early: hld up: stdy hdwy over 2f out: sn rdn: btn over 1f out* **11/2**
34-4 **8** *11* **Merchant Of Dubai**[19] 1842 11-8-13 **67**..........................(v) GrahamLee 4 27
(Jim Goldie) *midfield: drvn and outpcd over 2f out: sn btn* **12/1**
3-00 **9** *12* **Love Marmalade (IRE)**[9] 2093 6-9-6 **74**................(b[1]) ConnorBeasley 9 10
(Alistair Whillans) *led tl rdn and hdd over 2f out: sn wknd* **16/1**

2m 14.41s (2.41) **Going Correction** +0.35s/f (Good) **9** Ran SP% **116.2**
Speed ratings (Par 103): **104,101,100,93,93 92,92,83,73**
CSF £16.61 CT £206.02 TOTE £3.90: £1.60, £1.70, £6.40; EX 20.30 Trifecta £270.40.
Owner Lillies & Dubs Syndicate **Bred** Colman O'Flynn Jnr **Trained** Friarstown, Co. Kildare

FOCUS
This looked quite competitive on paper, but the winner took the race apart.

2363 BRITISH STALLION STUDS EBF TENNENT'S ROTHESAY STKS (LISTED RACE) (F&M) 1m 2f
4:20 (4:21) (Class 1) 4-Y-O+
£28,355 (£10,750; £5,380; £2,680; £1,345; £675) **Stalls** Low

Form RPR
11-1 **1** **Maleficent Queen**[21] 1786 4-9-0 96.................................. PhillipMakin 4 108
(Keith Dalgleish) *t.k.h: in tch: smooth hdwy over 2f out: edgd lft and led over 1f out: drvn and styd on strly fnl f* **3/1**[1]
2-14 **2** *2 ¾* **More Mischief**[18] 1855 4-9-0 96.. JoeyHaynes 1 103
(Jedd O'Keeffe) *cl up: led 3f out: rdn and hdd over 1f out: rallied: kpt on same pce fnl f* **9/2**[2]
453- **3** *5* **Namhroodah (IRE)**[236] 6708 4-9-0 96................................ DavidAllan 9 93
(James Tate) *hld up bhd ldng gp: effrt on outside over 2f out: chsd ldng pair over 1f out: edgd lft: no imp fnl f* **11/2**
23-5 **4** *2 ¾* **Elbereth**[28] 1569 5-9-0 95.. DarryllHolland 6 87
(Andrew Balding) *t.k.h: hld up: effrt and rdn over 2f out: outpcd fr over 1f out* **16/1**
34-2 **5** *8* **Brandybend (IRE)**[45] 1232 4-9-0 99.......................... ColmO'Donoghue 5 71
(Marco Botti) *s.i.s: hld up in midfield: effrt over 2f out: rdn and wknd wl over 1f out* **8/1**
0-15 **6** *6* **Haalan**[17] 1907 4-9-0 87.. TonyHamilton 12 59
(James Tate) *led 1f: chsd ldr: rdn and ev ch briefly 3f out: wknd appr 2f out* **33/1**
141- **7** *7* **Chain Of Daisies**[222] 7078 4-9-3 103............................ CathyGannon 14 48
(Henry Candy) *led after 1f: rdn and hdd 3f out: sn wknd* **6/1**
56-4 **8** *35* **Coreczka (IRE)**[30] 1540 5-9-0 71.................................... KierenFallon 13
(Miss Clare Louise Cannon, Ire) *hld up on outside: drvn and struggling 3f out: sn lost tch: t.o* **80/1**
13-0 **9** *48* **Persona Grata**[17] 1886 5-9-3 103.. GrahamLee 2
(Ed Walker) *s.i.s: hld up: rdn and lost pl over 3f out: sn struggling: t.o* **5/1**[3]
00-4 **10** *1 ½* **Loaves And Fishes**[22] 1757 4-9-0 88............................ DanielTudhope 8
(David O'Meara) *trckd ldrs tl lost pl and struggling over 3f out: sn lost tch: t.o* **16/1**

2m 13.02s (1.02) **Going Correction** +0.35s/f (Good) **10** Ran SP% **116.6**
Speed ratings (Par 111): **109,106,102,100,94 89,83,55,17,16**
CSF £16.29 TOTE £3.40: £1.20, £2.00, £2.30; EX 18.60 Trifecta £99.90.
Owner Weldspec Glasgow Limited **Bred** Kassala Limited **Trained** Carluke, S Lanarks

FOCUS
This was a well-run Listed race and they finished strung out like chasers. The first two have progressive profiles and the winner can make her mark in better races.

2364 JACKS ON FIRE H'CAP 5f
4:55 (4:56) (Class 3) (0-90,88) 4-Y-O+ **£7,762** (£2,310; £1,154; £577) **Stalls** Centre

Form RPR
3-1 **1** **Anonymous Lady (IRE)**[16] 1937 4-8-13 **80**..................(t) KierenFallon 5 88
(Adrian Paul Keatley, Ire) *dwlt: sn pushed along in tch: hdwy to ld over 1f out: kpt on wl u.p: jst hld on* **3/1**[1]
00-5 **2** *shd* **Classy Anne**[24] 1666 6-8-5 **75**.. JoeDoyle(3) 7 83
(Jim Goldie) *trckd ldrs gng wl: hdwy to dispute ld over 1f out: kpt on u.p ins fnl f: jst hld* **15/2**
00-0 **3** *2 ¼* **Lexi's Hero (IRE)**[14] 1968 8-9-0 **81**..............................(v) DavidNolan 1 81
(Richard Fahey) *trckd ldrs: effrt and rdn over 1f out: kpt on same pce ins fnl f* **8/1**
00-0 **4** *¾* **Desert Ace (IRE)**[24] 1672 5-9-2 **83**..........................(p) ConnorBeasley 6 80
(Michael Dods) *prom: rdn along 2f out: kpt on same pce fnl f* **11/2**[2]
00-5 **5** *2 ¾* **Jinky**[23] 1692 8-8-2 **69**.. JoeFanning 2 56
(Linda Perratt) *hld up: shkn up wl over 1f out: kpt on fnl f: nvr nrr* **14/1**
0-22 **6** *1* **Soie D'Leau**[18] 1848 4-9-7 **88**...................................... TonyHamilton 8 71
(Kristin Stubbs) *cl up: chal over 1f out: sn rdn: wknd ins fnl f* **3/1**[1]

00-4 **7** *1 ¾* **Blue Sonic**[23] 1693 6-8-2 **69** oh1 .... JamesSullivan 9 46
(Linda Perratt) *dwlt: hld up: rdn and outpcd 2f out: n.d after* **28/1**
6-60 **8** *1 ¼* **Rothesay Chancer**[24] 1666 8-8-11 **78** .... (p) GrahamLee 3 51
(Jim Goldie) *hld up in tch: drvn over 2f out: edgd lft and wknd over 1f out* **33/1**
11-3 **9** *1 ½* **Bapak Asmara (IRE)**[24] 1672 4-9-1 **82** .... TomEaves 4 49
(Kevin Ryan) *led tl rdn and hdd over 1f out: sn edgd lft and wknd* **13/2**[3]
1m 1.79s (2.39) **Going Correction** +0.675s/f (Yiel) **9** Ran SP% **114.6**
Speed ratings (Par 107): **107,106,103,102,97 96,93,91,88**
CSF £26.21 CT £163.76 TOTE £4.20: £1.60, £3.00, £2.70; EX 28.90 Trifecta £210.00.
Owner Adrian Paul Keatley & Mrs S Shiels **Bred** Aidan Sexton **Trained** Friarstown, Co. Kildare
FOCUS
An open sprint handicap.

2365 FRANKLIN & SONS APPRENTICE H'CAP — 1m 1f 20y
5:25 (5:25) (Class 6) (0-60,61) 4-Y-O+ **£2,587** (£770; £384; £192) **Stalls** Low

Form RPR
1 **Millefiori (IRE)**[25] 1661 4-8-2 **46** oh1 .... (p) RobbieDolan(5) 3 62+
(Adrian Paul Keatley, Ire) *dwlt: hld up: hdwy over 4f out: led over 2f out: hung lft and sn clr: kpt on strly fnl f: unchal* **4/1**[2]
053- **2** *3 ¾* **Penelope Pitstop**[159] 8182 4-8-0 **46** oh1 .... HayleyIrvine(7) 10 50
(Lee Smyth, Ire) *hld up bhd ldng gp: hdwy on wd outside over 3f out: chsd (clr) wnr over 1f out: kpt on fnl f: no imp* **25/1**
5-51 **3** *3 ¼* **Ghostly Arc (IRE)**[9] 2094 4-9-5 **61** 6ex .... AdamMcNamara(3) 7 59
(Noel Wilson) *led: rdn and hdd over 2f out: chsd wnr to over 1f out: sn outpcd* **5/2**[1]
4056 **4** *1 ¾* **Hydrant**[23] 1697 10-9-5 **58** .... AnnaHesketh 9 53
(Richard Guest) *trckd ldr: rdn over 2f out: hung lft and sn outpcd: n.d after* **5/1**[3]
00-4 **5** *2 ½* **Indian Giver**[37] 1382 8-9-3 **56** .... (b) RobJFitzpatrick 11 46
(John David Riches) *in tch: rdn along over 2f out: sn no imp* **14/1**
005- **6** *1 ¼* **The Name's Bond**[155] 2332 4-8-2 **46** oh1 .... CliffordLee(5) 6 33
(Keith Reveley) *hld up: rdn and outpcd over 3f out: stydo n fr over 1f out: nvr rchd ldrs* **25/1**
300- **7** *½* **Norville (IRE)**[89] 646 9-8-12 **54** .... (b) NatalieHambling(3) 4 40
(Lee Smyth, Ire) *prom: effrt and rdn over 2f out: wknd over 1f out* **7/1**
00-0 **8** *18* **Rioja Day (IRE)**[27] 1201 6-9-1 **57** .... (b) DanielleMooney(3) 2 9
(Jim Goldie) *hld up on ins: drvn and struggling over 3f out: sn btn* **8/1**
-000 **9** *3 ¼* **Honey Required**[49] 1145 4-8-4 **46** oh1 .... HollieDoyle(3) 5
(Alan Bailey) *hld up: struggling over 3f out: sn btn* **50/1**
04-0 **10** *¾* **Intensified (IRE)**[24] 1674 5-8-11 **50** .... NathanEvans 1
(Ruth Carr) *trckd ldrs: drvn along 3f out: wknd 2f out* **8/1**
/0-0 **11** *12* **Prince Of Time**[16] 1926 4-9-4 **60** .... CallumRodriguez(3) 8
(Richard Ford) *hld up in midfield on ins: struggling 4f out: sn btn: t.o* **40/1**
2m 4.75s (7.25) **Going Correction** +0.35s/f (Good) **11** Ran SP% **118.7**
Speed ratings (Par 101): **81,77,74,73,71 69,69,53,50,49 39**
CSF £105.45 CT £302.05 TOTE £5.50: £2.20, £5.90, £1.40; EX 116.20 Trifecta £713.20.
Owner Mrs F Hughes **Bred** Kevin J Molloy **Trained** Friarstown, Co. Kildare
FOCUS
An ordinary handicap.
T/Jkpt: Not won. T/Plt: £347.90 to a £1 stake. Pool: £56,707.93 - 118.97 winning units. T/Qpdt: £18.70 to a £1 stake. Pool: £5,597.32 - 221.10 winning units. **Richard Young**

2143 BATH (L-H)
Wednesday, May 18

OFFICIAL GOING: Good (8.8)
Wind: light breeze across Weather: sunny periods with occasional showers

2366 GREGG LATCHAMS SOLICITORS H'CAP — 1m 2f 46y
1:50 (1:50) (Class 6) (0-65,70) 3-Y-O **£2,264** (£673; £336; £168) **Stalls** Low

Form RPR
2056 **1** **Rockliffe**[22] 1740 3-8-11 **55** .... SilvestreDeSousa 1 62
(Mick Channon) *trckd ldrs: rdn wl over 2f out: led over 1f out: styd on wl fnl 120yds* **9/1**[3]
00-0 **2** *1 ¼* **Bigger And Better**[16] 1930 3-9-7 **65** .... SeanLevey 11 70
(Richard Hannon) *trckd ldrs: rdn to ld over 2f out: hdd over 1f out: no ex fnl 120yds* **12/1**
24-6 **3** *nk* **Ripoll (IRE)**[18] 1860 3-8-10 **61** .... (t) BenSanderson(7) 9 65
(Sylvester Kirk) *s.i.s: towards rr: nt clr run v briefly but hdwy over 2f out: wnt 3rd ent fnl f: styd on* **14/1**
3-22 **4** *1 ¾* **Funny Oyster (IRE)**[22] 1734 3-9-2 **60** .... (p) SteveDrowne 6 61
(George Baker) *mid-div: hdwy wl over 2f out: sn rdn: styd on but nt pce to get on terms* **11/1**
0531 **5** *nk* **Schoolboy Error (IRE)**[23] 1705 3-9-4 **62** .... WilliamCarson 12 62
(Jamie Osborne) *hld up towards rr: hdwy over 2f out: sn rdn: styd on but nt pce to get involved* **12/1**
00-1 **6** *nk* **Elocution**[16] 1918 3-9-4 **62** .... OisinMurphy 8 62
(Denis Coakley) *mid-div: rdn wl over 2f out: styd on fnl f: nvr trbld ldrs* **11/2**[2]
2-45 **7** *2 ¼* **The Juggler**[19] 1835 3-9-4 **62** .... (p) GeorgeBaker 4 57
(William Knight) *led: rdn and hdd over 2f out: wknd fnl f* **14/1**
600- **8** *1* **Palisade**[217] 7217 3-9-6 **64** .... LukeMorris 13 57
(Sir Mark Prescott Bt) *hld up towards rr: sme hdwy over 2f out: sn rdn: no further imp fnl f* **11/2**[2]
50-0 **9** *4 ½* **Lady Rocka**[22] 1734 3-8-9 **58** .... HectorCrouch(5) 2 43
(Amanda Perrett) *mid-div: rdn wl over 2f out: nvr threatened: fdd fnl f* **66/1**
36-0 **10** *1 ½* **Golden Isles (IRE)**[136] 29 3-8-13 **62** .... JosephineGordon(5) 3 44
(J S Moore) *trckd ldrs: rdn wl over 2f out: nvr threatened: wknd ent fnl f* **25/1**
0-61 **11** *½* **Pack It In (IRE)**[7] 2145 3-9-5 **70** 6ex .... JordanUys(7) 10 51
(Brian Meehan) *mid-div: hdwy to chse ldrs 2f out: sn rdn: wknd ent fnl f* **5/2**[1]
0-20 **12** *16* **Nutbourne Lad (IRE)**[18] 1860 3-9-1 **64** .... KieranShoemark(5) 7 15
(Amanda Perrett) *a towards rr* **25/1**
5-04 **13** *20* **Elegant Annie**[29] 1553 3-9-4 **62** .... RichardKingscote 5
(Jonathan Portman) *trckd ldrs: rdn 3f out: sn wknd* **50/1**
2m 12.48s (1.48) **Going Correction** +0.15s/f (Good) **13** Ran SP% **117.5**
Speed ratings (Par 97): **100,99,98,97,97 96,95,94,90,89 89,76,60**
CSF £107.01 CT £1504.92 TOTE £10.80: £3.20, £5.40, £3.40; EX 113.80 Trifecta £1169.40.
Owner Mrs Margaret Forsyth **Bred** Moyns Park Estate And Stud Ltd **Trained** West Ilsley, Berks

FOCUS
The rail was moved out around the bottom bend up to the 3f marker. Ten yards were added to distances of all races using the bottom bend. Rain overnight and in the run up to racing resulted in the ground easing, although both Silvestre De Sousa and Steve Drowne felt it was still riding "good". Little got into this moderate handicap.

2367 REDCLIFFE WELCOME HOME H'CAP — 1m 2f 46y
2:20 (2:20) (Class 5) (0-75,75) 4-Y-O+ **£3,105** (£924; £461; £230) **Stalls** Low

Form RPR
-012 **1** **Beausant**[5] 2205 4-9-1 **69** .... SteveDrowne 3 81+
(George Baker) *hld up in tch: stdy prog u.p fr over 2f out: sn hanging lft: chsd ldr ent fnl f: led cl home* **13/8**[1]
340- **2** *hd* **Man Look**[236] 6699 4-8-9 **63** .... OisinMurphy 1 74
(Andrew Balding) *awkward leaving stalls: sn led: pushed 4 l clr over 2f out: rdn over 1f out: no ex whn ct cl home* **7/2**[2]
102- **3** *5* **Clovelly Bay (IRE)**[150] 8319 5-9-7 **75** .... MartinDwyer 10 77
(Marcus Tregoning) *trckd ldrs: rdn wl over 2f out: styd on but nt pce to chal* **7/2**[2]
-335 **4** *2 ¾* **Bushel (USA)**[22] 1737 6-9-1 **72** .... EoinWalsh(3) 6 68
(Tony Newcombe) *hld up: struggling 4f out: hdwy over 1f out: styd on fnl f: nvr trbld ldrs* **14/1**
0-01 **5** *½* **Saint Helena (IRE)**[22] 1735 8-8-7 **64** .... (b) PhilipPrince(3) 7 59
(Mark Gillard) *s.i.s: hld up: plld hrd and tk clsr order after 2f: outpcd wl over 2f out: styd on fr over 1f out but no threat* **12/1**[3]
400 **6** *3 ½* **Uncle Dermot (IRE)**[16] 1916 8-9-2 **70** .... (p) RichardKingscote 9 59
(Brendan Powell) *hld up in tch: hdwy to trck ldr over 5f out: rdn over 2f out: fdd fnl f* **14/1**
-661 **7** *2 ½* **Mary Le Bow**[86] 676 5-8-4 **63** .... (t) CallumShepherd(5) 2 47
(Victor Dartnall) *trckd ldrs: rdn 3f out: wknd ent fnl f* **16/1**
-005 **8** *8* **Yeats Magic (IRE)**[8] 2129 4-9-6 **74** .... LukeMorris 8 43
(Ronald Harris) *hld up but in tch: racd keenly at times: trckd ldrs over 5f out: rdn 3f out: wknd over 1f out* **33/1**
2m 13.39s (2.39) **Going Correction** +0.15s/f (Good) **8** Ran SP% **112.4**
Speed ratings (Par 103): **96,95,91,89,89 86,84,78**
CSF £7.03 CT £16.28 TOTE £2.40: £1.20, £1.70, £1.20; EX 7.70 Trifecta £18.80.
Owner Beausant Partnership **Bred** Frank Brady **Trained** Manton, Wilts
FOCUS
Race run over 10yds further than advertised. No gallop on here, with the runner-up enjoying a very easy lead, and the winner's effort can be upgraded.

2368 BRAKES MAIDEN STKS — 1m 3f 144y
2:55 (2:55) (Class 5) 3-Y-O+ **£2,911** (£866; £432; £216) **Stalls** Low

Form RPR
2-2 **1** **Girling (IRE)**[19] 1826 3-8-6 0 .... SilvestreDeSousa 7 81+
(Ralph Beckett) *trckd clr ldr in clr 2nd: led jst over 2f out: sn in command: comf* **4/7**[1]
52 **2** *4 ½* **Mahfooz (IRE)**[25] 1651 3-8-8 0 .... MichaelJMMurphy(3) 5 75
(Charles Hills) *led: clr after 2f: rdn and hdd jst over 2f out: sn hld: kpt on same pce* **2/1**[2]
0-0 **3** *13* **Ocean Gale**[25] 1628 3-8-1 0 .... PatrickO'Donnell(5) 4 49
(Richard Price) *mid-div: lft 4th after 2f tl rdn wl over 2f out: regained wl hld 3rd ins fnl f* **100/1**
4 *2* **Rue Balzac (IRE)** 3-8-11 0 .... WilliamCarson 2 50
(Jamie Osborne) *hld up: rdn over 4f out: wnt hld 3rd over 2f out tl wknd ins fnl f* **14/1**
5 *16* **Irish Thistle (IRE)**[15] 2100 9-9-9 0 .... LucyKBarry(5) 6 25
(Dai Williams) *s.i.s: a in rr* **25/1**
006- **6** *8* **Miss Mittens**[329] 3507 4-9-9 0 .... TimmyMurphy 3 7
(Geoffrey Deacon) *a in rr* **100/1**
000- **7** *64* **Dramatic Voice**[204] 7532 3-8-6 0 .... LukeMorris 8
(Paul Cole) *chsd clr ldrs tl wknd qckly over 2f out: t.o* **50/1**
24 **P** **Celestra**[47] 1179 3-8-6 0 .... AdamBeschizza 1
(Alan King) *trcking ldrs whn lost action and p.u after 2f* **6/1**[3]
2m 31.56s (0.96) **Going Correction** +0.15s/f (Good)
WFA 3 from 4yo+ 17lb **8** Ran SP% **125.7**
Speed ratings (Par 103): **102,99,90,89,78 73,30,**
CSF £2.30 TOTE £1.50: £1.10, £1.10, £9.80; EX 2.90 Trifecta £97.10.
Owner Gillian, Lady Howard De Walden **Bred** Avington Manor Stud **Trained** Kimpton, Hants
FOCUS
Race run over 10yds further than advertised. This looked a match and they duly drew a long way clear, the runner-up going too fast in front and setting it up for the favourite.

2369 CRIMSON "CONFINED" H'CAP — 1m 3f 144y
3:30 (3:30) (Class 5) (0-70,70) 4-Y-O+ **£4,690** (£1,395; £697; £348) **Stalls** Low

Form RPR
/40- **1** **Sharjah (IRE)**[40] 1332 6-9-4 **67** .... (b) SilvestreDeSousa 8 74
(Andrew Slattery, Ire) *mde all: styd on wl: rdn out* **15/8**[1]
625- **2** *1 ¼* **Chantecler**[156] 3280 5-9-7 **70** .... LiamKeniry 1 74
(Neil Mulholland) *racd keenly: trckd ldrs: rdn to chse wnr over 2f out: kpt on but a being hld fnl f* **8/1**
-442 **3** *hd* **Favorite Girl (GER)**[23] 1711 8-9-0 **63** .... AndrewMullen 5 67
(Michael Appleby) *prom: rdn wl over 2f out: styd on same pce* **4/1**[2]
30-4 **4** *1 ¾* **Phantom River**[19] 1825 4-9-2 **65** .... WilliamTwiston-Davies 6 66
(Alan King) *trckd ldrs: rdn over 2f out: styd on same pce* **5/1**[3]
0045 **5** *shd* **Maverik**[23] 1699 8-9-2 **65** .... (t) CharlesBishop 7 66
(Ali Stronge) *stdd s: hdwy over 2f out: swtchd rt wl over 1f out: sn rdn: kpt on but nt pce to mount chal* **10/1**
565 **6** *4 ½* **Earthwindorfire**[30] 1529 5-9-4 **67** .... TimmyMurphy 4 60
(Geoffrey Deacon) *in tch: hdwy over 2f out: sn rdn: wknd ent fnl f* **7/1**
-606 **7** *12* **Sharp Sword (IRE)**[68] 899 5-9-5 **68** .... SamHitchcott 3 41
(Neil Mulholland) *s.i.s: nvr travelling: a detached in last* **12/1**
2m 31.5s (0.90) **Going Correction** +0.15s/f (Good) **7** Ran SP% **111.8**
Speed ratings (Par 103): **103,102,102,100,100 97,89**
CSF £16.82 CT £52.34 TOTE £2.80: £1.70, £3.10; EX 14.80 Trifecta £49.10.
Owner Mrs Sharon Slattery **Bred** John Connaughton **Trained** Thurles, Co Tipperary
■ Stewards' Enquiry : Andrew Mullen four-day ban: used whip above permitted levrl down the shoulder in the forehand (Jun 1-2,5-6)

FOCUS
Race run over 10yds further than advertised. No gallop on here and Silvestre de Sousa rode the other jockeys to sleep aboard the favourite.

2370 AVON VALLEY CLEANING H'CAP 1m 5f 22y
4:05 (4:05) (Class 6) (0-60,60) 4-Y-O+ **£2,264** (£673; £336; £168) **Stalls** High

Form RPR
-530 **1** **Stynes (IRE)**[28] 1578 6-8-5 **47**....(t) TomMarquand(3) 1 54
(Ali Stronge) *mid-div: hdwy over 2f out: sn rdn: led ent fnl f: hld on wl: drvn out* **6/1**[3]
00-0 **2** *nk* **Urban Space**[33] 1456 10-8-12 **54**....(t) DanielMuscutt(3) 8 61
(John Flint) *hld up towards rr: hdwy over 2f out: sn rdn: ev ch ent fnl f: kpt on wl* **8/1**
350- **3** *1 ¾* **Petrify**[184] 6999 6-8-8 **47**....(t) JimmyQuinn 3 52
(Bernard Llewellyn) *s.i.s: towards rr: nt clr run on inner 3f out: hdwy sn after: nt clr run and swtchd rt jst over 1f out: styd on wl ins fnl f* **20/1**
2120 **4** *1 ¼* **Shalambar (IRE)**[18] 1854 10-9-7 **60**....(v) LukeMorris 7 62
(Tony Carroll) *trckd ldrs: rdn over 2f out: led over 1f out tl ent fnl f: no ex* **10/1**
036- **5** *nk* **Alert**[26] 1613 4-9-6 **59**....(b) SilvestreDeSousa 2 61
(Andrew Slattery, Ire) *trckd ldrs: rdn to ld 2f out: hdd over 1f out: no ex ins fnl f* **3/1**[1]
1-15 **6** *1 ¼* **Captain George (IRE)**[47] 1182 5-9-3 **56**....(p) SteveDrowne 4 56
(Michael Blake) *towards rr: sn pushed along: hdwy over 2f out: sn drvn: styd on same pce fnl f* **6/1**[3]
00/0 **7** *3 ¼* **Hier Encore (FR)**[28] 1575 4-8-7 **46** oh1.... WilliamCarson 6 41
(David Menuisier) *mid-div: hdwy on outer 6f out: rdn to chse ldrs 3f out: fdd ins fnl f* **33/1**
60/- **8** *½* **Karl Marx (IRE)**[8] 2836 6-8-5 **47** oh1 ow1....(b) PhilipPrince(3) 11 42
(Mark Gillard) *disp ld tl drvn 3f out: kpt chsng ldrs tl fdd ins fnl f* **20/1**
0252 **9** *6* **Celestial Dancer (FR)**[47] 1182 4-8-9 **48**.... AndrewMullen 5 34
(Michael Appleby) *disp ld tl drvn ahd 3f out: hdd 2f out: wknd ent fnl f* **11/2**[2]
00-0 **10** *38* **Kenobe Star (IRE)**[19] 1826 4-9-6 **59**....(t) MartinLane 10
(David Dennis) *mid-div tl rdn and wknd over 2f out* **8/1**
500- **P** **Eastern Magic**[184] 5548 9-8-11 **50**.... WilliamTwiston-Davies 9
(Sarah Hollinshead) *hld up: effrt over 2f out: wknd over 1f out: p.u whn stmbld bdly and lost action fnl f* **15/2**

2m 55.91s (3.91) **Going Correction** +0.15s/f (Good) **11** Ran SP% **124.5**
Speed ratings (Par 101): **93,92,91,90,90 90,88,87,84,60**
CSF £55.23 CT £928.20 TOTE £9.40: £2.30, £3.20, £4.70; EX 88.10 Trifecta £810.40.
Owner EPDS Racing Partnership 18 **Bred** K & D McCormack **Trained** Eastbury, Berks

FOCUS
Race distance increased by 10yds. Lowly handicap form.

2371 KELLANDS/EBF STALLIONS NOVICE STKS (PLUS 10 RACE) 5f 11y
4:40 (4:40) (Class 4) 2-Y-O **£4,690** (£1,395; £697; £348) **Stalls** Centre

Form RPR
1 **Battaash (IRE)** 2-8-13 0.... MichaelJMMurphy(3) 9 88+
(Charles Hills) *unsettled in stalls and little slowly away: in tch: gd hdwy over 2f out: led over 1f out: drifted lft fnl f: readily* **14/1**
2 *4* **Leontes** 2-9-2 0.... OisinMurphy 4 74
(Andrew Balding) *s.i.s: last: hdwy over 2f out: chsd wnr ent fnl f: kpt on but no ch w wnr* **10/1**
6 **3** *½* **Mistime (IRE)**[7] 2162 2-8-11 0.... SilvestreDeSousa 8 67
(Mark Johnston) *hld up in tch: rdn and hdwy over 2f out: kpt on into 3rd fnl f but nt pce to get on terms* **7/1**
4 *1 ¼* **Nuclear Power** 2-9-2 0.... RichardKingscote 5 72
(Joseph Tuite) *hld up in tch: nt clr run on rails 2f out: squeezed through jst over 1f out: kpt on but nvr any threat* **2/1**[1]
34 **5** *1 ½* **The Nazca Lines (IRE)**[7] 2162 2-8-11 0.... CallumShepherd(5) 3 62
(John Quinn) *trckd ldrs: rdn over 2f out: kpt on same pce fnl f* **13/2**[3]
135 **6** *5* **Awesome Allan (IRE)**[14] 1965 2-9-3 0.... NoelGarbutt(3) 2 50
(David Evans) *uns rdr at s but sn ct: led: rdn over 2f out: hdd over 1f out: edgd sltly lft whn fading ent fnl f* **10/1**
7 *7* **Sans Souci Bay** 2-9-2 0.... SeanLevey 6 19
(Richard Hannon) *trckd ldrs: rdn over 2f out: wknd over 1f out* **5/2**[2]
0 **8** *shd* **Kodiac Moment (IRE)**[12] 1988 2-8-4 0.... JordanUys(7) 1 14
(Brian Meehan) *prom: rdn w ev ch fr over 2f out tl wl over 1f out: fading whn short of room and hmpd ent fnl f: rdr briefly lost iron* **20/1**
50 **U** **She's Rosanna**[13] 1976 2-8-11 0.... AdamBeschizza 7
(Steph Hollinshead) *rrd leaving stalls bef stumbling and unseating rdr* **66/1**

1m 4.2s (1.70) **Going Correction** +0.20s/f (Good) **9** Ran SP% **118.8**
Speed ratings (Par 95): **94,87,86,84,82 74,63,63,**
CSF £148.57 TOTE £16.40: £3.80, £3.30, £2.60; EX 113.90 Trifecta £708.80.
Owner Hamdan Al Maktoum **Bred** Ballyphilip Stud **Trained** Lambourn, Berks

FOCUS
Probably a fair little novice event and the winner was quite impressive.

2372 STREBEL FILLIES' H'CAP (DIV I) 5f 161y
5:15 (5:17) (Class 5) (0-70,76) 3-Y-O **£2,911** (£866; £432; £216) **Stalls** Centre

Form RPR
51-5 **1** **Belledesert**[33] 1452 3-9-7 **70**.... AdamBeschizza 6 78
(Steph Hollinshead) *trckd ldrs: rdn to chal 2f out: led ent fnl f: kpt on wl to assert fnl 120yds* **9/2**[3]
-651 **2** *2 ¾* **Zeeoneandonly (IRE)**[6] 2186 3-9-10 **76** 6ex....(v) PhilipPrince(3) 3 75
(David Evans) *led: rdn whn strly pressed fr over 2f out: hdd ent fnl f: kpt on but no ex fnl 120yds* **5/2**[1]
03-0 **3** *½* **Remember Me**[42] 1257 3-9-4 **67**.... SilvestreDeSousa 7 64
(Hughie Morrison) *mid-div: hdwy over 2f out: sn rdn: chsd ldng pair over 1f out: kpt on same pce* **4/1**[2]
40-6 **4** *1 ½* **Kingstreet Lady**[22] 1761 3-8-8 **57**.... OisinMurphy 8 49
(Richard Price) *trckd ldrs: rdn over 2f out: kpt on same pce fnl f* **25/1**
0-50 **5** *2 ¼* **African Showgirl**[19] 1829 3-8-13 **62**.... SteveDrowne 10 47
(George Baker) *sn pushed along towards rr: styd on but no threat fr over 1f out* **20/1**
6053 **6** *¾* **Allen's Folly**[7] 2143 3-8-2 **51** oh3.... KieranO'Neill 5 34
(Peter Hiatt) *prom: drvn wl over 2f out: wknd ent fnl f* **12/1**
100- **7** *3 ¼* **Prisom (IRE)**[140] 8391 3-9-1 **69**.... CallumShepherd(5) 1 41
(Gay Kelleway) *hld up in tch: effrt over 2f out: wknd over 1f out* **14/1**
660- **8** *6* **Turaathy (IRE)**[257] 6042 3-8-12 **64**.... EoinWalsh(3) 2 16
(Tony Newcombe) *s.i.s: a towards rr* **20/1**

562- **9** *shd* **Annie Salts**[183] 7877 3-9-2 **65**.... FergusSweeney 4 17
(Martyn Meade) *mid-div: hdwy 3f out: effrt over 2f out: wknd over 1f out* **4/1**[2]

1m 12.31s (1.11) **Going Correction** +0.20s/f (Good) **9** Ran SP% **114.5**
Speed ratings (Par 96): **100,96,95,93,90 89,85,77,77**
CSF £15.51 CT £48.23 TOTE £5.30: £1.80, £1.10, £1.90; EX 16.80 Trifecta £53.30.
Owner K Meredith, D Hodson, The Ocean Four **Bred** M Pyle & Mrs T Pyle **Trained** Upper Longdon, Staffs

FOCUS
Division one of a modest sprint, it was won in clear-cut fashion and looked the stronger leg with the winning time faster by 1.44sec.

2373 STREBEL FILLIES' H'CAP (DIV II) 5f 161y
5:50 (5:50) (Class 5) (0-70,70) 3-Y-O **£2,911** (£866; £432; £216) **Stalls** Centre

Form RPR
3 **1** **Inclination (IRE)**[33] 1451 3-9-0 **63**.... RyanTate 8 68+
(Clive Cox) *racd keenly: cl up: rdn to chal over 1f out: led briefly ent fnl f: kpt on wl to regain ld cl home* **15/8**[1]
41-3 **2** *hd* **Swirral Edge**[18] 1847 3-9-7 **70**.... SeanLevey 4 74
(David Brown) *hld up: gd hdwy over 1f out: tk narrow advantage jst ins fnl f: kpt on: hdd cl home* **7/2**[2]
1661 **3** *1* **Evening Starlight**[28] 1574 3-9-3 **66**.... RichardKingscote 5 67
(Ron Hodges) *trckd ldrs: rdn over 2f out: ev ch ent fnl f: no ex fnl 120yds* **8/1**
6600 **4** *½* **Pursuit Of Time**[9] 2107 3-7-11 **51** oh2....(p) NoelGarbutt(5) 9 50
(Michael Appleby) *s.i.s: sn trcking ldrs: rdn and ev ch 2f out: edgd lft ent fnl f: no ex fnl 120yds* **40/1**
-215 **5** *¾* **Iceaxe**[11] 2049 3-9-2 **65**.... LiamJones 7 62
(John Holt) *trckd ldr: rdn over 2f out: kpt on but nt pce to chal* **9/2**[3]
0-0 **6** *2* **Caitie (IRE)**[28] 1572 3-8-11 **65**....(b[1]) AaronJones(5) 6 55
(Paul Cole) *led: rdn and hdd ent fnl f: no ex* **10/1**
-354 **7** *¾* **Abberley Dancer (IRE)**[89] 638 3-9-3 **69**.... TomMarquand(3) 1 57
(J S Moore) *trckd ldr: rdn over 2f out: sn outpcd: n.d after* **17/2**
-116 **8** *5* **Powerful Dream (IRE)**[55] 1060 3-9-6 **69**.... OisinMurphy 2 40
(Ronald Harris) *cl up tl outpcd over 2f out* **12/1**

1m 13.75s (2.55) **Going Correction** +0.20s/f (Good) **8** Ran SP% **116.0**
Speed ratings (Par 96): **91,90,89,88,87 85,84,77**
CSF £8.61 CT £41.70 TOTE £3.10: £1.50, £1.10, £2.50; EX 10.10 Trifecta £27.30.
Owner James M Egan **Bred** Corduff Stud & T J Rooney **Trained** Lambourn, Berks

FOCUS
This looked the lesser of the two divisions and the time was significantly slower.
T/Plt: £343.70 to a £1 stake. Pool: £68,138.86 - 144.70 winning units. T/Qpdt: £88.10 to a £1 stake. Pool: £6,134.14 - 51.50 winning units. **Tim Mitchell**

1413 KEMPTON (A.W) (R-H)
Wednesday, May 18

OFFICIAL GOING: Polytrack: standard
Weather: Clear, virtually nil

2374 £10 FREE BET 32REDSPORT.COM APPRENTICE H'CAP 1m 3f (P)
5:55 (5:55) (Class 5) (0-70,70) 4-Y-O+ **£2,911** (£866; £432; £216) **Stalls** Low

Form RPR
160/ **1** **Sureness (IRE)**[30] 1099 6-9-4 **70**....(t) MeganNicholls(3) 3 79
(Charlie Mann) *hld up in rr: hdwy 4f out: gng wl 3f out: shkn up and led 2f out: kpt on wl ins fnl f* **25/1**
4611 **2** *1 ½* **Glasgow Central**[9] 2086 5-9-3 **66** 6ex.... JosephineGordon 7 72
(Phil McEntee) *settled in mid-div: rdn 2f out: styd on but hld by wnr* **4/1**[2]
405 **3** *1* **Viserion**[25] 1640 4-9-5 **68**....(p) GeorgeBuckell 1 72
(David Simcock) *chsd ldrs: rdn over 2f out: kpt on one pce ins fnl f* **7/2**[1]
0222 **4** *¾* **I'm Harry**[22] 1751 7-9-6 **69**....(vt) EdwardGreatrex 4 72
(George Baker) *hld up in rr: rdn over 2f out: one pce ins fnl f* **9/2**[3]
34-5 **5** *nk* **Lady Lunchalot (USA)**[89] 631 6-9-0 **63**....(p) HectorCrouch 5 65
(Laura Mongan) *in rr: rdn 4f out: styd on same pce fr over 1f out* **12/1**
2-52 **6** *¾* **Harlestone Hopes**[20] 1810 4-9-2 **65**....(p) KieranShoemark 8 66
(Ed Dunlop) *c across fr wd draw to ld: hdd after 6f: chsd ldr after: rdn over 2f out: wknd over 1f out* **5/1**
4500 **7** *1 ¾* **Dukes Meadow**[21] 1775 5-9-1 **67**.... RhiainIngram(3) 2 65
(Roger Ingram) *restrained leaving stalls: chsd ldrs: travelling wl over 2f out: shkn up and rdn 2f out: nt qckn and wknd fr over 1f out* **10/1**
14-0 **8** *12* **Taurian**[136] 30 5-9-4 **67**.... GaryMahon 6 43
(Ian Williams) *t.k.h: led after 6f: rdn over 2f out: squeezed up and hdd 2f out: wknd qckly and eased ins fnl f* **7/1**

2m 20.71s (-1.19) **Going Correction** -0.05s/f (Stan) **8** Ran SP% **110.2**
Speed ratings (Par 103): **102,100,100,99,99 98,97,88**
CSF £113.63 CT £420.85 TOTE £13.50: £4.70, £1.80, £1.70; EX 124.20 Trifecta £409.80.
Owner P Mott **Bred** Alberto Panetta **Trained** Upper Lambourn, Berks

FOCUS
Not strong form, even as apprentice handicaps go, and the outsider of the lot came home in front.

2375 32RED CASINO MEDIAN AUCTION MAIDEN STKS 7f (P)
6:25 (6:29) (Class 6) 3-4-Y-O **£2,264** (£673; £336; £168) **Stalls** Low

Form RPR
1 **Tarboosh** 3-9-3 0.... PatCosgrave 7 79+
(William Haggas) *chsd ldrs: gng wl ent st: nt clr run and swtchd lft over 1f out: rdn and picked up wl fnl 110yds: led fnl strides* **3/1**[1]
0-22 **2** *nk* **Destroyer**[18] 1859 3-9-3 76....(p) MartinDwyer 5 76
(William Muir) *led: nudged along over 2f out: rdn over 1f out: kpt on and hdd fnl strides* **6/1**[3]
3 *1 ½* **Crystallographer (IRE)** 3-8-12 0.... ShaneKelly 4 67
(David Lanigan) *wnt rt s: settled in mid-div on inner: rdn over 2f out: kpt on wl ins fnl f to take 3rd nr fin* **8/1**
6- **4** *shd* **Shadad (IRE)**[275] 5447 3-9-3 0.... FMBerry 14 72
(Ralph Beckett) *grad c across fr wd draw to press runner-up after 2f: stl disputing over 2f out: rdn and kpt on ins fnl f: lost 3rd nr fin* **15/2**
2-0 **5** *1 ¼* **Langham**[18] 1859 3-8-7 0.... JosephineGordon(5) 2 63
(Martyn Meade) *chsd ldrs: rdn over 2f out: ev ch over 1f out: wknd ins fnl f* **10/1**
05 **6** *hd* **Mr Andros**[18] 1859 3-9-3 0.... DavidProbert 8 68
(Andrew Balding) *settled in mid-div: rdn 2f out: rn green in st: styd on ins fnl f: improver* **14/1**
34- **7** *nk* **Gregarious (IRE)**[182] 7890 3-9-3 0.... JimCrowley 10 67
(Lucy Wadham) *in rr: c wd ent st: prog under hands and heels* **4/1**[2]
03- **8** *¾* **Mercifilly (FR)**[180] 7922 3-8-12 0....[1] LukeMorris 12 60
(Ed Walker) *mid-div: pushed along 3f out: no imp fr over 1f out* **16/1**

The Form Book, Raceform Ltd, Newbury, RG14 5SJ

9 2 1/4 **The Burning Man** 3-9-3 0 .... TomQueally 11 59+
(Charlie Fellowes) *rn green early and in rr: rdn along over 2f out: picked up and gd hdwy fr over 1f out: improver* **25/1**

3-40 10 1 1/2 **Maddys Dream**[23] 1701 3-9-0 70 .... SimonPearce(3) 13 55
(Lydia Pearce) *chsd ldrs: rdn 2f out: wknd ins fnl f* **33/1**

11 1 **Imperial State** 3-9-3 0 .... (t) TedDurcan 6 52
(George Scott) *in rr: rdn and no imp fr 2f out* **16/1**

12 4 **Gold Return (IRE)** 3-8-12 0 .... StevieDonohoe 3 36
(David Lanigan) *in rr: rdn over 3f out: sn hld and wknd* **25/1**

13 1 1/2 **Cool Angel (IRE)** 3-8-12 0 .... SamHitchcott 1 32
(Gary Moore) *hmpd s: settled in rr-div: rdn over 2f out: no imp and wknd fr over 1f out* **50/1**

14 7 **Pepper (IRE)** 3-8-9 0 .... MatthewCosham(3) 9 13
(Derek Shaw) *racd in mid-div: struggling ent st: rdn and wknd fr over 1f out* **125/1**

1m 25.7s (-0.30) **Going Correction** -0.05s/f (Stan) **14** Ran SP% **123.1**
Speed ratings (Par 101): **99,98,96,96,95 95,94,93,91,89 88,83,82,74**
CSF £20.40 TOTE £3.90: £1.60, £2.10, £3.60; EX 21.00 Trifecta £149.10.
Owner Hamdan Al Maktoum **Bred** Landmark Racing Limited **Trained** Newmarket, Suffolk
■ Stewards' Enquiry : Shane Kelly two-day ban: careless riding (Jun 1-2)

FOCUS
With the runner-up looking to run to his mark of 76, this was probably a fair maiden.

2376 BRITISH STALLION STUDS EBF NOVICE FILLIES' STKS (PLUS 10 RACE) 6f (P)
6:55 (7:00) (Class 5) 2-Y-O **£3,234** (£962; £481; £240) **Stalls** Low

Form RPR

4 1 **Ventura Blues (IRE)**[32] 1482 2-9-0 0 .... PatDobbs 11 79
(Richard Hannon) *chsd ldrs: nudged along 2f out: rdn over 1f out: led 1f out: pushed out* **8/1**

3 2 1 1/4 **Magical Forest (IRE)**[12] 2007 2-9-0 0 .... JamesDoyle 5 75
(Marco Botti) *led: rdn under 2f out: hdd 1f out: kpt on* **5/4**[1]

3 1 **Boost** 2-9-0 0 .... LukeMorris 4 72+
(Sir Mark Prescott Bt) *settled bhd ldrs on inner: rdn 2f out: swtchd off rail over 1f out: rn green tl picked up wl ins fnl f: improver* **2/1**[2]

4 4 **Cotinga** 2-9-0 0 .... FMBerry 6 60
(Ralph Beckett) *settled in rr: pushed along over 2f out: kpt on ins fnl f* **7/1**[3]

0 5 3 **Royal Melody**[12] 1988 2-8-9 0 .... HectorCrouch(5) 10 51
(Heather Main) *chsd ldrs: lugged rt and rn green over 2f out: lost pl and rdn: no ex fnl f* **50/1**

5 6 hd **Glenys The Menace (FR)**[22] 1749 2-9-0 0 .... KierenFox 8 50
(John Best) *chsd ldrs: rdn 2f out: hld fr over 1f out* **20/1**

7 1 **Isswara** 2-9-0 0 .... PaoloSirigu 7 47
(Marco Botti) *drvn along in last: ct up w pack after 4f: pushed along ent st: no ex and wknd* **20/1**

8 3/4 **Myredbush (IRE)** 2-9-0 0 .... JimCrowley 3 45
(Simon Dow) *settled bhd ldrs: pushed along 2f out: wknd fnl f* **25/1**

9 1 3/4 **Sweet Sienna** 2-9-0 0 .... RobertWinston 12 40
(Dean Ivory) *t.k.h in mid-div on outer: wknd fr over 1f out* **16/1**

1m 14.36s (1.26) **Going Correction** -0.05s/f (Stan) **9** Ran SP% **122.6**
Speed ratings (Par 90): **89,87,86,80,76 76,75,74,71**
CSF £18.97 TOTE £8.80: £3.10, £1.10, £1.40; EX 26.00 Trifecta £76.00.
Owner Middleham Park Racing Vi **Bred** George Kent **Trained** East Everleigh, Wilts

FOCUS
This had the look of a good fillies' novice race, which in its previous incarnation as a maiden, was taken by Cursory Glance in 2014. Experience told, with the winner and second both having their second starts, but the first four all look decent types.

2377 32RED H'CAP (LONDON MIDDLE DISTANCE SERIES QUALIFIER) 1m 3f (P)
7:25 (7:28) (Class 3) (0-95,93) 4-Y-O+
£7,158 (£2,143; £1,071; £535; £267; £134) **Stalls** Low

Form RPR

112- 1 **Almodovar (IRE)**[276] 5416 4-9-7 93 .... GeorgeBaker 13 113+
(David Lanigan) *led after 2f: mde all after: shkn up 2f out and sn stretched clr: impressive* **4/1**[3]

2-40 2 6 **Sarsted**[13] 1978 4-8-11 83 .... (b[1]) JimCrowley 3 88
(Hughie Morrison) *chsd ldrs and t.k.h: rdn 2f out: sme prog but no ch w easy wnr* **14/1**

62-2 3 1/2 **Higher Power**[25] 1633 4-8-11 83 .... TomQueally 4 87+
(James Fanshawe) *settled in mid-div: rdn 2f out: kpt on once pce* **7/2**[2]

013- 4 2 **Petrucci (IRE)**[212] 7348 4-8-12 84 .... TedDurcan 10 85
(Sir Michael Stoute) *chsd wnr in 2nd: rdn 2f out: wknd* **3/1**[1]

1111 5 1 1/2 **Tangramm**[68] 899 4-8-12 83 ow1 .... (p) RobertWinston 12 82
(Dean Ivory) *mid-div: rdn 2f out: no ex and wknd ins fnl f* **16/1**

221- 6 hd **Fallen For A Star**[166] 8108 4-8-12 84 .... [1] WilliamBuick 8 81+
(Luca Cumani) *fractious in stalls: led after 1f tl restrained bhd ldrs: rdn along 3f out: wknd ins fnl f* **7/1**

03P- 7 2 1/4 **London Citizen (USA)**[234] 6777 6-8-9 88 .... SamuelClarke(7) 5 81
(Chris Wall) *t.k.h in mid-div: rdn 2f out: sn hld and wknd ins fnl f* **25/1**

0-65 8 1 1/4 **Fiftyshadesfreed (IRE)**[21] 1797 5-9-0 86 .... (p) LiamKeniry 2 77
(George Baker) *settled in rr-div: tk clsr order over 3f out: rdn 2f out and sn no imp* **40/1**

421- 9 1/2 **Zamperini (IRE)**[201] 7593 4-8-13 85 .... FMBerry 6 75
(Mike Murphy) *in rr-div: rdn over 2f out: no ex fr over 1f out* **16/1**

5434 10 1 1/4 **Castilo Del Diablo (IRE)**[46] 1209 7-8-13 92 .... (p) SophieKilloran(7) 11 80
(David Simcock) *in rr: rdn over 2f out: sn hld* **14/1**

004- 11 4 1/2 **Adventure Seeker (IRE)**[256] 6107 5-9-4 90 .... (t) LukeMorris 1 70
(Ed Vaughan) *tk fierce hold early in rr: rdn over 2f out: fnd nil and wknd ins fnl f* **12/1**

2m 18.19s (-3.71) **Going Correction** -0.05s/f (Stan) **11** Ran SP% **118.8**
Speed ratings (Par 107): **111,106,106,104,103 103,101,101,100,99 96**
CSF £59.69 CT £217.51 TOTE £5.00: £1.90, £4.20, £1.80; EX 71.20 Trifecta £388.20.
Owner B E Nielsen **Bred** Bjorn Nielsen **Trained** Newmarket, Suffolk

FOCUS
A field featuring some fair types and some potential improvers, which was absolutely taken apart by the impressive winner.

2378 32RED.COM H'CAP (LONDON MILE SERIES QUALIFIER) 1m (P)
7:55 (7:57) (Class 4) (0-85,85) 4-Y-O+ **£4,690** (£1,395; £697; £348) **Stalls** Low

Form RPR

125/ 1 **Cape Icon**[711] 2983 5-9-2 80 .... AdamKirby 9 93+
(Clive Cox) *pressed ldr: pushed along over 2f out: str run to ld over 1f out: kpt on wl* **8/1**[3]

2101 2 2 1/4 **Welliesinthewater (IRE)**[23] 1702 6-9-0 78 .... (v) MartinLane 1 85
(Derek Shaw) *settled bhd ldrs in 3rd: rdn 2f out: kpt on ins fnl f tl wknd nr fin: hld on for 2nd* **16/1**

60-0 3 nse **Major Crispies**[12] 1990 5-9-7 85 .... GeorgeBaker 12 92
(James Eustace) *settled in mid-div on outer: gd prog over 2f out: rdn over 1f out: kpt on to press runner-up nr fin* **25/1**

2134 4 hd **Franco's Secret**[28] 1576 5-9-4 82 .... (v) CharlesBishop 6 88+
(Peter Hedger) *hld up in rr: stl plenty to do turning into st: rdn over 1f out and str run ins fnl f to press for placings: nvr nrr* **8/1**[3]

50-2 5 2 1/4 **Dutch Law**[21] 1775 4-9-4 82 .... RobertHavlin 3 83+
(Hughie Morrison) *nudged along on leaving stalls: mid-div: rdn 2f out: one pce ins fnl f* **4/1**[2]

355- 6 shd **Ruban (IRE)**[263] 5845 7-9-6 84 .... (t) PatCosgrave 8 85+
(Stuart Williams) *in rr: rdn 2f out: nudged along over 2f out: sme prog ins fnl f under hands and heels* **12/1**

0110 7 nk **Harry Holland**[21] 1797 4-9-4 82 .... (b[1]) MartinDwyer 11 82
(William Muir) *chsd ldrs: rdn 2f out: no ex ins fnl f* **16/1**

0000 8 1 1/4 **Pick A Little**[16] 1916 8-8-11 75 .... TimmyMurphy 4 72
(Michael Blake) *led: nudged along 2f out: sn rdn and hdd over 1f out: wknd ins fnl f* **100/1**

420- 9 3 **Iconic (IRE)**[226] 6979 4-9-5 83 .... WilliamBuick 13 74
(Henry Candy) *mid-div: rdn along 2f out: sn wknd* **20/1**

1- 10 1 1/4 **Important Point (USA)**[204] 7542 4-9-7 85 .... JamesDoyle 5 73
(Saeed bin Suroor) *settled in rr: sltly keen: pushed along over 2f out: no rspnse and eased ins fnl f* **7/4**[1]

516- 11 1 1/2 **King Torus (IRE)**[194] 7731 8-9-0 83 .... (v) CallumShepherd(5) 2 67
(Lee Carter) *mid-div on inner: rdn along over 2f out: no imp and wknd* **33/1**

3134 12 1 1/4 **Presumido (IRE)**[22] 1752 6-9-5 83 .... JimCrowley 10 64
(Simon Dow) *in rr: t.k.h: rdn 2f out: sn hld* **16/1**

1m 38.29s (-1.51) **Going Correction** -0.05s/f (Stan) **12** Ran SP% **116.5**
Speed ratings (Par 105): **105,102,102,102,100 100,99,98,95,94 92,91**
CSF £120.58 CT £3084.75 TOTE £9.70: £3.50, £3.90, £8.20; EX 139.20 Trifecta £2273.60.
Owner Mondial Racing & Robert Haim **Bred** J Bernstein & R Haim **Trained** Lambourn, Berks

FOCUS
A run-of-the-mill handicap and, with a number of these looking weighted up to their best, it was left to a horse to defy a near two-year absence to win.

2379 32RED ON THE APP STORE H'CAP 7f (P)
8:25 (8:27) (Class 6) (0-65,65) 4-Y-O+ **£2,264** (£673; £336; £168) **Stalls** Low

Form RPR

1100 1 **Eljaddaaf (IRE)**[16] 1928 5-9-5 65 .... RobertWinston 14 74
(Dean Ivory) *wnt lft s: in rr: swtchd to inner rail over 1f out: sn rdn and led ins fnl f: rdn out* **7/1**[2]

5005 2 1 3/4 **Straits Of Malacca**[19] 1838 5-9-3 63 .... LiamKeniry 3 67
(Simon Dow) *chsd ldr: rdn and led over 1f out: hdd 1f out: kpt on but hld by wnr* **16/1**

1166 3 1 **Misu Pete**[23] 1700 4-9-2 62 .... ShaneKelly 13 64
(Mark Usher) *chsd ldrs: rdn 2f out: kpt on wl between horses to grab 3rd nr fin* **14/1**

5055 4 nk **Ocean Legend (IRE)**[16] 1928 11-9-3 63 .... AdamKirby 7 65
(Tony Carroll) *chsd ldrs: lost pl in st and rdn 2f out: kpt on wl ins fnl f* **6/1**[1]

3-13 5 shd **Choral Clan (IRE)**[17] 1899 5-8-13 62 .... TomMarquand(3) 10 62
(Philip Mitchell) *in rr-div on outer: rdn 2f out and kpt on ins fnl f* **6/1**[1]

0560 6 nk **Cool Strutter (IRE)**[25] 1625 4-9-3 63 .... (b[1]) OisinMurphy 8 63
(Andrew Balding) *mid-div: rdn 2f out: gd prog on outer ins fnl f* **12/1**

5-45 7 nk **Miss Inga Sock (IRE)**[22] 1735 4-9-0 63 .... GeorgeDowning(3) 9 62
(Eve Johnson Houghton) *settled bhd ldrs: pushed along over 2f out: led briefly 2f out: hdd over 1f out: lost four plcd ins fnl f* **14/1**

1044 8 1/2 **Bookmaker**[7] 2153 6-9-3 63 .... (b) WilliamCarson 12 61
(John Bridger) *chsd ldrs: rdn 2f out: kpt on one pce* **12/1**

-060 9 3/4 **Swot**[16] 1928 4-9-5 65 .... (p) GeorgeBaker 6 61
(Roger Teal) *in rr: stl plenty to do turning in: pushed along over 1f out: no imp ins fnl f* **14/1**

4660 10 shd **Cascading Stars (IRE)**[26] 1595 4-9-5 65 .... LukeMorris 5 60
(Daniel Mark Loughnane) *in rr-div: rdn 2f out: sn hld* **8/1**[3]

15-0 11 1/2 **Monna Valley**[19] 1838 4-9-4 64 .... (t) PatCosgrave 1 58
(Stuart Williams) *mid-div: rdn 2f out: sn hld and wknd ins fnl f* **8/1**[3]

-502 12 3 1/2 **Yorkindred Spirit**[22] 1766 4-9-4 64 .... WilliamBuick 2 48
(Mark Johnston) *mid-div: rdn over 2f out: one pce and wknd* **12/1**

0-00 13 7 **Cloak And Degas (IRE)**[16] 1928 4-9-4 64 .... (v) MartinDwyer 4 30
(Tim McCarthy) *led: rdn and hdd 2f out: wknd qckly ins fnl f* **33/1**

354- 14 shd **Comparative**[161] 8158 4-9-2 62 .... JimCrowley 11 27
(Lydia Pearce) *pressed ldr: rdn 2f out: sn btn and eased ins fnl f* **12/1**

1m 25.15s (-0.85) **Going Correction** -0.05s/f (Stan) **14** Ran SP% **122.9**
Speed ratings (Par 101): **102,100,98,98,98 98,97,97,96,96 95,91,83,83**
CSF £116.71 CT £1585.31 TOTE £5.90: £4.80, £3.80, £3.90; EX 89.80 Trifecta £329.40.
Owner Wentdale Ltd & Mrs L A Ivory **Bred** Shadwell Estate Company Limited **Trained** Radlett, Herts

FOCUS
A weak handicap, where a case could have been made for most the field. They went a good pace and the finishers held sway.

2380 RACING UK IN GLORIOUS HD H'CAP 6f (P)
8:55 (8:57) (Class 6) (0-65,65) 4-Y-O+ **£2,264** (£673; £336; £168) **Stalls** Low

Form RPR

2-03 1 **Triple Dream**[32] 1496 11-9-4 62 .... OisinMurphy 11 69
(Milton Bradley) *broke wl fr wd draw: sn settled bhd clr ldrs: rdn 2f out: gd prog ins fnl f to ld fnl 100yds: kpt on* **14/1**

5120 2 nk **New Rich**[48] 1159 6-9-5 63 .... (b) JohnFahy 9 69
(Eve Johnson Houghton) *in rr: rdn w plenty to do over 2f out: str run ins fnl f to press wnr nr fin* **13/2**[3]

2341 3 2 **Bridge Builder**[42] 1261 6-9-7 65 .... (p) CharlesBishop 7 65+
(Peter Hedger) *chsd ldr: led 2f out: rdn and 3 l advantage 1f out: sn wkng: hdd 100yds out and lost 2nd cl home* **11/4**[1]

4462 4 shd **Only Ten Per Cent (IRE)**[42] 1261 8-9-2 63 .... AlistairRawlinson(3) 12 63
(J R Jenkins) *in rr: rdn 2f out: kpt on at one pce to press for 3rd nr fin* **12/1**

-235 5 1 1/4 **Ghost Train (IRE)**[48] 1159 7-9-3 61 .... (p) LukeMorris 8 57
(Tim McCarthy) *t.k.h in mid-div: rdn 2f out: kpt on* **8/1**

000 6 hd **Orlando Rogue (IRE)**[51] 1120 4-9-4 62 .... (p) LiamKeniry 10 57
(Conor Dore) *in rr: rdn 2f out: sme prog on rail tl wknd ins fnl f* **16/1**

6622 7 nk **Generalyse**[23] 1720 7-8-10 59 .... (p) JosephineGordon(5) 2 54
(Anabel K Murphy) *settled in mid-div on inner: rdn 2f out: one pce fnl f* **13/2**[3]

6-63 **8** *2 ¼* **Refuse Colette (IRE)**[20] 1811 7-9-5 **63**........................ WilliamCarson 3 51
(Mick Quinn) *settled bhd ldng pair in 3rd: rdn and ev ch over 2f out: wknd over 1f out* **10/1**

62-0 **9** *1* **Toni's A Star**[25] 1648 4-9-1 **62**.................................. GeorgeDowning(3) 6 47
(Tony Carroll) *led at gd pce: rdn over 2f out: hdd 2f out: wknd ins fnl f* **25/1**

020- **10** *½* **Malvia**[225] 7023 4-9-5 **63**.. AdamKirby 1 46
(Ian Williams) *mid-div: rdn over 2f out: sn one pce and wknd fnl f* **9/2**[2]

25-0 **11** *2 ½* **Essaka (IRE)**[25] 1648 4-9-2 **60**... JimCrowley 5 36
(Tony Carroll) *mid-div: rdn over 2f out: one pce and eased over 1f out* **25/1**

1m 12.32s (-0.78) **Going Correction** -0.05s/f (Stan) **11** Ran SP% **119.7**
Speed ratings (Par 101): **103,102,99,99,98 97,97,94,93,92 89**
CSF £104.05 CT £328.55 TOTE £6.60: £4.30, £4.30, £1.40; EX 89.20 Trifecta £515.20.
Owner J M Bradley **Bred** Hesmonds Stud Ltd **Trained** Sedbury, Gloucs

FOCUS

They went a really good pace in this very modest sprint handicap.
T/Plt: £591.60 to a £1 stake. Pool: £66,600.65 - 82.18 winning units. T/Qpdt: £303.00 to a £1 stake. pool: £6,765.12 - 16.52 winning units. **Cathal Gahan**

2381 - 2389a (Foreign Racing) - See Raceform Interactive

1854 GOODWOOD (R-H)

Thursday, May 19

OFFICIAL GOING: Good (7.5)

Wind: fresh against Weather: sunny

2390 NJS GROUP EBF NOVICE STKS (PLUS 10 RACE) 6f

1:50 (1:50) (Class 4) 2-Y-O **£5,175** (£1,540; £769; £384) **Stalls** High

Form RPR

1 **Yalta (IRE)** 2-9-2 0... WilliamBuick 4 90+
(Mark Johnston) *tall: lengthy: athletic: mde all: shkn up over 1f out: r.o wl: readily* **5/2**[2]

2 *2* **Repton (IRE)** 2-9-2 0... SeanLevey 2 84
(Richard Hannon) *w'like: leggy: s.i.s: sn trcking ldrs: rdn over 2f out: chal for 2nd ent fnl f: kpt on but a being readily hld by wnr* **14/1**[3]

1 **3** *nse* **Afandem (IRE)**[19] 1850 2-9-8 0.. RyanMoore 1 90
(Hugo Palmer) *athletic: trckd wnr: rdn over 2f out: jnd for 2nd ent fnl f: kpt on but a being hld by wnr: lost 2nd on nod* **1/2**[1]

4 *3 ¼* **Pleaseletmewin (IRE)** 2-9-2 0... FMBerry 5 74
(Ralph Beckett) *lengthy: s.i.s: cl up in 5th: rdn 2f out: kpt on but nt pce to get involved* **28/1**

5 **5** *23* **Son Castello (IRE)**[24] 1713 2-9-2 0.............................. JimmyFortune 3 5
(Brian Meehan) *tall: trckd ldrs: rdn over 2f out: wknd over 1f out* **40/1**

1m 12.91s (0.71) **Going Correction** +0.30s/f (Good) **5** Ran SP% **107.8**
Speed ratings (Par 95): **107,104,104,99,69**
CSF £29.01 TOTE £3.00: £2.50, £5.50; EX 22.50 Trifecta £23.80.
Owner Sheikh Hamdan bin Mohammed Al Maktoum **Bred** Darley **Trained** Middleham Moor, N Yorks

FOCUS

The first 2f of the 1m course was dolled out approximately 5 yards. The running rail from the 6f marker on the lower bend to the 2f marker in the straight had been dolled out approximately 6 yards, therefore increasing the distances of the 7f and 1m1f races by approximately 15 yards. Two horses totally dominated the market in the opener, but only one mattered throughout the final furlong.

2391 WINNEREVENTS.COM STKS (H'CAP) 7f

2:20 (2:20) (Class 2) (0-105,100) 4-Y-O+**£16,172** (£4,812; £2,405; £1,202) **Stalls** Low

Form RPR

001- **1** **Can't Change It (IRE)**[250] 6320 5-8-9 **88** ow1............(p) JamieSpencer 2 101+
(David Simcock) *in tch: tk cl order 3f out: nt clr run 2f out: qcknd up wl to ld 1f out: drifted rt: comf* **7/1**[3]

0600 **2** *2* **Emell**[12] 2027 6-9-7 **100**...(b) SeanLevey 3 106
(Richard Hannon) *trckd ldrs: rdn to chal wl over 1f out: ev ch ent fnl f: kpt on but nt gng pce of wnr* **8/1**

0043 **3** *½* **Arnold Lane (IRE)**[13] 1993 7-8-7 **86**........................ SilvestreDeSousa 5 91
(Mick Channon) *led: rdn 2f out: hdd ent fnl f: kpt on but no ex* **13/2**[2]

3-33 **4** *1 ½* **Cincuenta Pasos (IRE)**[17] 1929 5-8-1 **85**.............. EdwardGreatrex(5) 6 86
(Joseph Tuite) *hld up towards rr: hdwy but nt best of runs over 2f out: kpt on to go 4th ent fnl f but nt pce of ldrs* **12/1**

60-0 **5** *hd* **Czech It Out (IRE)**[19] 1856 6-8-10 **89**......................... CharlesBishop 13 89
(Amanda Perrett) *mid-div: hdwy to chse ldrs 2f out: edgd rt and kpt on same pce fnl f* **16/1**

0-00 **6** *1 ¼* **The Warrior (IRE)**[12] 2027 4-9-1 **94**.................................. RyanMoore 9 91+
(Amanda Perrett) *lw: hld up towards rr: nt clrest of runs 2f: hdwy over 1f out: kpt on fnl f but nt pce to threaten* **9/2**[1]

2306 **7** *hd* **Sirius Prospect (USA)**[19] 1856 8-9-5 **98**..................... RobertWinston 1 94
(Dean Ivory) *lw: trckd ldr: rdn over 2f out: one pce fnl f* **12/1**

0461 **8** *nk* **Russian Realm**[19] 1856 6-9-1 **94**.. ShaneKelly 10 90
(Richard Hughes) *in tch: rdn over 1f out: nt pce to get involved* **8/1**

00-0 **9** *½* **Pastoral Player**[15] 1959 9-8-2 **88**............................ CharlieBennett(7) 14 82
(Hughie Morrison) *hld up towards rr: rdn and stdy prog fr 2f out: kpt on same pce fnl f: nvr trbld ldrs* **33/1**

12-3 **10** *¾* **Scottish Glen**[12] 2033 10-9-0 **93**...................................... JimCrowley 12 85
(Patrick Chamings) *lw: hld up towards rr: rdn and hdwy over 2f out: nvr quite threatened: wknd ins fnl f* **12/1**

6-00 **11** *2 ¼* **Fox Trotter (IRE)**[91] 628 4-9-4 **97**................................ JimmyFortune 8 83
(Brian Meehan) *mid-div: rdn 2f out: no imp: wknd fnl f* **16/1**

0000 **12** *2 ½* **Anonymous John (IRE)**[68] 923 4-8-9 **88**.................... CathyGannon 7 67
(David Evans) *trckd ldr: rdn 2f out: wknd fnl f* **50/1**

000- **13** *3* **Red Avenger (USA)**[224] 7065 6-8-12 **96**..............(b) HectorCrouch(5) 11 67
(Gary Moore) *racd keenly: in tch: hdwy 3f out: sn rdn: wknd ent fnl f* **66/1**

06-0 **14** *8* **Enlace**[5] 2247 4-9-2 **95**... WilliamBuick 4 45
(Mark Johnston) *s.i.s: sn pushed along: a in rr* **8/1**

1m 28.01s (1.01) **Going Correction** +0.375s/f (Good) **14** Ran SP% **118.6**
Speed ratings (Par 109): **109,106,106,104,104 102,102,102,101,100 98,95,91,82**
CSF £60.57 CT £299.01 TOTE £7.50: £2.50, £2.90, £2.40; EX 64.00 Trifecta £440.60.
Owner Mrs Fitri Hay **Bred** Peter & Hugh McCutcheon **Trained** Newmarket, Suffolk

FOCUS

First 2f of the 1m course was dolled out approximately 5 yards. The running rail from the 6f marker on the lower bend to the 2f marker in the straight had been dolled out approximately 6 yards, increasing the distances of this race by approximately 15 yards. A decent handicap, but the early gallop didn't seem overly strong. It paid to be close to the leader. The winner carried over his improvement and is possibly worth a bit extra.

2392 CONSTRUCTION DAY STKS (H'CAP) 2m

2:55 (2:55) (Class 4) (0-85,83) 4-Y-O+ **£6,469** (£1,925; £962; £481) **Stalls** Low

Form RPR

3154 **1** **Albahar (FR)**[13] 1987 5-9-10 **83**....................................(p) WilliamBuick 12 95
(Chris Gordon) *slowly away: in last: pushed along and hdwy 3f out: sn trcking ldrs: led jst ins fnl f: styd on strly to draw clr: comf* **16/1**

00/1 **2** *4 ½* **Rayvin Black**[19] 1854 7-9-0 **78**.............................. EdwardGreatrex(5) 11 85
(Oliver Sherwood) *led: rdn over 2f out: hdd jst ins fnl f: styd on but no ex* **3/1**[2]

33-1 **3** *2* **Wolf Of Windlesham (IRE)**[26] 1038 4-8-4 **70**........... HectorCrouch(5) 9 75
(Stuart Edmunds) *lw: mid-div: hdwy 10f out to trck ldr: rdn over 3f out: hung rt and hld over 1f out: styd on same pce* **2/1**[1]

5130 **4** *3 ¾* **Spiritoftomintoul**[27] 1598 7-9-4 **80**........................(t) GeorgeDowning(3) 1 80
(Tony Carroll) *s.i.s: in last pair: stdy prog u.p fr 2f out: styd on fnl f: wnt 4th cl home* **33/1**

13-5 **5** *¾* **All For The Best (IRE)**[23] 1760 4-8-13 **74**........................(p) ShaneKelly 4 73
(Robert Stephens) *mid-div: rdn whn nt clr run on rails over 2f out: styd on ins fnl f: nvr trbld ldrs* **28/1**

35-5 **6** *shd* **Medburn Cutler**[19] 1854 6-8-9 **68**..............................(p) JamieSpencer 8 67
(Paul Henderson) *slowly away: in last trio tl gd hdwy 10f to trck ldr: rdn for brief chal over 3f out: hld over 1f out: no ex and lost 2 pls ins fnl f* **20/1**

4156 **7** *1 ¼* **Cotton Club (IRE)**[18] 1893 5-9-9 **82**.............................. FrederikTylicki 6 80
(Rod Millman) *nvr bttr than mid-div* **33/1**

50-2 **8** *1* **Snowy Dawn**[17] 1914 6-8-12 **71**..................................... RoystonFfrench 3 67
(Steph Hollinshead) *in tch: rdn to chse ldrs 3f out: fdd fnl f* **16/1**

15-3 **9** *4 ½* **Fitzwilly**[17] 1914 6-9-4 **77**.. SilvestreDeSousa 10 68
(Mick Channon) *mid-div: in last trio 9f out: rdn 3f out: sme prog past btn horses 2f out but nvr any threat* **5/1**[3]

40-0 **10** *2 ¼* **Arty Campbell (IRE)**[13] 1987 6-9-8 **81**............. WilliamTwiston-Davies 2 75
(Bernard Llewellyn) *trckd ldrs: rdn over 3f out: one pce whn nt clr run over 1f out: eased whn btn ins fnl f* **16/1**

130- **11** *20* **Brittleton**[202] 7597 4-9-4 **79**...(b) JimCrowley 5 43
(Harry Dunlop) *in tch: rdn in cl 3rd over 3f out: wknd over 2f out: eased fnl f* **25/1**

00-0 **12** *40* **See And Be Seen**[13] 1987 6-9-4 **77**.................................(p) LukeMorris 7
(Sylvester Kirk) *trckd ldr: rdn over 3f out: wknd 2f out: sn eased* **40/1**

500- **13** *8* **Kashgar**[230] 6896 7-8-12 **78**.......................................(t) GeorgeWood(7) 13
(Bernard Llewellyn) *mid-div tl wknd over 2f out: eased fr over 1f out* **20/1**

3m 34.62s (5.62) **Going Correction** +0.375s/f (Good)
WFA 4 from 5yo+ 2lb **13** Ran SP% **117.8**
Speed ratings (Par 105): **100,97,96,94,94 94,93,93,91,89 79,59,55**
CSF £57.73 CT £142.94 TOTE £12.00: £4.10, £1.40, £1.30; EX 72.20 Trifecta £230.20.
Owner Mrs Kate Digweed **Bred** Julien Leaunes **Trained** Morestead, Hampshire

FOCUS

Nothing more than a fair staying contest, in which the betting was dominated by a couple of well-above-average hurdlers. This was the winner's best run in Britain.

2393 WRIGHT JOINERY COMPANY STKS (H'CAP) 1m 1f

3:30 (3:30) (Class 4) (0-85,85) 3-Y-O

£6,225 (£1,864; £932; £466; £233; £117) **Stalls** Low

Form RPR

5-06 **1** **Bathos (IRE)**[12] 2029 3-9-7 **85**... WilliamBuick 5 92
(Mark Johnston) *lw: trckd ldrs: led 2f out: sn rdn: strly chal ent fnl f: kpt on wl to assert towards fin* **17/2**

34-2 **2** *½* **Thaqaffa (IRE)**[21] 1804 3-8-7 **71**................................... RoystonFfrench 6 77
(Marcus Tregoning) *cmpt: mid-div: hdwy 3f out: rdn and ev ch ent fnl f: drifted lft: no ex towards fin* **5/1**[2]

4-40 **3** *1 ½* **Bergholt (IRE)**[23] 1750 3-8-8 **72**..................................(p) JamieSpencer 9 75
(Philip Hide) *stdd s: in last: rdn and hdwy over 1f out: wnt 3rd ent fnl f: kpt on but nt pce to get on terms* **25/1**

4-23 **4** *2* **Scarlet Dragon**[12] 2029 3-9-1 **79**.................................... JimmyFortune 1 78+
(Eve Johnson Houghton) *racd keenly: mid-div on rails: nt clr run over 2f out: making gd hdwy whn stopped again ent fnl f: kpt on but no ch after* **5/1**[2]

4501 **5** *½* **Sark (IRE)**[27] 1602 3-8-10 **74**.. CathyGannon 2 72
(David Evans) *towards rr: sn nudged along: rdn 3f out: no real imp tl styd on fnl f: nvr trbld ldrs* **14/1**

3-31 **6** *¾* **Finelcity (GER)**[29] 1570 3-8-13 **77**.........................(b) SilvestreDeSousa 7 73
(Harry Dunlop) *led: rdn and hdd 2f out: kpt on tl no ex fnl 120yds* **6/1**[3]

0-10 **7** *1 ½* **Telegram**[13] 1992 3-9-4 **85**......................................(b[1]) TomMarquand(3) 8 78
(Richard Hannon) *lw: s.i.s: in last pair: pushed along over 4f out: rdn over 3f out: nvr gng pce to get on terms* **33/1**

61- **8** *nse* **Jim Dandy**[251] 6276 3-9-2 **80**........................... WilliamTwiston-Davies 10 72
(Alan King) *lw: mid-div: hdwy 3f out: rdn w ch 2f out: fdd ins fnl f* **7/1**

4124 **9** *shd* **Lord Huntingdon**[10] 2099 3-9-0 **78**................................... OisinMurphy 4 70
(Andrew Balding) *trckd ldr: chal 2f out: sn rdn: wknd ins fnl f* **11/1**

1-33 **10** *37* **Bedrock**[10] 2099 3-9-1 **79**.. RyanMoore 3
(William Haggas) *trckd ldrs: rdn over 2f out: appeared to lose action and sn eased: virtually p.u* **3/1**[1]

1m 58.4s (2.10) **Going Correction** +0.375s/f (Good) **10** Ran SP% **117.4**
Speed ratings (Par 101): **105,104,103,101,101 100,99,98,98,65**
CSF £51.06 CT £1032.12 TOTE £8.10: £2.40, £1.70, £6.80; EX 36.70 Trifecta £958.50.
Owner Sheikh Hamdan bin Mohammed Al Maktoum **Bred** Lofts Hall Stud **Trained** Middleham Moor, N Yorks

FOCUS

The first 2f of the 1m course was dolled out approximately 5 yards. The running rail from the 6f marker on the lower bend to the 2f marker in the straight had been dolled out approximately 6 yards, increasing this race distance by approximately 15 yards. An interesting race for 3yos, with many potentially open to improvement. A pb from the winner.

2394 VEOLIA HEIGHT OF FASHION STKS (LISTED RACE) (FILLIES) 1m 1f 192y

4:00 (4:00) (Class 1) 3-Y-O **£23,680** (£8,956; £4,476; £2,236) **Stalls** Low

Form RPR

3 **1** **Skiffle**[13] 1989 3-9-0 0.. WilliamBuick 4 104
(Charlie Appleby) *lw: broke wl: stdd into last trio: hdwy over 2f out: rdn to chse ldr over 1f out: styd on wl to ld towards fin* **5/1**[2]

1-2 **2** *1* **The Black Princess (FR)**[23] 1758 3-9-0 84.................. FrankieDettori 9 102
(John Gosden) *mid-div: hdwy over 3f out: led 2f out: sn rdn: no ex whn hdd towards fin* **13/8**[1]

01-5 **3** 7 **Play Gal**^{15} 1966 3-9-0 91... CathyGannon 1 88
(David Evans) *led: rdn and hdd 2f out: kpt on tl no ex fnl 150yds* **25/1**

0-51 **4** 4 **Visage Blanc**^{7} 2181 3-9-0 67... JFEgan 6 80
(Mick Channon) *in tch: hdwy over 4f out: rdn and ev ch over 2f out tl wl over 1f out: one pce after* **40/1**

3-2 **5** 5 **September Stars (IRE)**^{33} 1483 3-9-0 0... FMBerry 3 70
(Ralph Beckett) *tall: hld up: effrt to cl on ldrs over 2f out: nvr threatened: wknd fnl f* **6/1**^{3}

1- **6** hd **Zaakhir (IRE)**^{171} 8047 3-9-0 0... DarryllHolland 5 70
(Charles Hills) *tall: trckd ldr: pushed along over 3f out: rdn and hung lft over 2f out: no ex fnl f* **6/1**^{3}

4-10 **7** 2 **Mirsaalah**^{15} 1966 3-9-0 81... LukeMorris 2 66
(James Tate) *chsd ldrs: rdn and ev ch over 2f out: wknd jst over 1f out* **33/1**

10-4 **8** 4½ **Dessertoflife (IRE)**^{15} 1966 3-9-5 101... JoeFanning 7 62
(Mark Johnston) *trckd ldrs: rdn over 3f out: wknd jst over 1f out* **17/2**

1-1 **9** 7 **Cajoled (FR)**^{12} 2044 3-9-0 79...(t) RyanMoore 8 43
(George Scott) *str: swtg: s.i.s: effrt to cl on ldrs 3f out: nvr threatened: wknd over 1f out* **15/2**

2m 8.67s (0.57) **Going Correction** +0.375s/f (Good) **9** Ran SP% **114.9**
Speed ratings (Par 104): **112,111,105,102,98 98,96,93,87**
CSF £13.23 TOTE £5.80: £2.30, £1.10, £4.50; EX 12.70 Trifecta £297.00.
Owner Godolphin **Bred** Darley **Trained** Newmarket, Suffolk

FOCUS
This is usually a good race and seen as a stepping stone to the Oaks. Snow Fairy did the double in 2010, while Lady Of Dubai went on to finish third at Epsom last year. The pace seemed fair throughout and two came nicely clear, looking above the race standard, but the winner doesn't currently hold an entry in the fillies' Classic next month. The time was 27lb faster than the following maiden.

2395 BREEDERS BACKING RACING EBF MAIDEN FILLIES' STKS (PLUS 10 RACE) 1m 1f 192y
4:35 (4:36) (Class 5) 3-Y-O **£3,881** (£1,155; £577; £288) **Stalls** Low

Form RPR

0 **1** **Atone**^{27} 1608 3-9-0 0... RyanMoore 4 83+
(Sir Michael Stoute) *led for 2f: trckd ldrs: drvn over 2f out: chal ins fnl f: led fnl stride* **8/1**

4-6 **2** shd **Pleasure Dome**^{27} 1609 3-9-0 0... JimmyFortune 8 82
(Peter Chapple-Hyam) *prom: led 2f out: sn rdn: strly pressed and hld on to narrow advantage u.str.p fnl f: hdd fnl stride* **20/1**

2-4 **3** 2½ **High Hopes**^{27} 1609 3-9-0 0... JamieSpencer 6 78
(David Simcock) *led after 2f: rdn and hdd 2f out: kpt pressing wnr tl no ex fnl 100yds* **3/1**^{2}

05- **4** 6 **Zubeida**^{215} 7284 3-8-11 0... ThomasBrown$^{(3)}$ 10 65
(Ismail Mohammed) *leggy: hld up: hdwy 4f out: rdn over 2f out: styd on into 4th fnl f but nt pce of ldrs* **50/1**

3 **5** nk **Golden Reign (IRE)**^{37} 1392 3-9-0 0... PatCosgrave 1 64
(William Haggas) *s.i.s: sn mid-div: rdn wl over 2f out: nvr any imp* **4/5**^{1}

6 ½ **Maqueda (USA)** 3-9-0 0... JimCrowley 2 63
(Amanda Perrett) *str: trckd ldrs: rdn in hld 4th over 2f out: drifted lft over 1f out: fdd fnl f* **33/1**

0- **7** 2¾ **Al Egda**^{212} 7362 3-9-0 0... FrankieDettori 7 58
(John Gosden) *athletic: s.i.s: towards rr: rdn wl over 2f out: nvr any imp* **7/1**^{3}

8 ¾ **Talisa (IRE)** 3-9-0 0... JoeFanning 3 56+
(David Simcock) *w'like: s.i.s: towards rr: hdwy over 3f out: chal for 4th over 2f out tl wknd ent fnl f* **28/1**

0- **9** 2¾ **Lady Emma**^{208} 7472 3-9-0 0...^{1} RoystonFfrench 5 51
(Steph Hollinshead) *leggy: in tch tl outpcd and sltly short of room 3f out* **150/1**

5-0 **10** 1¾ **Onehelluvatouch**^{27} 1608 3-9-0 0... WilliamTwiston-Davies 9 47
(Philip Hide) *struggling 4f out: a towards rr* **66/1**

2m 11.06s (2.96) **Going Correction** +0.375s/f (Good) **10** Ran SP% **119.4**
Speed ratings (Par 96): **103,102,100,96,95 95,93,92,90,89**
CSF £143.66 TOTE £10.10: £2.70, £4.90, £1.50; EX 155.70 Trifecta £857.30.
Owner K Abdullah **Bred** Juddmonte Farms Ltd **Trained** Newmarket, Suffolk
■ Stewards' Enquiry : Pat Cosgrave one-day ban: careless riding (Jun 2)

FOCUS
A really interesting maiden which contained some fillies with some top-class pedigrees. The first three were clear and the form is rated around the third.

2396 SOUTHERN CRANES APPRENTICE STKS (H'CAP) 6f
5:05 (5:06) (Class 5) (0-70,70) 4-Y-O+ **£3,234** (£962; £481; £240) **Stalls** High

Form RPR

1445 **1** **Pour La Victoire (IRE)**^{16} 1946 6-9-4 70...(b) GeorgiaCox$^{(3)}$ 6 80
(Tony Carroll) *in tch: hdwy 2f out: rdn to ld fnl 120yds: r.o wl* **9/1**

00-4 **2** 1 **Pettochside**^{17} 1928 7-8-13 67... MitchGodwin$^{(5)}$ 5 74
(John Bridger) *lw: led: rdn wl over 1f out: hdd fnl 120yds: kpt on but no ex* **5/1**^{3}

0-60 **3** ½ **Regal Parade**^{12} 2028 12-9-7 70...(t) KieranShoemark 10 75
(Charlie Wallis) *hld up: swtchd to centre and hdwy 2f out: rdn over 1f out: kpt on to chse ldng pair fnl f: a being hld* **12/1**

-050 **4** 2 **Bahamian Sunrise**^{12} 2028 4-9-7 70... GeorgeBuckell 8 69
(John Gallagher) *broke wl: prom: rdn and ev ch over 1f out: kpt on same pce fnl f* **20/1**

-213 **5** ¾ **Lewisham**^{20} 1827 6-9-2 70... GeorgeWood$^{(5)}$ 3 66
(J R Jenkins) *trckd ldr: rdn w ev ch whn sltly short of room over 1f out: no ex fnl f* **11/4**^{1}

060- **6** nk **Captain Ryan**^{212} 7365 5-8-10 59... EdwardGreatrex 9 54
(Geoffrey Deacon) *hld up: racd keenly after 2f: rdn over 1f out: nt pce to get on terms* **25/1**

4140 **7** ½ **Harwoods Star (IRE)**^{12} 2028 6-9-0 70...(v) DavidEgan$^{(7)}$ 7 64
(John Butler) *s.i.s: towards rr: hdwy over 2f out: kpt on same pce fnl f* **20/1**

001 **8** ¾ **Summersault (IRE)**^{17} 1928 5-9-4 67... LucyKBarry 11 58
(Jamie Osborne) *mid-div: rdn over 2f out: hung lft whn btn over 1f out* **7/2**^{2}

02-5 **9** 1 **Oat Couture**^{36} 1419 4-9-4 67... HectorCrouch 4 55
(Henry Candy) *in tch: effrt 2f out: fdd ins fnl f* **14/1**

40-0 **10** 3¼ **Langley Vale**^{48} 1178 7-9-2 68...(p) KevinLundie$^{(3)}$ 1 46
(Roger Teal) *trckd ldrs: rdn and ev ch over 1f out: sn btn* **9/1**

1m 13.54s (1.34) **Going Correction** +0.30s/f (Good) **10** Ran SP% **113.3**
Speed ratings (Par 103): **103,101,101,98,97 96,96,95,93,89**
CSF £50.39 CT £553.84 TOTE £11.40: £4.10, £2.40, £4.80; EX 69.10 Trifecta £348.20.
Owner Curry House Corner **Bred** L Fox **Trained** Cropthorne, Worcs
■ Stewards' Enquiry : Georgia Cox caution: careless riding

FOCUS
A modest sprint handicap with a turd pb from the winner.
T/Plt: £121.40 to a £1 stake. Pool of £82937.23 - 498.60 winning tickets. T/Qpdt: £12.50 to a £1 stake. Pool of £8458.48 - 498.30 winning tickets. **Tim Mitchell**

2319 LINGFIELD (L-H)
Thursday, May 19

OFFICIAL GOING: Good (soft 7f to 7f 140yds)
Wind: light, half behind Weather: overcast

2397 MAIL NEWSPAPERS H'CAP 1m 3f 106y
2:00 (2:01) (Class 6) (0-60,66) 4-Y-O+ **£2,264** (£673; £336; £168) **Stalls** High

Form RPR

4311 **1** **Bamako Du Chatelet (FR)**^{2} 2326 5-9-4 60...(p) MarcMonaghan$^{(3)}$ 10 70
(Ian Williams) *hld up in tch in midfield: clsd to chse ldrs 4f out: rdn over 2f out: hdwy u.p to chse ldr over 1f out: led ins fnl f: styd on wl: rdn out* **1/1**^{1}

6112 **2** 1 **Glasgow Central**^{1} 2374 5-9-13 66 6ex... AdamKirby 2 74
(Phil McEntee) *chsd ldrs: clsd to ld and travelling strly over 2f out: sn rdn: drvn and hdd ins fnl f: styd on same pce after* **5/2**^{2}

0420 **3** 2 **Golden Thread**^{56} 1057 6-9-7 60... LiamJones 9 65
(Neil King) *hld up in tch in last trio: hdwy into midfield: hdwy into midfield and rdn over 3f out: 5th over 1f out: styd on to go 3rd ins fnl f: nvr getting on terms w ldng pair* **16/1**

53 **4** 3¼ **Forecast**^{20} 1824 4-9-5 58... TomQueally 7 58
(Martin Keighley) *t.k.h: chsd ldr: rdn and ev ch briefly over 2f out: outpcd over 1f out: kpt on same pce after* **8/1**^{3}

5-30 **5** 2¼ **Doctor Kehoe**^{10} 2105 4-9-7 60...(vt) SteveDrowne 6 56
(David Evans) *chsd ldrs: rdn over 2f out: outpcd and hld in 4th over 1f out: wknd ins fnl f* **12/1**

2333 **6** 5 **Les Gar Gan (IRE)**^{23} 1747 5-9-5 58...(be) StevieDonohoe 5 46
(Daniel Mark Loughnane) *hld up in tch in last trio: effrt over 2f out: modest hdwy to pass btn horses over 1f out: nvr threatened ldrs* **16/1**

-020 **7** 5 **Salient**^{19} 1854 12-9-0 53... KierenFox 4 33
(Michael Attwater) *led tl rdn and hdd over 2f out: sn outpcd: wknd over 1f out* **22/1**

400- **8** ¾ **Bollywood Dream**^{381} 1938 4-8-6 48...(p) DannyBrock$^{(3)}$ 8 27
(Peter Hedger) *stdd s: hld up in tch in last trio: effrt and stl lots to do 3f out: no prog: wl bhd over 1f out* **40/1**

060/ **9** 17 **Total Obsession**^{834} 484 9-8-2 46 oh1...(v) PaddyPilley$^{(5)}$ 1
(Mark Hoad) *in tch in midfield: rdn over 3f out: bhd fnl 2f* **66/1**

000- **10** 1¾ **Victoriously**^{328} 3614 4-9-7 60... MartinLane 11 9
(Andi Brown) *chsd ldrs for 4f: steadily lost pl: bhd over 3f out: lost tch over 2f out* **33/1**

2m 34.63s (3.13) **Going Correction** +0.15s/f (Good) **10** Ran SP% **120.4**
Speed ratings (Par 101): **94,93,91,89,87 84,80,80,67,66**
CSF £3.51 CT £24.15 TOTE £1.90: £1.10, £1.40, £4.20; EX 4.80 Trifecta £33.70.
Owner Macable Partnership **Bred** S N C Ecurie Jouenne Gerard **Trained** Portway, Worcs

FOCUS
Straight track at full width and the entire course had been verti-drained since the last meeting. Following 7mm of rain the previous day, the ground had eased to good (soft from 7f to 7f 140yds). A moderate handicap to start and a lopsided betting market, but it was the big two who fought out the finish. The third offers perspective.

2398 TELEGRAPH MAIDEN STKS 1m 3f 106y
2:30 (2:32) (Class 5) 3-Y-O+ **£2,911** (£866; £432; £216) **Stalls** High

Form RPR

1 **Jam Session (IRE)**^{41} 4-9-10 0... AdamKirby 8 78+
(Ian Williams) *hld up in tch in midfield: hdwy to chse ldrs and travelling wl over 3f out: rdn to ld over 1f out: sn clr: rdn out hands and heels fnl f: comf* **10/3**^{2}

0-0 **2** 2 **Chelsea's Boy (IRE)**^{23} 1739 3-8-9 0... JohnFahy 3 72
(Clive Cox) *chsd ldrs tl 8f out: in tch in midfield after: rdn and hdwy over 2f out: chsd clr wnr ins fnl f: r.o but no threat to wnr* **8/1**^{3}

0 **3** 5 **The Detainee**^{24} 1714 3-8-9 0... AdamBeschizza 4 64
(Jeremy Gask) *hld up in tch: shkn up over 2f out: hdwy and swtchd rt over 1f out: styd on ins fnl f: snatched 3rd last strides: no threat to ldrs* **50/1**

/30 **4** hd **Subordinate (GER)**^{23} 1739 7-9-10 0...(t) TimmyMurphy 6 63
(Emma Lavelle) *chsd ldrs: wnt 2nd 8f out tl led over 3f out: rdn and hdd over 1f out: sn outpce: lost 2nd and wknd ins fnl f* **12/1**

3 **5** ¾ **Sherdat (IRE)**^{24} 1704 3-8-4 0... HarryBentley 2 57
(Roger Varian) *chsd ldr tl 8f out: 4th and rdn over 3f out: no rspnse and plugged on same pce after* **4/9**^{1}

0-0 **6** 8 **Three Brothers (FR)**^{23} 1767 3-8-9 0... RyanClark 1 49
(Harry Dunlop) *led tl hdd and rdn over 3f out: wknd over 1f out* **50/1**

0/0 **7** nk **Intimidator (IRE)**^{10} 2098 5-9-7 0... DanielMuscutt$^{(3)}$ 7 48
(Miss Joey Ellis) *hld up in midfield: shkn up over 2f out: no hdwy: n.d* **80/1**

06-0 **8** 37 **Let's Confer**^{21} 1807 7-9-5 41...(t) RobertHavlin 10
(Michael Attwater) *in tch: chsd ldrs 8f out tl over 3f out: sn dropped out: t.o* **100/1**

0 **9** 26 **Pause For Applause**^{18} 1897 3-8-6 0...(p) DannyBrock$^{(3)}$ 9
(Jonathan Portman) *sn rdn along in rr: lost tch 5f out: t.o* **50/1**

2m 34.08s (2.58) **Going Correction** +0.15s/f (Good)
WFA 3 from 4yo+ 15lb **9** Ran SP% **119.2**
Speed ratings (Par 103): **96,94,90,90,90 84,84,57,38**
CSF £29.45 TOTE £3.50: £1.10, £2.00, £14.30; EX 24.90 Trifecta £986.50.
Owner A L R Morton **Bred** Haras De l'Hirondelle **Trained** Portway, Worcs
■ Buckle Street was withdrawn. Price at time of withdrawal 20/1. Rule 4 does not apply.

FOCUS
A weak maiden and, rather like the opener, only two mattered according to the market. With the long odds-on favourite running poorly it remains to be seen what the form amounts to. The winner may prove better than the bare form.

2399 NFRN (NATIONAL FEDERATION OF RETAIL NEWSAGENTS) H'CAP 1m 3f 106y
3:05 (3:05) (Class 4) (0-80,79) 4-Y-O+ **£4,690** (£1,395; £697; £348) **Stalls** High

Form RPR

03-2 **1** **Saumur**^{17} 1919 4-8-13 71... TomQueally 10 79
(Denis Coakley) *hld up in tch: rdn and hdwy over 2f out: chsd ldr jst over 1f out: styd on wl to ld last strides* **5/1**^{3}

0016 **2** hd **Moojaned (IRE)**^{4} 1717 5-9-4 79... PhilipPrince$^{(3)}$ 7 86
(David Evans) *led: rdn and hrd pressed but clr of field 3f out: forged ahd again over 1f out: styd on: hdd last strides* **15/2**

0011 **3** 3¾ **Astra Hall**[29] 1560 7-8-12 **75** .... GeorgeBuckell(5) 8 76
(Michael Appleby) *chsd ldrs: rdn 3f out: styd on and pressing ldrs jst over 1f out: no ex ins fnl f: wknd fnl 100yds* **7/1**

25-5 **4** 3¼ **Glens Wobbly**[21] 1810 8-8-12 **70** .... LiamJones 1 65
(Jonathan Geake) *sn bustled up to chse ldr: rdn to chal and clr w ldr 3f out: no ex over 1f out: wknd ins fnl f* **16/1**

40-4 **5** 1¼ **Forced Family Fun**[24] 1717 6-9-7 **79** .... SteveDrowne 9 72
(George Baker) *s.i.s: off the pce in last pair: lost tch over 3f out: hdwy and swtchd lft over 1f out: styd on fnl f: nvr trbld ldrs* **9/2**[2]

00-5 **6** *hd* **Prince Of Paris**[17] 1934 4-9-1 **73** .... RobertHavlin 5 66
(Roger Ingram) *in tch in midfield: rdn over 3f out: 5th and no imp 2f out: plugged on same pce after* **10/1**

3-32 **7** 4½ **Quality Song (USA)**[50] 1144 4-9-7 **79** .... PatDobbs 3 65
(Richard Hughes) *chsd ldrs tl lost pl over 4f out: rdn and no hdwy over 2f out: bhd over 1f out* **5/2**[1]

200- **8** 2½ **Perfect Rhythm**[235] 6778 5-8-4 **67** .... PaddyPilley(5) 2 49
(Patrick Chamings) *in tch in midfield: 4th and rdn over 2f out: no hdwy: wknd wl over 1f out* **14/1**

46-0 **9** *19* **Magical Thomas**[24] 1717 4-9-4 **76** .... LiamKeniry 4 26
(Neil Mulholland) *a in last pair and nvr on terms: lost tch over 3f out* **16/1**

2m 31.54s (0.04) **Going Correction** +0.15s/f (Good) **9** Ran SP% **115.2**
Speed ratings (Par 105): **105,104,102,99,98 98,95,93,79**
CSF £42.02 CT £262.60 TOTE £4.90: £2.00, £2.60, £2.20; EX 34.90 Trifecta £182.10.
Owner Sparkling Partners **Bred** Mrs C E Cone **Trained** West Ilsley, Berks

FOCUS
A fair handicap run at a good pace and the winning time was much faster than the two earlier races over the same trip. The winner is progressing.

2400 MENZIES DISTRIBUTION H'CAP — 1m 6f
3:40 (3:40) (Class 5) (0-70,70) 4-Y-O+ **£2,911** (£866; £432; £216) **Stalls** High

Form RPR

4-42 **1** **Onorina (IRE)**[19] 1854 4-9-3 **63** .... SamHitchcott 1 73
(Jim Boyle) *chsd ldrs: rdn to chal over 1f out: sustained duel w rival after: edgd lft: bumping w rival and led wl ins fnl f: kpt on: jst prevailed: fin 1st: plcd 2nd* **9/4**[1]

4-23 **2** *nse* **Ayr Of Elegance**[21] 1810 4-9-7 **67** .... GeorgeBaker 3 77
(Philip Hide) *led tl 8f out: handy: rdn to ld again 2f out: sustained duel w rival fr over 1f out: edgd rt: bumping w rival and hdd wl ins fnl f: rallied gamely cl home: jst hld: fin 2nd: awrdd the r* **11/4**[2]

0-46 **3** *6* **Starcrossed**[19] 1854 4-9-7 **67** .... (b) JohnFahy 7 69
(Eve Johnson Houghton) *t.k.h early: hld up in tch: effrt over 2f out: 4th and no imp whn edgd lft over 1f out: kpt on same pce to go 3rd wl ins fnl f* **8/1**

-603 **4** 1½ **Broughtons Berry (IRE)**[21] 1807 5-8-5 **51** oh3 .... MartinDwyer 8 51
(Willie Musson) *awkward leaving stalls and s.i.s: hld up in last pair but nvr settled: hdwy to ld 8f out: rdn and hdd 2f out: 3rd and btn 1f out: wknd ins fnl f: lost 3rd towards fin* **12/1**

-416 **5** ¾ **Rivers Run (IRE)**[90] 636 4-9-5 **70** .... PatrickO'Donnell(5) 6 68
(Ralph Beckett) *hld up in tch towards rr: effrt over 2f out: styd on same pce and no threat to ldrs fr over 1f out* **9/2**[3]

0504 **6** *5* **Star Anise (FR)**[22] 1778 5-8-0 **51** oh6 .... JosephineGordon(5) 4 42
(Paddy Butler) *taken down early: hld up in tch towards rr: effrt over 2f out: sn rdn and no imp: wknd fnl f* **33/1**

023- **7** 4½ **Voice Control (IRE)**[175] 8001 4-9-10 **70** .... TomQueally 9 55
(Laura Mongan) *mostly chsd ldr tl over 3f out: lost pl 2f out and sn wknd* **8/1**

1000 **8** *42* **Pao De Acuca (IRE)**[37] 1405 4-9-5 **65** .... (t) RenatoSouza 5
(Jose Santos) *stdd s: hld up in tch: lost tch 3f out: t.o and eased fnl f* **33/1**

3m 14.18s (4.18) **Going Correction** +0.15s/f (Good) **8** Ran SP% **111.4**
Speed ratings (Par 103): **94,93,90,89,89 86,83,59**
CSF £8.83 CT £39.79 TOTE £3.70: £1.60, £1.10, £2.50; EX 9.60 Trifecta £51.30.
Owner Sir David Prosser **Bred** J Hanly, T Stewart & A Stroud **Trained** Epsom, Surrey

FOCUS
A modest staying handicap, but a thrilling finish with the front pair getting very close to each other late on, and the result was decided in the stewards' room. The form is not too convincing.

2401 DAILY MIRROR - BEST FOR RACING H'CAP — 7f 140y
4:10 (4:11) (Class 5) (0-75,75) 4-Y-O+ **£2,911** (£866; £432; £216) **Stalls** Centre

Form RPR

0161 **1** **Flying Fantasy**[30] 1555 4-9-0 **73** .... AaronJones(5) 1 82
(Stuart Williams) *stdd s: hld up in tch: hdwy 3f out: rdn to chal wl over 1f out: hung lft after: led wl ins fnl f: hld on* **11/2**[2]

0-12 **2** *shd* **Black Caesar (IRE)**[22] 1780 5-9-0 **68** .... WilliamCarson 2 76
(Philip Hide) *hld up in tch: clsd to chse ldrs 1/2-way: led 2f out: sn rdn and hrd pressed: hung lft fr over 1f out: hdd wl ins fnl f: rallied u.p: jst hld* **7/1**[3]

0361 **3** *nse* **Duke Of North (IRE)**[7] 2187 4-8-0 **61** oh2 .... RhiainIngram(7) 8 69
(Jim Boyle) *hld up in tch in midfield: effrt and swtchd lft jst over 2f out: chsd ldng pair over 1f out: no imp tl r.o strly fnl 100yds: nt quite rch ldng pair* **15/2**

123- **4** *6* **Plauseabella**[300] 4581 5-8-7 **61** .... (p) MartinDwyer 9 54
(Stuart Kittow) *led: rdn and hdd 2f out: outpcd and btn 1f out: no ch w ldng trio and kpt on same pce after* **15/2**

45-4 **5** ¾ **Anastazia**[6] 2213 4-8-13 **72** .... (p) JosephineGordon(5) 10 63
(Paul D'Arcy) *chsd ldrs tl 1/2-way: shuffled bk and nt clr run over 2f out tl jst over 1f out: no ch w ldng trio and kpt on same pce after* **7/2**[1]

50-5 **6** ¾ **Wind In My Sails**[48] 1173 4-9-6 **74** .... LiamKeniry 4 63
(Ed de Giles) *stdd s: hld up in tch: clsd and swtchd lft jst over 2f out: rdn and no hdwy over 1f out: wknd ins fnl f* **8/1**

-416 **7** ¾ **Vale Of Iron (IRE)**[88] 663 4-8-13 **67** .... KierenFox 11 54
(John Best) *t.k.h: hld up in tch: shuffled bk and nt clr run over 2f out: ldng trio gng clr whn swtchd lft and stl nt clr run 1f out: n.d after* **9/1**

20/3 **8** *nk* **Mystic Jade**[13] 2001 4-9-6 **74** .... KieranO'Neill 3 61
(Richard Hannon) *chsd ldr tl jst over 2f out: outpcd u.p over 1f out: wknd ins fnl f* **10/1**

9 *6* **Severus (GER)**[221] 6-9-7 **75** .... DavidProbert 7 47
(Des Donovan, Ire) *hld up in tch towards rr: swtchd lft and effrt ent fnl 2f: no hdwy u.p over 1f out: wknd fnl f* **20/1**

-162 **10** *15* **Etaad (USA)**[36] 1416 5-9-1 **69** .... (b) GeorgeBaker 5 3
(Gary Moore) *stdd s: hld up in rr: shkn up 2f out: sn beate: eased ins fnl f* **8/1**

1m 30.7s (-1.60) **Going Correction** -0.10s/f (Good) **10** Ran SP% **119.7**
Speed ratings (Par 103): **104,103,103,97,97 96,95,95,89,74**
CSF £45.06 CT £300.72 TOTE £7.70: £2.90, £2.80, £2.50; EX 57.20 Trifecta £449.40.
Owner Happy Valley Racing & Breeding Limited **Bred** Hascombe And Valiant Studs **Trained** Newmarket, Suffolk

FOCUS
Another modest handicap. The runners raced towards the stands' rail early, but the first three all hung away to their left late on and ended up closer to the far rail. They finished clear and the winner carried over his AW improvement.

2402 NEWSSOLUTIONS CLAIMING STKS — 7f 140y
4:45 (4:47) (Class 6) 3-Y-O+ **£2,264** (£673; £336; £168) **Stalls** Centre

Form RPR

0503 **1** **Boycie**[7] 2184 3-8-4 70 .... (b) HollieDoyle(7) 4 77
(Richard Hannon) *chsd ldr tl 5f out: styd trcking ldrs: nt clr run over 2f out tl gap opened and ld over 1f out: rdn and asserted 1f out: r.o strly: readily* **8/1**

06- **2** *6* **Stoked (IRE)**[295] 4759 4-9-2 74 .... JosephineGordon(5) 3 63
(Chris Dwyer) *led: hdd 1/2-way: rdn 3f out: led again 2f out: hdd over 1f out: outpcd by wnr but kpt on for 2nd ins fnl f* **5/1**

02-1 **3** *2* **Faintly (USA)**[20] 1832 5-9-1 77 .... GeorgeDowning(3) 6 55
(Tony Carroll) *broke wl: stdd bk to chse ldrs: effrt and hung lft over 1f out: stl hanging and r.o same pce ins fnl f* **9/2**[3]

3000 **4** 2¼ **Clement (IRE)**[40] 1335 6-9-9 82 .... (v) CiaranMckee(5) 5 60
(John O'Shea) *stdd s: hld up in rr: hdwy to chse ldr 5f out: led 1/2-way: rdn and hdd 2f out: sn outpcd: 4th and wl hld fnl f* **8/1**

2336 **5** 1½ **Moonlight Venture**[21] 1818 5-9-8 77 .... (b) AdamKirby 8 50
(Conor Dore) *hld up in tch in midfield: rdn 3f out: little rspnse: rdn and btn 2f out* **2/1**[1]

4404 **6** *10* **Spiritual Star (IRE)**[8] 2150 7-9-5 72 .... (t) WilliamCarson 7 23
(Anthony Carson) *stdd s: hld up in tch last pair: clsd over 2f out: rdn 2f out: sn btn: bhd and eased ins fnl f* **4/1**[2]

-000 **7** *9* **All Or Nothin (IRE)**[30] 1544 7-8-13 52 .... PaddyPilley(5) 1
(Paddy Butler) *racd along towards centre: chsd ldrs: rdn 1/2-way: lost pl 2f out: sn wknd* **50/1**

1m 30.88s (-1.42) **Going Correction** -0.10s/f (Good)
WFA 3 from 4yo+ 12lb **7** Ran SP% **112.4**
Speed ratings (Par 101): **103,97,95,92,91 81,72**
CSF £45.38 TOTE £10.00: £4.50, £3.40; EX 65.90 Trifecta £271.00.
Owner Mrs V Hubbard & K T Ivory **Bred** Highclere Stud **Trained** East Everleigh, Wilts

FOCUS
Not a bad little claimer, but a slightly surprising result with those most favoured by the weights rather disappointing. The winner's effort could be rated higher.

2403 SMITHS NEWS FILLIES' H'CAP — 6f
5:15 (5:16) (Class 6) (0-65,65) 4-Y-O+ **£2,911** (£866; £432; £216) **Stalls** High

Form RPR

5322 **1** **One Big Surprise**[18] 1899 4-9-0 **58** .... ShaneKelly 4 72+
(Richard Hughes) *hld up in tch: clsd to trck ldr and gng wl over 1f out: swtchd rt ent fnl f: pushed into ld 150yds: sn rdn and asserted: r.o* **3/1**[1]

4-04 **2** *2* **Mrs Warren**[16] 1949 6-9-1 **59** .... SteveDrowne 6 63
(George Baker) *midfield: rdn over 2f out: hdwy u.p ent fnl f: wnt 2nd wl ins fnl f: kpt on* **10/1**

4243 **3** 1¼ **Colourfilly**[24] 1725 4-9-5 **63** .... (p) LiamJones 8 63
(Tom Dascombe) *led: rdn wl over 1f out: hdd 150yds out: no ex and outpcd after: lost 2nd wl ins fnl f* **7/1**

30-2 **4** ¾ **Darrell Rivers**[17] 1928 4-8-13 **64** .... MillyNaseb(7) 9 65
(Giles Bravery) *chsd ldrs tl lost pl and rdn over 2f out: swtchd lft and rallied over 1f out: keeping on whn nt clr run ins fnl f: kpt on towards fin: no threat to wnr* **7/2**[2]

-543 **5** *nk* **Two In The Pink (IRE)**[13] 2006 6-9-7 **65** .... AdamKirby 7 62
(Ralph J Smith) *sn niggled along towards rr: rdn over 2f out: styd on ins fnl f: nvr trbld ldrs* **6/1**

2-62 **6** ½ **Racing Angel (IRE)**[6] 2217 4-9-4 **62** .... WilliamCarson 2 58
(Mick Quinn) *chsd ldrs and racd towards centre: rdn 2f out: no ex over 1f out: wknd ins fnl f* **11/2**[3]

0554 **7** 1¼ **Mops Angel**[27] 1595 5-8-12 **59** .... (p) AlistairRawlinson(3) 5 51
(Michael Appleby) *s.i.s: bhd and sn rdn: sme prog over 1f out: no imp ins fnl f* **10/1**

244- **8** 3¾ **Regal Miss**[195] 7735 4-9-2 **65** .... PaddyPilley(5) 3 46
(Patrick Chamings) *chsd ldr tl over 1f out: sn btn: wknd fnl f* **16/1**

1m 10.73s (-0.47) **Going Correction** -0.10s/f (Good) **8** Ran SP% **113.5**
Speed ratings (Par 98): **99,96,94,93,93 92,90,85**
CSF £32.85 CT £192.87 TOTE £3.50: £1.50, £2.10, £2.60; EX 30.80 Trifecta £219.30.
Owner Withyslade **Bred** Withyslade **Trained** Upper Lambourn, Berkshire

FOCUS
A moderate fillies' handicap in which they stayed centre-to-nearside. There should be more to come from the winner.
T/Plt: £267.20 to a £1 stake. Pool of £61022.77 - 166.67 winning tickets. T/Qpdt: £33.90 to a £1 stake. Pool of £5767.11 - 125.70 winning tickets. **Steve Payne**

2264 RIPON (R-H)
Thursday, May 19

OFFICIAL GOING: Good to firm (good in places) changing to good after race 2 (6.45)
Wind: moderate 1/2 behind Weather: rain 1st 2

2404 COPT HEWICK FILLIES' NOVICE AUCTION STKS (PLUS 10 RACE) — 6f
6:15 (6:16) (Class 5) 2-Y-O **£3,234** (£962; £481; £240) **Stalls** High

Form RPR

1 **Appointed** 2-8-12 0 .... DavidAllan 3 76+
(Tim Easterby) *dwlt: in rr: outpcd over 3f out: gd hdwy over 1f out: r.o to ld last 100yds* **8/1**[3]

5 **2** ¾ **Melaniemillie**[28] 1583 2-8-7 0 .... JacobButterfield(3) 6 72
(Ollie Pears) *w ldr: upsides over 3f out: led over 1f out: hdd and no ex last 100yds* **12/1**

4 **3** 4½ **Best Bid (IRE)**[16] 1951 2-8-12 0 .... JasonHart 2 60
(John Quinn) *chsd ldrs: swtchd rt over 1f out: kpt on same pce to take 4th last 150yds* **17/2**

2641 **4** 2¾ **Zig Zag Girl**[4] 2266 2-8-10 0 .... FrannyNorton 8 50
(Scott Dixon) *led: hdd over 1f out: wknd fnl 150yds* **5/6**[1]

5 2¾ **Serenity Dove** 2-9-0 0 .... DougieCostello 1 46
(K R Burke) *chsd ldrs: outpcd and lost pl over 3f out* **20/1**

6 2¾ **Eva Gore** 2-8-10 0 .... PhillipMakin 7 34+
(David O'Meara) *in rr-div: outpcd over 3f out: brief effrt 2f out: sn wknd* **7/2**[2]

7 *nk* **Babalugats (IRE)** 2-8-10 0 .... AndrewMullen 4 33
(Tim Easterby) *chsd ldrs: outpcd and lost pl over 3f out* **28/1**

8 2 **Cheers All Round** 2-8-10 0 ShaneGray 5 27
(Henry Spiller) *dwlt: in rr: bhd fnl 3f* **50/1**
1m 12.99s (-0.01) **Going Correction** -0.175s/f (Firm) **8** Ran SP% **116.3**
Speed ratings (Par 90): **93,92,86,82,78 75,74,71**
CSF £93.60 TOTE £11.20: £3.90, £4.00, £3.20; EX 89.80 Trifecta £1363.20.
Owner Habton Farms **Bred** Lady Jennifer Green **Trained** Great Habton, N Yorks

FOCUS

The ground was described as good by a couple of jockeys, though David Allan said: "It is very loose on top".\n\x\x Only one of those with experience had shown themselves better than modest and few of the newcomers had compelling profiles so this was probably not a strong fillies' novice auction.

2405 SIS FILLIES' MAIDEN AUCTION STKS (PLUS 10 RACE) 1m 1f 170y

6:45 (6:47) (Class 4) 3-Y-O **£5,175** (£1,540; £769; £384) **Stalls** Low

Form RPR

4-0 1 **Arcamist**[37] 1392 3-8-11 0 MichaelJMMurphy(3) 1 73
(Charles Hills) *led: t.k.h: qcknd pce over 4f out: drvn over 2f out: edgd lft fnl f: fnd ex nr fin* **7/1**[3]

20-4 2 *nk* **Dot Green (IRE)**[13] 1989 3-9-0 82 SaleemGolam 2 72
(Mark H Tompkins) *dwlt: trckd ldr after 2f: effrt over 2f out: upsides over 1f out: no ex in clsng stages* **1/4**[1]

0-0 3 *5* **Sunshineandbubbles**[13] 1998 3-9-0 0 DaleSwift 4 62
(Daniel Mark Loughnane) *hld up in last: t.k.h: hdwy 4f out: sn drvn: one pce fnl 2f* **100/1**

23-6 4 *nse* **Just Fab (IRE)**[26] 1638 3-9-0 68 GrahamLee 3 62
(Ali Stronge) *trckd ldrs: drvn over 3f out: one pce whn edgd rt over 1f out* **6/1**[2]

2m 9.49s (4.09) **Going Correction** +0.175s/f (Good) **4** Ran SP% **107.8**
Speed ratings (Par 98): **90,89,85,85**
CSF £9.64 TOTE £6.60; EX 10.80 Trifecta £53.20.
Owner Mrs Julie Martin And David R Martin **Bred** Whitsbury Manor Stud And Mrs M E Slade **Trained** Lambourn, Berks

FOCUS

As weak a fillies' maiden auction as the size of the field might suggest and they went a steady pace in a race run over about 18 yards extra due to rails movement. Shaky form.

2406 LITTLETHORPE H'CAP 1m 6f

7:20 (7:20) (Class 4) (0-85,85) 4-Y-O+ **£5,175** (£1,540; £769; £384) **Stalls** High

Form RPR

16-1 1 **Always Resolute**[5] 2233 5-7-12 69 oh2 ow3 BenRobinson(7) 7 76+
(Brian Ellison) *hld up in last: hdwy on outside over 3f out: trcking ldrs over 2f out: shkn up to ld last 75yds: readily* **1/2**[1]

-642 2 *1 ¼* **Stormin Tom (IRE)**[13] 2018 4-8-0 69 ow1 RachelRichardson(5) 8 74
(Tim Easterby) *led after 1f: ducked lft over 10f out: hdd and no ex last 75yds* **15/2**[2]

232- 3 *1 ½* **Corona Borealis**[243] 6520 5-9-2 85 PhilDennis(5) 5 88
(Martin Todhunter) *hld up in rr: hdwy on ins over 3f out: chsng ldrs over 1f out: sn rdn: kpt on same pce last 150yds* **12/1**

-051 4 *hd* **Jan Smuts (IRE)**[13] 2018 8-8-3 72 (tp) NathanEvans(5) 2 75
(Wilf Storey) *mid-div: hdwy over 3f out: chsng ldrs over 1f out: kpt on same pce fnl 200yds* **14/1**

14-0 5 *5* **Skiddaw Valleys**[17] 1923 4-8-9 73 ShaneGray 6 69
(Alan Swinbank) *mid-div: hdwy to chse ldrs over 2f out: fdd fnl f* **25/1**

621- 6 *10* **Bulas Belle**[205] 7527 6-8-11 75 BarryMcHugh 1 57
(Grant Tuer) *led 1f: chsd ldrs: drvn 3f out: lost pl over 1f out* **33/1**

04-3 7 *3 ¾* **Kiwayu**[132] 103 7-8-2 66 (p) AndrewMullen 10 43
(Philip Kirby) *in rr: sn pushed along: drvn over 4f out: lost pl over 2f out* **9/1**[3]

40-0 8 *½* **Endless Credit (IRE)**[8] 2163 6-9-0 78 PJMcDonald 3 54
(Micky Hammond) *chsd ldrs: drvn over 3f out: lost pl 2f out* **33/1**

60-0 9 *1 ¼* **Perrault (IRE)**[14] 1972 4-9-4 82 (p) JackGarritty 9 56
(Richard Fahey) *chsd ldrs: clr 2nd whn carried lft over 10f out: drvn over 3f out: lost pl 2f out: eased nr fin* **16/1**

3m 4.53s (184.53) **9** Ran SP% **118.4**
CSF £4.95 CT £22.46 TOTE £1.50: £1.10, £2.20, £2.50; EX 6.00 Trifecta £43.40.
Owner Market Avenue Racing Club Ltd **Bred** Jarvis Associates **Trained** Norton, N Yorks

FOCUS

Race run over about 18 yards extra due to rails movement. A hot favourite who was officially 6lb well-in (less 2lb overweight) for a handicap over a new distance for Ripon, a race that was run at just a fair pace. The winner will still be well treated despite a rise.

2407 RIPONBET OUR PROFITS STAY IN RACING H'CAP 1m

7:50 (7:50) (Class 3) (0-95,90) 3-Y-O **£7,470** (£2,236; £1,118; £559; £279) **Stalls** Low

Form RPR

-012 1 **Dolphin Vista (IRE)**[19] 1867 3-9-5 88 TonyHamilton 2 97+
(Richard Fahey) *led 1f: trckd ldr: effrt over 3f out: led over 1f out: styd on wl: eased in clsng stages* **11/8**[1]

0-26 2 *3 ½* **Montsarrat (IRE)**[19] 1867 3-9-7 90 FrannyNorton 5 89
(Mark Johnston) *chsd ldrs: effrt over 3f out: rdn and hung rt over 1f out: kpt on to take modest 2nd last 75yds* **15/8**[2]

13-0 3 *hd* **Ninetta (IRE)**[35] 1438 3-9-2 85 PJMcDonald 6 84
(Ann Duffield) *led after 1f: drvn 2f out: sn hdd: kpt on same pce* **17/2**

2-15 4 *4* **Tawakkol**[19] 1867 3-9-2 85 GrahamLee 4 75
(Mark Johnston) *chsd ldrs: drvn and lost pl after 1f: hdwy over 3f out: chsng ldrs over 2f out: lost pl over 1f out* **5/1**[3]

22-0 5 *11* **Novinophobia**[12] 2029 3-8-8 77 GeorgeChaloner 7 42
(Richard Fahey) *in rr: drvn over 4f out: lost pl over 2f out: sn bhd* **20/1**

1m 41.3s (-0.10) **Going Correction** +0.175s/f (Good) **5** Ran SP% **108.8**
Speed ratings (Par 103): **107,103,103,99,88**
CSF £4.10 TOTE £1.80: £1.40, £2.30; EX 4.10 Trifecta £13.80.
Owner Y Nasib **Bred** Jim McDonald **Trained** Musley Bank, N Yorks

FOCUS

Nothing within 5lb of the ratings ceiling for this three-year-old handicap, which was run over around 18 yards extra due to rails movement and which lost much of its competitiveness thanks to the four withdrawals. The winner continues to progress.

2408 LADIES DAY 16TH JUNE BOOK NOW H'CAP 1m 4f 10y

8:25 (8:25) (Class 5) (0-70,71) 3-Y-O **£3,234** (£962; £481; £240) **Stalls** Low

Form RPR

6-21 1 **Regal Monarch**[9] 2126 3-9-10 71 6ex FrannyNorton 6 81+
(Mark Johnston) *sn trcking ldr: led 7f out: shkn up over 2f out: wnt clr over 1f out: eased fnl 75yds* **1/3**[1]

050- 2 *5* **Indulgent**[142] 8384 3-8-13 60 BarryMcHugh 1 56
(Tony Coyle) *t.k.h: trckd ldng pair: shkn up 6f out: drvn 3f out: tk modest 2nd over 1f out* **16/1**

0-51 3 *7* **Livella Fella (IRE)**[9] 2123 3-9-10 71 6ex PhillipMakin 5 61
(Keith Dalgleish) *t.k.h: led: hdd 7f out: chal over 2f out: wknd over 1f out: eased in clsng stages* **4/1**[2]

55-0 4 *2* **Sebastian's Wish (IRE)**[35] 1449 3-9-4 65 GeorgeChaloner 2 47
(Richard Whitaker) *chsd ldrs: drvn 4f out: lost pl over 2f out* **14/1**[3]

2m 39.53s (2.83) **Going Correction** +0.175s/f (Good) **4** Ran SP% **107.6**
Speed ratings (Par 99): **97,93,89,87**
CSF £6.51 TOTE £1.20; EX 7.20 Trifecta £7.90.
Owner East Layton Stud Ltd **Bred** A H Bennett **Trained** Middleham Moor, N Yorks

FOCUS

A couple of demonstrably in-form three-year-olds, both winners of handicaps in the past nine days, in a contest which was run over approximately 18 yards further due to rails movement. The winner is on the upgrade and value for extra.

2409 SHAROW APPRENTICE H'CAP 1m

8:55 (8:56) (Class 6) (0-60,60) 4-Y-O+ **£2,587** (£770; £384; £192) **Stalls** Low

Form RPR

0-00 1 **Curzon Line**[126] 179 7-9-2 60 NathanEvans(5) 15 74+
(Michael Easterby) *in tch: smooth hdwy on outside over 2f out: led last 150yds: v comf* **4/1**[2]

6033 2 *2 ¼* **Roger Thorpe**[12] 2046 7-9-5 58 MarcMonaghan 2 62
(Deborah Sanderson) *trckd ldrs: effrt on inner over 2f out: nt clr run and swtchd lft 1f out: styd on to take 2nd in clsng stages: no ch w wnr* **7/2**[1]

200- 3 *½* **Mowhoob**[241] 6601 6-8-11 55 DanielleMooney(5) 4 58
(David Nicholls) *sn chsng ldrs: hung lft and led over 1f out: hdd and no ex last 150yds* **20/1**

040 4 *1 ¼* **Outlaw Torn (IRE)**[2] 2330 7-9-6 59 (e) JacobButterfield 10 59
(Richard Guest) *w ldr: led over 6f out: hdd over 3f out: kpt on one pce appr fnl f* **15/2**

40-0 5 *2* **Midlight**[17] 1925 4-9-1 57 JoshDoyle(3) 3 52
(Richard Whitaker) *led tl over 6f out: led over 3f out tl over 1f out: one pce* **14/1**

56-6 6 *hd* **Bush Beauty (IRE)**[26] 1631 5-9-2 60 SophieKilloran(5) 13 55
(Eric Alston) *swtchd lft after s: in rr-div: hdwy over 2f out edgd rt over 1f out: kpt on one pce* **11/1**

6105 7 *3 ¼* **Miss Buckaroo (IRE)**[22] 1791 4-8-7 49 (b[1]) PhilDennis(3) 12 36
(James Given) *mid-div: hdwy over 3f out: edgd lft 2f out: nvr a factor* **33/1**

0-25 8 *¾* **Sooqaan**[64] 956 5-9-0 60 MathewStill(7) 7 46
(Antony Brittain) *mid-div: effrt over 2f out: nvr a factor* **7/1**[3]

0-04 9 *nse* **Vecheka (IRE)**[20] 1845 5-9-0 56 (p) CallumShepherd(3) 6 42
(Micky Hammond) *chsd ldrs: wknd over 1f out* **10/1**

44-0 10 *3 ¼* **Zingiber**[29] 1565 4-8-4 46 oh1 (t) NoelGarbutt(3) 8 24
(Wilf Storey) *bhd: sme hdwy over 2f out: edgd rt: wknd over 1f out* **28/1**

6-04 11 *6* **Al Furat (USA)**[16] 1952 8-8-2 46 oh1 (p) KieranSchofield(5) 14 10
(Ron Barr) *s.s: a in rr* **40/1**

-540 12 *¾* **Fairy Pools**[20] 1834 5-8-8 50 (b) RachelRichardson(3) 1 13
(Les Eyre) *mid-div: hdwy over 3f out: sn chsng ldrs: wknd fnl 2f* **28/1**

44-5 13 *3 ½* **Big Red**[36] 1412 4-8-2 46 oh1 RowanScott(5) 11 1
(Rebecca Bastiman) *s.s: detached in last: unruly and bucking after 1f: sn t.o: nvr on terms* **25/1**

-000 14 *¾* **Marmarus**[27] 1595 5-9-0 58 NatalieHambling(5) 9 11
(David Nicholls) *in rr: bhd fnl 2f* **50/1**

1m 42.5s (1.10) **Going Correction** +0.175s/f (Good) **14** Ran SP% **113.4**
Speed ratings (Par 101): **101,98,98,97,95 94,91,90,90,87 81,80,77,76**
CSF £14.40 CT £193.28 TOTE £4.30: £1.10, £1.70, £4.20; EX 19.50 Trifecta £232.40.
Owner Barry Burdett **Bred** Darley **Trained** Sheriff Hutton, N Yorks

■ I'm Super Too was withdrawn. Price at time of withdrawal 9/1. Rule 4 applies to all bets - deduct 10p in the pound.

FOCUS

Questions to answer for most of the runners in a typically uncompetitive 46-60 apprentice handicap, which was run at a stong pace over about 18 yards further than the advertised distance due to rail movement. The well treated winner can go in again.

T/Plt: £190.40 to a £1 stake. Pool of £53463.26 - 204.96 winning units. T/Qpdt: £2.20 to a £1 stake. Pool of £7176.05 - 2330.50 winning units. **Walter Glynn**

1603 SANDOWN (R-H)

Thursday, May 19

OFFICIAL GOING: Round course - good to firm (good in places); sprint course - good (good to firm in places)

Wind: Moderate, against Weather: Cloudy

2410 BETVICTOR MILLION POUND GOAL EBF NOVICE FILLIES' STKS (PLUS 10 RACE) 5f 6y

5:50 (5:51) (Class 5) 2-Y-O **£3,881** (£1,155; £577; £288) **Stalls** Low

Form RPR

1 **Grizzel (IRE)** 2-9-0 0 PatDobbs 1 77+
(Richard Hannon) *racd against rail: trckd ldrs: gap appeared and prog to ld jst ins fnl f: shkn up and r.o wl* **6/1**[3]

2 *¾* **Naafer** 2-9-0 0 AndreaAtzeni 8 74
(William Haggas) *trckd ldrs: plld out wd and prog over 1f out: chal and upsides wnr jst ins fnl f: shkn up and styd on but hld last 75yds* **4/1**[2]

3 *1 ¾* **Bithynia (IRE)** 2-9-0 0 JamesDoyle 4 68
(Hugo Palmer) *racd against rail: led 1f: shkn up 1/2-way: effrt to ld over 1f out but sn edgd lft: hdd and one pce jst ins fnl f* **11/8**[1]

45 4 *1* **Snoozy Sioux (IRE)**[13] 2007 2-8-11 0 TimClark(3) 5 64
(Martin Smith) *wl away: pressed ldrs: led 1/2-way to over 1f out: one pce* **33/1**

5 *1 ¾* **Night Law** 2-9-0 0 DavidProbert 9 58+
(Andrew Balding) *slowly away: rn green in last: pushed along and kpt on fnl f: nt disgracd* **20/1**

3 6 *2* **Fair Selene**[18] 1895 2-9-0 0 FrederikTylicki 10 51+
(Heather Main) *wnt lft s: in tch in rr: pushed along in last and btn wl over 1f out: passed two rivals nr fin* **16/1**

7 *nse* **Madame Bounty (IRE)** 2-9-0 0 AntonioFresu 6 51
(Ed Walker) *prom: led after 1f to 1/2-way: wknd 2f out* **25/1**

4 8 *2* **Whiteley (IRE)**[10] 2097 2-9-0 0 SilvestreDeSousa 2 44
(Mick Channon) *in tch in rr: no prog and wl btn whn short of room ins fnl f: fdd* **4/1**[2]

1m 3.01s (1.41) **Going Correction** +0.125s/f (Good) **8** Ran SP% **113.8**
Speed ratings (Par 90): **93,91,89,87,84 81,81,78**
CSF £29.22 TOTE £7.60: £1.90, £1.70, £1.10; EX 31.00 Trifecta £64.90.
Owner Merriebelle Irish Farm/Potensis B'Stock **Bred** Martin Butler **Trained** East Everleigh, Wilts

FOCUS
Round Course rail on outermost configuration, as per April 22 meeting, and out 3yds in home straight. 29 yards were added to all Round Course races. Likely this was a decent fillies' event, with a few noteworthy performances.

2411 BETVICTOR MILLION POUND GOAL YOUNG STAYERS H'CAP 1m 6f
6:25 (6:25) (Class 4) (0-85,85) 3-Y-O **£4,690** (£1,395; £697; £348) **Stalls** Low

Form RPR
21 **1** **Harbour Law**[18] 1897 3-9-7 **85** GeorgeBaker 2 94+
(Laura Mongan) *led 3f: trckd ldr: clsd to ld wl over 1f out: in command fnl f: rdn out* **7/2**[2]

3-33 **2** 1 1/2 **Rasasee (IRE)**[33] 1479 3-8-11 **75** LukeMorris 4 78
(Marco Botti) *t.k.h: hld up in 5th: pushed along 3f out: prog and drvn 2f out: chsd wnr ins fnl f: styd on but no imp* **14/1**

6-13 **3** nse **October Storm**[31] 1532 3-8-10 **74** SilvestreDeSousa 7 77
(Mick Channon) *hld up in last: rdn 3f out: no prog tl wl over 1f out: str run fnl f: nrly snatched 2nd* **6/1**

60-4 **4** 1 1/4 **Roderic's Secret (IRE)**[38] 1386 3-8-5 **69** KieranO'Neill 1 70
(David Menuisier) *t.k.h: trckd ldng pair: rdn and nt qckn over 2f out and sn lost pl: kpt on again fnl f* **25/1**

01-3 **5** 1 3/4 **City Of Ideas**[23] 1738 3-8-11 **75** JamesDoyle 8 74
(John Gosden) *trckd ldng trio: rdn wl over 2f out: tk 2nd over 1f out to ins fnl f: wknd* **2/1**[1]

6-62 **6** 3/4 **Le Tissier**[22] 1779 3-8-2 **66** oh1 CathyGannon 3 64
(Andrew Balding) *dwlt: t.k.h: hld up in 7th: pushed along over 3f out: effrt on inner over 2f out: no real prog after* **25/1**

62-2 **7** 3/4 **Argyle (IRE)**[31] 1532 3-8-6 **70** MartinDwyer 6 66
(William Muir) *t.k.h: pressed ldr: led after 3f: awkward bnd 5f out but stoked up and sn 3 l clr: hdd wl over 1f out: wknd fnl f: eased nr fin* **10/1**

5-11 **8** 10 **Recognition (IRE)**[20] 1835 3-8-8 **72** AndreaAtzeni 5 54
(Roger Varian) *t.k.h: hld up in 6th: shkn up 3f out and no prog: wknd 2f out: t.o* **4/1**[3]

3m 9.48s (4.98) **Going Correction** +0.30s/f (Good) **8** Ran SP% **113.3**
Speed ratings (Par 101): **97,96,96,95,94 93,93,87**
CSF £49.12 CT £280.78 TOTE £4.90: £1.50, £2.20, £2.10; EX 37.30 Trifecta £238.00.
Owner Mrs Jackie Cornwell **Bred** Hascombe And Valiant Studs **Trained** Epsom, Surrey

FOCUS
Race distance increased by 29yds. A useful 3yo handicap that saw a good effort from the winner. They didn't go much of a gallop early and finished in a bit of a bunch.

2412 BETVICTOR MILLION POUND GOAL H'CAP 1m 14y
6:55 (6:56) (Class 4) (0-85,85) 3-Y-O **£4,690** (£1,395; £697; £348) **Stalls** Low

Form RPR
461- **1** **Manson**[183] 7888 3-9-7 **85** JimCrowley 13 98+
(Dominic Ffrench Davis) *hld up in last: gng wl but stl there 2f out: plld out and gd prog over 1f out: str run and swept into the ld last 75yds: won gng away* **12/1**

44-1 **2** 1 1/4 **White Poppy (IRE)**[23] 1767 3-9-1 **79** OisinMurphy 2 85
(Andrew Balding) *led at mod pce: kicked on fr over 2f out: drvn and kpt on fr over 1f out: hdd and outpcd last 75yds* **14/1**

2-12 **3** nk **Shaan (IRE)**[15] 1960 3-9-7 **85** FrankieDettori 8 90
(Richard Hannon) *t.k.h: hld up bhd ldrs: rdn and prog 2f out: chsd ldr jst over 1f out to ins fnl f: kpt on* **5/1**[2]

3-1 **4** 1 **Limitless (IRE)**[24] 1714 3-9-7 **85** JamieSpencer 11 88+
(Jamie Osborne) *plld hrd: hld up towards rr: rdn and prog 2f out: disp 2nd jst over 1f out: one pce fnl f* **15/8**[1]

041- **5** 1/2 **Sky Ship**[173] 8037 3-9-4 **82** RyanMoore 3 84
(Sir Michael Stoute) *trckd ldng pair: rdn to dispute 2nd briefly over 1f out: one pce fnl f* **5/1**[2]

414- **6** 2 1/2 **Il Piccolo Grande (IRE)**[236] 6731 3-9-4 **82** LukeMorris 4 79
(James Tate) *t.k.h: trckd ldng pair: rdn over 2f out: lost pl u.p over 1f out: fdd* **20/1**

353- **7** shd **Mediciman**[211] 7397 3-9-0 **78** PatDobbs 9 74
(Henry Candy) *dwlt: hld up in last pair: urged along and no prog 3f out: kpt on fr over 1f out: n.d* **8/1**[3]

5-46 **8** 4 **Henry The Explorer (CAN)**[36] 1411 3-8-10 **74** SamHitchcott 12 60
(Jo Hughes) *trapped out wd in midfield: rdn and no prog over 2f out: wknd over 1f out* **66/1**

15-0 **9** 3 1/4 **Art Echo**[20] 1828 3-8-13 **77** RyanClark 6 56
(Jonathan Portman) *in tch in midfield: rdn wl over 2f out: no prog and sn struggling* **50/1**

5-21 **10** 3 **Pushaq (IRE)**[51] 1132 3-9-3 **81** AndreaAtzeni 7 53
(Marco Botti) *t.k.h: in tch on inner: rdn over 2f out: wknd qckly over 1f out* **16/1**

312- **11** nk **Show Me Again**[169] 8080 3-9-7 **85** SilvestreDeSousa 5 56
(David Dennis) *chsd ldr: rdn over 2f out: lost 2nd and wknd rapidly over 1f out* **16/1**

1m 45.13s (1.83) **Going Correction** +0.30s/f (Good) **11** Ran SP% **113.6**
Speed ratings (Par 101): **102,100,100,99,98 96,96,92,89,86 85**
CSF £159.37 CT £964.72 TOTE £9.60: £2.40, £4.90, £1.60; EX 141.80 Trifecta £1045.00.
Owner The Agincourt Partnership **Bred** Minster Stud **Trained** Lambourn, Berks

FOCUS
Race distance increased by 29yds. No great gallop on, in what was a fair 3yo handicap, so the winner did well to come from last. There's likely to be more to come from the winner.

2413 JOHN SUNLEY MEMORIAL H'CAP 1m 2f 7y
7:30 (7:30) (Class 3) (0-90,89) 3-Y-O **£7,439** (£2,213; £1,106; £553) **Stalls** Low

Form RPR
21-1 **1** **Primitivo**[6] 2209 3-9-5 **87** 6ex WilliamTwiston-Davies 8 99+
(Alan King) *hld up in last pair: prog on outer to ld 2f out: sn rdn clr: 3 l ahd ins fnl f: eased last 75yds* **7/4**[1]

52-2 **2** 1 **Midhmaar**[27] 1603 3-9-7 **89** AndreaAtzeni 6 95
(Owen Burrows) *trckd ldr: led over 2f out to 2f out: chsd wnr after but sn lft bhd: kpt on fnl f: flattered by proximity* **8/1**

44-5 **3** 3/4 **Yangtze**[26] 1639 3-8-0 **71** TomMarquand[(3)] 7 75
(Sir Michael Stoute) *hld up in last pair: shkn up over 2f out: hanging and rn green in last over 1f out: styd on fnl f: tk 3rd and nrst fin* **7/2**[2]

20-3 **4** 1/2 **New Caledonia (IRE)**[18] 1891 3-9-6 **88** JamesDoyle 3 91
(Mark Johnston) *led: shkn up and hdd over 2f out: one pce fr over 1f out* **9/2**

1 **5** 3/4 **Combative**[29] 1575 3-9-7 **89** RyanMoore 1 91
(Amanda Perrett) *trckd ldng pair: pushed along firmly over 2f out: rdn and no imp over 1f out: one pce* **4/1**[3]

-155 **6** 4 1/2 **Artful Mind**[48] 1185 3-8-0 **73** JosephineGordon[(5)] 5 66
(James Unett) *t.k.h: trckd ldng pair: tried to chal over 2f out: btn over 1f out: wknd fnl f* **50/1**

2m 13.46s (2.96) **Going Correction** +0.30s/f (Good) **6** Ran SP% **109.8**
Speed ratings (Par 103): **100,99,98,98,97 94**
CSF £15.69 CT £39.90 TOTE £2.50: £1.30, £2.60; EX 12.70 Trifecta £49.80.
Owner N Farrell, L Field, T Mellor & B Cognet **Bred** Mrs L H Field **Trained** Barbury Castle, Wilts

FOCUS
Race distance increased by 29yds. They didn't go particularly fast up front, but none the less this looks good handicap form, with the fast-improving winner value for much more than the winning margin. The second stepped up to beat the rest.

2414 BETVICTOR BREEDERS BACKING RACING EBF MAIDEN STKS 1m 2f 7y
8:00 (8:02) (Class 5) 3-4-Y-O **£3,881** (£1,155; £577; £288) **Stalls** Low

Form RPR
6- **1** **Shabeeb (USA)**[209] 7431 3-8-12 0 AndreaAtzeni 12 90+
(Roger Varian) *trckd ldrs in 5th: shkn up and clsd fr 2f out: rdn to ld ins fnl f: styd on and sn in command* **2/1**[1]

02- **2** 1 1/4 **Plenary (USA)**[187] 7863 3-8-12 0 SilvestreDeSousa 9 87
(Jeremy Noseda) *difficult to load into stall: trckd ldng pair: wnt 2nd over 2f out and sn pressed ldr: led briefly 1f out: outpcd ins fnl f but kpt on* **8/1**

02- **3** shd **High Shields (IRE)**[162] 8152 3-8-12 0 FMBerry 6 86
(Roger Charlton) *trckd ldr: led 3f out: rdn over 2f out: hdd 1f out: kpt on wl* **5/1**[3]

2 **4** 1 1/2 **Regicide (IRE)**[29] 1575 3-8-12 0 TomQueally 16 83
(James Fanshawe) *hld up early but prog to chse ldrs after 4f: clsd fr over 2f out and ch over 1f out: rdn and nt qckn sn after* **7/2**[2]

35 **5** 7 **William Hunter**[10] 2098 4-9-12 0 WilliamTwiston-Davies 7 70
(Alan King) *settled in midfield: pushed along vigorously fr over 2f out: nvr on terms but kpt on to take modest nr fin: could do bttr* **33/1**

6 nk **Madame Chow (IRE)** 3-8-7 0 OisinMurphy 1 64
(Ralph Beckett) *led to 3f out: sn btn: wknd over 1f out* **11/2**

0 **7** nse **Ma Peek (USA)**[23] 1739 3-8-12 0 JimmyFortune 8 69
(Brian Meehan) *hld up in midfield: pushed along firmly over 2f out and no prog: kpt on fnl f* **33/1**

8 2 3/4 **Profusion** 4-9-12 0 RyanMoore 4 64
(Sir Michael Stoute) *green preliminaries: trckd ldng trio: pushed along over 2f out: reminder sn after and wknd* **10/1**

9 1/2 **Royal Occassion** 4-9-12 0 SamHitchcott 5 63
(Jim Boyle) *nvr bttr than midfield: rdn and no real prog wl over 2f out* **50/1**

0 **10** hd **Balancing Time**[7] 2175 3-8-12 0 PatDobbs 10 62
(Amanda Perrett) *nvr bttr than midfield: shkn up and lft bhd over 2f out* **50/1**

0 **11** shd **Rowlestonerendezvu**[13] 2008 3-8-7 0 LukeMorris 15 57+
(Tony Carroll) *stdd s: hld up in rr: nudged along and no prog bhd rivals over 2f out: kpt on fnl f: could improve* **100/1**

0- **12** 3/4 **Imari Kid (IRE)**[209] 7431 3-8-12 0 LiamKeniry 14 60
(Gary Moore) *stdd s: hld up in last pair: pushed along over 2f out: no real prog and nvr involved* **66/1**

35 **13** 1/2 **Niceonecenturion**[17] 1930 3-8-12 0 JimCrowley 13 59
(William Knight) *stdd s: hld up in last pair: nudged along over 2f out: no real prog and nvr involved: could improve* **25/1**

14 10 **Tom's Rock (IRE)** 3-8-9 0 DanielMuscutt[(3)] 11 39
(John Butler) *s.s: a wl in rr: t.o* **66/1**

15 3 3/4 **Alfredo (IRE)**[20] 4-9-12 0 (t) TimmyMurphy 3 33
(Seamus Durack) *nvr bttr than midfield: rdn and wknd 3f out: t.o* **33/1**

2m 11.94s (1.44) **Going Correction** +0.30s/f (Good)
WFA 3 from 4yo 14lb **15** Ran SP% **128.4**
Speed ratings (Par 103): **106,105,104,103,98 97,97,95,95,95 95,94,94,86,83**
CSF £19.42 TOTE £3.10: £1.60, £3.10, £2.00; EX 20.30 Trifecta £101.10.
Owner Hamdan Al Maktoum **Bred** Shadwell Farm LLC **Trained** Newmarket, Suffolk

FOCUS
Race distance increased by 29yds. Traditionally a strong maiden, they went a fair gallop early, and it was won by a highly promising colt. The first four were clear and the form looks up to the race standard.

2415 BETVICTOR MILLION POUND GOAL FILLIES' H'CAP 1m 1f
8:35 (8:36) (Class 5) (0-75,75) 3-Y-O+ **£3,234** (£962; £481; £240) **Stalls** Low

Form RPR
335- **1** **Kath's Legacy**[140] 8409 3-8-7 **67** OisinMurphy 3 76
(Ben De Haan) *hld up in 4th: rdn and prog to chse clr ldr wl over 1f out: styd on wl to cl fnl f: led nr fin* **20/1**

30-0 **2** 1/2 **Ejayteekay**[19] 1859 3-8-10 **70** SilvestreDeSousa 6 78
(Hughie Morrison) *racd freely: led and clr w one rival after 3f: drew 8 l ahd 2f out: kpt on u.p after but hdd nr fin* **6/1**[2]

1-44 **3** 7 **Atwix**[30] 1552 4-9-12 **73** (b[1]) JimCrowley 8 68
(Lucy Wadham) *hld up in last pair: plld wd and rdn 2f out: prog to take 3rd fnl f: kpt on but no ch to threaten ldng pair* **8/1**[3]

4-30 **4** 2 3/4 **Apache Song**[23] 1739 3-8-10 **70** FrederikTylicki 9 57
(Rod Millman) *hld up in last pair: plld wd and reminder 2f out: prog and reminder over 1f out: tk 4th ins fnl f: kpt on quite wl* **14/1**

1- **5** 4 1/2 **Danilovna (IRE)**[182] 7905 3-9-0 **74** GeorgeBaker 5 51
(David Lanigan) *hld up towards rr and off the pce: shkn up over 2f out: limited prog to dispute modest 3rd jst over 1f out: nvr any ch and sn wknd* **10/11**[1]

243- **6** 4 **Forest Lakes (IRE)**[156] 8233 3-8-11 **71** JamieSpencer 2 39
(George Scott) *chsd clr ldng pair: rdn and no imp over 2f out: wknd wl over 1f out* **6/1**[2]

403- **7** 3/4 **Cooperess**[229] 6940 3-8-0 **60** oh3 KieranO'Neill 4 26
(Ali Stronge) *stdd s: plld hrd in midfield and off the pce: shkn up over 2f out: no prog and sn btn* **33/1**

-522 **8** 9 **Robins Pearl (FR)**[21] 1808 4-10-0 **75** DarryllHolland 7 23
(Harry Dunlop) *chsd ldr and clr of rest after 3f: rdn over 2f out: lost 2nd and wknd rapidly wl over 1f out: t.o* **8/1**[3]

1m 57.5s (1.80) **Going Correction** +0.30s/f (Good)
WFA 3 from 4yo 13lb **8** Ran SP% **117.5**
Speed ratings (Par 100): **104,103,97,94,90 87,86,78**
CSF £137.52 CT £1074.52 TOTE £16.30: £3.50, £1.60, £2.30; EX 80.00 Trifecta £558.40.
Owner Merv Cox **Bred** Merv Cox **Trained** Lambourn, Berks

FOCUS
Race distance increased by 29yds. They were strung out a long way from the finish in this modest fillies' handicap, with the runner-up making a bold bid for home, and the first two ended up well clear in a good time.
T/Plt: £670.00 to a £1 stake. Pool of £72220.56 - 78.68 winning tickets. T/Qpdt: £99.50 to a £1 stake. Pool of £6741.99 - 50.10 winning tickets. **Jonathan Neesom**

CARLISLE (R-H)

Friday, May 20

OFFICIAL GOING: Good to firm (good in places; 7.7)

Wind: Breezy, half against Weather: Overcast

2416 GET CARLISLE TIPS @BOOKIES.COM H'CAP 5f 193y

2:00 (2:01) (Class 5) (0-70,70) 4-Y-O+ **£2,911** (£866; £432; £216) **Stalls** Low

Form RPR

0-45 **1** **Kenny The Captain (IRE)**[20] 1869 5-9-5 **68**...........(b[1]) DuranFentiman 8 77
(Tim Easterby) *trckd ldrs: rdn to ld over 1f out: hld on wl fnl f* **13/2**[2]

5055 **2** 1 ¼ **Daylight**[7] 2201 6-9-1 **64**..............................(t) KeaganLatham 10 69+
(Michael Easterby) *midfield on wd outside: effrt and chsd wnr over 1f out: edgd rt and kpt on ins fnl f: nt pce to chal* **28/1**

0033 **3** ½ **Picks Pinta**[11] 2092 5-8-13 **67**..............................(p) PhilDennis[(5)] 3 70
(John David Riches) *prom: effrt whn n.m.r briefly wl over 1f out: swtchd lft and sn rdn: kpt on ins fnl f* **11/1**

21 **4** hd **Chaplin Bay (IRE)**[7] 2201 4-9-7 **70** 7ex.................... JamesSullivan 13 72+
(Ruth Carr) *sn niggled along in rr: rdn and hdwy on outside wl over 1f out: edgd rt and kpt on same pce wl ins fnl f* **7/4**[1]

0363 **5** 3 ¼ **Ancient Cross**[27] 1648 12-8-11 **65**...........................(bt) NathanEvans[(5)] 6 57
(Michael Easterby) *midfield: effrt and rdn 2f out: outpcd ins fnl f* **10/1**

3405 **6** 1 ¾ **National Service (USA)**[3] 2332 5-9-2 **65**.....................(tp) JoeFanning 4 51+
(Rebecca Menzies) *missed break: bhd: rdn and hdwy over 1f out: kpt on fnl f: nvr rchd ldrs* **11/1**

0-50 **7** ¾ **Ki Ki**[130] 146 4-8-13 **62**.. ConnorBeasley 7 46
(Bryan Smart) *in tch: drvn along over 2f out: wknd fnl f* **28/1**

100- **8** 2 ¼ **Caeser The Gaeser (IRE)**[220] 7190 4-8-4 **60**......... KieranSchofield[(7)] 9 37
(Nigel Tinkler) *bhd: rdn along 1/2-way: sme late hdwy: nvr on terms* **33/1**

5-40 **9** 1 **Coolcalmcollected (IRE)**[44] 1252 4-9-0 **63**...................... NeilFarley 11 37
(Andrew Crook) *in tch on outside: drvn and outpcd 2f out: sn btn* **100/1**

434- **10** 5 **Circuitous**[220] 7189 8-9-1 **64**..(v) JasonHart 12 22
(Keith Dalgleish) *prom: rdn over 2f out: wknd over 1f out* **12/1**

1605 **11** 4 ½ **Diatomic (IRE)**[31] 1549 4-8-12 **61**.................................(p) PJMcDonald 1 4
(Tom Dascombe) *towards rr: drvn along 1/2-way: nvr rchd ldrs* **25/1**

6160 **12** ½ **Lackaday**[20] 1869 4-9-2 **70**...(p) CallumShepherd[(5)] 5 12
(Mark Walford) *w ldr to over 2f out: rdn and wknd over 1f out* **16/1**

4101 **13** 1 ¾ **Razin' Hell**[66] 938 5-9-7 **70**..(v) BenCurtis 2 6
(John Balding) *led tl rdn and hdd over 1f out: sn wknd* **7/1**[3]

1m 12.99s (-0.71) **Going Correction** +0.025s/f (Good) **13** Ran SP% **116.2**

Speed ratings (Par 103): **105,103,102,102,98 95,94,91,90,83 77,77,74**

CSF £182.76 CT £2022.35 TOTE £9.60: £2.30, £5.20, £4.10; EX 205.60 Trifecta £2893.70.

Owner Reality Partnerships V **Bred** Joe Foley & John Grimes **Trained** Great Habton, N Yorks

FOCUS

Inside rail was moved out 6yds, from 1m start round Old Stable bend to 3f. The distance of this race was as advertised. There were differing views on the ground from jockeys, Joe Fanning feeling it was "just on the easy side of good" while Jason Hart felt it was "quick enough". Modest sprinting form, with the winner always well placed. He's rated to his best since last summer.

2417 COMPARE BEST ODDS @BOOKIES.COM EBF NOVICE STKS 5f

2:30 (2:33) (Class 5) 2-Y-O **£3,234** (£962; £481; £240) **Stalls** Low

Form RPR

1 **Tahoo (IRE)** 2-8-11 0.. JoeyHaynes 8 74+
(K R Burke) *in tch on outside: stdy hdwy over 1f out: shkn up to ld ins fnl f: qcknd clr: readily* **3/1**[2]

0 **2** 2 ¼ **Hope Against Hope (IRE)**[8] 2173 2-8-11 0...................... JoeFanning 2 66
(Mark Johnston) *led: rdn over 1f out: flashed tail ins fnl f: sn hdd: nt pce of wnr* **13/8**[1]

0 **3** 4 ½ **Jester Spirit (IRE)**[37] 1422 2-9-2 0... BenCurtis 6 55
(Tom Dascombe) *trckd ldr: rdn and edgd rt over 1f out: outpcd by first two fnl f* **10/1**

4 1 **Vatican Hill (IRE)** 2-9-2 0... TonyHamilton 5 51
(Richard Fahey) *hld up in tch on ins: rdn and effrt 2f out: sn no imp* **8/1**[3]

5 shd **Last Paradise (IRE)** 2-8-11 0.. PJMcDonald 1 46
(Ann Duffield) *trckd ldrs: rdn along over 2f out: wknd over 1f out* **9/1**

0 **6** ½ **Bellamay**[18] 1921 2-8-11 0... DuranFentiman 7 44
(John Weymes) *reluctant to enter stalls: dwlt and t.k.h in rr: effrt on outside 2f out: sn no imp* **66/1**

7 1 **Hotfill** 2-9-2 0.. GrahamGibbons 3 45
(David Barron) *dwlt: plld hrd and sn cl up: rdn and rn green 2f out: sn wknd* **8/1**[3]

8 ½ **Royal Celebration** 2-9-2 0.. ConnorBeasley 4 44
(Bryan Smart) *hld up bhd ldng gp: drvn over 2f out: sn no imp: btn fnl f* **12/1**

1m 3.59s (2.79) **Going Correction** +0.025s/f (Good) **8** Ran SP% **113.6**

Speed ratings (Par 93): **78,74,67,65,65 64,63,62**

CSF £8.14 TOTE £3.90: £1.50, £1.10, £3.30; EX 9.80 Trifecta £57.20.

Owner John Dance **Bred** Tally-Ho Stud **Trained** Middleham Moor, N Yorks

FOCUS

Race distance as advertised. The front two in the market dominated this ordinary novice event.

2418 FREE HORSE RACING BETS @BOOKIES.COM H'CAP 5f

3:05 (3:05) (Class 5) (0-70,70) 3-Y-O+ **£2,911** (£866; £432; £216) **Stalls** Low

Form RPR

0434 **1** **Windforpower (IRE)**[10] 2120 6-9-2 **60**............................(p) JoeFanning 7 66
(Tracy Waggott) *sn pushed along in rr: rdn and hdwy on outside over 1f out: led ins fnl f: idled: drvn out* **7/1**

01-3 **2** ½ **Anieres Boy**[13] 2053 4-9-1 **59**.. GrahamGibbons 3 63
(Michael Easterby) *t.k.h: cl up: led over 1f out to ins fnl f: kpt on towards fin* **15/8**[1]

6003 **3** ¾ **Oriental Relation (IRE)**[10] 2120 5-9-7 **70**...................(v) PhilDennis[(5)] 8 71
(James Given) *trckd ldrs on outside: effrt and ev ch over 1f out to ent fnl f: kpt on same pce last 100yds* **9/2**[2]

4-00 **4** nk **Tribesman**[18] 1922 3-9-3 **69**.. SamJames 4 67+
(Marjorie Fife) *prom: rdn along over 2f out: kpt on ins fnl f: nt pce to chal* **22/1**

1-40 **5** ½ **Danzeb (IRE)**[13] 2049 3-9-4 **70**... PJMcDonald 1 65
(Ann Duffield) *in tch on ins: effrt and rdn 2f out: sn edgd rt: plugged on fnl f: no imp* **11/2**

0626 **6** shd **Bronze Beau**[7] 2202 9-9-7 **65**..(tp) ShaneGray 2 63
(Kristin Stubbs) *led: rdn and hdd over 1f out: outpcd ins fnl f* **11/1**

223U **7** 3 ¾ **New Lease Of Life**[7] 2201 7-9-5 **63**...................................(v) JasonHart 5 62+
(Keith Dalgleish) *dwlt: sn rdn along in rr: hdwy u.p against far rail whn no room and hmpd appr fnl f: nt rcvr* **5/1**[3]

1m 2.31s (1.51) **Going Correction** +0.025s/f (Good)

WFA 3 from 4yo+ 8lb **7** Ran SP% **110.2**

Speed ratings (Par 103): **88,87,86,85,84 84,78**

CSF £19.08 CT £60.98 TOTE £7.00: £3.20, £1.30; EX 16.10 Trifecta £65.30.

Owner David Tate **Bred** Tally-Ho Stud **Trained** Spennymoor, Co Durham

■ Stewards' Enquiry : Shane Gray three-day ban: careless riding

FOCUS

Race distance as advertised. Plenty of pace on and the closers were favoured, so the runner-up therefore needs his effort upgrading. The winner built on his Beverly latest.

2419 EURO 2016 EXPERT TIPS @BOOKIES.COM MAIDEN FILLIES' STKS 7f 173y

3:40 (3:40) (Class 5) 3-Y-O+ **£2,911** (£866; £432; £216) **Stalls** Low

Form RPR

62- **1** **Wholesome (USA)**[237] 6751 3-8-12 0.......................... DougieCostello 5 78
(K R Burke) *dwlt: hld up in tch: checked after 3f: sn trcking ldrs: rdn and led over 1f out: kpt on wl fnl f* **6/4**[1]

00- **2** 1 ¾ **Lincoln Rocks**[292] 4898 3-8-12 0....................................... SamJames 2 74
(David O'Meara) *t.k.h: trckd ldrs: drvn and outpcd 3f out: rallied to chse wnr last 100yds: kpt on* **20/1**

222- **3** 2 **Prying Pandora (FR)**[223] 7123 3-8-12 75..................... TonyHamilton 9 69
(Richard Fahey) *t.k.h: pressed ldr: j. path after 3f: effrt and ev ch whn carried lft over 1f out: sn chsng wnr: edgd rt and lost 2nd ins fnl f: no ex* **2/1**[2]

4 4 **Lucky Violet (IRE)**[28] 4-9-10 0...........................[1] PJMcDonald 7 62
(Iain Jardine) *hld up in tch: rdn and outpcd over 2f out: edgd lft over 1f out: kpt on fnl f: no imp* **80/1**

05 **5** 6 **Penny Lane Forever**[27] 1628 3-8-12 0.............................. JackMitchell 6 45
(Roger Varian) *led: rdn and hung lft over 1f out: sn hdd: wknd ins fnl f* **5/2**[3]

006- **6** ¾ **Judith Gardenier**[242] 6583 4-9-10 37.......................... RoystonFfrench 3 46
(Iain Jardine) *hld up in tch: rdn and outpcd over 3f out: no imp fr 2f out* **100/1**

4 **7** nk **Table Manners**[22] 1814 4-9-7 0............................... MissEmmaSayer[(3)] 8 45
(Wilf Storey) *in tch on outside: drvn and outpcd over 3f out: btn fnl 2f* **8/1**

006- **8** 1 **Zruda**[159] 7679 5-9-10 43... JamesSullivan 1 43
(David Thompson) *t.k.h: in tch on ins: hmpd after 3f: rdn and outpcd over 3f out: sn btn* **100/1**

6 **9** 12 **Little Miss Nelly**[11] 2094 6-9-10 0..............................[1] ConnorBeasley 4 14
(Fred Watson) *s.i.s: bhd: struggling after 3f: nvr on terms* **125/1**

1m 40.6s (0.60) **Going Correction** +0.025s/f (Good)

WFA 3 from 4yo+ 12lb **9** Ran SP% **121.8**

Speed ratings (Par 100): **98,96,94,90,84 83,83,82,70**

CSF £33.90 TOTE £2.40: £1.10, £6.20, £1.10; EX 42.90 Trifecta £137.00.

Owner Hubert John Strecker **Bred** E Quinn, D Quinn, S Pierce Et Al **Trained** Middleham Moor, N Yorks

FOCUS

Race distance increased by 12yds. An ordinary maiden, run at a good gallop, and the form isn't worth much. The time was 18lb slower than the following handicap and the winner didn't match her standout 2yo form.

2420 PLAY MILLION POUND GOAL @BOOKIES.COM EBF FILLIES' H'CAP 7f 173y

4:10 (4:11) (Class 4) (0-85,84) 3-Y-O+ **£6,469** (£1,925; £962; £481) **Stalls** Low

Form RPR

03-3 **1** **Desert Haze**[25] 1714 3-8-5 **73**.. ShaneGray 5 79+
(Ralph Beckett) *t.k.h early: pressed ldr: ev ch and rdn whn carried lft over 1f out: rdr dropped whip ins fnl f: led last 100yds: pushed out* **2/1**[1]

-010 **2** ½ **Fidelma Moon (IRE)**[27] 1631 4-8-11 **72**................... JordanVaughan[(5)] 1 80
(K R Burke) *led: rdn and hung lft over 1f out: hdd ins fnl f: kpt on: hld nr fin* **12/1**

-060 **3** 1 ¼ **Alexandrakollontai (IRE)**[14] 2016 6-9-8 **78**.............(b) JamesSullivan 8 83
(Alistair Whillans) *bhd and sn niggled along: hdwy on outside over 1f out: kpt on ins fnl f: nt gng pce of first two* **22/1**

404- **4** ¾ **Renfrew Street**[198] 7702 3-8-7 **75**...................................... JoeFanning 9 75
(Mark Johnston) *dwlt: hld up on outside: rdn over 2f out: hdwy over 1f out: kpt on fnl f: no imp* **6/1**[3]

0-63 **5** 2 ½ **Breakable**[7] 2223 5-9-7 **82**.................................(p) RachelRichardson[(5)] 6 79
(Tim Easterby) *t.k.h: trckd ldrs: effrt and edgd rt over 1f out: outpcd fnl f* **11/4**[2]

115- **6** ½ **Al Shahaniya (IRE)**[237] 6757 3-9-0 **82**............................. PhillipMakin 3 75
(John Quinn) *dwlt: hld up in tch: hdwy over 2f out: rdn and outpcd over 1f out: sn outpcd* **13/2**

23-0 **7** 4 ½ **Hidden Treasures**[16] 1960 3-8-4 **72**............................. PatrickMathers 4 54
(Richard Fahey) *prom: rdn along over 2f out: wknd over 1f out* **22/1**

05-6 **8** 3 ½ **Forever A Lady (IRE)**[36] 1446 3-8-10 **78**.......................... JasonHart 7 52
(Keith Dalgleish) *prom: drvn along over 2f out: wknd over 1f out* **12/1**

1m 38.89s (-1.11) **Going Correction** +0.025s/f (Good)

WFA 3 from 4yo+ 12lb **8** Ran SP% **111.7**

Speed ratings (Par 102): **106,105,104,103,101 100,96,92**

CSF £25.97 CT £400.25 TOTE £2.80: £1.10, £2.60, £5.00; EX 32.20 Trifecta £388.30.

Owner H H Sheikh Mohammed Bin Khalifa Al Thani **Bred** Whatton Manor Stud & Robert Cornelius **Trained** Kimpton, Hants

■ Stewards' Enquiry : Jordan Vaughan one-day ban: careless riding (5 June)

FOCUS

Race distance increased by 12yds. A fair fillies' handicap and the winner can have her effort upgraded. The 1-2 were always the front pair.

2421 EURO 2016 FREE BETS @BOOKIES.COM H'CAP 6f 195y

4:45 (4:50) (Class 4) (0-80,79) 4-Y-O+ **£4,851** (£1,443; £721; £360) **Stalls** Low

Form RPR

5212 **1** **Surewecan**[11] 2091 4-8-11 **69**.. JoeFanning 4 77
(Mark Johnston) *dwlt: sn trcking ldrs: effrt and rdn over 1f out: led ins fnl f: hld on wl cl home* **10/3**[3]

50-0 **2** shd **Honeysuckle Lil (IRE)**[14] 2016 4-9-1 **73**............................ DavidAllan 5 80
(Tim Easterby) *in tch on outside: effrt and rdn 2f out: kpt on fnl f: jst hld* **10/1**

30-6 **3** ½ **Ralphy Boy (IRE)**[21] 1844 7-9-4 **76**................................. GrahamLee 2 81
(Alistair Whillans) *led at stdy pce: rdn and hrd pressed fr 2f out: edgd rt and hdd ins fnl f: one pce towards fin* **11/1**

22-5 **4** hd **Shootingsta (IRE)**[139] 24 4-9-7 **79**.......................(p) ConnorBeasley 3 84
(Bryan Smart) *t.k.h: trckd ldr: rdn and ev ch over 1f out to ins fnl f: kpt on: hld nr fin* **11/4**[1]

-220 **5** ½ **Gold Flash**6 2238 4-9-2 **74** (p) PhillipMakin 6 77
(Keith Dalgleish) *hld up in tch: rdn along 2f out: swtchd lft and kpt on ins fnl f* **3/1**2

01-4 **6** 2 **Chiswick Bey (IRE)**10 2121 8-9-0 **72** TonyHamilton 8 70
(Richard Fahey) *hld up in tch on ins: drvn and outpcd wl over 1f out: edgd rt: pluged on ins fnl f: no imp* **9/2**

1m 28.03s (0.93) **Going Correction** +0.025s/f (Good) **6** Ran SP% **110.4**
Speed ratings (Par 105): **95,94,94,94,93 91**
CSF £32.67 CT £306.21 TOTE £3.30: £2.10, £3.30; EX 30.50 Trifecta £169.30.
Owner Douglas Livingston **Bred** Christopher & Annabelle Mason **Trained** Middleham Moor, N Yorks

■ Royal Duchess was withdrawn. Price at time of withdrawal 9-1. Rule 4 applies to bets struck prior to withdrawal but not to SP bets - deduction 10p in the pound. New market formed.
■ Stewards' Enquiry : David Allan two-day ban: use of whip (5-6 June)

FOCUS
Race distance increased by 12yds. No great gallop on and a bunched finish. The winner is rated close to his 3yo form.

2422 FA CUP FINAL BETTING TIPS @BOOKIES.COM H'CAP 7f 173y
5:15 (5:16) (Class 5) (0-70,70) 3-Y-O **£2,911** (£866; £432; £216) **Stalls** Low

Form RPR

5464 **1** **Frap**22 1816 3-8-4 **58** RachelRichardson(5) 2 63+
(Richard Fahey) *dwlt hld up: gd hdwy against far rail over 1f out: kpt on wl fnl f to ld towards fin* **5/1**3

461- **2** hd **She's Electric (IRE)**225 7054 3-9-3 **66** PhillipMakin 4 70
(Keith Dalgleish) *t.k.h: trckd ldr: rdn and outpcd 2f out: rallied and led ins fnl f: kpt on: hdd towards fin* **5/1**3

-011 **3** 1½ **Ordinal**30 1574 3-9-5 **68** RoystonFfrench 5 68
(Mark Johnston) *led at ordinary gallop: rdn and qcknd over 2f out: hdd and no ex ins fnl f* **11/4**1

400- **4** ¾ **My Valentino (IRE)**289 5019 3-8-13 **62** JamesSullivan 7 60
(Dianne Sayer) *hld up in tch: drvn and outpcd over 2f out: kpt on fnl f: nt pce to chal* **16/1**

6 **5** 1¾ **Diamond Avalanche (IRE)**26 1673 3-9-7 **70** DavidNolan 8 64
(Patrick Holmes) *t.k.h: trckd ldrs: rdn and edgd rt 2f out: outpcd appr fnl f* **18/1**

6-22 **6** 1 **Fidra Bay (IRE)**26 1671 3-9-5 **68** NeilFarley 3 60
(Alan Swinbank) *trckd ldrs: rdn over 2f out: wknd ins fnl f* **3/1**2

550- **7** 2¼ **Oceanella (IRE)**217 7244 3-9-2 **65** DougieCostello 6 51
(K R Burke) *t.k.h: hld up in tch: rdn over 2f out: wknd over 1f out* **14/1**

-006 **8** hd **Mr Potter**18 1927 3-8-8 **57** (e) ConnorBeasley 1 43
(Richard Guest) *plld hrd: hld up: drvn over 2f out: sn no imp: btn over 1f out* **9/1**

1m 42.37s (2.37) **Going Correction** +0.025s/f (Good) **8** Ran SP% **112.8**
Speed ratings (Par 99): **89,88,87,86,84 83,81,81**
CSF £29.25 CT £81.04 TOTE £5.90: £2.20, £2.00, £1.10; EX 34.00 Trifecta £103.90.
Owner Dr Marwan Koukash **Bred** Kincorth Investments Inc **Trained** Musley Bank, N Yorks

FOCUS
Race distance increased by 12yds. Moderate handicap form, the pace was a steady one and the winner did well to come from off the pace. The winner built on his nursery form.
T/Plt: £138.80 to a £1 stake. Pool: £50,777.39 - 266.99 winning tickets T/Qpdt: £11.50 to a £1 stake. Pool: £4,942.95 - 315.67 winning tickets **Richard Young**

1951 CATTERICK (L-H)
Friday, May 20

OFFICIAL GOING: Good to firm (good in places; 8.7)
Wind: Moderate half behind Weather: Cloudy

2423 JUSTGIVING.COM/MARCIA-SANDERSON FOR MACMILLAN APPRENTICE H'CAP 5f
6:10 (6:11) (Class 6) (0-55,55) 4-Y-O+ **£2,264** (£673; £336; £168) **Stalls** Low

Form RPR

0000 **1** **Under Approval**13 2052 5-8-9 **46** oh1 (b) GemmaTutty(3) 2 57
(Karen Tutty) *racd towards inner: in tch: hdwy over 2f out: chsd ldrs over 1f out: rdn to ld ins fnl f: kpt on strly* **20/1**

-546 **2** 2½ **Compton River**13 2052 4-9-6 **54** PhilDennis 7 56
(Bryan Smart) *trckd ldrs: hdwy 2f out: rdn over 1f out: styng on whn swtchd lft ins fnl f: kpt on wl towards fin* **7/1**2

3053 **3** hd **Give Us A Belle (IRE)**3 2342 7-9-7 **55** (bt) PaddyPilley 6 56
(Christine Dunnett) *racd centre: led: rdn along wl over 1f out: drvn and edgd rt ins fnl f: sn hdd and kpt on same pce* **3/1**1

-000 **4** 1¼ **Incomparable**10 2120 11-8-8 **47** (p) NatalieHambling(5) 1 44
(Scott Dixon) *prom: chsd ldr 1/2-way: rdn along wl over 1f out: hld whn sltly hmpd ins fnl f* **28/1**

6025 **5** 1¼ **Lizzy's Dream**13 2052 8-9-4 **55** RowanScott(3) 10 47
(Rebecca Bastiman) *in tch: rdn along and sltly outpcd 2f out: styd on u.p fnl f: nrst fin* **12/1**

200- **6** shd **Lorimer's Lot (IRE)**189 7831 5-9-0 **53** (p) AdamMcNamara(5) 4 45
(Mark Walford) *in rr: pushed along 1/2-way: rdn 2f out: styd on appr fnl f: nrst fin* **10/1**

0200 **7** nk **Fuel Injection**32 1525 5-8-11 **50** KieranSchofield(5) 8 41
(Paul Midgley) *in rr: swtchd lft to inner rail 1/2-way: rdn 2f out: styd on appr fnl f: nrst fin* **10/1**

-000 **8** ¾ **Lydiate Lady**26 1676 4-9-4 **55** DavidParkes(3) 12 43
(Paul Green) *prom towards outer: rdn along 2f out: grad wknd* **11/1**

650- **9** 1 **Zebelini (IRE)**210 7437 4-8-13 **55** RobertDodsworth(8) 3 40
(Ollie Pears) *chsd ldr: rdn along over 2f out: wknd wl over 1f out* **9/1**

00-R **10** nse **A J Cook (IRE)**13 2052 6-9-0 **53** DanielleMooney(5) 11 37
(Ron Barr) *in rr: rdn along 2f out: n.d* **33/1**

0-00 **11** 1½ **Betty Boo (IRE)**14 2013 6-8-9 **46** oh1 CharlieBennett(3) 14 25
(Shaun Harris) *prom on outer: rdn along 1/2-way: sn wknd* **28/1**

00-0 **12** ¾ **Sunrise Dance**13 2052 7-8-12 **46** oh1 GeorgeBuckell 13 22
(Kenny Johnson) *a towards rr* **16/1**

630- **13** shd **Indastar**142 8399 6-8-13 **54** StephenCummins(7) 5 30
(Michael Herrington) *a towards rr* **8/1**3

040- **U** **Thornaby Princess**210 7437 5-9-2 **53** RobJFitzpatrick(3) 9
(Colin Teague) *stmbld and uns rdr s* **22/1**

59.63s (-0.17) **Going Correction** +0.075s/f (Good) **14** Ran SP% **117.6**
Speed ratings (Par 101): **104,100,99,97,95 95,95,93,92,92 89,88,88,**
CSF £143.07 CT £549.05 TOTE £28.10: £7.00, £2.80, £1.40; EX 222.30 Trifecta £1840.30.
Owner Grange Park Racing **Bred** Mickley Stud **Trained** Osmotherley, N Yorks

FOCUS
A low-grade sprint for apprentice riders with exposed performers and low-drawn horses dominating.

2424 IRISH STALLION FARMS EBF FILLIES' NOVICE STKS (PLUS 10 RACE) 5f
6:40 (6:40) (Class 5) 2-Y-O **£3,234** (£962; £481; £240) **Stalls** Low

Form RPR

423 **1** **Merry Banter**17 1951 2-9-0 0 GrahamGibbons 2 72
(Paul Midgley) *mde all: jnd and rdn wl over 1f out: drvn ent fnl f: kpt on gamely towards fin* **10/1**

2 1 **Flawlessly (FR)** 2-9-0 0 DanielTudhope 3 68
(James Bethell) *sn chsd wnr: smooth hdwy and cl up 2f out: chal over 1f out: rdn and ev ch ins fnl f: no ex towards fin* **13/8**1

0 **3** 7 **Clear As A Bell (IRE)**14 2007 2-9-0 0 DuranFentiman 4 43+
(Tim Easterby) *towards rr: hdwy 2f out: rdn and kpt on same pce appr fnl f* **100/1**

4 6 **Neigh Kid** 2-9-0 0 JasonHart 9 22
(Keith Dalgleish) *in rr: rdn along and hdwy 2f out: n.d* **12/1**

02 **5** 7 **Poppy Pivot (IRE)**17 1951 2-9-0 0 PJMcDonald 5
(Ann Duffield) *chsd ldrs: rdn along over 2f out: sn wknd* **13/2**3

6 1½ **Red Savina** 2-8-11 0 JoeDoyle(3) 7
(Kevin Ryan) *green and s.i.s: sn outpcd and a bhd* **25/1**

30 **7** ¾ **Born To Boogie**18 1921 2-9-0 0 TonyHamilton 1
(Chris Grant) *chsd ldrs on inner: rdn along over 2f out: sn wknd* **40/1**

B **Gabridan (IRE)** 2-9-0 0 GeorgeChaloner 6 +
(Richard Fahey) *trckd ldrs whn bdly hmpd and b.d 1/2-way* **10/1**

21 **F** **Wheneverwecan (IRE)**11 2090 2-9-4 0 JoeFanning 8
(Mark Johnston) *awkward and wnt rt s: chsd ldrs whn lost action and fell 1/2-way: fatally injured* **5/2**2

59.55s (-0.25) **Going Correction** +0.075s/f (Good) **9** Ran SP% **113.1**
Speed ratings (Par 90): **105,103,92,82,71 69,67, ,**
CSF £25.93 TOTE £12.60: £2.90, £1.80, £15.80; EX 29.40 Trifecta £858.40 Part won..
Owner H Thornton **Bred** Jeremy Green And Sons **Trained** Westow, N Yorks

FOCUS
A decent gallop to this handicap which went to a well-supported winner.

2425 BROOKLEIGH RIDING CENTRE (S) STKS 5f 212y
7:10 (7:11) (Class 6) 3-4-Y-O **£2,264** (£673; £336; £168) **Stalls** Low

Form RPR

0-00 **1** **I T Guru**4 2302 3-8-10 54 (t) BarryMcHugh 5 60
(Noel Wilson) *mde all: rdn over 1f out: drvn ins fnl f: kpt on wl towards fin* **12/1**

0441 **2** 1½ **Johnny B Goode (IRE)**13 2047 4-9-2 65 AdamMcNamara(7) 3 62
(Richard Fahey) *trckd wnr on inner: effrt over 2f out and sn pushed along: rdn over 1f out: swtchd rt and drvn ins fnl f: sn no imp* **1/1**1

05-0 **3** ¾ **Hadley**66 935 3-8-10 53 ConnorBeasley 4 53
(Tracy Waggott) *chsd ldrs: hdwy 2f out: rdn wl over 1f out: drvn ins fnl f: kpt on same pce* **10/1**

0300 **4** 2¼ **Castlerea Tess**34 1497 3-8-5 44 PatrickMathers 1 42
(Sarah Hollinshead) *towards rr: wd home turn and sn rdn: drvn and kpt on fr over 1f out: nrst fin* **16/1**

0-05 **5** 2¼ **Grenade**17 1953 4-8-12 44 PaulaMuir(7) 8 42
(Patrick Holmes) *t.k.h: hld up in tch: hdwy over 2f out: rdn wl over 1f out: sn one pce* **50/1**

00-0 **6** 1¼ **Letbygonesbeicons**13 2049 3-9-0 67 PJMcDonald 6 40
(Ann Duffield) *chsd wnr: rdn along 1/2-way: drvn and wknd 2f out* **5/2**2

5500 **7** 9 **Canford Crossing (IRE)**14 2015 3-8-10 63 (b1) RoystonFfrench 9 9
(David Nicholls) *chsd ldrs on outer: rdn along 1/2-way: sn outpcd and bhd* **8/1**3

0 **8** 2½ **Frenchie**28 1597 4-9-0 0 PaddyAspell 2
(Shaun Harris) *a in rr: bhd fnl 2f* **33/1**

1m 14.17s (0.57) **Going Correction** +0.20s/f (Good)
WFA 3 from 4yo 9lb **8** Ran SP% **117.3**
Speed ratings (Par 101): **104,102,101,98,95 93,81,78**
CSF £25.23 TOTE £17.50: £4.00, £1.10, £2.60; EX 28.00 Trifecta £200.30.There was no bid for the winner.
Owner John Blair **Bred** New Hall Stud **Trained** Middleham, N Yorks

FOCUS
An ordinary seller which was run over 12 yards further than the advertised distance.

2426 RACING UK PROFITS RETURNED TO RACING H'CAP 5f
7:40 (7:40) (Class 4) (0-80,86) 3-Y-O+ **£6,469** (£1,925; £962; £481) **Stalls** Low

Form RPR

00-0 **1** **Landing Night (IRE)**6 2261 4-9-8 **76** (p) PJMcDonald 2 85+
(Ann Duffield) *hmpd s: sn trcking ldrs: hdwy 2f out: chal over 1f out: rdn to ld ent fnl f: drvn and edgd lft last 110yds: kpt on* **13/2**

2-21 **2** ½ **First Bombardment**18 1922 3-9-0 **76** (p) DanielTudhope 1 79
(David O'Meara) *slt ld: jnd and rdn over 1f out: hdd ent fnl f: sn drvn and kpt on same pce* **9/4**1

0-00 **3** ¾ **Royal Brave (IRE)**14 2016 5-9-5 **73** BarryMcHugh 4 78+
(Rebecca Bastiman) *hld up: swtchd lft to inner and gd hdwy 2f out: chsd wnr on inner: and ev ch whn hmpd ins fnl f and again last 50yds: no ch after* **12/1**

2464 **4** ¾ **Desert Command**24 1744 6-9-5 **76** (v) MarcMonaghan(3) 6 77
(Robert Cowell) *clsd up: effrt 2f out: sn rdn: drvn over 1f out and sn one pce* **9/1**

0342 **5** nk **Flicka's Boy**5 2270 4-8-12 **73** AdamMcNamara(7) 3 73
(Tony Coyle) *sltly hmpd s and sn pushed along: swtchd rt to outer and hdwy 1/2-way: chsd ldr and rdn wl over 1f out: sn drvn: edgd lft and one pce* **11/4**2

2051 **6** ¾ **Rusty Rocket (IRE)**4 2305 7-9-13 **86** 6ex PaddyPilley(5) 5 83
(Paul Green) *trckd ldrs: pushed along over 2f out: sn rdn and wknd over 1f out* **9/2**3

200- **7** 9 **Native Falls (IRE)**293 4885 5-9-10 **78** ShaneGray 7 42
(Alan Swinbank) *prom: rdn along 2f out: sn wknd* **16/1**

59.33s (-0.47) **Going Correction** +0.075s/f (Good)
WFA 3 from 4yo+ 8lb **7** Ran SP% **112.5**
Speed ratings (Par 105): **106,105,104,102,102 101,86**
CSF £20.85 TOTE £8.10: £3.30, £1.60; EX 17.80 Trifecta £238.70.
Owner John Dance **Bred** Mrs Claire Doyle **Trained** Constable Burton, N Yorks

FOCUS
Mainly exposed performers in this 66-80 sprint in which the first three were drawn 1,2 and 4. The winner is rated close to last year's best.

2427 LESLIE PETCH FILLIES' H'CAP (2016 CATTERICK TWELVE FURLONG SERIES QUALIFIER) 1m 3f 214y

8:10 (8:10) (Class 5) (0-75,75) 4-Y-O+ **£3,234** (£962; £481; £240) **Stalls** Centre

Form RPR

364- **1** **Cartier (IRE)**[288] 5072 4-9-5 **73**..[1] JoeFanning 2 84+
(David Simcock) *hld up in rr: gd hdwy over 2f out: chsd ldr over 1f out: rdn and qcknd to ld ent fnl f: sn clr* **9/4**[2]

450- **2** *4* **Kip**[232] 6887 4-8-13 **67**.. SamJames 5 70
(David O'Meara) *led and sn clr: pushed along over 2f out: rdn over 1f out: hdd ent fnl f: sn drvn and kpt on same pce* **8/1**

012- **3** *4* **Carpe Vita (IRE)**[246] 6461 4-9-4 **72**........................ DanielTudhope 7 69
(David O'Meara) *trckd clr ldr: pushed along to take clsr order wl over 2f out: rdn wl over 1f out: sn btn* **10/11**[1]

606- **4** *6* **Multi Grain**[127] 5950 4-8-11 **65**.............................. PJMcDonald 1 52
(Micky Hammond) *trckd ldrs: pushed along 6f out: rdn along 4f out: drvn wl over 2f out and one pce* **7/1**[3]

2m 39.9s (1.00) **Going Correction** +0.20s/f (Good) **4** Ran SP% **106.8**
Speed ratings (Par 100): **104,101,98,94**
CSF £16.04 TOTE £2.30; EX 16.20 Trifecta £16.00.
Owner Al Asayl Bloodstock Ltd **Bred** Sheikh Sultan Bin Khalifa Al Nahyan **Trained** Newmarket, Suffolk

FOCUS
A fair gallop to this four-runner handicap which was run over 12 yards further than advertised. Modest fillies' form.

2428 RACING AGAIN 28TH MAY RATING RELATED MAIDEN STKS 7f

8:40 (8:41) (Class 6) 3-Y-O+ **£2,264** (£673; £336; £168) **Stalls** Low

Form RPR

50-4 **1** **Four Poets**[23] 1779 3-9-0 64.. RoystonFfrench 9 72
(David Simcock) *dwlt and bhd: hdwy 3f out: str run on outer wl over 1f out: rdn and styd on wl fnl f to ld last 50yds* **10/1**

3-32 **2** *2 1/4* **Rococoa (IRE)**[125] 211 3-9-0 64.................................... JoeFanning 4 66
(Ed Walker) *slt ld: rdn clr wl over 1f out: drvn ins fnl f: hdd and no ex last 50yds* **2/1**[1]

35-0 **3** *3/4* **Popsies Joy (IRE)**[39] 1381 3-9-0 64.......................... DuranFentiman 3 64
(Tim Easterby) *trckd ldrs: hdwy wl over 2f out: rdn to chse ldr wl over 1f out: drvn and kpt on same pce fnl f* **5/2**[2]

2400 **4** *2 1/2* **Intense Starlet (IRE)**[18] 1925 5-9-11 64........................ SamJames 8 61
(Marjorie Fife) *trckd ldrs: hdwy wl over 2f out: rdn wl over 1f out: drvn and one pce fnl f* **20/1**

-004 **5** *hd* **Canny Style**[25] 1725 3-8-11 63.. JoeDoyle(3) 6 57
(Kevin Ryan) *hld up in rr: hdwy on inner wl over 1f out: rdn and kpt on fnl f: nrst fin* **7/2**[3]

6-45 **6** *3/4* **Bradleysintown (IRE)**[39] 1379 3-9-0 60...................... ConnorBeasley 2 55
(Michael Dods) *cl up on inner: disp ld 1/2-way: rdn over 2f out: drvn wl over 1f out: grad wknd* **15/2**

0-00 **7** *nk* **Hashtag Frenzy**[24] 1768 3-8-7 35...............................(p) RowanScott(7) 1 54
(Rebecca Menzies) *chsd ldng pair on inner: rdn along 3f out: drvn 2f out and grad wknd* **100/1**

040- **8** *2* **Rose Eclair**[195] 7753 3-9-0 65.. JasonHart 5 48
(Tim Easterby) *towards rr: hdwy and in tch 1/2-way: rdn to chse ldrs over 2f out: sn drvn and wknd* **12/1**

0/0- **9** *20* **Mister York**[305] 4447 4-9-11 56.. PJMcDonald 10
(Antony Brittain) *s.i.s: a outpcd and bhd* **40/1**

1m 27.97s (0.97) **Going Correction** +0.20s/f (Good)
WFA 3 from 4yo+ 11lb **9** Ran SP% **120.9**
Speed ratings (Par 101): **102,99,98,95,95 94,94,92,69**
CSF £31.59 TOTE £6.80: £1.30, £1.60, £1.70; EX 49.40 Trifecta £114.50.
Owner Saeed Manana **Bred** Rabbah Bloodstock Limited **Trained** Newmarket, Suffolk

FOCUS
A maiden for horses rated 65 and below run over 12 yards further than advertised.
T/Plt: £111.70 to a £1 stake. Pool: £52,655.73 - 344.06 winning tickets T/Qpdt: £25.20 to a £1 stake. Pool: £3,839.03 - 112.5 winning tickets **Joe Rowntree**

2390 GOODWOOD (R-H)

Friday, May 20

OFFICIAL GOING: Good (7.6)
Wind: strong breeze across Weather: sunny

2429 SPITFIRE NOVICE AUCTION STKS 5f

1:50 (1:50) (Class 5) 2-Y-O **£3,234** (£962; £481; £240) **Stalls** High

Form RPR

1 **Quench Dolly** 2-8-8 0.. MichaelJMMurphy(3) 1 67
(John Gallagher) *cmpt: wnt rt and slowly away: sn trcking ldrs: rdn over 1f out: chal ent fnl f: led fnl 120yds: jst hld on* **8/1**

2 *nse* **Peachey Carnehan** 2-9-2 0.. FrannyNorton 2 72
(Mark Johnston) *str: pressed ldr: rdn over 1f out: led jst ins fnl f: hdd fnl 120yds: rallied wl nring fin: jst hld* **7/2**[3]

3 *1 1/2* **Zaatar (IRE)** 2-8-11 0.. CharlesBishop 3 61
(Mick Channon) *leggy: trckd ldrs: rdn 2f out: swtchd rt ent fnl f: kpt on to go 3rd cl home* **10/3**[2]

5 **4** *shd* **Latest Quest (IRE)**[7] 2204 2-9-2 0.................................. LukeMorris 5 66
(Sylvester Kirk) *w'like: medium-sized: led: rdn 2f out: hdd jst ins fnl f: kpt on but no ex fnl 100yds* **15/8**[1]

5 *1/2* **Apple Scruffs (IRE)** 2-9-2 0.. AdamBeschizza 6 64
(Michael Attwater) *str: bit bkwd: trckd ldrs: rdn 2f out: kpt on same pce fnl f* **33/1**

41 **6** *7* **Nazik**[10] 2125 2-9-4 0.. NoelGarbutt(5) 4 46
(David Evans) *cmpt: sn pushed along to chse ldrs: nvr gng pce to chal: fdd ins fnl f* **6/1**

1m 1.31s (1.11) **Going Correction** -0.125s/f (Firm) **6** Ran SP% **108.4**
Speed ratings (Par 93): **86,85,83,83,82 71**
CSF £33.20 TOTE £9.90: £4.20, £2.40; EX 37.00 Trifecta £108.50.
Owner Quench Racing Partnership **Bred** Mrs R J Gallagher **Trained** Chastleton, Oxon

FOCUS
The first 2f of the 1m course was dolled out approximately five yards, and the running rail from the 6f marker on the lower bend to the 2f marker in the straight was dolled out approximately six yards, adding approximately 15 yards to races over 7f, 1m and 1m3f. Parts of the 1m3f and 1m4f courses were watered overnight and there was 1mm of rain. Probably just ordinary form and it might be worth noting stalls 1-2-3 produced the first three finishers in that order, suggesting the stands' rail might have been best avoided.

2430 CHATEAU LA GORDONNE STKS (H'CAP) 7f

2:20 (2:20) (Class 4) (0-85,85) 4-Y-O+ **£6,469** (£1,925; £962; £481) **Stalls** Low

Form RPR

15-4 **1** **Arlecchino's Leap**[25] 1724 4-9-0 **78**................................(p) DavidProbert 1 85
(Mark Usher) *hld up: hdwy 2f out: rdn to chal ent fnl f: led fnl 100yds: kpt on wl* **7/1**[3]

-631 **2** *1/2* **Good Luck Charm**[24] 1746 7-8-5 **74**..........................(b) HectorCrouch(5) 5 79
(Gary Moore) *lw: hld up: hdwy 2f out: nt clr run briefly over 1f out: swtchd lft: r.o to hold ev ch ent fnl f: drifted rt: kpt on* **8/1**

01-0 **3** *nse* **Pharmaceutical (IRE)**[19] 1887 4-9-2 **80**........................ AdamBeschizza 2 85
(Stuart Williams) *stdd s: hdwy 2f out: nt clr run over 1f out: rdn to ld narrowly ins fnl f: hdd fnl 100yds: kpt on* **7/1**[3]

40-3 **4** *3/4* **Baltic Brave (IRE)**[13] 2032 5-9-7 **85**.................................. RyanMoore 7 88
(Hughie Morrison) *lw: trckd ldrs: rdn to ld over 1f out: hdd ins fnl f: kpt on same pce* **3/1**[1]

0-05 **5** *4 1/2* **Harlequin Striker (IRE)**[31] 1545 4-9-2 **80**...................... CharlesBishop 3 71
(Dean Ivory) *led: rdn 2f out: hdd over 1f out: no ex fnl 120yds* **7/1**[3]

-056 **6** *1* **Dutch Art Dealer**[37] 1418 5-9-4 **82**................................(p) JimCrowley 8 70
(Paul Cole) *pressed ldr: rdn and ev ch 2f out: wkng whn short of room ent fnl f* **7/2**[2]

0-06 **7** *3 1/4* **Live Dangerously**[17] 1946 6-8-7 **71** oh1........................ WilliamCarson 4 50
(John Bridger) *cl up: effrt over 1f out: wknd fnl f* **16/1**

040- **8** *1/2* **Cool Bahamian (IRE)**[163] 8163 5-9-5 **83**...........................(b) JohnFahy 6 61
(Eve Johnson Houghton) *cl up: effrt 2f out: wknd fnl f* **9/1**

1m 29.34s (2.34) **Going Correction** +0.50s/f (Yiel) **8** Ran SP% **111.7**
Speed ratings (Par 105): **106,105,105,104,99 98,94,93**
CSF £58.09 CT £401.94 TOTE £7.90: £2.80, £2.40, £2.80; EX 47.00 Trifecta £268.00.
Owner K Senior **Bred** J K Beckitt & Son **Trained** Upper Lambourn, Berks

FOCUS
This was run over 15 yards further than advertised. The leaders looked to be going up and down on the spot halfway up the straight, at which point the first three finishers, who raced in the last three places, arrived on the scene going strongly, suggesting the pace picked up prematurely. A small pb from the winner. with the second to form.

2431 GOODWOOD AERO CLUB FILLIES' STKS (H'CAP) 1m

2:55 (2:55) (Class 4) (0-80,80) 3-Y-O

£6,225 (£1,864; £932; £466; £233; £117) **Stalls** Low

Form RPR

1- **1** **Persuasive (IRE)**[198] 7700 3-9-7 **80**................................ FrankieDettori 1 91+
(John Gosden) *str: hld up in last pair but wl in tch: hdwy over 1f out: chal ent fnl f: led fnl 150yds: r.o wl: eased nring fin* **10/11**[1]

33-3 **2** *1 1/2* **Aristocratic**[25] 1701 3-9-4 **77**.. RyanMoore 2 84+
(Sir Michael Stoute) *trckd ldrs: rdn to ld ent fnl f: sn hdd: kpt on but nt pce of wnr fnl 120yds* **5/2**[2]

5-02 **3** *1 1/2* **Carpe Diem Lady (IRE)**[8] 2178 3-8-8 **67**.............................. JohnFahy 6 69
(Clive Cox) *lw: pressed ldr: rdn 2f out: ev ch ent fnl f: kpt on but nt pce of front pair* **11/2**[3]

54-0 **4** *hd* **Poster Girl**[24] 1758 3-8-12 **71**.. JimCrowley 4 73
(Jonathan Portman) *s.i.s: hld up in last pair but wl in tch: hdwy over 1f out: sn rdn: kpt on same pce fnl f* **20/1**

2-33 **5** *1* **Norse Magic**[24] 1758 3-9-0 **73**.. LukeMorris 7 73
(Sylvester Kirk) *lw: trckd ldrs: drvn over 2f out: kpt on ins fnl f but nt gng pce to get involved* **18/1**

0-00 **6** *hd* **Bay Of St Malo (IRE)**[8] 2181 3-8-9 **68**........................ KieranO'Neill 3 67
(Richard Hannon) *led: rdn 2f out: hdd ent fnl f: sn no ex* **33/1**

1m 43.2s (3.30) **Going Correction** +0.50s/f (Yiel) **6** Ran SP% **109.3**
Speed ratings (Par 98): **103,101,100,99,98 98**
CSF £3.12 TOTE £1.80: £1.40, £1.50; EX 3.80 Trifecta £7.50.
Owner Cheveley Park Stud **Bred** J F Tuthill **Trained** Newmarket, Suffolk

FOCUS
This was run over 15 yards further than advertised. A good fillies' handicap, two promising Cheveley Park-owned runners, who are entered in Group 1 company, finishing one-two and the third well in at the weights. It's hard to get behind the bare form but the first two are both capable of better.

2432 EBF STALLIONS COCKED HAT STKS (LISTED RACE) (C&G) 1m 3f

3:30 (3:30) (Class 1) 3-Y-O **£22,684** (£8,600; £4,304; £2,144) **Stalls** High

Form RPR

41-2 **1** **Algometer**[28] 1605 3-9-0 109.. JimCrowley 4 106
(David Simcock) *lw: trckd ldr: chal 3f out: sn rdn: led ins fnl f: styd on wl: rdn out* **13/8**[2]

1-2 **2** *1/2* **Prize Money**[19] 1891 3-9-0 101.. JamesDoyle 3 105
(Saeed bin Suroor) *lw: led at stdy pce: qcknd over 3f out: rdn over 1f out: hdd ins fnl f: styd on but no ex* **1/1**[1]

40-3 **3** *1/2* **Ormito (GER)**[15] 1974 3-9-0 97.. DavidProbert 2 104
(Andrew Balding) *lw: trckd ldrs: rdn wl over 1f out: tended to hang rt but styd on wl fnl f* **12/1**

1-14 **4** *21* **Speed Company (IRE)**[20] 1866 3-9-0 97.......................... RyanMoore 1 66
(John Quinn) *trckd ldrs: rdn wl over 2f out: wknd over 1f out* **8/1**[3]

2m 33.74s (7.24) **Going Correction** +0.50s/f (Yiel) **4** Ran SP% **106.9**
Speed ratings (Par 107): **93,92,92,77**
CSF £3.55 TOTE £2.70; EX 4.00 Trifecta £10.60.
Owner Miss K Rausing **Bred** Miss K Rausing **Trained** Newmarket, Suffolk

FOCUS
This was run over 15 yards further than advertised. This hasn't produced a Derby winner since Troy in 1979, but more recent winners include Rewilding (2010) and Storm The Stars (2015), who both then ran third at Epsom, while Masked Marvel (2011) landed the St Leger. The one-two in this year's race hold Derby entries. Algometer was a bit off his Sandown form with Prize Money rated to his handicap latest.

2433 EBF BREEDERS' SERIES FILLIES' H'CAP 1m 4f

4:00 (4:02) (Class 3) (0-90,90) 3-Y-O+ **£12,938** (£3,850; £1,924; £962) **Stalls** High

Form RPR

6-00 **1** **Tioga Pass**[20] 1855 5-10-0 **90**..(p) LukeMorris 3 98
(Paul Cole) *s.i.s: last: rdn and stdy prog fr 3f out: led jst ins fnl f: drifted sltly rt: styd on wl: drvn out* **11/1**

165- **2** *nk* **She Is No Lady**224 7076 4-9-11 **87** RyanMoore 2 94
(Ralph Beckett) *lw: trckd ldrs: rdn over 2f out: led over 1f out: hdd jst ins fnl f: edgd rt: styd on* **3/1**1
031- **3** *2 1/4* **Star Rider**203 7597 4-9-9 **85** (p) JimmyFortune 1 88
(Hughie Morrison) *trckd ldr: chal 3f out: sn rdn: ev ch over 1f out tl ent fnl f: styd on same pce* **7/1**
-313 **4** *nse* **Genuine Approval (IRE)**24 1759 3-8-0 **79** oh6 NickyMackay 5 81
(Jonathan Portman) *led: reminders over 3f out: drvn over 2f out: hdd over 1f out: disputing hld 3rd whn hmpd ins fnl f: styd on same pce* **16/1**
51-3 **5** *1 3/4* **Parnell's Dream**20 1853 4-8-11 **73** FMBerry 4 75
(Ralph Beckett) *hld up: hdwy 3f out: rdn to chse ldrs over 2f out: styng on at same pce in hld 5th whn hmpd ins fnl f* **6/1**3
31 **6** *2 3/4* **Hestina (FR)**18 1920 3-8-1 **80** CathyGannon 7 78
(Peter Chapple-Hyam) *lw: in tch: nt clr run and lost pl whn snatched up over 2f out: sn rdn: nt pce to get bk on terms: fdd fnl 120yds* **7/2**2
130- **7** *2* **Elysian Fields (GR)**295 4789 5-10-0 **90** PatDobbs 8 83
(Amanda Perrett) *trckd ldrs: chal over 2f out: sn rdn: fading whn short of room jst over 1f out* **9/1**
1-12 **8** *8* **Wavelet**109 420 4-8-10 **72** JimCrowley 6 52
(David Simcock) *in tch: effrt over 2f out: wknd over 1f out* **10/1**
100- **9** *41* **Novancia (IRE)**275 5514 4-9-6 **82** FrannyNorton 9
(Mark Johnston) *trckd ldr: rdn 3f out: wkng whn squeezed up jst over 2f out* **14/1**

2m 43.65s (5.25) **Going Correction** +0.50s/f (Yiel)
WFA 3 from 4yo+ 17lb **9** Ran SP% **114.0**
Speed ratings (Par 104): **102,101,100,100,99 97,95,90,63**
CSF £43.53 CT £251.62 TOTE £13.10: £3.30, £1.20, £2.30; EX 45.40 Trifecta £283.30.
Owner The Fairy Story Partnership **Bred** Deepwood Farm Stud **Trained** Whatcombe, Oxon

FOCUS
A decent fillies' handicap, although things got a bit messy in the straight. The winner is rated close to last year's best.

2434 LEVIN DOWN STKS (H'CAP) 6f
4:35 (4:35) (Class 2) (0-105,101) 3-Y-O+
£15,562 (£4,660; £2,330; £1,165; £582; £292) **Stalls** High

Form RPR
250- **1** *hd* **Go Far**154 8288 6-9-9 **97** (v) FMBerry 4 101
(Alan Bailey) *trckd ldrs: rdn wl over 1f out: drifted to centre fnl f: r.o wl fnl 120yds: wnt 2nd towards fin: jst failed: fin 2nd: awrdd the r* **16/1**
60-0 **2** *1* **Huntsmans Close**19 1887 6-9-12 **100** JamesDoyle 7 101
(Roger Charlton) *trckd ldrs: rdn and ev ch whn bdly hmpd jst over 1f out: carried rt fnl f: kpt on: fin on far side: hld towards fin: fin 3rd: plcd 2nd* **7/1**
33-2 **3** **Seeking Magic**19 1887 8-9-7 **95** (t) RyanTate 1 100
(Clive Cox) *swtchd lft sn after leaving stalls: mde all: drvn whn strly chal over 1f out: sn began to hang bdly rt: fin on far side: hld on: all out: fin 1st: disqualified and plcd 3rd* **11/4**1
0-01 **4** *hd* **Clear Spring (IRE)**7 2206 8-9-8 **101** 6ex KieranShoemark(5) 2 101
(John Spearing) *trckd ldr: rdn to chal over 1f out: sn hmpd: carried rt fnl f: fin on far rail: kpt on but hld towards fin* **9/2**2
0110 **5** *1* **Englishman**7 2206 6-9-2 **90** FrannyNorton 8 87
(Milton Bradley) *trckd ldr: rdn w ev ch over 1f out: kpt on same pce fnl f* **5/1**3
000- **6** *1 1/4* **Ruwaiyan (USA)**230 6948 7-9-13 **101** LukeMorris 5 94
(James Tate) *lw: hld up: rdn and hdwy over 1f out: kpt on same pce fnl f* **9/2**2
50-0 **7** *3* **Charles Molson**7 2206 5-9-9 **97** JimCrowley 6 81+
(Patrick Chamings) *trckd ldrs: rdn and ev ch whn bdly squeezed out jst over 1f out: no ch after and eased* **15/2**

1m 12.37s (0.17) **Going Correction** -0.125s/f (Firm) **7** Ran SP% **109.8**
Speed ratings (Par 109): **92,91,93,91,89 88,84**
CSF £110.60 CT £378.67 TOTE £13.20: £4.70, £3.40; EX 81.00.
Owner R West **Bred** Michael Turner **Trained** Newmarket, Suffolk
■ Stewards' Enquiry : Ryan Tate seven-day ban (3 Jun-9 Jun): careless riding

FOCUS
A controversial call from the stewards, who demoted the first-past-the-post Seeking Magic and placed him behind the third-past-the-post Huntsmans Close, and it's hard to agree with the decision under the rules. Seeking Magic, who initially led the field near the stands' rail, hung right from over a furlong out and badly squeezed up Charles Molson, who then interfered with Huntsmans Close, who then interfered with Clear Spring, with those four ending up on the far side of the track. However, while it did look bad, being such an untidy finish, many people will not go along with the key line from the stewards that the 'interference improved Seeking Magic's placing as it caused Huntsmans Close to lose considerable ground and momentum.' There was a length and a head between those two at the line and Seeking Magic traded long odds-on in the stewards' inquiry betting on Betfair, although he did drift a bit which is understandable considering the result wasn't announced for some 23 minutes. Seeking Magic is rated close to his old best.

2435 THREE FRIDAY NIGHTS STKS (H'CAP) 5f
5:05 (5:05) (Class 5) (0-70,70) 3-Y-O **£3,234** (£962; £481; £240) **Stalls** High

Form RPR
0-46 **1** **Wiley Post**8 2185 3-9-3 **69** (b) TomMarquand(3) 10 83
(Richard Hannon) *lw: hld up: rdn and hdwy over 1f out: led ent fnl f: r.o wl: comf* **7/1**
0-42 **2** *4* **Sir Theodore (IRE)**4 2288 3-9-3 **69** LouisSteward(3) 6 69
(Richard Spencer) *hld up: hdwy over 1f out: rdn to chal for 2nd whn hmpd ent fnl f: kpt on but nt pce of wnr* **2/1**1
6-52 **3** *1/2* **Dnaneer (IRE)**31 1554 3-8-7 **56** LukeMorris 2 54
(William Knight) *mid-div: hdwy 2f: sn rdn: disputing 3rd whn hung lft ent fnl f: kpt on same pce* **6/1**3
1-54 **4** *3/4* **Stormflower**18 1935 3-9-6 **69** LiamJones 8 65
(John Bridger) *chsd ldrs: rdn to ld over 1f out: hdd whn hung lft ent fnl f: kpt on same pce* **9/1**
-300 **5** *4 1/2* **Deer Song**18 1935 3-8-9 **58** (b) WilliamCarson 3 37
(John Bridger) *led: rdn over 2f out: hdd over 1f out: fdd ins fnl f* **25/1**
5204 **6** *nk* **Miss Phillyjinks (IRE)**24 1761 3-9-2 **65** (p) ShaneKelly 5 43
(Paul D'Arcy) *s.i.s: sn pushed along in last: nvr threatened to get on terms* **12/1**
340- **7** *2 3/4* **Chandresh**235 6806 3-9-0 **63** JimCrowley 1 31
(Robert Cowell) *chsd ldrs: rdn over 2f out: wknd fnl f* **10/1**
20-3 **8** *1 1/4* **Cherry Kool**22 1812 3-9-7 **70** FMBerry 7 34
(Stuart Williams) *prom: rdn over 2f out: ev ch over 1f out: wknd fnl f* **5/1**2
-600 **9** *8* **Silver Wings (IRE)**63 979 3-8-10 **66** (p) RhiainIngram(7) 9 1
(Roger Ingram) *mid-div: rdn over 2f out: sn wknd* **12/1**

58.54s (-1.66) **Going Correction** -0.125s/f (Firm) **9** Ran SP% **115.1**
Speed ratings (Par 99): **108,101,100,99,92 91,87,85,72**
CSF £21.31 CT £90.87 TOTE £8.30: £2.50, £1.30, £2.30; EX 29.80 Trifecta £226.50.
Owner Lady Whent **Bred** Lady Whent **Trained** East Everleigh, Wilts

FOCUS
A modest 3yo sprint and the field were spread out all over the place in the closing stages. The form is difficult to take too literally.
T/Plt: £865.90 to a £1 stake. Pool: £65,561.18 - 55.27 winning tickets T/Qpdt: £40.20 to a £1 stake Pool: £7,109.88 - 130.64 winning tickets **Tim Mitchell**

2029 HAYDOCK (L-H)
Friday, May 20

OFFICIAL GOING: Good to firm changing to good after race 4 (8.00)
Wind: moderate 1/2 against Weather: overcast, light rain

2436 APOLLOBET HAYDOCK PARK APPRENTICE TRAINING SERIES H'CAP (PART OF RACING EXCELLENCE INITIATIVE) 1m 2f 95y
6:30 (6:30) (Class 5) (0-70,68) 4-Y-O+ **£2,911** (£866; £432; £216) **Stalls** Centre

Form RPR
5363 **1** **Masterpaver**22 1802 5-9-6 **67** GaryMahon 1 77+
(Richard Fahey) *led: jnd over 3f out: styd on wl fnl f: eased nr fin* **7/4**1
1310 **2** *2* **La Havrese (FR)**34 1501 5-9-3 **64** JoshDoyle 2 68
(Lynn Siddall) *hld up in mid-div: hdwy to trck ldrs over 3f out: effrt 2f out: kpt on to take 2nd last 50yds* **8/1**3
1212 **3** *1* **My Lord**7 2210 8-9-0 **66** AledBeech(5) 5 68
(David Evans) *dwlt: t.k.h in rr: hdwy on outside over 3f out: hung rt and styd on fnl f: tk 3rd nr fin* **15/8**2
30-0 **4** *hd* **Cape Spirit (IRE)**24 1735 4-8-9 **56** (v1) EdwardGreatrex 4 58
(Andrew Balding) *mid-div: hdwy over 3f out: kpt on fnl f: tk 4th fnl strides* **12/1**
040- **5** *3/4* **Merchant Of Medici**217 7250 9-9-5 **66** CallumShepherd 6 66
(Micky Hammond) *trckd ldrs: upsides over 3f out: drvn over 2f out: fdd last 75yds* **8/1**3
0/0- **6** *1* **May's Boy**121 2465 8-8-7 **54** oh4 (p) GeorgiaCox 8 52
(James Moffatt) *chsd ldr: one pce fnl 2f* **40/1**
0-40 **7** *hd* **Anneani (IRE)**63 986 4-8-7 **54** oh5 NathanEvans 7 52
(Paul Green) *hld up in rr: t.k.h: hdwy on outer over 3f out: edgd lft over 1f out: fdd fnl 150yds* **16/1**

2m 14.4s (-1.10) **Going Correction** -0.15s/f (Firm) **7** Ran SP% **109.4**
Speed ratings (Par 103): **98,96,95,95,94 94,93**
CSF £14.78 CT £25.04 TOTE £2.50: £1.90, £3.30; EX 12.50 Trifecta £30.00.
Owner Mrs A M Riney **Bred** Mrs A M Riney **Trained** Musley Bank, N Yorks

FOCUS
Despite 9mm of rain on Thursday night the going was given as good to firm (GoingStick: 7.3). All races were run on the inner home straight. Race distance reduced by 5yds. A modest handicap run at a steady early gallop.

2437 EBF APOLLOBET DAILY RACING REFUNDS NEWCOMERS' MAIDEN STKS (PLUS 10 RACE) 5f
7:00 (7:00) (Class 4) 2-Y-O **£4,269** (£1,270; £634; £317) **Stalls** Centre

Form RPR
1 **Prince Of Cool** 2-9-5 0 TomEaves 5 80
(James Given) *mde all: drvn over 1f out: fnd ex clsng stages* **3/1**2
2 *1 1/4* **Pretty Vacant** 2-9-5 0 AndreaAtzeni 2 76
(Roger Varian) *sn w ldr: drvn over 2f out: cl 2nd over 1f out: edgd lft and kpt on same pce last 75yds* **8/1**
3 *4* **Hart Stopper** 2-9-5 0 JamieSpencer 1 61
(Michael Bell) *dwlt: outpcd in rr: hdwy over 2f out: wnt modest 3rd 1f out: edgd rt: one pce* **11/2**3
4 *3/4* **Bridal March** 2-9-0 0 FrannyNorton 3 53
(Mark Johnston) *w wnr: one pce over 1f out* **10/1**
5 *1 3/4* **Three C'S (IRE)** 2-9-5 0 GeorgeBaker 7 52
(David Dennis) *chsd ldrs: drvn over 2f out: outpcd over 1f out* **12/1**
6 *1 1/4* **Devilish Guest (IRE)** 2-9-5 0 SilvestreDeSousa 4 48
(Mick Channon) *dwlt: hdwy to chse ldrs over 3f out: drvn over 2f out: wknd fnl 150yds* **5/4**1

59.96s (-0.84) **Going Correction** -0.15s/f (Firm) **6** Ran SP% **112.7**
Speed ratings (Par 95): **100,98,91,90,87 85**
CSF £26.08 TOTE £4.10: £1.40, £4.10; EX 27.40 Trifecta £69.10.
Owner The Cool Silk Partnership **Bred** New Hall Stud **Trained** Willoughton, Lincs

FOCUS
Nothing to go on, but the race averages suggest this is usually a fair maiden, and the first two finished nicely clear.

2438 APOLLOBET CASH BACK IF 2ND ACHILLES STKS (LISTED RACE) 5f
7:30 (7:30) (Class 1) 3-Y-O+
£20,982 (£7,955; £3,981; £1,983; £995; £499) **Stalls** Centre

Form RPR
1-25 **1** **Take Cover**20 1862 9-9-8 110 DavidAllan 5 117
(David C Griffiths) *mde all: kpt on gamely fnl f: drvn out* **11/4**1
01-0 **2** *1 1/2* **Cotai Glory**20 1862 4-9-8 107 GeorgeBaker 3 112
(Charles Hills) *trckd ldrs: 2nd over 1f out: kpt on same pce last 100yds* **6/1**3
125- **3** *3/4* **Double Up**286 5129 5-9-4 107 (t) AndreaAtzeni 6 105+
(Roger Varian) *trckd ldrs: t.k.h: drvn over 2f out: sn hmpd: 3rd 1f out: kpt on same pce* **7/2**2
-440 **4** *1/2* **Line Of Reason (IRE)**20 1862 6-9-4 107 GrahamLee 8 103
(Paul Midgley) *hld up in mid-div: effrt 2f out: styd on wl last 150yds: tk 4th clsng stages* **11/1**
00-0 **5** *hd* **Kingsgate Native (IRE)**20 1862 11-9-4 107 TedDurcan 7 102
(Robert Cowell) *in rr: hdwy 2f out: edgd lft: kpt on fnl f: tk 5th clsng stages* **10/1**
03-3 **6** *1 3/4* **Canny Kool**16 1969 4-9-4 103 BenCurtis 1 96
(Brian Ellison) *w wnr: drvn over 2f out: fdd last 75yds* **25/1**
410- **7** *2 1/4* **Out Do**294 4818 7-9-4 109 (v) PhillipMakin 4 88
(David O'Meara) *mid-div: drvn to chse ldrs over 2f out: wknd fnl 150yds* **9/1**
0-11 **8** *1 1/4* **Encore D'Or**14 2003 4-9-4 96 MartinHarley 9 83
(Robert Cowell) *trckd ldrs: drvn over 2f out: sn edgd lft: wknd fnl f* **13/2**
50-0 **9** *1* **Moonraker**9 2159 4-9-4 101 SilvestreDeSousa 2 80
(Mick Channon) *dwlt: wnt lft s: in rr: reminders and wnt lft over 2f out: nvr a factor* **14/1**

58.41s (-2.39) **Going Correction** -0.15s/f (Firm) **9** Ran SP% **114.4**
Speed ratings (Par 111): **113,110,109,108,108 105,101,99,98**
CSF £19.33 TOTE £4.00: £1.40, £1.70, £2.20; EX 20.20 Trifecta £79.50.
Owner Norcroft Park Stud **Bred** Norcroft Park Stud **Trained** Bawtry, S Yorks

FOCUS
A competitive Listed event in which the two penalised runners finished first and second.

2439 APOLLOBET HOME OF CASHBACK OFFERS H'CAP 1m 3f 200y
8:00 (8:00) (Class 4) (0-85,85) 4-Y-O+ **£4,851** (£1,443; £721; £360) **Stalls** Centre

Form RPR
50/0 **1** **Sign Manual**[32] 1523 7-8-9 **73** ow1....................................(b) TomEaves 6 81
(Donald McCain) *mde all: qcknd pce over 3f out: kpt on gamely clsng stages* **16/1**
4-25 **2** *hd* **Hubertas**[20] 1852 4-8-12 **81**..................................(b) CallumShepherd[(5)] 11 88
(John Quinn) *t.k.h: sn trcking ldrs: drvn over 3f out: upsides and edgd lft 2f out: edgd lft fnl f: jst hld* **7/4**[1]
333- **3** *5* **Frederic Chopin**[218] 5749 5-8-10 **74**.................................. JackGarritty 8 73
(James Moffatt) *trckd ldrs: upsides 2f out: one pce whn n.m.r and fdd last 150yds* **12/1**
-010 **4** *¾* **Newera**[14] 1999 4-9-7 **85**..(p) GeorgeBaker 12 83+
(Tom Dascombe) *hld up towards rr: hdwy over 4f out: outpcd 3f out: kpt on to take modest 4th last 100yds* **15/8**[2]
4/4- **5** *2¼* **Fantasy King**[218] 5047 10-8-10 **74**...................................... GrahamLee 9 68
(James Moffatt) *sn trcking ldrs: effrt over 2f out: kpt on one pce fnl 2f* **9/1**[3]
221- **6** *2½* **Zenafire**[199] 7678 7-8-7 **71** oh4..(p) PaulQuinn 7 61
(Sarah Hollinshead) *hld up in rr: drvn and sme hdwy over 3f out: nvr a threat* **14/1**
/50- **7** *shd* **Brigadoon**[216] 3514 9-9-5 **83**... AndrewMullen 5 73
(Michael Appleby) *trckd ldrs: t.k.h: drvn over 3f out: wknd over 1f out* **16/1**
0-00 **8** *2¼* **Genres**[14] 2017 4-8-11 **75**.. NeilFarley 10 61
(Alan Swinbank) *hld up in rr: hdwy over 4f out: drvn over 3f out: sn outpcd: wknd over 1f out* **12/1**

2m 31.08s (-2.72) **Going Correction** -0.15s/f (Firm) **8** Ran SP% **115.0**
Speed ratings (Par 105): **103,102,99,99,97 95,95,94**
CSF £44.81 CT £364.31 TOTE £14.70: £4.30, £1.10, £2.10; EX 93.90 Trifecta £931.30.
Owner Graham & Carole Worsley **Bred** The Queen **Trained** Cholmondeley, Cheshire

FOCUS
Race distance reduced by 5yds. This was run at a steady early gallop and nothing got into it from behind.

2440 APOLLOBET BET ON LOTTERIES MAIDEN STKS 1m 3f 200y
8:30 (8:34) (Class 5) 3-Y-O+ **£2,911** (£866; £432; £216) **Stalls** Centre

Form RPR
1 **Corinthian** 3-8-11 0.. AndreaAtzeni 5 84+
(Roger Varian) *gave problems loading: sn chsng ldr: sn drvn along: reminders over 4f out: wnt 3rd over 2f out: styd on wl fnl f: led fnl strides* **7/2**[2]
0-5 **2** *nk* **Kaatskill Nap (FR)**[27] 1626 3-8-11 0................................ MartinDwyer 2 83
(David Menuisier) *dwlt: hdwy to chse ldrs after 3f: chal over 3f out: kpt on to ld narrowly clsng stages: hdd fnl strides* **10/1**
0-2 **3** *nk* **Superyacht (IRE)**[27] 1626 3-8-11 0.................................. TedDurcan 6 82
(Sir Michael Stoute) *led: shkn up over 2f out: rdn over 1f out: hdd and no ex clsng stages* **4/7**[1]
02- **4** *4* **Nodachi (IRE)**[215] 7309 3-8-6 0............................... EdwardGreatrex[(5)] 3 76
(Andrew Balding) *hld up: effrt over 4f out: sme hdwy over 2f out: one pce* **17/2**[3]
0 **5** *13* **Alcanar (USA)**[64] 968 3-8-11 0...................................... JamieSpencer 1 63
(Michael Bell) *trckd ldrs: 3rd over 5f out: drvn 4f out: wknd 2f out: eased last 100yds* **20/1**
0 **6** *9* **Gaelic Master (IRE)**[21] 1826 3-8-11 0.............. WilliamTwiston-Davies 4 41
(Michael Scudamore) *dwlt: in rr: outpcd over 3f out: lost pl over 2f out: bhd whn eased last 50yds* **100/1**

2m 33.53s (-0.27) **Going Correction** -0.15s/f (Firm) **6** Ran SP% **111.2**
Speed ratings (Par 103): **94,93,93,90,82 76**
CSF £34.74 TOTE £3.90: £1.90, £3.50; EX 27.90 Trifecta £45.10.
Owner Highclere Thoroughbred Racing(Gladstone) **Bred** Saleh Al Homaizi & Imad Al Sagar **Trained** Newmarket, Suffolk

FOCUS
Race distance reduced by 5yds. There was a thrilling finish to this maiden.

2441 APOLLOBET WEEKLY GOLF REFUNDS H'CAP 1m
9:00 (9:03) (Class 5) (0-75,75) 4-Y-O+ **£2,911** (£866; £432; £216) **Stalls** Low

Form RPR
-334 **1** **Just Be Lucky (IRE)**[14] 2010 4-9-1 **69**...........................(p) MartinHarley 1 86+
(Ivan Furtado) *trckd ldrs: nt clr run on inner fr over 2f out tl 1f out: styd on to ld last 50yds* **7/2**[2]
0-01 **2** *1¼* **Chosen Character (IRE)**[27] 1631 8-9-0 **73**............(vt) AnnaHesketh[(5)] 9 86
(Tom Dascombe) *led: hdd and no ex last 50yds* **9/2**[3]
2-04 **3** *6* **Know Your Name**[7] 2198 5-9-7 **75**.. NeilFarley 5 74
(Eric Alston) *trckd ldrs: kpt on same pce over 1f out: tk modest 3rd clsng stages* **6/1**
3020 **4** *1¼* **Sarmadee (IRE)**[14] 2010 4-9-6 **74**........................... SilvestreDeSousa 12 70
(Mick Channon) *sn chsng ldrs: 2nd over 6f out: kpt on one pce fnl f* **6/1**
30-6 **5** *hd* **Arms Around Me (IRE)**[24] 1756 4-8-13 **67**......................... TomEaves 6 63
(James Given) *hld up in rr: effrt 3f out: one pce fnl 2f* **40/1**
00-6 **6** *¾* **Mujazif (IRE)**[123] 239 6-8-13 **67**..................................(t) AndrewMullen 2 61
(Michael Appleby) *mid-div: effrt 4f out: sme hdwy over 2f out: nvr a factor* **3/1**[1]
40-0 **7** *1¼* **Almuhalab**[29] 1588 5-8-10 **64**... JamesSullivan 10 60+
(Ruth Carr) *trckd ldrs: effrt over 3f out: 5th and one pce whn bdly hmpd 100yds out: eased* **14/1**
145- **8** *1½* **Moonadee (IRE)**[262] 5981 4-9-4 **72**.. DaleSwift 8 60
(Daniel Mark Loughnane) *s.i.s: detached in rr: t.k.h: sme hdwy over 2f out: nvr on terms* **33/1**
6040 **9** *4* **Marmalad (IRE)**[34] 1502 4-8-6 **65** ow2.................(b) CallumShepherd[(5)] 7 44
(Shaun Lycett) *mid-div: drvn and hdwy on outside over 3f out: lost pl over 2f out* **25/1**
12-2 **10** *1¾* **Equleus**[135] 64 4-8-13 **67**... MartinLane 4 42
(Jeremy Gask) *s.i.s: in rr: drvn over 3f out: chsng ldrs over 2f out: lost pl over 1f out* **11/1**

1m 40.05s (-3.65) **Going Correction** -0.15s/f (Firm) **10** Ran SP% **118.2**
Speed ratings (Par 103): **112,110,104,103,103 102,101,99,95,94**
CSF £19.66 CT £94.08 TOTE £5.10: £2.20, £2.30, £2.40; EX 17.40 Trifecta £92.50.
Owner Charles Wentworth **Bred** Degner Limited **Trained** Wiseton, Nottinghamshire

FOCUS
Race distance reduced by 5yds. The first two pulled clear of the rest in this fair handicap.
T/Plt: £68.10 to a £1 stake. Pool: £64,569.24 - 691.91 winning units T/Qpdt: £13.70 to a £1 stake. Pool: £5,215.33 - 280.0 winning units **Walter Glynn**

2104 WOLVERHAMPTON (A.W) (L-H)
Friday, May 20

OFFICIAL GOING: Tapeta: standard
Wind: Fresh behind Weather: Cloudy

2442 GRAFITYP GROUP CELEBRATION H'CAP 7f 32y (Tp)
2:10 (2:12) (Class 6) (0-60,60) 4-Y-O+ **£2,264** (£673; £336; £168) **Stalls** High

Form RPR
1 **Capolavoro (FR)**[315] 5-9-7 **60**.. PatCosgrave 10 70+
(Robert Cowell) *chsd ldr tl led over 1f out: rdn out* **5/1**[2]
3103 **2** *1¾* **Little Indian**[9] 2155 6-9-5 **58**... FrederikTylicki 4 64
(J R Jenkins) *hld up: hdwy over 1f out: r.o to go 2nd wl ins fnl f: nt rch wnr* **5/1**[2]
0061 **3** *3* **Satchville Flyer**[18] 2081 5-8-12 **54**.................................. PhilipPrince[(3)] 6 52
(David Evans) *mid-div: rdn on outer over 2f out: hdwy over 1f out: hung lft ins fnl f: styd on same pce* **11/2**[3]
0625 **4** *1* **Colour My World**[28] 1595 6-9-3 **56**................(b) WilliamTwiston-Davies 8 52
(Ed McMahon) *led: rdn and hdd over 1f out: wknd ins fnl f* **10/3**[1]
4300 **5** *4* **Major Muscari (IRE)**[78] 799 8-9-6 **59**............................. MartinHarley 1 45
(Shaun Harris) *hld up: hdwy and nt clr run over 1f out: wknd ins fnl f* **16/1**
0-00 **6** *1* **Jebel Tara**[25] 1692 11-9-6 **59**..(bt) DaleSwift 9 42
(Alan Brown) *chsd ldrs: rdn over 2f out: wknd fnl f* **16/1**
0434 **7** *2½* **Lutine Charlie (IRE)**[11] 2087 9-8-11 **50**........................(p) TomQueally 12 27
(Emma Owen) *prom: rdn over 2f out: wknd over 1f out* **14/1**
300- **8** *3* **Henryhudsonbridge (USA)**[244] 6550 4-9-1 **57**............. EoinWalsh[(3)] 5 26
(Edward Bevan) *s.i.s: nt clr run over 1f out: nvr on terms* **33/1**
2-04 **9** *hd* **Beggers Luck**[114] 355 6-9-0 **53**.. HarryBentley 3 22
(Eric Wheeler) *mid-div: rdn and wknd over 1f out* **9/1**
500- **10** *5* **Verus Delicia (IRE)**[189] 7833 7-9-5 **58**................................ LiamKeniry 2 14
(Daniel Mark Loughnane) *hld up in tch: rdn over 2f out: wknd over 1f out* **10/1**
420- **11** *4½* **Jacksonfire**[285] 5176 4-8-4 **50**...................................(b) GeorgeWood[(7)] 7
(Michael Mullineaux) *s.s: outpcd* **33/1**

1m 28.56s (-0.24) **Going Correction** -0.05s/f (Stan) **11** Ran SP% **115.2**
Speed ratings (Par 101): **99,97,93,92,87 86,83,80,80,74 69**
CSF £29.55 CT £142.18 TOTE £4.90: £1.80, £2.10, £2.00; EX 34.30 Trifecta £188.50.
Owner Cyril Humphris & Partner **Bred** Cyril Humphris **Trained** Six Mile Bottom, Cambs

FOCUS
A modest handicap to start and not many ever got into it.

2443 GRAFITYP NV 70-YEAR CELEBRATION MEDIAN AUCTION MAIDEN STKS 1m 141y (Tp)
2:40 (2:41) (Class 5) 3-5-Y-O **£2,911** (£866; £432; £216) **Stalls** Low

Form RPR
2 **1** **Rebel Cause (IRE)**[24] 1767 3-8-12 0............... WilliamTwiston-Davies 7 82+
(Richard Spencer) *led: hdd over 6f out: chsd ldr tl over 4f out: rdn to ld over 1f out: r.o* **9/4**[1]
23- **2** *1½* **Invocation (FR)**[231] 6902 3-8-12 0.................................... MartinHarley 1 78+
(Alan King) *trckd ldrs: wnt 2nd over 4f out: led wl over 1f out: sn rdn and hdd: styd on same pce ins fnl f* **9/4**[1]
3 *4½* **Nobel Duke (IRE)** 3-8-12 0.. PatCosgrave 9 68+
(William Haggas) *chsd ldr tl led over 6f out: rdn and hdd wl over 1f out: edgd rt and no ex ins fnl f* **9/2**[3]
4 *1* **Brick Lane** 3-8-2 0.. JosephineGordon[(5)] 4 60+
(Robyn Brisland) *hld up: hdwy over 1f out: rn green ins fnl f: nt trble ldrs* **50/1**
0-3 **5** *¾* **Loveisreckless (IRE)**[23] 1798 3-8-7 0 ow3................(b) RobHornby[(3)] 6 62
(William Muir) *hmpd s: hld up: rdn over 2f out: r.o towards fin* **4/1**[2]
03 **6** *¾* **Swiftee (IRE)**[18] 1930 3-8-12 0.. TomEaves 3 62
(Ed Dunlop) *mid-div: n.m.r over 7f out: hdwy over 3f out: rdn over 1f out: wknd ins fnl f* **9/1**
6- **7** *1* **Bethnal Green**[492] 151 4-8-13 0.................................. GeorgeWood[(7)] 5 57
(Robyn Brisland) *sn prom: rdn over 2f out: wknd over 1f out* **50/1**
0 **8** *3½* **Spring In Kentucky**[18] 1930 4-9-6 0.................................. TomQueally 2 49?
(Daniel Kubler) *hld up: rdn over 2f out: a in rr* **66/1**
6 **9** *½* **Outback Guy (IRE)**[24] 1767 3-9-0 0 ow2.................................. DaleSwift 10 52?
(Kevin Frost) *s.i.s: hld up: rdn over 2f out: a bhd* **100/1**
00-0 **10** *4½* **Sunny Monday**[32] 1529 4-9-6 25.............................(b[1]) DannyBurton[(5)] 8 42?
(Emma Owen) *chsd ldrs: rdn over 3f out: wknd over 2f out* **100/1**

1m 49.55s (-0.55) **Going Correction** -0.05s/f (Stan)
WFA 3 from 4yo 13lb **10** Ran SP% **117.1**
Speed ratings (Par 103): **100,98,94,93,93 92,91,88,88,84**
CSF £7.28 TOTE £3.40: £1.20, £1.60, £1.90; EX 7.90 Trifecta £34.50.
Owner Rebel Racing III **Bred** Kildaragh Stud **Trained** Newmarket, Suffolk

FOCUS
An ordinary maiden and another race in which few ever got involved.

2444 GRAFITYP UK 25-YEAR CELEBRATION CLAIMING STKS 1m 1f 103y (Tp)
3:15 (3:15) (Class 6) 4-Y-O+ **£2,264** (£673; £336; £168) **Stalls** Low

Form RPR
-131 **1** **Marshgate Lane (USA)**[9] 2150 7-9-13 90.......................(p) LiamKeniry 6 89
(Neil Mulholland) *hld up: hdwy over 1f out: led and hung lft ins fnl f: r.o: comf* **1/1**[1]
3511 **2** *1¼* **Mr Red Clubs (IRE)**[24] 1762 7-9-3 75...........................(p) AndrewMullen 3 77
(Michael Appleby) *racd keenly: prom: trckd ldr over 7f out: rdn to ld over 1f out: hdd and unable qck ins fnl f* **5/1**[3]
0101 **3** *½* **Anton Chigurh**[25] 1707 7-8-10 73............................. PatrickVaughan[(7)] 1 76
(Tom Dascombe) *hld up: rdn and hdwy 1f out: styd on u.p* **8/1**
-350 **4** *½* **Ready (IRE)**[41] 1344 6-9-6 87..............................(p) JosephineGordon[(5)] 2 83
(Ivan Furtado) *plld hrd in 2nd pl tl over 7f out: remained handy: shkn up over 1f out: styd on same pce ins fnl f* **3/1**[2]
5103 **5** *1¾* **Vastly (USA)**[57] 1058 7-9-0 62...(t) TomQueally 4 69
(Sophie Leech) *led at stdy pce tl pushed along and qcknd over 2f out: rdn and hdd over 1f out: no ex ins fnl f* **16/1**

2m 0.85s (0.05) **Going Correction** -0.05s/f (Stan) **5** Ran SP% **108.7**
Speed ratings (Par 101): **97,95,95,95,93**
CSF £6.21 TOTE £1.70: £1.30, £2.30; EX 4.30 Trifecta £23.10.Marshgate Lane was subject to a Friendly claim of £13,000.
Owner The Affordable Partnership **Bred** Edmund A Gann **Trained** Limpley Stoke, Wilts

FOCUS
A fair claimer, but they went no pace early and it developed into a sprint from the home bend. All five runners were in a line across the track passing the furlong pole.

2445 HERMAN BOSMAN APPRECIATION H'CAP — 1m 4f 50y (Tp)
3:50 (3:50) (Class 5) (0-70,70) 4-Y-O+ **£2,911** (£866; £432; £216) **Stalls** Low

Form | | | | RPR
00-6 **1** **Azilian**[18] 1934 4-9-7 **70**.......(t) MartinHarley 7 81
(Paul Cole) *chsd ldrs: led over 3f out: rdn over 1f out: styd on wl* **11/2**[3]
010 **2** *4* **Shining Romeo**[8] 2174 4-9-1 **67**.......(t) TimClark[(3)] 6 72
(Denis Quinn) *hld up: hdwy on outer 3f out: chsd wnr over 2f out: rdn over 1f out: no ex ins fnl f* **22/1**
3313 **3** *nk* **Yasir (USA)**[34] 1500 8-8-5 **61**....... SophieKilloran[(7)] 4 66
(Sophie Leech) *s.i.s: hld up: hdwy on outer over 2f out: rdn over 1f out: styd on: nt rch ldrs* **9/2**[1]
1324 **4** *6* **Star Ascending (IRE)**[21] 1824 4-9-3 **66**.......(p) TomQueally 8 61
(Jennie Candlish) *chsd ldrs: rdn over 2f out: wknd fnl f* **5/1**[2]
2353 **5** *½* **Lions Charge (USA)**[23] 1796 9-9-0 **63**.......(tp) LiamKeniry 5 57
(Neil Mulholland) *hld up: pushed along and hdwy over 3f out: rdn over 2f out: wknd over 1f out* **6/1**
4423 **6** *18* **Comanche Chieftain (CAN)**[41] 1347 4-9-5 **68**.......(p) AndrewMullen 2 33
(Michael Appleby) *led 1f: remained w ldr tl led again 7f out: rdn and hdd over 3f out: wknd over 2f out* **13/2**
6020 **7** *11* **Wildomar**[41] 1347 7-8-8 **62**....... CiaranMckee[(5)] 3 10
(Peter Hiatt) *hld up: a in rr: rdn and wknd over 2f out* **28/1**
-562 **8** *7* **Horseguardsparade**[73] 864 5-9-7 **70**.......(p) WilliamTwiston-Davies 1 7
(Nigel Twiston-Davies) *mid-div: rdn over 4f out: wknd over 3f out* **9/2**[1]
0431 **9** *22* **Solarmaite**[25] 1711 7-9-0 **66**.......(b) RobHornby[(3)] 9
(Roy Bowring) *led after 1f: hdd 7f out: chsd ldr tl rdn over 3f out: wknd over 2f out* **11/1**

2m 37.9s (-2.90) **Going Correction** -0.05s/f (Stan) **9** Ran SP% **112.2**
Speed ratings (Par 103): **107,104,104,100,99 87,80,75,61**
CSF £110.39 CT £583.39 TOTE £5.80: £2.30, £4.80, £1.10; EX 86.30 Trifecta £982.30.
Owner The Fairy Story Partnership **Bred** Deepwood Farm Stud **Trained** Whatcombe, Oxon

FOCUS
An ordinary handicap and they went a scorching pace, with \bComanche Chieftain\p and \bSolarmaite\p taking each other on and cutting each other's throats as a result.

2446 ROSA VANLINGEN CELEBRATION H'CAP — 5f 216y (Tp)
4:20 (4:21) (Class 4) (0-85,85) 3-Y-O **£4,690** (£1,395; £697; £348) **Stalls** Low

Form | | | | RPR
16-3 **1** **Inland Sea (USA)**[44] 1267 3-9-4 **82**....... HarryBentley 5 88
(Richard Hannon) *a.p: hung rt over 2f out: rdn over 1f out: r.o u.p to ld nr fin* **2/1**[1]
2116 **2** *½* **Kyllukey**[24] 1763 3-8-12 **76**....... DarryllHolland 4 80
(Charles Hills) *chsd ldrs: wnt 2nd over 1f out: rdn to ld wl ins fnl hdd nr fin* **12/1**
02-5 **3** *nk* **Mutarajjil (IRE)**[19] 1894 3-8-10 **74**....... FrederikTylicki 6 77
(Roger Varian) *hld up: hdwy over 1f out: rdn and r.o ins fnl f* **11/4**[2]
410- **4** *½* **Symposium**[223] 7112 3-8-13 **77**....... PatCosgrave 3 78
(William Haggas) *hld up: hdwy over 1f out: rdn and edgd lft ins fnl f: r.o* **5/1**[3]
2132 **5** *¾* **Sir Dudley (IRE)**[14] 2002 3-9-7 **85**.......(b) TomEaves 1 84
(James Given) *sn chsng ldr: led 5f out: clr over 1f out: rdn and hdd wl ins fnl f* **10/1**
1404 **6** *nk* **Big Amigo (IRE)**[15] 1977 3-8-8 **72**.......(v) AndrewMullen 7 70
(Tom Dascombe) *s.i.s: hld up: plld hrd: rdn and hung lft fr over 1f out: r.o: nt rch ldrs* **11/1**
3-03 **7** *1* **Another Boy**[35] 1452 3-8-5 **74**.......(v) PatrickO'Donnell[(5)] 2 69
(Ralph Beckett) *s.i.s: hdwy over 1f out: rdn and nt clr run ins fnl f: nt trble ldrs* **10/1**
2560 **8** *2 ¾* **Furiant**[27] 1647 3-9-2 **80**....... AdrianNicholls 8 66
(Mark Johnston) *led 1f: chsd ldr: drvn along over 3f out: lost 2nd over 1f out: wknd ins fnl f* **33/1**

1m 13.56s (-0.94) **Going Correction** -0.05s/f (Stan) **8** Ran SP% **113.8**
Speed ratings (Par 101): **104,103,102,102,101 100,99,95**
CSF £27.15 CT £66.13 TOTE £2.60: £1.10, £3.10, £1.70; EX 26.80 Trifecta £100.40.
Owner H H Sheikh Mohammed Bin Khalifa Al Thani **Bred** Jane Johnson **Trained** East Everleigh, Wilts
■ Stewards' Enquiry : Darryll Holland two-day ban: use of whip (5-6 June)

FOCUS
A good 3yo sprint handicap and there was no hanging about. Winners should emerge from it.

2447 RENE COOLEN LONG SERVICE CELEBRATION H'CAP — 5f 20y (Tp)
4:55 (4:55) (Class 6) (0-55,55) 3-Y-O+ **£2,264** (£673; £336; £168) **Stalls** Low

Form | | | | RPR
0-42 **1** **Jack The Laird (IRE)**[23] 1794 3-8-13 **55**.......(b[1]) RobertWinston 1 63
(Dean Ivory) *sn pushed along to chse ldrs: rdn to ld ins fnl f: styd on: edgd lft towards fin* **13/8**[1]
0221 **2** *1 ¼* **Tasaaboq**[25] 1720 5-9-2 **55**.......(t) JosephineGordon[(5)] 3 62
(Phil McEntee) *sn pushed along towards rr: hdwy 2f out: rdn over 1f out: styd on* **7/2**[2]
3100 **3** *1 ¼* **Spray Tan**[18] 1913 6-9-0 **51**.......(b) GeorgeDowning[(3)] 4 53
(Tony Carroll) *chsd ldrs: rdn over 1f out: r.o* **28/1**
5332 **4** *nk* **Red Flute**[21] 1833 4-8-12 **49**.......(v) TimClark[(3)] 7 50
(Denis Quinn) *led: swtchd lft sn after s: hdd over 3f out: led again 2f out: sn rdn: hdd and no ex ins fnl f* **22/1**
00-5 **5** *½* **Fossa**[25] 1720 6-9-0 **55**....... BeckyBrisbourne[(7)] 2 54
(Mark Brisbourne) *s.i.s: hld up: swtchd rt over 1f out: rdn and r.o ins fnl f: nt rch ldrs* **11/1**
5050 **6** *2 ½* **Rat Catcher (IRE)**[25] 1720 6-8-13 **50**.......(p) RobHornby[(3)] 10 40
(Lisa Williamson) *hld up: rdn over 1f out: styd on ins fnl f: nvr nrr* **20/1**
0000 **7** *hd* **Willow Spring**[13] 2052 4-8-12 **46** oh1.......(b) MartinDwyer 6 35
(Conrad Allen) *s.i.s: hld up: hdwy 1/2-way: rdn over 1f out: wknd ins fnl f* **66/1**
6-32 **8** *¾* **John Joiner**[18] 1913 4-9-0 **53**.......(p) CiaranMckee[(5)] 5 40
(Peter Hedger) *chsd ldr tl led over 3f out: hdd 2f out: sn rdn: wknd ins fnl f* **7/1**[3]
2445 **9** *2 ½* **Very First Blade**[25] 1709 7-8-11 **52**.......(b) GeorgeWood[(7)] 11 30
(Michael Mullineaux) *prom on outer: pushed along 1/2-way: sn wknd* **28/1**
4214 **10** *1 ½* **Kuanyao (IRE)**[44] 1264 10-9-2 **55**.......(be) AnnStokell[(5)] 8 27
(Ann Stokell) *sn pushed along in rr: bhd fr 1/2-way* **25/1**
2541 **11** *3* **Blistering Dancer (IRE)**[26] 1676 6-8-12 **46**....... TomQueally 9 8
(Tony Carroll) *sn pushed along and prom: rdn and wknd over 1f out* **17/2**

1m 1.64s (-0.26) **Going Correction** -0.05s/f (Stan)
WFA 3 from 4yo+ 8lb **11** Ran SP% **113.0**
Speed ratings (Par 101): **100,98,96,95,94 90,90,89,85,82 78**
CSF £5.81 CT £105.87 TOTE £2.20: £1.10, £1.90, £4.80; EX 9.80 Trifecta £130.30.
Owner Michael & Heather Yarrow **Bred** E Mulryan **Trained** Radlett, Herts

FOCUS
A moderate sprint handicap.

2448 MR HERMAN BOSMAN SENIOR MEMORIAL APPRENTICE H'CAP — 1m 141y (Tp)
5:25 (5:26) (Class 6) (0-55,55) 4-Y-O+ **£2,264** (£673; £336; £168) **Stalls** Low

Form | | | | RPR
0423 **1** **Little Choosey**[24] 1768 6-9-2 **50**.......(bt) HollieDoyle 3 57
(Roy Bowring) *mid-div: hdwy over 2f out: rdn to ld ins fnl f: r.o* **15/2**
-632 **2** *1 ¾* **El Duque**[4] 2297 5-9-7 **55**.......(p) PatrickVaughan 10 58
(Bill Turner) *chsd ldr tl led over 2f out: rdn and hdd ins fnl f: styd on same pce* **4/1**[2]
0000 **3** *1 ¼* **Ocean Bentley (IRE)**[58] 1038 4-8-5 **46** oh1....... JoshuaBryan[(7)] 9 47
(Tony Carroll) *a.p: rdn over 1f out: styd on same pce fnl f* **40/1**
6346 **4** *2 ¾* **Luv U Lucky**[24] 1768 4-8-13 **47**.......(p) GeorgeWood 4 42
(Michael Appleby) *led: rdn and hdd over 2f out: wknd wl ins fnl f* **7/2**[1]
44-3 **5** *hd* **Edge (IRE)**[17] 1948 5-9-2 **50**....... JordanWilliams 12 45
(Bernard Llewellyn) *hld up: hmpd over 3f out: hdwy over 1f out: sn hung lft: swtchd rt and kpt on ins fnl f* **11/1**
6321 **6** *2* **Mount Cheiron (USA)**[23] 1791 5-9-4 **52**.......(p) CallumRodriguez 6 42
(Richard Ford) *chsd ldrs: rdn over 1f out: wknd ins fnl f* **5/1**[3]
000/ **7** *1 ¼* **Whitstable Native**[35] 5614 8-9-1 **49**.......(t) MillyNaseb 8 37
(Sophie Leech) *hld up: rdn over 1f out: n.d* **11/1**
6626 **8** *1* **Pipers Piping (IRE)**[31] 1556 10-9-2 **53**....... JaneElliott[(3)] 2 39
(Mandy Rowland) *hld up: nt clr run over 1f out: nvr nrr* **12/1**
0-50 **9** *¾* **Farang Jai Dee (IRE)**[34] 1495 4-8-7 **46** oh1....... GerO'Neill[(5)] 11 30
(Declan Carroll) *chsd ldrs: rdn over 3f out: wknd over 1f out* **33/1**
055- **10** *3 ¼* **Bold Grove**[263] 5932 4-9-0 **48**....... JoshQuinn 5 25
(Edward Bevan) *dwlt: hld up: hung rt over 3f out: sme hdwy over 2f out: sn wknd* **20/1**
0/00 **11** *3 ½* **Dutch Barney**[27] 1653 6-8-13 **47** oh1 ow1....... BeckyBrisbourne 1 17
(Mark Brisbourne) *mid-div: lost pl over 4f out: wknd 2f out* **25/1**
-146 **12** *7* **Diamond Runner (IRE)**[13] 2045 4-9-0 **53**.......(b) BenSanderson[(5)] 13 8
(Deborah Sanderson) *s.i.s: hld up: rdn and wknd over 2f out* **8/1**

1m 49.3s (-0.80) **Going Correction** -0.05s/f (Stan) **12** Ran SP% **120.1**
Speed ratings (Par 101): **101,99,98,95,95 93,92,91,91,88 85,79**
CSF £36.55 CT £1164.35 TOTE £8.40: £2.40, £1.40, £7.80; EX 51.40 Trifecta £917.00.
Owner K Nicholls **Bred** Mrs Sandra Fox **Trained** Edwinstowe, Notts

FOCUS
A moderate apprentice handicap full of horses who find it hard to win.
T/Jkpt: Part won. T/Plt: £16.10 to a £1 stake. Pool: £62,646.01 - 2,823.57 winning tickets T/Qpdt: £7.60 to a £1 stake. Pool: £5,506.65 - 535.00 winning tickets **Colin Roberts**

2449 - 2454a (Foreign Racing) - See Raceform Interactive

[2140] CHANTILLY (R-H)
Friday, May 20

OFFICIAL GOING: Turf: very soft; polytrack: standard

2455a PRIX VANTEAUX (GROUP 3) (3YO FILLIES) (TURF) — 1m 1f
1:15 (12:00) 3-Y-O **£29,411** (£11,764; £8,823; £5,882; £2,941)

| | | | RPR
1 **Zghorta Dance (FR)**[26] 1687 3-9-0 0....... IoritzMendizabal 6 104+
(J-C Rouget, France) *sn led: mde rest: rdn and qcknd over 1f out: styd on wl and a in control after: readily* **18/5**[3]
2 *2* **Azaelia (FR)**[40] 3-9-0 0....... Jean-BernardEyquem 1 100+
(Simone Brogi, France) *hld up in tch: angled out for clr run and rdn appr fnl f: styd on and wnt 2nd post: nvr nrr* **26/5**
3 *shd* **Dourdana (FR)**[24] 3-9-0 0....... ChristopheSoumillon 2 100
(A De Royer-Dupre, France) *midfield: rdn and effrt over 1f out: sn outpcd by wnr: styd on but hld fnl f: dropped to 3rd post* **6/4**[1]
4 *1 ½* **Asterina**[18] 3-9-0 0....... ThierryJarnet 7 97
(A De Royer-Dupre, France) *trckd wnr: rdn and effrt over 1f out: sn outpcd: fdd into 4th fnl f* **11/1**
5 *3* **Hiort (IRE)**[18] 3-9-0 0....... StephanePasquier 5 90
(P Bary, France) *hld up in rr: rdn 2f out: no imp and wl btn fnl f* **33/10**[2]
6 *nse* **Valenka (GER)**[32] 1541 3-9-0 0....... Pierre-CharlesBoudot 4 90
(M Munch, Germany) *t.k.h: trckd wnr on inner: rdn over 1f out: sn no ex and btn: wknd: dropped to last post* **41/5**

1m 57.46s (6.36) **6** Ran SP% **120.3**
WIN (incl. 1 euro stake): 4.60. PLACES: 2.30, 2.50. SF: 19.30.
Owner Ecurie I M Fares **Bred** Scea Haras De Manneville **Trained** Pau, France

2456a PRIX DES PASSEES (MAIDEN) (3YO COLTS & GELDINGS) (POLYTRACK) — 1m
1:45 (12:00) 3-Y-O **£9,191** (£3,676; £2,757; £1,838; £919)

| | | | RPR
1 **Honiara**[196] 7743 3-9-2 0....... ChristopheSoumillon 5 87
(Paul Cole) *w.w in 4th: tk clsr order on outer appr 1 1/2f out: qcknd to ld wl over 1f out: drvn ins fnl f: readily* **11/10**[1]
2 *1 ¼* **Dream Dy (FR)**[297] 3-9-2 0....... JulienAuge 9 84
(C Ferland, France) **13/5**[2]
3 *1 ¾* **Ardez (FR)**[73] 3-9-2 0....... TheoBachelot 7 80
(P Van De Poele, France) **16/1**
4 *1 ¼* **El Colombiano (FR)**[24] 3-8-10 0....... LukasDelozier[(6)] 1 77
(H-A Pantall, France) **71/10**
5 *½* **Right Charlie (FR)**[46] 3-9-2 0....... GeraldMosse 3 76
(J E Hammond, France) **13/1**
6 *9* **Akohol (IRE)**[43] 1311 3-9-2 0....... MaximeGuyon 10 55
(F Head, France) **7/2**[3]
7 *1 ¼* **Jona Black (FR)**[22] 1823 3-9-2 0.......(p) MorganDelalande 2 52
(W Delalande, France) **27/1**

WIN (incl. 1 euro stake): 2.10. PLACES: 1.20, 1.40, 1.90. DF: 2.80. SF: 4.60
Owner Meyrick Wright Asprey PJL Racing Wilcock **Bred** Scea Haras De Saint Pair
Trained Whatcombe, Oxon

 The Form Book, Raceform Ltd, Newbury, RG14 5SJ

^{2125}CHEPSTOW (L-H)

Saturday, May 21

OFFICIAL GOING: Soft

Wind: light 1/2 behind Weather: overcast, showers, becoming fine and dry

2457 THESUN.CO.UK/IRISH STALLION FARMS EBF NOVICE STKS 5f 16y

5:50 (5:51) (Class 5) 2-Y-O **£3,234** (£962; £481; £240) **Stalls** Centre

Form RPR

231 **1** **Tomily (IRE)**^{18} 1944 2-9-4 0 GaryMahon$^{(5)}$ 2 94+
(Richard Hannon) *mde all: edgd rt over 1f out: sn pushed clr: v easily* **2/5**^{1}

02 **2** *6* **Davarde (IRE)**^{9} 2180 2-9-2 0 JFEgan 5 65
(David Evans) *chsd wnr: drvn over 2f out: kpt on same pce: no ch w wnr* **11/4**^{2}

3 *hd* **Simmie (IRE)** 2-8-11 0 LiamKeniry 4 59
(Sylvester Kirk) *chsd ldng pair: drvn and outpcd over 2f out: kpt on and 3rd over 1f out: sn edgd lft: one pce* **33/1**

5 **4** *2 3/4* **Daffodil Mulligan**^{20} 1895 2-8-6 0 JosephineGordon$^{(5)}$ 3 49
(J S Moore) *chsd ldng pair: drvn and outpcd over 2f out: sltly hmpd 1f out: kpt on* **16/1**^{3}

5 *1* **Frozen Queen (IRE)** 2-8-6 0 KieranShoemark$^{(5)}$ 1 46
(J S Moore) *wnt lft s: sn outpcd and in rr: kpt on fnl 2f: nvr a factor* **25/1**

1m 2.33s (3.03) **Going Correction** +0.625s/f (Yiel) **5** Ran SP% **110.8**
Speed ratings (Par 93): **100,90,90,85,84**
CSF £1.79 TOTE £1.50: £1.10, £1.40; EX 1.60 Trifecta £7.90.
Owner Des Anderson **Bred** D J Anderson **Trained** East Everleigh, Wilts

FOCUS
Straightforward 2yo form with the useful winner dominating.

2458 FOLLOW @THESUNFOOTBALL FOR NON-STOP FOOTBALL COVERAGE H'CAP 5f 16y

6:20 (6:21) (Class 6) (0-55,55) 3-Y-O+ **£2,264** (£673; £336; £168) **Stalls** Centre

Form RPR

4345 **1** **Gilmer (IRE)**^{14} 2045 5-8-11 **50** NoelGarbutt$^{(5)}$ 13 61
(Laura Young) *towards rr: gd hdwy over 1f out: styd on strly to ld last 75yds* **11/1**

-003 **2** *2 1/4* **Spirit Of Rosanna**^{29} 1600 4-9-5 **53** (tp) AdamBeschizza 10 56
(Steph Hollinshead) *chsd ldrs: kpt on same pce last 75yds* **7/2**^{1}

2642 **3** *1 3/4* **Arizona Snow**^{95} 596 4-9-2 **55** (p) KieranShoemark$^{(5)}$ 4 52
(Ronald Harris) *chsd ldrs: kpt on same pce last 150yds* **12/1**

0664 **4** *nk* **Quantum Dot (IRE)**^{19} 1913 5-9-6 **54** (b) KieranO'Neill 1 50
(Ed de Giles) *racd alone far side: w ldrs: edgd rt over 1f out: kpt on same pce* **10/1**

10-0 **5** *hd* **Putemintheboot (IRE)**^{141} 3 3-8-5 **50** (t) PhilipPrince$^{(3)}$ 3 42
(David Evans) *racd centre: overall ldr: edgd lft and hdd last 75yds* **18/1**

4523 **6** *1 3/4* **Presto Boy**^{24} 1795 4-9-2 **50** ShaneKelly 9 39
(Richard Hughes) *mid-div: effrt over 2f out: nvr nr ldrs* **8/1**

0000 **7** *1* **Steel Rain**^{22} 1827 8-8-8 **47** (b) GaryMahon$^{(5)}$ 8 32
(Nikki Evans) *s.i.s: in rr: sme hdwy over 1f out: nvr a factor* **20/1**

0606 **8** *1* **Top Cop**^{43} 1319 7-8-13 **52** (p) JordanNason$^{(5)}$ 12 33
(Ronald Harris) *mid-div: hdwy over 2f out: sn chsng ldrs: wknd fnl f* **10/1**

6-02 **9** *1* **Blackdown Warrior**^{10} 2143 3-8-0 **47** AliceMills$^{(5)}$ 11 22
(Rod Millman) *wnt lft s: a towards rr* **5/1**^{2}

6566 **10** *3/4* **Louis Vee (IRE)**^{22} 1827 8-9-0 **53** (p) CiaranMckee$^{(5)}$ 15 28
(John O'Shea) *a in rr* **14/1**

0-00 **11** *nse* **Zebs Lad (IRE)**^{19} 1913 4-9-7 **55** (p) JFEgan 6 30
(Nikki Evans) *mid-div: lost pl 2f out: bhd whn eased clsng stages* **16/1**

05-5 **12** *4* **Secretfact**^{10} 2143 3-8-2 **49** JosephineGordon$^{(5)}$ 16 6
(Malcolm Saunders) *chsd ldrs: hung lft and lost pl over 2f out: bhd whn eased clsng stages* **6/1**^{3}

1m 2.14s (2.84) **Going Correction** +0.625s/f (Yiel) **12** Ran SP% **121.1**
WFA 3 from 4yo+ 8lb
Speed ratings (Par 101): **102,98,95,95,94 92,90,88,87,86 85,79**
CSF £50.37 CT £495.38 TOTE £12.40: £4.30, £1.90, £3.10; EX 81.50 Trifecta £950.10.
Owner Total Plumbing Supporters Club **Bred** Darley **Trained** Broomfield, Somerset

FOCUS
An ordinary maiden. The winner only needed to replicate last August's form.

2459 THE SUN FAVOURITE BRITAIN'S NO 1 RACING PULL-OUT MAIDEN AUCTION STKS 7f 16y

6:50 (6:54) (Class 5) 3-Y-O **£2,911** (£866; £432; £216) **Stalls** Centre

Form RPR

1 **Dynamic Girl (IRE)** 3-9-0 0 JFEgan 7 61
(Brendan Powell) *s.s: hdwy and 2nd over 2f out: led 1f out: edgd lft: hld on towards fin* **11/1**

430- **2** *nk* **Donttouchthechips (IRE)**^{207} 7540 3-9-0 65 JosephineGordon$^{(5)}$ 8 64
(Nikki Evans) *chsd ldrs: led over 3f out: hdd 1f out: kpt on towards fin* **10/1**

3 *1/2* **Hellavashock** 3-9-0 0 KieranShoemark$^{(5)}$ 4 63
(Giles Bravery) *chsd ldrs: kpt on towards fin* **12/1**

0 **4** *8* **Dltripleseven (IRE)**^{15} 2005 3-9-5 0 ShaneKelly 11 42
(Richard Hughes) *mid-div: hdwy to chse ldrs 3f out: wknd over 1f out* **10/1**

42 **5** *5* **Sciarra**^{27} 1673 3-8-7 0 LuluStanford$^{(7)}$ 2 24
(Michael Bell) *mid-div: wnt lft over 2f out: sn wknd* **5/2**^{1}

6 *6* **Shongololo (IRE)** 3-9-5 0 LiamKeniry 9 13
(Andrew Balding) *s.i.s: nvr on terms* **4/1**^{3}

00 **7** *11* **Rock Palm (IRE)**^{15} 2009 3-8-9 0 JennyPowell$^{(5)}$ 1
(Brendan Powell) *chsd ldrs: hung bdly lft and wknd 3f out: sn bhd and eased: lame* **7/1**

000- **8** *5* **Topsoil**^{222} 7166 3-9-0 0 JordanNason$^{(5)}$ 3
(Ronald Harris) *t.k.h: sn w ldrs: lost pl over 2f out: sn bhd* **66/1**

34-2 **9** *1 3/4* **Invigorate**^{23} 1806 3-9-5 69 (b^{1}) WilliamTwiston-Davies 6
(Harry Dunlop) *led: hdd over 3f out: lost pl over 2f out: sn bhd* **3/1**^{2}

1m 28.23s (5.03) **Going Correction** +0.625s/f (Yiel) **9** Ran SP% **121.8**
Speed ratings (Par 99): **96,95,95,85,80 73,60,55,53**
CSF £120.69 TOTE £11.60: £3.80, £2.70, £3.80; EX 94.10 Trifecta £660.50.
Owner Wajid Ali Abdul Qayyum **Bred** Swordlestown Stud **Trained** Upper Lambourn, Berks

FOCUS
An ordinary maiden.

2460 @SUNFAVE FOR YOUR LATEST RACING NEWS H'CAP 7f 16y

7:20 (7:21) (Class 4) (0-85,84) 4-Y-O+ **£5,175** (£1,540; £769; £384) **Stalls** Centre

Form RPR

3506 **1** **Sir Billy Wright (IRE)**^{28} 1634 5-9-1 **81** PhilipPrince$^{(3)}$ 1 90
(David Evans) *hld up: hdwy to chse ldrs over 2f out: led over 1f out: hung rt last 100yds: styd on* **7/1**^{3}

-605 **2** *1* **Peak Storm**^{26} 1724 7-8-8 **76** (p) CiaranMckee$^{(5)}$ 12 81
(John O'Shea) *s.i.s: hld up: hdwy over 2f out: kpt on to take 2nd last 100yds* **16/1**

0211 **3** *2 1/2* **Dilgura**^{20} 1898 6-9-4 **84** MatthewCosham$^{(3)}$ 6 83
(Stuart Kittow) *trckd ldrs: led 2f out: sn hdd: kpt on same pce* **11/4**^{1}

006 **4** *3 1/2* **Uncle Dermot (IRE)**^{3} 2367 8-8-7 **70** JFEgan 5 60
(Brendan Powell) *chsd ldrs: pushed along over 3f out: led briefly over 2f out: wknd last 150yds* **8/1**

4240 **5** *2 1/2* **Steal The Scene (IRE)**^{7} 2247 4-8-13 **81** GaryMahon$^{(5)}$ 8 64
(Richard Hannon) *hld up in rr: swtchd lft 4f out: sn chsng ldrs: rdr dropped whip over 1f out: sn wknd* **7/2**^{2}

5-20 **6** *1* **Gannicus**^{24} 1775 5-8-11 **74** (tp) ShaneKelly 10 55
(Brendan Powell) *chsd ldrs: hung lft and wknd over 1f out* **7/1**^{3}

5-11 **7** *10* **Evanescent (IRE)**^{23} 1818 7-9-5 **82** WilliamCarson 9 37
(Tony Carroll) *led tl over 2f out: sn lost pl and bhd: eased clsng stages* **9/1**

140- **8** *4 1/2* **Sarangoo**^{249} 6414 8-9-1 **78** CathyGannon 7 21
(Malcolm Saunders) *chsd ldrs: swtchd lft to stands' side: lost pl over 2f out: bhd whn eased clsng stages* **8/1**

01-0 **9** *3/4* **Popeswood (IRE)**^{19} 1929 4-9-5 **82** WilliamTwiston-Davies 3 23
(Ron Hodges) *in rr: bhd fnl 3f: bhd whn eased clsng stages* **9/1**

1m 26.36s (3.16) **Going Correction** +0.625s/f (Yiel) **9** Ran SP% **122.0**
Speed ratings (Par 105): **106,104,102,98,95 94,82,77,76**
CSF £116.25 CT £391.24 TOTE £9.90: £2.80, £3.60, £1.40; EX 106.40 Trifecta £543.50.
Owner Shropshire Wolves **Bred** Grangecon Stud **Trained** Pandy, Monmouths

FOCUS
A modest handicap, but sound form for the class.

2461 @SUNSPORT FOR ALL BREAKING SPORTS NEWS H'CAP 1m 2f 36y

7:50 (7:50) (Class 5) (0-70,67) 4-Y-O+ **£2,911** (£866; £432; £216) **Stalls** Low

Form RPR

323 **1** **Innoko (FR)**^{24} 1778 6-8-10 **59** GeorgeDowning$^{(3)}$ 4 66
(Tony Carroll) *trckd ldng pair: drvn 3f out: led over 1f out: drvn out* **7/2**^{3}

0-13 **2** *1 1/2* **Distant High**^{11} 2127 5-8-13 **64** (p) JosephineGordon$^{(5)}$ 7 68
(Richard Price) *sn chsng ldr: brought wd over 4f out: outpcd whn hung lft over 2f out: styd on to take 2nd clsng stages* **15/8**^{1}

2223 **3** *2 1/2* **Cartographic (USA)**^{35} 1501 4-9-3 **63** ShaneKelly 5 62
(David Evans) *trckd ldng pair: 2nd over 3f out: chal over 1f out: wknd last 100yds* **2/1**^{2}

5000 **4** *8* **Altaira**^{40} 1390 5-8-12 **58** WilliamCarson 3 41
(Tony Carroll) *led: rdn over 2f out: hdd over 1f out: sn wknd* **10/1**

4002 **5** *5* **Coup De Vent**^{11} 2127 5-8-9 **55** (be) CathyGannon 6 28
(John O'Shea) *awkward s: t.k.h in last: chsng ldrs 2f out: hung bdly lft: eased fnl f* **8/1**

2m 20.91s (10.31) **Going Correction** +0.975s/f (Soft) **5** Ran SP% **110.5**
Speed ratings (Par 103): **97,95,93,87,83**
CSF £10.55 TOTE £4.40: £2.00, £1.60; EX 13.60 Trifecta £26.60.
Owner Mill House Racing Syndicate **Bred** Marquise Soledad De Moratalla **Trained** Cropthorne, Worcs

FOCUS
A moderate handicap.

2462 DREAMTEAMFC.COM H'CAP 1m 4f 23y

8:20 (8:20) (Class 6) (0-55,55) 4-Y-O+ **£2,264** (£673; £336; £168) **Stalls** Low

Form RPR

0-02 **1** **Urban Space**^{3} 2370 10-9-3 **54** (t) DanielMuscutt$^{(3)}$ 1 63
(John Flint) *trckd ldrs: chal over 2f out: led 1f out: styd on* **3/1**^{1}

0-00 **2** *1 1/2* **Insight (IRE)**^{27} 1675 5-8-7 **46** oh1 (p) KieranShoemark$^{(5)}$ 14 53
(Steve Gollings) *chsd ldrs: 2nd 4f out: led over 2f out: hdd 1f out: kpt on same pce* **8/1**

3 *1 1/4* **Rolanna (IRE)**^{240} 6696 4-8-7 **46** oh1 (p) JosephineGordon$^{(5)}$ 16 51
(W J Martin, Ire) *mid-div: hdwy 3f out: chsng ldrs whn hung lft over 1f out: kpt on same pce* **9/1**

4436 **4** *1 1/2* **Ring Eye (IRE)**^{35} 1500 8-8-13 **52** CiaranMckee$^{(5)}$ 10 54
(John O'Shea) *hld up in rr: hdwy whn hmpd 2f out: styd on to take 4th last 150yds* **5/1**^{3}

0/60 **5** *4* **Seven Summits (IRE)**^{7} 870 9-8-12 **46** oh1 (b^{1}) ShaneKelly 4 42
(Sophie Leech) *s.i.s: sn mid-div: chsng ldrs over 3f out: edgd rt 2f out: wknd fnl f* **7/2**^{2}

625- **6** *7* **Mexican Mick**^{249} 6402 7-8-10 **49** (b) LucyKBarry$^{(5)}$ 3 34
(Peter Hiatt) *chsd ldrs: wknd over 2f out* **9/1**

2400 **7** *hd* **Foylesideview (IRE)**^{25} 1768 4-9-0 **48** CathyGannon 2 32
(Harry Chisman) *hld up in rr: t.k.h: rapid hdwy to ld 6f out: hdd over 2f out: lost pl over 1f out* **16/1**

0-04 **8** *6* **Scent Of Power**^{15} 2015 4-9-0 **51** ^{1} TimClark$^{(3)}$ 5 26
(Barry Leavy) *hld up in rr: nvr a factor* **10/1**

0060 **9** *23* **Renewing**^{22} 1830 5-8-7 **46** oh1 (v) GaryMahon$^{(5)}$ 6
(Roy Brotherton) *in rr: bhd and drvn 6f out: t.o whn eased 2f out* **25/1**

0500 **10** *10* **Teide Peak (IRE)**^{64} 981 7-8-13 **47** (tp) WilliamTwiston-Davies 15
(Grace Harris) *led tl 6f out: lost pl over 3f out: sn bhd: t.o whn eased 2f out* **20/1**

-630 **11** *27* **Castanea**^{101} 514 4-8-12 **46** oh1 KieranO'Neill 12
(Ronald Harris) *bhd: t.o whn eased 2f out: eventually completed* **16/1**

0-00 **12** *31* **Rebel Yell**^{42} 1343 4-8-12 **46** oh1 (vt) WilliamCarson 9
(Richard Price) *chsd ldrs: lost pl over 5f out: sn bhd: t.o whn eased 2f out* **33/1**

2m 49.75s (10.75) **Going Correction** +0.975s/f (Soft) **12** Ran SP% **127.4**
Speed ratings (Par 101): **103,102,101,100,97 92,92,88,73,66 48,28**
CSF £29.37 CT £207.17 TOTE £4.20: £1.90, £3.80, £3.20; EX 31.80 Trifecta £214.10.
Owner J L Flint **Bred** Winterbeck Manor Stud **Trained** Kenfig Hill, Bridgend

■ Stewards' Enquiry : Shane Kelly one-day ban; careless riding (5th June)

FOCUS
A weak handicap. The winner buuilt on last week's Bath run.

2463 FOLLOW @DREAMTEAMFC FOR LATEST FOOTBALL GOSSIP H'CAP 1m 4f 23y
8:50 (8:50) (Class 5) (0-75,75) 4-Y-O+ **£2,911** (£866; £432; £216) **Stalls** Low

Form RPR
-050 **1** **Bohemian Rhapsody (IRE)**[19] 1933 7-9-4 **72**.................. ShaneKelly 8 80
(Brendan Powell) *mid-div: remote 2nd over 6f out: led over 3f out: drvn out* **4/1**[2]
602/ **2** 1 ¾ **What A Scorcher**[16] 7304 5-9-1 **69**.......................... JFEgan 6 73
(Nikki Evans) *trckd ldrs: 2nd 3f out: kpt on same pce fnl f* **10/1**
20-6 **3** ¾ **Sunday Royal (FR)**[25] 1737 4-9-5 **73**.......................... SamHitchcott 4 76
(Harry Dunlop) *hld up in rr: chsng ldrs 4f out: 3rd 3f out: kpt on same pce fnl f* **13/2**
42-2 **4** 15 **Dizzey Heights (IRE)**[36] 1455 4-9-4 **72**.......................... CathyGannon 10 51
(Stuart Kittow) *s.s: in rr: reminders over 5f out: chsng ldrs over 4f out: lost pl over 2f out* **9/4**[1]
0561 **5** 4 ½ **Yul Finegold (IRE)**[22] 1824 6-9-7 **75**.......................... LiamKeniry 3 47
(Conor Dore) *led: wnt long way clr after 3f tl over 5f out: hdd over 3f out: lost pl 2f out* **7/1**
123- **6** 8 **Marengo**[237] 6778 5-9-0 **75**..........................(p) JordanWilliams[(7)] 2 34
(Bernard Llewellyn) *chsd clr ldr: drvn 4f out: lost pl over 3f out: sn bhd* **6/1**
7 19 **Endive**[220] 4-9-0 **68**.......................... AdamBeschizza 5
(Robert Stephens) *mid-div: lost pl and drvn over 5f out: sn bhd: t.o 3f out: eased fnl f* **9/2**[3]

2m 49.5s (10.50) **Going Correction** +0.975s/f (Soft) **7** Ran SP% **118.2**
Speed ratings (Par 103): **104,102,102,92,89 84,71**
CSF £43.92 CT £258.06 TOTE £6.10: £2.60, £3.70; EX 43.40 Trifecta £615.20.
Owner J Daniels **Bred** Sweetmans Bloodstock **Trained** Upper Lambourn, Berks

FOCUS
A modest handicap.
T/Plt: £400.20 to a £1 stake. Pool: £61,873.04 - 112.84 winning units. T/Qpdt: £165.30 to a £1 stake. Pool: £5,946.58 - 26.62 winning units. **Walter Glynn**

2429 GOODWOOD (R-H)
Saturday, May 21

OFFICIAL GOING: Good changing to good to soft after race 4 (4.00)
Wind: quite strong across Weather: rain, heavy at times

2464 AL BASTI EQUIWORLD FESTIVAL STKS (LISTED RACE) 1m 1f 192y
2:15 (2:15) (Class 1) 4-Y-O+
£28,355 (£10,750; £5,380; £2,680; £1,345; £675) **Stalls** Low

Form RPR
34-4 **1** **Decorated Knight**[24] 1774 4-9-0 107.......................... AndreaAtzeni 8 111
(Roger Charlton) *trckd ldrs: chal 2f out: sn rdn: led ent fnl f: kpt on wl: drifted rt towards fin* **4/1**[1]
006- **2** ½ **Educate**[208] 7509 7-9-0 96.......................... ThomasBrown 4 109
(Ismail Mohammed) *hld up in tch: hdwy over 2f out: nt clr run on heels of ldrs tl swtchd lft jst over 1f out: r.o wl fnl f: wnt 2nd cl home* **16/1**
32-3 **3** ½ **Black Cherry**[21] 1858 4-8-9 102.......................... JimmyFortune 6 103
(Richard Hannon) *sn led: dictated stdy pce: qcknd whn jnd over 2f out: hdd ent fnl f: drifted rt and no ex whn lost 2nd cl home* **10/1**
-443 **4** 1 ¾ **Master Carpenter (IRE)**[16] 1973 5-9-0 110.................. FrederikTylicki 3 105
(Rod Millman) *trckd ldr: chal 3f out: rdn whn pce qcknd over 2f out: kpt on same pce fnl f* **4/1**[1]
230/ **5** nk **Kings Fete**[616] 6329 5-9-0 104.......................... TedDurcan 1 104
(Sir Michael Stoute) *trckd ldrs: rdn over 1f out: kpt on same pce* **11/2**[3]
6-45 **6** 1 **Battalion (IRE)**[16] 1973 6-9-3 109..........................(p) PatDobbs 2 105
(William Haggas) *hld up: rdn over 1f out: nt pce to get involved* **5/1**[2]
0000 **7** 1 **Bossy Guest (IRE)**[38] 1425 4-9-0 106.......................... CharlesBishop 7 100
(Mick Channon) *hld up: hdwy over 3f out: effrt 2f out: fdd ent fnl f* **12/1**
101/ **8** 1 ¼ **Berkshire (IRE)**[582] 7243 5-9-0 112.......................... JimCrowley 5 97
(Paul Cole) *stdd s: racd keenly in last: hdwy over 3f out: effrt over 2f out: wknd over 1f out* **4/1**[1]

2m 14.56s (6.46) **Going Correction** +0.375s/f (Good) **8** Ran SP% **114.7**
Speed ratings (Par 111): **89,88,88,86,86 85,84,83**
CSF £67.71 TOTE £5.10: £1.80, £5.00, £2.20; EX 76.40 Trifecta £560.20.
Owner Saleh Al Homaizi & Imad Al Sagar **Bred** Saleh Al Homaizi & Imad Al Sagar **Trained** Beckhampton, Wilts

FOCUS
Good ground for this quality seven-race card, but the feeling among the jockeys who rode in the opener was that is was riding on the fast side. This opening Listed contest was a classy affair on paper but the form is tempered by the fact they they went such a steady gallop, resulting in most of the main protagonists racing quite keenly.

2465 INTRINSIC NEW FOR 2016 AT HEDGEHOLME STUD TAPSTER STKS (LISTED RACE) 1m 4f
2:50 (2:50) (Class 1) 4-Y-O+ **£29,600** (£11,195; £5,595; £2,795) **Stalls** High

Form RPR
312- **1** **Mount Logan (IRE)**[273] 5633 5-9-0 110.......................... AndreaAtzeni 4 106+
(Roger Varian) *trckd ldrs: chal over 1f out: sn rdn: tk narrow advantage ins fnl f: kpt on wl to edge ahd towards fin: rdn out* **2/1**[2]
224- **2** nk **Sweeping Up**[205] 7587 5-8-9 101..........................(t) JimmyFortune 3 100
(Hughie Morrison) *trckd ldrs: rdn to chal wl over 1f out: edgd rt: ev ch thrght fnl f: kpt on wl: jst hld* **12/1**
1-21 **3** ¾ **Noble Gift**[28] 1645 6-9-0 99.......................... CallumShepherd 2 104
(William Knight) *led: rdn 2f out: hld on gamely to narrow advantage tl hdd ins fnl f: no ex towards fin* **14/1**
06-0 **4** ½ **Eye Of The Storm (IRE)**[45] 1273 6-9-0 103.......................... PatDobbs 1 103+
(Amanda Perrett) *hld up 6th: hdwy over 1f out: kpt on wl fnl f wout having the clrest of runs: wnt 4th nring fin* **20/1**
11-2 **5** ½ **Bateel (IRE)**[21] 1855 4-8-9 99.......................... JimCrowley 6 97
(David Simcock) *hld up 5th: hdwy over 2f out: rdn and ev ch ent fnl f: no ex fnl 100yds* **5/4**[1]
521- **6** 6 **Mr Singh**[317] 4070 4-9-0 108.......................... RobertHavlin 5 93
(John Gosden) *trckd ldrs: effrt 2f out: wknd jst over 1f out* **11/2**[3]

2m 44.3s (5.90) **Going Correction** +0.375s/f (Good) **6** Ran SP% **112.3**
Speed ratings (Par 111): **95,94,94,93,93 89**
CSF £24.49 TOTE £2.70: £1.30, £5.00; EX 29.60 Trifecta £131.30.
Owner Sheikh Mohammed Obaid Al Maktoum **Bred** Ladyswood Stud & Canning Downs Stud Aus **Trained** Newmarket, Suffolk

FOCUS
It had been raining since just after the opening race. Another good quality Listed contest and this was run at a more even tempo, but they finished in a heap and it's hard to get overly excited about the overall form, despite the fact that it featured horses who have the potential to hold their own in better company.

2466 AL BASTI EQUIWORLD SUPPORTING GREATWOOD STKS (H'CAP) 7f
3:25 (3:26) (Class 2) 3-Y-O **£64,690** (£19,250; £9,620; £4,810) **Stalls** Low

Form RPR
3-11 **1** **Oh This Is Us (IRE)**[9] 2179 3-8-3 **86**.......................... TomMarquand[(3)] 2 95+
(Richard Hannon) *mid-div: hdwy over 2f out: rdn to ld jst ins fnl f: kpt on wl: drvn out* **9/2**[1]
6-13 **2** ½ **Haalick (IRE)**[57] 1071 3-9-7 **101**.......................... AndreaAtzeni 10 108+
(Roger Varian) *hld up bhd: rdn over 2f out: hdwy over 1f out: str run ins fnl f: wnt 2nd cl home: jst failed* **5/1**[2]
6-11 **3** hd **Tang Fleming**[16] 1975 3-8-6 **91**.......................... EdwardGreatrex[(5)] 1 97
(Andrew Balding) *trckd ldrs: rdn to ld briefly ent fnl f: kpt on wl* **5/1**[2]
21-2 **4** ½ **Arab Poet**[30] 1585 3-8-5 **85**.......................... JimmyQuinn 14 90+
(Sir Michael Stoute) *hld up towards rr: hdwy 2f out: rdn into cl 3rd jst ins fnl f: kpt on same pce fnl 120yds* **9/1**
1-15 **5** nk **Stamp Hill (IRE)**[21] 1865 3-8-6 **86**.......................... PatrickMathers 15 90
(Richard Fahey) *hld up towards rr: hdwy over 4f out into midfield: rdn 2f out: styd on wl ins fnl f* **25/1**
3-30 **6** ½ **Zhui Feng (IRE)**[21] 1864 3-9-6 **100**.......................... PatDobbs 11 103+
(Amanda Perrett) *mid-div: hdwy over 2f out: sn rdn: styd on ins fnl f but nvr threatening to get on terms* **10/1**
-231 **7** ¾ **Turbine (IRE)**[4] 2331 3-8-12 **92** 6ex.......................... FrannyNorton 9 93
(Mark Johnston) *led: rdn 2f out: hdd ent fnl f: no ex fnl 100yds* **7/1**[3]
2-23 **8** 1 ¼ **Alqubbah (IRE)**[14] 2042 3-8-13 **93**.......................... JimmyFortune 7 94+
(Ed Dunlop) *wnt rt s: hld up towards rr: hdwy over 3f out: squeezed up and lost pl over 2f out: styd on fnl f but nvr any threat* **10/1**
0-44 **9** hd **Dawaa**[21] 1851 3-8-10 **90**.......................... JimCrowley 4 87
(Mark Johnston) *mid-div: hdwy over 2f out: rdn to chse ldrs over 1f out: fdd fnl 120yds* **14/1**
24-1 **10** 2 ¾ **Noble Peace**[22] 1837 3-8-4 **84**.......................... CathyGannon 8 73
(Henry Candy) *racd keenly: trckd ldrs: rdn and ev ch 2f out: wknd ent fnl f* **20/1**
210- **11** ½ **Strong Challenge (IRE)**[298] 4724 3-8-12 **95**..................[1] KevinStott[(3)] 6 83
(Saeed bin Suroor) *hld up towards rr: hdwy 2f out: rdn ent fnl f: nvr threatened: wknd fnl 120yds* **14/1**
5-14 **12** 1 ¼ **Galesburg (IRE)**[23] 1817 3-8-1 **81**.......................... NickyMackay 12 66
(Mark Johnston) *trckd ldr: rdn over 2f out: wknd over 1f out* **28/1**
-241 **13** ¾ **Summer Icon**[9] 2177 3-8-10 **90**.......................... FrederikTylicki 13 73
(Mick Channon) *mid-div: hdwy over 4f out: effrt wl over 2f out: wknd over 1f out* **25/1**
6-30 **14** nk **Heraldic (USA)**[16] 1977 3-8-0 **80**.......................... CamHardie 5 62
(Mark Johnston) *trckd ldr: rdn over 2f out: wkng whn short of room ent fnl f* **50/1**

1m 28.05s (1.05) **Going Correction** +0.375s/f (Good) **14** Ran SP% **123.4**
Speed ratings (Par 105): **109,108,108,107,107 106,105,104,104,101 100,99,98,97**
CSF £25.31 CT £124.32 TOTE £4.80: £2.20, £1.60, £2.30; EX 31.60 Trifecta £88.80.
Owner Team Wallop **Bred** Herbertstown House Stud **Trained** East Everleigh, Wilts

FOCUS
The continuing rain was starting to have an effect on conditions, and the time of this contest, some 4sec slower than standard, suggested the going was now good at best. This was a fiercely competitive 3yo handicap featuring any number of horses who are likely to prove a good deal better than their current marks. They ended up right across the track in the straight and loads of these still held a chance as they went past the two-pole.

2467 AL BASTI EQUIWORLD DUBAI EBFSTALLIONS.COM FILLIES' NOVICE STKS (PLUS 10 RACE) 6f
4:00 (4:01) (Class 4) 2-Y-O **£5,175** (£1,540; £769; £384) **Stalls** High

Form RPR
2 **1** **Romantic View**[15] 1988 2-9-0 0.......................... MartinLane 7 87+
(Charlie Appleby) *mde all: qcknd clr fnl f: readily* **11/8**[1]
2 2 ¾ **Pepita (IRE)** 2-9-0 0.......................... PatDobbs 9 78
(Richard Hannon) *mid-div: hdwy 2f out: shkn up to chse wnr ins fnl f: kpt on but a being readily hld* **9/2**[3]
3 1 ¼ **Limelite (IRE)** 2-8-11 0.......................... TomMarquand[(3)] 2 74
(Richard Hannon) *sn trcking ldrs: rdn and ev ch 2f out: drifted lft over 1f out: kpt on but no ex fnl f* **12/1**
4 ¾ **Hellofahaste** 2-9-0 0.......................... FrederikTylicki 13 72
(Rod Millman) *trckd ldrs: rdn 2f out: kpt on same pce fnl f* **66/1**
5 2 ½ **Chica De La Noche** 2-9-0 0.......................... JimCrowley 6 64
(Simon Dow) *trckd ldrs: hmpd over 1f out: kpt on same pce fnl f* **50/1**
6 1 ¼ **Naifah (IRE)** 2-9-0 0.......................... JimmyQuinn 12 61
(John Gosden) *hld up: pushed along over 2f out: no imp tl styd on fnl f* **25/1**
7 2 **Swan Serenade** 2-9-0 0.......................... RyanClark 4 55
(Jonathan Portman) *trckd ldr: rdn and ev ch 2f out: hld over 1f out: wknd ins fnl f* **66/1**
7 dht **Shawami (IRE)** 2-9-0 0.......................... AndreaAtzeni 8 55
(Mick Channon) *mid-div tl wknd over 1f out* **14/1**
9 1 ¼ **Jasmincita (IRE)** 2-9-0 0.......................... SteveDrowne 1 51
(George Baker) *s.i.s: bhd: hdwy into midfield 2f out: no further imp fnl f* **33/1**
10 ½ **Moondust (IRE)** 2-9-0 0.......................... RobertHavlin 11 52+
(John Gosden) *racd keenly: trckd ldrs: rdn whn bdly hmpd over 1f out: no ch after* **5/2**[2]
11 2 **Masterfilly (IRE)** 2-9-0 0.......................... TedDurcan 5 43
(Ed Walker) *mid-div: rdn 2f out: wknd jst over 1f out* **20/1**
12 5 **Sukiwarrior (IRE)** 2-8-11 0.......................... MichaelJMMurphy[(3)] 10 28
(Charles Hills) *s.i.s: a towards rr* **25/1**

1m 14.29s (2.09) **Going Correction** +0.20s/f (Good) **12** Ran SP% **123.6**
Speed ratings (Par 92): **94,90,88,87,84 82,80,80,78,77 75,68**
CSF £7.76 TOTE £2.20: £1.10, £2.50, £2.80; EX 8.60 Trifecta £40.70.
Owner Godolphin **Bred** Darley **Trained** Newmarket, Suffolk

FOCUS
Some well-bred fillies on show but the winner, who had the advantage of a previous start, ran right away with this in the final furlong and looks quite smart. She could rate higher in a better grade.

2468 AL BASTI EQUIWORLD STKS (H'CAP) 1m 6f
4:35 (4:35) (Class 2) (0-105,101) 4-Y-O+ **£16,172** (£4,812; £2,405; £1,202) **Stalls** Low

Form RPR
22-0 **1** **Kinema (IRE)**[35] 1493 5-9-1 **95**.............................. PatDobbs 4 104+
(Ralph Beckett) *mid-div: hdwy 2f out: nt clrest of runs ent fnl f: squeezed through gap to ld fnl 120yds: asserting towards fin: comf* **11/2**[2]
315- **2** *1* **Monotype (IRE)**[317] 4070 4-8-9 **89**.............................. AndreaAtzeni 8 96
(Roger Varian) *trckd ldrs: rdn wl over 1f out: str chal ent fnl f: no ex fnl 100yds* **2/1**[1]
3105 **3** *nk* **Notarised**[28] 1645 5-9-7 **101**.............................. FrannyNorton 2 107
(Mark Johnston) *led: drvn and strly pressed fr 2f out: hld on to narrow advantage tl hdd fnl 120yds: no ex* **8/1**
0-25 **4** *1* **Gavlar**[28] 1642 5-8-8 **93**.............................. CallumShepherd(5) 7 97
(William Knight) *mid-div: hdwy over 3f out: rdn for str chal 2f out tl no ex ins fnl f* **10/1**
46 **5** *nse* **Cayirli (FR)**[14] 2024 4-8-11 **91**.............................. TimmyMurphy 11 95
(Seamus Durack) *trckd ldrs: hung rt whn rdn over 1f out: styd on fnl f but nt pce to get involved* **16/1**
13-0 **6** *9* **Scrutinise**[31] 1568 4-8-13 **93**.............................. JimCrowley 1 85
(Ed Dunlop) *mid-div: hdwy over 2f out: sn rdn to chse ldrs: wknd fnl f* **7/1**[3]
6443 **7** *4* **First Mohican**[17] 1963 8-9-7 **101**..............................(v[1]) JimmyFortune 9 87
(Alan King) *slowly away: bhd: hdwy over 3f out: sn rdn: nvr threatened: wknd fnl f* **10/1**
06 **8** *1 1/4* **Giant Redwood (IRE)**[14] 2025 4-8-2 **85**.............................. TomMarquand(3) 10 69
(Michael Bell) *trckd ldr tl rdn 3f out: sn btn* **22/1**
560- **9** *1 1/4* **Montaly**[315] 4163 5-8-10 **95**.............................. EdwardGreatrex(5) 3 77
(Andrew Balding) *towards rr: struggling over 4f out: nvr threatened* **9/1**
0-33 **10** *3/4* **Eton Rambler (USA)**[20] 1893 6-8-8 **88**.............................. SteveDrowne 6 69
(George Baker) *trckd ldrs: rdn over 2f out: wknd over 1f out* **20/1**
506- **11** *27* **Norab (GER)**[208] 7511 5-8-10 **90**.............................. JimmyQuinn 5 34
(Bernard Llewellyn) *wknd over 2f out: a towards rr* **40/1**
3m 8.32s (4.72) **Going Correction** +0.575s/f (Yiel) **11** Ran SP% **117.9**
Speed ratings (Par 109): **109,108,108,107,107 102,100,99,98,98 82**
CSF £16.47 CT £89.55 TOTE £6.10: £2.10, £1.30, £3.00; EX 23.70 Trifecta £130.80.
Owner R A Pegum **Bred** Rockhart Trading Ltd **Trained** Kimpton, Hants

FOCUS
The ground was changed to good to soft before this competitive staying handicap, which was run at what looked an even gallop, so the form looks sound enough. A group of five finished a long way clear.

2469 AL BASTI EQUIWORLD SUPPORTING BRITISH RACING STKS (VETERANS' H'CAP) 6f
5:10 (5:12) (Class 4) (0-80,80) 6-Y-O+ **£6,469** (£1,925; £962; £481) **Stalls** High

Form RPR
0-42 **1** **Pettochside**[2] 2396 7-8-1 **67**.............................. MitchGodwin(7) 2 81
(John Bridger) *mde all: qcknd clr over 1f out: easily* **7/4**[1]
516- **2** *3 3/4* **Joe Packet**[309] 4346 9-9-3 **76**.............................. RyanClark 1 78
(Jonathan Portman) *trckd wnr thrght: outpcd over 1f out: kpt on but sn no ch* **25/1**
5414 **3** *1/2* **Pretty Bubbles**[12] 2084 7-9-7 **80**..............................(v) FrederikTylicki 6 80
(J R Jenkins) *trckd wnr: rdn whn wnr qcknd clr over 1f out: kpt on same pce* **9/1**[3]
-112 **4** *1/2* **Elusive Ellen (IRE)**[19] 1929 6-9-5 **78**.............................. JimmyQuinn 10 77
(Brendan Powell) *trckd ldrs: rdn over 1f out: sn one pce* **11/2**[2]
-020 **5** *2 1/4* **Perfect Pastime**[19] 1928 8-8-9 **68**..............................(p) RobertHavlin 11 60
(Jim Boyle) *hld up towards rr: styd on fnl f: nvr trbld ldrs* **25/1**
4112 **6** *1/2* **Welease Bwian (IRE)**[17] 1964 7-8-12 **78**.............................. MillyNaseb(7) 4 68
(Stuart Williams) *mid-div: hdwy 2f out: sn rdn: one pce fnl f* **10/1**
0-60 **7** *nk* **Smoothtalkinrascal (IRE)**[31] 1566 6-9-2 **75**.............................. PatDobbs 5 64
(Peter Crate) *trckd ldrs: rdn 2f out: fdd fnl f* **11/1**
2464 **8** *1 1/4* **Head Space (IRE)**[22] 1827 8-8-7 **71**.............................. EdwardGreatrex(5) 7 56
(Brian Barr) *hld up: hdwy over 2f out: effrt over 1f out: wknd fnl f* **12/1**
-000 **9** *1* **Keep It Dark**[19] 1929 7-9-4 **77**.............................. JimCrowley 12 59
(William Knight) *a towards rr* **16/1**
-023 **10** *shd* **Lucky Di**[86] 713 6-9-1 **74**.............................. CharlesBishop 8 56
(Peter Hedger) *mid-div: rdn 2f out: sn wknd* **12/1**
0040 **11** *5* **Noble Deed**[14] 2028 6-8-11 **70**.............................. KierenFox 9 36
(Michael Attwater) *a bhd* **10/1**
1m 11.97s (-0.23) **Going Correction** +0.20s/f (Good) **11** Ran SP% **117.2**
Speed ratings: **109,104,103,102,99 99,98,96,95,95 88**
CSF £54.36 CT £313.12 TOTE £2.80: £1.50, £8.50, £1.90; EX 74.30 Trifecta £521.90.
Owner P Cook **Bred** New Hall Stud **Trained** Liphook, Hants

FOCUS
Probably not the deepest race for the grade but it was turned into a procession by the winner who spreadeagled these.

2470 AL BASTI EQUIWORLD EBF STALLIONS MAIDEN FILLIES' STKS (PLUS 10 RACE) 7f
5:45 (5:46) (Class 5) 3-Y-O
£3,735 (£1,118; £559; £279; £139; £70) **Stalls** Low

Form RPR
0- **1** **Out Of The Dark (IRE)**[331] 3547 3-8-11 0.............................. TomMarquand(3) 2 84
(Richard Hannon) *in tch: hdwy over 2f out: rdn to ld over 1f out: enough in hand and a holding on fnl f: rdn out* **16/1**
2 *nk* **Showreel** 3-9-0 0.............................. PatDobbs 4 83
(Amanda Perrett) *s.i.s: sn mid-div: hdwy 2f out: r.o wl fnl f: clsng on wnr at fin* **9/2**[2]
3 *2* **Rimraam** 3-9-0 0.............................. RobertHavlin 10 78
(John Gosden) *towards rr: hdwy fr 2f out: swtchd rt jst over 1f out: r.o fnl f* **10/1**
-2 **4** *nk* **Sweet Dragon Fly**[57] 1079 3-9-0 0.............................. JimCrowley 3 77+
(Paul Cole) *led: rdn over 2f out: hdd over 1f out: kpt on same pce* **5/2**[1]
5 *1 1/2* **Manaboo (USA)** 3-9-0 0.............................. MartinLane 9 73+
(Charlie Appleby) *racd keenly: mid-div tl hmpd and dropped in rr 6f out: sn pushed along: rdn for stdy prog fr 2f out: kpt on nicely fnl f* **10/1**
3 **6** *nk* **Nightingale Valley**[20] 1894 3-9-0 0.............................. FrederikTylicki 6 72
(Stuart Kittow) *mid-div: rdn 3f out: no imp tl r.o ins fnl f* **9/1**[3]
6- **7** *3/4* **Aghaany**[203] 7628 3-9-0 0.............................. AndreaAtzeni 7 70
(Roger Varian) *mid-div: rdn 2f out: styd on fnl f: nvr trbld ldrs* **9/2**[2]
8 *1 3/4* **Time To Exceed (IRE)** 3-9-0 0.............................. TedDurcan 5 65
(Henry Candy) *trckd ldrs: rdn 2f out: kpt on same pce fnl f* **33/1**
00- **9** *6* **Sparring Queen (USA)**[243] 6588 3-9-0 0.............................. OscarPereira 1 49
(Ralph Beckett) *trckd ldrs: rdn over 2f out: drifted lft: wknd ent fnl f* **33/1**
2- **10** *shd* **Zippy**[208] 7512 3-9-0 0.............................. JimmyFortune 13 49
(Daniel Kubler) *in tch: effrt 2f out: wknd fnl f* **11/1**
0 **11** *1* **Sixties Idol**[8] 2207 3-8-7 0.............................. KillianHennessy(7) 8 46
(Mick Channon) *hmpd on bnd 6f out: a towards rr* **33/1**
0 **12** *1/2* **Eisha Baby**[23] 1814 3-8-7 0.............................. HollieDoyle(7) 15 45
(Richard Hannon) *struggling over 3f out: a towards rr* **40/1**
06 **13** *1 1/2* **Lillyput (IRE)**[8] 2207 3-9-0 0.............................. CharlesBishop 12 41
(Mick Channon) *a towards rr* **25/1**
14 *hd* **St Mary'S** 3-8-9 0.............................. EdwardGreatrex(5) 14 40
(Andrew Balding) *s.i.s: racd green: a towards rr* **33/1**
0 **15** *3/4* **Sante (IRE)**[37] 1436 3-8-11 0.............................. MichaelJMMurphy(3) 11 38
(Charles Hills) *sn pressing ldr: rdn jst ins 3f out: wknd 2f out* **16/1**
1m 29.27s (2.27) **Going Correction** +0.575s/f (Yiel) **15** Ran SP% **131.3**
Speed ratings (Par 96): **110,109,107,107,105 104,104,102,95,95 94,93,91,91,90**
CSF £88.85 TOTE £23.30: £7.20, £2.50, £4.50; EX 193.80 Trifecta £3212.10.
Owner Mrs Boocock, Mrs Doyle, Mr Barry **Bred** D G Iceton **Trained** East Everleigh, Wilts

FOCUS
Probably just ordinary maiden form in truth, certainly in the context of maidens run at this track, but the front two pulled clear and there were some performance of note in behind.
T/Plt: £34.70 to a £1 stake. Pool: £108,846.54 - 2288.19 winning units. T/Qpdt: £6.60 to a £1 stake. Pool: £6,691.02 - 744.94 winning units. **Tim Mitchell**

2436 HAYDOCK (L-H)
Saturday, May 21

OFFICIAL GOING: Good to soft (soft in places) changing to soft after race 6 (4.45)
Wind: Light, half against Weather: Cloudy

2471 CHOICE TEACHERS H'CAP 1m 3f 200y
1:55 (1:56) (Class 3) (0-95,88) 3-Y-O **£9,337** (£2,796; £1,398; £699; £349) **Stalls** Centre

Form RPR
1-21 **1** **Red Verdon (USA)**[17] 1971 3-9-7 **88**.............................. GeorgeBaker 3 107+
(Ed Dunlop) *chsd ldrs: led on bit 2f out: shkn up over 1f out: styd on strly to sn go clr: eased down fnl 75yds* **10/11**[1]
1-03 **2** *5* **Rainbow Dreamer**[8] 2209 3-9-3 **84**.............................. WilliamTwiston-Davies 2 89
(Alan King) *chsd ldr: pushed along 4f out: chalng 3f out: sn led: rdn and hdd 2f out: sn no ch w wnr* **9/1**
-432 **3** *hd* **Emperor Napoleon**[8] 2209 3-8-10 **77**.............................. OisinMurphy 5 82
(Andrew Balding) *hld up pushed along 3f out: rdn and hung lft over 2f out: kpt on to chal for 2nd fnl f: no ch w wnr* **6/1**[3]
41-1 **4** *2 3/4* **Mainstream**[20] 1896 3-9-6 **87**.............................. StevieDonohoe 4 88
(Sir Michael Stoute) *stdd s: ref to settle: hld up: rdn over 2f out: edgd rt u.p over 1f out: no imp* **7/2**[2]
12-0 **5** *8* **Celebration Day (IRE)**[29] 1610 3-9-0 **81**.............................. GrahamLee 1 69
(Simon Crisford) *led: hdd wl over 2f out: n.m.r briefly whn u.p sn after: wknd over 1f out* **7/1**
2m 35.56s (1.76) **Going Correction** +0.225s/f (Good) **5** Ran SP% **111.4**
Speed ratings (Par 103): **103,99,99,97,92**
CSF £9.95 TOTE £1.90: £1.40, £2.40; EX 10.10 Trifecta £29.80.
Owner The Hon R J Arculli **Bred** Liberty Road Stables **Trained** Newmarket, Suffolk

FOCUS
All races run over the Stand Side Home Straight. The going continued to ease and was now good to soft, soft in places, resulting in a number of non-runners. Rail position on the bends meant the opening race was run over 1m4f 23yds.\n\x\x A decent 3yo handicap to start which has been won by some high-class performers in recent years, including the likes of Opinion Poll and Brown Panther. The winning time was 10.56sec outside standard, but quite apart from the softening ground it should be noted that they went a modest pace and the extra yardage should also be taken into account. The winning rider said: "It's good to soft, it's loose on top." Despite all of that, the winner could hardly have been more impressive.

2472 GPW RECRUITMENT H'CAP 2m 45y
2:30 (2:30) (Class 2) (0-100,95) 4-Y-O+ **£12,938** (£3,850; £1,924; £962) **Stalls** Low

Form RPR
00-2 **1** **My Reward**[28] 1642 4-9-5 **93**.............................. DavidAllan 3 100
(Tim Easterby) *mde all: rdn over 2f out: styd on gamely ins fnl f* **4/1**[2]
200- **2** *1 1/4* **Moscato**[224] 7115 5-9-7 **93**..............................(p) LukeMorris 9 98
(Sir Mark Prescott Bt) *sn chsd wnr: rdn and lugged lft whn chalng fr over 2f out: nt qckn ent fnl f: kpt on but no imp on wnr towards fin* **9/2**[3]
30-6 **3** *1 1/4* **Vive Ma Fille (GER)**[7] 2249 4-9-7 **95**.............................. PaulMulrennan 1 99
(Mark Johnston) *chsd ldrs: nt clr run on inner fr over 2f out: rdn over 1f out: kpt on same pce fnl 75yds* **9/1**
0/6 **4** *shd* **Matorico (IRE)**[9] 2194 5-8-12 **84**..............................(tp) GrahamLee 2 87+
(Jonjo O'Neill) *hld up: effrt over 2f out: stdy hdwy over 1f out: styd on towards fin: nt pce to chal* **9/4**[1]
1214 **5** *3 1/4* **Haines**[23] 1802 5-9-0 **89**.............................. RobHornby(3) 5 88
(Andrew Balding) *in tch: pushed along 3f out: one pce u.p fr over 1f out* **16/1**
11/0 **6** *2 1/2* **Venue**[17] 1967 6-9-4 **90**.............................. PaulHanagan 4 86
(Donald McCain) *racd keenly: hld up: rdn over 2f out: sn hung lft u.p: no imp on ldrs* **20/1**
60-4 **7** *1 1/4* **Saved By The Bell (IRE)**[28] 1642 6-9-6 **92**.............................. SamJames 6 87
(David O'Meara) *trckd ldrs: rdn over 3f out: lost pl over 2f out: n.d after* **9/1**
0-35 **8** *6* **Gabrial's King (IRE)**[17] 1967 7-9-6 **92**.............................. DavidNolan 8 80
(Richard Fahey) *hld up: rdn over 2f out: no imp: wl btn fnl f* **13/2**
3m 42.47s (8.17) **Going Correction** +0.225s/f (Good)
WFA 4 from 5yo+ 2lb **8** Ran SP% **112.9**
Speed ratings (Par 109): **88,87,86,86,85 83,83,80**
CSF £21.74 CT £149.71 TOTE £5.00: £1.70, £1.60, £2.90; EX 20.20 Trifecta £174.30.
Owner M J Macleod **Bred** Millsec Limited **Trained** Great Habton, N Yorks

FOCUS
Rail position on the bends meant this race was run over 2m 130yds. A decent staying handicap, but they dawdled for most of the way and it became a 3f sprint. It was therefore no coincidence that the first two held those position throughout and the closers had no chance. It's hard to be overly positive about the form.

2473 SILVER BOWL STKS (H'CAP) 1m
3:05 (3:05) (Class 2) 3-Y-O

£37,350 (£11,184; £5,592; £2,796; £1,398; £702) **Stalls** Low

Form RPR

31-1 **1** **Garcia**[30] 1585 3-8-11 **89** PaulHanagan 13 101+
(Richard Fahey) *in tch: effrt over 2f out: r.o to dispute ld ins fnl f: led fnl strides* **7/2**[1]

1-32 **2** *hd* **California Whip (USA)**[10] 2161 3-9-0 **92** SeanLevey 4 104+
(Richard Hannon) *in tch: rdn over 2f out: r.o to dispute ld ins fnl f: hdd fnl strides* **4/1**[2]

3-62 **3** *1 ¼* **Above N Beyond**[16] 1975 3-9-7 **99** (t) RichardKingscote 9 108
(Tom Dascombe) *led: rdn 2f out: hdd ins fnl f: kpt on u.p: hld nr fin* **12/1**

1323 **4** *4* **Mariee**[9] 2179 3-8-3 **81** AndrewMullen 11 81
(Mark Johnston) *chsd ldrs: rdn over 2f out: styd on same pce fnl f* **20/1**

23-1 **5** *3* **Wild Hacked (USA)**[19] 1931 3-8-4 **82** LukeMorris 3 75
(Marco Botti) *s.i.s: in rr: hld up: hdwy over 3f out: rdn to chse ldrs 2f out: one pce and no imp fnl f* **6/1**[3]

22-6 **6** *½* **Kingston Kurrajong**[15] 1994 3-8-11 **89** OisinMurphy 7 84+
(Andrew Balding) *hld up: rdn and nt clr run 2f out: kpt on ins fnl f: nvr able to chal* **33/1**

5-06 **7** *¾* **Explosive Power (IRE)**[21] 1851 3-8-10 **88** JoeyHaynes 12 78
(K R Burke) *midfield: pushed along over 4f out: no imp on ldrs* **50/1**

-365 **8** *¾* **Beaverbrook**[21] 1866 3-9-5 **97** AdamKirby 14 85
(Mark Johnston) *chsd ldrs: rdn over 2f out: sn outpcd: no imp after* **20/1**

01-2 **9** *2* **Another Touch**[21] 1851 3-9-2 **94** DavidNolan 2 78
(Richard Fahey) *midfield: pushed along and lost pl over 2f out: n.d after* **12/1**

5-21 **10** *2 ¼* **Shaiyem (IRE)**[14] 2029 3-8-8 **86** HarryBentley 10 65
(Richard Hannon) *racd keenly: hld up: rdn 2f out: nvr able to trble ldrs* **6/1**[3]

1-35 **11** *1 ¼* **Special Season**[57] 1071 3-9-5 **97** PatCosgrave 16 73
(William Haggas) *hld up: pushed along over 3f out: hdwy over 2f out: nt get to ldrs: wknd ins fnl f* **11/1**

-265 **12** *4 ½* **Ode To Evening**[16] 1975 3-9-6 **98** PaulMulrennan 15 63
(Mark Johnston) *chsd ldr tl rdn and lost pl over 2f out* **40/1**

44-0 **13** *50* **Still On Top**[16] 1975 3-9-2 **94** DavidAllan 6
(Tim Easterby) *in rr: pushed along over 3f out: eased whn wl btn 2f out: t.o* **25/1**

1m 44.36s (0.66) **Going Correction** +0.225s/f (Good) **13** Ran SP% **115.2**
Speed ratings (Par 105): **105,104,103,99,96 96,95,94,92,90 89,84,34**
CSF £14.79 CT £154.40 TOTE £4.10: £2.00, £2.10, £2.70; EX 17.10 Trifecta £130.80.
Owner Highclere Thoroughbred Racing (Pelham) **Bred** Highclere Stud **Trained** Musley Bank, N Yorks
■ Stewards' Enquiry : Sean Levey two-day ban (5-6 Jun): used whip above permitted level

FOCUS
Rail position on the bends meant this race was run over 1m 43yds. A warm renewal of the Silver Bowl as would be expected, with quite a few of these open to a lot more improvement and it was those types who dominated the market. Two of them fought out the finish and although the pair made contact in the very latter stages, the Stewards rightly allowed the result to stand. Unlike in the earlier races on the round course, the runners came up the centre in the straight and the first three pulled well clear. The unexposed winner built on his Beverley win.

2474 EBF STALLIONS CECIL FRAIL STKS (LISTED RACE) (FILLIES' & MARES) 6f
3:40 (3:40) (Class 1) 3-Y-O+

£26,653 (£10,105; £5,057; £2,519; £1,264; £634) **Stalls** Centre

Form RPR

20/0 **1** **Jane's Memory (IRE)**[17] 1969 4-9-3 95 RichardKingscote 5 106
(Rae Guest) *chsd ldrs: rdn 2f out: r.o to ld ins fnl f: in command nr fin* **20/1**

2-61 **2** *½* **Ridge Ranger (IRE)**[14] 2042 5-9-7 103 JasonHart 4 108
(Eric Alston) *prom: rdn 2f out: led over 1f out: hdd ins fnl f: hld nr fin* **3/1**[2]

350- **3** *¾* **Interception (IRE)**[217] 7278 6-9-3 108 GeorgeBaker 2 102
(David Lanigan) *hld up: hdwy over 2f out: rdn to chse ldrs over 1f out: styd on ins fnl f: nt quite pce of front two* **5/2**[1]

-042 **4** *1 ¾* **Marsh Hawk**[14] 2042 4-9-3 99 (b) SeanLevey 6 96
(Richard Hannon) *led: rdn and hdd over 1f out: stl cl up ins fnl f: no ex fnl 75yds* **4/1**[3]

35-0 **5** *3 ¾* **Priceless**[24] 1773 3-8-8 98 [1] LukeMorris 7 82
(Clive Cox) *missed break: in rr: rdn 3f out: sme hdwy over 1f out: nvr able to chal* **13/2**

12-4 **6** *17* **Imtiyaaz (IRE)**[14] 2042 4-9-3 93 HarryBentley 9 30
(Roger Varian) *in tch: rdn over 2f out: wknd wl over 1f out* **9/2**

0-00 **7** *7* **Souville**[14] 2042 5-9-3 88 (p) MartinHarley 11 7
(Chris Wall) *racd alone stands' side: in tch: rdn and wknd over 2f out: bhd over 1f out* **33/1**

1m 13.71s (-0.09) **Going Correction** +0.10s/f (Good)
WFA 3 from 4yo+ 9lb **7** Ran SP% **112.8**
Speed ratings (Par 108): **104,103,102,100,95 72,63**
CSF £77.03 TOTE £24.30: £6.80, £2.10; EX 129.00 Trifecta £730.40.
Owner P O'Neill **Bred** Knocklong House Stud **Trained** Newmarket, Suffolk

FOCUS
An interesting fillies' and mares' Listed sprint in which four of these had met in a similar event at Nottingham a fortnight earlier, but the result of this race was a surprise to most punters, with the change in the ground appearing to make all the difference. All bar one raced up the centre. The runner-up has been rated to form.

2475 TEMPLE STKS (GROUP 2) 5f
4:10 (4:11) (Class 1) 3-Y-O+

£56,710 (£21,500; £10,760; £5,360; £2,690; £1,350) **Stalls** Centre

Form RPR

05-1 **1** **Profitable (IRE)**[21] 1862 4-9-4 112 AdamKirby 12 120
(Clive Cox) *chsd ldrs travelling wl: drifted lft ins fnl f: sn led narrowly: r.o and continued to drift lft: a doing enough nr fin whn bmpd rival* **8/1**[3]

21- **2** *nk* **Mecca's Angel (IRE)**[274] 5600 5-9-1 120 PaulMulrennan 7 116
(Michael Dods) *w ldr: rdn to ld over 1f out: intimidated and carried lft ins fnl f: sn hdd narrowly: r.o u.p: hld whn bmpd nr fin* **1/1**[1]

10-3 **3** *2 ¼* **Waady (IRE)**[21] 1862 4-9-4 112 GrahamLee 2 111
(John Gosden) *hld up: rdn over 1f out: hdwy ins fnl f: r.o: gng on at fin* **9/1**

064- **4** *hd* **Pearl Secret**[230] 6971 7-9-4 109 OisinMurphy 5 110
(David Barron) *hld up: rdn and hdwy over 1f out: r.o ins fnl f: nt get to ldrs* **10/1**

0-46 **5** *nk* **Aeolus**[21] 1862 5-9-4 108 LukeMorris 10 109
(Ed Walker) *chsd ldrs: rdn over 2f out: nt qckn over 1f out: kpt on u.p ins fnl f* **18/1**

1-61 **6** *shd* **Kachy**[15] 1996 3-8-10 109 RichardKingscote 6 106
(Tom Dascombe) *chsd ldrs: rdn over 1f out: no ex fnl 50yds* **10/1**

-500 **7** *1 ¾* **Move In Time**[21] 1862 8-9-4 109 DavidNolan 13 103
(David O'Meara) *in tch: rdn 2f out: outpcd 1f out* **25/1**

3-35 **8** *hd* **Muthmir (IRE)**[56] 1104 6-9-4 114 PaulHanagan 3 102
(William Haggas) *hld up: rdn over 1f out: one pce ins fnl f* **7/1**[2]

4016 **9** *½* **Sir Maximilian (IRE)**[5] 2317 7-9-4 112 (p) PatCosgrave 11 100
(Ian Williams) *hld up: rdn 2f out: hdwy over 1f out: styd on u.p ins fnl f: no ex fnl 75yds and hmpd whn n.m.r* **16/1**

60-0 **10** *1 ¼* **Justineo**[21] 1862 7-9-4 105 (p) SeanLevey 16 96
(Robert Cowell) *led: rdn and hdd over 1f out: wknd ins fnl f* **50/1**

00-0 **11** *1 ¼* **Steps (IRE)**[21] 1862 8-9-4 112 (b) HarryBentley 1 91
(Roger Varian) *in rr: rdn 1/2-way: nvr a threat* **33/1**

59.4s (-1.40) **Going Correction** +0.10s/f (Good)
WFA 3 from 4yo+ 8lb **11** Ran SP% **121.7**
Speed ratings (Par 115): **115,114,110,110,110 109,107,106,106,104 102**
CSF £16.68 TOTE £8.40: £1.70, £1.10, £2.50; EX 22.20 Trifecta £162.50.
Owner A D Spence **Bred** Con Harrington **Trained** Lambourn, Berks
■ Stewards' Enquiry : Adam Kirby two-day ban (5-6 June): careless riding

FOCUS
This Group 2 sprint was affected by non-runners, though Take Cover and Cotai Glory ran in the Listed Achilles Stakes here last night when the ground was still on the quick side, and that decision was rather vindicated when they finished first and second. A decent line-up remained including two previous Group 1 winners, while six of these met in the Palace House Stakes at Newmarket three weeks ago, but punters only wanted to know about one horse. The race produced a thrilling finish, but things got tight between the first two when the winner hung away to his left late on and the Stewards again had to take a look. However, the result was allowed to stand and that looked the right decision.

2476 WALSH IBS H'CAP 6f
4:45 (4:46) (Class 3) (0-90,89) 4-Y-O+ **£8,086** (£2,406; £1,202; £601) **Stalls** Centre

Form RPR

121- **1** **Mehronissa**[245] 6540 4-9-7 **89** OisinMurphy 8 100+
(Ed Vaughan) *dwlt: hld up towards stands' side: angled to centre 3f out: pushed along and hdwy 2f out: rdn to chse ldr appr fnl f: led 110yds out: kpt on* **10/1**

05-3 **2** *1* **Shipyard (USA)**[15] 1990 7-9-4 **89** AlistairRawlinson(3) 5 97
(Michael Appleby) *led far side and overall ldr: rdn over 1f out: hdd 110yds out: one pce: 1st of 7 in gp* **8/1**[2]

00-4 **3** *nse* **Duke Cosimo**[21] 1869 6-8-9 **77** PJMcDonald 4 85
(Michael Herrington) *hld up far side: pushed along over 1f out: angled rt appr fnl f: sn rdn: kpt on: nrst fin: 2nd of 7 in gp* **9/1**[3]

6-50 **4** *1* **Snap Shots (IRE)**[17] 1968 4-9-3 **85** (t) RichardKingscote 2 90
(Tom Dascombe) *w ldr far side: rdn 2f out: no ex fnl 110yds: 3rd of 7 in gp* **14/1**

0-32 **5** *2 ½* **Ocean Sheridan (IRE)**[33] 1522 4-9-2 **84** PaulMulrennan 6 81
(Michael Dods) *dwlt: sn chsd ldrs far side: rdn 2f out: wknd ins fnl f: 4th of 7 in gp* **8/1**[2]

-000 **6** *1 ½* **Ballymore Castle (IRE)**[20] 1887 4-9-6 **88** DavidNolan 1 80
(Richard Fahey) *chsd ldrs far side: rdn 2f out: wknd ins fnl f: 5th of 7 in gp* **14/1**

5-30 **7** *½* **God Willing**[10] 2158 5-9-6 **88** (t) PatCosgrave 10 78
(Declan Carroll) *chsd ldr stands' side: rdn 2f out: sltly hmpd appr fnl f: edgd lft and wknd: 2nd of 6 in gp* **14/1**

200- **8** *shd* **Harwoods Volante (IRE)**[238] 6746 5-9-4 **86** SamJames 11 76
(David O'Meara) *in tch stands' side: rdn 2f out: edgd lft and wknd ins fnl f: 3rd of 6 in gpo* **20/1**

00-0 **9** *¾* **Meshardal (GER)**[15] 1997 6-9-1 **83** JamesSullivan 7 71
(Ruth Carr) *chsd ldrs far side: rdn 2f out: wknd fnl f: 6th of 7 in gp* **14/1**

1514 **10** *hd* **Fingal's Cave (IRE)**[15] 1997 4-9-0 **82** GrahamLee 12 69
(Mick Channon) *led gp towards stands' side: arnd l 2 l bhd ldrs on far side: rdn 2f out: sn wknd: 4th of 6 in gp* **5/1**[1]

3-00 **11** *nk* **Canyari (IRE)**[10] 2158 5-9-3 **85** PaulHanagan 15 71
(Richard Fahey) *hld up stands' side: rdn over 3f out: edgd lft fnl 2f: nvr threatened: 5th of 6 in gp* **5/1**[1]

4510 **12** *½* **Dinneratmidnight**[21] 1869 5-9-1 **83** (e) ConnorBeasley 13 67
(Richard Guest) *chsd ldr towards stands' side: rdn 2f out: wknd: last of 6 in gp* **16/1**

-463 **13** *10* **Mappin Time (IRE)**[28] 1650 8-9-1 **83** (b) DavidAllan 3 35
(Tim Easterby) *hld up far side: rdn over 2f out: sn wknd* **16/1**

1m 15.17s (1.37) **Going Correction** +0.425s/f (Yiel) **13** Ran SP% **117.8**
Speed ratings (Par 107): **107,105,105,104,100 98,98,98,97,96 96,95,82**
CSF £86.55 CT £754.49 TOTE £9.40: £3.40, £2.20, £4.70; EX 68.10 Trifecta £896.60.
Owner Salem Rashid **Bred** Carmel Stud **Trained** Newmarket, Suffolk

FOCUS
A decent sprint handicap. The field split into two early and those that raced more towards the far side were favoured.

2477 RACING UK NOW IN HD H'CAP 7f
5:20 (5:21) (Class 3) (0-95,94) 3-Y-O **£8,086** (£2,406; £1,202; £601) **Stalls** Low

Form RPR

-360 **1** **Calder Prince (IRE)**[79] 807 3-9-7 **94** RichardKingscote 6 102
(Tom Dascombe) *mde all: rdn over 2f out: kpt on wl* **16/1**

0-04 **2** *1 ¼* **Lagenda**[10] 2161 3-8-10 **83** (p) PaulMulrennan 8 87
(Kevin Ryan) *midfield: rdn and hdwy to chse ldr over 2f out: kpt on* **9/1**

40-5 **3** *¾* **Young John (IRE)**[21] 1851 3-8-9 **82** GrahamLee 3 84
(Richard Fahey) *in tch: rdn to chse ldr over 1f out: kpt on same pce ins fnl f* **14/1**

0-51 **4** *hd* **Fashaak (IRE)**[7] 2239 3-8-9 **82** SeanLevey 2 85+
(Richard Hannon) *midfield: pushed along and hdwy to chse ldr 2f out: drvn over 1f out: half bucked and rdr briefly unbalanced 1f out: one pce ins fnl f* **3/1**[1]

6-31 **5** *nk* **King Of Naples**[23] 1815 3-8-10 **90** GeorgeWood(7) 9 91
(James Fanshawe) *hld up: racd keenly: rdn and hdwy over 1f out: one pce ins fnl f* **9/2**[2]

5-31 **6** *1 ¾* **Viscount Barfield**[45] 1257 3-8-2 **75** oh1 JoeyHaynes 5 71
(Andrew Balding) *hld up: rdn and hdwy over 2f out: chsd ldr over 1f out: wknd fnl 110yds* **11/1**

100- **7** *2 ½* **Firedanser**[237] 6774 3-8-4 **77** JamesSullivan 4 67
(Richard Fahey) *trckd ldr: rdn over 2f out: wknd over 1f out* **20/1**

401- **8** *nk* **Majdool (IRE)**[234] 6853 3-9-4 **91** PaulHanagan 7 80
(Roger Varian) *trckd ldr: rdn over 2f out: wknd appr fnl f* **8/1**[3]

1512 **9** *nk* **Willsy**[21] 1847 3-8-4 **77** LukeMorris 10 65
(Mick Channon) *dwlt: hld up: rdn over 3f out: nvr threatened* **10/1**

31 **10** *61* **Rosenborg Rider (IRE)**[66] 952 3-8-6 **79** OisinMurphy 1 +
(Ralph Beckett) *in tch: lost pl over 4f out: sn dropped to rr: rdn over 3f out: sn wl bhd: eased* **9/2**[2]

1m 33.71s (3.01) **Going Correction** +0.55s/f (Yiel) **10** Ran SP% **117.2**
Speed ratings (Par 103): **104,102,101,101,101 99,96,95,95,25**
CSF £152.76 CT £2113.17 TOTE £16.40: £4.60, £3.30, £3.00; EX 167.00 Trifecta £1196.70.
Owner Peter Birbeck **Bred** Michael Pitt **Trained** Malpas, Cheshire
■ Stewards' Enquiry : James Sullivan The Veterinary Officer reported that upon inspection, FIREDANSER, was a gelding and not a colt as published in the racecard.
Sean Levey jockey said the colt bucked approaching the final furlong

FOCUS
Rail position on the bends meant this race was run over 7f 43yds and the going was changed to soft before this decent 3yo handicap. Again they came up the centre in the straight.
T/Jkpt: Not won. T/Plt: £91.60 to a £1 stake. Pool of £134167.34 - 1068.54 winning tickets. T/Qpdt: £25.20 to a £1 stake. Pool of £8907.06 - 260.80 winning tickets. **Darren Owen**

2247 NEWMARKET (R-H)

Saturday, May 21

OFFICIAL GOING: Good to firm (8.1)
Wind: medium, half behind Weather: light cloud, shower race 7

2478 ANDREW FLEET EBF STALLIONS NOVICE STKS (PLUS 10 RACE) 6f
1:50 (1:53) (Class 4) 2-Y-O **£4,528** (£1,347; £673; £336) **Stalls** High

Form RPR

4 **1** **Nibras Bounty (IRE)**[9] 2180 2-9-2 0 TomQueally 1 80
(Richard Hannon) *chsd ldr tl led ent fnl 3f: rdn and jnd 2f out: styd on u.p and forged ahd fnl 75yds: rdn out* **8/1**[3]

2 *1 ¼* **Evergate** 2-9-2 0 DarryllHolland 2 76
(Hugo Palmer) *hld up in last pair: hdwy to chse ldng pair over 3f out: clsd to chal and rdn 2f out: edgd lft over 1f out: no ex and wknd fnl 75yds* **6/4**[1]

3 *4 ½* **See The City (IRE)** 2-9-2 0 JoeFanning 5 63
(Mark Johnston) *racd keenly: led tl ent fnl 3f: 3rd and outpcd whn hung rt over 1f out: kpt on same pce and wl hld fnl f* **11/2**[2]

4 *1 ¾* **Native Prospect** 2-9-2 0 DavidProbert 6 58
(Andrew Balding) *awkward leaving stalls and s.i.s: rn green in last pair: 4th and outpcd 2f out: wl hld and kpt on same pce after* **33/1**

5 *5* **Phoenix Dawn** 2-9-2 0 MartinDwyer 3 43
(Brendan Powell) *chsd ldng pair: sn pushed along: lost pl over 3f out: bhd 2f out: rn green and wknd over 1f out* **100/1**

1m 13.94s (1.74) **Going Correction** +0.20s/f (Good) **5** Ran SP% **70.4**
Speed ratings (Par 95): **96,94,88,86,79**
CSF £7.83 TOTE £6.60: £2.50, £1.10; EX 8.80 Trifecta £14.10.
Owner Saeed H Al Tayer **Bred** Jim McDonald **Trained** East Everleigh, Wilts
■ Deningy was withdrawn.Price at time of withdrawal 6/4. Rule 4 applies to all bets- deduct 40p in the pound.

FOCUS
It was dry overnight but 3mm of water had been applied to the course on Friday afternoon. The going was given as good to firm (GoingStick: 8.1). Stands' side course in use. With \bDeningy\p, who created such a good impression on his debut at Ascot, playing up beforehand and withdrawn at the start, this proved weaker than expected. The first pair came clear.

2479 WESTMERE FARMS H'CAP 1m
2:20 (2:23) (Class 3) (0-90,90) 3-Y-O **£9,703** (£2,887; £1,443; £721) **Stalls** High

Form RPR

1-2 **1** **Chelsea Lad (IRE)**[28] 1623 3-9-6 **89** FergusSweeney 10 102+
(Martyn Meade) *hld up wl in tch in midfield: nt clr run jst over 2f: swtchd lft and bumping w rival over 1f out: in the clr and qcknd u.p 1f out: gd hdwy to ld 100yds out: r.o wl* **5/2**[1]

10-3 **2** *¾* **Barleysugar (IRE)**[23] 1809 3-9-3 **86** GrahamGibbons 5 95
(Sir Michael Stoute) *hld up in tch: swtchd rt and effrt over 2f out: hdwy u.p to ld and edgd lft jst ins fnl f: hdd 100yds out: styd on but nt quite pce of wnr* **6/1**

43-0 **3** *2 ½* **Jimenez (IRE)**[26] 1714 3-8-7 **76** JoeFanning 7 79
(Brian Meehan) *trckd ldng trio: nt clr run over 2f out: swtchd rt and hdwy over 1f out: chsng ldrs but struggling to qckn whn sltly impeded ins fnl f: kpt on same pce fnl 100yds* **12/1**

5-63 **4** *nk* **Storm Rising (IRE)**[7] 2237 3-9-7 **90** JamesDoyle 1 93+
(Richard Hannon) *wnt rt s: sn swtchd lft and in tch in rr: clsd and nt clr run over 2f out: swtchd rt and hdwy 1f out: nt clr run and swtchd rt again ins fnl f: styd on* **9/2**[3]

-000 **5** *2* **Essenaitch (IRE)**[15] 1992 3-8-11 **80** SaleemGolam 9 78
(David Evans) *hld up in tch in last pair: effrt and swtchd rt over 1f out: hdwy u.p 1f out: no ex and outpcd ins fnl f* **50/1**

2-1 **6** *2 ½* **War Story (IRE)**[26] 1701 3-9-2 **85** TomQueally 3 77
(Luca Cumani) *t.k.h: hld up wl in tch in midfield: clsd 3f out: rdn to ld over 1f out: hdd and pushed lft jst ins fnl f: sn wknd* **4/1**[2]

261- **7** *2 ½* **Dream Of Summer (IRE)**[184] 7902 3-8-8 **77** DavidProbert 4 63
(Andrew Balding) *t.k.h: led: rdn and hdd over 1f out: no ex and btn whn nt clr run and hmpd jst ins fnl f: wknd* **14/1**

1-23 **8** *1* **Zzoro (IRE)**[17] 1971 3-9-4 **87** DarryllHolland 2 71
(Charles Hills) *t.k.h: chsd ldrs: rdn jst over 2f out: struggling to qckn whn stmbld jst over 1f out: wknd ins fnl f* **9/1**

41-5 **9** *7* **Zealous (IRE)**[14] 2029 3-8-12 **81** MartinDwyer 6 49+
(Alan Swinbank) *chsd ldrs: rdn 2f out: losing pl whn bumping w wnr over 1f out: sn bhd: wknd fnl f* **16/1**

1m 38.37s (-0.23) **Going Correction** +0.20s/f (Good) **9** Ran SP% **113.2**
Speed ratings (Par 103): **109,108,105,105,103 100,98,97,90**
CSF £17.38 CT £148.62 TOTE £3.60: £1.70, £2.00, £3.10; EX 17.00 Trifecta £197.30.
Owner Richard Morecombe **Bred** Old Carhue & Graeng Bloodstock **Trained** Newmarket, Suffolk
■ Stewards' Enquiry : Fergus Sweeney three-day ban (5-7 June): careless riding.

FOCUS
A messy affair but an impressive winner.

2480 FRED MURFITT H'CAP 6f
2:55 (2:55) (Class 2) (0-105,97) 3-Y-O+ **£12,938** (£3,850; £1,924; £962) **Stalls** High

Form RPR

1-2 **1** **Yattwee (USA)**[21] 1865 3-9-4 **96** JamesDoyle 5 103
(Saeed bin Suroor) *chsd ldrs: rdn to chal 2f out: led over 1f out: edgd rt and 1f out: hdd ins fnl f: kpt on wl u.p to ld again last strides* **11/8**[1]

410- **2** *nk* **Sir Robert Cheval**[210] 7455 5-9-9 **95** LouisSteward(3) 3 103
(Robert Cowell) *trckd ldrs: effrt to chal over 1f out: bmpd 1f out: drvn to ld ins fnl f: edgd lft wl ins fnl f: hdd last strides* **10/1**

1-00 **3** *2* **Mujassam**[21] 1856 4-10-0 **97** (v) JackMitchell 7 99
(Roger Varian) *led: rdn 2f out: hdd over 1f out: 3rd and styd on same pce fnl f* **10/1**

0-25 **4** *4* **Solar Flair**[21] 1856 4-9-10 **93** (p) AmirQuinn 4 82
(William Knight) *w ldr: rdn and ev ch 2f out: 4th and outpcd whn edgd lft over 1f out: wknd ins fnl f* **7/1**[3]

15-0 **5** *2 ¾* **Whitman**[21] 1865 3-9-3 **95** JoeFanning 10 73
(Mark Johnston) *in tch in midfield: effrt 2f out: outpcd and unbalanced on downhill run over 1f out: sn hung rt and wknd fnl f* **12/1**

-062 **6** *1 ½* **Handsome Dude**[7] 2259 4-9-6 **89** (b) GrahamGibbons 6 64
(David Barron) *s.i.s: niggled along in last trio: rdn over 2f out: no imp and btn over 1f out: wknd fnl f* **4/1**[2]

00-0 **7** *2* **Highland Acclaim (IRE)**[10] 2158 5-9-4 **92** JoshDoyle(5) 2 61
(David O'Meara) *stdd and hmpd leaving stalls: t.k.h: hld up in tch towards rr: effrt 2f out: sn rdn and outpcd: wknd fnl f* **20/1**

6510 **8** *5* **Zac Brown (IRE)**[21] 1857 5-9-2 **90** AaronJones(5) 1 43
(Charlie Wallis) *stdd and wnt sharply lft s: hld up in tch: effrt 2f out: sn btn: bhd ins fnl f* **16/1**

000- **9** *shd* **Bahamian Heights**[161] 8205 5-9-0 **83** DavidProbert 9 35
(Robert Cowell) *in tch in midfield: rdn 2f out: outpcd and btn over 1f out: fdd ins fnl f* **16/1**

1m 12.02s (-0.18) **Going Correction** +0.20s/f (Good)
WFA 3 from 4yo+ 9lb **9** Ran SP% **117.0**
Speed ratings (Par 109): **109,108,105,100,96 94,92,85,85**
CSF £16.90 CT £104.53 TOTE £2.20: £1.10, £3.30, £2.80; EX 16.60 Trifecta £135.30.
Owner Godolphin **Bred** Darley **Trained** Newmarket, Suffolk

FOCUS
Nothing got into this from off the pace, the principals all close up from early on.

2481 PANTILE STUD FAIRWAY STKS (LISTED RACE) 1m 2f
3:30 (3:32) (Class 1) 3-Y-O **£20,982** (£7,955; £3,981; £1,983) **Stalls** High

Form RPR

2-52 **1** **Steel Of Madrid (IRE)**[14] 2029 3-9-3 98 TomQueally 3 105
(Richard Hannon) *chsd ldr tl 5f out: rdn and ev ch over 2f out: led ins fnl f: styd on wl to forge ahd fnl 75yds: rdn out* **3/1**[2]

2-12 **2** *1 ½* **Linguistic (IRE)**[15] 1994 3-9-3 103 JamesDoyle 4 102
(John Gosden) *trckd ldrs: clsd to chal over 2f out: rdn to ld over 1f out: edgd lft 1f out: hdd ins fnl f: no ex and outpcd fnl 75yds* **4/7**[1]

1-36 **3** *nse* **Tathqeef (USA)**[21] 1866 3-9-3 95 (p) DavidProbert 5 101
(John Gosden) *rousted along briefly leaving stalls: hld up in tch: hdwy to chse ldr 5f out: rdn to ld over 2f out: hdd over 1f out: stl ev ch whn squeezed for room 1f out: styd on same pce ins fnl f* **15/2**[3]

120- **4** *7* **Champagne City**[245] 6513 3-9-3 98 JoeFanning 1 88
(Mark Johnston) *led: hdd and rdn over 2f out: sn dropped out: wknd over 1f out* **14/1**

2m 9.77s (3.97) **Going Correction** +0.20s/f (Good) **4** Ran SP% **107.1**
Speed ratings (Par 107): **92,90,90,85**
CSF £5.15 TOTE £3.50; EX 4.10 Trifecta £8.00.
Owner Michael Pescod **Bred** Jeddah Bloodstock **Trained** East Everleigh, Wilts

FOCUS
The early pace wasn't searching and the race developed into a bit of a sprint-off between the first three.

2482 GALICUIX H'CAP 1m 4f
4:05 (4:05) (Class 2) (0-105,105) 4-Y-O+**£16,172** (£4,812; £2,405; £1,202) **Stalls** Centre

Form RPR

2300 **1** **John Reel (FR)**[17] 1967 7-9-0 **98** DarryllHolland 9 104
(David Evans) *chsd ldr: clsd to join ldr over 2f out: rdn 2f out: sustained chal and led wl ins fnl f: styd on* **14/1**

5100 **2** *¾* **Watersmeet**[20] 1885 5-9-0 **98** JoeFanning 5 103
(Mark Johnston) *led: rdn and jnd 2f out: sustained battle after and kpt on tl hdd and no ex wl ins fnl f* **8/1**

5443 **3** *nk* **Plutocracy (IRE)**[14] 2024 6-8-2 **91** HectorCrouch(5) 3 95+
(Gary Moore) *hld up in tch in last pair: effrt and hdwy 2f out: swtchd rt and chsd ldrs 1f out: ev ch ins fnl f: styd on same pce u.p fnl 100yds* **7/2**[3]

250- **4** *5* **Antiquarium (IRE)**[259] 6076 4-9-2 **100** JamesDoyle 4 96
(Charlie Appleby) *in tch in midfield: clsd to chse ldrs and rdn 2f out: drvn and no ex ent fnl f: wknd ins fnl f* **11/4**[1]

546- **5** *1* **Ajman Bridge**[273] 5641 6-9-7 **105** JackMitchell 7 100
(Roger Varian) *hld up in tch in midfield: effrt to chse ldrs and rdn 2f out: no ex u.p ent fnl f: wknd ins fnl f* **3/1**[2]

0-06 **6** *6* **Sennockian Star**[16] 1972 6-8-8 **92** (v) LiamJones 1 77
(Mark Johnston) *chsd ldrs: rdn and outpcd whn swtchd rt over 2f out: wknd over 1f out* **12/1**

345- **7** *30* **Felix Mendelssohn (IRE)**[266] 5869 5-9-5 **103** FergusSweeney 2 40
(David Simcock) *stdd s: hld up in tch in last pair: effrt over 2f out: sn btn: wl bhd and eased ins fnl f: t.o* **6/1**

2m 34.03s (2.03) **Going Correction** +0.20s/f (Good) **7** Ran SP% **113.6**
Speed ratings (Par 109): **101,100,100,96,96 92,72**
CSF £115.02 CT £481.55 TOTE £16.20: £6.50, £4.00; EX 140.80 Trifecta £708.50.
Owner Walters Plant Hire Ltd **Bred** Ecurie Biraben **Trained** Pandy, Monmouths

FOCUS
The re-positioning of the bend into the home straight increased the distance of this race by 9yds. A competitive middle-distance handicap.

2483 C J MURFITT LTD MAIDEN FILLIES' STKS (PLUS 10 RACE) 7f
4:40 (4:41) (Class 5) 3-Y-O **£3,881** (£1,155; £577; £288) **Stalls** High

Form RPR

4 **1** **Clear Water (IRE)**[37] 1436 3-9-0 0 JamesDoyle 14 85+
(Saeed bin Suroor) *chsd ldr and clr of field: clsd over 2f out: led over 1f out and sn rdn clr: r.o wl: readily* **15/8**[1]

5- **2** *4 ½* **Volition (IRE)**[278] 5438 3-9-0 0 GrahamGibbons 1 74+
(Sir Michael Stoute) *t.k.h: hld up in tch towards rr: pushed along and swtchd lft 2f out: hdwy over 1f out: styd on to go 2nd 100yds out: no ch w wnr* **9/1**

4-4 **3** *½* **Pietrafiore (IRE)**[15] 2009 3-9-0 0 JoeFanning 11 73
(Charlie Appleby) *hld up in tch in midfield: effrt and hdwy 2f out: no ch w wnr but kpt on u.p to go 3rd 100yds out* **5/2**[2]

4 *2 ¼* **Side Hill (USA)** 3-9-0 0 RobertTart 7 68+
(John Gosden) *s.i.s: rn green in rr: swtchd rt and hdwy over 1f out: styd on wl to pass btn horses ins fnl f: nvr trbld ldrs* **15/2**

0 **5** *hd* **Zabeel Princess**[29] 1597 3-9-0 0 .... JackMitchell 4 67
(Roger Varian) *led and sn clr: rdn and hdd over 1f out: sn btn: wknd and lost 3 pls fnl 100yds* **12/1**

4-6 **6** *1 3/4* **Nicarra (IRE)**[15] 2009 3-9-0 0 .... FergusSweeney 2 66+
(Henry Candy) *chsd ldrs: rdn and no imp on ldng pair 2f out: outpcd and btn whn short of room jst over 1f out: wknd ins fnl f* **7/1**[3]

0 **7** *hd* **Baileys Perle (IRE)**[9] 2177 3-9-0 0 .... IrineuGoncalves 13 63
(Chris Dwyer) *chsd ldng pair: rdn and no imp 2f out: lost pl and edgd rt jst over 1f out: wknd fnl f* **100/1**

8 *1 1/2* **Alaskan Breeze (IRE)** 3-9-0 0 .... MartinDwyer 8 59+
(Brian Meehan) *s.i.s: hld up in tch: outpcd over 2f out: pushed along and stmbld wl over 1f out: swtchd rt 1f out: n.d but kpt on steadily ins fnl f* **14/1**

9 *shd* **Luang Prabang (IRE)** 3-8-7 0 .... SamuelClarke(7) 12 59+
(Chris Wall) *wl in tch in midfield: pushed along and losing pl whn hmpd 2f out: wknd over 1f out* **33/1**

0 **10** *1 3/4* **Infiniti (IRE)**[9] 2177 3-9-0 0 .... SaleemGolam 5 55+
(Rae Guest) *t.k.h: rng green and hld up towards rr: rdn 2f out: struggling and outpcd over 1f out: wknd fnl f* **100/1**

0 **11** *17* **Purple Party (IRE)**[15] 2009 3-9-0 0 .... DarryllHolland 10 14
(George Margarson) *t.k.h: hld up in tch in midfield: rdn 2f out: sn btn: bhd fnl f* **100/1**

00 **12** *17* **Theydon Girls**[26] 1704 3-9-0 0 .... TomQueally 6
(Peter Charalambous) *t.k.h: midfield early tl stdd bk towards rr after 2f: lost tch 2f out: t.o* **100/1**

1m 25.83s (0.43) **Going Correction** +0.20s/f (Good) **12** Ran SP% **118.9**
Speed ratings (Par 96): **105,99,99,96,96 94,94,92,92,90 71,51**
CSF £20.12 TOTE £2.60: £1.20, £2.10, £1.80; EX 18.10 Trifecta £51.30.
Owner Godolphin **Bred** Darley **Trained** Newmarket, Suffolk

FOCUS
A fair maiden.

2484 MAINSTAY H'CAP — 1m 2f
5:15 (5:15) (Class 2) (0-100,96) 4-Y-0+ **£12,938** (£3,850; £1,924; £962) **Stalls** High

Form RPR

4035 **1** **Revolutionist (IRE)**[10] 2157 4-9-7 96 .... JamesDoyle 7 105
(Mark Johnston) *mde all: rdn 2f out: kpt on gamely u.p: forged ahd 100yds out: styd on: rdn out* **5/2**[1]

1000 **2** *1 1/2* **Master Of Finance (IRE)**[10] 2157 5-9-7 96 ....(b) JoeFanning 3 102
(Mark Johnston) *chsd wnr thrght: rdn 2f out: ev ch 2f out: wandered rt but stl ev ch 1f out: no ex and outpcd fnl 100yds* **20/1**

1-05 **3** *hd* **Franklin D (USA)**[91] 656 4-9-0 92 .... LouisSteward(3) 10 98
(Michael Bell) *stdd s: hld up in tch in last trio: hdwy over 2f out: rdn to chse ldrs and edgd lft over 1f out: kpt on u.p ins fnl f* **7/1**

00-5 **4** *3* **Forgotten Hero (IRE)**[20] 1885 7-9-5 94 ....(t) DougieCostello 4 94
(Kim Bailey) *stdd and bmpd s: t.k.h: hld up in tch in midfield: hdwy to chse ldrs 3f out: unable qck u.p over 1f out: styd on same pce fnl f* **12/1**

1553 **5** *1/2* **Dance Of Fire**[16] 1978 4-8-13 88 ....(p) DavidProbert 5 87
(Andrew Balding) *t.k.h: hld up in tch in midfield: effrt 2f out: no imp u.p over 1f out: one pce and hld and swtchd rt ins fnl f* **8/1**

4253 **6** *3 3/4* **Truth Or Dare**[17] 1959 5-9-3 92 .... MartinDwyer 9 83
(William Muir) *t.k.h: hld up in tch in midfield: rdn 2f out: sn outpcd and btn over 1f out: wknd fnl f* **10/1**

212- **7** *3/4* **High Baroque (USA)**[231] 6935 4-8-12 87 .... BarryMcHugh 6 77
(Richard Fahey) *chsd ldrs: rdn over 2f out: sn struggling and lost pl wl over 1f out: wknd fnl f* **10/1**

105- **8** *1 3/4* **Laurence**[211] 7426 4-9-1 90 .... TomQueally 2 76
(Luca Cumani) *t.k.h: chsd ldrs: rdn over 2f out: no ex and btn over 1f out: wknd ins fnl f* **5/1**[2]

6/ **9** *nk* **Vercingetorix (IRE)**[18] 6507 5-9-4 93 .... GrahamGibbons 1 79
(David Evans) *stdd s: hld up in tch in rr: rdn over 2f out: sn btn and no ch fnl 2f* **40/1**

221- **10** *nk* **Murgan**[220] 7221 4-9-0 89 .... DarryllHolland 8 74
(Peter Chapple-Hyam) *stdd s: hld up in tch in last pair: rdn over 2f out: sn btn: no ch fnl 2f* **6/1**[3]

2m 5.72s (-0.08) **Going Correction** +0.20s/f (Good) **10** Ran SP% **116.2**
Speed ratings (Par 109): **108,106,106,104,103 100,100,98,98,98**
CSF £58.62 CT £315.89 TOTE £3.90: £1.70, £4.20, £2.80; EX 41.40 Trifecta £414.30.
Owner Sheikh Hamdan bin Mohammed Al Maktoum **Bred** Darley **Trained** Middleham Moor, N Yorks

FOCUS
It proved hard to come from off the pace in this handicap, which was dominated from the front by the winner.
T/Plt: £141.50 to a £1 stake. Pool of £59845.36 - 308.65 winning tickets. T/Qpdt: £93.80 to a £1 stake. Pool of £3397.84 - 26.80 winning tickets. **Steve Payne**

2218 YORK (L-H)
Saturday, May 21

OFFICIAL GOING: Good (good to firm in places) changing to good after race 4 (3.50)
Wind: Fresh half behind Weather: Cloudy with showers

2485 TITANBET.CO.UK STKS (H'CAP) — 7f
2:05 (2:05) (Class 2) (0-110,105) 3-Y-0+
£18,675 (£5,592; £2,796; £1,398; £699; £351) **Stalls** Low

Form RPR

-000 **1** **Jallota**[15] 1993 5-9-9 103 .... JamieSpencer 4 112
(Charles Hills) *trckd ldrs: hdwy 2f out: rdn to chal ent fnl f: drvn to ld last 110yds: styd on wl* **9/2**[1]

-000 **2** *2 1/4* **Heaven's Guest (IRE)**[14] 2027 6-9-2 103 .... AdamMcNamara(7) 7 106
(Richard Fahey) *hld up in tch: hdwy 2f out: effrt and nt clr run jst over 1f out: swtchd rt and rdn ent fnl f: styd on wl towards fin* **14/1**

-645 **3** *nk* **Glen Moss (IRE)**[10] 2158 7-9-1 100 .... PhilDennis(5) 3 102
(Michael Dods) *prom: hdwy and cl up on inner 3f out: rdn to ld jst over 1f out: drvn and edgd rt ent fnl f: hdd last 110yds: kpt on same pce* **15/2**

0-30 **4** *2 1/4* **Fort Bastion (IRE)**[14] 2027 7-9-3 97 ....(b) PhillipMakin 6 93
(David O'Meara) *dwlt and in rr: hdwy 3f out: rdn wl over 1f out: kpt on fnl f: nrst fin* **13/2**[3]

0-03 **5** *1 1/4* **Lincoln (IRE)**[21] 1856 5-9-2 96 .... SilvestreDeSousa 1 89
(Mick Channon) *cl up: led wl over 1f out: sn rdn: hdd jst over 1f out: drvn and hld whn sltly hmpd ins fnl f* **5/1**[2]

03-6 **6** *1 1/4* **Salateen**[14] 2030 4-9-11 105 .... DanielTudhope 12 94
(David O'Meara) *slt ld: rdn along over 2f out: hdd wl over 1f out: drvn appr fnl f: sn wknd* **5/1**[2]

-335 **7** *1/2* **Georgian Bay (IRE)**[14] 2031 6-8-11 96 ....(v) JordanVaughan(5) 2 84
(K R Burke) *in tch: effrt over 2f out: rdn along wl over 1f out: no imp appr fnl f* **25/1**

60-0 **8** *3/4* **Room Key**[21] 1856 4-9-2 96 ....(b[1]) RobertWinston 13 82
(Eve Johnson Houghton) *a towards rr* **11/1**

550- **9** *1* **Cornwallville (IRE)**[30] 4-9-2 96 .... TomEaves 8 79
(David Loughnane) *in tch: pushed along 3f out: rdn over 2f out: sn wknd* **25/1**

04-0 **10** *2* **Valley Of Fire**[14] 2027 4-9-2 96 .... BenCurtis 5 74
(William Haggas) *midfield: rdn along 3f out: sn drvn and wknd fnl 2f* **20/1**

660- **11** *nse* **That Is The Spirit**[280] 5382 5-9-9 103 .... JackGarritty 10 81
(David O'Meara) *dwlt: rapid hdwy on outer and cl up after 1 1/2f: rdn along 3f out: wknd 2f out* **12/1**

0-56 **12** *8* **Hoof It**[10] 2158 9-9-2 96 .... KeaganLatham 11 52
(Michael Easterby) *dwlt: a bhd* **12/1**

1m 22.78s (-2.52) **Going Correction** -0.10s/f (Good) **12** Ran SP% **119.5**
Speed ratings (Par 109): **110,107,107,104,103 101,101,100,99,96 96,87**
CSF £66.75 CT £463.09 TOTE £5.40: £1.90, £4.00, £2.70; EX 65.50 Trifecta £531.80.
Owner Mrs Fitri Hay **Bred** Barry Walters **Trained** Lambourn, Berks

FOCUS
Racing on the traditional line and therefore no adjustment to race distances. There was a slight tailwind in the straight. Rain overnight and the general view from those who rode in the opener was that the ground was 'good'. An open handicap, the form of which looks decent.

2486 WEDDINGMATES.CO.UK GRAND CUP (LISTED RACE) — 1m 6f
2:40 (2:40) (Class 1) 4-Y-0+
£22,684 (£8,600; £4,304; £2,144; £1,076; £540) **Stalls** Low

Form RPR

11-1 **1** **Moonrise Landing (IRE)**[57] 1067 5-8-9 103 .... FMBerry 10 110
(Ralph Beckett) *hld up in tch: hdwy over 3f out: chsd ldrs 2f out: rdn to chal over 1f out: led ins fnl f: drvn out* **10/3**[2]

00- **2** *3/4* **Quest For More (IRE)**[200] 7697 6-9-0 109 ....(b) JamieSpencer 5 114
(Roger Charlton) *trckd ldrs: smooth hdwy over 3f out: sn cl up: led 2f out: rdn and edgd rt ent fnl f: sn hdd and drvn: no ex last 50yds* **7/2**[3]

0-00 **3** *7* **Angel Gabrial (IRE)**[17] 1967 7-9-0 104 .... GeorgeChaloner 3 104
(Richard Fahey) *trckd ldng pair: cl up over 3f out: sn rdn along and sltly outpcd 2f out: styd on u.p fnl f* **10/1**

63-3 **4** *3 3/4* **Twitch (IRE)**[21] 1855 4-8-9 97 ....(p) MarcMonaghan 9 94
(Hugo Palmer) *trckd ldr: cl up 1/2-way: led over 4f out: jnd and rdn 3f out: hdd 2f out: cl up and drvn tl wknd ent fnl f* **12/1**

5 *4 1/2* **The Minch (IRE)**[43] 5-9-0 0 .... DanielTudhope 6 93
(Jim Goldie) *hld up in rr: sme hdwy on outer over 2f out: sn rdn and plugged on fnl f* **12/1**

160- **6** *shd* **Seamour (IRE)**[196] 7757 5-9-0 99 .... BenCurtis 8 93
(Brian Ellison) *hld up in rr: hdwy wl over 2f out: sn rdn: plugged on fnl f* **12/1**

65-3 **7** *7* **Elidor**[15] 1995 6-9-0 106 .... SilvestreDeSousa 1 83
(Mick Channon) *in tch: hdwy 5f out: cl up on inner 3f out: rdn along 2f out: sn drvn and wknd* **11/4**[1]

61-6 **8** *31* **Captain Morley**[77] 843 5-9-0 99 .... TomEaves 4 39
(David Simcock) *hld up towards rr: effrt over 3f out: sn rdn and outpcd: bhd and eased over 1f out* **14/1**

0-21 **9** *8* **Havisham**[19] 1914 4-9-0 82 ....(p) SamHitchcott 7 28
(Andrew Balding) *led: rdn along and hdd over 4f out: sn wknd and bhd fr over 2f out* **40/1**

3m 0.03s (-0.17) **Going Correction** +0.175s/f (Good) **9** Ran SP% **113.2**
Speed ratings (Par 111): **107,106,102,100,97 97,93,76,71**
CSF £15.10 TOTE £3.80: £1.60, £1.40, £2.40; EX 13.30 Trifecta £70.50.
Owner P D Savill **Bred** Oak Hill Stud **Trained** Kimpton, Hants

FOCUS
Race distance as advertised. The rain set in prior to this contest, a decent Listed event in which they were soon quite well strung out in, and the front two came clear.

2487 FEDERATION OF BLOODSTOCK AGENTS STKS (H'CAP) — 1m 4f
3:15 (3:15) (Class 3) (0-90,91) 4-Y-0+ **£9,703** (£2,887; £1,443; £721) **Stalls** Centre

Form RPR

15-0 **1** **Forever Popular (USA)**[14] 2024 4-8-11 80 .... BenCurtis 3 92
(William Haggas) *trckd ldng pair: hdwy to ld over 2f out: sn rdn: drvn ins fnl f: kpt on wl towards fin* **11/1**

6-P6 **2** *1/2* **Yorkidding**[10] 2163 4-9-1 84 .... FMBerry 11 95
(Mark Johnston) *trckd ldng pair: hdwy 3f out: cl up 2f out: sn rdn to chal: drvn and ev ch ins fnl f: no ex towards fin* **12/1**

-11 **3** *4 1/2* **Walpole (IRE)**[19] 1934 4-8-13 82 .... JamieSpencer 6 86
(Hugo Palmer) *hld up in tch: hdwy over 3f out: chsd ldrs 2f out and sn rdn: drvn to chse ldng pair appr fnl f: kpt on same pce* **3/1**[2]

-252 **4** *nk* **Burano (IRE)**[16] 1978 7-9-6 89 .... PhillipMakin 8 93
(David O'Meara) *hld up in rr: hdwy on wd outside over 2f out: rdn over 1f out: styd on wl fnl f* **8/1**[3]

04-1 **5** *nse* **Shrewd**[35] 1135 6-9-6 89 .... RoystonFfrench 4 92
(Iain Jardine) *hld up in midfield: hdwy 3f out: rdn along over 2f out: drvn and kpt on fnl f* **14/1**

-004 **6** *2 3/4* **Maraakib (IRE)**[15] 2017 4-9-7 90 .... DanielTudhope 1 89
(David O'Meara) *hld up towards rr: hdwy on inner 3f out: chsd ldrs 2f out: sn rdn and ch: drvn and wknd appr fnl f* **16/1**

2-00 **7** *3 1/4* **Buonarroti (IRE)**[10] 2157 5-9-3 86 ....(v[1]) TomEaves 9 80
(Declan Carroll) *chsd ldrs: hdwy 4f out: rdn along over 2f out: drvn wl over 1f out: grad wknd* **33/1**

4 **8** *nk* **Time Of My Life (GER)**[20] 1880 5-9-1 84 .... JackGarritty 5 77
(Patrick Holmes) *hld up and in rr tl sme late hdwy* **25/1**

131 **9** *1 1/2* **Appeared**[10] 2163 4-9-8 91 .... SilvestreDeSousa 2 82
(Roger Varian) *trckd ldrs: hdwy 3f out: chal 2f out and ev ch: sn rdn and wknd appr fnl f* **15/8**[1]

30-1 **10** *5* **Braes Of Lochalsh**[21] 1852 5-8-4 76 ....(p) JoeDoyle(3) 7 59
(Jim Goldie) *trckd ldr: cl up over 4f out: rdn along wl over 3f out: sn wknd* **25/1**

0-03 **11** *1* **Cyril**[10] 1923 4-8-13 82 ....(p) ShaneGray 13 63
(Kevin Ryan) *led: rdn along over 3f out: hdd over 2f out: sn drvn and wknd* **33/1**

-632 **12** *8* **Salmon Sushi**[15] 2017 5-8-13 82 .... RobertWinston 12 51
(Tim Easterby) *a towards rr* **16/1**

2m 33.18s (-0.02) **Going Correction** +0.175s/f (Good) **12** Ran SP% **118.9**
Speed ratings (Par 107): **107,106,103,103,103 101,99,99,98,94 94,88**
CSF £130.41 CT £498.21 TOTE £11.40: £3.30, £3.10, £1.70; EX 172.20 Trifecta £602.40.
Owner Lael Stable **Bred** Mr And Mrs M Roy Jackson **Trained** Newmarket, Suffolk

FOCUS
Race distance as advertised. A decent handicap, run at a reasonable gallop, and the two fillies in the field dominated late on.

2488 TITANBET.CO.UK SPRING SPRINT (HANDICAP STKS) 5f
3:50 (3:51) (Class 2) (0-105,102) 3-Y-O+
£31,125 (£9,320; £4,660; £2,330; £1,165; £585) **Stalls** Centre

Form RPR
-526 **1** **Harry Hurricane**[8] 2206 4-9-3 **95** RobertWinston 9 103
(George Baker) *trckd ldrs: hdwy wl over 1f out: rdn to chal ent fnl f: drvn to ld last 150yds: hld on wl towards fin* **7/1**[3]
00-0 **2** *nk* **Bogart**[10] 2158 7-8-8 **86** (p) TomEaves 16 93
(Kevin Ryan) *prom: rdn over 1f out: ev ch ins fnl f: drvn and nt qckn towards fin* **12/1**
-514 **3** *nk* **Kimberella**[7] 2258 6-9-0 **92** RoystonFfrench 15 98
(David Nicholls) *in tch: hdwy on outer wl over 1f out: rdn ent fnl f: kpt on wl towards fin* **10/1**
030- **4** *nk* **Ninjago**[231] 6918 6-9-10 **102** DanielTudhope 1 107
(Paul Midgley) *in tch: gd hdwy 2f out: rdn over 1f out: chal ins fnl f and ev ch tl drvn and no ex towards fin* **16/1**
5100 **5** *1 1/4* **Normal Equilibrium**[9] 2188 6-8-10 **88** ShaneGray 5 89
(Robert Cowell) *led: rdn wl over 1f out: hdd ins fnl f: wknd* **25/1**
3316 **6** *1/2* **Royal Birth**[9] 2188 5-9-2 **94** (t) FMBerry 4 93
(Stuart Williams) *dwlt and in rr: hdwy wl over 1f out: rdn and kpt on wl fnl f: nrst fin* **13/2**[2]
00-0 **7** *nk* **Blaine**[7] 2258 6-8-11 **89** AdrianNicholls 14 87+
(David Nicholls) *hld up: hdwy wl over 1f out: sn rdn and kpt on fnl f: nrst fin* **25/1**
65-5 **8** *1* **Barnet Fair**[7] 2258 8-8-7 **88** JoeDoyle(3) 10 83+
(David Nicholls) *dwlt and in rr tl hdwy over 1f out: rdn and kpt on fnl f: fin* **12/1**
06-1 **9** *hd* **Bondi Beach Boy**[7] 2261 7-8-5 **83** ow1 GeorgeChaloner 3 78
(James Turner) *chsd ldr: rdn along wl over 1f out: sn wknd* **12/1**
6634 **10** *1/2* **Pearl Acclaim (IRE)**[7] 2261 6-8-3 **81** PaulQuinn 6 74
(David Nicholls) *trckd ldrs: effrt wl over 1f out: sn rdn and wknd ent fnl f* **20/1**
3302 **11** *nse* **Patrick (IRE)**[17] 1958 4-9-0 **92** JackGarritty 11 85
(Richard Fahey) *towards rr: hdwy 2f out: sn rdn and n.d* **8/1**
-400 **12** *3/4* **Related**[14] 2027 6-9-3 **95** (b) PhillipMakin 2 85
(Paul Midgley) *chsd ldr: rdn along 2f out: sn wknd* **12/1**
31-5 **13** *2* **Doctor Sardonicus**[9] 2188 5-9-0 **92** JamieSpencer 12 76
(David Simcock) *in tch: rdn along 2f out: sn drvn and wknd* **6/1**[1]
000- **14** *2* **Northgate Lad (IRE)**[238] 6747 4-9-0 **92** BenCurtis 8 70
(Brian Ellison) *a towards rr* **14/1**
0-10 **15** *1* **Arctic Feeling (IRE)**[9] 2188 8-8-11 **96** NatalieHambling(7) 7 70
(Richard Fahey) *dwlt: a in rr* **16/1**

57.86s (-1.44) **Going Correction** -0.025s/f (Good) **15** Ran SP% **122.0**
Speed ratings (Par 109): **110,109,109,108,106 105,105,103,103,102 102,101,98,94,93**
CSF £86.68 CT £861.88 TOTE £7.90: £3.00, £4.90, £2.70; EX 124.30 Trifecta £1650.10.
Owner PJL Racing **Bred** Selwood Bloodstock, Hoskins & Lowry **Trained** Manton, Wilts

FOCUS
Race distance as advertised. The ground was changed to good after this race. A typically competitive sprint for the track.

2489 YORKSHIRE REGIMENT EBF STALLIONS MEDIAN AUCTION NOVICE STKS (PLUS 10 RACE) 6f
4:20 (4:23) (Class 3) 2-Y-O
£7,439 (£2,213; £1,106; £553) **Stalls** High

Form RPR
1 **Broken Stones (IRE)** 2-9-2 0 JamieSpencer 3 89+
(Kevin Ryan) *towards rr whn j. path after 1f: hdwy 3f out: swtchd rt over 2f out and sn chsng ldng pair: styd on wl fnl f to ld last 100yds* **13/8**[1]
2 *1 1/2* **Megan Lily (IRE)** 2-8-11 0 JackGarritty 5 80+
(Richard Fahey) *led at gd pce: rdn along wl over 1f out: drvn and edgd lft ins fnl f: hdd and no ex last 100yds* **9/1**[3]
2 **3** *3 1/4* **Masham Star (IRE)**[9] 2193 2-9-2 0 FMBerry 8 75+
(Mark Johnston) *trckd ldr: cl up 1/2-way: chal 2f out and sn rdn: drvn and ev ch ent fnl f: kpt on same pce last 150yds* **7/4**[2]
4 *1 1/2* **Aventinus (IRE)** 2-8-13 0 MarcMonaghan(3) 9 70
(Hugo Palmer) *chsd ldng pair: rdn along and edgd lft 2f out: sn one pce* **20/1**
5 *1/2* **Looting** 2-8-13 0 JoeDoyle(3) 4 69
(David Brown) *chsd ldng pair: rdn along 2f out: sn one pce* **9/1**[3]
6 *4 1/2* **Ingleby Mackenzie** 2-9-2 0 SilvestreDeSousa 1 55
(Mick Channon) *dwlt and in rr: hdwy on outer wl over 2f out: sn rdn and n.d* **20/1**
7 *2* **Savea (IRE)** 2-9-2 0 DanielTudhope 7 49
(David O'Meara) *a towards rr* **25/1**
00 **8** *2* **Kilbaha Lady (IRE)**[19] 1921 2-8-11 0 TomEaves 2 38
(Nigel Tinkler) *chsd ldrs: rdn along over 2f out: sn wknd* **66/1**
9 *1 1/4* **Maazel (IRE)** 2-9-2 0 ShaneGray 10 40
(Roger Varian) *dwlt: a in rr* **25/1**

1m 12.31s (0.41) **Going Correction** -0.025s/f (Good) **9** Ran SP% **113.2**
Speed ratings (Par 97): **96,94,89,87,87 81,78,75,74**
CSF £14.12 TOTE £2.70: £1.10, £2.30, £1.10; EX 19.00 Trifecta £39.90.
Owner Matt & Lauren Morgan **Bred** Highpark Bloodstock Ltd **Trained** Hambleton, N Yorks
■ Party Tiger was withdrawn. Price at time of withdrawal 14-1. Rule 4 applies to all bets - deduction 5p in the pound.

FOCUS
Race distance as advertised. The second and third went charging off in this novice event, and the winner came through to win with a fair bit in hand.

2490 INFINITY TYRES BREEDERS BACKING RACING EBF FILLIES' STKS (H'CAP) 1m 2f 88y
4:55 (4:55) (Class 3) (0-90,90) 3-Y-O
£8,086 (£2,406; £1,202; £601) **Stalls** Low

Form RPR
010- **1** **Diploma**[225] 7073 3-9-7 **90** DanielTudhope 1 106
(Sir Michael Stoute) *trckd ldrs: hdwy on outer 3f out: led over 1f out: sn rdn and kpt on wl* **6/1**
2-11 **2** *3 1/4* **Sagely (IRE)**[6] 2269 3-9-3 **86** 6ex SilvestreDeSousa 6 96
(Ed Dunlop) *trckd ldng pair: hdwy over 3f out: led over 2f out: rdn and edgd lft 1 1/2f out: sn hdd: drvn and rallied ins fnl f: one pce last 110yds* **6/4**[1]
13-0 **3** *2* **Turning The Table (IRE)**[20] 1890 3-8-13 **82** JamieSpencer 4 88
(David Simcock) *dwlt: hld up in rr: hdwy wl over 2f out: rdn to chse ldrs over 1f out: kpt on same pce fnl f* **7/2**[2]
22-1 **4** *1 1/2* **Secret Sense (USA)**[44] 1289 3-8-9 **78** ow1 FMBerry 5 81
(Ralph Beckett) *hld up towards rr: hdwy 3f out: rdn along 2f out: chsd ldrs and drvn over 1f out: kpt on same pce* **4/1**[3]
23-2 **5** *6* **Dark Intention (IRE)**[15] 1998 3-8-1 **75** ow2 RachelRichardson(5) 2 67
(Lawrence Mullaney) *led: rdn along 3f out: hdd over 2f out: sn drvn and wknd* **12/1**
2-45 **6** *28* **Deodoro (USA)**[7] 2236 3-8-10 **79** PhillipMakin 3 18
(Mark Johnston) *trckd ldr: cl up over 4f out: rdn along over 3f out: sn wknd and bhd* **12/1**

2m 12.44s (-0.06) **Going Correction** +0.175s/f (Good) **6** Ran SP% **111.9**
Speed ratings (Par 100): **107,104,102,101,96 74**
CSF £15.43 TOTE £5.60: £2.40, £1.60; EX 14.50 Trifecta £35.30.
Owner The Queen **Bred** The Queen **Trained** Newmarket, Suffolk

FOCUS
Race distance as advertised. They were soon strung out in this useful fillies' handicap, the two outsiders racing clear, and the race produced quite a taking winner.

2491 JOHN WRIGHT ELECTRICAL GENTLEMAN AMATEUR RIDERS' STKS (H'CAP) 7f
5:25 (5:25) (Class 4) (0-80,78) 4-Y-O+
£6,239 (£1,935; £967; £484) **Stalls** Low

Form RPR
2-44 **1** **Mystic Miraaj**[28] 1625 4-11-4 **75** (b) MrWEasterby 15 86
(Tim Easterby) *trckd ldrs: hdwy 2f out: rdn to ld ent fnl f: edgd lft and kpt on wl towards fin* **5/1**[2]
4564 **2** *1 1/2* **Depth Charge (IRE)**[29] 1596 4-10-4 **68** (vt) MrBenjaminStephens(7) 7 75
(Kristin Stubbs) *in tch: hdwy over 2f out: rdn over 1f out: chal ins fnl f and ev ch tl no ex last 100yds* **25/1**
5040 **3** *3/4* **Classic Seniority**[15] 2016 4-11-4 **75** MrJohnDawson 8 80+
(Marjorie Fife) *towards rr: pushed along wl over 2f out: rdn and hdwy over 1f out: styd on strly fnl f* **25/1**
6046 **4** *2 1/2* **Midnight Rider (IRE)**[33] 1528 8-11-7 **78** (p) MrPMillman 12 76
(Rod Millman) *in tch: hdwy on inner to chse ldrs wl over 1f out: sn rdn and kpt on same pce fnl f* **16/1**
0425 **5** *hd* **Cliff (IRE)**[19] 1926 6-10-8 **68** (p) MrThomasGreatrex(3) 9 66
(Nigel Tinkler) *trckd ldrs: hdwy over 2f out: led wl over 1f out: rdn and hdd ent fnl f: sn drvn and grad wknd* **11/1**
1325 **6** *1* **Burning Blaze**[17] 1958 6-11-6 **77** MrRBirkett 5 72+
(Brian Ellison) *hld up: hdwy over 2f out: rdn wl over 1f out: kpt on fnl f* **10/1**[3]
00-6 **7** *3/4* **Order Of Service**[15] 2010 6-11-1 **77** MrRobertHooper(5) 14 70+
(Shaun Harris) *s.i.s and bhd: rdn and hdwy on inner 2f out: kpt on fnl f* **20/1**
5235 **8** *shd* **Indian Affair**[11] 2130 6-10-5 **69** (bt) MrJCJones(7) 10 62
(Milton Bradley) *prom: rdn along over 2f out: wknd over 1f out* **20/1**
0441 **9** *1* **Make On Madam (IRE)**[19] 1926 4-10-2 **66** MrJordanSwarbrick(7) 11 56
(Les Eyre) *chsd ldrs: rdn along over 2f out: grad wknd* **16/1**
14-0 **10** *2 1/2* **Baltic Prince (IRE)**[28] 1631 6-10-5 **67** MrBJames(5) 6 50
(Tony Carroll) *cl up: rdn along wl over 2f out: wknd wl over 1f out* **20/1**
20-0 **11** *1/2* **Gabrial The Tiger (IRE)**[7] 2259 4-10-13 **75** MrMEnnis(5) 18 57
(Richard Fahey) *sn led: rdn along over 2f out: hdd wl over 1f out: sn wknd* **20/1**
435- **12** *1* **Jack Luey**[199] 7710 9-11-7 **78** (p) MrTHamilton 2 57
(Lawrence Mullaney) *midfield: hdwy to chse ldrs on inner over 2f out: rdn wl over 1f out: sn wknd* **18/1**
1 **13** *nk* **Dutch Artist (IRE)**[18] 1953 4-11-6 **77** MrSWalker 1 55+
(David O'Meara) *hld up: a towards rr* **15/8**[1]
-262 **14** *1 1/4* **Dr Red Eye**[18] 1954 8-10-6 **68** (p) MrKLocking(5) 16 43
(Scott Dixon) *a towards rr* **12/1**
-600 **15** *2* **Ershaad (IRE)**[19] 1926 4-10-0 **64** oh2 MrJamesKendrick(7) 3 34
(Shaun Harris) *a in rr* **50/1**
3346 **16** *2* **Maureb (IRE)**[8] 2223 4-10-11 **71** (p) KaineWood(3) 17 35
(Tony Coyle) *cl up on outer: rdn along 2f out: drvn and wknd over 1f out* **14/1**
06-0 **17** *1 1/4* **Party Royal**[40] 1387 6-10-13 **70** MrDHDunsdon 13 31
(Nick Gifford) *a in rr* **33/1**

1m 25.87s (0.57) **Going Correction** -0.10s/f (Good) **17** Ran SP% **131.9**
Speed ratings (Par 105): **92,90,89,86,86 85,84,84,83,80 79,78,78,76,74 72,70**
CSF £137.24 CT £3029.69 TOTE £6.60: £1.70, £6.70, £6.60, £4.50; EX 180.60 Trifecta £3272.40.
Owner Richard Taylor & Philip Hebdon **Bred** Ashbrittle Stud **Trained** Great Habton, N Yorks

FOCUS
Race distance as advertised. The favourite ran no race in this amateur riders' handicap and the form is ordinary.
T/Plt: £34.70 to a £1 stake. Pool: £108,846.54 - 2288.19 winning units. T/Qpdt: £6.60 to a £1 stake. Pool: £6,691.02 - 744.94 winning units. **Joe Rowntree**

2492 - 2493a (Foreign Racing) - See Raceform Interactive

[1936] CURRAGH (R-H)
Saturday, May 21

OFFICIAL GOING: Round course - yielding; straight course - yielding to soft

2494a COLD MOVE EUROPEAN BREEDERS FUND MARBLE HILL STKS (LISTED RACE) 5f
4:30 (4:31) 2-Y-O
£26,029 (£8,382; £3,970; £1,764; £882; £441)

RPR
1 **Caravaggio (USA)**[33] 1534 2-9-3 0 RyanMoore 10 105+
(A P O'Brien, Ire) *chsd ldrs in 3rd on stands' rails: swtchd rt in 2nd appr fnl f: styd on wl under hands and heels to ld fnl 100yds: drew clr* **4/7**[1]
2 *2 1/4* **Mister Trader**[62] 1013 2-9-3 0 LeighRoche 8 97
(D J Bunyan, Ire) *attempted to make all: strly pressed ins fnl f: hdd fnl 100yds: kpt on wl in clr 2nd* **7/1**[3]
3 *4 1/4* **Ambiguity (IRE)**[10] 2165 2-9-3 0 DonnachaO'Brien 4 82
(A P O'Brien, Ire) *chsd ldr in 2nd: rdn and dropped to 3rd over 1f out: nt qckn w principals: kpt on same pce* **12/1**
4 *1 1/4* **Roly Poly (USA)**[26] 1729 2-8-12 0 SeamieHeffernan 2 72
(A P O'Brien, Ire) *sn chsd ldrs in 4th: nt qckn over 1f out: kpt on same pce fnl f* **5/1**[2]
5 *1 1/2* **Ready To Roc (IRE)**[36] 1465 2-9-3 0 ColinKeane 9 72
(J P Murtagh, Ire) *hld up: sme prog into 5th appr fnl f: kpt on same pce: nvr on terms* **8/1**

6 4 1/2 **Confrontational (IRE)** 2-9-3 0 ShaneFoley 3 56
(John Joseph Murphy, Ire) *hld up: pushed along in 5th after 1/2-way: no imp in 6th appr fnl f* **80/1**

7 nk **Hit The Bid**[13] 2066 2-9-3 0 PatSmullen 7 54
(D J Bunyan, Ire) *racd in rr for much of way: modest late hdwy wout ever threatening* **25/1**

8 2 3/4 **Hyzenthlay (IRE)**[34] 1506 2-8-12 0 AnaO'Brien 1 40
(A P O'Brien, Ire) *hld up: 7th 1/2-way on outer: no imp appr fnl f: eased ins fnl f* **20/1**

9 2 1/4 **The Mcgregornator (IRE)**[30] 1590 2-9-3 0 KierenFallon 6 36
(Adrian Paul Keatley, Ire) *hld up: pushed along bef 1/2-way: wknd qckly over 1f out: eased clsng stages* **33/1**

1m 2.22s (-0.68) **Going Correction** 0.0s/f (Good) **9** Ran SP% **124.4**
Speed ratings: **105,101,94,92,90 83,82,78,74**
CSF £5.84 TOTE £1.40: £1.02, £2.60, £3.50; DF 6.40 Trifecta £35.20.
Owner Mrs John Magnier & Michael Tabor & Derrick Smith **Bred** Windmill Manor Farms Inc Et Al **Trained** Cashel, Co Tipperary

FOCUS
A most impressive display from the winner here, stamping his class all over a decent bunch of juveniles.

2495a WEATHERBYS IRELAND GREENLANDS STKS (GROUP 2) 6f
5:05 (5:06) 4-Y-0+

£52,058 (£16,764; £7,941; £3,529; £1,764; £882)

RPR

1 **Mobsta (IRE)**[37] 1439 4-9-3 106 PatSmullen 1 110
(Mick Channon) *chsd ldrs: 4th at 1/2-way: rdn to press ldr in 2nd 1f out: led fnl 100yds: kpt on wl: all out* **14/1**

2 hd **Flight Risk (IRE)**[26] 1730 5-9-3 103 KevinManning 5 110
(J S Bolger, Ire) *led: strly pressed ent fnl f: hdd fnl 100yds: rallied wl: jst hld* **16/1**

3 1/2 **Dick Whittington (IRE)**[10] 2159 4-9-3 106 RyanMoore 6 108
(A P O'Brien, Ire) *sn trckd ldr in 2nd: rdn 2f out: dropped to 4th 1f out: kpt on again clsng stages into 3rd* **10/1**

4 1/2 **Maarek**[26] 1730 9-9-3 108 SeamieHeffernan 3 106+
(Miss Evanna McCutcheon, Ire) *hld up: rdn to take clsr order on outer over 1f out: wnt 3rd ins fnl f: kpt on same pce: dropped to 4th cl home* **8/1**[3]

5 shd **Don't Touch**[14] 2031 4-9-3 112 TonyHamilton 2 106+
(Richard Fahey) *chsd early ldrs: rdn over 2f out and nt qckn over 1f out in 5th: kpt on wl again clsng stages* **1/1**[1]

6 1 1/4 **Gordon Lord Byron (IRE)**[48] 1226 8-9-3 110 WayneLordan 4 102
(T Hogan, Ire) *hld up: pushed along over 2f out: sn no imp: kpt on wl ins fnl f into 6th cl home: nrst fin* **16/1**

7 3/4 **Fort Del Oro (IRE)**[26] 1730 4-9-0 107 BillyLee 7 97
(Edward Lynam, Ire) *chsd ldrs: 3rd at 1/2-way: travelled wl over 2f out: sn rdn and nt qckn 1f out: dropped to rr cl home* **11/4**[2]

1m 16.2s (0.70) **Going Correction** +0.425s/f (Yiel) **7** Ran SP% **115.3**
Speed ratings: **112,111,111,110,110 108,107**
CSF £200.15 TOTE £17.20: £4.50, £5.50; DF 164.90 Trifecta £1095.90.
Owner Billy Parish **Bred** P J Gleeson **Trained** West Ilsley, Berks

FOCUS
Neither of the market leaders covered themselves in glory in this steadily run affair.

2496a TATTERSALLS IRISH 2,000 GUINEAS (GROUP 1) 1m
5:40 (5:40) 3-Y-O

£125,735 (£41,911; £19,852; £8,823; £4,411; £2,205)

RPR

1 **Awtaad (IRE)**[19] 1938 3-9-0 106 ChrisHayes 5 122
(Kevin Prendergast, Ire) *sn settled in 5th: travelled wl to trck ldrs in 3rd 3f out: led under 2f out and sn pushed clr: styd on wl ins fnl f* **9/2**[3]

2 2 1/2 **Galileo Gold**[21] 1864 3-9-0 120 FrankieDettori 1 117
(Hugo Palmer) *trckd ldrs on inner in 4th: disp 3rd at 1/2-way: rdn over 2f out where n.m.r on inner: wnt 2nd 1f out: kpt on wl: nt rch wnr* **5/4**[1]

3 4 1/4 **Blue De Vega (GER)**[19] 1938 3-9-0 109 ColinKeane 6 106
(M D O'Callaghan, Ire) *hld up in 6th: rdn to chse ldrs in 4th under 2f out: wandered in 3rd appr fnl f: sn no ex w principals: kpt on same pce* **7/1**

4 1 3/4 **Bravery (IRE)**[33] 1538 3-9-0 94 DonnachaO'Brien 7 102
(A P O'Brien, Ire) *racd in 7th: rdn on inner under 2f out: swtchd lft in 5th appr fnl f: kpt on same pce into 4th fnl 150yds: nvr on terms* **33/1**

5 2 1/2 **Shogun (IRE)**[13] 2069 3-9-0 109 (b) ColmO'Donoghue 3 97
(A P O'Brien, Ire) *sn trckd ldrs in 3rd: disp 3rd at 1/2-way: sn rdn and nt qckn 2f out where dropped to rr: kpt on again clsng stages into 5th* **20/1**

6 2 1/4 **Air Vice Marshal (USA)**[21] 1864 3-9-0 112 SeamieHeffernan 2 92
(A P O'Brien, Ire) *led tl strly pressed 2f out and sn hdd: wknd fnl f* **10/1**

7 6 **Air Force Blue (USA)**[21] 1864 3-9-0 123 RyanMoore 8 78
(A P O'Brien, Ire) *racd in rr: pushed along under 2f out: sn no imp: eased ins fnl f* **4/1**[2]

8 3/4 **Sanus Per Aquam (IRE)**[224] 7114 3-9-0 110 KevinManning 4 76
(J S Bolger, Ire) *sn trckd ldr in 2nd: rdn and almost on terms under 3f out: wknd under 2f out and no imp whn sltly hmpd over 1f out: no ex* **16/1**

1m 45.26s (-0.74) **Going Correction** +0.325s/f (Good) **8** Ran SP% **117.8**
Speed ratings: **116,113,109,107,105 102,96,96**
CSF £10.88 CT £39.43; DF 13.50 Trifecta £57.30.
Owner Hamdan Al Maktoum **Bred** Shadwell Estate Company Limited **Trained** Friarstown, Co Kildare

FOCUS
There was an inkling that this group of milers were not a vintage lot, with The Gurkha not taking his chance, but it was hard not to be impressed by the winner's dismissal of the Newmarket hero.

2497a LANWADES STUD STKS (GROUP 2) (F&M) 1m
6:15 (6:16) 4-Y-0+

£52,058 (£16,764; £7,941; £3,529; £1,764; £882)

RPR

1 **Devonshire (IRE)**[62] 1016 4-9-0 107 BillyLee 4 110
(W McCreery, Ire) *chsd ldr in 2nd: rdn to ld under 3f out: pressed ent fnl f: styd on strly to extend advantage clsng stages* **4/1**[2]

2 2 **Irish Rookie (IRE)**[20] 1886 4-9-0 111 PatSmullen 5 105
(Martyn Meade) *hld up in 5th: travelled wl to take clsr order 2f out in 4th: rdn to chse ldr in 2nd 1f out: kpt on fnl 100yds* **3/1**[1]

3 3/4 **Hint Of A Tint (IRE)**[216] 7318 6-9-0 103 WayneLordan 7 103
(David Wachman, Ire) *racd on outer: quite keen and sn chsd ldrs in 3rd: rdn over 1f out: sn no imp on wnr: kpt on same pce* **10/1**

4 1 3/4 **Lucida (IRE)**[316] 4109 4-9-0 114 KevinManning 3 99
(J S Bolger, Ire) *settled off ldrs in 4th: rdn 2f out: no imp ent fnl f: kpt on same pce* **3/1**[1]

5 1 3/4 **Fluff (IRE)**[45] 1279 4-9-0 97 RyanMoore 6 95
(A P O'Brien, Ire) *racd in rr: rdn over 2f out: kpt on same pce into 5th ins fnl f: nvr on terms* **6/1**

6 2 3/4 **Queen Catrine (IRE)**[13] 2067 5-9-0 105 GaryCarroll 2 89
(G M Lyons, Ire) *sn led: hdd under 3f out: wknd fnl f* **20/1**

7 2 1/4 **Ainippe (IRE)**[19] 1939 4-9-0 106 ColinKeane 1 84
(G M Lyons, Ire) *hld up on inner: pushed along over 2f out: sn no imp: dropped to rr ent fnl f: eased clsng stages* **5/1**[3]

1m 46.2s (0.20) **Going Correction** +0.325s/f (Good) **7** Ran SP% **114.8**
Speed ratings: **112,110,109,107,105 103,100**
CSF £16.56 TOTE £4.50: £2.00, £2.10; DF 16.50 Trifecta £153.90.
Owner Godolphin **Bred** P Burns **Trained** Rathbride, Co Kildare

FOCUS
Again, the ground was critical to the outcome, and the chances are it ruined things for the highest-rated horse in the race.

2498 - (Foreign Racing) - See Raceform Interactive

PIMLICO (L-H)
Saturday, May 21

OFFICIAL GOING: Turf: good; dirt: muddy changing to sloppy after 17.51

2499a XPRESSBET.COM PREAKNESS STKS (GRADE 1) (3YO) (DIRT) 1m 1f 110y(D)
11:45 (12:00) 3-Y-O **£612,244** (£204,081; £112,244; £61,224; £30,612)

RPR

1 **Exaggerator (USA)**[14] 2063 3-9-0 0 KentJDesormeaux 5 122
(J Keith Desormeaux, U.S.A) **13/5**[2]

2 3 1/2 **Cherry Wine (USA)**[42] 1360 3-9-0 0 CoreyJLanerie 1 115
(Dale Romans, U.S.A) **173/10**

3 nse **Nyquist (USA)**[14] 2063 3-9-0 0 MarioGutierrez 3 115+
(Doug O'Neill, U.S.A) **7/10**[1]

4 1/2 **Stradivari (USA)**[34] 3-9-0 0 JohnRVelazquez 11 114
(Todd Pletcher, U.S.A) **8/1**[3]

5 1 **Lani (USA)**[14] 2063 3-9-0 0 YutakaTake 6 112
(Mikio Matsunaga, Japan) **30/1**

6 7 **Laoban (USA)**[42] 1360 3-9-0 0 FlorentGeroux 8 97
(Eric J Guillot, U.S.A) **67/1**

7 1 1/4 **Uncle Lino (USA)**[21] 3-9-0 0 FernandoHernandezPerez 2 95+
(Gary Sherlock, U.S.A) **35/1**

8 5 1/2 **Fellowship (USA)**[14] 3-9-0 0 (b) JoseLezcano 10 83
(Mark Casse, Canada) **58/1**

9 2 3/4 **Awesome Speed (USA)**[42] 3-9-0 0 JevianToledo 4 78+
(Alan E Goldberg, U.S.A) **52/1**

10 3/4 **Collected (USA)**[35] 3-9-0 0 (b) JavierCastellano 7 76+
(Bob Baffert, U.S.A) **14/1**

11 14 1/2 **Abiding Star (USA)**[14] 3-9-0 0 JDAcosta 9 47
(Edward Allard, U.S.A) **40/1**

1m 58.31s (2.72) **11** Ran SP% **123.3**
PARI-MUTUEL (all including 2 usd stake): WIN 7.20; PLACE (1-2) 3.20, 9.80; SHOW (1-2-3) 2.40, 4.20, 2.20; SF 88.40.
Owner Big Chief Racing LLC, Head Of Plains Partners LLC **Bred** Joseph B Murphy **Trained** USA

FOCUS
It was cold and rainy and the track was sloppy (sealed), which suited the winner. So too did a foolishly strong early pace, a first quarter of 22.38 the quickest in the history of the Preakness. At that point the first six finishers were positioned 8-10-2-5-11-6. It was a 0.52secs faster split than when American Pharoah powered through the mud in this race the previous year and they were slowing down from then on, going 46.56 (24.18), 1:11.97 (25.41), 1:38.19 (26.22). The winning Beyer speed figure was only 101.

2335 NOTTINGHAM (L-H)
Sunday, May 22

OFFICIAL GOING: Good (good to soft in places; 7.7)
Wind: light 1/2 against Weather: fine

2500 BRITISH STALLION STUDS EBF NOVICE STKS 5f 13y
2:20 (2:20) (Class 5) 2-Y-O **£3,881** (£1,155; £577; £288) **Stalls High**

Form RPR

1 **Silver Line (IRE)** 2-9-2 0 JamesDoyle 8 90+
(Saeed bin Suroor) *trckd ldrs: effrt 2f out: led over 1f out: hung lft and wnt clr last 150yds: easily* **6/5**[1]

2 3 1/2 **Bolt Phantom (USA)** 2-9-2 0 SilvestreDeSousa 3 74+
(Ismail Mohammed) *s.s: hdwy to chse ldrs over 3f out: wnt 2nd over 1f out: no ch w wnr* **6/4**[2]

3223 3 8 **Decadent Times (IRE)**[26] 1749 2-8-9 0 PatrickVaughan[(7)] 4 46
(Tom Dascombe) *wnt lft s: chsd ldr: led over 3f out: hdd over 1f out: sn wknd* **13/2**[3]

0 4 2 1/4 **Dark Hero (IRE)**[29] 1621 2-9-2 0 DarryllHolland 7 38
(Charles Hills) *led: t.k.h: hdd over 3f out: lost pl 2f out* **12/1**

0 U **Commander Blue**[12] 2119 2-9-2 0 JimCrowley 1
(Steph Hollinshead) *wnt lft s: chsd ldrs lost pl over 2f out: sn wl bhd: jinked lft and uns rdr fnl strides* **66/1**

59.97s (-1.53) **Going Correction** -0.125s/f (Firm) **5** Ran SP% **108.0**
Speed ratings (Par 93): **107,101,88,85,**
CSF £3.11 TOTE £2.00: £1.10, £1.40; EX 3.10 Trifecta £5.40.
Owner Godolphin **Bred** Ringfort Stud **Trained** Newmarket, Suffolk

FOCUS
Just 2mm of rain the previous day, and the going was given as good, good to soft in places (GoingStick: 7.7). Jockeys who rode in the first race suggested the ground on the straight course was riding good. The outer track was in use, and the rail was out 4yds on both bends. The two leaders set a good gallop in this novice race and the winner impressed in quickening clear. The form is fluid.

2501 MOST RELIABLE BET DG TAXIS H'CAP (DIV I) 1m 6f 15y
2:50 (2:50) (Class 5) (0-70,70) 4-Y-0+ **£3,234** (£962; £481; £240) **Stalls Low**

Form RPR

0-63 1 **Nam Hai (IRE)**[22] 1854 5-9-4 **67** WilliamTwiston-Davies 9 77+
(Kim Bailey) *wnt rt s: hld up in rr: effrt 4f out: led and dived lft 3f out: abt 4 l clr 1f out: drvn out towards fin* **5/2**[1]

-121 **2** ½ **Hurricane Volta (IRE)**^{25} 1778 5-9-1 **64**....................(p) CharlesBishop 4 69
(Peter Hedger) *s.i.s: hld up in rr: effrt and n.m.r 3f out: styd on to chse wnr last 100yds: clsng at fin* **10/1**

2300 **3** 1¼ **Scrafton**^{22} 1854 5-9-0 **66**.. GeorgeDowning$^{(3)}$ 3 69
(Tony Carroll) *hld up in mid-div: chsd wnr over 2f out: styd on same pce fnl f* **12/1**

6550 **4** nk **Dukes Den**^{5} 2326 5-8-5 **54**.. SilvestreDeSousa 7 57
(Mark Usher) *detached in last: effrt over 3f out: hung lft: styd on wl appr fnl f* **8/1**

46-6 **5** nk **Lady Of Yue**^{16} 1987 6-9-4 **67**.. JimmyQuinn 2 69
(Eugene Stanford) *trckd ldrs: effrt 3f out: kpt on fnl f* **5/1**^{3}

-P61 **6** 3½ **Christmas Hamper (IRE)**^{13} 2089 4-9-0 **63**........................ BenCurtis 5 61
(Michael Appleby) *chsd ldrs: upsides after 5f: led briefly 3f out: wknd fnl 150yds* **7/2**^{2}

31-6 **7** 12 **The Ducking Stool**^{53} 1156 9-9-7 **70**........................... AdamBeschizza 6 51
(Julia Feilden) *trckd ldrs: drvn over 3f out: lost pl over 2f out: bhd whn eased clsng stages* **25/1**

0631 **8** 2¾ **Tarakkom (FR)**^{12} 2131 4-8-11 **60**.................................. CathyGannon 1 37
(Peter Hiatt) *led: hdd over 3f out: lost pl over 2f out: bhd whn eased clsng stages* **9/1**

0-03 **9** 1¾ **Boldbob (IRE)**^{23} 1842 4-8-2 **51** oh6..........................(p) DuranFentiman 8 25
(Micky Hammond) *chsd ldrs: lost pl over 2f out: bhd whn eased clsng stages* **50/1**

3m 5.66s (-1.34) **Going Correction** -0.05s/f (Good) **9** Ran SP% **111.2**
Speed ratings (Par 103): **101,100,100,99,99 97,90,89,88**
CSF £26.94 CT £240.20 TOTE £3.20: £1.30, £2.50, £3.20; EX 22.50 Trifecta £208.70.
Owner This Horse Is For Sale Partnership **Bred** Micheal D Ryan **Trained** Andoversford, Gloucs

FOCUS
Race distance increased by approximately 24yds. This appeared to be run at a solid gallop (faster of the two divisions by 1.54sec) and the principals came from off the pace.

2502 MOST RELIABLE BET DG TAXIS H'CAP (DIV II) 1m 6f 15y

3:25 (3:26) (Class 5) (0-70,69) 4-Y-O+ **£3,234** (£962; £481; £240) **Stalls** Low

Form RPR

210- **1** **Atalan**^{209} 7520 4-9-5 **67**.. JimCrowley 8 76+
(Hughie Morrison) *trckd ldrs: led over 3f out: styd on wl: readily* **7/2**^{2}

46-3 **2** 2¾ **Hurry Home Poppa (IRE)**^{26} 1760 6-9-4 **66**..................... JoeFanning 7 71
(John Mackie) *hld up in mid-div: effrt 3f out: sn chsng wnr: kpt on: no imp* **15/8**^{1}

04-3 **3** 2¾ **Deepsand (IRE)**^{41} 1391 7-9-2 **64**...............................(tp) CharlesBishop 1 65
(Ali Stronge) *mid-div: reminders and chsd ldrs over 3f out: nt clr run and swtchd lft over 1f out: 3rd 1f out: kpt on one pce* **8/1**

0-40 **4** nk **Stanarley Pic**^{22} 1852 5-9-7 **69**.. NeilFarley 3 70
(Alan Swinbank) *t.k.h: led 1f: trckd ldrs: one pce fnl 2f* **5/1**^{3}

0002 **5** ½ **Medieval Bishop (IRE)**^{29} 1649 7-8-7 **58**..................(p) RobHornby$^{(3)}$ 4 58
(Tony Forbes) *led after 1f: hdd after 2f: chsd ldrs: outpcd over 2f out: kpt on fnl f* **12/1**

5625 **6** 1 **Thimaar (USA)**^{12} 2131 8-8-6 **54**....................................(b) KieranO'Neill 9 53
(Sarah Hollinshead) *hld up in rr: hdwy 7f out: chsng ldrs over 4f out: one pce fnl 2f* **16/1**

-312 **7** ½ **Lorelei**^{24} 1807 4-8-13 **61**.. MartinDwyer 2 59
(William Muir) *hld up in rr: effrt outside 4f out: outpcd over 2f out: kpt on fnl f* **15/2**

0000 **8** 6 **Opus Too (IRE)**^{24} 1807 5-7-9 **50** oh5.........................(tp) MillyNaseb$^{(7)}$ 6 40
(John Ryan) *trckd ldrs: led after 2f: hdd over 3f out: lost pl over 1f out* **100/1**

3m 7.2s (0.20) **Going Correction** -0.05s/f (Good) **8** Ran SP% **111.1**
Speed ratings (Par 103): **97,95,93,93,93 92,92,89**
CSF £9.83 CT £44.29 TOTE £4.50: £1.60, £1.10, £2.80; EX 12.50 Trifecta £53.70.
Owner The Fairy Story Partnership **Bred** Deepwood Farm Stud **Trained** East Ilsley, Berks

FOCUS
Race distance increased by approximately 24yds. This looked to be run at a steadier early gallop than the first division, and the time was 1.54sec slower.

2503 ODDS ON FAVOURITE DG TAXIS 01159500500 H'CAP 5f 13y

4:00 (4:00) (Class 6) (0-65,65) 3-Y-O **£2,587** (£770; £384; £192) **Stalls** High

Form RPR

60-5 **1** **Lady Joanna Vassa (IRE)**^{6} 2302 3-8-7 **51** oh2........ ConnorBeasley 11 57+
(Richard Guest) *w ldr: led over 1f out: edgd lft: drvn out* **7/2**^{1}

006- **2** 1¼ **Sacred Harp**^{283} 5290 3-9-3 **61**.......................................(t) OisinMurphy 6 63
(Stuart Williams) *trckd ldrs: effrt over 1f out: hung lft and wnt 2nd last 100yds: kpt on same pce* **5/1**^{3}

5332 **3** hd **Kiringa**^{6} 2302 3-8-2 **51** oh5... AaronJones$^{(5)}$ 8 52
(Robert Cowell) *dwlt: hld up on ins: nt clr run over 2f out: styd on fnl f: tk 3rd nr fin* **9/2**^{2}

3365 **4** nk **David's Beauty (IRE)**^{33} 1554 3-8-10 **54**...................(p) DougieCostello 7 54
(Brian Baugh) *led: hdd over 1f out: kpt on same pce last 150yds* **14/1**

2223 **5** 2½ **Hot Stuff**^{26} 1761 3-9-1 **62**.. GeorgeDowning$^{(3)}$ 4 53
(Tony Carroll) *trckd ldrs: edgd lft 1f out: wknd last 100yds* **11/2**

0-02 **6** 2¼ **Emerald Asset (IRE)**^{23} 1839 3-9-1 **59**..........................(p) GrahamLee 5 42
(Paul Midgley) *dwlt: towards rr: drvn over 2f out: sme hdwy and hung lft over 1f out: wknd last 150yds* **13/2**

5320 **7** 3 **Strictly Carter**^{5} 2337 3-9-6 **64**... FMBerry 2 36
(Alan Bailey) *chsd ldrs on outside: drvn and hung rt 2f out: wknd over 1f out* **11/2**

406- **8** 36 **Rio Glamorous**^{201} 7685 3-9-4 **62**...(t) JFEgan 3
(Roy Bowring) *half rrd s: sn chsng ldrs: drvn over 2f out: wkng whn n.m.r over 1f out: sn heavily eased: virtually p.u: t.o* **25/1**

1m 0.33s (-1.17) **Going Correction** -0.125s/f (Firm) **8** Ran SP% **111.7**
Speed ratings (Par 97): **104,102,101,101,97 93,88,31**
CSF £20.02 CT £76.87 TOTE £4.00: £1.20, £2.40, £1.50; EX 24.20 Trifecta £124.40.
Owner www.primelawns.co.uk **Bred** Tom Radley **Trained** Ingmanthorpe, W Yorks

FOCUS
A moderate sprint.

2504 JOSH "BANGER" GARRETT 21 TODAY H'CAP 5f 13y

4:35 (4:35) (Class 3) (0-95,101) 4-Y-O+ **£9,703** (£2,887; £1,443; £721) **Stalls** High

Form RPR

600- **1** **Tangerine Trees**^{226} 7091 11-8-11 **85**..........................(v) AndrewMullen 8 93
(Michael Appleby) *mde all: hld on gamely* **15/2**

-000 **2** ½ **Seve**^{18} 1968 4-8-9 **90** ow2..(t) PatrickVaughan$^{(7)}$ 6 96
(Tom Dascombe) *w wnr: t.k.h: drvn 2f out: no ex clsng stages* **16/1**

00-1 **3** ¾ **Lexington Abbey**^{46} 1272 5-9-7 **95**.. TomEaves 5 98
(Kevin Ryan) *trckd ldrs: effrt over 1f out: styd on to take 3rd nr fin* **5/2**^{1}

-343 **4** hd **Silvanus (IRE)**^{8} 2258 11-9-6 **94**.. GrahamLee 3 97
(Paul Midgley) *trckd ldrs: effrt over 1f out: styd on to take 4th nr fin* **11/1**

1012 **5** ½ **King Crimson**^{8} 2253 4-8-9 **83**.................................. SilvestreDeSousa 4 84
(Mick Channon) *chsd ldrs: drvn and outpcd over 1f out: swtchd rt over 1f out: styd on* **7/2**^{3}

4-11 **6** ¾ **Ladweb**^{30} 1601 6-8-2 **81** oh3..................................... PatrickO'Donnell$^{(5)}$ 7 79
(John Gallagher) *dwlt: sn chsng ldrs: drvn 2f out: one pce* **3/1**^{2}

-151 **7** 2¼ **Equally Fast**^{23} 1836 4-8-10 **84**..(b) MartinDwyer 1 74
(William Muir) *hood removed v late: wnt lft s: sn chsng ldrs: hung bdly lft over 1f out: lost pl and ended up alone far side* **8/1**

59.78s (-1.72) **Going Correction** -0.125s/f (Firm) **7** Ran SP% **112.9**
Speed ratings (Par 107): **108,107,106,105,104 103,100**
CSF £106.97 CT £381.73 TOTE £10.10: £3.70, £7.30; EX 112.60 Trifecta £593.60.
Owner Tangerine Trees Partnership **Bred** Mrs B A Matthews **Trained** Oakham, Rutland

FOCUS
A decent sprint handicap, and one for the old guard.

2505 LADIES NIGHT ON SATURDAY 2ND JULY MAIDEN FILLIES' STKS (PLUS 10 RACE) 1m 75y

5:05 (5:08) (Class 5) 3-Y-O **£3,881** (£1,155; £577; £288) **Stalls** Centre

Form RPR

23-2 **1** **Golden Stunner (IRE)**^{40} 1392 3-9-0 80.................................. FMBerry 4 85+
(Ralph Beckett) *hld up in tch: hdwy over 3f out: str run to ld last 150yds: wnt clr* **13/8**^{1}

4- **2** 2½ **Jawaayiz**^{178} 7997 3-9-0 0.. GrahamLee 14 77
(Simon Crisford) *chsd ldrs: drvn over 2f out: led appr fnl f: hdd and no ex last 150yds* **14/1**

02 **3** 3 **Malhama**^{29} 1628 3-9-0 0.. HarryBentley 10 70
(Roger Varian) *chsd ldrs: effrt over 2f out: kpt on same pce over 1f out* **7/1**

0-4 **4** 1 **Corpus Chorister (FR)**^{26} 1755 3-9-0 0....................... MartinDwyer 11 68
(David Menuisier) *chsd ldrs: drvn over 3f out: one pce fnl 2f* **20/1**

53- **5** nse **Triathlon (USA)**^{235} 6858 3-9-0 0..................................... TedDurcan 13 68+
(Sir Michael Stoute) *in rr: hdwy over 2f out: kpt on fnl f: nt rch ldrs* **6/1**^{3}

40 **6** 2 **Angelic Guest (IRE)**^{16} 1998 3-9-0 0......................... SilvestreDeSousa 9 63
(Mick Channon) *led: hdd appr fnl f: fdd* **14/1**

7 ¾ **Lolwah** 3-9-0 0.. JoeFanning 7 62+
(Sir Michael Stoute) *s.i.s: in rr: hdwy over 2f out: nvr a factor* **20/1**

5 **8** nk **Beauty Sleep (IRE)**^{16} 2009 3-9-0 0................................. PatCosgrave 8 61
(William Haggas) *mid-div: drvn over 3f out: one pce* **11/2**^{2}

0 **9** 1½ **Dance Band (IRE)**^{10} 2177 3-9-0 0.................................. JackMitchell 2 57
(Roger Varian) *in tch: hdwy over 2f out: fdd appr fnl f* **40/1**

0 **10** 1¾ **Zain Arion (IRE)**^{16} 2009 3-9-0 0................................... StevieDonohoe 1 53
(Charlie Fellowes) *dwlt: in rr: hdwy 5f out: fdd fnl 2f* **150/1**

0 **11** hd **Fire Jet (IRE)**^{16} 2009 3-9-0 0.. RoystonFfrench 5 53
(John Mackie) *in rr: hdwy 3f out: wknd over 1f out* **66/1**

12 7 **Arabian Night** 3-9-0 0.. RobertHavlin 3 37
(John Gosden) *s.i.s: in rr: drvn over 2f out: sn bhd* **14/1**

00- **13** 6 **Gaelic Angel (IRE)**^{221} 7212 3-9-0 0............. WilliamTwiston-Davies 12 23
(Michael Scudamore) *s.i.s: in rr: sme hdwy on outer over 3f out: hung rt and lost pl over 2f out: sn bhd* **100/1**

14 1 **Momentori** 3-9-0 0.. BenCurtis 15 21
(Scott Dixon) *mid-div: wd bnd after 2f: lost pl on outside over 2f out: sn bhd* **150/1**

1m 46.72s (-2.28) **Going Correction** -0.05s/f (Good) **14** Ran SP% **116.0**
Speed ratings (Par 96): **109,106,103,102,102 100,99,99,97,96 95,88,82,81**
CSF £25.01 TOTE £2.50: £1.40, £3.80, £2.10; EX 28.00 Trifecta £126.10.
Owner Sutong Pan **Bred** Fergus Cousins **Trained** Kimpton, Hants

FOCUS
Race distance increased by approximately 12yds. A fair maiden, won comfortably by the favourite.

2506 MERLIN INFLATABLES UK H'CAP 1m 75y

5:35 (5:36) (Class 5) (0-70,69) 3-Y-O **£3,234** (£962; £481; £240) **Stalls** Centre

Form RPR

444- **1** **Briyouni (FR)**^{212} 7423 3-9-4 **69**.. JoeDoyle$^{(3)}$ 7 81+
(Kevin Ryan) *trckd ldrs: smooth hdwy to ld over 2f out: abt 3 l clr whn idled last 75yds: drvn out nr fin* **11/4**^{1}

-523 **2** ¾ **Stars N Angels (IRE)**^{20} 1927 3-9-1 **63**...................(p) AndrewMullen 13 67
(Michael Appleby) *trckd ldrs: 2nd over 2f out: kpt on clsng stages* **6/1**^{3}

0-66 **3** nse **The King's Steed**^{23} 1828 3-9-5 **67**.. FMBerry 1 71
(Ralph Beckett) *mid-div: hdwy over 2f out: 3rd over 1f out: kpt on clsng stages* **8/1**

1430 **4** 2 **Specialv (IRE)**^{13} 2095 3-9-2 **64**......................................(p) BenCurtis 14 63
(Brian Ellison) *mid-divm: hdwy over 2f out: 4th over 1f out: kpt on same pce* **25/1**

066- **5** 2¼ **Chilli Jam**^{185} 7902 3-9-1 **63**.. KieranO'Neill 11 57
(Ed de Giles) *s.i.s: hdwy over 2f out: nvr a threat* **20/1**

45-6 **6** hd **L'Apogee**^{22} 1849 3-9-0 **62**... TonyHamilton 2 56
(Richard Fahey) *mid-div: hdwy over 2f out: kpt on one pce* **14/1**

055 **7** 1½ **Dwynant**^{25} 1798 3-9-2 **64**.. JohnFahy 9 54
(Kevin Frost) *chsd ldrs: wknd over 1f out* **50/1**

134 **8** ½ **Fable Of Arachne**^{25} 1777 3-8-13 **61**..............................(t) OisinMurphy 5 50
(Stuart Williams) *mid-div: hdwy over 3f out: one pce fnl 2f* **16/1**

56-2 **9** 1 **The Knave (IRE)**^{36} 1486 3-8-12 **60**......................... SilvestreDeSousa 15 47+
(Scott Dixon) *led: hdd over 2f out: wknd over 1f out* **11/2**^{2}

0-54 **10** 1 **Carlovian**^{25} 1792 3-8-9 **57**... JoeFanning 4 41
(Christopher Kellett) *prom: drvn 3f out: wknd over 1f out* **20/1**

0441 **11** 3¾ **Ubla (IRE)**^{11} 2152 3-9-4 **66**... DavidProbert 3 42
(Gay Kelleway) *in rr: effrt over 3f out: wknd 2f out* **14/1**

403- **12** 9 **Arlecchino's Rock**^{238} 6774 3-9-6 **68**..........................(p) LiamKeniry 10 23
(Mark Usher) *mid-div: effrt over 3f out: wknd over 2f out: eased whn bhd clsng stages* **12/1**

-342 **13** 2¾ **Masqueraded (USA)**^{95} 613 3-9-1 **68**...................... CharlesEddery$^{(5)}$ 6 17
(Gay Kelleway) *s.i.s: in rr: brief effrt over 2f out: sn lost pl: eased whn bhd clsng stages* **40/1**

4600 **14** 1 **Men United (FR)**^{8} 2255 3-9-0 **62**.. JFEgan 12 9+
(Roy Bowring) *t.k.h: sn w ldr: chal over 3f out: wknd over 2f out: sn heavily eased and bhd* **25/1**

1m 47.32s (-1.68) **Going Correction** -0.05s/f (Good) **14** Ran SP% **116.0**
Speed ratings (Par 99): **106,105,105,103,100 100,99,98,97,96 93,84,81,80**
CSF £15.39 CT £120.86 TOTE £3.80: £2.00, £1.80, £3.80; EX 20.30 Trifecta £156.90.
Owner Matt & Lauren Morgan **Bred** S C E A Elevage De La Croix De Place **Trained** Hambleton, N Yorks

FOCUS
Race distance increased by approximately 12yds. A modest handicap but a good performance from the winner.

2507 SAFE BET DG TAXIS 01159500500 H'CAP — 1m 2f 50y
6:05 (6:08) (Class 6) (0-65,65) 4-Y-O+ **£2,587** (£770; £384; £192) **Stalls** Low

Form — RPR
2660 **1** **Best Tamayuz**[50] 1202 5-9-2 **60** BenCurtis 13 — 70
(Scott Dixon) *chsd ldr: effrt over 2f out: led 1f out: drvn out* **9/1**
65-4 **2** 1 1/2 **Inflexiball**[29] 1640 4-8-13 **57** JoeFanning 14 — 64
(John Mackie) *hld up in mid-div: hdwy over 2f out: chsd wnr over 1f out: kpt on wl: nt rch wnr* **5/1**[1]
00-5 **3** 3 1/4 **Highlife Dancer**[19] 1947 8-9-2 **60** SilvestreDeSousa 12 — 61
(Mick Channon) *chsd ldrs: effrt over 3f out: hung lft: kpt on one pce over 1f out* **5/1**[1]
4-60 **4** nk **Storm Check**[29] 1631 4-8-9 **56** GeorgeDowning(3) 1 — 58
(Andrew Crook) *in rr: hdwy on ins and nt clr run over 2f out: nt clr run 1f out: styd on to take 4th nr fin* **20/1**
5 nk **Rockmount River (IRE)**[377] 7-9-0 **58** OisinMurphy 11 — 58
(David Bridgwater) *chsd ldrs: kpt on one pce fnl 2f* **12/1**
-454 **6** nse **Shaw Ting**[15] 2045 4-9-0 **58** (v[1]) AndrewMullen 10 — 58
(Michael Appleby) *led: hdd 1f out: one pce* **8/1**[3]
060 **7** nk **Last Wish (IRE)**[5] 2329 5-8-11 **55** (b[1]) ConnorBeasley 4 — 54
(Richard Guest) *prom: nt clr run 2f out: swtchd rt: styd on fnl f* **66/1**
1314 **8** 3 **Attain**[26] 1751 7-8-13 **62** (p) AaronJones(5) 7 — 55
(Julia Feilden) *in rr: hdwy over 2f out: edgd lft over 1f out: sn wknd* **8/1**[3]
9 3 3/4 **Annigoni (IRE)**[210] 7495 4-9-1 **59** JamesSullivan 15 — 45
(Ruth Carr) *in tch: hdwy 3f out: wknd over 1f out* **12/1**
3-00 **10** 4 **Mister Marcasite**[36] 1500 6-8-11 **55** PJMcDonald 16 — 34
(Antony Brittain) *mid-div: hdwy on outer 3f out: wknd over 1f out* **12/1**
2060 **11** 3/4 **My Mo (FR)**[9] 2205 4-9-3 **61** (p) LiamKeniry 8 — 38
(David Dennis) *chsd ldrs: rdn over 2f out: lost pl over 1f out* **25/1**
0-00 **12** 3 1/4 **First Sargeant**[31] 1588 6-9-2 **65** (p) JoshDoyle(5) 9 — 36
(Lawrence Mullaney) *rr-div: effrt 4f out: sn n.m.r: wknd over 2f out* **15/2**[2]
2406 **13** shd **Galuppi**[50] 1201 5-9-2 **60** (b) FMBerry 2 — 31
(J R Jenkins) *s.s: brief effrt on outer 3f out: sn wknd* **12/1**

2m 13.23s (-1.07) **Going Correction** -0.05s/f (Good) **13** Ran SP% **118.2**
Speed ratings (Par 101): **102,100,98,97,97 97,97,95,92,88 88,85,85**
CSF £51.90 CT £254.94 TOTE £10.30: £3.80, £2.00, £1.80; EX 69.90 Trifecta £351.70.
Owner P J Dixon & Partners **Bred** Rabbah Bloodstock Limited **Trained** Babworth, Notts

FOCUS
Race distance increased by approximately 12yds. An ordinary handicap but a bit of a gamble was landed.
T/Jkpt: £4,548.10 to a £1 stake. Pool: £393,418.00 - 86.50 winning tickets. T/Plt: £59.60 to a £1 stake. Pool: £84,878.78 - 1,039.31 winning tickets. T/Qpdt: £21.10 to £1 stake. Pool: £7,801.75 - 272.43 winning tickets. **Walter Glynn**

2508a (Foreign Racing) - See Raceform Interactive

2492 CURRAGH (R-H)
Sunday, May 22
OFFICIAL GOING: Round course - yielding to soft; straight course - soft

2509a TATTERSALLS IRISH 1,000 GUINEAS (GROUP 1) (FILLIES) — 1m
1:55 (1:56) 3-Y-O
£125,735 (£41,911; £19,852; £8,823; £4,411; £2,205)

RPR
1 **Jet Setting (IRE)**[21] 1888 3-9-0 106 ShaneFoley 10 — 119
(Adrian Paul Keatley, Ire) *pressed ldr in 2nd tl led after 3f: stl travelled wl 2f out: strly pressed ent fnl f and almost jnd fnl 100yds: rallied wl to hold on* **9/1**[3]
2 hd **Minding (IRE)**[21] 1888 3-9-0 120 RyanMoore 1 — 119+
(A P O'Brien, Ire) *chsd ldrs in 3rd: rdn to chse ldr in 2nd over 1f out: almost on terms fnl 100yds: kpt on wl: jst hld in clr 2nd* **4/11**[1]
3 10 **Now Or Never (IRE)**[14] 2068 3-9-0 110 KierenFallon 3 — 96
(M D O'Callaghan, Ire) *racd in mid-div: prog to chse ldrs in 4th under 2f out: wnt 3rd appr fnl f: sn no imp on principals: kpt on same pce* **13/2**[2]
4 2 1/4 **Czabo**[9] 2220 3-9-0 95 ColinKeane 14 — 90
(Mick Channon) *hld up towards rr: prog 2f out: wnt 4th ent fnl f: nvr on terms* **33/1**
5 1/2 **Cool Thunder (IRE)**[217] 7316 3-9-0 0 ChrisHayes 9 — 89
(Kevin Prendergast, Ire) *racd in rr: prog 2f out: rdn and no imp ent fnl f: kpt on same pce* **40/1**
6 1 1/4 **Radiantly**[14] 2068 3-9-0 101 BillyLee 2 — 86
(W McCreery, Ire) *hld up towards inner: pushed along in 5th under 2f out: wknd fr 1f out* **25/1**
7 1/2 **Tanaza (IRE)**[252] 6361 3-9-0 107 PatSmullen 11 — 85
(D K Weld, Ire) *chsd ldrs in 4th: prog to chse ldr in 2nd over 3f out: rdn and nt qckn in 3rd under 2f out: no ex* **16/1**
8 8 **Californiadreaming (IRE)**[11] 2171 3-9-0 83 (t) AnaO'Brien 7 — 67
(A P O'Brien, Ire) *hld up towards rr: nt qckn over 1f out: sn one pce* **100/1**
9 2 1/2 **Pretty Perfect (IRE)**[11] 2167 3-9-0 105 SeamieHeffernan 4 — 61
(A P O'Brien, Ire) *led tl hdd after 3f: rdn 3f out and sn wknd* **10/1**
10 18 **Coolmore (IRE)**[40] 1396 3-9-0 106 (p) ColmO'Donoghue 8 — 20
(A P O'Brien, Ire) *racd in mid-div: pushed along 1/2-way: sn dropped to rr and detached 2f out: eased* **16/1**

1m 42.46s (-3.54) **Going Correction** -0.125s/f (Firm) **10** Ran SP% **127.7**
Speed ratings: **112,111,101,99,99 97,97,89,86,68**
CSF £13.74 CT £33.54 TOTE £12.40: £2.00, £1.10, £1.80; DF 24.80 Trifecta £62.80.
Owner Adrian Paul Keatley **Bred** P Kelly **Trained** Friarstown, Co. Kildare

FOCUS
The rain prompted quite a few non-runners, and the ground would not have been ideal for all the participants.

2510a AIRLIE STUD GALLINULE STKS (GROUP 3) — 1m 2f
2:30 (2:30) 3-Y-O **£28,198** (£9,080; £4,301; £1,911; £955)

RPR
1 **Beacon Rock (IRE)**[14] 2069 3-9-3 108 RyanMoore 2 — 105+
(A P O'Brien, Ire) *mde all: strly pressed 2f out: styd on wl to reassert ins fnl f: kpt on strly: comf* **9/10**[1]
2 2 **Santa Monica**[9] 2226 3-9-0 88 DeclanMcDonogh 5 — 98+
(Charles O'Brien, Ire) *hld up in 4th: prog over 1f out: styd on wl ins fnl f into 2nd clsng stages: nrst fin* **25/1**

3 3/4 **Foxtrot Charlie (USA)**[314] 4215 3-9-3 0 PatSmullen 6 — 100
(D K Weld, Ire) *chsd ldr in 2nd: rdn to press wnr 2f out: no imp ins fnl f: dropped to 3rd clsng stages* **14/1**
4 shd **Housesofparliament (IRE)**[16] 1994 3-9-3 103 (t) SeamieHeffernan 7 — 99+
(A P O'Brien, Ire) *hld up in 3rd: rdn over 2f out: dropped to 4th ent fnl f: kpt on wl clsng stages to press for 3rd* **5/2**[2]
5 3/4 **Landofhopeandglory (IRE)**[15] 2036 3-9-3 101 MichaelHussey 1 — 98+
(A P O'Brien, Ire) *racd in rr thrght: kpt on wl ins fnl f: nvr on terms* **4/1**[3]

2m 17.12s (7.82) **Going Correction** +0.575s/f (Yiel) **5** Ran SP% **111.7**
Speed ratings: **91,89,88,88,88**
CSF £22.79 TOTE £1.50: £1.02, £8.90; DF 26.90 Trifecta £154.00.
Owner Derrick Smith & Mrs John Magnier & Michael Tabor **Bred** Remember When Syndicate **Trained** Cashel, Co Tipperary

FOCUS
Three of the five runners were from Ballydoyle, and as a trial for even the Irish Derby is probably won't amount to a great deal

2512a TATTERSALLS GOLD CUP (GROUP 1) — 1m 2f 110y
3:40 (3:43) 4-Y-O+
£108,455 (£34,926; £16,544; £7,352; £3,676; £1,838)

RPR
1 **Fascinating Rock (IRE)**[20] 1940 5-9-3 122 PatSmullen 4 — 125+
(D K Weld, Ire) *chsd ldr in 2nd: prog to ld over 2f out: rdn and styd on wl ins fnl f: gng away at fin* **9/4**[2]
2 3 3/4 **Found (IRE)**[20] 1940 4-9-0 120 RyanMoore 6 — 115
(A P O'Brien, Ire) *hld up: clsr to chse ldrs over 2f out: rdn to chse wnr in 2nd over 1f out: no imp ins fnl f* **8/15**[1]
3 1 1/2 **Success Days (IRE)**[20] 1940 4-9-3 112 ShaneFoley 8 — 115
(K J Condon, Ire) *led: c wd into st under 3f out and sn hung to stands' side where dropped to 4th: no imp over 1f out: kpt on same pce into 3rd ins fnl f* **8/1**[3]
4 4 1/4 **Bocca Baciata (IRE)**[11] 2167 4-9-0 108 ColmO'Donoghue 3 — 103
(Mrs John Harrington, Ire) *hld up on inner: much clsr to chse ldr in 2nd under 3f out: nt qckn in 3rd over 1f out: wknd into 4th ins fnl f* **25/1**
5 7 **Hot Sauce (IRE)**[20] 1940 4-9-0 97 KierenFallon 7 — 90
(John Joseph Murphy, Ire) *chsd ldrs in 3rd: rdn and nt qckn in 5th over 2f out: sn one pce* **100/1**
6 6 1/2 **The Steward (USA)**[20] 1940 5-9-3 96 (b) DeclanMcDonogh 5 — 80
(D K Weld, Ire) *bit slowly away and a in rr: rdn and detached over 2f out: nvr a factor* **150/1**

2m 20.72s (0.72) **Going Correction** +0.575s/f (Yiel) **6** Ran SP% **112.6**
Speed ratings: **120,117,116,113,108 103**
CSF £3.83 CT £4.81 TOTE £3.20: £1.90, £1.02; DF 4.40 Trifecta £6.80.
Owner Newtown Anner Stud Farm Ltd **Bred** Newtown Anner Stud **Trained** Curragh, Co Kildare

FOCUS
A convincing display from the winner here, conditions were perfect for him and there's little doubt that he's a top class performer when he gets an ease in the ground.

2511 - 2515a (Foreign Racing) - See Raceform Interactive

2073 CAPANNELLE (R-H)
Sunday, May 22
OFFICIAL GOING: Turf: good

2516a PREMIO CARLO D'ALESSIO (GROUP 3) (4YO+) (TURF) — 1m 4f
2:00 (12:00) 4-Y-O+ **£21,691** (£9,544; £5,205; £2,602)

RPR
1 **Time Chant**[217] 7330 4-8-9 0 DarioVargiu 3 — 103
(Stefano Botti, Italy) *w.w in fnl pair: hdwy bef 1/2-way to chse ldrs: wnt in pursuit of ldr wl over 2 1/2f out: styd on relentlessly u.p to ld ent fnl f: drvn out* **242/100**[2]
2 1/2 **Fanoulpifer**[336] 3443 5-8-9 0 CristianDemuro 4 — 102
(Stefano Botti, Italy) *led: kicked for home 3f out: rdn and rallied 2f out: hdd ent fnl f: styd on gamely u.p* **79/10**
3 5 **Refuse To Bobbin (IRE)**[35] 6-8-9 0 LucaManiezzi 7 — 94
(M Narduzzi, Italy) *settled in midfield: rdn and chsd ldrs fr 2f out: kpt on at same pce fnl f: nvr on terms* **133/10**
4 3/4 **Keshiro (IRE)**[63] 6-8-9 0 UmbertoRispoli 2 — 93
(Stefano Botti, Italy) *w.w towards rr: tk clsr order wl over 2 1/2f out: kpt on at one pce fr 1 1/2f out: n.d* **44/5**
5 1 **Dirgam (IRE)**[33] 1557 4-8-9 0 OlivierPeslier 6 — 91
(Y Durepaire, France) *w.w in fnl pair: rdn and prog 2f out: plugged on at same pce fnl f: nvr in contention* **87/100**[1]
6 12 **Targaryen (IRE)**[22] 6-8-9 0 (p) CarloFiocchi 1 — 72
(Luciano Vitabile, Italy) *chsd ldrs: rdn to hold pl 4f out: lost pl 3f out: sn wknd* **26/1**
7 8 **Shocking Blu**[35] 1516 4-8-9 0 (b) FabioBranca 8 — 59
(Stefano Botti, Italy) *chsd ldrs under a t.k.h: dropped into midfield bef 1/2-way: last and btn whn eased over 1 1/2f out* **129/10**
8 4 1/2 **Accino (GER)**[231] 4-8-9 0 (b) AndreaAtzeni 5 — 52
(R Rohne, Germany) *pressed ldr on outer: rdn and nt qckn 3f out: wknd fnl 1 1/2f* **76/10**[3]

2m 25.4s (-1.80) **8** Ran SP% **133.7**
WIN (incl. 1 euro stake): 3.41. PLACES: 1.56, 3.04, 3.54. DF: 17.42.
Owner Sandro Cardaioli **Bred** Massimo Parri **Trained** Italy

2517a DERBY SISAL MATCHPOINT (GROUP 2) (3YO COLTS & FILLIES) (TURF) — 1m 3f
4:55 (12:00) 3-Y-O **£238,970** (£105,147; £57,352; £28,676)

RPR
1 **Super Chic (IRE)**[28] 1686 3-9-2 0 DarioVargiu 5 — 105
(Il Cavallo In Testa, Italy) *hld up towards rr: smooth hdwy fr 4f out: led 1f out: drvn out* **28/1**
2 1/2 **Dee Dee D'Or (IRE)**[27] 3-9-2 0 CristianDemuro 1 — 105
(Stefano Botti, Italy) *hld up in rr: drvn and hdwy fr over 3f out: styd on fnl f: nt rch wnr* **15/4**[3]
3 nk **Full Drago (ITY)**[27] 3-9-2 0 UmbertoRispoli 3 — 104
(Stefano Botti, Italy) *disp ld tl hdd after 3f: rdn 3f out: ev ch 2f out: no ex ins fnl f* **30/1**
4 2 1/4 **Biz Heart (IRE)**[63] 3-9-2 0 (p) AndreaAtzeni 9 — 100
(Stefano Botti, Italy) *prom tl led after 3f: racd freely: rdn 2f out: drvn and hdd 1f out: wknd fnl f* **19/4**

The Form Book, Raceform Ltd, Newbury, RG14 5SJ

5 5 **Isfahan (GER)**21 1908 3-9-2 0 EduardoPedroza 4 91
(A Wohler, Germany) *towards rr of midfield: drvn and sme hdwy fr 3f out: wknd 1f out* **7/5**1
6 11 **Freedom Beel (IRE)**21 3-9-2 0 FabioBranca 7 71
(Stefano Botti, Italy) *midfield: effrt over 2f out: unable to chal: eased fnl f* **43/5**
7 6 **Poeta Diletto**28 1686 3-9-2 0 (p) CarloFiocchi 8 60
(Stefano Botti, Italy) *towards rr of midfield: dropped to rr 4f out: sn wl btn* **104/10**
8 1 1/2 **Presley (ITY)**42 3-9-2 0 SilvanoMulas 2 58
(Stefano Botti, Italy) *midfield: hdwy to trck ldrs 3f out: drvn and outpcd over 2f out: wknd fnl f* **16/1**
9 15 **True Solitaire (IRE)**42 1368 3-9-2 0 (p) LeighRoche 6 31
(D K Weld, Ire) *tk a t.k.h: disp ld tl hdd after 3f: drvn and outpcd over 3f out: sn btn and eased* **242/100**2
2m 14.9s (134.90) 9 Ran SP% **141.1**
WIN (incl. 1 euro stake): 28.76. PLACES: 8.10, 2.63. 7.70. DF: 315.10.
Owner Incolinx **Bred** Azienda Agricola La Morosina **Trained** Italy

2518a PREMIO TUDINI (GROUP 3) (3YO+) (TURF) 6f
5:35 (12:00) 3-Y-O+ **£23,529** (£10,352; £5,647; £2,823)

RPR
1 **Plusquemavie (IRE)**23 5-9-2 0 (b) GianpasqualeFois 8 102
(V Fazio, Italy) **2/1**1
2 nse **Pensierieparole**35 4-9-2 0 SilvanoMulas 7 102
(Il Cavallo In Testa, Italy) **76/10**
3 1 **Aquila Solitaria (IRE)**28 1685 3-8-4 0 DarioVargiu 4 94
(Il Cavallo In Testa, Italy) **81/10**
4 1/2 **Harlem Shake (IRE)**35 5-9-0 0 LucaManiezzi 10 95
(Marco Gasparini, Italy) **32/5**3
5 1/2 **Zapel**196 7766 3-8-7 0 UmbertoRispoli 14 94
(Stefano Botti, Italy) **164/10**
6 nse **Falest (IRE)**35 7-9-0 0 FedericoBossa 5 93
(D Crisanti, Italy) **128/10**
7 shd **Stright Way (ITY)**42 4-8-10 0 MarioSanna 9 89
(Endo Botti, Italy) **69/10**
8 1/2 **Trust You**196 7766 4-9-0 0 CristianDemuro 11 92
(Endo Botti, Italy) **48/10**2
9 nse **Evil Spell**42 4-8-10 0 (p) FabioBranca 1 87
(Endo Botti, Italy) **48/10**2
10 nse **Two Shades Of Grey (IRE)**14 5-9-0 0 MarcoMonteriso 12 91
(M Guarnieri, Italy) **92/10**
11 1/2 **Another Full Power (ITY)**23 7-9-0 0 (p) SalvatoreBasile 15 90
(M Grassi, Italy) **241/10**
12 8 **Time Shanakill (IRE)** 3-8-5 0 AndreaAtzeni 3 62
(Stefano Botti, Italy) **108/10**
13 1/2 **Alatan Blaze (ITY)**35 5-9-0 0 (p) CarloFiocchi 13 62
(Endo Botti, Italy) **69/10**
14 1 1/2 **Tamil Nadu**42 4-9-0 0 (p) SalvatoreSulas 2 58
(Andrea Renzi, Italy) **237/10**
15 3 **Princess Kay (IRE)**259 3-8-2 0 MarcelloBelli 6 43
(B Grizzetti & L Riccardi, Italy) **48/1**
1m 7.43s (-2.87)
WFA 3 from 4yo+ 9lb 15 Ran SP% **170.6**
WIN (incl. 1 euro stake): 2.98. PLACES: 1.60, 3.00, 2.86. DF: 29.98.
Owner Maestro **Bred** Allevamento Pian Di Neve **Trained** Italy

2519 - 2521a (Foreign Racing) - See Raceform Interactive

2358 AYR (L-H)
Monday, May 23

OFFICIAL GOING: Good to soft (good in places; 6.9)
Wind: Breezy, half against Weather: Cloudy, bright

2522 RACING UK NOW IN HD! MAIDEN STKS 1m 2f
2:00 (2:00) (Class 5) 3-Y-O+ **£2,911** (£866; £432; £216) **Stalls** Low

Form RPR
535- 1 **Navajo War Dance**220 7246 3-9-0 90 DougieCostello 4 80
(K R Burke) *trckd ldr: led gng wl over 2f out: rdn clr fr over 1f out* **8/11**1
34-6 2 4 **Torremar (FR)**30 1630 3-9-0 72 GrahamLee 6 72
(Kevin Ryan) *trckd ldrs: effrt and wnt 2nd over 2f out: drvn and hung lft over 1f out: sn no ch w wnr* **2/1**2
04 3 10 **Big Time Dancer (IRE)**17 2019 3-9-0 0 JamesSullivan 2 52
(Dianne Sayer) *t.k.h: hld up in tch: shkn up and hdwy 2f out: sn no imp* **20/1**
05 4 3 3/4 **Silva Samourai**14 2094 7-10-0 0 JoeyHaynes 1 46
(Susan Corbett) *led at modest gallop: rdn and hdd over 2f out: wknd over 1f out* **100/1**
0 5 6 **King Julien (IRE)**28 1715 3-8-11 0 JoeDoyle(3) 5 33
(John Ryan) *prom: drvn and struggling 3f out: btn fnl 2f* **13/2**3
6 2 1/4 **Shumaker (IRE)**30 1657 4-10-0 0 PaulMulrennan 3 29
(Noel C Kelly, Ire) *s.i.s: hld up: struggling wl over 2f out: sn wknd* **40/1**
2m 17.68s (5.68) **Going Correction** +0.50s/f (Yiel)
WFA 3 from 4yo+ 14lb 6 Ran SP% **112.8**
Speed ratings (Par 103): **97,93,85,82,78 76**
CSF £2.40 TOTE £1.60: £1.10, £2.00; EX 3.40 Trifecta £10.60.
Owner Geoffrey Bishop **Bred** G S Bishop **Trained** Middleham Moor, N Yorks

FOCUS
Drying conditions. The inside line was out three yards, adding nine yards to the race distance. An uncompetitive maiden. THe winner did not need to match his best.

2523 RACING UK DAY PASS NOW JUST £10 H'CAP 5f
2:30 (2:30) (Class 6) (0-65,65) 4-Y-O+ **£2,587** (£770; £384; £192) **Stalls** Low

Form RPR
0334 1 **Roy's Legacy**16 2052 7-8-6 57 CharlieBennett(7) 4 67
(Shaun Harris) *mde all: rdn over 1f out: edgd rt ins fnl f: kpt on strly* **8/1**
34-2 2 1 1/2 **Minty Jones**17 2013 7-8-7 51 (v) JoeyHaynes 7 56
(Michael Mullineaux) *dwlt: hld up: rdn and hdwy 1/2-way: hung lft and chsd wnr over 1f out: ch ins fnl f: sn no ex* **11/2**
0-64 3 3 1/2 **Bunce (IRE)**24 1843 8-9-7 65 PJMcDonald 6 57
(Linda Perratt) *hld up in tch: effrt and hdwy whn nt clr run briefly over 1f out: one pce fnl f* **5/1**3
-205 4 1 1/4 **Bahango (IRE)**24 1843 4-9-3 61 GrahamLee 5 49
(Patrick Morris) *t.k.h: pressed wnr to over 1f out: kpt on same pce fnl f* **10/1**
10-1 5 nk **Perfect Words (IRE)**16 2052 6-9-3 64 (p) JacobButterfield(3) 8 51
(Marjorie Fife) *in tch: effrt and pushed along over 2f out: one pce fr over 1f out* **4/1**2
-055 6 1 1/2 **Mystical King**5 2359 6-8-2 46 oh1 (p) JamesSullivan 2 27
(Linda Perratt) *in tch: rdn and hung lft 2f out: sn outpcd: n.d after* **14/1**
6-00 7 4 **It's Time For Bed**5 2360 4-8-2 46 RoystonFfrench 3 13
(Linda Perratt) *prom: drvn over 2f out: wknd over 1f out* **33/1**
-32 8 9 **Little Belter (IRE)**10 2202 4-8-13 57 (v) JoeFanning 1
(Keith Dalgleish) *dwlt: bhd: struggling over 2f out: sn wknd: eased whn btn fnl f* **9/4**1
1m 3.18s (3.78) **Going Correction** +0.80s/f (Soft) 8 Ran SP% **112.6**
Speed ratings (Par 101): **101,98,93,91,90 88,81,67**
CSF £49.66 CT £241.75 TOTE £10.20: £2.90, £2.40, £1.70; EX 55.50 Trifecta £470.00.
Owner S Mohammed, S Rowley & S Harris **Bred** A Christou **Trained** Carburton, Notts

FOCUS
A moderate sprint handicap. The winner is rated back towards this year's form.

2524 FOLLOW @RACING_UK ON TWITTER H'CAP 6f
3:05 (3:05) (Class 5) (0-75,75) 3-Y-O+ **£3,234** (£962; £481; £240) **Stalls** Low

Form RPR
2410 1 **Captain Scooby**22 1878 10-9-1 64 (b) JasonHart 6 70
(Richard Guest) *dwlt: hld up bhd ldng gp: stdy hdwy over 2f out: rdn to ld ins fnl f: hld on wl cl home* **25/1**
-432 2 hd **Go Go Green (IRE)**24 1843 10-9-6 72 JoeDoyle(3) 8 77
(Jim Goldie) *trckd ldrs gng wl: effrt and rdn ent fnl f: kpt on: jst hld* **16/1**
0-40 3 3/4 **Blue Sonic**5 2364 6-9-5 68 PaulMulrennan 1 71
(Linda Perratt) *dwlt: hld up: effrt nr side of gp over 1f out: kpt on fnl f: nrst fin* **33/1**
-454 4 1 1/2 **Vallarta (IRE)**22 1879 6-9-12 75 JamesSullivan 12 73
(Ruth Carr) *t.k.h: cl up: ev ch over 2f out: rdn and one pce fnl f* **5/1**3
50-1 5 1 3/4 **Mo Henry**28 1692 4-8-13 62 (p) JoeFanning 10 54
(Adrian Paul Keatley, Ire) *w ldr: led 1/2-way: rdn wl over 1f out: hung lft and hdd ins fnl f: wknd towards fin* **2/1**1
4-61 6 2 1/4 **Sir Domino (FR)**22 1879 4-9-12 75 GrahamLee 7 60
(Kevin Ryan) *trckd ldrs: rdn over 2f out: wknd over 1f out* **7/2**2
0-55 7 nk **Jinky**5 2364 8-9-6 69 GeorgeChaloner 3 53
(Linda Perratt) *in tch: rdn and outpcd wl over 1f out: n.d after* **14/1**
6-62 8 3 1/4 **Silver Streak (IRE)**17 2019 3-9-0 72 PJMcDonald 9 44
(Ann Duffield) *led to 1/2-way: rdn and wknd fr 2f out* **10/1**
145- 9 4 1/2 **Bop It**246 6558 7-9-9 72 DanielTudhope 2 31
(David O'Meara) *taken early to post: cl up: rdn over 2f out: wknd over 1f out: eased whn btn ins fnl f* **13/2**
-610 10 1 1/4 **Toledo**10 2200 3-8-12 70 SamJames 4 23
(Marjorie Fife) *in tch: drvn and lost pl over 2f out: sn struggling* **28/1**
1m 16.52s (4.12) **Going Correction** +0.80s/f (Soft)
WFA 3 from 4yo+ 9lb 10 Ran SP% **117.4**
Speed ratings (Par 103): **104,103,102,100,98 95,95,90,84,83**
CSF £368.18 CT £12750.06 TOTE £22.30: £4.90, £3.40, £4.10; EX 136.80 Trifecta £2287.50.
Owner The Captain Scooby Syndicate **Bred** Hellwood Stud Farm & Paul Davies (h'Gate) **Trained** Ingmanthorpe, W Yorks

FOCUS
It looked as though the leaders got racing plenty soon enough. The two oldest runners in the line-up, who were both waited with, came to the fore. THey are both rated to therir bests for the last couple of years.

2525 RACINGUK.COM H'CAP 1m
3:40 (3:42) (Class 6) (0-60,58) 4-Y-O+ **£2,587** (£770; £384; £192) **Stalls** Low

Form RPR
1 1 **Millefiori (IRE)**5 2365 4-8-8 45 (p) JoeFanning 2 72
(Adrian Paul Keatley, Ire) *prom: smooth hdwy to ld over 2f out: hung lft and drew clr fr over 1f out: v easily* **1/2**1
004- 2 10 **Drinks For Losers (IRE)**44 1349 5-8-5 45 JoeDoyle(3) 8 44
(Linda Perratt) *trckd ldrs: rdn over 2f out: chsd (clr) wnr over 1f out: kpt on: no imp* **14/1**
40-0 3 1 3/4 **Riponian**6 2330 6-9-0 51 TonyHamilton 3 46
(Susan Corbett) *t.k.h: led: hung rt thrght: c wd st: rdn and hdd over 2f out: sn one pce* **20/1**
40-0 4 shd **Bertha Burnett (IRE)**40 1412 5-8-12 49 GrahamLee 9 44
(Brian Rothwell) *prom: rdn along over 2f out: kpt on same pce fnl f* **33/1**
306- 5 4 **Modern Tutor**101 555 7-9-7 58 (t) DougieCostello 5 43
(Miss Nicole McKenna, Ire) *hld up: rdn along over 2f out: sn no imp* **18/1**
00-6 6 2 **Jubilee Song**17 2015 4-8-12 49 (b1) GeorgeChaloner 10 29
(Richard Whitaker) *hld up in tch: rdn and outpcd over 3f out: btn fnl 2f* **50/1**
0062 7 8 **Stanlow**27 1742 6-8-12 49 JoeyHaynes 6 10
(Michael Mullineaux) *hld up towards rr: drvn along over 3f out: btn over 2f out* **8/1**2
8 30 **Macalla (IRE)**11 7931 4-8-8 45 (p) PJMcDonald 1
(R Mike Smith) *dwlt: sn pushed along in rr: struggling fr 1/2-way: t.o* **9/1**
3503 9 10 **Mercury**21 1926 4-9-6 57 (p) PaulMulrennan 4
(Kevin Ryan) *cl up tl rdn and wknd over 2f out: t.o* **17/2**3
1m 45.26s (1.46) **Going Correction** +0.50s/f (Yiel) 9 Ran SP% **119.9**
Speed ratings (Par 101): **112,102,100,100,96 94,86,56,46**
CSF £9.91 CT £81.99 TOTE £1.30: £1.02, £3.80, £3.50; EX 11.70 Trifecta £107.60.
Owner Mrs F Hughes **Bred** Kevin J Molloy **Trained** Friarstown, Co. Kildare

FOCUS
This was run over nine yards further than advertised. It was desperately uncompetitive, with nothing able to go with the winner who was well ahead of her mark, and the third finishing in the money despite hanging to the stands' rail in the straight. The runners were spread all over the place in the closing stages. The winner was better than the impressive bare facts.

2526 RACING UK PROFITS RETURNED TO RACING H'CAP 1m 2f
4:15 (4:15) (Class 5) (0-70,70) 4-Y-O+ **£3,234** (£962; £481; £240) **Stalls** Low

Form RPR
00-3 1 **Cymraeg Bounty**30 1631 4-9-5 68 JoeFanning 4 81
(Iain Jardine) *t.k.h early: hld up in tch: effrt and shkn up over 2f out: edgd lft and led over 1f out: sn hrd pressed: hld on gamely fnl f* **5/2**1
3-52 2 shd **Henpecked**22 1881 6-8-13 62 ConnorBeasley 2 74
(Alistair Whillans) *t.k.h early: in tch: smooth hdwy to chal over 1f out: rdn ent fnl f: kpt on: jst hld* **3/1**2
5-20 3 6 **Testa Rossa (IRE)**14 2093 6-8-10 59 (v) GrahamLee 9 59
(Jim Goldie) *prom: hdwy to ld 3f out: rdn and hdd over 1f out: outpcd fnl f* **6/1**3

3350 **4** 1 3/4 **Sakhalin Star (IRE)**^{14} 2091 5-9-4 **67**....(e) JasonHart 6 63
(Richard Guest) *t.k.h early: hld up: effrt on outside over 2f out: rdn and no imp over 1f out* **6/1**^{3}

0-05 **5** 3 3/4 **Weapon Of Choice (IRE)**^{19} 1633 8-9-4 **70**....(tp) MissEmmaSayer$^{(3)}$ 8 59
(Dianne Sayer) *dwlt: hdwy to ld after 2f: rdn and hdd 3f out: outpcd fr 2f out* **9/1**

-430 **6** 3/4 **Gone With The Wind (GER)**^{14} 2091 5-9-1 **64**....(t) PaulMulrennan 5 51
(Rebecca Bastiman) *hld up: rdn along over 2f out: sn outpcd* **12/1**

4-00 **7** 2 3/4 **We'll Shake Hands (FR)**^{16} 2051 5-9-0 **70**....(v) CliffordLee$^{(7)}$ 1 52
(K R Burke) *t.k.h: prom: rdn over 2f out: edgd rt and wknd over 1f out* **7/1**

100- **8** 59 **Spokesperson (USA)**^{280} 5455 8-8-10 **59**.... JackGarritty 10
(Fred Watson) *led 2f: pressed ldr tl rdn and wknd over 2f out: sn lost tch: eased whn no ch: t.o* **25/1**

2m 17.75s (5.75) **Going Correction** +0.50s/f (Yiel) **8** Ran SP% **116.2**
Speed ratings (Par 103): **97,96,92,90,87 87,84,37**
CSF £10.33 CT £39.82 TOTE £3.40: £1.60, £1.50, £2.20; EX 11.50 Trifecta £42.30.
Owner M Andrews **Bred** Richard Evans **Trained** Carrutherstown, D'fries & G'way

FOCUS
This was run over nine yards further than advertised. An ordinary handicap in which the first two finished clear. The winner build on his recent stable debut.

2527 RACINGUK.COM/HD H'CAP 1m
4:45 (4:45) (Class 3) (0-95,95) 4-Y-O+ **£7,762** (£2,310; £1,154; £577) **Stalls** Low

Form RPR

03-0 **1** **Le Chat D'Or**^{56} 1122 8-8-9 **83**....(bt) PaulMulrennan 7 92
(Michael Dods) *hld up: effrt and plld out over 1f out: gd hdwy fnl f: led nr fin* **8/1**^{3}

1-23 **2** nk **Erik The Red (FR)**^{12} 2157 4-9-7 **95**.... ShaneGray 9 103
(Kevin Ryan) *stdd in rr: gd hdwy over 1f out: edgd lft: rdn to ld ins fnl f: kpt on: hdd nr fin* **7/4**^{1}

023- **3** 1 3/4 **Pintura**^{201} 7709 9-9-2 **90**....(b) PhillipMakin 1 94
(Alistair Whillans) *led at ordinary gallop: rdn over 1f out: hdd ins fnl f: kpt on same pce* **14/1**

-261 **4** 1/2 **Treasury Notes (IRE)**^{30} 1643 4-8-13 **87**.... DanielTudhope 2 90
(David O'Meara) *hld up in tch: rdn whn n.m.r and outpcd over 2f out: kpt on ins fnl f: nrst fin* **9/4**^{2}

60-0 **5** nk **Intiwin (IRE)**^{33} 1576 4-8-9 **83**.... TonyHamilton 5 85
(Richard Fahey) *trckd ldrs: rdn over 2f out: kpt on same pce fnl f* **8/1**^{3}

0202 **6** 1 1/4 **Abushamah (IRE)**^{9} 2256 5-8-7 **81**.... JamesSullivan 6 80
(Ruth Carr) *pressed ldr: rdn over 2f out: wknd appr fnl f* **8/1**^{3}

0-04 **7** 1 **Gworn**^{28} 1694 6-8-7 **81**....(p) PJMcDonald 3 78
(R Mike Smith) *prom: stdy hdwy gng wl over 2f out: rdn over 1f out: wknd ins fnl f* **11/1**

1m 46.1s (2.30) **Going Correction** +0.50s/f (Yiel) **7** Ran SP% **115.5**
Speed ratings (Par 107): **108,107,105,105,105 103,102**
CSF £22.96 CT £197.45 TOTE £9.80: £4.10, £1.50; EX 42.60 Trifecta £293.90.
Owner Dr Anne J F Gillespie **Bred** Dr A Gillespie **Trained** Denton, Co Durham

FOCUS
This was run over nine yards further than advertised. It was something of a muddling contest, run in a time 0.84sec slower than the well-handicapped Millefiori recorded in the earlier 0-60. The winner's best form since 2014.

2528 RACING UK H'CAP 7f 50y
5:15 (5:16) (Class 6) (0-60,60) 4-Y-O+ **£2,587** (£770; £384; £192) **Stalls** High

Form RPR

60-5 **1** **Joyful Star**^{14} 2096 6-8-11 **50**.... JackGarritty 9 59
(Fred Watson) *hld up: effrt whn nt clr run briefly over 2f out: hdwy to ld 1f out: pushed clr* **7/2**^{2}

0-04 **2** 3 **Goninodaethat**^{5} 2360 8-9-5 **58**.... PaulMulrennan 6 59
(Jim Goldie) *trckd ldrs: led over 2f out: rdn: edgd lft and hdd 1f out: kpt on: no ch w wnr* **7/2**^{2}

60-0 **3** 3 1/2 **Bushtiger (IRE)**^{24} 1845 4-8-7 **46** oh1.... JamesSullivan 1 38
(Ruth Carr) *bhd: rdn and hdwy on outside 2f out: kpt on fnl f: no imp* **20/1**

020- **4** 8 **Studio Star**^{230} 7009 4-8-7 **51**.... NathanEvans$^{(5)}$ 4 22
(Wilf Storey) *t.k.h: trckd ldrs on ins: rdn over 2f out: wknd over 1f out* **12/1**

21-0 **5** 3 1/2 **Outlaw Kate (IRE)**^{30} 1631 4-8-10 **49**....(p) JoeyHaynes 2 11
(Michael Mullineaux) *hld up in tch: rdn and outpcd over 2f out: btn over 1f out* **14/1**

0-00 **6** 1/2 **Call Me Crockett (IRE)**^{14} 2092 4-9-7 **60**....(p) RoystonFfrench 3 21
(Iain Jardine) *hld up: rdn over 2f out: sn no imp: btn over 1f out* **6/1**^{3}

3-00 **7** 4 1/2 **Takahiro**^{14} 2096 4-8-5 **47**....(b) JoeDoyle$^{(3)}$ 7
(Linda Perratt) *hld up in midfield on outside: stdy hdwy over 2f out: sn rdn: wknd over 1f out* **40/1**

135- **8** 4 1/2 **Elusive Gent (IRE)**^{38} 1464 9-8-10 **49**....(bt) TonyHamilton 5
(Miss Nicole McKenna, Ire) *pressed ldr: ev ch briefly 3f out: sn rdn: wknd 2f out* **8/1**

6152 **9** 22 **Emblaze**^{24} 1845 4-9-0 **58**.... PhilDennis$^{(5)}$ 8
(Bryan Smart) *t.k.h: led to over 2f out: drvn and wknd wl over 1f out* **3/1**^{1}

1m 36.63s (3.23) **Going Correction** +0.50s/f (Yiel) **9** Ran SP% **116.4**
Speed ratings (Par 101): **101,97,93,84,80 79,74,69,44**
CSF £16.36 CT £213.83 TOTE £4.20: £1.70, £1.90, £4.20; EX 17.70 Trifecta £289.60.
Owner F Watson **Bred** Rabbah Bloodstock Limited **Trained** Sedgefield, Co Durham

FOCUS
This was run over nine yards further than advertised. A moderate handicap and the favourite finished lame, but a likeable winner who built oh his reappearance. .
T/Plt: £101.80 to a £1 stake. Pool: £61,761.64 - 442.46 winning units. T/Qpdt: £44.00 to a £1 stake. Pool: £5,939.92 - 99.80 winning units. **Richard Young**

2416 CARLISLE (R-H)
Monday, May 23

OFFICIAL GOING: Good to firm (8.2)
Wind: fresh across Weather: fine

2529 APOLLOBET HOME OF CASHBACK OFFERS APPRENTICE TRAINING SERIES H'CAP 7f 173y
6:35 (6:35) (Class 5) (0-75,72) 4-Y-O+ **£2,911** (£866; £432; £216) **Stalls** Low

Form RPR

-000 **1** **Red Charmer (IRE)**^{21} 1926 6-9-2 **62**.... RowanScott 3 72
(Ann Duffield) *trckd ldr: rdn over 2f out: led jst ins fnl f: kpt on* **8/1**

5004 **2** 2 1/4 **Freight Train (IRE)**^{21} 1923 4-9-9 **72**.... GeorgeWood$^{(3)}$ 5 76
(Mark Johnston) *led: rdn 2f out: hdd jst ins fnl f: one pce* **15/8**^{2}

6-66 **3** 1 **Bush Beauty (IRE)**^{4} 2409 5-9-0 **60**.... SophieKilloran 1 62
(Eric Alston) *dwlt: hld up: rdn 2f out: kpt on ins fnl f* **11/2**^{3}

0-00 **4** 1 1/2 **Tanawar (IRE)**^{10} 2198 6-9-3 **66**....(b) AdamMcNamara$^{(3)}$ 2 64
(Ruth Carr) *trckd ldr: rdn over 2f out: no ex ins fnl f* **10/1**

34-2 **5** 3 1/2 **Newmarket Warrior (IRE)**^{26} 1785 5-9-9 **69**....(p) GeorgiaCox 7 62
(Iain Jardine) *hld up in tch: racd keenly: pushed along over 2f out: wknd ins fnl f* **13/8**^{1}

1m 40.05s (0.05) **Going Correction** 0.0s/f (Good) **5** Ran SP% **108.5**
Speed ratings (Par 103): **99,96,95,94,90**
CSF £22.71 TOTE £8.40: £5.00, £1.50; EX 31.00 Trifecta £125.70.
Owner I Farrington & R Chapman **Bred** Tally-Ho Stud **Trained** Constable Burton, N Yorks

FOCUS
It was dry overnight, although 4mm of water had been put on the course on Sunday afternoon. The going was given as good to firm (GoingStick: 8.2). The inside rail was out 6yds, from the mile start round the Old Stable bend to the 3f marker. Race distance increased by 12yds. The early gallop wasn't particularly strong in this apprentice handicap. The form is rated around the runner-up.

2530 APOLLOBET DAILY RACING REFUNDS NOVICE MEDIAN AUCTION STKS 5f
7:05 (7:08) (Class 5) 2-Y-O **£2,911** (£866; £432; £216) **Stalls** Low

Form RPR

2 **1** **Medici Banchiere**^{12} 2162 2-9-2 0.... DougieCostello 1 90
(K R Burke) *trckd ldng pair: pressed ldr gng wl 1/2-way: pushed along to ld over 1f out: r.o strly to go clr fnl f: impressive* **4/7**^{1}

5 **2** 10 **Galahad**^{14} 2090 2-9-2 0.... DavidNolan 5 54
(Richard Fahey) *hld up: sn pushed along: kpt on to go remote 2nd towards fin* **14/1**

4 **3** 1 1/2 **Major Jumbo**^{13} 2119 2-9-2 0.... TomEaves 2 49
(Kevin Ryan) *led narrowly: rdn whn hdd over 1f out: wknd fnl f: lost 2nd towards fin* **3/1**^{2}

4 12 **La Casa Tarifa (IRE)** 2-8-11 0.... FrannyNorton 3
(Mark Johnston) *s.i.s: sn pushed along in rr: bhd fnl 2f* **17/2**^{3}

0 **5** 6 **Redrosezorro**^{18} 1976 2-9-2 0.... JasonHart 4
(Eric Alston) *racd keenly: pressed ldr: lost pl 1/2-way: sn bhd* **25/1**

1m 0.55s (-0.25) **Going Correction** -0.125s/f (Firm) **5** Ran SP% **109.7**
Speed ratings (Par 93): **97,81,78,59,49**
CSF £9.79 TOTE £1.50: £1.20, £2.70; EX 7.70 Trifecta £12.50.
Owner Global Racing Club & Mrs E Burke **Bred** Mrs Sheila Oakes **Trained** Middleham Moor, N Yorks

FOCUS
The favourite set a pretty high standard and won easily. He looks worth his place at Royal Ascot and this form could be rated higher.

2531 APOLLOBET BET THROUGH YOUR MOBILE H'CAP (JOCKEY CLUB GRASSROOTS FLAT SPRINT SERIES QUALIFIER) 5f 193y
7:35 (7:36) (Class 4) (0-80,79) 4-Y-O+ **£5,175** (£1,540; £769; £384) **Stalls** Low

Form RPR

3021 **1** **Final Venture**^{10} 2202 4-9-3 **75**.... NeilFarley 9 85
(Alan Swinbank) *mde all: rdn over 2f out: pressed ent fnl f: hld on wl* **7/2**^{1}

0-40 **2** 1/2 **Manatee Bay**^{9} 2259 6-9-3 **75**....(v) FrannyNorton 8 83
(David Nicholls) *hld up in midfield: pushed along and sme hdwy 2f out: rdn and r.o wl fnl f: wnt 2nd towards fin* **4/1**^{2}

-000 **3** 1 **Apricot Sky**^{9} 2261 6-8-7 **72**.... DanielleMooney$^{(7)}$ 3 77
(David Nicholls) *chsd ldrs: rdn over 2f out: chal appr fnl f: no ex and lost 2nd towards fin* **25/1**

0050 **4** shd **Sunraider (IRE)**^{16} 2028 9-9-0 **72**.... GrahamLee 11 76
(Paul Midgley) *hld up: outpcd in rr over 3f out: stl plenty to do appr fnl f: r.o strly ins fnl f: nrst fin* **9/1**

30-0 **5** 1 **Fyrecracker (IRE)**^{9} 2259 5-9-3 **75**.... TomEaves 5 76
(Grant Tuer) *hld up: rdn and hdwy 2f out: kpt on fnl f* **40/1**

4-20 **6** 1/2 **Koptoon**^{16} 2028 4-8-13 **71**....(t) TonyHamilton 2 71
(Michael Appleby) *prom: rdn over 2f out: wknd fnl 110yds* **7/1**

0-00 **7** 1 3/4 **Meandmyshadow**^{16} 2050 8-9-0 **72**....(b) GrahamGibbons 14 66
(Alan Brown) *prom: rdn over 2f out: wknd ins fnl f* **25/1**

0-00 **8** 1 3/4 **Piazon**^{17} 2016 5-9-7 **79**....(p) ShaneGray 1 67
(Kevin Ryan) *dwlt: sn midfield on inner: rdn over 2f out: wknd ins fnl f* **14/1**

5-00 **9** shd **Eternitys Gate**^{9} 2238 5-9-3 **75**....(p) DanielTudhope 10 63
(David O'Meara) *midfield: rdn over 2f out: wknd ins fnl f* **11/2**^{3}

0-04 **10** 3 **Fuwairt (IRE)**^{9} 2238 4-9-6 **78**.... RaulDaSilva 13 57
(David Loughnane) *dwlt: sn midfield towards outer: rdn over 2f out: wknd fnl f* **8/1**

0-30 **11** 3 1/2 **Townsville**^{28} 1694 4-9-6 **78**.... JoeFanning 12 45
(Keith Dalgleish) *a towards rr* **22/1**

0-00 **12** 1 **Mercers Row**^{9} 2259 9-9-5 **77**.... DavidNolan 7 41
(Michael Herrington) *midfield: rdn and outpcd over 2f out: wknd over 1f out* **25/1**

1m 12.16s (-1.54) **Going Correction** -0.125s/f (Firm) **12** Ran SP% **116.2**
Speed ratings (Par 105): **105,104,103,102,101 100,98,96,96,92 87,86**
CSF £15.52 CT £300.91 TOTE £4.60: £1.80, £1.90, £8.50; EX 15.50 Trifecta £362.30.
Owner Brian Valentine **Bred** Newsells Park Stud **Trained** Melsonby, N Yorks

FOCUS
This sprint was run at a good pace and the winner, who led from the start, did well to hold the closers at bay. The winner built on his Hamilton win.

2532 APOLLOBET WEEKLY GOLF RETURNS H'CAP 7f 173y
8:05 (8:06) (Class 4) (0-80,80) 3-Y-O **£5,175** (£1,540; £769; £384) **Stalls** Low

Form RPR

12 **1** **Bargain Buy**^{33} 1572 3-9-6 **79**.... GrahamGibbons 3 84
(William Haggas) *in tch: hdwy over 2f out: rdn to ld narrowly wl over 1f out: hdd 50yds out: led again post* **9/4**^{1}

0-51 **2** shd **Quick N Quirky (IRE)**^{14} 2095 3-9-5 **78**....(t) DavidAllan 1 82
(Tim Easterby) *midfield: hdwy to chal strly 2f out: sn rdn: edgd ahd 50yds out: hdd post* **4/1**^{2}

44-2 **3** 3/4 **Deansgate (IRE)**^{41} 1400 3-8-13 **72**....(e^{1}) ConnorBeasley 7 74
(Julie Camacho) *s.i.s: hld up: racd keenly: pushed along over 3f out: rdn over 2f out: angled lft and hdwy over 1f out: kpt on fnl f* **14/1**

05-1 **4** nk **Island Flame (IRE)**^{29} 1671 3-8-9 **68**.... TonyHamilton 2 70+
(Richard Fahey) *trckd ldr: rdn over 2f out: kpt on same pce* **9/2**^{3}

10 **5** 2 1/4 **Fisher Green (IRE)**^{30} 1623 3-9-7 **80**.... PaulMulrennan 6 76
(Michael Dods) *trckd ldr: rdn over 2f out: wknd ins fnl f* **6/1**

403- **6** nk **Auxiliary**^{225} 7142 3-9-4 **77**.... DavidNolan 9 72
(Patrick Holmes) *hld up: pushed along 3f out: kpt on ins fnl f: nvr threatened* **28/1**

04-4 **7** nse **Muroor**^{25} 1815 3-8-13 **72**.... DanielTudhope 4 67
(David O'Meara) *led: rdn whn hdd wl over 1f out: wknd ins fnl f* **9/1**

-145 **8** 1 ¾ **He's A Dreamer (IRE)**[40] 1409 3-9-7 **80** PhillipMakin 5 71+
(David O'Meara) *s.i.s: sn in midfield racing keenly: hdwy on outer over 2f out: rdn 2f out: wknd ins fnl f* **12/1**

03-6 **9** 9 **Overhaugh Street**[28] 1691 3-8-13 **72** JasonHart 8 41
(Keith Dalgleish) *hld up: rdn over 4f out: sn struggling* **50/1**

1m 39.77s (-0.23) **Going Correction** 0.0s/f (Good) **9** Ran SP% **113.0**
Speed ratings (Par 101): **101,100,100,99,97 97,97,95,86**
CSF £10.80 CT £98.30 TOTE £2.80: £1.80, £1.50, £3.70; EX 12.50 Trifecta £123.50.
Owner Sheikh Rashid Dalmook Al Maktoum **Bred** Shane & Nicola O'Neill & R Kent **Trained** Newmarket, Suffolk

FOCUS
Race distance increased by 12yds. A competitive handicap in which the winenr carried forward his AW progress.

2533 APOLLOBET ONLINE GAMES AND CASINO H'CAP 6f 195y
8:35 (8:35) (Class 5) (0-70,70) 3-Y-O **£2,911** (£866; £432; £216) **Stalls** Low

Form RPR

12-4 **1** **Ponty Royale (IRE)**[32] 1584 3-8-13 **62** DavidAllan 1 66
(Tim Easterby) *racd keenly in midfield: pushed along and hdwy over 2f out: led over 1f out: sn rdn: kpt on wl* **3/1**[2]

55-6 **2** ¾ **Strummer (IRE)**[14] 2095 3-9-3 **66** TomEaves 9 68
(Kevin Ryan) *hld up in rr: gd hdwy over 2f out: rdn to chal 2f out: one pce towards fin* **11/1**

5-34 **3** nk **The Name's Paver**[26] 1788 3-9-4 **67** BarryMcHugh 5 68
(Noel Wilson) *trckd ldng pair: rdn over 2f out: kpt on* **10/1**

60-5 **4** 4 **Stormy Art (IRE)**[23] 1849 3-9-0 **63** PaulMulrennan 4 51
(Michael Dods) *hld up: rdn over 2f out: sme hdwy over 1f out: kpt on ins fnl f* **9/1**

0-35 **5** 3 ¾ **Oscar Hughes (IRE)**[25] 1815 3-8-11 **60** (p) ConnorBeasley 6 36
(Julie Camacho) *racd keenly: pressed ldr: hung lft on bnd 4f out: led narrowly over 2f out: hdd over 1f out: sn wknd* **25/1**

45-5 **6** nk **The Lynch Man**[26] 1788 3-9-7 **70** JasonHart 8 45
(John Quinn) *hld up: rdn over 2f out: one pce and nvr threatened* **4/1**[3]

2-50 **7** 2 ½ **Magical Lasso (IRE)**[29] 1671 3-9-1 **67** (b[1]) JoeDoyle[(3)] 7 34
(Kevin Ryan) *trckd ldng pair: rdn 3f out: wknd over 1f out* **22/1**

04-0 **8** 4 **Trikingdom**[29] 1667 3-8-6 **55** NeilFarley 3 9
(Alan Swinbank) *midfield: rdn over 2f out: hung rt over 1f out and wknd* **28/1**

61-2 **9** 2 ¼ **She's Electric (IRE)**[3] 2422 3-9-3 **66** PhillipMakin 2 13
(Keith Dalgleish) *led narrowly: rdn whn hdd over 2f out: wknd over 1f out* **9/4**[1]

1m 27.02s (-0.08) **Going Correction** 0.0s/f (Good) **9** Ran SP% **114.8**
Speed ratings (Par 99): **100,99,98,94,89 89,86,82,79**
CSF £34.23 CT £293.96 TOTE £4.20: £1.60, £2.60, £2.70; EX 35.80 Trifecta £242.90.
Owner Calvert, O'Neill & Partner **Bred** Tom Darcy And Vincent McCarthy **Trained** Great Habton, N Yorks

FOCUS
Race distance increased by 12yds. An ordinary handicap, but it was run at a decent gallop. The winner resumed her latter 2yo progress.

2534 APOLLOBET CASH BACK IF YOU'RE 2ND H'CAP 5f
9:05 (9:08) (Class 5) (0-75,73) 3-Y-O **£2,911** (£866; £432; £216) **Stalls** Low

Form RPR

1-56 **1** **Twentysvnthlancers**[57] 1112 3-9-0 **66** GrahamLee 6 69
(Paul Midgley) *mde all: a pressed by 2nd: rdn over 1f out: hld on wl* **8/1**

3-40 **2** nk **Lady Wootton**[9] 2255 3-8-7 **59** (b[1]) JoeFanning 4 61
(Keith Dalgleish) *pressed ldr: rdn 2f out: kpt on but a jst hld* **11/2**

6-53 **3** ½ **Wilde Extravagance (IRE)**[26] 1788 3-9-1 **67** ConnorBeasley 2 67
(Julie Camacho) *chsd ldng pair: rdn 2f out: kpt on* **9/2**[3]

006- **4** nk **Encantar**[220] 7261 3-9-6 **72** PJMcDonald 3 71
(Ann Duffield) *hld up: rdn and hdwy over 1f out: kpt on* **3/1**[2]

350- **5** nk **North Spirit (IRE)**[178] 8010 3-8-9 **61** SamJames 5 59
(David O'Meara) *chsd ldng pair: rdn 2f out: kpt on same pce* **9/1**

0-61 **6** 1 ½ **Crombay (IRE)**[16] 2050 3-9-7 **73** DavidAllan 7 65
(Tim Easterby) *chsd ldng pair on outer: rdn 1/2-way: wknd ins fnl f* **5/2**[1]

-000 **7** 6 **Zephyr Breeze**[57] 1111 3-9-1 **67** BarryMcHugh 1 38
(Noel Wilson) *hld up: rdn 1/2-way: sn wknd* **18/1**

1m 1.57s (0.77) **Going Correction** -0.125s/f (Firm) **7** Ran SP% **113.5**
Speed ratings (Par 99): **88,87,86,86,85 83,73**
CSF £49.86 TOTE £7.80: £2.60, £3.20; EX 48.00 Trifecta £229.30.
Owner Sandfield Racing **Bred** Bucklands Farm & Stud Ltd **Trained** Westow, N Yorks

FOCUS
A tight little sprint handicap. They finished in a bit of a heap but the pace held up. The winner is rated back to his 2yo form.

T/Plt: £139.20 to a £1 stake. Pool: £61,572.70 - 322.82 winning units. T/Qpdt: £38.50 to a £1 stake. Pool: £5,017.98 - 96.25 winning units. **Andrew Sheret**

2295 LEICESTER (R-H)
Monday, May 23

OFFICIAL GOING: Straight course - good to firm (good in places); round course - good (good to firm in places)
Wind: Light against Weather: Cloudy

2535 RAGDALE MAIDEN AUCTION STKS (DIV I) 6f
2:15 (2:16) (Class 5) 2-Y-O **£3,234** (£962; £481; £240) **Stalls** High

Form RPR

6 **1** **Baby Gal**[25] 1799 2-7-13 0 JosephineGordon[(5)] 1 68
(Giles Bravery) *chsd ldrs: rdn over 2f out: led wl over 1f out: r.o* **20/1**

2 1 ¼ **Bayston Hill** 2-8-11 0 LiamKeniry 8 71
(Mark Usher) *s.s: outpcd: hdwy over 1f out: r.o to go 2nd post: nt rch wnr* **50/1**

5 **3** nse **Spiritofedinburgh (IRE)**[42] 1384 2-8-13 0 StevieDonohoe 6 73
(Brendan Powell) *sn pushed along towards rr: hdwy over 1f out: rdn and ev ch ins fnl f: edgd rt and no ex towards fin* **10/1**

0 **4** 1 ½ **Global Revival (IRE)**[11] 2173 2-9-2 0 SilvestreDeSousa 4 72
(Ed Dunlop) *mid-div: pushed along over 3f out: hdwy 2f out: sn rdn: styd on same pce ins fnl f* **4/1**[2]

5 ½ **Mister Blue Sky (IRE)** 2-8-13 0 LukeMorris 3 67
(Sylvester Kirk) *chsd ldrs: rdn over 1f out: styd on same pce ins fnl f* **9/1**

6 ¾ **Equity** 2-8-13 0 RyanMoore 7 65+
(David Brown) *sn pushed along in rr: effrt and nt clr run over 1f out: r.o ins fnl f: nt trble ldrs* **9/4**[1]

7 ¾ **Angel's Acclaim (IRE)** 2-8-11 0 JimmyFortune 5 62
(Kevin Ryan) *trckd ldrs: rdn over 2f out: no ex fnl f* **9/2**[3]

8 1 ¾ **Notalot (IRE)** 2-9-2 0 (v[1]) WilliamCarson 12 60
(Michael Bell) *mid-div: hdwy over 3f out: rdn over 1f out: wknd ins fnl f* **25/1**

9 ¾ **Tigerfish (IRE)** 2-8-4 0 KieranO'Neill 10 46
(William Stone) *wnt rt s: mid-div: rdn 1/2-way: wknd wl over 1f out: nt clr run and swtchd rt ent fnl f* **20/1**

10 2 ¼ **Nudge Nudge** 2-8-9 0 MartinDwyer 9 44
(J S Moore) *sn pushed along in rr: nvr on terms* **66/1**

2 **11** ½ **Masquerade Bling (IRE)**[27] 1741 2-8-4 0 CamHardie 11 38
(Simon Hodgson) *chsd ldr tl rdn 2f out: wknd fnl f* **14/1**

5 **12** 3 ½ **Little Nosegay (IRE)**[58] 1086 2-8-4 0 CathyGannon 2 27
(David Evans) *led: rdn and hdd wl over 1f out: wknd fnl f* **16/1**

1m 14.16s (1.16) **Going Correction** -0.05s/f (Good) **12** Ran SP% **117.4**
Speed ratings (Par 93): **90,88,88,86,85 84,83,81,80,77 76,71**
CSF £740.73 TOTE £28.00: £4.60, £8.50, £3.10; EX 501.30 Trifecta £5215.60 Part won..
Owner G Wilding **Bred** G Wilding **Trained** Newmarket, Suffolk

FOCUS
The going was good to firm, good in places on the straight course and good, good to firm in places on the round course. A false rail from the top of the hill on the back straight to the winning line increased distances on the round course by about 17yds. This opening maiden proved a bit of a placepot-buster and those who raced more towards the centre of the track appeared favoured. Experience also counted with three of the first four having run before. It's been rated as ordinary form.

2536 RAGDALE MAIDEN AUCTION STKS (DIV II) 6f
2:45 (2:46) (Class 5) 2-Y-O **£3,234** (£962; £481; £240) **Stalls** High

Form RPR

4 **1** **Dr Julius No**[28] 1713 2-9-2 0 FMBerry 4 80
(Ralph Beckett) *mde all: rdn over 1f out: r.o u.p* **5/2**[2]

P6 **2** 2 ½ **Dolokhov**[51] 1203 2-8-9 0 (b[1]) LiamKeniry 11 66
(J S Moore) *a.p: rdn to chse wnr over 1f out: styd on same pce ins fnl f* **25/1**

3 1 **Mr Hobbs** 2-8-13 0 LukeMorris 1 67
(Sylvester Kirk) *s.i.s: hdwy 2f out: rdn over 1f out: no ex wl ins fnl f* **33/1**

4 1 **Top Hatter** 2-8-8 0 WilliamCarson 2 59
(Jamie Osborne) *hld up: plld hrd: hdwy and edgd lft 2f out: sn rdn: no ex ins fnl f* **2/1**[1]

5 shd **King Of Spades (FR)** 2-9-2 0 SilvestreDeSousa 5 66
(Mick Channon) *s.i.s: hdwy over 4f out: rdn over 2f out: styd on same pce fnl f* **11/1**

6 1 **Golden Slam** 2-8-11 0 AndreaAtzeni 8 58
(Roger Varian) *s.i.s: hdwy over 3f out: rdn over 1f out: no ex ins fnl f* **10/1**

30 **7** 3 **Madam Prancealot (IRE)**[49] 1233 2-8-6 0 CathyGannon 9 44
(David Evans) *sn pushed along in rr: kpt on ins fnl f: nvr nrr* **33/1**

6 **8** ¾ **Miss Monro (IRE)**[20] 1951 2-7-12 0 ow1 BenRobinson[(7)] 7 41+
(Brian Ellison) *prom: rdn over 2f out: wknd over 1f out* **66/1**

5 **9** ½ **Suetonius**[28] 1719 2-8-9 0 KieranO'Neill 10 43
(Ed McMahon) *w wnr tl rdn over 2f out: wknd over 1f out* **50/1**

6 **10** ¾ **Golden Guest**[11] 2173 2-9-2 0 TomQueally 3 48
(George Margarson) *chsd ldrs: hmpd 2f out: sn wknd* **6/1**[3]

11 4 **Girlofinkandstars (IRE)** 2-8-11 0 MartinDwyer 6 31+
(Rae Guest) *rrd s: outpcd* **8/1**

1m 13.82s (0.82) **Going Correction** -0.05s/f (Good) **11** Ran SP% **117.9**
Speed ratings (Par 93): **92,88,87,86,85 84,80,79,78,77 72**
CSF £71.09 TOTE £3.20: £2.00, £7.40, £5.70; EX 62.70 Trifecta £1846.70.
Owner Chelsea Thoroughbreds - Doctor No **Bred** Miss J Chaplin **Trained** Kimpton, Hants

FOCUS
The winning time was 0.34sec quicker than the first division. The action developed away from the stands' rail again.

2537 HICKLING (S) STKS 6f
3:20 (3:20) (Class 6) 3-5-Y-O **£2,264** (£673; £336; £168) **Stalls** High

Form RPR

2-13 **1** **Faintly (USA)**[4] 2402 5-9-6 77 (p) GeorgeDowning[(3)] 3 71
(Tony Carroll) *mde all: shkn up over 1f out: hung lft ins fnl f: styd on* **7/4**[1]

4412 **2** 1 **Johnny B Goode (IRE)**[3] 2425 4-9-9 65 PaulHanagan 10 68
(Richard Fahey) *hld up: rdn over 2f out: hdwy sn after: chsd wnr over 1f out: edgd rt ins fnl f: styd on* **5/2**[2]

4-00 **3** 4 **Diminutive (IRE)**[52] 1180 4-9-0 49 (p) StevieDonohoe 6 47
(Grace Harris) *prom: rdn over 1f out: no ex wl ins fnl f* **40/1**

0060 **4** 7 **Kenstone (FR)**[7] 2293 3-8-10 55 (p) SilvestreDeSousa 4 29
(David Dennis) *hld up: plld hrd: rdn over 2f out: nvr trbld ldrs* **10/1**

6423 **5** ½ **Arizona Snow**[2] 2458 4-9-0 55 (p) JordanNason[(5)] 2 30
(Ronald Harris) *chsd wnr: rdn over 2f out: lost 2nd over 1f out: wknd fnl f* **14/1**

00-0 **6** 1 ¾ **L'Es Fremantle (FR)**[143] 2 5-9-0 32 NoelGarbutt[(5)] 7 24
(Michael Chapman) *prom: racd keenly: rdn over 2f out: wknd wl over 1f out* **250/1**

6-06 **7** ¾ **Simply Black (IRE)**[21] 1913 5-8-9 54 (p) AnnStokell[(5)] 1 17
(Ann Stokell) *chsd ldrs: rdn over 2f out: wknd wl over 1f out* **66/1**

50-0 **8** nse **Dismantle (IRE)**[11] 2184 3-8-5 65 CathyGannon 5 15
(Grace Harris) *s.s: a bhd* **16/1**

-040 **9** ¾ **Robbian**[17] 2013 5-8-12 46 RPWalsh[(7)] 8 20
(Charles Smith) *prom: rdn over 2f out: wknd wl over 1f out* **100/1**

0005 **10** 2 ¼ **Alhella**[28] 1700 4-9-0 69 WilliamCarson 9 8
(Mick Quinn) *prom: rdn over 2f out: sn wknd* **4/1**[3]

1m 13.69s (0.69) **Going Correction** -0.05s/f (Good)
WFA 3 from 4yo+ 9lb **10** Ran SP% **111.9**
Speed ratings (Par 101): **93,91,86,77,76 74,73,72,71,68**
CSF £5.82 TOTE £2.60: £1.20, £1.30, £4.00; EX 6.40 Trifecta £129.70.
Owner J Babb **Bred** Juddmonte Farms Inc **Trained** Cropthorne, Worcs

FOCUS
An uncompetitive seller in which the first three pulled well clear. The winner was the pick of the weights.

2538 SWANNINGTON H'CAP 1m 1f 218y
3:55 (3:56) (Class 4) (0-85,85) 3-Y-O **£4,851** (£1,443; £721; £360) **Stalls** Low

Form RPR

61-6 **1** **Gershwin**[31] 1610 3-9-5 **83** GeorgeBaker 7 96+
(David Lanigan) *hld up: hdwy over 1f out: shkn up to ld wl ins fnl f: r.o: comf* **10/3**[2]

13-2 **2** ¾ **Banksea**[17] 1992 3-9-3 **81** RyanMoore 1 92
(Luca Cumani) *trckd ldrs: shkn up to ld over 1f out: rdn and hdd wl ins fnl f* **7/4**[1]

0-31 **3** *5* **Grapevine (IRE)**[14] 2099 3-8-11 **78** MichaelJMMurphy(3) 4 79
(Charles Hills) *s.i.s: hld up: plld hrd: hdwy over 2f out: rdn over 1f out: hung rt and no ex ins fnl f* **9/1**
3530 **4** *nse* **Lilbourne Prince (IRE)**[14] 2099 3-8-12 **76** SilvestreDeSousa 3 77
(David Evans) *led: rdn and hdd over 2f out: no ex ins fnl f* **16/1**
32-3 **5** *hd* **Sacred Trust**[30] 1653 3-9-0 **78** MartinHarley 6 79
(Hugo Palmer) *w ldr tl led over 2f out: rdn and hdd over 1f out: no ex ins fnl f* **8/1**
02-0 **6** *10* **Strathearn (IRE)**[29] 1671 3-8-3 **67** WilliamCarson 2 48
(Michael Bell) *hld up: hdwy 1/2-way: rdn over 2f out: wknd over 1f out* **50/1**
5-50 **7** *1 ½* **Taking Libertys**[18] 1975 3-9-4 **82** JimmyFortune 8 60
(Kevin Ryan) *hld up and a bhd* **40/1**
1-5 **8** *2* **Mutawaaly (IRE)**[41] 1398 3-9-7 **85** PaulHanagan 5 78
(Roger Varian) *chsd ldrs: rdn over 3f out: wknd over 1f out: eased* **7/2**[3]
2m 8.45s (0.55) **Going Correction** +0.225s/f (Good) **8** Ran SP% **113.1**
Speed ratings (Par 101): **106,105,101,101,101 93,92,90**
CSF £9.33 CT £44.97 TOTE £4.30: £1.40, £1.10, £2.50; EX 9.90 Trifecta £50.40.
Owner B E Nielsen **Bred** Haras De La Perelle **Trained** Newmarket, Suffolk
FOCUS
The false rail increased the race distance by about 17yds. A decent 3yo handicap and the first two are worth keeping onside. The form is rated around the fourth.

2539 SHARNFORD FILLIES' CONDITIONS STKS 7f
4:30 (4:30) (Class 3) 3-Y-O+ **£7,561** (£2,263; £1,131; £566; £282) **Stalls** High

Form RPR
140- **1** **Spangled**[241] 6707 4-9-0 97 AndreaAtzeni 4 108+
(Roger Varian) *mde all: qcknd over 2f out: shkn up over 1f out: edgd lft ins fnl f: r.o wl* **11/8**[2]
230- **2** *3 ½* **Opal Tiara (IRE)**[227] 7075 3-8-3 102 PaulHanagan 7 95
(Mick Channon) *chsd wnr: shkn up over 1f out: styd on same pce ins fnl f* **4/1**[3]
1400 **3** *1 ½* **Yeah Baby Yeah (IRE)**[14] 2115 3-7-10 82 RPWalsh(7) 6 91
(Gay Kelleway) *plld hrd and prom: pushed along over 2f out: outpcd wl over 1f out: styd on to go 3rd post* **33/1**
12-3 **4** *shd* **Thetis (IRE)**[10] 2220 3-8-3 102 JimmyQuinn 3 90
(Sir Michael Stoute) *hld up: plld hrd: trckd ldrs: rdn over 1f out: no ex ins fnl f* **5/4**[1]
00 **5** *36* **Striking Nigella**[20] 1953 6-8-9 0 NoelGarbutt(5) 2
(Michael Chapman) *sn pushed along in rr: bhd fr 1/2-way* **300/1**
1m 24.53s (-1.67) **Going Correction** -0.05s/f (Good)
WFA 3 from 4yo+ 11lb **5** Ran SP% **109.8**
Speed ratings (Par 104): **107,103,101,101,60**
CSF £7.19 TOTE £2.00: £1.10, £1.90; EX 5.90 Trifecta £55.20.
Owner Cheveley Park Stud **Bred** Cheveley Park Stud Ltd **Trained** Newmarket, Suffolk
FOCUS
Only three really mattered in this fillies' conditions event according to the market and it resulted in a powerful front-running performance from an older filly, who put the 3yos in their place. The time was only 6lb faster than the following 0-70 and the form pair disappointing, but the winner can prove better than the bare form.

2540 OLD DALBY H'CAP 7f
5:00 (5:00) (Class 5) (0-75,75) 4-Y-O+ **£3,234** (£962; £481; £240) **Stalls** High

Form RPR
005 **1** **Kestrel Dot Com**[27] 1765 4-9-2 **70** SilvestreDeSousa 5 83
(Chris Dwyer) *hld up: racd keenly: hdwy 1/2-way: rdn over 1f out: edgd rt and led ins fnl f: r.o* **9/1**
53-5 **2** *nk* **The Salmon Man**[30] 1632 4-8-13 **67** RyanMoore 2 79
(Brendan Powell) *prom: pushed along 4f out: rdn to ld over 1f out: edgd lft and hdd ins fnl f: unable qck nr fin* **13/8**[1]
2450 **3** *5* **Smokethatthunders (IRE)**[10] 2213 6-9-4 **72** StevieDonohoe 10 71
(James Unett) *hld up: hdwy u.p over 1f out: styd on same pce ins fnl f: wnt 3rd nr fin* **9/1**
000- **4** *1* **Unnoticed**[242] 6668 4-8-13 **67** LemosdeSouza 3 63
(Luca Cumani) *prom: chsd ldr 4f out: led wl over 1f out: rdn and hdd jst over 1f out: wknd wl ins fnl f* **7/2**[2]
10-6 **5** *3 ¾* **Ace Master**[9] 2238 8-9-7 **75** (b) JFEgan 8 61
(Roy Bowring) *led: clr 4f out: rdn and hdd wl over 1f out: wknd fnl f* **12/1**
0-50 **6** *6* **Ganymede**[11] 2187 5-9-0 **68** (v[1]) CharlesBishop 1 37
(Eve Johnson Houghton) *hld up: hdwy over 4f out: rdn over 2f out: wknd wl over 1f out* **17/2**[3]
100- **7** *2 ¾* **Free One (IRE)**[144] 8414 4-8-9 **68** JosephineGordon(5) 9 30
(Ivan Furtado) *sn pushed along in rr: rdn 1/2-way: wknd 2f out* **9/1**
0-00 **8** *20* **Living Leader**[21] 1928 7-8-8 **67** (tp) JennyPowell(5) 11
(Grace Harris) *chsd ldr 3f: sn rdn: wknd over 2f out* **33/1**
1m 25.03s (-1.17) **Going Correction** -0.05s/f (Good) **8** Ran SP% **111.5**
Speed ratings (Par 103): **104,103,97,96,92 85,82,59**
CSF £22.87 CT £134.99 TOTE £9.90: £1.90, £1.10, £2.30; EX 27.70 Trifecta £105.80.
Owner Mrs Nicola Thorne **Bred** Shadwell Estate Company Limited **Trained** Newmarket, Suffolk
FOCUS
An ordinary handicap in which the finish was fought out between the two least-exposed runners. An improved effort from the winner and the second, the first two clear.

2541 BREEDERS BACKING RACING EBF MAIDEN STKS 1m 60y
5:30 (5:32) (Class 5) 3-Y-O **£4,528** (£1,347; £673; £336) **Stalls** Low

Form RPR
0-5 **1** **Sabre Squadron (IRE)**[16] 2048 3-9-5 0 JimmyFortune 7 82+
(Peter Chapple-Hyam) *chsd ldr: shkn up over 2f out: led over 1f out: rdn out* **9/1**[3]
4 **2** *2 ¼* **Istanbul Bey**[25] 1800 3-9-5 0 PaulHanagan 4 77+
(William Haggas) *hld up in tch: shkn up over 2f out: chsd wnr ins fnl f: styd on same pce* **10/1**
3 *2 ½* **Al Neksh** 3-9-5 0 BenCurtis 5 71+
(William Haggas) *dwlt: hld up: plld hrd: hdwy over 2f out: rdn over 1f out: edgd rt and styd on ins fnl f* **4/1**[2]
0-2 **4** *1 ½* **Divisionist**[30] 1653 3-9-5 0 (t) RyanMoore 8 67
(Sir Michael Stoute) *trckd ldrs: rdn over 1f out: no ex ins fnl f* **8/11**[1]
0- **5** *nk* **Sir Pass I Am**[250] 6436 3-9-0 0 EdwardGreatrex(5) 2 67
(Andrew Balding) *hld up: pushed along over 2f out: r.o ins fnl f: nvr nrr* **28/1**
0- **6** *nk* **Equal Point**[221] 7237 3-9-5 0 MartinHarley 10 66
(William Knight) *led: rdn and hdd over 1f out: wknd wl ins fnl f* **100/1**
7 *nk* **Shargiah (IRE)** 3-9-5 0 JackMitchell 9 65+
(Roger Varian) *hld up: pushed along and hdwy over 2f out: wknd ins fnl f* **12/1**

0 **8** *1 ¼* **Perpetual Change (IRE)**[21] 1930 3-9-5 0 RyanTate 1 62+
(Clive Cox) *plld hrd and prom: rdn over 2f out: wknd fnl f* **33/1**
00 **9** *1 ¾* **Diamond Geyser (IRE)**[9] 2248 3-9-5 0 LemosdeSouza 3 58+
(Luca Cumani) *hld up: shkn up over 2f out: nvr on terms* **33/1**
6 **10** *nk* **Shrubland**[21] 1930 3-9-5 0 AntonioFresu 6 57
(Ed Walker) *mid-div: nt clr run and lost pl over 2f out: n.d after* **50/1**
1m 48.18s (3.08) **Going Correction** +0.225s/f (Good) **10** Ran SP% **117.0**
Speed ratings (Par 99): **93,90,88,86,86 86,85,84,82,82**
CSF £88.76 TOTE £10.20: £2.70, £2.90, £1.80; EX 71.80 Trifecta £361.60.
Owner Mrs Fitri Hay **Bred** Oak Hill Stud **Trained** Newmarket, Suffolk
FOCUS
The false rail increased the race distance by about 17yds. Not the most competitive of maidens with a lopsided betting market, but an interesting race and a few of these are likely to improve. The first two progressed.

2542 COPLOW H'CAP 7f
6:00 (6:00) (Class 6) (0-60,60) 4-Y-O+ **£2,264** (£673; £336; £168) **Stalls** High

Form RPR
00-0 **1** **Henryhudsonbridge (USA)**[3] 2442 4-9-1 **57** (b) RobHornby(3) 15 68
(Edward Bevan) *w ldrs: led over 5f out: rdn over 1f out: r.o* **33/1**
4553 **2** *2 ¼* **Top Offer**[14] 2096 7-9-5 **58** TimmyMurphy 12 63
(Patrick Morris) *hld up: hdwy over 1f out: wnt 2nd ins fnl f: nt rch wnr* **6/1**[2]
0103 **3** *2 ½* **First Excel**[17] 2013 4-9-5 **58** (b) JFEgan 16 56
(Roy Bowring) *plld hrd and prom: rdn and edgd rt over 1f out: styd on same pce ins fnl f* **8/1**
1001 **4** *nk* **The Happy Hammer (IRE)**[28] 1700 10-8-12 **51** WilliamCarson 1 48
(Eugene Stanford) *hld up: hdwy over 1f out: nt rch ldrs* **7/1**[3]
5531 **5** *½* **Hawk Moth (IRE)**[20] 1949 8-9-5 **58** (p) CathyGannon 5 54
(John Spearing) *dwlt: hld up: hdwy over 2f out: rdn over 1f out: no ex ins fnl f* **6/1**[2]
5540 **6** *nk* **Mops Angel**[4] 2403 5-9-3 **59** (p) AlistairRawlinson(3) 18 54
(Michael Appleby) *s.i.s: hld up: hdwy 1/2-way: rdn and edgd rt over 1f out: styd on same pce fnl f* **11/2**[1]
20-6 **7** *¾* **Zeteah**[26] 1791 6-8-10 **52** GeorgeDowning(3) 11 45
(Tony Carroll) *hld up: hdwy u.p over 1f out: nt rch ldrs* **16/1**
55-0 **8** *½* **Bold Grove**[3] 2448 4-8-6 **48** EoinWalsh(3) 7 40
(Edward Bevan) *hld up in tch: plld hrd: rdn over 1f out: wknd ins fnl f* **20/1**
22-0 **9** *3* **Man Of Music**[17] 2013 5-8-8 **47** StevieDonohoe 4 31
(Tony Carroll) *chsd ldrs: rdn over 2f out: wknd fnl f* **10/1**
00-0 **10** *2 ¾* **Monsieur Valentine**[125] 247 4-9-2 **60** PaddyPilley(5) 3 36
(Tony Carroll) *hld up in tch: rdn over 2f out: wknd fnl f* **9/1**
3060 **11** *5* **Dandys Perier (IRE)**[34] 1544 5-8-13 **57** JordanNason(5) 14 20
(Ronald Harris) *led: hdd over 5f out: rdn over 2f out: wknd over 1f out* **16/1**
50/0 **12** *nse* **Zafraaj**[22] 1899 5-8-9 **48** RyanTate 8 11
(Pat Murphy) *hld up: rdn 1/2-way: n.d* **20/1**
60-0 **13** *hd* **Imperial Link**[16] 2045 4-8-9 **53** CiaranMckee(5) 6 15
(John O'Shea) *s.i.s: hdwy over 5f out: rdn 1/2-way: wknd over 2f out* **25/1**
000- **14** *7* **Euroquip Boy (IRE)**[245] 6601 9-8-12 **56** NoelGarbutt(5) 17
(Michael Scudamore) *chsd ldrs: rdn over 2f out: wknd over 1f out* **20/1**
400- **15** *15* **Delysdream**[288] 5178 4-8-7 **49** (t) DannyBrock(3) 2
(Christine Dunnett) *prom: rdn 1/2-way: wknd over 2f out* **66/1**
1m 25.36s (-0.84) **Going Correction** -0.05s/f (Good) **15** Ran SP% **121.0**
Speed ratings (Par 101): **102,99,96,96,95 95,94,93,90,87 81,81,81,73,56**
CSF £206.74 CT £1777.60 TOTE £36.00: £10.20, £1.70, £2.50; EX 299.00 Trifecta £1258.50.
Owner E G Bevan **Bred** Eureka Thoroughbred Farm **Trained** Ullingswick, H'fords
FOCUS
A moderate if competitive handicap and something of a shock result.
T/Jkpt: Not won. T/Plt: £365.60 to a £1 stake. Pool: £77,681.03 - 155.10 winning units. T/Qpdt: £7.10 to a 31 stake. Pool: £9,801.08 - 1009.47 winning units. **Colin Roberts**

2309 WINDSOR (R-H)
Monday, May 23

OFFICIAL GOING: Good (7.3)
Wind: Light, behind Weather: Mostly fine

2543 SKY BET EBF STALLIONS NOVICE STKS (PLUS 10 RACE) 5f 10y
5:45 (5:47) (Class 4) 2-Y-O **£4,269** (£1,270; £634; £317) **Stalls** Low

Form RPR
4 **1** **Barrington (IRE)**[10] 2204 2-9-2 0 DarryllHolland 1 94
(Charles Hills) *s.i.s: rcvrd to ld after 1f: mde rest: firmly pushed clr fnl f* **2/1**[1]
4 **2** *6* **Super Julius**[16] 2023 2-9-2 0 ShaneKelly 3 72
(Eve Johnson Houghton) *led 1f: chsd wnr: on terms 2f out: kpt on and clr of rest but easily lft bhd fnl f* **8/1**[2]
3 *5* **Rapid Ranger** 2-9-2 0 JimCrowley 5 54
(Gary Moore) *chsd ldng pair 1/2-way but nt on terms: pushed along and lft further bhd fr over 1f out but hld on for 3rd* **8/1**[2]
4 *1 ¼* **Nicky Baby (IRE)** 2-9-2 0 RobertWinston 2 50+
(Dean Ivory) *outpcd in last: prog 2f out: keeping on against nr side rail and ch of 3rd whn short of room ins fnl f* **25/1**
5 *1 ¼* **Rising Eagle** 2-9-2 0 OisinMurphy 6 45
(Charles Hills) *sn pushed along to chse ldrs: outpcd bef 1/2-way* **22/1**[3]
64 **6** *¾* **Iftitah (IRE)**[7] 2295 2-9-2 0 LukeMorris 4 43
(George Peckham) *awkward s: effrt fr rr 1/2-way: rdn 2f out: hanging and nt run on after* **50/1**
0 **7** *5* **Silver Asset (IRE)**[30] 1635 2-9-2 0 AdamKirby 7 25
(Michael Wigham) *racd wd: chsd ldng pair to 1/2-way: sn wknd* **66/1**
1m 1.05s (0.75) **Going Correction** +0.225s/f (Good) **7** Ran SP% **67.2**
Speed ratings (Par 95): **103,93,85,83,81 80,72**
Irish Melody and Tropical Rock were withdrawn. Prices at time of withdrawal 50-1 and 10-11. Rule 4 applies to all bets - deduction 50p in the pound. CSF £4.55 TOTE £2.10: £1.30, £2.30; EX 5.90 Trifecta £14.20.
Owner Morecombe,Anderson,O'Callaghan,Sangster **Bred** C Marnane **Trained** Lambourn, Berks

FOCUS
The complexion of this novice event changed before the stalls opened with the hot favourite failing to load. There was no hanging about and the first pair dominated. The form is rated around the runner-up's debut, and might underplay the winner slightly.

2544 SKY BET MAIDEN STKS 6f
6:15 (6:15) (Class 5) 3-Y-O+ **£2,911** (£866; £432; £216) **Stalls** Low

Form RPR

3 **1** **Cold Snap (IRE)**[12] 2156 3-9-5 0 RobertHavlin 8 83+
(William Jarvis) *s.i.s: prog fr rr 1/2-way: trckd ldrs 2f out: plld out and shkn up over 1f out: clsd to ld last 100yds: rdn out* **7/1**[3]

6-3 **2** 3/4 **He's My Cracker**[22] 1892 3-9-5 0 AdamKirby 1 80
(Clive Cox) *chsd ldr: rdn to chal 2f out: led 1f out: hdd last 100yds: kpt on* **9/2**[2]

4-42 **3** 1 **Jayjinski (IRE)**[22] 1892 3-9-5 77 SeanLevey 3 77
(Richard Hannon) *led: gng strly 2f out: rdn over 1f out: hdd and one pce fnl f* **9/2**[2]

3-2 **4** 1 1/4 **Foresight (FR)**[23] 1849 3-9-5 0 JamieSpencer 5 73
(David Simcock) *trckd ldrs: shkn up against nr side rail 2f out: nt qckn and no imp over 1f out: one pce* **10/11**[1]

0- **5** 1 1/4 **Raising Sand**[242] 6672 4-10-0 0 HarryBentley 2 71+
(Roger Varian) *hld up in last trio: pushed along and prog over 1f out: tk 5th fnl f: keeping on but no ch whn eased last 75yds* **20/1**

0- **6** 4 **Guilded Rock**[349] 3017 3-9-5 0 OisinMurphy 4 56
(Stuart Kittow) *chsd ldng pair: urged along 1/2-way: lost pl and wknd wl over 1f out* **100/1**

3- **7** 2 1/4 **Broughtons Vision**[244] 6621 3-9-5 0 TomQueally 6 49
(Willie Musson) *hld up in last trio: in tch on outer 2f out: pushed along and wknd over 1f out* **20/1**

0-0 **8** 1/2 **Pacific Salt (IRE)**[44] 1337 3-9-5 0 FMBerry 7 47
(Roger Charlton) *chsd ldrs on outer: pushed along over 2f out: wknd over 1f out* **33/1**

6-0 **9** 8 **Pushy Lady**[22] 1892 3-8-9 0 AliceMills(5) 9 17
(Rod Millman) *sn pushed along in last: detached after 2f* **100/1**

1m 13.78s (0.78) **Going Correction** +0.225s/f (Good)
WFA 3 from 4yo 9lb **9** Ran SP% **115.7**
Speed ratings (Par 103): **103,102,100,99,97 92,89,88,77**
CSF £36.20 TOTE £9.80: £2.30, £2.00, £1.80; EX 41.60 Trifecta £173.40.
Owner P C J Dalby & R D Schuster **Bred** Yeguada De Milagro Sa **Trained** Newmarket, Suffolk

FOCUS
A fair sprint maiden. There was a bunched finish but the placed horses give it a straightforward look. It's rated around the third.

2545 KEITH HARTE WOBURN STUD H'CAP 1m 67y
6:45 (6:45) (Class 5) (0-75,75) 3-Y-O **£2,911** (£866; £432; £216) **Stalls** Low

Form RPR

-350 **1** **Outback Blue**[18] 1977 3-9-4 72 (t) ShaneKelly 6 82
(David Evans) *hld up in last: plld wd and gd prog fr 3f out: led 1f: sn rdn clr* **14/1**

55-0 **2** 2 1/4 **Impediment (IRE)**[31] 1602 3-8-10 64 (v[1]) TedDurcan 8 69
(Sir Michael Stoute) *hld up towards rr: prog over 2f out: drvn over 1f out: styd on to chse wnr ins fnl f: no imp* **10/1**

51 **3** 1 3/4 **London Glory**[25] 1806 3-9-5 73 GeorgeBaker 11 74+
(Chris Wall) *pressed ldr: hung lft bnd 6f out: led over 2f out gng strly: rdn over 1f out: sn hdd: fdd but clung on for 3rd* **7/1**[3]

040- **4** nse **Hardington**[159] 8246 3-9-3 71 FergusSweeney 12 72
(Alan King) *slowly away: hld up in last pair: prog 3f out: trying to cl but nt as qckly as wnr whn nt clr run briefly over 1f out: styd on and nrly snatched 3rd* **20/1**

56-6 **5** 1 3/4 **Pina**[30] 1622 3-8-6 63 TomMarquand(3) 9 60
(Roger Charlton) *trckd ldrs: rdn wl over 2f out: stl in tch over 1f out: one pce* **12/1**

-521 **6** hd **Frozen Force (IRE)**[26] 1777 3-9-7 75 JimCrowley 13 71
(Amanda Perrett) *wl plcd bhd ldrs: rdn over 2f out: no imp over 1f out: kpt on* **8/1**

00-3 **7** 2 1/2 **Master Of Heaven**[49] 1235 3-9-0 68 PatCosgrave 7 59
(Jim Boyle) *rdn in midfield 1/2-way: struggling in rr over 2f out: plugged on* **20/1**

-415 **8** 1/2 **Aldair**[16] 2044 3-9-4 72 SeanLevey 14 61
(Richard Hannon) *trapped out wd: in tch: rdn over 2f out: no prog over 1f out: wknd* **13/2**[2]

5-0 **9** 3 1/4 **Henshaw**[20] 1946 3-9-7 75 DarryllHolland 4 57
(Charles Hills) *hmpd s: t.k.h: hld up towards rr: rdn and no prog over 2f out* **25/1**

34-2 **10** 1 **Darksiteofthemoon (IRE)**[55] 1137 3-9-4 75 DanielMuscutt(3) 3 55
(Marco Botti) *hmpd s: t.k.h early: trckd ldrs: rdn over 2f out: wknd over 1f out* **9/1**

6-12 **11** 3 **Beauty Night**[16] 2044 3-9-5 73 AdamKirby 2 46+
(Clive Cox) *led: hanging lft bnd 5f out: drvn 3f out: hdd over 2f out: sn wknd* **11/4**[1]

-016 **12** 9 **Zebedee's Son (IRE)**[6] 2325 3-7-9 56 (p) RhiainIngram(7) 10 8
(Roger Ingram) *racd on outer towards rr: no prog over 2f out: sn wknd qckly* **50/1**

46-0 **13** 3 **Linguist (FR)**[39] 1429 3-9-2 70 LukeMorris 1 15
(Harry Dunlop) *wnt sharply lft s: chsd ldrs: rdn 3f out: wknd qckly 2f out* **66/1**

-445 **14** 39 **Total Power**[23] 1847 3-8-10 69 CallumShepherd(5) 5
(Brian Ellison) *chsd ldrs tl over 2f out: virtually p.u over 1f out* **16/1**

1m 46.64s (1.94) **Going Correction** +0.225s/f (Good) **14** Ran SP% **119.8**
Speed ratings (Par 99): **99,96,95,94,93 93,90,90,86,85 82,73,70,31**
CSF £137.99 CT £1077.18 TOTE £22.10: £6.00, £3.30, £1.90; EX 208.00 Trifecta £1828.30.
Owner Mrs Rachel Barnes **Bred** Grovewood Stud **Trained** Pandy, Monmouths

FOCUS
Race distance increased by 45yds. A competitive 3yo handicap run at a good pace. The winner improved on his AW form.

2546 WEATHERBYS PRIVATE BANK LEISURE STKS (LISTED RACE) 6f
7:15 (7:15) (Class 1) 3-Y-O+
£20,982 (£7,955; £3,981; £1,983; £995; £499) **Stalls** Low

Form RPR

014- **1** **The Tin Man**[219] 7278 4-9-0 112 TomQueally 7 119+
(James Fanshawe) *hld up in rr: smooth prog on outer over 2f out: tk 2nd over 1f out: led jst ins fnl f: shkn up and r.o wl: decisively* **3/1**[1]

00-3 **2** 2 **Watchable**[16] 2031 6-9-0 108 (v[1]) AdamKirby 5 112
(David O'Meara) *led against rail but pressed: kicked on fr 1/2-way: drvn over 1f out: hdd and outpcd jst ins fnl f* **9/1**

-420 **3** nk **Naadirr (IRE)**[58] 1104 5-9-0 109 (p) AndreaAtzeni 3 111
(Marco Botti) *hld up in rr: pushed along and no prog over 2f out: drvn over 1f out: styd on fnl f to take 3rd nr fin* **6/1**

120- **4** 3/4 **Strath Burn**[219] 7278 4-9-0 116 OisinMurphy 9 109
(Charles Hills) *hld up towards rr: prog on outer over 2f out but nt as qckly as wnr: drvn over 1f out: styd on same pce* **10/3**[2]

46-5 **5** 1 1/2 **King Of Rooks**[9] 2242 3-8-5 103 SilvestreDeSousa 4 102
(Richard Hannon) *pressed ldr: rdn over 2f out: lost 2nd over 1f out: one pce after* **10/1**

0-35 **6** 1 1/2 **Poyle Vinnie**[22] 1887 6-9-0 104 AndrewMullen 8 99
(Michael Appleby) *t.k.h: hld up bhd ldrs: waiting for room 2f out: rdn over 1f out: limited rspnse and sn no prog* **33/1**

40-0 **7** 1 1/4 **Code Red**[30] 1637 4-9-0 110 MartinDwyer 2 95
(William Muir) *hld up bhd ldrs: rdn 2f out: no prog over 1f out: wknd* **16/1**

/162 **8** 1/2 **Baccarat (IRE)**[16] 2031 7-9-0 109 JamesDoyle 10 93
(Charlie Appleby) *pressed ldrs on outer: rdn over 2f out: stl in tch over 1f out: fdd* **7/2**[3]

6-04 **9** 3 3/4 **Dutch Masterpiece**[19] 1969 6-9-4 105 (v) GeorgeBaker 1 85
(Gary Moore) *t.k.h: hld up in last: pushed along and no prog 2f out* **33/1**

10-0 **10** 3/4 **Humidor (IRE)**[23] 1862 9-9-0 103 PatCosgrave 6 79
(George Baker) *pressed ldng pair: rdn over 2f out: lost pl over 1f out and short of room sn after: wknd qckly ins fnl f* **66/1**

1m 11.64s (-1.36) **Going Correction** +0.225s/f (Good)
WFA 3 from 4yo+ 9lb **10** Ran SP% **116.9**
Speed ratings (Par 111): **118,115,114,113,111 109,108,107,102,101**
CSF £30.55 TOTE £4.00: £1.40, £2.80, £2.00; EX 32.50 Trifecta £200.30.
Owner Fred Archer Racing - Ormonde **Bred** Mrs Elizabeth Grundy **Trained** Newmarket, Suffolk

FOCUS
They didn't go that quickly in this Listed sprint. The winner impressed and is not far off the top domesstic sprinters. The runner-up is a fair benchmark.

2547 SKY BET WINDSOR SPRINT SERIES H'CAP (QUALIFIER FOR THE WINDSOR SPRINT SERIES FINAL) 6f
7:45 (7:47) (Class 3) (0-95,93) 4-Y-O+ **£7,439** (£2,213; £1,106; £553) **Stalls** Low

Form RPR

5-25 **1** **Ice Lord (IRE)**[17] 1990 4-9-1 **87** AdamKirby 10 96
(Clive Cox) *trckd ldrs: prog towards outer to ld jst over 1f out: drvn and hung rt ins fnl f: styd on* **5/2**[1]

6114 **2** 1 **Stellarta**[21] 1929 5-8-9 **81** DavidProbert 5 87
(Michael Blanshard) *hld up in last pair: prog over 1f out: rdn and trying to cl whn short of room ins fnl f: styd on wl to take 2nd nr fin* **25/1**

02-1 **3** 1/2 **Muir Lodge**[17] 1990 5-9-7 **93** (t) PatCosgrave 7 97
(George Baker) *hld up towards rr: pushed along over 2f out: prog u.p jst over 1f out: styd on to chse wnr wl ins fnl f: lost 2nd nr fin* **8/1**

16-0 **4** nk **Cartmell Cleave**[17] 1990 4-9-4 **90** TedDurcan 1 93
(Stuart Kittow) *trckd ldrs: chal 2f out: rdn to dispute ld briefly over 1f out: one pce fnl f* **9/1**

5-00 **5** 1 **Joey's Destiny (IRE)**[23] 1856 6-9-5 **91** LiamKeniry 3 91
(George Baker) *hld up in last: stl there and nudged along whn nt clr run over 1f out: swtchd lft ins fnl f: drvn fnl 120yds and fin w a flourish but too late to be involved* **14/1**

202 **6** 1 **Flowers On Venus (IRE)**[17] 1990 4-9-0 **86** AndreaAtzeni 2 83
(David Evans) *in tch in midfield: shkn up on inner 2f out: no real prog whn nt clr run jst ins fnl f: one pce after* **9/2**[3]

40-0 **7** nk **Cool Bahamian (IRE)**[3] 2430 5-8-11 **83** (b) JohnFahy 9 79
(Eve Johnson Houghton) *hld up: prog on outer over 3f out: in tch and drvn over 1f out: fdd* **33/1**

0-00 **8** 1/2 **My Dad Syd (USA)**[54] 1143 4-8-3 **75** SilvestreDeSousa 11 69
(Ian Williams) *free to post: pressed ldrs: rdn 2f out: disp ld briefly over 1f out: hld whn hmpd ins fnl f: wknd* **8/1**

21-2 **9** 3 3/4 **Francisco**[10] 2206 4-8-12 **89** GaryMahon(5) 8 71
(Richard Hannon) *pressed ldr to 2f out: wknd qckly over 1f out* **7/2**[2]

16-0 **10** 1/2 **Secret Missile**[58] 1090 6-9-6 **92** (b) FergusSweeney 4 73
(Gary Moore) *led: rdn and hdd over 1f out: wknd qckly* **66/1**

1m 13.1s (0.10) **Going Correction** +0.225s/f (Good) **10** Ran SP% **116.1**
Speed ratings (Par 107): **108,106,106,105,104 102,102,101,96,96**
CSF £70.88 CT £444.45 TOTE £3.50: £1.50, £4.60, £2.20; EX 55.50 Trifecta £542.70.
Owner Hintlesham Racing **Bred** Corduff Stud Ltd & J F Gribomont **Trained** Lambourn, Berks

FOCUS
A fair sprint handicap. Four of the first six came from the same Ascot race and the form is rated around the second.

2548 KENNET VALLEY THOROUGHBREDS MAIDEN AUCTION STKS 1m 2f 7y
8:15 (8:15) (Class 5) 3-Y-O **£2,911** (£866; £432; £216) **Stalls** Centre

Form RPR

4- **1** **Rockspirit (IRE)**[214] 7411 3-9-4 0 AndreaAtzeni 1 86+
(Marco Botti) *trckd ldng pair: shkn up to chal over 2f out: led over 1f out: rdn clr fnl f* **3/1**[2]

2-22 **2** 2 1/2 **Hepplewhite**[30] 1636 3-8-12 84 TomMarquand(3) 7 78
(Robert Eddery) *pressed ldr: upsides fr 1/2-way: drvn over 2f out: stl upsides over 1f out: one pce after* **5/4**[1]

4-25 **3** nk **Skeaping**[33] 1575 3-9-1 82 PatDobbs 2 77
(Richard Hannon) *mde most: rdn over 2f out: hdd over 1f out: edgd lft and nt qckn* **4/1**[3]

0 **4** 1/2 **Pastoral Music**[14] 2098 3-8-11 0 JimCrowley 4 72+
(Hughie Morrison) *hld up: trckd ldrs fr over 4f out: pushed along over 2f out: nvr cl enough to chal but reminder and styd on in encouraging style fnl f* **14/1**

6-2 **5** 1 1/4 **Admiral's Sunset**[19] 1962 3-8-6 0 LukeMorris 6 65+
(Hughie Morrison) *trckd ldrs: shkn up over 2f out: cl up but nt qckn over 1f out: fdd ins fnl f* **6/1**

4 **6** 6 **Touchdown Banwell (USA)**[46] 1294 3-8-13 0 DavidProbert 9 60
(Andrew Balding) *stdd s: hld up in last pair: lost tch w ldng gp 4f out: pushed along and tk remote 6th nr fin* **33/1**

7 3/4 **Tynecastle Park** 3-8-11 0 JackMitchell 5 56
(Robert Eddery) *dwlt: hld up in last pair: shkn up and lost tch w ldng gp 4f out: no ch after* **50/1**

00 **8** 2 **Placedela Concorde**[17] 2008 3-9-1 0 RobertTart 8 56
(Anthony Carson) *in tch towards rr to 4f out: sn struggling* **100/1**

30 **9** nk **Belle Of Seville**[11] 2183 3-8-1 0 SeanMooney(7) 3 48
(Dominic Ffrench Davis) *chsd ldrs to over 4f out: sn urged along and lost tch* **125/1**

2m 11.19s (2.49) **Going Correction** +0.225s/f (Good) **9** Ran SP% **117.1**
Speed ratings (Par 99): **99,97,96,96,95 90,89,88,88**
CSF £7.21 TOTE £4.90: £1.60, £1.20, £1.50; EX 10.00 Trifecta £31.30.
Owner Giuliano Manfredini **Bred** Patrick Byrnes **Trained** Newmarket, Suffolk

FOCUS
Race distance increased by 45yds. Not a bad 3yo maiden. There was a fair pace on and the placed horses set the standard. The winner may improve again.

2549 SKY BET H'CAP 1m 3f 135y
8:45 (8:46) (Class 4) (0-85,85) 4-Y-O+ **£4,690** (£1,395; £697; £348) **Stalls** Centre

Form RPR
22-1 **1** **Baadi**^{35} 1529 4-9-6 **84** AndreaAtzeni 4 93
(Charlie Fellowes) *sn trckd ldrs: wnt 2nd 4f out: rdn to chal 2f out: kpt on u.p to ld ins fnl f* **5/2**^{1}
0-01 **2** ¾ **Zambeasy**^{28} 1717 5-9-4 **82** JamieSpencer 3 90
(Philip Hide) *led at gd pce: pressed fr over 3f out: wandered in centre of trck but fought on gamely whn chal: hdd ins fnl f: kpt on* **5/1**^{3}
54-0 **3** ½ **Steppe Daughter (IRE)**^{33} 1568 5-9-1 **79** OisinMurphy 9 86
(Denis Coakley) *hld up wl in rr: effrt 3f out: prog 2f out: drvn and r.o to take 3rd ins fnl f: clsd on ldng pair nr fin* **20/1**
-652 **4** 2¼ **Sbraase**^{53} 1166 5-9-2 **80** LukeMorris 12 83
(James Tate) *slowly away: hld up wl in rr: effrt 3f out: sme prog 2f out: hrd rdn and styd on fr over 1f out: nt pce to chal* **12/1**
00-2 **5** *nk* **Priors Brook**^{21} 1934 5-8-9 **78** EdwardGreatrex$^{(5)}$ 2 81
(Andrew Balding) *prom: cl up 4f out and gng wl enough: drvn on wd outside over 2f out: one pce over 1f out* **4/1**^{2}
3-00 **6** 1¼ **New Strategy (IRE)**^{17} 2017 4-9-7 **85** (tp) JamesDoyle 5 86
(Saeed bin Suroor) *hld up towards rr: effrt 3f out: rdn over 2f out: kpt on one pce and nvr able to threaten* **9/1**
5526 **7** 1¾ **Ravenous**^{34} 1546 5-8-8 **72** KieranO'Neill 10 70
(Luke Dace) *wl in tch in midfield: rdn 3f out: no imp ldrs 2f out: plugged on fnl f* **16/1**
630- **8** 3¼ **Rydan (IRE)**^{180} 7977 5-9-7 **85** (v) JimCrowley 13 77
(Gary Moore) *hld up wl in rr: rdn 3f out: no prog and sn btn* **12/1**
0-54 **9** 3¼ **Biotic**^{21} 1933 5-9-4 **82** FrederikTylicki 6 68
(Rod Millman) *trckd ldrs: disp 2nd 4f out gng wl enough: rdn over 2f out: wknd wl over 1f out* **14/1**
210- **10** 1¾ **El Campeon**^{174} 8064 4-8-12 **76** HarryBentley 14 59
(Simon Dow) *sn in rr: effrt on outer 3f out: no prog 2f out: sn wknd* **25/1**
0023 **11** *43* **Mister Musicmaster**^{21} 1933 7-9-4 **82** GeorgeBaker 8
(Ron Hodges) *wl in tch in midfield: rdn 3f out: wknd qckly 2f out: eased and t.o* **16/1**
1123 **12** *22* **Weald Of Kent (USA)**^{76} 864 4-8-13 **77** (v) AndrewMullen 1
(Michael Appleby) *drvn to try to ld but had to chse ldr and often bustled along: lost 2nd and wknd rapidly 4f out: sn t.o* **50/1**

2m 30.51s (1.01) **Going Correction** +0.225s/f (Good) **12** Ran SP% **119.6**
Speed ratings (Par 105): **105,104,104,102,102 101,100,97,95,94 65,51**
CSF £14.36 CT £208.58 TOTE £3.60: £1.50, £2.20, £4.40; EX 18.00 Trifecta £522.40.
Owner Saleh Al Homaizi & Imad Al Sagar **Bred** Saleh Al Homaizi & Imad Al Sagar **Trained** Newmarket, Suffolk

FOCUS
Race distance increased by 45yds. They didn't hang around in this fair handicap and the form is sound.
T/Plt: £76.40 to a £1 stake. Pool: £99,025.56 - 945.81 winning units. T/Qpdt: £21.00 to a £1 stake. Pool: £9,364.27 - 329.96 winning units. **Jonathan Neesom**

2550 - (Foreign Racing) - See Raceform Interactive

2388 SAINT-CLOUD (L-H)
Monday, May 23

OFFICIAL GOING: Turf: heavy

2551a PRIX DE PONTARME (LISTED RACE) (3YO COLTS & GELDINGS) (TURF) 1m
1:50 (12:00) 3-Y-O **£20,220** (£8,088; £6,066; £4,044; £2,022)

RPR
1 **Time Warp**^{259} 6177 3-9-3 0 CristianDemuro 1 108
(Sir Mark Prescott Bt) *dwlt: sn rcvrd to ld after 100yds: mde rest: led field across to stands' side st: kicked fr home wl over 1 1/2f out: rdn whn pressed 1f out: styd on strly and asserted* **23/5**
2 *3* **Black Max (FR)**^{15} 3-8-13 0 FabriceVeron 3 97
(H-A Pantall, France) **21/10**^{2}
3 *2* **Siyounor (FR)**^{192} 7846 3-8-13 0 GregoryBenoist 5 93
(F-H Graffard, France) **18/5**^{3}
4 1¾ **Vedevani (FR)**^{33} 1580 3-9-3 0 AlexisBadel 4 92
(A De Royer-Dupre, France) **13/10**^{1}
5 *5* **Super Mac (FR)**^{24} 3-8-13 0 TonyPiccone 2 77
(Cedric Rossi, France) **18/1**

1m 47.85s (0.35) **5** Ran SP% **120.6**
WIN (incl. 1 euro stake): 5.60. PLACES: 2.40, 1.70. SF: 16.80.
Owner W E Sturt - Osborne House **Bred** Miss K Rausing **Trained** Newmarket, Suffolk

2343 WETHERBY (L-H)
Tuesday, May 24

OFFICIAL GOING: Good (7.8)
Wind: Fresh across Weather: Cloudy & cool

2552 BRITISH STALLION STUDS EBF NOVICE MEDIAN AUCTION STKS 5f 110y
5:40 (5:41) (Class 5) 2-Y-O **£3,234** (£962; £481; £240) **Stalls** High

Form RPR
0 **1** **Miss Rosina (IRE)**^{8} 2310 2-8-9 0 JoeFanning 6 67
(George Margarson) *prom: cl up 1/2-way: rdn and slt ld over 1f out: drvn and carried sltly rt ins fnl f: styd on to ld nr line* **16/1**
3 **2** *shd* **Dubai Knights (IRE)**^{10} 2235 2-9-0 0 PJMcDonald 2 72
(Ann Duffield) *cl up on inner: rdn and slt ld 2f out: drvn and edgd rt fnl f: hdd nr line* **11/8**^{1}
0 **3** ½ **La Haule Lady**^{13} 2162 2-8-9 0 GrahamLee 3 65
(Paul Midgley) *in tch: effrt and rdn wl over 1f out: styng on whn n.m.r and swtchd lft ins fnl f: fin strly* **28/1**
4 1¼ **Seebring (IRE)** 2-9-0 0 BenCurtis 7 66
(Brian Ellison) *towards rr: hdwy on outer 2f out: sn rdn: styd on fnl f* **12/1**
42 **5** *hd* **Vaux (IRE)**^{9} 2265 2-9-0 0 JoeyHaynes 4 66
(Ben Haslam) *s.i.s: sn chsng ldrs: cl up on outer over 3f out: rdn wl over 1f out: drvn and wknd ent fnl f* **9/4**^{2}
0 **6** *3* **Mr Enthusiastic**^{31} 1641 2-9-0 0 DavidAllan 5 56
(Noel Wilson) *slt ld: rdn along and hdd 2f out: drvn and wknd over 1f out* **40/1**
4 **7** *9* **Smiley Riley (IRE)**^{15} 2090 2-9-0 0 BarryMcHugh 1 26
(Tony Coyle) *chsd ldrs on inner: rdn along over 2f out: sn wknd* **14/1**
8 *36* **Private Matter** 2-9-0 0 TonyHamilton 9 +
(Richard Fahey) *prom on outer whn green and rn v wd turn 4f out: sn bhd and eased* **6/1**^{3}

1m 9.09s (3.09) **Going Correction** +0.10s/f (Good) **8** Ran SP% **113.3**
Speed ratings (Par 93): **83,82,82,80,80 76,64,16**
CSF £37.93 TOTE £13.70: £3.60, £1.10, £4.70; EX 49.90 Trifecta £808.30.
Owner Graham Lodge Partnership **Bred** Newtown Stud **Trained** Newmarket, Suffolk

FOCUS
No speed figures can be calculated for this track until there is sufficient data. Rail was set on innermost line and all race distances were as advertised. A modest novice event and the level of the form is fluid.

2553 SIXT CAR RENTAL H'CAP 1m
6:10 (6:13) (Class 6) (0-60,60) 3-Y-O **£2,587** (£770; £384; £192) **Stalls** High

Form RPR
0322 **1** **Simply Clever**^{29} 1705 3-9-2 **55** TomEaves 10 60
(David Brown) *hld up towards rr: pushed along 3f out: rdn wl over 1f out: swtchd lft and drvn appr fnl f: styd on wl towards fin to ld nr line* **12/1**
0060 **2** *nse* **Mr Potter**^{4} 2422 3-9-4 **57** (e) ConnorBeasley 12 62
(Richard Guest) *midfield: hdwy 3f out: chsd ldrs 2f out: rdn to ld jst over 1f out: drvn ins fnl f: hdd nr line* **16/1**
3-33 **3** *1* **Mango Chutney**^{9} 2271 3-9-6 **59** PhillipMakin 13 61
(John Davies) *hld up towards rr: stdy hdwy 3f out: chsd ldrs whn n.m.r over 1f out: sn rdn and ev ch ins fnl f: drvn and kpt on same pce towards fin* **15/2**^{3}
3-00 **4** 2¼ **Capital Gearing**^{38} 1486 3-9-3 **59** (b^{1}) LouisSteward$^{(3)}$ 14 56
(Henry Spiller) *dwlt and bhd: hdwy on outer wl over 2f out: rdn wl over 1f out: kpt on u.p fnl f* **22/1**
3-45 **5** *2* **Fine Example**^{22} 1927 3-9-6 **59** ShaneGray 7 51
(Kevin Ryan) *trckd ldr: cl up over 2f out: sn rdn to chal and ev ch tl drvn and wknd appr fnl f* **11/2**^{2}
66-1 **6** *nk* **Intalza (IRE)**^{26} 1819 3-8-13 **55** (p) JoeDoyle$^{(3)}$ 8 49
(Michael Herrington) *in tch on inner whn n.m.r and hmpd after 2f: effrt on inner over 2f out whn n.m.r: sn rdn and kpt on same pce* **12/1**
0-14 **7** ¾ **Tricky Dicky**^{30} 1670 3-9-6 **59** DuranFentiman 6 49
(Olly Williams) *led: rdn along over 2f out: drvn wl over 1f out: hdd appr fnl f: grad wknd* **10/1**
6-43 **8** 1½ **Miramonte Dancer (IRE)**^{15} 2095 3-9-7 **60** DavidAllan 9 46
(David C Griffiths) *in tch: hdwy over 2f out: rdn and hung lft over 1f out: sn drvn and btn* **9/2**^{1}
0-50 **9** 1¼ **Allfredandnobell (IRE)**^{8} 2308 3-9-7 **60** JoeyHaynes 4 43
(Micky Hammond) *nvr bttr than midfield* **10/1**
000- **10** *hd* **Any Guest (IRE)**^{263} 6036 3-9-2 **55** TomQueally 5 38
(George Margarson) *trckd ldrs: smooth hdwy to chse ldng pair over 2f out: rdn wl over 1f out: hld whn n.m.r appr fnl f: wknd* **11/2**^{2}
04-0 **11** *1* **Bulge Bracket**^{28} 1740 3-9-2 **55** (v^{1}) RichardKingscote 11 35
(Tom Dascombe) *a towards rr* **20/1**
600- **12** ¾ **Contendit**^{164} 8204 3-9-0 **53** GrahamGibbons 2 31
(Michael Easterby) *chsd ldrs on inner: rdn along wl over 2f out: sn wknd* **16/1**
00-0 **13** *3* **Mr Standfast**^{24} 1859 3-9-4 **57** TimmyMurphy 1 28
(Alan Phillips) *a in rr* **50/1**
60-0 **14** *35* **Mission Mars**^{30} 1670 3-9-1 **54** (v^{1}) DavidNolan 3
(Patrick Holmes) *chsd ldng pair: pushed along over 3f out: rdn wl over 2f out: sn wknd and bhd whn eased over 1f out* **66/1**

1m 42.51s (1.51) **Going Correction** +0.10s/f (Good) **14** Ran SP% **118.6**
Speed ratings (Par 97): **96,95,94,92,90 90,89,88,86,86 85,84,81,46**
CSF £180.95 CT £1019.82 TOTE £8.10: £2.60, £5.20, £3.00; EX 136.50 Trifecta £837.50.
Owner J R Atherton & Emma Byrne **Bred** Alan J McCabe **Trained** Averham Park, Notts

FOCUS
Race distance as advertised. A race that set up for the closers, with the leaders perhaps going a touch fast early. Very ordinary form.

2554 LIFE & STYLE H'CAP 5f 110y
6:45 (6:47) (Class 4) (0-85,85) 3-Y-O **£4,690** (£1,395; £697; £348) **Stalls** High

Form RPR
4-33 **1** **My Amigo**^{11} 2200 3-9-2 **80** PJMcDonald 4 91
(Ann Duffield) *trckd ldrs on inner: pushed along 1/2-way: hdwy 2f out: swtchd rt and rdn to chse ldr jst over 1f out: chal ins fnl f: led last 75yds: kpt on wl* **2/1**^{1}
2-23 **2** ¾ **Celebration**^{19} 1977 3-9-1 **79** (b^{1}) TonyHamilton 3 88
(Richard Fahey) *trckd ldng pair: hdwy on inner to ld 2f out: rdn ent fnl f: hdd and no ex last 75yds* **11/4**^{2}
3-65 **3** *2* **Midnight Malibu (IRE)**^{11} 2218 3-8-13 **77** DavidAllan 5 79
(Tim Easterby) *trckd ldrs: hdwy 2f out: rdn to chse ldr over 1f out: drvn and kpt on same pce fnl f* **9/1**
10-0 **4** *2* **Lydia's Place**^{11} 2218 3-9-2 **85** CallumShepherd$^{(5)}$ 6 81
(Richard Guest) *led: rdn along and hdd 2f out: drvn and hung rt over 1f out: grad wknd* **14/1**
0-00 **5** 1¼ **Farkle Minkus**^{11} 2200 3-9-1 **79** (p) PhillipMakin 9 71
(Keith Dalgleish) *cl up: rdn along over 2f out: sn drvn and wknd over 1f out* **20/1**
5-15 **6** *hd* **Pusey's Secret**^{26} 1812 3-8-10 **77** MichaelJMMurphy$^{(3)}$ 2 68
(John Gallagher) *outpcd and bhd: rdn along 1/2-way: kpt on u.p fnl f* **10/1**
2256 **7** ¾ **Kingsley Klarion (IRE)**^{19} 1977 3-9-5 **83** JoeFanning 7 72
(Mark Johnston) *chsd ldrs: rdn along 2f out: sn drvn and wknd* **9/1**
21- **8** 3¾ **Alkhor**^{344} 3235 3-9-5 **83** SeanLevey 10 59
(Richard Hannon) *a towards rr* **13/2**^{3}

1m 6.48s (0.48) **Going Correction** +0.10s/f (Good) **8** Ran SP% **113.9**
Speed ratings (Par 101): **100,99,96,93,92 91,90,85**
CSF £7.45 CT £37.63 TOTE £3.30: £1.50, £1.50, £1.50; EX 5.70 Trifecta £56.80.
Owner J Dance D & S Shewring M Tanner B Craig **Bred** Llety Farms **Trained** Constable Burton, N Yorks

FOCUS
Race distance as advertised. The right horses came to the fore in this useful sprint, which was made much more winnable when likely odds-on favourite Udontdodou came out earlier in the evening. The pace was good and the first two posted pbs.

2555 COURTYARD SPA BEST DRESSED LADY COMPETITION H'CAP 1m 1f
7:15 (7:15) (Class 5) (0-70,75) 4-Y-0+ **£2,911** (£866; £432; £216) **Stalls** High

Form RPR
3341 **1** **Just Be Lucky (IRE)**[4] 2441 4-9-12 **75** 6ex....................(p) MartinHarley 5 84+
(Ivan Furtado) *trckd ldng pair gng wl: smooth hdwy over 2f out: led on bit over 1f out: shkn up ins fnl f: kpt on* **11/8**[1]
3-44 **2** ¾ **Ingleby Spring (IRE)**[15] 2091 4-8-11 **60**........................ TonyHamilton 4 67
(Richard Fahey) *in tch: hdwy on outer wl over 1f out: rdn to chse wnr ins fnl f: kpt on* **12/1**
00-1 **3** 1 **Charles De Mille**[17] 2046 8-8-8 **57**.................................. PaulMulrennan 9 62
(Jedd O'Keeffe) *hld up in rr: hdwy wl over 2f out: effrt and n.m.r over 1f out: sn swtchd rt and rdn: kpt on wl towards fin* **10/1**
225 **4** 1¼ **Yulong Xiongba (IRE)**[81] 823 4-9-2 **65**...................... ConnorBeasley 8 67
(Julie Camacho) *prom: effrt on outer and cl up 3f out: rdn along 2f out: drvn over 1f out: grad wknd* **12/1**
0423 **5** ½ **Lightning Spree (IRE)**[11] 2198 4-9-4 **67**........................... ShaneGray 1 68
(Kevin Ryan) *slowly away and bhd: hdwy into midfield after 3f: in tch 4f out: pushed along wl over 2f out: sn rdn and kpt on same pce* **8/1**[2]
602- **6** ½ **Ronya (IRE)**[211] 7519 5-8-10 **59**................................ RoystonFfrench 10 59
(Tracy Waggott) *led: rdn along and hdd 2f out: sn drvn and grad wknd* **25/1**
00-0 **7** ½ **Framley Garth (IRE)**[31] 1632 4-9-0 **68**............... RachelRichardson(5) 14 67
(Patrick Holmes) *chsd ldrs on outer: rdn along over 2f out: sn one pce* **33/1**
3504 **8** hd **Sakhalin Star (IRE)**[1] 2526 5-9-4 **67**..................................(e) JasonHart 2 67
(Richard Guest) *trckd ldrs on inner: pushed along wl over 2f out: rdn and keeping on whn n.m.r on inner ent fnl f: sn swtchd rt and kpt on towards fin* **9/1**[3]
6-44 **9** 2 **Iftikaar (IRE)**[17] 2046 6-8-13 **62**..................................... AndrewMullen 15 56
(Philip Kirby) *trckd ldr: cl up 4f out: rdn to ld 2f out: drvn and hdd over 1f out: sn wknd* **20/1**
0-00 **10** nk **Moccasin (FR)**[34] 1561 7-8-11 **60**......................................(v) DavidAllan 3 53
(Geoffrey Harker) *a towards rr* **10/1**
6/0- **11** 1¼ **Judicious**[368] 2464 9-8-13 **62**.. DougieCostello 11 53
(Geoffrey Harker) *a towards rr* **50/1**
4-40 **12** ¾ **Stoneboat Bill**[31] 1632 4-9-4 **67**.. TomEaves 12 56
(Declan Carroll) *a in rr* **20/1**
0-06 **R** **Dreese (IRE)**[21] 1954 5-9-4 **70**.............................(p) JacobButterfield(3) 13
(Marjorie Fife) *ref to r* **40/1**

1m 54.93s (-0.07) **Going Correction** +0.10s/f (Good) **13** Ran SP% **117.5**
Speed ratings (Par 103): **104,103,102,101,100 100,100,99,98,97 96,96,**
CSF £16.44 CT £125.51 TOTE £2.30: £1.10, £3.60, £4.20; EX 22.80 Trifecta £166.50.
Owner Charles Wentworth **Bred** Degner Limited **Trained** Wiseton, Nottinghamshire

FOCUS
Race distance as advertised. Reasonable form for the level and there could be more to come from the winner..

2556 YORKSHIRE POST MAGAZINE H'CAP 1m 2f
7:50 (7:51) (Class 4) (0-85,85) 4-Y-0+ **£4,690** (£1,395; £697; £348) **Stalls** Centre

Form RPR
323- **1** **Swashbuckling (IRE)**[217] 7368 4-9-4 **82**...................... PaulMulrennan 3 92+
(Michael Wigham) *trckd ldrs on inner: swtchd rt and effrt ent fnl f: sn rdn to chal: kpt on wl to ld towards fin* **6/1**[3]
0-66 **2** nk **Innocent Touch (IRE)**[11] 2222 5-9-5 **83**....................... TonyHamilton 1 92
(Richard Fahey) *led: pushed along 2f out: rdn ent fnl f: sn jnd and drvn: hdd and no ex towards fin* **9/2**[1]
00-5 **3** 2½ **Eurystheus (IRE)**[17] 2043 7-8-12 **76**...............................(tp) TomQueally 5 80
(Michael Appleby) *trckd ldrs: hdwy on outer over 3f out: rdn 2f out: drvn and ch whn edgd lft over 1f out: kpt on same pce fnl f* **9/1**
0-26 **4** 1¼ **Spa's Dancer (IRE)**[19] 1978 9-9-7 **85**............................... GrahamLee 15 87
(James Eustace) *in tch: hdwy over 2f out: sn rdn and kpt on fnl f* **10/1**
52-0 **5** 1½ **Kapstadt (FR)**[28] 1001 6-9-0 **81**............................. GeorgeDowning(3) 13 80
(Ian Williams) *hld up in rr: hdwy wl over 2f out: sn rdn and kpt on fnl f* **9/1**
4-04 **6** hd **Rhythmical**[12] 2176 4-9-1 **79**..(b[1]) JoeFanning 14 77
(Mark Johnston) *hld up in rr: hdwy wl over 2f out: sn rdn and no imp fnl f* **7/1**
-430 **7** hd **Prendergast Hill (IRE)**[13] 2163 4-9-6 **84**........................... LiamKeniry 7 82
(Ed de Giles) *trckd ldrs: effrt over 2f out: rdn along whn n.m.r and swtchd rt over 1f out: sn drvn and btn* **5/1**[2]
46-0 **8** 2 **Plane Song (IRE)**[51] 1221 4-9-1 **79**...................................... BenCurtis 4 73
(Alan Swinbank) *t.k.h: hld up: a towards rr* **20/1**
4110 **9** shd **Rock Song**[17] 2043 7-8-11 **75**...................................... GrahamGibbons 6 69
(John Mackie) *trckd ldr: cl up 1/2-way: rdn along over 2f out: drvn wl over 1f out: sn wknd* **12/1**
640 **10** 2½ **Memory Cloth**[27] 1785 9-8-9 **73**.......................................(p) JackGarritty 8 62
(Micky Hammond) *trckd ldrs on inner: effrt over 2f out: rdn along and n.m.r over 1f out: sn btn* **16/1**
640- **11** 6 **Correggio**[227] 7125 6-9-2 **80**.. PJMcDonald 10 57
(Micky Hammond) *hld up in tch: rdn along wl over 2f out: sn outpcd and bhd* **33/1**

2m 9.32s (0.32) **Going Correction** +0.10s/f (Good) **11** Ran SP% **112.0**
Speed ratings (Par 105): **102,101,99,98,97 97,97,95,95,93 88**
CSF £31.42 CT £238.33 TOTE £7.80: £2.70, £2.10, £3.40; EX 43.10 Trifecta £377.90.
Owner Mrs T Lillingston & R Pegum **Bred** Mount Coote Stud And Richard Pegum **Trained** Newmarket, Suffolk

FOCUS
Race distance as advertised. No gallop on here and the first two were well placed. There's probably more to come from the winner.

2557 RACINGUK.COM/HD MEDIAN AUCTION MAIDEN STKS 1m
8:20 (8:21) (Class 6) 3-4-Y-0 **£2,587** (£770; £384; £192) **Stalls** High

Form RPR
42 **1** **High Draw (FR)**[28] 1755 3-9-2 0.................................... DougieCostello 6 84
(K R Burke) *chsd ldrs: pushed along 3f out: rdn to chal over 2f out: led wl over 1f out: sn drvn and edgd lft: kpt on fnl f* **7/4**[2]
0-32 **2** 1½ **Torch**[10] 2248 3-9-2 80.. SeanLevey 9 81
(Richard Hannon) *trckd ldng pair: hdwy and cl up 3f out: rdn along over 2f out: ev ch whn hmpd over 1f out: sn drvn and kpt on same pce ins fnl f* **13/8**[1]
35 **3** 6 **Excellent World (IRE)**[7] 2349 3-8-11 0........................... BarryMcHugh 4 62
(Tony Coyle) *led: pushed along 3f out: rdn over 2f out: hdd wl over 1f out: sn drvn and grad wknd* **12/1**
64 **4** ½ **Sir George Somers (USA)**[15] 2098 3-9-2 0...................... TedDurcan 8 66+
(Sir Michael Stoute) *chsd ldrs: rdn along over 2f out: sn drvn and kpt on same pce* **4/1**[3]
0- **5** 1¾ **Gilt Edged (IRE)**[234] 6930 3-8-11 0............................. ConnorBeasley 10 57
(Julie Camacho) *t.k.h: hld up in tch: effrt 3f out and sn pushed along: rdn 2f out and sn one pce* **66/1**
40 **6** 3¼ **Yours Forever**[27] 1798 3-8-11 0.. TomEaves 7 50
(Kevin Ryan) *trckd ldr: pushed along over 3f out: rdn over 2f out and sn wknd* **25/1**
7 3 **Hallux** 3-9-2 0.. GrahamGibbons 3 48
(David Barron) *s.i.s: a bhd* **14/1**
000- **8** 1 **Incus**[193] 7836 3-9-2 40.. LiamKeniry 5 45
(Ed de Giles) *a towards rr* **125/1**
0 **9** 2¼ **Ellerslie Joe**[17] 2048 4-10-0 0.. JamesSullivan 2 43
(Tom Tate) *in tch: rdn along 1/2-way: sn outpcd and bhd* **125/1**
00 **10** 8 **The Skipper's Cat**[32] 1597 4-9-4 0............................. GeorgeBuckell(5) 1 20
(Michael Appleby) *a bhd* **150/1**

1m 42.17s (1.17) **Going Correction** +0.10s/f (Good)
WFA 3 from 4yo 12lb **10** Ran SP% **116.4**
Speed ratings (Par 101): **98,96,90,90,88 85,82,81,78,70**
CSF £4.92 TOTE £2.10: £1.30, £1.10, £3.40; EX 5.30 Trifecta £32.20.
Owner Tim Dykes & Mrs E Burke **Bred** Assoc Aleyrion Bloodstock Ltd **Trained** Middleham Moor, N Yorks

FOCUS
Race distance as advertised. Little depth to this maiden and the big two in the market came clear after they went a decent gallop. The bare form has its limits.

2558 FAREWELL TO THE OLD MEMBERS STAND H'CAP 1m 6f
8:50 (8:50) (Class 6) (0-60,60) 4-Y-0+ **£2,587** (£770; £384; £192) **Stalls** Low

Form RPR
-160 **1** **Desktop**[21] 1955 4-9-5 **58**.. PJMcDonald 11 64
(Antony Brittain) *t.k.h: hld up towards rr: gd hdwy on outer wl over 2f out: rdn over 1f out: styd on to ld ins fnl f: drvn out* **9/1**[3]
23-0 **2** nk **Silver Shuffle (IRE)**[20] 1955 9-9-4 **60**..............(tp) MissEmmaSayer(3) 13 66
(Dianne Sayer) *hld up in rr: swtchd rt to outer 2 1/2f out: hdwy wl over 1f out: rdn and styd on strly fnl f* **20/1**
0-06 **3** ½ **Pertuis (IRE)**[21] 1955 10-9-7 **60**...................................(p) JackGarritty 14 65
(Micky Hammond) *hld up towards rr: hdwy 3f out: rdn to chse ldrs over 1f out: n.m.r and swtchd lft ent fnl f: kpt on wl towards fin* **12/1**
0-00 **4** nk **Midnight Warrior**[10] 2233 6-8-10 **54**.............................. PhilDennis(5) 12 59
(Ron Barr) *trckd ldrs: cl up 1/2-way: chal over 3f out: rdn to ld over 2f out: drvn and hdd ent fnl f: kpt on* **16/1**
0-00 **5** ¾ **Ullswater (IRE)**[21] 1955 8-9-1 **54**............................(tp) ConnorBeasley 6 58
(Philip Kirby) *trckd ldrs: hdwy on outer over 3f out: rdn to chal over 1f out: drvn and ev ch ent fnl f: kpt on same pce* **40/1**
66-5 **6** 1½ **Rockabilly Riot (IRE)**[24] 1674 6-9-7 **60**............................ GrahamLee 8 64
(Martin Todhunter) *hld up in midfield: hdwy 3f out: rdn wl over 1f out: chsd ldrs and n.m.r ent fnl f: kpt on towards fin* **10/1**
51-1 **7** nk **Major Rowan**[117] 368 5-9-4 **57**.. PhillipMakin 4 59
(John Davies) *hld up towards rr: rapid hdwy on outer to trck ldrs after 4f: effrt over 2f out: rdn and narrow ld briefly ent fnl f: sn hdd & wknd* **6/1**[2]
3554 **8** ¾ **Thankyou Very Much**[15] 2093 6-9-6 **59**........................(p) TedDurcan 10 60
(James Bethell) *awkward s and slowly away: bhd tl hdwy over 2f out: sn rdn and kpt on fnl f* **11/2**[1]
600- **9** 1 **Waltz Darling (IRE)**[165] 7679 8-9-2 **55**.............................. TomEaves 15 54
(Keith Reveley) *hld up: a towards rr* **14/1**
0-01 **10** hd **Solid Justice (IRE)**[30] 1674 5-9-1 **54**............................ JoeyHaynes 7 54
(Kenny Johnson) *chsd ldrs: rdn along wl over 2f out: drvn over 1f out: grad wknd* **20/1**
6-53 **11** nk **El Massivo (IRE)**[31] 1649 6-9-5 **58**.................................... BenCurtis 16 57
(Harriet Bethell) *prom: rdn along 3f out: wknd fnl 2f* **10/1**
3101 **12** shd **Frosty The Snowman (IRE)**[25] 1842 5-9-3 **56**............ JamesSullivan 3 55
(Ruth Carr) *a towards rr* **6/1**[2]
0-60 **13** ¾ **Moon Arc (IRE)**[29] 1697 4-9-4 **57**................................(p) TomQueally 2 58
(Keith Dalgleish) *midfield: effrt 3f out: sn rdn along and wknd 2f out* **20/1**
000- **14** 5 **Sigurd (GER)**[211] 7520 4-9-5 **58**... ShaneGray 5 49
(Kevin Ryan) *led: rdn along over 3f out: hdd over 2f out: sn drvn and wknd* **14/1**
033- **15** ½ **Perennial**[169] 7636 7-9-7 **60**.......................................(p) DougieCostello 1 50
(Philip Kirby) *in tch on inner: hdwy on inner 2f out and sn chsng ldrs: sn rdn and wknd ent fnl f* **16/1**

3m 8.74s (3.74) **Going Correction** +0.10s/f (Good) **15** Ran SP% **121.7**
Speed ratings (Par 101): **93,92,92,92,91 91,90,90,89,89 89,89,89,86,86**
CSF £183.86 CT £2177.77 TOTE £10.10: £3.30, £5.70, £5.60; EX 221.50 Trifecta £3442.40 Part won..
Owner Antony Brittain **Bred** Northgate Lodge Stud Ltd **Trained** Warthill, N Yorks

FOCUS
Race distance as advertised. Moderate staying form, although it's worth noting the first three here, who all came from the rear, had finished seventh, eighth and sixth respectively in the same Catterick handicap earlier in the month.
T/Plt: £29.60 to a £1 stake. Pool: £74,351.87 - 1,832.98 winning tickets. T/Qpdt: £3.40 to a £1 stake. Pool: £8,493.46 - 1,809.83 winning tickets. **Joe Rowntree**

2442 WOLVERHAMPTON (A.W) (L-H)
Tuesday, May 24

OFFICIAL GOING: Tapeta: standard
Wind: Light against Weather: Cloudy

2559 #FOLLOWUS ON TWITTER @WOLVESRACES H'CAP (DIV I) 5f 216y (Tp)
2:15 (2:15) (Class 6) (0-60,60) 3-Y-0 **£2,264** (£673; £336; £168) **Stalls** Low

Form RPR
000- **1** **Tulip Dress**[244] 6643 3-9-4 **57**.. RobertTart 6 62
(Anthony Carson) *mid-div: pushed along over 2f out: hdwy and nt clr run fr over 1f out tl wl ins fnl f: r.o to ld towards fin* **20/1**
050 **2** nk **The Lillster**[10] 2255 3-9-1 **57**................................. GeorgeDowning(3) 3 62
(Tony Carroll) *hld up: plld hrd: hdwy and nt clr run fr over 1f out tl swtchd lft wl ins fnl f: r.o* **15/2**
05-3 **3** hd **Whispering Wolf**[30] 1670 3-8-9 **51**.......................... JacobButterfield(3) 9 55
(Suzzanne France) *led: rdn and hung lft over 1f out: hdd towards fin* **11/1**

4-03 **4** *nk* **Pilgrims Path**[14] 2118 3-9-4 **57**....................................(p) KieranO'Neill 10 60
(Scott Dixon) *chsd ldrs: pushed along 1/2-way: rdn and hung lft fr over 1f out: ev ch wl ins fnl f: no ex towards fin* **11/1**

2262 **5** *3/4* **La Asomada**[14] 2118 3-9-2 **60**................................ JosephineGordon(5) 4 60
(David Barron) *w ldr: rdn and ev ch over 1f out: sn edgd lft: no ex towards fin* **4/1**[3]

-206 **6** *1* **Seaperle**[10] 2255 3-9-1 **54**.. DavidAllan 8 51+
(Tim Easterby) *dwlt: in rr: rdn over 1f out: r.o ins fnl f: nvr nrr* **10/3**[2]

300- **7** *1/2* **Windmills Girl**[225] 7160 3-9-5 **58**.. MartinLane 7 54
(Jeremy Gask) *hld up: rdn over 1f out: r.o ins fnl f: nvr on terms* **10/1**

-665 **8** *3/4* **Fiftytintsofsilver (IRE)**[15] 2083 3-8-7 **46** oh1.................... LukeMorris 2 40
(Gay Kelleway) *prom: nt clr run fr over 1f out: hmpd ins fnl f: nvr able to chal* **20/1**

6311 **9** *hd* **Bushwise (IRE)**[13] 2143 3-8-11 **50**..............................(p) FrannyNorton 5 50+
(Milton Bradley) *prom: shkn up over 1f out: cl up whn hmpd and eased wl ins fnl f* **3/1**[1]

0-00 **10** *4 1/2* **Kylla**[15] 2107 3-8-7 **46** oh1... DuranFentiman 1 26
(Shaun Harris) *hld up: rdn over 1f out: a in rr* **66/1**

1m 15.46s (0.96) **Going Correction** -0.075s/f (Stan) **10** Ran SP% **116.6**
Speed ratings (Par 97): **90,89,89,88,87 86,85,84,84,78**
CSF £159.53 CT £1792.40 TOTE £18.40: £3.40, £2.80, £3.20; EX 184.20 Trifecta £3798.20 Part won..
Owner Hugh & Mindi Byrne & Minster Stud **Bred** Minster Stud **Trained** Newmarket, Suffolk
■ Stewards' Enquiry : George Downing seven-day ban; improper riding (7th June-13th June)

FOCUS
A messy race with a bunched finish. It was the quicker division by 1.12sec. Ordinary form for the level.

2560 #FOLLOWUS ON TWITTER @WOLVESRACES H'CAP (DIV II) 5f 216y (Tp)
2:45 (2:46) (Class 6) (0-60,59) 3-Y-O **£2,264** (£673; £336; £168) **Stalls** Low

Form RPR

30-2 **1** **Jumeirah Star (USA)**[38] 1497 3-9-3 **55**..................(v1) AdamBeschizza 8 62
(Robert Cowell) *chsd ldrs: racd wd tl led over 4f out: rdn over 1f out: styd on* **3/1**[2]

0461 **2** *1 1/2* **Guapo Bay**[13] 2155 3-8-5 **50**...(b) TinaSmith(7) 1 53
(Richard Hannon) *a.p: chsd wnr over 2f out: rdn over 1f out: styd on same pce ins fnl f* **4/1**[3]

3 *5* **Minminwin (IRE)**[238] 6841 3-8-7 **45**.................................... LukeMorris 5 33
(Gay Kelleway) *chsd ldrs: drvn along over 3f out: styd on same pce fr over 1f out* **11/8**[1]

000- **4** *7* **Time Again**[178] 8033 3-8-13 **54**.. RobHornby(3) 6 21
(David Brown) *hld up: pushed along over 3f out: rdn and wknd over 2f out* **7/1**

046 **5** *1 1/4* **Bomber Etches**[82] 798 3-8-7 **45**...................................... KieranO'Neill 7 8
(Scott Dixon) *dwlt: sn pushed along in rr: rdn and wknd over 2f out* **16/1**

50-0 **6** *5* **Zophilly (IRE)**[29] 1725 3-9-7 **59**...(t) MartinLane 2 7
(Jeremy Gask) *led: hdd over 4f out: chsd wnr tl rdn over 2f out: wknd wl over 1f out* **12/1**

1m 14.58s (0.08) **Going Correction** -0.075s/f (Stan) **6** Ran SP% **113.2**
Speed ratings (Par 97): **96,94,87,78,76 69**
CSF £15.51 CT £22.29 TOTE £3.40: £1.30, £2.30; EX 13.30 Trifecta £23.90.
Owner Khalifa Dasmal & Partner **Bred** Circular Road Breeders **Trained** Six Mile Bottom, Cambs

FOCUS
Division two of this low-grade sprint handicap, and the slower by 1.12sec. The first two finished clear.

2561 AT THE RACES APP ON ANDROID MAIDEN STKS 5f 216y (Tp)
3:15 (3:15) (Class 5) 3-Y-O **£2,911** (£866; £432; £216) **Stalls** Low

Form RPR

24-3 **1** **Papa Luigi (IRE)**[12] 2186 3-9-5 73.................................... KieranO'Neill 4 78
(Richard Hannon) *led: hdd over 4f out: led again over 2f out: shkn up over 1f out: r.o: comf* **10/11**[1]

3-35 **2** *3 1/4* **Waneen (IRE)**[12] 2185 3-9-5 70... JFEgan 5 68
(Joseph Tuite) *chsd ldrs: rdn to chse wnr over 2f out: styd on same pce fnl f* **4/1**[3]

3 **3** *3 1/2* **Line Sport (IRE)**[18] 2019 3-9-5 0.................................... JamieSpencer 2 56
(Richard Fahey) *pushed along and in tch: hdwy u.p over 2f out: sn edgd lft: wnt 3rd over 1f out: styd on same pce* **3/1**[2]

4 *2 3/4* **Noble Act** 3-9-0 0.. SilvestreDeSousa 3 43
(Rae Guest) *dwlt: hld up: hdwy to dispute 3rd wl over 1f out: wknd fnl f* **7/1**

00-0 **5** *12* **Nefetari**[8] 2302 3-9-0 38.. JimmyQuinn 1 4
(Alan Brown) *prom: rdn whn hmpd over 2f out: sn wknd* **100/1**

0000 **6** *2 3/4* **Temujins Quest (IRE)**[7] 2333 3-9-5 0.............................. MartinLane 8
(Derek Shaw) *in tch and sn drvn along: hung lft over 5f out: led over 4f out: hdd over 2f out: wknd wl over 1f out* **150/1**

7 *11* **Ridge Pride (IRE)** 3-8-7 0... RowanScott(7) 6
(Rebecca Menzies) *in tch: hmpd over 5f out: rdn and wknd over 2f out* **40/1**

1m 13.46s (-1.04) **Going Correction** -0.075s/f (Stan) **7** Ran SP% **114.0**
Speed ratings (Par 99): **103,98,94,90,74 70,56**
CSF £5.00 TOTE £2.10: £1.40, £1.60; EX 6.00 Trifecta £11.00.
Owner Middleham Park Racing XLVIII **Bred** Gerry Flannery Developments Ltd **Trained** East Everleigh, Wilts

FOCUS
A pretty modest maiden, but the quickest of the 6f times on the day. The winner is rated back to his 2yo form.

2562 BLACK COUNTRY CHAMBER OF COMMERCE CLAIMING STKS 5f 20y (Tp)
3:45 (3:45) (Class 6) 3-Y-O+ **£2,264** (£673; £336) **Stalls** Low

Form RPR

5433 **1** **Come On Dave (IRE)**[68] 966 7-10-0 82.........................(v) AdamKirby 4 89
(John Butler) *mde all: qcknd over 1f out: rdn and edgd lft ins fnl f: styd on* **6/4**[1]

-505 **2** *1/2* **Long Awaited (IRE)**[8] 2305 8-9-0 85................(b) JosephineGordon(5) 3 78
(David Barron) *chsd wnr 1f: wnt 2nd again over 1f out: sn rdn: r.o* **15/8**[2]

/13- **3** *6* **Clumber Street**[413] 1234 5-9-5 81.. SeanLevey 5 57
(David Brown) *chsd wnr 4f out tl rdn over 1f out: wknd fnl f* **2/1**[3]

1m 1.45s (-0.45) **Going Correction** -0.075s/f (Stan) **3** Ran SP% **108.1**
Speed ratings (Par 101): **100,99,89**
CSF £4.46 TOTE £2.10; EX 3.40 Trifecta £4.90.Long Awaited was claimed by Mr C Dore for £8,000.
Owner Wildcard Racing Syndicate **Bred** Mrs Eithne Hamilton **Trained** Newmarket, Suffolk

FOCUS
Only three runners for this fair claimer, and they finished in market order. Not a race that taught us much.

2563 FOLLOW @ATTHERACES ON TWITTER H'CAP 1m 4f 50y (Tp)
4:15 (4:16) (Class 6) (0-65,64) 3-Y-O **£2,264** (£673; £336; £168) **Stalls** Low

Form RPR

0-21 **1** **Scarpeta (FR)**[14] 2124 3-9-2 **59**.. FrannyNorton 4 71+
(Mark Johnston) *mde all: pushed clr over 1f out: comf* **9/4**[1]

0240 **2** *5* **Frivolous Prince (IRE)**[35] 1551 3-8-5 **48**..................(vt) CathyGannon 2 52
(David Evans) *hld up: hdwy over 3f out: rdn to go 2nd ins fnl f: no ch w wnr* **8/1**

53-6 **3** *1* **Free Bounty**[31] 1619 3-9-2 **64**.................................. EdwardGreatrex(5) 8 66
(Philip McBride) *chsd ldrs: rdn over 2f out: edgd lft over 1f out: styd on same pce* **11/2**[3]

0-4 **4** *3/4* **Coarse Cut (IRE)**[29] 1718 3-9-6 **63**.. JohnFahy 1 64
(Eve Johnson Houghton) *chsd ldrs: rdn over 2f out: styd on same pce fr over 1f out* **11/1**

000- **5** *nk* **Mystique Heights**[192] 7863 3-9-3 **60**................................. LukeMorris 6 62
(Sir Mark Prescott Bt) *s.i.s: sn pushed along to go prom: chsd wnr over 8f out: shkn up at various stages after: rdn over 2f out: no ex and lost 2nd ins fnl f* **11/2**[3]

0-05 **6** *6* **Street Outlaw (IRE)**[31] 1651 3-9-5 **62**.................................. AdamKirby 5 53
(Daniel Mark Loughnane) *hld up: rdn over 5f out: wknd over 2f out* **7/1**

50U5 **7** *2 3/4* **Topalova**[14] 2123 3-8-13 **56**... SilvestreDeSousa 7 43
(Mark H Tompkins) *prom: rdn over 3f out: wknd over 1f out* **4/1**[2]

000- **8** *16* **Defiant Choice**[223] 7220 3-7-11 **45**............................... NoelGarbutt(5) 3 6
(Derek Shaw) *s.i.s: pushed along in rr thrght: rdn over 5f out: wknd over 2f out* **50/1**

2m 39.01s (-1.79) **Going Correction** -0.075s/f (Stan) **8** Ran SP% **115.4**
Speed ratings (Par 97): **102,98,98,97,97 93,91,80**
CSF £21.49 CT £88.84 TOTE £2.60: £1.10, £2.10, £2.20; EX 14.00 Trifecta £66.90.
Owner Brian Yeardley **Bred** Mme Michele Bliard **Trained** Middleham Moor, N Yorks

FOCUS
A modest handicap in which the progressive winner made all. He had the run of the race, and the runner-up helps with the level.

2564 FAMILY FUN DAY MONDAY 8TH AUGUST FILLIES' H'CAP 1m 4f 50y (Tp)
4:45 (4:45) (Class 5) (0-75,75) 4-Y-O+ **£2,911** (£866; £432; £216) **Stalls** Low

Form RPR

12-3 **1** **Ickymasho**[25] 1825 4-9-7 **75**... GeorgeBaker 3 85+
(Jonathan Portman) *mde all: qcknd over 2f out: shkn up over 1f out: styd on wl* **11/4**[1]

4235 **2** *3 1/4* **Hope You Dance (FR)**[13] 2149 4-8-12 **66**..................(p) JamieSpencer 1 70
(David Simcock) *hld up in tch: rdn over 2f out: styd on same pce ins fnl f: wnt 2nd nr fin* **4/1**[3]

22-4 **3** *hd* **Eager Beaver**[22] 1919 4-9-7 **75**.. MartinDwyer 2 79
(William Muir) *a.p: chsd wnr over 2f out: rdn over 1f out: edgd lft and no ex ins fnl f* **7/1**

6101 **4** *shd* **Bayan Kasirga (IRE)**[15] 2093 6-9-0 **75**.................. NatalieHambling(7) 8 79+
(Richard Fahey) *hmpd s: sn swtchd lft: hld up: hdwy and hung lft over 1f out: r.o: nrst fin* **7/2**[2]

0632 **5** *3* **Percys Princess**[13] 2149 5-8-4 **65**................................ GeorgeWood(7) 6 64
(Michael Appleby) *chsd ldrs: rdn over 2f out: wknd ins fnl f* **11/2**

10-0 **6** *2 3/4* **Rum Swizzle**[11] 2210 4-8-13 **67**... LukeMorris 4 62
(Harry Dunlop) *s.i.s and wnt rt s: hld up: rdn over 3f out: wknd over 1f out* **14/1**

550- **7** *nk* **Enchanted Moment**[225] 7173 4-9-0 **68**................................ TedDurcan 7 62
(Chris Wall) *chsd wnr after 1f tl rdn over 2f out: wknd fnl f* **16/1**

00-4 **8** *7* **Lady Clitico (IRE)**[9] 330 5-8-10 **71**.............................. RowanScott(7) 5 54
(Rebecca Menzies) *hld up: rdn over 3f out: wknd over 2f out* **22/1**

2m 38.88s (-1.92) **Going Correction** -0.075s/f (Stan) **8** Ran SP% **113.7**
Speed ratings (Par 100): **103,100,100,100,98 96,96,91**
CSF £13.73 CT £67.66 TOTE £4.00: £1.60, £1.90, £2.20; EX 12.70 Trifecta £52.90.
Owner C R Lambourne, M Forbes, D Losse **Bred** Allseasons Bloodstock **Trained** Upper Lambourn, Berks

FOCUS
A modest fillies' handicap, run in only a slightly quicker time than the preceding Class 6 handicap. The winner resumed her progress, with the next three to form.

2565 VISIT WOLVERHAMPTON-RACECOURSE.CO.UK H'CAP 1m 141y (Tp)
5:15 (5:15) (Class 4) (0-85,84) 3-Y-O **£4,690** (£1,395; £697; £348) **Stalls** Low

Form RPR

0-1 **1** **Dommersen (IRE)**[45] 1339 3-9-3 **80**................................ RobertHavlin 8 89+
(John Gosden) *s.i.s: rcvrd to go prom after 1f: chsd ldr over 6f out: led and hung rt fr over 2f out: rdn over 1f out: styd on* **7/2**[2]

440- **2** *1 1/2* **Winter Rose (IRE)**[227] 7112 3-9-6 **83**.............................. KieranO'Neill 5 88
(Richard Hannon) *plld hrd: trckd ldr 2f: remained handy: rdn over 1f out: hung lft ins fnl f: kpt on* **8/1**

1535 **3** *1 1/4* **Jintshi**[13] 2145 3-8-12 **75**... FrannyNorton 1 77
(Mark Johnston) *chsd ldrs: rdn over 2f out: styd on same pce ins fnl f* **7/1**[3]

1110 **4** *nse* **Pirate's Treasure**[32] 1602 3-9-3 **80**.............................. JamieSpencer 2 82
(James Tate) *hld up: plld hrd: hdwy and nt clr run over 1f out: sn rdn: styd on* **8/1**

51-4 **5** *3/4* **Ballard Down (IRE)**[18] 1992 3-9-7 **84**.............................. GeorgeBaker 3 84
(William Knight) *hld up: hdwy u.p and hung lft over 1f out: styd on same pce ins fnl f* **5/2**[1]

641- **6** *1 1/2* **Status Quo (IRE)**[238] 6834 3-9-0 **77**................................ LukeMorris 4 74
(Sir Mark Prescott Bt) *hld up: rdn over 2f out: styd on same pce fr over 1f out* **7/2**[2]

1236 **7** *13* **Winged Dancer**[48] 1267 3-8-13 **76**............................ SilvestreDeSousa 7 43
(Sylvester Kirk) *led: rdn and hdd over 2f out: wknd and eased fnl f* **14/1**

1m 49.52s (-0.58) **Going Correction** -0.075s/f (Stan) **7** Ran SP% **114.4**
Speed ratings (Par 101): **99,97,96,96,95 94,82**
CSF £30.87 CT £184.88 TOTE £4.80: £2.50, £3.40; EX 38.00 Trifecta £296.10.
Owner Al Mirqab Racing **Bred** The Lavington Stud **Trained** Newmarket, Suffolk

FOCUS
Fair handicap form, though the time was modest. A clear pb from the winner.

2566 VISIT ATTHERACES.COM H'CAP 1m 141y (Tp)
5:45 (5:45) (Class 6) (0-60,59) 4-Y-O+ **£2,264** (£673; £336; £168) **Stalls** Low

Form RPR

5/21 **1** **Barnaby Brook (CAN)**[89] 702 6-9-5 **57**.........................(b) LukeMorris 8 68
(Robyn Brisland) *chsd ldrs: rdn over 1f out: led ins fnl f: r.o wl* **11/4**[1]

0-00 **2** 2 1/2 **Filament Of Gold (USA)**[101] 569 5-8-12 **55**............. GaryMahon(5) 13 61
(Roy Brotherton) *chsd ldrs: lost pl over 3f out: rallied over 2f out: led over 1f out: rdn and hdd ins fnl f: styd on same pce* **22/1**

5503 **3** 3/4 **Miss Lillie**[15] 2087 5-9-7 **59**.. RobertWinston 7 63
(Roger Teal) *mid-div: pushed along and hdwy over 1f out: sn rdn: edgd lft ins fnl f: styd on to go 3rd nr fin* **6/1**[2]

3-05 **4** hd **Castle Talbot (IRE)**[13] 2144 4-9-4 **56**.............................(b[1]) ShaneKelly 2 60
(Richard Hughes) *led: rdn and hdd over 1f out: styd on same pce ins fnl f* **7/1**

066 **5** 2 **Zed Candy Girl**[34] 1565 6-9-7 **59**......................................(p) AdamKirby 3 59
(Daniel Mark Loughnane) *prom: chsd ldr over 2f out: rdn and ev ch over 1f out: no ex ins fnl f* **9/1**

5445 **6** 1 1/4 **Evervescent (IRE)**[38] 1500 7-9-4 **59**................................ EoinWalsh(3) 1 56
(Graeme McPherson) *hld up: hdwy over 1f out: sn rdn: wknd ins fnl f* **13/2**[3]

0324 **7** 1 1/4 **Diamonds A Dancing**[23] 1899 6-9-2 **59**..................(v) CiaranMckee(5) 9 53
(John O'Shea) *hld up: rdn over 2f out: nvr trbld ldrs* **10/1**

2410 **8** 1/2 **Ferryview Place**[67] 982 7-9-1 **53**............................(vt) StevieDonohoe 4 46
(Ian Williams) *hld up: rdn over 2f out: n.d* **12/1**

404 **9** 1/2 **Outlaw Torn (IRE)**[5] 2409 7-9-7 **59**.........................(e) PatrickMathers 11 51
(Richard Guest) *prom: chsd ldr over 6f out tl rdn over 2f out: wknd over 1f out* **8/1**

0456 **10** 2 1/2 **John Potts**[31] 1654 11-8-7 **45**..................................... SilvestreDeSousa 6 32
(Brian Baugh) *hld up: hdwy over 1f out: wknd ins fnl f* **10/1**

050- **11** 1/2 **Mixed Message (IRE)**[186] 7923 6-8-9 **50**............. RobHornby(3) 10 36
(Mandy Rowland) *s.i.s: hld up: rdn over 2f out: sn wknd* **25/1**

1m 49.63s (-0.47) **Going Correction** -0.075s/f (Stan) **11** Ran SP% **122.0**
Speed ratings (Par 101): **99,96,96,95,94 93,91,91,91,88 88**
CSF £76.05 CT £358.49 TOTE £2.40: £1.80, £8.30, £2.20; EX 73.10 Trifecta £316.40.
Owner Franconson Partners **Bred** Adena Springs **Trained** Newmarket, Suffolk

FOCUS
This moderate handicap was run at a solid pace. The third and fourth help with the level.
T/Plt: £137.20 to a £1 stake. Pool: £69,465.84 - 369.57 winning tickets. T/Qpdt: £6.80 to a £1 stake. Pool: £7,153.52 - 778.37 winning tickets. **Colin Roberts**

2567a (Foreign Racing) - See Raceform Interactive

2454 CHANTILLY (R-H)
Tuesday, May 24

OFFICIAL GOING: Turf: heavy; polytrack: standard

2568a PRIX D'ISPAHAN (GROUP 1) (4YO+) (TURF) 1m 1f
1:50 (12:00) 4-Y-O+ **£105,036** (£42,022; £21,011; £10,496; £5,257)

RPR

1 **A Shin Hikari (JPN)**[163] 8219 5-9-2 0................................ YutakaTake 3 126
(Masanori Sakaguchi, Japan) *disp ld on inner: hdd and trckd ldr after 2f: travelled strly thrght: eased into ld 2f out: shkn up and clr appr fnl f: easily* **74/10**

2 10 **Dariyan (FR)**[23] 1909 4-9-2 0................................ ChristopheSoumillon 4 111+
(A De Royer-Dupre, France) *w.w in midfield: shkn up to chse ldng pair wl over 2f out: styd on to go 2nd wl ins fnl f: no ch w wnr* **39/10**[2]

3 1 3/4 **Silverwave (FR)**[23] 1909 4-9-2 0.................................... MaximeGuyon 7 107+
(P Bary, France) *w.w in fnl trio between horses: bmpd under 3f out: rdn and prog 2f out: styd on u.p fr 1 1/2f out: tk 3rd cl home: nvr on terms* **10/1**

4 1/2 **Vadamos (FR)**[23] 1910 5-9-2 0........................... Pierre-CharlesBoudot 6 106
(A Fabre, France) *disp ld on outer: led after 2f and swtchd ins to rail: rdn and hdd 2f out: kpt on at same pce u.p: lost 2nd wl ins fnl f: dropped to 4th cl home* **42/10**[3]

5 2 **My Dream Boat (IRE)**[32] 1604 4-9-2 0........................... GeraldMosse 2 102
(Clive Cox) *t.k.h: hld up in fnl trio on inner: shkn up: angled out and bmpd under 3f out: last whn angled out ent fnl 2f: hrd rdn and styd on fr 1 1/2f out: nt pce to ever be in contention* **9/1**

6 3/4 **New Bay**[233] 6970 4-9-2 0.. VincentCheminaud 5 101
(A Fabre, France) *settled in midfield: abt 6 l 5th and niggled along over 2f out: sn labouring and wl btn ins fnl 1 1/2f* **6/4**[1]

7 2 1/2 **Mondialiste (IRE)**[163] 8218 6-9-2 0................................ DanielTudhope 8 95
(David O'Meara) *cl up on outer: rdn to hold pl over 2f out: sn wknd* **45/1**

8 1/2 **Wild Chief (GER)**[23] 1909 5-9-2 0.............................. AlexanderPietsch 9 94
(J Hirschberger, Germany) *hld up in fnl trio: hrd rdn 2 1/2f out and no imp: wl hld fnl 2f* **34/1**

9 dist **Erupt (IRE)**[177] 8042 4-9-2 0.................................... StephanePasquier 1
(F-H Graffard, France) *w.w in midfield: rdn and no imp 2 1/2f out: sn wknd: wl bhd whn eased fnl f* **20/1**

1m 53.29s (2.19) **9** Ran SP% **120.4**
WIN (incl. 1 euro stake): 8.40. PLACES: 2.60, 1.90, 2.30. DF: 21.20. SF: 39.00.
Owner Eishindo Co Ltd **Bred** K K Eishindo **Trained** Japan

FOCUS
Run at Chantilly as Longchamp is being redveloped. This was a good renewal of what has been a top-class race throughout the years was taken in devastating style by the Japanese-trained winner, who strode away from his rivals in the final stages while they toiled in his wake. He was always handy off a relatively slow pace.

2569 - (Foreign Racing) - See Raceform Interactive

2196 HAMILTON (R-H)
Wednesday, May 25

OFFICIAL GOING: Good to firm (good in places; 8.1)
Wind: Light, half against Weather: Overcast

2570 HIGHLAND SPRING WATER MANDORA NOVICE AUCTION STKS (£20,000 HIGHLAND SPRING WATER SERIES QUALIFIER) 6f 6y
2:00 (2:03) (Class 6) 2-Y-O **£2,911** (£866; £432; £216) **Stalls** High

Form RPR

3 **1** **Boundsy (IRE)**[32] 1641 2-8-13 0.................................... TonyHamilton 9 73
(Richard Fahey) *mde all against stands' rail: pushed along and hrd pressed fr over 1f out: hld on gamely towards fin* **9/1**

2 shd **Good Time Ahead (IRE)** 2-9-1 0................................... JackGarritty 1 74+
(Richard Fahey) *wnt rt s: hld up in midfield on outside: effrt and rdn over 1f out: hdwy to dispute ld last 50yds: jst hld* **14/1**

36 **3** 3/4 **Harome (IRE)**[13] 2193 2-9-0 0.. SamJames 2 71
(David Loughnane) *cl up: effrt and ev ch over 1f out to wl ins fnl f: kpt on same pce towards fin* **8/1**

4 1/2 **Teofonic (IRE)** 2-8-7 0.. JoeFanning 11 63+
(Mark Johnston) *sn pushed along bhd ldng bunch: rn green and outpcd over 3f out: hdwy over 1f out: kpt on ins fnl f* **8/1**

U **5** 3/4 **Showdance Kid**[8] 2344 2-9-1 0................................... DougieCostello 8 68
(K R Burke) *trckd ldrs: effrt and pushed along 2f out: kpt on same pce ins fnl f* **5/2**[1]

6 **6** 1/2 **Zebedee Cat (IRE)**[16] 2090 2-9-1 0.................................... GrahamLee 4 67
(Iain Jardine) *prom on outside: rdn along over 2f out: kpt on same pce fnl f* **33/1**

7 2 1/4 **Uncle Charlie (IRE)** 2-8-12 0.. PJMcDonald 3 57
(Ann Duffield) *noisy in paddock: rn green in rr: effrt and drvn 2f out: sn no imp* **7/1**[3]

2 **8** 1 3/4 **Bourbonisto**[11] 2235 2-8-12 0.. RaulDaSilva 7 52+
(Ben Haslam) *blindfold slow to remove and s.s: outpcd in rr: sme hdwy over 1f out: nvr on terms* **10/3**[2]

9 20 **Jock Talk (IRE)** 2-9-2 0.. TadhgO'Shea 6
(John Patrick Shanahan, Ire) *t.k.h: trckd ldrs: rdn over 2f out: wknd over 1f out: t.o* **20/1**

10 nse **Hot Gossip (IRE)** 2-8-6 0.. JamesSullivan 10
(Dianne Sayer) *dwlt: bhd and green: struggling after 2f: sn lost tch: t.o* **100/1**

1m 11.68s (-0.52) **Going Correction** -0.225s/f (Firm) **10** Ran SP% **111.7**
Speed ratings (Par 91): **94,93,92,92,91 90,87,85,58,58**
CSF £118.37 TOTE £8.30: £2.40, £3.80, £2.60; EX 97.40 Trifecta £1714.30.
Owner Kevin Mercer & Partner **Bred** Glenview House Stud **Trained** Musley Bank, N Yorks
■ Rag Tatter was withdrawn. Price at time of withdrawal 20-1. Rule 4 does not apply.

FOCUS
The ground had dried out slightly and was given as good to firm, good in places (from good). Rail on loop out 3yds, adding around 12yds to the last four races on the card. This looked an ordinary novice auction event beforehand, but a couple caught the eye and the race should produce a few winners. The winning time was 2.08sec outside standard and it resulted in a 1-2 for trainer Richard Fahey. The form is rated around the race average.

2571 HAMILTON PARK SUPPORTING RACING TO SCHOOL H'CAP 6f 6y
2:30 (2:32) (Class 6) (0-65,65) 3-Y-O+ **£2,911** (£866; £432; £216) **Stalls** High

Form RPR

1 **Born Innocent (IRE)**[23] 1942 3-8-6 **52**........................... TadhgO'Shea 3 62+
(John Patrick Shanahan, Ire) *hld up on outside: hdwy 2f out: led ent fnl f: drifted lft and pushed clr* **10/1**

5032 **2** 3 **Keene's Pointe**[12] 2201 6-9-12 **63**................................ TonyHamilton 4 66
(Kristin Stubbs) *hld up: rdn over 2f out: hdwy over 1f out: kpt on to take 2nd towards fin: nt gng pce to chal* **13/2**[2]

0-46 **3** shd **Spirit Of Wedza (IRE)**[36] 1555 4-9-9 **60**..................(p) ConnorBeasley 5 63
(Julie Camacho) *trckd ldrs: led over 1f out to ent fnl f: kpt on same pce last 100yds* **6/1**[1]

2215 **4** 1 3/4 **Bahamian Sunshine**[11] 2255 3-8-12 **65**..........(p) AdamMcNamara(7) 13 60
(Richard Fahey) *trckd ldrs: drvn and outpcd wl over 1f out: rallied ins fnl f: no imp* **6/1**[1]

4050 **5** 1 **Mighty Zip (USA)**[15] 2120 4-9-2 **60**.......................(p) LewisEdmunds(7) 6 54
(Kevin Ryan) *cl up: led over 2f out: rdn and hdd over 1f out: kpt on same pce fnl f* **22/1**

5354 **6** 1 1/4 **Danish Duke (IRE)**[12] 2202 5-9-9 **60**.........................(p) JamesSullivan 7 51
(Ruth Carr) *in tch: effrt over 2f out: rdn and edgd rt over 1f out: outpcd fnl f* **15/2**[3]

-361 **7** 1/2 **Gaelic Wizard (IRE)**[18] 2053 8-9-10 **61**........................(v) SamJames 11 50
(Karen Tutty) *midfield: rdn along over 2f out: no imp fr over 1f out* **15/2**[3]

4056 **8** 3 3/4 **National Service (USA)**[5] 2416 5-9-9 **65**..................(t) NathanEvans(5) 8 43+
(Rebecca Menzies) *missed break: hld up: shortlived effrt on outside 2f out: sn no imp* **13/2**[2]

0-03 **9** 1/2 **Spoken Words**[7] 2359 7-8-9 **46** oh1........................(b) PatrickMathers 12 22
(John David Riches) *trckd ldrs: drvn along over 2f out: wknd over 1f out* **28/1**

50-0 **10** 7 **Piccardo**[28] 1789 3-9-3 **63**... GeorgeChaloner 14 16
(Richard Fahey) *hld up: drvn along over 2f out: wknd wl over 1f out* **12/1**

414- **11** 17 **Sophistica (IRE)**[228] 7107 3-9-0 **60**.............................. RoystonFfrench 9
(Iain Jardine) *led and sn crossed to stands' rail: rdn and hdd over 2f out: wknd over 1f out: sn lost tch* **15/2**[3]

1m 10.48s (-1.72) **Going Correction** -0.225s/f (Firm)
WFA 3 from 4yo+ 9lb **11** Ran SP% **115.1**
Speed ratings (Par 101): **102,98,97,95,94 92,91,86,86,76 54**
CSF £72.04 CT £335.95 TOTE £14.30: £4.00, £2.30, £2.40; EX 96.40 Trifecta £495.20.
Owner Thistle Bloodstock Limited **Bred** Thistle Bloodstock Ltd **Trained** Kells, Co Kilkenny

FOCUS
A moderate sprint handicap and the unexposed winner was different gear. Those in behind help set a straightforward level.

2572 RACING TO SCHOOL H'CAP 5f 7y
3:05 (3:05) (Class 5) (0-75,81) 4-Y-O+ **£3,881** (£1,155; £577; £288) **Stalls** Centre

Form RPR

3-65 **1** **Imperial Legend (IRE)**[11] 2261 7-9-3 **71**............................ PaulQuinn 8 79
(David Nicholls) *hld up in tch: stdy hdwy over 1f out: whip knocked out of rdr's hand ins fnl f: sn led: comf* **13/2**[2]

00-4 **2** 1/2 **Ruby's Day**[18] 2050 7-9-2 **70**... TomEaves 2 76
(David Brown) *stdd s: hld up: hdwy over 1f out: effrt and chsd wnr wl ins fnl f: kpt on* **10/1**

-065 **3** 1/2 **Groundworker (IRE)**[22] 1956 5-8-11 **65**............................ GrahamLee 9 69
(Paul Midgley) *trckd ldrs: effrt: edgd rt and led over 1f out: hdd ins fnl f: kpt on same pce towards fin* **12/1**

0-52 **4** 1 **Classy Anne**[7] 2364 6-9-7 **75**...................................... DanielTudhope 3 76
(Jim Goldie) *t.k.h: cl up: led over 2f out to over 1f out: drvn and one pce ins fnl f* **15/8**[1]

2-56 **5** nk **Oriental Splendour (IRE)**[15] 2120 4-8-13 **67**........... JamesSullivan 11 67
(Ruth Carr) *dwlt: hld up: rdn and hdwy over 1f out: edgd rt and kpt on ins fnl f* **8/1**

0-00 **6** 4 **Tom Sawyer**[33] 1601 8-9-5 **73**..............................(b) ConnorBeasley 10 58
(Julie Camacho) *hld up: rdn over 2f out: edgd rt and outpcd wl over 1f out: sn no imp* **12/1**

/343 **7** nk **Pushkin Museum (IRE)**[26] 1843 5-9-3 **71**........................ DavidNolan 7 55
(Richard Fahey) *led to over 2f out: rdn and wknd over 1f out* **13/2**[2]

3111 **8** nk **Mitchum**[24] 1878 7-8-9 **68**...(p) PhilDennis(5) 4 51
(Ron Barr) *prom: rdn over 2f out: hung rt and wknd over 1f out* **15/2**[3]

2-00 **9** nk **Amber Crystal**[7] 2359 4-8-6 **60**.................................(b) PJMcDonald 1 42
(Linda Perratt) *cl up on far side of gp: drvn over 2f out: wknd over 1f out* **40/1**

58.76s (-1.24) **Going Correction** -0.225s/f (Firm) **9** Ran SP% **111.2**
Speed ratings (Par 103): **100,99,98,96,96 89,89,88,88**
CSF £65.40 CT £740.90 TOTE £8.10: £2.30, £2.10, £4.70; EX 69.70 Trifecta £1576.00.

Owner Gaga Syndicate **Bred** Newlands House Stud **Trained** Sessay, N Yorks

FOCUS

An ordinary sprint handicap in which the betting only wanted to know about one horse, but the market got it wrong. The winner is rated to his latter 2015 form.

2573 ST ANDREWS AMBULANCE H'CAP — 1m 1f 34y

3:40 (3:40) (Class 6) (0-60,57) 4-Y-O+ **£2,911** (£866; £432; £216) **Stalls** Low

Form RPR

11 **1** **Millefiori (IRE)**[2] 2525 4-9-1 **51** 6ex (p) TonyHamilton 6 68+
(Adrian Paul Keatley, Ire) *t.k.h in midfield: stdy hdwy over 2f out: swtchd rt and led over 1f out: nudged out: easily* **8/11**[1]

0-45 **2** *3* **Indian Giver**[7] 2365 8-9-1 **56** (b) RobJFitzpatrick(5) 1 62
(John David Riches) *trckd ldrs: led and rdn over 2f out: edgd both ways and hdd over 1f out: plugged on fnl f: no ch w easy wnr* **14/1**

0-60 **3** *4 ½* **Whip Up A Frenzy (IRE)**[98] 615 4-9-5 **55** AdamBeschizza 9 52
(Richard Rowe) *trckd ldrs: rdn along over 3f out: rallied: kpt on same pce fr 2f out* **8/1**[3]

00-0 **4** *nk* **Elle Dorado**[30] 1696 4-9-2 **52** RaulDaSilva 7 48
(David Loughnane) *s.i.s: hld up: rdn and outpcd over 3f out: rallied over 1f out: kpt on: nt pce to chal* **40/1**

004 **5** *3 ¼* **Question Of Faith**[16] 2094 5-9-1 **51** DavidNolan 4 41
(Martin Todhunter) *s.i.s: hld up: pushed along over 3f out: hdwy over 1f out: sn no imp* **25/1**

03-1 **6** *½* **Duke Of Yorkshire**[8] 2343 6-9-2 **57** (p) RachelRichardson(5) 2 46
(Tim Easterby) *led: rdn and hdd over 2f out: wknd over 1f out* **3/1**[2]

-040 **7** *3 ¼* **Al Furat (USA)**[6] 2409 8-8-4 **45** PhilDennis(5) 3 27
(Ron Barr) *dwlt: sn midfield: effrt and prom over 3f out: wknd fr 2f out* **50/1**

605- **8** *1 ½* **Tukitinyasok (IRE)**[211] 7538 9-8-11 **47** (p[1]) JamesSullivan 10 26
(Clive Mulhall) *pressed ldr: rdn over 2f out: outpcd and hld whn hung rt and hmpd over 1f out* **28/1**

26/0 **9** *4 ½* **Norfolk Sound**[16] 2093 5-9-3 **53** (t) GrahamLee 8 23
(Stuart Coltherd) *in tch: rdn over 3f out: wknd over 2f out* **50/1**

6/0- **10** *25* **Politico**[293] 5048 4-9-3 **53** SamJames 11
(Marjorie Fife) *hld up: rdn and struggling over 3f out: sn lost tch: t.o* **33/1**

1m 56.3s (-3.40) **Going Correction** -0.225s/f (Firm) **10** Ran SP% **117.3**
Speed ratings (Par 101): **106,103,99,99,96 95,92,91,87,65**
CSF £12.21 CT £51.09 TOTE £1.50: £1.10, £2.70, £2.30; EX 13.20 Trifecta £73.60.
Owner Mrs F Hughes **Bred** Kevin J Molloy **Trained** Friarstown, Co. Kildare

FOCUS

Rail movement added around 12yds to the race distance. A moderate handicap in which the betting was dominated by a pair who appeared to be well in and one of them scored with consummate ease. A step up from the runner-up.

2574 CADZOW CASTLE FILLIES' H'CAP — 1m 67y

4:15 (4:19) (Class 5) (0-70,70) 3-Y-O+ **£3,881** (£1,155; £577; £288) **Stalls** Low

Form RPR

-300 **1** **The Wee Barra (IRE)**[11] 2233 4-9-2 **61** (p) JoeDoyle(3) 1 69
(Kevin Ryan) *trckd ldr: rdn over 2f out: led ins fnl f: kpt on wl* **7/1**

23-0 **2** *1* **Star Of Spring (IRE)**[31] 1663 4-9-13 **69** RoystonFfrench 3 75
(Iain Jardine) *dwlt: t.k.h and sn prom: effrt and rdn 2f out: kpt on to take 2nd towards fin: nt rch wnr* **11/2**[3]

5-44 **3** *nk* **Bad Penny (IRE)**[19] 2011 3-8-10 **64** GrahamLee 8 66
(John Quinn) *hld up: hdwy on outside over 2f out: kpt on ins fnl f: nt pce to chal* **8/1**

244- **4** *shd* **Rosamaria (IRE)**[225] 7183 3-9-1 **69** JoeFanning 5 71
(Mark Johnston) *t.k.h: led: pushed along and edgd lft over 2f out: rdn over 1f out: hdd ins fnl f: no ex and lost two pls nr fin* **11/4**[1]

0-05 **5** *2 ¾* **Dark Crystal**[16] 2092 5-9-7 **63** JackGarritty 2 61
(Linda Perratt) *hld up: rdn along over 2f out: effrt and swtchd lft over 1f out: kpt on fnl f: no imp* **14/1**

6310 **6** *½* **Rock 'n Red (IRE)**[25] 1860 3-9-1 **69** TonyHamilton 6 63
(Ed Dunlop) *hld up in tch: rdn and effrt over 2f out edgd rt and outpcd fr over 1f out* **11/1**

40-1 **7** *2* **Haidees Reflection**[30] 1695 6-9-9 **65** DanielTudhope 7 60
(Jim Goldie) *trckd ldrs: rdn along over 2f out: outpcd whn n.m.r briefly over 1f out: wknd ins fnl f* **3/1**[2]

02-4 **8** *1 ½* **Chelabella**[28] 1798 3-9-2 **70** WilliamTwiston-Davies 9 56
(Michael Bell) *reluctant to go to post and walked to s: dwlt: hld up: drvn and outpcd over 2f out: sn btn* **10/1**

1m 46.4s (-2.00) **Going Correction** -0.225s/f (Firm)
WFA 3 from 4yo+ 12lb **8** Ran SP% **114.8**
Speed ratings (Par 100): **101,100,99,99,96 96,94,92**
CSF £45.17 CT £318.04 TOTE £9.10: £3.40, £2.00, £2.20; EX 51.30 Trifecta £390.30.
Owner Slaters Arms Racing Club **Bred** Gamra Partnership **Trained** Hambleton, N Yorks

FOCUS

Rail movement added around 12yds to the race distance. An ordinary fillies' handicap and a bit of a bunch finish. The winner was on a fair mark and is rated to form.

2575 ROA/RACING POST OWNERS JACKPOT H'CAP — 1m 3f 14y

4:45 (4:45) (Class 5) (0-70,70) 4-Y-O+ **£3,881** (£1,155; £577; £288) **Stalls** Low

Form RPR

5350 **1** **San Quentin (IRE)**[25] 1854 5-8-10 **64** JoshDoyle(5) 3 73
(David Loughnane) *hld up: stdy hdwy on outside to ld over 2f out: shkn up and clr over 1f out: edgd lft ins fnl f: comf* **8/1**

0-50 **2** *2* **Jammy Moment**[16] 2093 5-9-0 **63** PhillipMakin 5 68
(Keith Dalgleish) *hld up: hdwy to chse ldrs after 3f: effrt and ev ch briefly over 2f out: sn chsng wnr: kpt on fnl f: nt pce to chal* **6/1**[3]

3-30 **3** *½* **Lara Carbonara (IRE)**[12] 2198 4-9-0 **63** TadhgO'Shea 12 67
(John Patrick Shanahan, Ire) *chsd ldr: rdn and outpcd over 2f out: edgd lft and rallied over 1f out: kpt on ins fnl f: no imp* **17/2**

61-5 **4** *nk* **Celtic Power**[24] 1881 4-9-4 **67** DanielTudhope 10 70
(Jim Goldie) *hld up in tch: hdwy over 3f out: rdn and ev ch briefly over 2f out: kpt on same pce fnl f* **10/3**[1]

620- **5** *1 ¾* **Clear Spell (IRE)**[221] 7287 5-9-7 **70** [1] GrahamLee 7 71
(Alistair Whillans) *in tch: rdn and outpcd 3f out: kpt on fnl f: no imp* **5/1**[2]

36-0 **6** *1 ¼* **Tectonic (IRE)**[12] 2198 7-9-6 **69** (p) JasonHart 1 67
(Keith Dalgleish) *t.k.h: hld up: stdy hdwy over 2f out: shkn up over 1f out: wknd fnl f* **9/1**

60-3 **7** *2 ½* **Schmooze (IRE)**[24] 1881 7-8-10 **59** JackGarritty 4 53
(Linda Perratt) *hld up: drvn along and outpcd over 3f out: n.d after* **6/1**[3]

266- **8** *2 ¾* **Where's Tiger**[13] 4868 5-9-4 **67** JoeFanning 8 56
(Lucinda Russell) *led: rdn and hdd over 2f out: wknd wl over 1f out* **9/1**

0-05 **9** *hd* **New Colours**[16] 2089 5-8-7 **56** oh4 (p) JamesSullivan 11 45
(Linda Perratt) *hld up: drvn and struggling over 3f out: btn fnl 2f* **33/1**

2m 25.97s (0.37) **Going Correction** -0.225s/f (Firm) **9** Ran SP% **112.9**
Speed ratings (Par 103): **89,87,87,86,85 84,82,80,80**
CSF £53.90 CT £417.53 TOTE £7.90: £2.10, £2.20, £3.00; EX 56.30 Trifecta £428.00.
Owner Stephen Louch **Bred** London Thoroughbred Services Ltd **Trained** Market Drayton, Shropshire

FOCUS

Rail movement added around 12yds to the race distance. A modest handicap and they went a leisurely gallop. The winner is rated close to his AW form.

2576 BOOK NOW FOR SAINTS AND SINNERS H'CAP — 1m 1f 34y

5:15 (5:15) (Class 6) (0-65,64) 3-Y-O **£2,911** (£866; £432; £216) **Stalls** Low

Form RPR

0-02 **1** **Wotabreeze (IRE)**[23] 1927 3-8-13 **63** AdamMcNamara(7) 7 73
(John Quinn) *hld up in midfield: pushed along and outpcd after 3f: hdwy over 2f out: rdn to ld ins fnl f: r.o wl* **9/2**[2]

2 *1* **Northern Sky (IRE)**[16] 2112 3-8-9 **52** JoeFanning 3 60
(Adrian Paul Keatley, Ire) *prom: hdwy over 2f out: rdn and ev ch over 1f out to wl ins fnl f: kpt on* **6/4**[1]

60-6 **3** *nk* **Forecaster**[14] 2152 3-9-6 **63** WilliamTwiston-Davies 9 70
(Michael Bell) *early ldr: chsd ldr: led over 2f out: rdn and edgd rt over 1f out: hdd ins fnl f: one pce towards fin* **8/1**[3]

-603 **4** *3 ¾* **Weld Al Khawaneej (IRE)**[102] 565 3-9-3 **60** TomEaves 5 60
(Kevin Ryan) *t.k.h: hld up: effrt over 2f out: rdn and kpt on fnl f: nt rch ldrs* **16/1**

0-10 **5** *½* **Blushes (FR)**[30] 1725 3-9-6 **63** TonyHamilton 4 62
(Ed Dunlop) *hld up in tch: effrt over 2f out: sn rdn and edgd rt: outpcd ins fnl f* **16/1**

6445 **6** *3* **Rubis**[31] 1667 3-9-0 **57** (p) JackGarritty 12 50
(Richard Fahey) *t.k.h early: hld up: rdn along 3f out: edgd rt over 1f out: kpt on: no imp* **12/1**

00-4 **7** *hd* **My Valentino (IRE)**[5] 2422 3-9-2 **62** MissEmmaSayer(3) 11 54
(Dianne Sayer) *hld up: drvn and outpcd 1/2-way: rallied on outside over 3f out: edgd rt and outpcd over 1f out* **12/1**

0-30 **8** *2* **Sporty Yankee (USA)**[12] 2224 3-9-7 **64** (v[1]) DougieCostello 13 52
(K R Burke) *t.k.h: led: clr after 3f: rdn and hdd over 2f out: wknd over 1f out* **14/1**

0-10 **9** *1* **Croft Ranger (IRE)**[23] 1927 3-9-2 **64** (p) PhilDennis(5) 6 50
(Michael Dods) *dwlt: hld up: rdn along 3f out: sn outpcd: n.d after* **11/1**

30-0 **10** *3* **Lozah**[15] 2123 3-9-7 **64** RaulDaSilva 2 44
(David Loughnane) *midfield: drvn and outpcd over 3f out: sn btn* **66/1**

00-0 **11** *13* **Annie T**[35] 1562 3-8-2 **45** DuranFentiman 1
(Paul Midgley) *in tch on ins: drvn and struggling over 3f out: wknd over 2f out* **50/1**

1m 56.81s (-2.89) **Going Correction** -0.225s/f (Firm) **11** Ran SP% **114.9**
Speed ratings (Par 97): **103,102,101,98,98 95,95,93,92,89 78**
CSF £11.23 CT £51.41 TOTE £5.20: £2.70, £1.10, £2.20; EX 18.00 Trifecta £77.70.
Owner The New Century Partnership **Bred** Triermore Stud **Trained** Settrington, N Yorks

FOCUS

Rail movement added around 12yds to the race distance. A modest 3yo handicap though a few of these were likely to improve for the longer trip. They went a decent pace and the three market leaders pulled clear. The winner came from a decent Beverley race.

T/Jkpt: Not won. T/Plt: £2,918.90 to a £1 stake. Pool: £62,776.63 - 15.70 winning tickets T/Qpdt: £271.70 to a £1 stake. Pool: £6,498.78 - 17.70 winning tickets **Richard Young**

2374 KEMPTON (A.W) (R-H)

Wednesday, May 25

OFFICIAL GOING: Polytrack: standard

Wind: Almost nil Weather: Overcast

2577 32RED CASINO H'CAP (LONDON MILE SERIES QUALIFIER) — 1m (P)

6:20 (6:20) (Class 5) (0-75,75) 4-Y-O+ **£2,911** (£866; £432; £216) **Stalls** Low

Form RPR

2245 **1** **Pike Corner Cross (IRE)**[14] 2153 4-8-8 **62** OisinMurphy 7 71
(Ed de Giles) *towards rr: hdwy over 1f out: str run to ld fnl 50yds* **7/1**

-234 **2** *1* **Snappy Guest**[12] 2217 4-9-3 **71** AdamKirby 4 78
(George Margarson) *towards rr: rdn 4f out: swtchd rt and hdwy over 1f out: r.o to take 2nd fnl 50yds* **3/1**[1]

50-4 **3** *¾* **Hot Mustard**[23] 1916 6-9-0 **68** MartinDwyer 6 73
(William Muir) *t.k.h: led: kpt on u.p fnl 2f: hdd fnl 50yds* **10/1**

2 **4** *nk* **New Agenda**[71] 945 4-9-7 **75** TedDurcan 10 79
(Paul Webber) *chsd ldrs: hung rt and chal over 1f out: one pce fnl 75yds* **7/2**[2]

00-0 **5** *1 ¼* **Run With Pride (IRE)**[139] 82 6-9-5 **73** MartinLane 12 74
(Derek Shaw) *stdd s: bhd: rdn and swtchd to outer 2f out: styd on wl fr over 1f out* **16/1**

26-1 **6** *¾* **Roxie Lot**[49] 1262 4-8-9 **66** RobHornby(3) 1 66
(Pam Sly) *prom tl no ex fnl f* **12/1**

-022 **7** *½* **Thecornishbarron (IRE)**[13] 2174 4-8-12 **71** JosephineGordon(5) 2 69
(John Ryan) *in tch: rdn 3f out: styd on same pce* **13/2**[3]

2043 **8** *½* **Skidby Mill (IRE)**[8] 2324 6-9-3 **71** JimCrowley 8 68
(Laura Mongan) *chsd ldr tl outpcd over 2f out: sn btn* **14/1**

-000 **9** *½* **Secret Glance**[63] 1040 4-9-7 **75** PatDobbs 5 71
(Richard Rowe) *in tch: rdn over 2f out: sn btn* **20/1**

-300 **10** *1 ¼* **Rightway (IRE)**[44] 1390 5-9-2 **73** GeorgeDowning(3) 11 66
(Tony Carroll) *s.s: bhd: effrt over 2f out: n.d* **20/1**

2202 **11** *½* **Nasri**[30] 1700 10-8-12 **66** TomQueally 3 58
(Emma Owen) *mid-div: outpcd over 2f out: n.d after* **20/1**

4- **12** *4 ½* **Ost Wind**[275] 5695 4-9-5 **73** JimmyQuinn 13 54
(Michael Attwater) *mid-div tl lost pl over 2f out* **66/1**

1m 38.83s (-0.97) **Going Correction** 0.0s/f (Stan) **12** Ran SP% **118.2**
Speed ratings (Par 103): **104,103,102,101,100 99,99,98,98,97 96,92**
CSF £26.71 CT £214.71 TOTE £8.60: £3.80, £1.50, £4.40; EX 38.80 Trifecta £277.40.
Owner Tight Lines Partnership **Bred** Rockfield Farm **Trained** Ledbury, H'fords

FOCUS

A fair handicap.

2578 32RED ON THE APP STORE MAIDEN STKS — 7f (P)

6:50 (6:52) (Class 4) 3-Y-O+ **£3,042** (£3,042; £697; £348) **Stalls** Low

Form RPR

4 **1** **On The Bill (IRE)**^{23} 1931 3-9-3 0 SilvestreDeSousa 2 81
(Ed Dunlop) *prom: led 1f out: kpt on u.p fnl f: hld on to dead-heat* **9/2**^{2}

1 *dht* **Highland Dragon** 3-9-3 0 PatCosgrave 12 81+
(William Haggas) *dwlt: towards rr: rdn along and green 3f out: str run fnl f to dead-heat on line* **10/1**

3 *nse* **Run To The Hills (USA)** 3-9-3 0 StevieDonohoe 3 80+
(George Peckham) *dwlt: towards rr: hdwy over 1f out: fin wl: jst failed* **25/1**

4 *3/4* **Labyrinth (IRE)** 3-8-12 0 TedDurcan 9 73
(Sir Michael Stoute) *stdd s: hld up in midfield: hdwy over 1f out: styd on fnl f* **6/1**^{3}

5 *3/4* **Marbooh (IRE)** 3-9-3 0 PaulHanagan 1 76
(Charles Hills) *in tch on inner: rdn to chse ldrs 2f out: styd on same pce fnl f* **9/2**^{2}

0- **6** *1 1/2* **Sunset Dream (IRE)**^{300} 4790 3-8-12 0 PatDobbs 6 68
(Richard Hannon) *dwlt: bhd: hdwy on inner 2f out: no imp fnl f* **16/1**

0 **7** *3/4* **Roccor**^{19} 2004 3-8-5 0 MeganNicholls$^{(7)}$ 10 66
(Richard Hannon) *led at str pce tl 1f out: wknd fnl f* **40/1**

0 **8** *1 1/2* **Apache Myth**^{19} 2009 3-8-12 0 RyanTate 5 62
(James Eustace) *t.k.h: chsd ldrs tl wknd jst over 1f out* **33/1**

3 **9** *1/2* **Bond Trader**^{82} 824 3-9-3 0 AdamKirby 13 66+
(Clive Cox) *prom tl wknd over 1f out* **3/1**^{1}

20 **10** *2 1/2* **Emerald Loch**^{12} 2207 3-8-12 0 FMBerry 8 55
(Ralph Beckett) *chsd ldrs tl outpcd and btn over 2f out* **8/1**

0 **11** *3 3/4* **Pepper (IRE)**^{7} 2375 3-8-12 0 MartinLane 11 46
(Derek Shaw) *mid-div: rdn 3f out: sn outpcd* **100/1**

0 **12** *nk* **Frosty De Winter**^{24} 1894 3-9-3 0 LiamKeniry 4 50
(Chris Gordon) *dwlt: a towards rr: n.d fnl 2f* **100/1**

45 **13** *1 1/4* **Hidden Gem**^{30} 1723 3-8-12 0 LukeMorris 14 42
(Ed Walker) *a bhd* **20/1**

1m 25.2s (-0.80) **Going Correction** 0.0s/f (Stan) **13** Ran SP% **117.7**
Speed ratings (Par 105): **104,104,103,103,102 100,99,97,97,94 90,89,88**
WIN: HD £7.50, OTB £1.90; PL: HD £4.90, OTB £1.40, RTTH £8.70; EX: HD/OTB £32.00, OTB/HD £26.30; CSF: HD/OTB £25.48, OTB/HD £22.50; TF: HD/OTB/RTTH £793.20, OTB/HD/RTTH £404.70.
Owner M S Bloodstock Ltd **Bred** Mike Smith **Trained** Newmarket, Suffolk
Owner The Old Etonian Racing Syndicate **Bred** Val & Angela Leeson **Trained** Newmarket, Suffolk

FOCUS
A thrilling finish to this maiden, and the photo betting couldn't call it between the first three.

2579 £10 FREE BET AT 32REDSPORT.COM H'CAP 7f (P)
7:20 (7:21) (Class 4) (0-80,80) 4-Y-O+ **£4,690** (£1,395; £697; £348) **Stalls** Low

Form RPR

1230 **1** **Exalted (IRE)**^{23} 1928 5-8-7 66 (t) SilvestreDeSousa 13 75
(William Knight) *mde all: rdn over 2f out: edgd rt ins fnl f: hld on wl* **8/1**

4132 **2** *3/4* **Golden Wedding (IRE)**^{8} 2324 4-8-11 70 (p) CharlesBishop 6 77+
(Eve Johnson Houghton) *towards rr: hdwy over 1f out: carried lft ins fnl f: fin wl* **7/1**^{3}

0-32 **3** *3/4* **Sovereign Bounty**^{8} 2345 4-8-12 71 PaulMulrennan 2 76
(Jedd O'Keeffe) *chsd ldrs: rdn and carried rt over 1f out: kpt on* **4/1**^{1}

64-0 **4** *1/2* **Gothic Empire (IRE)**^{11} 2238 4-8-13 75 DanielMuscutt$^{(3)}$ 14 79
(James Fanshawe) *chsd wnr tl over 1f out: hrd rdn: edgd rt and lft: one pce* **14/1**

2-3 **5** *hd* **Mickey Haller (IRE)**^{29} 1765 4-9-2 75 JimmyFortune 1 79
(Brian Meehan) *t.k.h: prom: pressed wnr over 1f out tl squeezed for room on inner ins fnl f* **16/1**

44-0 **6** *nse* **Tournament**^{58} 1122 5-9-5 78 (t) JamieSpencer 9 81
(Seamus Durack) *travelled wl in midfield: shkn up over 1f out: carried lft ins fnl f: styd on* **4/1**^{1}

4-32 **7** *nk* **Mystical Sapphire**^{84} 780 6-9-5 78 GeorgeBaker 11 80
(Laura Mongan) *mid-div: effrt and sltly hmpd over 1f out: no imp fnl f* **9/1**

20 **8** *3/4* **Light From Mars**^{18} 2028 11-9-4 77 LukeMorris 10 77
(Ronald Harris) *bhd tl styd on u.p fr over 1f out* **20/1**

6306 **9** *1/2* **Majestic Myles (IRE)**^{18} 2033 8-9-5 78 OisinMurphy 5 77
(Lee Carter) *chsd ldrs tl hrd rdn and btn over 1f out* **20/1**

4261 **10** *1* **Justice First**^{30} 1724 4-9-7 80 MartinHarley 7 76
(Ed Dunlop) *towards rr: rdn 2f out: nvr able to chal* **11/2**^{2}

4520 **11** *2 1/2* **Among Angels**^{32} 1634 4-9-2 80 (p) EdwardGreatrex$^{(5)}$ 8 69
(Kevin Frost) *bhd: rdn and rn wd on bnd 3f out: nvr nr ldrs* **33/1**

314- **12** *nk* **Captain Marmalade (IRE)**^{319} 4156 4-8-11 70 KieranO'Neill 12 59
(Jimmy Fox) *stdd s and swtchd ins: a bhd* **66/1**

305- **13** *12* **Synodic (USA)**^{340} 3394 4-9-4 77 TimmyMurphy 4 33
(Seamus Durack) *a towards rr: no ch fnl 2f* **66/1**

1m 24.34s (-1.66) **Going Correction** 0.0s/f (Stan) **13** Ran SP% **117.0**
Speed ratings (Par 105): **109,108,107,106,106 106,106,105,104,103 100,100,86**
CSF £58.31 CT £267.84 TOTE £11.60: £3.80, £2.30, £2.00; EX 62.30 Trifecta £250.60.
Owner N J Roach **Bred** Rathbarry Stud **Trained** Patching, W Sussex
■ Stewards' Enquiry : Jimmy Fortune Fine: £140, failed to report at scales that gelding lost its action
Daniel Muscutt caution: careless riding

FOCUS
An open handicap but the winner dominated throughout.

2580 32RED.COM H'CAP (LONDON MIDDLE DISTANCE SERIES QUALIFIER) 1m 3f (P)
7:50 (7:50) (Class 4) (0-80,80) 3-Y-O **£4,690** (£1,395; £697; £348) **Stalls** Low

Form RPR

3-33 **1** **Real Dominion (USA)**^{24} 1897 3-9-7 80 DavidProbert 4 83
(Andrew Balding) *chsd ldrs: wnt 2nd over 3f out: chal and hanging rt whn bmpd over 1f out: cajoled to ld fnl 50yds* **7/2**^{3}

41-5 **2** *1/2* **Gold Faith (IRE)**^{35} 1571 3-9-5 78 FMBerry 2 80+
(Ralph Beckett) *hld up in last pair: rdn and hdwy 2f out: r.o to take 2nd nr fin* **3/1**^{2}

3243 **3** *nk* **Moueenn**^{19} 2012 3-8-9 75 CameronNoble$^{(7)}$ 5 76
(Roger Varian) *led at sedate pce: qckned 2f out: hrd rdn and veered lft over 1f out: hdd and one pce fnl 50yds* **16/1**

331- **4** *2 1/4* **Al Khafji**^{194} 7823 3-9-5 78 FrankieDettori 6 75
(Luca Cumani) *chsd ldr tl pushed along over 3f out: one pce appr fnl f* **5/4**^{1}

3-36 **5** *1* **Machine Learner**^{24} 1891 3-9-5 78 JamieSpencer 1 73
(Michael Bell) *chsd ldrs: rdn over 2f out: wknd over 1f out* **11/1**

-164 **6** *9* **Epsom Day (IRE)**^{37} 1532 3-9-1 74 (p) TomQueally 3 53
(Laura Mongan) *rrd s and missed break: t.k.h in rr: n.d fnl 2f* **25/1**

2m 25.76s (3.86) **Going Correction** 0.0s/f (Stan) **6** Ran SP% **109.7**
Speed ratings (Par 101): **85,84,84,82,82 75**
CSF £13.67 TOTE £4.90: £1.70, £2.40; EX 15.30 Trifecta £84.70.
Owner Mick and Janice Mariscotti **Bred** Kendall E Hansen, M D Racing Llc **Trained** Kingsclere, Hants

FOCUS
This handicap was run at a steady early pace and turned into a bit of a dash for the line.

2581 32RED H'CAP 6f (P)
8:20 (8:21) (Class 3) (0-90,90) 4-Y-O+
£7,158 (£2,143; £1,071; £535; £267; £134) **Stalls** Low

Form RPR

4034 **1** **Magnus Maximus**^{95} 657 5-9-6 89 MartinHarley 4 99
(Robyn Brisland) *mde all: rdn 2f out: hld on wl* **11/2**^{3}

120- **2** *1 1/4* **Memories Galore (IRE)**^{218} 7364 4-9-1 84 AdamKirby 3 90
(Harry Dunlop) *prom: chal over 1f out: one pce ins fnl f* **9/2**^{2}

5-50 **3** *3/4* **Mishaal (IRE)**^{31} 1672 6-9-7 90 PaulMulrennan 5 94
(Michael Herrington) *chsd wnr tl over 1f out: one pce* **9/1**

1143 **4** *nk* **Merhoob (IRE)**^{18} 2028 4-8-7 81 JosephineGordon$^{(5)}$ 11 84+
(John Ryan) *bhd: rdn over 2f out: nrest at fin* **7/1**

02 **5** *nk* **Pensax Lad (IRE)**^{33} 1601 5-9-2 88 GeorgeDowning$^{(3)}$ 2 90
(Ronald Harris) *chsd ldrs: hmpd after 1f: rdn 2f out: kpt on fnl f* **14/1**

3346 **6** *1/2* **Yeeoow (IRE)**^{19} 1990 7-8-13 82 JoeyHaynes 6 82
(K R Burke) *squeezed for room s: sn chsng ldrs: one pce fnl 2f* **6/1**

1300 **7** *nk* **Fleckerl (IRE)**^{32} 1650 6-9-7 90 (p) LiamKeniry 1 89
(Conor Dore) *dwlt: hld up: brief effrt over 1f out: nvr able to chal* **33/1**

006- **8** *hd* **Morache Music**^{226} 7163 8-9-6 89 JimCrowley 12 87
(Patrick Chamings) *bhd: sme hdwy on inner 2f out: no imp* **16/1**

5600 **9** *hd* **Varsovian**^{32} 1634 6-9-0 83 RenatoSouza 8 81
(Dean Ivory) *t.k.h towards rr: rdn 2f out: nvr rchd ldrs* **20/1**

1-10 **10** *nk* **The Big Lad**^{18} 2028 4-8-11 80 ShaneKelly 10 77
(Richard Hughes) *mid-div: hung rt over 2f out: towards rr and btn whn n.m.r over 1f out* **7/2**^{1}

1m 11.78s (-1.32) **Going Correction** 0.0s/f (Stan) **10** Ran SP% **112.8**
Speed ratings (Par 107): **108,106,105,104,104 103,103,103,102,102**
CSF £29.39 CT £216.73 TOTE £7.10: £2.30, £2.30, £2.70; EX 34.20 Trifecta £168.50.
Owner Franconson Partners **Bred** St Albans Bloodstock Llp **Trained** Newmarket, Suffolk

FOCUS
Very few got into this, with the pace holding up.

2582 RACINGUK.COM H'CAP 2m (P)
8:50 (8:51) (Class 4) (0-80,78) 4-Y-O+ **£4,690** (£1,395; £697; £348) **Stalls** Low

Form RPR

06-0 **1** **Royal Reef (IRE)**^{12} 2210 4-8-9 65 SilvestreDeSousa 4 73
(William Knight) *led for 4f: prom: rdn to ld again jst ins fnl f: jst hld on* **20/1**

40-4 **2** *nk* **Champagne Champ**^{33} 1598 4-9-5 75 FrederikTylicki 9 82
(Rod Millman) *mid-div: rdn 3f out: styd on wl fnl f: clsng at fin* **7/1**^{3}

1423 **3** *1 1/4* **Be My Sea (IRE)**^{25} 1852 5-9-8 76 WilliamCarson 8 81
(Tony Carroll) *prom: chal 2f out: one pce fnl f* **5/1**^{2}

00-1 **4** *nk* **Snow Conditions**^{63} 1039 5-9-0 68 JamieSpencer 5 73
(Philip Hide) *chsd ldrs: led over 2f out tl jst ins fnl f: no ex* **9/2**^{1}

3-15 **5** *1 1/4* **Kuriosa (IRE)**^{23} 1919 4-9-7 77 LukeMorris 11 80
(Marco Botti) *t.k.h in midfield: rdn 4f out: outpcd 2f out: styd on fnl f* **8/1**

120/ **6** *2* **Secure Cloud (IRE)**^{641} 5670 5-9-5 73 GeorgeBaker 3 74
(Lawney Hill) *s.s: bhd: rdn over 2f out: nrest at fin* **20/1**

0100 **7** *3/4* **Bazooka (IRE)**^{16} 2114 5-9-4 77 EdwardGreatrex$^{(5)}$ 2 77
(David Flood) *chsd ldrs tl wknd over 1f out* **40/1**

1210 **8** *1/2* **Fern Owl**^{30} 1717 4-9-4 74 JimCrowley 10 73
(Hughie Morrison) *towards rr: rdn over 2f out: nvr able to chal* **5/1**^{2}

46-3 **9** *hd* **Winter Spice (IRE)**^{117} 385 5-9-10 78 RyanTate 7 77
(Clive Cox) *s.s: bhd: effrt 2f out: n.d* **7/1**^{3}

5550 **10** *nk* **Alshan Fajer**^{30} 1717 6-9-8 76 AdamKirby 1 75
(J R Jenkins) *towards rr: hdwy on inner 2f out: wknd over 1f out* **20/1**

26- **11** *1 1/4* **Big McIntosh (IRE)**^{32} 6716 4-8-1 62 (t) JosephineGordon$^{(5)}$ 6 59
(John Ryan) *towards rr: effrt on inner 2f out: sn wknd* **12/1**

00-0 **12** *5* **Coup De Grace (IRE)**^{67} 234 7-8-12 66 ShaneKelly 12 57
(Pat Phelan) *prom: led after 4f tl over 2f out: wknd wl over 1f out* **20/1**

3m 29.08s (-1.02) **Going Correction** 0.0s/f (Stan)
WFA 4 from 5yo+ 2lb **12** Ran SP% **116.8**
Speed ratings (Par 105): **102,101,101,101,100 99,99,98,98,98 97,95**
CSF £142.07 CT £821.21 TOTE £17.70: £4.40, £2.40, £2.60; EX 56.70 Trifecta £4472.00 Part won..
Owner W J Knight **Bred** Herbertstown House Stud **Trained** Patching, W Sussex

FOCUS
It didn't pay to be too far off the pace in this staying handicap.
T/Plt: £266.80 to a £1 stake. Pool: £73,556.81 - 201.21 winning units. T/Qpdt: £33.30 to a £1 stake. Pool: £7,132.88 - 158.33 winning units. **Lee McKenzie**

^{2397}LINGFIELD (L-H)
Wednesday, May 25

OFFICIAL GOING: Good (good to soft in places; 7.6)
Wind: virtually nil Weather: overcast

2583 JOHN AND HAZEL PEEK 80TH BIRTHDAY NOVICE MEDIAN AUCTION STKS 5f
1:50 (1:51) (Class 5) 2-Y-O **£3,234** (£962; £481; £240) **Stalls** High

Form RPR

32 **1** **Rapacity Alexander (IRE)**^{19} 2007 2-8-11 0 JFEgan 2 85
(David Evans) *chsd ldr tl led after 1f: mde rest: drifting lft but gng clr 1f out: r.o strly: readily* **9/4**^{1}

4 **2** *3 1/4* **Diable D'Or (IRE)**^{12} 2203 2-9-2 0 ShaneKelly 4 78
(Eve Johnson Houghton) *chsd ldrs: wnt 2nd and effrt wl over 1f out: unable qck whn sltly hmpd and swtchd rt jst ins fnl f: kpt on same pce after* **11/4**^{2}

33 **3** *1 1/2* **El Torito (IRE)**^{14} 2147 2-9-2 0 PatCosgrave 5 73
(Jim Boyle) *hld up in tch in midfield: short of room 4f out: effrt and hdwy to chse ldng pair over 1f out: no imp whn hmpd jst ins fnl f: kpt on same pce after* **12/1**

3 **4** *3* **Zaatar (IRE)**^{5} 2429 2-8-11 0 SilvestreDeSousa 9 57
(Mick Channon) *hld up in tch in midfield: swtchd lft and rdn over 1f out: no ch w ldrs but kpt on to go modest 4th ins fnl f* **9/2**

5 *2 3/4* **Miss Gregarious** 2-8-11 0 IrineuGoncalves 8 47+
(Chris Dwyer) *in tch towards rr: swtchd lft and sme hdwy over 1f out: nvr on terms w ldrs: edging bk rt and kpt on same pce ins fnl f* **16/1**

5 **6** *1* **George Ravenscar**^{9} 2311 2-9-2 0 ...... HarryBentley 7 48
(Ed Vaughan) *led for 1f: chsd ldr tl unable qck u.p wl over 1f out: fdd ins fnl f* **33/1**

7 *3 ½* **Charlie Victor** 2-9-2 0 ...... AdamKirby 1 36
(Clive Cox) *s.i.s: sn rcvrd and in tch in midfield: rdn wl over 1f out: sn btn: wknd fnl f* **3/1**^{3}

8 *1 ¼* **Hi There Silver (IRE)** 2-9-2 0 ...... LiamKeniry 3 31
(Michael Madgwick) *hld up towards rr: outpcd 1/2-way: bhd over 1f out* **100/1**

9 *7* **Compton's Gee Wiz (IRE)** 2-8-4 0 ...... RhiainIngram$^{(7)}$ 6
(Brett Johnson) *dwlt: a outpcd in rr* **100/1**

1m 0.44s (2.24) **Going Correction** +0.35s/f (Good) **9** Ran SP% **119.1**
Speed ratings (Par 93): **96,90,88,83,79 77,72,70,58**
CSF £8.99 TOTE £3.30: £1.50, £1.20, £2.80; EX 9.90 Trifecta £64.90.
Owner Noel O'Callaghan **Bred** Aidan Fogarty **Trained** Pandy, Monmouths

FOCUS
All race distances were as advertised. The ground had dried a touch overnight and John Egan felt it was "real good ground" while Shane Kelly was of the opinion it was "on the dead side of good". The draw no longer has a great impact here, let alone when the ground is only good or softer, and that was again in evidence throughout the afternoon. The form horses came to the fore in what was an ordinary novice event. The winner paid a compliment to her Nottingham conqueror.

2584 FIRST TITLE INSURANCE PLC H'CAP 6f
2:20 (2:22) (Class 6) (0-60,60) 4-Y-0+ **£2,587** (£770; £384; £192) **Stalls** High

Form RPR

6140 **1** **Diamond Vine (IRE)**^{13} 2187 8-8-11 **50** ......(p) DavidProbert 6 57
(Ronald Harris) *dwlt: hld up in rr: hdwy 2f out: n.m.r over 1f out: wnt between rivals to chal ins fnl f: r.o wl u.p to ld fnl 50yds* **25/1**

5501 **2** *¾* **Pharoh Jake**^{26} 1833 8-9-5 **58** ...... WilliamCarson 13 63
(John Bridger) *hld up wl in tch in midfield: n.m.r over 1f out: swtchd lft and hdwy to chse ldrs 1f out: sn ev ch: led ins fnl f: edging lft: hdd and one pce fnl 50yds* **14/1**

3346 **3** *½* **Secret Witness**^{39} 1495 10-9-2 **58** ......(b) TomMarquand$^{(3)}$ 4 62
(Ronald Harris) *t.k.h: hld up towards rr: short of room and stmbld after 1f out: swtchd lft and hdwy over 1f out: drvn and ev ch ins fnl f: hung lft and styd on same pce after* **14/1**

1200 **4** *shd* **Multi Quest**^{28} 1794 4-8-11 **50** ......(v) SamHitchcott 15 55
(John E Long) *hld up in tch in midfield: effrt and n.m.r over 1f out: hdwy 1f out: r.o strly ins fnl f: nt rch ldrs* **20/1**

0334 **5** *¾* **Diamond Charlie (IRE)**^{16} 2088 8-9-6 **59** ......(p) JimCrowley 8 60
(Simon Dow) *hld up in tch towards rr: swtchd lft and hdwy over 1f out: rdn and ev ch jst ins fnl f: no ex and outpcd fnl 100yds* **12/1**

1344 **6** *1 ¼* **Blue Bounty**^{57} 1133 5-9-2 **55** ......(p) SaleemGolam 10 52
(Mark H Tompkins) *chsd ldrs tl led over 1f out: sn rdn: hdd ins fnl f: sn outpcd and wknd towards fin* **12/1**

0043 **7** *1 ¼* **Commanche**^{9} 2309 7-9-7 **60** ......(b) SilvestreDeSousa 16 59+
(Chris Dwyer) *hld up in tch in midfield: stuck bhd a wall of horses and nt clr run over 1f out: swtchd lft 1f out: kpt on ins fnl f: no threat to ldrs* **4/1**^{1}

6500 **8** *¾* **Multitask**^{36} 1544 6-8-9 **55** ...... GeorgeWood$^{(7)}$ 11 46
(Michael Madgwick) *t.k.h: hld up in tch in midfield: hdwy and rdn to chal over 1f out: carried lft and no ex jst ins fnl f: wknd fnl 100yds* **7/1**^{2}

0-60 **9** *½* **Piazza San Pietro**^{22} 1945 10-9-4 **57** ...... RichardKingscote 5 47
(Zoe Davison) *chsd ldrs: rdn and unable qck over 1f out: outpcd and btn 1f out: wknd ins fnl f* **50/1**

000- **10** *1* **Parisian Pyramid (IRE)**^{186} 7939 10-9-7 **60** ......(p) KierenFox 18 53+
(Lee Carter) *hld up in tch towards rr: stuck bhd wkng rival and nt clr run over 1f out: no threat to ldrs: kpt on ins fnl f* **10/1**

1216 **11** *2* **Chetan**^{70} 955 4-9-7 **60** ......(tp) LukeMorris 3 41
(Charlie Wallis) *taken down early: hld up in tch towards rr: effrt u.p jst over 2f out: no imp 1f out: wknd ins fnl f* **12/1**

0-55 **12** *½* **Fossa**^{5} 2447 6-8-9 **48** ...... RyanClark 9 30
(Mark Brisbourne) *chsd ldr tl wl over 1f out: stl pressing ldrs but unable qck over 1f out: btn whn short of room ent fnl f: wknd ins fnl f* **14/1**

2226 **13** *1 ¼* **Bertie Blu Boy**^{19} 2003 8-9-7 **60** ......(v) GeorgeBaker 14 35
(Lisa Williamson) *led tl hdd and rdn over 1f out: sn struggling: wknd fnl f* **7/1**^{2}

2212 **14** *3 ¾* **Tasaaboq**^{5} 2447 5-8-11 **55** ......(t) JosephineGordon$^{(5)}$ 1 19+
(Phil McEntee) *racd alone centre to far side: a towards rr: n.d* **8/1**^{3}

0015 **15** *1 ¼* **Picansort**^{22} 1950 9-9-4 **57** ...... ShaneKelly 12 41+
(Peter Crate) *hld up in tch towards rr: nt clrest of runs over 1f out: btn and eased ins fnl f* **12/1**

135- **16** *11* **Snow King (USA)**^{158} 8307 6-9-2 **55** ...... JFEgan 7
(Ted Powell) *midfield: rdn and struggling 1/2-way: bhd over 1f out* **20/1**

1m 14.11s (2.91) **Going Correction** +0.35s/f (Good) **16** Ran SP% **131.3**
Speed ratings (Par 101): **94,93,92,92,91 89,87,86,86,84 82,81,79,74,73 58**
CSF £353.20 CT £5262.81 TOTE £39.20: £7.80, £4.10, £4.30, £6.30; EX 683.10 Trifecta £4648.50 Part won..
Owner Ridge House Stables Ltd **Bred** Michael O'Mahony **Trained** Earlswood, Monmouths

FOCUS
Race distance as advertised. Plenty of pace on early here and there was nothing in the draw, two of the first three coming from well off the pace having been dropped in from low stalls. A messy race, and probably weak form.

2585 RACING WELFARE FILLIES' H'CAP (DIV I) 7f
2:50 (2:53) (Class 5) (0-70,70) 3-Y-0 **£3,234** (£962; £481; £240) **Stalls** High

Form RPR

1415 **1** **Figurante (IRE)**^{16} 2108 3-9-4 **67** ...... CathyGannon 4 76
(Jamie Osborne) *hld up in tch in midfield: effrt over 1f out: hdwy and str chal 1f out: sustained duel w rival after: edgd rt u.p ins fnl f: r.o wl to ld cl home* **6/1**

3-54 **2** *nse* **Make Music**^{24} 1898 3-9-1 **69** ...... EdwardGreatrex$^{(5)}$ 9 78
(Andrew Balding) *chsd ldrs tl wnt 2nd 1/2-way: led 2f out: rdn over 1f out: hrd pressed and wnt clr w wnr 1f out: carried rt ins fnl f: r.o wl: hdd cl home* **3/1**^{2}

34-3 **3** *4 ½* **Bonhomie**^{35} 1562 3-9-3 **66** ...... AndreaAtzeni 10 63
(Michael Bell) *chsd ldr tl 1/2-way: effrt 2f out: 3rd and unable qck ent fnl f: hung lft and wknd ins fnl f* **11/4**^{1}

0-00 **4** *1 ¼* **Harmony Day (IRE)**^{16} 2100 3-9-0 63 ...... PatDobbs 8 57
(Sylvester Kirk) *t.k.h: hld up in tch in rr: nt clrest of runs 2f out: hdwy jst over 1f out: no threat to ldrs but kpt on wl ins fnl f* **25/1**

1-50 **5** *1* **Shypen**^{32} 1638 3-9-7 **70** ...... AdamKirby 3 61
(George Margarson) *stdd and dropped in bhd after s: t.k.h: hld up towards rr: hdwy and swtchd sharply lft wl over 1f out: 4th and no imp 1f out: kpt on same pce after* **10/1**

1-60 **6** *6* **Foxinthehenhouse**^{49} 1257 3-9-2 **68** ...... TomMarquand$^{(3)}$ 5 44
(J R Jenkins) *sn led: hdd 2f out: sn u.p and outpcd: wknd fnl f* **25/1**

6-13 **7** *2* **Tigserin (IRE)**^{35} 1572 3-9-2 **65** ......^{1} SaleemGolam 7 36
(Giles Bravery) *taken down early: hld up in tch in midfield: effrt u.p jst over 1f out: little rspnse and btn over 1f out: racing awkwardly and wknd ins fnl f* **5/1**^{3}

00- **8** *nk* **Stylish Minerva**^{222} 7260 3-8-10 **59** ...... KieranO'Neill 2 29
(Richard Hannon) *dwlt and sltly hmpd leaving stalls: hld up in tch towards rr: effrt 2f out: sn rdn and no hdwy: wknd fnl f* **16/1**

0450 **9** *4 ½* **Katie Canford**^{42} 1420 3-8-6 **55** ...... WilliamCarson 1 13
(John Bridger) *t.k.h: hld up wl in tch in midfield: hdwy to chse ldrs 2f out: unable qck u.p over 1f out: wknd fnl f* **25/1**

1064 **10** *4 ½* **Timia**^{29} 1745 3-9-2 **65** ......(b^{1}) SilvestreDeSousa 6 11
(Ed Dunlop) *t.k.h: hld up in tch in midfield: rdn ent fnl 2f: sn struggling: lost pl over 1f out: bhd fnl f* **10/1**

1m 25.66s (2.36) **Going Correction** +0.35s/f (Good) **10** Ran SP% **118.2**
Speed ratings (Par 96): **100,99,94,93,92 85,83,82,77,72**
CSF £24.14 CT £60.62 TOTE £8.40: £2.60, £1.50, £1.30; EX 28.70 Trifecta £103.80.
Owner The Hon A Blyth **Bred** Mount Coote Stud **Trained** Upper Lambourn, Berks

FOCUS
Race distance as advertised. The first division of a modest handicap and the front two came clear. A step up on the winner's recent AW form.

2586 RACING WELFARE FILLIES' H'CAP (DIV II) 7f
3:25 (3:26) (Class 5) (0-70,69) 3-Y-0 **£3,234** (£962; £481; £240) **Stalls** High

Form RPR

0-14 **1** **Here's Two**^{16} 2108 3-9-4 **66** ...... GeorgeBaker 2 71
(Ron Hodges) *stdd s: t.k.h: hld up in tch in last pair: hdwy over 2f out: rdn to ld over 1f out: styd on wl ins fnl f: rdn out* **3/1**^{1}

536 **2** *1* **Phoenix Beat**^{25} 1859 3-9-6 **68** ......(p) DavidProbert 1 71
(Gay Kelleway) *in tch: rdn wl over 2f out: hdwy to chse ldrs jst over 1f out: styd on u.p to go 2nd fnl 50yds: nvr enough pce to chal ldr* **5/1**^{3}

2311 **3** *nk* **Broughtons Fancy**^{13} 2184 3-9-4 **69** ...... TomMarquand$^{(3)}$ 10 71
(Andrew Reid) *hld up in tch in midfield: effrt and carried rt jst over 2f out: hdwy u.p over 1f out: chsd wnr 1f out: styd on same pce and lost 2nd fnl 50yds* **7/2**^{2}

3605 **4** *¾* **Red Rose Riot (IRE)**^{28} 1792 3-8-8 **56** ...... MartinDwyer 3 56
(David Menuisier) *s.i.s: hld up in tch in last pair: rdn and hdwy ent fnl 2f: chsd ldrs and unable qck 1f out: pushed along and styd on same pce ins fnl f* **10/1**

-340 **5** *1 ¾* **Emily Goldfinch**^{54} 1183 3-9-2 **64** ...... SilvestreDeSousa 8 59
(Phil McEntee) *chsd ldr tl led 1/2-way: rdn and edgd rt jst over 2f out: hdd and unable qck over 1f out: wknd ins fnl f* **16/1**

0-00 **6** *3* **Boutan**^{25} 1860 3-9-5 **67** ...... SteveDrowne 7 55
(George Baker) *chsd ldrs: rdn and carried rt jst over 2f out: outpcd and btn over 1f out: wknd ins fnl f* **9/1**

54-4 **7** *14* **Himalayan Queen**^{35} 1572 3-9-0 **62** ...... ShaneKelly 6 26
(William Jarvis) *hld up in tch in midfield: effrt to chse ldrs ent fnl 2f: unable qck u.p and btn 1f out: wl hld and eased ins fnl f* **8/1**

41-0 **8** *11* **Pop Culture**^{32} 1630 3-9-3 **65** ...... RichardKingscote 5
(Jonathan Portman) *dwlt: in tch in midfield: outpcd and swtchd lft over 2f out: sn wknd and wl bhd fnl f* **10/1**

33-0 **9** *5* **Arctic Flower (IRE)**^{13} 2186 3-8-4 **52** ow1 ...... WilliamCarson 9
(John Bridger) *led tl 1/2-way: losing pl and bdly hmpd jst over 2f out: bhd after: t.o ins fnl f* **16/1**

1m 25.81s (2.51) **Going Correction** +0.35s/f (Good) **9** Ran SP% **114.9**
Speed ratings (Par 96): **99,97,97,96,94 91,75,62,56**
CSF £18.06 CT £54.13 TOTE £3.70: £1.60, £2.10, £2.00; EX 20.80 Trifecta £71.20.
Owner K Corcoran, John and Paul Frampton **Bred** D R Tucker **Trained** Charlton Mackrell, Somerset

FOCUS
Race distance as advertised. This looked the lesser of the two divisions and the time was 0.15sec slower than the first leg. The form seems sound, the winner close to her AW win two starts ago.

2587 MARTIN LAWRENCE 60TH BIRTHDAY CELEBRATION H'CAP 7f
4:00 (4:04) (Class 3) (0-90,88) 4-Y-0 **£7,246** (£2,168; £1,084; £542; £270) **Stalls** High

Form RPR

2-43 **1** **Felix Leiter**^{11} 2247 4-9-0 **88** ...... CliffordLee$^{(7)}$ 1 98
(K R Burke) *led and clr of field w rival: hdd 2f out: rdn and stl ev ch over 1f out: led again ins fnl f: sn clr and styd on strly: rdn out* **9/2**^{3}

4-53 **2** *2 ¼* **George Cinq**^{12} 2216 6-9-3 **87** ...... TomMarquand$^{(3)}$ 6 91
(George Scott) *pressing ldr and clr of field tl led 2f out: sn rdn: hdd ins fnl f: no ex: wknd but hld on for 2nd towards fin* **7/2**^{1}

0-P0 **3** *nk* **Passing Star**^{11} 2247 5-9-3 **87** ...... MichaelJMMurphy$^{(3)}$ 3 90
(Charles Hills) *chsd clr ldng pair: rdn ent fnl 2f: outpcd u.p over 1f out: rallied ins fnl f: styd on to press for 2nd cl home: no threat to wnr* **8/1**

000 **4** *nse* **Air Of York (IRE)**^{32} 1634 4-8-8 **78** ...... PhilipPrince$^{(3)}$ 11 81
(David Evans) *prom in main gp: rdn over 2f out: outpcd u.p over 1f out: rallied and styd on ins fnl f: no threat to wnr* **16/1**

315- **5** *1 ½* **Spiriting (IRE)**^{320} 4113 4-9-6 **87** ......(p) AndreaAtzeni 5 86
(Roger Varian) *hld up in midfield: swtchd lft and effrt jst over 2f out: chsd ldrs and drvn over 1f out: no imp: one pce and lost 2 pls ins fnl f* **4/1**^{2}

65-6 **6** *hd* **Misterioso (IRE)**^{11} 2247 4-9-4 **85** ...... WilliamCarson 2 84
(Jamie Osborne) *hld up in tch in midfield: effrt over 2f out: chsd ldrs and unable qck over 1f out: kpt on same pce ins fnl f* **8/1**

1530 **7** *6* **Shyron**^{18} 2033 5-9-5 **86** ...... AdamKirby 9 69
(George Margarson) *hld up in midfield: swtchd lft and effrt ent fnl 2f: no imp over 1f out: sn wknd* **8/1**

30-6 **8** *1 ¾* **Aqua Ardens (GER)**^{46} 1344 8-9-5 **86** ......(t) PatCosgrave 8 65
(George Baker) *sn niggled along in last trio: swtchd lft and effrt u.p jst over 2f out: sn struggling: wknd over 1f out* **12/1**

1-00 **9** *¾* **Popeswood (IRE)**^{4} 2460 4-9-1 **82** ...... RichardKingscote 4 59
(Ron Hodges) *v keen to post: stdd s: hld up in last pair: effrt ent fnl 2f: sn btn* **20/1**

05-0 **10** *shd* **Bold**^{24} 1887 4-8-11 **78** ......(t) OisinMurphy 10 54
(Stuart Williams) *stdd s: hld up in last pair: rdn ent fnl 2f: no rspnse and sn btn* **12/1**

1m 24.43s (1.13) **Going Correction** +0.35s/f (Good) **10** Ran SP% **119.8**
Speed ratings (Par 107): **107,104,104,104,102 102,95,93,92,92**
CSF £21.29 CT £128.62 TOTE £5.10: £1.70, £1.60, £2.80; EX 19.60 Trifecta £177.30.
Owner Tim Dykes & Mrs E Burke **Bred** Tibthorpe Stud **Trained** Middleham Moor, N Yorks

FOCUS
Race distance as advertised. Little got into this, the first two being in the front pair throughout. The winner confirmed Newmarket form with the third and sixth.

2588 FIRST TITLE INSURANCE PLC (S) STKS 1m 3f 106y
4:35 (4:37) (Class 6) 4-Y-O+ £2,587 (£770; £384; £192) Stalls High

Form RPR
1 **Hard Toffee (IRE)**15 5-9-0 0 JimCrowley 1 66
(Conrad Allen) *chsd ldng pair: clsd and travelling strly 3f out: led and rdn over 2f out: clr over 1f out: styd on* **3/1**2
-040 2 2 1/2 **Barren Brook**23 1933 9-9-0 70 LukeMorris 6 63
(Laura Mongan) *hld up in 4th: clsd to trck ldrs 4f out: nt clr run and shuffled bk 3f out: swtchd rt and rdn to chse wnr 2f out: hrd drvn and no imp 1f out* **1/2**1
65-0 3 7 **Shareni (IRE)**25 1854 7-9-0 65 LiamKeniry 3 51
(Zoe Davison) *chsd ldr: rdn and ev ch 3f out: sn outpcd: 3rd and wknd over 1f out* **16/1**
60/0 4 10 **Total Obsession**6 2397 9-8-4 42 (v) PaddyPilley(5) 5 30
(Mark Hoad) *bhd: clsd and in tch 4f out: effrt to chse ldrs over 2f out: sn struggling: wknd over 1f out* **33/1**
0350 5 17 **Claude Greenwood**8 2323 6-9-4 48 (b) RobertHavlin 2 12
(Linda Jewell) *led: rdn and hdd over 2f out: sn dropped out: bhd over 1f out: t.o* **8/1**3

2m 37.13s (5.63) **Going Correction** +0.625s/f (Yiel) **5 Ran SP% 111.6**
Speed ratings (Par 101): **104,102,97,89,77**
CSF £4.99 TOTE £3.40: £1.30, £1.10; EX 5.20 Trifecta £18.40.The winner was bought in for 6,400gns
Owner Miss Louise Allan **Bred** Marston Stud **Trained** Newmarket, Suffolk
■ Spring Overture was withdrawn. Price at time of withdrawal 33-1. Rule 4 does not apply.

FOCUS
Race distance as advertised. A seller lacking depth and the front pair drew clear. Shaky form.

2589 ROGER HOLMDEN MEMORIAL MEDIAN AUCTION MAIDEN STKS 1m 3f 106y
5:05 (5:09) (Class 6) 3-4-Y-O £2,587 (£770; £384; £192) Stalls High

Form RPR
22-0 1 **Tenzing Norgay**15 2126 3-8-11 62 (v1) LukeMorris 4 76+
(Sir Mark Prescott Bt) *in tch in midfield: smooth hdwy to ld over 2f out: sn rdn clr: in n.d over 1f out: eased wl ins fnl f* **15/8**2
2 5 **Swashbuckle** 3-8-11 0 LiamKeniry 5 64
(Andrew Balding) *s.i.s: hld up towards rr: effrt 3f out: rdn 2f out chsd clr wnr over 1f out: no imp but kpt on for clr 2nd* **7/4**1
00 3 4 1/2 **Sixties Idol**4 2470 3-8-6 0 SilvestreDeSousa 7 52
(Mick Channon) *hld up in last trio: rdn and rn green 3f out: stl green but hdwy to pass btn horses 1f out: wnt modest 3rd ins fnl f: no ch w wnr* **8/1**
4 4 2 **Gamesters Boy**21 1970 3-8-11 0 LiamJones 6 54
(Mark Brisbourne) *chsd ldr: rdn and ev ch 3f out: sn outpcd by wnr: 3rd and wl hld over 1f out: plugged on* **12/1**
05-0 5 1/2 **Trident Tested**55 1163 3-8-11 62 KierenFox 1 53
(John Best) *chsd ldng pair: rdn and unable qck over 2f out: 4th and wl btn over 1f out* **25/1**
50 6 25 **Tilsworth Phyllis**43 1400 4-9-7 0 1 LemosdeSouza 8 8
(J R Jenkins) *a bhd: lost tch over 3f out: t.o* **100/1**
64 7 1 1/2 **Tudor Icon**84 789 3-8-11 0 RichardKingscote 2 11
(Rae Guest) *racd keenly: led tl rdn and hdd over 2f out: sn dropped out: bhd and eased fnl f: t.o* **5/1**3

2m 35.58s (4.08) **Going Correction** +0.625s/f (Yiel)
WFA 3 from 4yo 15lb **7 Ran SP% 111.5**
Speed ratings (Par 101): **110,106,103,101,101 83,82**
CSF £5.23 TOTE £2.60: £1.10, £1.80; EX 5.50 Trifecta £21.20.
Owner J L C Pearce **Bred** J L C Pearce **Trained** Newmarket, Suffolk
■ Secret Shot was withdrawn. Price at time of withdrawal 66-1. Rule 4 does not apply.

FOCUS
Race distance as advertised. A very modest maiden and they finished strung out, but it was a much-improved effort by the winner and he looks one to keep onside in the short-term.

2590 INJURED JOCKEYS FUND H'CAP 1m 2f
5:35 (5:37) (Class 6) (0-55,61) 3-Y-O £2,587 (£770; £384; £192) Stalls Low

Form RPR
0-12 1 **Hint Of Grey (IRE)**15 2126 3-9-0 55 GeorgeWood(7) 4 62+
(Don Cantillon) *t.k.h: hld up wl in tch in midfield: effrt 2f out: rdn to ld over 1f out: clr ins fnl f: r.o wl: readily* **11/4**1
02-0 2 2 1/4 **Nanny Makfi**29 1740 3-9-1 49 FrederikTylicki 6 52
(Stuart Kittow) *hld up in midfield: effrt 2f out: swtchd rt and hdwy over 1f out: styd on wl ins fnl f: wnt 2nd nr fin* **22/1**
630- 3 nk **Its A Sheila Thing**166 8177 3-9-4 52 RobertHavlin 8 54
(Linda Jewell) *stdd s: t.k.h: hld up in tch in midfield: rdn and hdwy over 1f out: styd on wl ins fnl f* **66/1**
000- 4 nk **Final Choice**161 8251 3-9-3 51 GeorgeBaker 12 57+
(Roger Charlton) *v.s.a: hld up in rr: stl last over 3f out: swtchd rt over 2f out: hdwy and edging lft over 1f out: styd on wl ins fnl f* **3/1**2
00-3 5 hd **Becca Campbell (IRE)**29 1734 3-9-7 55 JohnFahy 9 56
(Eve Johnson Houghton) *led: rdn and hrd pressed 2f out: hdd over 1f out: styd on same pce ins fnl f: lost 3 pls nr fin* **25/1**
4-00 6 3/4 **Desert Tango**29 1740 3-8-10 51 CharlieBennett(7) 3 51
(Jonathan Portman) *chsd ldrs: u.p and ev ch 2f out tl unable qck ent fnl f: kpt on same pce ins fnl f* **50/1**
0561 7 1/2 **Rockliffe**7 2366 3-9-13 61 6ex JFEgan 5 60
(Mick Channon) *hld up wl in tch: effrt u.p and ev ch 2f out tl ent fnl f: styd on same pce ins fnl f* **9/2**3
-050 8 1 1/2 **French Legend**15 2126 3-8-12 51 EdwardGreatrex(5) 11 47
(Andrew Balding) *chsd ldrs: rdn ent fnl 2f: unable qck u.p over 1f out: wknd ins fnl f* **14/1**
-603 9 1 **Concur (IRE)**14 2148 3-9-1 49 JackMitchell 2 43
(Rod Millman) *chsd ldrs: unable qck u.p over 1f out: wknd ins fnl f* **16/1**
050- 10 1/2 **Bob's Boy**215 7431 3-9-7 55 RichardKingscote 13 48
(Jose Santos) *s.i.s: hld up in tch in last trio: effrt and swtchd rt over 1f out: no imp* **12/1**
0-02 11 1 1/4 **Gold Eliza (IRE)**14 2148 3-9-6 54 KieranO'Neill 7 45
(Richard Hannon) *s.i.s: hld up in tch: short of room 2f out: sn rdn and no hdwy* **8/1**
2-60 12 5 **Pivotal Dream (IRE)**36 1551 3-9-3 51 RyanClark 1 33
(Mark Brisbourne) *in tch in midfield: rdn and unable qck 2f: lost pl over 1f out: bhd fnl f* **25/1**

2m 17.34s (6.84) **Going Correction** +0.625s/f (Yiel) **12 Ran SP% 120.7**
Speed ratings (Par 97): **97,95,94,94,94 93,93,92,91,91 90,86**
CSF £33.72 CT £1655.95 TOTE £3.70: £1.60, £3.40, £7.40; EX 40.40 Trifecta £1535.80.
Owner Mrs Catherine Reed **Bred** Kildaragh Stud **Trained** Newmarket, Suffolk

FOCUS
Race distance as advertised. Just a moderate handicap and there was a bit of a bunch finish in behind the bang-in-form winner, who could do a bit better again.
T/Plt: £30.30 to a £1 stake. Pool: £64.203.59 - 1,545.46 winning tickets T/Qpdt: £1.90 to a £1 stake. Pool: £7,256.07 - 2,692.66 winning tickets **Steve Payne**

2591 - 2603a (Foreign Racing) - See Raceform Interactive

1958 CHELMSFORD (A.W) (L-H)
Thursday, May 26

OFFICIAL GOING: Polytrack: standard
Wind: virtually nil Weather: fine, light cloud

2604 THE CONQUER THE COURSE 16TH JULY EBF STALLIONS NOVICE STKS 6f (P)
2:20 (2:20) (Class 5) 2-Y-O £4,528 (£1,347; £673; £336) Stalls Centre

Form RPR
1 **Tailor's Row (USA)** 2-9-2 0 FrannyNorton 2 79+
(Mark Johnston) *broke fast: led for 1f: chsd ldr: rdn over 2f out: looked hld over 1f out: rallied to press ldr ins fnl f: styd on to ld towards fin* **9/4**1
213 2 1/2 **Kreb's Cycle (IRE)**19 2038 2-9-4 0 GaryMahon(5) 1 85
(Richard Hannon) *chsd ldr tl led after 1f: gng best 2f out: shkn up and looked in command w rdr looking arnd over 1f out: pushed along and drifted off of rail ins fnl f: hdd towards fin: nt enough time to respond and one pce* **7/2**2
3 4 **Kodiac Khan (IRE)** 2-9-2 0 JimCrowley 5 66
(Hugo Palmer) *dwlt: a 3rd: clsd and in tch whn rdn over 2f out: outpcd ent fnl f: wknd fnl 150yds* **9/4**1
4 3 1/4 **Al Hamdany (IRE)** 2-9-2 0 AndreaAtzeni 3 56
(Marco Botti) *s.i.s: rn green and sn rdn along in rr: swtchd rt over 1f out: wnt modest 4th 1f out: no imp* **6/1**3
542 5 6 **Vinnievanbaileys**17 2082 2-9-2 0 (b) LukeMorris 4 38
(Chris Dwyer) *dwlt: rdn along in 4th: reminders after 1f: drvn over 2f out: btn over 1f out: wknd* **8/1**

1m 14.14s (0.44) **Going Correction** +0.025s/f (Slow) **5 Ran SP% 109.2**
Speed ratings (Par 93): **98,97,92,87,79**
CSF £10.13 TOTE £2.90: £1.70, £1.10; EX 10.50 Trifecta £15.20.
Owner Sheikh Hamdan bin Mohammed Al Maktoum **Bred** Darley **Trained** Middleham Moor, N Yorks

FOCUS
The track had been power harrowed to 4 inches and gallop master finished to 2 inches. This looked a fair novice, although there are no race averages to go on.

2605 TITANBET.CO.UK H'CAP 1m 5f 66y(P)
2:50 (2:50) (Class 5) (0-70,76) 4-Y-O+ £5,175 (£1,540; £769; £384) Stalls Low

Form RPR
2514 1 **Sandy Cove**28 1810 5-9-4 67 RyanTate 7 75
(James Eustace) *hld up in tch in last quartet: effrt and hdwy on outer over 2f out: chsd ldrs over 1f out: styd on to ld ins fnl f: hld on gamely: rdn out* **10/1**
0-61 2 1/2 **Azilian**6 2445 4-9-13 76 6ex (t) MartinHarley 4 83
(Paul Cole) *chsd ldr: 3 l down and rdn over 2f out: styd on u.p to chal ins fnl f: kpt on wl u.p but a jst hld* **7/4**1
2033 3 1/2 **Unex Modigliani (IRE)**32 1675 7-8-7 56 (vt) MartinLane 3 62
(Derek Shaw) *hld up in last pair: effrt and stl plenty to do 3f out: hdwy u.p and switching rt over 1f out: chsd clr ldng trio ins fnl f: styd on strly fnl 100yds: nt quite rch ldrs* **12/1**
2-60 4 2 1/4 **County Wexford (IRE)**14 2174 5-8-8 60 DanielMuscutt(3) 6 63
(Miss Joey Ellis) *led: 3 l clr and rdn over 2f out: drvn over 1f out: hdd ins fnl f: no ex and styd on same pce fnl 100yds* **25/1**
0-06 5 7 **The Quarterjack**13 2210 7-8-13 67 KieranShoemark(5) 1 59
(Charlie Wallis) *stdd s: hld up in tch in last quartet: effrt over 2f out: no hdwy u.p over 1f out: wknd fnl f* **14/1**
-321 6 4 **Weld Arab (IRE)**11 606 5-9-4 67 1 LukeMorris 9 53
(Michael Blake) *in tch in midfield: rdn 5f out: drvn over 2f out: no imp and btn over 1f out: wknd fnl f* **14/1**
-114 7 1 1/4 **Avenue Des Champs**30 1760 4-9-0 66 DannyBrock(3) 5 51
(Jane Chapple-Hyam) *chsd ldrs: rdn over 2f out: unable qck and btn over 1f out: sn wknd* **10/3**2
32-2 8 1 **Rock Of Max**42 1434 4-9-4 70 (p) LouisSteward(3) 2 53
(Michael Bell) *in tch in midfield: n.m.r towards inner over 2f out: no hdwy u.p over 1f out: sn wknd* **6/1**3
0240 9 1 1/2 **Senor George (IRE)**30 1747 9-9-1 64 RyanClark 11 45
(Simon Hodgson) *stdd and dropped in bhd after s: hld up in rr: effrt over 2f out: no imp and btn over 1f out: wknd fnl f* **33/1**
0-44 P **Able Dash**42 1434 6-9-7 70 (v) TimmyMurphy 8
(Michael Blake) *in tch: rdn 5f out: lost pl qckly and bhd 4f out: lost tch and eased 3f out: p.u over 1f out* **10/1**

2m 53.96s (0.36) **Going Correction** +0.025s/f (Slow) **10 Ran SP% 119.7**
Speed ratings (Par 103): **99,98,98,97,92 90,89,88,87,**
CSF £28.61 CT £225.25 TOTE £12.00: £2.20, £1.50, £4.90; EX 38.20 Trifecta £323.80.
Owner Blue Peter Racing 12 **Bred** D J And Mrs Deer **Trained** Newmarket, Suffolk

FOCUS
A good effort from the winner, who didn't have the ideal trip but still got the best of the favourite, who in contrast had a charmed run. The winner has been rated back to his best.

2606 "THIS GIRL CAN" MAIDEN FILLIES' STKS 6f (P)
3:20 (3:25) (Class 5) 3-Y-O+ £5,175 (£1,540; £769; £384) Stalls Centre

Form RPR
3 1 **Kindly**20 2004 3-9-0 0 JimCrowley 6 77
(Simon Crisford) *mde all: rdn over 1f out: r.o wl ins fnl f: rdn out* **8/1**
3- 2 2 **Daring Day**254 6418 3-9-0 0 LukeMorris 2 71
(George Peckham) *chsd ldrs: effrt over 1f out: drvn 1f out: chsd wnr 100yds out: styd on same pce* **2/1**1
0-4 3 1/2 **May Rose (IRE)**20 2004 3-9-0 0 (t) AndreaAtzeni 10 69
(Marco Botti) *chsd ldr: rdn jst over 2f out: drvn over 1f out: lost 2nd and kpt on same pce ins fnl f* **12/1**
6 4 nk **Cliffhanger**31 1723 3-9-0 0 MartinHarley 1 68
(Paul Cole) *wnt rt s: in tch in midfield: effrt 2f out: swtchd rt ins fnl f: kpt on but nvr enough pce to threaten wnr* **20/1**
5-36 5 nk **Blue Geranium (IRE)**20 2004 3-9-0 77 FrankieDettori 5 67
(John Gosden) *in tch in midfield: effrt in 4th 2f out: drvn over 1f out: kpt on same pce ins fnl f* **9/4**2
- 6 4 1/2 **Dawreya (IRE)** 3-9-0 0 PaulHanagan 4 53
(Marcus Tregoning) *hld up in tch in last trio: effrt over 1f out: sn rdn and no imp: wknd ins fnl f* **4/1**3

00 **7** 1 1/4 **Eisha Baby**[5] 2470 3-8-7 0 .... MeganNicholls(7) 8 49
(Richard Hannon) *in tch in midfield: rdn over 2f out: lost pl and btn over 1f out: wknd ins fnl f* **40/1**

8 1 1/4 **Rebel Sky** 3-9-0 0 .... LemosdeSouza 9 45
(J R Jenkins) *stdd s: t.k.h: hld up in rr: effrt and swtchd rt over 1f out: sn btn: wknd fnl f* **100/1**

9 nk **Mabrokah** 3-9-0 0 ....[1] TomQueally 3 44
(William Haggas) *stdd s: t.k.h: hld up in last pair: effrt over 1f out: sn btn: wknd fnl f* **10/1**

1m 14.01s (0.31) **Going Correction** +0.025s/f (Slow)
WFA 3 from 4yo 9lb **9** Ran SP% **120.2**
Speed ratings (Par 100): **98,95,94,94,93 87,86,84,84**
CSF £25.22 TOTE £9.10: £1.90, £1.70, £2.70; EX 30.20 Trifecta £201.10.
Owner The Johnstone Catridge Partnership **Bred** D Curran **Trained** Newmarket, Suffolk

FOCUS
The pace held up here and it proved hard to challenge from behind. The winner confirmed Lingfield form with the third and fifth.

2607 BET AND WATCH AT TITANBET.CO.UK FILLIES' H'CAP 1m 2f (P)
3:50 (3:53) (Class 5) (0-70,63) 4-Y-0+ **£5,175** (£1,540; £769; £384) **Stalls** Low

Form RPR

4-55 **1** **Lady Lunchalot (USA)**[8] 2374 6-9-7 **63** ....(p) JimCrowley 6 72
(Laura Mongan) *hld up in tch: hdwy to chse ldrs over 2f out: rdn to chse ldr over 1f out: led 100yds out: sn clr: r.o wl* **9/2**

03-5 **2** 3 1/2 **Rustique**[15] 2151 4-9-6 **62** .... LukeMorris 5 64
(Ed Walker) *sn led: rdn over 1f out: drvn 1f out: hdd 100yds out: sn outpcd* **9/4**[1]

0025 **3** 2 **Coup De Vent**[5] 2461 5-8-13 **55** ....(be) TimmyMurphy 3 54
(John O'Shea) *taken down early: stdd and awkward leaving stalls: hld up in tch: hdwy on inner to chse ldrs 7f out: wnt 2nd over 2f out tl over 1f out: wknd ins fnl f* **14/1**

6-04 **4** 3 **Theydon Bois**[31] 1699 4-9-4 **60** ....(v) JimmyQuinn 2 53
(Peter Charalambous) *bmpd s: sn chsng ldr: rdn and lost pl over 2f out: wknd over 1f out* **8/1**

4-00 **5** 7 **Power Up**[124] 316 5-9-4 **60** .... MartinDwyer 4 40
(Jane Chapple-Hyam) *hld up in tch on outer: rdn over 2f out: sn struggling: wknd over 1f out* **7/2**[3]

34-5 **6** 2 1/2 **Titan Goddess**[28] 1805 4-9-3 **59** .... OisinMurphy 1 34
(Mike Murphy) *broke wl: led early: sn hdd and stdd bk into midfield: dropped to last and rdn 3f out: wknd wl over 1f out* **10/3**[2]

2m 8.6s **Going Correction** +0.025s/f (Slow) **6** Ran SP% **112.0**
Speed ratings (Par 100): **101,98,96,94,88 86**
CSF £14.99 TOTE £6.70: £4.20, £1.70; EX 13.50 Trifecta £61.80.
Owner Charlie's Starrs **Bred** Fred W Hertrich III **Trained** Epsom, Surrey
■ Stewards' Enquiry : Timmy Murphy two-day ban: used whip down shoulder in the forehand (Jun 9-10)

FOCUS
A messy race from a pace perspective. There are doubts about the form after tame efforts from the fourth to sixth.

2608 MONEY BACK 2ND AT TITANBET.CO.UK H'CAP 1m 2f (P)
4:20 (4:23) (Class 6) (0-55,61) 3-Y-O **£3,234** (£962; £481; £240) **Stalls** Low

Form RPR

00-4 **1** **Tyrannical**[23] 1948 3-9-3 **51** .... LukeMorris 9 56
(Sir Mark Prescott Bt) *drvn along early: hdwy into midfield and bk on bridle after 2f: gng clr in ldng quintet and drvn 2f out: styd on to ld 100yds out: rdn out* **6/4**[1]

6-23 **2** 1 **Go On Gal (IRE)**[31] 1705 3-8-10 **49** .... JosephineGordon(5) 10 52
(Julia Feilden) *chsd ldr: rdn and ev ch over 2f out: led 1f out: hdd and styd on same pce fnl 100yds* **5/1**[3]

0-00 **3** 1 3/4 **Britannia Boy**[14] 2184 3-8-9 **46** oh1 ....(p) DanielMuscutt(3) 2 46
(Mark Usher) *in tch in midfield: effrt and clr in ldng quintet over 2f out: chsng ldrs and swtchd lft over 1f out: kpt on same pce ins fnl f: wnt 3rd last strides* **66/1**

00-0 **4** nk **Bazzat (IRE)**[9] 2348 3-8-9 **46** oh1 ....(p) DannyBrock(3) 4 45
(John Ryan) *chsd ldrs: rdn and clr in ldng quintet ent fnl 2f: swtchd lft over 1f out: kpt on same pce ins fnl f* **40/1**

-644 **5** 1 1/2 **Aksum**[31] 1705 3-9-4 **52** .... GeorgiaCox 8 48
(Michael Bell) *sn led: rdn jst over 2f out: hdd 1f out: no ex: wknd wl ins fnl f* **8/1**

6253 **6** 9 **Never Say (IRE)**[20] 2015 3-8-13 **50** .... RobHornby(3) 5 29
(Jason Ward) *sn bhd: rdn wl over 2f out: sn lost tch w ldrs: no ch fnl 2f: fin lame* **7/1**

55-6 **7** nk **Nutzma**[31] 1705 3-8-13 **47** .... OisinMurphy 1 26
(Mike Murphy) *s.i.s: t.k.h: hld up in rr: rdn 3f out: sn btn: no ch fnl 2f* **20/1**

000- **8** 16 **Almost Spanish (IRE)**[278] 5617 3-8-12 **46** oh1 .... KieranO'Neill 3
(Scott Dixon) *chsd ldrs: rdn and lost pl rapidly over 2f out: wl bhd fnl f* **40/1**

33-0 **9** 21 **Captain Gerald**[30] 1768 3-9-5 **53** .... MartinHarley 13
(John Ryan) *hld up in last trio: rdn over 3f out: sn lost tch: t.o* **10/1**

50-2 **10** 4 1/2 **Melgate Melody**[10] 2308 3-9-2 **50** .... KeaganLatham 12
(Michael Easterby) *in tch in midfield tl lost pl qckly over 3f out: sn bhd: t.o* **7/2**[2]

2m 8.65s (0.05) **Going Correction** +0.025s/f (Slow) **10** Ran SP% **122.7**
Speed ratings (Par 97): **100,99,97,97,96 89,88,76,59,55**
CSF £9.70 CT £364.20 TOTE £2.40: £1.10, £1.60, £13.60; EX 9.10 Trifecta £619.10.
Owner Bunting-Osborne Hse,Sir P Vela,P Stanley **Bred** New England Stud & P J & P M Vela **Trained** Newmarket, Suffolk

FOCUS
A very weak race based on the third and fourth.

2609 DOWNLOAD THE TITANBET.CO.UK APP H'CAP (DIV I) 7f (P)
4:50 (4:51) (Class 6) (0-55,55) 3-Y-O+ **£3,234** (£962; £481; £240) **Stalls** Low

Form RPR

63-0 **1** **Sober Up**[128] 251 4-9-1 **46** oh1 .... MartinHarley 10 64
(Ivan Furtado) *mde all: rdn and wnt clr over 1f out: in n.d 1f out: eased towards fin: easily* **7/1**[3]

32-3 **2** 5 **Cadland Lad (IRE)**[36] 1574 3-8-8 **53** ....(t) DannyBrock(3) 3 53
(John Ryan) *dwlt and short of room sn after s: swtchd rt and hdwy on outer after 1f: chsd ldr 4f out: rdn and unable qck over 1f out: wl hld 2nd and kpt on same pce fnl f* **5/2**[1]

0235 **3** 1 **Assertive Agent**[29] 1794 6-9-8 **53** .... LukeMorris 1 54
(Tony Carroll) *t.k.h: hld up in tch: swtchd rt and effrt wl over 1f out: kpt on u.p ins fnl f: snatched 3rd cl home: no ch w wnr* **5/1**[2]

-200 **4** shd **Divine Touch**[31] 1705 3-8-0 **47** ....[1] PaddyPilley(5) 6 44
(Robert Eddery) *hld up in last trio: effrt on outer over 1f out: hdwy u.p over 1f out: styd on ins fnl f: no ch w wnr* **12/1**

4040 **5** nk **Ventura Falcon (IRE)**[15] 2148 3-8-13 **55** ....(p) KieranO'Neill 4 51
(Richard Hannon) *sn towards rr: rdn over 2f out: hdwy u.p over 1f out: kpt on ins fnl f: no ch w wnr* **7/1**[3]

5100 **6** 1/2 **Schottische**[31] 1695 6-9-10 **55** ....(p) RobertTart 9 54
(Alan Bailey) *chsd ldrs: effrt jst over 2f out: outpcd u.p over 1f out: wl hld and plugged on same pce fnl f: lost 3 pls towards fin* **16/1**

-660 **7** 3 1/2 **Muhtadim (IRE)**[32] 1676 4-8-12 **50** .... RPWalsh(7) 2 39
(Charles Smith) *hld up in tch in midfield: nt clrest of runs over 2f out: swtchd rt and effrt wl over 1f out: no imp: wknd ins fnl f* **40/1**

60-3 **8** 3 **Henry Grace (IRE)**[50] 1262 5-9-2 **52** ....(b) GaryMahon(5) 8 33
(Jimmy Fox) *wl in tch in midfield: rdn over 2f out: little rspnse and lost pl wl over 1f out: sn wknd* **5/1**[2]

5046 **9** 1 3/4 **Jonnie Skull (IRE)**[23] 1781 10-8-12 **48** ....(vt) JosephineGordon(5) 5 25
(Phil McEntee) *chsd ldr tl lost pl jst over 2f out: wknd over 1f out* **14/1**

6-24 **10** 6 **Jackpot**[30] 1742 6-9-1 **46** ....(p) StevieDonohoe 7 6
(Brendan Powell) *chsd ldrs: drvn over 2f out: sn struggling: wknd and bhd 1f out* **12/1**

1m 27.38s (0.18) **Going Correction** +0.025s/f (Slow)
WFA 3 from 4yo+ 11lb **10** Ran SP% **117.3**
Speed ratings (Par 101): **99,93,92,92,91 91,87,83,81,74**
CSF £24.97 CT £99.38 TOTE £9.10: £1.90, £1.70, £2.10; EX 26.50 Trifecta £173.60.
Owner The Giggle Factor Partnership **Bred** Mrs Elizabeth Grundy & Mrs Alice Cherry **Trained** Wiseton, Nottinghamshire

FOCUS
A moderate handicap, but the winner looks the type to go in again. The third and fourth help the level.

2610 DOWNLOAD THE TITANBET.CO.UK APP H'CAP (DIV II) 7f (P)
5:20 (5:20) (Class 6) (0-55,55) 3-Y-O+ **£3,234** (£962; £481; £240) **Stalls** Low

Form RPR

2132 **1** **Not Your Call (IRE)**[15] 2155 5-9-8 **53** .... KierenFox 5 68
(Lee Carter) *racd keenly: mde all: rdn and wnt clr over 1f out: in command and r.o wl fnl f* **11/4**[1]

0053 **2** 4 **Illusive Force (IRE)**[9] 2330 4-9-10 **55** ....(v) MartinLane 1 59
(Derek Shaw) *chsd ldrs: rdn to chse wnr 2f out: drvn and outpcd over 1f out: styd on same pce fnl f* **11/4**[1]

340 **3** 4 1/2 **Bold Max**[23] 1949 5-9-3 **48** ....(v) SamHitchcott 8 40
(Zoe Davison) *in tch in rr of main gp: rdn and hdwy on outer over 2f out: 3rd over 1f out: no imp after* **16/1**

406 **4** 1 **Star Of Kheleyf**[19] 2039 3-8-12 **54** .... AndrewMullen 7 39
(Michael Appleby) *hld up in tch in midfield: rdn over 2f out: no ch w wnr over 1f out: plugged on into 4th ins fnl f* **8/1**

55-0 **5** 3/4 **Carcharias (IRE)**[30] 1768 3-8-11 **53** .... RobHornby 4 36
(Ed de Giles) *in tch in rr of main gp: rdn over 2f out: sme hdwy on inner but no ch w wnr over 1f out: wl hld and plugged on same pce fnl f* **11/2**[2]

5220 **6** 3/4 **Dreaming Again**[36] 1578 6-8-11 **49** ....(b[1]) MitchGodwin(7) 3 34
(Jimmy Fox) *squeezed out sn after leaving stalls: detached in last: rdn 3f out: kpt on to pass btn horses ins fnl f: n.d* **7/1**

7 2 3/4 **Mistress Marinrio (IRE)**[111] 469 5-9-1 **46** oh1 ....(p) JohnFahy 9 24
(Kevin Frost) *t.k.h: chsd ldrs: rdn and struggling over 2f out: wknd over 1f out* **33/1**

060- **8** 5 **Grand Proposal**[148] 8393 4-9-5 **50** ....(p) LukeMorris 2 14
(Mike Murphy) *in tch in midfield: rdn over 3f out: drvn and no hdwy over 2f out: bhd and swtchd rt 1f out: wknd* **13/2**[3]

9 7 **Ace Of Arts (IRE)**[132] 203 4-9-1 **46** oh1 ....(t) MartinHarley 6
(P J F Murphy, Ire) *chsd wnr: drvn and unable qck over 2f out: lost 2nd 2f out: sn wknd* **20/1**

1m 26.93s (-0.27) **Going Correction** +0.025s/f (Slow)
WFA 3 from 4yo+ 11lb **9** Ran SP% **119.2**
Speed ratings (Par 101): **102,97,92,91,90 89,86,80,72**
CSF £10.17 CT £103.22 TOTE £3.20: £1.10, £1.60, £5.50; EX 10.30 Trifecta £69.50.
Owner Clear Racing **Bred** Castleton Lyons & Kilboy Estate **Trained** Epsom, Surrey

FOCUS
Very few got into this, with the pace holding up again. The time was the quicker of the two divisions by 0.45sec and this was a bit out of line with the winner's recent profile.
T/Plt: £37.30 to a £1 stake. Pool of £55512.59 - 1083.90 winning tickets. T/Qpdt: £7.40 to a £1 stake. Pool of £5374.18 - 534.55 winning tickets. **Steve Payne**

2471 HAYDOCK (L-H)
Thursday, May 26

OFFICIAL GOING: Good changing to good to soft after race 1 (2.00)
Wind: Light across Weather: Grey cloud and light showers

2611 GEORGE FORMBY'S BIRTHDAY NOVICE AUCTION STKS (PLUS 10 RACE) 5f
2:00 (2:00) (Class 4) 2-Y-O **£3,946** (£1,174; £586; £293) **Stalls** Centre

Form RPR

1 **Plata O Plomo** 2-9-2 0 .... BarryMcHugh 3 85+
(Tony Coyle) *walked to s early: qckly away and mde all: rdn clr and hung lft ent fnl f: styd on strly* **14/1**

32 **2** 2 **Northern Thunder (IRE)**[8] 2358 2-9-2 0 .... SeanLevey 5 76
(Richard Hannon) *trckd ldrs: effrt wl over 1f out: sn rdn and kpt on fnl f* **13/8**[1]

4 **3** shd **Gerrard's Return**[11] 2264 2-9-2 0 .... RichardKingscote 2 76
(Tom Dascombe) *trckd wnr: cl up over 2f out: rdn wl over 1f out: kpt on same pce fnl f* **12/1**

556 **4** 3 3/4 **Love Oasis**[13] 2219 2-8-11 0 .... JoeFanning 7 57
(Mark Johnston) *trckd wnr: pushed along 2f out: sn rdn and wknd appr fnl f* **5/1**[3]

5 1/2 **Major Cornwallis (IRE)** 2-9-2 0 .... TonyHamilton 1 60+
(Richard Fahey) *green: sn outpcd and rdn along in rr: styd on appr fnl f* **10/1**

6 2 1/4 **Suitcase 'N' Taxi** 2-9-2 0 .... DavidAllan 4 52
(Tim Easterby) *in tch: rdn along 2f out: sn wknd* **10/1**

7 1 3/4 **Burrishoole Abbey (IRE)** 2-9-2 0 .... DougieCostello 8 46
(K R Burke) *dwlt and wnt rt s: bhd: hdwy and in tch 1/2-way: rdn along 2f out: sn btn* **3/1**[2]

50U **8** 3 1/2 **She's Rosanna**[8] 2371 2-8-11 0 .... RoystonFfrench 6 28
(Steph Hollinshead) *in rr: rdn along 1/2-way: sn outpcd and bhd* **125/1**

1m 0.82s (0.02) **Going Correction** +0.075s/f (Good) **8** Ran SP% **113.1**
Speed ratings (Par 95): **102,98,98,92,91 88,85,79**
CSF £36.48 TOTE £19.80: £4.80, £1.10, £2.60; EX 44.90 Trifecta £482.50.

Owner Gap Personnel & Tony Coyle **Bred** Bumble Bloodstock Ltd **Trained** Norton, N Yorks

FOCUS
Following 4mm of rain overnight and another 2mm in the meantime the 'good to firm in places' was removed from the going description and it was now good all over. All races run over Inner Home Straight. Rail configuration on the bends meant that the last three races on the card were run over one yard further than advertised. Not the most competitive of juvenile events to start off with and the order didn't change much, but the winner looks a very good prospect. After riding in the opener Barry McHugh said: "It's on the easy side of good", while Joe Fanning said: "It's nearly good to soft".

2612 EBF APOLLOBET CASH BACK IF SECOND MAIDEN FILLIES' STKS (PLUS 10 RACE) 6f
2:30 (2:33) (Class 5) 2-Y-O £3,234 (£962; £481; £240) **Stalls** Centre

Form RPR

1 **Nasimi** 2-9-0 0 WilliamBuick 9 83+
(Charlie Appleby) *dwlt and wnt rt s: bhd: gd hdwy 2f out: rdn and str run to ld ins fnl f: sn clr: readily* **15/8**[1]

2 *3* **Nations Alexander (IRE)** 2-9-0 0 SeanLevey 3 72
(Richard Hannon) *cl up: effrt to ld wl over 1f out: rdn ent fnl f: sn hdd and drvn: kpt on same pce* **3/1**[2]

3 *hd* **Mia Cara** 2-9-0 0 DarryllHolland 5 71
(David Evans) *towards rr: hdwy 2f out: rdn over 1f out: styd on wl fnl f* **12/1**

444 4 *2 3/4* **Bonnie Arlene (IRE)**[17] 2082 2-9-0 0 JoeFanning 8 63
(Mark Johnston) *slt ld: rdn along 2f out: sn hdd and drvn: grad wknd* **16/1**

20 5 *4* **Playful Trickster (IRE)**[31] 1719 2-9-0 0 RichardKingscote 4 51
(Tom Dascombe) *towards rr: pushed along and hdwy 1/2-way: rdn to chse ldrs 2f out: sn drvn and one pce* **14/1**

5 6 *hd* **Sheppard's Gift**[11] 2265 2-9-0 0 DavidAllan 1 51
(Tim Easterby) *towards rr: hdwy and in tch 1/2-way: sn rdn along and wknd* **25/1**

6 7 *1/2* **Hazell Berry (IRE)**[29] 1793 2-9-0 0 SteveDrowne 2 49
(David Evans) *chsd ldrs: rdn along wl over 2f out: sn wknd* **25/1**

8 *nk* **Samran Says (IRE)** 2-9-0 0 TonyHamilton 7 48
(Richard Fahey) *cl up: rdn along and ev ch 2f out: sn drvn and wknd* **8/1**

9 *2 3/4* **Suraat (IRE)** 2-8-11 0 TomMarquand(3) 6 40
(George Scott) *trckd ldrs: rdn along over 2f out: sn wknd* **5/1**[3]

1m 15.52s (1.72) **Going Correction** +0.075s/f (Good) **9** Ran SP% **115.5**
Speed ratings (Par 90): **91,87,86,83,77 77,76,76,72**
CSF £7.40 TOTE £3.10: £1.50, £1.10, £5.10; EX 9.50 Trifecta £62.80.

Owner Godolphin **Bred** Darley **Trained** Newmarket, Suffolk

FOCUS
The ground was changed to good to soft before this race. A couple of the newcomers were well backed before this fillies' maiden, so it's probably worth viewing the form positively, and the winner was very impressive. She was value for a bit extra, with the fourth likely to be the key to the level.

2613 APOLLOBET BET THROUGH YOUR MOBILE H'CAP 6f
3:00 (3:01) (Class 4) (0-85,87) 4-Y-O+ £5,175 (£1,540; £769; £384) **Stalls** Centre

Form RPR

-504 1 **Snap Shots (IRE)**[5] 2476 4-9-7 85 (tp) RichardKingscote 4 96
(Tom Dascombe) *mde most: rdn over 1f out: kpt on strly* **6/1**[2]

0-00 2 *1 1/2* **Mass Rally (IRE)**[26] 1848 9-9-3 81 (b) PaulMulrennan 8 87
(Michael Dods) *hld up in rr: hdwy 2f out: nt clr run jst over 1f out and again ins fnl f: sn swtchd lft and rdn: fin wl* **9/1**

5061 3 *1/2* **Sir Billy Wright (IRE)**[5] 2460 5-9-6 87 6ex PhilipPrince(3) 11 92
(David Evans) *cl up: chal 2f out and ev ch: rdn ent fnl f: kpt on same pce* **15/2**[3]

4-20 4 *3/4* **Gold Club**[19] 2028 5-9-0 78 SeanLevey 15 80
(Ed McMahon) *dwlt and towards rr: hdwy on wd outside wl over 1f out: sn rdn and styd on ent fnl f: edgd lft and no imp last 100yds* **9/1**

50-1 5 *1 1/4* **Straightothepoint**[20] 2016 4-9-3 81 ConnorBeasley 2 79
(Bryan Smart) *cl up: ev ch 2f out and sn rdn: drvn appr fnl f and kpt on same pce* **15/2**[3]

-241 6 *1 1/2* **Explain**[12] 2259 4-9-6 84 JamesSullivan 6 77
(Ruth Carr) *midfield: pushed along 1/2-way: rdn and hdwy 2f out: drvn to chse ldrs over 1f out: sn edgd lft and wknd* **5/1**[1]

00-0 7 *1 1/4* **Signore Piccolo**[12] 2259 5-9-4 82 DanielTudhope 5 71
(David O'Meara) *chsd ldrs: rdn along wl over 1f out: wknd appr fnl f* **10/1**

6111 8 *1* **Point North (IRE)**[60] 1110 9-8-12 76 (b) DarryllHolland 3 62
(John Balding) *towards rr: hdwy and in tch over 2f out: rdn wl over 1f out: sn btn* **33/1**

0-60 9 *1/2* **Confessional**[12] 2259 9-9-7 85 (e) DavidAllan 14 70
(Tim Easterby) *cl up: rdn along 2f out: sn wknd* **12/1**

0-60 10 *1* **Navigate (IRE)**[38] 1530 4-9-7 85 (b[1]) FergusSweeney 13 66
(Martyn Meade) *a towards rr* **14/1**

0-30 11 *1* **The Hooded Claw (IRE)**[20] 1997 5-9-4 82 JasonHart 1 60
(Tim Easterby) *in tch on inner: hdwy to chse ldrs 1/2-way: rdn along 2f out: sn drvn and wknd* **20/1**

00-1 12 *5* **Kommander Kirkup**[26] 1869 5-8-13 82 PhilDennis(5) 10 44
(John Davies) *chsd ldrs: rdn along jst over 2f out: sn wknd* **11/1**

1m 13.3s (-0.50) **Going Correction** +0.075s/f (Good) **12** Ran SP% **114.0**
Speed ratings (Par 105): **106,104,103,102,100 98,97,95,95,93 92,85**
CSF £56.72 CT £415.05 TOTE £6.40: £2.60, £2.90, £2.30; EX 58.60 Trifecta £751.50.

Owner Gap Personnel **Bred** Tally-Ho Stud **Trained** Malpas, Cheshire

FOCUS
A competitive sprint handicap, but not that many got into it and the action unfolded centre-to-far side. The winner has been rated back to his best.

2614 APOLLOBET HOME OF CASHBACK OFFERS MAIDEN STKS 1m
3:30 (3:31) (Class 5) 3-Y-O+ £3,234 (£962; £481; £240) **Stalls** Low

Form RPR

1 **Lusory** 3-9-2 0 WilliamBuick 8 91+
(Charlie Appleby) *hld up in rr: green and pushed along after 3f: smooth hdwy on outer 3f out: chsd ldrs over 1f out: chal ins fnl f: led last 100yds: readily* **11/4**[1]

03-3 2 *1 1/4* **Perigee**[14] 2175 3-9-2 78 RobertHavlin 7 85
(John Gosden) *t.k.h early: trckd ldr: hdwy and cl up 3f out: rdn to ld 2f out: drvn ent fnl f: hdd and kpt on same pce last 100yds* **11/4**[1]

0- 3 *3 1/4* **Mujaamil**[209] 7592 3-9-2 0 PatCosgrave 4 78
(William Haggas) *trckd ldrs: hdwy wl over 2f out: rdn over 1f out: drvn and one pce fnl f* **11/4**[1]

3 4 *3 3/4* **Fashion Parade**[14] 2177 3-8-11 0 DarryllHolland 1 64
(Charles Hills) *chsd ldng pair on inner: rdn along over 2f out: sn one pce* **9/1**[3]

0 5 *3 1/2* **Proctor**[43] 1426 3-9-2 0 FergusSweeney 9 61
(Stuart Kittow) *hld up in rr: hdwy and n.m.r 2f out and again jst over 1f out: kpt on: nrst fin* **16/1**

0 6 *1 1/4* **Wallangarra**[19] 2048 3-9-2 0 AdamBeschizza 2 58
(Jeremy Gask) *chsd ldrs: rdn along wl over 2f out: sn one pce* **50/1**

0 7 *1 1/2* **Lobster Cocktail (IRE)**[20] 2005 3-9-2 0 RichardKingscote 3 55
(Ed Walker) *t.k.h early: chsd ldrs: rdn along wl over 2f out: grad wknd* **28/1**

24 8 *1 1/4* **Najd**[12] 2234 3-9-2 0 SeanLevey 6 52
(Richard Hannon) *led: pushed along and jnd 3f out: hdd 2f out: sn wknd* **8/1**[2]

0 9 *2 1/4* **Justice Lucky (USA)**[12] 2248 3-8-13 0 TomMarquand(3) 10 46
(David Elsworth) *dwlt: a towards rr* **50/1**

1m 42.12s (-1.58) **Going Correction** -0.10s/f (Good) **9** Ran SP% **114.4**
Speed ratings (Par 103): **103,101,98,94,91 90,88,87,85**
CSF £9.72 TOTE £4.00: £3.00, £1.40, £1.10; EX 10.60 Trifecta £27.80.

Owner Godolphin **Bred** Darley **Trained** Newmarket, Suffolk

FOCUS
Race run over 1m 1yd. An ordinary 3yo maiden dominated by the market principals, but the winner can go on to better things.

2615 APOLLOBET WEEKLY GOLF REFUNDS H'CAP 1m 3f 200y
4:00 (4:01) (Class 5) (0-70,70) 3-Y-O £3,234 (£962; £481; £240) **Stalls** Centre

Form RPR

4-62 1 **Marmajuke Bay**[31] 1718 3-9-7 70 (p) SteveDrowne 8 77+
(Mark Usher) *trckd ldrs: hdwy 3f out: rdn to ld over 1f out: kpt on strly* **9/1**

04-3 2 *2 1/4* **Kajaki (IRE)**[16] 2123 3-9-7 70 (p) ShaneGray 7 73
(Kevin Ryan) *trckd ldr: cl up 3f out: led jst over 2f out: sn rdn and hdd over 1f out: drvn and kpt on fnl f* **8/1**

0-55 3 *1/2* **Molten Gold**[20] 2000 3-9-6 69 PhillipMakin 2 71
(Andrew Balding) *trckd ldng pair on inner: hdwy over 2f out: rdn along wl over 1f out: drvn and kpt on same pce fnl f* **5/1**[2]

340 4 *1 1/2* **Muaither (IRE)**[99] 603 3-9-4 67 (b) RobertHavlin 4 67
(John Gosden) *hld up in tch: hdwy over 2f out and sn pushed along: rdn wl over 1f out: drvn and kpt on one pce fnl f* **7/1**[3]

0-66 5 *shd* **Lime And Lemon (IRE)**[29] 1798 3-9-3 69 TomMarquand(3) 9 69
(Philip McBride) *chsd ldrs: hdwy on outer over 3f out: cl up over 2f out and sn rdn: drvn wl over 1f out: plugged on one pce* **8/1**

0-10 6 *1* **Captain Peacock**[26] 1860 3-9-3 66 RichardKingscote 1 64
(William Knight) *led: jnd and pushed along 3f out: rdn and hdd jst over 2f out: sn drvn and wknd* **9/4**[1]

140- 7 *1* **Senza Una Donna**[238] 6881 3-9-3 66 (t) WilliamBuick 6 62
(Hughie Morrison) *a in rr* **5/1**[2]

60-4 8 *22* **Wayside Magic**[31] 1698 3-8-7 56 ConnorBeasley 5 17
(Michael Dods) *a in rr: rdn along 3f out: outpcd and bhd fnl 2f* **33/1**

2m 32.66s (-1.14) **Going Correction** -0.10s/f (Good) **8** Ran SP% **111.8**
Speed ratings (Par 99): **99,97,97,96,96 95,94,80**
CSF £74.18 CT £395.74 TOTE £10.50: £2.50, £2.20, £2.00; EX 53.50 Trifecta £418.50.

Owner The Ridgeway Alchemist's **Bred** The Welldiggers Partnership **Trained** Upper Lambourn, Berks

FOCUS
Race run over 1m3f 201yds. An ordinary 3yo handicap with previous winning form thin on the ground. The early pace was ordinary and it didn't pick up until inside the last half-mile.

2616 APOLLOBET ON LINE CASINO H'CAP (FOR LADY AMATEUR RIDERS) 1m 3f 200y
4:30 (4:31) (Class 5) (0-70,70) 4-Y-O+ £2,807 (£870; £435; £217) **Stalls** Centre

Form RPR

0-40 1 **Shalamzar (FR)**[17] 2093 7-10-6 69 (p) MissCWalton 8 77
(Micky Hammond) *hld up in rr: hdwy 3f out: in tch 2f out: rdn over 1f out: styd on strly to ld nr fin* **16/1**

142 2 *3/4* **Obboorr**[29] 1796 7-10-1 69 MissHDukes(5) 10 76
(Tim Fitzgerald) *trckd ldrs: hdwy 3f out: chsd ldrs 2f out: rdn over 1f out: slt ld last 100yds: hdd and no ex towards fin* **11/4**[1]

40-5 3 *1 1/2* **Merchant Of Medici**[6] 2436 9-10-0 66 (p) MissBeckySmith(3) 5 71
(Micky Hammond) *trckd ldr: hdwy and cl up over 3f out: led 2f out: rdn over 1f out: drvn and hdd last 100yds: no ex* **4/1**[3]

0-06 4 *2 1/4* **King Of Paradise (IRE)**[25] 1881 7-10-3 66 MissSBrotherton 1 67
(Eric Alston) *led: pushed along and jnd 3f out: rdn and hdd 2f out: drvn over 1f out: sn one pce* **10/3**[2]

506- 5 *3 3/4* **Smoky Hill (IRE)**[191] 7351 7-9-10 59 MissJoannaMason 6 54
(Tony Carroll) *chsd ldrs: rdn along over 2f out: sn no imp* **14/1**

62-6 6 *1/2* **Jersey Jewel (FR)**[27] 1825 4-10-2 70 MissCAGreenway(5) 7 64
(Tom Dascombe) *trckd ldng pair: hdwy 3f out: rdn along 2f out: drvn and wknd over 1f out* **6/1**

643- 7 *6* **The Yank**[189] 7909 7-9-13 67 MissPBridgwater(5) 4 52
(David Bridgwater) *chsd ldrs on inner: rdn along over 3f out: sn wknd* **17/2**

240- 8 *5* **Edas**[271] 5859 14-9-4 56 oh9 MissHelenCuthbert(3) 3 33
(Thomas Cuthbert) *a towards rr* **50/1**

060- 9 *2* **Flag Of Glory**[215] 7474 9-9-6 60 (b) MissMEdden(5) 2 33
(Peter Hiatt) *a in rr* **20/1**

006/ 10 *nk* **Peadar Miguel**[568] 7287 9-9-7 56 oh11 MissMMullineaux 9 29
(Michael Mullineaux) *a in rr* **66/1**

2m 34.88s (1.08) **Going Correction** -0.10s/f (Good) **10** Ran SP% **115.3**
Speed ratings (Par 103): **92,91,90,89,86 86,82,78,77,77**
CSF £58.66 CT £216.97 TOTE £15.60: £4.30, £1.50, £1.30; EX 91.90 Trifecta £512.90.

Owner Maybe The Last Time **Bred** H H The Aga Khan's Studs Sc **Trained** Middleham, N Yorks

FOCUS
Race run over 1m3f 201yds. A modest lady amateurs' event run at just a fair pace and the front four pulled clear. It was a 1-3 for trainer Micky Hammond.

T/Jkpt: Not won. T/Plt: £42.60 to a £1 stake. Pool of £69350.41 - 1187.17 winning tickets. T/Qpdt: £21.40 to a £1 stake. Pool of £5071.70 - 174.73 winning tickets. **Joe Rowntree**

2327 NEWCASTLE (A.W) (L-H)

Thursday, May 26

OFFICIAL GOING: Tapeta: standard

Wind: Breezy, half behind Weather: Overcast

2617 EBF STALLIONS/HMH CIVILS NORTH EAST NOVICE STKS (PLUS 10 RACE) 5f (Tp)

6:25 (6:26) (Class 4) 2-Y-O **£5,175** (£1,540; £769; £384) **Stalls** Centre

Form RPR

022 **1** **Poet's Society**[9] 2319 2-9-2 0 .... JamesDoyle 4 87
(Mark Johnston) *mde all: rdn: edgd lft and qcknd clr 2f out: rdn out fnl f: unchal* **7/4**[1]

02 **2** 3 **Tallinski (IRE)**[27] 1840 2-9-2 0 .... BenCurtis 9 76
(Brian Ellison) *in tch: effrt and pushed along 2f out: chsd (clr) wnr wl ins fnl f: kpt on: no imp* **11/2**[3]

3 1/2 **Kodicat (IRE)** 2-8-11 0 .... PaulMulrennan 1 69+
(Kevin Ryan) *chsd wnr: pushed along 2f out: one pce and lost 2nd wl ins fnl f* **15/8**[2]

4 3 **Heatongrad (IRE)** 2-9-2 0 .... TonyHamilton 3 64+
(Richard Fahey) *prom tl rdn and outpcd fr over 1f out* **16/1**

5 nse **Elegantly Bound (IRE)** 2-9-2 0 .... TomEaves 7 63+
(James Given) *dwlt: bhd and sn pushed along: hdwy fnl f: kpt on: nt pce to chal* **12/1**

6 3/4 **Vintage Dream (IRE)** 2-9-2 0 .... BarryMcHugh 8 61+
(Noel Wilson) *s.i.s: bhd and outpcd: sme late hdwy: nvr rchd ldrs* **28/1**

6 **7** 1/2 **Coverham (IRE)**[29] 1783 2-9-2 0 .... TedDurcan 6 59
(James Bethell) *chsd ldrs: rdn along 1/2-way: sn lost pl: btn over 1f out* **25/1**

5 **8** 4 **Ventura Secret (IRE)**[16] 2119 2-9-2 0 .... JackGarritty 5 45
(Tim Easterby) *t.k.h: prom tl rdn and wknd over 1f out* **20/1**

9 3 3/4 **Ey Up** 2-8-11 0 .... GrahamLee 2 26
(Paul Midgley) *rn green in rr: struggling 1/2-way: sn btn* **33/1**

58.84s (-0.66) **Going Correction** -0.10s/f (Stan) **9** Ran SP% **115.1**
Speed ratings (Par 95): **101,96,95,90,90 89,88,82,76**
CSF £11.19 TOTE £2.40: £1.02, £2.40, £1.50; EX 6.20 Trifecta £23.60.
Owner Sheikh Hamdan bin Mohammed Al Maktoum **Bred** Darley **Trained** Middleham Moor, N Yorks

■ Stewards' Enquiry : Paul Mulrennan caution: careless riding

FOCUS
There will be no speed figures at this track until there is sufficient data to calculate median times. The race distances have been remeasured following the inaugural meeting on the Tapeta at Newcastle. The track had been harrowed to a depth of 2.5 to 3 inches and reinstated with a Gallop Master. Winners should come out of this decent novice stakes, in which Poet's Society stepped up.

2618 ASCENT HOMES H'CAP 1m 2f 42y (Tp)

6:55 (6:56) (Class 5) (0-70,70) 4-Y-O+ **£5,175** (£1,540; £769; £384) **Stalls** High

Form RPR

-040 **1** **Briardale (IRE)**[24] 1923 4-9-7 **70** .... PJMcDonald 11 81
(James Bethell) *trckd ldrs: led over 2f out to appr fnl f: rallied and regained ld last 110yds: kpt on gamely u.p* **4/1**[1]

1125 **2** 1/2 **Rockwood**[32] 1664 5-9-6 **69** ....(v) PaulMulrennan 6 79
(Karen McLintock) *prom: smooth hdwy to ld appr fnl f: sn rdn: hdd last 110yds: kpt on same pce towards fin* **11/2**[2]

0000 **3** 3 1/4 **Hussar Ballad (USA)**[9] 2343 7-9-1 **64** .... DavidAllan 12 69+
(Antony Brittain) *missed break: hld up: hdwy over 2f out: nt clr run briefly over 1f out: kpt on wl to take 3rd towards fin: nt rch first two* **14/1**

2-00 **4** 3/4 **Mr Sundowner (USA)**[17] 2092 4-8-4 **60** ....(t) HollieDoyle(7) 10 62+
(Wilf Storey) *hld up: hdwy over 2f out: rdn to chse clr ldng pair over 1f out: one pce and lost 3rd pl towards fin* **25/1**

1-22 **5** 1/2 **Miss Ranger (IRE)**[27] 1825 4-8-13 **67** .... CallumShepherd(5) 8 68
(Brian Ellison) *hld up in tch: effrt and pushed along over 2f out: kpt on same pce fnl f* **4/1**[1]

3454 **6** 5 **Lean On Pete (IRE)**[30] 1762 7-9-1 **64** ....(p) GrahamGibbons 14 55
(Ollie Pears) *midfield on outside: drvn and effrt over 2f out: wknd over 1f out* **8/1**[3]

660- **7** 4 1/2 **Bling King**[236] 6933 7-8-11 **63** ....(p) KevinStott(3) 2 45
(Geoffrey Harker) *trckd ldrs: rdn over 2f out: wknd over 1f out* **12/1**

6-40 **8** hd **Chorus of Lies**[24] 1923 4-9-2 **65** .... JoeFanning 13 47
(Tracy Waggott) *led at ordinary gallop: rdn and hdd over 2f out: wknd over 1f out* **12/1**

/34- **9** nk **Amirli (IRE)**[235] 4008 5-9-7 **70** .... TomEaves 3 51
(Alistair Whillans) *hld up: rdn over 2f out: sme late hdwy: nvr rchd ldrs* **20/1**

00-5 **10** 3/4 **Ronald Gee (IRE)**[26] 1853 9-9-7 **70** .... DanielTudhope 5 50
(Jim Goldie) *cl up: rdn along over 3f out: wknd over 1f out* **16/1**

000- **11** nk **Exclusive Waters (IRE)**[19] 5943 6-9-1 **64** .... RobertWinston 7 43
(George Charlton) *t.k.h: hld up: rdn wl over 1f out: sn btn* **20/1**

60 **12** 1/2 **Champagne Rules**[45] 1391 5-9-7 **70** ....[1] PaddyAspell 9 48
(Sharon Watt) *hld up on outside: rdn over 2f out: drifted rt and wknd over 1f out* **33/1**

222- **13** 3/4 **Paddy's Rock (IRE)**[320] 4147 5-9-3 **66** .... JackGarritty 1 42
(Lynn Siddall) *hld up: drvn along 3f out: sn btn* **18/1**

5-06 **14** 3 3/4 **Carragold**[23] 1952 10-9-4 **67** .... GrahamLee 4 36
(Antony Brittain) *prom: rdn whn n.m.r briefly over 2f out: sn wknd* **25/1**

2m 9.69s (-0.71) **Going Correction** -0.025s/f (Stan) **14** Ran SP% **119.8**
Speed ratings (Par 103): **101,100,98,97,97 93,89,89,89,88 88,87,87,84**
CSF £22.68 CT £285.92 TOTE £5.40: £1.90, £2.50, £4.30; EX 32.10 Trifecta £321.30.
Owner J Carrick&Clarendon Thoroughbred Racing **Bred** Rabbah Bloodstock Limited **Trained** Middleham Moor, N Yorks

FOCUS
A modest handicap run at what looked an ordinary gallop, but the form seems sound enough and the winner has been rated back to his 3yo maiden win. The first two finished clear.

2619 MORPETH PRACTICE HORSEY MAIDEN STKS 1m 2f 42y (Tp)

7:30 (7:30) (Class 5) 3-Y-O **£4,528** (£1,347; £673; £336) **Stalls** High

Form RPR

63 **1** **Shraaoh (IRE)**[20] 2008 3-9-5 0 .... TedDurcan 5 97+
(Sir Michael Stoute) *sn trcking ldr: shkn up to ld over 1f out: pushed clr fr over 1f out: eased last 100yds: readily* **7/4**[2]

52-2 **2** 6 **Wave Reviews**[31] 1714 3-9-5 81 .... GrahamGibbons 4 85+
(William Haggas) *prom: effrt and pushed along over 2f out: chsd wnr over 1f out: sn one pce: eased whn hld ins fnl f* **6/4**[1]

00- **3** 1 3/4 **Great Thoughts (IRE)**[215] 7472 3-9-0 0 .... FrederikTylicki 6 74
(David Simcock) *s.i.s: hld up in tch: effrt and pushed along over 2f out: hdwy over 1f out: kpt on fnl f: no imp* **50/1**

4-2 **4** 1 1/2 **Exoteric**[22] 1970 3-9-5 0 .... JamesDoyle 1 76
(Charles Hills) *led at modest gallop: rdn and hdd over 2f out: wknd over 1f out* **7/2**[3]

0 **5** 5 **Askari**[14] 2175 3-9-5 0 .... JackMitchell 2 66
(Roger Varian) *trckd ldrs: rdn and hung lft over 2f out: wknd wl over 1f out* **16/1**

6 hd **Steely Rock** 3-9-5 0 .... JoeFanning 7 65
(Mark Johnston) *hld up: rdn and outpcd 4f out: no imp fr 2f out* **28/1**

4-4 **7** 3/4 **Sayedaati Saadati (IRE)**[32] 1662 3-9-5 0 .... DougieCostello 3 64
(David Simcock) *stdd in tch: rdn and outpcd over 2f out: btn over 1f out* **25/1**

2m 9.99s (-0.41) **Going Correction** -0.025s/f (Stan) **7** Ran SP% **113.7**
Speed ratings (Par 99): **100,95,93,92,88 88,87**
CSF £4.67 TOTE £2.80: £2.40, £1.10; EX 4.60 Trifecta £72.00.
Owner Al Shaqab Racing **Bred** Sunderland Holdings Inc **Trained** Newmarket, Suffolk

FOCUS
An interesting maiden, run in a very similar time to the preceding 60-70 handicap. The winner has progressed with each run and was impressive.

2620 SURGO CONSTRUCTION H'CAP 1m 5y (Tp)

8:05 (8:08) (Class 4) (0-85,85) 4-Y-O+ **£7,762** (£2,310; £865; £865) **Stalls** Centre

Form RPR

432- **1** **Firmament**[162] 8247 4-9-4 **85** .... ShelleyBirkett(3) 13 95+
(David O'Meara) *dwlt: hld up: smooth hdwy to ld over 1f out: hrd pressed fnl f: kpt on wl* **5/1**[1]

25-3 **2** shd **Hard To Handel**[16] 2121 4-9-4 **82** .... DanielTudhope 14 91+
(David O'Meara) *hld up: hdwy nr side of gp to press wnr over 1f out: edgd lft and ev ch ins fnl f: kpt on: jst hld* **5/1**[1]

1253 **3** 1 3/4 **Sands Chorus**[12] 2257 4-8-13 **77** .... TomEaves 2 82
(James Given) *taken early to post: cl up: rdn and ch over 1f out: kpt on same pce ins fnl f* **12/1**

3-30 **3** dht **Muhaafiz (IRE)**[15] 2163 4-8-12 **76** .... JamesDoyle 4 81
(David Brown) *led: rdn and hdd over 1f out: kpt on same pce ins fnl f* **6/1**[2]

133- **5** 1 1/2 **Zabeel Star (IRE)**[217] 5636 4-8-10 **77** .... JoeDoyle(3) 10 78
(Graeme McPherson) *hld up in tch: drvn and outpcd 2f out: rallied ins fnl f: kpt on* **33/1**

-604 **6** nk **Mukhayyam**[11] 2268 4-9-2 **85** .... RachelRichardson(5) 5 86
(Tim Easterby) *hld up in midfield: drvn and outpcd over 2f out: kpt on ins fnl f: nt pce to chal* **16/1**

2050 **7** nk **Eutropius (IRE)**[12] 2256 7-9-1 **79** .... JoeFanning 1 79+
(Alan Swinbank) *slowly away: hld up: effrt and pushed along over 2f out: kpt on fnl f: nrst fin* **16/1**

1126 **8** nse **Red Touch (USA)**[29] 1797 4-9-1 **82** .... AlistairRawlinson(3) 6 82
(Michael Appleby) *hld up in midfield: effrt over 2f out: edgd lft: no imp fr over 1f out* **14/1**

6-65 **9** 1 1/4 **Darrington**[20] 2017 4-9-3 **81** .... TonyHamilton 11 78
(Richard Fahey) *in tch: rdn over 2f out: wknd over 1f out* **8/1**[3]

-320 **10** 1 **One Pekan (IRE)**[98] 620 6-8-13 **84** .... DavidEgan(7) 8 78+
(Roger Varian) *missed break: hld up: hdwy on far side of gp over 2f out: no imp fr over 1f out* **12/1**

10-0 **11** 1 3/4 **Echo Of Lightning**[24] 1924 6-8-7 **76** ....(p) CallumShepherd(5) 9 66
(Brian Ellison) *chsd ldrs: rdn over 2f out: wknd over 1f out* **40/1**

/050 **12** 3 **Shouranour (IRE)**[9] 2331 6-8-11 **80** ....(p) JoshDoyle(5) 12 63
(Alan Brown) *hld up: rdn and outpcd over 2f out: n.d after* **28/1**

456- **13** 6 **Dream Walker (FR)**[209] 7598 7-8-8 **79** .... BenRobinson(7) 3 48
(Brian Ellison) *prom on far side of gp: outpcd and hung lft over 2f out: sn wknd* **20/1**

1m 37.97s (-0.63) **Going Correction** -0.10s/f (Stan) **13** Ran SP% **106.1**
Speed ratings (Par 105): **99,98,97,97,95 95,95,95,93,92 91,88,82**
WIN: £6.10 Firmament; PL: £1.70 Hard To Handel, £1.30 Sands Chorus, £2.30 Firmament; EXACTA: £27.40; CSF: £20.93; TC: £92.31, £50.30; TRIFECTA:£94.50, £86.30..
Owner Gallop Racing **Bred** Cheveley Park Stud Ltd **Trained** Upper Helmsley, N Yorks

■ Margaret's Mission was withdrawn. Price at time of withdrawal 5/1. Rule 4 applies to all bets - deduct 15p in the pound.

■ Stewards' Enquiry : Shelley Birkett two-day ban: used whip above permitted level (Jun 9-10)

FOCUS
David O'Meara had the first two in this ordinary handicap. Joint-favourites, they were draw 13 and 14 and came home down the centre of the track, but there appeared no bias with the next two home emerging from stalls 2 and 4. The race has been rated around the dead-heating thirds.

2621 CASTLE BUILDING SERVICES FILLIES' H'CAP 6f (Tp)

8:35 (8:35) (Class 4) (0-85,85) 4-Y-O+ **£7,762** (£2,310; £1,154; £577) **Stalls** Centre

Form RPR

1112 **1** **Baileys Mirage (FR)**[19] 2032 5-8-13 **77** ....(b) DavidAllan 9 90
(Chris Dwyer) *mde all: shkn up and qcknd over 1f out: kpt on wl fnl f: unchal* **11/2**[2]

-412 **2** 2 1/2 **Available (IRE)**[12] 2238 7-8-10 **74** ....(tp) JoeFanning 3 79
(John Mackie) *chsd ldr thrght: effrt and rdn over 1f out: kpt on same pce ins fnl f* **8/1**[3]

3-00 **3** 3 1/4 **Rural Celebration**[26] 1848 5-9-6 **84** .... DanielTudhope 4 79
(David O'Meara) *trckd ldrs: drvn along over 2f out: rallied: kpt on same pce ins fnl f* **28/1**

-250 **4** 3/4 **Childesplay**[20] 1990 5-9-7 **85** ....(p) GrahamLee 1 77
(Heather Main) *prom: rdn along 2f out: kpt on same pce fnl f* **10/1**

4143 **5** 1 1/4 **Pretty Bubbles**[5] 2469 7-9-2 **80** ....(v) FrederikTylicki 5 68
(J R Jenkins) *hld up in tch: effrt and hdwy over 1f out: kpt on fnl f: no imp* **11/1**

-006 **6** 1/2 **Gran Canaria Queen**[11] 2267 7-9-0 **83** .... RachelRichardson(5) 7 70
(Tim Easterby) *chsd ldrs: drvn and outpcd over 2f out: n.d after* **11/1**

630- **7** 3/4 **Savannah Beau**[259] 6248 4-9-3 **81** .... RobertWinston 6 65
(Marjorie Fife) *stdd s: hld up: rdn along wl over 1f out: sn no imp* **33/1**

1605 **8** hd **Three Gracez**[13] 2223 4-9-7 **85** .... SamJames 8 69
(Philip McBride) *hld up: pushed along and outpcd over 2f out: n.d after* **8/1**[3]

2/16 **9** 8 **Time Check (USA)**[20] 2016 4-9-4 **82** .... JamesDoyle 2 40
(Saeed bin Suroor) *hld up in tch: effrt and pushed along over 2f out: sn wknd: eased whn btn ins fnl f* **6/5**[1]

1m 10.91s (-1.59) **Going Correction** -0.10s/f (Stan) **9** Ran SP% **115.2**
Speed ratings (Par 102): **106,102,98,97,95 95,94,93,83**
CSF £48.62 CT £1130.30 TOTE £5.90: £1.90, £2.80, £6.10; EX 18.10 Trifecta £1064.30.
Owner G R Bailey Ltd (Baileys Horse Feeds) **Bred** Gr Baileys Ltd **Trained** Newmarket, Suffolk

FOCUS
A decent fillies' handicap. The pace held up and nothing got into it from the rear. The winner continues to progress.

2622 VISTAGE H'CAP 5f (Tp)
9:05 (9:05) (Class 5) (0-75,72) 3-Y-O+ **£5,175** (£1,540; £769; £384) **Stalls** Centre

Form RPR
51-1 **1** **Coto (IRE)**[9] 2334 4-9-3 **70** 6ex PaddyBradley[(7)] 5 79
(M J Tynan, Ire) *hld up: pushed along and hdwy over 1f out: hld on wl fnl f* **2/1**[1]

653 **2** *nk* **Orient Class**[36] 1559 5-9-4 **64** GrahamLee 8 72+
(Paul Midgley) *hld up in midfield: hdwy nr side of gp 2f out: ev ch fnl f: kpt on: jst hld* **6/1**[2]

4245 **3** *1* **Jaarih (IRE)**[26] 1874 4-9-12 **72** (p) PaulMulrennan 4 76
(Conor Dore) *in tch: hdwy far side of gp to ld over 1f out: rdn and hdd ins fnl f: kpt on same pce* **13/2**[3]

4341 **4** *3/4* **Windforpower (IRE)**[6] 2418 6-9-6 **66** 6ex (p) JoeFanning 1 67
(Tracy Waggott) *hld up on far side of gp: rdn over 2f out: hdwy over 1f out: kpt on fnl f* **12/1**

2-30 **5** *1/2* **Penny Royale**[16] 2120 4-9-7 **67** (b) DavidAllan 11 67
(Tim Easterby) *cl up: rdn and ev ch 2f out: kpt on same pce fnl f* **15/2**

540- **6** *1* **Innocently (IRE)**[149] 8389 5-9-7 **72** JoshDoyle[(5)] 3 68
(David O'Meara) *cl up: led briefly 2f out: rdn and outpcd fnl f* **16/1**

0016 **7** *1 1/2* **Coiste Bodhar (IRE)**[19] 2040 5-8-10 **63** NatalieHambling[(7)] 2 54
(Scott Dixon) *led to 2f out: rdn and wknd appr fnl f* **18/1**

0265 **8** *1/2* **Seamster**[32] 1668 9-9-12 **72** (bt) DanielTudhope 6 61
(David O'Meara) *chsd ldrs: drvn along over 2f out: wknd over 1f out* **16/1**

-325 **9** *1* **Noodles Blue Boy**[11] 2270 10-9-5 **72** (p) RobertDodsworth[(7)] 7 57
(Ollie Pears) *sn rdn along in rr: nvr able to chal* **20/1**

21-0 **10** *1* **Wilsons Ruby (IRE)**[13] 2200 3-8-13 **67** BenCurtis 10 46
(Brian Ellison) *dwlt: hld up nr side of gp: struggling over 2f out: sn btn* **8/1**

630- **11** *1* **Showbizzy**[227] 7167 3-8-11 **65** TonyHamilton 9 40
(Richard Fahey) *dwlt: hld up: struggling 1/2-way: sn btn* **25/1**

58.71s (-0.79) **Going Correction** -0.10s/f (Stan)
WFA 3 from 4yo+ 8lb **11** Ran SP% **117.2**
Speed ratings (Par 103): **102,101,99,98,97 96,93,93,91,89 88**
CSF £13.42 CT £66.87 TOTE £2.50: £1.10, £3.70, £3.20; EX 15.70 Trifecta £75.00.
Owner M J Tynan **Bred** Centaur Bloodstock Agency **Trained** Moyglass, Co Tipperary

FOCUS
A modest sprint handicap and straightforward form rated around the third.
T/Plt: £18.50 to a £1 stake. Pool of £78745.34 - 3091.02 winning tickets. T/Qpdt: £6.60 to a £1 stake. Pool of £6661.80 - 745.80 winning tickets. **Richard Young**

2410 SANDOWN (R-H)
Thursday, May 26

OFFICIAL GOING: Good to firm (good in places on round course; rnd 7.0, str 7.2)
Wind: Nil Weather: Fine, warm

2623 MARBANK CONSTRUCTION H'CAP (JOCKEY CLUB GRASSROOTS FLAT MIDDLE DISTANCE SERIES QUALIFIER) 1m 2f 7y
6:00 (6:01) (Class 5) (0-75,75) 4-Y-O+ **£3,234** (£962; £481; £240) **Stalls** Low

Form RPR
-011 **1** **Inniscastle Lad**[17] 2085 4-9-7 **75** (b) SilvestreDeSousa 1 83
(Ed Dunlop) *mde all: rdn for home 3f out: hrd pressed fr 2f out: jnd fnl f: fnd ex and battled on strly* **9/2**[1]

-110 **2** *1/2* **Bridge Of Sighs**[14] 2174 4-9-2 **70** FrankieDettori 9 77
(Martin Smith) *stdd s: hld up in last pair: prog 3f out: squeezed through to cl over 1f out: tk 2nd fnl f and upsides wnr: kpt on but nt qckn last 100yds* **6/1**[3]

00-3 **3** *1* **Choral Festival**[13] 2205 10-8-13 **67** WilliamCarson 6 73
(John Bridger) *hld up in last trio: nt clr run over 2f out tl swtchd lft over 1f out: r.o wl fnl f to take 3rd nr fin* **12/1**

5-31 **4** *3/4* **Speculator**[28] 1810 4-9-0 **68** ShaneKelly 11 72
(David Menuisier) *trckd ldng trio: rdn to press wnr jst over 2f out: upsides 1f out: sn lost 2nd and kpt on one pce: lost 3rd nr fin* **11/2**[2]

0345 **5** *2* **Top Diktat**[31] 1716 8-9-5 **73** RyanMoore 10 73
(Gary Moore) *trckd ldrs in 5th: lost pl and rdn over 2f out: drvn and kpt on fr over 1f out to dispute 4th briefly ins fnl f: no ch w ldrs* **13/2**

U005 **6** *1 3/4* **Isis Blue**[14] 2174 6-9-2 **70** (p) DavidProbert 2 66
(Rod Millman) *hld up in midfield: rdn wl over 2f out: n.m.r wl over 1f out: kpt on one pce and n.d* **8/1**

0-56 **7** *1 1/4* **Prince Of Paris**[7] 2399 4-9-5 **73** (tp) PatDobbs 5 67
(Roger Ingram) *trckd ldng pair: rdn and nt qckn on inner over 2f out: n.m.r after: wknd jst over 1f out* **12/1**

1240 **8** *3 1/2* **Saint Honore**[45] 1390 4-9-2 **70** JFEgan 7 57
(Pat Phelan) *in tch in midfield on outer: rdn over 3f out: kpt on u.p and stl in tch over 1f out: wknd ins fnl f: eased* **25/1**

230- **9** *1/2* **Sixties Love**[176] 8081 5-9-5 **73** PatSmullen 8 59
(Simon Dow) *awkward s: hld up in last pair: rdn and prog on outer over 2f out: disp 4th u.p 1f out but no ch: wknd* **14/1**

3464 **10** *2* **Karam Albaari (IRE)**[15] 2151 8-9-4 **72** (v[1]) AdamKirby 3 54
(J R Jenkins) *dwlt: in tch in midfield: pushed along 3f out: nt clr run on inner 2f out: no prog over 1f out: wknd* **16/1**

0-00 **11** *1* **Cornelious (IRE)**[14] 2174 4-9-2 **70** (p) FMBerry 4 50
(Clifford Lines) *chsd wnr: rdn over 3f out: lost 2nd jst over 2f out: wknd qckly over 1f out* **8/1**

2m 10.46s (-0.04) **Going Correction** 0.0s/f (Good) **11** Ran SP% **115.2**
Speed ratings (Par 103): **100,99,98,98,96 95,94,91,91,89 88**
CSF £30.17 CT £302.35 TOTE £4.60: £1.70, £2.30, £4.30; EX 19.80 Trifecta £305.40.
Owner E A L Dunlop **Bred** G Doyle & Lord Margadale **Trained** Newmarket, Suffolk
■ Stewards' Enquiry : Silvestre De Sousa four-day ban: used whip above permitted level (Jun 9-12)

FOCUS
The round course rail was on its innermost line and all race distances were as advertised. The ground was sightly quicker up the straight than on the Round course, a view backed up by David Probert who finished sixth in the opener, and GoingStick readings were as follows: Round 7.0; Straight 7.2. A modest handicap, run at a steady gallop early, and the winner made all under a well-judged ride.

2624 BETVICTOR MILLION POUND GOAL NATIONAL STKS (LISTED RACE) 5f 6y
6:35 (6:36) (Class 1) 2-Y-O
£14,744 (£5,590; £2,797; £1,393; £699; £351) **Stalls** Low

Form RPR
12 **1** **Global Applause**[12] 2240 2-9-0 0 RyanMoore 2 103
(Ed Dunlop) *racd against rail: mde virtually all: gng easily 2f out: stretched ahd over 1f out: drvn and edgd lft fnl f: styd on wl* **9/2**[3]

11 **2** *1 1/4* **Mehmas (IRE)**[12] 2240 2-9-0 0 FrankieDettori 6 99+
(Richard Hannon) *t.k.h: hld up in last pair: waiting for a gap 2f out: swtchd lft over 1f out: prog to take 2nd ins fnl f: r.o but nvr able to chal* **13/8**[1]

1 **3** *2* **Bohemian Flame (IRE)**[14] 2180 2-9-0 0 DavidProbert 1 91
(Andrew Balding) *s.i.s: chsd ldrs and racd against rail: shkn up 2f out: outpcd over 1f out: kpt on to take 3rd last 100yds: n.d* **25/1**

61 **4** *1 1/4* **Jule In The Crown**[10] 2310 2-8-9 0 SilvestreDeSousa 4 82
(Mick Channon) *taken steadily to post: pressed wnr: upsides over 3f out to over 1f out: hung lft u.p after: wknd and lost pl ins fnl f* **14/1**

1 **5** *5* **Chupalla**[61] 1087 2-8-9 0 WilliamBuick 5 64+
(Mark Johnston) *chsd ldng pair: pushed along after 2f: effrt to chal 2f out: sn btn: wknd fnl f* **15/8**[2]

421 **6** *1 1/2* **Copper Knight (IRE)**[22] 1965 2-9-0 0 PatSmullen 7 63+
(Hugo Palmer) *swvd lft s: t.k.h: hld up in last pair: shkn up 2f out: racd awkwardly and wknd over 1f out* **10/1**

1m 1.17s (-0.43) **Going Correction** 0.0s/f (Good) **6** Ran SP% **110.7**
Speed ratings (Par 101): **103,101,97,95,87 85**
CSF £11.93 TOTE £5.70: £3.00, £1.10; EX 13.70 Trifecta £95.40.
Owner Dr Johnny Hon **Bred** R F And S D Knipe **Trained** Newmarket, Suffolk

FOCUS
Race distance as advertised. A strong edition of a race that often has a bearing on the Royal meeting and the right two came to the fore, albeit they finished in a different order to when they met over 6f at Newbury last time. They didn't go a mad gallop and the winner was well placed on what may have been the fastest strip of ground under the rail. Global Applause confirmed his debut promise and a good effort from Mehmas too.

2625 BETVICTOR HENRY II STKS (GROUP 3) 2m 78y
7:05 (7:05) (Class 1) 4-Y-O+ **£36,861** (£13,975; £6,994; £3,484) **Stalls** Centre

Form RPR
414- **1** **Pallasator**[222] 7277 7-9-6 110 OisinMurphy 2 115
(Sir Mark Prescott Bt) *taken down early: hld up in 3rd: pushed along and prog to go 2nd 2f out: hrd rdn and clsd to ld 1f out: styd on wl and sn in command* **11/2**[3]

-444 **2** *2 1/4* **Suegioo (FR)**[13] 2221 7-9-2 108 (p) PaulHanagan 4 108
(Richard Fahey) *sn in last: chivvied along fr 5f out: no rspnse tl drvn and styd on fr over 1f out to take 2nd last 100yds: no threat to wnr* **10/1**

212- **3** *1 1/2* **Max Dynamite (FR)**[205] 7697 6-9-2 117 RyanMoore 1 106
(W P Mullins, Ire) *trckd ldr: pushed into ld over 2f out: pushed along more firmly and hdd 1f out: sn btn and lost 2nd last 100yds* **4/7**[1]

11-5 **4** *4* **Burmese**[29] 1772 4-9-0 108 WilliamBuick 3 101
(Marcus Tregoning) *led at stdy pce tl after 1/2-way: urged along over 3f out: hdd over 2f out: steadily fdd* **9/2**[2]

3m 43.12s (4.42) **Going Correction** 0.0s/f (Good)
WFA 4 from 6yo+ 2lb **4** Ran SP% **106.3**
Speed ratings (Par 113): **88,86,86,84**
CSF £39.55 TOTE £5.80; EX 22.60 Trifecta £42.80.
Owner Qatar Racing Limited **Bred** Newsells Park Stud **Trained** Newmarket, Suffolk

FOCUS
Race distance as advertised. A farce of a race with nothing wanting to lead and the runners dawdling for much of the first 1m4f of the contest. The form isn't worth much, yet it was a really encouraging reappearance from the penalised winner.

2626 BETVICTOR BRIGADIER GERARD STKS (GROUP 3) 1m 2f 7y
7:40 (7:44) (Class 1) 4-Y-O+
£36,861 (£13,975; £6,994; £3,484; £1,748; £877) **Stalls** Low

Form RPR
410- **1** **Time Test**[208] 7654 4-9-5 118 RyanMoore 7 124
(Roger Charlton) *hld up in last: prog over 2f out: clsd on ldng pair jst over 1f out: drvn to ld narrowly last 150yds: r.o wl and a jst holding runner-up* **3/1**[2]

3-22 **2** *nk* **Western Hymn**[21] 1973 5-9-0 115 FrankieDettori 1 118
(John Gosden) *dismntd and led to s: trckd ldng pair: wnt 2nd 2f out: rdn to ld jst over 1f out: hdd last 150yds: fought on wl but jst hld* **7/2**[3]

251- **3** *4 1/2* **Scottish (IRE)**[250] 6516 4-9-0 113 WilliamBuick 4 109
(Charlie Appleby) *led 1f: pressed ldr: rdn to ld again over 2f out: hdd jst over 1f out: readily lft bhd by ldng pair after* **7/1**

300- **4** *5* **Not So Sleepy**[207] 7668 4-9-0 104 (t) JimCrowley 5 99
(Hughie Morrison) *taken down early: hld up in last trio: pushed along and wl outpcd in last 2f out: shkn up jst over 1f out: tk modest 4th nr fin* **66/1**

00-0 **5** *3/4* **Niceofyoutotellme**[26] 1861 7-9-0 101 FMBerry 6 98
(Ralph Beckett) *t.k.h: hld up in last trio: rdn wl over 2f out: no prog and wknd over 1f out* **33/1**

11-0 **6** *4* **Intilaaq (USA)**[61] 1106 4-9-0 117 PaulHanagan 2 90
(Roger Varian) *led after 1f and set gd pce: rdn and hdd over 2f out: wknd qckly over 1f out* **5/4**[1]

6205 **7** *4 1/2* **Fire Fighting (IRE)**[13] 2222 5-9-0 106 (b) AdamKirby 3 81
(Mark Johnston) *chsd ldng trio: rdn 3f out: sn lost pl: wknd qckly wl over 1f out* **33/1**

2m 6.18s (-4.32) **Going Correction** 0.0s/f (Good) **7** Ran SP% **111.5**
Speed ratings (Par 113): **117,116,113,109,108 105,101**
CSF £13.08 TOTE £3.90: £1.60, £2.60; EX 11.80 Trifecta £43.30.
Owner K Abdullah **Bred** Juddmonte Farms Ltd **Trained** Beckhampton, Wilts

FOCUS
Race distance as advertised. A strong running of this, with two potential top-notchers heading up the betting and although the favourite disappointed, the form looks rock-solid with the penalised scorer beating last year's winner. They went overly fast early before the pace steadied. The winner recorded a personal best.

2627 HERON STKS (LISTED RACE) 1m 14y
8:15 (8:15) (Class 1) 3-Y-O **£20,982** (£7,955; £3,981; £1,983; £995) **Stalls** Low

Form RPR

45-6 **1** **Zonderland**[26] 1864 3-9-0 107 .... AdamKirby 4 108
(Clive Cox) *led 1f: trckd ldr: shkn up to chal 2f out: led over 1f out and sn rdn clr: styd on wl* **11/4**[2]

12-2 **2** 2¼ **Atlantic Sun**[20] 1991 3-9-0 97 .... SeanLevey 2 103
(Richard Hannon) *t.k.h: hld up bhd ldng pair: rdn 2f out: sltly awkward and nt qckn over 1f out: styd on to take 2nd ins fnl f: no imp on wnr* **7/1**

0-1 **3** ½ **Forge**[33] 1622 3-9-0 95 .... PatSmullen 6 101
(Sir Michael Stoute) *hld up bhd ldng pair: rdn 2f out: nt qckn over 1f out: disp 2nd ins fnl f: styd on* **11/8**[1]

1- **4** 1¾ **Royal Artillery (USA)**[216] 7423 3-9-0 0 ....(t) RyanMoore 5 97
(John Gosden) *hld up in last and sn detached: urged along over 3f out: rdn and rn green fr over 2f out: no prog tl styd on fnl f to take 4th nr fin* **7/2**[3]

20-0 **5** ½ **Cymric (USA)**[26] 1866 3-9-0 110 .... WilliamBuick 1 96
(John Gosden) *led after 1f: rdn and tried to go for home 2f out: hdd over 1f out: tightened up briefly and fdd ins fnl f* **12/1**

1m 42.53s (-0.77) **Going Correction** 0.0s/f (Good) **5** Ran SP% **111.2**
Speed ratings (Par 107): **103,100,100,98,98**
CSF £20.61 TOTE £3.30: £1.60, £3.30; EX 15.60 Trifecta £36.20.
Owner Cheveley Park Stud **Bred** Cheveley Park Stud Ltd **Trained** Lambourn, Berks
■ Stewards' Enquiry : Adam Kirby two-day ban: used whip in incorrect place (Jun 9-10)

FOCUS
Race distance as advertised. An interesting Listed event and every reason to believe this is good form for the level, even if they didn't go an overly fast gallop. The winner has been rated to his 2000 Guineas form.

2628 MET TRADERS H'CAP 1m 14y
8:45 (8:45) (Class 3) (0-95,95) 4-Y-O+
£7,470 (£2,236; £1,118; £559; £279; £140) **Stalls** Low

Form RPR

3-40 **1** **Chevallier**[29] 1775 4-8-2 81 oh1 .... JordanVaughan[(5)] 6 91
(K R Burke) *wl in tch: prog on outer over 2f out: rdn to dispute ld over 1f out: narrow ld ins fnl f: won on the nod* **12/1**

21/1 **2** shd **Jailawi (IRE)**[19] 2033 5-9-3 94 .... ThomasBrown[(3)] 12 103
(Ismail Mohammed) *wl in tch: prog on outer over 2f out: disp ld over 1f out: drvn and narrowly hdd ins fnl f: kpt on wl: jst pipped* **9/2**[2]

1-50 **3** 2¾ **Secret Art (IRE)**[13] 2216 6-9-4 92 .... WilliamBuick 4 95
(William Knight) *hld up off the pce in 10th: rdn and prog over 2f out: styd on to take 3rd fnl f: no imp on ldng pair* **10/1**

01/ **4** ½ **Heatstroke (IRE)**[582] 7371 4-8-13 87 .... JamieSpencer 9 89+
(Charles Hills) *stdd s: hld up in last pair and a long way off the pce: prog over 2f out: cajoled along and tried to cl over 1f out: nvr cl enough to threaten* **8/1**

2-40 **5** ½ **Highland Colori (IRE)**[26] 1856 8-9-7 95 ....(v[1]) DavidProbert 14 96
(Andrew Balding) *racd wd early: hld up in 9th and off the pce: prog and rdn on outer 2f out: kpt on fnl f: nvr gng pce to chal* **20/1**

326- **6** 3 **Postbag**[253] 6439 4-8-10 84 .... FergusSweeney 3 78
(Henry Candy) *trckd ldrs: rdn 2f out: drvn to dispute 3rd jst over 1f out: wknd ins fnl f* **12/1**

0-41 **7** ½ **Hulcolt (IRE)**[16] 2121 5-8-8 82 .... SilvestreDeSousa 8 75
(Ivan Furtado) *racd wd early: chsd ldr after 2f tl after 3f: styd prom tl rdn and lost pl fr 2f out: looked like dropping out but plugged on fnl f* **5/1**[3]

00-0 **8** nk **Directorship**[12] 2246 10-9-5 93 .... LiamKeniry 10 85
(Patrick Chamings) *hld up in 11th and off the pce: pushed along on inner 3f out: no prog tl shkn up and styd on fnl f: nvr involved* **25/1**

00-0 **9** 4 **Smaih (GER)**[12] 2247 4-8-13 87 .... WilliamCarson 11 70
(Jamie Osborne) *stdd s: hld up in last and a long way off the pce: swtchd lft wl over 1f out: sn rdn: modest late hdwy: nvr involved* **50/1**

001- **10** 1¾ **Ifwecan**[228] 7146 5-9-1 89 .... JimCrowley 7 68
(Martin Smith) *trckd ldr 2f and again over 2f out: rdn to chal wl over 1f out: sn wknd qckly* **25/1**

0000 **11** 1½ **El Tren (IRE)**[26] 1861 5-9-2 90 ....(v[1]) AdamBeschizza 5 65
(Michael Attwater) *a wl in rr: rdn and no prog over 2f out* **100/1**

6 **12** nk **Charlie Bear**[30] 1752 4-9-0 88 .... PatDobbs 13 63
(Jamie Osborne) *racd wd early: chsd ldr after 3f to over 2f out: sn wknd* **25/1**

0324 **13** 9 **Unforgiving Minute**[19] 2033 5-9-4 92 .... AdamKirby 1 46
(Gary Moore) *trckd ldrs: shkn up 3f out: wknd over 2f out: t.o* **14/1**

506- **14** 1 **Jacob Black**[260] 6205 5-9-6 94 .... FrankieDettori 2 67
(Keith Dalgleish) *led at gd pce: hdd & wknd rapidly over 1f out: eased and t.o* **3/1**[1]

1m 41.52s (-1.78) **Going Correction** 0.0s/f (Good) **14** Ran SP% **121.4**
Speed ratings (Par 107): **108,107,105,104,104 101,100,100,96,94 93,92,83,82**
CSF £61.32 CT £593.32 TOTE £13.50: £4.00, £1.90, £3.30; EX 69.60 Trifecta £818.70.
Owner Tim Dykes **Bred** Kincorth Investments Inc **Trained** Middleham Moor, N Yorks

FOCUS
Race distance as advertised. No hanging around here and the race set up for those coming from off the pace. The winner recorded a personal best.
T/Plt: £311.50 to a £1 stake. Pool of £82609.58 - 193.54 winning tickets. T/Qpdt: £101.00 to a £1 Pool of £5545.79 - 40.63 winning tickets. **Jonathan Neesom**

2629 - 2632a (Foreign Racing) - See Raceform Interactive

BADEN-BADEN (L-H)
Thursday, May 26

OFFICIAL GOING: Turf: good

2633a BADENER MEILE (GROUP 2) (3YO+) (TURF) 1m
4:10 (12:00) 3-Y-O+ **£29,411** (£7,261; £7,261; £2,941; £1,838)

RPR

1 **Royal Solitaire (IRE)**[25] 1907 4-8-13 0 .... DanielePorcu 2 105
(P Schiergen, Germany) *prom on inner: angled out and rdn to chal appr st: led ent fnl f: strly pressed but kpt on wl: drvn out* **48/10**[3]

2 ½ **Nymeria (GER)**[28] 1822 4-8-13 0 .... AndreasSuborics 7 104+
(Waldemar Hickst, Germany) *hld up: rdn into st: swtchd out and r.o fnl f: up to dead-heat for 2nd post but nt able to chal: nrst fin* **22/5**[2]

2 dht **Rosebay (GER)**[25] 5-8-13 0 .... AdriedeVries 9 104
(Markus Klug, Germany) *in tch: rdn 2f out: str chal fnl f: kpt on but jst hld: jnd for 2nd post* **71/10**

4 ½ **Felician (GER)**[18] 2074 8-9-2 0 .... AndreasHelfenbein 3 106+
(Ferdinand J Leve, Germany) *hld up in midfield: fanned out and rdn into st: r.o fnl f but nt quite pce to chal* **145/10**

5 3 **Mc Queen (FR)**[21] 4-9-2 0 .... StephenHellyn 4 99
(Yasmin Almenrader, Germany) *stdd and sn midfield: rdn into st: no ex and fdd fnl f* **36/5**

6 1 **Drummer (GER)**[18] 2074 4-9-2 0 .... DennisSchiergen 6 97
(P Schiergen, Germany) *sn midfield on inner: rdn into st: no ex and fdd fnl f* **141/10**

7 ¾ **Wildpark (GER)**[18] 2074 5-9-2 0 ....(b) FilipMinarik 1 95
(Melanie Sauer, Germany) *led: rdn into st: hdd ent fnl f: no ex and btn: wknd: eased towards fin* **13/10**[1]

8 10 **Quenby (USA)**[25] 4-8-13 0 .... EduardoPedroza 8 69
(A Wohler, Germany) *hld up: a in rr: fanned wd and rdn into st: sn lost tch and btn: eased* **132/10**

9 3¾ **Molly Le Clou (GER)**[46] 1376 4-9-2 0 ....(b) AlexanderPietsch 5 63
(J Hirschberger, Germany) *trckd ldr on outer: rdn bef st: sn btn: wknd and dropped to last: eased* **165/10**

1m 38.52s (-0.59) **9** Ran SP% **129.6**
WIN (incl. 10 euro stake) 58; PLACES 20, 17, 25; SF 97 (with Nymeria), 246 (with Rosebay).
Owner Gestut Ammerland **Bred** Janus Bloodstock Inc & Stilvi Compania Financiera **Trained** Germany

2366 BATH (L-H)
Friday, May 27

OFFICIAL GOING: Good to firm (firm in places)
Wind: light breeze across Weather: sunny

2634 M J CHURCH H'CAP 1m 5f 22y
2:00 (2:00) (Class 6) (0-60,60) 4-Y-O+ **£2,716** (£808; £404; £202) **Stalls** High

Form RPR

431U **1** **Dynamo (IRE)**[10] 2326 5-9-0 53 ....(t) ShaneKelly 10 63+
(Richard Hughes) *trckd ldr: swtchd rt 3f out: rdn to ld over 1f out: styd on wl: readily* **5/2**[1]

-156 **2** 1¾ **Captain George (IRE)**[9] 2370 5-9-3 56 ....(v) CharlesBishop 1 61
(Michael Blake) *mid-div: rdn and hdwy 2f out: chsd wnr ent fnl f: styd on but a being hld* **8/1**[3]

0 **3** 1¼ **Ballyfarsoon (IRE)**[69] 1004 5-8-12 51 ....(v) FMBerry 12 54
(Ian Williams) *trckd ldrs: rdn to ld over 2f out: hdd over 1f out: kpt on same pce* **8/1**[3]

5301 **4** ½ **Stynes (IRE)**[9] 2370 6-9-0 53 6ex ....(t) AdamKirby 3 56
(Ali Stronge) *mid-div: rdn and stdy hdwy fr over 2f out: wnt 4th ent fnl f: styd on* **9/2**[2]

20- **5** 2 **Surprise Us**[24] 8094 9-8-6 48 ow1 ....(p) PhilipPrince[(3)] 13 48
(Mark Gillard) *led: rdn 3f out: sn hdd: kpt on tl no ex fnl 120yds* **33/1**

06-0 **6** nk **Caerleon Kate**[31] 1748 4-8-7 46 oh1 ....(b[1]) KieranO'Neill 6 45
(Rod Millman) *trckd ldrs: rdn whn sltly hmpd 3f out: one pce fnl 2f* **66/1**

50-3 **7** hd **Petrify**[9] 2370 6-8-8 47 ....(t) JimmyQuinn 11 46
(Bernard Llewellyn) *s.i.s: in last pair: rdn and stdy prog fr over 2f out: styd on same pce fnl f* **8/1**[3]

5420 **8** 2 **Delagoa Bay (IRE)**[17] 2131 8-8-5 51 ow3 .... BenSanderson[(7)] 7 47
(Sylvester Kirk) *towards rr: rdn wl over 2f out: sme minor prog fnl f: nvr any danger* **25/1**

10-4 **9** 2¾ **Ragdollianna**[16] 2149 12-9-1 54 .... JFEgan 9 46
(Mark Hoad) *mid-div: rdn over 2f out: nvr threatened: fdd fnl 120yds* **16/1**

300- **10** shd **Lucky Diva**[248] 6630 9-8-9 55 ....(v) PatrickVaughan[(7)] 8 47
(Bill Turner) *slowly away: bhd: rdn and sme prog 2f out: wknd fnl f* **18/1**

-045 **11** shd **Rosie Royale (IRE)**[14] 2210 4-9-5 58 .... OisinMurphy 4 50
(Roger Teal) *a towards rr* **10/1**

60 **12** 5 **Arthur's Queen (FR)**[17] 2131 5-8-10 56 .... MeganNicholls[(7)] 5 41
(Carroll Gray) *mid-div tl 5f out: sn bhd* **20/1**

64- **13** 7 **Sailor Malan**[170] 8162 4-9-7 60 .... LukeMorris 2 35
(Gay Kelleway) *trckd ldrs: rdn over 3f out: wknd 2f out: eased fnl f* **14/1**

40-0 **14** 4 **Prince Of Cardamom (IRE)**[14] 2205 4-9-2 55 ....(p) DarrylHolland 14 25
(Jonathan Geake) *racd keenly: trckd ldrs: rdn over 3f out: wknd over 1f out: eased fnl f* **40/1**

2m 52.22s (0.22) **Going Correction** -0.025s/f (Good) **14** Ran SP% **122.5**
Speed ratings (Par 101): **98,96,96,95,94 94,94,93,91,91 91,88,83,81**
CSF £21.74 CT £146.86 TOTE £3.00: £1.20, £3.50, £3.20; EX 28.70 Trifecta £171.00.
Owner Foxtrot NH Racing Partnership X **Bred** Colm McEvoy **Trained** Upper Lambourn, Berkshire
■ Stewards' Enquiry : Shane Kelly caution; careless riding

FOCUS
The ground continued to dry out and was now good to firm, firm in places. Rail out around the bottom bend to the 3f marker, adding 10yds to race distances over 1m and beyond, including the opener. A moderate staying handicap to start. Fran Berry said it was "good, fast ground", while Shane Kelly described it as "quick".

2635 SIMONSTONE H'CAP 1m 5y
2:30 (2:30) (Class 6) (0-65,65) 4-Y-O+ **£2,716** (£808; £404; £202) **Stalls** Low

Form RPR

-044 **1** **Marcano (IRE)**[15] 2187 4-9-6 64 ....(t[1]) FrederikTylicki 8 76
(Rod Millman) *mid-div: gd hdwy over 2f out: led wl over 1f out: sn hrd pressed: rdn and edgd lft jst ins fnl f: kpt on wl to assert nring fin* **7/2**[2]

-015 **2** ¾ **Saint Helena (IRE)**[9] 2367 8-9-3 64 ....(b) PhilipPrince[(3)] 9 74
(Mark Gillard) *slowly away: bhd: rdn and hdwy fr over 2f out: str chal fr over 1f out: ev ch fnl f: no ex cl home* **8/1**

3024 **3** 2 **Lord Of The Storm**[18] 2085 8-9-5 63 .... LukeMorris 1 68
(Michael Attwater) *trckd ldrs: rdn for str chal fr 2f out: no ex ins fnl f* **15/2**

0-40 **4** 1¼ **Wahaab (IRE)**[113] 442 5-8-6 57 .... NicolaCurrie[(7)] 4 59
(Richard Hughes) *mid-div: hdwy 2f out: rdn ent fnl f: styd on but nt pce to chal* **12/1**

-523 **5** 7 **Knight Of The Air**[15] 2187 4-9-5 63 .... GeorgeBaker 5 49
(Mick Channon) *in tch: hdwy to chal 2f out: sn rdn and hld: drifted lft and fdd fnl f* **11/4**[1]

63-0 **6** 2 **Super Icon**[15] 2187 4-9-2 60 .... MartinDwyer 6 41
(Malcolm Saunders) *mid-div: rdn over 3f out: hdwy over 2f out: wknd over 1f out* **33/1**

-030 **7** 1½ **Nubar Boy**[16] 2153 9-9-5 **63**....(be) JFEgan 3 40
(Daniel Mark Loughnane) *disp ld tl wl over 1f out: sn wknd* **16/1**

6000 **8** ¾ **Wink Oliver**[32] 1700 4-9-7 **65**....(p) AdamKirby 7 40
(David Dennis) *trckd ldrs: rdn over 2f out: wknd over 1f out* **25/1**

050- **9** ¾ **Whistler Mountain**[220] 7368 4-9-2 **60**....(t[1]) OisinMurphy 10 34
(Brian Barr) *a towards rr* **25/1**

401 **10** 1 **Believe It (IRE)**[93] 696 4-9-3 **61**....(t) ShaneKelly 2 32
(Richard Hughes) *disp ld tl wl over 1f out: sn wknd* **9/2**[3]

500- **11** 25 **Rubheira**[203] 7735 4-8-7 **51** oh6....(b[1]) JimmyQuinn 11
(Paul Burgoyne) *racd keenly: a towards rr* **66/1**

0450 **12** 50 **Bailiwick**[60] 1120 5-9-2 **60**.... DarryllHolland 12
(Karen George) *hld up towards rr: appeared to lose action and eased fr over 2f out* **16/1**

1m 40.11s (-0.69) **Going Correction** -0.025s/f (Good) **12** Ran SP% **121.5**
Speed ratings (Par 101): **102,101,99,98,91 89,87,86,86,85 60,10**
CSF £31.54 CT £207.21 TOTE £4.70: £2.10, £2.30, £3.10; EX 33.50 Trifecta £273.80.
Owner The Links Partnership **Bred** David Barry **Trained** Kentisbeare, Devon

FOCUS
Rail movement added 10yds to race distance. A moderate handicap, but a fair pace thanks to a disputed lead.

2636 TARMAC FILLIES' H'CAP — 1m 5y
3:00 (3:02) (Class 5) (0-75,75) 4-Y-O+ **£3,234** (£962; £481; £240) **Stalls** Low

Form RPR

1142 **1** **Esteemable**[16] 2154 4-9-3 **74**.... DanielMuscutt(3) 2 83+
(James Fanshawe) *trckd ldrs: chal 2f out: led over 1f out: rdn clr fnl f: r.o wl* **11/4**[1]

63-3 **2** 2¼ **Hala Madrid**[25] 1932 4-9-6 **74**.... OisinMurphy 3 78
(Andrew Balding) *led: rdn and hdd over 1f out: kpt on but nt pce of wnr fnl f* **3/1**[2]

5356 **3** hd **Stosur (IRE)**[71] 967 5-9-7 **75**....(p) LukeMorris 6 79
(Gay Kelleway) *trckd ldr: rdn and ev ch 2f out: kpt on same pce fnl f* **7/2**[3]

-450 **4** 1 **Miss Inga Sock (IRE)**[9] 2379 4-8-9 **63**.... CharlesBishop 4 64
(Eve Johnson Houghton) *trckd ldrs: rdn to chal 2f out: kpt on same pce fnl f* **8/1**

10-6 **5** 4½ **Welsh Gem**[26] 1898 4-9-6 **74**.... AdamKirby 1 65
(Clive Cox) *hld up in cl 5th: rdn over 3f out: nvr threatened: fdd fnl f* **3/1**[2]

1m 40.66s (-0.14) **Going Correction** -0.025s/f (Good) **5** Ran SP% **110.0**
Speed ratings (Par 100): **99,96,96,95,91**
CSF £11.19 TOTE £2.90: £1.40, £2.20; EX 9.30 Trifecta £37.10.
Owner Mrs C R Philipson **Bred** Mrs M L Parry & P M Steele-Mortimer **Trained** Newmarket, Suffolk

FOCUS
Rail movement added 10yds to race distance. An ordinary little fillies' handicap and, with the pace a modest one, the time was 0.55sec slower than the preceding 0-65. The winner continues on the upgrade.

2637 SANCTUS LTD/BRITISH STALLION STUDS EBF NOVICE FILLIES' STKS (PLUS 10 RACE) — 5f 11y
3:30 (3:33) (Class 4) 2-Y-O **£4,528** (£1,347; £673; £336) **Stalls** Centre

Form RPR

2 **1** **Barroche (IRE)**[11] 2310 2-9-0 0.... AdamKirby 12 87+
(Clive Cox) *mde all: rdn clr over 1f out: r.o wl* **5/2**[1]

2 3¾ **Paco's Angel** 2-9-0 0.... ShaneKelly 9 74
(Richard Hughes) *in tch: hdwy 2f out: rdn to chse wnr jst over 1f out: kpt on nicely but nt pce to get on terms* **40/1**

4 **3** nk **Speed Freak**[11] 2310 2-9-0 0.... OisinMurphy 10 72
(Ralph Beckett) *trckd ldrs: rdn to chse wnr 2f out tl jst over 1f out: kpt on same pce* **3/1**[3]

4 1 **Giennah (IRE)** 2-9-0 0.... JimmyFortune 2 69+
(Brian Meehan) *towards rr: swtchd rt and drvn wl over 1f out: r.o wl fnl f: snatched 4th fnl strides* **20/1**

423 **5** shd **Tiggaliscious (IRE)**[11] 2310 2-9-0 0.... SeanLevey 4 68
(Richard Hannon) *mid-div: hdwy 2f out: sn rdn: kpt on but nt pce to get involved* **6/1**

6 1¼ **Star Catch** 2-9-0 0.... DarryllHolland 3 64+
(Charles Hills) *in tch: rdn 2f out: drifted lft fnl f: kpt on same pce* **11/4**[2]

44 **7** 1 **Primrose Place**[21] 2007 2-9-0 0.... KieranO'Neill 6 60
(Richard Hannon) *chsd ldrs: rdn over 2f out: hung rt over 1f out: wknd ins fnl f* **20/1**

61 **8** nk **Erica Bing**[16] 2147 2-9-3 0.... SamHitchcott 13 62
(Jo Hughes) *prom: rdn over 2f out: hld over 1f out: fdd ins fnl f* **33/1**

9 1¾ **Zambezi Queen (IRE)** 2-9-0 0.... LukeMorris 8 53
(Paul Cole) *outpcd early: a towards rr* **10/1**

10 2¼ **Nuptials (USA)** 2-9-0 0.... CharlesBishop 5 45
(Eve Johnson Houghton) *outpcd early: a towards rr* **66/1**

11 2½ **Seminole Dream (IRE)** 2-9-0 0.... JimmyQuinn 1 36
(Philip Kirby) *chsd ldrs tl wknd over 2f out* **66/1**

12 ½ **Pavela (IRE)** 2-9-0 0.... JFEgan 11 34
(Mick Channon) *sn outpcd: a towards rr* **33/1**

1m 1.14s (-1.36) **Going Correction** -0.375s/f (Firm) **12** Ran SP% **124.4**
Speed ratings (Par 92): **95,89,88,86,86 84,83,82,79,76 72,71**
CSF £119.03 TOTE £3.30: £1.20, £11.50, £1.60; EX 116.30 Trifecta £947.70.
Owner Wood Hall Stud Limited **Bred** T Kenny & P Byrne **Trained** Lambourn, Berks
■ Radar Love was withdrawn. Price at time of withdrawal 80-1. Rule 4 does not apply.

FOCUS
Quite an interesting novice fillies' event and the form should work out.

2638 BRISTOL AIRPORT H'CAP — 1m 3f 144y
4:00 (4:01) (Class 4) (0-85,83) 3-Y-O **£5,822** (£1,732; £865; £432) **Stalls** Low

Form RPR

2110 **1** **Manjaam (IRE)**[14] 2209 3-9-3 **79**.... LukeMorris 4 88+
(Ed Dunlop) *in tch: hdwy 2f out: rdn to ld over 1f out: styd on wl* **8/1**

4-10 **2** 2 **Snan (IRE)**[14] 2209 3-9-0 **76**.... SeanLevey 6 80
(Richard Hannon) *led for 1f: trckd ldr: rdn to ld jst over 2f out: hdd over 1f out: styd on but no ex fnl f* **10/1**

04-2 **3** ½ **Malmoosa (IRE)**[15] 2183 3-9-6 **82**.... JimmyFortune 5 85
(Brian Meehan) *hld up: rdn and hdwy fr 2f out: sn chsng ldng pair: styd on fnl f* **8/1**

5-14 **4** 7 **Against The Odds**[14] 2209 3-9-7 **83**.... JimCrowley 1 75
(Paul Cole) *trckd ldrs: nt clr run briefly twice over 2f out: rdn wl over 1f out: nt gng pce to mount chal: fdd ins fnl f* **3/1**[1]

-514 **5** ¾ **Visage Blanc**[8] 2394 3-8-12 **74**.... JFEgan 2 64
(Mick Channon) *in tch: rdn to chse ldrs over 2f out: fdd ins fnl f* **9/2**[2]

0-22 **6** 6 **Mawaany (IRE)**[31] 1739 3-9-1 **77**....(v) OisinMurphy 3 57
(Sir Michael Stoute) *rousted along leaving stalls: led after 1f: rdn and hdd jst over 2f out: sn btn* **5/1**[3]

43-1 **7** 3 **Tetradrachm**[21] 2000 3-9-6 **82**.... GeorgeBaker 7 66
(David Lanigan) *nvr really travelling in last: effrt over 2f out: nvr threatened: dismntd* **3/1**[1]

2m 28.54s (-2.06) **Going Correction** -0.025s/f (Good) **7** Ran SP% **116.2**
Speed ratings (Par 101): **105,103,103,98,98 94,92**
CSF £83.20 TOTE £8.50: £3.50, £5.80; EX 86.00 Trifecta £663.70.
Owner Mohammed Jaber **Bred** Ballylinch Stud **Trained** Newmarket, Suffolk

FOCUS
Rail movement added 10yds to race distance. Quite a decent middle-distance 3yo handicap and they finished well spread out. The winner resumed his AW progress.

2639 OCTAGON CONSULTANCY CLASSIFIED STKS — 1m 2f 46y
4:30 (4:32) (Class 6) 3-Y-O **£2,863** (£845; £422) **Stalls** Low

Form RPR

0-02 **1** **Bigger And Better**[9] 2366 3-9-0 65.... SeanLevey 7 71
(Richard Hannon) *trckd ldr: led over 2f out: sn rdn and strly pressed: hld on wl fnl f: all out* **5/4**[1]

50-4 **2** hd **Athlon (IRE)**[16] 2152 3-9-0 64.... ShaneKelly 6 71
(David Lanigan) *trckd ldrs: chal 2f out: rdn and ev ch thrght fnl f: kpt on: hld cl home* **11/4**[2]

06-5 **3** 1¾ **Cliffs Of Dover**[29] 1804 3-9-0 65.... DarryllHolland 1 67
(Charles Hills) *led: rdn and hdd over 2f out: kpt on same pce fnl f* **4/1**[3]

06-0 **4** 2½ **Centuro (USA)**[20] 2044 3-9-0 65....(p) FMBerry 2 63
(Jonjo O'Neill) *hmpd s: last but in tch: rdn over 2f out: wnt 4th over 1f out: styd on same pce fnl f* **16/1**

-443 **5** 5 **Asafoetida (IRE)**[50] 1297 3-9-0 64.... JimmyFortune 3 55
(Peter Chapple-Hyam) *hld up bhd ldrs: rdn over 2f out: nt pce to get on terms: appeared to lose action and eased ins fnl f* **7/1**

20-0 **6** 32 **Chempedak Bay (IRE)**[46] 1389 3-9-0 62....(b) LukeMorris 5
(Paul Cole) *hld up bhd ldrs: rdn over 3f out: wknd 2f out* **20/1**

2m 11.28s (0.28) **Going Correction** -0.025s/f (Good) **6** Ran SP% **114.3**
Speed ratings (Par 97): **97,96,95,93,89 63**
CSF £5.07 TOTE £2.00: £1.10, £2.00; EX 5.20 Trifecta £15.30.
Owner Carmichael Pryde **Bred** Cheveley Park Stud Ltd **Trained** East Everleigh, Wilts

FOCUS
Rail movement added 10yds to race distance. A moderate 3yo classified event contested by six maidens.

2640 M J CHURCH WASTE MANAGEMENT MEDIAN AUCTION MAIDEN STKS — 1m 2f 46y
5:00 (5:01) (Class 6) 3-4-Y-O **£2,716** (£808; £404; £202) **Stalls** Low

Form RPR

5- **1** **Dune Dancer (IRE)**[219] 7386 3-9-0 0.... ShaneKelly 1 79+
(David Lanigan) *hld up in tch: hdwy to chal 2f out: led over 1f out: styd on wl: rdn out* **5/2**[1]

4253 **2** ½ **Knights Table**[31] 1767 3-9-0 79.... LukeMorris 9 78
(James Tate) *trckd ldrs: led over 2f out: rdn and hdd over 1f out: ev ch fnl f: hld towards fin* **10/3**[2]

40-4 **3** 4 **Clever Bob (IRE)**[21] 2012 3-9-0 74.... JFEgan 6 70
(Joseph Tuite) *racd keenly: prom: rdn and ev ch fr over 2f out tl no ex ins fnl f* **9/1**

60 **4** 3 **Persaverance**[25] 1931 3-8-9 0.... HectorCrouch(5) 2 65
(Gary Moore) *hld up: rdn over 2f out: hdwy over 1f out: styd on but nt pce to get on terms* **50/1**

-403 **5** nk **Bergholt (IRE)**[8] 2393 3-9-0 72....(p) JimCrowley 7 64
(Philip Hide) *wnt rt leaving stalls: hld up: rdn wl over 2f out: hdwy over 1f out: styd on but nt pce to get on terms* **7/2**[3]

06 **6** 8 **Magnificent Madiba**[18] 2098 3-9-0 0.... JimmyFortune 5 49
(George Baker) *hld up: rdn 3f out: little imp* **20/1**

34 **7** 2½ **Playful Dude (USA)**[115] 428 3-9-0 0.... OisinMurphy 4 44
(Peter Chapple-Hyam) *hld up in tch: effrt over 2f out: nvr threatened: wknd over 1f out* **14/1**

-222 **8** 3 **Rain In The Face**[78] 892 3-9-0 75....(p) FMBerry 8 38
(Ralph Beckett) *led: rdn and hdd over 2f out: wknd over 1f out* **8/1**

4- **9** nk **Rehearse (IRE)**[254] 6437 3-9-0 0....[1] DarryllHolland 3 38
(Andrew Balding) *plld hrd: trckd ldrs: rdn over 2f out: wknd over 1f out* **12/1**

2m 10.13s (-0.87) **Going Correction** -0.025s/f (Good) **9** Ran SP% **116.1**
Speed ratings (Par 101): **102,101,98,96,95 89,87,84,84**
CSF £10.90 TOTE £3.50: £1.40, £1.10, £3.30; EX 12.70 Trifecta £82.40.
Owner Dick, Lockett, O'Connor & P Dean **Bred** Worksop Manor Stud **Trained** Newmarket, Suffolk

FOCUS
Rail movement added 10yds to race distance. A modest older-horse maiden with the runner-up's mark of 79 setting the benchmark.
T/Plt: £367.30 to a £1 stake. Pool: £65,245.91 - 129.65 winning tickets T/Qpdt: £80.90 to a £1 stake. Pool: £5,490.73 - 50.20 winning tickets **Tim Mitchell**

2288 BRIGHTON (L-H)
Friday, May 27

OFFICIAL GOING: Good (good to firm in places; 8.2)
Wind: light, behind Weather: fine, light cloud

2641 GENTING BELOW PRIVATE GAMING NOVICE STKS — 5f 59y
2:20 (2:20) (Class 5) 2-Y-O **£2,911** (£866; £432; £216) **Stalls** Centre

Form RPR

231 **1** **Monks Stand (USA)**[10] 2319 2-9-9 0....(p) RyanMoore 1 85
(Jeremy Noseda) *dwlt and pushed along early: in tch in 5th: effrt and swtchd lft 2f out: wnt between rivals to chal 1f out: rdn to ld ins fnl f: styd on strly and drew clr fnl 100yds* **2/5**[1]

33 **2** 2¾ **Princess Holly**[18] 2097 2-8-11 0....(p) AdamBeschizza 3 63
(Robert Cowell) *led: rdn over 1f out: hdd ins fnl f: styd on same pce after* **12/1**

43 **3** 1¾ **Zebspear (IRE)**[11] 2311 2-8-11 0.... EdwardGreatrex(5) 2 62
(Joseph Tuite) *trckd ldrs on inner: effrt ent fnl 2f: clsd u.p and pressing ldr over 1f out: no ex and outpcd fnl 150yds* **9/2**[2]

64 **4** ½ **Ortano (USA)**[12] 2265 2-9-2 0.... SilvestreDeSousa 4 60
(Mark Johnston) *racd keenly: chsd ldr: rdn 2f out: drvn and outpcd ent fnl f: styd on same pce after* **10/1**[3]

5 nk **Roman Legion (IRE)** 2-9-2 0.... RobertWinston 5 59+
(Dean Ivory) *s.i.s: rn green in detached last: drifting lft and clsd over 1f out: nt clr run and swtchd rt ins fnl f: styd on wl towards fin: no threat to wnr* **25/1**

6 3 ¾ **Angie Baby** 2-8-11 0 .... LiamKeniry 6 40
(J S Moore) *wl in tch in 4th: effrt and unable qck over 1f out: btn 1f out: wkng whn sltly hmpd ins fnl f* **66/1**

1m 2.31s (0.01) **Going Correction** +0.025s/f (Good) **6** Ran SP% **111.7**
Speed ratings (Par 93): **100,95,92,92,91 85**
CSF £6.58 TOTE £1.30: £1.10, £4.80; EX 6.70 Trifecta £14.50.

Owner Mrs Susan Roy **Bred** Blackstone Farm Llc **Trained** Newmarket, Suffolk

FOCUS
Following 2mm of overnight rain and another 3.5mm in the morning, the going was given as good, good to firm in places (GoingStick: 8.2). It didn't always look straightforward for the odds-on favourite here, but he was well on top at the line.

2642 GO CASINO PACKAGES H'CAP 5f 213y
2:50 (2:50) (Class 5) (0-75,73) 3-Y-O **£2,911** (£866; £432; £216) **Stalls** Centre

Form RPR

-06 **1** **Caitie (IRE)**[9] 2373 3-8-13 **65** .... (t) DavidProbert 7 71
(Paul Cole) *in tch in last pair: effrt u.p over 1f out: str run ins fnl f to ld last strides* **16/1**

05-5 **2** *hd* **Highly Sprung (IRE)**[51] 1258 3-9-7 **73** .... SilvestreDeSousa 3 78
(Mark Johnston) *led: rdn and qcknd 2f out: forged to ld 1f out: kpt on wl u.p: hdd last strides* **7/2**[2]

1-13 **3** *2* **Nag's Wag (IRE)**[11] 2314 3-9-5 **71** .... RyanMoore 2 70+
(George Baker) *trckd ldrs: effrt 2f out: drvn and cl up in 3rd whn n.m.r jst ins fnl f: styd on same pce after* **13/8**[1]

464- **4** *nse* **Magic Strike (IRE)**[301] 4812 3-9-1 **67** .... RyanTate 6 66
(Clive Cox) *chsd ldr: rdn and ev ch 2f out: unable qck and edgd lft 1f out: styd on same pce ins fnl f* **11/2**

1400 **5** *1* **Teversham**[34] 1638 3-8-10 **62** .... (p) IrineuGoncalves 4 58
(Chris Dwyer) *t.k.h: hld up in tch in midfield: rdn and hdwy over 1f out: cl 4th but unable qck 1f out: n.m.r on rail sn after: one pce fnl 150yds* **14/1**

-361 **6** *nk* **Al Sailiyah (IRE)**[11] 2288 3-9-1 **72** 6ex .... GaryMahon(5) 8 67
(Richard Hannon) *chsd ldrs: effrt 2f out: drvn and unable qck over 1f out: styd on same pce ins fnl f* **4/1**[3]

60-0 **7** *10* **Keiba (IRE)**[15] 2186 3-9-1 **67** .... TimmyMurphy 1 30
(Gary Moore) *taken down early: stdd s: t.k.h: hld up in last pair: pushed along wl over 1f out: sn btn: bhd and eased wl ins fnl f* **33/1**

1m 10.65s (0.45) **Going Correction** +0.025s/f (Good) **7** Ran SP% **111.2**
Speed ratings (Par 99): **98,97,95,95,93 93,79**
CSF £67.10 CT £139.02 TOTE £20.60: £8.70, £3.00; EX 91.60 Trifecta £259.80.

Owner A H Robinson **Bred** Lodge Park Stud **Trained** Whatcombe, Oxon

FOCUS
A modest handicap in which the winner has been rated back to her standout 2yo run.

2643 CABINS UK H'CAP 5f 213y
3:20 (3:20) (Class 4) (0-80,80) 4-Y-O+ **£4,690** (£1,395; £697; £348) **Stalls** Centre

Form RPR

4451 **1** **Pour La Victoire (IRE)**[8] 2396 6-8-4 **70** .... (b) GeorgiaCox(7) 7 81
(Tony Carroll) *chsd ldrs: effrt over 1f out: hdwy to ld jst ins fnl f: r.o strly: readily* **9/4**[1]

0052 **2** 2 ½ **Straits Of Malacca**[9] 2379 5-8-9 **68** .... LiamKeniry 1 71
(Simon Dow) *stdd after s: hld up in last pair: clsd 2f out: effrt to chse ldrs and rdn jst ins fnl f: chsd wnr 100yds: kpt on same pce after* **9/1**

5606 **3** ½ **Cool Strutter (IRE)**[9] 2379 4-8-8 **67** .... (b) DavidProbert 3 68
(Andrew Balding) *stdd after s: hld up in tch in midfield: clsd 2f out: styng on u.p whn nt clr run and swtchd rt ins fnl f: wnt 3rd cl home: no threat to wnr* **8/1**

-503 **4** *1* **Monumental Man**[11] 2290 7-9-6 **79** .... (p) AdamBeschizza 6 77
(Michael Attwater) *chsd ldr: rdn and ev ch over 1f out: led 1f out: sn hdd and outpcd: wknd fnl 100yds* **3/1**[2]

4320 **5** *1* **Veeraya**[44] 1415 6-8-7 **66** .... (bt) SilvestreDeSousa 5 61
(Julia Feilden) *stdd s: hld up in last pair: swtchd rt and effrt over 2f out: no imp tl styd on ins fnl f: nvr threatened ldrs* **9/2**[3]

650 **6** *nse* **Corporal Maddox**[21] 1997 9-9-4 **80** .... (p) GeorgeDowning(3) 4 75
(Ronald Harris) *in tch in midfield: hung rt bnd 4f out: rdn and no imp 2f out: styd on ins fnl f: no threat to wnr* **16/1**

-303 **7** *nse* **Great Expectations**[41] 1489 8-8-12 **71** .... (vt) WilliamCarson 2 66
(J R Jenkins) *chsd ldrs: effrt 2f out: hung lft and no imp over 1f out: wknd ins fnl f* **14/1**

5-00 **8** *6* **Quickaswecan**[48] 1341 5-8-12 **71** .... (t) RobertWinston 8 46
(Milton Bradley) *broke fast: led: rdn over 1f out: hdd 1f out: sn outpcd and short of room jst ins fnl f: wknd fnl 150yds* **20/1**

1m 9.52s (-0.68) **Going Correction** +0.025s/f (Good) **8** Ran SP% **112.4**
Speed ratings (Par 105): **105,101,101,99,98 98,98,90**
CSF £22.51 CT £136.23 TOTE £2.60: £1.10, £3.20, £2.50; EX 23.70 Trifecta £140.40.

Owner Curry House Corner **Bred** L Fox **Trained** Cropthorne, Worcs

FOCUS
A fair sprint handicap won easily by the favourite who has been rated similar to his Goodwood win.

2644 PREMIER GAMING EXPERIENCE H'CAP 1m 3f 196y
3:50 (3:50) (Class 5) (0-75,75) 3-Y-O **£2,911** (£866; £432; £216) **Stalls** High

Form RPR

22-1 **1** **Goldenfield (IRE)**[27] 1860 3-9-7 **75** .... (p) RyanMoore 1 86
(Gary Moore) *mde all: shkn up and readily asserted 2f out: in command and kpt on after: eased towards fin: unchal* **6/5**[1]

1424 **2** *6* **Jarir**[31] 1738 3-9-3 **74** .... TomMarquand(3) 5 75
(Richard Hannon) *stdd s: hld up in tch in rr: effrt in 4th 3f out: no ch w wnr over 1f out: styd on steadily to go 2nd 100yds out* **5/2**[2]

635 **3** 2 ½ **Summer Collection (IRE)**[31] 1739 3-9-2 **73** ...... MichaelJMMurphy(3) 4 70
(Charles Hills) *chsd ldng pair: effrt wl over 2f out: outpcd by wnr 2f out: bmpd and chsd clr wnr 1f out: no imp: lost 2nd 100yds out* **9/1**

5231 **4** 2 ½ **Dr Drey (IRE)**[91] 729 3-9-3 **71** .... WilliamCarson 2 64
(Jamie Osborne) *chsd wnr: rdn 4f out: outpcd 2f and wl hld whn hung lft over 1f out: lost 2nd 1f out and wknd ins fnl f* **9/2**[3]

0510 **5** *15* **Kemsing (IRE)**[21] 2012 3-9-2 **70** .... AdamBeschizza 3 39
(Julia Feilden) *hld up in tch in 4th: rdn over 3f out: sn struggling: wl bhd whn hung lft over 1f out* **16/1**

2m 33.05s (0.35) **Going Correction** +0.025s/f (Good) **5** Ran SP% **108.1**
Speed ratings (Par 99): **99,95,93,91,81**
CSF £4.22 TOTE £2.10: £1.30, £1.50; EX 4.00 Trifecta £12.20.

Owner Mr & Mrs W W Fleming **Bred** Gigginstown House Stud **Trained** Lower Beeding, W Sussex

FOCUS
A fair handicap won by a progressive 3yo.

2645 GENTING CASINO AMERICAN ROULETTE H'CAP 1m 1f 209y
4:20 (4:20) (Class 6) (0-65,64) 4-Y-O+ **£2,264** (£673; £336; £168) **Stalls** High

Form RPR

1122 **1** **Glasgow Central**[8] 2397 5-9-7 **64** .... SilvestreDeSousa 10 74
(Phil McEntee) *chsd ldrs: wnt 2nd 4f out: drvn to chal over 1f out: led: edgd lft and bmpd runner-up ins fnl f: kpt on and a holding runner-up after: rdn out* **2/1**[1]

2-56 **2** ½ **Pink Ribbon (IRE)**[24] 1947 4-8-12 **60** .... (p) EdwardGreatrex(5) 8 69
(Sylvester Kirk) *led after 1f: rdn 2f out: sn hrd pressed and drvn: hdd and bmpd ins fnl f: kpt on but a hld after* **7/1**[2]

35-4 **3** ¾ **Roy Rocket (FR)**[31] 1747 6-9-2 **59** .... AdamBeschizza 6 67
(John Berry) *stdd s: t.k.h: hld up in tch in last pair: clsd over 2f out: shkn up over 1f out: hdwy u.p to chse clr ldng pair ins fnl f: styd on wl fnl 100yds* **9/1**[3]

4000 **4** 2 ½ **Jazri**[87] 773 5-9-4 **61** .... (b) RobertWinston 7 64
(Milton Bradley) *stdd s: hld up in tch in last pair: hdwy over 2f out: rdn 2f out: chsd ldrs and drvn 1f out: no imp ins fnl f* **18/1**

-541 **5** 1 ¾ **Loving Your Work**[14] 2205 5-9-7 **64** .... RyanMoore 5 64
(Ken Cunningham-Brown) *t.k.h: chsd ldr after 1f tl 4f out: rdn 2f out: edging lft and unable qck over 1f out: wknd ins fnl f* **2/1**[1]

0-43 **6** *hd* **Lucky Dottie**[112] 461 5-8-2 **52** .... SophieRalston(7) 4 51
(Pat Phelan) *broke wl: sn stdd and hld up in tch in midfield: effrt 2f out: unable qck and outpcd over 1f out: hld whn swtchd rt 1f out: no imp after* **28/1**

0-53 **7** *nk* **Highlife Dancer**[5] 2507 8-8-10 **60** .... (v) KillianHennessy(7) 1 60
(Mick Channon) *hld up in tch in last trio: effrt on inner over 1f out: no imp and n.m.r 1f out: kpt on same pce ins fnl f* **10/1**

26-0 **8** 3 ¾ **Smile That Smile**[51] 1253 4-9-2 **62** .... TomMarquand(3) 9 53
(Mark H Tompkins) *hld up in tch in midfield: hdwy to chse ldrs and rdn over 2f out: unable qck and lost pl over 1f out: wknd fnl f* **22/1**

000 **9** *16* **Away In May**[32] 1715 5-8-7 **50** .... WilliamCarson 2 11
(John Spearing) *t.k.h: led tl hdd and stmbld after 1f: stdd bk into midfield but nvr settled: lost pl over 2f out: bhd whn swtchd rt over 1f out: wknd and eased ins fnl f* **66/1**

2m 4.58s (0.98) **Going Correction** +0.025s/f (Good) **9** Ran SP% **112.8**
Speed ratings (Par 101): **97,96,96,94,92 92,92,89,76**
CSF £16.42 CT £100.36 TOTE £2.60: £1.40, £2.50, £2.80; EX 16.20 Trifecta £65.30.

Owner Mrs Rebecca McEntee **Bred** Bolton Grange **Trained** Newmarket, Suffolk

FOCUS
This was run at a fairly sedate pace and few got into it.

2646 GENTING CASINO BLACK JACK H'CAP 7f 214y
4:50 (4:50) (Class 5) (0-70,70) 4-Y-O+ **£2,911** (£866; £432; £216) **Stalls** Centre

Form RPR

54-2 **1** **Lord Reason**[20] 2046 4-9-4 **67** .... SilvestreDeSousa 1 76
(John Butler) *t.k.h: chsd ldrs: styd against far rail fr 3f out: rdn to ld over 1f out: kpt on wl and a holding runner-up ins fnl f: drvn out* **10/3**[2]

6-01 **2** ¾ **He's My Boy (IRE)**[20] 2045 5-8-11 **67** .... GeorgeWood(7) 2 74
(James Fanshawe) *stdd s: hld up in last pair: hdwy over 2f out: rdn to chse wnr over 1f out: pressing wnr 1f out: kpt on u.p but a hld ins fnl f* **9/4**[1]

0-01 **3** 2 ¾ **Wordismybond**[18] 2087 7-9-4 **67** .... TimmyMurphy 7 68
(Richard Hughes) *t.k.h: chsd ldr: upsides over 2f out: rdn and unable qck jst over 1f out: 3rd and styd on same pce ins fnl f* **9/4**[1]

0-62 **4** 2 ¼ **George Baker (IRE)**[21] 2006 9-9-4 **67** .... LiamKeniry 3 63
(George Baker) *hld up in tch in midfield: nt clr run 2f out tl over 1f out: sn rdn and unable qck: kpt on ins fnl f: no threat to ldrs* **12/1**[3]

6245 **5** *nk* **Limerick Lord (IRE)**[32] 1707 4-8-12 **61** .... (p) AdamBeschizza 4 56
(Julia Feilden) *t.k.h: stdd bk into last pair after 1f: effrt u.p and drifted lft 2f out: swtchd rt 1f out: kpt on towards fin: nvr trbld ldrs* **12/1**[3]

000- **6** *nse* **Lady Hare (IRE)**[225] 7230 4-8-7 **61** ow1 .... DavidParkes(5) 5 56
(Ken Cunningham-Brown) *led: rdn and hdd over 1f out: 4th and btn 1f out: wknd ins fnl f* **33/1**

5444 **7** *5* **Ixelles Diamond (IRE)**[17] 2127 5-8-10 **62** .... TomMarquand(3) 6 45
(Andrew Reid) *chsd ldrs: rdn 3f out: lost pl and btn over 1f out: wknd fnl f* **12/1**[3]

1m 35.07s (-0.93) **Going Correction** +0.025s/f (Good) **7** Ran SP% **110.6**
Speed ratings (Par 103): **105,104,101,99,98 98,93**
CSF £10.49 CT £17.92 TOTE £4.00: £2.50, £1.10; EX 10.10 Trifecta £33.80.

Owner Greenstead Hall Racing Ltd **Bred** Greenstead Hall Racing Ltd **Trained** Newmarket, Suffolk

FOCUS
This was run at a steady early gallop. The winner has been rated back to his best.

2647 GENTING CASINO BRIGHTON H'CAP 6f 209y
5:20 (5:21) (Class 6) (0-60,60) 4-Y-O+ **£2,264** (£673; £336; £168) **Stalls** Centre

Form RPR

5315 **1** **Hawk Moth (IRE)**[4] 2542 8-9-2 **58** .... (p) TomMarquand(3) 1 67
(John Spearing) *hld up off the pce in main gp: swtchd rt and clsd 2f out: rdn to chse ldrs over 1f out: led ins fnl f: styd on strly* **7/2**[1]

0006 **2** 2 ¼ **Soaring Spirits (IRE)**[16] 2155 6-9-2 **55** .... (b) RobertWinston 8 58+
(Dean Ivory) *sn led and wnt clr w rival: rdn and wnt 3 l clr 2f out: drvn and hdd ins fnl f: styd on same pce after* **6/1**[3]

4323 **3** ½ **Wild Flower (IRE)**[24] 1949 4-8-6 **50** .... GaryMahon(5) 10 52
(Jimmy Fox) *hld up off the pce in main gp: rdn and effrt to chse clr ldng pair over 2f out: clsd u.p and pressing ldr ent fnl f: 3rd and styd on same pce after* **7/2**[1]

-435 **4** 2 ¾ **Tidal's Baby**[93] 696 7-9-1 **57** .... RobHornby(3) 6 51
(Lee Carter) *s.i.s: hld up wl off the pce in rr: swtchd rt and clsd 2f out: rdn and hdwy over 1f out: kpt on ins fnl f: nvr trbld ldrs* **9/1**

00-6 **5** *5* **Aye Aye Skipper (IRE)**[15] 2187 6-9-0 **58** .... (p) KieranShoemark(5) 7 39
(Ken Cunningham-Brown) *hld up off the pce in midfield: effrt over 2f out: drvn and no imp whn edgd lft ent fnl f: wknd ins fnl f* **6/1**[3]

0006 **6** *4* **Malih**[31] 1742 7-8-11 **50** .... DavidProbert 9 20
(Eric Wheeler) *s.i.s: hld up wl off the pce in last pair: effrt u.p over 2f out: no imp: plugged on to pass btn rivals ins fnl f* **20/1**

0055 **7** *5* **Just Marion (IRE)**[24] 1949 4-8-2 **46** oh1 .... PaddyPilley(5) 4 2
(James Grassick) *prom in main gp but nt on terms w ldrs: rdn over 2f out: wknd over 1f out: no ch whn swtchd rt ins fnl f* **25/1**

0-02 **8** *2* **Harry Bosch**[18] 2087 6-8-10 **49** .... (b) AdamBeschizza 11
(Julia Feilden) *sn wl clr w ldr tl rdn and btn 2f out: wknd over 1f out* **9/2**[2]

60-4 **9** *6* **Semille Obon**[28] 1837 4-8-11 **50**..(p) RyanTate 2
(Jamie Poulton) *prom in main gp tl 3f out: sn rdn and lost pl: bhd over 1f out* **40/1**

1m 22.16s (-0.94) **Going Correction** +0.025s/f (Good) 9 Ran SP% **112.2**
Speed ratings (Par 101): **106,103,102,99,94 89,83,81,74**
CSF £23.35 CT £77.17 TOTE £3.60: £1.30, £2.00, £1.50; EX 27.20 Trifecta £128.30.
Owner Kinnersley Partnership **Bred** Dr D Harron **Trained** Kinnersley, Worcs

FOCUS
The two leaders took each other on and this was run at a strong pace.
T/Plt: £60.80 to a £1 stake. Pool: £63,398.48 - 760.21 winning tickets T/Qpdt: £8.10 to a £1 stake. Pool: £5,604.32 - 507.05 winning tickets **Steve Payne**

2611 HAYDOCK (L-H)
Friday, May 27

OFFICIAL GOING: Good to soft (6.6)
Wind: almost nil Weather: fine, sunny and warm

2648 BRITISH STALLION STUDS EBF NOVICE STKS (PLUS 10 RACE) (DIV I) 6f
2:10 (2:11) (Class 4) 2-Y-0 **£4,269** (£1,270; £634; £317) **Stalls** High

Form RPR
1 **Mokarris (USA)** 2-9-2 0.. GrahamLee 3 87+
(Simon Crisford) *trckd ldrs: shkn up to ld appr fnl f: pushed out: v readily* **11/4**[2]

4 **2** *2* **Tafaakhor (IRE)**[15] 2193 2-9-2 0.. PaulHanagan 1 80
(Richard Hannon) *wnt rt s: chsd ldrs: led wl over 1f out: hdd appr fnl f: styd on same pce* **9/4**[1]

3 *3 ½* **Cajmere** 2-9-2 0.. RichardKingscote 5 70+
(Tom Dascombe) *trckd ldrs: wnt 3rd 1f out: kpt on same pce* **20/1**

4 *3 ¼* **Final Reckoning (IRE)** 2-9-2 0.. WilliamBuick 9 60+
(Charlie Appleby) *in rr: hdwy over 3f out: kpt on to take modest 4th 1f out* **4/1**[3]

6 **5** *2 ½* **Chickenfortea (IRE)**[14] 2196 2-9-2 0.................................. NeilFarley 10 52
(Eric Alston) *led: hdd wl over 1f out: wknd fnl f* **200/1**

6 *¾* **Ok By Me (IRE)** 2-8-11 0.. SteveDrowne 8 45
(David Evans) *sn drvn along in rr: hdwy over 2f out: styd on fnl f* **66/1**

7 *nk* **Rashford's Double (IRE)** 2-9-2 0................................ TonyHamilton 14 49+
(Richard Fahey) *wnt rt s: sn chsng ldrs: wknd over 1f out* **12/1**

06 **8** *3 ¾* **Graton**[11] 2301 2-9-2 0... DougieCostello 12 38
(K R Burke) *trckd ldrs: drvn over 2f out: wknd over 1f out* **100/1**

9 *1 ¼* **Juanito Chico (IRE)** 2-9-2 0... TomQueally 11 34
(William Jarvis) *dwlt: t.k.h in rr: hdwy over 3f out: sn chsng ldrs: lost pl over 1f out* **33/1**

10 *½* **The Big Short** 2-9-2 0.. JamesDoyle 2 33
(Charles Hills) *carried rt s: sn chsng ldrs: lost pl over 1f out* **10/1**

6 **11** *½* **Il Sicario (IRE)**[34] 1635 2-9-2 0...................................... JoeFanning 6 31
(Mark Johnston) *mid-div: drvn to chse ldrs over 2f out: wknd over 1f out* **16/1**

12 *1* **On Show (IRE)** 2-9-2 0.. GrahamGibbons 4 28
(David Brown) *sn drvn along and outpcd: bhd fnl 4f* **33/1**

13 *18* **Infatuated** 2-9-2 0.. PaulMulrennan 13
(Tim Easterby) *s.i.s: a last: wl bhd fnl 2f: t.o* **66/1**

1m 12.93s (-0.87) **Going Correction** -0.125s/f (Firm) 13 Ran SP% **115.2**
Speed ratings (Par 95): **100,97,92,88,85 84,83,78,76,76 75,74,50**
CSF £8.51 TOTE £4.50: £1.50, £1.20, £5.20; EX 11.80 Trifecta £186.00.
Owner Hamdan Al Maktoum **Bred** St Elias Stables LLC **Trained** Newmarket, Suffolk

FOCUS
All races were run over the Inner Home Straight. Race distance as advertised. The ground was again on the easy side and the big two in the market came nicely clear in what looked a decent novice contest, run in a time 0.3sec faster than the second leg.

2649 BRITISH STALLION STUDS EBF NOVICE STKS (PLUS 10 RACE) (DIV II) 6f
2:40 (2:44) (Class 4) 2-Y-0 **£4,269** (£1,270; £634; £317) **Stalls** High

Form RPR
2 **1** **Dream Of Dreams (IRE)**[44] 1422 2-9-2 0.................. JamieSpencer 10 89+
(Kevin Ryan) *led: hrd drvn over 1f out: carried lft last 100yds: fnd ex nr fin* **2/1**[1]

6 **2** *½* **Waqaas**[14] 2203 2-9-2 0.. PaulHanagan 12 88
(Charles Hills) *trckd ldrs: chal appr fnl f: upsides whn edgd lft last 100yds: no ex nr fin* **9/1**

2 **3** *1 ½* **Spiritous (USA)**[14] 2203 2-9-2 0.................................... JamesDoyle 4 83
(John Gosden) *trckd ldrs: effrt over 1f out: styd on same pce* **5/2**[2]

3 **4** *2 ¾* **Our Boy (IRE)**[14] 2203 2-9-2 0..................................... DanielTudhope 2 75
(David Evans) *in rr: hdwy over 2f out: kpt on same pce over 1f out* **7/1**

4 **5** *1 ¼* **Nuclear Power**[9] 2371 2-9-2 0.. TomQueally 14 71
(Joseph Tuite) *hld up in mid-div: hdwy over 2f out: sn chsng ldrs: wknd over 1f out* **16/1**

6 *½* **Majoris (IRE)** 2-9-2 0... WilliamBuick 5 70+
(Hugo Palmer) *dwlt: in rr: hdwy over 2f out: styd on fnl f* **13/2**[3]

7 *½* **Wigan Warrior** 2-9-2 0.. TomEaves 1 68
(David Brown) *mid-div: kpt on fnl 2f: nvr a factor* **100/1**

8 *1* **Buskin River (IRE)** 2-9-2 0.. JoeFanning 11 65
(Richard Hannon) *chsd ldrs: drvn over 2f out: edgd lft and wknd over 1f out* **25/1**

9 *1* **Eldorado Creek (IRE)** 2-9-2 0....................................... TonyHamilton 3 62
(Richard Fahey) *sn chsng ldrs: wknd over 1f out* **33/1**

56 **10** *3 ¾* **Glenys The Menace (FR)**[9] 2376 2-8-11 0.......................... KierenFox 7 46
(John Best) *prom: hung and lost pl over 3f out* **200/1**

11 *2 ¾* **Mutineer** 2-9-2 0... DougieCostello 9 43
(Daniel Kubler) *rrd s: in rr: sme hdwy over 2f out: sn wknd* **100/1**

12 *shd* **Hugging The Rails (IRE)** 2-9-2 0................................ PaulMulrennan 8 42
(Tim Easterby) *in rr: sme hdwy over 2f out: sn lost pl* **100/1**

13 *13* **These Are The Days (USA)** 2-9-2 0................................ SteveDrowne 6
(George Baker) *mid-div: lost pl over 2f out: sn bhd: b.b.v* **100/1**

14 *11* **Exciting Times** 2-9-2 0.. RichardKingscote 13
(Tom Dascombe) *s.i.s: in rr and sn drvn along: lost pl 3f out: wl bhd whn eased over 1f out* **33/1**

1m 13.23s (-0.57) **Going Correction** -0.125s/f (Firm) 14 Ran SP% **117.8**
Speed ratings (Par 95): **98,97,95,91,90 89,88,87,86,81 77,77,59,45**
CSF £20.01 TOTE £3.10: £1.50, £2.80, £1.10; EX 26.20 Trifecta £75.30.
Owner Saeed Suhail **Bred** Prostock Ltd **Trained** Hambleton, N Yorks

FOCUS
Race distance as advertised. The right horses came to the fore in the second division of this decent novice event, although the time was 0.3sec slower than the first leg.

2650 APOLLOBET BET ON LOTTERIES H'CAP 6f
3:10 (3:13) (Class 4) (0-80,80) 3-Y-0 **£5,175** (£1,540; £769; £384) **Stalls** High

Form RPR
00-0 **1** **Wayward Hoof**[22] 1977 3-9-2 **77**.................................... DougieCostello 6 85
(K R Burke) *w ldrs: led over 2f out: edgd lft fnl 75yds: hld on towards fin* **25/1**

3-13 **2** *½* **Bossipop**[20] 2049 3-8-12 **78**.............................(p) RachelRichardson(5) 9 85
(Tim Easterby) *hld up in mid-div: hdwy over 2f out: styd on to take 2nd last 75yds: n.m.r and no ex nr fin* **6/1**[2]

-231 **3** *1 ¼* **General Alexander (IRE)**[21] 2019 3-8-10 **78**........(p) BenRobinson(7) 12 80
(Brian Ellison) *mid-div: hdwy to chse ldrs over 2f out: edgd lft and kpt on same pce last 150yds* **10/1**

24-0 **4** *nk* **Alizoom (IRE)**[35] 1607 3-9-5 **80**...................................... HarryBentley 14 81
(Roger Varian) *stdd s: hld up towards rr: hdwy over 2f out: kpt on wl fnl f* **16/1**

-143 **5** *½* **Ice Age (IRE)**[21] 2002 3-9-4 **79**.. JohnFahy 17 78+
(Eve Johnson Houghton) *hld up towards rr: effrt and swtchd lft over 2f out: kpt on wl fnl f* **16/1**

40-0 **6** *hd* **Dark Defender**[13] 2251 3-9-5 **80**...................................... TomQueally 7 79
(Keith Dalgleish) *led: hdd over 2f out: crowded and wknd last 150yds* **15/2**

10-0 **7** *hd* **English Hero**[29] 1809 3-9-2 **77**.. MartinHarley 3 75
(William Knight) *chsd ldrs: one pce appr fnl f* **40/1**

6-45 **8** *1 ¼* **War Department (IRE)**[100] 612 3-9-3 **78**.......................... JamieSpencer 4 72
(Michael Bell) *stdd and swtchd rt s: hld up in rr: hdwy over 2f out: kpt on: nvr a threat* **16/1**

01- **9** *¾* **Times Legacy**[202] 7752 3-9-2 **77**.................................... JamesDoyle 15 69
(Peter Chapple-Hyam) *hld up in rr: effrt over 2f out: kpt on fnl f: nvr a factor* **5/1**[1]

20-0 **10** *½* **Mon Beau Visage (IRE)**[35] 1599 3-9-2 **77**..................... DanielTudhope 1 67
(David O'Meara) *chsd ldrs: lost pl over 1f out* **25/1**

-500 **11** *4* **Danecase**[13] 2239 3-9-5 **80**.. WilliamBuick 11 57
(David Dennis) *chsd ldrs: drvn over 2f out: wknd and eased fnl f* **11/1**

1-0 **12** *1 ¾* **Gowanless**[35] 1599 3-9-2 **77**...................................... PaulMulrennan 5 49
(Michael Dods) *chsd ldrs: lost pl over 1f out* **16/1**

1-0 **13** *2 ¼* **Dutch Gallery**[15] 2179 3-9-5 **80**............................ RichardKingscote 16 45
(Tom Dascombe) *hld up in rr: effrt over 2f out: nvr a factor* **13/2**[3]

3-11 **14** *7* **Avenue Of Stars**[30] 1788 3-9-3 **78**...............................(p) PaulHanagan 8 20
(Karen McLintock) *chsd ldrs: drvn over 3f out: lost pl over 2f out: bhd whn eased clsng stages* **8/1**

1m 12.88s (-0.92) **Going Correction** -0.125s/f (Firm) 14 Ran SP% **118.2**
Speed ratings (Par 101): **101,100,98,98,97 97,97,95,94,93 88,86,83,73**
CSF £163.74 CT £1627.73 TOTE £20.80: £5.40, £2.30, £2.60; EX 316.10 Trifecta £3325.90.
Owner Palatinate Racing A Chandler L Westwood **Bred** T A Scothern **Trained** Middleham Moor, N Yorks

FOCUS
Race distance as advertised. A fair handicap and, as in the two juvenile races, the action unfolded more towards the far side. The winner has been rated back to his early 2yo form.

2651 APOLLOBET DAILY RACING REFUNDS H'CAP 1m 2f 95y
3:40 (3:41) (Class 5) (0-75,75) 4-Y-0+ **£2,911** (£866; £432; £216) **Stalls** High

Form RPR
3631 **1** **Masterpaver**[7] 2436 5-8-13 **67**...................................... TonyHamilton 6 75
(Richard Fahey) *hld up in rr: effrt over 3f out: nt clr run over 2f out tl swtchd rt over 1f out: styd on wl to ld nr fin* **5/2**[1]

3302 **2** *nk* **Berrahri (IRE)**[16] 2151 5-9-5 **73**...................................... KierenFox 8 80
(John Best) *sn chsng ldr: led over 3f out: hdd and no ex nr fin* **9/1**

4-05 **3** *1 ½* **Oriental Tiger**[14] 2198 5-8-13 **67**.............................. RoystonFfrench 3 71
(Iain Jardine) *s.i.s: hld up in rr: effrt on ins and n.m.r over 3f out: chsng ldrs over 2f out: kpt on same pce fnl f* **7/1**

1-20 **4** *½* **Omotesando**[11] 2296 6-9-0 **75**.............................. CharlieBennett(7) 1 78
(Mark Brisbourne) *chsd ldrs: drvn over 3f out: kpt on one pce appr fnl f* **25/1**

0-43 **5** *nk* **Nonchalant**[18] 2093 5-9-7 **75**.....................................(v) DanielTudhope 5 78
(David O'Meara) *trckd ldrs: drvn upsides over 2f out: one pce fnl f* **6/1**

00-5 **6** *shd* **Hanseatic**[13] 2257 7-9-5 **73**.. GrahamGibbons 9 75
(Michael Easterby) *in rr: hdwy 6f out: drvn over 3f out: one pce over 1f out* **11/2**[3]

-000 **7** *8* **The Character (IRE)**[21] 1999 5-9-7 **75**..................(tp) RichardKingscote 4 62
(Tom Dascombe) *led: hdd over 3f out: lost pl over 1f out: edgd rt and eased clsng stages* **9/2**[2]

4-45 **8** *8* **The Third Man**[32] 1702 5-9-7 **75**...................................... TomQueally 7 47
(Henry Spiller) *hld up on outer: effrt 3f out: lost pl over 1f out: eased clsng stages* **20/1**

300- **9** *21* **Chief Spirit**[70] 8157 4-9-7 **75**...................................... PatCosgrave 2 7
(James Eustace) *sn chsng ldrs: reminders over 4f out: lost pl over 1f out: heavily eased last 100yds* **14/1**

2m 11.86s (-3.64) **Going Correction** -0.325s/f (Firm) 9 Ran SP% **114.2**
Speed ratings (Par 103): **101,100,99,99,98 98,92,86,69**
CSF £25.76 CT £138.97 TOTE £3.00: £1.10, £2.70, £2.90; EX 18.70 Trifecta £184.40.
Owner Mrs A M Riney **Bred** Mrs A M Riney **Trained** Musley Bank, N Yorks
■ Stewards' Enquiry : Kieren Fox two-day; used whip above permitted level (10th-11th July)

FOCUS
Race distance increased by 1yd. A modest handicap, but they went a fair clip and the favourite did well to win having got in a spot of bother.

2652 APOLLOBET BET THROUGH YOUR MOBILE H'CAP (JOCKEY CLUB GRASSROOTS MIDDLE DISTANCE SERIES QUALIFIER) 1m 2f 95y
4:10 (4:12) (Class 5) (0-70,70) 3-Y-0 **£2,911** (£866; £432; £216) **Stalls** High

Form RPR
50-0 **1** **Caponova (IRE)**[34] 1638 3-8-11 **60**............................ GrahamGibbons 3 69
(Tom Dascombe) *s.i.s: t.k.h: sn mid-div: hdwy over 2f out: edgd lft and styd on to ld clsng stages* **50/1**

-003 **2** *½* **Glance My Way (IRE)**[16] 2145 3-9-5 **68**............................ PatDobbs 2 76
(Richard Hannon) *chsd ldrs: nt clr run on inner over 2f out: led last 75yds: no ex and hdd clsng stages* **12/1**

3222 **3** *2* **Santiburi Spring**[16] 2152 3-9-2 **65**................................ KierenFox 11 69
(John Best) *led tl over 3f out: led over 1f out: hdd and kpt on same pce last 75yds* **20/1**

46-6 **4** *2* **Pinstripe**[21] 2012 3-9-4 **67**.. DanielTudhope 8 68
(Luca Cumani) *trckd ldrs: effrt over 1f out: one pce whn hmpd ins fnl 100yds* **3/1**[1]

0-1 **5** 3/4 **Maulesden May (IRE)**[29] 1816 3-9-7 **70**.......................... TomQueally 5 69
(Keith Dalgleish) *w ldr: led over 3f out: hdd over 1f out: wknd fnl 100yds* **14/1**

-031 **6** 1/2 **Monsieur Glory**[11] 2308 3-9-1 **64** 6ex.....................(v) RichardKingscote 10 62+
(Tom Dascombe) *trckd ldrs: nt clr run over 2f out: swtchd rt over 1f out: kpt on* **6/1**[3]

4-43 **7** 2 1/4 **Perceysvivace**[12] 2269 3-9-2 **65**.................................(p) TonyHamilton 13 59
(Richard Fahey) *trckd ldrs: hung lft over 1f out: sn wknd fnl 150yds* **10/1**

1-54 **8** 2 1/2 **Judicial Enquiry**[28] 1835 3-8-12 **61**.............................(p) JamieSpencer 7 50
(Ed Walker) *rr-div: reminders over 3f out: nt clr run over 2f out: wknd fnl f* **14/1**

5-00 **9** shd **Causey Arch (IRE)**[20] 2048 3-8-13 **62**......................... PaulMulrennan 4 51
(Michael Dods) *in rr: drvn over 3f out: sme hdwy over 2f out: nvr a factor* **25/1**

44-6 **10** 3 **Long Island**[38] 1553 3-8-1 **57**.. CharlieBennett(7) 6 40
(Mark Brisbourne) *n rr: hdwy on outer over 3f out: wknd over 1f out* **66/1**

00-4 **11** 3 1/4 **Clear Evidence**[17] 2122 3-9-5 **68**...................... WilliamTwiston-Davies 9 45
(Michael Bell) *trckd ldrs: t.k.h: effrt over 2f out: wknd fnl f* **11/1**

4-63 **12** 1 3/4 **Ripoll (IRE)**[9] 2366 3-8-12 **61**...(t) JamesDoyle 14 34
(Sylvester Kirk) *chsd ldrs: lost pl over 1f out: eased last 100yds* **4/1**[2]

206- **13** 9 **Callaghan (GER)**[251] 6522 3-9-6 **69**............................. DougieCostello 1 25
(Tom Gretton) *chsd ldrs: lost pl over 1f out: eased last 150yds* **50/1**

006- **14** 25 **Dark Avenue**[205] 7700 3-9-5 **68**.. MartinHarley 12
(William Knight) *trckd ldrs: drvn over 4f out: wknd 2f out: sn heavily eased: virtually p.u: t.o* **8/1**

2m 12.18s (-3.32) **Going Correction** -0.325s/f (Firm) **14** Ran SP% **122.9**
Speed ratings (Par 99): **100,99,98,96,95 95,93,91,91,89 86,85,77,57**
CSF £564.85 CT £11815.55 TOTE £70.40: £14.30, £3.30, £4.50; EX 1268.10 Trifecta £5315.70 Part won..
Owner Deva Racing Bushranger Partnership **Bred** Mr & Mrs T O'Brien **Trained** Malpas, Cheshire
■ Stewards' Enquiry : Graham Gibbons caution; careless riding

FOCUS
Race distance increased by 1yd. Modest form and there was a right old turn up. The race has been rated around the third.

2653 APOLLOBET HOME OF CASHBACK SPECIALS FILLIES' MAIDEN STKS 1m
4:40 (4:43) (Class 5) 3-Y-O+ **£2,911** (£866; £432; £216) **Stalls** Low

Form RPR

1 **Asama Blue (IRE)** 3-9-0 0.. PatCosgrave 2 83+
(William Haggas) *s.i.s: hdwy into mid-div over 6f out: trcking ldrs over 2f out: nt clr run over 1f out: 2nd last 100yds: str run to ld nr fin* **4/1**[3]

6- **2** nk **Laugh Aloud**[164] 8232 3-9-0 0..(t) WilliamBuick 12 79
(John Gosden) *trckd ldrs: led over 6f out: drvn over 2f out: hdd and no ex nr fin* **3/1**[1]

04- **3** 3 **Wall Of Light**[210] 7605 3-9-0 0................................ RichardKingscote 7 72
(Tom Dascombe) *w ldrs: effrt over 2f out: hung lft and kpt on same pce fnl f* **15/2**

04-0 **4** 3/4 **Sister Dude**[34] 1628 3-9-0 67.. DougieCostello 3 70
(K R Burke) *trckd ldrs: effrt over 2f out: kpt on same pce to take 4th last 100yds* **8/1**

4 **5** 1 3/4 **Idealist**[11] 2312 3-9-0 0.. HarryBentley 4 67
(Roger Varian) *trckd ldrs: n.m.r over 1f out: wkng whn sltly hmpd last 100yds* **7/2**[2]

0-5 **6** 1 3/4 **Heart Of An Angel**[15] 2177 3-8-11 0....................... LouisSteward(3) 11 62
(Philip McBride) *in rr: hdwy over 3f out: one pce fnl 2f* **7/1**

0 **7** 3/4 **Ray Of Light (IRE)**[32] 1723 3-9-0 0.. PatDobbs 6 60
(Richard Hannon) *led tl over 6f out: chsd ldrs: one pce fnl 2f* **20/1**

00- **8** 1 3/4 **Pacharana**[209] 7628 3-9-0 0.. DanielTudhope 8 59+
(Luca Cumani) *s.i.s: in rr: hdwy whn nt clr run 3f out: sn outpcd: kpt on appr fnl f* **12/1**

00- **9** 4 **Work (IRE)**[205] 7700 3-9-0 0.. JamieSpencer 1 46
(David Simcock) *dwlt: a towards rr* **33/1**

60 **10** 2 1/4 **Broadsword (IRE)**[34] 1653 4-9-12 0.................................. RyanPowell 5 44
(Kevin Frost) *chsd ldrs: lost pl over 2f out* **200/1**

1m 42.58s (-1.12) **Going Correction** -0.325s/f (Firm)
WFA 3 from 4yo 12lb **10** Ran SP% **118.5**
Speed ratings (Par 100): **92,91,88,87,86 84,83,81,77,75**
CSF £16.51 TOTE £5.40: £1.60, £1.60, £2.60; EX 17.90 Trifecta £156.80.
Owner Sir Peter Vela/Mrs D Nagle/Mrs J Magnier **Bred** Barronstown Stud **Trained** Newmarket, Suffolk

FOCUS
Race distance increased by 1yd. The front pair pulled clear in what was an ordinary maiden (fourth rated just 67) and the form looks muddling, with the winner very much the one to take from the race.

2654 APOLLOBET WEEKLY GOLF REFUNDS H'CAP 1m
5:10 (5:11) (Class 4) (0-80,81) 3-Y-O **£5,175** (£1,540; £769; £384) **Stalls** Low

Form RPR

3-23 **1** **Flyboy (IRE)**[43] 1449 3-9-6 **79**....................................... DanielTudhope 10 86+
(David O'Meara) *hld up in rr: hdwy on outside over 2f out: styd on wl fnl f: led fnl strides* **16/1**

25-1 **2** hd **Poet's Beauty (IRE)**[34] 1638 3-9-2 **78**.................(p) ThomasBrown(3) 12 84
(Ismail Mohammed) *trckd ldrs: t.k.h: chal 2f out: led narrowly last 100yds: hdd fnl strides* **11/1**

45-2 **3** nk **Shafafya**[34] 1630 3-9-3 **76**.. PaulHanagan 7 81
(Ed Dunlop) *hld up in mid-div: t.k.h: hdwy over 3f out: styd on wl fnl f* **12/1**

01-0 **4** hd **Constantino (IRE)**[16] 2161 3-9-5 **78**............................. TonyHamilton 4 83
(Richard Fahey) *trckd ldrs: drvn over 3f out: upsides last 75yds: no ex nr fin* **7/1**[3]

3-21 **5** nk **Town's History (USA)**[110] 496 3-9-4 **77**......................... JamesDoyle 14 81+
(Saeed bin Suroor) *mid-div: hdwy over 3f out: chsng ldrs over 1f out: kpt on same pce last 50yds* **8/1**

22-1 **6** 1 3/4 **Cambodia (IRE)**[18] 2109 3-9-3 **76**..................................... TedDurcan 6 76
(Chris Wall) *hld up in mid-div: hdwy over 2f out: chsng ldrs over 1f out: kpt on to take 6th last 50yds* **8/1**

-221 **7** 1 1/4 **Amazement (GER)**[12] 2271 3-9-8 **81** 6ex........................ MartinHarley 8 78
(James Tate) *trckd ldrs: led over 3f out: hdd & wknd last 100yds* **6/1**[2]

0-1 **8** 2 1/2 **Threat Assessed (IRE)**[17] 2128 3-9-7 **80**.......................... JohnFahy 5 71
(Clive Cox) *s.i.s: t.k.h: hdwy over 3f out: chsng ldrs over 1f out: fdd last 150yds* **4/1**[1]

-615 **9** 1/2 **Ronnie Baird**[23] 1971 3-9-5 **78**.................................(p) RobertHavlin 11 67
(Kristin Stubbs) *swtchd lft after s: led: hdd over 3f out: wknd appr fnl f* **50/1**

51-1 **10** hd **Mywayistheonlyway (IRE)**[27] 1847 3-9-4 **77**............. FergusSweeney 2 66
(Martyn Meade) *mid-div: drvn over 2f out: sn chsng ldrs: wknd over 1f out* **12/1**

6-1 **11** 1/2 **Huntlaw**[33] 1662 3-9-3 **76**.. JoeFanning 13 64+
(Mark Johnston) *s.i.s: in rr: hdwy on outside 3f out: chsng ldrs over 2f out: wknd over 1f out* **8/1**

5-04 **12** 3/4 **Not Touch**[15] 2185 3-9-1 **74**.. PatDobbs 1 60
(Richard Hannon) *s.i.s: hld up in rr: effrt on ins whn nt clr run 2f out: sn wknd* **25/1**

404 **13** hd **Zainat (IRE)**[20] 2044 3-9-1 **74**....................................... DougieCostello 9 59
(K R Burke) *in rr: hdwy over 4f out: chsng ldrs over 2f out: lost pl over 1f out* **28/1**

1m 41.1s (-2.60) **Going Correction** -0.325s/f (Firm) **13** Ran SP% **119.0**
Speed ratings (Par 101): **100,99,99,99,99 97,96,93,93,92 92,91,91**
CSF £177.88 CT £2196.01 TOTE £18.80: £4.40, £4.30, £4.50; EX 245.30 Trifecta £5216.80.
Owner George Murray **Bred** Micheal D Ryan **Trained** Upper Helmsley, N Yorks

FOCUS
Race distance increased by 1yd. Just a fair handicap, with a couple of the fancied runners disappointing, and there was little between the front five at the line, but there looked to be a few potential improvers in this.

2655 APOLLOBET ONLINE CASINO AND GAMES FILLIES' H'CAP 7f
5:45 (5:45) (Class 5) (0-70,70) 4-Y-O+ **£2,911** (£866; £432; £216) **Stalls** Low

Form RPR

2433 **1** **Colourfilly**[8] 2403 4-9-0 **63**..(p) RichardKingscote 8 72
(Tom Dascombe) *trckd ldr: led over 2f out: abt 3 l clr 1f out: drvn rt out* **9/2**[2]

3632 **2** 2 **Princess Peaches**[18] 2096 4-8-13 **62**.........................(p) JamieSpencer 4 66
(James Bethell) *chsd ldrs: wnt 2nd over 1f out: styd on same pce* **4/1**[1]

10-0 **3** 2 1/4 **Totally Magic (IRE)**[37] 1565 4-8-13 **62**......................... KeaganLatham 3 60
(Richard Whitaker) *trckd ldrs: 3rd over 1f out: kpt on same pce* **14/1**

-066 **4** shd **Cabal**[25] 1926 9-9-1 **67**...(v) KevinStott(3) 7 64
(Geoffrey Harker) *hld up in mid-div: hdwy to chse ldrs over 3f out: kpt on fnl f* **14/1**

1633 **5** shd **Binky Blue (IRE)**[31] 1754 4-9-5 **68**...................................... JoeFanning 6 65
(Daniel Mark Loughnane) *mid-div: hdwy and 3rd over 3f out: nt clr run 2f out: kpt on fnl f* **12/1**

0-24 **6** 1 1/4 **Darrell Rivers**[8] 2403 4-9-1 **64**....................................... TonyHamilton 11 58
(Giles Bravery) *trckd ldrs: effrt over 2f out: wknd towards fin* **9/2**[2]

4-24 **7** 3/4 **Zaria**[17] 2129 5-8-8 **60**...(p) ThomasBrown(3) 13 52
(Richard Price) *in rr: hdwy over 2f out: sn outpcd: kpt on fnl 75yds* **6/1**

1-12 **8** 7 **Pacolita (IRE)**[133] 191 4-9-7 **70**... PatDobbs 5 43
(Sylvester Kirk) *dwlt: stdd sn after s: hld up in rr: hdwy on ins over 2f out: edgd rt over 1f out: sn wknd* **5/1**[3]

6-50 **9** 1 1/4 **Pryers Princess**[10] 2332 4-9-0 **66**...........................(tp) LouisSteward(3) 9 35
(David C Griffiths) *s.i.s: in rr: hdwy over 2f out: lost pl over 1f out: sn bhd* **25/1**

000- **10** 19 **Clumber Place**[326] 3956 10-8-7 **56**....................................... ShaneGray 2
(John Balding) *led: hdd over 2f out: lost pl over 1f out: bhd whn heavily eased last 150yds* **25/1**

1m 27.34s (-3.36) **Going Correction** -0.325s/f (Firm) **10** Ran SP% **116.0**
Speed ratings (Par 100): **106,103,101,101,100 99,98,90,89,67**
CSF £22.75 CT £232.32 TOTE £6.20: £1.40, £1.40, £4.40; EX 21.60 Trifecta £238.00.
Owner Laurence Bellman **Bred** Michael E Broughton **Trained** Malpas, Cheshire

FOCUS
Race distance increased by 1yd. A race in which it paid to race handily and the winner has been rated a length up on her AW form.
T/Jkpt: Not won. T/Plt: £213.60 to a £1 stake. Pool: £81,756.80 - 279.31 winning tickets T/Qpdt: £153.30 to a £1 stake. Pool: £6,010.39 - 29.00 winning tickets **Walter Glynn**

2089 MUSSELBURGH (R-H)
Friday, May 27

OFFICIAL GOING: Good (7.4)
Wind: Light, half against Weather: Overcast

2656 DAIKIN APPLIED CLASSIC H'CAP 1m 4f 100y
6:40 (6:42) (Class 6) (0-65,65) 4-Y-O+ **£3,234** (£962; £481; £240) **Stalls** Low

Form RPR

30-3 **1** **Tourtiere**[33] 1674 8-9-0 **65**... HollieDoyle(7) 5 73
(Andrew Crook) *trckd ldr: smooth hdwy to ld over 2f out: shkn up over 1f out: kpt on wl fnl f* **9/2**[3]

0-62 **2** 1 **Sirpertan**[12] 1675 5-8-7 **51**.. SamJames 8 56
(Marjorie Fife) *trckd ldrs on outside: rdn over 2f out: rallied and chsd wnr over 1f out: kpt on ins fnl f* **7/2**[2]

10-5 **3** 1 1/2 **Fillydelphia (IRE)**[24] 1952 5-8-4 **55**................................. PaulaMuir(7) 7 58
(Patrick Holmes) *hld up: hdwy on outside over 2f out: rdn and hung rt over 1f out: kpt on fnl f: nrst fin* **12/1**

0024 **4** nk **San Cassiano (IRE)**[9] 2362 9-9-5 **63**..........................(p) JamesSullivan 3 66
(Ruth Carr) *led at ordinary gallop: rdn and hdd over 2f out: lost 2nd over 1f out: one pce fnl f* **3/1**[1]

000- **5** 7 **Neuf Des Coeurs**[242] 6819 5-9-6 **64**.............................. AndrewMullen 2 55
(Iain Jardine) *trckd ldrs: drvn along over 2f out: wknd appr fnl f* **10/1**

-050 **6** 2 3/4 **New Colours**[2] 2575 5-8-8 **52**...(p) PJMcDonald 4 39
(Linda Perratt) *hld up in tch: drvn and struggling over 2f out: sn btn* **16/1**

066- **7** 4 1/2 **Gunner Lindley (IRE)**[24] 4822 9-9-4 **62**...........................(v) JasonHart 9 42
(Stuart Coltherd) *hld up: struggling over 3f out: btn fnl 2f* **25/1**

-502 **P** **Jammy Moment**[2] 2575 5-9-5 **63**.. PhillipMakin 1
(Keith Dalgleish) *virtually ref to leave stalls: t.o whn consented to jump off and sn p.u* **7/2**[2]

2m 46.86s (4.86) **Going Correction** +0.35s/f (Good) **8** Ran SP% **114.1**
Speed ratings (Par 101): **97,96,95,95,90 88,85,**
CSF £20.56 CT £174.64 TOTE £5.80: £1.80, £1.30, £2.80; EX 21.90 Trifecta £233.00.
Owner G J Andrews **Bred** London Thoroughbred Services Ltd **Trained** Middleham Moor, N Yorks
■ Stewards' Enquiry : Sam James two-day ban; used whip above permitted level (10th-11th June)

FOCUS
Bottom bend out 2yds adding 7yds to all round course races. The pace steadied on the far side in this moderate handicap. The fourth sets the level.

2657 RACINGUK.COM MAIDEN STKS 7f 30y
7:10 (7:13) (Class 5) 3-Y-O+ **£3,234** (£962; £481; £240) **Stalls** Low

Form RPR

20-4 **1** **Weekend Offender (FR)**[26] 1883 3-9-3 78......................... GrahamLee 5 87
(Kevin Ryan) *pressed ldr: led gng wl over 2f out: pushed along over 1f out: drew clr fnl f* **2/1**[1]

32 **2** 5 **Haraz (IRE)**[10] 2349 3-9-3 81....(p) DavidNolan 2 73
(David O'Meara) *trckd ldrs: rdn over 2f out: chsd (clr) wnr ent fnl f: kpt on: no imp* **5/2**[2]

20-0 **3** nk **Dark Forest**[13] 2239 3-9-3 72.... JasonHart 4 72
(Simon West) *led at modest gallop: hdd and rdn over 2f out: rallied: lost 2nd ent fnl f: kpt on same pce* **15/2**

4 ½ **Glengarry** 3-9-3 0.... PhillipMakin 6 71+
(Keith Dalgleish) *s.i.s: hld up: stdy hdwy over 2f out: rdn and rn green over 1f out: kpt on same pce fnl f: bttr for r* **4/1**[3]

6 **5** 7 **Inner Knowing (IRE)**[81] 858 3-8-12 66....(v[1]) JoeyHaynes 7 47
(K R Burke) *t.k.h: trckd ldrs on outside: rdn over 2f out: carried hd high and wknd over 1f out* **14/1**

-000 **6** 10 **Trulove**[11] 2308 3-8-12 40.... PatrickMathers 1 20
(John David Riches) *dwlt: t.k.h and hld up in tch on ins: struggling over 2f out: sn btn* **125/1**

30 **7** ½ **Insurplus (IRE)**[13] 2234 3-9-0 0.... JoeDoyle(3) 3 23
(Jim Goldie) *hld up: rdn and outpcd over 4f out: n.d after: btn fnl 2f* **17/2**

1m 30.19s (1.19) **Going Correction** +0.35s/f (Good) 7 Ran SP% **111.7**
Speed ratings (Par 103): **107,101,100,100,92 80,80**
CSF £6.84 TOTE £3.20: £1.80, £1.30; EX 9.10 Trifecta £30.00.
Owner Matt & Lauren Morgan **Bred** Mathieu Daguzan-Garros Et Al **Trained** Hambleton, N Yorks

FOCUS
A modest maiden. Race distance increased by 7 yards. They went a routine pace and the form makes some sense with the winner belatedly building on his debut promise.

2658 BELMONT WALLYFORD H'CAP 5f
7:40 (7:41) (Class 3) (0-90,89) 3-Y-O+ **£12,938** (£3,850; £1,924; £962) **Stalls** High

Form RPR

-124 **1** **Bowson Fred**[23] 1964 4-9-5 **85**.... NathanEvans(5) 5 94
(Michael Easterby) *mde all: rdn over 1f out: hrd pressed fnl f: hld on wl* **9/2**[2]

21-0 **2** nk **Olivia Fallow (IRE)**[11] 2305 4-9-11 **86**.... GrahamLee 9 94+
(Paul Midgley) *prom: stdy hdwy and shkn up over 1f out: rdn and kpt on wl fnl f: tk 2nd nr fin: jst hld* **7/1**

-213 **3** nk **Paddy Power (IRE)**[14] 2218 3-9-3 **86**.... DavidNolan 1 90
(Richard Fahey) *prom: hdwy to press wnr over 1f out: drvn and ev ch ins fnl f: kpt on: no ex and lost 2nd nr fin* **4/1**[1]

0230 **4** 1 **Flash City (ITY)**[13] 2261 8-8-10 **71**....(p) JamesSullivan 6 74
(Ruth Carr) *dwlt: hld up: effrt and weaved through fr over 1f out: kpt on ins fnl f: nrst fin* **20/1**

06-0 **5** 1½ **Distant Past**[15] 2188 5-9-10 **88**....(p) JoeDoyle(3) 4 86
(Kevin Ryan) *t.k.h: hld up: hdwy on outside over 1f out: rdn and kpt on same pce ins fnl f* **13/2**

-422 **6** ½ **El Astronaute (IRE)**[14] 2218 3-9-6 **89**.... CamHardie 7 82
(John Quinn) *cl up: rdn over 1f out: outpcd ins fnl f* **5/1**[3]

4322 **7** shd **Go Go Green (IRE)**[4] 2524 10-8-11 **72**.... JasonHart 10 68
(Jim Goldie) *dwlt bhd and outpcd: kpt on fnl f: nvr on terms* **8/1**

5-05 **8** 1 **Rosina**[15] 2192 3-9-6 **89**.... PJMcDonald 3 78
(Ann Duffield) *bhd and outpcd: drvn along 2f out: sn no imp* **8/1**

5462 **9** 4 **Jebediah Shine**[11] 2305 4-9-7 **87**.... JoshDoyle(5) 8 65
(David O'Meara) *cl up tl rdn: edgd rt and wknd qckly 1f out* **9/1**

59.47s (-0.93) **Going Correction** 0.0s/f (Good)
WFA 3 from 4yo+ 8lb 9 Ran SP% **117.7**
Speed ratings (Par 107): **107,106,106,104,102 101,101,99,93**
CSF £36.71 CT £138.22 TOTE £4.90: £1.90, £2.50, £1.90; EX 49.60 Trifecta £207.60.
Owner Mrs A Jarvis **Bred** Mrs A Jarvis **Trained** Sheriff Hutton, N Yorks

FOCUS
A fair sprint handicap and the winner has been rated to his AW form.

2659 CANACCORD GENUITY H'CAP 1m 6f
8:10 (8:10) (Class 4) (0-80,80) 4-Y-O+ **£7,762** (£2,310; £1,154; £577) **Stalls** Low

Form RPR

01-0 **1** **Dominada (IRE)**[16] 2163 4-9-1 **79**.... CallumShepherd(5) 7 87
(Brian Ellison) *dwlt: sn trcking ldrs on outside: hdwy to ld over 2f out: rdn and edgd lft over 1f out: edgd rt ins fnl f: drvn out* **11/2**[3]

0-10 **2** 1¼ **Sisyphus**[15] 2194 4-9-5 **78**.... AndrewMullen 5 84
(Ollie Pears) *cl up: effrt and chsd wnr over 2f out: sn rdn: kpt on ins fnl f* **5/2**[2]

-043 **3** 2¼ **Triple Eight (IRE)**[24] 1955 8-8-6 **65**.... JoeyHaynes 4 68
(Philip Kirby) *hld up in tch: hdwy over 2f out: hung rt ins fnl f: kpt on same pce last 100yds* **10/1**

/0-4 **4** 4½ **Osaruveetil (IRE)**[20] 2051 5-9-7 **80**.... DavidNolan 6 77
(David O'Meara) *plld hrd: hld up: rdn along 3f out: hdwy u.p over 1f out: sn no imp* **13/8**[1]

02-4 **5** 4½ **Pass Muster**[33] 1665 9-8-10 **74**.... PhilDennis(5) 2 64
(Philip Kirby) *prom: drvn along 3f out: wknd over 1f out* **11/1**

111- **6** 7 **Wor Lass**[270] 5946 8-9-0 **78**.... AnnaHesketh(5) 1 59
(Susan Corbett) *hld up on ins: drvn and outpcd wl over 2f out: sn btn* **10/1**

100/ **7** 3½ **Discay**[16] 7496 7-9-7 **80**....(p) PJMcDonald 3 56
(Philip Kirby) *led at ordinary gallop: rdn and hdd over 2f out: sn lost pl and struggling* **25/1**

3m 8.11s (2.81) **Going Correction** +0.35s/f (Good) 7 Ran SP% **112.4**
Speed ratings (Par 105): **105,104,103,100,97 93,91**
CSF £18.97 TOTE £7.20: £3.10, £1.80; EX 22.50 Trifecta £188.30.
Owner Julie & Keith Hanson **Bred** Glending Bloodstock **Trained** Norton, N Yorks

FOCUS
Race distance increased by 7 yards. A modest staying handicap with the winner recording a personal best.

2660 BERNARDHUNTER CRANE HIRE H'CAP 7f 30y
8:40 (8:42) (Class 5) (0-70,70) 4-Y-O+ **£5,175** (£1,540; £769; £384) **Stalls** Low

Form RPR

4-13 **1** **Qaffaal (USA)**[34] 1652 5-9-1 **69**.... NathanEvans(5) 3 78+
(Michael Easterby) *t.k.h: hld up in tch: effrt over 2f out: rdn to ld ins fnl f: edgd lft: kpt on wl* **2/1**[1]

6200 **2** 1 **Atreus**[10] 2330 4-8-7 **56**....(p) JamesSullivan 5 62
(Michael Easterby) *cl up: led gng wl over 2f out: rdn over 1f out: hdd ins fnl f: kpt on same pce towards fin* **14/1**

0333 **3** 1¾ **Picks Pinta**[7] 2416 5-9-3 **66**....(b) PatrickMathers 1 67
(John David Riches) *s.i.s: hld up: hdwy on outside over 2f out: ev ch and rdn whn hung lft ent fnl f: sn edgd rt and one pce last 100yds* **7/2**[2]

54-3 **4** 1 **Courier**[10] 2347 4-9-1 **67**.... JacobButterfield(3) 7 66
(Marjorie Fife) *led: rdn and hdd over 2f out: rallied: kpt on same pce fnl f* **9/1**

5-56 **5** 2¾ **Rasaman (IRE)**[34] 1625 12-9-4 **70**.... JoeDoyle(3) 4 61
(Jim Goldie) *t.k.h early: hld up: rdn and outpcd over 2f out: sme late hdwy: no imp* **6/1**[3]

1030 **6** ½ **Azrur (IRE)**[28] 1841 6-9-7 **70**.... PhillipMakin 6 60
(Keith Dalgleish) *t.k.h: trckd ldrs tl rdn and wknd fr 2f out* **6/1**[3]

2444 **7** 1 **Kicking The Can (IRE)**[10] 2329 5-8-7 **56** oh3.... AndrewMullen 8 43
(David Thompson) *in tch: drvn over 2f out: wknd over 1f out* **10/1**

1m 30.68s (1.68) **Going Correction** +0.35s/f (Good) 7 Ran SP% **109.9**
Speed ratings (Par 103): **104,102,100,99,96 96,94**
CSF £28.53 CT £84.71 TOTE £2.20: £1.60, £5.60; EX 25.60 Trifecta £115.40.
Owner Calam & Holdsworth & M Burrows **Bred** Shadwell Farm LLC **Trained** Sheriff Hutton, N Yorks

FOCUS
Race distance increased by 7 yards. They went a solid pace in this moderate handicap which resulted in a 1-2 for trainer Michael Easterby. The runner-up set the standard.

2661 MACBET BEST ODDS GUARANTEED ALL RACES H'CAP 1m
9:10 (9:11) (Class 6) (0-65,64) 4-Y-O+ **£3,234** (£962; £481; £240) **Stalls** Low

Form RPR

0054 **1** **Adventureman**[18] 2092 4-8-13 **56**....(p) JamesSullivan 8 64
(Ruth Carr) *mde all at modest gallop: shkn up over 1f out: hld on wl last 100yds* **16/1**

-001 **2** nk **Curzon Line**[8] 2409 7-8-12 **60**.... NathanEvans(5) 6 67
(Michael Easterby) *in tch: smooth hdwy to chse wnr over 1f out: sn rdn: kpt on fnl f: jst hld* **11/10**[1]

0-13 **3** nk **Charles De Mille**[3] 2555 8-9-0 **57**.... GrahamLee 5 64
(Jedd O'Keeffe) *hld up in midfield: effrt and rdn 2f out: kpt on ins fnl f: hld nr fin* **7/2**[2]

60-5 **4** 4½ **Nelson's Bay**[10] 2329 7-8-9 **59**.... HollieDoyle(7) 7 55
(Wilf Storey) *hld up: hdwy on outside over 2f out: rdn and edgd rt over 1f out: kpt on fnl f: nt rch ldrs* **12/1**

/53- **5** ¾ **Exclusive Diamond**[459] 668 4-8-12 **55**.... PhillipMakin 3 49
(David O'Meara) *s.i.s: bhd: pushed along over 2f out: kpt on fnl f: nvr able to chal* **16/1**

1-35 **6** 1 **Opt Out**[18] 2091 6-9-7 **64**....(p) PJMcDonald 10 56
(Alistair Whillans) *s.i.s: hld up: rdn over 2f out: no imp fr over 1f out* **10/1**

6-00 **7** 1 **Cyflymder (IRE)**[115] 429 10-8-9 **52**.... JoeyHaynes 11 41
(David C Griffiths) *chsd ldrs: rdn over 2f out: wknd 1f out* **25/1**

-600 **8** 1¼ **Tiger's Home**[129] 246 6-9-0 **62**.... ShirleyTeasdale(5) 2 48
(Iain Jardine) *t.k.h: in tch: rdn over 2f out: edgd rt and wknd over 1f out* **40/1**

0-56 **9** 2¼ **Let Right Be Done**[18] 2091 4-9-6 **63**.... DavidNolan 1 44
(Linda Perratt) *chsd wnr: rdn over 2f out: wknd over 1f out* **22/1**

3-23 **10** 2¾ **Silver Duke (IRE)**[18] 2091 5-9-2 **62**....(b) JoeDoyle(3) 9 36
(Jim Goldie) *s.i.s: hld up: pushed along over 2f out: sn wknd: btn over 1f out* **6/1**[3]

1m 43.51s (2.31) **Going Correction** +0.35s/f (Good) 10 Ran SP% **123.3**
Speed ratings (Par 101): **102,101,101,96,96 95,94,92,90,87**
CSF £35.55 CT £86.59 TOTE £20.70: £3.00, £1.10, £1.80; EX 56.90 Trifecta £510.80.
Owner The Venturers & Mrs R Carr **Bred** Cheveley Park Stud Ltd **Trained** Huby, N Yorks

FOCUS
Race distance increased by 7 yards. It paid to race handily in this ordinary handicap and this is fair form for the grade with the first three clear.
T/Plt: £84.80 to a £1 stake. Pool: £58,050.31 - 499.27 winning tickets T/Qpdt: £19.50 to a £1 stake. Pool: £4,497.61 - 170.10 winning tickets **Richard Young**

[1783]PONTEFRACT (L-H)
Friday, May 27

OFFICIAL GOING: Good (8.2)
Wind: Virtually nil Weather: Fine & dry

2662 SOLUTIONS 4 CLEANING H'CAP 1m 4y
6:30 (6:30) (Class 5) (0-75,75) 4-Y-O+ **£3,234** (£962; £481; £240) **Stalls** Low

Form RPR

-000 **1** **Auspicion**[17] 2121 4-9-5 **73**.... AndrewElliott 3 82
(Tom Tate) *trckd ldng pair on inner: effrt and swtchd rt over 1f out: rdn to chal ins fnl f: led last 100yds: kpt on wl* **9/1**

05-5 **2** 1¼ **Stardrifter**[21] 2010 4-8-11 **72**.... AdamMcNamara(7) 5 78+
(Richard Fahey) *dwlt and in rr: swtchd rt to outer and gd hdwy over 1f out: n.m.r and swtchd rt again ent fnl f: sn rdn and styd on wl towards fin* **9/2**[1]

5-20 **3** shd **Lopes Dancer (IRE)**[33] 1664 4-9-6 **74**.... KierenFallon 1 80
(Alan Swinbank) *t.k.h early: trckd ldrs on inner: effrt and nt clr run over 1f out: swtchd rt and rdn jst ins fnl f: styd on wl towards fin* **9/2**[1]

-004 **4** nk **Talent Scout (IRE)**[25] 1926 10-8-7 **66**....(p) GemmaTutty(5) 2 71
(Karen Tutty) *set stdy pce: rdn and qcknd 2f out: drvn over 1f out: hdd last 100yds: kpt on same pce* **15/2**[3]

0-30 **5** 1¾ **Toga Tiger (IRE)**[102] 595 9-9-7 **75**.... LiamJones 9 76
(Kevin Frost) *in tch on outer: hdwy 2f out: rdn and edgd lft ent fnl f: sn drvn and kpt on towards fin* **25/1**

20-4 **6** ¾ **Le Laitier (FR)**[30] 1785 5-8-9 **63**.... BenCurtis 11 63
(Scott Dixon) *prom: cl up after 2f: chal over 2f out: rdn wl over 1f out: drvn appr fnl f and grad wknd* **25/1**

3-52 **7** ½ **Pumaflor (IRE)**[10] 2347 4-9-7 **75**.... GeorgeChaloner 6 73
(Richard Whitaker) *hld up towards rr: hdwy 3f out: rdn along 2f out: kpt on fnl f* **5/1**[2]

5-05 **8** ½ **Janaab (IRE)**[34] 1631 6-8-9 **68**....(t) RachelRichardson(5) 4 65
(Tim Easterby) *trckd ldrs: hdwy 3f out: rdn along wl over 1f out: sn drvn and one pce* **5/1**[2]

0-20 **9** 10 **Pivotman**[30] 1785 8-9-3 **71**....(bt) GrahamGibbons 8 45
(Michael Easterby) *midfield: hdwy to trck ldrs 4f out: rdn along 3f out: wknd wl over 1f out* **10/1**

0-50 **10** 2 **Osteopathic Remedy (IRE)**[13] 2256 12-9-5 **73**.... ConnorBeasley 7 43
(John Davies) *chsd ldrs: rdn along wl over 2f out: sn wknd* **20/1**

104- **11** 4 **Ivors Involvement (IRE)**[219] 7388 4-9-3 **71**.... TomEaves 10 31
(Tina Jackson) *dwlt: a in rr* **40/1**

1m 46.69s (0.79) **Going Correction** +0.20s/f (Good) 11 Ran SP% **115.4**
Speed ratings (Par 103): **104,102,102,102,100 99,99,98,88,86 82**
CSF £46.09 CT £208.70 TOTE £11.00: £3.80, £1.30, £2.20; EX 62.80 Trifecta £422.00.
Owner David Storey **Bred** Lael Stables **Trained** Tadcaster, N Yorks

FOCUS
The rail from the 6f start to the winning line was out by five yards adding approximately eight yards to all races. This was run at just an ordinary gallop and suited those ridden prominently. The winner ran his best race since joining Tom Tate.

2663 CONSTANT SECURITY SERVING YORKSHIRE RACECOURSES H'CAP 1m 4f 8y
7:00 (7:01) (Class 4) (0-80,80) 4-Y-O+ **£5,175** (£1,540; £769; £384) **Stalls** Low

Form RPR

5/36 **1** **Touch The Sky**[15] 2174 5-9-1 **74** ...... WilliamBuick 8 86+
(David Elsworth) *trckd ldng pair: hdwy and cl up over 3f out: led 2f out: sn rdn clr: kpt on strly* **4/1**[1]

4-46 **2** 3¼ **Medina Sidonia (IRE)**[27] 1852 4-8-8 **72** ......(p) RachelRichardson(5) 5 77
(Tim Easterby) *trckd ldrs: effrt over 2f out: sn rdn along and sltly outpcd over 1f out: drvn and kpt on fnl f* **8/1**

0-31 **3** shd **Russian Royale**[37] 1561 6-8-9 **75** ...... RowanScott(7) 1 79
(Micky Hammond) *dwlt and in rr: stdy hdwy over 3f out: rdn wl over 1f out: drvn and kpt on fnl f* **7/1**

-220 **4** 6 **Busy Street**[16] 2163 4-9-7 **80** ...... KierenFallon 4 75
(Alan Swinbank) *hld up in rr: hdwy on outer over 3f out: rdn along to chse ldrs 2f out: drvn over 1f out: sn one pce* **9/2**[2]

1-03 **5** 1½ **Dolphin Village (IRE)**[15] 2176 6-9-6 **79** ...... TomQueally 10 71
(Jane Chapple-Hyam) *hld up in rr: hdwy 3f out: rdn along outer to chse ldrs wl over 1f out: sn drvn and wknd* **10/1**

530- **6** 1 **Di's Gift**[224] 7254 7-8-13 **72** ......(e[1]) TomEaves 6 63
(Shaun Harris) *led: pushed along 3f out: rdn 2f out: sn hdd & wknd* **33/1**

1315 **7** 1 **Chilworth Bells**[10] 2328 4-8-13 **77** ...... JosephineGordon(5) 3 66
(David Barron) *trckd ldr on inner: rdn along 3f out: sn drvn and wknd* **6/1**[3]

20-3 **8** 6 **Poetic Verse**[20] 2051 6-9-0 **80** ...... AdamMcNamara(7) 2 60
(John Quinn) *a towards rr* **4/1**[1]

4503 **9** 21 **The Lock Master (IRE)**[13] 2233 9-8-8 **67** ......(p) LiamJones 7 13
(Michael Appleby) *trckd ldrs on outer: pushed along 4f out: rdn over 3f out: sn lost pl and bhd fnl 2f* **20/1**

2m 39.74s (-1.06) **Going Correction** +0.20s/f (Good) **9** Ran SP% **112.9**
Speed ratings (Par 105): **111,108,108,104,103 103,102,98,84**
CSF £35.31 CT £214.41 TOTE £4.10: £1.60, £2.90, £2.60; EX 34.00 Trifecta £311.10.
Owner Lordship Stud & Christopher Wright **Bred** Lordship Stud **Trained** Newmarket, Suffolk

FOCUS
Race distance increased by 8 yards. This was run at a medium gallop and provided an interesting and unexposed winner, who clearly has the potential to prove a bit better than this.

2664 EBF STALLIONS YOUNGSTERS CONDITIONS STKS (PLUS 10 RACE) 6f
7:30 (7:30) (Class 2) 2-Y-O **£12,450** (£3,728; £1,864; £932) **Stalls** Low

Form RPR

1 **1** **Yalta (IRE)**[8] 2390 2-9-2 0 ...... WilliamBuick 1 97+
(Mark Johnston) *sn led: quiuckened and pushed clr wl over 1f out: readily* **30/100**[1]

1 **2** 4½ **Wedding Dress**[30] 1793 2-8-11 0 ...... PatCosgrave 2 77
(David Brown) *trckd wnr on inner to 1/2-way: rdn over 2f out: drvn wl over 1f out: kpt on fnl f: no ch w wnr* **8/1**[3]

11 **3** hd **Orewa (IRE)**[17] 2119 2-9-2 0 ...... BenCurtis 4 81
(Brian Ellison) *hld up in rr: hdwy on outer wl over 2f out: rdn to chse wnr over 1f out: drvn ent fnl f: kpt on: no ch w wnr* **7/1**[2]

015 **4** 2¼ **Cullingworth (IRE)**[13] 2240 2-9-2 0 ...... JackGarritty 3 75
(Richard Fahey) *cl up: trckd wnr 1/2-way: rdn along jst over 2f out: drvn wl over 1f out: sn wknd* **12/1**

1m 17.92s (1.02) **Going Correction** +0.20s/f (Good) **4** Ran SP% **108.2**
Speed ratings (Par 99): **101,95,94,91**
CSF £3.28 TOTE £1.20; EX 3.50 Trifecta £8.00.
Owner Sheikh Hamdan bin Mohammed Al Maktoum **Bred** Darley **Trained** Middleham Moor, N Yorks

FOCUS
Race distance increased by 8 yards. Four previous winners in this conditions race for juveniles and a very interesting winner who is now Royal Ascot bound. The form could be rated higher.

2665 CONSTANT SECURITY SERVICES H'CAP 5f
8:00 (8:01) (Class 4) (0-85,85) 4-Y-O+ **£5,175** (£1,540; £769; £384) **Stalls** Low

Form RPR

-062 **1** **Stanghow**[10] 2346 4-9-0 **78** ...... PatCosgrave 10 86
(Antony Brittain) *trckd ldng pair: hdwy wl over 1f out: rdn to take slt ld 1f out: sn drvn and narrowly hdd ins fnl f: sn drvn and rallied to ld nr line* **12/1**

0-31 **2** shd **Majestic Hero (IRE)**[13] 2253 4-9-4 **82** ...... RichardKingscote 2 90
(Ronald Harris) *trckd ldr: cl up over 2f out: effrt to dispute ld over 1f out and ev ch: drvn to take slt ld ins fnl f: hdd and no ex nr line* **7/2**[1]

5-15 **3** 1¼ **Alpha Delphini**[13] 2259 5-9-5 **83** ...... ConnorBeasley 12 87+
(Bryan Smart) *hld up in rr: hdwy on outer wl over 1f out: rdn and styd on wl fnl f: nrst fin* **9/1**

6-10 **4** ¾ **Bondi Beach Boy**[6] 2488 7-9-4 **82** ...... GeorgeChaloner 3 83
(James Turner) *chsd ldrs: hdwy 2f out: rdn wl over 1f out: kpt on fnl f* **9/2**[2]

-603 **5** 1¼ **Singeur (IRE)**[10] 2346 9-9-2 **80** ...... BarryMcHugh 7 76
(Rebecca Bastiman) *chsd ldrs: rdn along wl over 1f out: drvn and kpt on same pce fnl f* **14/1**

0-04 **6** nk **Desert Ace (IRE)**[9] 2364 5-9-5 **83** ......(p) PaulMulrennan 6 78
(Michael Dods) *hld up towards rr: hdwy 2f out: effrt whn n.m.r ent fnl f: sn swtchd rt and rdn: no imp* **8/1**

0-06 **7** ¾ **Master Bond**[13] 2261 7-9-4 **82** ...... DanielTudhope 4 75+
(David O'Meara) *hld up towards rr: hdwy wl over 1f out: effrt whn n.m.r jst ins fnl f: one pce after* **7/1**

-304 **8** 1¼ **Kibaar**[11] 2305 4-9-7 **85** ...... TomEaves 1 73+
(Kevin Ryan) *trckd ldrs on inner: effrt whn nt clr run over 1f out: sn swtchd rt and rdn: no hdwy* **6/1**[3]

-016 **9** 1½ **Soul Brother (IRE)**[11] 2305 5-9-5 **83** ......(b) JackGarritty 9 69+
(Tim Easterby) *t.k.h: hld up in rr: effrt on inner whn nt clr run over 1f out: sn swtchd rt: no hdwy* **14/1**

35-0 **10** nk **Jack Lucy**[6] 2491 9-9-0 **78** ......(b) TomQueally 5 60
(Lawrence Mullaney) *led: jnd over 2f out: sn rdn: hdd over 1f out and sn wknd* **16/1**

00-0 **11** 13 **Native Falls (IRE)**[7] 2426 5-9-0 **78** ...... KierenFallon 11 13
(Alan Swinbank) *in tch on outer: rdn along over 2f out: sn outpcd and bhd* **40/1**

1m 3.53s (0.23) **Going Correction** +0.20s/f (Good) **11** Ran SP% **117.6**
Speed ratings (Par 105): **106,105,103,102,100 100,98,96,94,94 73**
CSF £53.80 CT £413.31 TOTE £14.20: £3.60, £1.80, £2.40; EX 62.40 Trifecta £557.80.
Owner Antony Brittain **Bred** Mel Brittain **Trained** Warthill, N Yorks

FOCUS
Race distance increased by 8 yards. Mainly exposed sorts in this sprint, but personal bests from the front two.

2666 ALAMO BUSINESS SYSTEMS FILLIES' H'CAP 1m 2f 6y
8:30 (8:31) (Class 5) (0-70,73) 3-Y-O+ **£3,234** (£962; £481; £240) **Stalls** Low

Form RPR

30-2 **1** **Peloponnese (FR)**[27] 1860 3-9-0 **70** ......(v[1]) TedDurcan 2 83
(Sir Michael Stoute) *trckd ldr: hdwy to ld 3f out: rdn clr over 1f out: kpt on wl* **10/11**[1]

35-1 **2** 5 **Kath's Legacy**[8] 2415 3-9-3 **73** 6ex ...... OisinMurphy 8 76
(Ben De Haan) *trckd ldrs: hdwy to chse wnr 2f out: sn rdn: swtchd lft and drvn ent fnl f: no imp* **4/1**[2]

0-60 **3** 1¾ **Pennerley**[21] 1989 3-8-10 **69** ...... ThomasBrown(3) 3 69
(James Eustace) *hld up in rr: hdwy on inner over 2f out: chsd ldrs over 1f out: sn rdn and kpt on same pce* **9/1**

4302 **4** 2¼ **The Dukkerer (IRE)**[10] 2343 5-9-4 **60** ...... TomEaves 4 56
(James Given) *led: pushed along over 3f out: sn hdd and rdn: drvn wl over 1f out: plugged on one pce* **16/1**

4-50 **5** 3 **Big Red**[8] 2409 4-9-0 **56** oh11 ...... BarryMcHugh 5 46
(Rebecca Bastiman) *chsd ldrs: rdn along over 2f out: drvn wl over 1f out: sn one pce* **40/1**

65-6 **6** 2½ **Kilim**[21] 2011 3-8-8 **64** ...... LemosdeSouza 1 48
(Luca Cumani) *trckd ldrs: effrt over 2f out: sn rdn along and wknd wl over 1f out* **15/2**[3]

35-0 **7** 1 **La Celebs Ville (IRE)**[31] 1758 3-9-0 **70** ......(p) RichardKingscote 10 52
(Tom Dascombe) *hld up: effrt and sme hdwy on outer over 2f out: rdn along wl over 1f out: sn wknd* **16/1**

44-0 **8** 6 **Royal Pearl**[17] 2123 3-7-13 **60** ...... NoelGarbutt(5) 6 30
(Tom Gretton) *v s.i.s and bhd: jnd field 1/2-way: rdn along wl over 2f out: sn outpcd and bhd* **50/1**

63-1 **U** **Sattelac**[32] 1698 3-8-10 **66** ...... TomQueally 9
(Keith Dalgleish) *stmbld and uns rdr s* **12/1**

2m 14.66s (0.96) **Going Correction** +0.20s/f (Good)
WFA 3 from 4yo+ 14lb **9** Ran SP% **118.0**
Speed ratings (Par 100): **104,100,98,96,94 92,91,86,**
CSF £4.78 CT £20.52 TOTE £1.70: £1.02, £2.00, £3.30; EX 4.90 Trifecta £36.70.
Owner Niarchos Family **Bred** Famille Niarchos **Trained** Newmarket, Suffolk

FOCUS
Race distance increased by 8 yards. A fair gallop to this fillies' handicap which produced a well-handicapped winner, but there is little depth to it with the first three finishing in the order to market expected.

2667 RONALD MCNALLY MEMORIAL MAIDEN STKS 6f
9:00 (9:03) (Class 5) 3-Y-O+ **£3,234** (£962; £481; £240) **Stalls** Low

Form RPR

2 **1** **Get Up And Dance**[13] 2234 3-9-0 0 ...... OisinMurphy 8 73+
(William Haggas) *trckd ldrs: smooth hdwy and cl up 2f out: led wl over 1f out: sn clr: readily* **1/1**[1]

6-30 **2** 5 **Dance Alone**[20] 2049 3-9-5 70 ......(p) TomEaves 4 62
(Kevin Ryan) *led: pushed along and jnd 2f out: sn hdd and rdn: drvn over 1f out: kpt on same pce* **5/1**[3]

2-20 **3** ½ **Mister Mischief**[20] 2049 3-9-5 68 ...... GrahamGibbons 2 60
(Paul Midgley) *in tch: effrt whn n.m.r on inner over 2f out: rdn to chse ldrs over 1f out: kpt on same pce* **10/3**[2]

06 **4** 5 **Portland Street (IRE)**[17] 2122 3-9-5 0 ...... PaulMulrennan 7 44
(Bryan Smart) *hld up towards rr: hdwy over 2f out: rdn whn swtchd lft over 1f out: sn no imp* **33/1**

6 **5** ¾ **Oyster Card**[24] 1953 3-9-2 0 ...... AlistairRawlinson(3) 1 42
(Michael Appleby) *towards rr: green and sn pushed along: rdn 1/2-way: hdwy on inner wl over 1f out: styd on fnl f: nrst fin* **25/1**

0-6 **6** nk **Man Of La Mancha (IRE)**[43] 1449 3-9-0 0 ......(t) RobJFitzpatrick(5) 9 41
(Ben Haslam) *s.i.s: a towards rr* **40/1**

7 1¾ **Lovin' Spoonful** 3-9-0 0 ......(b[1]) ConnorBeasley 6 30
(Bryan Smart) *green: sn rdn along and outpcd in rr tl sme late hdwy* **20/1**

8 4½ **Website**[247] 4-10-0 75 ......(p) PatCosgrave 3 23
(Robert Cowell) *chsd ldrs on inner: pushed along over 2f out: rdn wl over 1f out: drvn and hld whn hung bdly rt over 1f out: wknd* **7/1**

65 **9** 5 **Another Desperado (IRE)**[27] 1870 3-9-5 0 ...... BarryMcHugh 10 5
(Rebecca Bastiman) *chsd ldrs on outer: rdn along over 2f out: sn wknd* **66/1**

00- **10** 58 **Gettin' Lucky**[240] 6856 3-9-5 0 ......(v[1]) BenCurtis 5
(John Balding) *prom: rdn along 1/2-way: lost pl qckly and bhd whn eased wl over 1f out* **66/1**

1m 19.19s (2.29) **Going Correction** +0.20s/f (Good)
WFA 3 from 4yo 9lb **10** Ran SP% **119.2**
Speed ratings (Par 103): **92,85,84,78,77 76,74,68,61,**
CSF £6.15 TOTE £2.00: £1.10, £1.90, £1.70; EX 5.70 Trifecta £17.50.
Owner Qatar Racing & Clipper Logistics **Bred** Whitsbury Manor Stud **Trained** Newmarket, Suffolk

FOCUS
Race distance increased by 8 yards. A sprint maiden for older horses which lacked strength in depth, but it threw up an interesting winner who was building on debut promise..
T/Plt: £20.50 to a £1 stake. Pool: £66,476.87 - 2,359.34 winning tickets T/Qpdt: £3.50 to a £1 stake. Pool: £4,545.41 - 944.85 winning tickets **Joe Rowntree**

2118 BEVERLEY (R-H)
Saturday, May 28

OFFICIAL GOING: Good to firm (8.1)
Wind: Moderate behind Weather: Grey cloud

2668 SIGNUPBONUSES.CO.UK UK'S TOP GAMBLING SITES MEDIAN AUCTION MAIDEN STKS 5f
1:50 (1:50) (Class 5) 3-Y-O **£3,780** (£1,131; £565; £283; £141) **Stalls** Low

Form RPR

0-22 **1** **Geno (IRE)**[11] 2336 3-9-2 75 ......(b) JoeDoyle(3) 4 74
(Kevin Ryan) *mde all: rdn over 1f out: drvn ins fnl f: hld on wl towards fin* **1/1**[1]

-305 **2** 1¼ **Kingthistle**[19] 2095 3-9-5 65 ...... GrahamLee 1 70
(Michael Easterby) *hld up in rr: hdwy 2f out: rdn over 1f out: styd on wl fnl f* **8/1**

22-4 **3** ½ **Sunnyside Bob (IRE)**[28] 1870 3-9-5 77 ...... PhillipMakin 2 68
(David O'Meara) *chsd wnr: hdwy wl over 1f out: rdn and ev ch ent fnl f: sn drvn and kpt on same pce* **11/4**[2]

2 **4** 2 1/2 **Evenlode (IRE)**[28] 1870 3-9-5 0 GrahamGibbons 6 59
(David Barron) *towards rr: pushed along 1/2-way: rdn and sme hdwy wl over 1f out: drvn and no imp fnl f* **5/1**[3]

53 **5** 3 1/4 **Ryedale Rio (IRE)**[11] 2333 3-9-5 0 DavidAllan 5 47
(Tim Easterby) *trckd ldrs: hdwy to chse ldng pair over 2f out: sn rdn: wknd over 1f out* **12/1**

1m 1.65s (-1.85) **Going Correction** -0.35s/f (Firm) **5** Ran SP% **112.1**
Speed ratings (Par 99): **100,98,97,93,88**
CSF £9.92 TOTE £1.60: £1.20, £2.80; EX 9.30 Trifecta £29.10.
Owner Matt & Lauren Morgan **Bred** T Jones **Trained** Hambleton, N Yorks

FOCUS
The rail has been moved around the bottom bend, adding 18 yards to race distances on the Round course. A modest maiden that was dominated by the favourite. He didn't need to improve.

2669 BRIAN YEARDLEY CONTINENTAL TWO YEAR OLD TROPHY CONDITIONS STKS (PLUS 10 RACE) 5f
2:25 (2:26) (Class 2) 2-Y-O
£15,562 (£4,660; £2,330; £1,165; £582; £292) **Stalls** Low

Form RPR

1 **Prince Of Lir (IRE)** 2-8-9 0 LukeMorris 6 94+
(Robert Cowell) *cl up: effrt 2f out: rdn to ld jst over 1f out: kpt on strly fnl f* **6/1**

12 **2** 1 1/4 **The Last Lion (IRE)**[31] 1770 2-9-2 0 JoeFanning 7 96
(Mark Johnston) *in tch on outer: hdwy wl over 1f out: rdn to chal jst ins fnl f: ev ch tl drvn and nt qckn last 75yds* **9/4**[2]

13 **3** 2 1/4 **Rainbow Mist (IRE)**[13] 2264 2-9-0 0 PJMcDonald 5 86
(Ann Duffield) *towards rr: swtchd rt and hdwy on outer over 1f out: sn rdn and styd on wl towards fin* **10/1**

214 **4** 1/2 **Mailshot (USA)**[14] 2240 2-9-2 0 GrahamLee 4 86
(Mark Johnston) *slt ld: pushed along and hdd 2f out: sn rdn and kpt on same pce* **4/1**[3]

3 **5** shd **Logi (IRE)**[17] 2162 2-8-12 0 PatDobbs 1 82
(Richard Hannon) *cl up on inner: slt ld 2f out: sn rdn: hdd and hdd jst over 1f out: wknd* **7/4**[1]

614 **6** 8 **Springwood (IRE)**[16] 2173 2-9-2 0 TonyHamilton 2 57
(Richard Fahey) *a in rr* **16/1**

1m 1.37s (-2.13) **Going Correction** -0.35s/f (Firm) **6** Ran SP% **116.4**
Speed ratings (Par 99): **103,101,97,96,96 83**
CSF £20.84 TOTE £9.00: £3.30, £1.10; EX 28.60 Trifecta £108.00.
Owner The Cool Silk Partnership **Bred** Philip & Orla Hore **Trained** Six Mile Bottom, Cambs

FOCUS
Race distance as advertised. A useful conditions race that went to the newcomer, who is clearly decent. The time was 0.38secs faster than the following race for fillies.

2670 HILARY NEEDLER TROPHY FILLIES' CONDITIONS STKS (PLUS 10 RACE) 5f
3:00 (3:01) (Class 2) 2-Y-O
£15,562 (£4,660; £2,330; £1,165; £582; £292) **Stalls** Low

Form RPR

1 **1** **Grizzel (IRE)**[9] 2410 2-8-12 0 PatDobbs 2 93
(Richard Hannon) *hld up in rr: swtchd lft and hdwy over 1f out: n.m.r and swtchd rt ent fnl f: sn rdn and styd on strly last 150yds to ld nr fin* **5/2**[2]

21 **2** nk **Clem Fandango (FR)**[25] 1951 2-8-12 0 PhillipMakin 6 92
(Keith Dalgleish) *cl up: rdn to ld jst over 1f out: drvn ins fnl f: hdd and no ex towards fin* **6/1**

1 **3** 2 1/4 **Spin Doctor**[22] 2007 2-8-12 0 TonyHamilton 8 84
(Richard Fahey) *trckd ldng pair: hdwy on outer wl over 1f out: rdn appr fnl f: kpt on same pce* **7/2**[3]

12 **4** hd **Boater (IRE)**[15] 2219 2-8-12 0 JoeFanning 3 83
(Mark Johnston) *slt ld and gd pce: rdn 2f out: drvn and hdd over 1f out: wknd fnl f* **2/1**[1]

10 **5** 3 3/4 **Coolfitch (IRE)**[15] 2219 2-8-12 0 GrahamGibbons 4 71
(David O'Meara) *chsd ldrs: rdn along 2f out: sn drvn and wknd* **16/1**

4 **6** 2 1/4 **Indigo Beat**[14] 2254 2-8-12 0 PJMcDonald 7 61
(Ann Duffield) *a in rr* **33/1**

3 **7** 1 1/4 **Our Greta (IRE)**[24] 1965 2-8-12 0 LukeMorris 1 57
(Michael Appleby) *chsd ldrs on inner: rdn along 2f out: sn wknd* **14/1**

1m 1.75s (-1.75) **Going Correction** -0.35s/f (Firm) **7** Ran SP% **113.9**
Speed ratings (Par 96): **100,99,95,87,81 78,76**
CSF £17.68 TOTE £4.10: £1.40, £2.80; EX 21.00 Trifecta £61.50.
Owner Merriebelle Irish Farm/Potensis B'Stock **Bred** Martin Butler **Trained** East Everleigh, Wilts

FOCUS
Race distance as advertised. The front three came clear of the below-par favourite in what was a good little conditions race, the event getting back towards what it used to be following a good winner last year. The time was 0.38secs slower than the colts race previously.

2671 HAPPY BIRTHDAY GRAHAM HALLETT FILLIES' H'CAP 1m 1f 207y
3:35 (3:36) (Class 3) (0-95,90) 4-Y-O+
£7,158 (£2,143; £1,071; £535; £267; £134) **Stalls** Low

Form RPR

0-40 **1** **Loaves And Fishes**[10] 2363 4-9-5 **88** PhillipMakin 5 98
(David O'Meara) *led at sound pce: stdd 1/2-way: qcknd over 2f out: rdn clr over 1f out: drvn and kpt on wl towards fin* **6/1**

2 1 1/2 **Rosental**[246] 4-9-4 **90** KevinStott(3) 1 97+
(Luca Cumani) *hld up in tch: hdwy 2f out: swtchd lft and effrt over 1f out: swtchd rt and rdn ent fnl f: sn chsng wnr: drvn and no imp last 100yds* **9/4**[2]

2-02 **3** 3 1/4 **La Superba (IRE)**[14] 2236 4-9-5 **88** (p) GrahamLee 4 89
(David Elsworth) *trckd ldrs: hdwy over 2f out: rdn along wl over 1f out: sltly hmpd appr fnl f: kpt on same pce* **2/1**[1]

-526 **4** nk **Victoria Pollard**[12] 2313 4-8-10 **82** (p) RobHornby(3) 3 82
(Andrew Balding) *hld up in rr: hdwy over 2f out: effrt on outer and sltly hmpd over 1f out: rdn and kpt on one pce fnl f* **6/1**

-350 **5** 1 1/4 **Donna Graciosa (GER)**[27] 1880 4-8-7 **76** JoeFanning 6 73
(Mark Johnston) *trckd ldng pair: hdwy to chse wnr 1/2-way: rdn along over 2f out: drvn over 1f out: wknd ent fnl f* **11/2**[3]

0 **6** 4 **Shingwedzi (SAF)**[30] 1802 5-9-7 **90** (b) PatDobbs 2 79
(Ed Dunlop) *chsd wnr to 1/2-way: prom on inner: rdn along over 2f out: wknd wl over 1f out* **20/1**

2m 3.19s (-3.81) **Going Correction** -0.20s/f (Firm) **6** Ran SP% **112.8**
Speed ratings (Par 104): **107,105,103,102,101 98**
CSF £20.12 TOTE £8.40: £3.50, £1.70; EX 34.70 Trifecta £92.00.
Owner Nick Bradley Racing 15 **Bred** Whitley Stud **Trained** Upper Helmsley, N Yorks

FOCUS
Actual race distance 1m2f 5yds. No hanging around here but the front-running winner maintained the gallop. She built on last season's form for a different yard.

2672 ADVIEW.CO.UK CUP H'CAP 1m 1f 207y
4:10 (4:11) (Class 5) (0-75,74) 4-Y-O+ **£3,780** (£1,131; £565; £283; £141) **Stalls** Low

Form RPR

00-6 **1** **King Of The Celts (IRE)**[26] 1923 8-8-9 **67** RachelRichardson(5) 2 73
(Tim Easterby) *trckd ldr: hdwy over 2f out: rdn to chal on inner wl over 1f out: slt ld ent fnl f: sn drvn and hld on wl* **5/2**[1]

5315 **2** 1/2 **All You (IRE)**[11] 2347 4-9-5 **72** (v) PhillipMakin 9 77+
(David O'Meara) *hld up towards rr: gd hdwy 2f out: rdn over 1f out: chsd ldrs and n.m.r ins fnl f: squeezed through and kpt on strly towards fin* **9/2**[2]

-000 **3** hd **Mysterial**[14] 2233 6-8-7 **67** GerO'Neill(7) 4 71
(Declan Carroll) *t.k.h: led: clr 1/2-way: rdn along 2f out: edgd lft and hdd ent fnl f: kpt on wl u.p towards fin* **14/1**

26-0 **4** nk **Aneedh**[56] 1202 6-8-7 **63** (b) JoeDoyle(3) 6 66
(Clive Mulhall) *in tch: hdwy on inner 2f out: effrt and nt clr run ent fnl f: sn swtchd lft: rdn and n.m.r ins fnl f: kpt on* **12/1**

120- **5** 1/2 **Lopito De Vega (IRE)**[217] 7457 4-8-11 **64** DavidAllan 8 66
(David C Griffiths) *in tch: hdwy over 2f out: rdn to chse ldrs over 1f out: drvn and kpt on fnl f* **5/1**[3]

2-60 **6** nk **Captain Felix**[133] 215 4-9-7 **74** GrahamLee 3 76
(George Scott) *trckd ldrs: hdwy to chse ldng pair over 2f out: rdn and ev ch over 1f out: sn drvn and kpt on same pce* **9/1**

0330 **7** 2 3/4 **Dunquin (IRE)**[21] 2051 4-9-3 **70** PJMcDonald 7 66
(John Mackie) *trckd ldng pair: pushed along over 2f out: rdn wl over 1f out: grad wknd appr fnl f* **7/1**

0051 **8** 2 **Samsonite (IRE)**[22] 2015 4-8-11 **64** BarryMcHugh 1 56
(Tony Coyle) *hld up: a in rr* **8/1**

4350 **9** 2 **Cosmic Halo**[21] 2043 7-8-10 **63** TonyHamilton 5 51
(Richard Fahey) *stdd and swtchd rt s: hld up in rr: effrt and sme hdwy on outer over 2f out: rdn wl over 1f out: sn drvn and wknd* **16/1**

2m 4.96s (-2.04) **Going Correction** -0.20s/f (Firm) **9** Ran SP% **117.3**
Speed ratings (Par 103): **100,99,99,99,98 98,96,94,93**
CSF £13.79 CT £131.28 TOTE £3.30: £1.70, £1.40, £4.30; EX 11.70 Trifecta £271.80.
Owner Mrs B Oughtred **Bred** Gerrardstown House Stud **Trained** Great Habton, N Yorks

FOCUS
Actual race distance 1m2f 5yds. Run at a good gallop, the winner was well placed chasing the leader and the runner-up looked an unlucky loser. A bunch finish.

2673 BERYL AND JOE TURNER MEMORIAL H'CAP 1m 100y
4:45 (5:02) (Class 5) (0-70,70) 4-Y-O+ **£3,780** (£1,131; £565; £283; £141) **Stalls** Low

Form RPR

-602 **1** **Mr Cool Cash**[21] 2045 4-8-13 **65** PhilipPrince(3) 2 74
(Richard Guest) *trckd ldrs: hdwy on outer and cl up over 2f out: rdn to ld over 1f out: drvn ins fnl f: hld on wl towards fin* **4/1**[1]

5503 **2** hd **Lawyer (IRE)**[29] 1841 5-9-4 **67** GrahamGibbons 1 75
(David Barron) *chsd ldng pair: pushed along 2f out: rdn over 1f out: drvn and ev ch wl ins fnl f: no ex towards fin* **11/2**[2]

-550 **3** 1 **Save The Bees**[14] 2233 8-9-5 **68** TonyHamilton 3 73
(Declan Carroll) *t.k.h: led: rdn along 2f out: hdd over 1f out and sn drvn: kpt on u.p fnl f* **11/1**

6-00 **4** 1/2 **So It's War (FR)**[15] 2198 5-9-7 **70** (p) PhillipMakin 7 74+
(Keith Dalgleish) *in tch: hdwy 2f out: effrt and nt clr run ins fnl f: kpt on towards fin* **8/1**[3]

3-16 **5** 1 1/4 **John Caesar (IRE)**[31] 1785 5-9-1 **64** (t) BarryMcHugh 13 65+
(Rebecca Bastiman) *bhd: hdwy 2f out: swtchd to inner and rdn over 1f out: styd on wl fnl f: nrst fin* **20/1**

-000 **6** 1/2 **Tafahom (IRE)**[11] 2347 4-9-4 **67** LukeMorris 4 67
(Michael Easterby) *midfield: hdwy 3f out: rdn along 2f out: drvn over 1f out: kpt on fnl f* **33/1**

5030 **7** nse **Mercury**[5] 2525 4-8-5 **57** (b) JoeDoyle(3) 10 57
(Kevin Ryan) *in tch: hdwy 2f out: rdn to chse ldrs over 1f out: drvn and kpt on same pce fnl f* **16/1**

5-64 **8** 1 1/2 **Relight My Fire**[11] 2347 6-9-4 **67** (p) DavidAllan 8 64
(Tim Easterby) *hld up: hdwy 3f out: rdn to chse ldrs over 1f out: wknd fnl f* **4/1**[1]

3034 **9** 3 1/2 **The Firm (IRE)**[33] 1707 7-9-5 **68** (be) JoeFanning 9 56
(Daniel Mark Loughnane) *hld up: a towards rr* **14/1**

00-0 **10** 1/2 **Inspector Norse**[18] 2121 5-9-0 **68** RachelRichardson(5) 6 55
(Tim Easterby) *rrd s: a in rr* **20/1**

250- **11** 1 1/4 **Fazza**[218] 7427 9-9-0 **63** PaddyAspell 11 47
(Grant Tuer) *in tch: rdn along over 2f out: sn wknd* **33/1**

1011 **12** 1 3/4 **Ellaal**[19] 2091 7-9-5 **68** GrahamLee 5 48
(Ruth Carr) *trckd ldr: cl up 3f out: rdn along 2f out: sn drvn and wknd over 1f out* **4/1**[1]

1m 44.88s (-2.72) **Going Correction** -0.20s/f (Firm) **12** Ran SP% **122.8**
Speed ratings (Par 103): **105,104,103,103,102 101,101,100,96,96 94,93**
CSF £25.45 CT £193.77 TOTE £4.90: £1.70, £2.20, £3.60; EX 33.70 Trifecta £311.40.
Owner I Lawson **Bred** T G Holdcroft **Trained** Ingmanthorpe, W Yorks
■ Stewards' Enquiry : Graham Gibbons seven-day ban; used whip above the permitted level (11th-17th June)
Philip Prince four-day ban; used whip above the permitted level (11th-13th, 19th June)

FOCUS
Actual race distance 1m 118yds. A pretty moderate handicap, with those racing prominently favoured, and the winner showed a plucky attitude. He rates a length pb.

2674 CONSTANT SECURITY H'CAP 7f 100y
5:20 (5:36) (Class 5) (0-70,75) 3-Y-O **£3,780** (£1,131; £565; £283; £141) **Stalls** Low

Form RPR

5-03 **1** **Popsies Joy (IRE)**[8] 2428 3-9-0 **63** DuranFentiman 6 74
(Tim Easterby) *midfield: hdwy wl over 2f out: chsd ldr 1 1/2f out: sn rdn: styd on to ld last 120yds* **12/1**

-361 **2** 1 1/2 **Planetaria (IRE)**[12] 2306 3-9-4 **67** DavidAllan 12 74
(Garry Moss) *sn led and set str pce: rdn wl over 1f out: drvn ins fnl f: hdd and no ex last 120yds* **4/1**[2]

006- **3** 1 **Fort Jefferson**[220] 7394 3-8-9 **61** RobHornby(3) 4 66+
(Andrew Balding) *hld up in rr: hdwy on outer over 2f out: rdn wl over 1f out: kpt on fnl f* **9/1**

4641 **4** 2 1/4 **Frap**[8] 2422 3-8-8 **62** RachelRichardson(5) 2 61
(Richard Fahey) *chsd ldrs: hdwy over 2f out: nt clr run and swtchd rt wl over 1f out: sn rdn: styd on wl fnl f: nrst fin* **7/1**[3]

15-2 **5** 1/2 **Cote D'Azur**[11] 2322 3-9-10 **73** LukeMorris 10 71
(Sir Mark Prescott Bt) *chsd ldrs: hdwy wl over 2f out: rdn to chse ldng pair over 1f out: sn drvn and one pce* **15/8**[1]

-015 **6** 2 1/4 **Arcane Dancer (IRE)**[12] 2306 3-8-13 **62**........................(p) GrahamLee 5 54
(Lawrence Mullaney) *in tch: hdwy wl over 2f out: rdn along wl over 1f out: no imp appr fnl f* **12/1**

2-16 **7** nk **Be Kool (IRE)**[30] 1804 3-8-13 **69**.................................. BenRobinson(7) 3 60
(Brian Ellison) *bhd: hdwy over 2f out: swtchd rt to inner and rdn wl over 1f out: styd on fnl f: nrst fin* **8/1**

4-20 **8** 1 1/4 **Beverley Bullet**[26] 1927 3-9-1 **64**.............................. GrahamGibbons 13 52
(Les Eyre) *cl up: rdn 2f out: sn drvn and wknd over 1f out* **9/1**

10- **9** 3 1/4 **Colombe Bleu**[322] 4153 3-9-3 **66**.................................... BarryMcHugh 1 46
(Tony Coyle) *chsd ldng pair: rdn along over 2f out: wknd wl over 1f out* **25/1**

10- **10** 2 1/2 **Alpine Dream (IRE)**[261] 6241 3-9-6 **69**.............................. PJMcDonald 7 43
(Tim Easterby) *dwlt: a towards rr* **20/1**

504- **11** 7 **Tan Arabiq**[240] 6874 3-9-2 **68**.................................. MarcMonaghan(3) 11 24
(Michael Appleby) *chsd ldrs on outer: rdn along wl over 2f out: sn edgd rt and wknd* **25/1**

1m 31.7s (-2.10) **Going Correction** -0.20s/f (Firm) **11** Ran SP% **123.3**
Speed ratings (Par 99): **104,102,101,98,98 95,95,93,89,87 79**
CSF £98.80 CT £806.73 TOTE £24.40: £5.30, £1.90, £3.20; EX 162.90 Trifecta £1416.00.
Owner Reality Partnerships IV **Bred** Mrs Anna Giurta **Trained** Great Habton, N Yorks

FOCUS
Actual race distance 7f 118yds. Modest form but the pace was good, and the winner improved.
T/Plt: £189.00 to a £1 stake. Pool of £52998.83 - 204.66 winning tickets. T/Qpdt: £23.60 to a £1 stake. Pool of £3508.98 - 110.0 winning tickets. **Joe Rowntree**

[2423]CATTERICK (L-H)

Saturday, May 28

OFFICIAL GOING: Good (good to firm in places; 8.3)
Wind: Breezy, half against Weather: Overcast

2675 SCOOP6 IT'S A ROLLOVER NOVICE MEDIAN AUCTION STKS 5f
2:20 (2:20) (Class 5) 2-Y-O **£2,911** (£866; £432; £216) **Stalls** Low

Form RPR

51 **1** **Lawless Louis**[14] 2235 2-9-4 0.. JoshDoyle(5) 8 79
(David O'Meara) *cl up on outside: shkn up and led over 1f out: hld on wl ins fnl f* **3/1**[2]

4 **2** hd **Pulsating (IRE)**[22] 2014 2-8-11 0.. TomEaves 7 66
(Rebecca Menzies) *hld up in tch on outside: effrt and rdn over 1f out: chsd wnr ins fnl f: kpt on: jst hld* **14/1**

2 **3** 1 1/4 **Peachey Carnehan**[8] 2429 2-9-2 0............................... PaulMulrennan 2 67
(Mark Johnston) *led: rdn 1/2-way: hdd over 1f out: kpt on same pce ins fnl f* **4/6**[1]

6 **4** 1/2 **Traveltalk (IRE)**[11] 2344 2-9-2 0.. BenCurtis 3 65
(Brian Ellison) *prom: drvn and outpcd over 2f out: rallied over 1f out: kpt on same pce fnl f* **12/1**[3]

00 **5** 1 3/4 **Benidiction (IRE)**[15] 2196 2-8-11 0.............................. ConnorBeasley 1 54+
(Ann Duffield) *in tch: pushed along and outpcd 1/2-way: rallied fnl f: nt pce to chal* **66/1**

5 **6** 1 **Tough To Bear**[26] 1921 2-8-13 0.............................. JacobButterfield(3) 4 55
(Ollie Pears) *w ldrs tl rdn and outpcd over 1f out: btn ins fnl f* **25/1**

4 **7** shd **Neigh Kid**[8] 2424 2-8-11 0.. JasonHart 6 50
(Keith Dalgleish) *dwlt: t.k.h and sn trcking ldrs: rdn and hung lft over 1f out: sn wknd* **16/1**

1m 0.42s (0.62) **Going Correction** +0.175s/f (Good) **7** Ran SP% **110.6**
Speed ratings (Par 93): **102,101,99,98,96 94,94**
CSF £39.15 TOTE £4.30: £2.60, £6.80; EX 33.70 Trifecta £64.80.
Owner James Gaffney **Bred** Brendan Boyle & Ashbrittle Stud **Trained** Upper Helmsley, N Yorks

FOCUS
Not a particularly strong race overall but it still required a fairly useful effort from the winner to defy a penalty. The field finished rather compressed.

2676 SCOOP6 RACING'S MILLIONAIRE MAKER H'CAP 5f
2:55 (2:57) (Class 6) (0-60,60) 4-Y-O+ **£2,264** (£673; £336; £168) **Stalls** Low

Form RPR

2000 **1** **Fuel Injection**[8] 2423 5-8-9 **48**.. JackGarritty 12 57
(Paul Midgley) *trckd ldrs: effrt and wnt 2nd over 1f out: sn rdn and edgd lft: kpt on wl fnl f to ld cl home* **15/2**

00-6 **2** 1/2 **Lorimer's Lot (IRE)**[8] 2423 5-8-13 **52**...............................(p) JasonHart 6 59
(Mark Walford) *cl up: rdn to ld over 1f out: kpt on wl fnl f: hdd cl home* **8/1**

060- **3** 1/2 **Pavers Star**[172] 8149 7-9-4 **57**....................................(p) GeorgeChaloner 5 62
(Noel Wilson) *midfield: drvn along 1/2-way: hdwy over 1f out: edgd rt ins fnl f: kpt on* **25/1**

0-10 **4** nk **Lady Poppy**[21] 2052 6-9-0 **60**.................................... KieranSchofield(7) 4 64
(Jedd O'Keeffe) *in tch: rdn 1/2-way: kpt on fnl f: nrst fin* **9/2**[2]

2140 **5** shd **Kuanyao (IRE)**[8] 2447 10-8-11 **55**...............................(be) AnnStokell(5) 3 59
(Ann Stokell) *bhd and outpcd: hdwy over 1f out: swtchd rt and kpt on ins fnl f: nt pce to chal* **20/1**

0-00 **6** 1 **Sunrise Dance**[8] 2423 7-8-7 **46** oh1.............................. ConnorBeasley 8 46
(Kenny Johnson) *bhd: pushed along and effrt 1/2-way: kpt on fnl f: nvr rchd ldrs* **16/1**

-000 **7** hd **Kopassus (IRE)**[14] 2234 4-8-13 **57**..............................(b) JordanNason(5) 2 57
(Lawrence Mullaney) *bhd against far rail: drvn along 1/2-way: kpt on fnl f: n.d* **7/1**[3]

0-00 **8** 1 **Majestic Manannan (IRE)**[18] 2120 7-9-6 **59**............(v[1]) AndrewMullen 9 56+
(David Nicholls) *led at decent gallop: rdn and hdd over 1f out: wknd ins fnl f: eased towards fin* **11/1**

0-00 **9** nk **Steel City Boy (IRE)**[21] 2052 13-8-0 **46** oh1...................... RPWalsh(7) 1 41
(Shaun Harris) *sn pushed along bhd ldng gp: drvn along 1/2-way: no imp fr over 1f out* **66/1**

6364 **10** shd **Zipedeedodah (IRE)**[25] 1950 4-9-7 **60**......................(t) PaulMulrennan 7 56+
(Joseph Tuite) *dwlt: sn midfield on outside: effrt 2f out: no ex over 1f out: hld whn hmpd ins fnl f* **3/1**[1]

0004 **11** 1 **Incomparable**[8] 2423 11-8-7 **46**.......................................(p) BenCurtis 10 37+
(Scott Dixon) *towards rr on outside: drvn and struggling 1/2-way: nvr on terms* **16/1**

0001 **12** 1 **Under Approval**[8] 2423 5-8-7 **53**..............................(b) BenRobinson(7) 13 40+
(Karen Tutty) *missed break: bhd and outpcd: no ch fr 1/2-way* **9/1**

1m 0.79s (0.99) **Going Correction** +0.175s/f (Good) **12** Ran SP% **118.8**
Speed ratings (Par 101): **99,98,97,96,96 95,94,93,92,92 91,89**
CSF £65.12 CT £1458.22 TOTE £9.30: £2.50, £3.00, £6.70; EX 84.80 Trifecta £1401.90.
Owner Mrs Mandy Verity **Bred** Whitsbury Manor Stud & Pigeon House Stud **Trained** Westow, N Yorks

FOCUS
A modest handicap in which not many threatened to land a serious blow, the leading pair prominent throughout.

2677 SCOOP6 RESULTS AT TOTEPOOLLIVEINFO.COM H'CAP 7f
3:30 (3:31) (Class 4) (0-80,80) 4-Y-O+ **£5,175** (£1,540; £769; £384) **Stalls** Low

Form RPR

2450 **1** **Plucky Dip**[22] 1990 5-9-2 **78**.. DannyBrock(3) 8 88
(John Ryan) *in tch: hdwy to ld over 1f out: edgd lft u.p ins fnl f: kpt on wl* **13/2**

-222 **2** 1/2 **Jacbequick**[15] 2198 5-8-12 **76**.......................................(p) JoshDoyle(5) 1 85
(David O'Meara) *trckd ldrs: effrt and wnt 2nd over 1f out: ev ch whn n.m.r ins fnl f: kpt on: hld nr fin* **9/2**[2]

6-06 **3** 3 **Red Tycoon (IRE)**[14] 2259 4-9-2 **80**................................. PhilDennis(5) 9 81
(David Barron) *s.i.s: hld up: hdwy over 2f out: swtchd rt and chsd ldng pair over 1f out: kpt on same pce ins fnl f* **6/1**

2205 **4** shd **Gold Flash**[8] 2421 4-9-0 **73**.......................................(p) RoystonFfrench 5 73
(Keith Dalgleish) *hld up: pushed along after 2f: drvn and struggling wl over 2f out: gd hdwy on outside fnl f: fin wl* **12/1**

2620 **5** 3/4 **Dr Red Eye**[7] 2491 8-8-9 **68**..(p) BenCurtis 6 66
(Scott Dixon) *led: rdn and hdd over 1f out: sn outpcd* **11/1**

0055 **6** 1 **Energia Flavio (BRZ)**[14] 2256 5-8-11 **77**.............. AdamMcNamara(7) 4 73
(Richard Fahey) *hld up bhd ldng gp: drvn and outpcd wl over 2f out: kpt on fnl f: nvr able to chal* **4/1**[1]

000- **7** hd **Jubilee Brig**[232] 7093 6-9-5 **78**... NeilFarley 14 73
(Alan Swinbank) *s.i.s: hld up: rdn over 2f out: kpt on fnl f: no imp whn n.m.r cl home* **33/1**

1-00 **8** hd **Dutch Breeze**[11] 2345 5-9-4 **77**......................................(p) JackGarritty 2 71
(Tim Easterby) *in tch: drvn along over 2f out: wknd appr fnl f* **20/1**

2-00 **9** 1/2 **Trail Blaze (IRE)**[26] 1924 7-9-4 **77**.............................(b) KeaganLatham 10 70
(Kevin Ryan) *prom: wnt 2nd 3f out: sn rdn and ev ch: wknd over 1f out* **18/1**

221 **10** 1/2 **Tellovoi (IRE)**[19] 2092 8-9-0 **73**..(v) JasonHart 3 65
(Richard Guest) *missed break: bhd: drvn along over 2f out: no imp fr over 1f out* **11/2**[3]

00-0 **11** 10 **Aprovado (IRE)**[27] 1879 4-9-2 **75**............................(p) PaulMulrennan 12 40
(Michael Dods) *pressed ldr to 3f out: rdn and sn wknd* **33/1**

006- **12** 20 **Rodrigo De Torres**[242] 6831 9-9-7 **80**..............................(p) TomEaves 11
(Garry Moss) *in tch on outside: lost pl 1/2-way: strugling over 2f out: t.o* **22/1**

1m 27.29s (0.29) **Going Correction** +0.175s/f (Good) **12** Ran SP% **117.5**
Speed ratings (Par 105): **105,104,101,100,100 98,98,98,97,97 85,63**
CSF £33.78 CT £187.48 TOTE £10.80: £3.30, £1.80, £3.20; EX 49.30 Trifecta £160.30.
Owner Byron, Lavallin & Donnison **Bred** Cheveley Park Stud Ltd **Trained** Newmarket, Suffolk
■ Stewards' Enquiry : Danny Brock caution; careless riding

FOCUS
A fairly useful handicap which was run at a good pace. After rail movements the actual race distance was 7f 12yds. The winner is rated to last yea's turf form.

2678 SCOOP6 THREE WAYS TO WIN H'CAP 1m 7f 177y
4:05 (4:05) (Class 5) (0-70,70) 4-Y-O+ **£3,234** (£962; £481; £240) **Stalls** Low

Form RPR

-043 **1** **Roc De Prince**[19] 2089 7-8-8 **54**.................................(p) PaulMulrennan 3 64
(Keith Dalgleish) *trckd ldrs: wnt 2nd after 7f: led 3f out: shkn up and sn qcknd clr: kpt on wl fnl f: unchal* **11/4**[1]

0-60 **2** 4 **Nashville (IRE)**[25] 1955 7-8-11 **57**.. NeilFarley 4 62
(Andrew Crook) *hld up: rdn and hdwy over 2f out: chsd (clr) wnr over 1f out: kpt on fnl f: no imp* **20/1**

0-35 **3** 1 1/2 **Sherman McCoy**[38] 1561 10-9-3 **66**........................ JacobButterfield(3) 2 69
(Marjorie Fife) *led 1f: pressed ldr for 7f: cl up: rdn along and chsd (clr) wnr over 2f out to over 1f out: kpt on same pce* **5/1**

0-40 **4** 3 **Arthurs Secret**[67] 425 6-9-7 **67**..(b) JasonHart 1 67
(John Quinn) *in tch on ins: effrt and drvn along wl over 2f out: kpt on same pce fr over 1f out* **4/1**[3]

04-0 **5** 1 **Sthenic (FR)**[27] 1881 4-9-5 **67**......................................(p) JackGarritty 8 65
(Micky Hammond) *hld up in tch: pushed along and reminders over 4f out: drvn over 2f out: sn no imp* **20/1**

-533 **6** 27 **Singular Quest**[39] 1550 4-9-6 **68**.. BenCurtis 5 34
(Kevin Frost) *led after 1f and set stdy pce: hdd 3f out: sn lost pl and struggling: t.o* **7/2**[2]

4-32 **7** 7 **Dry Your Eyes (IRE)**[29] 1842 5-9-9 **69**........................ KeaganLatham 7 27
(David O'Meara) *hld up: rdn along on outside 3f out: struggling fnl 2f: t.o* **7/2**[2]

3m 34.08s (2.08) **Going Correction** +0.175s/f (Good)
WFA 4 from 5yo+ 2lb **7** Ran SP% **117.3**
Speed ratings (Par 103): **101,99,98,96,96 82,79**
CSF £57.72 CT £259.64 TOTE £3.00: £1.80, £3.00; EX 55.30 Trifecta £223.50.
Owner Equus Racing Club **Bred** Mrs James Wigan & London TB Services Ltd **Trained** Carluke, S Lanarks

FOCUS
After rail movements the actual race distance was 1m7f 201yds. An ordinary handicap which was run at a pretty sedate pace, the winner always having things under control after quickening clear off the home behind. The winner is rated close to last year's form.

2679 TOTEEXACTA PICK THE 1ST AND 2ND H'CAP 7f
4:40 (4:40) (Class 3) (0-90,88) 4-Y-O+ **£12,938** (£3,850; £1,924; £962) **Stalls** Low

Form RPR

33-1 **1** **Swift Approval (IRE)**[29] 1844 4-9-7 **88**..............................(p) TomEaves 8 97
(Kevin Ryan) *mde all: shkn up and qcknd 2f out: drvn and kpt on wl fnl f* **6/1**[2]

4340 **2** 1/2 **Big Time (IRE)**[56] 1195 5-9-5 **86**...............................(v[1]) RoystonFfrench 3 93
(David Nicholls) *t.k.h: trckd ldrs: effrt and chsd wnr 2f out: sn rdn: clsd fnl f: hld towards fin* **14/1**

-334 **3** 1 1/4 **Cincuenta Pasos (IRE)**[9] 2391 5-8-13 **85**................. NathanEvans(5) 14 89+
(Joseph Tuite) *hld up: rdn and hdwy on outside 2f out: kpt on ins fnl f: nrst fin* **8/1**

5-63 **4** nk **Beardwood**[14] 2259 4-9-1 **82**.. BenCurtis 12 85
(Brian Ellison) *midfield on outside: drvn and outpcd over 2f out: rallied fnl f: nt pce to chal* **11/2**[1]

50-0 **5** 1/2 **Green Howard**[38] 1563 8-9-4 **85**.................................... AndrewMullen 10 86
(Rebecca Bastiman) *hld up on outside: drvn along over 3f out: rallied over 2f out: hung lft over 1f out: kpt on same pce ins fnl f* **20/1**

00-0 **6** 1/2 **Regal Dan (IRE)**[28] 1848 6-9-6 **87**.. SamJames 11 87
(David O'Meara) *trckd ldrs: effrt and rdn over 2f out: no ex ins fnl f* **14/1**

-315 **7** *1* **Kalk Bay (IRE)**[22] 1997 9-9-2 **83**................................(t) KeaganLatham 15 80+
(Michael Easterby) *s.i.s: bhd: rdn over 3f out: hdwy on outside over 1f out: kpt on fnl f: no imp* **16/1**

00-1 **8** *nk* **Khelman (IRE)**[22] 1997 6-8-13 **87**........................... AdamMcNamara(7) 4 84
(Richard Fahey) *s.i.s: bhd and sn pushed along: hdwy over 1f out: kpt on fnl f: nvr on terms* **15/2**

-000 **9** *3/4* **Woody Bay**[14] 2257 6-8-13 **80**.. IanBrennan 5 75
(Mark Walford) *s.i.s: bhd: rdn over 3f out: sme late hdwy: nvr rchd ldrs* **14/1**

-000 **10** *nk* **Canyari (IRE)**[7] 2476 5-9-1 **82**...................................... GeorgeChaloner 1 76
(Richard Fahey) *hld up: rdn over 2f out: sme late hdwy: nvr on terms* **9/1**

-325 **11** *1/2* **Ocean Sheridan (IRE)**[7] 2476 4-9-2 **83**........................ PaulMulrennan 7 75
(Michael Dods) *midfield: drvn along over 2f out: hung lft and wknd over 1f out* **7/1**[3]

-005 **12** *1* **Edgar Balthazar**[13] 2268 4-9-5 **86**....................................(p) JasonHart 13 76
(Keith Dalgleish) *pressed wnr to 2f out: sn rdn and outpcd: btn ins fnl f* **12/1**

0-30 **13** *3/4* **Our Boy Jack (IRE)**[35] 1643 7-9-0 **81**................................ JackGarritty 6 69
(Richard Fahey) *hld up on ins: drvn along over 3f out: wknd fr 2f out* **16/1**

1-00 **14** *6* **Comino (IRE)**[14] 2256 5-8-7 **81**................................. LewisEdmunds(7) 9 52
(Kevin Ryan) *plld hrd: trckd ldrs tl rdn and wknd over 2f out* **25/1**

1m 26.84s (-0.16) **Going Correction** +0.175s/f (Good) **14** Ran SP% **123.1**
Speed ratings (Par 107): **107,106,105,104,104 103,102,102,101,100 100,99,98,91**
CSF £89.66 CT £708.28 TOTE £5.20: £1.80, £4.90, £4.10; EX 92.60 Trifecta £814.90.
Owner Middleham Park Racing XLIX **Bred** Mrs Jean Brennan **Trained** Hambleton, N Yorks

FOCUS
After rail movements the actual race distance was 7f 12yds. A useful front-running display from the winner, who clung on well after setting a good pace. The form is rated around the second.

2680 TOTETRIFECTA PICK THE 1,2,3 H'CAP 5f 212y
5:15 (5:15) (Class 5) (0-75,75) 4-Y-O+ **£3,234** (£962; £481; £240) **Stalls** Low

Form RPR

0001 **1** **Orion's Bow**[11] 2332 5-9-7 **75**...................................... RoystonFfrench 10 92
(David Nicholls) *hld up in midfield: shkn up over 2f out: qcknd to ld over 1f out: pushed clr: readily* **9/2**[2]

-402 **2** *3* **Manatee Bay**[5] 2531 6-9-7 **75**..(v) PaulQuinn 6 81
(David Nicholls) *t.k.h: hld up: rdn and hdwy over 1f out: chsd (clr) wnr ins fnl f: kpt on: no imp* **4/1**[1]

010- **3** *3/4* **Spirit Of Zeb (IRE)**[151] 8389 4-9-0 **75**................... AdamMcNamara(7) 8 79
(Richard Fahey) *chsd ldrs on outside: effrt and chsd wnr over 1f out to ins fnl f: edgd lft: one pce* **6/1**[3]

0-51 **4** *1 1/4* **Fantasy Justifier (IRE)**[18] 2130 5-9-4 **72**........................... TomEaves 3 72
(Ronald Harris) *t.k.h: chsd ldr: effrt and ev ch briefly over 1f out: no ex ins fnl f* **10/1**

0044 **5** *1* **Exotic Guest**[11] 2332 6-8-11 **65**....................................(p) JackGarritty 12 61
(Ruth Carr) *hld up: rdn along 2f out: kpt on fnl f: nt pce to chal* **10/1**

1600 **6** *1/2* **Lackaday**[8] 2416 4-9-0 **68**...(b) JasonHart 2 63
(Mark Walford) *in tch on ins: drvn over 2f out: one pce fr over 1f out* **16/1**

2345 **7** *1/2* **Jacob's Pillow**[27] 1879 5-9-4 **72**.................................... AndrewMullen 4 65
(Rebecca Bastiman) *chsd ldrs: drvn along over 2f out: rallied and ch briefly over 1f out: no ex fnl f* **12/1**

0-00 **8** *2* **Gabrial The Tiger (IRE)**[7] 2491 4-9-5 **73**.................. GeorgeChaloner 5 60
(Richard Fahey) *hld up in midfield on ins: drvn and outpcd over 2f out: sme late hdwy: n.d* **9/1**

0552 **9** *1 1/2* **Daylight**[8] 2416 6-8-11 **65**...(t) KeaganLatham 1 47
(Michael Easterby) *hld up: pushed along on ins over 2f out: no imp fr over 1f out: btn fnl f* **12/1**

0005 **10** *1/2* **Ypres**[18] 2120 7-8-10 **64**... BenCurtis 9 44
(Jason Ward) *t.k.h: hld up: rdn over 2f out: sn no imp* **16/1**

5340 **11** *1* **Llewellyn**[11] 2332 8-8-9 **68**...(b) PhilDennis(5) 7 45
(Declan Carroll) *led: rdn over 2f out: hdd over 1f out: sn wknd* **20/1**

40-0 **12** *2* **Solar Spirit (IRE)**[52] 1252 11-8-9 **63**............................... PaulMulrennan 11 34
(Tracy Waggott) *stdd s: rdn in rr over 2f out: sn btn* **20/1**

1m 13.34s (-0.26) **Going Correction** +0.175s/f (Good) **12** Ran SP% **117.3**
Speed ratings (Par 103): **108,104,103,101,100 99,98,96,94,93 92,89**
CSF £22.55 CT £106.62 TOTE £5.90: £1.90, £1.90, £3.00; EX 25.60 Trifecta £113.10.
Owner T J Swiers **Bred** Cheveley Park Stud Ltd **Trained** Sessay, N Yorks
■ Stewards' Enquiry : Jason Hart two-day ban; careless riding (11th-12th June)

FOCUS
After rail movements the actual race distance was exactly 6f. A one-sided handicap, the thriving winner blitzing his rivals. He looks better than ever. The second also caught the eye.

2681 TOTEPOOL LIKE US ON FACEBOOK MEDIAN AUCTION MAIDEN FILLIES' STKS 5f 212y
5:45 (5:48) (Class 6) 3-4-Y-O **£2,587** (£770; £384; £192) **Stalls** Low

Form RPR

1 **Sabrewing (IRE)** 3-9-0 0.. JackGarritty 2 79+
(Robert Cowell) *trckd ldrs: shkn up and green over 2f out: hdwy to ld ins fnl f: pushed out* **9/2**[3]

442- **2** *1/2* **Hyland Heather (IRE)**[232] 7087 3-9-0 78.................... GeorgeChaloner 5 77
(Richard Fahey) *pressed ldr: led over 2f out: rdn over 1f out: hdd ins fnl f: kpt on: hld nr fin* **5/4**[1]

032 **3** *4 1/2* **My Lucille (IRE)**[12] 2304 3-9-0 71.................................. AndrewMullen 3 63
(Tim Easterby) *t.k.h: led to over 2f out: hung lft and wknd over 1f out* **7/4**[2]

66 **4** *6* **Wishing Tree**[11] 2333 3-9-0 0... BenCurtis 1 44
(Brian Ellison) *in tch: drvn and outpcd over 2f out: btn over 1f out* **12/1**

5 *2* **Coquine** 3-9-0 0.. SamJames 4 37
(David O'Meara) *slowly away: rn green in rr: struggling 1/2-way: nvr on terms* **25/1**

1m 15.04s (1.44) **Going Correction** +0.175s/f (Good) **5** Ran SP% **110.5**
Speed ratings (Par 98): **97,96,90,82,79**
CSF £10.72 TOTE £5.70: £4.10, £1.10; EX 11.30 Trifecta £20.10.
Owner Qatar Racing Limited **Bred** Ms Theresa Killen **Trained** Six Mile Bottom, Cambs

FOCUS
A taking first effort from the well-bred winner, who overcame her inexperience to wear down an established rival.
T/Plt: £608.30 to a £1 stake. Pool of £54139.69 - 64.97 winning tickets. T/Qpdt: £59.60 to a £1 stake. Pool of £4475.18 - 55.50 winning tickets. **Richard Young**

1993 CHESTER (L-H)
Saturday, May 28

OFFICIAL GOING: Good (7.5)
Wind: Light, behind Weather: Fine

2682 BETWAY IRISH STALLION FARMS EBF NOVICE STKS (PLUS 10 RACE) 6f 18y
1:45 (1:46) (Class 4) 2-Y-O **£6,225** (£1,864; £932; £466; £233; £117) **Stalls** Low

Form RPR

1 **Scofflaw** 2-9-2 0.. DavidNolan 4 79+
(Richard Fahey) *chsd ldrs: effrt and swtchd lft jst over 1f out: r.o ins fnl f to ld fnl 110yds: in command after* **20/1**

2 **2** *3/4* **Havelock (IRE)**[32] 1736 2-9-2 0... WilliamBuick 1 77
(Mark Johnston) *led: rdn over 1f out: hdd fnl 110yds: hld nr fin* **9/4**[2]

5 **3** *2* **Arc Royal**[35] 1635 2-9-2 0.. RichardKingscote 2 71
(Tom Dascombe) *chsd ldrs: effrt over 1f out: n.m.r briefly on inner jst ins fnl f: styd on same pce after* **13/2**

1 **4** *1 1/2* **Cuppacoffee (IRE)**[13] 2265 2-9-1 0.............................. RowanScott(7) 3 73
(Ann Duffield) *w wnr: rdn over 1f out: nt qckn jst after: no ex fnl 110yds* **11/2**[3]

5 **5** *9* **Nordic Combined (IRE)**[11] 2335 2-9-2 0............................ ShaneGray 5 40
(Brian Ellison) *in rr of main gp: pushed along 1/2-way: outpcd jst after: nvr a threat* **66/1**

3 **6** *11* **Oceanus (IRE)**[15] 2204 2-9-2 0.................................. SilvestreDeSousa 6 7
(Ed Dunlop) *racd 3 wd chsng ldrs: pushed along 1/2-way: wknd over 2f out* **7/4**[1]

1U **7** *46* **Berkshire Boy (IRE)**[14] 2240 2-9-5 0................................. DavidProbert 7
(Andrew Balding) *missed break: rdn along to get gng: a wl bhd: t.o* **8/1**

1m 17.86s (4.06) **Going Correction** +0.475s/f (Yiel) **7** Ran SP% **113.2**
Speed ratings (Par 95): **91,90,87,85,73 58,**
CSF £63.86 TOTE £28.20: £8.10, £2.00; EX 62.50 Trifecta £684.30.
Owner P Timmins & A Rhodes Haulage **Bred** Mrs M E Slade **Trained** Musley Bank, N Yorks
■ Stewards' Enquiry : David Nolan caution; careless riding

FOCUS
There was 3mm of rain on Wednesday but it had been dry since. Nevertheless, Clerk of the course Andrew Morris said there was definitely moisture in the track. The going was given as good (GoingStick: 7.5), and after riding in the first race David Nolan agreed with that assessment, while William Buick said "There is a bit of ease in it." The entire length of the running rail was out by between 3 and 9yds. Actual race distance 6f 57yds (+39yds). A fair novice contest won nicely by the only newcomer in the line-up.

2683 BETWAY FILLIES' H'CAP 6f 18y
2:15 (2:16) (Class 3) (0-95,93) 3-Y-O+ **£14,006** (£4,194; £2,097; £1,048; £524; £263) **Stalls** Low

Form RPR

-402 **1** **Secret Hint**[15] 2223 5-9-8 **89**... DavidProbert 7 96
(Andrew Balding) *dwlt: hld up: hdwy 2f out: r.o to ld ins fnl f: pushed out nr fin* **11/2**

20-5 **2** *3/4* **Alsaaden**[23] 1977 3-8-9 **85**... TedDurcan 3 88
(Richard Hannon) *sn in rr: pushed along over 2f out: rdn over 1f out: hdwy ins fnl f: r.o to take 2nd nr fin: nt quite get to wnr* **6/1**

10-2 **3** *3/4* **Giddy**[13] 2267 3-8-3 **79**.. PatrickMathers 5 79
(Richard Fahey) *chsd ldrs: rdn over 1f out: led briefly jst ins fnl f: no ex nr fin* **7/2**[2]

05-0 **4** *1 3/4* **Lady Clair (IRE)**[43] 1453 3-9-3 **93**................................... JoeyHaynes 4 88
(K R Burke) *hld up: rdn over 1f out: kpt on u.p ins fnl f: nt gng pce to trble ldrs* **20/1**

5-00 **5** *2 1/4* **Plagiarism (USA)**[13] 2267 3-8-6 **82**................................ FrannyNorton 2 69
(Mark Johnston) *led: rdn over 2f out: hdd jst ins fnl f: wknd fnl 100yds* **10/1**

5-00 **6** *2* **Dutch Mist**[17] 2161 3-8-9 **85**.. ShaneGray 1 66
(Kevin Ryan) *chsd ldrs: effrt on inner over 1f out: sn no imp: one pce* **5/1**[3]

0-31 **7** *1/2* **Justice Angel (IRE)**[23] 1977 3-8-9 **85**........................ SilvestreDeSousa 6 64
(David Elsworth) *racd keenly: sn chsd ldr: moved upsides 4f out: rdn and lost 2nd over 1f out: wknd ins fnl f* **9/4**[1]

1m 16.54s (2.74) **Going Correction** +0.475s/f (Yiel)
WFA 3 from 5yo 9lb **7** Ran SP% **113.2**
Speed ratings (Par 104): **100,99,98,95,92 90,89**
CSF £36.92 TOTE £6.60: £2.90, £2.90; EX 43.90 Trifecta £163.50.
Owner John Drew & D H Caslon **Bred** George Strawbridge **Trained** Kingsclere, Hants

FOCUS
Actual race distance 6f 57yds (+39yds). This sprint handicap was run at a strong gallop and suited those ridden with a bit of patience. The winner matched her best form of last year.

2684 BETWAY H'CAP 7f 122y
2:50 (2:52) (Class 2) (0-105,105) 4-Y-O+ **£28,012** (£8,388; £4,194; £2,097; £1,048; £526) **Stalls** Low

Form RPR

0004 **1** **Sound Advice**[22] 1993 7-9-1 **99**...................................... RobertWinston 5 108
(Keith Dalgleish) *racd keenly: chsd ldrs: led 1f out: r.o ins fnl f: drvn out* **9/1**

1022 **2** *1* **Gabrial's Kaka (IRE)**[14] 2246 6-8-8 **92**.......................... FrannyNorton 6 99
(Richard Fahey) *midfield: rdn over 1f out: hdwy ins fnl f: sn tk 2nd: styd on towards fin: nt rch wnr* **4/1**[1]

0360 **3** *1/2* **Golden Steps (FR)**[15] 2206 5-9-0 **98**.............................. MartinHarley 8 103
(Marco Botti) *dwlt: hld up: rdn and hdwy over 1f out: r.o ins fnl f: nrst fin* **16/1**

0250 **4** *1/2* **Rene Mathis (GER)**[21] 2027 6-9-4 **102**............................ DavidNolan 4 106
(Richard Fahey) *chsd ldrs: rdn over 1f out: sn swtchd rt: nt qckn: styd on same pce towards fin* **14/1**

-010 **5** *1/2* **Predominance (IRE)**[21] 2027 4-8-12 **96**.......................(p) PatCosgrave 1 99
(William Haggas) *s.i.s: midfield: rdn over 1f out: hdwy ins fnl f: styd on towards fin: nt quite rch ldrs* **4/1**[1]

6222 **6** *1/2* **Capo Rosso (IRE)**[21] 2033 6-8-12 **96**...................... RichardKingscote 7 98
(Tom Dascombe) *led: rdn over 1f out: sn hdd: no ex fnl 100yds* **9/1**

50-0 **7** *nk* **Miracle Of Medinah**[21] 2027 5-8-11 **95**........................... LiamKeniry 3 96
(Mark Usher) *midfield: rdn ins fnl f: kpt on: nvr able to chal* **7/1**[2]

0-0 **8** *1 1/4* **Ocean Tempest**[56] 1196 7-8-11 **95**................................. DavidProbert 2 93
(John Ryan) *midfield: effrt over 1f out: n.m.r wl ins fnl f: kpt on same pce* **8/1**[3]

/12- **9** *shd* **Best Of Times**[372] 2454 4-9-7 **105** .... WilliamBuick 12 106+
(Saeed bin Suroor) *dwlt: hld up: swtchd rt and nt clr run over 1f out: effrt whn continually denied run ins fnl f: nvr able to cl* **10/1**

4-00 **10** *1/2* **Valley Of Fire**[7] 2485 4-8-7 **91** .... SilvestreDeSousa 10 87
(William Haggas) *chsd ldr: rdn and ev ch over 1f out: wknd fnl 100yds* **25/1**

420- **11** *hd* **Lulu The Zulu (IRE)**[322] 4150 8-9-1 **102** .... AlistairRawlinson(3) 11 98
(Michael Appleby) *dwlt: racd keenly: hld up in rr: pushed along 2f out: nvr a threat* **20/1**

0521 **12** *2 1/2* **Al Khan (IRE)**[10] 2361 7-8-8 **92** .... ShaneGray 9 81
(Kevin Ryan) *midfield: pushed along 2f out: bmpd 1f out: sn wknd* **16/1**

1m 35.46s (1.66) **Going Correction** +0.475s/f (Yiel) **12** Ran SP% **119.7**
Speed ratings (Par 109): **110,109,108,108,107 107,106,105,105,104 104,102**
CSF £45.31 CT £582.41 TOTE £11.00: £4.10, £2.40, £6.00; EX 61.20 Trifecta £1281.50.
Owner G L S Partnership **Bred** G L S Partnership **Trained** Carluke, S Lanarks

FOCUS
Actual race distance 7f 161yds (+39yds). The pace wasn't overly strong and it was an advantage to sit fairly handily. The winner is rated back to his best with the second to recent form.

2685 CHAMPIONS LEAGUE FINAL BETTING AT BETWAY H'CAP 1m 5f 89y
3:25 (3:25) (Class 3) (0-90,90) 4-Y-O+
£14,006 (£4,194; £2,097; £1,048; £524; £263) **Stalls** Low

Form RPR

63-0 **1** **Serena Grae**[143] 66 5-9-4 **87** .... PatCosgrave 6 94
(Marcus Tregoning) *wnt 2nd after 2f: rdn 3f out: led 1f out: r.o wl towards fin* **14/1**

2111 **2** *1 3/4* **Indira**[16] 2176 5-9-2 **90** .... JosephineGordon(5) 11 95
(John Berry) *chsd ldrs: effrt over 1f out: wnt 2nd ins fnl f: styd on: no imp on wnr towards fin* **7/1**[3]

5-11 **3** *nk* **Sir Chauvelin**[15] 2199 4-9-7 **90** .... WilliamBuick 7 94
(Jim Goldie) *hld up: pushed along on outer over 3f out: hdwy 2f out: styd on ins fnl f: hld nr fin* **6/1**[2]

-P62 **4** *nse* **Yorkidding**[7] 2487 4-9-5 **88** .... RichardKingscote 9 92+
(Mark Johnston) *hld up: wanted to lug lft over 1f out: str run ins fnl f: gng on at fin* **9/2**[1]

0P-0 **5** *3/4* **Gabrial's Star**[35] 1642 7-9-7 **90** ....(b) MartinHarley 3 93+
(Richard Fahey) *midfield: nt clr run over 1f out: hdwy ins fnl f: styd on: nt quite get to ldrs* **9/1**

1040 **6** *1 3/4* **Winterlude (IRE)**[27] 1893 6-9-7 **90** .... SilvestreDeSousa 12 90
(Jennie Candlish) *dwlt: midfield: nt clr run over 1f out and swtchd rt: styd on same pce ins fnl f* **8/1**

35/5 **7** *3/4* **Nabhan**[12] 2313 4-9-4 **87** .... DavidProbert 5 86
(Bernard Llewellyn) *hld up: hdwy 2f out: nt clr run jst ins fnl f: nvr able to chal* **25/1**

0004 **8** *1* **Be Perfect (USA)**[15] 2199 7-9-2 **85** ....(p) JamesSullivan 4 83
(Ruth Carr) *led: rdn over 1f out: sn hdd: wknd fnl 150yds* **7/1**[3]

43-3 **9** *1* **Trendsetter (IRE)**[22] 1999 5-9-2 **85** .... CamHardie 2 81
(John Quinn) *racd keenly: chsd ldr for 2f: remained prom: rdn over 1f out: no ex fnl 100yds* **6/1**[2]

06-0 **10** *1* **Norab (GER)**[7] 2468 5-9-2 **85** .... LiamKeniry 1 80
(Bernard Llewellyn) *in tch: effrt over 1f out: wknd fnl 150yds* **33/1**

0-42 **11** *4* **Zand (IRE)**[12] 2318 6-9-5 **88** .... FrannyNorton 10 77
(Mark Johnston) *racd keenly: hld up in rr: nt clr run over 2f out: nvr able to get on terms* **12/1**

1/06 **12** *17* **Venue**[7] 2472 6-9-4 **87** .... DavidNolan 8 50
(Donald McCain) *midfield: hdwy after 2f: sn chsd ldrs: lost pl 6f out: wknd over 2f out* **25/1**

2m 57.58s (4.88) **Going Correction** +0.475s/f (Yiel) **12** Ran SP% **117.9**
Speed ratings (Par 107): **103,101,101,101,101 100,99,99,98,97 95,84**
CSF £105.98 CT £661.75 TOTE £22.20: £6.20, £2.90, £2.10; EX 112.80 Trifecta £873.90.
Owner Mrs Heather Raw **Bred** Heather Raw **Trained** Whitsbury, Hants

FOCUS
Actual race distance 1m5f 158yds (+69yds). The gallop was an ordinary one here, and the winner got first run turning in. She resumed last year's progress back on turf.

2686 STELLAR GROUP MAIDEN STKS 7f 122y
4:00 (4:01) (Class 4) 3-Y-O+
£6,225 (£1,864; £932; £466; £233; £117) **Stalls** Low

Form RPR

2-22 **1** **Heir To A Throne (FR)**[18] 2122 3-9-2 83 .... ShaneGray 7 81
(Kevin Ryan) *racd keenly: chsd ldr: rdn over 2f out: led over 1f out: hld on gamely cl home* **11/4**[2]

3 **2** *hd* **Sehayli (IRE)**[38] 1577 3-9-2 0 .... PatCosgrave 5 80
(William Haggas) *in tch: effrt to take 2nd 1f out: r.o to chal ins fnl f: jst hld* **5/1**[3]

6-2 **3** *nk* **Loaded (IRE)**[17] 2156 3-9-2 0 .... DavidProbert 6 79+
(Andrew Balding) *racd keenly: hld up: rdn and str run ins fnl f: gng on at fin* **5/1**[3]

3 **4** *shd* **Edward Lewis**[15] 2207 3-9-2 0 .... RobertHavlin 2 79+
(John Gosden) *chsd ldrs: effrt over 1f out: ev ch ins fnl f: r.o: hld nr fin* **2/1**[1]

/20- **5** *5* **Billy Slater**[371] 2507 4-10-0 81 .... FrannyNorton 1 69
(Richard Fahey) *in rr: pushed along over 1f out: nvr able to trble ldrs* **7/1**

-433 **6** *1 1/2* **Ten Rocks**[122] 350 3-9-2 67 .... SilvestreDeSousa 4 62
(Lisa Williamson) *led: rdn and hdd over 1f out: wknd ins fnl f* **25/1**

05 **7** *6* **King Julien (IRE)**[5] 2522 3-8-11 0 .... JosephineGordon(5) 3 47
(John Ryan) *in tch: pushed along 3f out: wknd 2f out* **25/1**

1m 37.63s (3.83) **Going Correction** +0.475s/f (Yiel)
WFA 3 from 4yo 12lb **7** Ran SP% **113.5**
Speed ratings (Par 105): **99,98,98,98,93 91,85**
CSF £16.61 TOTE £4.30: £2.50, £2.60; EX 21.30 Trifecta £57.00.
Owner STS Racing Limited **Bred** S A R L Neustrian Associates **Trained** Hambleton, N Yorks

FOCUS
Actual race distance 7f 161yds (+39yds). A fair maiden, but they finished in a bit of a heap. The winner is rated only to form.

2687 RHS FLOWER SHOW TATTON PARK H'CAP 1m 4f 66y
4:35 (4:35) (Class 4) (0-85,85) 3-Y-O
£6,225 (£1,864; £932; £466; £233; £117) **Stalls** Low

Form RPR

56-1 **1** **Master Blueyes (IRE)**[15] 2224 3-9-1 **79** .... MartinHarley 7 87+
(Alan King) *racd keenly: broke wl: led early: prom: led wl over 1f out: sn rdn: r.o gamely ins fnl f: all out towards fin: jst hld on* **10/3**[2]

4-15 **2** *nse* **Gunnery (FR)**[15] 2209 3-9-7 **85** .... JamieSpencer 6 92
(Peter Chapple-Hyam) *midfield: hdwy 2f out: wnt 2nd over 1f out: r.o ins fnl f: str chal towards fin: jst failed* **11/4**[1]

5-15 **3** *1/2* **Hereawi**[35] 1636 3-8-12 **76** .... SilvestreDeSousa 4 82
(Ralph Beckett) *prom: rdn over 1f out: r.o ins fnl f trying to chal: hld nr fin* **7/2**[3]

15-2 **4** *1 3/4* **Engage (IRE)**[31] 1786 3-9-7 **85** .... TedDurcan 3 88
(Sir Michael Stoute) *s.i.s: hld up: hdwy 2f out: rdn over 1f out: styd on and edgd lft ins fnl f: no imp fnl 150yds* **6/1**

3-36 **5** *3* **Monaco Rose**[12] 2300 3-8-7 **71** oh5 .... PatrickMathers 1 69
(Richard Fahey) *hld up: rdn and hdwy over 1f out: kpt on ins fnl f: nvr able to trble ldrs* **20/1**

3212 **6** *5* **Second Serve (IRE)**[15] 2224 3-9-4 **82** .... JFEgan 5 72
(Mark Johnston) *sn led: rdn and hdd wl over 1f out: wknd fnl f* **11/2**

4-5U **7** *2 1/4* **Head High (IRE)**[15] 2224 3-8-10 **74** ....(p) ShaneGray 8 61
(Kevin Ryan) *chsd ldr after 2f tl rdn 2f out: wknd over 1f out* **33/1**

3233 **8** *8* **Four Mile Beach**[53] 1242 3-8-8 **72** .... FrannyNorton 2 46
(Mark Johnston) *a in rr: sn pushed along: nvr a threat* **14/1**

2m 42.75s (4.25) **Going Correction** +0.475s/f (Yiel) **8** Ran SP% **116.0**
Speed ratings (Par 101): **104,103,103,102,100 97,95,90**
CSF £13.19 CT £33.46 TOTE £5.10: £1.90, £1.10, £1.80; EX 17.20 Trifecta £79.20.
Owner The Barbury Lions **Bred** T Boylan **Trained** Barbury Castle, Wilts

FOCUS
Actual race distance 1m4f 126yds (+60yds). There was a close finish to this sound run handicap. The winner confirmed his York form.

2688 NIGHTINGALE HOUSE HOSPICE H'CAP 1m 2f 75y
5:10 (5:12) (Class 4) (0-85,84) 4-Y-O+
£6,225 (£1,864; £932; £466; £233; £117) **Stalls** High

Form RPR

1-34 **1** **Berlusca (IRE)**[113] 465 7-9-5 **82** .... DavidNolan 5 89
(David O'Meara) *hld up: hdwy over 1f out: r.o ins fnl f: led fnl strides* **16/1**

0-11 **2** *nk* **Bakht A Rawan (IRE)**[26] 1916 4-8-13 **76** .... SilvestreDeSousa 9 82
(Stuart Kittow) *midfield: hdwy over 1f out: r.o to ld wl ins fnl f: hdd fnl strides* **3/1**[1]

0-04 **3** *1 1/2* **Lord Franklin**[23] 1978 7-9-2 **79** .... TedDurcan 11 82
(Eric Alston) *chsd ldrs: rdn over 2f out: led ins fnl f: sn hdd: no ex fnl strides* **10/1**

15-0 **4** *nk* **Sellingallthetime (IRE)**[17] 2163 5-9-1 **83** ....(p) GeorgeBuckell(5) 6 85
(Michael Appleby) *midfield: rdn and hdwy over 1f out: styd on ins fnl f: nt gng pce of ldrs* **8/1**

643 **5** *1* **Corton Lad**[15] 2199 6-9-4 **84** ....(tp) LouisSteward(3) 4 84
(Keith Dalgleish) *midfield: rdn and hdwy over 1f out: kpt on ins fnl f: nt gng pce to chal* **11/2**[3]

1-40 **6** *nk* **Modernism**[23] 1978 7-9-7 **84** .... FrannyNorton 3 84
(Richard Fahey) *chsd ldr tl rdn over 1f out: stl ev ch jst ins fnl f: no ex fnl 75yds* **9/2**[2]

-030 **7** *3/4* **Cyril**[7] 2487 4-9-4 **81** ....(b[1]) ShaneGray 7 79
(Kevin Ryan) *racd keenly: led: rdn over 1f out: hdd ins fnl f: fdd fnl 75yds* **7/1**

0-00 **8** *1 1/4* **Character Onesie (IRE)**[14] 2257 4-8-11 **74** .... PatrickMathers 1 70
(Richard Fahey) *chsd ldrs: rdn and outpcd over 1f out: wl btn fnl 75yds* **10/1**

35-0 **9** *nk* **El Beau (IRE)**[22] 2017 5-9-2 **84** .... JosephineGordon(5) 10 79
(John Quinn) *hld up: pushed along 3f out: nt clr run and snatched up over 1f out: no threat after* **16/1**

0/00 **10** *3 1/4* **Novelty Seeker (USA)**[23] 1972 7-9-7 **84** .... JamesSullivan 8 73
(Michael Easterby) *in rr: rdn over 1f out: nvr a threat* **14/1**

2m 14.3s (3.10) **Going Correction** +0.475s/f (Yiel) **10** Ran SP% **118.8**
Speed ratings (Par 105): **106,105,104,104,103 103,102,101,101,98**
CSF £65.03 CT £525.04 TOTE £18.20: £5.30, £1.90, £2.60; EX 77.60 Trifecta £380.60.
Owner Peter R Ball **Bred** Value Bloodstock **Trained** Upper Helmsley, N Yorks

FOCUS
Actual race distance 1m2f 114yds (+39yds). The leader set an honest pace and it favoured the hold-up horses. Ordinary form for the grade, the winner back to his best.
T/Plt: £388.00 to a £1 stake. Pool of £99445.07 - 187.07 winning tickets. T/Qpdt: £29.80 to a £1 stake. Pool of £8088.21 - 200.75 winning tickets. **Darren Owen**

2648 HAYDOCK (L-H)
Saturday, May 28

OFFICIAL GOING: Good (7.6)
Wind: Almost nil Weather: Sunny spells

2689 £25 FREE BET AT 188BET.CO.UK H'CAP 1m
2:00 (2:00) (Class 3) (0-90,90) 4-Y-O+ **£8,086** (£2,406; £1,202; £601) **Stalls** Low

Form RPR

4111 **1** **Ice Slice (IRE)**[22] 2010 5-9-3 **86** .... RyanTate 1 96
(James Eustace) *mde all: rdn over 1f out: styd on gamely* **15/2**

-111 **2** *hd* **Clotilde**[26] 1932 4-9-3 **86** .... RyanMoore 13 95
(William Knight) *a.p: rdn over 1f out: chsd wnr ins fnl f: r.o* **13/2**[2]

03-1 **3** *1 1/2* **Rousayan (IRE)**[26] 1924 5-9-2 **85** .... DanielTudhope 9 91
(David O'Meara) *a.p: chsd wnr over 1f out tl rdn ins fnl f: styd on same pce* **7/1**[3]

03-5 **4** *1 3/4* **Mount Tahan (IRE)**[33] 1694 4-9-2 **85** .... JamieSpencer 14 87
(Kevin Ryan) *chsd wnr: rdn over 2f out: lost 2nd over 1f out: edgd lft and styd on same pce fnl f* **16/1**

0-43 **5** *1* **Strong Steps**[14] 2246 4-9-6 **89** ....(p) FrankieDettori 10 89
(Hugo Palmer) *hld up: hdwy u.p and edgd lft over 1f out: no ex ins fnl f* **7/2**[1]

56-0 **6** *2* **Home Cummins (IRE)**[28] 1871 4-9-6 **89** .... PaulHanagan 6 84
(Richard Fahey) *hld up: rdn over 2f out: styd on fr over 1f out: nt trble ldrs* **20/1**

-340 **7** *2 1/4* **Silvery Moon (IRE)**[17] 2157 9-9-7 **90** .... KierenFallon 12 80
(Tim Easterby) *hld up: racd keenly: rdn over 2f out: nvr on terms* **25/1**

3-05 **8** *3* **Gerry The Glover (IRE)**[11] 2331 4-9-4 **87** .... AndreaAtzeni 4 70
(Brian Ellison) *s.i.s: hld up: racd keenly: rdn over 2f out: n.d* **9/1**

13-2 **9** *shd* **Ghinia (IRE)**[32] 1757 5-9-1 **84** .... AdamKirby 7 67
(Pam Sly) *chsd ldrs: rdn over 2f out: wknd over 1f out* **9/1**

-300 **10** *3 3/4* **God Willing**[7] 2476 5-9-3 **86** ....(t) JimmyFortune 3 60
(Declan Carroll) *s.s: hld up: rdn over 2f out: sn wknd* **14/1**

1102 **11** *1* **Captain Revelation**[22] 1997 4-8-7 **83** .... PatrickVaughan(7) 2 55
(Tom Dascombe) *prom: rdn over 2f out: wknd over 1f out: eased* **16/1**

0-02 **12** *1/2* **Steel Train (FR)**[13] 2268 5-9-3 **89** .... ShelleyBirkett(3) 11 60
(David O'Meara) *hld up: nvr on terms* **16/1**

1-0 **13** *9* **Important Point (USA)**[10] 2378 4-9-2 **85**........................ JamesDoyle 8 35
(Saeed bin Suroor) *hld up: rdn over 2f out: sn wknd* **16/1**
1m 42.55s (-1.15) **Going Correction** +0.05s/f (Good) **13** Ran SP% **118.6**
Speed ratings (Par 107): **107,106,105,103,102 100,98,95,95,91 90,89,80**
CSF £55.22 CT £373.35 TOTE £8.50: £2.50, £2.70, £2.40; EX 63.30 Trifecta £262.60.
Owner The MacDougall Two **Bred** Kilfrush Stud **Trained** Newmarket, Suffolk

FOCUS
It was dry overnight and a warm day. All races were run on the stands' side home straight. This was run over 51yds further than advertised. The winner made all, posting another career best, and few got involved.

2690 188BET.CO.UK STKS (REGISTERED AS THE PINNACLE STAKES) (GROUP 3) (F&M) 1m 3f 200y

2:35 (2:35) (Class 1) 4-Y-O+

£35,727 (£13,545; £6,778; £3,376; £1,694; £850) **Stalls** Centre

Form RPR
12-3 **1** **Journey**[16] 2189 4-9-0 114.. FrankieDettori 6 108+
(John Gosden) *trckd ldr to 1/2-way: wnt 2nd again over 3f out: rdn to ld over 1f out: r.o* **1/1**[1]
24-2 **2** *1 ¼* **Sweeping Up**[7] 2465 5-9-0 101....................................(t) JimmyFortune 3 106
(Hughie Morrison) *led: clr 5f out tl over 3f out: rdn and hdd over 1f out: styd on same pce ins fnl f* **11/1**
35-6 **3** *3 ¼* **Miss Marjurie (IRE)**[28] 1855 6-9-0 109.......................... OisinMurphy 4 101+
(Denis Coakley) *hld up: hdwy over 2f out: rdn over 1f out: hung lft and no ex ins fnl f* **11/2**[3]
0 **4** *1 ¾* **Laganore (IRE)**[13] 2276 4-9-0 105...................................... KierenFallon 7 98+
(A J Martin, Ire) *hld up: pushed along and hdwy over 1f out: sn rdn and hung lft: no ex ins fnl f* **5/1**[2]
53-3 **5** *3 ¼* **Namhroodah (IRE)**[10] 2363 4-9-0 96.............................. AndreaAtzeni 1 93
(James Tate) *chsd ldrs: wnt 2nd 1/2-way tl over 3f out: rdn over 2f out: wknd over 1f out* **10/1**
402- **6** *1 ¼* **Lustrous**[259] 6306 5-9-0 105... PatSmullen 8 91
(David O'Meara) *hld up in tch: dropped in rr 1/2-way: hdwy 3f out: sn rdn: wknd over 1f out* **11/1**
201- **7** *6* **Mill Springs**[239] 6894 4-9-0 96... RobertHavlin 5 81
(John Gosden) *prom: rdn whn n.m.r over 2f out: wknd* **20/1**
2m 32.47s (-1.33) **Going Correction** +0.05s/f (Good) **7** Ran SP% **112.6**
Speed ratings (Par 113): **106,105,103,101,99 98,94**
CSF £12.97 TOTE £1.70: £1.10, £4.70; EX 14.60 Trifecta £50.50.
Owner George Strawbridge **Bred** George Strawbridge **Trained** Newmarket, Suffolk

FOCUS
This was run over 1m4f 31yds. The runner-up set a muddling pace and not many got involved. The winner is rated the best part of 10lb off last year's Gp 1 form.

2691 TIMEFORM JURY STKS (REGISTERED AS THE JOHN OF GAUNT STAKES) (GROUP 3) 7f

3:10 (3:10) (Class 1) 4-Y-O+

£35,727 (£13,545; £6,778; £3,376; £1,694; £850) **Stalls** Low

Form RPR
10-1 **1** **Home Of The Brave (IRE)**[35] 1637 4-9-0 115...............(t) JamesDoyle 6 118
(Hugo Palmer) *mde all: rdn over 1f out: r.o gamely* **9/4**[1]
0-02 **2** *nk* **Convey**[16] 2191 4-9-0 106..(p) RyanMoore 1 117
(Sir Michael Stoute) *a.p: nt clr run and shkn up over 1f out: chsd wnr ins fnl f: rdn and r.o wl* **6/1**[3]
43-1 **3** *2* **So Beloved**[21] 2030 6-9-0 113.. PatSmullen 4 112+
(David O'Meara) *trckd wnr tl over 4f out: remained handy: nt clr run over 1f out: styd on* **11/4**[2]
32-3 **4** *¾* **Breton Rock (IRE)**[36] 1606 6-9-0 113........................... JamieSpencer 9 110
(David Simcock) *pushed along into mid-div: hdwy 4f out: shkn up to chse wnr 2f out: sn rdn and ev ch: no ex wl ins fnl f* **6/1**[3]
5-04 **5** *1 ¾* **Dinkum Diamond (IRE)**[21] 2027 8-9-0 102..................... HarryBentley 3 105
(Henry Candy) *hld up: racd keenly: hdwy over 1f out: no imp ins fnl f* **33/1**
4-26 **6** *1 ½* **Tupi (IRE)**[17] 2159 4-9-0 109... AndreaAtzeni 8 101
(Richard Hannon) *plld hrd and prom: wnt 2nd over 4f out tl rdn 2f out: nt clr run and lost pl over 1f out: n.d afterwards* **14/1**
26-3 **7** *shd* **Here Comes When (IRE)**[35] 1637 6-9-0 109............... OisinMurphy 10 101
(Andrew Balding) *hld up: effrt over 2f out: styd on same pce fr over 1f out* **16/1**
06-6 **8** *2 ¼* **Adaay (IRE)**[36] 1606 4-9-0 113.. PaulHanagan 7 95
(William Haggas) *hld up: rdn over 2f out: nvr on terms* **15/2**
000- **9** *10* **Louis The Pious**[322] 4150 8-9-0 104................................... AdamKirby 5 68
(David O'Meara) *hld up: wknd over 2f out* **50/1**
1m 28.77s (-1.93) **Going Correction** +0.05s/f (Good) **9** Ran SP% **115.2**
Speed ratings (Par 113): **113,112,110,109,107 105,105,103,91**
CSF £16.28 TOTE £2.70: £1.10, £2.30, £1.60; EX 14.70 Trifecta £57.90.
Owner Godolphin **Bred** Earl Ecurie Du Grand Chene **Trained** Newmarket, Suffolk

FOCUS
This was run over 51yds further than advertised. A competitive Group 3, although the winner made all and it was hard to make up ground. The winner ran to form with the second improving on his latest.

2692 188BET SANDY LANE STKS (GROUP 2) 6f

3:45 (3:45) (Class 1) 3-Y-O

£51,039 (£19,350; £9,684; £4,824; £2,421; £1,215) **Stalls** Centre

Form RPR
11-1 **1** **Quiet Reflection**[48] 1374 3-8-11 109............................ DougieCostello 3 116
(K R Burke) *hld up: hdwy to ld 1f out: edgd lft and rdn clr: impressive* **7/1**
114- **2** *3 ¾* **Donjuan Triumphant (IRE)**[209] 7665 3-9-3 115............... RyanMoore 1 110
(Richard Fahey) *hld and pushed along 1/2-way: hdwy u.p over 1f out: styd on to go 2nd wl ins fnl f* **7/1**
1-11 **3** *hd* **Gifted Master (IRE)**[31] 1773 3-9-0 115.............................. PatSmullen 7 106
(Hugo Palmer) *sn led: rdn over 2f out: hdd over 1f out: styd on same pce ins fnl f* **5/4**[1]
32-0 **4** *nk* **Buratino (IRE)**[28] 1864 3-9-3 117....................................... JamesDoyle 2 108
(Mark Johnston) *hld up: hdwy over 2f out: rdn to ld and edgd rt over 1f out: sn hdd: styd on same pce* **11/2**[2]
211- **5** *2 ½* **La Rioja**[268] 6027 3-8-11 110.. OisinMurphy 5 94
(Henry Candy) *chsd ldrs: rdn over 1f out: wknd ins fnl f* **13/2**[3]
214- **6** *2* **Ajaya**[245] 6754 3-9-3 114... AndreaAtzeni 8 94
(William Haggas) *wnt rt s: sn chsng ldrs: rdn over 1f out: wknd ins fnl f* **8/1**
6032 **7** *½* **Gracious John (IRE)**[16] 2192 3-9-0 106.............................. AdamKirby 4 89
(David Evans) *led early: chsd ldr: rdn over 2f out: ev ch wl over 1f out: hmpd jst over 1f out: wknd ins fnl f* **16/1**
1m 10.57s (-3.23) **Going Correction** -0.175s/f (Firm) **7** Ran SP% **115.2**
Speed ratings (Par 111): **114,109,108,108,105 102,101**
CSF £54.47 TOTE £9.20: £3.60, £3.50; EX 56.70 Trifecta £233.40.
Owner Ontoawinner, Strecker & Burke **Bred** Springcombe Park Stud **Trained** Middleham Moor, N Yorks

FOCUS
The second running of this race as a Group 2 and there was an impressive winner who looks the form horse for the Commonwealth Cup. The time was 27lb faster than the following race.

2693 FREE SPINS AT 188BET CASINO H'CAP 6f

4:20 (4:22) (Class 4) (0-85,85) 3-Y-O **£5,498** (£1,636; £817; £408) **Stalls** Centre

Form RPR
1 **1** **Agree (IRE)**[40] 1524 3-9-2 **80**... AdamKirby 11 89+
(Brian Ellison) *hld up: pushed along 1/2-way: hdwy over 1f out: rdn to ld and hung lft wl ins fnl f: r.o* **6/1**[3]
242- **2** *1* **Andar**[230] 7141 3-8-13 **77**..(p) OisinMurphy 13 83
(Clive Cox) *stmbld s: sn chsng ldrs: led over 4f out: rdn and hung lft over 1f out: hdd and unable qck wl ins fnl f* **18/1**
41-6 **3** *1 ¼* **Nisser**[14] 2251 3-9-5 **83**... AndreaAtzeni 10 85+
(Richard Hannon) *hld up: pushed along over 2f out: nt clr run and swtchd rt ins fnl f: r.o to go 3rd nr fin: nt rch ldrs* **4/1**[2]
1 **4** *nk* **Mustallib (IRE)**[21] 2039 3-9-5 **83**..................................... PaulHanagan 7 84
(Charles Hills) *mid-div: hdwy over 2f out: rdn and ev ch over 1f out: styd on same pce ins fnl f* **3/1**[1]
41-0 **5** *nk* **Dollar Reward**[21] 2029 3-9-0 **78**... RyanMoore 2 78
(Sir Michael Stoute) *hld up: pushed along and hdwy 2f out: rdn over 1f out: styd on same pce ins fnl f* **7/1**
261- **6** *1* **Flying Pursuit**[203] 7753 3-9-7 **85**...................................... KierenFallon 14 82
(Tim Easterby) *a.p: rdn over 1f out: edgd lft and styd on same pce ins fnl f* **20/1**
40-3 **7** *1 ½* **Powerallied (IRE)**[22] 1996 3-9-6 **84**................................. JamesDoyle 4 76
(Richard Fahey) *chsd ldrs: rdn and ev ch over 1f out: hmpd ins fnl f: eased* **12/1**
1-51 **8** *1 ¾* **Belledesert**[10] 2372 3-9-0 **78**.. AdamBeschizza 8 65
(Steph Hollinshead) *prom: pushed along over 2f out: no ex fnl f* **16/1**
613- **9** *hd* **Force (IRE)**[226] 7235 3-9-3 **81**... DarryllHolland 3 70+
(Charles Hills) *hld up: running on whn nt clr run ins fnl f: eased* **16/1**
31-1 **10** *hd* **Dancing Years (IRE)**[42] 1487 3-9-0 **78**.......................... JimmyFortune 6 63
(Richard Fahey) *led: hdd over 4f out: remained handy: rdn and ev ch over 1f out: hmpd and wknd ins fnl f* **9/1**
0-00 **11** *2 ½* **Garden World (IRE)**[17] 2161 3-8-10 **74**.......................... HarryBentley 5 51
(Nigel Tinkler) *hld up: rdn and hung lft over 2f out: nt trble ldrs* **66/1**
0-66 **12** *1* **Be Bop Tango (FR)**[31] 1789 3-8-8 **72**............................ JoeyHaynes 12 46
(K R Burke) *stmbld s: hdwy 1/2-way: rdn and wknd over 1f out* **50/1**
6512 **13** *3 ¼* **Zeeoneandonly (IRE)**[10] 2372 3-8-6 **77**.................(vt) GeorgeWood(7) 9 41
(David Evans) *w ldrs: rdn and ev ch wl over 1f out: sn hung lft and wknd* **16/1**
1m 12.34s (-1.46) **Going Correction** -0.175s/f (Firm) **13** Ran SP% **120.6**
Speed ratings (Par 101): **102,100,99,98,98 96,94,92,92,92 88,87,83**
CSF £108.36 CT £393.98 TOTE £7.30: £2.80, £6.00, £2.10; EX 167.90 Trifecta £2515.20.
Owner Mrs J A Martin **Bred** Tally-Ho Stud **Trained** Norton, N Yorks

FOCUS
A decent 3yo sprint handicap. The first five were unexposed and the form is rated on the positive side.

2694 MOBILE BETTING AT 188BET H'CAP 1m 2f 95y

4:55 (4:55) (Class 4) (0-85,85) 3-Y-O **£5,498** (£1,636; £817; £408) **Stalls** Centre

Form RPR
2045 **1** **Clayton Hall (IRE)**[22] 2012 3-8-8 **72**.................................. KierenFallon 2 79
(Brian Ellison) *chsd ldr over 8f out: rdn to ld 1f out: styd on* **12/1**
1241 **2** *½* **Daisy Bere (FR)**[32] 1759 3-8-13 **77**................................... JoeyHaynes 6 83
(K R Burke) *a.p: led over 2f out: rdn and hdd 1f out: styd on same pce towards fin* **4/1**[2]
1-30 **3** *½* **Altarsheed (IRE)**[36] 1610 3-9-4 **82**................................. PaulHanagan 4 87
(Richard Hannon) *prom: rdn and nt clr run over 1f out: swtchd rt: r.o* **7/1**
424 **4** *2 ¼* **Justice Grace (IRE)**[38] 1577 3-8-12 **76**............................... RyanMoore 1 77
(Ralph Beckett) *led 1f: chsd ldrs: rdn over 2f out: styd on same pce ins fnl f* **4/1**[2]
1-42 **5** *3 ¼* **Rebel Lightning (IRE)**[19] 2099 3-8-12 **76**........ WilliamTwiston-Davies 9 71
(Richard Spencer) *hld up: rdn over 3f out: hdwy over 2f out: no ex ins fnl f* **5/1**[3]
1-65 **6** *6* **Zoffanys Pride (IRE)**[27] 1896 3-9-2 **80**........................(p) OisinMurphy 5 63
(Andrew Balding) *led after 1f: rdn and hdd over 2f out: wknd fnl f* **20/1**
5-10 **7** *3 ¾* **Gambit**[36] 1610 3-9-7 **85**... RichardKingscote 8 61+
(Tom Dascombe) *hld up: plld hrd: sme hdwy over 2f out: sn rdn: wknd over 1f out* **85/40**[1]
2m 16.18s (0.68) **Going Correction** +0.05s/f (Good) **7** Ran SP% **113.6**
Speed ratings (Par 101): **99,98,98,96,93 89,86**
CSF £58.24 CT £366.15 TOTE £14.30: £5.00, £2.80; EX 59.40 Trifecta £313.70.
Owner David W Armstrong **Bred** L Queally **Trained** Norton, N Yorks

FOCUS
This was run over 1m1f 141yds. A fair 3yo handicap, but the pace was muddling and it paid to be handy. The winner hadn't been progressing but this was better.

2695 BEST ODDS GUARANTEED AT 188BET H'CAP 7f

5:30 (5:31) (Class 4) (0-85,85) 3-Y-O **£5,498** (£1,636; £817; £408) **Stalls** Low

Form RPR
41- **1** **Booming Delight (IRE)**[238] 6930 3-9-6 **84**......................... RyanMoore 9 96+
(William Haggas) *mid-div: pushed along over 3f out: hdwy over 1f out: led and edgd lft 1f out: rdn out* **7/2**[2]
12-2 **2** *1* **Fighting Temeraire (IRE)**[14] 2239 3-9-7 **85**............. RobertWinston 12 92+
(Dean Ivory) *hld up: plld hrd early: pushed along and hdwy over 1f out: r.o to go 2nd nr fin: nt rch wnr* **5/1**[3]
56-1 **3** *nk* **George William**[50] 1324 3-8-9 **76**.............................. TomMarquand(3) 5 82
(Richard Hannon) *chsd ldrs: rdn over 1f out: r.o* **14/1**
21 **4** *1* **Maximian (IRE)**[28] 1849 3-9-5 **83**.................................. WilliamBuick 6 86
(Charlie Appleby) *a.p: rdn over 1f out: edgd lft ins fnl f: styd on same pce towards fin* **10/3**[1]
0-64 **5** *1 ¾* **Firesnake (IRE)**[15] 2200 3-8-5 **74**..........................(p) JordanVaughan(5) 4 73
(K R Burke) *chsd ldrs: rdn over 1f out: styd on same pce ins fnl f* **25/1**
0-1 **6** *½* **Showing Off (IRE)**[28] 1859 3-9-1 **79**................................ HarryBentley 2 76
(Henry Candy) *s.i.s and bmpd s: hld up: hdwy over 2f out: rdn over 1f out: styd on same pce ins fnl f* **7/1**

06-1 **7** *hd* **Red Artist**[32] 1763 3-9-7 **85** PaulHanagan 10 82
(Simon Crisford) *hld up: rdn over 2f out: r.o ins fnl f: nvr nrr* **9/1**

21 **8** *1¼* **Irish Optimism (IRE)**[33] 1691 3-9-0 **78** CamHardie 3 71
(John Quinn) *s.i.s and bmpd s: hld up: rdn over 2f out: nvr on terms* **25/1**

41-0 **9** *½* **Marshal Dan Troop (IRE)**[38] 1571 3-9-0 **78** JimmyFortune 1 73
(Peter Chapple-Hyam) *pushed along to join ldr after 1f tl rdn over 2f out: nt clr run ins fnl f: no ex* **33/1**

41-2 **10** *1½* **Captain Dion**[31] 1789 3-8-13 **77** PatSmullen 13 65
(Kevin Ryan) *chsd ldrs: rdn over 2f out: nt clr run over 1f out: wknd ins fnl f* **25/1**

-31 **11** *nk* **Golden Glimmer (IRE)**[22] 1998 3-9-7 **85** RichardKingscote 7 72
(Tom Dascombe) *led: jnd after 1f: wnt on again over 2f out: sn rdn and edgd lft: hdd 1f out: wknd ins fnl f* **8/1**

36-0 **12** *18* **Quoteline Direct**[14] 2239 3-8-9 **73** [1] KierenFallon 8 12
(Micky Hammond) *hld up: rdn and wknd over 2f out* **66/1**

14-0 **13** *nk* **Baltic Raider (IRE)**[53] 1243 3-9-1 **79** ConnorBeasley 11 17
(Michael Dods) *in rr: rdn over 3f out: wknd over 2f out* **40/1**

1m 29.78s (-0.92) **Going Correction** +0.05s/f (Good) **13** Ran SP% **120.7**
Speed ratings (Par 101): **107,105,105,104,102 101,101,100,99,97 97,76,76**
CSF £20.01 CT £231.29 TOTE £4.30: £1.80, £1.90, £3.90; EX 29.50 Trifecta £270.50.
Owner The Starship Partnership **Bred** T Hirschfeld **Trained** Newmarket, Suffolk

FOCUS
This was run over 51yds further than advertised. A fair handicap for 3yos which was well run, and the form is rated on the positive side.
T/Jkpt: Not won. T/Plt: £402.50 to a £1 stake. Pool of £152761.88 - 277.0 winning tickets.
T/Qpdt: £75.40 to a £ stake. Pool of £8724.43 - 85.60 winning tickets. **Colin Roberts**

2180 SALISBURY (R-H)
Saturday, May 28

OFFICIAL GOING: Good (good to soft in places; 7.8) changing to good after race 1 (5.50)
Wind: almost nil Weather: sunny

2696 IRISH STALLION FARMS BATHWICK TYRES EBF NOVICE STKS (PLUS 10 RACE) 5f
5:50 (5:51) (Class 4) 2-Y-O **£4,528** (£1,347; £673; £336) **Stalls** Low

Form RPR

2 **1** **Repton (IRE)**[9] 2390 2-9-2 0 SeanLevey 9 88
(Richard Hannon) *trckd ldr: led 2f out: r.o and in command fnl f: readily* **4/6**[1]

2 *1* **Second Thought (IRE)** 2-9-2 0 JimCrowley 10 82
(William Haggas) *s.i.s: in last pair: rdn and hdwy over 1f out: str run fnl 120yds: wnt 2nd towards fin: nt rch wnr* **4/1**[2]

3 *½* **Tallulah Rose** 2-8-11 0 SteveDrowne 3 76
(George Baker) *slowly away: sn in tch: swtchd lft 2f out: sn rdn: r.o to chse wnr ent fnl f: no ex whn lost 2nd cl home* **20/1**

2 **4** *1* **Leontes**[10] 2371 2-8-11 0 EdwardGreatrex(5) 5 77
(Andrew Balding) *trckd ldrs: swtchd lft and rdn 2f out: kpt on same pce fnl f* **5/1**[3]

210 **5** *¾* **Stringybark Creek**[14] 2240 2-9-3 0 PaddyPilley(5) 6 80
(Mick Channon) *in tch: effrt 2f out: keeping on at same pce and hld disputing 3rd whn rdr dropped whip ins fnl f* **10/1**

4 **6** *4½* **Crystal Secret**[40] 1527 2-8-11 0 WilliamCarson 7 53
(John Bridger) *led tl 2f out: wknd fnl f* **50/1**

6 **7** *nse* **Felstead Queen**[12] 2310 2-8-11 0 MartinDwyer 1 53
(Joseph Tuite) *trckd ldrs: rdn over 2f out: wknd fnl f* **33/1**

8 *½* **Fanfair** 2-8-11 0 TimmyMurphy 8 51
(Richard Hannon) *in last pair: rdn 2f out: nvr threatened* **16/1**

1m 1.96s (0.96) **Going Correction** -0.075s/f (Good) **8** Ran SP% **121.3**
Speed ratings (Par 95): **89,87,86,85,83 76,76,75**
CSF £3.96 TOTE £1.60: £1.10, £1.40, £4.10; EX 4.10 Trifecta £40.50.
Owner H Robin Heffer **Bred** Ringfort Stud **Trained** East Everleigh, Wilts

FOCUS
A fair maiden run at an honest pace.

2697 BATHWICK TYRES ANDOVER H'CAP 6f
6:20 (6:22) (Class 6) (0-65,65) 4-Y-O+ **£2,911** (£866; £432; £216) **Stalls** Low

Form RPR

3451 **1** **Gilmer (IRE)**[7] 2458 5-8-7 **56** NoelGarbutt(5) 4 66
(Laura Young) *hld up towards rr: rdn and hdwy fr over 1f out: str run ins fnl f: led towards fin* **12/1**

6-00 **2** *1* **Mad Endeavour**[18] 2130 5-8-12 **56** MartinLane 12 63
(Stuart Kittow) *a.p: rdn to ld 2f out: kpt on but no ex whn hdd towards fin* **11/1**[3]

3610 **3** *1* **Secret Look**[18] 2130 6-9-6 **64** MartinDwyer 2 68
(Ed McMahon) *chsd ldrs: rdn over 2f out: kpt on ins fnl f* **7/1**[2]

0U-3 **4** *1½* **Foxford**[40] 1533 5-8-9 **58** PaddyPilley(5) 6 58
(Patrick Chamings) *led tl rdn 2f out: kpt on tl no ex fnl 100yds* **20/1**

1202 **5** *¾* **New Rich**[10] 2380 6-9-7 **65** (b) JohnFahy 1 63
(Eve Johnson Houghton) *hld up towards rr: rdn and hdwy over 1f out: kpt on wl ins fnl f but nvr threatening to get on terms* **20/1**

3-04 **6** *¾* **Babyfact**[17] 2146 5-9-3 **61** GeorgeBaker 8 56
(Malcolm Saunders) *towards rr: hdwy 2f out: sn rdn: kpt on fnl f but nvr threatening to get involved* **7/1**[2]

3221 **7** *hd* **One Big Surprise**[9] 2403 4-9-7 **65** ShaneKelly 5 59
(Richard Hughes) *mid-div: nt best of runs twice over 1f out: nvr threatened* **2/1**[1]

0-06 **8** *2¼* **Bonjour Steve**[18] 2130 5-9-5 **63** (p) StevieDonohoe 13 51
(Richard Price) *chsd ldrs: rdn over 2f out: fdd ins fnl f* **16/1**

0240 **9** *1¼* **Mambo Spirit (IRE)**[18] 2130 12-8-13 **60** TimClark(3) 7 44
(Tony Newcombe) *dwlt: towards rr: sme minor late prog: nvr any danger* **33/1**

5-46 **10** *½* **Goadby**[22] 2013 5-8-10 **57** MichaelJMMurphy(3) 11 39
(John Holt) *dwlt: towards rr: rdn and sme hdwy 3f out: wknd fnl f* **12/1**

3054 **11** *nse* **Frangarry (IRE)**[33] 1720 4-8-13 **57** FMBerry 3 39
(Alan Bailey) *mid-div: effrt 2f out: wknd fnl f* **14/1**

644- **12** *8* **Vincenzo Coccotti (USA)**[260] 6281 4-9-3 **61** JimCrowley 14 19
(Ken Cunningham-Brown) *kpt wd 1st f: trckd ldrs after 2f: rdn over 2f out: wknd over 1f out* **14/1**

010 **13** *¾* **Spellmaker**[42] 1496 7-9-4 **65** EoinWalsh(3) 10 21
(Tony Newcombe) *mid-div: hdwy 3f out: effrt 2f out: sn wknd* **25/1**

6004 **14** *2¾* **Johnny Splash (IRE)**[52] 1269 7-9-3 **61** (v) JackMitchell 9 9
(Roger Teal) *chsd ldrs: rdn over 2f out: wknd over 1f out* **33/1**

1m 13.98s (-0.82) **Going Correction** -0.075s/f (Good) **14** Ran SP% **120.5**
Speed ratings (Par 101): **102,100,99,97,96 95,95,92,90,89 89,79,78,74**
CSF £127.93 CT £1025.81 TOTE £15.50: £4.00, £3.70, £3.30; EX 200.10 Trifecta £1675.40.
Owner Total Plumbing Supporters Club **Bred** Darley **Trained** Broomfield, Somerset

FOCUS
Prior to the second race the going was changed to good, from good, good to soft in places. The pace was sound for this open handicap.

2698 BATHWICK TYRES SALISBURY MAIDEN STKS 6f
6:50 (6:51) (Class 5) 3-Y-O+ **£3,557** (£1,058; £529; £264) **Stalls** Low

Form RPR

3-52 **1** **Gunmetal (IRE)**[15] 2207 3-9-2 77 MichaelJMMurphy(3) 7 89
(Charles Hills) *mde all: kpt on gamely: drvn out* **7/2**[3]

5-24 **2** *¾* **Dark Shot**[14] 2251 3-9-0 81 EdwardGreatrex(5) 8 86
(Andrew Balding) *chsd wnr thrght: drvn 2f out: styd on but a being hld fnl f* **9/4**[1]

0- **3** *2¾* **Malakky (IRE)**[352] 3074 3-9-5 0 JimCrowley 2 77
(Brian Meehan) *trckd ldrs: rdn over 2f out: styd on same pce* **8/1**

200- **4** *7* **Big Chill (IRE)**[252] 6535 4-10-0 79 GeorgeBaker 10 57
(Patrick Chamings) *mid-div: smooth hdwy over 3f out: rdn over 2f out: fnd little and edgd rt: fdd fnl f* **12/1**

662- **5** *hd* **Poet's Song (IRE)**[278] 5680 3-9-5 77 MartinDwyer 5 54
(Marcus Tregoning) *hmpd s: mid-div: rdn over 3f out: nvr any imp* **8/1**

6 *1* **The Invisible Dog (IRE)** 3-9-5 0 SeanLevey 6 51
(Richard Hannon) *wnt rt and bmpd leaving stalls: towards rr: rdn 3f out: nvr any imp on ldrs* **11/4**[2]

7 *5* **Where Next** 3-9-0 0 HectorCrouch(5) 1 35
(Henry Candy) *trckd ldrs: rdn over 2f out: wknd over 1f out* **40/1**

04 **8** *2* **Dltripleseven (IRE)**[7] 2459 3-9-5 0 ShaneKelly 3 29
(Richard Hughes) *a towards rr* **66/1**

9 *1¾* **Jaunty Joh (IRE)** 3-9-0 0 FergusSweeney 4 18
(Henry Candy) *hmpd s: mid-div: rdn wl over 2f out: wknd over 1f out* **33/1**

0 **10** *6* **Hodgkins Trust (IRE)**[14] 2234 3-9-0 0 DavidParkes(5) 9 4
(Jeremy Gask) *chsd ldrs tl wknd over 2f out* **66/1**

1m 12.93s (-1.87) **Going Correction** -0.075s/f (Good)
WFA 3 from 4yo 9lb **10** Ran SP% **117.9**
Speed ratings (Par 103): **109,108,104,95,94 93,86,84,81,73**
CSF £11.78 TOTE £4.00: £1.30, £1.20, £3.50; EX 15.00 Trifecta £67.70.
Owner Mrs J K Powell **Bred** Maurice Byrne **Trained** Lambourn, Berks

FOCUS
A truly run maiden in which it paid to race handy. The time was good and the winner improved.

2699 BATHWICK TYRES H'CAP 1m 6f 21y
7:20 (7:21) (Class 4) (0-85,84) 4-Y-O+ **£7,762** (£2,310; £1,154; £577) **Stalls** Far side

Form RPR

1 **Starchitect (IRE)**[23] 2583 5-9-5 **82** (bt) GeorgeBaker 11 91+
(David Pipe) *a.p: rdn for str chal 3f out: led over 1f out: styd on strly to assert ins fnl f* **15/8**[1]

2420 **2** *2¼* **Icebuster**[12] 2296 8-8-12 **75** FrederikTylicki 5 81
(Rod Millman) *trckd ldrs: rdn 3f out: styd on to go 2nd fnl 140yds but a being hld by wnr* **20/1**

4-21 **3** *1½* **Rideonastar (IRE)**[27] 1893 5-9-5 **82** MartinDwyer 9 86
(Brendan Powell) *led: rdn whn strly chal 3f out: hdd over 1f out: lost 2nd whn no ex fnl 140yds* **5/2**[2]

303- **4** *nse* **Oceane (FR)**[55] 6499 4-9-7 **84** FergusSweeney 10 88
(Alan King) *mid-div: rdn and stdy prog fr over 2f out: hung rt ent fnl f: styd on same pce* **7/1**[3]

32-0 **5** *¾* **Nigel**[22] 1987 4-8-13 **76** ShaneKelly 8 79
(Richard Hughes) *hld up towards rr: racd keenly: hdwy 3f out: sn rdn: styd on same pce fnl 2f* **12/1**

160- **6** *1¼* **Spice Fair**[77] 7564 9-9-6 **83** SteveDrowne 13 84
(Mark Usher) *hld up bhd: stl in last 2f out: styd on strly fnl f but nvr threatened to get involved* **20/1**

0-00 **7** *nse* **Lungarno Palace (USA)**[21] 2024 5-9-2 **82** (b) MichaelJMMurphy(3) 3 83
(John Gallagher) *trckd ldrs: rdn 4f out: fdd ins fnl f* **25/1**

24-0 **8** *1¼* **Daghash**[22] 1987 7-8-11 **79** KieranShoemark(5) 7 78
(Stuart Kittow) *hld up towards rr: rdn 3f out: sme late prog: nvr trbld ldrs* **28/1**

160- **9** *½* **Air Squadron**[229] 7165 6-9-2 **79** FMBerry 14 78
(Ralph Beckett) *mid-div: rdn 4f out: nt pce to get on terms: wknd fnl f* **7/1**[3]

60/4 **10** *5* **Doesyourdogbite (IRE)**[47] 1391 4-8-12 **75** JimCrowley 2 67
(Jonjo O'Neill) *chsd ldrs: rdn over 3f out: wknd over 1f out* **25/1**

42-6 **11** *11* **Sunny Future (IRE)**[26] 1914 10-8-12 **75** SeanLevey 4 51
(Malcolm Saunders) *racd keenly: hld up: mid-div over 5f out: wknd 2f out* **33/1**

3m 5.98s (-1.42) **Going Correction** +0.05s/f (Good) **11** Ran SP% **119.7**
Speed ratings (Par 105): **106,104,103,103,103 102,102,101,101,98 92**
CSF £48.30 CT £100.32 TOTE £2.30: £1.20, £4.90, £1.70; EX 37.00 Trifecta £145.60.
Owner Paul & Clare Rooney **Bred** Castleton Lyons & Kilboy Estate **Trained** Nicholashayne, Devon

FOCUS
They went a steady pace for this fair handicap and the first three were always prominent. There's more to come from the winner.

2700 BATHWICK TYRES BOURNEMOUTH H'CAP 1m 4f
7:50 (7:50) (Class 6) (0-65,65) 3-Y-O **£2,911** (£866; £432; £216) **Stalls** Low

Form RPR

0-52 **1** **The Graduate (IRE)**[17] 2145 3-9-2 **65** EdwardGreatrex(5) 7 78
(Andrew Balding) *mid-div: hdwy 5f out: rdn to chal 3f out: sn hung rt: led over 1f out: styd on wl to assert towards fin* **11/4**[1]

00-0 **2** *1* **Pongo Twistleton**[29] 1826 3-8-7 **51** WilliamCarson 2 63
(Jonjo O'Neill) *s.i.s: sn rousted along: led after 1f: drvn and hung lft fr over 2f out: narrowly hdd over 1f out: kpt on: hld nring fin* **33/1**

6610 **3** *6* **Harry's Endeavour**[18] 2126 3-9-4 **62** (p) TimmyMurphy 4 64
(Daniel Kubler) *mid-div: hdwy over 2f out: rdn to chse ldng pair over 1f out: styd on same pce ins fnl f* **14/1**

56-4 **4** *nk* **Scarlet Pimpernel**[54] 1235 3-9-0 **65** CharlieBennett(7) 6 67
(Hughie Morrison) *mid-div: rdn and hdwy over 1f out: styd on to go 4th ins fnl f: nvr threatened ldrs* **8/1**

16-4 **5** *2¼* **Masterson (IRE)**[18] 2126 3-9-4 **62** GeorgeBaker 12 62
(Mick Channon) *mid-div: hdwy over 2f out: sn rdn: chal for 3rd over 1f out: no ex fnl 100yds* **7/2**[2]

4356 **6** *3¾* **Howardian Hills (IRE)**[18] 2126 3-9-4 **62** SeanLevey 13 54
(Richard Hannon) *pushed along early to chse ldrs: rdn 3f out: wknd ent fnl f* **9/1**

00-0 **7** 4½ **Author's Dream**[29] 1826 3-8-13 **57**.......... JimCrowley 8 42
(William Knight) *s.i.s: bhd: rdn and hdwy 2f out: nvr threatened ldrs: wknd ent fnl f* **14/1**

00-0 **8** 5 **Hamilton Terrace**[19] 2098 3-8-11 **55**.......... FergusSweeney 10 32
(Henry Candy) *hld up towards rr: midfield over 5f out: rdn 3f out: wknd over 1f out* **25/1**

444- **9** 2 **Mystikana**[229] 7158 3-9-5 **63**.......... MartinDwyer 11 37
(Marcus Tregoning) *racd keenly: hld up bhd: sme late prog past btn horses: nvr any danger* **6/1**[3]

00-0 **10** 1 **Ancient World (USA)**[66] 1036 3-9-0 **61**.......... MichaelJMMurphy(3) 5 33
(Charles Hills) *mid-div: hdwy 5f out: rdn 3f out: sn wknd* **25/1**

-613 **11** 1¾ **Spinning Pearl (IRE)**[29] 1835 3-9-5 **63**.......... JohnFahy 1 32
(Eve Johnson Houghton) *trckd ldrs: rdn 3f out: wknd over 1f out* **12/1**

0-00 **12** ¾ **Charlie Parker (IRE)**[32] 1740 3-8-0 **51** oh6.......... SeanMooney(7) 3 19
(Dominic Ffrench Davis) *hld up: midfield 5f out: rdn 3f out: wknd 2f out* **66/1**

00-4 **13** 24 **Fateh (IRE)**[138] 139 3-8-9 **53**.......... MartinLane 9
(David Dennis) *racd keenly: led for 1f: pressed ldr: rdn over 3f out: sn wknd* **40/1**

2m 39.23s (1.23) **Going Correction** +0.05s/f (Good) **13** Ran SP% **119.9**
Speed ratings (Par 97): **97,96,92,92,90 88,85,81,80,79 78,78,62**
CSF £111.11 CT £1114.56 TOTE £3.30: £1.60, £7.10, £3.40; EX 103.10 Trifecta £2569.20.
Owner Mick and Janice Mariscotti **Bred** Daniel Chassagneux **Trained** Kingsclere, Hants

FOCUS
Plenty of unexposed types in this handicap which was run at an honest pace. The front two finished clear.

2701 BATHWICK TYRES FERNDOWN CLASSIFIED STKS 1m 1f 198y
8:20 (8:20) (Class 5) 3-Y-O **£3,234** (£962; £481; £240) **Stalls** Low

Form RPR

0-42 **1** **Panko (IRE)**[22] 2012 3-9-0 69.......... KieranO'Neill 7 75
(Ed de Giles) *trckd ldrs: led over 2f out: sn drvn whn strly chal: kpt on gamely fnl f: hld on wl* **6/1**[3]

65-6 **2** ¾ **Third Rock (IRE)**[21] 2044 3-9-0 68..........(v[1]) StevieDonohoe 2 73
(Sir Michael Stoute) *trckd ldrs: rdn for str chal fr over 2f out: ev ch ent fnl f: hld towards fin* **3/1**[1]

004- **3** 1 **Thahab Ifraj (IRE)**[213] 7561 3-8-11 68.......... ThomasBrown(3) 1 71
(Ismail Mohammed) *in tch: rdn to chse ldng pair over 1f out: styd on same pce ins fnl f* **7/2**[2]

0-02 **4** 3 **Ejayteekay**[9] 2415 3-8-11 74..........[1] CharlieBennett(7) 4 69
(Hughie Morrison) *led: rdn and hdd over 2f out: sn one pce* **3/1**[1]

0-55 **5** ¾ **City By The Bay**[22] 2005 3-8-9 68.......... GaryMahon(5) 3 64
(Richard Hannon) *trckd ldrs: rdn over 2f out: sn one pce* **6/1**[3]

20-0 **6** 2¾ **Touch Of Color**[35] 1638 3-9-0 67.......... FMBerry 6 58
(Clive Cox) *hld up: outpcd 3f out: nvr threatened* **16/1**

01- **7** 2½ **Hermarna (IRE)**[229] 7159 3-9-0 68.......... MartinLane 8 53
(Harry Dunlop) *in tch: effrt 3f out: wknd jst over 1f out* **12/1**

2m 13.38s (3.48) **Going Correction** +0.05s/f (Good) **7** Ran SP% **114.4**
Speed ratings (Par 99): **88,87,86,84,83 81,79**
CSF £24.32 TOTE £7.10: £2.90, £1.90; EX 30.90 Trifecta £127.60.
Owner Simon Treacher **Bred** Jennifer & Evelyn Cullen **Trained** Ledbury, H'fords

FOCUS
An open contest run at a steady pace. The winner's Chepstow run had been franked since.
T/Plt: £61.00 to a £1 stake. Pool of £63367.48 - 757.70 winning tickets. T/Qpdt: £15.50 to a £1 stake. Pool of £6136.82 - 292.32 winning tickets. **Tim Mitchell**

2702 - 2710a (Foreign Racing) - See Raceform Interactive

2633 BADEN-BADEN (L-H)
Saturday, May 28

OFFICIAL GOING: Turf: good

2711a ITTLINGEN DERBY TRIAL (GROUP 3) (3YO) (TURF) 1m 2f
3:50 (12:00) 3-Y-O **£23,529** (£8,823; £4,411; £2,205; £1,470)

RPR

1 **Wai Key Star (GER)**[12] 3-9-2 0.......... EduardoPedroza 1 109
(A Wohler, Germany) *chsd ldng pair on inner: rdn to chal ldr 1 1/2f out: led appr fnl f: drvn clr* **68/10**[3]

2 2¾ **El Loco (GER)**[34] 1689 3-9-2 0.......... AdriedeVries 2 103
(Markus Klug, Germany) *led: kicked 2 l clr 2 1/2f out: rdn whn pressed 1 1/2f out: hdd appr fnl f: no ex* **11/10**[1]

3 4¾ **Noble House (GER)**[27] 3-9-2 0.......... AndreasSuborics 6 94
(Mario Hofer, Germany) *w.w towards rr: last and scrubbed along whn outpcd 3f out: styd on u.p to chse ldng pair fr 1 1/2f out: kpt on at same pce fnl f: nvr on terms* **127/10**

4 2¼ **San Salvador (GER)**[23] 3-9-2 0.......... AndreasHelfenbein 8 89
(Andreas Lowe, Germany) *w.w towards rr: no imp whn rdn 2f out: plugged on fr over 1f out: nvr in contention* **13/5**[2]

5 ½ **Nimrod (IRE)**[48] 3-9-2 0.......... DennisSchiergen 5 88
(P Schiergen, Germany) *hld up in rr: prog 2 1/2f out: sn hrd rdn: no further hdwy fr 2f out* **94/10**

6 shd **Nacar (GER)**[27] 1908 3-9-2 0.......... KoenClijmans 3 88
(Mario Hofer, Germany) *chsd ldng pair on outer: 3rd and hrd rdn under 2f out: sn btn and dropped away* **107/10**

7 3¾ **Volcancito (SWI)**[13] 3-9-2 0.......... JozefBojko 4 80
(A Wohler, Germany) *pressed ldr: rdn and nt qckn 2 1/2f out: grad fdd ins fnl 2f* **157/10**

8 nk **Capitano (GER)**[34] 1689 3-9-2 0.......... AlexanderPietsch 7 80
(J Hirschberger, Germany) *w.w towards rr: outpcd and scrubbed along fr 2f out: sn bhd* **81/10**

2m 4.23s (-0.76) **8** Ran SP% **130.7**
WIN (incl. 10 euro stake): 78. PLACES: 16, 11, 21. SF: 154.
Owner Stall Salzburg **Bred** Gestut Park Wiedingen **Trained** Germany

2712 - 2715a (Foreign Racing) - See Raceform Interactive

2164 NAAS (L-H)
Sunday, May 29

OFFICIAL GOING: Good

2716a OWENSTOWN STUD STKS (LISTED RACE) 7f
2:35 (2:37) 3-Y-O+
£20,606 (£6,636; £3,143; £1,397; £698; £349)

RPR

1 **Anamba**[245] 6791 3-8-9 104.......... WilliamBuick 1 102+
(M Halford, Ire) *chsd ldrs: 7th 1/2-way: pushed along and hdwy far side fr over 2f out to ld over 1f out: rdn clr and kpt on wl* **3/1**[1]

2 2 **Hasanour (USA)**[115] 455 6-9-11 100.......... ShaneFoley 3 106
(M Halford, Ire) *hld up: 11th appr st: hdwy gng wl fr over 2f out to chse ldrs in 5th over 1f out: r.o into 2nd and kpt on wl: nvr on terms* **16/1**

3 1¾ **Sevenleft (IRE)**[58] 1190 3-9-0 95.......... GaryCarroll 7 97
(Ms Sheila Lavery, Ire) *led: rdn 1 1/2f out and hdd u.p over 1f out: sn no imp on wnr u.p in 3rd and kpt on same pce clsng stages* **33/1**

4 hd **Orcia (IRE)**[35] 1680 4-9-6 98.......... ConorHoban 4 95
(M Halford, Ire) *cl up on inner early: 3rd 1/2-way: rdn 1 1/2f out and no imp on wnr u.p in 4th ins fnl f: kpt on same pce* **50/1**

5 ¾ **The Happy Prince (IRE)**[9] 2450 4-9-11 101..........(t) RyanMoore 5 98+
(A P O'Brien, Ire) *chsd ldrs: 5th 1/2-way: rdn in 6th over 1f out and no imp on ldrs ins fnl f: kpt on same pce* **5/1**[2]

6 ½ **Tennessee Wildcat (IRE)**[337] 3669 6-10-0 102.......... ColinKeane 8 100+
(G M Lyons, Ire) *settled in rr: sme hdwy gng wl over 2f out: rdn into 7th 1f out and kpt on u.p ins fnl f: nvr trbld ldrs* **20/1**

7 3¼ **Fainleog (IRE)**[19] 2132 5-9-6 76.......... AdrianO'Shea 13 83
(Mrs A M O'Shea, Ire) *cl up on outer: 2nd 1/2-way: rdn in 2nd fr 2f out and no ex u.p in 5th ent fnl f: one pce after and wknd into 7th clsng stages where eased* **100/1**

8 1¼ **Embiran (IRE)**[27] 1938 3-9-0 102.......... PatSmullen 2 81
(D K Weld, Ire) *hld up in tch: short of room on inner and checked after 2f where dropped to rr: last into st: sme hdwy under 2f out: rdn in mod 9th ins fnl f and kpt on one pce* **3/1**[1]

9 3 **In My Pocket (IRE)**[21] 2067 4-9-11 104.......... DeclanMcDonogh 6 77
(John M Oxx, Ire) *chsd ldrs early: pushed along in 10th appr st and no imp: one pce fnl 2f* **7/1**

10 6½ **Yuften**[41] 1536 5-9-11 108.......... ConnorKing 12 59
(J P Murtagh, Ire) *in tch on outer early: 8th 1/2-way: rdn and no ex fr over 2f out: one pce after* **13/2**[3]

11 nk **Taisce Naisiunta (IRE)**[217] 7492 3-8-9 99.......... KevinManning 14 49
(J S Bolger, Ire) *sn chsd ldrs: 4th 1/2-way: rdn over 2f out and sn no ex: wknd over 1f out* **25/1**

12 1 **Assume (IRE)**[224] 7318 4-9-6 101.......... WayneLordan 9 51
(David Wachman, Ire) *hld up: 9th 1/2-way: pushed along under 2f out and no imp over 1f out: eased ins fnl f* **25/1**

13 shd **Gussy Goose (IRE)**[27] 1939 4-9-6 95..........(v) BillyLee 10 50
(David Wachman, Ire) *towards rr and pushed along early: pushed along into st and no imp fr under 3f out* **33/1**

14 3¾ **Lily's Rainbow (IRE)**[42] 1509 4-9-9 102.......... LeighRoche 11 43
(Mrs Denise Foster, Ire) *hld up in mid-div: pushed along in 6th appr st and sn no ex u.p: wknd fnl 2f* **20/1**

1m 23.39s (-4.11)
WFA 3 from 4yo+ 11lb **14** Ran SP% **124.4**
CSF £53.25 TOTE £3.60: £1.40, £5.40, £7.90; DF 56.90 Trifecta £2773.20.
Owner Godolphin **Bred** Darley **Trained** Doneany, Co Kildare

FOCUS
A mixed message or two from the form, but it was a rough enough race and the winner did it well.

2717a COOLMORE WAR COMMAND ROCHESTOWN (C & G) STKS (LISTED RACE) 6f
3:10 (3:11) 2-Y-O **£28,198** (£9,080; £4,301; £1,911; £955)

RPR

1 **Peace Envoy (FR)**[27] 1936 2-9-3 0.......... RyanMoore 6 101
(A P O'Brien, Ire) *sn led: pressed gng wl 1 1/2f out: lost action briefly and jinked sltly rt jst ins fnl f: sn rdn and kpt on wl u.p clsng stages* **15/8**[2]

2 ½ **Lundy**[21] 2066 2-9-3 0.......... DonnachaO'Brien 5 99
(A P O'Brien, Ire) *trckd ldrs tl clsr in 2nd bef 1/2-way: pushed along in cl 2nd 1 1/2f out: sn rdn and kpt on wl clsng stages wout matching wnr* **7/2**[3]

3 2¼ **Moritzburg**[18] 2165 2-9-3 0.......... WilliamBuick 2 92+
(M Halford, Ire) *sltly hmpd s and settled in rr: tk clsr order in 4th bef 1/2-way: pushed along over 2f out: rdn and no imp on ldrs over 1f out: kpt on same pce into 3rd wl ins fnl f: nvr trbld ldrs* **8/1**

4 ¾ **Bective (IRE)**[56] 1223 2-9-3 0.......... RonanWhelan 4 90
(J F Levins, Ire) *hld up bhd ldrs: last bef 1/2-way: rdn ent fnl f and kpt on u.p between horses into nvr nrr 4th cl home: nvr trbld ldrs* **66/1**

5 hd **Hakeem (FR)**[12] 2335 2-9-3 0.......... HarryBentley 1 89
(Richard Hannon) *broke wl and wnt sltly rt s: sn settled bhd ldr tl dropped to 3rd bef 1/2-way: rdn 1 1/2f out where n.m.r on inner: no ex u.p ins fnl f and one pce clsng stages where dropped to rr* **11/8**[1]

1m 13.06s (-0.14) **5** Ran SP% **111.7**
CSF £8.92 TOTE £2.30: £1.02, £1.90; DF 6.70 Trifecta £22.10.
Owner Mrs John Magnier & Michael Tabor & Derrick Smith **Bred** Team Hogdala A B **Trained** Cashel, Co Tipperary

FOCUS
A tactical contest with O'Brien father and son dominating, but plenty was taken away from this race by the withdrawal of \bPsychedelic Funk\p

2718a COOLMORE STUD EUROPEAN BREEDERS FUND FILLIES' SPRINT STKS (LISTED RACE) 6f
3:40 (3:43) 2-Y-O
£28,198 (£9,080; £4,301; £1,911; £955; £477)

RPR

1 **Cuff (IRE)**[18] 2164 2-9-0 0.......... RyanMoore 9 102+
(A P O'Brien, Ire) *w ldrs: swtchd lft in 3rd under 2f out and hdwy far side to ld over 1f out: drvn clr ins fnl f and kpt on wl: comf* **11/4**[1]

2 3 **Yulong Baobei (IRE)**[11] 2381 2-9-0 0.......... ShaneFoley 10 92
(M Halford, Ire) *wnt sltly rt s: chsd ldr: rn freely early: rdn in cl 2nd over 1f out and sn no imp on wnr: kpt on same pce ins fnl f where edgd sltly lft: jst hld 2nd* **7/1**[3]

3 shd **Seafront**16 2211 2-9-0 0 ChrisHayes 6 92
(James Tate) *towards rr: tk clsr order under 2f out: rdn in 8th over 1f out and r.o wl ins fnl f: jst failed for 2nd: nt trble easy wnr* **33/1**

4 1/2 **Wayside Flower**18 2164 2-9-0 0 ColinKeane 5 90
(G M Lyons, Ire) *chsd ldrs: 6th 1/2-way: tk clsr order under 2f out: sn rdn in 4th and no imp on wnr u.p in 3rd briefly: kpt on same pce ins fnl f* **10/3**2

5 hd **Magical Fire (IRE)**18 2164 2-9-0 0 BillyLee 2 90
(M D O'Callaghan, Ire) *dwlt: hld up towards rr early: tk clsr order in mid-div after 1/2-way: rdn in 6th 1 1/2f out and no imp on wnr ent fnl f: kpt on same pce* **14/1**

6 hd **Oh Grace (IRE)**18 2164 2-9-0 0 KevinManning 13 89
(J S Bolger, Ire) *mid-div: rdn in 7th over 1f out and no imp on wnr ins fnl f: kpt on u.p clsng stages* **16/1**

7 1 1/2 **Pepita (IRE)**8 2467 2-9-0 0 PatDobbs 11 85
(Richard Hannon) *dwlt: hld up towards rr: rdn over 1f out and kpt on u.p ins fnl f: nvr nrr* **10/1**

8 hd **Spy Ring (IRE)**9 2449 2-9-0 0 KierenFallon 7 86
(M D O'Callaghan, Ire) *dwlt: settled in mid-div: tk clsr order fr 1/2-way: rdn in 5th over 1f out and no imp on wnr disputing 3rd briefly wl ins fnl f where hmpd: no imp after and eased clsng stages* **8/1**

9 1 1/4 **Melesina (IRE)**24 1976 2-9-0 0 TonyHamilton 8 80
(Richard Fahey) *settled in rr: rdn over 1f out and kpt on one pce u.p ins fnl f: nvr nrr* **50/1**

10 2 **Hyzenthlay (IRE)**8 2494 2-9-0 0 AnaO'Brien 12 74
(A P O'Brien, Ire) *mid-div: rdn and no ex 2f out: wknd fnl f* **50/1**

11 nk **Megan Lily (IRE)**8 2489 2-9-0 0 JackGarritty 4 73
(Richard Fahey) *broke wl to ld narrowly far side: rdn and hdd over 1f out: sn no ex and wknd ins fnl f* **7/1**3

12 6 **Elizabeth Browning (IRE)** 2-9-0 0 SeamieHeffernan 1 55
(A P O'Brien, Ire) *chsd ldrs: 4th 1/2-way: short of room on inner over 2f out where checked and sn dropped towards rr: no imp trailing in rr ent fnl f: eased ins fnl f* **20/1**

13 4 1/2 **Tilly Trotter (IRE)**58 1187 2-9-0 0 PatSmullen 3 42
(D K Weld, Ire) *rrd and dislodged rdr bef s: loaded wout rdr: chsd ldrs: 5th 1/2-way: no ex under 2f out and sn wknd: eased ins fnl f* **25/1**

1m 11.33s (-1.87) **13** Ran SP% **123.0**
CSF £21.85 TOTE £2.80: £1.10, £2.20, £8.20; DF 14.00 Trifecta £219.00.
Owner Mrs John Magnier & Michael Tabor & Derrick Smith **Bred** Massarra Syndicate **Trained** Cashel, Co Tipperary

FOCUS
Certainly an interesting race and it was another rough one. The winner didn't escape it but in the end she was certainly impressive.

2719a BAR ONE RACING LACKEN STKS (GROUP 3) 6f
4:15 (4:15) 3-Y-O
£28,198 (£9,080; £4,301; £1,911; £955; £477)

RPR

1 **Only Mine (IRE)**14 2272 3-9-0 101 GaryCarroll 1 111
(Joseph G Murphy, Ire) *settled in cl 2nd far side tl disp fr 1/2-way: led over 2f out and rdn clr over 1f out: styd on wl* **16/1**

2 2 3/4 **Washington DC (IRE)**14 2272 3-9-3 112 (t) RyanMoore 5 105+
(A P O'Brien, Ire) *hld up: gng wl and swtchd rt in 6th over 1f out: r.o wl into 2nd ins fnl 150yds wout ever troubling wnr clsng stages* **1/1**1

3 2 1/2 **Aclaim (IRE)**45 1442 3-9-3 94 PatSmullen 7 97
(Martyn Meade) *wnt sltly rt s: chsd ldrs: cl 3rd at 1/2-way: rdn over 1f out and sn no imp on wnr: kpt on same pce in 3rd wl ins fnl f* **4/1**3

4 1/2 **Erysimum (IRE)**12 2351 3-9-0 92 BillyLee 4 92
(W McCreery, Ire) *broke wl to sn ld narrowly: jnd fr 1/2-way and hdd over 2f out: sn rdn and no imp bhd ldrs 1f out: kpt on same pce* **20/1**

5 1/2 **Smash Williams (IRE)**226 7275 3-9-3 111 KevinManning 2 94
(J S Bolger, Ire) *hld up bhd ldrs: cl 4th at 1/2-way: rdn and no ex 1 1/2f out: kpt on same pce ins fnl f* **11/4**2

6 hd **Waterloo Bridge (IRE)**14 2272 3-9-3 104 (t) SeamieHeffernan 6 93
(A P O'Brien, Ire) *on toes befhand: hld up: 5th 1/2-way: tk clsr order 1 1/2f out where rdn: no imp on wnr u.p in 2nd briefly ent fnl f: one pce wl ins fnl f* **20/1**

7 6 1/2 **Al Qahwa (IRE)**273 5915 3-9-3 100 WilliamBuick 3 72
(M Halford, Ire) *dwlt and in rr thrght: pushed along bef 1/2-way and no imp* **33/1**

1m 9.93s (-3.27) **7** Ran SP% **115.0**
CSF £32.93 TOTE £23.60: £5.00, £1.02; DF 57.20 Trifecta £241.90.
Owner Mrs C C Regalado-Gonzalez **Bred** Mrs C L Weld **Trained** Fethard, Co Tipperary

FOCUS
An up-to-scratch renewal that produced a surprise winner who was rated 11lb inferior to the runner-up coming here. There appeared to be no fluke about it.

2720 - 2721a (Foreign Racing) - See Raceform Interactive

2710 BADEN-BADEN (L-H)
Sunday, May 29

OFFICIAL GOING: Turf: good

2722a SILBERNE PEITSCHE (GROUP 3) (3YO+) (TURF) 6f
2:00 (12:00) 3-Y-O+ **£23,529** (£8,823; £4,411; £2,205; £1,470)

RPR

1 **Shining Emerald**24 5-9-6 0 EduardoPedroza 8 108+
(A Wohler, Germany) *chsd ldrs: 2 l 3rd and rdn 1f out: styd on wl u.p to ld 75yds out and asserted* **7/10**1

2 1 **Daring Match (GER)**24 5-9-6 0 AlexanderPietsch 9 105
(J Hirschberger, Germany) *pressed ldr: cl 2nd and rdn over 2f out: virtually upsides 1f out: responded to press and led 125yds out: hdd fnl 75yds: no ex* **131/10**

3 hd **Donnerschlag**24 6-9-6 0 (b) MarcLerner 11 104
(Jean-Pierre Carvalho, Germany) *led main gp of nine in centre: led overall and c stands' side 2 1/2f out: hdd fnl 125yds: no ex* **17/2**

4 1 3/4 **Forgino (GER)**24 5-9-6 0 AdriedeVries 4 99+
(T Potters, Germany) *dwlt: in rr: wl adrift and rdn over 1 1/2f out: styd on wl fnl f: nrest at fin* **132/10**

5 1/2 **Making Trouble (GER)**28 4-9-6 0 FilipMinarik 6 97+
(Melanie Sauer, Germany) *settled in midfield: rdn and nt qckn fr 2f out: kpt on at same pce fnl f* **10/1**

6 hd **Prince Orpen (FR)**24 5-9-6 0 JozefBojko 10 97
(Helena Blazkova, Czech Republic) *chsd ldng pair: 4th and hrd rdn over 1f out: one pce u.p fnl f* **238/10**

7 3/4 **Flashy Approach**24 6-9-6 0 EugenFrank 7 94
(P Bradik, Germany) *racd in midfield: nt qckn u.p wl over 1 1/2f out: one pce fr over 1f out* **26/1**

8 2 3/4 **Fly First**24 7-9-6 0 AndreasHelfenbein 2 85
(Ferdinand J Leve, Germany) *w.w towards rr: rdn and no imp 2f out: wl hld fnl f* **81/10**2

9 5 **Never Compromise (FR)**19 2141 3-8-11 0 IanFerguson 1 67
(Henk Grewe, Germany) *a in fnl pair: nvr in contention* **126/10**

10 7 **Gamgoom**65 1066 5-9-6 0 AndreasSuborics 3 47
(Mario Hofer, Germany) *racd alone stands' side and led overall: hdd 2 1/2f out: wknd wl over 1f out and eased ins fnl f* **41/5**3

1m 11.12s (0.83)
WFA 3 from 4yo+ 9lb **10** Ran SP% **129.5**
WIN (incl. 10 euro stake): 17. PLACES: 12, 24, 20. SF: 128.
Owner Jaber Abdullah **Bred** Rabbah Bloodstock Limited **Trained** Germany

2723a GROSSER PREIS DER BADISCHEN WIRTSCHAFT (GROUP 2) (4YO+) (TURF) 1m 3f
3:50 (12:00) 4-Y-O+ **£29,411** (£11,397; £5,882; £2,941; £1,838)

RPR

1 **Iquitos (GER)**35 4-9-0 0 NormanRichter 9 113
(H-J Groschel, Germany) *hld up in rr: drvn and gd hdwy fr over 2f out: led 1f out: styd on wl: rdn out* **112/10**

2 2 **Articus (FR)**35 4-9-0 0 StephenHellyn 10 109
(Waldemar Hickst, Germany) *hld up in rr: rdn and hdwy fr 3f out: ev ch over 1f out: kpt on: nt pce of wnr* **67/10**3

3 2 1/4 **Ito (GER)**21 2075 5-9-6 0 FilipMinarik 5 111
(Jean-Pierre Carvalho, Germany) *led: drvn 2f out: hdd 1f out: no ex fnl f* **4/5**1

4 3/4 **Devastar (GER)**35 4-9-0 0 AdriedeVries 2 104
(Markus Klug, Germany) *trckd ldrs: drvn: edgd rt and unable qck 2f out: short of room 1f out: kpt on same pce* **159/10**

5 1 3/4 **Early Morning (GER)**21 2075 7-8-10 0 IanFerguson 4 97
(Dr A Bolte, Germany) *midfield: rdn over 2f out: nt quite able to chal: wknd steadily fnl f* **196/10**

6 2 3/4 **Eric (GER)**21 2075 5-9-0 0 AlexanderPietsch 1 96
(C Von Der Recke, Germany) *midfield: rdn over 2f out: sltly hmpd over 1f out: wknd 1f out* **26/1**

7 1 **Nightflower (IRE)**182 8042 4-9-3 0 DennisSchiergen 8 97
(P Schiergen, Germany) *chsd ldr: effrt 3f out: wkng whn bmpd under 2f out: sn btn* **23/10**2

8 12 **Fair Mountain (GER)**21 2075 4-9-0 0 EduardoPedroza 7 73
(A Wohler, Germany) *in tch: rdn and unable qck 3f out: wl btn 2f out: eased* **115/10**

2m 17.32s (-1.95) **8** Ran SP% **129.5**
WIN (incl. 10 euro stake): 122. PLACES: 18, 16, 12. SF: 796..
Owner Stall Mulligan **Bred** Frau Dr Erika Buhmann **Trained** Germany

2550 SAINT-CLOUD (L-H)
Sunday, May 29

OFFICIAL GOING: Turf: good to soft

2724a PRIX DE SAINT-GERMAIN-DES-PRES (CLAIMER) (2YO) (TURF) 6f
1:05 (12:00) 2-Y-O **£8,455** (£3,382; £2,536; £1,691; £845)

RPR

1 **Efichope (FR)** 2-8-8 0 (p) MickaelForest 4 63
(A Chopard, France) **22/1**

2 nk **Sheila's Lad (IRE)**33 1741 2-9-1 0 ChristopheSoumillon 6 69
(J S Moore) *t.k.h: chsd ldrs: rdn 1 1/2f out: styd on u.p ins fnl f: nt quite rch wnr* **6/4**1

3 snk **Heavens Stream (FR)**22 2-9-1 0 (b) StephanePasquier 9 69
(Y Gourraud, France) **42/10**3

4 snk **Fast Kar (IRE)**16 2-8-11 0 EddyHardouin 5 64
(Matthieu Palussiere, France) **71/10**

5 1/2 **Eblouis Moi (FR)** 2-9-1 0 Pierre-CharlesBoudot 7 67
(A Giorgi, Italy) **17/5**2

6 snk **Sowgay (FR)**48 2-8-11 0 (b) AdrienFouassier 8 62
(C Plisson, France) **40/1**

7 3/4 **Sisterleon Davis (FR)**9 2454 2-8-11 0 (p) SylvainRuis 2 60
(C Plisson, France) **14/1**

8 1/2 **Kidane Traou Land (FR)**48 2-8-11 0 (p) RichardJuteau 1 58
(C Plisson, France) **25/1**

9 2 **Hot N Sassy (IRE)**19 2125 2-8-8 0 (p) IoritzMendizabal 10 49
(J S Moore) *sltly outpcd early: nudged along in fnl pair: last and no imp whn rdn 2 1/2f out: sme mod prog late on: nvr a factor* **19/1**

10 4 **Chababa Rosetgri (FR)**22 2-8-11 0 RonanThomas 3 40
(H De Nicolay, France) **32/1**

1m 19.0s (2.20) **10** Ran SP% **119.6**
WIN (incl. 1 euro stake): 23.00; PLACES: 3.50, 1.30, 1.80; DF: 22.90; SF: 77.70.
Owner Alain Chopard **Bred** Mlle S Brel **Trained** France

2725a PRIX VICOMTESSE VIGIER (GROUP 2) (4YO+) (TURF) 1m 7f 110y
1:35 (12:00) 4-Y-O+ **£54,485** (£21,029; £10,036; £6,691)

RPR

1 **Vazirabad (FR)**64 1102 4-9-2 0 ChristopheSoumillon 2 120+
(A De Royer-Dupre, France) *hld up towards rr: clsd on outer over 1 1/2f out: virtually upsides ldr and shkn up 1f out: styd on to ld fnl 110yds and asserted* **2/7**1

2 3/4 **Fly With Me (FR)**35 1688 6-8-11 0 (p) MaximeGuyon 3 112
(E Libaud, France) *trckd ldr under a tight hold: shkn up to chal 2f out: led wl over 1 1/2f out: pressed fr over 1 1/2f out: rallied u.p: hdd fnl 110yds: no ex* **9/2**2

3 1 1/4 **Manatee**64 1102 5-9-0 0 MickaelBarzalona 4 114
(A Fabre, France) *led: rdn and raised tempo over 2f out: hdd wl over 1 1/2f out: styd on at same pce fnl f* **15/2**3

4 4 **Walzertakt (GER)**[14] 2286 7-9-0 0 IoritzMendizabal 1 109
(Jean-Pierre Carvalho, Germany) *in rr: nvr really travelling smoothly: nudged along 1/2-way: rdn 2 1/2f out but no imp: plugged on at one pce: nvr in contention* **22/1**

3m 35.96s (-2.74)
WFA 4 from 5yo+ 1lb 4 Ran SP% **112.1**
WIN (incl. 1 euro stake); 1.40; PLACES: 1.10, 1.10; SF: 2.40.
Owner H H Aga Khan **Bred** S C E A Haras De Son Altesse L'Aga Khan **Trained** Chantilly, France

FOCUS
This was slowly run with a sprint finish. All four are rated to their recent form.

2726a PRIX CLEOPATRE (GROUP 3) (3YO FILLIES) (TURF) 1m 2f 110y
3:00 (12:00) 3-Y-O **£29,411** (£11,764; £8,823; £5,882; £2,941)

RPR

1 **Highlands Queen (FR)**[56] 3-8-9 0 StephanePasquier 2 110
(Y Gourraud, France) *led early: sn hdd and w.w in tch: qcknd to ldr over 1 1/2f out: draw clr fr over 1f out: comf* **6/1**[3]

2 5 **Mango Tango (FR)**[35] 3-8-9 0 LouisBeuzelin 4 100
(P Bary, France) *hld up in rr: chsd Apple Betty in gp of two on stands' side st: sn rdn and styd on to take 2nd ins fnl f: no ch w wnr* **11/1**

3 1 1/4 **Apple Betty (IRE)**[29] 1877 3-8-10 0 ow1 ChristopheSoumillon 5 99
(J-C Rouget, France) *t.k.h and sn plld way to ld: restrained towards rr whn hdd after 1 1/2f: led one rival over to stands' side ent st over 2 1/2f out: hdd in gp 1 1/2f out: kpt on at same pce fnl f* **8/11**[1]

4 nk **Gargotiere (FR)**[20] 2115 3-8-9 0 AlexisBadel 1 97
(H-F Devin, France) *cl up: led after 1 1/2f: hdd bef 1/2-way and remained cl up: readily outpcd by eventual wnr fr wl over 1f out and wknd* **5/2**[2]

5 2 **Indecence Choisie (FR)**[41] 1541 3-8-10 0 ow1 OlivierPeslier 3 94
(C Ferland, France) *restrained in 2nd: led bef 1/2-way: led gp of three on ins rail ent st over 2 1/2f out: hdd over 1 1/2f out: sn outpcd by eventual wnr wl over 1f out: wknd* **12/1**

2m 17.41s (-2.19) 5 Ran SP% **116.8**
WIN (incl. 1 euro stake): 6.50; PLACES: 3.50, 4.20; SF: 32.80.
Owner Mme Nathalie Kerjean **Bred** S.C.E.A. Domaine De L'Argos **Trained** France

2727a PRIX CORRIDA (GROUP 2) (4YO+ FILLIES & MARES) (TURF) 1m 2f 110y
3:35 (12:00) 4-Y-O+ **£54,485** (£21,029; £10,036; £6,691; £3,345)

RPR

1 **Speedy Boarding**[17] 2189 4-8-10 0 FrederikTylicki 6 114
(James Fanshawe) *chsd ldng trio: shkn up to hold pl wl over 2 1/2f out: sn drvn and styd on to ld 1 1/2f out: r.o gamely u.p fnl f: a holding runner-up* **4/1**[2]

2 1/2 **Siljan's Saga (FR)**[28] 1909 6-9-1 0 TheoBachelot 5 118
(J-P Gauvin, France) *settled in midfield on inner: cl 5th and travelling wl appr 2f out: nt clr run and angled out appr 1 1/2f out: r.o u.p to chse ldr ins fnl f: nvr quite on terms* **11/2**[3]

3 2 1/2 **Candarliya (FR)**[35] 1688 4-9-1 0 ChristopheSoumillon 1 113
(A De Royer-Dupre, France) *w.w towards rr: rdn and prog whn n.m.r 2f out: styd on u.p fr wl over 1f out: chsd ldng pair ins fnl f: run petered out last 110yds* **5/4**[1]

4 1 1/4 **Contribution**[31] 1822 4-8-10 0 VincentCheminaud 8 106+
(A Fabre, France) *w.w in fnl trio: hrd rdn on outer 2f out: kpt on u.p fr wl over 1f out: nt pce to get in contention* **11/2**[3]

5 1 1/4 **Sassella (IRE)**[31] 1822 4-8-10 0 MaximeGuyon 7 103
(A Fabre, France) *w.w in midfield on outer: hrd rdn in 5th 2f out: plugged on at one pce* **18/1**

6 nk **Beautiful Heroine (IRE)**[31] 1822 5-8-13 0 GregoryBenoist 2 106
(F-H Graffard, France) *led early: hdd after 100yds: trckd ldr on inner: rdn and nt qckn wl over 1 1/2f out: sn btn* **16/1**

7 3/4 **Ame Bleue**[31] 1822 4-8-10 0 Pierre-CharlesBoudot 10 101
(A Fabre, France) *w.w in fnl pair: rdn and effrt over 2f out: plugged on fr over 1f out: nvr a factor* **16/1**

8 3 1/2 **Bourree (GER)**[62] 4-8-13 0 EddyHardouin 11 97
(Andreas Lowe, Germany) *hld up towards rr on outer: rdn and no imp fr 2f out: nvr in contention* **14/1**

9 1 3/4 **Thank You Bye Bye (FR)**[31] 1822 4-8-10 0 OlivierPeslier 4 91
(J-P Gauvin, France) *t.k.h: chsd ldr on outer: rdn and wknd ins fnl 1 1/2f* **22/1**

10 1 1/4 **Amazona (GER)**[31] 1822 4-8-10 0 IoritzMendizabal 3 89
(Jean-Pierre Carvalho, Germany) *led after 100yds: hdd 1 1/2f out: sn wknd* **33/1**

11 20 **Stone Roses (FR)**[40] 1557 4-8-10 0 MickaelBarzalona 9 50
(F Head, France) *outpcd in rr early: last and pushed along 3f out: sn t.o* **20/1**

2m 16.17s (-3.43) 11 Ran SP% **131.0**
WIN (incl. 1 euro stake): 8.60; PLACES: 2.10, 1.70, 1.30; DF: 21.90; SF: 50.30.
Owner Helena Springfield Ltd **Bred** Meon Valley Stud **Trained** Newmarket, Suffolk

FOCUS
This was well run.

1516 SAN SIRO (R-H)
Sunday, May 29

OFFICIAL GOING: Turf: heavy

2728a GRAN PREMIO DI MILANO (GROUP 2) (4YO+) (TURF) 1m 4f
3:15 (12:00) 4-Y-O+ **£64,338** (£28,308; £15,441; £7,720)

RPR

1 **Dylan Mouth (IRE)**[203] 7767 5-9-4 0 FrankieDettori 6 116+
(Marco Botti) *mde all: drvn clr wl over 1f out: won easing down* **4/11**[1]

2 5 1/2 **Circus Couture (IRE)**[21] 2073 4-9-2 0 FabioBranca 5 102
(Stefano Botti, Italy) *chsd ldrs: rdn and nt qckn 2f out: styd on to take 2nd fnl f: no ch w wnr* **4/11**[1]

3 2 3/4 **Novano (GER)**[28] 4-9-2 0 RobertHavlin 7 98
(Waldemar Hickst, Germany) *chsd ldrs: wnt 2nd bef 1/2-way: rdn and no imp on ldr 1 1/2f out: grad lft* **19/5**[3]

4 hd **Touch Of Genius (IRE)**[29] 4-9-2 0 LucaManiezzi 3 97+
(Josef Vana, Czech Republic) *settled in 5th: rdn and effrt 1 1/2f out: plugged on at one pce fnl f* **85/40**[2]

5 2 3/4 **Taratchi (FR)**[25] 4-9-2 0 AntoineHamelin 2 93
(J Parize, France) *chsd ldr: rdn and wknd wl over 2f out* **189/10**

6 dist **Lovato (GER)**[14] 2286 4-9-2 0 DanielePorcu 1
(P Schiergen, Germany) *a bhd: t.o fr over 2f out* **19/5**[3]

2m 35.9s (4.40) 6 Ran SP% **225.3**
WIN (incl. 1 euro stake): 1.38. PLACES: 1.46, 1.61. DF: 2.51.
Owner Scuderia Effevi SRL **Bred** Azienda Agricola Mariano **Trained** Newmarket, Suffolk

2729a PREMIO CARLO VITTADINI (GROUP 3) (3YO+) (TURF) 1m
3:50 (12:00) 3-Y-O+ **£26,838** (£11,808; £6,441; £3,220)

RPR

1 **Kaspersky (IRE)**[21] 2073 5-9-5 0 UmbertoRispoli 4 106
(Endo Botti, Italy) *mde all: a in clr ld: drvn fr 2f out: unchal* **85/40**[2]

2 2 3/4 **Greg Pass (IRE)**[28] 4-9-5 0 DarioVargiu 1 100
(Il Cavallo In Testa, Italy) *midfield: stdy hdwy fr 4f out: rdn 2f out: kpt on wl but no imp on wnr* **79/50**[1]

3 2 **Tamarind Cove (IRE)**[28] 4-9-5 0 LucaManiezzi 8 95+
(Josef Vana, Czech Republic) *hld up towards rr: rdn and kpt on steadily fr 3f out: tk 3rd clsng stages: nrst fin* **59/20**[3]

4 1/2 **Azzeccagarbugli (IRE)**[168] 3-8-7 0 AndreaAtzeni 2 91
(Stefano Botti, Italy) *chsd ldr: rdn and outpcd 3f out: plugged on: lost 3rd clsng stages* **106/10**

5 2 **Porsenna (IRE)**[21] 2073 6-9-5 0 SilvanoMulas 5 89
(Stefano Botti, Italy) *hld up in rr: rdn fr 3f out: kpt on steadily but n.d* **116/10**

6 2 1/2 **Azari**[49] 4-9-5 0 FrankieDettori 6 84
(Il Cavallo In Testa, Italy) *trckd ldrs: rdn and outpcd over 3f out: steadily wknd* **156/10**

7 12 **Saint Bernard**[21] 2073 7-9-5 0 SalvatoreSulas 3 56
(Simone Langiano, Italy) *hld up towards rr: drvn and unable qck 3f out: eased whn btn over 1f out* **78/10**

1m 41.9s (-0.20)
WFA 3 from 4yo+ 12lb 7 Ran SP% **130.0**
WIN (incl. 1 euro stake): 3.13. PLACES: 1.62, 1.46. DF: 3.93.
Owner Allevamento La Nuova Sbarra **Bred** Allevamento La Nuova Sbarra **Trained** Italy

2730a OAKS D'ITALIA (GROUP 2) (3YO FILLIES) (TURF) 1m 3f
5:15 (12:00) 3-Y-O **£136,029** (£59,852; £32,647; £16,323)

RPR

1 **Nepal (GER)** 3-8-11 0 MichaelCadeddu 8 105+
(Dr A Bolte, Germany) **219/10**

2 2 3/4 **Gambissara (FR)**[22] 3-8-11 0 BertrandFlandrin 2 100
(Lennart Hammer-Hansen, Germany) **28/1**

3 4 1/2 **Son Macia (GER)**[42] 3-8-11 0 DanielePorcu 3 92
(Andreas Lowe, Germany) **13/1**

4 2 1/2 **A Raving Beauty (GER)**[24] 1986 3-8-11 0 AntoineHamelin 4 88
(A Wohler, Germany) **129/10**

5 2 **Valuta Pregiata**[35] 1685 3-8-11 0 CarloFiocchi 11 84
(Stefano Botti, Italy) **31/1**

6 2 **Edya**[22] 3-8-11 0 DarioVargiu 6 80
(Stefano Botti, Italy) **68/10**[3]

7 4 **Miss Steff (IRE)** 3-8-11 0 UmbertoRispoli 10 73
(Stefano Botti, Italy) **9/1**

8 dist **Dry Your Eyes (ITY)**[22] 3-8-11 0 NicolaPinna 7
(Stefano Botti, Italy) **91/10**

9 12 **Page One (FR)**[22] 3-8-11 0 MarioEsposito 12
(M Arienti, Italy) **83/1**

10 2 **Responsibleforlove (IRE)**[22] 3-8-11 0 FrankieDettori 9
(Endo Botti, Italy) **6/5**[1]

11 1/2 **Cassina De Pomm (ITY)**[231] 7156 3-8-11 0 AndreaAtzeni 5
(Stefano Botti, Italy) **61/20**[2]

12 7 **Extremely Vintage (IRE)**[56] 3-8-11 0 MarioSanna 1
(Endo Botti, Italy) **6/5**[1]

13 2 **Conselice**[35] 1685 3-8-11 0 SilvanoMulas 14
(Stefano Botti, Italy) **74/10**

14 2 **Victim Of Love (ITY)**[35] 1685 3-8-11 0 FabioBranca 13
(Stefano Botti, Italy) **91/10**

2m 23.5s (4.90) 14 Ran SP% **196.6**
WIN (incl. 1 euro stake): 22.85. PLACES: 6.11, 8.82, 4.51. DF: 511.84.
Owner Stall Seseke **Bred** M Ruhl **Trained** Germany

2731 - (Foreign Racing) - See Raceform Interactive

2535 LEICESTER (R-H)
Monday, May 30

OFFICIAL GOING: Good to firm (good in places on the round course)
Wind: Light against Weather: Overcast

2732 TOTEPLACEPOT PLAY EVERY DAY NOVICE MEDIAN AUCTION STKS 5f
2:10 (2:10) (Class 5) 2-Y-O **£3,881** (£1,155; £577; £288) **Stalls** High

Form RPR

2 1 **Pretty Vacant**[10] 2437 2-9-2 0 AndreaAtzeni 3 82+
(Roger Varian) *mde virtually all: rdn over 1f out: r.o* **4/7**[1]

2 2 **Rosebride** 2-8-11 0 PaulHanagan 5 67+
(Richard Fahey) *hld up: pushed along 1/2-way: hdwy over 1f out: edgd rt and r.o to go 2nd post: nt rch wnr* **10/1**

3 nk **The Daley Express (IRE)** 2-9-2 0 DaleSwift 6 71
(Ed McMahon) *pushed along in early: hdwy over 3f out: rdn to chse wnr and edgd lft fnl f: styd on: lost 2nd post* **20/1**

04 4 3 **Misty Moo**[13] 2335 2-8-6 0 GeorgeBuckell(5) 2 55
(Michael Appleby) *w wnr: rdn and ev ch over 1f out: wknd wl ins fnl f* **50/1**

40 5 1/2 **Cosmic Beau (IRE)**[28] 1915 2-9-2 0 (v) RichardKingscote 7 58
(Tom Dascombe) *prom: plld hrd: jnd wnr over 3f out tl rdn wl over 1f out: wknd ins fnl f* **14/1**

6 hd **Mums The Word** 2-8-11 0 TedDurcan 1 52
(Richard Hannon) *wnt rt s: hung rt fr 1/2-way: hdwy over 1f out: wknd ins fnl f* **4/1**[2]

7 1 1/2 **Goodwood Crusader (IRE)** 2-9-2 0 RyanMoore 4 52
(Richard Hughes) *chsd ldrs: shkn up and edgd rt over 1f out: wknd fnl f* **8/1**[3]

6 8 7 **Jet Setter (IRE)**[35] 1713 2-9-2 0 RobertHavlin 8 27
(Brian Meehan) *prom tl rdn and wknd over 1f out* **25/1**

1m 1.35s (1.35) **Going Correction** +0.125s/f (Good) 8 Ran SP% **121.1**
Speed ratings (Par 93): **94,90,90,85,84 84,82,70**
CSF £8.31 TOTE £1.50: £1.10, £2.80, £4.20; EX 6.90 Trifecta £69.20.

Owner Miss C A Baines **Bred** D R Botterill **Trained** Newmarket, Suffolk

FOCUS

The going was officially good to firm, good in places on the round course. An ordinary juvenile contest to start and fairly straightforward for the hot favourite.

2733 TOTEJACKPOT PLAY EVERY DAY (S) STKS 1m 1f 218y

2:45 (2:45) (Class 6) 3-5-Y-O **£2,587** (£770; £384; £192) **Stalls** Low

Form RPR

-040 **1** **Scent Of Power**[9] 2462 4-8-9 49 GeorgeWood(7) 3 60
(Barry Leavy) *hld up in tch: plld hrd: led over 2f out: rdn clr over 1f out* **10/1**

46-6 **2** *3* **Yankee Mail (FR)**[61] 1157 4-9-2 70 DougieCostello 7 54
(K R Burke) *hld up: hdwy over 3f out: sn rdn: hung rt and chsd wnr over 1f out: styd on same pce ins fnl f* **13/8**[1]

5050 **3** *3 ¾* **Arsenale (GER)**[32] 1654 5-8-13 45 AlistairRawlinson(3) 5 47
(Michael Appleby) *led 2f: chsd ldrs: outpcd over 2f out: styd on ins fnl f: wnt 3rd nr fin* **14/1**

0-00 **4** *½* **Imperial Link**[7] 2542 4-8-11 53 (p) CiaranMckee(5) 4 46
(John O'Shea) *w ldr: led 8f out: rdn and hdd over 2f out: no ex fr over 1f out* **33/1**

2000 **5** *6* **Hannington**[55] 900 5-9-7 74 (tp) DaleSwift 1 40
(Barry Brennan) *s.i.s: hld up: sme hdwy u.p over 1f out: wknd fnl f* **4/1**[3]

3420 **6** *2 ¾* **Masqueraded (USA)**[8] 2506 3-8-0 68 (p) RPWalsh(7) 2 34
(Gay Kelleway) *trckd ldrs: wnt 2nd over 5f out tl over 3f out: sn rdn: wknd over 1f out* **7/1**

6-05 **7** *6* **Jersey Roy**[40] 1573 3-8-7 65 PaulHanagan 6 22
(Richard Fahey) *plld hrd: w ldrs: hung lft fr over 4f out: rdn over 3f out: wknd wl over 1f out* **7/2**[2]

2m 10.09s (2.19) **Going Correction** +0.125s/f (Good)
WFA 3 from 4yo+ 14lb **7** Ran SP% **111.5**
Speed ratings (Par 101): **96,93,90,90,85 83,78**
CSF £25.46 TOTE £13.00: £4.30, £1.80; EX 33.80 Trifecta £282.40.
Owner Cops & Robbers **Bred** Minster Stud **Trained** Forsbrook, Staffs

FOCUS

A moderate seller, with few coming into this in much form, and official ratings went out of the window.

2734 TOTEQUADPOT FOUR PLACES IN FOUR RACES H'CAP 1m 60y

3:20 (3:21) (Class 4) (0-80,80) 4-Y-O+ **£6,469** (£1,925; £962; £481) **Stalls** Low

Form RPR

0-06 **1** **Normandy Knight**[17] 2198 4-8-12 **71** PaulHanagan 5 81
(Richard Fahey) *mid-div: hdwy and swtchd lft over 2f out: rdn to join ldr over 1f out: styd on to ld post* **6/1**[3]

5-23 **2** *nk* **Ttainted Love**[18] 2174 4-9-2 **75** (p) TedDurcan 1 84
(Chris Wall) *chsd ldrs: rdn to ld over 1f out: edgd rt ins fnl f: hdd post* **4/1**[2]

5006 **3** *1 ¾* **Dubai Dynamo**[15] 2268 11-9-7 **80** AndrewElliott 6 85
(Ruth Carr) *hld up: swtchd lft and hdwy over 1f out: r.o: nt rch ldrs* **10/1**

0000 **4** *3* **Pick A Little**[12] 2378 8-8-5 **71** MitchGodwin(7) 7 69
(Michael Blake) *chsd ldrs tl led over 5f out: rdn and hdd over 1f out: no ex ins fnl f* **28/1**

6052 **5** *1 ¼* **Peak Storm**[9] 2460 7-8-13 **77** (p) CiaranMckee(5) 4 72
(John O'Shea) *s.i.s: hld up: nt clr run over 2f out: hdwy over 1f out: nrst fin* **22/1**

33-2 **6** *2 ¾* **Terhaal (IRE)**[42] 1521 4-9-5 **78** RyanMoore 12 67
(David O'Meara) *mid-div: pushed along and hdwy over 2f out: rdn over 1f out: wknd ins fnl f* **9/4**[1]

05-0 **7** *¾* **Mister Music**[52] 1318 7-9-6 **79** (v) AndreaAtzeni 3 66
(Robert Eddery) *s.i.s: hld up: hdwy u.p over 1f out: wknd ins fnl f* **6/1**[3]

2-03 **8** *9* **Hickster (IRE)**[23] 2043 5-9-1 **79** CallumShepherd(5) 8 52
(Roy Bowring) *led: hdd over 5f out: chsd ldr: rdn over 2f out: wknd over 1f out: eased* **8/1**

00-0 **9** *6* **Free One (IRE)**[7] 2540 4-8-4 **68** JosephineGordon(5) 10 21
(Ivan Furtado) *hld up: rdn over 2f out: wknd wl over 1f out* **33/1**

20-0 **10** *5* **Cosmic Ray**[16] 2256 4-9-2 **75** DougieCostello 9 16
(Daniel Mark Loughnane) *w ldr tl hung lft over 5f out: remained handy: rdn over 3f out: wknd over 2f out* **50/1**

066- **11** *4* **Nona Blu**[343] 3447 4-8-7 **66** NickyMackay 2
(Michael Wigham) *prom tl rdn and wknd over 2f out* **33/1**

1m 45.06s (-0.04) **Going Correction** +0.125s/f (Good) **11** Ran SP% **115.2**
Speed ratings (Par 105): **105,104,102,99,98 95,95,86,80,75 71**
CSF £27.90 CT £240.59 TOTE £6.90: £1.90, £1.90, £3.20; EX 29.60 Trifecta £286.80.
Owner Mrs H Steel **Bred** Al-Baha Bloodstock **Trained** Musley Bank, N Yorks

FOCUS

A fair handicap and a true pace with a couple in here who like to force it. The winner was building on his 3yo form.

2735 TOTEEXACTA PICK THE 1ST AND 2ND EBF MAIDEN FILLIES' STKS 1m 3f 183y

3:55 (3:56) (Class 4) 3-Y-O+ **£5,822** (£1,732; £865; £432) **Stalls** Low

Form RPR

5/ **1** **Lady Of Camelot (IRE)**[542] 8036 4-9-13 0 [1] RobertHavlin 11 93+
(John Gosden) *hld up in tch: chsd ldr over 2f out: led over 1f out: shkn up and styd on wl* **16/1**

22 **2** *1 ¾* **Ajman Princess (IRE)**[24] 1989 3-8-10 0 AndreaAtzeni 2 89
(Roger Varian) *led 1f: trckd ldr: racd keenly: lost 2nd 5f out: remained handy: led over 3f out: hdd over 1f out: styd on same pce ins fnl f* **2/1**[2]

3 *¾* **Ruscombe** 3-8-10 0 TedDurcan 1 88+
(Sir Michael Stoute) *s.i.s: hld up: hdwy over 1f out: r.o: nt rch ldrs* **8/1**[3]

33-2 **4** *5* **Moorside**[26] 1966 3-8-10 96 RyanMoore 4 80
(Charles Hills) *trckd ldrs: wnt 2nd 5f out: pushed along over 3f out: lost 2nd over 2f out: no ex fr over 1f out* **4/6**[1]

33-6 **5** *4 ½* **Denham Sound**[18] 2183 3-8-5 75 HectorCrouch(5) 9 73
(Henry Candy) *led after 1f: hdd over 3f out: sn rdn: wkng whn hung rt fr over 1f out* **20/1**

65 **6** *shd* **Gloryette**[17] 2215 3-8-10 0 FrederikTylicki 7 73+
(Ed Dunlop) *hld up: pushed along over 2f out: nvr on terms* **28/1**

64 **7** *1* **Heavensfield**[17] 2215 3-8-10 0 DougieCostello 3 71
(Mark H Tompkins) *prom: rdn over 3f out: wknd 2f out* **66/1**

64 **8** *shd* **Edge Of Reason**[16] 2260 3-8-10 0 AntonioFresu 10 72
(Ed Walker) *hld up: plld hrd: rdn over 2f out: n.d* **50/1**

9 *13* **Pray For Paris** 3-8-10 0 FergusSweeney 5 50
(Martyn Meade) *s.i.s: hld up: rdn: hung rt and wknd over 2f out* **20/1**

0- **10** *33* **Respectability**[378] 2343 4-9-10 0 JoeDoyle(3) 6
(Ivan Furtado) *hld up: hdwy over 5f out: rdn and wknd 3f out* **66/1**

2m 33.27s (-0.63) **Going Correction** +0.125s/f (Good)
WFA 3 from 4yo 17lb **10** Ran SP% **128.2**
Speed ratings (Par 102): **107,105,105,102,99 98,98,98,89,67**
CSF £50.99 TOTE £18.10: £3.50, £1.30, £2.60; EX 73.20 Trifecta £415.60.
Owner Yasushi Rokuroda **Bred** Taihei Stud Farm **Trained** Newmarket, Suffolk

FOCUS

A well above-average older fillies' maiden as a couple of these had already shown some very smart form and there were also a couple of nicely bred newcomers.

2736 TOTEPOOL CHIP & PIN BETTING H'CAP 6f

4:25 (4:26) (Class 3) (0-95,92) 3-Y-O

£12,450 (£3,728; £1,864; £932; £466; £234) **Stalls** High

Form RPR

31-6 **1** **Taneen (USA)**[16] 2242 3-9-4 **89** PaulHanagan 1 105+
(Roger Varian) *wnt rt s: hld up: hdwy 2f out: led over 1f out: shkn up: edgd rt and qcknd clr: eased nr fin* **11/4**[2]

00-4 **2** *4 ½* **Madrinho (IRE)**[24] 1991 3-9-7 **92** RyanMoore 10 93
(Richard Hannon) *hld up: hdwy u.p over 1f out: r.o to go 2nd post: no ch w wnr* **6/1**[3]

51- **3** *nse* **Bounce**[243] 6851 3-9-5 **90** FergusSweeney 4 91+
(Henry Candy) *trckd ldrs: led 2f out: rdn: hung lft and hdd over 1f out: sn outpcd* **9/1**

1325 **4** *2 ¼* **Sir Dudley (IRE)**[10] 2446 3-8-4 **80** (b) PhilDennis(5) 6 74
(James Given) *chsd ldr tl rdn over 2f out: no ex fr over 1f out* **16/1**

301- **5** *2 ½* **Tawdheef (IRE)**[220] 7432 3-9-6 **91** RobertHavlin 5 77+
(Simon Crisford) *prom: pushed along and lost pl after 1f: rdn over 2f out: r.o towards fin* **5/2**[1]

1203 **6** *1 ¼* **Buying Trouble (USA)**[16] 2242 3-8-13 **84** BenCurtis 9 66
(David Evans) *edgd rt s: prom: rdn over 2f out: wknd over 1f out* **6/1**[3]

256- **7** *2* **Ejaazah (IRE)**[261] 6307 3-9-3 **88** TedDurcan 2 63
(Richard Hannon) *chsd ldrs: rdn over 2f out: wknd over 1f out* **25/1**

10-6 **8** *½* **Mont Kiara (FR)**[24] 1996 3-9-2 **90** JoeDoyle(3) 3 64
(Kevin Ryan) *led 4f: sn rdn and wknd* **18/1**

0-05 **9** *5* **Zebstar (IRE)**[24] 1996 3-9-0 **90** (p) JosephineGordon(5) 8 48
(James Unett) *hmpd s: hld up: rdn 1/2-way: wknd over 2f out* **33/1**

0-24 **10** *1 ¼* **Handytalk (IRE)**[38] 1607 3-8-12 **83** FrederikTylicki 7 37
(Rod Millman) *mid-div: rdn 1/2-way: wknd over 2f out* **12/1**

1m 11.82s (-1.18) **Going Correction** +0.125s/f (Good) **10** Ran SP% **119.4**
Speed ratings (Par 103): **112,106,105,102,99 97,95,94,87,86**
CSF £20.44 CT £137.31 TOTE £4.20: £1.90, £1.60, £3.00; EX 19.50 Trifecta £102.20.
Owner Hamdan Al Maktoum **Bred** Haymarket Farm & Machmer Hall **Trained** Newmarket, Suffolk

FOCUS

A warm 3yo sprint handicap, won last year by the subsequent dual Group-race winner Magical Memory. They finished well spread out with this year's winner taking it apart, and he too could be a Pattern-class sprinter in the making.

2737 FOLLOW @TOTEPOOL ON TWITTER FILLIES' H'CAP 7f

4:55 (4:55) (Class 4) (0-80,79) 4-Y-O+ **£6,301** (£1,886; £943; £472; £235) **Stalls** High

Form RPR

0603 **1** **Alexandrakollontai (IRE)**[10] 2420 6-9-5 **77** (b) ConnorBeasley 6 88
(Alistair Whillans) *s.s: hld up: hdwy over 2f out: led over 1f out: edgd rt and rdn clr ins fnl f* **11/2**

6-22 **2** *5* **Gleaming Girl**[21] 2084 4-8-7 **72** SophieKilloran(7) 1 70
(David Simcock) *hld up: racd keenly: hdwy 4f out: rdn and ev ch over 1f out: styng on same pce whn edgd lft wl ins fnl f* **9/2**[3]

0-24 **3** *¾* **Azagal (IRE)**[17] 2223 5-9-1 **78** RachelRichardson(5) 2 73
(Tim Easterby) *trckd ldrs: plld hrd: rdn and ev ch over 1f out: styd on same pce fnl f* **7/4**[1]

000- **4** *½* **Appleberry (IRE)**[182] 8050 4-9-2 **79** JosephineGordon(5) 4 73
(Michael Appleby) *led: rdn and hdd over 1f out: no ex ins fnl f* **8/1**

6-23 **5** *2 ¾* **Exoplanet Blue**[31] 1838 4-9-0 **72** FergusSweeney 3 64
(Henry Candy) *trckd ldr: rdn and ev ch over 1f out: styng on same pce whn hmpd and eased wl ins fnl f* **5/2**[2]

1m 26.55s (0.35) **Going Correction** +0.125s/f (Good) **5** Ran SP% **109.6**
Speed ratings (Par 102): **103,97,96,95,92**
CSF £28.43 TOTE £6.40: £2.90, £1.70; EX 23.60 Trifecta £67.80.
Owner Chris Spark & William Orr **Bred** Sean O'Sullivan **Trained** Newmill-On-Slitrig, Borders
■ Stewards' Enquiry : Sophie Killoran caution: careless riding

FOCUS

An ordinary fillies' handicap, especially with the non-runners, and recent winning form was thin on the ground. All five were in a line across the track passing the furlong pole, but the winner bolted up. The winner is rated to her best but with reservations.

2738 COLLECT YOUR TOTEPOOL WINNINGS AT BETFRED SHOPS APPRENTICE H'CAP 1m 3f 183y

5:25 (5:27) (Class 6) (0-65,65) 4-Y-O+ **£3,234** (£962; £481; £240) **Stalls** Low

Form RPR

-304 **1** **Safira Menina**[14] 2313 4-9-6 **64** NatalieHambling(3) 4 73
(Martin Smith) *hld up: hdwy over 1f out: led ins fnl f: r.o wl* **6/1**[3]

14-2 **2** *2 ¾* **Flutterbee**[27] 1947 4-9-7 **65** (p) GeorgeWood(3) 3 70
(George Baker) *hld up in tch: edgd rt over 1f out: led ins fnl f: sn hdd and unable qck* **9/4**[1]

6325 **3** *¾* **Percys Princess**[6] 2564 5-9-7 **62** PaddyBradley 6 65
(Michael Appleby) *led: hdd 4f out: remained w ldr: rdn over 2f out: led again over 1f out: hdd ins fnl f: styd on same pce* **8/1**

4405 **4** *1 ½* **Nolecce**[21] 2110 9-8-5 **53** WilliamCox(7) 7 54
(Tony Forbes) *chsd ldr 4f: remained handy: rdn over 2f out: nt clr run over 1f out: styd on same pce ins fnl f* **20/1**

-055 **5** *nk* **Saint Thomas (IRE)**[33] 1796 9-9-0 **55** DavidParkes 1 58
(John Mackie) *trckd ldrs: effrt and nt clr run over 1f out: styd on same pce ins fnl f* **11/1**

0056 **6** *nk* **Surround Sound**[36] 1674 6-9-3 **58** (tp) AdamMcNamara 8 58
(Tim Easterby) *trckd ldrs: plld hrd: wnt 2nd 8f out: led 4f out: rdn and hdd over 1f out: no ex ins fnl f* **9/1**

042- **7** *2 ¼* **Doubly Clever (IRE)**[37] 2890 4-9-4 **62** MitchGodwin(3) 9 58
(Michael Blake) *hld up: rdn over 3f out: hung rt over 1f out: n.d* **5/2**[2]

6203 **R** **Easydoesit (IRE)**[21] 2110 8-9-0 **55** (p) GeorgiaCox 2
(Tony Carroll) *c out of the stalls slowly: wnt one stride: ref to r and uns rdr* **20/1**

R/R- **R** **Royal Trooper (IRE)**[507] 97 10-9-4 **62** BeckyBrisbourne(3) 5
(Mark Brisbourne) *ref to r* **66/1**

2m 41.02s (7.12) **Going Correction** +0.125s/f (Good) **9** Ran SP% **114.1**
Speed ratings (Par 101): **81,79,78,77,77 77,75, ,**
CSF £19.21 CT £108.34 TOTE £8.00: £2.30, £1.30, £1.80; EX 19.10 Trifecta £124.10.

Owner Four Winds Racing Partnership **Bred** Hascombe And Valiant Studs **Trained** Newmarket, Suffolk

FOCUS

A modest apprentice handicap and plenty of drama at the start with Royal Trooper refusing to race yet again and Easydoesit unseating his rider soon after exiting the stalls. The winner is rated close to last year's best.

T/Plt: £79.50 to a £1 stake. Pool: £74,733.62 - 685.92 winning tickets. T/Qpdt: £24.20 to £1 stake. Pool: £6,675.83 - 203.40 winning tickets. **Colin Roberts**

2301 REDCAR (L-H)

Monday, May 30

OFFICIAL GOING: Good to firm (good in places; 8.6)

Wind: Fresh against Weather: Overcast, odd shower

2739 RACINGUK.COM NOVICE AUCTION STKS 5f

12:45 (12:50) (Class 5) 2-Y-O **£3,234** (£962; £481; £240) **Stalls** Centre

Form				RPR
42	1		**Whiteandgold**[17] 2196 2-8-8 0 ow1 PaulMulrennan 7 (Bryan Smart) *mde all: pushed along over 1f out: edgd lft: kpt on* **11/10**[1]	72
02	2	1 3/4	**Hope Against Hope (IRE)**[10] 2417 2-8-10 0 JoeFanning 8 (Mark Johnston) *chsd ldr: rdn 2f out: kpt on* **7/2**[2]	66
5	3	2	**Trois Bon Amis (IRE)**[42] 1520 2-9-1 0 DavidAllan 3 (Tim Easterby) *trckd ldr: rdn 2f out: one pce fnl f* **14/1**	64
	4	shd	**Yorkshiredebut (IRE)** 2-8-8 0 JamesSullivan 10 (Paul Midgley) *sn chsd ldr: rdn 2f out: one pce fnl f* **16/1**	56
0	5	1 1/4	**Belle's Angel (IRE)**[13] 2344 2-8-9 0 PJMcDonald 9 (Ann Duffield) *hld up: sn pushed along: kpt on ins fnl f: nrst fin* **10/1**	53+
	6	shd	**Mary Brady** 2-8-12 0 ow1 PhillipMakin 6 (David O'Meara) *midfield: pushed along 3f out: one pce and nvr threatened* **7/1**[3]	55+
	7	1 1/4	**Whisper A Word (IRE)** 2-8-7 0 CamHardie 5 (Tim Easterby) *sn pushed along in rr: sme hdwy over 1f out: nvr threatened* **33/1**	46
	8	9	**Irish Melody (IRE)** 2-8-8 0 NathanEvans(5) 2 (Bill Turner) *dwlt and wnt lft s: a in rr* **12/1**	19
06	9	6	**Bellamay**[10] 2417 2-8-6 0 DuranFentiman 4 (John Weymes) *midfield: rdn 3f out: sn wknd* **100/1**	

1m 0.94s (2.34) **Going Correction** +0.175s/f (Good) **9 Ran SP% 115.6**

Speed ratings (Par 93): **88,85,82,81,79 79,77,63,53**

CSF £4.89 TOTE £2.10: £1.30, £1.30, £2.80; EX 5.70 Trifecta £32.80.

Owner Crossfields Racing **Bred** Crossfields Bloodstock Ltd **Trained** Hambleton, N Yorks

FOCUS

It was dry overnight and the going was officially good to firm, good in places (GoingStick: 8.9). This is likely to prove ordinary form, but the winner has the scope to rate higher.

2740 HIGH DEFINITION ON RACING UK MEDIAN AUCTION MAIDEN STKS 6f

1:15 (1:18) (Class 5) 3-Y-O **£3,234** (£962; £481; £240) **Stalls** Centre

Form				RPR
4	1		**Bahamian Dollar**[13] 2349 3-9-2 0 EoinWalsh(3) 6 (James Tate) *trckd ldr: led 2f out: sn pushed along: rdn ins fnl f: kpt on* **9/4**[2]	84
424-	2	1 1/4	**David's Duchess (IRE)**[317] 4391 3-9-0 83 TonyHamilton 11 (Richard Fahey) *dwlt: midfield: hdwy 2f out: pushed along to chal appr fnl f: rdn ins fnl f: one pce* **6/5**[1]	75
	3	3 3/4	**Hilary J** 3-9-0 0 PJMcDonald 9 (Ann Duffield) *in tch: pushed along to chse ldr over 1f out: rdn ent fnl f: wknd fnl 110yds* **9/2**[3]	63
	4	3 1/4	**A Fitting Finale** 3-9-0 0 TomEaves 5 (Kevin Ryan) *dwlt: hld up: pushed along over 4f out: kpt on fnl f* **12/1**	53+
0-0	5	2	**Tarnend Lass**[14] 2303 3-9-0 0 (t) DavidAllan 1 (Tim Easterby) *trckd ldr: rdn and ev ch 2f out: wknd over 1f out* **25/1**	46
	6	4	**Tell The Stars** 3-8-11 0 JacobButterfield(3) 2 (Ollie Pears) *dwlt: sn midfield: pushed along 3f out: wknd over 1f out* **33/1**	33
00-	7	2 1/4	**Shudbeme**[250] 6655 3-9-5 0 DuranFentiman 8 (Neville Bycroft) *s.i.s: a towards rr* **100/1**	31
-00	8	1 3/4	**Lowrie**[14] 2303 3-9-0 0 PatrickMathers 4 (John David Riches) *led: edgd lft fr 3f out: hdd 2f out: wknd* **100/1**	21
40-0	9	1/2	**Emilie Bronte**[14] 2302 3-9-0 53 JoeFanning 7 (Chris Fairhurst) *prom: rdn over 2f out: sn wknd* **20/1**	19

1m 13.46s (1.66) **Going Correction** +0.175s/f (Good) **9 Ran SP% 115.6**

Speed ratings (Par 99): **95,93,88,84,81 76,73,70,70**

CSF £5.09 TOTE £3.30: £1.20, £1.10, £1.80; EX 6.00 Trifecta £16.90.

Owner Saeed Manana **Bred** Burns Farm Stud **Trained** Newmarket, Suffolk

■ L C Saloon was withdrawn. Price at time of withdrawal 25-1. Rule 4 does not apply.

FOCUS

A fair maiden. The winner built on his debut and the second is rated close to form.

2741 CONGRATULATIONS GOLDEN TICKET WINNER ELIZABETH GARSTANG (S) STKS 7f

1:45 (1:52) (Class 6) 3-5-Y-O **£2,587** (£770; £384; £192) **Stalls** Centre

Form				RPR
3004	1		**Castlerea Tess**[10] 2425 3-8-5 44 PatrickMathers 9 (Sarah Hollinshead) *s.i.s: hld up: pushed along and hdwy over 2f out: led appr fnl f: kpt on pushed out* **25/1**	51
2040	2	1	**Tancred (IRE)**[13] 2342 5-9-13 62 (p) PaulMulrennan 4 (Conor Dore) *dwlt: hld up: pushed along and hdwy over 2f out: rdn over 1f out: wnt 2nd 110yds out: kpt on* **8/1**	63
0-06	3	1	**Letbygonesbeicons**[10] 2425 3-8-6 63 RowanScott(7) 2 (Ann Duffield) *midfield: angled to outer over 1f out: rdn and kpt on* **12/1**	53
-306	4	1	**Mr Lucas (IRE)**[32] 1819 3-8-10 45 (v) JoeFanning 12 (Peter Niven) *chsd ldrs: rdn over 2f out: one pce fnl f* **16/1**	48
6322	5	1/2	**El Duque**[10] 2448 5-9-5 55 (p) NathanEvans(5) 5 (Bill Turner) *pressed ldr: rdn to ld over 1f out: hdd appr fnl f: wknd fnl 110yds* **2/1**[1]	53+
-500	6	2	**Farang Jai Dee (IRE)**[10] 2448 4-9-7 43 (b) JFEgan 6 (Declan Carroll) *midfield: rdn 3f out: no imp* **33/1**	45
001	7	1	**I T Guru**[10] 2425 3-8-13 59 (t) BarryMcHugh 7 (Noel Wilson) *led narrowly: rdn whn hdd over 1f out: wknd fnl f* **11/1**	41+
0-00	8	3	**Bold Spirit**[40] 1565 5-9-10 59 (vt) DavidAllan 8 (Declan Carroll) *chsd ldrs: rdn over 3f out: wknd fnl 2f* **7/1**[3]	37
3-60	9	3	**Overhaugh Street**[7] 2532 3-8-10 72 (v[1]) JoeyHaynes 1 (Keith Dalgleish) *hld up: rdn over 3f out: sn struggling* **11/2**[2]	22
6	10	8	**Miss Macchiato (IRE)**[36] 1662 3-8-5 0 (p) PJMcDonald 10 (Ann Duffield) *chsd ldrs: rdn over 3f out: lost pl qckly and bhd* **14/1**	
000-	11	1 1/4	**Miss Mozaico**[182] 8055 3-8-5 30 PaulQuinn 13 (Richard Whitaker) *s.i.s: a towards rr* **50/1**	

1m 27.67s (3.17) **Going Correction** +0.175s/f (Good)

WFA 3 from 4yo+ 11lb **11 Ran SP% 109.7**

Speed ratings (Par 101): **88,86,85,84,84 81,80,77,73,64 63**

CSF £187.07 TOTE £20.90: £6.00, £2.30, £3.20; EX 299.90 Trifecta £3416.20.There was no bid for the winner.

Owner Graham Brothers Racing Partnership **Bred** Graham Brothers Racing Partnership **Trained** Upper Longdon, Staffs

■ Sekuras Girl was withdrawn. Price at time of withdrawal 14-1. Rule 4 applies to all bets - deduction 5p in the pound.

FOCUS

This ordinary seller was run at a good pace and it suited those ridden patiently.

2742 RACING UK PROFITS RETURNED TO RACING H'CAP 5f

2:15 (2:21) (Class 5) (0-75,75) 3-Y-O **£3,234** (£962; £481; £240) **Stalls** Centre

Form				RPR
1-03	1		**Laughton**[13] 2337 3-9-3 71 ShaneGray 16 (Kevin Ryan) *hld up: pushed along and gd hdwy over 1f out: led ins fnl f: edgd lft: kpt on* **6/1**[1]	81+
40-0	2	1 1/4	**Silver Sands (IRE)**[63] 1126 3-8-9 63 JasonHart 17 (Tim Easterby) *chsd ldrs: rdn 2f out: kpt on* **20/1**	69
5-06	3	1	**Mininggold**[13] 2334 3-8-12 66 JackGarritty 9 (Tim Easterby) *in tch: rdn 2f out: kpt on* **16/1**	68
656-	4	shd	**Sandra's Secret (IRE)**[213] 7601 3-9-0 68 DavidAllan 14 (Les Eyre) *pressed ldr: rdn to ld 2f out: hdd ins fnl f: no ex* **20/1**	70
31	5	hd	**Semana Santa**[59] 1181 3-9-4 72 GrahamGibbons 10 (David Barron) *led narrowly: rdn whn hdd 2f out: no ex ins fnl f* **8/1**[2]	73
413-	6	3/4	**Harmonic Wave (IRE)**[227] 7243 3-9-0 75 RowanScott(7) 15 (Ann Duffield) *midfield: pushed along over 1f out: kpt on fnl f* **16/1**	73
1-04	7	3/4	**Fruit Salad**[23] 2049 3-8-13 67 JoeFanning 13 (James Bethell) *dwlt: sn midfield: pushed along 2f out: one pce* **10/1**	63
4-06	8	nse	**Roll On Rory**[28] 1922 3-9-4 72 (p) AndrewMullen 8 (Jason Ward) *prom: rdn 1/2-way: no ex ins fnl f* **20/1**	67
3-55	9	1	**Searanger (USA)**[28] 1922 3-8-11 65 PJMcDonald 11 (Ann Duffield) *hld up: rdn 1/2-way: kpt on ins fnl f: nvr threatened* **25/1**	57
000-	10	1/2	**French**[240] 6931 3-9-7 75 GrahamLee 3 (Antony Brittain) *midfield: rdn 2f out: nvr threatened* **10/1**	65
556-	11	hd	**Dyllan (IRE)**[232] 7142 3-9-5 73 JamesSullivan 6 (Ruth Carr) *dwlt: hld up: rdn and sme hdwy appr fnl f: nvr threatened* **10/1**	62
14-0	12	1/2	**Lady Nayef**[30] 1847 3-9-4 72 JFEgan 5 (John Butler) *midfield: rdn 1/2-way: wknd over 1f out* **14/1**	59
3-00	13	2	**Baby Ballerina**[33] 1788 3-8-12 66 (p) PaulMulrennan 7 (Brian Ellison) *a towards rr* **14/1**	46
03-5	14	7	**First Rate**[13] 2333 3-9-6 74 HarryBentley 1 (Roger Varian) *chsd ldrs: rdn 2f out: sn wknd* **9/1**[3]	29
041-	15	4 1/2	**Tawayna (IRE)**[286] 5491 3-9-2 70 [1] PhillipMakin 4 (David O'Meara) *midfield: rdn 1/2-way: wknd over 1f out* **8/1**[2]	9
-650	16	1 3/4	**Jazz Legend (USA)**[28] 1922 3-9-2 70 (b[1]) TomEaves 2 (James Given) *midfield: rdn 3f out: sn wknd and bhd* **25/1**	3

59.36s (0.76) **Going Correction** +0.175s/f (Good) **16 Ran SP% 120.9**

Speed ratings (Par 99): **100,98,96,96,95 94,93,93,91,91 90,89,86,75,68 65**

CSF £130.95 CT £1891.66 TOTE £5.20: £1.70, £4.20, £4.30, £4.30; EX 141.00 Trifecta £2456.60.

Owner Mrs Angie Bailey **Bred** Skymarc Farm Inc **Trained** Hambleton, N Yorks

FOCUS

An open sprint handicap. They came up the centre of the track before fanning out, and those drawn high dominated. Those drawn in the bottom seven stalls finished in the last seven places, but the form makes a fair bit of sense around 2-3-4-5-6.

2743 MARKET CROSS JEWELLERS H'CAP 1m 2f

2:50 (2:50) (Class 4) (0-80,80) 4-Y-O+ **£4,851** (£1,443; £721; £360) **Stalls** Low

Form				RPR
4-52	1		**Grand Canyon (IRE)**[12] 2362 4-8-12 71 PhillipMakin 9 (David O'Meara) *s.i.s: hld up: pushed along and gd hdwy over 1f out: rdn to ld ins fnl f: kpt on* **7/2**[2]	79
0665	2	3/4	**Kiwi Bay**[12] 2362 11-9-1 74 PaulMulrennan 6 (Michael Dods) *s.i.s: hld up: short of room on inner over 2f out tl over 1f out: swtchd rt ent fnl f: r.o wl: gaining at fin* **16/1**	81+
0606	3	nse	**Peterhouse (USA)**[13] 2328 4-9-1 74 (p) JFEgan 2 (Jason Ward) *dwlt: sn midfield: rdn over 2f out: hdwy over 1f out: styd on* **7/1**[3]	80
5503	4	3/4	**Save The Bees**[2] 2673 8-8-9 68 NeilFarley 11 (Declan Carroll) *led: rdn over 2f out: hdd ins fnl f: no ex* **17/2**	73
2410	5	3/4	**Farham (USA)**[20] 2121 4-8-13 72 TonyHamilton 3 (Richard Fahey) *trckd ldng pair: rdn over 2f out: one pce fnl f* **9/1**	75
0-06	6	3 3/4	**Muqarred (USA)**[14] 2296 4-8-11 75 JoshDoyle(5) 5 (David Loughnane) *hld up: rdn over 2f out: nvr threatened ldrs* **20/1**	71
-000	7	1 1/4	**Artful Prince**[13] 2347 6-9-0 73 (b) TomEaves 7 (James Given) *midfield: hdwy over 2f out: rdn and ev ch over 1f out: wknd ins fnl f* **12/1**	66
3123	8	2	**Moonday Sun (USA)**[14] 2296 7-9-5 78 (p) GrahamLee 4 (John Butler) *trckd ldng pair: racd keenly: rdn 3f out: wknd over 1f out* **8/1**	67
6406	9	3 1/4	**Moonlightnavigator (USA)**[16] 2257 4-9-7 80 JoeFanning 8 (John Quinn) *midfield towards outer: rdn over 3f out: wknd fnl 2f* **16/1**	63
102-	10	1 1/2	**Taraz**[262] 6267 4-9-6 79 HarryBentley 10 (Roger Varian) *prom: rdn over 3f out: wknd 2f out* **11/4**[1]	59

2m 6.57s (-0.53) **Going Correction** -0.025s/f (Good) **10 Ran SP% 116.3**

Speed ratings (Par 105): **101,100,100,99,99 96,95,93,90,89**

CSF £57.92 CT £374.96 TOTE £4.70: £1.90, £5.50, £2.30; EX 59.30 Trifecta £482.50.

Owner Sir Robert Ogden **Bred** Sir Robert Ogden **Trained** Upper Helmsley, N Yorks

FOCUS

The first three came from off the pace in this fair handicap. The winner continues to improve.

2744 RACING UK ZETLAND GOLD CUP H'CAP 1m 2f

3:25 (3:25) (Class 2) (0-105,104) 3-Y-O+ **£16,172** (£4,812; £2,405; £1,202) **Stalls** Low

Form				RPR
0351	1		**Revolutionist (IRE)**[9] 2484 4-9-10 100 JoeFanning 10 (Mark Johnston) *trckd ldr: led over 3f out: rdn over 2f out: kpt on wl* **8/1**[3]	112
24-1	2	1 1/4	**Central Square (IRE)**[21] 2098 4-9-0 90 HarryBentley 2 (Roger Varian) *in tch: trckd ldr 3f out: rdn over 2f out: kpt on* **9/4**[1]	99+

-023 **3** 3/4 **Swift Emperor (IRE)**[15] 2268 4-8-13 **89**............................ PhillipMakin 9 96
(David Barron) *midfield: hdwy over 2f out: rdn to chal over 1f out: one pce ins fnl f* **8/1**[3]

0426 **4** *nk* **Snoano**[29] 1885 4-8-13 **89**.. GrahamLee 8 95
(Tim Easterby) *midfield: rdn and hdwy over 2f out: kpt on* **25/1**

-311 **5** *1 1/4* **Tawdeea**[13] 2328 4-9-1 **91**.. SamJames 6 97+
(David O'Meara) *hld up in midfield: pushed along and hdwy on inner over 2f out: bit short of room appr fnl f and swtchd lft: bit short of room again 110yds: one pce* **10/1**

-400 **6** *3/4* **Birdman (IRE)**[18] 2191 6-9-9 **104**................................... JoshDoyle(5) 11 106
(David O'Meara) *hld up: rdn 3f out: kpt on ins fnl f: nvr threatened ldrs* **33/1**

-616 **7** *1/2* **Hit The Jackpot (IRE)**[19] 2157 7-9-5 **98**.................... ShelleyBirkett(3) 4 99+
(David O'Meara) *midfield: yet to be asked for effrt whn hmpd over 1f out and lost pl: no ch after* **20/1**

10-1 **8** *1* **Dance King**[24] 2017 6-8-13 **89**..(tp) DavidAllan 1 88
(Tim Easterby) *s.i.s: hld up: rdn over 3f out: nvr threatened* **12/1**

23-0 **9** *4* **Fattsota**[17] 2222 8-9-12 **102**.. DavidNolan 3 93
(David O'Meara) *trckd ldr: rdn over 3f out: wknd over 1f out* **25/1**

1-2 **10** *21* **Winter House**[23] 2037 4-9-1 **91**................................(p) PaulMulrennan 13 40
(Saeed bin Suroor) *hld up: pushed along over 5f out: rdn 4f out: sn wknd: eased* **11/4**[2]

01-4 **11** *1/2* **English Summer**[25] 1972 9-9-2 **92**...........................(t) GeorgeChaloner 5 40
(Richard Fahey) *in tch: rdn over 4f out: wknd over 3f out: eased* **33/1**

12 *27* **Eternal**[409] 1539 4-9-5 **95**... JFEgan 7
(Declan Carroll) *led: rn wd on bnd 5f out: hdd over 3f out: hung rt: eased and t.o* **50/1**

2m 4.23s (-2.87) **Going Correction** -0.025s/f (Good) **12** Ran SP% **116.7**
Speed ratings (Par 109): **110,109,108,108,107 106,106,105,102,85 84,63**
CSF £23.87 CT £152.67 TOTE £8.80: £2.90, £1.40, £2.70; EX 31.40 Trifecta £170.50.
Owner Sheikh Hamdan bin Mohammed Al Maktoum **Bred** Darley **Trained** Middleham Moor, N Yorks

FOCUS
A good-quality handicap run at a decent gallop. The winner and second have been rated as improvers.

2745 COME RACING AGAIN TOMORROW H'CAP (DIV I) 1m 6f 19y
4:00 (4:00) (Class 6) (0-65,65) 4-Y-O+ **£2,587** (£770; £384; £192) **Stalls** Low

Form RPR

24-0 **1** **Dew Pond**[24] 2018 4-9-5 **63**.. DavidAllan 5 74
(Tim Easterby) *hld up in midfield: pushed along and gd hdwy over 2f out: led appr fnl f: rdn and styd on wl* **3/1**[2]

220- **2** *2 1/2* **Ingleby Hollow**[238] 6982 4-9-7 **65**............................... GrahamGibbons 2 73
(David O'Meara) *trckd ldr: led over 12f out: rdn over 2f out: hdd appr fnl f: one pce fnl 110yds* **11/4**[1]

-055 **3** *3 1/4* **Cape Hideaway**[16] 2233 4-9-0 **58**......................................(p) JasonHart 7 62
(Mark Walford) *trckd ldr: rdn to chal over 2f out: one pce in 3rd fr over 1f out* **13/2**

36-0 **4** *1* **Noble Reach**[123] 368 5-8-3 **47**...(p) CamHardie 8 49
(Lawrence Mullaney) *led: hdd over 12f out: trckd ldr: rdn and outpcd over 3f out: plugged on again fr over 1f out* **12/1**

0/00 **5** *1/2* **No Not Yet**[23] 2048 4-8-4 **48**.. AndrewMullen 9 50
(Michael Dods) *hld up in rr: pushed along over 4f out: plugged on fr over 1f out: nvr threatened* **22/1**

00-2 **6** *1 1/4* **Exclusive Contract (IRE)**[21] 2089 5-9-1 **62**......... JacobButterfield(3) 11 62
(Ollie Pears) *midfield: rdn and hdwy over 3f out: wknd over 1f out* **11/2**[3]

605- **7** *3/4* **Rocky Two (IRE)**[27] 5765 6-8-2 **46** oh1............................ JoeyHaynes 3 45
(Philip Kirby) *midfield: rdn over 3f out: no imp* **20/1**

00-0 **8** *3/4* **Waltz Darling (IRE)**[6] 2558 8-8-6 **55**................................ JoshDoyle(5) 6 54
(Keith Reveley) *hld up: rdn over 3f out: nvr threatened* **8/1**

-000 **9** *4* **That Be Grand**[16] 2233 5-8-2 **46**................................(p) DuranFentiman 4 39
(Shaun Harris) *in tch: rdn 4f out: wknd over 2f out* **33/1**

30-5 **10** *2* **La Fritillaire**[48] 1405 4-8-8 **52** ow2...................................... TomEaves 12 42
(James Given) *hld up in midfield: rdn over 3f out: sn wknd* **14/1**

3m 6.08s (1.38) **Going Correction** -0.025s/f (Good) **10** Ran SP% **117.9**
Speed ratings (Par 101): **95,93,91,91,90 90,89,89,87,85**
CSF £11.52 CT £49.79 TOTE £3.60: £1.50, £1.30, £2.50; EX 12.00 Trifecta £70.90.
Owner Ashfield Caravan Park **Bred** Pollards Stables **Trained** Great Habton, N Yorks

FOCUS
A modest handicap, but the winner was well backed and it was the faster of the two divisions by 0.42sec. The winner was rated a minor improver on last year's form.

2746 COME RACING AGAIN TOMORROW H'CAP (DIV II) 1m 6f 19y
4:30 (4:30) (Class 6) (0-65,65) 4-Y-O+ **£2,587** (£770; £384; £192) **Stalls** Low

Form RPR

4-30 **1** **Kiwayu**[11] 2406 7-9-6 **64**..(p) AndrewMullen 12 69
(Philip Kirby) *midfield: hdwy 3f out: rdn to ld 2f out: strly pressed fr appr fnl f: hld on wl* **4/1**[3]

05-0 **2** *nk* **District Attorney (IRE)**[6] 1626 7-8-3 **47**...................... DuranFentiman 8 52
(Chris Fairhurst) *hld up: stdy hdwy fr 3f out: rdn to chal strly appr fnl f: kpt on: jst hld* **28/1**

1010 **3** *shd* **Frosty The Snowman (IRE)**[6] 2558 5-8-12 **56**........... JamesSullivan 5 60
(Ruth Carr) *midfield inner: trckd ldrs 3f out: rdn 2f out: nt a much room towards inner: styd on ins fnl f* **10/3**[2]

460- **4** *1 1/2* **Pencaitland**[227] 7262 4-8-2 **46**...................................... PatrickMathers 2 49
(Noel Wilson) *hld up in midfield: hdwy 3f out: rdn and ev ch 2f out: one pce fginal f* **10/1**

525- **5** *nk* **Bowdler's Magic**[26] 6786 9-9-7 **65**.................................. DavidNolan 11 67
(David Thompson) *hld up in midfield: hdwy 3f out: rdn to chse ldr over 1f out: one pce fnl f* **5/2**[1]

0620 **6** *15* **Symbolist (IRE)**[42] 1523 4-9-3 **61**...................................(v) GrahamLee 3 44
(John Norton) *trckd ldr: rdn to chal over 2f out: wknd wl over 1f out* **7/1**

6/00 **7** *3* **Private Dancer**[14] 2307 5-8-5 **49**...................................... BarryMcHugh 6 28
(Ron Barr) *racd keenly: led: rdn whn hdd 2f out: wknd* **25/1**

020- **8** *3 1/4* **Strikemaster (IRE)**[269] 6067 10-8-6 **50**........................(t) PJMcDonald 10 25
(Lee James) *a in rr* **16/1**

30/0 **9** *31* **Wild Hill Boy**[13] 2330 6-8-2 **46**.. JoeyHaynes 9
(David C Griffiths) *trckd ldr: rdn over 5f out: sn wknd* **25/1**

566- **10** *5* **Belle Peinture (FR)**[90] 7678 5-8-2 **46** oh1........................ CamHardie 7
(Alan Lockwood) *in tch: trckd ldr over 6f: rdn over 3f out: sn wknd: eased* **33/1**

3m 6.5s (1.80) **Going Correction** -0.025s/f (Good) **10** Ran SP% **113.2**
Speed ratings (Par 101): **93,92,92,91,91 83,81,79,61,59**
CSF £112.30 CT £409.61 TOTE £5.30: £2.00, £7.50, £1.70; EX 145.00 Trifecta £1125.60.
Owner Mrs Jayne Sivills **Bred** Fittocks Stud **Trained** East Appleton, N Yorks

FOCUS
This looked the weaker of the two divisions, and it was also the slower of the two, by 0.42sec. Compressed finish, straightforward form; winner class dropper, only needed to match this year's Tapeta form to take this.
T/Plt: £133.80 to a £1 stake. Pool: £70,740.51 - 385.95 winning tickets T/Qpdt: £100.80 to a £1 stake. Pool: £4,666.83 - 34.25 winning tickets **Andrew Sheret**

2543 WINDSOR (R-H)
Monday, May 30

OFFICIAL GOING: Good to firm (good in places; 7.8)
Wind: light, across Weather: overcast

2747 SKY BET NOVICE AUCTION STKS (DIV I) 6f
1:50 (1:51) (Class 5) 2-Y-O **£3,557** (£1,058; £529; £264) **Stalls** Low

Form RPR

1 **Groupie** 2-8-8 0.. TomMarquand(3) 2 73+
(Richard Hannon) *broke wl: sn stdd bk and trckd ldrs tl led over 2f out: pushed clr over 1f out: rn green and edgd lft ins fnl f: pressed but holding rivals towards fin: pushed out* **7/2**[2]

5 **2** *nk* **Espresso Freddo (IRE)**[13] 2319 2-9-2 0.......................... LukeMorris 8 77
(Sir Mark Prescott Bt) *chsd ldr: rdn and chsd wnr over 2f out: hung rt over 1f out: rallied to press wnr wl ins fnl f: kpt on but hld towards fin* **10/1**

3 *hd* **High Acclaim (USA)** 2-9-2 0...................................... SamHitchcott 9 77
(Roger Teal) *dwlt: sn rcvrd to trckd ldrs: wnt 3rd over 2f out: drvn over 1f out: styd on to press wnr wl ins fnl f: kpt on but hld towards fin* **20/1**

4 *3 1/2* **Cj Parker** 2-8-11 0.. JackMitchell 7 61+
(Jim Boyle) *s.i.s: pushed along in rr early: swtchd lft and hdwy over 1f out: chsd clr ldng trio ins fnl f: kpt on but no threat to ldrs* **20/1**

5 *3* **What A Boy** 2-8-12 0.. FMBerry 1 53+
(Ralph Beckett) *dwlt: in tch in last trio: rdn over 2f out: hdwy into midfield but no imp over 1f out: wknd ins fnl f* **11/10**[1]

6 *1/2* **Doneraile (IRE)** 2-9-0 0.. WilliamCarson 4 54
(Robert Eddery) *in tch in midfield: rdn over 2f out: outpcd and btn over 1f out: wknd ins fnl f* **20/1**

7 *3/4* **Tullinahoo (IRE)** 2-9-0 0.. OisinMurphy 5 51
(Denis Coakley) *s.i.s: in tch in last trio: rdn over 2f out: no hdwy and wl hld whn nt clr run jst ins fnl f* **5/1**[3]

8 *nk* **Born To Please** 2-8-7 0.. KieranO'Neill 3 43
(Mark Usher) *t.k.h: hld up in tch in midfield: rdn over 2f out: sn struggling: wknd over 1f out* **25/1**

5 **9** *5* **Battle Of Wits (IRE)**[19] 2147 2-8-12 0............................ DarryllHolland 6 33
(J S Moore) *sn led: hdd over 2f out and sn lost pl: bhd fnl f* **28/1**

1m 14.5s (1.50) **Going Correction** +0.075s/f (Good) **9** Ran SP% **117.2**
Speed ratings (Par 93): **93,92,92,87,83 83,82,81,74**
CSF £33.10 TOTE £4.30: £1.50, £1.70, £5.20; EX 21.90 Trifecta £461.20.
Owner Mrs J K Powell **Bred** John M Troy **Trained** East Everleigh, Wilts

FOCUS
The inner of the straight was dolled out 16yds at 6f and 8yds at the winning line, and the top bend was out 12yds from its normal inner configuration, adding 48yds to race distances over 1m-plus. This is probably just ordinary form, but the race should produce winners.

2748 SKY BET NOVICE AUCTION STKS (DIV II) 6f
2:20 (2:22) (Class 5) 2-Y-O **£3,557** (£1,058; £529; £264) **Stalls** Low

Form RPR

5 **1** **High On Love (IRE)**[17] 2211 2-8-11 0.......................... StevieDonohoe 3 73
(Charlie Fellowes) *mde all: rdn over 1f out: styd on wl under mainly hands and heels riding ins fnl f* **11/8**[1]

2 *3/4* **Fastar (IRE)** 2-9-0 0.. JimmyFortune 6 74+
(Brian Meehan) *s.i.s: hld up in tch towards rr: swtchd lft and hdwy 2f out: rdn and hdwy over 1f out: drvn to chse wnr ins fnl f: kpt on but a hld fnl 100yds* **11/1**

3 *1* **Fair Power (IRE)** 2-9-0 0.. LukeMorris 9 71
(Sylvester Kirk) *in tch: effrt over 2f out: hdwy to chse ldrs and drvn 1f out: wnt 3rd ins fnl f: styd on but no imp* **16/1**

0 **4** *2 1/2* **At The Beach**[18] 2173 2-9-2 0...................................... TimmyMurphy 2 65
(Richard Hannon) *hld up in tch in midfield: nt clr run on inner 2f out: swtchd lft and squeezing through jst over 1f out: kpt on same pce ins fnl f* **7/1**[3]

5 *1 1/4* **Brexit** 2-8-7 0.. KieranO'Neill 8 53
(Pat Phelan) *chsd ldrs: rdn over 2f out: drvn and unable qck over 1f out: wknd ins fnl f* **33/1**

6 *1 1/4* **Liberatum** 2-9-0 0.. WilliamBuick 7 56
(Hugo Palmer) *chsd ldrs: effrt and rdn to chse wnr wl over 1f out tl outpcd and lost pl jst ins fnl f: wknd fnl 100yds* **4/1**[2]

3 **7** *4 1/2* **Kings Heart (IRE)**[18] 2173 2-9-2 0................................ SteveDrowne 4 44
(Mark Usher) *chsd wnr: rdn ent fnl 2f: lost 2nd wl over 1f out and sn outpcd: wknd fnl f* **4/1**[2]

8 *3 1/4* **Chamasay** 2-8-12 0.. DarryllHolland 1 31
(J S Moore) *s.i.s: a in rr: nvr on terms* **16/1**

9 *7* **Lady Parker (IRE)** 2-8-7 0.. JohnFahy 5 5
(J S Moore) *v.s.a: a wl bhd* **50/1**

1m 15.18s (2.18) **Going Correction** +0.075s/f (Good) **9** Ran SP% **116.2**
Speed ratings (Par 93): **88,87,85,82,80 79,73,68,59**
CSF £18.71 TOTE £2.60: £1.40, £2.60, £3.50; EX 18.80 Trifecta £120.50.
Owner Equine Enthusiasts **Bred** Ms Ethel Anne Moloney **Trained** Newmarket, Suffolk

FOCUS
A similar-looking standard to the first division.

2749 SKY BET H'CAP 1m 67y
2:55 (2:55) (Class 5) (0-75,78) 3-Y-O **£3,557** (£1,058; £529; £264) **Stalls** Low

Form RPR

3-23 **1** **Quebee**[24] 2009 3-9-6 **74**.. AdamKirby 1 86
(Clive Cox) *dwlt: hld up in tch in midfield: hdwy over 2f out: rdn to ld ent and edgd rt ent fnl f: r.o strly and drew clr fnl 150yds: readily* **4/1**[2]

3501 **2** *4* **Outback Blue**[7] 2545 3-9-10 **78** 6ex.................................(t) ShaneKelly 4 81
(David Evans) *hld up in tch in midfield: swtchd lft and hdwy 2f out: squeezed between rivals and pressing ldrs jst over 1f out: 2nd but outpcd by wnr ins fnl f* **7/2**[1]

53-4 **3** *1 1/4* **Charmy**[21] 2109 3-9-2 **70**..[1] OisinMurphy 7 70
(Andrew Balding) *wl in tch in midfield: effrt over 2f out: drvn to ld over 1f out: sn hdd and unable qck: styd on same pce ins fnl f* **10/1**

410- **4** *1/2* **Lord Kelvin (IRE)**[264] 6208 3-9-7 **75**................................ JamieSpencer 6 74
(Charles Hills) *dwlt: hld up towards rr: swtchd lft and effrt 2f out: hdwy u.p and wnt lft 1f out: kpt on ins fnl f no ch w wnr* **12/1**

00-5 **5** ½ **Silhouette (IRE)**[17] 2207 3-9-2 **70**.......................... TimmyMurphy 2 68
(Daniel Kubler) *chsd ldrs: nt clr run on inner 2f out: swtchd lft and hdwy jst ins fnl f: styd on: no threat to wnr* **10/1**

000- **6** 1 **Free Passage**[213] 7592 3-9-0 **68**.......................... MartinHarley 9 63
(Henry Candy) *hld up in last quartet: swtchd lft ent fnl 2f: hdwy over 1f out: pushed lft 1f out: kpt on same pce ins fnl f* **10/1**

54-2 **7** ¾ **Wafi Star (IRE)**[32] 1800 3-9-1 **74**.......................... EdwardGreatrex(5) 10 68+
(Simon Crisford) *t.k.h: chsd ldrs: rdn 1/2-way: chsd ldr 3f out tl out: struggling whn slt hmpd and lost pl over 1f out: wknd ins fnl f* **8/1**[3]

0-20 **8** ¾ **Premier Currency (IRE)**[21] 2099 3-9-5 **73**.......................... FMBerry 3 65
(Mike Murphy) *led: rdn 3f out: drvn and hdd 1f out: sn btn: wknd fnl f* **25/1**

33-0 **9** nk **Hygrove Percy**[34] 1738 3-9-4 **72**.......................... LiamKeniry 12 63
(Neil Mulholland) *hld up in tch towards rr: nt clr run on inner over 2f out: swtchd lft but all ch had gone jst over 1f out: no imp* **25/1**

-210 **10** ½ **Siri**[18] 2178 3-9-6 **74**.......................... SilvestreDeSousa 13 64+
(Mick Channon) *hld up in last quartet: swtchd lft jst over 2f out: nt clr run over 1f out: wl hld and nt given a hrd time ins fnl f* **10/1**

21-4 **11** 6 **Marcle (IRE)**[35] 1703 3-8-11 **65**.......................... KieranO'Neill 5 41
(Ed de Giles) *chsd ldr tl 3f: lost pl u.p 2f out: sn wknd* **20/1**

0-10 **12** 2 **Gunman**[13] 2341 3-8-10 **67**.......................... TomMarquand(3) 14 39
(Richard Hannon) *in tch in midfield: effrt on outer but no imp over 2f out: wknd over 1f out* **20/1**

0-30 **13** 3 **Master Of Heaven**[7] 2545 3-9-0 **68**.......................... PatCosgrave 8 33
(Jim Boyle) *midfield: rdn 3f out: hung lft and btn 2f out: wknd over 1f out* **20/1**

-400 **P** **Maddys Dream**[12] 2375 3-8-10 **67**.......................... SimonPearce(3) 11
(Lydia Pearce) *sn dropped to rr: bhd whn hung lft 1/2-way: sn eased: p.u and dismntd over 2f out* **50/1**

1m 46.86s (2.16) **Going Correction** +0.35s/f (Good) **14** Ran SP% **121.3**
Speed ratings (Par 99): **103,99,97,97,96 95,95,94,93,93 87,85,82,**
CSF £16.45 CT £137.99 TOTE £4.80: £1.80, £1.60, £2.70; EX 17.30 Trifecta £214.00.
Owner Martin A Collins **Bred** M A Collins **Trained** Lambourn, Berks

FOCUS
This was run over 48yds further than advertised. A competitive handicap run at a good pace, and the winner made big improvement.

2750 SKY BET MAIDEN STKS 5f 10y

3:30 (3:30) (Class 5) 3-Y-O+ **£3,881** (£1,155; £577; £288) **Stalls** Low

Form RPR

32- **1** **Spanish City**[269] 6065 3-9-5 0.......................... WilliamBuick 3 78+
(Roger Varian) *t.k.h: hld up wl in tch: nt clr run and swtchd lft wl over 1f out: clsng and swtchd lft again jst over 1f out: sn chalng u.p: led 100yds out: r.o strly* **5/6**[1]

4-23 **2** 1¼ **Just Glamorous (IRE)**[14] 2288 3-9-5 70.......................... LukeMorris 5 73
(Ronald Harris) *sn in tch in midfield: effrt to chse ldr over 1f out: drvn and ev ch 1f out: led ins fnl f: sn hdd and styd on same pce fnl 100yds* **9/2**[3]

0-20 **3** ¾ **Verne Castle**[18] 2186 3-9-5 73.......................... DavidProbert 8 70
(Andrew Balding) *chsd ldr tl led 4f out: drvn over 1f out: hdd and no ex u.p ins fnl f: styd on same pce fnl 100yds* **8/1**

-423 **4** 3¼ **Jayjinski (IRE)**[7] 2544 3-9-5 77..........................(b[1]) SeanLevey 2 59
(Richard Hannon) *in tch in last trio: swtchd lft and hdwy over 2f out: clsng and rdn to chse ldrs whn pushed lft jst over 2f out: wknd ins fnl f* **5/2**[2]

43-4 **5** 3 **Westbourne Grove (USA)**[34] 1753 3-9-5 59..........................(p) MartinHarley 4 48
(Robert Cowell) *broke fast: led but v keen: hdd after 2f: chsng ldrs whn nt clr run and swtchd lft over 1f out: sn rdn and no imp 1f out: wknd ins fnl f* **16/1**

6-46 **6** 2½ **Frank Sandatra**[74] 970 3-9-5 49.......................... ShaneKelly 6 39
(Peter Crate) *mostly chsd ldr tl rdn and unable qck over 1f out: sn btn: wknd ins fnl f* **33/1**

050 **7** 1½ **Flashy King (IRE)**[40] 1577 3-9-5 35.......................... OisinMurphy 7 33
(Joseph Tuite) *sn dropped towards rr: rdn 3f out: wknd over 1f out* **80/1**

0 **8** 6 **Willyegolassiego**[13] 2321 3-9-0 0.......................... LiamKeniry 1 7
(Neil Mulholland) *s.i.s: a bhd* **66/1**

1m 0.81s (0.51) **Going Correction** +0.075s/f (Good) **8** Ran SP% **124.0**
Speed ratings (Par 103): **98,96,94,89,84 80,78,68**
CSF £5.92 TOTE £1.90: £1.02, £1.90, £2.10; EX 7.30 Trifecta £24.00.
Owner Merry Fox Stud Limited **Bred** Merry Fox Stud Limited **Trained** Newmarket, Suffolk
■ Stewards' Enquiry : William Buick four-day ban: careless riding (Jun 13,19-21)

FOCUS
An ordinary sprint maiden but a promising winner. This has been rated around the 2nd to his handicap latest.

2751 SKY BET WINDSOR SPRINT SERIES H'CAP (QUALIFIER FOR THE WINDSOR SPRINT SERIES FINAL) 5f 10y

4:05 (4:05) (Class 2) (0-105,102) 3-Y-O **£12,938** (£3,850; £1,924; £962) **Stalls** Low

Form RPR

0-13 **1** **A Momentofmadness**[54] 1271 3-8-2 **83**..........................[1] JimmyQuinn 5 91
(Charles Hills) *taken down early and led to post: t.k.h: chsd ldng pair: wnt 2nd 3f out: rdn to chal over 1f out: edgd lft 1f out: led wl ins fnl f: r.o strly* **10/1**

5110 **2** 1½ **Just That Lord**[17] 2218 3-8-5 **86**.......................... LukeMorris 7 89
(Bill Turner) *led and crossed to rail after 2f: rdn and hrd pressed over 1f out: edgd lft u.p 1f out: hdd and one pce fnl 150yds* **3/1**[2]

1-13 **3** ½ **Gwendolyn (GER)**[30] 1872 3-8-2 **83** oh1.......................... KieranO'Neill 1 84
(Robert Cowell) *dwlt: in tch in midfield: effrt and n.m.r over 1f out: swtchd rt and rdn ent fnl f: styd on to snatch 3rd nr fin* **14/1**

2421 **4** ½ **Discreet Hero (IRE)**[17] 2218 3-8-4 **85** ow1..........(t) SilvestreDeSousa 6 84
(Simon Crisford) *stdd s: hld up in tch in rr: effrt jst over 2f out: hdwy and drvn to chse ldrs over 1f out: unable qck 1f out: wknd towards fin* **10/11**[1]

216- **5** 3½ **Point Of Woods**[219] 7460 3-8-6 **87**.......................... JohnFahy 2 74
(Ralph Beckett) *sn dropped to last pair and sltly impeded after 1f: rdn 2f out: no imp* **12/1**

2250 **6** 11 **Field Of Vision (IRE)**[66] 1070 3-9-7 **102**.......................... GeorgeBaker 4 49
(Joseph Tuite) *chsd ldr for 2f: rdn over 1f out: sn btn: wknd fnl f* **9/1**[3]

1m 0.54s (0.24) **Going Correction** +0.075s/f (Good) **6** Ran SP% **110.8**
Speed ratings (Par 105): **101,98,97,97,91 73**
CSF £38.76 TOTE £12.10: £3.10, £2.10; EX 43.50 Trifecta £238.00.
Owner Tony Wechsler & Ann Plummer **Bred** D R Tucker **Trained** Lambourn, Berks
■ Stewards' Enquiry : Silvestre De Sousa Fine: £140, weighed-in 1lb heavy

FOCUS
The winner built on his AW win, with the 2nd similar to his C&D success.

2752 MR & MRS NEWMAN GOLDEN WEDDING ANNIVERSARY H'CAP 1m 2f 7y

4:35 (4:36) (Class 3) (0-95,92) 4-Y-O+ **£7,439** (£2,213; £1,106; £553) **Stalls** Centre

Form RPR

6-06 **1** **Master Of Irony (IRE)**[37] 1643 4-8-13 **84**..........................(v) OisinMurphy 7 96+
(Ralph Beckett) *stdd after s: hld up in tch in last pair: wnt far side 4f out: rdn and hdwy over 1f out: led ins fnl f: sn clr and r.o strly: readily* **6/1**

5-44 **2** 3¼ **Croquembouche (IRE)**[17] 2222 7-9-3 **88**.......................... JamieSpencer 5 93
(Ed de Giles) *led: wnt far side 4f out: rdn over 2f out: drvn over 1f out: hdd ins fnl f: outpcd by wnr but hld on for 2nd ins fnl f* **5/1**[3]

-005 **3** ½ **Passover**[23] 2037 5-9-2 **92**.......................... EdwardGreatrex(5) 1 96
(Andrew Balding) *t.k.h: sn chsng ldr: wnt far side 4f out: rdn over 2f out: unable qck over 1f out: styd on same pce ins fnl f* **25/1**

2213 **4** 3 **Perfect Cracker**[25] 1972 8-9-4 **89**.......................... AdamKirby 2 87
(Clive Cox) *broke wl: sn stdd bk and chsd ldng trio: effrt over 2f out: chsd ldr over 1f tl 1f out: sn btn: wknd ins fnl f* **9/1**

/2-4 **5** 1¼ **Shakopee**[17] 2214 4-9-1 **86**.......................... SilvestreDeSousa 3 82+
(Luca Cumani) *t.k.h: hld up in tch: styd nr side 4f out: effrt 2f out: no imp and btn over 1f out: wknd ins fnl f* **7/2**[2]

3-25 **6** 1 **American Artist (IRE)**[25] 1972 4-9-7 **92**.......................... WilliamBuick 8 86
(Roger Varian) *t.k.h: hld up in tch in midfield: wnt far side 4f out: rdn over 2f out: no imp and btn whn edgd rt jst over 1f out: wknd ins fnl f* **11/4**[1]

6/0 **7** shd **Vercingetorix (IRE)**[9] 2484 5-9-5 **90**.......................... ShaneKelly 4 83
(David Evans) *stdd s: hld up in tch in last pair: styd nr side 4f out: rdn 2f out: no imp: wknd fnl f* **66/1**

310- **8** 1½ **Shell Bay (USA)**[232] 7145 4-9-5 **90**.......................... SeanLevey 9 80
(Richard Hannon) *chsd ldrs: wnt far side 4f out: rdn and unable qck over 2f out: lost pl over 1f out: bhd ins fnl f* **9/1**

3-56 **9** ½ **Illusive (IRE)**[24] 2017 5-8-13 **87**..........................(vt[1]) TomMarquand(3) 6 76
(George Scott) *t.k.h: hld up in tch towards rr: wnt far side 4f out: effrt u.p over 2f out: no imp and btn over 1f out: wknd fnl f* **17/2**

2m 10.2s (1.50) **Going Correction** +0.35s/f (Good) **9** Ran SP% **115.7**
Speed ratings (Par 107): **108,105,105,102,101 100,100,99,99**
CSF £36.12 CT £699.14 TOTE £7.00: £2.30, £2.10, £3.50; EX 39.50 Trifecta £714.80.
Owner Qatar Racing Ltd & Partner **Bred** Tinnakill Bloodstock **Trained** Kimpton, Hants

FOCUS
This was run over 48yds further than advertised. The majority of these surprisingly went far side in the straight, led by the runner-up. The two who stayed near side were never in it. Improved form from the winner and there's a case for rating this even higher.

2753 SKY BET FILLIES' H'CAP 1m 3f 135y

5:05 (5:05) (Class 4) (0-85,84) 4-Y-O+ **£4,851** (£1,443; £721; £360) **Stalls** Centre

Form RPR

03-2 **1** **Stockhill Diva**[35] 1717 6-9-5 **82**.......................... FMBerry 5 94+
(Brendan Powell) *chsd ldng pair: swtchd lft to far side and effrt over 2f out: led over 1f out: sn clr and r.o strly fnl f: easily* **15/8**[1]

0-26 **2** 7 **Graceland (FR)**[24] 1999 4-9-7 **84**.......................... JamieSpencer 4 84
(Michael Bell) *stdd s: hld up in last pair: swtchd lft to far side and effrt over 2f out: sn rdn: wnt 2nd but no ch w wnr 1f out: kpt on* **5/2**[2]

64-1 **3** nk **Cartier (IRE)**[10] 2427 4-9-2 **79**.......................... SeanLevey 2 79
(David Simcock) *stdd s: hld up in last pair: swtchd lft to far side and effrt over 2f out: drvn no imp over 1f out: 3rd and kpt on same pce fnl f* **11/4**[3]

/26- **4** 1¼ **Northern Meeting (IRE)**[19] 4551 6-8-13 **76**..........................(p) ShaneKelly 3 74
(Robert Stephens) *led: rdn 3f out and styd nr side: hdd over 1f out: sn outpcd: wknd fnl f* **14/1**

0-13 **5** 6 **Hound Music**[28] 1919 4-8-12 **75**.......................... MartinHarley 1 63
(Jonathan Portman) *chsd ldr: styd nr side and rdn 3f out: dropped to rr and btn over 1f out: wknd* **13/2**

2m 32.28s (2.78) **Going Correction** +0.35s/f (Good) **5** Ran SP% **110.0**
Speed ratings (Par 102): **104,99,99,98,94**
CSF £6.84 TOTE £2.80: £1.60, £1.40; EX 5.90 Trifecta £14.30.
Owner Mrs M Fairbairn & E Gadsden **Bred** Mrs M Fairbairn And E Gadsden **Trained** Upper Lambourn, Berks

FOCUS
This was run over 48yds further than advertised. Three of the five runners went far side in the straight and they finished 1-2-3, although they were the first three in the market. Another improved performance from the winner.

2754 SKY BET TOP PRICE EVERY FAVOURITE H'CAP 6f

5:35 (5:35) (Class 4) (0-85,85) 4-Y-O+ **£4,851** (£1,443; £721; £360) **Stalls** Low

Form RPR

0-00 **1** **Rio Ronaldo (IRE)**[37] 1634 4-9-3 **81**.......................... JamieSpencer 7 92+
(Mike Murphy) *stdd s: hld up in rr: clsd gng wl over 1f out: squeezed through and chsd ldrs 1f out: pushed along and str run ins fnl f to ld cl home* **14/1**

43-5 **2** ½ **Pixeleen**[56] 1237 4-9-0 **78**.......................... OisinMurphy 9 87
(Malcolm Saunders) *chsd ldrs: rdn to ld 2f out: drvn over 1f out: kpt on wl ins fnl f: hdd and unable qck cl home* **16/1**

46-0 **3** 3 **Spring Fling**[45] 1453 5-9-6 **84**.......................... MartinHarley 2 83
(Henry Candy) *t.k.h: hld up in tch in midfield: hdwy over 2f out: rdn to chse ldr wl over 1f out: no ex and btn ins fnl f: wknd fnl 75yds* **7/1**[3]

566 **4** ½ **Baddilini**[12] 2361 6-8-11 **75**..........................(p) FMBerry 4 73
(Alan Bailey) *towards rr: hdwy u.p over 1f out: kpt on ins fnl f: nvr trbld ldrs* **25/1**

1/24 **5** 1¼ **Jaywalker (IRE)**[14] 2290 5-8-12 **76**.......................... SilvestreDeSousa 3 70
(Mick Channon) *chsd ldrs: effrt 2f out: drvn to chse ldrs but unable qck over 1f out: wknd ins fnl f* **7/1**[3]

-232 **6** 1½ **Upstaging**[14] 2290 4-9-0 **78**..........................(b) LukeMorris 14 67
(Paul Cole) *s.i.s: sn rdn and sn rcvrd to r in tch in midfield: hdwy to chse ldrs and drvn over 1f out: btn 1f out: wknd ins fnl f* **11/2**[2]

2-00 **7** 3¼ **Syrian Pearl**[16] 2247 5-8-8 **79**.......................... SamuelClarke(7) 10 58+
(Chris Wall) *s.i.s: bhd and pushed along: rdn and hdwy 2f out: no imp over 1f out: wknd fnl f* **10/1**

-050 **8** ¾ **Kinglami**[28] 1929 7-8-13 **82**..........................(v) EdwardGreatrex(5) 5 58
(John O'Shea) *in tch in midfield: rdn ent fnl 2f: unable qck and btn 1f out: wknd fnl f* **16/1**

00-5 **9** nse **Royal Mezyan (IRE)**[16] 2253 5-9-3 **81**.......................... GeorgeBaker 12 57
(Henry Spiller) *hld up towards rr: hdwy 2f out: short of room and no hdwy over 1f out: wknd fnl f* **25/1**

114 **10** 2½ **Bouclier (IRE)**[40] 1566 6-9-3 **81**.......................... WilliamCarson 13 49
(Tony Carroll) *in tch in midfield: rdn 2f out: losing pl and n.m.r over 1f out: sn wknd* **3/1**[1]

120- **11** *3* **Nocturn**[307] 4727 7-9-7 **85**....(p) DavidProbert 8 43
(Ronald Harris) *led tl 1/2-way: rdn over 2f out: lost pl over 1f out: sn wknd* **40/1**

0-00 **12** *2 1/4* **Field Game**[17] 2206 4-8-13 **84**....(bt[1]) CharlieBennett[(7)] 16 35
(Hughie Morrison) *taken down early: chsd ldr tl led 1/2-way: rdn and hdd 2f out: lost pl over 1f out: sn wknd* **16/1**

00-5 **13** *3/4* **Sydney Ruffdiamond**[30] 1857 4-9-7 **85**.... ShaneKelly 1 34
(Richard Hughes) *stdd and grad moving lft to far rail after s: effrt 2f out: no hdwy over 1f out: sn wknd and eased wl ins fnl f* **10/1**

-110 **14** *13* **Evanescent (IRE)**[9] 2460 7-9-4 **82**.... RobertWinston 11
(Tony Carroll) *chsd ldrs: rdn over 2f out: losing pl whn bdly hmpd 2f out: wl bhd after: t.o and eased ins fnl f* **25/1**

0-11 **15** *23* **Fear Or Favour (IRE)**[14] 2309 5-9-2 **80**.... WilliamBuick 15
(George Scott) *in tch in midfield: squeezed out and bdly hmpd 2f out: dropped to rr and eased after: t.o* **15/2**

1m 12.5s (-0.50) **Going Correction** +0.075s/f (Good) **15** Ran SP% **133.6**
Speed ratings (Par 105): **106,105,101,100,99 97,92,91,91,88 84,81,80,62,32**
CSF £234.07 CT £1768.14 TOTE £21.90: £6.30, £4.70, £3.60; EX 320.00 Trifecta £5940.90.
Owner The Castaways **Bred** Knocktoran Stud & Kildaragh Stud **Trained** Westoning, Beds

FOCUS
They all raced far side in this well-contested sprint handicap. A length pb from the winner and runner-up.
T/Jkpt: Not won. T/Plt: £168.60 to a £1 stake. Pool of £82797.03 - 358.39 winning tickets T/Qpdt: £26.10 to a £1 stake. Pool of £7115.74 - 201.50 winning units. **Steve Payne**

2755a (Foreign Racing) - See Raceform Interactive

2732 LEICESTER (R-H)
Tuesday, May 31

OFFICIAL GOING: Good to firm (good in places on round course) (abandoned after race 2 due to unsafe ground)
Wind: Fresh against Weather: Overcast turning to rain after race 2

2756 BRITISH STALLION STUDS EBF MAIDEN STKS (PLUS 10 RACE) (DIV I) 6f
2:00 (2:02) (Class 4) 2-Y-O **£4,528** (£1,347; £673; £336) **Stalls** High

Form RPR

1 **Thunder Snow (IRE)** 2-9-5 0.... JamesDoyle 2 84+
(Saeed bin Suroor) *hld up: pushed along over 2f out: hdwy over 1f out: r.o to ld wl ins fnl f: sn clr: readily* **4/1**[3]

2 *1 1/4* **Parys Mountain (IRE)** 2-9-5 0.... SilvestreDeSousa 6 80+
(Charles Hills) *chsd ldrs: led over 1f out: rdn: edgd lft and hdd wl ins fnl f: styd on same pce* **16/1**

2 **3** *1 1/4* **Evergate**[10] 2478 2-9-5 0.... DarryllHolland 9 77
(Hugo Palmer) *w ldr tl led over 3f out: rdn and hdd over 1f out: styd on same pce wl ins fnl f* **2/1**[1]

4 *1/2* **Arzaak (IRE)** 2-9-5 0.... PaulHanagan 13 75+
(Owen Burrows) *free to post: hld up: racd keenly: hdwy over 1f out: r.o: nt rch ldrs* **20/1**

2 **5** *3/4* **Juan Horsepower**[20] 2147 2-9-5 0.... SeanLevey 8 73
(Richard Hannon) *led: hdd over 3f out: rdn over 1f out: n.m.r ins fnl f: styd on same pce* **14/1**

6 *nk* **Hyde Park** 2-9-5 0.... FrankieDettori 4 72+
(John Gosden) *hld up: pushed along and hdwy over 2f out: no ex wl ins fnl f* **9/4**[2]

7 *6* **Apex King (IRE)** 2-9-5 0.... GeorgeBaker 1 54
(Ed Dunlop) *s.i.s: in rr: styd on fr over 1f out: nvr on terms* **20/1**

8 *1 1/2* **Drochaid** 2-9-5 0.... LiamKeniry 3 49
(Andrew Balding) *s.i.s: outpcd: sme late hdwy* **66/1**

9 *nk* **Bongrace (IRE)** 2-9-0 0.... ShaneGray 5 43
(Kevin Ryan) *chsd ldrs: rdn over 2f out: wknd wl over 1f out* **66/1**

10 *3 1/4* **Jumira Prince (IRE)** 2-9-5 0.... AndreaAtzeni 11 39
(Roger Varian) *s.i.s: hdwy over 4f out: rdn and wknd 2f out* **9/1**

11 *7* **General Allenby** 2-9-5 0.... PatDobbs 7 18
(Henry Tett) *sn outpcd* **100/1**

06 **12** *3 3/4* **Heavenly Cry**[48] 1422 2-9-0 0.... NoelGarbutt[(5)] 12 6
(Denis Quinn) *sn pushed along in rr: sme hdwy 1/2-way: rdn and wknd over 2f out* **200/1**

1m 13.25s (0.25) **Going Correction** +0.05s/f (Good) **12** Ran SP% **120.6**
Speed ratings (Par 95): **100,98,96,96,95 94,86,84,84,79 70,65**
CSF £62.14 TOTE £6.80: £2.20, £4.90, £1.20; EX 72.90 Trifecta £275.70.
Owner Godolphin **Bred** Darley **Trained** Newmarket, Suffolk

FOCUS
The going was the same as for the previous day's meeting - good to firm, good in places on the round course. The first division of an interesting maiden with a couple having already shown decent ability up against some expensive debutants. This race was won by the high-class miler Toormore three years ago and a few winners should emerge from this contest, with the first six pulling clear.

2757 BRITISH STALLION STUDS EBF MAIDEN STKS (PLUS 10 RACE) (DIV II) 6f
2:30 (2:31) (Class 4) 2-Y-O **£4,528** (£1,347; £673; £336) **Stalls** High

Form RPR

1 **Rodaini (USA)** 2-9-5 0.... SilvestreDeSousa 5 79+
(Simon Crisford) *w ldrs: racd keenly: rdn over 1f out: r.o to ld nr fin* **5/6**[1]

2 *nse* **Magillen (IRE)** 2-9-5 0.... FrankieDettori 10 79+
(Charles Hills) *hld up in tch: rdn over 1f out: ev ch wl ins fnl f: r.o* **5/1**[2]

5 **3** *nk* **Prerogative (IRE)**[24] 2023 2-9-5 0.... PatDobbs 8 78
(Richard Hannon) *led: rdn over 1f out: hdd nr fin* **10/1**

4 *3* **Thammin** 2-9-5 0.... PaulHanagan 2 69+
(Owen Burrows) *hld up: racd keenly: hdwy 2f out: rdn ins fnl f: styd on* **16/1**

5 **5** *hd* **Await The Storm (IRE)**[30] 1889 2-9-5 0.... JimmyFortune 11 67
(Brian Meehan) *w ldrs: rdn over 1f out: styd on same pce ins fnl f* **16/1**

6 *nk* **Outre Mer (IRE)** 2-9-5 0.... JamesDoyle 4 66+
(John Gosden) *mid-div: hdwy over 1f out: sn rdn: styd on: nt rch ldrs* **14/1**

7 *1/2* **Black Trilby (IRE)** 2-9-5 0.... AdamKirby 3 65+
(Clive Cox) *w ldrs tl rdn over 1f out: no ex ins fnl f* **15/2**[3]

0 **8** *1/2* **Maazel (IRE)**[10] 2489 2-9-5 0.... AndreaAtzeni 9 63
(Roger Varian) *s.i.s: hld up: racd keenly: shkn up over 1f out: r.o ins fnl f: nvr nrr* **50/1**

9 *1/2* **Forster Square (IRE)** 2-9-5 0.... PatrickMathers 7 62
(Richard Fahey) *trckd ldrs: arced keenly: rdn over 2f out: styd on same pce fnl f* **40/1**

10 *shd* **White Chin (IRE)** 2-9-5 0.... RichardKingscote 6 61
(Tom Dascombe) *s.i.s: hld up: shkn up over 1f out: styd on: nt trble ldrs* **66/1**

11 *3 1/2* **Melcano** 2-9-0 0.... DarryllHolland 12 45
(David Evans) *in rr: hdwy 1/2-way: shkn up over 2f out: outpcd fr wl over 1f out* **100/1**

12 *22* **Jackman** 2-9-2 0.... GeorgeDowning[(3)] 1
(Tony Carroll) *sn pushed along in rr: bhd fr 1/2-way* **100/1**

1m 14.76s (1.76) **Going Correction** +0.05s/f (Good) **12** Ran SP% **118.4**
Speed ratings (Par 95): **90,89,89,85,85 84,84,83,82,82 78,48**
CSF £4.94 TOTE £1.80: £1.30, £2.00, £2.50; EX 6.60 Trifecta £35.40.
Owner Abdullah Saeed Al Naboodah **Bred** Greenwood Lodge Farm **Trained** Newmarket, Suffolk

FOCUS
Pace muddling first 2f, field in a heap as a result and loads of these finishing with something left; winner should rate higher. The runner-up slipped and fell on the bend after the winning post and as a result the rest of the meeting was abandoned.

2758 SAFFRON 3-Y-O FILLIES' H'CAP 6f
() (Class 5) (0-75,) 3-Y-O £

2759 CORONATION FILLIES' H'CAP 7f
() (Class 4) (0-85,) 3-Y-O £

2760 STATHERN CLAIMING STKS 7f
() (Class 5) 3-Y-O £

2761 BRITISH STALLION STUDS EBF NOVICE STKS (PLUS 10 RACE) 5f
() (Class 4) 2-Y-O £

2762 JENNINGSBET H'CAP 5f
() (Class 5) (0-75,) 4-Y-O+ £

2763 OADBY H'CAP 1m 1f 218y
() (Class 6) (0-65,) 3-Y-O £

T/Plt: £1.50 to a £1 stake. Pool: £51,498.00 - 34,157.95 winning tickets. **Colin Roberts**

2583 LINGFIELD (L-H)
Tuesday, May 31

OFFICIAL GOING: Polytrack: standard
Wind: Fresh, against Weather: Overcast

2764 BRITISH STALLION STUDS EBF FILLIES' NOVICE STKS (PLUS 10 RACE) 6f 1y(P)
5:50 (5:52) (Class 5) 2-Y-O **£3,881** (£1,155; £577; £288) **Stalls** Low

Form RPR

43 **1** **Lexington Sky (IRE)**[18] 2211 2-9-0 0.... KieranO'Neill 1 78
(Richard Hannon) *mde virtually all: pushed into def ld wl over 1f out: shkn up whn pressed fnl f: kpt on wl* **11/4**[2]

2 **2** *nk* **Naafer**[12] 2410 2-9-0 0.... PaulHanagan 6 77+
(William Haggas) *t.k.h early: trckd ldrs: shkn up to go 2nd over 1f out: rdn to chal fnl f: kpt on but hld nr fin* **2/5**[1]

3 *1 1/4* **Turanga Leela** 2-9-0 0.... HarryBentley 2 73
(Tom Dascombe) *w wnr to 2f out: lost 2nd over 1f out: kpt on steadily fnl f* **14/1**[3]

4 *2* **Scudding (USA)** 2-9-0 0....[1] StevieDonohoe 7 67
(Charlie Fellowes) *racd in 6th: pushed along over 2f out: prog to take 4th jst over 1f out: shkn up and kpt on fnl f* **20/1**

5 *4 1/2* **Miss Reignier** 2-9-0 0.... SteveDrowne 5 54
(Michael Blanshard) *hld up in last pair: outpcd over 2f out: pushed along and nt on terms after* **66/1**

6 *hd* **Ablaze** 2-9-0 0.... LiamKeniry 8 53
(Laura Mongan) *t.k.h: prog on outer to join ldng pair after 2f: rdn 2f out: sn wknd* **100/1**

7 *2 1/4* **Driver's Girl (USA)** 2-9-0 0.... LukeMorris 3 47
(Marco Botti) *chsd ldrs: pushed along bef 1/2-way: fdd fr 2f out* **14/1**[3]

8 *9* **Surfina** 2-9-0 0.... OisinMurphy 4 20
(Dean Ivory) *slowly away: rn green and a in last pair: wknd over 2f out: t.o* **16/1**

1m 13.4s (1.50) **Going Correction** -0.025s/f (Stan) **8** Ran SP% **124.6**
Speed ratings (Par 90): **89,88,86,84,78 78,75,63**
CSF £4.55 TOTE £3.70: £1.30, £1.02, £2.50; EX 6.10 Trifecta £23.70.
Owner Middleham Park Racing CXIV **Bred** Stephanie Hanly **Trained** East Everleigh, Wilts

FOCUS
An uncompetitive contest run at a steady pace.

2765 INJURED JOCKEYS FUND H'CAP 6f 1y(P)
6:20 (6:21) (Class 5) (0-70,70) 4-Y-O+ **£2,911** (£866; £432; £216) **Stalls** Low

Form RPR

-031 **1** **Triple Dream**[13] 2380 11-9-2 **65**.... OisinMurphy 8 72
(Milton Bradley) *mde virtually all: hrd pressed fr 2f out: kpt on wl and hld on wl nr fin* **8/1**[3]

0522 **2** *hd* **Straits Of Malacca**[4] 2643 5-9-2 **65**....(p) HarryBentley 5 71
(Simon Dow) *trckd ldrs: effrt on inner over 1f out: str chal ins fnl f: nt qckn last strides* **9/2**[1]

0122 **3** *nk* **Colourbearer (IRE)**[36] 1712 9-9-0 **68**....(t) KieranShoemark[(5)] 6 73
(Charlie Wallis) *t.k.h: pressed ldr: chal and upsides 2f out: nt go by and lost 2nd fnl f: kpt on nr fin* **10/1**

0404 **4** *1* **Noverre To Go (IRE)**[21] 2130 10-8-7 **56**....(p) LukeMorris 4 58
(Ronald Harris) *trckd ldrs: rdn and nt qckn over 1f out: kpt on ins fnl f to take 4th nr fin* **10/1**

-300 **5** *shd* **Ripinto (IRE)**[18] 2213 4-9-0 **70**....(v[1]) RhiainIngram[(7)] 7 72
(Jim Boyle) *wl in tch: urged along 2f out: hanging and nt qckn over 1f out: kpt on ins fnl f* **7/1**[2]

4000 **6** *nk* **Swiss Cross**[35] 1746 9-9-1 **64**....(bt) StevieDonohoe 2 68+
(Phil McEntee) *towards rr: prog on inner over 1f out to chse ldng trio fnl f: nowhere to go after and nvr able to chal: lost pl nr fin* **8/1**[3]

-030 **7** *1* **Hipz (IRE)**[29] 1928 5-8-13 **62**.... LiamKeniry 10 59
(Laura Mongan) *pressed ldng pair: stl upsides 2f out: lost 3rd jst over 1f out: fdd* **20/1**

0-06 **8** *hd* **Jungle Bay**[28] 1945 9-9-6 **69**....(b) JoeFanning 9 66
(Jane Chapple-Hyam) *dwlt: prog out v wd to press ldrs after 2f: rdn 2f out: fdd fnl f* **8/1**[3]

222- **9** *hd* **Dunnscotia**[296] 5176 4-9-4 **67**..(t) WilliamCarson 3 63
(Paul Webber) *s.i.s: hld up in last pair: pushed along over 2f out: nt clr run v briefly wl over 1f out and swtchd out wd: kpt on fnl f: nvr involved* **7/1**[2]

420 **10** ½ **Agerzam**[43] 1533 6-8-10 **62**..(b) TomMarquand(3) 11 56
(Ronald Harris) *sn pushed along in last pair fr wd draw: nvr able to mde any real prog: kpt on nr fin* **16/1**

4640 **11** ¾ **Head Space (IRE)**[10] 2469 8-9-5 **68**.................................. JimmyQuinn 1 60
(Brian Barr) *towards rr: pushed along on inner over 2f out: no prog over 1f out: fdd fnl f* **8/1**[3]

1m 11.93s (0.03) **Going Correction** -0.025s/f (Stan) **11** Ran SP% **116.5**
Speed ratings (Par 103): **98,97,97,96,95 95,94,93,93,92 91**
CSF £43.44 CT £368.12 TOTE £7.30: £2.80, £2.20, £2.00; EX 27.30 Trifecta £57.40.
Owner J M Bradley **Bred** Hesmonds Stud Ltd **Trained** Sedbury, Gloucs

FOCUS
The pace was honest for this open handicap. The 1-2-3 all have better back form and the ageing winner is rated a length up on his Kempton, his best since March last year.

2766 COME TO COUNTRYSIDE DAY JUNE 4 H'CAP 1m 4f (P)
6:50 (6:50) (Class 5) (0-70,69) 3-Y-O **£2,911** (£866; £432; £216) **Stalls** Low

Form RPR

2-01 **1** **Tenzing Norgay**[6] 2589 3-9-6 **68** 6ex.................................(v) LukeMorris 4 81+
(Sir Mark Prescott Bt) *racd freely: mde all: drew clr 2f out: 6 l clr 1f out: eased fnl 100yds* **4/11**[1]

2050 **2** 1½ **Gabster (IRE)**[21] 2126 3-9-0 **62**.. OisinMurphy 3 66
(Amanda Perrett) *hld up in last: gng wl enough jst over 2f out: stuck bhd chsng pair tl swtchd rt over 1f out: qckly tk 2nd and r.o to cl on eased down wnr: no ch to threaten* **5/1**[2]

336 **3** 4½ **Hongkong Adventure**[17] 2260 3-9-6 **68**........................... PatCosgrave 2 64
(Rae Guest) *dwlt: sn disp 2nd pl: reminder 5f out: drvn 3f out: lost 2nd and fdd over 1f out* **8/1**[3]

3010 **4** 1½ **Kelvin Hall**[15] 2300 3-9-7 **69**.. JoeFanning 1 63
(Mark Johnston) *disp 2nd pl: rdn wl over 2f out: sn lft bhd by wnr: fdd over 1f out* **10/1**

2m 31.33s (-1.67) **Going Correction** -0.025s/f (Stan) **4** Ran SP% **110.2**
Speed ratings (Par 99): **104,103,100,99**
CSF £2.70 TOTE £1.20; EX 2.80 Trifecta £6.60.
Owner J L C Pearce **Bred** J L C Pearce **Trained** Newmarket, Suffolk

FOCUS
A hard race to rate with 3-4 below form, the 2nd getting stuck behind them turning in and the winner eased last 1/2 furlong or so.

2767 RETRAINING OF RACEHORSES MAIDEN FILLIES' STKS 1m 2f (P)
7:20 (7:24) (Class 5) 3-Y-O+ **£2,911** (£866; £432; £216) **Stalls** Low

Form RPR

6 **1** **Haddajah (IRE)**[25] 1989 3-8-12 0.................................... FrankieDettori 2 82+
(Sir Michael Stoute) *led 1f: chsd ldr to 7f out: rdn 3f out: effrt on inner 2f out: led over 1f out but sn hrd pressed: flashed tail but kpt on wl* **4/5**[1]

0-2 **2** *nk* **Julia Dream**[19] 2182 3-8-12 0... PatCosgrave 10 81
(William Haggas) *t.k.h: hld up in midfield: shkn up and prog over 2f out: rdn to press wnr over 1f out: chal ins fnl f: kpt on but hld nr fin* **3/1**[2]

42- **3** 2¾ **Bretoncelles (FR)**[194] 7905 3-8-12 0.................................. LukeMorris 4 76
(Harry Dunlop) *trckd ldrs: rdn over 2f out: effrt on inner over 1f out: chsd ldng pair ins fnl f: no imp* **16/1**

4 *nk* **Mazalto (IRE)** 3-8-9 0.. MarcMonaghan(3) 12 75+
(Hugo Palmer) *towards rr: rdn 3f out: no prog tl styd on fr over 1f out: tk 4th ins fnl f: kpt on* **66/1**

5 1 **Elraazy** 3-8-12 0.. PaulHanagan 3 73+
(John Gosden) *s.s: hld up in last: stl there 2f out: pushed along and styd on quite takingly fr over 1f out* **6/1**[3]

36- **6** ½ **Up To You (USA)**[183] 8048 3-8-12 0................................ NickyMackay 6 72
(John Gosden) *t.k.h: trckd ldr 7f out to 2f out: wknd over 1f out* **20/1**

0- **7** *nk* **Ceecubed (IRE)**[230] 7219 3-8-12 0................................ OisinMurphy 13 71
(Jeremy Noseda) *sweeping prog fr wd draw to ld after 1f: hdd over 1f out: steadily wknd* **66/1**

8 2 **Tenerezza (IRE)** 3-8-12 0.. ShaneKelly 11 67
(David Lanigan) *hld up in rr: pushed along over 2f out: one pce and no real prog over 1f out* **50/1**

4 **9** ½ **Brick Lane**[11] 2443 3-8-12 0... JimmyQuinn 5 66
(Robyn Brisland) *trckd ldrs: rdn in 4th pl 3f out: lost pl and fdd fr 2f out* **66/1**

10 *nk* **Always Summer** 3-8-9 0..[1] DanielMuscutt(3) 7 66
(James Fanshawe) *settled wl in rr: pushed along over 3f out: no great prog after* **50/1**

35 **11** 2¼ **Sherdat (IRE)**[12] 2398 3-8-12 0....................................... HarryBentley 8 61
(Roger Varian) *racd on outer: chsd ldrs: rdn and lost pl over 2f out: steadily wknd* **16/1**

2m 5.23s (-1.37) **Going Correction** -0.025s/f (Stan)
WFA 3 from 4yo 14lb **11** Ran SP% **119.8**
Speed ratings (Par 100): **104,103,101,101,100 100,99,98,97,97 95**
CSF £3.16 TOTE £1.90: £1.10, £1.60, £3.30; EX 4.50 Trifecta £23.00.
Owner Al Shaqab Racing **Bred** Sunderland Holding Inc & R P Blds Ltd **Trained** Newmarket, Suffolk
■ Skadi (100-1) and Sweeping Beauty (100-1) were withdrawn. Rule 4 does not apply.

FOCUS
A muddling fillies' maiden, field rather compressed and downfield runners are likely to limit this in time.

2768 CANTERING CUISINE H'CAP 5f 6y(P)
7:50 (7:52) (Class 4) (0-80,80) 4-Y-O+ **£4,690** (£1,395; £697; £348) **Stalls** High

Form RPR

0032 **1** **Desert Strike**[32] 1838 10-8-13 **72**....................................(p) LiamKeniry 3 79
(Conor Dore) *fast away: led: drvn 2f out: edgd rt over 1f out and sn hdd: rallied to ld last 75yds* **5/1**[3]

6032 **2** *nk* **Mossgo (IRE)**[14] 2342 6-8-11 **70**....................................(t) KierenFox 5 76
(John Best) *trckd ldng pair: clsd on inner to ld jst over 1f out: sn drvn: kpt on but hdd last 75yds* **7/1**

0150 **3** ½ **Picansort**[6] 2584 9-8-11 **70**...(b) ShaneKelly 7 74
(Peter Crate) *t.k.h: hld up bhd ldrs: stl keen jst over 2f out: rdn and nt qckn over 1f out: styd on ins fnl f to take 3rd last stride* **14/1**

5-21 **4** *shd* **Shackled N Drawn (USA)**[24] 2040 4-9-6 **79**.............. HarryBentley 10 83
(Peter Hedger) *dwlt: hld up in last pair: prog wl over 1f out: rdn to chse ldng pair ins fnl f: kpt on but nvr quite able to chal: lost 3rd last stride* **7/2**[1]

3345 **5** *hd* **Diamond Charlie (IRE)**[6] 2584 8-9-0 **73**.....................(p) LukeMorris 6 76
(Simon Dow) *s.i.s: t.k.h in last: hmpd after 1f: stl last 2f out: drvn and styd on ins fnl f: gaining at fin* **8/1**

0200 **6** 1 **Temple Road (IRE)**[52] 1341 8-8-11 **70**.........................(bt) OisinMurphy 2 70
(Milton Bradley) *hld up towards rr: gng wl on inner over 1f and looked a threat: rdn and fnd little fnl f: wl hld whn n.m.r nr fin* **10/1**

2221 **7** ½ **Elusivity (IRE)**[28] 1956 8-9-7 **80**..(p) JoeFanning 9 78
(Conor Dore) *pressed wnr to wl over 1f out: fdd ins fnl f* **5/1**[3]

416- **8** *hd* **Free To Love**[232] 7170 4-9-0 **76**.......................................[1] TomMarquand(3) 8 73
(Charles Hills) *racd on outer: chsd ldrs: rdn 1/2-way: sn lost pl: wl over 1f out: kpt on* **4/1**[2]

58.82s (0.02) **Going Correction** -0.025s/f (Stan) **8** Ran SP% **114.9**
Speed ratings (Par 105): **98,97,96,96,96 94,93,93**
CSF £39.71 CT £458.52 TOTE £7.20: £2.50, £2.60, £3.90; EX 52.70 Trifecta £724.60.
Owner Andrew Page **Bred** Mrs Mary Rowlands **Trained** Hubbert's Bridge, Lincs

FOCUS
An open sprint handicap that saw a bunched finish, with the winner making a minor step up on his recent runs.

2769 RYAN VEHICLES H'CAP 1m 1y(P)
8:20 (8:21) (Class 6) (0-65,65) 4-Y-O+ **£2,264** (£673; £336; £168) **Stalls** High

Form RPR

-135 **1** **Choral Clan (IRE)**[13] 2379 5-9-4 **62**................................... JackMitchell 5 71
(Philip Mitchell) *trckd ldrs: shkn up and prog jst over 2f out: rdn and r.o fr over 1f out to ld last 75yds* **6/1**[2]

010 **2** ½ **Believe It (IRE)**[4] 2635 4-9-3 **61**.. ShaneKelly 4 69
(Richard Hughes) *wl plcd: prog to go 3rd over 2f out: chsd ldr over 1f out: hrd rdn to chal and upsides 100yds out: jst outpcd* **7/2**[1]

3613 **3** ½ **Duke Of North (IRE)**[12] 2401 4-8-13 **64**.................. RhiainIngram(7) 11 71
(Jim Boyle) *trapped out wd early: prog to go prom after 2f: chsd ldr 3f out: rdn to ld 2f out: hdd and no ex last 75yds* **8/1**

6264 **4** ¾ **Little Lord Nelson**[33] 1805 4-9-1 **64**............................(t) AaronJones(5) 7 69
(Stuart Williams) *hld up in midfield: rdn and prog along w wnr over 2f out: styd on same pce fr over 1f out to take 4th ins fnl f* **7/1**[3]

5310 **5** 2 **Al's Memory (IRE)**[14] 2324 7-9-6 **64**................................. PatCosgrave 6 64
(David Evans) *pressed ldr to 3f out: steadily lost pl u.p* **10/1**

0353 **6** ½ **For Shia And Lula (IRE)**[20] 2153 7-9-5 **63**........................ LukeMorris 1 62
(Daniel Mark Loughnane) *led: rdn and hdd 2f out: steadily wknd* **12/1**

2565 **7** ½ **Red Unico (IRE)**[64] 1124 4-9-5 **63**.................................... OisinMurphy 3 61
(Brian Barr) *t.k.h: hld up bhd ldrs: rdn and lost pl over 2f out: n.d after* **16/1**

1260 **8** ½ **Gunner Moyne**[20] 2153 4-9-0 **63**.................................. HectorCrouch(5) 9 59
(Gary Moore) *stdd s: hld up in last pair: pushed along in last over 2f out: mod late prog: nvr involved* **25/1**

5501 **9** *nk* **Runaiocht (IRE)**[32] 1834 6-9-2 **60**.................................(b) JimmyQuinn 2 56
(Paul Burgoyne) *plld hrd: cl up bhd ldrs: rdn over 2f out: wknd over 1f out* **6/1**[2]

5435 **10** 1½ **Two In The Pink (IRE)**[12] 2403 6-9-0 **65**.................... PaddyBradley(7) 8 57
(Ralph J Smith) *hld up in last trio: rdn 3f out: no prog and wl btn over 1f out* **10/1**

500- **11** *nk* **Kawaii**[174] 8158 4-8-13 **60**... TimClark(3) 12 51
(Martin Smith) *trapped out v wd early: towards rr whn able to gain cover 1/2-way: rdn over 2f out: no prog* **50/1**

5000 **12** *nse* **Dukes Meadow**[13] 2374 5-9-7 **65**....................................... SteveDrowne 10 56
(Roger Ingram) *slowly away: mostly in last trio: rdn over 2f out: brief prog over 1f out: fdd fnl f* **10/1**

1m 36.97s (-1.23) **Going Correction** -0.025s/f (Stan) **12** Ran SP% **121.1**
Speed ratings (Par 101): **105,104,104,103,101 100,100,99,99,97 97,97**
CSF £27.84 CT £176.99 TOTE £6.90: £2.60, £2.30, £2.50; EX 38.20 Trifecta £220.20.
Owner Bob Harris & Patricia Mitchell **Bred** L Queally **Trained** Kingston Lisle, Oxfordshire

FOCUS
An open handicap run at a decent pace.

2770 RACING WELFARE H'CAP 7f 1y(P)
8:50 (8:51) (Class 5) (0-70,69) 3-Y-O **£2,911** (£866; £432; £216) **Stalls** Low

Form RPR

6-26 **1** **Kafoo**[29] 1917 3-9-1 **63**.. PaulHanagan 6 69
(Ed Dunlop) *pushed up to ld and mde virtually all: hrd pressed fnl f: jst hld on* **4/1**[2]

531- **2** *shd* **Wakame (IRE)**[195] 7887 3-8-13 **61**.................................. PatCosgrave 4 67
(Ed de Giles) *trckd ldng pair: wnt 2nd on inner over 1f out: str chal fnl f: jst failed* **6/1**[3]

1323 **3** ½ **Music Major**[14] 2325 3-8-8 **56**.. LukeMorris 3 60+
(Michael Attwater) *hld up in midfield: rdn over 2f out: prog over 1f out: tk 3rd ins fnl f: kpt on but unable to chal* **3/1**[1]

-641 **4** 1 **Packing (IRE)**[34] 1792 3-9-2 **64**...................................... WilliamCarson 8 66
(Jamie Osborne) *trckd ldrs: shkn up and cl enough over 1f out: kpt on same pce fnl f* **7/1**

45-5 **5** ¾ **Aberlady (USA)**[24] 2050 3-9-6 **68**.............................(b[1]) StevieDonohoe 10 68
(Sir Michael Stoute) *stdd fr wd draw and hld up in last pair: rdn 2f out: styd on u.p fr jst over 1f out: nrst fin but no ch* **6/1**[3]

-330 **6** *nk* **Ginger Joe**[34] 1788 3-9-5 **67**.. SeanLevey 5 66
(David Brown) *chsd wnr: rdn over 2f out: lost 2nd over 1f out: fdd ins fnl f* **10/1**

4-15 **7** 2¼ **False Id**[47] 1431 3-9-3 **68**... TomMarquand(3) 9 61
(Robert Eddery) *in rr: brought wd 1/2-way and racd awkwardly: rdn over 2f out: wl hld over 1f out: one pce* **8/1**

3-06 **8** ½ **Vallance Road**[114] 495 3-8-12 **67**................................. SamuelClarke(7) 7 58
(Robyn Brisland) *a in rr: shkn up and no prog 2f out* **12/1**

44-0 **9** 1½ **Mr Marchwood**[19] 2186 3-9-7 **69**.. LiamKeniry 1 56
(Sylvester Kirk) *hld up in last trio: shkn up over 1f out: no prog and nvr involved* **33/1**

1m 24.65s (-0.15) **Going Correction** -0.025s/f (Stan) **9** Ran SP% **116.9**
Speed ratings (Par 99): **99,98,98,97,96 95,93,92,91**
CSF £28.66 CT £82.00 TOTE £6.00: £2.30, £2.10, £1.20; EX 34.90 Trifecta £238.10.
Owner Hamdan Al Maktoum **Bred** Shadwell Estate Company Limited **Trained** Newmarket, Suffolk

FOCUS
Some unexposed types in this handicap which was run at a steady pace. It paid to race handy. The winner is rated close to his penultimate form.

T/Plt: £23.80 to a £1 stake. Pool: £47,765.00 - 2,000.67 winning tickets. T/Qpdt: £13.00 to a £1 stake. Pool: £3,091.00 - 236.76 winning tickets. **Jonathan Neesom**

2739 REDCAR (L-H)

Tuesday, May 31

OFFICIAL GOING: Good to firm (9.3)

Wind: Strong against Weather: Heavy grey cloud

2771 IRISH STALLION FARMS EBF FILLIES' NOVICE MEDIAN AUCTION STKS (PLUS 10 RACE) 6f

2:20 (2:20) (Class 5) 2-Y-O **£3,234** (£962; £481; £240) **Stalls** Centre

Form				RPR
	1		**Cheval Blanche (USA)** 2-9-0 0 JamieSpencer 4 (Michael Bell) *towards rr: gd hdwy on inner over 2f out: chsd ldr jst ins fnl f: sn rdn and kpt on strly to ld nr line* **4/1**2	71+
40	2	shd	**Mightaswellsmile**18 2219 2-9-0 0 TomEaves 2 (James Given) *led: rdn clr over 1f out: drvn and edgd lft ins fnl f: hdd and no ex nr line* **11/2**3	71
	3	1	**Coping Stone** 2-9-0 0 GrahamGibbons 6 (David Brown) *in tch: hdwy 1/2-way: chsd ldr over 1f out: sn rdn and kpt on same pce fnl f* **13/2**	67
	4	1	**Local Artist (IRE)** 2-9-0 0 PhillipMakin 3 (John Quinn) *towards rr: hdwy over 2f out: rdn over 1f out: styd on fnl f: nrst fin* **11/1**	64
	5	1/2	**Island Vision (IRE)** 2-9-0 0 FrederikTylicki 10 (David Simcock) *towards rr: swtchd rt to outer and gd hdwy over 2f out: rdn to chse ldrs over 1f out: kpt on same pce fnl f* **11/1**	63
00	6	hd	**Roys Dream**25 2007 2-9-0 0 TonyHamilton 5 (Kristin Stubbs) *prom: rdn along 2f out: drvn over 1f out: grad wknd* **28/1**	62
5	7	1	**Lady Cristal (IRE)**17 2254 2-9-0 0 JoeyHaynes 7 (K R Burke) *trckd ldrs: rdn along 2f out: sn one pce* **7/2**1	59
	8	hd	**Wakened (IRE)** 2-9-0 0 PJMcDonald 9 (Tom Dascombe) *towards rr: swtchd rt and racd wd over 2f out: hdwy wl over 1f out: sn rdn and no imp* **9/1**	58
	9	1 3/4	**Flawed Diamond (FR)** 2-9-0 0 DougieCostello 12 (K R Burke) *a towards rr* **18/1**	53
40	10	1	**Tranquil Tracy**16 2265 2-8-11 0 JacobButterfield(3) 1 (John Norton) *cl up: rdn along over 2f out: sn wknd* **80/1**	49
	11	3 3/4	**Lil's Affair (IRE)** 2-9-0 0 PaulMulrennan 13 (Bryan Smart) *chsd ldrs: rdn along over 2f out: sn wknd* **12/1**	37
6	12	5	**Queens Parade (IRE)**43 1520 2-9-0 0 JamesSullivan 8 (Sharon Watt) *a towards rr* **100/1**	21
	13	10	**Miss Island Ruler** 2-9-0 0 PaddyAspell 15 (Shaun Harris) *a bhd* **100/1**	

1m 15.14s (3.34) **Going Correction** +0.35s/f (Good) **13 Ran SP% 117.2**

Speed ratings (Par 90): **91,90,89,88,87 87,85,85,83,82 77,70,57**

CSF £25.52 TOTE £3.50: £1.30, £3.10, £3.00; EX 28.80 Trifecta £134.50.

Owner The Hon Mrs J M Corbett & C Wright **Bred** Klawervlei Stud **Trained** Newmarket, Suffolk

FOCUS

It was dry overnight and the going was given as good to firm (GoingStick: 9.3). There was a strong wind against the runners in the straight. There were one or two interesting newcomers and one of them came through.

2772 HIGH DEFINITION RACING UK MAIDEN H'CAP 1m 6f 19y

2:50 (2:51) (Class 6) (0-65,62) 3-Y-O **£2,385** (£704; £352) **Stalls** Low

Form				RPR
00-4	1		**Dusky Raider (IRE)**38 1619 3-9-7 62 PaulMulrennan 9 (Michael Dods) *prom: cl up 5f out: chal 3f out: led 2f out and sn rdn: drvn along on inner ent fnl f: kpt on gamely towards fin* **5/1**	66
0023	2	nk	**Mikro Polemistis (IRE)**21 2124 3-8-12 53 BenCurtis 4 (Brian Ellison) *hld up and bhd: hdwy 4f out: swtchd rt to outer and gd hdwy wl over 2f out: chal wl over 1f out: rdn and ev ch whn edgd persistently lft ins fnl f: no ex towards fin* **9/2**3	57
0043	3	nse	**Falcon's Fire (IRE)**15 2308 3-8-13 54 PhillipMakin 7 (Keith Dalgleish) *hld up and bhd: stdy hdwy over 3f out: trckd ldrs over 2f out: rdn to chal over 1f out: drvn and ev ch ins fnl f: no ex nr fin* **7/2**2	58
00-6	4	hd	**Hazely**36 1698 3-8-6 47 PJMcDonald 10 (James Bethell) *trckd ldrs: hdwy over 3f out: cl up 2f out: sn rdn: drvn and ev ch ent fnl f tl no ex towards fin* **22/1**	51
-400	5	4 1/2	**Tred Softly (IRE)**21 2124 3-9-2 57 (b1) TomEaves 1 (John Quinn) *trckd ldrs: smooth hdwy 3f out: effrt 2f out and sn rdn: drvn over 1f out and sn one pce* **28/1**	55
-422	6	3	**Adherence**14 2348 3-9-5 60 BarryMcHugh 3 (Tony Coyle) *led: pushed along 4f out: rdn 3f out: hdd 2f out and grad wknd* **5/2**1	54
60-0	7	2	**Kerry Icon**15 2308 3-8-7 48 RoystonFfrench 6 (Iain Jardine) *t.k.h early: hld up: a towards rr* **14/1**	39
5650	8	hd	**Ready Steady (USA)**36 1698 3-8-9 50 RaulDaSilva 8 (David Loughnane) *trckd ldrs on inner: pushed along over 3f out: sn rdn and wknd wl over 2f out* **100/1**	41
40-0	9	14	**Miss Marina Bay**21 2124 3-9-0 55 RyanPowell 2 (Sir Mark Prescott Bt) *hld up towards rr: pushed along over 4f out: sn rdn: drvn 3f out and sn bhd* **8/1**	28

3m 7.04s (2.34) **Going Correction** +0.125s/f (Good) **9 Ran SP% 112.2**

Speed ratings (Par 97): **98,97,97,97,95 93,92,92,84**

CSF £26.40 CT £87.15 TOTE £5.90: £1.40, £1.60, £2.00; EX 25.30 Trifecta £121.70.

Owner A Wynn Williams & D Graham **Bred** Spratstown Bloodstock Ltd **Trained** Denton, Co Durham

FOCUS

A moderate staying handicap, and the first four finished in a heap.

2773 JACK AND DORIS OWENS MEMORIAL H'CAP 1m

3:20 (3:24) (Class 5) (0-70,73) 4-Y-O+ **£2,911** (£866; £432; £216) **Stalls** Centre

Form				RPR
6026	1		**Shamaheart (IRE)**14 2345 6-9-7 70 (p) DavidAllan 11 (Geoffrey Harker) *t.k.h: hld up: effrt whn nt clr run wl over 1f out: rdn and gd hdwy to ld wl ins fnl f: hld on wl* **8/1**3	79+
6-03	2	nse	**City Of Night (IRE)**14 2329 4-8-8 57 (e) ConnorBeasley 10 (Julie Camacho) *dwlt: hld up: gd hdwy on nr side of gp to dispute ld ins fnl f: kpt on wl: jst hld* **12/1**	65
0-34	3	1/2	**Ferdy (IRE)**38 1632 7-8-7 56 oh2 PJMcDonald 17 (Paul Green) *hld up: hdwy over 2f out: rdn to dispute ld briefly ins fnl f: kpt on: hld nr fin* **25/1**	63
5032	4	1	**Lawyer (IRE)**3 2673 5-9-4 67 GrahamGibbons 5 (David Barron) *t.k.h: hld up in rr: n.m.r 1/2-way: effrt and rdn over 1f out: kpt on same pce last 100ds* **7/2**1	72
0-00	5	1/2	**Almuhalab**11 2441 5-8-13 62 JamesSullivan 1 (Ruth Carr) *prom: effrt and ev ch over 1f out to ins fnl f: kpt on same pce last 100yds* **8/1**3	65
4-25	6	1/2	**Newmarket Warrior (IRE)**8 2529 5-9-6 69 (p) RoystonFfrench 18 (Iain Jardine) *t.k.h: hld up: stdy hdwy over 2f out: rdn over 1f out: kpt on same pce ins fnl f* **20/1**	71
5-00	7	nk	**Zeshov (IRE)**21 2121 5-9-5 68 BarryMcHugh 3 (Rebecca Bastiman) *hld up: hdwy on far side of gp to ld over 1f out: hdd ins fnl f: sn no ex* **14/1**	69
4255	8	shd	**Cliff (IRE)**10 2491 6-9-5 68 TonyHamilton 13 (Nigel Tinkler) *trckd ldrs: rdn along over 1f out: outpcd ins fnl f* **12/1**	69
3-00	9	1/2	**Inshaa**14 2347 4-9-7 70 GrahamLee 9 (Michael Herrington) *hld up in tch: rdn along appr fnl f: sn outpcd* **9/1**	70
5-00	10	hd	**Grandest**75 964 5-8-1 57 BenRobinson(7) 15 (Brian Ellison) *missed break: bhd tl hdwy over 1f out: kpt on fnl f: nt pce to chal* **20/1**	57
540	11	1	**Robero**96 703 4-9-1 64 BenCurtis 8 (Brian Ellison) *t.k.h: in tch: effrt on far side of gp over 1f out: wknd ins fnl f* **4/1**2	61
-100	12	1	**Thello**14 2329 4-8-7 56 oh1 JasonHart 16 (Nigel Tinkler) *t.k.h: in tch tl rdn and wknd over 1f out* **50/1**	51
50-0	13	2 3/4	**Euro Mac**15 2303 4-8-7 56 oh11 DuranFentiman 4 (Neville Bycroft) *dwlt: t.k.h in rr: hdwy over 2f out: rdn and wknd fnl f* **66/1**	44
230-	14	1	**Broctune Papa Gio**347 3365 9-8-12 64 JoeDoyle(3) 6 (Keith Reveley) *t.k.h: cl up: effrt and rdn over 1f out: wknd fnl f* **20/1**	50
000-	15	1/2	**Ella's Delight (IRE)**228 7256 6-9-0 63 DavidNolan 12 (Martin Todhunter) *midfield: pushed along and lost pl over 1f out: sn btn* **50/1**	48
-000	16	1 1/4	**First Sargeant**9 2507 6-9-2 65 (p) DougieCostello 7 (Lawrence Mullaney) *slowly away: sn rcvrd and led after 1f: drvn and hdd over 1f out: sn btn* **33/1**	47
000-	17	4	**Slim Chance (IRE)**255 6545 7-9-1 64 AndrewElliott 14 (Simon West) *t.k.h: led 1f: cl up tl rdn and wknd over 1f out* **66/1**	36

1m 40.47s (3.87) **Going Correction** +0.35s/f (Good) **17 Ran SP% 124.5**

Speed ratings (Par 103): **94,93,93,92,91 91,91,91,90,90 89,88,85,84,84 82,78**

CSF £90.84 CT £2397.78 TOTE £9.10: £2.00, £3.70, £5.30, £1.60; EX 41.70 Trifecta £2189.00.

Owner A S Ward **Bred** Gus Roche **Trained** Thirkleby, N Yorks

FOCUS

This handicap was dominated by those ridden patiently out the back. The winner is rated back to his best.

2774 RACING UK HD ON SKY432 MEDIAN AUCTION MAIDEN STKS 1m 2f

3:50 (3:53) (Class 5) 3-5-Y-O **£2,911** (£866; £432; £216) **Stalls** Low

Form				RPR
63-	1		**Guy Fawkes**169 8225 3-9-0 0 GrahamGibbons 6 (William Haggas) *trckd ldr: led after 2f: pushed clr 2f out: readily* **2/1**1	88+
4	2	3 1/4	**Zanjabeel**35 1767 3-9-0 0 (t) GrahamLee 9 (Simon Crisford) *trckd wnr after 2f: rdn along over 12f out: drvn wl over 1f out: sn no imp* **9/4**2	74
03	3	3	**Dream Factory (IRE)**27 1961 3-9-0 0 JFEgan 2 (Marco Botti) *hld up in tch: hdwy 3f out: rdn along over 2f out: kpt on appr fnl f: nrst fin* **14/1**	68
252	4	4	**Kings Gold (IRE)**14 2327 3-9-0 75 PaulMulrennan 3 (Michael Dods) *hld up in rr: hdwy 3f out: rdn along 2f out: sn drvn and n.d* **5/1**3	60
0-6	5	3/4	**Next Train's Gone**41 1575 3-9-0 0 JackGarritty 8 (James Eustace) *chsd ldrs: rdn along over 3f out: sn drvn and wknd* **16/1**	59
52-0	6	1 3/4	**Like No Other**21 2123 3-9-0 70 DavidAllan 10 (Les Eyre) *a towards rr* **33/1**	55
	7	3/4	**Princesse Eva (FR)**322 3-8-9 72 FrederikTylicki 1 (James Fanshawe) *chsd ldrs: effrt over 3f out: rdn along wl over 2f out: sn wknd* **13/2**	49
	8	27	**Daleside** 3-8-9 0 JamieSpencer 4 (Michael Bell) *dwlt and a in rr: outpcd and bhd fnl 2f* **14/1**	
0-3	9	32	**Ballycoyle Girl (IRE)**29 1920 3-8-9 0 DuranFentiman 7 (Tony Coyle) *led 2f: chsd ldng pair: pushed along 1/2-way: rdn and lost pl over 3f out: sn bhd* **150/1**	

2m 6.64s (-0.46) **Going Correction** +0.125s/f (Good) **9 Ran SP% 116.9**

Speed ratings (Par 103): **106,103,101,97,97 95,95,73,48**

CSF £6.78 TOTE £3.00: £1.30, £1.40, £3.60; EX 8.70 Trifecta £59.60.

Owner The Queen **Bred** The Queen **Trained** Newmarket, Suffolk

FOCUS

This proved straightforward for the favourite, who looks a useful handicapper in the making. The 2nd and 3rd are rated close to their AW maiden form.

2775 RACING UK IN GLORIOUS HD H'CAP 5f

4:20 (4:20) (Class 4) (0-85,85) 4-Y-O+ **£6,469** (£1,925; £962; £481) **Stalls** Centre

Form				RPR
4-40	1		**Fredricka**17 2261 5-9-4 82 JasonHart 6 (David Barron) *trckd ldrs: hdwy over 1f out: chal ins fnl f: rdn to ld last 75yds* **8/1**	89
-400	2	hd	**Lexington Place**17 2258 6-9-6 84 JamesSullivan 5 (Ruth Carr) *t.k.h early: hld up in tch: hdwy over 1f out: rdn to chal ins fnl f: ev ch tl no ex nr line* **5/1**2	90
-003	3	shd	**Bashiba (IRE)**15 2305 5-9-0 78 (t) TomEaves 2 (Nigel Tinkler) *dwlt and wnt rt s: in rr: hdwy 2f out: nt clr run and swtchd rt ent fnl f: sn rdn and styd on strly towards fin* **7/1**3	84
0-00	4	1 1/4	**Captain Dunne (IRE)**17 2261 11-8-10 79 RachelRichardson(5) 7 (Tim Easterby) *led: rdn ent fnl f: hdd last 75yds: hld whn n.m.r nr fin* **11/1**	80
0-01	5	1 3/4	**Landing Night (IRE)**11 2426 4-9-1 79 (p) PJMcDonald 8 (Ann Duffield) *t.k.h early: trckd ldrs: chsd ldr over 2f out: rdn over 1f out: drvn and wknd fnl f* **7/1**3	74
0516	6	1/2	**Rusty Rocket (IRE)**11 2426 7-9-5 83 PaulMulrennan 11 (Paul Green) *cl up: rdn along 2f out: sn drvn and wknd* **17/2**	76
230/	7	3	**Ziggy Lee**640 5925 10-9-0 78 DougieCostello 1 (Lawrence Mullaney) *chsd ldrs on outer: rdn along wl over 1f out: sn wknd* **66/1**	61
6-43	8	1	**Just Us Two (IRE)**17 2261 4-9-7 85 JamieSpencer 4 (Robert Cowell) *trckd ldrs: effrt wl over 1f out: sn rdn and btn* **13/8**1	64

59.52s (0.92) **Going Correction** +0.35s/f (Good) **8 Ran SP% 111.2**

Speed ratings (Par 105): **106,105,105,103,100 99,95,93**

CSF £44.88 CT £285.43 TOTE £8.50: £3.20, £1.50, £1.90; EX 49.40 Trifecta £336.00.

Owner Ron Hull **Bred** J C Parsons & J J Gilmartin **Trained** Maunby, N Yorks

FOCUS
Once again, with the strong headwind working against those in the front rank, the finish was contested by those who had been held up and got plenty of cover. The winner is rated back to her best.

2776 RACING UK PROFITS RETURNED TO RACING H'CAP (DIV I) 6f
4:50 (4:51) (Class 5) (0-70,70) 3-Y-O **£2,911** (£866; £432; £216) **Stalls** Centre

Form RPR
-664 **1** **In My Place**[14] 2336 3-9-0 **63**........(p) TonyHamilton 11 67
(Richard Fahey) *hld up towards rr: swtchd rt to outer and hdwy wl over 1f out: rdn to chal and hung lft ent fnl f: edgd lft and led last 120yds: kpt on* **7/1**
600- **2** *nk* **Reinforced**[228] 7253 3-8-7 **56**........ ConnorBeasley 2 59
(Michael Dods) *trckd ldrs: hdwy 2f out: rdn to chal over 1f out: slt ld appr fnl f: hdd last 120yds: kpt on* **10/1**
-402 **3** *nk* **Lady Wootton**[8] 2534 3-8-10 **59**........(b) JamieSpencer 9 61
(Keith Dalgleish) *hld up towards rr: hdwy whn nt clr run and swtchd lft over 1f out: rdn and hdwy ent fnl f: sn ev ch tl drvn and no ex towards fin* **5/1**[3]
6-50 **4** *2 1/4* **King's Currency**[17] 2255 3-8-8 **57**........ TomEaves 10 52
(Jedd O'Keeffe) *in rr: swtchd lft and hdwy over 1f out: sn rdn and styd on wl fnl f: nrst fin* **20/1**
0-36 **5** *nse* **Dream Farr (IRE)**[30] 1894 3-9-6 **69**........(t) AntonioFresu 7 64
(Ed Walker) *in tch: hdwy 2f out: rdn to chal ent fnl f: sn drvn and kpt on same pce* **4/1**[2]
534 **6** *2 1/2* **Bromley Cross (IRE)**[45] 1494 3-9-4 **67**........ BenCurtis 5 54
(Brian Ellison) *trckd ldrs: hdwy and cl up 2f out: rdn over 1f out: hmpd ent fnl f: sn one pce* **12/1**
-352 **7** *1 1/2* **Waneen (IRE)**[7] 2561 3-9-7 **70**........ JFEgan 3 52
(Joseph Tuite) *led: pushed along over 2f out: rdn wl over 1f out: drvn and hdd appr fnl f: wknd* **7/2**[1]
40-0 **8** *3/4* **Rose Eclair**[11] 2428 3-9-0 **63**........ DavidAllan 6 43
(Tim Easterby) *cl up: rdn along 2f out: wkng whn hmpd ent fnl f* **12/1**
06-4 **9** *1 1/4* **The Armed Man**[31] 1849 3-9-2 **65**........ AndrewElliott 4 41
(Chris Fairhurst) *cl up: chal over 2f out: rdn wl over 1f out: drvn and hld whn hmpd ent fnl f* **10/1**
265- **10** *4 1/2* **Cautionary Note**[252] 6613 3-8-11 **60**........ RoystonFfrench 8 21
(Nigel Tinkler) *chsd ldrs: rdn along over 2f out: sn drvn and wknd* **33/1**

1m 14.58s (2.78) **Going Correction** +0.35s/f (Good) **10** Ran SP% **112.7**
Speed ratings (Par 99): **95,94,94,91,91 87,85,84,83,77**
CSF £72.13 CT £388.51 TOTE £8.00: £2.70, £3.30, £1.70; EX 101.90 Trifecta £595.60.
Owner A Rhodes Haulage And P Timmins **Bred** Sean Gorman **Trained** Musley Bank, N Yorks
■ Stewards' Enquiry : Ben Curtis two-day ban: careless riding (Jun 19-20)

FOCUS
Following the pattern set in the earlier races on the straight track, getting plenty of cover proved crucial as they ran into a strong headwind.

2777 RACING UK PROFITS RETURNED TO RACING H'CAP (DIV II) 6f
5:20 (5:26) (Class 5) (0-70,70) 3-Y-O **£2,911** (£866; £432; £216) **Stalls** Centre

Form RPR
0-03 **1** **Laila Honiwillow**[17] 2255 3-8-9 **58**........ JackGarritty 11 66
(Jedd O'Keeffe) *trckd ldrs: hdwy to ld wl over 1f out: sn rdn: drvn and edgd lft ins fnl f: kpt on wl towards fin* **9/2**[3]
6-00 **2** *nk* **East Street Revue**[31] 1847 3-8-8 **57**........(b[1]) DuranFentiman 4 64
(Tim Easterby) *in tch: hdwy on outer over 1f out: sn rdn and styd on to chal ins fnl f: drvn and no ex towards fin* **20/1**
40-6 **3** *1* **Lady Nahema (IRE)**[48] 1420 3-9-0 **63**........ PJMcDonald 1 67
(Ann Duffield) *hld up in rr: hdwy 2f out: sn swtchd rt to outer and rdn over 1f out: chal ent fnl f and rdr dropped whip: kpt on* **18/1**
21-3 **4** *nse* **Rose Marmara**[14] 2334 3-9-7 **70**........ JamieSpencer 6 75
(Richard Fahey) *towards rr: hdwy wl over 1f out: sn rdn and styd on wl fnl f: nrst fin* **2/1**[1]
-331 **5** *nk* **Mr Orange (IRE)**[17] 2255 3-8-12 **61**........ GrahamGibbons 10 64
(Paul Midgley) *trckd ldrs: hdwy over 2f out and sn cl up: rdn and ev ch over 1f out: drvn ent fnl f: wknd* **11/4**[2]
655 **6** *2 3/4* **Bit Of A Quirke**[24] 2039 3-8-10 **59**........ JasonHart 7 53
(Mark Walford) *prom: rdn along over 2f out: sn drvn and wknd* **14/1**
5-04 **7** *10* **Arize (IRE)**[17] 2255 3-9-2 **65**........ TomEaves 9 27
(David Brown) *led: pushed along 3f out: rdn and hdd 2f out: sn drvn and hung bdly lft over 1f out: bhd and eased after* **8/1**
5-33 **P** **Penny Pot Lane**[14] 2336 3-9-4 **67**........ GeorgeChaloner 3
(Richard Whitaker) *plld hrd and cl up tl lost pl qckly after 1 1/2f: lost action and p.u* **7/1**

1m 13.41s (1.61) **Going Correction** +0.35s/f (Good) **8** Ran SP% **118.5**
Speed ratings (Par 99): **103,102,101,101,100 97,83,**
CSF £88.10 CT £1501.23 TOTE £6.20: £2.50, £5.70, £3.50; EX 89.50 Trifecta £1354.50.
Owner Caron & Paul Chapman **Bred** J P Coggan **Trained** Middleham Moor, N Yorks
■ Its Only Mossy (9-2) was withdrawn. Rule 4 applies to bets struck at board prices prior to withdrawal not to SP bets. Deduction - 15p in the pound. New market formed.

FOCUS
In contrast to previous races on the straight track, the hold-up horses did not come through to dominate, a steady gallop probably being the reason. The winner was better than the bare form last time and reversed placings with the 5th.

2778 WATCH RACING UK IN HD AMATEUR RIDERS' MAIDEN H'CAP 6f
5:55 (6:00) (Class 6) (0-65,62) 4-Y-O+ **£2,305** (£709; £354) **Stalls** Centre

Form RPR
5465 **1** **Giant Spark**[24] 2053 4-10-10 **58**........ MrSWalker 6 79+
(Paul Midgley) *prom: hdwy to ld over 2f out: clr whn shkn up over 1f out: eased ins fnl f: readily* **6/4**[1]
0-02 **2** *9* **Poolstock**[13] 2359 4-10-1 **56**........(p) MissSEDods[(7)] 10 50
(Michael Dods) *prom: effrt and chsd (clr) wnr over 1f out: kpt on fnl f: no imp* **9/2**[2]
4004 **3** *3 1/4* **Intense Starlet (IRE)**[11] 2428 5-11-0 **62**........ MrJohnDawson 2 46
(Marjorie Fife) *prom: pushed along over 2f out: kpt on same pce fr over 1f out* **14/1**
30-4 **4** *1 3/4* **Isntshesomething**[35] 1754 4-10-4 **55**........ KaineWood[(3)] 8 34
(Richard Guest) *led tl rdn and hdd over 2f out: no ex and lost 2nd over 1f out* **8/1**
5462 **5** *3/4* **Compton River**[11] 2423 4-10-3 **54**........ MrThomasGreatrex[(3)] 13 31
(Bryan Smart) *awkward s: hld up: stdy hdwy 1/2-way: rdn and hung lft wl over 1f out: sn no imp* **7/1**[3]
040 **6** *1* **Vecheka (IRE)**[12] 2409 5-10-1 **54**........(v[1]) MrJoeWright[(5)] 12 28
(Micky Hammond) *slowly away: sn in tch: rdn and outpcd over 2f out: n.d after* **9/1**
6355 **7** *nk* **Natalia**[35] 1768 7-9-7 **48** oh3........(v) DrMVoikhansky[(7)] 5 21
(Sarah Hollinshead) *s.i.s: bhd and outpcd: pushed along and hung lft over 2f out: sn no imp* **14/1**
4-63 **8** *1 1/4* **Charlie's Approval (IRE)**[24] 2047 4-10-1 **49**........(v[1]) MissCWalton 14 18
(Ben Haslam) *hld up: pushed along over 2f out: sn outpcd: btn over 1f out* **20/1**
000 **9** *2 1/4* **Abonos (IRE)**[37] 1676 4-9-9 **48** oh3........ MissPBridgwater[(5)] 3 10
(Simon West) *cl up tl rdn and wknd 2f out* **66/1**
0-66 **10** *9* **Island Express (IRE)**[81] 902 9-10-0 **48** oh1........(tp) MissADeniel 11
(Ann Stokell) *midfield: pushed along and struggling 1/2-way: sn btn* **100/1**

1m 15.31s (3.51) **Going Correction** +0.35s/f (Good) **10** Ran SP% **112.4**
Speed ratings (Par 101): **90,78,73,71,70 69,68,66,63,51**
CSF £7.47 CT £65.71 TOTE £2.40: £1.40, £1.70, £3.10; EX 8.20 Trifecta £58.10.
Owner Frank Brady **Bred** Frank Brady **Trained** Westow, N Yorks
■ Grenade (25-1) was withdrawn not under orders. Rule 4 does not apply.

FOCUS
This moderate amateur riders' handicap proved one-sided. The winner stood out on his profile and routed these.
T/Jkpt: Not won. T/Plt: £81.50 to a £1 stake. Pool: £54,640.33 - 489.32 winning tickets. T/Qpdt: £19.20 to a £1 stake. Pool: £5,557.76 - 213.80 winning tickets. **Joe Rowntree & Richard Young**

2559 WOLVERHAMPTON (A.W) (L-H)
Tuesday, May 31

OFFICIAL GOING: Tapeta: standard
Wind: moderate against Weather: overcast, showers

2779 FOLLOW AT THE RACES ON TWITTER NOVICE STKS (PLUS 10 RACE) 5f 216y (Tp)
6:10 (6:12) (Class 4) 2-Y-O **£3,946** (£1,174; £586; £293) **Stalls** Low

Form RPR
4 **1** **Pleaseletmewin (IRE)**[12] 2390 2-9-2 0........ FMBerry 4 82
(Ralph Beckett) *chsd ldrs: rdn 2f out: chal ent fnl f: kpt on: led post* **6/4**[1]
3 **2** *shd* **Zamjar**[14] 2319 2-9-2 0........ SilvestreDeSousa 2 81
(Ed Dunlop) *trckd ldr: rdn over 1f out: led narrowly 1f out: kpt on: hdd post* **15/8**[2]
0512 **3** *2 3/4* **Who Told Jo Jo (IRE)**[25] 2014 2-9-0 0........ NathanEvans[(5)] 6 76
(Bill Turner) *led: rdn 2f out: hdd 1f out: no ex* **14/1**
2 **4** *nk* **Sidewinder (IRE)**[43] 1520 2-9-2 0........ RichardKingscote 5 72
(Tom Dascombe) *dwlt: hld up: rdn wl over 1f out: kpt on ins fnl f: nvr threatened ldrs* **3/1**[3]
2 **5** *3 3/4* **Conistone**[17] 2254 2-8-11 0........ TedDurcan 3 56
(James Bethell) *in tch: rdn over 2f out: wknd appr fnl f* **8/1**
4 **6** *7* **Valley Lodge**[15] 2311 2-8-13 0........ ShelleyBirkett[(3)] 1 40
(Julia Feilden) *s.i.s: hld up: rdn over 2f out: sn wknd* **66/1**

1m 15.08s (0.58) **Going Correction** -0.125s/f (Stan) **6** Ran SP% **119.1**
Speed ratings (Par 95): **91,90,87,86,81 72**
CSF £5.05 TOTE £2.50: £1.50, £1.70; EX 8.00 Trifecta £37.90.
Owner R Roberts **Bred** Ballykilbride Stud **Trained** Kimpton, Hants

FOCUS
This novice event proved a lively betting heat. It was run at a modest pace and the two market leaders came clear. Improvement from the first two, with the 3rd/4th helping to set the opening level.

2780 DOWNLOAD THE AT THE RACES APP MAIDEN STKS 7f 32y (Tp)
6:40 (6:42) (Class 5) 3-Y-O **£3,040** (£904; £452; £226) **Stalls** High

Form RPR
46- **1** **Mickey (IRE)**[285] 5565 3-9-5 0........(t) RichardKingscote 5 83+
(Tom Dascombe) *trckd ldng pair: pushed along and qcknd to ld 1f out: sn clr: comf* **1/1**[1]
6-4 **2** *3 3/4* **Shadad (IRE)**[13] 2375 3-9-5 0........ FMBerry 7 72
(Ralph Beckett) *trckd ldng pair: rdn over 2f out: kpt on to go 2nd 110yds out: no ch w wnr* **11/4**[2]
0 **3** *1 1/2* **Tom's Rock (IRE)**[12] 2414 3-9-5 0........ RobertHavlin 1 68
(John Butler) *dwlt: hld up in midfield: pushed along over 2f out: hdwy over 1f out: styd on to go 3rd 50yds out* **125/1**
64 **4** *1 1/4* **Fly True**[15] 2303 3-9-0 0........ MartinLane 4 60
(Jeremy Gask) *pressed ldr: rdn 2f out: led appr fnl f: hdd 1f out: wknd* **20/1**
4 **5** *1 1/2* **Check 'Em Tuesday (IRE)**[36] 1723 3-9-0 0........ DaleSwift 2 56
(Daniel Mark Loughnane) *led narrowly: rdn over 2f out: hdd appr fnl f: wknd* **25/1**
6 *2 3/4* **Dasheen** 3-9-5 0........ FrannyNorton 9 54
(Mark Johnston) *hld up: pushed along 3f out: nvr threatened* **16/1**[3]
0- **7** *6* **Excellent Alibi**[276] 5851 3-9-5 0........(t) DavidProbert 3 37
(Andrew Balding) *dwlt: a towards rr* **22/1**
60 **8** *1 3/4* **Outback Guy (IRE)**[11] 2443 3-9-5 0........ LiamJones 6 33
(Kevin Frost) *midfield: rdn over 2f out: sn wknd* **125/1**

1m 27.55s (-1.25) **Going Correction** -0.125s/f (Stan) **8** Ran SP% **97.1**
Speed ratings (Par 99): **102,97,96,94,92 89,82,80**
CSF £2.26 TOTE £1.70: £1.10, £1.10, £4.60; EX 3.10 Trifecta £103.50.
Owner Mrs Janet Lowe & Tom Dascombe **Bred** Viscountess Brookeborough **Trained** Malpas, Cheshire
■ Istiqlaal (3-1) was withdrawn. Rule 4 applies to all bets. Deduction - 25p in the pound.

FOCUS
They went a fair pace in this modest maiden. no depth,

2781 BLACK COUNTRY CHAMBER OF COMMERCE H'CAP 1m 4f 50y (Tp)
7:10 (7:10) (Class 6) (0-60,60) 4-Y-O+ **£2,587** (£770; £384; £192) **Stalls** Low

Form RPR
1 **Lady Makfi (IRE)**[231] 7206 4-8-13 **52**........ MartinHarley 7 60+
(Johnny Farrelly) *hld up: pushed along and gd hdwy over 1f out: rdn to ld 1f out: edgd lft ins fnl f: kpt on* **28/1**
0-62 **2** *1 1/2* **Weardiditallgorong**[20] 2144 4-9-1 **54**........(b) DavidProbert 5 61
(Des Donovan, Ire) *hld up in midfield: hdwy 2f out: rdn to chal appr fnl f: kpt on: hmpd nr fin* **7/2**[1]
5040 **3** *1 1/4* **Chauvelin**[22] 2110 5-8-7 **46** oh1........(b) FrannyNorton 2 50
(Richard Guest) *slowly away: sn rcvrd to trck ldrs: led over 1f out: sn rdn: hdd 1f out: one pce* **7/1**
3125 **4** *1/2* **Happy Jack (IRE)**[28] 1578 5-9-0 **53**........(b) PatDobbs 12 56
(Michael Wigham) *midfield: hdwy to trck ldr gng wl 2f out: rdn appr fnl f: one pce* **5/1**[2]

-320 **5** 5 **Head Coach**[18] 2205 4-9-2 **58**.....(p) DannyBrock(3) 8 53
(Jane Chapple-Hyam) *hld up: pushed along and sme hdwy over 2f out: rdn over 1f out: sn no further imp* **7/1**

6034 **6** 10 **Broughtons Berry (IRE)**[12] 2400 5-8-9 **48**..... SilvestreDeSousa 3 30
(Willie Musson) *prom: led over 7f out: rdn over 3f out: hdd over 1f out: wknd* **6/1**

5260 **7** 2 3/4 **Well Owd Mon**[22] 2110 6-8-12 **51**.....(p) SamHitchcott 10 26
(Sarah Hollinshead) *slowly away: hld up: rdn over 3f out: minor hdwy over 2f out: wknd over 1f out* **25/1**

2-04 **8** 6 **Street Art (IRE)**[57] 1239 4-9-0 **53**..... TedDurcan 6 18
(Mike Murphy) *hld up: rdn over 2f out: sn wknd* **11/1**

3-06 **9** nk **Super Icon**[4] 2635 4-9-7 **60**..... MartinDwyer 9 25
(Malcolm Saunders) *sn trckd ldrs: rdn 3f out: wknd over 1f out* **25/1**

0626 **10** 10 **Invincible Wish (IRE)**[20] 2144 4-9-4 **60**..... RobHornby(3) 4 9
(Trevor Wall) *trckd ldrs: rdn over 3f out: sn wknd* **11/2**[3]

-000 **11** 38 **Strawberryfields**[42] 1547 4-8-0 **46** oh1.....(p) MitchGodwin(7) 1
(Des Donovan, Ire) *led: hdd over 7f: lost pl qckly over 4f out: sn wl bhd: eased* **100/1**

2m 37.71s (-3.09) **Going Correction** -0.125s/f (Stan) **11** Ran SP% **114.0**
Speed ratings (Par 101): **105,104,103,102,99 92,91,87,86,80 54**
CSF £117.71 CT £782.17 TOTE £28.60: £6.30, £1.40, £2.60; EX 229.50 Trifecta £1571.40.
Owner The Lansdowners **Bred** Coleman Bloodstock Limited **Trained** Enmore, Somerset

FOCUS
A weak handicap that looked wide open.

2782 VISIT ATTHERACES.COM H'CAP — 2m 119y (Tp)
7:40 (7:42) (Class 4) (0-85,84) 4-Y-O+ **£4,851** (£1,443; £721; £360) **Stalls** Low

Form RPR

0-10 **1** **Stonecutter (IRE)**[38] 1642 5-9-10 **84**..... RichardKingscote 9 92
(James Unett) *trckd ldr: rdn over 2f out: led ins fnl f: edgd lft: styd on* **5/1**[2]

3241 **2** 1 1/2 **Zakatal**[35] 1766 10-9-6 **80**..... MartinHarley 11 86
(Rebecca Menzies) *led at stdy pce: qcknd pce over 2f out: hdd ins fnl f: kpt on* **12/1**

3/11 **3** 1 1/4 **Minstrels Gallery (IRE)**[22] 2105 7-9-1 **75**..... JimCrowley 8 80
(Lucy Wadham) *trckd ldr: rdn over 2f out: one pce* **5/2**[1]

/2-0 **4** 1 **Mister Bob (GER)**[22] 2105 7-8-7 **68**.....(p) TedDurcan 6 71
(James Bethell) *midfield: pushed along over 2f out: bit short of room appr fnl f: swtchd rt: styd on wl: wnt 4th nr fin* **20/1**

/0-1 **5** nk **Planetoid (IRE)**[29] 1177 8-9-8 **82**.....(b) TimmyMurphy 10 85
(Jim Best) *in tch: rdn over 2f out: one pce: lost 4th nr fin* **16/1**

3646 **6** 3/4 **Communicator**[38] 1642 8-9-7 **81**.....(v) DavidProbert 3 83
(Andrew Balding) *midfield: rdn over 2f out: one pce and nvr threatened* **8/1**

0-00 **7** 1/2 **Arty Campbell (IRE)**[12] 2392 6-8-11 **78**..... JoshuaBryan(7) 5 79
(Bernard Llewellyn) *hld up: rdn over 2f out: kpt on ins fnl f: nvr threatened* **12/1**

1304 **8** 1/2 **Spiritoftomintoul**[12] 2392 7-9-2 **79**.....(t) GeorgeDowning(3) 1 80
(Tony Carroll) *hld up: rdn over 2f out: nvr threatened* **12/1**

35-3 **9** 1/2 **Full Day**[61] 1166 5-9-0 **79**.....(p) CallumShepherd(5) 2 79
(Brian Ellison) *hld up: nvr threatened* **6/1**[3]

4123 **10** 1/2 **Heart Locket**[42] 1552 4-8-6 **73**..... NathanEvans(5) 7 73
(Michael Easterby) *in tch: rdn over 2f out: wknd fnl f* **14/1**

00-0 **11** 5 **Kashgar**[12] 2392 7-8-10 **75**.....(t) RachealKneller(5) 4 69
(Bernard Llewellyn) *dwlt: a in rr* **50/1**

3m 43.25s (-0.45) **Going Correction** -0.125s/f (Stan)
WFA 4 from 5yo+ 2lb **11** Ran SP% **113.0**
Speed ratings (Par 105): **96,95,94,94,94 93,93,93,93,92 90**
CSF £60.96 CT £182.45 TOTE £7.40: £3.10, £1.20, £1.90; EX 56.50 Trifecta £133.40.
Owner Northern Line Racing Ltd **Bred** Gigginstown House Stud **Trained** Wolverhampton, West Midlands

FOCUS
Not a bad staying handicap. They were strung out early, but didn't go quick and it paid to race handily.

2783 FOLLOW AT THE RACES ON INSTAGRAM FILLIES' H'CAP — 1m 141y (Tp)
8:10 (8:13) (Class 5) (0-75,75) 3-Y-O+ **£3,040** (£904; £452; £226) **Stalls** Low

Form RPR

4-43 **1** **Pietrafiore (IRE)**[10] 2483 3-8-12 **72**..... WilliamBuick 4 79+
(Charlie Appleby) *hld up in midfield: rdn and hdwy over 1f out: led 110yds out: kpt on* **15/8**[1]

-141 **2** 3/4 **Bocking End (IRE)**[22] 2108 3-8-11 **74**..... LouisSteward(3) 2 79
(Michael Bell) *led: rdn over 1f out: hung rt appr fnl f: hdd 110yds out: one pce* **5/1**[3]

61-5 **3** 1 3/4 **Crowning Glory (FR)**[19] 2178 3-8-9 **69**..... FMBerry 7 70
(Ralph Beckett) *in tch: rdn over 2f out: kpt on same pce* **7/1**

5-01 **4** 1 1/4 **Lady Bayside**[21] 2129 8-8-12 **64**..... JosephineGordon(5) 8 64
(Malcolm Saunders) *hld up: rdn over 2f out: styd on ins fnl f: wnt 4th post* **28/1**

03-4 **5** hd **My Favourite Thing**[49] 1392 3-9-0 **74**..... AndreaAtzeni 1 72
(Roger Varian) *trckd ldr: rdn over 2f out: wknd fnl 110yds* **3/1**[2]

6610 **6** shd **Mary Le Bow**[13] 2367 5-8-11 **63**.....(t) CallumShepherd(5) 9 62
(Victor Dartnall) *dwlt and swtchd lft s: hld up: rdn and hdwy on inner over 1f out: no ex fnl 110yds* **16/1**

05-0 **7** 1/2 **Happy Tidings**[19] 2177 3-9-1 **75**..... RichardKingscote 6 71
(Tom Dascombe) *trckd ldr: rdn over 2f out: wknd ins fnl f* **16/1**

-225 **8** 6 **Divine Joy**[47] 1429 3-8-11 **71**.....(b1) LiamJones 3 53
(Marco Botti) *midfield: rdn over 2f out: wknd over 1f out* **11/1**

1m 48.8s (-1.30) **Going Correction** -0.125s/f (Stan)
WFA 3 from 5yo+ 13lb **8** Ran SP% **112.5**
Speed ratings (Par 100): **100,99,97,96,96 96,95,90**
CSF £11.16 CT £52.26 TOTE £2.80: £1.20, £1.50, £2.20; EX 12.50 Trifecta £47.20.
Owner Godolphin **Bred** Darley **Trained** Newmarket, Suffolk

FOCUS
A modest fillies' handicap, made up of six 3yos. It was run at a fair enough pace and the winner built on her maiden promise.

2784 AT THE RACES VIRGIN 535 H'CAP — 1m 141y (Tp)
8:40 (8:44) (Class 6) (0-60,60) 3-Y-O **£2,587** (£770; £384; £192) **Stalls** Low

Form RPR

0-11 **1** **Therthaar**[35] 1768 3-9-2 **58**..... ThomasBrown(3) 7 71+
(Ismail Mohammed) *midfield: pushed along and stdy hdwy on outer fr 2f out: led 1f out: edgd lft: kpt on to go clr* **6/5**[1]

0341 **2** 4 1/2 **Ada Misobel (IRE)**[36] 1710 3-8-9 **53**.....(p) CallumShepherd(5) 5 55
(Roy Bowring) *trckd ldrs: rdn 3f out: ev ch over 1f out: one pce and no ch w wnr ins fnl f* **18/1**

006- **3** shd **Hymn For The Dudes**[302] 4929 3-8-11 **50**.....(t) MartinHarley 6 52
(John Berry) *trckd ldrs: shuffled bk a bit 2f out: short of room over 1f out: swtchd lft appr fnl f: rdn and kpt on* **25/1**

60-0 **4** 1/2 **Cape Crystal (IRE)**[22] 2108 3-8-13 **59**.....(b1) ManuelFernandes(7) 9 60
(Sir Mark Prescott Bt) *midfield towards outer: hdwy to trck ldrs over 3f out: rdn over 2f out: one pce fnl f* **18/1**

-040 **5** 1 1/4 **Elegant Annie**[13] 2366 3-9-2 **55**..... RyanClark 4 53
(Jonathan Portman) *led: rdn over 2f out: hdd 1f out: wknd ins fnl f* **66/1**

-110 **6** 1 **Free To Roam (IRE)**[29] 1927 3-9-1 **54**..... DavidProbert 1 50
(Philip McBride) *hld up: rdn over 2f out: kpt on ins fnl f* **9/1**

000- **7** 2 **A Boy Named Sue**[288] 5453 3-8-7 **46** oh1..... PatrickMathers 10 38
(Peter Niven) *hld up: rdn over 2f out: sme late hdwy: nvr threatened* **14/1**

06-6 **8** 1 1/2 **Alzebarh (IRE)**[14] 2321 3-8-11 **57**..... GeorgeWood(7) 2 46
(James Fanshawe) *midfield: rdn over 2f out: wknd fnl f* **16/1**

4-65 **9** 4 1/2 **Swansway**[18] 2212 3-9-7 **60**.....(v1) RichardKingscote 11 39
(Tom Dascombe) *prom: rdn over 2f out: wknd over 1f out: eased* **11/2**[2]

00-6 **10** 12 **Baz's Boy**[32] 1829 3-8-7 **46**..... SamHitchcott 12
(John Flint) *dwlt: a in rr* **33/1**

006 **11** 6 **Dream Trader (IRE)**[25] 2005 3-9-7 **60**.....(v1) AndreaAtzeni 13 1
(Roger Varian) *in tch: pushed along and lost pl 3f out: sn wknd: eased* **7/1**[3]

056 **12** 9 **Chapess**[27] 1961 3-9-1 **57**..... LouisSteward(3) 8
(Philip McBride) *hld up: rdn over 4f: sn btn: t.o* **33/1**

1m 47.98s (-2.12) **Going Correction** -0.125s/f (Stan) **12** Ran SP% **117.6**
Speed ratings (Par 97): **104,100,99,99,98 97,95,94,90,79 74,66**
CSF £25.72 CT £378.89 TOTE £2.10: £1.30, £4.00, £3.70; EX 23.10 Trifecta £702.00.
Owner Sultan Ali **Bred** Cheveley Park Stud Ltd **Trained** Newmarket, Suffolk

FOCUS
This moderate 3yo handicap was all about the highly progressive winner, and the form in behind is straightforward.

2785 FOLLOW @ATTHERACES ON TWITTER H'CAP — 5f 20y (Tp)
9:10 (9:11) (Class 6) (0-65,65) 3-Y-O+ **£2,587** (£770; £384; £192) **Stalls** Low

Form RPR

650 **1** **Dutch Archer**[31] 1849 3-9-4 **65**..... RichardKingscote 9 70
(Jeremy Gask) *hld up in midfield: pushed along and gd hdwy over 1f out: r.o: led post* **13/2**[3]

0-41 **2** hd **Roaring Rory**[21] 2118 3-9-1 **65**.....(p) JacobButterfield(3) 5 69
(Ollie Pears) *pressed ldr: rdn 2f out: led 1f out: kpt on: hdd post* **9/2**[2]

2-00 **3** nse **Toni's A Star**[13] 2380 4-9-0 **60**..... GeorgiaCox(7) 7 67
(Tony Carroll) *midfield: rdn 1/2-way: hdwy over 1f out: r.o fnl f: jst failed* **12/1**

0533 **4** 1 **Give Us A Belle (IRE)**[11] 2423 7-9-1 **59**.....(vt) PaddyPilley(5) 1 62
(Christine Dunnett) *led: rdn 1/2-way: hung rt over 1f out: hdd 1f out: no ex* **10/1**

4156 **5** 1/2 **Eland Ally**[22] 2088 8-9-1 **59**.....(p) JosephineGordon(5) 10 61
(Anabel K Murphy) *swtchd lft jst after s: hld up racing keenly: rdn 2f out: kpt on ins fnl f: nrst fin* **16/1**

5610 **6** 1 **Your Gifted (IRE)**[14] 2334 9-9-12 **65**.....(v) RaulDaSilva 3 63
(Lisa Williamson) *trckd ldng pair: rdn 2f out: wknd fnl 110yds* **8/1**

0506 **7** 3/4 **Rocket Rob (IRE)**[32] 1833 10-9-6 **59**..... MartinDwyer 2 54
(Willie Musson) *slowly away: hld up in rr: rdn 2f out: nvr threatened* **14/1**

0-21 **8** 1 1/4 **Lucky Clover**[29] 1913 5-9-9 **62**..... MartinHarley 6 53
(Malcolm Saunders) *trckd ldng pair: rdn 2f out: short of room ent fnl f: wknd* **7/2**[1]

035- **9** 1 3/4 **Manipura**[162] 8330 3-9-2 **63**..... MartinLane 4 45
(Derek Shaw) *midfield: rdn 1/2-way: wknd over 1f out* **16/1**

0042 **U** **Quality Art (USA)**[36] 1721 8-9-8 **64**..... RobHornby(3) 8
(Simon Hodgson) *uns rdr leaving stalls* **13/2**[3]

1m 1.48s (-0.42) **Going Correction** -0.125s/f (Stan)
WFA 3 from 4yo+ 8lb **10** Ran SP% **113.4**
Speed ratings (Par 101): **98,97,97,96,95 93,92,90,87,**
CSF £34.79 CT £341.25 TOTE £7.70: £2.70, £2.00, £3.40; EX 36.20 Trifecta £363.40.
Owner A J Edwards & S Dobb **Bred** Limestone And Tara Studs **Trained** Stockbridge, Hants

FOCUS
An ordinary sprint handicap, run at a frantic pace. The winner's latest course form not far off this, with the 4th one of those to help guide level.
T/Plt: £15.50 to a £1 stake. Pool: £81,999.20 - 3,847.51 winning tickets. T/Qpdt: £7.10 to a £1 stake. Pool: £6,412.14 - 663.41 winning tickets. **Andrew Sheret**

2604 CHELMSFORD (A.W) (L-H)
Wednesday, June 1

OFFICIAL GOING: Polytrack: standard
Wind: medium, half against Weather: cloudy, drizzly rain at times

2786 BET TOTEPLACEPOT AT BETFRED.COM EBF NOVICE STKS (PLUS 10 RACE) — 5f (P)
6:10 (6:10) (Class 4) 2-Y-O **£4,528** (£1,347; £673; £336) **Stalls** Low

Form RPR

63 **1** **Mistime (IRE)**[14] 2371 2-8-11 0..... SilvestreDeSousa 3 74
(Mark Johnston) *chsd ldr: swtchd lft and effrt over 1f out: drvn 1f out: styd on strly to ld fnl 75yds: sn in command: eased cl home* **4/1**[3]

16 **2** 1 3/4 **Gerrard's Fur Coat**[23] 2104 2-9-1 0..... MartinHarley 4 72
(Tom Dascombe) *led: c towards centre and rdn over 1f out: drvn ins fnl f: hdd and one pce fnl 75yds* **16/1**

41 **3** 3/4 **Mr Scaramanga**[23] 2082 2-9-6 0..... TomMarquand(3) 5 77
(Richard Hannon) *stmbld leaving stalls: rcvrd into midfield and pushed rt 4f out: effrt in 3rd over 1f out: styd on fnl 100yds: no threat to wnr* **3/1**[2]

04 **4** 2 3/4 **Dark Hero (IRE)**[10] 2500 2-9-2 0..... WilliamBuick 2 60
(Charles Hills) *chsd ldrs: pushed along and unable qck over 1f out: styd on same pce ins fnl f* **20/1**

5 1/2 **Kamra (USA)** 2-9-2 0..... FrankieDettori 6 62+
(Jeremy Noseda) *wnt rt s and slowly away: rn green in rr: hung rt bnd 4f out: rdn over 2f out: sme hdwy in centre over 1f out: no imp and styd on same pce ins fnl f* **5/6**[1]

6 1/2 **Precious Plum** 2-8-6 0..... JosephineGordon(5) 1 52
(Chris Dwyer) *t.k.h: hld up in tch: short of room and wnt rt 4f out: rdn over 1f out: unable qck and styd on same pce ins fnl f* **50/1**

1m 1.0s (0.80) **Going Correction** 0.0s/f (Stan) **6** Ran SP% **112.2**
Speed ratings (Par 95): **93,90,89,84,83 83**
CSF £56.65 TOTE £5.20: £2.20, £6.10; EX 35.90 Trifecta £92.80.
Owner J M Brown **Bred** Ennistown Stud **Trained** Middleham Moor, N Yorks

FOCUS
Track had been power harrowed to 4 inches and gallop mastered to 2 inches to maintain a going description of standard after significant rainfall. Despite two previous winners and a well-backed newcomer, this looks to be just modest juvenile form.

2787 BET TOTEJACKPOT AT BETFRED.COM H'CAP 5f (P)
6:40 (6:41) (Class 3) (0-90,91) 4-Y-O+ **£9,703** (£2,887; £1,443; £721) **Stalls** Low

Form RPR
1241 **1** **Bowson Fred**[5] 2658 4-9-5 **91** 6ex NathanEvans(5) 1 102
(Michael Easterby) *taken down early and mounted on crse: mde all: rdn and qcknd over 1f out: in command and r.o strly fnl f: readily* **5/2**[1]

1126 **2** 2 **Welease Bwian (IRE)**[11] 2469 7-8-6 **78** (v) AaronJones(5) 2 82
(Stuart Williams) *dwlt: sn rcvrd to chse ldng pair: effrt to chse wnr over 1f out: styd on but no imp ins fnl f* **12/1**

46-4 **3** 1 1/4 **Escalating**[18] 2253 4-8-7 **77** TomMarquand(3) 4 77
(Michael Appleby) *t.k.h: chsd ldng trio: effrt u.p over 1f out: wnt 3rd 1f out: styd on same pce ins fnl f* **7/2**[2]

4510 **4** 1 **Top Boy**[18] 2253 6-8-13 **80** (v) MartinLane 8 76
(Derek Shaw) *stdd and short of room leaving stalls: sn swtchd lft and hld up in tch in last quartet: effrt over 1f out: styd on ins fnl f: no threat to wnr* **10/1**

5004 **5** hd **Dynamo Walt (IRE)**[26] 2003 5-9-1 **82** (v) AdamBeschizza 9 77
(Derek Shaw) *stdd s: hld up in tch in last quartet: effrt and hdwy over 1f out: styd on ins fnl f: no threat to wnr* **16/1**

2611 **6** 1 1/4 **Saved My Bacon (IRE)**[34] 1803 5-8-12 **79** SilvestreDeSousa 11 70
(Chris Dwyer) *taken down early: stdd s: hld up in tch in rr: hdwy u.p over 1f out: styd on ins fnl f: nvr trbld ldrs* **7/1**[3]

25 **7** hd **Pensax Lad (IRE)**[7] 2581 5-9-4 **88** GeorgeDowning(3) 7 78
(Ronald Harris) *in tch in midfield: drvn and unable qck over 1f out: styd on same pce and no imp ins fnl f* **25/1**

0/0- **8** 3/4 **Immediate**[235] 4-9-7 **88** JamieSpencer 6 75
(Robert Cowell) *hld up in tch in last quartet: effrt ent fnl f: unable qck and no imp ins fnl f* **20/1**

-600 **9** 1 3/4 **Stocking**[17] 2267 4-9-0 **81** (b) HarryBentley 5 62
(Roger Varian) *in tch in midfield: rdn and no hdwy over 1f out: wknd ins fnl f* **16/1**

-000 **10** shd **Lucky Beggar (IRE)**[20] 2188 6-9-6 **87** WilliamBuick 3 68
(Charles Hills) *taken down early: chsd wnr tl unable qck u.p and lost pl over 1f out: wknd ins fnl f* **7/2**[2]

59.22s (-0.98) **Going Correction** 0.0s/f (Stan) **10** Ran SP% **122.7**
Speed ratings (Par 107): **107,103,101,100,99 97,97,96,93,93**
CSF £36.95 CT £109.09 TOTE £3.70: £1.30, £4.90, £1.60; EX 53.50 Trifecta £194.20.
Owner Mrs A Jarvis **Bred** Mrs A Jarvis **Trained** Sheriff Hutton, N Yorks

FOCUS
A competitive sprint handicap and, even though nothing got into it from off the pace, the suspicion is that it represents decent form for the grade. The favourite is better than ever.

2788 BET TOTEQUADPOT AT BETFRED.COM H'CAP 6f (P)
7:10 (7:10) (Class 2) (0-100,97) 3-Y-O **£12,938** (£3,850; £1,924; £962) **Stalls** Centre

Form RPR
-250 **1** **Sign Of The Kodiac (IRE)**[26] 1996 3-9-5 **95** TomEaves 2 103
(James Given) *mde all: rdn over 1f out: sustained duel w runner-up tl forged ahd wl ins fnl f: styd on: rdn out* **12/1**

1610 **2** 1 **Suqoor**[18] 2251 3-9-2 **92** [1] SilvestreDeSousa 11 96
(Chris Dwyer) *sn prom: jnd ldr 4f out: rdn over 1f out: sustained duel w wnr after tl no ex and one pce wl ins fnl f* **6/1**[3]

-116 **3** 3/4 **Willytheconqueror (IRE)**[19] 2232 3-9-7 **97** MartinDwyer 3 99
(William Muir) *chsd ldrs: wnt 3rd over 2f out: effrt over 1f out: swtchd rt ins fnl f: styd on u.p but nvr enough pce to chal* **8/1**

40-5 **4** 3 **Elronaq**[18] 2250 3-9-6 **96** PaulHanagan 8 88+
(Charles Hills) *sn bhd: wl off the pce and rdn 3f out: hdwy 1f out: styd on wl ins fnl f: wnt 4th last strides: nvr trbld ldrs* **10/1**

321 **5** nk **Musdam (USA)**[16] 2298 3-8-6 **82** StevieDonohoe 6 73+
(Sir Michael Stoute) *off the pce in last pair: rdn over 2f out: hdwy over 1f out: chsd clr ldng trio 1f out: kpt on but nvr threatening ldrs: lost 4th last strides* **4/1**[2]

6-31 **6** nk **Inland Sea (USA)**[12] 2446 3-8-10 **86** HarryBentley 1 76+
(Richard Hannon) *midfield: rdn and outpcd over 3f out: effrt u.p on inner over 1f out: kpt on ins fnl f: no threat to ldrs* **4/1**[2]

32-3 **7** 1 3/4 **Vibrant Chords**[48] 1442 3-8-12 **88** JamesDoyle 7 73+
(Henry Candy) *chsd ldr early: short of room hmpd and dropped to midfield after 1f: effrt in 5th over 2f out: no hdwy u.p over 1f out: wl hld fnl f* **11/4**[1]

-116 **8** hd **Ticking Away**[40] 1607 3-8-10 **86** SeanLevey 9 70
(David Brown) *sn chsng ldr tl lost 2nd 4f out: 4th and rdn over 2f out: lost pl and btn over 1f out: wknd fnl f* **20/1**

1m 12.06s (-1.64) **Going Correction** 0.0s/f (Stan) **8** Ran SP% **113.6**
Speed ratings (Par 105): **110,108,107,103,103 102,100,100**
CSF £80.40 CT £621.32 TOTE £12.80: £3.00, £2.30, £2.00; EX 77.10 Trifecta £639.20.
Owner The Cool Silk Partnership **Bred** Mrs Claire Doyle **Trained** Willoughton, Lincs

FOCUS
Despite a couple of early morning defections, this had all the hallmarks of a good sprint handicap for 3yos. However, once again, it proved impossible to make up any ground from off the pace and is form to treat with a degree of caution, although it's been rated at face value.

2789 BET TOTEEXACTA AT BETFRED.COM FILLIES' H'CAP 1m (P)
7:40 (7:43) (Class 2) (0-100,95) 3-Y-O+ **£12,938** (£3,850; £1,924; £962) **Stalls** Low

Form RPR
1-1 **1** **Persuasive (IRE)**[12] 2431 3-8-9 **87** FrankieDettori 1 98+
(John Gosden) *wl in tch in midfield: wnt 4th and swtchd rt wl over 1f out: pushed along and qcknd to ld 150yds out: sn in command: eased cl home: comf* **9/4**[1]

0-32 **2** 1 3/4 **Barleysugar (IRE)**[11] 2479 3-8-12 **90** RyanMoore 2 97
(Sir Michael Stoute) *led tl 5f out: drvn and ev ch over 1f out: led 1f out: sn hdd and outpcd by wnr but battled on to hold 2nd ins fnl f* **3/1**[2]

34-1 **3** 1/2 **Mise En Rose (USA)**[28] 1960 3-9-0 **92** WilliamBuick 4 98
(Charlie Appleby) *chsd ldrs: effrt to chal over 1f out: drvn ent fnl f: outpcd by wnr and kpt on same pce ins fnl f* **9/4**[1]

2254 **4** 1 **Bint Dandy (IRE)**[25] 2026 5-10-0 **95** (b) SilvestreDeSousa 8 102
(Chris Dwyer) *sn w ldr: led 5f out: rdn and hrd pressed over 1f out: hdd 1f out: kpt on same pce ins fnl f* **20/1**

6253 **5** 3 1/4 **Subtle Knife**[23] 2084 7-8-10 **82** JosephineGordon(5) 3 81
(Giles Bravery) *hld up in last pair: rdn over 3f out: styd on ins fnl f: nvr trbld ldrs* **50/1**

1111 **6** nk **Lucy The Painter (IRE)**[21] 2154 4-9-5 **86** HarryBentley 7 85
(Ed de Giles) *in tch in midfield: effrt in 5th and nt clrest of runs wl over 1f out: sn outpcd: wknd ins fnl f* **10/1**[3]

5-1 **7** 3 3/4 **Malmostosa**[37] 1723 3-8-5 **83** LukeMorris 6 70
(Marco Botti) *hld up in tch in 7th: effrt over 2f out: no imp u.p over 1f out: wknd ins fnl f* **12/1**

204- **8** 6 **Chiringuita (USA)**[221] 7471 3-8-13 **91** TedDurcan 9 64
(James Bethell) *sn chsng ldrs: u.p and lost pl over 2f out: wknd over 1f out: bhd fnl f* **28/1**

61-0 **9** nse **Veena (FR)**[46] 1476 3-8-8 **86** ow1 JamieSpencer 5 59
(David Simcock) *stdd after s: a in rr: rdn wl over 2f out: no prog: wl btn over 1f out* **25/1**

1m 37.55s (-2.35) **Going Correction** 0.0s/f (Stan)
WFA 3 from 4yo+ 11lb **9** Ran SP% **117.3**
Speed ratings (Par 96): **111,109,108,107,104 104,100,94,94**
CSF £8.97 CT £16.36 TOTE £3.20: £1.60, £1.10, £1.10; EX 10.20 Trifecta £21.70.
Owner Cheveley Park Stud **Bred** J F Tuthill **Trained** Newmarket, Suffolk

FOCUS
Four came into this with a win next to their name and it looks like strong form for the fillies' division, with the winner doing it nicely. There's more to come from her.

2790 BET TOTETRIFECTA AT BETFRED.COM MAIDEN STKS (PLUS 10 RACE) 1m (P)
8:10 (8:14) (Class 4) 3-Y-O **£8,086** (£2,406; £1,202; £601) **Stalls** Low

Form RPR
0-2 **1** **Silent Attack**[16] 2298 3-9-5 0 JamesDoyle 6 88+
(Saeed bin Suroor) *hld up wl in tch in midfield: clsd and nt clr run 2f out tl swtchd lft jst over 1f out: racd awkwardly but sn chalng: led wl ins fnl f: sn in command: comf* **5/4**[1]

5-4 **2** 1 1/4 **Autocratic**[39] 1639 3-9-5 0 RyanMoore 1 82
(Sir Michael Stoute) *t.k.h: trckd ldrs: rdn to ld over 1f out: drvn 1f out: hdd and styd on same pce wl ins fnl f* **5/4**[1]

06- **3** 1/2 **Calvados Spirit**[215] 7592 3-9-5 0 MartinDwyer 7 81
(William Muir) *hld up in tch in midfield: gd hdwy on outer over 2f out: drvn and ev ch over 1f out: styd on same pce ins fnl f* **12/1**[2]

4 **4** 1 3/4 **Predetermined (IRE)**[19] 2207 3-9-5 0 DavidProbert 10 77
(Andrew Balding) *t.k.h: hld up in tch in midfield: swtchd rt and effrt wl over 1f out: styd on same pce ins fnl f* **16/1**

0 **5** 6 **Imperial State**[14] 2375 3-9-5 0 (t) TedDurcan 8 63
(George Scott) *hld up in midfield but nt on terms w ldrs: clsd 3f out: shkn up and swtchd rt over 1f out: no threat to ldrs but styd on steadily ins fnl f* **66/1**

0- **6** 2 1/2 **Regal Gait (IRE)**[310] 4705 3-9-5 0 HarryBentley 12 57
(Simon Dow) *chsd ldrs: rdn 3f out: lost pl and btn over 1f out: sn wknd* **66/1**

3 **6** dht **Wasseem (IRE)**[34] 1806 3-9-0 0 (t) EdwardGreatrex(5) 15 57
(Simon Crisford) *chsd ldr: rdn to ld wl over 1f out: sn hdd and outpcd: wknd ins fnl f* **20/1**

05 **8** 4 **Alcanar (USA)**[12] 2440 3-9-5 0 WilliamCarson 11 48+
(Michael Bell) *stdd s: hld up wl in tch in last quartet: shkn up over 4f out: tk hold of bit and keen over 3f out: nudged along and sme hdwy but hanging lft over 1f out: no ch but kpt on steadily ins fnl f* **66/1**

5 **9** nse **Jabbaar**[15] 2320 3-9-5 0 PaulHanagan 13 49
(Owen Burrows) *chsd ldrs: rdn and lost pl over 2f out: wknd over 1f out* **14/1**[3]

4 **10** hd **Skara Mae (IRE)**[96] 735 3-9-0 0 WilliamBuick 3 45
(Charles Hills) *led: rdn and hdd wl over 1f out: sn outpcd and btn: no ch whn eased ins fnl f* **33/1**

65 **11** nse **Patent**[15] 2340 3-9-5 0 SeanLevey 16 48+
(Richard Hannon) *wl off the pce in last quartet: no ch but kpt on steadily ins fnl f: n.d* **33/1**

0 **12** 8 **Isostatic**[20] 2177 3-9-0 0 MartinLane 14 24
(Rae Guest) *a off the pce in last quartet: n.d* **66/1**

13 2 **Victorious Laugh (IRE)** 3-9-5 0 LukeMorris 5 25
(Marco Botti) *s.i.s: rn green in rr: n.d* **33/1**

6 **14** 3 3/4 **Sid Sweeney**[23] 2109 3-9-0 0 CharlesEddery(5) 9 16
(Gay Kelleway) *t.k.h: dropped to last after 2f: lost tch over 2f out* **100/1**

00 **15** 9 **Missed The Cut**[20] 2175 3-9-5 0 SilvestreDeSousa 2
(Michael Wigham) *midfield early but nvr on terms w ldrs: dropped to rr qp: 5f out: t.o fnl f* **66/1**

1m 39.11s (-0.79) **Going Correction** 0.0s/f (Stan) **15** Ran SP% **131.2**
Speed ratings (Par 101): **103,101,101,99,93 91,91,87,86,86 86,78,76,72,63**
CSF £2.71 TOTE £2.50: £1.30, £1.10, £4.00; EX 4.50 Trifecta £23.60.
Owner Godolphin **Bred** Ship Commodities **Trained** Newmarket, Suffolk

FOCUS
Not as competitive as the field-size made it look with punters only wanting to know about the front two in the market. They were soon strung out, with the first four coming clear.

2791 COLLECT TOTEPOOL WINNINGS AT BETFRED SHOPS H'CAP 1m 2f (P)
8:40 (8:45) (Class 4) (0-80,80) 4-Y-O+ **£8,086** (£2,406; £1,202; £601) **Stalls** Low

Form RPR
1335 **1** **Whoopsy Daisy**[26] 1999 4-9-0 **73** MartinDwyer 3 80
(Jane Chapple-Hyam) *trckd ldrs: clsd and nt clr run over 2f out: swtchd lft and effrt over 1f out: rdn to ld 1f out: drvn and edgd rt ins fnl f: styd on* **5/1**[3]

1656 **2** 1 **Buckland Beau**[37] 1716 5-9-7 **80** StevieDonohoe 4 85
(Charlie Fellowes) *hld up in tch in last trio: clsd over 2f out: swtchd rt and drvn to chse ldrs over 1f out: wnt 2nd 100yds out: kpt on* **5/1**[3]

-532 **3** hd **Taper Tantrum (IRE)**[22] 2121 4-9-6 **79** JamieSpencer 2 84
(Michael Bell) *chsd ldrs: wnt 2nd 7f out: hrd drvn over 2f out: unable qck over 1f out: styd on same pce ins fnl f* **7/2**[1]

60/1 **4** 1 **Sureness (IRE)**[14] 2374 6-8-9 **75** (t) MeganNicholls(7) 5 78
(Charlie Mann) *in tch in midfield: effrt on outer over 2f out: kpt on ins fnl f: nvr threatening wnr* **11/1**

20-5 **5** 1 1/2 **Compton Mill**[16] 2296 4-9-2 **75** (t) RyanMoore 6 75
(Hughie Morrison) *chsd ldr for 3f out: lost pl and pushed along over 3f out: rallied u.p and chsd ldrs over 1f out: no ex and btn whn swtchd lft ins fnl f: wknd towards fin* **9/2**[2]

3622 **6** 1/2 **Patriotic (IRE)**[37] 1722 8-9-2 **75** (p) SilvestreDeSousa 7 74
(Chris Dwyer) *wnt rt s and bustled along early: in tch in last trio: short of room 7f out: rdn over 2f out: styd on ins fnl f: nvr trbld ldrs* **7/1**

2233 **7** 2 1/2 **Free Running (IRE)**[21] 2154 4-8-9 **73** EdwardGreatrex(5) 1 67
(Simon Crisford) *sn led and set stdy gallop: rdn and qcknd over 1f out: hdd 1f out: sn outpcd and btn: wknd ins fnl f* **8/1**

5112 **8** 3 3/4 **Mr Red Clubs (IRE)**[12] 2444 7-8-11 **75**..................(p) GeorgeBuckell(5) 8 61
(Michael Appleby) *pushed rt s: sn chsng ldng trio: lost pl u.p over 1f out: wknd ins fnl f* **16/1**

2600 **9** 9 **U S Navy Seal (USA)**[19] 2214 4-9-7 **80**................................(v) JFEgan 9 48
(J R Jenkins) *hld up in last trio: rdn over 2f out: sn outpcd: bhd and hung rt over 1f out* **14/1**

2m 7.69s (-0.91) **Going Correction** 0.0s/f (Stan) **9** Ran SP% **118.2**
Speed ratings (Par 105): **103,102,102,101,100 99,97,94,87**
CSF £31.01 CT £99.90 TOTE £6.20: £2.30, £2.40, £1.50; EX 33.20 Trifecta £118.00.
Owner Mrs Charles Cyzer **Bred** C A Cyzer **Trained** Dalham, Suffolk

FOCUS
A wide open, fair handicap, but probably not as competitive as it first looked with a number of these looking weighted up to their best form.

2792 CCR LADIES DAY 16TH JUNE H'CAP 1m 6f (P)
9:10 (9:11) (Class 6) (0-65,60) 4-Y-O+ **£3,234** (£962; £481; £240) **Stalls** Low

Form RPR

12 **1** **Eurato (FR)**[29] 1955 6-9-7 **60**...(p) RyanMoore 6 70
(Steve Gollings) *hld up in tch in midfield: clsd and travelling strly over 2f out: pushed along and led over 1f out: sn clr: easily* **1/1**[1]

3242 **2** 7 **What A Party (IRE)**[16] 2292 4-9-4 **57**.................................(p) LukeMorris 1 58
(Gay Kelleway) *chsd ldrs: rdn over 2f out: drvn over 1f out: chsd clr wnr ins fnl f: kpt on but no ch w wnr* **14/1**

4060 **3** 1 1/2 **Galuppi**[10] 2507 5-9-7 **60**..(p) FrederikTylicki 4 59
(J R Jenkins) *hld up in tch in rr: rdn and hdwy over 1f out: chsd wnr over 1f out: no imp: lost 2nd and kpt on same pce ins fnl f* **25/1**

0645 **4** 3/4 **Investissement**[36] 1748 10-8-5 **49**.....................(tp) JosephineGordon(5) 2 47
(Paddy Butler) *hld up in tch in midfield: rdn over 2f out: no ch w wnr and kpt on same pce ins fnl f* **25/1**

0333 **5** 1 1/4 **Unex Modigliani (IRE)**[6] 2605 7-9-3 **56**.........................(vt) MartinLane 3 52
(Derek Shaw) *rdn along in rr: hdwy to chse ldr and bk on bridle after 3f: rdn to ld and hung lft wl over 1f out: sn hdd and btn: wknd ins fnl f* **3/1**[2]

5425 **6** 3 1/2 **My Tringaling (IRE)**[16] 2292 4-8-9 **53**........................... AaronJones(5) 8 45
(Stuart Williams) *led: rdn over 2f out: hdd wl over 1f out and sn btn: wknd* **14/1**

03-6 **7** 18 **Grey's Angel**[28] 1962 4-9-7 **60**.................................... SilvestreDeSousa 5 28
(Philip McBride) *chsd ldr for 3f: styd chsng ldrs tl lost pl u.p over 2f out: bhd fnl f* **14/1**

600- **8** 23 **Beyond Argument (IRE)**[251] 6672 4-9-2 **55**.............(p) JamieSpencer 7
(David Simcock) *hld up in last pair: rdn 5f out: lost tch over 2f out: eased over 1f out: t.o* **6/1**[3]

3m 4.22s (1.02) **Going Correction** 0.0s/f (Stan) **8** Ran SP% **117.0**
Speed ratings (Par 101): **97,93,92,91,91 89,78,65**
CSF £18.55 CT £217.12 TOTE £1.90: £1.02, £3.30, £9.00; EX 10.60 Trifecta £124.70.
Owner Northern Bloodstock Racing **Bred** Wertheimer & Frere **Trained** Scamblesby, Lincs

FOCUS
An extremely moderate race which the favourite took with ease.
T/Plt: £145.30 to a £1 stake. Pool: £69,351.78 - 348.22 winning units. T/Qpdt: £16.40 to a £1 stake. Pool: £7,851.34 - 352.36 winning units. **Steve Payne**

2500 NOTTINGHAM (L-H)
Wednesday, June 1

OFFICIAL GOING: Good to firm (good in places; 8.3)
Wind: Fresh behind Weather: Overcast

2793 TOTEPLACEPOT EBF STALLIONS MAIDEN FILLIES' STKS (PLUS 10 RACE) 5f 13y
2:00 (2:05) (Class 5) 2-Y-O **£3,234** (£962; £481; £240) **Stalls** Centre

Form RPR

1 **Bletchley** 2-9-0 0.. OisinMurphy 12 81+
(Ralph Beckett) *racd nr stands' rail: towards rr: hdwy 2f out: sn swtchd lft towards centre and rdn over 1f out: styd on strly fnl f to ld nr fin* **25/1**

5 **2** nk **Reeh (IRE)**[26] 1988 2-9-0 0.. PaulHanagan 4 80
(John Gosden) *racd centre: t.k.h and led: rdn clr over 1f out: edgd lft wl ins fnl f: hdd and no ex towards fin* **13/8**[1]

0 **3** 2 1/4 **Madame Bounty (IRE)**[13] 2410 2-9-0 0............................ LukeMorris 1 72
(Ed Walker) *racd centre: chsd ldng pair: rdn along and hdwy to chse ldr wl over 1f out: kpt on same pce fnl f* **25/1**

2 **4** 2 1/4 **Broadhaven Honey (IRE)**[16] 2295 2-9-0 0...................... MartinDwyer 7 64
(Ed McMahon) *racd centre: chsd ldr: rdn along over 2f out: drvn wl over 1f out and one pce* **9/2**[3]

5 1 **Alice's Dream** 2-9-0 0.. AndreaAtzeni 10 60+
(Marco Botti) *dwlt and sltly hmpd s: sn swtchd lft and towards rr: hdwy on outer 2f out: styd on fnl f: nrst fin* **14/1**

6 3/4 **Cool Echo** 2-9-0 0.. FrederikTylicki 3 57
(J R Jenkins) *towards rr: hdwy 1/2-way: rdn along wl over 1f out: kpt on fnl f* **100/1**

46 **7** nse **Mesmeric Moment**[53] 1342 2-9-0 0................................. AdamKirby 11 57
(David Evans) *racd stands' rail: prom: rdn along over 2f out: sn wknd* **33/1**

00 **8** 1 1/2 **Kodiac Moment (IRE)**[14] 2371 2-9-0 0......................... JimmyFortune 8 52
(Brian Meehan) *chsd ldrs centre: pushed along 1/2-way: sn rdn and wknd* **50/1**

9 1/2 **How's Lucy** 2-8-11 0.. DannyBrock(3) 5 50
(Jane Chapple-Hyam) *chsd ldrs centre: rdn along 1/2-way: sn wknd* **50/1**

10 nse **Parlance (IRE)** 2-9-0 0.. RyanMoore 9 50
(Sir Michael Stoute) *green and awkward s: a in rr* **7/2**[2]

11 11 **Digital Revolution** 2-9-0 0... DavidAllan 6 10
(Antony Brittain) *in rr: rdn along and outpcd 2f out: sn hung bdly lft to far rail and bhd* **100/1**

1m 0.34s (-1.16) **Going Correction** -0.15s/f (Firm) **11** Ran SP% **101.7**
Speed ratings (Par 90): **103,102,98,95,93 92,92,90,89,89 71**
CSF £50.99 TOTE £21.00: £4.70, £1.10, £3.90; EX 54.20 Trifecta £1203.10.
Owner Qatar Racing Limited **Bred** Qatar Bloodstock Ltd **Trained** Kimpton, Hants
■ Pellucid was withdrawn. Price at time of withdrawal 6-1. Rule 4 applies to all bets - deduction 10p in the pound.

FOCUS
Outer track used and all distances as advertised. After 1mm of overnight rain, the ground remained officially on the faster side of good. Plenty of drama before the start of this fillies maiden, with Kodiac Moment getting kicked by Broadhaven Honey, Mesmeric Moment unshipping Adam Kirby and the well-backed Pellucid withdrawn having spread a plate.

2794 TOTEJACKPOT FILLIES' H'CAP 6f 15y
2:30 (2:31) (Class 5) (0-75,75) 4-Y-O+ **£3,234** (£962; £481; £240) **Stalls** Centre

Form RPR

36-2 **1** **Darma (IRE)**[49] 1419 4-9-0 **73**................................ JosephineGordon(5) 2 80
(Martyn Meade) *wnt rt s: racd centre: prom: overall ldr over 2f out: rdn over 1f out: drvn ins fnl f: kpt on wl* **3/1**[1]

-000 **2** hd **Meandmyshadow**[9] 2531 8-9-4 **72**...............................(b) DaleSwift 10 78
(Alan Brown) *racd nr stands' rail: overall ldr: hdd and pushed along over 2f out: rdn over 1f out: drvn: edgd lft and rallied ins fnl f: jst hld* **10/1**

-002 **3** 2 1/4 **Mrs Biggs**[25] 2050 4-8-11 **65**.. PaulHanagan 3 64
(Declan Carroll) *sltly hmpd s and in rr: pushed along 1/2-way: rdn 2f out: styd on wl appr fnl f* **6/1**[3]

21-0 **4** 1 1/4 **Princess Tansy**[18] 2253 4-9-2 **75**............................... GeorgeBuckell(5) 4 70
(David Simcock) *racd centre: trckd ldrs: hdwy to chse wnr centre over 2f out: rdn wl over 1f out: drvn and kpt on same pce fnl f* **10/1**

10-0 **5** 3 **Lolita**[19] 2217 4-9-6 **74**.. FrannyNorton 1 59
(J R Jenkins) *chsd ldrs on wd outside: rdn along 2f out: sn drvn and wknd over 1f out* **10/1**

20-5 **6** 1 **East Coast Lady (IRE)**[19] 2217 4-9-6 **74**...................... FrederikTylicki 9 56
(William Stone) *racd nr stands' rail: trckd ldr: pushed along 1/2-way: rdn over 2f out: sn drvn and wknd* **4/1**[2]

0-64 **7** 1 1/4 **Margrets Gift**[32] 1872 5-9-5 **73**..(p) DavidAllan 6 51
(Tim Easterby) *hmpd s: in rr and swtchd rt to r stands' rail: a bhd* **7/1**

50-0 **8** 1 **Two Turtle Doves (IRE)**[136] 230 10-7-10 **57** oh3 ow1.. JaneElliott(7) 8 32
(Michael Mullineaux) *carried lft s: chsd ldrs: rdn along over 2f out: sn wknd* **50/1**

-003 **9** 2 1/4 **Sakhee's Rose**[110] 543 6-8-6 **60**.................................(b) MartinDwyer 7 28
(Ed McMahon) *hmpd s: racd towards stands' rail: a in rr* **10/1**

1m 13.06s (-1.64) **Going Correction** -0.15s/f (Firm) **9** Ran SP% **110.1**
Speed ratings (Par 100): **104,103,100,99,95 93,92,90,87**
CSF £31.18 CT £156.96 TOTE £3.40: £1.60, £2.70, £1.50; EX 34.60 Trifecta £292.40.
Owner David Caddy **Bred** Di Lualdi Lucia & C **Trained** Newmarket, Suffolk

FOCUS
A run-of-the-mill fillies' sprint with one of the few runners in the line up coming here off a good run landing the spoils.

2795 EBF STALLIONS TOTEQUADPOT FILLIES' H'CAP 1m 75y
3:00 (3:01) (Class 4) (0-80,80) 3-Y-O **£6,469** (£1,925; £962; £481) **Stalls** Centre

Form RPR

1- **1** **Eternally**[204] 7788 3-9-3 **76**.. RobertHavlin 3 81+
(John Gosden) *trckd ldrs: smooth hdwy over 2f out: led over 1f out: sn rdn and kpt on towards fin* **7/2**[1]

1 **2** 1/2 **Pure Art**[42] 1577 3-9-4 **77**.. FMBerry 11 81+
(Ralph Beckett) *hld up in rr: swtchd rt and hdwy wl over 1f out: sn nt clr run and hmpd: rdn and styd on strly fnl f* **5/1**[2]

4-42 **3** 1 **Perfect Quest**[26] 2011 3-8-5 **64**.. RyanTate 2 64
(Clive Cox) *dwlt: hdwy on inner to chse ldrs after 1f: effrt and hdwy over 2f out: rdn over 1f out: drvn and kpt on wl fnl f* **7/1**[3]

4-66 **4** nk **Nicarra (IRE)**[11] 2483 3-8-10 **69**.................................. FergusSweeney 13 68
(Henry Candy) *hld up towards rr: hdwy 3f out: rdn along wl over 1f out: kpt on wl fnl f* **20/1**

00-6 **5** nk **Cleverconversation (IRE)**[20] 2179 3-8-13 **75**............. DannyBrock(3) 1 74
(Jane Chapple-Hyam) *led: pushed along 3f out: rdn over 2f out: hdd over 1f out: drvn and kpt on same pce fnl f* **12/1**

-214 **6** nk **Intermittent**[20] 2181 3-9-5 **78**.. GeorgeBaker 5 78+
(Roger Charlton) *hld up and bhd: swtchd rt to outer and hdwy 3f out: chsd ldrs whn rdn: edgd lft and hmpd over 1f out: kpt on fnl f* **8/1**

51-3 **7** shd **Little Kipling**[20] 2178 3-8-8 **67**... OisinMurphy 7 65
(Stuart Williams) *prom: trckd ldr 1/2-way: cl up 3f out: rdn along 2f out: drvn over 1f out: kpt on same pce* **8/1**

0-50 **8** 1 1/4 **Dora's Field (IRE)**[35] 1798 3-8-12 **71**............................... PatCosgrave 4 66
(Ed Dunlop) *hld up: hdwy on inner 3f out: rdn to chse ldrs 2f out: sn drvn and no imp fnl f* **16/1**

2-15 **9** 1 **Wings Of Esteem (IRE)**[26] 2011 3-8-12 **71**................. DougieCostello 6 64
(K R Burke) *t.k.h: trckd ldrs: effrt 3f out: rdn along 2f out: sn drvn and one pce* **20/1**

12-3 **10** nse **Indigo**[28] 1960 3-8-5 **69**.. JosephineGordon(5) 10 61
(Mark Usher) *in tch on outer: hdwy 5f out: chsd ldng pair 3f out: rdn and edgd rt wl over 1f out: sn drvn and wknd* **25/1**

50-5 **11** 13 **Salvo**[20] 2179 3-9-7 **80**.. StevieDonohoe 8 43
(Charlie Fellowes) *hld up towards rr: effrt and sme hdwy 3f out: rdn over 2f out: sn btn* **8/1**

436- **12** 4 **So Much Fun (IRE)**[239] 7019 3-9-1 **77**...................... ThomasBrown(3) 12 30
(Ismail Mohammed) *hld up towards rr: swtchd rt to outer and sme hdwy 3f out: rdn along over 2f out: sn wknd* **33/1**

1m 46.94s (-2.06) **Going Correction** -0.15s/f (Firm) **12** Ran SP% **114.6**
Speed ratings (Par 98): **108,107,106,106,105 105,105,104,103,103 90,86**
CSF £18.15 CT £116.61 TOTE £4.00: £1.40, £2.70, £2.00; EX 18.00 Trifecta £79.10.
Owner Cheveley Park Stud **Bred** Cheveley Park Stud Ltd **Trained** Newmarket, Suffolk
■ Stewards' Enquiry : Josephine Gordon two-day ban: careless riding (Jun 21-22)

FOCUS
An interesting race featuring several unexposed fillies and the winner filled that category having won her AW maiden last season.

2796 TOTETRIFECTA PICK THE 1,2,3 H'CAP 1m 75y
3:30 (3:30) (Class 2) (0-110,108) 3-Y-O+**£16,172** (£4,812; £2,405; £1,202) **Stalls** Centre

Form RPR

126- **1** **Spirit Raiser (IRE)**[250] 6707 5-9-4 **98**......................... FrederikTylicki 9 105+
(James Fanshawe) *trckd ldng pair: hdwy and cl up 3f out: led wl over 1f out: rdn ins fnl f: kpt on wl* **4/1**[2]

0-30 **2** 1 1/2 **Off Art**[21] 2157 6-8-11 **94**......................................(p) RachelRichardson(5) 2 99
(Tim Easterby) *led: pushed along over 2f out: hdd and rdn wl over 1f out: kpt on wl u.p fnl f* **6/1**

-040 **3** nse **Express Himself (IRE)**[20] 2191 5-9-6 **100**........................ JimCrowley 1 103+
(Ed McMahon) *dwlt and in rr: swtchd rt and hdwy whn n.m.r wl over 1f out: sn rdn: kpt on wl fnl f* **7/2**[1]

0-00 **4** 2 **Room Key**[11] 2485 4-9-2 **94**... JamieSpencer 3 94
(Eve Johnson Houghton) *hld up towards rr: hdwy on outer 2 1/2f out: rdn and sltly hmpd over 1f out: drvn: edgd lft and kpt on same pce fnl f* **12/1**

65-6 **5** 1 ½ **Spark Plug (IRE)**[18] 2246 5-9-10 **104** JimmyFortune 4 99
(Brian Meehan) *trckd ldrs: effrt over 2f out: rdn over 1f out: sn drvn and kpt on one pce* **5/1**[3]

-304 **6** 1 ¾ **Fort Bastion (IRE)**[11] 2485 7-9-2 **96** (b) PhillipMakin 6 87
(David O'Meara) *trckd ldrs: hdwy on outer and cl up 3f out: shkn up 2f out: sn rdn and wknd* **11/2**

0-60 **7** 2 **Two For Two (IRE)**[20] 2191 8-9-3 **97** RaulDaSilva 5 83
(David Loughnane) *trckd ldr: cl up 3f out: rdn along 2f out: sn ev ch: drvn over 1f out and sn wknd* **22/1**

-006 **8** 1 ½ **The Warrior (IRE)**[13] 2391 4-9-2 **94** (t) PatDobbs 7 78
(Amanda Perrett) *dwlt: a in rr* **10/1**

1m 46.42s (-2.58) **Going Correction** -0.15s/f (Firm) **8** Ran SP% **109.7**
Speed ratings (Par 109): **110,108,108,106,104 103,101,99**
CSF £25.70 CT £83.71 TOTE £4.60: £1.30, £2.10, £1.20; EX 31.00 Trifecta £117.90.
Owner Lord Vestey **Bred** Stowell Park Stud **Trained** Newmarket, Suffolk

FOCUS
A good-quality handicap, run at a stop-start pace, with the winner making a pleasing seasonal reappearance. The form is rated around the second.

2797 EBF STALLIONS TOTEEXACTA NOTTINGHAMSHIRE OAKS STKS (LISTED RACE) (F&M) 1m 2f 50y
4:00 (4:00) (Class 1) 4-Y-0+

£23,818 (£9,030; £4,519; £2,251; £1,129; £567) **Stalls** Low

Form RPR

3-54 **1** **Elbereth**[14] 2363 5-9-0 95 OisinMurphy 6 102
(Andrew Balding) *trckd ldr: cl up over 3f out: led wl over 2f out: rdn wl over 1f out: drvn and kpt on wl towards fin* **8/1**

55-1 **2** hd **Tears Of The Sun**[36] 1743 5-9-0 95 AdamKirby 5 101
(Clive Cox) *hld up in rr: hdwy wl over 2f out: swtchd lft to inner and effrt wl over 1f out: sn swtchd rt and rdn: drvn and styd on strly fnl f: jst failed* **10/1**

12-1 **3** 2 ¼ **Weetles**[37] 1716 4-9-0 87 RyanTate 12 97
(Clive Cox) *hld up towards rr: hdwy on wd outside over 2f out: rdn to chse ldrs and hung bdly rt ent fnl f: sn drvn and kpt on* **6/1**[3]

32-6 **4** nk **Sound Of Freedom (IRE)**[46] 1475 4-9-0 0 JimCrowley 3 96
(Marco Botti) *trckd ldrs: hdwy over 2f out: rdn along wl over 1f out: kpt on fnl f* **3/1**[1]

-251 **5** hd **Sagaciously (IRE)**[18] 2236 4-9-0 95 RichardKingscote 4 96
(Ed Dunlop) *hld up towards rr: hdwy on inner wl over 2f out: rdn to chse wnr over 1f out: sn drvn and wknd fnl f* **7/2**[2]

02-0 **6** 3 ¼ **California (IRE)**[32] 1855 4-9-0 94 RobertHavlin 10 89
(John Gosden) *in tch on outer: effrt 3f out and sn pushed along rdn 2f out and sn no imp* **6/1**[3]

20-0 **7** nk **Pamona (IRE)**[32] 1855 4-9-0 97 (v[1]) AndreaAtzeni 2 89
(Luca Cumani) *trckd ldrs: hdwy 3f out: rdn over 2f out: sn drvn and btn* **8/1**

024- **8** 11 **Ceaseless (IRE)**[325] 4181 4-9-0 87 DavidAllan 11 67
(James Tate) *cl up on outer: rdn along 3f out: sn wknd* **22/1**

600- **9** 2 ¾ **Forte**[294] 5278 4-9-0 99 PhillipMakin 1 61
(David O'Meara) *led: rdn along over 3f out: hdd wl over 2f out: sn wknd* **25/1**

2m 11.99s (-2.31) **Going Correction** -0.15s/f (Firm) **9** Ran SP% **115.3**
Speed ratings (Par 111): **107,106,105,104,104 102,101,93,90**
CSF £84.20 TOTE £9.90: £2.80, £2.70, £1.60; EX 95.20 Trifecta £519.00.
Owner David Taylor **Bred** David Taylor **Trained** Kingsclere, Hants

FOCUS
The feature race on the card but although it was competitive enough, it is probably ordinary form for Listed level. A length pb from the winner.

2798 TOTESWINGER THREE WAYS TO WIN H'CAP 1m 6f 15y
4:30 (4:30) (Class 5) (0-70,67) 3-Y-0 **£2,911** (£866; £432; £216) **Stalls** Low

Form RPR

-660 **1** **Aristocles (IRE)**[16] 2300 3-9-6 **66** (p) JimCrowley 4 74
(Sir Michael Stoute) *trckd ldng pair: hdwy 4f out: cl up 3f out: rdn to chal 2f out: led appr fnl f: sn drvn and kpt on wl towards fin* **7/1**

-211 **2** ½ **Scarpeta (FR)**[8] 2563 3-9-5 **65** 6ex FrannyNorton 8 72
(Mark Johnston) *led: pushed along and jnd over 2f out: rdn wl over 1f out: hdd appr fnl f: drvn and rallied last 120yds: no ex towards fin* **6/5**[1]

1124 **3** 2 **Kalamata**[15] 2348 3-9-7 **67** AndreaAtzeni 5 71
(Roger Varian) *dwlt: trckd ldrs: hdwy over 3f out: cl up over 2f out: rdn and ev ch over 1f out: drvn ins fnl f: kpt on same pce* **9/2**[3]

00-0 **4** 12 **Palisade**[14] 2366 3-9-2 **62** (p) LukeMorris 6 49
(Sir Mark Prescott Bt) *trckd ldr: pushed along over 4f out: rdn 3f out: sn drvn and wknd fnl 2f* **11/4**[2]

30-6 **5** 27 **Provoking (USA)**[44] 1532 3-9-7 **67** AdamKirby 2 16
(David Evans) *t.k.h: hld up in rr: sme hdwy over 4f out: rdn along over 3f out: sn outpcd and bhd* **20/1**

3m 8.26s (1.26) **Going Correction** -0.15s/f (Firm) **5** Ran SP% **107.6**
Speed ratings (Par 99): **94,93,92,85,70**
CSF £15.33 TOTE £7.80: £3.10, £1.10; EX 22.90 Trifecta £74.10.
Owner Athos Christodoulou **Bred** A Christodoulou **Trained** Newmarket, Suffolk
■ Stewards' Enquiry : Jim Crowley four-day ban: careless riding (Jun 19-22)

FOCUS
Three non-runners took away some of the interest from a good race for the grade but it still produced an exciting finish and the winner relished his first crack at this trip.

2799 TOTEPOOLLIVEINFO.COM "HANDS AND HEELS" APPRENTICE SERIES H'CAP 1m 2f 50y
5:00 (5:03) (Class 6) (0-65,65) 4-Y-0+ **£2,264** (£673; £336; £168) **Stalls** Low

Form RPR

4231 **1** **Little Choosey**[12] 2448 6-8-10 **54** (tp) HollieDoyle 4 60
(Roy Bowring) *trckd ldr: hdwy and cl up 3f out: rdn to ld over 1f out: hld on wl towards fin* **4/1**[2]

4-22 **2** nk **Flutterbee**[2] 2738 4-9-7 **65** (p) GeorgeWood 1 70
(George Baker) *hld up in rr: hdwy wl over 2f out: effrt over 1f out: rdn to chse wnr ins fnl f and sn ev ch: no ex towards fin* **6/4**[1]

00-0 **3** 3 ¼ **Miningrocks (FR)**[65] 1120 4-8-10 **54** HarryBurns 8 53
(Declan Carroll) *led: jnd 3f out: rdn along 2f out: sn hdd: kpt on same pce fnl f* **20/1**

04-3 **4** 4 **Qibtee (FR)**[15] 2343 6-9-4 **62** BenRobinson 2 53
(Les Eyre) *hld up in rr: hdwy on outer over 2f out: rdn wl over 1f out: sn one pce* **8/1**[3]

0000 **5** 1 ¾ **Vivre La Reve**[36] 1735 4-8-12 **56** RobertDodsworth 6 44
(James Unett) *t.k.h early: trckd ldrs on outer: hdwy over 3f out: rdn along over 2f out: sn wknd* **33/1**

0-04 **6** ½ **Elle Dorado**[7] 2573 4-8-8 **52** AdamMcNamara 3 39
(David Loughnane) *trckd ldng pair on inner: pushed along over 3f out: rdn over 2f out: sn wknd* **10/1**

2m 16.19s (1.89) **Going Correction** -0.05s/f (Good) **6** Ran SP% **87.9**
Speed ratings (Par 101): **90,89,87,83,82 82**
CSF £6.25 CT £31.56 TOTE £3.20: £1.60, £1.50; EX 7.60 Trifecta £33.20.
Owner K Nicholls **Bred** Mrs Sandra Fox **Trained** Edwinstowe, Notts
■ Ifan was withdrawn. Price at times of withdrawal 11-4. Rule 4 applies to all bets - deduction 25p in the pound.

FOCUS
The withdrawal of second favourite Ifan at the start on veterinary advice further weakened a low-key end to proceedings.
T/Jkpt: Not won. T/Plt: £55.50 to a £1 stake. Pool: £72,814.7 - 957.58 winning tickets T/Qpdt: £12.50 to a £1 stake. Pool: £5,575.4 - 327.74 winning tickets **Joe Rowntree**

2404 RIPON (R-H)
Wednesday, June 1

OFFICIAL GOING: Good (8.2)
Wind: Fresh, half against Weather: Overcast, cold

2800 BRITISH STALLION STUDS EBF NOVICE STKS 5f
6:30 (6:37) (Class 5) 2-Y-0 **£3,881** (£1,155; £577; £288) **Stalls** High

Form RPR

1 **Shamsaya (IRE)** 2-8-11 0 GrahamLee 4 77+
(Simon Crisford) *trckd ldrs: effrt and shkn up 2f out: led ins fnl f: kpt on wl nr fin* **7/2**[2]

0 **2** ½ **Computable**[21] 2162 2-9-2 0 DavidAllan 8 80+
(Tim Easterby) *t.k.h: trckd ldrs: smooth hdwy to ld over 1f out: sn rdn and rn green: hdd ins fnl f: kpt on: hld nr fin* **15/8**[1]

3 2 **Savannah's Dream** 2-8-11 0 PhillipMakin 7 68+
(David O'Meara) *dwlt and wnt rt s: in tch: effrt and rn green over 1f out: kpt on same pce ins fnl f* **5/1**[3]

2 **4** 3 ¾ **Flawlessly (FR)**[12] 2424 2-8-11 0 PJMcDonald 5 54
(James Bethell) *led against stands' rail: pushed along whn faltered over 1f out: sn hdd: wknd ins fnl f* **15/8**[1]

45 **5** 3 **Kahrab (IRE)**[19] 2196 2-9-2 0 JoeFanning 3 49
(Mark Johnston) *dwlt and wnt rt s: sn cl up: rdn over 2f out: wknd over 1f out* **16/1**

0 **6** 3 ½ **Newgate Sioux**[16] 2301 2-8-11 0 BarryMcHugh 1 31
(Tony Coyle) *s.i.s: sn wl bhd: nvr on terms* **150/1**

7 3 ¼ **Doctor Dynamite (IRE)** 2-9-2 0 DuranFentiman 6 24
(Tim Easterby) *upset in stalls: s.v.s: a wl bhd* **50/1**

1m 1.61s (1.61) **Going Correction** +0.175s/f (Good) **7** Ran SP% **117.0**
Speed ratings (Par 93): **94,93,90,84,79 73,68**
CSF £10.94 TOTE £4.80: £2.60, £1.30; EX 12.30 Trifecta £40.00.
Owner Saeed H Al Tayer **Bred** Rabbah Bloodstock Limited **Trained** Newmarket, Suffolk

FOCUS
Rail on bend from back straight to home straight was dolled out by 2yds, adding about 4yds to races on the round course. The course had avoided the rain and Joe Fanning described the going as "good, fast ground". A fair novice event that went to one of the newcomers. All bar the runner-up spent a long time standing in the stalls after Yorkshire Bounty got loose.

2801 EURA AUDIT UK H'CAP 1m
7:00 (7:04) (Class 5) (0-70,75) 3-Y-0 **£3,234** (£962; £481; £240) **Stalls** Low

Form RPR

0-53 **1** **Carnageo (FR)**[15] 2341 3-9-5 **68** TonyHamilton 9 80
(Richard Fahey) *trckd ldr: led gng wl 2f out: edgd rt and rdn clr fnl f: readily* **15/2**[2]

602 **2** 6 **Mr Potter**[8] 2553 3-8-6 **55** (e) ConnorBeasley 5 53
(Richard Guest) *taken early to post: t.k.h: hld up in tch: blkd after 1f: effrt and rdn 2f out: edgd rt and chsd (clr) wnr 1f out: kpt on: no imp* **15/2**[2]

5-36 **3** nk **Saxon Gold (IRE)**[16] 2308 3-8-7 **56** (p) SamJames 8 54
(John Davies) *led at ordinary gallop against ins rail: rdn and hdd 2f out: lost 2nd 1f out: kpt on same pce* **25/1**

-603 **4** nk **Mecca's Missus (IRE)**[16] 2306 3-8-12 **61** (p) PaulMulrennan 12 58
(Michael Dods) *t.k.h: hld up towards rr: effrt on outside over 2f out: sn rdn: edgd rt and kpt on same pce fnl f* **9/1**[3]

44-1 **5** 1 ½ **Briyouni (FR)**[10] 2506 3-9-9 **75** 6ex JoeDoyle(3) 1 69
(Kevin Ryan) *plld hrd: in tch: n.m.r after 1f: effrt and rdn over 2f out: sn no rspnse: btn fnl f* **8/15**[1]

-500 **6** hd **Allfredandnobell (IRE)**[8] 2553 3-8-8 **57** JoeyHaynes 6 50
(Micky Hammond) *hld up: rdn on outside over 2f out: hdwy whn nt clr run briefly over 1f out: nvr able to chal* **20/1**

50-4 **7** 6 **Someone Exciting**[16] 2304 3-8-5 **54** JamesSullivan 2 33
(David Thompson) *plld hrd: hld up: rdn along and outpcd 3f out: nvr on terms* **33/1**

50-0 **8** 1 ¾ **Oceanella (IRE)**[12] 2422 3-8-11 **60** DougieCostello 4 35
(K R Burke) *t.k.h: prom: n.m.r after 1f: rdn along 3f out: hung rt and wknd 2f out* **20/1**

00-0 **9** nse **The Resdev Way**[16] 2308 3-8-2 **51** oh2 PaulQuinn 7 26
(Richard Whitaker) *plld hrd: hld up in tch on outside: hmpd after 1f: effrt and ev ch briefly over 2f out: wknd over 1f out* **66/1**

4-05 **10** 21 **Blagger**[37] 1698 3-8-2 **51** oh6 (bt[1]) PatrickMathers 3
(Richard Guest) *taken early to post: s.i.s: t.k.h early in rr: lost tch fr 3f out: t.o* **100/1**

1m 42.53s (1.13) **Going Correction** +0.175s/f (Good) **10** Ran SP% **117.6**
Speed ratings (Par 99): **101,95,94,94,92 92,86,84,84,63**
CSF £55.82 CT £1343.89 TOTE £9.60: £2.10, £2.00, £3.70; EX 41.50 Trifecta £376.80.
Owner The Up For Anything Syndicate **Bred** Viktor Timoshenko **Trained** Musley Bank, N Yorks

FOCUS
Race distance increased by 4yds. A few of these wanted to be on the pace, resulting in scrimmaging rounding the first bend, and little got into it, with the favourite disappointing.

2802 RIPON FARM SERVICES H'CAP 6f
7:30 (7:32) (Class 4) (0-85,83) 3-Y-0 **£4,851** (£1,443; £721; £360) **Stalls** High

Form RPR

6-10 **1** **Brilliant Vanguard (IRE)**[21] 2161 3-9-2 **78** PaulMulrennan 4 86
(Kevin Ryan) *cl up: led gng wl over 2f out: rdn over 1f out: hld on wl cl home* **5/1**[2]

06-3 **2** shd **Rantan (IRE)**[143] 131 3-9-2 **78** PhillipMakin 10 85
(David Barron) *hld up: effrt and hdwy on outside over 1f out: kpt on wl u.p fnl f: jst hld* **12/1**

10- **3** 1 1/4 **Mustique (IRE)**[256] 6514 3-9-3 **79** TonyHamilton 9 82+
(Richard Fahey) *in tch: stdy hdwy over 2f out: effrt and chsd wnr over 1f out to ins fnl f: kpt on same pce towards fin* **8/1**

16-2 **4** 1 **Flowing Clarets**[39] 1647 3-9-2 **78** JackGarritty 11 78
(Richard Fahey) *hld up: stdy hdwy and swtchd rt over 2f out: effrt and disp 2nd pl over 1f out: kpt on same pce ins fnl f* **3/1**[1]

5-41 **5** 1/2 **Van Gerwen**[25] 2049 3-8-11 **73** JasonHart 8 71
(Les Eyre) *dwlt: sn midfield: rdn over 2f out: rallied: kpt on same pce ins fnl f* **7/1**[3]

15-0 **6** 3 1/2 **Spike (IRE)**[19] 2218 3-8-12 **74** GrahamGibbons 3 61
(David Barron) *dwlt and wnt rt s: sn swtchd lft and hld up: hdwy whn nt clr run briefly over 1f out: kpt on fnl f: nt pce to chal* **16/1**

140- **7** 1 1/2 **Market Choice (IRE)**[242] 6931 3-9-6 **82** ConnorBeasley 5 64
(Michael Dods) *hld up: rdn and outpcd over 2f out: kpt on fnl f: nvr able to chal* **11/1**

0-61 **8** 3/4 **Dodgy Bob**[19] 2200 3-9-6 **82** (p) ShaneGray 2 62
(Kevin Ryan) *cl up on outside: rdn over 2f out: wknd over 1f out* **8/1**

0-00 **9** 1 1/2 **Mon Beau Visage (IRE)**[5] 2650 3-9-1 **77** (p) DavidNolan 6 52
(David O'Meara) *cl up: led after 2f to over 2f out: rdn and wknd over 1f out* **14/1**

52-4 **10** 1 1/4 **Never In Doubt**[38] 1669 3-8-13 **75** GeorgeChaloner 15 46
(Richard Whitaker) *racd against stands' rail: led 2f: cl up tl rdn and wknd 2f out* **12/1**

502- **11** 1/2 **Cuppatee (IRE)**[207] 7753 3-8-9 **71** PJMcDonald 7 40
(Ann Duffield) *hld up: shkn up and outpcd 2f out: sn btn* **25/1**

1m 14.0s (1.00) **Going Correction** +0.175s/f (Good) **11** Ran SP% **116.5**
Speed ratings (Par 101): **100,99,98,96,96 91,89,88,86,84 84**
CSF £63.06 CT £482.20 TOTE £5.80: £2.30, £3.70, £2.00; EX 81.10 Trifecta £529.50.
Owner J C G Chua & C K Ong **Bred** Frank Moynihan **Trained** Hambleton, N Yorks

FOCUS
Race distance as advertised. Fair sprinting form, with a few unexposed contenders in this.

2803 DIRECTORS CUP (H'CAP) 6f
8:00 (8:03) (Class 3) (0-95,95) 4-Y-O+ **£7,439** (£2,213; £1,106; £553) **Stalls** High

Form RPR

0-43 **1** **Duke Cosimo**[11] 2476 6-8-4 **78** PJMcDonald 1 89
(Michael Herrington) *hld up: hdwy on outside wl over 1f out: led ins fnl f: rdn and r.o wl* **5/1**[2]

0-03 **2** 1 **Red Pike (IRE)**[21] 2158 5-9-6 **94** PaulMulrennan 13 102
(Bryan Smart) *led against stands' rail: rdn along over 1f out: hdd and flashed tail ins fnl f: one pce towards fin* **10/3**[1]

-450 **3** 2 **Mississippi**[32] 1848 7-8-7 **81** (p) BarryMcHugh 7 83+
(Paul Midgley) *hld up: shkn up and stdy hdwy over 1f out: chsd ldng pair wl ins fnl f: nvr nrr* **7/1**[3]

0240 **4** 1/2 **Intense Style (IRE)**[21] 2158 4-9-2 **90** DavidAllan 14 90
(Les Eyre) *trckd ldrs: rdn along 2f out: kpt on same pce ins fnl f* **10/1**

0-00 **5** 1/2 **Meshardal (GER)**[11] 2476 6-8-7 **81** JamesSullivan 2 79
(Ruth Carr) *hld up in tch on outside: effrt and pushed along over 1f out: kpt on same pce fnl f* **14/1**

4-10 **6** 1 1/4 **Tumblewind**[18] 2258 6-8-13 **87** GeorgeChaloner 10 81+
(Richard Whitaker) *dwlt: hld up against stands' rail: no room fr 1/2-way tl last 100yds: nt rcvr* **25/1**

4630 **7** 1 **Mappin Time (IRE)**[11] 2476 8-8-2 **81** ow1 (b) RachelRichardson(5) 8 72+
(Tim Easterby) *hld up nr stands' rail: no room fr 1/2-way tl ins fnl f: nt rcvr* **25/1**

-060 **8** 3/4 **Adam's Ale**[20] 2188 7-8-9 **83** DougieCostello 12 72
(Mark Walford) *prom: drvn over 2f out: wknd over 1f out* **12/1**

00-0 **9** 2 **Fast Act (IRE)**[18] 2258 4-9-4 **95** JoeDoyle(3) 3 77
(Kevin Ryan) *spd on outside tl rdn and wknd over 1f out* **40/1**

00-0 **10** 1/2 **Eccleston**[39] 1644 5-9-5 **93** (v) PhillipMakin 9 74+
(David O'Meara) *hld up: nt clr run over 2f out to over 1f out: sn rdn and no imp* **5/1**[2]

6-00 **11** hd **Grandad's World (IRE)**[18] 2258 4-9-2 **90** (p) TonyHamilton 5 70
(Richard Fahey) *trckd ldrs: rdn over 2f out: wknd over 1f out* **20/1**

0-00 **12** 1 1/4 **Highland Acclaim (IRE)**[11] 2480 5-9-0 **88** DavidNolan 6 64
(David O'Meara) *dwlt: hld up in tch: drvn along over 2f out: sn wknd* **22/1**

1m 12.77s (-0.23) **Going Correction** +0.175s/f (Good) **12** Ran SP% **111.6**
Speed ratings (Par 107): **108,106,104,103,102 101,99,98,96,95 95,93**
CSF £18.09 CT £101.98 TOTE £5.10: £1.90, £1.60, £2.00; EX 22.40 Trifecta £139.00.
Owner Stuart Herrington **Bred** Cheveley Park Stud Ltd **Trained** Cold Kirby, N Yorks

FOCUS
Race distance as advertised. The right horses came to the fore late on in what was a good sprint, predictably run in a quicker time than the 3yo race 30 mins earlier. The form is rated around the runner-up, with the winner's best run since August 2014.

2804 SIS MAIDEN STKS 1m 1f 170y
8:30 (8:33) (Class 5) 3-Y-O+ **£2,911** (£866; £432; £216) **Stalls** Low

Form RPR

4 **1** **Indulged**[26] 2008 3-8-9 0 TomQueally 6 82+
(James Fanshawe) *prom: shkn up and rn green 2f out: hdwy to ld appr fnl f: edgd rt and pushed out fnl f: comf* **7/4**[2]

5-2 **2** nk **Fastnet Tempest (IRE)**[19] 2197 3-9-0 0 JoeFanning 3 84
(William Haggas) *t.k.h: trckd ldr: led gng wl 3f out: rdn and hdd appr fnl f: rallied: hld towards fin* **4/7**[1]

3 **3** 8 **Throckley**[25] 2048 5-9-13 0 SamJames 8 71+
(John Davies) *t.k.h: hld up: rdn over 3f out: rallied to chse clr ldng pair 1f out: no imp* **10/1**

4 3/4 **Aislabie (FR)** 3-9-0 0 JasonHart 5 66
(Mark Walford) *t.k.h: trckd ldrs: rdn and outpcd over 3f out: kpt on fnl f: no imp* **40/1**

5 2 1/4 **Ecoute (IRE)**[38] 3-9-0 0 [1] GrahamLee 1 61
(Mick Channon) *t.k.h: led at modest gallop: rdn and hdd 3f out: rallied: wknd over 1f out* **9/1**[3]

-000 **6** 6 **Don't Tell Nik (IRE)**[15] 2327 3-8-9 40 RaulDaSilva 7 44?
(David Loughnane) *t.k.h: hld up: rdn and outpcd over 3f out: btn fnl 2f* **125/1**

7 20 **Charm Park**[381] 6-9-13 0 TonyHamilton 9 9
(Geoffrey Harker) *slowly away: hdwy to tag onto main gp after 3f: rdn and lost tch over 3f out: t.o* **100/1**

2m 5.38s (-0.02) **Going Correction** +0.175s/f (Good)
WFA 3 from 5yo+ 13lb **7** Ran SP% **123.3**
Speed ratings (Par 103): **107,106,100,99,97 93,77**
CSF £3.43 TOTE £2.80: £1.10, £1.10; EX 3.80 Trifecta £9.90.
Owner Cheveley Park Stud **Bred** Cheveley Park Stud Ltd **Trained** Newmarket, Suffolk

FOCUS
Race distance increased by 4yds. The big two dominated and both look worth keeping on side.

2805 RIPON RACES SUPPORTS RACING WELFARE H'CAP 2m
9:00 (9:01) (Class 5) (0-75,74) 4-Y-O+ **£3,234** (£962; £481; £240) **Stalls** High

Form RPR

6422 **1** **Stormin Tom (IRE)**[13] 2406 4-8-13 **70** RachelRichardson(5) 5 80+
(Tim Easterby) *mde all: set ordinary gallop but clr to 1/2-way: shkn up and qcknd clr over 2f out: kpt on wl fnl f: eased nr fin: unchal* **15/8**[1]

5012 **2** 2 3/4 **Hallstatt (IRE)**[15] 2338 10-8-13 **67** (t) JoeDoyle(3) 2 72
(John Mackie) *prom: effrt and chsd (clr) wnr over 2f out: kpt on fnl f: nt pce to chal* **11/1**

3-32 **3** 1 3/4 **Rock On Bollinski**[32] 1852 6-9-8 **73** (p) BenCurtis 7 76
(Brian Ellison) *hld up in tch on outside: rdn over 3f out: kpt on fr 2f out: nrst fin* **4/1**[3]

12-3 **4** hd **Carpe Vita (IRE)**[12] 2427 4-9-6 **72** DavidNolan 6 75
(David O'Meara) *hld up in tch on ins: effrt whn nt clr run 3f out tl swtchd rt and effrt over 1f out: no imp fnl f* **7/2**[2]

2244 **5** 2 1/4 **Northside Prince (IRE)**[26] 2018 10-9-4 **69** NeilFarley 9 69
(Alan Swinbank) *trckd ldrs: effrt and rdn wl over 2f out: wknd over 1f out* **12/1**

03/0 **6** 4 **Daliance (IRE)**[20] 2194 7-9-7 **72** (b) TonyHamilton 1 67
(Noel Williams) *chsd wnr: rdn and lost 2nd over 2f out: wknd over 1f out* **16/1**

41-0 **7** 5 **La Bacouetteuse (FR)**[38] 1665 11-9-5 **70** (b) DavidAllan 3 59
(Iain Jardine) *dwlt: t.k.h in rr: rdn and outpcd over 3f out: nvr on terms* **13/2**

3m 35.33s (3.53) **Going Correction** +0.175s/f (Good)
WFA 4 from 6yo+ 1lb **7** Ran SP% **112.2**
Speed ratings (Par 103): **98,96,95,95,94 92,90**
CSF £22.86 CT £73.30 TOTE £2.70: £2.30, £5.40; EX 22.80 Trifecta £92.00.
Owner Three Jolly Farmers **Bred** Mill House, Donald, Fowlston & McStay **Trained** Great Habton, N Yorks

FOCUS
Race distance increased by 4yds. A modest staying handicap that was dominated by the front-running favourite.
T/Plt: £88.40 to a £1 stake. Pool: £73,806.17 - 609.04 winning units. T/Qpdt: £10.70 to a 31 stake. Pool: £7,296.82 - 502.10 winning units. **Richard Young**

2567 CHANTILLY (R-H)
Wednesday, June 1

OFFICIAL GOING: Turf: heavy; polytrack: standard

2806a PRIX DU BOIS DE PERTHE (CLAIMER) (5YO+) (POLYTRACK) 1m 1f 110y
3:20 (12:00) 5-Y-O+ **£6,985** (£2,794; £2,095; £1,397; £698)

RPR

1 **Kingspone (FR)**[12] 5-9-1 0 GregoryBenoist 10 83
(Mme P Butel, France) **78/10**

2 4 **Theo Danon (GER)**[22] 8-8-11 0 EddyHardouin 4 71
(Mario Hofer, Germany) **19/5**[2]

3 1 1/4 **Lykastos (IRE)**[12] 6-9-2 0 (b) Pierre-CharlesBoudot 7 73
(J Phelippon, France) **76/10**[3]

4 shd **New Outlook (USA)**[26] 8-9-3 0 NicolasLarenaudie(5) 5 79
(F Chappet, France) **27/10**[1]

5 1/2 **Orphic (FR)**[26] 7-9-6 0 RonanThomas 1 76
(J Phelippon, France) **9/1**

6 5 **Bonnoption**[135] 5-8-8 0 SylvainRuis 12 54
(R Le Gal, France) **18/1**

7 snk **Freud (FR)**[67] 1089 6-9-6 0 ChristopheSoumillon 3 66
(Ian Williams) *dwlt sltly: sn settled in midfield: rdn over 2f out: outpcd by ldrs over 1f out: no ex and fdd fnl f* **79/10**

8 1 **Nalon**[65] 5-8-9 0 MlleIsisMagnin(6) 9 59
(J-M Lefebvre, France) **20/1**

9 3 **Warrigal (IRE)**[363] 5259 6-9-6 0 (b) GlenBraem 6 57
(Leo Braem, Belgium) **27/1**

10 hd **Marmaris (FR)**[34] 7-8-8 0 AntoineHamelin 13 45
(C Lerner, France) **24/1**

11 4 1/2 **Full Pelt (USA)**[23] 8-9-1 0 (b) NorbertJeanpierre 8 43
(L Van Cauwenberghe, Belgium) **63/1**

12 dist **Kalahari Soldier (GER)**[22] 5-8-13 0 ow2 (p) OlivierPeslier 2
(Mario Hofer, Germany) **11/1**

13 15 **Lara Karay (FR)** 5-8-8 0 MarcelloBartoli 14
(Gianluca Bietolini, Italy) **90/1**

WIN (incl. 1 euro stake): 8.80. PLACES: 2.60, 2.10, 2.70. DF: 17.20. SF: 45.00
Owner Mme G Villedey & Elmina Sas **Bred** Ecurie Valencia **Trained** France

2570 HAMILTON (R-H)
Thursday, June 2

OFFICIAL GOING: Good to firm (8.7)
Wind: Light, half behind Weather: Sunny, warm

2807 LOCKTON COMPANIES 50TH ANNIVERSARY NOVICE AUCTION STKS (£20,000 HIGHLAND SPRING SERIES QUALIFIER) 5f 7y
2:00 (2:00) (Class 5) 2-Y-O **£3,557** (£1,058; £529; £264) **Stalls** High

Form RPR

363 **1** **Harome (IRE)**[8] 2570 2-9-1 0 SamJames 6 72
(David Loughnane) *mde all: rdn over 1f out: edgd lft ins fnl f: hld on wl* **4/1**[3]

4231 **2** nk **Merry Banter**[13] 2424 2-9-1 0 GrahamLee 3 71
(Paul Midgley) *cl up: rdn along 2f out: kpt on ins fnl f: jst hld* **7/4**[1]

4 **3** nk **La Casa Tarifa (IRE)**[10] 2530 2-8-8 0 JoeFanning 5 65
(Mark Johnston) *trckd ldrs: effrt and rdn over 1f out: checked ins fnl f: kpt on fin: improve* **9/1**

20 **4** 1 1/2 **Bourbonisto**[8] 2570 2-8-13 0 JoeyHaynes 7 62
(Ben Haslam) *dwlt: chsd ldng gp: rdn along over 2f out: effrt over 1f out: kpt on same pce ins fnl f* **11/4**[2]

5 3 **Inglorious** 2-8-13 0 RoystonFfrench 2 52+
(Keith Dalgleish) *noisy in preliminaries: s.i.s: rn green in rr: outpcd tl sme late hdwy: bttr for r* **8/1**

40 **6** *nk* **Neigh Kid**^{5} 2675 2-8-6 0 ShaneGray 1 44
(Keith Dalgleish) *wnt rt s: t.k.h and sn cl up: hung rt thrght: wknd over 1f out* **16/1**

59.63s (-0.37) **Going Correction** -0.025s/f (Good) **6** Ran SP% **110.0**
Speed ratings (Par 93): **101,100,100,97,92 92**
CSF £10.98 TOTE £5.90: £2.90, £1.50; EX 12.10 Trifecta £63.70.
Owner R G Fell **Bred** Limestone & Tara Studs **Trained** Market Drayton, Shropshire

FOCUS
The watered ground was given as good to firm (GoingStick: 8.7). The rail on the loop was out 3yds. Modest novice form.

2808 WATCH RACING UK IN HD APPRENTICE H'CAP 5f 7y
2:30 (2:30) (Class 6) (0-65,65) 4-Y-O+ **£2,911** (£866; £432; £216) **Stalls** High

Form RPR

3341 **1** **Roy's Legacy**^{10} 2523 7-9-0 **63** 6ex CharlieBennett$^{(5)}$ 10 69
(Shaun Harris) *cl up: led 1/2-way: rdn and edgd rt over 1f out: hld on wl ins fnl f* **12/1**

20 **2** *¾* **Little Belter (IRE)**^{10} 2523 4-8-10 **57** (v) EdwardGreatrex$^{(3)}$ 1 60
(Keith Dalgleish) *checked s: sn led on outside: hdd 1/2-way: rallied: kpt on ins fnl f: hld nr fin* **8/1**

-532 **3** *shd* **See Vermont**^{23} 2120 8-9-2 **65** (p) RowanScott$^{(5)}$ 5 68
(Rebecca Bastiman) *hld up: effrt and hdwy on outside over 1f out: kpt on ins fnl f: hld nr fin* **6/1**^{2}

1100 **4** *nk* **Boxing Shadows**^{57} 1255 6-9-0 **65** BenRobinson$^{(7)}$ 9 67
(Les Eyre) *hld up against stands' rail: rdn along 2f out: kpt on ins fnl f: nrst fin* **12/1**

0-15 **5** *½* **Perfect Words (IRE)**^{10} 2523 6-9-6 **64** JacobButterfield 6 64
(Marjorie Fife) *w ldrs: rdn along 2f out: kpt on same pce ins fnl f* **12/1**

-220 **6** *½* **Chookie's Lass**^{16} 2334 5-8-13 **64** (p) CliffordLee$^{(7)}$ 2 62
(Keith Dalgleish) *dwlt: sn cl up on outside: rdn and ch over 1f out: one pce ins fnl f* **7/1**^{3}

00-6 **7** *½* **Classic Flyer**^{141} 159 4-9-6 **64** (p) ShelleyBirkett 4 60
(David O'Meara) *in tch: drvn along over 2f out: kpt on same pce fnl f* **10/1**

0653 **8** *hd* **Groundworker (IRE)**^{8} 2572 5-9-2 **65** AdamMcNamara$^{(5)}$ 3 61
(Paul Midgley) *early ldr: w ldrs: rdn over 2f out: kpt on same pce fnl f* **15/8**^{1}

0010 **9** *nk* **Under Approval**^{5} 2676 5-8-6 **53** (b) GemmaTutty$^{(3)}$ 7 48
(Karen Tutty) *dwlt: bhd: pushed along and outpcd 1/2-way: kpt on fnl f: no imp* **12/1**

-000 **10** *10* **It's Time For Bed**^{10} 2523 4-8-0 **47** oh1 ow1 PhilDennis$^{(3)}$ 8 6
(Linda Perratt) *in tch: drvn along 1/2-way: sn struggling: lost tch ins fnl f* **100/1**

59.48s (-0.52) **Going Correction** -0.025s/f (Good) **10** Ran SP% **113.5**
Speed ratings (Par 101): **103,101,101,101,100 99,98,98,97,81**
CSF £101.58 CT £650.10 TOTE £11.60: £3.10, £2.00, £1.90; EX 70.70 Trifecta £577.00.
Owner S Mohammed, S Rowley & S Harris **Bred** A Christou **Trained** Carburton, Notts

FOCUS
A modest sprint.

2809 NEILSLAND AND EARNOCK JULIAN WATSON MEMORIAL MAIDEN STKS 6f 6y
3:00 (3:04) (Class 5) 3-Y-O+ **£3,881** (£1,155; £577; £288) **Stalls** Centre

Form RPR

32- **1** **Birkdale (IRE)**^{360} 2977 3-9-5 0 GrahamLee 7 73+
(David O'Meara) *racd away fr main gp: mde all: pushed along fr 2f out: edgd rt and kpt on wl fnl f: comf* **1/1**^{1}

-506 **2** *1 ¼* **Take Charge**^{26} 2049 3-9-5 71 ShaneGray 3 68
(David Brown) *led main centre gp: rdn along 2f out: kpt on fnl f: nt pce of wnr* **5/2**^{2}

45- **3** *¾* **Full Of Promise**^{208} 7751 3-9-0 0 GeorgeChaloner 6 61
(Richard Fahey) *cl up centre: rdn and edgd both ways over 1f out: kpt on same pce ins fnl f* **8/1**^{3}

00- **4** *½* **Prairie Impulse**^{352} 3254 3-9-0 0 PJMcDonald 1 59
(Ann Duffield) *prom: rdn and effrt 2f out: kpt on same pce ins fnl f* **16/1**

4 **5** *¾* **Lucky Violet (IRE)**^{13} 2419 4-9-8 0 RoystonFfrench 4 59
(Iain Jardine) *s.i.s: bhd and green: hdwy over 1f out: kpt on fnl f: no imp* **25/1**

0- **6** *4 ½* **Abu Khadra (IRE)**^{208} 7752 3-9-5 0 DavidNolan 2 47
(Richard Fahey) *fly j. s: hld up: rdn and hung rt over 2f out: wknd over 1f out* **8/1**^{3}

7 *5* **Lord Bopper (IRE)** 3-9-0 0 RobJFitzpatrick$^{(5)}$ 5 31
(Ben Haslam) *prom: drvn and outpcd over 3f out: hung lft over 2f out: sn wknd* **40/1**

1m 11.44s (-0.76) **Going Correction** -0.025s/f (Good)
WFA 3 from 4yo 8lb **7** Ran SP% **113.0**
Speed ratings (Par 103): **104,102,101,100,99 93,87**
CSF £3.51 TOTE £1.60: £1.10, £2.10; EX 4.20 Trifecta £12.60.
Owner David W Armstrong **Bred** R N Auld **Trained** Upper Helmsley, N Yorks

FOCUS
Just an ordinary maiden and the winner probably didn't need to improve.

2810 ALEX FERGUSSON MEMORIAL H'CAP 1m 67y
3:30 (3:35) (Class 6) (0-65,65) 4-Y-O+ **£2,911** (£866; £432; £216) **Stalls** Low

Form RPR

0001 **1** **Red Charmer (IRE)**^{10} 2529 6-9-4 **62** PJMcDonald 1 75+
(Ann Duffield) *trckd ldrs: smooth hdwy to ld over 2f out: shkn up and qcknd clr over 1f out: readily* **6/4**^{1}

6-00 **2** *3 ½* **British Embassy (IRE)**^{16} 2347 4-9-2 **65** EdwardGreatrex$^{(5)}$ 9 68
(David Loughnane) *t.k.h: trckd ldrs: effrt over 3f out: hung rt and chsd wnr 2f out: kpt on fnl f: nt pce to chal* **20/1**

-442 **3** *¾* **Ingleby Spring (IRE)**^{9} 2555 4-8-9 **60** AdamMcNamara$^{(7)}$ 5 61
(Richard Fahey) *hld up: rdn and outpcd 4f out: rallied 2f out: kpt on fnl f: nt pce to chal* **11/4**^{2}

0466 **4** *nk* **Incurs Four Faults**^{16} 2330 5-8-8 **52** JasonHart 3 53
(Keith Dalgleish) *t.k.h: led to over 2f out: kpt on same pce fr over 1f out* **6/1**^{3}

0-03 **5** *1 ¼* **Bushtiger (IRE)**^{10} 2528 4-8-2 **46** oh1 JamesSullivan 2 44
(Ruth Carr) *stdd s: hld up: effrt against far rail wl over 2f out: swtchd lft and kpt on fnl f: nvr rchd ldrs* **18/1**

-305 **6** *nse* **I'm Super Too (IRE)**^{31} 1925 9-8-8 **57** GemmaTutty$^{(5)}$ 4 55
(Karen Tutty) *midfield: rdn along over 2f out: no imp fr over 1f out* **8/1**

0-00 **7** *8* **Rioja Day (IRE)**^{15} 2365 6-8-10 **54** (v) JoeFanning 6 33
(Jim Goldie) *hld up: drvn and outpcd 4f out: n.d after* **14/1**

5400 **8** *hd* **Fairy Pools**^{14} 2409 5-8-4 **48** PatrickMathers 8 27
(Les Eyre) *hld up on outside: drvn along over 3f out: wknd fr 2f out* **66/1**

1-05 **9** *¾* **Outlaw Kate (IRE)**^{10} 2528 4-8-0 **49** (p) PhilDennis$^{(5)}$ 7 26
(Michael Mullineaux) *chsd ldr to over 3f out: hung rt and wknd 2f out* **50/1**

1m 45.08s (-3.32) **Going Correction** -0.30s/f (Firm) **9** Ran SP% **112.2**
Speed ratings (Par 101): **104,100,99,99,98 98,90,89,89**
CSF £35.42 CT £76.68 TOTE £2.50: £1.30, £5.00, £1.70; EX 32.70 Trifecta £85.00.
Owner I Farrington & R Chapman **Bred** Tally-Ho Stud **Trained** Constable Burton, N Yorks

FOCUS
Race distance increased by 12yds. This proved straightforward for the unpenalised winner.

2811 WEATHERBYS PRIVATE BANK HAMILTONIAN H'CAP 1m 1f 34y
4:00 (4:00) (Class 4) (0-80,76) 4-Y-O+ **£6,469** (£1,925; £962; £481) **Stalls** Low

Form RPR

-303 **1** **Muhaafiz (IRE)**^{7} 2620 4-9-7 **76** (p) ShaneGray 7 89
(David Brown) *trckd ldrs: effrt and rdn over 1f out: led ins fnl f: qcknd clr: eased nr fin* **10/3**^{2}

6-40 **2** *3 ¾* **Belle Travers**^{21} 2174 4-9-4 **73** DavidNolan 9 78
(Richard Fahey) *pressed ldr: rdn over 2f out: led over 1f out to ins fnl f: kpt on: nt pce of wnr* **11/1**

-230 **3** *¾* **Silver Duke (IRE)**^{6} 2661 5-8-7 **62** (b) JoeFanning 8 65
(Jim Goldie) *s.i.s: hld up: rdn over 2f out: kpt on fnl f to take 3rd cl home: nrst fin* **14/1**

6261 **4** *nse* **Archie's Advice**^{32} 1884 5-9-5 **74** JasonHart 5 77
(Keith Dalgleish) *in tch on outside: effrt over 2f out: drvn and outpcd over 1f out: kpt on ins fnl f* **4/1**^{3}

4146 **5** *shd* **Archipeligo**^{24} 2093 5-9-3 **72** (p) RoystonFfrench 3 75
(Iain Jardine) *hld up in tch: drvn and outpcd over 3f out: rallied over 2f out: kpt on ins fnl f* **8/1**

0110 **6** *1* **Ellaal**^{5} 2673 7-8-13 **68** JamesSullivan 6 69
(Ruth Carr) *led: rdn over 2f out: hdd over 1f out: outpcd ins fnl f* **9/1**

3152 **7** *¾* **All You (IRE)**^{5} 2672 4-9-3 **72** (v) SamJames 2 71
(David O'Meara) *hld up: effrt and pushed along over 2f out: no imp fr over 1f out* **9/4**^{1}

6-06 **8** *4 ½* **Tectonic (IRE)**^{8} 2575 7-9-0 **69** (p) GrahamLee 4 58
(Keith Dalgleish) *hld up in tch on ins: stdy hdwy and rdn over 1f out: wknd ins fnl f* **25/1**

1m 55.94s (-3.76) **Going Correction** -0.30s/f (Firm) **8** Ran SP% **113.8**
Speed ratings (Par 105): **104,100,100,99,99 98,98,94**
CSF £38.68 CT £449.44 TOTE £4.80: £3.10, £4.60, £4.70; EX 49.90 Trifecta £466.10.
Owner J C Fretwell **Bred** Mrs Anne McDonnell **Trained** Averham Park, Notts

FOCUS
Race distance increased by 12yds. A fair handicap taken in good style by the winner.

2812 WEATHERBYS PRIVATE BANK H'CAP 6f 6y
4:30 (4:30) (Class 5) (0-70,70) 4-Y-O+ **£3,881** (£1,155; £577; £288) **Stalls** Centre

Form RPR

-300 **1** **Inexes**^{16} 2345 4-9-7 **70** SamJames 4 75
(Marjorie Fife) *dwlt: sn prom: rdn to ld appr fnl f: hld on wl towards fin* **10/3**^{2}

0322 **2** *nk* **Keene's Pointe**^{8} 2571 6-9-0 **63** JoeFanning 6 67
(Kristin Stubbs) *dwlt: bhd: outpcd over 3f out: rallied over 1f out: wnt 2nd towards fin: jst hld* **2/1**^{1}

0-00 **3** *½* **Star Cracker (IRE)**^{16} 2332 4-9-0 **63** (p) JasonHart 7 65
(Jim Goldie) *w ldrs: rdn and edgd lft over 1f out: kpt on ins fnl f: hld nr fin* **8/1**

-006 **4** *½* **Pabusar**^{18} 2270 8-8-5 **54** (v) PJMcDonald 2 55
(Micky Hammond) *prom: effrt and rdn 2f out: kpt on same pce ins fnl f* **16/1**

6306 **5** *nk* **Gold Beau (FR)**^{16} 2332 6-8-13 **65** (p) JacobButterfield$^{(3)}$ 5 65
(Kristin Stubbs) *sn chsd along bhd ldng gp: hdwy over 1f out: kpt on ins fnl f: no imp* **11/2**

-603 **6** *1 ¾* **Salvatore Fury (IRE)**^{20} 2202 6-9-4 **67** (p) GrahamLee 3 61
(Keith Dalgleish) *t.k.h: led to appr fnl f: no ex ins fnl f* **7/2**^{3}

-000 **7** *2* **Amber Crystal**^{8} 2572 4-8-8 **57** GeorgeChaloner 8 45
(Linda Perratt) *w ldrs: rdn over 2f out: wknd fnl f* **33/1**

-000 **8** *shd* **Takahiro**^{10} 2528 4-8-2 **51** oh4 JamesSullivan 1 39
(Linda Perratt) *bhd: drvn and outpcd 1/2-way: nvr a factor* **100/1**

1m 11.6s (-0.60) **Going Correction** -0.025s/f (Good) **8** Ran SP% **114.9**
Speed ratings (Par 103): **103,102,101,101,100 98,95,95**
CSF £10.49 CT £47.61 TOTE £3.50: £1.40, £1.40, £1.40; EX 12.20 Trifecta £59.70.
Owner 21st Century Racing **Bred** Meon Valley Stud **Trained** Stillington, N Yorks

FOCUS
An ordinary sprint which suited those ridden with a bit of patience.

2813 D M HALL H'CAP 1m 5f 15y
5:00 (5:00) (Class 6) (0-65,70) 4-Y-O+ **£2,911** (£866; £432; £216) **Stalls** Low

Form RPR

03 **1** **Ballyfarsoon (IRE)**^{6} 2634 5-8-7 **51** (b^{1}) PJMcDonald 1 57
(Ian Williams) *t.k.h: trckd ldrs: drvn and outpcd over 2f out: rallied over 1f out: kpt on wl to ld nr fin* **6/1**^{3}

3501 **2** *nk* **San Quentin (IRE)**^{8} 2575 5-9-7 **70** 6ex EdwardGreatrex$^{(5)}$ 5 76
(David Loughnane) *hld up in last pl: smooth hdwy on outside 3f out: led and edgd lft over 1f out: kpt on fnl f: hdd nr fin* **7/2**^{2}

20-2 **3** *hd* **Ingleby Hollow**^{3} 2745 4-9-7 **65** DavidNolan 6 71
(David O'Meara) *led: rdn over 2f out: edgd lft and hdd over 1f out: kpt on ins fnl f* **5/2**^{1}

30-3 **4** *¾* **Hero's Story**^{38} 1697 6-8-11 **55** JoeFanning 3 60
(Jim Goldie) *hld up in tch: rdn over 2f out: rallied over 1f out: kpt on ins fnl f: hld nr fin* **7/1**

-010 **5** *1 ¾* **Solid Justice (IRE)**^{9} 2558 5-8-10 **54** JoeyHaynes 8 56
(Kenny Johnson) *trckd ldr to over 2f out: kpt on same pce u.p fnl f* **16/1**

25-0 **6** *½* **Stoneham**^{21} 498 5-8-13 **57** RoystonFfrench 10 58
(Iain Jardine) *prom: drvn and outpcd over 2f out: kpt on ins fnl f: nt pce to chal* **13/2**

0-30 **7** *1 ¾* **Schmooze (IRE)**^{8} 2575 7-9-1 **59** GeorgeChaloner 2 58
(Linda Perratt) *hld up: drvn and outpcd over 3f out: kpt on fnl f: no imp* **22/1**

40-4 **8** *3 ¾* **Byronegetonefree**^{24} 2089 5-8-2 **46** oh1 PatrickMathers 7 39
(Stuart Coltherd) *hld up on outside: drvn and outpcd over 2f out: btn over 1f out* **16/1**

502P **R** **Jammy Moment**^{6} 2656 5-9-5 **63** GrahamLee 9
(Keith Dalgleish) *ref to r* **12/1**

2m 49.18s (-4.72) **Going Correction** -0.30s/f (Firm) **9** Ran SP% **114.7**
Speed ratings (Par 101): **102,101,101,101,100 99,99,96,**
CSF £27.10 CT £65.79 TOTE £7.50: £1.80, £1.40, £1.10; EX 38.70 Trifecta £113.50.
Owner Patrick Kelly **Bred** A O'Sullivan **Trained** Portway, Worcs

FOCUS
Race distance increased by 12yds. They finished in a bit of a heap in this modest handicap.

T/Plt: £35.30 to a £1 stake. Pool: £52,944.65 - 1,093.03 winning tickets. T/Qpdt: £7.80 to a £1 stake. Pool: £4,547.34 - 429.02 winning tickets. **Richard Young**

[2577]KEMPTON (A.W) (R-H)

Thursday, June 2

OFFICIAL GOING: Polytrack: standard

Wind: strong half-against Weather: cloudy

2814 RACINGUK.COM APPRENTICE H'CAP — 1m 3f (P)

5:40 (5:42) (Class 6) (0-65,65) 4-Y-O+ — **£2,264** (£673; £336; £168) **Stalls** Low

Form — RPR

43/0 **1** **Eugenic**[16] 2323 5-8-4 **51** ... LuluStanford[(3)] 1 — 56
(Rod Millman) *hld up in rr: stl plenty to do ent st: rdn and swtchd to outer over 2f out: str run ins fnl f to ld nr fin* **10/1**

231 **2** *nk* **Innoko (FR)**[12] 2461 6-9-4 **62** ... GeorgiaCox 2 — 67
(Tony Carroll) *in tch in rr-div: rdn in centre 2f out: kpt on wl ins fnl f to take 2nd post* **3/1**[2]

3504 **3** *1/2* **Dalaki (IRE)**[24] 2105 5-9-7 **65** ... (b) HollieDoyle 8 — 69
(Des Donovan, Ire) *led after 2f at slow pce: rdn on rail over 2f out: kpt on ins fnl f tl hdd and lost two pls nr fin* **2/1**[1]

1114 **4** *1* **Celtic Ava (IRE)**[78] 951 4-9-3 **61** ... PaddyBradley 6 — 64
(Pat Phelan) *hld up in rr-div but in tch: w wnr ent st: rdn 2f out: nt qckn tl ins fnl f: kpt on wl* **11/2**

-222 **5** *hd* **Flutterbee**[1] 2799 4-9-2 **65** ... (p) JordanUys[(5)] 7 — 67
(George Baker) *chsd ldrs: t.k.h: rdn 2f out: nt qckn over 1f out: kpt on ins fnl f* **5/1**[3]

6400 **6** *1/2* **Opera Buff**[16] 2326 7-8-13 **57** ... (p) CharlesEddery 4 — 58
(Rae Guest) *led for 2f: chsd ldr after: rdn over 2f out: wknd ins fnl f* **14/1**

040- **7** *6* **Royal Etiquette (IRE)**[185] 8052 9-9-0 **58** ... (tp) MeganNicholls 5 — 49
(Lawney Hill) *missed break and lost several l: grad mde up grnd and chsd ldr by 1/2-way: rdn 2f out: lost tch ent fnl f* **20/1**

-600 **8** *3* **Heat Storm (IRE)**[24] 2110 5-7-11 **46** oh1 ... (t) RobertDodsworth[(5)] 3 — 33
(James Unett) *t.k.h early: ct on heels and had to check after 5f: prog outside to chse ldrs ent st: rdn 2f out: sn no ex* **100/1**

2m 24.34s (2.44) **Going Correction** -0.05s/f (Stan) — **8** Ran SP% **111.9**
Speed ratings (Par 101): **89,88,88,87,87 87,82,80**
CSF £38.43 CT £84.07 TOTE £11.40: £2.60, £1.20, £1.30; EX 36.40 Trifecta £124.50.
Owner Chris Scott **Bred** M S Saunders And Chris Scott **Trained** Kentisbeare, Devon
■ Stewards' Enquiry : Hollie Doyle four-day ban: used whip above permitted level (Jun 19-22)

FOCUS
A low-grade apprentice handicap and the early pace was very steady.

2815 32RED ON THE APP STORE MAIDEN STKS (DIV I) — 1m 4f (P)

6:10 (6:12) (Class 5) 3-Y-O+ — **£2,911** (£866; £432; £216) **Stalls** Centre

Form — RPR

32 **1** **Muntahaa (IRE)**[27] 2008 3-8-13 0 ... PaulHanagan 3 — 97+
(John Gosden) *settled bhd ldrs: upsides gng wl 3f out: shkn up and hung rt into rival over 2f out: sn led: rdn and wnt clr fnl f: impressive* **4/7**[1]

6 **2** *6* **Marmelo**[20] 2208 3-8-13 0 ... FergusSweeney 4 — 85
(Hughie Morrison) *settled in mid-div: rdn 2f out: prog over 1f out: kpt on ins fnl f: no ch w wnr* **12/1**

23- **3** *3 3/4* **Alyssa**[222] 7467 3-8-8 0 ... FMBerry 9 — 74
(Ralph Beckett) *in rr early: tk clsr order on outer by 1/2-way: rdn over 2f out: rn green 2f out: styd on ins fnl f: gng on at fin* **3/1**[2]

0-0 **4** *6* **Dostoyevsky (IRE)**[20] 2208 3-8-13 0 ... (b[1]) TomQueally 1 — 69
(David Lanigan) *led: pressed over 2f out whn bmpd by wnr: sn brushed aside: wknd over 1f out* **6/1**[3]

0 **5** *1/2* **Marshall Aid (IRE)**[21] 2175 3-8-13 0 ... (t) JamieSpencer 10 — 69
(Hugo Palmer) *chsd ldrs: rdn over 2f out: kpt on one pce* **50/1**

0 **6** *2 1/4* **Leaping**[21] 2183 3-8-8 0 ... AndreaAtzeni 8 — 60
(Roger Charlton) *chsd ldrs on outside of pack: rn green bnd: rdn over 2f out: wknd fnl f* **20/1**

03 **7** *2 3/4* **The Detainee**[14] 2398 3-8-13 0 ... AdamBeschizza 11 — 61
(Jeremy Gask) *rn green early: in rr and nudged along: wknd fr 2f out* **50/1**

56 **8** *9* **Sisania (IRE)**[20] 2215 3-8-8 0 ... LiamJones 5 — 41
(Marco Botti) *s.s: in rr: in last ent st: wknd fr 2f out* **100/1**

9 *41* **Tractive Effort** 3-8-13 0 ... RobertHavlin 7
(Michael Attwater) *mid-div: rdn to hold pl after 5f: bhd ent st* **100/1**

0 **10** *1 1/4* **Charioteer**[24] 2098 3-8-13 0 ... PatCosgrave 6
(Ed Dunlop) *in rr and rn green: nudged along most of way: rdn ent st: sn btn* **50/1**

2m 30.67s (-3.83) **Going Correction** -0.05s/f (Stan) — **10** Ran SP% **123.3**
Speed ratings (Par 103): **110,106,103,99,99 97,95,89,62,61**
CSF £10.20 TOTE £1.50: £1.02, £3.50, £1.10; EX 9.00 Trifecta £21.40.
Owner Hamdan Al Maktoum **Bred** Shadwell Estate Company Limited **Trained** Newmarket, Suffolk

FOCUS
The first division of an interesting 3yo maiden and an easy winner, with the rest strung out behind. It was 8l faster than division two and has been rated fairly positively.

2816 32RED ON THE APP STORE MAIDEN STKS (DIV II) — 1m 4f (P)

6:40 (6:42) (Class 5) 3-Y-O+ — **£2,911** (£866; £432; £216) **Stalls** Centre

Form — RPR

45 **1** **Point Of View (IRE)**[21] 2175 3-8-13 0 ... AndreaAtzeni 4 — 90+
(Roger Varian) *chsd ldr: t.k.h: stl on bit gng wl 2f out: sn rdn and led: kpt on wl ins fnl f: a holding runner-up* **5/4**[1]

34 **2** *nk* **Mazaz (IRE)**[37] 1739 3-8-13 0 ... (t) RobertHavlin 1 — 89
(John Gosden) *chsd ldrs: cl up over 2f out: rdn and ev ch 2f out: kpt on to chse wnr fnl f: a hld* **3/1**[2]

2-53 **3** *7* **Magnum (IRE)**[17] 2291 3-8-13 80 ... (b) JimmyFortune 5 — 77
(Brian Meehan) *chsd ldrs: pushed along 3f out: rdn and kpt on same pce fr over 1f out* **7/1**[3]

0 **4** *3 1/2* **Vanishing Point**[20] 2208 3-8-13 0 ... DavidProbert 3 — 72
(Andrew Balding) *in rr: rdn over 2f out: kpt on ins fnl f: gng on at fin* **66/1**

4-4 **5** *1/2* **Scottish Summit (IRE)**[47] 1483 3-8-13 0 ... TedDurcan 8 — 71
(Sir Michael Stoute) *chsd ldrs: rdn 2f out: sn hld and kpt on* **8/1**

-55 **6** *1/2* **Kesselring**[20] 2208 3-8-13 0 ... SeanLevey 10 — 70
(Richard Hannon) *led: rdn and hdd over 2f out: wknd after* **20/1**

04 **7** *1 3/4* **Eastern Lady (IND)**[21] 2182 3-8-8 0 ... SilvestreDeSousa 9 — 62
(William Knight) *in rr: rdn 3f out: sme prog 2f out: no ex fr 1f out* **12/1**

8 *24* **Midnight Mystic** 3-8-8 0 ... JamieSpencer 2 — 24
(Michael Bell) *hood removed late: in last most of way: pushed along over 4f out: rdn ent st whn sn btn* **25/1**

9 *1/2* **Beauchamp Pasha** 3-8-13 0 ... LukeMorris 7 — 28
(Harry Dunlop) *reluctant to load: in rr: rdn along 8f out: c bk on bit nt long after: pushed along 3f out: sn no ex* **100/1**

6 **10** *1/2* **Mister Showman**[32] 1897 3-8-13 0 ... RyanClark 6 — 27
(Jonathan Portman) *mid-div: pushed along on bnd: rdn fr 4f out: sn wknd ent st* **100/1**

2m 31.57s (-2.93) **Going Correction** -0.05s/f (Stan) — **10** Ran SP% **112.8**
Speed ratings (Par 103): **107,106,102,99,99 99,97,81,81,81**
CSF £4.47 TOTE £2.10: £1.20, £1.20, £2.40; EX 5.80 Trifecta £19.30.
Owner Sheikh Mohammed Obaid Al Maktoum **Bred** Rabbah Bloodstock Limited **Trained** Newmarket, Suffolk
■ Stewards' Enquiry : Ted Durcan caution: careless riding

FOCUS
The second leg of this maiden was run 0.9secs slower than the first, but the market leaders came clear. The form is rated on the positive side.

2817 IRISH STALLION FARMS EBF NOVICE FILLIES' STKS (PLUS 10 RACE) — 6f (P)

7:10 (7:11) (Class 5) 2-Y-O — **£3,234** (£962; £481; £240) **Stalls** Low

Form — RPR

1 **Sibilance** 2-9-0 0 ... FMBerry 1 — 79
(Ralph Beckett) *sn led: shkn up ent 2f out: qcknd up over 1f out: kpt on wl* **8/1**[3]

2 *1 1/2* **Stop The Wages (IRE)** 2-9-0 0 ... JimmyFortune 3 — 75
(Brian Meehan) *settled in mid-div on inner: rdn over 2f out: kpt on wl ins fnl f* **66/1**

3 **3** *nse* **Boost**[15] 2376 2-9-0 0 ... LukeMorris 7 — 74
(Sir Mark Prescott Bt) *half-rrd leaving stalls: nudged into mid-div after: rdn 2f out: no immediate rspnse tl kpt on wl ins fnl f to press runner-up nr fin* **4/7**[1]

4 *1/2* **Bee Case** 2-9-0 0 ... JimCrowley 4 — 73+
(Hugo Palmer) *in rr: swtchd wd ent st: stl plenty to do: drvn along 2f out: gd prog ins fnl f: bttr for run* **10/1**

5 *hd* **Tiburtina (IRE)** 2-9-0 0 ... PatDobbs 5 — 72
(Sylvester Kirk) *chsd ldrs: rdn 2f out: stl there tl wknd ins fnl f* **66/1**

6 *1/2* **Hawana (USA)** 2-9-0 0 ... WilliamBuick 8 — 71+
(John Gosden) *settled bhd ldrs: nudged along over 2f out: kpt on wl tl wknd fnl 110yds* **5/1**[2]

7 *2 1/4* **Halinka (IRE)** 2-9-0 0 ... AndreaAtzeni 9 — 64
(Roger Varian) *mid-div on outer: gng wl over 2f out: rdn 2f out: one pce after* **12/1**

8 *hd* **Penny Green** 2-9-0 0 ... RyanTate 12 — 63
(James Eustace) *in rr: rdn 2f out: wknd fnl f* **66/1**

9 *5* **Textured (IRE)** 2-9-0 0 ... TedDurcan 2 — 48
(Sir Michael Stoute) *missed break and rn green in rr: nvr involved* **16/1**

10 *shd* **Lucky Return** 2-9-0 0 ... DavidProbert 6 — 48
(Des Donovan, Ire) *chsd ldr: rdn 2f out: lost pl and wknd qckly fr over 1f out* **100/1**

1m 15.13s (2.03) **Going Correction** -0.05s/f (Stan) — **10** Ran SP% **119.6**
Speed ratings (Par 90): **84,82,81,81,81 80,77,77,70,70**
CSF £407.26 TOTE £13.10: £3.20, £9.50, £1.02; EX 230.90 Trifecta £5106.30 Part won. Pool: £6,808.52 - 0.34 winning tickets..
Owner Nigel & Carolyn Elwes **Bred** Aylesfield Farms Stud **Trained** Kimpton, Hants

FOCUS
Inexperienced fillies but some major stables represented in this juvenile maiden and an all-the-way winner.

2818 32RED CASINO H'CAP — 7f (P)

7:40 (7:41) (Class 4) (0-85,85) 3-Y-O — **£4,690** (£1,395; £697; £348) **Stalls** Low

Form — RPR

1-45 **1** **Wimpole Hall**[19] 2239 3-8-13 **77** ... SilvestreDeSousa 1 — 83
(William Jarvis) *settled in mid-div: nudged along over 2f out: pushed along 2f out: jinked sltly rt sn after: rdn and picked up wl ins fnl f to ld nr fin* **5/1**[3]

2222 **2** *1/2* **Ice Royal (IRE)**[84] 887 3-9-6 **84** ... JamieSpencer 5 — 89+
(Jamie Osborne) *nudged along leaving stalls: in rr: prog and rdn 2f out: kpt on wl to take 2nd ins fnl f* **4/1**[1]

1-16 **3** *1/2* **Irish Eclare (IRE)**[27] 2002 3-8-10 **77** ... MichaelJMMurphy[(3)] 8 — 81
(Charles Hills) *chsd ldr: shkn up and led over 1f out: kpt on tl wknd and lost two pls nr fin* **20/1**

-316 **4** *nse* **Viscount Barfield**[12] 2477 3-8-9 **73** ... DavidProbert 13 — 77+
(Andrew Balding) *in rr: rdn 2f out: kpt on wl between horses ins fnl f to press for placings* **15/2**

313 **5** *1/2* **Rocket Power**[82] 924 3-9-1 **79** ... LukeMorris 7 — 81
(James Tate) *in rr: rdn 2f out: kpt on wl tl fr over 1f out: one pce wl ins fnl f* **8/1**

-360 **6** *2 1/2* **Colonel Bossington (IRE)**[22] 2156 3-8-11 **75** ... JimCrowley 9 — 70
(William Knight) *settled in mid-div: rdn over 2f out: sn hld* **25/1**

-514 **7** *nk* **Fashaak (IRE)**[12] 2477 3-9-4 **82** ... SeanLevey 4 — 77
(Richard Hannon) *chsd ldr: rdn over 2f out: wknd fnl f* **9/2**[2]

512- **8** *2* **Art Collection (FR)**[196] 7896 3-9-7 **85** ... GeorgeBaker 10 — 74
(Gary Moore) *hld up in rr: rdn 2f out: sn btn* **33/1**

31- **9** *6* **Graceful James (IRE)**[176] 8152 3-9-2 **80** ... KieranO'Neill 6 — 53
(Jimmy Fox) *t.k.h in mid-div: rdn over 2f out: wknd fnl f* **6/1**

1-3 **10** *nk* **D'Niro (IRE)**[37] 1750 3-9-0 **78** ... OisinMurphy 11 — 50
(Harry Dunlop) *tk fierce hold on way to post: sn led fr outside draw: clr ldr 1/2-way: rdn 2f out: hdd & wknd over 1f out* **10/1**

-210 **11** *7* **Saeedan (IRE)**[19] 2239 3-9-0 **78** ... WilliamBuick 3 — 31
(Marco Botti) *in rr: rdn 2f out: sn btn* **16/1**

1m 25.04s (-0.96) **Going Correction** -0.05s/f (Stan) — **11** Ran SP% **118.5**
Speed ratings (Par 101): **103,102,101,101,101 98,98,95,88,88 80**
CSF £24.91 CT £379.60 TOTE £6.30: £2.40, £2.30, £7.80; EX 32.80 Trifecta £341.10.
Owner Ms E L Banks **Bred** R F And S D Knipe **Trained** Newmarket, Suffolk
■ Stewards' Enquiry : Jamie Spencer two-day ban: used whip without allowing gelding sufficient time to respond (Jun 19-20)

FOCUS
A decent and competitive looking 3yo handicap and a close finish.

2819 £10 FREE BET AT 32REDSPORT.COM H'CAP (LONDON MILE SERIES QUALIFIER) 1m (P)
8:10 (8:12) (Class 3) (0-90,90) 4-Y-O+
£7,158 (£2,143; £1,071; £535; £267; £134) **Stalls** Low

Form RPR
2-35 **1** **Bastille Day**[20] 2214 4-8-9 **78** WilliamBuick 12 87
(David Elsworth) *chsd ldr: rdn over 2f out: kpt on wl ins fnl f to get up on line* **6/1**[3]
60- **2** *nse* **Countermeasure**[263] 6368 4-8-10 **79** AndreaAtzeni 11 88
(Roger Charlton) *led after 1f: rdn 2f out: kpt on wl tl hdd fnl strides* **5/1**[2]
0-03 **3** *3/4* **Major Crispies**[15] 2378 5-9-2 **85** GeorgeBaker 5 92
(James Eustace) *settled in mid-div and t.k.h: prog over 2f out: rdn and kpt on wl fnl f: nrst fin* **9/1**
1344 **4** *1/2* **Franco's Secret**[15] 2378 5-8-13 **82** (v) CharlesBishop 3 88+
(Peter Hedger) *in rr: swtchd fr centre to inner over 1f out: gd prog on rail to press for placings: nrst fin* **8/1**
130- **5** *1 3/4* **Up In Lights (IRE)**[208] 7756 4-9-5 **88** TomQueally 6 90+
(James Fanshawe) *settled in rr-div: shkn up and nudged along over 2f out: rdn ins fnl f: gng on at fin* **4/1**[1]
4314 **6** *3/4* **Jodies Jem**[29] 1959 6-9-0 **86** TomMarquand(3) 2 86
(William Jarvis) *mid-div on inner: rdn over 2f out: one pce and wknd nr fin* **10/1**
55-6 **7** *1/2* **Ruban (IRE)**[15] 2378 7-9-0 **83** (t) AdamBeschizza 9 82
(Stuart Williams) *settled in mid-div: rdn 2f out: kpt on one pce* **16/1**
0000 **8** *2 1/2* **Complicit (IRE)**[19] 2246 5-9-7 **90** (t) LukeMorris 7 83
(Paul Cole) *chsd ldrs: t.k.h: rdn over 2f out: kpt on between horses tl wknd fnl f* **6/1**[3]
202- **9** *2* **Yamllik**[364] 2877 4-8-13 **82** FMBerry 8 71
(Brian Barr) *in rr and tk fierce hold: rdn over 3f out: sn hld and wknd* **66/1**
5-00 **10** *hd* **Fire Ship**[19] 2246 7-9-7 **90** SilvestreDeSousa 1 78
(William Knight) *in rr on inner: rdn over 2f out: sn wknd* **12/1**
5/ **11** *10* **Vocaliser (IRE)**[61] 4658 4-8-12 **81** LiamKeniry 4 46
(Robin Dickin) *led briefly: chsd ldrs after and t.k.h: rdn and wknd qckly fr 2f out* **66/1**
40/0 **12** *3 1/2* **Storm King**[29] 1959 7-9-2 **85** OisinMurphy 13 42
(David C Griffiths) *in rr: rapid prog after 5f to press ldrs: rdn 2f out: wknd qckly after* **50/1**
003- **13** *4 1/2* **Zugzwang (IRE)**[320] 4371 5-9-7 **90** JamieSpencer 10 37
(Ed de Giles) *settled in mid-div: rdn 2f out: sn wknd* **33/1**
1m 37.85s (-1.95) **Going Correction** -0.05s/f (Stan) **13** Ran SP% **116.9**
Speed ratings (Par 107): **107,106,106,105,103 103,102,100,98,98 88,84,80**
CSF £34.69 CT £278.44 TOTE £7.60: £2.60, £2.40, £3.10; EX 38.40 Trifecta £353.50.
Owner Lordship Stud & David Elsworth **Bred** New England Stud And Partners **Trained** Newmarket, Suffolk

FOCUS
The feature race and another competitive contest that produced a desperate finish.

2820 32RED.COM H'CAP 2m (P)
8:40 (8:42) (Class 4) (0-85,85) 4-Y-O+ **£4,690** (£1,395; £697; £348) **Stalls** Low

Form RPR
4233 **1** **Be My Sea (IRE)**[8] 2582 5-9-1 **76** WilliamCarson 3 84
(Tony Carroll) *racd mostly in 3rd: rdn 3f out: led 1f out: kpt on wl ins fnl f* **2/1**[1]
1/14 **2** *hd* **Knight's Parade (IRE)**[17] 1417 6-8-12 **76** (t) DannyBrock(3) 5 83
(Sarah Humphrey) *in rr: rdn over 3f out: picked up wl fr over 1f out to chal wnr: hld* **16/1**
6-01 **3** *3 1/2* **Royal Reef (IRE)**[8] 2582 4-8-9 **71** 6ex SilvestreDeSousa 6 74
(William Knight) *settled in 2nd tl rdn to take up ld 4f out: hdd 1f out: lost two pls nr ins fnl f* **9/4**[2]
060 **4** *11* **Giant Redwood (IRE)**[12] 2468 4-9-6 **82** JamieSpencer 4 71
(Michael Bell) *settled in disp last: rdn 4f out: one pce* **7/1**
1 **5** *2 3/4* **An Fear Ciuin (IRE)**[51] 1405 5-8-6 **74** (p) CallumRodriguez(7) 7 60
(Richard Ford) *led: hdd 4f out: rdn 3f out: wknd* **5/1**[3]
001- **6** *3 3/4* **Thunder Pass (IRE)**[267] 6207 5-9-7 **85** (t) TomMarquand(3) 1 67
(David Pipe) *racd in 4th: rdn 4f out: wknd fr over 2f out* **7/1**
3m 27.37s (-2.73) **Going Correction** -0.05s/f (Stan)
WFA 4 from 5yo+ 1lb **6** Ran SP% **111.7**
Speed ratings (Par 105): **104,103,102,96,95 93**
CSF £31.29 TOTE £2.60: £1.50, £6.60; EX 27.70 Trifecta £70.10.
Owner Gary Attwood **Bred** Sunderland Holdings Inc **Trained** Cropthorne, Worcs

FOCUS
This stayers' handicap was run at an even pace early and they finished strung out.

2821 32RED H'CAP 7f (P)
9:10 (9:11) (Class 4) (0-80,80) 4-Y-O+ **£4,690** (£1,395; £697; £348) **Stalls** Low

Form RPR
24-2 **1** **Mutamid**[38] 1707 4-9-1 **74** SilvestreDeSousa 6 85
(Ismail Mohammed) *led early: mde all after: rdn over 2f out: kpt finding and styd on wl ins fnl f* **2/1**[1]
0 **2** *2* **Severus (GER)**[14] 2401 6-8-13 **72** DavidProbert 9 77
(Des Donovan, Ire) *settled in rr-div: nudged along on bnd to take clsr order bhd ldrs ent st: rdn 2f out: kpt on wl to hold 2nd spot* **66/1**
0566 **3** *1/2* **Dutch Art Dealer**[13] 2430 5-9-7 **80** (b) JamieSpencer 8 84+
(Paul Cole) *dropped out leaving stalls and hld up in rr: ct bhd wall of horses ent st: rdn and swtchd to inner 2f out: kpt on wl to chal for 2nd: nrst fin* **5/2**[2]
1001 **4** *nk* **Eljaddaaf (IRE)**[15] 2379 5-8-12 **71** RobertWinston 13 74
(Dean Ivory) *in rr: stl plenty to do over 2f out: shuffled along over 1f out: kpt on ins fnl f: nvr nrr* **7/2**[3]
0554 **5** *hd* **Ocean Legend (IRE)**[15] 2379 11-7-10 **62** MitchGodwin(7) 3 64
(Tony Carroll) *cl up chsng ldrs: rdn over 1f out: wknd ins fnl f* **14/1**
2160 **6** *1 3/4* **Chetan**[8] 2584 4-8-9 **68** (tp) LukeMorris 10 66
(Charlie Wallis) *chsd ldr: rdn over 1f out: nt qckn and wknd fnl f* **25/1**
2020 **7** *2 1/4* **Nasri**[8] 2577 10-8-0 **66** GeorgeWood(7) 7 58
(Emma Owen) *chsd ldrs on outer: nudged into st: lost pl over 2f out: kpt on past btn horses at one pce ins fnl f* **33/1**
0065 **8** *1/2* **Renounce (IRE)**[17] 2309 4-8-5 **67** (t) DannyBrock(3) 11 57
(Charlie Wallis) *mid-div on outer: swtchd wd and rdn over 2f out: one pce* **25/1**
3-02 **9** *3/4* **Red Cossack (CAN)**[23] 2129 5-8-12 **71** (t) WilliamCarson 1 59
(Paul Webber) *t.k.h settled in last four: rdn over 2f out on inner: sn wknd* **20/1**
3365 **10** *1/2* **Moonlight Venture**[14] 2402 5-9-4 **77** (b) LiamKeniry 4 64
(Conor Dore) *settled on rail bhd ldrs: rdn over 2f out: losing pl and lft bhd fr 2f out* **33/1**
102 **11** *nk* **Perfect Alchemy (IRE)**[27] 2001 5-9-5 **78** OisinMurphy 2 64
(Patrick Chamings) *mid-div: rdn and outpcd fr over 2f out: wknd qckly ins fnl f* **14/1**
1m 24.75s (-1.25) **Going Correction** -0.05s/f (Stan) **11** Ran SP% **117.3**
Speed ratings (Par 105): **105,102,102,101,101 99,97,96,95,95 94**
CSF £169.35 CT £353.71 TOTE £3.10: £1.40, £7.20, £1.40; EX 68.20 Trifecta £668.80.
Owner Saeed Manana **Bred** Woodcote Stud Ltd **Trained** Newmarket, Suffolk

FOCUS
A fair handicap that was run 0.29 secs faster than the earlier race over the trip for 3yos.
T/Plt: £18.10 to a £1 stake. Pool: £69,691.40 - 2795.84 winning tickets. T/Qpdt: £10.30 to a £1 stake. Pool: £6,282.29 - 447.48 winning tickets. **Cathal Gahan**

2764 LINGFIELD (L-H)
Thursday, June 2

OFFICIAL GOING: Soft (good to soft in places in places; 6.1)
Wind: medium, against Weather: overcast

2822 JOHN & JOAN GOODALL MEMORIAL NOVICE MEDIAN AUCTION STKS 6f
2:10 (2:11) (Class 5) 2-Y-O **£3,234** (£962; £481; £240) **Stalls** Centre

Form RPR
6 **1** **Golden Slam**[10] 2536 2-9-2 0 AndreaAtzeni 15 71
(Roger Varian) *mde all: rdn over 1f out: hung lft ins fnl f: hld on u.p towards fin* **9/2**[3]
2 *shd* **Haulani (USA)** 2-9-2 0 WilliamTwiston-Davies 11 71
(Philip Hide) *hld up: effrt 2f out: hdwy and drvn to chse wnr over 1f out: ev ch ins fnl f: r.o* **11/4**[1]
3 *1 1/2* **Sixties Habana** 2-9-2 0 CharlesBishop 2 66+
(Mick Channon) *in tch in midfield: effrt and swtchd lft 2f out: rdn and hdwy to chse ldng pair 1f out: styd on same pce ins fnl f* **25/1**
4 *nk* **Bobby Vee** 2-8-6 0 CharlesEddery(5) 10 60
(Dean Ivory) *hld up in midfield: rdn over 2f out: hdwy and swtchd rt over 1f out: styd on ins fnl f: nvr trbld ldrs* **25/1**
0 **5** *3/4* **Met By Moonlight**[21] 2180 2-8-11 0 DavidProbert 1 58
(Ron Hodges) *stdd and swtchd rt after s: rn green in rr: gng lft and hdwy over 1f out: clsng and swtchd lft ent fnl f: kpt on ins fnl f: nvr trbld ldrs* **100/1**
6 *2 3/4* **Moneyoryourlife** 2-9-2 0 PatDobbs 12 55+
(Richard Hannon) *stdd s: hld up in rr: effrt and pushed along jst over 2f out: rdn and hdwy into midfield over 1f out: kpt on same pce ins fnl f: nvr trbld ldrs* **8/1**
4 **7** *1 1/2* **A Sure Welcome**[16] 2344 2-8-13 0 TomMarquand(3) 9 50
(John Spearing) *wl in tch in midfield: effrt to chse ldrs 2f out: unable qck u.p over 1f out: wknd ins fnl f* **14/1**
8 *hd* **Noble Attitude (FR)** 2-9-2 0 KierenFox 4 50
(John Best) *chsd ldrs: unable qck u.p over 1f out: wknd ins fnl f* **8/1**
9 *1 3/4* **Winning Bid** 2-9-2 0 PatCosgrave 6 44
(Harry Dunlop) *s.i.s: rn green in rr: j. path 5f out: pushed along and sme hdwy over 1f out: n.d but kpt on steadily ins fnl f* **33/1**
2 **10** *1/2* **Affordability**[24] 2104 2-9-2 0 LukeMorris 3 43
(Daniel Mark Loughnane) *chsd ldr: rdn 2f out: drvn and lost 2nd over 1f out: sn btn: wknd and wl hld whn eased ins fnl f* **6/1**
11 *1* **If I Say So** 2-8-11 0 JosephineGordon(5) 14 40
(J S Moore) *in tch in midfield: rdn 2f out: unable qck and lost pl over 1f out: wknd fnl f* **66/1**
6 **12** *6* **Ingleby Mackenzie**[12] 2489 2-9-2 0 SilvestreDeSousa 8 22
(Mick Channon) *in tch in midfield: rdn and lost pl jst over 2f out: wl btn over 1f out: eased wl ins fnl f* **4/1**[2]
13 *12* **Quandary Peak** 2-8-11 0 LiamKeniry 13
(J S Moore) *dwlt: rcvrd to chse ldrs after 2f: lost pl qckly over 2f out: wl bhd over 1f out* **66/1**
0 **14** *7* **Lilly Ballerina (IRE)**[31] 1915 2-8-8 0 GeorgeDowning(3) 5
(Tony Carroll) *in tch in midfield tl lost pl qckly over 2f out: t.o fnl f* **100/1**
1m 18.03s (6.83) **Going Correction** +0.90s/f (Soft) **14** Ran SP% **123.6**
Speed ratings (Par 93): **90,89,87,87,86 82,80,80,78,77 76,68,52,42**
CSF £17.09 TOTE £4.60: £1.30, £1.70, £10.30; EX 19.60 Trifecta £371.70.
Owner Biddestone Racing Partnership XIX **Bred** Whitsbury Manor Stud **Trained** Newmarket, Suffolk

FOCUS
Following 5mm of rain the previous day and another 2.5mm overnight, the going was soft, good to soft in places (from good, good to soft in places) resulting in a few non-runners. After the first race Luke Morris said "It's soft", while Liam Keniry said "It's soft mainly." An ordinary novice median auction event to start in which they raced centre-to-nearside. It was rather a messy contest, but a few caught the eye.

2823 188BET HORSE RACING CHARTER FILLIES' H'CAP (DIV I) 7f
2:40 (2:41) (Class 5) (0-70,70) 3-Y-O **£3,234** (£962; £481; £240) **Stalls** Centre

Form RPR
0-20 **1** **Black Bess**[27] 2002 3-9-7 **70** PatCosgrave 3 83+
(Jim Boyle) *stdd after s: hld up in tch: clsd gng wl over 2f out: rdn and qcknd to ld over 1f out: sn clr and in command: heavily eased towards fin* **5/1**[2]
3113 **2** *3 1/2* **Broughtons Fancy**[8] 2586 3-9-3 **69** TomMarquand(3) 10 69+
(Andrew Reid) *broke wl: stdd bk to trck ldrs: nt clr run jst over 2f out tl fnlly enough room and hdwy to go 2nd 1f out: r.o for clr 2nd: no ch w wnr* **11/10**[1]
046- **3** *6* **In Ken's Memory**[238] 7054 3-9-4 **67** JFEgan 4 51
(John Butler) *chsd ldr: rdn jst over 2f out: 2nd and outpcd by wnr over 1f out: lost wl hld 2nd 1f out: wknd ins fnl f* **9/1**
0-03 **4** *1 1/4* **Wilspa's Magic (IRE)**[23] 2128 3-8-11 **60** DavidProbert 5 41
(Ron Hodges) *in tch in rr: pushed along 1/2-way: swtchd lft and hdwy u.p 2f out: outpcd by wnr over 1f out: wknd ins fnl f* **10/1**
6-31 **5** *7* **Belle Mare Plage**[134] 258 3-9-2 **65** OisinMurphy 2 28
(Stuart Williams) *in rr: rdn and struggling 1/2-way: rallied u.p 2f out: sn no imp and wknd over 1f out* **17/2**
2-04 **6** *4* **Abaco Ridge**[32] 1892 3-9-3 **66** FMBerry 7 19
(Ralph Beckett) *led: rdn and hdd over 2f out: sn btn and flashed tail u.p: wknd* **13/2**[3]

0-00 **7** *21* **Artisandra (FR)**[20] 2212 3-8-2 **51** oh1 (v1) LukeMorris 1
(William Knight) *racd along in centre: chsd ldrs tl rdn and btn 2f out: sn dropped out: wl bhd and eased ins fnl f: t.o* **20/1**

1m 29.35s (6.05) **Going Correction** +0.90s/f (Soft) **7** Ran SP% **112.0**
Speed ratings (Par 96): **101,97,90,88,80 76,52**
CSF £10.46 CT £45.68 TOTE £5.50: £2.90, £1.20; EX 12.40 Trifecta £55.40.
Owner The Clean Sweep Partnership **Bred** Paddock Space **Trained** Epsom, Surrey

FOCUS
A modest fillies' handicap and another messy event. They finished well spread out and this was a case of contrasting fortunes for the two market leaders. All bar the complete outsider came nearside.

2824 188BET HORSE RACING CHARTER FILLIES' H'CAP (DIV II) 7f
3:10 (3:12) (Class 5) (0-70,70) 3-Y-O **£3,234** (£962; £481; £240) **Stalls** Centre

Form RPR
-542 **1** **Make Music**[8] 2585 3-9-6 **69** DavidProbert 9 78
(Andrew Balding) *led tl 1/2-way: pressed ldr tl led again and gng best over 1f out: rdn to assert and drifted lft ent fnl f: r.o and drew clr ins fnl f: comf* **4/5**[1]

5362 **2** *2 1/4* **Phoenix Beat**[8] 2586 3-9-5 **68** LukeMorris 3 71
(Gay Kelleway) *chsd ldrs: rdn 1/2-way: drvn to chse wnr 1f out: unable qck and one pce fnl 100yds* **7/2**[2]

3110 **3** *2 1/2* **Bushwise (IRE)**[9] 2559 3-8-11 **60** (p) SilvestreDeSousa 5 57
(Milton Bradley) *stdd after s: t.k.h: hld up in tch towards rr: hdwy u.p over 1f out: wnt 3rd ins fnl f: sn outpcd* **12/1**

-130 **4** *3 1/2* **Tigserin (IRE)**[8] 2585 3-8-11 **65** KieranShoemark(5) 4 53
(Giles Bravery) *chsd ldr tl led 1/2-way: rdn and hdd over 1f out: lost 2nd and btn 1f out: sn wknd* **10/1**[3]

-050 **5** *1 1/4* **Tamara Love (IRE)**[38] 1703 3-8-13 **62** (t) AdamBeschizza 6 46
(Stuart Williams) *dwlt: sn rcvrd and in tch in midfield: rdn 1/2-way: lost pl and btn over 1f out: wknd fnl f* **33/1**

-420 **6** *2 1/4* **She's All Mine**[20] 2212 3-9-1 **64** KieranO'Neill 7 42
(Richard Hannon) *in tch in midfield: rdn over 2f out: lost pl and bhd over 1f out: wknd* **12/1**

3540 **7** *nk* **Abberley Dancer (IRE)**[15] 2373 3-8-13 **67** JosephineGordon(5) 1 45
(J S Moore) *stdd s: t.k.h: hld up in tch towards rr: hdwy over 2f out: chsd ldrs but unable qck u.p over 1f out: fdd ins fnl f* **22/1**

-600 **8** *2 1/4* **Sweet Temptation (IRE)**[16] 2322 3-9-7 **70** OisinMurphy 8 42
(Stuart Williams) *stdd s: hld up in tch in rr: effrt 2f out: sn btn: bhd fnl f* **14/1**

1m 29.89s (6.59) **Going Correction** +0.90s/f (Soft) **8** Ran SP% **116.2**
Speed ratings (Par 96): **98,95,92,88,87 84,84,81**
CSF £3.80 CT £18.27 TOTE £1.80: £1.10, £2.50, £2.20; EX 4.20 Trifecta £19.20.
Owner Mrs I A Balding **Bred** Brook Stud Bloodstock Ltd **Trained** Kingsclere, Hants

FOCUS
The betting had a rather lopsided look to it in this division, but the market got it spot on. The winning time was just over half a second slower than the first leg.

2825 £25 FREE BET AT 188BET (S) STKS 1m 3f 106y
3:40 (3:41) (Class 6) 3-Y-O **£2,587** (£770; £384; £192) **Stalls** High

Form RPR
5-05 **1** **Trident Tested**[8] 2589 3-9-0 62 KierenFox 8 57
(John Best) *taken down early: mde virtually all: rdn 2f out: drvn and forged ahd jst over 1f out: styd on and drew clr fnl f* **7/4**[1]

3004 **2** *3 3/4* **Lady Fontenail**[21] 2184 3-8-4 46 (p) AliceMills(5) 1 45
(Rod Millman) *broke wl sn stdd bk into 3rd and t.k.h: effrt to chse wnr 2f out: stl pressing ldr but looking hld whn swtchd rt 1f out: sn btn: plugged on* **4/1**[3]

4206 **3** *7* **Masqueraded (USA)**[3] 2733 3-9-8 68 (v) LukeMorris 5 47
(Gay Kelleway) *chsd ldr: rdn over 2f out: 3rd and outpcd 2f out: wknd over 1f out* **9/2**

4 *7* **Buachaillnaheirean (IRE)** 3-9-0 0 AdamBeschizza 7 28
(Christine Dunnett) *restless in stalls: slowly away: hld up in tch in last pair: rdn 4f out: sn outpcd: no ch fnl 2f: plugged on fnl f to go modest 4th cl home* **11/1**

640 **5** *1/2* **Tudor Icon**[8] 2589 3-8-9 0 CharlesEddery(5) 6 27
(Rae Guest) *stdd after s: t.k.h: hld up in last pair: effrt in 4th 2f out: sn btn and wknd over 1f out: eased and lost modest 4th cl home* **3/1**[2]

0000 **6** *7* **Cappy Brown**[44] 1548 3-9-0 42 (p) FMBerry 4 16
(Alan Bailey) *in tch in midfield: rdn 3f out: sn struggling: wknd 2f out* **25/1**

2m 47.55s (16.05) **Going Correction** +0.90s/f (Soft) **6** Ran SP% **111.7**
Speed ratings (Par 97): **77,74,69,64,63 58**
CSF £9.01 TOTE £3.20: £2.40, £2.00; EX 9.20 Trifecta £37.00.Buachaillnaheirean was bought by Mr Neil King for £5000
Owner Curtis & Williams Bstk, Paine & Malt **Bred** Curtis & Williams Bloodstock **Trained** Oad Street, Kent

FOCUS
A moderate seller run in a very slow time and not form to get carried away with.

2826 188BET.CO.UK MAIDEN AUCTION STKS 1m 3f 106y
4:10 (4:10) (Class 5) 3-Y-O **£3,234** (£962; £481; £240) **Stalls** High

Form RPR
02 **1** **Talent To Amuse (IRE)**[20] 2215 3-9-2 0 AndreaAtzeni 2 84+
(Roger Varian) *chsd ldr: effrt 2f out: rdn and clsd to chal ent fnl f: led ins fnl f: sn in command: pushed out: readily* **4/5**[1]

-253 **2** *2 1/2* **Skeaping**[10] 2548 3-9-4 82 PatDobbs 5 81
(Richard Hannon) *sn led: rdn 2f out: jnd and drvn ent fnl f: hdd ins fnl f: sn btn and kpt on same pce after* **3/1**[2]

3 *13* **Embroidery (IRE)** 3-9-2 0 SamHitchcott 1 58
(Harry Dunlop) *chsd ldng pair: rdn wl over 2f out: sn struggling and outpcd 2f out: wknd over 1f out* **66/1**[3]

23-2 **4** *3 1/2* **Invocation (FR)**[13] 2443 3-9-4 77 FergusSweeney 4 54
(Alan King) *restless in stalls: stdd s: hld up in tch in rr: effrt in 4th over 2f out: sn outpcd: wknd over 1f out* **3/1**[2]

5 *16* **Petite Jack** 3-9-0 0 LiamJones 3 23
(Neil King) *in tch in 4th: rdn 3f out: sn dropped to rr and lost tch: t.o fnl f* **100/1**

2m 41.24s (9.74) **Going Correction** +0.90s/f (Soft) **5** Ran SP% **108.0**
Speed ratings (Par 99): **100,98,88,86,74**
CSF £3.38 TOTE £1.90: £1.20, £1.70; EX 3.20 Trifecta £28.10.
Owner J Shack **Bred** Gerard Mulligan **Trained** Newmarket, Suffolk

FOCUS
An uncompetitive maiden.

2827 188BET H'CAP 1m 1f
4:40 (4:41) (Class 4) (0-80,78) 4-Y-O+ **£5,175** (£1,540; £769; £384) **Stalls** Low

Form RPR
112- **1** **Inke (IRE)**[266] 6250 4-9-4 **75** (p) PatCosgrave 10 83
(Jim Boyle) *hld up in last quartet: plenty to do and effrt 3f out: hdwy 2f out: styd on u.p to chse ldr 1f out: led ins fnl f: forged clr fnl 100yds: rdn out* **4/1**[2]

-060 **2** *2 1/4* **Live Dangerously**[13] 2430 6-8-11 **68** WilliamCarson 4 71
(John Bridger) *taken down early: hld up in last pair: plenty to do and effrt over 3f out: shifting lft and hdwy u.p 2f out: chsd ldrs 1f out: kpt on steadily: snatched 2nd last strides* **16/1**

-060 **3** *shd* **Firestorm (GER)**[16] 2324 5-9-3 **74** RobertHavlin 5 76
(Michael Attwater) *chsd ldrs: 3rd and travelling wl over 3f out: effrt ent fnl 2f: styd on same pce u.p fr over 1f out* **6/1**

-530 **4** *shd* **World Record (IRE)**[20] 2213 6-8-6 **63** JFEgan 1 65+
(Mick Quinn) *led and sn clr: rdn over 2f out: stl 3 l clr and drvn over 1f out: hdd ins fnl f: no ex: lost 2 pls last strides* **13/2**

-603 **5** *3 1/4* **Woofie (IRE)**[22] 2150 4-9-2 **73** (b) JimCrowley 6 68
(Laura Mongan) *chsd ldr: rdn over 2f out: little imp u.p: lost 2nd 1f out: sn wknd* **5/1**[3]

4350 **6** *hd* **Charlies Mate**[16] 2324 5-9-6 **77** KierenFox 3 72
(John Best) *hld up off the pce in last quartet: plenty to do and rdn over 3f out: sme prog jst over 1f out: plugged on ins fnl f: nvr threatening ldrs* **8/1**

-624 **7** *2* **Molten Lava (IRE)**[21] 2174 4-9-4 **75** (b) LukeMorris 2 65
(Paul Cole) *chsd ldrs: cl enough in 4th over 3f out: rdn and no rspnse over 2f out: lost pl over 1f out: wl btn fnl f* **3/1**[1]

10-0 **8** *1 1/2* **Champagne Bob**[21] 2187 4-8-7 **67** TomMarquand(3) 9 54
(Richard Price) *a off the pce in last pair: rdn over 3f out: no imp: n.d* **11/1**

2m 3.37s (6.77) **Going Correction** +0.90s/f (Soft) **8** Ran SP% **114.6**
Speed ratings (Par 105): **105,103,102,102,99 99,97,96**
CSF £63.61 CT £381.80 TOTE £4.00: £1.40, £5.70, £2.00; EX 67.90 Trifecta £548.10.
Owner Harrier Racing 2 **Bred** Barbara Prendergast **Trained** Epsom, Surrey

FOCUS
A fair handicap and they went a very solid pace, so the form looks sound enough for the grade.

2828 EPSOM DERBY FESTIVAL BETTING AT 188BET H'CAP 1m 1f
5:10 (5:10) (Class 6) (0-60,60) 3-Y-O **£2,587** (£770; £384; £192) **Stalls** Low

Form RPR
3-00 **1** **Captain Gerald**[7] 2608 3-8-9 **53** (p) JosephineGordon(5) 5 58
(John Ryan) *mde all: rdn over 1f out: kpt on and a holding rivals ins fnl f: pushed out fnl 100yds* **16/1**

0-04 **2** *1* **Buzz Lightyere**[17] 2293 3-9-7 **60** JimCrowley 2 63
(Michael Attwater) *in tch in midfield: effrt to chse ldrs 2f out: drvn and styd on to chse wnr ins fnl f: kpt on but a hld after* **11/2**[3]

4-00 **3** *3/4* **Outback Princess**[30] 1948 3-8-4 **48** HectorCrouch(5) 3 50
(Gary Moore) *chsd ldr: rdn wl over 1f out: kpt on u.p: lost 2nd and styd on same pce ins fnl f* **20/1**

0160 **4** *1 3/4* **Zebedee's Son (IRE)**[10] 2545 3-9-3 **56** (p) MartinLane 8 54
(Roger Ingram) *in tch in midfield: effrt to chse ldrs 2f out: styd on same pce ins fnl f* **14/1**

60-0 **5** *8* **Lazizah**[16] 2325 3-8-11 **57** TylerSaunders(7) 4 39
(Marcus Tregoning) *stdd s: hld up in tch: effrt on inner over 2f out: sn outpcd: wl hld over 1f out: swtchd rt ins fnl f* **16/1**

000 **6** *1 1/4* **Rising Sunshine (IRE)**[20] 2207 3-9-7 **60** KieranO'Neill 1 40
(Richard Hannon) *chsd ldrs: rdn over 2f out: struggling 2f out and sn lost pl: wknd fnl f* **4/1**[2]

000- **7** *2* **Dusty Raven**[177] 8144 3-9-6 **59** LukeMorris 9 35
(Sir Mark Prescott Bt) *stdd s: t.k.h: early: hld up in tch in rr of main gp: rdn over 3f out: no hdwy: wl btn fnl 2f* **3/1**[1]

-450 **8** *3 1/2* **The Juggler**[15] 2366 3-9-7 **60** [1] GeorgeBaker 12 29
(William Knight) *stdd and dropped in bhd after s: hld up in detached last: effrt and stl plenty to do over 2f out: no prog: wl: btn fnl 2f* **3/1**[1]

0-0 **9** *30* **Compton Sky (USA)**[37] 1740 3-8-12 **51** SamHitchcott 11
(Jo Hughes) *racd wd: chsd ldrs tl lost pl qckly 3f out: sn bhd: t.o* **33/1**

2m 7.07s (10.47) **Going Correction** +0.90s/f (Soft) **9** Ran SP% **111.5**
Speed ratings (Par 97): **89,88,87,85,78 77,75,72,46**
CSF £96.62 CT £1742.96 TOTE £15.90: £3.40, £2.20, £5.90; EX 119.90 Trifecta £1867.60.
Owner John Ryan Racing Partnership **Bred** Nell Kent **Trained** Newmarket, Suffolk

FOCUS
A moderate 3yo handicap with the nine remaining runners having a combined record of 1-56 coming into it. There were a couple in here that looked as though they might improve for going handicapping, but they failed to fire.

2829 FREE SPINS AT 188BET CASINO H'CAP 1m 3f 106y
5:45 (5:46) (Class 6) (0-60,61) 3-Y-O **£2,587** (£770; £384; £192) **Stalls** High

Form RPR
6-35 **1** **Hearty (IRE)**[17] 2300 3-9-5 **58** JimCrowley 4 65
(Jeremy Noseda) *chsd ldrs tl wnt 2nd 7f out: upsides ldr 6f out tl led over 3f out: edgd lft over 2f out: hdd and rdn 2f out: styd w ldr: drvn to ld again ins fnl f: styd on gamely* **3/1**[2]

-121 **2** *3/4* **Hint Of Grey (IRE)**[8] 2590 3-9-1 **61** 6ex GeorgeWood(7) 7 67
(Don Cantillon) *hld up in tch in midfield: shuffled bk to last pair 6f out: hdwy over 2f out: rdn to chse ldng pair 2f out: chsd wnr wl ins fnl f: styd on but nvr getting to wnr* **1/1**[1]

4356 **3** *2 1/4* **Dor's Law**[37] 1758 3-9-7 **60** RobertWinston 6 63
(Dean Ivory) *t.k.h: hld up in rr early: hdwy into midfield 7f out: rdn and hdwy to ld 2f out: drvn over 1f out: hdd ins fnl f: no ex and btn wl ins fnl f: wknd towards fin* **9/1**

0-04 **4** *3* **Bazzat (IRE)**[7] 2608 3-8-5 **47** oh1 ow1 (p) DannyBrock(3) 5 45
(John Ryan) *chsd ldr tl 7f out: styd prom: rdn and struggling to qckn over 2f out: 4th and outpcd 2f out: kpt on same pce and wl hld after* **12/1**

0000 **5** *hd* **Monpazier (IRE)**[17] 2308 3-8-7 **46** oh1 (p) MartinLane 9 44
(K R Burke) *restless in stalls: hld up in tch: effrt over 2f out: no imp tl styd on ins fnl f: nvr trbld ldrs* **28/1**

660 **6** *1* **Dilly Daydream (IRE)**[20] 2212 3-8-12 **56** JosephineGordon(5) 2 52
(Giles Bravery) *in tch in midfield: effrt over 2f out: 5th and no imp over 1f out: styd on same pce and wl hld after* **25/1**

000- **7** *2 1/2* **Madame Claud**[198] 7878 3-9-3 **56** GeorgeBaker 3 48
(Hughie Morrison) *stdd s: hld up in tch in rr: effrt and hung lft ent fnl 2f: no hdwy and wl hld whn nt clr run ent fnl f* **6/1**[3]

050- **8** 3 1/4 **Royal Mighty**[226] 7353 3-8-4 **50** SamuelClarke(7) 1 38
(Jane Chapple-Hyam) *led tl over 3f out: losing pl whn hmpd over 2f out: bhd over 1f out* **33/1**
2m 42.92s (11.42) **Going Correction** +0.90s/f (Soft) **8** Ran SP% **117.2**
Speed ratings (Par 97): **94,93,91,89,89 88,86,84**
CSF £6.42 CT £22.67 TOTE £4.20: £1.90, £1.02, £2.70; EX 7.60 Trifecta £35.30.
Owner Miss Yvonne Jacques **Bred** Ronan Fitzpatrick **Trained** Newmarket, Suffolk
FOCUS
Another moderate 3yo handicap, and again all bar one of these were maidens going into it.
T/Plt: £43.70 to a £1 stake. Pool: £56,093.29 - 936.43 winning tickets. T/Qpdt: £8.50 to a £1 stake. Pool: £4,155.13 - 357.7 winning tickets. **Steve Payne**

2800 RIPON (R-H)
Thursday, June 2

OFFICIAL GOING: Good (good to firm in places; 8.3)
Wind: moderate 1/2 against Weather: overcast becoming fine

2830 BRITISH STALLION STUDS EBF NOVICE STKS 6f
2:20 (2:21) (Class 5) 2-Y-O **£3,881** (£1,155; £577; £288) **Stalls** High

Form RPR
1 **Fayez (IRE)** 2-9-2 0 HarryBentley 3 84+
(David O'Meara) *s.s: hdwy to chse ldrs over 2f out: edgd lft and led appr fnl f: drvn out* **14/1**
2 1 1/2 **Jacquard (IRE)** 2-9-2 0 FrannyNorton 2 80+
(Mark Johnston) *hmpd s: swtchd lft after s: led after 1f: hdd appr fnl f: styd on same pce fnl 75yds* **6/4**[2]
50 **3** 5 **Mulwith (IRE)**[33] 1850 2-9-2 0 GrahamGibbons 5 65
(David Barron) *t.k.h in rr: swtchd rt over 2f out: kpt on to take modest 3rd last 75yds* **66/1**
3 **4** 3/4 **Dalton**[15] 2358 2-9-2 0 PhillipMakin 9 65
(David O'Meara) *hmpd s: trckd ldrs: nt clr run on ins over 1f out: kpt on same pce fnl f* **11/8**[1]
5 2 1/4 **Expenditure (IRE)** 2-9-2 0 BarryMcHugh 6 56
(Jedd O'Keeffe) *chsd ldrs: effrt over 2f out: wknd fnl f* **33/1**
50 **6** 1/2 **Yes You (IRE)**[27] 2007 2-8-11 0 TomEaves 4 49
(James Given) *wnt rt s: sn chsng ldrs on outside: swtchd rt 1f out: sn wknd* **28/1**
7 nk **Dream Team** 2-9-2 0 PaulMulrennan 10 53
(Michael Dods) *hmpd s: outpcd and drvn along in last: hdwy over 2f out: nvr a factor* **20/1**
8 6 **Scotch Myst** 2-9-2 0 TonyHamilton 1 35
(Richard Fahey) *swvd rt s: sn chsng ldrs: wknd over 1f out* **10/1**[3]
9 3 1/4 **Regal Decree** 2-9-2 0 JackGarritty 7 25
(Jedd O'Keeffe) *mid-div: sme hdwy over 2f out: wknd over 1f out* **22/1**
0 **10** 13 **Ey Up**[7] 2617 2-8-11 0 DougieCostello 8
(Paul Midgley) *wnt lft s: led 1f: chsd ldrs: lost pl over 1f out: eased whn bhd* **66/1**
1m 14.29s (1.29) **Going Correction** +0.05s/f (Good) **10** Ran SP% **116.3**
Speed ratings (Par 93): **93,91,84,83,80 79,79,71,66,49**
CSF £33.71 TOTE £18.90: £3.50, £1.10, £10.40; EX 42.20 Trifecta £833.90.
Owner Sheikh Abdullah Almalek Alsabah **Bred** Miss Siobhan Ryan **Trained** Upper Helmsley, N Yorks
FOCUS
Rail on bend from back straight to home straight dolled out by 2yds, adding about 4 yards to races on the round course. The front pair came clear in what was an ordinary novice contest.

2831 FOLLOW @RIPONRACES ON TWITTER H'CAP 1m 1f 170y
2:50 (2:58) (Class 5) (0-70,75) 3-Y-O **£3,234** (£962; £481; £240) **Stalls** Low

Form RPR
5-65 **1** **Mr Grumpy**[58] 1242 3-8-13 **62** PhillipMakin 3 67+
(Keith Dalgleish) *dwlt: sn trcking ldrs: shkn up to ld wl over 1f out: edgd rt: pushed out: readily* **9/2**[2]
-021 **2** 3 **Wotabreeze (IRE)**[8] 2576 3-9-1 **69** 6ex NathanEvans(5) 2 68
(John Quinn) *dwlt: hdwy to chse ldrs over 3f out: edgd lft over 2f out: kpt on to take 2nd clsng stages: no imp* **5/6**[1]
5-66 **3** 3/4 **L'Apogee**[11] 2506 3-8-13 **62** TonyHamilton 7 60
(Richard Fahey) *led after 1f: hdd over 1f out: kpt on same pce* **6/1**[3]
60-5 **4** 3/4 **Becky The Thatcher**[18] 2269 3-9-3 **66** JackGarritty 5 62
(Micky Hammond) *sn trcking ldrs: t.k.h: effrt over 2f out: kpt on same pce fnl f* **10/1**
6-16 **5** hd **Intalza (IRE)**[9] 2553 3-8-3 **55** (p) JoeDoyle(3) 4 51
(Michael Herrington) *led 1f: trckd ldrs: effrt over 2f out: kpt on same pce appr fnl f* **15/2**
06-5 **6** nk **Calypso Delegator (IRE)**[18] 2271 3-8-4 **58** ow3 CallumShepherd(5) 6 53
(Micky Hammond) *unruly and uns rdr 3 times bef being loaded: in last: hdwy over 3f out: kpt on same pce fnl 2f: nvr a threat* **25/1**
2m 6.33s (0.93) **Going Correction** +0.05s/f (Good) **6** Ran SP% **111.7**
Speed ratings (Par 99): **98,95,95,94,94 94**
CSF £8.62 CT £20.47 TOTE £5.30: £2.50, £1.10; EX 9.70 Trifecta £24.70.
Owner Straightline Construction Ltd **Bred** Lord Halifax **Trained** Carluke, S Lanarks
FOCUS
Race distance increased by 4yds. Not a bad little race with a well-handicapped winner beating the penalised favourite.

2832 RIPONBET OUR PROFITS STAY IN RACING H'CAP 1m 1f 170y
3:20 (3:22) (Class 4) (0-85,85) 4-Y-O+ **£4,851** (£1,443; £721; £360) **Stalls** Low

Form RPR
435 **1** **Corton Lad**[5] 2688 6-9-6 **84** (tp) PhillipMakin 7 92
(Keith Dalgleish) *trckd ldrs: edgd lft after 1f: hmpd appr fnl f: styd on to ld clsng stages* **11/2**[3]
21-6 **2** nk **Count Montecristo (FR)**[23] 2121 4-9-3 **81** TomEaves 5 88
(Kevin Ryan) *dwlt: t.k.h: sn led: edgd lft over 1f out: hdd and no ex clsng stages* **3/1**[2]
50-4 **3** 1 1/2 **Rotherwick (IRE)**[20] 2216 4-9-7 **85** (t) MartinHarley 6 89
(Paul Cole) *trckd ldrs: drvn and hung rt over 1f out: hmpd appr fnl f: kpt on same pce* **15/8**[1]
2000 **4** 1 1/4 **Polar Forest**[16] 2328 6-9-0 **83** (e) CallumShepherd(5) 1 84
(Richard Guest) *sn trcking ldrs: edgd lft over 2f out: carried lft appr fnl f: kpt on last 100yds* **10/1**
0-53 **5** 1 1/2 **Eurystheus (IRE)**[9] 2556 7-8-9 **76** (tp) AlistairRawlinson(3) 3 74
(Michael Appleby) *in rr: hmpd after 1f: effrt over 3f out: hung rt over 1f out: kpt on: nvr a threat* **6/1**
1-02 **6** 3 3/4 **Bogardus (IRE)**[134] 256 5-7-9 **66** PaulaMuir(7) 4 57
(Patrick Holmes) *in rr: hmpd after 1f: effrt over 3f out: kpt on fnl f: nvr a threat* **11/1**
20 **7** 12 **Invictus (GER)**[27] 2017 4-9-7 **85** JackGarritty 2 51
(Micky Hammond) *led early: t.k.h: trckd ldrs: effrt over 3f out: lost pl 2f out: bhd whn eased clsng stages* **18/1**
2m 4.47s (-0.93) **Going Correction** +0.05s/f (Good) **7** Ran SP% **112.1**
Speed ratings (Par 105): **105,104,103,102,101 98,88**
CSF £21.44 TOTE £5.20: £2.10, £1.90; EX 22.00 Trifecta £82.10.
Owner J Hutton **Bred** Frank Brady And Brian Scanlon **Trained** Carluke, S Lanarks
■ Stewards' Enquiry : Phillip Makin two-day ban: careless riding (Jun 19-20)
Jack Garritty gelding wore earplugs to the start which were then removed
FOCUS
Race distance increased by 4yds. A pretty ordinary race for the level and little got into it from off the pace.

2833 WEATHERBYS VAT SERVICES H'CAP 1m
3:50 (3:50) (Class 3) (0-95,95) 4-Y-O+ **£7,439** (£2,213; £1,106; £553) **Stalls** Low

Form RPR
2614 **1** **Treasury Notes (IRE)**[10] 2527 4-8-13 **87** MartinHarley 8 96+
(David O'Meara) *hld up towards rr: hdwy 3f out: nt clr run over 1f out: hmpd: squeezed through and r.o to ld clsng stages* **7/2**[2]
3003 **2** 1/2 **Lat Hawill (IRE)**[16] 2331 5-9-7 **95** PhillipMakin 1 102
(Keith Dalgleish) *dwlt: sn trcking ldrs: nt clr run over 2f out: squeezed through to ld last 150yds: hdd and no ex clsng stages* **6/1**
6-01 **3** 3/4 **Get Knotted (IRE)**[19] 2256 4-9-0 **88** (p) PaulMulrennan 3 93
(Michael Dods) *led early: trckd ldr: chal over 2f out: led appr fnl f: wnt lft and hdd last 150yds: kpt on same pce* **7/1**
-635 **4** nk **Wilde Inspiration (IRE)**[33] 1871 5-9-2 **90**[1] ConnorBeasley 4 94
(Julie Camacho) *trckd ldrs: chal over 2f out: rdn over 1f out: hmpd last 150yds: styd on same pce* **3/1**[1]
0-00 **5** 1 3/4 **Glenalmond (IRE)**[27] 1993 4-8-11 **85** (p) DougieCostello 2 85
(K R Burke) *s.i.s: reminders and sn led: rdn over 2f out: hdd appr fnl f: wknd nr fin* **12/1**
0216 **6** 1 3/4 **Taysh (USA)**[19] 2256 4-8-11 **85** BenCurtis 6 81
(Michael Appleby) *t.k.h in rr: effrt over 3f out: chsng ldrs over 1f out: sn fdd* **15/2**
000- **7** 1 1/2 **Brazos (IRE)**[264] 6313 5-9-7 **95** DavidAllan 7 88+
(James Tate) *hld up in rr: t.k.h: effrt on ins 3f out: nt clr run 2f out: hung rt over 1f out: sn fdd* **4/1**[3]
1m 40.04s (-1.36) **Going Correction** +0.05s/f (Good) **7** Ran SP% **113.5**
Speed ratings (Par 107): **108,107,106,106,104 102,101**
CSF £24.08 CT £137.38 TOTE £4.40: £2.50, £2.60; EX 14.50 Trifecta £34.00.
Owner T Proctor **Bred** Ammerland Verwaltung Gmbh & Co Kg **Trained** Upper Helmsley, N Yorks
FOCUS
Race distance increased by 4yds. An interesting handicap, with several well-handicapped on old form. The form is rated around the third and fourth.

2834 MICHAEL PADLEY MEMORIAL H'CAP 6f
4:20 (4:21) (Class 5) (0-70,70) 3-Y-O **£2,911** (£866; £432; £216) **Stalls** High

Form RPR
0-40 **1** **Round The Island**[17] 2302 3-8-9 **58** (p) PaulQuinn 10 66+
(Richard Whitaker) *mid-div: swtchd lft over 2f out: kpt on to ld last 150yds: drvn out* **20/1**
0-51 **2** 3/4 **Lady Joanna Vassa (IRE)**[11] 2503 3-8-6 **55** 6ex ConnorBeasley 2 59
(Richard Guest) *swtchd lft after s: chsd ldrs: led over 1f out: hdd and no ex last 150yds* **9/2**[3]
-535 **3** nk **Mustn't Grumble (IRE)**[38] 1721 3-8-11 **60** (p) MartinHarley 12 65+
(Ivan Furtado) *chsd ldrs: nt clr run over 2f out: nt clr run: hung rt and swtchd rt 1f out: styd on* **5/1**
2-61 **4** 1 1/4 **Secret Clause**[16] 2337 3-9-0 **66** AlistairRawlinson(3) 4 65+
(Michael Appleby) *wnt rt s: rr-div: hdwy on outer over 2f out: chsng ldrs over 1f out: kpt on same pce last 100yds* **4/1**[2]
0-45 **5** 3 **Highway Robber**[39] 1673 3-8-0 **54** ow1 RachelRichardson(5) 5 43
(Wilf Storey) *in rr: hdwy and edgd rt over 1f out: kpt on same pce* **16/1**
4-10 **6** 1 3/4 **Undertow (IRE)**[113] 519 3-9-3 **66** DougieCostello 3 50
(K R Burke) *dwlt: in rr: effrt on outer and hung rt over 2f out: chsng ldrs over 1f out: kpt on same pce* **14/1**
1-63 **7** 1 **Sarabi**[140] 181 3-9-0 **63** (p) DaleSwift 7 44
(Scott Dixon) *led after 1f: hdd over 1f out: wknd fnl 150yds* **16/1**
-422 **8** 4 1/2 **Sir Theodore (IRE)**[13] 2435 3-9-4 **70** LouisSteward(3) 1 36
(Richard Spencer) *chsd ldrs on outer: wknd over 1f out* **11/4**[1]
4404 **9** nk **Red Chatterbox (IRE)**[109] 578 3-8-3 **52** DuranFentiman 8 17
(Scott Dixon) *mid-div: hdwy over 2f out: lost pl over 1f out* **40/1**
4330 **10** 2 **Wishsong**[16] 2336 3-9-2 **70** AnnaHesketh(5) 6 29
(David Nicholls) *mid-div: drvn to chse ldrs on outer over 2f out: wknd over 1f out* **11/1**
5-60 **11** 4 1/2 **Caymus**[31] 1922 3-8-13 **62** (e[1]) BarryMcHugh 9 6
(Tracy Waggott) *led 1f: chsd ldrs: lost pl over 1f out* **66/1**
1m 13.58s (0.58) **Going Correction** +0.05s/f (Good) **11** Ran SP% **117.0**
Speed ratings (Par 99): **98,97,96,94,90 88,87,81,80,78 72**
CSF £106.18 CT £541.30 TOTE £21.70: £6.80, £1.90, £2.10; EX 171.50 Trifecta £1242.10.
Owner Robin Dollar & David Horner **Bred** R Dollar, T Adams & G F Pemberton **Trained** Scarcroft, W Yorks
FOCUS
Race distance as advertised. A moderate sprint, although the first two are unexposed.

2835 SIS MAIDEN STKS 1m
4:50 (4:51) (Class 5) 3-Y-O **£2,911** (£866; £432; £216) **Stalls** Low

Form RPR
340- **1** **House Of Commons (IRE)**[272] 6051 3-9-5 83 MartinHarley 11 80+
(Paul Cole) *trckd ldrs: led on bit over 1f out: pushed out clsng stages* **4/6**[1]
2 1/2 **Imperial Focus (IRE)** 3-9-2 0 JoeDoyle(3) 4 76
(Simon Waugh) *mid-div: hdwy and swtchd lft over 2f out: chsng ldrs over 1f out: kpt on to take 2nd nr fin* **150/1**
3 1/2 **Apres Midi (IRE)** 3-9-0 0 DougieCostello 5 70
(K R Burke) *chsd ldrs: drvn over 3f out: 2nd and edgd rt appr fnl f: styd on same pce* **7/1**
34 **4** 5 **Proven Point (IRE)**[67] 1113 3-9-5 0 BarryMcHugh 6 63
(Tony Coyle) *wnt lft s: led: hdd over 3f out: wkng whn n.m.r on inner 1f out* **4/1**[2]
06 **5** 1 1/2 **Cliff Edge (IRE)**[16] 2340 3-9-5 0 HarryBentley 3 60+
(Roger Varian) *s.i.s: hdwy over 2f out: kpt on same pce* **6/1**[3]
00 **6** hd **Catskill Mountains (IRE)**[16] 2320 3-9-5 0 JackMitchell 10 59+
(Roger Varian) *in rr: hdwy 3f out: edgd rt over 1f out: one pce* **16/1**

00- **7** 1 1/4 **Fast Operator (IRE)**[253] 6655 3-8-7 0 .... KieranSchofield(7) 9 51
(Nigel Tinkler) *hmpd s: mid-div: effrt 3f out: kpt on one pce* **200/1**
8 5 **Hightime Girl** 3-9-0 0 ....(t) DaleSwift 2 40
(David Loughnane) *s.i.s: hdwy on ins over 2f out: wknd over 1f out* **50/1**
0 **9** 1/2 **Hallux**[9] 2557 3-9-5 0 .... GrahamGibbons 8 44
(David Barron) *hmpd s: mid-div: hdwy 3f out: fdd over 1f out* **20/1**
606- **10** 3 3/4 **Invincible Bond**[339] 3707 3-9-5 35 .... JackGarritty 13 35
(Simon Waugh) *rr-div: brief effrt whn hmpd 2f out: sn wknd* **200/1**
00- **11** nse **Bahrikate**[352] 3267 3-9-0 0 .... TomEaves 7 30
(Michael Herrington) *wnt rt s: trckd ldr: led over 3f out: hdd and lost pl over 1f out* **200/1**
0 **12** 7 **Beadlam (IRE)**[23] 2122 3-9-0 0 .... RaulDaSilva 12 14
(David Loughnane) *s.i.s: brief effrt on outside over 2f out: sn lost pl and bhd* **200/1**
00- **13** 5 **Take In Time**[257] 6521 3-9-0 0 .... NathanEvans(5) 1 7
(Michael Easterby) *chsd ldrs: lost pl over 2f out* **200/1**

1m 41.82s (0.42) **Going Correction** +0.05s/f (Good) **13** Ran SP% **122.5**
Speed ratings (Par 99): **99,98,98,93,91 91,90,85,84,80 80,73,68**
CSF £245.76 TOTE £1.60: £1.10, £13.00, £2.40; EX 55.70 Trifecta £583.70.
Owner Mrs Fitri Hay **Bred** Sunderlans, Monceaux & Prodhomme **Trained** Whatcombe, Oxon

FOCUS
Race distance increased by 4yds. A maiden lacking depth, two of the newcomers, one of which was 150-1, bustled up the favourite, the trio clear.

2836 LADIES DAY 16TH JUNE BOOK NOW H'CAP 1m 4f 10y
5:20 (5:21) (Class 5) (0-70,70) 4-Y-O+ **£3,234** (£962; £481; £240) **Stalls** Centre

Form RPR
50-2 **1** **Kip**[13] 2427 4-9-4 67 .... HarryBentley 12 77
(David O'Meara) *trckd ldrs: led appr fnl f: drvn out* **10/1**
320 **2** 2 1/2 **Wishing Well**[27] 2018 4-9-2 65 .... JackGarritty 8 71
(Micky Hammond) *hld up in mid-div: hdwy 3f out: chsng ldrs over 1f out: kpt on to take 2nd nr fin* **7/1**
04-6 **3** nk **Arrowtown**[42] 1586 4-9-7 70 .... GrahamGibbons 2 75+
(Michael Easterby) *wnt lft s: hld up in rr: effrt and nt clr run on inner over 3f out: nt clr run and swtchd lft 2f out: styd on appr fnl f: tk 3rd nr fin* **4/1**[1]
-600 **4** 1 **Moon Arc (IRE)**[9] 2558 4-8-8 57 ....(p) ConnorBeasley 13 60
(Keith Dalgleish) *trckd ldr: led over 2f out: hdd appr fnl f: kpt on same pce* **16/1**
/02- **5** 4 1/2 **Bright Applause**[407] 1588 8-9-2 65 .... BarryMcHugh 11 61
(Tracy Waggott) *chsd ldrs: wknd over 1f out* **20/1**
4215 **6** 1/2 **Mcvicar**[24] 2093 7-9-0 63 ....(p) PhillipMakin 4 58
(John Davies) *mid-div: effrt over 2f out: one pce* **4/1**[1]
0010 **7** nk **Gabrial The Terror (IRE)**[21] 2194 6-9-5 68 ....(p) TonyHamilton 3 63
(Richard Fahey) *hld up in rr: pushed along 6f out: kpt on fnl 2f: nvr a factor* **6/1**[3]
-000 **8** 3/4 **Indian Chief (IRE)**[24] 2093 6-9-2 65 .... PaulMulrennan 5 59+
(Rebecca Bastiman) *hld up in rr: effrt on ins over 3f out: nt clr at any stage: eased over 1f out* **16/1**
00 **9** 1 **Champagne Rules**[7] 2618 5-9-7 70 .... PaddyAspell 7 62
(Sharon Watt) *rr-div: hdwy over 4f out: lost pl over 1f out* **50/1**
10-0 **10** 1 1/2 **Captain Swift (IRE)**[17] 2296 5-9-7 70 .... TomEaves 9 60
(John Mackie) *chsd ldrs: drvn over 4f out: lost pl over 1f out* **12/1**
30-3 **11** 2 1/2 **Moon Over Rio (IRE)**[43] 1560 5-8-13 62 .... AndrewElliott 1 48
(Ben Haslam) *led: hdd over 2f out: lost pl over 1f out* **11/2**[2]
5-00 **R** **Rolen Sly**[135] 251 7-8-2 51 oh6 .... DuranFentiman 6
(Neville Bycroft) *ref to r: lft at s* **50/1**

2m 35.47s (-1.23) **Going Correction** +0.05s/f (Good) **12** Ran SP% **119.4**
Speed ratings (Par 103): **106,104,104,103,100 100,99,99,98,97 96,**
CSF £77.78 CT £330.89 TOTE £9.50: £3.20, £2.50, £2.20; EX 104.30 Trifecta £645.00.
Owner Chris Napthine **Bred** Carwell Equities Ltd **Trained** Upper Helmsley, N Yorks

FOCUS
Race distance increased by 4yds. A race dominated by the girls, with the front four clear, and a race that should produce winners at a similar level.
T/Jkpt: Not won. T/Plt: £86.20 to a £1 stake. Pool: £65,036.75 - 550.22 winning tickets. T/Qpdt: £23.90 to a £1 stake. Pool: £5,872.69 - 181.76 winning tickets. **Walter Glynn**

2837 - 2843a (Foreign Racing) - See Raceform Interactive

[1846]FONTAINEBLEAU
Thursday, June 2

OFFICIAL GOING: Turf: heavy

2844a PRIX DES VERNES (CLAIMER) (2YO) (TURF) 6f
11:40 (12:00) 2-Y-O **£6,985** (£2,794; £2,095; £1,397; £698)

RPR
1 **Frozen Queen (IRE)**[12] 2457 2-8-8 0 .... IoritzMendizabal 2 60
(J S Moore) *mde all: sltly awkward thrght: hung lft u.p fnl f but kpt on and a doing enough* **4/1**[3]
2 nk **Zahiria (FR)** 2-8-11 0 ....(p) AntoineHamelin 6 62
(A Chopard, France) **17/10**[1]
3 1 1/2 **Kite Davis (FR)** 2-9-1 0 ....(p) RichardJuteau 1 62
(C Plisson, France) **27/10**[2]
4 1/2 **Freeze Fly (IRE)**[57] 1284 2-9-1 0 .... CristianDemuro 4 60
(J-V Toux, France) **58/10**
5 3/4 **Highgate (FR)**[43] 1579 2-8-11 0 .... FabriceVeron 5 54
(F-X De Chevigny, France) **56/10**
6 3/4 **Evidence Sarthoise (FR)**[56] 2-8-8 0 .... LudovicBoisseau(3) 3 52
(C Plisson, France) **15/1**

WIN (incl. 1 euro stake): 5.00. PLACES: 1.90, 1.50, Csf: 11.50
Owner A D Crook & J S Moore **Bred** Hyde Park Stud **Trained** Upper Lambourn, Berks

[2634]BATH (L-H)
Friday, June 3

OFFICIAL GOING: Good to firm (good in places; 8.7)
Wind: almost nil Weather: sunny

2845 GRAZE BAR BREWERY AND CHOPHOUSE H'CAP 5f 11y
6:00 (6:02) (Class 6) (0-60,60) 4-Y-O+ **£2,587** (£770; £384; £192) **Stalls** Centre

Form RPR
60-6 **1** **Captain Ryan**[15] 2396 5-9-4 57 .... TimmyMurphy 4 66
(Geoffrey Deacon) *trckd ldr: led over 1f out: kpt on wl: rdn out* **3/1**[1]
00-0 **2** 3/4 **Jaganory (IRE)**[24] 2130 4-9-7 60 ....(p) PatCosgrave 6 66
(Christopher Mason) *trckd ldrs: rdn and ev ch over 1f out: kpt on but no ex ins fnl f* **8/1**
-320 **3** 1/2 **John Joiner**[14] 2447 4-8-11 53 .... MichaelJMMurphy(3) 2 58
(Peter Hedger) *mid-div: hdwy 2f out: rdn ent fnl f: kpt on but no ex towards fin* **9/2**[2]
24-0 **4** 1/2 **Mc Diamond (IRE)**[32] 1913 4-8-13 59 .... GeorgeWood(7) 7 62
(Michael Mullineaux) *mid-div: rdn over 2f out: no imp tl r.o ins fnl f: wnt 4th cl home* **16/1**
5605 **5** 3/4 **Catalinas Diamond (IRE)**[32] 1913 8-9-6 59 ....(t) AdamKirby 10 62
(Pat Murphy) *hld up: hdwy 2f out: trcking ldrs whn bdly short of room jst over 1f out: kpt on but nt pce to mount chal ins fnl f* **6/1**[3]
1003 **6** 3/4 **Spray Tan**[14] 2447 6-8-9 51 ....(b) GeorgeDowning(3) 1 48
(Tony Carroll) *mid-div: hdwy 2f out: sn rdn and short of room: kpt on same pce fnl f* **14/1**
6060 **7** 3/4 **Top Cop**[13] 2458 7-8-6 50 ....(p) JordanNason(5) 3 45
(Ronald Harris) *chsd ldr: rdn over 2f out: no ex ins fnl f* **14/1**
-060 **8** nk **Simply Black (IRE)**[11] 2537 5-8-11 55 ow1 ....(p) AnnStokell(5) 5 49
(Ann Stokell) *slowly away: sn rousted along to ld: rdn and hdd over 1f out: fdd fnl f* **66/1**
5236 **9** 2 1/4 **Presto Boy**[13] 2458 4-8-3 49 .... DavidEgan(7) 11 40
(Richard Hughes) *awkward leaving stalls: bhd: little imp whn short of room and bdly hmpd ent fnl f: no ch after* **7/1**
5-50 **10** 1 1/2 **Burnt Cream**[133] 292 9-8-13 52 ....(t) MartinHarley 9 32
(Martin Bosley) *hld up: effrt over 1f out: wknd fnl f* **10/1**
640- **11** 3/4 **Indian Tim**[264] 6344 4-8-0 46 oh1 .... LuluStanford(7) 8 23
(Milton Bradley) *in tch: rdn and hdwy over 2f out: wknd ent fnl f* **12/1**

1m 2.49s (-0.01) **Going Correction** -0.10s/f (Good) **11** Ran SP% **118.6**
Speed ratings (Par 101): **96,94,94,93,92 90,89,89,85,83 81**
CSF £27.69 CT £108.63 TOTE £4.00: £1.70, £2.80, £1.50; EX 32.30 Trifecta £159.00.
Owner A Lomax, B Mortimer, W H & J Simpson **Bred** Mrs C Lloyd **Trained** Compton, Berks

FOCUS
A low-grade sprint handicap featuring a number of multiple course winners and one of them justified favouritism.

2846 BATH ALES GEM H'CAP 5f 161y
6:30 (6:31) (Class 5) (0-75,75) 3-Y-O+ **£2,911** (£866; £432; £216) **Stalls** Centre

Form RPR
-206 **1** **Koptoon**[11] 2531 4-9-9 71 .... FMBerry 1 85
(Jo Hughes) *mid-div: hdwy over 1f out: led ins fnl f: r.o strly: readily* **10/1**
0504 **2** 3 3/4 **Bahamian Sunrise**[15] 2396 4-9-2 69 .... GeorgeBuckell(5) 10 71
(John Gallagher) *led: rdn over 1f out: hdd ins fnl f: nt pce of wnr* **12/1**
606 **3** 1 3/4 **Ambitious Icarus**[17] 2346 7-9-13 75 ....(e) ConnorBeasley 9 71
(Richard Guest) *towards rr of midfield: rdn over 2f out: hdwy over 1f out: r.o fnl f* **11/1**
0032 **4** 1 1/2 **Ginzan**[23] 2146 8-9-13 75 .... MartinHarley 3 66
(Malcolm Saunders) *trckd ldrs: rdn whn swtchd rt over 1f out: kpt on same pce fnl f* **10/1**
35-0 **5** 3/4 **Magical Daze**[27] 2028 4-9-11 73 .... JackMitchell 2 61
(Sylvester Kirk) *prom: rdn 2f out: no ex ins fnl f* **14/1**
010 **6** nse **Summersault (IRE)**[15] 2396 5-9-0 67 .... LucyKBarry(5) 4 55
(Jamie Osborne) *in tch: rdn over 2f out sn one pce* **6/1**[1]
066- **7** 3/4 **Archimedes (IRE)**[216] 7637 3-9-2 72 .... KieranO'Neill 12 56
(Robert Cowell) *in tch: effrt 2f out: wknd fnl f* **15/2**[3]
46-1 **8** 1/2 **Edged Out**[35] 1827 6-9-6 75 .... GeorgeWood(7) 5 59
(Christopher Mason) *trckd ldrs: rdn over 2f out: wknd fnl f* **7/1**[2]
5125 **9** 3 **Picket Line**[27] 2028 4-9-12 74 .... TimmyMurphy 11 48
(Geoffrey Deacon) *mid-div: rdn over 2f out: wknd over 1f out* **7/1**[2]
3-34 **10** 1/2 **Quite A Story**[123] 424 4-9-8 70 .... PatCosgrave 14 43
(Patrick Chamings) *mid-div: effrt over 2f out: wknd over 1f out* **12/1**
3200 **11** nk **Quintus Cerialis (IRE)**[18] 2290 4-9-13 75 ....(p) AdamKirby 7 47
(Clive Cox) *s.i.s: a towards rr* **12/1**
513- **12** 1 3/4 **Jan Steen (IRE)**[212] 7702 3-9-4 74 .... TomQueally 8 38
(Denis Coakley) *a towards rr* **12/1**
4633 **13** 2 1/4 **Divine Call**[86] 872 9-9-2 67 ....(v) MichaelJMMurphy(3) 6 25
(Milton Bradley) *slowly away: a towards rr* **33/1**
-430 **14** 1 1/4 **Dominium (USA)**[27] 2028 9-9-8 75 ....(b) DavidParkes(5) 13 29
(Jeremy Gask) *sn struggling: a in rr* **12/1**

1m 9.94s (-1.26) **Going Correction** -0.10s/f (Good)
WFA 3 from 4yo+ 8lb **14** Ran SP% **125.6**
Speed ratings (Par 103): **104,99,96,94,93 93,92,91,87,87 86,84,81,79**
CSF £130.23 CT £1400.51 TOTE £11.70: £3.30, £5.30, £4.20; EX 206.70 Trifecta £1136.10.
Owner Richard and Nicola Hunt **Bred** Bearstone Stud Ltd **Trained** Lambourn, Berks

FOCUS
Open betting for a competitive sprint handicap.

2847 BATH ALES HOP POLE/BRITISH STALLION STUDS EBF NOVICE STKS 5f 11y
7:00 (7:02) (Class 5) 2-Y-O **£3,234** (£962; £481; £240) **Stalls** Centre

Form RPR
1 **Big Time Baby (IRE)** 2-9-2 0 ....(t) LiamJones 4 84
(Tom Dascombe) *trckd ldrs: rdn over 1f out: r.o ins fnl f to ld fnl 75yds* **9/2**[2]
2 1/2 **Kodiline (IRE)** 2-9-2 0 .... AdamKirby 5 82
(Clive Cox) *trckd ldr: led over 1f out: sn rdn: kpt on but no ex whn hdd fnl 75yds* **4/7**[1]
3 3 **Second Nature** 2-9-2 0 .... MartinHarley 9 71
(James Tate) *trckd ldrs: rdn 2f out: sn edgd sltly lft: kpt on ins fnl f: wnt 3rd towards fin* **16/1**
55 **4** nk **Captain Hawk**[16] 2358 2-8-13 0 .... MichaelJMMurphy(3) 2 70
(Charles Hills) *led: rdn and hdd over 1f out: no ex fnl 120yds* **7/1**[3]
5 1/2 **Desert Mark (IRE)** 2-9-2 0 .... KieranO'Neill 1 68
(Richard Hannon) *trckd ldrs: rdn 2f out: kpt on same pce fnl f* **16/1**
6 3/4 **Farleigh Mac** 2-8-13 0 .... RobHornby(3) 3 66+
(Andrew Balding) *mid-div: chsng ldrs whn squeezed up sltly ent fnl f: fdd* **33/1**
20 **7** nk **Masquerade Bling (IRE)**[11] 2535 2-8-11 0 .... RyanClark 6 59
(Simon Hodgson) *in tch: rdn 2f out: sn one pce* **50/1**
P65 **8** 1 **Spin Top**[22] 2180 2-9-2 0 .... ShaneKelly 10 61
(Joseph Tuite) *sn outpcd in rr* **33/1**
9 1 1/4 **Pursuing Steed** 2-9-2 0 .... TomQueally 8 56
(John Gallagher) *s.i.s: a towards rr* **25/1**
4 **10** 3/4 **Restore (IRE)**[17] 2319 2-9-2 0 .... TimmyMurphy 7 54
(Richard Hannon) *s.i.s: a in last pair* **8/1**

1m 2.54s (0.04) **Going Correction** -0.10s/f (Good) **10** Ran SP% **128.9**
Speed ratings (Par 93): **95,94,89,88,88 86,86,84,82,81**
CSF £8.07 TOTE £8.40: £2.40, £1.10, £3.60; EX 16.70 Trifecta £106.50.

The Form Book, Raceform Ltd, Newbury, RG14 5SJ

Owner Jones & Owen Promotions Ltd **Bred** Paul & Billy McEnery **Trained** Malpas, Cheshire
FOCUS
This juvenile novice stakes was run fractionally slower than the opening handicap.

2848 BATH ALES SUMMER'S HARE MAIDEN FILLIES' STKS 5f 161y
7:30 (7:31) (Class 5) 3-Y-O+ £3,234 (£962; £481; £240) Stalls Centre

Form RPR
-24 1 **Sweet Dragon Fly**[13] 2470 3-9-0 0 MartinHarley 2 87
(Paul Cole) *trckd ldr: rdn to ld ent fnl f: r.o wl to draw clr: comf* 1/1[1]
22- 2 4 **Sirajiah (IRE)**[303] 5005 3-9-0 0 PatCosgrave 5 74
(William Haggas) *led: rdn and hdd ent fnl f: kpt on but nt pce of wnr* 2/1[2]
3 3 1/4 **Land Of Dubai (IRE)** 3-9-0 0 AdamKirby 7 63+
(Clive Cox) *chsd ldrs: rdn over 2f out: kpt on to go 3rd ins fnl f but nt pce of front pair* 7/1[3]
0-0 4 1 **Dream Dana (IRE)**[18] 2294 3-9-0 0 TimmyMurphy 6 60
(Jamie Osborne) *slowly away: sn prom: rdn over 1f out: sn drifted lft and hld: fdd ins fnl f* 50/1
33- 5 5 **Artists Model (IRE)**[184] 8074 3-9-0 0 FMBerry 9 43
(Henry Candy) *in tch: effrt over 2f out: nt quite pce to get on terms: fdd fnl f* 10/1
0 6 1 **Staffa (IRE)**[33] 1894 3-9-0 0 TomQueally 3 40
(Denis Coakley) *s.i.s: towards rr: hdwy 2f out: rdn ent fnl f: sn wknd* 33/1
0-60 7 2 1/4 **Tally's Song**[37] 1795 3-8-11 35 RobHornby(3) 8 33
(Grace Harris) *broke wl: trckd ldrs: rdn 2f out: wknd ent fnl f* 100/1
0-0 8 10 **Romantic Angel (USA)**[18] 2298 3-8-11 0 ThomasBrown(3) 1
(Ismail Mohammed) *s.i.s: a towards rr* 33/1
9 6 **Blue Silk** 3-8-9 0 KieranShoemark(5) 4
(Roger Charlton) *slowly away: racd keenly: sn mid-div: rdn over 2f out: wknd wl over 1f out* 14/1
5- 10 17 **Beyond The Edge**[318] 4476 4-9-1 0 GeorgeWood(7) 10
(Christopher Mason) *sn outpcd in rr* 66/1

1m 10.4s (-0.80) **Going Correction** -0.10s/f (Good)
WFA 3 from 4yo 8lb 10 Ran SP% **121.9**
Speed ratings (Par 100): **101,95,91,90,83 82,79,65,57,35**
CSF £3.23 TOTE £1.90: £1.10, £1.30, £1.90; EX 4.10 Trifecta £14.60.
Owner Mrs Fitri Hay **Bred** Newsells Park Stud **Trained** Whatcombe, Oxon
FOCUS
Quite an interesting 3yo fillies' maiden run 0.46 secs slower than the earlier handicap over the trip. The market leaders dominated.

2849 BATH ALES HARE FOUNDATION H'CAP 1m 5y
8:00 (8:00) (Class 6) (0-65,65) 4-Y-O+ £2,587 (£770; £384; £192) Stalls Low

Form RPR
0152 1 **Saint Helena (IRE)**[7] 2635 8-9-6 64 (b) FMBerry 10 75
(Mark Gillard) *slowly away: sn in tch: led 2f out: styd on wl fnl f: rdn out* 13/8[1]
0600 2 3 **Last Wish (IRE)**[12] 2507 5-8-8 52 (b) ConnorBeasley 8 56
(Richard Guest) *s.i.s: towards rr: rdn and hdwy over 2f out: chsd wnr over 1f out: kpt on but a being comf hld* 10/1
0455 3 5 **Maverik**[16] 2369 8-9-5 63 (t) PatCosgrave 5 55
(Ali Stronge) *led: rdn and hdd 2f out: sn hld: no ex fnl f* 3/1[2]
4005 4 2 3/4 **Bognor (USA)**[22] 2187 5-9-7 65 (v[1]) AdamKirby 9 50
(Michael Attwater) *trckd ldrs: rdn and ev ch 2f out: sn hld: kpt on same pce fnl f* 8/1[3]
566- 5 2 **Avon Scent**[249] 6812 6-7-9 46 oh1 (p) RPWalsh(7) 2 26
(Christopher Mason) *trckd ldrs: rdn over 2f out: sn one pce* 25/1
1002 6 1 **The Tichborne (IRE)**[35] 1832 8-9-1 64 (b) DannyBurton(5) 1 42
(Roger Teal) *s.i.s: towards rr: rdn 3f out: sme hdwy 2f out: no further imp fnl f* 10/1
330- 7 9 **Delaire**[191] 7986 4-8-12 63 GeorgeWood(7) 7 19
(Martin Bosley) *in tch: rdn over 2f out: wknd over 1f out* 10/1
/ 8 1 3/4 **Moss Street**[44] 3940 6-8-8 55 (bt) DanielMuscutt(3) 6 7
(John Flint) *pressed ldr: rdn 3f out: sn hld: wknd wl over 1f out* 14/1
60-0 9 nk **Kaaber (USA)**[18] 2309 5-7-13 50 (b) MitchGodwin(3) 3
(Roy Brotherton) *trckd ldrs: rdn 3f out: wknd wl over 1f out* 50/1
00-0 10 5 **Orbit The Moon (IRE)**[24] 2130 8-9-1 62 (tp) RobHornby(3) 4
(Grace Harris) *a towards rr* 20/1

1m 41.12s (0.32) **Going Correction** +0.075s/f (Good) 10 Ran SP% **118.7**
Speed ratings (Par 101): **101,98,93,90,88 87,78,76,76,71**
CSF £19.42 CT £48.42 TOTE £2.50: £1.30, £2.90, £1.60; EX 21.20 Trifecta £89.10.
Owner Adrian Hosie **Bred** Frank O'Malley **Trained** Holwell, Dorset
■ Stewards' Enquiry : R P Walsh two-day ban (19-20 June): careless riding
FOCUS
Rail movements added 10yds to the race distance. A moderate handicap but a decisive winner.

2850 BATH ALES SALAMANDER H'CAP 1m 5f 22y
8:30 (8:30) (Class 6) (0-65,65) 4-Y-O+ £2,587 (£770; £384; £192) Stalls High

Form RPR
4-00 1 **Blue Top**[20] 1831 7-7-10 47 (v[1]) HollieDoyle(7) 2 53
(Dai Burchell) *trckd ldr: led 6f out: qcknd 5 l clr 3f out: sn rdn: enough in hand and a holding on fnl f: drvn out* 14/1
-463 2 3/4 **Starcrossed**[15] 2400 4-9-7 65 (b) JohnFahy 9 70
(Eve Johnson Houghton) *rousted along leaving stalls: sn led: hdd 6f out: chsd wnr tl outpcd over 2f out: rallied over 1f out: styd on to take 2nd cl home but a being hld by wnr* 10/1
31U1 3 nk **Dynamo (IRE)**[7] 2634 5-9-1 59 6ex (t) ShaneKelly 7 63
(Richard Hughes) *trckd ldrs: rdn to chse wnr over 2f out: styd on same pce fnl f: lost 2nd cl home* 6/4[1]
-021 4 2 3/4 **Urban Space**[13] 2462 10-8-10 57 (t) DanielMuscutt(3) 4 57
(John Flint) *trckd ldrs: outpcd over 2f out: styd on again fr over 1f out but nvr any threat* 13/2[3]
520- 5 2 **Grams And Ounces**[25] 8317 9-8-11 62 (t) GeorgeWood(7) 3 59
(Grace Harris) *hld up in tch: rdn over 2f out: sn one pce* 10/1
00-0 6 1 3/4 **Perfect Rhythm**[15] 2399 5-9-2 65 PaddyPilley(5) 1 60
(Patrick Chamings) *hld up: hdwy over 2f out: sn rdn: chal for 3rd over 1f out: fdd fnl f* 16/1
0-30 7 2 1/4 **Petrify**[7] 2634 6-8-3 47 (t) KieranO'Neill 5 38
(Bernard Llewellyn) *hld up in tch: drvn over 2f out: nvr threatened: fdd fnl f* 9/1
3352 8 2 1/2 **Helmsman (IRE)**[35] 1846 4-9-0 58 AdamKirby 8 46
(J S Moore) *trckd ldrs: rdn wl over 2f out: wknd jst over 1f out* 9/2[2]
0/-0 9 25 **Karl Marx (IRE)**[16] 2370 6-7-9 46 oh1 RPWalsh(7) 6
(Mark Gillard) *a detached in last: struggling 7f out: wknd 2f out: eased* 33/1

2m 52.23s (0.23) **Going Correction** +0.075s/f (Good) 9 Ran SP% **115.2**
Speed ratings (Par 101): **102,101,101,99,98 97,95,94,79**
CSF £144.23 CT £335.13 TOTE £22.70: £3.30, £2.50, £1.20; EX 106.40 Trifecta £1401.30 Part won..
Owner B M G Group **Bred** Mrs Joan M Langmead **Trained** Briery Hill, Blaenau Gwent
■ Stewards' Enquiry : Hollie Doyle four-day ban (23-26 Jun): used whip above permitted level
FOCUS
Rail movements added 10yds to the race distance. Another low-grade contest but the early pace was was quite decent. It produced a surprise winner.

2851 BATH ALES BARNSEY H'CAP 1m 2f 46y
9:00 (9:01) (Class 6) (0-60,58) 3-Y-O £2,264 (£673; £336; £168) Stalls Low

Form RPR
00-5 1 **Desert Cross**[23] 2148 3-9-3 54 FMBerry 8 59
(Jonjo O'Neill) *racd keenly: in tch: hdwy over 2f out: rdn over 1f out: styd on wl fnl f: led fnl strides* 11/1
00-4 2 hd **Final Choice**[9] 2590 3-8-9 51 KieranShoemark(5) 1 56
(Roger Charlton) *dwlt: towards rr: hdwy over 2f out: rdn over 1f out: led ent fnl f: ct cl home* 15/8[1]
06-6 3 nse **Ochos Rios**[48] 1484 3-9-5 56 AdamKirby 3 61
(David Evans) *chsd ldr: sltly outpcd wl over 2f out: styd on wl fnl f: nrly snatched 2nd fnl stride* 3/1[2]
005 4 1 **Dalavand (IRE)**[17] 2325 3-9-7 58 TimmyMurphy 2 61
(Jamie Osborne) *trckd ldrs: rdn 2f out: styd on but nt clrest of runs ins fnl f* 16/1
-020 5 3/4 **Gold Eliza (IRE)**[9] 2590 3-8-10 54 HollieDoyle(7) 5 59+
(Richard Hannon) *hld up towards rr: rdn whn nt clr run over 1f out: hdwy ent fnl f: styng on wl but denied clr run bhd ldrs fnl 75yds* 8/1[3]
0-50 6 nk **Monday Club**[17] 2325 3-9-1 57 [1] JosephineGordon(5) 4 58
(Dominic Ffrench Davis) *hld up towards rr: hdwy over 2f out: rdn over 1f out: styd on same pce ins fnl f* 9/1
000- 7 2 **Maer Rocks (IRE)**[170] 8245 3-9-1 52 PatCosgrave 12 49
(Marcus Tregoning) *led: rdn and hdd over 2f out: kpt on w ev ch tl no ex ins fnl f* 14/1
6-64 8 nk **Patanjali (IRE)**[23] 2148 3-9-5 56 TomQueally 10 53
(Eve Johnson Houghton) *trckd ldrs: led over 2f out: sn rdn: hdd ent fnl f: wknd* 8/1[3]
0-00 9 1 3/4 **Rosie's Vision**[17] 2325 3-8-9 51 RachealKneller(5) 9 44
(Mark Usher) *stdd s: a in rr* 25/1
00-0 10 1 1/4 **Russian Rascal**[35] 1826 3-8-11 48 [1] ShaneKelly 11 39
(Stuart Kittow) *mid-div: rdn over 2f out: wknd over 1f out* 25/1

2m 15.85s (4.85) **Going Correction** +0.075s/f (Good) 10 Ran SP% **120.6**
Speed ratings (Par 97): **83,82,82,82,81 81,79,79,77,76**
CSF £33.08 CT £80.80 TOTE £13.10: £2.90, £1.60, £1.60; EX 39.40 Trifecta £360.00.
Owner P Hickey **Bred** W T , R T & N S Whittle **Trained** Cheltenham, Gloucs
FOCUS
Rail movements added 10yds to the race distance. A very moderate 3yo handicap, but it produced a blanket finish.
T/Plt: £26.80 to a £1 stake. Pool: £59,433.03 - 1615.97 winning units T/Qpdt: £2.20 to a £1 stake. Pool: £6,000.67 - 1976.45 winning units **Tim Mitchell**

2675 CATTERICK (L-H)
Friday, June 3

OFFICIAL GOING: Good to firm (8.6)
Wind: Light, half behind Weather: Overcast

2852 BRITISH STALLION STUDS EBF NOVICE STKS 5f
1:50 (1:51) (Class 5) 2-Y-O £3,234 (£962; £481; £240) Stalls Low

Form RPR
1 **Queen Kindly** 2-8-11 0 JamieSpencer 4 82+
(Richard Fahey) *prom: smooth hdwy to chse ldr 1/2-way: shkn up to ld ins fnl f: qcknd clr: readily* 2/5[1]
4 2 5 **Katebird (IRE)**[20] 2235 2-8-11 0 JoeFanning 3 59
(Mark Johnston) *led: clr 1/2-way: sn rdn: hdd ins fnl f: no ch w ready wnr* 7/2[2]
3 1 1/4 **Best Away (FR)** 2-9-2 0 JamesSullivan 6 60
(Ruth Carr) *bhd and sn pushed along: hdwy over 1f out: kpt on: nvr nrr* 80/1
4 4 **Coco La Belle (IRE)** 2-8-11 0 DavidAllan 5 40
(Tim Easterby) *dwlt: rn green in rr: rdn whn hung lft over 1f out: nvr able to chal* 28/1
5 1 **Wild Approach (IRE)** 2-9-2 0 GrahamLee 1 42
(Robert Cowell) *chsd ldr to 1/2-way: rn green and wknd over 1f out* 9/1[3]
6 4 1/2 **Trick Of The Lyte (IRE)** 2-9-2 0 JasonHart 2 25
(John Quinn) *chsd ldrs: lost pl over 3f out: drifted rt and struggling fr 1/2-way* 18/1

1m 0.27s (0.47) **Going Correction** +0.025s/f (Good) 6 Ran SP% **113.6**
Speed ratings (Par 93): **97,89,87,80,79 71**
CSF £2.21 TOTE £1.30: £1.10, £1.60; EX 2.70 Trifecta £51.00.
Owner Jaber Abdullah **Bred** Rabbah Bloodstock Limited **Trained** Musley Bank, N Yorks
FOCUS
Following a dry night the going remained good to firm and all race distances were as advertised. Only one of the six runners in this novice event had previous experience, but all eyes were on one of the five newcomers and she didn't disappoint.

2853 DINE AND VIEW AT CATTERICK RACES (S) STKS 1m 5f 175y
2:25 (2:25) (Class 6) 4-Y-O+ £2,264 (£673; £336; £168) Stalls Low

Form RPR
-206 1 **The Kid**[73] 1028 5-8-12 73 (p) DougieCostello 2 70+
(John Quinn) *t.k.h: trckd ldrs: shkn up and squeezed through to ld ins fnl f: pushed out: comf* 2/1[2]
-635 2 1/2 **Sinakar (IRE)**[28] 2018 5-8-10 73 JoshDoyle(5) 5 72
(David O'Meara) *trckd ldrs: rdn to ld over 2f out: edgd lft: hdd ins fnl f: kpt on: hld nr fin* 4/7[1]
00 3 3 **Desert Sensation (IRE)**[20] 2260 4-8-12 0 (t) JoeFanning 4 65
(Tracy Waggott) *pressed ldr: led 1/2-way: rdn and hdd over 2f out: rallied and ev ch tl outpcd last 100yds* 33/1
4400 4 15 **Monzino (USA)**[31] 1952 8-9-1 37 GrahamLee 6 45
(Michael Chapman) *hld up: pushed along over 6f out: drvn and outpcd 4f out: n.d after* 200/1

0-00 **5** *18* **Troy Boy**[25] 2089 6-8-12 37.......... BarryMcHugh 1 15
(Rebecca Bastiman) *led at ordinary gallop: cl up tl rdn and wknd over 3f out* **100/1**

33-0 **P** **Perennial**[10] 2558 7-8-12 60..........(p) AndrewMullen 3
(Philip Kirby) *hld up in tch: drvn and struggling 1/2-way: lost tch whn p.u and dismntd over 2f out* **12/1**[3]

3m 3.41s (-0.19) **Going Correction** +0.025s/f (Good) **6** Ran SP% **109.1**
Speed ratings (Par 101): **101,100,99,90,80**
CSF £3.25 TOTE £3.60: £1.10, £1.10; EX 4.60 Trifecta £14.90.The winner was bought in for 4,500gns. Desert Sensation was claimed by R. D. P. Newland for £6,000. Sinakar was claimed by Mr Conor Dore for £6,000.
Owner D Ward **Bred** D Boocock **Trained** Settrington, N Yorks

FOCUS
A poor seller which was a match according to the market, but a tenuous link with Epsom as three of the six runners were sired by Derby winners.

2854 LIONWELD KENNEDY H'CAP 5f
3:00 (3:00) (Class 5) (0-70,68) 3-Y-O **£2,911** (£866; £432; £216) **Stalls** Low

Form RPR

-021 **1** **Black Grass**[44] 1558 3-8-9 61.......... NathanEvans(5) 4 76
(Michael Easterby) *mde all: pushed along over 1f out: hld on wl fnl f* **3/1**[2]

2210 **2** *1* **Fumbo Jumbo (IRE)**[17] 2334 3-9-7 68.......... DavidAllan 2 79
(Garry Moss) *taken early to post: cl up: drvn along 1/2-way: kpt on fnl f: hld towards fin* **13/2**[3]

31-1 **3** *2 1/4* **Show Palace**[18] 2302 3-9-2 63.......... GrahamLee 5 66
(Jennie Candlish) *hld up in tch: hdwy to chse ldrs over 1f out: sn rdn: edgd lft ins fnl f: kpt on same pce* **15/8**[1]

-004 **4** *3 1/2* **Tribesman**[14] 2418 3-9-7 68.......... SamJames 6 58
(Marjorie Fife) *hld up: pushed along 1/2-way: hdwy and hung lft over 1f out: no imp fnl f* **10/1**

50-5 **5** *3 1/4* **North Spirit (IRE)**[11] 2534 3-9-0 61.......... GrahamGibbons 8 40
(David O'Meara) *cl up on outside: rdn along 1/2-way: wknd over 1f out* **12/1**

6-06 **6** *3* **Dark Confidant (IRE)**[25] 2106 3-9-1 62.......... JasonHart 1 30
(Richard Guest) *chsd ldrs: drvn along 1/2-way: wknd over 1f out* **9/1**

46-0 **7** *2 1/4* **Irish Cailin (IRE)**[18] 2302 3-8-11 58.......... PaulMulrennan 3 18
(Paul Midgley) *t.k.h: in tch: drvn and outpcd 1/2-way: btn over 1f out* **20/1**

-503 **8** *4* **Cool Silk Boy (IRE)**[92] 797 3-9-6 67.......... TomEaves 7 12
(James Given) *dwlt: hld up: hdwy on outside 1/2-way: wknd wl over 1f out* **16/1**

1m 0.05s (0.25) **Going Correction** +0.025s/f (Good) **8** Ran SP% **110.5**
Speed ratings (Par 99): **99,97,93,88,83 78,74,68**
CSF £21.16 CT £41.92 TOTE £3.20: £1.30, £1.50, £1.30; EX 23.30 Trifecta £59.20.
Owner T Dewhirst, L Folwell, S Hull & D Swales **Bred** M W Easterby **Trained** Sheriff Hutton, N Yorks

FOCUS
An ordinary 3yo sprint handicap, but several were vying for the early lead so the pace was decent.

2855 EBF STALLIONS BREEDING WINNERS FILLIES' H'CAP 7f
3:35 (3:35) (Class 4) (0-80,78) 3-Y-O+ **£6,469** (£1,925; £962; £481) **Stalls** Low

Form RPR

16-0 **1** **Invermere**[41] 1623 3-9-1 75.......... TonyHamilton 6 80
(Richard Fahey) *pressed ldr: rdn and led over 1f out: hrd pressed fnl f: hld on wl* **6/1**[3]

0-21 **2** *nk* **Blue Jacket (USA)**[25] 2096 5-8-11 61.......... JamesSullivan 8 69
(Dianne Sayer) *prom on outside: effrt and hdwy over 1f out: rdn and ch ins fnl f: edgd lft: kpt on to take 2nd cl home* **10/1**

0-26 **3** *hd* **Hawatif (IRE)**[23] 2161 3-9-4 78.......... JoeFanning 4 82
(Mark Johnston) *led at stdy gallop: rdn and hdd over 1f out: rallied: kpt on fnl f: hld nr fin* **2/1**[1]

1 **4** *1 3/4* **Owaseyf (USA)**[18] 2303 3-9-1 75.......... HarryBentley 1 77+
(Roger Varian) *trckd ldrs on ins: effrt whn nt clr run over 1f out to last 100yds: kpt on same pce towards fin* **2/1**[1]

0-60 **5** *4 1/2* **Fleurtille**[17] 2332 7-8-12 62..........(p) DougieCostello 3 53
(Ray Craggs) *hld up in tch: drvn along over 2f out: no imp over 1f out: btn fnl f* **66/1**

-243 **6** *5* **Azagal (IRE)**[4] 2737 5-10-0 78.......... DavidAllan 2 55
(Tim Easterby) *s.s: bhd: drvn over 2f out: sn btn* **4/1**[2]

1m 26.76s (-0.24) **Going Correction** +0.025s/f (Good)
WFA 3 from 4yo+ 10lb **6** Ran SP% **111.5**
Speed ratings (Par 102): **102,101,101,99,94 88**
CSF £57.97 CT £157.16 TOTE £5.70: £1.80, £2.10; EX 42.20 Trifecta £186.50.
Owner Mcculloch Bloodstock Ltd **Bred** The Lavington Stud **Trained** Musley Bank, N Yorks

FOCUS
A fair fillies' handicap, but a messy race.

2856 FREE MONTH TRIAL RACING UK H'CAP 5f 212y
4:10 (4:10) (Class 6) (0-65,65) 3-Y-O+ **£2,587** (£770; £384; £192) **Stalls** Low

Form RPR

10-0 **1** **Bondi Beach Babe**[17] 2334 6-9-13 64..........(p) TomEaves 5 75
(James Turner) *mde all: rdn and qcknd clr 2f out: kpt on wl fnl f: unchal* **8/1**

3635 **2** *1 1/2* **Ancient Cross**[14] 2416 12-9-9 60..........(bt) GrahamGibbons 1 68
(Michael Easterby) *dwlt: sn midfield: effrt against far rail whn nt clr run over 1f out: rcvrd and chsd wnr ins fnl f: kpt on: no imp* **3/1**[1]

4064 **3** *1 1/4* **Prigsnov Dancer (IRE)**[31] 1956 11-9-2 60.......... RowanScott(7) 11 62
(Deborah Sanderson) *hld up towards rr: hdwy on outside 2f out: edgd lft and kpt on fnl f: nrst fin* **28/1**

2155 **4** *nk* **Iceaxe**[16] 2373 3-9-5 64.......... RoystonFfrench 9 63
(John Holt) *midfield: rdn and hdwy 2f out: kpt on ins fnl f* **7/2**[2]

0506 **5** *3/4* **Rat Catcher (IRE)**[14] 2447 6-8-11 48..........(p) LemosdeSouza 3 47
(Lisa Williamson) *bhd: rdn and hdwy over 2f out: kpt on ins fnl f: nt pce to chal* **40/1**

5500 **6** *nk* **Kyllach Me (IRE)**[17] 2332 4-9-4 60..........(b) PhilDennis(5) 2 58
(Bryan Smart) *t.k.h: trckd ldrs on ins: wnt 2nd over 2f out: rdn and edgd lft over 1f out: outpcd ins fnl f* **9/1**

0402 **7** *2 3/4* **Tancred (IRE)**[4] 2741 5-9-11 62..........(b) JamesSullivan 6 51
(Conor Dore) *bhd and sn pushed along: hdwy over 1f out: edgd lft: kpt on: n.d* **7/1**[3]

-000 **8** *1 1/4* **Bold Spirit**[4] 2741 5-9-8 59..........(bt) DavidAllan 7 45
(Declan Carroll) *trckd wnr to over 2f out: rdn and wknd over 1f out* **10/1**

650- **9** *2* **Horsforth**[295] 5291 4-9-11 62.......... BarryMcHugh 8 42
(Tony Coyle) *prom: drvn along over 2f out: wknd over 1f out* **25/1**

4650 **10** *hd* **City Of Angkor Wat (IRE)**[18] 2309 6-10-0 65..........(p) PaulMulrennan 10 44
(Conor Dore) *midfield on outside: rdn over 2f out: sn struggling: eased whn hld ins fnl f* **8/1**

000- **11** *14* **Dark Castle**[316] 4540 7-9-11 62.......... PJMcDonald 12
(Micky Hammond) *dwlt and wnt rt s: bhd: struggling 1/2-way: sn lost tch* **22/1**

1m 13.39s (-0.21) **Going Correction** +0.025s/f (Good)
WFA 3 from 4yo+ 8lb **11** Ran SP% **115.1**
Speed ratings (Par 101): **102,100,98,97,96 96,92,91,88,88 69**
CSF £30.18 CT £656.30 TOTE £10.00: £3.30, £1.10, £9.30; EX 36.20 Trifecta £605.20.
Owner G R Turner & H Turner **Bred** G R & H Turner **Trained** Norton-le-Clay, N Yorks

FOCUS
A moderate handicap and not many got into it.

2857 START YOUR RACING UK FREE TRIAL H'CAP 5f 212y
4:55 (4:55) (Class 4) (0-85,82) 4-Y-O+ **£5,175** (£1,540; £769; £384) **Stalls** Low

Form RPR

0004 **1** **Luis Vaz De Torres (IRE)**[35] 1844 4-9-2 77.......... TomEaves 8 88
(Richard Fahey) *trckd ldrs: wnt 2nd 1/2-way: effrt and rdn 2f out: led ins fnl f: kpt on wl* **18/1**

6521 **2** *1* **Best Trip (IRE)**[20] 2238 9-9-2 82.......... NathanEvans(5) 11 89
(Marjorie Fife) *led and sn crossed to ins rail: rdn over 1f out: hdd ins fnl f: no ex towards fin* **13/2**

4022 **3** *1 1/2* **Manatee Bay**[6] 2680 6-9-0 75..........(v) PaulQuinn 7 78+
(David Nicholls) *t.k.h: hld up towards rr: pushed along and effrt 2f out: kpt on wl fnl f: nt rch first two* **4/1**[2]

214 **4** *shd* **Chaplin Bay (IRE)**[14] 2416 4-8-11 72.......... JamesSullivan 3 74+
(Ruth Carr) *hld up: rdn over 2f out: hdwy over 1f out: kpt on: nrst fin* **3/1**[1]

15-4 **5** *1 1/2* **Foreign Diplomat**[144] 142 4-9-7 82.......... GrahamGibbons 5 79
(David O'Meara) *t.k.h: prom against ins rail: rdn over 2f out: one pce ins fnl f: lost two pls nr fin* **7/1**

2-00 **6** *3/4* **Be Bold**[33] 1879 4-9-2 77.......... BarryMcHugh 4 72
(Rebecca Bastiman) *t.k.h: in tch: rdn over 2f out: outpcd fnl f* **66/1**

4-00 **7** *shd* **Free Zone**[34] 1874 7-9-0 80..........(v) JoshDoyle(5) 2 75
(David O'Meara) *hld up: rdn along over 2f out: kpt on ins fnl f: nvr able to chal* **18/1**

1060 **8** *2 3/4* **Clubland (IRE)**[50] 1444 7-9-1 81.......... AaronJones(5) 1 67
(Roy Bowring) *dwlt: bhd: effrt and drvn along over 2f out: no imp fr over 1f out* **20/1**

46-5 **9** *hd* **Nezar (IRE)**[20] 2238 5-8-12 78..........(v) CallumShepherd(5) 10 63
(John Quinn) *dwlt: sn midfield on outside: effrt over 2f out: edgd rt and wknd over 1f out* **11/2**[3]

505- **10** *2 3/4* **Compton Park**[273] 6045 9-9-7 82..........(t) DavidAllan 6 58
(Les Eyre) *dwlt: t.k.h in rr: hung rt bnd over 3f out: rdn and no imp fr 2f out* **11/1**

0-00 **11** *8* **Native Falls (IRE)**[7] 2665 5-9-1 76.......... ShaneGray 9 27
(Alan Swinbank) *trckd ldr to 1/2-way: rdn and wknd qckly 2f out: eased whn btn ins fnl f* **40/1**

1m 12.72s (-0.88) **Going Correction** +0.025s/f (Good) **11** Ran SP% **113.8**
Speed ratings (Par 105): **106,104,102,102,100 99,99,95,95,91 81**
CSF £124.57 CT £567.25 TOTE £13.90: £3.60, £2.50, £2.00; EX 104.50 Trifecta £621.80.
Owner Lets Go Racing 1 **Bred** Peter Molony **Trained** Musley Bank, N Yorks

FOCUS
A fair sprint handicap and the pace was strong, but another race where few got themselves into a winning position.

2858 WE WILL MISS YOU MARION MAIDEN STKS 1m 3f 214y
5:30 (5:31) (Class 5) 3-Y-O+ **£3,234** (£962; £481; £240) **Stalls** Centre

Form RPR

/44- **1** **Snow Prince**[133] 7721 5-10-0 0.......... PJMcDonald 3 77
(Steve Gollings) *trckd ldrs: rdn over 4f out: rallied: led ins fnl f: styd on wl* **18/1**

5-33 **2** *3/4* **Ice Galley (IRE)**[20] 2260 3-8-13 74.......... TomEaves 6 76
(Kevin Ryan) *wnt lft s: led: rdn over 2f out: hdd ins fnl f: kpt on: hld nr fin* **3/1**[2]

3 *10* **Ifandbutwhynot (IRE)**[48] 10-10-0 0.......... DavidAllan 2 60
(Tim Easterby) *hld up in tch: stdy hdwy over 5f out: effrt and rdn over 2f out: outpcd fnl f* **7/1**

4 *1 1/4* **Pearl Phoenix (FR)** 6-10-0 0.......... JasonHart 4 58
(John Quinn) *trckd ldr: carried wd bnd after 3f: ev ch over 4f out to over 2f out: wknd appr fnl f: broke down and dismntd after line* **7/2**[3]

5 *50* **Lady Broome**[36] 5-9-9 0..........(p) DougieCostello 1
(John David Riches) *dwlt: bhd: hmpd 1/2-way: sn lost tch: t.o* **125/1**

06- **6** *2* **The Winningtipster**[250] 6781 3-8-13 0.......... JoeyHaynes 7
(Susan Corbett) *prom 3f: sn lost pl: struggling over 5f out: t.o* **125/1**

-322 **7** *76* **School Fete (IRE)**[28] 2000 3-8-10 80..........(v[1]) LouisSteward(3) 5
(Michael Bell) *hmpd s: in tch: rdn and lost pl jst bef 1/2-way: sn lost tch: virtually p.u fnl 3f* **1/1**[1]

F **Trinity House (IRE)**[24] 4-10-0 0..........(tp) PaddyAspell 8
(Michael Smith) *slowly away and wnt bdly rt sn after s: hld up: stdy hdwy and in tch whn clipped heels and fell jst bef 1/2-way* **125/1**

2m 37.96s (-0.94) **Going Correction** +0.025s/f (Good)
WFA 3 from 4yo+ 15lb **8** Ran SP% **117.4**
Speed ratings (Par 103): **104,103,96,96,62 61,10,**
CSF £73.92 TOTE £19.50: £4.20, £1.40, £2.00; EX 86.00 Trifecta £408.60.
Owner C Johnstone **Bred** West Lodge Stud **Trained** Scamblesby, Lincs

FOCUS
No shortage of incident in this maiden with the two early leaders getting into a spot of bother taking the opening bend, \bTrinity House\p coming down around 7f from home and the fourth horse sadly going wrong near the line.
T/Plt: £35.00 to a £1 stake. Pool: £42,688.36 - 890.34 winning tickets T/Qpdt: £24.10 to a £1 stake. Pool: £3,026.27 - 92.90 winning tickets **Richard Young**

2233 DONCASTER (L-H)
Friday, June 3

OFFICIAL GOING: Good to firm (8.1)
Wind: Light half against Weather: Cloudy

2859 NAPOLEONS CASINOS & RESTAURANTS SHEFFIELD SUPPORTING WPCC H'CAP 1m 4f
6:10 (6:10) (Class 5) (0-75,75) 3-Y-O **£5,175** (£1,540; £769; £384) **Stalls** Low

Form RPR

2-55 **1** **Euchen Glen**[21] 2197 3-9-6 74.......... GrahamLee 1 83+
(Jim Goldie) *hld up: hdwy over 2f out: n.m.r and swtchd rt over 1f out: rdn to chal ins fnl f: led last 75yds* **20/1**

50-5 **2** 1 1/4 **Nucky Thompson**[18] 2291 3-9-3 **71**.................. WilliamTwiston-Davies 5 78
(Richard Spencer) *trckd ldrs: hdwy 3f out: rdn to ld over 1f out: jnd and drvn ins fnl f: hdd and no ex last 75yds* **28/1**

51 **3** 3 3/4 **West Coast Flyer**[101] 687 3-9-7 **75**.............................. JamieSpencer 4 76
(David Simcock) *hld up: hdwy on outer over 2f out: rdn wl over 1f out: kpt on fnl f* **11/4**[2]

02-4 **4** 5 **Hammer Gun (USA)**[37] 1784 3-9-6 **74**............................ TedDurcan 3 67
(Sir Michael Stoute) *trckd ldng pair: hdwy on inner and cl up 3f out: rdn along 2f out: drvn and one pce fr over 1f out* **7/2**[3]

-011 **5** 5 **Tenzing Norgay**[3] 2766 3-9-6 **74** 12ex...........................(v) RyanPowell 6 59
(Sir Mark Prescott Bt) *trckd ldr: cl up over 3f out: led wl over 2f out: rdn along 2f out: hdd over 1f out: sn btn* **11/8**[1]

2-34 **6** 25 **Templier (IRE)**[77] 980 3-9-7 **75**... JoeFanning 2 20
(Mark Johnston) *led: rdn along over 3f out: hdd wl over 2f out: sn drvn and wknd* **9/1**

2m 38.99s (4.09) **Going Correction** +0.35s/f (Good) **6** Ran SP% **109.2**
Speed ratings (Par 99): **100,99,96,93,90 73**
CSF £341.55 CT £1859.17 TOTE £21.70: £8.80, £9.70; EX 124.70 Trifecta £805.70.
Owner W M Johnstone **Bred** W M Johnstone **Trained** Uplawmoor, E Renfrews

FOCUS
The round course was railed out from 1m2f until joining the straight, adding about 6yds. An interesting little handicap featuring a couple of last time out winners, although the two outsiders came from off the pace to dominate the finish.

2860 ORIGINBROADBAND.COM SUPPORTING WESTON PARK CANCER CHARITY FILLIES' H'CAP 1m 2f 60y

6:40 (6:41) (Class 5) (0-70,73) 4-Y-0+ **£4,528** (£1,347; £673; £336) **Stalls** Low

Form RPR

-120 **1** **Wavelet**[14] 2433 4-9-7 **70**.. JamieSpencer 5 78
(David Simcock) *trckd ldr: hdwy to ld over 2f out: rdn and hung lft over 1f out: drvn out* **7/2**[1]

312- **2** 1 1/2 **Putaringonit (IRE)**[171] 8228 4-9-7 **70**.................................. MartinLane 2 74
(Jeremy Gask) *hld up: hdwy 3f out: effrt whn nt clr run over 1f out: sn rdn and chsd wnr ins fnl f: no imp towards fin* **4/1**[2]

02-6 **3** 1 1/4 **Ronya (IRE)**[10] 2555 5-8-10 **59**.................................... RoystonFfrench 7 61
(Tracy Waggott) *sn led: rdn along over 3f out: hdd over 2f out: drvn and n.m.r over 1f out: kpt on same pce* **9/1**

0-44 **4** hd **Phantom River**[16] 2369 4-9-0 **63**....................(p) WilliamTwiston-Davies 6 64
(Alan King) *hld up: hdwy on outer 3f out: rdn along and sltly outpcd wl over 1f out: drvn and kpt on fnl f* **9/2**[3]

3102 **5** nse **La Havrese (FR)**[14] 2436 5-8-10 **64**................................ JoshDoyle(5) 3 66
(Lynn Siddall) *hld up in rr: hdwy over 3f out: swtchd lft to inner and effrt 2f out: styng on whn hmpd over 1f out: sn swtchd rt and kpt on same pce* **7/2**[1]

0-04 **R** **Dalmarella Dancer (IRE)**[17] 2343 5-8-11 **65**.......... JordanVaughan(5) 4
(K R Burke) *ref to r tk no part* **4/1**[2]

2m 14.39s (4.99) **Going Correction** +0.35s/f (Good) **6** Ran SP% **112.6**
Speed ratings (Par 100): **94,92,91,91,91**
CSF £17.73 CT £112.86 TOTE £3.30: £1.40, £2.80; EX 13.10 Trifecta £76.90.
Owner Miss K Rausing **Bred** Miss K Rausing **Trained** Newmarket, Suffolk

FOCUS
The round course was railed out from 1m2f until joining the straight, adding about 6yds. An average fillies' handicap run at a slow pace and there was some scrimmaging in the home straight.

2861 BUCKINGHAM INSURANCE FIGHTING CANCER WITH WPCC MAIDEN STKS 1m (S)

7:10 (7:12) (Class 5) 3-Y-0 **£4,204** (£1,251; £625; £312) **Stalls** Low

Form RPR

4 **1** **El Hayem (IRE)**[48] 1474 3-9-5 0.. JoeFanning 11 90
(Sir Michael Stoute) *towards rr: smooth hdwy on outer over 3f out: chsd ldrs 2f out: rdn to ld over 1f out: kpt on wl* **25/1**

3 **2** 1 3/4 **Burguillos**[21] 2208 3-9-5 0.............................. WilliamTwiston-Davies 12 86
(Alan King) *trckd ldrs: effrt wl over 1f out: rdn to chse wnr ins fnl f: kpt on* **13/2**

0- **3** 1 1/2 **Fidaawy**[252] 6711 3-9-5 0.. TedDurcan 4 82+
(Sir Michael Stoute) *dwlt and bhd: hdwy 2f out: rdn over 1f out: styd on wl fnl f: nrst fin* **3/1**[2]

5-2 **4** 1 **Silk Cravat**[32] 1931 3-9-5 0.. MartinLane 1 80
(Simon Crisford) *led: pushed along 2f out: sn rdn: hdd over 1f out: sn drvn and grad wknd* **2/1**[1]

0-0 **5** 1/2 **Wannabe Friends**[22] 2175 3-9-5 0............................... JamieSpencer 6 79+
(Luca Cumani) *in tch: effrt 2f out: sn rdn and kpt on same pce* **33/1**

02 **6** 1 3/4 **Azizaan**[17] 2340 3-9-5 0... HarryBentley 13 75
(Roger Varian) *chsd ldr: cl up over 2f out: rdn wl over 1f out: sn wknd* **8/1**

4 **7** 2 1/4 **Egyptian (USA)**[17] 2320 3-9-5 0.. GrahamLee 7 69
(Jeremy Noseda) *in tch: pushed along wl over 2f out: rdn wl over 1f out and sn wknd* **25/1**

8 nk **Ya Jammeel** 3-9-5 0... TonyHamilton 2 68
(Richard Fahey) *midfield: pushed along over 3f out: rdn along wl over 2f out: n.d* **25/1**

522 **9** 1/2 **Raven's Corner (IRE)**[17] 2320 3-9-5 83.......................... RobertHavlin 5 67
(John Gosden) *chsd ldng pair: rdn 2f out: wknd over 1f out* **9/2**[3]

0- **10** 1/2 **Sautter**[226] 7395 3-9-5 0.. PaulMulrennan 14 66
(Peter Chapple-Hyam) *a towards rr* **40/1**

00 **11** 1 1/4 **Zain Arion (IRE)**[12] 2505 3-9-0 0................................ StevieDonohoe 10 58
(Charlie Fellowes) *a in rr* **100/1**

00 **12** 2 **Glorious Legend (IRE)**[21] 2208 3-9-5 0........................ GeorgeBaker 8 58
(Ed Walker) *dwlt: a in rr* **100/1**

0 **13** 12 **Momentori**[12] 2505 3-9-0 0.. BenCurtis 9 24
(Scott Dixon) *a towards rr* **150/1**

1m 40.98s (1.68) **Going Correction** +0.275s/f (Good) **13** Ran SP% **120.5**
Speed ratings (Par 99): **102,100,98,97,97 95,93,92,92,91 90,88,76**
CSF £174.35 TOTE £22.80: £5.30, £2.40, £2.00; EX 215.70 Trifecta £1859.30 Part won..
Owner Al Shaqab Racing **Bred** Denis Brosnan **Trained** Newmarket, Suffolk

FOCUS
Some of the bigger yards were represented for this competitive maiden in which some of the main fancies disappointed. They came down the middle and went an honest gallop. The form is rated slightly positively.

2862 BLUE LINE TAXIS BARNSLEY SUPPORTING WPCC H'CAP 7f

7:40 (7:41) (Class 3) (0-95,94) 4-Y-0+ **£12,291** (£3,657; £1,827; £913) **Stalls** Low

Form RPR

1012 **1** **Welliesinthewater (IRE)**[16] 2378 6-8-0 **78**..............(v) NoelGarbutt(5) 14 86
(Derek Shaw) *trckd ldrs: hdwy 3f out: cl up 2f out: rdn to ld and hung rt ent fnl f: sn drvn and kpt on wl towards fin* **22/1**

4501 **2** 3/4 **Plucky Dip**[6] 2677 5-8-8 **84** 6ex....................................... DannyBrock(3) 10 90
(John Ryan) *trckd ldrs: hdwy over 2f out: rdn and ev ch over 1f out: drvn ins fnl f: no ex towards fin* **8/1**

0613 **3** 3/4 **Sir Billy Wright (IRE)**[8] 2613 5-8-9 **85**.......................... PhilipPrince(3) 11 89
(David Evans) *sn prom: led over 2f out: rdn over 1f out: hdd ent fnl f: sn drvn and kpt on same pce* **8/1**

000 **4** nk **Fox Trotter (IRE)**[15] 2391 4-9-7 **94**................................ JoeFanning 4 97
(Brian Meehan) *dwlt and in rr: hdwy wl over 2f out: rdn wl over 1f out: styd on wl fnl f: nrst fin* **12/1**

1-2 **5** 1/2 **Rouge Nuage (IRE)**[21] 2213 6-8-3 **76**............................. JimmyQuinn 7 78
(Conrad Allen) *trckd ldrs: effrt 2f out: sn rdn: drvn and kpt on same pce fnl f* **16/1**

-000 **6** 3/4 **Highland Acclaim (IRE)**[2] 2803 5-9-1 **88**....................... HarryBentley 16 88+
(David O'Meara) *dwlt and t.k.h in rr: hdwy 3f out: rdn over 1f out: kpt on fnl f: nrst fin* **22/1**

230- **7** 1 3/4 **Big Whiskey (IRE)**[158] 8380 6-9-6 **93**................................ KierenFox 3 88
(John Best) *in tch: hdwy 2f out and sn rdn: drvn and no imp fnl f* **12/1**

00-0 **8** hd **Northgate Lad (IRE)**[13] 2488 4-9-3 **90**............................... BenCurtis 2 85
(Brian Ellison) *dwlt: sn in tch: hdwy on inner to chse ldrs 1/2-way: rdn along 2f out: drvn over 1f out: grad wknd* **22/1**

0-05 **9** 3/4 **Burn The Boats (IRE)**[30] 1959 7-9-1 **88**.......................... MartinLane 5 81
(Mike Murphy) *led: hdd over 2f out and sn rdn along: drvn over 1f out: wknd fnl f* **16/1**

-313 **10** 1/2 **Hakam (USA)**[16] 2361 4-8-9 **82**.. GrahamLee 12 73
(Charles Hills) *nvr bttr than midfield* **15/2**[3]

0-40 **11** 1/2 **Free Code (IRE)**[27] 2027 5-9-3 **90**............................ GrahamGibbons 17 80
(David Barron) *cl up on outer: rdn along over 2f out: sn wknd* **7/1**[2]

5-60 **12** 1/2 **Fiftyshadesofgrey (IRE)**[34] 1856 5-9-7 **94**......................(t) LiamKeniry 6 82
(George Baker) *dwlt: a towards rr* **9/1**

00-0 **13** nse **Hawkeyethenoo (IRE)**[23] 2158 10-8-10 **88**................ HectorCrouch(5) 9 76+
(Jim Goldie) *towards rr: swtchd lft to far rail over 2f out: in tch and rdn wl over 1f out: sn btn* **12/1**

4-21 **14** 2 1/4 **Slemy (IRE)**[17] 2345 5-8-6 **79**...................................... JamesSullivan 15 61
(Ruth Carr) *plld hrd: a in rr* **6/1**[1]

-000 **15** 2 1/2 **Ingleby Angel (IRE)**[22] 2191 7-9-7 **94**........................ RoystonFfrench 18 69
(Colin Teague) *midfield on outer: rdn along over 3f out: sn lost pl and bhd* **66/1**

1m 26.8s (0.50) **Going Correction** +0.275s/f (Good) **15** Ran SP% **120.2**
Speed ratings (Par 107): **108,107,106,105,105 104,102,102,101,100 100,99,99,97,94**
CSF £181.48 CT £1553.19 TOTE £20.50: £6.00, £3.10, £3.60; EX 281.90 Trifecta £810.00 Part won..
Owner Shawthing Racing Partnership **Bred** Brendan Ryan **Trained** Sproxton, Leics

FOCUS
A competitive handicap in which it proved difficult to come from off the pace. They raced down the middle.

2863 WELDRICKS PHARMACY IN SUPPORT OF WESTON PARK H'CAP 5f

8:10 (8:11) (Class 4) (0-85,85) 3-Y-0+ **£5,175** (£1,540; £769; £384) **Stalls** Low

Form RPR

3-60 **1** **Oh So Sassy**[20] 2253 6-9-12 **83**...................................... GeorgeBaker 10 95
(Chris Wall) *racd wd: in tch: hdwy over 2f out: rdn to ld over 1f out: sn clr* **9/2**[3]

2304 **2** 2 3/4 **Flash City (ITY)**[7] 2658 8-9-0 **71**................................(p) JamesSullivan 9 73
(Ruth Carr) *in rr: hdwy 2f out: rdn over 1f out: styd on fnl f* **12/1**

-312 **3** 1 1/4 **Majestic Hero (IRE)**[7] 2665 4-9-11 **82**........................ JamieSpencer 4 80
(Ronald Harris) *racd towards far side rail: cl up: rdn 2f out and ev ch: drvn over 1f out and kpt on same pce* **9/4**[1]

-342 **4** 2 1/4 **Socialites Red**[32] 1922 3-8-9 **73**... BenCurtis 2 60
(Scott Dixon) *chsd ldrs towards far side: rdn along over 2f out: drvn over 1f out: kpt on fnl f* **8/1**

6340 **5** nk **Pearl Acclaim (IRE)**[13] 2488 6-9-9 **80**............................ TomEaves 5 68
(David Nicholls) *chsd ldrs: rdn along 2f out: sn drvn and wknd over 1f out* **10/1**

0051 **6** shd **Pearl Noir**[19] 2270 6-8-7 **67**...(b) TimClark(3) 8 55
(Scott Dixon) *chsd ldr: led over 3f out: rdn 2f out: drvn and hdd over 1f out: wknd* **20/1**

31 **7** 4 1/2 **Alsvinder**[17] 2333 3-9-7 **85**.. HarryBentley 12 54
(David O'Meara) *sn rdn along and outpcd: a in rr* **7/2**[2]

0-30 **8** 1 **Grand Beauty (IRE)**[18] 2305 4-9-12 **83**.......................[1] GrahamLee 6 51
(Robert Cowell) *in tch: rdn along 2f out: sn wknd* **16/1**

160- **9** 1 1/4 **Royal Acquisition**[164] 8347 6-9-7 **78**........................ FrederikTylicki 7 42
(Ivan Furtado) *racd centre: chsd ldrs: rdn along 2f out: sn wknd* **16/1**

59.64s (-0.86) **Going Correction** 0.0s/f (Good)
WFA 3 from 4yo+ 7lb **9** Ran SP% **115.6**
Speed ratings (Par 105): **106,101,99,96,95 95,88,86,84**
CSF £56.79 CT £152.35 TOTE £5.10: £1.40, £3.90, £1.50; EX 68.30 Trifecta £279.70.
Owner The Eight Of Diamonds **Bred** Mrs C J Walker **Trained** Newmarket, Suffolk

FOCUS
A sprint handicap featuring a couple of improving 3yo's taking on their elders, though it was their elders who held sway. They went a good gallop.

2864 SUN H'CAP 7f

8:40 (8:42) (Class 5) (0-70,70) 3-Y-0 **£4,204** (£1,251; £625; £312) **Stalls** Low

Form RPR

604- **1** **Tripartite (IRE)**[220] 7531 3-9-3 **66**...................................... MartinLane 4 74
(Jeremy Gask) *chsd ldrs: hdwy 2f out: rdn to chal over 1f out: drvn ins fnl f: led last 75yds* **25/1**

2154 **2** 1/2 **Bahamian Sunshine**[9] 2571 3-8-9 **65**.................(p) AdamMcNamara(7) 8 71
(Richard Fahey) *prom: hdwy and cl up 1/2-way: rdn to ld wl over 1f out: drvn ins fnl f: hdd and no ex last 75yds* **10/1**

0-26 **3** 1/2 **Mithqaal (USA)**[17] 2322 3-9-3 **66**................................... JoeFanning 13 74+
(Owen Burrows) *midfield: effrt on outer 2f out and sn rdn: swtchd lft ent fnl f: styd on strly towards fin* **13/2**[3]

-424 **4** nk **Dark Command**[18] 2306 3-8-11 **60**...........................(p) PaulMulrennan 11 64
(Michael Dods) *towards rr: hdwy 3f out: chsd ldrs over 1f out: sn rdn and styd on fnl f: nrst fin* **5/1**[2]

552- **5** 1/2 **El Principe**[219] 7553 3-8-11 **60**...[1] DavidAllan 14 62
(Les Eyre) *prom: cl up 1/2-way: rdn 2f out and ev ch tl drvn over 1f out and kpt on same pce* **16/1**

00-6 **6** 1 1/4 **Bryght Boy**[20] 2234 3-9-0 **63**.. AntonioFresu 1 62
(Ed Walker) *dwlt and in rr: hdwy 1/2-way: in tch and rdn over 1f out: no imp fnl f* **11/1**

40- **7** 1 1/4 **Epeius (IRE)**[238] 7092 3-9-6 **69**...................................... JoeyHaynes 18 65
(Ben Haslam) *chsd ldrs: rdn along over 2f out: grad wknd* **14/1**

0045 **8** 2 1/2 **Canny Style**[14] 2428 3-8-11 **60**.. GrahamLee 9 49
(Kevin Ryan) *towards rr: hdwy over 2f out: sn rdn and no imp* **20/1**

04-4 **9** *1* **Rebel Raiser**[36] 1806 3-9-5 **68** (b[1]) WilliamTwiston-Davies 5 54
(Richard Spencer) *cl up: led 3f out: rdn and hdd wl over 1f out: sn drvn and wknd appr fnl f* **20/1**

00-5 **10** *nk* **Whitkirk**[24] 2122 3-8-6 **55** JamesSullivan 15 40+
(Jedd O'Keeffe) *in rr tl sme late hdwy* **40/1**

65 **11** *2* **Diamond Avalanche (IRE)**[14] 2422 3-9-5 **68** BenCurtis 7 48
(Patrick Holmes) *chsd ldrs: rdn along wl over 2f out: sn wknd* **25/1**

5405 **12** *2 1/4* **Le Manege Enchante (IRE)**[25] 2106 3-9-0 **63** TonyHamilton 3 37
(Derek Shaw) *dwlt: a towards rr* **50/1**

-343 **13** *3 1/4* **The Name's Paver**[11] 2533 3-9-4 **67** (p) BarryMcHugh 12 32
(Noel Wilson) *a in rr* **14/1**

3-05 **14** *5* **Claymore (IRE)**[17] 2322 3-9-7 **70** GeorgeBaker 10 22
(David Lanigan) *a towards rr* **11/4**[1]

0550 **15** *1/2* **Dwynant**[12] 2506 3-9-1 **64** RyanPowell 19 14
(Kevin Frost) *led: pushed along and hdd 3f out: sn rdn and wknd* **33/1**

060- **16** *hd* **Mancinello (IRE)**[197] 7902 3-8-7 **63** JordanUys(7) 20 13
(Brian Meehan) *cl up on outer: rdn along 3f out: sn drvn and wknd* **25/1**

500- **17** *38* **St Dunstan (IRE)**[213] 7673 3-8-9 **58** TomEaves 17
(John Quinn) *a in rr: outpcd and bhd fnl 2f* **25/1**

1m 27.48s (1.18) **Going Correction** +0.275s/f (Good) **17** Ran SP% **125.6**
Speed ratings (Par 99): **104,103,102,102,101 100,99,96,95,94 92,89,86,80,79 79,36**
CSF £238.25 CT £1918.81 TOTE £42.00: £7.90, £2.60, £2.40, £1.70; EX 553.40 Trifecta £1134.40 Part won..
Owner The Salt House Syndicate **Bred** Tally-Ho Stud **Trained** Stockbridge, Hants

FOCUS
The finale was a competitive 3yo handicap in which those racing towards the far side held the edge.
T/Plt: £10,288.90 to a £1 stake. Pool: £68,358.11 - 4.85 winning units T/Qpdt: £51.70 to a £1 stake. Pool: £8,995.01 - 128.7 winning units **Joe Rowntree**

1566 EPSOM (L-H)
Friday, June 3

OFFICIAL GOING: Good to soft (overall 6.4; home straight: stands' side 6.4; far side 6.0)
Wind: light, half against Weather: overcast

2865 INVESTEC WOODCOTE STKS (LISTED RACE) 6f
2:00 (2:01) (Class 1) 2-Y-O
£28,355 (£10,750; £5,380; £2,680; £1,345; £675) **Stalls** High

Form RPR

12 **1** **Legendary Lunch (IRE)**[18] 2311 2-9-0 0 PatDobbs 3 94
(Richard Hannon) *str: stdd s: trckd ldrs: styd against far rail st: pushed along and qcknd to ld over 1f out: almost 2 l clr 1f out: drvn ins fnl f: hdd last strides: led again on the nod on post* **5/2**[1]

21 **2** *nse* **Danielsflyer (IRE)**[16] 2358 2-9-0 0 PhillipMakin 7 94
(David Barron) *str: hld up in 5th: swtchd rt and effrt 2f out: hdwy u.p to chse wnr ins fnl f: str run to ld last strides: hdd on the nod on post* **10/1**[3]

11 **3** *2* **Sea Of Snow (USA)**[18] 2311 2-8-9 0 WilliamBuick 5 83
(Mark Johnston) *w'like: led: hdd and rdn over 2f out: drvn and unable qck over 1f out: styd on same pce ins fnl f* **4/1**[2]

1 **4** *3/4* **Hyperfocus (IRE)**[41] 1635 2-9-0 0 JamesDoyle 1 86
(Hugo Palmer) *tall: w ldr tl led over 2f out: sn rdn: hdd and unable qck over 1f out: lost 2nd and styd on same pce ins fnl f* **4/1**[2]

1 **5** *1 3/4* **Tibr (USA)**[27] 2038 2-9-0 0 RyanMoore 6 80
(Ed Dunlop) *trckd ldrs: effrt and pressing ldrs 2f out: unable qck over 1f out: wknd ins fnl f* **5/2**[1]

411 **6** *9* **Sayesse**[22] 2173 2-9-0 0 SilvestreDeSousa 4 53
(Mick Channon) *stdd s: hld up in last: effrt 2f out: no imp and btn over 1f out: wknd fnl f* **16/1**

1m 13.55s (4.15) **Going Correction** +0.55s/f (Yiel) **6** Ran SP% **112.1**
Speed ratings (Par 101): **94,93,91,90,87 75**
CSF £27.46 TOTE £3.30: £1.90, £4.20; EX 26.40 Trifecta £152.30.
Owner The Rat Pack Partnership 2016 **Bred** Johnston King **Trained** East Everleigh, Wilts

FOCUS
It was dry overnight and the going was given as good to soft (GoingStick: 6.4 (Home straight: stands' side 6.4; far side 6.0). The rail was out by up to 4.5yds from the 1m marker to the winning post. Race distance increased by 6yds. This had been moved from its usual slot on Derby day. It looked a useful bunch on paper, but they didn't go that quick and the first pair were well clear at the finish. The winning time suggested ground more on the soft side. As is often the case for the Woodcote, the form is rated as just below par for the grade.

2866 INVESTEC WEALTH & INVESTMENT STKS (H'CAP) 1m 2f 18y
2:35 (2:37) (Class 2) 4-Y-O+
£31,125 (£9,320; £4,660; £2,330; £1,165; £585) **Stalls** Low

Form RPR

-100 **1** **Imshivalla (IRE)**[27] 2026 5-8-6 **88** PaulHanagan 1 97
(Richard Fahey) *swtg: broke wl: stdd to trck ldng pair and travelled strly: wnt 2nd over 2f out: sn chalng: rdn to ld over 1f out: in command and styd on strly fnl f* **25/1**

00-2 **2** *1 1/4* **Gold Prince (IRE)**[21] 2214 4-8-3 **90** EdwardGreatrex(5) 4 96
(Sylvester Kirk) *lw: led: rdn and clr w wnr 2f out: hdd over 1f out: unable qck and styd on same pce fnl f* **16/1**

0-30 **3** *1 1/4* **What About Carlo (FR)**[29] 1972 5-9-4 **100** JimmyFortune 3 104
(Eve Johnson Houghton) *lw: hld up in tch in midfield: effrt over 2f out: hdwy to chse clr ldng pair over 1f out: styd on and steadily clsd ins fnl f: nvr threatening ldrs* **9/2**[2]

-111 **4** *6* **Dark Red (IRE)**[29] 1972 4-8-13 **95** RyanMoore 5 87
(Ed Dunlop) *dwlt: hld up in tch: effrt over 2f out: hdwy u.p 2f out: drvn to go 3rd briefly wl over 1f out: 4th and no imp fr over 1f out* **7/4**[1]

-412 **5** *1 3/4* **Felix De Vega (IRE)**[29] 1972 4-8-11 **93** CamHardie 9 81
(Michael Easterby) *sn chsng ldr tl dropped to 3rd and rdn over 2f out: outpcd 2f out: 5th and wl hld over 1f out: plugged on* **12/1**

2050 **6** *hd* **Fire Fighting (IRE)**[8] 2626 5-9-10 **106** (b) FMBerry 6 94
(Mark Johnston) *hld up in tch in last trio: effrt ent fnl 2f: drvn over 1f out: no threat to ldrs but plugged on to pass btn horses ins fnl f* **10/1**

0-10 **7** *1* **Darshini**[29] 1972 4-8-9 **91** (p) AndreaAtzeni 7 77
(Sir Michael Stoute) *swtg: hld up in tch in last trio: effrt over 3f out: no imp and outpcd 2f out: wl hld and plugged on same pce after* **10/1**

-066 **8** *1 1/2* **Sennockian Star**[13] 2482 6-8-8 **90** FrannyNorton 2 73
(Mark Johnston) *in tch in midfield: rdn 3f out: lost pl and btn 2f out: wknd over 1f out* **14/1**

21/0 **9** *1 3/4* **Pasaka Boy**[27] 2024 6-8-8 **90** RichardKingscote 8 69
(Jonathan Portman) *hld up in tch in midfield: effrt whn n.m.r over 2f out: sn rdn and outpcd: wl btn over 1f out* **10/1**

0002 **10** *2 1/4* **Master Of Finance (IRE)**[13] 2484 5-9-1 **97** (b) SilvestreDeSousa 10 72
(Mark Johnston) *dwlt: steadily rcvrd on outer to chse ldng trio 7f out: swtchd rt and rdn over 3f out: lost pl and btn 2f out: bhd and eased wl ins fnl f* **8/1**[3]

2m 12.63s (2.93) **Going Correction** +0.55s/f (Yiel) **10** Ran SP% **117.0**
Speed ratings (Par 109): **110,109,108,103,101 101,100,99,98,96**
CSF £372.48 CT £2135.13 TOTE £30.10: £5.60, £5.10, £1.70; EX 462.50 Trifecta £5097.80.
Owner Pow Partnership **Bred** M Fahy & Rathbarry Stud **Trained** Musley Bank, N Yorks

FOCUS
Race distance increased by 19yds. A good handicap, but few got into it, with the pace holding up. The first two have unconvincing profiles.

2867 INVESTEC DIOMED STKS (GROUP 3) 1m 114y
3:10 (3:10) (Class 1) 3-Y-O+
£39,697 (£15,050; £7,532; £3,752; £1,883; £945) **Stalls** Low

Form RPR

5535 **1** **Tullius (IRE)**[42] 1604 8-9-5 110 (v[1]) JimmyFortune 1 113
(Andrew Balding) *lw: hld up in tch: effrt and hdwy over 2f out: chsd ldr wl over 1f out: styd on to chal 100yds: r.o wl u.p to ld last stride* **5/2**[1]

4-41 **2** *shd* **Decorated Knight**[13] 2464 4-9-5 109 AndreaAtzeni 11 112
(Roger Charlton) *dwlt: hld up in tch in last pair: effrt over 1f out: hdwy to chse ldng pair over 1f out: styd on u.p to chal 100yds out: led towards fin: hdd last stride* **7/2**[2]

-340 **3** *hd* **Custom Cut (IRE)**[26] 2067 7-9-10 114 DavidNolan 5 117
(David O'Meara) *led: rdn over 2f out: drvn ent fnl f: hrd pressed 100yds out: battled on gamely tl hdd and lost 2 pls towards fin* **8/1**

2265 **4** *4 1/2* **Sovereign Debt (IRE)**[33] 1910 7-9-8 112 RyanMoore 3 104
(David Nicholls) *stdd s: hld up in tch in rr: swtchd lft and effrt on inner over 2f out: nt clr run and shuffled bk jst over 2f out: swtchd rt 2f out: hdwy to chse clr ldng trio 1f out: kpt on but nvr any ch of chalng* **4/1**[3]

03-4 **5** *3 3/4* **Celestial Path (IRE)**[26] 2074 4-9-5 105 LukeMorris 4 93
(Sir Mark Prescott Bt) *lw: in tch in midfield: rdn over 3f out: drvn and unable qck over wl over 1f out* **10/1**

0110 **6** *3* **Sea Of Flames**[22] 2190 3-8-7 101 SilvestreDeSousa 2 84
(David Elsworth) *taken down early: chsd ldr for 1f: chsd ldrs after: rdn and unable qck over 2f out: lost pl and bhd over 1f out* **8/1**

6-10 **7** *2* **Fanciful Angel (IRE)**[99] 720 4-9-5 107 FrankieDettori 7 81
(Marco Botti) *taken down early: dwlt: rcvrd to chse ldr and t.k.h after 1f: rdn over 2f out: lost 2nd wl over 1f out and sn lost pl: wknd fnl f* **15/2**

1m 47.9s (1.80) **Going Correction** +0.55s/f (Yiel)
WFA 3 from 4yo+ 12lb **7** Ran SP% **113.9**
Speed ratings (Par 113): **114,113,113,109,106 103,101**
CSF £11.28 TOTE £3.50: £2.10, £2.50; EX 14.80 Trifecta £61.30.
Owner Kennet Valley Thoroughbreds VI **Bred** Sc Archi Romani **Trained** Kingsclere, Hants
■ Stewards' Enquiry : Ryan Moore The Stewards found the jockey guilty of careless riding and cautioned him as to his future conduct in races.
Frankie Dettori vet reported that a post-race examination of the gelding failed to reveal any abnormalities.

FOCUS
Race distance increased by 19yds. This edition of the Group 3 Diomed was hit by non-runners. There was a sound pace on and it produced a desperate three-way finish. The form makes sense, the winner rated to the balance of last year's best.

2868 INVESTEC MILE (H'CAP) 1m 114y
3:45 (3:47) (Class 2) (0-105,99) 4-Y-O+
£24,900 (£7,456; £3,728; £1,864; £932; £468) **Stalls** Low

Form RPR

6-02 **1** **Examiner (IRE)**[34] 1861 5-9-0 **92** OisinMurphy 7 100
(Stuart Williams) *lw: hld up in tch in rr: swtchd rt and hdwy over 2f out: chsd ldrs over 1f out: drvn and chal jst ins fnl f: r.o wl to ld 50yds out: r.o* **11/2**[3]

-302 **2** *1/2* **Instant Attraction (IRE)**[34] 1871 5-9-7 **99** JackGarritty 5 106
(Jedd O'Keeffe) *nodded leaving stalls: sn chsng ldrs: rdn to chal over 2f out: drvn over 1f out: led ent fnl f: kpt on wl tl hdd and one pce fnl 50yds* **6/1**

-614 **3** *1 1/4* **Miss Van Gogh**[20] 2236 4-8-11 **89** PaulHanagan 3 93
(Richard Fahey) *t.k.h: hld up in tch in midfield: rdn and hdwy to ld 2f out: drvn over 1f out: hdd ent fnl f: no ex and outpcd fnl 75yds* **8/1**

3-3 **4** *1 1/4* **Alcatraz (IRE)**[39] 1716 4-8-5 **83** (t) FrannyNorton 2 84+
(George Baker) *lw: t.k.h: wl in tch in midfield: nt clrest of runs over 2f out: swtchd rt and effrt 2f out: drvn over 1f out: styd on same pce ins fnl f* **5/1**[2]

-645 **5** *nk* **Cordite (IRE)**[27] 2032 5-8-6 **84** SamHitchcott 9 84
(Jim Boyle) *taken down early: sn pushed up to chse ldr: led 7f out: rdn over 2f out: hdd 2f out: unable qck u.p over 1f out: kpt on same pce ins fnl f* **33/1**

0101 **6** *hd* **Spring Offensive (IRE)**[19] 2268 4-8-13 **91** GeorgeChaloner 4 91+
(Richard Fahey) *t.k.h: hld up in tch in midfield: nt clr run and shuffled bk 5f out: hdwy and nt clr run again over 2f out tl hdwy u.p 1f out: styd on ins fnl f: nvr threatening ldrs* **12/1**

100- **7** *shd* **Persun**[223] 7473 4-8-6 **84** LukeMorris 11 84
(Mick Channon) *hld up in tch in last trio: rdn and hdwy over 1f out: drvn ent fnl f: styd on same pce and no imp fnl 150yds* **16/1**

00-1 **8** *1* **Fieldsman (USA)**[20] 2247 4-8-13 **91** JamesDoyle 10 88+
(George Scott) *in tch in midfield: hdwy on outer to chse ldr 6f out tl c to stands' side 3f out: sn u.p: unable qck 2f out: hld and styd on same pce fnl f* **14/1**

03-4 **9** *1 1/4* **Melvin The Grate (IRE)**[139] 221 6-9-0 **92** DavidProbert 6 87
(Andrew Balding) *s.i.s: hld up in tch in rr: hdwy over 2f out: rdn and chsd ldrs over 1f out: no ex and btn 1f out: wknd ins fnl f* **10/1**

0-62 **10** *11* **Jack's Revenge (IRE)**[21] 2216 8-8-11 **89** (bt) SteveDrowne 12 58
(George Baker) *stdd s: hld up in tch: hdwy over 2f out: no ex u.p over 1f out: sn btn: wknd qckly and eased ins fnl f* **14/1**

2321 **11** *3* **Dutch Uncle**[27] 2037 4-8-9 **87** SilvestreDeSousa 8 49
(Ed Dunlop) *in tch in midfield: nt handle downhill run 5f out: rdn 3f out: sn lost pl and btn 2f out: bhd fnl f* **9/2**[1]

2140 **12** *4* **Bold Prediction (IRE)**[28] 1993 6-8-7 **90** EdwardGreatrex(5) 1 43
(Ed Walker) *led for 1f: chsd ldr tl 6f out: styd handy tl lost pl u.p over 2f out: bhd fnl f* **25/1**

1m 48.93s (2.83) **Going Correction** +0.55s/f (Yiel) **12** Ran SP% **118.4**
Speed ratings (Par 109): **109,108,107,106,106 105,105,104,103,94 91,87**
CSF £38.48 CT £266.75 TOTE £6.90: £2.40, £2.60, £2.90; EX 46.50 Trifecta £327.00.
Owner DJM Racing **Bred** River Downs Stud **Trained** Newmarket, Suffolk

■ Stewards' Enquiry : Edward Greatrex trainer's rep said the gelding was unsuited by the going which was good to soft and would prefer a faster surface.

David Probert two-day ban (19-20 June): used whip above shoulder height

Luke Morris two-day ban (19-20 June): used whip above shoulder height

Silvestre De Sousa trainer said the gelding was unsuited by the ground which was good to soft and would prefer a faster surface.

FOCUS

Race distance increased by 19yds. An open handicap. A pb from the winner with another solid effort from the second.

2869 INVESTEC OAKS (GROUP 1) (FILLIES) — 1m 4f 10y

4:30 (4:32) (Class 1) 3-Y-O

£269,372 (£102,125; £51,110; £25,460; £12,777; £6,412) **Stalls** Centre

Form — RPR

1-12 **1** **Minding (IRE)**[12] 2509 3-9-0 119 RyanMoore 4 118+
(A P O'Brien, Ire) *lw: hld up in rr: hdwy and midfield 8f out: short of room, dropped to 8th and hmpd st: sn swtchd lft: swtchd rt and qcknd smartly to chse ldr over 2f out: rdn to ld over 1f out: in command and styd on fnl f* **10/11**[1]

31-2 **2** 1 3/4 **Architecture (IRE)**[27] 2035 3-9-0 97 FrankieDettori 9 115
(Hugo Palmer) *lw: hld up in tch towards rr: wnt 3rd and travelling wl st: rdn and qcknd to ld over 2f out: hdd over 1f out: hld and styd on same pce after for clr 2nd* **12/1**

1-24 **3** 8 **Harlequeen**[23] 2160 3-9-0 102 SilvestreDeSousa 5 102
(Mick Channon) *hld up in tch in rr: swtchd rt over 4f out: cl 6th and edgd lft st: effrt to chse ldrs over 2f out: 3rd 2f out: sn outpcd by ldng pair: wl hld but clr 3rd fr over 1f out: kpt on* **14/1**

1 **4** 14 **Somehow (IRE)**[30] 1966 3-9-0 98 SeamieHeffernan 6 80
(A P O'Brien, Ire) *led: rdn and hdd over 2f out: outpcd 2f out and sn btn: wknd and battling for modest 4th fnl f* **7/1**[3]

31 **5** hd **Skiffle**[15] 2394 3-9-0 103 WilliamBuick 8 79
(Charlie Appleby) *lw: hld up in tch in last trio: smooth hdwy on outer 4f out: wnt 2nd and travelling wl st: rdn to press ldr briefly 2f out: sn btn: wknd and battling for modest 4th fnl f* **6/1**[2]

4-1 **6** 9 **Seventh Heaven (IRE)**[27] 2035 3-9-0 98 ColmO'Donoghue 7 65
(A P O'Brien, Ire) *swtg: chsd ldrs: rdn 4f out: 7th and losing pl whn squeezed for room and hmpd st: lost tch over 2f out: t.o* **20/1**

12-6 **7** 19 **Turret Rocks (IRE)**[33] 1888 3-9-0 110 KevinManning 1 35
(J S Bolger, Ire) *in tch in midfield: chsd ldrs 8f out: 4th and rdn st: sn dropped out and bhd: t.o* **10/1**

2105 **8** 24 **Australian Queen**[23] 2160 3-9-0 90 JamesDoyle 3
(David Elsworth) *lw: jnd ldr over 10f out tl 5th and dropping out qckly st: sn bhd and lost tch over 2f out: t.o* **50/1**

1-3 **P** **Diamonds Pour Moi**[30] 1966 3-9-0 95 OisinMurphy 2
(Ralph Beckett) *t.k.h: w ldrs early: steadily lost pl: in tch in last pair 6f out: dropped to last and eased 5f out: sn p.u and dismntd over 2f out* **12/1**

2m 42.66s (3.76) **Going Correction** +0.55s/f (Yiel) **9** Ran SP% **117.0**
Speed ratings (Par 110): **109,107,102,93,93 87,74,58,**
CSF £13.91 CT £100.06 TOTE £1.90: £1.20, £2.60, £2.90; EX 14.80 Trifecta £127.60.

Owner Derrick Smith & Mrs John Magnier & Michael Tabor **Bred** Orpendale, Chelston & Wynatt **Trained** Cashel, Co Tipperary

■ Stewards' Enquiry : Silvestre De Sousa The Stewards found Dettori in guilty of careless riding in that he had allowed his horse to drop in towards the rail and cautioned him as to his future conduct in races.

FOCUS

Race distance increased by 19yds. A weak Oaks on paper, with only two previous Group winners in attendance and the Musidora winner So Mi Dar missing out through injury. It got messy as they turned for home and the race fell apart from there, with the first pair coming well clear. The first three came from the back. The form has been rated as up to scratch although Minding was a little off her Guineas win.

2870 INVESTEC SURREY STKS (LISTED RACE) — 7f

5:15 (5:15) (Class 1) 3-Y-O

£22,684 (£8,600; £4,304; £2,144; £1,076; £540) **Stalls** Low

Form — RPR

0-1 **1** **Smuggler's Moon**[21] 2207 3-9-0 79 JimmyFortune 6 109+
(Brian Meehan) *stdd s: hld up in rr: swtchd rt and effrt 2f out: str run and edging lft over 1f out: chal ent fnl f: led 150yds out: sn in command but rn green in front: eased nr fin* **14/1**

26-5 **2** 3/4 **Make Fast**[27] 2034 3-8-9 96 DavidProbert 2 98
(Andrew Balding) *hld up in tch: nt clrest of runs over 2f out: effrt 2f out: outpcd by ldng trio over 1f out: rallied and styd on strly ins fnl f: wnt 2nd 50yds out: nvr getting to wnr* **11/1**

33-5 **3** 1 **Raucous**[51] 1424 3-9-0 104 RyanMoore 7 100
(William Haggas) *in tch in midfield: effrt to chse clr ldr 2f out: styd on and pressing ldng pair whn short of room and hmpd 1f out: kpt on same pce u.p ins fnl f* **7/1**

-132 **4** nk **Haalick (IRE)**[13] 2466 3-9-4 104 AndreaAtzeni 1 103+
(Roger Varian) *lw: awkward leaving stalls and s.i.s: hld up in tch: nt clr run on inner over 2f out: swtchd rt 2f out and again over 1f out: 5th and plenty to do 1f out: styd on wl fnl 100yds: nvr gng to rch ldrs* **13/8**[1]

0-23 **5** 1 **Scrutineer (IRE)**[20] 2250 3-9-0 102 SilvestreDeSousa 8 97
(Mick Channon) *chsd ldr tl rdn to ld over 2f out: clr and hung lft over 1f out: hrd pressed and drvn 1f out: hdd 150yds out: no ex: wknd wl ins fnl f* **3/1**[2]

2-00 **6** 5 **Justice Law (IRE)**[23] 2161 3-9-0 91 OisinMurphy 5 83
(David Elsworth) *dwlt: sn in tch in midfield: rdn over 2f out: sn outpcd and btn: wknd over 1f out* **16/1**

3130 **7** nk **Bear Faced**[70] 1071 3-9-0 98 LukeMorris 4 82
(Sir Mark Prescott Bt) *chsd ldrs: rdn over 3f out: drvn and lost pl 2f out: sn wknd* **25/1**

3601 **8** 7 **Calder Prince (IRE)**[13] 2477 3-9-0 99 RichardKingscote 3 64
(Tom Dascombe) *led tl rdn and hdd over 2f out: unable qck u.p and lost 2nd wl over 1f out: wknd over 1f out* **6/1**[3]

1m 27.01s (3.71) **Going Correction** +0.55s/f (Yiel) **8** Ran SP% **114.6**
Speed ratings (Par 107): **100,99,98,97,96 90,90,82**
CSF £154.09 TOTE £13.70: £3.00, £2.90, £2.20; EX 134.30 Trifecta £1338.10.

Owner Manton Thoroughbreds **Bred** Bugley Stud (alchemilla) Partnership **Trained** Manton, Wilts

FOCUS

Race distance increased by 12yds. An interesting Listed race and a fine performance from the winner, who showed a smart turn of foot. The time was only similar to the following handicap.

2871 INVESTEC SPECIALIST BANK STKS (H'CAP) — 7f

5:50 (5:52) (Class 2) (0-100,98) 3-Y-O

£18,675 (£5,592; £2,796; £1,398; £699; £351) **Stalls** Low

Form — RPR

-354 **1** **King's Pavilion (IRE)**[29] 1975 3-8-11 88 FrannyNorton 3 96
(Mark Johnston) *hld up in tch: swtchd rt and effrt over 2f out: hdwy and hanging lft over 1f out: chal ins fnl f: led 50yds: r.o wl* **10/1**

-155 **2** 1/2 **Stamp Hill (IRE)**[13] 2466 3-8-9 86 GeorgeChaloner 5 93
(Richard Fahey) *lw: chsd ldrs: wnt 2nd and edgd lft ent fnl 2f: rdn to ld over 1f out: drvn 1f out: hdd and one pce fnl 50yds* **7/2**[1]

240- **3** 2 **Qeyaadah (IRE)**[267] 6244 3-9-0 91 PaulHanagan 4 92
(Ed Dunlop) *t.k.h: hld up in tch in midfield: rdn and hdwy 2f out: chsng ldrs and sltly hmpd jst over 1f out: 3rd and styd on same pce ins fnl f* **12/1**

23-0 **4** 1 3/4 **Reputation (IRE)**[23] 2161 3-8-5 82 CamHardie 1 79
(John Quinn) *chsd ldr tl over 2f out: short of room ent fnl 2f: drvn and unable qck over 1f out: wknd ins fnl f* **15/2**

5-20 **5** 7 **Candelisa (IRE)**[34] 1851 3-9-7 98 JackGarritty 7 76
(Jedd O'Keeffe) *sn dropped to last pair: effrt wl over 2f out: no imp: plugged on to pass btn horses ins fnl f: nvr trbld ldrs* **12/1**

21-1 **6** 2 **Happy Call**[28] 2002 3-8-3 85 (v) EdwardGreatrex[(5)] 8 57
(Simon Crisford) *lw: led: rdn and hdd over 1f out: sn drvn and btn: fdd fnl f* **6/1**[3]

412- **7** 2 1/4 **Harry Champion**[168] 8286 3-7-13 81 JosephineGordon[(5)] 2 47
(Hugo Palmer) *chsd ldrs early: stdd bk into midfield: pushed along on downhill run 4f out: rdn over 2f out: sn btn: wknd over 1f out* **8/1**

-634 **8** 3/4 **Storm Rising (IRE)**[13] 2479 3-8-13 90 SeanLevey 9 54
(Richard Hannon) *in tch: rdn and no rspnse over 2f out: sn lost pl and wknd over 1f out* **9/2**[2]

02-1 **9** 3/4 **Short Work**[33] 1894 3-8-0 82 (p) PatrickO'Donnell[(5)] 6 44
(Ralph Beckett) *lunged forward prematurely and hit stalls gate: s.i.s: nvr gng wl in rr: lost tch 2f out* **15/2**

1m 27.02s (3.72) **Going Correction** +0.55s/f (Yiel) **9** Ran SP% **113.8**
Speed ratings (Par 105): **100,99,97,95,87 84,82,81,80**
CSF £44.33 CT £428.50 TOTE £12.30: £3.50, £1.80, £3.40; EX 54.30 Trifecta £489.30.

Owner Sheikh Hamdan bin Mohammed Al Maktoum **Bred** Darley **Trained** Middleham Moor, N Yorks

FOCUS

Race distance increased by 12yds. A competitive heat. They got racing for home plenty soon enough and the time was similar to the previous Listed race.

T/Jkpt: Not won. T/Plt: £339.40 to a £1 stake. Pool: £237,815.64 - 511.39 winning tickets T/Qpdt: £30.70 to a £1 stake. Pool: £19,968.17 - 480.10 winning tickets **Steve Payne**

2464 GOODWOOD (R-H)

Friday, June 3

OFFICIAL GOING: Good (good to firm in places; 7.9)

Wind: Moderate, half behind Weather: Fine

2872 ROA/RACING POST OWNERS JACKPOT AMATEUR RIDERS' STKS (H'CAP) — 1m 1f

6:20 (6:23) (Class 5) (0-70,70) 4-Y-O+ **£3,119** (£967; £483; £242) **Stalls** Low

Form — RPR

-562 **1** **Pink Ribbon (IRE)**[7] 2645 4-10-4 60 (p) MissSBrotherton 11 69
(Sylvester Kirk) *prom in chsng gp: led wl over 1f out: hld on wl* **11/2**[2]

4506 **2** 1/2 **Goodwood Moonlight**[17] 2323 4-9-6 51 (p) MrThomasGreatrex[(3)] 14 59
(Ian Williams) *mid-div: hdwy 2f out: chal ins fnl f: r.o* **12/1**

4-30 **3** 1 1/4 **China Girl (IND)**[31] 1947 4-10-6 67 MrJDoe[(5)] 12 72
(William Knight) *mid-div: hdwy over 2f out: styd on fnl f* **20/1**

0-50 **4** 2 1/2 **Byrd In Hand (IRE)**[17] 2323 9-9-2 51 oh3 (v) MissTannyaBagoban[(7)] 6 51
(John Bridger) *led tl wl over 1f out: one pce* **33/1**

20-6 **5** 1/2 **Collodi (GER)**[41] 1640 7-10-7 68 MissPBridgwater[(5)] 2 67
(David Bridgwater) *s.s: bhd: hdwy over 2f out: nrest at fin* **16/1**

0004 **6** 1 1/2 **Jazri**[7] 2645 5-9-12 61 (b) MrJCJones[(7)] 8 56
(Milton Bradley) *dwlt: bhd tl styd on fnl 2f* **16/1**

0-01 **7** 1 1/2 **Space War**[28] 2006 9-10-9 65 (t) MissJoannaMason 5 57
(Michael Easterby) *chsd ldrs: effrt 2f out: no ex fnl f* **10/1**

013- **8** hd **Dubawi Light**[191] 7973 5-10-7 70 WilliamClarke[(7)] 7 62+
(Gary Moore) *towards rr: hmpd over 4f out: styng on at fin* **8/1**[3]

0-51 **9** 1/2 **Victor's Bet (SPA)**[33] 1899 7-10-8 69 MissEllaSmith[(5)] 1 59
(Ralph J Smith) *mid-div: hmpd over 4f out: rdn 3f out: nvr nr ldrs* **5/2**[1]

4540 **10** 1 **Cadeaux Pearl**[72] 1047 8-9-4 51 MrKLocking[(5)] 4 39
(Scott Dixon) *chsd ldr: chal 2f out: sn wknd* **50/1**

16-6 **11** 1 1/4 **Kissy Suzuki**[152] 30 4-10-4 62 MissGDucker[(7)] 10 52
(Hughie Morrison) *chsd ldrs tl wknd 2f out* **14/1**

0440 **12** 3/4 **Bookmaker**[16] 2379 6-10-4 61 ow2 (b) MrRyanBird[(3)] 13 47
(John Bridger) *nvr trbld ldrs* **20/1**

0-42 **13** 24 **Estibdaad (IRE)**[86] 875 6-10-3 64 (t) MissMBryant[(5)] 15
(Paddy Butler) *a bhd: no ch fnl 3f* **40/1**

6-00 **14** 29 **Party Royal**[13] 2491 6-10-13 69 (p) MrDHDunsdon 9
(Nick Gifford) *a bhd: hmpd over 4f out: t.o and eased fnl 3f: lame* **25/1**

2233 **P** **Cartographic (USA)**[13] 2461 4-10-0 61 KatherineGlenister[(5)] 3
(David Evans) *chsd ldrs tl lost pl and p.u over 4f out: fatally injured* **8/1**[3]

1m 57.43s (1.13) **Going Correction** -0.025s/f (Good) **15** Ran SP% **122.1**
Speed ratings (Par 103): **93,92,91,89,88 87,86,85,85,84 83,82,61,35,**
CSF £64.30 CT £848.25 TOTE £6.20: £2.40, £2.90, £7.60; EX 70.80 Trifecta £2321.80.

Owner Mrs Michelle Cousins **Bred** Ann & Joe Hallinan **Trained** Upper Lambourn, Berks

■ Stewards' Enquiry : Miss P Bridgwater four-day ban (tba): used whip above permitted level

FOCUS

The first 2f of the mile course were dolled out 2yds, adding 12yds to the finale, but otherwise all race distances were as advertised. The pace to this reasonably competitive opening amateur riders' handicap was decent without being destructively strong.

2873 BREEDERS BACKING RACING EBF NOVICE STKS — 6f

6:50 (6:53) (Class 5) 2-Y-O **£3,234** (£962; £481; £240) **Stalls** High

Form — RPR

1 **Boynton (USA)** 2-9-2 0 WilliamBuick 6 88+
(Charlie Appleby) *in tch: effrt and rn green over 1f out: shkn up and led ins fnl f: pushed out* **9/2**[3]

2 nk **Mutawatheb (IRE)** 2-9-2 0 PatDobbs 7 87+
(Richard Hannon) *prom: led over 1f out tl ins fnl f: kpt on* **6/4**[1]

3 ¾ **Rebel De Lope** 2-9-2 0 .... DarryllHolland 9 85+
(Charles Hills) *s.i.s and rdn s: sn in tch: effrt 2f out: styd on wl fnl f* **14/1**

2 4 2 ¼ **Montataire (IRE)**[19] 2264 2-9-2 0 .... JamesDoyle 10 78
(Mark Johnston) *led tl over 1f out: one pce* **3/1**[2]

0 5 2 **Challow (IRE)**[21] 2203 2-9-2 0 .... JimCrowley 8 72
(Sylvester Kirk) *chsd ldr tl outpcd fnl 2f* **8/1**

6 3 ¼ **Racemaker** 2-9-2 0 .... CharlesBishop 3 62
(Mick Channon) *hld up in rr: rdn over 2f out: n.d* **33/1**

0 7 4 **Brise De Mer (FR)**[21] 2203 2-9-2 0 .... SteveDrowne 2 50
(George Baker) *a towards rr: rdn and btn 2f out* **25/1**

8 1 ½ **Muirsheen Durkin** 2-9-2 0 .... FergusSweeney 5 46
(Tom Dascombe) *a bhd* **28/1**

9 13 **Legendoire (IRE)** 2-9-2 0 .... MartinDwyer 4 7
(John Gallagher) *mid-div: rdn over 2f out: sn wknd* **33/1**

1m 11.3s (-0.90) **Going Correction** -0.125s/f (Firm) **9** Ran SP% **114.1**
Speed ratings (Par 93): **101,100,99,96,93 89,84,82,64**
CSF £11.08 TOTE £5.30: £1.50, £1.50, £3.10; EX 13.20 Trifecta £95.10.
Owner Godolphin **Bred** Twin Creeks Farm **Trained** Newmarket, Suffolk

FOCUS
In all likelihood a fair juvenile novice sprint, and newcomers filled the podium. The first three can all do better than the bare form.

2874 DERRIES LOWER NOVICE STKS (IN MEMORY OF FRED AND NORMA DUDLEY) 5f
7:20 (7:22) (Class 5) 2-Y-O **£3,234** (£962; £481; £240) **Stalls** High

Form RPR

1 **Kachess** 2-8-11 0 .... RichardKingscote 3 80+
(Tom Dascombe) *chsd ldr travelling strly: led 2f out: shkn up and qcknd clr fnl f: comf* **5/2**[2]

2 3 **Waqt (IRE)** 2-9-2 0 .... MartinDwyer 1 74
(Marcus Tregoning) *outpcd in rr: hdwy over 1f out: r.o to take 2nd ins fnl f* **12/1**

3 ½ **Apamurra (USA)** 2-8-11 0 .... WilliamBuick 6 67
(Mark Johnston) *towards rr: hdwy over 1f out: r.o* **11/8**[1]

332 4 1 ¾ **Princess Holly**[7] 2641 2-8-11 0 ....(p) SilvestreDeSousa 5 61
(Robert Cowell) *led tl 2f out: no ex fnl f* **6/1**

5 5 ½ **Apple Scruffs (IRE)**[14] 2429 2-9-2 0 .... AdamBeschizza 4 64
(Michael Attwater) *prom tl no ex over 1f out* **16/1**

4 6 shd **Top Hatter**[11] 2536 2-8-11 0 .... WilliamCarson 2 59
(Jamie Osborne) *in tch tl rdn and btn over 1f out* **9/2**[3]

58.2s (-2.00) **Going Correction** -0.125s/f (Firm) **6** Ran SP% **116.7**
Speed ratings (Par 93): **111,106,105,102,101 101**
CSF £31.41 TOTE £3.60: £1.90, £4.30; EX 31.30 Trifecta £88.10.
Owner David Lowe **Bred** Liam Sheridan **Trained** Malpas, Cheshire

FOCUS
Just the six runners but a decent winning time, and the first three all look potentially very useful. The winner will be worth her place up in grade.

2875 EBF STALLIONS BREEDING WINNERS FILLIES' STKS (H'CAP) 6f
7:50 (7:52) (Class 3) (0-90,90) 3-Y-O+ **£9,703** (£2,887; £1,443; £721) **Stalls** High

Form RPR

10-1 1 **Dancing Star**[22] 2185 3-8-10 **80** .... DavidProbert 2 94+
(Andrew Balding) *chsd ldr: led over 2f out: in control fnl f: comf* **5/2**[1]

2036 2 2 ¾ **Buying Trouble (USA)**[4] 2736 3-9-0 **84** .... DarryllHolland 4 89
(David Evans) *bhd: shkn up and hdwy over 1f out: r.o wl to take 2nd nr fin* **8/1**

1142 3 nk **Stellarta**[11] 2547 5-9-5 **81** .... SteveDrowne 9 87
(Michael Blanshard) *mid-div: hdwy over 1f out: kpt on same pce fnl f* **10/1**

100- 4 ¾ **Rosie's Premiere (IRE)**[236] 7143 4-10-0 **90** .... RobertWinston 8 93
(Dean Ivory) *prom: hrd rdn over 1f out: one pce* **22/1**

5-30 5 3 ¼ **Links Drive Lady**[32] 1929 8-9-6 **85** .... JackDuern(3) 10 78
(Dean Ivory) *dwlt: towards rr: effrt 2f out: nvr able to chal* **10/1**

601- 6 1 **Kassia (IRE)**[242] 6978 3-9-2 **86** .... SilvestreDeSousa 6 74+
(Mick Channon) *dwlt: hld up: effrt and in tch whn nt clr run over 1f out: n.d after* **9/2**[3]

10-5 7 ½ **Haley Bop (IRE)**[59] 1243 3-9-2 **86** .... WilliamBuick 1 72
(Mark Johnston) *in tch tl rdn and btn over 1f out* **10/1**

00-1 8 1 **Marmalady (IRE)**[34] 1857 6-9-10 **86** .... RichardKingscote 3 71
(Robert Cowell) *chsd ldrs: chal over 2f out: hung rt: wknd over 1f out* **4/1**[2]

2603 9 8 **Penny Dreadful**[19] 2267 4-8-11 **73** ....(p) LukeMorris 7 32
(Scott Dixon) *led tl over 2f out: wknd over 1f out* **20/1**

1m 10.27s (-1.93) **Going Correction** -0.125s/f (Firm)
WFA 3 from 4yo+ 8lb **9** Ran SP% **114.2**
Speed ratings (Par 104): **107,103,102,101,97 96,95,94,83**
CSF £22.96 CT £170.41 TOTE £3.80: £1.70, £2.90, £2.50; EX 26.30 Trifecta £133.50.
Owner J C Smith **Bred** Littleton Stud **Trained** Kingsclere, Hants
■ Stewards' Enquiry : Jack Duern three-day ban (19-21 June): careless riding

FOCUS
A well-contested fillies' handicap for the feature event, and a winning time 1.03 seconds quicker than that of the earlier novice stakes despite them not appearing to go off all that hard early.

2876 RUSSIAN ORIGINAL STANDARD STKS (H'CAP) 1m 4f
8:20 (8:22) (Class 5) (0-75,75) 4-Y-O+ **£3,234** (£962; £481; £240) **Stalls** High

Form RPR

0/14 1 **Sureness (IRE)**[2] 2791 6-9-0 **75** ....(t) MeganNicholls(7) 6 84
(Charlie Mann) *w ldr: hrd rdn and led 1f out: styd on wl* **11/2**[3]

110 2 3 **Rose Above**[69] 1092 4-9-4 **72** .... OisinMurphy 2 76
(Andrew Balding) *hld up in rr: hdwy on bit to ld over 2f out: hdd 1f out: one pce ins fnl f* **7/2**[2]

3111 3 3 ½ **Bamako Du Chatelet (FR)**[15] 2397 5-8-13 **67** ....(p) JamesDoyle 3 65
(Ian Williams) *trckd ldrs tl outpcd fnl 2f* **1/1**[1]

10-0 4 4 ½ **Onda District (IRE)**[28] 1999 4-9-0 **75** .... CallumRodriguez(7) 1 66
(Richard Ford) *in tch tl wknd and hung lft 2f out* **10/1**

603- 5 3 ¾ **Concord (IRE)**[282] 5756 4-9-0 **68** .... MartinDwyer 5 53
(Marcus Tregoning) *slt ld tl over 2f out: wknd wl over 1f out* **7/1**

000/ 6 ¾ **Art History (IRE)**[1017] 5640 8-9-1 **69** .... LukeMorris 4 53
(Zoe Davison) *hld up in 5th: outpcd 4f out: sn struggling* **33/1**

2m 42.72s (4.32) **Going Correction** -0.025s/f (Good) **6** Ran SP% **112.1**
Speed ratings (Par 103): **84,82,79,76,74 73**
CSF £24.69 TOTE £6.40: £2.70, £2.30; EX 30.10 Trifecta £76.50.
Owner P Mott **Bred** Alberto Panetta **Trained** Upper Lambourn, Berks

FOCUS
Just 8lb between these on official ratings but still not that strong a contest for the grade, and with the favourite disappointing it took less winning than it might.

2877 SISTER BLISS MAIDEN FILLIES' STKS 1m
8:50 (8:52) (Class 5) 3-Y-O+ **£3,234** (£962; £481; £240) **Stalls** Low

Form RPR

5 1 **Manaboo (USA)**[13] 2470 3-9-0 0 .... WilliamBuick 2 94+
(Charlie Appleby) *trckd ldrs gng wl: led over 1f out: pushed out* **11/4**[2]

2 1 ½ **Wilamina (IRE)** 3-9-0 0 .... FergusSweeney 6 89
(Martyn Meade) *hld up in 5th: hdwy over 1f out: r.o to take 2nd ins fnl f* **25/1**

0-2 3 1 ½ **Delve (IRE)**[22] 2177 3-9-0 0 .... RichardKingscote 3 85
(Sir Michael Stoute) *t.k.h: prom: rdn to press ldrs over 1f out: one pce* **11/10**[1]

4 5 **Entrench** 3-9-0 0 .... JimCrowley 1 73+
(Amanda Perrett) *s.s: t.k.h in 6th: styng on at fin* **12/1**

0- 5 1 **Karisma (IRE)**[315] 4573 3-9-0 0 .... JamesDoyle 9 71+
(Roger Varian) *racd freely: led tl wknd over 1f out* **16/1**

00 6 6 **Midnight Mood**[22] 2182 3-9-0 0 .... SamHitchcott 4 56
(Dominic Ffrench Davis) *bhd: rdn 3f out: nvr trbld ldrs* **66/1**

4 7 ½ **Poole Belle (IRE)**[22] 2177 3-9-0 0 .... OisinMurphy 7 55
(Henry Candy) *chsd ldr tl wknd 2f out* **12/1**

3 8 5 **Irrevocable (IRE)**[18] 2312 3-9-0 0 .... JimmyFortune 5 43
(Roger Charlton) *s.s: a bhd* **9/2**[3]

1m 38.39s (-1.51) **Going Correction** -0.025s/f (Good) **8** Ran SP% **119.1**
Speed ratings (Par 100): **106,104,103,98,97 91,90,85**
CSF £67.76 TOTE £4.00: £1.70, £4.60, £1.10; EX 80.90 Trifecta £276.20.
Owner Godolphin **Bred** Darley **Trained** Newmarket, Suffolk

FOCUS
Actual race distance 1m12yds. Some potentially nice prospects on show, and the second favourite obliged with a good bit in hand.
T/Plt: £176.20 to a £1 stake. Pool: £59,011.83 - 244.48 winning units T/Qpdt: £25.80 to a £1 stake. Pool: £5437.44 - 155.37 winning units **Lee McKenzie**

2878 - 2880a (Foreign Racing) - See Raceform Interactive

2066 LEOPARDSTOWN (L-H)
Friday, June 3

OFFICIAL GOING: Good to firm

2881a SEAMUS & ROSEMARY MCGRATH MEMORIAL SAVAL BEG STKS (LISTED RACE) 1m 6f
7:35 (7:35) 4-Y-O+ **£21,257** (£6,845; £3,242; £1,441; £720)

RPR

1 **Order Of St George (IRE)**[264] 6363 4-9-12 124 .... DonnachaO'Brien 4 112+
(A P O'Brien, Ire) *dwlt and sltly impeded s: hld up in 4th: gng wl appr st and hdwy on outer into 2nd 1 1/2f out where rdn 3 l adrift of ldr: styd on strly to ld ins fnl f and drew clr: easily* **2/7**[1]

2 4 ½ **Fact Or Folklore (IRE)**[41] 1659 4-9-0 94 .... BillyLee 2 89
(W McCreery, Ire) *attempted to make all: drvn over 3 l clr fr 2f out: reduced advantage u.p over 1f out and hdd u.p ins fnl f: no ch w easy wnr: kpt on same pce* **6/1**[2]

3 2 ¼ **Modem**[12] 2514 6-9-5 80 ....(p) NGMcCullagh 3 91
(Mrs John Harrington, Ire) *settled bhd ldr: disp 2nd at 1/2-way: rdn in 2nd into st and no imp on ldrs u.p in 3rd over 1f out: kpt on same pce* **20/1**

4 2 **Botany Bay (IRE)**[12] 2514 4-9-5 86 .... DeclanMcDonogh 6 88+
(Charles O'Brien, Ire) *w.w in rr: last at 1/2-way: rdn detached in rr over 3f out and no imp into st: kpt on fr 2f out into mod 4th 1f out: nvr trbld ldrs* **10/1**

5 9 ½ **Silwana (IRE)**[19] 2275 5-9-3 103 ....(p) ShaneFoley 5 76
(Takashi Kodama, Ire) *wnt lft s: settled bhd ldr: disp 2nd at 1/2-way: rdn in 3rd into st and sn no imp on ldr u.p in 4th: no ex and wknd to rr 1f out: eased ins fnl f* **7/1**[3]

3m 0.99s (-0.01) **Going Correction** +0.175s/f (Good) **5** Ran SP% **118.4**
Speed ratings: **107,104,103,102,96**
CSF £3.19 TOTE £1.20: £1.02, £2.60; DF 2.30 Trifecta £15.20.
Owner L J Williams/Mrs J Magnier/M Tabor/D Smith **Bred** Paget Bloodstock **Trained** Cashel, Co Tipperary

FOCUS
Overall, a weak Saval Beg as the favourite probably frightened off any meaningful opposition, and despite market unease he did it more or less as expected.

2883a KING GEORGE V CUP (LISTED RACE) 1m 4f
8:35 (8:35) 3-Y-O **£19,522** (£6,286; £2,977; £1,323; £661; £330)

RPR

1 **The Major General (IRE)**[12] 2515 3-9-3 86 ....(b) MichaelHussey 2 99+
(A P O'Brien, Ire) *chsd ldrs: 3rd 5f out: rdn to chal in 2nd over 1f out and kpt on wl u.p between horses to ld wl ins fnl f: all out clsng stages: kpt on wl* **11/1**

2 ½ **Claudio Monteverdi (IRE)**[44] 1567 3-9-3 98 ....(t) DonnachaO'Brien 3 98+
(A P O'Brien, Ire) *disp early tl settled bhd ldr after 2f: cl 2nd 5f out: rdn 2f out and dropped to 3rd 1 1/2f out: kpt on again to chal in 2nd wl ins fnl f: kpt on wl wout matching wnr cl home* **11/8**[1]

3 nk **Lieutenant General (IRE)**[26] 2069 3-9-3 99 .... PBBeggy 4 98+
(A P O'Brien, Ire) *dwlt and settled towards rr: 5th 5f out: rdn into 2nd 1 1/2f out and clsd u.p to chal on outer wl ins fnl f where flashed tail: wnt 3rd cl home: nrst fin* **13/2**[3]

4 ½ **Siamsaiocht (IRE)**[9] 2595 3-8-12 91 ....(b) RonanWhelan 6 92
(J S Bolger, Ire) *disp early tl led after 2f: narrow advantage 5f out: rdn clr fr 2f out: reduced advantage u.p over 1f out and hdd wl ins fnl f: no ex cl home where dropped to 4th* **8/1**

5 2 **Zalfana (IRE)**[236] 7150 3-8-12 0 .... PatSmullen 5 89
(D K Weld, Ire) *chsd ldrs: 4th 5f out: rdn in 4th fr over 3f out and no imp on ldrs u.p in 5th 1 1/2f out: kpt on same pce ins fnl f* **11/4**[2]

6 shd **Santa Monica**[12] 2510 3-8-12 100 .... DeclanMcDonogh 1 89
(Charles O'Brien, Ire) *dwlt and settled in rr: last 5f out: tk clsr order on outer appr st: rdn and no imp on ldrs over 1f out: kpt on same pce ins fnl f* **7/1**

2m 39.41s (4.11) **Going Correction** +0.175s/f (Good) **6** Ran SP% **114.0**
Speed ratings: **93,92,92,92,90 90**
CSF £27.47 TOTE £11.70: £3.40, £1.20; DF 32.80 Trifecta £117.00.
Owner Magnier Tabor Smith Jooste Kantor **Bred** J S Bolger **Trained** Cashel, Co Tipperary

FOCUS
This looked a weak enough Listed race beforehand with one or two having questionable ratings, time will tell how good it was.

2882 - 2884a (Foreign Racing) - See Raceform Interactive

^{2859}DONCASTER (L-H)

Saturday, June 4

OFFICIAL GOING: Good to firm (8.2) (watered)
Wind: Virtually nil Weather: Cloudy & warm

2885 DAILY PRICE BOOSTS AT LADBROKES EBF STALLIONS NOVICE FILLIES' STKS (PLUS 10 RACE) 6f 110y

1:55 (1:59) (Class 5) 2-Y-O **£3,881** (£1,155; £577; £288) **Stalls** High

Form RPR

1 **Dainty Dandy (IRE)** 2-9-0 0 SamJames 1 77
(David O'Meara) *mde all: rdn wl over 1f out: styd on wl fnl f: jinked rt nr fin* **12/1**

6 **2** *1* **Naifah (IRE)**^{14} 2467 2-9-0 0 RobertHavlin 3 74
(John Gosden) *hld up towards rr: hdwy over 2f out: rdn to chse ldrs over 1f out: kpt on wl fnl f: tk 2nd on line* **12/1**

3 *hd* **Dubai Elegance** 2-9-0 0 JamesDoyle 9 74+
(Saeed bin Suroor) *hld up in rr: hdwy 3f out: rdn to chse ldrs over 1f out: chsd wnr ins fnl f: hld whn n.m.r and swtchd lft nr fin: lost 2nd on line* **3/1**^{2}

32 **4** *3/4* **Magical Forest (IRE)**^{17} 2376 2-9-0 0 MartinHarley 2 72
(Marco Botti) *trckd ldng pair: effrt to chse wnr over 1f out: sn rdn: drvn and kpt on same pce fnl f* **7/2**^{3}

0 **5** *5* **Quantum Field (USA)**^{51} 1437 2-9-0 0 HarryBentley 7 58
(David Brown) *chsd ldrs: rdn along over 2f out: sn drvn and wknd* **22/1**

533 **6** *1* **Hi Milady (IRE)**^{33} 1915 2-9-0 0 FMBerry 4 55
(Dominic Ffrench Davis) *cl up: rdn along 2f out: sn drvn and wknd* **20/1**

7 *6* **Illaunmore (USA)** 2-9-0 0 NickyMackay 5 39
(John Gosden) *a towards rr* **12/1**

8 *2 3/4* **Just Heather (IRE)** 2-9-0 0 PaddyAspell 8 31
(John Wainwright) *dwlt: a in rr* **100/1**

9 *3/4* **High Excitement (USA)** 2-8-11 0 MichaelJMMurphy$^{(3)}$ 6 29
(Charles Hills) *dwlt: rapid hdwy on outer to trck ldrs after 2f: cl up 1/2-way: rdn along wl over 2f out: sn wknd* **7/4**^{1}

1m 21.03s (1.13) **Going Correction** -0.075s/f (Good) **9** Ran SP% **116.8**
Speed ratings (Par 90): **90,88,88,87,82 80,74,70,70**
CSF £141.53 TOTE £15.50: £3.40, £3.00, £1.10; EX 165.00 Trifecta £978.30.
Owner Nick Bradley Racing 7 **Bred** Laurence Kennedy **Trained** Upper Helmsley, N Yorks

FOCUS
The official going was good to firm (watered). Rail out from 1m2f point on the round course to where it joins the straight, adding around 6yds to race distances on the round course. An interesting novice fillies' event to start in which the betting was dominated by a couple of debutants, but it was another of the newcomers who proved too good.

2886 LADBROKES MAIDEN STKS 5f

2:30 (2:31) (Class 5) 3-Y-O+ **£2,098** (£2,098; £481; £240) **Stalls** High

Form RPR

23- **1** **Futoon (IRE)**^{232} 7244 3-8-11 0 JoeDoyle$^{(3)}$ 10 74
(Kevin Ryan) *prom: cl up 2f out: rdn over 1f out: led ent fnl f: sn drvn and kpt on: jnd on line* **11/4**^{1}

24 **1** *dht* **Evenlode (IRE)**^{7} 2668 3-9-5 0 FMBerry 11 79
(David Barron) *chsd ldrs on outer: rdn along and cl up 2f out: drvn ent fnl f: kpt on wl to join ldr on line* **9/1**

6 **3** *1 3/4* **Princess Momoka**^{19} 2298 3-9-0 0 HarryBentley 2 68+
(Roger Varian) *chsd ldrs: rdn over 1f out: drvn and kpt on fnl f* **4/1**^{3}

4 *hd* **Primanora** 3-8-11 0 AlistairRawlinson$^{(3)}$ 5 67+
(Michael Appleby) *sn led: hdd 2f out and sn rdn: green and hung lft to far rail ent fnl f: grad wknd* **14/1**

4 **5** *2 1/4* **Lightfeet (USA)**^{52} 1414 3-9-5 0 AdamBeschizza 6 64
(Jeremy Gask) *dwlt: sn trcking ldrs: effrt 2f out and sn rdn: drvn and kpt on same pce fnl f* **7/1**

2-04 **6** *1* **Dacoity**^{18} 2337 3-9-5 72 PatrickMathers 7 60
(Richard Fahey) *chsd ldrs: rdn along 2f out: sn drvn and one pce* **3/1**^{2}

7 *1 1/2* **Vale Of Flight (IRE)** 3-9-0 0 DavidProbert 1 50
(Rae Guest) *cl up on outer: pushed along over 3f out: sn rdn along and wknd over 2f out* **14/1**

8 *nk* **Shesthedream (IRE)** 3-9-0 0^{1} SamJames 9 49
(David O'Meara) *dwlt: a towards rr* **16/1**

55- **9** *8* **Perfectly Fair**^{253} 6720 3-9-0 0 DuranFentiman 12 20
(Simon West) *a towards rr* **50/1**

0-0 **10** *13* **Hazel's Song**^{39} 1765 4-9-2 0 (t^{1}) AnnaHesketh$^{(5)}$ 4
(Steph Hollinshead) *chsd ldrs: rdn along 1/2-way: sn wknd* **100/1**

1m 0.15s (-0.35) **Going Correction** -0.075s/f (Good)
WFA 3 from 4yo 7lb **10** Ran SP% **116.3**
Speed ratings (Par 103): **99,99,96,95,92 90,88,87,75,54**
WIN: Futoon 1.60, Evenlode 5.40; PL: F 1.70 , E 2.80, P M 2.10; EX: E/F 23.00, F/E 14.30; CSF: E/F/PM 16.95, F/E/PM 14.17; TF: E/F/PM 87.20, F/E/PM 59.70.
Owner Course & Distance Racing **Bred** Melchior Bloodstock & Partners **Trained** Hambleton, N Yorks
Owner Harrowgate Bloodstock Ltd **Bred** Paul Starr **Trained** Maunby, N Yorks

FOCUS
An ordinary older-horse sprint maiden which favoured those that raced on or near the pace. The first two couldn't be separated by the judge.

2887 DOWNLOAD THE LADBROKES APP H'CAP 1m 6f 132y

3:05 (3:05) (Class 5) (0-70,67) 4-Y-O+ **£3,881** (£1,155; £577; £288) **Stalls** Low

Form RPR

6-32 **1** **Hurry Home Poppa (IRE)**^{13} 2502 6-9-6 67 FrannyNorton 3 74
(John Mackie) *trckd ldrs: hdwy 3f out: led 2f out and sn rdn: drvn ins fnl f: kpt on wl towards fin* **9/2**^{2}

1212 **2** *3/4* **Hurricane Volta (IRE)**^{13} 2501 5-9-4 65 (p) CharlesBishop 2 71
(Peter Hedger) *trckd ldrs on inner: hdwy 3f out: n.m.r and swtchd rt over 1f out: sn rdn to chse wnr: drvn ins fnl f: kpt on* **11/4**^{1}

06-6 **3** *1 3/4* **Ivanhoe**^{18} 2338 6-9-4 65 DavidProbert 7 69
(Michael Blanshard) *hld up in rr: hdwy wl over 2f out: rdn wl over 1f out: drvn ins fnl f: kpt on same pce* **10/1**

P616 **4** *3/4* **Christmas Hamper (IRE)**^{13} 2501 4-8-13 63 AlistairRawlinson$^{(3)}$ 5 66
(Michael Appleby) *led: rdn along 3f out: hdd 2f out: sn drvn and one pce fnl f* **5/1**^{3}

-6P0 **5** *5* **Mr Snoozy**^{47} 1523 7-9-3 67 RobHornby$^{(3)}$ 1 63
(Mark Walford) *trckd ldr: pushed along wl over 3f out: rdn wl over 2f out: drvn and wknd wl over 1f out* **8/1**

5043 **6** *1 1/4* **Dalaki (IRE)**^{2} 2814 5-8-11 65 (b) HollieDoyle$^{(7)}$ 6 59
(Des Donovan, Ire) *dwlt: a in rr* **13/2**

1144 **7** *15* **Midtech Star (IRE)**^{33} 1914 4-9-2 63 (v) JamesDoyle 4 37
(Ian Williams) *trckd ldr: effrt over 3f out: rdn along wl over 2f out: drvn and wknd wl over 1f out: eased fnl f* **11/2**

3m 12.98s (5.58) **Going Correction** +0.25s/f (Good) **7** Ran SP% **110.4**
Speed ratings (Par 103): **95,94,93,93,90 89,81**
CSF £16.05 TOTE £4.70: £2.90, £1.60; EX 13.80 Trifecta £113.30.
Owner D Ward **Bred** Kilcarn Stud **Trained** Church Broughton , Derbys

FOCUS
Rail movement added about 6yds to race distance. A modest staying handicap and the pace was ordinary. It's rated around the front four.

2888 LADBROKES H'CAP 1m 4f

3:40 (3:40) (Class 4) (0-85,85) 4-Y-O+ **£5,175** (£1,540; £769; £384) **Stalls** Low

Form RPR

00-0 **1** **Odeon**^{24} 2163 5-8-10 77 JoeDoyle$^{(3)}$ 8 84
(James Given) *led and sn clr: pushed along and jnd 3f out: rdn 2f out and sn hdd: drvn and rallied gamely ins fnl f to ld again last 100yds* **5/1**^{3}

-242 **2** *1 3/4* **Life Less Ordinary (IRE)**^{24} 2163 4-9-4 82 WilliamCarson 2 86
(Jamie Osborne) *hld up in rr: smooth hdwy over 3f out: rdn to ld wl over 1f out: drvn and hung lft ins fnl f: hdd and no ex last 100yds* **2/1**^{1}

-435 **3** *3/4* **Nonchalant**^{8} 2651 5-8-10 74 (v) DavidProbert 3 77
(David O'Meara) *hld up in rr: hdwy 2f out: rdn over 1f out: styd on to chse ldng pair ins fnl f: kpt on same pce* **4/1**^{2}

0-00 **4** *1 1/4* **Chebsey Beau**^{28} 2051 6-8-10 74 RobertHavlin 1 75
(John Quinn) *trckd ldrs: hdwy 3f out: rdn along 2f out: sn drvn and kpt on one pce* **33/1**

210 **5** *1 1/4* **Biff Johnson (IRE)**^{18} 2328 4-9-4 82 (p) FMBerry 7 81
(Keith Dalgleish) *hld up in tch: hdwy on wd outside 3f out: rdn to chse ldrs 2f out: drvn and wknd over 1f out* **8/1**

0042 **6** *3* **Freight Train (IRE)**^{12} 2529 4-8-8 72 FrannyNorton 4 66
(Mark Johnston) *trckd clr ldr: tk clsr order 3f out: chal over 2f out and ev ch tl rdn and wknd over 1f out* **6/1**

02-3 **7** *17* **Clovelly Bay (IRE)**^{17} 2367 5-8-6 75 ow2 TylerSaunders$^{(7)}$ 6 44
(Marcus Tregoning) *t.k.h: trckd ldrs: pushed along 3f out: rdn 2f out: sn wknd* **6/1**

2m 35.9s (1.00) **Going Correction** +0.25s/f (Good) **7** Ran SP% **112.6**
Speed ratings (Par 105): **106,104,104,103,102 100,89**
CSF £14.97 CT £42.63 TOTE £6.50: £3.60, £1.80; EX 18.20 Trifecta £60.70.
Owner Alex Owen **Bred** Northmore Stud **Trained** Willoughton, Lincs

FOCUS
Rail movement added about 6yds to race distance. A fair middle-distance handicap and with a few in here that like to force it a decent pace was always likely. The form is rated around the third.

2889 BET IN PLAY WITH LADBROKES CLASSIFIED STKS 1m 2f 60y

4:15 (4:15) (Class 3) 3-Y-O **£7,762** (£2,310; £1,154; £577) **Stalls** Low

Form RPR

6-1 **1** **Shabeeb (USA)**^{16} 2414 3-9-3 89 HarryBentley 5 99
(Roger Varian) *awkward s: sn trcking ldng pair: hdwy 4f out: chsd clr ldr over 2f out: rdn and edgd lft 2f out: led 1 1/2f out: sn rdn clr* **11/10**^{1}

-262 **2** *6* **Montsarrat (IRE)**^{16} 2407 3-9-3 90 JamesDoyle 4 88
(Mark Johnston) *led: rdn clr over 3f out: drvn and hdd 1 1/2f out: kpt on same pce* **9/2**^{3}

11-4 **3** *nk* **Danehill Kodiac (IRE)**^{21} 2244 3-9-3 87 PatDobbs 2 87
(Richard Hannon) *trckd ldr: pushed along and outpcd 3f out: rdn over 2f out: kpt on u.p fnl f* **11/4**^{2}

0-10 **4** *1 3/4* **Royal Reserve**^{29} 1992 3-9-3 85 FMBerry 3 84
(William Muir) *in rr: hdwy over 3f out: rdn to chse ldrs over 2f out: drvn wl over 1f out and one pce* **12/1**

5-41 **5** *9* **Tap The Honey**^{18} 2327 3-8-12 83 JordanVaughan$^{(5)}$ 1 67
(K R Burke) *trckd ldrs: hdwy on inner over 3f out: rdn along over 2f out: sn drvn and btn* **10/1**

2m 11.5s (2.10) **Going Correction** +0.25s/f (Good) **5** Ran SP% **109.3**
Speed ratings (Par 103): **101,96,95,94,87**
CSF £6.31 TOTE £1.80: £1.10, £2.90; EX 5.40 Trifecta £9.90.
Owner Hamdan Al Maktoum **Bred** Shadwell Farm LLC **Trained** Newmarket, Suffolk

FOCUS
Rail movement added about 6yds to race distance. A small field for this decent 3yo classified event, but they went a fair pace and the winner was impressive. It's rated around the second.

2890 CASH OUT AVAILABLE AT LADBROKES FILLIES' H'CAP 7f

5:10 (5:11) (Class 3) (0-95,92) 4-Y-O+ **£8,409** (£2,502; £1,250; £625) **Stalls** High

Form RPR

2160 **1** **Lavetta**^{22} 2223 4-8-10 81 DarryllHolland 2 88
(Alan Swinbank) *t.k.h: trckd ldr: hdwy 2f out: sn rdn: drvn ins fnl f: styd on wl to ld last 50yds* **8/1**

1155 **2** *nk* **Moon River (IRE)**^{28} 2026 4-8-10 81 RobertHavlin 1 87
(Michael Appleby) *led: rdn over 1f out: drvn ins fnl f: hdd and no ex last 50yds* **2/1**^{1}

5-00 **3** *3/4* **Mothers Finest (IRE)**^{23} 2191 4-9-7 92 (t) JamesDoyle 3 96
(K R Burke) *trckd ldrs: hdwy on outer over 2f out and sn cl up: rdn to chal over 1f out: drvn and ev ch ins fnl f: kpt on same pce* **2/1**^{1}

-635 **4** *1 3/4* **Breakable**^{15} 2420 5-8-11 82 (p) DuranFentiman 5 81
(Tim Easterby) *trckd ldrs: hdwy over 2f out: rdn wl over 1f out: drvn appr fnl f: one pce* **9/2**^{2}

00-1 **5** *1 3/4* **Lyfka**^{26} 2084 4-8-13 84 (t) MartinHarley 4 79
(Paul Cole) *dwlt: hld up in rr: rdn along 2f out: sn btn* **13/2**^{3}

1m 26.91s (0.61) **Going Correction** -0.075s/f (Good) **5** Ran SP% **109.3**
Speed ratings (Par 104): **93,92,91,89,87**
CSF £23.97 TOTE £10.30: £4.30, £1.50; EX 23.00 Trifecta £89.20.
Owner Guy Reed Racing **Bred** G Reed **Trained** Melsonby, N Yorks

FOCUS
Again just the five runners for this quite valuable fillies' handicap and the pace was ordinary. The winner is rated to form.

2891 TRACK YOUR FOOTBALL ACCA WITH LADBROKES H'CAP 1m (R)

5:40 (5:43) (Class 4) (0-85,85) 3-Y-O **£5,175** (£1,540; £769; £384) **Stalls** High

Form RPR

3-14 **1** **Limitless (IRE)**^{16} 2412 3-9-7 85 WilliamCarson 6 101
(Jamie Osborne) *dwlt and hld up in rr: gd hdwy on outer over 2f out: rdn to ld and hung bdly rt appr fnl f: c rt to stands' rail: drvn out* **5/1**^{2}

1- **2** *2* **Next Stage**[192] 7980 3-9-4 **82**..........[1] JamesDoyle 2 94+
(Saeed bin Suroor) *dwlt: hld up in tch: hdwy 1/2-way: pushed along to chse ldrs over 2f out: effrt and ev ch whn bdly hmpd appr fnl f: sn swtchd lft and rdn: drvn and kpt on fnl f* **11/8**[1]

45-1 **3** *3 ¾* **Easter Mate (IRE)**[95] 770 3-9-2 **80**..........(p) FMBerry 12 83+
(Ralph Beckett) *hld up in rr: hdwy wl over 2f out: styng on whn n.m.r and hmpd jst over 1f out: sn rdn and kpt on* **20/1**

651- **4** *¾* **Storm Ahead (IRE)**[159] 8377 3-9-1 **82**.......... JoeDoyle(3) 14 83+
(Marcus Tregoning) *hld up towards rr: hdwy 2f out: styng on wl whn hmpd jst over 1f out: kpt on fnl f* **25/1**

43-1 **5** *4* **Dubai's Secret**[19] 2299 3-9-5 **83**.......... PatDobbs 8 75+
(Richard Hannon) *dwlt and hld up in rr: hdwy 2f out: styng on whn hmpd jst over 1f out: kpt on same pce after* **12/1**

4463 **6** *1* **Young Christian**[19] 2307 3-8-8 **72**.......... AndrewElliott 4 62+
(Tom Tate) *led: rdn along 2f out: hdd whn bdly hmpd appr fnl f: one pce after* **66/1**

160- **7** *1 ¾* **Le Roi Du Temps (USA)**[225] 7421 3-8-13 **77**.......... DarryllHolland 3 63+
(Ivan Furtado) *prom: cl up 2f out: rdn and ev ch whn bdly hmpd appr fnl f: wknd after* **33/1**

-231 **8** *¾* **Flyboy (IRE)**[8] 2654 3-9-4 **82**.......... SamJames 13 66+
(David O'Meara) *hld up: hdwy 2f out: rdn to chse ldrs whn bdly hmpd appr fnl f: nt rcvr* **7/1**[3]

23-5 **9** *hd* **Absolute Zero (IRE)**[19] 2299 3-8-13 **77**..........[1] HarryBentley 11 61+
(Roger Varian) *chsd ldrs: rdn along wl over 1f out: hld whn hmpd appr fnl f* **14/1**

10-6 **10** *1 ¾* **Experto Crede (IRE)**[37] 1809 3-9-5 **83**.......... AntonioFresu 9 63+
(Ed Walker) *trckd ldrs: hdwy 2f out: rdn whn hmpd appr fnl f: wknd after* **10/1**

13-6 **11** *nk* **Ormskirk**[22] 2200 3-9-1 **79**.......... DaleSwift 10 58
(Brian Ellison) *chsd ldrs: pushed along 3f out: rdn 2f out: grad wknd* **50/1**

2-05 **12** *¾* **Novinophobia**[16] 2407 3-8-9 **73**.......... GeorgeChaloner 1 50
(Richard Fahey) *cl up on outer: rdn along over 2f out: wknd over 1f out* **50/1**

12-0 **13** *3 ¾* **Show Me Again**[16] 2412 3-9-7 **85**.......... MartinHarley 7 54
(David Dennis) *hld up: hdwy 2f out: sn rdn and n.d* **66/1**

441 **14** *19* **Heart Of Lions (USA)**[18] 2321 3-9-6 **84**.......... RobertHavlin 5 9+
(John Gosden) *chsd ldrs: pushed along wl over 3f out: rdn and lost pl wl over 2f out: sn bhd and eased* **10/1**

1m 38.68s (-1.02) **Going Correction** -0.075s/f (Good) **14** Ran SP% **122.3**
Speed ratings (Par 101): **102,100,96,95,91 90,88,88,87,86 85,85,81,62**
CSF £11.71 CT £135.70 TOTE £7.20: £1.80, £1.40, £4.90; EX 17.00 Trifecta £192.40.
Owner Michael Buckley & Michael Watt **Bred** Ballylinch Stud **Trained** Upper Lambourn, Berks

FOCUS
A fair 3yo handicap with 12 of the 14 runners previous winners, but one of roughest races seen in a while with the first past the post wiping out several of his rivals when running diagonally to his right coming to the last furlong. The Stewards allowed the result to stand with the winning margin likely the crucial factor, but the connections of several of the beaten horses have every right to feel aggrieved. The 1-2 look way ahead of their marks.
T/Plt: £57.20 to a £1 stake. Pool: £67,633.79 - 861.96 winning tickets. T/Qpdt: £10.90 to a £1 stake. Pool: £4,164.88 - 281.98 winning tickets. **Joe Rowntree**

2865 EPSOM (L-H)
Saturday, June 4

OFFICIAL GOING: Good to soft (overall 6.4, stands' 6.4, far 6.3)
Wind: light, half against Weather: mainly overcast, odd brighter spell

2892 INVESTEC PRIVATE BANKING H'CAP STKS (H'CAP) 1m 2f 18y
2:00 (2:01) (Class 2) (0-105,96) 3-Y-O

£31,125 (£9,320; £4,660; £2,330; £1,165; £585) **Stalls** Low

Form RPR

-220 **1** **Gawdawpalin (IRE)**[21] 2244 3-8-0 **75**.......... KieranO'Neill 14 89
(Sylvester Kirk) *chsd ldng trio: swtchd lft and rdn to ld over 2f out: sn qcknd clr: in n.d and drifting rt ins fnl f: rdn out* **25/1**

10-0 **2** *2 ¾* **Goodwood Zodiac (IRE)**[29] 1992 3-8-8 **83**.......... FrederikTylicki 15 92+
(William Knight) *hld up off the pce in last trio: rdn and effrt over 2f out: gd hdwy over 1f out: chsd wnr ins fnl f: styd on wl but nvr threatening wnr* **33/1**

135 **3** *1 ¼* **High Grounds (IRE)**[30] 1974 3-9-4 **93**.......... JamieSpencer 3 99
(Charles Hills) *hld up in last quartet: swtchd lft and effrt over 2f out: hdwy and switching rt over 1f out: wnt 3rd 100yds out: styd on but nvr threatening wnr* **16/1**

4-31 **4** *1* **Poet's Word (IRE)**[29] 2008 3-8-12 **87**.......... RyanMoore 2 91+
(Sir Michael Stoute) *lw: wl in tch in midfield: effrt over 2f out: hdwy to battle for placings over 1f out: chsd clr wnr 1f out: kpt on but no imp: lost 2 pls ins fnl f* **9/4**[1]

3-50 **5** *hd* **Percy Street**[35] 1866 3-9-6 **95**.......... DougieCostello 12 99
(K R Burke) *s.i.s: sn rcvrd and in tch in midfield: effrt over 2f out: hdwy to battle for placings ent fnl f: no real imp and kpt on same pce ins fnl f* **33/1**

-234 **6** *6* **Scarlet Dragon**[16] 2393 3-8-1 **79**.......... TomMarquand(3) 5 71
(Eve Johnson Houghton) *in tch in midfield: effrt over 2f out: sn outpcd and no imp whn squeezed for room over 1f out: wl hld and plugged on same pce after* **20/1**

1420 **7** *2 ¼* **Soldier In Action (FR)**[21] 2244 3-9-3 **92**.......... AdamKirby 8 80
(Mark Johnston) *chsd ldrs: wnt 2nd 7f out: rdn and ev ch 3f out: sn outpcd by wnr in 2nd: no imp u.p and lost 2nd 1f out: wknd ins fnl f* **14/1**

1-16 **8** *2 ¾* **Prince Of Arran**[21] 2244 3-8-9 **84**..........(v) TomQueally 13 66
(Charlie Fellowes) *swtg: s.i.s: sn rcvrd and in tch in midfield: rdn ent fnl 2f: sn outpcd and btn: wknd over 1f out* **14/1**

-111 **9** *2 ½* **Medburn Dream**[36] 1828 3-8-7 **82**.......... RichardKingscote 7 59
(Paul Henderson) *led: rdn and hdd over 2f out: sn outpcd: wknd over 1f out* **15/2**[3]

15-2 **10** *1 ¾* **Cartago**[21] 2244 3-9-5 **94**.......... FrankieDettori 4 68
(John Gosden) *hld up in tch in midfield: effrt jst over 2f out: no rspnse and struggling whn sltly hmpd over 1f out: sn wknd* **9/2**[2]

21-3 **11** *¾* **Dark Devil (IRE)**[30] 1975 3-8-11 **86**.......... PaulHanagan 9 58
(Richard Fahey) *hld up off the pce in rr: rdn and no hdwy over 2f out: no ch whn swtchd lft over 1f out* **11/1**

20-4 **12** *1 ¼* **Champagne City**[14] 2481 3-9-7 **96**.......... SilvestreDeSousa 10 66
(Mark Johnston) *a towards rr: rdn and no hdwy over 2f out: wknd wl over 1f out* **20/1**

-061 **13** *4 ½* **Bathos (IRE)**[16] 2393 3-9-1 **90**.......... WilliamBuick 11 51
(Mark Johnston) *lw: a towards rr: rdn over 3f out: sn struggling: wknd wl over 1f out* **14/1**

-316 **14** *1 ¾* **Finelcity (GER)**[16] 2393 3-8-0 **75**..........(b) JimmyQuinn 6 32
(Harry Dunlop) *chsd ldr tl 7f out: styd handy: rdn to press ldrs briefly over 2f out: sn outpcd and btn: wknd wl over 1f out* **33/1**

221 **15** *48* **Banish (USA)**[18] 2320 3-8-9 **84**..........(p) OisinMurphy 1
(Hugo Palmer) *athletic: lw: restless in stalls: trckd ldrs tl rdn and lost pl qckly 3f out: sn bhd: t.o and virtually p.u fnl f* **20/1**

2m 10.21s (0.51) **Going Correction** +0.35s/f (Good) **15** Ran SP% **121.9**
Speed ratings (Par 105): **111,108,107,107,106 102,100,98,96,94 94,93,89,88,49**
CSF £651.68 CT £12776.58 TOTE £28.40: £7.40, £11.50, £5.20; EX 1248.90 Trifecta £7107.40 Part won..

Owner H Balasuriya **Bred** L Queally **Trained** Upper Lambourn, Berks

FOCUS
This May was the wettest at Epsom since 2007 - rain was recorded on only six days but there 88mm, including 22.5mm on the Tuesday of Derby week. It was dry overnight into Oaks day and again into Derby day, but this time there was a heavy dew. The going was again given as good to soft, but it was a gradually warming day so drying conditions, and there was fresh ground with the rail, which was out for the Oaks card, at the innermost configuration. All distances as advertised. The likes of Lailani (2002), Stage Gift (2006), Conduit (2008) and Dandino (2010) all won this before winning at Group level, but there have been some ordinary editions as well. The 1st (25-1), 2nd (33-1) and 5th (33-1) did much of their racing out wide. The form makes a fair bit of sense.

2893 PRINCESS ELIZABETH STKS (SPONSORED BY INVESTEC) (GROUP 3) (F&M) 1m 114y
2:35 (2:35) (Class 1) 3-Y-O+

£39,697 (£15,050; £7,532; £3,752; £1,883; £945) **Stalls** Low

Form RPR

-005 **1** **Epsom Icon**[21] 2245 3-8-8 97.......... SilvestreDeSousa 4 104
(Mick Channon) *hld up in 4th: clsd and rdn to press ldr over 2f out: drvn to ld over 1f out: 2 l clr 1f out: styd on strly: rdn out* **8/1**[2]

2 *3 ½* **Sayana (FR)**[29] 2020 4-9-6 109.......... ChristopheSoumillon 7 98
(A De Royer-Dupre, France) *lengthy: lw: stdd after s: hld up off the pce last pair: clsd and effrt jst over 2f out: hdwy and hung lft over 1f out: wnt 3rd jst ins fnl f: kpt on but no ch w wnr: wnt 2nd last strides* **1/2**[1]

33-6 **3** *hd* **Rosie Cotton (IRE)**[10] 2603 4-9-6 98..........(tp) MickaelBarzalona 2 97
(Mme Pia Brandt, France) *w'like: swtg: chsd ldng pair: effrt jst over 2f out: hdwy u.p over 1f out: chsd clr wnr 1f out: kpt on but no ch w wnr: lost 2nd last strides* **9/1**[3]

1232 **4** *½* **Oakley Girl**[35] 1858 4-9-6 100.......... OisinMurphy 1 96
(Stuart Williams) *hld up off the pce in last trio: effrt 2f out: clsd and swtchd rt over 1f out: styd on u.p ins fnl f: no threat to wnr* **10/1**

20-0 **5** *1* **Merry Me (IRE)**[63] 1207 5-9-6 95.......... JamieSpencer 5 94
(Andrew Balding) *chsd ldr: clsd and rdn to ld over 2f out: drvn and hdd over 1f out: lost 2nd 1f out: kpt on same pce ins fnl f* **12/1**

-401 **6** *8* **Loaves And Fishes**[7] 2671 4-9-6 94.......... PaulHanagan 3 76
(David O'Meara) *led: clr 5f out: rdn and hdd over 2f out: wknd over 1f out* **25/1**

3-00 **P** **Persona Grata**[17] 2363 5-9-6 103.......... GeorgeBaker 6
(Ed Walker) *hld up off the pce in last trio: effrt 2f out: hung lft and no hdwy over 1f out: sn eased: plld and dismntd ins fnl f* **20/1**

1m 47.29s (1.19) **Going Correction** +0.35s/f (Good)
WFA 3 from 4yo+ 12lb **7** Ran SP% **113.2**
Speed ratings (Par 113): **108,104,104,104,103 96,**
CSF £12.22 TOTE £8.20: £2.70, £1.10; EX 17.10 Trifecta £74.40.

Owner Epsom Stars Racing I **Bred** Norman Court Stud **Trained** West Ilsley, Berks

FOCUS
Not a strong Group 3, with the favourite a bit disappointing, but there was a decisive winner who has been given some credit.

2894 QUEEN ELIZABETH II CORONATION CUP (SPONSORED BY INVESTEC) (GROUP 1) 1m 4f 10y
3:10 (3:20) (Class 1) 4-Y-O+

£226,840 (£86,000; £43,040; £21,440; £10,760; £5,400) **Stalls** Centre

Form RPR

1-11 **1** **Postponed (IRE)**[70] 1107 5-9-0 124.......... AndreaAtzeni 3 126+
(Roger Varian) *lw: hld up in 3rd: 3rd and travelling wl st: chsd clr ldr over 2f out: clsd smoothly and nudged into ld over 1f out: sn in command and r.o strly: v easily* **8/11**[1]

-312 **2** *4 ½* **Found (IRE)**[13] 2512 4-8-11 120.......... RyanMoore 4 114
(A P O'Brien, Ire) *hld up in midfield: 6th st: trckd wnr through over 2f out: 3rd and drvn over 1f out: no ch w wnr: kpt on to go 2nd wl ins fnl f* **3/1**[2]

226- **3** *1 ¼* **Roseburg (IRE)**[265] 6371 5-9-0 106.......... JackMitchell 1 115
(Roger Varian) *led: clr tl stdd gallop 6f out: stretched clr again over 3f out: rdn and hdd over 1f out: sn brushed aside by wnr: kpt on same pce and lost 2nd wl ins fnl f* **50/1**

11-2 **4** *1 ¾* **Simple Verse (IRE)**[35] 1863 4-8-11 116.......... OisinMurphy 7 109
(Ralph Beckett) *hld up in midfield: 5th st: effrt in 4th 2f out: sn hung lft and no imp: kpt on ins fnl f: no ch w wnr* **5/1**[3]

40-3 **5** *shd* **Second Step (IRE)**[22] 2221 5-9-0 118.......... JamieSpencer 8 112
(Luca Cumani) *stdd s: hld up in last pair: 7th st: swtchd rt and effrt 2f out: sme hdwy over 1f out: kpt on ins fnl f: no ch w wnr* **16/1**

4434 **6** *4* **Master Carpenter (IRE)**[14] 2464 5-9-0 110.......... FrederikTylicki 6 105
(Rod Millman) *stdd s: hld up in rr: 8th st: rdn over 2f out: sn btn: no ch whn hung lft over 1f out* **40/1**

66-2 **7** *½* **Arabian Queen (IRE)**[34] 1886 4-8-11 116.......... SilvestreDeSousa 5 102
(David Elsworth) *chsd ldr: 2nd st: rdn and lost pl over 2f out: wknd over 1f out* **8/1**

1-55 **8** *33* **Star Storm (IRE)**[21] 2241 4-9-0 103.......... TomQueally 2 52
(James Fanshawe) *in tch: 4th st: sn rdn and lost pl over 2f out: wl bhd and virtually p.u ins fnl f: t.o* **33/1**

2m 43.54s (4.64) **Going Correction** +0.35s/f (Good) **8** Ran SP% **123.9**
Speed ratings (Par 117): **98,95,94,93,92 90,89,67**
CSF £3.57 CT £62.11 TOTE £1.60: £1.02, £1.60, £11.80; EX 3.40 Trifecta £127.10.

Owner Sheikh Mohammed Obaid Al Maktoum **Bred** St Albans Bloodstock Llp **Trained** Newmarket, Suffolk

FOCUS
Race distance as advertised. A strong edition of the race, but the favourite's pacemaker Roseburg set a go-stop-go gallop, which didn't suit all, indeed the 50-1 shot wasn't beaten far for second. Still, it was a really impressive performance from the top-class Postponed, who is rated to form. There are a few doubts with some of the others not running their races.

2895 INVESTEC CORPORATE BANKING "DASH" (HERITAGE H'CAP) 5f
3:45 (3:50) (Class 2) 3-Y-O+
£61,590 (£18,540; £9,270; £4,620; £2,320; £1,170) **Stalls** High

Form RPR

3046 **1** **Caspian Prince (IRE)**[100] 723 7-9-6 **104**................(t) RobertWinston 17 113
(Dean Ivory) *chsd ldrs tl led 2f out: drvn ins fnl f: jst hld on:all out* **11/1**

5143 **2** *shd* **Kimberella**[14] 2488 6-8-8 **92**.. FrederikTylicki 19 102+
(David Nicholls) *lw: anticipated s and v.s.a: in rr: rdn and clsng qckly whn swtchd lft 1f out: chsd wnr 100yds: r.o strly: jst failed* **10/1**

0321 **3** *1 3/4* **Duke Of Firenze**[23] 2188 7-8-11 **95** 4ex............................ DavidAllan 20 96
(David C Griffiths) *lw: towards rr: hdwy on stands' rail over 1f out: rdn 1f out: styd on wl: swtchd lft wl ins fnl f: wnt 3rd last strides: nt rch ldrs* **6/1**[2]

1-25 **4** *shd* **Mukaynis (IRE)**[31] 1968 5-8-6 **90**....................................(b) ShaneGray 18 91
(Kevin Ryan) *midfield: rdn and hdwy 2f out: clsng and swtchd lft 1f out: styd on wl ins fnl f: nt rch ldrs* **10/1**

0-50 **5** *shd* **Blithe Spirit**[31] 1968 5-8-6 **90**.. JFEgan 14 91
(Eric Alston) *chsd ldr for 2f: wnt 2nd again jst over 1f out: no ex u.p and lost 2nd 100yds out: lost 2 pls last strides* **33/1**

3-21 **6** *1* **Seeking Magic**[15] 2434 8-8-11 **95**.................................(t) OisinMurphy 16 92
(Clive Cox) *taken down early: hld up in midfield: effrt over 1f out: nudged sltly lefy jst over 1f out: hdwy ins fnl f: styd on: nt rch ldrs* **9/1**[3]

4164 **7** *3/4* **Boom The Groom (IRE)**[71] 1066 5-9-3 **101**...................... AdamKirby 2 95+
(Tony Carroll) *in tch in midfield: effrt to chse ldrs and carried lft over 1f out: no ex jst ins fnl f: wknd wl ins fnl f* **14/1**

500- **8** *nk* **Lathom**[260] 6495 3-8-7 **98**.. KierenFallon 8 88+
(David O'Meara) *in tch in midfield: hdwy and switching lft ent fnl f: kpt on ins fnl f: no threat to ldrs* **33/1**

1005 **9** *nse* **Normal Equilibrium**[14] 2488 6-8-5 **89**............................ SamHitchcott 7 82+
(Robert Cowell) *in tch in midfield: effrt 2f out: no imp u.p over 1f out: kpt on again ins fnl f: no threat to ldrs* **25/1**

0-20 **10** *hd* **Monsieur Joe (IRE)**[19] 2317 9-9-10 **108**........................... GrahamLee 4 100+
(Paul Midgley) *in tch in midfield: lost pl and dropped to rr 1/2-way: rallying whn sltly hmpd ent fnl f: styd on: nvr gng to rch ldrs* **14/1**

0006 **11** *nk* **Green Door (IRE)**[21] 2258 5-8-11 **98**...................(v) TomMarquand[(3)] 13 89
(Robert Cowell) *chsd ldrs: drvn and unable qck over 1f out: edging lft ins fnl f: wknd fnl 75yds* **20/1**

-122 **12** *2* **Roudee**[31] 1968 4-8-12 **96**.. RichardKingscote 10 80
(Tom Dascombe) *chsd ldrs: rdn and unable qck over 1f out: wknd ins fnl f* **11/1**

0-00 **13** *1/2* **Humidor (IRE)**[12] 2546 9-8-12 **103**............................ GeorgeWood[(7)] 11 85
(George Baker) *taken down early and led to post: v.s.a: bhd: styd on to pass btn horses ins fnl f: n.d* **20/1**

00/0 **14** *2 1/2* **Hay Chewed (IRE)**[35] 1862 5-9-1 **99**............................... MartinDwyer 9 72
(Conrad Allen) *led: edgd rt after 1f: hdd 2f out: sn hung lft and btn 1f out: wknd ins fnl f* **16/1**

5261 **15** *3* **Harry Hurricane**[14] 2488 4-9-1 **99** 4ex............................ SteveDrowne 1 61
(George Baker) *in tch in midfield: rdn and no hdwy over 1f out: wknd fnl f* **10/1**

143 **16** *1/2* **Sandfrankskipsgo**[29] 2003 7-8-4 **88**................................. JimmyQuinn 3 49
(Peter Crate) *chsd ldrs: rdn over 1f out: sn struggling: losing pl whn short of room jst ins fnl f: wknd* **50/1**

12-2 **17** *2* **Maljaa**[31] 1969 4-9-9 **107**..(b) PaulHanagan 6 60
(Roger Varian) *lw: a towards rr: n.d* **5/1**[1]

55.99s (0.29) **Going Correction** +0.35s/f (Good)
WFA 3 from 4yo+ 7lb **17 Ran SP% 125.3**
Speed ratings (Par 109): **111,110,108,107,107 106,104,104,104,104 103,100,99,95,90 89,86**
CSF £109.42 CT £522.32 TOTE £14.40: £4.00, £2.90, £1.70, £2.80; EX 124.40 Trifecta £597.00.

Owner Stephen Louch **Bred** Ballygallon Stud Ltd **Trained** Radlett, Herts

FOCUS
Fast and furious as usual and those racing near to the stands' rail were massively favoured, with the first six home drawn 14 upwards. The runner-up looked an unlucky loser having anticipated the start. The winner is rated to a better view of his form.

2896 INVESTEC DERBY (GROUP 1) (ENTIRE COLTS & FILLIES) 1m 4f 10y
4:30 (4:35) (Class 1) 3-Y-O
£876,169 (£332,175; £166,242; £82,812; £41,560; £20,857) **Stalls** Centre

Form RPR

1 **1** **Harzand (IRE)**[55] 1370 3-9-0 110.. PatSmullen 9 124+
(D K Weld, Ire) *str: in tch in midfield: 8th st: rdn and hdwy to chse ldr over 2f out: led over 1f out: pressed jst ins fnl f: fnd ex u.p and styd on wl to assert fnl 100yds: rdn out* **13/2**[3]

1 **2** *1 1/2* **US Army Ranger (IRE)**[30] 1974 3-9-0 108...................... RyanMoore 15 122+
(A P O'Brien, Ire) *lw: hld up in last trio: 16th st: nt clrest of runs 3f out: swtchd rt over 2f out and gd hdwy to chse clr ldng pair over 1f out: hung lft and clsd to press wnr jst ins fnl f: no ex wl ins fnl f* **7/2**[1]

4-23 **3** *1 1/4* **Idaho (IRE)**[27] 2069 3-9-0 108.................................... SeamieHeffernan 8 119
(A P O'Brien, Ire) *swtg: hld up in tch in midfield: 5th st: rdn and qcknd to ld over 2f out: hdd and drvn over 1f out: lost 2nd but stl cl enough jst ins fnl f: no ex 100yds out: wknd towards fin* **14/1**

311 **4** *5* **Wings of Desire**[23] 2190 3-9-0 114................................ FrankieDettori 13 111
(John Gosden) *hld up in last quartet: 12th st: rdn and hdwy over 2f out: 4th and no imp over 1f out: styd on same pce ins fnl f* **6/1**[2]

-421 **5** *3* **Humphrey Bogart (IRE)**[28] 2036 3-9-0 105...................... SeanLevey 2 106
(Richard Hannon) *stdd s: hld up in last quartet: 15th st: rdn and hdwy over 2f out: 5th and edging lft over 1f out: no imp: wl hld and plugged on same pce ins fnl f* **25/1**

-211 **6** *1* **Red Verdon (USA)**[14] 2471 3-9-0 102.................... SilvestreDeSousa 16 107+
(Ed Dunlop) *niggled in rr early: hld up in last: 14th st: gd hdwy on inner whn rn into heels and hmpd over 2f out: trying to rally whn nt clr run and swtchd lft over 1f out: rdn and wnt 6th 1f out: kpt on: no ch w ldrs* **20/1**

1-21 **7** *2* **Algometer**[15] 2432 3-9-0 106.. JimCrowley 4 101
(David Simcock) *swtg: s.i.s and bustled along leaving stalls: hld up towards rr: 11th st: rdn and hdwy over 2f out: no imp and btn over 1f out: wknd fnl f* **33/1**

2-11 **8** *2* **Cloth Of Stars (IRE)**[27] 2076 3-9-0 109................. MickaelBarzalona 14 98
(A Fabre, France) *str: lw: t.k.h: chsd ldr: 2nd st: rdn to ld over 2f out: sn hdd and outpcd: wknd u.p over 1f out* **8/1**

12-2 **9** *nse* **Massaat (IRE)**[35] 1864 3-9-0 116.................................... PaulHanagan 11 98
(Owen Burrows) *t.k.h: chsd ldrs: 3rd st: rdn 3f out: sn struggling and outpcd 2f out: wknd over 1f out* **11/1**

2-13 **10** *3* **Across The Stars (IRE)**[28] 2036 3-9-0 103...................... KierenFallon 6 93
(Sir Michael Stoute) *str: in tch in midfield: nt handle downhill run and lost pl 4f out: 10th st: plenty to do and swtchd rt 2f out: no ch but plugged on to pass btn horses ins fnl f* **25/1**

25-2 **11** *3* **Deauville (IRE)**[23] 2190 3-9-0 113..............................(t) JamieSpencer 12 89
(A P O'Brien, Ire) *hld up in tch in midfield: 9th st: effrt towards inner over 2f out: outpcd u.p 2f out: wknd over 1f out* **14/1**

6-21 **12** *1 1/4* **Ulysses (IRE)**[22] 2208 3-9-0 98.. AndreaAtzeni 3 87
(Sir Michael Stoute) *athletic: lw: hld up in tch in midfield: 7th st: sn swtchd rt and effrt u.p: no imp 2f out: wknd over 1f out* **8/1**

-134 **13** *6* **Biodynamic (IRE)**[30] 1974 3-9-0 94.............................. DougieCostello 7 77
(K R Burke) *in tch in midfield: jostled over 10f out: hdwy 5f out and 6th st: rdn 3f out and sn dropped out: wl bhd over 1f out* **100/1**

14-2 **14** *7* **Port Douglas (IRE)**[30] 1974 3-9-0 111................(bt) ColmO'Donoghue 10 66
(A P O'Brien, Ire) *led: drvn and hdd over 2f out: sn lost pl and wl btn: wl bhd over 1f out: t.o* **16/1**

-325 **15** *7* **Shogun (IRE)**[14] 2496 3-9-0 109................................ DonnachaO'Brien 5 55
(A P O'Brien, Ire) *lw: in tch in midfield: stuck bhd struggling rival and shuffled bk to rr on downhill run 4f out: 13th st: sn bhd and lost tch 2f out: t.o and eased ins fnl f* **33/1**

1-51 **16** *11* **Moonlight Magic**[27] 2069 3-9-0 111................................. KevinManning 1 37
(J S Bolger, Ire) *athletic: chsd ldrs: 4th st: sn rdn and dropped out rapidly: wl bhd 2f out: t.o and eased fnl f* **14/1**

2m 40.09s (1.19) **Going Correction** +0.35s/f (Good) **16 Ran SP% 125.6**
Speed ratings (Par 113): **110,109,108,104,102 102,100,99,99,97 95,94,90,85,81 73**
CSF £28.06 CT £323.98 TOTE £8.40: £2.60, £2.10, £5.40; EX 39.50 Trifecta £532.60.

Owner H H Aga Khan **Bred** His Highness The Aga Khan's Studs S C **Trained** Curragh, Co Kildare

FOCUS
Four horses were supplemented for 75,000GBP, and 54,500GBP from each payment was added to the prize fund, making this the most valuable race ever staged in Britain. Plenty of connections were keen to have a go, as the field lacked an obvious star, but the right types dominated and the feeling is this will prove to be at least an okay Derby. The form has been rated up to standard with Harzand extending his ballysax superiority over Idaho. There was a 1-2-3 for Ireland, and the first seven finishers were waited with off a quick early pace.

2897 INVESTEC ASSET FINANCE STKS (H'CAP) 1m 4f 10y
5:15 (5:16) (Class 2) (0-100,100) 4-Y-O+
£18,675 (£5,592; £2,796; £1,398; £699; £351) **Stalls** Centre

Form RPR

30-2 **1** **Green Light**[19] 2313 5-8-8 **87**..(v) OisinMurphy 16 97+
(Ralph Beckett) *taken down early: hld up in rr: gd hdwy over 3f out: swtchd lft 2f out and rdn to ld over 1f out: clr and edgd lft 1f out: styd on: rdn out* **16/1**

130- **2** *2 1/4* **Polarisation**[183] 6270 4-9-7 **100**.................................... WilliamBuick 14 106
(Charlie Appleby) *lw: chsd ldng trio: effrt over 2f out: rdn and ev ch 2f out: unable qck w wnr over 1f out: chsd wnr over 1f out: styd on same pce ins fnl f* **16/1**

03/2 **3** *1 1/4* **Repeater**[14] 2498 7-7-11 **83**..................................(b) KillianLeonard[(7)] 17 87
(Miss Amanda Mooney, Ire) *hld up in midfield: clsd to trck ldrs over 3f out: effrt and rdn over 1f out: styd on same pce ins fnl f: wnt 3rd towards fin* **12/1**

24-1 **4** *1/2* **Iftiraaq (IRE)**[17] 1737 5-7-11 **81**.........................(p) JosephineGordon[(5)] 5 84
(Seamus Durack) *chsd ldrs tl wnt 2nd 4f out tl led 3f out: sn rdn: hdd and unable qck w wnr over 1f out: kpt on same pce ins fnl f* **20/1**

14-2 **5** *1 3/4* **Duretto**[28] 2024 4-9-1 **94**.. JimCrowley 6 94
(Andrew Balding) *lw: wl in tch in midfield: swtchd lft and effrt over 2f out: rdn and hdwy to chal 2f out: unable qck w wnr over 1f out: wknd ins fnl f* **4/1**[1]

-252 **6** *1 3/4* **Hubertas**[15] 2439 4-7-10 **82**......................................(b) GeorgeWood[(7)] 2 80
(John Quinn) *wl in tch in midfield: hdwy to chse ldrs over 3f out: rdn and unable qck over 2f out: swtchd rt wl over 1f out: wl hld and plugged on same pce fr over 1f out* **25/1**

561- **7** *1 1/2* **Karraar**[265] 6355 5-8-13 **92**..(p) PaulHanagan 10 87
(William Haggas) *hld up towards rr: effrt and switching rt 3f out: sme hdwy u.p over 1f out: plugged on ins fnl f: nvr trbld ldrs* **13/2**[3]

-000 **8** *nk* **Buonarroti (IRE)**[14] 2487 5-8-5 **84**................................(v) NeilFarley 15 79
(Declan Carroll) *hld up wl off the pce in rr: hdwy on outer over 3f out: drvn and no hdwy 2f out: plugged on same pce and wl hld after* **40/1**

0-13 **9** *7* **Barwick**[19] 2313 8-8-11 **90**... SteveDrowne 7 74
(George Baker) *niggled along in rr early: off the pce in last quintet: prog over 2f out but nvr on terms w ldrs: wknd fnl f* **8/1**

4355 **10** *4* **Blue Surf**[49] 1475 7-9-6 **99**.. AndreaAtzeni 4 76
(Amanda Perrett) *in tch in midfield: effrt over 2f out: sn drvn and no imp 2f out: wknd over 1f out* **10/1**

013- **11** *nk* **Ladurelli (IRE)**[220] 7556 4-8-8 **87**................................... JamieSpencer 8 64
(Paul Cole) *in tch in midfield: effrt 2f out: sn outpcd u.p: wknd fnl f* **12/1**

560/ **12** *1 3/4* **Stars Over The Sea (USA)**[147] 3379 5-9-1 **94**...... RichardKingscote 11 68
(Mark Johnston) *led tl 3f out: sn u.p and lost pl: wknd over 1f out* **25/1**

-122 **13** *7* **Whinging Willie (IRE)**[45] 1568 7-8-4 **83**......................(v) SamHitchcott 9 46
(Gary Moore) *a towards rr: rdn 5f out: bhd 3f out: sn lost tch* **14/1**

10-0 **14** *5* **Shell Bay (USA)**[5] 2752 4-8-11 **90**.................................. SeanLevey 13 45
(Richard Hannon) *a in rr: lost tch 2f out* **33/1**

110- **15** *21* **Senrima (IRE)**[308] 4856 4-8-9 **88**...................................... MartinDwyer 3 9
(Brian Meehan) *midfield tl lost pl and bhd over 3f out: lost tch 2f out: eased fnl f: t.o* **25/1**

P624 **16** *20* **Yorkidding**[7] 2685 4-8-9 **88**.................................... SilvestreDeSousa 1
(Mark Johnston) *wl in tch in midfield: rdn 6f out: lost pl and bhd 3f out: t.o and eased fnl f* **11/2**[2]

5-03 **17** *shd* **Hardstone (USA)**[21] 2249 5-8-13 **92**................................ GrahamLee 12
(Michael Dods) *chsd ldr tl 4f out: sn dropped out: t.o and eased fnl f* **25/1**

2m 41.81s (2.91) **Going Correction** +0.35s/f (Good) **17 Ran SP% 128.3**
Speed ratings (Par 109): **104,102,101,101,100 99,98,97,93,90 90,89,84,81,67 53,53**
CSF £241.05 CT £3199.23 TOTE £19.00: £3.40, £3.90, £3.20, £4.30; EX 282.90 Trifecta £4406.80.

Owner Sceptre **Bred** Brightwalton Stud **Trained** Kimpton, Hants

■ Stewards' Enquiry : Sam Hitchcott jockey said gelding was never travelling.
Sean Levey jockey said gelding was never travelling.

FOCUS
Race distance as advertised. No great gallop on in this useful handicap, although the winner did come from the rear. The winner still has some potential.

2898 INVESTEC ASSET MANAGEMENT STKS (H'CAP) 6f
5:50 (5:51) (Class 2) (0-100,100) 4-Y-O+
£18,675 (£5,592; £2,796; £1,398; £699; £351) **Stalls** High

Form RPR

0-00 **1** **Blaine**[14] 2488 6-8-8 **87**.....(b) KierenFallon 4 104
(David Nicholls) *midfield: rdn and clsd over 1f out: burst between rivals to ld jst ins fnl f: sn clr: r.o strly: readily* **8/1**[2]

0-50 **2** 4 1/2 **Shared Equity**[42] 1627 5-9-7 **100**..... GrahamLee 8 103
(Jedd O'Keeffe) *lw: led: rdn and forged ahd over 1f out: hdd and immediately outpcd by wnr ins fnl f: battled on gamely to hold 2nd* **6/1**[1]

0100 **3** nk **Perfect Pasture**[29] 1993 6-9-6 **99**.....(v) SeanLevey 17 101
(Michael Easterby) *hld up in midfield: effrt u.p over 1f out: drvn and chsd ldrs 1f out: no ch w wnr but kpt on to go 3rd towards fin* **25/1**

5643 **4** 3/4 **Waseem Faris (IRE)**[35] 1857 7-8-3 **87**..... JosephineGordon(5) 5 87
(Joseph Tuite) *taken down early: restless in stalls: chsd ldrs: rdn over 2f out: chsd ldr over 1f out tl outpcd by wnr and kpt on same pce ins fnl f* **33/1**

1105 **5** 2 3/4 **Englishman**[15] 2434 6-8-10 **89**..... DougieCostello 1 80
(Milton Bradley) *stdd s: hld up in tch in midfield: effrt on inner over 2f out: drvn and kpt on same pce fr over 1f out* **11/1**[3]

26-0 **6** 1 **George Bowen (IRE)**[24] 2158 4-9-5 **98**..... JamieSpencer 11 86+
(Richard Fahey) *stdd s: hld up wl off the pce in rr: switching rt and effrt but stl plenty to do 2f out: hdwy u.p over 1f out: styd on ins fnl f: nvr trbld ldrs* **6/1**[1]

-025 **7** 2 1/4 **Iseemist (IRE)**[28] 2042 5-9-4 **97**..... ShaneGray 16 77
(John Gallagher) *broke wl to press ldrs fr wd draw: 3rd and outpcd over 2f out: drvn and btn over 1f out: wknd fnl f* **20/1**

003- **8** 1/2 **Ashpan Sam**[235] 7178 7-9-0 **100**..... GeorgeWood(7) 14 79
(David W Drinkwater) *w ldr tl no ex u.p and btn over 1f out: wknd ins fnl f* **12/1**

-100 **9** 1 1/2 **Arctic Feeling (IRE)**[14] 2488 8-9-2 **95**..... JimmyQuinn 3 72
(Richard Fahey) *hld up off the pce towards rr: rdn and hdwy u.p over 1f out: keeping on but no ch w wnr whn nt clr run and eased ins fnl f* **25/1**

5244 **10** 1 1/2 **Boomerang Bob (IRE)**[84] 923 7-8-12 **96**..... LucyKBarry(5) 15 65
(Jamie Osborne) *s.i.s: off the pce towards rr: wd bnd over 3f out: rdn 2f out: styd on ins fnl f: nvr trbld ldrs* **20/1**

-000 **11** nk **Valley Of Fire**[7] 2684 4-8-10 **89**..... MartinDwyer 7 57
(William Haggas) *midfield: rdn and lost pl over 3f out: n.d after* **16/1**

10-2 **12** hd **Ghalib (IRE)**[21] 2247 4-9-3 **96**..... AndreaAtzeni 12 66
(Ed Walker) *midfield: effrt and rdn 2f out: sn no imp: wl hld and eased ins fnl f* **6/1**[1]

40-4 **13** 2 1/2 **Zanetto**[24] 2158 6-9-3 **96**..... SilvestreDeSousa 2 56
(John Quinn) *lw: midfield: effrt towards inner over 2f out: sn no imp: wknd over 1f out* **8/1**[2]

2554 **14** shd **Barracuda Boy (IRE)**[28] 2031 6-9-6 **99**..... RichardKingscote 6 58
(Tom Dascombe) *squeezed for room and dropped to rr sn after s: a in rr: effrt and sltly hmpd over 1f out: wl btn after* **16/1**

6-00 **15** 3/4 **Secret Missile**[12] 2547 6-8-9 **88**.....(b) FergusSweeney 9 45
(Gary Moore) *taken down early: in tch in midfield: rdn and lost pl jst over 2f out: bhd and eased ins fnl f* **50/1**

0-00 **16** 3/4 **Charles Molson**[15] 2434 5-9-3 **96**..... JimCrowley 10 51
(Patrick Chamings) *a towards rr: drvn and no rspnse 2f out: wl btn over 1f out* **20/1**

-005 **17** 3 3/4 **Joey's Destiny (IRE)**[12] 2547 6-8-11 **90**..... LiamKeniry 13 33
(George Baker) *midfield: bdly hmpd and lost pl 4f out: bhd and rdn 2f out: no hdwy: wl bhd ins fnl f* **16/1**

1m 10.23s (0.83) **Going Correction** +0.35s/f (Good) **17** Ran SP% **125.6**
Speed ratings (Par 109): **108,102,101,100,96 95,92,91,89,87 87,87,83,83,82 81,76**
CSF £51.27 CT £1223.20 TOTE £9.40: £2.20, £2.40, £7.50, £9.00; EX 92.00 Trifecta £1742.60.
Owner Lady O'Reilly **Bred** Toby Barker **Trained** Sessay, N Yorks

FOCUS
Race distance as advertised. A race that is often ultra-competitive, there was no hanging around and a clear-cut winner emerged.
T/Jkpt: Not won. T/Plt: £1,364.50 to a £1 stake. Pool: £361,072.30 - 193.17 winning tickets.
T/Qpdt: £43.00 to a £1 stake. Pool: £37,098.86 - 637.87 winning tickets. **Steve Payne**

2822 LINGFIELD (L-H)
Saturday, June 4

OFFICIAL GOING: Turf course - good (good to soft in places); all-weather - polytrack: standard
Wind: Moderate, against Weather: Hazy sun

2899 £25 FREE BET AT 188BET AMATEUR RIDERS' H'CAP 1m 2f (P)
5:45 (5:48) (Class 6) (0-60,63) 4-Y-O+ **£2,495** (£774; £386; £193) **Stalls** Low

Form RPR

620- **1** **City Ground (USA)**[247] 6878 9-11-0 **60**..... MissSBrotherton 1 71
(Michael Appleby) *mde all: qcknd clr over 1f out: comf* **7/2**[2]

0621 **2** 2 1/4 **Engai (GER)**[65] 1165 10-10-0 **53**..... MissPBridgwater(7) 12 59
(David Bridgwater) *s.s: towards rr: hdwy and wd on bnd 2f out: styd on to take 2nd nr fin* **10/1**

/211 **3** hd **Barnaby Brook (CAN)**[11] 2566 6-11-0 **63**.....(b) MrPMillman(3) 5 67
(Robyn Brisland) *prom: outpcd over 2f out: styd on fnl f* **13/8**[1]

4100 **4** 1 1/4 **Ferryview Place**[11] 2566 7-10-6 **52**.....(p) MrSWalker 3 54
(Ian Williams) *in tch: effrt over 2f out: drvn to chse ldrs over 1f out: one pce* **8/1**[3]

0460 **5** 1/2 **Jonnie Skull (IRE)**[9] 2609 10-9-9 **46**.....(t) MrThomasGreatrex(5) 2 47
(Phil McEntee) *chsd wnr tl no ex ins fnl f* **16/1**

000- **6** 3 1/2 **Goal (IRE)**[20] 7962 8-10-4 **53**.....(v) BrodieHampson(3) 11 47
(Sally Randell) *dwlt: sn in midfield: hdwy to join ldrs 3f out: wknd over 1f out* **20/1**

0344 **7** 3 3/4 **Candesta (USA)**[18] 2323 6-10-4 **53**.....(tp) MrRBirkett(3) 10 40
(Julia Feilden) *chsd ldrs tl wknd over 1f out* **8/1**[3]

-565 **8** 3/4 **Bond Mystery**[5] 2955 4-9-7 **46** oh1..... MrWillPettis(7) 8 32
(Natalie Lloyd-Beavis) *sn rdn along in midfield: no hdwy fnl 3f* **33/1**

63-6 **9** 11 **Tseo**[143] 161 4-10-6 **59**..... MrRobertHooper(7) 13 24
(David Brown) *in tch on outer tl wknd 3f out* **20/1**

0050 **10** 3 3/4 **Ron Waverly (IRE)**[39] 1748 6-9-10 **49** oh1 ow3.....(t) MissMBryant(7) 6 7
(Paddy Butler) *a bhd* **50/1**

60-0 **11** 2 **Flag Of Glory**[9] 2616 9-10-4 **57**.....(p) MissMEdden(7) 14 11
(Peter Hiatt) *prom tl wknd 4f out* **33/1**

6535 **12** 1/2 **Je T'Aime Encore**[78] 876 4-9-11 **48**..... MissPFuller(5) 9
(Gay Kelleway) *towards rr: modest effrt on inner over 3f out: sn wknd* **16/1**

0/04 **13** 9 **Total Obsession**[10] 2588 9-9-7 **46** oh1.....(v) MrJPearce(7) 4
(Mark Hoad) *s.i.s: a bhd* **66/1**

2m 6.13s (-0.47) **Going Correction** -0.075s/f (Stan) **13** Ran SP% **122.3**
Speed ratings (Par 101): **98,96,96,95,94 91,88,88,79,76 74,74,67**
CSF £36.27 CT £79.07 TOTE £5.80: £2.00, £2.20, £1.10; EX 52.40 Trifecta £40.80.
Owner Mrs D R Brotherton **Bred** Mrs E Scott Jr & Mrs L Macelree **Trained** Oakham, Rutland
■ Ballyheigue was withdrawn. Price at time of withdrawal 25-1 Rule 4 does not apply.

FOCUS
A low-grade amateur riders' race on Polytrack and the winner made all.

2900 188BET.CO.UK H'CAP 1m 2f (P)
6:20 (6:20) (Class 5) (0-75,75) 3-Y-O **£3,234** (£962; £481; £240) **Stalls** Low

Form RPR

5216 **1** **Frozen Force (IRE)**[12] 2545 3-9-2 **75**..... KieranShoemark(5) 4 80
(Amanda Perrett) *chsd ldr: hrd rdn over 1f out: led ins fnl f: drvn out* **12/1**

15 **2** 3/4 **Mighty Lady**[18] 2339 3-9-5 **73**..... WilliamTwiston-Davies 13 77+
(Robyn Brisland) *stdd s: t.k.h in rr: hdwy and weaved through fnl 2f: clsng on wnr whn hmpd nr fin: r.o* **33/1**

31-2 **3** nk **Mayasa (IRE)**[149] 85 3-9-7 **75**.....(b) DavidAllan 1 78
(James Tate) *led tl over 1f out: kpt on u.p* **8/1**[3]

35-0 **4** nk **Pourquoi Non (IRE)**[35] 1860 3-8-11 **65**..... OisinMurphy 11 67
(Denis Coakley) *t.k.h: prom on outer: slt ld over 1f out tl ins fnl f: one pce* **14/1**

4242 **5** hd **Jarir**[8] 2644 3-9-3 **74**.....(b[1]) TomMarquand(3) 3 76
(Richard Hannon) *in tch: rdn over 2f out: styd on fnl f* **7/2**[1]

1-3 **6** 1/2 **Shufoog**[29] 2011 3-8-10 **71**..... GeorgiaCox(7) 2 73+
(William Haggas) *chsd ldrs: hmpd on inner over 2f out: one pce fnl f* **7/2**[1]

22-4 **7** nk **So Celebre (GER)**[31] 1971 3-9-5 **73**..... AdamKirby 6 73
(Ian Williams) *mid-div: rdn to chse ldrs over 1f out: one pce fnl f* **7/1**[2]

4-66 **8** hd **Ride The Lightning**[22] 2209 3-9-6 **74**..... TomQueally 7 74+
(Brian Meehan) *dwlt: sn in midfield: effrt on inner and n.m.r 1f out: nvr able to chal* **8/1**[3]

1-32 **9** 3/4 **Brave Archibald (IRE)**[19] 2291 3-9-4 **72**..... MartinLane 9 71
(Paul Cole) *towards rr: rdn over 2f out: styd on fnl f* **10/1**

1146 **10** hd **Palpitation (IRE)**[25] 2123 3-8-11 **70**..... AaronJones(5) 5 68
(David Brown) *prom tl wknd over 1f out* **20/1**

3-60 **11** 2 **Knight Commander**[36] 1828 3-9-3 **71**..... FrederikTylicki 10 65
(William Knight) *dwlt: bhd: effrt and wd into st: nvr trbld ldrs* **20/1**

01-6 **12** 19 **Davey Boy**[66] 1155 3-9-3 **74**..... LouisSteward(3) 8 30
(Michael Bell) *in tch on outer: rdn 4f out: wknd 2f out* **33/1**

2m 5.42s (-1.18) **Going Correction** -0.075s/f (Stan) **12** Ran SP% **118.0**
Speed ratings (Par 99): **101,100,100,99,99 99,99,98,98,98 96,81**
CSF £363.06 CT £3316.95 TOTE £14.80: £5.20, £4.40, £2.40; EX 517.10 Trifecta £2884.00 Part won..
Owner A D Spence **Bred** J Kenny **Trained** Pulborough, W Sussex
■ Stewards' Enquiry : David Allan two-day ban; used whip above the permitted level (19th-20th June)

FOCUS
This fair 3yo handicap was run 0.71 secs faster than the preceding amateurs' contest but resulted in a blanket finish.

2901 GORMAN GAMBLE H'CAP 1m 3f 106y
6:50 (6:50) (Class 6) (0-55,55) 4-Y-O+ **£2,587** (£770; £384; £192) **Stalls** High

Form RPR

0/00 **1** **Catharina**[42] 1654 4-8-12 **46**..... RenatoSouza 6 55+
(Dean Ivory) *t.k.h: chsd ldrs: led over 2f out: clr fnl f: easily* **20/1**

-000 **2** 6 **Spinning Rose**[121] 445 4-9-6 **54**..... RobertWinston 5 53
(Dean Ivory) *s.s: sn in tch: chal 2f out: one pce appr fnl f* **5/1**[3]

4000 **3** nk **Foylesideview (IRE)**[14] 2462 4-9-0 **48**..... SteveDrowne 10 47
(Harry Chisman) *stdd s: towards rr: rdn and styd on fnl 2f: nvr nrr* **7/1**

0006 **4** 1 1/4 **Shirataki (IRE)**[26] 2110 8-8-11 **50**..... HectorCrouch(5) 9 47
(Peter Hiatt) *s.s: hld up in rr: hdwy 2f out: hrd rdn over 1f out: styd on same pce* **6/1**

4-56 **5** 3 **Megalala (IRE)**[39] 1747 15-9-4 **52**..... WilliamTwiston-Davies 3 44
(John Bridger) *pressed ldr: rdn over 4f out: lost 2nd over 2f out: sn outpcd* **4/1**[2]

00 **6** 9 **Spring In Kentucky**[15] 2443 4-9-7 **55**..... TimmyMurphy 8 32
(Daniel Kubler) *in tch tl hrd rdn and wknd 2f out* **12/1**

06-6 **7** 4 **Miss Mittens**[17] 2368 4-8-12 **46** oh1..... OisinMurphy 7 17
(Geoffrey Deacon) *s.s: a bhd* **20/1**

-605 **8** 1 **Sheikh The Reins (IRE)**[18] 2323 7-9-0 **48**..... KierenFox 4 17
(John Best) *prom tl wknd over 2f out* **3/1**[1]

00-0 **9** 3 1/4 **Suzi Icon**[25] 2127 4-9-7 **55**..... JFEgan 2 19
(John Butler) *led tl over 2f out: sn wknd* **8/1**

2m 36.56s (5.06) **Going Correction** +0.475s/f (Yiel) **9** Ran SP% **116.8**
Speed ratings (Par 101): **100,95,95,94,92 85,82,82,79**
CSF £118.15 CT £778.15 TOTE £19.60: £4.50, £2.00, £2.30; EX 167.30 Trifecta £963.70.
Owner K T Ivory **Bred** Kathryn Joy Lees **Trained** Radlett, Herts

FOCUS
The first of the turf races and the going was Good, good to soft in places. A very moderate contest and a surprise winner.

2902 ALAN PARFITT MEMORIAL MAIDEN AUCTION STKS 5f
7:20 (7:24) (Class 5) 2-Y-O **£3,234** (£962; £481; £240) **Stalls** Centre

Form RPR

3 **1** **Simmie (IRE)**[14] 2457 2-8-6 0..... EdwardGreatrex(5) 7 70
(Sylvester Kirk) *chsd ldrs: effrt over 2f out: led ins fnl f: all out* **7/2**[3]

32 **2** shd **Kody Ridge (IRE)**[19] 2289 2-9-5 0..... MartinLane 2 78
(David Dennis) *w ldrs: led over 1f out tl ins fnl f: rallied wl nr fin* **6/1**

0 **3** 7 **Swan Serenade**[14] 2467 2-8-13 0..... RyanClark 8 47
(Jonathan Portman) *chsd ldrs: effrt over 2f out: no ex fnl f* **10/1**

5 **4** 1 1/4 **Papa Delta**[19] 2295 2-9-0 0..... GeorgeDowning(3) 6 46
(Tony Carroll) *w ldrs: rdn over 2f out: wknd 1f out* **20/1**

5 2 1/2 **Marquee Club** 2-9-3 0..... TimmyMurphy 9 37
(Jamie Osborne) *rn green and sn wl bhd: sme late hdwy* **10/1**

6 **6** 3/4 **Angie Baby**[8] 2641 2-8-11 0..... LiamKeniry 4 29
(J S Moore) *led tl wknd over 1f out* **20/1**

7 1 1/4 **Champagne Queen** 2-9-0 0..... OisinMurphy 5 27
(Rae Guest) *outpcd: a bhd* **10/3**[2]

8 3 ¾ **Biologist (IRE)** 2-8-7 0 GeorgiaCox[7] 1 14+
(William Haggas) *missed break and wnt lft s: lost 10 l: a t.o* **5/2**[1]
1m 1.31s (3.11) **Going Correction** +0.60s/f (Yiel) 8 Ran SP% **115.9**
Speed ratings (Par 93): **99,98,87,85,81 80,78,72**
CSF £25.13 TOTE £4.70: £1.30, £2.00, £2.20; EX 20.00 Trifecta £143.10.
Owner Neil Simpson **Bred** D Ryan, D S Ryan & R A Williams **Trained** Upper Lambourn, Berks
■ Stewards' Enquiry : Liam Keniry one-day ban; not kept straight from the stalls (19th June)

FOCUS
An ordinary looking juvenile maiden in which the market leaders were well beaten.

2903 DES KELLY MEMORIAL H'CAP 6f
7:50 (7:53) (Class 4) (0-85,85) 4-Y-O+ **£5,175** (£1,540; £769; £384) **Stalls** Centre

Form RPR
0-00 **1** **Cool Bahamian (IRE)**[12] 2547 5-9-3 **81** (b) JohnFahy 2 89
(Eve Johnson Houghton) *sn outpcd in rr: hdwy 2f out: led ins fnl f: drvn out* **10/1**
2610 **2** ½ **Justice First**[10] 2579 4-8-9 **80** HarryBurns[7] 5 86
(Ed Dunlop) *outpcd in rr: hdwy over 1f out: r.o to press wnr fnl 100yds: jst hld* **11/1**
545- **3** 1 ½ **Silver Rainbow (IRE)**[198] 7907 4-9-4 **85** MichaelJMMurphy[3] 3 87
(Charles Hills) *prom: chal 2f out: hrd rdn: one pce fnl f* **8/1**
1124 **4** *shd* **Elusive Ellen (IRE)**[14] 2469 6-9-0 **78** JimmyQuinn 4 79+
(Brendan Powell) *s.i.s: outpcd in rr: hdwy and swtchd lft wl over 1f out: r.o fnl f* **6/1**[3]
434 **5** *1* **Merhoob (IRE)**[10] 2581 4-9-3 **81** AdamKirby 6 79
(John Ryan) *chsd ldrs: slt ld 2f out tl ins fnl f: no ex* **3/1**[1]
6560 **6** ½ **Heartsong (IRE)**[21] 2238 7-8-9 **78** PatrickO'Donnell[5] 7 74
(John Gallagher) *outpcd towards rr: hdwy and nt clr run 2f out: swtchd rt over 1f out: nvr able to chal* **20/1**
25-0 **7** 2 ½ **It Must Be Faith**[140] 213 6-9-2 **85** (p) GeorgeBuckell[5] 1 73
(Michael Appleby) *w ldrs in centre tl wknd fnl f* **12/1**
0-06 **8** *11* **Flexible Flyer**[21] 2253 7-9-2 **80** SilvestreDeSousa 8 33
(Chris Dwyer) *disp ld tl wknd 2f out: bhd and eased 1f out* **7/2**[2]
5100 **9** 1 ½ **Zac Brown (IRE)**[14] 2480 5-9-7 **85** FrederikTylicki 10 33
(Charlie Wallis) *anticipated s: disp ld on stands' rail tl wknd 2f out* **8/1**
1m 13.84s (2.64) **Going Correction** +0.60s/f (Yiel) 9 Ran SP% **113.6**
Speed ratings (Par 105): **106,105,103,103,101 101,97,83,81**
CSF £111.40 CT £921.68 TOTE £15.20: £4.10, £3.50, £2.50; EX 143.40 Trifecta £958.60.
Owner L R Godfrey & R F Johnson Houghton **Bred** Kildaragh Stud **Trained** Blewbury, Oxon

FOCUS
The feature race, a decent sprint handicap but a contest where the principals came from off the pace.

2904 188BET MAIDEN FILLIES' STKS 7f
8:20 (8:20) (Class 5) 3-Y-O+ **£3,234** (£962; £481; £240) **Stalls** Centre

Form RPR
64 **1** **Cliffhanger**[9] 2606 3-8-11 0 TomMarquand[3] 7 77
(Paul Cole) *towards rr: hdwy 2f out: led 1f out: pushed out* **20/1**
2 **2** 1 ¾ **Aflame**[33] 1930 3-9-0 0 TedDurcan 2 72
(Sir Michael Stoute) *chsd ldrs: led 2f out tl 1f out: kpt on same pce* **10/11**[1]
3 1 ¾ **Andanotherone (IRE)** 3-9-0 0 SilvestreDeSousa 1 67
(Simon Crisford) *outpcd towards rr: hdwy to press ldrs 2f out: one pce fnl f* **7/1**[3]
0 **4** 3 ¼ **Time To Exceed (IRE)**[14] 2470 3-9-0 0 FergusSweeney 9 59
(Henry Candy) *t.k.h: prom: led 3f out tl 2f out: btn over 1f out* **12/1**
55- **5** *1* **Blue Moon Rising (IRE)**[236] 7160 3-9-0 0 WilliamTwiston-Davies 6 56
(Michael Bell) *t.k.h in midfield: rdn and no hdwy fnl 2f* **8/1**
0-0 **6** *3* **Color Force (IRE)**[23] 2177 3-9-0 0 RobertWinston 4 49
(Gay Kelleway) *bhd: sme hdwy 3f out: wknd 2f out* **50/1**
00 **7** 2 ¾ **Dance Band (IRE)**[13] 2505 3-9-0 0 JackMitchell 10 41
(Roger Varian) *led for over 1f: lost pl 3f out: btn in midfield whn hmpd over 2f out* **16/1**
8 *2* **Excellent Sounds** 3-9-0 0 JimmyFortune 3 36
(Hughie Morrison) *bhd: sme hdwy over 2f out: sn wknd* **28/1**
9 *6* **Oasis Moon** 3-9-0 0 OisinMurphy 5 21
(William Haggas) *a bhd* **9/2**[2]
10 *8* **Ms Arsenal**[11] 4-9-10 0 JFEgan 8 4
(Giles Bravery) *s.s: t.k.h: hdwy to ld over 5f out: hdd 3f out: sn wknd* **33/1**
1m 26.9s (3.60) **Going Correction** +0.60s/f (Yiel)
WFA 3 from 4yo 10lb 10 Ran SP% **120.9**
Speed ratings (Par 100): **103,101,99,95,94 90,87,85,78,69**
CSF £39.18 TOTE £16.50: £5.30, £1.10, £2.60; EX 66.10 Trifecta £314.90.
Owner Frank Stella **Bred** Whitsbury Manor Stud **Trained** Whatcombe, Oxon

FOCUS
Several major yards represented in this fillies' maiden but a surprise winner.

2905 FRENCH OPEN TENNIS AT 188BET FILLIES' H'CAP 5f
8:50 (8:50) (Class 5) (0-70,69) 3-Y-O+ **£3,234** (£962; £481; £240) **Stalls** Centre

Form RPR
0025 **1** **Pucon**[37] 1811 7-9-11 **66** (p) LiamKeniry 3 77
(Roger Teal) *mde all: clr over 1f out: easily* **10/1**
00-0 **2** *5* **Beau Mistral (IRE)**[43] 1600 7-9-0 **58** GeorgeDowning[3] 5 51
(Tony Carroll) *in tch: rdn over 2f out: chsd wnr over 1f out: no imp* **8/1**
3-03 **3** 1 ¾ **Remember Me**[17] 2372 3-9-4 **66** JimmyFortune 1 50
(Hughie Morrison) *s.i.s: outpcd in rr: hdwy 2f out: no imp fnl f* **3/1**[2]
3323 **4** *2* **Kiringa**[13] 2503 3-8-3 **51** JimmyQuinn 4 28
(Robert Cowell) *prom: chsd wnr 2f out tl hrd rdn and wknd over 1f out* **6/1**
3616 **5** 1 ½ **Al Sailiyah (IRE)**[8] 2642 3-9-4 **69** TomMarquand[3] 2 40
(Richard Hannon) *chsd ldrs: hrd rdn 2f out: sn wknd* **9/4**[1]
550 **6** 3 ¾ **Secret Sonnet**[43] 1597 3-8-5 **53** AdamBeschizza 7 11
(Stuart Williams) *a outpcd* **14/1**
3-04 **7** ¾ **Ulfah Dream**[18] 2334 3-9-2 **67** DanielMuscutt[3] 6 22
(Marco Botti) *chsd wnr tl wknd 2f out* **5/1**[3]
59.99s (1.79) **Going Correction** +0.60s/f (Yiel)
WFA 3 from 7yo 7lb 7 Ran SP% **113.6**
Speed ratings (Par 100): **109,101,98,95,92 86,85**
CSF £83.05 TOTE £10.70: £4.00, £4.30; EX 53.70 Trifecta £398.60.
Owner J A Redmond **Bred** J Redmond **Trained** Great Shefford, Berks
■ Stewards' Enquiry : Adam Beschizza £650.00 fine; attempted to weigh out wearing a safety vest which had been modified.

FOCUS
This modest fillies handicap was run 1.32 secs faster than the earlier juvenile maiden and the two older mares were first home.
T/Plt: £950.10 to a £1 stake. Pool: £45,163.31 - 34.70 winning tickets. T/Qpdt: £33.20 to a £1 stake. Pool: £5,163.68 - 114.95 winning tickets. **Lee McKenzie**

2656 MUSSELBURGH (R-H)
Saturday, June 4

OFFICIAL GOING: Good to firm (8.8) (watered)
Wind: Fresh behind Weather: Sunny

2906 RACINGUK.COM H'CAP 7f 30y
1:40 (1:41) (Class 5) (0-70,69) 3-Y-O+ **£3,234** (£962; £481; £240) **Stalls** Low

Form RPR
0113 **1** **Ordinal**[15] 2422 3-9-3 **68** JoeFanning 12 75+
(Mark Johnston) *mde all: pushed along 2f out: rdn ins fnl f: kpt on wl* **5/2**[1]
00-6 **2** *2* **Desire**[22] 2201 4-9-0 **62** (p) AdamMcNamara[7] 1 68
(Richard Fahey) *in tch: rdn and hdwy to chse ldr 2f out: kpt on but a hld* **10/1**
2002 **3** *2* **Atreus**[8] 2660 4-9-3 **58** (p) GrahamGibbons 2 59
(Michael Easterby) *in tch: rdn over 2f out: kpt on* **6/1**[2]
00 **4** *nk* **Longroom**[47] 1524 4-8-12 **53** BarryMcHugh 3 53
(Noel Wilson) *midfield: rdn and hdwy 2f out: kpt on fnl f* **50/1**
0-00 **5** ¾ **Just Paul (IRE)**[26] 2091 6-9-3 **58** JackGarritty 6 56
(Micky Hammond) *hld up: rdn over 2f out: sme hdwy over 1f out: kpt on ins fnl f: nvr threatened* **12/1**
5532 **6** 1 ½ **Top Offer**[12] 2542 7-8-13 **59** PhilDennis[5] 5 53
(Patrick Morris) *hld up: rdn 2f out: kpt on ins fnl f: nvr threatened* **6/1**[2]
-565 **7** ½ **Rasaman (IRE)**[8] 2660 12-9-12 **67** PaulMulrennan 8 59+
(Jim Goldie) *hld up in rr: pushed along 2f out: n.m.r over 1f out tl jst ins fnl f: kpt on fnl 75yds: nvr able to chal* **12/1**
-560 **8** 1 ¾ **Let Right Be Done**[8] 2661 4-9-5 **60** DavidNolan 11 48
(Linda Perratt) *trckd ldr: rdn over 2f out: wknd fnl f* **25/1**
-356 **9** 1 ¾ **Opt Out**[8] 2661 6-9-8 **63** (p) PJMcDonald 7 46
(Alistair Whillans) *hld up in rr: pushed along over 2f out: nvr threatened* **7/1**[3]
34-0 **10** 1 ¼ **Circuitous**[15] 2416 8-9-7 **62** (p) TomEaves 10 42
(Keith Dalgleish) *trckd ldr: rdn over 2f out: wknd fnl f* **22/1**
0000 **11** *6* **Takahiro**[2] 2812 4-8-9 **50** oh5 (p) JamesSullivan 4 13
(Linda Perratt) *s.i.s: sn in midfield racing keenly: rdn over 2f out: wknd* **100/1**
1-20 **12** *7* **She's Electric (IRE)**[12] 2533 3-9-4 **69** PhillipMakin 9 9
(Keith Dalgleish) *hld up in midfield towards outer: rdn over 2f out: sn wknd* **8/1**
1m 26.43s (-2.57) **Going Correction** -0.35s/f (Firm)
WFA 3 from 4yo+ 10lb 12 Ran SP% **116.4**
Speed ratings (Par 103): **100,97,95,95,94 92,91,89,87,86 79,71**
CSF £27.28 CT £139.45 TOTE £3.20: £1.30, £3.40, £2.40; EX 24.40 Trifecta £165.00.
Owner Sheikh Hamdan bin Mohammed Al Maktoum **Bred** Darley **Trained** Middleham Moor, N Yorks

FOCUS
Ground very much on the quick side, which was confirmed by the time of this opening handicap. The went a good gallop but nothing could get in a blow on the leader, who is one to keep on the right side of for now. The form is rated around the second to fourth.

2907 RACING UK PROFITS RETURNED TO RACING H'CAP 1m
2:15 (2:18) (Class 3) (0-90,87) 3-Y-O **£12,938** (£3,850; £1,924; £962) **Stalls** Low

Form RPR
0012 **1** **Billy Roberts (IRE)**[26] 2095 3-8-10 **76** ConnorBeasley 4 85
(Richard Guest) *mde all: rdn over 2f out: strly pressed 2f out tl 1f out: kpt on wl fnl f* **10/1**
1 **2** 1 ¾ **Blair House (IRE)**[18] 2340 3-9-7 **87** PhillipMakin 9 94+
(Charlie Appleby) *dwlt: hld up towards outer: pushed along over 4f out: rdn over 2f out: hdwy over 1f out: r.o ins fnl f: wnt 2nd nr fin* **2/1**[1]
0-41 **3** ½ **Weekend Offender (FR)**[8] 2657 3-9-3 **83** TomEaves 10 86
(Kevin Ryan) *midfield: rdn over 2f out: hdwy over 1f out: wnt 2nd jst ins fnl f: kpt on: lost 2nd nr fin* **9/1**
00-4 **4** 1 ¼ **Miniaturist (FR)**[19] 2299 3-8-11 **77** PaulMulrennan 5 77
(Mark Johnston) *hld up in midfield: racd keenly: rdn over 2f out: sme hdwy over 1f out: kpt on ins fnl f* **10/1**
10-0 **5** *nk* **Worlds His Oyster**[24] 2161 3-8-9 **80** CallumShepherd[5] 8 79
(John Quinn) *prom: rdn over 2f out: outpcd over 1f out: plugged on fnl f* **28/1**
-512 **6** *hd* **Quick N Quirky (IRE)**[12] 2532 3-9-0 **80** (b[1]) JasonHart 7 78
(Tim Easterby) *trckd ldrs: rdn to chal strly 2f out: wknd ins fnl f* **16/1**
0-32 **7** 3 ¾ **Midnight Macchiato (IRE)**[23] 2179 3-8-13 **79** PatCosgrave 6 67+
(David Brown) *s.i.s: hld up: n.m.r on inner 5f out: swtchd lft wl over 1f out: sn rdn: nvr threatened* **5/1**[2]
6-10 **8** 1 ¼ **Huntlaw**[8] 2654 3-8-12 **78** JoeFanning 1 63
(Mark Johnston) *dwlt: sn trckd ldrs: rdn over 2f out: wknd fnl f* **13/2**[3]
3235 **9** 2 ¼ **Steccando (IRE)**[18] 2327 3-8-11 **77** BenCurtis 3 56
(Alan Swinbank) *dwlt: sn midfield: rdn over 2f out: wknd over 1f out* **25/1**
66-2 **10** *6* **Ocean Ready (USA)**[80] 958 3-8-5 **71** LukeMorris 11 34
(Sir Mark Prescott Bt) *hld up: bmpd over 5f out: rdn over 3f out: sn btn* **13/2**[3]
0-01 **11** 3 ¾ **Back To Bond**[18] 2349 3-8-8 **74** TonyHamilton 2 26
(Richard Fahey) *prom: rdn 3f out: sn wknd* **33/1**
1m 38.12s (-3.08) **Going Correction** -0.35s/f (Firm) 11 Ran SP% **121.0**
Speed ratings (Par 103): **101,99,98,97,97 97,93,92,89,83 80**
CSF £30.63 CT £201.27 TOTE £11.40: £3.10, £1.10, £3.40; EX 42.70 Trifecta £538.40.
Owner www.primelawns.co.uk **Bred** Burgage Stud **Trained** Ingmanthorpe, W Yorks

FOCUS
A competitive 3yo handicap but once again the pace held up and it was very hard for those that came from off the pace to make a meaningful challenge. The third and fourth offer substance to the form.

2908 EBFSTALLIONS.COM EDINBURGH CASTLE STKS (A CONDITIONS RACE) (PLUS 10 RACE) 5f
2:50 (2:51) (Class 2) 2-Y-O
£15,562 (£4,660; £2,330; £1,165; £582; £292) **Stalls** High

Form RPR
1 **1** **Kocollada (IRE)**[21] 2254 2-8-7 0 TonyHamilton 6 83
(Richard Fahey) *dwlt: hld up: angled rt to outer 2f out: sn pushed along appr fnl f: kpt on pushed out: led towards fin: shade cosily* **7/1**
0221 **2** *nk* **Poet's Society**[9] 2617 2-8-12 0 PaulMulrennan 5 87
(Mark Johnston) *led narrowly: rdn 2f out: kpt on: hdd towards fin* **3/1**[1]
124 **3** *nk* **Boater (IRE)**[7] 2670 2-8-7 0 JoeFanning 2 81
(Mark Johnston) *pressed ldr: rdn 2f out: kpt on* **7/2**[2]

511 **4** *1 1/4* **Lawless Louis**[7] 2675 2-8-12 0 PhillipMakin 4 81
(David O'Meara) *trckd ldng pair: rdn 1/2-way: one pce fnl f* **13/2**
323 **5** *1 3/4* **Kodi Da Capo (IRE)**[21] 2254 2-8-7 0 JasonHart 3 70
(Keith Dalgleish) *hld up in tch: rdn 2f out: nvr threatened* **28/1**
21 **6** *2 3/4* **Chevalier Du Lac (IRE)**[18] 2344 2-8-12 0 CamHardie 7 65
(John Quinn) *dwlt: hld up in tch: rdn 2f out: wknd appr fnl f* **11/2**
1 **7** *nk* **Tahoo (IRE)**[15] 2417 2-8-7 0 PJMcDonald 1 59
(K R Burke) *sn chsd ldrs towards outer: rdn 2f out: wknd appr fnl f* **4/1**[3]
58.15s (-2.25) **Going Correction** -0.475s/f (Firm) **7** Ran SP% **111.9**
Speed ratings (Par 99): **99,98,98,96,93 88,88**
CSF £27.01 TOTE £7.10: £3.40, £1.50; EX 44.50 Trifecta £120.10.
Owner Sheikh Rashid Dalmook Al Maktoum **Bred** Mrs O M E McKeever **Trained** Musley Bank, N Yorks

FOCUS
A cracking sprint and Royal Ascot would have to be on the agenda for the winner, and possibly one or two of the others.

2909 EDINBURGH GIN EDINBURGH CUP (H'CAP) 1m 4f 100y
3:25 (3:26) (Class 3) (0-90,87) 3-Y-O
£37,350 (£11,184; £5,592; £2,796; £1,398; £702) **Stalls** Low

Form RPR
12-0 **1** **Dal Harraild**[43] 1610 3-9-7 **87** PatCosgrave 1 97
(William Haggas) *trckd ldr: rdn over 2f out: led appr fnl f: kpt on wl* **12/1**
04-4 **2** *2 1/4* **St Michel**[19] 2300 3-8-3 **69** LukeMorris 4 75+
(Sir Mark Prescott Bt) *in tch: pushed along over 3f out: edgd lft over 2f out: sn drvn: styd on fnl f: wnt 2nd towards fin* **5/1**[3]
-211 **3** *nk* **Regal Monarch**[16] 2408 3-8-11 **77** JoeFanning 7 83
(Mark Johnston) *led: rdn over 2f out: hdd appr fnl f: one pce: lost 2nd towards fin* **7/2**[1]
4-53 **4** *1* **Yangtze**[16] 2413 3-8-7 **73** StevieDonohoe 3 77+
(Sir Michael Stoute) *dwlt: hld up: pushed along over 2f out: angled rt and hdwy 2f out: styd on fnl f* **9/2**[2]
-242 **5** *1 1/4* **Juste Pour Nous**[21] 2252 3-9-4 **84** PaulMulrennan 11 86
(Mark Johnston) *midfield: pushed along and hdwy 3f out: rdn over 1f out: one pce ins fnl f* **10/1**
52-3 **6** *1 1/4* **West Drive (IRE)**[22] 2224 3-9-2 **82** GrahamGibbons 8 82
(Roger Varian) *trckd ldr: rdn over 2f out: sltly hmpd appr fnl f: wknd* **6/1**
3114 **7** *nse* **Project Bluebook (FR)**[22] 2224 3-8-10 **76** JasonHart 9 76
(John Quinn) *hld up: rdn over 2f out: sme hdwy over 1f out: nvr threatened* **16/1**
2451 **8** *nk* **Tartan Bute**[18] 2348 3-8-7 **73** AndrewMullen 2 73
(Mark Johnston) *hld up: rdn over 2f out: sme hdwy over 1f out: nvr threatened* **25/1**
22 **9** *5* **Sunglider (IRE)**[20] 2271 3-8-13 **79** PhillipMakin 13 71
(David O'Meara) *hld up: nvr threatened* **20/1**
3222 **10** *9* **Zeehan**[23] 2181 3-8-8 **74** PJMcDonald 6 51
(Clive Cox) *in tch: rdn 3f out: sn wknd* **14/1**
6-31 **11** *4* **Blakeney Point**[19] 2300 3-8-7 **73** JoeyHaynes 10 44
(Roger Charlton) *hld up in midfield: pushed along over 3f out: sn wknd* **9/1**
5-30 **12** *30* **Picture Painter (IRE)**[29] 1992 3-8-7 **73** JamesSullivan 5
(Jim Goldie) *midfield: wnt in snatches: rdn over 4f out: wknd over 3f out: eased* **66/1**
2m 38.82s (-3.18) **Going Correction** -0.35s/f (Firm) **12** Ran SP% **120.8**
Speed ratings (Par 103): **96,94,94,93,92 91,91,91,88,82 79,59**
CSF £71.11 CT £262.12 TOTE £12.90: £3.20, £1.90, £2.00; EX 90.40 Trifecta £433.30.
Owner St Albans Bloodstock Limited **Bred** St Albans Bloodstock Llp **Trained** Newmarket, Suffolk
■ Stewards' Enquiry : Joe Fanning two-day ban; used whip above the permitted level (19th-20th June)

FOCUS
A red-hot handicap run at what looked a strong gallop and the overall time was under standard, so this is strong 3yo handicap form. The winner was a big improvement.

2910 RACING UK DAY PASS JUST £10 H'CAP 7f 30y
4:00 (4:02) (Class 3) (0-90,92) 4-Y-O+ **£12,938** (£3,850; £1,924; £962) **Stalls** Low

Form RPR
3150 **1** **Kalk Bay (IRE)**[7] 2679 9-8-8 **82** (t) NathanEvans(5) 11 91
(Michael Easterby) *hld up in rr: rdn and gd hdwy on outer wl over 1f out: led 1f out: kpt on wl* **12/1**
3402 **2** *1 1/2* **Big Time (IRE)**[7] 2679 5-9-5 **88** (v) RoystonFfrench 2 91
(David Nicholls) *in tch: rdn over 2f out: kpt on fnl f: wnt 2nd 50yds out* **8/1**
50-2 **3** *3/4* **Alejandro (IRE)**[17] 2361 7-9-2 **85** DavidNolan 6 86
(David O'Meara) *trckd ldng pair: rdn over 2f out: swtchd lft ent fnl f: kpt on* **6/1**[3]
2-10 **4** *1 1/2* **Exchequer (IRE)**[35] 1856 5-9-7 **90** PatCosgrave 10 87
(David Brown) *led narrowly: hdd over 4f out: rdn to ld again over 2f out: hdd 1f out: no ex* **6/1**[3]
-441 **5** *2* **Mystic Miraaj**[14] 2491 4-8-11 **80** (b) JasonHart 1 72
(Tim Easterby) *dwlt: sn midfield: rdn over 2f out: no imp* **5/1**[2]
3-11 **6** *3/4* **Swift Approval (IRE)**[7] 2679 4-9-9 **92** (p) TomEaves 5 82
(Kevin Ryan) *in tch on inner: rdn over 2f out: no imp* **4/1**[1]
0-63 **7** *1* **Ralphy Boy (IRE)**[15] 2421 7-8-7 **76** PJMcDonald 8 63
(Alistair Whillans) *trckd ldng pair: rdn over 2f out: wknd fnl f* **14/1**
3256 **8** *1 1/4* **Burning Blaze**[14] 2491 6-8-7 **76** BenCurtis 12 59
(Brian Ellison) *pressed ldr: led over 4f out: rdn over 3f out: hdd over 2f out: wknd over 1f out* **25/1**
40-0 **9** *8* **Santefisio**[38] 1797 10-9-3 **86** (b) PhillipMakin 9 48
(Keith Dalgleish) *hld up: rdn 3f out: wknd over 1f out* **16/1**
0-50 **10** *2* **Redvers (IRE)**[29] 1990 8-8-13 **82** (p) BarryMcHugh 4 38
(Noel Wilson) *a towards rr* **33/1**
6-14 **11** *13* **Bahama Moon (IRE)**[42] 1643 4-9-3 **86** GrahamGibbons 3 7
(David Barron) *swtchd rt s: a in rr* **5/1**[2]
1m 25.0s (-4.00) **Going Correction** -0.35s/f (Firm) course record **11** Ran SP% **120.0**
Speed ratings (Par 107): **108,106,105,103,101 100,99,98,88,86 71**
CSF £106.80 CT £656.74 TOTE £16.50: £3.60, £1.60, £3.00; EX 148.50 Trifecta £2163.80.
Owner Linda Folwell, Steve Hull & David Swales **Bred** Wentworth Racing **Trained** Sheriff Hutton, N Yorks

FOCUS
Another competitive handicap run at a strong gallop and they smashed the course record here. The winner is rated back to his best.

2911 RACING UK NOW IN HD H'CAP 1m 4f 100y
4:55 (4:55) (Class 4) (0-80,77) 4-Y-O+ **£6,469** (£1,925; £962; £481) **Stalls** Low

Form RPR
41-6 **1** **Hillgrove Angel (IRE)**[17] 2362 4-8-13 **69** RoystonFfrench 3 78
(Iain Jardine) *in tch: rdn and hdwy over 2f out: led over 1f out: kpt on* **10/1**
-046 **2** *1/2* **Rhythmical**[11] 2556 4-9-7 **77** (b) JoeFanning 4 85
(Mark Johnston) *midfield: pushed along and hdwy 2f out: bmpd sltly appr fnl f: sn rcvrd to chse ldr: kpt on* **13/8**[1]
0-00 **3** *3/4* **Endless Credit (IRE)**[16] 2406 6-9-5 **75** PJMcDonald 2 82
(Micky Hammond) *led: rdn over 2f out: hdd over 1f out: plugged on* **16/1**
4-05 **4** *hd* **Skiddaw Valleys**[16] 2406 4-9-1 **71** BenCurtis 7 77
(Alan Swinbank) *hld up in tch: rdn and hdwy 2f out: edgd rt appr fnl f: kpt on same pce* **9/2**[3]
-462 **5** *2 1/2* **Medina Sidonia (IRE)**[8] 2663 4-8-12 **73** (p) RachelRichardson(5) 1 75
(Tim Easterby) *trckd ldr: rdn over 2f out: grad wknd fnl f* **5/2**[2]
400- **6** *2 3/4* **Hallingham**[15] 6820 6-8-9 **65** (v) LukeMorris 6 63
(Chris Gordon) *trckd ldr: pushed along over 4f out: rdn over 2f out: wknd fnl f* **14/1**
0-50 **7** *2 1/4* **Ronald Gee (IRE)**[9] 2618 9-8-6 **67** PhilDennis(5) 5 61
(Jim Goldie) *stdd s: hld up in rr: rdn over 3f out: nvr threatened* **20/1**
2m 45.06s (3.06) **Going Correction** -0.35s/f (Firm) **7** Ran SP% **111.3**
Speed ratings (Par 105): **75,74,74,74,72 70,69**
CSF £25.33 TOTE £13.60: £4.40, £1.10; EX 36.10 Trifecta £149.70.
Owner JAB **Bred** Carrigbeg Stud Co Ltd **Trained** Carruthertown, D'fries & G'way

FOCUS
A weak 0-80 handicap on paper with most of these coming here out of form, and the overall time was around 7 secs slower than the only other race run over this trip on the card.

2912 TOP ODDS FOR EURO2016 AT MACBETSPORTS.CO.UK APPRENTICE H'CAP 1m 6f
5:30 (5:30) (Class 5) (0-70,70) 4-Y-O+ **£3,234** (£962; £481; £240) **Stalls** Low

Form RPR
001- **1** **Impulsive American**[44] 6240 4-9-4 **67** (b) AdamMcNamara(5) 4 79+
(David Pipe) *hld up in tch: pushed along over 4f out: hdwy 3f out: rdn to ld appr fnl f: styd on wl* **11/10**[1]
6-53 **2** *3 3/4* **Aldreth**[29] 2018 5-9-6 **67** NathanEvans(3) 2 74
(Michael Easterby) *trckd ldr: rdn to ld over 3f out: hdd appr fnl f: kpt on but sn no ch w wnr* **11/4**[2]
03/2 **3** *2 1/2* **Frederic**[28] 2051 5-9-9 **70** CallumShepherd(3) 3 73
(Micky Hammond) *dwlt: sn trckd ldr: rdn over 3f out: plugged on* **5/1**[3]
-000 **4** *shd* **Love Marmalade (IRE)**[17] 2362 6-9-7 **70** RowanScott(5) 1 73
(Alistair Whillans) *led: rdn whn hdd over 2f out: no ex fnl f* **8/1**
433- **5** *8* **Slipper Satin (IRE)**[226] 6877 6-9-6 **67** (t) RachelRichardson(3) 5 59
(Simon West) *hld up: hdwy to trck ldr over 7f out: rdn 3f out: wknd over 1f out* **12/1**
0506 **6** *nk* **New Colours**[8] 2656 5-8-4 **51** oh1 (p) PhilDennis(3) 6 42
(Linda Perratt) *in tch: rdn 3f out: wknd over 1f out* **33/1**
3m 0.98s (-4.32) **Going Correction** -0.35s/f (Firm) **6** Ran SP% **112.7**
Speed ratings (Par 103): **98,95,94,94,89 89**
CSF £4.36 TOTE £1.80: £1.10, £2.20; EX 5.20 Trifecta £7.30.
Owner Mrs Jo Tracey **Bred** David Brocklehurst **Trained** Nicholashayne, Devon

FOCUS
A modest staying event and the well-backed favourite, who won over hurdles at this track over the winter, handled the much quicker conditions to justify the support. He's rated a bit higher for this win than his Flat form would suggest.
T/Plt: £152.10 to a £1 stake. Pool: £63,737.90 - 305.82 winning tickets. T/Qpdt: £43.30 to a £1 stake. Pool: £3,575.06 - 60.98 winning tickets. **Andrew Sheret**

2617 NEWCASTLE (A.W) (L-H)
Saturday, June 4

OFFICIAL GOING: Tapeta: standard
Wind: Breezy, half against Weather: Fine, dry

2913 NESTLE/EBF STALLIONS NOVICE STKS 6f (Tp)
6:10 (6:13) (Class 5) 2-Y-O **£3,881** (£1,155; £577; £288) **Stalls** Centre

Form RPR
4 **1** **White Royale (USA)**[38] 1783 2-8-11 0 KeaganLatham 12 75
(Kevin Ryan) *mde all: pushed along 2f out: styd on strly fnl f* **16/1**
33 **2** *1* **Rapid Rise (IRE)**[22] 2196 2-9-2 0 PatCosgrave 5 77
(David Brown) *trckd wnr: effrt and rdn over 2f out: kpt on same pce last 100yds* **12/1**
34 **3** *1/2* **Another Angel (IRE)**[35] 1850 2-9-2 0 PaulMulrennan 10 76
(Michael Dods) *t.k.h: in tch: stdy hdwy over 2f out: effrt and plld out over 1f out: pushed along and kpt on fnl f* **7/2**[2]
02 **4** *4* **Tawny Port**[19] 2301 2-9-2 0 TomEaves 3 64
(James Given) *prom: drvn and edgd lft over 2f out: outpcd fnl f* **11/1**
5 *1 1/4* **Black Isle Boy (IRE)** 2-8-11 0 JoshDoyle(5) 8 60+
(David O'Meara) *in tch: rdn whn hung lft to far rail over 2f out: no imp fr over 1f out* **10/1**[3]
1 **6** *hd* **Tailor's Row (USA)**[9] 2604 2-9-9 0 FrannyNorton 7 66
(Mark Johnston) *trckd ldrs: drvn along over 2f out: checked over 1f out: wknd fnl f* **5/4**[1]
04 **7** *nk* **Global Revival (IRE)**[12] 2535 2-9-2 0 CamHardie 2 58+
(Ed Dunlop) *bhd: pushed along 1/2-way: hdwy over 1f out: kpt on: nvr nr to chal* **16/1**
4 **8** *3 3/4* **Vatican Hill (IRE)**[15] 2417 2-9-2 0 TonyHamilton 4 47
(Richard Fahey) *midfield: rdn whn carried lft over 2f out: sn outpcd: btn fnl f* **25/1**
9 *nse* **Foxy Boy** 2-9-2 0 ConnorBeasley 1 47+
(Michael Dods) *s.i.s: rn green in rr: sme hdwy over 1f out: nvr able to chal* **33/1**
6 **10** *shd* **Geego**[20] 2264 2-9-2 0 PatrickMathers 11 47
(Richard Fahey) *bhd: pushed along 1/2-way: shortlived effrt wl over 1f out: sn btn* **50/1**
11 *3/4* **Urban Spirit (IRE)** 2-9-2 0 JackGarritty 14 44
(Jedd O'Keeffe) *hld up: drvn and outpcd over 2f out: sn wknd* **50/1**
12 *7* **Operational** 2-9-2 0 JamesSullivan 9 23
(Jedd O'Keeffe) *bhd: drvn and struggling over 3f out: sn btn* **40/1**
13 *4 1/2* **Generous Times** 2-8-11 0 AndrewMullen 6
(Chris Grant) *bhd: struggling over 3f out: nvr on terms* **100/1**
1m 12.56s (0.06) **Going Correction** +0.05s/f (Slow) **13** Ran SP% **117.7**
Speed ratings (Par 93): **101,99,99,93,92 91,91,86,86,86 85,75,69**
CSF £181.89 TOTE £17.50: £3.10, £2.20, £1.70; EX 310.40 Trifecta £1482.50 Part won..
Owner Highbank Stud **Bred** High Bank Syndicate **Trained** Hambleton, N Yorks

FOCUS
There will be no speed figures at this track until there is sufficient data to calculate median times. An interesting novices' event but the placed horses have already been beaten twice in maidens and the warm favourite proved disappointing, so it's hard to get too excited about the form. Nothing really got into it from off the pace.

2914 PARKLANDS GOLF CLUB MAIDEN STKS 1m 2f 42y (Tp)
6:40 (6:41) (Class 5) 3-Y-O+ **£3,881** (£1,155; £577; £288) **Stalls** High

Form RPR
4 **1** **Huge Future**[21] 2248 3-8-11 0 KevinStott[(3)] 9 89+
(Saeed bin Suroor) *hld up on outside: smooth hdwy 3f out: shkn up to ld appr fnl f: pushed out: comf* **4/5**[1]
3 **2** *2* **Gibbs Hill (GER)**[18] 2327 3-9-0 0 PaulMulrennan 3 82
(Roger Varian) *chsd ldr: smooth hdwy to ld over 2f out: rdn and hdd appr fnl f: kpt on same pce* **7/2**[2]
3 *3 1/4* **Kensington Star** 3-9-0 0 (v[1]) PatCosgrave 4 75
(Simon Crisford) *s.s: bhd: reminders and green over 4f out: hdwy to chse ldrs whn edgd lft over 1f out: kpt on same pce fnl f* **5/1**[3]
02 **4** *6* **Corroyer (IRE)**[37] 1815 3-9-0 0 CamHardie 1 63
(John Quinn) *trckd ldrs: rdn along over 1f out: outpcd fnl f* **10/1**
0 **5** *10* **Rockery (IRE)**[108] 603 3-8-9 0 FrannyNorton 5 38
(Ed Dunlop) *hld up towards rr: pushed along over 2f out: sn outpcd: no imp fr over 1f out* **20/1**
0 **6** *1 3/4* **Brother Khee**[19] 2307 5-9-10 0 (vt) MissEmmaSayer[(3)] 2 41
(Wilf Storey) *t.k.h early: trckd ldrs tl wknd wl over 1f out* **100/1**
7 *1* **Social Media** 3-8-9 0 TomEaves 7 33
(Ed Dunlop) *hld up on ins: drvn along over 2f out: sn n.d: btn over 1f out* **9/1**
0 **8** *2 1/2* **Percy's Endeavour**[18] 2327 3-8-9 0 JasonHart 8 28
(Mark Walford) *led tl rdn and hdd over 2f out: wknd wl over 1f out* **80/1**
9 *9* **Adrakhan (FR)**[17] 5-9-6 0 HollieDoyle[(7)] 6 16
(Wilf Storey) *bhd: struggling over 3f out: sn btn* **50/1**

2m 10.28s (-0.12) **Going Correction** +0.075s/f (Slow)
WFA 3 from 5yo 13lb **9** Ran SP% **122.5**
Speed ratings (Par 103): **103,101,98,94,86 84,83,81,74**
CSF £4.14 TOTE £1.70: £1.10, £1.30, £1.80; EX 4.70 Trifecta £12.80.
Owner Godolphin **Bred** W And R Barnett Ltd **Trained** Newmarket, Suffolk

FOCUS
This might not be bad maiden form as the winner looks potentially quite smart and the placed horses look well up to winning a maiden. They were in a different league to the others. The winner is sure to do much better than the bare form.

2915 VELUX WHITE WINDOW H'CAP 1m 2f 42y (Tp)
7:10 (7:11) (Class 6) (0-65,64) 4-Y-O+ **£3,234** (£962; £481; £240) **Stalls** High

Form RPR
5020 **1** **Yorkindred Spirit**[17] 2379 4-9-7 **64** (v) FrannyNorton 4 75+
(Mark Johnston) *hld up: smooth hdwy on outside over 2f out: shkn up to ld over 1f out: pushed clr: readily* **11/1**
53-5 **2** *3 1/2* **Exclusive Diamond**[8] 2661 4-8-7 **55** JoshDoyle[(5)] 11 59
(David O'Meara) *hld up: rdn and hdwy over 2f out: chsd (clr) wnr ins fnl f: kpt on: no imp* **9/2**[2]
0-35 **3** *hd* **Cool Music (IRE)**[69] 1114 6-8-13 **56** PatCosgrave 6 60
(Antony Brittain) *hld up in midfield: effrt and rdn whn n.m.r briefly 2f out: kpt on fnl f: nt pce to chal* **8/1**
254 **4** *2* **Yulong Xiongba (IRE)**[11] 2555 4-9-7 **64** ConnorBeasley 8 64
(Julie Camacho) *led at ordinary gallop: hdd 3f out: rallied and ev ch over 1f out: outpcd and lost two pls ins fnl f* **4/1**[1]
040 **5** *1/2* **Outlaw Torn (IRE)**[11] 2566 7-8-11 **57** (e) PhilipPrince[(3)] 9 56
(Richard Guest) *t.k.h early: trckd ldr: led 3f out to over 1f out: rdn and outpcd fnl f* **11/1**
20-5 **6** *1* **Life Knowledge (IRE)**[18] 2330 4-9-1 **58** DavidNolan 5 55
(Patrick Holmes) *trckd ldrs: effrt and drvn along wl over 1f out: outpcd fnl f* **8/1**
4546 **7** *3/4* **Lean On Pete (IRE)**[9] 2618 7-9-5 **62** (e) GrahamGibbons 3 58
(Ollie Pears) *t.k.h: hld up in midfield: effrt against far rail wl over 1f out: no ex and eased last 100yds* **7/1**[3]
51-0 **8** *1/2* **Glasgon**[18] 2329 6-9-3 **60** JackGarritty 1 55
(Ray Craggs) *in tch: rdn and outpcd over 2f out: sme late hdwy: nvr rchd ldrs* **16/1**
0 **9** *3/4* **Annigoni (IRE)**[13] 2507 4-8-13 **56** JamesSullivan 14 49
(Ruth Carr) *prom: drvn along over 2f out: wknd fnl f* **14/1**
0-65 **10** *1 1/2* **Arms Around Me (IRE)**[15] 2441 4-9-7 **64** TomEaves 13 54
(James Given) *hld up: rdn along 3f out: no imp fr 2f out* **16/1**
42-0 **11** *6* **Gabrial's Hope (FR)**[18] 2343 7-9-0 **57** TonyHamilton 10 36
(Tracy Waggott) *t.k.h: hld up on ins: struggling over 2f out: sn btn* **33/1**
60-0 **12** *nk* **Bling King**[9] 2618 7-9-3 **60** (p) PaulMulrennan 12 38
(Geoffrey Harker) *s.i.s: hld up: struggling over 2f out: sn btn* **16/1**
00-6 **13** *14* **Stradater (IRE)**[26] 2089 7-9-0 **57** JasonHart 7 9
(Sandy Thomson) *s.i.s: bhd: struggling over 3f out: sn lost tch* **33/1**

2m 11.18s (0.78) **Going Correction** +0.075s/f (Slow) **13** Ran SP% **119.8**
Speed ratings (Par 101): **99,96,96,94,94 93,92,92,91,90 85,85,74**
CSF £60.00 CT £425.71 TOTE £10.90: £3.30, £2.50, £3.00; EX 58.30 Trifecta £956.40.
Owner Paul Robert York **Bred** Ed's Stud Ltd **Trained** Middleham Moor, N Yorks

FOCUS
Weak handicap form in truth, with most of these coming with risks attached. The winner was impressive but she's fairly exposed and it's unlikely she's as far ahead of her mark as this run suggests.

2916 J.T.DOVE BUILDING MATERIALS H'CAP 2m 56y (Tp)
7:40 (7:41) (Class 6) (0-65,65) 4-Y-O+ **£3,234** (£962; £481; £240) **Stalls** Low

Form RPR
0-40 **1** **Byronegetonefree**[2] 2813 5-8-5 **46** oh1 PatrickMathers 6 53
(Stuart Coltherd) *in tch: hdwy to ld over 3f out: rdn over 1f out: kpt on strly fnl f* **12/1**
1-61 **2** *2 1/4* **Nonagon**[34] 1881 5-9-0 **62** (t) HollieDoyle[(7)] 10 66
(Wilf Storey) *hld up: stdy hdwy on outside to chse wnr over 2f out: rdn and hung lft over 1f out: kpt on same pce fnl f* **5/1**[2]
26- **3** *1* **Politbureau**[283] 5740 9-9-7 **62** PJMcDonald 11 65
(Micky Hammond) *hld up: rdn over 2f out: hdwy over 1f out: kpt on fnl f: nt pce to chal* **14/1**
346- **4** *3/4* **Salford Dream**[341] 3706 7-8-8 **49** PaulMulrennan 3 51
(Pauline Robson) *prom on ins: drvn and outpcd over 2f out: rallied ins fnl f: no imp* **7/1**
25-5 **5** *1/2* **Bowdler's Magic**[5] 2746 9-9-10 **65** DavidNolan 1 67
(David Thompson) *hld up on ins: drvn along over 2f out: effrt over 1f out: sn no imp* **6/1**[3]
4050 **6** *1 1/4* **Yorkshireman (IRE)**[32] 1955 6-8-5 **46** oh1 (b) FrannyNorton 4 46
(Lynn Siddall) *hld up: rdn along over 2f out: kpt on fnl f: nt pce to chal* **10/1**
5504 **7** *hd* **Dukes Den**[13] 2501 5-8-11 **52** (p) GrahamGibbons 13 54
(Mark Usher) *in tch: hdwy to chse wnr briefly over 2f out: edgd lft and one pce whn n.m.r appr fnl f: eased whn hld last 100yds* **5/1**[2]
6- **8** *15* **Papagayo (IRE)**[307] 4913 4-9-2 **58** TomEaves 2 40
(Barry Murtagh) *t.k.h: hld up: rdn over 2f out: sn wknd* **20/1**
-0P3 **9** *20* **Apollo Eleven (IRE)**[26] 2105 7-9-8 **63** (p) AndrewMullen 7 21
(Michael Appleby) *cl up: led over 4f out to over 3f out: rdn and wknd over 2f out: t.o* **7/2**[1]
500- **10** *36* **Bygones For Coins (IRE)**[11] 2951 8-8-5 **46** oh1 (b[1]) ConnorBeasley 9
(Kenny Johnson) *led to over 4f out: sn lost pl and struggling: t.o* **40/1**
020- **11** *dist* **Goldan Jess (IRE)**[201] 7871 12-9-8 **63** PaddyAspell 5
(Philip Kirby) *in tch on outside: lost pl bef 1/2-way: sn lost tch: virtually p.u fnl 4f* **20/1**

3m 33.69s (-1.51) **Going Correction** +0.075s/f (Slow)
WFA 4 from 5yo+ 1lb **11** Ran SP% **117.8**
Speed ratings (Par 101): **106,104,104,104,103 103,103,95,85,67**
CSF £69.43 CT £864.10 TOTE £15.80: £4.20, £2.70, £2.20; EX 108.40 Trifecta £3163.00 Part won..
Owner Coltherd Conchar **Bred** Mrs A M Sturges **Trained** Selkirk, Borders
■ Stewards' Enquiry : Hollie Doyle three-day ban; careless riding (27th-29th June)

FOCUS
Low-grade stuff and, given the winner was a longstanding maiden who hadn't ever even been placed previously, it's hard to get excited about this form.

2917 LRB PLUMBING & HEATING H'CAP 1m 5y (Tp)
8:10 (8:14) (Class 4) (0-85,85) 3-Y-O+ **£6,145** (£1,828; £913; £456) **Stalls** Centre

Form RPR
1-10 **1** **Replenish (FR)**[24] 2161 3-9-2 **84** TonyHamilton 14 92+
(James Fanshawe) *hld up: shkn up over 2f out: hdwy to ld appr fnl f: edgd lft last 100yds: kpt on wl* **11/4**[1]
5-16 **2** *1 1/4* **Push Me (IRE)**[18] 2347 9-9-6 **77** RoystonFfrench 6 85
(Iain Jardine) *hld up: hdwy far side 2f out: chsd wnr ins fnl f: kpt on* **8/1**
5-32 **3** *2 1/4* **Hard To Handel**[9] 2620 4-10-0 **85** DavidNolan 9 88
(David O'Meara) *hld up in tch: shkn up over 2f out: effrt and chsd ldrs ins fnl f: r.o* **7/2**[2]
2533 **4** *1/2* **Sands Chorus**[9] 2620 4-9-6 **77** TomEaves 5 79
(James Given) *cl up: drvn along over 2f out: kpt on same pce fnl f* **7/1**[3]
-0U0 **5** *1 3/4* **Musaaid (IRE)**[32] 1954 4-8-13 **75** NathanEvans[(5)] 8 73
(Michael Easterby) *t.k.h early: led tl rdn and hdd appr fnl f: sn outpcd* **33/1**
610 **6** *3/4* **Dusky Dawn**[22] 2223 4-9-7 **78** BenCurtis 12 74
(Alan Swinbank) *hld up: pushed along and hdwy over 2f out: kpt on fnl f: no imp* **25/1**
1-04 **7** *1 1/4* **Buccaneers Vault (IRE)**[18] 2345 4-9-8 **79** PaulMulrennan 3 72
(Michael Dods) *hld up: shkn up and hdwy over 1f out: kpt on fnl f: nt pce to chal* **10/1**
2-00 **8** *1 3/4* **Border Bandit (USA)**[25] 2121 8-9-1 **72** (p) BarryMcHugh 1 61
(Tracy Waggott) *in tch: drvn along over 2f out: wknd over 1f out* **66/1**
52-0 **9** *1* **Mustaqqil (IRE)**[30] 1978 4-9-6 **80** ShelleyBirkett[(3)] 10 67
(David O'Meara) *hld up: rdn over 2f out: sme hdwy over 1f out: nvr rchd ldrs* **25/1**
0330 **10** *nk* **Gurkha Friend**[18] 2331 4-9-7 **78** JackGarritty 11 64
(Karen McLintock) *hld up in midfield: pushed along whn nt clr run over 2f out: sn rdn and outpcd* **10/1**
4013 **11** *2 1/2* **Viewpoint (IRE)**[22] 2214 7-10-0 **85** AndrewMullen 13 65
(Michael Appleby) *in tch: drvn along over 2f out: sn wknd* **10/1**
/16- **12** *7* **Symbolic Star (IRE)**[406] 1650 4-9-4 **80** PhilDennis[(5)] 2 44
(Barry Murtagh) *in tch: drvn along over 2f out: wknd wl over 1f out* **100/1**
-300 **13** *6* **Heraldic (USA)**[14] 2466 3-9-1 **83** FrannyNorton 7 30
(Mark Johnston) *cl up tl rdn and lost pl over 2f out: sn struggling* **12/1**

1m 38.28s (-0.32) **Going Correction** +0.05s/f (Slow)
WFA 3 from 4yo+ 11lb **13** Ran SP% **120.6**
Speed ratings (Par 105): **103,101,99,99,97 96,95,93,92,92 89,82,76**
CSF £24.47 CT £83.89 TOTE £3.60: £1.80, £3.30, £1.80; EX 31.60 Trifecta £73.80.
Owner Mac & Friends **Bred** S A Franklin Finance **Trained** Newmarket, Suffolk

FOCUS
A competitive 0-85 handicap won by a progressive 3yo, with the front two nicely clear. The form fits.

2918 NORTHUMBERLAND GOLF COURSE H'CAP 7f 14y (Tp)
8:40 (8:42) (Class 5) (0-70,70) 4-Y-O+ **£3,881** (£1,155; £577; £288) **Stalls** Centre

Form RPR
400 **1** **Robero**[4] 2773 4-9-6 **69** BenCurtis 8 78+
(Brian Ellison) *in tch: smooth hdwy to ld over 2f out: rdn over 1f out: kpt on wl fnl f* **7/2**[1]
0664 **2** *3/4* **Cabal**[8] 2655 9-9-2 **65** (v) FrannyNorton 5 71
(Geoffrey Harker) *hld up: effrt and hdwy wl over 1f out: sn rdn: wnt 2nd wl ins fnl f: kpt on* **16/1**
5642 **3** *hd* **Depth Charge (IRE)**[14] 2491 4-9-7 **70** (vt) TonyHamilton 2 75
(Kristin Stubbs) *hld up in midfield: hdwy to chse wnr over 1f out: sn rdn: lost 2nd and no ex wl ins fnl f* **17/2**
-004 **4** *2 1/4* **Tanawar (IRE)**[12] 2529 6-9-2 **65** (b) JamesSullivan 4 64
(Ruth Carr) *hld up: stdy hdwy over 2f out: rdn over 1f out: kpt on same pce ins fnl f* **25/1**
1663 **5** *1 3/4* **Misu Pete**[17] 2379 4-8-13 **62** GrahamGibbons 10 57
(Mark Usher) *in tch: effrt and drvn along 2f out: no imp fnl f* **13/2**[3]
3251 **6** *hd* **Foie Gras**[37] 1805 6-9-3 **66** (p) ConnorBeasley 7 60
(Chris Dwyer) *s.i.s: hld up: rdn over 2f out: kpt on fnl f: nt pce to chal* **10/1**
5302 **7** *1 1/4* **Grey Destiny**[18] 2330 6-8-11 **60** PJMcDonald 6 51
(Antony Brittain) *s.i.s: hld up: rdn over 2f out: no imp fr over 1f out* **8/1**
3300 **8** *4* **Royal Holiday (IRE)**[22] 2198 9-9-7 **70** (p) SamJames 1 50
(Marjorie Fife) *led to over 2f out: rdn and wknd over 1f out* **20/1**
050- **9** *1 1/4* **One Man Army**[309] 4838 4-9-3 **66** PaulMulrennan 12 43
(Julia Brooke) *hld up: rdn over 2f out: no imp over 1f out* **33/1**
6021 **10** *1/2* **Mr Cool Cash**[7] 2673 4-9-2 **68** PhilipPrince[(3)] 13 51
(Richard Guest) *prom: hdwy to dispute 2nd pl briefly over 1f out: wknd ins fnl f: eased* **9/2**[2]
-036 **11** *1/2* **Danot (IRE)**[34] 1884 4-9-0 **68** PhilDennis[(5)] 11 42
(Jedd O'Keeffe) *cl up: rdn and ev ch over 2f out: wknd over 1f out* **12/1**
-120 **12** *5* **Afkar (IRE)**[111] 581 8-9-6 **69** (p) JasonHart 9 29
(Mandy Rowland) *trckd ldrs: rdn and ev ch over 2f out: wknd over 1f out* **33/1**

233- **13** *nse* **Charava (IRE)**[235] 7189 4-9-1 **64** ow2.............................. DavidNolan 14 24
(Patrick Holmes) *hld up towards rr: rdn and hung lft over 2f out: wknd wl over 1f out* **16/1**

000- **14** *16* **Lothair (IRE)**[232] 7256 7-8-13 **65**.............................. JacobButterfield(3) 3
(Alan Swinbank) *t.k.h and sddle sn slipped forward: cl up tl lost pl qckly over 2f out: sn lost tch* **66/1**

1m 25.89s (-0.31) **Going Correction** +0.05s/f (Slow) **14** Ran SP% **119.9**
Speed ratings (Par 103): **103,102,101,99,97 97,95,91,89,89 88,82,82,64**
CSF £58.11 CT £465.10 TOTE £4.40: £2.00, £4.10, £3.10; EX 69.00 Trifecta £452.70.
Owner Alan Zheng **Bred** Mrs P C Burton & R J Lampard **Trained** Norton, N Yorks

FOCUS
The market got this ordinary handicap spot on as \bRobero\p was well-backed to land his first handicap. He's rated in line with a better view of his AW form.

2919 PARKLANDS MINI GOLF & DRIVING RANGE H'CAP 5f (Tp)
9:10 (9:12) (Class 6) (0-65,67) 3-Y-O+ **£3,234** (£962; £481; £240) **Stalls** Centre

Form RPR

3411 **1** **Roy's Legacy**[2] 2808 7-9-4 **62**.................................. CharlieBennett(7) 12 71
(Shaun Harris) *prom: pushed along and hdwy to ld over 1f out: rdn and hld on wl fnl f* **13/2**[2]

4-46 **2** *½* **Whispering Soul (IRE)**[19] 2302 3-8-4 **48**....................(b) PJMcDonald 3 52
(Ann Duffield) *t.k.h: in tch: stdy hdwy over 2f out: rdn over 1f out: chsd wnr ins fnl f: clsng at fin* **14/1**

30-0 **3** *1* **Indastar**[15] 2423 6-9-2 **53**.. TomEaves 14 57
(Michael Herrington) *taken early to post: led to over 1f out: rallied: lost 2nd and no ex ins fnl f* **25/1**

532 **4** *hd* **Orient Class**[9] 2622 5-9-9 **67**................................. AdamMcNamara(7) 2 70+
(Paul Midgley) *prom: effrt and rdn on far side over 1f out: kpt on same pce ins fnl f* **3/1**[1]

3414 **5** *nk* **Windforpower (IRE)**[9] 2622 6-9-13 **64**.......................(p) BarryMcHugh 5 66
(Tracy Waggott) *prom: drvn along over 2f out: rallied: kpt on same pce fnl f* **16/1**

00-0 **6** *2½* **Sea Of Green**[17] 2359 4-9-4 **55**...................................... PaulMulrennan 8 48
(Jim Goldie) *hld up: pushed along and hdwy 2f out: rdn and no imp fnl f* **18/1**

4101 **7** *nse* **Captain Scooby**[12] 2524 10-9-4 **55**.................................(b) JasonHart 6 48
(Richard Guest) *bhd and sn pushed along: hdwy fnl f: kpt on: nvr able to chal* **10/1**[3]

0-62 **8** *¾* **Lorimer's Lot (IRE)**[7] 2676 5-8-11 **53**............... RachelRichardson(5) 10 43
(Mark Walford) *hld up towards rr: rdn along 1/2-way: no imp fr over 1f out* **20/1**

14-0 **9** *½* **Sophistica (IRE)**[10] 2571 3-9-1 **59**.............................. RoystonFfrench 9 44
(Iain Jardine) *s.i.s: hld up: pushed along wl over 1f out: sn no imp* **22/1**

0-20 **10** *2* **Whipphound**[18] 2342 8-9-6 **57**....................................... JamesSullivan 11 38
(Ruth Carr) *towards rr: pushed along 1/2-way: sn no imp* **20/1**

1-32 **11** *½* **Anieres Boy**[15] 2418 4-9-9 **60**...................................... GrahamGibbons 7 39
(Michael Easterby) *cl up: rdn along 1/2-way: wknd over 1f out* **3/1**[1]

4-04 **12** *3* **Emerald Bay**[19] 2302 3-9-2 **60**.. RaulDaSilva 4 25
(Ivan Furtado) *cl up: drvn along over 2f out: wknd wl over 1f out* **11/1**

59.62s (0.12) **Going Correction** +0.05s/f (Slow)
WFA 3 from 4yo+ 7lb **12** Ran SP% **116.3**
Speed ratings (Par 101): **101,100,98,98,97 93,93,92,91,88 87,82**
CSF £85.66 CT £2154.35 TOTE £8.50: £2.20, £4.80, £3.90; EX 115.20 Trifecta £2924.00.
Owner S Mohammed, S Rowley & S Harris **Bred** A Christou **Trained** Carburton, Notts
■ Mayfield Girl was withdrawn. Price at time of withdrawal 22-1. Rule 4 does not apply.

FOCUS
A modest sprint but the winner, although fully exposed, came here in grand form and was able to complete the hat-trick.
T/Plt: £115.60 to a £1 stake. Pool: £50,642.64 - 319.60 winning tickets. T/Qpdt: £45.50 to a £1 stake. Pool: £4,959.66 - 80.60 winning tickets. **Richard Young**

2920 - 2922a (Foreign Racing) - See Raceform Interactive

2508 CURRAGH (R-H)
Saturday, June 4

OFFICIAL GOING: Good to firm (watered)

2923a TRM BALLYOGAN STKS (GROUP 3) (F&M) 6f
6:00 (6:00) 3-Y-O+

£27,330 (£8,801; £4,169; £1,852; £926; £463)

RPR

1 **Divine (IRE)**[28] 2042 5-9-6 100....................................... RonanWhelan 6 115
(Mick Channon) *racd in mid-div: 5th at 1/2-way: qcknd wl between horses to ld appr fnl f and sn clr: styd on wl* **12/1**

2 *3½* **Fort Del Oro (IRE)**[14] 2495 4-9-6 107....................................... BillyLee 4 104
(Edward Lynam, Ire) *hld up: 7th at 1/2-way: swtchd rt over 1f out into 3rd 1f out: kpt on wl into 2nd fnl 100yds: nt trble wnr* **11/4**[1]

3 *½* **Only Mine (IRE)**[6] 2719 3-9-1 107....................................... GaryCarroll 8 104
(Joseph G Murphy, Ire) *sn led: rdn over 2f out: hdd appr fnl f and sn no match for wnr: kpt on same pce and dropped to 3rd fnl 100yds* **7/2**[2]

4 *½* **Diamond Fields (IRE)**[20] 2272 3-8-12 96..................... WayneLordan 1 99+
(T Stack, Ire) *racd towards rr: pushed along bef 1/2-way: no imp in 8th 2f out: kpt on wl ins fnl f into 4th cl home: nrst fin* **16/1**

5 *2* **Marsha (IRE)**[21] 2251 3-8-12 100.............................. DeclanMcDonogh 7 93
(Sir Mark Prescott Bt) *t.k.h early to chse ldrs in 3rd: clsr to press ldrs under 2f out: nt qckn appr fnl f: sn one pce* **4/1**[3]

6 *2* **Fine Blend (IRE)**[23] 2192 3-8-12 98.................................. ChrisHayes 2 86
(William Muir) *racd in mid-div towards outer: 6th at 1/2-way: rdn over 2f out to take clsr order: nt qckn ins fnl f: wknd* **25/1**

7 *½* **Byzantium**[28] 2042 4-9-6 100... RobbieDowney 5 87
(Edward Lynam, Ire) *chsd ldrs in 4th: trckd ldrs 2f out: rdn and nt qckn appr fnl f: sn no ex* **40/1**

8 *1¾* **Ainippe (IRE)**[14] 2497 4-9-9 104.................................. ColinKeane 9 84
(G M Lyons, Ire) *racd in rr: no imp and detached 2f out: kpt on ins fnl f: nvr a threat* **9/2**

9 *3¾* **Most Beautiful**[20] 2272 3-8-12 100.................................(b[1]) ConnorKing 3 67
(David Wachman, Ire) *sn trckd ldr in 2nd: pressed ldr over 2f out: sn rdn and wknd qckly over 1f out: eased clsng stages* **10/1**

1m 12.21s (-3.29) **Going Correction** -0.25s/f (Firm)
WFA 3 from 4yo+ 8lb **9** Ran SP% **116.0**
Speed ratings: **111,106,105,105,102 99,99,96,91**
CSF £45.38 TOTE £13.20: £4.00, £1.30, £1.40; DF 44.70 Trifecta £265.90.
Owner M Al-Qatami & K M Al-Mudhaf **Bred** Yeomanstown Stud **Trained** West Ilsley, Berks

FOCUS
This was the second running of this Group 3 at the Curragh. It used to take place at Leopardstown prior to that. A reasonably competitive renewal of the race with seven of the nine runners rated 100 or higher. The pace was extremely generous throughout and it suited closers. The winner sprinted clear once finding daylight.

2924a TRI EQUESTRIAN SILVER STKS (LISTED RACE) 1m 2f
6:30 (6:30) 3-Y-O+

£20,389 (£6,566; £3,110; £1,382; £691; £345)

RPR

1 **Portage (IRE)**[252] 6755 4-9-9 100....................................... ShaneFoley 2 102
(M Halford, Ire) *chsd ldrs in 3rd: niggled along 3f out: rdn to press ldr in 2nd under 2f out: led appr fnl f and pushed clr: kpt on wl* **7/4**[1]

2 *1* **Chemical Charge (IRE)**[567] 7798 4-9-9 0........................... ColinKeane 1 100+
(G M Lyons, Ire) *hld up in 4th: pushed along 3f out: no imp 2f out in 5th: kpt on wl ins fnl f into 2nd clsng stages: nrst fin* **3/1**[3]

3 *2¼* **Sir Isaac Newton**[47] 1536 4-9-9 106.......................... EmmetMcNamara 3 96+
(A P O'Brien, Ire) *bit slowly away and settled towards rr: pushed along in 4th 2f out: chsd clr ldr ins fnl f: no imp and dropped to 3rd fnl 100yds* **5/2**[2]

4 *4½* **General Macarthur (USA)**[43] 1615 3-8-10 91..........(t) MichaelHussey 6 86
(A P O'Brien, Ire) *led: qcknd 3f out: strly pressed under 2f out: hdd appr fnl f: sn no ex and wknd ins fnl f* **14/1**

5 *hd* **St Gallen (IRE)**[18] 2350 3-8-10 85.............................. NGMcCullagh 4 85
(John Joseph Murphy, Ire) *sn in rr: pushed along 3f out: no imp under 2f out: kpt on one pce fnl f* **10/1**

6 *½* **Duchess Andorra (IRE)**[6] 2721 5-9-4 86.......................(p) ConnorKing 5 80
(J P Murtagh, Ire) *trckd ldr in 2nd: rdn and nt qckn 2f out: wknd appr fnl f* **12/1**

2m 8.25s (-1.05) **Going Correction** +0.025s/f (Good)
WFA 3 from 4yo+ 13lb **6** Ran SP% **113.4**
Speed ratings: **105,104,102,98,98 98**
CSF £7.46 TOTE £2.20: £1.10, £1.70; DF 6.90 Trifecta £14.60.
Owner Godolphin **Bred** Barbara Prendergast **Trained** Doneany, Co Kildare

FOCUS
A small field but the market spoke loud and clear. The winner was the subject of strong support and the original favourite, \bSir Issac Newton\p drifted all the way out to 5-2. The gallop was generous throughout and the winner was value for more than the winning margin.

2925 - 2926a (Foreign Racing) - See Raceform Interactive

2316 DEAUVILLE (R-H)
Saturday, June 4

OFFICIAL GOING: Turf: soft

2927a PRIX DU PALAIS-ROYAL (GROUP 3) (3YO+) (STRAIGHT) (TURF) 7f
2:45 (12:00) 3-Y-O+ **£29,411** (£11,764; £8,823; £5,882; £2,941)

RPR

1 **Attendu (FR)**[20] 2283 3-8-10 0....................................... MaximeGuyon 5 113+
(C Laffon-Parias, France) *settled in 3rd: angled out and rdn appr fnl 1 1/2f: chal outside two rivals wl over 1f out: led ins fnl f: r.o u.p: asserted last 75yds* **13/2**[3]

2 *2* **Esoterique (IRE)**[174] 8218 6-9-7 0...................... Pierre-CharlesBoudot 1 112
(A Fabre, France) *trckd ldr: angled out to chal between horses wl over 1f out: led narrowly 1f out: sn hdd and kpt on at same pce under driving: wl hld fnl 75yds* **8/11**[1]

3 *3* **Territories (IRE)**[231] 7280 4-9-11 0......................... VincentCheminaud 3 108+
(A Fabre, France) *t.k.h: hld up in rr: clsd in 4th and rdn 1f out: styd on at same pce fnl f: nt pce to trble front two* **3/1**[2]

4 *1½* **Dhevanafushi**[26] 2117 3-8-8 0....................................... FabriceVeron 4 93
(H-A Pantall, France) *hld up in fnl pair: scrubbed along appr 2f out: sn rdn and no real imp appr fnl f: kpt on at same pce: nvr in contention* **14/1**

5 *½* **Love Spirit**[39] 1769 6-9-4 0.. OlivierPeslier 2 96
(J Baudron, France) *led at a decent gallop: rdn 1 1/2f out: hdd 1f out and no ex: grad dropped away* **13/2**[3]

1m 26.65s (-1.65)
WFA 3 from 4yo+ 10lb **5** Ran SP% **116.2**
WIN (incl. 1 euro stake): 5.50. PLACES: 1.70, 1.10. SF: 16.00.
Owner Wertheimer & Frere **Bred** Wertheimer & Frere **Trained** Chantilly, France

2928a PRIX DES LILAS (LISTED RACE) (3YO FILLIES) (STRAIGHT) (TURF) 1m (R)
3:20 (12:00) 3-Y-O **£20,220** (£8,088; £6,066; £4,044; £2,022)

RPR

1 **Czabo**[13] 2509 3-8-13 0.. MaximeGuyon 5 104+
(Mick Channon) *hld up bhd ldr: shkn up and qcknd to ld wl over 1 1/2f out: sn rdn and virtually jnd ent fnl f: r.o u.p: asserted fnl 75yds* **93/10**

2 *1¼* **Come Alive**[20] 2282 3-8-13 0.................................. VincentCheminaud 4 101
(A Fabre, France) *a cl up: chsd ldr wl over 1 1/2f out: virtually upsides ent fnl f: no ex last 75yds* **13/10**[1]

3 *snk* **Magnolea (IRE)**[26] 2116 3-8-13 0.............................. IoritzMendizabal 7 101
(J-C Rouget, France) **44/5**

4 *snk* **Robanne**[34] 1888 3-8-13 0.. GeraldMosse 3 100
(William Knight) *wnt lft s and bmpd rival: hld up in rr: hdwy on outside wl over 1 1/2f out: styd on ins fnl f: run flattened out late on: nvr on terms* **9/1**

5 *hd* **Classe Vendome (FR)**[41] 1687 3-8-13 0................ StephanePasquier 2 100
(N Clement, France) **18/1**

6 *hd* **Saimaa (IRE)**[46] 3-8-13 0.................................. Pierre-CharlesBoudot 1 99
(H-F Devin, France) **69/10**[3]

7 *3* **Qatar Power (FR)**[26] 2116 3-8-13 0.............................. OlivierPeslier 8 92
(F Head, France) **42/10**[2]

8 *¾* **Denga (IRE)**[33] 3-8-13 0.. TheoBachelot 9 91
(S Wattel, France) **17/2**

1m 42.01s (1.21) **8** Ran SP% **121.1**
WIN (Incl. 1 euro stake): 10.30. PLACES: 2.50, 1.40, 2.20. DF: 12.10. SF: 23.60.
Owner Norman Court Stud **Bred** Norman Court Stud **Trained** West Ilsley, Berks

2872 GOODWOOD (R-H)

Sunday, June 5

OFFICIAL GOING: Good to firm (8.0)

Wind: light, half behind Weather: sunny

2929 SUNDAY SCHOOL MAIDEN STKS 1m 1f 192y

1:50 (1:51) (Class 5) 3-Y-O+ **£3,234** (£962; £481; £240) **Stalls** Low

Form RPR

02-3 **1** **High Shields (IRE)**[17] 2414 3-9-0 85........................ RichardKingscote 9 91
(Roger Charlton) *mde all: 3 l clr and rdn 2f out: styd on wl and a maintaining advantage: comf* **5/2**[1]

0-2 **2** 2 3/4 **Stratum**[60] 1270 3-9-0 0........................ RobertHavlin 11 85
(John Gosden) *chsd wnr thrght: 3 l down and rdn ent fnl 2f: drvn over 1f out: no imp on wnr but kpt on for clr 2nd* **9/2**[2]

3 5 **Frontiersman** 3-9-0 0........................ WilliamBuick 4 75+
(Charlie Appleby) *hld up in tch in midfield: effrt over 2f out: no imp: rn green: hung rt but hdwy over 1f out: wnt 3rd ins fnl f: kpt on but no threat to ldrs* **5/2**[1]

5 **4** 1 **Desert Way (IRE)**[30] 1989 3-8-9 0........................ FMBerry 2 68
(Ralph Beckett) *chsd ldng pair: rdn 3f out: sn outpcd u.p and wl hld over 1f out: plugged on same pce and lost 4th ins fnl f* **9/2**[2]

00 **5** 8 **Balancing Time**[17] 2414 3-9-0 0........................ JimCrowley 7 57
(Amanda Perrett) *chsd ldng trio: outpcd and rdn 2f out: wl btn and wandered lft ent fnl f: wknd fnl f* **50/1**

6 1 **Cape Cova (IRE)** 3-9-0 0........................ TomQueally 5 55+
(John Gosden) *s.i.s: rn green in rr: rdn 6f out: lost tch w ldrs 3f out: sn u.p and hdwy over 1f out: no ch but styd on to pass btn horses ins fnl f* **20/1**

7 1/2 **Intercepted** 3-9-0 0........................ ShaneKelly 12 54+
(David Lanigan) *hld up in last quartet: rdn 4f out: sn outpcd and wl hld 3f out: prog over 1f out: no ch but kpt on to pass btn horses ins fnl f* **33/1**

5 **8** 1/2 **Hills Of Rome (IRE)**[37] 1826 3-9-0 0........................ PatDobbs 3 53
(Richard Hannon) *in tch in midfield: rdn 3f out and sn struggling: wl btn over 1f out: wknd fnl f* **9/1**[3]

0 **9** 1/2 **Dancing Rainbow (GR)**[24] 2182 3-8-4 0........................ HectorCrouch(5) 1 47
(Amanda Perrett) *in tch in midfield: rdn 3f out: sn struggling and wl btn over 1f out: wknd ins fnl f* **66/1**

00 **10** 15 **Wassail**[24] 2183 3-8-9 0........................ LiamKeniry 8 17
(Ed de Giles) *stdd after s: hld up in last trio: rdn over 2f out: sn struggling and hung lft: t.o ins fnl f* **200/1**

11 1 **Mybrotherjohnny**[187] 5-9-13 0........................[1] CharlesBishop 6 21
(Jamie Poulton) *t.k.h: in tch in midfield: rdn 3f out: sn btn: fading and hung lft over 1f out: t.o ins fnl f* **125/1**

12 3/4 **Wun Destination**[33] 7-9-3 0........................ DannyBurton(5) 10 14
(John Panvert) *v s.i.s: a towards rr: rdn 5f out: struggling u.p over 3f out: bhd fnl 2f: t.o* **150/1**

2m 7.6s (-0.50) **Going Correction** 0.0s/f (Good)
WFA 3 from 5yo+ 13lb **12** Ran SP% **116.6**
Speed ratings (Par 103): **102,99,95,95,88 87,87,87,86,74 73,73**
CSF £13.50 TOTE £3.70: £1.60, £1.40, £1.20; EX 15.50 Trifecta £53.00.
Owner Michael Pescod **Bred** Rabbah Bloodstock Limited **Trained** Beckhampton, Wilts

FOCUS

Good to firm ground for a seven-race card. This looked a reasonable maiden on paper but the front two filled those places throughout, nothing else got into it and they finished quite well strung out. The winner and fourth set the standard.

2930 LIZ JONES CELEBRATING 30 YEARS' NSPCC FUNDRAISING STKS (H'CAP) 1m 3f

2:20 (2:20) (Class 5) (0-75,75) 4-Y-O+ **£3,234** (£962; £481; £240) **Stalls** High

Form RPR

-006 **1** **Jacob Cats**[24] 2176 7-9-7 75........................(v) FrederikTylicki 5 83
(William Knight) *dwlt: hld up in rr: effrt on inner 2f out: hdwy u.p over 1f out: lft in ld ins fnl f: r.o strly: rdn out* **10/3**[1]

4160 **2** 1 1/4 **Vale Of Iron (IRE)**[17] 2401 4-8-13 67........................ KierenFox 3 73
(John Best) *stdd s: hld up in last pair: swtchd lft over 3f out: rdn: hdwy and drifted rt over 1f out: lft w ev ch ins fnl f: chsd wnr and r.o same pce ins fnl f* **11/2**

-260 **3** 1 3/4 **Classic Mission**[107] 640 5-8-8 69........................(v) CharlieBennett(7) 6 72
(Jonathan Portman) *chsd ldr: clsd to join ldr and travelling strly 3f out: shkn up to ld jst over 2f out: 2 l clr whn hung bdly lft over 1f out: stl hanging and hdd ins fnl f: styd on same pce fnl 100yds* **12/1**

1631 **4** 2 3/4 **Solveig's Song**[20] 2292 4-8-2 56 oh1........................(p) JimmyQuinn 8 54
(Steve Woodman) *chsd ldrs: effrt over 2f out: drvn 2f out: chsd ldr over 1f out: lft w ev ch ins fnl f: sn btn: wknd fnl 100yds* **7/1**

0-33 **5** 4 **Choral Festival**[10] 2623 10-9-0 68........................ WilliamCarson 2 59
(John Bridger) *hld up in midfield: effrt 2f: sn u.p and outpcd: wl hld and plugged on same pce ins fnl f* **4/1**[2]

5615 **6** hd **Yul Finegold (IRE)**[15] 2463 6-9-7 75........................ PaulMulrennan 1 65
(Conor Dore) *led: hdd and rdn jst over 2f out: no ex u.p and btn over 1f out: wknd fnl f* **5/1**

2136 **7** 6 **Karnage (IRE)**[67] 1144 4-9-5 73........................(b) TimmyMurphy 7 53
(Daniel Kubler) *chsd ldrs: effrt 2f out: sn short of room and unable qck u.p over 1f out: wknd fnl f* **9/2**[3]

2m 26.11s (-0.39) **Going Correction** 0.0s/f (Good) **7** Ran SP% **113.5**
Speed ratings (Par 103): **101,100,98,96,93 93,89**
CSF £21.50 CT £192.74 TOTE £4.40: £2.80, £2.70; EX 21.90 Trifecta £191.50.
Owner Canisbay Bloodstock **Bred** Highclere Stud **Trained** Patching, W Sussex

FOCUS

Race increased by 12yds. Not a strong race, even for this grade, and although the first two home came from the back, the pace didn't look overly strong. The third horse probably would have won but he's thrown it away before and he did so again.

2931 HARRIET THE PINT SIZED FIGHTER MEMORIAL VETERANS' STKS (H'CAP) 5f

2:55 (2:55) (Class 4) (0-85,88) 6-Y-O+ **£6,469** (£1,925; £962; £481) **Stalls** High

Form RPR

-600 **1** **Confessional**[10] 2613 9-9-4 82........................(e) JackGarritty 9 90
(Tim Easterby) *hld up in last trio: nt clr run jst over 2f out: hdwy and swtchd rt over 1f out: drvn and styd on to ld wl ins fnl f: hld on: drvn out* **4/1**[2]

0-00 **2** nk **Emjayem**[32] 1964 6-8-12 76........................ JimCrowley 6 83
(Ed McMahon) *chsd ldng pair: effrt 1f out: chsd clr wnr and swtchd rt jst ins fnl f: drvn and styd on to chal wl ins fnl f: r.o but hld towards fin* **8/1**

-421 **3** 1/2 **Pettochside**[15] 2469 7-8-4 75........................ MitchGodwin(7) 11 80
(John Bridger) *hld up in last trio: pushed along jst over 1f out: rdn and hdwy ins fnl f: clsng and sltly impeded wl ins fnl f: gng on fin: nvr quite getting to ldrs* **7/2**[1]

5052 **4** 1/2 **Long Awaited (IRE)**[12] 2562 8-9-3 81........................(b) PaulMulrennan 10 84
(Conor Dore) *sn bhd: rdn jst over 1f out: hdwy u.p ins fnl f: styd on strly fnl 100yds: nt quite rch ldrs* **12/1**

3501 **5** 1 3/4 **Powerful Wind (IRE)**[19] 2342 7-8-13 77........................ RichardKingscote 2 74
(Charlie Wallis) *led and sn arnd 3 l clr: rdn 1f out: tiring and hung lft ins fnl f: hdd wl ins fnl f: fading towards fin* **9/2**[3]

6-41 **6** 3/4 **Whitecrest**[33] 1950 8-8-8 72........................ LukeMorris 4 66
(John Spearing) *midfield: rdn 1/2-way: kpt on same pce ins fnl f* **8/1**

0322 **7** 1/2 **Mossgo (IRE)**[5] 2768 6-8-6 70........................(t) KierenFox 7 62
(John Best) *hood removed after leaving stall but lost little grnd: hld up in last trio: nt clr run over 1f out: swtchd lft and kpt on ins fnl f: no ch w ldrs* **7/1**

0266 **8** 3/4 **Royal Bajan (USA)**[19] 2342 8-8-2 69........................(v) TomMarquand(3) 5 59
(Robert Cowell) *chsd clr ldr and clr of field: rdn jst over 1f out: lost 2nd jst ins fnl f: sn wknd* **16/1**

6013 **9** 1 1/4 **Ask The Guru**[27] 2088 6-8-2 66 oh2........................(p) JimmyQuinn 8 51
(Michael Attwater) *midfield: effrt over 1f out: carried rt ent fnl f: sn btn and wknd ins fnl f* **16/1**

57.31s (-2.89) **Going Correction** -0.425s/f (Firm) **9** Ran SP% **114.6**
Speed ratings: **106,105,104,103,101 99,99,97,95**
CSF £35.60 CT £122.30 TOTE £5.80: £1.80, £1.90, £1.40; EX 47.90 Trifecta £235.80.
Owner Bearstone Stud Limited **Bred** Bearstone Stud Ltd **Trained** Great Habton, N Yorks
■ Stewards' Enquiry : Jack Garritty caution: careless riding

FOCUS

\bPowerful Wind\p went off like the clappers here and he set it up for the closers who arrived in the final furlong. The first two home were both on very long losing runs so this veterans' contest wouldn't be form to go wild about. The runner-up is rated to his best.

2932 MAYWAL STKS (H'CAP) 2m

3:30 (3:30) (Class 3) (0-90,89) 4-Y-O+ **£9,703** (£2,887; £1,443; £721) **Stalls** Low

Form RPR

650/ **1** **Galizzi (USA)**[169] 7106 5-9-9 88........................(t) WilliamBuick 5 98+
(Charlie Appleby) *sn chsng ldr: clsd to join ldr and clr of field 5f out: rdn to ld 3f out: clr and drifted rt over 1f out: styd on strly: eased cl home* **4/1**[2]

1560 **2** 4 **Cotton Club (IRE)**[17] 2392 5-8-6 78........................ GeorgeWood(7) 2 82
(Rod Millman) *hld up in midfield: effrt over 3f out: chsd wnr over 2f out: unable qck and edgd rt over 1f out: styd on same pce ins fnl f* **12/1**

64-0 **3** 3/4 **King Calypso**[35] 1893 5-8-5 75........................ EdwardGreatrex(5) 1 78+
(Denis Coakley) *stdd s: hld up in last trio: swtchd lft and effrt but plenty to do over 3f out: edgd rt and hdwy u.p over 1f out: stl edging rt but styd on wl ins fnl f: no ch w wnr* **9/1**

3-50 **4** 2 **Percy Veer**[30] 1987 4-9-7 87........................ PatDobbs 7 88
(Sylvester Kirk) *chsd ldrs after 2f: rdn over 2f out: 4th and outpcd whn nt clr run and swtchd lft over 1f out: no ch w wnr but kpt on u.p ins fnl f* **16/1**

0501 **5** 1/2 **Bohemian Rhapsody (IRE)**[15] 2463 7-8-11 76........................ ShaneKelly 3 76
(Brendan Powell) *midfield: 6th and plenty to do whn rdn 4f out: drvn and sme prog over 1f out: styd on u.p ins fnl f: no threat to wnr* **14/1**

2-12 **6** 1 **Seaside Sizzler**[30] 1987 9-9-9 88........................ GeorgeBaker 4 87
(William Knight) *chsd ldr early: sn settled in midfield: effrt in 5th 4f out: drvn to go 3rd but no imp on wnr wl over 1f out: wknd ins fnl f* **5/2**[1]

-003 **7** nk **Wordiness**[30] 1987 8-9-7 86........................ SilvestreDeSousa 6 88+
(David Evans) *stdd s: hld up wl off the pce in rr: plenty to do and rdn over 3f out: hdwy whn nt clr run and hmpd over 1f out: hung rt 1f out: nt clrest of runs and nt given a hrd time ins fnl f: eased nr fin* **5/1**[3]

2-20 **8** 7 **Shades Of Silver**[30] 1987 6-9-10 89........................ JimCrowley 8 79
(Ed de Giles) *led: clr w wnr 5f out: rdn and hdd 5f out: wknd u.p over 1f out* **10/1**

-232 **9** 2 1/4 **Ayr Of Elegance**[17] 2400 4-8-6 72........................(p) HarryBentley 9 59
(Philip Hide) *stdd s: hld up off the pce in last trio: effrt over 3f out: drvn and no imp 2f out: wl bhd ins fnl f* **9/1**

3m 28.38s (-0.62) **Going Correction** -0.425s/f (Firm)
WFA 4 from 5yo+ 1lb **9** Ran SP% **114.6**
Speed ratings (Par 107): **101,99,98,97,97 96,96,93,92**
CSF £50.29 CT £406.21 TOTE £4.80: £2.30, £4.60, £3.30; EX 61.20 Trifecta £413.60.
Owner Godolphin **Bred** Darley **Trained** Newmarket, Suffolk
■ Stewards' Enquiry : George Wood caution: careless riding.

FOCUS

A strongly run staying handicap which produced an impressive and improved winner.

2933 CAPPAGH BUILDING A BETTER FUTURE (S) STKS 5f

4:00 (4:00) (Class 4) 2-Y-O **£6,469** (£1,925; £962; £481) **Stalls** High

Form RPR

520 **1** **Billy's Boots**[34] 1915 2-8-13 0........................ SilvestreDeSousa 2 64
(Mick Channon) *led and grad moved across to stands' rail: rdn ent fnl 2f: drvn and hdd over 1f out: rallied u.p to ld again 100yds out: styd on: eased cl home* **5/2**[1]

0 **2** 1/2 **The Night Is Ours (IRE)**[30] 1988 2-8-3 0........................ JosephineGordon(5) 7 57
(J S Moore) *in tch in midfield: dropped to last pair after 2f: effrt u.p over 1f out: hdwy 1f out: styd on wl to go 2nd wl ins fnl f* **16/1**

50 **3** 1 1/4 **Little Nosegay (IRE)**[13] 2535 2-8-5 0........................ TomMarquand(3) 1 53
(David Evans) *wnt rt s: sn rcvrd to chse ldr: led over 1f out: sn rdn: drifted rt ins fnl f: hdd 100yds out: no ex: lost 2nd and wknd wl ins fnl f* **12/1**

00 **4** 1 1/2 **Patrouille De Nuit (IRE)**[32] 1965 2-8-13 0........................ PaulMulrennan 3 52
(J S Moore) *bmpd s: in rr: effrt over 1f out: hdwy ins fnl f: styd on wl fnl 100yds: nvr trbld ldrs* **8/1**

55 **5** 1 **Secret Coin (IRE)**[26] 2125 2-8-8 0........................ WilliamCarson 5 44
(Jamie Osborne) *chsd ldrs: rdn wl over 1f out: 3rd and unable qck u.p 1f out: wknd ins fnl f* **7/2**[2]

2 **6** 1 3/4 **Trust The Indian**[38] 1813 2-8-13 0........................ LukeMorris 4 42
(Bill Turner) *bmpd s: in tch in midfield: rdn 1/2-way: no imp u.p over 1f out: wknd ins fnl f* **9/2**[3]

020 **7** 2 1/2 **Black Redstart**[30] 2007 2-8-1 0........................ GeorgeWood(7) 6 28
(Alan Bailey) *awkward leaving stalls: in tch in rr: hdwy and switching rt fr 4f out: midfield and rdn ent fnl 2f: no ex and btn jst over 1f out: wknd ins fnl f* **5/1**

58.97s (-1.23) **Going Correction** -0.425s/f (Firm) **7** Ran SP% **110.3**
Speed ratings (Par 95): **92,91,89,86,85 82,78**
CSF £39.23 TOTE £2.90: £3.00, £6.20; EX 37.70 Trifecta £314.80.Billy's boots was bought in for £7,000
Owner M Channon **Bred** Mike Channon Bloodstock Ltd **Trained** West Ilsley, Berks

FOCUS
A valuable seller, so a huge opportunity for some horses that are unlikely to be winning races of this value in the future. The form is rated as above par for the grade.

2934 BETFRED SUPPORTS THE NSPCC STKS (H'CAP) 7f
4:35 (4:35) (Class 3) (0-90,88) 3-Y-O+ **£9,703** (£2,887; £1,443; £721) **Stalls** Low

Form RPR
0433 **1** **Arnold Lane (IRE)**[17] 2391 7-9-12 **86** SilvestreDeSousa 2 96
(Mick Channon) *mde all: set stdy gallop tl grad increased pce fr 1/2-way and clr over 2f out: 3 l clr and drvn over 1f out: r.o wl: rdn out* **7/2**[1]

-255 **2** 2 1/4 **Easy Tiger**[22] 2247 4-9-6 **80** MartinDwyer 14 84
(William Muir) *t.k.h: sn chsng ldr: rdn over 2f out: no imp on wnr: kpt on gamely to hold 2nd fnl f* **10/1**

0-20 **3** 1/2 **Outback Ruler (IRE)**[22] 2246 4-9-10 **84** JohnFahy 1 87
(Clive Cox) *t.k.h: chsd ldng pair: rdn over 2f out: drvn and no imp on wnr over 1f out: battling for 2nd and kpt on same pce ins fnl f* **11/1**

1-03 **4** nk **Pharmaceutical (IRE)**[16] 2430 4-9-8 **82** AdamBeschizza 3 84
(Stuart Williams) *t.k.h: hld up in tch in midfield: nt clr run wl over 1f out tl swtchd lft jst over 1f out: battling for 2nd but no imp on wnr ins fnl f: kpt on same pce fnl 100yds* **13/2**[2]

0-53 **5** 1 3/4 **Young John (IRE)**[15] 2477 3-8-11 **81** TonyHamilton 5 74
(Richard Fahey) *stdd and swtchd rt after s: sn in tch in midfield: effrt on inner over 1f out: no imp and styd on same pce ins fnl f* **9/1**

3343 **6** 1 1/4 **Cincuenta Pasos (IRE)**[8] 2679 5-9-6 **85** EdwardGreatrex(5) 13 79+
(Joseph Tuite) *hld up in tch in last quartet: hdwy u.p over 1f out: kpt on ins fnl f: nvr trbld ldrs* **10/1**

5-41 **7** 1 1/4 **Arlecchino's Leap**[16] 2430 4-9-7 **81** (p) LiamKeniry 15 71
(Mark Usher) *stdd after s and swtchd rt to r on inner rail: hdwy into midfield 5f out: nt clr run 2f out: swtchd lft and effrt u.p over 1f out: no imp ins fnl f* **20/1**

-122 **8** nk **Black Caesar (IRE)**[17] 2401 5-8-10 **70** WilliamCarson 4 59
(Philip Hide) *t.k.h: chsd ldng trio: rdn over 2f out: drvn: unable qck and lost pl over 1f out: wknd ins fnl f* **7/1**[3]

0-60 **9** 1 **Aqua Ardens (GER)**[11] 2587 8-9-11 **85** (t) SteveDrowne 11 72
(George Baker) *hld up in tch in last quartet: effrt ent fnl 2f: rdn and no hdwy over 1f out: nvr trbld ldrs* **33/1**

0050 **10** 3/4 **Athletic**[22] 2247 7-9-4 **81** (v) TomMarquand(3) 12 66
(Andrew Reid) *stdd and swtchd rt s: t.k.h: hld up in tch in last quartet: effrt 2f out: sn drvn and no hdwy: nvr trbld ldrs* **25/1**

4-00 **11** 4 1/2 **Carnival King (IRE)**[22] 2247 4-9-10 **84** (b[1]) JimCrowley 9 57
(Brian Meehan) *hld up in midfield: rdn over 2f out: lost pl and bhd whn edgd rt over 1f out: wknd fnl f* **9/1**

4-20 **12** 3 3/4 **Goring (GER)**[30] 1993 4-9-11 **85** WilliamBuick 6 47
(Eve Johnson Houghton) *hld up in tch in midfield: wd bnd over 3f out: rdn 2f out: no hdwy and lost pl over 1f out: wknd fnl f* **7/1**[3]

1m 25.63s (-1.37) **Going Correction** 0.0s/f (Good)
WFA 3 from 4yo+ 10lb **12** Ran SP% **118.6**
Speed ratings (Par 107): **107,104,103,103,101 100,98,98,97,96 91,86**
CSF £38.28 CT £359.37 TOTE £4.70: £1.90, £3.10, £3.80; EX 32.90 Trifecta £199.00.

Owner J Mitchell **Bred** Lynn Lodge Stud **Trained** West Ilsley, Berks

FOCUS
Race increased by 12yds. An open handicap on paper but the draw played a big part in proceedings as the early pace was very steady, and track position proved crucial. The winner's effort is worth more at face value.

2935 NSPCC CHARITY RACEDAY STKS (H'CAP) 7f
5:10 (5:10) (Class 5) (0-75,75) 3-Y-O **£3,234** (£962; £481; £240) **Stalls** Low

Form RPR
00-4 **1** **Penwortham (IRE)**[27] 2095 3-9-6 **74** TonyHamilton 3 83
(Richard Fahey) *t.k.h: hld up in midfield: clsd on inner and swtchd lft over 1f out: sn rdn and pressed ldr ins fnl f: r.o u.p to ld wl ins fnl f: rdn out* **6/1**

4-31 **2** 1/2 **Frenchman (FR)**[30] 2005 3-9-4 **75** MichaelJMMurphy(3) 1 82
(Charles Hills) *racd keenly: led: rdn 2f out: drvn and pressed ins fnl f: hdd and styd on same pce wl ins fnl f* **3/1**[2]

4151 **3** 2 **Figurante (IRE)**[11] 2585 3-9-3 **71** WilliamCarson 6 73
(Jamie Osborne) *hld up in last pair: rdn and swtchd lft over 2f out: swtchd rt and hdwy u.p over 1f out: wnt 3rd 1f out: styd on ins fnl f: nvr enough pce to chal ldrs* **5/1**[3]

30-4 **4** 2 **Zabdi**[79] 978 3-9-1 **69** PatDobbs 8 66
(Richard Hannon) *hld up in last pair: effrt 2f out: sme hdwy whn nt clr run ent fnl f: sn swtchd lft and wnt 4th ins fnl f: kpt on same pce: nvr trbld ldrs* **12/1**

4-22 **5** 6 **Thaqaffa (IRE)**[17] 2393 3-9-7 **75** (p) MartinDwyer 4 55
(Marcus Tregoning) *chsd ldrs: clsd to press ldrs over 2f out: rdn 2f out: sn drvn and unable qck: btn 1f out: wknd fnl f* **9/4**[1]

5140 **6** 2 3/4 **Rhythm And Blues**[36] 1847 3-9-4 **72** JohnFahy 5 45
(Clive Cox) *hld up in last pair: effrt over 2f out: no hdwy and swtchd lft over 1f out: wknd fnl f* **10/1**

0-13 **7** 2 1/2 **Staintondale Lass (IRE)**[19] 2322 3-9-6 **74** HarryBentley 7 40
(Ed Vaughan) *chsd ldr: rdn 2f out: sn edgd lft and unable qck: btn over 1f out: wknd fnl f* **10/1**

1m 26.32s (-0.68) **Going Correction** 0.0s/f (Good) **7** Ran SP% **112.6**
Speed ratings (Par 99): **103,102,100,97,91 87,85**
CSF £23.54 CT £95.48 TOTE £6.50: £4.10, £1.40; EX 22.40 Trifecta £129.10.

Owner Richard Fahey Ebor Racing Club Ltd **Bred** Kilfeacle Stud **Trained** Musley Bank, N Yorks

■ Stewards' Enquiry : Michael J M Murphy two-day ban: used whip above permitted level (Jun 19-20)

FOCUS
Race increased by 12yds. This doesn't strike as anything other than ordinary form for the grade but there are reasons to be hopeful with a few of these and it may produce a couple of winners in the near future.

T/Jkpt: £6,670.30 to a £1 stake. Pool: £286,823.36 - 43.00 winnin gunits. T/Plt: £114.30 to a £1 stake. Pool: £117,739.23 - 751.92 winning units. T/Qpdt: £71.30 to a £1 stake. Pool: £8,172.24 - 84.80 winning units. **Steve Payne**

2936 - 2942a (Foreign Racing) - See Raceform Interactive

2806 CHANTILLY (R-H)
Sunday, June 5

OFFICIAL GOING: Turf: soft

2943a PRIX DU GROS-CHENE (GROUP 2) (3YO+) (TURF) 5f
1:20 (12:00) 3-Y-O+ **£54,485** (£21,029; £10,036; £6,691; £3,345)

RPR
1 **Son Cesio (FR)**[20] 2317 5-9-3 0 VincentCheminaud 7 115
(H-A Pantall, France) *w.w towards rr: shkn up and chsd ldrs fr 1 1/2f out: hrd rdn and r.o to ld ins fnl f: hld on gamely u.p* **9/4**[1]

2 snk **Catcall (FR)**[12] 7-9-3 0 OlivierPeslier 6 114
(P Sogorb, France) *cl up on outer: rdn to ld under 1 1/2f out: hdd ins fnl f: rallied u.p but a hld* **6/1**

3 2 **Finsbury Square (IRE)**[20] 2317 4-9-3 0 (b) ChristopheSoumillon 8 107
(F Chappet, France) *w.w in rr: rdn and hdwy on outer fr 1 1/2f out: styd on to go 3rd wl ins fnl f: run flattened out last 100yds: nvr trbld front two* **3/1**[2]

4 hd **Iffranesia (FR)**[36] 1862 6-9-0 0 StephanePasquier 3 104
(Robert Cowell) *led: hdd under 1 1/2f out: one pce u.p fnl f* **12/1**

5 shd **Maarek**[15] 2495 9-9-3 0 SeamieHeffernan 5 106+
(Miss Evanna McCutcheon, Ire) *dwlt: racd in fnl trio: drvn along to hold pl bef 1/2-way: kpt on u.p fr over 1f out: nt pce to get involved* **9/2**[3]

6 1 1/2 **Damila (FR)**[23] 2232 3-8-7 0 FabriceVeron 2 95
(H-A Pantall, France) *broke wl: trckd ldr: rdn and nt qckn wl over 1f out: wknd late on* **16/1**

7 3 **Ride Like The Wind (IRE)**[20] 2317 4-9-3 0 MickaelBarzalona 1 90
(F Head, France) *w.w in tch on stands' rail: rdn and no imp 1 1/2f out: wknd ins fnl f* **7/1**

8 1 **Mirza**[20] 2317 9-9-3 0 (p) IoritzMendizabal 4 86
(Rae Guest) *chsd ldr: outpcd and scrubbed along wl over 1 1/2f out: wknd fnl f* **12/1**

59.58s (1.28) **Going Correction** +0.60s/f (Yiel)
WFA 3 from 4yo+ 7lb **8** Ran SP% **122.0**
Speed ratings: **113,112,109,109,109 106,101,100**
WIN (incl. 1 euro stake): 2.70. PLACES: 1.10, 1.50, 1.20. DF: 9.60. SF: 16.10.
Owner Yves Borotra **Bred** Yves Borotra **Trained** France

2944a PRIX DE ROYAUMONT (GROUP 3) (3YO FILLIES) (TURF) 1m 4f
1:55 (12:00) 3-Y-O **£29,411** (£11,764; £8,823; £4,411; £4,411)

RPR
1 **The Juliet Rose (FR)**[26] 2142 3-9-0 0 StephanePasquier 6 100+
(N Clement, France) *racd alone in centre early and led overall: jnd main gp after 2f: kicked for home over 2f out: sn rdn and r.o: styd on strly fnl f: a in command* **6/4**[1]

2 1 1/2 **Al Wathna**[26] 2142 3-9-0 0 GregoryBenoist 4 98
(J-C Rouget, France) *trckd ldrs on outer: rdn to chse ldr fr 2f out: styd on u.p: a hld by wnr* **9/2**[3]

3 nk **Armande (IRE)**[20] 3-9-0 0 Pierre-CharlesBoudot 3 98+
(A Fabre, France) *hld up in fnl pair: n.m.r whn pce qcknd over 2f out: swtchd ins and nt clr run whn snatched up appr fnl f: stdd and angled out: styd on wl fnl 150yds: nvr nrr* **4/1**[2]

4 1/2 **Jollify (IRE)**[23] 3-9-0 0 MickaelBarzalona 2 97
(A Fabre, France) *led main gp of five: trckd ldr after 2f: rdn and nt qckn whn tempo increased over 2f out: kpt on at same pce fnl 1 1/2f* **12/1**

4 dht **Tres Rock Glory (IRE)**[31] 1986 3-9-0 0 AurelienLemaitre 1 97
(F Head, France) *cl up on inner: hrd rdn under 2f out: chsd ldr ins fnl f: dropped away last 100yds* **4/1**[2]

6 3 1/2 **Pakora (FR)**[36] 1877 3-9-0 0 FrankieDettori 5 91
(P Sogorb, France) *hld up in fnl pair: rdn and nt qckn ent fnl 2f: wl btn whn eased fnl 100yds* **9/1**

2m 41.22s (10.22) **Going Correction** +0.60s/f (Yiel) **6** Ran SP% **115.9**
Speed ratings: **89,88,87,87,87 85**
WIN (incl. 1 euro stake): 2.70. PLACES: 1.30, 1.80. SF: 7.30.
Owner Mayfair Speculators Sarl & Equifrance Holdings **Bred** Guy Heald **Trained** Chantilly, France

FOCUS
It proved hard to make ground in the sprint to the line.

2945a PRIX DE SANDRINGHAM (GROUP 2) (3YO FILLIES) (TURF) 1m
2:30 (12:00) 3-Y-O **£54,485** (£21,029; £10,036; £6,691; £3,345)

RPR
1 **Volta (FR)**[27] 2116 3-8-11 0 Pierre-CharlesBoudot 3 113+
(F-H Graffard, France) *hld up towards rr: moved into midfield fr 1/2-way: rdn and styd on to chal between horses under 1 1/2f out: led appr fnl f: qcknd clr: comf* **9/4**[1]

2 4 **Besotted (IRE)**[36] 1875 3-8-11 0 FrankieDettori 6 104
(P Sogorb, France) *cl up on outer: nt qckn whn rdn 1 1/2f out: styd on to chse ldr ins fnl f: readily outpcd by wnr: jst hld on for 2nd* **9/2**[3]

3 hd **Aim To Please (FR)**[21] 2282 3-8-11 0 GeraldMosse 7 104
(F Doumen, France) *hld up in rr: hdwy and n.m.r under 1 1/2f out: nt clr run ent fnl f: swtchd ins and styd on wl fnl 150yds: jst missed 2nd* **20/1**

4 3/4 **Rosay (IRE)**[36] 1875 3-8-11 0 CristianDemuro 8 102
(J-C Rouget, France) *w.w in fnl pair: rdn and no imp wl over 1 1/2f out: styd on fnl f: nt pce to get on terms* **8/1**

5 hd **Powder Snow (USA)**[27] 2116 3-8-11 0 MickaelBarzalona 4 101
(H-A Pantall, France) *t.k.h: hld up in midfield: rdn and kpt on fr 1 1/2f out: nt pce to get involved* **14/1**

6 1 3/4 **High Quality (IRE)**[35] 3-8-11 0 VincentCheminaud 2 97
(A Fabre, France) *chsd ldr: rdn to chal over 1 1/2f out: wknd ins fnl f* **10/1**

7 nk **Zayva (FR)**[25] 3-8-11 0 ChristopheSoumillon 9 97
(A De Royer-Dupre, France) *hld up towards rr: rdn and no imp fr 2f out: nvr in contention* **4/1**[2]

8 3/4 **Prairie Pearl (FR)**[28] 3-8-11 0 OlivierPeslier 5 95
(H-A Pantall, France) *led: rdn whn chal over 1 1/2f out: hdd over 1f out: wknd ins fnl f* **12/1**

9 14 **Sasparella (FR)**[21] 2282 3-8-11 0 MaximeGuyon 1 63
(C Laffon-Parias, France) *t.k.h: hld up in tch on inner: rdn and outpcd 1 1/2f out: wknd fnl f* **11/2**

1m 39.0s (1.00) **Going Correction** +0.60s/f (Yiel) **9** Ran SP% **123.7**
Speed ratings: **119,115,114,114,113 112,111,111,97**
WIN (incl. 1 euro stake): 3.00. PLACES: 1.30, 1.70, 4.40. DF: 5.90. SF: 10.30.
Owner Ecurie Salabi **Bred** T, Mme D & A De La Heronniere **Trained** France

FOCUS
The second to eighth set the standard.

2946a PRIX DU JOCKEY CLUB (GROUP 1) (3YO COLTS & FILLIES) (TURF) 1m 2f 110y

3:15 (12:00) 3-Y-O **£630,220** (£252,132; £126,066; £62,977; £31,544)

RPR

1 **Almanzor (FR)**[26] 2140 3-9-2 0 Jean-BernardEyquem 7 117
(J-C Rouget, France) *w.w in midfield: rdn and hdwy fr 2f out: styd on strly u.p to ld ent fnl f: drvn out* **20/1**

2 1 1/2 **Zarak (FR)**[21] 2283 3-9-2 0 ChristopheSoumillon 16 114+
(A De Royer-Dupre, France) *w.w in fnl pair: tk clsr order 3f out: styng on whn nt clr run 1 1/2f out: styd on wl u.p fnl f: nt rch wnr* **7/1**

3 1 3/4 **Dicton**[21] 2283 3-9-2 0 OlivierPeslier 13 111
(Gianluca Bietolini, Italy) *hld up towards rr: swtchd outside and hdwy 2f out: styd on wl u.p fnl f: nt pce to get on terms* **10/1**

4 1 1/4 **Talismanic**[13] 2550 3-9-2 0 MickaelBarzalona 11 109
(A Fabre, France) *led: hdd after 2f and remained cl up on outer: hrd rdn to chse ldr 1 1/2f out: styd on to ld briefly and narrowly over 1f out: hdd ent fnl f: no ex* **20/1**

5 shd **Apilobar (FR)**[28] 2076 3-9-2 0 CristianDemuro 17 108
(F Vermeulen, France) *hld up in rr: hdwy on inner 2 1/2f out: styd on u.p fr 1 1/2f out: nvr plcd to chal* **33/1**

6 3/4 **Golden Bridge (FR)**[29] 3-9-2 0 DavidMorisson 6 107
(C Gourdain, France) *t.k.h: hld up in fnl 3rd: towards rr and nt clr run under 2 1/2f out: swtchd ins and styd on wl u.str.p fr 1 1/2f out: nrest at fin* **100/1**

7 1/2 **Royal Julius (IRE)**[21] 2281 3-9-2 0 ThierryJarnet 3 106
(A De Watrigant, France) *hld up in midfield: n.m.r 2f out: rdn and effrt wl over 1f out: kpt on at one pce fnl f: nvr in contention* **50/1**

8 1 1/2 **Mekhtaal**[21] 2281 3-9-2 0 GregoryBenoist 15 103
(J-C Rouget, France) *hld up towards rr: last and rdn over 1 1/2f out: mde up grnd past btn horses fr wl over 1f out: nvr trbld ldrs* **9/2**[2]

9 1 1/2 **Raseed**[46] 1582 3-9-2 0 AurelienLemaitre 4 100
(F Head, France) *trckd ldrs: rdn and outpcd 1 1/2f out: dropped away ins fnl f* **10/1**

10 1 **Bravery (IRE)**[15] 2496 3-9-2 0 RyanMoore 14 98
(A P O'Brien, Ire) *w.w towards rr of midfield: rdn and no imp on outer fr 2 1/2f out: styd on late but nvr seen w a ch* **12/1**

11 2 **Robin Of Navan (FR)**[28] 2076 3-9-2 0 TonyPiccone 2 94
(Harry Dunlop) *virtually upsides ldr: led after 2f: kicked for home appr 2f out: hdd over 1f out: sn wknd* **13/2**

12 snk **Ventura Storm (IRE)**[21] 2281 3-9-2 0 GeraldMosse 9 94
(Richard Hannon) *w.w in midfield on outer: rdn and no imp 2f out: sn wknd* **40/1**

13 nse **Floodlight (USA)**[26] 2140 3-9-2 0 Pierre-CharlesBoudot 8 94
(A Fabre, France) *w.w in midfield: rdn and btn wl over 1 1/2f out* **33/1**

14 1 **Black Sea (IRE)**[24] 2190 3-9-2 0 SeamieHeffernan 1 92
(A P O'Brien, Ire) *t.k.h: hld up in tch on inner: 4th and rdn 2f out but no imp: wknd fnl f* **25/1**

15 2 1/2 **Imperial Aviator**[22] 2244 3-9-2 0 OisinMurphy 5 87
(Roger Charlton) *trckd ldrs between horses: rdn and nt qckn fr 2f out: sn wknd* **6/1**[3]

16 2 **Foundation (IRE)**[24] 2190 3-9-2 0 FrankieDettori 12 83
(John Gosden) *trckd ldrs on outer: rdn and no imp 2 1/2f out: wknd wl over 1f out and eased* **4/1**[1]

2m 11.62s (2.82) **Going Correction** +0.60s/f (Yiel) 16 Ran SP% **128.8**
Speed ratings: **113,111,110,109,109 109,108,107,106,105 104,104,104,103,101 100**
WIN (incl. 1 euro stake): 20.60. PLACES: 5.30, 3.20, 3.30. DF: 76.30. SF: 168.30.
Owner Ecurie Antonio Caro & Gerard Augustin-Normand **Bred** Haras D'Etreham **Trained** Pau, France

FOCUS
The British and Irish runners disappointed in what looked a rank-ordinary Prix du Jockey Club.

2947a GRAND PRIX DE CHANTILLY (GROUP 2) (4YO+) (TURF) 1m 4f

4:00 (12:00) 4-Y-O+ **£54,485** (£21,029; £10,036; £6,691; £3,345)

RPR

1 **One Foot In Heaven (IRE)**[28] 2077 4-8-11 0 ChristopheSoumillon 3 110+
(A De Royer-Dupre, France) *plld hrd: hld up towards rr: shkn up and tk clsr order fr 2f out: smoothly jnd ldrs appr 1f out and qckly led: drvn out and wl on top cl home* **1/1**[1]

2 3/4 **Garlingari (FR)**[35] 1909 5-9-2 0 StephanePasquier 7 114
(Mme C Barande-Barbe, France) *cl up bhd ldrs: rdn to chal 1 1/2f out: w ldrs appr fnl f: styd on u.p fnl f: nt muster pce of wnr* **4/1**[2]

3 snk **Harlem**[28] 2077 4-8-11 0 VincentCheminaud 1 109+
(A Fabre, France) *clsd up on inner: rdn and struggling wl over 1 1/2f out: rallying whn n.m.r 1f out: angled out and styd on wl fnl 125yds: jst missed 2nd* **10/1**

4 1 1/2 **Guignol (GER)**[42] 4-8-11 0 Pierre-CharlesBoudot 8 107
(Jean-Pierre Carvalho, Germany) *led: hdd 1/2-way and remained cl up: rdn and outpcd by ldrs wl over 1f out: kpt on at same pce fnl f* **25/1**

5 1 **Sumbal (IRE)**[35] 1909 4-8-11 0 OisinMurphy 5 105
(F-H Graffard, France) *t.k.h: hld up in fnl pair: hrd rdn to hold pl over 2f out: styd on u.p fnl f: nrest at fin* **8/1**

6 snk **Ayrad (IRE)**[22] 2241 5-8-11 0 AndreaAtzeni 4 105
(Roger Charlton) *trckd ldr: 2nd and pushed along wl over 1 1/2f out: grad dropped away ins fnl f* **6/1**[3]

7 2 **Grey Lion (IRE)**[28] 2077 4-8-11 0 MaximeGuyon 2 102
(A Fabre, France) *a towards rr: rdn and no imp wl over 1 1/2f out: wl hld fnl f* **16/1**

8 19 **Ming Dynasty (FR)**[35] 1909 4-9-2 0 UmbertoRispoli 6 76
(M Delzangles, France) *plld hrd: hld up in rr: rapid move rnd whole field to ld 1/2-way: rdn and hdd over 1f out: sn wknd and eased* **12/1**

2m 35.53s (4.53) **Going Correction** +0.60s/f (Yiel) 8 Ran SP% **121.9**
Speed ratings: **108,107,107,106,105 105,104,91**
WIN (incl. 1 euro stake): 2.50. PLACES: 1.10, 1.40, 1.50. DF: 4.30. SF: 6.70.
Owner Fair Salinia Ltd **Bred** Craigavon Agro Ltd **Trained** Chantilly, France

FOCUS
This became a sprint up the straight.

2948a PRIX DU BOIS BRANDIN (H'CAP) (3YO) (TURF) 1m

4:35 (12:00) 3-Y-O

£20,735 (£8,382; £6,176; £3,970; £2,426; £1,544)

RPR

1 **Livinginafantasy (FR)**[65] 3-8-9 0 TheoBachelot 1 78
(S Wattel, France) **152/10**

2 shd **Enjoy The Silence (FR)**[29] 3-8-11 0 RonanThomas 14 79
(C Boutin, France) **56/1**

3 snk **Babel's Book (FR)**[45] 3-9-2 0 (p) Jean-BernardEyquem 9 84
(F-H Graffard, France) **33/1**

4 1 1/2 **Feel Alive (FR)** 3-8-9 0 StephanePasquier 4 74
(F Rohaut, France) **15/1**

5 1/2 **Eternal Army (FR)**[28] 3-9-4 0 Pierre-CharlesBoudot 2 81
(H-A Pantall, France) **27/10**[1]

6 nse **Normandy Kitten (USA)**[28] 3-9-1 0 (p) CristianDemuro 11 78
(Gianluca Bietolini, Italy) **53/10**[2]

7 1 1/4 **Donuts Reyor (FR)**[13] 3-9-1 0 MickaelBarzalona 10 75
(Y Barberot, France) **76/10**[3]

8 hd **Kenfay (FR)**[28] 3-8-13 0 (b) ThierryThulliez 5 73
(Y Gourraud, France) **11/1**

9 hd **Mon Bisou (IRE)**[23] 3-8-11 0 UmbertoRispoli 12 70
(G Botti, France) **25/1**

10 shd **Rappelle Moi (FR)**[28] 3-9-4 0 AnthonyCrastus 13 77
(D Prod'Homme, France) **21/1**

11 2 1/2 **Jaaref (IRE)**[34] 3-9-0 0 GeraldMosse 8 68
(J E Hammond, France) **11/1**

12 2 1/2 **Rashawn (FR)**[28] 3-9-2 0 FabriceVeron 16 64
(H-A Pantall, France) **14/1**

13 10 **War Reporter (FR)**[34] 3-8-11 0 (p) MaximeGuyon 3 36
(F Rossi, France) **20/1**

14 1 1/4 **Great Dora (FR)**[18] 2389 3-9-2 0 (p) GregoryBenoist 7 38
(S Wattel, France) **75/1**

15 6 **Texada**[34] 3-8-9 0 VincentCheminaud 6 17
(Mme C Head-Maarek, France) **37/1**

16 11 **Honiara**[16] 2456 3-9-4 0 ChristopheSoumillon 15
(Paul Cole) *a towards rr: wl bhd fnl 2f* **9/1**

1m 41.43s (3.43) 16 Ran SP% **122.1**
WIN (incl. 1 euro stake): 16.20. PLACES: 5.00, 15.40, 10.40. DF: 500.00. SF: 795.90.
Owner Mme I Corbani & Sarl Jedburgh Stud **Bred** Mme I Corbani & Sarl Jedburgh Stud **Trained** France

1376 DUSSELDORF (R-H)

Sunday, June 5

OFFICIAL GOING: Turf: good to soft

2949a WEMPE 96. GERMAN 1000 GUINEAS (GROUP 2) (3YO FILLIES) (TURF) 1m

4:10 (12:00) 3-Y-O **£51,470** (£20,588; £11,029; £5,882; £2,941)

RPR

1 **Hawksmoor (IRE)**[20] 2316 3-9-2 0 (b) JamesDoyle 1 102
(Hugo Palmer) *trckd ldrs on inner: angled out and rdn 1 1/2f out: styd on to ld under 1f out: r.o fnl f: rdn out* **6/5**[1]

2 1/2 **Shy Witch (GER)**[36] 3-9-2 0 IanFerguson 3 101
(H-J Groschel, Germany) *hld up towards rr: swtchd outside and hdwy 2f out: rdn and r.o wl fr over 1f out: nvr quite on terms* **99/10**

3 3/4 **Dynamic Lips (IRE)**[28] 3-9-2 0 AndreasHelfenbein 5 99
(Andreas Lowe, Germany) *hld up in midfield: hdwy wl over 1 1/2f out: 5th and rdn appr fnl f: styd on u.p: wnt 3rd cl home* **243/10**

4 3/4 **Monaco Show (FR)**[36] 3-9-2 0 StephenHellyn 6 97
(A Wohler, Germany) *w.w in midfield: rdn and hdwy 2f out: styd on strly fnl f: nrest at fin* **26/1**

5 hd **Milenia (GER)**[31] 3-9-2 0 EugenFrank 4 97
(Markus Klug, Germany) *hld up in midfield: rdn to chse ldrs fr 1 1/2f out: kpt on at same pce u.p fnl f* **55/1**

6 nse **Double Dream (FR)**[49] 1513 3-9-2 0 EduardoPedroza 9 97
(A Wohler, Germany) *led: rdn and rallied whn pressed wl over 1f out: hdd ent fnl f: no ex* **44/5**[3]

7 nk **Princess Asta (FR)**[18] 2389 3-9-2 0 AndreasSuborics 10 96
(Mario Hofer, Germany) *hld up towards rr: hdwy 2f out: styd on ins fnl f: nvr trbld ldrs* **51/1**

8 3/4 **Dhaba (GER)**[49] 1513 3-9-2 0 AdriedeVries 15 94
(Markus Klug, Germany) *w.w in fnl trio: rdn and hdwy on ins wl over 1 1/2f out: styd on ins fnl f: snatched up whn nt clr run last 75yds* **47/10**[2]

9 1/2 **Rebel Surge (IRE)**[23] 2220 3-9-2 0 WilliamTwiston-Davies 16 93
(Richard Spencer) *a towards rr: rdn and btn fr 2f out* **56/1**

10 3/4 **Walun (GER)**[36] 3-9-2 0 DanielePorcu 14 92
(P Schiergen, Germany) *w.w towards rr: rdn and effrt 1 1/2f out: plugged on at same pce fnl f* **246/10**

11 1/2 **Kenrivash (FR)**[35] 3-9-2 0 AntoineHamelin 11 90
(Henk Grewe, Germany) *cl up on outer: nt qckn u.p wl over 1 1/2f out: sn wknd* **30/1**

12 shd **Parvaneh (IRE)**[20] 2315 3-9-2 0 MarcLerner 2 90
(Waldemar Hickst, Germany) *racd in midfield: pushed along bef 1/2-way: no imp: wknd wl over 1f out* **9/1**

13 1/2 **Lips Planet (GER)**[36] 3-9-2 0 FilipMinarik 7 89
(Andreas Lowe, Germany) *settled in midfield: rdn and wknd wl over 1 1/2f out* **41/1**

14 1 1/2 **Near England (IRE)**[36] 3-9-2 0 MartinSeidl 13 86
(Markus Klug, Germany) *w.w in midfield on outer: rdn and btn fr 1 1/2f out* **98/10**

15 1/2 **Redenca (GER)**[36] 3-9-2 0 JozefBojko 8 84
(A Wohler, Germany) *a in fnl f: wknd u.p ins fnl 1 1/2f* **195/10**

16 2 1/4 **La Merced (GER)**[49] 1513 3-9-2 0 (b) DennisSchiergen 12 79
(P Schiergen, Germany) *chsd ldrs: rdn and wknd ins fnl 2f* **235/10**

1m 37.3s (-3.86) 16 Ran SP% **133.2**
WIN (incl. 10 euro stake): 22. PLACES: 13, 27, 37, 34. SF: 175.
Owner Lael Stable **Bred** Tenuta Genzianella **Trained** Newmarket, Suffolk

FOCUS
A tight finish and it's likely some of these were flattered.

2950 - 2951a (Foreign Racing) - See Raceform Interactive

2284 LES LANDES
Monday, May 30

OFFICIAL GOING: Turf: firm
Wind: Moderate, across away from stand Weather: Fine

2952a GEOFFREY EDWARDS MEMORIAL H'CAP — 1m 4f
3:00 (3:05) 3-Y-O+ **£1,780** (£640; £380)

RPR

1 **Black Night (IRE)**[15] 4-10-9 0 ShaunPayne 6 69
(J Moon, Jersey) *hld up: hdwy fr 1/2-way: wnt 2nd over 2f out: led over 1f out: rdn out* **4/1**[2]

2 3 ½ **Mr Opulence**[15] 7-8-10 0 TimClark 7 36
(T Le Brocq, Jersey) *trckd ldrs: lost pl 1/2-way: kpt on again fr 3f out: wnt 2nd wl ins fnl f* **5/1**[3]

3 nk **King Kenny**[15] 11-8-5 0 NoraLooby 3 31
(Mrs A Corson, Jersey) *hld up: hdwy fr 4f out: kpt on one pce to go 3rd wl ins fnl f* **12/1**

4 2 **Aussie Lyrics (FR)**[15] 6-10-2 0 AliceMills 4 52
(Mrs C Gilbert, Jersey) *trckd ldr: 2 l 2nd and travelling wl 3f out: sn rdn and fnd little u.p* **1/1**[1]

5 1 **Wicked Tara**[28] 2080 6-8-9 0 oh11 ow4 PhilipPrince 5 30
(Natalie Lloyd-Beavis) *led: nt handle turn and briefly rdn over 7f out: hdd over 1f out: wknd nr fin* **6/1**

6 8 **Spring Dixie (IRE)**[15] 4-9-11 0 JemmaMarshall 1 33
(Mrs A Malzard, Jersey) *mid-div: hdwy to go 3rd briefly 1/2-way: wknd 2f out* **17/2**

7 8 **Bowl Imperior**[225] 7327 4-10-8 0 MattieBatchelor 2 31
(Mrs A Malzard, Jersey) *hld up: outpcd fr 4f out: n.d* **11/2**

8 dist **Foiled**[28] 6-8-6 0 oh16 ow1 RyanClark 8
(Jan Coomer, Guernsey) *trckd ldr: rdn and lost pl 1/2-way: t.o* **33/1**

Owner Mrs Anne Moon **Bred** Manister House Stud **Trained** St-Martin, Jersey

2953a LA VALLETTE 2016 JERSEY BULLET H'CAP — 5f 110y
3:40 (3:44) 3-Y-O+ **£2,380** (£860; £510)

RPR

1 **Country Blue (FR)**[15] 2284 7-10-0 0 (p) MattieBatchelor 2 50
(Mrs A Malzard, Jersey) *chsd ldr: led over 2f out: jst hld on: all out* **2/1**[2]

2 hd **Valmina**[15] 2284 9-10-12 0 NickSlatter 3 61
(K Kukk, Jersey) *chsd ldrs in 4th: hdwy fr 2f out: wnt 2nd 1f out: kpt on wl: jst failed* **7/4**[1]

3 shd **Purley Queen (IRE)**[15] 2284 7-10-2 0 (p) AliceMills 4 51
(Mrs C Gilbert, Jersey) *pressed ldr: sltly outpcd on bnd over 2f out: rallied and ev ch fnl f: no ex* **2/1**[2]

4 3 **Chester'slittlegem (IRE)**[15] 2284 7-8-5 0 oh4 (p) NoraLooby 1 16
(Mrs A Corson, Jersey) *outpcd: kpt on same pce fr 2f out: nrest at fin* **8/1**[3]

5 5 **Kersivay**[309] 10-8-5 0 oh9 JemmaMarshall 5
(Mrs A Malzard, Jersey) *outpcd: nvr able to chal* **12/1**

6 2 **Hurricane Alert**[28] 1913 4-10-1 0 RyanClark 6 17
(Natalie Lloyd-Beavis) *led tl over 2f out: sn wknd* **9/1**

Owner A Taylor **Bred** Mme S Rangler & R Freih **Trained** St Ouen, Jersey

2954a WHITSUN H'CAP MILE — 1m 100y
4:15 (4:15) 3-Y-O+ **£1,780** (£640; £380)

RPR

1 **Benoordenhout (IRE)**[15] 5-10-5 0 TimClark 4 54
(T Le Brocq, Jersey) *mde virtually all: briefly jnd ins fnl f: rallied gamely: drvn out* **5/2**[1]

2 1 ½ **Pas D'Action**[15] 2284 8-10-5 0 (p) JemmaMarshall 3 51
(Mrs A Malzard, Jersey) *hld up: hdwy fr 4f out: drvn to briefly join ldr ins fnl f: no ex fnl 100yds* **4/1**

3 2 ½ **Brown Velvet**[15] 2284 4-10-5 0 PhilipPrince 6 45
(K Kukk, Jersey) *cl 2nd: ev ch 2f out: no ex and lost 2nd over 1f out* **11/2**

4 3 **Tax Reform (IRE)**[15] 2284 6-9-9 0 RyanClark 2 29
(Natalie Lloyd-Beavis) *hld up: unable to chal fr 2f out* **11/4**[2]

5 5 **Lucifers Shadow (IRE)**[15] 2285 7-9-10 0 (v) AliceMills 1 19
(Mrs C Gilbert, Jersey) *trckd ldrs: unable to chal fr 2f out: wknd* **3/1**[3]

6 2 **Engaging Smile**[15] 2284 4-10-12 0 RichardCondon 5 30
(J Moon, Jersey) *trckd ldrs: outpcd fr 4f out: wknd* **14/1**

Owner S M Smith **Bred** Prof C Green **Trained** Jersey

2955a THE CRAWFORD FAMILY H'CAP — 1m 2f
4:50 (4:50) (0-55,0) 3-Y-O+ **£1,780** (£640; £380)

RPR

1 **Hawaiian Freeze**[15] 1517 7-10-5 0 RichardCondon 5 37
(J Moon, Jersey) *mid-div: hdwy 3f out: led 2f out: drvn out* **8/1**

2 hd **Lady Petrus**[15] 11-8-9 0 oh3 ow4 (p) PhilipPrince 9 13
(K Kukk, Jersey) *hld up: hdwy fr over 2f out: kpt on wl: jst failed* **16/1**

3 1 ½ **Grey Panel (FR)**[15] 2285 8-10-0 0 TimClark 4 29
(T Le Brocq, Jersey) *mid-div: kpt on fr 3f out: ev ch over 1f out: no ex* **5/1**[3]

4 2 **Carrera**[15] 2285 6-10-5 0 MattieBatchelor 1 30
(Mrs A Malzard, Jersey) *mid-div: hdwy fr over 2f out: nt rch ldrs* **4/1**[2]

5 4 **Bond Mystery**[15] 2285 4-10-2 0 RyanClark 3 19
(Natalie Lloyd-Beavis) *bhd tl mod late hdwy through btn horses* **9/1**

6 3 **Captain James (FR)**[15] 2285 6-10-0 0 AliceMills 8 11
(Mrs C Gilbert, Jersey) *pressed ldr: led 5f out: hdd & wknd 2f out* **5/4**[1]

7 2 ½ **Steely**[15] 8-10-12 0 (p) NickSlatter 2 18
(K Kukk, Jersey) *led: set str pce: rdn 6f out: hdd & wknd 5f out* **4/1**[2]

8 8 **Frankki M**[15] 2284 6-8-5 0 MissMHooper 6
(Mrs A Corson, Jersey) *sn bhd* **16/1**

9 6 **Fast Freddie**[15] 2285 12-9-1 0 NoraLooby 7
(Mrs A Corson, Jersey) *pressed ldr tl wknd rapidly 3f out* **10/1**

10 6 **Albecq**[15] 2285 4-10-3 0 JemmaMarshall 10
(Mrs A Malzard, Jersey) *a bhd* **8/1**

Owner Mrs Anne Moon **Bred** Mrs D O Joly **Trained** St-Martin, Jersey

2522 AYR (L-H)
Monday, June 6

OFFICIAL GOING: Good to firm (8.5)
Wind: light against Weather: sunny

2956 EBF/TOTEPLACEPOT AVAILABLE AT EVERY MEETING NOVICE STKS — 6f
2:00 (2:01) (Class 5) 2-Y-O **£3,234** (£962; £481; £240) **Stalls** Low

Form RPR

23 1 **Masham Star (IRE)**[16] 2489 2-9-2 0 JoeFanning 6 85+
(Mark Johnston) *sn pressed ldr: pushed along to ld wl over 1f out: kpt on: comf* **2/5**[1]

5 2 4 **Heir Of Excitement (IRE)**[21] 2301 2-9-2 0 PaulMulrennan 1 73
(Kevin Ryan) *led: hdd wl over 1f out: sn rdn: one pce and no ch w wnr* **10/1**[3]

0 3 1 ½ **Wigan Warrior**[10] 2649 2-9-2 0 TomEaves 4 69
(David Brown) *chsd ldng pair: rdn over 2f out: kpt on same pce* **6/1**[2]

4 shd **Bear Essentials (IRE)** 2-9-2 0 SamJames 2 68
(David O'Meara) *chsd ldng pair: pushed along over 2f out: kpt on same pce* **10/1**[3]

0 5 9 **Seminole Dream (IRE)**[10] 2637 2-8-11 0 DougieCostello 5 36+
(Philip Kirby) *chsd ldng pair: pushed along over 2f out: sn wknd* **150/1**

0 6 7 **Hollywood Harry (IRE)**[35] 1921 2-9-2 0 PhillipMakin 3 20+
(Keith Dalgleish) *s.i.s: hld up in tch: pushed along 1/2-way: sn wknd* **28/1**

1m 11.52s (-0.88) **Going Correction** -0.225s/f (Firm) **6** Ran SP% **108.0**
Speed ratings (Par 93): **96,90,88,88,76 67**
CSF £4.77 TOTE £1.20: £1.10, £4.70; EX 4.40 Trifecta £10.80.
Owner 3 Batterhams and a Reay **Bred** Petra Bloodstock Agency Ltd **Trained** Middleham Moor, N Yorks

FOCUS
Watered ground but a warm, drying day. The inside rail was out 3yds. An uncompetitive juvenile contest, but a decent winner with probably more to come.

2957 TOTEJACKPOT AVAILABLE EVERY DAY MEDIAN AUCTION MAIDEN STKS — 1m
2:30 (2:33) (Class 5) 3-4-Y-O **£3,234** (£962; £481; £240) **Stalls** Low

Form RPR

1 **Nicholas T**[33] 4-10-0 0 PaulMulrennan 3 79+
(Jim Goldie) *stdd s: hld up in tch on inner: angled rt 2f out: pushed along and hdwy to chse ldr appr fnl f: kpt on: led towards fin* **6/1**[2]

4 2 ½ **Glengarry**[10] 2657 3-9-3 0 PhillipMakin 2 75+
(Keith Dalgleish) *trckd ldng pair: pushed along to ld over 1f out: rdn ins fnl f: one pce: hdd towards fin* **8/13**[1]

3 3 **Archippos** 3-9-3 0 DougieCostello 8 68
(Philip Kirby) *trckd ldng pair: rdn and outpcd 2f out: kpt on ins fnl f: wnt 3rd nr fin* **33/1**

6 4 ¾ **Dasheen**[6] 2780 3-9-3 0 JoeFanning 7 66
(Mark Johnston) *prom: rdn to ld 2f out: hdd over 1f out: no ex ins fnl f* **12/1**

5 4 ½ **Action Pursuits** 3-9-3 0 TonyHamilton 4 55
(Adrian Paul Keatley, Ire) *in tch: rdn over 2f out: wknd over 1f out* **8/1**

25-0 6 hd **Bay Mirage (IRE)**[21] 2307 3-9-0 75 JoeDoyle(3) 1 55
(Kevin Ryan) *led: rdn whn hdd 2f out: sn wknd* **7/1**[3]

1m 40.87s (-2.93) **Going Correction** -0.325s/f (Firm)
WFA 3 from 4yo 11lb **6** Ran SP% **110.4**
Speed ratings (Par 103): **101,100,97,96,92 92**
CSF £9.87 TOTE £8.30: £2.70, £1.10; EX 11.40 Trifecta £118.90.
Owner W M Johnstone **Bred** W M Johnstone **Trained** Uplawmoor, E Renfrews
■ Stewards' Enquiry : Dougie Costello two-day ban: used whip above permitted level (Jun 20-21)

FOCUS
This was run over 9yds further than advertised. A modest maiden.

2958 TOTEQUADPOT FOUR PLACES IN FOUR RACES H'CAP — 1m 2f
3:00 (3:00) (Class 6) (0-60,58) 4-Y-O+ **£2,264** (£673; £336; £168) **Stalls** Low

Form RPR

-203 1 **Testa Rossa (IRE)**[14] 2526 6-9-7 **58** (v) PaulMulrennan 2 67
(Jim Goldie) *midfield: smooth hdwy on inner over 2f out: led appr fnl f: pushed clr: comf* **7/2**[3]

-000 2 4 ½ **Grandest**[6] 2773 5-9-6 **57** BenCurtis 9 57
(Brian Ellison) *slowly away: hld up: rdn and hdwy on outer over 2f out: wnt 2nd ins fnl f: kpt on but no ch w wnr* **11/4**[1]

4 3 2 ¼ **Hydrant**[19] 2365 10-9-5 **56** JoeFanning 4 52
(Richard Guest) *led: rdn over 2f out: hdd appr fnl f: lost 2nd ins fnl f: no ex* **10/3**[2]

-452 4 nk **Indian Giver**[12] 2573 8-9-1 **57** (p) RobJFitzpatrick(5) 3 53
(John David Riches) *chsd ldr: rdn 3f out: sn one pce* **6/1**

06-6 5 3 ¼ **Judith Gardenier**[17] 2419 4-8-8 **45** RoystonFfrench 6 34
(Iain Jardine) *midfield: rdn over 3f out: wknd fnl f* **18/1**

4-00 6 1 ¼ **Intensified (IRE)**[19] 2365 5-8-10 **47** (p) JamesSullivan 1 34
(Ruth Carr) *chsd ldr: rdn 3f out: wknd appr fnl f* **20/1**

05-6 7 4 ½ **The Name's Bond**[19] 2365 4-8-8 **45** TomEaves 7 24
(Keith Reveley) *hld up: pushed along over 3f out: wknd appr fnl f* **22/1**

-000 8 1 ¼ **Moccasin (FR)**[13] 2555 7-9-6 **57** (b[1]) TonyHamilton 8 33
(Geoffrey Harker) *in tch on outer: pushed along and lost pl over 3f out: wknd fnl 2f* **10/1**

2m 7.84s (-4.16) **Going Correction** -0.325s/f (Firm) **8** Ran SP% **109.7**
Speed ratings (Par 101): **103,99,97,97,94 93,90,89**
CSF £12.38 CT £30.39 TOTE £3.70: £1.30, £1.80, £1.40; EX 14.60 Trifecta £43.70.
Owner Mr & Mrs Gordon Grant **Bred** Hugo Merry And Khalid Al-Mudhaf **Trained** Uplawmoor, E Renfrews

FOCUS
This was run over 9yds further than advertised. A moderate handicap, but the winner has a good record here and has been rated to a career best.

2959 TOTEEXACTA PICK THE 1ST AND 2ND H'CAP — 1m 1f 20y
3:30 (3:30) (Class 5) (0-75,75) 4-Y-O+ **£3,234** (£962; £481; £240) **Stalls** Low

Form RPR

0-31 1 **Cymraeg Bounty**[14] 2526 4-9-4 **72** JoeFanning 4 84+
(Iain Jardine) *racd keenly: trckd ldr: led over 3f out: pushed clr over 2f out: rdn over 1f out: kpt on* **7/4**[1]

-066 2 2 ½ **Muqarred (USA)**[7] 2743 4-9-7 **75** (p) SamJames 3 79
(David Loughnane) *led: hdd over 3f out: sn rdn: kpt on but no ch w wnr* **12/1**

111 **3** 3/4 **Millefiori (IRE)**[12] 2573 4-9-0 **68**....(p) TonyHamilton 8 70
(Adrian Paul Keatley, Ire) *midfield: rdn and hdwy over 2f out: disp 2nd ent fnl f: no ex towards fin* **7/2**[2]

2303 **4** 1 1/4 **Silver Duke (IRE)**[4] 2811 5-8-8 **62**....(b) JamesSullivan 7 62
(Jim Goldie) *s.i.s: hld up in rr: rdn 3f out: sme hdwy 2f out: drvn appr fnl f: one pce* **12/1**

6652 **5** 3/4 **Kiwi Bay**[7] 2743 11-9-6 **74**.... PaulMulrennan 6 72
(Michael Dods) *midfield: rdn over 2f out: no imp* **5/1**[3]

-340 **6** 2 1/2 **Beautiful Stranger (IRE)**[19] 2362 5-9-5 **73**....(p) PhillipMakin 9 65
(Keith Dalgleish) *in tch: rdn over 2f out: wknd fnl f* **7/1**

30-4 **7** 5 **Remember Rocky**[42] 1697 7-8-7 **66**....(p) AnnaHesketh(5) 5 47
(Lucy Normile) *hld up: pushed along over 4f out: rdn over 2f out: wknd over 1f out* **10/1**

1m 54.82s (-2.68) **Going Correction** -0.325s/f (Firm) **7** Ran SP% **112.2**
Speed ratings (Par 103): **98,95,95,94,93 91,86**
CSF £23.22 CT £66.05 TOTE £2.20: £1.50, £4.90; EX 33.00 Trifecta £175.80.
Owner M Andrews **Bred** Richard Evans **Trained** Carrutherstown, D'fries & G'way

FOCUS
This was run over 9yds further than advertised. The 1st and 2nd raced 2nd and 1st for much of the way. The winner was building on his previous win.

2960 TOTETRIFECTA PICK THE 1, 2, 3 H'CAP 7f 50y
4:00 (4:01) (Class 5) (0-75,75) 4-Y-O+ **£3,234** (£962; £481; £240) **Stalls** High

Form RPR
0105 **1** **Favourite Treat (USA)**[19] 2361 6-9-4 **72**....(e) JamesSullivan 1 82
(Ruth Carr) *in tch: rdn and hdwy to chse ldr appr fnl f: led ins fnl f: kpt on* **16/1**

2121 **2** 1 3/4 **Surewecan**[17] 2421 4-9-3 **71**.... JoeFanning 3 76
(Mark Johnston) *led: hdd over 5f out: chsd ldr: led again over 1f out: sn rdn: hdd ins fnl f: one pce* **4/1**[1]

1422 **3** hd **Eastern Dragon (IRE)**[48] 1546 6-9-3 **71**.... RoystonFfrench 7 76
(Iain Jardine) *midfield: rdn over 2f out: hdwy appr fnl f: kpt on* **4/1**[1]

2054 **4** hd **Gold Flash**[9] 2677 4-9-4 **72**....(p) PhillipMakin 6 76
(Keith Dalgleish) *midfield: rdn over 2f out: hdwy towards outer over 1f out: kpt on fnl f* **4/1**[1]

-200 **5** shd **Mustaqbal (IRE)**[20] 2347 4-9-2 **70**....(p) PaulMulrennan 8 75
(Michael Dods) *hld up: pushed along over 2f out: hdwy over 1f out: bit short of room ent fnl f and again ins fnl f: kpt on fnl 110yds* **5/1**[2]

5-30 **6** 3/4 **Sophisticated Heir (IRE)**[27] 1521 6-9-0 **75**....(b) AdamMcNamara(7) 2 77
(David Loughnane) *hld up: pushed along over 2f out: short of room jst ins fnl f: swtchd rt: kpt on fnl 75yds: nvr able to chal* **12/1**[3]

-055 **7** 1 1/2 **Dark Crystal**[12] 2574 5-8-8 **62**.... GeorgeChaloner 5 60
(Linda Perratt) *chsd ldr: rdn over 2f out: wknd ins fnl f* **16/1**

0-10 **8** 1 3/4 **Haidees Reflection**[12] 2574 6-8-11 **65**.... TomEaves 9 59
(Jim Goldie) *hld up: rdn over 2f out: nvr threatened* **14/1**

-042 **9** 1 3/4 **Goninodaethat**[14] 2528 8-8-5 **59**.... CamHardie 4 48
(Jim Goldie) *racd keenly: led over 5f out: sn clr: reduced advantage over 2f out: rdn whn hdd over 1f out: wknd ins fnl f* **20/1**

6-00 **10** 2 1/4 **Gambino (IRE)**[24] 2198 6-9-1 **72**.... JoeDoyle(3) 10 55
(John David Riches) *midfield: rdn over 2f out: wknd over 1f out* **12/1**[3]

1m 30.34s (-3.06) **Going Correction** -0.325s/f (Firm) **10** Ran SP% **115.2**
Speed ratings (Par 103): **104,102,101,101,101 100,98,96,94,92**
CSF £78.20 CT £319.84 TOTE £12.60: £2.80, £1.90, £2.90; EX 77.00 Trifecta £279.50.
Owner Paul Saxton & The Bottom Liners **Bred** Fares Farm Inc **Trained** Huby, N Yorks

FOCUS
This was run over 9yds further than advertised. The keen-going Goninodaethat blasted clear early on, but was ignored by the others. Ordinary form.

2961 TOTEPOOL HAPPY RETIREMENT MALCOLM KNOWLES H'CAP 6f
4:30 (4:32) (Class 4) (0-80,80) 4-Y-O+ **£5,175** (£1,540; £769; £384) **Stalls** Low

Form RPR
-002 **1** **Intisaab**[30] 2028 5-9-4 **80**....(p) ShelleyBirkett(3) 8 89
(David O'Meara) *hld up in tch: rdn and hdwy 2f out: led appr fnl f: kpt on* **11/4**[1]

0-15 **2** 3/4 **Mo Henry**[14] 2524 4-8-3 **62**....(v) JoeFanning 7 68
(Adrian Paul Keatley, Ire) *hld up in tch: rdn and hdwy over 1f out: ev ch ent fnl f: kpt on* **11/4**[1]

0403 **3** nk **Classic Seniority**[16] 2491 4-9-2 **75**.... SamJames 4 80
(Marjorie Fife) *pressed ldr: rdn over 2f out: kpt on* **11/2**[3]

-003 **4** shd **Star Cracker (IRE)**[4] 2812 4-8-4 **63**.... CamHardie 6 67
(Jim Goldie) *trckd ldng pair: rdn 2f out: kpt on* **12/1**

4544 **5** 2 3/4 **Vallarta (IRE)**[14] 2524 6-9-1 **74**.... JamesSullivan 2 70
(Ruth Carr) *led narrowly: rdn 2f out: hdd appr fnl f: wknd ins fnl f* **3/1**[2]

3220 **6** 1 1/2 **Go Go Green (IRE)**[10] 2658 10-9-0 **73**.... PaulMulrennan 5 64
(Jim Goldie) *s.i.s: hld up: rdn over 2f out: nvr threatened* **12/1**

-550 **7** 7 **Jinky**[14] 2524 8-8-8 **67**.... TomEaves 1 35
(Linda Perratt) *trckd ldng pair: rdn over 2f out: wknd over 1f out* **28/1**

1m 10.16s (-2.24) **Going Correction** -0.225s/f (Firm) **7** Ran SP% **112.6**
Speed ratings (Par 105): **105,104,103,103,99 97,88**
CSF £10.24 CT £36.69 TOTE £2.90: £1.60, £2.40; EX 12.00 Trifecta £54.70.
Owner Stuart Graham **Bred** Shadwell Estate Company Limited **Trained** Upper Helmsley, N Yorks

FOCUS
A fair and well-run sprint handicap with the winner recording a personal best.

2962 TOTEPOOLLIVEINFO.COM H'CAP (FOR LADY AMATEUR RIDERS) 1m 5f 13y
5:00 (5:00) (Class 6) (0-65,65) 4-Y-O+ **£2,183** (£677; £338; £169) **Stalls** Low

Form RPR
0/0- **1** **Van Mildert (IRE)**[92] 140 7-8-11 **46** oh1....(p) MissAWaugh(5) 1 52
(Kenneth Slack) *mde all: rdn over 2f out: strly pressed over 1f out: edgd rt jst ins fnl f: hld on wl* **10/1**

0403 **2** 2 **Chauvelin**[6] 2781 5-9-2 **46** oh1....(b) MissADeniel 7 49
(Richard Guest) *hld up: hdwy over 3f out: rdn to chal over 1f out: bmpd sltly jst ins fnl f: sn drvn: hung lft and one pce fnl 75yds* **15/8**[1]

0045 **3** 3 1/2 **Question Of Faith**[12] 2573 5-9-5 **49**.... MissSBrotherton 4 47
(Martin Todhunter) *hld up in tch: hdwy to trck ldr 7f out: rdn over 2f out: one pce in 3rd fr over 1f out* **7/2**[3]

0433 **4** 3 **Triple Eight (IRE)**[10] 2659 8-10-0 **65**....(p) MissJAHeneghan(7) 2 58
(Philip Kirby) *in tch: rdn 3f out: wknd fnl f* **3/1**[2]

4-40 **5** 3 1/2 **Merchant Of Dubai**[19] 2362 11-10-7 **65**.... MrsCBartley 6 53
(Jim Goldie) *trckd ldr: rdn 3f out: wknd over 1f out* **9/2**

2m 53.42s (-0.58) **Going Correction** -0.325s/f (Firm) **5** Ran SP% **109.3**
Speed ratings (Par 101): **88,86,84,82,80**
CSF £28.69 TOTE £9.30: £3.90, £1.30; EX 33.30 Trifecta £148.00.
Owner Mrs Evelyn Slack **Bred** Chesters Stud Ltd **Trained** Hilton, Cumbria

FOCUS
This was run over 18yds further than advertised. A low-grade handicap and not form to be positive about with the winner given a soft lead.

T/Plt: £19.30 to a £1 stake. Pool: £67,496.42 - 2546.42 winning units. T/Qpdt: £11.50 to a £1 stake. Pool: £5,009.26 - 321.10 winning units. **Andrew Sheret**

2641 BRIGHTON (L-H)
Monday, June 6

OFFICIAL GOING: Good to firm changing to good to firm (firm in places) after race 1 (2.15)
Wind: virtually nil Weather: sunny and warm

2963 REGIS REMOVALS BRIGHTON SUPPORTS DVLCC NOVICE AUCTION STKS 5f 213y
2:15 (2:15) (Class 5) 2-Y-O **£3,234** (£962; £481; £240) **Stalls** Low

Form RPR
5 **1** **Spirit Of Sarwan (IRE)**[25] 2173 2-9-1 0.... AdamBeschizza 6 72
(Julia Feilden) *hld up in tch in midfield: hdwy u.p over 1f out: led 100yds out: r.o strly* **9/1**

2 **2** 1 **Bayston Hill**[14] 2535 2-9-1 0.... LiamKeniry 8 69
(Mark Usher) *stdd s: hld up in tch in last trio: effrt jst over 2f out: rdn and ev ch over 1f out tl no ex and one pce fnl 100yds* **10/3**[2]

0 **3** hd **Irish Melody (IRE)**[7] 2739 2-9-1 0....(p) JFEgan 2 68
(Bill Turner) *led: rdn 2f out: hrd pressed and drvn over 1f out: hdd and one pce fnl 100yds* **66/1**

23 **4** 1 **Peachey Carnehan**[9] 2675 2-9-2 0.... SilvestreDeSousa 5 66
(Mark Johnston) *chsd ldr: drvn and ev ch over 1f tl no ex 100yds: wknd towards fin* **2/1**[1]

5 **5** 2 1/2 **Roman Legion (IRE)**[10] 2641 2-9-1 0.... RobertWinston 7 58
(Dean Ivory) *dwlt and swtchd lft after s: hld up in tch in last trio: effrt 2f out: sn chalng and rdn: hung lft and no ex 100yds out: sn btn and eased towards fin* **4/1**[3]

6 1 3/4 **Amathyst** 2-8-10 0.... LukeMorris 1 48
(Michael Appleby) *sn chsng ldrs: moving rt and barging match w rival jst over 2f out: unable qck u.p over 1f out: wknd ins fnl f* **7/1**

0361 **7** shd **King Of Castilla**[28] 2104 2-9-2 0....(t) CallumShepherd(5) 3 58
(Gay Kelleway) *t.k.h: in tch in midfield: carried rt: n.m.r and barging match w rival jst over 2f out: drvn and no hdwy over 1f out: wknd ins fnl f* **8/1**

0 **8** 3 1/4 **Myredbush (IRE)**[19] 2376 2-8-10 0.... JimCrowley 4 38
(Simon Dow) *dropped to rr 4f out: rdn and no hdwy 2f out: wknd fnl f* **25/1**

1m 10.33s (0.13) **Going Correction** -0.10s/f (Good) **8** Ran SP% **115.4**
Speed ratings (Par 93): **95,93,93,92,88 86,86,81**
CSF £39.50 TOTE £11.70: £2.80, £1.30, £7.90; EX 47.00 Trifecta £980.40.
Owner Mr & Mrs George Bhatti **Bred** John Fallon **Trained** Exning, Suffolk

FOCUS
The going was good to firm (GoingStick: 9.0) and the rail was dolled out from the 4 1/2f point to the 3 1/2f marker, adding 4yds to each race distance. A modest novice event.

2964 KIWI RECRUITMENT CHICHESTER SUPPORTS DVLCC H'CAP 5f 213y
2:45 (2:45) (Class 6) (0-60,59) 3-Y-O+ **£2,587** (£770; £384; £192) **Stalls** Low

Form RPR
0062 **1** **Soaring Spirits (IRE)**[10] 2647 6-9-8 **55**....(b) RobertWinston 8 66
(Dean Ivory) *sn led and mde rest: rdn over 1f out: asserted u.p 1f out: styd on strly and drew clr ins fnl f* **9/4**[1]

0/ **2** 2 1/2 **Bounty Pursuit**[274] 4-9-9 **56**....[1] LukeMorris 6 60
(Michael Appleby) *sn chsng ldrs: rdn ent fnl 2f: styd on u.p to press ldrs 1f out: chsd wnr and kpt on same pce ins fnl f* **11/2**[3]

056 **3** 1 1/4 **Canford Belle**[26] 2143 3-9-1 **56**.... JimCrowley 5 54
(Amanda Perrett) *in tch in midfield: effrt over 1f out: chsd ldng trio 1f out: swtchd rt ins fnl f: styd on u.p to go 3rd towards fin: no threat to wnr* **16/1**

0430 **4** 3/4 **Commanche**[12] 2584 7-9-12 **59**....(b) SilvestreDeSousa 4 57
(Chris Dwyer) *led briefly: sn hdd and chsd wnr for over 1f out: wnt 2nd again and swtchd rt ent fnl 2f: drvn and pressing wnr over 1f out tl no ex and lost 2nd ins fnl f: wknd fnl 75yds* **3/1**[2]

-550 **5** 2 1/4 **Fossa**[12] 2584 6-8-13 **46**.... RyanClark 7 37
(Mark Brisbourne) *dwlt: sn rcvrd and in tch in midfield: hdwy 2f out: rdn and no imp in 4th over 1f out: wknd ins fnl f* **20/1**

1401 **6** 1/2 **Diamond Vine (IRE)**[12] 2584 8-9-6 **53**....(p) DavidProbert 3 42
(Ronald Harris) *sn dropped to last pair and rdn along: drvn over 1f out: plugged on ins fnl f: nvr trbld ldrs* **9/1**

5-00 **7** 1 1/2 **Essaka (IRE)**[19] 2380 4-9-7 **57**.... GeorgeDowning(3) 1 42
(Tony Carroll) *stdd and awkward leaving stalls: slowly away and t.k.h in rr: clsd in centre 3f out: rdn and no hdwy over 1f out: wknd fnl f* **7/1**

5415 **8** 2 3/4 **Cuban Queen (USA)**[26] 2155 3-8-12 **53**....(p) SteveDrowne 2 28
(Jeremy Gask) *in tch in last trio: effrt 2f out: sn btn: wknd over 1f out* **10/1**

00-0 **9** 8 **Rubheira**[10] 2635 4-8-12 **45**....(b) JimmyQuinn 9
(Paul Burgoyne) *taken down early: racd keenly: hdwy to chse wnr over 4f out tl ent fnl 2f: sn pushed rt and lost pl: bhd over 1f out: eased wl ins fnl f* **66/1**

1m 9.34s (-0.86) **Going Correction** -0.10s/f (Good)
WFA 3 from 4yo+ 8lb **9** Ran SP% **114.9**
Speed ratings (Par 101): **101,97,96,95,92 91,89,85,75**
CSF £14.93 CT £157.23 TOTE £3.00: £1.20, £2.40, £3.50; EX 18.70 Trifecta £173.10.
Owner Mrs Doreen Carter **Bred** Kevin & Meta Cullen **Trained** Radlett, Herts

FOCUS
Race distance increased by 4yds. A moderate sprint handicap in which the winner was suited by the drop back in trip.

2965 KSL ACCOUNTS CHICHESTER SUPPORTS DVLCC H'CAP 1m 1f 209y
3:15 (3:15) (Class 5) (0-75,75) 4-Y-O+ **£2,911** (£866; £432; £216) **Stalls** High

Form RPR
2-05 **1** **Nigel**[9] 2699 4-9-7 **75**.... ShaneKelly 1 84
(Richard Hughes) *mde all: rdn over 1f out: asserting whn hung rt and rdn 1f out: styd on wl and in command fnl 150yds: pushed out fnl 100yds* **9/4**[2]

4-21 **2** 2 1/4 **Lord Reason**[10] 2646 4-9-4 **72**.... SilvestreDeSousa 4 76
(John Butler) *hld up in tch in 4th: effrt over 2f out: rdn to chse wnr over 1f out: struggling to qckn and swtchd lft 1f out: styd on same pce ins fnl f* **11/8**[1]

10-0 **3** 1 1/2 **The Gay Cavalier**[35] 1933 5-8-9 **70**....(t) JonathanFisher(7) 3 71
(John Ryan) *stdd s: hld up off the pce in last pair: clsd and in tch 5f out: nt clr run and swtchd lft 2f out: hdwy to chse ldng pair 1f out: swtchd rt and kpt on ins fnl f* **14/1**

1/00 **4** 3 **New Street (IRE)**[30] 2043 5-9-7 **75**....(v[1]) TimmyMurphy 2 70
(Jim Best) *hld up off the pce in last pair: clsd and in tch 5f out: rdn and no hdwy over 1f out: wl hld and styd on same pce fnl f* **20/1**

256- **5** *shd* **Persian Breeze**[34] 7826 4-9-7 **75**..............................(b[1]) JimCrowley 7 70
(Lucy Wadham) *chsd wnr tl wl over 1f out: sn u.p and unable qck: wl hld and kpt on same pce ins fnl f* **7/1**

-062 **6** *nse* **Deluxe**[34] 1949 4-8-7 **61**.. JFEgan 6 56
(Pat Phelan) *t.k.h: chsd ldng pair: effrt on inner over 2f out: outpcd over 1f out: wl hld and styd on same pce fnl f* **6/1**[3]

2m 2.59s (-1.01) **Going Correction** -0.10s/f (Good) **6** Ran SP% **111.1**
Speed ratings (Par 103): **100,98,97,94,94 94**
CSF £5.60 TOTE £2.60: £1.90, £1.40; EX 5.80 Trifecta £33.40.
Owner Normandie Stud Ltd **Bred** Normandie Stud Ltd **Trained** Upper Lambourn, Berkshire

FOCUS
Race distance increased by 4yds. This was dominated from the start by the winner, who couldn't have had things much easier in front.

2966 LUV CARPETS BOGNOR REGIS SUPPORTS DVLCC H'CAP 1m 3f 196y
3:45 (3:45) (Class 4) (0-85,85) 4-Y-O+ **£4,690** (£1,395; £697; £348) **Stalls** High

Form RPR

-152 **1** **Knight Music**[25] 2176 4-9-6 **84**.. RobertHavlin 2 89
(Michael Attwater) *mde all: rdn over 2f out: sustained duel w runner-up after: r.o wl and a jst holding rival ins fnl f: rdn out* **6/4**[1]

4-03 **2** *shd* **Steppe Daughter (IRE)**[14] 2549 5-9-2 **80**....................... OisinMurphy 5 84
(Denis Coakley) *chsd wnr after 1f: rdn and ev ch over 1f out: sustained duel w wnr after: r.o wl but a jst hld ins fnl f* **6/4**[1]

30-0 **3** *¾* **Rydan (IRE)**[14] 2549 5-9-5 **83**..(v) TomQueally 6 86
(Gary Moore) *chsd wnr for 1f: trckd ldrs after: effrt ent fnl 2f: drvn over 1f out: styd on u.p fnl 100yds: nvr quite enough pce to chal ldrs* **4/1**[2]

152- **4** *1* **Echo Brava**[175] 5938 6-9-7 **85**.. TimmyMurphy 4 86
(Jim Best) *stdd s: hld up in tch in rr: effrt 2f out: rdn and unable qck 1f out: styd on same pce ins fnl f* **11/1**[3]

2m 39.57s (6.87) **Going Correction** -0.10s/f (Good) **4** Ran SP% **108.3**
Speed ratings (Par 105): **73,72,72,71**
CSF £3.97 TOTE £2.50; EX 3.70 Trifecta £6.20.
Owner The Attwater Partnership **Bred** Mr & Mrs A E Pakenham **Trained** Epsom, Surrey

FOCUS
Race distance increased by 4yds. This was run at a steady gallop and developed into a bit of a sprint with the order hardly changing.

2967 BUSINESS PULSE HORSHAM SUPPORTS DVLCC H'CAP 1m 1f 209y
4:15 (4:16) (Class 6) (0-55,56) 3-Y-O **£2,264** (£673; £336; £168) **Stalls** High

Form RPR

0-00 **1** **Lady Rocka**[19] 2366 3-9-7 **54**..(b[1]) JimCrowley 7 59
(Amanda Perrett) *chsd ldng trio: effrt 2f out: styd on u.p over 1f out: led wl ins fnl f: gng away at fin: rdn out* **12/1**

0500 **2** *1 ¾* **French Legend**[12] 2590 3-9-2 **49**....................................... OisinMurphy 1 51
(Andrew Balding) *chsd ldr tl 5f out: styd prom: drvn and hdwy over 1f out: led 1f out: hdd and one pce wl ins fnl f* **8/1**[3]

0 **3** *nk* **Princess Zoffany (IRE)**[31] 2005 3-9-1 **48**....................... KieranO'Neill 4 49
(Jimmy Fox) *hld up in tch in midfield: effrt over 2f out: hdwy u.p over 1f out: chsd ldrs 1f out: styd on same pce ins fnl f* **50/1**

0-35 **4** *nk* **Becca Campbell (IRE)**[12] 2590 3-9-7 **54**........................(p) JohnFahy 6 55
(Eve Johnson Houghton) *dwlt and rdn along early: in tch in midfield: hdwy u.p over 1f out: kpt on same pce ins fnl f* **10/1**

0-41 **5** *nk* **Tyrannical**[11] 2608 3-9-7 **54**.. LukeMorris 5 54
(Sir Mark Prescott Bt) *chsd ldrs: wnt 2nd 5f out: rdn and ev ch over 2f out: edgd rt and unable qck over 1f out: cl 3rd and edgd bk lft u.p 1f out: styd on same pce ins fnl f* **11/10**[1]

-630 **6** *¾* **Mischief Maisy (IRE)**[27] 2126 3-9-7 **54**............................. ShaneKelly 8 53
(Amanda Perrett) *hld up in tch in midfield: effrt over 1f out: drvn 1f out: styd on fnl 100yds: nvr enough pce to threaten ldrs* **33/1**

-000 **7** *3 ½* **Pour Pavot (IRE)**[103] 700 3-9-2 **54**.......................... HectorCrouch[(5)] 2 46
(Gary Moore) *stdd s: t.k.h: hld up in tch in last trio: effrt 2f out: sn rdn and ho hdwy: plugging on but wl hld whn nt clr run and swtchd rt ins fnl f* **16/1**

-001 **8** *hd* **Captain Gerald**[4] 2828 3-9-4 **56** 6ex..................(p) JosephineGordon[(5)] 3 48
(John Ryan) *led: rdn wl over 1f out: drvn and hdd 1f out: sn btn and wknd fnl 100yds* **11/2**[2]

-003 **9** *10* **Ron's Ballad**[48] 1548 3-8-5 **45**..................................... GeorgeWood[(7)] 10 18
(Michael Madgwick) *stdd and dropped in bhd after s: hld up in tch in last trio: effrt 2f out: drvn and no hdwy over 1f out: wknd fnl f* **14/1**

0-04 **10** *6* **Broughtons Mystery**[20] 2325 3-9-7 **54**.................... SilvestreDeSousa 9 15
(Willie Musson) *stdd s: hld up in tch in rr: rdn over 2f out: sme hdwy u.p over 1f out: sn btn: wknd fnl f* **10/1**

2m 2.36s (-1.24) **Going Correction** -0.10s/f (Good) **10** Ran SP% **117.4**
Speed ratings (Par 97): **100,98,98,98,97 97,94,94,86,81**
CSF £105.06 CT £4579.68 TOTE £15.10: £2.90, £2.10, £11.70; EX 133.50 Trifecta £7907.30 Part won..
Owner Coombelands Racing Syndicate **Bred** Mrs J Chandris **Trained** Pulborough, W Sussex

FOCUS
Race distance increased by 4yds. A moderate handicap with the principals all in a heap. Modest form.

2968 ENVITIA HORSHAM SUPPORTS DVLCC FILLIES' H'CAP 7f 214y
4:45 (4:45) (Class 5) (0-70,70) 3-Y-O **£2,911** (£866; £432; £216) **Stalls** Low

Form RPR

-006 **1** **Bay Of St Malo (IRE)**[17] 2431 3-9-2 **65**........................... KieranO'Neill 4 74
(Richard Hannon) *chsd ldr tl rdn to ld over 1f out: r.o wl and in command ins fnl f: rdn out* **9/1**

-023 **2** *2 ½* **Carpe Diem Lady (IRE)**[17] 2431 3-9-7 **70**............................. JohnFahy 8 73
(Clive Cox) *rrd as stalls opened: sn rcvrd and t.k.h in midfield: effrt u.p 2f out: hdwy to chse wnr 1f out: styd on same pce ins fnl f* **3/1**[1]

666- **3** *1 ¼* **Cacica**[181] 8144 3-9-5 **68**..................................... WilliamTwiston-Davies 7 68
(George Scott) *chsd ldrs: effrt over 1f out: unable qck and styd on same pce ins fnl f* **7/1**

6445 **4** *¾* **Aksum**[11] 2608 3-7-10 **52** oh1 ow1.............................. GeorgeWood[(7)] 13 50
(Michael Bell) *t.k.h: chsd ldrs: edgd lft u.p over 1f out: kpt on same pce ins fnl f* **6/1**[3]

406 **5** *1 ¼* **Angelic Guest (IRE)**[15] 2505 3-8-12 **68**.................. KillianHennessy[(7)] 6 64
(Mick Channon) *hld up in tch in midfield: rdn and hdwy towards inner over 1f out: nt clr run and swtchd rt ins fnl f: styd on but no threat to wnr* **12/1**

-320 **6** *1 ¼* **Last Star Falling (IRE)**[21] 2306 3-9-3 **66**.............(p) SilvestreDeSousa 9 59
(Henry Spiller) *led: drvn and hdd over 1f out: no ex and wknd ins fnl f* **9/1**

4-60 **7** *½* **Long Island**[10] 2652 3-8-1 **55** ow2............................. PaddyPilley[(5)] 5 47
(Mark Brisbourne) *s.i.s: hld up in last pair: rdn and sme hdwy over 1f out: swtchd rt and kpt on ins fnl f: nvr trbld ldrs* **25/1**

14-0 **8** *½* **Pinch A Kiss**[61] 1257 3-9-3 **66**.. RyanClark 10 56
(Jonathan Portman) *in tch towards rr: effrt u.p 2f out: sn drvn and no hdwy: wl hld fnl f* **25/1**

-332 **9** *11* **Fun For All**[105] 675 3-9-6 **69**... LukeMorris 3 34
(James Tate) *wl in tch in midfield: effrt over 2f out: hung lft and wknd over 1f out: bhd and eased wl ins fnl f* **7/1**

3551 **P** **Heads You Win**[21] 2293 3-9-1 **64**................................ TimmyMurphy 12
(Jamie Osborne) *stdd after s: hld up in last pair: effrt 2f out: sn hung lft and btn: eased and p.u ins fnl f: dismntd* **11/2**[2]

1m 34.64s (-1.36) **Going Correction** -0.10s/f (Good) **10** Ran SP% **115.1**
Speed ratings (Par 96): **102,99,98,97,96 95,94,94,83,**
CSF £35.68 CT £200.23 TOTE £10.20: £2.70, £1.50, £2.50; EX 42.10 Trifecta £334.60.
Owner Coriolan Partnership **Bred** T Purcell & K Purcell **Trained** East Everleigh, Wilts

FOCUS
Race distance increased by 4yds. A modest fillies' event.

2969 DAME VERA LYNN CHILDREN'S CHARITY APPRENTICE H'CAP 6f 209y
5:15 (5:17) (Class 6) (0-55,54) 3-Y-O+ **£2,264** (£673; £336; £168) **Stalls** Low

Form RPR

-565 **1** **Ettie Hart (IRE)**[21] 2293 3-8-8 **53**...................... KillianHennessy[(5)] 4 59
(Mick Channon) *mde all: rdn over 1f out: hrd pressed jst ins fnl f: styd on wl: rdn out* **11/2**[3]

5102 **2** *½* **Ashford Island**[21] 2293 3-8-6 **51**................................ KevinLundie[(5)] 12 56
(Mike Murphy) *hld up in tch: rdn and hdwy over 1f out: chal jst ins fnl f: kpt on but a hld* **5/1**[2]

560- **3** *3 ¼* **Frank Bridge**[301] 5218 3-8-7 **50**.................................. AaronJones[(3)] 11 46
(Eve Johnson Houghton) *in tch in midfield: effrt and n.m.r ent fnl 2f: hdwy 1f out: styd on to go 3rd wl ins fnl f: no threat to ldng pair* **20/1**

543- **4** *¾* **The Reel Way (GR)**[309] 4901 5-9-5 **49**........................ DanielMuscutt 5 47
(Patrick Chamings) *chsd ldrs: effrt on inner to chse wnr 2f out tl 1f out: sn btn: wknd and lost 3rd wl ins fnl f* **8/1**

2004 **5** *nse* **Divine Touch**[11] 2609 3-8-1 **46**................................. GeorgeWood[(5)] 13 40
(Robert Eddery) *hld up in tch towards rr: effrt u.p over 1f out: styd on ins fnl f: no threat to ldrs* **10/1**

1233 **6** *1 ¼* **Israfel**[83] 947 3-8-11 **54**.. LucyKBarry[(3)] 10 44
(Jamie Osborne) *chsd ldr tl 4f out: rdn 2f out: unable qck and losing pl whn short of room 1f out: wknd ins fnl f* **10/1**

000/ **7** *shd* **Birikyno**[857] 411 5-9-4 **48**.. RobHornby 9 42
(Matthew Salaman) *stdd s: hld up in tch in midfield: effrt on inner whn nt clr run and swtchd rt over 1f out: keeping on same pce whn nt clr run and no hdwy 100yds out* **25/1**

624- **8** *1 ½* **Deftera Lad (IRE)**[273] 6169 4-9-4 **53**........................ PaddyBradley[(5)] 3 43
(Pat Phelan) *chsd ldrs: wnt 2nd 4f out tl 2f out: sn u.p and unable qck: wknd ins fnl f* **7/1**

-354 **9** *11* **Comadoir (IRE)**[40] 1781 10-9-1 **45**..........................(p) ThomasBrown 14 5
(Paul Burgoyne) *hld up in last pair: effrt wl over 1f out: sn btn: bhd and eased wl ins fnl f* **12/1**

000- **10** *7* **Overstone Lass (IRE)**[235] 7232 4-8-10 **45**.............. MeganNicholls[(5)] 2
(John Spearing) *sn bhd: edgd lft and no hdwy u.p over 1f out: bhd and eased ins fnl f* **50/1**

3233 **U** **Wild Flower (IRE)**[10] 2647 4-9-1 **50**.........................[1] MitchGodwin[(5)] 8
(Jimmy Fox) *in tch in midfield whn clipped heels: stmbld and uns rdr 5f out* **10/3**[1]

1m 22.61s (-0.49) **Going Correction** -0.10s/f (Good)
WFA 3 from 4yo+ 10lb **11** Ran SP% **115.2**
Speed ratings (Par 101): **98,97,93,92,92 91,91,89,76,68**
CSF £31.68 CT £520.71 TOTE £7.20: £2.10, £2.10, £6.20; EX 38.30 Trifecta £516.60.
Owner Lord Ilsley Racing (Marsden Syndicate) **Bred** Lynn Lodge Stud **Trained** West Ilsley, Berks
■ Killian Hennessy's first winner in Britain.
■ Stewards' Enquiry : Killian Hennessy four-day ban: used whip above permitted level (Jun 20-23)

FOCUS
Race distance increased by 4yds. An ordinary handicap with the winner showing good speed.
T/Jkpt: Not won. T/Plt: £335.50 to a £1 stake. Pool: £78,520.86 - 170.85 winning units. T/Qpdt: £90.80 to a £1 stake. Pool: £5,689.38 - 46.35 winning units. **Steve Payne**

2662 PONTEFRACT (L-H)
Monday, June 6

OFFICIAL GOING: Good to firm (8.7)
Wind: Light half against Weather: Fine & dry

2970 HUDDERSFIELD GIANTS NOVICE AUCTION FILLIES' STKS (PLUS 10 RACE) 6f
6:45 (6:47) (Class 5) 2-Y-O **£3,234** (£962; £481; £240) **Stalls** Low

Form RPR

4 **1** **Teofonic (IRE)**[12] 2570 2-8-12 0.................................. FrannyNorton 6 78+
(Mark Johnston) *towards rr: gd hdwy over 2f out: trckd ldrs over 1f out: rdn to ld ins fnl f: sn clr* **7/4**[1]

6 **2** *5* **Eva Gore**[18] 2404 2-8-10 0... JackGarritty 1 61+
(David O'Meara) *trckd ldr: hdwy 2f out: led wl over 1f out: rdn ent fnl f: sn hdd and kpt on same pce* **9/1**

3 *nk* **Snuggy (IRE)** 2-8-12 0...................................... GrahamGibbons 2 62+
(David Barron) *dwlt and in rr: gd hdwy over 2f out: chsd ldrs on inner over 1f out: sn rdn and kpt on same pce* **7/1**[3]

5 **4** *4* **Serenity Dove**[18] 2404 2-9-0 0...................................... JoeyHaynes 5 52
(K R Burke) *chsd ldrs: rdn along 2f out: drvn over 1f out: no imp* **15/2**

0 **5** *3 ¼* **Babalugats (IRE)**[18] 2404 2-8-10 0................................... DavidAllan 9 38
(Tim Easterby) *in tch: pushed along and outpcd 1/2-way: hdwy on outer wl over 1f out: sn rdn and kpt on* **40/1**

6 *3* **London Grammar (IRE)** 2-9-0 0.. JasonHart 8 33
(John Quinn) *dwlt: a towards rr* **20/1**

56 **7** *4* **Sheppard's Gift**[11] 2612 2-9-0 0.............................(b[1]) DuranFentiman 10 21
(Tim Easterby) *sn led: rdn along over 2f out: hdd wl over 1f out: sn drvn and wknd* **50/1**

8 *2 ¼* **Not Now Nadia (IRE)** 2-9-0 0.................................... ConnorBeasley 7 15
(Michael Dods) *chsd ldrs: rdn along over 2f out: sn wknd* **16/1**

00 **9** *14* **Red Shanghai (IRE)**[34] 1951 2-8-10 0.......................... RichardKingscote 4
(Tom Dascombe) *chsd ldng pair: rdn along 2f out: sn drvn and wknd* **20/1**

10 *35* **Shelneverwalkalone** 2-8-10 0.. BarryMcHugh 3
(Ivan Furtado) *dwlt: sn in tch on inner: pushed along over 2f out: sn rdn and wknd* **33/1**

P **Poker Alice** 2-9-0 **0** JimmyFortune 11
(Peter Chapple-Hyam) *sn outpcd and bhd whn lost action and p.u after 2f* **7/2**[2]

1m 19.34s (2.44) **Going Correction** +0.20s/f (Good) **11** Ran SP% **115.6**
Speed ratings (Par 90): **91,84,83,78,74 70,64,61,43,**
CSF £16.81 TOTE £2.60: £1.10, £2.50, £2.20; EX 19.10 Trifecta £86.90.
Owner Kingsley Park 5 **Bred** Floors Farming And Dominic Burke **Trained** Middleham Moor, N Yorks

FOCUS
The rail was been dolled out 5yds from the 6f bend adding approximately 8yds to all races. A strongly run race early, but the form lacks depth.

2971 TONY BETHELL MEMORIAL H'CAP (ROUND 3 OF THE PONTEFRACT STAYERS CHAMPIONSHIP 2016) 2m 1f 22y
7:15 (7:20) (Class 4) (0-80,80) 4-Y-O+ **£5,175** (£1,540; £769; £384) **Stalls** Low

Form RPR

21-6 **1** **Bulas Belle**[18] 2406 6-9-4 **74** BarryMcHugh 4 86
(Grant Tuer) *mde all: rdn clr 2f out: styd on strly* **16/1**

04-0 **2** *5* **Waterclock (IRE)**[25] 2194 7-9-6 **76** (p) PJMcDonald 11 81
(Micky Hammond) *hld up towards rr: niggled along bef 1/2-way: rdn along 5f out: hdwy over 3f out: drvn wl over 1f out: styd on: no ch w wnr* **7/2**[1]

4-00 **3** *2* **Daghash**[9] 2699 7-9-2 **77** KieranShoemark[(5)] 1 80
(Stuart Kittow) *hld up towards rr: hdwy on outer 5f out: pushed along to chse ldrs 3f out: rdn wl over 1f out: kpt on* **4/1**[2]

-564 **4** *4* **Riptide**[20] 2338 10-8-10 **66** RichardKingscote 12 64
(Michael Scudamore) *prom: rdn along 3f out: drvn wl over 1f out: kpt on same pce* **15/2**

-250 **5** *3* **Tuscan Gold**[31] 2018 9-9-2 **72** PaulHanagan 2 67
(Micky Hammond) *hld up and bhd: hdwy 4f out: rdn along over 2f out: sn drvn and plugged on one pce* **9/2**[3]

00/0 **6** *4 ½* **Hartside (GER)**[2] 1253 7-8-13 **69** (v) DougieCostello 8 59
(Peter Winks) *chsd ldrs: hdwy over 4f out: rdn along over 3f out: drvn over 2f out and sn btn* **16/1**

16/6 **7** *9* **Lexi's Boy (IRE)**[45] 1598 8-9-10 **80** (tp) DavidNolan 10 60
(Donald McCain) *trckd wnr: pushed along over 3f out: rdn along over 2f out: drvn wl over 1f out: grad wknd* **25/1**

-602 **8** *5* **Nashville (IRE)**[9] 2678 7-8-5 **61** oh4 NeilFarley 3 36
(Andrew Crook) *hld up: a in rr* **20/1**

-320 **9** *4 ½* **Madam Lilibet (IRE)**[34] 1955 7-8-9 **65** JoeyHaynes 6 35
(Sharon Watt) *chsd ldrs: pushed along over 7f out: rdn along over 4f out: sn wknd* **25/1**

/142 **10** *1 ½* **Knight's Parade (IRE)**[4] 2820 6-9-3 **76** (t) DannyBrock[(3)] 7 44
(Sarah Humphrey) *hld up towards rr: hdwy and in tch 1/2-way: chsd ldrs on outer 4f out: rdn along 3f out: sn drvn and wknd* **13/2**

6013 **11** *30* **Topaling**[41] 1766 5-8-10 **66** SaleemGolam 5 1
(Mark H Tompkins) *trckd ldrs on inner: effrt 4f out: rdn along 3f out: sn drvn and wknd* **33/1**

3m 49.22s (4.62) **Going Correction** +0.20s/f (Good) **11** Ran SP% **112.7**
Speed ratings (Par 105): **97,94,93,91,90 88,84,81,79,78 64**
CSF £65.29 CT £271.85 TOTE £16.50: £3.70, £1.90, £1.80; EX 111.60 Trifecta £562.70.
Owner E Tuer **Bred** E Tuer **Trained** Birkby, N Yorks
■ The first training success for Grant Tuer.

FOCUS
Rail movement added 8 yards to race distance. Mainly exposed sorts in this long-distance handicap which was run at a modest gallop resulted in a runaway winner.

2972 MR WOLF SPRINT H'CAP 6f
7:45 (7:46) (Class 3) (0-90,86) 3-Y-O
£9,337 (£2,796; £1,398; £699; £349; £175) **Stalls** Low

Form RPR

-006 **1** **Dutch Mist**[9] 2683 3-9-1 **80** (b[1]) KeaganLatham 10 87
(Kevin Ryan) *dwlt and hld up in rr: gd hdwy on outer wl over 1f out: rdn to chal ins fnl f: led nr fin* **16/1**

4-05 **2** *nk* **Gallipoli (IRE)**[23] 2251 3-9-6 **85** TonyHamilton 4 91+
(Richard Fahey) *hld up in tch: hdwy on inner whn n.m.r wl over 1f out: sn rdn and squeezed through ins fnl f: kpt on wl towards fin* **3/1**[1]

-132 **3** *nk* **Bossipop**[10] 2650 3-8-11 **81** (p) RachelRichardson[(5)] 5 86
(Tim Easterby) *hld up in rr: gd hdwy over 2f out: sn cl up: rdn to ld jst over 1f out: drvn ins fnl f: hdd and no ex towards fin* **5/1**[3]

-415 **4** *shd* **Van Gerwen**[5] 2802 3-8-8 **73** DavidAllan 6 78
(Les Eyre) *trckd ldrs: hdwy over 2f out: rdn to chal over 1f out: ev ch: drvn ins fnl f: no ex towards fin* **11/2**

0-01 **5** *shd* **Wayward Hoof**[10] 2650 3-9-2 **81** DougieCostello 7 85
(K R Burke) *trckd ldrs: hdwy 2f out and sn cl up: rdn over 1f out and ev ch: drvn ins fnl f: no ex towards fin* **9/1**

1450 **6** *22* **He's A Dreamer (IRE)**[14] 2532 3-8-13 **78** [1] GrahamGibbons 1 12
(David O'Meara) *cl up on inner: rdn to ld 2f out: sn drvn: hdd over 1f out: sn wknd and eased* **10/1**

300- **7** *½* **Gin In The Inn (IRE)**[247] 6931 3-9-1 **80** JackGarritty 3 12
(Richard Fahey) *slt ld: rdn along and hdd 2f out: sn wknd* **8/1**

0-1 **8** *28* **Aleef (IRE)**[26] 2156 3-9-5 **84** PaulHanagan 9
(Charles Hills) *t.k.h: cl up: rdn along over 2f out: sn wknd and bhd* **4/1**[2]

1m 17.03s (0.13) **Going Correction** +0.20s/f (Good) **8** Ran SP% **113.1**
Speed ratings (Par 103): **107,106,106,106,105 76,75,38**
CSF £62.47 CT £283.30 TOTE £17.80: £4.60, £1.70, £1.50; EX 72.10 Trifecta £317.70.
Owner The Springfield Partnership **Bred** Palmerston Bloodstock Ltd **Trained** Hambleton, N Yorks

FOCUS
Rail movement added 8 yards to race distance. A decent sprint for 3yos which produced a bunch finish between five who were a long way clear of the other three, who went off very hard.

2973 WAKEFIELD TRINITY WILDCATS H'CAP 1m 2f 6y
8:15 (8:16) (Class 4) (0-80,80) 3-Y-O **£5,175** (£1,540; £769; £384) **Stalls** Low

Form RPR

04-4 **1** **Renfrew Street**[17] 2420 3-9-1 **74** FrannyNorton 3 87+
(Mark Johnston) *trckd ldng pair: effrt on inner and nt clr run over 1f out: swtchd rt and rdn ent fnl f: qcknd to ld last 100yds: sn clr* **11/4**[2]

2412 **2** *2 ½* **Daisy Bere (FR)**[9] 2694 3-9-6 **79** JoeyHaynes 6 84
(K R Burke) *trckd ldng pair: hdwy wl over 1f out: rdn to ld ent fnl f: sn edgd lft: hdd and kpt on same pce last 100yds* **10/3**[3]

15-4 **3** *2* **Sepal (USA)**[33] 1960 3-9-3 **76** GrahamGibbons 2 79+
(Charles Hills) *sn led: rdn wl over 1f out: hdd ent fnl f: sn drvn and kpt on one pce* **5/2**[1]

44-4 **4** *3* **Rosamaria (IRE)**[12] 2574 3-8-10 **69** RichardKingscote 8 64
(Mark Johnston) *trckd ldr: cl up 1/2-way: rdn along 2f out: sn drvn and wknd appr fnl f* **10/1**

-500 **5** *¾* **Taking Libertys**[14] 2538 3-9-5 **78** KeaganLatham 1 72
(Kevin Ryan) *hld up in rr: hdwy over 2f out: sn rdn along: drvn and no imp fnl f* **5/1**

2-06 **6** *4* **Like No Other**[6] 2774 3-8-11 **70** (v[1]) DavidAllan 5 56
(Les Eyre) *hld up in tch: pushed along wl over 2f out: rdn wl over 1f out: sn wknd* **14/1**

2m 12.82s (-0.88) **Going Correction** +0.20s/f (Good) **6** Ran SP% **110.7**
Speed ratings (Par 101): **111,109,107,105,104 101**
CSF £11.93 CT £22.99 TOTE £3.10: £2.00, £1.90; EX 11.30 Trifecta £31.00.
Owner Douglas Livingston **Bred** D Curran **Trained** Middleham Moor, N Yorks
■ Stewards' Enquiry : Joey Haynes caution: careless riding

FOCUS
Rail movement added 8 yards to race distance. A 1m2f handicap for 3yos run at a medium gallop.

2974 CASTLEFORD TIGERS H'CAP 6f
8:45 (8:45) (Class 5) (0-70,75) 3-Y-O+ **£3,234** (£962; £481; £240) **Stalls** Low

Form RPR

6-53 **1** **Consistant**[27] 2130 8-9-1 **60** EoinWalsh[(3)] 5 69
(Brian Baugh) *in tch: hdwy over 2f out: rdn to ld over 1f out: drvn ins fnl f: kpt on wl towards fin* **16/1**

4500 **2** *½* **Teetotal (IRE)**[30] 2053 6-9-0 **56** GrahamGibbons 4 63
(Nigel Tinkler) *t.k.h early: trckd ldrs: effrt to chse wnr over 1f out: drvn to chal ins fnl f: ev ch tl no ex towards fin* **15/2**[2]

2061 **3** *1 ½* **Koptoon**[3] 2846 4-10-5 **75** 6ex DougieCostello 12 78+
(Jo Hughes) *hld up in rr: swtchd rt to outer and gd hdwy 2f out: rdn to chse ldng pair ins fnl f: sn edgd lft and no imp towards fin* **9/4**[1]

3235 **4** *2 ¼* **Spice Mill (IRE)**[53] 1435 3-9-0 **67** AlistairRawlinson[(3)] 2 60
(Michael Appleby) *hld up: hdwy 2f out: rdn to chse ldrs whn n.m.r 1f out: sn swtchd lft to inner: kpt on* **12/1**

-305 **5** *½* **Penny Royale**[11] 2622 4-9-9 **65** (b) DavidAllan 11 59
(Tim Easterby) *trckd ldrs on outer: clsd up 1/2-way: led over 2f out: rdn and hdd over 1f out: sn drvn and grad wknd* **16/1**

40-4 **6** *nk* **Geoff Potts (IRE)**[26] 2156 3-9-6 **70** RichardKingscote 7 61
(Jeremy Gask) *in tch on outer: hdwy 2f out: rdn along wl over 1f out: kpt on same pce fnl f* **17/2**[3]

20-0 **7** *nk* **Tavener**[44] 1648 4-10-0 **70** DavidNolan 9 62
(David O'Meara) *midfield: hdwy wl over 1f out: rdn and hung bdly lft ent fnl f: sn drvn and no imp* **16/1**

560 **8** *1 ¾* **Clon Rocket (IRE)**[20] 2336 3-8-11 **68** MeganEllingworth[(7)] 1 55
(John Holt) *dwlt and towards rr: sme hdwy wl over 1f out: sn rdn and n.d* **33/1**

00-0 **9** *nk* **Caeser The Gaeser (IRE)**[17] 2416 4-8-9 **58** KieranSchofield[(7)] 10 43
(Nigel Tinkler) *dwlt and in rr: hdwy 2f out: sn rdn and n.d* **40/1**

1010 **10** *1 ¼* **Captain Scooby**[2] 2919 10-9-10 **66** (b) JasonHart 13 47
(Richard Guest) *hld up in rr: effrt whn nt clr run wl over 1f out: no hdwy after* **20/1**

0000 **11** *4 ½* **Bold Spirit**[3] 2856 5-9-3 **59** (t) TonyHamilton 3 26
(Declan Carroll) *led: pushed along and hdd over 2f out: sn rdn and wknd* **25/1**

0000 **12** *1 ½* **Kopassus (IRE)**[9] 2676 4-8-9 **56** (p) JordanNason[(5)] 14 18
(Lawrence Mullaney) *a in rr* **33/1**

-000 **13** *2 ¾* **Slingsby**[31] 2016 5-9-7 **68** (b) NathanEvans[(5)] 15 21
(Michael Easterby) *prom: rdn along 1/2-way: sn wknd* **20/1**

-302 **14** *12* **Dance Alone**[10] 2667 3-9-5 **69** (p) TomEaves 16
(Kevin Ryan) *chsd ldrs: rdn 2f out: sn wknd* **14/1**

002- **15** *4 ½* **Red Harry (IRE)**[178] 8179 4-10-0 **70** (t) PJMcDonald 8
(David C Griffiths) *chsd ldrs: rdn along over 2f out: sn wknd* **9/1**

1m 17.45s (0.55) **Going Correction** +0.20s/f (Good)
WFA 3 from 4yo+ 8lb **15** Ran SP% **116.8**
Speed ratings (Par 103): **104,103,101,98,97 97,96,94,94,92 86,84,80,64,58**
CSF £115.48 CT £385.83 TOTE £17.30: £4.80, £2.30, £1.60; EX 154.00 Trifecta £545.40.
Owner Miss J A Price **Bred** Bearstone Stud Ltd **Trained** Audley, Staffs

FOCUS
Rail movement added 8 yards to race distance. A mixture of some unexposed 3yos taking on older exposed horses in this sprint. The pace wasn't strong and the first two were always well to the fore.

2975 FEATHERSTONE ROVERS H'CAP 5f
9:15 (9:15) (Class 5) (0-75,75) 4-Y-O+ **£3,234** (£962; £481; £240) **Stalls** Low

Form RPR

-000 **1** **Eternitys Gate**[14] 2531 5-9-4 **72** DavidNolan 6 79
(Ivan Furtado) *mde most: rdn wl over 1f out: drvn ins fnl f: hld on gamely* **5/1**[3]

-565 **2** *nk* **Oriental Splendour (IRE)**[12] 2572 4-8-12 **66** JamesSullivan 2 72
(Ruth Carr) *t.k.h: trckd ldrs: hdwy wl over 1f out: n.m.r ent fnl f: sn drvn and ev ch: kpt on* **13/2**

1004 **3** *hd* **Boxing Shadows**[4] 2808 6-8-11 **65** PJMcDonald 3 70
(Les Eyre) *trckd ldng pair: hdwy 2f out: rdn to chal over 1f out: drvn and ev ch ins fnl f: no ex towards fin* **8/1**

-003 **4** *nse* **Royal Brave (IRE)**[17] 2426 5-9-5 **73** BarryMcHugh 4 78+
(Rebecca Bastiman) *hld up towards rr: hdwy on inner over 1f out: rdn and n.m.r ins fnl f: squeezed through and kpt on wl towards fin* **4/1**[1]

6063 **5** *1 ¼* **Ambitious Icarus**[3] 2846 7-9-7 **75** (e) JasonHart 5 76
(Richard Guest) *hld up in rr: hdwy on outer wl over 1f out: rdn to chse ldrs ins fnl f: drvn: edgd lft and no imp last 75yds* **5/1**[3]

0033 **6** *1* **Oriental Relation (IRE)**[17] 2418 5-9-1 **69** (v) TomEaves 11 66
(James Given) *cl up: disp ld 2f out: sn rdn: drvn ent fnl f: fdd* **12/1**

3425 **7** *1* **Flicka's Boy**[17] 2426 4-9-5 **73** DuranFentiman 8 66
(Tony Coyle) *hld up towards rr: hdwy 2f out: rdn to chse ldrs ent fnl f: sn drvn and kpt on same pce* **16/1**

40-6 **8** *nse* **Innocently (IRE)**[11] 2622 5-8-11 **70** (v) JoshDoyle[(5)] 1 63
(David O'Meara) *chsd ldng pair: rdn along wl over 1f out: drvn ent fnl f: grad wknd* **9/2**[2]

-006 **9** *½* **Tom Sawyer**[12] 2572 8-9-2 **70** (b) ConnorBeasley 7 61
(Julie Camacho) *dwlt and towards rr: effrt and sme hdwy 2f out: sn rdn and n.d* **20/1**

1m 3.73s (0.43) **Going Correction** +0.20s/f (Good) **9** Ran SP% **114.3**
Speed ratings (Par 103): **104,103,103,103,101 99,97,97,97**
CSF £36.98 CT £256.94 TOTE £5.80: £2.10, £2.30, £3.30; EX 41.20 Trifecta £319.90.
Owner Mrs June Bownes **Bred** Cheveley Park Stud Ltd **Trained** Wiseton, Nottinghamshire
■ Stewards' Enquiry : David Nolan two-day ban: used whip above permitted level (Jun 20-21)

FOCUS
Rail movement added 8 yards to race distance. Exposed sorts in this 5f handicap which was run at a fair gallop and produced a bunch finish. The form is probably ordinary.

T/Plt: £75.70 to a £1 stake. Pool: £76,922.13 - 741.39 winning units. T/Qpdt: £25.00 to a £1 stake. Pool: £5,668.63 - 167.16 winning units. **Joe Rowntree**

2747 WINDSOR (R-H)

Monday, June 6

OFFICIAL GOING: Good (good to firm in places)

Wind: Almost nil Weather: Sunny, very warm

2976 DAILY PRICE BOOSTS AT LADBROKES EBF STALLIONS NOVICE STKS (PLUS 10 RACE) 6f

6:00 (6:02) (Class 4) 2-Y-O **£4,269** (£1,270; £634; £317) **Stalls** Low

Form RPR

1 **Bin Battuta** 2-9-2 0 JamesDoyle 1 85+
(Saeed bin Suroor) *trckd ldrs: pushed along over 2f out: swtchd to outer and prog over 1f out: led jst ins fnl f: sn drew clr* **6/4**1

2 3 1/4 **Sakurajima (IRE)** 2-9-2 0 DarryllHolland 8 72
(Charles Hills) *t.k.h: trckd ldrs: prog 2f out: drvn to chal and upsides 1f out: outpcd fnl f* **14/1**

3 1 1/2 **Big Lachie** 2-9-2 0 WilliamCarson 6 68
(Jamie Osborne) *t.k.h: hld up tl plld way through to ld over 2f out: rdn and hdd jst ins fnl f: fdd* **25/1**

4 3/4 **Himself** 2-8-13 0 TomMarquand(3) 10 65
(Richard Hannon) *chsd ldr to 1/2-way: rdn wl over 1f out: hanging and one pce after* **6/1**3

5 1/2 **Harbour Master** 2-9-2 0 WilliamBuick 3 64+
(Jamie Osborne) *fractious bef ent stall and also in it: restrained s and hld up in detached last: reminders jst over 1f out: styd on fnl f: nrst fin* **10/1**

0 6 2 **Bara Brith**72 1086 2-8-8 0 PhilipPrince(3) 9 53
(David Evans) *led to over 2f out: wkng whn short of room over 1f out* **66/1**

7 1/2 **Silent Echo** 2-9-2 0 GeorgeBaker 2 56
(Roger Charlton) *t.k.h: trckd ldrs: pushed along 2f out: steadily wknd over 1f out* **2/1**2

60 8 2 1/4 **Golden Guest**14 2536 2-9-2 0 TomQueally 4 50
(George Margarson) *t.k.h: hld up towards rr: pushed along and no prog 2f out: wknd* **20/1**

1m 14.04s (1.04) **Going Correction** -0.05s/f (Good) 8 Ran SP% **113.5**
Speed ratings (Par 95): **91,86,84,83,83 80,79,76**
CSF £23.10 TOTE £2.10: £1.50, £3.50, £4.90; EX 21.80 Trifecta £198.40.
Owner Godolphin **Bred** Darley **Trained** Newmarket, Suffolk

FOCUS
Inner of straight dolled out 16yds at 6f and 8yds at the winning line. Top bend dolled out 12yds from normal inner configuration, adding 48yds to race distances of 1m-plus. A hot, sunny day and the ground would have been quickening all the time, with the consensus amongst jockeys being that it was on the fast side. This had the looked of a decent novice event and was won in good style by the well-bred favourite.

2977 LADBROKES CELEBRATING ROYAL WINDOR'S 150TH ANNIVERSARY CLAIMING STKS 1m 2f 7y

6:30 (6:30) (Class 5) 3-Y-O+ **£2,911** (£866; £432; £216) **Stalls** Centre

Form RPR

2123 1 **My Lord**17 2436 8-9-1 72 AledBeech(7) 4 71+
(David Evans) *t.k.h: hld up in last pair: smooth prog 2f out: led 1f out: drvn clr* **2/1**1

/01- 2 3 1/4 **Mount Shamsan**76 7674 6-9-9 75 GeorgeBaker 2 66
(Gary Moore) *trckd ldr: rdn and nt qckn over 2f out and sn lost pl: kpt on u.p to take 2nd again nr fin* **7/2**2

0005 3 1/2 **Hannington**7 2733 5-9-1 74 (tp) CharlieBennett(7) 8 64
(Barry Brennan) *led at mod pce: kicked on 3f out: hdd and one pce 1f out* **20/1**3

4046 4 nk **Spiritual Star (IRE)**18 2402 7-9-6 70 (t) RobertTart 7 61
(Anthony Carson) *hld up in last pair: rdn and no prog over 2f out: hdwy jst ins fnl f: one pce last 100yds* **7/2**2

0-60 5 3 **Lily Edge**126 412 7-9-0 44 WilliamCarson 5 49
(John Bridger) *trckd ldrs: rdn to chal against nr side rail fr 2f out tl wknd fnl f* **25/1**

16-0 6 3 3/4 **King Torus (IRE)**19 2378 8-9-5 81 (p) CallumShepherd(5) 3 52
(Lee Carter) *trckd ldrs: rdn over 2f out: lost pl and wknd over 1f out* **7/2**2

2m 13.45s (4.75) **Going Correction** +0.125s/f (Good)
WFA 3 from 5yo+ 13lb 6 Ran SP% **108.6**
Speed ratings (Par 103): **86,83,83,82,80 77**
CSF £8.59 TOTE £2.30: £1.50, £2.10; EX 8.70 Trifecta £62.30.My Lord was claimed by Mr P. Butler £6000; Spiritual Star was claimed by Mr L. A. Carter for £4000
Owner Mrs I M Folkes **Bred** Mrs Monica Teversham **Trained** Pandy, Monmouths

FOCUS
Race distance increased by 48yds. Nearly all of these had either stamina or well being to prove, the one exception being the favourite and he duly won with loads to spare.

2978 DOWNLOAD THE LADBROKES APP H'CAP 1m 2f 7y

7:00 (7:01) (Class 4) (0-85,85) 4-Y-O+ **£4,690** (£1,395; £697; £348) **Stalls** Centre

Form RPR

31-5 1 **Oasis Spear**40 1775 4-9-5 **83** GeorgeBaker 5 92+
(Chris Wall) *led 2f but t.k.h and then hld up jst bhd ldrs: rdn to chal 2f out: led over 1f out: drvn and steadily asserted fnl f* **7/4**1

4300 2 1 1/2 **Prendergast Hill (IRE)**13 2556 4-9-4 **82** JamesDoyle 9 87
(Ed de Giles) *pressed ldr over 8f out: led 3f out: drvn and hrd pressed 2f out: hdd over 1f out: kpt on wl but readily hld last 100yds* **7/2**2

0-00 3 nk **Smaih (GER)**11 2628 4-9-6 **84** WilliamCarson 1 88
(Jamie Osborne) *hld up towards rr: clsd on ldrs 2f out: swtchd lft and drvn over 1f out: tk 3rd fnl f and styd on* **16/1**

33-6 4 3/4 **Sahara (IRE)**44 1624 4-8-11 **75** TedDurcan 7 80+
(Chris Wall) *hld up in last pair: stl last but gng wl 2f out: pushed along whn rn into trble over 1f out: light reminder and styd on in gd style to take 4th nr fin* **16/1**

134- 5 1 1/4 **Thames Knight**238 7172 4-8-5 **76** TylerSaunders(7) 2 76
(Marcus Tregoning) *trckd ldrs: pushed along 2f out: lost pl over 1f out: one pce fnl f* **10/1**

-540 6 hd **Biotic**14 2549 5-9-3 **81** FrederikTylicki 6 81
(Rod Millman) *hld up in tch: effrt on outer over 2f out: in tch over 1f out but one pce u.p after: wknd last 75yds* **8/1**3

-100 7 2 **Craftsmanship (FR)**37 1861 5-9-3 **84** (p) TomMarquand(3) 8 80
(Robert Eddery) *hld up in last pair: urged along over 3f out: effrt on outer and in tch over 1f out: wknd fnl f* **8/1**3

100- 8 11 **Gold Sands (IRE)**270 6245 4-9-7 **85** LukeMorris 4 65
(James Tate) *led after 2f to 3f out: wknd u.p 2f out* **8/1**3

2m 8.77s (0.07) **Going Correction** +0.125s/f (Good) 8 Ran SP% **112.8**
Speed ratings (Par 105): **104,102,102,101,100 100,99,90**
CSF £7.51 CT £68.48 TOTE £2.20: £1.10, £1.70, £4.30; EX 9.50 Trifecta £104.20.
Owner Ms Aida Fustoq **Bred** Deerfield Farm **Trained** Newmarket, Suffolk
■ Stewards' Enquiry : William Carson caution: careless riding

FOCUS
Race distance increased by 48yds. Run at an ordinary gallop, the favourite won despite not looking happy on the ground and can leave this form behind in time.

2979 BET IN PLAY WITH LADBROKES H'CAP 1m 3f 135y

7:30 (7:30) (Class 3) (0-95,95) 4-Y-O+ **£7,439** (£2,213; £1,106; £553) **Stalls** Centre

Form RPR

13-0 1 **First Sitting**44 1620 5-9-7 **95** JamesDoyle 4 106
(Chris Wall) *hld up in 4th: smooth prog to trck ldr 3f out: led wl over 1f out: rdn clr sn after: v readily* **10/3**2

13P/ 2 5 **Ruwasi**590 7440 5-8-8 **82** LukeMorris 6 85
(James Tate) *t.k.h: hld up in last: prog on inner 3f out to chal 2f out: hrd rdn to chse wnr after: lft bhd fnl f* **14/1**

0053 3 3/4 **Passover**7 2752 5-8-13 **92** EdwardGreatrex(5) 1 94
(Andrew Balding) *led: drew clr bnd 6f out: c bk to rivals 3f out: drvn and hdd wl over 1f out: sn in 3rd and one pce* **9/2**3

111- 4 1 1/2 **Sparring (IRE)**191 8038 4-9-4 **92** (p) WilliamBuick 5 92
(Charlie Appleby) *trckd ldng pair: pushed along 5f out: tried to cl u.p over 2f out: nvr gng pce to threaten* **1/1**1

0-66 5 31 **Archangel Raphael (IRE)**47 1569 4-9-7 **95** SilvestreDeSousa 2 43
(Amanda Perrett) *trckd ldr to 3f out: sn wknd: eased over 1f out: t.o* **17/2**

2m 28.55s (-0.95) **Going Correction** +0.125s/f (Good) 5 Ran SP% **108.5**
Speed ratings (Par 107): **108,104,104,103,82**
CSF £37.83 TOTE £4.20: £1.90, £3.20; EX 32.60 Trifecta £91.10.
Owner Bringloe & Clarke **Bred** Juddmonte Farms Ltd **Trained** Newmarket, Suffolk

FOCUS
Race distance increased by 48yds. A race that set up for the closers, with the favourite disappointing.

2980 CASH OUT AVAILABLE AT LADBROKES MAIDEN STKS 6f

8:00 (8:02) (Class 5) 3-Y-O+ **£2,911** (£866; £432; £216) **Stalls** Low

Form RPR

0-5 1 **Raising Sand**14 2544 4-9-13 0 AndreaAtzeni 8 86+
(Roger Varian) *trckd ldrs: wnt 2nd over 2f out: clsd and shkn up to ld jst ins fnl f: pushed out* **10/3**2

-242 2 1 1/2 **Dark Shot**9 2698 3-9-5 81 DavidProbert 5 79
(Andrew Balding) *mde most: def advantage over 2f out: drvn and hdd jst ins fnl f: nt qckn* **4/9**1

3 2 1/4 **Waseefa**264 6449 3-8-7 0 DavidEgan(7) 9 67
(John Butler) *hld up: prog over 2f out: tk 3rd over 1f out: nudged along and styd on steadily fnl f* **16/1**

3-40 4 4 1/2 **Angie's Girl**20 2337 3-9-0 66 JohnFahy 7 53
(Clive Cox) *hld up in tch: gng wl whn nt clr run over 2f out: sn outpcd: shkn up and styd on to take 4th fnl f* **7/1**3

36 5 6 **Olympic Duel (IRE)**20 2349 3-9-5 0 WilliamCarson 1 38
(Peter Hiatt) *in tch: pushed along 1/2-way: outpcd fr 2f out: no ch after* **14/1**

50- 6 1/2 **Cliffmeena (IRE)**199 7921 3-9-0 0 KieranO'Neill 12 32
(Alex Hales) *hld up in rr: effrt on outer over 2f out: wknd over 1f out* **33/1**

06 7 9 **Bertie Bishop**41 1765 4-9-10 0 DanielMuscutt(3) 10 10
(Brian McMath) *outpcd and sn rdn in last: t.o* **66/1**

00 8 3 3/4 **Purple Party (IRE)**16 2483 3-9-0 0 DarryllHolland 2
(George Margarson) *w ldr to over 2f out: sn wknd: t.o* **100/1**

0-6 9 1/2 **Guilded Rock**14 2544 3-9-5 0 MartinDwyer 3
(Stuart Kittow) *w to over 2f out: wknd rapidly: t.o* **25/1**

10 9 **Gorgeous (FR)** 3-9-0 0 LukeMorris 11
(Tony Carroll) *pushed along and outpcd after 2f: wl bhd after: t.o* **33/1**

1m 12.62s (-0.38) **Going Correction** -0.05s/f (Good)
WFA 3 from 4yo 8lb 10 Ran SP% **129.6**
Speed ratings (Par 103): **100,98,95,89,81 80,68,63,62,50**
CSF £5.65 TOTE £4.60: £1.50, £1.02, £4.80; EX 6.60 Trifecta £48.90.
Owner Castle Down Racing & Mrs H Varian **Bred** Meon Valley Stud **Trained** Newmarket, Suffolk

FOCUS
Race distance as advertised. Very little depth to this sprint maiden.

2981 TRACK YOUR FOOTBALL ACCA WITH LADBROKES CLASSIFIED STKS 6f

8:30 (8:31) (Class 5) 3-Y-O **£2,911** (£866; £432; £216) **Stalls** Low

Form RPR

4-31 1 **Papa Luigi (IRE)**13 2561 3-8-11 73 TomMarquand(3) 2 88
(Richard Hannon) *trckd ldr: led 2f out and qckly in command: clr fnl f: comf* **3/1**1

-155 2 3 3/4 **September Issue**31 2002 3-9-0 75 LukeMorris 7 76
(Gay Kelleway) *hld up in midfield: waiting for room over 2f out: prog over 1f out: urged along and styd on to take 2nd nr fin* **14/1**

-156 3 1/2 **Pusey's Secret**13 2554 3-8-11 75 (b1) MichaelJMMurphy(3) 1 74
(John Gallagher) *taken down early: chsd ldrs: drvn 2f out: chsd wnr ins fnl f: no imp and lost 2nd nr fin* **33/1**

03-3 4 nk **Hitman**25 2185 3-8-11 75 RobHornby(3) 5 73
(William Muir) *hld up in rr: prog against rail fr 2f out: styd on fnl f to press for a pl nr fin* **5/1**2

5-52 5 1/2 **Highly Sprung (IRE)**10 2642 3-9-0 75 WilliamBuick 11 72+
(Mark Johnston) *towards rr: rdn and effrt on outer over 1f out: kpt on but n.d* **8/1**

251- 6 1/2 **Sir Roger Moore (IRE)**163 8355 3-9-0 75 JFEgan 9 70
(John Butler) *led to 2f out: sn no ch w wnr: lost 2nd and fdd ins fnl f* **14/1**

01-5 7 hd **Pine Ridge**35 1935 3-9-0 75 JohnFahy 12 70+
(Clive Cox) *prom on outer: shkn up over 2f out: styd w ch of pl tl fdd ins fnl f* **17/2**

4-02 8 2 1/4 **Athollblair Boy (IRE)**20 2337 3-9-0 74 SilvestreDeSousa 10 62+
(Nigel Tinkler) *hld up in rr: reminders fr over 1f out: modest prog and nvr involved* **6/1**3

-030 9 shd **Another Boy**17 2446 3-9-0 74 (v) FMBerry 8 62
(Ralph Beckett) *hld up in rr: pushed along over 1f out: modest prog and reminder fnl f: nvr involved* **12/1**

3-05 10 3 1/4 **Equistar**25 2186 3-9-0 73 FrederikTylicki 4 52
(Jonathan Portman) *prom: rdn 2f out: lost pl over 1f out: eased whn no ch* **14/1**

03-0 **11** *8* **Cautious Optimism**[39] 1809 3-9-0 75............................... MartinDwyer 3 26
(William Muir) *rousted to go prom but racd awkwardly: wknd wl over 2f out: t.o* **25/1**
4-20 **12** *6* **Darksiteofthemoon (IRE)**[14] 2545 3-9-0 74.................. AndreaAtzeni 6 7
(Marco Botti) *a in rr: wknd 2f out: t.o* **18/1**
1m 12.52s (-0.48) **Going Correction** -0.05s/f (Good) **12** Ran SP% **117.3**
Speed ratings (Par 99): **101,96,95,94,94 93,93,90,90,85 75,67**
CSF £47.24 TOTE £3.80: £1.80, £3.50, £4.40; EX 45.50 Trifecta £1478.30.
Owner Middleham Park Racing XLVIII **Bred** Gerry Flannery Developments Ltd **Trained** East Everleigh, Wilts

FOCUS
Race distance as advertised. Little got into this, with the well-backed favourite, who recorded a personal best, winning with plenty in hand having been well placed throughout.

2982 LADBROKES H'CAP 5f 10y
9:00 (9:00) (Class 4) (0-85,83) 3-Y-O **£4,690** (£1,395; £697; £348) **Stalls** Low

Form RPR
10- **1** **Moondyne Joe (IRE)**[324] 4391 3-9-1 **77**.................. SilvestreDeSousa 1 84
(K R Burke) *pushed up to ld: rdn over 1f out: hdd ins fnl f: hrd drvn and rallied to ld nr fin* **9/2**[3]
10-2 **2** *nk* **Silken Skies (IRE)**[21] 2314 3-9-1 **77**................................ JamesDoyle 7 83
(Clive Cox) *hld up: prog over 2f out: chsd wnr over 1f out: drvn to ld ins fnl f: hdd nr fin* **3/1**[2]
120- **3** *1 ½* **This Is For You**[254] 6741 3-9-1 **77**.................................... OisinMurphy 6 78
(Andrew Balding) *t.k.h: hld up in tch: effrt over 1f out: rdn and styd on to take 3rd nr fin: nvr able to chal* **10/1**
-461 **4** *¾* **Wiley Post**[17] 2435 3-9-1 **80**......................................(b) TomMarquand(3) 2 78
(Richard Hannon) *trckd ldrs: wnt 2nd over 2f out and sn rdn to chal: nt qckn u.str.p over 1f out and lost 2nd: one pce* **5/2**[1]
33-0 **5** *2 ½* **Storm Melody**[35] 1935 3-8-13 **75**.. FMBerry 5 64
(Jonjo O'Neill) *s.i.s: hld up in detached last: pushed along over 1f out: kpt on steadily: nvr involved* **8/1**
0-34 **6** *5* **Adham (IRE)**[134] 322 3-9-7 **83**... LukeMorris 4 54
(James Tate) *pressed wnr to over 2f out: sn wknd* **12/1**
1-04 **7** *10* **Dheban (IRE)**[24] 2218 3-9-4 **80**.. WilliamBuick 3 15
(Richard Hannon) *pressed ldrs: lost pl 1/2-way: sn wknd: t.o* **7/1**
59.83s (-0.47) **Going Correction** -0.05s/f (Good) **7** Ran SP% **112.1**
Speed ratings (Par 101): **101,100,98,96,92 84,68**
CSF £17.65 CT £124.65 TOTE £5.10: £2.40, £2.30; EX 21.20 Trifecta £108.80.
Owner J Burley & Mrs E Burke **Bred** Thomas Hassett **Trained** Middleham Moor, N Yorks

FOCUS
Race distance as advertised. The right horses came to the fore, with the winner, a northern raider, well backed following a jockey change.
T/Plt: £70.90 to a £1 stake. Pool: £93,894.99 - 965.44 winning units. T/Qpdt: £23.60 to a £1 stake. Pool: £7,239.84 - 226.07 winning units. **Jonathan Neesom**

2983 - 2989a (Foreign Racing) - See Raceform Interactive

2899 LINGFIELD (L-H)
Tuesday, June 7

OFFICIAL GOING: Turf - good to soft (good in places) (abandoned after race 1 (5.50) due to unsafe ground); aw course - polytrack: standard
Wind: Nil Weather: Fine but sultry

2990 MPRO5 MOBILISE EVERYTHING FILLIES' NOVICE STKS (PLUS 10 RACE) 6f
5:50 (5:54) (Class 5) 2-Y-O **£3,234** (£962; £481; £240) **Stalls** Centre

Form RPR
4 **1** **Cotinga**[20] 2376 2-9-0 0.. FMBerry 4 73
(Ralph Beckett) *dwlt: sn chsd ldrs: pushed along over 2f out: prog to go 2nd over 1f out: drvn and styd on wl to ld last strides* **8/1**
0 **2** *shd* **Her Terms**[32] 1988 2-9-0 0.. PatCosgrave 7 73
(William Haggas) *r against rail: cl up: smooth prog to ld over 1f out: drvn and hung lft fnl f: kpt on but hdd last stride* **6/1**[3]
05 **3** *7* **Royal Melody**[20] 2376 2-9-0 0... LukeMorris 3 52
(Heather Main) *prom: led over 2f out to over 1f out: readily lft bhd by ldng pair after but clr of rest* **100/1**
4 *5* **Ginger Truffle** 2-9-0 0.. TomQueally 8 37
(Brett Johnson) *dwlt: mostly in last: pushed along and passed wkng rivals fr 2f out despite running green* **100/1**
5 *4 ½* **Rebecca Rocks** 2-9-0 0.. HarryBentley 6 23
(Henry Candy) *chsd ldrs: rdn over 2f out: steadily wknd* **7/2**[2]
5 **6** *10* **Chica De La Noche**[17] 2467 2-9-0 0.................................. JimCrowley 1
(Simon Dow) *racd on wd outside: nvr quite on terms w ldrs fr 1/2-way: wknd rapidly wl over 1f out* **8/1**
3 **7** *5* **Limelite (IRE)**[17] 2467 2-9-0 0.. RyanMoore 5
(Richard Hannon) *mde most to over 2f out: wknd and heavily eased: t.o* **11/8**[1]
6 **8** *¾* **Toy Theatre**[37] 1889 2-9-0 0.. JoeFanning 2
(Mark Johnston) *racd towards outer: in tch to 1/2-way: wknd rapidly over 2f out: t.o* **6/1**[3]
1m 16.03s (4.83) **Going Correction** +0.65s/f (Yiel) **8** Ran SP% **117.1**
Speed ratings (Par 90): **93,92,83,76,70 57,50,49**
CSF £56.28 TOTE £11.20: £3.10, £2.40, £6.00; EX 51.60 Trifecta £1274.90.
Owner Larksborough Stud Limited **Bred** Larksborough Stud Limited **Trained** Kimpton, Hants

FOCUS
Following 9.2mm of rainfall during the afternoon, the going on the turf course was given as good to soft, good in places (GoingStick: 7.7). The straight course was narrowed by 4yds on the stands' side rail. They finished well strung out behind the first two in this fillies' novice race. Because of false patches of ground around five and a half furlongs out the next three races on the card, all due to take place on the turf course, were abandoned.

2991 HOSPICE IN WEALD (S) STKS 6f
() (Class 6) 3-Y-O+ £

2992 MPRO5.COM H'CAP 7f 140y
() (Class 6) (0-55,) 4-Y-O+ £

2993 MPRO5 MAIDEN STKS 7f 140y
() (Class 5) 3-Y-O+ £

2994 MPRO5 HEALTHCARE FILLIES' H'CAP 1m 4f (P)
7:50 (7:50) (Class 4) (0-80,80) 4-Y-O+ **£5,175** (£1,540; £769; £384) **Stalls** High

Form RPR
1-35 **1** **Parnell's Dream**[18] 2433 4-8-13 **72**.. FMBerry 4 79+
(Ralph Beckett) *trckd ldr: rdn over 2f out: drvn to ld jst ins fnl f: styd on wl* **3/1**[2]
3-21 **2** *¾* **Saumur**[19] 2399 4-9-3 **76**... TomQueally 6 81
(Denis Coakley) *hld up in 4th: prog to chse ldng pair over 2f out: drvn to chal on outer over 1f out: kpt on to take 2nd last 75yds: a hld* **7/2**[3]
2-43 **3** *½* **Eager Beaver**[14] 2564 4-9-2 **75**... MartinDwyer 8 79
(William Muir) *t.k.h: led at mod pce: kicked on 3f out: hdd and one pce jst ins fnl f* **12/1**
5264 **4** *1 ¼* **Victoria Pollard**[10] 2671 4-9-7 **80**..................................(p) DavidProbert 2 82+
(Andrew Balding) *stdd s: hld up in last pair: shkn up over 2f out: prog on inner over 1f out: styd on to take 4th but no ch to threaten* **6/1**
0 **5** *½* **Endive**[17] 2463 4-8-4 **63**... LukeMorris 1 64
(Robert Stephens) *chsd ldng pair tl rdn and lost pl over 2f out: n.d after: plugged on* **33/1**
4-00 **6** *1* **Taurian**[20] 2374 5-8-6 **65**... SilvestreDeSousa 5 65
(Ian Williams) *t.k.h: hld up in 5th: rdn over 2f out: no prog* **8/1**
0462 **7** *nk* **Rhythmical**[3] 2911 4-9-4 **77**..(b) JoeFanning 7 76
(Mark Johnston) *s.s: sn in 6th: shkn up over 2f out: no prog wl over 1f out and btn after* **5/2**[1]
30-0 **8** *1* **Sixties Love**[12] 2623 5-8-12 **71**... JimCrowley 3 69
(Simon Dow) *s.s: hld up in last: shkn up over 2f out: no prog* **14/1**
2m 32.33s (-0.67) **Going Correction** +0.075s/f (Slow) **8** Ran SP% **118.5**
Speed ratings (Par 102): **105,104,104,103,103 102,102,101**
CSF £14.61 CT £111.01 TOTE £4.40: £1.40, £1.60, £2.80; EX 21.60 Trifecta £134.80.
Owner Mr and Mrs David Aykroyd **Bred** Mr & Mrs David Aykroyd **Trained** Kimpton, Hants

FOCUS
A steadily run fillies' handicap, and it paid to race close to the pace. The first two are steadily on the upgrade.

2995 CRIMSON TIDE 20TH ANNIVERSARY H'CAP 1m 7f 169y(P)
8:20 (8:20) (Class 5) (0-75,75) 4-Y-O+ **£3,234** (£962; £481; £240) **Stalls** High

Form RPR
4-00 **1** **Saborido (USA)**[36] 1914 10-9-10 **75**..............................(b) JimCrowley 1 83
(Amanda Perrett) *mde all: set mod pce tl sent for home wl over 2f out: drvn and styd on fr over 1f out: essentially unchal* **5/1**
-134 **2** *1 ¾* **Tempuran**[35] 1947 7-9-5 **70**... RyanMoore 5 76
(David Bridgwater) *trckd wnr: rdn over 2f out: nt qckn over 1f out: kpt on same pce u.p* **7/4**[1]
5500 **3** *4 ½* **Alshan Fajer**[13] 2582 6-9-10 **75**.. FrederikTylicki 3 76
(J R Jenkins) *slowly away: t.k.h: hld up in last: no ch once pce lifted over 2f out: styd on fnl f to take 3rd nr fin* **7/1**
2405 **4** *½* **Peeps**[40] 1807 4-8-5 **57**... JoeFanning 2 57
(Mark H Tompkins) *dwlt: trckd ldng pair: rdn over 2f out: one pce and no imp after: lost 3rd nr fin* **12/1**
-135 **5** *1* **Kawartha**[39] 1824 4-9-1 **67**... TomQueally 6 66
(Robert Stephens) *hld up in 4th: outpcd and no ch once pce lifted over 2f out: no imp on ldrs after* **7/2**[2]
3620 **6** *nk* **Todd**[73] 1092 6-9-7 **72**.. SilvestreDeSousa 7 73+
(Anabel K Murphy) *hld up in 5th: outpcd and no ch once pce lifted over 2f out: trying to make hdwy on inner but no ch whn nt clr run ins fnl f* **4/1**[3]
3m 27.79s (2.09) **Going Correction** +0.075s/f (Slow)
WFA 4 from 6yo+ 1lb **6** Ran SP% **115.4**
Speed ratings (Par 103): **97,96,93,93,93 92**
CSF £14.79 TOTE £6.00: £2.70, £1.40; EX 16.60 Trifecta £73.20.
Owner Mrs Amanda Perrett **Bred** R D Hubbard And R Masterson **Trained** Pulborough, W Sussex

FOCUS
A lack of pace resulted in this staying handicap developing into a bit of a dash for the line. The winner has been rated close to his latter 2015 form.

2996 7,000,000 TO 1 H'CAP 1m 2f (P)
8:50 (8:50) (Class 5) (0-70,70) 4-Y-O+ **£3,234** (£962; £481; £240) **Stalls** Low

Form RPR
40-0 **1** **Fearless Lad (IRE)**[146] 164 6-8-12 **61**................................ KierenFox 3 69
(John Best) *hld up in last pair: rdn and gd prog on outer over 1f out: r.o to ld last 100yds: sn clr* **7/1**
5203 **2** *1 ½* **Pearly Prince**[27] 2151 4-9-6 **69**..............................(e[1]) SilvestreDeSousa 5 72
(Peter Hedger) *slowly away: hld up in last pair: cajoled along over 2f out: racing awkwardly whn nt clr run briefly over 1f out: trying to mount an effrt whn nt clr run again briefly ins fnl f: r.o to take 2nd last stride* **3/1**[1]
6-20 **3** *shd* **What A Dandy (IRE)**[136] 316 5-9-4 **67**......................(p) PatCosgrave 7 71
(Jim Boyle) *led 2f: chsd ldr to 1/2-way: drvn 3f out: responded fr over 1f out and led briefly 150yds out: outpcd last 100yds* **5/1**
0102 **4** *1 ½* **Shining Romeo**[18] 2445 4-9-4 **67**....................................... LukeMorris 1 68
(Denis Quinn) *trckd ldr 2f and again fr 1/2-way: rdn to ld wl over 1f out: idled in front and hdd 150yds out: sn lost pl* **4/1**[3]
5414 **5** *1 ¾* **Owners Day**[22] 2292 6-9-6 **69**... LiamKeniry 2 66
(Neil Mulholland) *chsd ldrs: rdn over 3f out: tried to cl on inner over 1f out: fdd fnl f* **11/1**
31-5 **6** *2* **Nosey Barker (IRE)**[124] 448 4-9-7 **70**..........................(p) KieranO'Neill 6 63
(Richard Hannon) *slowly away: rapid prog to ld after 2f: drvn and hdd wl over 1f out: wknd* **7/2**[2]
/304 **7** *1 ¾* **Subordinate (GER)**[19] 2398 7-9-4 **67**............................(t) TimmyMurphy 4 57
(Emma Lavelle) *trckd ldrs: shkn up over 2f out: no rspnse and wknd over 1f out* **8/1**
2m 4.63s (-1.97) **Going Correction** +0.075s/f (Slow) **7** Ran SP% **115.8**
Speed ratings (Par 103): **110,108,108,107,106 104,103**
CSF £29.01 CT £115.79 TOTE £8.40: £3.80, £2.20; EX 33.90 Trifecta £113.00.

Owner Mrs Jackie Jones **Bred** Brittas House Stud & Lynch Bages & Samac **Trained** Oad Street, Kent

FOCUS

This was run at a sound pace and the first two came from the back of the field. The winner is rated back to form.

T/Plt: £25.20 to a £1 stake. Pool: £78,761.88 - 2,279.37 winning tickets. T/Qpdt: £2.70 to a £1 stake. Pool: £6,841.76 - 1,829.21 winning tickets. **Jonathan Neesom**

[2696] SALISBURY (R-H)

Tuesday, June 7

OFFICIAL GOING: Good to firm (good in places; 8.4)

Wind: almost nil Weather: humid

2997 BATHWICK TYRES NOVICE AUCTION STKS 6f

2:15 (2:16) (Class 5) 2-Y-O **£3,557** (£1,058; £529; £264) **Stalls** Low

Form RPR

4 **1** **Hellofahaste**[17] 2467 2-8-7 0 FrederikTylicki 10 74
(Rod Millman) *lt-f: mid-div: lost pl 3f out: rdn 2f out: sn swtchd lft: r.o strly fnl f: led cl home: readily* **9/4**[1]

3 **2** ½ **Mr Hobbs**[15] 2536 2-8-9 0 EdwardGreatrex(5) 1 80
(Sylvester Kirk) *tall: trckd ldr: rdn to ld over 1f out: kpt on but no ex whn hdd cl home* **10/3**[2]

3 1¼ **Ariena (IRE)** 2-8-7 0 JohnFahy 5 69+
(Clive Cox) *str: mid-div: rdn over 2f out: hdwy over 1f out: chsd ldr briefly jst ins fnl f: kpt on* **13/2**

4 3 **Affair** 2-8-7 0 PaulHanagan 8 60+
(Hughie Morrison) *w'like: swtg: sn pushed along towards rr: nt clr run briefly over 2f out: hdwy over 1f out: r.o wl to go 4th ins fnl f: nt rch ldrs* **16/1**

0 **5** 1½ **Waves (IRE)**[42] 1736 2-8-9 0 ShaneKelly 6 57
(Eve Johnson Houghton) *prom: rdn over 2f out: one pce fnl f* **100/1**

6 1½ **Angel Down** 2-9-2 0 OisinMurphy 4 60
(Henry Candy) *str: mid-div: rdn over 3f out: kpt on fnl f but nvr gng pce to get involved* **9/1**

50 **7** 1¼ **Battle Of Wits (IRE)**[8] 2747 2-8-7 0 JosephineGordon(5) 11 52
(J S Moore) *w'like: trckd ldrs: rdn over 2f out: one pce fnl f* **100/1**

8 ½ **Broughtons Story** 2-9-0 0 StevieDonohoe 7 53
(Willie Musson) *cmpt: bit bkwd: s.i.s: bhd: kpt on past btn horses fnl f: nvr trbld ldrs* **66/1**

6 **9** 1½ **Moneyoryourlife**[5] 2822 2-8-12 0 PatDobbs 13 46
(Richard Hannon) *lengthy: mid-div: effrt over 2f out: wknd fnl f* **6/1**[3]

10 ¾ **Woodukheleyfit** 2-8-9 0 TomMarquand(3) 2 44
(Sylvester Kirk) *led: rdn and hdd over 1f out: wknd fnl f* **16/1**

0 **11** shd **Hawridge Glory (IRE)**[43] 1713 2-9-0 0 RobertHavlin 12 45
(Rod Millman) *mid-div: rdn over 2f out: wknd over 1f out* **33/1**

12 shd **Famous Dynasty (IRE)** 2-8-12 0 DavidProbert 3 43
(Michael Blanshard) *w'like: s.i.s: a towards rr* **66/1**

13 7 **Kath's Boy (IRE)** 2-9-0 0 WilliamCarson 9 24
(Tony Carroll) *str: bit bkwd: s.i.s: a towards rr* **33/1**

4 **14** 1½ **Skilful Lord (IRE)**[27] 2147 2-9-2 0 MartinDwyer 14 22
(Stuart Kittow) *cmpt: towards rr: sme hdwy over 3f out: rdn over 2f out: sn wknd* **20/1**

1m 15.82s (1.02) **Going Correction** +0.025s/f (Good) **14** Ran SP% **118.8**

Speed ratings (Par 93): **94,93,91,87,85 83,82,81,79,78 78,78,68,66**

CSF £8.72 TOTE £3.00: £1.40, £2.00, £3.10; EX 9.30 Trifecta £45.30.

Owner J F S Laws **Bred** Mrs J E Laws **Trained** Kentisbeare, Devon

FOCUS

Rail erected up to 20ft off permanent far-side rail between 6f and 2f out. Both Frederik Tylicki and Edward Greatrex felt the ground was "good". Quite an ordinary novice event but a useful effort from the winner, who came from an unpromising position.

2998 BATHWICK TYRES MAIDEN STKS (DIV I) 6f 212y

2:45 (2:45) (Class 5) 3-Y-O+ **£3,557** (£1,058; £529; £264) **Stalls** Centre

Form RPR

1 **Open 'n Shut** 3-9-4 0 AndreaAtzeni 8 84+
(Roger Varian) *cmpt: mid-div: swtchd lft over 2f out: sn rdn: hdwy over 1f out: r.o strly fnl f: led fnl stride* **14/1**

2-3 **2** hd **Ehtiraas**[24] 2248 3-9-4 0 PaulHanagan 4 83
(Owen Burrows) *lengthy: trckd ldr: chal 2f out: sn hrd rdn: led fnl 140yds: hdd fnl stride* **10/11**[1]

22-0 **3** ¾ **Gold Trade (IRE)**[26] 2179 3-9-4 80 (p) WilliamBuick 3 81
(Hugo Palmer) *led: rdn whn strly pressed 2f out: hdd fnl 140yds: kpt on but no ex* **6/1**[3]

6 **4** 1½ **The Invisible Dog (IRE)**[10] 2698 3-9-4 0 SeanLevey 12 77+
(Richard Hannon) *str: lw: mid-div: hdwy ent fnl f: kpt on to go 4th fnl 120yds: nt pce of ldrs* **12/1**

3- **5** 4 **See You When (IRE)**[361] 3113 3-9-4 0 PatDobbs 13 66+
(Richard Hannon) *hld up towards rr: hdwy over 1f out: kpt on nicely ins fnl f but nvr any threat* **5/1**[2]

46- **6** ¾ **Awesome Quality (USA)**[283] 5851 3-9-4 0 GeorgeBaker 2 64
(James Tate) *mid-div: swtchd lft over 2f out: sn rdn and edgd rt: kpt on ins fnl f but nvr gng pce to get on terms* **25/1**

3-0 **7** 1¾ **Broughtons Vision**[15] 2544 3-9-4 0 StevieDonohoe 11 59
(Willie Musson) *lengthy: mid-div: outpcd and lost pl 2f out: styng on whn sltly hmpd ent fnl f but nvr any threat* **66/1**

00 **8** hd **Rowlestonerendezvu**[19] 2414 3-8-13 0 WilliamCarson 7 54+
(Tony Carroll) *str: s.i.s: bhd: sme late prog: nvr any threat* **150/1**

P3- **9** shd **Cause And Effect (IRE)**[230] 7387 3-9-4 0 FMBerry 1 59
(Ralph Beckett) *str: rdn over 2f out: nvr bttr than mid-div* **14/1**

0 **10** ½ **Where Next**[10] 2698 3-9-4 0 MartinHarley 6 57
(Henry Candy) *w'like: trckd ldrs: rdn to chse ldng pair over 2f out tl wknd ent fnl f* **66/1**

30 **11** 4 **Nightingale Valley**[17] 2470 3-8-13 0 MartinDwyer 10 41
(Stuart Kittow) *trckd ldr: rdn over 2f out: wknd over 1f out* **12/1**

12 50 **Twilight Pursuits** 3-8-13 0 RyanClark 9
(Natalie Lloyd-Beavis) *unf: sn pushed along towards rr: wknd 3f out: eased over 1f out* **200/1**

1m 28.36s (-0.24) **Going Correction** +0.025s/f (Good)

WFA 3 from 5yo 10lb **12** Ran SP% **120.0**

Speed ratings (Par 103): **102,101,100,99,94 93,91,91,91,90 86,29**

CSF £27.43 TOTE £17.60: £3.80, £1.10, £2.10; EX 39.90 Trifecta £187.90.

Owner The Open'n Shut Partnership **Bred** J B J Richards **Trained** Newmarket, Suffolk

FOCUS

No great gallop on here and the winner did well to overcome two horses with experience, both of whom got first run, on debut. The race has been rated around the third.

2999 BATHWICK TYRES MAIDEN STKS (DIV II) 6f 212y

3:15 (3:16) (Class 5) 3-Y-O+ **£3,557** (£1,058; £529; £264) **Stalls** Centre

Form RPR

2-0 **1** **Mamillius**[25] 2207 3-9-4 0 SteveDrowne 4 89
(George Baker) *tall: lw: trckd ldr: led 2f out: sn rdn: kpt on wl to assert fnl f: comf* **11/1**

5 **2** 3¼ **Marbooh (IRE)**[13] 2578 3-9-4 0 PaulHanagan 6 80
(Charles Hills) *trckd ldrs: rdn to chse ldng pair 2f out: kpt on to go 2nd fnl 140yds but no ch w wnr* **9/2**[3]

0-0 **3** 1¾ **Khor Al Udaid**[36] 1931 3-9-4 0 (b) RobertHavlin 2 75
(John Gosden) *led: rdn whn hdd 2f out: kpt pressing wnr tl no ex ins fnl f: lost 2nd fnl 140yds* **11/1**

-223 **4** ¾ **Dubai Mission (IRE)**[22] 2298 3-9-4 78 SeanLevey 1 73
(Richard Hannon) *in tch: rdn wl over 1f out: sn swtchd lft: kpt on same pce fnl f* **3/1**[2]

4 **5** ½ **Horrah**[45] 1622 3-9-4 0 GeorgeBaker 8 72+
(Roger Charlton) *lengthy: stmbld bdly leaving stalls: towards rr: midfield 3f out: rdn 2f out: styd on but no threat fnl f* **15/8**[1]

30 **6** 1 **Bond Trader**[13] 2578 3-9-4 0 JohnFahy 12 69+
(Clive Cox) *swtg: towards rr: sme hdwy 2f out: sn rdn: styd on fnl f* **20/1**

50 **7** hd **Heiba (IRE)**[24] 2234 4-10-0 0 (t) AndreaAtzeni 3 72
(Charlie Fellowes) *cmpt: mid-div: rdn over 2f out: kpt on same pce* **25/1**

00 **8** ½ **Roccor**[13] 2578 3-8-13 0 PatDobbs 14 62
(Richard Hannon) *racd keenly: towards rr: sme late prog: nvr a danger* **25/1**

0 **9** 1 **Dream Free**[25] 2207 3-9-4 0 ShaneKelly 7 64
(David Lanigan) *str: lw: s.i.s: sn rousted along into mid-div: rdn over 1f out: no imp: fdd fnl 100yds* **25/1**

0 **10** 4½ **Tasteofexcellence (IRE)**[32] 2005 3-8-10 0 PhilipPrince(3) 5 47
(Roger Ingram) *leggy: trckd ldr: rdn wl over 2f out: sn wknd* **100/1**

0 **11** 1¾ **Jaunty Joh (IRE)**[10] 2698 3-8-13 0 MartinHarley 10 42
(Henry Candy) *a towards rr* **66/1**

0 **12** 1 **Signal Hill (IRE)**[21] 2320 3-9-4 0 OisinMurphy 13 45
(Andrew Balding) *str: s.i.s: a towards rr* **33/1**

00- **13** 13 **Mcelligott (IRE)**[295] 5453 3-8-11 0 RhiainIngram(7) 9 10
(Richard Price) *cls cpld: mid-div tl wknd 2f out* **250/1**

14 dist **Endzinano** 3-8-10 0 RobHornby(3) 11
(Simon Hodgson) *cmpt: a towards rr: eased fr over 2f out* **200/1**

1m 28.03s (-0.57) **Going Correction** +0.025s/f (Good)

WFA 3 from 4yo 10lb **14** Ran SP% **117.3**

Speed ratings (Par 103): **104,100,98,97,96 95,95,94,93,88 86,85,70,**

CSF £54.13 TOTE £10.10: £3.30, £1.50, £3.70; EX 58.30 Trifecta £836.70.

Owner The Mamillius Partnership **Bred** East Bloodstock & Mr S Graham **Trained** Manton, Wilts

FOCUS

An unsatisfactory maiden, with little getting into it from off the pace and the well-backed favourite disappointing after a notable stumble exiting the stalls. The time was faster than the first division.

3000 SHARP'S DOOM BAR H'CAP 5f

3:45 (3:45) (Class 5) (0-70,68) 3-Y-O **£3,234** (£962; £481; £240) **Stalls** Low

Form RPR

3-00 **1** **Entertaining Ben**[22] 2288 3-9-7 **68** (p) MartinDwyer 9 75
(William Muir) *trckd ldrs: rdn to ld over 1f out: kpt on wl fnl f* **25/1**

-314 **2** 2¼ **Showmethewayavrilo**[29] 2106 3-9-7 **68** MartinHarley 3 67
(Malcolm Saunders) *chsd ldrs: rdn and ev ch over 1f out: kpt on but no ex ins fnl f* **13/2**[3]

142 **3** nk **Justice Lady (IRE)**[36] 1935 3-9-2 **63** MartinLane 6 61+
(David Elsworth) *missed break: racd too freely and trcking ldrs after 2f: rdn and ev ch over 1f out: no ex fnl f: jst hld on for 3rd* **6/4**[1]

0-05 **4** nse **Puteminthebooot (IRE)**[17] 2458 3-7-11 **49** (t) NoelGarbutt(5) 8 47
(David Evans) *sn outpcd in last pair: r.o wl fnl f: nrly snatched 3rd fnl stride* **16/1**

0-64 **5** 1¾ **Kingstreet Lady**[20] 2372 3-8-8 **55** JFEgan 7 46
(Richard Price) *in tch: rdn over 2f out: kpt on but nt pce to get on terms* **16/1**

1-00 **6** 1½ **Star Jeanie**[26] 2185 3-9-6 **67** PatDobbs 5 53
(Richard Hannon) *sn outpcd in last pair: kpt on ins fnl f but nvr any threat* **13/2**[3]

4500 **7** ¾ **Katie Canford**[13] 2585 3-8-4 **51** (b[1]) WilliamCarson 4 34
(John Bridger) *chsd ldrs: rdn over 2f out: wknd fnl f* **25/1**

06-2 **8** ¾ **Sacred Harp**[16] 2503 3-9-0 **61** (t) OisinMurphy 1 42
(Stuart Williams) *cl up: effrt 2f out: wknd fnl f* **9/2**[2]

62-0 **9** 5 **Annie Salts**[20] 2372 3-8-11 **63** (t) JosephineGordon(5) 2 26
(Martyn Meade) *led: rdn and hdd over 1f out: wknd fnl f* **12/1**

1m 2.12s (1.12) **Going Correction** +0.025s/f (Good) **9** Ran SP% **112.0**

Speed ratings (Par 99): **92,88,87,87,85 82,81,80,72**

CSF £172.05 CT £401.60 TOTE £19.60: £5.20, £2.40, £1.10; EX 121.90 Trifecta £463.00.

Owner Berkeley, Edginton, Niven **Bred** C J Mills **Trained** Lambourn, Berks

FOCUS

As in the previous race, the favourite compromised her chance leaving the stalls and the form doesn't look up to much, with two of the other fancied runners disappointing also.

3001 EBF STALLIONS BREEDING WINNERS MARGADALE FILLIES' H'CAP 1m 1f 198y

4:15 (4:15) (Class 4) (0-85,81) 3-Y-O+ **£7,762** (£2,310; £1,154; £577) **Stalls** Low

Form RPR

4-12 **1** **White Poppy (IRE)**[19] 2412 3-9-1 **81** OisinMurphy 3 98
(Andrew Balding) *pushed along leaving stalls: trckd ldrs: rdn to chal fr over 2f out: led narrowly jst over 1f out: styd on wl fnl 120yds* **2/1**[1]

4-1 **2** 1¾ **Sightline**[55] 1406 3-8-11 **77** PatDobbs 6 90
(Ralph Beckett) *hmpd sn after s: trckd ldr: led over 3f out: rdn whn strly pressed over 2f out: narrowly hdd jst over 1f out: styd on but no ex fnl 120yds* **3/1**[2]

1-52 **3** 7 **Perceived**[22] 2296 4-9-6 **73** MartinHarley 1 73
(Henry Candy) *in tch: rdn to chse ldng pair 2f out: styd on but nvr gng pce to get on terms* **12/1**

01-5 **4** ½ **Natural Beauty**[31] 2035 3-8-10 **76** (t) RobertHavlin 5 74
(John Gosden) *hmpd sn after s: in tch: rdn to dispute hld 3rd 2f out: styd on but nvr gng pce to get on terms w front pair* **11/1**

0-35 **5** 1¾ **Loveisreckless (IRE)**[18] 2443 3-7-13 **70** (b) JosephineGordon(5) 9 65
(William Muir) *s.i.s: sn in tch: chal for hld 3rd 2f out tl no ex ins fnl f* **16/1**

4-30 **6** *1 ½* **Justice Lass (IRE)**[24] 2239 3-8-12 **78**................................ MartinLane 7 70
(David Elsworth) *jinked lft sn after s: hld up in last pair: hdwy over 3f out: sn rdn: one pce fnl 2f* **14/1**

2-12 **7** *35* **Bombilate (USA)**[21] 2339 3-8-12 **78**................................ WilliamBuick 4
(Charlie Appleby) *lw: trckd ldrs: effrt over 3f out: wknd over 2f out: eased* **5/1**[3]

41-4 **8** *3 ¾* **Sunscape (IRE)**[21] 2339 3-8-6 **72**................................ PaulHanagan 8
(Hughie Morrison) *slowly away: racd too freely and sn led: rn wd on bnd over 6f out: hdd over 3f out: sn hld: wknd and eased 2f out* **10/1**

3-55 **9** *3 ¾* **Miss Minuty**[113] 595 4-9-5 **79**................................ GeorgeWood(7) 2
(Alexandra Dunn) *a towards rr: eased whn btn fnl 2f* **33/1**

2m 8.44s (-1.46) **Going Correction** +0.025s/f (Good)
WFA 3 from 4yo 13lb **9** Ran SP% **115.6**
Speed ratings (Par 102): **106,104,99,98,97 96,68,65,62**
CSF £7.92 CT £54.99 TOTE £3.00: £1.10, £1.80, £3.10; EX 10.50 Trifecta £67.40.
Owner Qatar Racing Limited **Bred** John Malone **Trained** Kingsclere, Hants

FOCUS
Two progressive and well handicapped types came clear in what was a decent fillies' handicap.

3002 ROA/RACING POST OWNERS JACKPOT H'CAP 1m 4f
4:45 (4:45) (Class 5) (0-70,70) 4-Y-O+ **£3,234** (£962; £481; £240) **Stalls** Low

Form RPR

-463 **1** **Blenheim Warrior**[25] 2210 4-9-2 **65**................................ AndreaAtzeni 10 73
(Richard Hughes) *trckd ldr: led over 2f out: drvn whn drifting lft over 1f out: jst hld on* **10/11**[1]

0450 **2** *hd* **Rosie Royale (IRE)**[11] 2634 4-8-8 **57**................................ OisinMurphy 5 64
(Roger Teal) *trckd ldrs: rdn over 1f out: styd on wl clsng stages: jst failed* **20/1**

-314 **3** *1 ½* **Speculator**[12] 2623 4-9-5 **68**................................ ShaneKelly 7 73
(David Menuisier) *mid-div: hdwy whn short of room over 3f out: rdn 2f out: chal jst over 1f out: no ex fnl 120yds* **5/1**[2]

253 **4** *2* **Oratorio's Joy (IRE)**[27] 2149 6-9-5 **68**................................ WilliamCarson 6 70
(Jamie Osborne) *mid-div: hdwy over 3f out: rdn over 2f out: mounting chal whn bdly squeezed out jst over 1f out: hld after* **14/1**

2400 **5** *¾* **Senor George (IRE)**[12] 2605 9-8-13 **62**................................ RyanClark 2 62
(Simon Hodgson) *hld up: rdn 3f out: hdwy over 2f out: styd on fnl f but nt pce to get involved* **50/1**

3354 **6** *hd* **Bushel (USA)**[20] 2367 6-9-4 **70**................................ EoinWalsh(3) 1 70
(Tony Newcombe) *trckd ldrs tl lost pl 6f out: in tch: rdn wl over 2f out: styd on but nt pce to get bk on terms* **8/1**[3]

-560 **7** *2 ¼* **Prince Of Paris**[12] 2623 4-9-7 **70**................................(t) PatDobbs 4 66
(Roger Ingram) *hld up: hdwy 3f out: sn rdn: nvr threatened: fdd ins fnl f* **12/1**

6400 **8** *8* **Kay Sera**[53] 1456 8-8-9 **61**................................ RobHornby(3) 8 44
(Tony Newcombe) *hld up: hdwy over 3f out: effrt over 2f out: wknd fnl f* **22/1**

3-22 **9** *8* **Start Seven**[109] 630 4-9-6 **69**................................ JFEgan 9 40
(Joseph Tuite) *led tl over 2f out: sn wknd* **16/1**

243- **10** *52* **Dylan's Storm (IRE)**[18] 5257 4-9-4 **67**................................(t) MartinDwyer 11
(David Dennis) *in tch tl wknd over 3f out: virtually p.u* **50/1**

2m 38.63s (0.63) **Going Correction** +0.025s/f (Good) **10** Ran SP% **113.4**
Speed ratings (Par 103): **98,97,96,95,95 94,93,88,82,48**
CSF £26.08 CT £62.71 TOTE £1.70: £1.10, £4.70, £2.20; EX 24.40 Trifecta £126.60.
Owner Saleh Al Homaizi & Imad Al Sagar **Bred** Saleh Al Homaizi & Imad Al Sagar **Trained** Upper Lambourn, Berkshire
■ Stewards' Enquiry : Andrea Atzeni three-day ban: careless riding (Jun 21-23)
Martin Dwyer trainer's rep said gelding had a breathing problem

FOCUS
The pace slowed right up once they'd jostled for early positions in this modest handicap and Andrea Atzeni's ride was the difference in winning and losing for the favourite.

3003 MOLSON COORS H'CAP 6f 212y
5:15 (5:15) (Class 6) (0-60,60) 3-Y-O **£2,911** (£866; £432; £216) **Stalls** Low

Form RPR

00-0 **1** **R Bar Open (FR)**[29] 2106 3-9-6 **60**................................ RobertWinston 12 67
(Dean Ivory) *towards rr: hdwy 2f out: sn rdn: r.o wl fnl f: led towards fin* **16/1**

0-51 **2** *nk* **Moi Aussie**[29] 2107 3-9-2 **56**................................ MartinDwyer 10 62
(Ed McMahon) *lw: prom: led over 3f out: rdn 2f out: no ex whn hdd towards fin* **5/1**[1]

00-6 **3** *2 ¾* **Constable Clouds (USA)**[22] 2293 3-9-3 **57**................(v[1]) GeorgeBaker 9 56
(Gary Moore) *led tl over 3f out: sn rdn: styd on same pce fnl f* **6/1**[2]

-604 **4** *nk* **Harmony Bay (IRE)**[13] 2585 3-9-6 **60**................................ PatDobbs 2 58
(Sylvester Kirk) *mid-div: hdwy over 2f out: sn rdn: chsd ldr ent fnl f: kpt on same pce* **5/1**[1]

21-2 **5** *3 ½* **Bahamian Boy**[29] 2083 3-8-10 **57**................................ CharlieBennett(7) 13 46
(Hughie Morrison) *dwlt: bhd: trying to make hdwy on rails whn nt clr run over 3f out: rdn 2f out: nt pce to get involved* **6/1**[2]

-500 **6** *3* **Indie Music**[29] 2108 3-8-12 **59**................................ BenSanderson(7) 3 39
(Sylvester Kirk) *swtg: nvr bttr than mid-div* **17/2**[3]

00-6 **7** *2* **Lucia Sciarra**[76] 1045 3-8-11 **56**................................ JosephineGordon(5) 6 31
(Giles Bravery) *trckd ldrs: rdn over 2f out: wknd ent fnl f* **20/1**

60-0 **8** *½* **Turaathy (IRE)**[20] 2372 3-9-3 **60**................................ EoinWalsh(3) 11 34
(Tony Newcombe) *s.i.s: towards rr: sme late prog: nvr a factor* **20/1**

5-05 **9** *2 ¾* **Smile Of Approval (IRE)**[26] 2184 3-9-3 **60**................................ DannyBrock(3) 1 26
(Jonathan Portman) *mid-div: rdn over 2f out: nvr any imp: wknd ins fnl f* **33/1**

00-0 **10** *shd* **Stylish Minerva**[13] 2585 3-8-13 **56**................................ TomMarquand(3) 14 22
(Richard Hannon) *s.i.s: a towards rr* **14/1**

-505 **11** *10* **African Showgirl**[20] 2372 3-9-5 **59**................................ SteveDrowne 5
(George Baker) *a towards rr* **16/1**

055 **12** *nk* **Plymouth Mo**[104] 697 3-9-5 **59**................................ OisinMurphy 4
(Rod Millman) *chsd ldrs tl wknd 2f out* **10/1**

0400 **13** *¾* **Straduff (IRE)**[52] 1497 3-9-1 **58**................................ MichaelJMMurphy(3) 7
(J S Moore) *mid-div tl wknd 2f out* **25/1**

1m 29.29s (0.69) **Going Correction** +0.025s/f (Good) **13** Ran SP% **116.3**
Speed ratings (Par 97): **97,96,93,93,89 85,83,82,79,79 68,67,67**
CSF £87.04 CT £545.22 TOTE £16.70: £5.00, £2.20, £3.30; EX 131.50 Trifecta £1593.60.
Owner The Macaroni Beach Society **Bred** Dream With Me Stable Inc **Trained** Radlett, Herts

FOCUS
Moderate sprinting form won by an improver.

3004 LITTLETON STUD RACING EXCELLENCE APPRENTICE H'CAP (WHIPS SHALL BE CARRIED BUT NOT USED) 6f
5:45 (5:46) (Class 5) (0-75,74) 4-Y-O+ **£3,234** (£962; £481; £240) **Stalls** Low

Form RPR

00-0 **1** **Monarch Maid**[22] 2290 5-9-4 **69**................................ LuluStanford(3) 7 79
(Peter Hiatt) *mde all: kpt on wl: pushed out* **10/1**

50-2 **2** *1 ½* **Doctor Bong**[26] 2187 4-9-4 **73**................................(p) JoshuaBryan(7) 10 78
(Andrew Balding) *lw: chsd wnr: rdn over 2f out: kpt on but a being hld fnl f* **11/4**[1]

-404 **3** *shd* **Wahaab (IRE)**[11] 2635 5-8-2 **57**................................ NicolaCurrie(7) 9 62
(Richard Hughes) *in tch: pushed along fr 2f out: r.o ins fnl f: nrly snatched 2nd fnl strides* **6/1**[3]

6133 **4** *hd* **Duke Of North (IRE)**[7] 2769 4-9-2 **64**................................ RhiainIngram 11 68
(Jim Boyle) *chsd ldrs: pushed along over 2f out: kpt on ins fnl f* **4/1**[2]

63-0 **5** *12* **Oeil De Tigre (FR)**[24] 2253 5-9-10 **72**................................ GeorgiaCox 1 38
(Tony Carroll) *chsd wnr: pushed along over 2f out: wknd ent fnl f* **12/1**

-640 **6** *1* **Brazen Spirit**[97] 782 4-9-9 **74**................................(v) JoshQuinn(3) 4 36
(Clive Cox) *dwlt: last but sn in tch: wknd over 1f out* **16/1**

116/ **7** *8* **Molly Jones**[656] 5595 7-8-7 **60**................................ SeanMooney(5) 3
(Matthew Salaman) *chsd ldrs tl wknd 2f out* **33/1**

1m 15.67s (0.87) **Going Correction** +0.05s/f (Good) **7** Ran SP% **86.6**
Speed ratings (Par 103): **96,94,93,93,77 76,65**
CSF £21.28 CT £70.17 TOTE £9.60: £3.10, £1.60; EX 22.50 Trifecta £111.90.
Owner Carl Demczak **Bred** Oakhill Stud **Trained** Hook Norton, Oxon
■ Pandar (11-4) was withdrawn. Rule 4 applies to all bets. Deduction - 25p in the pound.

FOCUS
No whips allowed here and very little happened in the race, the winner being kept rolling in front.
T/Plt: £9.40 to a £1 stake. Pool: £76,773.17 - 5,908.25 winning tickets. T/Qpdt: £10.60 to a £1 stake. Pool: £5,277.72 - 367.20 winning tickets. **Tim Mitchell**

3005 - (Foreign Racing) - See Raceform Interactive

2724 SAINT-CLOUD (L-H)
Tuesday, June 7

OFFICIAL GOING: Turf: soft

3006a PRIX DE VILLE-D'AVRAY (CLAIMER) (2YO) (TURF) 6f
1:50 (12:00) 2-Y-O **£9,926** (£3,970; £2,977; £1,985; £992)

RPR

1 **Erica Bing**[11] 2637 2-8-13 0................................ MaximeGuyon 12 76
(Jo Hughes) *mde all: broke wl fr wd draw and led: sn swtchd ins to rail: rowed along and kicked for home 2 1/2f out: 2 l clr and rdn 1 1/2f out: drew clr fnl f* **14/1**

2 *2* **Sheila's Lad (IRE)**[9] 2724 2-9-1 0................................ IoritzMendizabal 1 72
(D Windrif, France) **59/10**[3]

3 *½* **Efichope (FR)**[9] 2724 2-8-8 0................................(p) JulienAuge 5 64
(A Chopard, France) **10/1**

4 *nk* **Elusiva (FR)**[23] 2280 2-8-13 0 ow2................(p) Pierre-CharlesBoudot 11 68
(P Sogorb, France) **11/5**[1]

5 *2 ½* **Decale** 2-9-1 0................................ ChristopheSoumillon 9 62
(K Borgel, France) **11/2**[2]

6 *4* **Echapee Divine (FR)**[31] 2-8-11 0................................(b[1]) OlivierPeslier 8 46
(T Lemer, France) **33/1**

7 *¾* **Barlongueta (IRE)** 2-9-1 0................................ VincentCheminaud 4 48
(M Delcher Sanchez, France) **52/1**

8 *½* **Fast Kar (IRE)**[9] 2724 2-8-8 0................................ EddyHardouin 7 39
(Matthieu Palussiere, France) **13/1**

9 *¾* **Decapulse (IRE)**[42] 2-8-13 0................................ CristianDemuro 3 42
(J-V Toux, France) **63/10**

10 *snk* **Chababa Rosetgri (FR)**[9] 2724 2-8-11 0................(p) RonanThomas 6 40
(H De Nicolay, France) **43/1**

11 *¾* **Rainbow Black**[23] 2280 2-9-5 0................................ PierreBazire(3) 10 48
(A Giorgi, Italy) **74/10**

12 *2 ½* **Silver Top (FR)** 2-8-11 0................................ AntoineHamelin 2 30
(M Nigge, France) **30/1**

1m 18.39s (1.59) **12** Ran SP% **120.0**
WIN (incl. 1 euro stake): 15.70. PLACES: 4.40, 2.50, 3.40. DF: 55.40. SF: 118.40..
Owner Richard Kent & Jo Hughes **Bred** Mickley Stud & Sue Shone **Trained** Lambourn, Berks

3007a PRIX DE FRENEUSE (CLAIMER) (3YO FILLIES) (TURF) 1m
2:55 (12:00) 3-Y-O **£8,455** (£3,382; £2,536; £1,691; £845)

RPR

1 **Blonville (FR)**[22] 3-8-11 0................................ OlivierPeslier 2 74
(H-A Pantall, France) **12/5**[1]

2 *5* **Singaraja (FR)**[243] 3-8-6 0................................ MlleLauraGrosso(5) 1 62
(K Borgel, France) **15/1**

3 *1 ½* **Rip Van Suzy (IRE)**[27] 2172 3-9-4 0................................ MaximeGuyon 6 66
(Jo Hughes) *hld up bhd ldng trio: rdn to hold pl wl over 2 1/2f out: styng on sn after whn sltly impeded: chsd wnr fr 1 1/2f out: grad lft bhd by wnr ent fnl f: fdd and dropped to 3rd fnl 100yds* **71/10**

4 *snk* **Des Annees Folles (FR)**[30] 3-9-1 0................................ MickaelBarzalona 3 62
(Y Barberot, France) **39/10**[2]

5 *shd* **Zip Code (FR)**[8] 3-9-1 0................................ IoritzMendizabal 8 62
(Robert Collet, France) **53/10**[3]

6 *1 ½* **Diaspora (FR)**[173] 3-8-9 0................................(p) MlleIsisMagnin(6) 9 59
(C Escuder, France) **13/1**

7 *nse* **Pepite Noire (FR)**[79] 3-9-1 0................................ ChristopheSoumillon 7 58
(K Borgel, France) **67/10**

8 *8* **Lila Mahyana (FR)**[13] 2602 3-9-5 0................................ EddyHardouin 5 44
(C Boutin, France) **54/10**

1m 48.28s (0.78) **8** Ran SP% **120.0**
WIN (incl. 1 euro stake): 3.40. PLACES: 1.70, 3.40, 2.50. DF: 16.10. SF: 26.00..
Owner H H Sheikh Abdulla Bin Khalifa Al Thani **Bred** Franklin Finance S.A. **Trained** France

2668 BEVERLEY (R-H)

Wednesday, June 8

OFFICIAL GOING: Good to firm (8.1)

Wind: Light, across Weather: Fine & dry

3008 ETTON CLAIMING STKS 5f

2:00 (2:02) (Class 6) 2-Y-O **£2,587** (£770; £384; £192) **Stalls** Low

Form RPR

50 **1** **Suetonius**[16] 2536 2-8-7 0 JoeFanning 4 62
(Ed McMahon) *led: rdn along wl over 1f out and sn jnd: hdd narrowly ins fnl f: drvn and rallied wl to ld again nr fin* **7/1**

005 **2** *nse* **Benidiction (IRE)**[11] 2675 2-8-10 0 PJMcDonald 7 65
(Ann Duffield) *trckd wnr: hdwy and cl up 1 1/2f out: rdn to take narrow advantage ins fnl f: sn drvn: hdd nr fin* **7/1**

32 **3** *2 3/4* **Springforth**[24] 2266 2-8-7 0 GeorgeChaloner 6 52+
(Richard Fahey) *dwlt: sn trcking ldrs: rdn over 1f out: drvn and no imp fnl f* **7/4**[1]

4 **4** *3* **Charlie Beer Punt (IRE)**[50] 1543 2-9-1 0 LiamJones 8 49
(Tom Dascombe) *cl up on outer: rdn along 2f out: sn drvn and wknd over 1f out* **7/2**[2]

56 **5** *nse* **Tough To Bear**[11] 2675 2-8-8 0 (p) JacobButterfield(3) 2 45
(Ollie Pears) *trckd wnr on inner: effrt 2f out and sn rdn: drvn over 1f out and sn one pce* **6/1**[3]

034 **6** *3 1/4* **Eid Rose**[24] 2266 2-8-6 0 BenCurtis 5 28
(Scott Dixon) *in tch: rdn along 1/2-way: n.d* **14/1**

7 *4 1/2* **Fair Skies (IRE)** 2-8-7 0 LemosdeSouza 1 13
(Ivan Furtado) *sn outpcd and a in rr* **12/1**

1m 3.16s (-0.34) **Going Correction** -0.325s/f (Firm) **7** Ran SP% **112.2**

Speed ratings (Par 91): **89,88,84,79,79 74,67**

CSF £51.73 TOTE £8.10: £3.10, £3.30; EX 49.30 Trifecta £174.10.The winner was claimed by Mr Claes Bjorling for £6,000.

Owner Mrs Fiona Williams **Bred** Mrs F S Williams **Trained** Lichfield, Staffs

■ Fire Engine was withdrawn. Price at time of withdrawal 25-1. Rule 4 does not apply.

FOCUS

Race distance was as advertised. The going was good to firm and had been watered. Joe Fanning described it as "beautiful ground". A modest juvenile claimer where the pair who fought out a close finish were the first two throughout.

3009 RACING UK IN HD H'CAP (DIV I) 5f

2:30 (2:32) (Class 6) (0-65,65) 3-Y-O+ **£2,587** (£770; £384; £192) **Stalls** Low

Form RPR

3-30 **1** **Bond Bombshell**[22] 2334 3-8-12 **61** JoshDoyle(5) 3 68
(David O'Meara) *cl up on inner: led 2f out: rdn clr over 1f out: kpt on* **13/2**[3]

6266 **2** *1* **Bronze Beau**[19] 2418 9-9-13 **64** (tp) JoeFanning 6 70
(Kristin Stubbs) *slt ld: pushed along and hdd 2f out: sn rdn: styd on u.p fnl f* **9/1**

0/2 **3** *1* **Bounty Pursuit**[2] 2964 4-9-5 **56** AndrewMullen 11 59+
(Michael Appleby) *hld up: hdwy wl over 1f out: sn rdn: styd on fnl f: nrst fin* **4/1**[1]

0-05 **4** *1 1/4* **Nefetari**[15] 2561 3-8-2 **46** oh1 (p) JimmyQuinn 12 41
(Alan Brown) *wnt lft s: sn chsng ldng pair: rdn wl over 1f out: drvn and kpt on same pce fnl f* **100/1**

-412 **5** *3/4* **Roaring Rory**[8] 2785 3-9-4 **65** (p) JacobButterfield(3) 7 58
(Ollie Pears) *midfield: rdn along and sltly outpcd over 2f out: styng on whn n.m.r ent fnl f: swtchd lft and drvn: kpt on towards fin* **4/1**[1]

5323 **6** *nk* **See Vermont**[6] 2808 8-10-0 **65** (p) PaulMulrennan 9 60
(Rebecca Bastiman) *towards rr: hdwy on outer over 1f out: rdn and kpt on fnl f* **5/1**[2]

3610 **7** *1* **Gaelic Wizard (IRE)**[14] 2571 8-9-5 **61** (v) GemmaTutty(5) 4 55
(Karen Tutty) *towards rr: sme hdwy on inner whn n.m.r over 1f out: n.d* **8/1**

40-U **8** *3/4* **Thornaby Princess**[19] 2423 5-9-2 **53** RoystonFfrench 8 41
(Colin Teague) *chsd ldrs: rdn 2f out: sn drvn and wknd over 1f out* **33/1**

-250 **9** *1 1/4* **Tinsill**[29] 2120 5-8-9 **53** KieranSchofield(7) 1 37
(Nigel Tinkler) *in tch: rdn along 2f out: sn btn* **14/1**

-040 **10** *3/4* **Emerald Bay**[4] 2919 3-9-2 **60** RaulDaSilva 2 38
(Ivan Furtado) *chsd ldrs: rdn 2f out: wknd over 1f out* **9/1**

0-00 **11** *5* **Emilie Bronte**[9] 2740 3-8-9 **53** AndrewElliott 5 13
(Chris Fairhurst) *sn outpcd and a in rr* **28/1**

-000 **12** *2* **George Bailey (IRE)**[32] 2052 4-8-13 **50** BarryMcHugh 10 6
(Suzzanne France) *stmbld s: a in rr* **25/1**

1m 1.89s (-1.61) **Going Correction** -0.325s/f (Firm)

WFA 3 from 4yo+ 7lb **12** Ran SP% **119.0**

Speed ratings (Par 101): **99,97,95,93,92 92,90,89,87,86 78,74**

CSF £62.04 CT £270.90 TOTE £5.50: £2.60, £2.60, £2.40; EX 67.30 Trifecta £1259.70.

Owner Trendy Ladies **Bred** Mrs P M A Avison **Trained** Upper Helmsley, N Yorks

■ Stewards' Enquiry : Raul Da Silva two-day ban: careless riding (Jun 22-23)

FOCUS

A modest sprint handicap where they went a fast pace and it proved impossible to come from behind. The winner has a good record here.

3010 RACING UK IN HD H'CAP (DIV II) 5f

3:00 (3:01) (Class 6) (0-65,64) 3-Y-O+ **£2,587** (£770; £384; £192) **Stalls** Low

Form RPR

2-52 **1** **Burtonwood**[42] 1790 4-9-7 **64** RowanScott(7) 1 72
(Julie Camacho) *trckd ldng pair on inner: swtchd lft and hdwy over 1f out: rdn to take narrow advantage ent fnl f: kpt on* **10/3**[2]

230- **2** *1/2* **Kinloch Pride**[179] 8196 4-9-1 **51** (p) BarryMcHugh 3 57
(Noel Wilson) *sn led: rdn along wl over 1f out: drvn and hdd narrowly ent fnl f: kpt on wl* **12/1**

-042 **3** *3/4* **Poppy In The Wind**[22] 2334 4-9-10 **60** (v) DaleSwift 6 63
(Alan Brown) *midfield: effrt 2f out and sn rdn: styng on whn n.m.r ent fnl f: sn swtchd lft and drvn: fin strly* **9/2**[3]

0-02 **4** *1/2* **Silver Sands (IRE)**[9] 2742 3-9-6 **63** DavidAllan 5 61
(Tim Easterby) *trckd ldng pair: effrt 2f out and sn rdn drvn over 1f out and kpt on same pce* **5/2**[1]

040- **5** *1 1/2* **Midnight Robbery**[221] 7641 3-9-3 **60** PaulMulrennan 2 53
(Bryan Smart) *cl up on inner: disp ld 1/2-way: rdn wl over 1f out: ev ch tl drvn ent fnl f and grad wknd* **14/1**

006- **6** *4 1/2* **Knockamany Bends (IRE)**[229] 7437 6-9-4 **54** (p) PaddyAspell 7 34
(John Wainwright) *chsd ldrs: rdn along 2f out: sn drvn and one pce* **33/1**

0040 **7** *nk* **Incomparable**[11] 2676 11-8-9 **45** (p) BenCurtis 8 24
(Scott Dixon) *a towards rr* **14/1**

-000 **8** *nse* **Majestic Manannan (IRE)**[11] 2676 7-9-7 **57** AndrewMullen 9 35
(David Nicholls) *hmpd s and t.k.h early: a towards rr* **14/1**

6-40 **9** *3/4* **Go Charlie**[142] 241 5-8-11 **47** LemosdeSouza 4 23
(Lisa Williamson) *t.k.h: a in rr* **25/1**

0-40 **10** *1 1/2* **Rise Up Singing**[23] 2302 3-8-2 **45** RaulDaSilva 12 12
(Colin Teague) *wnt rt s: a in rr* **66/1**

4145 **11** *2 1/4* **Windforpower (IRE)**[4] 2919 6-10-0 **64** (p) JoeFanning 11 26
(Tracy Waggott) *hmpd s: a in rr* **8/1**

1m 1.68s (-1.82) **Going Correction** -0.325s/f (Firm)

WFA 3 from 4yo+ 7lb **11** Ran SP% **116.9**

Speed ratings (Par 101): **101,100,99,98,95 88,88,88,86,84 80**

CSF £42.14 CT £187.06 TOTE £4.40: £1.80, £3.50, £1.90; EX 55.10 Trifecta £178.40.

Owner Judy & Richard Peck & Partner **Bred** Brightwalton Stud **Trained** Norton, N Yorks

FOCUS

Another modest sprint handicap run at a good clip (this was run 0.21s faster than the first division). Unlike in the first division the leaders came back to the field.

3011 WEATHERBYS HAMILTON H'CAP 1m 100y

3:30 (3:30) (Class 4) (0-80,79) 4-Y-O+ **£5,040** (£1,508; £754; £377; £188) **Stalls** Low

Form RPR

2222 **1** **Jacbequick**[11] 2677 5-9-2 **79** (v) JoshDoyle(5) 10 86
(David O'Meara) *mde most: rdn wl over 1f out: drvn ins fnl f: hld on gamely towards fin* **6/1**[3]

044- **2** *nk* **Rocket Ronnie (IRE)**[177] 8227 6-9-0 **72** DaleSwift 9 78
(Ed McMahon) *stdd s and hld up in rr: hdwy wl over 1f out: rdn and nt clr run ins fnl f: swtchd lft last 100yds and fin strly* **14/1**

-536 **3** *hd* **Simply Shining (IRE)**[26] 2216 6-8-13 **78** AdamMcNamara(7) 6 84
(Richard Fahey) *trckd ldrs: hdwy over 2f out: chsd wnr over 1f out: sn rdn: drvn and chal ent fnl f: ev ch tl no ex towards fin* **7/2**[1]

10 **4** *hd* **Dutch Artist (IRE)**[18] 2491 4-9-5 **77** DavidNolan 4 82
(David O'Meara) *trckd ldrs on inner: hdwy over 2f out: rdn over 1f out: n.m.r and swtchd lft ins fnl f: drvn and keeping on whn bmpd nr fin* **11/2**[2]

3004 **5** *1* **Final**[25] 2256 4-9-0 **72** JoeFanning 2 77
(Mark Johnston) *hld up towards rr: hdwy over 2f out: chsd ldrs whn carried rt over 1f out and sn swtchd to inner: gd hdwy ins fnl f and ev ch whn nt clr run and hmpd last 50yds: nt rcvr* **6/1**[3]

3-51 **6** *3/4* **Victoire De Lyphar (IRE)**[23] 2297 9-9-0 **72** (e) PaulMulrennan 7 73
(Ruth Carr) *prom: trckd wnr after 2f: rdn along wl over 1f out: drvn ent fnl f: grad wknd* **10/1**

0-51 **7** *3 1/2* **Nonno Giulio (IRE)**[22] 2347 5-9-7 **79** PJMcDonald 1 72
(David Loughnane) *in tch: effrt over 2f out: rdn along wl over 1f out: sn btn* **11/2**[2]

400- **8** *2 3/4* **Shadowtime**[247] 6981 11-8-7 **65** AndrewMullen 5 52
(Tracy Waggott) *t.k.h: trckd ldrs: hdwy over 2f out: rdn wl over 1f out: sn edgd rt and wknd* **40/1**

20-5 **9** *3* **Lopito De Vega (IRE)**[11] 2672 4-8-6 **64** BenCurtis 3 44
(David C Griffiths) *hld up: rdn along wl over 2f out: sn wknd* **7/1**

600- **10** *1 1/2* **Thornaby Nash**[276] 6131 5-9-7 **79** GrahamGibbons 8 55
(Colin Teague) *a bhd* **50/1**

1m 43.99s (-3.61) **Going Correction** -0.325s/f (Firm) **10** Ran SP% **114.2**

Speed ratings (Par 105): **105,104,104,104,103 102,99,96,93,91**

CSF £84.28 CT £337.17 TOTE £7.20: £2.30, £3.40, £1.20; EX 46.60 Trifecta £357.60.

Owner Cherry Garth Racing **Bred** Russ Wake **Trained** Upper Helmsley, N Yorks

FOCUS

The race was run over 18yds further than advertised. A fair race where once more it paid to be up with the pace and on the rail.

3012 MEGAN O'MEARA 19TH BIRTHDAY H'CAP 1m 1f 207y

4:00 (4:01) (Class 5) (0-70,70) 4-Y-O+ **£3,780** (£1,131; £565; £283; £141) **Stalls** Low

Form RPR

0003 **1** **Mysterial**[11] 2672 6-9-1 **68** PhilDennis(5) 3 78
(Declan Carroll) *set str gallop and clr: stdd 1/2-way: qcknd 2 1/2f out: rdn over 1f out: kpt on strly* **10/1**

0201 **2** *2 1/2* **Yorkindred Spirit**[4] 2915 4-9-8 **70** 6ex (v) JoeFanning 4 75+
(Mark Johnston) *hld up towards rr: hdwy on wd outside over 2f out: rdn over 1f out: sn drvn and kpt on* **11/2**

-513 **3** *nse* **Ghostly Arc (IRE)**[21] 2365 4-9-0 **62** BarryMcHugh 7 67
(Noel Wilson) *chsd wnr: rdn wl over 1f out: drvn appr fnl f: kpt on* **11/2**

0555 **4** *3 3/4* **Saint Thomas (IRE)**[9] 2738 9-8-7 **55** PJMcDonald 5 52
(John Mackie) *trckd ldrs: hdwy over 2f out: rdn along wl over 1f out: sn drvn and one pce* **5/1**[3]

604 **5** *1 1/4* **Lostock Hall (IRE)**[32] 2043 4-9-6 **68** BenCurtis 1 63
(K R Burke) *trckd ldrs on inner: effrt 3f out: rdn along over 2f out: drvn wl over 1f out and sn one pce* **3/1**[1]

0-61 **6** *1/2* **King Of The Celts (IRE)**[11] 2672 8-9-2 **69** RachelRichardson(5) 2 63
(Tim Easterby) *hld up in tch: effrt over 2f out: sn rdn and n.d* **4/1**[2]

04 **7** *11* **Truly**[23] 2307 5-9-4 **66** GrahamGibbons 6 38
(Colin Teague) *plld hrd: chsd ldrs: rdn along wl over 2f out: sn wknd* **33/1**

3001 **8** *2* **The Wee Barra (IRE)**[14] 2574 4-8-12 **63** (p) JoeDoyle(3) 8 31
(Kevin Ryan) *stmbld s: a in rr* **8/1**

0/04 **9** *3 3/4* **Rising Rainbow**[23] 2297 5-8-2 **50** oh5 (b) RaulDaSilva 9 10
(Ivan Furtado) *t.k.h: hld up: a in rr* **66/1**

2m 3.69s (-3.31) **Going Correction** -0.325s/f (Firm) **9** Ran SP% **117.1**

Speed ratings (Par 103): **100,98,97,94,93 93,84,83,80**

CSF £64.89 CT £338.60 TOTE £13.30: £3.70, £2.20, £1.90; EX 86.70 Trifecta £698.50.

Owner Mrs Sarah Bryan **Bred** Ladyswood, Canning Down & D Farrington **Trained** Malton, N Yorks

FOCUS

The race distance was 18yds further than advertised. A moderate handicap where the winner, who has been rated to his best, was sent on a long way out.

3013 BEVERLEY FOLK FESTIVAL HERE NEXT WEEK H'CAP 7f 100y

4:30 (4:31) (Class 5) (0-70,70) 4-Y-O+ **£3,780** (£1,131; £565; £283; £141) **Stalls** Low

Form RPR

0-01 **1** **Barwah (USA)**[22] 2329 5-8-4 **53** AndrewMullen 5 62
(Peter Niven) *in tch: hdwy over 2f out: rdn over 1f out: chsd ldr appr fnl f: drvn and styd on wl to ld last 80yds* **10/1**

-004 **2** *1 3/4* **So It's War (FR)**[11] 2673 5-9-7 **70** (p) PhillipMakin 4 75
(Keith Dalgleish) *hld up towards rr: hdwy over 2f out: effrt and n.m.r over 1f out: sn swtchd rt to inner and rdn: styd on wl fnl f* **4/1**[1]

0044 **3** *1/2* **Talent Scout (IRE)**[12] 2662 10-8-11 **65** GemmaTutty(5) 10 69
(Karen Tutty) *chsd ldrs: hdwy 2f out: rdn wl over 1f out: styd on wl u.p fnl f* **10/1**

0-51 **4** *1* **Joyful Star**[16] 2528 6-8-9 **58** ow1 PaulMulrennan 9 59+
(Fred Watson) *hld up and bhd: hdwy on inner wl over 1f out: sn rdn squeezed through ins fnl f: nrst fin* **13/2**[3]

0300 **5** *½* **Mercury**[11] 2673 4-8-4 **56** (b) JoeDoyle(3) 8 56
(Kevin Ryan) *led and sn clr at str gallop: pushed along wl over 1f out: rdn appr fnl f: hdd & wknd last 80yds* **10/1**

0332 **6** *nk* **Roger Thorpe**[20] 2409 7-8-9 **58** CamHardie 2 57
(Deborah Sanderson) *chsd ldrs: rdn along 2f out: drvn over 1f out: kpt on one pce* **5/1**[2]

1000 **7** *1* **Thello**[8] 2773 4-8-6 **55** PJMcDonald 7 52
(Nigel Tinkler) *in tch: rdn along over 2f out: sn one pce* **20/1**

0-00 **8** *1* **White Flag**[32] 2053 5-8-2 **56** ow1 RachelRichardson(5) 12 50
(Tim Easterby) *a towards rr* **25/1**

4-00 **9** *2* **Baltic Prince (IRE)**[18] 2491 6-9-3 **66** JoeFanning 3 55
(Tony Carroll) *sn chsng clr ldr: rdn and hdwy over 2f out: drvn over 1f out: wknd appr fnl f* **9/1**

4410 **10** *1* **Make On Madam (IRE)**[18] 2491 4-9-3 **66** GrahamGibbons 6 53
(Les Eyre) *dwlt: a in rr* **7/1**

0-06 **11** *14* **Playboy Bay**[23] 2307 4-8-3 **57** (p) PhilDennis(5) 11 9
(Ron Barr) *a towards rr* **66/1**

0-46 **12** *¾* **Le Laitier (FR)**[12] 2662 5-8-13 **62** BenCurtis 1 12
(Scott Dixon) *chsd ldng pair: rdn along over 2f out: sn wknd* **8/1**

1m 30.98s (-2.82) **Going Correction** -0.325s/f (Firm) **12** Ran SP% **121.0**
Speed ratings (Par 103): **103,101,100,99,98 98,97,96,93,92 76,75**
CSF £49.92 CT £429.55 TOTE £12.20: £3.80, £1.50, £3.80; EX 52.70 Trifecta £605.80.
Owner Keep The Faith Partnership **Bred** Shadwell Farm LLC **Trained** Barton-le-Street, N Yorks

FOCUS
The race was run over 18yds further than advertised. A competitive handicap where the front runner went very hard and the race changed complexion late on. The winner has been rated to her AW form.

3014 SKIDBY MAIDEN STKS 7f 100y
5:00 (5:00) (Class 5) 3-Y-O+ **£3,780** (£1,131; £565; £283; £141) **Stalls** Low

Form RPR

00-2 **1** **Lincoln Rocks**[19] 2419 3-8-12 77 PhillipMakin 8 72
(David O'Meara) *mde all: rdn over 1f out: drvn and kpt on wl fnl f* **5/2**[2]

2 *1¾* **Al Hawraa** 3-8-9 0 JoeDoyle(3) 3 67+
(Kevin Ryan) *hld up: hdwy over 2f out: rdn to chse wnr whn jst ins fnl f: sn edgd rt and no imp* **10/1**

32 **3** *7* **Sehayli (IRE)**[11] 2686 3-9-3 0 GrahamGibbons 11 54+
(William Haggas) *sn trcking wnr: pushed along 3f out: rdn 2f out: sn drvn: wandered and one pce* **8/11**[1]

-060 **4** *½* **Bazula (IRE)**[22] 2333 3-9-3 36 (b[1]) AndrewMullen 1 53
(Tim Easterby) *chsd ldrs on inner: hdwy over 2f out: rdn wl over 1f out: sn drvn and one pce* **50/1**

00- **5** *nse* **Ring Of Art**[183] 8144 3-9-3 0 GeorgeChaloner 5 53+
(Richard Fahey) *towards rr: sme hdwy wl over 2f out: rdn and edgd lft wl over 1f out: plugged on u.p fnl f* **8/1**[3]

030- **6** *2* **Bigbadboy (IRE)**[183] 8144 3-9-3 52 CamHardie 2 48
(Clive Mulhall) *chsd ldrs: rdn along over 2f out: drvn wl over 1f out: sn wknd* **50/1**

5056 **7** *2* **Ksenia (IRE)**[29] 2118 3-8-5 45 KieranSchofield(7) 9 38
(Nigel Tinkler) *t.k.h: nvr bttr then midfield* **80/1**

05 **8** *4* **Indibeau**[23] 2303 4-9-8 0 DavidAllan 10 32
(Garry Moss) *chsd ldrs: rdn along 3f out: drvn over 2f out: sn wknd* **16/1**

000- **9** *16* **Sunnyhills Belford**[285] 5815 3-8-12 49 (p) BarryMcHugh 4
(Noel Wilson) *chsd ldrs: hdwy on wd outside over 3f out: rdn over 2f out: sn wknd* **80/1**

46- **10** *18* **Breton Blues**[339] 3929 6-9-13 0 PaulMulrennan 6
(Fred Watson) *s.i.s: a outpcd and bhd* **50/1**

400- **U** **Big Larry (IRE)**[256] 6759 3-9-3 49 IanBrennan 7
(Nigel Tinkler) *towards rr whn stmbld and uns rdr over 4f out* **50/1**

1m 31.39s (-2.41) **Going Correction** -0.325s/f (Firm)
WFA 3 from 4yo+ 10lb **11** Ran SP% **122.9**
Speed ratings (Par 103): **100,98,90,89,89 87,84,80,61,41**
CSF £28.04 TOTE £3.40: £1.30, £2.60, £1.10; EX 29.00 Trifecta £59.00.
Owner Peter Smith P C Coaches Limited **Bred** James Ortega Bloodstock **Trained** Upper Helmsley, N Yorks

FOCUS
The race was run over 18yds further than advertised. A maiden that seemed to revolve around two, but the favourite ran disappointingly and the race lacks depth.

3015 COTTINGHAM H'CAP (BEVERLEY MIDDLE DISTANCE SERIES) 1m 4f 16y
5:30 (5:37) (Class 6) (0-60,58) 3-Y-O **£2,587** (£770; £384; £192) **Stalls** Low

Form RPR

3146 **1** **Rainbow Lad (IRE)**[29] 2124 3-9-2 **53** BenCurtis 5 60
(Michael Appleby) *trckd ldrs: hdwy over 3f out: led over 2f out: bdly hmpd by loose horse on inner 1 1/2f out: sn rdn: carried lft and hmpd by loose horse ins fnl f: kpt on wl towards fin* **13/2**[2]

0433 **2** *1½* **Falcon's Fire (IRE)**[8] 2772 3-9-3 **54** PhillipMakin 4 58
(Keith Dalgleish) *hld up towards rr: hdwy 3f out: chsd ldrs over 1f out: rdn whn hmpd ins fnl f: kpt on towards fin* **11/4**[1]

-600 **3** *shd* **Chestnut Storm (IRE)**[43] 1740 3-9-3 **54** PaulMulrennan 7 57
(Ed Dunlop) *hld up in rr: hdwy over 2f out: rdn over 1f out: styd on ins fnl f* **7/1**[3]

-050 **4** *1½* **Citadel**[29] 2124 3-8-8 **45** (v) AndrewMullen 2 46
(John Wainwright) *t.k.h: trckd ldrs: hdwy over 2f out: rdn wl over 1f out: kpt on u.p fnl f* **40/1**

000- **5** *¾* **Lady Turpin (IRE)**[239] 7180 3-9-2 **53** GeorgeChaloner 6 53
(Richard Fahey) *hld up towards rr: hdwy on outer wl over 2f out: rdn to chse ldrs over 1f out: drvn: carried lft and kpt on same pce fnl f* **16/1**

500- **6** *nk* **Primobella**[211] 7788 3-9-7 **58** DaleSwift 10 60
(Ed McMahon) *chsd ldrs: hdwy over 2f out: rdn to chal jst over 1f out: ev ch whn hmpd ins fnl f: nt rcvr* **10/1**

0-00 **7** *1* **Kerry Icon**[8] 2772 3-8-11 **48** PJMcDonald 3 46
(Iain Jardine) *hld up in rr: hdwy 2f out: sn rdn and plugged on fnl f* **22/1**

500 **8** *6* **High On Light**[41] 1814 3-8-13 **50** DavidAllan 8 38
(Tim Easterby) *a towards rr* **8/1**

50-2 **9** *7* **Indulgent**[20] 2408 3-9-6 **57** BarryMcHugh 12 34
(Tony Coyle) *prom: rdn along over 2f out: sn drvn and wknd* **15/2**

6500 **10** *10* **Ready Steady (USA)**[8] 2772 3-8-13 **50** GrahamGibbons 9 11
(David Loughnane) *cl up: lft in ld after 1 1/2f: hdd over 5f out: rdn along 3f out: wknd over 2f out: sn bhd and eased* **66/1**

-004 **11** *1¼* **Jon H The Lawman (IRE)**[23] 2308 3-8-8 **45** (b[1]) JimmyQuinn 11 4+
(Ronald Thompson) *in tch on outer: rapid hdwy to ld over 5f out: rdn along and hdd over 2f out: sn wknd* **20/1**

45-0 **U** **Goodknight Percy (IRE)**[29] 2124 3-9-3 **57** (p) JoeDoyle(3) 1
(Kevin Ryan) *led: hung bdly lft bnd after 1 1/2f and uns rdr* **7/1**[3]

2m 37.69s (-2.11) **Going Correction** -0.325s/f (Firm) **12** Ran SP% **115.9**
Speed ratings (Par 97): **94,93,92,91,91 91,90,86,81,75 74,**
CSF £23.11 CT £130.33 TOTE £8.20: £2.70, £1.40, £2.70; EX 29.10 Trifecta £131.60.
Owner Infinity Racing **Bred** Rathbarry Stud **Trained** Oakham, Rutland

FOCUS
The race was run over 18yds further than advertised. A low-key and messy finale that was enlivened by the antics of a loose horse.
T/Jkpt: Not won. T/Plt: £382.20 to a £1 stake. Pool: £67,877.84. 129.63 winning tickets. T/Qpdt: £31.50 to a £1 stake. Pool: £5,419.60. 127.30 winning tickets. **Joe Rowntree**

2807 HAMILTON (R-H)
Wednesday, June 8

OFFICIAL GOING: Good to firm changing to good to firm (firm in places) after race 2 (6.45)
Wind: Light, half against Weather: Sunny, warm

3016 HAMILTON-PARK.CO.UK AMATEUR RIDERS' H'CAP 6f 6y
6:15 (6:16) (Class 6) (0-60,64) 4-Y-O+ **£2,807** (£870; £435; £217) **Stalls** Centre

Form RPR

6352 **1** **Ancient Cross**[5] 2856 12-11-0 **60** (bt) MissJoannaMason 2 70
(Michael Easterby) *hld up: hdwy on outside over 1f out: led ins fnl f: rdn out* **11/2**[2]

4651 **2** *nk* **Giant Spark**[8] 2778 4-11-4 **64** 6ex MrSWalker 6 73
(Paul Midgley) *trckd ldrs: led and rdn over 2f out: hdd ins fnl f: kpt on towards fin* **5/6**[1]

5540 **3** *2¾* **Bogsnog (IRE)**[21] 2360 6-10-6 **55** KaineWood(3) 1 56
(Kristin Stubbs) *prom: effrt and hung lft over 1f out: outpcd by first two ins fnl f* **16/1**

0-03 **4** *2¾* **Saltarello (IRE)**[53] 1495 4-10-10 **59** MissBeckySmith(3) 4 52
(Marjorie Fife) *prom: rdn and outpcd 2f out: edgd rt over 1f out: no imp fnl f* **12/1**

0001 **5** *nk* **Hab Reeh**[21] 2359 8-10-6 **52** (p) MissSBrotherton 5 44
(Ruth Carr) *led to over 2f out: rdn and wknd over 1f out* **17/2**[3]

-006 **6** *3¾* **Reflation**[22] 2329 4-10-2 **55** (p) MissCADods(7) 9 35
(Michael Dods) *in tch: rdn over 2f out: edgd rt and wknd wl over 1f out* **25/1**

0-00 **7** *nk* **Two Turtle Doves (IRE)**[7] 2794 10-10-7 **53** MissMMullineaux 3 33
(Michael Mullineaux) *cl up: rdn 1/2-way: outpcd whn hmpd over 1f out: sn btn* **66/1**

3-66 **8** *1½* **Yair Hill (IRE)**[30] 2096 8-10-3 **52** (p) MissHelenCuthbert(3) 8 27
(Thomas Cuthbert) *hld up on nr side of gp: pushed along and outpcd over 2f out: n.d after* **28/1**

0540 **9** *3½* **Frangarry (IRE)**[11] 2697 4-10-2 **55** (v[1]) MissJCooley(7) 7 20
(Alan Bailey) *dwlt: hld up: stdy hdwy over 3f out: rdn and wknd 2f out* **14/1**

055- **10** *3¼* **Jessie Allan (IRE)**[312] 4863 5-10-0 **46** oh1 MrsCBartley 10
(Jim Goldie) *bhd on nr side of gp: struggling over 3f out: btn over 2f out* **50/1**

1m 11.15s (-1.05) **Going Correction** -0.25s/f (Firm) **10** Ran SP% **111.5**
Speed ratings (Par 101): **97,96,92,89,88 83,83,81,76,72**
CSF £9.64 CT £66.54 TOTE £6.30: £2.20, £1.02, £4.30; EX 11.60 Trifecta £73.20.
Owner M W Easterby **Bred** Darley **Trained** Sheriff Hutton, N Yorks
■ Stewards' Enquiry : Kaine Wood caution: careless riding

FOCUS
Rail out 3yds on the loop. The main action developed down the centre in this moderate sprint handicap, confined to amateur riders. The first pair came clear and the form looks straightforward.

3017 TAGGARTS LANARKSHIRE H'CAP 5f 7y
6:45 (6:46) (Class 5) (0-70,70) 3-Y-O **£3,881** (£1,155; £577; £288) **Stalls** Centre

Form RPR

-002 **1** **East Street Revue**[8] 2777 3-8-8 **57** (b) DuranFentiman 3 79
(Tim Easterby) *s.i.s: hld up in tch: hdwy to ld over 1f out: pushed clr fnl f: readily* **5/1**[2]

023 **2** *7* **Lady Wootton**[8] 2776 3-8-11 **60** (b) DougieCostello 4 57
(Keith Dalgleish) *w ldrs: rdn and ev ch over 1f out: kpt on fnl f: nt ch w ready wnr* **11/2**[3]

3052 **3** *2¼* **Kingthistle**[11] 2668 3-9-2 **70** NathanEvans(5) 7 59
(Michael Easterby) *hld up in tch: drvn over 2f out: kpt on ins fnl f: nt pce to chal* **9/4**[1]

1440 **4** *shd* **Jess**[32] 2050 3-9-2 **65** ShaneGray 5 53
(Kevin Ryan) *led: rdn over 2f out: hdd over 1f out: kpt on same pce fnl f* **7/1**

3200 **5** *1¾* **Strictly Carter**[17] 2503 3-9-0 **63** ow1 (v[1]) RobertTart 6 45
(Alan Bailey) *cl up: drvn along over 2f out: no ex over 1f out* **11/1**

-026 **6** *1½* **Emerald Asset (IRE)**[17] 2503 3-8-9 **58** (p) JackGarritty 2 35
(Paul Midgley) *cl up: rdn along over 2f out: wknd over 1f out* **10/1**

3-00 **7** *3* **Alba Dawn (IRE)**[21] 2359 3-8-7 **56** (b) JasonHart 9 22
(Keith Dalgleish) *bhd on nr side of gp: drvn and outpcd over 2f out: n.d after* **20/1**

0-00 **8** *1¾* **Sneakin'Pete**[21] 2360 3-8-2 **51** oh6 JamesSullivan 8 11
(Linda Perratt) *dwlt: hld up: struggling over 2f out: sn btn* **100/1**

65 **9** *9* **Lilliard (IRE)**[26] 2200 3-9-2 **65** TadhgO'Shea 1
(John Patrick Shanahan, Ire) *hld up in tch: drvn and struggling over 2f out: eased whn btn fnl f: fatally injured* **6/1**

57.77s (-2.23) **Going Correction** -0.25s/f (Firm) **9** Ran SP% **112.8**
Speed ratings (Par 99): **107,95,92,92,89 86,82,79,64**
CSF £31.72 CT £77.76 TOTE £4.10: £1.20, £1.60, £1.70; EX 16.40 Trifecta £45.50.
Owner S A Heley **Bred** Habton Farms & A Heley **Trained** Great Habton, N Yorks

FOCUS
They again they kept to the middle in this modest 3yo sprint handicap. The second sets the level, meaning a big personal best from the winner.

3018 FREE MONTH TRIAL OF RACING UK H'CAP 1m 3f 14y
7:15 (7:16) (Class 6) (0-65,64) 4-Y-O+ **£2,911** (£866; £432; £216) **Stalls** High

Form RPR

000- **1** **The Blue Banana (IRE)**[260] 6619 7-8-7 **50** JamesSullivan 8 57
(Grant Tuer) *hld up: pushed along and hdwy over 3f out: drvn over 2f out: led wl ins fnl f: kpt on wl* **14/1**

-303 **2** *nk* **Lara Carbonara (IRE)**[14] 2575 4-9-6 **63** TadhgO'Shea 9 70
(John Patrick Shanahan, Ire) *trckd ldrs: rdn over 2f out: rallied and ev ch wl ins fnl f: jst hld* **7/2**[2]

-064 **3** 1 ¾ **King Of Paradise (IRE)**[13] 2616 7-9-7 **64** .... JasonHart 3 68
(Eric Alston) *led: rdn 3f out: hdd wl ins fnl f: kpt on same pce* **5/2**[1]

4664 **4** 1 **Incurs Four Faults**[6] 2810 5-8-9 **52** .... ConnorBeasley 1 54
(Keith Dalgleish) *wnt lft s: t.k.h: trckd ldr: effrt and rdn over 2f out: ev ch over 1f out: one pce ins fnl f* **4/1**[3]

-300 **5** 3 **Schmooze (IRE)**[6] 2813 7-8-13 **56** .... JackGarritty 6 53
(Linda Perratt) *hld up: drvn and outpcd 1/2-way: hdwy over 1f out: kpt on fnl f: no imp* **8/1**

06-4 **6** 9 **Multi Grain**[19] 2427 4-9-4 **61** .... TomEaves 2 44
(Micky Hammond) *carried lft s: hld up in tch: outpcd 1/2-way: no imp fr over 3f out* **14/1**

5556 **7** 7 **Cosmic Tigress**[25] 2233 5-9-0 **57** .... DougieCostello 4 29
(John Quinn) *blkd s: t.k.h in tch: rdn and wknd over 2f out* **5/1**

2m 21.43s (-4.17) **Going Correction** -0.325s/f (Firm) **7** Ran SP% **111.9**
Speed ratings (Par 101): **102,101,100,99,97 91,85**
CSF £59.60 CT £164.33 TOTE £18.20: £6.40, £2.10; EX 69.10 Trifecta £215.90.
Owner ARC Racing Yorkshire X **Bred** Tally-Ho Stud **Trained** Birkby, N Yorks
■ Stewards' Enquiry : James Sullivan two-day ban: used whip above permitted level (Jun 22-23)

FOCUS
Race distance increased by 12yds. Predictably there was no hanging around in this moderate handicap and it saw a cracking finish. The winner has been rated towards the best of last year.

3019 TAGGARTS LAND ROVER MAIDEN STKS 1m 1f 34y
7:45 (7:45) (Class 5) 3-Y-O+ **£3,881** (£1,155; £577; £288) **Stalls** Low

Form RPR

1 **Bachelorhood** 3-9-2 0 .... TomEaves 1 76
(Charlie Appleby) *in tch: hdwy over 3f out: rdn and ev ch over 1f out: led ins fnl f: kpt on wl* **11/10**[1]

053- **2** 1 ¼ **Carbon Dating (IRE)**[117] 4-10-0 86 .... TadhgO'Shea 6 75
(John Patrick Shanahan, Ire) *t.k.h: chsd ldrs on outside: led over 3f out: rdn 2f out: hdd ins fnl f: one pce* **9/4**[2]

04 **3** 1 ¾ **Jessica Jo (IRE)**[26] 2197 3-8-11 0 .... FrannyNorton 5 64
(Mark Johnston) *t.k.h early: chsd ldr: effrt and pushed along over 3f out: ev ch over 1f out to ins fnl f: no ex towards fin* **13/2**

4 18 **Eez Eh (IRE)** 3-9-2 0 .... DougieCostello 2 30
(Keith Dalgleish) *s.i.s: hld up: outpcd and green over 3f out: btn fnl 2f* **11/2**[3]

6 **5** 1 ¼ **Ogwen Valley Girl**[44] 1708 5-9-2 0 ....(b[1]) MrLewisStones(7) 3 24
(Michael Mullineaux) *led: clr after 2f: rdn and hdd over 3f out: sn wknd* **200/1**

1m 56.94s (-2.76) **Going Correction** -0.325s/f (Firm)
WFA 3 from 4yo+ 12lb **5** Ran SP% **107.6**
Speed ratings (Par 103): **99,97,96,80,79**
CSF £3.60 TOTE £2.00: £1.10, £1.50; EX 5.30 Trifecta £12.80.
Owner Godolphin **Bred** Darley **Trained** Newmarket, Suffolk

FOCUS
Race distance increased by 12yds. An ordinary maiden, run at a solid pace.

3020 FOLLOW @HAMILTONPARKRC ON TWITTER H'CAP 1m 67y
8:15 (8:17) (Class 6) (0-60,60) 3-Y-O+ **£2,911** (£866; £432; £216) **Stalls** Low

Form RPR

-113 **1** **Bajan Rebel**[32] 2045 5-9-6 **57** .... NathanEvans(5) 4 65
(Michael Easterby) *chsd ldr: effrt and rdn 2f out: led ins fnl f: hung lft: kpt on wl* **7/2**[1]

6034 **2** nk **Weld Al Khawaneej (IRE)**[14] 2576 3-9-3 **60** .... TomEaves 7 64
(Kevin Ryan) *hld up in tch: stdy hdwy over 2f out: effrt and swtchd lft 1f out: chsd wnr wl ins fnl f: hung lft: jst hld* **13/2**[2]

3 1 ½ **Jocks Wa Hae (IRE)**[37] 1942 3-8-4 **47** oh1 ow1 .... TadhgO'Shea 2 48+
(John Patrick Shanahan, Ire) *slowly away: bhd: hdwy on outside 3f out: rdn 2f out: kpt on fnl f: hld whn checked nr fin: improve* **7/1**[3]

0-03 **4** nk **Riponian**[16] 2525 6-9-2 **48** .... JoeyHaynes 1 51
(Susan Corbett) *led: qcknd clr over 3f out: hdd ins fnl f: kpt on same pce* **7/1**[3]

3006 **5** 1 ½ **Togetherwecan (IRE)**[30] 2087 4-9-4 **50** ....(b[1]) FrannyNorton 11 49
(Mark Johnston) *s.i.s: hld up: pushed along 3f out: hdwy over 1f out: kpt on fnl f: nrst fin* **16/1**

0620 **6** nk **Stanlow**[16] 2525 6-9-3 **49** ....(v) RobertTart 6 48
(Michael Mullineaux) *hld up: effrt and pushed along over 3f out: hdwy over 1f out: kpt on fnl f: no imp* **14/1**

6000 **7** shd **Tiger's Home**[12] 2661 6-9-8 **59** .... ShirleyTeasdale(5) 3 57
(Iain Jardine) *prom: drvn along over 2f out: outpcd fnl f* **20/1**

0-55 **8** ¾ **Ryan The Giant**[120] 509 3-8-6 **49** .... ConnorBeasley 8 43
(Keith Dalgleish) *midfield on outside: drvn and outpcd 3f out: edgd rt over 1f out: kpt on: no imp* **9/1**

-035 **9** 1 **Bushtiger (IRE)**[6] 2810 4-9-0 **46** oh1 .... JamesSullivan 14 40
(Ruth Carr) *t.k.h in midfield on outside: drvn and outpcd over 2f out: n.d after* **12/1**

0-64 **10** ½ **Chookie Valentine**[84] 958 3-8-9 **52** .... JasonHart 9 42
(Keith Dalgleish) *trckd ldrs: rdn over 2f out: wknd ins fnl f* **9/1**

-400 **11** 6 **Anneani (IRE)**[19] 2436 4-9-3 **49** .... ShaneGray 10 28
(Paul Green) *s.i.s: bhd: struggling over 3f out: nvr on terms* **12/1**

0240 **12** 1 **Dark Illustrator**[50] 1551 3-8-9 **52** .... NeilFarley 12 25
(Alan Swinbank) *hld up in midfield: drvn and outpcd over 3f out: btn fnl 2f* **25/1**

1m 46.37s (-2.03) **Going Correction** -0.325s/f (Firm)
WFA 3 from 4yo+ 11lb **12** Ran SP% **117.1**
Speed ratings (Par 101): **97,96,95,94,93 93,93,92,91,90 84,83**
CSF £24.63 CT £152.26 TOTE £3.70: £1.70, £1.70, £2.30; EX 24.20 Trifecta £238.00.
Owner Julian Rooney **Bred** Aldridge Racing Partnership **Trained** Sheriff Hutton, N Yorks

FOCUS
Race distance increased by 12yds. This looked an ordinary handicap, but it proved a real test at the distance.

3021 TAGGARTS JAGUAR H'CAP 6f 6y
8:45 (8:45) (Class 4) (0-80,83) 4-Y-O+ **£6,469** (£1,925; £962; £481) **Stalls** Centre

Form RPR

211 **1** **Final Venture**[16] 2531 4-9-7 **80** .... NeilFarley 4 92
(Alan Swinbank) *mde all: rdn over 1f out: kpt on wl fnl f* **7/2**[1]

6060 **2** 1 ½ **Cosmic Chatter**[22] 2346 6-9-0 **73** ....(p) JamesSullivan 10 80
(Ruth Carr) *hld up: pushed along and outpcd over 2f out: hdwy over 1f out: wnt 2nd wl ins fnl f: nt pce of wnr* **11/1**

10-3 **3** nk **Spirit Of Zeb (IRE)**[11] 2680 4-8-9 **75** .... AdamMcNamara(7) 8 81
(Richard Fahey) *trckd wnr: drvn and outpcd over 1f out: kpt on ins fnl f* **7/2**[1]

6031 **4** ¾ **Alexandrakollontai (IRE)**[9] 2737 6-9-10 **83** 6ex ......(b) ConnorBeasley 5 87
(Alistair Whillans) *dwlt: bhd: rdn over 2f out: kpt on fnl f: nrst fin* **15/2**

-451 **5** hd **Kenny The Captain (IRE)**[19] 2416 5-8-13 **72** ....(b) DuranFentiman 7 75
(Tim Easterby) *t.k.h: cl up: effrt and chsd wnr over 1f out to wl ins fnl f: no ex* **11/2**[2]

6036 **6** 1 ½ **Salvatore Fury (IRE)**[6] 2812 6-8-3 **67** ....(p) NathanEvans(5) 3 65
(Keith Dalgleish) *prom: effrt and shkn up over 1f out: outpcd fnl f* **11/1**

0504 **7** 1 **Sunraider (IRE)**[16] 2531 9-8-13 **72** .... JackGarritty 2 67
(Paul Midgley) *in tch on outside: rdn and outpcd over 2f out: n.d after* **7/1**[3]

0-05 **8** 6 **Fyrecracker (IRE)**[16] 2531 5-9-1 **74** .... TomEaves 9 50
(Grant Tuer) *in tch tl rdn and wknd fr 2f out* **8/1**

1m 9.95s (-2.25) **Going Correction** -0.25s/f (Firm) **8** Ran SP% **111.9**
Speed ratings (Par 105): **105,103,102,101,101 99,98,90**
CSF £41.09 CT £142.07 TOTE £2.70: £1.02, £5.60, £1.90; EX 43.20 Trifecta £258.30.
Owner Brian Valentine **Bred** Newsells Park Stud **Trained** Melsonby, N Yorks

FOCUS
This modest sprint was run at a routine pace and the winner, who continues on the upgrade, dictated.

3022 AUCHINRAITH H'CAP 5f 7y
9:15 (9:16) (Class 6) (0-55,55) 4-Y-O+ **£2,911** (£866; £432; £216) **Stalls** Centre

Form RPR

4450 **1** **Very First Blade**[19] 2447 7-8-13 **47** ow1 ....(p) RobertTart 5 56
(Michael Mullineaux) *cl up: rdn 2f out: led wl ins fnl f: r.o* **8/1**

0001 **2** ¾ **Fuel Injection**[11] 2676 5-9-3 **51** .... JackGarritty 4 57
(Paul Midgley) *trckd ldrs: rdn to ld appr fnl f: hdd wl ins fnl f: no ex* **11/4**[1]

0064 **3** 1 ½ **Pabusar**[6] 2812 8-9-6 **54** ....(v) DavidNolan 7 55+
(Micky Hammond) *dwlt: bhd: drvn along over 2f out: kpt on fnl f: nt rch first two* **11/4**[1]

1405 **4** 1 **Kuanyao (IRE)**[11] 2676 10-9-2 **55** ....(be) AnnStokell(5) 8 52
(Ann Stokell) *dwlt: bhd on nr side of gp: pushed along and effrt over 2f out: edgd rt over 1f out: kpt on: no imp* **9/1**

00-0 **5** 2 ¼ **Henry Morgan**[51] 1525 9-9-6 **54** .... TomEaves 2 43
(David Brown) *led tl rdn and hdd appr fnl f: sn outpcd* **9/2**[2]

040- **6** 3 **Ya Boy Sir (IRE)**[239] 7190 9-9-0 **48** ....(p) RoystonFfrench 1 26
(Iain Jardine) *stdd bhd ldng gp: rdn along wl over 1f out: sn wknd* **13/2**[3]

0000 **7** 1 ¼ **It's Time For Bed**[6] 2808 4-8-12 **46** oh1 .... JamesSullivan 3 20
(Linda Perratt) *prom tl rdn and wknd over 1f out* **28/1**

000- **8** 8 **Bannock Town**[254] 6815 5-8-7 **46** oh1 ....(p) NathanEvans(5) 6
(Linda Perratt) *prom: drvn and outpcd 1/2-way: sn struggling* **66/1**

59.24s (-0.76) **Going Correction** -0.25s/f (Firm) **8** Ran SP% **110.9**
Speed ratings (Par 101): **96,94,92,90,87 82,80,67**
CSF £28.47 CT £72.89 TOTE £10.80: £2.70, £1.10, £1.50; EX 48.60 Trifecta £166.80.
Owner Ogwen Valley Racing **Bred** L R Owen **Trained** Alpraham, Cheshire

FOCUS
It paid to race prominently in this weak sprint handicap. The winner has been rated back to his turf best.
T/Plt: £18.90 to a £1 stake. Pool: £61,269.72. 2,355.63 winning tickets T/Qpdt: £11.40 to a £1 stake. Pool: £4,890.50. 316.80 winning tickets. **Richard Young**

2689 HAYDOCK (L-H)
Wednesday, June 8

OFFICIAL GOING: Good to firm (firm in places) (7.4)
Wind: light, half against Weather: fine

3023 APOLLOBET HOME OF CASHBACK OFFERS MAIDEN STKS 1m
2:10 (2:10) (Class 5) 3-Y-O+ **£2,911** (£866; £432; £216) **Stalls** Low

Form RPR

3 **1** **Al Neksh**[16] 2541 3-9-1 0 .... FrankieDettori 2 85
(William Haggas) *dwlt sltly: mde most: rdn and strly pressed 2f out: styd on fnl f: pushed out and in command fnl 110yds* **5/6**[1]

2 1 **Most Celebrated (IRE)** 3-9-1 0 .... JamesDoyle 1 82
(Saeed bin Suroor) *dwlt: hld up in tch: rdn over 2f out: styd on wl fnl f: wnt 2nd 75yds out* **5/1**[3]

3 1 ¼ **Song Of Namibia (IRE)** 5-9-12 0 .... RyanMoore 3 82
(Sir Michael Stoute) *trckd ldng pair: pushed along and hdwy to chal strly 2f out: rdn over 1f out: no ex fnl 110yds* **9/2**[2]

4 6 **Tarseekh** 3-9-1 0 .... PaulHanagan 5 64
(Roger Varian) *hld up in tch: rdn along and rn green over 3f out: nvr threatened* **6/1**

0-0 **5** ¾ **Simply Me**[55] 1438 3-8-10 0 .... RichardKingscote 7 57
(Tom Dascombe) *prom: rdn over 2f out: wknd over 1f out* **12/1**

6 ¾ **Justice Pleasing** 3-9-1 0 .... JackGarritty 6 61
(David Loughnane) *dwlt: hld up: rdn over 2f out: nvr threatened* **100/1**

1m 40.04s (-3.66) **Going Correction** -0.40s/f (Firm)
WFA 3 from 5yo 11lb **6** Ran SP% **112.4**
Speed ratings (Par 103): **102,101,99,93,93 92**
CSF £5.51 TOTE £1.60: £1.10, £2.60; EX 5.40 Trifecta £12.80.
Owner Al Shaqab Racing **Bred** The Pocock Family **Trained** Newmarket, Suffolk

FOCUS
All races run over the Inner Home Straight. Allowing for rail movement on bends the actual race distance was 7f 218yds. A total of 8mm of water had been put on the track every day since Saturday, but the ground remained fast, with Frankie Dettori saying: "It is good to firm throughout. I suspect it will get a bit quicker throughout the day." \n\x\x Quite an interesting maiden, with some leading connections represented, and three useful types came clear.

3024 LONGINES IRISH CHAMPIONS WEEKEND EBF NOVICE FILLIES' STKS (PLUS 10 RACE) 6f
2:40 (2:40) (Class 5) 2-Y-O **£3,234** (£962; £481; £240) **Stalls** Centre

Form RPR

1 **Fair Eva** 2-9-0 0 .... RyanMoore 6 96+
(Roger Charlton) *pushed along and rn green first 1f: sn midfield: smooth hdwy fr 3f out to ld gng wl 2f out: pushed clr fr over 1f out: impressive* **1/1**[1]

2 **2** 4 **Nations Alexander (IRE)**[13] 2612 2-9-0 0 .... SeanLevey 7 78
(Richard Hannon) *trckd ldr: chal 2f out: rdn over 1f out: kpt on but sn no ch w wnr* **7/2**[2]

3 2 **Miss Infinity (IRE)** 2-9-0 0 .... FrannyNorton 1 72
(Mark Johnston) *led: hdd 2f out: sn rdn: kpt on same pce* **16/1**

0 **4** 4 ½ **Jasmincita (IRE)**[18] 2467 2-9-0 0 .... SteveDrowne 5 59
(George Baker) *outpcd in rr tl kpt on fr over 1f out: wnt 4th towards fin* **33/1**

3 **5** ½ **Kodicat (IRE)**[13] 2617 2-9-0 0 .... TomEaves 3 57
(Kevin Ryan) *in tch: rdn over 2f out: one pce* **5/1**[3]

3 **6** *nk* **Mia Cara**[13] 2612 2-9-0 0 DarryllHolland 8 56
(David Evans) *dwlt: sn in tch: rdn over 2f out: one pce* **12/1**

B **7** *6* **Gabridan (IRE)**[19] 2424 2-9-0 0 TonyHamilton 4 38
(Richard Fahey) *hld up: sn pushed along: a towards rr* **25/1**

8 *3 3/4* **Riviere Argentee (FR)** 2-9-0 0 DougieCostello 9 27
(K R Burke) *in tch: rdn over 2f out: wknd* **50/1**

9 *4 1/2* **Hazy Manor (IRE)** 2-9-0 0 RichardKingscote 2 13
(Tom Dascombe) *hld up: rdn over 3f out: sn wknd and sn bhd* **20/1**

1m 13.11s (-0.69) **Going Correction** -0.10s/f (Good) **9** Ran SP% **116.0**
Speed ratings (Par 90): **100,94,92,86,85 84,76,71,65**
CSF £4.32 TOTE £1.90: £1.10, £1.70, £3.70; EX 6.20 Trifecta £33.20.
Owner K Abdullah **Bred** Juddmonte Farms Ltd **Trained** Beckhampton, Wilts

FOCUS
Race distance as advertised. Likely a useful novice with the winner impressing on debut.

3025 APOLLOBET ONLINE GAMES AND CASINO H'CAP 1m 6f
3:10 (3:10) (Class 4) (0-85,77) 3-Y-O **£5,175** (£1,540; £769; £384) **Stalls** Low

Form RPR
-102 **1** **Snan (IRE)**[12] 2638 3-9-7 **77** (p) FrankieDettori 1 82
(Richard Hannon) *in tch: rdn over 2f out: led narrowly wl over 1f out: edgd lft appr fnl f: hld on wl fnl 110yds* **9/4**[1]

-133 **2** *1/2* **October Storm**[20] 2411 3-9-6 **76** SilvestreDeSousa 4 80
(Mick Channon) *hld up: rdn over 3f out: hdwy 2f out: swtchd rt over 1f out: styd on fnl f: wnt 2nd towards fin* **7/2**[2]

4-32 **3** *nk* **Kajaki (IRE)**[13] 2615 3-9-0 **70** (p) TomEaves 3 74
(Kevin Ryan) *led at stdy pce: qcknd pce over 3f out: rdn whn jnd over 2f out: hdd wl over 1f out: remained cl up: one pce and lost 2nd towards fin* **8/1**

-332 **4** *nk* **Rasasee (IRE)**[20] 2411 3-9-7 **77** AndreaAtzeni 2 80
(Marco Botti) *racd keenly: hld up in tch: rdn 3f out: hdwy 2f out: ev ch appr fnl f: no ex fnl 50yds* **9/2**

0-44 **5** *4* **Roderic's Secret (IRE)**[20] 2411 3-8-13 **69** PaulHanagan 6 67
(David Menuisier) *racd keenly: trckd ldr: rdn to chal strly over 2f out: lost pl whn sltly hmpd appr fnl f: wknd* **9/1**

4510 **6** *2 1/2* **Tartan Bute**[4] 2909 3-9-3 **73** FrannyNorton 5 67
(Mark Johnston) *midfield: pushed along over 5f out: rdn over 3f out: wknd over 1f out* **4/1**[3]

3m 1.89s (-0.11) **Going Correction** -0.40s/f (Firm) **6** Ran SP% **112.3**
Speed ratings (Par 101): **84,83,83,83,81 79**
CSF £10.33 TOTE £3.10: £1.20, £2.30; EX 11.60 Trifecta £34.10.
Owner Al Shaqab Racing **Bred** Slow Sand Syndicate **Trained** East Everleigh, Wilts

FOCUS
Allowing for rail movement on bends the actual race distance was 1m5f 218yds. A muddling race with a tight finish and not form to put much trust in.

3026 APOLLOBET DAILY RACING REFUNDS H'CAP 1m
3:40 (3:40) (Class 3) (0-90,87) 3-Y-O **£8,086** (£2,406; £1,202; £601) **Stalls** Low

Form RPR
3-10 **1** **Galvanize (USA)**[38] 1891 3-9-0 **80** RyanMoore 7 89
(Sir Michael Stoute) *hld up: pushed along and hdwy on outer over 2f out: led over 1f out: rdn and kpt on fnl f* **6/1**

12-0 **2** *3* **Albernathy**[28] 2161 3-9-7 **87** WilliamBuick 4 89+
(Charlie Appleby) *racd keenly: trckd ldr towards outer: rdn 2f out: edgd lft over 1f out: kpt on same pce fnl f* **13/8**[1]

021- **3** *hd* **Sunnua (IRE)**[235] 7284 3-8-10 **76** PatrickMathers 2 78
(Richard Fahey) *in tch: rdn over 2f out: styd on fnl f* **25/1**

-531 **4** *1 1/2* **Carnageo (FR)**[7] 2801 3-8-8 **74** 6ex TonyHamilton 6 73
(Richard Fahey) *trckd ldr: rdn over 2f out: sltly hmpd over 1f out: kpt on same pce ins fnl f* **7/2**[2]

33-0 **5** *nk* **Eqleem**[28] 2161 3-9-6 **86** PaulHanagan 5 84
(Mark Johnston) *led: rdn over 2f out: hdd over 1f out: wknd ins fnl f* **13/2**

-423 **6** *3 1/4* **Aleko**[33] 1992 3-8-12 **78** JamesDoyle 1 76+
(Mark Johnston) *in tch: pushed along over 2f out: nvr much room on inner: hmpd ins fnl f: eased* **4/1**[3]

1m 39.87s (-3.83) **Going Correction** -0.40s/f (Firm) **6** Ran SP% **111.8**
Speed ratings (Par 103): **103,100,99,98,98 94**
CSF £16.13 TOTE £8.00: £4.10, £1.10; EX 19.40 Trifecta £145.20.
Owner Flaxman Stables Ireland Ltd **Bred** Flaxman Holdings Limited **Trained** Newmarket, Suffolk

FOCUS
Allowing for rail movement on bends the actual race distance was 7f 218yds. A fair handicap won in good style by an improver, although there were excuses for the fancied beaten runners.

3027 APOLLOBET BET THROUGH YOUR MOBILE H'CAP 1m 3f 200y
4:10 (4:10) (Class 3) (0-95,94) 4-Y-O+ **£8,086** (£2,406; £1,202; £601) **Stalls** Centre

Form RPR
40-1 **1** **King Bolete (IRE)**[32] 2024 4-9-7 **94** AndreaAtzeni 3 107+
(Roger Varian) *mde all: pushed along over 2f out: pressed over 1f out: kpt on pushed out: a doing enough* **4/7**[1]

3115 **2** *1/2* **Tawdeea**[9] 2744 4-9-4 **91** SamJames 4 103
(David O'Meara) *hld up in tch in 4th: clsr 3f out: rdn to chal over 1f out: kpt on but a hld* **11/4**[2]

12-4 **3** *6* **Perestroika**[32] 2024 4-9-1 **88** FergusSweeney 2 90
(Henry Candy) *trckd ldr in 2nd: rdn over 2f out: wknd over 1f out* **6/1**[3]

00-0 **4** *2 3/4* **Novancia (IRE)**[19] 2433 4-8-7 **80** (b[1]) FrannyNorton 1 78
(Mark Johnston) *in tch in 3rd: pushed along over 3f out: rdn 2f out: wknd fnl f* **25/1**

2m 29.02s (-4.78) **Going Correction** -0.40s/f (Firm) **4** Ran SP% **108.5**
Speed ratings (Par 107): **99,98,94,92**
CSF £2.42 TOTE £1.40; EX 2.50 Trifecta £3.10.
Owner Sheikh Mohammed Obaid Al Maktoum **Bred** Ship Commodities International **Trained** Newmarket, Suffolk

FOCUS
Allowing for rail movement on bends the actual race distance was 1m3f 198yds. Run at a steady gallop, the winner enjoyed an easy lead and they finished in market order, with the front pair clear.

3028 APOLLOBET WEEKLY GOLF RETURNS MAIDEN STKS 1m 3f 200y
4:40 (4:41) (Class 5) 3-Y-O+ **£2,911** (£866; £432; £216) **Stalls** Centre

Form RPR
32 **1** **Forth Bridge**[38] 1897 3-8-13 0 RyanMoore 2 86
(Michael Bell) *led: rdn over 2f out: hdd narrowly over 1f out: rallied to ld again ins fnl f: styd on* **7/4**[2]

02-2 **2** *1/2* **Plenary (USA)**[20] 2414 3-8-13 86 SilvestreDeSousa 3 85
(Jeremy Noseda) *racd keenly in tch: hdwy 3f out: rdn to ld narrowly over 1f out: hdd ins fnl f: sn no ex* **10/11**[1]

0 **3** *4* **Queen Of The Stars**[26] 2215 3-8-8 0 PaulHanagan 1 74
(William Haggas) *s.i.s: hld up: pushed along and hdwy over 2f out: sn 3rd: styd on* **12/1**

4 *20* **Daily News** 3-8-13 0 AndreaAtzeni 6 47
(Roger Varian) *dwlt: sn trckd ldr: rdn over 2f out: sn wknd* **6/1**[3]

44 **5** *1 3/4* **Gamesters Boy**[14] 2589 3-8-13 0 DarryllHolland 4 44
(Mark Brisbourne) *trckd ldr: rdn over 2f out: wknd* **100/1**

00 **6** *36* **Secret Shot**[98] 778 4-10-0 0 FergusSweeney 7
(David Dennis) *hld up in tch: rdn over 3f out: sn wknd and t.o* **150/1**

2m 30.67s (-3.13) **Going Correction** -0.40s/f (Firm)
WFA 3 from 4yo+ 15lb **6** Ran SP% **112.4**
Speed ratings (Par 103): **94,93,91,77,76 52**
CSF £3.67 TOTE £2.90: £1.50, £1.10; EX 3.70 Trifecta £18.90.
Owner The Queen **Bred** The Queen **Trained** Newmarket, Suffolk

FOCUS
Allowing for rail movement on bends the actual race distance was 1m3f 198yds. Quite a good maiden, two useful types drawing a few lengths clear of a promising filly, with the rest nowhere.

3029 APOLLOBET BET ON LOTTERIES H'CAP 7f
5:10 (5:11) (Class 4) (0-85,85) 3-Y-O **£5,175** (£1,540; £769; £384) **Stalls** Low

Form RPR
6-13 **1** **George William**[11] 2695 3-9-2 **80** SeanLevey 10 87
(Richard Hannon) *midfield on outer: rdn over 2f out: hdwy over 1f out: chal ins fnl f: edgd lft: kpt on: led towards fin* **9/2**[2]

-042 **2** *1/2* **Lagenda**[18] 2477 3-9-4 **85** (p) KevinStott[(3)] 5 91
(Kevin Ryan) *trckd ldng pair: rdn over 2f out: led narrowly over 1f out: edgd lft 75yds out: kpt on: hdd towards fin* **7/1**

1 **3** *2 1/4* **Tarboosh**[21] 2375 3-9-1 **79** PaulHanagan 8 79+
(William Haggas) *racd keenly in midfield: smooth hdwy over 2f out: rdn to chal over 1f out: no ex fnl 110yds* **2/1**[1]

1-00 **4** *1 3/4* **Dutch Gallery**[12] 2650 3-8-11 **75** AndreaAtzeni 1 70
(Tom Dascombe) *led narrowly: hdd over 4f out: remained cl up: rdn over 2f out: no ex ins fnl f* **9/1**

41 **5** *nse* **Normandie Lady**[49] 1562 3-8-13 **77** TonyHamilton 2 72
(Richard Fahey) *dwlt: hld up: rdn over 2f out: styd on ins fnl f* **6/1**[3]

-440 **6** *2 1/2* **Peak Hill**[32] 2044 3-8-9 **73** SamJames 4 61
(David Evans) *in tch: rdn over 2f out: grad wknd over 1f out* **20/1**

033- **7** *shd* **Fang**[249] 6929 3-8-12 **76** (bt[1]) RyanMoore 7 64
(Brian Meehan) *racd keenly: w ldr on outside: led over 4f out: c up centre in st: rdn over 2f out: hdd over 1f out: wknd fnl f* **8/1**

1- **8** *8* **Next Life**[252] 6850 3-9-6 **84** JamesDoyle 6 50
(Saeed bin Suroor) *restless in stall: dwlt: hld up in rr: rdn over 2f out: wknd over 1f out: eased ins fnl f* **7/1**

1m 26.68s (-4.02) **Going Correction** -0.40s/f (Firm) **8** Ran SP% **116.7**
Speed ratings (Par 101): **106,105,102,100,100 97,97,88**
CSF £36.50 CT £82.66 TOTE £4.50: £1.50, £2.20, £1.20; EX 33.70 Trifecta £130.50.
Owner Lady Coventry & Partners **Bred** Rachel Countess Of Coventry **Trained** East Everleigh, Wilts

FOCUS
Allowing for rail movement on bends the actual race distance was 6f 218yds. A decent 3yo handicap and the form looks rock-solid with the winner recording a personal best.
T/Plt: £9.20 to a £1 stake. Pool: £55,526.53. 4,402.41 winning tickets. T/Qpdt: £7.60 to a £1 stake. Pool: £2,608.88. 253.30 winning tickets. **Andrew Sheret**

2814 KEMPTON (A.W) (R-H)
Wednesday, June 8

OFFICIAL GOING: Polytrack: standard
Wind: nil Weather: scattered showers early, cloudy after

3030 RACINGUK.COM APPRENTICE H'CAP (JOCKEY CLUB GRASSROOTS FLAT MIDDLE DISTANCE SERIES QUALIFIER) 1m (P)
6:00 (6:00) (Class 5) (0-75,75) 4-Y-O+ **£2,911** (£866; £432; £216) **Stalls** Low

Form RPR
3-32 **1** **Hala Madrid**[12] 2636 4-9-11 **74** EdwardGreatrex 8 82
(Andrew Balding) *sn led: mde all after: sltly hmpd runner-up after 2f: wound up over 2f out: rdn 2f out: kpt on wl fnl f: pushed out* **8/1**[3]

0-40 **2** *1 1/2* **Warofindependence (USA)**[26] 2213 4-9-12 **75** (v[1]) HectorCrouch 3 80
(Alan Bailey) *chsd ldrs: hmpd by wnr on rail after 2f and in turn hmpd rival: rdn 2f out: tk 2nd over 1f out: kpt on ins fnl f: no imp on ldr* **8/1**[3]

0600 **3** *1/2* **Swot**[21] 2379 4-8-11 **63** (p) KevinLundie[(3)] 1 67
(Roger Teal) *settled in mid-div: rdn on inner 2f out: grad drifted off rail ins fnl f: styd on fnl f to press runner-up nr fin* **20/1**

5010 **4** *1* **Runaiocht (IRE)**[8] 2769 6-8-11 **60** (b) CallumShepherd 12 62
(Paul Burgoyne) *t.k.h in rr: c to inner rail and rdn 2f out: styd on past wkng horses over 1f out* **10/1**

10-6 **5** *1/2* **With Approval (IRE)**[28] 2151 4-9-5 **68** KieranShoemark 10 68
(Laura Mongan) *chsd ldr: rdn 2f out: kpt on one pce fnl f* **25/1**

3-41 **6** *1/2* **Classical Rose**[22] 2324 4-9-6 **74** GeorgeWood[(5)] 6 73
(Charlie Fellowes) *settled bhd ldrs: rdn 2f out and nt qckn: one pce fr over 1f out* **2/1**[1]

-606 **7** *3/4* **Captain Felix**[11] 2672 4-9-5 **73** [1] CameronNoble[(5)] 7 71
(George Scott) *settled in mid-div: tk clsr order 4f out: rdn over 2f out sn hld* **9/1**

3000 **8** *nk* **Rightway (IRE)**[14] 2577 5-9-4 **70** MeganNicholls[(3)] 5 67
(Tony Carroll) *in rr: rdn 2f out: wknd fnl f* **12/1**

3150 **9** *2 3/4* **Gavarnie Encore**[50] 1544 4-8-8 **57** PaddyPilley 9 48
(Michael Blanshard) *broke wl and sn restrained: in rr-div on outer at 1/2-way: rdn along over 3f out: sn hld in ent st* **9/1**

2035 **10** *3 1/2* **West Leake (IRE)**[40] 1834 10-8-7 **56** GaryMahon 11 38
(Paul Burgoyne) *racd out wd in mid-div: pushed along and c wd into st: rdn over 2f out: wknd fnl f* **20/1**

420- **11** *7* **Mazaaher**[261] 6600 6-9-2 **72** TommyO'Connor[(7)] 2 38
(Owen Burrows) *mid-div: hmpd clipped heels and nrly fell after 2f: in rr after and t.k.h: btn and eased in st* **7/1**[2]

1m 39.77s (-0.03) **Going Correction** -0.05s/f (Stan) **11** Ran SP% **118.2**
Speed ratings (Par 103): **98,96,96,95,94 94,93,92,90,86 79**
CSF £68.73 CT £1272.07 TOTE £7.40: £3.10, £3.30, £8.40; EX 81.80 Trifecta £1751.60.
Owner N M Watts **Bred** Bishop Wilton Stud **Trained** Kingsclere, Hants
■ Stewards' Enquiry : Edward Greatrex six-day ban: careless riding (Jun 22-27)

FOCUS
This was run at a steady tempo and the winner dictated throughout.

3031 GOFFS LONDON SALE/KEMPTON BREEZE-UP 12-13 JUNE 2016 H'CAP 1m 3f (P)
6:30 (6:31) (Class 6) (0-55,55) 4-Y-O+ **£2,264** (£673; £336; £168) **Stalls** Low

Form RPR
000 **1** **Munsarim (IRE)**[22] 2326 9-9-7 **55**......(v) KierenFox 1 62
(Lee Carter) *settled in rr: gng wl ent st: twice hmpd over 2f out: shkn up and kpt on wl over 1f out: chal between horses fnl f: led fnl 110yds: pushed out* **8/1**[3]

0655 **2** 1 ¼ **First Summer**[32] 2046 4-9-5 **53**...... MartinHarley 2 58
(Shaun Harris) *chsd ldrs: swtchd lft off rail and hmpd wnr over 2f out: rdn 2f out: led jst over 1f out: drvn ent fnl f: hdd 110yds out: kpt on* **6/1**[2]

0-04 **3** 2 ½ **Cape Spirit (IRE)**[19] 2436 4-9-2 **55**......(v) EdwardGreatrex[(5)] 6 56
(Andrew Balding) *in rr: stl wl off the pce whn rdn ent st: hdwy over 1f out: kpt on wl to take 3rd fnl strides: nrst fin* **5/1**[1]

5233 **4** nk **Top Pocket**[49] 1578 4-9-0 **51**...... DanielMuscutt[(3)] 12 52
(Michael Madgwick) *in rr on outer: rdn over 2f out: kpt on wl to press for 3rd nr fin* **6/1**[2]

514/ **5** hd **Barnacle**[1065] 4147 7-8-12 **46** oh1......(v) StevieDonohoe 9 46
(Emma Owen) *chsd ldrs on inner: rdn over 2f out: led 2f out: hdd jst over 1f out: wknd ins fnl f and lost two pls nr fin* **40/1**

-054 **6** 1 ½ **Castle Talbot (IRE)**[15] 2566 4-9-0 **55**...... StephenCummins[(7)] 13 53
(Richard Hughes) *settled in mid-div: rdn over 2f out on outer: drifted into centre ins fnl f: kpt on* **9/1**

2530 **7** ¾ **Awesome Rock (IRE)**[65] 1239 7-8-5 **46**...... RhiainIngram[(7)] 3 43
(Roger Ingram) *in rr: pushed along over 2f out on rail: kpt on under hands and heels fnl f* **20/1**

5250 **8** ½ **Fitzwilliam**[36] 1948 4-8-13 **52**...... PaddyPilley[(5)] 4 49
(Mick Channon) *in rr: ct on heels ent st: squeezed up 3f out: rdn on outer over 2f out: gng on at fin* **12/1**

6531 **9** 1 **Vivo Per Lei (IRE)**[22] 2323 4-8-13 **54**...... GeorgeWood[(7)] 11 48
(Dr Jon Scargill) *settled in mid-div: rdn on inner over 2f out: kpt on one pce* **6/1**[2]

0620 **10** 6 **Rezwaan**[22] 2323 9-9-3 **51**......(b) ShaneKelly 10 39
(Murty McGrath) *pushed along leaving stalls to ld: increased pce over 3f out: sn rdn: hdd 2f out and wknd qckly fnl f* **10/1**

00-0 **11** 9 **Bollywood Dream**[20] 2397 4-8-12 **46** oh1......(v[1]) CharlesBishop 8 16
(Peter Hedger) *chsd ldrs: rdn and wknd fr over 2f out* **33/1**

0-5 **12** 6 **Surprise Us**[12] 2634 9-8-12 **46**......(p) OisinMurphy 14 7
(Mark Gillard) *chsd ldrs: rdn 2f out: wknd fnl f: t.o* **20/1**

500- **13** 9 **My Renaissance**[204] 7216 6-8-12 **51**......(t) CallumShepherd[(5)] 5
(Ben Case) *in rr: niggled along at 1/2-way: rdn and wknd qckly 2f out: t.o* **20/1**

2m 21.6s (-0.30) **Going Correction** -0.05s/f (Stan) **13** Ran SP% **117.1**
Speed ratings (Par 101): **99,98,96,96,95 94,94,93,93,88 82,77,71**
CSF £50.03 CT £267.65 TOTE £11.50: £4.00, £1.70, £1.70; EX 77.70 Trifecta £675.90.
Owner Wackey Racers Harefield **Bred** Shadwell Estate Company Limited **Trained** Epsom, Surrey
■ Stewards' Enquiry : Martin Harley caution: careless riding

FOCUS
A moderate handicap in which the leaders wound things up from some way out.

3032 32RED/BRITISH STALLION STUDS EBF NOVICE STKS 6f (P)
7:00 (7:00) (Class 5) 2-Y-O **£3,234** (£962; £481; £240) **Stalls** Low

Form RPR
5 **1** **Morning Suit (USA)**[46] 1621 2-9-2 0...... RichardKingscote 2 77
(Mark Johnston) *sltly hmpd s: chsd ldr: shkn up 2f out: upsides ldr whn wnt sltly rt and leaned on runner-up over 1f out: rdn and sn led 1f out: pushed out fnl f and sltly drifted rt: comf* **1/1**[1]

0 **2** 2 ¼ **Cappananty Con**[25] 2235 2-9-2 0...... RobertWinston 5 70
(Dean Ivory) *led at slow pce: niggled along over 2f out: rdn 2f out: hdd 1f out: kpt on to hold 2nd fnl 110yds* **9/1**[3]

3 nk **Ahead Of Time** 2-9-2 0...... MartinHarley 1 69
(David Simcock) *settled bhd ldrs: rdn on inner over 2f out: nt qckn tl over 1f out: kpt on wl to press for 2nd fnl 110yds* **5/2**[2]

6 **4** 4 ½ **Control Centre (IRE)**[30] 2082 2-9-2 0...... PatDobbs 7 56
(Richard Hannon) *settled in rr: rdn 2f out: ev ch over 1f out: sn lft bhd and rdn out hands and heels* **9/1**[3]

0 **5** ¾ **Zamadance**[26] 2204 2-8-13 0...... TomMarquand[(3)] 3 54
(Sylvester Kirk) *wnt rt s: settled bhd ldrs: niggled along over 2f out: rdn 2f out: lft bhd ent fnl f: hands and heels after* **16/1**

3 **6** 13 **Padleyourowncanoe**[22] 2335 2-9-2 0...... SteveDrowne 4 15
(Daniel Mark Loughnane) *in rr: scrubbed along to hold tch most of way: rdn over 3f out: sn hld and eased over 1f out* **14/1**

1m 13.99s (0.89) **Going Correction** -0.05s/f (Stan) **6** Ran SP% **111.1**
Speed ratings (Par 93): **92,89,88,82,81 64**
CSF £10.79 TOTE £1.80: £1.10, £4.50; EX 9.40 Trifecta £26.10.
Owner Sheikh Hamdan bin Mohammed Al Maktoum **Bred** Darley **Trained** Middleham Moor, N Yorks

FOCUS
A fair novice race.

3033 32RED ON THE APP STORE H'CAP (LONDON MIDDLE DISTANCE SERIES QUALIFIER) 1m 3f (P)
7:30 (7:30) (Class 5) (0-70,70) 3-Y-O **£2,911** (£866; £432; £216) **Stalls** Low

Form RPR
5-60 **1** **Sixties Groove (IRE)**[33] 2005 3-9-0 **63**...... JimCrowley 5 77+
(Jeremy Noseda) *settled bhd ldrs: gng wl over 2f out: shkn up and led wl over 1f out: drifted sltly lft ins fnl f: kpt finding to hold off runner-up* **9/2**[3]

505 **2** 1 **Hayward Field (IRE)**[22] 2321 3-9-1 **64**...... HarryBentley 9 76+
(Roger Varian) *settled in mid-div and t.k.h: tk clsr order over 2f out: sn rdn and kpt on to chal wnr fnl f: hld fnl 110yds* **4/1**[2]

0534 **3** 4 ½ **Multigifted**[30] 2083 3-8-1 **57**...... GeorgeWood[(7)] 2 61
(Michael Madgwick) *mid-div: rdn over 2f out: one pce fr 1f out and sn no ch as front pair plld clr ins fnl f* **33/1**

003- **4** 2 ¼ **Tyrell (IRE)**[247] 6985 3-8-9 **58**...... WilliamTwiston-Davies 3 58+
(Alan King) *settled on mid-div on inner: scrubbed along 5f out: rdn over 2f out: styd on one pce* **4/1**[2]

00-5 **5** 3 ¼ **Mystique Heights**[15] 2563 3-8-9 **58**...... LukeMorris 14 52
(Sir Mark Prescott Bt) *pressed ldr for first 6f tl led: rdn and hdd wl over 1f out: one pce and wknd fr over 1f out* **10/1**

604 **6** 1 ½ **Persaverance**[12] 2640 3-8-13 **67**...... HectorCrouch[(5)] 6 58+
(Gary Moore) *in rr: rdn over 2f out: one pce* **16/1**

-021 **7** 1 **Bigger And Better**[12] 2639 3-9-4 **67**...... PatDobbs 8 57
(Richard Hannon) *pressed ldrs tl settled bhd ldrs after 4f: rdn over 2f out: sn wknd* **7/2**[1]

64-0 **8** nse **Fandango (GER)**[44] 1714 3-9-2 **65**......[1] AdamBeschizza 12 55
(Jeremy Gask) *in rr: niggled along to hold tch on bnd 4f out: rdn over 2f out: kpt on one pce* **33/1**

-044 **9** 1 ¼ **Bazzat (IRE)**[6] 2829 3-7-11 **51** oh6...... NoelGarbutt[(5)] 1 38
(John Ryan) *mid-div: rdn and wknd fr 3f out* **16/1**

06-0 **10** 10 **Calliope**[23] 2291 3-9-1 **64**...... OisinMurphy 11 33
(Andrew Balding) *s.s and taken to rail after 1f: settled in rr: rdn and wknd fr over 3f out* **25/1**

5-35 **11** 41 **Hijran (IRE)**[43] 1759 3-9-2 **65**......(v[1]) StevieDonohoe 7
(Charlie Fellowes) *led tl hdd after 6f: settled bhd ldrs on rail after: niggled along on bnd over 3f out: rdn over 2f out: wknd fnl f: t.o* **20/1**

00-6 **12** 19 **Horatia The Fleet**[130] 402 3-8-4 **53**...... MartinDwyer 4
(Willie Musson) *mid-div on outer: rdn out wd over 3f out: wknd fr 2f out: t.o* **100/1**

2m 18.92s (-2.98) **Going Correction** -0.05s/f (Stan) **12** Ran SP% **116.7**
Speed ratings (Par 99): **108,107,104,102,100 98,98,98,97,89 60,46**
CSF £21.17 CT £530.13 TOTE £5.60: £2.40, £1.80, £5.30; EX 27.60 Trifecta £589.00.
Owner Mrs Susan Roy **Bred** Minch Bloodstock **Trained** Newmarket, Suffolk

FOCUS
The first two finished nicely clear here and the form looks sound for the level.

3034 32RED.COM FILLIES' H'CAP 7f (P)
8:00 (8:00) (Class 4) (0-85,85) 3-Y-O **£4,690** (£1,395; £697; £348) **Stalls** Low

Form RPR
214 **1** **Battlement**[27] 2178 3-8-11 **75**......(p) FMBerry 5 82+
(Roger Charlton) *hld up in rr under restraint and t.k.h: rdn 2f out: kpt on wl fr over 1f in sustained battled w runner-up tl led 1f out: asserted fnl 110yds* **11/4**[2]

40-2 **2** ¾ **Winter Rose (IRE)**[15] 2565 3-9-7 **85**...... PatDobbs 6 89
(Richard Hannon) *led after 2f: rdn 2f out: kpt on in sustained duel w wnr fr over 1f out: hdd 1f out: kpt on wl tl wnr asserted fnl 110yds* **11/2**

1-P **3** nk **Nassuvian Pearl**[53] 1476 3-8-7 **71**......[1] OisinMurphy 1 74+
(Ralph Beckett) *sltly awkward ldng stalls: taken bk and settled in rr: rdn on outer over 2f out: kpt on wl fnl f: nvr nrr* **5/1**[3]

212 **4** 1 ½ **Semra (USA)**[55] 1432 3-8-11 **75**...... LukeMorris 4 74
(Marco Botti) *in rr: upsides and rdn 2f out: kpt on one pce* **11/1**

21- **5** 1 ¼ **Dutch Destiny**[240] 7161 3-9-3 **81**...... PatCosgrave 3 77
(William Haggas) *t.k.h: led after 1f: hdd after 2f and settled bhd ldr: rdn 2f out: sn no ex and wknd* **13/8**[1]

3-00 **6** 4 ½ **Unilit (IRE)**[32] 2042 3-9-7 **85**......(t) JFEgan 2 69
(David Evans) *led early: hdd sn after and restrained bhd ldrs: swtchd to inner: rdn 2f out: wknd fnl f* **20/1**

1m 26.86s (0.86) **Going Correction** -0.05s/f (Stan) **6** Ran SP% **109.9**
Speed ratings (Par 98): **93,92,91,90,88 83**
CSF £17.05 TOTE £2.80: £1.50, £3.50; EX 16.30 Trifecta £51.00.
Owner K Abdullah **Bred** Juddmonte Farms Ltd **Trained** Beckhampton, Wilts

FOCUS
An interesting fillies' handicap, but a steady early pace meant it turned into a bit of a sprint in the straight.

3035 32RED CASINO H'CAP 7f (P)
8:30 (8:30) (Class 4) (0-80,80) 4-Y-O+ **£4,690** (£1,395; £697; £348) **Stalls** Low

Form RPR
5140 **1** **Mezmaar**[56] 1418 7-9-2 **75**...... PatCosgrave 12 84
(Kevin Morgan) *in rr and racd freely early: tk clsr order over 2f out: swtchd off rail to centre over 1f out: styd on strly to ld 110yds: won gng away* **15/2**[3]

5663 **2** 1 **Dutch Art Dealer**[6] 2821 5-9-7 **80**......(b) LukeMorris 4 86
(Paul Cole) *awkward leaving stalls and rousted along early: in rr: stl in rr over 2f out: swtchd to inner rail over 1f out and rdn: kpt on fnl f* **3/1**[1]

46-5 **3** ½ **Avalanche Express**[70] 1151 4-8-11 **70**...... MartinDwyer 8 75
(William Muir) *hld up in mid-div: rdn 2f out: kpt on wl between horses over 1f out: styd on and tk 3rd fnl strides* **12/1**

2301 **4** nk **Exalted (IRE)**[14] 2579 5-8-13 **72**......(t) JimCrowley 2 76+
(William Knight) *chsd ldrs: rdn 2f out: led 2f out: hdd under 1f out: wknd and lost two pls nring fin* **4/1**[2]

-156 **5** shd **Bank Of Gibraltar**[22] 2324 4-9-3 **79**......(p) TomMarquand[(3)] 6 83
(Richard Hughes) *hld up in rr: clr run up rail ent st: rdn 2f out: ev ch 1f out and briefly led under 1f out: hdd 110yds out: wknd and lost three pls nr fin* **8/1**

-320 **6** 3 ¼ **Mystical Sapphire**[14] 2579 6-9-5 **78**...... GeorgeBaker 1 73
(Laura Mongan) *chsd ldrs: stl gng wl 2f out: shuffled along fr over 1f out: hands and heel fnl f* **8/1**

6000 **7** 1 **Varsovian**[14] 2581 6-9-7 **80**...... RenatoSouza 3 72
(Dean Ivory) *chsd ldrs: rdn along over 2f out: nt qckn: sme prog ins fnl f* **16/1**

0200 **8** 3 ½ **Nasri**[6] 2821 10-8-7 **66**...... JFEgan 10 49
(Emma Owen) *rousted along fr wd draw to ld after 2f: niggled along over 2f out: rdn and hdd 2f out: wknd and eased fnl f* **33/1**

0-05 **9** 2 **Run With Pride (IRE)**[14] 2577 6-8-11 **70**...... MartinLane 9 47
(Derek Shaw) *in rr: rdn along over 2f out: no imp fr wl over 1f out: eased fnl f* **10/1**

6220 **10** 1 **Silver Bid (USA)**[25] 2253 4-8-11 **70**...... FMBerry 7 45
(Alan Bailey) *chsd ldrs on outer: lost pl over 2f and rdn: one pce: eased fnl f* **10/1**

1m 24.98s (-1.02) **Going Correction** -0.05s/f (Stan) **10** Ran SP% **113.7**
Speed ratings (Par 105): **103,101,101,100,100 97,95,91,89,88**
CSF £29.44 CT £273.88 TOTE £7.60: £2.80, £1.80, £2.60; EX 33.90 Trifecta £479.40.
Owner Roemex Ltd **Bred** Denford Stud Ltd **Trained** Gazeley, Suffolk

FOCUS
The pace collapsed late on and the first three were three of the four who were held up at the back of the field in the early stages.

3036 £10 FREE BET AT 32REDSPORT.COM H'CAP 6f (P)
9:00 (9:01) (Class 5) (0-75,79) 3-Y-O **£2,911** (£866; £432; £216) **Stalls** Low

Form RPR
-311 **1** **Papa Luigi (IRE)**[2] 2981 3-9-7 **79** 6ex...... GaryMahon[(5)] 1 92
(Richard Hannon) *sn led: increased pce 4f out: shkn up 2f out: rdn 1f out: drifted fr centre to inner rail under whip: stened up and pushed out fnl 110yds: ld reduced nr fin* **10/11**[1]

-126 **2** ¾ **Baron Bolt**[37] 1935 3-9-5 **72**......(p) LukeMorris 2 81
(Paul Cole) *hld up bhd ldrs: rdn jst over 2f: no imp on wnr tl kpt on wl ins fnl f to reduce ld cl home* **14/1**

2-30 **3** 4 **Mazzini**[23] 2298 3-9-6 **73** FrederikTylicki 11 69+
(James Fanshawe) *hld up in rr: stl nr rr 3f out: niggled along to cl over 2f out: drvn 2f out: str run on outer to take 3rd nr fin* **3/1**[2]

2104 **4** ¾ **Roseale (IRE)**[33] 2002 3-9-6 **73** MartinLane 6 67
(Jeremy Gask) *settled in mid-div: rdn over 2f out: kpt on one pce: lost 3rd nr fin* **20/1**

35-2 **5** ¾ **Jack Nevison**[56] 1414 3-9-7 **74** FergusSweeney 10 65
(Henry Candy) *settled in rr of mid-div: swtchd to inner and rdn 2f out: sme prog past btn horses fr 1f out* **20/1**

1645 **6** 1 ¼ **Thee And Me (IRE)**[22] 2336 3-8-9 **69** KevinLundie[(7)] 5 56
(Mike Murphy) *hld up in rr: niggled along over 3f out: rdn on inner over 2f out: hands and heel ins fnl f* **25/1**

502- **7** nk **Burningfivers (IRE)**[236] 7248 3-9-4 **71** JFEgan 8 57
(Joseph Tuite) *in rr-div: rdn 2f out: kpt on one pce past btn horses ins fnl f* **33/1**

031- **8** 1 ½ **Tesoro (IRE)**[173] 8287 3-9-2 **69** RobertWinston 4 51
(Dean Ivory) *chsd ldrs: rdn over 2f out: one pce fr 1f out: wknd* **12/1**[3]

44-0 **9** ¾ **The Burnham Mare (IRE)**[23] 2314 3-8-10 **70**(p) HollieDoyle[(7)] 9 49
(J S Moore) *chsd ldrs: rdn over 2f out: no imp and one pce fr over 1f out: wknd fnl f* **33/1**

41-0 **10** 2 ½ **Murdanova (IRE)**[146] 171 3-9-6 **73** JohnFahy 12 44
(Kevin Frost) *in rr: niggled along over 3f out to take clsr order: rdn 2f out: sn hld and wknd* **33/1**

520- **11** 1 **Equinette (IRE)**[252] 6850 3-9-5 **72** JimCrowley 3 40
(Amanda Perrett) *chsd ldr: shkn up over 2f out: no rspnse and ease fnl f* **20/1**

0 **12** ½ **Medicean El Diablo**[33] 2002 3-8-13 **66** KieranO'Neill 7 32
(Jimmy Fox) *wnt lft leaving stalls: in rr: drifted wd ent st: scrubbed along over 2f out: nvr involved* **33/1**

1m 11.93s (-1.17) **Going Correction** -0.05s/f (Stan) **12** Ran SP% **121.6**
Speed ratings (Par 99): **105,104,98,97,96 95,94,92,91,88 86,86**
CSF £14.15 CT £29.53 TOTE £1.70: £1.10, £3.90, £1.10; EX 14.10 Trifecta £65.80.
Owner Middleham Park Racing XLVIII **Bred** Gerry Flannery Developments Ltd **Trained** East Everleigh, Wilts

FOCUS
The favourite dominated from the outset here.
T/Plt: £202.00 to a £1 stake. Pool: £67,764.27. 244.86 winning tickets. T/Qpdt: £18.10 to a £1 stake. Pool: £6,972.55. 284.84 winning tickets. **Cathal Gahan**

YARMOUTH (L-H)

Wednesday, June 8

OFFICIAL GOING: Good to firm (good in back straight and bends; 7.8)
Wind: breezy Weather: some sunshine early; becoming decidedly cool after; 16 degrees

3037 BRITISH STALLION STUDS EBF NOVICE STKS (PLUS 10 RACE) 5f 42y
2:20 (2:28) (Class 4) 2-Y-O **£4,657** (£1,386; £692; £346) **Stalls** Centre

Form RPR

1 **Ardad (IRE)** 2-9-2 0 RobertHavlin 7 84+
(John Gosden) *free to s: stdd and missed break: effrt 1/2-way: rdn to ld jst ins fnl f: kpt on stoutly* **3/1**[2]

2 1 **Seed Corn** 2-8-11 0 PatCosgrave 5 75
(William Haggas) *pressed ldr: rdn to ld 2f out: hdd jst ins fnl f: nt qckn fnl 100yds* **9/4**[1]

3 1 ¾ **Maakaasib** 2-9-2 0 AdamKirby 6 74
(Simon Crisford) *racd keenly: cl up: rdn wl over 1f out: nt qckn ins fnl f* **10/3**[3]

4 1 ¼ **Kyllang Rock (IRE)** 2-9-2 0 LukeMorris 2 70
(James Tate) *missed break: effrt whn stmbld 2f out: nt chal ldrs after but kpt on nicely clsng stage* **25/1**

01 **5** ½ **Miss Rosina (IRE)**[15] 2552 2-9-0 0 TomQueally 8 66
(George Margarson) *kpt hanging rt: racd freely in ld for 3f: drvn and no ex over 1f out* **9/1**

0 **6** 1 ¼ **Rose Berry**[38] 1889 2-8-11 0 FrederikTylicki 4 58
(Chris Dwyer) *pressed ldrs: rdn over 2f out: btn over 1f out* **11/1**

7 3 ½ **Seprani** 2-8-11 0 SamHitchcott 1 46
(Mrs Ilka Gansera-Leveque) *missed break: effrt 1/2-way: drvn and wknd wl over 1f out* **50/1**

1m 0.49s (-2.21) **Going Correction** -0.525s/f (Hard) **7** Ran SP% **103.0**
Speed ratings (Par 95): **96,94,91,89,88 86,81**
CSF £8.16 TOTE £3.40: £1.80, £2.10; EX 11.20 Trifecta £26.30.
Owner Abdullah Saeed Al Naboodah **Bred** Tally-Ho Stud **Trained** Newmarket, Suffolk
■ Golden Easter was withdrawn. Price at time of withdrawal 6-1. Rule 4 applies to all bets - deduction 10p in the pound.

FOCUS
This was the first meeting to take place at Yarmouth since last September's big three-day fixture was abandoned halfway through, with remedial work having taken place on the area of the track just after the winning line in the meantime. The going was officially good to firm, good on the back straight and on both bends. The winning jockey in the opener said: "It's good, fast ground and very fair." A fair novice event to start and a very volatile betting market. The finish was dominated by newcomers.

3038 JOHN KEMP 4 X 4 CENTRE OF NORFOLK FILLIES' H'CAP 6f 3y
2:50 (2:54) (Class 5) (0-75,75) 3-Y-O+ **£3,067** (£905; £453) **Stalls** Centre

Form RPR

-505 **1** **Shypen**[14] 2585 3-8-6 **68** JaneElliott[(7)] 2 76
(George Margarson) *pressed ldrs on outer: led wl over 1f out: clr ins fnl f: hld on wl* **12/1**

02-5 **2** 1 ¼ **Hillside Dream (IRE)**[56] 1423 3-9-5 **74** LukeMorris 3 78
(James Tate) *bhd and sn shkn up: drvn and clsd fr 2f out: sn n.m.r: chsd wnr over 1f out: edgd lft: styd on wl but a hld* **9/1**

5-33 **3** 2 **Lajatico**[41] 1815 3-9-0 **69** FrederikTylicki 11 67
(Ed Vaughan) *chsd ldrs on stands' rail: drvn to chal 2f out: hld in 3rd pl fnl f* **7/1**[3]

003 **4** 3 **Shahaama**[32] 2039 3-8-5 **60** JFEgan 4 48
(Mick Channon) *pressed ldr but sn drvn along: rdn and racd awkwardly 2f out: btn over 1f out* **15/2**

361- **5** ½ **Olympic Runner**[200] 7937 3-9-6 **75** PatCosgrave 1 61
(William Haggas) *nvr bttr than midfield: rdn and btn over 1f out* **7/2**[1]

-365 **6** ¾ **Blue Geranium (IRE)**[13] 2606 3-9-6 **75** RobertHavlin 6 59
(John Gosden) *midfield: rdn wl over 1f out: kpt on same pce* **8/1**

-630 **7** 2 ½ **Refuse Colette (IRE)**[21] 2380 7-9-9 **70**(v) WilliamCarson 8 48
(Mick Quinn) *led at str pce tl drvn and hdd wl over 1f out: lost pl qckly* **10/1**

0-05 **8** 1 ½ **Lolita**[7] 2794 4-9-8 **74** JosephineGordon[(5)] 9 47
(J R Jenkins) *chsd ldrs tl drvn and wknd over 2f out* **16/1**

3405 **9** 5 **Emily Goldfinch**[14] 2586 3-8-7 **62** DavidProbert 5 17
(Phil McEntee) *nvr on terms: t.o* **16/1**

5-45 **10** 8 **Anastazia**[20] 2401 4-9-9 **70** ShaneKelly 7 2
(Paul D'Arcy) *no ch fr 1/2-way: t.o and eased* **5/1**[2]

00 **11** 3 ¼ **Baileys Perle (IRE)**[18] 2483 3-8-10 **65** MartinLane 10
(Chris Dwyer) *last away and rdn: nvr gng wl: t.o* **22/1**

1m 9.82s (-4.58) **Going Correction** -0.525s/f (Hard) course record
WFA 3 from 4yo+ 8lb **11** Ran SP% **117.2**
Speed ratings (Par 100): **109,107,104,100,100 99,95,93,87,76 72**
CSF £115.12 CT £836.62 TOTE £12.90: £3.70, £2.90, £2.40; EX 139.70 Trifecta £1482.60.
Owner F Butler **Bred** F Butler **Trained** Newmarket, Suffolk

FOCUS
An ordinary fillies' handicap, but they went a cracking pace and took 0.08sec off the 6f course record.

3039 THURLOW NUNN VAUXHALL DEALER OF GREAT YARMOUTH FILLIES' H'CAP 1m 3y
3:20 (3:22) (Class 3) (0-90,90) 3-Y-O **£7,439** (£2,213; £1,106; £553) **Stalls** Centre

Form RPR

3-13 **1** **Singyoursong (IRE)**[30] 2108 3-8-2 **71** KieranO'Neill 6 78
(David Simcock) *towards rr: rdn and effrt 2f out: sustained run fnl f: kpt on gamely to ld nr fin* **3/1**[1]

4003 **2** hd **Yeah Baby Yeah (IRE)**[16] 2539 3-9-2 **85** AdamKirby 8 91
(Gay Kelleway) *settled wl and taken steadily in last tl rdn 3f out: gd run to ld wl over 1f out: hrd drvn fnl f: worn down cl home* **33/1**

65-2 **3** 1 ½ **Blossomtime**[38] 1898 3-9-7 **90** MartinLane 7 92
(Charlie Appleby) *a in same pl: rdn and outpcd over 1f out: rallied 1f out: no imp on ldng pair ins fnl f* **11/2**[3]

121 **4** ½ **Bargain Buy**[16] 2532 3-8-13 **82** PatCosgrave 5 83
(William Haggas) *racd keenly and pressed ldr: rdn over 1f out: nt qckn fnl f* **3/1**[1]

1031 **5** 1 ½ **World's Greatest (USA)**[26] 2212 3-8-2 **71** oh1(t) LukeMorris 4 68
(Stuart Williams) *t.k.h: pressed ldrs tl rdn 2f out: no ex over 1f out* **4/1**[2]

-104 **6** 1 **Alyaa (IRE)**[39] 1867 3-7-13 **73** NoelGarbutt[(5)] 3 68
(Conrad Allen) *plld hrd: led tl rdn and hdd wl over 1f out: sn lost pl* **12/1**

0-65 **7** ¾ **Cleverconversation (IRE)**[7] 2795 3-8-3 **75** DannyBrock[(3)] 2 68
(Jane Chapple-Hyam) *swishing tail leaving stalls: chsd ldrs: rdn over 2f out: no rspnse: btn over 1f out* **6/1**

1m 36.33s (-4.27) **Going Correction** -0.525s/f (Hard) **7** Ran SP% **110.3**
Speed ratings (Par 100): **100,99,98,97,96 95,94**
CSF £83.41 CT £486.82 TOTE £3.90: £2.50, £6.90; EX 76.00 Trifecta £335.60.
Owner Saeed Jaber **Bred** Rabbah Bloodstock Limited **Trained** Newmarket, Suffolk

FOCUS
A decent 3yo fillies' handicap, but the early pace didn't look anything special and a couple were inclined to take a grip.

3040 HAVEN SEASHORE HOLIDAY PARK H'CAP 6f 3y
3:50 (3:50) (Class 6) (0-55,55) 4-Y-O+ **£2,264** (£673; £336; £168) **Stalls** Centre

Form RPR

232 **1** **Wedgewood Estates**[42] 1795 5-9-6 **54** AdamKirby 6 63
(Tony Carroll) *chsd ldrs: rdn to ld wl over 1f out: sn clr: rdn out whn in command ins fnl f* **13/2**[2]

3310 **2** 2 ¾ **Malaysian Boleh**[22] 2332 6-9-6 **54**(b) JamieSpencer 7 55
(Shaun Lycett) *bhd: last at 1/2-way: sn racing awkwardly: decided to run on ins fnl f and fin strly to snatch 2nd: no ch w wnr* **9/4**[1]

2120 **3** nk **Tasaaboq**[14] 2584 5-9-1 **54**(t) JosephineGordon[(5)] 12 54
(Phil McEntee) *effrt 1/2-way: rdn to chal for 2nd over 1f out: chsd wnr vainly after: lost 2nd nr fin* **17/2**

5410 **4** ½ **Blistering Dancer (IRE)**[19] 2447 6-9-2 **50** JFEgan 10 48
(Tony Carroll) *led: drvn and hdd wl over 1f out: kpt on same pce whn duelling for wl hld 2nd ins fnl f* **8/1**[3]

2004 **5** 2 ¼ **Multi Quest**[14] 2584 4-9-3 **51**(v) SamHitchcott 2 43
(John E Long) *chsd ldrs on outer: sn drvn along: no ex over 1f out* **8/1**[3]

0255 **6** 1 ¼ **Lizzy's Dream**[19] 2423 8-9-6 **54** TomQueally 3 42
(Rebecca Bastiman) *racd keenly and pressed ldrs: rdn 2f out: no ex wl over 1f out* **14/1**

3446 **7** shd **Blue Bounty**[14] 2584 5-9-5 **53**(p) SaleemGolam 11 41
(Mark H Tompkins) *cl up and t.k.h: rdn 2f out: btn wl over 1f out* **13/2**[2]

6600 **8** 4 **Muhtadim (IRE)**[13] 2609 4-8-12 **46** MartinLane 14 22
(Charles Smith) *cl up tl drvn and fdd 2f out* **50/1**

0000 **9** 1 ½ **Willow Spring**[19] 2447 4-8-7 **46** oh1 NoelGarbutt[(5)] 1 17
(Conrad Allen) *nvr on terms* **40/1**

600- **10** 1 ¼ **Get Prancer**[308] 5007 4-8-12 **46** oh1 FrederikTylicki 4 13
(J R Jenkins) *struggling fr 1/2-way* **25/1**

0000 **11** 3 ½ **Marmarus**[20] 2409 5-9-7 **55**(p) RobertHavlin 9 12
(David Nicholls) *s.s: nvr gng wl in rr: t.o* **16/1**

00-0 **12** 3 ¾ **Delysdream**[16] 2542 4-8-12 **46** oh1(bt[1]) DavidProbert 15
(Christine Dunnett) *chsd ldrs: rdn 3f out: sn struggling: t.o* **25/1**

1m 11.17s (-3.23) **Going Correction** -0.525s/f (Hard) **12** Ran SP% **114.8**
Speed ratings (Par 101): **100,96,95,95,92 90,90,85,83,81 76,71**
CSF £19.96 CT £128.26 TOTE £6.80: £2.40, £1.50, £2.80; EX 26.60 Trifecta £92.40.
Owner Wedgewood Estates **Bred** Wedgewood Estates **Trained** Cropthorne, Worcs

FOCUS
A competitive handicap, but a moderate one. The entire field were inclined to race towards the stands' rail on this occasion. The winner has been rated to his best.

3041 GROSVENOR CASINO OF GREAT YARMOUTH MAIDEN H'CAP 1m 3f 104y
4:20 (4:20) (Class 6) (0-65,64) 4-Y-O+ **£2,975** (£885; £442; £221) **Stalls** Low

Form RPR

3-22 **1** **Longside**[25] 2233 4-9-4 **64** ThomasBrown[(3)] 2 70
(James Eustace) *trckd ldng pair: pushed into ld 2f out: 3 l clr 1f out: comf* **2/5**[1]

-005 **2** 4 ½ **Troy Boy**[5] 2853 6-7-9 **46** oh1(p) RPWalsh[(7)] 4 41
(Rebecca Bastiman) *led: rdn over 3f out: hdd 2f out: in vain pursuit of wnr after* **50/1**

00-6 **3** ½ **Moncarno**[26] 2205 6-9-2 **59** WilliamCarson 7 54
(John Best) *t.k.h and pressed ldrs: 3rd and u.p 2f out: awkward hd carriage and fnd nil after: plugged on* **18/1**

0/00 **4** ¾ **Intimidator (IRE)**[20] 2398 5-9-0 **57** RobertHavlin 6 51
(Miss Joey Ellis) *hld up in 5th pl: rdn over 2f out: fnd little: plodded into 4th ins fnl f* **10/1**[3]

0603 **5** 1 **Galuppi**[7] 2792 5-8-13 **56**(p) FrederikTylicki 1 48
(J R Jenkins) *hld up last: rdn over 2f out: nvr making any sort of imp* **9/2**[2]

64-0 **6** *3* **Sailor Malan**[12] 2634 4-8-12 **55**.. DavidProbert 3 42
(Gay Kelleway) *pressed ldr: chal over 3f out: drvn and wknd tamely over 2f out* **16/1**

2m 29.61s (0.91) **Going Correction** +0.15s/f (Good) **6** Ran SP% **111.8**
Speed ratings (Par 101): **102,98,98,97,97 94**
CSF £25.81 TOTE £1.40: £1.20, £9.40; EX 12.80 Trifecta £26.30.
Owner Park Lodge Racing **Bred** Juddmonte Farms Ltd **Trained** Newmarket, Suffolk

FOCUS
A very modest maiden handicap in which only two mattered according to the betting, but they went in very different directions in the market and the race panned out accordingly. Weak form.

3042 FOLLOW TWITTER AT GREAT YARMOUTH RACECOURSE H'CAP 1m 2f 23y
4:50 (4:50) (Class 5) (0-75,75) 3-Y-O **£2,911** (£866; £432; £216) **Stalls** Low

Form RPR

00-2 **1** **Prosecute (FR)**[26] 2212 3-9-4 **72**.................................... JamieSpencer 8 79+
(David Simcock) *stdd s: hld up last in slow r tl 4f out: effrt 2f out: drvn to ld fnl 100yds: styd on wl* **2/1**[1]

644- **2** *1/2* **Long Call**[226] 7518 3-9-3 **71**.. MartinLane 4 75
(Charlie Appleby) *t.k.h trcking ldrs: led 2f out: sn rdn: hdd 100yds out: jst hld after* **5/1**[2]

6-14 **3** *nk* **Jive Time**[28] 2145 3-9-7 **75**.. AdamKirby 7 78
(James Tate) *trckd ldrs: rdn 3f out: kpt on wout quite threatening ins fnl f* **12/1**

40-0 **4** *1* **Guns Of Leros (USA)**[33] 2008 3-9-3 **71**.......................... GeorgeBaker 5 72+
(Gary Moore) *hld up and bhd: rdn 3f out: mde grnd qckly ins fnl f: styd on nicely* **6/1**[3]

023 **5** *1 3/4* **Malhama**[17] 2505 3-9-5 **73**...[1] JackMitchell 3 71
(Roger Varian) *t.k.h: prom: rdn and n.m.r 2f out: swtchd rt: one pce fnl f* **13/2**

6-50 **6** *1 3/4* **Royal Mahogany (IRE)**[25] 2248 3-8-12 **66**...................... TomQueally 9 60
(Luca Cumani) *led at stdy pce: drvn and hdd 2f out: sn lost pl* **22/1**

0-64 **7** *1 3/4* **Lady Blanco (USA)**[62] 1289 3-8-7 **61**...........................[1] DavidProbert 2 52
(Andrew Balding) *towards rr: rdn over 2f out: no imp fr over 1f out* **14/1**

-436 **8** *nk* **Harlequin Rock**[26] 2212 3-8-9 **63**................................... WilliamCarson 6 53
(Mick Quinn) *t.k.h and pressed ldr tl rdn over 2f out: plugged on same pce after* **28/1**

000 **9** *1* **Western Prince**[25] 2248 3-9-6 **74**..................................... RobertHavlin 1 62
(John Gosden) *t.k.h in rr: rdn over 2f out: btn over 1f out* **7/1**

2m 10.89s (0.39) **Going Correction** +0.15s/f (Good) **9** Ran SP% **112.3**
Speed ratings (Par 99): **104,103,103,102,101 99,98,98,97**
CSF £11.26 CT £91.23 TOTE £2.50: £1.10, £1.40, £3.30; EX 11.00 Trifecta £87.10.
Owner Highclere Thoroughbred Racing(Earl Grey) **Bred** S C E A Haras Du Ma **Trained** Newmarket, Suffolk

FOCUS
An ordinary 3yo handicap. They went no pace early and it developed into a sprint.

3043 ANNUAL BADGES AT GREAT YARMOUTH RACECOURSE APPRENTICE H'CAP (DIV I) 1m 3y
5:20 (5:21) (Class 6) (0-55,55) 4-Y-O+ **£2,264** (£673; £336; £168) **Stalls** Centre

Form RPR

0-36 **1** **Honey Badger**[50] 1547 5-9-3 **54**...............................(v[1]) AaronJones(3) 8 62+
(Eugene Stanford) *towards rr: effrt wl over 1f out: sn wnt 3rd: pushed along sltly to ld fnl 75yds: sn asserted* **4/1**[2]

06-0 **2** *2* **Gypsy Major**[22] 2323 4-9-7 **55**...................................(b) MarcMonaghan 5 58
(Garry Moss) *sn 2nd: rdn to ld 2f out: hdd and outpcd fnl 75yds* **12/1**

4605 **3** *2 1/2* **Jonnie Skull (IRE)**[4] 2899 10-8-9 **46**................(vt) JosephineGordon(3) 7 43
(Phil McEntee) *led: rdn 3f out: hdd 2f out: plugged on gamely although wl hld in fnl f* **6/1**[3]

00-3 **4** *1 1/4* **Mowhoob**[20] 2409 6-9-2 **55**...................................... DanielleMooney(5) 3 49
(David Nicholls) *slowly away: sn rcvrd to press ldrs: 4th and rdn 1f out: nt qckn after* **7/2**[1]

260 **5** *1 1/4* **Ted's Brother (IRE)**[30] 2096 8-9-7 **55**.............................(e) RobHornby 6 46
(Richard Guest) *pressed ldrs tl rdn and btn over 1f out: kpt on steadily fnl 100yds* **10/1**

0003 **6** *shd* **Ocean Bentley (IRE)**[19] 2448 4-8-6 **47** oh1 ow1......... JoshuaBryan(7) 1 38
(Tony Carroll) *midfield: rdn over 3f out: brief effrt: btn 2f out* **11/1**

6050 **7** *1 3/4* **Frantical**[22] 2323 4-8-13 **52**...(p) GeorgiaCox(5) 4 39
(Tony Carroll) *dwlt: in rr and reminders after 2f: nvr travelling* **6/1**[3]

-020 **8** *4 1/2* **Harry Bosch**[12] 2647 6-9-1 **49**.....................................(b) ShelleyBirkett 9 25
(Julia Feilden) *cl up tl rdn and fdd wl over 1f out* **15/2**

0066 **9** *hd* **Malih**[12] 2647 7-8-8 **47**.. MitchGodwin(5) 2 22
(Eric Wheeler) *struggling fnl 3f* **28/1**

/60- **10** *33* **Magic Ice**[509] 177 6-8-5 **46** oh1.. DavidEgan(7) 10
(John Berry) *t.k.h early: cl up tl lost pl 1/2-way: sn floundering bdly and t.o: b.b.v* **28/1**

1m 36.87s (-3.73) **Going Correction** -0.525s/f (Hard) **10** Ran SP% **114.6**
Speed ratings (Par 101): **97,95,92,91,90 89,88,83,83,50**
CSF £50.22 CT £281.06 TOTE £3.80: £1.40, £3.90, £1.80; EX 48.70 Trifecta £389.00.
Owner Mrs Deborah Black **Bred** Mrs Deborah Black **Trained** Newmarket, Suffolk

FOCUS
The first division of a moderate apprentice handicap. A personal best from the winner.

3044 ANNUAL BADGES AT GREAT YARMOUTH RACECOURSE APPRENTICE H'CAP (DIV II) 1m 3y
5:50 (5:51) (Class 6) (0-55,55) 4-Y-O+ **£2,264** (£673; £336; £168) **Stalls** Centre

Form RPR

3-52 **1** **Rustique**[13] 2607 4-9-7 **55**... ThomasBrown 9 64
(Ed Walker) *trckd ldrs gng wl: delayed effrt tl clsd to ld over 1f out: sn in command but looked idling and kpt up to work* **6/4**[1]

6300 **2** *3 1/4* **Rosie Crowe (IRE)**[103] 730 4-8-9 **48**...................(v) CharlieBennett(5) 10 49
(Shaun Harris) *cl up: rdn 2f out: w wnr briefly over 1f out: wl hld by her ins fnl f* **9/1**

4360 **3** *2 1/4* **Gulland Rock**[36] 1949 5-9-0 **55**...................................... LukeCarson(7) 2 51
(Anthony Carson) *a abt same pl: rdn 2f out: wknd ins fnl f* **6/1**[3]

6-00 **4** *3* **Nifty Kier**[43] 1742 7-8-9 **46** oh1.............................. JosephineGordon(3) 1 35
(Phil McEntee) *led: rdn 3f out: hdd over 1f out: wknd fnl f* **6/1**[3]

0-60 **5** *nk* **Zeteah**[16] 2542 6-9-2 **50**.. MichaelJMMurphy 6 38
(Tony Carroll) *towards rr: rdn 3f out: nvr trbld ldrs after* **7/2**[2]

4056 **6** *13* **General Tufto**[44] 1707 11-8-7 **46** oh1......................(b) SophieKilloran(5) 8
(Charles Smith) *bhd: rdn 1/2-way: no rspnse and sn struggling: t.o and eased 1f out* **33/1**

506- **7** *hd* **Madam Mai Tai**[278] 6070 4-8-13 **47**.................................. DannyBrock 7
(Rebecca Bastiman) *prom: rdn sn after 1/2-way: struggling fnl 3f: t.o and eased 1f out* **16/1**

1m 36.91s (-3.69) **Going Correction** -0.525s/f (Hard) **7** Ran SP% **109.6**
Speed ratings (Par 101): **97,93,91,88,88 75,75**
CSF £14.63 CT £56.66 TOTE £2.20: £1.30, £4.30; EX 14.40 Trifecta £69.50.
Owner Dubai Thoroughbred Racing **Bred** D Lancaster-Smith & Moreton Manor Stud **Trained** Upper Lambourn, Berks

FOCUS
The runners came up the middle of the track this time. The winning time was fractionally slower than the first division.
T/Plt: £183.50 to a £1 stake. Pool: £65,261.36. 259.61 winning tickets. T/Qpdt: £29.00 to a £1 stake. Pool: £4,904.48. 124.85 winning tickets. **Iain Mackenzie**

3045 - 3051a (Foreign Racing) - See Raceform Interactive

3023 HAYDOCK (L-H)
Thursday, June 9

OFFICIAL GOING: Good to firm (firm in places; 7.5)
Wind: light 1/2 against Weather: overcast, humid

3052 RACINGUK.COM/FREETRIAL HAYDOCK PARK APPRENTICE TRAINING SERIES H'CAP 1m 3f 200y
6:45 (6:46) (Class 5) (0-70,70) 4-Y-O+ **£3,234** (£962; £481; £240) **Stalls** Centre

Form RPR

-053 **1** **Oriental Tiger**[13] 2651 5-9-6 **67**............................... AdamMcNamara(3) 6 76
(Iain Jardine) *s.s: t.k.h in rr: stmbld after 2f: hdwy over 3f out: 3rd over 2f out: 2nd on ins 1f out: led last 150yds: drvn out* **9/4**[1]

4364 **2** *1 1/2* **Ring Eye (IRE)**[19] 2462 8-8-4 **53** ow1.............................. CliffordLee(5) 4 60
(John O'Shea) *chsd ldr: effrt on ins to ld over 3f out: edgd rt over 1f out: hdd last 150yds: kpt on same pce* **9/2**[3]

3003 **3** *4 1/2* **Scrafton**[18] 2501 5-9-7 **65**... NathanEvans 1 64
(Tony Carroll) *led: hdd over 3f out: wknd last 150yds* **9/2**[3]

0-53 **4** *10* **Merchant Of Medici**[14] 2616 9-9-7 **65**...................(p) CallumShepherd 7 48
(Micky Hammond) *trckd ldrs: drvn and outpcd over 3f out: modest 4th over 1f out: nvr a threat* **7/2**[2]

13/5 **5** *3/4* **Another Lincolnday**[33] 2051 5-9-12 **70**.............................. PhilDennis 8 52
(Michael Herrington) *hld up in rr: drvn 3f out: lost pl over 1f out* **5/1**

4-34 **6** *2 1/4* **Qibtee (FR)**[8] 2799 6-8-13 **62**...................................(b) BenRobinson(5) 2 41
(Les Eyre) *s.i.s: t.k.h: hdwy to trck ldr over 6f out: lost pl over 1f out* **20/1**

2m 30.6s (-3.20) **Going Correction** -0.375s/f (Firm) **6** Ran SP% **110.8**
Speed ratings (Par 103): **95,94,91,84,83 82**
CSF £12.29 CT £38.35 TOTE £3.30: £2.00, £2.80; EX 10.30 Trifecta £34.10.
Owner A Barclay **Bred** James Thom And Sons **Trained** Carrutherstown, D'fries & G'way

FOCUS
Allowing for rail movements on bends, the distances on the round course were 2 yards shorter than advertised. Following a warm and dry spell, 37mm of irrigation had been applied to the track since last weekend. Mainly exposed types in a modest handicap. The gallop soon steadied and the first two pulled clear in the closing stages. The winer built on his previous form.

3053 RIPPONDEN SILK MILL ARE BACK AGAIN H'CAP 1m 2f 95y
7:15 (7:15) (Class 5) (0-70,69) 3-Y-O **£3,234** (£962; £481; £240) **Stalls** Centre

Form RPR

0-01 **1** **Caponova (IRE)**[13] 2652 3-9-3 **65**............................. RichardKingscote 5 72+
(Tom Dascombe) *hld up in rr: t.k.h: hdwy over 3f out: hung lft and led appr fnl f: drvn out* **13/8**[1]

5315 **2** *1 1/2* **Schoolboy Error (IRE)**[22] 2366 3-9-0 **62**....................... WilliamCarson 4 65
(Jamie Osborne) *trckd ldrs: drvn over 3f out: n.m.r and swtchd rt over 1f out: kpt on to take 2nd last 100yds* **11/4**[2]

603 **3** *shd* **Raven Banner (IRE)**[24] 2304 3-8-10 **63**................. CallumShepherd(5) 1 66
(Daniel Mark Loughnane) *stdd s: hld up in rr: hdwy on ins 4f out: edgd rt 3f out: styd on to take 3rd last 50yds* **12/1**

3-65 **4** *2* **Forgiving Flower**[44] 1758 3-9-3 **65**................................ DougieCostello 2 64
(K R Burke) *led: qcknd pce over 5f out: hdd appr fnl f: wknd clsng stages* **5/1**[3]

1556 **5** *8* **Artful Mind**[21] 2413 3-9-7 **69**... DavidNolan 7 53
(James Unett) *trckd ldr: wknd fnl f: eased clsng stages* **5/1**[3]

34-0 **6** *20* **Chesham Rose (IRE)**[132] 384 3-8-0 **53**.......................... NoelGarbutt(5) 3
(Dave Roberts) *t.k.h: sn trcking ldrs: drvn over 4f out: lost pl over 2f out: sn wl bhd* **22/1**

2m 11.99s (-3.51) **Going Correction** -0.375s/f (Firm) **6** Ran SP% **110.1**
Speed ratings (Par 99): **99,97,97,96,89 73**
CSF £6.01 TOTE £2.00: £1.10, £1.90; EX 6.60 Trifecta £21.30.
Owner Deva Racing Bushranger Partnership **Bred** Mr & Mrs T O'Brien **Trained** Malpas, Cheshire

FOCUS
Rail movements reduced the official distance by 2yds. A modest handicap in which the gallop to the home straight was on the steady side. The winner progressed from his C&D latest.

3054 BRIAN PELL'S 65TH BIRTHDAY NOVICE STKS (PLUS 10 RACE) 7f
7:45 (7:46) (Class 4) 2-Y-O **£3,946** (£1,174; £586; £293) **Stalls** Low

Form RPR

1 **Frankuus (IRE)** 2-9-2 0.. JoeFanning 6 85+
(Mark Johnston) *chsd ldrs: effrt over 2f out: hung lft and led appr fnl f: styd on wl clsng stages* **4/1**[3]

53 **2** *1 3/4* **Arc Royal**[12] 2682 2-9-2 0... RichardKingscote 8 80
(Tom Dascombe) *swtchd lft after s: sn w ldr: led over 2f out: hdd appr fnl f: styd on same pce last 100yds* **8/1**

3 *nk* **Devil's Bridge (IRE)** 2-9-2 0... SteveDrowne 4 79+
(Richard Hannon) *dwlt: in rr: drvn and hdwy over 3f out: wnt 3rd last 100yds: styd on clsng stages* **7/2**[2]

24 **4** *3 1/4* **Sidewinder (IRE)**[9] 2779 2-9-2 0.................................... WilliamCarson 3 71
(Tom Dascombe) *led: hdd over 2f out: wknd fnl f* **16/1**

5 **5** *1* **Looting**[19] 2489 2-9-2 0.. GrahamGibbons 2 68
(David Brown) *wnt lft and bmpd s: t.k.h: trckd ldrs: wknd fnl f* **13/2**

6 *3* **Never A Word (USA)** 2-9-2 0... WilliamBuick 5 60+
(Charlie Appleby) *n.m.r sn after s: in last: effrt over 3f out: hung bdly lft fnl f: eased last 75yds* **7/4**[1]

7 *1/2* **Midnight Man (FR)** 2-9-2 0... DougieCostello 1 59+
(K R Burke) *wnt rt and bmpd s: in rr: hdwy to chse ldrs over 2f out: wknd over 1f out* **50/1**

8 *2 1/4* **Reinstorm** 2-9-2 0... TonyHamilton 7 52
(Richard Fahey) *in rr: sme hdwy 4f out: lost pl over 1f out* **25/1**

1m 27.86s (-2.84) **Going Correction** -0.375s/f (Firm) **8** Ran SP% **114.7**
Speed ratings (Par 95): **101,99,98,94,93 90,89,87**
CSF £35.74 TOTE £4.70: £1.80, £2.20, £2.30; EX 31.90 Trifecta £161.70.
Owner Hussain Lootah & Ahmad Al Shaikh **Bred** Ballylinch Stud **Trained** Middleham Moor, N Yorks

The Form Book, Raceform Ltd, Newbury, RG14 5SJ

FOCUS
Rail movements reduced the length of this race by 2yds. An interesting maiden in which the gallop was a reasonable one and this race should throw up winners, as it usually does.

3055 ANDREW & JULIE LOVE TENERIFE H'CAP — 1m
8:15 (8:15) (Class 3) (0-95,94) 4-Y-O+ **£8,086** (£2,406; £1,202; £601) **Stalls** Low

Form / RPR

2226 **1** **Capo Rosso (IRE)**[12] 2684 6-9-7 **94**....... RichardKingscote 10 103
(Tom Dascombe) *chsd ldr: led over 6f out: drvn and styd on strly fnl 2f* **5/1**[2]

0-46 **2** 2 1/4 **Archie (IRE)**[34] 1993 4-9-1 **88**....... JoeFanning 1 92
(Clive Cox) *trckd ldrs: t.k.h: chsd wnr over 1f out: styd on same pce* **6/1**[3]

2010 **3** 3/4 **Supersta**[33] 2027 5-9-1 **88**.......(p) AndrewMullen 6 90
(Michael Appleby) *prom: t.k.h: chsng ldrs and hung lft over 1f out: kpt on same pce* **10/1**

0-03 **4** nk **What Say You (IRE)**[44] 1757 4-8-12 **85**....... DougieCostello 2 87
(K R Burke) *mid-div: hdwy on ins over 3f out: n.m.r and kpt on same pce fnl f: eased nr fin* **8/1**

0-05 **5** 1 1/4 **Intiwin (IRE)**[17] 2527 4-8-9 **82**....... TonyHamilton 8 81
(Richard Fahey) *chsd ldrs: hung lft and one pce over 1f out* **12/1**

0-0 **6** nk **He's No Saint**[25] 2268 5-9-3 **90**.......(v) DavidNolan 3 88
(David O'Meara) *led tl over 6f out: kpt on one pce over 1f out* **16/1**

3400 **7** 1/2 **Silvery Moon (IRE)**[12] 2689 9-9-1 **88**....... DavidAllan 4 85
(Tim Easterby) *in rr: hdwy on inner over 2f out: n.m.r over 1f out: kpt on same pce* **16/1**

3-35 **8** 1 1/4 **Outer Space**[33] 2033 5-9-4 **91**....... WilliamCarson 7 85
(Jamie Osborne) *s.i.s: in rr: hdwy over 2f out: n.m.r over 1f out: kpt on one pce* **16/1**

444- **9** nk **Heisman (IRE)**[244] 7088 5-9-0 **87**.......(t) SteveDrowne 5 80
(George Baker) *mid-div: drvn over 2f out: nvr a factor* **9/2**[1]

-510 **10** nk **Finn Class (IRE)**[23] 2331 5-9-4 **91**....... PaulMulrennan 9 83
(Michael Dods) *prom early: in rr after 2f: sme hdwy over 2f out: nvr a factor* **8/1**

04-0 **11** 14 **Emirates Airline**[35] 1978 4-9-2 **89**.......(p) WilliamBuick 11 49
(Saeed bin Suroor) *swtchd lft after s: hld up in rr: sme hdwy on outside over 2f out: lost pl over 1f out: bhd whn heavily eased last 100yds* **8/1**

1m 38.97s (-4.73) **Going Correction** -0.375s/f (Firm) **11** Ran SP% **116.9**
Speed ratings (Par 107): **108,105,105,104,103 103,102,101,101,100 86**
CSF £34.91 CT £296.06 TOTE £7.30: £2.30, £2.70, £2.70; EX 43.40 Trifecta £340.80.
Owner Deva Racing Red Clubs Partnership **Bred** Michael Wiley **Trained** Malpas, Cheshire

FOCUS
Rail movements reduced the official distance by 2yds. Mainly exposed sorts in a decent handicap. The gallop was fair but those held up weren't seen to best effect. The winner is rated back to his best.

3056 STEVE & LIAM NEAL'S SUPER SPRINT H'CAP — 5f
8:45 (8:45) (Class 4) (0-85,84) 3-Y-O+ **£5,336** (£1,588; £793; £396) **Stalls** Centre

Form / RPR

6-26 **1** **Major Pusey**[24] 2290 4-9-2 **75**....... MichaelJMMurphy(3) 7 85
(John Gallagher) *led: jnd over 1f out: fnd ex towards fin* **6/1**[3]

4002 **2** 3/4 **Lexington Place**[9] 2775 6-10-0 **84**....... JamesSullivan 5 91
(Ruth Carr) *dwlt: hld up in last: hdwy 2f out: nt clr run and swtchd rt 1f out: styd on to take 2nd post* **11/4**[1]

-005 **3** shd **Plagiarism (USA)**[12] 2683 3-9-2 **79**....... WilliamBuick 3 83
(Mark Johnston) *n.m.r sn after s: towards rr: hdwy on outside over 2f out: upsides over 1f out: kpt on same pce last 75yds* **8/1**

1510 **4** 1 1/4 **Equally Fast**[18] 2504 4-9-11 **84**.......(b) RobHornby(3) 4 86
(William Muir) *wnt bdly lft after 100yds and collided: trckd ldrs: kpt on same pce last 150yds* **13/2**

0033 **5** 1/2 **Bashiba (IRE)**[9] 2775 5-9-7 **77**.......(t) GrahamGibbons 2 77
(Nigel Tinkler) *w ldrs: bdly bmpd after 100yds: almost upsides over 1f out: kpt on same pce* **4/1**[2]

0-42 **6** hd **Ruby's Day**[15] 2572 7-9-2 **72**....... TomEaves 8 72
(David Brown) *chsd ldrs: kpt on same pce over 1f out* **11/1**

-060 **7** 1/2 **Master Bond**[13] 2665 7-9-10 **80**....... DavidNolan 6 78
(David O'Meara) *chsd ldrs: one pce over 1f out* **13/2**

-640 **8** 1 1/2 **Margrets Gift**[8] 2794 5-9-3 **73**.......(p) DavidAllan 9 65
(Tim Easterby) *drvn to chse ldrs 1/2-way: fdd appr fnl f* **16/1**

1m 0.11s (-0.69) **Going Correction** +0.025s/f (Good)
WFA 3 from 4yo+ 7lb **8** Ran SP% **112.9**
Speed ratings (Par 105): **106,104,104,102,101 101,100,98**
CSF £22.30 CT £132.82 TOTE £6.90: £2.40, £1.40, £2.60; EX 33.20 Trifecta £182.90.
Owner C R Marks (banbury) **Bred** C R Marks (Banbury) **Trained** Chastleton, Oxon

FOCUS
The race distance was as advertised. A useful handicap in which the field raced in the centre. The gallop was not a breakneck one for a sprint. A length pb from the winner.

3057 MOGS ON YET ANOTHER STAG DO H'CAP — 1m 2f 95y
9:15 (9:15) (Class 4) (0-80,80) 4-Y-O+ **£5,336** (£1,588; £793; £396) **Stalls** Centre

Form / RPR

3-02 **1** **Demonstration (IRE)**[23] 2328 4-9-7 **80**.......(p) JoeFanning 4 86
(William Jarvis) *mde all: qcknd pce over 5f out: drvn over 2f out: hld on all out clsng stages* **13/2**

-264 **2** 1/2 **Jolievitesse (FR)**[29] 2163 4-9-3 **76**....... JoeyHaynes 3 81
(K R Burke) *hld up in rr: hdwy on ins 4f out: chsng ldrs and n.m.r over 2f out: kpt on to take 2nd post* **7/2**[2]

0111 **3** nse **Inniscastle Lad**[14] 2623 4-9-6 **79**.......(b) WilliamBuick 7 84
(Ed Dunlop) *trckd wnr: drvn over 3f out: styd on same pce fnl 150yds* **5/1**[3]

2-05 **4** 1 1/4 **Kapstadt (FR)**[16] 2556 6-9-6 **79**....... PaulMulrennan 5 82
(Ian Williams) *hld up: sn trcking ldrs: effrt over 3f out: kpt on one pce fnl f* **13/2**

5-52 **5** nk **Stardrifter**[13] 2662 4-9-0 **73**....... TonyHamilton 6 75
(Richard Fahey) *hld up in rr: hdwy over 6f out: drvn 3f out: chsng ldrs over 1f out: one pce* **3/1**[1]

-043 **6** 1 **Lord Franklin**[12] 2688 7-9-5 **78**....... JasonHart 2 78
(Eric Alston) *hld up: sn trcking ldrs: nt clr run and swtchd lft over 1f out: fdd clsng stages* **12/1**

0000 **7** 2 1/4 **The Character (IRE)**[13] 2651 5-8-13 **72**....... RichardKingscote 1 68
(Tom Dascombe) *chsd ldrs: lost pl over 2f out: no threat after* **11/2**

2m 10.68s (-4.82) **Going Correction** -0.375s/f (Firm) **7** Ran SP% **113.6**
Speed ratings (Par 105): **104,103,103,102,102 101,99**
CSF £29.00 TOTE £6.70: £3.00, £2.30; EX 28.70 Trifecta £174.90.
Owner P C J Dalby & R D Schuster **Bred** Floors Farming, S Roy & Admington Hall **Trained** Newmarket, Suffolk

FOCUS
Rail movements reduced the length of this race by 2yds. A fair handicap in which the gallop was steady until the 3f marker and this bare form doesn't look reliable. A turf pb from the winner.

T/Plt: £62.60 to a £1 stake. Pool: £69,118.41 - 805.94 winning units. T/Qpdt: £22.00 to a £1 stake. Pool: £5,064.65 - 170.03 winning units. **Walter Glynn**

2240 NEWBURY (L-H)
Thursday, June 9

OFFICIAL GOING: Good to firm (7.2)
Wind: almost nil Weather: sunny

3058 BE WISER INSURANCE NOVICE STKS (PLUS 10 RACE) — 6f 110y
2:00 (2:03) (Class 4) 2-Y-O **£4,043** (£1,203; £601; £300) **Stalls** Centre

Form / RPR

1 **Aardwolf (USA)** 2-9-2 0....... JamesDoyle 12 81+
(Mark Johnston) *a.p: led 2f out: sn rdn: jst hld on* **5/1**[3]

2 shd **Sea Fox (IRE)** 2-9-2 0....... FMBerry 8 81+
(David Evans) *mid-div: rdn 2f out: no imp tl r.o ent fnl f: fin strly: jst failed* **12/1**

3 hd **Ronald R (IRE)** 2-9-2 0....... JamieSpencer 11 80+
(Michael Bell) *s.i.s: towards rr: hdwy 2f out: r.o wl ins fnl f: wnt 2nd briefly fnl 100yds: clsng on wnr at fin* **16/1**

4 1 1/4 **Asaas (USA)** 2-9-2 0....... AndreaAtzeni 4 77+
(Roger Varian) *led tl rdn 2f out: kpt on same pce fnl f* **9/2**[2]

5 1/2 **Bacchus** 2-9-2 0....... JimmyFortune 5 75+
(Brian Meehan) *trckd ldrs: rdn and ev ch fr 2f out tl edgd lft ent fnl f: no ex fnl 140yds* **25/1**

6 shd **Dourado (IRE)** 2-9-2 0....... RyanMoore 3 75+
(Richard Hannon) *s.i.s: sn mid-div: hdwy over 2f out: rdn over 1f out: kpt on same pce ins fnl f* **11/4**[1]

7 1 **Pillar Of Society (IRE)** 2-9-2 0....... PatDobbs 7 72+
(Richard Hannon) *racd keenly: trckd ldrs: rdn over 2f out: sn one pce* **25/1**

8 1/2 **Hurricane Rush (IRE)** 2-9-2 0....... DarryllHolland 13 71+
(Charles Hills) *s.i.s: towards rr: styd on fnl f: nvr a factor* **16/1**

9 1 1/2 **Sufrah (USA)** 2-9-2 0....... FrankieDettori 6 67
(Brian Meehan) *mid-div: rdn and hdwy 2f out: wknd ins fnl f* **12/1**

10 hd **Sfumato** 2-9-2 0....... GeorgeBaker 2 66+
(Roger Charlton) *trckd ldrs: rdn over 2f out: wknd ins fnl f* **9/2**[2]

11 2 **Permanent** 2-9-2 0....... TimmyMurphy 1 60
(Daniel Kubler) *slowly away and jinked lft: a towards rr* **66/1**

5 **12** 9 **Phoenix Dawn**[19] 2478 2-9-2 0....... MartinDwyer 15 35
(Brendan Powell) *mid-div tl wknd 2f out* **50/1**

13 3 3/4 **Poetic Force (IRE)** 2-9-2 0....... JimCrowley 10 25
(Jonathan Portman) *towards rr of midfield: sme hdwy over 3f out: wknd over 1f out* **33/1**

1m 18.7s (-0.60) **Going Correction** -0.175s/f (Firm) **13** Ran SP% **120.9**
Speed ratings (Par 95): **96,95,95,94,93 93,92,91,90,89 87,77,73**
CSF £61.29 TOTE £5.50: £2.00, £3.30, £3.80; EX 76.40 Trifecta £896.00.
Owner Sheikh Hamdan bin Mohammed Al Maktoum **Bred** Darley **Trained** Middleham Moor, N Yorks

FOCUS
Race distance as advertised. Jockeys felt the ground was 'beautiful'. A race that threw up some smart performers when it was run as a maiden, most notably Toronado, and plenty of these look capable of making up into useful performers. However the race is rated at the bottom end of the race averages. They went quite a good pace and the closers nearly benefited.

3059 CROSSLAND EBF STALLIONS MAIDEN FILLIES' STKS (PLUS 10 RACE) — 1m (S)
2:30 (2:33) (Class 4) 3-Y-O **£5,336** (£1,588; £793; £396) **Stalls** Centre

Form / RPR

6-0 **1** **Aghaany**[19] 2470 3-9-0 0....... AndreaAtzeni 1 83+
(Roger Varian) *a.p: led 2f out: sn rdn: kpt on wl fnl f* **6/1**

4 **2** 3/4 **Side Hill (USA)**[19] 2483 3-9-0 0....... JamesDoyle 7 81
(John Gosden) *led tl rdn 2f out: kpt on gamely fnl f but a being hld by wnr* **10/3**[2]

5-2 **3** hd **Volition (IRE)**[19] 2483 3-9-0 0....... RyanMoore 4 80
(Sir Michael Stoute) *s.i.s: mid-div: hdwy 3f out: rdn to dispute 2nd ent fnl f: kpt on but no ex nring fin* **2/1**[1]

4 1 3/4 **Entsar (IRE)** 3-9-0 0....... FrankieDettori 10 75+
(William Haggas) *mid-div: hdwy over 2f out: sn rdn to chse ldrs: kpt on same pce fnl f* **8/1**

2 **5** 1 3/4 **Dame Judi (IRE)**[24] 2312 3-9-0 0....... JamieSpencer 12 71
(Simon Crisford) *prom: rdn and ev ch 2f out: disputing 2nd ent fnl f: no ex fnl 120yds* **11/2**[3]

0 **6** 2 1/4 **Alaskan Breeze (IRE)**[19] 2483 3-9-0 0....... JimmyFortune 11 66
(Brian Meehan) *s.i.s: towards rr: rdn and hdwy over 1f out: styd on fnl f but n.d to ldrs* **33/1**

000 **7** 3/4 **Rock Palm (IRE)**[19] 2459 3-9-0 0....... MartinDwyer 13 64
(Brendan Powell) *trckd ldrs: rdn 3f out: wknd fnl f* **100/1**

0- **8** nk **Limonata (IRE)**[276] 6163 3-9-0 0....... OisinMurphy 2 63+
(Henry Candy) *mid-div tl outpcd 4f out: in last pair ent fnl f: no ch whn styd on fnl 120yds* **33/1**

0- **9** 1/2 **Aurora Gray**[210] 7811 3-9-0 0....... PatDobbs 3 62
(Hughie Morrison) *little slowly away: sn trcking ldrs: rdn over 2f out: wknd fnl f* **33/1**

10 nk **Sycara (IRE)** 3-9-0 0.......[1] JimCrowley 5 61
(Jeremy Noseda) *s.i.s: sn mid-div: rdn over 2f out: nvr threatened: fdd fnl f* **25/1**

0 **11** 1 **Encore Moi**[24] 2312 3-9-0 0....... FMBerry 8 59
(Marco Botti) *hld up towards rr: rdn over 2f out: nvr any real imp: fdd ins fnl f* **40/1**

12 2 1/2 **Chandon Elysees** 3-8-9 0....... HectorCrouch(5) 14 53
(Gary Moore) *mid-div: rdn 2f out: sn wknd* **100/1**

13 1 **Corella (IRE)** 3-9-0 0....... JohnFahy 6 50+
(Clive Cox) *racd keenly: mid-div: rdn 2f out: wknd fnl f* **50/1**

1m 39.88s (0.18) **Going Correction** -0.175s/f (Firm) **13** Ran SP% **116.2**
Speed ratings (Par 98): **92,91,91,89,87 85,84,84,83,83 82,79,78**
CSF £24.06 TOTE £6.30: £1.80, £1.50, £1.40; EX 28.30 Trifecta £120.70.
Owner Hamdan Al Maktoum **Bred** Shadwell Estate Company Limited **Trained** Newmarket, Suffolk

FOCUS
Race distance as advertised. Not much pace on for what was a useful fillies' maiden, but the right horses still came to the fore. The winner was a big improver from his Goodwood race that has worked out well.

3060 LORD WEINSTOCK MEMORIAL EBF STALLIONS STKS (LISTED RACE) (FILLIES) 1m 2f 6y
3:05 (3:06) (Class 1) 3-Y-O

£28,355 (£10,750; £5,380; £2,680; £1,345; £675) **Stalls** Centre

Form RPR

4-1 **1** **Abingdon (USA)**[34] 1989 3-9-0 87 RyanMoore 8 98+
(Sir Michael Stoute) *trckd ldr: led 3f out: rdn ent fnl f: styd on and a holding on: drvn out* **2/1**[2]

10 **2** ½ **Beauly**[26] 2245 3-9-0 90 [1] JamesDoyle 1 96
(Charles Hills) *trckd ldrs: chsd wnr 2f out: sn rdn: styd on wl towards fin but a being hld* **9/1**[3]

3-1 **3** 4 ½ **Snow Moon**[34] 2009 3-9-0 90 FrankieDettori 9 87+
(John Gosden) *stdd to last after 4f: rdn and stdy prog fr over 2f out: wnt 3rd jst ins fnl f: nvr any threat to front pair* **10/11**[1]

1350 **4** 1 ¾ **Motdaw**[26] 2244 3-9-0 78 OisinMurphy 6 84
(Mick Channon) *hld up bhd ldrs: rdn over 2f out: kpt on fnl f but nvr gng pce to get involved* **66/1**

01-5 **5** 1 **Tiptree (IRE)**[39] 1890 3-9-0 93 JamieSpencer 5 82
(Luca Cumani) *hld up bhd ldrs: rdn 2f out: chal for 3rd briefly ent fnl f: no ex fnl 75yds* **9/1**[3]

1-53 **6** 2 ½ **Play Gal**[21] 2394 3-9-0 91 JFEgan 4 77
(David Evans) *led: pushed along over 4f out: rdn and hdd 2f out: no ex fnl f* **20/1**

4-62 **7** 10 **Pleasure Dome**[21] 2395 3-9-0 82 JimmyFortune 3 58
(Peter Chapple-Hyam) *trckd ldrs: rdn over 2f out: sn wknd* **50/1**

2m 5.47s (-3.33) **Going Correction** -0.175s/f (Firm) 7 Ran SP% **113.9**
Speed ratings (Par 104): **106,105,102,100,99 97,89**
CSF £19.34 TOTE £3.00: £1.60, £3.30; EX 19.50 Trifecta £35.70.
Owner Ballymacoll Stud **Bred** Ballymacoll Stud **Trained** Newmarket, Suffolk

FOCUS
Race distance increased by 14yds. An unsatisfactory race, with there being little pace on and the duel between the two well-bred, highly promising market leaders failing to materialise. Nonetheless, the winner is highly promising. The form is rated around the runner-up to her C&D latest.

3061 COMAX H'CAP 1m (S)
3:40 (3:42) (Class 4) (0-85,85) 4-Y-O+ **£6,469** (£1,925; £962; £481) **Stalls** Centre

Form RPR

20-0 **1** **Iconic (IRE)**[22] 2378 4-9-3 81 OisinMurphy 12 90+
(Henry Candy) *led nrside gp: overall ldr whn gps merged over 2f out: jst hld on: all out* **25/1**

230- **2** hd **Weld Al Emarat**[293] 5602 4-9-7 85 JamieSpencer 13 93
(Simon Crisford) *swtchd to centre after 2f: trckd ldrs: rdn 2f out: kpt on wl fnl f: jst hld* **7/2**[1]

2601 **3** nk **Exceeding Power**[27] 2213 5-8-0 71 GeorgeWood(7) 5 78
(Martin Bosley) *racd centre: trckd ldrs: rdn 2f out: kpt on wl ins fnl f* **8/1**

32-6 **4** ½ **Ataman (IRE)**[33] 2043 4-8-13 77 JamesDoyle 2 83
(Chris Wall) *racd centre: mid-div: rdn and hdwy fr 2f out: wnt 4th ins fnl f: kpt on* **11/2**[2]

0-25 **5** 1 ¾ **Dutch Law**[22] 2378 4-9-4 82 (b) JimCrowley 8 84
(Hughie Morrison) *racd centre: mid-div: smooth hdwy 2f out: swtchd rt for effrt ent fnl f: nt qckn* **6/1**[3]

0-04 **6** hd **Cricklewood Green (USA)**[23] 2324 5-8-12 76 PatDobbs 4 77
(Sylvester Kirk) *racd centre: mid-div: hdwy 2f out: sn rdn: kpt on same pce fnl f* **8/1**

6-24 **7** ½ **Squire**[47] 1633 5-9-1 79 AndreaAtzeni 15 79
(Michael Attwater) *racd nrside: mid-div: rdn over 1f out: kpt on fnl f: nvr a threat* **9/1**

0-34 **8** 1 **Baltic Brave (IRE)**[20] 2430 5-9-7 85 RyanMoore 14 83
(Hughie Morrison) *racd centre: hld up: swtchd lft for effrt over 1f out: nvr goi ng pce to get on terms* **12/1**

2504 **9** nse **Childesplay**[14] 2621 5-9-5 83 (p) FrankieDettori 10 80
(Heather Main) *racd nrside: nvr bttr than mid-div* **25/1**

6101 **10** ¾ **Jack Of Diamonds (IRE)**[43] 1797 7-9-5 83 RobertWinston 9 79
(Roger Teal) *racd nrside: stdd s: hdwy 2f out: sn rdn: nt pce to get involved* **14/1**

-206 **11** 2 **Gannicus**[19] 2460 5-8-9 73 (tp) LiamKeniry 1 64
(Brendan Powell) *racd centre: a towards rr* **25/1**

-604 **12** ½ **Edge Of Heaven**[29] 2154 4-9-4 82 GeorgeBaker 11 72
(Jonathan Portman) *racd nrside: trckd ldr: rdn and edgd lft fr 2f out: wknd fnl f* **40/1**

1100 **13** 54 **Harry Holland**[22] 2378 4-9-3 81 (b) MartinDwyer 7
(William Muir) *led centre gp tl wknd qckly over 2f out* **16/1**

1m 37.1s (-2.60) **Going Correction** -0.175s/f (Firm) 13 Ran SP% **118.3**
Speed ratings (Par 105): **106,105,105,105,103 103,102,101,101,100 98,98,44**
CSF £106.54 CT £816.56 TOTE £32.60: £6.40, £2.20, £4.10; EX 220.20 Trifecta £843.30.
Owner First Of Many And Turner **Bred** Noel O'Callaghan **Trained** Kingston Warren, Oxon

FOCUS
Race distance as advertised. A messy race in the early stages, with two horses establishing a lead, albeit well away from each other, and it took a while for a few of the runners, most notably the runner-up, to decide which one to chase, with them establishing into two groups. The winner can do better than the bare form.

3062 BE WISER INSURANCE "RESTRICTED" H'CAP 7f (S)
4:10 (4:13) (Class 5) (0-75,75) 3-Y-O **£3,234** (£962; £481; £240) **Stalls** Centre

Form RPR

0-60 **1** **Blackout (FR)**[29] 2161 3-9-7 75 PatDobbs 13 89
(Richard Hannon) *s.i.s: towards rr: stdy prog fr 3f out: rdn over 1f out: str run ent fnl f: led fnl 120yds: rdn out* **20/1**

5-35 **2** nk **Generalship (IRE)**[26] 2248 3-9-4 72 (b) JamesDoyle 4 85
(John Gosden) *trckd ldrs: rdn to chal 2f out: led ent fnl f: kpt on but no ex whn hdd fnl 120yds* **11/4**[1]

235- **3** 2 ¾ **Red Tea**[202] 7921 3-8-13 67 FMBerry 2 75+
(Peter Hiatt) *s.i.s: hld up: sme prog whn nt clr run briefly wl over 1f out: r.o strly fnl f: snatched 3rd fnl strides* **12/1**

0-34 **4** nk **Shadow Game**[23] 2322 3-9-4 72 FrannyNorton 5 77
(Mark Johnston) *led: rdn and hdd ent fnl f: kpt on same pce* **8/1**

31-5 **5** nk **Izmir (IRE)**[47] 1630 3-9-5 73 RyanMoore 3 77
(William Haggas) *mid-div: hdwy 2f out: sn rdn: wnt 3rd over 1f out: no ex fnl 120yds* **3/1**[2]

024- **6** 1 ¼ **Kitaaby (IRE)**[285] 5851 3-9-7 75 JimmyFortune 7 76
(Brian Meehan) *trckd ldrs: rdn 2f out: one pce fnl f* **12/1**

03-0 **7** 2 **Arlecchino's Rock**[18] 2506 3-9-0 68 [1] LiamKeniry 9 63
(Mark Usher) *racd keenly: hld up: swtchd rt 2f out: sn rdn: sme late prog but nvr any threat* **25/1**

060 **8** 1 ½ **Lillyput (IRE)**[19] 2470 3-8-8 62 JFEgan 10 53
(Mick Channon) *nvr bttr than mid-div* **25/1**

4624 **9** 2 ¼ **Lucky Louie**[28] 2186 3-8-13 67 RobertWinston 12 56
(Roger Teal) *trckd ldrs: effrt 2f out: wknd ins fnl f* **7/1**[3]

0-00 **10** ½ **Show Legend**[24] 2299 3-9-5 73 JamieSpencer 1 57
(Michael Bell) *mid-div: rdn 2f out: nvr threatened: wknd ins fnl f* **25/1**

F00- **11** ½ **Lorelina**[161] 8409 3-8-6 65 EdwardGreatrex(5) 6 48
(Andrew Balding) *mid-div tl outpcd 2f out: no threat after* **20/1**

01-0 **12** 1 ¾ **Desirable**[28] 2185 3-8-9 63 OisinMurphy 14 41
(Hughie Morrison) *prom tl hung lft and wknd 2f out* **66/1**

006 **13** 1 ½ **Attitude Rocks**[78] 1036 3-8-8 62 JohnFahy 8 36
(Clive Cox) *s.i.s: a towards rr* **20/1**

1m 23.79s (-1.91) **Going Correction** -0.175s/f (Firm) 13 Ran SP% **118.0**
Speed ratings (Par 99): **103,102,99,99,98 97,95,93,90,90 89,87,85**
CSF £68.60 CT £739.73 TOTE £20.60: £5.30, £1.60, £3.60; EX 106.90 Trifecta £2111.80.
Owner Martin Hughes & Michael Kerr-Dineen **Bred** S A R L Haras Du Logis Saint Germain **Trained** East Everleigh, Wilts

FOCUS
Race distance as advertised. A fairly modest handicap and, as in the previous race, one of the outsiders came more towards the stands' side to narrowly deny the favourite. The winner finally built on his maiden win last year.

3063 INSURE WISER H'CAP 1m 4f 5y
4:45 (4:46) (Class 5) (0-70,70) 3-Y-O **£3,234** (£962; £481; £240) **Stalls** Centre

Form RPR

3404 **1** **Muaither (IRE)**[14] 2615 3-9-2 65 (b) FrankieDettori 2 74
(John Gosden) *mid-div: hdwy over 4f out: rdn to chse ldr 2f out: led ins fnl f: styd on wl* **13/2**[3]

6-25 **2** ¾ **Admiral's Sunset**[17] 2548 3-9-5 68 GeorgeBaker 3 75
(Hughie Morrison) *led: rdn 2f out: battled on gamely: hdd ins fnl f: styd on but no ex* **8/1**

350 **3** 1 ¾ **Niceonecenturion**[21] 2414 3-9-6 69 JimCrowley 9 73
(William Knight) *hld up towards rr: hdwy 4f out: rdn over 2f out: wnt 3rd over 1f out: styd on* **9/1**

05-4 **4** 1 ¾ **Zubeida**[21] 2395 3-9-5 68 JamesDoyle 12 69+
(Ismail Mohammed) *mid-div: wandered u.p and lost pl over 2f out: styd on ins fnl f: wnt 4th fnl strides* **14/1**

6-53 **5** hd **Cliffs Of Dover**[13] 2639 3-9-1 64 FMBerry 7 65
(Charles Hills) *hld up towards rr: rdn and hdwy fr 3f out: wnt 4th ent fnl f: styd on same pce* **8/1**

5-52 **6** nk **Duck A L'Orange (IRE)**[24] 2300 3-9-7 70 JamieSpencer 11 71
(Michael Bell) *hld up bhd: rdn and hdwy fr 2f out: styd on fnl f but nt pce to get on terms* **5/1**[2]

-553 **7** 2 **Molten Gold**[14] 2615 3-9-6 69 RyanMoore 8 66
(Andrew Balding) *hld up towards rr: hdwy 4f out: rdn to chse ldrs over 2f out: fdd ins fnl f* **4/1**[1]

44-0 **8** 1 ¾ **Mystikana**[12] 2700 3-8-7 63 (b[1]) TylerSaunders(7) 1 58
(Marcus Tregoning) *racd keenly: trckd ldrs: chal gng wl over 3f out tl rdn 2f out: sn hld: fdd ins fnl f* **66/1**

0-16 **9** 1 **Elocution**[22] 2366 3-8-11 60 OisinMurphy 5 53
(Denis Coakley) *trckd ldrs: rdn over 2f out: wknd over 1f out* **10/1**

6-63 **10** 1 **Ochos Rios**[6] 2851 3-8-7 56 JFEgan 10 47
(David Evans) *stmbld leaving stalls: mid-div: rdn 3f out: nvr any imp: wknd fnl f* **14/1**

003 **11** 4 ½ **Sixties Idol**[15] 2589 3-8-7 56 LiamKeniry 6 40
(Mick Channon) *mid-div tl rdn over 3f out: wknd 2f out* **33/1**

2314 **12** ½ **Dr Drey (IRE)**[13] 2644 3-9-7 70 JimmyFortune 14 53
(Jamie Osborne) *trckd ldr: rdn over 3f out: wknd 2f out* **16/1**

2m 33.0s (-2.50) **Going Correction** -0.175s/f (Firm) 12 Ran SP% **115.0**
Speed ratings (Par 99): **101,100,99,98,98 97,96,95,94,94 91,90**
CSF £55.90 CT £468.95 TOTE £7.50: £2.70, £3.00, £3.60; EX 57.20 Trifecta £603.30.
Owner Al Shaqab Racing **Bred** New England, Myriad & Mount Coote **Trained** Newmarket, Suffolk
■ Stewards' Enquiry : Tyler Saunders one-day ban: weighed in 2lb heavy (23 June)

FOCUS
Race distance increased by 14yds. They went a solid gallop in this ordinary handicap and were spread across the track in the straight. The form is rated on the positive side.

3064 WISER ACADEMY AMATEUR RIDERS' H'CAP 1m 2f 6y
5:15 (5:20) (Class 5) (0-70,69) 4-Y-O+ **£3,119** (£967; £483; £242) **Stalls** Centre

Form RPR

456/ **1** **Good Of Luck**[19] 322 7-10-2 60 (p) MrThomasGreatrex(3) 6 75+
(Warren Greatrex) *hld up bhd: hdwy 3f out: rdn 2f out: led ent fnl f: styd on strly: rdn out* **7/1**[3]

20-1 **2** 3 ½ **City Ground (USA)**[5] 2899 9-10-11 66 6ex MissSBrotherton 13 74
(Michael Appleby) *trckd ldrs: rdn 3f out: ev ch over 1f out tl ent fnl f: styd on but nt pce of wnr* **15/8**[1]

0-05 **3** 2 **Silver Alliance**[31] 2085 8-10-10 65 (b[1]) MrRBirkett 8 70+
(Julia Feilden) *trckd ldrs early: midfield after 2f: hdwy 4f out: led 3f out: rdn and hdd ent fnl f: no ex* **16/1**

0-65 **4** 3 **Collodi (GER)**[6] 2872 7-10-8 68 (p) MissPBridgwater(5) 10 67
(David Bridgwater) *slowly away: towards rr: gd hdwy 4f out: ev ch 3f out: rdn and drifted rt wl over 1f out: styd on same pce fnl f* **12/1**

2224 **5** 2 ½ **I'm Harry**[22] 2374 7-11-0 69 (vt) MrSWalker 2 63
(George Baker) *hld up towards rr: hdwy 4f out: rdn over 2f out: styd on same pce* **8/1**

5- **6** 2 ¾ **Three Colours Red (IRE)**[34] 6794 4-10-4 66 (tp) MrBHicks(7) 5 55
(Warren Greatrex) *mid-div: rdn over 3f out: styd on same pce fnl 2f: nvr trbld ldrs* **7/1**[3]

0046 **7** 13 **Jazri**[6] 2872 5-9-12 60 (b) MrJCJones(7) 15 24
(Milton Bradley) *nvr bttr than mid-div* **16/1**

0-06 **8** 9 **Rum Swizzle**[16] 2564 4-10-6 64 (v[1]) MissPFuller(3) 9 11
(Harry Dunlop) *chsd ldrs: rdn over 4f out: ev ch 3f out: sn wknd* **33/1**

-510 **9** ½ **Victor's Bet (SPA)**[6] 2872 7-10-9 69 MissEllaSmith(5) 4 15
(Ralph J Smith) *towards rr: rapid hdwy on outer to dispute ld over 6f out: rdn 4f out: hdd 3f out: sn wknd* **6/1**[2]

0004 **10** 4 **Altaira**[19] 2461 5-10-0 55 MissJoannaMason 3
(Tony Carroll) *led tl 6f out: disp over 4f out tl 3f out: wknd qckly* **33/1**

2-03 **11** 1 **Azure Amour (IRE)**[29] 2144 4-10-1 56 MrPMillman 14
(Rod Millman) *mid-div tl 4f out: sn bhd* **16/1**

-006 **12** *14* **Alketios (GR)**[34] 2006 5-10-0 **62**.............................. MissGLDouble[(7)] 12
(Chris Gordon) *trckd ldrs: disp ld 6f out tl 4f out: sn wknd* **33/1**

2m 6.62s (-2.18) **Going Correction** -0.175s/f (Firm) **12** Ran SP% **119.3**
Speed ratings (Par 103): **101,98,96,94,92 90,79,72,72,68 68,56**
CSF £20.21 CT £202.81 TOTE £7.60: £2.40, £1.30, £4.90; EX 23.60 Trifecta £426.20.
Owner Bernard & Jane Panton **Bred** Mrs G Slater **Trained** Upper Lambourn, Berks

FOCUS
Race distance increased by 14yds. They got racing a long way out in this amateur riders' event and the race set up for the closers. A Flat pb from the winner.
T/Plt: £426.60 to a £1 stake. Pool: £69,486.97 - 118.89 winning units. T/Qpdt: £137.60 to a £1 stake. Pool: £4,444.51 - 23.90 winning units. **Tim Mitchell**

2793 NOTTINGHAM (L-H)
Thursday, June 9

OFFICIAL GOING: Good to firm (good in places) changing to good to firm after race 2 (2.20)
Wind: Virtually nil Weather: Fine & dry

3065 BRITISH STALLION STUDS EBF NOVICE STKS 6f 15y
1:50 (1:50) (Class 5) 2-Y-0 **£3,234** (£962; £481; £240) **Stalls** High

Form RPR
1 **Blue Point (IRE)** 2-9-2 0.. WilliamBuick 5 85+
(Charlie Appleby) *cl up: led ent fnl f: green and sn edgd lft: pushed out: readily* **6/4**[2]

42 **2** *½* **Tafaakhor (IRE)**[13] 2648 2-9-2 0.. PaulHanagan 9 80
(Richard Hannon) *slt ld: rdn along over 1f out: hdd ent fnl f: sn drvn and edgd lft: kpt on* **4/6**[1]

5 **3** *2 ¾* **Mister Blue Sky (IRE)**[17] 2535 2-9-2 0.............................. LukeMorris 6 72
(Sylvester Kirk) *trckd ldrs: swtchd lft and effrt over 1f out: sn rdn and kpt on same pce* **16/1**[3]

00 **4** *2* **Maazel (IRE)**[9] 2757 2-9-2 0.. HarryBentley 1 66
(Roger Varian) *hld up: hdwy on outer 2f out: rdn over 1f out: no imp fnl f* **50/1**

5 **5** *8* **Rising Eagle**[17] 2543 2-8-13 0.............................. MichaelJMMurphy[(3)] 3 42
(Charles Hills) *t.k.h: trckd ldrs: effrt 2f out: rdn wl over 1f out: sn edgd rt and wknd* **66/1**

6 *3 ¼* **Spun Gold** 2-9-2 0.. AdamKirby 4 32
(Luca Cumani) *green: hld up in rr: pushed along 2f out: sn outpcd and eased* **25/1**

1m 13.82s (-0.88) **Going Correction** -0.30s/f (Firm) **6** Ran SP% **113.2**
Speed ratings (Par 93): **93,92,88,86,75 71**
CSF £2.83 TOTE £2.30: £1.30, £1.10; EX 3.00 Trifecta £10.10.
Owner Godolphin **Bred** Oak Lodge Bloodstock **Trained** Newmarket, Suffolk

FOCUS
The ground was officially good to firm, good in places (watered). Outer track in operation with the rail set out 2yds on the home bend, adding around 6yds to race distances on the round course. An interesting novice event to start. It was a two-horse race according to the market and that is how it panned out, with the winning time 3.22sec outside standard. The form is rated on the cautious side.

3066 CARLING CUSTOMER MAIDEN STKS 1m 75y
2:20 (2:21) (Class 5) 3-Y-O+ **£2,911** (£866; £432; £216) **Stalls** Centre

Form RPR
0 **1** **Staunch**[23] 2340 3-9-2 0.. AdamKirby 3 90+
(Clive Cox) *midfield: hdwy over 3f out: chsd ldng pair over 1f out: rdn to ld ins fnl f: kpt on strly* **8/1**

3-32 **2** *3 ¼* **Perigee**[14] 2614 3-9-2 80.. RobertHavlin 6 82
(John Gosden) *trckd ldrs: cl up 3f out: led 2f out and sn rdn: drvn and hdd ins fnl f: kpt on same pce* **1/1**[1]

3-03 **3** *1 ½* **Jimenez (IRE)**[19] 2479 3-9-2 76.. JoeFanning 8 78
(Brian Meehan) *sn trcking ldr: effrt over 2f out and sn rdn along: drvn over 1f out: kpt on same pce* **7/2**[2]

0- **4** *½* **Eljeemi (IRE)**[219] 7673 3-9-2 0.................................... GrahamGibbons 1 77
(William Haggas) *led: pushed along 3f out: hdd 2f out: sn drvn and grad wknd* **6/1**[3]

5 *2 ½* **Heart Of Oak** 3-8-11 0.. LukeMorris 9 66
(George Peckham) *in tch: hdwy to chse ldrs 3f out: rdn along over 2f out: drvn wl over 1f out: kpt on one pce* **33/1**

5-6 **6** *½* **Master Gunner (USA)**[28] 2175 3-9-2 0.............................. TedDurcan 4 70
(Sir Michael Stoute) *in tch: effrt over 3f out and sn pushed along: rdn over 2f out: sn drvn and plugged on one pce* **7/1**

60 **7** *6* **Shrubland**[17] 2541 3-9-2 0.. RichardKingscote 10 55
(Ed Walker) *dwlt: a in rr* **66/1**

0 **8** *12* **Keyman (IRE)**[23] 2320 3-9-2 0.. MartinLane 5 26
(Jeremy Gask) *a in rr* **100/1**

9 *7* **Out Of The Ashes** 3-9-2 0... PaulMulrennan 2 10
(Philip McBride) *a in rr* **100/1**

0-0 **10** *½* **Respectability**[10] 2735 4-9-8 0.. TomEaves 7 6
(Ivan Furtado) *prom: pushed along over 4f out: rdn wl over 3f out and sn wknd* **100/1**

1m 44.49s (-4.51) **Going Correction** -0.30s/f (Firm)
WFA 3 from 4yo 11lb **10** Ran SP% **117.0**
Speed ratings (Par 103): **110,106,105,104,102 101,95,83,76,76**
CSF £16.65 TOTE £8.70: £2.20, £1.02, £1.70; EX 19.70 Trifecta £79.50.
Owner Cheveley Park Stud **Bred** Cheveley Park Stud Ltd **Trained** Lambourn, Berks

FOCUS
Rail movement added around 6yds to race distance. Not the most competitive of maidens, but they went a good pace and the winner did it nicely. The form is rated around the second and third.

3067 FREE MONTH TRIAL OF RACING UK H'CAP 1m 6f 15y
2:50 (2:50) (Class 6) (0-60,60) 4-Y-O+ **£2,264** (£673; £336; £168) **Stalls** Low

Form RPR
5-04 **1** **Duke Of Diamonds**[37] 1955 4-8-13 **55**...................... ShelleyBirkett[(3)] 12 64
(Julia Feilden) *trckd ldrs: swtchd rt and hdwy 3f out: rdn to ld wl over 1f out: clr ins fnl f: styd on strly* **7/1**[3]

/0-4 **2** *4* **Impeccability**[26] 1136 6-8-7 **46** oh1........................(p) RoystonFfrench 9 48
(John Mackie) *prom: hdwy to ld wl over 2f out: sn rdn: hdd and drvn wl over 1f out: kpt on same pce* **20/1**

0-50 **3** *¾* **La Fritillaire**[10] 2745 4-8-11 **50**.. TomEaves 16 51
(James Given) *prom: pushed along 3f out: rdn 2f out: sn drvn and kpt on same pce* **20/1**

0103 **4** *nk* **Frosty The Snowman (IRE)**[10] 2746 5-9-2 **55**.......... JamesSullivan 17 55
(Ruth Carr) *trckd ldrs on outer: hdwy over 4f out: pushed along 3f out: rdn 2f out: drvn and kpt on fnl f* **5/1**[2]

06-0 **5** *hd* **Lineman**[77] 1057 6-9-6 **59**..(v) KieranO'Neill 4 59+
(Sarah Hollinshead) *hld up towards rr: hdwy on outer wl over 2f out: rdn wl over 1f out: kpt on: nrst fin* **22/1**

-005 **6** *½* **Ullswater (IRE)**[16] 2558 8-8-9 **53**................................(tp) PhilDennis[(5)] 5 53
(Philip Kirby) *hld up towards rr: hdwy on outer wl over 2f out: rdn along wl over 1f out: kpt on fnl f: nrst fin* **16/1**

-046 **7** *3 ½* **Black Iceman**[98] 796 8-8-4 **46** oh1............................ SimonPearce[(3)] 3 41
(Lydia Pearce) *bhd tl sme late hdwy* **33/1**

5 **8** *¾* **Irish Thistle (IRE)**[22] 2368 9-9-7 **60**................................ PaulMulrennan 1 54
(Dai Williams) *a towards rr* **16/1**

5-02 **9** *shd* **District Attorney (IRE)**[10] 2746 7-8-8 **47**.................. DuranFentiman 15 41
(Chris Fairhurst) *a towards rr* **16/1**

230- **10** *1 ½* **Ginger Fizz**[15] 1248 9-9-7 **60**.......................................(tp) LukeMorris 7 52
(Ben Case) *a towards rr* **15/2**

1601 **11** *½* **Desktop**[16] 2558 4-9-7 **60**.. PJMcDonald 10 51
(Antony Brittain) *in tch: pushed along over 3f out: rdn wl over 2f out: sn btn* **3/1**[1]

0005 **12** *¾* **Farrah's Choice**[31] 2086 4-8-2 **46** oh1............................ PaddyPilley[(5)] 8 36
(James Grassick) *led: rdn along 4f out: hdd wl over 2f out: sn drvn and wknd* **66/1**

6-04 **13** *1 ¾* **Noble Reach**[10] 2745 5-8-5 **49** ow2..........................(p) JordanNason[(5)] 2 37
(Lawrence Mullaney) *in tch on inner: pushed along over 3f out: rdn wl over 2f out: sn wknd* **10/1**

2-45 **14** *9* **Hall Of Beauty**[147] 170 4-8-9 **48**.................................... AndrewMullen 14 24
(Michael Appleby) *midfield: hdwy on outer to trck ldrs after 5f: chsd ldng pauir over 4f out: rdn along over 3f out: sn wknd* **9/1**

3m 4.99s (-2.01) **Going Correction** -0.30s/f (Firm) **14** Ran SP% **121.0**
Speed ratings (Par 101): **93,90,90,90,90 89,87,87,87,86 86,85,84,79**
CSF £147.08 CT £2676.16 TOTE £9.10: £2.80, £6.20, £7.40; EX 166.50 Trifecta £2243.30.
Owner Carol Bushnell & Partners **Bred** Barry Walters Farms **Trained** Exning, Suffolk

FOCUS
Rail movement added around 6yds to race distance. The going was changed to good to firm all over before this race.\n\x\x A moderate staying handicap and nothing got into it from off the pace, with the winner proving different gear. Ordinary form behind.

3068 START YOUR RACING UK FREE TRIAL H'CAP 6f 15y
3:25 (3:26) (Class 3) (0-90,89) 4-Y-O+
£7,470 (£2,236; £1,118; £559; £279; £140) **Stalls** High

Form RPR
-444 **1** **Growl**[26] 2259 4-9-5 **87**.. PaulHanagan 8 100
(Richard Fahey) *trckd ldrs: hdwy over 2f out: rdn to ld over 1f out: hung lft ins fnl f: kpt on* **7/2**[1]

3-52 **2** *1* **Pixeleen**[10] 2754 4-8-10 **78**...................................... RichardKingscote 5 88+
(Malcolm Saunders) *trckd ldrs: effrt whn nt clr run over 1f out: sn swtchd lft to outer and rdn ent fnl f: sn chsng wnr: kpt on* **5/1**[2]

21-0 **3** *2 ½* **Little Palaver**[27] 2206 4-9-6 **88**... AdamKirby 2 90
(Clive Cox) *cl up: rdn along 2f out and ev ch tl drvn and kpt on same pce fnl f* **20/1**

026 **4** *½* **Flowers On Venus (IRE)**[17] 2547 4-9-4 **86**............. GrahamGibbons 10 88+
(David Evans) *prom: n.m.r and lost pl 2f out: sn rdn and styd on fnl f* **6/1**[3]

00-0 **5** *shd* **Bahamian Heights**[19] 2480 5-8-13 **81**............................ LukeMorris 1 81
(Robert Cowell) *trckd ldrs: hdwy on outer 1/2-way: cl up 2f out: sn rdn and kpt on same pce fnl f* **50/1**

-011 **6** *1* **Upavon**[24] 2290 6-7-13 **74**......................................(t) MillyNaseb[(7)] 4 71
(Stuart Williams) *rrd and dwlt s: towards rr: hdwy over 1f out: kpt on fnl f* **6/1**[3]

5-00 **7** *1 ¼* **It Must Be Faith**[5] 2903 6-9-3 **85**.................................... MartinLane 6 78
(Michael Appleby) *led: rdn along 2f out: hdd over 1f out and grad wknd* **16/1**

6-04 **8** *¾* **Cartmell Cleave**[17] 2547 4-9-7 **89**.....................................(t) TedDurcan 7 79
(Stuart Kittow) *dwlt: a towards rr* **5/1**[2]

2416 **9** *2 ¼* **Explain**[14] 2613 4-9-2 **84**.. JamesSullivan 11 67
(Ruth Carr) *hld up: a towards rr* **8/1**

223- **10** *8* **Bushephalus (IRE)**[368] 2966 4-8-6 **74**.............................. JoeFanning 9 31
(Ivan Furtado) *dwlt: sn in tch: pushed along over 2f out: sn rdn and wknd over 1f out* **16/1**

1m 11.76s (-2.94) **Going Correction** -0.30s/f (Firm) **10** Ran SP% **113.7**
Speed ratings (Par 107): **107,105,102,101,101 100,98,97,94,83**
CSF £20.07 CT £306.86 TOTE £4.00: £1.50, £1.90, £4.30; EX 20.70 Trifecta £175.70.
Owner Dr Marwan Koukash **Bred** Kincorth Investments Inc **Trained** Musley Bank, N Yorks

FOCUS
A decent sprint handicap in which they went a good pace, but they spurned the nearside rail and all the action unfolded up the middle. The winner is rated back to his best.

3069 DOOM BAR SUMMER H'CAP (DIV I) 6f 15y
4:00 (4:03) (Class 6) (0-65,65) 3-Y-O+ **£2,264** (£673; £336; £168) **Stalls** High

Form RPR
-322 **1** **Rococoa (IRE)**[20] 2428 3-9-6 **65**.. LukeMorris 12 76+
(Ed Walker) *trckd ldrs: hdwy and cl up over 2f out: led 1 1/2f out: sn rdn clr: kpt on strly* **9/2**[1]

0445 **2** *2 ½* **Exotic Guest**[12] 2680 6-9-12 **63**................................(p) JamesSullivan 15 68
(Ruth Carr) *swtchd lft s: hld up and bhd: hdwy over 2f out: effrt whn n.m.r wl over 1f out: sn rdn: styd on strly fnl f* **5/1**[2]

-006 **3** *2* **Jebel Tara**[20] 2442 11-9-12 **63**.......................................(bt) DaleSwift 1 62
(Alan Brown) *cl up: ev ch 2f out: sn rdn and kpt on same pce fnl f* **18/1**

-500 **4** *nse* **Pryers Princess**[13] 2655 4-9-11 **62**................................ PJMcDonald 4 61
(David C Griffiths) *towards rr: hdwy over 2f out: rdn along wl over 1f out: chsd ldrs appr fnl f: sn drvn and kpt on same pce* **33/1**

0-40 **5** *½* **Hamish McGonagain**[24] 2302 3-9-0 **59**........................(p) MartinLane 2 54
(Jeremy Gask) *wnt rt s: hld up towards rr: hdwy on wd outside wl over 1f out: sn rdn and styd on fnl f* **20/1**

6103 **6** *1 ¼* **Secret Look**[12] 2697 6-9-13 **64**.....................................(p) AdamKirby 11 58
(Ed McMahon) *chsd ldrs: rdn along wl over 1f out: sn drvn and one pce fnl f* **9/2**[1]

-626 **7** *nse* **Comparinka**[46] 1670 3-8-10 **55**................................(p) KieranO'Neill 5 46
(Scott Dixon) *chsd ldrs: rdn along wl over 1f out: sn drvn and one pce* **33/1**

6000 **8** *¾* **Ershaad (IRE)**[19] 2491 4-9-2 **58**.............................. CharlieBennett[(5)] 3 49
(Shaun Harris) *dwlt and sltly hmpd s: in rr: hdwy on outer wl over 1f out: sn rdn and no imp ins fnl f* **50/1**

1033 **9** *nk* **First Excel**[17] 2542 4-9-3 **57**......................................(b) RobHornby[(3)] 6 47
(Roy Bowring) *prom: cl up 1/2-way: rdn along wl over 1f out: grad wknd* **8/1**[3]

652- **10** *2* **Desert River (IRE)**[243] 7107 3-9-3 **62**............................ JoeyHaynes 13 44
(Mark H Tompkins) *a towards rr* **18/1**

-004 **11** *nk* **Dalalah**[22] 2359 3-8-5 **50** ConnorBeasley 7 31
(Richard Guest) *nvr bttr than midfield* **16/1**

0232 **12** *hd* **Atrayu (IRE)**[31] 2107 3-9-4 **63** GrahamGibbons 10 44
(Paul D'Arcy) *slt ld: rdn along 2f out: hdd 1 1/2f out: sn wknd* **5/1**[2]

0-00 **13** *3 1/4* **Piccardo**[15] 2571 3-9-1 **60** JackGarritty 8 31
(Richard Fahey) *midfield: rdn along 2f out: sn wknd* **25/1**

5006 **14** *10* **Farang Jai Dee (IRE)**[10] 2741 4-8-9 **46** oh1 (b) DavidAllan 9
(Declan Carroll) *t.k.h: a towards rr* **50/1**

54-0 **15** *20* **Comparative**[22] 2379 4-9-9 **60** (v[1]) PaulMulrennan 14
(Lydia Pearce) *dwlt: a in rr: outpcd and bhd whn eased over 1f out* **16/1**

1m 12.27s (-2.43) **Going Correction** -0.30s/f (Firm)
WFA 3 from 4yo+ 8lb **15** Ran SP% **121.5**
Speed ratings (Par 101): **104,100,98,97,97 95,95,94,94,91 91,90,86,73,46**
CSF £24.56 CT £383.82 TOTE £4.80: £1.90, £2.10, £6.30; EX 22.80 Trifecta £448.30.
Owner Elaine Chivers & Merlin Racing **Bred** Tally-Ho Stud **Trained** Upper Lambourn, Berks

FOCUS
The first division of a moderate sprint handicap, won well by an unexposed 3yo filly. The form makes sense.

3070 DOOM BAR SUMMER H'CAP (DIV II) — 6f 15y
4:30 (4:32) (Class 6) (0-65,64) 3-Y-O+ **£2,264** (£673; £336; £168) **Stalls** High

Form RPR

-460 **1** **Goadby**[12] 2697 5-9-7 **57** RoystonFfrench 8 65
(John Holt) *cl up: rdn over 1f out: led jst ins fnl f: drvn out* **14/1**

5221 **2** *1* **Fortinbrass (IRE)**[45] 1712 6-9-2 **59** LewisEdmunds(5) 5 64
(John Balding) *prom: effrt wl over 1f out: rdn and ev ch ins fnl f: kpt on* **12/1**

3546 **3** *3/4* **Danish Duke (IRE)**[15] 2571 5-9-8 **58** (p) JamesSullivan 6 61
(Ruth Carr) *led: rdn over 1f out: drvn and hdd ins fnl f: kpt on* **8/1**[2]

0-00 **4** *1/2* **Etienne Gerard**[27] 2217 4-9-13 **63** (p) AndrewMullen 12 64+
(Nigel Tinkler) *hld up towards rr: hdwy 2f out: rdn over 1f out: styd on fnl f: nrst fin* **12/1**

2-32 **5** *shd* **Cadland Lad (IRE)**[14] 2609 3-8-6 **53** (t) DannyBrock(3) 9 52
(John Ryan) *chsd ldrs: rdn and ch over 1f out: sn drvn and kpt on same pce* **6/1**[1]

5-00 **6** *1/2* **Bold Grove**[17] 2542 4-8-6 **45** EoinWalsh(3) 11 44
(Edward Bevan) *dwlt and bhd: hdwy on outer over 2f out: sn rdn and styd on fnl f: nrst fin* **12/1**

2-50 **7** *1* **Oat Couture**[21] 2396 4-10-0 **64** TedDurcan 14 60
(Henry Candy) *hld up towards rr: hdwy on outer 1/2-way: in tch and rdn 2f out: kpt on one pce* **8/1**[2]

4666 **8** *3/4* **Potternello (IRE)**[52] 1533 4-9-5 **62** KillianHennessy(7) 7 56
(Mick Channon) *trckd ldrs: effrt wl over 1f out: sn rdn and wknd appr fnl f* **8/1**[2]

6000 **9** *1/2* **Men United (FR)**[18] 2506 3-8-12 **59** RobHornby(3) 10 50
(Roy Bowring) *t.k.h: hld up: a towards rr* **14/1**

4-22 **10** *1 1/2* **Minty Jones**[17] 2523 7-9-2 **52** (b) HarryBentley 3 40
(Michael Mullineaux) *chsd ldrs: rdn 2f out: sn wknd* **8/1**[2]

0320 **11** *2* **Monsieur Jimmy**[23] 2332 4-8-12 **48** (b) DavidAllan 1 30
(Declan Carroll) *dwlt: a in rr* **8/1**[2]

0-40 **12** *2 3/4* **Tallulah Fleur**[26] 2234 3-8-4 **48** JoeyHaynes 2 20
(Ann Duffield) *chsd ldrs on wd outside: rdn along over 2f out: sn drvn and wknd* **33/1**

0223 **13** *2* **Krazy Paving**[38] 1913 4-9-5 **55** (b) LukeMorris 4 23
(Anabel K Murphy) *towards rr: rdn along over 2f out: sn wknd* **10/1**[3]

1m 12.88s (-1.82) **Going Correction** -0.30s/f (Firm)
WFA 3 from 4yo+ 8lb **13** Ran SP% **118.3**
Speed ratings (Par 101): **100,98,97,97,96 96,94,93,93,91 88,84,82**
CSF £170.51 CT £1445.29 TOTE £16.80: £4.30, £3.40, £3.10; EX 224.60 Trifecta £2707.10.
Owner Cleartherm Glass Sealed Units Ltd **Bred** D R Botterill **Trained** Peckleton, Leics

FOCUS
This was even more open than the first division according to the betting. The race was dominated by those that raced handily with the first three home forcing the tempo throughout. The winning time was 0.61sec slower than the first leg. The winner is rated to last year's peak.

3071 RACING UK FREE TRIAL LIMITED TIME FILLIES' H'CAP (GRASSROOTS MIDDLE DISTANCE SERIES QUALIFIER) — 1m 2f 50y
5:05 (5:06) (Class 5) (0-75,75) 3-Y-O **£2,911** (£866; £432; £216) **Stalls** Low

Form RPR

043- **1** **Pure Fantasy**[192] 8048 3-9-3 **71** WilliamTwiston-Davies 2 79+
(Roger Charlton) *hld up: hdwy 3f out: trckd ldrs 2f out: effrt and n.m.r over 1f out: sn squeezed through and rdn to chal ins fnl f: led last 100yds: readily* **11/4**[2]

4-01 **2** *1 3/4* **Arcamist**[21] 2405 3-9-4 **75** MichaelJMMurphy(3) 4 79
(Charles Hills) *led: pushed along over 2f out: rdn wl over 1f out: jnd and drvn jst ins fnl f: hdd and no ex last 100yds* **7/1**[3]

6 **3** *2 1/2* **Della Valle (GER)**[23] 2339 3-9-6 **74** TedDurcan 7 73
(Mike Murphy) *hld up in rr: hdwy on outer wl over 2f out: rdn over 1f out: drvn and styd on fnl f* **25/1**

2-03 **4** *hd* **Shadow Spirit**[23] 2339 3-9-6 **74** AdamKirby 5 73
(James Eustace) *trckd ldrs: hdwy and cl up 3f out: rdn along 2f out: drvn and edgd rt over 1f out: sn one pce* **6/4**[1]

006- **5** *1* **All The Rage**[258] 6720 3-8-9 **63** LukeMorris 1 60
(Sir Mark Prescott Bt) *chsd ldng pair: hdwy 3f out: rdn 2f out: drvn over 1f out and sn one pce* **11/4**[2]

2m 10.83s (-3.47) **Going Correction** -0.30s/f (Firm) **5** Ran SP% **109.7**
Speed ratings (Par 96): **101,99,97,97,96**
CSF £20.23 TOTE £4.10: £2.20, £2.40; EX 18.10 Trifecta £60.00.
Owner The Queen **Bred** The Queen **Trained** Beckhampton, Wilts

FOCUS
Rail movement added around 6yds to race distance. An ordinary 3yo fillies' handicap but the winner looks to have more to offer..

3072 RACINGUK.COM/FREETRIAL H'CAP — 1m 2f 50y
5:35 (5:36) (Class 6) (0-60,59) 4-Y-O+ **£2,264** (£673; £336; £168) **Stalls** Low

Form RPR

1035 **1** **Vastly (USA)**[20] 2444 7-9-0 **52** (t) LukeMorris 9 58
(Sophie Leech) *trckd ldng pair cl up 3f out: rdn to chal over 1f out: drvn ins fnl f: led last 100yds* **12/1**

3024 **2** *1/2* **The Dukkerer (IRE)**[13] 2666 5-9-7 **59** TomEaves 14 64
(James Given) *trckd ldr: cl up 3f out: rdn to ld over 1f out: drvn ins fnl f: hdd and no ex last 100yds* **9/1**

2311 **3** *1 1/2* **Little Choosey**[8] 2799 6-8-9 **54** (tp) HollieDoyle(7) 5 58
(Roy Bowring) *trckd ldrs: hdwy 3f out: effrt over 1f out and ev ch whn nt clr run: swtchd rt and rdn ent fnl f: kpt on* **3/1**[1]

-012 **4** *nk* **Sexy Secret**[50] 1578 5-9-0 **55** (p) SimonPearce(3) 10 57
(Lydia Pearce) *led: pushed along over 2f out: rdn and hdd over 1f out: sn drvn and grad wknd* **16/1**

4-16 **5** *1 1/2* **Master Of Song**[134] 346 9-9-3 **58** (p) RobHornby(3) 15 57+
(Roy Bowring) *hld up and bhd: hdwy on wd outside over 3f out: rdn wl over 1f out: chsd ldrs appr fnl f: kpt on* **25/1**

3140 **6** *1* **Attain**[18] 2507 7-9-4 **59** (p) ShelleyBirkett(3) 8 56
(Julia Feilden) *in tch: hdwy to trck ldrs 3f out: rdn along wl over 1f out: drvn and no imp fnl f* **10/1**

0-03 **7** *1/2* **Miningrocks (FR)**[8] 2799 4-9-2 **54** TedDurcan 4 50
(Declan Carroll) *plld hrd: hld up in rr: hdwy 2f out: styd on wl fnl f: nrst fin* **14/1**

-305 **8** *1/2* **Doctor Kehoe**[21] 2397 4-9-6 **58** (vt) AdamKirby 3 53
(David Evans) *trckd ldrs on inner: effrt 3f out: rdn along 2f out: sn drvn and one pce* **8/1**

-530 **9** *1/2* **Highlife Dancer**[13] 2645 8-8-13 **58** (v) KillianHennessy(7) 6 52
(Mick Channon) *hld up: hdwy 3f out: rdn along over 2f out: no imp* **7/1**[3]

66-0 **10** *shd* **Belle Peinture (FR)**[10] 2746 5-8-7 **45** (b[1]) CamHardie 2 39
(Alan Lockwood) *in rr: effrt and n.m.r on inner over 2f out: swtchd markedly rt to outer over 1f out: kpt on fnl f* **50/1**

1050 **11** *1/2* **Miss Buckaroo (IRE)**[21] 2409 4-8-10 **48** (b) JamesSullivan 7 41
(James Given) *chsd ldrs: rdn along on inner over 2f out: drvn wl over 1f out: wknd appr fnl f* **40/1**

40-0 **12** *nk* **Royal Etiquette (IRE)**[7] 2814 9-9-6 **58** (vt) WilliamTwiston-Davies 11 50
(Lawney Hill) *a towards rr* **20/1**

6002 **13** *nk* **Last Wish (IRE)**[6] 2849 5-9-0 **52** (b) ConnorBeasley 13 44
(Richard Guest) *chsd ldrs: rdn along wl over 2f out: sn drvn and wknd* **6/1**[2]

300- **14** *2 1/2* **Kantara Castle (IRE)**[194] 8040 5-8-11 **49** (tp) RoystonFfrench 1 36
(John Mackie) *in rr: sme hdwy 3f out: sn rdn along and wknd* **9/1**

2m 13.36s (-0.94) **Going Correction** -0.30s/f (Firm) **14** Ran SP% **125.2**
Speed ratings (Par 101): **91,90,89,89,87 87,86,86,85,85 85,85,85,83**
CSF £116.53 CT £418.39 TOTE £15.60: £4.00, £3.50, £1.40; EX 158.70 Trifecta £624.70.
Owner Out Of Bounds Racing Club **Bred** Juddmonte Farms Inc **Trained** Elton, Gloucs

FOCUS
Rail movement added around 6yds to race distance. A moderate handicap to end with and again it paid to be handy. The winner had previously looked better on the AW.
T/Jkpt: Not won. T/Plt: £138.30 to a £1 stake. Pool: £56,720.63 - 299.22 winning units. T/Qpdt: £141.40 to a £1 stake. Pool: £3,651.30 - 19.10 winning units. **Joe Rowntree**

3037 YARMOUTH (L-H)
Thursday, June 9

OFFICIAL GOING: Good to firm (good in back straight and on both bends; 8.0)
Wind: light, behind Weather: sunny

3073 SEADELL SHOPS AND CHALETS AT HEMSBY FILLIES' NEWCOMERS' MAIDEN STKS (PLUS 10 RACE) (DIV I) — 6f 3y
2:10 (2:13) (Class 5) 2-Y-O **£3,622** (£1,078; £538; £269) **Stalls** Centre

Form RPR

1 **Soul Silver (IRE)** 2-9-0 0 MartinHarley 9 77+
(David Simcock) *in tch in midfield: effrt to chse ldr wl over 1f out: rdn and styd on to chal jst ins fnl f: pushed along and fnd enough to ld cl home* **4/1**[3]

2 *nk* **Salla** 2-8-11 0 ThomasBrown(3) 1 76+
(Ismail Mohammed) *in tch: hdwy to ld 2f out: shkn up ent fnl f: hrd pressed ins fnl f: rdn and kpt on fnl 150yds tl hdd and no ex cl home* **2/1**[1]

3 *2* **On Her Toes (IRE)** 2-9-0 0 PatCosgrave 8 70+
(William Haggas) *trckd ldrs: rdn over 2f out: 3rd and unable qck whn sltly short of room and swtchd lft over 1f out: styd on same pce ins fnl f* **5/2**[2]

4 *2 1/4* **Ruby Woo** 2-9-0 0 AdamBeschizza 6 63
(Stuart Williams) *s.i.s: sn rcvrd and in tch in midfield: effrt to chse clr ldng trio wl over 1f out: kpt on but no imp fnl f* **8/1**

5 *1* **Party Nights** 2-8-7 0 GabrieleMalune(7) 2 60
(Luca Cumani) *t.k.h: led for 1f: chsd ldr tl 2f out: sn outpcd and styd on same pce fr over 1f out* **18/1**

6 *1 3/4* **Sandwood Bay** 2-9-0 0 SaleemGolam 7 55+
(Mark H Tompkins) *s.i.s: hld up in tch in rr of main gp: pushed and along and sme hdwy 2f out: 6th and kpt on same pce fr over 1f out* **25/1**

7 *2* **Gentle Whisper** 2-9-0 0 StevieDonohoe 3 49
(Charlie Fellowes) *s.i.s: sn rcvrd and in tch in midfield: rdn over 2f out: sn outpcd and lost pl: wl hld and kpt on same pce after* **14/1**

8 *6* **Artsteelwork** 2-9-0 0 AntonioFresu 4 31
(Denis Quinn) *t.k.h: chsd ldr tl led after 1f out: hdd 2f out: sn lost pl: wknd over 1f out* **66/1**

9 *1/2* **Cadela Rica** 2-9-0 0 DavidProbert 5 30
(Gay Kelleway) *s.i.s: hld up in tch in rr of main gp: rdn ent fnl 2f: sn outpcd: wknd over 1f out* **25/1**

10 *4 1/2* **Twaddle** 2-8-7 0 LuluStanford(7) 10 16
(Alan Coogan) *s.i.s: pushed along in detached last thrght: lost tch over 1f out* **66/1**

1m 12.46s (-1.94) **Going Correction** -0.525s/f (Hard) **10** Ran SP% **115.6**
Speed ratings (Par 90): **91,90,87,84,83 81,78,70,69,63**
CSF £11.95 TOTE £4.60: £1.20, £1.30, £1.50; EX 12.10 Trifecta £42.50.
Owner Qatar Racing Limited **Bred** Lisieux Stud & Irish National Stud **Trained** Newmarket, Suffolk

FOCUS
The track wasn't watered after Wednesday's comeback card and following this opener Martin Harley descibed it as "lovely ground", although Stevie Donohoe called it "fast." No previous form to go on in this, but it was the quicker division by 0.86sec.

3074 SEADELL SHOPS AND CHALETS AT HEMSBY FILLIES' NEWCOMERS' MAIDEN STKS (PLUS 10 RACE) (DIV II) — 6f 3y
2:40 (2:43) (Class 5) 2-Y-O **£3,622** (£1,078; £538; £269) **Stalls** Centre

Form RPR

1 **Urban Fox** 2-9-0 0 MartinHarley 3 76
(James Tate) *trckd ldrs tl wnt 2nd over 2f out: rdn to ld over 1f out: flashed tail u.p but asserted ins fnl f: r.o strly* **11/2**

2 *1 1/2* **Rosabelle** 2-9-0 0 RobertTart 4 72
(Alan Bailey) *led: rdn 2f out: hdd over 1f out: kpt on same pce ins fnl f* **20/1**

3 *1* **Preobrajenska** 2-9-0 0[1] WilliamCarson 5 69
(Michael Bell) *in tch in midfield: effrt to chse ldng pair over 1f out: styd on same pce ins fnl f* **4/1**[3]

4 1 1/4 **Jumping Around (IRE)** 2-9-0 0 PatCosgrave 8 65+
(William Haggas) *sltly hmpd leaving stalls: hld up in tch in midfield: pushed along and effrt over 1f out: hdwy 1f out: kpt on ins fnl f: no threat to wnr* **9/4**[1]

5 nk **Dubara** 2-9-0 0 TomQueally 7 64+
(Luca Cumani) *stdd and wnt rt leaving stalls: hld up in tch in last pair: pushed along over 1f out: hdwy 1f out: kpt on ins fnl f: nvr trbld ldrs* **7/2**[2]

6 3 **Newz Watch** 2-9-0 0 LiamJones 6 55
(Mick Quinn) *t.k.h: chsd ldrs: 4th and unable qck u.p over 1f out: wknd fnl f* **33/1**

7 1/2 **Saxagogo** 2-8-11 0 DanielMuscutt(3) 2 53
(George Scott) *in tch in midfield: effrt to chse ldrs over 1f out: no ex u.p: wknd ins fnl f* **10/1**

8 1/2 **Lady Kaviar (IRE)** 2-9-0 0 RyanPowell 9 52
(George Margarson) *t.k.h: chsd ldr tl over 2f out: sn rdn and lost pl: wknd fnl f* **14/1**

9 2 1/2 **Cambridge Favorite** 2-9-0 0 SaleemGolam 1 44
(Mrs Ilka Gansera-Leveque) *uns rdr and galloped loose to post: s.i.s: in tch in rr: effrt and hung lft 2f out: sn btn* **50/1**

1m 13.32s (-1.08) **Going Correction** -0.525s/f (Hard) **9** Ran SP% **113.8**
Speed ratings (Par 90): **86,84,82,81,80 76,75,75,71**
CSF £104.08 TOTE £5.60: £1.50, £3.40, £1.80; EX 93.50 Trifecta £702.70.
Owner Saeed Manana **Bred** Mascalls Stud **Trained** Newmarket, Suffolk

FOCUS
They didn't go much pace in this newcomers' race and the tme was 0.86sec slower than the opener.

3075 INJURED JOCKEYS FUND (S) STKS 7f 3y
3:15 (3:15) (Class 6) 2-Y-O **£2,264** (£673; £336) **Stalls** Centre

Form RPR
3 1 **Sixties Habana**[7] 2822 2-8-13 0 CharlesBishop 2 61+
(Mick Channon) *t.k.h: mde all: nudged along and wnt clr over 1f out: r.o wl: easily* **1/8**[1]

0 2 3 1/2 **Nudge Nudge**[17] 2535 2-8-8 0 JosephineGordon(5) 1 49
(J S Moore) *hld up in cl 3rd: wnt 2nd and rdn over 2f out: outpcd and btn over 1f out: kpt on same pce for clr 2nd* **20/1**[3]

3 24 **Fast Watch**[29] 2164 2-8-8 0 JackMitchell 3
(Jose Santos) *t.k.h: trckd wnr tl over 2f out: sn rdn and outpcd: 3rd and wl btn over 1f out: eased ins fnl f* **8/1**[2]

1m 26.07s (-0.53) **Going Correction** -0.525s/f (Hard) **3** Ran SP% **104.8**
Speed ratings (Par 91): **82,78,50**
CSF £3.32 TOTE £1.10; EX 3.10 Trifecta £2.10.Sixties Habana was bought by Leigh Place Stud for 13,600gns
Owner Norman Court Racing I **Bred** Norman Court Stud & Mike Channon B/S Ltd **Trained** West Ilsley, Berks

FOCUS
A non-event, and not a race to dwell on.

3076 THURLOW NUNN VAUXHALL DEALER OF GREAT YARMOUTH FILLIES' H'CAP 1m 2f 23y
3:50 (3:50) (Class 5) (0-70,76) 4-Y-O+ **£2,911** (£866; £432; £216) **Stalls** Low

Form RPR
00-6 1 **Mercy Me**[42] 1810 4-8-13 **62** RyanPowell 5 67
(John Ryan) *stdd s: hld up in midfield: clsd to trck ldrs 4f out: rdn to ld over 1f out: edgd lft u.p and hrd pressed ins fnl f: duelled w runner-up fnl 100yds: r.o and hld on cl home* **17/2**

6-62 2 hd **Yankee Mail (FR)**[10] 2733 4-9-7 **70** PatCosgrave 7 74
(Gay Kelleway) *stdd s: hld up in last pair: clsd and trcking ldrs 3f out: effrt over 1f out: wnt between rivals to chal and carried lft ins fnl f: duelled w wnr fnl 100yds: r.o: jst hld cl home* **7/1**[3]

2422 3 3 3/4 **What A Party (IRE)**[8] 2792 4-8-8 **57** (p) DavidProbert 2 54
(Gay Kelleway) *led: rdn and hdd 2f out: kpt on u.p tl no ex ins fnl f: outpcd fnl 100yds* **7/2**[2]

1201 4 nk **Wavelet**[6] 2860 4-9-8 **76** 6ex GeorgeBuckell(5) 1 72
(David Simcock) *chsd ldr: rdn to ld 2f out: sn hdd: stl pressing ldr tl lost 2nd: squeezed for room and hmpd ins fnl f: nt rcvr: sn lost 3rd and wl hld fnl 100yds* **6/5**[1]

-044 5 6 **Theydon Bois**[14] 2607 4-8-8 **57** (p[1]) JimmyQuinn 4 41
(Peter Charalambous) *chsd ldrs: shkn up 4f out: drvn and lost pl over 2f out: wknd over 1f out* **7/1**[3]

225- 6 27 **Broughtons Harmony**[162] 8394 4-9-6 **69** TomQueally 3
(Willie Musson) *stdd s: hld up in rr: effrt 3f out: rdn and no hdwy over 2f out: wl btn and eased fnl f* **16/1**

2m 8.98s (-1.52) **Going Correction** -0.175s/f (Firm) **6** Ran SP% **109.1**
Speed ratings (Par 100): **99,98,95,95,90 69**
CSF £59.39 TOTE £11.30: £4.20, £2.70; EX 81.90 Trifecta £262.10.
Owner G Smith-Bernal & A Dee **Bred** Aston Mullins Stud **Trained** Newmarket, Suffolk

FOCUS
Very ordinary fillies' form, rated negatively.

3077 YOUR MORTGAGE SOLUTIONS AT GORLESTON 15TH ANNIVERSARY H'CAP 1m 3f 104y
4:20 (4:20) (Class 4) (0-85,85) 3-Y-O+ **£4,690** (£1,395; £697; £348) **Stalls** Low

Form RPR
31-2 1 **Lord George (IRE)**[64] 1260 3-8-11 **82** TomQueally 2 94+
(James Fanshawe) *hld up in tch: smooth hdwy to join ldrs on bit 2f out: nudged into ld over 1f out: pressed and rdn ins fnl f: hdd towards fin: rallied u.p to ld again cl home* **1/1**[1]

6524 2 shd **Sbraase**[17] 2549 5-9-8 **79** PatCosgrave 5 90
(James Tate) *hld up in tch: chsd ldrs over 1f out: trckd wnr 1f out: rdn hands and heels to chal ins fnl f: hit once w whip and led towards fin: hdd and no ex cl home* **5/1**[2]

0-30 3 3 1/4 **Goodwood Mirage (IRE)**[28] 2176 6-9-11 **85** LouisSteward(3) 4 91
(Michael Bell) *chsd ldr after 2f tl led 9f out: rdn ent fnl 2f: hdd over 1f out: no ex ins fnl f: wknd fnl 100yds* **12/1**

3-40 4 5 **Shahbar**[26] 2244 3-8-10 **81** MartinHarley 1 78
(Marco Botti) *chsd ldr for 2f: styd chsng ldrs: wnt 2nd again 6f out: rdn and ev ch over 2f out: no ex over 1f out: wknd ins fnl f* **11/2**[3]

0220 5 5 **Thecornishbarron (IRE)**[15] 2577 4-9-0 **71** JackMitchell 7 60
(John Ryan) *stdd after s: hld up in rr: shkn up and effrt 3f out: drvn and no hdwy over 2f out: wknd over 1f out* **13/2**

0426 6 1 3/4 **Freight Train (IRE)**[5] 2888 4-9-1 **72** LiamJones 3 58
(Mark Johnston) *led for 3f: chsd ldr tl 6f out: struggling u.p over 2f out: wknd over 1f out* **12/1**

2m 25.12s (-3.58) **Going Correction** -0.175s/f (Firm)
WFA 3 from 4yo+ 14lb **6** Ran SP% **110.8**
Speed ratings (Par 105): **106,105,103,99,96 95**
CSF £6.13 TOTE £1.80: £1.30, £1.80; EX 5.00 Trifecta £23.10.
Owner Fred Archer Racing - Bend Or **Bred** Sarl Elevage Du Haras De Bourgeauville **Trained** Newmarket, Suffolk

FOCUS
A modest handicap run at an ordinary gallop. The winner was back to the level of his maiden win.

3078 BURLINGTON PALM HOTEL OF GREAT YARMOUTH H'CAP 7f 3y
4:55 (4:57) (Class 6) (0-65,65) 4-Y-O+ **£2,264** (£673; £336; £168) **Stalls** Centre

Form RPR
4122 1 **Johnny B Goode (IRE)**[17] 2537 4-9-0 **63** JosephineGordon(5) 3 71
(Chris Dwyer) *taken down early: hld up in tch: hdwy over 2f out: rdn to chse ldng pair over 1f out: styd on u.p to chse ldr 50yds: kpt on to ld on post* **5/1**[2]

4660 2 nse **Pyla (IRE)**[38] 1926 4-9-6 **64** LemosdeSouza 13 72
(Denis Quinn) *stdd after s: hld up in tch in rr: hdwy to chse ldr jst over 2f out: rdn and ev ch over 1f out: led 1f out: kpt on steadily u.p: jnd cl home: hdd on post* **7/1**[3]

3-01 3 1 1/4 **Sober Up**[14] 2609 4-8-13 **57** (p) MartinHarley 10 61
(Ivan Furtado) *chsd ldrs: j. path over 5f out: sn led: rdn 2f out: hdd 1f out: no ex and btn whn lost 2nd fnl 50yds: keeping on same pce and hld whn n.m.r nr fin* **5/2**[1]

0006 4 1/2 **Swiss Cross**[9] 2765 9-9-6 **64** (bt) StevieDonohoe 4 67
(Phil McEntee) *dwlt: hld up in tch in rr: rdn and hdwy 2f out: chsd ldng trio ent fnl f: styd on: nvr enough pce to rch ldrs* **11/1**

020- 5 3 1/4 **Royal Caper**[252] 6886 6-8-12 **59** DanielMuscutt(3) 7 53
(Miss Joey Ellis) *in tch in midfield: effrt u.p jst over 2f out: drvn and unable qck over 1f out: wknd ins fnl f* **25/1**

5-00 6 2 1/4 **Monna Valley**[22] 2379 4-8-13 **62** (t) AaronJones(5) 9 50
(Stuart Williams) *chsd ldrs: rdn and unable qck ent fnl 2f: outpcd and btn over 1f out: wknd fnl f* **17/2**

654- 7 nse **Decisive (IRE)**[238] 7232 4-8-12 **56** RobertTart 12 44
(Anthony Carson) *hld up in tch: hdwy to chse ldrs 3f out: rdn and unable qck 2f out: sn btn: wknd fnl f* **16/1**

-440 8 2 **Makhfar (IRE)**[57] 1415 5-9-0 **58** (v) AdamBeschizza 6 41
(Kevin Morgan) *dwlt: in tch towards rr: hdwy 1/2-way: rdn and unable qck over 2f out: drvn and btn over 1f out: wknd fnl f* **8/1**

0400 9 18 **Marmalad (IRE)**[20] 2441 4-9-3 **61** KierenFallon 11
(Shaun Lycett) *in tch: hdwy to chse ldr 1/2-way tl over 2f out: sn struggling and wknd over 1f out: wl btn and eased ins fnl f* **20/1**

0-00 10 3 **Harbour Patrol (IRE)**[23] 2347 4-9-5 **63** TomQueally 2
(Rebecca Bastiman) *led for 2f: lost pl 1/2-way: bhd 2f out: wl bhd and eased ins fnl f* **11/1**

0050 11 1 1/4 **Alhella**[17] 2537 4-9-7 **65** PatCosgrave 1
(Mick Quinn) *hld up in tch towards rr: effrt over 2f out: sn btn: wl bhd and eased ins fnl f* **33/1**

-400 12 1 1/4 **Coolcalmcollected (IRE)**[20] 2416 4-8-12 **59** LouisSteward(3) 8
(Andrew Crook) *chsd ldrs tl lost pl 1/2-way: sn bhd: eased ins fnl f* **33/1**

1m 23.73s (-2.87) **Going Correction** -0.525s/f (Hard) **12** Ran SP% **116.4**
Speed ratings (Par 101): **95,94,93,92,89 86,86,84,63,60 58,57**
CSF £37.24 CT £107.74 TOTE £5.70: £1.80, £2.50, £1.50; EX 40.40 Trifecta £84.60.
Owner Mrs C M Goode **Bred** Noel Brosnan **Trained** Newmarket, Suffolk

FOCUS
The first four came clear in this moderate handicap. The winner is rated up slightly on this year's selling form.

3079 RIVERSIDE RENTALS OF HORNING H'CAP 1m 3y
5:25 (5:26) (Class 4) (0-80,80) 3-Y-O **£4,690** (£1,395; £697; £348) **Stalls** Centre

Form RPR
-260 1 **Zain Emperor (IRE)**[23] 2336 3-8-13 **72** (v[1]) StevieDonohoe 10 82
(Charlie Fellowes) *hld up in tch in midfield: rdn and effrt to chse ldrs wl over 1f out: led jst ins fnl f: r.o strly: rdn out* **14/1**

-215 2 2 1/2 **Town's History (USA)**[13] 2654 3-9-2 **78** KevinStott(3) 2 82
(Saeed bin Suroor) *in tch in midfield: clsd to trck ldrs 1/2-way: rdn to chse ldr wl over 1f out: ev ch 1f out: chsd wnr and r.o same pce ins fnl f* **2/1**[1]

050- 3 1 **Melabi (IRE)**[250] 6924 3-9-4 **77** [1] PatCosgrave 7 79
(William Haggas) *stdd s: hld up in tch in last pair: effrt u.p over 1f out: wnt 4th 1f out: styd on u.p to go 3rd wl ins fnl f: no threat to wnr* **11/2**[3]

1-10 4 1 3/4 **Mywayistheonlyway (IRE)**[13] 2654 3-9-4 **77** FergusSweeney 4 74
(Martyn Meade) *chsd ldr tl rdn to ld 2f out: drvn over 1f out: hdd jst ins fnl f: wknd fnl 100yds* **8/1**

-450 5 4 **War Department (IRE)**[13] 2650 3-8-10 **76** LuluStanford(7) 6 64
(Michael Bell) *dwlt: t.k.h and sn rcvrd to chse ldrs: drvn and btn over 1f out: wknd fnl f* **18/1**

0-44 6 2 1/2 **Miniaturist (FR)**[5] 2907 3-9-4 **77** LiamJones 5 59
(Mark Johnston) *led: rdn and hdd 2f out: sn drvn and unable qck: btn 1f out: wknd fnl f* **7/2**[2]

1-00 7 3 **Marshal Dan Troop (IRE)**[12] 2695 3-9-3 **76** JackMitchell 8 51
(Peter Chapple-Hyam) *stdd s: hld up in tch in last trio: effrt jst over 2f out: sn drvn and no hdwy over 1f out: wknd fnl f* **16/1**

1-20 8 8 **Cryptic (IRE)**[23] 2322 3-9-2 **75** TomQueally 1 30
(Luca Cumani) *hld up in tch in last trio: effrt over 2f out: no hdwy and sn btn: wl bhd and eased ins fnl f* **15/2**

633- 9 22 **Ocean Eleven**[215] 7745 3-9-7 **80** KierenFallon 9
(John Ryan) *chsd ldrs early: lost pl and midfield whn rdn 1/2-way: dropped to rr over 2f out: eased over 1f out: t.o* **20/1**

1m 35.75s (-4.85) **Going Correction** -0.525s/f (Hard) **9** Ran SP% **116.4**
Speed ratings (Par 101): **103,100,99,97,93 91,88,80,58**
CSF £42.71 CT £182.02 TOTE £23.70: £5.30, £1.30, £2.10; EX 87.90 Trifecta £617.90.
Owner Asaad Al Banwan **Bred** Kevin J Molloy **Trained** Newmarket, Suffolk

FOCUS
A fair handicap lacking improvers, but it was sound run. A length pb from the winner.

3080 TRAFALGAR RESTAURANT AT GREAT YARMOUTH RACECOURSE CLASSIFIED STKS 1m 3y
6:00 (6:01) (Class 6) 3-Y-O **£2,264** (£673; £336; £168) **Stalls** Centre

Form RPR
000- 1 **Mia Tesoro (IRE)**[226] 7534 3-9-0 57 [1] StevieDonohoe 15 64
(Charlie Fellowes) *hld up in tch in rr: clsd 1/2-way: chsd ldrs and swtchd rt wl over 1f out: rdn to ld over 1f out: styd on* **12/1**

04-0 **2** *1* **Port Paradise**[143] 242 3-8-7 59................................ SamuelClarke[(7)] 13 62
(William Jarvis) *chsd ldrs tl led over 2f out: hdd over 1f out: kpt on but a hld ins fnl f* **8/1**[3]

6-00 **3** *1 1/4* **Golden Isles (IRE)**[22] 2366 3-8-9 60.................. JosephineGordon[(5)] 14 59
(J S Moore) *in tch towards rr and niggled along early: hdwy 1/2-way: rdn to chse ldr jst over 2f out: stl cl enough in 3rd and drvn over 1f out: styd on same pce ins fnl f* **18/1**

0-04 **4** *1/2* **Fol O'Yasmine**[24] 2294 3-9-0 60.. PatCosgrave 8 57
(William Haggas) *hld up wl in tch in midfield: effrt to chse ldrs 2f out: drvn and edgd lft over 1f out: styd on same pce ins fnl f* **5/2**[1]

300 **5** *nk* **General Hazard (IRE)**[27] 2207 3-8-11 60.................. LouisSteward[(3)] 5 57
(Michael Bell) *hld up in tch towards rr: hdwy over 2f out: chsd ldrs and drvn over 1f out: styd on same pce u.p ins fnl f* **16/1**

00-0 **6** *3 3/4* **Any Guest (IRE)**[16] 2553 3-9-0 54.................................... RyanPowell 4 49
(George Margarson) *w ldr: rdn over 2f out: unable qck and outpcd whn sltly hmpd over 1f out: wknd fnl f* **16/1**

0-00 **7** *6* **Mistymoistymorning (IRE)**[28] 2178 3-9-0 60...........(b[1]) KierenFallon 16 34
(John Ryan) *in tch towards rr: pushed along and hdwy over 3f out: rdn and outpcd whn sltly hmpd wl over 1f out: wl btn 1f out* **9/1**

00-0 **8** *2 1/2* **Mr Turner**[43] 1784 3-9-0 58.. SaleemGolam 11 27
(Mark H Tompkins) *t.k.h: hld up in tch in midfield: rdn over 2f out: sn outpcd: wl btn and plugged on same pce fr over 1f out* **20/1**

0-02 **9** *hd* **Gladys Cooper (IRE)**[23] 2325 3-9-0 57.......................... AntonioFresu 3 27
(Ed Walker) *hld up in tch in midfield: effrt over 2f out: racd awkwardly u.p and btn over 1f out: sn wknd* **12/1**

00-1 **10** *6* **Tulip Dress**[16] 2559 3-9-0 60.. RobertTart 1 12
(Anthony Carson) *stdd s: hld up in rr: effrt 3f out: sn struggling: wl btn over 1f out* **14/1**

-004 **11** *3/4* **Capital Gearing**[16] 2553 3-9-0 57...................................(b) TomQueally 2 11
(Henry Spiller) *dwlt: sn rcvrd to chse ldrs: rdn and no rspnse over 2f out: wknd over 1f out* **14/1**

6300 **12** *1/2* **Serendib's Glory (IRE)**[31] 2107 3-9-0 57.................(t) AdamBeschizza 9 9
(Julia Feilden) *led tl rdn and hdd over 2f out: sn btn: wknd over 1f out* **50/1**

6022 **13** *2 1/2* **Mr Potter**[8] 2801 3-9-0 60..(e) PatrickMathers 6 3
(Richard Guest) *taken down early: hld up in tch in midfield: rdn over 2f out: sn btn* **11/2**[2]

5-00 **14** *50* **Sakhastic**[46] 1670 3-8-11 43..................................(b) DanielMuscutt[(3)] 10
(Christine Dunnett) *dwlt: a in rr: rdn 3f out: lost tch and virtually p.u over 1f out: t.o* **66/1**

1m 36.95s (-3.65) **Going Correction** -0.525s/f (Hard) **14** Ran SP% **119.0**
Speed ratings (Par 97): **97,96,94,94,93 90,84,81,81,75 74,74,71,21**
CSF £102.28 TOTE £16.50: £5.60, £4.50, £5.80; EX 124.50 Trifecta £1085.50.
Owner Deron Pearson **Bred** D Pearson **Trained** Newmarket, Suffolk

FOCUS
This low-grade classified stakes was confined to horses who had won no more than once. High draws came out on top, as they tended to on the straight track over the two days of the fixture. Ordinary form for the grade.
T/Plt: £41.20 to a £1 stake. Pool: £49,356.66 - 874.34 winning units. T/Qpdt: £10.70 to a £1 stake. Pool: £3,874.55 - 266.20 winning units. **Steve Payne**

3081 - 3083a (Foreign Racing) - See Raceform Interactive

2878 LEOPARDSTOWN (L-H)
Thursday, June 9

OFFICIAL GOING: Good to firm

3084a CORAL.IE GLENCAIRN STKS (LISTED RACE) 1m
7:25 (7:25) 3-Y-O+
£20,606 (£6,636; £3,143; £1,397; £698; £349)

RPR

1 **Foxtrot Charlie (USA)**[18] 2510 3-8-12 99.......................... PatSmullen 3 101
(D K Weld, Ire) *sn chsd ldrs: 4th 1/2-way: gng wl bhd ldrs in 5th under 2f out and impr between horses to chal in 2nd over 1f out: rdn to ld far side ins fnl 150yds and kpt on wl* **11/4**[2]

2 *1* **Tennessee Wildcat (IRE)**[11] 2716 6-9-9 102.................... ColinKeane 6 102+
(G M Lyons, Ire) *hld up in tch: 5th 1/2-way: gng wl into st and impr on outer fr 2f out to chal over 1f out: sn rdn in 3rd and no imp on wnr wl ins fnl f: kpt on to snatch 2nd fnl stride* **5/2**[1]

3 *nse* **Orcia (IRE)**[11] 2716 4-9-4 96.. ShaneFoley 4 97
(M Halford, Ire) *prom: sn settled bhd ldr in 2nd: gng wl and clsr in 2nd 3f out: pushed along into st and led over 1f out: sn rdn and strly pressed: hdd ins fnl 150yds and no ex cl home: denied 2nd fnl stride* **6/1**

4 *1 1/2* **Yufuen**[11] 2716 5-9-9 104.. ConnorKing 5 98
(J P Murtagh, Ire) *chsd ldrs: 3rd 1/2-way: rdn 1 1/2f out and no imp on ldrs u.p in 4th ins fnl f: kpt on same pce* **9/1**

5 *1 1/4* **Elleval (IRE)**[98] 812 6-9-9 106..............................(p) ColmO'Donoghue 8 95
(David Marnane, Ire) *settled in rr: last at 1/2-way: pushed along into st and sme hdwy fr 2f out: rdn in 7th ins fnl f and kpt on same pce into nvr nrr 5th clsng stages* **11/2**[3]

6 *shd* **Current State (IRE)**[11] 2721 4-9-4 82.................................... BillyLee 1 90
(T Stack, Ire) *towards rr: 7th 1/2-way: gng wl into st and tk clsr order in 6th over 1f out: sn rdn and no imp on ldrs u.p in 5th wl ins fnl f: kpt on same pce and dropped to 6th clsng stages* **20/1**

7 *3 3/4* **Pour Deux (IRE)**[18] 2511 4-9-4 86.......................... DeclanMcDonogh 2 81
(John M Oxx, Ire) *sn led: over 2 l clr bef 1/2-way: rdn into st w reduced advantage and hdd over 1f out: wknd* **25/1**

8 *nk* **Hurricane Cass (IRE)**[22] 2386 4-9-9 92........................ WayneLordan 7 86
(T Stack, Ire) *hld up in tch: 6th 1/2-way: rdn on outer into st and sn no imp u.p in rr: one pce fnl f* **8/1**

1m 42.17s (0.97) **Going Correction** +0.35s/f (Good)
WFA 3 from 4yo+ 11lb **8** Ran SP% **114.6**
Speed ratings: **109,108,107,106,105 105,101,101**
CSF £10.11 TOTE £2.70: £1.30, £1.10, £1.90; DF 7.10 Trifecta £38.00.
Owner Calumet Farm **Bred** Calumet Farm **Trained** Curragh, Co Kildare

FOCUS
A competitive Listed heat where everything probably had some sort of chance, but it was a good performance from the winner considering his inexperience. The order didn't change that much.

3085 - 3087a (Foreign Racing) - See Raceform Interactive

2262 BELMONT PARK (L-H)
Thursday, June 9

OFFICIAL GOING: Dirt: fast; turf: good

3088a BELMONT CORONATION INVITATIONAL STKS (LISTED RACE) (4YO+ FILLIES & MARES) (TURF) 1m 7f 110y
8:07 (12:00) 4-Y-O+
£78,911 (£27,210; £13,605; £6,802; £4,081; £2,721)

RPR

1 **Suffused**[68] 4-8-2 0.. JoseLOrtiz 2 100
(William Mott, U.S.A) **48/10**[3]

2 *4 3/4* **Achnaha (IRE)**[41] 5-8-4 0.. JavierCastellano 1 95
(George Weaver, U.S.A) **63/20**[2]

3 *3* **Generosidade (URU)**[41] 6-8-8 0............................ TiagoJosuePereira 5 96
(Paulo H Lobo, Brazil) **2/1**[1]

4 *1 1/4* **Brandybend (IRE)**[22] 2363 4-8-2 0................................ FlorentGeroux 3 89
(Marco Botti) *led: rdn and strly pressed early in st: hdd over 1f out: no ex and btn sn after: wknd* **53/10**

5 *3 3/4* **Al Khazaaliya (USA)**[491] 4-8-4 0............................ JohnRVelazquez 6 87
(Todd Pletcher, U.S.A) **66/10**

6 *9 3/4* **Return To Grace (USA)**[41] 4-8-5 0 ow3.......................(b) JoelRosario 4 76
(Mark Casse, Canada) **26/5**

Owner Juddmonte Farms Inc **Bred** Juddmonte Farms Ltd **Trained** USA

3089 - (Foreign Racing) - See Raceform Interactive

2927 DEAUVILLE (R-H)
Thursday, June 9

OFFICIAL GOING: Turf: good

3090a PRIX HAMPTON (LISTED RACE) (3YO+) (TURF) 5f
5:10 (12:00) 3-Y-O+ **£19,117** (£7,647; £5,735; £3,823; £1,911)

RPR

1 **Justineo**[19] 2475 7-9-2 0.. Pierre-CharlesBoudot 6 108
(Robert Cowell) *mde all: broke wl and led: shkn up whn pressed over 2f out: drvn 1 1/2f out and responded: edgd lft and styd on wl fnl f* **63/10**[2]

2 *hd* **The Right Man**[48] 1618 4-9-2 0.......................... Francois-XavierBertras 2 107
(D Guillemin, France) **11/10**[1]

3 *1 1/2* **Porthilly (FR)**[203] 7910 6-8-13 0... AlexisBadel 9 99
(J E Hammond, France) **16/1**

4 *shd* **Pupa Di Saronno (FR)**[24] 2317 5-8-13 0.......................... FabriceVeron 4 99
(H-A Pantall, France) **14/1**

5 *3/4* **Muharaaj (IRE)**[66] 5-9-2 0..(p) AntoineHamelin 5 99
(Mlle M-L Mortier, France) **31/1**

6 *nk* **Gengis (FR)**[24] 2317 6-9-5 0.. UmbertoRispoli 1 101
(G Doleuze, France) **10/1**

7 *shd* **Royal Prize**[10] 6-9-2 0..(b) GregoryBenoist 3 97
(Mme M Bollack-Badel, France) **67/10**[3]

8 *1/2* **Spanish Romance (IRE)**[51] 3-8-6 0............................ CristianDemuro 7 90
(E J O'Neill, France) **24/1**

9 *snk* **Elabela (IRE)**[222] 7662 6-8-13 0.. GeraldMosse 8 92
(J E Hammond, France) **11/1**

10 *4* **Artplace (IRE)**[16] 6-9-2 0......................................(b) DelphineSantiago 10 81
(Carina Fey, France) **9/1**

57.83s (0.33)
WFA 3 from 4yo+ 7lb **10** Ran SP% **121.4**
WIN (incl. 1 euro stake): 7.30. PLACES: 2.00, 1.20, 3.10. DF: 6.20. SF: 14.50.
Owner Saleh Al Homaizi & Imad Al Sagar **Bred** Saleh Al Homaizi & Imad Al Sagar **Trained** Six Mile Bottom, Cambs

3091a (Foreign Racing) - See Raceform Interactive

3092a PRIX DURBAR (CONDITIONS) (4YO) (TURF) 1m 4f 110y
7:10 (12:00) 4-Y-O **£10,294** (£4,117; £3,088; £2,058; £1,029)

RPR

1 **Lindblad (GER)**[14] 4-9-6 0.. CristianDemuro 9 92
(Waldemar Hickst, Germany) **13/10**[1]

2 *1* **Notte D'Oro (IRE)**[59] 4-8-10 0.................................. MickaelBarzalona 1 81
(Mme Pia Brandt, France) **17/5**[2]

3 *hd* **Khozabad (FR)**[205] 7885 4-9-0 0.......................... Pierre-CharlesBoudot 3 84
(J-M Lefebvre, France) **5/1**[3]

4 *2* **Jam Session (IRE)**[21] 2398 4-9-6 0.............................. UmbertoRispoli 4 87
(Ian Williams) *disp ld on inner: narrow advantage whn rdn 2f out: strly pressed and hdd ins fnl f: no ex after and dropped to 4th* **68/10**

5 *1/2* **Aimless Lady (FR)**[8] 4-8-10 0.. MaximeGuyon 2 76
(F Vermeulen, France) **81/10**

6 *3* **Theomour (FR)**[213] 4-9-3 0.. IoritzMendizabal 7 78
(Mlle B Renk, France) **9/1**

7 *1 1/2* **Anna Lou (FR)**[121] 4-8-10 0.................................. AnthonyCaramanolis 6 69
(B Drieux, France) **54/1**

8 *10* **Simbel (IRE)**[424] 1361 4-8-10 0.. GeraldMosse 8 53
(F Doumen, France) **39/1**

2m 44.14s (-2.26) **8** Ran SP% **121.0**
WIN (incl. 1 euro stake): 2.30. PLACES: 1.10, 1.30, 1.30. DF: 5.10. SF: 8.90.
Owner Gerd Apel **Bred** G Apel **Trained** Germany

2457 CHEPSTOW (L-H)
Friday, June 10

OFFICIAL GOING: Good to firm (firm in places) changing to good to soft after race 2 (6.20)
Wind: almost nil Weather: rain, clearing after race 3 (6.55)

3093 TRADE CENTRE WALES/EBF NOVICE STKS (PLUS 10 RACE) 6f 16y
5:50 (5:55) (Class 4) 2-Y-O **£4,851** (£1,443; £721; £360) **Stalls** Centre

Form RPR

14 **1** **Sterling Silva (IRE)**[44] 1770 2-9-3 0.............................. GaryMahon[(5)] 2 81
(Richard Hannon) *chsd ldrs: led 3f out: jnd 2f out: sn rdn: r.o wl fnl f* **7/2**[2]

35 **2** ½ **Logi (IRE)**[13] 2669 2-9-2 0 PatDobbs 1 74
(Richard Hannon) *prom: chal 2f out: rdn appr fnl f: sn outpcd by wnr: clsng cl home* **3/1**[1]

3 *nk* **Hedging (IRE)** 2-8-11 0 EdwardGreatrex(5) 13 73
(Eve Johnson Houghton) *towards rr: pushed along after 2f: hdwy over 1f out: kpt on wl towards fin* **16/1**

4 ½ **Alcazar** 2-9-2 0 SaleemGolam 12 71
(David Simcock) *mid-div: rdn and hdwy over 2f out: r.o wl ins fnl f* **7/2**[2]

5 *nk* **Bazwind (IRE)** 2-9-2 0 PatCosgrave 5 70
(David Evans) *towards rr: rdn and hdwy 1/2-way: sn edgd lft: one pce ins fnl f* **20/1**

43 **6** ¾ **Gerrard's Return**[15] 2611 2-9-2 0 LiamJones 8 68
(Tom Dascombe) *wnt rt leaving stalls: sn prom: rdn and hung lft 2f out: one pce ins fnl f* **8/1**

06 **7** 12 **Bara Brith**[4] 2976 2-8-4 0 AledBeech(7) 10 27
(David Evans) *chsd ldrs tl lost pl over 2f out: no ch after but gng on fin* **50/1**

0 **8** ¾ **Asfaar (IRE)**[56] 1454 2-9-2 0 TedDurcan 9 30
(Brian Meehan) *hmpd leaving stalls: rdn over 2f out: a towards rr* **10/1**

6 **9** 1½ **Devilish Guest (IRE)**[21] 2437 2-9-2 0 GeorgeBaker 7 25
(Mick Channon) *cl up: led after 1f to 3f out: sn rdn: wknd over 1f out* **6/1**[3]

10 3½ **Radar Love (IRE)** 2-8-11 0 LiamKeniry 6 10
(J S Moore) *mid-div: rdn 3f out: wknd 2f out* **50/1**

6 **11** *hd* **Rock On Dandy (FR)**[29] 2180 2-9-2 0 LukeMorris 3 14
(Harry Dunlop) *mid-div: rdn over 3f out: bhd fnl 2f* **33/1**

P **Noble Kind** 2-8-8 0 PhilipPrince(3) 4
(David Evans) *wnt lft s: bhd: hung rt after 2f: edgd lft 1/2-way: no ch whn p.u over 2f out: fatally injured* **33/1**

1m 13.63s (1.63) **Going Correction** +0.075s/f (Good) **12** Ran SP% **124.4**
Speed ratings (Par 95): **92,91,90,90,89 88,72,71,69,65 64,**
CSF £14.55 TOTE £3.60: £1.30, £1.20, £4.30; EX 15.30 Trifecta £215.20.
Owner Middleham Park Racing XVII **Bred** Kildaragh Stud **Trained** East Everleigh, Wilts

FOCUS
All race distances as advertised. Heavy rain prior to racing and during the opener and times suggested it had got into the ground. A fair novice and a one-two for Richard Hannon. The winner matched his pre-race mark.

3094 CHEPSTOWMACHINESALES.CO.UK FOR KUBOTA MINI EXCAVATORS MAIDEN FILLIES' STKS 1m 4f 23y

6:20 (6:24) (Class 5) 3-Y-O+ **£3,234** (£962; £481; £240) **Stalls** Low

Form RPR

6 **1** **Dubka**[29] 2182 3-8-10 0 TedDurcan 2 80+
(Sir Michael Stoute) *trckd ldrs: wnt 2nd over 5f out: rdn over 2f out: styd on u.p to ld ins fnl f: r.o* **7/4**[2]

-0 **2** 2 **Eyeshine**[49] 1609 3-8-10 0 RobertHavlin 7 77+
(John Gosden) *sn led: rdn over 1f out: hdd ins fnl f: no ex* **13/8**[1]

3 2 **Tobouggaloo**[44] 5-9-11 0 LiamKeniry 8 74
(Stuart Kittow) *s.i.s: in rr: pushed along and clsd 4f out: rdn over 2f out: kpt on to go 3rd ins fnl f* **14/1**

02/2 **4** ½ **What A Scorcher**[20] 2463 5-9-6 71 EdwardGreatrex(5) 4 73
(Nikki Evans) *mid-div: rdn and hdwy 4f out: outpcd by ldrs over 1f out: one pce and lost 3rd ins fnl f* **10/1**

5 7 **Notice (IRE)** 3-8-10 0 SaleemGolam 9 62
(David Simcock) *mid-div: clsd 4f out: rdn whn briefly short of room 3f out: wknd over 1f out* **12/1**

6 2¾ **Martha McCandles**[438] 5-9-11 0 GeorgeBaker 6 57+
(Alan King) *chsd ldrs: rdn over 2f out: wknd fnl f* **33/1**

0 **7** 1¼ **Lily Trotter**[29] 2183 3-8-10 0 PatDobbs 10 55
(Ralph Beckett) *towards rr: rdn and struggling 4f out: styd on fnl 2f: nvr nr ldrs* **7/1**[3]

0-3 **8** ½ **Shine**[37] 1962 3-8-10 0 LukeMorris 12 55
(Jonathan Portman) *chsd ldrs: pushed along 5f out: wknd over 1f out* **25/1**

9 14 **Hortense Mancini**[218] 7-9-8 0 TimClark(3) 11 32
(Mark Bradstock) *rdn 5f out: a in rr* **100/1**

0 **10** 12 **Bonchard**[49] 1609 3-8-10 0 LiamJones 1 13
(Emma Owen) *t.k.h: trckd ldr: lost 2nd over 5f out: sn rdn: wknd 3f out: t.o* **66/1**

2m 38.92s (-0.08) **Going Correction** +0.20s/f (Good)
WFA 3 from 5yo+ 15lb **10** Ran SP% **119.7**
Speed ratings (Par 100): **108,106,105,105,100 98,97,97,88,80**
CSF £5.02 TOTE £2.90: £1.10, £1.30, £3.60; EX 6.30 Trifecta £38.10.
Owner Sir Evelyn De Rothschild **Bred** Southcourt Stud **Trained** Newmarket, Suffolk

FOCUS
Race distance as advertised. The ground was changed to good to soft following this race. A pretty ordinary maiden and two well-bred fillies from top yards fought out the finish. The race can be judged around the 71-rated fourth.

3095 HICKS LOGISTICS H'CAP 1m 2f 36y

6:55 (6:55) (Class 5) (0-75,71) 4-Y-O+ **£2,911** (£649; £649) **Stalls** Low

Form RPR

434- **1** **Shalimah (IRE)**[277] 6167 4-9-7 71 (v) RyanTate 3 77
(Clive Cox) *mde virtually all: jnd 3f out: sn rdn: styd on gamely u.p fnl f: asserted fnl 50yds* **6/5**[1]

2312 **2** 1 **Innoko (FR)**[8] 2814 6-8-12 62 LukeMorris 2 66
(Tony Carroll) *trckd wnr: rdn to chal over 2f out: ev ch u.p tl no ex fnl 50yds: jnd for 2nd on line* **2/1**[2]

-132 **2** *dht* **Distant High**[20] 2461 5-8-7 64 (p) GeorgeWood(7) 1 68
(Richard Price) *dwlt: hld up in tch in last: clsd 4f out: rdn over 2f out: ev ch over 1f out tl unable qck ins fnl f: tk share of 2nd on line* **9/4**[3]

2m 13.09s (2.49) **Going Correction** +0.20s/f (Good) **3** Ran SP% **109.6**
Speed ratings (Par 103): **98,97,97**
Ex: Shalimah & Distant High £2.00, Shalimah & Innoko £1.50; CSF: Shalimah & Distant High £2.05, Shalimah & Innoko £1.93 TF:S&DH&I: 2.10, S&I&DH: 2.20 TOTE £2.10.
Owner Mrs Christine Craddock **Bred** Yeomanstown Stud **Trained** Lambourn, Berks

FOCUS
Race distance as advertised. Just the three runners but still a fair gallop set courtesy of the winner. He's rated to his 3yo form.

3096 CCF FILLIES' H'CAP 1m 14y

7:30 (7:30) (Class 5) (0-70,68) 4-Y-O+ **£2,911** (£866; £432; £216) **Stalls** Centre

Form RPR

-014 **1** **Lady Bayside**[10] 2783 8-8-12 64 JosephineGordon(5) 6 73
(Malcolm Saunders) *a.p: rdn over 2f out: led appr fnl f: r.o wl to assert fnl 100yds* **5/1**[3]

23-4 **2** 2 **Plauseabella**[22] 2401 5-8-13 60 (p) TedDurcan 3 64
(Stuart Kittow) *led: racd alone towards far side 2f: rdn and hdd appr fnl f: no ex fnl 100yds* **7/2**[1]

-240 **3** 2¾ **Zaria**[14] 2655 5-8-5 59 (p) GeorgeWood(7) 8 57
(Richard Price) *chsd ldrs: rdn over 2f out: kpt on fnl f: tk 3rd on post* **4/1**[2]

6600 **4** *hd* **Cascading Stars (IRE)**[23] 2379 4-9-2 63 GeorgeBaker 1 60
(Daniel Mark Loughnane) *hld up: rdn and hdwy 2f out: chsd ldng pair over 1f out but no further imp: lost 3rd post* **7/1**

5 1 **Untapped Spectrum (IRE)**[28] 2228 4-8-0 52 (p) NoelGarbutt(5) 4 47
(W J Martin, Ire) *rrd s: t.k.h in rr: hdwy and prom after 3f: rdn and outpcd by ldrs 2f out: kpt on same pce* **7/2**[1]

0253 **6** 6 **Coup De Vent**[15] 2607 5-8-6 53 (be) LukeMorris 7 34
(John O'Shea) *t.k.h towards rr: rdn 3f out: wknd over 1f out* **14/1**

340- **7** 3¼ **Secret Lightning (FR)**[256] 6818 4-9-5 66 MartinLane 5 40
(Michael Appleby) *t.k.h: trckd ldrs: rdn 3f out: wknd over 1f out* **11/2**

1m 36.71s (0.51) **Going Correction** +0.075s/f (Good) **7** Ran SP% **115.7**
Speed ratings (Par 100): **100,98,95,95,94 88,84**
CSF £23.33 TOTE £5.20: £2.20, £2.30; EX 22.60 Trifecta £66.30.
Owner M S Saunders **Bred** M Saunders & T Bostwick **Trained** Green Ore, Somerset

FOCUS
Race distance as advertised. Little got into this modest handicap in which the winner sowed her best form since 2014..

3097 MCL LOGISTICS H'CAP 7f 16y

8:00 (8:00) (Class 5) (0-75,75) 4-Y-O+ **£2,911** (£866; £432; £216) **Stalls** Centre

Form RPR

0000 **1** **Secret Glance**[16] 2577 4-9-7 75 AdamBeschizza 9 84
(Richard Rowe) *mde all: shkn up over 1f out: sn drew clr: easily* **20/1**

00-5 **2** 3½ **Gold Hunter (IRE)**[24] 2345 6-9-5 73 TedDurcan 4 73
(Steve Flook) *chsd ldrs: wnt 2nd 3f out: rdn 2f out: sn outpcd by wnr but kpt on to hold 2nd* **9/2**[2]

1322 **3** ¾ **Golden Wedding (IRE)**[16] 2579 4-9-5 73 (p) CharlesBishop 7 70
(Eve Johnson Houghton) *mid-div: hdwy 3f out: sn rdn: wnt 3rd 2f out: kpt on same pce fnl f* **5/1**[3]

0-04 **4** 1 **Port Lairge**[45] 1746 6-8-9 66 (v) MichaelJMMurphy(3) 8 60
(John Gallagher) *mid-div: rdn and clsd 3f out: one pce and no imp on ldrs fnl 2f* **10/1**

-203 **5** 1 **Never To Be (USA)**[52] 457 5-8-8 67 (t) GaryMahon(5) 10 59
(Nikki Evans) *towards rr: rdn over 3f out: hdwy 2f out: styd on same pce fnl f* **50/1**

0-01 **6** 2¾ **Henryhudsonbridge (USA)**[18] 2542 4-8-6 63 (b) EoinWalsh(3) 11 48+
(Edward Bevan) *racd alone stands' side: prom: rdn and lost pl over 2f out: wknd fnl f* **7/1**

0/30 **7** 2 **Mystic Jade**[22] 2401 4-9-5 73 PatDobbs 6 52
(Richard Hannon) *s.i.s: in rr: rdn 1/2-way: no real imp: wknd over 1f out* **8/1**

2-13 **8** 6 **Double Czech (IRE)**[31] 2129 5-9-3 71 (v) DavidProbert 2 35
(Patrick Chamings) *chsd ldrs: rdn 3f out: wknd over 1f out* **7/2**[1]

0204 **9** 2¾ **Sarmadee (IRE)**[21] 2441 4-9-5 73 GeorgeBaker 3 30
(Mick Channon) *hld up: rdn over 2f out: wknd over 1f out* **9/2**[2]

-000 **10** 33 **Living Leader**[18] 2540 7-8-6 65 (p) EdwardGreatrex(5) 5
(Grace Harris) *chsd ldrs: rdn 3f out: wknd over 1f out: virtually p.u fnl f: t.o* **16/1**

1m 22.21s (-0.99) **Going Correction** +0.075s/f (Good) **10** Ran SP% **120.6**
Speed ratings (Par 103): **108,104,103,102,100 97,95,88,85,47**
CSF £111.51 TOTE £17.30: £3.80, £1.90, £2.10; EX 165.90 Trifecta £421.30.
Owner Mrs Susan McCarthy **Bred** S L Edwards **Trained** Sullington, W Sussex

FOCUS
Race distance as advertised. Bit of an upset here in an ordinary handicap. The winner is rated back to his Pontefract form.

3098 FUSELAND ELECTRICAL AND MECHANICAL SERVICES H'CAP 6f 16y

8:35 (8:35) (Class 5) (0-70,70) 3-Y-O+ **£2,911** (£866; £432; £216) **Stalls** Centre

Form RPR

4511 **1** **Gilmer (IRE)**[13] 2697 5-9-0 61 NoelGarbutt(5) 3 73+
(Laura Young) *s.s: in rr: rdn and hdwy over 2f out: swtchd rt over 1f out: str burst to ld wl ins fnl f* **7/2**[1]

0-02 **2** ¾ **Jaganory (IRE)**[7] 2845 4-9-4 60 (p) PatCosgrave 11 67
(Christopher Mason) *chsd ldrs: rdn over 2f out: ev ch ins fnl f: tk 2nd nr fin* **11/2**[3]

055 **3** ½ **Swendab (IRE)**[28] 2202 8-9-6 67 (v) CiaranMckee(5) 1 72
(John O'Shea) *led: rdn over 2f out: edgd lft over 1f out: hdd wl ins fnl f* **16/1**

5043 **4** 1¼ **Glastonberry**[30] 2146 8-9-9 70 JosephineGordon(5) 9 71
(Geoffrey Deacon) *chsd ldrs: rdn over 2f out: unable qck fnl f* **11/2**[3]

2350 **5** *shd* **Indian Affair**[20] 2491 6-9-11 67 (bt) RoystonFfrench 16 68
(Milton Bradley) *chsd ldrs: rdn over 2f out: sn sltly outpcd by principals: kpt on fnl f* **6/1**

00-0 **6** 1¼ **Verus Delicia (IRE)**[21] 2442 7-9-4 63 MichaelJMMurphy(3) 8 60
(Daniel Mark Loughnane) *towards rr: rdn over 2f out: hdwy over 1f out: one pce fnl f* **16/1**

-236 **7** ½ **Born To Finish (IRE)**[29] 2186 3-9-2 66 (p) MartinLane 14 61+
(Jeremy Gask) *s.i.s: towards rr: rdn over 3f out: hdwy over 1f out: nudged along and no imp on ldrs fnl f* **9/2**[2]

200 **8** ½ **Agerzam**[10] 2765 6-9-6 62 (p) DavidProbert 5 56
(Ronald Harris) *mid-div: hdwy 1/2-way: rdn over 2f out: ev ch over 1f out: wknd ins fnl f* **14/1**

0-00 **9** 2 **Firgrove Bridge (IRE)**[34] 2040 4-9-8 64 AdamBeschizza 17 51
(Steph Hollinshead) *wnt to post early: s.i.s: in rr: rdn 1/2-way: no imp* **20/1**

4044 **10** 5 **Noverre To Go (IRE)**[10] 2765 10-9-7 63 (p) LukeMorris 4 34
(Ronald Harris) *t.k.h: chsd ldrs: rdn over 2f out: wknd over 1f out* **8/1**

1m 11.98s (-0.02) **Going Correction** +0.075s/f (Good)
WFA 3 from 4yo+ 8lb **10** Ran SP% **119.8**
Speed ratings (Par 103): **103,102,101,99,99 97,97,96,93,87**
CSF £23.44 CT £283.28 TOTE £4.10: £2.00, £2.20, £3.40; EX 23.00 Trifecta £359.20.
Owner Total Plumbing Supporters Club **Bred** Darley **Trained** Broomfield, Somerset

FOCUS
Race distance as advertised. The action unfolded centre-to-stands' side in this moderate sprint. The winner rates a bit better than the bare form.

3099 LONGCROFT H'CAP 2m 49y

9:10 (9:10) (Class 6) (0-65,64) 4-Y-O+ **£2,264** (£673; £336; £168) **Stalls** Low

Form RPR

0214 **1** **Urban Space**[7] 2850 10-9-0 57 (t) TimClark(3) 3 63
(John Flint) *chsd ldrs: rdn over 2f out: hung rt over 1f out: led ins fnl f: hld on wl* **6/1**[3]

/363 **2** *nk* **Prince Of Islay (IRE)**[31] 2131 5-8-10 **50**......................(b) RobertHavlin 10 56
(Amanda Perrett) *prom: led after 4f tl 1/2-way: styd cl up: led again over 3f out: sn drvn: hdd ins fnl f: kpt on* **5/1**[2]

0-44 **3** *1 1/2* **Madame Lafite**[42] 1831 4-9-7 **62**.. GeorgeBaker 9 66
(Jonathan Portman) *s.s: hld up in rr: hdwy over 3f out: rdn over 2f out: hung lft after: styd on to go 3rd ins fnl f* **9/2**[1]

-044 **4** *nk* **Agreement (IRE)**[31] 2131 6-9-0 **59**.......................(b) EdwardGreatrex[(5)] 6 62
(Nikki Evans) *a.p: rdn over 3f out: styd on: unable qck and lost 3rd ins fnl f* **12/1**

00-0 **5** *2 3/4* **Lucky Diva**[14] 2634 9-8-6 **53**....................................(p) PatrickVaughan[(7)] 2 53
(Bill Turner) *mid-div: hdwy 4f out: rdn over 2f out: wknd fnl f* **20/1**

0-66 **6** *1* **Taste The Wine (IRE)**[16] 2131 10-9-4 **58**...................... DavidProbert 12 57
(Bernard Llewellyn) *hld up: stdy hdwy over 3f out: rdn over 2f out: one pce fnl f* **9/1**

6256 **7** *3* **Thimaar (USA)**[19] 2502 8-8-7 **52**..........................(b) JosephineGordon[(5)] 4 47
(Sarah Hollinshead) *t.k.h: led 4f: styd cl up: rdn 3f out: outpcd over 1f out* **10/1**

3-22 **8** *1* **Fuzzy Logic (IRE)**[31] 2131 7-8-5 **52**.............................(b) WilliamCox[(7)] 8 46
(Bernard Llewellyn) *hld up towards rr: rdn 4f out: styd on same pce fnl 2f* **5/1**[2]

1204 **9** *11* **Shalambar (IRE)**[23] 2370 10-9-5 **59**.................................(v) LiamKeniry 5 40
(Tony Carroll) *s.i.s: in rr: hdwy after 6f: rushed up to ld 1/2-way: rdn and hdd over 3f out: wknd 2f out* **12/1**

6220 **10** *15* **Golly Miss Molly**[27] 2233 5-9-10 **64**.................................(b) LukeMorris 1 27
(Jeremy Gask) *mid-div: dropped towards rr 1/2-way: rdn 6f out: wknd 2f out: t.o* **7/1**

355- **11** *1* **Casila (IRE)**[300] 5398 4-9-5 **60**.................................(p) RoystonFfrench 11 22
(Ann Duffield) *chsd ldrs: rdn 4f out: wknd 3f out: t.o* **12/1**

3m 41.09s (2.19) **Going Correction** +0.20s/f (Good)
WFA 4 from 5yo+ 1lb **11** Ran SP% **125.2**
Speed ratings (Par 101): **102,101,101,100,99 99,97,97,91,84 83**
CSF £38.66 CT £153.98 TOTE £7.10: £2.60, £2.20, £1.90; EX 50.00 Trifecta £347.70.
Owner J L Flint **Bred** Winterbeck Manor Stud **Trained** Kenfig Hill, Bridgend

FOCUS
Race distance as advertised. A weak staying handicap that was run at a decent gallop. The first three dictate a very modest level.
T/Plt: £23.10 to a £1 stake. Pool: £57,338.61 - 1,809.56 winning tickets T/Qpdt: £14.80 to a £1 stake. Pool: £4,229.50 - 210.74 winning tickets **Richard Lowther**

2929 GOODWOOD (R-H)

Friday, June 10

OFFICIAL GOING: Good (good to firm in places on round course)
Wind: light, across Weather: overcast

3100 FREE MONTH TRIAL OF RACING UK NOVICE AUCTION STKS (PLUS 10 RACE) 6f
6:10 (6:12) (Class 4) 2-Y-O **£5,175** (£1,540; £769; £384) **Stalls** High

Form RPR

631 **1** **Mistime (IRE)**[9] 2786 2-9-3 0.. JoeFanning 5 84
(Mark Johnston) *mde all: rdn over 1f out: styd on wl and drew clr ins fnl f: rdn out* **7/1**

5 **2** *2 1/2* **King Of Spades (FR)**[18] 2536 2-9-2 0.............................. MartinHarley 8 76
(Mick Channon) *hld up wl in tch in midfield: effrt and drvn over 1f out: swtchd rt ins fnl f: styd on and wnt 2nd last strides: no threat to wnr* **13/2**

22 **3** *hd* **Tap Tap Boom**[31] 2125 2-9-2 0.. SteveDrowne 1 75
(George Baker) *pressed wnr: drvn over 1f out: no ex and btn ins fnl f: wknd towards fin and lost 2nd last strides* **13/2**

2 **4** *1 3/4* **Fastar (IRE)**[11] 2748 2-9-2 0.. JimmyFortune 6 70+
(Brian Meehan) *restless in stalls: awkward leaving stalls and s.i.s: hld up in last pair: clsd over 2f out: swtchd rt and effrt to chse ldrs over 1f out: 4th and no ex 1f out: wknd fnl 100yds* **2/1**[1]

5 *2* **Herm (IRE)** 2-9-2 0.. JFEgan 2 64
(David Evans) *s.i.s: sn rcvrd and in tch in midfield: chsd ldrs 4f out: unable qck u.p over 1f out: wknd ins fnl f* **33/1**

41 **6** *5* **Reign On**[25] 2295 2-9-8 0.. FMBerry 4 55
(Ralph Beckett) *t.k.h: trckd ldr for 2f: styd handy in midfield: effrt and drvn over 1f out: fnd little and sn btn: wknd fnl f* **4/1**[2]

7 *3/4* **Fire Brigade** 2-8-13 0... LouisSteward[(3)] 3 46+
(Michael Bell) *s.i.s: rn green and pushed along in detached last early: clsd 1/2-way: in tch in midfield and rdn over 1f out: sn btn: wknd fnl f* **9/2**[3]

1m 12.08s (-0.12) **Going Correction** -0.025s/f (Good) **7** Ran SP% **113.6**
Speed ratings (Par 95): **99,95,95,93,90 83,82**
CSF £50.02 TOTE £6.80: £2.80, £3.80; EX 38.70 Trifecta £211.30.
Owner J M Brown **Bred** Ennistown Stud **Trained** Middleham Moor, N Yorks

FOCUS
The first 2f of the mile course was dolled out 5 yards increasing distances of 7f and 1m races by 12 yards. The top bend was out 3 yards increasing distances of the 1m2f/1m4f races by 8 yards. The going was good, good to firm in places on the round course. This opening novice auction was run at a fair pace and the winner scored in good style under a positive ride. The third looks the best guide.

3101 FEDERATION OF BLOODSTOCK AGENTS APPRENTICE STKS (H'CAP) 7f
6:45 (6:45) (Class 4) (0-85,85) 4-Y-O+ **£5,175** (£1,540; £769; £384) **Stalls** Low

Form RPR

0-00 **1** **Pastoral Player**[22] 2391 9-9-7 **85**........................ CharlieBennett[(5)] 7 93
(Hughie Morrison) *taken down early: stdd s: hld up in tch in rr: effrt 2f out: hdwy 1f out: chsd ldr ins fnl f: r.o under hands and heels riding to ld last strides* **13/2**

2552 **2** *hd* **Easy Tiger**[5] 2934 4-9-7 **80**.. LouisSteward 4 87
(William Muir) *led for 1f: chsd ldr after tl led on bit wl over 1f out: rdn over 1f out: drvn ins fnl f: kpt on u.p: hdd last strides* **5/4**[1]

2405 **3** *1 1/2* **Steal The Scene (IRE)**[20] 2460 4-9-1 **79**...................... HollieDoyle[(5)] 2 82
(Richard Hannon) *hld up in tch: effrt and swtchd lft over 1f out: nt clrst of runs and swtchd bk rt ent fnl f: styd on u.p to go 3rd towards fin* **4/1**[2]

5-66 **4** *1/2* **Misterioso (IRE)**[16] 2587 4-9-7 **83**.................................. LucyKBarry[(3)] 6 85
(Jamie Osborne) *awkward leaving stalls: t.k.h and sn rcvrd to trck ldrs: effrt to chse ldr over 1f out: unable qck 1f out: kpt on same pce and lost 2 pls ins fnl f* **11/2**[3]

-260 **5** *1 1/2* **Royal Normandy**[28] 2217 4-8-11 **70**.................................(b) RobHornby 1 68
(Andrew Balding) *trckd ldrs: effrt on inner over 2f out: no imp u.p over 1f out: wknd ins fnl f* **12/1**

-100 **6** *1* **The Big Lad**[16] 2581 4-8-12 **78**.................................. StephenCummins[(7)] 8 73
(Richard Hughes) *wnt rt s: pushed along and hdwy to ld after 1f: rdn and hdd wl over 1f out: outpcd over 1f out: wknd ins fnl f* **8/1**

0-50 **7** *5* **Welsh Inlet (IRE)**[29] 2187 8-8-8 **67**.................................... DannyBrock 5 48
(John Bridger) *hld up in tch in last pair: effrt 2f out: no prog u.p over 1f out: wknd fnl f* **25/1**

1m 26.91s (-0.09) **Going Correction** +0.025s/f (Good) **7** Ran SP% **115.8**
Speed ratings (Par 105): **101,100,99,98,96 95,89**
CSF £15.53 CT £37.41 TOTE £7.50: £2.90, £1.30; EX 19.60 Trifecta £64.20.
Owner The Pursuits Partnership **Bred** Whitsbury Manor Stud & Pigeon House Stud **Trained** East Ilsley, Berks
■ Stewards' Enquiry : Lucy K Barry caution; careless riding

FOCUS
Rail movement added 12yds to race distance. The pace was not very strong and there was a tight finish in this fair handicap. The winner is rated to his best during the past year.

3102 SIR ERIC PARKER MEMORIAL STKS (H'CAP) 1m 1f 192y
7:20 (7:21) (Class 3) (0-90,84) 3-Y-O **£9,703** (£2,887; £1,443; £721) **Stalls** Low

Form RPR

-303 **1** **Altarsheed (IRE)**[13] 2694 3-9-6 **83**.................................... FrankieDettori 4 91
(Richard Hannon) *hld up in rr: effrt on inner over 2f out: nt clr run and switching lft over 1f out: hdwy and 4th whn changed legs and qcknd ins fnl f: led fnl 50yds: sn in command and eased cl home* **9/2**

-341 **2** *3/4* **Paling**[25] 2291 3-9-0 **77**.. WilliamTwiston-Davies 3 84
(Roger Charlton) *hld up in tch: n.m.r ent fnl 2f: rdn and hdwy over 1f out: led jst ins fnl f: hdd and one pce fnl 50yds* **4/1**[3]

3234 **3** *1 3/4* **Mariee**[20] 2473 3-9-4 **81**.. JoeFanning 1 84
(Mark Johnston) *sn led: hdd after 2f: chsd ldr tl rdn to ld wl over 1f out: hdd jst ins fnl f: styd on same pce after* **7/2**[2]

15 **4** *hd* **Sam Missile (IRE)**[40] 1891 3-9-4 **84**............................ DanielMuscutt[(3)] 2 87
(James Fanshawe) *t.k.h: trckd ldrs: effrt wl over 2f out: styd on same pce fnl f* **3/1**[1]

5304 **5** *7* **Lilbourne Prince (IRE)**[18] 2538 3-8-12 **75**.............................. JFEgan 6 64
(David Evans) *broke wl: sn stdd and hld up in last pair: effrt over 2f out: no hdwy over 1f out: wknd fnl f* **10/1**

2-05 **6** *3 1/2* **Celebration Day (IRE)**[20] 2471 3-9-2 **79**......................(v[1]) JimCrowley 5 61
(Simon Crisford) *led after 2f: rdn and hdd over 1f out: wknd fnl f* **9/2**

2m 7.67s (-0.43) **Going Correction** +0.025s/f (Good) **6** Ran SP% **112.7**
Speed ratings (Par 103): **102,101,100,99,94 91**
CSF £22.64 TOTE £4.70: £2.50, £2.30; EX 18.40 Trifecta £43.70.
Owner Hamdan Al Maktoum **Bred** L Montgomery **Trained** East Everleigh, Wilts
■ Stewards' Enquiry : Jim Crowley jockey said gelding stumbled shortly after the start and hung right-handed.

FOCUS
Rail movement added 8yds to race distance. TThis decent handicap was a race of changing fortunes in the closing stages. There are positives to be taken from the first four.

3103 RUSSIAN STANDARD ORIGINAL STKS (H'CAP) 1m 4f
7:50 (7:50) (Class 4) (0-85,82) 3-Y-O **£6,469** (£1,925; £962; £481) **Stalls** High

Form RPR

0-02 **1** **Chelsea's Boy (IRE)**[22] 2398 3-8-13 **74**................................ JohnFahy 2 80
(Clive Cox) *hld up wl in tch: effrt on inner over 2f out: hdwy over 1f out: chal ins fnl f to ld towards fin* **8/1**

02-4 **2** *shd* **Nodachi (IRE)**[21] 2440 3-9-0 **75**.. OisinMurphy 6 80
(Andrew Balding) *chsd ldr tl rdn to ld over 2f out: drvn ent fnl f: hdd and one pce fnl 50yds* **9/2**[3]

2126 **3** *2 1/2* **Second Serve (IRE)**[13] 2687 3-9-7 **82**................................ JoeFanning 1 85+
(Mark Johnston) *led: rdn and hdd over 2f out: rallied u.p over 1f out: cl 3rd and styng on whn squeezed for room and snatched up ins fnl f: nt rcvr and one pce after* **3/1**[2]

5015 **4** *1/2* **Sark (IRE)**[22] 2393 3-9-0 **75**.. JFEgan 4 75
(David Evans) *hld up in tch in rr: effrt on outer 3f out: hdwy to press ldrs 2f out: no ex 1f out: wknd wl ins fnl f* **15/2**

31-4 **5** *4 1/2* **Al Khafji**[16] 2580 3-9-2 **77**.. FrankieDettori 3 70
(Luca Cumani) *broke wl: sn stdd and hld up in tch: dropped to rr and nt clrest of runs over 2f out: effrt and hung rt over 1f out: kpt on same pce fnl f* **5/2**[1]

-016 **6** *3/4* **Michael's Mount**[25] 2291 3-8-12 **73**...................................... FMBerry 5 65
(Ed Dunlop) *t.k.h: chsd ldrs after 1f: rdn and hdwy to chal over 2f out: no ex and btn 1f out: wknd ins fnl f* **9/2**[3]

2m 39.84s (1.44) **Going Correction** +0.025s/f (Good) **6** Ran SP% **112.8**
Speed ratings (Par 101): **96,95,94,93,90 90**
CSF £43.10 TOTE £8.10: £3.80, £2.40; EX 34.70.
Owner Dave Dawes **Bred** Rockhart Trading Ltd **Trained** Lambourn, Berks
■ Stewards' Enquiry : Oisin Murphy caution; careless riding
John Fahy four-day ban; used whip above permitted level (24th-27th June)

FOCUS
Rail movement added 8yds to race distance. An ordinary gallop and all six runners had a chance approaching the final furlong, but the first two pulled clear in the end. The winner built on his maiden form.

3104 BESPOKE PROPERTIES MAIDEN STKS 1m
8:25 (8:26) (Class 5) 3-Y-O **£3,234** (£962; £481; £240) **Stalls** Low

Form RPR

0- **1** **Tukhoom (IRE)**[266] 6501 3-9-2 0.................................. LouisSteward[(3)] 7 84+
(Marcus Tregoning) *sn stdd and hld up off the pce in last: smooth hdwy to chse ldrs 2f out: rdn to ld 1f out: styd on strly* **5/1**[3]

22-4 **2** *3 1/2* **Van Dyke**[51] 1575 3-9-5 76.. FMBerry 3 73
(Hughie Morrison) *wnt lft s: chsd ldrs: rdn to ld 2f out: drvn and hdd 1f out: outpcd by wnr but kpt on for clr 2nd fnl f* **9/4**[2]

3 **3** *2 1/4* **Daafik**[24] 2340 3-9-5 0.. FrankieDettori 5 68
(Simon Crisford) *t.k.h early: stdd into last pair after 1f: nt clr run 3f out: rdn and hdwy to chse ldrs 2f out: drvn and outpcd over 1f out: wl hld and kpt on same pce fnl f* **5/6**[1]

0-0 **4** *3/4* **Imari Kid (IRE)**[22] 2414 3-9-0 0.................................... HectorCrouch[(5)] 4 66
(Gary Moore) *stdd and awkward leaving stalls: plld hrd: chsd ldrs after 2f: swtchd lft and effrt over 2f out: no ex over 1f out: wknd ins fnl f* **22/1**

0 **5** *3 1/2* **Cadeaux Boxer**[29] 2175 3-9-5 0.. OisinMurphy 2 57
(Martin Smith) *stdd s: t.k.h: hdwy to ld after 2f: rdn and hdd 2f out: outpcd and btn over 1f out: wknd fnl f* **25/1**

0-6 **6** *19* **Equal Point**[18] 2541 3-9-5 0.. MartinHarley 1 12
(William Knight) *sn led: hdd after 2f: chsd ldr tl lost pl qckly ent fnl 2f: wl bhd 1f out* **20/1**

1m 39.05s (-0.85) **Going Correction** +0.025s/f (Good) **6** Ran SP% **114.9**
Speed ratings (Par 99): **105,101,99,98,95 76**
CSF £16.66 TOTE £6.70: £3.50, £1.80; EX 19.90 Trifecta £24.50.
Owner Hamdan Al Maktoum **Bred** Kabansk Ltd & Rathbarry Stud **Trained** Whitsbury, Hants

The Form Book, Raceform Ltd, Newbury, RG14 5SJ

FOCUS
Rail movement added 12yds to race distance. The odds-on favourite was disappointing in this maiden but the other Hamdan Al Maktoum-owned runner was impressive and they finished quite well strung out.

3105 MISTA JAM STKS (H'CAP) 6f

9:00 (9:00) (Class 4) (0-85,83) 3-Y-O **£5,175** (£1,540; £769; £384) **Stalls** High

Form RPR

4-21 **1** **Very Honest (IRE)**[35] 2004 3-9-4 **80**................................ OisinMurphy 5 87
(Brett Johnson) *racd nr stands' rail: w ldr: ev ch and hung rt over 1f out: led 1f out: stl hanging but hld on wl fnl f: rdn out* **8/1**[3]

0-06 **2** ½ **Calypso Choir**[41] 1865 3-9-5 **81**.. JimCrowley 3 86
(Sylvester Kirk) *racd in centre: sn led: shkn up over 1f out: hdd and rdn 1f out: kpt on but a jst hld ins fnl f* **8/1**[3]

1-63 **3** 1 **Nisser**[13] 2693 3-9-7 **83**.. SeanLevey 8 85
(Richard Hannon) *racd in centre: wnt rt and bmpd s: hld up in last trio: swtchd rt and effrt 2f out: drvn over 1f out: styd on wl fnl 100yds: nt rch ldrs* **15/8**[1]

4-10 **4** *hd* **Noble Peace**[20] 2466 3-9-6 **82**.. FergusSweeney 1 83
(Henry Candy) *racd in centre: in tch in midfield: rdn 2f out: no imp tl hdwy ins fnl f: styd on wl fnl 100yds: nt rch ldrs* **5/1**[2]

21-3 **5** 1 **Go On Go On Go On**[135] 344 3-9-3 **79**............................ JohnFahy 2 77
(Clive Cox) *chsd ldrs: swtchd lft and racd between main gp and wnr on stands' rail: effrt over 1f out: short of room jst ins fnl f: sn hung rt: bmpd rival and lost 3rd 100yds out: wknd towards fin* **8/1**[3]

1-00 **6** 1¾ **Quick March**[35] 2002 3-9-1 **77**.. FMBerry 6 69
(Roger Charlton) *racd in centre: wnt lft and bmpd rival s: hld up in last trio: effrt 2f out: kpt on but nvr enough pce to chal* **12/1**

-115 **7** ½ **Bring On A Spinner**[25] 2314 3-8-4 **71**.......................... AaronJones[(5)] 4 62
(Stuart Williams) *racd in centre: chsd ldrs: rdn and lost pl 2f out: hld and kpt on same pce ins fnl f* **9/1**

6-12 **8** 2 **Ower Fly**[56] 1452 3-9-0 **83**.. MeganNicholls[(7)] 7 67
(Richard Hannon) *racd in centre: squeezed out s: hld up in rr: effrt 2f out: no hdwy: bhd fnl f* **8/1**[3]

1m 11.63s (-0.57) **Going Correction** -0.025s/f (Good) **8** Ran SP% **113.6**
Speed ratings (Par 101): **102,101,100,99,98 96,95,92**
CSF £68.35 CT £169.91 TOTE £7.70: £2.60, £2.50, £1.10; EX 71.90 Trifecta £311.00.
Owner J Daniels, B R Johnson and Omni **Bred** Darley **Trained** Epsom, Surrey

FOCUS
The winner raced alone near the stands' rail in this interesting handicap. The first two dominated and the winner is rated as improving,.
T/Plt: £381.00 to a £1 stake. Pool: £48,184.72 - 92.31 winning tickets T/Qpdt: £45.60 to a £1 stake. Pool: £4,518.56 - 73.24 winning tickets **Steve Payne**

2623 SANDOWN (R-H)

Friday, June 10

OFFICIAL GOING: Good (good to firm in places; 7.3)
Wind: Almost nil Weather: Fine, warm

3106 VISIT SRI LANKA/EBF STALLIONS NOVICE STKS 5f 6y

1:45 (1:46) (Class 5) 2-Y-O **£3,881** (£1,155; £577; £288) **Stalls** Low

Form RPR

1 **Somebody To Love (IRE)** 2-8-11 0................................ RyanMoore 7 85+
(Richard Hannon) *awkward s and s.i.s: detached in last early: stl last and waiting for a gap jst over 1f out: str prog fnl f: led 100yds out: stormed clr: quite impressive debut* **5/1**[3]

2 2¼ **Blue Suede (IRE)** 2-8-11 0.. KieranO'Neill 8 77
(Richard Hannon) *t.k.h: trckd ldng pair: chal over 1f out: led jst ins fnl f: hanging and rn green after: hdd and outpcd last 100yds* **33/1**

3 *hd* **Mutawakked (IRE)** 2-9-2 0.. JimmyFortune 3 81+
(Brian Meehan) *chsd ldng trio: pushed along 1/2-way: rdn over 1f out: styd on ins fnl f: nrly tk 2nd but nvr gng pce to chal* **4/1**[2]

4 2 **Vote** 2-8-11 0.. RyanTate 5 69
(James Eustace) *in tch in rr against rail: pushed along and prog to chse ldng pair fnl f: cl up whn hmpd 120yds out: nt rcvr but kpt on nr fin* **33/1**

3 **5** ½ **Apamurra (USA)**[7] 2874 2-8-11 0................................... WilliamBuick 2 67
(Mark Johnston) *trckd ldr: led wl over 1f out gng easily: rdn and hdd jst ins fnl f: wknd* **7/4**[1]

0 **6** 2¼ **Sans Souci Bay**[23] 2371 2-9-2 0.. SeanLevey 6 64+
(Richard Hannon) *in tch in rr: shkn up and no real prog whn checked briefly 1f out* **10/1**

7 *hd* **Hilario** 2-9-2 0.. GeraldMosse 4 63
(Charles Hills) *in tch in rr: pushed along 1/2-way: no prog over 1f out* **6/1**

0 **8** 11 **White Chin (IRE)**[10] 2757 2-9-2 0.............................. RichardKingscote 1 24
(Tom Dascombe) *led to wl over 1f out: wknd rapidly: t.o* **8/1**

1m 2.26s (0.66) **Going Correction** 0.0s/f (Good) **8** Ran SP% **113.4**
Speed ratings (Par 93): **94,90,90,86,86 82,82,64**
CSF £136.46 TOTE £5.10: £1.80, £3.90, £1.50; EX 82.50 Trifecta £439.00.
Owner Magnier, Mrs Shanahan, Tabor **Bred** Roundhill Stud **Trained** East Everleigh, Wilts

FOCUS
The ground had dried out a little and was now good, good to firm in places. Rail out up to 5yds from 1m1f to winning post, adding 21yds to race distances on round course. Sprint course at full width. This useful novice event was quite a messy affair, but a remarkable performance from the winner.

3107 SRI LANKA: PARADISE ISLAND/EBF STALLIONS FILLIES' H'CAP 1m 14y

2:20 (2:20) (Class 4) (0-85,84) 3-Y-O **£6,469** (£1,925; £962; £481) **Stalls** Low

Form RPR

3-31 **1** **Desert Haze**[21] 2420 3-8-13 **76**.. FMBerry 7 87+
(Ralph Beckett) *trckd ldr after 2f: chal gng easily over 2f out: led over 1f out: rdn out to assert last 100yds* **5/4**[1]

210- **2** 1½ **Giveaway Glance**[258] 6757 3-8-13 **76**........................ FergusSweeney 3 84+
(Alan King) *hld up in last: nt clr run 2f out and swtchd lft: shkn up and prog over 1f out: styd on wl to take 2nd last strides* **16/1**

1412 **3** *nk* **Bocking End (IRE)**[10] 2783 3-8-12 **75**............................ RyanMoore 6 82
(Michael Bell) *led after 1f: drvn and pressed over 2f out: hdd over 1f out: kpt on tl no ex last 100yds: lost 3rd fnl strides* **11/2**[3]

0-1 **4** 1 **Out Of The Dark (IRE)**[20] 2470 3-9-3 **83**.................. TomMarquand[(3)] 2 88
(Richard Hannon) *hld up in 6th: rdn over 2f out: tending to hang rt but prog to chse clr ldng pair wl over 1f out: kpt on but lost 3rd ins fnl f* **4/1**[2]

04-3 **5** 2¾ **Wall Of Light**[14] 2653 3-8-8 **71**.................................. RichardKingscote 5 69
(Tom Dascombe) *chsd ldng trio: shkn up and no prog over 2f out: wl btn over 1f out: fdd fnl f* **12/1**

62-1 **6** ¾ **Wholesome (USA)**[21] 2419 3-9-7 **84**............................ DougieCostello 1 81
(K R Burke) *taken down early: t.k.h: hld up in 5th: pushed along over 2f out: no prog and nvr involved* **7/1**

0-24 **7** 2¼ **Stylistik**[45] 1750 3-8-12 **75**.. KieranO'Neill 4 66
(Luke Dace) *led 1f: sn in 3rd: rdn wl over 2f out: lost pl and wknd wl over 1f out* **11/1**

1m 44.67s (1.37) **Going Correction** +0.10s/f (Good) **7** Ran SP% **114.2**
Speed ratings (Par 98): **97,95,95,94,91 90,88**
CSF £23.88 TOTE £1.90: £1.10, £6.40; EX 18.60 Trifecta £59.20.
Owner H H Sheikh Mohammed Bin Khalifa Al Thani **Bred** Whatton Manor Stud & Robert Cornelius **Trained** Kimpton, Hants

FOCUS
Rail movement added 21yds to race distance. A fair handicap featuring some progressive 3yo fillies, though the pace was nothing special and those at the front looked favoured. The level of the form is set around the third.

3108 AMAZING SRI LANKA/EBFSTALLIONS.COM MAIDEN STKS 7f 16y

2:55 (2:56) (Class 5) 2-Y-O **£3,881** (£1,155; £577; £288) **Stalls** Low

Form RPR

1 **Monticello (IRE)** 2-9-5 0.. JoeFanning 6 78+
(Mark Johnston) *mde all: rdn 2f out: pressed over 1f out: styd on wl and a holding runner-up ins fnl f* **5/2**[2]

2 ½ **Celestial Spheres (IRE)** 2-9-5 0...................................... WilliamBuick 3 77+
(Charlie Appleby) *trckd ldng trio: wnt 2nd 2f out: shkn up over 1f out and sn tried to chal: styd on but a hld fnl f* **2/1**[1]

3 2½ **Wefait (IRE)** 2-9-5 0.. RyanMoore 1 70+
(Richard Hannon) *in tch in 5th: shkn up 3f out: nvr able to threaten ldrs but kpt on to take 3rd fnl f* **10/3**[3]

60 **4** ½ **Ingleby Mackenzie**[8] 2822 2-9-5 0................................ CharlesBishop 2 69
(Mick Channon) *chsd ldng pair to over 2f out: sn pushed along: outpcd over 1f out: kpt on fnl f: nt disgracd* **22/1**

5 *nk* **Manolito De Madrid (GER)** 2-9-5 0............................ DavidProbert 4 68+
(Andrew Balding) *plld hrd early: hld up in last: effrt and in tch 2f out: outpcd and rn green over 1f out: kpt on wl last 100yds* **10/1**

6 ½ **Star Maker** 2-9-5 0.. JimCrowley 7 66+
(Sylvester Kirk) *hld up in 6th: effrt on outer and cl enough 2f out: rn green and outpcd over 1f out: kpt on* **10/1**

7 2¾ **Baker Street** 2-9-5 0.. RichardKingscote 5 59+
(Tom Dascombe) *chsd wnr to 2f out: wknd rapidly fnl f* **12/1**

1m 33.05s (3.55) **Going Correction** +0.10s/f (Good) **7** Ran SP% **115.2**
Speed ratings (Par 93): **83,82,79,79,78 78,74**
CSF £8.08 TOTE £3.50: £1.70, £1.30; EX 9.50 Trifecta £26.60.
Owner Dr J Walker **Bred** Mrs C Regalado-Gonzalez **Trained** Middleham Moor, N Yorks

FOCUS
Rail movement added 21yds to race distance. An interesting maiden with six of the seven runners newcomers, but they went no pace and with the winner enjoying the run of things, this form would be far from certain to be confirmed should any these meet each other again in the future. The winner could do no more than win well.

3109 GEORGE LINDON-TRAVERS MEMORIAL H'CAP 1m 2f 7y

3:30 (3:30) (Class 3) (0-90,90) 4-Y-O+ **£7,439** (£2,213; £1,106; £553) **Stalls** Low

Form RPR

133- **1** **Bermondsey**[268] 6440 4-8-13 **82**.. RyanMoore 12 97
(Luca Cumani) *hld up in 6th: prog on outer wl over 2f out: led wl over 1f out: hanging rt but sn clr: rdn out: decisively* **11/2**[2]

-650 **2** 5 **Fiftyshadesfreed (IRE)**[23] 2377 5-9-2 **85**..................(p) JimmyFortune 7 90
(George Baker) *hld up in last trio: prog on outer over 2f out: rdn to take 2nd jst over 1f out: styd on but no ch w wnr* **25/1**

-240 **3** 1¾ **Solo Hunter**[36] 1978 5-9-1 **89**..............................(b) JosephineGordon[(5)] 9 91
(Martyn Meade) *chsd ldrs in 5th: rdn wl over 2f out: nvr gng pce to chal but styd on fr over 1f out to take 3rd ins fnl f* **10/1**

-115 **4** 1¼ **Berkeley Vale**[24] 2324 5-8-8 **77**..............................(v) RichardKingscote 8 76
(Roger Teal) *trckd ldng trio: rdn over 2f out: pressed for 2nd pl over 1f out: one pce after* **20/1**

356- **5** 1 **Regulation (IRE)**[34] 8093 7-9-7 **90**................................ DougieCostello 1 87
(Neil King) *hld up in 9th: pushed along fr over 2f out: kpt on steadily to take 5th nr fin: nt disgracd* **25/1**

31-0 **6** 1¾ **Harold Lloyd**[39] 1933 4-8-10 **79**.................................. FergusSweeney 5 73
(Henry Candy) *led after 2f and maintained str pce: hdd wl over 1f out: sn wknd* **9/1**

21-0 **7** 1¾ **Zamperini (IRE)**[23] 2377 4-9-2 **85**.. FMBerry 4 75
(Mike Murphy) *v awkward s: hld up in last trio: pushed along 3f out: nvr a factor but shkn up and passed a few fr over 1f out* **9/1**

033- **8** 1 **River Dart (IRE)**[258] 6734 4-9-0 **83**.............................. RoystonFfrench 10 71
(Marcus Tregoning) *in tch in 7th: rdn 3f out: no prog 2f out: one pce* **14/1**

4-00 **9** 1 **Silver Dixie (USA)**[25] 2296 6-8-6 **75**..............................(p) JoeFanning 11 61
(Peter Hedger) *slowly away: hld up in last: shkn up over 2f out: no meaningful prog and nvr involved* **33/1**

-061 **10** 2¾ **Master Of Irony (IRE)**[11] 2752 4-9-7 **90** 6ex..................(v) OisinMurphy 6 71
(Ralph Beckett) *hld up in 8th: shkn up 3f out: no prog and sn struggling: wl btn fnl 2f* **9/4**[1]

000- **11** 3 **Extremity (IRE)**[251] 6942 5-9-4 **87**.................................... WilliamBuick 3 62
(Hugo Palmer) *led 2f out: chsd ldr to over 2f out: wknd wl over 1f out: eased* **11/1**

-442 **12** 1¼ **Croquembouche (IRE)**[11] 2752 7-9-5 **88**............................ JimCrowley 2 60
(Ed de Giles) *chsd ldng pair to over 2f out: wknd and sn eased* **7/1**[3]

2m 8.34s (-2.16) **Going Correction** +0.10s/f (Good) **12** Ran SP% **118.1**
Speed ratings (Par 107): **112,108,106,105,104 103,102,101,100,98 95,94**
CSF £141.26 CT £1345.53 TOTE £6.10: £2.50, £8.60, £3.40; EX 183.40 Trifecta £1797.90.
Owner Fittocks Stud **Bred** Fittocks Stud **Trained** Newmarket, Suffolk

FOCUS
Rail movement added 21yds to race distance. A decent handicap and, with the pace a strong one, this looks rock-solid form. The runner-up helps with the standard.

3110 SRI LANKA: SOMETHING FOR EVERYONE H'CAP 1m 2f 7y

4:05 (4:05) (Class 4) (0-80,80) 3-Y-O **£4,690** (£1,395; £697; £348) **Stalls** Low

Form RPR

0-11 **1** **Shabbah (IRE)**[35] 2012 3-9-6 **79**.. RyanMoore 8 89+
(Sir Michael Stoute) *trckd ldr: pushed firmly into the ld 2f out: drvn to assert fnl f: styd on wl* **8/11**[1]

-215 **2** 1½ **Both Sides**[27] 2244 3-9-6 **79**.. DavidProbert 9 84
(Andrew Balding) *hld up in 5th: prog to trck ldng pair over 2f out and sn pushed along: rdn over 1f out: styd on to take 2nd last 100yds: unable to chal* **5/1**[2]

16 **3** ½ **White Shaheen**[48] 1623 3-9-0 76 RobHornby(3) 3 80
(William Muir) *chsd ldng pair to over 2f out: sn shkn up: rdn over 1f out: styd on to take 3rd nr fin* **8/1**[3]

6-55 **4** ¾ **Banham (USA)**[45] 1738 3-8-10 72 (b1) KieranShoemark(3) 5 74
(Roger Charlton) *pushed up to ld: rdn and hdd 2f out: kpt on but lost 2 pls last 100yds* **10/1**

4035 **5** 6 **Bergholt (IRE)**[14] 2640 3-9-0 73 (p) RichardKingscote 4 63
(Philip Hide) *stdd s: hld up in last: reminders fr 2f out: tk modest 5th fnl f: nvr in it* **14/1**

11-0 **6** 1 **Sheila's Treat (IRE)**[35] 1992 3-8-10 69 TomQueally 6 57
(Denis Coakley) *t.k.h early: hld up in 6th: shkn up and in tch over 2f out: wknd over 1f out* **20/1**

-602 **7** ½ **Cape Banjo (USA)**[24] 2321 3-9-1 79 PatrickO'Donnell(5) 7 66
(Ralph Beckett) *chsd ldng trio: rdn on outer over 2f out: sn lost pl and wknd* **20/1**

61-0 **8** 7 **Jim Dandy**[22] 2393 3-9-7 80 WilliamTwiston-Davies 10 53
(Alan King) *hld up in 7th: rdn and no prog over 2f out: wknd over 1f out* **11/1**

2m 10.35s (-0.15) **Going Correction** +0.10s/f (Good) **8 Ran SP% 119.3**
Speed ratings (Par 101): **104,102,102,101,97 96,95,90**
CSF £5.04 CT £16.09 TOTE £1.70: £1.10, £1.50, £2.50; EX 5.40 Trifecta £23.20.
Owner Abdullah Saeed Al Naboodah **Bred** Sunderland Holdings Inc **Trained** Newmarket, Suffolk

FOCUS
Rail movement added 21yds to race distance. A fair 3yo handicap, but they didn't go much of a pace with three of the first four home always up there, but even so that quartet pulled well clear. The form has been rated slightly positively. The time was just over two seconds slower than the older horses in the preceding 0-90 handicap.

3111 BECK H'CAP — 7f 16y
4:40 (4:41) (Class 5) (0-75,76) 3-Y-O £3,234 (£962; £481; £240) **Stalls** Low

Form RPR

0300 **1** **Another Boy**[4] 2981 3-9-1 74 (p) PatrickO'Donnell(5) 9 78
(Ralph Beckett) *trckd ldng pair: shkn up 3f out: rdn to chal 2f out: narrow ld 1f out: hld on wl* **11/1**

1 **2** hd **Dynamic Girl (IRE)**[20] 2459 3-8-10 64 [1] OisinMurphy 6 67
(Brendan Powell) *t.k.h: trckd ldr: led 2f out: narrowly hdd 1f out: fought on wl but jst hld nr fin* **6/1**[3]

-201 **3** ½ **Black Bess**[8] 2823 3-9-8 76 6ex RyanMoore 3 78
(Jim Boyle) *trckd ldrs: pushed along fr 2f out: rdn and styd on fnl f on inner: gaining at fin* **7/2**[2]

010- **4** ¾ **Palenville (IRE)**[357] 3341 3-9-7 75 JimCrowley 7 77+
(Simon Crisford) *hld up in last trio: prog over 2f out: clsd on ldng pair over 1f out: sn rdn and nt qckn: kpt on same pce after* **3/1**[1]

1R10 **5** hd **Beleave**[77] 1071 3-9-2 70 [1] KieranO'Neill 5 69
(Luke Dace) *taken down early: rrd jst bef stalls opened: trckd ldrs: cl enough fr 2f out: rdn and nt qckn over 1f out: one pce after* **16/1**

00-4 **6** 1 **Reaver (IRE)**[31] 2128 3-8-11 65 TomQueally 8 62
(Eve Johnson Houghton) *hld up in last: rdn 2f out: styd on fr over 1f out: nrst fin but nvr able to threaten* **25/1**

2100 **7** shd **Siri**[11] 2749 3-9-6 74 CharlesBishop 1 70+
(Mick Channon) *no room on inner after 2f and dropped to rr: tried to make prog fr over 2f out gng wl but nvr a clr run: pushed along and one pce fnl f* **16/1**

056- **8** 6 **Peter Park**[234] 7370 3-9-6 74 JohnFahy 4 54
(Clive Cox) *led: rdn and hdd 2f out: wknd qckly over 1f out* **10/1**

-645 **9** 4½ **Firesnake (IRE)**[13] 2695 3-9-0 73 (p) JordanVaughan(5) 2 41
(K R Burke) *trckd ldrs: shkn up 2f out: wknd qckly over 1f out* **7/1**

4046 **10** 8 **Big Amigo (IRE)**[21] 2446 3-9-3 71 RichardKingscote 10 18
(Tom Dascombe) *swvd lft s: in tch on outer tl wknd over 2f out: t.o* **8/1**

1m 31.0s (1.50) **Going Correction** +0.10s/f (Good) **10 Ran SP% 118.2**
Speed ratings (Par 99): **95,94,94,93,93 91,91,85,79,70**
CSF £76.60 CT £289.72 TOTE £12.30: £3.20, £2.10, £1.40; EX 92.50 Trifecta £535.10.
Owner Mrs Philip Snow & Partners **Bred** Mrs P Snow & Partners **Trained** Kimpton, Hants
■ Stewards' Enquiry : Patrick O'Donnell two-day ban; used whip above permitted level (24th-25th June)

FOCUS
Rail movement added 21yds to race distance. A modest handicap and the principals finishing in a heap suggests the form is not strong, but a stirring finish. A length pb from the winner.
T/Plt: £160.00 to a £1 stake. Pool: £64,972.32 - 296.28 winning tickets T/Qpdt: £10.40 to a £1 stake. Pool: £5,092.83 - 359.61 winning tickets **Jonathan Neesom**

2485 YORK (L-H)
Friday, June 10

OFFICIAL GOING: Good (7.6)
Wind: Virtually nil Weather: Grey cloud

3112 MEL BRITTAIN EBF NOVICE STKS (PLUS 10 RACE) — 5f
2:00 (2:00) (Class 3) 2-Y-O £6,792 (£2,021; £1,010; £505) **Stalls** High

Form RPR

1 **Angel Meadow** 2-8-11 0 PJMcDonald 9 78+
(Micky Hammond) *dwlt and bhd: gd hdwy over 2f out: rdn over 1f out: styd on strly fnl f to ld nr line* **66/1**

2 hd **Dundunah (USA)** 2-8-11 0 GrahamGibbons 1 77+
(David O'Meara) *cl up: green and pushed along 2f out: rdn and edgd lft over 1f out: chal ins fnl f: drvn to ld last 100yds: edgd lft and hdd nr line* **2/1**[1]

3 2½ **Eltanin (IRE)** 2-9-2 0 CamHardie 11 73
(John Quinn) *green and towards rr: hdwy 2f out: rdn wl over 1f out: kpt on wl fnl f* **12/1**[3]

4 ¾ **Rubiesnpearls** 2-8-11 0 TonyHamilton 2 65
(Richard Fahey) *towards rr: pushed along over 2f out: sn rdn: styd on u.p fnl f* **14/1**

6 **5** shd **Emerald Secret (IRE)**[27] 2235 2-8-11 0 PaulMulrennan 4 65
(Paul Midgley) *slt ld: hdd 1/2-way: cl up and rdn wl over 1f out: drvn and kpt on same pce fnl f* **22/1**

02 **6** hd **Computable**[9] 2800 2-9-2 0 DavidAllan 10 69
(Tim Easterby) *cl up: led 1/2-way: rdn ins fnl f: hdd: edgd lft and wknd qckly last 100yds* **2/1**[1]

7 ¾ **Franca Florio (IRE)** 2-8-11 0 JamieSpencer 5 62+
(Kevin Ryan) *hld up in rr: hdwy whn nt clr run wl over 1f out: sn swtchd rt and rdn: kpt on fnl f* **8/1**[2]

8 6 **Used To Be** 2-9-2 0 BenCurtis 3 45
(K R Burke) *chsd ldrs: rdn 2f out: wknd appr fnl f* **20/1**

9 2 **Precious Skye (IRE)** 2-8-11 0 KeaganLatham 8 33
(David O'Meara) *dwlt: a towards rr* **20/1**

4 **10** 1 **Yorkshiredebut (IRE)**[11] 2739 2-8-11 0 JamesSullivan 7 29
(Paul Midgley) *t.k.h: trckd ldrs: rdn 2f out: sn wknd* **14/1**

11 nk **Maggi May (IRE)** 2-8-11 0 TomEaves 6 28
(David Brown) *trckd ldrs: rdn along 2f out: sn wknd* **20/1**

1m 1.01s (1.71) **Going Correction** +0.20s/f (Good) **11 Ran SP% 118.9**
Speed ratings (Par 97): **94,93,89,88,88 88,86,77,74,72 71**
CSF £188.83 TOTE £57.80: £11.50, £1.20, £4.00; EX 332.90 Trifecta £2978.40.
Owner David Green **Bred** M Zipfel **Trained** Middleham, N Yorks

FOCUS
Fair form in this novice event. Newcomers filled the first four places and they all left the impression they'll improve next time. The winner was a big price but this was no fluke. The pace was sound.

3113 888SPORT.COM (H'CAP) — 1m 2f 88y
2:35 (2:35) (Class 3) (0-95,95) 4-Y-O+ £12,938 (£3,850; £1,924; £481; £481) **Stalls** Low

Form RPR

00-0 **1** **Pandora (IRE)**[34] 2026 4-9-7 95 [1] PhillipMakin 8 102
(David O'Meara) *s.i.s and lost 5 l s: jnd field after 2f: hdwy 3f out: rdn wl over 1f out: styd on strly on wd outside fnl f to ld nr fin* **8/1**

0-54 **2** ¾ **Forgotten Hero (IRE)**[20] 2484 7-9-4 92 (t) KierenFallon 12 97
(Kim Bailey) *hld up towards rr: hdwy 3f out: chsd ldrs 2f out: rdn over 1f out: chal ins fnl f: sn drvn and ev ch: kpt on to ld briefly last 30yds: hdd and no ex nr fin* **6/1**[3]

0046 **3** nk **Maraakib (IRE)**[20] 2487 4-9-1 89 DavidNolan 1 94
(David O'Meara) *led: qcknd clr over 2f out: rdn wl over 1f out: drvn ins fnl f: hdd and no ex last 30yds* **15/2**

6046 **4** ¾ **Mukhayyam**[15] 2620 4-8-4 83 RachelRichardson(5) 5 86
(Tim Easterby) *in tch: hdwy over 3f out: chsd ldrs 2f out: sn rdn: drvn ent fnl f: kpt on same pce* **16/1**

0-30 **4** dht **Empress Ali (IRE)**[30] 2157 5-8-13 87 JamesSullivan 7 90
(Tom Tate) *trckd ldr: pushed along 3f out: rdn 2f out: drvn ent fnl f: kpt on same pce* **8/1**

/000 **6** ¾ **Novelty Seeker (USA)**[13] 2688 7-8-3 82 NathanEvans(5) 9 84
(Michael Easterby) *hld up in tch: hdwy over 3f out: chsd ldrs 2f out: sn rdn: drvn and kpt on same pce fnl f* **20/1**

6613 **7** 9 **Intrude**[90] 920 4-8-11 85 MartinDwyer 11 69
(David Simcock) *hld up: a in rr* **8/1**

3031 **8** hd **Muhaafiz (IRE)**[8] 2811 4-8-8 82 6ex (p) ShaneGray 3 65
(David Brown) *t.k.h early: trckd ldrs: hdwy over 2f out: rdn wl over 1f out: drvn and kpt on same pce fnl f* **6/1**[3]

05-0 **9** 9 **Laurence**[20] 2484 4-9-0 88 AndreaAtzeni 4 53
(Luca Cumani) *trckd ldrs: hdwy over 3f out: effrt 2f out: sn rdn and wknd: eased fnl f* **11/2**[2]

-650 **10** 2¼ **Darrington**[15] 2620 4-8-6 80 PaulHanagan 6 41
(Richard Fahey) *trckd ldng pair: effrt one wd outside 3f out: rdn along over 2f out: sn drvn and btn: bhd whn eased over 1f out* **5/1**[1]

2m 13.41s (0.91) **Going Correction** +0.30s/f (Good) **10 Ran SP% 116.4**
Speed ratings (Par 107): **108,107,107,106,106 105,98,98,91,89**
CSF £55.28 CT £378.09 TOTE £7.60: £2.70, £2.20, £2.80; EX 28.30 Trifecta £192.40.
Owner Sir Robert Ogden **Bred** Sir Robert Ogden **Trained** Upper Helmsley, N Yorks

FOCUS
A few of the market leaders performed below expectations in this useful contest, but that shouldn't take anything away from the performance of the top weight, who did well to prevail after starting slowly and being held up in a race which appeared to be run at no more than a modest gallop until the final 4f. The third and fourth are the best guides to the form.

3114 SKF ROUS (S) STKS — 6f
3:10 (3:11) (Class 3) 2-Y-O £7,762 (£2,310; £1,154; £577) **Stalls** High

Form RPR

52 **1** **Melaniemillie**[22] 2404 2-8-6 0 JacobButterfield(3) 5 72
(Ollie Pears) *prom: trckd ldr 4f out: swtchd lft over 2f out: led wl over 1f out: rdn clr ent fnl f: kpt on strly* **7/2**[2]

40 **2** 3½ **Smiley Riley (IRE)**[17] 2552 2-9-0 0 BarryMcHugh 7 67
(Tony Coyle) *led 2f: prom: rdn to chse wnr over 1f out: drvn and no imp fnl f* **33/1**

5201 **3** 4 **Billy's Boots**[5] 2933 2-9-0 0 FrannyNorton 10 55
(Mick Channon) *towards rr: hdwy 1/2-way: rdn wl over 1f out: drvn and kpt on fnl f* **13/2**

416 **4** nk **Nazik**[21] 2429 2-9-0 0 PaulMulrennan 8 54
(David Evans) *trckd ldrs: pushed along 2f out: sn rdn: drvn and kpt on one pce fnl f* **10/1**

5 **5** ¾ **Major Cornwallis (IRE)**[15] 2611 2-9-0 0 PaulHanagan 11 51
(Richard Fahey) *trckd ldrs: hdwy over 2f out: rdn along wl over 1f out: sn one pce* **5/2**[1]

6 ½ **Mr Skinnylegs** 2-9-0 0 BenCurtis 1 50
(Brian Ellison) *in tch on outer: hdwy 2f out: drvn to chse ldrs and edgd rt over 1f out: sn wknd* **16/1**

13 **7** 3½ **Baltic Beau**[26] 2265 2-9-0 0 TonyHamilton 4 39
(Richard Fahey) *slowly away: a in rr* **10/1**

060 **8** 1 **Graton**[14] 2648 2-9-0 0 JoeyHaynes 3 36
(K R Burke) *chsd ldrs on outer: rdn along over 2f out: sn drvn and wknd* **25/1**

9 3¼ **Elements Legacy** 2-9-0 0 (v1) AndrewMullen 9 27
(K R Burke) *slowly away: a in rr* **20/1**

433 **10** ½ **Zebspear (IRE)**[14] 2641 2-9-0 0 KierenFallon 2 25
(Joseph Tuite) *prom: led after 2f: swtchd rt to stands' rail over 2f out: rdn and hdd wl over 1f out: sn drvn and wknd* **11/2**[3]

560 **11** 4½ **Sheppard's Gift**[4] 2970 2-8-9 0 (b) DavidAllan 12 7
(Tim Easterby) *a towards rr* **33/1**

1m 14.82s (2.92) **Going Correction** +0.20s/f (Good) **11 Ran SP% 118.1**
Speed ratings (Par 97): **88,83,78,77,76 75,71,69,65,64 58**
CSF £122.15 TOTE £4.50: £1.60, £7.00, £2.40; EX 112.50 Trifecta £960.50.
Owner John H Sissons **Bred** John H Sissons **Trained** Norton, N Yorks

FOCUS
A fair effort from the winner to readily land this quite valuable seller.

3115 JIGSAW SPORTS BRANDING (H'CAP) — 7f
3:45 (3:48) (Class 3) (0-90,90) 4-Y-O+ £7,439 (£2,213; £1,106; £553) **Stalls** Low

Form RPR

4033 **1** **Classic Seniority**[4] 2961 4-8-6 75 JamesSullivan 4 87
(Marjorie Fife) *midfield: hdwy and in tch over 2f out: rdn to chse ldrs over 1f out: drvn to ld wl ins fnl f: kpt on* **16/1**

-013 **2** 1¼ **Get Knotted (IRE)**[8] 2833 4-9-5 88 (p) PaulMulrennan 1 97
(Michael Dods) *prom: effrt to chse ldr wl over 1f out: ev ch ins fnl f: sn drvn and kpt on* **9/1**

2-31 **3** 1 ¾ **Normandy Barriere (IRE)**[34] 2028 4-9-2 **85** TomEaves 2 89
(Nigel Tinkler) *in tch: hdwy over 2f out: rdn to chse ldrs over 1f out: drvn and ev ch ins fnl f: kpt on* **13/2**[2]

-040 **4** 1 ½ **Fuwairt (IRE)**[18] 2531 4-8-8 **77** PJMcDonald 18 77
(David Loughnane) *hld up and bhd: hdwy on inner wl over 2f out: rdn wl over 1f out: styd on fnl f: nrst fin* **50/1**

5212 **5** ½ **Best Trip (IRE)**[7] 2857 9-8-13 **82** RobertWinston 8 81
(Marjorie Fife) *led: rdn clr wl over 2f out: drvn jst over 1f out: hdd wl ins fnl f: fdd* **16/1**

1255 **6** ½ **Nuno Tristan (USA)**[86] 960 4-9-0 **90** AdamMcNamara(7) 12 88
(Richard Fahey) *towards rr: hdwy on wd outside 3f out: rdn and edgd lft 2f out: drvn to chse ldrs over 1f out: kpt on same pce* **20/1**

-320 **7** 1 ½ **Brigliadoro (IRE)**[69] 1204 5-9-0 **83** AndreaAtzeni 16 76+
(Philip McBride) *hld up and bhd: hdwy over 2f out: sn rdn and styd on wl fnl f: nrst fin* **20/1**

3300 **8** *nk* **Gurkha Friend**[6] 2917 4-8-9 **78** PaulHanagan 17 71+
(Karen McLintock) *towards rr: hdwy over 2f out: rdn wl over 1f out: kpt on fnl f: nrst fin* **25/1**

4022 **9** 1 ¼ **Big Time (IRE)**[6] 2910 5-9-5 **88** (v) KierenFallon 7 77+
(David Nicholls) *midfield: hdwy and in tch whn nt clr run and hmpd 2f out: sn rdn and no imp* **11/2**[1]

0-06 **10** *2* **Regal Dan (IRE)**[13] 2679 6-8-11 **85** JoshDoyle(5) 6 69
(David O'Meara) *in tch: rdn along 2f out: sn drvn and grad wknd* **8/1**

0-23 **11** 2 ¼ **Alejandro (IRE)**[6] 2910 7-9-2 **85** DavidNolan 15 63
(David O'Meara) *chsd ldr: rdn along 2f out: sn wknd* **15/2**[3]

-050 **12** ½ **Purple Rock (IRE)**[44] 1797 4-8-4 **78** (t) NathanEvans(5) 9 54
(Michael Easterby) *nvr bttr than midfield* **20/1**

664 **13** *nse* **Baddilini**[11] 2754 6-8-1 **75** (p) PaddyPilley(5) 3 51
(Alan Bailey) *towards rr: hdwy on inner and in tch 3f out: rdn along over 2f out: sn wknd* **33/1**

0-05 **14** *hd* **Green Howard**[13] 2679 8-9-1 **84** CamHardie 19 60
(Rebecca Bastiman) *a towards rr* **33/1**

4503 **15** 1 ¼ **Mississippi**[9] 2803 7-8-12 **81** BarryMcHugh 14 53
(Paul Midgley) *a towards rr* **25/1**

4415 **16** *8* **Mystic Miraaj**[6] 2910 4-8-11 **80** (b) DavidAllan 13 31
(Tim Easterby) *chsd ldrs: rdn along 3f out: sn wknd* **8/1**

3-54 **17** *22* **Mount Tahan (IRE)**[13] 2689 4-9-2 **85** JamieSpencer 5
(Kevin Ryan) *chsd ldrs: rdn along wl over 2f out: wknd and lost action wl over 1f out: sn eased* **12/1**

001- **18** *18* **Rex Imperator**[274] 6248 7-9-7 **90** PhillipMakin 11
(David O'Meara) *hld up in rr: effrt over 2f out: no hdwy and lost action wl over 1f out: sn eased* **20/1**

1m 25.73s (0.43) **Going Correction** +0.25s/f (Good) **18** Ran SP% **126.7**
Speed ratings (Par 107): **107,105,103,101,101 100,99,98,97,94 92,91,91,91,90 80,55,35**
CSF £136.10 CT £712.75 TOTE £21.30: £3.60, £2.90, £1.80, £11.30; EX 231.20 Trifecta £5225.90.
Owner D & S Woodall **Bred** E Cantillon, D Cantillon & A Driver **Trained** Stillington, N Yorks

FOCUS
A fairly useful handicap which was run at a good pace. The first three were drawn low and the second looks the best guide.

3116 EBF BREEDERS' SERIES FILLIES' (H'CAP) 6f

4:20 (4:20) (Class 2) (0-100,100) 3-Y-O+
£18,675 (£5,592; £2,796; £1,398; £699; £351) **Stalls** Centre

Form RPR

145- **1** **Mayfair Lady**[251] 6931 3-8-13 **100** AdamMcNamara(7) 6 111
(Richard Fahey) *mde all: rdn over 1f out: kpt on strly* **5/1**[3]

-440 **2** 2 ½ **Dawaa**[20] 2466 3-8-9 **89** FrannyNorton 5 92
(Mark Johnston) *a chsng wnr: rdn over 1f out: drvn ins fnl f: no imp* **8/1**

21-1 **3** 1 ¼ **Mehronissa**[20] 2476 4-9-7 **93** JamieSpencer 4 94+
(Ed Vaughan) *dwlt and in rr: swtchd rt to stands' rail and hdwy 2f out: rdn over 1f out: styd on fnl f: nrst fin* **9/2**[2]

-003 **4** *1* **Rural Celebration**[15] 2621 5-8-11 **83** GrahamGibbons 1 81
(David O'Meara) *trckd ldrs: pushed along over 2f out: rdn wl over 1f out: kpt on same pce* **20/1**

5-04 **5** ¾ **Lady Clair (IRE)**[13] 2683 3-8-10 **90** JoeyHaynes 2 83
(K R Burke) *trckd ldrs: pushed along 2f out: sn rdn and kpt on same pce* **25/1**

0-04 **6** 1 ¼ **Love Island**[26] 2267 7-9-2 **88** (t) GeorgeChaloner 3 79
(Richard Whitaker) *hld up: swtchd lft to outer and hdwy wl over 1f out: rdn and kpt on fnl f* **10/1**

-106 **7** *nse* **Tumblewind**[9] 2803 6-9-1 **87** PaulQuinn 7 78
(Richard Whitaker) *hld up: effrt and nt clr run 2f out and again over 1f out: swtchd lft and rdn ent fnl f: kpt on* **20/1**

0066 **8** 2 ¾ **Gran Canaria Queen**[15] 2621 7-8-4 **81** oh1 (b) RachelRichardson(5) 10 63
(Tim Easterby) *trckd ldrs: rdn 2f out: sn drvn and wknd* **20/1**

0-23 **9** *nk* **Giddy**[13] 2683 3-8-1 **81** oh2 PatrickMathers 8 60
(Richard Fahey) *trckd ldng pair: rdn along over 2f out: wknd wl over 1f out* **15/2**

-230 **10** 1 ½ **Alqubbah (IRE)**[20] 2466 3-8-13 **93** PaulHanagan 9 68
(Ed Dunlop) *hld up in tch: rdn and edgd lft 2f out: drvn and edgd lft again over 1f out: sn btn* **7/2**[1]

56-0 **P** **Queen's Pearl (IRE)**[34] 2042 4-9-6 **92** AndreaAtzeni 11
(Roger Varian) *in tch on outer: hdwy to chse ldrs over 2f out: rdn and lost action wl over 1f out: sn eased and p.u* **17/2**

1m 11.64s (-0.26) **Going Correction** +0.20s/f (Good)
WFA 3 from 4yo+ 8lb **11** Ran SP% **117.7**
Speed ratings (Par 96): **109,105,104,102,101 100,99,96,95,93**
CSF £41.71 CT £194.64 TOTE £6.10: £2.60, £3.30, £1.90; EX 48.90 Trifecta £295.40.
Owner Mrs H Steel **Bred** Mrs H Steel **Trained** Musley Bank, N Yorks

FOCUS
Some useful fillies lined up here but it turned out to be a one-sided affair, the impressive all-the-way winner never looking in trouble, few ever threatening to land a serious blow. A pb from the winner, albeit helped by the jockey's claim.

3117 RUSH HAIR YORK OPENING 18TH JUNE (H'CAP) 1m 6f

4:50 (4:52) (Class 3) (0-90,89) 4-Y-O+ **£7,439** (£2,213; £1,106; £553) **Stalls** Low

Form RPR

4-15 **1** **Shrewd**[20] 2487 6-9-7 **89** MartinDwyer 11 99
(Iain Jardine) *hld up and bhd: hdwy on wd outside over 2f out: rdn over 1f out: styd on strly to ld ins fnl f: kpt on strly* **12/1**

05-3 **2** 3 ¼ **Rite To Reign**[29] 2194 5-9-6 **88** GrahamGibbons 12 93
(Philip McBride) *hld up towards rr: hdwy wl over 2f out: rdn wl over 1f out: styd on fnl f* **8/1**[3]

1-5 **3** 1 ½ **Sign Of A Victory (IRE)**[34] 2024 7-9-6 **88** JamieSpencer 2 91
(Nicky Henderson) *trckd ldrs: hdwy over 2f out: rdn to chse ldr ent fnl f: sn drvn and kpt on same pce* **11/8**[1]

-143 **4** *1* **Two Jabs**[30] 2163 6-9-3 **85** AndrewMullen 3 87
(Michael Appleby) *ledd: pushed along over 3f out: rdn over 2f out: hdd wl over 1f out: grad wknd* **5/1**[2]

-000 **5** 2 ½ **Lungarno Palace (USA)**[13] 2699 5-8-12 **80** (b) PaulHanagan 1 78
(John Gallagher) *chsd ldrs: rdn along on inner 3f out: drvn 2f out and grad wknd* **14/1**

1-65 **6** 1 ¼ **Swaheen**[40] 1880 4-9-6 **88** ConnorBeasley 4 84
(Julie Camacho) *hld up towards rr: effrt 3f out and sn rdn: drvn and sme hdwy over 1f out: n.d* **12/1**

0-00 **7** 2 ½ **Min Alemarat (IRE)**[37] 1967 5-9-6 **88** DavidAllan 8 81
(Tim Easterby) *chsd ldr: pushed along wl over 3f out: rdn wl over 2f out: wknd over 1f out* **50/1**

-313 **8** *9* **Russian Royale**[14] 2663 6-8-8 **76** PJMcDonald 5 56
(Micky Hammond) *hld up: hdwy 4f out: chsd ldrs 3f out: rdn along 2f out: sn drvn and btn* **20/1**

0-45 **9** *8* **Resiliency (IRE)**[27] 2249 5-9-2 **84** RobertWinston 9 53
(Michael Appleby) *in tch: hdwy to chse ldrs 4f out: rdn along 3f out: sn wknd* **8/1**[3]

-401 **10** *3* **Shalamzar (FR)**[15] 2616 7-8-4 **72** (p) DuranFentiman 6 37
(Micky Hammond) *hld up: a in rr* **40/1**

6-54 **P** **Vilman (IRE)**[41] 1852 4-8-11 **79** (p) KierenFallon 10
(Simon West) *trckd ldrs: hdwy over 4f out: cl up 3f out: led wl over 1f out: drvn and hdd whn lost action and p.u qckly ins fnl f: fatally injured* **16/1**

3m 5.6s (5.40) **Going Correction** +0.30s/f (Good) **11** Ran SP% **118.1**
Speed ratings (Par 107): **96,94,93,92,91 90,89,84,79,77**
CSF £103.18 CT £218.27 TOTE £12.20: £3.30, £2.30, £1.40; EX 65.00 Trifecta £211.10.
Owner Tapas Partnership **Bred** Darley **Trained** Carrutherstown, D'fries & G'way

FOCUS
A useful performance from the winner, who continues to go the right way. The pace was a good one and the leading pair both come from towards the rear. The winner is rated back to his old Flat best.

3118 RIPLEYCOLLECTION.COM APPRENTICE (H'CAP) 1m 4f

5:20 (5:23) (Class 4) (0-80,80) 4-Y-O+ **£6,469** (£1,925; £962; £481) **Stalls** Centre

Form RPR

053 **1** **Viserion**[23] 2374 4-8-11 **68** (p) GeorgeBuckell(3) 10 79
(David Simcock) *hld up towards rr: gd hdwy on outer 3f out: chsd ldrs 2f out: rdn to ld appr fnl f and sn hung lft: jnd and drvn ins fnl f: kpt on gamely towards fin* **9/1**

-222 **2** ¾ **I Am Not Here (IRE)**[34] 2043 5-8-13 **70** CallumShepherd(3) 3 80
(Brian Ellison) *hld up in rr: stdy hdwy wl over 2f out: chsd ldrs over 1f out: chal jst ins fnl f: sn rdn and ev ch tl drvn: no ex towards fin* **3/1**[1]

-301 **3** *4* **Kiwayu**[11] 2746 7-8-13 **70** 6ex (p) PhilDennis(3) 14 74
(Philip Kirby) *hld up: hdwy over 3f out: rdn to chse ldrs whn n.m.r and hmpd over 1f out: drvn and kpt on fnl f* **18/1**

5310 **4** ½ **Dark Diamond (IRE)**[11] 1296 6-8-5 **62** (b) JordanNason(3) 4 65
(Michael Chapman) *trckd ldr: led 4f out: rdn over 2f out: hdd and drvn whn n.m.r and hmpd appr fnl f: kpt on same pce* **50/1**

4625 **5** *1* **Medina Sidonia (IRE)**[6] 2911 4-9-2 **73** (p) RachelRichardson(3) 1 74
(Tim Easterby) *trckd ldrs on inner: pushed along 4f out: rdn over 2f out: styd on u.p to chse ldrs ent fnl f: sn one pce* **8/1**[3]

60-3 **6** 1 ¾ **Itlaaq**[38] 1952 10-9-2 **75** (t) DanielleMooney(5) 5 73
(Michael Easterby) *hld up in rr: hdwy on inner 3f out: pushed along 2f out: sn rdn and kpt on fnl f* **20/1**

0-21 **7** *nse* **Kip**[8] 2836 4-9-2 **73** 6ex JoshDoyle(3) 9 71
(David O'Meara) *hld up towards rr: hdwy 3f out: rdn along 2f out: n.m.r over 1f out: n.d* **4/1**[2]

1266 **8** ¾ **Next Edition (IRE)**[35] 2018 8-8-12 **66** (p) JoeDoyle 8 63
(Philip Kirby) *hld up towards rr: hdwy 3f out: rdn along on outer to chse ldrs whn n.m.r and hmpd over 1f out: sn drvn and one pce* **14/1**

300- **9** *7* **Kisumu**[101] 4018 4-8-6 **67** CliffordLee(7) 11 53
(Micky Hammond) *hld up towards rr: effrt and sme hdwy 3f out: rdn along 2f out: n.d* **33/1**

413- **10** ¾ **Chant (IRE)**[370] 2946 6-8-13 **72** RowanScott(5) 12 57
(Ann Duffield) *trckd ldrs: hdwy and cl up over 3f out: led wl over 2f out and sn rdn clr: drvn and hdd appr fnl f: wknd* **20/1**

0-40 **11** *nk* **Lady Clitico (IRE)**[17] 2564 5-9-3 **71** (p) JacobButterfield 2 55
(Rebecca Menzies) *in tch: rdn along over 3f out: sn wknd* **28/1**

0-40 **12** 1 ½ **Arabian Oasis**[24] 2328 4-9-2 **75** AdamMcNamara(5) 6 57
(Philip Kirby) *dwlt: a in rr* **33/1**

6-21 **13** *8* **Tamayuz Magic (IRE)**[34] 2051 5-9-8 **79** (b) NathanEvans(3) 13 48
(Michael Easterby) *chsd ldrs: rdn along on outer 3f out: drvn over 2f out and sn wknd* **4/1**[2]

50-0 **14** *6* **Brigadoon**[21] 2439 9-9-12 **80** AlistairRawlinson 7 39
(Michael Appleby) *led: rdn along over 4f out: sn hdd & wknd* **25/1**

2m 35.19s (1.99) **Going Correction** +0.30s/f (Good) **14** Ran SP% **122.7**
Speed ratings (Par 105): **105,104,101,101,100 99,99,99,94,93 93,92,87,83**
CSF £33.85 CT £497.92 TOTE £10.00: £3.20, £1.60, £5.60; EX 41.70 Trifecta £691.20.
Owner The Charlie Finan Crowd **Bred** Sheikh Sultan Bin Khalifa Al Nahyan **Trained** Newmarket, Suffolk

FOCUS
They went hard up front in this apprentice event, setting it up for those coming from off the pace. The winner was an improver up in trip.
T/Jkpt: Not won. T/Plt: £170.00 to a £1 stake. Pool: £111,283.58 - 477.65 winning tickets T/Qpdt: £20.70 to a £1 stake. Pool: £9,415.13 - 335.34 winning tickets **Joe Rowntree**

3088 BELMONT PARK (L-H)

Friday, June 10

OFFICIAL GOING: Dirt: fast; turf: firm

3119a NEW YORK STKS (GRADE 2) (4YO+ FILLIES & MARES) (TURF) 1m 2f (T)

10:14 (12:00) 4-Y-O+
£187,074 (£68,027; £40,816; £20,408; £10,204; £6,802)

RPR

1 **Dacita (CHI)**[55] 1503 4-8-11 0 (b) IradOrtizJr 2 113
(Chad C Brown, U.S.A) **49/10**[3]

2 ¾ **Sea Calisi (FR)**[34] 4-8-9 0 JoseLOrtiz 1 110
(Chad C Brown, U.S.A) **4/5**[1]

3 ½ **Guapaza (CHI)**[34] 4-8-3 0 JohnRVelazquez 7 103
(Chad C Brown, U.S.A) **63/10**

4 1 1/2 **Trophee (FR)**167 5-8-5 0 ow2 .... JoelRosario 3 102
(Christophe Clement, U.S.A) **132/10**
5 3 **Kyllachy Queen (IRE)**40 1886 4-8-4 0 ow1 .... JuniorAlvarado 6 95
(Marco Botti) **37/1**
6 nse **Photo Call (IRE)**69 5-8-11 0 .... JavierCastellano 5 101
(Todd Pletcher, U.S.A) **18/5**2
7 3 1/2 **Havana Moon (USA)**33 2077 4-8-3 0 .... FlorentGeroux 4 86
(M Delzangles, France) **44/1**
2m 1.46s (0.17) **7 Ran SP% 119.8**

Owner Sheep Pond Partners & Bradley Thoroughbreds **Bred** Haras Paso Nevado **Trained** USA

1357 COMPIEGNE (L-H)
Friday, June 10

OFFICIAL GOING: Turf: soft

3120a PRIX D'EULALIE (CONDITIONS) (3YO) (TURF) 1m
2:15 (12:00) 3-Y-O **£8,823** (£3,529; £2,647; £1,764; £882)

RPR
1 **Lefortovo (FR)**26 2287 3-9-0 0 .... MickaelBarzalona 1 83
(Jo Hughes) *hld up in tch on inner: clsd and rdn to chal ent fnl f: kpt on wl and led towards fin: shade cosily* **83/10**
2 1 1/4 **Proudofyou (USA)**46 3-8-7 0 .... PierreBazire(3) 5 76
(Gianluca Bietolini, Italy) **23/1**
3 hd **Sweet Charity (FR)**41 1877 3-9-1 0 .... StephanePasquier 4 81
(N Clement, France) **2/1**1
4 3/4 **Thisvi**18 3-8-8 0 .... TonyPiccone 7 72
(E Lellouche, France) **11/1**
5 1/2 **Matara (FR)**23 2389 3-9-1 0 .... OlivierPeslier 2 78
(H-A Pantall, France) **6/1**2
6 2 **Elide (IRE)**40 3-8-13 0 .... ChristopheSoumillon 3 71
(P Bary, France) **2/1**1
7 snk **So Funny (USA)**23 2389 3-8-10 0 .... MaximeGuyon 6 68
(F Head, France) **15/2**3
8 4 **Akbulat** 3-8-11 0 .... BauyrzhanMurzabayev 8 60
(A Savujev, Czech Republic) **38/1**
\n\x\x PARI-MUTUEL (all including 1 euro stake): WIN 9.30; PLACE 2.50, 3.70, 1.50;
Owner L Ormsby, H Downs, R Bedford & J Hughes **Bred** Ecurie Haras De Beauvoir **Trained** Lambourn, Berks

2845 BATH (L-H)
Saturday, June 11

OFFICIAL GOING: Firm (10.9)
Wind: almost nil Weather: showers

3121 TOTESCOOP6 ROLLOVER BET NOW H'CAP 1m 3f 144y
1:45 (1:45) (Class 5) (0-70,70) 4-Y-O+ **£3,299** (£981; £490; £245) **Stalls** Low

Form RPR
40-2 1 **Man Look**24 2367 4-9-4 **67** .... LiamKeniry 7 77+
(Andrew Balding) *mde all: pushed clr wl over 2f out: heavily eased towards fin* **10/11**1
5141 2 3 1/4 **Sandy Cove**16 2605 5-9-4 **67** .... RyanTate 1 70
(James Eustace) *trckd wnr tl rdn over 2f out: styd on to regain 2nd fnl f but no ch w easy wnr* **3/1**2
0065 3 1/2 **Dark Amber**32 2127 6-8-13 **67** .... (p) EdwardGreatrex(5) 6 69
(Brendan Powell) *trckd ldrs: rdn to chse wnr over 2f out: nt pce to mount chal: no ex whn lost 2nd ins fnl f* **7/2**3
4005 4 15 **Senor George (IRE)**4 3002 9-8-13 **62** .... RyanClark 4 39
(Simon Hodgson) *s.i.s: chsd ldrs: rdn 3f out: wknd over 1f out* **9/1**
2m 29.84s (-0.76) **Going Correction** -0.15s/f (Firm) **4 Ran SP% 109.6**
Speed ratings (Par 103): **96,93,93,83**
CSF £3.97 TOTE £1.70; EX 3.30 Trifecta £4.60.
Owner C C Buckley **Bred** Hunscote House Farm Stud **Trained** Kingsclere, Hants

FOCUS
Officially firm ground but there had been some rain before racing and they were kicking the top off. The jockeys reported it to be good, fast ground. This was a depleted field and they went a dawdle early, so this was a bit of a non event in truth. They sprinted from the home turn and the leader was much the best placed. The runner-up looks the best guide.

3122 TOTESCOOP6 MILLIONAIRE MAKER/EBF STALLIONS NOVICE FILLIES' STKS (PLUS 10 RACE) 5f 11y
2:20 (2:21) (Class 4) 2-Y-O **£4,819** (£1,434; £716; £358) **Stalls** Centre

Form RPR
3 1 **Tallulah Rose**14 2696 2-9-0 0 .... SteveDrowne 7 78
(George Baker) *trckd ldrs: swtchd rt ins fnl f: qcknd up smartly whn asked fnl 120yds: led cl home* **7/2**3
1 2 3/4 **Groupie**12 2747 2-9-0 0 .... TomMarquand(3) 8 78
(Richard Hannon) *prom: led 2f out: sn rdn: kpt on fnl f: hdd cl home* **11/4**2
3 3 1/2 **Turanga Leela**11 2764 2-9-0 0 .... LiamKeniry 10 73
(Tom Dascombe) *trckd ldrs: chal 2f out: sn rdn: ev ch fnl f: kpt on* **10/1**
4 4 1/2 **Giennah (IRE)**15 2637 2-9-0 0 .... JimmyFortune 1 71
(Brian Meehan) *led tl rdn 2f out: ev ch fnl f: no ex nring fin* **9/4**1
0 5 2 1/2 **Halinka (IRE)**9 2817 2-9-0 0 .... JackMitchell 9 62
(Roger Varian) *cl up: rdn over 2f out: fdd ins fnl f* **8/1**
644 6 3 1/4 **Princess Way (IRE)**46 1741 2-8-9 0 .... EdwardGreatrex(5) 3 51
(David Evans) *sn outpcd: nvr on terms* **25/1**
5 7 1/2 **Joshlee (IRE)**33 2097 2-9-0 0 .... ShaneKelly 2 49
(Richard Hughes) *chsd ldrs: rdn over 2f out: wknd fnl f* **8/1**
8 10 **Kadi (IRE)** 2-9-0 0 .... AdamBeschizza 5 13+
(Joseph Tuite) *rrd leaving stalls: nvr rcvrd and a bhd* **25/1**
1m 2.01s (-0.49) **Going Correction** -0.05s/f (Good) **8 Ran SP% 118.7**
Speed ratings (Par 92): **101,99,99,98,94 89,88,72**
CSF £14.20 TOTE £5.00: £1.70, £1.20, £4.70; EX 15.50 Trifecta £80.10.
Owner The Bailye Baker Partnership **Bred** Floors Farming & The Duke Of Devonshire **Trained** Manton, Wilts

FOCUS
A really interesting fillies' novices' event in which several came here on the back of a promising debut run.

3123 TOTEQUADPOT FOUR PLACES IN FOUR RACES H'CAP 5f 161y
2:55 (2:55) (Class 4) (0-80,80) 3-Y-O+ **£4,690** (£1,395; £697; £348) **Stalls** Centre

Form RPR
0324 1 **Ginzan**8 2846 8-9-2 **75** .... GeorgeBaker 6 83
(Malcolm Saunders) *hld up: hdwy 2f out: led ent fnl f: r.o wl: rdn out* **3/1**1
16-0 2 1 1/4 **Free To Love**11 2768 4-9-2 **75** .... SteveDrowne 1 79
(Charles Hills) *led: rdn and hdd ent fnl f: kpt on but no ex* **4/1**2
2635 3 3/4 **Secret Asset (IRE)**36 2003 11-9-5 **78** .... (v) LukeMorris 4 80
(Lisa Williamson) *chsd ldrs: rdn 2f out: kpt on ins fnl f but nt pce to get on terms* **14/1**
113- 4 2 **Silverrica (IRE)**243 7170 6-9-0 **76** .... TomMarquand(3) 5 71
(Malcolm Saunders) *chsd ldrs: rdn and ev ch over 1f out: kpt on same pce fnl f* **7/1**
0464 5 1 **Midnight Rider (IRE)**21 2491 8-8-10 **76** .... GeorgeWood(7) 2 68
(Rod Millman) *in tch rdn wl over 2f out: nt pce to get on terms* **4/1**2
5034 6 nse **Monumental Man**15 2643 7-9-5 **78** .... (v1) AdamBeschizza 7 69
(Michael Attwater) *prom: rdn and ev ch over 2f out tl over 1f out: fdd ent fnl f* **5/1**3
-110 7 6 **Fear Or Favour (IRE)**12 2754 5-9-4 **80** .... (v1) MarcMonaghan(3) 8 52
(George Scott) *sn rousted along in last: a outpcd* **11/2**
1m 10.04s (-1.16) **Going Correction** -0.05s/f (Good) **7 Ran SP% 116.2**
Speed ratings (Par 105): **105,103,102,99,98 98,90**
CSF £15.68 CT £144.23 TOTE £3.80: £2.50, £2.60; EX 18.70 Trifecta £171.50.
Owner Paul Nicholas **Bred** Hedsor Stud **Trained** Green Ore, Somerset

FOCUS
They appeared to go quite hard in this competitive handicap and that set things up nicely for a closer. The winner's best since her Brighton win last year.

3124 TOTEEXACTA PICK THE FIRST & SECOND H'CAP 1m 5y
3:30 (3:30) (Class 3) (0-90,87) 4-Y-O+ **£7,439** (£2,213; £1,106; £553) **Stalls** Low

Form RPR
00-6 1 **Gratzie**35 2026 5-9-7 **87** .... GeorgeBaker 1 98
(Mick Channon) *hld up: hdwy over 2f out: shkn up to ld ent fnl f: r.o wl: readily* **11/4**1
4423 2 3 3/4 **Van Huysen (IRE)**33 2085 4-7-11 **70** .... GeorgeWood(7) 5 72
(Dominic Ffrench Davis) *s.i.s: in last: hdwy over 2f out: rdn but nt clrest of runs fr wl over 1f out tl jst ins fnl f: kpt on to go 2nd cl home: no ch w wnr* **4/1**2
0525 3 nk **Peak Storm**12 2734 7-8-6 **77** .... (p) EdwardGreatrex(5) 4 78
(John O'Shea) *trckd ldrs: rdn 2f out: chal for hld 2nd ent fnl f: kpt on* **12/1**
0230 4 1/2 **Mister Musicmaster**19 2549 7-8-8 **81** .... MeganNicholls(7) 7 81
(Ron Hodges) *trckd ldrs: rdn over 2f out: led over 1f out: hdd ent fnl f: no ex fnl 120yds* **9/1**3
0-43 5 1 **Hot Mustard**17 2577 6-8-5 **74** .... TomMarquand(3) 3 71
(William Muir) *chsd ldr: rdn to chal over 2f out: ev ch over 1f out: no ex ins fnl f* **4/1**2
004 6 1 1/4 **Air Of York (IRE)**17 2587 4-8-5 **78** .... AledBeech(7) 2 72
(David Evans) *in tch: effrt over 2f out: nt pce to threaten* **11/1**
-012 7 3 **Chosen Character (IRE)**22 2441 8-8-10 **76** .... (vt) LiamKeniry 6 63
(Tom Dascombe) *led: rdn over 2f out: hdd over 1f out: wknd ins fnl f* **4/1**2
1m 38.02s (-2.78) **Going Correction** -0.15s/f (Firm) **7 Ran SP% 112.7**
Speed ratings (Par 107): **107,103,102,102,101 100,97**
CSF £13.46 TOTE £3.60: £2.30, £2.80; EX 20.40 Trifecta £139.00.
Owner David Hudd & Chris Wright **Bred** John Troy & Robert Levitt **Trained** West Ilsley, Berks

FOCUS
A strongly run 0-90 handicap but six of the field were rated lower than 81, so this wouldn't have been the strongest race for the grade and the winner was easily the classiest in the field. She was close to confirming last year's Listed form.

3125 TOTEPOOLLIVEINFO.COM H'CAP 1m 5y
4:05 (4:05) (Class 5) (0-70,70) 4-Y-O+ **£3,203** (£946; £473) **Stalls** Low

Form RPR
0-56 1 **Wind In My Sails**23 2401 4-9-7 **70** .... LiamKeniry 11 78
(Ed de Giles) *hld up: hdwy over 2f out: led over 1f out: kpt on wl: pushed out* **7/2**3
5235 2 1 **Knight Of The Air**15 2635 4-8-7 **61** .... PaddyPilley(5) 4 67
(Mick Channon) *trckd ldrs: rdn to ld over 1f out: sn hdd: kpt on but hld fnl 120yds: barged nring fin* **3/1**2
6 3 3/4 **Zephyros (GER)**39 1949 5-8-3 **59** .... GeorgeWood(7) 2 64+
(David Bridgwater) *in tch: hdwy over 2f out: swtchd lft over 1f out: rdn and keeping on in cl 3rd but hld whn squeezed up on rails nring fin* **5/2**1
204- 4 1 **Bobby Benton (IRE)**82 1767 5-9-4 **67** .... (v1) TimmyMurphy 5 68
(Jim Best) *hld up: hdwy 2f out: sn rdn: kpt on fnl f* **16/1**
2635 5 1 **Caledonia Laird**36 2006 5-9-4 **67** .... RyanClark 6 66
(Jo Hughes) *broke wl: trckd ldrs: rdn 2f out: kpt on but nt pce to mount chal* **7/1**
3240 6 4 1/2 **Diamonds A Dancing**18 2566 6-8-2 **56** .... (be) EdwardGreatrex(5) 9 44
(John O'Shea) *hld up: rdn over 2f out: nvr any imp* **8/1**
0-00 7 3/4 **Prince Of Cardamom (IRE)**15 2634 4-8-3 **52** .... (p) RyanTate 8 38
(Jonathan Geake) *sn led: rdn and hdd over 1f out: wknd fnl f* **25/1**
6060 8 3/4 **Sharp Sword (IRE)**24 2369 5-8-12 **64** .... TomMarquand(3) 7 49
(Neil Mulholland) *s.i.s: sn upsides ldr: rdn over 2f out: wknd over 1f out* **14/1**
1m 40.08s (-0.72) **Going Correction** -0.15s/f (Firm) **8 Ran SP% 115.8**
Speed ratings (Par 103): **97,96,95,94,93 88,88,87**
CSF £14.68 CT £30.30 TOTE £4.80: £2.10, £1.10, £1.30; EX 18.50 Trifecta £29.60.
Owner John Manser **Bred** Meon Valley Stud **Trained** Ledbury, H'fords
■ Stewards' Enquiry : Paddy Pilley three-day ban; careless riding (25th-27th June)

FOCUS
It started raining before this race and rain falling on firm ground sometimes causes problems here but they went a good gallop and there were no problems on the bends. The pace fell apart and the finish was dominated by hold-up horses. Sound form, the winner back to his best.

3126 TOTETRIFECTA PICK THE 1,2,3 H'CAP 5f 161y
4:40 (4:41) (Class 5) (0-70,68) 3-Y-O **£3,067** (£905; £453) **Stalls** Centre

Form RPR
31 1 **Inclination (IRE)**24 2373 3-9-6 **67** .... RyanTate 6 76
(Clive Cox) *hld up: hdwy 2f out: wnt 3rd ent fnl f: sn rdn: r.o wl to ld cl home* **7/4**1
0034 2 nk **Shahaama**3 3038 3-8-8 **60** .... PaddyPilley(5) 7 68
(Mick Channon) *trckd ldrs: led 2f out: sn rdn: edgd lft: kpt on but no ex whn hdd cl home* **5/1**

3142 **3** 1 1/2 **Showmethewayavrilo**[4] 3000 3-9-4 **68**.................... TomMarquand(3) 5 71
(Malcolm Saunders) *trckd ldrs: swtchd lft over 1f out: rdn to chal ent fnl f: tight for room but kpt on tl no ex fnl 75yds* **7/2**[2]
-033 **4** 7 **Remember Me**[7] 2905 3-9-4 **65**...........................(b[1]) GeorgeBaker 4 45
(Hughie Morrison) *led tl rdn 2f out: sn hld: wknd fnl f* **4/1**[3]
5000 **5** 15 **Mostashreqah**[30] 2186 3-9-3 **64**...........................(t) LiamKeniry 8
(Milton Bradley) *prom: rdn over 2f out: wknd over 1f out* **50/1**
-450 **6** 4 **Tim The Taxi**[33] 2107 3-8-6 **58**.............................. EdwardGreatrex(5) 2
(David Evans) *in tch: rdn 3f out: wknd over 1f out* **16/1**
60-0 **7** 19 **Mancinello (IRE)**[8] 2864 3-8-13 **60**.............................. TimmyMurphy 3
(Brian Meehan) *sn outpcd: a in rr* **25/1**

1m 10.73s (-0.47) **Going Correction** -0.05s/f (Good) **7 Ran SP% 106.9**
Speed ratings (Par 99): **101,100,98,89,69 63,38**
CSF £9.46 CT £19.82 TOTE £2.20: £1.10, £2.70; EX 10.20 Trifecta £30.00.
Owner James M Egan **Bred** Corduff Stud & T J Rooney **Trained** Lambourn, Berks
■ Jumeirah Star was withdrawn. Price at time of withdrawal 9/1. Rule 4 applies to all bets- deduct 10p in the pound.

FOCUS
They appeared to go a decent gallop here and this was a true test. The front three pulled clear and the form looks sound enough for the grade. The winner rates back to her debut figure.

3127 COLLECT TOTEPOOL WINNINGS AT BETFRED SHOPS MAIDEN STKS 5f 11y
5:15 (5:15) (Class 5) 3-Y-O+ **£2,911** (£866; £432; £216) **Stalls** Centre

Form RPR
330- **1** **Cosmopolitan Girl (IRE)**[185] 8155 3-8-11 70........... TomMarquand(3) 2 77
(Robert Cowell) *trckd ldr: led over 1f out: rdn clr ent fnl f: comf* **4/1**[3]
42-2 **2** 3 1/4 **Andar**[14] 2693 3-9-5 80...(p) RyanTate 5 71
(Clive Cox) *sn pushed along to chse ldng pair: rdn over 1f out: kpt on to go 2nd ins fnl f: nvr any threat to wnr* **1/2**[1]
-203 **3** 3/4 **Verne Castle**[12] 2750 3-9-5 70.................................. LiamKeniry 4 68
(Andrew Balding) *led: rdn and hdd over 1f out: no ex ins fnl f* **3/1**[2]
00 **4** 9 **Hodgkins Trust (IRE)**[14] 2698 3-8-12 0...................... GeorgeWood(7) 3 37
(Jeremy Gask) *a outpcd in detached last* **50/1**

1m 1.23s (-1.27) **Going Correction** -0.05s/f (Good)
WFA 3 from 4yo 7lb **4 Ran SP% 113.6**
Speed ratings (Par 103): **108,102,101,87**
CSF £6.98 TOTE £6.30; EX 7.90 Trifecta £11.60.
Owner Saleh Al Homaizi & Imad Al Sagar **Bred** Corrin Stud & Dream Ahead Syndicate **Trained** Six Mile Bottom, Cambs

FOCUS
This looked a one-sided maiden on paper with \bAndar\p setting a clear standard on official ratings, but he's proving expensive to follow and his colours were lowered by a filly rated 10lb inferior. She's rated to a better view of her early 2yo form.
T/Plt: £27.70 to a £1 stake. Pool of £46257.19 - 1217.59 winning tickets. T/Qpdt: £6.50 to a £1 stake. Pool of £3178.66 - 361.44 winning tickets. **Tim Mitchell**

2682 CHESTER (L-H)
Saturday, June 11

OFFICIAL GOING: Good (7.1) changing to soft after race 3 (3.25)
Wind: light 1/2 behind Weather: fine, thunder storm after race 2 (2.50)

3128 HALEWOOD INTERNATIONAL NOVICE STKS (PLUS 10 RACE) 5f 16y
2:15 (2:17) (Class 4) 2-Y-O **£6,225** (£1,864; £932; £466; £233; £117) **Stalls** High

Form RPR
42 **1** **Super Julius**[19] 2543 2-9-2 0... JohnFahy 1 86+
(Eve Johnson Houghton) *mde all: shkn up over 1f out: wnt clr last 150yds: readily* **7/2**[2]
2 **2** 3 3/4 **Carson City**[32] 2119 2-9-2 0.. TonyHamilton 4 73
(Richard Fahey) *trckd ldrs: drvn to chse wnr over 1f out: kpt on same pce: no imp* **7/4**[1]
25 **3** 1 1/2 **Four Dragons**[37] 1976 2-8-11 0.............................. RichardKingscote 9 62
(Tom Dascombe) *mid-div: outpcd over 2f out: swtchd ins and hdwy over 1f out: kpt on wl to take 3rd nr fin* **10/1**
45 **4** 1/2 **Amlak**[29] 2219 2-8-11 0.. SeanLevey 8 60
(Richard Hannon) *trckd ldrs: effrt over 1f out: kpt on same pce* **7/2**[2]
5123 **5** 2 1/4 **Who Told Jo Jo (IRE)**[11] 2779 2-8-12 0................. PatrickVaughan(7) 3 60
(Bill Turner) *chsd wnr: wknd fnl f* **5/1**[3]
05 **6** hd **Redrosezorro**[19] 2530 2-9-2 0.....................................(b[1]) PatrickMathers 5 56
(Eric Alston) *trckd ldrs: t.k.h: kpt on same pce over 1f out* **50/1**
162 **7** 4 1/2 **Gerrard's Fur Coat**[10] 2786 2-9-0 0.............................. LiamJones 6 38
(Tom Dascombe) *chsd ldrs: drvn over 2f out: wknd appr fnl f* **16/1**
65 **8** 7 **Chickenfortea (IRE)**[15] 2648 2-9-2 0.............................. TedDurcan 10 15
(Eric Alston) *in rr: outpcd and lost pl over 3f out: sn bhd* **33/1**
06 **9** 8 **Newgate Sioux**[10] 2800 2-8-11 0.............................. BarryMcHugh 7
(Tony Coyle) *dwlt: swtchd lft after s: a detached in last* **150/1**

1m 1.28s (0.28) **Going Correction** +0.10s/f (Good) **9 Ran SP% 118.0**
Speed ratings (Par 95): **101,95,92,91,88 87,80,69,56**
CSF £10.25 TOTE £5.80: £1.90, £1.10, £3.40; EX 12.10 Trifecta £63.70.
Owner B Miller **Bred** T R G Vestey **Trained** Blewbury, Oxon

FOCUS
There had been 13mm of rain since Thursday evening and the going was given as good (GoingStick: 7.1). The running rail was on the very inside so all distances were as advertised. Not a bad novice race.

3129 CRABBIE'S H'CAP 1m 4f 66y
2:50 (2:50) (Class 4) (0-85,87) 4-Y-O+ **£7,781** (£2,330; £1,165; £582; £291; £146) **Stalls** High

Form RPR
23-6 **1** **Marengo**[21] 2463 5-8-10 **74**...(p) StevieDonohoe 4 81
(Bernard Llewellyn) *dwlt: in rr: drvn and hdwy to ld over 5f out: hld on towards fin* **22/1**
406 **2** 1/2 **Modernism**[14] 2688 7-9-4 **82**.. TonyHamilton 5 88
(Richard Fahey) *trckd ldrs: nt clr run 2f out: styd on wl fnl f: tk 2nd last 75yds* **5/1**[3]
21-6 **3** 1 **Zenafire**[22] 2439 7-8-3 **67**...(p) PatrickMathers 1 71
(Sarah Hollinshead) *dwlt: sn trcking ldrs: t.k.h: effrt over 2f out: sn outpcd: hdwy over 1f out: styd on wl to take 3rd nr fin* **12/1**
3-30 **4** nk **Trendsetter (IRE)**[14] 2685 5-9-6 **84**.............................. SeanLevey 2 88
(John Quinn) *trckd ldrs: chal over 2f out: kpt on same pce last 150yds* **5/2**[1]
5/50 **5** 2 1/4 **Nabhan**[14] 2685 4-9-2 **87** ow2.................................. JordanWilliams(7) 10 87
(Bernard Llewellyn) *mid-div: effrt over 3f out: kpt on one pce over 1f out* **16/1**
0104 **6** 1/2 **Newera**[22] 2439 4-9-7 **85**.......................................(p) RichardKingscote 11 85
(Tom Dascombe) *hld up in rr: outpcd over 4f out: hdwy on outer 2f out: kpt on: nvr a threat* **13/2**
-012 **7** 2 1/2 **Bertie Moon**[69] 1222 6-8-10 **77**...............................(v[1]) SimonPearce(3) 6 73
(Lydia Pearce) *chsd ldr: led after 1f: hdd after 3f: chal over 2f out: wknd fnl f* **10/1**
-204 **8** 1 3/4 **Omotesando**[15] 2651 6-8-5 **74**.................................... CharlieBennett(5) 8 67
(Mark Brisbourne) *led 1f: led after 3f: hdd over 5f out: wkng whn n.m.r on inner over 1f out* **18/1**
0100 **9** 2 1/2 **Gabrial The Terror (IRE)**[9] 2836 6-8-3 **67**...............(p) FrannyNorton 12 56
(Richard Fahey) *s.i.s: swtchd lft after s: in rr: lost pl over 4f out* **12/1**
5-04 **10** nk **Sellingallthetime (IRE)**[14] 2688 5-8-13 **82**...........(p) GeorgeBuckell(5) 7 70
(Michael Appleby) *in rr: hdwy over 6f out: drvn over 3f out: lost pl over 1f out* **9/2**[2]

2m 41.65s (3.15) **Going Correction** +0.10s/f (Good) **10 Ran SP% 116.7**
Speed ratings (Par 105): **93,92,92,91,90 89,88,87,85,85**
CSF £128.80 CT £1407.44 TOTE £15.80: £3.80, £2.20, £4.00; EX 221.70 Trifecta £1080.90.
Owner Mrs Beth Williams **Bred** Lilly Hall Farm **Trained** Fochriw, Caerphilly

FOCUS
A bit of a messy race pace-wise, and a bold piece of race-riding won it for the winner. He rates a small pb, with the runner-up close to form.

3130 RED SQUARE VODKA H'CAP 7f 122y
3:25 (3:27) (Class 3) (0-90,86) 3-Y-O **£12,450** (£3,728; £1,864; £932; £466; £234) **Stalls** High

Form RPR
41 **1** **Morando (FR)**[40] 1930 3-9-10 **86**...................................... HarryBentley 4 98+
(Roger Varian) *coltish in paddock: trckd ldr: led over 1f out: styd on strly: readily* **6/4**[1]
-154 **2** 3 1/2 **Tawakkol**[23] 2407 3-9-6 **82**... FrannyNorton 3 85
(Mark Johnston) *trckd ldrs: effrt over 2f out: chsd wnr and hung bdly rt over 1f out: kpt on: no imp* **7/1**
41-5 **3** 3/4 **Sky Ship**[23] 2412 3-9-1 **82**.............................. JosephineGordon(5) 9 83
(Sir Michael Stoute) *trckd ldrs on outside: outpcd 2f out: styd on fnl f* **9/2**[2]
5012 **4** 1/2 **Outback Blue**[12] 2749 3-9-3 **79**.....................................(t) BarryMcHugh 6 79
(David Evans) *in rr: hdwy on ins over 4f out: kpt on fnl f* **12/1**
13-0 **5** 1 **Force (IRE)**[14] 2693 3-9-5 **81**.................................. RichardKingscote 10 78
(Charles Hills) *s.i.s: hld up in rr: hdwy on outer over 1f out: kpt on same pce* **16/1**
-060 **6** hd **Explosive Power (IRE)**[21] 2473 3-9-9 **85**......................... JoeyHaynes 2 82
(K R Burke) *led: drvn over 3f out: hdd over 1f out: wknd fnl 150yds* **13/2**[3]
-160 **7** 1 1/4 **Be Kool (IRE)**[14] 2674 3-8-6 **68**...................................... BenCurtis 5 62
(Brian Ellison) *half-rrd s: hld up in rr: t.k.h: hdwy over 2f out: one pce over 1f out* **25/1**
6414 **8** 7 **Frap**[14] 2674 3-8-0 **62**.. PatrickMathers 8 38
(Richard Fahey) *in rr: hdwy into mid-div over 4f out: lost pl over 1f out: eased whn bhd in clsng stages* **25/1**
0-52 **9** 1 1/2 **Alsaaden**[14] 2683 3-9-10 **86**... SeanLevey 7 58
(Richard Hannon) *chsd ldrs: effrt over 2f out: lost pl over 1f out: eased whn bhd in clsng stages* **17/2**

1m 40.91s (7.11) **Going Correction** +0.525s/f (Yiel) **9 Ran SP% 115.8**
Speed ratings (Par 103): **85,81,80,80,79 79,77,70,69**
CSF £12.57 CT £37.73 TOTE £2.60: £1.40, £2.90, £2.80; EX 15.60 Trifecta £51.50.
Owner H H Sheikh Mohammed Bin Khalifa Al Thani **Bred** Guy Pariente Holding Sprl **Trained** Newmarket, Suffolk

FOCUS
Torrential rain began to hit the course before this race, and soon afterwards the going was officially changed to soft. A good 3yo handicap won by a smart type. Not many got involved.

3131 WILLOW WATER H'CAP 5f 16y
4:00 (4:02) (Class 3) (0-95,92) 3-Y-O **£9,337** (£2,796; £1,398; £699; £349; £175) **Stalls** High

Form RPR
-232 **1** **Celebration**[18] 2554 3-8-11 **82**.....................................(p) PatrickMathers 2 91
(Richard Fahey) *w ldr: effrt over 1f out: kpt on to ld in clsng stages* **3/1**[2]
-312 **2** nk **Reflektor (IRE)**[37] 1977 3-9-7 **92**.............................. RichardKingscote 1 100
(Tom Dascombe) *led: drvn 1f out: hdd and no ex in clsng stages* **1/1**[1]
0-30 **3** 1 3/4 **Powerallied (IRE)**[14] 2693 3-8-13 **84**.............................. JoeyHaynes 3 86
(Richard Fahey) *trckd ldrs: effrt on inner and n.m.r over 1f out: styd on same pce last 150yds* **6/1**[3]
16-5 **4** 2 1/4 **Point Of Woods**[12] 2751 3-8-13 **84**.................................. JohnFahy 4 78
(Ralph Beckett) *hld up towards rr: effrt over 1f out: kpt on same pce: nvr a threat* **20/1**
1-36 **5** hd **Curtain Call**[29] 2218 3-8-7 **78**.. BarryMcHugh 6 71
(Richard Fahey) *chsd ldrs: drvn 2f out: one pce over 1f out* **16/1**
3424 **6** 2 3/4 **Socialites Red**[8] 2863 3-7-12 **74** oh1 ow1.............. JosephineGordon(5) 5 57
(Scott Dixon) *wnt rt s: w ldrs: drvn 2f out: hung rt and wknd last 100yds* **18/1**
10- **7** 4 1/2 **Appleton**[275] 6244 3-9-3 **88**.. HarryBentley 7 55
(David O'Meara) *s.i.s: wl outpcd and sn drvn along: nvr on terms* **7/1**

1m 3.16s (2.16) **Going Correction** +0.525s/f (Yiel) **7 Ran SP% 117.7**
Speed ratings (Par 103): **103,102,99,96,95 91,84**
CSF £6.68 CT £16.00 TOTE £4.70: £2.20, £1.50; EX 9.30 Trifecta £25.40.
Owner Bearstone Stud Limited **Bred** Bearstone Stud Ltd **Trained** Musley Bank, N Yorks

FOCUS
Few got into this, with the first two dominating throughout. The winner improved again to deny the second.

3132 JJ WHITLEY FILLIES' H'CAP 7f 122y
4:35 (4:37) (Class 4) (0-80,78) 4-Y-O+ **£6,225** (£1,864; £932; £466; £233; £117) **Stalls** High

Form RPR
-663 **1** **Bush Beauty (IRE)**[19] 2529 5-7-9 **59** oh1.................. SophieKilloran(7) 4 73
(Eric Alston) *stdd s: hld up in rr: t.k.h: hdwy and nt clr run 2f out: swtchd rt: 2nd over 1f out: led last 150yds: wnt clr* **8/1**
30-5 **2** 7 **Celtic Sixpence (IRE)**[50] 1600 8-8-12 **69** ow2.................. RobertTart 1 66
(Nick Kent) *chsd ldr: led over 1f out: hdd and kpt on same pce last 150yds* **5/1**[2]
0-02 **3** 2 1/4 **Honeysuckle Lil (IRE)**[22] 2421 4-9-3 **74**..................(p) DuranFentiman 3 68+
(Tim Easterby) *chsd ldrs: bdly hmpd 2f out: swtchd rt: kpt on to take modest 3rd clsng stages* **5/1**[2]

0102 **4** *1 3/4* **Fidelma Moon (IRE)**[22] 2420 4-9-2 **73** JoeyHaynes 6 60
(K R Burke) *led: hdd over 4f out: edgd lft 2f out: one pce* **6/1**[3]
650- **5** *1 3/4* **Trulee Scrumptious**[261] 6668 7-8-2 **62** (v) RosieJessop(3) 2 44
(Peter Charalambous) *hld up towards rr: effrt over 3f out: one pce fnl 2f* **9/1**
0-62 **6** *2 3/4* **Desire**[7] 2906 4-8-7 **64** (p) PatrickMathers 9 39
(Richard Fahey) *swtchd lft after s: mid-div over 3f out: drvn over 2f out: fdd over 1f out* **9/1**
5136 **7** *2* **Queen Aggie (IRE)**[110] 670 6-9-7 **78** BenCurtis 5 48
(Tony Carroll) *hld up in rr: effrt and c wd over 2f out: nvr a factor* **12/1**
3460 **8** *6* **Maureb (IRE)**[21] 2491 4-8-13 **70** (p) BarryMcHugh 8 25
(Tony Coyle) *chsd ldrs: led over 4f out: hdd over 1f out: sn wknd* **20/1**
4331 **9** *29* **Colourfilly**[15] 2655 4-8-11 **68** (p) RichardKingscote 7
(Tom Dascombe) *chsd ldrs: drvn 3f out: lost pl 2f out: sn heavily eased: virtually p.u: t.o* **5/2**[1]

1m 38.65s (4.85) **Going Correction** +0.95s/f (Soft) **9** Ran SP% **119.8**
Speed ratings (Par 102): **113,106,103,102,100 97,95,89,60**
CSF £49.54 CT £225.57 TOTE £7.90: £2.40, £3.40, £2.50; EX 69.70 Trifecta £510.60.
Owner D Charlesworth **Bred** Lynn Lodge Stud **Trained** Longton, Lancs

FOCUS
They finished well strung out here, the winner improving hugely for the soft ground. The pace was strong and it remains to be seen if the winner can repeat this.

3133 TSINGTAO CHINESE BEER H'CAP — 6f 18y
5:10 (5:11) (Class 4) (0-85,85) 4-Y-O+
£7,781 (£2,330; £1,165; £582; £291; £146) **Stalls** High

Form RPR
0-03 **1** **Lexi's Hero (IRE)**[24] 2364 8-9-2 **80** (v) PatrickMathers 2 89
(Richard Fahey) *mde all: drvn over 1f out: hld on towards fin* **7/2**[1]
-000 **2** *nk* **Ballesteros**[28] 2238 7-9-2 **80** RobertTart 12 88
(Richard Fahey) *mid-div: hdwy over 2f out: chsd wnr over 1f out: no ex in clsng stages* **20/1**
-006 **3** *1 1/2* **Deauville Prince (FR)**[36] 1997 6-9-5 **83** (vt) RichardKingscote 10 86
(Tom Dascombe) *hld up in rr: hdwy on outside 2f out: styd on fnl f: tk 3rd nr fin* **11/1**
-503 **4** *nse* **Mishaal (IRE)**[17] 2581 6-9-4 **82** BarryMcHugh 8 85
(Michael Herrington) *chsd ldrs 3rd 1f out: kpt on same pce* **14/1**
5-03 **5** *3/4* **Fast Dancer (IRE)**[36] 1997 4-9-6 **84** TedDurcan 3 85+
(Joseph Tuite) *in rr: hdwy 2f out: kpt on same pce fnl f* **4/1**[2]
2-00 **6** *1 3/4* **Personal Touch**[28] 2247 7-8-10 **79** GeorgeBuckell(5) 9 74
(Michael Appleby) *mid-div: hdwy over 2f out: kpt on one pce* **10/1**
0-15 **7** *3 1/2* **Straightothepoint**[16] 2613 4-9-3 **81** JohnFahy 4 65+
(Bryan Smart) *chsd ldrs: edgd rt and lost pl over 1f out* **4/1**[2]
-300 **8** *2* **The Hooded Claw (IRE)**[16] 2613 5-9-1 **79** (p) DuranFentiman 5 56
(Tim Easterby) *chsd ldrs: lost pl over 1f out* **12/1**
400- **9** *8* **Foxtrot Knight**[236] 7343 4-9-2 **80** JoeyHaynes 1 32+
(Ruth Carr) *half-rrd s: detached in last: brief effrt 2f out: eased and bhd in clsng stages* **8/1**[3]
00-0 **10** *1 1/4* **Harwoods Volante (IRE)**[21] 2476 5-9-7 **85** (p) KeaganLatham 6 33
(David O'Meara) *chsd wnr: upsides 3f out: wknd over 1f out: sn eased* **10/1**

1m 18.6s (4.80) **Going Correction** +0.95s/f (Soft) **10** Ran SP% **119.0**
Speed ratings (Par 105): **106,105,103,103,102 100,95,92,82,80**
CSF £76.37 CT £724.94 TOTE £4.80: £2.20, £4.30, £3.40; EX 38.70 Trifecta £400.90.
Owner Dr Marwan Koukash **Bred** T J Pabst **Trained** Musley Bank, N Yorks
■ Stewards' Enquiry : Patrick Mathers four-day ban: use of whip (25-28 June)

FOCUS
A competitive sprint, and a one-two for the Fahey stable and owner Dr Marwan Koukash. The winner's best form since last summer.
T/Plt: £75.60 to a £1 stake. Pool of £58699.23 - 566.37 winning tickets. T/Qpdt: £12.60 to a £1 stake. Pool of £4036.06 - 235.80 winning tickets. **Walter Glynn**

2756 LEICESTER (R-H)
Saturday, June 11

OFFICIAL GOING: Soft (heavy in the dips)
Wind: virtually nil Weather: overcast, muggy

3134 EBF OLD MOUT FILLIES' NOVICE STKS (PLUS 10 RACE) — 6f
6:10 (6:10) (Class 4) 2-Y-O
£4,528 (£1,347; £673; £336) **Stalls** High

Form RPR
41 **1** **Ventura Blues (IRE)**[24] 2376 2-9-6 0 PatDobbs 1 83+
(Richard Hannon) *travelled strly: pressed ldr tl pushed into ld and qcknd ent fnl f: sn in command and r.o strly: easily* **6/4**[1]
4 **2** *3 1/4* **Bridal March**[22] 2437 2-9-0 0 FrannyNorton 5 67
(Mark Johnston) *led: rdn and hdd ent fnl f: outpcd by wnr but kpt on for clr 2nd ins fnl f* **5/1**
3 *2 1/4* **Clef** 2-9-0 0 TonyHamilton 6 61
(Richard Fahey) *stdd s: t.k.h: trckd ldrs: rdn and unable qck over 1f out: 3rd and styd on same pce ins fnl f* **7/2**[3]
0 **4** *1* **Wakened (IRE)**[11] 2771 2-9-0 0 LiamJones 3 58
(Tom Dascombe) *dwlt: in tch in 4th: rdn wl over 1f out: unable qck and btn 1f out* **3/1**[2]
5 *8* **Bathtub Stella (USA)** 2-8-7 0 PatrickVaughan(7) 8 34
(Tom Dascombe) *dwlt: a in last: rdn over 2f out: sn struggling: bhd over 1f out* **20/1**

1m 15.29s (2.29) **Going Correction** +0.25s/f (Good) **5** Ran SP% **108.7**
Speed ratings (Par 92): **94,89,86,85,74**
CSF £9.05 TOTE £1.90: £1.10, £2.30; EX 7.90 Trifecta £11.40.
Owner Middleham Park Racing Vi **Bred** George Kent **Trained** East Everleigh, Wilts

FOCUS
Torrential rain on Friday caused a going chance to soft, heavy in places, and there were a raft of non-runners.\n\x\x Four absentees in the opener, won in good style by the previous winner in the field.

3135 JOHN SMITHS EXTRA SMOOTH CLAIMING STKS — 1m 1f 218y
6:40 (6:40) (Class 6) 3-4-Y-O
£2,587 (£770; £384; £192) **Stalls** Low

Form RPR
40-0 **1** **Senza Una Donna**[16] 2615 3-9-1 64 (t) RobertHavlin 6 71
(Hughie Morrison) *stdd s: hld up in last pair: clsd and nt clr run 3f out: wnt 3rd over 2f out: rdn to chal over 1f out: led wl ins fnl f: hld on: rdn out* **5/2**[2]
0401 **2** *hd* **Scent Of Power**[12] 2733 4-8-9 57 HollieDoyle(7) 1 60
(Barry Leavy) *hld up in tch pair: clsd to chse ldrs over 3f out: wnt 2nd over 2f out: rdn to ld over 1f out: hdd wl ins fnl f: kpt on but hld towards fin* **7/1**[3]
3150 **3** *shd* **Chilworth Bells**[15] 2663 4-9-6 75 JosephineGordon(5) 7 68
(David Barron) *dwlt and bustled along leaving stalls: in tch in midfield: rdn and hdwy to chse ldrs 4f out: 4th and outpcd u.p 2f out: hung rt over 1f out: rallied to go 3rd ins fnl f: styd on wl: nt quite rch ldrs* **11/8**[1]
2-06 **4** *4* **Mollie's Girl (IRE)**[46] 1759 3-8-1 65 FrannyNorton 2 49
(Michael Appleby) *chsd ldrs tl lost pl u.p 3f out: outpcd and wl hld 2f out: no threat to ldrs but kpt on again fnl f* **7/1**[3]
-004 **5** *2 1/4* **Imperial Link**[12] 2733 4-8-9 48 (p) CiaranMckee(5) 8 46
(John O'Shea) *t.k.h: led: rdn 2f out: hdd over 1f out and sn btn: wknd fnl f* **25/1**
0-11 **6** *16* **Frivolous Lady (IRE)**[115] 613 3-7-9 65 (v) NoelGarbutt(5) 3 13
(David Evans) *in tch in midfield: rdn and lost pl over 3f out: bhd fnl 2f* **7/1**[3]
000- **7** *2 1/2* **Virtual Song**[180] 8225 3-7-7 36 RPWalsh(7) 10 8
(Barry Leavy) *chsd ldr: rdn and lost pl over 2f out: sn btn: fdd over 1f out* **66/1**

2m 12.6s (4.70) **Going Correction** +0.55s/f (Yiel)
WFA 3 from 4yo 13lb **7** Ran SP% **113.5**
Speed ratings (Par 101): **103,102,102,99,97 84,82**
CSF £19.86 TOTE £3.20: £1.70, £2.40; EX 20.70 Trifecta £38.30.Chilworth Bells was claimed by C Dore for £12000.
Owner Castle Down Racing **Bred** Meon Valley Stud **Trained** East Ilsley, Berks

FOCUS
A modest claimer but run at a solid pace and it produced an exciting three-way finish.

3136 ASHLEY BARBER MEMORIAL H'CAP — 5f
7:10 (7:10) (Class 5) (0-70,70) 3-Y-O+
£3,234 (£962; £481; £240) **Stalls** High

Form RPR
-626 **1** **Racing Angel (IRE)**[23] 2403 4-9-6 **62** WilliamCarson 1 72
(Mick Quinn) *chsd ldng pair: swtchd rt and clsd 2f out: rdn to ld over 1f out: sn edgd lft: clr and styd on wl ins fnl f: rdn out* **10/3**[3]
2662 **2** *2 3/4* **Bronze Beau**[3] 3009 9-9-3 **64** (tp) JosephineGordon(5) 5 64
(Kristin Stubbs) *taken down early: led and set fast gallop: rdn and hdd over 1f out: hld by wnr and kpt on same pce ins fnl f* **13/8**[1]
20-0 **3** *1* **Malvia**[24] 2380 4-8-11 **60** (b[1]) MitchGodwin(7) 8 57
(Ian Williams) *dwlt: sn outpcd in rr: rdn 1/2-way: awkward hd carriage u.p: no imp tl styd on ins fnl f: snatched 3rd last strides: nvr trbld ldrs* **8/1**
30-0 **4** *nk* **Showbizzy**[16] 2622 3-8-13 **62** TonyHamilton 4 54
(Richard Fahey) *sn outpcd in 4th: rdn wl over 1f out: sme prog and swtchd rt ins fnl f: kpt on same pce fnl 100yds* **7/1**
6644 **5** *2 1/2* **Quantum Dot (IRE)**[21] 2458 5-8-11 **53** (b) PatCosgrave 3 39
(Ed de Giles) *w ldr: rdn ent fnl 2f: 3rd and btn ent fnl f: wknd ins fnl f* **11/4**[2]

1m 1.23s (1.23) **Going Correction** +0.25s/f (Good)
WFA 3 from 4yo+ 7lb **5** Ran SP% **111.5**
Speed ratings (Par 103): **100,95,94,93,89**
CSF £9.34 TOTE £4.10: £2.10, £1.60; EX 7.40 Trifecta £24.50.
Owner YNWA Partnership **Bred** Ms N O'Reilly **Trained** Newmarket, Suffolk

FOCUS
With the top three in the weights all non-runners this was a modest event but they went fast early and the winner did it easily.

3137 FOSTERS SUPER CHILLED H'CAP — 7f
7:40 (7:40) (Class 4) (0-80,79) 3-Y-O+ **£6,301** (£1,886; £943; £472; £235) **Stalls** High

Form RPR
3-00 **1** **Hidden Treasures**[22] 2420 3-8-9 **70** TonyHamilton 3 73
(Richard Fahey) *led tl 1/2-way: rdn: edgd lft and sltly outpcd over 1f out: squeezed for room 1f out: rallied gamely u.p ins fnl f: led towards fin* **10/1**
1611 **2** *nk* **Flying Fantasy**[23] 2401 4-9-6 **76** AaronJones(5) 9 82
(Stuart Williams) *t.k.h: w ldr tl led 1/2-way: rdn 2f out: hdd over 1f out: hung lft ent fnl f: ev ch ins fnl f: kpt on* **11/4**[2]
4503 **3** *1/2* **Smokethatthunders (IRE)**[19] 2540 6-9-5 **70** StevieDonohoe 7 75
(James Unett) *hld up in tch in rr: effrt and swtchd rt ent fnl f: sn chalng: drvn to ld wl ins fnl f: hdd and no ex towards fin* **5/1**[3]
-1 **4** *shd* **Ebony N Ivory**[41] 1892 3-9-3 **78** HarryBentley 2 78
(Roger Varian) *t.k.h: pressed ldrs: rdn to ld and hung lft over 1f out: hdd wl ins fnl f: styd on same pce towards fin* **1/1**[1]
-000 **5** *5* **Piazon**[19] 2531 5-9-11 **76** KeaganLatham 5 67
(Kevin Ryan) *taken down early: t.k.h: trckd ldrs: effrt over 1f out: no ex 1f out: wknd ins fnl f* **12/1**

1m 27.01s (0.81) **Going Correction** +0.25s/f (Good)
WFA 3 from 4yo+ 10lb **5** Ran SP% **110.1**
Speed ratings (Par 105): **105,104,104,103,98**
CSF £36.86 TOTE £11.00: £5.10, £1.90; EX 27.30 Trifecta £82.80.
Owner Andrew Tinkler **Bred** Redgate Bloodstock Ltd **Trained** Musley Bank, N Yorks

FOCUS
Another much-reduced field but an exciting finish in a race that changed complexion dramatically in the final furlong.

3138 HEINEKEN EXTRA COLD H'CAP — 6f
8:10 (8:10) (Class 4) (0-80,80) 3-Y-O
£6,469 (£1,925; £962) **Stalls** High

Form RPR
4-04 **1** **Alizoom (IRE)**[15] 2650 3-9-7 **80** HarryBentley 2 84
(Roger Varian) *chsd ldr: rdn to ld over 1f out: r.o wl: rdn out* **2/1**[2]
1- **2** *1* **Sainted**[217] 7751 3-9-3 **76** PatCosgrave 3 77
(William Haggas) *t.k.h: led: rdn and hdd over 1f out: rn green and edgd rt ent fnl f: kpt on again fnl 50yds* **8/13**[1]
1-03 **3** *3/4* **Early Bird (IRE)**[35] 2050 3-8-13 **72** TonyHamilton 7 70
(Richard Fahey) *stdd s: hld up in tch in 3rd: effrt over 1f out: styd on same pce ins fnl f* **6/1**[3]

1m 14.19s (1.19) **Going Correction** +0.25s/f (Good) **3** Ran SP% **109.5**
Speed ratings (Par 101): **102,100,99**
CSF £3.80 TOTE £2.80; EX 3.50 Trifecta £3.20.
Owner Khalifa Dasmal & A Merza **Bred** M Gittins **Trained** Newmarket, Suffolk

FOCUS
Just three went to post after the non-runners and the winner put his experience to good use in toppling the unexposed odds-on favourite.

3139 STRONGBOW CLOUDY APPLE H'CAP 1m 3f 183y
8:40 (8:40) (Class 5) (0-75,80) 4-Y-O+ **£3,234** (£962; £481; £240) **Stalls** Low

Form RPR
04-1 **1** **The New Pharaoh (IRE)**[29] 2210 5-9-3 **71**...................... GeorgeBaker 7 80+
(Chris Wall) *hld up in 3rd: wnt 2nd over 1f out: effrt an 1 l down 1f out: edging lft whn hit w whip: looked hld up r.o under hands and heels riding fnl 75yds: led last stride* **4/7**[1]
355 **2** *shd* **William Hunter**[23] 2414 4-9-2 **70**...................... WilliamTwiston-Davies 1 78
(Alan King) *chsd ldr: clsd 3f out: rdn to ld over 2f out: drvn over 1f out: looked to be holding wnr tl pressed and no ex towards fin: hdd last stride* **7/2**[2]
0025 **3** *4 1/2* **Medieval Bishop (IRE)**[20] 2502 7-7-10 **57**.................(p) HollieDoyle(7) 6 58
(Tony Forbes) *racd keenly: led and clr tl rdn 3f out: hdd over 2f out: 3rd and outpcd fnl f* **12/1**
3041 **4** *5* **Safira Menina**[12] 2738 4-8-13 **70**.. TimClark(3) 2 63
(Martin Smith) *s.i.s: hld up in rr: effrt over 2f out: no imp: wl btn 1f out* **11/2**[3]

2m 39.41s (5.51) **Going Correction** +0.55s/f (Yiel) **4** Ran SP% **109.0**
Speed ratings (Par 103): **103,102,99,96**
CSF £2.90 TOTE £1.40; EX 2.80 Trifecta £6.90.
Owner Ms Aida Fustoq **Bred** Deerfield Farm **Trained** Newmarket, Suffolk

FOCUS
A modest event run at a steady pace but it produced another tight finish, the unexposed pair pulling clear of their rivals.

3140 STRONGBOW DARK FRUITS H'CAP 5f
9:10 (9:12) (Class 6) (0-60,66) 3-Y-O **£2,587** (£770; £384; £192) **Stalls** High

Form RPR
3654 **1** **David's Beauty (IRE)**[20] 2503 3-9-0 **53**......................... PatCosgrave 12 59
(Brian Baugh) *in tch in midfield: effrt to chse ldr wl over 1f out: drvn and ev ch ins fnl f: led and edgd rt ins fnl f: hld on wl: rdn out* **3/1**[2]
5353 **2** *shd* **Mustn't Grumble (IRE)**[9] 2834 3-9-10 **63**...(p) WilliamTwiston-Davies 13 69
(Ivan Furtado) *stdd s: hld up in tch: effrt to chse ldrs over 1f out: ev ch ins fnl f: edgd rt towards fin: jst hld* **9/4**[1]
-054 **3** *2 3/4* **Putemintheboot (IRE)**[4] 3000 3-8-10 **49**.....................(t) DarryllHolland 8 45
(David Evans) *led: rdn wl over 1f out: drvn and hdd ins fnl f: wknd wl ins fnl f* **7/2**[3]
6650 **4** *2 3/4* **Fiftytintsofsilver (IRE)**[18] 2559 3-8-0 **46** oh1................... RPWalsh(7) 6 32
(Gay Kelleway) *awkward leaving stalls and slowly away: bhd: hdwy to pass btn rivals ins fnl f: styd on: nvr trbld ldrs* **10/1**
0400 **5** *1 3/4* **Vocalise**[32] 2118 3-8-2 **46** oh1.. NoelGarbutt(5) 3 26
(Charles Smith) *in tch in midfield: rdn over 2f out: unable qck and btn over 1f out: wknd ins fnl f* **25/1**
3236 **6** *1* **Justice Rock**[46] 1745 3-9-2 **60**..........................(v) JosephineGordon(5) 2 36
(Phil McEntee) *taken down early: chsd ldrs tl 2f out: lost pl u.p and btn over 1f out: wknd ins fnl f* **9/2**
6066 **7** *7* **Barnsdale**[53] 1554 3-8-0 **46** oh1.......................... MeganEllingworth(7) 11
(John Holt) *chsd ldrs: rdn 1/2-way: lost pl 2f out: bhd ins fnl f* **25/1**

1m 1.81s (1.81) **Going Correction** +0.25s/f (Good) **7** Ran SP% **113.0**
Speed ratings (Par 97): **95,94,90,86,83 81,70**
CSF £9.93 CT £22.81 TOTE £3.00: £3.40, £1.10; EX 11.20 Trifecta £30.00.
Owner G B Hignett **Bred** Miss Sinead Looney **Trained** Audley, Staffs

FOCUS
A weak finale but another close finish on the night, the winner looking the more resolute of the pair that fought it out.
T/Plt: £122.60 to a £1 stake. Pool of £38286.18 - 227.90 winning tickets. T/Qpdt: £29.50 to a £1 stake. Pool of £3143.19 - 78.81 winning tickets. **Steve Payne**

2990 LINGFIELD (L-H)
Saturday, June 11

OFFICIAL GOING: Good to soft (soft in places) changing to soft after race 1 (5.50)
Wind: Light, behind; becoming almost nil after race 2 Weather: Unsettled, some rain

3141 BET ON ENGLAND-V-RUSSIA WITH LADBROKES H'CAP 1m 2f
5:50 (5:50) (Class 6) (0-60,60) 3-Y-O **£2,587** (£770; £384; £192) **Stalls** Low

Form RPR
2402 **1** **Frivolous Prince (IRE)**[18] 2563 3-8-6 **48**...........(vt) KieranShoemark(3) 9 55
(David Evans) *hld up in rr: hdwy 3f out: led over 1f out: rdn and styd on* **8/1**
6-45 **2** *1 3/4* **Masterson (IRE)**[14] 2700 3-9-0 **60**........................... KillianHennessy(7) 6 64
(Mick Channon) *prom: led briefly wl over 1f out: kpt on same pce* **3/1**[1]
-000 **3** *1 1/2* **Rosie's Vision**[8] 2851 3-8-10 **49**....................................... SteveDrowne 4 50
(Mark Usher) *t.k.h in midfield: outpcd 4f out: styd on u.p fnl 2f* **33/1**
6054 **4** *nk* **Red Rose Riot (IRE)**[17] 2586 3-9-2 **55**.............................. ShaneKelly 2 56
(David Menuisier) *t.k.h: in tch: stmbld on bnd over 3f out: rdn to press ldrs over 1f out: one pce* **15/2**[3]
-006 **5** *1/2* **Fishergate**[115] 612 3-9-7 **60**.. AdamBeschizza 3 60
(Richard Rowe) *led for 2f: prom tl no ex 1f out* **20/1**
66-5 **6** *3* **Chilli Jam**[20] 2506 3-9-7 **60**.. KieranO'Neill 5 54
(Ed de Giles) *t.k.h: in tch on outer: clsd on ldrs 4f out: wknd over 1f out* **4/1**[2]
000- **7** *nk* **Boychick (IRE)**[173] 8323 3-9-0 **56**.........................(b[1]) ThomasBrown(3) 1 50
(Ed Walker) *s.i.s: nvr trbld ldrs* **14/1**
5-00 **8** *3* **Onehelluvatouch**[23] 2395 3-9-2 **55**..................................... AdamKirby 8 43
(Philip Hide) *prom: led after 2f tl 7f out: led wl over 2f out tl wknd wl over 1f out* **10/1**
0044 **9** *1 1/4* **Fun Money**[53] 1551 3-9-0 **53**... PaulMulrennan 7 39
(Ed Dunlop) *towards rr: effrt and nt clr run over 2f out: n.d after* **12/1**
0-04 **10** *16* **Cape Crystal (IRE)**[11] 2784 3-9-6 **59**.......................(b) LukeMorris 10 16
(Sir Mark Prescott Bt) *t.k.h: prom: led 7f out tl wl over 2f out: sn wknd* **4/1**[2]

2m 18.98s (8.48) **Going Correction** +0.75s/f (Yiel) **10** Ran SP% **119.0**
Speed ratings (Par 97): **96,94,93,93,92 90,90,87,86,73**
CSF £32.95 CT £770.68 TOTE £9.30: £2.70, £1.20, £11.60; EX 43.30 Trifecta £2306.90.
Owner Wayne Clifford **Bred** Seamus Fox **Trained** Pandy, Monmouths

FOCUS
A very weak handicap won by a 48-rated gelding who was 0-14 coming into this, so hardly form to get excited about.

3142 BET ON TONIGHT'S FOOTBALL AT LADBROKES H'CAP 1m 2f
6:20 (6:20) (Class 5) (0-70,67) 4-Y-O+ **£3,234** (£962; £481; £240) **Stalls** Low

Form RPR
0/0- **1** **Song And Dance Man**[495] 387 6-9-2 **65**...................... DannyBrock(3) 1 73
(Jane Chapple-Hyam) *dwlt: sn trcking ldrs: led 2f out: rdn out* **20/1**
-603 **2** *2 1/4* **Whip Up A Frenzy (IRE)**[17] 2573 4-8-7 **53**................ AdamBeschizza 2 57
(Richard Rowe) *led tl 2f out: kpt on u.p* **7/1**
-622 **3** *1 1/4* **Weardiditallgorong**[11] 2781 4-9-2 **62**..............................(b) AdamKirby 7 63
(Des Donovan, Ire) *hld up in rr: effrt over 2f out: styd on fnl f* **5/2**[1]
-013 **4** *2 3/4* **Wordismybond**[15] 2646 7-9-7 **67**.. ShaneKelly 3 63
(Richard Hughes) *t.k.h: trckd ldrs: hrd rdn 2f out: wknd over 1f out* **7/2**[3]
4-00 **5** *2* **Racing Knight (IRE)**[28] 2233 4-9-2 **62**........................... PaulMulrennan 6 54
(David Evans) *pressed ldr tl 3f out: sn wknd* **3/1**[2]
-551 **6** *hd* **Lady Lunchalot (USA)**[16] 2607 6-9-7 **67**............................... LukeMorris 5 58
(Laura Mongan) *dwlt: hld up in 5th: rdn 4f out: wknd over 2f out* **9/2**

2m 17.17s (6.67) **Going Correction** +0.75s/f (Yiel) **6** Ran SP% **111.2**
Speed ratings (Par 103): **103,101,100,98,96 96**
CSF £140.88 TOTE £18.40: £8.50, £4.50; EX 124.40 Trifecta £586.50.
Owner Miss Charlie McPhillips **Bred** Paulyn Ltd **Trained** Dalham, Suffolk

FOCUS
The ground was changed to soft before this race. Danny Brock took this modest handicap by the scruff of the neck early in the straight and his mount rewarded the positive tactics by seeing his rivals off.

3143 CASH OUT ON YOUR APP WITH LADBROKES FILLIES' NOVICE MEDIAN AUCTION STKS (PLUS 10 RACE) 5f
6:50 (6:51) (Class 5) 2-Y-O **£2,587** (£770; £384; £192) **Stalls** Low

Form RPR
1 **Mrs Danvers** 2-9-0 0.. RyanClark 1 86+
(Jonathan Portman) *chsd ldrs: led wl over 1f out: clr fnl f: easily* **33/1**
2 **2** *3 1/4* **Paco's Angel**[15] 2637 2-9-0 0.. ShaneKelly 7 74
(Richard Hughes) *disp ld tl wl over 1f out: sn outpcd by wnr* **11/10**[1]
33 **3** *6* **Alwalaa (IRE)**[26] 2295 2-9-0 0.. PaulMulrennan 5 53
(Mark Johnston) *chsd ldrs: rdn 1/2-way: outpcd fnl 2f* **5/1**[3]
105 **4** *2* **Coolfitch (IRE)**[14] 2670 2-9-7 0... FMBerry 3 53
(David O'Meara) *racd freely: disp ld tl wl over 1f out: sn wknd* **11/4**[2]
5 *1* **Highland Dream (IRE)** 2-9-0 0.. AdamKirby 8 42
(Clive Cox) *a abt same pl: n.d fnl 2f* **10/1**
6 *1 3/4* **Sweet Amazement** 2-9-0 0.. SteveDrowne 4 36
(Mark Usher) *dwlt: outpcd towards rr: sme hdwy 2f out: wknd over 1f out* **16/1**
0 **7** *4* **Lucky Return**[9] 2817 2-9-0 0.. KieranO'Neill 2 21
(Des Donovan, Ire) *rring in stalls: dwlt: outpcd: sn wl bhd* **25/1**
8 *9* **My Dear Baby (IRE)** 2-9-0 0.. AdamBeschizza 6
(Robert Cowell) *s.s: outpcd: a wl bhd* **12/1**

1m 0.49s (2.29) **Going Correction** +0.60s/f (Yiel) **8** Ran SP% **120.4**
Speed ratings (Par 90): **105,99,90,87,85 82,76,61**
CSF £74.26 TOTE £34.20: £7.90, £1.02, £2.40; EX 135.80 Trifecta £569.40.
Owner Turf Club 2014 **Bred** M A Burton & Connie Hopper **Trained** Upper Lambourn, Berks

FOCUS
Those with form set a decent standard in this novice event but they were all blown away by a newcomer sent off at an unfancied 33-1.

3144 DOWNLOAD THE LADBROKES APP H'CAP 6f
7:20 (7:20) (Class 4) (0-80,80) 3-Y-O+ **£5,175** (£1,540; £769; £384) **Stalls** Low

Form RPR
60-2 **1** **Shanghai Glory (IRE)**[30] 2186 3-9-6 **80**................................ FMBerry 2 95
(Charles Hills) *prom: led over 1f out: rdn clr* **10/11**[1]
-531 **2** *5* **Lightning Charlie**[43] 1838 4-9-10 **79**...................... KieranShoemark(3) 4 80
(Amanda Perrett) *chsd ldr: rdn 3f out: one pce appr fnl f* **5/1**[3]
1224 **3** *3 1/2* **Cultured Knight**[26] 2314 3-9-3 **77**...................................... ShaneKelly 3 65
(Richard Hughes) *hld up: effrt over 2f out: wnt 3rd and hrd rdn over 1f out: no imp* **10/3**[2]
3030 **4** *3/4* **Great Expectations**[15] 2643 8-9-3 **69**............................(vt) AdamKirby 6 56
(J R Jenkins) *chsd ldrs: hrd rdn 2f out: one pce* **10/1**
-060 **5** *nk* **Jungle Bay**[11] 2765 9-8-12 **67**..................................(b) DannyBrock(3) 5 53
(Jane Chapple-Hyam) *led after 1f tl wknd over 1f out* **16/1**
20-0 **6** *1 1/4* **Evening Attire**[49] 1634 5-9-8 **74**....................................... RyanPowell 1 56
(William Stone) *in tch: rdn after 2f: sn outpcd* **10/1**

1m 13.86s (2.66) **Going Correction** +0.75s/f (Yiel)
WFA 3 from 4yo+ 8lb **6** Ran SP% **116.2**
Speed ratings (Par 105): **112,105,100,99,99 97**
CSF £6.36 TOTE £1.70: £1.10, £3.30; EX 6.80 Trifecta £12.90.
Owner Kangyu Int Racing (HK) Ltd & F Ma **Bred** Owenstown Stud **Trained** Lambourn, Berks

FOCUS
Not a very competitive 0-80 handicap and the well-backed favourite bolted in.

3145 BEST PRICES ON THE FOOTBALL AT LADBROKES MEDIAN AUCTION MAIDEN STKS 7f
7:50 (7:53) (Class 6) 3-4-Y-O **£2,587** (£770; £384; £192) **Stalls** Low

Form RPR
1 **Miss Carbonia (IRE)** 3-8-8 0................................ ThomasBrown(3) 10 79+
(Ismail Mohammed) *reluctant to enter stalls: in tch: effrt over 2f out: led 1f out: rdn out* **12/1**
523 **2** *3 1/2* **Compas Scoobie**[25] 2349 3-9-2 74.................................... JackMitchell 9 75
(Roger Varian) *led on stands' rail tl 1f out: one pce* **9/4**[1]
4 **3** *6* **Hilltop Ranger (IRE)**[42] 1859 3-8-11 0.............................. SteveDrowne 5 55
(Daniel Kubler) *dwlt: outpcd and bhd: styd on to take 3rd ins fnl f* **4/1**[3]
40 **4** *5* **Brick Lane**[11] 2767 3-8-11 0.. FMBerry 4 43
(Robyn Brisland) *prom tl wknd wl over 1f out* **7/1**
5 *5* **Dream Voice (IRE)** 3-8-8 0... EoinWalsh(3) 8 30
(James Tate) *dwlt: rn green in rr: hdwy 3f out: wknd 2f out* **10/1**
-233 **6** *4 1/2* **California Lad**[33] 2098 3-9-2 76.................................(v) LukeMorris 2 24
(Harry Dunlop) *prom in centre: j. path after 2f: wknd over 2f out* **5/2**[2]
6-0 **7** *13* **Bethnal Green**[22] 2443 4-9-0 0................................ LuluStanford(7) 3
(Robyn Brisland) *chsd ldrs in centre tl wknd 3f out* **20/1**
8 *5* **Monique Rosa (FR)** 3-8-4 0... JordanUys(7) 1
(George Baker) *s.s: sn in tch towards far side: wknd 1/2-way: bhd and eased fnl 3f* **25/1**

1m 28.71s (5.41) **Going Correction** +0.90s/f (Soft)
WFA 3 from 4yo 10lb **8** Ran SP% **117.2**
Speed ratings (Par 101): **105,101,94,88,82 77,62,57**
CSF £40.42 TOTE £14.20: £2.90, £1.50, £1.80; EX 49.30 Trifecta £210.60.

Owner Sheikh Juma Dalmook Al Maktoum **Bred** Mrs Elizabeth O'Leary **Trained** Newmarket, Suffolk

FOCUS

A modest maiden and conditions played a big part, with the field finishing strung out like three-mile chasers.

3146 BET NOW WITH THE LADBROKES APP H'CAP — 7f

8:20 (8:22) (Class 6) (0-55,55) 3-Y-O+ **£2,587** (£770; £384; £192) **Stalls** Low

Form RPR

-000 **1** **Zebs Lad (IRE)**[21] 2458 4-9-0 **52**....(p) MeganNicholls(7) 9 65
(Nikki Evans) *mid-div: hdwy 3f out: led wl over 1f out: rdn clr* **20/1**

5651 **2** 4 ½ **Ettie Hart (IRE)**[5] 2969 3-8-5 **53**.... KillianHennessy(7) 12 51
(Mick Channon) *disp ld: led after 2f tl wl over 1f out: sn outpcd* **15/8**[1]

0-06 **3** 8 **Lucky Leyf**[73] 1139 4-9-8 **53**.... FMBerry 10 35
(Philip Hide) *chsd ldrs tl outpcd fnl 2f* **8/1**[3]

1032 **4** nse **Little Indian**[22] 2442 6-9-10 **55**.... AdamKirby 2 37
(J R Jenkins) *in tch far side: effrt and hrd rdn over 2f out: edgd rt: no imp* **9/2**[2]

0240 **5** 1 **Espoir**[25] 2325 3-8-11 **52**....(v) ShaneKelly 1 27
(David Evans) *prom far side tl edgd rt and btn 2f out* **17/2**

0604 **6** 1 ¼ **Kenstone (FR)**[19] 2537 3-8-9 **50**....(p) LukeMorris 5 22
(David Dennis) *chsd ldrs: rdn 4f out: outpcd fnl 3f* **14/1**

2360 **7** ¾ **Presto Boy**[8] 2845 4-8-11 **49**.... NicolaCurrie(7) 4 23
(Richard Hughes) *t.k.h towards rr: hdwy over 2f out: wknd wl over 1f out* **16/1**

0-00 **8** 3 ½ **Links Bar Marbella (IRE)**[31] 2148 3-8-8 **49** ow3....(b1) KierenFox 13 10
(Eric Wheeler) *mid-div on stands' rail: outpcd fnl 3f* **20/1**

0-00 **9** 1 ¼ **Captain Joey (IRE)**[24] 2359 3-8-6 **47**.... KieranO'Neill 7
(Charles Hills) *sn outpcd towards rr* **16/1**

6100 **10** 3 ½ **Chandrayaan**[43] 1834 9-9-2 **47**....(v) SamHitchcott 6
(John E Long) *outpcd: sn rdn along: a bhd* **33/1**

000- **11** 3 ¼ **Born To Fly (IRE)**[12] 7440 5-9-1 **49**.... DannyBrock(3) 11
(Christine Dunnett) *in tch: rdn 4f out: wknd 3f out* **18/1**

00-0 **12** 13 **Soiree**[56] 1497 3-8-3 **51**....(b1) LuluStanford(7) 3
(Eve Johnson Houghton) *disp ld for 2f: lost pl 4f out: sn bhd* **22/1**

2624 **13** hd **Intimately**[52] 1574 3-8-13 **54**.... RyanClark 8
(Jonathan Portman) *prom tl wknd 3f out* **12/1**

1m 30.0s (6.70) **Going Correction** +1.05s/f (Soft)
WFA 3 from 4yo+ 10lb **13** Ran SP% **122.8**
Speed ratings (Par 101): **103,97,88,88,87 86,85,81,79,75 72,57,57**
CSF £56.66 CT £321.93 TOTE £22.70: £7.50, £1.40, £3.70; EX 99.10 Trifecta £1128.90.
Owner Dragon Racing **Bred** Tally-Ho Stud **Trained** Pandy, Monmouths

FOCUS

A weak handicap despite the big field and the action unfolded towards the stands side once again, with very little getting into it from off the pace.

3147 TRACK YOUR ACCA WITH LADBROKES MAIDEN STKS — 6f

8:50 (8:50) (Class 5) 3-Y-O+ **£3,234** (£962; £481) **Stalls** Low

Form RPR

6-32 **1** **He's My Cracker**[19] 2544 3-9-0 80.... AdamKirby 4 81
(Clive Cox) *mde all: rdn and qcknd 2f out: edgd rt ins fnl f: hld on wl* **4/7**[1]

062- **2** 2 **Catchment**[241] 7211 3-8-9 77.... FMBerry 3 73
(Amanda Perrett) *trckd wnr: rdn 2f out: kpt on same pce: hld whn n.m.r fnl 50yds* **15/8**[2]

3 1 ¼ **Gift From God** 3-9-0 0.... KieranO'Neill 1 71
(Hugo Froud) *a 3rd: rdn and one pce fnl 2f* **10/1**[3]

1m 18.19s (6.99) **Going Correction** +1.20s/f (Soft) **3** Ran SP% **107.5**
Speed ratings (Par 103): **101,98,96**
CSF £1.93 TOTE £1.40; EX 2.00 Trifecta £2.30.
Owner Paul & Clare Rooney **Bred** Richard Kent **Trained** Lambourn, Berks

FOCUS

Just three runners but reasons to be hopeful for the future for all three.
T/Plt: £158.00 to a £1 stake. Pool of £38115.66 - 176.05 winning tickets. T/Qpdt: £4.30 to a £1 stake. Pool of £3958.16 - 674.70 winning tickets. **Lee McKenzie**

2906 MUSSELBURGH (R-H)

Saturday, June 11

OFFICIAL GOING: Good (7.9)

Wind: Light, half against Weather: Overcast

3148 MADELEINE CUP EBF STALLIONS MAIDEN STKS (PLUS 10 RACE) — 5f

2:00 (2:00) (Class 4) 2-Y-O **£4,204** (£1,251; £625; £312) **Stalls** High

Form RPR

50 **1** **Ventura Secret (IRE)**[16] 2617 2-9-5 0.... DavidAllan 1 75
(Tim Easterby) *prom on outside: effrt and rdn over 1f out: led wl ins fnl f: kpt on wl* **11/2**[3]

2 ½ **Liquid (IRE)** 2-9-5 0.... PhillipMakin 7 73
(David Barron) *dwlt: sn prom: swtchd rt 1/2-way: led gng wl over 1f out: sn rdn: hdd and no ex wl ins fnl f: bttr for r* **9/5**[1]

3 nk **Alicante Dawn** 2-9-5 0.... ConnorBeasley 3 72
(Bryan Smart) *s.i.s: rn green in rr: rdn and hdwy over 1f out: edgd rt and kpt on ins fnl f: nrst fin* **8/1**

42 **4** 2 ½ **Katebird (IRE)**[8] 2852 2-9-0 0.... JoeFanning 5 58
(Mark Johnston) *t.k.h early led: rdn over 2f out: hdd over 1f out: outpcd ins fnl f* **5/2**[2]

0 **5** 2 **Samran Says (IRE)**[16] 2612 2-9-0 0.... JackGarritty 4 51
(Richard Fahey) *t.k.h early: cl up: rdn along 2f out: wknd ins fnl f* **6/1**

6 **6** 7 **Red Savina**[22] 2424 2-9-0 0.... ShaneGray 2 26
(Kevin Ryan) *cl up: rdn along and struggling over 2f out: sn btn* **10/1**

59.75s (-0.65) **Going Correction** -0.15s/f (Firm) **6** Ran SP% **114.2**
Speed ratings (Par 95): **99,98,97,93,90 79**
CSF £16.30 TOTE £6.20: £3.10, £1.40; EX 16.40 Trifecta £101.60.
Owner Middleham Park Racing LXI & Partner **Bred** Audrey Frances Stynes **Trained** Great Habton, N Yorks

FOCUS

A fair juvenile maiden with a number of major northern-based yards represented, but experience counted in the end.

3149 STOBO CASTLE LADIES DAY GOLD CUP (A H'CAP) — 2m

2:35 (2:36) (Class 4) (0-85,82) 4-Y-O+ **£12,938** (£3,850; £1,924; £962) **Stalls** High

Form RPR

1-41 **1** **Sweet Selection**[25] 2338 4-9-4 **77**.... PJMcDonald 14 86+
(Hughie Morrison) *trckd ldrs: rdn and outpcd over 4f out: rallied to ld over 1f out: kpt on strly fnl f* **11/2**[2]

-532 **2** 2 **Aldreth**[7] 2912 5-8-4 **67**....(p) NathanEvans(5) 12 74
(Michael Easterby) *hld up in midfield: effrt and hdwy over 2f out: chsd wnr ins fnl f: kpt on: no imp* **13/2**[3]

4221 **3** ¾ **Stormin Tom (IRE)**[10] 2805 4-8-12 **76**.... RachelRichardson(5) 10 82
(Tim Easterby) *led and clr: rdn 3f out: hdd over 1f out: no ex and lost 2nd pl ins fnl f* **9/1**

01-1 **4** 1 ¼ **Impulsive American**[7] 2912 4-8-8 **74**....(b) AdamMcNamara(7) 6 78+
(David Pipe) *hld up and bhd: rdn along over 3f out: gd hdwy on outside over 1f out: edgd rt and kpt on fnl f: nt pce to chal* **2/1**[1]

1-61 **5** 1 **Hillgrove Angel (IRE)**[7] 2911 4-8-12 **71**.... ConorHoban 7 74
(Iain Jardine) *hld up on ins: drvn along over 3f out: plugged on fr 2f out: no imp* **12/1**

43/1 **6** 1 ½ **Almost Gemini (IRE)**[67] 1244 7-8-12 **73**....(b) KevinStott(3) 4 74
(Kenneth Slack) *hld up in midfield: rdn and outpcd over 3f out: rallied over 1f out: kpt on fnl f: no imp* **7/1**

11-6 **7** 1 **Wor Lass**[15] 2659 8-9-1 **78**.... AnnaHesketh(5) 8 78
(Susan Corbett) *chsd wnr: effrt over 3f out: lost 2nd and edgd lft 2f out: wknd fnl f* **28/1**

0-00 **8** nk **Perrault (IRE)**[23] 2406 4-9-4 **77**....(p) JackGarritty 3 77
(Richard Fahey) *hld up in tch: effrt on ins over 3f out: rdn and wknd wl over 1f out* **25/1**

1540 **9** 1 ¾ **Gabrial The Duke (IRE)**[36] 1999 6-9-10 **82**....(b) GeorgeChaloner 2 80
(Richard Fahey) *s.i.s: sn drvn along in rr: struggling over 2f out: n.d after* **16/1**

0514 **10** nk **Jan Smuts (IRE)**[23] 2406 8-8-9 **72**....(tp) PhilDennis(5) 1 69
(Wilf Storey) *hld up in midfield: short-lived effrt over 3f out: sn rdn: wknd over 2f out* **33/1**

5-30 **11** 2 **Full Day**[11] 2782 5-9-2 **79**....(p) CallumShepherd(5) 5 74
(Brian Ellison) *hld up: drvn and outpcd over 3f out: nvr on terms* **16/1**

2-45 **12** 2 ¾ **Pass Muster**[15] 2659 9-9-0 **72**....(p) PhillipMakin 11 63
(Philip Kirby) *s.i.s: bhd: struggling over 3f out: sn btn* **33/1**

1-54 **13** 14 **Celtic Power**[17] 2575 4-8-7 **66**.... JoeFanning 13 41
(Jim Goldie) *s.i.s: sn in tch on outside: rdn over 3f out: sn wknd: t.o* **25/1**

3m 31.47s (-2.03) **Going Correction** -0.025s/f (Good)
WFA 4 from 5yo+ 1lb **13** Ran SP% **121.0**
Speed ratings (Par 105): **104,103,102,102,101 100,100,100,99,99 98,96,89**
CSF £39.13 CT £320.47 TOTE £7.10: £2.50, £2.10, £2.90; EX 55.90 Trifecta £725.50.
Owner Paul Brocklehurst **Bred** S A Douch **Trained** East Ilsley, Berks

FOCUS

The rails were at their innermost and distances were as advertised. A nice prize and a competitive staying handicap won by an improving sort.

3150 WILLIAM HILL SCOTTISH TARTAN TROPHY (A CONSOLATION FOR SCOTTISH SPRINT CUP) (H'CAP) — 5f

3:10 (3:12) (Class 3) 4-Y-O+ **£25,876** (£7,700; £3,848; £1,924) **Stalls** High

Form RPR

4-60 **1** **Meadway**[30] 2188 5-9-10 **90**....(p) ConnorBeasley 4 100
(Bryan Smart) *mde all: swtchd lft sn after s to r jst off stands' rail: rdn and edgd rt over 1f out: hld on wl fnl f* **20/1**

1-02 **2** 1 **Olivia Fallow (IRE)**[15] 2658 4-9-2 **85**.... JoeDoyle(3) 15 91+
(Paul Midgley) *trckd ldrs against stands' rail: effrt and rdn over 1f out: chsd wnr ins fnl f: kpt on* **7/2**[1]

3040 **3** 1 ¼ **Kibaar**[15] 2665 4-9-2 **85**.... KevinStott(3) 2 87
(Kevin Ryan) *cl up: drvn along over 1f out: kpt on same pce ins fnl f* **25/1**

3405 **4** nk **Pearl Acclaim (IRE)**[8] 2863 6-9-0 **80**....(p) PaulQuinn 1 81
(David Nicholls) *chsd ldrs on outside: rdn along 2f out: kpt on same pce fnl f* **11/1**

0621 **5** hd **Stanghow**[15] 2665 4-9-4 **84** 6ex.... PhillipMakin 5 84
(Antony Brittain) *cl up: rdn along 2f out: outpcd ins fnl f* **12/1**

-524 **6** ¾ **Classy Anne**[17] 2572 6-8-13 **79**.... JoeFanning 11 76
(Jim Goldie) *hld up towards rr: hdwy after 2f: rdn 2f out: kpt on ins fnl f* **11/1**

5-50 **7** ½ **Barnet Fair**[21] 2488 8-9-6 **86**.... FrederikTylicki 7 82
(David Nicholls) *in tch: effrt and rdn over 1f out: outpcd ins fnl f* **11/2**[3]

2206 **8** nse **Go Go Green (IRE)**[5] 2961 10-8-6 **72**.... GeorgeChaloner 8 67
(Jim Goldie) *dwlt: sn in midfield: drvn along 1/2-way: edgd rt and one pce appr fnl f* **16/1**

5-32 **9** nk **Shipyard (USA)**[21] 2476 7-9-7 **90**.... AlistairRawlinson(3) 6 84+
(Michael Appleby) *dwlt: hld up on outside: hdwy 1/2-way: rdn over 1f out: sn no imp* **9/2**[2]

-015 **10** ¾ **Landing Night (IRE)**[11] 2775 4-8-13 **79**....(p) PJMcDonald 12 71
(Ann Duffield) *hld up stands' rail: rdn 2f out: no imp fnl f* **22/1**

4345 **11** nk **Merhoob (IRE)**[7] 2903 4-9-1 **81**.... RoystonFfrench 10 72+
(John Ryan) *dwlt: bhd: rdn along after 2f: nvr rchd ldrs* **10/1**

6-05 **12** ½ **Distant Past**[15] 2658 5-9-8 **88**....(p) ShaneGray 9 77
(Kevin Ryan) *hld up: rdn along 1/2-way: sn no imp: btn over 1f out* **12/1**

0034 **13** ¾ **Star Cracker (IRE)**[5] 2961 4-8-0 **66** oh3....(p) RaulDaSilva 3 52
(Jim Goldie) *bhd on outside: drvn along 1/2-way: sn n.d: btn over 1f out* **20/1**

-643 **14** hd **Bunce (IRE)**[19] 2523 8-8-2 **68** oh1 ow2.... AndrewMullen 13 53
(Linda Perratt) *bhd against stands' rail: drvn along over 2f out: sn struggling* **50/1**

/-40 **15** ½ **Clergyman**[26] 2305 4-8-11 **77**.... NeilFarley 14 61
(Rebecca Bastiman) *dwlt and wnt rt s: bhd and sn rdn along: nvr on terms* **33/1**

58.66s (-1.74) **Going Correction** -0.15s/f (Firm) **15** Ran SP% **125.4**
Speed ratings (Par 107): **107,105,103,102,102 101,100,100,100,98 98,97,96,96,95**
CSF £85.82 CT £1880.92 TOTE £26.50: £8.20, £2.10, £8.50; EX 171.70 Trifecta £3609.20.
Owner Michael Moses & Terry Moses **Bred** Bond Thoroughbred Corporation **Trained** Hambleton, N Yorks

FOCUS
The consolation race for the following Sprint Cup but a good handicap in its own right. Unusually here, four of the first five came from a low draw.

3151 WILLIAM HILL SCOTTISH SPRINT CUP (A HERITAGE H'CAP) 5f
3:45 (3:49) (Class 2) 4-Y-O+
£62,250 (£18,640; £9,320; £4,660; £2,330; £1,170) **Stalls** High

Form RPR
4461 **1** **Hoofalong**[44] 1801 6-8-5 **94**........(b) NathanEvans(5) 16 105
(Michael Easterby) *in tch: effrt and swtchd rt over 1f out: led ins fnl f: rdn out* **16/1**
1-03 **2** *1 1/4* **Thesme**[30] 2188 4-8-8 **92**........RoystonFfrench 4 99+
(Nigel Tinkler) *cl up: rdn along 1/2-way led over 1f out to ins fnl f: kpt on* **10/1**
3213 **3** *1 1/2* **Duke Of Firenze**[7] 2895 7-9-2 **100**........DavidAllan 9 101
(David C Griffiths) *s.i.s: hld up: hdwy whn nt clr run wl over 1f out to ins fnl f: kpt on: nt pce of first two* **10/1**
1432 **4** *1/2* **Kimberella**[7] 2895 6-8-9 **93**........FrederikTylicki 17 92
(David Nicholls) *in tch: rdn over 2f out: kpt on ins fnl f* **3/1**[1]
-000 **5** *1 1/4* **Desert Law (IRE)**[30] 2188 8-9-2 **100**........MartinLane 13 95+
(Paul Midgley) *rdr lost iron briefly s: hld up: nt clr run over 1f out: rdn and kpt on fnl f: nt pce to chal* **22/1**
400- **6** *1 1/2* **Robot Boy (IRE)**[231] 7461 6-8-13 **97**........PhillipMakin 7 86
(David Barron) *in tch: effrt and rdn over 1f out: outpcd ins fnl f* **11/1**
0060 **7** *hd* **Green Door (IRE)**[7] 2895 5-8-12 **96**........(v) JackGarritty 8 85
(Robert Cowell) *s.i.ss: hld up: nt clr run 1/2-way: sn rdn: kpt on fnl f: nrst fin* **20/1**
-200 **8** *nk* **Monsieur Joe (IRE)**[7] 2895 9-9-7 **108**........JoeDoyle(3) 10 96
(Paul Midgley) *midfield: rdn and outpcd over 2f out: no imp fr over 1f out* **16/1**
6001 **9** *nk* **Confessional**[6] 2931 9-8-7 **91** 6ex........(e) GeorgeChaloner 3 78
(Tim Easterby) *prom on outside: drvn along 1/2-way: no ex fr over 1f out* **28/1**
3166 **10** *1/2* **Royal Birth**[21] 2488 5-8-8 **92**........(t) ConorHoban 11 77
(Stuart Williams) *midfield: drvn along 1/2-way: one pce whn hmpd over 1f out: sn n.d* **10/1**
00-1 **11** *3/4* **Tangerine Trees**[20] 2504 11-8-7 **91** 6ex........(v) AndrewMullen 12 73
(Michael Appleby) *cl up: rdn along 1/2-way: wknd appr fnl f* **20/1**
100- **12** *3/4* **Secretinthepark**[259] 6732 6-8-4 **93**........(p) CallumShepherd(5) 6 72
(Robert Cowell) *bhd: drvn along over 2f out: nvr able to chal* **25/1**
-401 **13** *3/4* **Judicial (IRE)**[28] 2258 4-9-0 **98**........(e) ConnorBeasley 14 75
(Julie Camacho) *rrd and lost grnd s: bhd: effrt on outside 1/2-way: no imp over 1f out: sn btn* **7/1**[2]
-220 **14** *1* **Fast Track**[30] 2188 5-8-10 **94**........JoeFanning 5 67
(David Barron) *bhd: drvn along over 3f out: nvr on terms* **20/1**
2642 **15** *1/2* **Red Baron (IRE)**[28] 2258 7-9-2 **100**........NeilFarley 2 71
(Eric Alston) *led at str gallop: rdn and hdd over 1f out: sn btn* **10/1**
3434 **16** *hd* **Silvanus (IRE)**[20] 2504 11-8-10 **94**........PJMcDonald 1 65
(Paul Midgley) *midfield on outside: rdn over 2f out: wknd over 1f out* **33/1**
0-11 **17** *nk* **See The Sun**[31] 2158 5-8-4 **93**........RachelRichardson(5) 15 62
(Tim Easterby) *chsd ldrs: rdn 1/2-way: nt clr run over 1f out: wknd ins fnl f* **9/1**[3]

57.77s (-2.63) **Going Correction** -0.15s/f (Firm) **17** Ran SP% **132.8**
Speed ratings (Par 109): **115,113,110,109,107 105,105,104,104,103 102,100,99,98,97 97,96**
CSF £164.71 CT £1780.31 TOTE £19.70: £3.70, £2.50, £2.60, £2.40; EX 255.50 Trifecta £5918.30.
Owner A Chandler, L Westwood, D & Y Blunt **Bred** D F Spence **Trained** Sheriff Hutton, N Yorks
■ Stewards' Enquiry : Nathan Evans two-day ban: careless riding (25-26 June)

FOCUS
The feature race and a high class sprint that was run 0.89 secs faster than the preceding consolation race. Hold-up horses were more involved here and the winner posted a surprise pb.

3152 WILLIAM HILL FILLIES AND MARES (A H'CAP) 1m
4:20 (4:20) (Class 3) (0-90,87) 3-Y-O+ **£12,938** (£3,850; £1,924; £962) **Stalls** Low

Form RPR
0-50 **1** **Haley Bop (IRE)**[8] 2875 3-8-13 **83**........JoeFanning 5 91
(Mark Johnston) *in tch: effrt over 2f out: carried lft over 1f out: led ins fnl f: pushed out* **10/1**
-360 **2** *2* **Rosy Morning (IRE)**[26] 2305 3-8-2 **72**........RaulDaSilva 7 75
(Mark Johnston) *led: rdn and hung lft over 1f out: hdd ins fnl f: kpt on same pce* **33/1**
10-1 **3** *1/2* **Lil Sophella (IRE)**[29] 2223 7-9-8 **81**........JackGarritty 8 86
(Patrick Holmes) *s.i.s: hld up: hdwy over 2f out: rdn and chsd stands' side pair ins fnl f: no imp* **6/1**
6-06 **4** *hd* **Home Cummins (IRE)**[14] 2689 4-9-7 **87**........AdamMcNamara(7) 2 91
(Richard Fahey) *prom: drvn and outpcd over 3f out: rallied over 1f out: kpt on fnl f: no imp* **5/1**[2]
21 **5** *1 3/4* **Catalan (IRE)**[26] 2307 3-8-8 **78**........PJMcDonald 3 75
(Hughie Morrison) *trckd ldrs: effrt and rdn over 2f out: edgd lft and outpcd over 1f out* **4/1**[1]
0-26 **6** *1 1/2* **Hidden Rebel**[28] 2236 4-9-7 **80**........ConnorBeasley 1 77
(Alistair Whillans) *t.k.h: hld up in tch: drvn and over 2f out: outpcd over 1f out* **11/2**[3]
5-60 **7** *1 3/4* **Forever A Lady (IRE)**[22] 2420 3-8-5 **75**........AndrewMullen 10 65
(Keith Dalgleish) *sn pushed along and cl up: rdn 3f out: wknd over 1f out* **25/1**
3-46 **8** *1* **Bell Heather (IRE)**[26] 2299 3-8-9 **79**........GeorgeChaloner 9 67
(Richard Fahey) *trckd ldrs: rdn along 3f out: wknd 2f out* **7/1**
-162 **9** *6* **Push Me (IRE)**[7] 2917 9-9-8 **81**........RoystonFfrench 4 58
(Iain Jardine) *hld up: rdn and outpcd over 2f out: n.d after* **4/1**[1]
6106 **10** *7* **Dusky Dawn**[7] 2917 4-9-3 **76**........NeilFarley 6 37
(Alan Swinbank) *hld up in tch: effrt over 3f out: wknd over 2f out* **16/1**

1m 39.56s (-1.64) **Going Correction** -0.025s/f (Good)
WFA 3 from 4yo+ 11lb **10** Ran SP% **120.6**
Speed ratings (Par 107): **107,105,104,104,102 101,99,98,92,85**
CSF £292.82 CT £2156.98 TOTE £11.70: £3.50, £8.30, £2.50; EX 148.50 Trifecta £3113.30.
Owner Abdulla Al Mansoori **Bred** Mighty Universe Ltd **Trained** Middleham Moor, N Yorks
■ Stewards' Enquiry : Raul Da Silva caution: careless riding

FOCUS
Not a bad fillies' handicap run at a fair pace.

3153 KILCO (INTERNATIONAL) LEADERS IN FARM HYGIENE H'CAP 7f 30y
4:55 (4:57) (Class 5) (0-70,70) 3-Y-O+ **£3,234** (£962; £481; £240) **Stalls** Low

Form RPR
-000 **1** **Gabrial The Tiger (IRE)**[14] 2680 4-9-7 **70**........AdamMcNamara(7) 1 81
(Richard Fahey) *mde all at decent gallop: rdn and edgd lft 2f out: hld on wl fnl f* **5/2**[1]
-000 **2** *1 3/4* **Cyflymder (IRE)**[15] 2661 10-8-9 **51** oh2........DavidAllan 2 57
(David C Griffiths) *trckd ldrs: rdn over 2f out: wnt 2nd appr fnl f: kpt on* **16/1**
446- **3** *hd* **My Two Scoops**[236] 7336 3-9-2 **68**........PJMcDonald 7 69+
(Ann Duffield) *hld up: hdwy and rdn over 2f out: kpt on fnl f: nrst fin* **6/1**[3]
0023 **4** *3/4* **Atreus**[7] 2906 4-8-11 **58**........(p) NathanEvans(5) 10 61
(Michael Easterby) *chsd wnr: rdn over 2f out: lost 2nd appr fnl f: sn no ex* **6/1**[3]
0646 **5** *3 3/4* **Honcho (IRE)**[29] 2217 4-9-11 **70**........JoeDoyle(3) 5 63
(John Ryan) *in tch: effrt over 2f out: rdn and no imp wl over 1f out* **12/1**
-006 **6** *2 1/2* **Call Me Crockett (IRE)**[19] 2528 4-9-3 **59**........(p) JoeFanning 12 46
(Iain Jardine) *hld up in midfield: pushed along over 2f out: sn no imp* **20/1**
-212 **7** *2* **Blue Jacket (USA)**[8] 2855 5-9-3 **62**........MissEmmaSayer(3) 6 43
(Dianne Sayer) *stdd s: hld up: hdwy over 2f out: rdn and wknd fnl f* **10/3**[2]
04-5 **8** *2 3/4* **Amy Blair**[123] 510 3-8-3 **55**........AndrewMullen 8 25
(Keith Dalgleish) *t.k.h early: hld up: drvn and outpcd over 2f out: sn btn* **18/1**
2-26 **9** *3 1/2* **Andaz**[110] 679 3-9-0 **69**........JacobButterfield(3) 4 29
(Marjorie Fife) *reluctant to enter stalls and restless whn loaded: s.i.s: bhd: struggling whn hmpd 3f out: nvr on terms* **20/1**
2012 **10** *7* **Lucky Lodge**[25] 2332 6-9-11 **67**........(p) PhillipMakin 11 12
(Antony Brittain) *hld up: drvn and edgd rt 3f out: sn wknd* **17/2**
-600 **11** *40* **Final Spring (IRE)**[26] 2302 3-8-0 **52** oh7........[1] RaulDaSilva 3
(Jim Goldie) *in tch: struggling over 3f out: sn struggling: t.o* **66/1**

1m 29.22s (0.22) **Going Correction** -0.025s/f (Good)
WFA 3 from 4yo+ 10lb **11** Ran SP% **120.6**
Speed ratings (Par 103): **97,95,94,93,89 86,84,81,77,69 23**
CSF £45.77 CT £231.29 TOTE £3.50: £1.70, £5.50, £1.80; EX 47.60 Trifecta £337.70.
Owner Dr Marwan Koukash **Bred** Kenneth Heelan **Trained** Musley Bank, N Yorks

FOCUS
An ordinary handicap run at a frantic early pace and few got involved from behind.

3154 GAYNOR WINYARD H'CAP 1m 4f 100y
5:25 (5:27) (Class 6) (0-65,62) 4-Y-O+ **£3,234** (£962; £481; £240) **Stalls** Low

Form RPR
000- **1** **Tonto's Spirit**[12] 4512 4-8-4 **45**........AndrewMullen 5 52
(Kenneth Slack) *mde all: rdn over 2f out: hld on wl fnl f* **2/1**[1]
0566 **2** *2 1/4* **Surround Sound**[12] 2738 6-9-1 **56**........(tp) DavidAllan 4 59
(Tim Easterby) *hld up: hdwy over 2f out: effrt and chsd wnr over 1f out: kpt on fnl f: nt rch wnr* **5/2**[2]
00-5 **3** *2 3/4* **Neuf Des Coeurs**[15] 2656 5-9-7 **62**........(p) RoystonFfrench 8 61
(Iain Jardine) *trckd ldrs: prom: effrt over 2f out: no ex over 1f out* **6/1**
0-53 **4** *1* **Fillydelphia (IRE)**[15] 2656 5-8-6 **54**........PaulaMuir(7) 1 51
(Patrick Holmes) *hld up in tch: hdwy to chse wnr over 2f out to over 1f out: sn no ex* **7/2**[3]
060- **5** *2 3/4* **Gold Chain (IRE)**[14] 5140 6-9-2 **60** ow1........(tp) MissEmmaSayer(3) 6 53
(Dianne Sayer) *hld up in tch: rdn on outside over 2f out: no imp over 1f out* **12/1**
5066 **6** *2 1/4* **New Colours**[7] 2912 5-8-2 **48**........(p) PhilDennis(5) 2 37
(Linda Perratt) *chsd wnr to over 2f out: sn lost pl: btn fnl f* **11/1**

2m 44.57s (2.57) **Going Correction** -0.025s/f (Good) **6** Ran SP% **114.4**
Speed ratings (Par 101): **90,88,86,86,84 82**
CSF £7.51 CT £23.91 TOTE £3.00: £1.90, £1.50; EX 7.10 Trifecta £17.80.
Owner A Slack **Bred** Mrs J M Quy **Trained** Hilton, Cumbria

FOCUS
A moderate contest to end with and another all-the-way winner.
T/Plt: £348.80 to a £1 stake. Pool of £67888.95 - 142.08 winning tickets. T/Qpdt: £56.90 to a £1 stake. Pool of £5524.20 - 71.80 winning tickets. **Richard Young**

3106 SANDOWN (R-H)
Saturday, June 11

OFFICIAL GOING: Good to firm (good in places on sprint course; round 7.6, sprint 7.4)
Wind: Moderate, against Weather: Cloudy, warm

3155 BETSTARS.UK BEST ODDS ENGLAND V RUSSIA H'CAP 7f 16y
1:40 (1:40) (Class 3) (0-95,91) 3-Y-O
£9,337 (£2,796; £1,398; £699; £349; £175) **Stalls** Low

Form RPR
-222 **1** **Destroyer**[24] 2375 3-8-7 **77**........(p) SamHitchcott 2 83
(William Muir) *chsd ldrs in 5th: rdn over 2f out: clsd over 1f out: drvn ahd ins fnl f: hld on* **25/1**
-530 **2** *hd* **London Protocol (FR)**[31] 2161 3-8-10 **85**........JordanVaughan(5) 5 90
(K R Burke) *t.k.h: disp ld 1f: pressed ldr after tl led over 2f out: hung lft fr over 1f out: hdd ins fnl f: kpt on wl: jst hld* **9/1**
2-16 **3** *1/2* **War Story (IRE)**[21] 2479 3-9-1 **85**........AdamKirby 6 89
(Luca Cumani) *hld up in last trio: rdn over 2f out: prog over 1f out: chal fnl f: styd on same pce nr fin* **4/1**[2]
2-10 **4** *1 1/4* **Short Work**[8] 2871 3-8-12 **82**........(p) FMBerry 9 82
(Ralph Beckett) *dwlt: hld up in last: rdn 3f out: no prog tl jst over 1f out: styd on but nvr able to chal* **14/1**
1-24 **5** *nk* **Arab Poet**[21] 2466 3-9-2 **86**........RyanMoore 3 85
(Sir Michael Stoute) *t.k.h: trckd ldng trio: rdn 2f out: tried to chal over 1f out: nt qckn jst ins fnl f: one pce after* **5/4**[1]
5120 **6** *nk* **Willsy**[21] 2477 3-8-7 **77**........(v[1]) OisinMurphy 4 76
(Mick Channon) *hld up in last trio: rdn over 2f out: no prog tl styd on ins fnl f: nrst fin* **33/1**
-213 **7** *nk* **Dream Mover (IRE)**[42] 1851 3-9-3 **87**........FrankieDettori 8 85
(Marco Botti) *in tch in 6th: rdn over 2f out: nvr able to cl on ldrs but kpt on same pce* **7/1**[3]
01-0 **8** *shd* **Majdool (IRE)**[21] 2477 3-9-7 **91**........AndreaAtzeni 7 89
(Roger Varian) *disp ld 1f: trckd ldng pair after: rdn 2f out: sltly impeded fr over 1f out: fdd ins fnl f* **10/1**

-140 **9** 1 ½ **Galesburg (IRE)**[21] 2466 3-8-8 **78**................................ PaulMulrennan 1 72
(Mark Johnston) *won battle for ld after 1f: hdd over 2f out: styd on terms tl wknd fnl f* **20/1**

1m 29.98s (0.48) **Going Correction** +0.125s/f (Good) **9** Ran SP% **114.3**
Speed ratings (Par 103): **102,101,101,99,99 99,98,98,96**
CSF £224.94 CT £1104.87 TOTE £27.30: £5.60, £3.10, £1.60; EX 324.60 Trifecta £2382.70.
Owner Capt J Appoo, Quaintance, Clark, Moore **Bred** Whitsbury Manor Stud **Trained** Lambourn, Berks

FOCUS
Sprint Course at full width. Round Course railed out up to 5yds from 1m1f to winning post - adding 21yds to all Round Course race distances. A couple of these wanted to lead early and, with a surprise winner, the form looks ordinary.

3156 BETSTARS.UK FOR HORSE RACING H'CAP 1m 1f
2:10 (2:11) (Class 3) (0-90,88) 3-Y-O

£12,450 (£3,728; £1,864; £932; £466; £234) **Stalls** Low

Form RPR
0-10 **1** **Threat Assessed (IRE)**[15] 2654 3-8-13 **80**................ PaulMulrennan 10 90
(Clive Cox) *hld up in tch: prog 2f out: drvn to chal ins fnl f: styd on wl to ld last strides* **12/1**

0-11 **2** *hd* **Dommersen (IRE)**[18] 2565 3-9-5 **86**................................ FrankieDettori 4 95
(John Gosden) *hld up in tch: prog 2f out: rdn to ld jst ins fnl f: sn pressed: kpt on but hdd last strides* **5/1**[2]

3-15 **3** 1 ½ **Wild Hacked (USA)**[21] 2473 3-9-1 **82**............................. AndreaAtzeni 6 88
(Marco Botti) *prom: wnt 2nd over 2f out: rdn to ld over 1f out: hdd and one pce jst ins fnl f* **9/2**[1]

4-60 **4** 1 ½ **Brorocco**[52] 1575 3-8-7 **74**.. OisinMurphy 5 77
(Andrew Balding) *hld up in last: gd prog on inner wl over 1f out: threatened to cl on ldrs jst ins fnl f: one pce after* **25/1**

410- **5** 3 ¼ **Cosmeapolitan**[245] 7113 3-9-1 **82**.......................... WilliamTwiston-Davies 3 78
(Alan King) *hld up in last pair: rdn and prog jst over 2f out: cl 5th jst ins fnl f: wknd* **20/1**

1-43 **6** 7 **Chester Street**[26] 2299 3-8-13 **80**..................................(b[1]) RyanMoore 1 60
(Roger Charlton) *led: tried to stretch for home over 2f out: hdd over 1f out: wknd and eased* **9/2**[1]

01 **7** 2 ¼ **Star Blaze**[28] 2248 3-9-1 **82**.. MartinHarley 8 57
(Mick Channon) *chsd ldrs: u.p wl over 2f out: wknd wl over 1f out* **9/2**[1]

2 35 **8** 5 **Sacred Trust**[19] 2538 3-8-11 **78**... FMBerry 7 42
(Hugo Palmer) *prom: rdn 3f out: carried lft and hmpd over 2f out: sn wknd* **9/1**[3]

421 **9** 1 ¼ **High Draw (FR)**[18] 2557 3-8-11 **83**........................... JordanVaughan[(5)] 9 44
(K R Burke) *pressed ldr tl hung lft over 2f out: sn wknd qckly* **5/1**[2]

1m 55.31s (-0.39) **Going Correction** +0.125s/f (Good) **9** Ran SP% **114.2**
Speed ratings (Par 103): **106,105,104,103,100 94,92,87,86**
CSF £70.07 CT £316.00 TOTE £14.20: £4.20, £1.90, £1.70; EX 78.80 Trifecta £979.30.
Owner Alan G Craddock **Bred** Roundhill Stud **Trained** Lambourn, Berks

FOCUS
Race distance increased by 21yds. A useful 3yo handicap, although a couple of the fancied runners disappointed.

3157 BETSTARS BY POKERSTARS H'CAP 1m 14y
2:45 (2:46) (Class 2) (0-100,98) 3-Y-O+

£21,787 (£6,524; £3,262; £1,631; £815; £409) **Stalls** Low

Form RPR
6-30 **1** **Mutamakkin (USA)**[42] 1861 4-9-7 **91**................................ RyanMoore 7 102+
(Sir Michael Stoute) *hld up in last: stl there jst over 2f out: prog and squeezed through to chse clr ldr jst over 1f out: drvn and r.o wl to ld last strides* **11/4**[1]

-053 **2** ¾ **Franklin D (USA)**[21] 2484 4-9-6 **93**........................(v[1]) LouisSteward[(3)] 3 102
(Michael Bell) *led: drew clr wl over 2f out: stl 3 l ld 1f out: idled fnl f: hdd last strides* **7/1**

3541 **3** 1 ¼ **King's Pavilion (IRE)**[8] 2871 3-8-12 **93**................................ FMBerry 11 95
(Mark Johnston) *sn hld up towards rr: rdn over 2f out: effrt on outer to chse clr ldr briefly over 1f out: kpt on same pce fnl f* **11/2**[3]

-503 **4** *nk* **Secret Art (IRE)**[16] 2628 6-9-8 **92**.................................... MartinHarley 4 96
(William Knight) *hld up in last trio: rdn 2f out: kpt on fr over 1f out: pressed for 3rd nr fin* **9/1**

0610 **5** 2 ¼ **Mr Bossy Boots (IRE)**[35] 2027 5-9-2 **91**.............(t) PatrickO'Donnell[(5)] 1 90
(Ralph Beckett) *chsd ldrs: rdn wl over 2f out: no imp on ldr over 1f out: fdd* **16/1**

2650 **6** 1 **Ode To Evening**[21] 2473 3-9-1 **96**................................ PaulMulrennan 6 90
(Mark Johnston) *chsd ldr: drvn wl over 2f out: lost 2nd and wandered over 1f out: fdd* **14/1**

024- **7** 3 ¼ **Laidback Romeo (IRE)**[274] 6286 4-9-0 **84**........................ AdamKirby 9 73
(Clive Cox) *hld up in last trio: effrt on outer and drvn over 2f out: no prog whn sltly intimidated and swvd lft over 1f out: wknd* **6/1**

0121 **8** 14 **Dolphin Vista (IRE)**[23] 2407 3-9-0 **95**............................ FrankieDettori 2 49
(Richard Fahey) *in tch: rdn wl over 2f out: wknd over 1f out: heavily eased: t.o* **7/2**[2]

200- **9** 18 **The Rectifier (USA)**[196] 8034 9-10-0 **98**........................(t) OisinMurphy 8 14
(Seamus Durack) *t.k.h: pressed ldrs: rdn over 2f out: sn wknd: heavily eased and t.o* **16/1**

1m 42.32s (-0.98) **Going Correction** +0.125s/f (Good)
WFA 3 from 4yo+ 11lb **9** Ran SP% **119.5**
Speed ratings (Par 109): **109,108,106,106,103 102,99,85,67**
CSF £23.52 CT £102.40 TOTE £4.10: £1.40, £2.50, £2.10; EX 24.80 Trifecta £137.30.
Owner Hamdan Al Maktoum **Bred** Helen K Groves Revokable Trust **Trained** Newmarket, Suffolk

FOCUS
Race distance increased by 21yds. Again there was competition for the lead and the closers were favoured, so the runner-up needs his effort upgrading.

3158 BETSTARS.UK SCURRY STKS (LISTED RACE) 5f 6y
3:20 (3:21) (Class 1) 3-Y-O

£20,982 (£7,955; £3,981; £1,983; £995; £499) **Stalls** Low

Form RPR
35-1 **1** **Easton Angel (IRE)**[30] 2192 3-8-12 103........................... PaulMulrennan 8 110+
(Michael Dods) *trckd ldrs: coasting 2f out: asked to ld 1f out and qckly drew clr: comf* **2/1**[1]

1163 **2** 2 ¼ **Willytheconqueror (IRE)**[10] 2788 3-9-0 97........................ MartinDwyer 4 103
(William Muir) *hld up in 5th: pushed along and waiting for a gap over 1f out: r.o to take 2nd last 100yds: no ch w wnr* **8/1**

23-2 **3** 1 ½ **Ornate**[158] 45 3-9-0 110.. RyanMoore 5 98
(William Haggas) *pressed ldng pair: led wl over 1f out: drvn and hdd 1f out: no ch w wnr and lost 2nd last 100yds* **3/1**[2]

305- **4** ½ **Soapy Aitken**[294] 5642 3-9-0 98.. AdamKirby 9 96
(Clive Cox) *hld up in 6th: plld out wd and effrt over 1f out: drvn and kpt on one pce after* **16/1**

1-44 **5** ½ **Dhahmaan (IRE)**[28] 2242 3-9-3 100............................... FrankieDettori 6 97
(Marco Botti) *settled in last: pushed along and nt clr run over 1f out: modest prog fnl f: nvr gng pce to be involved* **6/1**

2-25 **6** 2 **Lil's Joy (IRE)**[29] 2232 3-8-9 101.. OisinMurphy 2 82
(Giles Bravery) *led 100yds: w ldr: led briefly 2f out: fdd fnl f* **10/1**

121- **7** 6 **Shaden (IRE)**[266] 6514 3-9-0 106.. AndreaAtzeni 1 65
(George Scott) *pushed up to ld after 100yds against rail: hdd 2f out: wknd rapidly fnl f* **11/2**[3]

1m 0.32s (-1.28) **Going Correction** +0.025s/f (Good) **7** Ran SP% **114.1**
Speed ratings (Par 107): **111,107,105,104,103 100,90**
CSF £18.68 TOTE £2.10: £1.30, £4.50; EX 22.20 Trifecta £139.10.
Owner Al Shaqab Racing & Ritchie Fiddes **Bred** James Waldron **Trained** Denton, Co Durham

FOCUS
Race distance as advertised. The favourite proved different class to these and is rated back to her Queen Mary form, but this was not the strongest of Listed races.

3159 BETSTARS.UK MONEY BACK IF ENGLAND LOSE H'CAP (JOCKEY CLUB GRASSROOTS SPRINT SERIES QUALIFIER) 5f 6y
3:55 (3:58) (Class 4) (0-80,81) 4-Y-O+ **£5,175** (£1,540; £769; £384) **Stalls** Low

Form RPR
/245 **1** **Jaywalker (IRE)**[12] 2754 5-9-5 **76**................................ CharlesBishop 10 85
(Mick Channon) *spd fr wd draw to press ldr: led 2f out: drvn out and styd on wl fnl f* **11/2**[3]

-261 **2** 1 **Major Pusey**[2] 3056 4-9-7 **81** 6ex........................ MichaelJMMurphy[(3)] 3 86
(John Gallagher) *led against rail: rdn and hdd 2f out: chsd wnr after: kpt on but a hld: jst lasted for 2nd* **4/1**[1]

262- **3** *shd* **Costa Filey**[207] 7882 5-8-10 **67**.. OisinMurphy 7 72
(Ed Vaughan) *wl in tch: rdn and prog over 1f out: disp 2nd ins fnl f: styd on and nrly snatched 2nd* **14/1**

420- **4** *shd* **Ejbaar**[249] 7017 4-9-5 **76**.. RyanMoore 9 80+
(Robert Cowell) *towards rr: rdn 2f out: prog over 1f out: r.o wl nr fin and nrly grabbed a pl* **10/1**

5000 **5** ¾ **Captain Bob (IRE)**[28] 2253 5-9-6 **77**................................ AdamKirby 12 79+
(Robert Cowell) *stdd s: hld up in rr and swtchd to rail: gng bttr than most 2f out: shuffled along over 1f out: kpt on steadily fnl f: one to nte* **9/1**

0130 **6** ¾ **Ask The Guru**[6] 2931 6-8-7 **64**.......................................(p) JimmyQuinn 2 63
(Michael Attwater) *prom against rail: rdn over 1f out: kpt on fnl f* **18/1**

4511 **7** *nse* **Pour La Victoire (IRE)**[15] 2643 6-8-12 **76**................(b) GeorgiaCox[(7)] 1 75
(Tony Carroll) *s.s: pushed along and detached in last: taken to outer 1/2-way: styd on wl fnl f: nrst fin* **9/2**[2]

5060 **8** ¾ **Rocket Rob (IRE)**[11] 2785 10-8-3 **60**............................ KieranO'Neill 13 56
(Willie Musson) *hld up in rr on outer: pushed along 2f out: kpt on fr over 1f out: nvr gng pce to threaten* **20/1**

0-04 **9** ½ **Tagula Night (IRE)**[26] 2309 10-9-4 **78**.......................(vt) JackDuern[(3)] 5 72
(Dean Ivory) *chsd ldrs towards outer: rdn 2f out: no imp 1f out: fdd ins fnl f* **8/1**

-600 **10** 1 **Smoothtalkinrascal (IRE)**[21] 2469 6-9-1 **72**...................(t) FMBerry 6 63
(Peter Crate) *s.i.s: wl in rr: u.p in last over 1f out: no great prog after* **12/1**

3220 **11** 1 ¼ **Mossgo (IRE)**[6] 2931 6-9-1 **72**..(t) KierenFox 8 58
(John Best) *chsd ldrs: rdn 2f out: sn lost pl and btn* **20/1**

0000 **12** 3 ¼ **Keep It Dark**[21] 2469 7-9-3 **74**.. MartinHarley 4 48
(William Knight) *prom to 2f out: wknd* **14/1**

1m 1.0s (-0.60) **Going Correction** +0.025s/f (Good) **12** Ran SP% **119.6**
Speed ratings (Par 105): **105,103,103,103,101 100,100,99,98,97 95,89**
CSF £27.99 CT £295.22 TOTE £7.10: £2.80, £2.50, £4.40; EX 32.00 Trifecta £325.70.
Owner Insignia Racing (Crest) **Bred** Kilfrush Stud **Trained** West Ilsley, Berks

FOCUS
Race distance as advertised. Just a fair sprint and little got into it from off the pace.

3160 BETSTARS.UK IT'S A GAME CHANGER/EBF STALLIONS MAIDEN STKS 1m 2f 7y
4:30 (4:33) (Class 5) 3-Y-O **£3,881** (£1,155; £577; £288) **Stalls** Low

Form RPR
5-42 **1** **Autocratic**[10] 2790 3-9-5 78.. RyanMoore 8 94+
(Sir Michael Stoute) *chsd ldng pair: shkn up wl over 2f out: clsd to go 2nd over 1f out: rdn to ld last 150yds: styd on wl* **3/1**[2]

05 **2** 2 **Makzeem**[36] 2008 3-9-5 0.................................... WilliamTwiston-Davies 6 90
(Roger Charlton) *led 1f: trckd ldr: led over 2f out: drvn over 1f out: hdd and one pce last 150yds* **3/1**[2]

2 **3** 3 ½ **New World Power (JPN)**[29] 2208 3-9-5 0........................ OisinMurphy 14 83
(Roger Varian) *led after 1f: hdd and shkn up over 2f out: nt qckn and lost 2nd over 1f out: one pce* **6/4**[1]

4 2 **Stanley** 3-9-5 0.. AdamKirby 9 79
(Luca Cumani) *wl in tch: pushed along to take 4th 2f out but nt on terms w ldrs: kpt on same pce after* **16/1**

5 1 ¾ **Sir Valentine (GER)** 3-9-5 0.. MartinHarley 7 75+
(Alan King) *dwlt: wl in rr: shkn up 3f out: prog fr 2f out: styd on same pce fnl f* **50/1**

6 **6** ¾ **Henry Croft**[49] 1626 3-9-5 0.. NickyMackay 1 74
(John Gosden) *trckd ldng pair: shkn up and steadily wknd fr over 2f out* **12/1**[3]

5-0 **7** 1 ½ **Alquffaal**[45] 1784 3-9-5 0.. KieranO'Neill 10 71
(Roger Varian) *hld up in last trio: rdn wl over 2f out: nvr a factor but kpt on fr over 1f out* **50/1**

00 **8** 1 ¼ **Ma Peek (USA)**[23] 2414 3-9-5 0....................................... FrankieDettori 2 68
(Brian Meehan) *chsd ldrs: shkn up wl over 2f out: no prog wl over 1f out: fdd* **25/1**

0 **9** ¾ **Faction**[33] 2098 3-8-12 0.. JoshuaBryan[(7)] 5 67
(Andrew Balding) *in tch: fly-leapt after 3f: shkn up wl over 2f out: no prog* **66/1**

10 1 **Lost The Moon** 3-9-0 0.. SaleemGolam 4 60
(Mark H Tompkins) *in tch in midfield: rdn and no prog over 2f out: wknd fnl f* **100/1**

05 **11** *nk* **Askari**[16] 2619 3-9-5 0.. AndreaAtzeni 12 64
(Roger Varian) *nvr bttr than midfield: u.p wl over 2f out: sn btn* **33/1**

60- **12** 16 **Rod Of Iron**[215] 7777 3-9-2 0...................................... DanielMuscutt[(3)] 3 32
(Michael Madgwick) *dwlt: a in rr: sltly impeded after 3f: wknd over 2f out: t.o* **100/1**

6 **13** 1 ½ **Madame Chow (IRE)**[23] 2414 3-9-0 0.................................... FMBerry 11 24
(Ralph Beckett) *stdd into last trio: shkn up and wknd over 2f out: t.o* **16/1**

0- **14** ½ **Sirdaal (USA)**[260] 6711 3-9-5 0 PaulMulrennan 13 28
(Owen Burrows) *restrained into last sn after s: rdn 3f out: no prog: t.o* **50/1**

2m 9.69s (-0.81) **Going Correction** +0.125s/f (Good) **14** Ran SP% **125.6**
Speed ratings (Par 99): **108,106,103,102,100 100,98,97,97,96 96,83,82,81**
CSF £12.59 TOTE £4.10: £1.40, £1.50, £1.40; EX 14.70 Trifecta £30.30.
Owner Cheveley Park Stud **Bred** Cheveley Park Stud Ltd **Trained** Newmarket, Suffolk

FOCUS
Race distance increased by 21yds. This had the look of a good maiden and the big three in the market, all prominent throughout, duly dominated.

3161 SPIN AND BET FOR X10 ODDS H'CAP 1m 6f
5:05 (5:07) (Class 4) (0-85,83) 4-Y-O+ **£5,822** (£1,732; £865; £432) **Stalls** Low

Form RPR

/361 **1** **Touch The Sky**[15] 2663 5-9-5 **81** OisinMurphy 6 89
(David Elsworth) *led: shkn up over 2f out: rdn and hdd 1f out: edgd lft but rallied to ld again last 100yds: hld on wl* **6/4**[1]

-213 **2** *nk* **Rideonastar (IRE)**[14] 2699 5-9-6 **82** RyanMoore 1 89
(Brendan Powell) *trckd ldng pair: shkn up over 2f out: drvn and clsd to ld 1f out: kpt on but hdd and jst hld last 100yds* **15/8**[2]

66-2 **3** *3* **Desdichado**[46] 1760 4-9-4 **80** FMBerry 2 83
(Ralph Beckett) *hld up in last: shkn up and effrt over 2f out: cl enough over 1f out: fdd ins fnl f* **4/1**[3]

5-30 **4** *hd* **Fitzwilly**[23] 2392 6-8-13 **75** (v[1]) CharlesBishop 9 78
(Mick Channon) *t.k.h early: trckd ldr: chal over 2f out: rdn and fnd nil wl over 1f out: sn lost 2nd and btn* **10/1**

6-65 **5** *2* **Lady Of Yue**[20] 2501 6-7-10 **65** MillyNaseb[(7)] 7 65
(Eugene Stanford) *hld up in 4th: dropped to last 2f out and outpcd: nvr on terms after* **14/1**

3m 9.72s (5.22) **Going Correction** +0.125s/f (Good) **5** Ran SP% **110.5**
Speed ratings (Par 105): **90,89,88,88,86**
CSF £4.63 TOTE £2.20: £1.20, £1.50; EX 4.00 Trifecta £8.20.
Owner Lordship Stud & Christopher Wright **Bred** Lordship Stud **Trained** Newmarket, Suffolk

FOCUS
Race distance increased by 21yds. They dawdled for this 1m6f handicap and the winner and favourite was perfectly placed at the head of affairs.
T/Plt: £69.60 to a £1 stake. Pool: £97,037.11 - 1,017.25 winning units T/Qpdt: £7.00 to a £1 stake. Pool: £7,385.69 - 773.24 winning units **Jonathan Neesom**

3112 YORK (L-H)
Saturday, June 11

OFFICIAL GOING: Good to soft (good in places; 6.8)
Wind: Virtually nil Weather: Cloudy

3162 QUEEN MOTHER'S CUP (LADY AMATEUR RIDERS) (H'CAP) 1m 4f
1:50 (1:51) (Class 3) (0-95,90) 3-Y-O+ **£12,478** (£3,870; £1,934; £968) **Stalls** Centre

Form RPR

4264 **1** **Snoano**[12] 2744 4-10-7 **89** MissEEasterby[(6)] 8 98
(Tim Easterby) *midfield: hdwy on wd outside wl over 2f out: rdn to ld 1 1/2f out and sn edgd lft: kpt on* **11/1**

6311 **2** ½ **Masterpaver**[15] 2651 5-9-6 **74** MissFMcSharry[(6)] 7 82
(Richard Fahey) *cl up: led over 2f out: hdd 1 1/2f out and sn rdn: drvn and rallied ins fnl f: ev ch tl no ex towards fin* **8/1**[3]

00-0 **3** 2½ **Tapis Libre**[31] 2163 8-10-3 **79** MissJoannaMason 6 83
(Michael Easterby) *trckd ldrs: hdwy 3f out: chsd ldr 2f out: rdn over 1f out: drvn and kpt on same pce fnl f* **16/1**

6115 **4** ½ **Nietzsche**[29] 2224 3-9-0 **77** BrodieHampson 4 80
(Brian Ellison) *midfield: hdwy 3f out: rdn to chse ldrs wl over 1f out: drvn and kpt on same pce fnl f* **8/1**[3]

1-41 **5** 2¼ **Nayel (IRE)**[31] 2157 4-10-13 **89** MsKWalsh 10 89
(Richard Hannon) *trckd ldrs: hdwy 3f out: chsd ldrs 2f out: sn rdn and kpt on one pce fnl f* **4/1**[1]

1-40 **6** *hd* **English Summer**[12] 2744 9-10-8 **90** (t) MissEmilyBullock[(6)] 13 89+
(Richard Fahey) *hld up towards rr: hdwy wl over 2f out: rdn over 1f out: styd on wl fnl f: nrst fin* **20/1**

4-00 **7** ½ **Mistiroc**[29] 2199 5-11-0 **90** (p) MissGAndrews 2 89
(John Quinn) *trckd ldrs: hdwy 3f out: rdn wl over 1f out: drvn and one pce appr fnl f* **14/1**

0-30 **8** *shd* **Blue Hussar (IRE)**[29] 2222 5-10-11 **87** (p) MissCWalton 3 86
(Micky Hammond) *trckd ldrs: hdwy to chse ldng pair over 3f out: rdn 2f out: drvn over 1f out and sn one pce* **14/1**

-230 **9** ¾ **Intense Tango**[28] 2249 5-10-11 **87** MissHayleyMoore 12 84
(K R Burke) *midfield: hdwy wl over 2f out: rdn along wl over 1f out: sn one pce* **20/1**

2524 **10** *nk* **Burano (IRE)**[21] 2487 7-10-7 **89** MrsShaunaCurtis[(6)] 11 86
(David O'Meara) *a towards rr* **10/1**

30-5 **11** *1* **Sikandar (IRE)**[29] 2199 4-10-1 **80** (tp) MissLWilson[(3)] 15 75
(Brian Ellison) *dwlt: a towards rr* **25/1**

6240 **12** 3¼ **Yorkidding**[7] 2897 4-10-10 **86** MissBeckySmith 1 76
(Mark Johnston) *led: pushed along over 3f out: rdn wl over 2f out: sn hdd & wknd* **9/1**

03-4 **13** *nse* **Oceane (FR)**[14] 2699 4-10-8 **84** (p) MissSBrotherton 9 74
(Alan King) *a towards rr* **7/1**[2]

412- **14** *41* **Dhaular Dhar (IRE)**[219] 6786 14-10-1 **77** MrsCBartley 14 1
(Jim Goldie) *a towards rr* **33/1**

0/01 **P** **Sign Manual**[22] 2439 7-9-10 **75** (b) MissAMcCain[(3)] 5
(Donald McCain) *cl up: rdn along over 4f out: lost action and p.u qckly wl over 3f* **20/1**

2m 34.25s (1.05) **Going Correction** +0.125s/f (Good)
WFA 3 from 4yo+ 15lb **15** Ran SP% **122.4**
Speed ratings (Par 107): **101,100,99,98,97 97,96,96,96,95 95,93,93,65,**
CSF £89.58 CT £1429.31 TOTE £13.20: £4.20, £3.20, £6.50; EX 139.20 Trifecta £3057.10.
Owner M J Macleod **Bred** Minster Stud **Trained** Great Habton, N Yorks

FOCUS
Rail alignment moved to provide fresh ground on home bend. The race distance was reduced by 42yds. This was a strong race of its type and there was no hanging around, which put the majority out of their comfort zone. The winner was back to his best.

3163 BETSTARS.UK HOME OF SPIN & BET STKS (H'CAP) 7f
2:25 (2:25) (Class 2) (0-105,102) 3-Y-O+
£24,900 (£7,456; £3,728; £1,864; £932; £468) **Stalls** Low

Form RPR

-431 **1** **Felix Leiter**[17] 2587 4-8-13 **94** CliffordLee[(7)] 9 104
(K R Burke) *mde all: rdn clr wl over 1f out: kpt on strly* **11/2**[2]

0000 **2** 1¼ **Valley Of Fire**[7] 2898 4-8-12 **86** PatCosgrave 7 93
(William Haggas) *hld up towards rr: hdwy wl over 2f out: chsd ldrs wl over 1f out: drvn ent fnl f: kpt on* **16/1**

6-50 **3** *shd* **Alfred Hutchinson**[30] 2191 8-9-10 **98** (p) JimCrowley 2 104
(David O'Meara) *trckd ldng pair: hdwy to chse wnr over 2f out: rdn along wl over 1f out: drvn fnl f: kpt on* **7/1**

1-02 **4** 2½ **Withernsea (IRE)**[49] 1627 5-9-9 **97** TomEaves 10 97
(Richard Fahey) *hld up in tch: hdwy wl over 2f out: sn pushed along: rdn wl over 1f out: drvn fnl f and kpt on one pce* **5/1**[1]

-035 **5** *nse* **Lincoln (IRE)**[21] 2485 5-9-6 **94** JFEgan 5 94
(Mick Channon) *plld hrd: trckd ldrs: hdwy 3f out: chsd wnr wl over 1f out: sn drvn and wknd ins fnl f* **13/2**[3]

20-0 **6** *shd* **Lulu The Zulu (IRE)**[14] 2684 8-9-12 **100** DarryllHolland 3 99
(Michael Appleby) *hld up towards rr: hdwy on inner over 2f out: rdn to chse ldrs over 1f out: drvn and kpt on one pce fnl f* **10/1**

4021 **7** 2¾ **Secret Hint**[14] 2683 5-9-3 **91** DavidProbert 4 83
(Andrew Balding) *hld up in rr: swtchd rt to outer and gd hdwy jst over 2f out: rdn to chse ldrs over 1f out: sn edgd lft and btn* **5/1**[1]

5300 **8** 1¼ **Shyron**[17] 2587 5-8-2 **83** JaneElliott[(7)] 11 72
(George Margarson) *dwlt: a in rr* **25/1**

60-0 **9** *5* **That Is The Spirit**[21] 2485 5-9-12 **100** DavidNolan 12 75
(David O'Meara) *chsd wnr: rdn along 3f out: wknd jst over 2f out* **8/1**

-003 **10** *18* **Mujassam**[21] 2480 4-9-9 **97** (b[1]) PaulHanagan 8 23
(Roger Varian) *trckd ldrs: effrt 3f out and sn rdn: drvn 2f out: sn wknd and bhd whn eased fnl f* **7/1**

1m 26.66s (1.36) **Going Correction** +0.425s/f (Yiel) **10** Ran SP% **117.0**
Speed ratings (Par 109): **109,107,107,104,104 104,101,99,94,73**
CSF £89.27 CT £639.52 TOTE £6.70: £2.40, £4.40, £2.70; EX 104.50 Trifecta £1806.40.
Owner Tim Dykes & Mrs E Burke **Bred** Tibthorpe Stud **Trained** Middleham Moor, N Yorks

FOCUS
This good-quality handicap looked competitive, but the winner stole a march 3f out and wasn't for catching. He continues on the upgrade.

3164 BEST WESTERN HOTELS GANTON STKS (LISTED RACE) 1m
3:00 (3:00) (Class 1) 3-Y-O+
£22,684 (£8,600; £4,304; £2,144; £1,076; £540) **Stalls** Low

Form RPR

223- **1** **Mutakayyef**[245] 7118 5-9-7 112 PatCosgrave 5 113+
(William Haggas) *trckd ldrs: smooth hdwy 3f out: cl up 2f out: led ent fnl f: sn rdn and kpt on: readily* **11/4**[1]

2654 **2** *1* **Sovereign Debt (IRE)**[8] 2867 7-9-12 111 DarryllHolland 11 115
(David Nicholls) *led after 1f: pushed along 2f out: rdn and jnd over 1f out: hdd ent fnl f: sn drvn and kpt on* **14/1**

425/ **3** 1¼ **Muwaary**[698] 4278 5-9-7 112 PaulHanagan 3 107+
(John Gosden) *hld up in rr: hdwy over 2f out: rdn over 1f out: styd on strly fnl f: nrst fin* **4/1**[2]

0001 **4** *nk* **Jallota**[21] 2485 5-9-7 110 JamieSpencer 4 106
(Charles Hills) *trckd ldrs: hdwy over 2f out: rdn to chse ldrs over 1f out: drvn and kpt on fnl f* **5/1**[3]

0546 **5** 1¼ **Gabrial (IRE)**[28] 2243 7-9-7 110 WilliamBuick 1 103
(Richard Fahey) *t.k.h early: towards rr: pushed along and sltly outpcd 3f out: hdwy 2f out and sn chsng ldrs: rdn over 1f out: kpt on* **6/1**

10-0 **6** *nse* **Baraweez (IRE)**[30] 2191 6-9-7 105 DaleSwift 6 103
(Brian Ellison) *led 1f: chsd ldr: effrt and cl up over 2f out: rdn wl over 1f out: drvn and kpt on same pce fnl f* **16/1**

7 3½ **Red Napoleon (USA)**[280] 6118 4-9-7 0 JamesDoyle 7 95
(Ralph Beckett) *in tch: effrt and sme hdwy on outer wl over 2f out: rdn along wl over 1f out: sn btn* **16/1**

-012 **8** 1½ **You're Fired (IRE)**[35] 2030 5-9-7 108 DougieCostello 2 91
(K R Burke) *hld up: hdwy on outer 3f: chsd ldrs 2f out: sn rdn and wknd* **6/1**

0-46 **9** 1¾ **Oracolo (IRE)**[30] 2191 4-9-7 91 FergusSweeney 8 87
(David Simcock) *trckd ldng pair: pushed along 3f out: rdn over 2f out: grad wknd* **28/1**

3-66 **10** *1* **Top Notch Tonto (IRE)**[37] 1973 6-9-7 107 (b[1]) TomEaves 9 85
(Brian Ellison) *hld up in rr: hdwy on outer 3f out: rdn along over 2f out: sn wknd* **10/1**

1m 39.31s (0.31) **Going Correction** +0.425s/f (Yiel) **10** Ran SP% **122.9**
Speed ratings (Par 111): **103,102,100,100,99 99,95,94,92,91**
CSF £46.94 TOTE £4.10: £1.60, £3.20, £1.70; EX 48.40 Trifecta £201.70.
Owner Hamdan Al Maktoum **Bred** Cheveley Park Stud Ltd **Trained** Newmarket, Suffolk

FOCUS
The race distance was reduced by 24yds. This Listed event was run at an uneven pace and it paid to race handily. The winner didn't need to match his best.

3165 888SPORT CHARITY SPRINT (H'CAP) 6f
3:35 (3:36) (Class 2) (0-105,102) 3-Y-O
£62,250 (£18,640; £9,320; £4,660; £2,330; £1,170) **Stalls** Centre

Form RPR

2-33 **1** **Mr Lupton (IRE)**[28] 2251 3-9-7 **102** JamieSpencer 2 115
(Richard Fahey) *hld up in rr towards far side: stdy hdwy on inner over 2f out: effrt ent fnl f: sn swtchd rt and rdn to chse ldr: drvn and styd on wl to ld nr fin* **10/1**

0-11 **2** ½ **Dancing Star**[8] 2875 3-8-8 **89** DavidProbert 4 100
(Andrew Balding) *racd towards far side: prom: cl up 3f out: led wl over 1f out: rdn clr jst over 1f out: drvn ins fnl f: hdd and no ex towards fin* **6/1**[2]

1211 **3** 4½ **Ikerrin Road (IRE)**[42] 1865 3-8-9 **90** CamHardie 1 87
(John Quinn) *racd towards far side: prom: effrt 2f out and ev ch: sn rdn: drvn and kpt on same pce fnl f* **9/1**[3]

6-30 **4** *nk* **Venturous (IRE)**[28] 2251 3-9-2 **97** WilliamBuick 12 93
(Charlie Appleby) *trckd ldrs: hdwy 2f out: rdn over 1f out: drvn and kpt on same pce fnl f* **10/1**

1123 **5** *1 ¼* **Kadrizzi (FR)**[78] 1070 3-9-6 **101** RobertWinston 3 93
(Dean Ivory) *racd towards far side: in tch: pushed along and sltly outpcd 2f out: sn rdn: chsd ldrs and swtchd lft jst ins fnl f: styd on* **16/1**

1-13 **6** *hd* **Aclaim (IRE)**[13] 2719 3-9-2 **97** FergusSweeney 7 88+
(Martyn Meade) *hld up in rr: hdwy 2f out: effrt and n.m.r over 1f out: swtchd lft and rdn ent fnl f: kpt on* **6/1**[2]

00-0 **7** *1 ¼* **Lathom**[7] 2895 3-9-1 **96** JimCrowley 6 83
(David O'Meara) *trckd ldrs towards far side: effrt 2f out: rdn whn n.m.r over 1f out: drvn and one pce fnl f* **20/1**

2501 **8** *2 ¼* **Sign Of The Kodiac (IRE)**[10] 2788 3-8-13 **94** TomEaves 11 74
(James Given) *racd centre: led: rdn along 2f out: sn hdd and drvn: grad wknd* **28/1**

-11 **9** *¾* **Udontdodou**[26] 2314 3-8-8 **89** JasonHart 13 67+
(Richard Guest) *racd centre: trckd ldr: cl up 1/2-way: effrt 2f out and sn shkn up: rdn over 1f out and sn one pce* **4/1**[1]

0-42 **10** *hd* **Madrinho (IRE)**[12] 2736 3-8-11 **92** TomQueally 10 69+
(Richard Hannon) *towards rr whn n.m.r and lost pl 1/2-way: sn rdn and sme late hdwy* **16/1**

6-50 **11** *1* **Twin Sails**[28] 2242 3-9-1 **96** PatCosgrave 8 70
(Dean Ivory) *chsd ldrs centre: rdn along 2f out: sn wknd* **25/1**

4-00 **12** *nk* **Still On Top**[21] 2473 3-8-9 **90** JamesSullivan 18 63
(Tim Easterby) *a towards rr* **20/1**

0320 **13** *nse* **Taexali (IRE)**[27] 2272 3-8-13 **94** TadhgO'Shea 15 67
(John Patrick Shanahan, Ire) *a towards rr* **25/1**

01-5 **14** *1 ¼* **Tawdheef (IRE)**[12] 2736 3-8-10 **91** RobertHavlin 9 60
(Simon Crisford) *a towards rr* **14/1**

3534 **15** *nk* **Sixties Sue**[41] 1882 3-8-8 **89** JFEgan 17 57
(Mick Channon) *in tch: rdn along over 2f out: sn wknd* **33/1**

0-54 **16** *¾* **Elronaq**[10] 2788 3-8-13 **94** PaulHanagan 20 59
(Charles Hills) *racd towards stands' side: chsd ldrs: rdn along over 2f out: sn wknd* **22/1**

5-04 **17** *15* **Riflescope (IRE)**[36] 1996 3-9-2 **97** JamesDoyle 14 14
(Mark Johnston) *midfield: rdn along 1/2-way: sn wknd* **25/1**

1m 11.86s (-0.04) **Going Correction** +0.425s/f (Yiel) **17** Ran SP% **127.0**
Speed ratings (Par 105): **114,113,107,106,105 105,103,100,99,99 97,97,97,95,95 94,74**
CSF £62.66 CT £420.63 TOTE £11.20: £3.00, £1.70, £2.90, £2.60; EX 55.50 Trifecta £961.30.
Owner N D Kershaw **Bred** Ms E O'Neill **Trained** Musley Bank, N Yorks

FOCUS
A fiercely competitive 3yo sprint handicap, taken last year by subsequent Group 1 winner Twilight Son. Being drawn low was a big advantage and the first pair drew well clear.

3166 ICE CO SUPPORTING MACMILLAN STKS (H'CAP) 1m 208y

4:10 (4:12) (Class 4) (0-80,85) 4-Y-O+ **£7,762** (£2,310; £1,154; £577) **Stalls** Low

Form RPR

0000 **1** **Woody Bay**[14] 2679 6-9-5 **78** DougieCostello 4 87
(Mark Walford) *trckd ldrs: hdwy 3f out: rdn wl over 1f out: chal ent fnl f: sn drvn and kpt on gamely to ld nr line* **16/1**

-535 **2** *shd* **Eurystheus (IRE)**[9] 2832 7-9-2 **75** (tp) TomQueally 9 84
(Michael Appleby) *trckd ldng trio: wd to centre home turn: slt ld over 2f out: rdn and edgd lft over 1f out: drvn ins fnl f: hdd nr line* **11/1**

0001 **3** *hd* **Auspicion**[15] 2662 4-9-3 **76** AndrewElliott 13 84
(Tom Tate) *trckd ldng pair on inner: hdwy 3f out: chal over 1f out: sn rdn and ev ch: drvn ins fnl f: no ex nr fin* **10/1**[3]

1252 **4** *2* **Rockwood**[16] 2618 5-9-0 **73** (v) JamieSpencer 3 76
(Karen McLintock) *in tch: hdwy on bit 3f out: trckd ldrs over 2f out: shkn up wl over 1f out: sn rdn and kpt on same pce* **8/1**[2]

2221 **5** *nk* **Jacbequick**[3] 3011 5-9-7 **85** 6ex (v) JoshDoyle[(5)] 15 88
(David O'Meara) *cl up: wd to centre home turn: rdn 2f out and ev ch: drvn whn sltly hmpd and swtchd rt appr fnl f: kpt on* **13/2**[1]

00 **6** *hd* **Tadaany (IRE)**[28] 2257 4-9-5 **78** JimCrowley 18 80+
(David O'Meara) *hld up in rr: hdwy wl over 2f out: rdn wl over 1f out: styd on fnl f: nrst fin* **33/1**

0500 **7** *¾* **Eutropius (IRE)**[16] 2620 7-9-4 **77** DarryllHolland 1 78+
(Alan Swinbank) *hld up towards rr: hdwy wl over 2f out: rdn and styd on fnl f: nrst fin* **16/1**

/030 **8** *1* **Torrid**[28] 2256 5-9-7 **80** [1] CamHardie 10 78
(Michael Easterby) *hld up towards rr: hdwy over 2f out: sn rdn and kpt on fnl f* **10/1**[3]

3-26 **9** *3 ¼* **Terhaal (IRE)**[12] 2734 4-9-5 **78** SamJames 20 69
(David O'Meara) *a towards rr* **12/1**

1-34 **10** *1 ¾* **Trinity Star (IRE)**[28] 2257 5-9-4 **77** (p) TomEaves 17 64
(Michael Dods) *dwlt: a towards rr* **16/1**

210 **11** *nse* **Tellovoi (IRE)**[14] 2677 8-9-0 **73** (v) JasonHart 8 60
(Richard Guest) *led: styd nr inner rail home st: rdn along and hdd wl over 2f out: sn wknd* **33/1**

1-46 **12** *nse* **Chiswick Bey (IRE)**[22] 2421 8-8-5 **71** NatalieHambling[(7)] 19 57
(Richard Fahey) *a towards rr* **25/1**

0500 **13** *2 ¼* **Shouranour (IRE)**[16] 2620 6-9-4 **77** (p) DaleSwift 5 58
(Alan Brown) *a towards rr* **14/1**

56-0 **14** *4* **Dream Walker (FR)**[16] 2620 7-9-4 **77** (p) TadhgO'Shea 6 49
(Brian Ellison) *dwlt: a in rr* **16/1**

40-0 **15** *1 ¼* **Correggio**[18] 2556 6-8-11 **77** RowanScott[(7)] 14 46
(Micky Hammond) *a towards rr* **25/1**

-061 **16** *9* **Normandy Knight**[12] 2734 4-9-2 **75** PaulHanagan 16 24
(Richard Fahey) *chsd ldrs: rdn along 3f out: sn drvn and wknd* **8/1**[2]

-200 **17** *nk* **Pivotman**[15] 2662 8-8-11 **70** JamesSullivan 7 18
(Michael Easterby) *midfield: hdwy on inner to chse ldrs 3f out: rdn over 2f out: sn drvn and wknd* **33/1**

4353 **18** *8* **Nonchalant**[7] 2888 5-9-1 **74** (v) DavidNolan 11 3
(David O'Meara) *chsd ldrs: rdn along 3f out: sn wknd* **10/1**[3]

1m 51.73s (-0.27) **Going Correction** +0.425s/f (Yiel) **18** Ran SP% **125.6**
Speed ratings (Par 105): **106,105,105,103,103 103,102,101,99,97 97,97,95,91,90 82,82,75**
CSF £175.28 CT £1913.68 TOTE £23.10: £4.90, £2.70, £3.20, £2.60; EX 235.20 Trifecta £3022.80.
Owner P C Thompson **Bred** Cheveley Park Stud Ltd **Trained** Sherriff Hutton, N Yorks

FOCUS
The race distance was reduced by 35yds. It doesn't come much more open than this fair handicap. Again a low draw proved an advantage and, despite them being strung out early, few landed a blow from off the pace. Sound form.

3167 REG GRIFFIN APPRECIATION EBF STALLIONS MAIDEN STKS (PLUS 10 RACE) 6f

4:45 (4:47) (Class 3) 2-Y-O **£7,762** (£2,310; £1,154; £577) **Stalls** High

Form RPR

1 **Marie Of Lyon** 2-9-0 0 PaulHanagan 8 80+
(Richard Fahey) *trckd ldrs: green pushed along and sltly outpcd 2f out: hdwy ent fnl f: sn rdn and styd on wl to ld last 100yds* **4/1**[3]

4 **2** *1 ½* **Final Reckoning (IRE)**[15] 2648 2-9-5 0 WilliamBuick 4 81
(Charlie Appleby) *cl up: rdn to ld appr jst over 1f out: drvn ins fnl f: hdd and no ex last 100yds* **3/1**[2]

3 *hd* **Starlight Romance (IRE)** 2-9-0 0 DavidNolan 3 75+
(Richard Fahey) *towards rr: pushed along and green 2f out: hdwy over 1f out: styd on strly fnl f* **14/1**

2 **4** *1 ¼* **Jacquard (IRE)**[9] 2830 2-9-5 0 JamesDoyle 1 76
(Mark Johnston) *led: rdn wl over 1f out: drvn and hdd appr fnl f: fdd* **7/4**[1]

5 *1* **Mister Moosah (IRE)** 2-9-5 0 RobertWinston 2 73
(Micky Hammond) *trckd ldrs: hdwy 2f out: sn rdn and ch tl drvn and one pce ent fnl f* **16/1**

6 *1 ½* **Nautical Haven** 2-9-5 0 TomEaves 6 69
(Kevin Ryan) *trckd ldrs: hdwy to chse ldng pair over 2f out: rdn wl over 1f out: grad wknd* **12/1**

3 **7** *3* **Cajmere**[15] 2648 2-9-5 0 JimCrowley 11 60
(Tom Dascombe) *in tch on outer: hdwy 2f out: sn chsng ldrs: rdn over 1f out: sn one pce* **8/1**

6 **8** *6* **Allux Boy (IRE)**[36] 2014 2-9-5 0 TomQueally 10 42
(Nigel Tinkler) *in tch to 1/2-way: sn outpcd* **40/1**

0 **9** *6* **My Girl Maisie (IRE)**[30] 2193 2-9-0 0 JasonHart 7 19
(Richard Guest) *a towards rr* **20/1**

10 *7* **Zarkavon** 2-9-0 0 JamesSullivan 5
(John Wainwright) *a towards rr* **50/1**

11 *1* **Nyx** 2-9-0 0 JFEgan 9
(Richard Guest) *a in rr* **33/1**

1m 14.16s (2.26) **Going Correction** +0.35s/f (Good) **11** Ran SP% **124.8**
Speed ratings (Par 97): **98,96,95,94,92 90,86,78,70,61 60**
CSF £17.04 TOTE £5.30: £1.80, £1.70, £3.30; EX 20.60 Trifecta £195.30.
Owner Clipper Logistics **Bred** Limestone Stud **Trained** Musley Bank, N Yorks

FOCUS
Not a bad 2yo maiden. Predictably the main action developed near the far rail. THe winner and third, both trained by Richard Fahey, look likely improvers.

3168 CHARLES HENRY MEMORIAL STKS (H'CAP) 6f

5:20 (5:24) (Class 4) (0-80,86) 3-Y-O+ **£7,762** (£2,310; £1,154; £577) **Stalls** Centre

Form RPR

2-10 **1** **Pomme De Terre (IRE)**[42] 1869 4-9-10 **79** (b) TomEaves 3 90
(Michael Dods) *in tch far side: hdwy over 2f out: rdn over 1f out: styd on to ld ins fnl f: drvn out* **14/1**

0021 **2** *1 ½* **Intisaab**[5] 2961 5-10-0 **86** 6ex (p) ShelleyBirkett[(3)] 18 92+
(David O'Meara) *racd towards stands' side: hld up in rr: gd hdwy wl over 1f out: rdn ent fnl f: sn drvn and kpt on* **13/2**[2]

6-43 **3** *nk* **Escalating**[10] 2787 4-9-7 **76** (tp) WilliamBuick 5 83+
(Michael Appleby) *hld up far side: hdwy wl over 1f out: rdn and styd on wl fnl f* **5/1**[1]

-050 **4** *½* **Art Obsession (IRE)**[28] 2238 5-9-6 **75** DougieCostello 11 78
(Paul Midgley) *racd towards centre: sn led: rdn and edgd lft wl over 1f out: drvn and hdd ins fnl f: kpt on* **25/1**

5355 **5** *¾* **Rich Again (IRE)**[25] 2346 7-9-7 **76** (b) JamesDoyle 9 77
(James Bethell) *racd towards far side: hld up in tch: hdwy wl over 1f out: sn rdn and styd on fnl f* **10/1**

00-0 **6** *nk* **Amood (IRE)**[25] 2345 5-9-4 **73** AndrewElliott 4 73
(Simon West) *racd towards far side: hld up: hdwy 2f out: n.m.r and swtchd rt to centre over 1f out: sn rdn and styd on* **25/1**

-000 **7** *1 ¼* **Dutch Breeze**[14] 2677 5-9-6 **75** (p) DavidNolan 17 71
(Tim Easterby) *racd towards stands' side: trckd ldrs: hdwy 2f out: sn rdn and ev ch tl drvn and kpt on same pce fnl f* **33/1**

0400 **8** *shd* **Whozthecat (IRE)**[28] 2259 9-9-8 **77** JFEgan 8 73
(Declan Carroll) *cl up far side: rdn along 2f out: grad wknd* **16/1**

0/0- **9** *1 ½* **Naggers (IRE)**[392] 2273 5-9-5 **74** RobertWinston 10 65
(Paul Midgley) *swtchd towards far side s: chsd ldrs: rdn along 2f out: grad wknd* **9/1**

45-0 **10** *1 ¼* **Bop It**[19] 2524 7-8-11 **71** (p) JoshDoyle[(5)] 6 58
(David O'Meara) *racd towards far side: chsd ldrs: rdn along wl over 1f out: sn drvn and wknd* **16/1**

-403 **11** *nk* **Mon Brav**[28] 2238 9-9-5 **74** TomQueally 14 60
(Brian Ellison) *a towards rr far side* **12/1**

6300 **12** *1* **Mappin Time (IRE)**[10] 2803 8-9-9 **78** (b) JasonHart 7 61
(Tim Easterby) *a towards rr far side* **20/1**

-060 **13** *1 ¾* **Mime Dance**[28] 2259 5-9-5 **74** SamJames 20 51
(David O'Meara) *racd towards stands' rail: trckd ldrs: rdn along over 2f out: sn wknd* **33/1**

0002 **14** *1* **Meandmyshadow**[10] 2794 8-9-6 **75** (b) DaleSwift 12 49
(Alan Brown) *racd towards stands' side: prom: rdn along over 2f out: sn drvn and wknd* **20/1**

-063 **15** *2 ¼* **Red Tycoon (IRE)**[14] 2677 4-9-3 **79** RowanScott[(7)] 15 46
(David Barron) *racd towards stands' side: a in rr* **12/1**

6035 **16** *½* **Singeur (IRE)**[15] 2665 9-9-11 **80** CamHardie 16 45
(Rebecca Bastiman) *racd towards stands' side: a towards rr* **33/1**

-131 **17** *3 ¼* **Faintly (USA)**[19] 2537 5-9-6 **75** (p) JamesSullivan 1 30
(Ruth Carr) *racd nr far rail: in tch: hdwy to chse ldrs 1/2-way: rdn along 2f out: sn wknd* **16/1**

1600 **18** *2 ¼* **Uptight (FR)**[58] 1444 4-9-7 **76** (p) JamieSpencer 2 24
(Kevin Ryan) *chsd ldrs far side: rdn along over 2f out: sn wknd* **16/1**

0000 **19** *hd* **Canyari (IRE)**[14] 2679 5-9-11 **80** (p) PaulHanagan 19 27
(Richard Fahey) *racd nr stands' rail: a bhd* **8/1**[3]

1m 13.07s (1.17) **Going Correction** +0.425s/f (Yiel) **19** Ran SP% **131.8**
Speed ratings (Par 105): **106,104,103,102,101 101,99,99,97,96 95,94,92,90,87 87,82,79,79**
CSF £99.47 CT £548.09 TOTE £14.60: £3.20, £2.00, £2.20, £6.30; EX 113.20 Trifecta £300.20.
Owner Dunham Trading Ltd **Bred** Mcmahon Thoroughbreds Ltd **Trained** Denton, Co Durham

FOCUS
In keeping with the meeting bias this fair sprint handicap suited those racing towards the far rail. The winner resumed his progress.
T/Jkpt: Not won. T/Plt: £604.40 to a £1 stake. Pool: £194,292.66 - 234.65 winning tickets T/Qpdt: £31.50 to a £1 stake. Pool: £13,676.46 - 321.02 winning tickets **Joe Rowntree**

3169 - 3177a (Foreign Racing) - See Raceform Interactive

[3119]BELMONT PARK (L-H)

Saturday, June 11

OFFICIAL GOING: Dirt: fast; turf: firm

3178a LONGINES JUST A GAME STKS (GRADE 1) (4YO+ FILLIES & MARES) (TURF) 1m (T)

8:58 (12:00) 4-Y-O+

£255,102 (£88,435; £47,619; £31,292; £20,408; £13,605)

RPR

1 **Celestine (USA)**[70] 4-8-9 0 JuniorAlvarado 8 119
(William Mott, U.S.A) *chsd ldr: travelled strly thrght: rdn and qcknd up smartly to ld over 1f out: impressive* **15/2**

2 3 ¾ **Recepta (USA)**[28] 5-8-5 0 JohnRVelazquez 2 106
(James J Toner, U.S.A) *racd in mid-div on inner: rdn for effrt over 1f out: kpt on wl fnl f but no match for wnr* **77/20**[2]

3 1 **Mrs McDougal (USA)**[56] 4-8-5 0 JoseLOrtiz 7 104+
(Chad C Brown, U.S.A) *racd in mid-div: rdn and unable qck 2f out: kpt on wl fnl f to grab 3rd in dying strides* **71/20**[1]

4 nk **Lady Lara (IRE)**[70] 5-8-9 0 JoseLezcano 13 107
(William Mott, U.S.A) *trckd ldrs: rdn 2f out to chal: r.o one pce fnl f: lost 3rd dying strides* **207/10**

5 nk **Faufiler (IRE)**[36] 5-8-1 0 DraydenVanDyke 10 98
(H Graham Motion, U.S.A) *hld up in mid-div: rdn to chal 1f out: kpt on one pce fnl f but unable to chal* **73/10**[3]

6 nk **Prize Exhibit**[36] 4-8-5 0 (b) FlavienPrat 6 102
(James Cassidy, U.S.A) *hld up in mid-div: rdn along 2f out: swtchd out 1f out but nvr able to chal* **57/1**

7 ½ **Rainha Da Bateria (USA)**[35] 4-8-2 0 ow1 (b) JavierCastellano 12 97
(Chad C Brown, U.S.A) *hld up in rr: swtchd wdst of all to chal and rdn 2f out: r.o one pce fnl f: nrst fin* **111/10**

8 hd **Strike Charmer (USA)**[28] 6-8-5 0 ow2 (b) JoelRosario 1 100
(Mark Hennig, U.S.A) *racd in mid-div: pushed along for effrt 2f out whn hmpd: kpt on again whn hmpd again ins fnl f* **14/1**

9 nse **La Berma (IRE)**[36] 4-8-1 0 VictorEspinoza 4 96
(James Cassidy, U.S.A) *led: rdn and hdd over 1f out: wknd ins fnl f* **44/1**

10 1 **Lexie Lou (CAN)**[13] 5-8-5 0 JulienRLeparoux 11 98
(Mark Casse, Canada) *racd in 3rd: pushed along over 2f out: rdn for effrt and wknd 1f out: eased* **178/10**

11 1 **Tapitry (USA)**[28] 4-8-1 0 FlorentGeroux 3 91
(Claude McGaughey III, U.S.A) *hld up in last: rdn for effrt 2f out: kpt on one pce fnl f but nvr able to chal* **195/10**

12 nk **Irish Rookie (IRE)**[21] 2497 4-8-1 0 IradOrtizJr 9 91
(Martyn Meade) *hld up in rr: gd hdwy over 3f out: swtchd wd to chal and rdn 2f out: showed little rspnse: wknd and eased down ins fnl f* **87/10**

13 1 ¾ **My Miss Sophia (USA)**[28] 5-8-4 0 ow3 MikeESmith 5 90
(William Mott, U.S.A) *chsd ldrs: rdn along to chal 2f out: failed to respond and wknd qckly: eased down* **98/10**

1m 31.64s (-2.96) **13** Ran SP% **119.7**
PARI-MUTUEL (all including 2 usd stake): WIN 17.00; PLACE (1-2) 8.50, 5.40; SHOW (1-2-3) 5.70, 3.90, 3.60; SF 101.50.
Owner James A Bryan Jr **Bred** Phoenix Rising Farms **Trained** USA

3179 - 3180a (Foreign Racing) - See Raceform Interactive

3181a BELMONT STKS (GRADE 1) (3YO) (DIRT) 1m 4f (D)

11:37 (12:00) 3-Y-O

£544,217 (£190,476; £102,040; £68,027; £40,816; £30,612)

RPR

1 **Creator (USA)**[35] 2063 3-9-0 0 (b) IradOrtizJr 13 119
(Steven Asmussen, U.S.A) **164/10**

2 nse **Destin (USA)**[35] 2063 3-9-0 0 (b) JavierCastellano 2 119
(Todd Pletcher, U.S.A) **84/10**

3 1 ½ **Lani (USA)**[21] 2499 3-9-0 0 YutakaTake 10 117
(Mikio Matsunaga, Japan) **122/10**

4 2 ½ **Governor Malibu (USA)**[28] 3-9-0 0 (b) JoelRosario 1 113
(Christophe Clement, U.S.A) **171/10**

5 2 ¼ **Stradivari (USA)**[21] 2499 3-9-0 0 JohnRVelazquez 5 109
(Todd Pletcher, U.S.A) **66/10**[3]

6 ¾ **Brody's Cause (USA)**[35] 2063 3-9-0 0 LuisSaez 12 108
(Dale Romans, U.S.A) **189/10**

7 1 **Cherry Wine (USA)**[21] 2499 3-9-0 0 CoreyJLanerie 3 106
(Dale Romans, U.S.A) **103/10**

8 1 **Gettysburg (USA)**[16] 3-9-0 0 PacoLopez 6 105
(Steven Asmussen, U.S.A) **55/1**

9 ½ **Suddenbreakingnews (USA)**[35] 2063 3-9-0 0 MikeESmith 4 104
(Donnie K Von Hemel, U.S.A) **26/5**[2]

10 1 ½ **Trojan Nation (USA)**[35] 2063 3-9-0 0 AaronTGryder 9 101
(Patrick Gallagher, U.S.A) **66/1**

11 3 **Exaggerator (USA)**[21] 2499 3-9-0 0 KentJDesormeaux 11 97
(J Keith Desormeaux, U.S.A) **29/20**[1]

12 1 ½ **Seeking The Soul (USA)**[13] 3-9-0 0 FlorentGeroux 7 94
(Dallas Stewart, U.S.A) **55/1**

13 1 ½ **Forever D'Oro (USA)**[13] 3-9-0 0 JoseLOrtiz 8 92
(Dallas Stewart, U.S.A) **65/1**

2m 28.51s (-0.45) **13** Ran SP% **120.0**
PARI-MUTUEL (all including 2 usd stake): WIN 34.80; PLACE (1-2) 14.60, 9.40; SHOW (1-2-3) 9.40, 6.20, 6.60; SF 269.20.
Owner WinStar Farm LLC & Bobby Flay **Bred** Mt Brilliant Broodmares I LLC **Trained** USA

FOCUS
The Kentucky Derby winner Nyquist was absent due to sickness, but the Preakness winner Exaggerator was back for more, and plenty of familiar names from the first two legs of the Triple Crown lined up in opposition. The winner's stablemate Gettysburg, who is in the same ownership and had only recently been switched from Todd Pletcher's stable, took them along in 24.09, 48.48 (24.39), 1:13.28 (24.80), and to a mile in 1:37.96 (24.68), before giving way to Destin on the turn into the straight. The winning time was 2:28.51.

[2943]CHANTILLY (R-H)

Saturday, June 11

OFFICIAL GOING: Turf: good; polytrack: standard

3182a PRIX LA FLECHE (LISTED RACE) (2YO) (TURF) 5f

4:35 (12:00) 2-Y-O **£20,220** (£8,088; £6,066; £4,044; £2,022)

RPR

1 **Rapacity Alexander (IRE)**[17] 2583 2-8-13 0 MickaelBarzalona 8 97
(David Evans) *mde all: gd early spd: 2 l clr whn rdn 2f out: r.o wl despite reduced advantage fnl f and a doing enough* **39/10**[2]

2 ¾ **Sans Equivoque (GER)**[35] 2-8-13 0 ThierryJarnet 5 94
(D Guillemin, France) **36/5**

3 ½ **Fixette (IRE)**[22] 2454 2-8-13 0 Pierre-CharlesBoudot 3 93
(F-H Graffard, France) *rrd s: sn midfield: rdn 2f out: kpt on wl for 3rd fnl f but nt pce to chal* **39/10**[2]

4 ½ **Bomba (FR)**[47] 2-8-13 0 JohanVictoire 7 91
(Charley Rossi, France) **26/5**[3]

5 1 **Merci Patron (FR)**[17] 2601 2-9-2 0 JulianResimont 6 90
(N Caullery, France) **16/1**

6 hd **Cosachope (FR)**[44] 1821 2-8-13 0 ChristopheSoumillon 2 86
(P Sogorb, France) **14/5**[1]

7 nk **Cavaprun (FR)**[44] 1820 2-9-2 0 GregoryBenoist 1 88
(C Baillet, France) **69/10**

8 9 **Defi Chope (FR)** 2-8-13 0 EddyHardouin 9 53
(C Boutin, France) **54/1**

9 7 **Zahiria (FR)**[9] 2844 2-8-13 0 (p) AntoineHamelin 4 28
(P Adda, France) **24/1**

58.4s (0.10) **9** Ran SP% **119.8**
WIN (incl. 1 euro stake): 4.90. PLACES: 2.10, 2.30, 1.50. DF: 20.00. SF: 41.20.
Owner Noel O'Callaghan **Bred** Aidan Fogarty **Trained** Pandy, Monmouths

3183a PRIX PAUL DE MOUSSAC (GROUP 3) (3YO COLTS & GELDINGS) (TURF) 1m

5:35 (12:00) 3-Y-O **£29,411** (£11,764; £8,823; £5,882; £2,941)

RPR

1 **Zelzal (FR)**[27] 2283 3-8-10 0 GregoryBenoist 8 115+
(J-C Rouget, France) *hld up: pushed along and hdwy over 1f out: qcknd smartly to reel in ldr fnl f and led towards fin: drew clr: comf* **10/3**[3]

2 2 ½ **Moon Trouble (IRE)**[27] 2283 3-8-10 0 MickaelBarzalona 4 107
(F Head, France) *led and sn wnt clr: rdn over 1f out: clsd down fnl f and hdd towards fin: no ex w wnr after but kpt on wl enough for 2nd* **7/1**

3 2 **Degas (GER)**[26] 2315 3-8-10 0 AdriedeVries 7 102
(Markus Klug, Germany) *hld up: last whn sltly hmpd ent fnl f: r.o towards fin and up for 3rd post but n.d* **5/2**[2]

4 hd **Hurricane (FR)**[86] 972 3-8-10 0 ChristopheSoumillon 1 102
(J-C Rouget, France) *trckd clr ldr: rdn to try and cl over 1f out: sn no imp: kpt on same pce fnl f: lost 3rd post* **9/4**[1]

5 shd **Siyounor (FR)**[19] 2551 3-8-10 0 Pierre-CharlesBoudot 5 102
(F-H Graffard, France) *restrained and sn in midfield on inner: rdn 2f out: kpt on same pce and n.d* **11/1**

6 snk **Kourkan (FR)**[34] 3-8-10 0 ThierryJarnet 3 101
(J-M Beguigne, France) *dwlt sltly: hld up: rdn over 1f out: hung rt u.p and plugged on wout threatening fnl f* **10/1**

7 3 **Ankle (FR)**[32] 2140 3-8-10 0 MaximeGuyon 2 94
(C Ferland, France) *restrained in midfield: nt clrest of runs in st but no real imp anyway and nvr threatened* **16/1**

8 2 **Golden Nino (FR)**[40] 3-8-10 0 FabriceVeron 6 90
(H-A Pantall, France) *t.k.h: midfield: rdn and effrt to chse ldr 2f out: outpcd over 1f out: wkng whn short of room ent fnl f: sn dropped to last* **16/1**

1m 35.43s (-2.57) **8** Ran SP% **124.1**
WIN (incl. 1 euro stake): 3.30 (Zelzal coupled with Siyounor). PLACES: 1.50, 1.90, 1.50. DF: 12.90. SF: 17.60.
Owner Al Shaqab Racing **Bred** Viktor Timoshenko **Trained** Pau, France

3184a PRIX DE LA GARINNELLE (CLAIMER) (4YO+) (POLYTRACK) 1m 6f

6:35 (12:00) 4-Y-O+ **£8,455** (£3,382; £2,536; £1,691; £845)

RPR

1 **Prophets Pride**[22] 6-8-11 0 (b) ChristopheSoumillon 2 68
(F Vermeulen, France) **17/10**[1]

2 3 **Gentleshaw (FR)**[31] 7-8-11 0 MaximeGuyon 14 64
(W Mongil, Germany) **15/1**

3 snk **Azilian**[16] 2605 4-9-8 0 MickaelBarzalona 10 75
(Paul Cole) *led: hdd bef 1/2-way and trckd new ldr: rdn to chal again early in st: readily outpcd by wnr over 1f out: styd on for wl hld 3rd fnl f* **41/5**

4 hd **Dagobert Duke**[66] 6-9-3 0 MathieuPelletan(5) 1 75
(C Boutin, France) **17/1**

5 shd **Tikiouine (FR)**[10] 4-8-6 0 MlleIsisMagnin(5) 6 63
(J-M Lefebvre, France) **38/1**

6 1 ¼ **Portalay (FR)**[31] 5-8-11 0 StephanePasquier 4 62
(Rod Collet, France) **12/1**

7 ¾ **Kingspone (FR)**[10] 2806 5-9-1 0 GregoryBenoist 11 65
(Mme P Butel, France) **56/10**[2]

8 hd **Special Request (FR)**[22] 9-9-1 0 Pierre-CharlesBoudot 7 64
(N Caullery, France) **74/10**[3]

9 1 ½ **Jason Bournes (FR)**[22] 9-8-4 0 ClementLecoeuvre(7) 8 58
(E Lellouche, France) **35/1**

10 hd **Art Of Zapping (FR)**[79] 5-9-5 0 (b) FredericSpanu 3 66
(T Castanheira, France) **43/5**

11 snk **Zoria Katiba (FR)**[7] 4-9-2 0 (p) ThibaultSpeicher(3) 9 66
(Mlle A Voraz, France) **50/1**

12 3 **Chene Boppe (FR)**[20] 6-8-13 0 JeremieMonteiro(5) 5 61
(J-M Baudrelle, France) **70/1**

13 1 ½ **Pretorius (FR)**[116] 10-8-8 0 PierreBazire(3) 13 51
(G Taupin, France) **17/1**

14 dist **Experimentalist**[230] 8-9-2 0 (b) GlenBraem 12
(Leo Braem, Belgium) **57/1**

WIN (incl. 1 euro stake): 2.70. PLACES: 1.40, 4.00, 3.00. DF: 24.80. SF: 40.20
Owner Jan Romel **Bred**\x\x Rabbah Bloodstock Limited **Trained** France

[2885]DONCASTER (L-H)

Sunday, June 12

OFFICIAL GOING: Good to soft (good in places) changing to good to soft after race 1 (2.00) changing to soft after race 3 (3.00)

Wind: Virtually nil Weather: Heavy cloud and showers

3185 YWPF H'CAP 1m (R)

2:00 (2:00) (Class 4) (0-80,78) 4-Y-O+ **£5,175** (£1,540; £769; £384) **Stalls** Low

Form RPR

0-56 **1** **Hanseatic**[16] 2651 7-9-1 **72**.. CamHardie 7 80
(Michael Easterby) *trckd ldng pair: hdwy over 2f out and sn chsng ldr: rdn to chal ins fnl f: led last 100yds: drvn out* **7/2**[1]

-520 **2** ½ **Pumaflor (IRE)**[16] 2662 4-9-4 **75**................................ GeorgeChaloner 4 82
(Richard Whitaker) *led: pushed along 2f out: rdn over 1f out: jnd and drvn ins fnl f: hdd and no ex last 100yds* **9/2**[2]

0-03 **3** 2 **Spryt (IRE)**[26] 2345 4-9-2 **78**.. JoshDoyle(5) 9 80
(David O'Meara) *hld up: hdwy wl over 2f out: rdn to chse ldng pair over 1f out: drvn and no imp fnl f* **7/2**[1]

3-30 **4** shd **Red Paladin (IRE)**[42] 1884 6-9-1 **72**..............................(p) JoeFanning 6 74
(Kristin Stubbs) *hld up in rr: hdwy over 2f out: rdn over 1f out: kpt on fnl f* **11/2**

0-60 **5** 4 ½ **Order Of Service**[22] 2491 6-9-6 **77**................................. PaddyAspell 3 69
(Shaun Harris) *chsd ldrs: rdn along over 2f out: drvn wl over 1f out: grad wknd* **8/1**

2642 **6** 5 **Stun Gun**[81] 1047 6-7-13 **61**...(p) NoelGarbutt(5) 8 41
(Derek Shaw) *trckd ldr: pushed along 3f out: rdn over 2f out and sn wknd* **16/1**

6640 **7** 6 **Baddilini**[2] 3115 6-9-2 **73**...(p) FMBerry 2 39
(Alan Bailey) *trckd ldrs: rdn along 3f out: sn outpcd and bhd* **5/1**[3]

1m 42.6s (2.90) **Going Correction** +0.50s/f (Yiel) **7** Ran SP% **111.7**

Speed ratings (Par 105): **105,104,102,102,97 92,86**

CSF £18.40 CT £56.43 TOTE £4.50: £2.40, £1.80; EX 17.90 Trifecta £68.60.

Owner Blunt, Brook, Hull, Chandler & Westwood **Bred** Juddmonte Farms Ltd **Trained** Sheriff Hutton, N Yorks

FOCUS

Good to soft, good in places going for this seven-race card. The round course was railed out from 1m2f until the round meets the straight, adding 6yds to races 5, 6 and 7.\n\x\x This looked a very open little handicap on paper, with questions surrounding all of the runners.

3186 PROJECT POLAR BRITISH STALLION STUDS EBF NOVICE FILLIES' STKS (PLUS 10 RACE) 7f

2:30 (2:30) (Class 5) 2-Y-O **£3,881** (£1,155; £577; £288) **Stalls** Centre

Form RPR

1 **Calare (IRE)** 2-9-0 0.. JamesDoyle 4 76+
(Charlie Appleby) *hld up: gd hdwy 2f out: chal over 1f out: qcknd to ld ent fnl f: sn edgd lft and clr: readily* **1/1**[1]

2 2 ¼ **Conqueress (IRE)** 2-9-0 0..................................... RichardKingscote 3 70
(Tom Dascombe) *trckd ldng pair: hdwy to chse ldr wl over 1f out: rdn ent fnl f: kpt on same pce* **12/1**

3 ¾ **Pantera Negra (IRE)** 2-9-0 0....................................... PaulMulrennan 2 68+
(Ed Dunlop) *hld up: green and pushed along over 2f out: rdn and hdwy over 1f out: kpt on fnl f* **13/2**[3]

4444 **4** 2 **Bonnie Arlene (IRE)**[17] 2612 2-9-0 0................................ JoeFanning 1 63
(Mark Johnston) *led: pushed along 2f out: rdn over 1f out: hdd & wknd ent fnl f* **12/1**

12 **5** 6 **Wedding Dress**[16] 2664 2-9-7 0.. PatCosgrave 5 54
(David Brown) *trckd ldr: pushed along 2f out: rdn wl over 1f out: sn drvn and wknd* **2/1**[2]

1m 30.84s (4.54) **Going Correction** +0.50s/f (Yiel) **5** Ran SP% **112.1**

Speed ratings (Par 90): **94,91,90,88,81**

CSF £13.77 TOTE £1.80: £1.10, £5.40; EX 12.00 Trifecta £43.30.

Owner Godolphin **Bred** Darley **Trained** Newmarket, Suffolk

FOCUS

Not the deepest novice event for this track, especially with Wedding Dress, who brought the best form to the table, proving very disappointing. However, the first three home were all newcomers and they clearly have potential.

3187 HARBON ELECTRICAL SERVICES H'CAP 1m (R)

3:00 (3:01) (Class 4) (0-85,82) 3-Y-O **£5,175** (£1,540; £769; £384) **Stalls** Low

Form RPR

1-50 **1** **Zealous (IRE)**[22] 2479 3-9-4 **79**..................................... DarryllHolland 10 86
(Alan Swinbank) *trckd ldrs: hdwy 3f out: chsd ldng pair 2f out: rdn over 1f out: led jst ins fnl f: sn drvn and hld on wl towards fin* **9/1**

21 **2** shd **Rebel Cause (IRE)**[23] 2443 3-9-6 **81**............... WilliamTwiston-Davies 7 87
(Richard Spencer) *in tch: hdwy on outer over 3f out: trckd ldrs over 2f out: rdn to chal over 1f out: drvn ins fnl f and ev ch: kpt on* **6/1**[3]

1-04 **3** 1 ¾ **Constantino (IRE)**[16] 2654 3-9-5 **80**................................. JamesDoyle 3 82
(Richard Fahey) *hld up: pushed along and outpcd 3f out: rdn over 2f out: hdwy to chse ldrs whn hung bdly lft over 1f out: drvn and kpt on fnl f* **7/4**[1]

0-50 **4** 1 ¾ **Holy Grail (IRE)**[28] 2267 3-9-4 **82**.............................. LouisSteward(3) 9 80
(Simon West) *led: rdn along over 2f out: jnd and drvn over 1f out: hdd jst ins fnl f: grad wknd* **25/1**

-100 **5** 1 ¼ **Al Hamd (IRE)**[31] 2179 3-9-5 **80**...............................(p) PaulMulrennan 11 75
(Ed Dunlop) *chsd ldr: rdn along over 2f out: drvn wl over 1f out: sn wknd* **20/1**

2-15 **6** 1 **With Pleasure**[136] 366 3-9-2 **77**... PhillipMakin 8 70
(David O'Meara) *hld up and bhd: hdwy over 2f out: sn rdn: kpt on fnl f* **16/1**

310 **7** 3 ¾ **Rosenborg Rider (IRE)**[22] 2477 3-9-4 **79**............................ FMBerry 1 63
(Ralph Beckett) *stdd s and hld up in rr: sme late hdwy* **10/1**

34-0 **8** 4 ½ **Gregarious (IRE)**[25] 2375 3-9-0 **75**.............................. DougieCostello 4 49
(Lucy Wadham) *in tch on inner: hdwy to chse ldrs 3f out: rdn over 2f out: sn drvn and wknd* **11/2**[2]

2100 **9** 5 **Abareeq**[36] 2029 3-9-7 **82**.. JoeFanning 2 44
(Mark Johnston) *trckd ldrs: pushed along 3f out: rdn over 2f out: sn btn* **9/1**

-210 **10** 11 **Pushaq (IRE)**[24] 2412 3-9-5 **80**..............................(p) RichardKingscote 5 17
(Marco Botti) *trckd ldng pair: effrt over 3f out: rdn along wl over 2f out: sn wknd* **16/1**

1m 42.08s (2.38) **Going Correction** +0.50s/f (Yiel) **10** Ran SP% **115.5**

Speed ratings (Par 101): **108,107,106,104,103 102,98,93,88,77**

CSF £61.53 CT £141.88 TOTE £10.70: £3.20, £2.50, £1.10; EX 67.10 Trifecta £198.50.

Owner Mrs J Porter **Bred** Knocklong House Stud **Trained** Melsonby, N Yorks

FOCUS

This looked wide open on paper, despite the presence of a short-priced favourite, but the early gallop looked steady and several raced keenly. Although a few of these probably have more to offer, this form might not be particularly reliable.

3188 YORKSHIRE WILDLIFE PARK H'CAP 6f

3:30 (3:32) (Class 3) (0-95,95) 3-Y-O+ **£7,762** (£2,310; £1,154; £577) **Stalls** Centre

Form RPR

2404 **1** **Intense Style (IRE)**[11] 2803 4-9-7 **88**................................ DavidAllan 12 97
(Les Eyre) *trckd ldrs: hdwy wl over 1f out: rdn to ld jst ins fnl f: drvn and kpt on wl towards fin* **10/1**

-532 **2** ½ **George Cinq**[18] 2587 6-9-7 **88**.. JamesDoyle 7 95
(George Scott) *hld up towards rr: gd hdwy wl over 1f out: rdn and styd on strly fnl f* **6/1**[2]

0-00 **3** ½ **Eccleston**[11] 2803 5-9-10 **91**..(v) SamJames 1 96
(David O'Meara) *towards rr: pushed along 2f out: rdn over 1f out: styd on wl fnl f* **10/1**

-005 **4** ¾ **Meshardal (GER)**[11] 2803 6-8-11 **78**.............................. JamesSullivan 5 81
(Ruth Carr) *in tch: hdwy wl over 2f out: sn prom: rdn over 1f out: wknd ins fnl f* **8/1**[3]

0626 **5** ¾ **Handsome Dude**[22] 2480 4-9-8 **89**................................(b) PhillipMakin 6 90
(David Barron) *trckd ldrs: hdwy over 2f out: rdn over 1f out: drvn and kpt on same pce fnl f* **8/1**[3]

6-03 **6** ¾ **Spring Fling**[13] 2754 5-9-2 **83**..................................... FergusSweeney 11 81+
(Henry Candy) *trckd ldrs: hdwy 1/2-way: led over 2f out: rdn and hung bdly lft to far rail over 1f out: hdd jst ins fnl f: kpt on same pce* **9/2**[1]

-560 **7** 1 ¼ **Hoof It**[22] 2485 9-9-7 **93**... NathanEvans(5) 16 87
(Michael Easterby) *trckd ldrs: cl up on outer 1/2-way: rdn wl over 1f out: grad wknd appr fnl f* **6/1**[2]

140- **8** hd **El Viento (FR)**[177] 8288 8-9-3 **91**...........................(v) AdamMcNamara(7) 4 85
(Richard Fahey) *t.k.h: chsd ldrs: rdn along 2f out: sn drvn and wknd* **28/1**

430- **9** ½ **Fendale**[267] 6515 4-9-11 **92**.. PaulMulrennan 13 84
(Michael Dods) *in rr tl styd on fnl 2f* **12/1**

0006 **10** 4 **Highland Acclaim (IRE)**[9] 2862 5-9-4 **85**........................ DavidNolan 15 64
(David O'Meara) *in tch: rdn 2f out: sn drvn and btn* **14/1**

0-02 **11** 16 **Bogart**[22] 2488 7-9-7 **88**...(p) TomEaves 3 16
(Kevin Ryan) *cl up: led after 2f: rdn and hdd over 2f out: sn wknd* **17/2**

0-00 **12** 18 **Masamah (IRE)**[39] 1968 10-9-7 **88**..........................(p) GeorgeChaloner 2
(Patrick Morris) *slt ld 2f: cl up: rdn along 1/2-way: sn wknd* **66/1**

1m 16.15s (2.55) **Going Correction** +0.60s/f (Yiel) **12** Ran SP% **117.0**

Speed ratings (Par 107): **107,106,105,104,103 102,101,100,100,94 73,49**

CSF £67.98 CT £633.65 TOTE £13.40: £4.10, £2.30, £4.00; EX 81.60 Trifecta £722.50.

Owner RP Racing Ltd **Bred** J S Bolger & John Corcoran **Trained** Catwick, N Yorks

FOCUS

The ground was changed to soft ahead of this race after half an hour of sustained heavy rain. A wide-open sprint handicap.

3189 INTO AFRICA CLASSIFIED STKS 1m 2f 60y

4:05 (4:05) (Class 5) 3-Y-O **£3,881** (£1,155; £577; £288) **Stalls** Low

Form RPR

5-14 **1** **Island Flame (IRE)**[20] 2532 3-9-0 68...........................[1] PatrickMathers 5 76
(Richard Fahey) *hld up in rr: hdwy on outer 3f out: rdn to ld wl over 1f out: sn edgd lft and clr: kpt on strly* **13/2**

033- **2** 6 **Signed And Sealed**[228] 7561 3-9-0 69................................ JoeFanning 2 65
(Mark Johnston) *led: rdn along over 2f out: hdd wl over 1f out: sn drvn and kpt on same pce* **4/1**[3]

0-02 **3** 5 **Arithmetic (IRE)**[27] 2306 3-9-0 70...................................... JamesDoyle 4 61
(Charles Hills) *trckd ldr: hdwy 3f out: pushed along 2f out: sn rdn: swtchd rt and drvn appr fnl f: sn one pce* **13/8**[1]

-421 **4** 8 **Panko (IRE)**[15] 2701 3-9-0 69... KieranO'Neill 1 40
(Ed de Giles) *trckd ldng pair: hdwy on inner 3f out: rdn along 2f out: sn drvn and wknd* **7/4**[2]

2m 18.47s (9.07) **Going Correction** +0.60s/f (Yiel) **4** Ran SP% **107.8**

Speed ratings (Par 99): **87,82,78,73**

CSF £28.38 TOTE £7.60; EX 25.30 Trifecta £46.40.

Owner Northumbria Leisure Ltd **Bred** Christopher Maye **Trained** Musley Bank, N Yorks

FOCUS

A modest little classified stakes that was won just over two furlongs out when Patrick Mathers swept to the front on his mount, as his rivals all struggled to find a change of gear.

3190 SAFARI VILLAGE MAIDEN STKS 1m 4f

4:40 (4:40) (Class 5) 3-Y-O+ **£3,881** (£1,155; £577; £288) **Stalls** Low

Form RPR

5 **1** **Dawn Horizons**[31] 2183 3-8-7 0... JoeFanning 9 88+
(William Haggas) *hld up in tch: smooth hdwy over 4f out: cl up 2f out: sn led and pushed clr: readily* **15/8**[2]

42 **2** 3 ¾ **Withhold**[29] 2260 3-8-12 0... JamesDoyle 8 83
(Charles Hills) *trckd ldr: hdwy 3f out: chal over 2f out: rdn to ld briefly 2f out: sn hdd and drvn: kpt on: no ch w wnr* **11/8**[1]

3 6 **London Prize**[72] 5-9-13 0... PaulMulrennan 2 73
(Ian Williams) *led and sn clr: pushed along 3f out: rdn over 2f out: hdd 2f out: sn drvn and kpt on one pce* **8/1**

645 **4** 6 **Rosette**[29] 2260 4-9-8 0.. DarryllHolland 1 59
(Alan Swinbank) *trckd ldrs: pushed along 4f out: rdn along over 3f out: sn one pce* **25/1**

05 **5** 4 ½ **Marshall Aid (IRE)**[10] 2815 3-8-12 0.......................................(t) FMBerry 7 57
(Hugo Palmer) *trckd ldrs: effrt over 3f out: rdn along wl over 2f out: sn drvn and outpcd* **14/1**

6- **6** 6 **Lee Bay**[221] 7707 3-8-12 0... NickyMackay 4 47
(John Gosden) *hld up: a bhd* **11/2**[3]

00-0 **7** ½ **Defiant Choice**[19] 2563 3-8-7 40................................... NoelGarbutt(5) 6 46
(Derek Shaw) *a bhd* **200/1**

2m 40.13s (5.23) **Going Correction** +0.60s/f (Yiel)

WFA 3 from 4yo+ 15lb **7** Ran SP% **114.4**

Speed ratings (Par 103): **106,103,99,95,92 87,86**

CSF £4.82 TOTE £2.50: £1.60, £1.60; EX 4.80 Trifecta £16.20.

Owner A E Oppenheimer **Bred** Hascombe And Valiant Studs **Trained** Newmarket, Suffolk

FOCUS
Not much depth to this maiden and they finished well strung out, although conditions would have played their part in that. The winner looks potentially very smart and the runner-up will probably be winning soon.

3191 WILDLIFE ADVENTURE APPRENTICE H'CAP — 1m 6f 132y
5:10 (5:11) (Class 5) (0-70,70) 4-Y-O+ — **£3,881** (£1,155; £577; £288) **Stalls** Low

Form — RPR

4-01 **1** **Dew Pond**[13] 2745 4-9-8 **69**... RachelRichardson[(3)] 9 — 79
(Tim Easterby) *hld up in tch: hdwy 5f out: chsd ldng pair 3f out: rdn to ld over 1f out: drvn clr fnl f: kpt on* **5/1**[1]

1-60 **2** *3 ¾* **The Ducking Stool**[21] 2501 9-9-11 **69**... ShelleyBirkett 6 — 74
(Julia Feilden) *trckd ldrs: hdwy 5f out: cl up 3f out: effrt 2f out: sn rdn to chal and ev ch tl drvn and kpt on same pce ins fnl f* **14/1**

-404 **3** *2 ¼* **Stanarley Pic**[21] 2502 5-9-5 **68**... MeganNicholls[(5)] 4 — 70
(Alan Swinbank) *hld up: hdwy on outer to trck ldrs 5f out: effrt 3f out: sn rdn along and sltly outpcd: drvn and kpt on fnl f* **6/1**[3]

0-60 **4** *nk* **Bridey's Lettuce (IRE)**[29] 2233 4-9-2 **63**... JosephineGordon[(3)] 11 — 65+
(Ivan Furtado) *trckd ldr: cl up 1/2-way: led over 4f out: rdn along 3f out: drvn and hdd over 1f out: grad wknd* **8/1**

4-33 **5** *¾* **Deepsand (IRE)**[21] 2502 7-9-2 **63**...(tp) EdwardGreatrex[(3)] 10 — 64
(Ali Stronge) *s.i.s and bhd: hdwy 1/2-way: chsd ldrs 3f out: rdn over 2f out: sn drvn and kpt on same pce* **11/2**[2]

30-6 **6** *18* **Di's Gift**[16] 2663 7-9-7 **70**... CharlieBennett[(5)] 3 — 47
(Shaun Harris) *hld up: sme hdwy over 4f out: rdn along over 3f out: n.d* **13/2**

0-00 **7** *1 ¼* **Waltz Darling (IRE)**[13] 2745 8-8-7 **51** oh1... JoeDoyle 8 — 27
(Keith Reveley) *hld up towards rr: sme hdwy over 4f out: rdn along over 3f out: n.d* **9/1**

-004 **8** *¾* **Midnight Warrior**[19] 2558 6-8-7 **54**... PhilDennis[(3)] 2 — 29
(Ron Barr) *led: rdn along and hdd over 4f out: sn wknd* **16/1**

-526 **9** *37* **Harlestone Hopes**[25] 2374 4-9-2 **65**...(p) HarryBurns[(5)] 1
(Ed Dunlop) *in tch: pushed along bef 1/2-way: sn lost pl and bhd fnl 4f* **13/2**

305- **10** *51* **In Vino Veritas (IRE)**[190] 8121 5-8-11 **58**... JoshDoyle[(3)] 7
(Lynn Siddall) *trckd ldrs: rdn along 6f out: sn wknd and bhd fnl 4f* **10/1**

3m 19.27s (11.87) **Going Correction** +0.70s/f (Yiel) — **10** Ran SP% **115.8**
Speed ratings (Par 103): **96,94,92,92,92 82,81,81,61,34**
CSF £73.98 CT £429.86 TOTE £5.00: £2.00, £3.90, £2.20; EX 71.60 Trifecta £480.60.
Owner Ashfield Caravan Park **Bred** Pollards Stables **Trained** Great Habton, N Yorks

FOCUS
A wide open apprentice riders' handicap but it was won quite authoritatively by the only last-time-out winner in the contest.
T/Jkpt: Not won. T/Plt: £70.00 to a £1 stake. Pool: £101,747.53 - 1,060.36 winning tickets T/Qpdt: £17.80 to a £1 stake. Pool: £6,419.00 - 265.91 winning tickets **Joe Rowntree**

2997 SALISBURY (R-H)
Sunday, June 12

OFFICIAL GOING: Good to firm changing to good after race 1 (2.15)
Wind: mild breeze against Weather: showers

3192 BLIND AND TRACK SERVICE H'CAP — 1m 4f
2:15 (2:15) (Class 4) (0-85,87) 4-Y-O+ — **£5,175** (£1,540; £769; £384) **Stalls** Low

Form — RPR

22-1 **1** **Red Cardinal (IRE)**[47] 1739 4-9-5 **82**... JamieSpencer 2 — 95+
(David Simcock) *travelled wl thrght: trckd ldrs: led 2f out: drifted rt: sn clr: easily* **8/11**[1]

251- **2** *6* **Faithful Mount**[210] 7165 7-9-7 **84**... PatDobbs 6 — 87
(Ian Williams) *trckd ldrs: stirrup leather broke after 3f: continued wout stirrups: chsd wnr fr over 1f out but a being hld* **4/1**[2]

3035 **3** *1 ¾* **Agent Gibbs**[31] 2176 4-9-6 **83**... TonyHamilton 4 — 83
(John O'Shea) *trckd ldrs: rdn 2f out: kpt on same pce fnl f* **8/1**[3]

0056 **4** *2* **Isis Blue**[17] 2623 6-7-13 **69**...(p) GeorgeWood[(7)] 3 — 66
(Rod Millman) *trckd ldrs: rdn 2f out: one pce fnl f* **10/1**

0162 **5** *¾* **Moojaned (IRE)**[24] 2399 5-8-12 **82**... AledBeech[(7)] 5 — 78
(David Evans) *led tl rdn 2f out: sn one pce* **9/1**

2m 35.76s (-2.24) **Going Correction** -0.025s/f (Good) — **5** Ran SP% **108.1**
Speed ratings (Par 105): **106,102,100,99,99**
CSF £3.71 TOTE £1.50: £1.10, £2.30; EX 3.70 Trifecta £12.30.
Owner Walters Plant Hire Ltd **Bred** Lynch Bages Ltd **Trained** Newmarket, Suffolk

FOCUS
A fair handicap with a progressive winner.

3193 MANOR FARM BUTCHERS H'CAP — 5f
2:45 (2:45) (Class 4) (0-85,88) 3-Y-O+ — **£5,175** (£1,540; £769; £384) **Stalls** Low

Form — RPR

-131 **1** **A Momentofmadness**[13] 2751 3-9-10 **88**... AndreaAtzeni 7 — 92
(Charles Hills) *trckd ldrs: rdn 2f out: no immediate imp tl r.o ins fnl f: led cl home* **1/1**[1]

0125 **2** *nk* **King Crimson**[21] 2504 4-9-12 **83**... CharlesBishop 5 — 89
(Mick Channon) *led: rdn 2f out: 2 l up ent fnl f: kpt on but no ex whn hdd cl home* **6/1**[2]

-116 **3** *nk* **Ladweb**[21] 2504 6-9-4 **78**... MichaelJMMurphy[(3)] 4 — 83
(John Gallagher) *in tch: rdn 2f out: kpt on ins fnl f: wnt 3rd cl home* **7/1**[3]

4644 **4** *¾* **Desert Command**[23] 2426 6-9-0 **74**...(b[1]) MarcMonaghan[(3)] 6 — 76
(Robert Cowell) *trckd ldr: rdn 2f out: nt pce to chal: no ex whn losing 2 pls fnl 120yds* **7/1**[3]

500- **5** *1 ¼* **Newton's Law (IRE)**[183] 8205 5-9-3 **81**...(t) JordanUys[(7)] 1 — 79
(Brian Meehan) *s.i.s: in last pair: rdn and sme hdwy 2f out: drifted lft and rt fnl f: no ex fnl 120yds* **11/1**

0146 **6** *¾* **Taajub (IRE)**[99] 835 9-9-13 **84**... ShaneKelly 2 — 79
(Peter Crate) *wnt lft s: trckd ldr: rdn 2f out: nt gng pce to get on terms: no ex fnl f* **14/1**

40-6 **7** *3 ½* **Noble Asset**[39] 1964 5-9-10 **81**... OisinMurphy 3 — 63
(Milton Bradley) *s.i.s: in last pair: rdn 2f out: wknd jst over 1f out* **12/1**

1m 1.03s (0.03) **Going Correction** +0.175s/f (Good)
WFA 3 from 4yo+ 7lb — **7** Ran SP% **112.0**
Speed ratings (Par 105): **106,105,105,103,101 100,95**
CSF £7.03 CT £26.39 TOTE £2.00: £1.40, £2.20; EX 6.90 Trifecta £21.20.
Owner Tony Wechsler & Ann Plummer **Bred** D R Tucker **Trained** Lambourn, Berks
■ Stewards' Enquiry : Marc Monaghan seven-day ban: used whip above permitted level (Jun 26-Jul 2)

FOCUS
This was run at a good sprint tempo and the form should stand up.

3194 WATERAID MILDREN CONSTRUCTION MAIDEN FILLIES' STKS (PLUS 10 RACE) — 1m 1f 198y
3:15 (3:17) (Class 5) 3-Y-O — **£3,557** (£1,058; £529; £264) **Stalls** Low

Form — RPR

1 **Playful Sound** 3-9-0 0... WilliamBuick 4 — 82+
(Sir Michael Stoute) *mid-div: swtchd lft and hdwy over 2f out: sn rdn: styd on wl fnl f: led cl home* **14/1**

4- **2** *nk* **Statuesque**[256] 6857 3-9-0 0... TedDurcan 10 — 81
(Sir Michael Stoute) *led: rdn over 1f out: 2 l clr ent fnl f: hdd cl home* **7/1**[2]

2 **3** *shd* **Trainnah**[37] 2009 3-9-0 0... FrankieDettori 9 — 81
(William Haggas) *s.i.s: sn mid-div: hdwy over 3f out: rdn over 2f out: styd on wl w wnr to go 3rd ins fnl f: nrly snatched 2nd fnl stride* **15/8**[1]

0 **4** *2 ½* **Adalene**[51] 1608 3-9-0 0... OisinMurphy 14 — 76
(David Simcock) *mid-div: rdn 2f out: styd on fnl f but nt pce to get on terms* **25/1**

0 **5** *hd* **Brief Visit**[37] 2009 3-9-0 0... DavidProbert 11 — 76
(Andrew Balding) *trckd ldrs: rdn to chal briefly over 2f out: styd on tl no ex ins fnl f* **100/1**

33 **6** *nk* **Taffeta Lady**[30] 2215 3-9-0 0...(p) JimCrowley 5 — 75
(Lucy Wadham) *hld up towards rr: hdwy over 2f out: sn rdn: styd on but nt pce to get involved* **10/1**[3]

5 **7** *4* **Tangba**[31] 2182 3-9-0 0... AndreaAtzeni 1 — 67
(Roger Varian) *trckd ldrs: rdn 3f out: one pce fnl 2f* **7/1**[2]

0 **8** *¾* **Disquotational**[51] 1609 3-9-0 0... JamieSpencer 8 — 66
(David Simcock) *hld up towards rr: sme prog u.p 2f out: no further imp fnl f* **33/1**

0 **9** *3 ½* **Tenerezza (IRE)**[12] 2767 3-9-0 0... ShaneKelly 12 — 59
(David Lanigan) *trckd ldrs: rdn over 2f out: wknd ent fnl f* **66/1**

0 **10** *2* **Pixel (IRE)**[27] 2312 3-9-0 0... JFEgan 13 — 55
(Jeremy Noseda) *mid-div: rdn over 3f out: wknd over 1f out* **40/1**

11 *1 ¾* **Staplehurst (IRE)** 3-9-0 0... TimmyMurphy 3 — 51
(Geoffrey Deacon) *s.i.s: a towards rr* **100/1**

0-0 **12** *hd* **Lady Emma**[24] 2395 3-9-0 0... AdamBeschizza 7 — 51
(Steph Hollinshead) *mid-div: reminders over 4f out: wknd 2f out* **200/1**

2m 10.71s (0.81) **Going Correction** +0.175s/f (Good) — **12** Ran SP% **88.7**
Speed ratings (Par 96): **103,102,102,100,100 100,97,96,93,92 90,90**
CSF £57.63 TOTE £11.70: £3.50, £1.10, £1.10; EX 58.50 Trifecta £123.50.
Owner Newsells Park Stud **Bred** Newsells Park Stud **Trained** Newmarket, Suffolk
■ Malmoosa was withdrawn. Price at time of withdrawal 5/2. Rule 4 applies to all bets - deduction 25p in the pound.

FOCUS
A decent maiden, typical of the course. The second and third had run well on their debuts, so the form looks solid. The pace was ordinary until quickening 3f from home.

3195 BRITISH STALLION STUDS EBF CATHEDRAL STKS (LISTED RACE) — 6f
3:45 (3:48) (Class 1) 3-Y-O+
£23,818 (£9,030; £4,519; £2,251; £1,129; £567) **Stalls** Low

Form — RPR

1-15 **1** **Don't Touch**[22] 2495 4-9-5 112... TonyHamilton 6 — 116
(Richard Fahey) *trckd ldr: rdn 2f out: led ent fnl f: a holding on: drvn out* **7/2**[2]

13-3 **2** *nk* **Danzeno**[32] 2159 5-9-5 113... FrankieDettori 10 — 115
(Michael Appleby) *hld up towards rr: hdwy over 2f out: rdn over 1f out: str run fnl f: wnt 2nd towards fin: nt quite rch wnr* **5/2**[1]

0-32 **3** *1 ¼* **Watchable**[20] 2546 6-9-5 110...(v) AdamKirby 9 — 111
(David O'Meara) *led: rdn 2f out: edgd lft and hdd ent fnl f: kpt on but no ex* **10/1**

111/ **4** *1* **Charming Thought**[604] 7239 4-9-5 116...(t) WilliamBuick 1 — 108
(Charlie Appleby) *mid-div: pushed along whn swtchd lft over 1f out: rdn and kpt on nicely wout ever threatening fnl f: wnt 4th cl home* **11/2**

-014 **5** *½* **Clear Spring (IRE)**[23] 2434 8-9-5 102... ShaneKelly 2 — 106
(John Spearing) *trckd ldrs: rdn 2f out: kpt on but nt pce to mount chal* **66/1**

20-4 **6** *nse* **Strath Burn**[20] 2546 4-9-5 116... OisinMurphy 3 — 106
(Charles Hills) *trckd ldrs: rdn 2f out: nvr quite threatened: kpt on same pce fnl f* **5/1**[3]

420- **7** *1 ¼* **Burnt Sugar (IRE)**[281] 6075 4-9-5 106...(b) PatDobbs 7 — 102
(Richard Hannon) *mid-div: rdn 2f out: nt pce to get involved* **20/1**

0-00 **8** *1* **Moonraker**[23] 2438 4-9-5 98... GeorgeBaker 4 — 99
(Mick Channon) *hld up towards rr: rdn 2f out: swtchd rt over 1f out: little imp* **50/1**

130- **9** *1* **Polybius**[211] 7856 5-9-5 108... TedDurcan 8 — 96
(David Lanigan) *hld up towards rr: rdn 2f out: nvr any imp* **22/1**

4203 **10** *¾* **Naadirr (IRE)**[20] 2546 5-9-5 109...(p) AndreaAtzeni 5 — 93
(Marco Botti) *mid-div: rdn 2f out: wknd ent fnl f* **9/1**

0-05 **11** *6* **Kingsgate Native (IRE)**[23] 2438 11-9-5 106... PaulHanagan 11 — 74
(Robert Cowell) *mid-div: rdn 2f out: sn wknd* **33/1**

1m 13.93s (-0.87) **Going Correction** +0.175s/f (Good) — **11** Ran SP% **117.4**
Speed ratings (Par 111): **112,111,109,108,107 107,106,104,103,102 94**
CSF £11.93 TOTE £4.70: £1.80, £1.30, £2.90; EX 13.40 Trifecta £87.80.
Owner Nicholas Wrigley & Kevin Hart **Bred** Cheveley Park Stud Ltd **Trained** Musley Bank, N Yorks

FOCUS
A quality Listed contest, with several Group-class contestants, run at a solid pace.

3196 TOBY BALDING MEMORIAL NOVICE STKS (PLUS 10 RACE) — 6f
4:20 (4:20) (Class 3) 2-Y-O — **£9,703** (£2,887; £1,443; £721) **Stalls** Low

Form — RPR

6 **1** **Farleigh Mac**[9] 2847 2-9-2 0... DavidProbert 10 — 79
(Andrew Balding) *racd keenly: prom: rdn to ld ent fnl f: jst hld on* **6/1**[3]

2 *nse* **Salouen (IRE)** 2-9-2 0... PatDobbs 4 — 79
(Sylvester Kirk) *s.i.s: in last trio: hdwy 2f out: r.o wl ins fnl f: jst failed* **16/1**

3 *3 ½* **Bengal Lancer** 2-9-2 0... TonyHamilton 8 — 68+
(Ian Williams) *outpcd towards rr: hdwy 2f out: kpt on to go 3rd fnl 100yds: nt pce of front pair* **66/1**

42 **4** *1 ¼* **Diable D'Or (IRE)**[18] 2583 2-9-2 0... RobertWinston 1 — 65
(Eve Johnson Houghton) *led: rdn and hdd ent fnl f: no ex fnl 120yds* **11/4**[1]

5 *7* **Poet's Princess** 2-8-11 0... JimCrowley 2 — 39+
(Hughie Morrison) *dwlt: bhd: styd on fnl f but nvr any threat* **20/1**

022 **6** *1 ¼* **Davarde (IRE)**[22] 2457 2-9-2 0... JFEgan 6 — 40
(David Evans) *trckd ldrs: rdn over 2f out: wknd over 1f out* **17/2**

0 **7** *5* **The Big Short**[16] 2648 2-9-2 0 .... WilliamBuick 3 25
(Charles Hills) *trckd ldrs: rdn over 2f out: wknd over 1f out* **6/1**[3]

8 *2 ¼* **Zebby Sizz (IRE)** 2-9-2 0 .... SeanLevey 9 18
(Richard Hannon) *in tch: effrt over 2f out: sn wknd* **13/2**

21 **9** *7* **Mister Sunshine (IRE)**[27] 2289 2-9-8 0 .... AdamKirby 7
(Clive Cox) *trckd ldrs: rdn over 2f out: hung lft and qckly btn* **3/1**[2]

1m 15.24s (0.44) **Going Correction** +0.175s/f (Good) **9** Ran SP% **116.2**
Speed ratings (Par 97): **104,103,99,97,88 86,79,76,67**
CSF £95.80 TOTE £6.80: £2.30, £4.20, £6.20; EX 106.20 Trifecta £4304.20.
Owner Farleigh Racing **Bred** Farleigh Court Racing Partnership **Trained** Kingsclere, Hants

FOCUS
This is likely to prove an above-average novice event and there should be several future winners in the line-up.

3197 RON DURRANT 80TH BIRTHDAY CELEBRATION FILLIES' H'CAP 6f 212y
4:55 (4:55) (Class 5) (0-75,75) 3-Y-0+ **£3,234** (£962; £481; £240) **Stalls** Low

Form RPR

2 **1** **Stars N Angels (IRE)**[21] 2506 3-8-7 **64** .... (p) OisinMurphy 5 68
(Michael Appleby) *mde virtually all: kpt on wl: rdn out* **13/8**[1]

0421 **2** *1 ¼* **First Experience**[37] 2001 5-9-5 **71** .... (p) CallumShepherd(5) 6 76
(Lee Carter) *trckd ldrs: rdn to chse wnr over 1f out: kpt on but a being hld fnl f* **7/1**

-206 **3** *nk* **Greenfyre (IRE)**[26] 2337 3-8-8 **68** .... TomMarquand(3) 1 68
(Richard Hannon) *broke wl: sn stdd to trck wnr: rdn 2f out: kpt on same pce fnl f* **13/2**

-222 **4** *¾* **Gleaming Girl**[13] 2737 4-9-4 **72** .... SophieKilloran(7) 2 74
(David Simcock) *awkward leaving stalls: trckd ldrs: rdn 2f out: kpt on same pce fnl f* **5/1**[3]

1042 **5** *1 ¼* **Secret Insider (USA)**[74] 1155 3-9-4 **75** .... WilliamBuick 4 70
(Hugo Palmer) *trckd ldrs: effrt over 2f out: sn hld: kpt on same pce fnl f* **9/4**[2]

1m 30.46s (1.86) **Going Correction** +0.175s/f (Good)
WFA 3 from 4yo+ 10lb **5** Ran SP% **111.4**
Speed ratings (Par 100): **96,94,94,93,91**
CSF £13.20 TOTE £2.30: £1.50, £3.00; EX 12.80 Trifecta £52.00.
Owner C L Bacon **Bred** Doc Bloodstock **Trained** Oakham, Rutland

FOCUS
The winner dictated a weak pace which turned into a sprint in the last quarter-mile, making the form potentially unreliable.

3198 LITTLETON STUD RACING EXCELLENCE APPRENTICE H'CAP (WHIPS SHALL BE CARRIED BUT NOT USED) 1m
5:25 (5:25) (Class 6) (0-60,60) 3-Y-O **£2,911** (£866; £432; £216) **Stalls** Low

Form RPR

0405 **1** **Elegant Annie**[12] 2784 3-9-0 **53** .... LuluStanford 4 59
(Jonathan Portman) *mid-div: hdwy 2f out: led ent fnl f: r.o wl: readily* **8/1**

5-06 **2** *2 ¼* **Moon Over Mobay**[34] 2108 3-9-0 **60** .... JoshuaBryan(7) 7 61
(Andrew Balding) *hld up: struggling 1/2-way: hdwy 2f out: styd on to chse wnr ins fnl f but a being readily hld* **10/3**[1]

3440 **3** *2 ¼* **Nidnod**[54] 1548 3-8-11 **53** .... MitchGodwin(3) 5 49
(John Bridger) *prom: carried to stands' side 3f out: drifted bk to centre and ev ch briefly ent fnl f: sn hld: kpt on same pce* **14/1**

5002 **4** *2 ½* **Lady McGuffy (IRE)**[31] 2184 3-8-9 **53** .... (t) AledBeech(5) 3 43
(David Evans) *mid-div: hdwy to ld 3f out: hdd ent fnl f: no ex* **5/1**[3]

-034 **5** *4 ½* **Wilspa's Magic (IRE)**[10] 2823 3-8-12 **58** .... WilliamCox(7) 1 37
(Ron Hodges) *led tl drifted to stands' side 3f out: one pce and hld after* **12/1**

6030 **6** *3* **Concur (IRE)**[18] 2590 3-8-7 **49** .... (p) GeorgeWood(3) 6 21
(Rod Millman) *trckd ldrs: rdn 3f out: wknd fnl f* **11/2**

03-0 **7** *2 ¼* **Cooperess**[24] 2415 3-8-11 **55** .... CliffordLee(5) 10 21
(Ali Stronge) *slowly away: in last trio: hdwy over 3f out to trck ldrs: wknd ent fnl f* **10/1**

00-3 **8** *1* **Ormering**[34] 2083 3-8-10 **49** .... RhiainIngram 8 13
(Roger Teal) *trckd ldrs: effrt 3f out: wknd over 1f out* **20/1**

040- **9** *1* **Unsuspected Girl (IRE)**[250] 7013 3-9-3 **56** .... SophieKilloran 9 17
(David Simcock) *hld up: hdwy over 3f out: effrt over 2f out: wknd over 1f out* **4/1**[2]

5005 **10** *2* **Thief Of Hearts**[47] 1764 3-8-7 **49** .... (p[1]) PatrickVaughan(3) 2 6
(Bill Turner) *trckd ldrs: rdn 3f out: wknd over 1f out* **33/1**

1m 45.25s (1.75) **Going Correction** +0.175s/f (Good) **10** Ran SP% **117.4**
Speed ratings (Par 97): **98,95,93,91,86 83,81,80,79,77**
CSF £35.10 CT £374.85 TOTE £7.70: £3.00, £1.60, £4.60; EX 36.40 Trifecta £523.60.
Owner Tom Edwards & Partners **Bred** Qatar Bloodstock Ltd **Trained** Upper Lambourn, Berks

FOCUS
A typically modest race of its type, run at a medium pace, and the runners used the full width of the track.
T/Plt: £27.70 to a £1 stake. Pool: £73,729.82 - 1,936.13 winning tickets T/Qpdt: £23.40 to a £1 stake. Pool: £5,838.97 - 184.52 winning tickets **Tim Mitchell**

3199 - 3200a (Foreign Racing) - See Raceform Interactive

2449 CORK (R-H)
Sunday, June 12

OFFICIAL GOING: Sprint course - yielding to soft; round course - yielding (good to yielding in places)

3201a CORAL.IE MIDSUMMER SPRINT STKS (LISTED RACE) 5f
3:20 (3:20) 3-Y-O+ **£20,606** (£6,636; £3,143; £1,397; £698)

RPR

1 **Spirit Quartz (IRE)**[27] 2317 8-9-9 108 .... (p) PatSmullen 7 103+
(Robert Cowell) *chsd ldrs: 4th 1/2-way: impr gng wl fr 1/2-way to ld narrowly 1 1/2f out: sn rdn and jnd briefly ins fnl f: kpt on wl u.p w narrow advantage to assert cl home* **5/4**[2]

2 *½* **Ardhoomey (IRE)**[23] 2450 4-9-9 104 .... ColinKeane 5 101
(C M Lyons, Ire) *settled bhd ldrs: effrt on outer 1 1/2f out: almost on terms ent fnl f: sn rdn in cl 2nd and disp briefly ins fnl f: kpt on wl wout matching wnr clsng stages* **11/10**[1]

3 *4 ¼* **Faintleog (IRE)**[8] 2922 5-9-4 76 .... AdrianO'Shea 2 81
(Mrs A M O'Shea, Ire) *broke wl to ld briefly tl sn hdd and settled in cl 2nd: rdn after 1/2-way and sn lost pl: no imp on ldrs u.p in 4th 1 1/2f out: kpt on one pce ins fnl f* **14/1**

4 *1 ¼* **Little Sweetheart (IRE)**[15] 2704 5-9-4 72 .... DannyGrant 3 76
(Patrick J Flynn, Ire) *sn led: narrow advantage at 1/2-way: rdn and hdd 1 1/2f out: no ex in 3rd ent fnl f and sn wknd* **25/1**

5 *½* **Dikta Del Mar (SPA)**[23] 2450 4-9-4 95 .... ShaneFoley 4 75
(T Hogan, Ire) *in rr thrght: pushed along 2f out and no imp on ldrs ent fnl f: kpt on one pce* **10/1**[3]

57.88s (-1.32)
WFA 3 from 4yo+ 7lb **5** Ran SP% **111.7**
CSF £3.01 TOTE £2.30: £1.20, £1.10; DF 2.80 Trifecta £10.40.
Owner Ecurie La Boetie **Bred** Ballygallon Stud Ltd **Trained** Six Mile Bottom, Cambs

FOCUS
A fairly average renewal of this Listed sprint, which not surprisingly went for export.

3202a CORAL.IE MUNSTER OAKS STKS (GROUP 3) (F&M) 1m 4f
3:55 (3:57) 3-Y-O+
£32,536 (£10,477; £4,963; £2,205; £1,102; £551)

RPR

1 **Pretty Perfect (IRE)**[21] 2509 3-8-9 104 .... ColmO'Donoghue 7 106
(A P O'Brien, Ire) *sn led and mde rest: over 1 l clr at 1/2-way: rdn over 2f out and extended advantage u.p 1 1/2f out: styd on strly ins fnl f: comf* **3/1**[2]

2 *4* **Shamreen (IRE)**[18] 2595 3-8-9 99 .... (v[1]) PatSmullen 5 100
(D K Weld, Ire) *chsd ldrs: 4th 1/2-way: tk clsr order bhd ldrs under 3f out: rdn into 2nd over 1f out and no imp on clr wnr: kpt on same pce ins fnl f* **11/8**[1]

3 *2 ¼* **Best In The World (IRE)**[32] 2160 3-8-9 96 .... MichaelHussey 9 96
(A P O'Brien, Ire) *dwlt sltly and in rr early: 8th 1/2-way: hdwy fr over 3f out to chse ldrs over 2f out where rdn: sn swtchd and wnt 4th between horses 1f out: no imp on wnr in 3rd ins fnl f: kpt on same pce* **20/1**

4 *2 ½* **Twitch (IRE)**[22] 2486 4-9-9 97 .... (p) ChrisHayes 2 91
(Hugo Palmer) *pushed along early to sn trck ldr in 2nd: rdn 3f out and no imp on wnr u.p in 3rd over 1f out: lost pl ins fnl f and kpt on one pce clsng stages* **8/1**

5 *½* **Siamsaiocht (IRE)**[9] 2883 3-8-9 92 .... (p) KevinManning 1 92
(J S Bolger, Ire) *settled in mid-div: disp 5th at 1/2-way: rdn in 5th under 3f out and no imp on wnr u.p ent fnl f: kpt on one pce* **11/1**

6 *¾* **Avenante**[22] 2498 4-9-9 90 .... DeclanMcDonogh 6 89
(John M Oxx, Ire) *pushed along in 2nd early tl sn settled bhd ldrs in 3rd: racd keenly: rdn on outer in 4th over 2f out and no ex 1 1/2f out where dropped to 6th: one pce after* **14/1**

7 *1 ¾* **Gallope (IRE)**[28] 2276 4-9-9 80 .... ShaneFoley 8 87
(Mrs Prunella Dobbs, Ire) *on toes befhand: hld up: last at 1/2-way: rdn under 3f out and sme modest hdwy u.p into 7th 1f out: kpt on one pce* **66/1**

8 *4 ¾* **How High The Moon (IRE)**[32] 2167 3-8-9 98 .... SeamieHeffernan 4 80
(A P O'Brien, Ire) *hld up in mid-div: disp 5th at 1/2-way: pushed along in 6th over 4f out and no ex u.p fr under 3f out: one pce after and wknd into 8th 1f out* **6/1**[3]

9 *3* **French Blue**[18] 2595 3-8-9 88 .... WayneLordan 3 75
(W McCreery, Ire) *in rr of mid-div: 7th 1/2-way: rdn in 8th over 2f out and no imp: sn dropped to rr* **20/1**

2m 36.09s (-11.81)
WFA 3 from 4yo 15lb **9** Ran SP% **118.5**
CSF £7.54 TOTE £3.80: £1.70, £1.02, £2.50; DF 8.20 Trifecta £71.00.
Owner Michael Tabor & Derrick Smith & Mrs John Magnier **Bred** Milanova Syndicate **Trained** Cashel, Co Tipperary

FOCUS
Disappointing she may have been in the Irish 1000 Guineas, but the winner was impressive here in making all and the Irish Oaks looks the logical target

3203 - 3206a (Foreign Racing) - See Raceform Interactive

2286 HOPPEGARTEN (R-H)
Sunday, June 12

OFFICIAL GOING: Turf: good

3207a DIANA-TRIAL (GROUP 2) (3YO FILLIES) (TURF) 1m 2f
3:50 (12:00) 3-Y-O **£29,411** (£11,397; £5,882; £2,941; £1,838)

RPR

1 **Meergorl (GER)**[28] 3-9-2 0 .... FrederikTylicki 13 100
(R Dzubasz, Germany) *settled in midfield: clsd 2 1/2f out: rdn to chal under 1 1/2f out: r.o u.p in sustained dual fr over 1f out: led fnl strides* **17/2**

2 *nk* **Pagella (GER)**[76] 3-9-2 0 .... AlexanderPietsch 9 99
(J Hirschberger, Germany) *settled towards rr: hdwy on outer appr 2f out: led under 1 1/2f out: hrd pressed by eventual wnr fr over 1f out: r.o u.p: hdd fnl strides* **11/2**[2]

3 *3 ½* **Kasalla (GER)** 3-9-2 0 .... MartinSeidl 8 92
(Markus Klug, Germany) *w.w towards rr: hdwy sn after 1/2-way: 5th and rdn 2 1/2f out: nt clr run and angled out 2f out: swtchd bk ins and styd to go 3rd wl ins fnl f: nt rch front two* **57/10**[3]

4 *¾* **Night Music (GER)** 3-9-2 0 .... EduardoPedroza 11 91
(A Wohler, Germany) *w.w towards rr: scrubbed along and prog 2 1/2f out: styd on wl fnl f: tk 4th cl home: nvr on terms* **19/5**[1]

5 *¾* **Mary Sun (FR)**[34] 2115 3-9-2 0 .... IoritzMendizabal 5 89
(Henk Grewe, Germany) *led: hrd rdn whn pressed over 1 1/2f out: hdd sn after: no ex* **147/10**

6 *½* **Wild Approach (GER)**[28] 3-9-2 0 .... FilipMinarik 6 88
(Melanie Sauer, Germany) *chsd ldr: rdn and nt qckn wl over 2f out: one pce fnl f* **32/5**

7 *3 ½* **Lopera (GER)** 3-9-2 0 .... DanielePorcu 7 81
(P Schiergen, Germany) *t.k.h: cl up: 2nd and hrd rdn over 1 1/2f out: wknd ins fnl f* **79/10**

8 *2* **La Dynamite (IRE)**[56] 3-9-2 0 .... AdriedeVries 12 77
(Markus Klug, Germany) *tk v str hold: wnt wd first bnd: hld up in midfield: chsd ldrs bef 1/2-way: rdn and wknd fr 2f out* **19/5**[1]

9 *1 ¾* **Cockney Blue** 3-9-2 0 .... FranciscoDaSilva 4 74
(Malgorzata Fabianska, Poland) *hld up in fnl pair: last and rdn 2 1/2f out: passed btn horses late on: nvr a factor* **43/1**

10 *½* **Whole Lotta Rosie (GER)**[15] 2710 3-9-2 0 .... StephenHellyn 3 73
(M Rulec, Germany) *hld up in fnl pair: rdn and no imp 2f out: wl hld whn eased ins fnl f* **21/1**

11 *¾* **Always Hope (GER)** 3-9-2 0 .... AndreasHelfenbein 10 71
(Andreas Lowe, Germany) *cl up: outpcd and rdn 2 1/2f out: sn wknd* **172/10**

12 *1* **Dalmatian Sea (GER)**[238] 7323 3-9-2 0.................... MichaelCadeddu 1 69
(A Wohler, Germany) *w.w in midfield: rdn and btn over 2f out: sn wknd* **45/1**

2m 4.5s (-2.20) **12** Ran SP% **128.1**
WIN (incl. 10 euro stake): 95. PLACES: 26, 22, 23. SF: 569.
Owner Gestut Gorlsdorf **Bred** Gestut Gorlsdorf **Trained** Germany

[2529]CARLISLE (R-H)

Monday, June 13

OFFICIAL GOING: Good (good to soft in places)
Wind: Light, half behind Weather: Overcast

3208 MOLSON COORS NOVICE AUCTION STKS 5f 193y
2:00 (2:02) (Class 5) 2-Y-O **£2,911** (£866; £432; £216) **Stalls** Low

Form RPR
U5 **1** **Showdance Kid**[19] 2570 2-9-2 0.................................. DougieCostello 3 75+
(K R Burke) *dwlt: t.k.h and sn in tch: drvn along 2f out: kpt on wl fnl f to ld last 25yds* **4/1**[1]
4 **2** *1/2* **Local Artist (IRE)**[13] 2771 2-8-11 0.................................. JasonHart 6 67
(John Quinn) *chsd ldrs: effrt and wnt 2nd over 1f out: drvn and ev ch ins fnl f: kpt on: hld cl home* **7/1**[3]
3 *1/2* **Alfie's Angel (IRE)** 2-9-2 0.................................. LukeMorris 7 70+
(Bryan Smart) *in tch on outside: drvn and outpcd over 3f out: rallied on outside over 1f out: kpt on wl fnl f to take 3rd cl home: improve* **18/1**
31 **4** *nse* **Boundsy (IRE)**[19] 2570 2-9-2 0.................................. AdamMcNamara[(7)] 5 75
(Richard Fahey) *led: rdn along 2f out: hdd and no ex last 25yds* **9/2**[2]
53 **5** *3 1/2* **Kroy**[38] 2014 2-9-2 0.................................. AndrewMullen 9 60
(Ollie Pears) *hld up: rdn along over 2f out: kpt on fnl f: nvr able to chal* **16/1**
6 *nse* **Harbour Belle** 2-8-11 0.................................. PaulMulrennan 12 54+
(Michael Dods) *hld up: shkn up over 1f out: styd on steadily fnl f: nvr nr to chal* **28/1**
7 *3/4* **Our Boy John (IRE)** 2-9-2 0.................................. GeorgeChaloner 11 57
(Richard Fahey) *hld up on outside: drvn along over 2f out: no imp fr over 1f out* **20/1**
6 **8** *3/4* **Equity**[21] 2535 2-9-2 0.................................. TomEaves 2 55
(David Brown) *trckd ldrs: rdn over 2f out: wknd fnl f* **4/1**[1]
3 **9** *1 1/4* **He's A Toff (IRE)**[27] 2344 2-9-2 0.................................. TomQueally 8 51
(Tim Easterby) *s.i.s: hld up: pushed along over 2f out: nvr rchd ldrs* **12/1**
10 *1/2* **Little Miss Lola** 2-8-11 0.................................. NeilFarley 1 45
(Alan Swinbank) *dwlt: t.k.h and sn midfield on ins: rdn along over 2f out: wknd over 1f out* **11/1**
0 **11** *3/4* **Doctor Dynamite (IRE)**[12] 2800 2-9-2 0.................................. AndrewElliott 10 47+
(Tim Easterby) *s.i.s: rn green in rr: nvr on terms* **100/1**
025 **12** *7* **Poppy Pivot (IRE)**[24] 2424 2-8-11 0.................................. PJMcDonald 4 21
(Ann Duffield) *chsd ldr tl rdn and wknd over 1f out* **12/1**

1m 14.65s (0.95) **Going Correction** +0.05s/f (Good) **12** Ran SP% **114.7**
Speed ratings (Par 93): **95,94,93,93,88 88,87,86,85,84 83,74**
CSF £30.22 TOTE £5.40: £2.30, £2.70, £4.00; EX 36.90 Trifecta £607.70.
Owner Hambleton Racing Ltd Trio & E Burke **Bred** Natton House Thoroughbreds & Mark Woodall **Trained** Middleham Moor, N Yorks

FOCUS
The ground had dried out a little and was now good, good to soft in places. The inside rail had been moved out 6yds around the Old Stable and 3yds up the home straight, adding 14yds to race distances on the round course. An ordinary novice auction to start, but a tight finish with four in a line across the track nearing the post. Andrew Elliott said the ground was "on the good side of soft - more good", while Neil Farley described conditions as "just on the easy side."

3209 MOLSON COORS MAIDEN FILLIES' STKS 5f 193y
2:30 (2:32) (Class 5) 3-Y-O+ **£2,911** (£866; £432; £216) **Stalls** Low

Form RPR
3 **1** **Red Box**[28] 2294 3-9-0 0.................................. LukeMorris 8 86+
(Sir Mark Prescott Bt) *hld up: pushed along and hung rt over 2f out: rallied over 1f out: led wl ins fnl f: pushed out* **13/8**[1]
24-2 **2** *2* **David's Duchess (IRE)**[14] 2740 3-9-0 80.................. GeorgeChaloner 4 79
(Richard Fahey) *led at decent gallop: rdn and clr over 1f out: hdd and no ex wl ins fnl f* **9/4**[2]
22 **3** *1* **Brockholes**[28] 2303 3-9-0 0.................................. PJMcDonald 7 76
(Ann Duffield) *in tch: pushed along over 2f out: hung rt and chsd clr ldr over 1f out: kpt on same pce wl ins fnl f* **11/2**[3]
35- **4** *6* **Andalusite**[384] 2590 3-9-0 0.................................. RoystonFfrench 3 57
(Ed McMahon) *chsd ldrs: rdn over 2f out: outpcd over 1f out* **10/1**
0323 **5** *3 3/4* **My Lucille (IRE)**[16] 2681 3-9-0 70.................................. JasonHart 5 45
(Tim Easterby) *t.k.h: trckd ldrs: rdn along over 2f out: wknd over 1f out* **9/1**
6 **6** *2* **Tell The Stars**[14] 2740 3-9-0 0.................................. AndrewMullen 9 38
(Ollie Pears) *s.i.s: bhd: pushed along and outpcd over 3f out: n.d after* **80/1**
00- **7** *1* **Gabbys Lad (IRE)**[294] 5697 3-9-0 0.................................. NeilFarley 10 35
(Eric Alston) *chsd ldrs on outside: outpcd and struggling over 2f out: sn btn* **150/1**
4 **8** *4* **A Fitting Finale**[14] 2740 3-9-0 0.................................. TomEaves 2 22
(Kevin Ryan) *dwlt: hld up: pushed along and edgd rt over 2f out: sn btn* **25/1**
36 **9** *8* **Anna Barkova (IRE)**[28] 2304 3-9-0 0.................................. DougieCostello 1
(K R Burke) *dwlt: chsd ldng gp: rdn and edgd rt over 2f out: sn btn* **14/1**

1m 13.24s (-0.46) **Going Correction** +0.05s/f (Good) **9** Ran SP% **115.7**
Speed ratings (Par 100): **105,102,101,93,88 85,84,78,68**
CSF £5.35 TOTE £2.70: £1.20, £1.30, £2.00; EX 6.50 Trifecta £14.10.
Owner Cheveley Park Stud **Bred** Cheveley Park Stud Ltd **Trained** Newmarket, Suffolk

FOCUS
An ordinary and uncompetitive 3yo fillies' maiden, though the majority of these had already shown ability. They finished well spread out and the runner-up's mark of 80 sets the benchmark.

3210 MOLSON COORS H'CAP (DIV I) 5f 193y
3:00 (3:03) (Class 5) (0-70,69) 3-Y-O+ **£2,911** (£866; £432; £216) **Stalls** Low

Form RPR
-463 **1** **Spirit Of Wedza (IRE)**[19] 2571 4-9-2 60.........................(p) JoeDoyle[(3)] 7 73
(Julie Camacho) *t.k.h: mde all: rdn and clr wl over 1f out: kpt on wl fnl f: unchal* **9/2**[2]
4452 **2** *3 3/4* **Exotic Guest**[4] 3069 6-9-8 63..(p) TomEaves 12 64+
(Ruth Carr) *hld up: hdwy on outside 2f out: edgd rt and chsd (clr) wnr ins fnl f: kpt on: no imp* **10/3**[1]
65 **3** *1/2* **Inner Knowing (IRE)**[17] 2657 3-8-13 62...................(p) DougieCostello 5 59
(K R Burke) *chsd clr ldng pair: effrt and wnt 2nd over 2f out to ins fnl f: sn no ex* **18/1**
3222 **4** *1 3/4* **Keene's Pointe**[11] 2812 6-9-6 64.................................. ShelleyBirkett[(3)] 3 58
(Kristin Stubbs) *hld up: rdn and hdwy over 1f out: kpt on fnl f: nt pce to chal* **13/2**
-063 **5** *1 3/4* **Mininggold**[14] 2742 3-9-3 66.................................. JasonHart 10 52
(Tim Easterby) *in tch: effrt and rdn over 2f out: wknd ins fnl f* **11/1**
6322 **6** *hd* **Princess Peaches**[17] 2655 4-9-1 63..................(p) AdamMcNamara[(7)] 8 51
(James Bethell) *hld up bhd ldng gp: effrt over 2f out: sn outpcd: no imp fnl f* **5/1**[3]
043 **7** *nk* **Big Time Dancer (IRE)**[21] 2522 3-8-7 56 ow1........(p) GeorgeChaloner 1 41
(Dianne Sayer) *sn pushed along to chse wnr: rdn and outpcd 2f out: btn fnl f* **12/1**
3333 **8** *3/4* **Picks Pinta**[17] 2660 5-9-7 67..................................(p) RobJFitzpatrick[(5)] 9 51
(John David Riches) *dwlt: hld up: effrt and rdn over 2f out: wknd over 1f out* **9/2**[2]
6050 **9** *12* **Diatomic (IRE)**[24] 2416 4-9-3 58..(p) LukeMorris 2 4
(Tom Dascombe) *sn pushed along and in tch: rdn and struggling over 2f out: sn wknd* **25/1**

1m 13.48s (-0.22) **Going Correction** +0.05s/f (Good)
WFA 3 from 4yo+ 8lb **9** Ran SP% **114.6**
Speed ratings (Par 103): **103,98,97,95,92 92,92,91,75**
CSF £19.72 CT £245.08 TOTE £6.00: £2.20, £1.50, £5.50; EX 22.00 Trifecta £339.30.
Owner Owners Group 005 **Bred** N Hartery **Trained** Norton, N Yorks

FOCUS
The first division of a modest sprint handicap and few ever got into it. The winner has been rated back to his best.

3211 MOLSON COORS H'CAP (DIV II) 5f 193y
3:30 (3:32) (Class 5) (0-70,69) 3-Y-O+ **£2,911** (£866; £432; £216) **Stalls** Low

Form RPR
6641 **1** **In My Place**[13] 2776 3-8-10 66..............................(p) AdamMcNamara[(7)] 9 73+
(Richard Fahey) *bhd: in last and outpcd 1/2-way: gd hdwy on outside over 1f out: qcknd to ld ins fnl f: kpt on strly* **3/1**[1]
-300 **2** *1 1/2* **Mallymkun**[27] 2345 4-9-3 63.................................. JordanVaughan[(5)] 12 67
(K R Burke) *hld up in tch on outside: smooth hdwy over 2f out: effrt and ev ch over 1f out to ins fnl f: kpt on: nt pce of wnr* **12/1**
0063 **3** *shd* **Jebel Tara**[4] 3069 11-9-8 63..(bt) DaleSwift 11 67
(Alan Brown) *trckd ldrs: led over 2f out to ins fnl f: kpt on same pce towards fin* **6/1**[2]
0000 **4** *1* **Lydiate Lady**[24] 2423 4-8-12 53.................................. JoeFanning 8 53
(Paul Green) *hld up in midfield: pushed along over 2f out: kpt on fnl f: nt gng pce to chal* **11/1**
3065 **5** *1 3/4* **Gold Beau (FR)**[11] 2812 6-9-6 64..............................(v) ShelleyBirkett[(3)] 6 59
(Kristin Stubbs) *trckd ldrs: effrt and n.m.r wl over 1f out: sn rdn: kpt on same pce fnl f* **8/1**
3425 **6** *hd* **Viva Verglas (IRE)**[68] 1264 5-9-12 67..........................(b) LukeMorris 10 61
(Daniel Mark Loughnane) *bhd: rdn along 1/2-way: hdwy over 1f out: kpt on fnl f: nt gng pce to chal* **9/1**
00-0 **7** *1* **Slim Chance (IRE)**[13] 2773 7-9-6 61.................................. AndrewElliott 7 52
(Simon West) *dwlt: bhd: rdn over 2f out: hung lft and hdwy ins fnl f: n.d* **20/1**
0-00 **8** *1/2* **Kodimoor (IRE)**[37] 2049 3-9-4 67.................................. DougieCostello 5 54
(Christopher Kellett) *bhd: rdn along over 2f out: no imp fr over 1f out* **50/1**
-040 **9** *1* **Percy's Gal**[27] 2332 5-9-7 67.................................. GemmaTutty[(5)] 1 62
(Karen Tutty) *wnt lft s: hld up in midfield: effrt whn n.m.r briefly over 1f out: sn wknd* **8/1**
-200 **10** *1/2* **Whipphound**[9] 2919 8-9-1 56.................................. PaulMulrennan 3 41
(Ruth Carr) *pressed ldr: rdn over 2f out: wknd fnl f* **16/1**
-405 **11** *1 1/2* **Danzeb (IRE)**[24] 2418 3-9-6 69..(p) PJMcDonald 2 47
(Ann Duffield) *blkd s: t.k.h: in tch: effrt and hanging rt whn nt clr run briefly over 1f out: sn wknd* **7/1**[3]
0-50 **12** *nk* **Spring Bird**[62] 1402 7-9-5 60.................................. NeilFarley 4 39
(Alan Swinbank) *led to over 2f out: cl up tl wknd fnl f* **33/1**

1m 13.88s (0.18) **Going Correction** +0.05s/f (Good)
WFA 3 from 4yo+ 8lb **12** Ran SP% **115.6**
Speed ratings (Par 103): **100,98,97,96,94 93,92,91,90,89 87,87**
CSF £38.95 CT £179.41 TOTE £2.80: £1.30, £3.40, £2.40; EX 49.40 Trifecta £459.20.
Owner A Rhodes Haulage And P Timmins **Bred** Sean Gorman **Trained** Musley Bank, N Yorks
■ Stewards' Enquiry : Dale Swift caution; careless riding

FOCUS
The winning time was 0.4sec slower than the first division. An amazing winning performance from the favourite and this didn't look a case of the pace collapsing, which makes his effort even more remarkable.

3212 THURSBY (JOCKEY CLUB GRASSROOTS FLAT MIDDLE DISTANCE SERIES QUAL) H'CAP 1m 1f
4:00 (4:00) (Class 5) (0-70,70) 4-Y-O+ **£2,911** (£866; £432; £216) **Stalls** Low

Form RPR
0000 **1** **Artful Prince**[14] 2743 6-9-4 70..(b) JoeDoyle[(3)] 4 78
(James Given) *hld up: hdwy over 2f out: led over 1f out: drifted rt ins fnl f: bmpd rival towards fin: hld on wl* **11/4**[1]
0-00 **2** *nk* **Framley Garth (IRE)**[20] 2555 4-8-11 67.......................... PaulaMuir[(7)] 10 74
(Patrick Holmes) *t.k.h early: hld up in tch: effrt over 1f out: chsd wnr ins fnl f: bmpd towards fin: kpt on: jst hld* **16/1**
5034 **3** *3* **Save The Bees**[14] 2743 8-8-12 68.................................. GerO'Neill[(7)] 5 68
(Declan Carroll) *led: rdn over 2f out: hdd over 1f out: edgd rt and kpt on same pce ins fnl f* **11/4**[1]
/0-0 **4** *3/4* **Judicious**[20] 2555 9-8-8 57.................................. JoeFanning 9 56
(Geoffrey Harker) *hld up: hdwy on outside 2f out: edgd rt and kpt on same pce ins fnl f* **12/1**
00 **5** *3/4* **Annigoni (IRE)**[9] 2915 4-8-3 52..(p) LukeMorris 2 49
(Ruth Carr) *hld up in tch: drvn and outpcd over 2f out: rallied fnl f: no imp* **9/1**
-060 **6** *1 1/2* **Tectonic (IRE)**[11] 2811 7-9-2 65..(p) JasonHart 3 61
(Keith Dalgleish) *t.k.h: hld up in tch: effrt against far rail wl over 1f out: wknd fnl f* **10/1**
05-0 **7** *2 1/2* **Haymarket**[49] 1697 7-9-0 68.................................. GarryWhillans[(5)] 1 56
(R Mike Smith) *chsd ldrs: rdn over 2f out: wknd over 1f out* **7/1**[3]
-000 **8** *1/2* **Inshaa**[13] 2773 4-9-0 68.................................. JoshDoyle[(5)] 6 55
(Michael Herrington) *t.k.h: chsd ldr: drvn over 2f out: wknd over 1f out* **6/1**[2]

1m 59.13s (1.53) **Going Correction** +0.25s/f (Good) **8** Ran SP% **112.8**
Speed ratings (Par 103): **103,102,100,99,98 97,95,94**
CSF £49.17 CT £131.50 TOTE £3.40: £1.40, £4.50, £1.30; EX 44.20 Trifecta £144.30.
Owner Ingram Racing **Bred** Graham Wilson **Trained** Willoughton, Lincs

FOCUS
Rail movement added 14yds to race distance. A modest handicap run at an ordinary pace and things got tight between the first two near the line. The Stewards had a look, but allowed the result to stand. The winner was on a good mark.

3213 BRITISH STALLION STUDS EBF FILLIES' H'CAP 6f 195y
4:30 (4:32) (Class 4) (0-80,80) 3-Y-O **£6,469** (£1,925; £962; £481) **Stalls** Low

Form RPR

15-6 **1** **Al Shahaniya (IRE)**[24] 2420 3-9-0 **80** AdamMcNamara[(7)] 7 87
(John Quinn) *hld up in midfield: rdn over 2f out: hdwy over 1f out: led wl ins fnl f: kpt on strly* **12/1**

-031 **2** 1 1/4 **Popsies Joy (IRE)**[16] 2674 3-8-10 **69** JasonHart 4 73
(Tim Easterby) *hld up in midfield: effrt and hung rt over 2f out: led over 1f out to wl ins fnl f: kpt on same pce* **13/2**[3]

5-20 **3** hd **Dominannie (IRE)**[35] 2095 3-8-6 **65** NeilFarley 12 68
(Alan Swinbank) *hld up on outside: rdn along over 2f out: kpt on fnl f: nrst fin* **25/1**

213- **4** 1 1/2 **Company Asset (IRE)**[277] 6241 3-9-7 **80** TomEaves 1 79
(Kevin Ryan) *hld up: rdn over 2f out: hdwy over 1f out: kpt on same pce wl ins fnl f* **10/1**

310 **5** 2 **Bint Arcano (FR)**[76] 1137 3-8-10 **72** JoeDoyle[(3)] 11 66
(Julie Camacho) *t.k.h: hld up: rdn over 2f out: hdwy fnl f: no imp* **10/1**

16-0 **6** 3/4 **Zaina Rizeena**[32] 2179 3-9-4 **77** GeorgeChaloner 10 69+
(Richard Fahey) *t.k.h: led: rdn over 2f out: hdd over 1f out: sn wknd* **9/1**

0-22 **7** 1 3/4 **Bad Girl Caoimhe (IRE)**[54] 1562 3-8-6 **70** CallumShepherd[(5)] 5 57
(Brian Ellison) *dwlt: bhd: rdn over 2f out: effrt whn nt clr run briefly over 1f out: kpt on: nt pce to chal* **5/1**[1]

61 **8** 1/2 **Connemera Queen**[28] 2304 3-8-12 **71** RoystonFfrench 2 57
(Tracy Waggott) *in tch on ins: drvn and outpcd over 2f out: n.d after* **33/1**

531- **9** 2 3/4 **Ambriel (IRE)**[269] 6490 3-9-5 **78** PaulMulrennan 3 56
(Michael Dods) *pressed ldr: rdn over 2f out: wknd over 1f out* **8/1**

4-04 **10** hd **Sister Dude**[17] 2653 3-8-6 **70** JordanVaughan[(5)] 9 48
(K R Burke) *racd wd: hld up in tch: rdn over 2f out: wknd wl over 1f out* **9/1**

3-04 **11** nse **Florenza**[30] 2239 3-9-0 **73** AndrewElliott 8 51
(Chris Fairhurst) *plld hrd early: hld up in tch: struggling over 2f out: sn btn* **12/1**

14-0 **12** 2 **Rio's Cliffs**[30] 2239 3-9-5 **78** JoeFanning 6 50
(Martyn Meade) *t.k.h: trckd ldrs tl rdn and wknd over 1f out* **11/2**[2]

1m 28.47s (1.37) **Going Correction** +0.25s/f (Good) **12** Ran SP% **116.8**
Speed ratings (Par 98): **102,100,100,98,96 95,93,92,89,89 89,87**
CSF £86.74 CT £1954.08 TOTE £11.90: £3.90, £2.00, £8.90; EX 83.80 Trifecta £2269.30.
Owner Al Shaqab Racing **Bred** L Montgomery **Trained** Settrington, N Yorks
■ Stewards' Enquiry : Neil Farley two-day ban: used whip above permitted level (Jun 27-28)

FOCUS
Rail movement added 14yds to race distance. Quite a decent 3yo fillies' handicap, won by an unexposed type, and they went a good pace.

3214 RACING UK H'CAP 7f 173y
5:00 (5:00) (Class 5) (0-70,70) 4-Y-O+ **£2,911** (£866; £432; £216) **Stalls** Low

Form RPR

4200 **1** **McDelta**[48] 1735 6-8-4 **57** ow1 (p) CallumShepherd[(5)] 10 65
(Ian Williams) *hld up: drvn and outpcd over 3f out: rallied over 1f out: styd on wl fnl f to ld towards fin* **9/2**[1]

-343 **2** 1 **Ferdy (IRE)**[13] 2773 7-8-8 **57** PJMcDonald 3 62
(Paul Green) *hld up: smooth hdwy over 2f out: rdn to ld ins fnl f: kpt on: hdd and no ex towards fin* **6/1**[3]

-650 **3** nk **Arms Around Me (IRE)**[9] 2915 4-8-11 **60** TomEaves 12 64
(James Given) *hld up: drvn and outpcd over 2f out: swtchd lft and hdwy over 1f out: kpt on fnl f: nrst fin* **11/1**

0023 **4** 1/2 **Mrs Biggs**[12] 2794 4-8-9 **65** GerO'Neill[(7)] 9 68
(Declan Carroll) *hld up in midfield: effrt over 2f out: kpt on ins fnl f* **12/1**

00-0 **5** 1/2 **Lothair (IRE)**[9] 2918 7-9-2 **65** JoeFanning 8 67
(Alan Swinbank) *chsd ldng pair: effrt and rdn over 2f out: outpcd ins fnl f* **20/1**

-616 **6** 1 **Call Out Loud**[43] 1899 4-9-4 **67** (t) AndrewMullen 11 66+
(Michael Appleby) *blindfold slow to remove and s.s: sn rcvrd and in tch: hung rt and led wl over 1f out: rdn and hdd ins fnl f: sn wknd* **7/1**

6642 **7** 1 1/2 **Cabal**[9] 2918 9-9-2 **65** (v) JasonHart 1 61
(Geoffrey Harker) *t.k.h: hld up in tch: drvn over 2f out: wknd over 1f out* **7/1**

0443 **8** 1 **Talent Scout (IRE)**[5] 3013 10-8-11 **65** GemmaTutty[(5)] 4 58
(Karen Tutty) *t.k.h: pressed wnr: rdn over 2f out: wknd over 1f out* **9/2**[1]

1106 **9** 11 **Ellaal**[11] 2811 7-9-4 **67** PaulMulrennan 6 34
(Ruth Carr) *led at str gallop: rdn and hdd wl over 1f out: sn lost pl: eased whn btn ins fnl f* **11/2**[2]

1m 41.46s (1.46) **Going Correction** +0.25s/f (Good) **9** Ran SP% **111.8**
Speed ratings (Par 103): **102,101,100,100,99 98,97,96,85**
CSF £29.91 CT £274.30 TOTE £5.90: £2.30, £2.00, £3.80; EX 32.30 Trifecta £262.00.
Owner Jim Mellon & Partners **Bred** Roden House Stud **Trained** Portway, Worcs
■ Stewards' Enquiry : Callum Shepherd caution: careless riding

FOCUS
Rail movement added 14yds to race distance. An ordinary handicap and the leaders went off far too quick. The first three home occupied the last three positions at halfway.

3215 WATCH RACING UK ON 3 DEVICES H'CAP 1m 3f 39y
5:30 (5:31) (Class 5) (0-70,66) 3-Y-O **£2,911** (£866; £432; £216) **Stalls** High

Form RPR

05-4 **1** **Silva Eclipse**[27] 2327 3-9-6 **65** PaulMulrennan 4 72+
(Jedd O'Keeffe) *t.k.h early: trckd ldrs: effrt and wnt 2nd 3f out: hung rt and led appr fnl f: styd on wl* **4/1**[2]

0-04 **2** 1 3/4 **Palisade**[12] 2798 3-9-0 **59** (v[1]) LukeMorris 5 63
(Sir Mark Prescott Bt) *dwlt: sn led: rdn over 2f out: hdd appr fnl f: kpt on same pce* **7/2**[1]

065- **3** 1 1/4 **Young Tom**[222] 7707 3-8-11 **56** AndrewMullen 7 58
(Michael Appleby) *t.k.h early: hld up in tch: effrt and edgd rt 2f out: kpt on fnl f: nt gng pce to chal* **9/2**[3]

3-1U **4** 1 **Sattelac**[17] 2666 3-9-7 **66** TomQueally 1 66
(Keith Dalgleish) *chsd ldr to 3f out: rdn and one pce fr over 1f out* **5/1**

6-56 **5** 3 1/4 **Calypso Delegator (IRE)**[11] 2831 3-8-5 **55** CallumShepherd[(5)] 6 49
(Micky Hammond) *hld up: rdn and outpcd 3f out: rallied fnl f: no imp* **12/1**

0-40 **6** hd **My Valentino (IRE)**[19] 2576 3-9-1 **60** TomEaves 3 54
(Dianne Sayer) *slowly away: hld up: rdn and outpcd over 3f out: plugged on fnl f: no imp* **9/1**

0104 **7** 2 1/2 **Kelvin Hall**[13] 2766 3-9-4 **63** JoeFanning 8 52
(Mark Johnston) *hld up: effrt and hung rt 2f out: sn wknd* **7/1**

61-6 **8** 7 **Heaven Scent**[27] 2348 3-9-6 **65** PJMcDonald 2 52
(Ann Duffield) *hld up in tch: rdn over 3f out: wknd wl over 1f out* **11/1**

2m 29.71s (6.61) **Going Correction** +0.25s/f (Good) **8** Ran SP% **115.6**
Speed ratings (Par 99): **85,83,82,82,79 79,77,77**
CSF £18.66 CT £64.95 TOTE £5.20: £1.90, £1.10, £2.30; EX 20.80 Trifecta £125.10.
Owner Geoff & Sandra Turnbull **Bred** R F Broad **Trained** Middleham Moor, N Yorks

FOCUS
Rail movement added 14yds to race distance. A modest 3yo handicap to end with and the first four pulled clear.
T/Jkpt: Not won. T/Plt: £50.40 to a £1 stake. Pool: £70,714.78 - 1,024.09 winning tickets T/Qpdt: £17.40 to a £1 stake. Pool: £6,880.56 - 291.00 winning tickets **Richard Young**

3065 NOTTINGHAM (L-H)
Monday, June 13

OFFICIAL GOING: Soft (6.0)
Wind: almost nil Weather: light rain

3216 EURO 2016 BETTING AT 188BET NOVICE MEDIAN AUCTION STKS 5f 13y
6:40 (6:40) (Class 5) 2-Y-O **£3,067** (£905; £453) **Stalls** Centre

Form RPR

0 **1** **Private Matter**[20] 2552 2-9-2 0 TonyHamilton 5 85+
(Richard Fahey) *mde all: shkn up and wnt clr 1f out: v easily* **11/4**[2]

0 **2** 6 **Notalot (IRE)**[21] 2535 2-9-2 0 (v) WilliamTwiston-Davies 4 58
(Michael Bell) *chsd ldrs: drvn over 2f out: hung rt and 2nd 1f out: no ch w wnr* **3/1**[3]

3 2 **Cupid's Arrow (IRE)** 2-9-2 0 JamesSullivan 3 51
(Ruth Carr) *wnt lft s: t.k.h: sn w ldrs: edgd lft 2f out: one pce* **14/1**

4 2 **Geraldine (GER)** 2-8-11 0 SilvestreDeSousa 7 39
(Stuart Williams) *trckd ldrs: effrt over 2f out: wknd appr fnl f* **7/4**[1]

5 1 3/4 **Miss Florence** 2-8-8 0 TomMarquand[(3)] 1 32+
(David Barron) *carried lft s: sn w ldrs: drvn over 2f out: hung lft: wknd over 1f out* **7/1**

1m 3.58s (2.08) **Going Correction** +0.30s/f (Good) **5** Ran SP% **107.2**
Speed ratings (Par 93): **95,85,82,79,76**
CSF £10.61 TOTE £4.40: £1.30, £1.70; EX 10.30 Trifecta £70.90.
Owner Cheveley Park Stud **Bred** Cheveley Park Stud Ltd **Trained** Musley Bank, N Yorks

FOCUS
Outer track used. Rail set out 2yds on the home bend adding approximately 6yds to races 4, 5 and 6. Testing ground and they came across to race stands' side. There won't be many easier juvenile winners this season, but they looked ordinary in behind.

3217 £25 FREE BET AT 188BET "RESTRICTED" H'CAP 5f 13y
7:10 (7:11) (Class 5) (0-75,75) 4-Y-O+ **£2,835** (£848; £424; £212; £105) **Stalls** Centre

Form RPR

50-4 **1** **Rainbow Orse**[29] 2270 4-9-1 **69** (p) SilvestreDeSousa 5 79
(Robert Cowell) *w ldr: led over 2f out: edgd lft over 1f out: drvn out* **5/1**[2]

5652 **2** 1 1/4 **Oriental Splendour (IRE)**[7] 2975 4-8-12 **66** JamesSullivan 2 71
(Ruth Carr) *hld up in mid-div: effrt over 2f out: chsd wnr fnl f: styd on same pce* **8/1**

-204 **3** 1/2 **One Boy (IRE)**[27] 2346 5-9-7 **75** (p) TonyHamilton 3 78
(Richard Fahey) *trckd ldrs: drvn and hung rt over 1f out: kpt on same pce* **5/1**[2]

-003 **4** hd **Musharrif**[31] 2217 4-9-7 **75** StevieDonohoe 9 78+
(Declan Carroll) *in rr-div: kpt on wl fnl f* **7/1**[3]

0635 **5** 1/2 **Ambitious Icarus**[7] 2975 7-9-6 **74** (e) PatrickMathers 10 75
(Richard Guest) *dwlt: in rr: nt clr run on inner over 3f out: swtchd lft 2f out: chsng ldrs 1f out: kpt on same pce* **5/1**[2]

0-02 **6** hd **Beau Mistral (IRE)**[9] 2905 7-7-11 **58** RPWalsh[(7)] 4 58
(Tony Carroll) *led tl over 2f out: fdd fnl 150yds* **16/1**

45 **7** nk **Indian Tinker**[41] 1945 7-8-12 **66** (p) JimCrowley 6 65
(Robert Cowell) *gave problems in stalls: half rrd and slowly away: in rr: hdwy on outer over 2f out: chsng ldrs over 1f out: kpt on one pce* **9/2**[1]

600- **8** 1/2 **Storm Lightning**[248] 7082 7-9-2 **73** DanielMuscutt[(3)] 7 70
(Mark Brisbourne) *chsd ldrs: outpcd over 1f out: kpt on fnl 100yds* **33/1**

-060 **9** 2 **Bonjour Steve**[16] 2697 5-8-4 **61** (v[1]) TomMarquand[(3)] 1 51
(Richard Price) *chsd ldrs: wknd over 1f out* **8/1**

1m 2.47s (0.97) **Going Correction** +0.30s/f (Good) **9** Ran SP% **111.7**
Speed ratings (Par 103): **104,102,101,100,100 99,99,98,95**
CSF £42.41 CT £205.48 TOTE £5.00: £1.60, £2.40, £1.70; EX 43.80 Trifecta £97.20.
Owner G Johnson **Bred** D R Botterill **Trained** Six Mile Bottom, Cambs

FOCUS
Race distance as advertised. They again headed for the stands' rail and the winner, who was recording a personal best, was always up on the speed near to the rail.

3218 188BET.CO.UK FILLIES' H'CAP 6f 15y
7:40 (7:41) (Class 4) (0-85,78) 3-Y-O+ **£4,851** (£1,443; £721; £360) **Stalls** Centre

Form RPR

200 **1** **Emerald Loch**[19] 2578 3-8-4 **67** (p) PatrickO'Donnell[(5)] 6 79
(Ralph Beckett) *trckd ldrs: effrt over 2f out: led over 1f out: forged clr fnl 75yds* **6/1**

25-1 **2** 2 1/2 **Cersei**[46] 1814 3-9-5 **77** JimCrowley 5 81
(David Simcock) *dwlt: hld up in rr: swtchd lft over 2f out: w wnr over 1f out: styd on same pce last 100yds* **11/8**[1]

00-4 **3** 2 1/2 **Appleberry (IRE)**[14] 2737 4-9-13 **77** SilvestreDeSousa 7 75
(Michael Appleby) *trckd ldr: t.k.h: drvn over 2f out: one pce fnl f* **5/1**[3]

44-1 **4** 1 3/4 **Evangelical**[48] 1761 3-9-6 **78** TonyHamilton 3 68
(Richard Fahey) *half-rrd s: in rr: effrt over 2f out: chsng ldrs over 1f out: sn wknd* **11/4**[2]

520 **5** shd **Misu Moneypenny**[27] 2334 3-8-12 **70** JamesSullivan 2 60
(Scott Dixon) *led: hdd over 1f out: sn wknd* **14/1**

1m 16.75s (2.05) **Going Correction** +0.30s/f (Good)
WFA 3 from 4yo+ 8lb **5** Ran SP% **106.4**
Speed ratings (Par 102): **98,94,91,89,88**
CSF £13.83 TOTE £6.60: £2.30, £1.90; EX 16.70 Trifecta £55.00.
Owner J C Smith **Bred** Littleton Stud **Trained** Kimpton, Hants

FOCUS
Race distance as advertised. Fairly ordinary sprinting form, but an unexposed winner.

3219 188BET H'CAP 1m 2f 50y
8:10 (8:10) (Class 4) (0-85,81) 4-Y-O+ **£4,851** (£1,443; £721; £360) **Stalls** Low

Form RPR
-054 **1** **Kapstadt (FR)**[4] 3057 6-9-5 **79** FrannyNorton 3 91
(Ian Williams) *led: qcknd pce over 3f out: drvn over 2f out: rdn clr fnl f* **3/1**[2]

6601 **2** *7* **Best Tamayuz**[22] 2507 5-8-5 **65** JamesSullivan 5 64
(Scott Dixon) *trckd ldrs: t.k.h: effrt over 3f out: outpcd over 2f out: styd on and swtchd rt 75yds out: tk modest 2nd post* **8/1**

-112 **3** *nse* **Bakht A Rawan (IRE)**[16] 2688 4-9-3 **77** SilvestreDeSousa 4 76
(Stuart Kittow) *trckd ldrs: 2nd over 8f out: upsides over 3f out: sn drvn: fdd fnl f* **11/10**[1]

51-0 **4** *1 1/4* **Optima Petamus**[27] 2328 4-9-6 **80** TonyHamilton 1 76
(Patrick Holmes) *trckd ldrs: effrt over 3f out: edgd rt over 2f out: one pce* **9/1**

0-41 **5** *22* **Aldeburgh**[37] 2043 7-9-7 **81** WilliamTwiston-Davies 2 35
(Nigel Twiston-Davies) *hld up in last: effrt over 3f out: lost pl 2f out: sn bhd: heavily eased fnl f* **5/1**[3]

2m 19.8s (5.50) **Going Correction** +0.45s/f (Yiel) **5** Ran SP% **110.4**
Speed ratings (Par 105): **96,90,90,89,71**
CSF £24.34 TOTE £3.20: £2.20, £4.20; EX 20.90 Trifecta £49.50.
Owner Anchor Men **Bred** Charles Barel **Trained** Portway, Worcs

FOCUS
Race distance increased by 6yds. Run at a steady gallop, the winner made nearly all the running and came right away. Not form to put much faith in, though, given the ground.

3220 ROYAL ASCOT 10% REFUND AT 188BET H'CAP 1m 75y
8:40 (8:40) (Class 6) (0-65,65) 4-Y-O+ **£2,264** (£673; £336; £168) **Stalls** Centre

Form RPR
0-66 **1** **Mujazif (IRE)**[24] 2441 6-9-7 **65** (p) SilvestreDeSousa 8 77
(Michael Appleby) *mid-div: effrt 4f out: led 3f out: drvn clr over 1f out: eased clsng stages* **15/8**[1]

5040 **2** *3 1/2* **Sakhalin Star (IRE)**[20] 2555 5-9-7 **65** (e) FrannyNorton 10 68
(Richard Guest) *mid-div: hdwy on outer over 3f out: chsd wnr over 1f out: kpt on: no imp* **9/2**[2]

-400 **3** *1 3/4* **Stoneboat Bill**[20] 2555 4-9-6 **64** TonyHamilton 12 63
(Declan Carroll) *s.i.s: hld up in rr: hdwy 3f out: 3rd over 1f out: kpt on same pce* **8/1**[3]

-505 **4** *3 1/2* **Big Red**[17] 2666 4-7-9 **46** oh1 RPWalsh(7) 5 37
(Rebecca Bastiman) *rr-div: hdwy on outside over 3f out: modest 4th 1f out: one pce* **50/1**

-002 **5** *4* **British Embassy (IRE)**[11] 2810 4-9-7 **65** SamJames 14 47
(David Loughnane) *led to post: trckd ldrs on outer: upsides over 2f out: wknd appr fnl f* **14/1**

0-00 **6** *3/4* **Champagne Bob**[11] 2827 4-9-3 **64** TomMarquand(3) 3 44
(Richard Price) *s.i.s: rr-div: reminders and hdwy over 3f out: one pce fnl 2f* **16/1**

0054 **7** *3* **Bognor (USA)**[10] 2849 5-9-5 **63** (v) WilliamTwiston-Davies 4 36
(Michael Attwater) *drvn to chse ldrs: lost pl over 1f out* **20/1**

0541 **8** *3/4* **Adventureman**[17] 2661 4-9-3 **61** (p) JamesSullivan 6 32
(Ruth Carr) *led 1f: chsd ldrs: wknd over 1f out* **12/1**

-4 **9** *3* **Dolphin Rock**[43] 1884 9-8-12 **63** (b) CallumRodriguez(7) 1 27
(Richard Ford) *w ldr: led after 1f: hdd 3f out: edgd rt and wknd over 1f out* **8/1**[3]

0532 **10** *7* **Illusive Force (IRE)**[18] 2610 4-8-11 **55** (v) MartinLane 9
(Derek Shaw) *chsd ldrs: drvn over 3f out: lost pl 2f out: eased clsng stages* **20/1**

520- **11** *12* **Zain Time**[230] 7539 4-8-9 **53** StevieDonohoe 13
(Charlie Fellowes) *s.i.s: in rr: lost pl over 3f out: sn wl bhd* **10/1**

1m 52.03s (3.03) **Going Correction** +0.45s/f (Yiel) **11** Ran SP% **116.0**
Speed ratings (Par 101): **102,98,96,93,89 88,85,84,81,74 62**
CSF £9.19 CT £54.14 TOTE £2.30: £1.10, £2.10, £2.90; EX 11.20 Trifecta £53.50.
Owner The Horse Watchers **Bred** Wardstown Stud Ltd **Trained** Oakham, Rutland

FOCUS
Race distance increased by 6yds. A modest handicap, but they went a good gallop and it very much set up for the closers. There was another clear-cut winner, who was a mid-80s horse last year.

3221 ROYAL ASCOT EXTRA PLACES AT 188BET H'CAP 1m 6f 15y
9:10 (9:10) (Class 5) (0-75,75) 4-Y-O+ **£2,911** (£866; £432; £216) **Stalls** Low

Form RPR
353- **1** **Jack Bear**[210] 7871 5-8-10 **64** SilvestreDeSousa 9 77+
(Harry Whittington) *stdd s: t.k.h: sn trckd ldrs: effrt over 3f out: led over 2f out: forged clr over 1f out: eased clsng stages* **5/2**[2]

0/00 **2** *5* **Hier Encore (FR)**[26] 2370 4-7-9 **56** oh11 RPWalsh(7) 5 60
(David Menuisier) *hld up in rr: hdwy over 3f out: nt clr run on inner 2f out: wnt 2nd 1f out: no ch w wnr* **50/1**

5620 **3** *4 1/2* **Horseguardsparade**[24] 2445 5-8-9 **70** (p) KillianHennessy(7) 6 68
(Nigel Twiston-Davies) *rr-div: hdwy over 5f out: chsng ldrs and hung lft over 2f out: kpt on one pce to take modest 3rd last 100yds* **12/1**

/113 **4** *hd* **Minstrels Gallery (IRE)**[13] 2782 7-9-7 **75** JimCrowley 4 73
(Lucy Wadham) *led after 1f: hdd over 2f out: fdd fnl f* **11/4**[3]

1-10 **5** *1 1/2* **Maoi Chinn Tire (IRE)**[27] 2338 9-9-6 **74** TimmyMurphy 7 70
(Jennie Candlish) *hld up in rr: sme hdwy on outside over 3f out: hung lft: kpt on fnl 2f: nvr a factor* **8/1**

0130 **6** *5* **Topaling**[7] 2971 5-8-12 **66** StevieDonohoe 2 55
(Mark H Tompkins) *sn trcking ldrs: lost pl over 2f out* **25/1**

-631 **7** *6* **Nam Hai (IRE)**[22] 2501 5-9-4 **72** WilliamTwiston-Davies 1 54
(Kim Bailey) *led 1f: hld up in mid-div: hdwy 4f out: edgd lft and wknd over 1f out* **9/4**[1]

50-0 **8** *11* **Sakhra**[35] 2110 5-7-11 **56** oh11 NoelGarbutt(5) 10 23
(Mark Brisbourne) *chsd ldrs: drvn over 4f out: lost pl over 3f out: sn bhd* **33/1**

3m 17.46s (10.46) **Going Correction** +0.45s/f (Yiel) **8** Ran SP% **113.6**
Speed ratings (Par 103): **88,85,82,82,81 78,75,69**
CSF £116.70 CT £1263.69 TOTE £3.70: £1.90, £10.90, £4.50; EX 54.10 Trifecta £1171.30.
Owner Joe Bear Racing **Bred** S M Ransom **Trained** Sparsholt, Oxfordshire

FOCUS
Race distance increased by 6yds. A modest staying handicap won by what was clearly a very well-handicapped horse.
T/Plt: £121.40 to a £1 stake. Pool: £44,581.00 - 369.20 winning tickets T/Qpdt: £37.30 to a £1 stake. Pool: £3,373.00 - 90.20 winning tickets **Walter Glynn**

2254 THIRSK (L-H)
Monday, June 13

OFFICIAL GOING: Good to firm (good in places; 9.6) racing abandoned after race 3 (3.15) due to unsafe bend
Wind: Virtually nil Weather: Heavy grey cloud

3222 BEST ODDS GUARANTEED AT 188BET MAIDEN AUCTION STKS (DIV I) 6f
2:15 (2:17) (Class 5) 2-Y-O **£2,911** (£866; £432; £216) **Stalls** High

Form RPR
1 **Miss Sugars** 2-8-9 0 ow1 JamieSpencer 6 65+
(David Simcock) *towards rr: pushed along 2f out: hdwy over 1f out: rdn and styd on strly ins fnl f to ld last stride* **11/4**[1]

2 *shd* **Princeofthequeen (USA)** 2-9-1 0 SamJames 4 71
(David O'Meara) *trckd ldng pair: hdwy and cl up 1/2-way: rdn to ld over 1f out: drvn ins fnl f: hdd last stride* **9/1**

6 **3** *3/4* **Suitcase 'N' Taxi**[18] 2611 2-8-13 0 DavidAllan 9 67
(Tim Easterby) *cl up: effrt 2f out: sn chal and rdn over 1f out: ev ch ins fnl f: drvn and no ex towards fin* **5/1**[3]

6 **4** *1/2* **Vintage Dream (IRE)**[18] 2617 2-9-1 0 BarryMcHugh 8 67
(Noel Wilson) *led: pushed along 2f out: rdn and hdd over 1f out: kpt on same pce* **4/1**[2]

60 **5** *nk* **Miss Monro (IRE)**[21] 2536 2-8-8 0 BenCurtis 10 59
(Brian Ellison) *trckd ldrs: swtchd lft and hdwy 2f out: rdn and ch whn n.m.r appr fnl f: sn drvn and kpt on same pce* **20/1**

6 *4* **African Grey** 2-9-1 0 (b[1]) PhillipMakin 2 54+
(David Barron) *wnt lft s and in rr: hdwy on outer 1/2-way: chsd ldrs wl over 1f out: sn rdn: green and wandered: wknd fnl f* **4/1**[2]

05 **7** *2 1/2* **Belle's Angel (IRE)**[14] 2739 2-8-2 0 RowanScott(7) 5 41
(Ann Duffield) *chsd ldrs: pushed along 1/2-way: sn rdn along and outpcd fnl 2f* **13/2**

8 *1 3/4* **Sheepscar Lad (IRE)** 2-9-2 0 TonyHamilton 7 42
(Nigel Tinkler) *s.i.s: a in rr* **14/1**

1m 13.98s (1.28) **Going Correction** -0.10s/f (Good) **8** Ran SP% **118.1**
Speed ratings (Par 93): **87,86,85,85,84 79,76,73**
CSF £29.67 TOTE £3.50: £1.50, £2.40, £1.80; EX 25.10 Trifecta £105.40.
Owner Tick Tock Partnership **Bred** Chippenham Lodge Stud **Trained** Newmarket, Suffolk

FOCUS
Almost certainly just a run-of-the-mill maiden, but the winner deserves credit for getting up having run green/met trouble and has the potential to go on to better things.

3223 BEST ODDS GUARANTEED AT 188BET MAIDEN AUCTION STKS (DIV II) 6f
2:45 (2:48) (Class 5) 2-Y-O **£2,911** (£866; £432; £216) **Stalls** High

Form RPR
1 **Pellucid** 2-8-11 0 JamieSpencer 8 81+
(David Simcock) *t.k.h early: hld up: smooth hdwy over 2f out cl up over 1f out: qcknd and led on bit ent fnl f: readily* **9/4**[1]

35 **2** *2* **In First Place**[33] 2162 2-9-2 0 TonyHamilton 1 75
(Richard Fahey) *trckd ldrs: cl up 1/2-way: rdn and ev ch over 1f out: drvn and kpt on same pce fnl f* **5/2**[2]

6 **3** *2 1/4* **Mary Brady**[14] 2739 2-8-10 0 SamJames 6 62
(David O'Meara) *cl up: led 2f out: rdn over 1f out: hdd ent fnl f: sn one pce* **20/1**

53 **4** *2 1/2* **Trois Bon Amis (IRE)**[14] 2739 2-9-1 0 DavidAllan 10 60
(Tim Easterby) *led: pushed along and hdd 2f out: rdn over 1f out: sn wknd* **17/2**

55 **5** *1 3/4* **Nordic Combined (IRE)**[16] 2682 2-8-13 0 BenCurtis 2 53
(Brian Ellison) *in tch on outer: pushed along wl over 2f out: rdn wl over 1f out: sn one pce* **100/1**

432 **6** *1 1/4* **Jollydee (IRE)**[27] 2344 2-8-8 0 BarryMcHugh 7 44
(Paul Midgley) *trckd ldrs on inner: rdn along 2f out: grad wknd* **7/1**

0 **7** *1 1/4* **Kazanan (IRE)**[51] 1621 2-8-10 0 ConnorBeasley 5 42
(Michael Dods) *chsd ldrs: pushed along 1/2-way: sn rdn and outpcd fnl 2f* **22/1**

4 **8** *1 1/4* **Servo (IRE)**[28] 2301 2-9-0 0 DarryllHolland 9 42
(Alan Swinbank) *t.k.h: chsd ldrs: effrt over 2f out: sn rdn and wknd* **6/1**[3]

9 *1* **Royal Icon** 2-8-9 0 ShaneGray 4 34
(Kevin Ryan) *a towards rr* **25/1**

10 *1/2* **Pontecarlo Boy** 2-8-10 0 JacobButterfield(3) 3 37
(Richard Whitaker) *s.i.s: green and a in rr* **40/1**

1m 12.68s (-0.02) **Going Correction** -0.10s/f (Good) **10** Ran SP% **113.0**
Speed ratings (Par 93): **96,93,90,87,84 83,81,79,78,77**
CSF £7.16 TOTE £3.20: £1.50, £1.30, £4.90; EX 9.10 Trifecta £97.50.
Owner Mrs Julia Annable **Bred** El Catorce Partnership **Trained** Newmarket, Suffolk

FOCUS
A really taking performance from the impressive winner who looks a cut above the average maiden auction winner.

3224 £25 FREE BET AT 188BET H'CAP 1m
3:15 (3:19) (Class 5) (0-70,70) 3-Y-O **£3,557** (£1,058; £529; £264) **Stalls** Low

Form RPR
-034 **1** **Palmerston**[34] 2123 3-9-1 **67** AlistairRawlinson(3) 14 76
(Michael Appleby) *in tch: hdwy 1/2-way: trckd ldrs 3f out: led wl over 1f out: sn rdn and edgd lft: drvn ins fnl f: kpt on* **11/1**

06-3 **2** *1/2* **Fort Jefferson**[16] 2674 3-8-13 **62** DavidProbert 1 70+
(Andrew Balding) *hld up towards rr: hdwy 1/2-way: chsd ldrs over 1f out: rdn and styd on wl fnl f* **11/4**[1]

0-50 **3** *3/4* **Whitkirk**[10] 2864 3-8-4 **53** JoeyHaynes 2 59
(Jedd O'Keeffe) *hld up: hdwy 1/2-way: chsd ldrs whn swtchd rt over 1f out: sn rdn and ev ch on outer: drvn and kpt on same pce fnl f* **33/1**

55-4 **4** *1 1/2* **Pickett's Charge**[29] 2269 3-9-7 **70** BarryMcHugh 5 72+
(Tony Coyle) *hld up towards rr: hdwy over 2f out: n.m.r wl over 1f out: sn rdn and styd on wl fnl f: nrst fin* **14/1**

-333 **5** *3/4* **Mango Chutney**[20] 2553 3-8-11 **60** PhillipMakin 8 61
(John Davies) *hld up: hdwy 3f out: rdn along 2f out: styd on fnl f: nrst fin* **8/1**

00-0 **6** *shd* **A Boy Named Sue**[13] 2784 3-7-11 **51** oh6 NathanEvans(5) 15 51
(Peter Niven) *trckd ldng pair: pushed along over 2f out: rdn over 1f out: n.m.r and swtchd rt ent fnl f: sn drvn and kpt on same pce* **25/1**

64-3 **7** *hd* **Kirkham**[53] 1584 3-9-4 **67** .... ConnorBeasley 13 67
(Julie Camacho) *cl up: led over 3f out: rdn along over 2f out: hdd wl over 1f out and grad wknd* **15/2**[3]

4244 **8** *½* **Dark Command**[10] 2864 3-8-11 **60** .... (p) JamesSullivan 6 61+
(Michael Dods) *t.k.h early: trckd ldng pair on inner: effrt 2f out and sn rdn: drvn appr fnl f and sn one pce* **6/1**[2]

6-00 **9** *¾* **Quoteline Direct**[16] 2695 3-9-6 **69** .... JackGarritty 4 66
(Micky Hammond) *hld up towards rr: hdwy wl over 2f out: rdn over 1f out: swtchd rt ins fnl f: kpt on: nrst fin* **40/1**

5-56 **10** *1 ¾* **The Lynch Man**[21] 2533 3-9-5 **68** .... CamHardie 9 61
(John Quinn) *towards rr: hdwy over 2f out: rdn wl over 1f out: n.d* **25/1**

0-54 **11** *½* **Stormy Art (IRE)**[21] 2533 3-8-6 **60** .... PhilDennis(5) 3 51
(Michael Dods) *trckd ldrs: stmbld bdly bnd after 3f but hld position: effrt 2f out: sn pushed along and n.m.r: fdd fnl f* **20/1**

4304 **12** *nse* **Specialv (IRE)**[22] 2506 3-9-0 **63** .... (p) BenCurtis 10 61+
(Brian Ellison) *a towards rr* **12/1**

04-0 **13** *7* **Fastnet Prince (IRE)**[136] 376 3-9-1 **64** .... (t) DarryllHolland 12 39
(David Evans) *a towards rr* **10/1**

4-40 **14** *2 ¾* **Muroor**[21] 2532 3-9-7 **70** .... DavidNolan 11 38
(David O'Meara) *led: pushed along and hdd 3f out: sn rdn and wknd 2f out* **12/1**

00-0 **15** *18* **Shudbeme**[14] 2740 3-8-3 **52** oh6 ow1 .... (p) DuranFentiman 7
(Neville Bycroft) *a in rr: outpcd and bhd fr over 2f out* **100/1**

6340 **S** **Deben**[28] 2306 3-8-6 **55** .... (p) ShaneGray 16
(Kevin Ryan) *in rr whn slipped up on home turn* **25/1**

1m 39.43s (-0.67) **Going Correction** -0.10s/f (Good) **16** Ran SP% **126.0**
Speed ratings (Par 99): **99,98,97,96,95 95,95,94,93,92 91,91,84,81,63**
CSF £39.60 CT £1064.14 TOTE £13.60: £3.70, £1.10, £7.60, £3.80; EX 59.00 Trifecta £2392.60.

Owner Infinity Racing **Bred** Carwell Equities Ltd **Trained** Oakham, Rutland
■ Stewards' Enquiry : Jack Garritty three-day ban: careless riding (Jun 27-29)

FOCUS
A modest handicap, but the winner has the potential to go on from this now his stable has found the key to him, while the runner-up also shaped well. They went very steady around the turn, the jockeys clearly concerned about the surface, and the remainder of the meeting was abandoned after one slipped and unseated exiting the bend.

3225 188BET.CO.UK FILLIES' H'CAP 1m 4f
() (Class 5) (0-70,) 3-Y-O+ £

3226 DOUG HALL 70TH BIRTHDAY H'CAP 6f
() (Class 6) (0-65,) 3-Y-O £

3227 ROYAL ASCOT 10% REFUND AT 188BET MAIDEN FILLIES' STKS 1m
() (Class 5) 3-Y-O+ £

3228 188BET H'CAP 1m 4f
() (Class 6) (0-65,) 4-Y-O+ £

3229 ROYAL ASCOT EXTRA PLACES AT 188BET H'CAP 7f
() (Class 5) (0-75,) 3-Y-O £

T/Plt: £3.90 to a £1 stake. Pool: £63,593.19 - 11,872.58 winning tickets T/Qpdt: £1.90 to a £1 stake. Pool: £5,290.59 - 1,996.74 winning tickets **Joe Rowntree**

2976 WINDSOR (R-H)
Monday, June 13

OFFICIAL GOING: Good to soft (good in places) changing to soft after race 2 (6.20)
Wind: Light, behind Weather: Overcast becoming bright

3230 DAILY PRICE BOOSTS AT LADBROKES APPRENTICE H'CAP 1m 3f 135y
5:50 (5:51) (Class 6) (0-65,64) 4-Y-O+ £2,264 (£673; £336; £168) **Stalls** Centre

Form RPR

14-0 **1** **Merry Dancer (IRE)**[31] 2210 4-9-3 **58** .... MitchGodwin(3) 6 65
(Patrick Chamings) *pressed ldr: lft in ld over 5f out to 4f out: drvn over 2f out: chal over 1f out: kpt on to ld last 75yds* **9/2**[3]

0165 **2** *nk* **Turnbury**[16] 1747 5-9-8 **60** .... (p) MeganNicholls 11 67
(Nikki Evans) *led: hung lft bnd over 5f out and hdd: regained ld 4f out: hrd pressed fr 2f out: kpt on wl but hdd last 75yds* **14/1**

3313 **3** *½* **Tommys Geal**[28] 2292 4-9-8 **63** .... GeorgeWood(3) 5 69
(Michael Madgwick) *in tch: rdn wl over 2f out: clsd to chal jst over 1f out: kpt on but a jst hld* **5/1**

-04R **4** *2 ¼* **Dalmarella Dancer (IRE)**[10] 2860 5-9-7 **64** .... CliffordLee(5) 4 67
(K R Burke) *rel to r and much tail swishing early: sn in tch: prog on wd outside 3f out: on terms 2f out: nt qckn over 1f out: fdd* **15/2**

5621 **5** *2 ½* **Pink Ribbon (IRE)**[10] 2872 4-9-12 **64** .... (p) GeorgiaCox 3 63
(Sylvester Kirk) *chsd ldrs: rdn over 3f out: tried to cl fr 2f out: wknd fnl f* **4/1**[2]

0000 **6** *1* **Rail Dancer**[73] 1173 4-9-8 **60** .... DavidParkes 1 57
(Richard Rowe) *in tch in rr: rdn 4f out: styd alone against nr side rail fr 3f out: nvr on terms w ldrs after* **7/2**[1]

1144 **7** *3 ½* **Celtic Ava (IRE)**[11] 2814 4-9-8 **60** .... PaddyBradley 7 51
(Pat Phelan) *hld up in midfield: clsd on ldrs on outer 3f out gng wl: shkn up and nt qckn 2f out: lost pl over 1f out and then short of room: wknd* **7/1**

33-P **8** *29* **Duc De Seville (IRE)**[14] 1047 4-9-4 **56** .... (b) AnnaHesketh 2
(Michael Chapman) *dwlt: pushed along after 2f: nvr gng wl: wknd over 4f out: t.o* **33/1**

0306 **F** **Machiavelian Storm (IRE)**[27] 2326 4-8-7 **45** .... LuluStanford 9
(Richard Mitchell) *trckd ldng pair: lft in 2nd pl over 5f out to 4f out: rdn and sing to lost pl whn stmbld and fell 2f out* **20/1**

2m 35.3s (5.80) **Going Correction** +0.55s/f (Yiel) **9** Ran SP% **115.7**
Speed ratings (Par 101): **102,101,101,99,98 97,95,75,**
CSF £64.85 CT £327.22 TOTE £5.50: £2.20, £3.60, £2.20; EX 74.80 Trifecta £422.70.
Owner Caroline Ellis And Matthew Hunt **Bred** Heather Raw **Trained** Baughurst, Hants
■ Stewards' Enquiry : Mitch Godwin four-day ban: used whip above permitted level (Jun 27-30)

FOCUS
The inner running rail had been moved for this meeting to provide completely fresh ground. Inner of straight at normal inner configuration, making straight maximum width. Top bend dolled out 3yds from normal inner configuration, adding 10yds to race distances of 1m-plus. It was a damp day and the turf was cutting up in this opening handicap for apprentice riders. The main action developed away from the stands' rail.

3231 LADBROKES EBF STALLIONS NOVICE STKS 5f 10y
6:20 (6:21) (Class 5) 2-Y-O £3,234 (£962; £481; £240) **Stalls** Low

Form RPR

333 **1** **El Torito (IRE)**[19] 2583 2-9-2 0 .... SamHitchcott 5 77
(Jim Boyle) *pushed along early: in tch: prog to chse ldr wl over 1f out: drvn to ld last 150yds: styd on wl* **9/4**[2]

03 **2** *1 ½* **Compton Lane**[32] 2180 2-9-2 0 .... FrederikTylicki 2 72
(Rod Millman) *led against nr side rail: rdn over 1f out: hdd and one pce last 150yds* **7/4**[1]

56 **3** *4 ½* **George Ravenscar**[19] 2583 2-9-2 0 .... HarryBentley 1 55
(Ed Vaughan) *cl up: disp 2nd briefly wl over 1f out: lft bhd by ldng pair u.p jst over 1f out* **8/1**

4 *¾* **Sheila's Palace** 2-8-11 0 .... JohnFahy 6 48
(J S Moore) *s.i.s: in tch in last pair: pushed along and sme prog over 1f out: rdn and kpt on fnl f: n.d* **20/1**

0 **5** *1 ¾* **Hi There Silver (IRE)**[19] 2583 2-9-2 0 .... LiamKeniry 7 46
(Michael Madgwick) *chsd ldr to wl over 1f out: wknd* **66/1**

6 *1 ¾* **Jashma (IRE)** 2-9-2 0 .... ShaneKelly 8 40
(Richard Hughes) *s.i.s: sn trckd ldrs: shkn up 2f out: rdn and wknd over 1f out* **7/2**[3]

00 **7** *3 ¼* **Silver Asset (IRE)**[21] 2543 2-9-2 0 .... RobertHavlin 3 28
(Michael Wigham) *hld up in last pair: rdn and wknd on outer wl over 1f out* **40/1**

1m 2.19s (1.89) **Going Correction** +0.325s/f (Good) **7** Ran SP% **109.2**
Speed ratings (Par 93): **97,94,87,86,83 80,75**
CSF £5.90 TOTE £2.80: £1.80, £1.40; EX 6.40 Trifecta £18.80.
Owner The 'In Recovery' Partnership **Bred** Mary F Fogarty **Trained** Epsom, Surrey

FOCUS
The two market leaders dominated the finish of this modest novice event.

3232 DOWNLOAD THE LADBROKES APP (S) STKS 6f
6:50 (6:52) (Class 5) 2-Y-O £2,911 (£866; £432; £216) **Stalls** Low

Form RPR

460 **1** **Mesmeric Moment**[12] 2793 2-8-6 0 .... SamHitchcott 1 57
(David Evans) *racd against nr side rail: mde all: rdn over 1f out: kpt on wl fnl f* **5/1**[3]

0 **2** *¾* **Born To Please**[14] 2747 2-8-6 0 .... KieranO'Neill 7 55
(Mark Usher) *in tch in rr: shkn up over 2f out: stl only 7th and u.p over 1f out: r.o fnl f: fin wl to take 2nd nr fin* **25/1**

2013 **3** *nk* **Billy's Boots**[3] 3114 2-9-2 0 .... GeorgeBaker 2 64
(Mick Channon) *pressed wnr: rdn wl over 1f out: stl chalng fnl f: no ex last 100yds and lost 2nd nr fin* **7/4**[1]

405 **4** *¾* **Cosmic Beau (IRE)**[14] 2732 2-8-11 0 .... (t) RichardKingscote 6 57
(Tom Dascombe) *fractious bef s: settled in rr: rdn and prog jst over 2f out: chsd ldng pair over 1f out and cl enough: nt qckn fnl f and lost 3rd nr fin* **7/2**[2]

26 **5** *5* **Trust The Indian**[8] 2933 2-8-8 0 .... (p) TimClark(3) 3 42
(Bill Turner) *trckd ldrs: cl 3rd over 2f out: sn rdn: wknd over 1f out* **22/1**

004 **6** *1 ½* **Patrouille De Nuit (IRE)**[8] 2933 2-8-11 0 .... LiamKeniry 8 37
(J S Moore) *wl in tch: disp 3rd over 2f out: sn rdn: wknd over 1f out* **12/1**

4660 **7** *1 ¼* **Hot N Sassy (IRE)**[15] 2724 2-8-3 0 .... DannyBrock(3) 5 28
(J S Moore) *in tch: effrt on outer 1/2-way: wknd over 1f out* **16/1**

8 *8* **Luduamf (IRE)** 2-8-11 0 .... SeanLevey 4 9
(Richard Hannon) *s.i.s and rn green: in tch in last to over 2f out: wknd* **5/1**[3]

0 **9** *49* **Compton's Gee Wiz (IRE)**[19] 2583 2-8-6 0 .... MartinDwyer 9
(Brett Johnson) *pressed ldng pair to 1/2-way: wknd rapidly: t.o* **66/1**

1m 15.57s (2.57) **Going Correction** +0.325s/f (Good) **9** Ran SP% **115.2**
Speed ratings (Par 93): **95,94,93,92,85 83,82,71,6**
CSF £118.51 TOTE £5.50: £2.10, £4.40, £1.10; EX 115.70 Trifecta £504.80.There was no bid for the winner. Billy's Boots Mr A. S. Reid £8,000. Born To Please Mr M. D. I. Usher was subject a Friendly claim of £8,000.
Owner Mark Benton **Bred** M J Benton **Trained** Pandy, Monmouths

FOCUS
A typically moderate 2yo seller rated around the third.

3233 BET IN PLAY WITH LADBROKES H'CAP 6f
7:20 (7:21) (Class 4) (0-85,83) 4-Y-O+ £4,690 (£1,395; £697; £348) **Stalls** Low

Form RPR

-305 **1** **Links Drive Lady**[10] 2875 8-9-4 **83** .... JackDuern(3) 7 91
(Dean Ivory) *dwlt: towards rr: prog over 2f out: chsd ldr over 1f out: styd on to ld ins fnl f: rdn out* **9/2**[3]

16-2 **2** *1* **Joe Packet**[23] 2469 9-9-0 **76** .... RyanClark 1 81
(Jonathan Portman) *w ldr: led against nr side rail over 2f out: def advantage over 1f out: hdd and no ex ins fnl f* **8/1**

2326 **3** *nk* **Upstaging**[14] 2754 4-9-1 **77** .... (p) MartinHarley 12 81
(Paul Cole) *in tch: prog over 2f out: rdn to take 3rd over 1f out: styd on but nvr quite able to chal* **5/2**[1]

5140 **4** *1 ½* **Fingal's Cave (IRE)**[23] 2476 4-9-6 **82** .... GeorgeBaker 9 81
(Mick Channon) *settled in last pair: shkn up over 2f out: rdn and no prog tl r.o to take 4th ins fnl f: clsd on ldrs but too late to threaten* **3/1**[2]

0-50 **5** *6* **Sydney Ruffdiamond**[14] 2754 4-9-6 **82** .... (p) ShaneKelly 5 62
(Richard Hughes) *trckd ldrs: cl 4th and rdn jst over 2f out: wknd over 1f out* **8/1**

14-0 **6** *1* **Captain Marmalade (IRE)**[19] 2579 4-8-8 **70** .... KieranO'Neill 11 47
(Jimmy Fox) *stdd s: hld up in last: pushed along over 2f out: reminder over 1f out: modest prog and nvr involved* **25/1**

0524 **7** *3 ½* **Long Awaited (IRE)**[8] 2931 8-9-5 **81** .... (b) LiamKeniry 6 46
(Conor Dore) *mde most to over 2f out: edgd lft and wknd* **14/1**

-300 **8** *7* **Invincible Diamond (IRE)**[49] 1724 4-8-12 **77** .... DannyBrock(3) 2 20
(J S Moore) *w ldrs to 1/2-way: lost pl rapidly* **20/1**

4264 **9** *5* **Burning Thread (IRE)**[73] 1175 9-9-0 **83** .... (b) AdamMcLean(7) 8 10
(David Elsworth) *w ldrs on outer to over 2f out: wknd qckly over 1f out* **25/1**

1m 14.04s (1.04) **Going Correction** +0.325s/f (Good) **9** Ran SP% **113.1**
Speed ratings (Par 105): **106,104,104,102,94 92,88,78,72**
CSF £37.83 CT £107.65 TOTE £5.60: £1.80, £2.90, £1.30; EX 41.70 Trifecta £163.10.
Owner Cynthia Smith & Radlett Racing **Bred** Peter Webb **Trained** Radlett, Herts

FOCUS
A fair sprint handicap in which the principals were nicely clear at the finish. The winner has a good record here and the placed horses give it a straightforward look.

3234 CASH OUT AVAILABLE AT LADBROKES H'CAP 1m 67y
7:50 (7:51) (Class 4) (0-80,80) 4-Y-O+ **£4,690** (£1,395; £697; £348) **Stalls** Low

Form RPR

055 **1** **Harlequin Striker (IRE)**[24] 2430 4-9-5 **78** RobertWinston 3 88
(Dean Ivory) *trckd ldng pair: wnt 2nd 3f out: rdn 2f out: led 1f out: drvn out and kpt on wl* **10/1**

-054 **2** 1¼ **Shifting Star (IRE)**[47] 1780 11-8-8 **67** (vt) WilliamCarson 12 74
(John Bridger) *led: racd against nr side rail in st: rdn 2f out: hdd 1f out: kpt on but hld after* **22/1**

3-52 **3** ¾ **The Salmon Man**[21] 2540 4-8-13 **72** FMBerry 2 77
(Brendan Powell) *in tch in midfield: pushed along over 3f out: rdn and prog to take 3rd over 1f out: clsd on ldng pair fnl f: one pce last 100yds* **11/4**[2]

-232 **4** ¾ **Ttainted Love**[14] 2734 4-9-5 **78** (p) TedDurcan 4 82
(Chris Wall) *hld up in midfield: gng bttr than many over 2f out: nt clr run briefly wl over 1f out: shkn up and styd on to take 4th ins fnl f: nrst fin* **10/3**[3]

-000 **5** 1½ **Popeswood (IRE)**[19] 2587 4-9-6 **79** RichardKingscote 8 79
(Ron Hodges) *s.i.s: hld up in last trio: pushed along over 2f out: sme prog over 1f out and rdn: kpt on but nvr able to threaten* **25/1**

1-23 **6** 2 **Mezzotint (IRE)**[41] 1946 7-9-5 **78** OisinMurphy 10 74
(Lee Carter) *hld up in last trio: pushed along 2f out: sme prog nr side fnl f and shkn up: nvr involved* **12/1**

0602 **7** 2¼ **Live Dangerously**[11] 2827 6-8-10 **69** LiamJones 9 59
(John Bridger) *sltly awkward s: plld hrd and sn chsd ldng trio: lost pl and rdn 2f out: wknd* **20/1**

45 **8** 3¾ **Bunbury**[42] 1931 4-9-1 **74** ShaneKelly 5 56
(Richard Hughes) *hld up: prog on wd outside to trck ldrs 3f out: drvn 2f out: sn wknd* **2/1**[1]

02-0 **9** 1¾ **Yamlik**[11] 2819 4-9-7 **80** FrederikTylicki 6 58
(Brian Barr) *chsd ldr to 3f out: sn lost pl u.p* **25/1**

05-0 **10** 2½ **Synodic (USA)**[19] 2579 4-8-11 **70** JackMitchell 7 42
(Seamus Durack) *stdd s: hld up in last: pushed along 4f out: no prog and sn btn* **100/1**

1m 44.72s (0.02) **Going Correction** +0.15s/f (Good) **10** Ran SP% **117.7**
Speed ratings (Par 105): **105,103,103,102,100 98,96,92,91,88**
CSF £205.11 CT £788.71 TOTE £10.30: £2.80, £5.50, £1.70; EX 208.50 Trifecta £1718.30.
Owner Harlequin Direct Ltd **Bred** John Doyle **Trained** Radlett, Herts

FOCUS
Race distance inceased by 10yds. A modest handicap where racing handily proved an advantage.

3235 TRACK YOUR FOOTBALL ACCA WITH LADBROKES MAIDEN STKS 1m 2f 7y
8:20 (8:24) (Class 5) 3-Y-O+ **£2,911** (£866; £432; £216) **Stalls** Centre

Form RPR

3-22 **1** **Rex Bell (IRE)**[49] 1715 3-9-1 80 (p) RobertHavlin 14 84
(John Gosden) *mde all: racd against nrside rail st: clr 2f out: comf* **11/4**[1]

2 3 **Endless Acres (IRE)** 3-9-1 0 ShaneKelly 7 78
(Charlie Fellowes) *in tch in midfield: rdn 3f out: prog to take 2nd 1f out: no ch w wnr* **50/1**

30 **3** 1¼ **Pointel (FR)**[31] 2208 3-9-1 0 FrederikTylicki 9 76
(James Fanshawe) *prom: rdn over 2f out: kpt on same pce* **4/1**[2]

56- **4** nk **Maroc**[234] 7442 3-9-1 0 MartinHarley 1 75
(Paul Cole) *chsd wnr: rdn over 2f out: lost 2f and one pce fnl f* **33/1**

0- **5** 1½ **The Otmoor Poet**[191] 8123 3-9-1 0 FergusSweeney 11 72
(Alan King) *towards rr: pushed along over 3f out: prog 2f out: kpt on same pce* **100/1**

6 1¼ **Divine Quickstep (IRE)** 3-8-10 0 TedDurcan 12 64
(Sir Michael Stoute) *hld up: prog 1/2-way: shkn up and outpcd over 2f out: kpt on* **14/1**

7 1¾ **Fashion Design (IRE)** 3-8-10 0 RichardKingscote 5 61+
(Sir Michael Stoute) *rn green in rr: struggling 4f out: kpt on* **16/1**

0-5 **7** dht **Sir Pass I Am**[21] 2541 3-8-10 0 EdwardGreatrex(5) 15 66
(Andrew Balding) *hmpd in rr after 3f: pushed along over 3f out: styd on fr over 1f out* **16/1**

9 shd **Ex Lover** 3-9-1 0 AndreaAtzeni 4 69+
(Roger Varian) *dwlt: sn prom: rdn 3f out: wl hld whn bmpd over 1f out* **11/4**[1]

10 ¾ **Tam O'Shanter (IRE)** 3-9-1 0 JamesDoyle 3 69+
(Charlie Appleby) *prom: disp 2nd pl over 3f out to 2f: hld whn bmpd over 1f out* **13/2**[3]

65- **11** 1½ **Rubensian**[226] 7638 3-9-1 0 SaleemGolam 2 61
(David Simcock) *hld up in last pair: shkn up and no prog over 2f out* **25/1**

12 1¼ **Contingency** 3-8-10 0 JackMitchell 10 54
(Stuart Williams) *hld up in last pair: pushed along and no prog over 2f out* **80/1**

13 10 **Falak (IRE)** 3-9-1 0 HarryBentley 8 39
(Roger Varian) *rn green in rr: wd bnd 5f out: t.o* **17/2**

0 **14** 7 **Ravens Heart (IRE)**[42] 1930 4-10-0 0 RenatoSouza 6 26
(Dean Ivory) *lost midfield pl 1/2-way: sn bhd t.o* **66/1**

2m 13.04s (4.34) **Going Correction** +0.55s/f (Yiel) **14** Ran SP% **128.1**
WFA 3 from 4yo 13lb
Speed ratings (Par 103): **104,101,100,100,99 98,96,96,96,96 94,93,85,80**
CSF £179.89 TOTE £3.70: £1.40, £11.20, £2.80; EX 207.20 Trifecta £1421.90.
Owner Lady Bamford **Bred** Lady Bamford **Trained** Newmarket, Suffolk
■ Skadi was withdrawn. Price at time of withdrawal 150-1 Rule 4 does not apply.

FOCUS
Race distance inceased by 10yds. The all-the-way winner had the run of the race.

3236 BEST ODDS GUARANTEED AT LADBROKES H'CAP 1m 2f 7y
8:50 (8:51) (Class 5) (0-70,70) 3-Y-O **£2,911** (£866; £432; £216) **Stalls** Centre

Form RPR

0-42 **1** **Athlon (IRE)**[17] 2639 3-9-3 **66** GeorgeBaker 10 78
(David Lanigan) *trckd ldrs: wnt 2nd over 2f out: led over 1f out: hrd pressed fnl f: jst hld on* **3/1**[1]

-300 **2** hd **Sporty Yankee (USA)**[19] 2576 3-8-5 **61** CliffordLee(7) 14 72
(K R Burke) *towards rr: prog over 2f out: chsd wnr over 1f out: str chal fnl f: jst hld* **14/1**

2641 **3** 7 **Betsalottie**[27] 2325 3-8-13 **62** WilliamCarson 2 63
(John Bridger) *led: rdn and hdd over 1f out: heavily eased last 75yds* **10/1**

40-4 **4** 3¾ **Hardington**[21] 2545 3-9-7 **70** FergusSweeney 15 60
(Alan King) *hld up: prog to chse ldrs 3f out: fdd over 1f out* **4/1**[2]

-423 **5** 1¾ **Perfect Quest**[12] 2795 3-9-1 **64** RyanTate 9 50
(Clive Cox) *lost pl and struggling in rr 1/2-way: renewed effrt over 2f out: n.d over 1f out* **15/2**[3]

-663 **6** ¾ **The King's Steed**[22] 2506 3-9-5 **68** FMBerry 11 53
(Ralph Beckett) *t.k.h: prom tl wknd 2f out* **4/1**[2]

-300 **7** 1¼ **Master Of Heaven**[14] 2749 3-9-0 **63** (t) JackMitchell 13 45
(Jim Boyle) *dwlt: detached in last tl 1/2-way: effrt on outer 3f out: sn btn* **25/1**

50-5 **8** 4 **Pretty Jewel**[33] 2152 3-9-0 **63** AndreaAtzeni 3 37
(James Tate) *a towards rr: struggling over 3f out* **14/1**

2-66 **9** 6 **Ede's The Mover**[74] 1163 3-8-6 **62** SophieRalston(7) 7 24
(Pat Phelan) *lost pl 1/2-way: bhd over 2f out* **33/1**

40-6 **10** ½ **Compton Lady (IRE)**[49] 1703 3-8-10 **62** (p) ThomasBrown(3) 12 23
(Ismail Mohammed) *chsd ldr to over 2f out: wknd rapidly* **25/1**

036 **11** 8 **Swiftee (IRE)**[24] 2443 3-9-7 **70** FrederikTylicki 1 15
(Ed Dunlop) *chsd ldr tl wknd rapidly over 2f out* **8/1**

2m 11.76s (3.06) **Going Correction** +0.55s/f (Yiel) **11** Ran SP% **120.9**
Speed ratings (Par 99): **109,108,103,100,98 98,97,94,89,88 82**
CSF £47.99 CT £385.87 TOTE £4.30: £1.50, £4.40, £2.70; EX 53.90 Trifecta £459.00.
Owner The Athlon Partnership **Bred** Thomas Maher **Trained** Newmarket, Suffolk

FOCUS
Race distance inceased by 10yds. A modest 3yo handicap, run at a routine pace, though the time compared favourably with the previous maiden.
T/Plt: £89.90 to a £1 stake. Pool: £89,627.62 - 727.33 winning tickets T/Qpdt: £24.00 to a £1 stake. Pool: £8,523.33 - 262.19 winning tickets **Jonathan Neesom**

3237 - 3241a (Foreign Racing) - See Raceform Interactive

2023 ASCOT (R-H)
Tuesday, June 14

OFFICIAL GOING: Soft (stands' side 6.7, centre 6.5, far side 6.7, round 6.1)
Wind: light, half against Weather: showers drying up but staying cloudy

3242 QUEEN ANNE STKS (BRITISH CHAMPIONS SERIES) (GROUP 1) 1m (S)
2:30 (2:37) (Class 1) 4-Y-O+
£340,260 (£129,000; £64,560; £32,160; £16,140; £8,100) **Stalls** Centre

Form RPR

211- **1** **Tepin (USA)**[38] 5-8-11 121 (t) JulienRLeparoux 12 120
(Mark Casse, Canada) *lengthy: lw: a.p: effrt over 2f out: rdn to ld over 1f out: edgd rt ins fnl f: kpt on wl and a doing enough towards fin* **11/2**[2]

-141 **2** ½ **Belardo (IRE)**[31] 2243 4-9-0 119 JamesDoyle 2 122
(Roger Varian) *hld up: hdwy over 2f out: 2nd and chalng over 1f out: r.o for press ins fnl f: a hld* **9/2**[1]

430- **3** 1¼ **Lightning Spear**[241] 7281 5-9-0 115 OisinMurphy 13 119
(David Simcock) *hld up: hdwy 2f out: rdn over 1f out: chsd ldrs ins fnl f: r.o towards fin but nt pce of front two* **20/1**

0-15 **4** ¾ **Toormore (IRE)**[31] 2243 5-9-0 119 WilliamBuick 14 117
(Richard Hannon) *midfield: hdwy 2f out: styd on ins fnl f and lugged rt: nt pce to get to ldrs* **12/1**

21-2 **5** 1¾ **Ervedya (FR)**[44] 1910 4-8-11 115 ChristopheSoumillon 9 110
(J-C Rouget, France) *hld up: hdwy over 2f out: rdn over 1f out: no imp tl styd on nr fin: nt get to ldrs* **9/2**[1]

10-3 **6** shd **Amazing Maria (IRE)**[44] 1886 5-8-11 117 OlivierPeslier 7 110
(David O'Meara) *chsd ldrs: rdn over 2f out: nt qckn ins fnl f: styd on same pce u.p fnl 100yds* **20/1**

10-0 **7** ½ **Kodi Bear (IRE)**[31] 2243 4-9-0 116 AdamKirby 3 112
(Clive Cox) *chsd clr ldr: rdn to ld over 2f out: hdd over 1f out: no ex fnl 100yds* **9/1**

0-02 **8** 2¾ **Cougar Mountain (IRE)**[37] 2067 5-9-0 113 (tp) RyanMoore 6 106
(A P O'Brien, Ire) *hld up in rr: rdn and hdwy over 1f out: kpt on ins fnl f: no imp* **20/1**

22-3 **9** 1 **Endless Drama (IRE)**[31] 2243 4-9-0 116 ColinKeane 10 103
(G M Lyons, Ire) *lw: chsd ldrs: rdn over 2f out: hung rt and nt qckn over 1f out: one pce and btn fnl f* **11/2**[2]

10 3 **A Shin Erwin (IRE)**[20] 2603 5-9-0 102 CristianDemuro 11 96
(Hidemasa Nakao, Japan) *str: s.i.s: in rr: pushed along 3f out: plugged on fnl f: nvr a threat* **66/1**

20-0 **11** nk **Mondialiste (IRE)**[21] 2568 6-9-0 118 PatSmullen 8 96
(David O'Meara) *swtg: racd keenly: in tch: rdn over 2f out: sn wknd* **25/1**

3-00 **12** 13 **Barchan (USA)**[31] 2243 4-9-0 80 JackMitchell 4 66
(Roger Varian) *led: clr after 2f: rdn and stl 6 l clr 3f out: hdd over 2f out: wknd over 1f out* **200/1**

04-2 **13** 1 **Esoterique (IRE)**[10] 2927 6-8-11 119 Pierre-CharlesBoudot 1 61
(A Fabre, France) *midfield: rdn over 2f out: wknd over 1f out: eased whn wl btn ins fnl f* **7/1**[3]

1m 43.98s (3.18) **Going Correction** +0.625s/f (Yiel) **13** Ran SP% **117.4**
Speed ratings (Par 117): **109,108,107,106,104 104,104,101,100,97 97,84,83**
CSF £27.32 CT £480.04 TOTE £4.40: £1.90, £2.10, £6.10; EX 24.80 Trifecta £752.70.
Owner Robert E Masterson **Bred** Machmer Hall **Trained** North America
■ The first winner in Britain for both Mark Casse and Julien Leparoux.

FOCUS
A wretched run of weather in the week leading up to this year's meeting, including a deluge of half a month's expected rainfall in one evening last Friday, meant it was soft all over on the opening day for the first time since 1971. There was a further 4mm overnight and plenty arrived in the lead up to the Queen Anne. James Doyle, aboard the runner-up, said afterwards "it's soft, but they are getting through it." The running rail on the round course was positioned approx 6yds out from the 1m4f start, decreasing to 3yds out about 9f out to the home straight. This was the most open-looking edition of this Group 1 mile contest for some time. They shunned either rail, but congregated more towards the far side and there was a solid pace on courtesy of Godolphin's pacemaker Barchan. The form looks strong rated around the runner-up, although the going played a big part.

3243 COVENTRY STKS (GROUP 2) 6f
3:05 (3:10) (Class 1) 2-Y-O
£85,065 (£32,250; £16,140; £8,040; £4,035; £2,025) **Stalls** Centre

Form RPR

1 **1** **Caravaggio (USA)**[24] 2494 2-9-1 0 RyanMoore 13 115+
(A P O'Brien, Ire) *racd in centre: hld up towards rr: hdwy and swtchd rt ent fnl 2f: chsd ldr and rdn over 1f out: drifting rt but str run to ld jst ins fnl f: r.o strly and drew clr: impressive: 1st of 9 in gp* **13/8**[1]

112 **2** 2¼ **Mehmas (IRE)**[19] 2624 2-9-1 0 FrankieDettori 1 107
(Richard Hannon) *lw: racd far side: chsd ldrs: wnt 2nd overall and travelling wl over 2f out: rdn to ld over 1f out: hdd jst ins fnl f: outpcd by wnr but styd on for clr 2nd: 1st of 9 in gp* **8/1**[3]

3 2 1/2 **Psychedelic Funk**[34] 2165 2-9-1 0 .... ColinKeane 8 100
(G M Lyons, Ire) *str: lw: racd far side: chsd ldrs: effrt 2f out: chsd ldrs and drvn over 1f out: 3rd and outpcd ent fnl f: wl hld by ldng pair but hld on gamely for 3rd ins fnl f: 2nd of 9 in gp* **9/2**[2]

1 4 hd **Medieval (IRE)**[32] 2203 2-9-1 0 .... JamieSpencer 2 99
(Paul Cole) *w'like: str: racd far side: s.i.s: bhd: pushed along after 2f: hdwy u.p and swtchd lft over 1f out: styd on and battling for 3rd ins fnl f: no threat to ldng pair: 3rd of 9 in gp* **25/1**

5 shd **Van Der Decken**[23] 2508 2-9-1 0 .... WayneLordan 6 99
(P Twomey, Ire) *cmpt: lw: racd far side: in tch in midfield: effrt 2f out: hdwy over 1f out: wnt 4th 1f out: styd on and battling for 3rd ins fnl f: no threat to ldng pair: 4th of 9 in gp* **16/1**

1 6 3 1/2 **Thunder Snow (IRE)**[14] 2756 2-9-1 0 .... JamesDoyle 9 88
(Saeed bin Suroor) *gd sort; athletic; lw: racd in centre: swtchd lft after s: hld up towards rr: hdwy into midfield after 2f: rdn and hdwy to ld gp jst over 2f out and chsd ldrs overall: 5th and outpcd over 1f out: wknd ins fnl f: 2nd of 9 in gp* **12/1**

2311 7 4 **Monks Stand (USA)**[18] 2641 2-9-1 0 ....(p) JimCrowley 12 76
(Jeremy Noseda) *str: racd in centre: midfield overall: effrt u.p over 2f out: no imp and btn over 1f out: wknd fnl f: 3rd of 9 in gp* **66/1**

11 8 1/2 **Yalta (IRE)**[18] 2664 2-9-1 0 .... WilliamBuick 4 75
(Mark Johnston) *racd far side: overall ldr tl rdn and hdd over 1f out: sn btn: fdd ins fnl f: 5th of 9 in gp* **10/1**

9 1/2 **Silvertoni (USA)**[40] 2-8-12 0 ....(bt) JoseValdiviaJr 19 70
(Wesley A Ward, U.S.A) *tall: racd in centre: led gp but only midfield overall: rdn and lost pl wl over 2f out: wknd over 1f out: 4th of 9 in gp* **25/1**

2 10 nse **Parys Mountain (IRE)**[14] 2756 2-9-1 0 .... AndreaAtzeni 16 73
(Charles Hills) *w'like: leggy: racd in centre: t.k.h: prom in gp and midfield overall: rdn over 2f out: sn struggling: wknd over 1f out: 5th of 9 in gp* **50/1**

12 11 1 **Stoneyford Lane (IRE)**[41] 1965 2-9-1 0 .... RoystonFfrench 18 70
(Steph Hollinshead) *cls cpld: racd in centre: towards rr: effrt over 2f out: sn struggling: wknd over 1f out: 6th of 9 in gp* **50/1**

P62 12 hd **Dolokhov**[22] 2536 2-9-1 0 ....(b) LiamKeniry 3 70
(J S Moore) *lengthy: racd far side: sn dropped towards rr: nvr trbld ldrs: 6th of 9 in gp* **100/1**

521 13 nk **Rusumaat (IRE)**[29] 2301 2-9-1 0 .... JoeFanning 5 69
(Mark Johnston) *cmpt: racd far side: t.k.h: chsd overall ldr tl over 2f out: sn struggling u.p: wknd over 1f out: 7th of 9 in gp* **33/1**

2 14 2 **Lundy**[16] 2717 2-9-1 0 .... DonnachaO'Brien 7 63
(Joseph Patrick O'Brien, Ire) *str: racd far side: t.k.h: hld up in midfield: effrt over 2f out: no imp and hung lft over 1f out: sn wknd: 8th of 9 in gp* **33/1**

15 4 1/2 **Grand Coalition (IRE)**[10] 2920 2-9-1 0 .... PatSmullen 10 49
(J P Murtagh, Ire) *unf: racd in centre: t.k.h: chsd gp ldr and midfield overall: rdn to ld gp wl over 2f out: sn lost gp ld and struggling: wknd wl over 1f out: 7th of 9 in gp* **40/1**

1 16 2 1/4 **Mokarris (USA)**[18] 2648 2-9-1 0 .... PaulHanagan 14 42
(Simon Crisford) *athletic: racd in centre: t.k.h: hld up in midfield: clsd to chse gp ldrs over 2f out: sn rdn and struggling: wknd wl over 1f out: 8th of 9 in gp* **8/1**[3]

41 17 hd **Nibras Bounty (IRE)**[24] 2478 2-9-1 0 .... SeanLevey 15 42
(Richard Hannon) *athletic: racd in centre: in tch in midfield: rdn to press gp ldrs over 2f out: sn struggling: wl over 1f out: 8th of 9 in gp* **66/1**

18 6 **Garth Rockett** 2-9-1 0 .... MartinDwyer 17 24
(Brendan Powell) *w'like: str: racd in centre: a bhd: 9th of 9 in gp* **100/1**

1m 16.36s (1.86) **Going Correction** +0.625s/f (Yiel) **18 Ran SP% 126.1**
Speed ratings (Par 105): **112,109,105,105,105 100,95,94,93,93 92,92,91,89,83 80,79,71**
CSF £13.90 CT £56.55 TOTE £2.40: £1.30, £2.60, £1.90; EX 15.80 Trifecta £56.80.
Owner Mrs John Magnier & Michael Tabor & Derrick Smith **Bred** Windmill Manor Farms Inc Et Al **Trained** Cashel, Co Tipperary

FOCUS
Every reason to believe this was a good edition of the race, although soft ground clearly wasn't ideal for these youngsters and it's likely most of them were affected negatively in one way or another by the going. They split into two groups, the larger group racing towards the stands' side, and that's where the winner came from, but the next four home emerged from the far side group, which held the advantage from an early stage , and that makes the performance of the favourite, who had them chase them down, all the more taking.

3244 KING'S STAND STKS (BRITISH CHAMPIONS SERIES & GLOBAL SPRINT CHALLENGE) (GROUP 1) 5f

3:40 (3:46) (Class 1) 3-Y-O+

£226,840 (£86,000; £43,040; £21,440; £10,760; £5,400) **Stalls** Centre

Form RPR

5-11 1 **Profitable (IRE)**[24] 2475 4-9-4 117 .... AdamKirby 8 118+
(Clive Cox) *lw: chsd ldrs: rdn to ld over 1f out: edgd lft ins fnl f: kpt on gamely and finding for press nr fin* **4/1**[2]

1-02 2 nk **Cotai Glory**[25] 2438 4-9-4 107 .... GeorgeBaker 18 117
(Charles Hills) *in tch: clsd over 1f out: sn in 2nd pl: r.o to chal strly ins fnl f: hld nr fin* **33/1**

-300 3 1 **Goken (FR)**[34] 2159 4-9-4 105 .... JamieSpencer 9 113+
(Kevin Ryan) *hld up in rr: hdwy and nt clr run over 1f out: swtchd lft ins fnl f: r.o strly: clsng on front two nr fin* **50/1**

1242 4 nk **Jungle Cat (IRE)**[45] 1862 4-9-4 113 .... WilliamBuick 14 112
(Charlie Appleby) *lw: midfield: rdn over 2f out: hdwy over 1f out: chsd ldrs ins fnl f: styd on same pce nr fin* **14/1**

0-33 5 nk **Waady (IRE)**[24] 2475 4-9-4 112 .... PaulHanagan 20 111
(John Gosden) *swtg: midfield: rdn and hdwy over 1f out: chsd ldrs ins fnl f: styd on: hld nr fin* **8/1**[3]

1-06 6 hd **Medicean Man**[101] 841 10-9-4 106 ....(tp) RichardKingscote 17 110
(Jeremy Gask) *hld up: swtchd lft 2f out: hdwy over 1f out: styd on ins fnl f: nt quite pce to get to ldrs* **50/1**

10-0 7 2 **Out Do**[25] 2438 7-9-4 109 ....(v) PhillipMakin 2 103
(David O'Meara) *s.i.s: hld up: hdwy whn gng ok 2f out: rdn to chse ldrs over 1f out: one pce nr fin* **50/1**

5000 8 3/4 **Move In Time**[24] 2475 8-9-4 107 ....(v) DavidNolan 15 101
(David O'Meara) *swtg: towards rr: hdwy 2f out: plld out to lft over 1f out: kpt on u.p ins fnl f: no imp on ldrs* **33/1**

15-0 9 nk **Mongolian Saturday (USA)**[44] 1911 6-9-4 115 .... FlorentGeroux 19 99
(Enebish Ganbat, U.S.A) *str: dismntd and reluctant to go to post: led: rdn and hdd over 2f out: continued to chse ldrs over 1f out: no ex fnl 100yds* **16/1**

-465 10 3/4 **Aeolus**[24] 2475 5-9-4 108 .... LukeMorris 7 97
(Ed Walker) *lw: in tch: rdn over 2f out: chsd ldrs over 1f out: no ex fnl 75yds* **25/1**

-251 11 1/2 **Take Cover**[25] 2438 9-9-4 111 .... DavidAllan 1 95
(David C Griffiths) *gd spd and racd alone on far side: stl there over 1f out: styd on u.p and edgd lft ins fnl f: one pce fnl 75yds* **20/1**

25-3 12 1 1/2 **Double Up**[25] 2438 5-9-4 107 ....(t) AndreaAtzeni 4 90
(Roger Varian) *lw: hld up: effrt 2f out: hdwy over 1f out: one pce and no imp ins fnl f* **25/1**

0160 13 1 3/4 **Sir Maximilian (IRE)**[24] 2475 7-9-4 111 ....(p) JamesDoyle 6 83
(Ian Williams) *chsd ldrs: rdn over 2f out: nt qckn over 1f out: fdd fnl 150yds* **33/1**

64-4 14 1 **Pearl Secret**[24] 2475 7-9-4 109 .... OisinMurphy 13 80
(David Barron) *hld up: rdn over 1f out: nvr a threat* **9/1**

-120 15 1 **Lancelot Du Lac (ITY)**[45] 1862 6-9-4 108 .... RobertWinston 10 76
(Dean Ivory) *chsd ldrs: rdn to ld over 1f out: hdd over 1f out: sn wknd: eased whn btn wl ins fnl f* **33/1**

21-2 16 nk **Mecca's Angel (IRE)**[24] 2475 5-9-1 120 .... PaulMulrennan 5 72
(Michael Dods) *swtg: prom: rdn over 2f out: u.p and btn whn n.m.r and hmpd twice over 1f out: eased ins fnl f* **6/4**[1]

0/00 17 9 **Hay Chewed (IRE)**[10] 2895 5-9-1 97 .... MartinDwyer 12 40
(Conrad Allen) *chsd ldrs: rdn over 2f out: sn wknd* **100/1**

1m 2.69s (2.19) **Going Correction** +0.625s/f (Yiel)
WFA 3 from 4yo+ 7lb **17 Ran SP% 124.8**
Speed ratings (Par 117): **107,106,104,104,103 103,100,99,98,97 96,94,91,89,88 87,73**
CSF £140.97 CT £5953.35 TOTE £4.60: £1.80, £10.30, £13.90; EX 158.10 Trifecta £4651.70.
Owner A D Spence **Bred** Con Harrington **Trained** Lambourn, Berks

FOCUS
Another highly competitive King's Stand. They went a frantic pace, with the main action developing down the middle, and the first pair had the finish to themselves. Straightforward enough form.

3245 ST JAMES'S PALACE STKS (BRITISH CHAMPIONS SERIES) (GROUP 1) (ENTIRE COLTS) 1m (R)

4:20 (4:25) (Class 1) 3-Y-O

£226,840 (£86,000; £43,040; £21,440; £10,760; £5,400) **Stalls** Low

Form RPR

3-12 1 **Galileo Gold**[24] 2496 3-9-0 120 .... FrankieDettori 7 124
(Hugo Palmer) *t.k.h: chsd ldr: effrt over 2f out: clsd and rdn to ld over 1f out: jst over 2 l clr 1f out: drvn ins fnl f: styd on and a doing enough: rdn out* **6/1**[3]

1 2 1 1/4 **The Gurkha (IRE)**[30] 2283 3-9-0 120 ....(t) RyanMoore 1 122+
(A P O'Brien, Ire) *stdd s: t.k.h: hld up in 6th: effrt 2f out: clsng whn short of room: hmpd and swtchd lft ent fnl f: wnt 4 l 3rd 150yds out: r.o wl u.p to go 2nd towards fin: nvr getting to wnr* **4/5**[1]

11 3 1/2 **Awtaad (IRE)**[24] 2496 3-9-0 120 .... ChrisHayes 3 120
(Kevin Prendergast, Ire) *lengthy: lw: stdd after s: t.k.h: hld up in 5th: effrt 2f out: wnt 3rd and edgd rt u.p jst over 1f out: wnt 2nd and jst over 2 l down ent fnl f: styd on same pce fnl f: lost 2nd towards fin* **5/2**[2]

0-05 4 5 **Cymric (USA)**[19] 2627 3-9-0 105 .... JamesDoyle 6 108
(John Gosden) *lw: led: rdn ent fnl 2f: hdd over 1f out and unable qck: 4th and btn 1f out: wknd ins fnl f* **66/1**

110- 5 3 **Emotionless (IRE)**[248] 7114 3-9-0 117 .... WilliamBuick 2 101
(Charlie Appleby) *lw: stdd s: hld up in last: effrt 2f out: sn drvn and no imp: plugged on to go modest 5th towards fin: nvr trbld ldrs* **10/1**

-602 6 1 **First Selection (SPA)**[30] 2283 3-9-0 109 .... JimCrowley 4 99
(Simon Crisford) *t.k.h: hld up in midfield: wnt 3rd 6f out tl lost pl u.p and sltly hmpd jst over 1f out: wknd ins fnl f* **33/1**

2-32 7 31 **Ehtiraas**[7] 2998 3-9-0 0 .... PaulHanagan 5 28
(Owen Burrows) *t.k.h: chsd ldng pair for 2f: in tch in midfield after tl dropped to rr jst over 2f out: sn btn: t.o and virtually p.u ins fnl f* **100/1**

1m 44.01s (3.31) **Going Correction** +0.725s/f (Yiel) **7 Ran SP% 112.9**
Speed ratings (Par 113): **112,110,110,105,102 101,70**
CSF £11.05 CT £14.70 TOTE £5.40: £2.50, £1.10; EX 11.30 Trifecta £19.20.
Owner Al Shaqab Racing **Bred** Brian O'Rourke **Trained** Newmarket, Suffolk

FOCUS
Race distance increased by 3yds. A race that brought together the winners of the English, Irish and French 2,000 Guineas but we didn't get the definitive answer as to who is the best, for the winner was very much best placed of the trio and the favourite was denied a run and forced to switch. The pace was a fair one, not overly strong.

3246 ASCOT STKS (H'CAP) 2m 4f

5:00 (5:01) (Class 2) (0-100,100) 4-Y-O+

£49,800 (£14,912; £7,456; £3,728; £1,864; £936) **Stalls** Low

Form RPR

1 **Jennies Jewel (IRE)**[23] 2514 9-9-3 **93** .... RonanWhelan 2 104
(Jarlath P Fahey, Ire) *mde all: rdn over 2f out: kpt on gamely ins fnl f: hld on wl* **6/1**[2]

650/ 2 nk **Qewy (IRE)**[67] 7144 6-9-10 **100** .... JamesMcDonald 10 110+
(Charlie Appleby) *lw: hld up: hdwy 3f out: swtchd lft over 2f out: styd on strly ins fnl f: edgd rt: wnt 2nd ins fnl 100yds: pressed wnr nr fin but jst hld* **33/1**

01-0 3 1 3/4 **Mill Springs**[17] 2690 4-9-3 **96** .... FrankieDettori 6 104
(John Gosden) *trckd ldrs: rdn over 2f out: wnt 2nd wl over 1f out: tried to chal ins fnl f: no ex nr fin* **25/1**

00-2 4 2 1/4 **Moscato**[24] 2472 5-9-4 **94** ....(p) LukeMorris 17 100
(Sir Mark Prescott Bt) *chsd ldrs: wnt 2nd after 5f: lost 2nd 7f out: rdn to regain 2nd pl over 2f out tl wl over 1f out: kpt on u.p ins fnl f: one pce fnl 75yds* **18/1**

60-0 5 3 3/4 **Montaly**[24] 2468 5-9-4 **94** .... DavidProbert 18 96
(Andrew Balding) *midfield: rdn and hdwy 3f out: chsd ldrs 2f out: styd on same pce ins fnl f* **33/1**

0-00 6 1 3/4 **Totalize**[41] 1967 7-9-0 **95** .... CallumShepherd(5) 7 96
(Brian Ellison) *hld up in midfield: rdn and hdwy over 2f out: styd on ins fnl f: nt rch ldrs* **16/1**

1/ 7 1/2 **Pique Sous (FR)**[24] 2498 9-9-8 **98** ....(t) RyanMoore 9 98+
(W P Mullins, Ire) *midfield: nt clr run 3f out: hdwy whn swtchd lft 2f out: styd on ins fnl f: nt rch ldrs* **15/2**[3]

060/ 8 3 1/4 **Penglai Pavilion (USA)**[91] 7447 6-9-5 **95** .... JamesDoyle 20 92
(Charlie Appleby) *s.i.s: racd keenly: hld up: u.p 3f out: hdwy over 1f out: kpt on ins fnl f: nvr able to trble ldrs* **16/1**

50/1 9 1 1/4 **Galizzi (USA)**[9] 2932 5-9-1 **91** 3ex ....(t) WilliamBuick 1 87
(Charlie Appleby) *lw: midfield: hmpd on bnd after 7f: rdn over 2f out: sme hdwy over 1f out: one pce ins fnl f* **8/1**

4 10 2 3/4 **Wolfcatcher (IRE)**[31] 2249 4-9-0 **93** ....(p) AdamKirby 14 86
(Charlie Appleby) *in tch: rdn 4f out: chsd ldrs over 2f out: wknd ins fnl f* **25/1**

0-40 **11** *6* **Saved By The Bell (IRE)**[24] 2472 6-9-2 **92**........................ DavidNolan 3 79
(David O'Meara) *chsd ldrs: hmpd on bnd after 7f: rdn over 3f out: wknd over 2f out* **66/1**

0113 **12** *3/4* **Mirsaale**[44] 1880 6-9-7 **97**........................(p) JoeFanning 19 83
(Keith Dalgleish) *in tch: chsd ldrs after 5f: wnt 2nd 7f out: rdn and lost 2nd over 2f out: wknd over 1f out* **20/1**

46/ **13** *4 1/2* **Sempre Medici (FR)**[46] 3619 6-9-1 **91**........................ MartinHarley 16 73
(W P Mullins, Ire) *midfield: effrt over 2f out: rdn and wknd over 1f out* **8/1**

56/1 **14** *14* **No Heretic**[41] 1967 8-9-7 **97**........................ JamieSpencer 8 65
(Nicky Henderson) *lw: s.i.s: hld up in rr: hmpd on bnd after 7f: u.p over 2f out: no imp: eased whn btn ins fnl f* **12/1**

4/ **15** *2 1/2* **Chartbreaker (FR)**[56] 5-9-2 **92**........................(p) SamHitchcott 15 57
(Chris Gordon) *chsd ldr for 5f: remained handy: pushed along over 5f out: wknd over 2f out* **50/1**

1-3 **16** *1* **Silver Concorde**[41] 1967 8-9-9 **99**........................ PatSmullen 5 63
(D K Weld, Ire) *midfield: hmpd on bnd after 7f: hdwy 3f out: chsd ldrs 2f out: wknd over 1f out* **5/1**[1]

66-0 **17** *9* **Le Maitre Chat (USA)**[41] 1967 5-9-2 **92**........................(p) PaulHanagan 13 47
(Ian Williams) *in rr: u.p over 3f out: edgd rt whn trying to plug on over 1f out: nvr a threat* **14/1**

1110 **18** *10* **Sunblazer (IRE)**[81] 1067 6-9-7 **97**........................(t) WilliamTwiston-Davies 4 42
(Kim Bailey) *s.i.s: in rr: u.p over 3f out: no imp: eased whn wl btn over 1f out: t.o* **66/1**

/31- **19** *2* **Eshtiaal (USA)**[17] 1984 6-9-1 **91**........................(tp) FMBerry 11 34
(Gordon Elliott, Ire) *hld up: u.p over 3f out: eased whn wl btn over 1f out: t.o* **20/1**

432- **20** *43* **Hassle (IRE)**[23] 6749 7-9-10 **100**........................(p) OisinMurphy 12
(Dr Richard Newland) *midfield: rdn over 3f out: wknd over 2f out: eased whn wl btn over 1f out: t.o* **14/1**

4m 34.7s (9.90) **Going Correction** +0.725s/f (Yiel)
WFA 4 from 5yo+ 3lb **20** Ran SP% **131.0**
Speed ratings (Par 109): **109,108,108,107,105 105,104,103,103,101 99,99,97,91,90 90,86,82,82,64**
CSF £210.37 CT £4653.01 TOTE £6.40: £1.60, £8.50, £6.30, £4.40; EX 271.70 Trifecta £7027.00.
Owner A N McIntyre **Bred** E Sexton C Bailey And N McIntyre **Trained** Monasterevin, Co. Kildare
■ The first winner at the royal meeting for both Jarlath Fahey and Ronan Whelan.

FOCUS
Race distance increased by 17yds. A competitive staying handicap as usual and a game front-running performance from the winner, who recorded a Flat personal best albeit in line with her improved jumps form.

3247 WINDSOR CASTLE STKS (LISTED RACE) 5f
5:35 (5:37) (Class 1) 2-Y-O

£45,368 (£17,200; £8,608; £4,288; £2,152; £1,080) **Stalls** Centre

Form RPR

1 **1** **Ardad (IRE)**[6] 3037 2-9-3 0........................ RobertHavlin 1 104+
(John Gosden) *tall: racd far side: hld up in tch: clsd to trck ldrs and swtchd lft over 1f out: rdn and qcknd to ld jst over 1f out: clr and r.o strly fnl f: readily: 1st of 12 in gp* **20/1**

3 **2** *3 1/4* **Savannah's Dream**[13] 2800 2-8-12 0........................ PhillipMakin 6 87
(David O'Meara) *lengthy: racd far side: hld up in tch in midfield: effrt and clsd 2f out: swtchd rt and chsd ldrs jst over 1f out: styd on u.p to snatch 2nd on post: no threat to wnr: 2nd of 12 in gp* **100/1**

3 *nse* **Pedestal (IRE)**[19] 2629 2-9-3 0........................ RyanMoore 8 92
(A P O'Brien, Ire) *str: racd far side: hld up in tch towards rr: effrt and swtchd rt over 1f out: nt clrest of runs and swtchd bk lft jst over 1f out: hdwy to chse clr wnr 100yds: no imp: lost 2nd on post: 3rd of 12 in gp* **14/1**

23 **4** *1/2* **Full Intention**[40] 1976 2-9-3 0........................ RichardKingscote 24 90
(Tom Dascombe) *racd in centre: chsd gp ldr and chsd ldrs overall: led gp and rdn over 2f out: drifting rt and unable qck over 1f out: kpt on same pce ins fnl f: 1st of 10 in gp* **33/1**

5 *hd* **Callender (IRE)**[30] 2273 2-9-3 0........................ ChrisHayes 19 89
(P J Prendergast, Ire) *lengthy: racd in centre: s.i.s: in rr: swtchd rt and rdn 2f out: hdwy u.p over 1f out: styd on wl ins fnl f: nvr trbld ldrs: 2nd of 10 in gp* **50/1**

21 **6** *3/4* **Pretty Vacant**[15] 2732 2-9-3 0........................ AndreaAtzeni 3 87
(Roger Varian) *leggy: racd far side: hld up in tch towards rr: gd hdwy over 2f out: chsd ldrs and rdn over 1f out: unable qck and one pce ins fnl f: 4th of 12 in gp* **25/1**

2 **7** *nk* **Yulong Baobei (IRE)**[16] 2718 2-8-12 0........................ ShaneFoley 2 81
(M Halford, Ire) *str: racd far side: racd keenly: chsd ldr: rdn to ld over 1f out: sn hdd and unable qck: edgd lft and one pce ins fnl f: 5th of 12 in gp* **16/1**

3 **8** *1* **Just An Idea (IRE)**[35] 2125 2-9-3 0........................ MartinHarley 18 82
(Harry Dunlop) *w'like: racd in centre: chsd gp ldrs and in tch overall: rdn ent fnl 2f: drifting rt and unable qck over 1f out: kpt on same pce ins fnl f: 3rd of 10 in gp* **100/1**

31 **9** *hd* **Top Score**[30] 2264 2-9-3 0........................(p) JamesDoyle 17 81
(Saeed bin Suroor) *racd in centre: midfield: effrt 2f out: sme hdwy u.p ent fnl f: styd on u.p but no threat to wnr ins fnl f: 4th of 10 in gp* **33/1**

24 **10** *shd* **Leontes**[17] 2696 2-9-3 0........................ DavidProbert 11 81
(Andrew Balding) *w'like: leggy: racd far side: sn pushed along in rr: sme hdwy u.p over 1f out: kpt on same pce ins fnl f: nvr trbld ldrs: 6th of 12 in gp* **66/1**

2105 **11** *hd* **Stringybark Creek**[17] 2696 2-9-3 0........................ GeorgeBaker 13 80
(Mick Channon) *racd in centre: stdd after s: bhd: rdn and swtchd rt over 1f out: styd on wl ins fnl f: nvr trbld ldrs: 5th of 10 in gp* **100/1**

1 **12** *2 1/4* **Battaash (IRE)**[27] 2371 2-9-3 0........................ PaulHanagan 23 72+
(Charles Hills) *athletic: racd in centre: unruly and rring in stalls: in tch in midfield: effrt 2f out: unable qck over 1f out: wknd ins fnl f: 6th of 10 in gp* **11/1**

2 **13** *2 1/4* **Bolt Phantom (USA)**[23] 2500 2-9-3 0........................ SeanLevey 14 64
(Ismail Mohammed) *w'like: racd in centre: stdd after s: midfield: effrt 2f out: no hdwy u.p over 1f out: wknd fnl f: 7th of 10 in gp* **25/1**

1 **14** *2* **Fayez (IRE)**[12] 2830 2-9-3 0........................ HarryBentley 12 57
(David O'Meara) *tall: racd far side: s.i.s: bhd: rdn 2f out: swtchd rt jst over 1f out: swtchd bk lft and kpt on to pass btn horses ins fnl f: nvr trbld ldrs: 7th of 12 in gp* **25/1**

2311 **15** *nk* **Tomily (IRE)**[24] 2457 2-9-3 0........................ PatDobbs 5 56
(Richard Hannon) *racd far side: chsd ldrs: rdn 2f out: lost pl and btn over 1f out: wknd ins fnl f: 8th of 12 in gp* **13/2**[3]

16 *1/2* **Big City Dreamin (USA)**[67] 2-8-12 0........................(bt) FrankieDettori 7 49
(Wesley A Ward, U.S.A) *str: lw: racd far side: overall ldr tl rdn and hdd over 1f out: sn btn: fdd and eased ins fnl f: 9th of 12 in gp* **6/1**[2]

17 *1/2* **Drafted (USA)**[48] 2-9-3 0........................(bt) WilliamBuick 10 52
(Eoin Harty, U.S.A) *cmpt: racd far side: dwlt: in tch towards rr: drvn 2f out: swtchd lft and no imp over 1f out: wknd ins fnl f: 10th of 12 in gp* **7/1**

3 **18** *1/2* **Ambiguity (IRE)**[24] 2494 2-9-3 0........................ DonnachaO'Brien 16 50
(Joseph Patrick O'Brien, Ire) *str: racd in centre: a towards rr: rdn and no hdwy 2f out: bhd fnl f: 8th of 10 in gp* **33/1**

3 **19** *3/4* **Big Lachie**[8] 2976 2-9-3 0........................ WilliamCarson 21 48
(Jamie Osborne) *w'like: str: racd in centre: midfield: effrt jst over 2f out: sn drvn and no hdwy wknd over 1f out: 9th of 10 in gp* **100/1**

2 **20** *4* **Mister Trader**[24] 2494 2-9-3 0........................ PatSmullen 4 33
(D J Bunyan, Ire) *tall: racd far side: racd keenly: chsd ldrs: rdn 2f out: sn btn and lost pl over 1f out: bhd ins fnl f: 11th of 12 in gp* **11/4**[1]

4216 **21** *2* **Copper Knight (IRE)**[19] 2624 2-9-3 0........................(b[1]) JimCrowley 9 26
(Hugo Palmer) *racd far side: wl in tch in midfield: rdn 2f out: sn btn: bhd ins fnl f: 12th of 12 in gp* **16/1**

11 **22** *6* **Kananee (USA)**[34] 2162 2-9-3 0........................ JamesMcDonald 20 5
(Saeed bin Suroor) *lw: racd in centre: led gp and chsd ldrs overall: lost gp ld and rdn over 2f out: lost pl qckly over 1f out: bhd and eased ins fnl f: 10th of 10 in gp* **16/1**

1m 2.56s (2.06) **Going Correction** +0.625s/f (Yiel) **22** Ran SP% **132.0**
Speed ratings (Par 101): **108,102,102,101,101 100,99,98,98,97 97,93,90,87,86 85,85,84,83,76 73,63**
CSF £1299.79 CT £25345.51 TOTE £32.60: £7.40, £30.70, £4.50; EX 3341.90 Trifecta £23624.90 Part won..
Owner Abdullah Saeed Al Naboodah **Bred** Tally-Ho Stud **Trained** Newmarket, Suffolk
■ Robert Havlin's first Royal Ascot winner.

FOCUS
This turned out to be more open than the market suggested and, although clearly not a strong race, despite the time being fractionally quicker than the King's Stand, it was hard not to be taken by the winners dominance. They split into two group and the low-drawn runners, racing on the far side, were favoured with the winner coming from stall one.
T/Jkpt: Not won. T/Plt: £1,219.40 to a £1 stake. Pool: £549,555.56 - 328.97 winning tickets.
T/Qpdt: £402.80 to a £1 stake. Pool: £29,829.22 - 54.80 winning tickets.
Darren Owen & Steve Payne

3008 BEVERLEY (R-H)

Tuesday, June 14

OFFICIAL GOING: Good (7.6)
Wind: Moderate half behind Weather: Cloudy

3248 HORSE COMES FIRST NOVICE MEDIAN AUCTION STKS 7f 100y
6:40 (6:43) (Class 5) 2-Y-O **£3,780** (£1,131; £565; £283; £141) **Stalls** Low

Form RPR

2 **1** **Roar (IRE)**[28] 2335 2-9-2 0........................ BenCurtis 7 70
(Brian Ellison) *sn led: rdn wl over 1f out: drvn and edgd lft ins fnl f: kpt on* **2/1**[1]

2 *3/4* **Bear Valley (IRE)** 2-9-2 0........................ FrannyNorton 6 68+
(Mark Johnston) *trckd wnr: green and niggled along over 2f out: effrt over 1f out: n.m.r and swtchd rt ins fnl f: kpt on* **9/4**[2]

3 *1 1/4* **Mayleen (IRE)** 2-8-11 0........................ JamesSullivan 8 60+
(Ann Duffield) *s.i.s and in rr: hdwy on inner 2f out: rdn over 1f out: styd on fnl f: nrst fin* **16/1**

60 **4** *1* **Il Sicario (IRE)**[18] 2648 2-9-2 0........................ DarryllHolland 3 63
(Mark Johnston) *trckd ldng pair: hdwy to chse wnr 3f out: rdn to chal over 1f out: ev ch tl drvn ins fnl f: kpt on same pce* **6/1**

5 *1* **Miss Bates** 2-8-11 0........................ PJMcDonald 5 55+
(Ann Duffield) *towards rr: hdwy over 2f out: rdn to chse ldrs over 1f out: kpt on same pce fnl f* **5/1**[3]

6 *1* **Breakwater Bay (IRE)** 2-9-2 0........................ DuranFentiman 2 58
(Tim Easterby) *trckd ldrs: hdwy over 2f out: chsd ldrs and rdn wl over 1f out: one pce appr fnl f* **25/1**

060 **7** *11* **Heavenly Cry**[14] 2756 2-8-11 0........................ NoelGarbutt[(5)] 4 32
(Denis Quinn) *trckd ldrs: hdwy over 3f out: rdn along on outer 2f out: sn wknd* **66/1**

1m 36.43s (2.63) **Going Correction** -0.175s/f (Firm) **7** Ran SP% **106.3**
Speed ratings (Par 93): **77,76,74,73,72 71,58**
CSF £5.81 TOTE £2.70: £1.40, £1.70; EX 4.40 Trifecta £33.20.
Owner K Strangeway & J M Basquill **Bred** Wollemie Park Stud **Trained** Norton, N Yorks
■ Balance Sheet was withdrawn. Price at time of withdrawal 8-1. Rule 4 applies to all bets - deduction 10p in the pound.

FOCUS
This was a juvenile novice run over 7f118yds, so quite a stiff test. The time was slow and the form is probably no more than ordinary.

3249 BEVERLEY ANNUAL BADGEHOLDERS MAIDEN FILLIES' STKS 7f 100y
7:10 (7:10) (Class 5) 3-Y-O+ **£3,780** (£1,131; £565; £283; £141) **Stalls** Low

Form RPR

4-2 **1** **Jawaayiz**[23] 2505 3-8-12 0........................ SilvestreDeSousa 6 71+
(Simon Crisford) *trckd ldng pair: hdwy over 2f out: sn chsng ldr: chal over 1f out: rdn and slt ld appr fnl f: drvn and kpt on wl towards fin* **30/100**[1]

53 **2** *1 3/4* **Sonnet (IRE)**[29] 2303 3-8-12 0........................ DarryllHolland 1 66+
(Charles Hills) *trckd ldr: led 5f out: jnd 2f out and sn rdn: drvn and hdd appr fnl f: kpt on same pce* **10/3**[2]

6-44 **3** *3 1/4* **The Excel Queen (IRE)**[47] 1819 3-8-12 56........................ DuranFentiman 8 58
(Tony Coyle) *slt ld: hdd 5f out and cl up: rdn along over 2f out: drvn wl over 1f out and sn wknd* **12/1**

00 **4** *1 3/4* **Beadlam (IRE)**[12] 2835 3-8-12 0........................ JoeyHaynes 4 54
(David Loughnane) *towards rr: pushed along 3f out: rdn over 2f out: hdwy over 1f out: sn no imp* **66/1**

5 *3 1/4* **Candy Express** 3-8-12 0........................ JamesSullivan 5 46
(Clive Mulhall) *dwlt and in rr: hdwy on inner whn nt clr run wl over 1f out: rdn and styd on fnl f* **50/1**

0-5 **6** *nk* **Gilt Edged (IRE)**[21] 2557 3-8-9 0........................ JoeDoyle[(3)] 2 45
(Julie Camacho) *trckd ldrs: pushed along 3f out: rdn 2f out: sn drvn and grad wknd* **10/1**[3]

0- **7** *1* **Lady Chara**[384] 2598 3-8-12 0........................ PJMcDonald 3 42
(Ann Duffield) *dwlt and towards rr: hdwy 1/2-way: chsd ldrs wl over 2f out: rdn wl over 1f out: grad wknd* **20/1**

5 **8** *3 1/2* **Coquine**[17] 2681 3-8-7 0........................ JoshDoyle[(5)] 7 34
(David O'Meara) *chsd ldrs: rdn along 3f out: wknd over 2f out* **16/1**

1m 33.32s (-0.48) **Going Correction** -0.175s/f (Firm) **8** Ran SP% **130.9**
Speed ratings (Par 100): **95,93,89,87,83 83,82,78**
CSF £2.28 TOTE £1.30: £1.02, £1.20, £2.80; EX 2.30 Trifecta £7.50.
Owner Hamdan Al Maktoum **Bred** D R Botterill **Trained** Newmarket, Suffolk

FOCUS
An uncompetitive maiden run at just an ordinary gallop and the proximity of the third holds the form back. The race distance was 18 yards further than advertised.

3250 BRITISH STALLION STUDS LAURENT PERRIER EVENING EBF CONDITIONS STKS 5f
7:40 (7:44) (Class 3) 3-Y-O+

£8,715 (£2,609; £1,304; £652; £326; £163) **Stalls** Low

Form				RPR
4404	**1**		**Line Of Reason (IRE)**[25] 2438 6-9-7 106 MartinLane 1 (Paul Midgley) *trckd ldrs on inner: hdwy 1 1/2f out: sn swtchd lft and chal: rdn to ld jst ins fnl f: drvn out* **2/1**[1]	111
-032	**2**	1 1/4	**Red Pike (IRE)**[13] 2803 5-9-3 96 TomEaves 3 (Bryan Smart) *led: jnd and rdn over 1f out: hdd jst ins fnl f: drvn and kpt on same pce* **4/1**[2]	102
40-0	**3**	6	**Pipers Note**[52] 1644 6-9-3 98 GeorgeChaloner 4 (Richard Whitaker) *trckd ldrs: hdwy to chse ldr 1/2-way: rdn wl over 1f out: grad wknd* **5/1**[3]	80
5-06	**4**	1/2	**Another Wise Kid (IRE)**[73] 1197 8-9-0 99 DougieCostello 2 (Paul Midgley) *chsd ldrs: pushed along and outpcd 1/2-way: rdn wl over 1f out: kpt on fnl f* **10/1**	76
0-00	**5**	2 1/2	**Foxy Forever (IRE)**[131] 450 6-9-0 97 ConnorBeasley 5 (Michael Wigham) *stmbld s and in rr: hdwy on inner wl over 1f out: rdn and kpt on fnl f* **10/1**	67
5540	**6**	2 3/4	**Barracuda Boy (IRE)**[10] 2898 6-9-3 97 SilvestreDeSousa 6 (Tom Dascombe) *wnt lft s: sn chsng ldrs rdn along over 2f out: drvn wl over 1f out: sn wknd* **7/1**	60
3-36	**7**	1 1/4	**Canny Kool**[25] 2438 4-8-7 102 BenRobinson(7) 7 (Brian Ellison) *wnt lft s: in tch: rdn along 2f out: sn wknd* **11/2**	52

1m 0.08s (-3.42) **Going Correction** -0.425s/f (Firm) course record **7** Ran SP% **116.1**
Speed ratings (Par 107): **110,108,98,97,93 89,87**
CSF £10.47 TOTE £2.80: £1.70, £1.40; EX 6.40 Trifecta £55.50.
Owner Taylor's Bloodstock Ltd **Bred** Corduff Stud Ltd, J Corcoran & J Judd **Trained** Westow, N Yorks

FOCUS
A conditions sprint in which the winner and runner-up broke the track record and pulled well clear of the remainder.

3251 ALAN WOOD CONSULTANT OF CHOICE FILLIES' H'CAP 1m 4f 16y
8:10 (8:10) (Class 4) (0-80,80) 3-Y-O+ **£5,040** (£1,508; £754; £377; £188) **Stalls** Low

Form				RPR
3134	**1**		**Genuine Approval (IRE)**[25] 2433 3-8-10 80 DannyBrock(3) 6 (Jonathan Portman) *trckd ldr: cl up 3f out: chal 2f out: rdn over 1f out: led ent fnl f: sn drvn and kpt on wl* **8/1**	87
4-41	**2**	nk	**Renfrew Street**[8] 2973 3-8-13 80 6ex FrannyNorton 2 (Mark Johnston) *set stdy pce: qcknd over 3f out: sn jnd: pushed along 2f out: sn rdn: hdd ent fnl f: drvn and rallied last 100yds: no ex towards fin* **1/1**[1]	86
-210	**3**	3 1/2	**Kip**[4] 3118 4-9-1 72 JoshDoyle(5) 5 (David O'Meara) *t.k.h: trckd ldrs: effrt and n.m.r over 2f out: chsd ldrs over 1f out: sn rdn and kpt on same pce* **15/2**[3]	72
31-3	**4**	3/4	**Purple Magic**[33] 2181 3-8-5 72 PJMcDonald 8 (Michael Bell) *trckd ldng pair on outer: rdn along over 2f out: drvn over 1f out: sn one pce* **11/2**[2]	71
656	**5**	1/2	**Gloryette**[15] 2735 3-8-6 73 SilvestreDeSousa 4 (Ed Dunlop) *t.k.h: trckd ldrs on inner: effrt over 2f out: sn rdn and wknd over 1f out* **11/2**[2]	71
1014	**6**	nk	**Bayan Kasirga (IRE)**[21] 2564 6-9-2 75 AdamMcNamara(7) 3 (Richard Fahey) *dwlt and in rr: effrt 2f out: sn rdn and no imp* **14/1**	73
-225	**7**	1 3/4	**Miss Ranger (IRE)**[19] 2618 4-9-1 67 (p) BenCurtis 7 (Brian Ellison) *hld up: sme hdwy on outer 3f out: rdn along over 2f out: drvn over 1f out: sn one pce* **16/1**	62

2m 41.02s (1.22) **Going Correction** -0.175s/f (Firm)
WFA 3 from 4yo+ 15lb **7** Ran SP% **116.2**
Speed ratings (Par 102): **88,87,85,84,84 84,83**
CSF £17.05 CT £65.59 TOTE £8.40: £2.80, £1.60; EX 11.90 Trifecta £115.20.
Owner The Genuine Partnership **Bred** Rossenarra Bloodstock Limited **Trained** Upper Lambourn, Berks

FOCUS
A muddling gallop to this handicap which was run over 18 yards further than advertised. It was run to suit the prominent racers and the first pair, who were in the first two throughout, finished clear of the rest.

3252 BEVERLEY FOLK FESTIVAL HERE THIS WEEKEND H'CAP 1m 100y
8:40 (8:44) (Class 5) (0-75,75) 3-Y-O+ **£3,780** (£1,131; £565; £283; £141) **Stalls** Low

Form				RPR
10-4	**1**		**Lord Kelvin (IRE)**[15] 2749 3-9-2 74 SilvestreDeSousa 9 (Charles Hills) *trckd ldrs: swtchd lft to outer 2f out: sn cl up: rdn and edgd lft ent fnl f: drvn to ld last 75yds: kpt on* **3/1**[1]	79
6063	**2**	hd	**Peterhouse (USA)**[15] 2743 4-10-0 75 BenCurtis 4 (Jason Ward) *hld up and bhd: gd hdwy 3f out: effrt on outer 2f out: rdn to chal over 1f out: ev ch ins fnl f: sn drvn and kpt on* **11/2**[3]	82
0-10	**3**	nk	**Toboggan's Fire**[61] 1446 3-9-2 74 PJMcDonald 2 (Ann Duffield) *trckd ldrs: pushed along over 2f out: rdn wl over 1f out: swtchd to inner and drvn ins fnl f: squeezed through and ev ch: no ex nr fin* **10/1**	77
0662	**4**	1/2	**Muqarred (USA)**[8] 2959 4-9-12 73 (p) SamJames 1 (David Loughnane) *led: jnd and rdn 2f out: drvn over 1f out: hdd and no ex last 75yds* **13/2**	78
5353	**5**	2 1/2	**Jintshi**[21] 2565 3-9-0 72 FrannyNorton 6 (Mark Johnston) *trckd ldrs: rapid hdwy on outer to chse ldng pair over 3f out: rdn along wl over 1f out: drvn and ev ch ent fnl f: wknd last 150yds* **5/1**[2]	68
4-23	**6**	1	**Deansgate (IRE)**[22] 2532 3-9-0 72 (e) ConnorBeasley 10 (Julie Camacho) *hld up towards rr: hdwy 2f out: rdn over 1f out: ev ch ent fnl f: sn drvn and one pce* **6/1**	66
0-00	**7**	1 1/4	**Echo Of Lightning**[19] 2620 6-9-6 74 BenRobinson(7) 3 (Brian Ellison) *chsd ldr: hdwy and cl up over 2f out: rdn wl over 1f out: drvn and wknd fnl f* **12/1**	68

1m 45.28s (-2.32) **Going Correction** -0.175s/f (Firm)
WFA 3 from 4yo+ 11lb **7** Ran SP% **101.5**
Speed ratings (Par 103): **104,103,103,103,100 99,98**
CSF £15.16 CT £87.70 TOTE £2.70: £1.80, £2.60; EX 15.80 Trifecta £43.50.
Owner Mrs Fitri Hay **Bred** Glashare House Stud **Trained** Lambourn, Berks
■ Tellovoi and Venutius were withdrawn. Prices at time of withdrawals 8-1 and 14-1 respectively. Rule 4 applies to all bets - deduction 15p in the pound.
■ Stewards' Enquiry : Ben Curtis two-day ban: used whip above permitted level (Jun 28-29)
Silvestre De Sousa two-day ban: used whip above permitted level (Jun 28-29)

FOCUS
A tightly-knit handicap reduced to seven runners with one absentee and a further two withdrawn at the start. It was run at a medium gallop over 18 yards further than advertised, the seven were virtually in line abreast coming to the final furlong and a length covered the first four home.

3253 RACING UK FREE ONE MONTH TRIAL H'CAP 1m 1f 207y
9:10 (9:10) (Class 6) (0-65,65) 4-Y-O+ **£2,587** (£770; £384; £192) **Stalls** Low

Form				RPR
43	**1**		**Hydrant**[8] 2958 10-8-12 56 ConnorBeasley 9 (Richard Guest) *chsd clr ldr: led 3f out: rdn over 1f out: drvn and styd on strly fnl f* **7/2**[1]	65
-165	**2**	3 1/4	**John Caesar (IRE)**[17] 2673 5-9-6 64 (t) BarryMcHugh 7 (Rebecca Bastiman) *hld up and bhd: hdwy on outer over 2f out: rdn to chse ldrs over 1f out: drvn to chse wnr ins fnl f: no imp* **6/1**	67
6-00	**3**	2 1/2	**Morocco**[28] 2329 7-8-8 52 (e[1]) JoeyHaynes 8 (Karen Tutty) *chsd ldrs: hdwy 3f out: sn chsng wnr: rdn along wl over 1f out: drvn and one pce fnl f* **12/1**	50
0025	**4**	1 1/4	**British Embassy (IRE)**[1] 3220 4-9-7 65 SamJames 3 (David Loughnane) *led: clr after 3f: hdd 3f out and sn rdn: drvn wl over 1f out: grad wknd* **4/1**[2]	61
0000	**5**	3 1/2	**First Sargeant**[14] 2773 6-9-2 60 (p) SilvestreDeSousa 1 (Lawrence Mullaney) *hld up towards rr: hdwy over 2f out: rdn to chse ldrs wl over 1f out: sn btn* **5/1**[3]	49
100/	**6**	3/4	**Think**[510] 7284 9-8-2 46 oh1 (tp) JamesSullivan 5 (Clive Mulhall) *chsd ldrs: rdn along over 2f out: sn drvn and outpcd* **33/1**	34
000-	**7**	shd	**Christmas Light**[252] 7008 9-8-8 52 CamHardie 2 (Alan Lockwood) *a towards rr* **25/1**	40
550-	**8**	25	**Dont Tell Chris (FR)**[266] 6617 4-8-9 56 ShelleyBirkett(3) 6 (David O'Meara) *in tch: hdwy on outer to chse ldrs over 3f out: rdn over 2f out: sn wknd and bhd whn eased fnl f* **4/1**[2]	
5460	**U**		**Lean On Pete (IRE)**[10] 2915 7-8-6 50 PJMcDonald 4 (Ollie Pears) *stmbld and uns rdr s* **15/2**	

2m 5.74s (-1.26) **Going Correction** -0.175s/f (Firm) **9** Ran SP% **119.4**
Speed ratings (Par 101): **98,95,93,92,89 89,88,68,**
CSF £25.87 CT £231.20 TOTE £4.80: £1.70, £2.50, £3.60; EX 31.80 Trifecta £328.10.
Owner Mrs Alison Guest **Bred** Lord Halifax **Trained** Ingmanthorpe, W Yorks

FOCUS
A low-grade handicap run at a decent gallop. The distance was 18 yards further than advertised.
T/Plt: £8.40 to a £1 stake. Pool: £51,680.32 - 4,468.82 winning tickets. T/Qpdt: £6.40 to a £1 stake. Pool: £4,089.95 - 467.16 winning tickets. **Joe Rowntree**

2963 BRIGHTON (L-H)
Tuesday, June 14

OFFICIAL GOING: Good to firm
Wind: Fresh, half against Weather: Fine

3254 IRISH STALLION FARMS EBF NOVICE MEDIAN AUCTION STKS 5f 213y
5:50 (5:50) (Class 5) 2-Y-O **£3,234** (£962; £481; £240) **Stalls** Low

Form				RPR
13	**1**		**Afandem (IRE)**[26] 2390 2-9-6 0 MarcMonaghan(3) 8 (Hugo Palmer) *racd freely: led tl 2f out: rallied and led over 1f out: drvn clr* **2/5**[1]	89
61	**2**	2 1/2	**Baby Gal**[22] 2535 2-8-13 0 JosephineGordon(5) 1 (Giles Bravery) *trckd ldrs: led 2f out tl over 1f out: one pce ins fnl f* **12/1**	77
6	**3**	4 1/2	**Racemaker**[11] 2873 2-9-2 0 CharlesBishop 3 (Mick Channon) *dwlt: hld up in 5th: rdn and no imp fnl 2f* **16/1**	61+
440	**4**	2 3/4	**Primrose Place**[18] 2637 2-8-11 0 KieranO'Neill 4 (Richard Hannon) *chsd wnr tl wknd 2f out* **10/1**[3]	48
	5	hd	**Dangerous Ends** 2-9-2 0 KierenFox 2 (Brett Johnson) *dwlt: sn outpcd and bhd* **50/1**	52
52	**6**	6	**Espresso Freddo (IRE)**[15] 2747 2-9-2 0 RyanPowell 5 (Sir Mark Prescott Bt) *dwlt: sn prom: wknd qckly 2f out* **9/2**[2]	34

1m 10.86s (0.66) **Going Correction** +0.125s/f (Good) **6** Ran SP% **114.2**
Speed ratings (Par 93): **100,96,90,87,86 78**
CSF £7.04 TOTE £1.50: £1.10, £3.80; EX 5.50 Trifecta £29.50.
Owner Hamad Rashed Bin Ghedayer **Bred** Rabbah Bloodstock Limited **Trained** Newmarket, Suffolk

FOCUS
Problems with the irrigation system meant that the ground could not be watered, and the going was understandably quick. Rail movements added 8 yards to the distance of each race. An uncompetitive novice event and the long odds-on winner wasn't overly impressive in getting the job done.

3255 ROC SOLUTIONS - OFFICIAL ELECTRICAL&SECURITY PARTNER H'CAP 7f 214y
6:20 (6:20) (Class 6) (0-60,59) 4-Y-O+ **£2,264** (£673; £336; £168) **Stalls** Low

Form				RPR
3225	**1**		**El Duque**[15] 2741 5-8-12 55 (p) HectorCrouch(5) 2 (Bill Turner) *chsd ldr: led over 1f out: rdn out* **4/1**[3]	62
63	**2**	1 1/2	**Zephyros (GER)**[3] 3125 5-9-0 59 GeorgeWood(7) 4 (David Bridgwater) *chsd ldrs: rdn 2f out: styd on to take 2nd ins fnl f* **6/4**[1]	62
4510	**3**	1 1/2	**Fairy Mist (IRE)**[34] 2155 9-9-1 53 (b) AdamBeschizza 6 (John Bridger) *in tch: outpcd and hrd rdn 2f out: styd on fnl f* **8/1**	53
U106	**4**	hd	**Palace Moon**[46] 1834 11-9-5 57 (t) KierenFox 3 (Michael Attwater) *trckd ldrs gng wl: rdn 2f out: styd on same pce* **16/1**	56
6053	**5**	1	**Jonnie Skull (IRE)**[6] 3043 10-8-2 45 (vt) JosephineGordon(5) 1 (Phil McEntee) *led: 3 l ahd 1/2-way: rdn 3f out: edgd lft and hdd over 1f out: wknd fnl f* **8/1**	42
0613	**6**	9	**Satchville Flyer**[25] 2442 5-8-11 49 PatCosgrave 5 (David Evans) *stdd s: plld hrd in rr: promising hdwy on inner over 2f out: n.m.r whn edgd lft and hit rail 1f out: eased* **10/3**[2]	49+

1m 37.69s (1.69) **Going Correction** +0.125s/f (Good) **6** Ran SP% **111.2**
Speed ratings (Par 101): **96,94,93,92,91 82**
CSF £10.25 TOTE £5.30: £2.20, £1.30; EX 14.30 Trifecta £40.10.
Owner Mrs Tracy Turner **Bred** John James **Trained** Sigwells, Somerset

The Form Book, Raceform Ltd, Newbury, RG14 5SJ

FOCUS
Race run over 8 yards further than advertised. A low-grade handicap and a bit of a messy race.

3256 JOHN SMITH'S RACEDAY 3RD AUGUST H'CAP 1m 1f 209y
6:50 (6:51) (Class 6) (0-60,60) 3-Y-O **£2,264** (£673; £336; £168) **Stalls** High

Form RPR
5002 **1** **French Legend**[8] 2967 3-8-5 **49**.................... EdwardGreatrex(5) 1 60
(Andrew Balding) *mde all: 3 l ahd 1/2-way: rdn and styd on wl fnl 2f: comf* **6/1**[3]
0-05 **2** 4½ **Lazizah**[12] 2828 3-8-13 **55**....................[1] LouisSteward(3) 7 57
(Marcus Tregoning) *mid-div: hdwy 3f out: chsd wnr over 1f out: no imp* **12/1**
-452 **3** 1¾ **Masterson (IRE)**[3] 3141 3-9-0 **60**.................... KillianHennessy(7) 11 59
(Mick Channon) *hld up in rr: styd on in centre fnl 2f: nvr nrr* **9/4**[1]
054 **4** ¾ **Dalavand (IRE)**[11] 2851 3-9-5 **58**.................... TimmyMurphy 10 55
(Jamie Osborne) *bhd: rdn and hdwy 2f out: styd on same pce* **12/1**
001 **5** 4½ **Lady Rocka**[8] 2967 3-9-2 **60** 6ex....................(b) HectorCrouch(5) 3 49
(Amanda Perrett) *prom: chsd wnr 4f out tl wknd over 1f out* **7/1**
-042 **6** 2½ **Buzz Lightyere**[12] 2828 3-9-7 **60**.................... KierenFox 6 44
(Michael Attwater) *chsd ldrs tl outpcd fnl 2f* **9/2**[2]
0205 **7** 1½ **Gold Eliza (IRE)**[11] 2851 3-9-1 **54**.................... KieranO'Neill 9 35
(Richard Hannon) *hld up in rr: hdwy 3f out: wknd over 1f out* **10/1**
5000 **8** 7 **Katie Canford**[7] 3000 3-8-12 **51**.................... AdamBeschizza 5 19
(John Bridger) *in tch tl rdn and wknd 3f out* **25/1**
00-0 **9** 2½ **Dusty Raven**[12] 2828 3-9-4 **57**....................(p) RyanPowell 8 20
(Sir Mark Prescott Bt) *a towards rr: bhd and rdn fnl 5f* **16/1**
606 **10** 13 **Dilly Daydream (IRE)**[12] 2829 3-8-9 **53**..........(b[1]) JosephineGordon(5) 4
(Giles Bravery) *chsd wnr tl 4f out: wknd 3f out* **16/1**

2m 3.45s (-0.15) **Going Correction** +0.125s/f (Good) **10** Ran SP% **115.8**
Speed ratings (Par 97): **105,101,100,99,95 93,92,87,85,74**
CSF £74.87 CT £209.93 TOTE £7.00: £2.00, £3.70, £1.40; EX 96.00 Trifecta £430.90.
Owner J C Smith **Bred** Littleton Stud **Trained** Kingsclere, Hants

FOCUS
Race run over 8 yards further than advertised. Not a bad event for the grade and the winner was stepping up on recent form.

3257 FROSTS LADIES DAY 4TH AUGUST FILLIES' H'CAP 1m 1f 209y
7:20 (7:21) (Class 4) (0-80,75) 4-Y-O+ **£4,690** (£1,395; £697; £348) **Stalls** High

Form RPR
-622 **1** **Yankee Mail (FR)**[5] 3076 4-8-11 **65**.................... PatCosgrave 4 74
(Gay Kelleway) *hld up: effrt over 1f out: hung lft and led ins fnl f: styd on* **10/3**[3]
2-31 **2** 1¾ **Ickymasho**[21] 2564 4-9-7 **75**.................... LukeMorris 3 81
(Jonathan Portman) *disp ld: led after 3f: edgd rt over 1f out: hdd ins fnl f: one pce* **9/4**[2]
3563 **3** 3¾ **Stosur (IRE)**[18] 2636 5-9-7 **75**....................(p) TimmyMurphy 1 73
(Gay Kelleway) *hld up: effrt 2f out: one pce* **6/1**
-321 **4** 1½ **Hala Madrid**[6] 3030 4-9-1 **74**.................... EdwardGreatrex(5) 5 80+
(Andrew Balding) *disp ld for 3f: pressed ldr tl bdly squeezed and snatched up jst ins fnl f: nt rcvr* **13/8**[1]

2m 3.63s (0.03) **Going Correction** +0.125s/f (Good) **4** Ran SP% **106.2**
Speed ratings (Par 102): **104,102,99,98**
CSF £10.56 TOTE £4.30; EX 8.90 Trifecta £31.80.
Owner Ms G Kelleway & R Mortlock **Bred** Haras D'Etreham **Trained** Exning, Suffolk

FOCUS
Race run over 8 yards further than advertised. This fair handicap for fillies was run in a slightly slower time than the preceding 46-60 event and the winner was on a good mark.

3258 CHECKATRADE RACEDAY 5TH AUGUST H'CAP 6f 209y
7:50 (7:51) (Class 6) (0-65,65) 4-Y-O+ **£2,264** (£673; £336; £168) **Stalls** Low

Form RPR
0546 **1** **Castle Talbot (IRE)**[6] 3031 4-9-1 **59**....................(p) ShaneKelly 7 65
(Richard Hughes) *chsd ldrs: rdn over 2f out: styd on to ld nr fin* **7/2**[2]
2025 **2** hd **New Rich**[17] 2697 6-9-7 **65**....................(b) JohnFahy 1 70
(Eve Johnson Houghton) *led: kpt on u.p fnl 2f: ct nr fin* **7/1**
-042 **3** 1¾ **Mrs Warren**[26] 2403 6-9-2 **60**.................... SteveDrowne 4 60
(George Baker) *blindfold removed late: dwlt: hld up towards rr: hdwy and nt clr run over 1f out: swtchd rt: styd on fnl f* **9/2**
2352 **4** nk **Knight Of The Air**[3] 3125 4-8-12 **61**.................... PaddyPilley(5) 3 60
(Mick Channon) *trckd ldr: shkn up over 1f out: lost 2nd and one pce ins fnl f* **9/4**[1]
3151 **5** nk **Hawk Moth (IRE)**[18] 2647 8-9-5 **63**....................(p) LukeMorris 2 62
(John Spearing) *hld up: effrt and hrd rdn over 1f out: styd on fnl f* **4/1**[3]
4020 **6** 4 **Tancred (IRE)**[11] 2856 5-9-3 **61**....................(p) LiamKeniry 6 49
(Conor Dore) *in tch: rdn 3f out: wknd over 1f out* **16/1**
440- **7** 3 **Gotasinggotadance**[258] 6848 4-8-2 **46** oh1.................... KieranO'Neill 5 26
(Philip Hide) *stdd s: t.k.h in rr: no imp whn hung lft over 1f out* **33/1**

1m 24.34s (1.24) **Going Correction** +0.125s/f (Good) **7** Ran SP% **112.5**
Speed ratings (Par 101): **97,96,94,94,94 89,86**
CSF £26.74 TOTE £3.90: £2.60, £3.50; EX 33.50 Trifecta £154.10.
Owner Gerry Dolan **Bred** Herbertstown & Diomed **Trained** Upper Lambourn, Berkshire

FOCUS
Race run over 8 yards further than advertised. Modest handicap form with the principals finishing in a heap..

3259 FORD SUMMER FESTIVAL RUN 16TH JULY H'CAP 5f 213y
8:20 (8:20) (Class 5) (0-70,70) 3-Y-O+ **£2,911** (£866; £432; £216) **Stalls** Low

Form RPR
240 **1** **Najd**[19] 2614 3-9-2 **69**.................... TomMarquand(3) 3 76
(Richard Hannon) *hld up in 5th: nt clr run over 1f out: hdwy over 1f out: led ins fnl f: rdn out* **7/2**[2]
1 **2** 1 **Capolavoro (FR)**[25] 2442 5-9-11 **67**.................... PatCosgrave 4 73
(Robert Cowell) *pressed ldr: led 2f out tl ins fnl f: unable qck* **11/10**[1]
0400 **3** 2¾ **Noble Deed**[24] 2469 6-9-11 **67**....................(b) KierenFox 5 64
(Michael Attwater) *bhd: rdn over 2f out: effrt and hung lft over 1f out: styd on fnl f* **7/1**[3]
3400 **4** hd **Showtime Star**[96] 894 6-10-0 **70**.................... LukeMorris 6 67
(Gay Kelleway) *towards rr: outpcd 2f out: styd on fnl f* **7/1**[3]
6220 **5** 2¼ **Generalyse**[27] 2380 7-9-3 **59**....................(v) TimmyMurphy 2 48
(Anabel K Murphy) *t.k.h: prom on inner: chal 2f out: hrd rdn over 1f out: wknd fnl f* **16/1**
-000 **6** 3 **Quickaswecan**[18] 2643 5-9-10 **66**....................(t) RyanTate 1 46
(Milton Bradley) *led tl 2f out: wknd 1f out* **12/1**
2142 **7** 7 **Compton Prince**[96] 889 7-8-13 **55**....................(b) LiamKeniry 8 12
(Milton Bradley) *prom on outer tl wknd 2f out: eased whn wl btn fnl f* **12/1**

1m 10.43s (0.23) **Going Correction** +0.125s/f (Good)
WFA 3 from 5yo+ 8lb **7** Ran SP% **116.1**
Speed ratings (Par 103): **103,101,98,97,94 90,81**
CSF £7.99 CT £24.36 TOTE £4.20: £1.60, £1.40; EX 9.90 Trifecta £42.20.
Owner Al Shaqab Racing **Bred** Mrs D O'Brien **Trained** East Everleigh, Wilts

FOCUS
Race run over 8 yards further than advertised. The first two came down the centre in this ordinary sprint handicap, but the pair remain unexposed.

3260 OXFAM TRAILWALKER CHALLENGE 22ND-24TH JULY H'CAP 5f 59y
8:50 (8:51) (Class 6) (0-60,58) 3-Y-O+ **£2,264** (£673; £336; £168) **Stalls** Low

Form RPR
4035 **1** **Our Lord**[28] 2342 4-9-12 **58**.................... LukeMorris 2 64
(Bill Turner) *mde all: hld on wl fnl f: gamely* **15/8**[1]
1503 **2** nk **Picansort**[14] 2768 9-9-11 **57**.................... ShaneKelly 3 62
(Peter Crate) *hld up in 6th: hdwy 2f out: str chal fnl f: jst hld* **11/4**[2]
-400 **3** ½ **Go Charlie**[6] 3010 5-9-1 **47**.................... LemosdeSouza 5 50
(Lisa Williamson) *s.s: bhd: rdn 2f out: styd on wl fnl f* **17/2**
0600 **4** ¾ **Simply Black (IRE)**[11] 2845 5-8-12 **49**....................(p) AnnStokell(5) 4 49
(Ann Stokell) *hld up in 5th: rdn and hung lft over 1f out: styd on* **16/1**
00-5 **5** shd **Fabulous Flyer**[49] 1753 3-8-11 **50**.................... AdamBeschizza 7 47
(Jeremy Gask) *dwlt: t.k.h: sn prom on outer: chal 2f out: no ex ins fnl f* **8/1**
2224 **6** ½ **Imjin River (IRE)**[50] 1709 9-8-13 **45**....................(tp) PatCosgrave 6 43
(William Stone) *prom tl no ex fnl f* **8/1**
1565 **7** 1¾ **Eland Ally**[14] 2785 8-9-12 **58**....................(b) KieranO'Neill 1 50
(Anabel K Murphy) *dwlt: sn prom on inner: rdn 3f out: wknd 1f out* **6/1**[3]

1m 3.56s (1.26) **Going Correction** +0.125s/f (Good)
WFA 3 from 4yo+ 7lb **7** Ran SP% **114.4**
Speed ratings (Par 101): **94,93,92,91,91 90,87**
CSF £7.17 TOTE £3.10: £1.60, £1.60; EX 8.40 Trifecta £44.40.
Owner Mrs M S Teversham **Bred** Mrs Monica Teversham **Trained** Sigwells, Somerset

FOCUS
Race run over 8 yards further than advertised. They finished in a heap in this very moderate sprint handicap and the winner had an easy time of it early.
T/Plt: £68.10 to a £1 stake. Pool: £43,748.87 - 468.61 winning tickets. T/Qpdt: £51.80 to a £1 stake. Pool: £3,828.48 - 54.60 winning tickets. **Lee McKenzie**

3222 THIRSK (L-H)
Tuesday, June 14

OFFICIAL GOING: Good (good to firm in places; 8.8)
Wind: almost nil Weather: fine and sunny

3261 BRITISH STALLION STUDS 188BET EBF FILLIES' NOVICE STKS (PLUS 10 RACE) 6f
2:10 (2:10) (Class 5) 2-Y-O **£3,881** (£1,155; £577; £288) **Stalls** High

Form RPR
1 **Lady In Question (IRE)** 2-9-0 0.................... TonyHamilton 11 75
(Richard Fahey) *in rr: hdwy over 2f out: swtchd lft over 1f out: styd on to ld towards fin* **17/2**
2 nk **Peach Pavlova (IRE)** 2-9-0 0.................... PJMcDonald 8 74
(Ann Duffield) *chsd ldrs: led last 150yds: hdd and no ex towards fin* **16/1**
3 3½ **Screen Angel (IRE)** 2-9-0 0.................... GeorgeChaloner 1 64+
(Richard Fahey) *w ldrs: led over 1f out: hdd last 150yds: kpt on same pce* **12/1**
4 hd **Harbour Lightning** 2-9-0 0.................... JamesSullivan 10 63
(Ann Duffield) *s.i.s: rr-div: hdwy over 2f out: swtchd lft over 1f out: kpt on same pce* **66/1**
5 1¾ **Seduce Me** 2-9-0 0.................... DougieCostello 2 58+
(K R Burke) *w ldrs: edgd rt and wknd appr fnl f* **20/1**
6 nk **Hope Solo (IRE)** 2-9-0 0.................... JasonHart 6 63
(Tim Easterby) *s.i.s: in rr: hdwy and nt clr run over 1f out: keeping on whn bdly hmpd 150yds out* **40/1**
402 **7** nse **Mightaswellsmile**[14] 2771 2-9-0 0.................... TomEaves 12 60
(James Given) *led: hdd over 1f out: wkng whn n.m.r on inner 150yds out* **4/1**[2]
43 **8** 1 **Speed Freak**[18] 2637 2-9-0 0.................... ShaneGray 4 54
(Ralph Beckett) *wnt lft s: rr-div: effrt 2f out: nvr a factor* **2/1**[1]
3 **9** ¾ **Snuggy (IRE)**[8] 2970 2-9-0 0.................... SamJames 9 51
(David Barron) *chsd ldrs: lost pl over 1f out* **11/2**[3]
10 3 **Booshbash (IRE)** 2-9-0 0.................... SilvestreDeSousa 7 42+
(Ed Dunlop) *wnt rt s: in rr: sme hdwy over 2f out: reminders and sn wnt rt: sn lost pl* **17/2**
4 **11** 3 **Coco La Belle (IRE)**[11] 2852 2-9-0 0.................... DuranFentiman 3 33
(Tim Easterby) *hmpd s: t.k.h: sn mid-div: drvn 3f out: lost pl wl over 1f out: sn eased* **33/1**

1m 12.87s (0.17) **Going Correction** -0.10s/f (Good) **11** Ran SP% **115.0**
Speed ratings (Par 90): **94,93,88,88,86 85,85,84,83,79 75**
CSF £125.98 TOTE £8.40: £3.70, £5.80, £2.60; EX 166.20 Trifecta £2024.50.
Owner Ms Amie Canham **Bred** M Phelan **Trained** Musley Bank, N Yorks

FOCUS
Following the abandonment of the previous day's card after three races, this meeting had to pass an 8.30 inspection. The going was good, good to firm in places and the track had been watered overnight with 12mm on the bottom bend, 10mm on the top bend and 3mm on the straights. Home bend dolled out 6yds, adding about 20yds to the distances of races on the round course. An open fillies' novice event to start and the jockeys reported the ground to be on the soft side of good, with Dougie Costello describing it as "good to soft, a bit dead."

3262 ROYAL ASCOT 10% REFUND AT 188BET H'CAP 7f
2:45 (2:46) (Class 5) (0-70,70) 3-Y-O+ **£3,234** (£962; £481; £240) **Stalls** Low

Form RPR
001 **1** **Robero**[10] 2918 4-9-8 **64**.................... BenCurtis 16 76+
(Brian Ellison) *trckd ldrs on outer: led over 1f out: drvn out* **7/2**[1]
054- **2** 1¾ **Dark Wonder (IRE)**[166] 8411 4-9-6 **62**....................(p) TomEaves 3 69
(Ivan Furtado) *chsd ldrs: swtchd rt over 1f out: styd on to take 2nd last 75yds* **12/1**
4-34 **3** 1 **Courier**[18] 2660 4-9-7 **66**.................... JacobButterfield(3) 14 70
(Marjorie Fife) *trckd ldr: led briefly 2f out: kpt on same pce* **11/1**
0044 **4** nk **Tanawar (IRE)**[10] 2918 6-9-8 **64**....................(b) JamesSullivan 12 67+
(Ruth Carr) *swtchd lft after s: hld up in rr: hdwy over 2f out: kpt on fnl f: tk 4th clsng stages* **12/1**

-005 **5** *1* **Just Paul (IRE)**[10] 2906 6-9-1 **57**................................(p) PJMcDonald 11 58
(Micky Hammond) *in rr: hdwy over 2f out: hung lft and one pce over 1f out* **10/1**[3]
2550 **6** *2 1/2* **Cliff (IRE)**[14] 2773 6-9-10 **66**....................................... SilvestreDeSousa 9 60
(Nigel Tinkler) *in rr on outer: drvn over 3f out: hdwy over 2f out: hung lft: one pce* **7/2**[1]
6006 **7** *hd* **Lackaday**[17] 2680 4-9-10 **66**..(p) JasonHart 13 60
(Mark Walford) *led: hdd 2f out: fdd appr fnl f* **18/1**
0-54 **8** *4 1/2* **Nelson's Bay**[18] 2661 7-8-7 **56**.. HollieDoyle(7) 4 37
(Wilf Storey) *s.i.s: hld up in rr: nt clr run over 2f out: wknd over 1f out* **11/1**
0-50 **9** *1* **Alans Pride (IRE)**[28] 2343 4-9-3 **59**..........................(p) ConnorBeasley 5 38
(Michael Dods) *in tch: dropped to rr over 2f out: sme hdwy over 2f out: wknd over 1f out* **13/2**[2]
0043 **10** *1/2* **Intense Starlet (IRE)**[14] 2778 5-9-4 **60**........................... SamJames 10 37
(Marjorie Fife) *uns rdr and led to post: trckd ldrs: wknd over 1f out: sn eased* **33/1**
5364 **11** *2 3/4* **Kadooment Day (IRE)**[49] 1764 3-8-11 **68**........... JordanVaughan(5) 15 34
(K R Burke) *in tch on outer: effrt over 2f out: sn wknd* **16/1**
00-0 **12** *7* **Ella's Delight (IRE)**[14] 2773 6-9-4 **60**............................. BarryMcHugh 1 11
(Martin Todhunter) *s.i.s: hdwy over 5f out: lost pl over 2f out: eased whn bhd clsng stages* **50/1**

1m 27.22s (0.02) **Going Correction** +0.10s/f (Good)
WFA 3 from 4yo+ 10lb **12** Ran SP% **115.0**
Speed ratings (Par 103): **103,101,99,99,98 95,95,90,89,88 85,77**
CSF £46.34 CT £424.39 TOTE £3.70: £1.80, £3.70, £4.80; EX 28.30 Trifecta £345.50.
Owner Alan Zheng **Bred** Mrs P C Burton & R J Lampard **Trained** Norton, N Yorks

FOCUS
Rail movement added about 20yds to race distance. A modest handicap and it was imperative to be handy, with the first three in the first four positions throughout.

3263 THEAKSTON BEST BITTER H'CAP 1m 4f
3:20 (3:20) (Class 4) (0-80,80) 4-Y-O+ **£4,851** (£1,443; £721; £360) **Stalls** High

Form RPR
6-00 **1** **Plane Song (IRE)**[21] 2556 4-9-2 **75**........................ SilvestreDeSousa 6 84+
(Alan Swinbank) *trckd ldrs: effrt over 3f out: led and edgd lft over 1f out: drvn rt out* **7/2**[2]
-003 **2** *1/2* **Endless Credit (IRE)**[10] 2911 6-9-2 **75**........................... PJMcDonald 2 83
(Micky Hammond) *led: edgd rt and hdd over 1f out: kpt on wl: no ex nr fin* **13/2**[3]
4-16 **3** *4* **Lady Lekki (IRE)**[38] 2051 4-8-13 **72**................................. JoeyHaynes 5 74
(Ben Haslam) *chsd ldrs: pushed along over 5f out: hmpd and swtchd rt over 1f out: kpt on one pce* **15/2**
441- **4** *nk* **Trevisani (IRE)**[244] 7213 4-9-7 **80**....................................(b) TedDurcan 1 81
(David Lanigan) *s.s: hld up in rr: plld wd 3f out: sn rdn and hung lft: styd on clsng stages* **9/4**[1]
0-30 **5** *1/2* **Poetic Verse**[18] 2663 6-9-5 **78**....................................... DougieCostello 4 78
(John Quinn) *chsd ldrs: effrt 3f out: one pce over 1f out* **15/2**
0-04 **6** *2* **Novancia (IRE)**[6] 3027 4-9-7 **80**...................................... FrannyNorton 7 78
(Mark Johnston) *swtchd lft after s: in rr: effrt over 3f out: no imp: eased nr fin* **7/1**
20-0 **7** *1/2* **Cloud Monkey (IRE)**[5] 2163 6-9-4 **77**............................ BarryMcHugh 8 73
(Martin Todhunter) *half-rrd s: hld up in rr: t.k.h: sme hdwy over 2f out: wknd fnl f* **12/1**

2m 39.59s (3.39) **Going Correction** +0.10s/f (Good) **7** Ran SP% **110.0**
Speed ratings (Par 105): **92,91,89,88,88 87,86**
CSF £24.03 CT £146.94 TOTE £3.60: £1.10, £3.60; EX 23.00 Trifecta £92.70.
Owner Brian Valentine **Bred** Ballymacoll Stud Farm Ltd **Trained** Melsonby, N Yorks

FOCUS
Rail movement added about 20yds to race distance. A fair handicap, but the pace was ordinary. The race has been rated around the runner-up.

3264 STALLIONS BREEDING WINNERS 188BET.CO.UK EBF MAIDEN STKS 1m
3:55 (3:56) (Class 5) 3-Y-O+ **£3,881** (£1,155; £577; £288) **Stalls** Low

Form RPR
45 **1** **Idealist**[18] 2653 3-8-12 0.. FrederikTylicki 4 75
(Roger Varian) *w ldr: led after 1f: drvn over 2f out: edgd rt and hld on clsng stages* **4/1**[2]
56 **2** *1/2* **Warrior Prince**[31] 2248 3-9-3 0................................ SilvestreDeSousa 9 79
(Ed Dunlop) *led 1f: chsd wnr: drvn upsides over 2f out: no ex towards fin* **6/4**[1]
2 **3** *1/2* **Imperial Focus (IRE)**[12] 2835 3-9-0 0............................... JoeDoyle(3) 2 78
(Simon Waugh) *trckd ldrs: effrt over 2f out: swtchd ins and styd on fnl 100yds* **4/1**[2]
36 **4** *4 1/2* **Wasseem (IRE)**[13] 2790 3-9-3 0......................................(t) MartinLane 6 67
(Simon Crisford) *trckd ldrs: effrt 3f out: fdd fnl f* **6/1**[3]
45 **5** *1 3/4* **Lucky Violet (IRE)**[12] 2809 4-9-4 0......................... ShirleyTeasdale(5) 5 61+
(Iain Jardine) *mid-div: stdy hdwy 3f out: kpt on to take modest 5th 1f out* **33/1**
6 *2 3/4* **Al Nasser Alwashik** 3-9-3 0... SamJames 11 56
(David Loughnane) *s.i.s: sn bhd: hdwy and hung lft over 2f out: tk modest 6th clsng stages* **66/1**
4- **7** *1 1/4* **Royal Acclaim (IRE)**[358] 3453 4-10-0 0......................... BarryMcHugh 1 56
(Rebecca Bastiman) *mid-div: drvn 3f out: sn chsng ldrs: wknd fnl f* **80/1**
8 *5* **Western Way (IRE)**[7] 7-10-0 0.. TedDurcan 8 44
(Don Cantillon) *s.s: a towards rr hanging lft thrght* **12/1**
9 *16* **Scarlet Wings** 3-8-12 0.. BenCurtis 3
(K R Burke) *s.i.s: sn bhd: t.o* **18/1**

1m 41.53s (1.43) **Going Correction** +0.10s/f (Good)
WFA 3 from 4yo+ 11lb **9** Ran SP% **112.9**
Speed ratings (Par 103): **93,92,92,87,85 83,81,76,60**
CSF £10.06 TOTE £4.60: £1.70, £1.10, £1.50; EX 12.20 Trifecta £17.20.
Owner Cheveley Park Stud **Bred** Cheveley Park Stud Ltd **Trained** Newmarket, Suffolk
■ Stewards' Enquiry : Shirley Teasdale 14-day ban: failed to take all reasonable and permissable measures to obtain best possible placing (Jun 28-Jul 9,11-12)

FOCUS
Rail movement added about 20yds to race distance. A modest older-horse maiden and the order barely changed.

3265 ROYAL ASCOT EXTRA PLACES AT 188BET H'CAP (DIV I) 6f
4:35 (4:35) (Class 4) (0-85,85) 3-Y-O+ **£4,851** (£1,443; £721; £360) **Stalls** High

Form RPR
0011 **1** **Orion's Bow**[17] 2680 5-10-0 **85**.. BarryMcHugh 4 102+
(David Nicholls) *trckd ldrs: led on bit appr fnl f: pushed clr: v readily* **11/4**[1]
-525 **2** *3 1/4* **Highly Sprung (IRE)**[8] 2981 3-8-10 **75**.......................... FrannyNorton 1 80
(Mark Johnston) *w ldr: led briefly 2f out: kpt on: no ch w wnr* **11/2**[2]
-002 **3** *1* **Mass Rally (IRE)**[19] 2613 9-9-6 **82**.................................(b) PhilDennis(5) 9 86
(Michael Dods) *hood removed v late: dwlt: hld up towards rr: hdwy on outside over 2f out: chsng ldng pair over 1f out: edgd lft: kpt on same pce* **11/2**[2]
04-0 **4** *1 1/2* **York Glory (USA)**[48] 1787 8-9-2 **73**.............................. JamesSullivan 5 72
(Ruth Carr) *s.s: hld up in rr: hdwy 2f out: kpt on to take modest 4th clsng stages* **14/1**
0044 **5** *1 1/2* **Tribesman**[11] 2854 3-8-1 **66**.. CamHardie 2 58
(Marjorie Fife) *mid-div: hdwy on outer over 2f out: one pce over 1f out* **25/1**
0-00 **6** *3/4* **Signore Piccolo**[19] 2613 5-9-4 **80**................................(p) JoshDoyle(5) 10 72
(David O'Meara) *trckd ldrs: effrt over 2f out: edgd lft over 1f out: one pce* **13/2**[3]
0600 **7** *1 3/4* **Adam's Ale**[13] 2803 7-9-9 **80**.. DougieCostello 6 66
(Mark Walford) *mid-div: swtchd outside to chse ldrs over 2f out: wknd appr fnl f* **8/1**
05-0 **8** *2 3/4* **Compton Park**[11] 2857 9-9-7 **78**.. PJMcDonald 8 55
(Les Eyre) *dwlt: hld up towards rr: sme hdwy over 2f out: wknd over 1f out* **18/1**
0-60 **9** *2 1/2* **Fast Shot**[48] 1787 8-8-13 **75**................................ RachelRichardson(5) 11 44
(Tim Easterby) *in rr: drvn over 2f out: nvr a factor* **7/1**
-000 **10** *2 3/4* **Native Falls (IRE)**[11] 2857 5-9-1 **72**................................ NeilFarley 3 33
(Alan Swinbank) *swtchd lft after s: led: hdd 2f: sn lost pl* **50/1**

1m 10.68s (-2.02) **Going Correction** -0.10s/f (Good)
WFA 3 from 5yo+ 8lb **10** Ran SP% **112.1**
Speed ratings (Par 105): **109,104,103,101,99 98,96,92,89,85**
CSF £16.65 CT £77.12 TOTE £3.20: £1.20, £1.90, £1.90; EX 16.70 Trifecta £41.50.
Owner T J Swiers **Bred** Cheveley Park Stud Ltd **Trained** Sessay, N Yorks

FOCUS
The first division of a fair sprint handicap, but quite a few of these have seen better days and it proved one-way traffic for the in-form favourite.

3266 ROYAL ASCOT EXTRA PLACES AT 188BET H'CAP (DIV II) 6f
5:10 (5:10) (Class 4) (0-85,85) 3-Y-O+ **£4,851** (£1,443; £721; £360) **Stalls** High

Form RPR
0-05 **1** **Eastern Racer (IRE)**[45] 1848 4-9-9 **80**................................(p) DaleSwift 7 89
(Brian Ellison) *dwlt: jnd ldrs after 2f: led over 1f out: fnd ex clsng stages* **5/1**[3]
5-45 **2** *1 1/4* **Foreign Diplomat**[11] 2857 4-9-10 **81**................................... SamJames 5 86
(David O'Meara) *hld up: smooth hdwy to trck ldrs over 2f out: upsides over 1f out: edgd lft and styd on same pce last 50yds* **7/1**
01 **3** *3/4* **The Commendatore**[28] 2336 3-9-0 **79**..............................(b) JasonHart 8 80+
(David Barron) *hld up in rr: hdwy and swtchd outside over 2f out: upsides over 1f out: kpt on same pce last 75yds* **3/1**[1]
0223 **4** *nk* **Manatee Bay**[11] 2857 6-9-6 **77**...(v) PaulQuinn 1 79
(David Nicholls) *mid-div: effrt over 2f out: upsides over 1f out: kpt on same pce fnl 100yds* **13/2**
10-3 **5** *6* **Mustique (IRE)**[13] 2802 3-9-1 **80**...................................... TonyHamilton 4 60
(Richard Fahey) *t.k.h: trckd ldrs: lost pl over 1f out* **10/3**[2]
23-0 **6** *1 3/4* **Bushephalus (IRE)**[5] 3068 4-9-3 **74**......................... SilvestreDeSousa 3 51
(Ivan Furtado) *swtchd rt after s: led: hdd over 1f out: sn wknd: eased clsng stages* **10/1**
-430 **7** *13* **Ravenhoe (IRE)**[43] 1922 3-8-7 **72**....................................... MartinLane 9 5
(Mark Johnston) *awkward s: chsd ldrs after 1f: drvn 3f out: lost pl 2f out: eased whn bhd clsng stages* **8/1**

1m 11.26s (-1.44) **Going Correction** -0.10s/f (Good)
WFA 3 from 4yo+ 8lb **7** Ran SP% **110.8**
Speed ratings (Par 105): **105,103,102,101,93 91,74**
CSF £36.42 CT £116.24 TOTE £5.90: £3.50, £4.40; EX 49.90 Trifecta £154.80.
Owner Mrs J A Martin **Bred** Tally-Ho Stud **Trained** Norton, N Yorks

FOCUS
The winning time was just over half a second slower than the first division. A personal best from the winner.

3267 EBF STALLIONS BEST ODDS GUARANTEED AT 188BET MAIDEN STKS 7f
5:45 (5:46) (Class 5) 3-Y-O **£3,881** (£1,155; £577; £288) **Stalls** Low

Form RPR
1 **Takatul (USA)** 3-9-2 0.. MichaelJMMurphy(3) 9 84+
(Charles Hills) *s.i.s: in rr: drvn over 3f out: swtchd outside over 1f out: styd on to ld last 150yds* **11/2**[3]
0-3 **2** *1 3/4* **Malakky (IRE)**[17] 2698 3-9-5 0... TedDurcan 11 72
(Brian Meehan) *restless in stalls: trckd ldrs: led briefly 1f out: no ex* **5/4**[1]
65 **3** *3 1/4* **Enjoy Life (IRE)**[29] 2304 3-9-0 0... ShaneGray 3 58
(Kevin Ryan) *trckd ldrs: led 2f out: hdd 1f out: kpt on same pce* **20/1**
6-5 **4** *hd* **Ballyer Rallyer (IRE)**[36] 2109 3-9-5 0.................................... DaleSwift 1 63
(Daniel Mark Loughnane) *s.s: t.k.h: sn trcking ldrs: edgd rt over 1f out: kpt on towards fin* **50/1**
03-4 **5** *4* **Joyful Day (IRE)**[155] 145 3-9-5 69.................................. TonyHamilton 2 52
(Robert Cowell) *led: hdd over 2f out: grad wknd* **7/1**
4- **6** *hd* **Qortaaj**[220] 7752 3-9-5 0... SamJames 6 51
(David Loughnane) *trckd ldrs: swtchd rt 2f out: wknd over 1f out* **11/1**
0- **7** *9* **Fleeting Dream (IRE)**[238] 7360 3-9-0 0.......................... FrederikTylicki 10 22
(William Haggas) *s.i.s: in rr: nvr on terms* **5/2**[2]
0 **8** *1/2* **Lord Bopper (IRE)**[12] 2809 3-9-0 0............................ RobJFitzpatrick(5) 5 26
(Ben Haslam) *trckd ldrs: t.k.h: lost pl over 1f out* **100/1**
00 **9** *32* **Cecile Royale**[49] 1753 3-9-0 0.. SaleemGolam 4
(Stuart Williams) *s.i.s: in rr: wl bhd fnl 2f: t.o* **66/1**

1m 28.32s (1.12) **Going Correction** +0.10s/f (Good) **9** Ran SP% **118.4**
Speed ratings (Par 99): **97,95,91,91,86 86,75,75,38**
CSF £13.00 TOTE £6.60: £2.20, £1.10, £4.80; EX 15.00 Trifecta £211.80.
Owner Hamdan Al Maktoum **Bred** Shadwell Farm LLC **Trained** Lambourn, Berks

FOCUS
Rail movement added about 20yds to race distance. A modest and uncompetitive 3yo maiden and not form to get carried away with outside of the winner.

3268 US OPEN GOLF AT 188BET H'CAP 5f
6:15 (6:15) (Class 6) (0-65,65) 3-Y-O+ **£2,726** (£805; £402) **Stalls** High

Form RPR
0160 **1** **Coiste Bodhar (IRE)**[19] 2622 5-9-4 **62**................. NatalieHambling(7) 6 69
(Scott Dixon) *mde virtually all: hotly pressed fnl f: fnd ex nr fin* **16/1**
-630 **2** *nk* **Sarabi**[12] 2834 3-9-4 **62**...(p) DaleSwift 9 65
(Scott Dixon) *w ldrs: upsides fnl f: no ex nr fin* **20/1**

2650 **3** *hd* **Seamster**[19] **2622** 9-9-5 **56**....(t) SamJames 1 61
(David Loughnane) *led two others centre: w ldrs edgd rt over 1f out: no ex clsng stages* **16/1**

-155 **4** 1 ¾ **Perfect Words (IRE)**[12] **2808** 6-9-9 **63**.... JacobButterfield(3) 10 62+
(Marjorie Fife) *chsd ldrs: kpt on same pce fnl f* **18/1**

1-13 **5** ½ **Show Palace**[11] **2854** 3-9-5 **63**.... DougieCostello 16 58+
(Jennie Candlish) *mid-div stands' side: effrt over 2f out: hung lft over 1f out: kpt on fnl 100yds* **3/1**[1]

2054 **6** 1 ¾ **Bahango (IRE)**[22] **2523** 4-9-1 **59**....(p) AdamMcNamara(7) 5 50
(Patrick Morris) *chsd ldrs: fdd fnl f* **28/1**

0043 **7** ½ **Boxing Shadows**[8] **2975** 6-10-0 **65**.... TonyHamilton 13 54+
(Les Eyre) *in rr: hdwy 2f out: kpt on: nt rch ldrs* **10/1**

-620 **8** 2 ¼ **Lorimer's Lot (IRE)**[10] **2919** 5-9-1 **52**....(p) JasonHart 7 33
(Mark Walford) *s.i.s: hdwy over 2f out: hung lft: wknd over 1f out* **20/1**

-320 **9** 1 **Anieres Boy**[10] **2919** 4-9-4 **60**.... NathanEvans(5) 15 37
(Michael Easterby) *mid-div: drvn over 2f out: sn outpcd* **9/2**[2]

05-0 **10** 1 ¼ **Kingfisher Girl**[31] **2255** 3-8-6 **53**.... TimClark(3) 3 23
(Michael Appleby) *racd w two others centre: chsd ldr that gp: lost pl over 1f out* **50/1**

3055 **11** ¾ **Penny Royale**[8] **2974** 4-9-9 **65**....(b) RachelRichardson(5) 2 35
(Tim Easterby) *racd w two others centre: chsd ldr that gp: wknd over 1f out* **6/1**[3]

60-3 **12** 1 ¼ **Pavers Star**[17] **2676** 7-9-6 **57**....(p) BarryMcHugh 14 23
(Noel Wilson) *chsd ldrs: wknd over 1f out* **25/1**

-600 **13** 2 ½ **Caymus**[12] **2834** 3-8-7 **56**.... PhilDennis(5) 4 10
(Tracy Waggott) *s.i.s: swtchd lft after s: sn w ldrs: lost pl over 1f out* **80/1**

632 **14** 33 **Mighty Bond**[59] **1490** 4-8-12 **49**.... FrederikTylicki 12
(Tracy Waggott) *towards rr: lost pl and wl bhd over 2f out: sn eased: virtually p.u: t.o* **7/1**

59.06s (-0.54) **Going Correction** -0.10s/f (Good)
WFA 3 from 4yo+ 7lb **14** Ran SP% **116.1**
Speed ratings (Par 101): **100,99,99,96,95 92,92,88,86,84 83,81,77,24**
CSF £306.04 CT £5219.18 TOTE £22.80: £6.10, £5.30, £6.60; EX 219.10 Trifecta £5596.90 Part won..
Owner Yvonne Lowe & W A Robinson **Bred** C Amerian **Trained** Babworth, Notts
■ Stewards' Enquiry : Natalie Hambling two-day ban: used whip above permitted level (Jun 28-29)

FOCUS
A moderate but open sprint handicap to end. The majority of the runners came up the nearside while three, including the third, came up the centre. This was a race dominated by those that raced up with the pace and it resulted in a 1-2 for trainer Scott Dixon.
T/Plt: £825.00 to a £1 stake. Pool: £47,095.62 - 41.67 winning tickets. T/Qpdt: £18.50 to a £1 stake. Pool: £4,213.61 - 167.90 winning tickets. **Walter Glynn**

3242 ASCOT (R-H)
Wednesday, June 15

OFFICIAL GOING: Soft (stands' side 6.6, centre 6.5, far side 6.4, round 5.8)
Wind: Light, across Weather: Sunny Intervals and showers

3269 JERSEY STKS (GROUP 3) 7f
2:30 (2:35) (Class 1) 3-Y-O
£51,039 (£19,350; £9,684; £4,824; £2,421; £1,215) **Stalls** Centre

Form RPR

1-23 **1** **Ribchester (IRE)**[46] **1864** 3-9-6 113.... WilliamBuick 7 118
(Richard Fahey) *travelled strly thrght: trckd ldrs: clsd to press ldrs 2f out: rdn and qcknd to ld ent fnl f: r.o strly: rdn out* **7/1**[2]

1-11 **2** 2 ¼ **Thikriyaat (IRE)**[32] **2250** 3-9-1 103.... PaulHanagan 17 107+
(Sir Michael Stoute) *hld up towards rr: swtchd rt over 2f out: swtchd bk lft and effrt ent fnl 2f: drifting rt and hdwy ent fnl f: styd on strly ins fnl f to snatch 2nd last strides: no threat to wnr* **8/1**[3]

0-13 **3** *hd* **Forge**[20] **2627** 3-9-1 101.... RyanMoore 3 106
(Sir Michael Stoute) *swtg: hld up in midfield: effrt to chse ldrs over 1f out: clsd 3rd but unable qck ent fnl f: chsd clr wnr wl ins fnl f: no imp and lost 2nd last strides* **12/1**

23-1 **4** ½ **Ibn Malik (IRE)**[63] **1424** 3-9-1 111.... JamesMcDonald 2 105
(Charles Hills) *travelled strly: trckd ldr tl led 2f out: sn drvn: hdd ent fnl f: nt gng pce of wnr and kpt on same pce ins fnl f: lost 2 pls wl ins fnl f* **8/1**[3]

-112 **5** 1 **Remarkable**[32] **2242** 3-9-1 98....(b) RobertHavlin 10 102+
(John Gosden) *hld up towards rr: gd hdwy 2f out: chsng ldrs and rdn whn hung rt over 1f out: swtchd lft ent fnl f: stl wanting to hang rt and one pce ins fnl f: nt clrest of runs towards fin* **8/1**[3]

11 **6** 2 ½ **Castle Harbour**[35] **2161** 3-9-1 98.... FrankieDettori 9 96+
(John Gosden) *lw: hld up in tch towards rr: hdwy over 2f out: chsd ldrs and rdn over 1f out: unable qck and btn 1f out: wknd ins fnl f* **5/1**[1]

1324 **7** 1 ¼ **Haalick (IRE)**[12] **2870** 3-9-1 104....(v[1]) AndreaAtzeni 1 93
(Roger Varian) *s.i.s: sn rcvrd and in tch in midfield after 2f: rdn and hdwy 2f out: unable qck over 1f out: wknd ins fnl f* **12/1**

3-53 **8** *nk* **Raucous**[12] **2870** 3-9-1 104....(p) JimCrowley 13 92
(William Haggas) *in tch in midfield: effrt 2f out: unable qck u.p and edging rt over 1f out: wknd ins fnl f* **50/1**

-113 **9** *nse* **Gifted Master (IRE)**[18] **2692** 3-9-4 115.... PatSmullen 5 95
(Hugo Palmer) *led: hdd 2f out: sn u.p and no ex: lost pl and btn jst over 1f out: wknd ins fnl f* **7/1**[2]

3-15 **10** 4 ½ **C Note (IRE)**[49] **1773** 3-9-1 99.... ColmO'Donoghue 8 80
(Martyn Meade) *lw: chsd ldrs: rdn jst over 2f out: sn struggling and btn over 1f out: wknd ins fnl f* **25/1**

11-2 **11** 3 ½ **Light Music**[39] **2034** 3-8-12 98.... PatCosgrave 14 68
(William Haggas) *stdd and wnt lft s: t.k.h: hld up in tch towards rr: hdwy into midfield after 2f: rdn and no imp 2f out: sn btn and wknd fnl f* **14/1**

55-1 **12** 1 ¾ **Ross Castle (IRE)**[33] **2232** 3-9-4 105....(t) TonyPiccone 4 69
(Matthieu Palussiere, France) *bhd: u.p and drifting rt over 2f out: plugged on to pass btn horses over 1f out: nvr trbld ldrs* **40/1**

-235 **13** 1 ¼ **Scrutineer (IRE)**[12] **2870** 3-9-1 102.... SilvestreDeSousa 12 63
(Mick Channon) *t.k.h: hld up wl in tch in midfield: rdn jst over 2f out: sn struggling and btn over 1f out: wknd fnl f* **28/1**

0- **14** 2 ¼ **Bolting (USA)**[37] **2117** 3-9-1 101.... StephanePasquier 6 57
(F-H Graffard, France) *athletic: t.k.h: hld up in tch in midfield: rdn and lost pl jst over 2f out: bhd over 1f out* **25/1**

6010 **15** *nk* **Calder Prince (IRE)**[12] **2870** 3-9-1 99.... RichardKingscote 15 57
(Tom Dascombe) *lw: chsd ldrs: rdn over 2f out: sn drvn and lost pl: wknd over 1f out* **66/1**

3-14 **16** 4 **Steady Pace**[125] **539** 3-9-1 111.... JamesDoyle 11 46
(Saeed bin Suroor) *swtchd rt s and t.k.h early: in tch in midfield: rdn 3f out: sn struggling and lost pl: no ch over 1f out* **25/1**

20-0 **17** 4 ½ **Herald The Dawn (IRE)**[46] **1864** 3-9-6 112.... KevinManning 18 39
(J S Bolger, Ire) *wl in tch in midfield: clsd to chse ldrs 1/2-way: rdn and lost pl over 2f out: sn wl btn and bhd over 1f out* **16/1**

33-0 **18** 11 **Ocean Eleven**[6] **3079** 3-9-1 80....(p) RobertWinston 20 6
(John Ryan) *a in rr: rdn 3f out: sn wl btn: t.o and eased ins fnl f* **150/1**

1 **19** ¾ **Toliman**[37] **2117** 3-9-1 104....(p) Pierre-CharlesBoudot 16 4
(A & G Botti, Italy) *w'like: in tch in midfield: lost pl and rdn over 2f out: bhd wl over 1f out: t.o and eased ins fnl f* **66/1**

1m 28.49s (0.89) **Going Correction** +0.35s/f (Good) **19** Ran SP% **126.0**
Speed ratings (Par 109): **108,105,105,104,103 100,99,98,98,93 89,87,86,83,83 78,73,61,60**
CSF £57.99 CT £698.94 TOTE £6.90: £2.80, £3.30, £4.50; EX 64.50 Trifecta £1246.00.
Owner Godolphin **Bred** A Thompson & M O'Brien **Trained** Musley Bank, N Yorks

FOCUS
The running rail on the round course was positioned approx 6yds out from the 1m4f start decreasing to 3yds out about 9f out to the home straight. The course saw no rain after racing on the opening day until a heavy shower about an hour prior to the Jersey Stakes. Rider James Doyle said: "It is the same as yesterday" and Jim Crowley said: "After that shower, it is the same as yesterday." This looked typically wide open, but the form horses generally came to the fore, with those racing in the far side group faring best, and it makes sense. The level is a bit fluid, but the runner-up has been rated to form for now.

3270 QUEEN MARY STKS (GROUP 2) (FILLIES) 5f
3:05 (3:11) (Class 1) 2-Y-O
£62,381 (£23,650; £11,836; £5,896; £2,959; £1,485) **Stalls** Centre

Form RPR

1 **Lady Aurelia (USA)**[55] 2-9-0 0....(b) FrankieDettori 14 123+
(Wesley A Ward, U.S.A) *tall: str: mde all: qcknd clr over 1f out: pushed out and r.o strly ins fnl f: impressive* **2/1**[1]

2 7 **Al Johrah**[26] **2454** 2-9-0 0.... GregoryBenoist 8 98
(H-F Devin, France) *str: lw: midfield: hdwy 2f out: rdn to go 2nd 1f out: styd on but no ch w wnr fnl f* **9/2**[2]

212 **3** 2 ½ **Clem Fandango (FR)**[18] **2670** 2-9-0 0.... PhillipMakin 1 89
(Keith Dalgleish) *leggy: in tch: effrt 2f out: sn chsd ldrs: nt qckn over 1f out: kpt on for press ins fnl f but a hld* **16/1**

11 **4** ½ **Kocollada (IRE)**[11] **2908** 2-9-0 0.... JamieSpencer 9 87
(Richard Fahey) *cmpt: stdd s: hld up in rr: rdn 2f out: hdwy over 1f out: styd on ins fnl f: gng on at fin but nt pce to rch ldrs* **16/1**

31 **5** *hd* **Simmie (IRE)**[11] **2902** 2-9-0 0.... PatDobbs 7 86
(Sylvester Kirk) *w'like: hld up in rr: hdwy whn carried rt over 1f out: styd on ins fnl f: gng on at fin but nt pce to rch ldrs* **100/1**

21 **6** 2 ¼ **Barroche (IRE)**[19] **2637** 2-9-0 0.... AdamKirby 15 78
(Clive Cox) *lengthy: chsd ldrs: wnt 2nd 2f out: rdn and outpcd by wnr appr fnl f: lost 2nd 1f out: no ex fnl 100yds* **14/1**

2110 **7** 1 ½ **Stormy Clouds (IRE)**[33] **2219** 2-9-0 0.... SeanLevey 4 73
(Richard Hannon) *midfield: rdn over 2f out: struggling to go pce of ldrs over 1f out: styd on towards fin: nvr able to trble ldrs* **33/1**

4 **8** *nse* **Roly Poly (USA)**[25] **2494** 2-9-0 0.... RyanMoore 5 73
(A P O'Brien, Ire) *str: lw: hld up: carried rt and hmpd over 1f out: hdwy sn after: kpt on ins fnl f: nvr able to trble ldrs* **8/1**

2 **9** 3 ¼ **Madam Dancealot (IRE)**[41] **1976** 2-9-0 0.... PatSmullen 2 61
(Joseph Tuite) *chsd ldrs: pushed along 1/2-way: wknd over 1f out* **25/1**

1 **10** *hd* **Kachess**[12] **2874** 2-9-0 0.... RichardKingscote 3 60
(Tom Dascombe) *athletic: chsd wnr: rdn and lost 2nd 2f out: jinked lft whn u.p and losing pl over 1f out: wl btn ins fnl f* **13/2**[3]

1 **11** *hd* **Quench Dolly**[26] **2429** 2-9-0 0.... MichaelJMMurphy 13 60
(John Gallagher) *midfield: effrt to chse ldrs 2f out: rdn and outpcd over 1f out* **100/1**

52 **12** 2 ¼ **Reeh (IRE)**[14] **2793** 2-9-0 0.... PaulHanagan 6 52
(John Gosden) *racd keenly: in tch: rdn and wknd over 1f out* **33/1**

614 **13** 1 ½ **Jule In The Crown**[20] **2624** 2-9-0 0.... SilvestreDeSousa 16 46
(Mick Channon) *lw: hld up: hdwy 2f out: rdn over 1f out: sn wknd* **20/1**

321 **14** ¾ **Camargue**[40] **1988** 2-9-0 0.... WilliamBuick 12 43
(Mark Johnston) *lw: chsd ldrs: pushed along 2f out: outpcd whn edgd rt over 1f out: sn wknd* **12/1**

041 **15** 1 ½ **Vona (IRE)**[33] **2219** 2-9-0 0.... JackGarritty 17 38
(Richard Fahey) *hld up: pushed along 2f out: no imp: eased whn wl btn ins fnl f* **25/1**

16 ½ **Spiaggia (IRE)**[22] 2-9-0 0.... TonyPiccone 10 36
(F Chappet, France) *str: lw: chsd ldrs: pushed along 2f out: wknd over 1f out: eased whn wl btn ins fnl f* **25/1**

1 **17** 4 **Katrine (IRE)**[40] **2014** 2-9-0 0.... JoeFanning 11 22
(Mark Johnston) *leggy: hmpd and squeezed out s: midfield: lost pl 2f out: eased whn wl btn ins fnl f* **33/1**

1m 0.14s (-0.36) **Going Correction** +0.35s/f (Good) **17** Ran SP% **129.2**
Speed ratings (Par 102): **116,104,100,100,99 96,93,93,88,88 87,84,81,80,78 77,70**
CSF £9.43 CT £127.82 TOTE £2.60: £1.50, £2.30, £5.60; EX 13.00 Trifecta £180.60.
Owner Stonestreet Stables LLC/G Bolton/P Leidel **Bred** Stonestreet Thoroughbred Holdings LLC **Trained** North America

FOCUS
Debatable just how strong a Group 2 this was, but all the hype around the US raider proved spot on and the favourite blew her rivals away in the style of a top-class sprinting juvenile. They raced in one large group down the centre. It's been rated a sensational performance, and on a part of the track that was largely avoided as it was perceived to be a tad slower. This year's domestic 2yo fillies to date look well below par and the third has been rated in line with her Beverley effort.

3271 DUKE OF CAMBRIDGE STKS (GROUP 2) (F&M) 1m (S)
3:40 (3:44) (Class 1) 4-Y-O+
£99,242 (£37,625; £18,830; £9,380; £4,707; £2,362) **Stalls** Centre

Form RPR

0-1 **1** **Usherette (IRE)**[45] **1886** 4-9-3 117.... MickaelBarzalona 10 119+
(A Fabre, France) *hld up in tch in midfield: clsd to join ldrs and travelling strly 2f out: rdn to ld 1f out: qcknd clr 1f out: r.o strly: eased cl home: comf* **9/4**[1]

35 **2** 2 ¼ **Furia Cruzada (CHI)**[45] **1886** 4-9-0 109.... PatSmullen 7 111
(John Gosden) *stdd after s: hld up in tch in last quintet: rdn and hdwy over 1f out: rdn to chse clr wnr and edgd rt 1f out: r.o but no imp* **20/1**

12-1 **3** *shd* **Always Smile (IRE)**[34] **2191** 4-9-0 110.... JamesDoyle 13 110+
(Saeed bin Suroor) *lw: stdd s: hld up in tch in rr: swtchd lft and effrt ent fnl 2f: hdwy u.p jst over 1f out: styd on strly and battling for 2nd towards fin: no threat to wnr* **9/2**[2]

432- **4** 1 **Miss Temple City (USA)**[61] **1472** 4-9-5 110....(t) RyanMoore 9 113
(H Graham Motion, U.S.A) *stdd after s: t.k.h: hld up in tch in last quintet: swtchd rt and nt clr run jst over 2f out: hdwy u.p over 1f out: battling for placings 1f out: kpt on same pce fnl f* **12/1**

12-0 **5** *shd* **Jazzi Top**[45] 1886 4-9-0 115 FrankieDettori 2 108
(John Gosden) *t.k.h: chsd ldrs: effrt to press ldrs 2f out: chsd wnr and drvn over 1f out: unable qck and lost 2nd 1f out: styd on same pce after* **7/1**[3]

36-4 **6** *½* **Lucida (IRE)**[25] 2497 4-9-0 113 KevinManning 8 107
(J S Bolger, Ire) *stdd after s: t.k.h: hld up in tch towards rr: swtchd rt and effrt jst over 2f out: hdwy u.p over 1f out: chsng ldrs whn sltly impeded and swtchd lft 1f out: kpt on same pce after* **10/1**

2-33 **7** *¾* **Black Cherry**[25] 2464 4-9-0 102 PatDobbs 1 105
(Richard Hannon) *hld up in tch in midfield: effrt u.p 2f out: unable qck over 1f out: no imp and kpt on same pce ins fnl f* **50/1**

-023 **8** *1 ½* **Excilly**[104] 809 4-9-0 103 RichardKingscote 6 102
(Tom Dascombe) *broke wl: sn stdd and hld up wl in tch in midfield: switching rt and effrt 2f out: no imp u.p 1f out: kpt on same pce after* **100/1**

0-10 **9** *nk* **Maimara (FR)**[45] 1910 4-9-0 108 GregoryBenoist 5 101
(M Delzangles, France) *t.k.h: led: sn hdd and chsd ldr: rdn ent fnl 2f: unable qck and lost pl over 1f out: wknd ins fnl f* **12/1**

0-21 **10** *hd* **Devonshire (IRE)**[25] 2497 4-9-3 109 WilliamBuick 14 103
(W McCreery, Ire) *stdd s: hld up in tch in midfield: effrt and rdn 2f out: unable qck over 1f out: kpt on same pce fnl f* **8/1**

26-1 **11** *1 ¼* **Blond Me (IRE)**[46] 1858 4-9-0 107 DavidProbert 3 98
(Andrew Balding) *t.k.h: hld up in tch in midfield: swtchd rt and effrt ent fnl 2f: no hdwy u.p over 1f out: wknd ins fnl f* **11/1**

2544 **12** *3 ¼* **Bint Dandy (IRE)**[14] 2789 5-9-0 87 (b) FrederikTylicki 12 90
(Chris Dwyer) *chsd ldrs: rdn ent fnl 2f: unable qck and lost pl over 1f out: wknd fnl f* **100/1**

40-1 **13** *2* **Spangled**[23] 2539 4-9-0 100 AndreaAtzeni 4 85
(Roger Varian) *t.k.h: sn led and set stdy gallop: rdn 2f out: sn hdd and outpcd: wknd fnl f* **20/1**

1240 **14** *17* **Volunteer Point (IRE)**[39] 2034 4-9-0 102 SilvestreDeSousa 11 46
(Mick Channon) *taken down early: stdd after s: t.k.h: hld up in tch in last quintet: rdn ent fnl 2f: sn btn: bhd and eased ins fnl f* **50/1**

1m 43.33s (2.53) **Going Correction** +0.60s/f (Yiel) **14** Ran SP% **120.8**
Speed ratings (Par 115): **111,108,108,107,107 107,106,104,104,104 103,99,97,80**
CSF £57.27 CT £200.55 TOTE £2.80: £1.60, £6.90, £1.80; EX 63.00 Trifecta £448.60.
Owner Godolphin SNC **Bred** Darley **Trained** Chantilly, France

FOCUS
This year's Duke of Cambridge may not have been the most competitive and there was just a routine pace on down the centre, but the form still looks rock solid for the division. The winner was quite impressive, and the form makes sense, with the seventh and eighth rated close to form.

3272 PRINCE OF WALES'S STKS (BRITISH CHAMPIONS SERIES) (GROUP 1) 1m 2f
4:20 (4:20) (Class 1) 4-Y-O+

£425,325 (£161,250; £80,700; £40,200; £20,175; £10,125) **Stalls** Low

Form RPR

1-15 **1** **My Dream Boat (IRE)**[22] 2568 4-9-0 117 AdamKirby 3 123
(Clive Cox) *lw: hld up: rdn and swtchd lft over 2f out: hdwy sn after: wnt 2nd over 1f out: r.o strly ins fnl f: hung lft and led towards fin* **16/1**

3122 **2** *nk* **Found (IRE)**[11] 2894 4-8-11 120 RyanMoore 5 119
(A P O'Brien, Ire) *in tch: effrt 2f out: led sn after: edgd rt whn running on over 1f out: hdd towards fin* **4/1**[2]

-222 **3** *3 ½* **Western Hymn**[20] 2626 5-9-0 115 FrankieDettori 6 115
(John Gosden) *chsd ldr tl pushed along 2f out: rdn and ev ch wl over 1f out: nt qckn: kpt on ins fnl f but nt gng pce of front two* **12/1**

236- **4** *¾* **The Grey Gatsby (IRE)**[277] 6337 5-9-0 122 JamieSpencer 1 114
(Kevin Ryan) *lw: chsd ldrs: rdn over 2f out: ev ch wl over 1f out: nt qckn: styd on same pce ins fnl f* **10/1**[3]

-113 **5** *nk* **Tryster (IRE)**[81] 1106 5-9-0 115 (p) WilliamBuick 2 113
(Charlie Appleby) *hld up in rr: rdn over 2f out: hung lft whn outpcd over 1f out: hung rt whn trying to keep on ins fnl f: wl hld* **12/1**

1-1 **6** *shd* **A Shin Hikari (JPN)**[22] 2568 5-9-0 129 YutakaTake 4 113
(Masanori Sakaguchi, Japan) *lengthy: lw: led: rdn 2f out: sn hdd: kpt on same pce and wl hld ins fnl f* **8/13**[1]

2m 11.38s (3.98) **Going Correction** +0.825s/f (Soft) **6** Ran SP% **112.3**
Speed ratings (Par 117): **117,116,113,113,113 113**
CSF £77.05 TOTE £19.30: £8.20, £2.60; EX 73.20 Trifecta £314.60.
Owner Paul & Clare Rooney **Bred** Patrick Monahan **Trained** Lambourn, Berks

FOCUS
Race distance increased by 10yds. No great gallop on here and the race turned into a huge anti-climax, with the high-profile favourite running miles below his best and the race going to the complete outsider. With the favourite disappointing, the race has been rated as a standard renewal, with the runner-up helping to set the level.

3273 ROYAL HUNT CUP (HERITAGE H'CAP) 1m (S)
5:00 (5:01) (Class 2) 3-Y-O+

£108,937 (£32,620; £16,310; £8,155; £4,077; £2,047) **Stalls** Centre

Form RPR

25-1 **1** **Portage (IRE)**[11] 2924 4-9-5 105 5ex JamesDoyle 4 115
(M Halford, Ire) *lw: racd far side: chsd ldr: rdn and ev ch over 1f out: led 1f out: styd on wl and forged ahd fnl 100yds: rdn out* **10/1**[3]

12-1 **2** *1 ¼* **Librisa Breeze**[67] 1344 4-8-11 97 RobertWinston 26 104+
(Dean Ivory) *racd in centre tl gps merged 3f out: hld up towards rr: hdwy and hung rt over 1f out: str chal 1f out: no ex and outpcd by wnr fnl 100yds* **8/1**[2]

22-0 **3** *nk* **Mitchum Swagger**[53] 1637 4-9-8 108 GeorgeBaker 20 114+
(David Lanigan) *racd far side: hld up in rr: swtchd rt 2f out: clsd and nt clr run over 1f out: wnt between rivals and hdwy ent fnl f: r.o strly u.p fnl 150yds: swtchd lft towards fin: nt rch ldrs* **14/1**

-021 **4** *½* **Azraff (IRE)**[32] 2246 4-8-13 99 AndreaAtzeni 10 104+
(Marco Botti) *racd far side: in tch in midfield: effrt and nt clr run over 1f out: sn swtchd lft and hdwy: rdn to chse ldrs jst ins fnl f: kpt on* **20/1**

0352 **5** *½* **Battle Of Marathon (USA)**[49] 1774 4-9-10 110 (p) AdamKirby 2 114
(John Ryan) *racd far side: effrt 2f out: hdwy and drvn to chse ldrs 1f out: kpt on same pce fnl 150yds: hld whn sltly hmpd towards fin* **25/1**

0000 **6** *½* **Bossy Guest (IRE)**[25] 2464 4-9-4 104 SilvestreDeSousa 19 107
(Mick Channon) *racd far side: stdd s: hld up towards rr: hdwy jst over 2f out: nt clr run jst over 1f out: rdn and styd on ins fnl f: nt rch ldrs* **50/1**

3022 **7** *hd* **Instant Attraction (IRE)**[12] 2868 5-8-13 99 JackGarritty 12 101
(Jedd O'Keeffe) *racd far side: chsd ldrs: rdn over 2f out: unable qck u.p over 1f out: styd on same pce ins fnl f* **16/1**

00-1 **8** *nk* **Early Morning (IRE)**[56] 1576 5-8-12 98 GeraldMosse 7 100
(Harry Dunlop) *racd far side: led: rdn 2f out: drvn and hdd 1f out: no ex u.p: wknd fnl 100yds* **50/1**

34-1 **9** *½* **Carry On Deryck**[118] 628 4-9-6 106 JamesMcDonald 25 106+
(Saeed bin Suroor) *lw: racd in centre tl gps merged 3f out: in tch in midfield: effrt 2f out: hdwy u.p and hanging rt over 1f out: styd on: nt rch ldrs* **20/1**

-305 **10** *hd* **Earth Drummer (IRE)**[39] 2027 6-8-12 98 ShaneKelly 5 98
(David Loughnane) *racd far side: hld up in tch in midfield: effrt 2f out: n.m.r jst over 1f out: rdn and kpt on ins fnl f: no threat to ldrs* **25/1**

0054 **11** *nk* **Glory Awaits (IRE)**[34] 2191 6-8-13 99 (b) JamieSpencer 9 99+
(David Simcock) *racd far side: stdd s: hld up in rr: swtchd rt and effrt 2f out: nt clr run over 1f out: hdwy u.p ins fnl f: r.o wl u.p: no threat to ldrs* **22/1**

5-65 **12** *½* **Spark Plug (IRE)**[14] 2796 5-9-4 104 (p) SeanLevey 11 102+
(Brian Meehan) *racd far side: hld up in rr: nt clr run 2f out: stl bhd and hdwy jst over 1f out: clsng whn nt clr run again and swtchd lft ins fnl f: r.o strly: no threat to ldrs* **33/1**

66-3 **13** *nk* **Mr Owen (USA)**[45] 1910 4-9-9 109 OisinMurphy 14 106
(F Rohaut, France) *racd far side: hld up in rr: nt clr run 2f out: swtchd lft over 1f out: sn edging rt but clsng: kpt on ins fnl f: no threat to ldrs* **20/1**

-002 **14** *nse* **Hasanour (USA)**[17] 2716 6-9-0 100 ShaneFoley 8 97
(M Halford, Ire) *lw: racd far side: wl in tch in midfield: effrt over 1f out: rdn and unable qck jst over 1f out: wknd wl ins fnl f* **25/1**

4-25 **15** *½* **Donncha (IRE)**[34] 2191 5-8-12 101 TomMarquand(3) 31 97
(Robert Eddery) *lw: racd centre tl gps merged 3f out: stmbld leaving stalls: hld up in rr: hdwy over 2f out: u.p and carried rt over 1f out: no ex and wknd ins fnl f* **10/1**[3]

-445 **16** *½* **Man Of Harlech**[74] 1196 5-9-0 100 DavidProbert 15 95
(Andrew Balding) *racd far side: in tch in midfield: unable qck u.p over 1f out: hld and styd on same pce fnl f* **28/1**

-031 **17** *½* **Secret Brief (IRE)**[74] 1196 4-9-4 104 WilliamBuick 3 98
(Charlie Appleby) *racd far side: wl in tch in midfield: effrt 2f out: rdn and unable qck over 1f out: sn btn: wknd ins fnl f* **12/1**

6002 **18** *hd* **Emell**[27] 2391 6-9-1 101 (b) PatDobbs 16 94+
(Richard Hannon) *racd far side: in tch in midfield: shuffled bk towards rr and nt clr run 2f out: sme hdwy and nt clr run again jst ins fnl f: swtchd rt and kpt on fnl 100yds: no threat to ldrs* **50/1**

-405 **19** *1* **Boomshackerlacker (IRE)**[118] 628 6-8-13 99 PatCosgrave 32 90
(George Baker) *racd in centre tl gps merged 3f out: stdd s: hld up towards rr: effrt 2f out: no real imp u.p over 1f out: kpt on same pce fnl f* **33/1**

4156 **20** *1 ¼* **Captain Cat (IRE)**[49] 1774 7-9-2 107 (b) EdwardGreatrex(5) 27 95
(Roger Charlton) *racd in centre tl gps merged 3f out: in tch in midfield: effrt 2f out: no hdwy u.p over 1f out: wknd ins fnl f* **33/1**

4-10 **21** *hd* **Gm Hopkins**[32] 2243 5-9-12 112 RobertHavlin 18 100+
(John Gosden) *lw: racd far side: hld up in rr: nt clr run 2f out: all ch had gone but sme late hdwy ins fnl f: nvr trbld ldrs* **12/1**

-022 **22** *2 ¾* **Convey**[18] 2691 4-9-6 106 (p) RyanMoore 33 87
(Sir Michael Stoute) *racd in centre tl gps merged 3f out: stdd s: hld up in rr: effrt 2f out: sn rdn and edging rt: no prog and wl hld fnl f: nvr a threat* **13/2**[1]

26-1 **23** *½* **Spirit Raiser (IRE)**[14] 2796 5-9-3 103 5ex FrederikTylicki 22 83
(James Fanshawe) *racd in centre tl gps merged 3f out: wl in tch in midfield: rdn over 2f out: unable qck and btn whn sltly impeded over 1f out: wknd ins fnl f* **20/1**

6-50 **24** *1* **Hors De Combat**[34] 2191 5-8-11 104 GeorgeWood(7) 6 82
(James Fanshawe) *racd far side: wl in tch in midfield: rdn jst over 2f out: unable qck and lost pl over 1f out: wknd ins fnl f* **20/1**

434- **25** *1 ½* **Basem**[266] 6639 5-9-10 110 JimmyFortune 30 85
(Saeed bin Suroor) *racd in centre tl gps merged 3f out: prom in gp and in tch in midfield overall: rdn 2f out: sn struggling and lost pl over 1f out: wknd fnl f* **22/1**

-300 **26** *3 ½* **Balty Boys (IRE)**[34] 2191 7-9-0 105 (b) CallumShepherd(5) 1 71
(Brian Ellison) *racd far side: chsd ldrs: rdn and lost pl over 2f out: bhd over 1f out* **14/1**

1446 **27** *6* **Solar Deity (IRE)**[95] 920 7-8-13 99 PatSmullen 21 52
(Jane Chapple-Hyam) *lw: racd far side: in tch in midfield: rdn and lost pl over 2f out: in rr whn nt clr run and hmpd 2f out: sn bhd* **50/1**

110- **28** *19* **Algaith (USA)**[249] 7118 4-9-6 106 PaulHanagan 23 15
(Owen Burrows) *racd centre tl gps merged 3f out: led gp and chsd ldrs overall tl over 2f out: lost pl 2f out: bhd and eased ins fnl f* **66/1**

1m 43.01s (2.21) **Going Correction** +0.60s/f (Yiel) **28** Ran SP% **142.9**
Speed ratings (Par 109): **112,110,110,109,109 108,108,108,107,107 107,106,106,106,106 105,105,104,103,102 102,99,99,98,9**
CSF £74.04 CT £1192.58 TOTE £10.80: £3.10, £2.40, £3.40, £9.20; EX 100.90 Trifecta £1833.70.
Owner Godolphin **Bred** Barbara Prendergast **Trained** Doneany, Co Kildare
■ The first Irish-trained Hunt Cup winner since 1966, and Michael Halford's first Royal Ascot winner.

FOCUS
One of the most competitive handicaps of the Flat season. This year the field just didn't want to know the stands' side and those drawn low were at a big advantage. The form looks decent rated around the fifth.

3274 SANDRINGHAM H'CAP (LISTED RACE) (FILLIES) 1m (S)
5:35 (5:39) (Class 1) (0-110,107) 3-Y-O

£45,368 (£17,200; £8,608; £4,288; £2,152; £1,080) **Stalls** Centre

Form RPR

1-11 **1** **Persuasive (IRE)**[14] 2789 3-8-9 95 FrankieDettori 17 107+
(John Gosden) *lw: in tch: impr over 2f out: led wl over 1f out: edgd rt appr fnl f whn running on: pushed out: r.o wl towards fin* **11/4**[1]

-24 **2** *1 ¼* **Diamond Fields (IRE)**[11] 2923 3-8-11 97 WayneLordan 24 105+
(T Stack, Ire) *hld up: hdwy 2f out: nt clr run over 1f out: continued to prog ins fnl f: r.o to take 2nd post: nt rch wnr* **33/1**

220- **3** *nse* **Sharaakah (IRE)**[250] 7073 3-8-7 93 oh3 JoeFanning 20 100
(Ed Dunlop) *racd keenly: hld up in midfield: hdwy 2f out: swtchd lft whn nt clr run over 1f out: wnt 2nd and hung rt appr fnl f: r.o: nt rch wnr: lost 2nd post* **25/1**

-426 **4** *1 ¾* **Radiantly**[24] 2509 3-9-0 100 BillyLee 12 103
(W McCreery, Ire) *hld up: rdn whn swtchd rt and hdwy over 2f out: cl up chsng ldrs over 1f out: styd on u.p ins fnl f: a hld* **20/1**

10-1 **5** *1 ½* **Diploma**[25] 2490 3-9-0 100 RyanMoore 23 100+
(Sir Michael Stoute) *midfield: hdwy over 2f out: rdn to chse ldrs over 1f out: styd on ins fnl f: nt rch ldrs* **13/2**[3]

2-1 **6** *1 ¼* **Anamba**[17] 2716 3-9-4 104 WilliamBuick 8 101
(M Halford, Ire) *midfield: hdwy over 2f out: rdn and ev ch wl over 1f out: sn unable to go pce of wnr: no ex fnl 110yds* **5/1**[2]

6-52 **7** 3 3/4 **Make Fast**[12] 2870 3-8-12 **98** .... DavidProbert 7 86
(Andrew Balding) *lw: hld up: rdn and nt clr run over 1f out: styd on ins fnl f: unable to rch ldrs* **10/1**

-236 **8** shd **Light Up Our World (IRE)**[35] 2160 3-9-0 **100** .... PatDobbs 6 88
(Richard Hannon) *hld up in midfield: rdn and hdwy over 2f out: nt clr run over 1f out: styd on u.p ins fnl f: nvr able to chal* **33/1**

50-0 **9** 1/2 **Gypsy Eyes (IRE)**[32] 2245 3-8-7 **93** oh3 .... RichardKingscote 21 80
(Charles Hills) *unruly gng to post: racd keenly: trckd ldrs: rdn over 2f out: ch over 1f out: nt qckn: styd on same pce ins fnl f* **33/1**

-030 **10** 3/4 **Great Page (IRE)**[39] 2042 3-8-13 **99** .... SeanLevey 2 84
(Richard Hannon) *prom: rdn and ev ch 2f out: outpcd over 1f out: kpt on same pce ins fnl f* **20/1**

52-1 **11** 1/2 **Dolce Strega (IRE)**[44] 1939 3-9-0 **100** .... PatSmullen 16 84
(W McCreery, Ire) *unf: racd keenly in midfield: rdn over 2f out: unable to go pce over 1f out: kpt on ins fnl f: nvr trbld ldrs* **10/1**

-650 **12** shd **Rebel Surge (IRE)**[10] 2949 3-8-7 **93** oh2 .... TomMarquand 25 77
(Richard Spencer) *hld up: rdn over 2f out: hdwy over 1f out: kpt on ins fnl f: nvr trbld ldrs* **40/1**

0032 **13** 1 **Yeah Baby Yeah (IRE)**[7] 3039 3-8-7 **93** oh8 .... JohnRVelazquez 9 74
(Gay Kelleway) *hld up: carried rt over 2f out: nt clr run on rail over 1f out: kpt on ins fnl f: n.d* **50/1**

5 **14** nse **Classe Vendome (FR)**[11] 2928 3-8-9 **95** .... StephanePasquier 5 76
(N Clement, France) *midfield: rdn and hdwy 2f out: edgd rt u.p over 1f out: wknd and eased ins fnl f* **22/1**

4-13 **15** 1/2 **Mise En Rose (USA)**[14] 2789 3-8-7 **93** .... MickaelBarzalona 11 73
(Charlie Appleby) *prom: rdn and ev ch 2f out: outpcd over 1f out: wl btn ins fnl f* **14/1**

1-34 **16** 1/2 **Quality Time (IRE)**[39] 2034 3-8-9 **95** .... JamesMcDonald 18 74
(Saeed bin Suroor) *led: rdn and hdd wl over 1f out: sn wknd* **25/1**

30-2 **17** 4 1/2 **Opal Tiara (IRE)**[23] 2539 3-8-12 **98** .... OisinMurphy 4 67
(Mick Channon) *midfield: effrt over 2f out: u.p whn n.m.r and hmpd over 1f out: sn eased* **33/1**

10-2 **18** 4 1/2 **Aljuljalah (USA)**[33] 2220 3-8-13 **99** .... AndreaAtzeni 14 57
(Roger Varian) *midfield: pushed along over 2f out: wknd over 1f out: eased whn btn ins fnl f* **14/1**

120- **19** 3/4 **Alamode**[235] 7471 3-9-0 **100** .... (p) MartinDwyer 26 56
(Marcus Tregoning) *racd alone on nr side: prom: stl wl there over 3f out: u.p and wknd over 2f out* **33/1**

15-0 **20** 4 1/2 **Blue Bayou**[45] 1888 3-9-7 **107** .... (t) JimmyFortune 22 53
(Brian Meehan) *prom: rdn over 2f out: sn edgd lft u.p and wknd* **33/1**

3215 **21** 23 **Pure Diamond**[46] 1858 3-9-3 **103** .... JamesDoyle 3
(Saeed bin Suroor) *midfield: in tch whn rdn over 2f out: wknd qckly: eased whn wl btn over 1f out* **25/1**

1m 44.27s (3.47) **Going Correction** +0.60s/f (Yiel) **21** Ran SP% **135.6**
Speed ratings (Par 104): **106,104,104,102,101 100,96,96,95,95 94,94,93,93,92 92,87,83,82,78 55**
CSF £116.71 CT £2060.01 TOTE £3.00: £1.30, £9.70, £6.00, £5.90; EX 229.60 Trifecta £9585.80.
Owner Cheveley Park Stud **Bred** J F Tuthill **Trained** Newmarket, Suffolk
■ Planchart was withdrawn. Price at time of withdrawal 33-1. Rule 4 does not apply

FOCUS
Usually a strong handicap, it was on in good style by a future Group-race filly. They raced centre-to-far side in the one group, with only one of the outsiders Alamode coming stands' side. The fourth has been rated to form.
T/Jkpt: Not won. T/Plt: £165.00 to a £1 stake. Pool: £505,613.10 - 2,236.47 winning tickets
T/Qpdt: £53.60 to a £1 stake. Pool: £30,405.44 - 419.06 winning tickets
Steve Payne & Darren Owen

2786 CHELMSFORD (A.W) (L-H)
Wednesday, June 15

OFFICIAL GOING: Polytrack: standard
Wind: Fresh, behind Weather: Cloudy with sunny spells

3275 PERRIN & ROWE EBF FILLIES' NOVICE STKS (PLUS 10 RACE) 7f (P)
6:10 (6:10) (Class 5) 2-Y-O **£4,528** (£1,347; £673; £336) **Stalls** Low

Form RPR

5 **1** **Island Vision (IRE)**[15] 2771 2-9-0 0 .... MartinHarley 4 79
(David Simcock) *chsd ldrs: rdn over 1f out: r.o to ld wl ins fnl f* **5/1**[3]

20 **2** nk **Pepita (IRE)**[17] 2718 2-9-0 0 .... KieranO'Neill 2 78
(Richard Hannon) *led: rdn and hung rt fr over 1f out: hdd wl ins fnl f* **10/11**[1]

41 **3** 1/2 **Teofonic (IRE)**[9] 2970 2-9-4 0 .... MartinLane 1 82
(Mark Johnston) *chsd ldr: wnt upsides over 5f out tl rdn over 3f out: hmpd ins fnl f: styd on u.p* **2/1**[2]

4 **4** 4 **Cj Parker**[16] 2747 2-9-0 0 .... JackMitchell 5 66
(Jim Boyle) *hld up: rdn over 3f out: styd on: nt rch ldrs* **16/1**

5 28 **Ciel Rouge** 2-8-11 0 .... DannyBrock(3) 3
(Charlie Wallis) *chsd ldrs: sn pushed along: lost pl over 4f out: bhd fr 1/2-way* **50/1**

1m 27.95s (0.75) **Going Correction** -0.05s/f (Stan) **5** Ran SP% **110.2**
Speed ratings (Par 90): **93,92,92,87,55**
CSF £10.16 TOTE £6.40: £2.80, £1.10; EX 12.80 Trifecta £17.80.
Owner Sheikh Juma Dalmook Al Maktoum **Bred** Black Crow Syndicate **Trained** Newmarket, Suffolk
■ Stewards' Enquiry : Kieran O'Neill caution: careless riding

FOCUS
A fair fillies' novice race run at an ordinary pace.

3276 JEM PARTNERS CHASE H'CAP 1m 2f (P)
6:40 (6:41) (Class 4) (0-80,79) 4-Y-O+ **£8,086** (£2,406; £1,202; £601) **Stalls** Low

Form RPR

4232 **1** **Van Huysen (IRE)**[4] 3124 4-8-12 **75** .... JosephineGordon(5) 5 84
(Dominic Ffrench Davis) *chsd ldr: rdn over 1f out: led ins fnl f: styd on* **9/2**[3]

5323 **2** hd **Taper Tantrum (IRE)**[14] 2791 4-9-4 **79** .... (v[1]) LouisSteward(3) 1 87
(Michael Bell) *led: rdn over 2f out: hdd ins fnl f: styd on* **11/4**[1]

3351 **3** 1 3/4 **Whoopsy Daisy**[14] 2791 4-9-4 **76** .... DarryllHolland 6 80+
(Jane Chapple-Hyam) *chsd ldrs: rdn over 1f out: styd on same pce* **3/1**[2]

1102 **4** 6 **Bridge Of Sighs**[20] 2623 4-9-1 **73** .... FMBerry 7 65+
(Martin Smith) *s.i.s: hld up: rdn over 2f out: n.d* **9/2**[3]

6000 **5** nk **U S Navy Seal (USA)**[14] 2791 4-9-5 **77** .... TimmyMurphy 4 69
(J R Jenkins) *hld up: racd keenly: rdn over 1f out: wknd fnl f* **25/1**

2012 **6** 2 1/2 **Yorkindred Spirit**[7] 3012 4-8-13 **71** .... (v) MartinLane 3 58
(Mark Johnston) *hld up: rdn over 4f out: wknd fnl f* **8/1**

0-44 **7** 6 **Tyrsal (IRE)**[151] 212 5-8-3 **66** .... PaddyPilley(5) 2 41
(Clifford Lines) *hld up: hdwy on outer over 4f out: rdn and wknd over 1f out* **10/1**

2m 8.2s (-0.40) **Going Correction** -0.05s/f (Stan) **7** Ran SP% **112.1**
Speed ratings (Par 105): **99,98,97,92,92 90,85**
CSF £16.57 TOTE £5.50: £2.60, £1.90; EX 18.30 Trifecta £56.50.
Owner Prof C D Green **Bred** Prof C Green **Trained** Lambourn, Berks

FOCUS
With the pace holding up, very few got into this. A small personal best from the winner.

3277 PMV ESSEX H'CAP 5f (P)
7:10 (7:10) (Class 2) (0-105,97) 3-Y-O+ **£12,938** (£3,850; £1,924; £962) **Stalls** Low

Form RPR

1660 **1** **Royal Birth**[4] 3151 5-9-6 **94** .... (t) AaronJones(5) 7 107
(Stuart Williams) *chsd ldrs: rdn to ld ins fnl f: edgd rt: r.o* **7/2**[3]

2411 **2** 1 1/2 **Bowson Fred**[14] 2787 4-9-9 **97** .... NathanEvans(5) 4 105
(Michael Easterby) *led: rdn and hdd ins fnl f: styd on same pce* **3/1**[2]

-110 **3** 3/4 **Encore D'Or**[26] 2438 4-9-13 **96** .... MartinHarley 5 101
(Robert Cowell) *chsd ldrs: rdn over 1f out: styd on same pce ins fnl f* **5/2**[1]

0045 **4** 3/4 **Dynamo Walt (IRE)**[14] 2787 5-8-5 **79** .... (v) NoelGarbutt(5) 2 82
(Derek Shaw) *chsd ldrs: rdn 1/2-way: styd on same pce ins fnl f* **12/1**

4/60 **5** 1 1/2 **Shamshon (IRE)**[34] 2188 5-10-0 **97** .... WilliamCarson 6 94
(Jamie Osborne) *hld up: rdn over 1f out: r.o towards fin: nt trble ldrs* **20/1**

3612 **6** 3 1/2 **Brother Tiger**[90] 966 7-9-10 **93** .... FMBerry 1 78
(David C Griffiths) *pushed along to chse ldr: wnt upsides over 3f out: rdn and ev ch over 1f out: wknd ins fnl f* **5/1**

0050 **7** 3/4 **Normal Equilibrium**[11] 2895 6-9-0 **86** .... LouisSteward(3) 9 68
(Robert Cowell) *a in rr: rdn over 1f out: wknd fnl f* **16/1**

2560 **8** 3 1/4 **Kingsley Klarion (IRE)**[22] 2554 3-9-0 **90** .... MartinLane 8 57
(Mark Johnston) *dwlt: outpcd* **16/1**

58.51s (-1.69) **Going Correction** -0.05s/f (Stan)
WFA 3 from 4yo+ 7lb **8** Ran SP% **116.7**
Speed ratings (Par 109): **111,108,107,106,103 98,97,91**
CSF £14.81 CT £30.36 TOTE £4.40: £2.10, £1.10, £1.60; EX 19.00 Trifecta £49.70.
Owner The Morley Family **Bred** Old Mill Stud & S Williams & J Parry **Trained** Newmarket, Suffolk

FOCUS
There was a disputed pace here and that set things up for a closer. The winner has a progressive profile on the AW and this was another step up.

3278 DEVITT INSURANCE 80TH ANNIVERSARY FILLIES' H'CAP 1m 6f (P)
7:40 (7:41) (Class 2) (0-105,94) 4-Y-O+ **£12,938** (£3,850; £1,924; £962) **Stalls** Low

Form RPR

65-2 **1** **She Is No Lady**[26] 2433 4-9-3 **90** .... FMBerry 4 98+
(Ralph Beckett) *a.p: shkn up over 2f out: led over 1f out: rdn and edgd lft ins fnl f: styd on wl* **3/1**[2]

3-01 **2** 2 **Serena Grae**[18] 2685 5-8-9 **85** .... MichaelJMMurphy(3) 7 90
(Marcus Tregoning) *a.p: hmpd after 2f: chsd ldr over 3f out: led over 2f out: rdn and hdd over 1f out: styd on same pce ins fnl f* **7/1**

1230 **3** 2 1/2 **Heart Locket**[15] 2782 4-7-11 **75** oh4 .... NathanEvans(5) 1 77
(Michael Easterby) *hld up: hdwy over 1f out: sn rdn: styd on same pce ins fnl f* **12/1**

5-01 **4** 3/4 **Forever Popular (USA)**[25] 2487 4-8-12 **85** .... PatCosgrave 5 85
(William Haggas) *hld up: hdwy over 3f out: rdn over 1f out: styd on same pce* **6/4**[1]

31-6 **5** 1/2 **Mediation**[44] 1933 4-8-9 **82** .... HarryBentley 6 82
(Roger Varian) *led 7f: chsd ldr tl over 3f out: rdn over 1f out: styd on same pce* **6/1**[3]

-262 **6** 25 **Graceland (FR)**[16] 2753 4-8-5 **83** .... JosephineGordon(5) 8 48
(Michael Bell) *s.i.s: racd keenly: rcvrd to go 2nd after 1f: led 9f out: rdn and hdd over 2f out: wknd over 1f out* **7/1**

2m 59.96s (-3.24) **Going Correction** -0.05s/f (Stan) **6** Ran SP% **112.0**
Speed ratings (Par 96): **107,105,104,104,103 89**
CSF £23.20 CT £214.63 TOTE £3.60: £2.00, £2.80; EX 23.20 Trifecta £131.80.
Owner D & J Newell **Bred** Derek & Judith Newell **Trained** Kimpton, Hants
■ Stewards' Enquiry : Michael J M Murphy jockey said mare clipped heels when running freely on the first bend
Josephine Gordon jockey sdaid filly ran too freely

FOCUS
Not a bad fillies' handicap and the race has been rated around the third.

3279 MCCARTHY 50 YEARS AND STILL RUNNING H'CAP 6f (P)
8:10 (8:12) (Class 3) (0-95,95) 4-Y-O+ **£9,703** (£2,887; £1,443; £721) **Stalls** Centre

Form RPR

51R1 **1** **Gentlemen**[42] 1958 5-9-0 **93** .... JosephineGordon(5) 5 102
(Phil McEntee) *s.i.s: hld up: hdwy over 1f out: sn rdn: r.o to ld wl ins fnl f* **9/2**[2]

2440 **2** 1 **Boomerang Bob (IRE)**[11] 2898 7-9-6 **94** .... WilliamCarson 8 99
(Jamie Osborne) *hld up: hdwy over 1f out: sn rdn: r.o to go 2nd post* **7/1**

1121 **3** shd **Baileys Mirage (FR)**[20] 2621 5-8-11 **85** .... (b) SilvestreDeSousa 2 90
(Chris Dwyer) *led 5f out: rdn over 1f out: hdd wl ins fnl f* **3/1**[1]

0341 **4** 1/2 **Magnus Maximus**[21] 2581 5-9-5 **93** .... MartinHarley 4 96
(Robyn Brisland) *led 1f: chsd ldr: rdn over 1f out: styd on same pce ins fnl f* **3/1**[1]

-001 **5** 1/2 **Crew Cut (IRE)**[44] 1929 8-8-1 **80** .... AaronJones(5) 1 81
(Stuart Williams) *prom: rdn over 1f out: styd on same pce ins fnl f* **6/1**[3]

1-20 **6** 2 3/4 **Francisco**[23] 2547 4-9-1 **89** .... KieranO'Neill 6 82
(Richard Hannon) *plld hrd and prom: rdn over 2f out: lost pl wl over 1f out* **8/1**

1m 12.04s (-1.66) **Going Correction** -0.05s/f (Stan) **6** Ran SP% **106.1**
Speed ratings (Par 107): **109,107,107,106,106 102**
CSF £30.32 CT £87.84 TOTE £4.90: £2.20, £3.00; EX 32.50 Trifecta £149.30.
Owner Eventmaker Racehorses **Bred** Mrs Eleanor Kent **Trained** Newmarket, Suffolk
■ Burn The Boats was withdrawn. Price at time of withdrawal was 10-1. Rule 4 applies to all bets - deduction 5p in the pound.

FOCUS
A good sprint. The two leaders were caught in the closing stages by the two who had been held up out the back. The winner has improved with each run this year.

3280 CHELMSFORD RACECOURSE SUPPORTING HAVENS HOSPICES H'CAP 6f (P)
8:40 (8:41) (Class 6) (0-65,65) 3-Y-O **£3,234** (£962; £481; £240) **Stalls** Centre

Form RPR

52-0 **1** **Desert River (IRE)**[6] 3069 3-9-4 **62** .... DarryllHolland 4 66+
(Mark H Tompkins) *plld hrd and prom: stdd and lost pl over 4f out: hdwy over 1f out: swtchd rt ins fnl f: rdn and r.o to ld post* **5/1**[3]

0-04 **2** *shd* **Dream Dana (IRE)**[12] 2848 3-9-5 **63** .... TimmyMurphy 8 66
(Jamie Osborne) *led after 1f: rdn and hdd over 1f out: r.o* **20/1**

000- **3** *hd* **Poplar**[217] 7795 3-8-12 **56** .... MartinHarley 3 58
(Robyn Brisland) *chsd ldrs: led over 1f out: sn rdn: hdd post* **6/1**

425 **4** *3/4* **Sciarra**[25] 2459 3-9-6 **64** .... OisinMurphy 1 64
(Michael Bell) *hld up: rdn over 2f out: r.o ins fnl f: nt rch ldrs* **7/2**[2]

2046 **5** *hd* **Miss Phillyjinks (IRE)**[26] 2435 3-9-6 **64** .... (b) ShaneKelly 2 63
(Paul D'Arcy) *hld up: hdwy over 1f out: sn rdn: styd on* **8/1**

4050 **6** *1* **Le Manege Enchante (IRE)**[12] 2864 3-9-2 **60** .... (p) MartinLane 5 56
(Derek Shaw) *s.i.s: hld up: rdn over 1f out: styd on: nt trble ldrs* **8/1**

0-66 **6** *dht* **Curious Fox**[50] 1753 3-8-13 **57** .... WilliamCarson 6 53
(Anthony Carson) *led 1f: chsd ldrs: rdn over 2f out: n.m.r and no ex ins fnl f* **20/1**

4005 **8** *2* **Teversham**[19] 2642 3-9-7 **65** .... (p) SilvestreDeSousa 7 55
(Chris Dwyer) *plld hrd and prom: wnt 2nd over 3f out: rdn and hung lft over 1f out: no ex ins fnl f* **9/4**[1]

1m 14.36s (0.66) **Going Correction** -0.05s/f (Stan) **8** Ran SP% **115.7**
Speed ratings (Par 97): **93,92,92,91,91 90,90,87**
CSF £94.88 CT £609.89 TOTE £7.30: £1.80, £3.30, £1.60; EX 62.90 Trifecta £769.20.
Owner Pat Swayne and Partner **Bred** Kassala Limited **Trained** Newmarket, Suffolk

FOCUS
The early pace was steady and plenty raced keenly. The two leaders had it between them until joined and passed in the dying strides.

3281 TODAY'S TALENT, TOMORROW'S SUCCESS MAIDEN AUCTION STKS — 1m 2f (P)
9:10 (9:13) (Class 5) 3-Y-O — **£5,175** (£1,540; £769; £384) **Stalls** Low

Form — RPR

0-42 **1** **Dot Green (IRE)**[27] 2405 3-9-0 80 .... DarryllHolland 1 72+
(Mark H Tompkins) *hld up in tch: racd keenly: shkn up to ld over 1f out: hung lft ins fnl f: sn clr* **15/8**[2]

-332 **2** *3 1/2* **Archimento**[30] 2307 3-9-5 82 .... SilvestreDeSousa 3 70
(Ed Dunlop) *trckd ldrs: wnt 2nd over 5f out: ev ch fr over 2f out: sn rdn: hung lft and no ex ins fnl f* **5/6**[1]

46 **3** *nk* **Touchdown Banwell (USA)**[23] 2548 3-9-5 0 .... LiamKeniry 5 69
(Andrew Balding) *led after 1f: rdn and hdd over 1f out: edgd rt and styd on same pce ins fnl f* **20/1**

344 **4** *1 3/4* **Proven Point (IRE)**[13] 2835 3-9-5 73 .... BarryMcHugh 2 68+
(Tony Coyle) *led 1f: chsd ldr tl over 5f out: remained handy: hmpd over 2f out: styd on same pce fr over 1f out* **5/1**[3]

0-0 **5** *12* **On Budget (IRE)**[34] 2175 3-9-5 0 .... RobertTart 4 42
(Anthony Carson) *hld up: hdwy over 4f out: rdn and wknd over 1f out* **50/1**

2m 7.43s (-1.17) **Going Correction** -0.05s/f (Stan) **5** Ran SP% **112.7**
Speed ratings (Par 99): **102,99,98,97,87**
CSF £3.91 TOTE £3.40: £1.50, £1.10; EX 4.90 Trifecta £21.70.
Owner Dahab Racing **Bred** J & S Quigley **Trained** Newmarket, Suffolk

FOCUS
A fair but muddling maiden. The form has been rated around the fourth.
T/Plt: £111.40 to a £1 stake. Pool: £48,660.84. 318.65 winning tickets. T/Qpdt: 33.80 to a £1 stake. Pool: £6,028.39. 131.69 winning tickets. **Colin Roberts**

3016 HAMILTON (R-H)
Wednesday, June 15

OFFICIAL GOING: Good to soft (good in places; 8.3)
Wind: Breezy, half against Weather: Overcast

3282 RACINGUK.COM/FREETRIAL NOVICE AUCTION STKS — 5f 7y
2:10 (2:11) (Class 5) 2-Y-O — **£3,881** (£1,155; £577; £288) **Stalls** High

Form — RPR

3235 **1** **Kodi Da Capo (IRE)**[11] 2908 2-8-11 0 .... JasonHart 8 71
(Keith Dalgleish) *fly-jmpd s: t.k.h: led: rdn and edgd rt over 1f out: hdd ins fnl f: rallied gamely to regain ld on line* **7/2**[3]

14 **2** *shd* **Cuppacoffee (IRE)**[18] 2682 2-9-2 0 .... RowanScott(7) 5 83
(Ann Duffield) *cl up: rdn along 2f out: led ins fnl f: kpt on: hdd on line* **4/1**

42 **3** *1 1/4* **Pulsating (IRE)**[18] 2675 2-8-11 0 .... PJMcDonald 7 66
(Rebecca Menzies) *dwlt: in tch: effrt on outside and rdn over 1f out: kpt on same pce ins fnl f* **5/2**[1]

216 **4** *1/2* **Chevalier Du Lac (IRE)**[11] 2908 2-9-2 0 .... AdamMcNamara(7) 4 76
(John Quinn) *trckd ldrs: drvn along 2f out: kpt on same pce ins fnl f* **3/1**[2]

62 **5** *1 1/4* **Eva Gore**[9] 2970 2-8-6 0 .... JoshDoyle(5) 3 60
(David O'Meara) *prom: effrt and drvn along over 1f out: outpcd ins fnl f* **10/1**

6 *1* **Rita's Girl** 2-8-11 0 .... BenCurtis 6 56+
(K R Burke) *dwlt: bhd and sn outpcd: sme late hdwy: nvr on terms* **22/1**

1m 0.14s (0.14) **Going Correction** +0.10s/f (Good) **6** Ran SP% **109.2**
Speed ratings (Par 93): **102,101,99,99,97 95**
CSF £16.65 TOTE £4.40: £2.10, £1.90; EX 20.70 Trifecta £48.50.
Owner Equus I **Bred** Tally-Ho Stud **Trained** Carluke, S Lanarks

FOCUS
The rail on the the loop had been moved to provide fresh ground, which added 24yds to races over a mile-plus. Good to soft, good in places, was the official description of the ground, with the time of the first suggesting it was moving towards just good ground. Two penalised colts took on four maiden fillies in this ordinary novice auction. They seemed to go a decent clip, but the pace dominated and it resulted in a tight finish.

3283 BRITISH STALLION STUDS EBF MAIDEN STKS (A £20,000 HIGHLAND SPRING WATER SERIES QUALIFIER) — 6f 6y
2:45 (2:45) (Class 5) 2-Y-O — **£3,557** (£1,058; £529; £264) **Stalls** High

Form — RPR

1 **Love Dreams (IRE)** 2-9-2 0 .... FrannyNorton 3 79+
(Mark Johnston) *mde all and sn crossed to stands' side: shkn up and qcknd clr over 1f out: eased towards fin: promising* **9/2**[3]

2 *2* **What's The Story** 2-9-2 0 .... TomQueally 10 70+
(Keith Dalgleish) *s.i.s: rn green in rr: hdwy swtchd rt 2f out: kpt on wl fnl f to take 2nd cl home: no ch w wnr: bttr for r* **8/1**

32 **3** *hd* **Dubai Knights (IRE)**[22] 2552 2-9-5 0 .... PJMcDonald 5 72
(Ann Duffield) *trckd ldrs: rdn and wnt 2nd over 1f out: kpt on fnl f: no ex and lost 2nd cl home* **5/2**[1]

4 **4** *3/4* **Heatongrad (IRE)**[20] 2617 2-9-5 0 .... DavidNolan 7 70+
(Richard Fahey) *in tch: effrt and rdn over 1f out: kpt on ins fnl f: nt gng pce to chal* **4/1**[2]

44 **5** *1 3/4* **Tagur (IRE)**[33] 2196 2-9-5 0 .... TomEaves 2 65
(Kevin Ryan) *trckd ldrs: effrt and drvn along over 1f out: no ex ins fnl f* **8/1**

66 **6** *5* **Zebedee Cat (IRE)**[21] 2570 2-9-5 0 .... JoeyHaynes 1 50
(Iain Jardine) *pressed ldr tl rdn and lost 2nd appr fnl f: sn wknd* **11/1**

7 *2 3/4* **Klaremount (IRE)** 2-9-2 0 .... DougieCostello 4 39
(K R Burke) *dwlt: hld up in midfield: rdn and green over 2f out: wknd over 1f out* **14/1**

8 *1 1/4* **Chochenyo** 2-9-2 0 .... PaulMulrennan 9 35
(Bryan Smart) *s.i.s: sn niggled along towards rr: outpcd over 2f out: n.d after* **20/1**

9 *4 1/2* **Fully Focussed (IRE)** 2-8-11 0 .... JamesSullivan 6 16
(Ann Duffield) *bhd: rdn and hung rt over 2f out: sn wknd* **25/1**

10 *1 1/2* **Shake And Bakes** 2-9-2 0 .... SamJames 8 17
(Marjorie Fife) *s.s: bhd: rdn along 2f out: sn wknd* **33/1**

1m 12.37s (0.17) **Going Correction** +0.10s/f (Good) **10** Ran SP% **115.5**
Speed ratings (Par 93): **102,99,99,98,95 89,85,83,77,75**
CSF £38.78 TOTE £4.90: £1.70, £2.90, £1.40; EX 38.30 Trifecta £87.90.
Owner Crone Stud Farms Ltd **Bred** John O'Connor **Trained** Middleham Moor, N Yorks

FOCUS
The four with experience didn't look to set an unattainable level for the newcomers to aim for and two colts making their debut managed to finish 1-2, with both showing good promise for the future.

3284 SAM COLLINGWOOD-CAMERON H'CAP — 6f 6y
3:20 (3:21) (Class 5) (0-75,75) 3-Y-O+ — **£3,881** (£1,155; £577; £288) **Stalls** High

Form — RPR

5 **1** **Ionization (IRE)**[28] 2383 3-9-2 **71** .... TadhgO'Shea 6 81+
(John Patrick Shanahan, Ire) *trckd ldrs: pushed along and swtchd rt over 1f out: qckndto ld ins fnl f: comf* **9/2**[3]

-616 **2** *2 3/4* **Sir Domino (FR)**[23] 2524 4-9-7 **75** .... (b[1]) AdamMcNamara(7) 2 79
(Kevin Ryan) *fly-jmpd s: sn led: rdn and clr over 1f out: edgd lft and hdd ins fnl f: no ex* **4/1**[2]

3001 **3** *1/2* **Inexes**[13] 2812 4-9-11 **72** .... SamJames 4 74
(Marjorie Fife) *prom: effrt and chsd (clr) wnr over 1f out to ins fnl f: kpt on same pce* **7/1**

2144 **4** *1 1/4* **Chaplin Bay (IRE)**[12] 2857 4-9-11 **72** .... JamesSullivan 8 70
(Ruth Carr) *s.i.s: hld up: rdn and hdwy on outside over 1f out: kpt on same pce ins fnl f* **11/4**[1]

1-32 **5** *3/4* **Swirral Edge**[28] 2373 3-9-4 **73** .... TomEaves 3 67
(David Brown) *hld up in tch gonig wl: nt clr run over 2f out to over 1f out: rdn and one pce fnl f* **8/1**

-000 **6** *6* **Mercers Row**[23] 2531 9-9-13 **74** .... DavidNolan 1 50
(Michael Herrington) *dwlt: hld up: rdn over 2f out: sn no imp* **20/1**

5600 **7** *4* **Furiant**[26] 2446 3-9-6 **75** .... (b[1]) FrannyNorton 5 37
(Mark Johnston) *early ldr: w ldr: rdn over 2f out: wknd over 1f out* **10/1**

2-1 **8** *5* **Doeadeer (IRE)**[104] 791 3-9-2 **71** .... TomQueally 7 17
(Keith Dalgleish) *wnt lft s: sn w ldrs: rdn over 2f out: wknd over 1f out* **17/2**

1m 12.07s (-0.13) **Going Correction** +0.10s/f (Good)
WFA 3 from 4yo+ 8lb **8** Ran SP% **112.8**
Speed ratings (Par 103): **104,100,99,98,97 89,83,77**
CSF £22.20 CT £122.81 TOTE £5.80: £1.60, £2.20, £2.50; EX 30.00 Trifecta £177.50.
Owner Thistle Bloodstock Limited **Bred** Thistle Bloodstock Limited **Trained** Kells, Co Kilkenny

FOCUS
A fair sprint handicap. Finishers held sway after a decent pace was set and the time was 0.3sec quicker then the preceding juvenile maiden. The race has been rated around the third.

3285 FOLLOW @HAMILTONPARKRC ON TWITTER H'CAP — 1m 67y
3:55 (3:56) (Class 5) (0-70,70) 3-Y-O — **£3,881** (£1,155; £577; £288) **Stalls** Low

Form — RPR

3612 **1** **Planetaria (IRE)**[18] 2674 3-9-7 **70** .... DavidAllan 8 81
(Garry Moss) *mde all at ordinary gallop: rdn 2f out: hld on wl fnl f* **10/3**[1]

-651 **2** *3/4* **Mr Grumpy**[13] 2831 3-9-7 **70** .... JasonHart 2 79
(Keith Dalgleish) *trckd ldrs: rdn 3f out: effrt and edgd lft 2f out: sn edgd rt: kpt on to take 2nd towards fin* **9/2**[2]

-134 **3** *1* **Carbutt's Ridge (IRE)**[120] 597 3-8-5 **54** .... (v) BenCurtis 6 61
(K R Burke) *pressed ldr: rdn over 2f out: kpt on same pce last 100yds: lost 2nd towards fin* **16/1**

0342 **4** *1 3/4* **Weld Al Khawaneej (IRE)**[7] 3020 3-8-11 **60** .... ShaneGray 3 63
(Kevin Ryan) *s.i.s: hld up: stdy hdwy over 2f out: sn rdn: kpt on fnl f: nt pce to chal* **5/1**[3]

1 **5** *2* **Born Innocent (IRE)**[21] 2571 3-8-12 **61** .... TadhgO'Shea 7 59
(John Patrick Shanahan, Ire) *hld up in tch: rdn and outpcd over 2f out: no imp over 1f out* **11/2**

0-15 **6** *2 3/4* **Maulesden May (IRE)**[19] 2652 3-9-7 **70** .... TomQueally 4 62
(Keith Dalgleish) *t.k.h early: prom: effrt and rdn 3f out: wknd over 1f out* **7/1**

3221 **7** *1 1/2* **Simply Clever**[22] 2553 3-8-10 **59** .... TomEaves 1 47
(David Brown) *t.k.h: hld up in tch: drvn and outpcd over 2f out: sn btn* **8/1**

6034 **8** *shd* **Mecca's Missus (IRE)**[14] 2801 3-8-7 **61** .... (p) PhilDennis(5) 5 49
(Michael Dods) *t.k.h: hld up: rdn over 2f out: sn btn* **10/1**

1m 48.32s (-0.08) **Going Correction** -0.10s/f (Good) **8** Ran SP% **111.9**
Speed ratings (Par 99): **96,95,94,92,90 87,86,86**
CSF £17.43 CT £203.61 TOTE £3.90: £1.40, £1.70, £4.10; EX 20.70 Trifecta £290.80.
Owner Pinnacle Four Partnership **Bred** Fastnet Stud Ltd **Trained** Wynyard, Stockton-On-Tees

FOCUS
It proved hard to make up ground in this pretty competitive but modest handicap, with the winner making all. They raced over 24yds further than advertised.

3286 BOTHWELL CASTLE H'CAP — 1m 67y
4:35 (4:35) (Class 4) (0-80,80) 3-Y-O+ — **£6,469** (£1,925; £962; £481) **Stalls** Low

Form — RPR

0063 **1** **Dubai Dynamo**[16] 2734 11-10-0 **80** .... JamesSullivan 7 89
(Ruth Carr) *hld up: pushed along and outpcd over 3f out: rallied on outside over 2f out: led wl ins fnl f: edgd lft: rdn out* **8/1**

2614 **2** *1 1/2* **Archie's Advice**[13] 2811 5-9-7 **73** .... JasonHart 10 79
(Keith Dalgleish) *hld up towards rr: hdwy on outside to ld over 1f out: sn rdn: hdd wl ins fnl f: no ex* **7/1**

-344 **3** *1 1/4* **Shadow Game**[6] 3062 3-8-9 **72** .... AndrewElliott 5 72
(Mark Johnston) *prom: drvn and outpcd over 1f out: rallied ins fnl f: tk 3rd towards fin: nt pce of first two* **7/2**[1]

-513 **4** *3/4* **Livella Fella (IRE)**[27] 2408 3-8-8 **71** .... AndrewMullen 2 69
(Keith Dalgleish) *led: rdn over 2f out: edgd lft and hdd over 1f out: outpcd ins fnl f* **14/1**

-043 **5** *1 1/2* **Know Your Name**[26] 2441 5-9-2 **75** .... RowanScott(7) 6 73
(Eric Alston) *hld up in midfield: smooth hdwy over 2f out: rdn and ev ch over 1f out: wknd ins fnl f* **6/1**[3]

20-5 **6** *1 ½* **Billy Slater**[18] 2686 4-9-13 **79**........................ GeorgeChaloner 9 74
(Richard Fahey) *s.i.s: hld up: pushed along over 3f out: hdwy whn nt clr run over 2f out to over 1f out: sn no imp* **22/1**

006 **7** *1* **Tadaany (IRE)**[4] 3166 4-9-12 **78**........................(p) SamJames 8 70
(David O'Meara) *prom: rdn over 2f out: wknd wl over 1f out* **4/1**[2]

60-0 **8** *10* **Gun Case**[45] 1884 4-9-6 **72**........................ TomEaves 1 41
(Alistair Whillans) *hld up on ins: effrt and pushed along over 2f out: wknd over 1f out* **33/1**

6150 **9** *hd* **Ronnie Baird**[19] 2654 3-8-12 **75**........................(p) DougieCostello 4 41
(Kristin Stubbs) *pressed ldr: rdn along 3f out: wknd wl over 1f out* **9/1**

5-00 **10** *5* **Haymarket**[2] 3212 7-8-11 **68**........................ GarryWhillans(5) 3 25
(R Mike Smith) *chsd ldrs: drvn along over 3f out: wknd 2f out* **10/1**

1m 46.51s (-1.89) **Going Correction** -0.10s/f (Good)
WFA 3 from 4yo+ 11lb **10** Ran SP% **113.2**
Speed ratings (Par 105): **105,103,102,101,100 98,97,87,87,82**
CSF £61.00 CT £237.54 TOTE £7.90: £2.50, £2.50, £1.60; EX 45.80 Trifecta £370.00.
Owner The Bottom Liners **Bred** T K & Mrs P A Knox **Trained** Huby, N Yorks

FOCUS
The best race on the card was a wide-open handicap where 24yds were added to the official distance. The closers held sway, with the race changing complexion completely in the last 2f.

3287 SAINTS & SINNERS WITH BEN HAENOW NEXT WEEK H'CAP 1m 1f 34y
5:10 (5:16) (Class 6) (0-60,60) 3-Y-O+ **£2,911** (£866; £432; £216) **Stalls** Low

Form RPR

3 **1** **Jocks Wa Hae (IRE)**[7] 3020 3-8-3 **47** oh1 ow1........................ TadhgO'Shea 4 59+
(John Patrick Shanahan, Ire) *chsd ldr 2f: cl up: rdn and outpcd over 3f out: rallied 2f out: led ins fnl f: sn clr: pricked ears nr fin: comf* **2/1**[1]

-000 **2** *2 ¼* **Causey Arch (IRE)**[19] 2652 3-9-0 **58**........................(p) TomEaves 13 64
(Michael Dods) *led at decent gallop: rdn over 2f out: hdd ins fnl f: kpt on: nt pce of wnr* **14/1**

-663 **3** *2* **L'Apogee**[13] 2831 3-9-2 **60**........................ GeorgeChaloner 12 62
(Richard Fahey) *prom: hdwy to press ldr after 2f: rdn along and ev ch 3f out: kpt on same pce ins fnl f* **8/1**[2]

6644 **4** *2 ¾* **Incurs Four Faults**[7] 3018 5-9-5 **51**........................ JasonHart 5 50
(Keith Dalgleish) *hld up: stdy hdwy over 3f out: rdn over 2f out: edgd rt and kpt on same pce ins fnl f* **8/1**[2]

4524 **5** *nk* **Indian Giver**[9] 2958 8-9-6 **57**........................(p) RobJFitzpatrick(5) 9 55
(John David Riches) *in tch: drvn and outpcd over 2f out: kpt on fnl f: nt pce to chal* **10/1**[3]

0-00 **6** *½* **Galilee Chapel (IRE)**[29] 2330 7-8-7 **46**........................(b) RowanScott(7) 3 43
(Alistair Whillans) *hld up: rdn and outpcd 4f out: rallied 2f out: edgd rt: kpt on fnl f: no imp* **14/1**

605 **7** *4 ½* **Ted's Brother (IRE)**[7] 3043 8-9-9 **55**........................(e) BenCurtis 6 43
(Richard Guest) *missed break: hld up: shortlived effrt over 2f out: edgd rt and no further imp over 1f out* **16/1**

-165 **8** *½* **Intalza (IRE)**[13] 2831 3-8-6 **53**........................(p) JoeDoyle(3) 1 38
(Michael Herrington) *reluctant to enter stalls: prom: drvn along 4f out: wknd 2f out* **10/1**[3]

664- **9** *9* **Arriella**[225] 7681 4-9-0 **46**........................ SamJames 7 15
(John Davies) *s.i.s: bhd: drvn and struggling 4f out: nvr on terms* **50/1**

04-2 **10** *hd* **Drinks For Losers (IRE)**[23] 2525 5-9-0 **46**........................ JamesSullivan 8 15
(Linda Perratt) *hld up on ins: rdn and struggling wl over 2f out: sn btn* **20/1**

-000 **11** *shd* **Rioja Day (IRE)**[13] 2810 6-8-13 **50**........................(b) PhilDennis(5) 10 18
(Jim Goldie) *hld up: outpcd and drvn along 4f out: sn btn* **33/1**

0-56 **12** *7* **Life Knowledge (IRE)**[11] 2915 4-9-11 **57**........................ DougieCostello 14 11
(Patrick Holmes) *prom: drvn and outpcd over 3f out: btn fnl 2f* **14/1**

-550 **13** *4 ½* **Ryan The Giant**[7] 3020 3-8-5 **49**........................(p) PatrickMathers 11
(Keith Dalgleish) *hld up: rdn and outpcd over 5f out: shortlived effrt over 3f out: sn btn* **14/1**

00-6 **14** *6* **Macmidnight**[45] 1883 4-8-9 **46** oh1........................(t) GarryWhillans(5) 2
(Donald Whillans) *s.i.s: bhd: struggling 4f out: sn btn* **100/1**

1m 58.19s (-1.51) **Going Correction** -0.10s/f (Good)
WFA 3 from 4yo+ 12lb **14** Ran SP% **116.9**
Speed ratings (Par 101): **102,100,98,95,95 95,91,90,82,82 82,76,72,66**
CSF £29.93 CT £190.39 TOTE £2.60: £1.50, £3.30, £2.30; EX 28.80 Trifecta £163.00.
Owner Thistle Bloodstock Limited **Bred** Thistle Bloodstock Ltd **Trained** Kells, Co Kilkenny

FOCUS
A desperately weak race where not many got involved and the winner looks a good bit ahead of his mark. It took place over 24yds further than advertised.

3288 HAMILTON-PARK.CO.UK APPRENTICE H'CAP 1m 4f 14y
5:45 (5:45) (Class 6) (0-60,60) 4-Y-O+ **£2,911** (£866; £432; £216) **Stalls** Low

Form RPR

4032 **1** **Chauvelin**[9] 2962 5-8-7 **46**........................(b) EoinWalsh 1 55
(Richard Guest) *dwlt and blkd s: hld up: hdwy to chse ldr over 2f out: edgd lft ins fnl f: kpt on to ld post* **7/1**

3612 **2** *nse* **Henry Smith**[29] 2326 4-9-2 **60**........................(be) RobJFitzpatrick(5) 2 69
(Garry Moss) *dwlt and bmpd s: hld up: hdwy to ld over 3f out: rdn over 2f out: kpt on fnl f: hdd last stride* **11/2**[3]

0-34 **3** *5* **Hero's Story**[13] 2813 6-9-2 **55**........................ JoeDoyle 6 56
(Jim Goldie) *hld up in tch: rdn over 2f out: edgd rt over 1f out: kpt on fnl f: nt rch first two* **4/1**[2]

421/ **4** *¾* **Sleepy Haven (IRE)**[115] 2237 6-9-1 **59**........................(t) AdamMcNamara(5) 3 59
(Jennie Candlish) *trckd ldrs: drvn and ev ch briefly over 3f out: plugged on same pce fr 2f out* **6/4**[1]

6004 **5** *1* **Moon Arc (IRE)**[13] 2836 4-8-13 **55**........................(p) JoshDoyle(3) 9 53
(Keith Dalgleish) *in tch: effrt and rdn over 2f out: outpcd fr over 1f out* **7/1**

0056 **6** *1 ¾* **Ullswater (IRE)**[6] 3067 8-8-11 **53**........................(tp) PhilDennis(3) 7 48
(Philip Kirby) *t.k.h: cl up: rdn and ev ch over 3f out: wknd over 1f out* **14/1**

04-0 **7** *11* **Lightning Steps**[52] 1674 4-8-6 **52** ow3........................ CliffordLee(7) 4 30
(Declan Carroll) *t.k.h: led at modest gallop: rdn and hdd over 3f out: wknd fr 2f out* **18/1**

2m 38.64s (0.04) **Going Correction** -0.10s/f (Good) **7** Ran SP% **112.3**
Speed ratings (Par 101): **95,94,91,91,90 89,81**
CSF £42.87 CT £173.60 TOTE £9.10: £4.10, £2.60; EX 27.70 Trifecta £124.60.
Owner Mrs Alison Guest **Bred** Mr & Mrs A E Pakenham **Trained** Ingmanthorpe, W Yorks
■ Stewards' Enquiry : Rob J Fitzpatrick four-day ban: used whip above permitted level (Jun 29-Jul 1 & 3)

FOCUS
A good finish to this modest apprentice handicap, in which the front two pulled well clear in a race that was 24yds further than advertised.
T/Plt: £47.10 to a £1 stake. Pool: £48,133.33 - 746.00 winning tickets T/Qpdt: £9.60 to a £1 stake. Pool: £3,446.80 - 263.80 winning tickets **Richard Young**

2830 RIPON (R-H)
Wednesday, June 15

OFFICIAL GOING: Good (good to soft in places; 7.7)
Wind: Moderate, half against Weather: Fine

3289 SAM BROWN APPRENTICE H'CAP 6f
6:30 (6:30) (Class 6) (0-65,65) 3-Y-O+ **£3,234** (£962; £481; £240) **Stalls** High

Form RPR

4-00 **1** **Royal Connoisseur (IRE)**[32] 2238 5-10-0 **65**........................ HayleyIrvine 2 74
(Richard Fahey) *mde all: jnd 1f out: fnd ex nr fin* **3/1**[2]

462 **2** *½* **Whispering Soul (IRE)**[11] 2919 3-8-6 **51**........................(b) LiamLewis-Salter 7 57
(Ann Duffield) *trckd ldrs: t.k.h: upsides fnl f: no ex clsng stages* **15/2**

0-40 **3** *2* **Secret City (IRE)**[56] 1565 10-9-9 **60**........................ TommyO'Connor 3 62
(Rebecca Bastiman) *carried rt s: in rr: swtchd lft after s: hdwy and edgd rt over 1f out: kpt on to take 3rd post* **18/1**

5-33 **4** *shd* **Whispering Wolf**[22] 2559 3-8-7 **52**........................ JoshuaBryan 9 51
(Suzzanne France) *mid-div: edgd rt over 2f out: upsides over 1f out: kpt on same pce* **7/1**

-000 **5** *shd* **Hashtag Frenzy**[26] 2428 3-8-2 **47** oh1 ow1........................(p) KimberleyVanderVegt 5 46
(Rebecca Menzies) *chsd ldrs on outside: reminders over 2f out: kpt on same pce appr fnl f* **33/1**

0450 **6** *2 ¼* **Canny Style**[12] 2864 3-8-13 **58**........................(b[1]) LewisEdmunds 8 50
(Kevin Ryan) *trckd ldrs: upsides over 2f out: wknd appr fnl f* **5/1**[3]

00-4 **7** *6* **Prairie Impulse**[13] 2809 3-9-4 **63**........................ WilliamCox 4 37
(Ann Duffield) *wnt rt s: chsd ldrs on outside: effrt and edgd rt over 2f out: hung lft and lost pl over 1f out* **14/1**

0643 **8** *1 ¾* **Pabusar**[7] 3022 8-9-2 **53**........................(tp) LaurenSteade 11 24
(Micky Hammond) *chsd ldrs: drvn over 2f out: lost pl over 1f out* **12/1**

5002 **R** **Teetotal (IRE)**[9] 2974 6-9-5 **56**........................ DavidEgan 10
(Nigel Tinkler) *ref to r: tk no part* **11/4**[1]

1m 14.84s (1.84) **Going Correction** +0.125s/f (Good)
WFA 3 from 4yo+ 8lb **9** Ran SP% **115.2**
Speed ratings (Par 101): **92,91,88,88,88 85,77,75,**
CSF £25.79 CT £345.55 TOTE £3.90: £1.40, £2.70, £4.50; EX 27.50 Trifecta £416.90.
Owner S & G Clayton, A Blower **Bred** Mrs Sheila Morrissey **Trained** Musley Bank, N Yorks
■ Hayley Irvine's first winner.
■ Stewards' Enquiry : Kimberley Van der Vegt one-day ban: weighed in without girth (Jun 29)

FOCUS
A race for apprentices who hadn't ridden a winner, with the leaders coming up the middle of the track.

3290 BONDGATE NOVICE FILLIES' STKS (PLUS 10 RACE) 5f
7:00 (7:07) (Class 5) 2-Y-O **£2,911** (£866; £432; £216) **Stalls** High

Form RPR

2 **1** **Rosebride**[16] 2732 2-9-0 0........................ TonyHamilton 4 68
(Richard Fahey) *wnt rt s: w ldrs: led over 1f out: pushed out* **5/2**[1]

2 *¾* **Climax** 2-9-0 0........................ FrannyNorton 2 65+
(Mark Johnston) *wnt rt s: chsd ldrs: green and wnt lft over 2f out: swtchd rt over 1f out: kpt on same pce clsng stages* **14/1**[3]

3 *1 ½* **My Cherry Blossom** 2-9-0 0........................ DavidNolan 12 60
(Tim Easterby) *chsd ldrs: nt clr run and swtchd rt appr fnl f: r.o* **33/1**

521 **4** *shd* **Melaniemillie**[5] 3114 2-8-11 0........................ JacobButterfield(3) 6 60
(Ollie Pears) *w ldr: led briefly 2f out: kpt on same pce* **5/2**[1]

50 **5** *1* **Shadow Wing (IRE)**[40] 2007 2-9-0 0........................ JoeyHaynes 3 56
(Tom Dascombe) *carried rt s: mid-div: hdwy over 2f out: kpt on same pce fnl f* **50/1**

50 **6** *2 ¾* **Limbrick**[32] 2235 2-9-0 0........................ PJMcDonald 1 46
(Ann Duffield) *carried rt s: sn chsng ldrs: one pce appr fnl f* **80/1**

7 *nk* **Tael O' Gold** 2-9-0 0........................ RoystonFfrench 7 45
(Iain Jardine) *mid-div: sn drvn along: kpt on fnl f: nvr a threat* **40/1**

421 **8** *1* **Whiteandgold**[16] 2739 2-9-4 0........................ PaulMulrennan 11 45
(Bryan Smart) *gave problems loading: restless in stalls: led: hdd 2f out: wknd appr fnl f* **7/2**[2]

05 **9** *½* **Seminole Dream (IRE)**[9] 2956 2-9-0 0........................ ConnorBeasley 5 40
(Philip Kirby) *mid-div: sn drvn along: kpt on fnl f: nvr a factor* **150/1**

10 *nk* **Xenon** 2-9-0 0........................ RyanPowell 8 38
(Sir Mark Prescott Bt) *mid-div: sme hdwy 2f out: nvr a factor: eased nr fin* **16/1**

11 *3 ¾* **Ocelot** 2-9-0 0........................ DuranFentiman 10 25
(Tim Easterby) *gave problems loading: restless in stalls: s.s: a bhd: nvr on terms* **7/2**[2]

12 *2 ½* **Can Can Dream** 2-9-0 0........................ CamHardie 13 16
(Olly Williams) *s.v.s: a detached in last* **100/1**

1m 1.44s (1.44) **Going Correction** +0.125s/f (Good) **12** Ran SP% **124.4**
Speed ratings (Par 90): **93,91,89,89,87 83,82,81,80,79 73,69**
CSF £42.81 TOTE £3.10: £1.10, £3.60, £9.80; EX 30.20 Trifecta £848.20.
Owner Cheveley Park Stud **Bred** Cheveley Park Stud Ltd **Trained** Musley Bank, N Yorks

FOCUS
Probably an average juvenile maiden in which there was plenty of trouble loading the runners into the stalls and some had a wait of around eight minutes. The winner has been rated to her debut form.

3291 RIPON-RACES.CO.UK FILLIES' H'CAP 1m 1f 170y
7:30 (7:30) (Class 4) (0-85,85) 3-Y-O+ **£5,175** (£1,540; £769; £384) **Stalls** Low

Form RPR

5-23 **1** **Shafafya**[19] 2654 3-8-8 **78**........................ PaulMulrennan 5 87+
(Ed Dunlop) *hld up in last: hdwy on ins over 3f out: nt clr run over 2f out: swtchd lft and 2nd over 1f out: styd on to ld last 75yds: readily* **6/4**[1]

-402 **2** *2* **Belle Travers**[13] 2811 4-9-3 **74**........................ TonyHamilton 4 80
(Richard Fahey) *sn chsng ldrs: led 3f out: hdd and no ex last 75yds* **8/1**

-456 **3** *1 ¾* **Deodoro (USA)**[25] 2490 3-8-5 **75**........................ FrannyNorton 6 76
(Mark Johnston) *chsd ldrs: drvn 3f out: edgd rt and one pce fnl 150yds* **7/1**

21-0 **4** *2 ¾* **All About Time**[32] 2236 4-10-0 **85**........................ DavidNolan 1 82
(David O'Meara) *dwlt: sn chsng ldrs: drvn 3f out: wknd over 1f out* **5/1**[3]

3-03 **5** *8* **Ninetta (IRE)**[27] 2407 3-9-1 **85**........................ PJMcDonald 3 64
(Ann Duffield) *led: hdd 3f out: lost pl over 1f out* **7/2**[2]

40-0 **6** *7* **Secret Lightning (FR)**[5] 3096 4-8-9 **66**........................(p) AndrewMullen 2 32
(Michael Appleby) *trckd ldrs: t.k.h: drvn over 3f out: edgd lft: lost pl 2f out* **16/1**

2m 5.01s (-0.39) **Going Correction** +0.125s/f (Good)
WFA 3 from 4yo 13lb **6** Ran SP% **108.4**
Speed ratings (Par 102): **106,104,103,100,94 88**
CSF £13.06 TOTE £2.10: £1.60, £3.60; EX 11.30 Trifecta £34.20.

Owner Hamdan Al Maktoum **Bred** Shadwell Estate Company Limited **Trained** Newmarket, Suffolk

FOCUS

Race run over 4yds further than advertised. A medium gallop to this fillies' handicap in which several were in fair form and the winner came from last to first. The runner-up has been rated to form.

3292 WELLS MEMORIAL CHALLENGE TROPHY H'CAP 6f

8:00 (8:01) (Class 3) (0-95,87) 3-Y-O **£7,561** (£2,263; £1,131; £566; £282) **Stalls** High

Form RPR

61-6 **1** **Flying Pursuit**[18] 2693 3-9-4 **84**.. DavidAllan 3 93
(Tim Easterby) *in rr: effrt and nt clr run 2f out: swtchd lft: upsides over 1f out: led last 150yds: drvn out* **8/1**

1323 **2** 3/4 **Bossipop**[9] 2972 3-8-10 **81**................................(p) RachelRichardson(5) 5 88+
(Tim Easterby) *dwlt: hld up in rr: hdwy on ins and nt clr run over 1f out: styd on appr fnl f: tk 2nd last 75yds: no ex* **9/2**[2]

-331 **3** 1 1/2 **My Amigo**[22] 2554 3-9-6 **86**.. PJMcDonald 4 88
(Ann Duffield) *awkward s: hdwy to chse ldrs over 4f out: led over 1f out: hdd last 150yds: kpt on same pce* **3/1**[1]

2133 **4** 4 **Paddy Power (IRE)**[19] 2658 3-9-7 **87**................................ DavidNolan 8 76
(Richard Fahey) *trckd ldrs: swtchd rt and led over 2f out: hdd over 1f out: wknd fnl f* **5/1**[3]

1131 **5** 1 1/2 **Ordinal**[11] 2906 3-8-8 **74**.. FrannyNorton 6 58
(Mark Johnston) *w ldrs: wknd over 1f out* **11/2**

-101 **6** 2 1/4 **Brilliant Vanguard (IRE)**[14] 2802 3-9-3 **83**................ PaulMulrennan 7 60
(Kevin Ryan) *upset in stalls: led: hdd over 2f out: sn lost pl* **5/1**[3]

-050 **7** nk **Rosina**[19] 2658 3-8-12 **85**.. SophieKilloran(7) 2 61
(Ann Duffield) *trckd ldrs: t.k.h: wknd over 1f out* **20/1**

6-24 **8** 1 3/4 **Flowing Clarets**[14] 2802 3-8-12 **78**................................ TonyHamilton 1 49
(Richard Fahey) *t.k.h: trckd ldrs: lost pl over 3f out* **10/1**

1m 12.7s (-0.30) **Going Correction** +0.125s/f (Good) **8** Ran SP% **116.9**

Speed ratings (Par 103): **107,106,104,98,96 93,93,90**

CSF £44.77 CT £134.21 TOTE £10.10: £2.90, £1.80, £1.30; EX 51.70 Trifecta £197.50.

Owner Ontoawinner, M Hulin & Partner **Bred** Crossfields Bloodstock Ltd **Trained** Great Habton, N Yorks

FOCUS

A competitive sprint for 3yos run at a sound gallop, but the form might be misleading for the early leaders dropped away and the first two came from well off the pace. Another pb from the winner, with the third rated to his Wetherby latest.

3293 SIS MAIDEN STKS 6f

8:30 (8:33) (Class 5) 3-Y-O **£2,911** (£866; £432; £216) **Stalls** High

Form RPR

26- **1** **Tanaasub (IRE)**[221] 7752 3-9-0 0................................ PaulMulrennan 10 72+
(Robert Cowell) *mde all stands' side: shkn up appr fnl f: pushed clr: readily* **5/2**[2]

2 2 3/4 **Eisha Flower (USA)** 3-9-0 0.. TonyHamilton 5 63+
(Richard Fahey) *mid-div: green and drvn after 2f: hdwy over 2f out: chsd wnr over 1f out: no imp* **9/4**[1]

06 **3** nk **Noah Amor (IRE)**[40] 2019 3-9-5 0.................................. FrannyNorton 3 67
(David Nicholls) *trckd ldrs on outside: swtchd lft over 4f out: wnt 3rd 1f out: kpt on* **20/1**

5-6 **4** 4 1/2 **Ss Vega**[58] 1524 3-9-0 0.. PJMcDonald 6 48
(James Bethell) *sn outpcd and in rr: sme hdwy over 1f out: wnt modest 4th last 150yds* **9/1**[3]

650 **5** 3 1/4 **Another Desperado (IRE)**[19] 2667 3-9-5 39............... AndrewMullen 7 42
(Rebecca Bastiman) *chsd ldrs: outpcd over 2f out: no threat after* **100/1**

535 **6** 1 3/4 **Ryedale Rio (IRE)**[18] 2668 3-9-5 68.................................. DavidAllan 4 37
(Tim Easterby) *chsd wnr: drvn over 2f out: wknd fnl f* **9/1**[3]

5062 **7** 3 **Take Charge**[13] 2809 3-9-5 71.. ShaneGray 2 27
(David Brown) *wnt rt s: towards rr: hdwy on outside over 2f out: lost pl over 1f out* **5/2**[2]

00-0 **8** 1/2 **Take In Time**[13] 2835 3-9-5 0.. KeaganLatham 1 26
(Michael Easterby) *hood removed v late: dwlt and carried rt s: a outpcd and in rr* **100/1**

1m 13.2s (0.20) **Going Correction** +0.125s/f (Good) **8** Ran SP% **114.7**

Speed ratings (Par 99): **103,99,98,92,88 86,82,81**

CSF £8.52 TOTE £2.80: £1.30, £1.10, £4.50; EX 9.10 Trifecta £60.30.

Owner Abdulla Al Mansoori **Bred** J F Tuthill **Trained** Six Mile Bottom, Cambs

■ Flummoxed was withdrawn. Price at time of withdrawal 33-1. Rule 4 does not apply.

FOCUS

There were varied abilities in this sprint maiden in which the first three finished clear. The winner has been rated to her 2yo debut run.

3294 IT'S LADIES DAY TOMORROW H'CAP 1m 4f 10y

9:00 (9:01) (Class 5) (0-75,74) 4-Y-O+ **£3,234** (£962; £481; £240) **Stalls** Centre

Form RPR

-054 **1** **Skiddaw Valleys**[11] 2911 4-9-4 **71**.................................... TonyHamilton 8 78
(Alan Swinbank) *trckd ldrs: chal over 3f out: styd on to ld last 50yds* **7/1**

3202 **2** 1/2 **Wishing Well**[13] 2836 4-8-12 **65**.. TomEaves 2 71
(Micky Hammond) *hld up in mid-div: hdwy 4f out: sn drvn: 3rd 1f out: swtchd lft and styd on to take 2nd nr fin* **13/2**

0-31 **3** 3/4 **Tourtiere**[19] 2656 8-8-6 **68**.. HollieDoyle(7) 7 73
(Andrew Crook) *led: hdd and no ex last 50yds* **5/1**[3]

-521 **4** hd **Grand Canyon (IRE)**[16] 2743 4-9-7 **74**............................ PhillipMakin 3 79
(David O'Meara) *hld up towards rr: shkn up over 6f out: hdwy 4f out: rdn over 2f out: styd on fnl f* **5/4**[1]

3/23 **5** 1 3/4 **Frederic**[11] 2912 5-9-3 **70**.. PJMcDonald 6 72
(Micky Hammond) *drvn early to chse ldrs: chal over 3f out: one pce over 1f out* **9/2**[2]

06-0 **6** 2 1/2 **Tiger Twenty Two**[12] 1588 5-8-7 **60**.............................. AndrewMullen 5 58
(Brian Rothwell) *chsd ldrs: drvn over 4f out: one pce fnl 2f* **22/1**

34-0 **7** 27 **Walk Like A Giant**[164] 33 5-9-3 **70**........................(p) PaulMulrennan 4 25
(Julia Brooke) *chsd ldrs: drvn over 4f out: wknd 3f out: bhd whn eased clsng stages: t.o* **20/1**

000- **8** shd **Fledermaus (IRE)**[236] 7428 6-8-7 **60**..............................(t) CamHardie 1 15
(Tina Jackson) *s.i.s: in rr: drvn over 6f out: lost pl 3f out: bhd whn eased clsng stages* **50/1**

2m 39.15s (2.45) **Going Correction** +0.125s/f (Good) **8** Ran SP% **116.2**

Speed ratings (Par 103): **96,95,95,95,93 92,74,74**

CSF £50.59 CT £249.62 TOTE £8.90: £2.30, £2.00, £1.90; EX 52.90 Trifecta £277.40.

Owner John Wills **Bred** J R Wills **Trained** Melsonby, N Yorks

FOCUS

Race run over 4yds further than advertised. No more than a fair gallop to this 1m4f handicap in which the winner and third had the run of the race. The form looks believeable for now, with the front five all within 2lb of these marks in recent starts.

T/Plt: £97.20 to a £1 stake. Pool: £57,412.94. 431.14 winning tickets. T/Qpdt: £15.70 to a £1 stake. Pool: £5,356.42. 251.96 winning tickets. **Walter Glynn**

3269 ASCOT (R-H)

Thursday, June 16

OFFICIAL GOING: Soft (stands' side7.2, centre 6.7, far side 7.0, round 6.3)

Wind: light, across Weather: overcast

3295 NORFOLK STKS (GROUP 2) 5f

2:30 (2:30) (Class 1) 2-Y-O

£56,710 (£21,500; £10,760; £5,360; £2,690; £1,350) **Stalls** Centre

Form RPR

1 **1** **Prince Of Lir (IRE)**[19] 2669 2-9-1 0................................ LukeMorris 10 107
(Robert Cowell) *cmpt: lw: hld up in tch: pushed along over 2f out: rdn and hdwy over 1f out: rn to ld fnl 150yds: in control cl home* **8/1**

122 **2** 1/2 **The Last Lion (IRE)**[19] 2669 2-9-1 0................................ JoeFanning 8 105
(Mark Johnston) *lw: chsd ldrs: rdn to ld wl over 1f out: hdd fnl 150yds: kpt on u.p: hld nr fin* **20/1**

1 **3** nk **Silver Line (IRE)**[25] 2500 2-9-1 0.................................. JamesDoyle 11 104
(Saeed bin Suroor) *unf: scope: in rr: swtchd lft over 2f out: hdwy wl over 1f out: chalng ent fnl f: styd on: hld nr fin* **7/2**[2]

1 **4** 1/2 **Peace Envoy (FR)**[18] 2717 2-9-1 0................................ RyanMoore 6 102
(A P O'Brien, Ire) *str: hld up: hdwy 2f out: chsd ldrs ins fnl f: styd on: nt quite pce to get to ldrs: no further imp nr fin* **9/2**[3]

121 **5** 1 1/2 **Global Applause**[21] 2624 2-9-1 0................................ FrankieDettori 4 97
(Ed Dunlop) *swtg: in tch: effrt 2f out: ev ch over 1f out: nt qckn: styd on same pce u.p ins fnl f* **3/1**[1]

121 **6** 1 1/4 **Legendary Lunch (IRE)**[13] 2865 2-9-1 0............................ PatDobbs 9 92
(Richard Hannon) *lw: hld up: pushed along over 2f out: hdwy 1f out: styd on ins fnl f: gng on at fin* **7/1**

1 **7** shd **Big Time Baby (IRE)**[13] 2847 2-9-1 0....................(t) RichardKingscote 3 92
(Tom Dascombe) *w'like: w ldrs: led over 2f out: rdn and hdd wl over 1f out: fdd fnl 100yds* **16/1**

45 **8** 2 1/2 **Nuclear Power**[20] 2649 2-9-1 0.. TomQueally 7 83
(Joseph Tuite) *leggy: in rr: sn pushed along: hdwy u.p over 1f out: kpt on ins fnl f: nt gng pce to trble ldrs* **66/1**

9 2 1/4 **Red Lodge (USA)**[20] 2-8-12 0..............................(bt) JohnRVelazquez 5 72
(Wesley A Ward, U.S.A) *tall: str: lw: racd keenly: chsd ldrs: rdn over 1f out: wknd ins fnl f* **8/1**

1 **10** nk **Prince Of Cool**[27] 2437 2-9-1 0.. TomEaves 1 74
(James Given) *leggy: chsd ldrs tl rdn and wknd over 1f out* **25/1**

1 **11** 2 3/4 **Plata O Plomo**[21] 2611 2-9-1 0...................................... BarryMcHugh 2 64
(Tony Coyle) *cmpt: walked to post: led: hdd over 2f out: rdn and wknd over 1f out* **20/1**

1m 1.17s (0.67) **Going Correction** +0.25s/f (Good) **11** Ran SP% **120.9**

Speed ratings (Par 105): **104,103,102,101,99 97,97,93,89,89 84**

CSF £161.51 CT £534.21 TOTE £10.50: £2.60, £4.70, £1.80; EX 167.40 Trifecta £670.20.

Owner The Cool Silk Partnership **Bred** Philip & Orla Hore **Trained** Six Mile Bottom, Cambs

FOCUS

Another dry night and only a brief shower or two prior to racing. There was fresh ground on the inside of the round course from the 1m4f start to the 9f marker. Rider James Doyle remarked after the opener: "It is similar to yesterday and a bit dead".\n\x\x This was a typical Norfolk. Unsurprisingly they stuck down the middle, although the principals made their efforts more towards the stands' side. The fourth has been rated to his Irish mark.

3296 TERCENTENARY STKS (FORMERLY THE HAMPTON COURT STAKES) (GROUP 3) 1m 2f

3:05 (3:06) (Class 1) 3-Y-O

£51,039 (£19,350; £9,684; £4,824; £2,421; £1,215) **Stalls** Low

Form RPR

11-1 **1** **Hawkbill (USA)**[47] 1866 3-9-0 106.................................... WilliamBuick 2 112
(Charlie Appleby) *swtg: racd keenly early: chsd ldng pair: clsd to press ldrs 3f out: ev ch 2f out: rdn to ld over 1f out: drvn clr ins fnl f: styd on: rdn out* **11/2**[3]

1-22 **2** 1 1/4 **Prize Money**[27] 2432 3-9-0 101.. JamesDoyle 4 109
(Saeed bin Suroor) *chsd ldr: rdn to press ldr 3f out: drvn to ld wl over 1f out: sn hdd: a hld by wnr but kpt on u.p for clr 2nd fnl f* **4/1**[1]

3 2 3/4 **Long Island Sound (USA)**[30] 2352 3-9-0 102...............(t) RyanMoore 7 104+
(A P O'Brien, Ire) *str: lw: t.k.h early: hld up in last trio: effrt over 2f out: hdwy u.p to chse clr ldng pair 1f out: kpt on steadily but nvr a threat to ldrs* **9/2**[2]

-521 **4** 1 3/4 **Steel Of Madrid (IRE)**[26] 2481 3-9-0 104............................ PatDobbs 6 100
(Richard Hannon) *lw: t.k.h: hld up in midfield: effrt ent fnl f: battling for 3rd but no imp on ldrs over 1f out: 4th and kpt on same pce ins fnl f* **12/1**

1-4 **5** 3/4 **Royal Artillery (USA)**[21] 2627 3-9-0 99.....................(tp) AndreaAtzeni 3 98+
(John Gosden) *tall: lw: t.k.h: chsd ldng trio: effrt ent fnl 2f: edging rt and no imp u.p jst over 1f out: wl hld and styd on same pce fnl f* **14/1**

-424 **6** shd **Race Day (IRE)**[33] 2250 3-9-0 98.. MartinLane 9 98
(Saeed bin Suroor) *led: rdn over 2f out: hdd wl over 1f out: sn dropped to 3rd and outpcd: wknd ins fnl f* **33/1**

1-23 **7** 3 **Blue De Vega (GER)**[26] 2496 3-9-4 107............................ KierenFallon 1 96
(M D O'Callaghan, Ire) *w'like: stdd s: hld up in midfield: effrt u.p jst over 2f out: no imp: wknd ins fnl f: eased towards fin* **11/2**[3]

1-2 **8** 1 1/4 **Abdon**[47] 1866 3-9-0 102.. FrankieDettori 8 89
(Sir Michael Stoute) *lw: stdd s: t.k.h: hld up in last pair: effrt jst over 2f out: no hdwy and wl btn 1f out: eased wl ins fnl f* **4/1**[1]

21 **9** 1/2 **Mulk**[43] 1970 3-9-0 90.. PaulHanagan 5 88
(Sir Michael Stoute) *t.k.h: early: hld up in rr: effrt 2f out: no hdwy and wl btn over 1f out* **10/1**

2m 9.59s (2.19) **Going Correction** +0.50s/f (Yiel) **9** Ran SP% **115.3**

Speed ratings (Par 109): **111,110,107,106,105 105,103,102,101**

CSF £27.75 CT £107.35 TOTE £6.60: £2.30, £1.60, £1.60; EX 26.20 Trifecta £146.30.

Owner Godolphin **Bred** Helen K Groves Revokable Trust **Trained** Newmarket, Suffolk

FOCUS
The rail on the round course was positioned approximately 3yds out from around the 9f point to the home straight, adding about 9yds to the distance of this race. This was somewhat tactical, only the three Godolphin runners ever really involved, and a number of these were not seen to best effect. The front-running sixth was a doubtful stayer but has been rated close to form nevertheless.

3297 RIBBLESDALE STKS (GROUP 2) (FILLIES) 1m 4f
3:40 (3:40) (Class 1) 3-Y-O

£113,420 (£43,000; £21,520; £10,720; £5,380; £2,700) **Stalls** Low

Form RPR

3 **1** **Even Song (IRE)**[46] 1890 3-9-0 95 RyanMoore 5 108+
(A P O'Brien, Ire) *lw: midfield: checked after 4f: hdwy over 2f out: led over 1f out: r.o ins fnl f: edgd rt towards fin whn in command* **15/8**[1]

222 **2** 1 1/2 **Ajman Princess (IRE)**[17] 2735 3-9-0 86 [1] AndreaAtzeni 4 105
(Roger Varian) *chsd ldrs: chalng over 1f out: nt qckn: styd on u.p ins fnl f: nt pce of wnr* **33/1**

1-22 **3** 1 **The Black Princess (FR)**[28] 2394 3-9-0 101 WilliamBuick 11 103+
(John Gosden) *racd keenly: hld up: rdn whn bmpd over 2f out: hdwy over 1f out: edgd rt ins fnl f: styd on wl: nt quite get to ldrs* **8/1**

15-4 **4** nk **Queen's Trust**[33] 2245 3-9-0 96 OlivierPeslier 10 103+
(Sir Michael Stoute) *hld up in rr: rdn over 2f out: hdwy over 1f out: r.o ins fnl f: gng on at fin* **12/1**

2-21 **5** hd **Shall We (IRE)**[35] 2183 3-9-0 89 TedDurcan 12 102
(Sir Michael Stoute) *racd keenly: led: rdn and hdd over 1f out: kpt on u.p ins fnl f but nt pce of ldrs* **25/1**

-131 **6** hd **We Are Ninety (IRE)**[33] 2245 3-9-0 98 JimCrowley 6 102+
(Hugo Palmer) *lw: midfield: rdn and swtchd lft over 2f out: hdwy over 1f out: styd on ins fnl f: one pce nr fin* **16/1**

1 **7** 1 3/4 **Sovereign Parade (IRE)**[35] 2182 3-9-0 89 RobertHavlin 7 99+
(John Gosden) *unf: scope: lw: hld up: u.p and outpcd over 2f out: styd on ins fnl f: nt pce to trble ldrs* **7/1**[3]

1-22 **8** shd **Architecture (IRE)**[13] 2869 3-9-0 114 FrankieDettori 13 99
(Hugo Palmer) *in tch: effrt over 2f out: no imp u.p over 1f out: one pce fnl 150yds* **3/1**[2]

21-2 **9** 1 1/2 **Chicadoro**[46] 1890 3-9-0 100 FMBerry 3 97
(Ralph Beckett) *racd keenly: in tch: chalng over 1f out: sn outpcd u.p: fdd ins fnl f* **12/1**

10 1/2 **Olala (GER)**[37] 2142 3-9-0 94 AntoineHamelin 2 96
(M Figge, Germany) *leggy: swtg: midfield: rdn and hdwy over 1f out to chse ldng bunch: kpt on same pce and no imp ins fnl f* **25/1**

314 **11** 3/4 **Capricious Cantor (IRE)**[40] 2035 3-9-0 86 SilvestreDeSousa 14 95
(Ed Dunlop) *racd keenly: hld up: rdn over 2f out: sn outpcd: kpt on ins fnl f: eased whn no ch towards fin* **50/1**

0-40 **12** hd **Dessertoflife (IRE)**[28] 2394 3-9-0 99 JoeFanning 1 94
(Mark Johnston) *swtg: missed break: racd keenly: hld up: rdn over 2f out: no imp* **50/1**

102 **13** nk **Beauly**[7] 3060 3-9-0 90 JamieSpencer 9 94
(Charles Hills) *chsd ldr: rdn whn c fairly wd into st over 2f out: sn lost 2nd: wknd 1f out* **25/1**

0-1 **14** nk **Rocaverde (IRE)**[55] 1609 3-9-0 86 PatSmullen 8 93
(Ralph Beckett) *lw: prom: pushed along over 2f out and carried lft: wknd over 1f out* **33/1**

2m 39.74s (7.24) **Going Correction** +0.50s/f (Yiel) **14** Ran SP% **126.0**
Speed ratings (Par 108): **95,94,93,93,93 92,91,91,90,90 89,89,89,89**
CSF £85.72 CT £439.80 TOTE £2.80: £1.50, £7.00, £2.60; EX 64.20 Trifecta £561.00.
Owner Mrs John Magnier **Bred** Barronstown Stud **Trained** Cashel, Co Tipperary
■ Stewards' Enquiry : Jim Crowley caution: careless riding

FOCUS
This looked an open Ribblesdale. They went an uneven pace until it lifted around 3f out, and fanned across into the middle inside the final furlong. The compressed finish limits the level of the form.

3298 GOLD CUP IN HONOUR OF THE QUEEN'S 90TH BIRTHDAY (BRITISH CHAMPIONS SERIES) (GROUP 1) 2m 4f
4:20 (4:21) (Class 1) 4-Y-O+

£226,840 (£86,000; £43,040; £21,440; £10,760; £5,400) **Stalls** Low

Form RPR

11-1 **1** **Order Of St George (IRE)**[13] 2881 4-9-0 124 RyanMoore 10 121+
(A P O'Brien, Ire) *str: swtg: hld up in midfield: clsd 6f out: wl in tch but short of room and jostling 5f out: switching lft and effrt bnd over 2f out: str run in st to ld over 1f out: styd on strly and drew clr ins fnl f: impressive* **10/11**[1]

02-1 **2** 3 **Mizzou (IRE)**[50] 1772 5-9-2 111 AndreaAtzeni 1 117
(Luca Cumani) *lw: hld up in midfield: wnt prom in chsng gp and clsd on ldrs 6f out: rdn and effrt 3f out: chsd ldrs 2f out: chsd wnr ent fnl f: no threat to wnr but styd on for clr 2nd* **10/1**

3-10 **3** 2 1/4 **Sheikhzayedroad**[82] 1107 7-9-2 112 MartinHarley 12 115
(David Simcock) *hld up in last sextet: clsd 6f out: in tch whn nt clr run on inner and hmpd 3f out: swtchd lft and hdwy u.p over 2f out: 6th and styng but hanging rt over 1f out: stl hanging bdly but r.o to go 3rd fnl 100yds* **40/1**

13-0 **4** 2 3/4 **Mille Et Mille**[53] 1688 6-9-2 111 (t) ThierryThulliez 18 112
(C Lerner, France) *t.k.h early: chsd ldrs tl led after 2f: wnt clr 12f out tl 5f out: rdn and kicked on again over 2f out: drvn and hdd over 1f out: 3rd and btn 1f out: kpt on same pce* **33/1**

1-54 **5** 2 1/4 **Burmese**[21] 2625 4-9-0 108 (p) WilliamBuick 13 110
(Marcus Tregoning) *hld up in midfield: clsd and pushed along 6f out: hdwy to chse ldrs 4f out: rdn over 2f out: no ex and outpcd over 1f out: wl hld and plugged on same pce fnl f* **40/1**

11-3 **6** 1 1/4 **Flying Officer (USA)**[50] 1772 6-9-2 115 FrankieDettori 6 109
(John Gosden) *lw: prom in chsng gp: clsd 6f out: rdn to chse ldr 3f out tl no ex u.p over 1f out: 4th and btn 1f out: wknd ins fnl f* **7/1**[2]

-221 **7** nk **Clever Cookie**[34] 2221 8-9-2 113 (p) PJMcDonald 17 108
(Peter Niven) *stdd and swtchd rt after s: hld up in last pair: clsd 6f out: wl in tch but stuck bhd a wall of horses 3f out: swtchd rt and effrt over 2f out: sme hdwy over 1f out: kpt on ins fnl f: n.d* **8/1**[3]

4442 **8** nk **Suegioo (FR)**[21] 2625 7-9-2 108 (p) PaulHanagan 4 108
(Richard Fahey) *hld up in last sextet: clsd 6f out but stuck wd: stl bhd and effrt over 2f out: moving rt and hdwy over 1f out: styd on to pass btn rivals ins fnl f: n.d* **50/1**

20-4 **9** 1/2 **Kicky Blue (GER)**[53] 1688 6-8-13 106 MickaelBarzalona 16 105
(T Clout, France) *leggy: hld up in last sextet: clsd 6f out: hdwy 4f out: chsd ldrs and rdn over 2f out: 7th and no ex u.p over 1f out: wknd fnl f* **50/1**

12-3 **10** 6 **Max Dynamite (FR)**[21] 2625 6-9-2 116 PatSmullen 9 102
(W P Mullins, Ire) *hld up in midfield: clsd 6f out: wl in tch whn short of room and bdly hmpd on inner 3f out: swtchd rt and tried to rally u.p over 2f out: no prog: wl hld over 1f out* **7/1**[2]

2-01 **11** 13 **Wasir (GER)**[32] 2286 4-9-0 107 UmbertoRispoli 5 89
(A Wohler, Germany) *swtg: prom in chsng gp: hmpd 8f out: clsd 6f out: beginning to struggle and jostling w wnr 5f out: lost pl u.p wl over 2f out: no ch after: eased ins fnl f* **66/1**

14-1 **12** 12 **Pallasator**[21] 2625 7-9-2 112 OisinMurphy 7 77
(Sir Mark Prescott Bt) *swtg: taken down early: hld up in midfield: clsd 6f out: wl in tch whn short of room and jostling 3f out: effrt u.p over 2f out: no hdwy and sn btn: eased ins fnl f: t.o* **12/1**

430- **13** 1 1/2 **Fun Mac (GER)**[235] 7502 5-9-2 108 (t) JamesDoyle 2 75
(Hughie Morrison) *prom in chsng gp: clsd 6f out: swtchd lft and effrt u.p 3f out: unable qck and btn ent fnl 2f: wl bhd and eased fnl f: t.o* **33/1**

24-4 **14** 3/4 **Tiberian (FR)**[39] 2077 4-9-0 109 AdrienFouassier 8 74
(Alain Couetil, France) *str: hld up in last sextet: clsd 6f out: in tch and effrt on outer bnd over 2f out: sn btn: wl bhd and eased fnl f: t.o* **66/1**

46-2 **15** 17 **Scotland (GER)**[40] 2025 5-9-2 109 [1] JamieSpencer 15 57
(Andrew Balding) *swtg: stdd s: hld up in rr: hdwy into midfield after 3f: clsd 6f out: swtchd lft and effrt over 2f out: sn btn: wl bhd and eased fnl f: t.o* **20/1**

55-0 **16** 30 **The Twisler**[32] 2286 4-9-0 104 SilvestreDeSousa 11 27
(Jane Chapple-Hyam) *chsd ldr: pushed along and clsd 6f out: rdn and lost 2nd 3f out: drvn and wandered over 2f out: sn btn and eased t.o* **100/1**

445/ **17** 31 **Griraz (FR)**[247] 11-9-2 84 (t) DonnachaO'Brien 14
(David Pipe) *stdd s: hld up in last sextet: hdwy on outer 10f out: wnt prom in chsng gp 8f out: clsd 6f out: lost pl over 4f out: bhd and lost tch over 2f out: eased: t.o* **100/1**

4m 26.21s (1.41) **Going Correction** +0.50s/f (Yiel)
WFA 4 from 5yo+ 2lb **17** Ran SP% **129.7**
Speed ratings (Par 117): **117,115,114,113,112 112,112,112,111,109 104,99,98,98,91 79,67**
CSF £11.00 CT £266.46 TOTE £1.90: £1.02, £3.60, £15.60; EX 12.50 Trifecta £296.50.
Owner L J Williams/Mrs J Magnier/M Tabor/D Smith **Bred** Paget Bloodstock **Trained** Cashel, Co Tipperary

FOCUS
Actual race distance 2m4f 9yds. Probably not a great Gold Cup, but there hasn't been a bigger field since 1900, if ever, and we saw a high-class winner. The fourth set a rather stop-start pace and they stacked up before the home turn. The winner did not need to match his Irish St Leger form to win this. The fourth and fifth have been rated close to their marks.

3299 BRITANNIA STKS (HERITAGE H'CAP) (C&G) 1m (S)
5:00 (5:03) (Class 1) (0-105,101) 3-Y-O

£74,700 (£22,368; £11,184; £5,592; £2,796; £1,404) **Stalls** Centre

Form RPR

-141 **1** **Limitless (IRE)**[12] 2891 3-9-1 **95** JamieSpencer 12 110+
(Jamie Osborne) *tall: str: lw: started awkwardly: racd far side: hld up: hdwy and swtchd rt over 2f out: led overall wl over 1f out: rdn and hung rt ins fnl f: all out nr fin: 1st of 18 in gp* **13/2**[3]

3-05 **2** shd **Abe Lincoln (USA)**[36] 2161 3-8-12 **92** (p) JimCrowley 18 104
(Jeremy Noseda) *racd far side: in midfield: hdwy over 2f out: wnt 2nd over 1f out: r.o strly ins fnl f: jst failed: 2nd of 18 in gp* **20/1**

-322 **3** 2 1/4 **California Whip (USA)**[26] 2473 3-9-3 **97** SeanLevey 23 104+
(Richard Hannon) *lw: swtchd lft early to r in stands' side gp: hld up: swtchd lft and hdwy 2f out: rdn over 1f out: r.o ins fnl f: led gp fnl 100yds: edgd rt towards fin: hld by front two: 1st of 10 in gp* **12/1**

-310 **4** 1 1/4 **Arcanada (IRE)**[42] 1975 3-8-13 **93** MartinHarley 30 97
(Tom Dascombe) *racd stands' side: led gp and wl on terms w other side: rdn over 1f out: hdd in gp fnl 100yds: no ex towards fin: 2nd of 10 in gp* **66/1**

1-21 **5** shd **Yattwee (USA)**[26] 2480 3-9-6 **100** JamesDoyle 27 104
(Saeed bin Suroor) *racd stands' side: trckd ldrs: effrt over 2f out: ev ch in gp over 1f out: styd on ins fnl f: 3rd of 10 in gp* **20/1**

41-1 **6** 1 1/2 **Booming Delight (IRE)**[19] 2695 3-8-12 **92** RyanMoore 9 92
(William Haggas) *tall: lengthy: lw: racd far side: trckd ldrs: led overall 2f out: sn hdd: unable to go pce of ldrs over 1f out: styd on same pce ins fnl f: 3rd of 18 in gp* **11/2**[1]

62-3 **7** 1 1/4 **Zodiakos (IRE)**[47] 1867 3-8-6 **89** MarcMonaghan[(3)] 28 86
(Hugo Palmer) *racd stands' side: chsd ldrs: rdn over 2f out: nt qckn over 1f out: styd on same pce ins fnl f: 4th of 10 in gp* **25/1**

31-1 **8** 1 **Folkswood**[47] 1867 3-9-4 **98** WilliamBuick 17 93
(Charlie Appleby) *swtg: racd far side: chsd ldrs: rdn over 2f out: styd on same pce ins fnl f: 4th of 18 in gp* **6/1**[2]

15-1 **9** nk **Taurean Star (IRE)**[41] 1992 3-8-6 **89** DanielMuscutt[(3)] 20 83
(Michael Bell) *racd far side: hld up: hdwy over 2f out: rdn over 1f out: styd on ins fnl f: nt pce of ldrs: 5th of 18 in gp* **20/1**

1106 **10** nk **Sea Of Flames**[13] 2867 3-9-6 **100** SilvestreDeSousa 22 94
(David Elsworth) *swtchd lft early to r in stands' side gp: midfield: effrt to chse ldrs over 2f out: one pce ins fnl f: 5th of 10 in gp* **50/1**

-306 **11** 1 1/4 **Zhui Feng (IRE)**[26] 2466 3-9-5 **99** TomQueally 19 90
(Amanda Perrett) *lw: racd far side: towards rr: rdn over 2f out: hdwy over 1f out: kpt on ins fnl f: nvr able to trble ldrs: 6th of 18 in gp* **33/1**

4-21 **12** 3/4 **Mustashry**[40] 2048 3-9-1 **95** PaulHanagan 14 84
(Sir Michael Stoute) *racd far side: midfield: rdn and hdwy over 2f out: sn ch: unable to go pce of ldrs over 1f out: kpt on same pce ins fnl f: 7th of 18 in gp* **12/1**

15-0 **13** nk **Wall Of Fire (IRE)**[30] 2331 3-8-10 **90** (b) PatSmullen 31 78
(Hugo Palmer) *lw: racd stands' side: midfield: effrt over 2f out: sn chsd ldrs: no imp over 1f out: one pce ins fnl f: 6th of 10 in gp* **33/1**

4-16 **14** hd **Carrington (FR)**[33] 2237 3-8-11 **91** MartinLane 26 79
(Charlie Appleby) *s.s: racd stands' side: hld up: rdn and edgd rt whn hdwy 3f out: chsd ldrs 2f out: one pce over 1f out: 7th of 10 in gp* **50/1**

4 **15** 1/2 **Pacodali (IRE)**[14] 2840 3-9-2 **96** (p) GeorgeBaker 10 83
(J P Murtagh, Ire) *racd far side: hld up: swtchd rt and hdwy 2f out: unable to go pce of ldrs over 1f out: kpt on u.p but no imp ins fnl f: 8th of 18 in gp* **25/1**

1-11 **16** 3/4 **Garcia**[26] 2473 3-9-1 **95** TonyHamilton 21 80
(Richard Fahey) *racd far side: midfield: rdn 3f out: kpt on u.p over 1f out: nvr able to trble ldrs: 9th of 18 in gp* **8/1**

3-54 **17** 2 3/4 **Palawan**[55] 1605 3-9-1 **95** PatDobbs 25 74
(Richard Hannon) *racd stands' side: hld up: swtchd lft over 2f out: sn rdn: no imp: 8th of 10 in gp* **40/1**

-111 **18** *nk* **Oh This Is Us (IRE)**[26] 2466 3-8-9 **92**........................ TomMarquand(3) 3 70
(Richard Hannon) *racd far side: midfield: rdn and hdwy over 2f out: sn chsd ldrs: kpt on same pce and no imp fr over 1f out: 10th of 18 in gp* **20/1**

61-1 **19** *5* **Manson**[28] 2412 3-8-12 **92**.. OisinMurphy 11 59
(Dominic Ffrench Davis) *racd far side: midfield: rdn over 2f out: no hdwy over 1f out: n.d after: 11th of 18 in gp* **12/1**

20 *3 ½* **Monarch (IRE)**[22] 2591 3-9-0 **97**........................(t) DonnachaO'Brien(3) 29 56
(A P O'Brien, Ire) *unf: racd stands' side: trckd ldrs: rdn 3f out: wknd over 2f out: 9th of 10 in gp* **25/1**

3 **21** *3 ¾* **Sevenleft (IRE)**[18] 2716 3-9-4 **98**....................................... GaryCarroll 16 48
(Ms Sheila Lavery, Ire) *str: lw: racd far side: led overall: rdn over 2f out: hdd wl over 1f out: sn wknd: 12th of 18 in gp* **50/1**

10-6 **22** *nse* **Mikmak**[55] 1603 3-8-8 **88**.. SamHitchcott 5 38
(William Muir) *racd far side: trckd ldrs: rdn over 2f out: wknd over 1f out: 13th of 18 in gp* **50/1**

-623 **23** *hd* **Above N Beyond**[26] 2473 3-9-7 **101**.......................(t) RichardKingscote 4 50
(Tom Dascombe) *racd far side: in tch: rdn 3f out: wknd over 1f out: 14 of 18 in gp* **33/1**

-144 **24** *3* **Speed Company (IRE)**[27] 2432 3-8-12 **97**........... EdwardGreatrex(5) 32 39
(John Quinn) *s.i.s: racd stands' side: hld up: rdn and hung rt 2f out: nvr a threat: 10th of 10 in gp* **33/1**

1-23 **25** *2 ¾* **Monteverdi (FR)**[36] 2161 3-8-10 **90**.. FMBerry 7 26
(Jamie Osborne) *racd far side: hld up: carried rt and rdn over 2f out: nvr a threat: 15th of 18 in gp* **20/1**

5413 **26** *2* **King's Pavilion (IRE)**[5] 3157 3-8-13 **93**..................(p) JamesMcDonald 1 25
(Mark Johnston) *racd far side: prom: pushed along 1/2-way: rdn 3f out: wknd over 2f out: eased whn wl btn over 1f out: 16th of 18 in gp* **25/1**

2-22 **27** *3 ½* **Fighting Temeraire (IRE)**[19] 2695 3-8-9 **89**............. RobertWinston 24 12
(Dean Ivory) *swtchd rt early: racd far side: hld up: rdn over 2f out: nvr a threat: eased whn wl btn over 1f out: 17th of 18 in gp* **14/1**

21-3 **28** *2 ½* **Predilection (USA)**[68] 1338 3-9-5 **99**............................ FrankieDettori 13 17
(John Gosden) *str: racd far side: midfield: rdn and wknd qckly 3f out: eased whn wl btn over 1f out: 18th of 18 in gp* **16/1**

1m 40.42s (-0.38) **Going Correction** +0.25s/f (Good) **28 Ran SP% 152.5**
Speed ratings: **111,110,108,107,107 105,104,103,103,102 101,100,100,100,99 99,96,96,91,87 83,83,83,80,77 75,7**
CSF £143.07 CT £1640.72 TOTE £8.90: £2.90, £7.80, £3.50, £20.50; EX 339.30 Trifecta £4442.90.
Owner Michael Buckley & Michael Watt **Bred** Ballylinch Stud **Trained** Upper Lambourn, Berks
■ Perkunas was withdrawn. Price at time of withdrawal 50/1.Rule 4 does not apply.

FOCUS
This looked extremely competitive as usual. There was a decent pace on, with the winner coming from last to first, and there seemed no real bias this time. The third is a cracking benchmark. The third, fourth and fifth have been rated close to their marks.

3300 KING GEORGE V STKS (H'CAP) 1m 4f
5:35 (5:35) (Class 1) (0-105,99) 3-Y-O
£56,025 (£16,776; £8,388; £4,194; £2,097; £1,053) **Stalls** Low

Form RPR

1-11 **1** **Primitivo**[28] 2413 3-9-3 **95**................................ WilliamTwiston-Davies 11 108
(Alan King) *hld up in tch in midfield: swtchd lft and clsd on bit over 2f out: rdn to ld 2f out: hung lft but styd on strly fnl f: rdn out* **13/2**[3]

35-4 **2** *3 ¼* **Platitude**[41] 1994 3-9-7 **99**.. RyanMoore 18 107
(Sir Michael Stoute) *styd wd early: hld up towards rr: hdwy 3f out: swtchd lft and hdwy on outer over 2f out: wnt 3rd and hung rt wl over 1f out: chsd wnr and stl hanging over 1f out: racing on inner rail and r.o same pce ins fnl f* **12/1**

1-30 **3** *3* **Harrison**[35] 2190 3-9-1 **93**.. SilvestreDeSousa 6 96
(Mick Channon) *chsd ldrs: rdn to ld over 2f out: hdd and drvn 2f out: 3rd and no ex over 1f out: stl clr 3rd but wknd ins fnl f* **8/1**

1 **4** *2 ½* **The Major General (IRE)**[13] 2883 3-9-4 **99**....(b) DonnachaO'Brien(3) 13 102+
(A P O'Brien, Ire) *hld up towards rr: stuck bhd a wall of horses over 2f out tl swtchd lft over 1f out: r.o strly ins fnl f: snatched 4th last stride: no ch w ldrs* **14/1**

1-43 **5** *hd* **Danehill Kodiac (IRE)**[12] 2889 3-8-9 **87**............................ SeanLevey 5 86
(Richard Hannon) *chsd ldr for 4f: styd prom: rdn over 2f out: getting outpcd and swtchd rt wl over 1f out: wl hld and kpt on same pce ins fnl f: lost 4th last strides* **33/1**

21-5 **6** *½* **Paris Protocol**[55] 1610 3-9-1 **93**.. PatDobbs 14 91
(Richard Hannon) *lw: stdd s: hld up in rr: hdwy on inner 3f out: chsd ldrs and rdn over 2f out: outpcd and battling for btn 4th over 1f out: wknd ins fnl f* **12/1**

1154 **7** *1 ½* **Nietzsche**[5] 3162 3-8-0 **78** oh1.. JoeyHaynes 1 73
(Brian Ellison) *towards rr: effrt and swtchd lft over 2f out: edging rt but hdwy to pass btn horses over 1f out: kpt on but no ch w ldrs fnl f* **33/1**

2-22 **8** *2 ½* **Midhmaar**[28] 2413 3-8-12 **90**... PaulHanagan 10 81
(Owen Burrows) *dwlt: hld up towards rr: nt clr run over 2f out: effrt u.p 2f out: sme hdwy to pass btn horses over 1f out: no ch w ldrs* **20/1**

40-0 **9** *hd* **Ocean Jive**[110] 756 3-9-0 **92**.. JimmyFortune 8 83
(Brian Meehan) *towards rr: effrt on inner 3f out: sme prog on inner but nt threatening ldrs whn short of room and hmpd wl over 1f out: no hdwy after: wknd fnl f* **33/1**

2425 **10** *2 ¾* **Juste Pour Nous**[12] 2909 3-8-6 **84**......................... RichardKingscote 16 71
(Mark Johnston) *styd wd early: chsd ldrs: wnt 2nd 8f out tl over 2f out: lost pl u.p over 1f out: wknd fnl f* **25/1**

21-2 **11** *½* **Lovell**[55] 1610 3-9-1 **93**.. WilliamBuick 7 79
(Charlie Appleby) *lw: t.k.h: wl in tch in midfield: rdn and lost pl whn short of room ent fnl 2f out: rdn and no hdwy over 1f out: sn wknd* **6/1**[2]

1263 **12** *2 ½* **Second Serve (IRE)**[6] 3103 3-8-4 **82**.............................. JoeFanning 12 64
(Mark Johnston) *a towards rr: rdn and effrt on outer over 2f out: no prog: wknd wl over 1f out* **33/1**

451 **13** *2 ¾* **Point Of View (IRE)**[14] 2816 3-8-12 **90**.......................... AndreaAtzeni 17 68
(Roger Varian) *styd wd early: in tch in midfield: effrt to chse ldrs over 2f out: rdn and struggling to qckn whn short of room 2f out: wknd over 1f out* **14/1**

35-1 **14** *2 ¼* **Navajo War Dance**[24] 2522 3-8-12 **90**....................... DougieCostello 15 64
(K R Burke) *t.k.h: led tl rdn and hdd over 2f out: losing pl and hmpd wl over 1f out: sn wknd and bhd fnl f* **33/1**

631 **15** *4* **Shraaoh (IRE)**[21] 2619 3-8-13 **91**...................................... FrankieDettori 4 59
(Sir Michael Stoute) *str: lw: hld up in tch in midfield: n.m.r over 2f out: nt clr run and hmpd wl over 1f out: no ch after: bhd and eased ins fnl f* **5/2**[1]

63-1 **F** **Guy Fawkes**[16] 2774 3-8-10 **88**... PatSmullen 3
(William Haggas) *dwlt: hld up towards rr: lost action: stmbld and fell after 2f: fatally injured* **7/1**

2m 34.51s (2.01) **Going Correction** +0.50s/f (Yiel) **16 Ran SP% 131.8**
Speed ratings: **113,110,108,107,107 106,105,104,103,102 101,100,98,96,94**
CSF £82.79 CT £641.64 TOTE £7.40: £1.90, £3.50, £2.50, £3.10; EX 86.90 Trifecta £997.20.
Owner N Farrell, L Field, T Mellor & B Cognet **Bred** Mrs L H Field **Trained** Barbury Castle, Wilts

FOCUS
Actual race distance 1m4f 9yds. A typically open edition of this event, run at a decent gallop, and this is solid handicap form. It was 5.23sec faster than the slowly run Ribblesdale. The first two raced wide apart in the final furlong. The race was marred by a fatal injury to Guy Fawkes early on. Another decent pb from the winner, while the third has been rated to form.
T/Jkpt: Not won. T/Plt: £298.60 to a £1 stake. Pool of £522603.60 - 1277.26 winning tickets.
T/Qpdt: £51.30 to a £1 stake. Pool of £34184.46 - 492.80 winning tickets.
Darren Owen & Steve Payne

3275 CHELMSFORD (A.W) (L-H)
Thursday, June 16

OFFICIAL GOING: Polytrack: standard
Wind: Light across Weather: Cloudy

3301 DEBENHAMS PERSONAL SHOPPER NOVICE AUCTION STKS 6f (P)
1:50 (1:52) (Class 5) 2-Y-O
£5,175 (£1,540; £769; £384) **Stalls** Centre

Form RPR

4 **1** **Scudding (USA)**[16] 2764 2-8-11 0.................................. StevieDonohoe 6 65
(Charlie Fellowes) *disp ld to 1/2-way: sn pushed along: rdn to ld over 1f out: styd on* **7/2**[2]

2 *½* **Quick Thought (IRE)** 2-8-11 0... JimmyQuinn 4 64
(Dr Jon Scargill) *trckd ldrs: plld hrd: rdn and ev ch ins fnl f: unable qck nr fin* **33/1**

04 **3** *1 ¼* **At The Beach**[17] 2748 2-9-2 0.. KieranO'Neill 5 65
(Richard Hannon) *chsd ldrs: rdn over 2f out: nt clr run over 1f out: r.o* **5/1**

4 *3 ¾* **Enigmatic (IRE)** 2-9-2 0.. WilliamCarson 1 57+
(Jamie Osborne) *hld up: rdn and hmpd over 1f out: sn swtchd rt: r.o towards fin* **5/1**

5 *½* **Praneleya (IRE)** 2-8-11 0.. SaleemGolam 3 47
(Marco Botti) *s.i.s: hld up in tch: rdn and hung lft over 1f out: styd on same pce* **9/2**[3]

0 **6** *hd* **Tennessee Rose (IRE)**[50] 1793 2-8-11 0.........................(t) LiamJones 7 47
(Tom Dascombe) *disp ld tl wnt on 1/2-way: rdn and hdd over 1f out: wknd ins fnl f* **25/1**

7 *7* **Baileys Showgirl (FR)** 2-8-11 0.................................. FrederikTylicki 2 26+
(Mark Johnston) *rrd s and lost all ch: a wl bhd* **5/2**[1]

8 *1* **Blast Of Faith (IRE)** 2-9-2 0... RyanTate 8 28
(Richard Hughes) *s.i.s: in rr: rdn over 2f out: sn wknd* **12/1**

1m 14.17s (0.47) **Going Correction** 0.0s/f (Stan) **8 Ran SP% 116.8**
Speed ratings (Par 93): **96,95,93,88,88 87,78,77**
CSF £102.50 TOTE £3.80: £1.50, £8.90, £1.80; EX 144.80 Trifecta £718.80.
Owner William McAlpin **Bred** Greenwood Lodge Farm Inc **Trained** Newmarket, Suffolk

FOCUS
An ordinary juvenile novice contest. The favourite was rearing up when the starter let the field go which was most unsatisfactory. They went a respectable gallop at best on standard Polytrack.

3302 OLIVERS PLANTS LTD H'CAP 2m (P)
2:20 (2:21) (Class 5) (0-70,70) 4-Y-O+
£5,175 (£1,540; £769; £384) **Stalls** Low

Form RPR

23-0 **1** **Voice Control (IRE)**[28] 2400 4-9-4 **67**.................................. LiamKeniry 9 75
(Laura Mongan) *hld up: hdwy over 3f out: rdn to ld over 1f out: flashed tail u.p: styd on* **33/1**

3335 **2** *1 ½* **Unex Modigliani (IRE)**[15] 2792 7-8-1 **55**..................(vt) NoelGarbutt(5) 5 61
(Derek Shaw) *hld up: hdwy over 2f out: rdn and nt clr run over 1f out: styd on* **16/1**

2352 **3** *4* **Hope You Dance (FR)**[23] 2564 4-9-3 **66**.....................(p) MartinDwyer 2 67
(David Simcock) *hld up: rdn over 2f out: hdwy: nt clr run and swtchd rt over 1f out: r.o to go 3rd wl ins fnl f: nt rch ldrs* **8/1**

121 **4** *2 ¼* **Eurato (FR)**[15] 2792 6-9-0 **70**...............................(p) AdamMcNamara(7) 6 69
(Steve Gollings) *hld up: hdwy over 4f out: rdn over 2f out: wknd fnl f* **2/1**[1]

36-P **5** *hd* **Front Five (IRE)**[63] 1434 4-9-6 **69**...................................... TimmyMurphy 7 67
(Martin Bosley) *chsd clr ldr tl too clsr order over 5f out: led 4f out: rdn and hdd over 1f out: wknd ins fnl f* **20/1**

0-14 **6** *2* **Snow Conditions**[22] 2582 5-9-5 **68**.................................. WilliamCarson 8 64
(Philip Hide) *chsd ldrs: wnt upsides over 4f out: rdn over 1f out: wknd fnl f* **8/1**

1342 **7** *1* **Tempuran**[9] 2995 7-9-7 **70**... AdamKirby 1 65+
(David Bridgwater) *led: wnt clr after 2f tl c bk to the field over 5f out: hdd 4f out: rdn over 2f out: edgd lft over 1f out: sn wknd* **11/4**[2]

-205 **8** *11* **Danglydontask**[30] 2338 5-8-5 **59**.......................... JosephineGordon(5) 3 41
(David Arbuthnot) *mid-div: rdn over 3f out: wknd over 2f out* **5/1**[3]

-065 **P** **The Quarterjack**[21] 2605 7-8-13 **65**...................... KieranShoemark(3) 10
(Charlie Wallis) *mid-div: pushed along over 4f out: rdn and wknd over 2f out: p.u fnl f* **20/1**

3m 29.97s (-0.03) **Going Correction** 0.0s/f (Stan) **9 Ran SP% 117.2**
Speed ratings (Par 103): **100,99,97,96,96 95,94,89,**
CSF £467.07 CT £4585.18 TOTE £36.70: £4.80, £3.50, £2.70; EX 495.50 Trifecta £5128.60 Part won..
Owner Mrs P J Sheen **Bred** Ballymacoll Stud Farm Ltd **Trained** Epsom, Surrey

FOCUS
A modest staying handicap. They went a muddling gallop. The winner has been rated back to his best for now.

3303 POWER TESTING LTD 50TH ANNIVERSARY H'CAP 1m (P)
2:55 (2:56) (Class 3) (0-90,90) 4-Y-O+
£9,703 (£2,887; £1,443; £721) **Stalls** Low

Form RPR

-435 **1** **Strong Steps**[19] 2689 4-9-1 **89**...........................(p) JosephineGordon(5) 4 98
(Hugo Palmer) *chsd ldrs: rdn to ld ins fnl f: jst hld on* **3/1**[2]

32-1 **2** *nk* **Firmament**[21] 2620 4-9-3 **89**.. ShelleyBirkett(3) 5 97+
(David O'Meara) *n.m.r after s: hld up: hdwy over 1f out: r.o wl: nt quite rch wnr* **4/1**[3]

1400 **3** *1* **Bold Prediction (IRE)**[13] 2868 6-8-13 **89**............. AdamMcNamara(7) 3 95
(Ed Walker) *led: rdn and hdd 1f out: styd on same pce towards fin* **14/1**

25/1 **4** *1 ½* **Cape Icon**[29] 2378 5-9-4 **87**.. AdamKirby 11 90+
(Clive Cox) *trckd ldrs: plld hrd: rdn over 1f out: styd on same pce ins fnl f* **9/4**[1]

-033 **5** *nk* **Major Crispies**[14] 2819 5-9-2 **85** RyanTate 10 87
(James Eustace) *w ldr: rdn and ev ch over 1f out: no ex ins fnl f* **10/1**

1000 **6** *1/2* **Craftsmanship (FR)**[10] 2978 5-9-1 **84** FrederikTylicki 7 85+
(Robert Eddery) *hld up: pushed along over 2f out: r.o towards fin: nvr nrr* **14/1**

60 **7** *3/4* **Charlie Bear**[21] 2628 4-9-2 **85** WilliamCarson 6 84
(Jamie Osborne) *hld up: racd keenly: hdwy u.p over 1f out: nt trble ldrs* **25/1**

6410 **8** *2* **Street Force (USA)**[34] 2213 5-8-13 **85** (tp) AlistairRawlinson(3) 9 79
(Michael Appleby) *hld up in tch: racd keenly: rdn over 1f out: wknd ins fnl f* **33/1**

-P03 **9** *nk* **Passing Star**[22] 2587 5-9-1 **87** MichaelJMMurphy(3) 8 81
(Charles Hills) *prom: rdn over 2f out: wknd fnl f* **7/1**

03-0 **10** *3 1/2* **Zugzwang (IRE)**[14] 2819 5-9-7 **90** LiamKeniry 2 76
(Ed de Giles) *hld up: rdn over 1f out: nvr on terms* **50/1**

-050 **11** *1/2* **Run With Pride (IRE)**[8] 3035 6-7-11 **71** oh1 NoelGarbutt(5) 1 56
(Derek Shaw) *s.s: hdwy u.p 2f out: edgd lft over 1f out: wknd fnl f* **33/1**

1m 39.24s (-0.66) **Going Correction** 0.0s/f (Stan) **11** Ran SP% **122.4**
Speed ratings (Par 107): **103,102,101,100,99 99,98,96,96,92 92**
CSF £15.73 CT £150.86 TOTE £3.90: £1.60, £1.70, £3.70; EX 19.80 Trifecta £143.80.
Owner Al Shaqab Racing **Bred** Exors Of The Late J Ellis **Trained** Newmarket, Suffolk

FOCUS
A decent handicap. They went a proper gallop. The third has been rated to form and sets the standard.

3304 BENTLEY ESSEX H'CAP — 1m 2f (P)
3:30 (3:31) (Class 3) (0-95,94) 4-Y-O+ **£9,703** (£2,887; £1,443; £721) **Stalls** Low

Form RPR

100- **1** **Primogeniture (IRE)**[246] 7222 5-9-1 **88** TimmyMurphy 3 93
(Mary Hambro) *chsd ldrs: rdn over 1f out: r.o to ld wl ins fnl f* **66/1**

12 **2** *hd* **Burcan (FR)**[63] 1430 4-8-8 **81** JimmyQuinn 5 86
(Jeremy Noseda) *chsd ldr: rdn and edgd lft over 1f out: r.o* **5/2**[1]

/1-2 **3** *nk* **Street Artist (IRE)**[36] 2150 6-8-12 **85** PatCosgrave 8 89
(David Nicholls) *led at stdy pce tl qcknd over 2f out: rdn over 1f out: hdd wl ins fnl f* **8/1**

0660 **4** *1* **Sennockian Star**[13] 2866 6-9-0 **87** (v) FrederikTylicki 6 89+
(Mark Johnston) *prom: lost pl after 2f: rdn over 1f out: r.o ins fnl f: nt rch ldrs* **5/1**[3]

0130 **5** *shd* **Viewpoint (IRE)**[12] 2917 7-8-6 **84** JosephineGordon(5) 4 86+
(Michael Appleby) *s.i.s: hld up: rdn over 1f out: r.o ins fnl f: nt rch ldrs* **14/1**

6130 **6** *1 1/2* **Intrude**[6] 3113 4-9-7 **94** MartinDwyer 7 95+
(David Simcock) *s.i.s: hld up: effrt and nt clr run over 1f out: r.o towards fin: nvr nrr* **7/1**

2134 **7** *1/2* **Perfect Cracker**[17] 2752 8-9-4 **91** AdamKirby 2 89
(Clive Cox) *trckd ldrs: racd keenly: rdn over 1f out: no ex ins fnl f* **8/1**

13-0 **8** *nk* **Ladurelli (IRE)**[12] 2897 4-8-12 **85** (t) WilliamCarson 1 83
(Paul Cole) *hld up in tch: rdn over 1f out: no ex ins fnl f* **9/2**[2]

0205 **9** *9* **Emerald (ITY)**[34] 2216 4-9-1 **88** DarryllHolland 9 68
(Marco Botti) *hld up: hdwy over 2f out: hmpd and wknd wl over 1f out* **8/1**

2m 7.07s (-1.53) **Going Correction** 0.0s/f (Stan) **9** Ran SP% **117.4**
Speed ratings (Par 107): **106,105,105,104,104 103,103,102,95**
CSF £231.22 CT £1541.03 TOTE £45.50: £5.50, £1.60, £2.10; EX 161.70 Trifecta £1238.80.
Owner Mrs Richard Hambro **Bred** V B Shirke, K N Dhunjibhoy & B M Desai **Trained** Bourton-on-the-Hill, Gloucs

FOCUS
A good handicap. They went a steady gallop. Muddling form, with the runner-up rated to his latest effort.

3305 TIPTREE "GIN AND JAM" MEDIAN AUCTION MAIDEN FILLIES' STKS — 1m 2f (P)
4:05 (4:08) (Class 4) 3-4-Y-O **£8,086** (£2,406; £1,202; £601) **Stalls** Low

Form RPR

1 **Blind Faith (IRE)** 3-9-0 0 AdamKirby 1 70
(Luca Cumani) *trckd ldrs: racing keenly at 1/2-way: rdn to ld ins fnl f: r.o wl* **7/4**[1]

2 *1 1/2* **Potters Lady Jane**[70] 4-9-7 0 JosephineGordon(5) 4 67
(Lucy Wadham) *chsd ldr: rdn to ld over 1f out: edgd lft and hdd ins fnl f: styd on same pce* **5/1**[3]

35 **3** *1 1/4* **Golden Reign (IRE)**[28] 2395 3-9-0 0 PatCosgrave 3 65
(William Haggas) *led at stdy pce tl qcknd over 2f out: rdn and hdd over 1f out: no ex ins fnl f* **7/4**[1]

-355 **4** *nk* **Loveisreckless (IRE)**[9] 3001 3-9-0 70 (b) MartinDwyer 5 64
(William Muir) *s.i.s: pushed along and looked reluctant early then hld up after 1f: shkn up over 2f out: kpt on ins fnl f* **9/2**[2]

5 *1/2* **Cross Cave** 3-9-0 0 FrederikTylicki 2 63
(Emma Owen) *s.v.s: rcvrd to latch on to the rr of the field over 8f out: pushed along and hdwy over 1f out: no ex ins fnl f* **16/1**

2m 10.72s (2.12) **Going Correction** 0.0s/f (Stan)
WFA 3 from 4yo 12lb **5** Ran SP% **113.5**
Speed ratings (Par 102): **91,89,88,88,88**
CSF £11.41 TOTE £3.10: £2.40, £3.00; EX 12.90 Trifecta £30.70.
Owner Christopher Wright & Miss Emily Asprey **Bred** B Kennedy **Trained** Newmarket, Suffolk

FOCUS
An modest little fillies' maiden. They went a particularly steady gallop. The bare form is modest, if a little fluid.

3306 SIMPLY RED HERE ON 1ST JULY H'CAP — 1m 6f (P)
4:45 (4:46) (Class 4) (0-85,75) 3-Y-O **£8,086** (£2,406; £1,202; £601) **Stalls** Low

Form RPR

4-42 **1** **St Michel**[12] 2909 3-9-2 **70** LukeMorris 6 79+
(Sir Mark Prescott Bt) *wnt prom after 1f: chsd ldr over 2f out: shkn up to ld over 1f out: edgd lft ins fnl f: styd on wl: comf* **10/11**[1]

2112 **2** *2 1/4* **Scarpeta (FR)**[15] 2798 3-9-0 **68** FrederikTylicki 3 72
(Mark Johnston) *led: rdn and hdd over 1f out: styd on same pce ins fnl f* **9/2**[2]

-365 **3** *1 1/2* **Monaco Rose**[19] 2687 3-8-12 **66** PatCosgrave 4 68
(Richard Fahey) *hld up: nt clr run over 2f out: hdwy over 1f out: sn rdn: no imp ins fnl f* **7/1**

033 **4** *2 1/2* **Dream Factory (IRE)**[16] 2774 3-9-2 **70** AdamKirby 7 68
(Marco Botti) *hld up: reminder over 7f out: drvn along 3f out: hdwy u.p over 1f out: shied at rivals whip sn after: hung lft and styd on same pce* **10/1**

-110 **5** *2 1/2* **Recognition (IRE)**[28] 2411 3-9-4 **72** JackMitchell 1 67
(Roger Varian) *hld up: effrt and nt clr run over 1f out: edgd lft and wknd ins fnl f* **5/1**[3]

640 **6** *3 3/4* **Heavensfield**[17] 2735 3-9-7 **75** DarryllHolland 2 65
(Mark H Tompkins) *trckd ldrs: shkn up over 2f out: wknd over 1f out* **25/1**

1646 **7** *16* **Epsom Day (IRE)**[22] 2580 3-9-4 **72** RyanTate 5 39
(Laura Mongan) *chsd ldr tl rdn over 2f out: wknd over 1f out* **20/1**

3m 1.86s (-1.34) **Going Correction** 0.0s/f (Stan) **7** Ran SP% **117.4**
Speed ratings (Par 101): **103,101,100,99,98 95,86**
CSF £5.69 TOTE £1.80: £1.20, £2.40; EX 5.90 Trifecta £21.80.
Owner J L C Pearce **Bred** J L C Pearce **Trained** Newmarket, Suffolk

FOCUS
A fair 3yo staying handicap, but once again they went a modest gallop. The runner-up has been rated to form.

3307 "CONQUER THE COURSE" ON 16TH JULY H'CAP — 5f (P)
5:20 (5:21) (Class 5) (0-70,70) 3-Y-O+ **£5,175** (£1,540; £769; £384) **Stalls** Low

Form RPR

40-3 **1** **Ada Lovelace**[44] 1950 6-9-7 **70** (p) RhiainIngram(7) 5 80
(John Gallagher) *hld up: hdwy wl over 1f out: swtchd rt sn after: r.o to ld wl ins fnl f* **8/1**

1220 **2** *2* **More Spice (IRE)**[30] 2342 4-9-9 **70** (v) AaronJones(5) 1 73
(Robert Cowell) *led: hung rt 1/2-way: rdn over 1f out: hdd and unable qck wl ins fnl f* **5/2**[1]

-365 **3** *1 3/4* **Dream Farr (IRE)**[16] 2776 3-9-7 **69** (b[1]) LukeMorris 2 64
(Ed Walker) *s.i.s: in rr: effrt and nt clr run over 1f out: rdn: hung lft and r.o to go 3rd wl ins fnl f: nt rch ldrs* **11/4**[2]

3430 **4** *nk* **Pushkin Museum (IRE)**[22] 2572 5-9-7 **70** AdamMcNamara(7) 9 65
(Richard Fahey) *hld up: pushed along over 3f out: r.o u.p ins fnl f: nt rch ldrs* **5/1**[3]

2006 **5** *nk* **Temple Road (IRE)**[16] 2768 8-9-12 **68** (bt) PatCosgrave 4 62
(Milton Bradley) *chsd ldrs: rdn over 1f out: wknd wl ins fnl f* **10/1**

4111 **6** *1/2* **Roy's Legacy**[12] 2919 7-9-6 **67** CharlieBennett(5) 6 60
(Shaun Harris) *chsd ldr tl rdn over 1f out: wknd ins fnl f* **7/1**

35-0 **7** *1 1/4* **Manipura**[16] 2785 3-8-7 **60** (p) NoelGarbutt(5) 8 46
(Derek Shaw) *s.i.s: bhd: rdn over 1f out: nt trble ldrs* **33/1**

0-60 **8** *1* **Classic Flyer**[14] 2808 4-9-3 **62** (v) ShelleyBirkett(3) 7 46
(David O'Meara) *chsd ldrs: rdn over 1f out: wknd fnl f* **12/1**

5334 **9** *3/4* **Give Us A Belle (IRE)**[16] 2785 7-8-11 **58** (bt) PaddyPilley(5) 3 40
(Christine Dunnett) *chsd ldrs: rdn whn hmpd over 1f out: wknd fnl f* **12/1**

59.54s (-0.66) **Going Correction** 0.0s/f (Stan)
WFA 3 from 4yo+ 6lb **9** Ran SP% **122.9**
Speed ratings (Par 103): **105,101,99,98,98 97,95,93,92**
CSF £30.29 CT £73.07 TOTE £10.50: £2.90, £1.20, £2.00; EX 36.60 Trifecta £194.30.
Owner D A Clark **Bred** D A Clark **Trained** Chastleton, Oxon

FOCUS
A modest sprint handicap. They went a decent gallop. The runner-up has been rated close to form.
T/Plt: £312.10 to a £1 stake. Pool of £31261.51 - 73.12 winning tickets. T/Qpdt: £26.90 to a £1 stake. Pool of £2950.53 - 81.0 winning tickets. **Colin Roberts**

3134 LEICESTER (R-H)
Thursday, June 16

3308 Meeting Abandoned - waterlogged

3141 LINGFIELD (L-H)
Thursday, June 16

OFFICIAL GOING: Polytrack: standard
Wind: Moderate, behind; becoming light, behind from race 5 Weather: Cloudy

3314 RETRAINING OF RACEHORSES FILLIES' H'CAP — 1m 1y(P)
5:50 (5:50) (Class 5) (0-70,69) 4-Y-O+ **£3,234** (£962; £481; £240) **Stalls** High

Form RPR

6-34 **1** **Carolinae**[34] 2205 4-9-0 **62** StevieDonohoe 1 72+
(Charlie Fellowes) *chsd ldrs: wnt 2nd 2f out: led ins fnl f: rdn out* **6/4**[1]

-446 **2** *1 1/4* **Tabla**[115] 667 4-9-4 **66** AmirQuinn 7 73
(Lee Carter) *led: hrd rdn and hdd ins fnl f: one pce* **12/1**

-401 **3** *3 1/2* **Legal Art**[30] 2330 4-8-12 **60** JimmyQuinn 5 59
(Brian Ellison) *in tch: effrt over 2f out: one pce* **4/1**[2]

4350 **4** *2* **Two In The Pink (IRE)**[16] 2769 6-9-1 **63** AdamBeschizza 3 57
(Ralph J Smith) *in tch: rdn over 2f out: no ex over 1f out* **9/1**

6335 **5** *nk* **Binky Blue (IRE)**[20] 2655 4-9-4 **66** LiamKeniry 6 60
(Daniel Mark Loughnane) *hld up in 6th: pushed along and swtchd rt 1f out: styd on fnl f* **8/1**

0430 **6** *hd* **Skidby Mill (IRE)**[22] 2577 6-9-4 **69** KieranShoemark(3) 8 62
(Laura Mongan) *chsd ldr on outer tl 2f out: wknd over 1f out* **9/2**[3]

000- **7** *5* **Just Isla**[199] 8046 6-8-9 **57** (p) DavidProbert 4 39
(Michael Blanshard) *a bhd* **20/1**

-100 **8** *3 1/2* **Ballroom Angel**[58] 1556 4-8-2 **50** KieranO'Neill 2 24
(Philip Hide) *dwlt: a bhd* **20/1**

1m 36.77s (-1.43) **Going Correction** -0.075s/f (Stan) **8** Ran SP% **116.5**
Speed ratings (Par 100): **104,102,99,97,96 96,91,88**
CSF £22.45 CT £60.34 TOTE £2.40: £1.10, £3.70, £2.10; EX 18.00 Trifecta £134.50.
Owner Saeed bel Obaida **Bred** Meon Valley Stud **Trained** Newmarket, Suffolk

FOCUS
An ordinary fillies' handicap. A length pb from the runner-up.

3315 AVENSYS NOVICE STKS — 6f 1y(P)
6:20 (6:22) (Class 5) 2-Y-O **£3,234** (£962; £481; £240) **Stalls** High

Form RPR

3 **1** **High Acclaim (USA)**[17] 2747 2-9-2 0 FergusSweeney 4 80
(Roger Teal) *hld up in 5th: effrt over 2f out: clsd on clr ldr and led jst ins fnl f: pushed clr* **3/1**[2]

3 **2** *2 1/4* **Fair Power (IRE)**[17] 2748 2-9-2 0 DavidProbert 8 73
(Sylvester Kirk) *mid-div: hdwy to chse ldrs over 1f out: styd on same pce* **8/1**

25 **3** *shd* **Juan Horsepower**[16] 2756 2-9-2 0 KieranO'Neill 9 73
(Richard Hannon) *hld up in 4th: effrt over 2f out: styd on same pce fnl f* **4/1**[3]

2 **4** *3/4* **Haulani (USA)**[14] 2822 2-9-2 0 LiamKeniry 1 71
(Philip Hide) *chsd clr ldr tl over 1f out: one pce* **2/1**[1]

5 *3/4* **Thomas Cranmer (USA)** 2-9-2 0 LiamJones 7 68
(Mark Johnston) *dwlt: rn green and rdn along in rr: sme hdwy on outer 3f out: wd and hanging on fnl bnd: styd on* **20/1**

2 6 shd **Rajar**[68] 1342 2-8-11 0 TimmyMurphy 6 63
(Richard Hannon) *chsd ldrs tl 3f out: btn whn rn wd on fnl bnd: kpt on fnl f* **8/1**

7 2 1/4 **Buxted Dream (USA)** 2-9-2 0 ShaneKelly 5 61
(Luca Cumani) *dwlt: nvr trbld ldrs* **16/1**

0 8 3 1/4 **Noble Attitude (FR)**[14] 2822 2-9-2 0 KierenFox 10 52
(John Best) *s.s: a bhd* **25/1**

9 2 **Roundabout Magic (IRE)** 2-8-13 0 KieranShoemark(3) 3 46
(Simon Dow) *led at fast pce: sn clr: hdd & wknd rapidly jst ins fnl f* **66/1**

10 2 1/2 **Rockaria** 2-9-2 0 WilliamCarson 2 38
(Philip Hide) *dwlt: rdn 1/2-way: a towards rr* **66/1**

1m 11.55s (-0.35) **Going Correction** -0.075s/f (Stan) **10** Ran SP% **118.0**
Speed ratings (Par 93): **99,96,95,94,93 93,90,86,83,80**
CSF £26.60 TOTE £3.90: £1.40, £2.20, £1.60; EX 36.60 Trifecta £121.50.
Owner Excel Racing **Bred** Regis Farms Lp **Trained** Great Shefford, Berks

FOCUS
A fair novice race.

3316 CRYSTAL PALACE FOOTBALL CLUB H'CAP 5f 6y(P)
6:50 (6:51) (Class 6) (0-65,64) 4-Y-O+ **£2,587** (£770; £384; £192) **Stalls** High

Form RPR

0000 1 **Dusty Blue**[68] 1334 4-8-9 **55** (t) GeorgeDowning(3) 5 66
(Tony Carroll) *s.i.s: bdly outpcd in rr: c wd and rapid hdwy over 1f out: str run to ld wl ins fnl f: won gng away* **4/1**[1]

3324 2 2 1/4 **Red Flute**[27] 2447 4-8-3 **49** (v) TimClark(3) 2 52
(Denis Quinn) *sn led and set gd pce: hrd rdn and hdd wl ins fnl f: no ex* **8/1**

042U 3 3/4 **Quality Art (USA)**[16] 2785 8-9-4 **64** RobHornby(3) 4 64
(Simon Hodgson) *bhd: rdn 2f out: styd on wl fnl f* **14/1**

3640 4 nk **Zipedeedodah (IRE)**[19] 2676 4-9-3 **60** OisinMurphy 8 59
(Joseph Tuite) *chsd ldrs on outer: effrt and wd on fnl bnd: kpt on fnl f* **5/1**[3]

5012 5 hd **Pharoh Jake**[22] 2584 8-9-2 **59** WilliamCarson 3 57
(John Bridger) *broke wl: n.m.r and lost pl after 1f: hdwy on inner over 1f out: kpt on* **9/2**[2]

6445 6 hd **Quantum Dot (IRE)**[5] 3136 5-8-10 **53** (b) KieranO'Neill 6 51
(Ed de Giles) *chsd ldr tl over 1f out: one pce* **8/1**

4460 7 hd **Blue Bounty**[8] 3040 5-9-2 **59** (p) SaleemGolam 1 56
(Mark H Tompkins) *chsd ldrs: wnt 2nd over 1f out tl no ex ins fnl f* **4/1**[1]

1306 8 3 **Ask The Guru**[5] 3159 6-9-7 **64** (p) JimmyQuinn 7 50
(Michael Attwater) *in tch in 5th tl wknd over 1f out* **7/1**

58.3s (-0.50) **Going Correction** -0.075s/f (Stan) **8** Ran SP% **116.2**
Speed ratings (Par 101): **101,97,96,95,95 95,94,89**
CSF £36.76 CT £408.62 TOTE £3.30: £1.40, £2.20, £3.80; EX 37.00 Trifecta £461.70.
Owner M Chung **Bred** Denford Stud Ltd **Trained** Cropthorne, Worcs

FOCUS
A competitive sprint handicap on paper, but a bit of a gamble was landed. Straightforward form.

3317 HEART FM (S) STKS 5f 6y(P)
7:20 (7:21) (Class 6) 3-Y-O+ **£2,587** (£770; £384; £192) **Stalls** High

Form RPR

13-3 1 **Clumber Street**[23] 2562 5-8-9 78 KieranShoemark(3) 5 64
(David Brown) *dwlt: t.k.h: prom: led over 1f out: drvn out* **5/2**[2]

5032 2 nk **Picansort**[2] 3260 9-9-8 70 (b) ShaneKelly 7 73
(Peter Crate) *hld up in 6th: effrt and wd st: clsd on wnr fnl f: r.o* **7/4**[1]

000 3 1 1/4 **Agerzam**[6] 3098 6-9-3 60 (p) LukeMorris 4 64
(Ronald Harris) *short of room after 100yds: hld up in 5th on inner: hdwy on rail over 1f out: one pce fnl 100yds* **11/4**[3]

0-60 4 1 1/4 **Angel Flores (IRE)**[36] 2155 5-8-7 56 OisinMurphy 2 49
(Lee Carter) *chsd ldrs: outpcd 2f out: kpt on fnl f* **7/1**

-466 5 1 **Frank Sandatra**[17] 2750 3-8-6 49 JohnFahy 6 48
(Peter Crate) *stmbld s: led tl over 1f out: no ex fnl f* **20/1**

-056 6 3 1/2 **No Body's Fool**[31] 2288 3-8-1 42 KieranO'Neill 1 31
(Michael Madgwick) *chsd ldr tl 3f out: wknd over 1f out* **66/1**

0500 7 8 **Flashy King (IRE)**[17] 2750 3-8-6 40 JimmyQuinn 3 7
(Joseph Tuite) *s.i.s: racd wd: outpcd* **66/1**

58.63s (-0.17) **Going Correction** -0.075s/f (Stan)
WFA 3 from 5yo+ 6lb **7** Ran SP% **111.8**
Speed ratings (Par 101): **98,97,95,93,91 86,73**
CSF £6.93 TOTE £3.20: £1.60, £1.60; EX 7.00 Trifecta £13.10.The winner was bought by L Carter for 3,400gns.
Owner J C Fretwell **Bred** Denis Barry **Trained** Averham Park, Notts

FOCUS
Ordinary selling form. The runner-up helps with setting the opening level.

3318 INJURED JOCKEYS FUND FILLIES' H'CAP 1m 4f (P)
7:50 (7:50) (Class 5) (0-70,70) 3-Y-O **£3,234** (£962; £481; £240) **Stalls** Low

Form RPR

640 1 **Edge Of Reason**[17] 2735 3-9-7 **70** AntonioFresu 4 75
(Ed Walker) *lost 8 l s: plld hrd: hdwy to ld after 3f: set modest pce: qcknd and rn wd on fnl bnd: styd on wl fnl f* **10/1**

06-5 2 1 1/4 **All The Rage**[7] 3071 3-9-0 **63** LukeMorris 5 66
(Sir Mark Prescott Bt) *plld hrd: chsd ldr most of way: chalng whn carried wd on fnl bnd: kpt on u.p* **7/2**[1]

50-2 3 1 1/2 **Matidia**[64] 1410 3-8-12 **66** PatrickO'Donnell(5) 8 67
(Ralph Beckett) *led after 1f tl after 3f: prom: kpt on same pce fnl 2f* **7/1**[3]

3106 4 1/2 **Rock 'n Red (IRE)**[22] 2574 3-9-6 **69** SilvestreDeSousa 7 69
(Ed Dunlop) *t.k.h in midfield: rdn over 2f out: styd on fnl f* **7/1**[3]

5343 5 hd **Multigifted**[8] 3033 3-8-1 **57** GeorgeWood(7) 6 57+
(Michael Madgwick) *t.k.h in rr: rdn over 2f out: styd on wl fnl f* **8/1**

1212 6 nse **Hint Of Grey (IRE)**[14] 2829 3-8-13 **62** LiamKeniry 2 62
(Don Cantillon) *t.k.h: led for 1f: chsd ldrs: one pce fnl 2f* **4/1**[2]

-603 7 hd **Pennerley**[20] 2666 3-9-5 **68** RyanTate 1 67
(James Eustace) *t.k.h in midfield: effrt on inner in st: styd on same pce* **7/1**[3]

20-5 8 2 3/4 **Permera**[37] 2124 3-8-9 **58** SaleemGolam 3 53
(Mark H Tompkins) *in tch tl outpcd and btn over 1f out* **12/1**

0232 9 nk **Mikro Polemistis (IRE)**[16] 2772 3-8-4 **53** (p) JimmyQuinn 9 48
(Brian Ellison) *a bhd* **25/1**

6-30 10 2 1/4 **Purple Raven**[54] 1619 3-8-13 **69** KillianHennessy(7) 10 60
(Michael Bell) *sn towards rr on outer: n.d fnl 3f* **14/1**

2m 35.53s (2.53) **Going Correction** -0.075s/f (Stan) **10** Ran SP% **118.1**
Speed ratings (Par 96): **88,87,86,85,85 85,85,83,83,82**
CSF £45.62 CT £268.37 TOTE £10.40: £2.60, £2.50, £2.00; EX 64.30 Trifecta £723.40.
Owner The Forest Partners **Bred** Churchill Bloodstock Investments Ltd **Trained** Upper Lambourn, Berks

FOCUS
A modest handicap run at a dawdling pace, but a good performance from the winner given all that went wrong for her.

3319 RACING WELFARE H'CAP 1m 1y(P)
8:20 (8:29) (Class 6) (0-60,60) 3-Y-O **£2,587** (£770; £384; £192) **Stalls** High

Form RPR

0405 1 **Ventura Falcon (IRE)**[21] 2609 3-9-1 **54** SilvestreDeSousa 7 59
(Richard Hannon) *chsd ldrs: led 1f out: all out* **8/1**

00-0 2 hd **Sparring Queen (USA)**[26] 2470 3-9-4 **57** FMBerry 4 62
(Ralph Beckett) *cl up: pressed ldrs over 1f out: str chal fnl f: r.o* **9/2**[3]

0-00 3 1/2 **Pacific Salt (IRE)**[24] 2544 3-8-13 **55** [1] KieranShoemark(3) 1 58+
(Roger Charlton) *hld up in midfield: rdn over 2f out: fin wl* **12/1**

0-63 4 1/2 **Constable Clouds (USA)**[9] 3003 3-9-4 **57** (v) GeorgeBaker 5 59
(Gary Moore) *prom: led briefly over 1f out: kpt on u.p* **3/1**[1]

6-60 5 1 1/2 **Alzebarh (IRE)**[16] 2784 3-9-1 **54** TomQueally 10 53
(James Fanshawe) *mid-div: effrt and wd into st: kpt on same pce fnl f* **16/1**

0006 6 3/4 **Rising Sunshine (IRE)**[14] 2828 3-9-5 **58** KieranO'Neill 3 55
(Richard Hannon) *prom: rdn over 2f out: one pce* **6/1**

4051 7 nse **Elegant Annie**[4] 3198 3-9-0 **53** RyanClark 11 50
(Jonathan Portman) *towards rr on outer: carried wd into st: nvr rchd ldrs* **7/2**[2]

5-05 8 1 3/4 **Carcharias (IRE)**[21] 2610 3-8-11 **50** LiamKeniry 2 42
(Ed de Giles) *sn led and racd freely: hrd rdn over 2f out: hdd over 1f out: wknd fnl f* **20/1**

000 9 3/4 **Pacohontas**[57] 1577 3-8-13 **55** JackDuern(3) 8 46
(Dean Ivory) *sn bhd: styng on at fin* **25/1**

606- 10 1/2 **Ambuscade**[183] 8243 3-9-0 **53** OisinMurphy 12 42
(Hughie Morrison) *towards rr on outer: pushed wdr on bnd after 3f: swtchd ins and effrt over 2f out: no imp over 1f out* **20/1**

-600 11 1 3/4 **Home Again**[73] 1238 3-9-7 **60** KierenFox 6 45
(Lee Carter) *a towards rr* **25/1**

1m 38.02s (-0.18) **Going Correction** -0.075s/f (Stan) **11** Ran SP% **121.6**
Speed ratings (Par 97): **97,96,96,95,94 93,93,91,91,90 88**
CSF £43.04 CT £444.96 TOTE £8.80: £2.80, £1.90, £3.60; EX 89.50 Trifecta £501.40.
Owner Middleham Park Racing LI & Peter Barker **Bred** Jim McDonald **Trained** East Everleigh, Wilts
■ Tamara Love was withdrawn. Price at time of withdrawal 20/1. Rule 4 does not apply.

FOCUS
A moderate contest run at a sound pace.

3320 CANTERING CUISINE H'CAP 6f 1y(P)
8:50 (8:59) (Class 6) (0-65,65) 3-Y-O+ **£2,587** (£770; £384; £192) **Stalls** Low

Form RPR

53-5 1 **Hepworth Marble (IRE)**[36] 2156 3-9-7 **65** GeorgeBaker 1 69
(Gary Moore) *mde all: hrd rdn ins fnl f: hld on wl* **3/1**[2]

52 2 shd **Wattaboutsteve**[52] 1709 5-8-9 **46** AdamBeschizza 2 52
(Ralph J Smith) *prom: drvn to chal on inner ins fnl f: n.m.r: r.o wl* **7/1**

000 3 1 **Whaleweigh Station**[38] 2087 5-9-12 **63** LemosdeSouza 9 66
(J R Jenkins) *chsd ldrs: rdn over 2f out: kpt on fnl f* **16/1**

0064 4 nk **Swiss Cross**[7] 3078 9-9-13 **64** (bt) SilvestreDeSousa 3 66
(Phil McEntee) *dwlt: towards rr: n.m.r on inner on bnd after 1f: rdn and hdwy over 1f out: styd on fnl f* **15/8**[1]

4150 5 2 **Cuban Queen (USA)**[10] 2964 3-8-9 **53** OisinMurphy 10 47
(Jeremy Gask) *bhd: rdn 2f out: styd on wl fnl f* **9/1**

3463 6 1/2 **Secret Witness**[22] 2584 10-9-7 **58** (b) LukeMorris 4 52
(Ronald Harris) *in tch: rdn 3f out: no imp over 1f out* **11/2**[3]

635- 7 1 3/4 **Suitsus**[276] 6381 5-9-11 **62** TimmyMurphy 8 51
(Geoffrey Deacon) *sn bhd: nvr rchd ldrs* **16/1**

600- 8 1 3/4 **Interchoice Star**[187] 8206 11-9-3 **57** (p) AlistairRawlinson(3) 6 41
(Ray Peacock) *chsd wnr tl wknd over 1f out* **50/1**

0-55 9 3 **Nelson's Pride**[31] 2294 5-8-2 **46** oh1 (t) RhiainIngram(7) 7 21
(Roger Ingram) *mid-div tl outpcd and dropped to rr 2f out* **33/1**

1m 11.21s (-0.69) **Going Correction** -0.075s/f (Stan)
WFA 3 from 5yo+ 7lb **9** Ran SP% **114.3**
Speed ratings (Par 101): **101,100,99,99,96 95,93,91,87**
CSF £24.12 CT £286.83 TOTE £4.70: £1.90, £2.60, £4.70; EX 27.80 Trifecta £321.80.
Owner R A Green **Bred** Mrs Sheila O'Ryan **Trained** Lower Beeding, W Sussex
■ Stewards' Enquiry : Silvestre De Sousa used whip without giving gelding time to respond 5th suspension in 6mths (18-day ban, 6 days deferred until 24 Aug: 1 Jul-13 Jul)

FOCUS
An ordinary sprint handicap.
T/Plt: £151.70 to a £1 stake. Pool of £50364.97 - 242.32 winning tickets. T/Qpdt: £80.20 to a £1 stake. Pool of £5159.17 - 47.60 winning tickets. **Lee McKenzie**

3289 RIPON (R-H)
Thursday, June 16

OFFICIAL GOING: Good (good to soft in places; 7.9)
Wind: moderate 1/2 against Weather: overcast, light showers

3321 BRITISH STALLION STUDS EBF NOVICE STKS 6f
2:10 (2:13) (Class 5) 2-Y-O **£3,881** (£1,155; £577; £288) **Stalls** High

Form RPR

1 **White Tower (IRE)** 2-9-2 0 FrannyNorton 3 78
(Mark Johnston) *w ldrs: effrt 2f out: styd on to ld last 75yds* **2/1**[2]

32 2 3/4 **Zamjar**[16] 2779 2-9-2 0 PhillipMakin 8 76
(Ed Dunlop) *led: rdn over 1f out: hdd and no ex last 75yds* **15/8**[1]

55 3 1 1/4 **Await The Storm (IRE)**[16] 2757 2-9-2 0 (b[1]) HarryBentley 6 72
(Brian Meehan) *w ldrs: t.k.h: rdn over 1f out: wknd nr fin* **9/2**[3]

4 2 **Ocean Princess (IRE)** 2-8-11 0 PaulMulrennan 7 61+
(Michael Dods) *trckd ldrs: effrt over 2f out: edgd rt over 1f out: kpt on same pce: will improve* **14/1**

5 4 1/2 **Spanish Beauty** 2-8-8 0 JacobButterfield(3) 9 48
(Ollie Pears) *s.s: bhd: hdwy over 2f out: nvr on terms* **50/1**

6 nse **Babouska** 2-8-11 0 CamHardie 4 47
(Michael Easterby) *chsd ldrs: drvn over 2f out: wknd over 1f out* **80/1**

4 7 7 **Bear Essentials (IRE)**[10] 2956 2-9-2 0 SamJames 2 31
(David O'Meara) *wnt rt s: mid-div: reminders over 2f out: lost pl over 1f out* **5/1**

8 3/4 **Lucy's Law (IRE)** 2-8-11 0 AndrewElliott 1 24
(Tom Tate) *wnt rt s: outpcd in rr: sn drvn along: lost pl 2f out* **50/1**

1m 14.41s (1.41) **Going Correction** +0.05s/f (Good) **8** Ran SP% **114.8**
Speed ratings (Par 93): **92,91,89,86,80 80,71,70**
CSF £6.17 TOTE £3.30: £1.10, £1.10, £2.30; EX 5.90 Trifecta £24.50.

The Form Book, Raceform Ltd, Newbury, RG14 5SJ

Owner Sheikh Hamdan bin Mohammed Al Maktoum **Bred** Darley **Trained** Middleham Moor, N Yorks

FOCUS
The going remained the same as for the previous evening's meeting - officially good, good to soft in places and the winning rider in the opener said it was on the soft side of good. Rail on bend from back straight to home straight out 2yds, adding 4yds to distance of races on the round course. An ordinary novice event to start and not very competitive according to the betting. The first three dominated the race from the outset. The opening level is fluid.

3322 SIS CLAIMING STKS — 6f
2:45 (2:46) (Class 5) 3-Y-O+ **£2,911** (£866; £432; £216) **Stalls** High

Form RPR
6-50 **1** **Nezar (IRE)**[13] 2857 5-8-11 75........................ NathanEvans(5) 6 78
(John Quinn) *trckd ldrs: effrt 2f out: led last 150yds: pushed out* **11/10**[1]
1433 **2** 2 ¼ **Hit The Lights (IRE)**[32] 2270 6-8-6 68..................(v) DanielleMooney(7) 1 68
(David Nicholls) *w ldr: t.k.h: w ldr: led over 3f out: drvn 2f out: hdd and no ex last 150yds* **7/2**[3]
6100 **3** 1 ¼ **Gaelic Wizard (IRE)**[8] 3009 8-8-9 61........................(v) GemmaTutty(5) 4 65
(Karen Tutty) *w ldrs: kpt on same pce fnl f* **12/1**
5240 **4** 1 ¾ **Long Awaited (IRE)**[3] 3233 8-9-2 81..........................(b) PaulMulrennan 2 61
(Conor Dore) *trckd ldrs: swtchd rt 2f out: sn upsides: wknd fnl 75yds* **9/4**[2]
005 **5** 26 **Striking Nigella**[24] 2539 6-8-0 0.............................. RobertDodsworth(7) 7
(Michael Chapman) *s.i.s: sn bhd nand drvn along: t.o 2f out* **100/1**
1m 13.26s (0.26) **Going Correction** +0.05s/f (Good)
WFA 3 from 5yo+ 7lb **5** Ran SP% **109.3**
Speed ratings (Par 103): **100,97,95,93,58**
CSF £5.27 TOTE £2.10: £1.10, £1.90; EX 5.20 Trifecta £18.30.Nezar was claimed by B R Millman for £10,000
Owner Maxilead Limited **Bred** Edgeridge Ltd And Glenvale Stud **Trained** Settrington, N Yorks
■ Hadleywas withdrawn. Price at time of withdrawal 28/1. Rule 4 does not apply.

FOCUS
A wide range of abilities in this modest claimer, which was reduced by one when Hadley was withdrawn after going down in his stall. Trainers David Nicholls and John Quinn had won seven of the last ten runnings between them and their representatives dominated the finish this time. The third is the key to the level, while the winner has been rated to his reappearance form.

3323 SANLAM PRIVATE WEALTH H'CAP — 1m 4f 10y
3:20 (3:20) (Class 4) (0-80,77) 3-Y-O **£4,851** (£1,443; £721; £360) **Stalls** Low

Form RPR
0-25 **1** **Lord Yeats**[50] 1784 3-9-7 **77**.. JackGarritty 4 87
(Jedd O'Keeffe) *mde all: drvn 3f out: styd on wl: unchal* **12/1**
0-23 **2** 1 ¾ **Injam (IRE)**[54] 1636 3-9-6 **76**...................................... PaulMulrennan 2 82
(Jedd O'Keeffe) *trckd wnr: effrt 4f out: kpt on same pce fnl f* **11/4**[2]
5052 **3** nk **Hayward Field (IRE)**[8] 3033 3-8-8 **64**............................ HarryBentley 5 70+
(Roger Varian) *hld up in rr: effrt over 3f out: hdwy over 2f out: 3rd 1f out: kpt on same pce* **6/4**[1]
0-54 **4** 3 ¼ **Becky The Thatcher**[14] 2831 3-8-8 **64**........................ DuranFentiman 1 64
(Micky Hammond) *trckd ldrs: t.k.h: effrt over 2f out: fdd fnl f* **33/1**
31 **5** 2 ¾ **Isharah (USA)**[108] 768 3-9-5 **75**.................................... FrannyNorton 6 71
(Mark Johnston) *hmpd and dropped bk to detached last sn after s: pushed along over 4f out: kpt on fnl 2f: nvr a factor* **4/1**[3]
2-40 **6** 1 ½ **So Celebre (GER)**[12] 2900 3-9-2 **72**................................ DavidNolan 3 66
(Ian Williams) *trckd ldrs: effrt over 2f out: wknd over 1f out* **8/1**
45-4 **7** ¾ **Airton**[64] 1410 3-8-6 **67**.. NathanEvans(5) 7 59
(James Bethell) *wnt rt s: mid-div: racd wd: drvn over 3f out: wknd fnl 2f* **16/1**
2m 37.27s (0.57) **Going Correction** +0.05s/f (Good) **7** Ran SP% **114.3**
Speed ratings (Par 101): **100,98,98,96,94 93,93**
CSF £45.02 TOTE £13.40: £5.40, £1.90; EX 60.90 Trifecta £165.90.
Owner Geoff & Sandra Turnbull **Bred** Geoff & Sandra Turnbull **Trained** Middleham Moor, N Yorks

FOCUS
Rail movement added 4yds to race distance. A fair 3yo handicap even though only one of the seven runners had won before and, not for the first time at this track, the winner was in the ideal position out in front. It resulted in a 1-2 for trainer Jedd O'Keeffe. The runner-up has been rated to the better view of his Doncaster form.

3324 LADIES DAY H'CAP — 1m 1f
3:55 (3:56) (Class 3) (0-90,90) 4-Y-O **£7,246** (£2,168; £1,084; £542; £270) **Stalls** Low

Form RPR
20-3 **1** **Salieris Mass**[41] 2017 4-9-6 **89**.. FrannyNorton 7 100+
(Mark Johnston) *sn chsng ldrs: 2nd over 4f out: drvn over 3f out: styd on fnl f: led fnl strides* **9/4**[1]
5334 **2** nk **Sands Chorus**[12] 2917 4-8-2 **76**.. PhilDennis(5) 6 83
(James Given) *led: qcknd pce over 3f out: drvn over 1f out: hdd fnl strides* **4/1**[3]
014 **3** 3 ½ **Gulf Of Poets**[31] 2296 4-8-3 **77**...................................... NathanEvans(5) 5 76
(Michael Easterby) *trckd ldr: n.m.r on inner over 1f out: kpt on same pce* **7/2**[2]
2-50 **4** 1 **Indy (IRE)**[47] 1871 5-9-0 **90**.. RowanScott(7) 1 87
(David Barron) *sn trcking ldrs: drvn over 2f out: kpt on fnl f* **11/2**
3200 **5** ½ **One Pekan (IRE)**[21] 2620 6-8-7 **83**..........................(p) CameronNoble(7) 2 79
(Roger Varian) *hld up towards rr: hdwy to trck ldrs over 4f out: kpt on same pce over 1f out: eased fnl strides* **7/1**
-020 **6** 30 **Steel Train (FR)**[19] 2689 5-9-0 **88**.................................... JoshDoyle(5) 3 18
(David O'Meara) *hld up in rr: t.k.h: hdwy over 3f out: lost pl 2f out: sn bhd: eased in clsng stages: t.o* **8/1**
1m 54.86s (0.16) **Going Correction** +0.05s/f (Good) **6** Ran SP% **112.0**
Speed ratings (Par 107): **101,100,97,96,96 69**
CSF £11.41 TOTE £3.00: £1.80, £2.00; EX 10.00 Trifecta £23.90.
Owner Newsells Park Stud **Bred** Selwood B/S, Tuely, Tuely & Herridge **Trained** Middleham Moor, N Yorks

FOCUS
Rail movement added 4yds to race distance. A decent handicap albeit recent winning form was thin on the ground. They went an even pace and the order changed very little, except right at the end where it matters the most. A length pb from the runner-up, with the third rated close to his latest effort.

3325 BEAUMONT ROBINSON LADIES' DERBY H'CAP (LADY AMATEUR RIDERS) — 1m 4f 10y
4:35 (4:35) (Class 6) (0-65,65) 4-Y-O+ **£3,119** (£967; £483; £242) **Stalls** Low

Form RPR
-063 **1** **Pertuis (IRE)**[23] 2558 10-10-2 **60**....................................(p) MissCWalton 3 69
(Micky Hammond) *s.i.s: hdwy 8f out: 2nd and edgd lft over 1f out: styd on to ld last 100yds* **12/1**
0321 **2** ½ **Chauvelin**[1] 3288 5-9-2 **46**..(b) MissADeniel 1 54+
(Richard Guest) *s.s: t.k.h in rr: hdwy to trck ldrs over 4f out: led over 2f out: wandered and hdd last 100yds* **4/1**[2]
4534 **3** ¾ **Vedani (IRE)**[21] 2110 7-9-9 **53**.. MissJoannaMason 6 60+
(Tony Carroll) *mid-div: hdwy 5f out: chsng ldrs over 3f out: styd on wl fnl 150yds: tk 3rd nr fin* **8/1**
/53- **4** 1 **Oliver's Gold**[12] 5204 8-9-0 **47**..........................(p) MissRMcDonald(3) 8 52
(Mark Walford) *hld up in mid-div: hdwy over 3f out: chsng ldrs over 1f out: keeping on same pce whn sltly hmpd 1f out* **9/2**[3]
0244 **5** ½ **San Cassiano (IRE)**[20] 2656 9-10-4 **62**..................(p) MissSBrotherton 5 67
(Ruth Carr) *led 1f: trckd ldr: led briefly 3f out: kpt on same pce fnl f* **3/1**[1]
-534 **6** 5 **Merchant Of Medici**[7] 3052 9-10-4 **65**..................... MissBeckySmith(3) 7 62
(Micky Hammond) *chsd ldrs: one pce over 1f out* **12/1**
/0-1 **7** 3 **Van Mildert (IRE)**[10] 2962 7-9-4 **51** 6ex....................(p) MissAWaugh(3) 2 43
(Kenneth Slack) *led after 1f: hdd over 2f out: wknd over 1f out* **13/2**
60-4 **8** 1 ½ **Pencaitland**[17] 2746 4-8-11 **46**...................................... MissLWilson(5) 10 35
(Noel Wilson) *chsd ldrs: lost pl over 1f out* **20/1**
0200 **9** hd **Rainford Glory (IRE)**[30] 2343 6-9-8 **57**....................(p) MissHDukes(5) 9 46
(Tim Fitzgerald) *mid-div: hdwy over 6f out: sn chsng ldrs: wknd over 1f out* **20/1**
0000 **10** 2 ½ **That Be Grand**[17] 2745 5-9-2 **46** oh1............................... MrsCBartley 11 31
(Shaun Harris) *chsd ldrs: drvn over 4f out: lost pl over 2f out* **33/1**
400- **11** 6 **Kheskianto (IRE)**[212] 5484 10-9-2 **46** oh1............(t) MissMMullineaux 12 21
(Michael Chapman) *in rr: drvn 6f out: bhd fnl 2f* **100/1**
2m 40.03s (3.33) **Going Correction** +0.05s/f (Good) **11** Ran SP% **116.5**
Speed ratings (Par 101): **90,89,89,88,88 84,82,81,81,80 76**
CSF £56.83 CT £415.78 TOTE £11.20: £3.40, £2.10, £2.60; EX 85.40 Trifecta £377.30.
Owner M H O G **Bred** Killeen Castle Stud **Trained** Middleham, N Yorks

FOCUS
Rail movement added 4yds to race distance. A moderate handicap for lady amateurs, but a truly run race and the first five came clear.

3326 NORTH ORMESBY WMC TONY BENNETT MEMORIAL H'CAP — 5f
5:10 (5:11) (Class 5) (0-75,75) 3-Y-O+ **£3,234** (£962; £481; £240) **Stalls** High

Form RPR
0003 **1** **Apricot Sky**[24] 2531 6-9-9 **72**.. FrannyNorton 6 83
(David Nicholls) *chsd ldrs: led appr fnl f: drvn out* **10/3**[1]
324 **2** 1 ¾ **Orient Class**[12] 2919 5-9-4 **67**....................................... JackGarritty 5 72
(Paul Midgley) *hld up in mid-div: hdwy and n.m.r over 1f out: styd on to take 2nd last 150yds: no ex* **6/1**[2]
3042 **3** ¾ **Flash City (ITY)**[13] 2863 8-8-9 **71**............................(b[1]) JamesSullivan 1 73
(Ruth Carr) *carried rt s: in rr: swtchd lft after s: hld up in rr: hdwy to trck ldrs whn n.m.r over 1f out: styd on same pce last 100yds* **10/3**[1]
5312 **4** shd **Henley**[44] 1956 4-9-7 **70**.. RoystonFfrench 7 72
(Tracy Waggott) *led: t.k.h: hdd appr fnl f: kpt on same pce* **13/2**[3]
3450 **5** 1 **Jacob's Pillow**[19] 2680 5-9-7 **70**...................................... AndrewMullen 3 68
(Rebecca Bastiman) *mid-div: hdwy on outer to chse ldrs over 2f out: hung rt: fdd towards fin* **7/1**
13-6 **6** hd **Harmonic Wave (IRE)**[17] 2742 3-8-12 **74**........................ RowanScott(7) 4 69
(Ann Duffield) *hld up towards rr: hdwy over 2f out: chsng ldrs whn n.m.r over 1f out: kpt on same pce* **7/1**
0-00 **7** ¾ **Aprovado (IRE)**[19] 2677 4-9-12 **75**............................(p) PaulMulrennan 9 70
(Michael Dods) *chsd ldrs: dropped bk over 2f out: effrt and swtchd rt 1f out: kpt on* **18/1**
1160 **8** shd **Sir Geoffrey (IRE)**[61] 1481 10-8-7 **56**...............................(b) CamHardie 8 50
(Scott Dixon) *w ldr: one pce over 1f out* **25/1**
6100 **9** 12 **Toledo**[24] 2524 3-8-12 **67**...(p) SamJames 2 16
(Marjorie Fife) *wnt rt s: sn chsng ldrs on outer: wknd over 1f out: eased whn bhd* **28/1**
59.49s (-0.51) **Going Correction** +0.05s/f (Good)
WFA 3 from 4yo+ 6lb **9** Ran SP% **111.3**
Speed ratings (Par 103): **106,103,102,101,100 99,98,98,79**
CSF £22.15 CT £68.52 TOTE £5.00: £2.00, £2.40, £1.10; EX 21.10 Trifecta £63.40.
Owner The Wayward Lads & David Padgett **Bred** Mrs James Bethell **Trained** Sessay, N Yorks

FOCUS
A modest sprint handicap. The runner-up has been rated to his AW latest, and the fourth close to form.

3327 STRAY FM CELEBRATING LADIES DAY H'CAP — 1m
5:45 (5:45) (Class 5) (0-75,75) 4-Y-O+ **£2,911** (£866; £432; £216) **Stalls** Low

Form RPR
0324 **1** **Lawyer (IRE)**[16] 2773 5-9-1 **69**... PhillipMakin 7 78
(David Barron) *trckd ldrs: nt clr run over 2f out: shkn up to ld 1f out: drvn out* **6/1**[2]
4223 **2** 1 ¼ **Eastern Dragon (IRE)**[10] 2960 6-9-3 **71**...................... RoystonFfrench 4 77
(Iain Jardine) *hld up in mid-div: hdwy over 2f out: chsng ldrs over 1f out: kpt on to take 2nd nr fin* **9/2**[1]
0261 **3** hd **Shamaheart (IRE)**[16] 2773 6-9-5 **73**..........................(p) FrannyNorton 1 79
(Geoffrey Harker) *s.i.s: hdwy and nt clr run over 2f out: chsng ldrs over 1f out: kpt on to take 3rd fnl strides* **15/2**[3]
-540 **4** hd **Nelson's Bay**[2] 3262 7-8-2 **56**.. CamHardie 9 61
(Wilf Storey) *hld up in rr: effrt over 2f out: styd on fnl f: tk 4th fnl strides* **33/1**
0U05 **5** ½ **Musaaid (IRE)**[12] 2917 4-9-0 **73**................................... NathanEvans(5) 12 77
(Michael Easterby) *t.k.h: racd wd: sn trcking ldrs: led over 2f out: hdd 1f out: kpt on same pce* **10/1**
-050 **6** 3 **Janaab (IRE)**[20] 2662 6-8-12 **66**..(t) DavidAllan 11 63
(Tim Easterby) *chsd ldrs: drvn over 2f out: one pce appr fnl f* **9/2**[1]
-000 **7** 1 ½ **Trail Blaze (IRE)**[19] 2677 7-9-4 **75**................................(b) JoeDoyle(3) 10 69
(Kevin Ryan) *swtchd rt after s: led: drvn over 3f out: hdd over 2f out: wknd fnl f* **9/2**[1]
0304 **8** ½ **Illustrious Prince (IRE)**[30] 2330 9-8-8 **62**..................(p) ConnorBeasley 8 54
(Julie Camacho) *mid-div: drvn over 3f out: wknd over 1f out* **20/1**
-500 **9** 2 ¾ **Osteopathic Remedy (IRE)**[20] 2662 12-8-10 **69**........... PhilDennis(5) 6 55
(John Davies) *mid-div: effrt over 2f out: edgd rt and lost pl over 1f out* **25/1**
0510 **10** 1 **Samsonite (IRE)**[19] 2672 4-8-9 **63**................................. DuranFentiman 3 47
(Tony Coyle) *mid-div: drvn to chse ldrs over 3f out: wknd over 1f out* **20/1**
0360 **11** 1 ½ **Danot (IRE)**[12] 2918 4-8-13 **67**... JackGarritty 2 47
(Jedd O'Keeffe) *chsd ldr: led briefly 3f out: lost pl over 1f out* **9/1**
04-0 **12** 28 **Ivors Involvement (IRE)**[20] 2662 4-9-1 **69**..................... PaulMulrennan 5
(Tina Jackson) *t.k.h in rr: bhd fnl 2f: eased whn t.o in clsng stages* **50/1**
1m 40.97s (-0.43) **Going Correction** +0.05s/f (Good) **12** Ran SP% **118.0**
Speed ratings (Par 103): **104,102,102,102,101 98,97,96,94,93 91,63**
CSF £30.66 CT £210.63 TOTE £6.70: £2.00, £1.60, £2.70; EX 22.80 Trifecta £149.30.
Owner John Knotts **Bred** Drumlin Bloodstock **Trained** Maunby, N Yorks

FOCUS
Rail movement added 4yds to race distance. An ordinary handicap to end with and the two leaders may have gone off too quick. The second and third helps set the standard.
T/Plt: £40.90 to a £1 stake. Pool of £49069.41 - 874.37 winning tickets. T/Qpdt: £21.50 to a £1 stake. Pool of £2753.78 - 94.70 winning tickets. **Walter Glynn**

3328 - 3331a (Foreign Racing) - See Raceform Interactive

3081 LEOPARDSTOWN (L-H)

Thursday, June 16

OFFICIAL GOING: Soft

3332a OLIVER BRADY MEMORIAL SHABRA BALLYCORUS STKS (GROUP 3) 7f 20y
7:55 (8:01) 3-Y-O+

£27,330 (£8,801; £4,169; £1,852; £926; £463)

RPR

1 **Dick Whittington (IRE)**26 2495 4-9-9 105 SeamieHeffernan 4 109+
(A P O'Brien, Ire) *chsd ldrs on inner in 3rd: rdn to chse ldr in 2nd under 2f out: led ent fnl f and sn forged clr: comf* **7/4**2

2 2 3/4 **Al Mohalhal (IRE)**5 3175 3-9-0 94 (p) KevinManning 3 99
(J S Bolger, Ire) *led: qcknd 2 l clr under 2f out: hdd ent fnl f: nt pce of wnr but kpt on wl in clr 2nd* **12/1**

3 4 3/4 **Dont Bother Me (IRE)**39 2070 6-9-9 98 (t) RonanWhelan 6 88
(Niall Moran, Ire) *chsd ldrs in 4th: pushed along under 3f out: wnt 3rd over 1f out: sn no imp on principals: kpt on same pce* **9/1**

4 1 1/4 **Kelinni (IRE)**40 2030 8-9-9 109 ShaneGray 5 85
(Kevin Ryan) *t.k.h to trck ldr in 2nd tl rdn and nt qckn under 2f out: sn dropped to 4th and no ex appr fnl f* **13/8**1

5 nk **Gordon Lord Byron (IRE)**26 2495 8-9-12 107 WayneLordan 1 87
(T Hogan, Ire) *hld up in 5th: sme hdwy on outer 2f out: sn no imp in rr: kpt on one pce into 5th fnl 100yds: scoped wrong* **11/2**3

6 2 1/2 **Corail (IRE)**80 1127 4-9-6 92 ChrisHayes 2 74
(P D Deegan, Ire) *racd in rr tl shortlived effrt in 5th under 2f out: no imp appr fnl f: dropped to rr fnl 100yds* **33/1**

1m 32.92s (4.22)
WFA 3 from 4yo+ 9lb **6** Ran SP% **110.5**
CSF £20.97 TOTE £2.80: £1.40, £3.60; DF 20.50 Trifecta £180.10.
Owner Michael Tabor & Derrick Smith & Mrs John Magnier **Bred** Swordlestown Stud **Trained** Cashel, Co Tipperary

FOCUS
A pretty impressive performance from the winner, easily his best performance since his juvenile days, and it will be interesting to see if he can come back to that sort of level. The runner-up is rated to his best.

3333 - 3335a (Foreign Racing) - See Raceform Interactive

3295 ASCOT (R-H)

Friday, June 17

OFFICIAL GOING: Good to soft (soft in places on round course; stands' side 7.5, centre 7.0, far side 7.3, round 5.9)
Wind: Almost nil Weather: Fine

3336 ALBANY STKS (GROUP 3) (FILLIES) 6f
2:30 (2:33) (Class 1) 2-Y-O

£45,368 (£17,200; £8,608; £4,288; £2,152; £1,080) **Stalls** Centre

Form RPR

1 **Brave Anna (USA)**27 2492 2-9-0 0 SeamieHeffernan 16 103
(A P O'Brien, Ire) *str: awkward leaving stalls and s.i.s: towards rr: rdn and effrt 2f out: clsng and drifting rt u.p over 1f out: led 1f out: strly pressed towards fin: hld on cl home* **16/1**

1 **2** shd **Bletchley**16 2793 2-9-0 0 OisinMurphy 4 103
(Ralph Beckett) *str: lw: s.i.s: hld up in rr: hdwy ent fnl 2f: chsd ldrs and drvn jst over 1f out: chsd wnr ins fnl f: styd on strly fnl 75yds: jst hld* **16/1**

1 **3** 1/2 **Queen Kindly**14 2852 2-9-0 0 JamieSpencer 14 101
(Richard Fahey) *leggy: towards rr: rdn 2f out: hdwy u.p jst over 1f out: str run to press ldng pair 100yds out: kpt on but hld towards fin* **13/2**3

1 **4** 1/2 **Create A Dream (USA)**51 1770 2-9-0 0 (b) FrankieDettori 15 100
(Wesley A Ward, U.S.A) *lw: racd alone nrest to stands' rail: chsd ldr tl 1/2-way: lost pl but stl in tch: rdn and hdwy over 1f out: pressed ldrs and drvn ins fnl f: kpt on same pce towards fin* **11/2**2

1 **5** 1 **Cuff (IRE)**19 2718 2-9-0 0 RyanMoore 2 97
(A P O'Brien, Ire) *str: swtg: t.k.h: chsd ldrs: wnt 2nd wl over 1f out: ev ch u.p over 1f out: no ex ins fnl f: wknd fnl 75yds* **2/1**1

1 **6** 2 **Kilmah**35 2211 2-9-0 0 RichardKingscote 7 91+
(Mark Johnston) *athletic: mde most: rdn wl over 1f out: hdd 1f out: no ex u.p and wknd fnl 100yds* **12/1**

1 **7** 1 3/4 **Dainty Dandy (IRE)**13 2885 2-9-0 0 MartinHarley 10 85
(Paul Cole) *w'like: in tch in midfield: stl travelling wl 2f out: shkn up over 1f out: sn drvn and unable qck: wknd ins fnl f* **33/1**

400 **8** 1/2 **Melesina (IRE)**19 2718 2-9-0 0 PaulHanagan 6 84
(Richard Fahey) *midfield and sn niggled along: rdn and outpcd 2f out: rallied and styd on to pass btn horses 1f out: kpt on but no threat to ldrs* **100/1**

113 **9** 2 3/4 **Sea Of Snow (USA)**14 2865 2-9-0 0 JamesDoyle 13 76
(Mark Johnston) *sn chsng ldrs: rdn 2f out: unable qck u.p and btn ent fnl f: wknd* **33/1**

51 **10** 3/4 **High On Love (IRE)**18 2748 2-9-0 0 StevieDonohoe 3 73
(Charlie Fellowes) *w'like: in rr: effrt 2f out: hung rt and no imp over 1f out: wl hld and plugged on same pce fnl f* **50/1**

6 **11** shd **Oh Grace (IRE)**8 3081 2-9-0 0 (p) KevinManning 1 73
(J S Bolger, Ire) *w'like: wnt rt s: sn chsng ldrs: wnt 2nd 1/2-way tl wl over 1f out: sn lost pl u.p: wknd fnl f* **20/1**

1 **12** 2 1/4 **Cheval Blanche (USA)**17 2771 2-9-0 0 JamesMcDonald 5 66
(Michael Bell) *cmpt: hld up in tch in midfield: effrt 2f out: unable qck u.p and btn: wknd fnl f* **66/1**

11 **13** 4 1/2 **Grizzel (IRE)**20 2670 2-9-0 0 PatDobbs 8 53
(Richard Hannon) *cmpt: chsd ldrs: rdn ent fnl 2f: sn struggling and lost pl: wknd over 1f out* **13/2**3

23 **14** 1 **Perfect Madge (IRE)**35 2219 2-9-0 0 PatSmullen 9 50
(Kevin Ryan) *a towards rr: rdn 2f out: sn btn* **20/1**

13 **15** 3 1/2 **Spin Doctor**20 2670 2-9-0 0 TonyHamilton 11 39
(Richard Fahey) *w'like: in tch in midfield: rdn ent fnl 2f: sn btn: wknd over 1f out* **25/1**

21 **16** 2 1/4 **Romantic View**27 2467 2-9-0 0 WilliamBuick 12 33
(Charlie Appleby) *hld up in tch in midfield: hdwy to chse ldrs 3f out: rdn ent fnl 2f: sn lost pl and btn whn wandered u.p over 1f out: bhd and eased ins fnl f* **11/1**

1m 15.2s (0.70) **Going Correction** +0.275s/f (Good) **16** Ran SP% **126.9**
Speed ratings (Par 100): **106,105,105,104,103 100,98,97,93,92 92,89,83,82,77 74**
CSF £239.89 CT £1926.52 TOTE £19.30: £5.00, £3.70, £2.30; EX 339.90 Trifecta £3778.30.
Owner Mrs E M Stockwell **Bred** Mrs E Stockwell **Trained** Cashel, Co Tipperary
■ Stewards' Enquiry : Seamie Heffernan nine-day ban (1-9 July): used whip above permitted level
Oisin Murphy four-day ban (1&3-5 July): used whip above permitted level

FOCUS
There was only 1.5mm of rain late on Thursday evening and it had been dry since, so the going had quickened up to good to soft in the Straight (GoingStick: Stands' side: 7.5, Centre: 7.0, Far side: 7.3) and good to soft, soft in places on the Round course (GoingStick: 5.9). The temporary rail in place on the Round course over the previous three days had been removed to provide fresh ground, and all distances were as advertised. A pretty open Albany, and the pace was good, the principals coming from well back. It's been rated an ordinary renewal.

3337 KING EDWARD VII STKS (GROUP 2) (C&G) 1m 4f
3:05 (3:05) (Class 1) 3-Y-O

£122,210 (£46,332; £23,187; £11,550; £5,796; £2,909) **Stalls** Low

Form RPR

-130 **1** **Across The Stars (IRE)**13 2896 3-9-0 103 FrankieDettori 4 111
(Sir Michael Stoute) *swtg: trckd ldrs: effrt over 2f out: carried lft and led narrowly over 1f out: r.o and in command cl home* **7/1**3

-341 **2** 1 1/4 **Beacon Rock (IRE)**26 2510 3-9-0 108 RyanMoore 2 109
(A P O'Brien, Ire) *racd keenly: led at stdy pce: shkn up on bnd over 2f out: sn pressed: edgd lft u.p and hdd narrowly over 1f out: r.o: no ex cl home* **7/2**1

321 **3** hd **Muntahaa (IRE)**15 2815 3-9-0 94 PaulHanagan 5 108+
(John Gosden) *tall: lengthy: lw: midfield: rdn and nt qckn over 2f out: effrt over 1f out: prog for press whn intimidated by rival ins fnl f: r.o cl home gng on at fin* **10/1**

34 **4** 3/4 **Housesofparliament (IRE)**26 2510 3-9-0 103 (t) SeamieHeffernan 6 107
(A P O'Brien, Ire) *midfield: nt clr run 2f out: effrt whn swtchd lft wl over 1f out: swtchd rt ent fnl f: styd on: nt gng pce of ldrs* **16/1**

31-2 **5** 1 **Carntop**41 2036 3-9-0 104 (p) FMBerry 3 106
(Ralph Beckett) *racd keenly: chsd ldr for 1f: trckd ldrs after: chalng 2f out: carried sltly lft 1f out: nt qckn ent fnl f: no ex fnl 75yds* **9/2**2

4215 **6** hd **Humphrey Bogart (IRE)**13 2896 3-9-0 105 SeanLevey 1 106
(Richard Hannon) *hld up: rdn over 2f out: effrt over 1f out: styd on ins fnl f: nvr able to chal* **7/1**3

7 1 **Lustrous Light (IRE)**20 2709 3-9-0 0 ColinKeane 7 104
(G M Lyons, Ire) *medium-sized: str: hld up: effrt over 2f out: jinked lft over 1f out: kpt on ins fnl f: nvr trbld ldrs* **12/1**

-122 **8** hd **Linguistic (IRE)**27 2481 3-9-0 103 (b1) WilliamBuick 8 104+
(John Gosden) *lw: s.i.s: hld up in rr: swtchd lft arnd the field over 2f out: hdwy over 1f out: nt get to ldrs: outpcd ins fnl f: hung rt after: no ex fnl 75yds* **7/1**3

10 **9** 6 **Choreographer (IRE)**36 2190 3-9-0 97 AndreaAtzeni 9 94
(Roger Varian) *racd keenly: chsd ldr after 1f: rdn and ev ch 2f out: nt qckn u.p over 1f out: wknd ins fnl f* **9/2**2

2m 35.18s (2.68) **Going Correction** +0.275s/f (Good) **9** Ran SP% **118.8**
Speed ratings (Par 111): **102,101,101,100,99 99,99,98,94**
CSF £32.70 CT £250.48 TOTE £7.80: £2.30, £1.60, £3.60; EX 37.00 Trifecta £390.30.
Owner Saeed Suhail **Bred** Hascombe And Valiant Studs **Trained** Newmarket, Suffolk

FOCUS
A tricky King Edward VII and very open according to the market. The Derby form was represented by the fifth and tenth from that race and the form of the Epsom Classic did receive something of a boost. However, it was something of a messy race with the field only going a moderate gallop, which only increased turning for home, and a time 6.58sec outside standard is slow even allowing for the ground. Several of these were inclined to take a strong hold early, but the winner was probably the main sufferer as he pulled for quite a long way. The level is a bit fluid. It's been rated around the bottom end of the race standard, with the field compressed at the finish.

3338 COMMONWEALTH CUP (GROUP 1) 6f
3:40 (3:40) (Class 1) 3-Y-O

£243,853 (£92,450; £46,268; £23,048; £11,567; £5,805) **Stalls** Centre

Form RPR

1-11 **1** **Quiet Reflection**20 2692 3-9-0 117 DougieCostello 8 113
(K R Burke) *stdd after s: hld up in tch in midfield: clsd and travelling strly over 1f out: chsd ldrs and effrt ent fnl f: rdn and qcknd to ld 100yds out: r.o strly* **7/4**1

-616 **2** 1 **Kachy**27 2475 3-9-3 109 RichardKingscote 3 113
(Tom Dascombe) *lw: sn chsng ldr and racd sltly away fr rivals towards far side: led 1/2-way: began to hang lft ent fnl 2f: wnt bdly lft over 1f out: racing against stands' rails whn hdd 100yds out: one pce after* **14/1**

-012 **3** 1/2 **Washington DC (IRE)**19 2719 3-9-3 109 (t) RyanMoore 6 111
(A P O'Brien, Ire) *t.k.h: chsd ldng pair: wnt 2nd 2f out: sn drvn and ev ch ent fnl f: styd on same pce fnl 100yds* **8/1**

11-5 **4** 1 **La Rioja**20 2692 3-9-0 110 OisinMurphy 12 105
(Henry Candy) *in tch in midfield: effrt u.p over 1f out: chsd ldrs 1f out: styd on same pce ins fnl f* **11/1**

26-0 **5** hd **Illuminate (IRE)**47 1888 3-9-0 113 PatDobbs 4 105
(Richard Hannon) *chsd ldng trio: effrt 2f out: drvn and unable qck over 1f out: styd on same pce fnl f* **14/1**

3-51 **6** hd **Cheikeljack (FR)**71 1308 3-9-3 110 VincentCheminaud 2 107
(H-A Pantall, France) *tall: lengthy: racd sltly away fr rivals towards far side: hld up towards rr: stdy hdwy 1/2-way: effrt 2f: chsd ldrs and drvn over 1f out: styd on same pce ins fnl f* **7/1**3

-206 **7** 3/4 **Waterloo Bridge (IRE)**19 2719 3-9-3 100 (t) SeamieHeffernan 7 105
(A P O'Brien, Ire) *lw: dwlt: hld up in tch towards rr: effrt 2f out: drvn and unable qck over 1f: styd on same pce ins fnl f* **33/1**

-120 **8** 1/2 **Dream Dubai**34 2242 3-9-3 106 AdamKirby 9 103
(Sylvester Kirk) *stdd after s: midfield tl eased bk into last trio after 2f: rdn 2f out: no imp tl styd on ins fnl f: nvr trbld ldrs* **16/1**

14-2 **9** 1 1/4 **Donjuan Triumphant (IRE)**20 2692 3-9-3 115 SilvestreDeSousa 11 99
(Richard Fahey) *s.i.s: hld up in last pair: effrt wl over 1f out: sn drvn: edging rt and no imp ent fnl f: kpt on same pce after* **5/1**2

5-31 **10** 7 **Log Out Island (IRE)**34 2242 3-9-3 110 JamesDoyle 5 77
(Richard Hannon) *taken down early: led tl 1/2-way: rdn and lost 2nd 2f out: lost pl and bhd 1f out: wknd and eased wl ins fnl f* **7/1**3

1m 14.5s **Going Correction** +0.275s/f (Good) **10** Ran SP% **119.6**
Speed ratings (Par 113): **111,109,109,107,107 107,106,105,103,94**
CSF £30.63 CT £168.43 TOTE £2.50: £1.40, £4.60, £2.80; EX 28.50 Trifecta £190.40.

Owner Ontoawinner, Strecker & Burke **Bred** Springcombe Park Stud **Trained** Middleham Moor, N Yorks

FOCUS

On paper this was perhaps not quite as strong a race as last year's inaugural running, but the winner is a smart young sprinter capable of taking on her elders. The winner did not need to repeat her Sandy Lane Stakes form to win. The runner-up has been rated as running a pb.

3339 CORONATION STKS (BRITISH CHAMPIONS SERIES) (GROUP 1) (FILLIES) 1m (R)

4:20 (4:22) (Class 1) 3-Y-O

£226,840 (£86,000; £43,040; £21,440; £10,760; £2,700) **Stalls** Low

Form RPR

3-13 **1** **Qemah (IRE)**[33] 2282 3-9-0 110 GregoryBenoist 11 114
(J-C Rouget, France) *str: racd keenly on outer early: hld up: hdwy over 1f out: r.o to ld ins fnl f: in command towards fin* **6/1**

23-1 **2** *1 3/4* **Nemoralia (USA)**[35] 2220 3-9-0 112 OlivierPeslier 9 110
(Jeremy Noseda) *hld up in midfield: nt clr run and hmpd over 2f out: rdn whn swtchd lft and hdwy over 1f out: styd on to take 2nd fnl 75yds: nt trble wnr: jst hld on for 2nd post* **4/1**[2]

-330 **3** *shd* **Alice Springs (IRE)**[33] 2282 3-9-0 111 RyanMoore 3 110+
(A P O'Brien, Ire) *hld up: nt clr run over 2f out: sn swtchd lft: nt clr run over 1f out w plenty of work to do: hdwy ent fnl f: r.o strly: fin wl* **8/1**

-213 **4** *3/4* **Now Or Never (IRE)**[26] 2509 3-9-0 109 KierenFallon 8 108
(M D O'Callaghan, Ire) *str: midfield: hdwy 3f out: rdn to ld wl over 1f out: sn wnt rt under driving: hdd ins fnl f: lost 2nd fnl 75yds: no ex* **16/1**

-223 **5** *3/4* **Promising Run (USA)**[37] 2160 3-9-0 107 JamesDoyle 5 107
(Saeed bin Suroor) *in tch: effrt on inner to chse ldrs 2f out: styd on ins fnl f: nt pce to mount serious chal* **33/1**

20-1 **6** *3/4* **Ashadihan**[41] 2034 3-9-0 104 JamieSpencer 7 105
(Kevin Ryan) *in rr: pushed along over 3f out: rdn and hdwy over 1f out: kpt on ins fnl f: nt gng pce to chal* **33/1**

-101 **6** *dht* **Jet Setting (IRE)**[26] 2509 3-9-0 120 ShaneFoley 4 105
(Adrian Paul Keatley, Ire) *led: rdn and hdd wl over 1f out: stl cl up chsng ldrs ent fnl f: no ex and fdd fnl 75yds* **9/4**[1]

14-0 **8** *2* **Tanaza (IRE)**[26] 2509 3-9-0 106 PatSmullen 2 103+
(D K Weld, Ire) *leggy: midfield: nt clr run over 2f out and lost pl: effrt whn nt clr run and hmpd over 1f out: rallied and prog ins fnl f: nt clr run again fnl 75yds: sn eased* **20/1**

-152 **9** *1 3/4* **Nathra (IRE)**[33] 2282 3-9-0 110 FrankieDettori 13 99+
(John Gosden) *s.i.s: sn chsd ldrs: n.m.r over 2f out: nt qckn over 1f out: eased whn no ex fnl 75yds* **5/1**[3]

3-34 **10** *3/4* **Besharah (IRE)**[33] 2282 3-9-0 114 AndreaAtzeni 6 94
(William Haggas) *hld up: rdn and no imp whn nt clr run and hmpd over 1f out: n.d after* **16/1**

1-42 **11** *nk* **Fireglow**[37] 2160 3-9-0 110 WilliamBuick 12 94
(Mark Johnston) *chsd ldr: rdn and ev ch 2f out: u.p and nt qckning whn n.m.r and hmpd over 1f out: sn lost pl: n.d after: eased whn btn fnl 75yds* **16/1**

0-11 **12** *2 1/2* **Marenko**[62] 1476 3-9-0 105 SeanLevey 1 88
(Richard Hannon) *lw: trckd ldrs: effrt 2f out: wknd over 1f out* **50/1**

1441 **13** *1 1/4* **Czabo**[13] 2928 3-9-0 99 SilvestreDeSousa 10 85
(Mick Channon) *lw: midfield: hdwy over 3f out: rdn and lost pl over 2f out: n.d after* **33/1**

1m 40.56s (-0.14) **Going Correction** +0.275s/f (Good) **13** Ran SP% **126.0**
Speed ratings (Par 110): **111,109,109,108,107 106,106,104,103,102 102,99,98**
CSF £30.45 CT £208.44 TOTE £7.50: £2.60, £2.10, £2.60; EX 33.20 Trifecta £279.80.
Owner Al Shaqab Racing **Bred** Ecurie Cadran Bissons Sas lei **Trained** Pau, France

FOCUS

Unlike in the St James's Palace earlier in the week where the winners of the English, Irish and French 2,000 Guineas' were all present, only the winner of the Irish 1,000 Guineas turned up here, though the form of the other two Classics was well represented. The pace was a fair one, without being anything special, and a few didn't enjoy the clearest of runs, but the winner was still impressive. A small pb from the winner, while the fourth and fifth help set the standard.

3340 DUKE OF EDINBURGH STKS (H'CAP) 1m 4f

5:00 (5:00) (Class 2) (0-105,105) 3-Y-O+

£49,800 (£14,912; £7,456; £3,728; £1,864; £936) **Stalls** Low

Form RPR

2-01 **1** **Kinema (IRE)**[27] 2468 5-9-4 99 FMBerry 19 109
(Ralph Beckett) *hld up in last quartet: plenty to do and swtchd lft over 2f out: str run to chse clr ldng trio over 1f out: sustained run to chse ldr and edging rt ins fnl f: led and bmpd runner-up 50yds out: r.o* **8/1**[3]

/0-1 **2** *1 1/4* **Elite Army**[41] 2025 5-9-10 105 JamesDoyle 13 113+
(Saeed bin Suroor) *lw: racd keenly: chsd ldrs: wnt 2nd 7f out: rdn and effrt to press ldr 2f out: led 2f out: drvn clr ent fnl f: tiring and edging rt ins fnl f: hdd 50yds out: bmpd and wknd cl home* **9/2**[1]

30/5 **3** *nk* **Kings Fete**[27] 2464 5-9-9 104 RyanMoore 15 114+
(Sir Michael Stoute) *swtg: stdd s: hld up in last pair: swtchd rt over 2f out: gd hdwy and swtchd rt over 1f out: swtchd lft and chalng between rivals whn squeezed and snatched up 50yds out: swtchd lft and rallied cl home* **13/2**[2]

3-01 **4** *2 3/4* **First Sitting**[11] 2979 5-9-4 99 4ex GeorgeBaker 9 103
(Chris Wall) *wl in tch in midfield: chsd ldrs 4f out: effrt in 3rd over 2f out: keeping on same pce whn edgd rt and sltly hmpd wl ins fnl f* **14/1**

13-2 **5** *1/2* **Fabricate**[35] 2199 4-9-2 97 (p) PatSmullen 7 100
(Michael Bell) *swtg: hld up towards rr: swtchd lft and effrt but stl plenty to do over 2f out: hdwy over 1f out: styd on steadily ins fnl f: nvr enough pce to rch ldrs* **8/1**[3]

6/0- **6** *nk* **A Soldier's Life (IRE)**[278] 6372 5-9-4 99 JamesMcDonald 16 101
(Charlie Appleby) *racd keenly: chsd ldr tl led after 2f: rdn and hdd 2f out: no ex u.p and lost 2nd ins fnl f: plugged on same pce after* **25/1**

4-13 **7** *4* **Top Tug (IRE)**[35] 2222 5-9-5 100 FergusSweeney 5 96
(Alan King) *swtg: hld up in midfield: effrt u.p over 2f out: 7th and no imp ent fnl f: wl hld and plugged on same pce after* **16/1**

/01- **8** *3/4* **Rare Rhythm**[267] 6679 4-9-2 97 WilliamBuick 17 101+
(Charlie Appleby) *swtg: hld up towards rr: clsd whn nt clr run and hmpd jst over 2f out: rdn and over 1f out: styd on ins fnl f: no ch w ldrs* **13/2**[2]

35/ **9** *hd* **Ivan Grozny (FR)**[62] 2035 6-9-6 101 MartinHarley 10 95
(W P Mullins, Ire) *hld up towards rr: effrt whn nt clr run and swtchd lft over 1f out: hdwy u.p over 1f out: 8th and no imp 1f out: plugged on same pce after* **10/1**

45-0 **10** *1 1/2* **Felix Mendelssohn (IRE)**[27] 2482 5-9-3 98 JamieSpencer 14 90
(David Simcock) *stdd and dropped in bhd after s: hld up in rr: stl last of main gp over 2f out: swtchd rt and hdwy u.p 1f out: kpt on: no ch w ldrs* **33/1**

0-65 **11** *2 1/2* **Windshear**[75] 1219 5-9-9 104 SeanLevey 18 92
(Richard Hannon) *hld up towards rr: swtchd rt and effrt on inner over 2f out: no imp u.p over 1f out: sn wknd* **33/1**

3-14 **12** *2* **Cymro (IRE)**[42] 1995 4-9-9 104 RichardKingscote 22 89
(Tom Dascombe) *styd wd early: chsd ldrs: wnt 3rd 4f out: rdn and lost 3rd over 2f out: wknd over 1f out* **8/1**[3]

21-3 **13** *8* **Missed Call (IRE)**[41] 2025 6-9-4 99 TomQueally 21 71
(James Fanshawe) *hld up in midfield: effrt bnd over 2f out: outpcd u.p 2f out: sn wknd* **20/1**

-350 **14** *nk* **Quarterback (GER)**[106] 811 4-9-8 103 (p) PatDobbs 4 75
(Rune Haugen) *wl in tch in midfield: rdn over 2f out: sn struggling and lost pl jst over 2f out: wknd over 1f out* **50/1**

46-5 **15** *nk* **Ajman Bridge**[27] 2482 6-9-9 104 (b) AndreaAtzeni 6 75
(Roger Varian) *lw: hld up in midfield: effrt over 2f out: sn drvn and unable qck: wknd over 1f out* **16/1**

1053 **16** *3 1/4* **Notarised**[27] 2468 5-9-6 101 SilvestreDeSousa 2 67
(Mark Johnston) *lw: dwlt and bustled along early: midfield: effrt towards inner whn nt clr run and hmpd 2f out: no ch after: eased ins fnl f* **25/1**

3001 **17** *6* **John Reel (FR)**[27] 2482 7-9-6 101 AdamKirby 1 57
(David Evans) *midfield: rdn over 2f out: losing pl and towards rr whn squeezed for room and hmpd wl over 1f out: no ch after: eased ins fnl f* **40/1**

000- **18** *5* **Faithful Creek (IRE)**[237] 7470 4-9-2 97 (bt) JimmyFortune 20 45
(Brian Meehan) *hld up in midfield: rdn over 2f out: sn lost pl: wknd wl over 1f out: eased ins fnl f* **50/1**

2-63 **19** *99* **Hamelin (IRE)**[76] 1209 6-9-7 102 (v) FrankieDettori 3
(George Scott) *lw: t.k.h: led for 2f: chsd ldr tl 7f out: styd prom tl lost pl 4f out: sn bhd: eased fnl 2f: t.o* **20/1**

2m 32.59s (0.09) **Going Correction** +0.275s/f (Good) **19** Ran SP% **135.2**
Speed ratings (Par 109): **110,109,108,107,106 106,103,103,103,102 100,99,93,93,93 91,87,84,18**
CSF £42.78 CT £265.13 TOTE £10.30: £2.70, £2.00, £2.40, £3.60; EX 62.50 Trifecta £488.20.
Owner The Ashes **Bred** Rockhart Trading Ltd **Trained** Kimpton, Hants
■ Stewards' Enquiry : F M Berry seven-day ban (1-7 Jul): failing to take sufficient timely corrective action

FOCUS

A highly competitive handicap run at a good pace. The winner had to survive a stewards' enquiry after badly hampering the third close home. A length pb from the runner-up, with the fourth rated close to his Windsor win.

3341 QUEEN'S VASE (LISTED RACE) 2m

5:35 (5:36) (Class 1) 3-Y-O

£51,039 (£19,350; £9,684; £4,824; £2,421; £1,215) **Stalls** Low

Form RPR

1 **Sword Fighter (IRE)**[37] 2169 3-9-3 0 ColmO'Donoghue 4 103
(A P O'Brien, Ire) *leggy: sn led: mde rest: rdn whn pressed over 2f out: styd on and kpt finding for press ins fnl f: game* **33/1**

211 **2** *3/4* **Harbour Law**[29] 2411 3-9-3 91 GeorgeBaker 13 102
(Laura Mongan) *broke wl: led early: chsd ldr: rdn to chal 2f out: styd on ins fnl f: hld nr fin* **8/1**

3 *3/4* **Twilight Payment (IRE)**[20] 2709 3-9-3 0 (p) KevinManning 19 101
(J S Bolger, Ire) *angular: racd keenly: in tch: pushed along and lost pl over 5f out: outpcd 3f out: edgd rt ent fnl 2f: styd on strly ins fnl f: edgd lft fnl 110yds: gng on at fin* **20/1**

-445 **4** *nk* **Landofhopeandglory (IRE)**[26] 2510 3-9-3 0 RyanMoore 11 101+
(A P O'Brien, Ire) *lw: midfield: hdwy whn hung rt over 2f out: rdn and swtchd lft over 1f out: wanted to lug rt bhd ldrs ins fnl f: styd on: run flattened out fnl strides* **10/3**[1]

5- **5** *1/2* **Ebediyin (IRE)**[37] 2169 3-9-3 0 PatSmullen 6 100
(D K Weld, Ire) *athletic: lw: in tch: trcking ldrs gng wl 3f out: rdn to chal over 1f out: no ex fnl 75yds* **4/1**[2]

-152 **6** *1 3/4* **Gunnery (FR)**[20] 2687 3-9-3 88 JamieSpencer 15 98
(Peter Chapple-Hyam) *hld up: hdwy on inner 3f out: rdn over 2f out: plld out ent fnl 2f: edgd lft whn styng on ins fnl f: sltly checked fnl 110yds: eased whn unable to rch ldrs towards fin* **9/1**

1 **7** *2* **The Tartan Spartan (IRE)**[48] 1873 3-9-3 0 TadhgO'Shea 17 96
(John Patrick Shanahan, Ire) *tall: midfield: rdn 4f out: outpcd over 3f out: prog and styd on u.p over 1f out: clsng towards fin: nt rch ldrs* **33/1**

2-21 **8** *2* **Girling (IRE)**[30] 2368 3-8-12 82 FMBerry 3 89
(Ralph Beckett) *chsd ldrs: rdn 3f out: outpcd wl over 1f out: styd on same pce ins fnl f* **14/1**

3650 **9** *2 1/4* **Beaverbrook**[27] 2473 3-9-3 95 WilliamBuick 5 91
(Mark Johnston) *hmpd s: hld up: stdy prog u.p fr 2f out: nvr able to trble ldrs* **33/1**

4200 **10** *hd* **Soldier In Action (FR)**[13] 2892 3-9-3 90 JoeFanning 10 91
(Mark Johnston) *chsd ldrs: ev ch 3f out: rdn over 2f out: nt qckn: one pce fr over 1f out* **16/1**

0-33 **11** *6* **Ormito (GER)**[28] 2432 3-9-3 100 DavidProbert 1 83
(Andrew Balding) *restless in stalls: midfield: effrt 4f out: edgd lft u.p whn chsng ldng bunch 2f out: flashed tail over 1f out whn no imp: wknd ins fnl f* **5/1**[3]

12 *1 1/4* **Cole Porter (IRE)**[40] 2072 3-9-3 87 (tp) SeamieHeffernan 18 82
(A P O'Brien, Ire) *leggy: scope: lw: hld up: rdn and outpcd over 2f out: plugged on fr over 1f out: nvr a threat* **16/1**

0-11 **13** *10* **Opposition**[34] 2252 3-9-3 84 FrankieDettori 12 70+
(Ed Dunlop) *tall: racd keenly in midfield: prog to chse ldrs 4f out: rdn 2f out: wknd over 1f out* **10/1**

6-31 **14** *14* **Daphne**[35] 2215 3-8-12 84 PatCosgrave 14 48
(William Haggas) *hld up: struggling over 3f out: t.o* **20/1**

15 *13* **Saga Sprint (IRE)**[15] 2837 3-8-12 0 KierenFallon 8 32
(J R Finn, Ire) *chsd ldrs: pushed along over 5f out: wknd over 3f out: eased whn wl btn fnl 2f: t.o* **66/1**

16 *3* **Birthplace (IRE)**[26] 2513 3-9-3 0 (tp) AnaO'Brien 7 34
(Joseph Patrick O'Brien, Ire) *hld up: struggling 3f out: nvr a threat: t.o* **50/1**

050 **17** *1 1/2* **King Julien (IRE)**[20] 2686 3-9-3 58 AdamKirby 9 32
(John Ryan) *a in rr: u.p 1/2-way: toiling 3f out: t.o* **100/1**

-533 **18** *1 3/4* **Magnum (IRE)**[15] 2816 3-9-3 80 (b) JimmyFortune 16 30
(Brian Meehan) *hld up: pushed along over 5f out: struggling to keep up 3f out: t.o* **40/1**

3m 34.55s (5.55) **Going Correction** +0.275s/f (Good) **18** Ran SP% **133.6**
Speed ratings (Par 107): **97,96,96,96,95 94,93,92,91,91 88,88,83,76,69 68,67,66**
CSF £284.24 CT £5447.72 TOTE £50.70: £10.50, £3.00, £8.80; EX 577.30 Trifecta £19847.00 Part won..
Owner Michael Tabor & Derrick Smith & Mrs John Magnier **Bred** Glenvale Stud **Trained** Cashel, Co Tipperary

FOCUS
This might have been expected to have been an even greater test of stamina for these 3yos than usual in the ground, but they didn't go a great pace and the 1-2 passing the post on the first circuit were also the 1-2 at the end of the contest. Aidan O'Brien was winning this race for the fifth time in ten years. The level is fluid, with a wide range of abilities on show. It's been rated around the first two to the race standard.
T/Jkpt: Not won. T/Plt: £1,251.10 to a £1 stake. Pool: £508,784.25 - 296.86 winning tickets
T/Qpdt: £98.40 to a £1 stake. Pool: £38,243.28 - 287.46 winning tickets
Steve Payne & Darren Owen

2956 AYR (L-H)
Friday, June 17

OFFICIAL GOING: Good (7.7)
Wind: Almost nil Weather: Overcast

3342 TENNENT'S BLACK T AMATEUR RIDERS' H'CAP 1m 2f
6:30 (6:31) (Class 6) (0-65,64) 4-Y-O+ **£3,119** (£967; £483; £242) **Stalls** Low

Form RPR
0065 **1** **Togetherwecan (IRE)**[9] [3020] 4-9-7 **50**..........(b) MissEmmaBedford(7) 8 61
(Mark Johnston) *t.k.h early: hld up in tch: lost pl after 4f: gd hdwy on outside to ld 2f out: edgd lft and pushed clr fr over 1f out* **12/1**
0010 **2** *6* **The Wee Barra (IRE)**[9] [3012] 4-10-6 **63**....................(p) MissHTLees(7) 7 63
(Kevin Ryan) *cl up: led after 2f: pushed along and hdd 2f out: plugged on fnl f: nt gng pce of wnr* **10/1**
2031 **3** *2 1/4* **Testa Rossa (IRE)**[11] [2958] 6-11-0 **64** 6ex......................(v) MrsCBartley 2 59
(Jim Goldie) *hld up in tch: stdy hdwy over 3f out: effrt and swtchd rt wl over 1f out: sn no imp* **5/2**[1]
05-0 **4** *1 1/4* **Poor Duke (IRE)**[140] [388] 6-9-11 **47**........................ MissMMullineaux 5 40
(Michael Mullineaux) *trckd ldrs: rdn over 2f out: kpt on same pce fr over 1f out* **33/1**
0003 **5** *1* **Hussar Ballad (USA)**[22] [2618] 7-11-0 **64**.................. MissSBrotherton 6 55
(Antony Brittain) *s.i.s: t.k.h: stdy hdwy over 3f out: effrt whn checked briefly wl and outpcd wl over 1f out: n.d after* **7/2**[2]
-000 **6** *1 1/4* **Whitchurch**[41] [2045] 4-10-1 **54**..........................(p) MrThomasGreatrex(3) 4 43
(Philip Kirby) *bhd and sn detached: effrt and hdwy on outside over 2f out: no further imp appr fnl f* **4/1**[3]
3021 **7** *8* **Quadriga (IRE)**[71] [1295] 6-9-8 **51**........................... MissJAHeneghan(7) 3 24
(Philip Kirby) *trckd ldrs: rdn over 3f out: wknd 2f out* **12/1**
3-16 **8** *nk* **Duke Of Yorkshire**[23] [2573] 6-10-6 **61**...................(p) MissEEasterby(5) 9 34
(Tim Easterby) *led 2f: w ldr: rdn over 3f out: wknd over 2f out* **5/1**
2m 11.75s (-0.25) **Going Correction** -0.125s/f (Firm) **8** Ran SP% **114.9**
Speed ratings (Par 101): **96,91,89,88,87 86,80,79**
CSF £123.38 CT £398.21 TOTE £12.60: £3.40, £2.70, £1.30; EX 72.80 Trifecta £438.60.
Owner Douglas Livingston **Bred** Soc Finanza Locale Consulting Srl **Trained** Middleham Moor, N Yorks
■ Stewards' Enquiry : Mrs C Bartley jockey was found guilty of careless riding and was cautioned as to her future conduct
FOCUS
A low-grade handicap for amateur riders run over 15 yards further than advertised. The pace was fair and it produced a runaway winner who's rated a minor pb.

3343 HEVERLEE MAIDEN STKS 1m 1f 20y
7:05 (7:06) (Class 5) 3-Y-O+ **£3,881** (£1,155; £577; £288) **Stalls** Low

Form RPR
2532 **1** **Knights Table**[21] [2640] 3-9-3 79..................................... PaulMulrennan 1 81+
(James Tate) *mde all: shkn up 2f out: kpt on strly fnl f* **13/8**[1]
3 **2** *1 3/4* **Apres Midi (IRE)**[15] [2835] 3-8-12 0.................................. JoeyHaynes 7 72+
(K R Burke) *trckd ldrs: effrt and chsd wnr over 1f out: edgd lft: kpt on ins fnl f: hld towards fin* **2/1**[2]
45- **3** *3 3/4* **Jaameh (IRE)**[231] [7592] 3-9-3 0... JasonHart 5 69+
(Mark Johnston) *trckd ldr: rdn over 2f out: edgd lft and kpt on same pce fr over 1f out* **9/2**[3]
0 **4** *2 1/4* **You'll Do**[144] [331] 3-8-12 0.. GarryWhillans(5) 6 64
(Maurice Barnes) *dwlt: t.k.h: hld up in tch: effrt on outside over 2f out: edgd lft and no imp over 1f out* **66/1**
4 **5** *1 3/4* **Eez Eh (IRE)**[9] [3019] 3-9-3 0... PhillipMakin 2 60
(Keith Dalgleish) *trckd ldrs: drvn along and outpcd over 2f out: n.d after* **25/1**
0 **6** *hd* **Ya Jammeel**[14] [2861] 3-9-3 0.. DavidNolan 8 60+
(Richard Fahey) *bhd: drvn and outpcd over 3f out: sme late hdwy: nvr on terms* **7/1**
34 **7** *hd* **Sophie P**[53] [1691] 3-8-12 0... TomEaves 3 54+
(R Mike Smith) *t.k.h: hld up in tch: effrt whn nt clr run over 2f out: rdn and wknd appr fnl f* **14/1**
6 **8** *15* **Shumaker (IRE)**[25] [2522] 4-10-0 0...................................... JackGarritty 4 27
(Noel C Kelly, Ire) *hld up: drvn and outpcd over 3f out: sn struggling: t.o* **80/1**
1m 56.3s (-1.20) **Going Correction** -0.125s/f (Firm)
WFA 3 from 4yo 11lb **8** Ran SP% **115.4**
Speed ratings (Par 103): **100,98,95,93,91 91,91,77**
CSF £5.10 TOTE £2.40: £1.02, £1.40, £2.10; EX 5.00 Trifecta £12.60.
Owner Saeed Manana **Bred** Ashbrittle Stud **Trained** Newmarket, Suffolk
FOCUS
An older horse maiden featuring a couple of interesting, unexposed sorts. It was run over 15 yards further than advertised and it was run at just a medium gallop. The winner is rated in line with his best efforts.

3344 MENABREA H'CAP 7f 50y
7:40 (7:42) (Class 5) (0-75,81) 3-Y-O+ **£3,881** (£1,155; £577; £288) **Stalls** High

Form RPR
0331 **1** **Classic Seniority**[7] [3115] 4-10-3 **81** 6ex................ JacobButterfield(3) 11 88
(Marjorie Fife) *prom: rdn and hdwy to ld over 1f out: hld on gamely fnl f* **10/3**[1]
0544 **2** *nk* **Gold Flash**[11] [2960] 4-9-11 **72**..(b) PhillipMakin 1 78
(Keith Dalgleish) *dwlt: sn in tch: effrt and rdn over 1f out: chsd wnr wl ins fnl f: jst hld* **4/1**[2]
1051 **3** *nk* **Favourite Treat (USA)**[11] [2960] 6-9-10 **78** 6ex...(e) AdamMcNamara(7) 5 83
(Ruth Carr) *hld up in tch on outside: hdwy to chse wnr over 1f out: lost 2nd and no ex wl ins fnl f* **5/1**[3]
-514 **4** *1 1/2* **Joyful Star**[9] [3013] 6-8-10 **57**.. JackGarritty 3 58
(Fred Watson) *dwlt: hld up: rdn 2f out: kpt on fnl f: nt pce to chal* **4/1**[2]
-050 **5** *3/4* **Novinophobia**[13] [2891] 3-8-12 **68**... TomEaves 9 64+
(Richard Fahey) *led: rdn and hdd over 1f out: kpt on same pce fnl f* **10/1**
3560 **6** *1 1/2* **Opt Out**[13] [2906] 6-9-1 **62**...(p) CamHardie 6 57
(Alistair Whillans) *s.i.s: hld up: rdn on outside over 2f out: no imp fr over 1f out* **22/1**
-250 **7** *hd* **Sooqaan**[29] [2409] 5-8-11 **58**... KeaganLatham 7 53
(Antony Brittain) *trckd ldr: drvn over 2f out: wknd over 1f out* **22/1**
-630 **8** *2* **Ralphy Boy (IRE)**[13] [2910] 7-10-0 **75**..................................... JasonHart 2 64
(Alistair Whillans) *trckd ldrs: rdn along over 2f out: wknd over 1f out* **8/1**
0420 **9** *2 1/2* **Goninodaethat**[11] [2960] 8-8-12 **59**................................... PaulMulrennan 4 41
(Jim Goldie) *plld hrd: hld up: rdn along 2f out: sn wknd* **16/1**
1m 32.08s (-1.32) **Going Correction** -0.125s/f (Firm)
WFA 3 from 4yo+ 9lb **9** Ran SP% **114.5**
Speed ratings (Par 103): **102,101,101,99,98 97,96,94,91**
CSF £16.50 CT £63.78 TOTE £4.50: £1.60, £1.70, £1.60; EX 19.70 Trifecta £60.10.
Owner D & S Woodall **Bred** E Cantillon, D Cantillon & A Driver **Trained** Stillington, N Yorks
FOCUS
Quite a competitive 7f handicap with several coming into the race in good form. It was run over 15 yards further and the pace was reasonable. The winner confirmed his York latest.

3345 MAGNERS H'CAP 1m 5f 13y
8:10 (8:12) (Class 3) (0-90,89) 4-Y-O+ **£9,056** (£2,695; £1,346; £673) **Stalls** Low

Form RPR
2222 **1** **I Am Not Here (IRE)**[7] [3118] 5-8-2 **70**................................ JoeyHaynes 1 80+
(Brian Ellison) *chsd clr ldng trio: hdwy over 2f out: effrt and led over 1f out: pushed clr fnl f* **2/1**[1]
0-10 **2** *3 3/4* **Braes Of Lochalsh**[27] [2487] 5-8-8 **76**........................... PaulMulrennan 2 80
(Jim Goldie) *hld up: drvn along 3f out: hdwy over 1f out: kpt on to take 2nd nr fin: no ch w wnr* **7/1**
0040 **3** *1/2* **Be Perfect (USA)**[20] [2685] 7-9-0 **82**................................(p) JackGarritty 6 85
(Ruth Carr) *pressed ldr: led gng wl over 2f out: sn rdn: hdd over 1f out: one pce fnl f: lost 2nd nr fin* **7/1**
P-05 **4** *nk* **Gabrial's Star**[20] [2685] 7-9-0 **89**............................(b) AdamMcNamara(7) 4 92
(Richard Fahey) *s.i.s: hld up: rdn along wl over 2f out: kpt on fnl f: nvr able to chal* **3/1**[2]
0004 **5** *3/4* **Love Marmalade (IRE)**[13] [2912] 6-8-2 **70** oh2.................... CamHardie 5 72
(Alistair Whillans) *trckd ldrs: drvn along over 2f out: outpcd fnl f* **22/1**
0-01 **6** *3* **Odeon**[13] [2888] 5-8-13 **81**.. TomEaves 7 78
(James Given) *led: rdn and hdd over 2f out: wknd fnl f* **7/1**
-110 **7** *25* **Fast Pick (IRE)**[37] [2163] 4-8-8 **76**.......................................(p) JasonHart 3 36
(Keith Dalgleish) *bhd: rdn fr 1/2-way: lost tch fr 3f out: t.o* **6/1**[3]
2m 53.22s (-0.78) **Going Correction** -0.125s/f (Firm) **7** Ran SP% **114.5**
Speed ratings (Par 107): **97,94,94,94,93 91,76**
CSF £16.72 TOTE £2.60: £1.50, £2.90; EX 13.40 Trifecta £82.70.
Owner Koo's Racing Club **Bred** John Reilly **Trained** Norton, N Yorks
FOCUS
A fair staying handicap, run over 30 yards further than advertised, and it was run at a good gallop with the field soon strung out. It's rated around the runner-up.

3346 TENNENT'S H'CAP 6f
8:45 (8:47) (Class 3) (0-95,95) 3-Y-O+ **£9,056** (£2,695; £1,346; £673) **Stalls** High

Form RPR
0212 **1** **Intisaab**[6] [3168] 5-9-2 **86** 6ex.......................................(p) ShelleyBirkett(3) 1 97+
(David O'Meara) *hld up: rdn and hdwy over 1f out: led ins fnl f: pushed out* **5/2**[1]
50-0 **2** *3/4* **Cornwallville (IRE)**[27] [2485] 4-9-8 **94**................................ JoshDoyle(5) 3 102
(David Loughnane) *hld up in tch: hdwy to ld over 1f out: hdd ins fnl f: kpt on: hld nr fin* **14/1**
-431 **3** *3 1/2* **Duke Cosimo**[16] [2803] 6-9-2 **83**... TomEaves 2 80
(Michael Herrington) *hld up in tch: effrt and rdn over 1f out: kpt on ins fnl f: nt pce of first two* **7/2**[2]
0-00 **4** *1 1/2* **Gamesome (FR)**[37] [2158] 5-10-0 **95**.................................. PaulMulrennan 4 87
(Paul Midgley) *w ldr: rdn along 2f out: outpcd fnl f* **11/2**[3]
00-0 **5** *2* **Above The Rest (IRE)**[55] [1627] 5-9-9 **90**............................ PhillipMakin 8 76
(David Barron) *led to over 1f out: sn drvn and outpcd* **7/2**[2]
0-00 **6** *1/2* **Fast Act (IRE)**[16] [2803] 4-9-6 **90**.. KevinStott(3) 6 74
(Kevin Ryan) *trckd ldrs: rdn along over 1f out: sn btn* **18/1**
0-00 **7** *1* **Hawkeyethenoo (IRE)**[14] [2862] 10-8-12 **86**........(t) AdamMcNamara(7) 7 67
(Jim Goldie) *missed break: hld up: rdn on outside over 1f out: sn btn* **7/1**
1/0- **8** *3/4* **Star Citizen**[384] [2710] 4-9-3 **84**.. JackGarritty 5 62
(Fred Watson) *dwlt: t.k.h and sn chsng ldr: rdn and ev ch over 1f out: wknd fnl f* **50/1**
1m 10.43s (-1.97) **Going Correction** -0.125s/f (Firm) **8** Ran SP% **114.8**
Speed ratings (Par 107): **108,107,102,100,97 97,95,94**
CSF £39.44 CT £120.25 TOTE £3.00: £1.40, £3.60, £1.40; EX 27.90 Trifecta £102.00.
Owner Stuart Graham **Bred** Shadwell Estate Company Limited **Trained** Upper Helmsley, N Yorks
FOCUS
An interesting 6f handicap and though the early pace wasn't that strong, the time was just 0.43 seconds slower than standard. Another pb from the winner.

3347 CALEDONIA BEST H'CAP 1m 2f
9:15 (9:16) (Class 4) (0-85,85) 3-Y-O+ **£6,469** (£1,925; £962; £481) **Stalls** Low

Form RPR
-551 **1** **Euchen Glen**[14] [2859] 3-8-10 **79**..................................... PaulMulrennan 2 89+
(Jim Goldie) *t.k.h: hld up in tch: no room fr 2f out: swtchd rt and nt clr run 1f out: swtchd lft and qcknd to ld last 50 nyd: kpt on strly* **4/1**[3]
-040 **2** *1/2* **Gworn**[25] [2527] 6-9-8 **79**.. JackGarritty 5 85
(R Mike Smith) *prom: effrt and pushed along over 1f out: led ent fnl f: hdd last 50yds: kpt on* **8/1**
105 **3** *1/2* **Biff Johnson (IRE)**[13] [2888] 4-9-9 **80**.........................(b[1]) PhillipMakin 1 85
(Keith Dalgleish) *trckd ldrs: rdn over 1f out: kpt on ins fnl f* **14/1**
-662 **4** *nk* **Innocent Touch (IRE)**[24] [2556] 5-9-7 **85**.............. AdamMcNamara(7) 7 89
(Richard Fahey) *pressed ldrs: led 2f out: hdd ent fnl f: kpt on same pce* **11/4**[2]
-510 **5** *3 3/4* **Freewheel (IRE)**[31] [2324] 6-9-7 **78**....................................... CamHardie 8 75
(Garry Moss) *hld up: drvn along on outside over 2f out: kpt on fnl f: nt gng pce to chal* **7/1**
00-0 **6** *1 1/4* **Arantes**[35] [2198] 5-8-10 **72**..(p) JoshDoyle(5) 6 66
(R Mike Smith) *dwlt: hld up: rdn along and effrt 2f out: one pce fnl f* **28/1**
-412 **7** *5* **Renfrew Street**[3] [3251] 3-8-11 **80** 6ex.................................. JasonHart 3 64
(Mark Johnston) *led at ordinary gallop: rdn and hdd 2f out: wknd fnl f* **2/1**[1]
2m 8.99s (-3.01) **Going Correction** -0.125s/f (Firm)
WFA 3 from 4yo+ 12lb **7** Ran SP% **113.7**
Speed ratings (Par 105): **107,106,106,105,102 101,97**
CSF £34.58 CT £403.49 TOTE £5.20: £2.50, £3.70; EX 34.40 Trifecta £283.50.
Owner W M Johnstone **Bred** W M Johnstone **Trained** Uplawmoor, E Renfrews

The Form Book, Raceform Ltd, Newbury, RG14 5SJ

FOCUS
Quite a competitive handicap run over 15 yards further than advertised run at a fair gallop. The winner was value for a bit extra.
T/Plt: £34.40 to a £1 stake. Pool: £48454.19 - 1026.86 winsing units. T/Qpdt: £18.10 to a £1 stake. Pool: £3901.25 - 158.90 winning units. **Richard Young**

3100 GOODWOOD (R-H)
Friday, June 17

OFFICIAL GOING: Soft
Wind: Almost nil Weather: Heavy thundery showers

3348 NYETIMBER CLASSIC CUVEE APPRENTICE STKS (H'CAP) 1m 1f 192y
6:10 (6:10) (Class 5) (0-75,73) 3-Y-O **£3,234** (£962; £481; £240) **Stalls** Low

Form RPR
-556 **1** **Kesselring**[15] 2816 3-9-9 **73**.................................... MeganNicholls(3) 2 85
(Richard Hannon) *led for 2f: disp ld after and led field to stands' rail: led again over 2f out: drvn clr ins fnl f* **3/1**[2]
5-04 **2** 6 **Kismet Hardy**[45] 1946 3-9-10 **71**.................................... GaryMahon 3 71
(Richard Hannon) *in tch: rdn 3f out: chsd wnr over 1f out: no imp* **4/1**[3]
000- **3** 2 **Sennockian Song**[221] 7777 3-9-7 **71**.................... RobJFitzpatrick(3) 5 67
(Mark Johnston) *cl up: rdn to chse wnr over 2f out: lost 2nd and one pce appr fnl f* **5/1**
6-64 **4** 3/4 **Pinstripe**[21] 2652 3-9-1 **67**.................................... GabrieleMalune(5) 1 62
(Luca Cumani) *in tch: effrt over 2f out: hrd rdn and btn over 1f out* **6/4**[1]
0502 **5** 6 **Gabster (IRE)**[17] 2766 3-8-12 **62**.................................(p) GeorgiaCox(3) 7 45
(Amanda Perrett) *s.i.s: hdwy to dispute ld after 2f and led field to stands' rail: wknd over 2f out* **8/1**
2m 19.38s (11.28) **Going Correction** +1.125s/f (Soft) **5** Ran SP% **112.8**
Speed ratings (Par 99): **99,94,92,92,87**
CSF £15.29 TOTE £3.60: £1.90, £2.40; EX 14.80 Trifecta £48.00.
Owner R J McCreery **Bred** Stowell Hill Ltd **Trained** East Everleigh, Wilts

FOCUS
The going was soft after rain during the afternoon and rail movements added 8yds to the race distance. A modest 3yo apprentice handicap and the field came stands' side in the straight. Tricky form to rate.

3349 NYETIMBER BLANC DE BLANCS STKS (H'CAP) 6f
6:45 (6:45) (Class 5) (0-70,70) 4-Y-O+ **£3,234** (£962; £481; £240) **Stalls** High

Form RPR
-002 **1** **Mad Endeavour**[20] 2697 5-8-9 **58**.................................... MartinLane 3 69
(Stuart Kittow) *racd in centre: w ldr: led 1/2-way: drvn out* **7/2**[2]
-603 **2** 2 3/4 **Regal Parade**[29] 2396 12-9-4 **70**.............................(t) KieranShoemark(3) 5 72
(Charlie Wallis) *hld up in centre: rdn and hdwy 2f out: chsd wnr fnl f: kpt on same pce* **9/2**[3]
12 **3** 1 1/2 **Capolavoro (FR)**[3] 3259 5-9-4 **67**.................................... JimCrowley 7 64
(Robert Cowell) *prom in centre: chsd wnr over 2f out tl 1f out: no ex* **7/4**[1]
4354 **4** 1/2 **Tidal's Baby**[21] 2647 7-8-6 **55**.................................... JimmyQuinn 4 51
(Lee Carter) *racd in centre: hld up: effrt over 2f out: one pce* **7/1**
0-60 **5** 6 **Feeling Easy (IRE)**[41] 2028 4-9-5 **68**.................................... WilliamCarson 1 45
(Robert Eddery) *chsd ldrs in centre: hung lft and wknd over 2f out* **9/1**
0-00 **6** 8 **Langley Vale**[29] 2396 7-9-1 **64**.................................(p) RobertWinston 8 15
(Roger Teal) *led on stands' rail tl 1/2-way: wknd wl over 1f out* **12/1**
22-0 **7** 11 **Dunnscotia**[17] 2765 4-9-4 **67**.................................(t) TedDurcan 9
(Paul Webber) *chsd ldr on stands' rail: rdn 1/2-way: sn wknd* **14/1**
1m 15.37s (3.17) **Going Correction** +0.625s/f (Yiel) **7** Ran SP% **113.6**
Speed ratings (Par 103): **103,99,97,96,88 78,63**
CSF £19.28 CT £35.28 TOTE £4.70: £2.10, £2.60; EX 23.40 Trifecta £70.80.
Owner Reg Gifford **Bred** S R Hope **Trained** Blackborough, Devon

FOCUS
An ordinary sprint handicap in which the market leaders dominated, but the time suggested the ground was soft. A pb from the winner but this form might not be that reliable.

3350 NYETIMBER ROSE MAIDEN FILLIES' STKS 1m 1f
7:15 (7:16) (Class 5) 3-Y-O+ **£3,234** (£962; £481; £240) **Stalls** Low

Form RPR
2-3 **1** **Alyday**[53] 1723 3-9-0 0.................................... TedDurcan 2 84+
(Sir Michael Stoute) *hld up in rr: hdwy 2f out: drvn to ld over 1f out: rdn clr fnl f* **2/1**[1]
50 **2** 2 1/2 **Beauty Sleep (IRE)**[26] 2505 3-9-0 0.................................... RobertWinston 6 77
(William Haggas) *led and set sedate pce: hrd rdn and hdd over 1f out: one pce* **7/1**
-3 **3** 2 1/4 **Ecureuil (IRE)**[36] 2182 3-8-11 0.................................... MarcMonaghan(3) 4 72
(Hugo Palmer) *hld up: hdwy and rdn over 2f out: one pce appr fnl f* **9/4**[2]
0 **4** 6 **Sleeplessinseattle**[42] 2008 3-9-0 0.................................... FrederikTylicki 1 59
(James Fanshawe) *cl up tl wknd 2f out* **11/2**
4 **5** 8 **Entrench**[14] 2877 3-9-0 0.................................... JimCrowley 3 41
(Amanda Perrett) *stdd s: hdwy to press ldr after 2f: hrd rdn and wknd 2f out* **9/2**[3]
6 3 1/2 **Just For Show (IRE)** 3-9-0 0.................................... WilliamCarson 5 34
(Shaun Lycett) *s.s: sn chsng ldrs: wknd over 2f out* **22/1**
2m 6.5s (10.20) **Going Correction** +1.125s/f (Soft) **6** Ran SP% **114.5**
Speed ratings (Par 100): **99,96,94,89,82 79**
CSF £16.80 TOTE £2.60: £1.50, £3.70; EX 15.70 Trifecta £34.90.
Owner Sir Evelyn De Rothschild **Bred** Southcourt Stud **Trained** Newmarket, Suffolk

FOCUS
Rail movements added 10yds to the race distance and they again came stands' side in the straight. Quite an interesting fillies' maiden with some good yards represented, but despite a steady gallop they finished well spread out. The form is set loosely around the second.

3351 RUSSIAN STANDARD ORIGINAL STKS (H'CAP) 1m 6f
7:50 (7:50) (Class 3) (0-95,94) 4-Y-O+
£9,337 (£2,796; £1,398; £699; £349; £175) **Stalls** Low

Form RPR
300- **1** **Boite (IRE)**[69] 4742 6-9-0 **87**.................................... MartinLane 6 100+
(Warren Greatrex) *trckd ldrs: led over 3f out: clr over 1f out: easily* **10/1**
15-2 **2** 5 **Monotype (IRE)**[27] 2468 4-9-4 **91**.................................... AndreaAtzeni 7 96
(Roger Varian) *chsd ldrs: rdn 3f out: wnt 2nd ins fnl f: nt trble wnr* **11/10**[1]
31-3 **3** 1 1/4 **Star Rider**[28] 2433 4-8-12 **85**.................................(p) JimCrowley 11 88
(Hughie Morrison) *trckd ldr: chal 3f out: outpcd fnl 2f: lost 2nd ins fnl f* **10/3**[2]
60-6 **4** 3 1/2 **Spice Fair**[20] 2699 9-8-10 **83**.................................... SteveDrowne 8 81
(Mark Usher) *hld up in rr: rdn and sme hdwy 2f out: nvr rchd ldrs* **14/1**
3235 **5** 1 3/4 **Scarlet Minstrel**[47] 1893 4-8-0 **78**.................................(p) EdwardGreatrex(5) 3 74
(Andrew Balding) *t.k.h in 5th: rdn to chse ldrs 3f out: wknd 1f out* **8/1**
12-0 **6** 10 **Mark Hopkins**[47] 1893 4-9-2 **89**.................................... DavidProbert 1 71
(David Elsworth) *a towards rr: n.d fnl 3f* **13/2**[3]
6-00 **7** 15 **Norab (GER)**[20] 2685 5-8-7 **80**.................................(p) JimmyQuinn 9 41
(Bernard Llewellyn) *led: hrd rdn over 4f out: hdd over 3f out: sn wknd* **40/1**
110- **8** 9 **All Talk N No Do (IRE)**[325] 4726 5-9-7 **94**.................(tp) TimmyMurphy 4 42
(Seamus Durack) *a towards rr: no ch fnl 3f* **16/1**
3m 16.54s (12.94) **Going Correction** +1.125s/f (Soft) **8** Ran SP% **119.2**
Speed ratings (Par 107): **108,105,104,102,101 95,87,82**
CSF £22.49 CT £48.48 TOTE £12.70: £3.00, £1.10, £1.30; EX 26.50 Trifecta £87.70.
Owner Mrs T Brown **Bred** Eledy Srl **Trained** Upper Lambourn, Berks

FOCUS
Rail movements added 8yds to the race distance. One of the feature races and a decent staying contest featuring several unexposed types. The gallop looked sound and it resulted in a runaway winner. He is rated back to his best.

3352 NYETIMBER DEMI-SEC FILLIES' STKS (H'CAP) 1m 4f
8:25 (8:26) (Class 3) (0-90,89) 3-Y-O+ **£9,703** (£2,887; £1,443; £721) **Stalls** High

Form RPR
0-21 **1** **Peloponnese (FR)**[21] 2666 3-8-4 **79**.................................(v) JoeFanning 7 101+
(Sir Michael Stoute) *pressed ldr: led 2f out: drvn clr over 1f out: easily* **13/8**[1]
3504 **2** 5 **Motdaw**[8] 3060 3-8-3 **78**.................................... JFEgan 3 87
(Mick Channon) *t.k.h: trckd ldrs: wnt 2nd 2f out: sn outpcd* **10/1**
-433 **3** 4 1/2 **Eager Beaver**[10] 2994 4-8-11 **75**.................................... RobHornby(3) 5 77
(William Muir) *led: qcknd 5f out: hrd rdn and hdd 2f out: sn btn* **8/1**
-023 **4** 4 **La Superba (IRE)**[20] 2671 4-9-13 **88**.................................(p) JimCrowley 2 83
(David Elsworth) *dwlt: hld up in rr: rdn 3f out: 4th and no imp whn edgd rt fnl f* **7/1**
/141 **5** 9 **Sureness (IRE)**[14] 2876 6-8-13 **81**.................................(t) MeganNicholls(7) 4 62
(Charlie Mann) *dwlt: hld up in 5th: effrt 3f out: wknd 2f out* **7/1**
4-23 **6** 3 3/4 **Lovely Memory (IRE)**[34] 2236 4-9-9 **89**.................(v[1]) EdwardGreatrex(5) 1 64
(Saeed bin Suroor) *in tch tl wknd 2f out* **7/2**[2]
2m 51.25s (12.85) **Going Correction** +1.125s/f (Soft)
WFA 3 from 4yo+ 14lb **6** Ran SP% **116.4**
Speed ratings (Par 104): **102,98,95,93,87 84**
CSF £8.91 TOTE £2.40: £1.60, £2.40; EX 9.00 Trifecta £43.90.
Owner Niarchos Family **Bred** Famille Niarchos **Trained** Newmarket, Suffolk

FOCUS
Rail movements added 8yds to the race distance. A decent fillies' handicap run at an ordinary pace before it quickened from the turn at the top of the hill. The finished strung out behind the easy winner, who is value for extra.

3353 BASEMENT JAXX STKS (H'CAP) 6f
8:55 (8:55) (Class 5) (0-70,70) 3-Y-O **£3,408** (£1,006; £503) **Stalls** High

Form RPR
0342 **1** **Shahaama**[6] 3126 3-8-11 **60**.................................... FrederikTylicki 7 69+
(Mick Channon) *trckd ldrs gng wl: rdn to ld over 1f out: drvn out* **9/4**[1]
-061 **2** 1/2 **Caitie (IRE)**[21] 2642 3-9-5 **68**.................................(t) DavidProbert 3 73
(Paul Cole) *dwlt: hld up in 5th: rdn and hdwy over 1f out: chsd wnr fnl 50yds: clsng at fin* **5/1**
1554 **3** 1/2 **Iceaxe**[14] 2856 3-9-1 **64**.................................... JoeFanning 2 67
(John Holt) *led tl wl over 1f out: kpt on u.p* **11/4**[2]
-544 **4** 1 3/4 **Stormflower**[28] 2435 3-8-12 **68**.................................... MitchGodwin(7) 4 66
(John Bridger) *t.k.h: pressed ldr: led briefly wl over 1f out: one pce* **4/1**[3]
-150 **5** 2 **False Id**[17] 2770 3-9-4 **67**.................................(p) WilliamCarson 1 58
(Robert Eddery) *prom tl outpcd wl over 1f out* **8/1**
0300 **6** 22 **Tahiti One**[37] 2148 3-8-0 **54**.................................... EdwardGreatrex(5) 6
(Tony Carroll) *dwlt: a last: rdn 1/2-way: no ch fnl 2f* **10/1**
1m 16.13s (3.93) **Going Correction** +0.625s/f (Yiel) **6** Ran SP% **114.3**
Speed ratings (Par 99): **98,97,96,94,91 62**
CSF £14.23 CT £31.26 TOTE £3.20: £1.60, £2.70; EX 15.40 Trifecta £20.30.
Owner M Al-Qatami & K M Al-Mudhaf **Bred** D J And Mrs Deer **Trained** West Ilsley, Berks

FOCUS
This low-grade 3yo sprint, dominated by fillies, was run 0.76secs slower than the earlier contest over the trip, although it had rained between those races. Sound enough form.
T/Plt: £59.00 to a £1 stake. Pool: £30,664.00 - 519.50 winning units. T/Qpdt: £2.90 to a £1 stake. Pool: £2,880.00 - 961.80 winning units. **Lee McKenzie**

2478 NEWMARKET (R-H)
Friday, June 17

OFFICIAL GOING: Good to soft
Wind: Fresh behind Weather: Cloudy with sunny spells

3354 TAYLOR WIMPEY APPRENTICE H'CAP 1m
5:50 (5:51) (Class 5) (0-70,70) 4-Y-O+ **£3,234** (£962; £481; £240) **Stalls** High

Form RPR
-126 **1** **Theydon Thunder**[78] 1165 4-8-3 **52**.................................... GeorgeWood(5) 6 64
(Peter Charalambous) *a.p: led over 1f out: sn rdn: r.o wl: eased nr fin* **9/1**
1006 **2** 3 3/4 **Schottische**[22] 2609 6-8-2 **53**.................................(p) LiamLewis-Salter(7) 2 56
(Alan Bailey) *mid-div: hdwy over 2f out: rdn over 1f out: styd on to go 2nd wl ins fnl f* **33/1**
6-16 **3** 3/4 **Roxie Lot**[23] 2577 4-9-8 **66**.................................... CallumShepherd 12 67
(Pam Sly) *hld up: hdwy over 2f out: rdn to chse wnr over 1f out: styd on same pce fnl f* **9/1**
2644 **4** 1 1/2 **Little Lord Nelson**[17] 2769 4-9-0 **63**.................................(tp) MillyNaseb(5) 10 61
(Stuart Williams) *hld up: pushed along over 3f out: hdwy over 1f out: sn rdn: styd on same pce fnl f* **4/1**[1]
0535 **5** shd **Jonnie Skull (IRE)**[3] 3255 10-8-7 **51** oh6.................(t) JosephineGordon 9 49
(Phil McEntee) *chsd ldrs: rdn over 2f out: styd on same pce fr over 1f out* **16/1**
-060 **6** 1 1/4 **Tommy's Secret**[42] 2010 6-9-9 **70**.................................... CharlieBennett(3) 7 65
(Jane Chapple-Hyam) *hld up: rdn over 3f out: nt trble ldrs* **11/2**[3]
1024 **7** 1 3/4 **Shining Romeo**[10] 2996 4-9-4 **67**.................................... PatrickVaughan(5) 3 58
(Denis Quinn) *s.i.s: rcvrd to go prom after 1f: rdn over 2f out: wknd over 1f out* **5/1**[2]
5304 **8** 1 1/2 **World Record (IRE)**[15] 2827 6-9-5 **63**.................................... AaronJones 1 50
(Mick Quinn) *led: hdd over 4f out: led again over 2f out tl over 1f out: wknd fnl f* **4/1**[1]
1406 **9** 6 **Attain**[8] 3072 7-8-8 **59**.................................(p) LiamDoran(7) 8 32
(Julia Feilden) *hld up: rdn over 3f out: wknd over 2f out* **11/1**

-004 **10** *nk* **Nifty Kier**[9] 3044 7-8-1 **52** oh6 ow1 .... GeorgiaDobie(7) 4 25
(Phil McEntee) *chsd ldrs: wnt 2nd over 5f out tl led over 4f out: hdd over 2f out: wknd over 1f out* **50/1**
1620 **11** *12* **Etaad (USA)**[29] 2401 5-9-11 **69** ....(b) HectorCrouch 5 14
(Gary Moore) *s.i.s: wnt mid-div over 6f out: rdn and wknd over 2f out* **20/1**
1m 40.12s (0.12) **Going Correction** +0.20s/f (Good) **11** Ran SP% **115.9**
Speed ratings (Par 103): **107,103,102,101,100 99,97,96,90,90 78**
CSF £271.59 CT £2771.86 TOTE £10.80: £3.00, £8.60, £2.70; EX 401.80 Trifecta £1916.90.
Owner pcracing.co.uk **Bred** Mill Farm Stud **Trained** Newmarket, Suffolk

FOCUS
Far-side track used. The repositioning of the bend into the home straight increased the distance of the 1m2f races by 22 yards. This was the first meeting of the season on the July Course here, and the going was good to soft. The leaders set a good gallop up the centre of the track in this minor handicap and the winner scored in emphatic style from off the pace. He built on his AW form under a top claimer.

3355 HENBRANDT LTD IMPORTER OF HARLEQUIN BRAND H'CAP 1m 2f
6:20 (6:21) (Class 4) (0-85,82) 3-Y-O **£5,175** (£1,540; £769; £384) **Stalls** Centre

Form RPR
21-0 **1** **Baydar**[42] 1992 3-9-7 **82** .... JackMitchell 2 95+
(Hugo Palmer) *s.i.s: hld up: hdwy over 2f out: led and edgd rt ins fnl f: r.o wl* **7/2**[1]
2-60 **2** *2* **Percy's Romance**[36] 2178 3-8-3 **69** .... JosephineGordon(5) 9 78
(Sir Michael Stoute) *s.i.s: hld up: hdwy over 2f out: led over 1f out: hdd ins fnl f: styd on same pce* **9/1**
0-44 **3** *5* **Corpus Chorister (FR)**[26] 2505 3-8-8 **69** .... MartinDwyer 3 68
(David Menuisier) *hmpd s: sn chsng ldrs: rdn and ev ch over 1f out: wknd ins fnl f* **6/1**
-322 **4** *1 3/4* **Torch**[24] 2557 3-9-2 **80** .... TomMarquand(3) 5 76
(Richard Hannon) *sn prom: rdn and hung lft fr over 2f out: wknd fnl f* **4/1**[2]
-450 **5** *2 1/4* **Loading (IRE)**[32] 2291 3-9-3 **78** .... KieranO'Neill 8 69
(Richard Hannon) *hld up: hdwy over 2f out: rdn and wknd over 1f out* **12/1**
0000 **6** *1/2* **Western Prince**[9] 3042 3-8-13 **74** .... RobertHavlin 6 64
(John Gosden) *led: rdn and hdd over 1f out: wknd fnl f* **14/1**
126 **7** *4* **Albert Boy (IRE)**[33] 2269 3-8-3 **71** .... NatalieHambling(7) 4 53
(Scott Dixon) *wnt rt s: racd keenly in 2nd: rdn over 2f out: wknd over 1f out* **10/1**
31-0 **8** *2 3/4* **Nessita**[56] 1602 3-9-0 **75** ....(p) HarryBentley 7 52
(Hugo Palmer) *prom: racd keenly: rdn over 2f out: wknd over 1f out* **11/1**
41-6 **9** *13* **Status Quo (IRE)**[24] 2565 3-9-2 **77** .... LukeMorris 1 28
(Sir Mark Prescott Bt) *hld up: rdn and wknd over 2f out* **5/1**[3]
2m 6.8s (1.30) **Going Correction** +0.30s/f (Good) **9** Ran SP% **115.0**
Speed ratings (Par 101): **106,104,100,99,97 96,93,91,81**
CSF £35.23 CT £182.77 TOTE £4.40: £1.50, £3.10, £2.20; EX 36.30 Trifecta £167.00.
Owner V I Araci **Bred** Fittocks Stud **Trained** Newmarket, Suffolk

FOCUS
Race distance increased by 22 yards. An interesting handicap involving several unexposed types. They went a decent pace and the first two, who came from the back, pulling well clear. The winner built on his taking 2yo maiden win.

3356 NGK SPARK PLUGS NOVICE STKS (PLUS 10 RACE) 6f
6:55 (6:56) (Class 4) 2-Y-O **£3,946** (£1,174; £586; £293) **Stalls** High

Form RPR
23 **1** **Spiritous (USA)**[21] 2649 2-9-2 0 .... JamesDoyle 5 85
(John Gosden) *chsd ldr tl shkn up to ld over 1f out: edgd rt ins fnl f: rdn out* **7/4**[1]
2 *hd* **Hathiq (IRE)** 2-9-2 0 .... SilvestreDeSousa 2 84
(Owen Burrows) *s.i.s: hld up: hdwy over 1f out: rdn to chse wnr ins fnl f: r.o* **11/2**
3 *1 1/4* **Nobly Born** 2-9-2 0 .... RobertHavlin 6 81
(John Gosden) *trckd ldrs: nt clr run over 1f out: r.o* **12/1**
1 **4** *1* **Aardwolf (USA)**[8] 3058 2-9-8 0 .... JamesMcDonald 7 84
(Mark Johnston) *led: rdn: edgd rt and hdd over 1f out: no ex wl ins fnl f* **5/1**[3]
5 *nk* **Thaaqib** 2-8-13 0 .... TomMarquand(3) 4 77
(Charles Hills) *chsd ldrs: shkn up over 2f out: styd on same pce fnl f* **5/2**[2]
6 *2* **Fortune Of War** 2-9-2 0 .... MartinDwyer 1 71
(Jane Chapple-Hyam) *s.i.s: hld up: shkn up over 2f out: nt trble ldrs* **25/1**
7 *3/4* **Gaia Princess (IRE)** 2-8-11 0 .... WilliamTwiston-Davies 3 64
(Gary Moore) *hld up: sme hdwy over 2f out: rdn over 1f out: no ex fnl f* **33/1**
1m 14.61s (2.11) **Going Correction** +0.30s/f (Good) **7** Ran SP% **111.5**
Speed ratings (Par 95): **97,96,95,93,93 90,89**
CSF £11.29 TOTE £2.60: £1.50, £2.60; EX 11.10 Trifecta £64.60.
Owner Godolphin **Bred** Don Alberto Corporation **Trained** Newmarket, Suffolk

FOCUS
The pace was not very strong and they finished in a bit of a bunch in this novice, but the leading form contender came out on top and there was plenty of promise from some newcomers. The winner came from a good Haydock maiden.

3357 ELECTRONIC METALWORK SERVICES H'CAP 1m
7:30 (7:30) (Class 5) (0-75,81) 3-Y-O **£3,234** (£962; £481; £240) **Stalls** High

Form RPR
-601 **1** **Blackout (FR)**[8] 3062 3-9-13 **81** 6ex .... JamesDoyle 4 92
(Richard Hannon) *hld up: hdwy over 2f out: led over 1f out: drvn out* **3/1**[1]
2-1 **2** *2 1/4* **Feed The Goater (FR)**[32] 2294 3-9-0 **71** .... TomMarquand(3) 12 77
(Richard Hannon) *hld up: hdwy over 2f out: rdn and edgd rt over 1f out: styd on to go 2nd wl ins fnl f* **7/2**[2]
4-15 **3** *1* **Briyouni (FR)**[16] 2801 3-9-7 **75** .... ShaneGray 2 79
(Kevin Ryan) *chsd ldr tl led over 2f out: rdn and hdd over 1f out: edgd rt and no ex ins fnl f* **9/2**[3]
03-0 **4** *3* **Mercifilly (FR)**[30] 2375 3-8-13 **67** .... LukeMorris 3 64
(Ed Walker) *hld up: shkn up 1/2-way: hdwy u.p 2f out: wknd wl ins fnl f* **10/1**
600- **5** *1 3/4* **Mamoo**[185] 8234 3-8-6 **60** .... MartinDwyer 7 53
(Mike Murphy) *s.i.s: hld up: nt clr run fr over 2f out tl styd on ins fnl f: nvr trbld ldrs* **33/1**
-460 **6** *1* **Henry The Explorer (CAN)**[29] 2412 3-9-3 **71** .... PaulHanagan 1 61
(Jo Hughes) *hld up: hdwy u.p over 2f out: wknd over 1f out* **28/1**
00-6 **7** *8* **Free Passage**[18] 2749 3-8-7 **66** .... HectorCrouch(5) 11 38
(Henry Candy) *chsd ldrs tl rdn and wknd over 1f out* **8/1**
44-0 **8** *1* **Pacommand**[42] 1992 3-9-1 **72** .... DanielMuscutt(3) 9 42
(Marco Botti) *prom: rdn over 2f out: wknd over 1f out* **20/1**
36-0 **9** *2* **So Much Fun (IRE)**[16] 2795 3-9-6 **74** ....(p) SilvestreDeSousa 8 39
(Ismail Mohammed) *hld up in tch: rdn over 2f out: wknd over 1f out* **20/1**
641 **10** *1* **Cliffhanger**[13] 2904 3-9-7 **75** .... MartinHarley 5 38+
(Paul Cole) *hld up: effrt over 2f out: wknd over 1f out* **8/1**
60 **11** *9* **Rupert Boy (IRE)**[62] 1486 3-8-6 **60** ....(b) KieranO'Neill 6 2
(Scott Dixon) *led: rdn and hdd over 2f out: wknd wl over 1f out* **40/1**
1m 40.48s (0.48) **Going Correction** +0.30s/f (Good) **11** Ran SP% **115.1**
Speed ratings (Par 99): **109,106,105,102,101 100,92,91,89,88 79**
CSF £12.03 CT £46.34 TOTE £3.80: £1.50, £1.90, £2.00; EX 16.00 Trifecta £60.20.
Owner Martin Hughes & Michael Kerr-Dineen **Bred** S A R L Haras Du Logis Saint Germain **Trained** East Everleigh, Wilts

FOCUS
The went a decent pace and the favourite scored in good style under a hold-up ride. The winner may do better still.

3358 OMA (WEST AFRICA) SHIPPING & LOGISTICS H'CAP 7f
8:00 (8:02) (Class 3) (0-95,95) 3-Y-O+ **£9,056** (£2,695; £1,346; £673) **Stalls** High

Form RPR
3-35 **1** **Namhroodah (IRE)**[20] 2690 4-10-0 **95** .... LukeMorris 5 104
(James Tate) *racd centre: hld up: pushed along and hdwy over 2f out: rdn over 1f out: hung lft ins fnl f: r.o u.p to ld post: 1st of 12 in gp* **14/1**
-255 **2** *nk* **Dutch Law**[8] 3061 4-9-1 **82** .... WilliamTwiston-Davies 14 90
(Hughie Morrison) *s.i.s: chsd ldr far side: rdn and hung rt fr over 2f out: led that pair over 1f out: led overall u.p wl ins fnl f: hdd post: 1st of 2 that side* **5/1**[1]
2-30 **3** *shd* **Scottish Glen**[29] 2391 10-9-6 **92** .... HectorCrouch(5) 4 99
(Patrick Chamings) *racd centre: hld up: hdwy over 1f out: rdn to ld ins fnl f: sn hdd: r.o: 2nd of 12 in gp* **25/1**
01-0 **4** *1/2* **Ifwecan**[22] 2628 5-9-8 **89** .... PaulHanagan 2 95
(Martin Smith) *racd centre: chsd ldrs: led that gp 1/2-way: overall ldr 3f out: rdn over 1f out: hdd ins fnl f: styd on: 3rd of 12 in gp* **33/1**
-405 **5** *2* **Highland Colori (IRE)**[22] 2628 8-9-12 **93** ....(v) LiamKeniry 6 94
(Andrew Balding) *racd centre: chsd ldrs: rdn and ev ch over 1f out: edgd lft and no ex wl ins fnl f: 4th of 12 in gp* **12/1**
00-0 **6** *3/4* **Brazos (IRE)**[15] 2833 5-9-12 **93** .... MartinHarley 11 92
(James Tate) *racd centre: chsd ldrs: rdn and ev ch wl over 1f out: styd on same pce ins fnl f: 5th of 12 in gp* **12/1**
-254 **7** *1* **Solar Flair**[27] 2480 4-9-11 **92** .... JamesDoyle 10 88
(William Knight) *led centre gp to 1/2-way: remained handy: rdn and ev ch over 1f out: no ex ins fnl f: 6th of 12 in gp* **8/1**[3]
5-60 **8** *nse* **Ruban (IRE)**[15] 2819 7-8-6 **78** ....(t) AaronJones(5) 3 74
(Stuart Williams) *racd centre: hld up: hdwy over 2f out: rdn over 1f out: styd on same pce fnl f: 7th of 12 in gp* **11/1**
12- **9** *hd* **Shwaimsa (IRE)**[280] 6279 3-8-12 **88** .... KieranO'Neill 9 80
(Richard Hannon) *racd centre: hld up: hdwy over 2f out: rdn over 1f out: styd on same pce fnl f: 8th of 12 in gp* **9/1**
0244 **10** *nk* **Bertiewhittle**[34] 2247 8-9-2 **88** .... JosephineGordon(5) 12 82
(David Barron) *racd centre: prom: shkn up over 2f out: no ex ins fnl f: 9th of 12 in gp* **8/1**[3]
06-0 **11** *hd* **Morache Music**[23] 2581 8-9-3 **87** .... DanielMuscutt(3) 1 81
(Patrick Chamings) *racd centre: hld up: hdwy over 2f out: rdn over 1f out: no ex fnl f: 10th of 12 in gp* **33/1**
4331 **12** *2* **Arnold Lane (IRE)**[12] 2934 7-9-11 **92** 6ex .... SilvestreDeSousa 13 80
(Mick Channon) *overall ldr far side 4f: sn rdn: hung rt and hdd that side over 1f out: wknd ins fnl f: last of 2 that side* **8/1**[3]
-000 **13** *1 1/2* **Field Game**[18] 2754 4-8-13 **80** ....(t) RobertHavlin 7 64
(Hughie Morrison) *racd centre: hld up: effrt over 2f out: wknd fnl f: 11th of 12 in gp* **25/1**
0004 **14** *7* **Fox Trotter (IRE)**[14] 2862 4-9-13 **94** .... HarryBentley 8 60
(Brian Meehan) *racd centre: s.i.s: hld up: hdwy over 2f out: rdn and wknd over 1f out: last of 12 in gp* **7/1**[2]
1m 26.33s (0.63) **Going Correction** +0.30s/f (Good)
WFA 3 from 4yo+ 9lb **14** Ran SP% **116.5**
Speed ratings (Par 107): **108,107,107,106,104 103,102,102,102,102 101,99,97,89**
CSF £76.74 CT £1782.21 TOTE £14.70: £4.80, £2.50, £5.70; EX 109.30 Trifecta £2345.90.
Owner Saeed Manana **Bred** Gevi International Bv **Trained** Newmarket, Suffolk

FOCUS
There was a tight finish in this good handicap and the runners were spread across the track. The form is set around the third.

3359 BREEDERS BACKING RACING EBF MAIDEN STKS (PLUS 10 RACE) 1m 2f
8:35 (8:38) (Class 4) 3-Y-O **£5,498** (£1,636; £817; £408) **Stalls** Centre

Form RPR
5- **1** **Natural Scenery**[342] 4152 3-9-0 0 .... JamesDoyle 11 78+
(Saeed bin Suroor) *a.p: edgd rt over 1f out: led ins fnl f: pushed out: edgd lft towards fin* **2/1**[1]
6 **2** *1* **Cape Cova (IRE)**[12] 2929 3-9-5 0 .... TomQueally 9 79+
(John Gosden) *hld up: pushed along and hdwy on outer over 2f out: rdn and hung rt over 1f out: r.o to go 2nd nr fin* **22/1**
032 **3** *nk* **Lexington Law (IRE)**[36] 2175 3-9-2 80 .... TomMarquand(3) 10 78
(Richard Hannon) *chsd ldr: rdn and ev ch over 1f out: styd on* **9/2**[2]
2-22 **4** *1 1/4* **Plenary (USA)**[9] 3028 3-9-5 86 .... SilvestreDeSousa 2 76
(Jeremy Noseda) *led: rdn over 1f out: hdd ins fnl f: styd on same pce* **2/1**[1]
5 *1/2* **Dharoos (IRE)** 3-9-5 0 .... PaulHanagan 7 75+
(John Gosden) *hld up: rdn over 3f out: r.o ins fnl f: nt trble ldrs* **7/1**[3]
3 **6** *1 1/2* **Hellavashock**[27] 2459 3-9-5 0 .... AdamBeschizza 4 72
(Giles Bravery) *chsd ldrs: rdn whn hmpd over 1f out: styd on same pce* **25/1**
6 **7** *nk* **Astrosecret**[77] 1179 3-9-0 0 .... SaleemGolam 6 66
(Mark H Tompkins) *hld up: nt clr run over 2f out: hdwy over 1f out: styd on same pce fnl f* **66/1**
0 **8** *2* **Tynecastle Park**[25] 2548 3-9-5 0 .... JackMitchell 8 67
(Robert Eddery) *s.i.s: hld up: rdn over 1f out: n.d* **50/1**
0- **9** *1* **Lisala (FR)**[185] 8232 3-9-0 0 .... LukeMorris 3 60
(George Peckham) *hld up in tch: racd keenly: rdn over 1f out: wknd ins fnl f* **50/1**
10 *1 1/4* **Teofilo Wolf** 3-9-0 0 .... ThomasBrown 1 58
(Ismail Mohammed) *plld hrd and prom: rdn over 2f out: hmpd and wknd 1f out* **12/1**
11 *43* **Astrowizard** 3-9-5 0 .... DarryllHolland 5
(Mark H Tompkins) *hld up: rdn and wknd over 2f out* **100/1**
2m 10.49s (4.99) **Going Correction** +0.30s/f (Good) **11** Ran SP% **119.6**
Speed ratings (Par 101): **92,91,90,89,89 88,88,86,85,84 50**
CSF £54.86 TOTE £2.70: £1.20, £5.10, £1.50; EX 44.50 Trifecta £178.30.
Owner Godolphin **Bred** Darley **Trained** Newmarket, Suffolk

FOCUS
Race distance increased by 22 yards. One of the market leaders scored with authority in this decent maiden, but the form is a bit muddling and might not prove reliable.

3360 32RED.COM H'CAP 5f
9:05 (9:05) (Class 5) (0-75,75) 3-Y-O **£3,234** (£962; £481; £240) **Stalls** High

Form RPR
0021 **1** **East Street Revue**[9] 3017 3-8-11 **65** 6ex....................(b) DuranFentiman 2 84
(Tim Easterby) *hld up: hdwy at 1/2-way: led over 1f out: rdn clr* **7/2**[3]
1423 **2** *4 ½* **Justice Lady (IRE)**[10] 3000 3-8-9 **63**........................ SilvestreDeSousa 3 66
(David Elsworth) *plld hrd: led 4 out: rdn: hung rt and hdd over 1f out: no ex fnl f* **9/4**[1]
6-20 **3** *2 ½* **Sacred Harp**[10] 3000 3-8-0 **61**.......................................(t[1]) MillyNaseb[(7)] 5 55
(Stuart Williams) *hld up: hdwy over 1f out: wknd ins fnl f* **16/1**
-221 **4** *½* **Geno (IRE)**[20] 2668 3-9-7 **75**..(p) ShaneGray 6 67
(Kevin Ryan) *led 1f: chsd ldr: rdn 1/2-way: wknd ins fnl f* **7/2**[3]
2005 **5** *2 ½* **Strictly Carter**[9] 3017 3-8-3 **62**..........................(b[1]) JosephineGordon[(5)] 1 45
(Alan Bailey) *sn pushed along to chse ldrs: rdn 1/2-way: wknd over 1f out* **16/1**
531- **6** *½* **Consulting**[219] 7795 3-9-7 **75**.. HarryBentley 7 56
(Martyn Meade) *prom tl rdn: edgd lft and wknd over 1f out* **3/1**[2]
59.89s (0.79) **Going Correction** +0.30s/f (Good) **6** Ran SP% **112.0**
Speed ratings (Par 99): **105,97,93,93,89 88**
CSF £11.75 TOTE £4.20: £2.30, £1.50; EX 11.10 Trifecta £131.40.
Owner S A Heley **Bred** Habton Farms & A Heley **Trained** Great Habton, N Yorks

FOCUS
A well-treated runner had no trouble defying a penalty in this sprint handicap and this was a pb.
T/Plt: £288.80 to a £1 stake. Pool: £55,435.39 - 140.10 winning units. T/Qpdt: £32.10 to a £1 stake. Pool: £5,917.56 - 136.40 winning units. **Colin Roberts**

2771 REDCAR (L-H)
Friday, June 17

OFFICIAL GOING: Good changing to good to soft after race 3 (2.55)
Wind: light against Weather: overcast, drizzle from 3rd

3361 ROYAL ASCOT EXTRA PLACES AT 188BET (S) STKS 7f
1:50 (1:51) (Class 6) 2-Y-O **£2,385** (£704; £352) **Stalls** Centre

Form RPR
53 **1** **Areyoutheway (IRE)**[33] 2266 2-8-11 0........................(v) FrannyNorton 5 65
(Tom Dascombe) *led narrowly: rdn whn hdd ent fnl f: kpt on: led again nr fin* **15/8**[2]
323 **2** *nk* **Springforth**[9] 3008 2-8-11 0.. GeorgeChaloner 2 64
(Richard Fahey) *pressed ldr: rdn to ld narrow ent fnl f: one pce and hdd nr fin* **7/4**[1]
5 **3** *1 ¾* **Last Paradise (IRE)**[28] 2417 2-8-6 0.............................. PJMcDonald 4 54
(Ann Duffield) *dwlt: hld up: rdn and hdwy to chse ldng pair over 1f out: kpt on same pce* **11/2**[3]
0 **4** *4* **Elements Legacy**[7] 3114 2-8-5 0 ow1........................(v) CliffordLee[(7)] 6 50
(K R Burke) *trckd ldng pair: rdn over 2f out: wknd fnl f* **10/1**
0 **5** *3* **Generous Times**[13] 2913 2-8-6 0.................................... ConnorBeasley 3 36
(Chris Grant) *racd keenly: trckd ldng pair: rdn over 2f out: wknd over 1f out* **33/1**
604 **6** *½* **The Fossil**[50] 1813 2-8-11 0...(v) BenCurtis 1 39
(Tom Dascombe) *hld up: rdn over 2f out: wknd over 1f out* **9/1**
1m 28.72s (4.22) **Going Correction** +0.35s/f (Good) **6** Ran SP% **108.6**
Speed ratings (Par 91): **89,88,86,82,78 78**
CSF £5.13 TOTE £2.90: £1.40, £1.50; EX 5.50 Trifecta £14.00.There was no bid for the winner. Last Paradise was claimed by Mr T. Vaughan for £6,000. Springforth was subject of a Friendly claim of £6,000.
Owner The Roaring Twenties **Bred** Vincent Hannon **Trained** Malpas, Cheshire

FOCUS
Good ground, and no changes to race distances. A moderate opener, in which the first two were up there all the way. The winner is rated back to his debut figure.

3362 EURO 2016 BETTING AT 188BET MAIDEN STKS 1m 2f
2:20 (2:24) (Class 5) 3-Y-O+ **£2,911** (£866; £432; £216) **Stalls** Low

Form RPR
42 **1** **Istanbul Bey**[25] 2541 3-9-2 0.. BenCurtis 5 85+
(William Haggas) *trckd ldr: led on bit 4f out: pushed along over 2f out: drew clr fr appr fnl f: eased towards fin* **4/7**[1]
2 *4* **Miss Galidora (IRE)** 3-8-11 0... SamJames 8 68
(David O'Meara) *hld up in midfield: hdwy over 3f out: rdn over 2f out: kpt on to go 2nd fnl 50yds* **8/1**
3 *¾* **Dubawi Hundred (IRE)** 3-9-2 0....................................... DavidAllan 10 72
(James Tate) *midfield: hdwy to trck ldr over 3f out: rdn over 2f out: no ch w wnr over 1f out: no ex and lost 2nd fnl 50yds* **11/2**[3]
4 *1 ¾* **Dawn Flight (IRE)** 3-9-2 0... PJMcDonald 2 68
(John Davies) *dwlt: sn in tch racing keenly: rdn 3f out: one pce* **33/1**
6 **5** *4* **Steely Rock**[22] 2619 3-9-2 0.. FrannyNorton 9 60
(Mark Johnston) *sn led: pushed along whn hdd 4f out: sn outpcd and dropped to rr: plugged on again fnl f* **5/1**[2]
6 *hd* **Snappydresser** 3-8-11 0.. RoystonFfrench 1 55
(Tracy Waggott) *slowly away: hld up: pushed along and minor hdwy over 2f out: nvr threatened* **100/1**
7 *6* **Hellracer** 3-9-2 0... ConnorBeasley 3 48
(Bryan Smart) *trckd ldr: rdn 3f out: wknd fnl 2f* **16/1**
36 **8** *2 ¾* **Jasper Jay**[33] 2271 3-9-2 0... DuranFentiman 7 42
(Tony Coyle) *got loose bef: hld up: rdn over 3f out: sn wknd* **33/1**
2m 13.3s (6.20) **Going Correction** 0.0s/f (Good) **8** Ran SP% **119.6**
WFA 3 from 5yo 12lb
Speed ratings (Par 103): **75,71,71,69,66 66,61,59**
CSF £6.65 TOTE £1.40: £1.02, £2.50, £1.80; EX 7.60 Trifecta £20.70.
Owner Simon Munir & Isaac Souede **Bred** Arbib Bloodstock Partnership **Trained** Newmarket, Suffolk

FOCUS
A steadily-run maiden which lacked depth. The winner was much the best although the second favourite disappointed.

3363 188BET.CO.UK H'CAP 1m 2f
2:55 (2:58) (Class 5) (0-70,68) 4-Y-O+ **£2,911** (£866; £432; £216) **Stalls** Low

Form RPR
531 **1** **Viserion**[7] 3118 4-9-2 **68**...(p) GeorgeBuckell[(5)] 9 77+
(David Simcock) *hld up: rdn over 3f out: hdwy on outer over 2f out: styd on: led nr fin* **9/4**[1]
0254 **2** *nk* **British Embassy (IRE)**[3] 3253 4-9-4 **65**............................. SamJames 3 73
(David Loughnane) *racd keenly: trckd ldr: rdn over 2f out: led 1f out: kpt on: hdd nr fin* **11/1**
2-63 **3** *2* **Ronya (IRE)**[14] 2860 5-8-10 **57**...................................... RoystonFfrench 5 61
(Tracy Waggott) *led: hdd 7f out: chsd ldr: rdn to ld again 2f out: hdd 1f out: no ex* **14/1**
2-00 **4** *1 ½* **Gabrial's Hope (FR)**[13] 2915 7-8-8 **55**............................. FrannyNorton 4 56
(Tracy Waggott) *racd keenly in midfield: pushed along 2f out: kpt on fnl f* **33/1**
-004 **5** *½* **Mr Sundowner (USA)**[22] 2618 4-8-5 **59**.....................(t) HollieDoyle[(7)] 11 59
(Wilf Storey) *in tch: rdn over 2f out: one pce* **16/1**
2-00 **6** *2* **Diletta Tommasa (IRE)**[116] 676 6-9-1 **62**.........................(p) DaleSwift 6 58
(Daniel Mark Loughnane) *hld up: rdn over 3f out: kpt on fnl f: nvr threatened* **25/1**
12-5 **7** *shd* **Le Deluge (FR)**[155] 173 6-9-2 **63**...................................(t) PJMcDonald 8 59
(Micky Hammond) *prom: led 7f out: clr over 5f out tl over 3f out: rdn whn hdd 2f out: sn wknd* **8/1**[3]
0-34 **8** *1 ¼* **Mowhoob**[9] 3043 6-8-1 **55**.. DanielleMooney[(7)] 10 48
(David Nicholls) *hld up: pushed along over 2f out: nvr threatened* **22/1**
633/ **9** *3 ¼* **Gold Show**[801] 1362 7-8-13 **60**... BarryMcHugh 1 47
(Grant Tuer) *trckd ldr: rdn 3f out: wknd over 1f out* **25/1**
0531 **10** *½* **Oriental Tiger**[8] 3052 5-9-6 **67**.. DanielTudhope 12 53
(Iain Jardine) *midfield: rdn 3f out: wknd over 1f out* **5/2**[2]
510- **11** *10* **Jan De Heem**[245] 7258 6-8-13 **60**..................................(p) JamesSullivan 7 26
(Tina Jackson) *midfield: rdn 3f out: wknd over 1f out* **33/1**
2m 6.26s (-0.84) **Going Correction** 0.0s/f (Good) **11** Ran SP% **109.3**
Speed ratings (Par 103): **103,102,101,99,99 97,97,96,94,93 85**
CSF £22.96 CT £250.29 TOTE £2.80: £1.30, £2.70, £3.40; EX 24.50 Trifecta £158.30.
Owner Tick Tock Partnership **Bred** Sheikh Sultan Bin Khalifa Al Nahyan **Trained** Newmarket, Suffolk
■ Day Of The Eagle was withdrawn. Price at time of withdrawal 33-1. Rule 4 does not apply.

FOCUS
Modest handicap form, but it was well run. There's more to come fom the winner.

3364 PINNACLE RACING SYNDICATE SHARES NOW AVAILABLE H'CAP (PINNACLE CUP MILE SERIES QUALIFIER) 1m
3:30 (3:32) (Class 3) (0-90,90) 3-Y-O+ **£7,439** (£2,213; £1,106; £553) **Stalls** Centre

Form RPR
2026 **1** **Abushamah (IRE)**[25] 2527 5-9-4 **80**............................... JamesSullivan 2 89
(Ruth Carr) *dwlt: hld up: pushed along and hdwy over 1f out: led ins fnl f: kpt on pushed out* **7/1**
2343 **2** *2 ½* **Mariee**[7] 3102 3-8-9 **81**... FrannyNorton 3 82
(Mark Johnston) *led narrowly: rdn 2f out: hdd ins fnl f: one pce* **9/4**[1]
2210 **3** *½* **Amazement (GER)**[21] 2654 3-8-9 **81**.................................. DavidAllan 6 81
(James Tate) *trckd ldng pair: rdn 2f out: kpt on ins fnl f* **5/2**[2]
0556 **4** *hd* **Energia Flavio (BRZ)**[20] 2677 5-9-0 **76**..................... GeorgeChaloner 1 78
(Richard Fahey) *pressed ldr: rdn 3f out: no ex and lost 3nd nr fin* **11/1**
0000 **5** *3* **Ingleby Angel (IRE)**[14] 2862 7-9-9 **90**.......................... NathanEvans[(5)] 5 85
(Colin Teague) *trckd ldng pair: rdn over 2f out: grad wknd over 1f out* **28/1**
3-13 **6** *2 ¼* **Rousayan (IRE)**[20] 2689 5-9-11 **87**.................................. DanielTudhope 7 77
(David O'Meara) *trckd ldng pair: rdn over 2f out: wknd ins fnl f* **10/3**[3]
0004 **7** *1 ¾* **Polar Forest**[15] 2832 6-9-6 **82**....................................(e) ConnorBeasley 8 68
(Richard Guest) *hld up: rdn over 2f out: wknd over 1f out* **16/1**
1m 39.82s (3.22) **Going Correction** +0.35s/f (Good)
WFA 3 from 5yo+ 10lb **7** Ran SP% **112.6**
Speed ratings (Par 107): **97,94,94,93,90 88,86**
CSF £22.44 CT £49.80 TOTE £6.50: £3.00, £1.60; EX 30.40 Trifecta £93.50.
Owner Grange Park Racing & Mrs R Carr **Bred** Shadwell Estate Company Limited **Trained** Huby, N Yorks

FOCUS
The official going was changed to good to soft before this race. The pace was reasonable for this decent handicap and the bare form could be rated higher.

3365 FREE MONTH TRIAL OF RACING UK H'CAP 1m 2f
4:05 (4:07) (Class 4) (0-80,80) 3-Y-O **£4,851** (£1,443; £721; £360) **Stalls** Low

Form RPR
42-1 **1** **Muzdawaj**[55] 1653 3-9-7 **80**... BenCurtis 1 88+
(William Haggas) *hld up in rr: pushed along and hdwy 2f out: rdn to ld ins fnl f: edgd lft: kpt on wl* **1/1**[1]
5-1 **2** *1 ¼* **Dune Dancer (IRE)**[21] 2640 3-9-7 **80**................................. ShaneKelly 4 85
(David Lanigan) *hld up in tch: pushed along and hdwy over 2f out: rdn over 1f out: kpt on: wnt 2nd towards fin* **7/4**[2]
4-62 **3** *nk* **Torremar (FR)**[25] 2522 3-8-10 **72**................................... JoeDoyle[(3)] 3 76
(Kevin Ryan) *led: rdn 2f out: hdd ins fnl f: no ex and lost 2nd towards fin* **8/1**[3]
-430 **4** *4* **Perceysvivace**[21] 2652 3-8-5 **64**.................................(p) PatrickMathers 5 60
(Richard Fahey) *trckd ldr: rdn over 2f out: wknd ins fnl f* **16/1**
-415 **5** *1 ¾* **Tap The Honey**[13] 2889 3-8-12 **78**................................ CliffordLee[(7)] 6 71
(K R Burke) *trckd ldr: rdn over 2f out: wknd ins fnl f* **16/1**
2m 7.89s (0.79) **Going Correction** 0.0s/f (Good) **5** Ran SP% **109.2**
Speed ratings (Par 101): **96,95,94,91,90**
CSF £2.91 TOTE £1.90: £1.10, £1.10; EX 3.30 Trifecta £7.00.
Owner Hamdan Al Maktoum **Bred** Shadwell Estate Company Limited **Trained** Newmarket, Suffolk

FOCUS
A fair handicap. The third set a decent pace for the first part of the race before slowing it down on the approach to the home turn. The winner is on the upgrade.

3366 CELEBRATE THE LIFE OF JOE NEWTON H'CAP (DIV I) 1m
4:45 (4:47) (Class 5) (0-70,75) 3-Y-O+ **£2,911** (£866; £432; £216) **Stalls** Centre

Form RPR
2005 **1** **Mustaqbal (IRE)**[11] 2960 4-9-9 **70**.............................(p) PhilDennis[(5)] 10 79
(Michael Dods) *in tch: trckd ldrs gng wl over 1f out: swtchd rt appr fnl f: rdn and edgd lft to join ldr 110yds out: pushed out to ld towards fin* **13/2**[3]
6420 **2** *½* **Cabal**[4] 3214 9-9-9 **65**...(v) FrannyNorton 4 73
(Geoffrey Harker) *midfield: pushed along and hdwy over 1f out: led ins fnl f: sn jnd: kpt on: hdd towards fin* **8/1**
-256 **3** *1 ¾* **Newmarket Warrior (IRE)**[17] 2773 5-9-12 **68**.......(p) RoystonFfrench 14 72
(Iain Jardine) *hld up in midfield: pushed along over 1f out: kpt on wl fnl f: nrst fin* **8/1**
-005 **4** *2* **Almuhalab**[17] 2773 5-9-5 **61**.. JamesSullivan 9 60
(Ruth Carr) *midfield: hdwy over 1f out: rdn to chal ent fnl f: one pce* **11/2**[2]
-455 **5** *½* **Highway Robber**[15] 2834 3-7-8 **53**................................. HollieDoyle[(7)] 1 49
(Wilf Storey) *midfield: rdn over 2f out: kpt on* **20/1**

-032 **6** ½ **City Of Night (IRE)**17 2773 4-9-4 60....................(e) ConnorBeasley 2 57
(Julie Camacho) *hld up in rr: rdn and hdwy over 1f out: one pce ins fnl f* **7/2**1

0156 **7** shd **Arcane Dancer (IRE)**20 2674 3-8-9 61....................(p) DavidAllan 11 56
(Lawrence Mullaney) *prom: rdn over 1f out: wknd ins fnl f* **15/2**

06-0 **8** ½ **Jordan James (IRE)**75 1216 3-9-3 69.................... BenCurtis 8 63
(Brian Ellison) *led narrowly: rdn 2f out: hdd ins fnl f: wknd* **33/1**

326 **9** 1½ **Top Offer**13 2906 7-9-3 59.................... ShaneKelly 6 51
(Patrick Morris) *hld up: pushed along 2f out: nvr threatened* **10/1**

0-30 **10** nk **Lady Canford (IRE)**54 1671 3-8-12 64.................... PJMcDonald 5 53
(James Bethell) *in tch: rdn over 2f out: wknd fnl f* **16/1**

-060 **11** ¾ **Playboy Bay**9 3013 4-9-1 57....................(v) AndrewMullen 3 47
(Ron Barr) *hld up: nvr threatened* **66/1**

30-0 **12** nk **Broctune Papa Gio**17 2773 9-9-3 62.................... JoeDoyle(3) 7 51
(Keith Reveley) *prom: rdn over 2f out: wknd over 1f out* **16/1**

0/0- **13** 6 **Luvlylynnthomas**428 1447 4-8-9 51 oh6.................... RaulDaSilva 12 26
(Micky Hammond) *midfield: rdn over 2f out: wknd over 1f out* **100/1**

1m 40.8s (4.20) **Going Correction** +0.35s/f (Good)
WFA 3 from 4yo+ 10lb **13** Ran SP% **116.0**
Speed ratings (Par 103): **93,92,90,88,88 87,87,87,85,85 84,84,78**
CSF £54.43 CT £436.29 TOTE £8.30: £2.60, £3.30, £3.20; EX 73.60 Trifecta £510.70.
Owner M J K Dods **Bred** Shadwell Estate Company Limited **Trained** Denton, Co Durham

FOCUS
Modest handicap form, with a small pb from the winner.

3367 CELEBRATE THE LIFE OF JOE NEWTON H'CAP (DIV II) 1m
5:20 (5:22) (Class 5) (0-70,70) 3-Y-O+ **£2,911** (£866; £432; £216) **Stalls** Centre

Form RPR

42-4 **1** **Weather Front (USA)**35 2212 3-9-3 69.................... DavidAllan 12 77+
(James Tate) *dwlt: hld up: pushed along whn hmpd over 1f out: swtchd rt: sn gd hdwy: rdn ins fnl f: kpt on wl: led 75yds out* **3/1**2

544 **2** 1¼ **Yulong Xiongba (IRE)**13 2915 4-9-7 63.................... ConnorBeasley 13 70
(Julie Camacho) *trckd ldr: rdn 2f out: led appr fnl f: hdd 75yds out: one pce* **12/1**

0012 **3** 1 **Curzon Line**21 2661 7-9-7 68.................... NathanEvans(5) 11 73
(Michael Easterby) *prom: led 4f out: pushed along whn hdd appr fnl f: sn rdn: edgd lft and one pce fnl 110yds* **9/4**1

6423 **4** ½ **Depth Charge (IRE)**13 2918 4-10-0 70....................(vt) ShaneKelly 1 74
(Kristin Stubbs) *hld up: pushed along and hdwy 2f out: bit short of room over 1f out: rdn and kpt on fnl f* **8/1**

-034 **5** nse **Saltarello (IRE)**9 3016 4-9-3 59.................... SamJames 10 62
(Marjorie Fife) *midfield: rdn over 1f out: kpt on fnl f* **20/1**

-521 **6** 1 **Rustique**9 3044 4-8-13 55.................... AntonioFresu 8 56
(Ed Walker) *midfield: rdn over 2f out: one pce* **11/2**3

0-00 **7** 1½ **Bling King**13 2915 7-9-4 60....................(p) FrannyNorton 3 58
(Geoffrey Harker) *in tch: rdn 2f out: wknd fnl 50yds* **20/1**

4306 **8** 1½ **Gone With The Wind (GER)**25 2526 5-9-6 62........(t) AndrewMullen 14 56
(Rebecca Bastiman) *hld up: rdn 2f out: nvr threatened* **25/1**

50-0 **9** nse **Fazza**20 2673 9-9-4 60.................... PaddyAspell 9 54
(Grant Tuer) *hld up: nvr threatened* **25/1**

0-40 **10** ½ **Someone Exciting**16 2801 3-8-1 53 oh2 ow1.................... PatrickMathers 5 44
(David Thompson) *hld up in midfield: rdn over 2f out: wknd fnl f* **40/1**

000 **11** 3½ **Border Bandit (USA)**13 2917 8-9-11 67....................(p) RoystonFfrench 7 52
(Tracy Waggott) *midfield: rdn over 2f out: wknd over 1f out* **16/1**

10-0 **12** 7 **Colombe Bleu**20 2674 3-8-11 63.................... BarryMcHugh 4 30
(Tony Coyle) *trckd ldr: rdn 3f out: wknd over 1f out* **50/1**

660- **13** 7 **Orobas (IRE)**296 5739 4-8-4 51 oh5.................... PhilDennis(5) 6 4
(Ron Barr) *sn led: hdd 4f out: sn rdn: wknd over 2f out* **100/1**

1m 39.35s (2.75) **Going Correction** +0.35s/f (Good)
WFA 3 from 4yo+ 10lb **13** Ran SP% **118.4**
Speed ratings (Par 103): **100,98,97,97,97 96,94,93,93,92 89,82,75**
CSF £34.95 CT £96.50 TOTE £3.50: £1.60, £3.50, £1.60; EX 38.50 Trifecta £113.60.
Owner Saif Ali **Bred** Kirsten Rausing **Trained** Newmarket, Suffolk

FOCUS
The quicker division by 1.45sec, this went to an unexposed three-year-old. Sound form.

3368 188BET MAIDEN H'CAP 5f
5:55 (5:57) (Class 5) (0-70,70) 3-Y-O+ **£2,911** (£866; £432; £216) **Stalls** Centre

Form RPR

0-00 **1** **Rose Eclair**17 2776 3-8-12 60....................(b1) DavidAllan 2 68
(Tim Easterby) *chsd ldr: rdn 2f out: led appr fnl f: edgd rt: kpt on* **10/1**

0523 **2** 1¼ **Kingthistle**9 3017 3-9-3 70.................... NathanEvans(5) 5 73
(Michael Easterby) *prom: rdn 2f out: kpt on* **5/1**2

0266 **3** shd **Emerald Asset (IRE)**9 3017 3-8-10 58.................... PJMcDonald 7 61
(Paul Midgley) *hld up: pushed along 1/2-way: rdn over 1f out: r.o fnl f: nrst fin* **14/1**

0-05 **4** nk **Tarnend Lass**18 2740 3-8-3 51 oh1....................(t) PatrickMathers 12 53
(Tim Easterby) *chsd ldrs: rdn 1/2-way: kpt on fnl f* **33/1**

56-0 **5** ½ **Dyllan (IRE)**18 2742 3-9-8 70.................... JamesSullivan 8 70
(Ruth Carr) *racd keenly in tch: rdn to chse ldr appr fnl f: n.m.r and swtchd lft 110yds out: one pce* **15/2**

6-40 **6** ½ **The Armed Man**17 2776 3-9-0 62.................... AndrewElliott 4 60
(Chris Fairhurst) *dwlt: hld up: rdn 1/2-way: kpt on fnl f: nvr threatened ldrs* **16/1**

4625 **7** ½ **Compton River**17 2778 4-8-6 53.................... PhilDennis(5) 9 51
(Bryan Smart) *trckd ldrs: rdn over 1f out: no ex fnl 110yds* **12/1**

30-2 **8** ¾ **Kinloch Pride**9 3010 4-8-9 51....................(p) BarryMcHugh 11 46
(Noel Wilson) *w ldr: rdn 1/2-way: wknd ins fnl f* **7/1**3

5346 **9** hd **Bromley Cross (IRE)**17 2776 3-9-3 65....................(p) BenCurtis 1 58
(Brian Ellison) *led narrowly: rdn 2f out: hdd appr fnl f: wknd ins fnl f* **10/1**

-022 **10** 1½ **Poolstock**17 2778 4-9-0 56....................(p) ConnorBeasley 3 45
(Michael Dods) *chsd ldrs: rdn 1/2-way: wknd fnl f* **9/2**1

020 **11** 2 **Ay Up Audrey**32 2304 5-8-10 52.................... AndrewMullen 10 34
(Rebecca Bastiman) *dwlt: sn pushed along: a towards rr* **33/1**

0/44 **12** 4½ **Douglas Bank (IRE)**41 2040 4-9-10 66....................(b) RyanPowell 6 32
(Roy Bowring) *chsd ldrs: lost pl 1/2-way: wknd over 1f out* **9/1**

59.91s (1.31) **Going Correction** +0.35s/f (Good)
WFA 3 from 4yo+ 6lb **12** Ran SP% **113.4**
Speed ratings (Par 103): **103,101,100,100,99 98,97,96,96,94 90,83**
CSF £56.70 CT £709.25 TOTE £11.10: £3.20, £1.60, £4.30; EX 82.30 Trifecta £1605.30.
Owner James Bowers **Bred** J Bowers **Trained** Great Habton, N Yorks
■ Stewards' Enquiry : Connor Beasley trainer said the gelding was unsuited by the good to soft going which was too soft for the gelding on this occasion.

FOCUS
A very moderate handicap. The winner is rated back to her 2yo form.
T/Plt: £29.00 to a £1 stake. Pool: £31,929.92 - 802.76 winning tickets T/Qpdt: £19.70 to a £1 stake. Pool: £3,255.18 - 121.97 winning tickets **Andrew Sheret**

3369 - 3375a (Foreign Racing) - See Raceform Interactive

3089 DEAUVILLE (R-H)
Friday, June 17

OFFICIAL GOING: Turf: soft; polytrack: standard

3376a PRIX DE BRETIGNY (CLAIMER) (5YO+) (POLYTRACK) 7f 110y
11:00 (11:00) 5-Y-O+ **£6,985** (£2,794; £2,095; £1,397; £698)

RPR

1 **Asulaman (GER)**38 9-8-11 0....................(b) AurelienLemaitre 7 80
(S Cerulis, France) **98/10**

2 1¼ **For Ever (FR)**18 5-9-1 0....................(b) AntoineHamelin 3 81
(Y Barberot, France) **9/1**

3 1 **Serez (IRE)**38 6-9-2 0....................(b) MickaelBarzalona 1 80
(Charley Rossi, France) **20/1**

4 shd **Menardais (FR)**47 1910 7-9-10 0.................... JeffersonSmith(3) 5 91
(T Castanheira, France) **11/5**2

5 hd **Louvain (FR)**32 7-9-1 0....................(b) EddyHardouin 2 78
(G Nicot, France) **11/1**

6 ¾ **Stormy Ride (IRE)**24 5-9-4 0....................(b) MaximeGuyon 4 79
(E Libaud, France) **57/10**3

7 1½ **Silverheels (IRE)**58 1576 7-9-5 0....................(b) ChristopheSoumillon 6 76
(Paul Cole) *hld up: rdn 2f out: nt qckn* **9/5**1

8 2 **Onirique (IRE)**10 5-9-1 0....................(p) StephanePasquier 8 67
(D Windrif, France) **14/1**

Owner Baron Yvan Del Marmol **Bred** Gestut Elsetal **Trained** France
WIN (incl. 1 euro stake): 10.80. PLACES: 3.90, 3.60, 5.30. DF: 35.10. SF: 75.10

3377a PRIX GIRL FRIEND (CONDITIONS) (4YO+) (POLYTRACK) 1m 1f 110y
12:00 (12:00) 4-Y-O+ **£12,132** (£4,852; £3,639; £2,426; £1,213)

RPR

1 **The Captain (FR)**38 5-8-8 0....................(p) EmmanuelEtienne(6) 6 94
(P Van De Poele, France) **48/10**

2 ½ **Sainte Amarante (FR)**14 4-8-10 0.................... TheoBachelot 5 89
(Yves de Nicolay, France) **42/10**3

3 snk **Hawke (IRE)**22 4-9-0 0....................(b) MaximeGuyon 7 93
(Mme Pia Brandt, France) **12/1**

4 2½ **Magneticjim (IRE)**23 2603 4-9-0 0.................... ChristopheSoumillon 2 88
(P Bary, France) **31/10**2

5 nk **Simba (FR)**14 8-9-0 0.................... ThierryThulliez 3 87
(C Lerner, France) **7/1**

6 1¾ **Waikika (FR)**22 5-8-10 0.................... ThierryJarnet 4 80
(Y Barberot, France) **9/1**

7 shd **Berkshire (IRE)**27 2464 5-9-0 0.................... GeraldMosse 1 83
(Paul Cole) *hld up: a in rr: rdn 3f out: no imp in st: nvr a factor* **12/5**1

WIN (incl. 1 euro stake): 5.80. PLACES: 2.50, 2.40. SF: 25.20
Owner Antoine Sauty De Chalon **Bred** A Sauty De Chalon **Trained** France

3378 - 3379a (Foreign Racing) - See Raceform Interactive

2952 LES LANDES
Friday, June 17

OFFICIAL GOING: Turf: firm
Wind: Moderate, across towards stand Weather: Cloudy

3380a QUILTER CHEVIOT H'CAP 7f
7:40 (7:40) 3-Y-O+ **£2,380** (£860; £510)

RPR

1 **Pas D'Action**18 2954 8-9-13 0....................(p) JemmaMarshall 1 53
(Mrs A Malzard, Jersey) *hld up: rdn to chal fr 2f out: led wl ins fnl f: drvn out* **11/4**2

2 ½ **Benoordenhout (IRE)**18 2954 5-10-2 0.................... TimClark 2 55
(T Le Brocq, Jersey) *led: hdd and no ex wl ins fnl f* **15/8**1

3 ½ **First Cat**33 2285 9-9-1 0.................... PhilipPrince 4 39
(K Kukk, Jersey) *trckd ldrs: rdn to chal fr 2f out: no ex* **8/1**

4 ½ **Valmina**18 2953 9-10-12 0....................(p) NickSlatter 5 62
(K Kukk, Jersey) *t.k.h: trckd ldr: ev ch inisde fnl f: one pce* **13/2**

5 ½ **Jackpot**22 2609 6-9-3 0 ow1....................(p) RichardCondon 3 38
(Brendan Powell) *hld up: outpcd fr 2f out: kpt on nr fin* **3/1**3

6 ¾ **Chapeau Bleu (IRE)**33 2284 4-9-13 0.................... MarkQuinlan 6 46
(Mrs C Gilbert, Jersey) *trckd ldrs: outpcd fr 2f out: btn ins fnl f* **7/1**

7 5 **Spanish Bounty**33 2284 11-9-8 0.................... MattieBatchelor 7 27
(Mrs A Malzard, Jersey) *s.s: a bhd* **7/1**

Owner J Jamouneau **Bred** Jenny Hall Bloodstock Ltd **Trained** St Ouen, Jersey

3381a LIBERATION BREWERY H'CAP 1m 4f
8:50 (8:53) 3-Y-O+ **£1,780** (£640; £380)

RPR

1 **Mr Opulence**18 2952 7-9-3 0.................... TimClark 8 42
(T Le Brocq, Jersey) *distant 2nd: squeezed and lost pl over 7f out: hdwy over 3f out: rdn to ld wl ins fnl f: all out* **2/1**1

2 1 **King Kenny**18 2952 11-8-12 0.................... NoraLooby 2 35
(Mrs A Corson, Jersey) *prom in main pack: wnt 2nd over 7f out: led 3f out: hung rt u.p fr 1f out: no ex* **11/2**3

3 1 **Spring Overture**52 1739 4-8-6 0 oh14 ow1.................... MissCRobinson 9 28
(Brendan Powell) *t.k.h: hld up: outpcd over 7f out: kpt on same pce fr 2f out* **7/1**

4 5 **Engaging Smile**18 2954 4-9-13 0.................... RichardCondon 3 41
(J Moon, Jersey) *led: sn clr: c bk to field 5f out: hdd 3f out: wknd* **10/1**

5 nk **Captain James (FR)**18 2955 6-8-8 0.................... AliceMills 1 21
(Mrs C Gilbert, Jersey) *hld up: unable to chal fr 2f out* **11/4**2

6 1 **Carrera**18 2955 6-9-1 0.................... MissMHooper 6 27
(Mrs A Malzard, Jersey) *hld up: hdwy 4f out: nvr able to chal* **13/2**

7 10 **Bowl Imperior**18 2952 4-10-12 0.................... MattieBatchelor 7 36
(Mrs A Malzard, Jersey) *hld up: drvn and lost pl over 4f out: sn btn* **11/2**3

8 4 **Albecq**18 2955 4-8-10 0.................... JemmaMarshall 5
(Mrs A Malzard, Jersey) *sn bhd* **14/1**

Owner S M Smith **Bred** Miss Victoria Haigh **Trained** Jersey

3336 ASCOT (R-H)

Saturday, June 18

OFFICIAL GOING: Good to soft (stands' side 7.8, centre 7.6, far side 7.6, round 6.4)

Wind: Virtually nil Weather: Overcast

3382 CHESHAM STKS (LISTED RACE) 7f

2:30 (2:32) (Class 1) 2-Y-O

£45,368 (£17,200; £8,608; £4,288; £2,152; £1,080) **Stalls** Centre

Form RPR

1 **Churchill (IRE)**[27] 2508 2-9-3 0 RyanMoore 8 100+
(A P O'Brien, Ire) *wl-made: lw: chsd ldrs: led over 2f out: rdn and drifted lft fr over 1f out: r.o wl and in command towards fin* **8/11**[1]

2 **2** ½ **Isomer (USA)**[36] 2204 2-9-3 0 JamieSpencer 10 99+
(Andrew Balding) *lengthy: lw: midfield: pushed along 4f out: hdwy 2f out: chsd wnr over 1f out: r.o to chal ins fnl f: hld nr fin* **25/1**

1 **3** 1 **Cunco (IRE)**[36] 2204 2-9-3 0 RobertHavlin 14 96+
(John Gosden) *athletic: str: keen to post: chsd ldrs: rdn and nt qckn 2f out: r.o fnl 150yds: gng on at fin* **7/2**[2]

413 **4** ½ **Mr Scaramanga**[17] 2786 2-9-3 0 PatDobbs 11 95
(Richard Hannon) *in tch: rdn and outpcd over 2f out: rallied and prog ins fnl f: styd on: nt pce to chal* **50/1**

1 **5** ½ **Frankuus (IRE)**[9] 3054 2-9-3 0 JoeFanning 12 94+
(Mark Johnston) *tall: lengthy: led: rdn and hdd over 2f out: nt qckn over 1f out but stl wl there: styd on same pce fnl 150yds* **15/2**[3]

013 **6** 1¼ **Thora Barber**[35] 2240 2-8-12 0 AndreaAtzeni 15 86
(David Evans) *racd keenly: chsd ldr to 1/2-way: sn rdn: nt qckn 2f out: kpt on u.p ins fnl f: edgd rt fnl 100yds and no ex* **40/1**

5 **7** ½ **Aiming For Rio (FR)**[9] 3091 2-8-12 0 MickaelBarzalona 6 84+
(Matthieu Palussiere, France) *leggy: midfield: nt clr run over 2f out: hdwy over 1f out: sn chalng: no ex fnl 75yds* **14/1**

41 **8** 1½ **Admiralty Arch**[37] 2193 2-9-3 0 JimmyFortune 4 86
(Richard Hannon) *in tch: effrt over 2f out: nt qckn over 1f out: one pce ins fnl f: no ex fnl 150yds* **20/1**

0 **9** 3 **Eldorado Creek (IRE)**[22] 2649 2-9-3 0 DavidNolan 9 78
(Richard Fahey) *str: hld up in rr: rdn and struggling to go pce 2f out: hdwy ins fnl f: styd on: nt pce to rch ldrs* **66/1**

10 ¾ **Justice Frederick (IRE)**[12] 2983 2-9-3 0 DonnachaO'Brien 7 76
(Paul D'Arcy) *leggy: hld up: effrt and impr over 2f out: chsd ldng bunch over 1f out: no real imp: wl btn fnl 100yds* **40/1**

2 **11** 1¼ **Magillen (IRE)**[18] 2757 2-9-3 0 FrankieDettori 2 73
(Charles Hills) *str: lw: hld up in midfield: hdwy 2f out: outpcd over 1f out: eased whn btn ins fnl f* **16/1**

231 **12** 9 **Masham Star (IRE)**[12] 2956 2-9-3 0 AdamKirby 3 51
(Mark Johnston) *racd keenly: hld up: hdwy 3f out: chalng 2f out: wknd over 1f out* **33/1**

13 13 **Filudo (FR)** 2-9-3 0 DanielTudhope 13 18
(David O'Meara) *lengthy: racd keenly in tch: rdn and wknd over 2f out: lft wl bhd over 1f out* **50/1**

1m 29.57s (1.97) **Going Correction** +0.30s/f (Good) **13** Ran SP% **126.3**
Speed ratings (Par 101): **100,99,98,97,97 95,95,93,90,89 87,77,62**
CSF £33.34 CT £58.17 TOTE £1.90: £1.02, £6.70, £1.80; EX 22.80 Trifecta £72.50.
Owner Michael Tabor & Derrick Smith & Mrs John Magnier **Bred** Liberty Bloodstock **Trained** Cashel, Co Tipperary

FOCUS

Race distances were as advertised, the temporary rail on the round course having been removed after racing on Thursday. There was just half a millimetre of rain overnight and good to soft was generally agreed by the jockeys as the right description of underfoot conditions. The opening time in a race run at an ordinary gallop was almost 4sec slower than standard. This looked a good renewal of the Chesham on paper, although they finished rather compressed. The race is confined to the progeny of stallions who won over 1m2f or further; that includes Frankel, whose representatives finished third and fifth. The far side of the group appeared disadvantaged, with high numbers dominating. It's hard to get too enthusiastic about the bare form but the winner was well backed and it'll be a surprise if he doesn't do better again.

3383 WOLFERTON H'CAP (LISTED RACE) 1m 2f

3:05 (3:05) (Class 1) (0-110,109) 4-Y-O+

£45,368 (£17,200; £8,608; £4,288; £2,152; £1,080) **Stalls** Low

Form RPR

64-3 **1** **Sir Isaac Newton**[14] 2924 4-9-0 **102** RyanMoore 5 111
(A P O'Brien, Ire) *swtg: stdd s: travelled strly in midfield: swtchd rt and effrt over 2f out: rdn to ld over 1f out: drvn and styd on ins fnl f: drvn out* **7/1**

141- **2** ½ **Second Wave (IRE)**[175] 8359 4-9-0 **102** [1] AdamKirby 8 110
(Charlie Appleby) *stdd after s: t.k.h: hld up in rr: swtchd lft and effrt over 2f out: hdwy u.p over 1f out: styd on strly to go 2nd 50yds: nvr quite getting to wnr* **20/1**

3511 **3** ¾ **Revolutionist (IRE)**[19] 2744 4-9-3 **105** JamesMcDonald 15 112+
(Mark Johnston) *lw: in tch in midfield but stuck wd: clsd to chse ldrs and rdn ent fnl 2f: drvn to chse wnr 1f out: kpt on but a hld: lost 2nd and one pce fnl 50yds* **9/1**

1-60 **4** hd **Arthenus**[35] 2246 4-8-12 **100** (p) FrederikTylicki 14 106
(James Fanshawe) *stdd s: hld up in rr: effrt on outer over 2f out: hdwy but stl only 9th over 1f out: styd on strly ins fnl f to go 4th nr fin: nvr quite getting to ldrs* **12/1**

06-2 **5** ¾ **Educate**[28] 2464 7-9-6 **108** MickaelBarzalona 6 113
(Ismail Mohammed) *hld up towards rr: sme prog 1/2-way: effrt on inner to chse ldrs 2f out: drvn over 1f out: kpt on same pce ins fnl f* **16/1**

12-0 **6** 2¾ **Best Of Times**[21] 2684 4-9-3 **105** JamesDoyle 13 104+
(Saeed bin Suroor) *chsd ldrs: wnt 2nd over 2f out: sn rdn and chalng: led wl over 1f out: sn drvn and hdd: changed legs: faltered and lost 2nd 1f out: wknd ins fnl f* **4/1**[1]

0506 **7** ½ **Fire Fighting (IRE)**[15] 2866 5-9-2 **104** (b) JoeFanning 12 102
(Mark Johnston) *dwlt and bustled along early: towards rr: swtchd rt and effrt over 2f out: hdwy u.p to chse ldrs over 1f out: kpt on same pce ins fnl f* **25/1**

-213 **8** nse **Noble Gift**[28] 2465 6-9-2 **104** CallumShepherd 9 102
(William Knight) *taken down early: t.k.h early: chsd ldr tl led travelling strly 3f out: rdn over 2f out: hdd wl over 1f out and drvn: no ex ent fnl f: wknd ins fnl f* **33/1**

1-11 **9** ½ **Maleficent Queen**[31] 2363 4-9-4 **106** PhillipMakin 16 103
(Keith Dalgleish) *swtg: hld up in tch in midfield: effrt jst over 2f out: no imp tl styd on steadily ins fnl f: nvr gng pce to get involved* **9/2**[2]

456 **10** 9 **Battalion (IRE)**[28] 2464 6-9-5 **107** (p) PatCosgrave 7 86
(William Haggas) *fly j. as stalls opened and slowly away: towards rr: swtchd rt and effrt over 2f out: no imp u.p over 1f out: wknd fnl f* **25/1**

00-4 **11** hd **Not So Sleepy**[23] 2626 4-9-2 **104** (t) JimCrowley 4 83
(Hughie Morrison) *taken down early: t.k.h early: chsd ldrs: rdn and unable qck over 2f out: wknd over 1f out* **25/1**

-245 **12** nk **Maverick Wave (USA)**[85] 1069 5-9-7 **109** RobertHavlin 2 87
(John Gosden) *hld up in midfield: rdn 3f out: struggling and lost pl over 2f out: wl btn over 1f out* **20/1**

-303 **13** 15 **What About Carlo (FR)**[15] 2866 5-8-12 **100** JimmyFortune 3 48
(Eve Johnson Houghton) *fly j. as stalls opened and s.i.s: bustled along and sn rcvrd to chse ldrs: rdn and lost pl over 2f out: sn btn: wknd qckly over 1f out: eased ins fnl f* **20/1**

2-22 **14** 8 **Pacify**[38] 2157 4-9-0 **102** (v[1]) FMBerry 10 34
(Ralph Beckett) *lw: hld up towards rr: effrt jst over 2f out: sn btn and bhd: eased ins fnl f: t.o* **6/1**[3]

11-4 **15** 17 **Oceanographer**[48] 1885 4-9-0 **102** (p) WilliamBuick 1
(Charlie Appleby) *swtg: racd keenly: led tl rdn and hdd 3f out: lost pl and bhd 2f out: eased fnl f: t.o* **8/1**

2m 7.59s (0.19) **Going Correction** +0.30s/f (Good) **15** Ran SP% **128.4**
Speed ratings (Par 111): **111,110,110,109,109 107,106,106,106,99 98,98,86,80,66**
CSF £147.95 CT £1303.97 TOTE £7.10: £2.20, £6.60, £3.20; EX 153.40 Trifecta £3181.20.
Owner Derrick Smith & Mrs John Magnier & Michael Tabor **Bred** Newsells Park Stud **Trained** Cashel, Co Tipperary

FOCUS

A wide open, classy handicap, with no horse in the line-up rated below 100. The winner has been rated back to his best.

3384 HARDWICKE STKS (GROUP 2) 1m 4f

3:40 (3:43) (Class 1) 4-Y-O+

£127,597 (£48,375; £24,210; £12,060; £6,052; £3,037) **Stalls** Low

Form RPR

3-11 **1** **Dartmouth**[43] 1995 4-9-1 114 OlivierPeslier 4 121
(Sir Michael Stoute) *midfield: plld out and hdwy jst over 2f out: rdn to ld narrowly jst over 1f out: edgd rt whn duelling w rival ins fnl f: r.o gamely* **10/1**

1-40 **2** hd **Highland Reel (IRE)**[55] 1690 4-9-1 119 SeamieHeffernan 8 120
(A P O'Brien, Ire) *swtg: racd keenly on outer: chsd ldrs: wnt 2nd to chal 2f out and rdr dropped whip: carried hd to one side whn carried rt and duelling w wnr ins fnl f: r.o u.p: jst hld* **6/1**[2]

12-1 **3** 3¼ **Almodovar (IRE)**[31] 2377 4-9-1 107 GeorgeBaker 7 115
(David Lanigan) *lw: led: rdn and hdd jst over 1f out: unable to go w front pair fnl 100yds: styd on same pce* **9/1**

12-1 **4** 3¾ **Mount Logan (IRE)**[28] 2465 5-9-1 110 AndreaAtzeni 10 109
(Roger Varian) *swtg: s.i.s: hld up: rdn and hdwy over 2f out: chsd ldng trio over 1f out: styd on ins fnl f: no imp* **16/1**

53-1 **5** 3¾ **Beautiful Romance**[37] 2189 4-8-12 112 JamesDoyle 6 100
(Saeed bin Suroor) *lw: hld up: swtchd lft and rdn over 2f out: hdwy over 1f out: kpt on ins fnl f: nt pce to trble ldrs* **6/1**[2]

33-2 **6** 3 **Wicklow Brave**[43] 1995 7-9-1 112 WilliamBuick 2 98
(W P Mullins, Ire) *missed break: bhd: nvr really travelling wl: plugged on u.p over 1f out: nvr a threat* **16/1**

1-24 **7** 1 **Simple Verse (IRE)**[14] 2894 4-8-12 115 OisinMurphy 5 93
(Ralph Beckett) *lw: racd keenly: chsd ldr: pushed along 3f out: rdn and lost 2nd 2f out: wknd over 1f out* **7/1**[3]

13-1 **8** 4 **Exosphere**[49] 1863 4-9-1 119 RyanMoore 1 90
(Sir Michael Stoute) *midfield: rdn and nt pick up over 2f out: sn wknd: wl btn over 1f out* **6/4**[1]

30-1 **9** 1¼ **Astronereus (IRE)**[35] 2241 5-9-1 111 PatDobbs 3 88
(Amanda Perrett) *chsd ldrs: rdn over 2f out: wknd wl over 1f out* **20/1**

2m 32.06s (-0.44) **Going Correction** +0.30s/f (Good) **9** Ran SP% **116.7**
Speed ratings (Par 115): **113,112,110,108,105 103,103,100,99**
CSF £69.37 CT £566.43 TOTE £7.30: £2.20, £1.80, £3.10; EX 62.30 Trifecta £563.20.
Owner The Queen **Bred** Darley **Trained** Newmarket, Suffolk

■ Stewards' Enquiry : Olivier Peslier the jockey was cautioned as to his future conduct.

FOCUS

Another warm edition of the Hardwicke Stakes. The first two came close together and the result was confirmed only after a stewards' enquiry. Sir Michael Stoute has now won this event ten times, including seven of the last eleven runnings, and has had the last two beaten favourites too. The runner-up sets the standard.

3385 DIAMOND JUBILEE STKS (BRITISH CHAMPIONS SERIES & GLOBAL SPRINT CHALLENGE) (GROUP 1) 6f

4:20 (4:21) (Class 1) 4-Y-O+

£340,260 (£129,000; £64,560; £32,160; £16,140; £8,100) **Stalls** Centre

Form RPR

12-5 **1** **Twilight Son**[38] 2159 4-9-3 117 RyanMoore 3 118
(Henry Candy) *t.k.h: chsd ldng pair: effrt over 1f out: wnt 2nd and ev ch ent fnl f: r.o to ld 50yds out: rdn out* **7/2**[3]

32-4 **2** nk **Gold-Fun (IRE)**[48] 1911 7-9-3 119 (v) ChristopheSoumillon 5 117
(Richard Gibson, Hong Kong) *lengthy: str: hld up in tch in midfield: clsd and nt clr run over 1f out: gap opened and hdwy u.p 1f out: r.o wl u.p fnl 100yds: snatched 2nd last stride* **7/1**

0-15 **3** shd **Signs Of Blessing (IRE)**[33] 2317 5-9-3 113 OlivierPeslier 6 117
(F Rohaut, France) *sn led: rdn over 1f out: drvn jst ins fnl f: hdd 50yds out: kpt on but hld cl home: lost 2nd last stride* **25/1**

3-11 **4** hd **Magical Memory (IRE)**[38] 2159 4-9-3 114 FrankieDettori 10 116+
(Charles Hills) *stdd s: hld up in tch in rr: swtchd lft over 1f out: sn rdn and qcknd to press ldr ins fnl f: no ex and one pce towards fin* **3/1**[1]

0-22 **5** shd **Suedois (FR)**[38] 2159 5-9-3 111 DanielTudhope 4 116
(David O'Meara) *hld up in tch in last pair: rdn and hdwy over 1f out: drvn and ev ch ins fnl f: styd on same pce towards fin* **12/1**

/15- **6** 2 **Undrafted (USA)**[70] 6-9-3 118 JohnRVelazquez 2 110
(Wesley A Ward, U.S.A) *t.k.h: hld up chsng ldrs: effrt over 1f out: drvn and unable qck ent fnl f: styd on same pce after* **8/1**

7 2½ **Holler (AUS)**[86] 3-9-3 117 (bt) JamesMcDonald 9 102
(J O'Shea, Australia) *str: broke wl: sn hdd and chsd ldr: rdn over 1f out: drvn and lost 2nd ent fnl f: wknd fnl 150yds* **12/1**

14-1 **8** ¾ **The Tin Man**[26] 2546 4-9-3 115 TomQueally 8 99+
(James Fanshawe) *stdd s: t.k.h: hld up in tch in midfield: effrt over 1f out: struggling to qckn whn sltly impeded jst ins fnl f: sn wknd* **10/3**[2]

0-30 **9** 3¾ **Mattmu**[38] 2159 4-9-3 110 (p) DavidAllan 1 87
(Tim Easterby) *str: in tch in midfield: rdn wl over 1f out: sn outpcd and bhd 1f out: wknd* **20/1**

1m 13.84s (-0.66) **Going Correction** +0.30s/f (Good)
WFA 3 from 4yo+ 7lb **9** Ran SP% **117.9**
Speed ratings (Par 117): **116,115,115,115,115 112,109,108,103**
CSF £28.96 CT £534.75 TOTE £4.50: £1.60, £2.50, £6.90; EX 30.20 Trifecta £399.00.
Owner Godfrey Wilson & Cheveley Park Stud **Bred** Mrs C R D Wilson **Trained** Kingston Warren, Oxon

FOCUS
A smaller field than usual, and it was a real international affair, with the best of the British taken on by last year's winner from the USA, and by contenders from Hong Kong, Australia and France. The form is questionable, however, as the pace was modest, it paid to race handily, and they finished in a heap. The third is the key to the form and has been rated as running a small pb.

3386 WOKINGHAM STKS (HERITAGE H'CAP) 6f

5:00 (5:00) (Class 2) (0-110,109) 3-Y-O+

£108,937 (£32,620; £16,310; £8,155; £4,077; £2,047) **Stalls** Centre

Form RPR

0-00 **1** **Outback Traveller (IRE)**[42] 2027 5-9-1 **100** MartinHarley 28 112+
(Robert Cowell) *lw: trckd ldrs nr side travelling wl: gps merged over 2f out: rdn over 1f out: qcknd to ld ins fnl f: edgd rt fnl 100yds: kpt on gamely nr fin* **10/1**[3]

1-12 **2** hd **Brando**[37] 2188 4-9-2 **101** TomEaves 11 112+
(Kevin Ryan) *midfield in far side gp: hdwy whn gps merged over 2f out: rdn to chal over 1f out: r.o for press ins fnl f: jst hld* **7/1**[1]

6453 **3** 1½ **Glen Moss (IRE)**[28] 2485 7-9-1 **100** PhillipMakin 26 107
(Michael Dods) *lw: chsd ldr on nr side: gps merged over 2f out: led over 1f out: hdd ins fnl f: styd on same pce towards fin* **25/1**

31-5 **4** ¾ **Absolutely So (IRE)**[42] 2030 6-9-10 **109** OisinMurphy 6 113
(Andrew Balding) *lw: in tch on far side: pushed along whn gps merged over 2f out: hdwy over 1f out: r.o ins fnl f: nt quite pce of ldrs* **25/1**

10-3 **5** 1 **Buckstay (IRE)**[42] 2027 6-9-10 **109** (p) JamieSpencer 1 110+
(Peter Chapple-Hyam) *stdd s: hld up in rr on far side: gps merged over 2f out: swtchd lft and hdwy over 1f out: r.o ins fnl f: nt rch ldrs* **10/1**[3]

20-0 **6** nk **Burnt Sugar (IRE)**[6] 3195 4-9-7 **106** (b) JamesMcDonald 27 106
(Richard Hannon) *hld up on nr side: gps merged over 2f out: rdn and hdwy whn edgd rt over 1f out: r.o ins fnl f: nt rch ldrs* **20/1**

-111 **7** nse **Spring Loaded (IRE)**[84] 1090 4-9-1 **100** ShaneKelly 14 100
(Paul D'Arcy) *hld up on far side: gps merged over 2f out: hdwy 2f out: rdn and chsd ldrs over 1f out: styd on ins fnl f* **12/1**

24-0 **8** ½ **Toofi (FR)**[37] 2188 5-9-4 **103** AndreaAtzeni 30 101
(Robert Cowell) *hld up on nr side: edgd rt whn gps merged over 2f out: hdwy over 1f out: r.o ins fnl f: no further imp nr fin* **8/1**[2]

-000 **9** ½ **Jack Dexter**[38] 2159 7-9-3 **102** FMBerry 8 99
(Jim Goldie) *midfield on far side: gps merged over 2f out: sn nt clr run: rdn and hdwy over 1f out: styd on ins fnl f: nt rch ldrs* **25/1**

-502 **10** nk **Shared Equity**[14] 2898 5-9-1 **100** DavidNolan 7 96
(Jedd O'Keeffe) *racd on far side: prom: gps merged over 2f out: led 2f out: rdn and hdd over 1f out: styd on same pce fnl 100yds* **16/1**

2532 **11** hd **Mutawathea**[42] 2027 5-8-12 **102** (p) EdwardGreatrex(5) 3 97
(Simon Crisford) *racd on far side: chsd ldrs: rdn whn gps merged over 2f out: effrt over 1f out: r.o towards fin* **20/1**

-024 **12** ½ **Coulsty (IRE)**[42] 2030 5-9-7 **109** (b[1]) TomMarquand(3) 19 102
(Richard Hannon) *lw: midfield on far side: rdn and hdwy whn gps merged over 2f out: styd on ins fnl f: one pce fnl 50yds: nt rch ldrs* **28/1**

-045 **13** nk **Dinkum Diamond (IRE)**[21] 2691 8-8-12 **102** HectorCrouch(5) 13 94
(Henry Candy) *racd on far side: trckd ldrs: rdn whn gps merged over 2f out: stl wl there over 1f out: no ex fnl 150yds* **33/1**

-356 **14** ¾ **Poyle Vinnie**[26] 2546 6-9-2 **104** AlistairRawlinson(3) 10 94
(Michael Appleby) *lw: prom on far side: led whn gps merged over 2f out: sn hdd: no ex fnl 100yds* **33/1**

-565 **15** nk **The Happy Prince (IRE)**[20] 2716 4-9-2 **101** (t) RyanMoore 20 90
(A P O'Brien, Ire) *lw: midfield on nr side: swtchd rt whn gps merged over 2f out: hdwy over 1f out: kpt on ins fnl f: nt rch ldrs: one pce fnl 75yds* **7/1**[1]

0-10 **16** nk **Accession (IRE)**[42] 2027 7-8-8 **100** GeorgeWood(7) 4 88
(Charlie Fellowes) *lw: in tch on far side: gps merged over 2f out: rdn and nt qckn 2f out: styd on same pce ins fnl f* **40/1**

-000 **17** ½ **Humidor (IRE)**[14] 2895 9-9-4 **103** PatCosgrave 2 90
(George Baker) *edgy: midfield on far side: gps merged over 2f out: rdn over 1f out: no imp* **66/1**

1640 **18** 1 **Boom The Groom (IRE)**[14] 2895 5-9-2 **101** WilliamCarson 18 81
(Tony Carroll) *prom on far side: rdn whn gps merged over 2f out: wknd over 1f out* **50/1**

-266 **18** dht **Tupi (IRE)**[21] 2691 4-9-10 **109** (b[1]) PatDobbs 23 89
(Richard Hannon) *in tch on nr side: gps merged over 2f out: rdn and outpcd wl over 1f out: kpt on same pce ins fnl f* **20/1**

5600 **20** shd **Stepper Point**[65] 1439 7-9-4 **103** (p) SamHitchcott 21 83
(William Muir) *racd nr side gp: overall ldr: gps merged and hdd over 2f out: wknd over 1f out* **66/1**

0-03 **21** 1¼ **Huntsmans Close**[29] 2434 6-9-1 **100** JamesDoyle 9 76
(Roger Charlton) *swtg: racd far side in midfield: gps merged over 2f out: sn rdn: no hdwy over 1f out* **16/1**

50-3 **22** nse **Interception (IRE)**[28] 2474 6-9-8 **107** GeorgeBaker 12 83
(David Lanigan) *swtg: racd in far side gp: gps merged over 2f out: rdn over 1f out: no hdwy tl tried to keep on ins fnl f: nvr able to get nr ldrs* **12/1**

-200 **23** nk **Majestic Moon (IRE)**[42] 2027 6-8-10 **100** GeorgeBuckell(5) 17 75
(John Gallagher) *lw: prom on far side: rdn whn gps merged over 2f out: wknd over 1f out* **40/1**

30-4 **24** 1 **Ninjago**[28] 2488 6-9-3 **102** AdamKirby 24 74
(Paul Midgley) *racd nr side: hld up: gps merged over 2f out: rdn wl over 1f out: nvr a threat* **14/1**

03-0 **25** 1 **Ashpan Sam**[14] 2898 7-9-1 **100** LukeMorris 15 68
(David W Drinkwater) *racd far side: led gp: hdd whn gps merged over 2f out: rdn and wknd over 1f out* **66/1**

-504 **26** 3¼ **B Fifty Two (IRE)**[36] 2206 7-9-1 **100** DarryllHolland 5 58
(Charles Hills) *racd far side: hld up: outpcd 1/2-way: gps merged over 2f out: nvr a threat* **33/1**

3-66 **27** 3¼ **Salateen**[28] 2485 4-9-3 **102** DanielTudhope 25 50
(David O'Meara) *in tch on nr side: rdn and wknd whn gps merged over 2f out* **25/1**

4451 **28** 3¼ **Flash Fire (IRE)**[42] 2027 4-9-10 **109** WilliamBuick 16 46
(Charlie Appleby) *racd in far side gp: in tch: chsng ldrs whn gps merged over 2f out: wknd over 1f out: eased whn btn ins fnl f* **20/1**

1m 14.05s (-0.45) **Going Correction** +0.30s/f (Good) **28** Ran SP% **146.1**
Speed ratings (Par 109): **115,114,112,111,110 110,109,109,108,108 107,107,106,105,105 105,104,103,103,102 101,101,100,99**
CSF £70.23 CT £1811.71 TOTE £10.50: £2.50, £2.60, £12.00, £7.10; EX 95.00 Trifecta £5397.70.
Owner Lordship Stud & Mrs J Morley **Bred** Tally-Ho Stud **Trained** Six Mile Bottom, Cambs

FOCUS
There was just a 9lb spread in this high-class handicap and, remarkably, a mark of 100 was required to get a run. The field divided into three groups before merging at around the two pole, the winner coming out of a bunch of nine who raced towards the stands' side. The third helps set the standard, while the fourth has been rated to his Listed winning form.

3387 QUEEN ALEXANDRA STKS (CONDITIONS RACE) 2m 5f 159y

5:35 (5:37) (Class 2) 4-Y-O+

£49,800 (£14,912; £7,456; £3,728; £1,864; £936) **Stalls** Low

Form RPR

211/ **1** **Commissioned (IRE)**[94] 7242 6-9-2 97 (p) AdamKirby 15 103+
(Gordon Elliott, Ire) *hld up in tch in midfield: effrt to chse ldrs over 2f out: rdn to chse ldr over 1f out: led 1f out: styd on strly* **12/1**

465 **2** 1¾ **Cayirli (FR)**[28] 2468 4-9-0 91 TimmyMurphy 13 101
(Seamus Durack) *led after 2f tl after 4f: chsd ldr tl 12f out: styd prom: rdn to ld 2f out: hdd over 1f out: edgd rt and styd on same pce fnl f* **40/1**

200- **3** 3¾ **Clondaw Warrior (IRE)**[63] 7277 9-9-2 108 RyanMoore 16 98+
(W P Mullins, Ire) *lw: stdd s: hld up in last quartet: effrt over 2f out: gd hdwy u.p over 1f out: chsd clr ldng pair jst ins fnl f: styd on: nvr threatened ldrs* **7/2**[1]

23-4 **4** 1½ **Oriental Fox (GER)**[42] 2025 8-9-5 108 JoeFanning 6 100
(Mark Johnston) *t.k.h: hld up in tch in midfield: effrt over 2f out: hdwy u.p over 1f out: wnt 4th jst ins fnl f: styd on: nvr threatened ldrs* **7/2**[1]

126 **5** 2 **Sandro Botticelli (IRE)**[52] 1772 4-9-3 107 FrankieDettori 9 98
(John Ryan) *lw: hld up in midfield: clsd 5f out: swtchd lft effrt 2f out: 7th and keeping but nt threatening ldrs whn nt clr run ent fnl f: gap opened and r.o fnl 100yds to snatch 5th last stride* **8/1**

10-1 **6** shd **Amour De Nuit (IRE)**[45] 1963 4-9-3 106 LukeMorris 11 98
(Sir Mark Prescott Bt) *t.k.h: wl in tch in midfield: effrt to over 2f out: sn drvn and ev ch tl no ex over 1f out: wknd ins fnl f* **6/1**[2]

4430 **7** 1¼ **First Mohican**[28] 2468 8-9-2 101 JimmyFortune 4 94
(Alan King) *s.i.s: hld up towards rr: hdwy 4f out: pushed lft and effrt over 2f out: no imp u.p over 1f out: plugged on same pce ins fnl f* **40/1**

5 **8** nk **The Minch (IRE)**[28] 2486 5-9-2 0 DanielTudhope 20 93
(Jim Goldie) *stdd and dropped in after s: hld up towards rr: hdwy into midfield after 6f: effrt on outer over 2f out: no imp tl kpt on steadily ins fnl f: nvr trbld ldrs* **16/1**

-126 **9** nk **Seaside Sizzler**[13] 2932 9-9-2 88 JimCrowley 3 93
(William Knight) *chsd ldrs: effrt to chse ldr 3f out: ev ch over 2f out tl no ex over 1f out: lost 3rd and btn 1f out: wknd ins fnl f* **33/1**

1-34 **10** 1 **Pinzolo**[107] 793 5-9-2 101 WilliamBuick 14 92
(Charlie Appleby) *stdd s: hld up in rr: effrt over 2f out: sme hdwy and edging rt over 1f out: nvr trbld ldrs* **16/1**

11-2 **11** 1½ **Magic Circle (IRE)**[48] 1893 4-9-0 90 FMBerry 5 91
(Ralph Beckett) *lw: hld up in tch in midfield: nt clrest of runs: swtchd lft and effrt over 2f out: no hdwy over 1f out: wknd fnl f* **7/1**[3]

30-5 **12** 2 **Tommy Docc (IRE)**[107] 793 4-9-0 93 PhillipMakin 2 89
(Keith Dalgleish) *led for 2f: styd chsng ldrs tl 6th and outpcd u.p 2f out: wknd over 1f out* **40/1**

13 4 **Agenor (GER)**[66] 5-9-2 84 AlexanderPietsch 18 85
(C Von Der Recke, Germany) *stdd s: hld up in rr: effrt on outer over 2f out: no imp: wl btn over 1f out: n.d* **66/1**

1-05 **14** ¾ **Grumeti**[37] 2194 8-9-2 88 AdamBeschizza 7 85
(Alan King) *hld up towards rr: effrt 2f out: sn drvn and no prog: wl btn fnl f* **25/1**

500- **15** 4 **Simenon (IRE)**[245] 7277 9-9-2 102 MartinHarley 17 81
(W P Mullins, Ire) *t.k.h: hld up in midfield: hdwy to chse ldr after 3f: led after 4f tl rdn and hdd 2f out: lost pl and btn over 1f out: fdd fnl f* **16/1**

-200 **16** 48 **Shades Of Silver**[13] 2932 6-9-2 87 JamieSpencer 12 38
(Ed de Giles) *chsd ldrs: wnt 3nd 12f out tl 3f out: lost pl and bhd 2f out: sn eased: t.o* **50/1**

1-01 **17** 4½ **Frosty Berry**[73] 1273 7-9-2 103 ShaneGray 1 34
(Ed de Giles) *prom early: sn settled bk into midfield: effrt over 2f out: sn struggling: wknd over 1f out: eased fnl f: t.o* **20/1**

-210 **18** hd **Havisham**[28] 2486 4-9-0 82 OisinMurphy 8 34
(Andrew Balding) *hld up in rr: rdn 4f out: no hdwy: lost tch 2f out: eased fnl f: t.o* **50/1**

5m 0.77s (11.37) **Going Correction** +0.30s/f (Good)
WFA 4 from 5yo+ 2lb **18** Ran SP% **132.0**
Speed ratings (Par 109): **91,90,89,88,87 87,87,87,87,86 86,85,83,83,82 64,63,63**
CSF £455.68 CT £2063.84 TOTE £15.50: £4.40, £12.60, £2.00; EX 611.10 Trifecta £3360.10.
Owner Nick Bradley Racing Nineteen Partnership **Bred** Kilfrush Stud **Trained** Longwood, Co Meath

FOCUS
This was not the extreme stamina test it could have been as the pace was fairly steady for a long way and plenty raced keenly. A small Flat pb from the winner.
T/Jkpt: Not won. T/Plt: £1,080.30 to a £1 stake. Pool: £533,428.56 - 360.43 winning units
T/Qpdt: £150.10 to a £1 stake. Pool: £39,104.18 - 192.68 winning units
Darren Owen & Steve Payne

3342 AYR (L-H)

Saturday, June 18

OFFICIAL GOING: Good to firm (good in places; 8.0)
Wind: Almost nil Weather: Cloudy, bright

3388 ARNOLD CLARK BRITISH STALLION STUDS EBF NOVICE STKS (PLUS 10 RACE) 6f

1:50 (1:51) (Class 4) 2-Y-O **£4,528** (£1,347; £673; £336) **Stalls** High

Form RPR

3 **1** **Miss Infinity (IRE)**[10] 3024 2-8-11 0 PaulMulrennan 2 85+
(Mark Johnston) *mde all: pushed along and clr over 1f out: edgd lft and kpt on strly fnl f: unchal* **9/2**[2]

2 2¾ **Smokey Lane (IRE)** 2-9-2 0 SamJames 5 81
(David Evans) *chsd wnr thrght: rdn along 2f out: kpt on fnl f: nt pce to chal* **16/1**

0154 **3** *2 3/4* **Cullingworth (IRE)**[22] 2664 2-9-1 0........................ NatalieHambling(7) 4 78
(Richard Fahey) *dwlt: hld up: pushed along 1/2-way: rdn and hdwy over 1f out: kpt on fnl f: nrst fin* **9/1**

3 **4** *1 1/2* **Rebel De Lope**[15] 2873 2-8-13 0........................ MichaelJMMurphy(3) 6 68
(Charles Hills) *missed break: hld up: hdwy on outside 1/2-way: rdn wl over 1f out: sn no imp: edgd lft and btn ins fnl f* **8/13**[1]

5 *6* **Oceanic (IRE)** 2-9-2 0........................ JasonHart 8 48
(John Quinn) *dwlt and wnt rt s: hld up: hdwy over 2f out: rdn and wknd over 1f out* **8/1**[3]

03 **6** *3 3/4* **La Haule Lady**[25] 2552 2-8-11 0........................ JackGarritty 7 31
(Paul Midgley) *chsd ldrs tl rdn and wknd over 2f out* **22/1**

0 **7** *7* **Scotch Myst**[16] 2830 2-9-2 0........................ GeorgeChaloner 3 14
(Richard Fahey) *trckd ldrs: rdn and hung lft over 2f out: sn wknd* **22/1**

1m 12.79s (0.39) **Going Correction** +0.075s/f (Good) **7** Ran SP% **115.8**
Speed ratings (Par 95): **100,96,92,90,82 77,68**
CSF £69.60 TOTE £5.10: £2.80, £8.30; EX 67.50 Trifecta £394.00.
Owner Mrs Jane Newett **Bred** Desert Star Phoenix Jvc **Trained** Middleham Moor, N Yorks

FOCUS
The going was good to firm, good in places. A fair novice contest run at a sound pace. A nice step forward from the winner, with the third rated to his best bar his Newbury run.

3389 SUNSPORT H'CAP 1m
2:20 (2:22) (Class 3) (0-95,92) 3-Y-O
£9,337 (£2,796; £1,398; £699; £349; £175) **Stalls** Low

Form RPR

3-46 **1** **Timeless Art (IRE)**[35] 2239 3-8-5 **76**........................ JoeyHaynes 3 81
(K R Burke) *s.i.s: hld up in rr: hdwy on outside to ld over 1f out: rdn and hld on wl towards fin* **9/4**[1]

5-05 **2** *hd* **Whitman**[28] 2480 3-9-7 **92**........................ PaulMulrennan 2 96
(Mark Johnston) *led: rdn and hdd over 1f out: rallied and ev ch fnl f: hld nr fin* **8/1**

322 **3** *nk* **Haraz (IRE)**[22] 2657 3-8-6 **77**........................ JamesSullivan 4 80
(David O'Meara) *unruly bef s: hld up: hdwy against far rail 2f out: sn rdn: kpt on wl fnl f* **10/1**

2310 **4** *1* **Flyboy (IRE)**[14] 2891 3-8-11 **82**........................ SamJames 1 83
(David O'Meara) *prom: drvn and outpcd wl over 1f out: kpt on ins fnl f: nt pce to chal* **7/2**[3]

0121 **5** *nk* **Billy Roberts (IRE)**[14] 2907 3-8-11 **82**........................ ConnorBeasley 6 82
(Richard Guest) *t.k.h early: pressed ldr: ev ch over 2f out to over 1f out: no ex ins fnl f* **5/2**[2]

6-50 **6** *1 3/4* **Doubly Motivated (IRE)**[45] 1966 3-8-12 **86**....... MichaelJMMurphy(3) 5 82
(Charles Hills) *t.k.h: trckd ldrs: rdn over 2f out: edgd lft and outpcd fr over 1f out* **9/1**

1m 42.19s (-1.61) **Going Correction** -0.225s/f (Firm) **6** Ran SP% **111.8**
Speed ratings (Par 103): **99,98,98,97,97 95**
CSF £19.96 TOTE £3.10: £1.40, £3.50; EX 22.60 Trifecta £188.20.
Owner Owners For Owners: Timeless Art **Bred** Sarl Elevage Du Haras De Bourgeauville **Trained** Middleham Moor, N Yorks

FOCUS
Due to rail movements the actual race distance was 1m 21yds. Not a strong contest for the grade but it produced an exciting finish. The third has been rated to form.

3390 SCOTTISH SUN ON SUNDAY H'CAP 1m
2:55 (2:55) (Class 2) (0-105,102) 4-Y-O+
£18,675 (£5,592; £2,796; £1,398; £699; £351) **Stalls** Low

Form RPR

0222 **1** **Gabrial's Kaka (IRE)**[21] 2684 6-8-12 **93**........................ GeorgeChaloner 7 101
(Richard Fahey) *hld up: effrt and rdn whn n.m.r briefly over 2f out: hdwy over 1f out: led wl ins fnl f: kpt on wl* **8/1**

0403 **2** *hd* **Express Himself (IRE)**[17] 2796 5-9-5 **100**........................ MartinDwyer 10 107
(Ed McMahon) *s.s: hld up: rdn: hdwy and weaved through fr over 1f out: chal wl ins fnl f: jst hld* **5/1**[1]

00-3 **3** *1* **Margaret's Mission (IRE)**[42] 2026 5-8-4 **85**........................ JamesSullivan 6 90
(Jim Goldie) *reluctant to enter stalls: hld up: rdn 3f out: hdwy on outside to ld over 1f out: edgd lft and hdd wl ins fnl f: no ex* **10/1**

0041 **4** *3/4* **Sound Advice**[21] 2684 7-9-7 **102**........................ RobertWinston 11 105
(Keith Dalgleish) *hld up in tch: smooth hdwy to ld over 2f out: rdn and hdd over 1f out: kpt on same pce fnl f* **12/1**

6141 **5** *3/4* **Treasury Notes (IRE)**[16] 2833 4-8-11 **92**........................ SamJames 5 94
(David O'Meara) *hld up: hdwy on ins over 2f out: sn rdn: kpt on ins fnl f: nt pce to chal* **11/2**[2]

0132 **6** *3/4* **Get Knotted (IRE)**[8] 3115 4-8-11 **92**........................(p) PaulMulrennan 8 92
(Michael Dods) *prom chsng gp: stdy hdwy and cl up over 2f out: rdn and edgd lft over 1f out: sn one pce* **8/1**

-600 **7** *2 1/2* **Two For Two (IRE)**[17] 2796 8-8-13 **94**........................ JoeyHaynes 9 88
(David Loughnane) *hld up: hdwy on outside and ev ch wl over 1f out: outpcd fnl f* **20/1**

3046 **8** *1/2* **Fort Bastion (IRE)**[17] 2796 7-8-9 **95**........................(v) JoshDoyle(5) 2 88
(David O'Meara) *s.i.s: hld up: rdn whn n.m.r briefly over 2f out: no imp fr over 1f out* **10/1**

0032 **9** *1* **Lat Hawill (IRE)**[16] 2833 5-9-2 **97**........................ ConnorBeasley 1 88
(Keith Dalgleish) *hld up in midfield: drvn along over 2f out: sn outpcd: n.d after* **12/1**

-302 **10** *nk* **Off Art**[17] 2796 6-9-0 **95**........................(p) JackGarritty 3 85
(Tim Easterby) *chsd clr ldng pair to bef 1/2-way: rdn over 2f out: lost pl wl over 1f out* **10/1**

0233 **11** *4 1/2* **Swift Emperor (IRE)**[19] 2744 4-8-9 **90**........................ JasonHart 4 70
(David Barron) *disp ld at str pce to over 2f out: wknd over 1f out* **13/2**[3]

2261 **12** *14* **Capo Rosso (IRE)**[9] 3055 6-9-4 **99**........................ RichardKingscote 12 46
(Tom Dascombe) *set str gallop: hdd over 2f out: sn struggling: eased whn no ch fnl f* **11/1**

1m 39.98s (-3.82) **Going Correction** -0.225s/f (Firm) **12** Ran SP% **123.4**
Speed ratings (Par 109): **110,109,108,108,107 106,104,103,102,102 97,83**
CSF £49.78 CT £418.03 TOTE £9.30: £3.20, £2.20, £3.30; EX 63.90 Trifecta £990.40.
Owner Dr Marwan Koukash **Bred** Dave Orme **Trained** Musley Bank, N Yorks

FOCUS
Due to rail movements the actual race distance was 1m 21yds. They went a fierce pace for this decent handicap which suited the closers. A pb from the runner-up, who had the race run to suit.

3391 NEWS SCOTLAND H'CAP 1m 2f
3:30 (3:31) (Class 3) (0-95,92) 4-Y-O+ **£9,703** (£2,887; £1,443; £721) **Stalls** Low

Form RPR

4-12 **1** **Central Square (IRE)**[19] 2744 4-9-7 **92**........................ PaulMulrennan 2 100+
(Roger Varian) *trckd ldrs: rdn and outpcd over 2f out: rallied over 1f out: led last 50yds: rdn out* **5/6**[1]

1 **2** *1/2* **Nicholas T**[12] 2957 4-8-5 **76**........................ JamesSullivan 3 83
(Jim Goldie) *unruly bef s: t.k.h: hld up in tch: rdn over 2f out: hdwy over 1f out: led briefly ins fnl f: hdd last 50yds: edgd rt and no ex* **9/2**[2]

4351 **3** *1/2* **Corton Lad**[16] 2832 6-9-1 **86**........................(tp) RobertWinston 7 92
(Keith Dalgleish) *pressed ldr: rdn over 2f out: hdd over 1f out: rallied: no ex wl ins fnl f* **7/1**

0402 **4** *nk* **Gworn**[1] 3347 6-8-8 **79**........................ ConnorBeasley 4 84
(R Mike Smith) *hld up in tch: smooth hdwy over 1f out: rdn and kpt on same pce ins fnl f* **8/1**

6/00 **5** *1* **Vercingetorix (IRE)**[19] 2752 5-9-2 **87**........................ JasonHart 1 90?
(David Evans) *hld up in last pl: rdn along 3f out: kpt on fnl f: nt pce to chal* **25/1**

5240 **6** *1* **Burano (IRE)**[7] 3162 7-9-3 **88**........................(v[1]) SamJames 6 89
(David O'Meara) *prom: rdn over 2f out: wknd appr fnl f* **6/1**[3]

1200 **7** *8* **Spes Nostra**[65] 1445 8-9-2 **87**........................(b) MartinDwyer 5 72
(Iain Jardine) *led: rdn over 2f out: hdd over 1f out: sn wknd* **25/1**

2m 9.14s (-2.86) **Going Correction** -0.225s/f (Firm) **7** Ran SP% **118.3**
Speed ratings (Par 107): **102,101,101,100,100 99,92**
CSF £5.34 TOTE £1.70: £1.10, £2.60; EX 5.50 Trifecta £14.10.
Owner Clipper Logistics **Bred** Mrs Cherry Faeste **Trained** Newmarket, Suffolk

FOCUS
Due to rail movements the actual race distance was 1m2f 21yds. A fair handicap run at a sound pace. The third helps set the standard, with the fourth close to the previous night's form.

3392 SCOTTISH SUN/BRITISH STALLION STUDS EBF LAND O'BURNS FILLIES' STKS (LISTED RACE) 5f
4:10 (4:10) (Class 1) 3-Y-O+
£28,355 (£10,750; £5,380; £2,680; £1,345; £675) **Stalls** High

Form RPR

3-25 **1** **Marsha (IRE)**[14] 2923 3-8-12 **100**........................ PaulMulrennan 9 109+
(Sir Mark Prescott Bt) *plld hrd: hld up: smooth hdwy over 1f out: led gng wl ins fnl f: qcknd clr on bit w ears pricked: v readily* **7/4**[1]

0-36 **2** *2 1/2* **Fine Blend (IRE)**[14] 2923 3-9-2 **97**........................ MartinDwyer 3 99
(William Muir) *s.i.s: sn pushed along in rr: hdwy over 1f out: chsd (clr) wnr wl ins fnl f: nt pce to chal* **12/1**

0362 **3** *nk* **Buying Trouble (USA)**[15] 2875 3-8-12 **85**........................ JasonHart 5 94
(David Evans) *hld up in tch: effrt and drvn along over 1f out: kpt on ins fnl f* **20/1**

-612 **4** *nk* **Ridge Ranger (IRE)**[28] 2474 5-9-8 **103**........................ NeilFarley 8 99
(Eric Alston) *cl up: rdn and led over 1f out: hdd ins fnl f: kpt on same pce towards fin* **5/2**[2]

-334 **5** *1* **Shadow Hunter (IRE)**[37] 2192 3-8-12 **94**........................ RobertWinston 1 89
(Paul D'Arcy) *dwlt: hld up: rdn and effrt on outside over 1f out: kpt on fnl f: no imp* **10/1**

-022 **6** *1/2* **Olivia Fallow (IRE)**[7] 3150 4-9-4 **88**........................ JackGarritty 4 89
(Paul Midgley) *hld up bhd ldng gp: rdn and effrt on wd outside over 1f out: no imp fnl f* **8/1**

0-55 **7** *1/2* **Shrill**[34] 2272 3-8-12 **92**........................ BillyLee 2 86
(W McCreery, Ire) *trckd ldrs: rdn along wl over 1f out: wknd ins fnl f* **6/1**[3]

1-11 **8** *5* **Coto (IRE)**[23] 2622 4-9-4 **75**........................ RichardKingscote 10 70
(M J Tynan, Ire) *chsd ldrs tl rdn and wknd over 1f out* **25/1**

4620 **9** *3/4* **Jebediah Shine**[22] 2658 4-9-4 **88**........................ SamJames 6 67
(David O'Meara) *chsd ldrs: rdn over 2f out: wknd over 1f out* **33/1**

5-40 **10** *3/4* **Silk Bow**[106] 821 3-8-12 **78**........................ JamesSullivan 7 62
(James Given) *led tl hdd over 1f out: sn wknd* **50/1**

58.33s (-1.07) **Going Correction** +0.075s/f (Good)
WFA 3 from 4yo+ 6lb **10** Ran SP% **120.6**
Speed ratings (Par 108): **111,107,106,106,104 103,102,94,93,92**
CSF £24.58 TOTE £2.90: £1.10, £3.40, £4.60; EX 29.80 Trifecta £377.70.
Owner Elite Racing Club **Bred** Elite Racing Club **Trained** Newmarket, Suffolk

FOCUS
Not the strongest renewals of this Listed contest but they went a decent gallop and the winner did it very impressively. The sixth has been rated close to the balance of her form.

3393 SLATERS H'CAP 5f
4:50 (4:59) (Class 3) (0-95,92) 3-Y-O+ **£9,703** (£2,887; £1,443; £721) **Stalls** High

Form RPR

0022 **1** **Lexington Place**[9] 3056 6-9-5 **85**........................ JamesSullivan 7 92
(Ruth Carr) *stdd in last pl: effrt and hdwy over 1f out: rdn ins fnl f: kpt on wl to ld cl home* **4/1**[2]

50-0 **2** *nk* **Dragon King (IRE)**[35] 2259 4-9-8 **88**........................ PaulMulrennan 5 94
(Michael Dods) *trckd ldrs gng wl: rdn to ld ins fnl f: kpt on: hdd cl home* **3/1**[1]

-401 **3** *hd* **Fredricka**[18] 2775 5-9-4 **84**........................ JasonHart 1 89
(David Barron) *hld up in tch: effrt and hdwy over 1f out: kpt on u.p fnl f: hdd cl home* **9/1**

4226 **4** *1 1/4* **El Astronaute (IRE)**[22] 2658 3-9-3 **89**........................ RobertWinston 2 88
(John Quinn) *led: rdn along 2f out: hdd ins fnl f: kpt on same pce* **9/2**[3]

4340 **5** *1* **Silvanus (IRE)**[7] 3151 11-9-12 **92**........................ JackGarritty 3 89
(Paul Midgley) *trckd ldrs: effrt and rdn over 1f out: kpt on same pce ins fnl f* **14/1**

5246 **6** *shd* **Classy Anne**[7] 3150 6-8-12 **78**........................ GeorgeChaloner 4 75
(Jim Goldie) *trckd ldrs: rdn along 2f out: kpt on same pce appr fnl f* **9/1**

15-0 **7** *3 3/4* **Sahreej (IRE)**[35] 2251 3-9-1 **90**........................ MichaelJMMurphy(3) 8 71
(Charles Hills) *t.k.h: disp ld to over 1f out: sn rdn: wknd fnl f* **6/1**

58.75s (-0.65) **Going Correction** +0.075s/f (Good)
WFA 3 from 4yo+ 6lb **7** Ran SP% **104.1**
Speed ratings (Par 107): **108,107,107,105,103 103,97**
CSF £13.55 CT £71.42 TOTE £3.80: £2.30, £1.80; EX 15.40 Trifecta £71.40.
Owner Mrs Marion Chapman **Bred** Christopher & Annabelle Mason **Trained** Huby, N Yorks
■ Seve (7-1) was withdrawn. Rule 4 applies to all bets. Deduction - 10p in the pound.

FOCUS
An open sprint handicap run at a fair pace. They finished in a bunch. The third helps set the standard, while the fourth has been rated close to form.

3394 GLASGOW PRESTWICK AIRPORT H'CAP 6f
5:25 (5:25) (Class 4) (0-80,79) 3-Y-O+ **£5,175** (£1,540; £769; £384) **Stalls** High

Form RPR

1-34 **1** **Rose Marmara**[18] 2777 3-8-12 **70**........................ GeorgeChaloner 2 84
(Richard Fahey) *in tch: hdwy to ld over 1f out: edgd lft and pushed clr fnl f* **5/1**[3]

5445 **2** *5* **Vallarta (IRE)**[12] 2961 6-9-7 **72**........................ JamesSullivan 9 72
(Ruth Carr) *dwlt: hld up: effrt and swtchd rt over 1f out: hdwy to chse (clr) wnr ins fnl f: no imp* **7/2**[2]

1162 **3** 1 1/4 **Kyllukey**[29] [2446] 3-9-4 **79** MichaelJMurphy(3) 10 73
(Charles Hills) *w ldrs: rdn 2f out: kpt on same pce fnl f* **8/1**

0-06 **4** 1 **Dark Defender**[22] [2650] 3-9-7 **79** (b1) RobertWinston 5 70
(Keith Dalgleish) *t.k.h: hld up in tch: hdwy and ev ch wl over 1f out: kpt on same pce fnl f* **5/2**1

2-10 **5** nk **Off The Scale (IRE)**[49] [1869] 4-9-0 **72** BenRobinson(7) 8 64
(Brian Ellison) *prom: hdwy and ev ch 2f out: rdn and outpcd ins fnl f* **14/1**

4000 **6** 1 **Whozthecat (IRE)**[7] [3168] 9-9-3 **75** GerO'Neill(7) 1 64
(Declan Carroll) *prom: rdn and edgd lft over 1f out: sn no ex* **13/2**

4122 **7** 3/4 **Available (IRE)**[23] [2621] 7-9-13 **78** (tp) ConnorBeasley 11 64
(John Mackie) *cl up: led over 2f out to over 1f out: wknd ins fnl f* **13/2**

56-5 **8** 7 **Fray**[56] [1624] 5-9-11 **76** JackGarritty 7 40
(Jim Goldie) *dwlt and sn wl bhd: nvr on terms* **16/1**

1310 **9** 4 1/2 **Faintly (USA)**[7] [3168] 5-9-7 **72** (p) PaulMulrennan 3 21
(Ruth Carr) *led to over 2f out: sn rdn and wknd* **16/1**

1m 12.18s (-0.22) **Going Correction** +0.075s/f (Good)
WFA 3 from 4yo+ 7lb **9** Ran SP% **123.7**
Speed ratings (Par 105): **104,97,95,94,93 92,91,82,76**
CSF £24.69 CT £144.79 TOTE £6.40: £2.20, £1.60, £2.60; EX 28.40 Trifecta £186.80.
Owner Jaber Abdullah **Bred** Rabbah Bloodstock Limited **Trained** Musley Bank, N Yorks

FOCUS
They went a sound pace for this open handicap. It's been rated around the runner-up.
T/Plt: £238.60 to a £1 stake. Pool: £60,243.03 - 184.30 winning tickets. T/Qpdt: £11.60 to a £1 stake. Pool: £5,186.41 - 330.32 winning tickets. **Richard Young**

3052 HAYDOCK (L-H)

Saturday, June 18

OFFICIAL GOING: Good to soft (soft in places; 6.3)
Wind: light 1/2 against Weather: fine

3395 BETFRED "LOOKING FORWARD TO CORRS" H'CAP 1m 2f 95y
6:30 (6:30) (Class 5) (0-75,75) 3-Y-O+ **£3,234** (£962; £481; £240) **Stalls** Centre

Form RPR

-011 **1** **Caponova (IRE)**[9] [3053] 3-8-11 **70** LiamJones 2 78+
(Tom Dascombe) *dwlt: hld up towards rr: effrt and plld wd over 3f out: styd on appr fnl f: str run to ld fnl strides* **3/1**2

-661 **2** nk **Mujazif (IRE)**[5] [3220] 6-9-5 **71** 6ex (p) PaddyPilley(5) 1 78
(Michael Appleby) *trckd ldng pair: effrt over 3f out: styd on to ld last 150yds: hdd and no ex fnl strides* **5/4**1

313- **3** 2 1/4 **Azzir (IRE)**[234] [7564] 4-9-8 **74** JordanVaughan(5) 3 77
(K R Burke) *trckd ldrs: t.k.h: effrt 3f out: kpt on same pce fnl f* **10/3**3

20-5 **4** nk **Clear Spell (IRE)**[24] [2575] 5-9-1 **69** RowanScott(7) 5 71
(Alistair Whillans) *s.v.s: hdwy and in tch over 7f out: drvn over 4f out: styd on appr fnl f* **12/1**

2040 **5** 1 **Omotesando**[7] [3129] 6-9-7 **73** CharlieBennett(5) 6 73
(Mark Brisbourne) *led: qcknd pce over 4f out: rdn over 2f out: hdd over 1f out: one pce* **11/1**

0000 **6** 2 1/4 **Rightway (IRE)**[10] [3030] 5-9-4 **68** GeorgeDowning(3) 7 64
(Tony Carroll) *trckd ldr: led over 1f out: hdd last 150yds: wknd clsng stages* **25/1**

2m 18.12s (2.62) **Going Correction** 0.0s/f (Good)
WFA 3 from 4yo+ 12lb **6** Ran SP% **112.4**
Speed ratings (Par 103): **89,88,86,86,85 84**
CSF £7.19 CT £11.59 TOTE £4.10: £1.90, £1.20; EX 9.00 Trifecta £17.00.
Owner Deva Racing Bushranger Partnership **Bred** Mr & Mrs T O'Brien **Trained** Malpas, Cheshire

FOCUS
All races on Inner Home Straight. A fair handicap and they went a sensible gallop on ground officially described as good to soft, soft in places. Race run over 3yds further than advertised. The third has been rated to form.

3396 BETFRED "VISIT OUR SHOPS ON COURSE" NOVICE STKS (PLUS 10 RACE) 5f
7:00 (7:00) (Class 4) 2-Y-O **£3,946** (£1,174; £586; £293) **Stalls** Centre

Form RPR

0 **1** **Queen Celeste (IRE)**[35] [2254] 2-8-11 0 FrannyNorton 3 60
(Mark Johnston) *mde all: t.k.h: abt 4 l clr 2f out: drvn over 1f out: edgd lft: jst lasted* **5/4**1

46 **2** hd **Valley Lodge**[18] [2779] 2-9-2 0 BarryMcHugh 2 64
(Julia Feilden) *dwlt: sn chsng wnr: drvn over 2f out: kpt on wl fnl f: jst hld* **14/1**

0 **3** 6 **Forster Square (IRE)**[18] [2757] 2-9-2 0 TonyHamilton 4 43
(Richard Fahey) *in rr: drvn 3f out: sn outpcd: tk modest 3rd last 100yds* **6/4**2

03 **4** 1/2 **Jester Spirit (IRE)**[29] [2417] 2-9-2 0 LiamJones 1 41
(Tom Dascombe) *sn drvn along: outpcd over 2f out: wandered: lost modest 3rd last 100yds* **4/1**3

1m 5.23s (4.43) **Going Correction** +0.40s/f (Good) **4** Ran SP% **111.1**
Speed ratings (Par 95): **80,79,70,69**
CSF £14.92 TOTE £2.00; EX 16.70 Trifecta £23.70.
Owner Lowther Racing Stewart McDonald &Partner **Bred** Yeomanstown Stud & Doc Bloodstock **Trained** Middleham Moor, N Yorks

FOCUS
An ordinary little juvenile novice contest. They went a respectable gallop. It'll take time for this form to settle.

3397 BETFRED TV EBF FILLIES' H'CAP (JOCKEY CLUB GRASSROOTS FLAT SPRINT SERIES QUALIFIER) 5f
7:35 (7:35) (Class 4) (0-80,80) 3-Y-O+ **£6,469** (£1,925; £962; £481) **Stalls** Centre

Form RPR

6-06 **1** **Guishan**[130] [508] 6-9-8 **79** TimClark(3) 5 90
(Michael Appleby) *w ldrs: led over 2f out: fnd ex clsng stages* **5/1**3

-040 **2** 1/2 **Fruit Salad**[19] [2742] 3-8-0 **65** NathanEvans(5) 2 72
(James Bethell) *chsd ldrs towards far side: drvn upsides over 1f out: no ex clsng stages* **7/2**2

-003 **3** 1 **Toni's A Star**[18] [2785] 4-8-3 **62** PaddyPilley(5) 6 67
(Tony Carroll) *in rr stands' side: hdwy over 2f out: chsng ldrs over 1f out: hung lft: kpt on same pce last 150yds* **15/2**

23-1 **4** 2 1/2 **Futoon (IRE)**[14] [2886] 3-9-4 **78** FrannyNorton 3 72
(Kevin Ryan) *chsd ldrs: upsides over 1f out: fdd last 100yds* **3/1**1

-026 **5** 1/2 **Beau Mistral (IRE)**[5] [3217] 7-8-0 **61** oh3 RPWalsh(7) 4 56
(Tony Carroll) *dwlt: hdwy over 2f out: chsng ldrs over 1f out: one pce* **7/1**

30-0 **6** 1 1/2 **Savannah Beau**[23] [2621] 4-9-12 **80** BarryMcHugh 7 69
(Marjorie Fife) *dwlt: hld up towards rr: hdwy over 2f out: nvr trbld ldrs* **8/1**

-616 **7** 1 **Crombay (IRE)**[26] [2534] 3-8-13 **73** DuranFentiman 1 57
(Tim Easterby) *w ldrs towards far side: wknd appr fnl f* **12/1**

22-1 **8** 2 1/4 **By Rights**[159] [146] 5-8-13 **70** GeorgeDowning(3) 8 48
(Tony Carroll) *racd stands' side: led tl over 2f out: lost pl over 1f out* **9/1**

1m 2.15s (1.35) **Going Correction** +0.40s/f (Good)
WFA 3 from 4yo+ 6lb **8** Ran SP% **117.0**
Speed ratings (Par 102): **105,104,102,98,97 95,93,90**
CSF £23.45 CT £132.21 TOTE £6.20: £1.90, £1.50, £2.50; EX 29.80 Trifecta £198.80.
Owner Brian D Cantle **Bred** B D Cantle **Trained** Oakham, Rutland

FOCUS
The feature contest was a fairly decent fillies' handicap. They went a proper gallop. The third has been rated close to her recent form.

3398 BETFRED "FOLLOW US ON TWITTER" H'CAP 1m
8:05 (8:05) (Class 4) (0-85,85) 4-Y-O+ **£4,851** (£1,443; £721; £360) **Stalls** Low

Form RPR

0120 **1** **Chosen Character (IRE)**[7] [3124] 8-8-12 **76** (vt) FrannyNorton 6 85
(Tom Dascombe) *mde all: drvn over 1f out: hld on gamely* **7/4**1

6-00 **2** 1/2 **Dream Walker (FR)**[7] [3166] 7-8-11 **75** (t) BenCurtis 10 83
(Brian Ellison) *trckd ldng pair: drvn 3f out: 2nd appr fnl f: hung lft: no ex clsng stages* **5/1**2

4060 **3** 2 1/4 **Moonlightnavigator (USA)**[19] [2743] 4-9-0 **78** DougieCostello 8 81
(John Quinn) *chsd wnr: drvn 3f out: keeping on one pce whn n.m.r 150yds out* **6/1**

000- **4** hd **Intensical (IRE)**[252] [7130] 5-9-1 **79** RaulDaSilva 1 81+
(Ivan Furtado) *s.i.s: hld up: hdwy over 3f out: nt clr run over 2f out: edgd lft over 1f out: plld wd 150yds out: kpt on same pce* **7/1**

-000 **5** 2 3/4 **Character Onesie (IRE)**[21] [2688] 4-8-8 **72** TonyHamilton 5 68
(Richard Fahey) *trckd ldng pair: one pce whn n.m.r on inner over 1f out* **5/1**2

1360 **6** 4 **Queen Aggie (IRE)**[7] [3132] 6-8-10 **77** GeorgeDowning(3) 7 64
(Tony Carroll) *stdd s: hld up in rr: t.k.h: hdwy 4f out: effrt over 2f out: wknd over 1f out* **14/1**

1013 **7** 1/2 **Anton Chigurh**[29] [2444] 7-8-9 **73** LiamJones 3 59
(Tom Dascombe) *s.s: in rr: plld wd and sme hdwy over 3f out: lost pl over 1f out* **11/2**3

1m 42.68s (-1.02) **Going Correction** 0.0s/f (Good) **7** Ran SP% **118.5**
Speed ratings (Par 105): **105,104,102,102,99 95,94**
CSF £11.53 CT £44.24 TOTE £2.80: £2.00, £2.80; EX 12.80 Trifecta £49.70.
Owner Aykroyd And Sons Ltd **Bred** Moyglare Stud Farm Ltd **Trained** Malpas, Cheshire

FOCUS
Race run over 3yds further than advertised. A decent handicap, the second race on the round course and, off a decent gallop, they clocked a time more akin to plain good to soft ground. The runner-up has been rated to his late 2015 form.

3399 BETFRED TWEET US YOUR PHOTOS H'CAP 1m
8:35 (8:36) (Class 4) (0-80,79) 3-Y-O **£4,851** (£1,443; £721; £360) **Stalls** Low

Form RPR

-330 **1** **Bedrock**[30] [2393] 3-9-7 **79** (p) TonyHamilton 6 85+
(William Haggas) *led after 1f: drvn 2f out: edgd rt and hld on all out clsng stages* **9/4**2

5-00 **2** hd **La Celebs Ville (IRE)**[22] [2666] 3-8-8 **66** LiamJones 4 70
(Tom Dascombe) *trckd ldrs: effrt over 3f out: kpt on and edgd lft clsng stages: jst hld* **8/1**

4-44 **3** 1 1/4 **Rosamaria (IRE)**[12] [2973] 3-8-10 **68** FrannyNorton 1 71+
(Mark Johnston) *chsd ldrs: nt clr run over 2f out: tried to squeeze between horses whn bdly hmpd and snatched up nr fin* **4/1**3

1040 **4** 8 **Custard The Dragon**[56] [1638] 3-8-9 **67** BenCurtis 2 50
(John Mackie) *led 1f: chsd wnr: wkng whn short of room on inner over 1f out* **6/1**

14 **5** 8 **Ultimate Star**[35] [2237] 3-9-7 **79** DougieCostello 5 43
(David Simcock) *dwlt: hdwy to chse ldrs over 3f out: rdn over 2f out: hung lft and lost pl over 1f out: lame* **13/8**1

1m 43.94s (0.24) **Going Correction** 0.0s/f (Good) **5** Ran SP% **114.3**
Speed ratings (Par 101): **98,97,96,88,80**
CSF £19.49 TOTE £2.60: £1.40, £3.40; EX 21.30 Trifecta £110.60.
Owner Highclere Thoroughbred Racing(Gladstone) **Bred** Highclere Stud & Ors Bloodstock **Trained** Newmarket, Suffolk

FOCUS
Race run over 3yds further than advertised. A fairly decent 3yo handicap. They went a respectable gallop. The runner-up has been rated close to his C&D form at two.

3400 BETFRED WIN RACECOURSE TICKETS ON TWITTER MAIDEN STKS 1m
9:05 (9:07) (Class 5) 3-Y-O+ **£2,911** (£866; £432; £216) **Stalls** Low

Form RPR

1 **Tomahawk Kid** 3-8-13 0 GeorgeDowning(3) 1 70+
(Ian Williams) *s.s and fly-leaping early: hdwy after 2f: shkn up 4f out: hdwy over 1f out: styd on and edgd lft to ld nr fin* **8/1**

64 **2** nk **Dasheen**[12] [2957] 3-9-2 0 FrannyNorton 3 69
(Mark Johnston) *led: drvn over 2f out: hdd and no ex nr fin* **13/8**1

3 1 3/4 **Angrywhitepyjamas (IRE)** 3-9-2 0 DougieCostello 2 65
(William Muir) *dwlt: in rr: effrt over 3f out: styd on fnl f: tk 3rd clsng stages* **2/1**2

6- **4** 1 1/4 **Three Times A Lord**[501] [401] 4-9-12 0 LemosdeSouza 5 64
(Ivan Furtado) *trckd ldr: t.k.h: chal over 2f out: wknd fnl 75yds* **8/1**

6 **5** 4 **Justice Pleasing**[10] [3023] 3-9-2 0 JoeyHaynes 6 52
(David Loughnane) *uns rdr and led rdrless to post: restless in stalls: trckd ldng pair: t.k.h: effrt 3f out: wknd fnl f* **4/1**3

1m 47.69s (3.99) **Going Correction** 0.0s/f (Good)
WFA 3 from 4yo 10lb **5** Ran SP% **113.7**
Speed ratings (Par 103): **80,79,77,76,72**
CSF £22.26 TOTE £8.30: £3.50, £1.40; EX 24.80 Trifecta £37.30.
Owner Phil Mousley **Bred** Phil Mousley **Trained** Portway, Worcs

FOCUS
An ordinary maiden. They went a modest gallop. The level is fluid.
T/Plt: £127.60 to a £1 stake. Pool: £46,273.64 - 264.56 winning tickets. T/Qpdt: £31.20 to a £1 stake. Pool: £3,852.64 - 91.10 winning tickets. **Walter Glynn**

3314 LINGFIELD (L-H)

Saturday, June 18

OFFICIAL GOING: Polytrack: standard

Wind: mild breeze against Weather: overcast

3401 HEART FM H'CAP — 1m 2f (P)

5:45 (5:45) (Class 6) (0-52,52) 3-Y-O+ **£2,587** (£770; £384; £192) **Stalls** Low

Form / RPR

-565 **1** **Megalala (IRE)**[14] 2901 15-8-13 50 MitchGodwin(7) 14 — 56
(John Bridger) *mde all: kpt on v gamely whn strly chal fr 2f out: asserting nring fin* **16/1**

5403 **2** 3/4 **Understory (USA)**[32] 2323 9-9-6 50 RyanTate 8 — 55
(Tim McCarthy) *trckd ldr: chal over 3f out: rdn and ev ch fr wl over 1f out: no ex towards fin* **3/1**[1]

50-0 **3** 2 **Bob's Boy**[24] 2590 3-8-10 52 (p) JackMitchell 12 — 53
(Jose Santos) *squeezed up s: sn mid-div: hdwy over 4f out: rdn to chse ldng pair 2f out: styd on but nt pce to chal fnl f* **5/1**[2]

0045 **4** nk **Imperial Link**[7] 3135 4-8-13 48 (p) CiaranMckee(5) 1 — 48
(John O'Shea) *mid-div: rdn and hdwy over 1f out: styd on fnl f* **8/1**

60-0 **5** 2 3/4 **Grand Proposal**[23] 2610 4-9-0 47 [1] KieranShoemark(3) 10 — 42
(Mike Murphy) *in tch: rdn 3f out: one pce fnl 2f* **20/1**

2500 **6** 3/4 **Fitzwilliam**[10] 3031 4-9-0 51 KillianHennessy(7) 11 — 45
(Mick Channon) *squeezed up s: towards rr: styd on fr over 1f out: nvr trbld ldrs* **7/1**[3]

6200 **7** nse **Rezwaan**[10] 3031 9-9-6 50 (p) TomQueally 13 — 43
(Murty McGrath) *trckd ldrs: rdn 2f out: nt pce to get on terms: no ex towards fin* **16/1**

2/0- **8** 3/4 **Ding Ding**[20] 68 5-9-8 52 RobertHavlin 6 — 44
(Sheena West) *a mid-div* **16/1**

4200 **9** 1 1/4 **Clock On Tom**[20] 1578 6-9-7 51 LiamKeniry 7 — 41
(Denis Quinn) *hld up towards rr: rdn 2f out: sme minor prog fnl f: nvr trbld ldrs* **10/1**

600- **10** nk **Summerling (IRE)**[246] 7263 5-9-1 48 DannyBrock(3) 2 — 37
(Phil McEntee) *rdn 2f out: nvr bttr than mid-div* **7/1**[3]

-046 **11** 1 1/2 **Standing Strong (IRE)**[41] 672 8-8-10 47 (p) MeganNicholls(7) 9 — 33
(Zoe Davison) *s.i.s: a towards rr* **25/1**

024- **12** 7 **Lettuce Snow (IRE)**[233] 7583 4-9-5 52 RobHornby(3) 4 — 25
(Geoffrey Deacon) *mid-div: rdn 3f out: wknd 2f out* **8/1**

50-0 **13** 23 **Spice Boat**[115] 701 4-8-11 46 CallumShepherd(5) 3
(Paddy Butler) *trckd ldrs: rdn 3f out: wknd 2f out* **50/1**

2m 5.85s (-0.75) **Going Correction** -0.075s/f (Stan)
WFA 3 from 4yo+ 12lb — **13** Ran SP% **126.2**
Speed ratings (Par 101): **100,99,97,97,95 94,94,94,93,92 91,86,67**
CSF £66.03 CT £293.45 TOTE £14.60: £6.20, £1.40, £2.50; EX 62.70 Trifecta £807.70.
Owner Trevor Wallace **Bred** Joseph Gallagher **Trained** Liphook, Hants

FOCUS
A very weak handicap run at a steady pace and this was dominated by those that raced to the fore early. The form isn't worth much but that won't matter a jot to connections of remarkable veteran Megalaa who registered a 20th career success on his 133 start. Ordinary form.

3402 HARRIS & BAILEY H'CAP — 1m 2f (P)

6:15 (6:16) (Class 6) (0-55,65) 4-Y-O+ **£2,587** (£770; £384; £192) **Stalls** Low

Form / RPR

1351 **1** **Choral Clan (IRE)**[18] 2769 5-9-7 65 JackMitchell 3 — 70
(Philip Mitchell) *mid-div: hdwy on inner 2f out: rdn ent fnl f: led fnl 80yds: r.o wl* **3/1**[2]

4-0 **2** nk **Ost Wind**[24] 2577 4-9-4 65 RobHornby(3) 8 — 69
(Michael Attwater) *trckd ldr: rdn over 2f out: led briefly fnl 120yds: kpt on but no ex cl home* **25/1**

0-61 **3** shd **Mercy Me**[9] 3076 4-9-7 65 RyanPowell 1 — 69
(John Ryan) *hld up towards rr: rdn and hdwy over 1f out: sn swtchd rt: r.o strly fnl f: jst hld* **9/2**[3]

2-00 **4** 1 **Chella Thriller (SPA)**[38] 2153 7-9-3 61 WilliamTwiston-Davies 2 — 63
(Ralph J Smith) *led: rdn over 2f out: hdd fnl 120yds: no ex* **16/1**

-005 **5** nse **Power Up**[23] 2607 5-8-11 58 DannyBrock(3) 11 — 60
(Jane Chapple-Hyam) *sn trcking ldr: rdn over 2f out: nt quite pce to mount chal: kpt on* **14/1**

0-01 **6** 1 1/2 **Fearless Lad (IRE)**[11] 2996 6-9-7 65 KierenFox 5 — 66
(John Best) *hld up in last: stl last pair u.p over 1f out: r.o strly wout ever threatening to rch ldrs fnl f* **2/1**[1]

360- **7** 1 1/2 **Santadelacruze**[247] 7230 7-8-12 56 (b) RobertHavlin 4 — 53
(Mark Hoad) *mid-div: hdwy 2f out: sn rdn: nt pce to get on terms: fdd fnl 100yds* **25/1**

-605 **8** 3/4 **Lily Edge**[12] 2977 7-7-9 46 oh1 (b) MitchGodwin(7) 6 — 41
(John Bridger) *towards rr of mid-div: rdn over 2f out: nvr threatened* **16/1**

400/ **9** 6 **Magnus Romeo**[258] 2805 5-9-1 62 (t) KieranShoemark(3) 7 — 46
(Johnny Farrelly) *mid-div tl wknd 2f out* **50/1**

55/0 **10** nk **Aramadyh**[33] 2292 5-9-4 62 TomQueally 10 — 45
(Jim Best) *struggling over 5f out: a towards rr* **33/1**

550- **11** nk **Wally's Wisdom**[201] 8046 4-8-9 58 CallumShepherd(5) 9 — 41
(Lee Carter) *racd keenly: trckd ldrs: rdn over 2f out: wknd fnl f* **7/1**

2m 5.4s (-1.20) **Going Correction** -0.075s/f (Stan) — **11** Ran SP% **120.0**
Speed ratings (Par 101): **101,100,100,99,99 98,97,96,92,91 91**
CSF £83.25 CT £343.62 TOTE £3.70: £1.40, £8.30, £1.90; EX 84.30 Trifecta £840.00.
Owner Bob Harris & Patricia Mitchell **Bred** L Queally **Trained** Kingston Lisle, Oxfordshire

FOCUS
A competitive heat for the grade with three last time-out winners but, as with the first race, the pace was once again pretty steady. The leader kicked for home off the bend and the closers only really got competitive in the final half furlong. The principals dictate the level.

3403 IMTECH H'CAP — 1m 4f (P)

6:45 (6:45) (Class 5) (0-75,74) 4-Y-O+ **£3,234** (£962; £481; £240) **Stalls** Low

Form / RPR

1602 **1** **Vale Of Iron (IRE)**[13] 2930 4-9-1 68 KierenFox 8 — 77
(John Best) *racd keenly: hld up: hdwy to trck ldr 6f out: led 2f out: clr ent fnl f: readily* **2/1**[1]

/004 **2** 3 1/4 **New Street (IRE)**[12] 2965 5-9-6 73 (v) WilliamTwiston-Davies 7 — 77
(Jim Best) *hld up: rdn and hdwy over 1f out: r.o fnl f: wnt 2nd cl home: no ch w wnr* **20/1**

4640 **3** 1/2 **Karam Albaari (IRE)**[23] 2623 8-9-3 70 (v) FrederikTylicki 3 — 73
(J R Jenkins) *slowly away: in last pair: rdn and hdwy over 1f out: chal for 2nd ent fnl f: kpt on* **9/1**

5260 **4** nse **Ravenous**[26] 2549 5-9-4 71 KieranO'Neill 1 — 74
(Luke Dace) *cl up: rdn to chse wnr but hld ent fnl f: no ex towards fin* **7/2**[2]

1503 **5** 3 3/4 **Chilworth Bells**[7] 3135 4-9-7 74 LiamKeniry 6 — 71
(Conor Dore) *trckd ldr tl 6f out: rdn over 2f out: nt pce to threaten* **10/1**

0-06 **6** nse **Perfect Rhythm**[15] 2850 5-9-3 70 PatCosgrave 5 — 67
(Patrick Chamings) *trckd ldrs: jinked off rails over 4f out: rdn over 2f out: chal for 2nd over 1f out: no ex fnl f* **6/1**

0603 **7** hd **Firestorm (GER)**[16] 2827 5-9-7 74 RobertHavlin 2 — 71
(Michael Attwater) *led tl 2f out: sn rdn: lost 2nd ent fnl f: no ex fnl 120yds* **9/2**[3]

143/ **8** 17 **Amantius**[768] 2207 7-8-7 63 KieranShoemark(3) 4 — 32
(Johnny Farrelly) *trckd ldrs: struggling to hold pl whn pushed wd 2f out: sn wknd* **20/1**

2m 31.22s (-1.78) **Going Correction** -0.075s/f (Stan) — **8** Ran SP% **116.6**
Speed ratings (Par 103): **102,99,99,99,96 96,96,85**
CSF £46.41 CT £291.72 TOTE £3.10: £1.30, £4.30, £3.00; EX 62.10 Trifecta £502.90.
Owner Lingfield Park Owners Group I **Bred** Knockainey Stud & Storway Ltd **Trained** Oad Street, Kent

■ Stewards' Enquiry : Kieran Shoemark jockey said the gelding lost action and hung right-handed on the final bend. The Veterinary Officer reported that a post-race examination of the gelding failed to reveal any abnormalities.
Kieren Fox jockey was found guilty of careless riding and was cautioned as to his future conduct in races.

FOCUS
A run of the mill handicap on paper but it threw up a very impressive winner, with his rivals in a bit of a heap in behind. The third has been rated to his penultimate 1m2f form here.

3404 KEN & MOYRA'S 50TH GOLDEN WEDDING ANNIVERSARY MAIDEN AUCTION STKS — 7f 1y(P)

7:20 (7:21) (Class 6) 2-Y-O **£2,587** (£770; £384; £192) **Stalls** Low

Form / RPR

0 **1** **Quandary Peak**[16] 2822 2-8-3 0 DannyBrock(3) 5 — 64+
(J S Moore) *mid-div: rdn and hdwy over 1f out: led fnl 120yds: r.o wl* **66/1**

22 **2** 3/4 **Bayston Hill**[12] 2963 2-9-1 0 LiamKeniry 6 — 71
(Mark Usher) *trckd ldrs: rdn over 2f out: ch ent fnl f: kpt on* **7/2**[2]

42 **3** nk **Bridal March**[7] 3134 2-8-9 0 JoeFanning 11 — 64
(Mark Johnston) *trckd ldr: chal over 2f out: rdn to ld ent fnl f: hdd fnl 120yds: kpt on but no ex cl home* **6/4**[1]

0 **4** 1/2 **Winning Bid**[16] 2822 2-9-0 0 PatCosgrave 2 — 68
(Harry Dunlop) *chsd ldrs: rdn over 2f out: kpt on ins fnl f* **14/1**

0 **5** 1 3/4 **If I Say So**[16] 2822 2-8-9 0 MarcMonaghan(3) 9 — 61
(J S Moore) *mid-div: hdwy over 2f out: hung rt and lost pl home turn: styd on but no threat fnl f* **50/1**

6 1 **Rake's Progress** 2-8-12 0 LukeMorris 7 — 58
(Heather Main) *hld up: rdn and hdwy over 1f out: r.o fnl f* **16/1**

55 **7** nk **Apple Scruffs (IRE)**[15] 2874 2-9-0 0 AdamBeschizza 10 — 60
(Michael Attwater) *s.i.s: sn mid-div: rdn over 2f out: no imp* **16/1**

4 **8** hd **Bobby Vee**[16] 2822 2-8-4 0 CharlesEddery(5) 1 — 54
(Dean Ivory) *led: rdn whn pressed 2f out: hdd ent fnl f: wknd fnl 120yds* **5/1**[3]

5 **9** 2 1/4 **Rinky Dink Dawn (IRE)**[71] 1316 2-8-11 0 KieranO'Neill 3 — 50
(J S Moore) *mid-div: hdwy on inner 2f out: sn rdn: nvr threatened: wknd fnl 120yds* **33/1**

10 1 **Georgio (GER)** 2-8-12 0 RobHornby(3) 4 — 51
(Andrew Balding) *a towards rr* **7/1**

11 3 1/2 **Otomo** 2-8-12 0 WilliamTwiston-Davies 8 — 39
(Philip Hide) *a towards rr* **25/1**

1m 25.36s (0.56) **Going Correction** -0.075s/f (Stan) — **11** Ran SP% **120.1**
Speed ratings (Par 91): **93,92,91,91,89 88,87,87,84,83 79**
CSF £289.21 TOTE £49.80: £12.60, £1.90, £1.10; EX 553.50 Trifecta £2343.70.
Owner Kieron Badger & J S Moore **Bred** Mr And Mrs R Newman **Trained** Upper Lambourn, Berks

FOCUS
This didn't look a bad maiden on paper as those to have run had showed a reasonable level of form, and some of the newcomers impressed in the prelims. The runner-up helps set the initial level.

3405 JOHN MAYNE 50TH BIRTHDAY CELEBRATION H'CAP — 7f 1y(P)

7:50 (7:51) (Class 4) (0-85,84) 4-Y-O+ **£5,175** (£1,540; £769; £384) **Stalls** Low

Form / RPR

3450 **1** **Merhoob (IRE)**[7] 3150 4-9-2 79 RyanPowell 1 — 88
(John Ryan) *mid-div: hdwy over 1f out: str chal fnl 140yds: led fnl stride* **6/1**[3]

5222 **2** shd **Straits Of Malacca**[18] 2765 5-8-3 66 (p) NickyMackay 3 — 74
(Simon Dow) *trckd ldrs: rdn over 1f out: led fnl 140yds: kpt on: hdd fnl stride* **16/1**

212 **3** 1 1/4 **Surewecan**[12] 2960 4-8-9 72 JoeFanning 6 — 77
(Mark Johnston) *trckd ldrs: rdn to ld v briefly jst ins fnl f: kpt on same pce* **5/1**[2]

60-1 **4** hd **Acclio (IRE)**[42] 2032 5-9-3 80 LukeMorris 4 — 84
(James Tate) *s.i.s: sn mid-div: rdn whn hung lft over 1f out: hdwy ent fnl f: kpt on to go 4th but nvr threatening to get on terms* **6/4**[1]

5040 **5** 3/4 **Childesplay**[9] 3061 5-9-0 80 (p) TomMarquand(3) 10 — 82
(Heather Main) *led after 1f: rdn 2f out: hdd jst ins fnl f: no ex* **8/1**

06 **6** nk **Corporal Maddox**[22] 2643 9-9-1 78 (p) RobertHavlin 5 — 79
(Ronald Harris) *mid-div: rdn and hdwy over 1f out: kpt on ins fnl f* **18/1**

0-15 **7** 1/2 **Lyfka**[14] 2890 4-9-7 84 (tp) RyanTate 7 — 84
(Paul Cole) *hld up: rdn w plenty to do over 1f out: r.o wl fnl f but nvr threatening to get involved* **16/1**

5053 **8** 2 3/4 **Robert The Painter (IRE)**[33] 2297 8-8-6 74 (b) CallumShepherd(5) 8 — 66
(Lee Carter) *led for 1f: trckd ldr: rdn over 2f out: wknd ins fnl f* **16/1**

00-4 **9** 5 **Big Chill (IRE)**[21] 2698 4-9-1 78 PatCosgrave 9 — 57
(Patrick Chamings) *in tch: effrt 2f out: wknd over 1f out* **20/1**

0464 **P** **Spiritual Star (IRE)**[12] 2977 7-9-3 80 KierenFox 2
(Lee Carter) *stdd s: last: b.b.v 2f out: sn p.u* **12/1**

1m 22.9s (-1.90) **Going Correction** -0.075s/f (Stan) — **10** Ran SP% **117.4**
Speed ratings (Par 105): **107,106,105,105,104 104,103,100,94,**
CSF £97.33 CT £529.75 TOTE £6.60: £1.90, £2.60, £1.60; EX 107.40 Trifecta £226.40.
Owner Gerry McGladery **Bred** Airlie Stud **Trained** Newmarket, Suffolk

FOCUS
Reasonably competitive stuff and the pace looked even. Plenty had their chance in the straight but the result wasn't decided until right on the line. The third has been rated close to his recent turf form.

3406 SAMWORTH BROTHERS MAIDEN STKS — 6f 1y(P)

8:20 (8:23) (Class 5) 3-Y-O+ **£3,234** (£962; £481; £240) **Stalls** Low

Form / RPR

22- **1** **Gravity Flow (IRE)**[271] 6589 3-9-0 0 PatCosgrave 6 — 84+
(William Haggas) *led after 1f: rdn over 1f out: kpt on wl to assert fnl f* **7/4**[2]

632- **2** 2¼ **Ballylare**[329] 4622 3-9-5 0 KierenFox 3 80
(John Best) *trckd ldrs: rdn 2f out: chsd wnr jst ins fnl f: kpt on but a being hld* **14/1**

22 **3** *nk* **Aflame**[14] 2904 3-9-0 0 TedDurcan 5 74
(Sir Michael Stoute) *led for 1f: pressed ldr: rdn over 1f out: hld ent fnl f: sn lost 2nd: kpt on same pce* **5/4**[1]

3-2 **4** 1¾ **Daring Day**[23] 2606 3-9-0 0 LukeMorris 9 68
(George Peckham) *trckd ldrs: rdn over 2f out: kpt on same pce fnl f* **6/1**[3]

0-4 **5** 1½ **Sexton Blake (IRE)**[43] 2005 3-9-0 0 HectorCrouch(5) 1 69
(Gary Moore) *mid-div: rdn over 2f out: kpt on but nt pce to get involved* **12/1**

0 **6** 4½ **Oasis Moon**[14] 2904 3-9-0 0 JoeFanning 2 49
(William Haggas) *in tch: effrt over 1f out: wknd fnl f* **18/1**

00 **7** 4 **Pepper (IRE)**[24] 2578 3-8-11 0 MatthewCosham(3) 4 36
(Derek Shaw) *sn struggling towards rr: nvr on terms* **100/1**

8 14 **German Whip** 3-9-5 0 TomQueally 7
(Gary Moore) *s.i.s: a outpcd in last pair* **25/1**

00 **F** **Frosty De Winter**[24] 2578 3-9-5 0 LiamKeniry 8
(Chris Gordon) *hld up: pushed along and making hdwy whn stmbld and fell over 2f out: fatally injured* **100/1**

B **Squire Hockey** 3-9-5 0 WilliamTwiston-Davies 10
(Gary Moore) *s.i.s: sn outpcd in last: sme prog whn b.d over 2f out* **50/1**

1m 11.17s (-0.73) **Going Correction** -0.075s/f (Stan) **10** Ran SP% **122.5**
Speed ratings (Par 103): **101,98,97,95,93 87,81,63, ,**
CSF £27.89 TOTE £2.90: £2.00, £3.40, £1.10; EX 28.00 Trifecta £57.00.
Owner Sheikh Juma Dalmook Al Maktoum **Bred** Eimear Mulhern & Abbeville Stud **Trained** Newmarket, Suffolk

FOCUS
Probably no more than an ordinary maiden in truth but the winner looks quite useful and she saw off rivals who had run to a reasonable level previously, so the form has a sound feel to it. It's been rated around the third.

3407 BEST DAD IN THE WORLD H'CAP 5f 6y(P)
8:50 (8:53) (Class 5) (0-75,75) 3-Y-O+ **£3,234** (£962; £481; £240) **Stalls** High

Form RPR

1044 **1** **Roseale (IRE)**[10] 3036 3-9-4 72 AdamBeschizza 2 78
(Jeremy Gask) *trckd ldrs: rdn to ld ent fnl f: r.o: a holding on* **6/1**

-232 **2** ½ **Just Glamorous (IRE)**[19] 2750 3-9-2 70 LukeMorris 4 74
(Ronald Harris) *trckd ldrs: rdn and r.o wl ins fnl f: wnt 2nd fnl 100yds: a being hld by wnr* **7/2**[1]

0321 **3** 1¼ **Desert Strike**[18] 2768 10-9-8 75 (p) HectorCrouch(5) 1 77
(Conor Dore) *led: rdn and hdd ent fnl f: kpt on same pce* **5/1**[3]

3335 **4** 4½ **Fine 'n Dandy (IRE)**[45] 1964 5-9-8 70 FrederikTylicki 3 55
(J R Jenkins) *pressed ldr: rdn and ev ch 2f out: sn hld: wknd ins fnl f* **10/1**

1-04 **5** ½ **Princess Tansy**[17] 2794 4-9-7 74 GeorgeBuckell(5) 8 58
(David Simcock) *rrd leaving stalls: outpcd in last: nvr on terms* **16/1**

-300 **6** 2¾ **Case Key**[47] 1935 3-9-5 73 DarryllHolland 6 45
(Charles Hills) *sn outpcd in last trio: n.d* **4/1**[2]

2-16 **7** *hd* **Aragon Knight**[33] 2314 3-9-4 75 TomMarquand(3) 7 46
(Heather Main) *chsd ldrs: rdn over 2f out: wknd over 1f out* **11/2**

453 **8** 6 **Jaarih (IRE)**[23] 2622 4-9-10 72 (p) TomQueally 5 23
(Conor Dore) *sn outpcd in last pair: nvr on terms* **8/1**

58.11s (-0.69) **Going Correction** -0.075s/f (Stan)
WFA 3 from 4yo+ 6lb **8** Ran SP% **114.6**
Speed ratings (Par 103): **102,101,99,92,91 86,86,76**
CSF £27.38 CT £112.72 TOTE £5.60: £2.20, £1.60, £1.90; EX 21.50 Trifecta £82.10.
Owner The Sutton Veny Syndicate **Bred** Mrs Sandra McCarthy **Trained** Stockbridge, Hants

FOCUS
Competitive enough for the grade but they were an exposed bunch and even the two 3yo's that finished first and second have had plenty of goes in handicaps already. The third has been rated close to his latest form.
T/Plt: £28.10 to a £1 stake. Pool: £60,110.40 - 1,556.41 winning tickets. T/Qpdt: £6.70 to a £1 stake. Pool: £6,900.64 - 754.49 winning tickets. **Tim Mitchell**

3354 NEWMARKET (R-H)
Saturday, June 18

OFFICIAL GOING: Good to soft
Wind: Fresh behind Weather: Overcast

3408 ROYAL ASCOT BETTING AT 188BET EBF STALLIONS NOVICE STKS (PLUS 10 RACE) 7f
1:40 (1:40) (Class 4) 2-Y-O **£4,528** (£1,347; £673; £336) **Stalls** High

Form RPR

0 **1** **Apex King (IRE)**[18] 2756 2-9-2 0 DavidProbert 2 84
(Ed Dunlop) *chsd ldrs: rdn over 2f out: str run wl ins fnl f to ld last strides* **5/1**[2]

6 **2** *nk* **Hyde Park**[18] 2756 2-9-2 0 NickyMackay 4 83
(John Gosden) *led to 1/2-way: led again over 1f out: rdn and edgd lft ins fnl f: hdd last strides* **4/6**[1]

41 **3** 1¼ **Pleaseletmewin (IRE)**[18] 2779 2-9-8 0 JohnFahy 6 86
(Ralph Beckett) *w ldr tl led 1/2-way: rdn over 2f out: hdd over 1f out: no ex towards fin* **7/1**[3]

4 4 **Londinium** 2-9-2 0 HarryBentley 3 70
(Mark Johnston) *s.i.s: in rr: rdn over 2f out: styd on to go 4th ins fnl f: nvr nrr* **16/1**

5 3 **Metronomic (IRE)** 2-9-2 0 SilvestreDeSousa 8 62
(Richard Hannon) *s.i.s: hld up: hdwy over 2f out: sn rdn and edgd lft: wknd over 1f out* **14/1**

6 ½ **Opening Time** 2-9-2 0 SeanLevey 7 60
(Richard Hannon) *chsd ldrs: rdn over 2f out: wknd over 1f out* **20/1**

7 2¾ **Farook (IRE)** 2-9-2 0 PaulHanagan 5 53
(Charles Hills) *chsd ldrs tl rdn and wknd over 1f out* **8/1**

0 **8** 23 **Twaddle**[9] 3073 2-8-4 0 SophieScardifield(7) 1
(Alan Coogan) *s.i.s: a in rr: wknd over 2f out* **100/1**

1m 27.51s (1.81) **Going Correction** +0.25s/f (Good) **8** Ran SP% **118.6**
Speed ratings (Par 95): **99,98,97,92,89 88,85,59**
CSF £9.04 TOTE £9.70: £2.10, £1.02, £1.80; EX 15.60 Trifecta £67.80.
Owner Mohammed Jaber **Bred** Dr W O'Brien **Trained** Newmarket, Suffolk

FOCUS
Far-side track in use. Repositioning of the bend into the home straight increased the distance of the 1m5f race by 22yds. There was just 1.5mm of rain overnight and the going remained good to soft. The winning time of the opener was 4.51sec outside standard and Nicky Mackay said: "It's soft", while Paul Hanagan said: "It's proper good to soft." They went no pace early in this ordinary novice event, but the placed horses got racing from some way out and that may have played into the hands of the winner. The level is a bit fluid.

3409 EURO 2016 BETTING AT 188BET H'CAP 1m 5f
2:10 (2:11) (Class 5) (0-75,78) 4-Y-O+ **£3,881** (£1,155; £577; £288) **Stalls** High

Form RPR

0061 **1** **Jacob Cats**[13] 2930 7-9-10 78 (v) SilvestreDeSousa 11 88
(William Knight) *s.i.s: hld up: hdwy over 2f out: rdn to ld over 1f out: styd on wl* **9/1**

-351 **2** 2 **Parnell's Dream**[11] 2994 4-9-7 75 SeanLevey 5 82
(Ralph Beckett) *chsd ldrs: wnt 2nd 3f out: led 2f out: rdn and hdd over 1f out: no ex wl ins fnl f* **9/2**[2]

6-11 **3** 1 **Always Resolute**[30] 2406 5-9-5 73 DaleSwift 7 79
(Brian Ellison) *hld up: hdwy over 2f out: sn rdn: styd on same pce ins fnl f* **13/8**[1]

62-4 **4** ¾ **Kristjano (GER)**[35] 2233 4-9-1 69 (p) TedDurcan 2 73
(Chris Wall) *chsd ldrs: rdn over 2f out: styd on same pce ins fnl f* **6/1**[3]

4502 **5** 3¼ **Rosie Royale (IRE)**[11] 3002 4-8-6 60 KieranO'Neill 8 60
(Roger Teal) *hld up: hdwy over 4f out: rdn over 1f out: styd on same pce* **20/1**

10-1 **6** ½ **Atalan**[27] 2502 4-9-4 72 FergusSweeney 1 71
(Hughie Morrison) *led: rdn and hung lft fr over 2f out: sn hdd: wknd ins fnl f* **6/1**[3]

3U-0 **7** 1½ **Satanic Beat (IRE)**[21] 2296 7-9-4 72 StevieDonohoe 3 69
(Phil Middleton) *prom: rdn over 2f out: sn hung lft: ev ch over 1f out: wknd ins fnl f* **50/1**

4006 **8** 1 **Opera Buff**[16] 2814 7-7-11 56 oh1 (p) NoelGarbutt(5) 4 51
(Rae Guest) *chsd ldr: pushed along over 4f out: lost 2nd 3f out: wknd fnl f* **40/1**

102 **9** 2½ **Rose Above**[15] 2876 4-9-7 75 DavidProbert 10 66
(Andrew Balding) *hld up: racd keenly: nt clr run over 2f out: rdn over 1f out: wknd fnl f* **10/1**

2m 50.49s (6.49) **Going Correction** +0.25s/f (Good) **9** Ran SP% **113.1**
Speed ratings (Par 103): **90,88,88,87,85 85,84,83,82**
CSF £47.30 CT £98.79 TOTE £6.80: £2.80, £2.20, £1.02; EX 31.70 Trifecta £138.80.
Owner Canisbay Bloodstock **Bred** Highclere Stud **Trained** Patching, W Sussex

FOCUS
Repositioning of the bend into the home straight increased race distance by 22yds. An ordinary handicap and the pace was modest, resulting in a time 10.49sec outside standard. The field made straight for the centre of the track after turning in and all nine runners were within a length or so of each other passing the 2f pole, though the first four eventually pulled clear. A small pb from the runner-up.

3410 £25 FREE BET AT 188BET EBF STALLIONS FILLIES' H'CAP 1m
2:45 (2:46) (Class 4) (0-85,87) 3-Y-O+ **£6,469** (£1,925; £962; £481) **Stalls** High

Form RPR

3-21 **1** **Golden Stunner (IRE)**[27] 2505 3-8-11 83 PatrickO'Donnell(5) 3 93
(Ralph Beckett) *racd centre: hld up: hdwy to chse ldr over 3f out: led 2f out: rdn ins fnl f: jst hld on* **11/4**[1]

41-6 **2** *nse* **Rostova (USA)**[43] 1992 3-9-0 81 TedDurcan 6 90
(Sir Michael Stoute) *swtchd to r centre 7f out: chsd ldrs: rdn and ev ch fr over 1f out: r.o: jst failed* **11/2**

11 **3** 2¼ **Mukaabra**[37] 2178 3-8-12 79 PaulHanagan 2 83
(James Tate) *racd centre: hld up: hdwy over 2f out: rdn and hung lft over 1f out: styd on same pce ins fnl f* **3/1**[2]

1-45 **4** 1 **Zest (IRE)**[43] 1992 3-8-13 83 DanielMuscutt(3) 1 85
(James Fanshawe) *stdd s: racd centre: hld up: hdwy over 2f out: rdn over 1f out: styd on same pce ins fnl f* **4/1**[3]

-306 **5** 1 **Justice Lass (IRE)**[11] 3001 3-8-10 77 SilvestreDeSousa 8 76
(David Elsworth) *chsd ldr tl swtchd to ld centre gp 7f out: overall ldr 6f out: rdn and hdd 2f out: no ex ins fnl f* **12/1**

0-56 **6** 6 **East Coast Lady (IRE)**[17] 2794 4-9-1 72 DavidProbert 7 59
(William Stone) *s.i.s: sn rcvrd to be overall ldr far side: lft to r alone 7f out: hdd 6f out: remained up w the pce tl rdn over 2f out: hung rt over 1f out: wknd fnl f* **33/1**

0-22 **7** 7 **Winter Rose (IRE)**[10] 3034 3-9-6 87 SeanLevey 5 56
(Richard Hannon) *racd centre: plld hrd: trckd ldr in centre tl pushed along over 3f out: wknd over 1f out* **10/1**

26-6 **8** 83 **Postbag**[23] 2628 4-9-12 83 FergusSweeney 4
(Henry Candy) *racd centre: hld up: hdwy 1/2-way: rdn and wknd over 2f out: eased over 1f out* **14/1**

1m 40.26s (0.26) **Going Correction** +0.25s/f (Good)
WFA 3 from 4yo 10lb **8** Ran SP% **113.4**
Speed ratings (Par 102): **108,107,105,104,103 97,90,7**
CSF £17.98 CT £47.27 TOTE £3.60: £1.60, £1.90, £1.10; EX 21.70 Trifecta £80.40.
Owner Sutong Pan **Bred** Fergus Cousins **Trained** Kimpton, Hants

FOCUS
Not a bad fillies' handicap. The 3yo generation had dominated recent runnings of the race and did so again. All bar one raced up the centre of the track. The level is a bit fluid, but the third has been rated close to her 1m win on the Rowley Mile, with the fourth to form.

3411 188BET.CO.UK EBF STALLIONS MAIDEN STKS (PLUS 10 RACE) (DIV I) 1m
3:20 (3:23) (Class 4) 3-Y-O **£5,498** (£1,636; £817; £408) **Stalls** High

Form RPR

1 **Permission** 3-8-11 0 DanielMuscutt(3) 6 89+
(James Fanshawe) *hld up: hdwy and nt clr run over 2f out: chsd ldr over 1f out: shkn up to ld ins fnl f: qcknd clr: easily* **14/1**

5220 **2** 4 **Raven's Corner (IRE)**[15] 2861 3-9-5 83 NickyMackay 10 81
(John Gosden) *chsd ldr tl led over 2f out: rdn and hdd ins fnl f: no ex* **4/1**[2]

3 1 **Mubajal** 3-9-5 0 PaulHanagan 2 79+
(Owen Burrows) *hld up: rdn over 2f out: styd on to go 3rd wl ins fnl f* **2/1**[1]

05 **4** 1 **Rockery (IRE)**[14] 2914 3-8-7 0 HarryBurns(7) 4 71
(Ed Dunlop) *led over 5f: sn rdn: no ex fnl f* **40/1**

3-5 **5** *nk* **See You When (IRE)**[11] 2998 3-9-5 0 SeanLevey 5 76
(Richard Hannon) *hld up in tch: racd keenly: rdn and edgd lft over 1f out: no ex fnl f* **2/1**[1]

03 **6** 4½ **Tom's Rock (IRE)**[18] 2780 3-9-5 0 JimmyQuinn 3 65
(John Butler) *prom: rdn and hung lft over 1f out: wknd fnl f* **25/1**

7 6 **Stamford Raffles** 3-9-5 0 JackMitchell 7 52
(Stuart Williams) *hld up: pushed along over 2f out: sn wknd* **33/1**

The Form Book, Raceform Ltd, Newbury, RG14 5SJ

8 3 1/4 **Donnerhall (IRE)** 3-9-5 0 SilvestreDeSousa 11 44
(Simon Crisford) *s.i.s: sn prom: rdn and wknd over 2f out* **7/1**[3]

00 **9** 3 1/4 **King Of Arts (IRE)**[40] 2109 3-9-5 0 HarryBentley 12 37
(David Simcock) *chsd ldrs: rdn over 2f out: wknd over 1f out* **66/1**

00 **10** 3 1/4 **Infiniti (IRE)**[28] 2483 3-9-0 0 SaleemGolam 9 24
(Rae Guest) *hld up: wknd over 2f out* **66/1**

0 **11** 10 **Fearless Poppy**[72] 1289 3-8-11 0 DannyBrock[(3)] 8
(Christine Dunnett) *prom: pushed along 1/2-way: wknd over 2f out* **100/1**

1m 41.54s (1.54) **Going Correction** +0.25s/f (Good) **11** Ran SP% **119.0**
Speed ratings (Par 101): **102,98,97,96,95 91,85,81,78,75 65**
CSF £67.83 TOTE £16.40: £3.20, £1.70, £1.30; EX 85.40 Trifecta £443.70.
Owner Mrs J Scott, J F Dean & Lady Trenchard **Bred** Glebe Stud, J F Dean & Lady Trenchard **Trained** Newmarket, Suffolk

FOCUS
An ordinary 3yo maiden with only one of these having shown much ability on turf before, though there were a couple of interesting newcomers and one of them left quite an impression. The runner-up has been rated close to his AW form for now.

3412 188BET.CO.UK EBF STALLIONS MAIDEN STKS (PLUS 10 RACE) (DIV II) 1m

4:00 (4:01) (Class 4) 3-Y-O **£5,498** (£1,636; £817; £408) **Stalls** High

Form RPR

2 **1** **Wilamina (IRE)**[15] 2877 3-9-0 0 FergusSweeney 10 94+
(Martyn Meade) *mde all: rdn over 1f out: styd on wl* **3/1**[2]

6-2 **2** 3 1/2 **Laugh Aloud**[22] 2653 3-9-0 0 (t) NickyMackay 5 86
(John Gosden) *mid-div: hdwy over 2f out: chsd wnr over 1f out: sn rdn: styd on same pce ins fnl f* **10/1**

4- **3** 5 **Great Order (USA)**[267] 6711 3-9-5 0 DavidProbert 4 80
(Saeed bin Suroor) *awkward s: hld up: rdn over 2f out: styd on to go 3rd ins fnl f: nvr nrr* **5/6**[1]

06-3 **4** 1 **Calvados Spirit**[17] 2790 3-9-5 77 PaulHanagan 11 77
(William Muir) *w wnr: rdn and ev ch over 2f out: wknd fnl f* **8/1**[3]

0 **5** 1 1/2 **Shargiah (IRE)**[26] 2541 3-9-5 0 HarryBentley 9 74
(Roger Varian) *chsd ldrs: rdn over 2f out: wknd over 1f out* **33/1**

05 **6** 1 1/4 **Imperial State**[17] 2790 3-9-5 0 (t) TedDurcan 1 71
(George Scott) *hld up: rdn over 2f out: wknd over 1f out* **100/1**

5 **7** 1 1/2 **Heart Of Oak**[9] 3066 3-9-0 0 StevieDonohoe 3 62
(George Peckham) *trckd ldrs: plld hrd: rdn over 2f out: wknd over 1f out* **66/1**

8 3 1/4 **Zwayyan** 3-9-5 0 SilvestreDeSousa 6 60+
(William Haggas) *dwlt: hld up: rdn over 1f out: hung lft fnl f: n.d* **12/1**

9 1 **Gomez** 3-9-5 0 SaleemGolam 2 61
(Rae Guest) *hld up: sme hdwy whn hung bdly lft fr over 1f out: almost p.u ins fnl f* **100/1**

00 **10** 1 **Lobster Cocktail (IRE)**[23] 2614 3-9-5 0 AntonioFresu 8 55
(Ed Walker) *s.i.s: hld up: rdn and wknd 2f out* **100/1**

11 9 **Istiqlaal** 3-9-5 0 MartinLane 7 35
(Charlie Appleby) *chsd ldrs: pushed along 3f out: wknd 2f out* **16/1**

1m 39.86s (-0.14) **Going Correction** +0.25s/f (Good) **11** Ran SP% **120.7**
Speed ratings (Par 101): **110,106,101,100,99 97,96,93,92,91 82**
CSF £33.53 TOTE £4.30: £1.40, £2.60, £1.10; EX 26.30 Trifecta £60.00.
Owner Ladyswood Stud **Bred** John Boden And Willie Kane **Trained** Newmarket, Suffolk

FOCUS
A few more of these had shown fair turf form than in the first division and again there were a couple of interesting and very expensive newcomers, though they both flopped. The winning time was 1.86sec faster than the first leg and the field finished well spread out. The runner-up has been rated as improving slightly on her latest run.

3413 188BET H'CAP 5f

4:40 (4:40) (Class 2) (0-105,103) 3-Y-O **£12,938** (£3,850; £1,924; £962) **Stalls** High

Form RPR

5010 **1** **Sign Of The Kodiac (IRE)**[7] 3165 3-8-6 **91** JoeDoyle[(3)] 1 97
(James Given) *w ldr tl led 4f out: rdn over 1f out: r.o gamely* **9/2**

0-60 **2** nk **Mont Kiara (FR)**[19] 2736 3-8-4 **86** HarryBentley 2 91
(Kevin Ryan) *hld up: hdwy over 1f out: sn rdn: r.o* **8/1**

133 **3** 1/2 **Gwendolyn (GER)**[19] 2751 3-8-2 **84** oh2 KieranO'Neill 6 87
(Robert Cowell) *hld up: racd keenly: hdwy over 1f out: rdn and ev ch ins fnl f: unable qck towards fin* **6/1**

6-20 **4** 1 3/4 **Lady Macapa**[37] 2192 3-8-12 **94** SilvestreDeSousa 3 91
(William Knight) *trckd ldrs: plld hrd: rdn over 1f out: styd on same pce* **7/2**[2]

0-00 **5** nk **Lathom**[7] 3165 3-8-12 **94** PaulHanagan 4 90
(David O'Meara) *led 1f: chsd wnr: rdn over 1f out: no ex ins fnl f* **4/1**[3]

6-55 **6** nk **King Of Rooks**[26] 2546 3-9-7 **103** SeanLevey 5 98
(Richard Hannon) *chsd ldrs: rdn over 1f out: no ex ins fnl f* **3/1**[1]

1m 0.35s (1.25) **Going Correction** +0.25s/f (Good) **6** Ran SP% **110.8**
Speed ratings (Par 105): **100,99,98,95,95 94**
CSF £36.83 TOTE £5.30: £2.50, £4.10; EX 38.20 Trifecta £176.70.
Owner The Cool Silk Partnership **Bred** Mrs Claire Doyle **Trained** Willoughton, Lincs

FOCUS
A warm 3yo sprint handicap despite the small field, but they didn't go a mad pace and the winner was always in the ideal position. A turf pb from the winner, with the third rated in line with the better view of his latest form.

3414 MOBILE BETTING AT 188BET H'CAP 6f

5:20 (5:22) (Class 4) (0-85,90) 3-Y-O+ **£5,175** (£1,540; £769; £384) **Stalls** High

Form RPR

-000 **1** **Syrian Pearl**[19] 2754 5-9-3 **76** TedDurcan 7 86+
(Chris Wall) *hld up: hdwy and nt clr run over 1f out: r.o u.p to ld nr fin* **12/1**

0-21 **2** hd **Shanghai Glory (IRE)**[7] 3144 3-9-10 **90** SilvestreDeSousa 4 96
(Charles Hills) *a.p: rdn to ld ins fnl f: edgd lft and hdd nr fin* **15/8**[1]

-664 **3** shd **Misterioso (IRE)**[8] 3101 4-9-9 **82** MartinLane 1 90
(Jamie Osborne) *hld up: rdn over 1f out: r.o wl ins fnl f: nt quite get there* **14/1**

-034 **4** 3/4 **Pharmaceutical (IRE)**[13] 2934 4-9-9 **82** SeanLevey 14 88
(Stuart Williams) *hld up: hdwy over 1f out: r.o* **10/1**

0005 **5** 1 1/2 **Captain Bob (IRE)**[7] 3159 5-9-4 **77** JimmyQuinn 8 78
(Robert Cowell) *chsd ldrs: rdn over 1f out: ev ch whn hung lft ins fnl f: styd on same pce* **8/1**[3]

1320 **6** shd **Dandyleekie (IRE)**[35] 2238 4-9-4 **80** ShelleyBirkett[(3)] 9 80
(David O'Meara) *prom: rdn over 1f out: styd on* **12/1**

1100 **7** 3/4 **Evanescent (IRE)**[19] 2754 7-9-6 **79** DavidProbert 6 77
(Tony Carroll) *hld up: pushed along over 2f out: r.o ins fnl f: nvr nrr* **66/1**

-040 **8** 1 1/4 **Tagula Night (IRE)**[7] 3159 10-8-13 **75** (vt) JackDuern[(3)] 13 69
(Dean Ivory) *led: rdn over 2f out: hung lft over 1f out: hdd and no ex ins fnl f* **33/1**

-413 **9** nk **Jordan Sport**[35] 2239 3-9-4 **84** PaulHanagan 12 75
(Richard Fahey) *plld hrd and prom: rdn over 1f out: no ex ins fnl f* **7/2**[2]

4330 **10** 1 **Showboating (IRE)**[80] 1153 8-9-5 **85** LewisEdmunds[(7)] 11 75
(John Balding) *chsd ldrs: rdn over 2f out: no ex fnl f* **40/1**

2003 **11** 3/4 **Vimy Ridge**[66] 1427 4-9-7 **80** (p) RobertTart 5 68
(Alan Bailey) *chsd ldr: rdn over 2f out: wknd ins fnl f* **33/1**

6102 **12** 1 1/4 **Justice First**[14] 2903 4-9-2 **82** HarryBurns[(7)] 3 66
(Ed Dunlop) *hld up: rdn over 1f out: n.d* **25/1**

-001 **13** 7 **Cool Bahamian (IRE)**[14] 2903 5-9-12 **85** (b) JohnFahy 2 46
(Eve Johnson Houghton) *hld up: wknd over 1f out* **25/1**

1m 13.1s (0.60) **Going Correction** +0.25s/f (Good)
WFA 3 from 4yo+ 7lb **13** Ran SP% **116.8**
Speed ratings (Par 105): **106,105,105,104,102 102,101,99,99,98 97,95,86**
CSF £31.96 CT £342.94 TOTE £13.20: £2.80, £1.40, £3.90; EX 47.60 Trifecta £775.00.
Owner The Clodhoppers **Bred** Jeremy Green And Sons **Trained** Newmarket, Suffolk

FOCUS
A fair sprint handicap, though something of a lopsided betting market with a warm favourite. The winner, third and fourth came from the very back of the field, suggesting the leaders may have gone off too quick. The winner has been rated back to form, with the runner-up confirming his recent improvement.

3415 BEST ODDS GUARANTEED AT 188BET H'CAP 7f

5:55 (5:55) (Class 4) (0-85,85) 3-Y-O **£5,175** (£1,540; £769; £384) **Stalls** High

Form RPR

-521 **1** **Gunmetal (IRE)**[21] 2698 3-9-5 **83** SteveDrowne 10 92
(Charles Hills) *led centre gp: overall ldr over 2f out: rdn over 1f out: jst hld on* **3/1**[1]

1-05 **2** nk **Dollar Reward**[21] 2693 3-8-13 **77** TedDurcan 7 85
(Sir Michael Stoute) *racd centre: a.p: rdn to chse wnr over 1f out: nt quite get there* **5/1**[3]

0-60 **3** 2 1/4 **Experto Crede (IRE)**[14] 2891 3-9-3 **81** AntonioFresu 1 83
(Ed Walker) *racd centre: hld up: rdn over 2f out: hung lft and r.o ins fnl f: nt rch ldrs* **9/1**

-633 **4** 2 **Nisser**[8] 3105 3-9-5 **83** SeanLevey 9 80
(Richard Hannon) *racd centre: chsd wnr tl rdn over 1f out: no ex ins fnl f* **10/3**[2]

0-05 **5** hd **Worlds His Oyster**[14] 2907 3-9-1 **79** MartinLane 8 75
(John Quinn) *racd centre: hld up: rdn over 3f out: styd on ins fnl f: nvr trbld ldrs* **10/1**

12-0 **6** 3/4 **Edification**[37] 2179 3-9-5 **83** FergusSweeney 11 77
(Martyn Meade) *s.i.s: racd alone far side: sn rcvrd to ld overall: rdn and hdd over 2f out: edgd rt and wknd ins fnl f* **20/1**

-451 **7** 2 1/2 **Wimpole Hall**[16] 2818 3-9-2 **80** SilvestreDeSousa 12 67
(William Jarvis) *racd centre: chsd ldrs: rdn over 2f out: wknd over 1f out* **11/2**

0-00 **8** 50 **English Hero**[22] 2650 3-8-12 **76** HarryBentley 5
(William Knight) *racd centre: rdr had trble w his nrside iron as sn as they lft the stalls: in rr: kicked both feet out of the irons over 4f out: sn lost tch* **12/1**

1m 26.8s (1.10) **Going Correction** +0.25s/f (Good) **8** Ran SP% **111.7**
Speed ratings (Par 101): **103,102,100,97,97 96,93,36**
CSF £17.34 CT £116.72 TOTE £4.30: £1.40, £2.10, £3.00; EX 20.40 Trifecta £149.80.
Owner Mrs J K Powell **Bred** Maurice Byrne **Trained** Lambourn, Berks

FOCUS
A fair 3yo handicap in which again one went far side, while the rest came centre-to-nearside. The third has been rated to his best.
T/Plt: £24.70 to a £1 stake. Pool: £60,046.30 - 1,769.13 winning tickets. T/Qpdt: £15.90 to a £1 stake. Pool: £3,757.92 - 174.00 winning tickets. **Colin Roberts**

3361 REDCAR (L-H)

Saturday, June 18

OFFICIAL GOING: Good to soft (7.8)
Wind: Light against Weather: Overcast, sunny after 4th

3416 EBF STALLIONS ROYAL ASCOT BETTING AT 188BET NOVICE STKS 6f

1:35 (1:37) (Class 5) 2-Y-O **£3,234** (£962; £481; £240) **Stalls** Centre

Form RPR

60 **1** **Allux Boy (IRE)**[7] 3167 2-8-11 0 RachelRichardson[(5)] 8 67
(Nigel Tinkler) *mde all: pushed along over 1f out: strly pressed ent fnl f: rdn and hld on wl* **50/1**

6 **2** nk **London Grammar (IRE)**[12] 2970 2-8-11 0 CamHardie 6 61
(John Quinn) *prom: rdn 2f out: chal strly ent fnl f: kpt on but a jst hld* **20/1**

60 **3** 2 1/4 **Coverham (IRE)**[23] 2617 2-9-2 0 KeaganLatham 7 59
(James Bethell) *trckd ldrs: pushed along over 1f out: rdn ins fnl f: kpt on* **25/1**

0 **4** 4 **Foxy Boy**[14] 2913 2-9-2 0 AndrewMullen 10 47
(Michael Dods) *prom: rdn 2f out: grad wknd over 1f out* **10/1**

5 2 3/4 **Snookered (IRE)** 2-8-9 0 AdamMcNamara[(7)] 2 39
(Richard Fahey) *dwlt: sn in tch: rdn and outpcd over 2f out: no threat after* **4/1**[2]

6 2 **Bahkit (IRE)** 2-9-2 0 BenCurtis 5 33
(Alan Swinbank) *hld up: pushed along over 2f out: nvr threatened* **16/1**

7 1/2 **Bajan Spice (IRE)** 2-8-11 0 PJMcDonald 12 26
(Ann Duffield) *dwlt: sn in tch: rdn over 2f out: wknd over 1f out* **7/1**[3]

8 shd **Party Tiger** 2-9-2 0 TonyHamilton 4 31
(Richard Fahey) *s.i.s: sn prom racing keenly: rdn 2f out: wknd appr fnl f* **15/8**[1]

1m 14.79s (2.99) **Going Correction** +0.15s/f (Good) **8** Ran SP% **92.8**
Speed ratings (Par 93): **86,85,82,77,73 70,70,70**
CSF £479.36 TOTE £35.30: £9.00, £3.00, £5.20; EX 679.50 TRIFECTA Not won..
Owner M Webb **Bred** Victor Stud Bloodstock Ltd **Trained** Langton, N Yorks
■ Morning Suit (3-1) was withdrawn. Rule 4 applies to all bets. Deduction - 25p in the pound.

FOCUS
Good to soft ground and no changes to race distances. Cam Hardie said: "The ground is on the slow side of good," while Andrew Mullen said: "It is on the dead side". The opener was a moderate novice for juveniles which sparked a lively betting heat. This probably lacked depth and it's been rated at a low level for now, but it's fluid.

3417 TEESSIDE HOSPICE FASHION SHOW H'CAP (DIV I) 1m 6f 19y
2:05 (2:05) (Class 6) (0-65,68) 4-Y-O+ **£2,749** (£818; £408; £204) **Stalls** Low

Form RPR
-050 **1** **Balmusette**[32] 2338 7-8-10 **54** BarryMcHugh 6 61
(Keith Reveley) *trckd ldrs: rdn 3f out: hung lft over 2f out: chal ins fnl f: styd on: led towards fin* **5/1**[3]
3013 **2** *hd* **Kiwayu**[8] 3118 7-9-10 **68** (p) AndrewMullen 4 75
(Philip Kirby) *hld up: hdwy over 2f out: rdn over 1f out: chal ins fnl f: kpt on* **9/4**[1]
0431 **3** *hd* **Roc De Prince**[21] 2678 7-9-2 **60** (p) GrahamGibbons 9 66
(Keith Dalgleish) *prom: rdn to ld 3f out: strly pressed ins fnl f: one pce and hdd towards fin* **4/1**[2]
5540 **4** *1 1/2* **Thankyou Very Much**[25] 2558 6-8-8 **57** (p) NathanEvans(5) 11 62
(James Bethell) *hld up: rdn and hdwy on outer over 2f out: chsd ldrs appr fnl f: no ex fnl 110yds* **8/1**
-040 **5** *1 1/4* **Noble Reach**[9] 3067 5-8-2 **46** oh1 CamHardie 5 49
(Lawrence Mullaney) *led: rdn whn hdd 3f out: remained cl up: one pce fnl f* **16/1**
/005 **6** *nk* **No Not Yet**[19] 2745 4-8-2 **46** PatrickMathers 2 49
(Michael Dods) *trckd ldrs: rdn 3f out: sn one pce* **10/1**
0506 **7** *1 1/2* **Yorkshireman (IRE)**[14] 2916 6-8-2 **46** oh1 (b) FrannyNorton 10 47
(Lynn Siddall) *midfield: rdn over 2f out: no imp* **25/1**
6-3 **8** *1/2* **Politbureau**[14] 2916 9-9-7 **65** (p) PJMcDonald 3 65
(Micky Hammond) *racd keenly in midfield on inner: rdn over 2f out: in tch over 1f out: wknd ins fnl f* **7/1**
-020 **9** *14* **District Attorney (IRE)**[9] 3067 7-8-4 **48** DuranFentiman 8 30
(Chris Fairhurst) *hld up: pushed along over 3f out: wknd 2f out* **25/1**

3m 5.7s (1.00) **Going Correction** +0.15s/f (Good) **9** Ran SP% **113.7**
Speed ratings (Par 101): **103,102,102,101,101 101,100,99,91**
CSF £16.36 CT £47.84 TOTE £6.10: £1.90, £1.40, £1.50; EX 18.50 Trifecta £88.60.
Owner Mr & Mrs W J Williams **Bred** W J & Mrs M Williams **Trained** Lingdale, Redcar & Cleveland

FOCUS
This was stronger than the second division of this moderate staying handicap, in which it paid to race prominently. Straightforward form.

3418 TEESSIDE HOSPICE FASHION SHOW H'CAP (DIV II) 1m 6f 19y
2:40 (2:40) (Class 6) (0-65,65) 4-Y-O+ **£2,749** (£818; £408; £204) **Stalls** Low

Form RPR
5-06 **1** **Stoneham**[16] 2813 5-8-11 **55** RoystonFfrench 4 62
(Iain Jardine) *midfield: rdn and hdwy 2f out: sn chsd ldr: led 110yds out: styd on* **4/1**[3]
0553 **2** *3/4* **Cape Hideaway**[19] 2745 4-9-0 **58** (p) DougieCostello 7 64
(Mark Walford) *led: hdd 11f out: trckd ldr: rdn over 2f out: led again over 1f out: hdd 110yds out: one pce* **9/2**
-404 **3** *3/4* **Arthurs Secret**[21] 2678 6-9-7 **65** (v) CamHardie 3 70
(John Quinn) *in tch: rdn 3f out: ev ch over 1f out: one pce ins fnl f* **7/2**[2]
3-0P **4** *3/4* **Perennial**[15] 2853 7-8-6 **55** (p) PhilDennis(5) 5 59
(Philip Kirby) *hld up: hdwy on inner 3f out: rdn to chse ldrs 2f out: one pce fnl f* **18/1**
-400 **5** *2 1/4* **Chorus of Lies**[23] 2618 4-9-4 **62** BarryMcHugh 9 63
(Tracy Waggott) *racd keenly: trckd ldr: led 11f out: rdn 3f out: hdd over 1f out: wknd ins fnl f* **12/1**
-612 **6** *1* **Nonagon**[14] 2916 5-8-12 **63** (t) AdamMcNamara(7) 6 63
(Wilf Storey) *hld up: pushed along and sme hdwy 3f out: rdn over 2f out: wknd ins fnl f* **5/2**[1]
/00- **7** *1 1/2* **Danzella**[231] 7640 4-8-2 **46** oh1 DuranFentiman 10 44
(Chris Fairhurst) *hld up: nvr threatened* **33/1**
055- **8** *10* **Keep Up (GER)**[7] 7543 4-8-3 **47** (p) AndrewMullen 8 32
(Philip Kirby) *in tch: rdn over 3f out: sn lost pl and bhd* **16/1**

3m 9.2s (4.50) **Going Correction** +0.15s/f (Good) **8** Ran SP% **110.8**
Speed ratings (Par 101): **93,92,92,91,90 89,89,83**
CSF £20.85 CT £64.24 TOTE £5.20: £1.60, £1.50, £1.80; EX 19.80 Trifecta £75.30.
Owner The Dregs Of Humanity & Partner **Bred** Norman Court Stud **Trained** Carrutherstown, D'fries & G'way

FOCUS
This looked weaker than the first division, run in a time over three seconds slower. Once again it proved best to be up with the pace. Straightforward form, with the winner rated close to last year's turf peak.

3419 H JARVIS 138TH ANNIVERSARY H'CAP 7f
3:15 (3:18) (Class 3) (0-90,88) 4-Y-O+ **£7,762** (£2,310; £1,154; £577) **Stalls** Centre

Form RPR
2556 **1** **Nuno Tristan (USA)**[8] 3115 4-9-6 **87** TonyHamilton 6 98
(Richard Fahey) *hld up: gd hdwy 2f out: led appr fnl f: kpt on wl pushed out* **7/1**[3]
0404 **2** *2 1/4* **Fuwairt (IRE)**[8] 3115 4-8-9 **76** JFEgan 1 81
(David Loughnane) *hld up: pushed along and gd hdwy over 1f out: rdn to chal appr fnl f: one pce and no ch w wnr ins fnl f* **10/1**
-634 **3** *nk* **Beardwood**[21] 2679 4-9-1 **82** BenCurtis 9 86
(Brian Ellison) *midfield: rdn over 2f out: styd on wl fnl f* **4/1**[1]
2166 **4** *1 1/2* **Taysh (USA)**[16] 2833 4-9-3 **84** PatrickMathers 10 84
(Michael Appleby) *chsd ldr: rdn over 2f out: kpt on same pce* **8/1**
-510 **5** *nk* **Nonno Giulio (IRE)**[10] 3011 5-8-12 **79** PJMcDonald 2 78
(David Loughnane) *led: rdn over 2f out: hdd appr fnl f: grad wknd* **16/1**
2436 **6** *hd* **Azagal (IRE)**[15] 2855 5-8-4 **76** RachelRichardson(5) 11 75
(Tim Easterby) *midfield: wnt prom over 3f out: rdn over 3f out: wknd ins fnl f* **16/1**
400 **7** *shd* **Free Code (IRE)**[15] 2862 5-9-7 **88** GrahamGibbons 5 90+
(David Barron) *hld up: pushed along 2f out: short of room ins fnl f: swtchd rt: kpt on* **8/1**
0-40 **8** *1* **My Name Is Rio (IRE)**[61] 1522 6-9-5 **86** AndrewMullen 13 82
(Michael Dods) *hld up: rdn over 2f out: sme hdwy over 1f out: nvr threatened* **12/1**
-210 **9** *1/2* **Slemy (IRE)**[15] 2862 5-8-7 **79** NathanEvans(5) 4 73
(Ruth Carr) *midfield: rdn over 2f out: wknd ins fnl f* **9/2**[2]
200- **10** *2 1/2* **Zacynthus (IRE)**[231] 7635 8-9-2 **83** RoystonFfrench 3 71
(John Balding) *in tch: rdn over 2f out: wknd fnl f* **33/1**
0-10 **11** *3/4* **Khelman (IRE)**[21] 2679 6-8-12 **86** AdamMcNamara(7) 8 72
(Richard Fahey) *trckd ldr: rdn over 3f out: wknd over 1f out* **10/1**
-000 **12** *6* **Free Zone**[15] 2857 7-8-10 **77** DougieCostello 12 46
(David O'Meara) *hld up: rdn 3f out: sn btn* **33/1**

1m 25.4s (0.90) **Going Correction** +0.15s/f (Good) **12** Ran SP% **116.4**
Speed ratings (Par 107): **100,97,97,95,95 94,94,93,92,90 89,82**
CSF £73.83 CT £321.80 TOTE £7.90: £2.40, £2.60, £1.70; EX 72.30 Trifecta £456.60.
Owner Nick Bradley Racing 16 **Bred** Galleria Bloodstock & Samac **Trained** Musley Bank, N Yorks

FOCUS
A competitive handicap in which 4yos have done well down the years, and it was that age-group who triumphed once more. They went a good gallop, suiting those coming from off the pace, and the form should be viewed in a positive light, a number of well handicapped runners coming to the fore. The winner has been rated to his AW form, and the third close to his recent form.

3420 MARKET CROSS JEWELLERS H'CAP 5f
3:50 (3:53) (Class 4) (0-85,84) 3-Y-O **£6,469** (£1,925; £962; £481) **Stalls** Centre

Form RPR
0211 **1** **Black Grass**[15] 2854 3-7-12 **66** NathanEvans(5) 9 80
(Michael Easterby) *mde all: rdn over 1f out: kpt on wl to draw clr ins fnl f* **5/2**[1]
-653 **2** *3* **Midnight Malibu (IRE)**[25] 2554 3-8-13 **76** DuranFentiman 12 79
(Tim Easterby) *chsd ldr: rdn 2f out: swtchd lft appr fnl f: kpt on but no ch w wnr* **12/1**
-561 **3** *1 1/2* **Twentysvnthlancers**[26] 2534 3-8-5 **68** PJMcDonald 10 66
(Paul Midgley) *hld up: rdn 3f out: hdwy 2f out: kpt on fnl f* **10/1**
0-50 **4** *1 1/2* **Excessable**[36] 2218 3-9-1 **83** (t) RachelRichardson(5) 5 75+
(Tim Easterby) *hld up: pushed along and hdwy on outside over 1f out: kpt on* **5/1**[2]
3254 **5** *1* **Sir Dudley (IRE)**[19] 2736 3-8-10 **78** (b) PhilDennis(5) 6 67
(James Given) *dwlt: sn chsd ldr: rdn over 2f out: wknd ins fnl f* **13/2**
1-00 **6** *1/2* **Gowanless**[22] 2650 3-8-10 **73** (p) CamHardie 1 60+
(Michael Dods) *hld up: rdn over 2f out: sme hdwy on wd outside over 1f out: nvr threatened* **22/1**
0-04 **7** *1* **Lydia's Place**[25] 2554 3-9-3 **83** EoinWalsh(3) 8 66
(Richard Guest) *prom: rdn over 2f out: wknd appr fnl f* **10/1**
-212 **8** *3/4* **First Bombardment**[29] 2426 3-9-0 **77** (p) GrahamGibbons 11 58
(David O'Meara) *in tch: rdn over 2f out: wkng whn hmpd ins fnl f* **11/2**[3]
40-0 **9** *3/4* **Market Choice (IRE)**[17] 2802 3-9-2 **79** AndrewMullen 2 57
(Michael Dods) *sn outpcd in rr: a bhd* **16/1**
0-40 **10** *nk* **New Road Side**[36] 2218 3-8-13 **76** BarryMcHugh 3 53
(Tony Coyle) *chsd ldrs: rdn over 2f out: wknd over 1f out* **16/1**

58.76s (0.16) **Going Correction** +0.15s/f (Good) **10** Ran SP% **115.9**
Speed ratings (Par 101): **104,99,96,94,92 92,90,89,88,87**
CSF £34.53 CT £224.83 TOTE £3.00: £1.10, £3.20, £3.40; EX 30.90 Trifecta £174.00.
Owner T Dewhirst, L Folwell, S Hull & D Swales **Bred** M W Easterby **Trained** Sheriff Hutton, N Yorks

FOCUS
A fair sprint handicap and an impressive winner, who was up there from the start. The runner-up has been rated close to form.

3421 188BET CLAIMING STKS 7f
4:30 (4:31) (Class 5) 3-Y-O+ **£3,072** (£914; £456; £228) **Stalls** Centre

Form RPR
-612 **1** **Layla's Hero (IRE)**[51] 1818 9-9-5 78 (b) AndrewMullen 11 80
(David Nicholls) *in tch: hdwy to trck ldr over 2f out: rdn to ld appr fnl f: kpt on* **5/1**[3]
00-6 **2** *1* **Balducci**[33] 2297 9-9-5 88 (b[1]) PJMcDonald 13 77
(David Loughnane) *led: rdn 2f out: hdd appr fnl f: kpt on* **11/1**
2560 **3** *1 1/4* **Burning Blaze**[14] 2910 6-9-11 75 BenCurtis 1 80
(Brian Ellison) *hld up: rdn and hdwy over 2f out: kpt on* **5/1**[3]
-516 **4** *2* **Victoire De Lyphar (IRE)**[10] 3011 9-9-1 70 (e) NathanEvans(5) 4 70
(Ruth Carr) *in tch: rdn over 2f out: one pce* **10/3**[1]
-300 **5** *3 1/2* **Our Boy Jack (IRE)**[21] 2679 7-9-1 79 (p) AdamMcNamara(7) 3 63
(Richard Fahey) *in tch: rdn over 2f out: wknd over 1f out* **7/2**[2]
1-61 **6** *2 3/4* **Smart Mover (IRE)**[52] 1789 3-8-9 74 CamHardie 8 49
(John Quinn) *hld up in tch: rdn over 2f out: wknd over 1f out* **7/1**
3650 **7** *nk* **Moonlight Venture**[16] 2821 5-9-4 75 (b) KevinStott(3) 6 54
(Conor Dore) *hld up: nvr threatened* **9/1**
-050 **8** *1/2* **Jersey Roy**[19] 2733 3-8-7 62 PatrickMathers 7 45
(Richard Fahey) *in tch: rdn over 2f out: sn wknd* **25/1**
0000 **9** *3* **Shearian**[50] 1845 6-9-3 54 (p) RoystonFfrench 10 41
(Tracy Waggott) *prom: rdn 3f out: wknd over 1f out* **50/1**
000- **10** *4 1/2* **Wisteria**[317] 5052 4-8-9 44 (t) GarryWhillans(5) 2 26
(Susan Corbett) *a towards rr* **100/1**
00-0 **11** *12* **Sarafina**[14] 1550 4-8-11 40 (b[1]) DougieCostello 5
(David Thompson) *v.s.a: a detached* **100/1**
00 **12** *8* **Frenchie**[29] 2425 4-9-0 0 PaddyAspell 9
(Shaun Harris) *midfield: rdn over 3f out: sn wknd: t.o* **100/1**

1m 25.94s (1.44) **Going Correction** +0.15s/f (Good)
WFA 3 from 4yo+ 9lb **12** Ran SP% **118.2**
Speed ratings (Par 103): **97,95,94,92,88 85,84,84,80,75 61,52**
CSF £57.25 TOTE £5.50: £1.80, £3.20, £1.80; EX 44.80 Trifecta £343.00.
Owner D Nicholls **Bred** Epona Bloodstock Ltd **Trained** Sessay, N Yorks

FOCUS
A fair claimer for the grade. The winner was another on the card to have raced up the stands' rail. The winner has been rated to his recent level in a straightforward claimer. There were no claims.

3422 EURO 2016 BETTING AT 188BET MEDIAN AUCTION MAIDEN STKS 6f
5:10 (5:10) (Class 5) 3-5-Y-O **£3,072** (£914; £456; £228) **Stalls** Centre

Form RPR
2-03 **1** **Operative**[35] 2234 3-9-2 75 KevinStott(3) 8 83
(Ed de Giles) *trckd ldrs: led over 2f out: sn rdn: drvn over 1f out: kpt on* **3/1**[1]
3 **2** *2* **Hilary J**[19] 2740 3-9-0 0 [1] PJMcDonald 6 72
(Ann Duffield) *midfield: rdn over 2f out: hdwy over 1f out: chsd wnr ins fnl f: kpt on same pce* **17/2**
26 **3** *3 3/4* **Coronation Day**[37] 2177 3-9-0 0 DougieCostello 9 60
(James Tate) *prom: led briefly wl over 2f out: rdn 2f out: wknd ins fnl f* **10/3**[2]
24-0 **4** *1/2* **Questo**[32] 2346 4-9-12 72 RoystonFfrench 7 65
(Tracy Waggott) *hld up: rdn over 2f out: kpt on ins fnl f: nvr threatened* **7/1**
-024 **5** *1* **Silver Sands (IRE)**[10] 3010 3-9-5 67 AndrewElliott 1 60
(Tim Easterby) *hld up: rdn over 2f out: nvr threatened* **7/1**
-046 **6** *3/4* **Dacoity**[14] 2886 3-8-12 72 AdamMcNamara(7) 4 57
(Richard Fahey) *prom: rdn over 2f out: wknd over 1f out* **9/2**[3]

6-20 **7** 1 1/2 **Run Rio Run (IRE)**42 2049 3-9-5 68 AndrewMullen 3 53
(Michael Dods) *led: rdn whn hdd wl over 2f out: sn wknd* **14/1**
00 **8** 10 **Hallux**16 2835 3-9-5 0 GrahamGibbons 2 21
(David Barron) *hld up: rdn over 3f out: sn bhd: eased ins fnl f* **25/1**
1m 11.56s (-0.24) **Going Correction** +0.15s/f (Good)
WFA 3 from 4yo 7lb **8** Ran SP% **112.3**
Speed ratings (Par 103): **107,104,99,98,97 96,94,81**
CSF £27.77 TOTE £5.00: £1.10, £2.90, £2.00; EX 22.30 Trifecta £216.50.
Owner Gwyn & Samantha Powell & Partner **Bred** Whitsbury Manor Stud **Trained** Ledbury, H'fords

FOCUS
A weak maiden, but they went a good pace. The runner-up has been rated as building on her debut.

3423 188BET.CO.UK H'CAP 5f
5:50 (5:52) (Class 6) (0-65,65) 3-Y-O **£2,749** (£818; £408; £204) **Stalls** Centre

Form RPR
-550 **1** **Searanger (USA)**19 2742 3-9-4 **62** PJMcDonald 4 69
(Ann Duffield) *hld up towards far side: rdn 2f out: hdwy over 1f out: led 75yds out: kpt on* **13/2**
-301 **2** 3/4 **Bond Bombshell**10 3009 3-9-0 **65** AdamMcNamara(7) 7 69
(David O'Meara) *prom towards stands' side: rdn 1/2-way: led wl over 1f out: hdd 75yds out: edgd lft and one pce* **5/13**
00-3 **3** 3/4 **Chip Or Pellet**33 2302 3-8-3 **47** AndrewMullen 10 49
(Nigel Tinkler) *prom towards stands' side: rdn 2f out: hung lft fnl f but kpt on* **7/22**
512 **4** 1/2 **Lady Joanna Vassa (IRE)**16 2834 3-8-11 **58** EoinWalsh(3) 5 58
(Richard Guest) *dwlt: sn chsd ldrs towards far side: rdn 2f out: kpt on* **5/21**
0000 **5** 1/2 **Men United (FR)**9 3070 3-8-13 **57** (t) JFEgan 6 56
(Roy Bowring) *hld up in centre: rdn and hdwy over 1f out: keeping whn short of room 50yds out* **9/1**
664 **6** 1 1/2 **Wishing Tree**21 2681 3-8-10 **57** KevinStott(3) 9 50
(Brian Ellison) *outpcd in rr towards stands' side tl kpt on fnl f* **16/1**
40-5 **7** 1 **Midnight Robbery**10 3010 3-8-9 **58** PhilDennis(5) 2 47
(Bryan Smart) *w ldr towards far side: rdn 2f out: wknd ins fnl f* **14/1**
4-00 **8** 1 3/4 **Sophistica (IRE)**14 2919 3-8-13 **57** RoystonFfrench 8 40
(Iain Jardine) *dwlt: hld up towards stands' side: nvr threatened* **14/1**
45-0 **9** hd **Lady Elizabeth (IRE)**156 181 3-8-13 **57** (p) RyanClark 1 39
(Scott Dixon) *led narrowly towards far side: rdn whn hdd wl over 1f out: sn wknd* **20/1**
-000 **10** 1 1/4 **Kylla**25 2559 3-8-2 **46** oh1 CamHardie 3 23
(Shaun Harris) *chsd ldrs towards far side: rdn 2f out: wknd appr fnl f* **50/1**
-000 **11** 3 1/4 **Lowrie**19 2740 3-8-2 **46** oh1 PatrickMathers 12 12
(John David Riches) *chsd ldrs towards stands' side: rdn 1/2-way: wknd fnl f* **50/1**
59.67s (1.07) **Going Correction** +0.15s/f (Good) **11** Ran SP% **118.7**
Speed ratings (Par 97): **97,95,94,93,93 90,89,86,85,83 78**
CSF £38.81 CT £136.20 TOTE £7.30: £2.90, £1.80, £1.30; EX 37.60 Trifecta £246.00.
Owner ICM Racing & John Dance **Bred** Phoenix Rising Farms **Trained** Constable Burton, N Yorks

FOCUS
An interesting little sprint featuring some unexposed types, and the main contenders dominated. They split into two groups, where the far side provided both a stronger pace and the eventual winner. The runner-up has been rated near her Beverley win.
T/Plt: £3,710.90 to a £1 stake. Pool: £54,698.57 - 10.76 winning tickets. T/Qpdt: £13.80 to a £1 stake. Pool: £4,563.02 - 243.30 winning tickets. **Andrew Sheret**

3424 - 3427a (Foreign Racing) - See Raceform Interactive

DOWN ROYAL (R-H)
Saturday, June 18

OFFICIAL GOING: Good

3428a MAGNERS ULSTER DERBY (PREMIER H'CAP) 1m 4f 106y
4:35 (4:36) 3-Y-O
£43,382 (£13,970; £6,617; £2,941; £1,470; £735)

RPR
1 **Stellar Mass (IRE)**14 2926 3-9-6 **92** KevinManning 3 100+
(J S Bolger, Ire) *hld up in tch: 6th 1/2-way: rdn to chal 1 1/2f out and led ent fnl f: drvn clr ins fnl f and styd on wl* **9/22**
2 1 3/4 **Manjaam (IRE)**22 2638 3-9-0 **86** WayneLordan 5 91
(Ed Dunlop) *sn chsd ldrs: 4th 1/2-way: rdn on inner under 2f out and short of room bhd ldrs 1 1/2f out where dropped to 5th: swtchd ins fnl f and r.o wl into 2nd: nt trble wnr* **10/31**
3 2 1/2 **Lieutenant General (IRE)**15 2883 3-9-12 **98** ColmO'Donoghue 4 99
(A P O'Brien, Ire) *w.w towards rr: 8th 1/2-way: impr bhd ldrs gng wl under 2f out: n.m.r and sltly hmpd over 1f out: sn rdn in 5th and r.o between horses into 3rd cl home: nvr trbld ldrs* **9/22**
4 nk **Power Struggle (IRE)**20 2720 3-8-8 **80** (t) ChrisHayes 6 81
(A Oliver, Ire) *hld up: 7th 1/2-way: swtchd lft to outer and rdn 2f out: sn bmpd sltly and no imp on ldrs ent fnl f: kpt on ins fnl f: nvr trbld ldrs* **16/1**
5 nk **Zalfana (IRE)**15 2883 3-9-6 **92** PatSmullen 9 92
(D K Weld, Ire) *chsd ldrs: 3rd 1/2-way: rdn almost on terms 2f out and no ex u.p over 1f out: one pce fnl f* **8/1**
6 1 3/4 **Tonkinese**14 2925 3-9-6 **92** (tp) ShaneFoley 1 89
(M Halford, Ire) *settled bhd ldr in 2nd: rdn to ld briefly over 1f out tl sn hdd & wknd qckly ins fnl f* **13/23**
7 1 1/2 **Raconteur**21 2709 3-8-10 **82** DeclanMcDonogh 8 77
(W McCreery, Ire) *chsd ldrs: 5th 1/2-way: tk clsr order on outer 2f out where edgd sltly lft and bmpd rival: sn no ex u.p in 6th: one pce fnl f* **8/1**
8 2 **Lex Talionis (IRE)**10 3050 3-7-11 **76** oh1 (p) KillianLeonard(7) 7 68
(J F Levins, Ire) *hld up: last at 1/2-way: short of room and checked on inner over 4f out: rdn in rr over 3f out and no imp: kpt on one pce fnl 2f* **12/1**
9 3 1/4 **Spader (IRE)**35 2244 3-9-0 **86** ColinKeane 2 73
(G M Lyons, Ire) *led: over 1 l clr at 1/2-way: stl gng wl over 2f out: rdn under 2f out and hdd u.p over 1f out: wknd qckly and eased ins fnl f* **13/23**
2m 47.09s (8.99) **9** Ran SP% **121.9**
CSF £21.17 CT £73.77 TOTE £5.10: £1.40, £1.40, £2.10; DF 20.30 Trifecta £86.70.
Owner Mrs June Judd **Bred** Tinnakill House & Alan Byrne **Trained** Coolcullen, Co Carlow

FOCUS
An up-to-scratch renewal. The field were rated between 76 and 98. The winner looks a Group horse in the making once again. The early pace was quite strong thanks to \bSpader\p but Colin Keane tried to slow the tempo after a few furlongs. The third and fourth help with the standard.

3429 - 3432a (Foreign Racing) - See Raceform Interactive

2970 PONTEFRACT (L-H)
Sunday, June 19

OFFICIAL GOING: Good to firm (good in places; 8.7)
Wind: light 1/2 behind Weather: overcast, light rain last 2

3433 TOTEPOOL LIKE US ON FACEBOOK EBF STALLIONS NOVICE FILLIES' STKS (PLUS 10 RACE) 6f
2:10 (2:10) (Class 5) 2-Y-O **£4,528** (£1,347; £673; £336) **Stalls** Low

Form RPR
1 **Fancy Day (IRE)** 2-9-0 0 FrannyNorton 3 72+
(Mark Johnston) *w ldr: led over 2f out: pushed out: readily* **10/33**
2 2 **Miss Sheridan (IRE)** 2-9-0 0 CamHardie 9 66
(Michael Easterby) *led tl over 2f out: kpt on same pce to regain 2nd last 75yds* **22/1**
06 **3** nk **Savannah Slew**44 2007 2-9-0 0 TomEaves 6 65
(James Given) *hld up on outer: hdwy over 2f out: chsd wnr over 1f out: kpt on same pce* **12/1**
5 **4** 1 1/4 **Alice's Dream**18 2793 2-9-0 0 AndreaAtzeni 1 61
(Marco Botti) *chsd ldrs: effrt over 2f out: sn outpcd: kpt on fnl f* **13/81**
5 3/4 **Rainbow Chimes (IRE)** 2-9-0 0 PJMcDonald 4 59
(Ann Duffield) *chsd ldrs: outpcd over 2f out: kpt on fnl f* **3/12**
6 2 1/2 **Lucrezia** 2-9-0 0 TedDurcan 2 52
(Sir Michael Stoute) *dwlt: effrt over 2f out: sn outpcd: nvr a threat* **5/1**
7 2 1/4 **Beau Strata (IRE)** 2-9-0 0 JamesSullivan 5 45
(Clive Mulhall) *stdd s: hld up in rr: effrt over 2f out: nvr a factor* **50/1**
60 **8** 10 **Queens Parade (IRE)**19 2771 2-9-0 0 PaddyAspell 10 15
(Sharon Watt) *chsd ldrs: lost pl wl ocver 1f out: eased whn bhd clsng stages* **100/1**
1m 18.69s (1.79) **Going Correction** -0.025s/f (Good) **8** Ran SP% **117.8**
Speed ratings (Par 90): **87,84,83,82,81 77,74,61**
CSF £67.91 TOTE £4.10: £1.40, £4.50, £2.60; EX 71.30 Trifecta £688.10.
Owner Sheikh Hamdan bin Mohammed Al Maktoum **Bred** Darley **Trained** Middleham Moor, N Yorks

FOCUS
The going was given as good to firm, good in places (GoingStick: 8.7). The rail was dolled out 15 feet from the 6f bend to the winning post, adding approximately 8yds to all races. Mostly newcomers in this line-up and the chances are the race will throw up a winner or two. The opening level is fluid.

3434 @TOTEPOOL FOLLOW US ON TWITTER MAIDEN AUCTION STKS 1m 4f 8y
2:40 (2:41) (Class 5) 3-Y-O **£4,528** (£1,347; £673; £336) **Stalls** Low

Form RPR
3 **1** **Pumblechook**57 1651 3-9-1 0 JimCrowley 4 77
(Lucy Wadham) *led 2f: trckd ldr: drvn to ld over 1f out: kpt on* **8/111**
04 **2** 2 1/4 **Pastoral Music**27 2548 3-8-11 0 AndreaAtzeni 5 69
(Hughie Morrison) *trckd ldrs: effrt over 2f out: chsd wnr fnl f: kpt on same pce* **2/12**
3 1 1/2 **Waiting For Richie** 3-9-0 0 JamesSullivan 2 70
(Tom Tate) *dwlt: detached in rr: wnt modest 4th over 2f out: kpt on fnl f: tk 3rd post* **10/13**
00 **4** nse **Charioteer**17 2815 3-9-0 0 (b1) SilvestreDeSousa 1 70
(Ed Dunlop) *drvn leaving stalls: sn chsng ldr: led after 2f: qcknd pce over 5f out: drvn 3f out: hdd 2f out: one pce* **12/1**
06 **5** 45 **Gaelic Master (IRE)**30 2440 3-8-13 0 DougieCostello 3
(Michael Scudamore) *led rdrless to post: dwlt: sn trcking ldrs: drvn 4f out: lost pl over 2f out: sn bhd: eased over 1f out: sn t.o: eventually completed* **50/1**
2m 41.96s (1.16) **Going Correction** -0.025s/f (Good) **5** Ran SP% **110.0**
Speed ratings (Par 99): **95,93,92,92,62**
CSF £2.39 TOTE £1.60: £1.10, £1.50; EX 2.30 Trifecta £5.90.
Owner Christopher W T Johnston **Bred** Castlemartin Sky & Skymarc Farm **Trained** Newmarket, Suffolk

FOCUS
Race distance increased by approximately 8yds. An ordinary maiden.

3435 TOTEPOOL CHIP & PIN BETTING H'CAP 1m 2f 6y
3:10 (3:11) (Class 3) (0-90,90) 3-Y-O+
£12,450 (£3,728; £1,864; £932; £466; £234) **Stalls** Low

Form RPR
3-22 **1** **Banksea**27 2538 3-8-13 **87** AndreaAtzeni 3 98+
(Luca Cumani) *trckd ldrs: t.k.h: stdd after 2f into mid-div: hdwy over 2f out: led and edgd lft over 1f out: drvn out* **11/101**
-100 **2** 2 1/4 **Darshini**16 2866 4-10-0 **90** TedDurcan 6 96
(Sir Michael Stoute) *chsd ldrs: effrt over 3f out: chsd wnr appr fnl f: kpt on same pce* **12/1**
0-10 **3** 1/2 **Dance King**20 2744 6-9-13 **89** (tp) PaulMulrennan 7 94
(Tim Easterby) *dwlt in rr: drvn over 3f out: hdwy over 2f out: 3rd appr fnl f: kpt on same pce* **10/1**
20-1 **4** 3 1/2 **Arrowzone**37 2216 5-9-12 **88** SilvestreDeSousa 1 86
(Ivan Furtado) *trckd ldrs: hmpd and dropped bk over 1f out: styd on to take 4th clsng stages* **11/42**
0406 **5** 1 1/2 **Winterlude (IRE)**22 2685 6-9-12 **88** (p) TomQueally 8 83
(Jennie Candlish) *w ldr: led briefly and wnt lft wl over 1f out: wknd fnl f* **20/1**
4105 **6** 1/2 **Farham (USA)**20 2743 4-8-9 **71** TonyHamilton 4 65
(Richard Fahey) *hld up in rr: effrt over 2f out: kpt on: nvr a threat* **16/1**
200 **7** 4 1/2 **Invictus (GER)**17 2832 4-9-7 **83** PJMcDonald 2 68
(Micky Hammond) *mid-div: reminders 3f out: sn lost pl* **40/1**
0463 **8** nk **Maraakib (IRE)**9 3113 4-10-0 **90** DanielTudhope 5 74
(David O'Meara) *led: hdd wl over 1f out: wkng whn hmpd appr fnl f* **8/13**
2m 11.46s (-2.24) **Going Correction** -0.025s/f (Good)
WFA 3 from 4yo+ 12lb **8** Ran SP% **115.3**
Speed ratings (Par 107): **107,105,104,102,100 100,96,96**
CSF £16.70 CT £91.64 TOTE £1.90: £1.10, £2.80, £3.30; EX 13.30 Trifecta £67.40.
Owner Leonidas Marinopoulos **Bred** Hascombe And Valiant Studs **Trained** Newmarket, Suffolk

FOCUS
Race distance increased by approximately 8yds. Not a bad handicap, and the winner can rate higher still.

3436 TOTEPOOL PONTEFRACT CASTLE STKS (LISTED RACE) 1m 4f 8y
3:40 (3:40) (Class 1) 4-Y-O+

£22,684 (£8,600; £4,304; £2,144; £1,076; £540) **Stalls** Low

Form RPR

120- **1** **Loving Things**[254] 7078 4-8-10 95 MartinLane 8 104+
(Luca Cumani) *trckd ldrs: effrt over 2f out: swtchd ins over 1f out: led last 150yds: drvn out* **9/1**

P0-0 **2** 1 3/4 **Yarrow (IRE)**[50] 1855 4-8-10 92 TedDurcan 9 101
(Sir Michael Stoute) *hld up towards rr: effrt on outer over 2f out: chsng ldrs over 1f out: styd on to take 2nd nr fin* **28/1**

-111 **3** 3/4 **Barsanti (IRE)**[37] 2222 4-9-1 105 AndreaAtzeni 1 105
(Roger Varian) *drvn early to chse ldrs: drvn and 2nd over 2f out: led briefly appr fnl f: edgd lft and kpt on same pce last 150yds* **1/1**[1]

4-22 **4** 2 1/4 **Sweeping Up**[22] 2690 5-8-10 105 (t) JimCrowley 5 97
(Hughie Morrison) *w ldr: led 3f out: sn drvn: hdd over 1f out: wknd last 75yds* **4/1**[2]

1-60 **5** 3/4 **Captain Morley**[29] 2486 5-9-1 99 TomEaves 2 100
(David Simcock) *hld up in mid-div: hdwy over 3f out: kpt on same pce fnl f:* **33/1**

-400 **6** *nk* **Monaleen (IRE)**[50] 1855 5-8-10 90 PaulMulrennan 6 95
(Ian Williams) *hld up in rr: hdwy over 3f out: chsng ldrs over 1f out: keeping one pce whn edgd lft 75yds out* **100/1**

6160 **7** 1/2 **Hit The Jackpot (IRE)**[20] 2744 7-9-1 97 DanielTudhope 10 99
(David O'Meara) *swtchd lft after s: hld up in rr: hdwy on outside over 2f out: sn drvn: kpt on one pce over 1f out* **25/1**

02-6 **8** *nk* **Lustrous**[22] 2690 5-8-10 103 GrahamGibbons 3 94
(David O'Meara) *led: hdd over 1f out: wkng whn n.m.r and eased clsng stages* **10/1**

5-30 **9** 2 1/4 **Elidor**[29] 2486 6-9-1 106 SilvestreDeSousa 7 99
(Mick Channon) *trckd ldrs: t.k.h: 3rd 2f out: sn wknd: hmpd 75yds out: eased* **11/2**[3]

2m 37.05s (-3.75) **Going Correction** -0.025s/f (Good) 9 Ran SP% **115.7**
Speed ratings (Par 111): **111,109,109,107,107 107,106,106,105**
CSF £218.47 TOTE £11.80: £2.90, £5.70, £1.02; EX 257.40 Trifecta £751.60.
Owner Normandie Stud Ltd **Bred** Normandie Stud Ltd **Trained** Newmarket, Suffolk

FOCUS
Race distance increased by approximately 8yds. There was an easy winner of this Listed race, but it didn't go the way the market expected.

3437 TOTEPOOLLIVEINFO.COM PONTEFRACT CUP (H'CAP) (ROUND 4 OF PONTEFRACT STAYERS CHAMPIONSHIP 2016) 2m 1f 216y
4:10 (4:11) (Class 4) (0-85,85) 4-Y-O+ **£6,469** (£1,925; £962; £481) **Stalls** Low

Form RPR

2-00 **1** **Wind Place And Sho**[38] 2194 4-9-9 85 RyanTate 2 95
(James Eustace) *trckd ldrs: 2nd over 1f out: led and edgd lft appr fnl f: edgd rt and drvn clr* **4/1**[2]

5644 **2** 6 **Riptide**[13] 2971 10-8-5 66 oh1 FrannyNorton 10 69
(Michael Scudamore) *in rr: hdwy 10f out: kpt on to chse clr wnr last 75yds* **16/1**

0604 **3** 1 **Giant Redwood (IRE)**[17] 2820 4-9-2 78 DavidNolan 5 80
(Michael Bell) *chsd ldrs: 3rd over 1f out: kpt on same pce* **20/1**

6164 **4** *nk* **Christmas Hamper (IRE)**[15] 2887 4-8-4 66 oh4 (p) AndrewMullen 8 68
(Michael Appleby) *chsd ldr: drvn over 3f out: led and edgd lft 2f out: sn hdd: kpt on same pce* **20/1**

3200 **5** 1 1/2 **Madam Lilibet (IRE)**[13] 2971 7-8-5 66 oh2 JoeyHaynes 12 66
(Sharon Watt) *rn in snatches: sn drvn along: hdwy after 6f: chsng ldrs over 3f out: kpt on appr fnl f* **40/1**

0/06 **6** 1 1/4 **Hartside (GER)**[13] 2971 7-8-0 66 oh1 NathanEvans(5) 4 65
(Peter Winks) *chsd ldrs: drvn over 4f out: reminders 3f out: one pce* **25/1**

0-00 **7** 2 **See And Be Seen**[31] 2392 6-9-0 75 (p) SilvestreDeSousa 7 72
(Sylvester Kirk) *swtchd lft s: hld up in rr: nt clr on inner over 3f out: swtchd outside over 2f out: chsng ldrs over 1f out: hld whn eased clsng stages* **7/2**[1]

4043 **8** 7 **Stanarley Pic**[7] 3191 5-8-0 68 MeganNicholls(7) 11 57
(Alan Swinbank) *t.k.h: trckd ldrs after 3f: lost pl over 1f out: eased clsng stages* **12/1**[3]

0122 **9** 1 1/4 **Hallstatt (IRE)**[18] 2805 10-8-3 67 (t) JoeDoyle(3) 9 55
(John Mackie) *mid-div: effrt 4f out: wknd over 1f out* **16/1**

4-02 **10** 1 **Waterclock (IRE)**[13] 2971 7-9-0 75 (p) PJMcDonald 3 62
(Micky Hammond) *in rr: drvn over 5f out: bhd fnl 2f* **4/1**[2]

1-61 **11** 3 **Bulas Belle**[13] 2971 6-9-6 81 BarryMcHugh 1 64
(Grant Tuer) *led: hdd and hmpd 2f out: sn lost pl: eased clsng stages* **7/2**[1]

0 **12** 1 **Gran Paradiso (IRE)**[36] 2260 4-8-8 70 (p) TomEaves 13 52
(Micky Hammond) *hld up in rr: reminders over 5f out: bhd fnl 2f* **33/1**

3m 58.81s (2.61) **Going Correction** -0.025s/f (Good)
WFA 4 from 5yo+ 1lb 12 Ran SP% **122.7**
Speed ratings (Par 105): **93,90,89,89,89 88,87,84,83,83 82,81**
CSF £62.71 CT £1172.32 TOTE £5.00: £2.00, £4.20, £6.50; EX 66.00 Trifecta £1211.70.
Owner Harold Nass **Bred** Rockville Pike Partnership **Trained** Newmarket, Suffolk
■ Stewards' Enquiry : Andrew Mullen caution: careless riding

FOCUS
Race distance increased by approximately 8yds. This was run at a good gallop and the winner took it with some ease.

3438 TOTEPOOL RACING'S BIGGEST SUPPORTER FILLIES' H'CAP 1m 4y
4:40 (4:40) (Class 4) (0-85,85) 3-Y-O+ **£6,469** (£1,925; £962; £481) **Stalls** Low

Form RPR

1421 **1** **Esteemable**[23] 2636 4-9-6 80 DanielMuscutt(3) 6 87
(James Fanshawe) *hld up in mid-div: nt clr run on inner over 2f out tl chsd ldr over 1f out: styd on to ld last 75yds* **4/1**[2]

3602 **2** 1/2 **Rosy Morning (IRE)**[8] 3152 3-8-6 73 FrannyNorton 1 77
(Mark Johnston) *led: drvn over 2f out: hdd and no ex last 75yds* **9/2**[3]

00-0 **3** *nk* **Persun**[16] 2868 4-9-13 84 SilvestreDeSousa 8 89
(Mick Channon) *hld up towards rr: hdwy over 2f out: chsng ldrs whn swtchd rt over 1f out: kpt on wl to take 3rd post* **4/1**[2]

5363 **4** *shd* **Simply Shining (IRE)**[11] 3011 6-9-0 78 AdamMcNamara(7) 4 83
(Richard Fahey) *chsd ldrs: effrt 3f out: kpt on same pce fnl f* **7/2**[1]

3-20 **5** 6 **Ghinia (IRE)**[22] 2689 5-9-10 84 RobHornby(3) 5 75
(Pam Sly) *chsd ldrs:: drvn over 2f out: wknd fnl f* **11/2**

06 **6** 4 **Shingwedzi (SAF)**[22] 2671 5-9-11 85 KieranShoemark(3) 3 67
(Ed Dunlop) *hld up in rr: hdwy on outside 2f out: wknd fnl f* **33/1**

0-21 **7** 3 1/2 **Lincoln Rocks**[11] 3014 3-8-9 76 SamJames 7 48
(David O'Meara) *w ldr: drvn over 2f out: wknd over 1f out: eased clsng stages* **13/2**

1m 44.04s (-1.86) **Going Correction** -0.025s/f (Good)
WFA 3 from 4yo+ 10lb 7 Ran SP% **112.1**
Speed ratings (Par 102): **108,107,107,107,101 97,93**
CSF £21.26 CT £74.46 TOTE £5.10: £3.40, £3.30; EX 25.80 Trifecta £73.90.
Owner Mrs C R Philipson **Bred** Mrs M L Parry & P M Steele-Mortimer **Trained** Newmarket, Suffolk

FOCUS
Race distance increased by approximately 8yds. An open fillies' handicap.

3439 TOTEPOOL COLLECT YOUR WINNINGS AT BETFRED SHOPS H'CAP 6f
5:10 (5:13) (Class 5) (0-75,75) 3-Y-O **£3,881** (£1,155; £577; £288) **Stalls** Low

Form RPR

-060 **1** **Roll On Rory**[20] 2742 3-9-1 69 (p) BenCurtis 2 78
(Jason Ward) *chsd ldrs: drvn 2f out: styd on to ld clsng stages* **8/1**

5252 **2** 3/4 **Highly Sprung (IRE)**[5] 3265 3-9-7 75 FrannyNorton 9 82
(Mark Johnston) *w ldr: led over 2f out: hdd and no ex clsng stages* **3/1**[1]

3315 **3** 1 1/4 **Mr Orange (IRE)**[19] 2777 3-8-7 61 (p) BarryMcHugh 13 64+
(Paul Midgley) *racd wd: chsd ldrs: swtchd lft after 1f out: styd on same pce fnl 150yds* **12/1**

5600 **4** 1 3/4 **Clon Rocket (IRE)**[13] 2974 3-8-5 66 MeganEllingworth(7) 1 63
(John Holt) *s.i.s: in rr: hdwy on ins and swtchd lft over 1f out: sn chsng ldrs: one pce fnl 150yds* **16/1**

45-3 **5** 2 1/2 **Full Of Promise**[17] 2809 3-8-10 64 TonyHamilton 5 53
(Richard Fahey) *in rr: swtchd rt over 1f out: styd on last 100yds* **12/1**

6-4 **6** 1 3/4 **Encantar**[27] 2534 3-9-4 72 (p) PJMcDonald 11 56
(Ann Duffield) *swtchd lft after s: in rr: hdwy over 2f out: kpt on one pce over 1f out.* **16/1**

31 **7** 2 1/4 **Kindly**[24] 2606 3-9-7 75 JimCrowley 12 52+
(Simon Crisford) *racd w: w ldrs: swtchd lft after 1f: wknd fnl f* **13/2**[2]

2-43 **8** 2 3/4 **Sunnyside Bob (IRE)**[22] 2668 3-9-5 73 DanielTudhope 4 41
(David O'Meara) *led: hdd over 2f out: lost pl over 1f out* **7/1**[3]

00-0 **9** 1 1/4 **French**[20] 2742 3-9-4 72 DavidNolan 3 36
(Antony Brittain) *chsd ldrs: hung lft and lost pl over 1f out* **16/1**

-020 **10** 11 **Athollblair Boy (IRE)**[13] 2981 3-9-6 74 SilvestreDeSousa 10
(Nigel Tinkler) *chsd ldrs: drvn over 2f out: sn lost pl: eased whn bhd clsng stages* **9/1**

1m 16.77s (-0.13) **Going Correction** -0.025s/f (Good) 10 Ran SP% **105.0**
Speed ratings (Par 99): **99,98,96,94,90 88,85,81,80,65**
CSF £26.52 CT £216.40 TOTE £9.50: £2.90, £1.50, £3.20; EX 34.20 Trifecta £318.50.
Owner P Adams, P Clarke, T Wickins, J Sutton **Bred** Stuart Matheson **Trained** Middleham, N Yorks
■ Spike and Indian Pursuit were withdrawn. Prices at time of withdrawal 9-1 and 16-1. Rule 4 applies to all bets - deduction 10p in the pound.

FOCUS
Race distance increased by approximately 8yds. This sprint handicap was run at a good gallop.
T/Jkpt: £143,314.60 to a £1 stake. Pool: £143,314.60 - 1 winning ticket. T/Plt: £76.50 to a £1 stake. Pool: £79,932.93 - 762.15 winning tickets. T/Qpdt: £24.60 to a £1 stake. Pool: £7,262.43 - 218.00 winning tickets. **Walter Glynn**

3440 - 3447a (Foreign Racing) - See Raceform Interactive

BRO PARK (L-H)
Sunday, June 19

OFFICIAL GOING: Turf: good to soft

3448a TAITTINGERS BLOOMERS' VASE (LISTED RACE) (4YO+ FILLIES & MARES) (TURF) 1m
11:45 (12:00) 4-Y-O+ **£24,115** (£8,038; £4,019; £2,411; £1,607)

RPR

1 **Ray**[273] 6575 4-9-2 0 KevinStott 2 90
(Jessica Long, Sweden) **199/10**

2 1 1/4 **Subtle Knife**[18] 2789 7-9-2 0 JosephineGordon 6 87
(Giles Bravery) *a cl up: rdn and ev ch over 1f out: styd on u.p fnl f* **137/10**

3 2 **Hoku (IRE)**[273] 6575 5-9-2 0 ManuelSantos 1 82
(Bent Olsen, Denmark) **19/10**[2]

4 1 1/4 **Arabda**[724] 5-9-2 0 Per-AndersGraberg 7 80
(Patrick Wahl, Sweden) **10/9**[1]

5 1/2 **Ikc Moneypenny (USA)** 4-9-2 0 NelsonDeSouza 4 78
(Cathrine Erichsen, Norway) **13/1**

6 3/4 **Antigua (SWE)**[644] 6386 4-9-2 0 JacobJohansen 5 77
(Tommy Gustafsson, Sweden) **144/10**

7 9 **Zarzuela (DEN)**[399] 6-9-2 0 ElioneChaves 3 56
(Niels Petersen, Norway) **89/20**[3]

\n\x\x PARI-MUTUEL (all including 1sek stake): WIN 20.94; PLACE 3.15, 2.54, 1.73;
Owner Chess Racing Ab **Bred** Chess Racing Ab **Trained** Sweden

3449a STOCKHOLMS STORA PRIS (GROUP 3) (4YO+) (TURF) 1m 1f
4:35 (12:00) 4-Y-O+ **£56,270** (£20,096; £10,450; £6,430; £3,215)

RPR

1 **Coprah**[14] 8-9-2 0 NelsonDeSouza 12 100
(Cathrine Erichsen, Norway) **45/1**

2 1/2 **Amie Noire (GER)**[245] 5-8-13 0 Jan-ErikNeuroth 1 96
(Wido Neuroth, Norway) **226/10**

3 1/2 **Icecapada (IRE)**[49] 1907 4-8-13 0 ElioneChaves 10 95
(Niels Petersen, Norway) **17/5**[2]

4 1 **Berling (IRE)**[29] 9-9-2 0 DinaDanekilde 6 96
(Jessica Long, Sweden) **29/4**[3]

5 *nk* **Diplomat (GER)**[42] 2073 5-9-2 0 MartinHarley 11 95
(Mario Hofer, Germany) **11/10**[1]

6 2 **Avon Pearl**[14] 7-9-2 0 (b) CarlosLopez 5 91
(Rune Haugen) **106/10**

7 1 1/4 **El Abandonado (SWE)**[220] 5-9-2 0 (b) ManuelSantos 4 88
(Maria Sandh, Sweden) **63/1**

8 1 1/2 **Jubilance (IRE)**[273] 6576 7-9-2 0 JacobJohansen 8 85
(Bent Olsen, Denmark) **54/1**

9 3/4 **Probably (IRE)**[29] 6-9-2 0 (p) KevinStott 7 84
(Rune Haugen) **178/10**

10 1/2 **Captain America (SWE)**[220] 6-9-2 0 (b) OliverWilson 3 83
(Annike Bye Hansen, Norway) **37/1**

11 ½ **Einsteins Folly (IRE)**[14] 6-9-2 0 MrFredrikJanetzky 9 82
(Jessica Long, Sweden) **225/10**
12 3½ **Silver Ocean (USA)**[47] 1957 8-9-2 0 Per-AndersGraberg 2 74
(Niels Petersen, Norway) **15/2**

PARI-MUTUEL (all including 1sek stake): WIN 45.62; PLACE 8.04, 5.14, 2.51; SF 883.09
Owner IKC Racing **Bred** Grasshopper 2000 Ltd **Trained** Norway

3182 CHANTILLY (R-H)

Sunday, June 19

OFFICIAL GOING: Turf: soft

3450a PRIX DU LYS LONGINES (GROUP 3) (3YO) (TURF) 1m 4f

1:55 (1:55) 3-Y-O **£29,411** (£11,764; £8,823; £5,882; £2,941)

RPR

1 **Spring Master**[27] 2550 3-8-11 0 OlivierPeslier 5 104
(P Bary, France) *trckd ldr on outer: virtually upsides ldr fr 1/2-way: nudged along to ld appr 2f out: sn rdn and edgd rt 1 1/2f out: r.o gamely u.p fnl f: jst hld on* **7/4**[1]
2 shd **Golden Valentine (FR)**[26] 2569 3-8-8 0 AurelienLemaitre 6 101
(F Head, France) *w.w in rr: swtchd outside and hdwy wl over 2f out: styd on u.p to chal 125yds out: sustained run to line: jst failed* **11/4**[2]
3 3½ **Al Haram (FR)**[45] 1986 3-8-11 0 GregoryBenoist 1 98
(E Lellouche, France) *trckd ldrs on inner: angled out to chsd ldr between horses 1 1/2f out: kpt on at same pce fnl f: nvr trbld front two* **7/1**
4 3 **Canessar (FR)**[41] 3-8-11 0 ChristopheSoumillon 4 94
(M Delzangles, France) *w.w in fnl pair: trckd ldng pair on outer fr 1/2-way: rdn and nt qckn ins fnl 2f: one pce under hands and heels fr 1f out* **3/1**[3]
5 1¾ **Mahari (IRE)**[27] 2550 3-8-11 0 Pierre-CharlesBoudot 3 92
(A Fabre, France) *led: virtually jnd 1/2-way: rdn 2 1/2f out: hdd appr 2f out: wknd fnl f* **5/1**

2m 33.94s (2.94) **Going Correction** +0.30s/f (Good) **5 Ran SP% 117.2**
Speed ratings: **102,101,99,97,96**
WIN (incl. 1 euro stake): 2.90. PLACES: 1.40, 1.40. SF: 5.80.
Owner Ecurie Jean-Louis Bouchard **Bred** Haras Du Mezeray **Trained** Chantilly, France

3451a PRIX BERTRAND DU BREUIL LONGINES (GROUP 3) (4YO+) (TURF) 1m

2:30 (2:30) 4-Y-O+ **£29,411** (£11,764; £8,823; £5,882; £2,941)

RPR

1 **Pas De Deux (GER)**[28] 6-9-0 0 AntoineCoutier 5 107
(Yasmin Almenrader, Germany) *chsd ldrs on outer: 4th and rowed along 2f out: styd on u.p fr 1 1/2f out to chal ent fnl f: r.o to ld 125yds out: drvn out* **25/1**
2 ¾ **Impassable (IRE)**[232] 7654 4-8-13 0 MaximeGuyon 7 104+
(C Laffon-Parias, France) *w.w in fnl trio on outer: hdwy over 1 1/2f out: r.o fnl f: nt rch wnr* **3/1**[2]
3 snk **Sea Front (FR)**[44] 2020 5-8-8 0 VincentCheminaud 4 99+
(E Libaud, France) *hld up in fnl trio: hdwy wl over 1 1/2f out: styd on ins fnl f: nt pce to chal* **8/1**[3]
4 nk **Stillman (FR)**[49] 1910 5-8-11 0 (b) OlivierPeslier 8 101
(P Khozian, France) *led: rdn ins fnl 2f and rallied: chal ent fnl f: hdd 125yds out: no ex* **16/1**
5 hd **Territories (IRE)**[15] 2927 4-8-11 0 MickaelBarzalona 6 101+
(A Fabre, France) *w.w in rr: hdwy on outer 2f out: cl 5th and rdn 1f out: styd on same pce fnl f* **4/6**[1]
6 nk **Hello My Love (FR)**[26] 5-8-11 0 EddyHardouin 2 100
(Carina Fey, France) *chsd ldr on inner: angled out and rdn 2f out: kpt on at one pce fnl f* **50/1**
7 4 **Incahoots**[49] 1910 4-8-8 0 AurelienLemaitre 1 88
(F Head, France) *settled in midfield on inner: cl 3rd and rdn wl over 2f out: sn btn and wknd fnl f* **33/1**

1m 37.64s (-0.36) **Going Correction** +0.30s/f (Good) **7 Ran SP% 110.7**
Speed ratings: **113,112,112,111,111 111,107**
WIN (incl. 1 euro stake): 24.30. PLACES: 7.90, 3.00, 2.70. DF: 62.00. SF: 151.40.
Owner Dirk Von Mitzlaff **Bred** Dirk Von Mitzlaff **Trained** Germany

3452a PRIX DE DIANE LONGINES (GROUP 1) (3YO FILLIES) (TURF) 1m 2f 110y

3:15 (3:15) 3-Y-O **£420,147** (£168,088; £84,044; £41,985; £21,029)

RPR

1 **La Cressonniere (FR)**[35] 2282 3-9-0 0 CristianDemuro 9 112+
(J-C Rouget, France) *midfield early: sn hld up towards rr: hdwy on outer over 2f out: str run to ld appr 1f out: drvn and r.o fnl f: readily* **11/4**[1]
2 ½ **Left Hand**[34] 2316 3-9-0 0 (p) MaximeGuyon 1 111
(C Laffon-Parias, France) *t.k.h: hld up towards rr on inner: moved into midfield 1/2-way: rdn and clsd fr 2f out: chsd ldng pair 1 1/2f out: jnd ldrs and immediately hdd by eventual wunner appr 1f out: r.o gamely u.p* **50/1**
3 1¼ **Volta (FR)**[14] 2945 3-9-0 0 ChristopheSoumillon 12 109+
(F-H Graffard, France) *t.k.h: hld up in midfield: dropped toward rr bef 1/2-way: swtchd outside and hdwy whn hmpd and lost momentum 2f out: styd on u.p fnl f: wnt 3rd 70yds out: nt trble front two* **11/2**
4 ½ **Azaelia (FR)**[30] 2455 3-9-0 0 Jean-BernardEyquem 13 108
(Simone Brogi, France) *w.w towards rr on inner: prog sn after 1/2-way: chsng ldng gp whn nt clr run and snatched up wl over 1 1/2f out: angled bk ins and styd on between horses fnl f: nt pce to chal* **66/1**
5 ¾ **Coolmore (IRE)**[28] 2509 3-9-0 0 (p) SeamieHeffernan 2 106
(A P O'Brien, Ire) *sn led on inner: drvn 2l clr 3f out: hrd rdn and hdd appr 1f out: kpt on at one pce* **33/1**
6 nk **Ballydoyle (IRE)**[49] 1888 3-9-0 0 RyanMoore 15 106
(A P O'Brien, Ire) *w.w in fnl trio: last and rdn 2f out: styd on u.p fr 1 1/2f out: run flattened out fnl 100yds: nvr on terms* **7/2**[2]
7 shd **Zghorta Dance (FR)**[30] 2455 3-9-0 0 IoritzMendizabal 4 105
(J-C Rouget, France) *settled in midfield: chsd ldng quarter fr 3f out: rdn and edgd lft to bump rival over 2f out: hrd rdn and kpt on at same pce fnl f* **25/1**
8 snk **Swiss Range**[49] 1890 3-9-0 0 FrankieDettori 3 105
(John Gosden) *t.k.h: hld up in tch: angled out to chse ldr 2f out: nvr able to chal u.p and edgd lft 1 1/2f out: lft bhd by ldrs ins fnl f: fin 9th: plcd 8th* **4/1**[3]
9 ½ **Jemayel (IRE)**[34] 2316 3-9-0 0 GregoryBenoist 10 104
(J-C Rouget, France) *w.w towards rr: prog into midfield bef 1/2-way: rdn and nt qckn 2 1/2f out: keeping on u.p whn hmpd and snatched up appr fnl f: kpt on fnl 100yds: nvr in contention: fin 10th: plcd 9th* **20/1**
10 11 **Gysoave (FR)**[19] 3-9-0 0 TheoBachelot 5 83
(Waldemar Hickst, Germany) *chaded ldrs: rdn and nt qckn whn hmpd over 2f out: plugged on at same pce: fin 11th: plcd 10th* **100/1**
11 hd **Camprock (FR)**[34] 2316 3-9-0 0 MickaelBarzalona 14 82
(Mme Pia Brandt, France) *hld up in fnl pair: rdn and short-lived effrt over 1 1/2f out: sn btn: fin 12th: plcd 11th* **16/1**
12 snk **Happy Approach (FR)**[26] 2569 3-9-0 0 AntoineHamelin 7 82
(M Nigge, France) *chsd ldrs on outer: wnt 2nd sn after 1/2-way: rdn and nt qckn fr 2f out: wknd ins fnl 1 1/2f: fin 13th: plcd 12th* **100/1**
13 ½ **The Juliet Rose (FR)**[14] 2944 3-9-0 0 StephanePasquier 8 81
(N Clement, France) *cl up on outer: struggling and rdn 2 1/2f out: heavily bmpd over 2f out: wl hld whn hmpd by faller wl under 1 1/2f out: sn eased: fin 14th: plcd 13th* **18/1**
D shd **Highlands Queen (FR)**[21] 2726 3-9-0 0 WilliamBuick 6 105
(Y Gourraud, France) *hld up in midfield: hrd rdn and effrt whn edgd rt wl over 1 1/2f out causing interference: kpt on at one pce u.p fnl f: fin 8th: disqualified and plcd last* **14/1**
P **Tierra Del Fuego (FR)**[34] 2316 3-9-0 0 (p) OlivierPeslier 16
(G E Mikhalides, France) *a among bkmakers: dropped away qckly and lost action over 3f out: sn p.u* **100/1**
U **Armande (IRE)**[14] 2944 3-9-0 0 Pierre-CharlesBoudot 11
(A Fabre, France) *settled towards rr: clsd fr 2f out: midfield and effrt between horses whn bdly hmpd and uns rdr wl under 1 1/2f out* **20/1**

2m 9.45s (0.65) **Going Correction** +0.30s/f (Good) **16 Ran SP% 124.8**
Speed ratings: **109,108,107,107,106 106,106,106,105,97 97,97,97, ,106**
WIN (incl. 1 euro stake): 3.80. PLACES: 1,80, 5.10, 2.50. DF: 60.70. SF: 93.90.
Owner Ecurie Antonio Caro & Gerard Augustin-Normand **Bred** Franklin Finance **Trained** Pau, France

FOCUS
This year's renewal of the French Classic looked well up to scratch with viable challengers from Britain and Ireland up against a strong home defence. Before Star Of Seville last year, the seven previous winners of the Diane had gone into the race unbeaten and that trend resumed here, but this was a very rough race with one filly pulled up, another losing her rider, and plenty of trouble up the home straight including a chain reaction started by horses angling for a run passing the 2f pole. The pace didn't look anything special.

2315 COLOGNE (R-H)

Sunday, June 19

OFFICIAL GOING: Turf: soft

3453a OPPENHEIM-UNION-RENNEN (GROUP 2) (3YO) (TURF) 1m 3f

3:50 (12:00) 3-Y-O **£29,411** (£11,397; £5,882; £2,941; £1,838)

RPR

1 **Boscaccio (GER)**[34] 3-9-2 0 DennisSchiergen 7 105
(Christian Sprengel, Germany) *hld up in midfield: hdwy wl over 2 1/2f out: rdn to chal 2f out: led over 1 1/2f out: r.o u.p fnl f* **7/5**[1]
2 ¾ **El Loco (GER)**[22] 2711 3-9-2 0 AdriedeVries 3 104
(Markus Klug, Germany) *settled in midfield on inner: clsd to chse ldrs fr 4f out: eased into ld 2 1/2f out: hrd pressed 2f out: hdd over 1 1/2f out: r.o gamely u.p fnl f* **22/5**[3]
3 ¾ **Dschingis Secret (GER)**[34] 3-9-2 0 MartinSeidl 5 103
(Markus Klug, Germany) *hld up in fnl pair: hdwy under 3f out: styd on wl fnl 1 1/2f: nrest at fin* **207/10**
4 6 **Berghain (IRE)**[49] 1908 3-9-2 0 AlexanderPietsch 9 92
(J Hirschberger, Germany) *racd in rr: last and rdn over 2f out: swtchd outside and styd on fr 1 1/2f out: nt pce to trble ldrs* **138/10**
5 2 **Savoir Vivre (IRE)**[29] 3-9-2 0 (b) FrederikTylicki 4 88
(Jean-Pierre Carvalho, Germany) *settled in midfield on outer: rdn and nt qckn 2f out: plugged on at one pce* **13/5**[2]
6 8 **San Salvador (GER)**[22] 2711 3-9-2 0 AndreasHelfenbein 10 74
(Andreas Lowe, Germany) *a towards rr: rdn and wl btn fnl 2f* **228/10**
7 ¾ **Bora Rock (IRE)**[34] 3-9-2 0 MrVinzenzSchiergen 1 73
(P Schiergen, Germany) *led under a t.k.h: hdd 2 1/2f out: wknd ins fnl 2f* **239/10**
8 19 **Light Of Air (FR)**[29] 3-9-2 0 (b) JozefBojko 6 38
(A Wohler, Germany) *chsd ldr on outer: rdn and wknd fr 2 1/2f out: t.o* **229/10**
9 7 **Cashman (FR)** 3-9-2 0 EduardoPedroza 2 26
(A Wohler, Germany) *tk v t.k.h: hld up in tch: wknd u.p over 2f out: t.o* **52/1**

2m 21.03s (0.23) **9 Ran SP% 113.6**
WIN (incl. 10 euro stake): 24. PLACES: 12, 14, 23. SF: 94.
Owner R Hupe & Friends **Bred** Stiftung Gestut Fahrhof **Trained** Germany

FOCUS
This was rather slowly run.

3454 - (Foreign Racing) - See Raceform Interactive

2728 SAN SIRO (R-H)

Sunday, June 19

OFFICIAL GOING: Turf: good to soft

3455a PREMIO DEL GIUBILEO (GROUP 3) (3YO+) (TURF) 1m 1f

5:00 (12:00) 3-Y-O+ **£21,691** (£9,544; £5,205; £2,602)

RPR

1 **Greg Pass (IRE)**[21] 2729 4-9-4 0 DarioVargiu 5 104
(Il Cavallo In Testa, Italy) *t.k.h: rdn to ld under 2f out: hdd ent fnl f: rallied u.p: led again 75yds out: sn asserted* **143/20**
2 1¾ **Voice Of Love (IRE)**[21] 3-8-7 0 AntonioFresu 6 99
(Stefano Botti, Italy) *hld up in fnl trio: hdwy to go 4th wl over 2f out: sustained run to ld ent fnl f: r.o u.p: hdd fnl 75yds: no ex* **2/5**[1]
3 1½ **Circus Couture (IRE)**[21] 2728 4-9-6 0 UmbertoRispoli 4 99
(Stefano Botti, Italy) *drvn to ld: kicked 3l clr wl over 3f out: sn rdn: hdd under 2f out: sn outpcd by ldrs: gng on again fin* **2/5**[1]
4 3½ **Rogue Runner (GER)**[113] 757 4-9-4 0 CarloFiocchi 2 90
(P Schiergen, Germany) *chsd ldrs: hrd rdn and nt qckn fr 2 1/2f out: kpt on at same pce* **26/5**[2]

5 2 1/2 **Brex Drago (ITY)**[63] 4-9-6 0 NicolaPinna 1 86
(Stefano Botti, Italy) *hld up in fnl trio: hdwy to chse ldrs fr 2 1/2f out: rdn and no imp 2f out: one pce fnl f* **193/10**

6 1/2 **Poeta Diletto**[28] 2517 3-8-9 0 SilvanoMulas 7 84
(Stefano Botti, Italy) *t.k.h: hld up in midfield: rdn and no imp 2f out: one pce fnl f* **107/10**

7 nk **Felician (GER)**[24] 2633 8-9-6 0 PatCosgrave 8 85
(Ferdinand J Leve, Germany) *outpcd in rr: rdn and short-lived effrt 2 1/2f out: sn no further imp: plugged on at same pce* **61/10**[3]

8 dist **Azari**[21] 2729 4-9-4 0 MarioEsposito 3
(Il Cavallo In Testa, Italy) *chsd ldrs: rdn and no hdwy 3f out: wknd and eased ins fnl 2f: t.o* **37/1**

1m 53.0s (-4.90)
WFA 3 from 4yo+ 11lb 8 Ran SP% **201.4**
WIN (incl. 1 euro stake): 8.13. PLACES: 1.17, 1.02, 1.63. DF: 4.79.
Owner Incolinx **Bred** Valdirone Soc Ag Sas Di Lualdi Lucia & C **Trained** Italy

3093 CHEPSTOW (L-H)

Monday, June 20

3456 Meeting Abandoned - waterlogged

3230 WINDSOR (R-H)

Monday, June 20

OFFICIAL GOING: Soft (heavy in places)
Wind: Moderate, behind Weather: Sunny

3463 CLICSARGENT.ORG.UK NEWCOMERS' MAIDEN STKS 6f
5:50 (5:54) (Class 5) 2-Y-O **£2,911** (£866; £432; £216) **Stalls** Low

Form RPR

1 **South Seas (IRE)** 2-9-5 0 OisinMurphy 3 93+
(Andrew Balding) *pressed ldrs: pushed into ld 2f out: rdn over 1f out and sn drew rt away: styd on strly* **7/4**[1]

2 8 **Winning Ways (IRE)** 2-9-5 0 PatCosgrave 1 69+
(William Haggas) *racd against nr side rail: mde most: shkn up and hdd 2f out: clr of rest but no ch w wnr 1f out: eased* **7/2**[3]

3 4 1/2 **Plato's Kode (IRE)** 2-9-5 0 GeorgeBaker 16 56
(Seamus Durack) *racd on outer: w ldrs to jst over 2f out: kpt on for 3rd but no ch w ldng pair over 1f out* **16/1**

4 1 1/4 **Act Of Freedom (IRE)** 2-9-5 0 JamesDoyle 4 52
(Charlie Appleby) *chsd ldrs: rdn over 2f out: sn wl outpcd and no ch* **3/1**[2]

5 1/2 **Just Maybe** 2-9-5 0 HarryBentley 11 50
(Mike Murphy) *dwlt: in tch in rr to over 2f out: sn outpcd* **40/1**

6 1 **Eternal Dream** 2-9-5 0 MartinHarley 8 47
(William Knight) *w ldrs to over 2f out: wknd* **16/1**

7 nk **Broughtons Knight** 2-9-5 0 StevieDonohoe 9 46
(Willie Musson) *dwlt: a in rr: no ch fnl 2f* **66/1**

8 1 1/4 **Quothquan (FR)** 2-8-12 0 GeorgeWood[(7)] 2 43
(Michael Madgwick) *in tch: rdn and effrt to chse ldrs 1/2-way: wknd 2f out* **100/1**

9 4 **Raj Balaraaj (GER)** 2-9-5 0 SteveDrowne 14 31
(George Baker) *dwlt: spd on outer to 1/2-way: wknd qckly* **20/1**

10 4 1/2 **Glory Of Paris (IRE)** 2-9-5 0 FrederikTylicki 10 17
(Rod Millman) *spd over 2f: sn lost pl and bhd* **25/1**

1m 15.92s (2.92) **Going Correction** +0.625s/f (Yiel) 10 Ran SP% **108.9**
Speed ratings (Par 93): **105,94,88,86,86 84,84,82,77,71**
CSF £6.61 TOTE £2.60: £1.10, £1.30, £3.00; EX 8.30 Trifecta £58.60.
Owner Qatar Racing Limited **Bred** Stonepark Farms **Trained** Kingsclere, Hants
■ Private Mission was withdrawn.Price at time of withdrawal 12/1. Rule 4 applies to all bets - deduct 5p in the pound.

FOCUS
Inner of straight at normal inner configuration, making straight maximum width. Top bend dolled out 3yds from normal inner configuration, adding 10yds to race distances of 1m. Jockeys reported the ground as very soft, but said runners were getting through it. This had the look of a decent maiden and was won in taking style by the well-backed favourite. He's a smart prospect.

3464 CLIC SARGENT MAIDEN STKS 1m 67y
6:20 (6:22) (Class 5) 3-Y-O+ **£2,911** (£866; £432; £216) **Stalls** Low

Form RPR

0 1 **Lolwah**[29] 2505 3-8-13 0 TedDurcan 2 71+
(Sir Michael Stoute) *hld up in midfield: waiting for a gap over 2f out: prog over 1f out: n.m.r but got through ins fnl f and r.o to ld nr fin* **2/1**[1]

36 2 hd **Major Assault**[49] 1931 3-9-4 0 AdamKirby 5 74
(Clive Cox) *settled in rr: urged along and gd prog jst over 2f out: drvn ahd jst over 1f out: kpt on but hdd nr fin* **3/1**[2]

3 1 **Singapore Sling** 3-9-4 0 TomQueally 6 72
(James Fanshawe) *hld up wl in rr: swtchd to wd outside and prog over 2f out: clsd to chal over 1f out: nt qckn ins fnl f* **6/1**[3]

-0 4 1 **Gatillo**[68] 1421 3-9-4 0 JimmyQuinn 9 70
(George Margarson) *in rr: pushed along and stl green 1/2-way: prog on outer 3f out: reminders to chal over 1f out: hld and one pce fnl f* **25/1**

0 5 1 1/2 **Royal Hero**[38] 2207 3-9-4 0 GeorgeBaker 7 66
(Amanda Perrett) *mde most: rdn over 2f out: hdd and fdd jst over 1f out* **16/1**

6 6 3 **Shongololo (IRE)**[30] 2459 3-9-4 0 OisinMurphy 1 60
(Andrew Balding) *t.k.h: trckd ldng pair: rdn over 2f out: wknd over 1f out* **8/1**

7 5 **Skiff** 4-10-0 0 JimCrowley 12 51
(Brendan Powell) *dwlt: sn prom: on terms on outer over 2f out: wknd over 1f out* **14/1**

8 1/2 **Monologue (IRE)**[62] 3-9-4 0 RyanClark 4 48
(Simon Hodgson) *chsd ldrs: waiting for a gap over 2f out: sn rdn and wknd over 1f out* **66/1**

00 9 1/2 **Ravens Heart (IRE)**[7] 3235 4-10-0 0 RenatoSouza 10 49
(Dean Ivory) *w ldr to over 2f out: sn wknd u.p* **100/1**

0- 10 nk **Helfire**[308] 5460 3-8-8 0 CharlieBennett[(5)] 13 41
(Hughie Morrison) *free to post: dwlt: a in rr: shoved along 1/2-way: sn btn* **7/1**

0 11 1/2 **Mybrotherjohnny**[15] 2929 5-10-0 0 CharlesBishop 11 47
(Jamie Poulton) *dwlt: sn chsd ldrs: wd bnd over 5f out: prog on outer to chal jst over 2f out: wknd rapidly over 1f out* **66/1**

12 22 **Thenoblepranks ter (IRE)** 7-9-9 0 DannyBurton[(5)] 14
(Emma Owen) *dwlt: last and lost tch 1/2-way: t.o* **80/1**

1m 50.13s (5.43) **Going Correction** +0.625s/f (Yiel)
WFA 3 from 4yo+ 10lb 12 Ran SP% **117.8**
Speed ratings (Par 103): **97,96,95,94,93 90,85,84,84,84 83,61**
CSF £7.58 TOTE £2.90: £1.10, £1.50, £2.30; EX 9.40 Trifecta £31.60.
Owner Abdullah Saeed Al Naboodah **Bred** G B Balding & Cheveley Park Stud **Trained** Newmarket, Suffolk

FOCUS
Race distance increased by 10yds. A pretty ordinary maiden, run at a steady enough gallop and in a slow time, but the winning favourite can rate better than the form.

3465 SKY BET TOP PRICE EVERY FAVOURITE H'CAP 1m 67y
6:50 (6:51) (Class 4) (0-85,84) 3-Y-O **£4,690** (£1,395; £697; £348) **Stalls** Low

Form RPR

1132 1 **Sir Roderic (IRE)**[35] 2299 3-9-3 **80** FrederikTylicki 2 86
(Rod Millman) *trckd ldng pair: rdn to cl over 2f out: led wl over 1f out: edgd lft sn after: drvn out and kpt on* **3/1**[1]

2532 2 1 1/4 **Skeaping**[18] 2826 3-9-3 **80** SeanLevey 1 83
(Richard Hannon) *pressed ldr: led briefly 2f out: pressing wnr whn sltly impeded jst over 1f out: one pce after* **8/1**

421- 3 nse **Rock Steady (IRE)**[237] 7540 3-9-1 **78** WilliamTwiston-Davies 8 81
(Roger Charlton) *stdd s: hld up in last trio: lot to do once ldrs kicked on over 3f out: reminders and prog 2f out: tk 3rd fnl f: pushed along and nrly snatched 2nd* **8/1**

1-45 4 2 3/4 **Ballard Down (IRE)**[27] 2565 3-9-7 **84** GeorgeBaker 6 81
(William Knight) *hld up in last trio: hanging lft fr 1/2-way: sme prog fr 2f out but hung lft and nvr able to threaten* **11/2**[3]

1110 5 1 1/2 **Medburn Dream**[16] 2892 3-9-5 **82** OisinMurphy 7 76
(Paul Henderson) *racd freely: led to 2f out: steadily wknd* **3/1**[1]

40-1 6 13 **House Of Commons (IRE)**[18] 2835 3-9-6 **83** JamieSpencer 4 48
(Paul Cole) *chsd ldrs: rdn 3f out: sn btn: wknd 2f out: t.o* **9/2**[2]

1206 7 2 **Willsy**[9] 3155 3-8-12 **75** (v) SilvestreDeSousa 3 38
(Mick Channon) *slowly away: a in rr: wknd over 2f out: t.o* **14/1**

1m 47.8s (3.10) **Going Correction** +0.625s/f (Yiel) 7 Ran SP% **112.5**
Speed ratings (Par 101): **109,107,107,104,103 90,88**
CSF £26.54 CT £170.96 TOTE £4.00: £1.80, £4.70; EX 28.40 Trifecta £207.30.
Owner The Links Partnership **Bred** Thomas G Cooke **Trained** Kentisbeare, Devon

FOCUS
Race distance increased by 10yds. A couple of these wanted to lead and the pace was reasonable enough. Only ordinary form, though, the winner taking another step forward.

3466 SKY BET ROYAL WINDSOR SPRINT SERIES H'CAP (A QUALIFIER FOR THE WINDSOR SPRINT SERIES FINAL) 6f
7:20 (7:20) (Class 3) (0-95,90) 3-Y-O **£7,439** (£2,213; £1,106; £553) **Stalls** Low

Form RPR

-535 1 **Young John (IRE)**[15] 2934 3-8-11 **80** JamieSpencer 3 89
(Richard Fahey) *mde virtually all: swtchd to far rail 1/2-way: hrd rdn 2f out: sn clr: in n.d after: eased last 50yds* **3/1**[1]

-000 2 2 3/4 **English Hero**[2] 3415 3-8-7 **76** HarryBentley 1 77
(William Knight) *hld up nr side: rdn 2f out: swtchd between rivals and led gp over 1f out: kpt on but no ch w wnr* **8/1**

-240 3 3/4 **Handytalk (IRE)**[21] 2736 3-8-10 **79** FrederikTylicki 4 78
(Rod Millman) *pressed nr side ldr: rdn over 2f out: no ch w wnr over 1f out: kpt on nr fin* **6/1**

435 4 1 3/4 **Ice Age (IRE)**[24] 2650 3-8-9 **78** JohnFahy 7 71
(Eve Johnson Houghton) *racd w wnr out wd to over 3f out then c towards nr side gp and on terms: drvn in centre over 2f out: one pce after* **13/2**

-315 5 6 **King Of Naples**[30] 2477 3-8-13 **89** GeorgeWood[(7)] 8 64
(James Fanshawe) *hld up on nr side: rdn and effrt over 2f out: wknd over 1f out* **10/3**[2]

6102 6 3 3/4 **Suqoor**[19] 2788 3-9-7 **90** SilvestreDeSousa 5 54
(Chris Dwyer) *mde most on nr side to over 1f out: wknd* **7/2**[3]

1m 15.43s (2.43) **Going Correction** +0.625s/f (Yiel) 6 Ran SP% **109.0**
Speed ratings (Par 103): **108,104,103,101,93 88**
CSF £24.70 CT £119.78 TOTE £3.80: £2.00, £2.50; EX 18.50 Trifecta £88.20.
Owner Mrs A M Riney **Bred** Carpet Lady Partnership **Trained** Musley Bank, N Yorks

FOCUS
Race distance as advertised. There was an immediate split on exiting the stalls, with the winner and fourth staying down the middle, but only the favourite went far side in the straight and it resulted in a clear victory. The form has been rated at face value.

3467 CLIC SARGENT FILLIES' H'CAP 1m 2f 7y
7:50 (7:50) (Class 4) (0-85,82) 3-Y-O+ **£4,806** (£1,511; £813) **Stalls** Centre

Form RPR

63 1 **Della Valle (GER)**[11] 3071 3-8-8 **74** HarryBentley 6 83
(Mike Murphy) *hld up in 3rd: prog to ld 2f out: shkn up over 1f out: wl in command and pushed out* **9/1**

41 2 4 1/2 **Indulged**[19] 2804 3-9-2 **82** TomQueally 5 83
(James Fanshawe) *led: shkn up whn pressed 3f out: rdn and hdd 2f out: one pce and wl hld over 1f out* **4/6**[1]

12-1 3 10 **Inke (IRE)**[18] 2827 4-9-12 **80** (p) PatCosgrave 2 66
(Jim Boyle) *trckd ldr: rdn to chal 3f out: sn btn off and dropped to 3rd: eased whn no ch last 150yds* **11/4**[2]

04R4 R **Dalmarella Dancer (IRE)**[7] 3230 5-8-5 **64** JordanVaughan[(5)] 1
(K R Burke) *led to post: ref to r* **7/1**[3]

2m 14.48s (5.78) **Going Correction** +0.625s/f (Yiel)
WFA 3 from 4yo+ 12lb 4 Ran SP% **109.2**
Speed ratings (Par 102): **101,97,89,**
CSF £16.17 TOTE £7.20; EX 15.70 Trifecta £26.70.
Owner Borgatti & Moir **Bred** Gestut Ammerland **Trained** Westoning, Beds

FOCUS
Race distance increased by 10yds. Two key non-runners, one refusing to race and a labouring favourite, so safe to say this form is worth little, although the race has been rated at face value. They headed far side.

3468 MAHJACKS DIY 50TH ANNIVERSARY H'CAP 1m 3f 135y
8:20 (8:21) (Class 5) (0-75,75) 3-Y-O **£2,911** (£866; £432; £216) **Stalls** Centre

Form RPR

3002 1 **Sporty Yankee (USA)**[7] 3236 3-8-7 **61** JoeyHaynes 4 70
(K R Burke) *hld up in last pair: prog over 2f out: rdn to ld over 1f out: hd at awkward angle but hld on u.p* **11/4**[1]

-600 2 nk **Knight Commander**[16] 2900 3-8-13 **67** FrederikTylicki 8 76
(William Knight) *hld up in last: prog over 2f out: hrd rdn to take 2nd 1f out: str chal last 100yds: jst hld* **18/1**

-601 **3** 2 3/4 **Sixties Groove (IRE)**[12] 3033 3-9-3 **71** JimCrowley 1 76
(Jeremy Noseda) *trckd ldrs: clsd to ld wl over 3f out and tk field to far side: rdn and hdd over 1f out: one pce u.p* **11/4**[1]
3-44 **4** 5 **Folly Bergere (IRE)**[59] 1608 3-9-7 **75** RyanTate 9 71
(James Eustace) *trckd ldrs: shkn up 3f out: steadily wknd fr 2f out* **6/1**[3]
5530 **5** 8 **Molten Gold**[11] 3063 3-9-0 **68** OisinMurphy 5 51
(Andrew Balding) *trckd ldrs: rdn to chse ld 3f out to over 2f out: wknd* **9/2**[2]
0-43 **6** 13 **Clever Bob (IRE)**[24] 2640 3-9-5 **73** JFEgan 2 36
(Joseph Tuite) *pressed ldr: upsides over 3f out: lost pl and pushed along over 2f out: sn wknd and eased* **16/1**
2220 **7** 48 **Zeehan**[16] 2909 3-9-6 **74** AdamKirby 6
(Clive Cox) *mde most to wl over 3f out: wknd rapidly and sn t.o* **7/1**

2m 37.65s (8.15) **Going Correction** +0.625s/f (Yiel) 7 Ran SP% **109.4**
Speed ratings (Par 99): **97,96,94,91,86 77,45**
CSF £47.79 CT £133.52 TOTE £3.40: £1.70, £5.10; EX 38.70 Trifecta £122.00.
Owner The Mount Racing Club & Mrs E Burke **Bred** Brandywine Farm **Trained** Middleham Moor, N Yorks

FOCUS
Race distance increased by 10yds. A modest handicap, with a few of them struggling on the ground, and they again headed far side. The pace was a fair one and those held up came to the fore.

3469 SKY BET H'CAP 5f 10y
8:50 (8:51) (Class 6) (0-65,65) 3-Y-O+ **£2,587** (£770; £384; £192) **Stalls** Low

Form RPR
3203 **1** **John Joiner**[17] 2845 4-8-10 **52** JosephineGordon(3) 6 61
(Peter Hedger) *trckd ldrs: rdn 2f out: led over 1f out: drvn out and kpt on fnl f* **11/2**
4341 **2** 3/4 **Oscars Journey**[74] 1299 6-9-12 **65** (v) FrederikTylicki 2 71
(J R Jenkins) *pressed ldrs: styd alone nr side fr 3f out: styd on terms and kpt on fnl f* **5/1**[3]
4104 **3** nk **Blistering Dancer (IRE)**[12] 3040 6-8-11 **50** JoeyHaynes 4 55
(Tony Carroll) *chsd ldr: rdn to ld 2f out: hdd over 1f out: kpt on same pce fnl f* **10/1**
U-34 **4** 1/2 **Foxford**[23] 2697 5-8-10 **56** MitchGodwin(7) 10 59
(Patrick Chamings) *prom: rdn over 2f out: n.m.r between rivals over 1f out: kpt on same pce fnl f* **7/2**[2]
42U3 **5** 1 **Quality Art (USA)**[4] 3316 8-9-8 **64** RobHornby(3) 9 64
(Simon Hodgson) *dwlt: hld up in rr: prog on outer 2f out to chse ldrs jst over 1f out: nt qckn fnl f* **12/1**
6660 **6** 2 1/2 **Potternello (IRE)**[11] 3070 4-9-7 **60** (v) SilvestreDeSousa 12 51
(Mick Channon) *dwlt: in tch in rr: rdn over 2f out: no imp on ldrs over 1f out* **3/1**[1]
0-00 **7** 3/4 **Secret Bird (IRE)**[41] 2130 4-9-7 **60** RobertWinston 7 48
(Dean Ivory) *settled in rr: rdn 2f out: no prog and btn over 1f out* **9/1**
5546 **8** 2 3/4 **Salvado (IRE)**[81] 1164 6-8-0 **46** oh1 RhiainIngram(7) 3 24
(Tony Carroll) *pushed along in last pair after 2f: nvr on terms* **33/1**
3005 **9** 2 1/2 **Deer Song**[31] 2435 3-8-10 **55** (b) WilliamCarson 13 22
(John Bridger) *led: tk all but one of field to far side 3f out: drvn and hdd 2f out: wknd* **16/1**
000- **10** hd **Rich Harvest (USA)**[185] 8290 11-8-3 **47** oh1 ow1 JordanVaughan(5) 8 15
(Ray Peacock) *in tch in rr to 2f out: wknd* **100/1**

1m 3.08s (2.78) **Going Correction** +0.625s/f (Yiel)
WFA 3 from 4yo+ 6lb 10 Ran SP% **115.9**
Speed ratings (Par 101): **102,100,100,99,97 93,92,88,84,84**
CSF £32.95 CT £223.23 TOTE £5.60: £1.80, £2.00, £2.60; EX 41.90 Trifecta £240.30.
Owner Mrs S Lynch & A Lomax **Bred** Mrs J McMahon **Trained** Hook, Hampshire

FOCUS
Race distance as advertised. All bar the runner-up raced far side and there was little in it. A fractional pb from the winner.
T/Plt: £455.90 to a £1 stake. Pool of £79300.73 - 126.97 winning tickets. T/Qpdt: £288.50 to a £1 stake. Pool of £5770.09 -14.80 winning tickets. **Jonathan Neesom**

2779 WOLVERHAMPTON (A.W) (L-H)
Monday, June 20

OFFICIAL GOING: Tapeta: standard
Wind: Light across Weather: Cloudy with sunny spells

3470 VISIT ATTHERACES.COM AMATEUR RIDERS' (S) STKS 1m 4f 50y (Tp)
6:10 (6:10) (Class 6) 4-Y-O+ **£2,183** (£507; £507; £169) **Stalls** Low

Form RPR
3133 **1** **Yasir (USA)**[19] 2445 8-11-4 61 MrsClaireHardwick 1 69
(Sophie Leech) *hld up: hdwy on outer over 2f out: led wl over 1f out: rdn and edgd lft ins fnl f: jst over a l up whn lft clr wl ins fnl f* **4/1**[2]
00-6 **2** 6 **Goal (IRE)**[4] 2899 8-10-12 51 (vt) BrodieHampson 3 53
(Sally Randell) *mid-div: hdwy over 5f out: rdn over 1f out: wkng whn hmpd wl ins fnl f* **20/1**
0-00 **2** dht **Flag Of Glory**[16] 2899 9-10-7 55 MissMEdden(5) 5 53
(Peter Hiatt) *led: rdn and hdd wl over 1f out: wknd ins fnl f* **50/1**
35/0 **4** 1 1/4 **Kuda Huraa (IRE)**[27] 1586 8-10-12 77 (b) MissHBethell 11 51
(Harriet Bethell) *hld up: pushed along over 5f out: hdwy over 1f out: nvr nrr* **9/1**[3]
422/ **5** 1 1/2 **Jazzy Lady (IRE)**[46] 499 5-10-4 74 MissHayleyMoore(3) 2 44
(Jim Best) *chsd ldrs: hmpd over 2f out: rdn and edgd lft over 1f out: wknd fnl f* **9/1**[3]
311- **6** 3 3/4 **Ventura Castle**[13] 2056 4-10-9 73 (bt) MissPFuller(3) 12 43
(Jamie Snowden) *chsd ldr after 1f: tl pushed along and nt clr run over 2f out: rdn over 1f out: sn wknd* **16/1**
5336 **7** 1 1/2 **Singular Quest**[23] 2678 4-10-9 67 (p) MrThomasGreatrex(3) 4 41
(Kevin Frost) *hld up in tch: rdn over 3f out: wknd over 1f out* **3/1**[1]
0000 **8** 7 **Pao De Acuca (IRE)**[19] 2400 4-11-4 60 (t) MrFTett 7 35
(Jose Santos) *chsd ldrs tl rdn and wknd over 2f out* **20/1**
0-00 **9** 9 **Kenobe Star (IRE)**[22] 2370 4-10-12 56 (p) MrSWalker 9 15
(David Dennis) *mid-div: rdn over 3f out: wknd over 2f out* **12/1**
064 **10** 7 **Shirataki (IRE)**[16] 2901 8-10-13 49 MissMollyKing(5) 10 10
(Peter Hiatt) *s.s: hld up: rdn and wknd over 2f out* **20/1**
04/0 **11** 1/2 **It's A Mans World**[16] 1222 10-10-7 58 MissLWilson(5) 8
(Brian Ellison) *hld up: bhd fnl 5f* **25/1**
6-60 **U** **Kissy Suzuki**[17] 2872 4-10-0 65 MrGRoberts(7) 6 73+
(Hughie Morrison) *hld up: pushed along 7f out: hdwy over 3f out: chsd wnr and hung lft fr over 1f out: hmpd wl ins fnl f: swtchd rt and jst over a l down whn sddled slipped and uns rdr* **3/1**[1]

2m 42.26s (1.46) **Going Correction** 0.0s/f (Stan) 12 Ran SP% **123.7**
Speed ratings (Par 101): **95,91,91,90,89 86,85,81,75,70 70,**
PL: Goal £7.00, £1.60, Flag Of Glory £9.20, £1.60 ; EX: Y/F £113.20, Y/G £47.60; CSF: Y/F £105.18, Y/G £44.91; TRIFECTA: Y/F/G £1317.10, Y/G/4 £1294.50. TOTE £5.20.There was no bid for the winner. Kissy Suzuki was subject to a friendly claim.
Owner Mike Harris Racing Club **Bred** Shadwell Farm LLC **Trained** Elton, Gloucs
■ A winner on her first Flat ride for Clare Hart.
■ Stewards' Enquiry : Mrs Claire Hardwick two-day ban: careless riding (Jul 7-8)
Mr G Roberts six-day ban: careless riding (Jul 7,13,16,20,21,23)

FOCUS
A modest seller for amateur riders and there was late drama. A step up from the winner but there's every chance Kissy Suzuki would have won.

3471 FOLLOW @ATTHERACES ON TWITTER H'CAP 5f 20y (Tp)
6:40 (6:40) (Class 5) (0-75,75) 3-Y-O **£3,105** (£924; £461; £230) **Stalls** Low

Form RPR
2111 **1** **Black Grass**[2] 3420 3-9-4 **72** 6ex CamHardie 3 79
(Michael Easterby) *mde all: set stdy pce tl qcknd over 1f out: rdn and edgd rt ins fnl f: r.o* **10/11**[1]
501 **2** 3/4 **Dutch Archer**[20] 2785 3-9-0 **68** RichardKingscote 5 72
(Jeremy Gask) *chsd wnr: rdn and ev ch ins fnl f: carried rt and unable qck nr fin* **5/2**[2]
003- **3** 1 **Mysterious Glance**[251] 7191 3-9-1 **69** DaleSwift 7 70
(Ed McMahon) *hld up: rdn over 1f out: r.o to go 3rd wl ins fnl f: nt trble ldrs* **14/1**
-001 **4** nk **Entertaining Ben**[13] 3000 3-9-6 **74** (p) MartinDwyer 2 74
(William Muir) *trckd ldrs: shkn up over 1f out: styd on same pce ins fnl f* **6/1**[3]
64-4 **5** 3 1/4 **Majestic Girl (IRE)**[67] 1435 3-8-7 **61** LukeMorris 6 49
(Robert Cowell) *s.i.s: pushed along in rr early: rdn over 1f out: sn outpcd* **11/1**

1m 2.72s (0.82) **Going Correction** 0.0s/f (Stan) 5 Ran SP% **110.2**
Speed ratings (Par 99): **93,91,90,89,84**
CSF £3.40 TOTE £1.80: £1.10, £1.70; EX 2.50 Trifecta £12.20.
Owner T Dewhirst, L Folwell, S Hull & D Swales **Bred** M W Easterby **Trained** Sheriff Hutton, N Yorks
■ Stewards' Enquiry : Cam Hardie caution: careless riding

FOCUS
A fair 3yo sprint handicap. The winner is thriving at present.

3472 DOWNLOAD THE AT THE RACES APP NOVICE STKS (PLUS 10 RACE) 5f 216y (Tp)
7:10 (7:11) (Class 4) 2-Y-O **£3,946** (£1,174; £586; £293) **Stalls** Low

Form RPR
24 **1** **Jacquard (IRE)**[9] 3167 2-9-0 0 FrannyNorton 4 87
(Mark Johnston) *mde virtually all: shkn up over 1f out: styd on wl: eased nr fin* **10/11**[1]
32 **2** 2 1/4 **Mr Hobbs**[13] 2997 2-9-0 0 LukeMorris 7 80
(Sylvester Kirk) *hld up: hdwy over 3f out: rdn to chse wnr and hung lft fr over 1f out: no imp ins fnl f* **7/4**[2]
0133 **3** 8 **Billy's Boots**[7] 3232 2-8-11 0 TomMarquand(3) 5 56
(Andrew Reid) *chsd ldrs: rdn over 1f out: wknd fnl f* **14/1**
4 1 1/2 **Gentleman Giles (IRE)** 2-9-0 0 TimmyMurphy 3 52
(Jamie Osborne) *prom: lost pl over 3f out: swtchd rt over 2f out: nt clr run wl over 1f out: n.d after: will improve* **20/1**
3610 **5** shd **King Of Castilla**[14] 2963 2-9-3 0 (t) RichardKingscote 6 54
(Gay Kelleway) *hld up: swtchd rt over 2f out: slipped wl over 1f out: sn rdn and hung lft: nvr trbld ldrs* **6/1**[3]
6 1 3/4 **Aberdonian** 2-9-0 0 NickyMackay 1 46
(Jeremy Gask) *s.i.s: nvr on terms* **33/1**
60 **7** 1 1/4 **Hazell Berry (IRE)**[25] 2612 2-8-6 0 PhilipPrince(3) 2 37
(David Evans) *broke wl: nt clr run and lost pl sn after s: pushed along 1/2-way: wknd over 2f out* **50/1**
8 1/2 **Arthurthedelegator** 2-9-0 0 PaulMulrennan 9 41
(Oliver Greenall) *s.i.s: sn rcvrd to chse ldrs: wknd wl over 1f out* **25/1**
0 **9** 12 **Fair Skies (IRE)**[12] 3008 2-9-0 0 LemosdeSouza 8 5
(Ivan Furtado) *chsd wnr tl rdn wl over 1f out: sn wknd* **50/1**

1m 14.48s (-0.02) **Going Correction** 0.0s/f (Stan) 9 Ran SP% **125.2**
Speed ratings (Par 95): **100,97,86,84,84 81,80,79,63**
CSF £2.85 TOTE £1.70: £1.10, £1.50, £3.10; EX 3.30 Trifecta £12.90.
Owner Sheikh Hamdan bin Mohammed Al Maktoum **Bred** Darley **Trained** Middleham Moor, N Yorks

FOCUS
Little depth to this maiden and the two market leaders were dominant. The form could be rated a few lengths better.

3473 JOIN THE BLACK COUNTRY CHAMBER OF COMMERCE CLAIMING STKS 5f 216y (Tp)
7:40 (7:41) (Class 5) 3-Y-O **£3,105** (£924; £461; £230) **Stalls** Low

Form RPR
1132 **1** **Broughtons Fancy**[18] 2823 3-8-5 66 TomMarquand(3) 4 61
(Andrew Reid) *disp ld tl wnt on over 1f out: sn rdn: styd on* **6/5**[1]
6440 **2** 1/2 **Silver Springs (IRE)**[34] 2322 3-8-4 65 ow1 PhilipPrince(3) 1 59
(David Evans) *w wnr tl rdn over 1f out: rallied and ev ch ins fnl f: r.o* **7/2**[3]
6046 **3** 1/2 **Kenstone (FR)**[9] 3146 3-8-9 47 (p) LukeMorris 7 59
(David Dennis) *chsd ldrs: rdn and hung lft over 1f out: r.o* **25/1**
6504 **4** 2 1/2 **Fiftytintsofsilver (IRE)**[9] 3140 3-7-10 45 RPWalsh(7) 2 46
(Gay Kelleway) *chsd ldrs: rdn over 2f out: no ex ins fnl f* **50/1**
6456 **5** nk **Thee And Me (IRE)**[12] 3036 3-8-6 67 KevinLundie(7) 6 55
(Mike Murphy) *prom: rdn over 2f out: styd on same pce fnl f* **9/4**[2]
0 **6** 1 1/2 **Moving Robe (IRE)**[39] 2177 3-8-5 0 (b[1]) NoelGarbutt(5) 8 47
(Conrad Allen) *prom: racd keenly: rdn over 2f out: hung lft over 1f out: styd on same pce* **33/1**
2366 **7** 2 1/2 **Justice Rock**[9] 3140 3-8-5 57 (be) CallumShepherd(5) 5 40
(Phil McEntee) *s.i.s: in rr: rdn over 2f out: wandered over 1f out: nvr on terms* **16/1**
55-4 **8** hd **Piccacard**[167] 48 3-8-6 49 AndrewMullen 3 35
(Michael Appleby) *sn pushed along in rr: rdn over 2f out: wknd over 1f out* **25/1**

1m 14.48s (-0.02) **Going Correction** 0.0s/f (Stan) 8 Ran SP% **116.9**
Speed ratings (Par 99): **100,99,98,95,94 92,89,89**
CSF £5.74 TOTE £2.10: £1.10, £1.50, £3.90; EX 5.50 Trifecta £65.20.Fiftytintsofsilver was claimed by Horses First Racing Limited for £5000.

Owner A S Reid **Bred** Michael E Broughton **Trained** Mill Hill, London NW7

FOCUS
A modest claimer in which it paid to race handily. The form could flatter the third.

3474 AT THE RACES SKY 415 H'CAP 7f 32y (Tp)
8:10 (8:11) (Class 6) (0-60,60) 3-Y-O+ **£2,393** (£712; £355; £177) **Stalls** High

Form RPR
5320 **1** **Illusive Force (IRE)**[7] 3220 4-9-5 **55**................................(v) MartinLane 3 63
(Derek Shaw) *hld up in tch: chsd ldr over 2f out: sn rdn: led ins fnl f: styd on* **13/2**[3]
006 **2** *nk* **Orlando Rogue (IRE)**[33] 2380 4-9-10 **60**..................(p) PaulMulrennan 2 67
(Conor Dore) *chsd ldrs: rdn over 2f out: chsd wnr wl ins fnl f: r.o* **8/1**
1321 **3** *1 ¾* **Not Your Call (IRE)**[25] 2610 5-9-10 **60**................................ KierenFox 10 63+
(Lee Carter) *led: rdn over 1f out: hdd ins fnl f: styd on same pce* **5/2**[1]
0600 **4** *½* **Dandys Perier (IRE)**[28] 2542 5-9-2 **57**......................... JordanNason(5) 6 59
(Ronald Harris) *hld up: hdwy 4f out: rdn over 2f out: styd on* **33/1**
0-06 **5** *1 ½* **Verus Delicia (IRE)**[10] 3098 7-9-6 **56**............................... LukeMorris 12 54
(Daniel Mark Loughnane) *hld up: hdwy and nt clr run 2f out: sn rdn: styd on same pce ins fnl f* **20/1**
5520 **6** *nse* **Daylight**[23] 2680 6-9-7 **57**...(t) CamHardie 4 55
(Michael Easterby) *hld up: rdn over 2f out: hdwy over 1f out: nt rch ldrs* **9/1**
644- **7** *½* **Magician Coutinho**[317] 5164 4-9-7 **57**.......................... DanielTudhope 7 54
(David O'Meara) *s.i.s: hld up: rdn over 2f out: hung lft and r.o ins fnl f: nvr nrr* **3/1**[2]
0665 **8** *nse* **Zed Candy Girl**[27] 2566 6-9-1 **58**..............................(p) PaddyBradley(7) 1 55
(Daniel Mark Loughnane) *broke wl: sn lost pl pl: hdwy u.p over 1f out: no ex wl ins fnl f* **15/2**
5406 **9** *2* **Mops Angel**[28] 2542 5-9-6 **56**.......................................(p) AndrewMullen 8 48
(Michael Appleby) *hld up: rdn over 2f out: nvr on terms* **9/1**
0040 **10** *1 ¾* **Johnny Splash (IRE)**[23] 2697 7-9-7 **60**..................(v) TomMarquand(3) 9 47
(Roger Teal) *prom: chsd ldr 5f out tl rdn over 2f out: wknd ins fnl f* **20/1**
26-5 **11** *6* **Rafaaf (IRE)**[58] 1648 8-9-2 **57**................................... CiaranMckee(5) 11 30
(Richard Phillips) *chsd ldrs: rdn over 2f out: wknd wl over 1f out* **20/1**
5461 **12** *23* **Ciaras Cookie (IRE)**[102] 895 4-8-13 **52**.............. AlistairRawlinson(3) 5
(Mandy Rowland) *chsd ldr 2f: rdn over 3f out: sn wknd* **25/1**

1m 29.44s (0.64) **Going Correction** 0.0s/f (Stan) **12** Ran SP% **130.9**
Speed ratings (Par 101): **96,95,93,93,91 91,90,90,88,86 79,53**
CSF £59.00 CT £174.48 TOTE £11.90: £3.80, £4.50, £1.30; EX 78.30 Trifecta £328.60.
Owner Brian Johnson (Northamptonshire) **Bred** Kilshannig Stud **Trained** Sproxton, Leics

FOCUS
A modest handicap and a close finish. The winner reversed Chelmsford form with the third.

3475 FOLLOW AT THE RACES ON INSTAGRAM MEDIAN AUCTION MAIDEN STKS 1m 141y (Tp)
8:40 (8:41) (Class 5) 3-Y-O **£3,105** (£924; £461; £230) **Stalls** Low

Form RPR
6-42 **1** **Shadad (IRE)**[20] 2780 3-9-5 76.. FMBerry 5 78
(Ralph Beckett) *mde all: rdn over 1f out: sn edgd rt: styd on u.p: wnt lft towards fin* **4/1**
2-42 **2** *¾* **Van Dyke**[10] 3104 3-9-5 75.. LukeMorris 7 76
(Hughie Morrison) *a.p: chsd wnr 3f out: rdn over 1f out: styd on u.p* **11/4**[2]
3 **3** *3* **Crystallographer (IRE)**[33] 2375 3-9-0 0........................... ShaneKelly 8 65
(David Lanigan) *a.p: rdn over 1f out: hung lft and no ex ins fnl f* **3/1**[3]
3-24 **4** *1 ½* **Invocation (FR)**[18] 2826 3-9-5 77................................... PaulMulrennan 4 67
(Alan King) *hld up: hdwy over 2f out: rdn over 1f out: styd on same pce* **6/1**
0 **5** *1 ¼* **Princesse Eva (FR)**[20] 2774 3-8-11 70.....................[1] DanielMuscutt(3) 3 59
(James Fanshawe) *hld up in tch: shkn up over 2f out: no ex ins fnl f* **16/1**
0 **6** *1 ½* **Gold Return (IRE)**[33] 2375 3-9-0 0.......................... RichardKingscote 1 56
(David Lanigan) *hld up: shkn up and edgd lft over 1f out: nvr on terms* **50/1**
63 **7** *½* **Naqdy**[42] 2109 3-9-5 0.. PaulHanagan 9 60
(William Haggas) *s.i.s: hdwy 6f out: rdn whn nt clr run over 2f out: wknd over 1f out* **9/4**[1]
00 **8** *nk* **Private Jet**[56] 1714 3-9-5 0.. DarryllHolland 10 60
(Charles Hills) *s.i.s: hdwy to chse wnr 7f out: rdn and lost 2nd 3f out: wknd over 1f out* **50/1**
0- **9** *8* **Fire Empress**[327] 4749 3-8-11 0............................... MatthewCosham(3) 2 38
(James Unett) *hld up: nvr on terms* **100/1**
06-0 **10** *9* **Invincible Bond**[18] 2835 3-9-2 42...................................... JoeDoyle(3) 6 24
(Simon Waugh) *s.i.s: hld up: pushed along over 3f out: wknd over 2f out* **100/1**

1m 49.18s (-0.92) **Going Correction** 0.0s/f (Stan) **10** Ran SP% **128.5**
Speed ratings (Par 99): **104,103,100,99,98 96,96,96,89,81**
CSF £17.28 TOTE £7.00: £1.70, £1.10, £2.00; EX 23.10 Trifecta £85.30.
Owner H H Sheikh Mohammed Bin Khalifa Al Thani **Bred** Barronstown Stud **Trained** Kimpton, Hants

FOCUS
A fair maiden in which the favourite ran well below expectations. The winner had the run of things.

3476 WATCH TODAY'S REPLAYS ON THE ATR APP H'CAP 1m 141y (Tp)
9:10 (9:11) (Class 6) (0-65,63) 4-Y-O+ **£2,393** (£712; £355; £177) **Stalls** Low

Form RPR
0351 **1** **Vastly (USA)**[11] 3072 7-9-7 **63**...(t) LukeMorris 7 71
(Sophie Leech) *s.i.s: hld up: nt clr run over 2f out: hdwy over 1f out: rdn to ld and edgd lft wl ins fnl f: r.o* **7/2**[2]
000- **2** *1 ¼* **What Usain**[247] 7294 4-9-6 **62**.......................................(v) DanielTudhope 3 67
(David O'Meara) *hld up in tch: plld hrd: nt clr run over 1f out: rdn and ev ch whn edgd lft ins fnl f: styd on same pce* **9/4**[1]
-002 **3** *nk* **Filament Of Gold (USA)**[27] 2566 5-8-8 **55**................(p) GaryMahon(5) 5 60
(Roy Brotherton) *chsd ldrs: led over 1f out: rdn and hdd wl ins fnl f: styd on same pce* **7/2**[2]
6106 **4** *hd* **Mary Le Bow**[20] 2783 5-9-1 **62**.............................(t) CallumShepherd(5) 4 66
(Victor Dartnall) *hld up: hdwy over 1f out: rdn and ev ch whn n.m.r ins fnl f: styd on same pce* **4/1**[3]
0-00 **5** *2* **Free One (IRE)**[21] 2734 4-9-4 **63**..........................(b1) TomMarquand(3) 8 63
(Ivan Furtado) *hld up: pushed along over 3f out: styd on fr over 1f out: nt rch ldrs* **12/1**
0000 **6** *2* **Mr Frankie**[40] 2153 5-8-12 **57**.....................................(p) JoeDoyle(3) 2 53
(Richard Phillips) *chsd ldr tl led 3f out: rdn and hdd over 1f out: sn edgd lft and no ex* **20/1**
0066 **7** *4* **Call Me Crockett (IRE)**[9] 3153 4-9-1 **57**....................(p) AndrewMullen 1 45
(Iain Jardine) *plld hrd and prom: rdn over 2f out: wknd fnl f* **14/1**
0300 **8** *7* **Nubar Boy**[24] 2635 9-9-5 **61**..(p) DaleSwift 6 34
(Daniel Mark Loughnane) *led: rdn and hdd 3f out: ev ch wl over 1f out: hmpd and wknd ent fnl f* **16/1**

1m 49.25s (-0.85) **Going Correction** 0.0s/f (Stan) **8** Ran SP% **120.2**
Speed ratings (Par 101): **103,101,101,101,99 97,94,88**
CSF £12.54 CT £30.27 TOTE £3.80: £1.70, £1.40, £1.30; EX 12.10 Trifecta £45.50.
Owner Out Of Bounds Racing Club **Bred** Juddmonte Farms Inc **Trained** Elton, Gloucs

FOCUS
A modest handicap run at a decent pace. Straightforward form.
T/Plt: £15.30 to a £1 stake. Pool of £73864.34 - 3516.78 winning tickets. T/Qpdt: £4.00 to a £1 stake. Pool of £7805.63 - 1438.57 winning tickets. **Colin Roberts**

3248 BEVERLEY (R-H)
Tuesday, June 21

OFFICIAL GOING: Good (7.2)
Wind: Light across Weather: Cloudy with sunny periods

3477 RACING UK IN GLORIOUS HD NOVICE AUCTION STKS 7f 100y
2:00 (2:01) (Class 5) 2-Y-O **£3,780** (£1,131; £565; £283; £141) **Stalls** Low

Form RPR
1 **Proud Archi (IRE)** 2-9-3 0.. PaulMulrennan 3 76+
(Michael Dods) *hld up towards rr: hdwy over 2f out: shkn up over 1f out: chsd ldr ins fnl f: sn green and edgd lft: styd on to ld last 100yds* **9/4**[1]
51 **2** *¾* **Spirit Of Sarwan (IRE)**[15] 2963 2-9-6 0...................... AdamBeschizza 8 77
(Julia Feilden) *sn led: rdn along over 1f out: jnd and drvn ins fnl f: hdd last 100yds: kpt on same pce* **9/4**[1]
0 **3** *1 ¾* **Muirsheen Durkin**[18] 2873 2-8-13 0......................(p) RichardKingscote 5 66
(Tom Dascombe) *trckd ldrs: hdwy 2f out: rdn to chse ldng pair ent fnl f: kpt on same pce* **7/2**[2]
4 *6* **Steel Helmet (IRE)** 2-9-5 0... BenCurtis 7 58+
(Brian Ellison) *dwlt: green and bhd: pushed along and hdwy 2f out: rdn and kpt on fnl f* **9/1**
54 **5** *¾* **Serenity Dove**[15] 2970 2-8-12 0.. JoeyHaynes 4 49
(K R Burke) *chsd ldr: pushed along 3f out: rdn over 2f out: sn drvn and wknd over 1f out* **8/1**[3]
05 **6** *2* **Babalugats (IRE)**[15] 2970 2-8-1 0........................ RachelRichardson(5) 6 38
(Tim Easterby) *chsd ldng pair: rdn along over 2f out: sn wknd* **25/1**
0 **7** *1* **Mr C (IRE)**[37] 2264 2-9-0 0.. JacobButterfield(3) 1 47
(Ollie Pears) *towards rr: sme hdwy over 2f out: sn rdn along and n.d* **66/1**
65 **8** *1 ½* **Powerless (IRE)**[46] 2014 2-8-11 0.. DavidAllan 2 37
(Tim Easterby) *trckd ldrs on inner: hdwy to chse ldng pair 3f out: rdn over 2f out: sn wknd* **20/1**

1m 34.76s (0.96) **Going Correction** -0.10s/f (Good) **8** Ran SP% **115.0**
Speed ratings (Par 93): **90,89,87,80,79 77,76,74**
CSF £7.23 TOTE £3.30: £1.20, £1.10, £1.60; EX 8.40 Trifecta £34.50.
Owner Eagle Racing **Bred** Robert Allcock **Trained** Denton, Co Durham

FOCUS
The official going remained good and the riders in the first race agreed. Rail around bottom bend moved to its narrowest position, adding 18yds to distances of races on the round course, including this opening contest. A modest novice auction event and quite a test for these 2yos with the winning time 4.66sec outside standard.

3478 WATCH LIVE RACING AND BET WITH RACING UK H'CAP (DIV I) 7f 100y
2:30 (2:30) (Class 5) (0-70,70) 3-Y-O+ **£3,780** (£1,131; £565; £283; £141) **Stalls** Low

Form RPR
3443 **1** **Shadow Game**[6] 3286 3-9-5 **70**... JoeFanning 4 81+
(Mark Johnston) *trckd ldrs: hdwy over 2f out: rdn to chse ldr over 1f out: styd on to ld ins fnl f* **2/1**[1]
-640 **2** *2 ¼* **Relight My Fire**[24] 2673 6-9-10 **66**.......................................(p) DavidAllan 6 74
(Tim Easterby) *led: rdn clr wl over 1f out: drvn and hdd ins fnl f: kpt on same pce* **5/1**[2]
4100 **3** *1 ¼* **Make On Madam (IRE)**[13] 3013 4-9-9 **65**................. GrahamGibbons 1 70
(Les Eyre) *in tch on inner: hdwy 2f out: rdn and n.m.r over 1f out: swtchd lft and drvn: kpt on towards fin* **12/1**
31-2 **4** *1* **Wakame (IRE)**[21] 2770 3-8-12 **63**....................................... ShaneGray 13 63
(Ed de Giles) *chsd ldrs: pushed along and outpcd 3f out: sn rdn: kpt on fnl f* **11/1**
0-00 **5** *¾* **Lozah**[27] 2576 3-8-8 **59**...(bt1) SamJames 3 57+
(David Loughnane) *in rr: hdwy over 2f out: rdn wl over 1f out: styd on fnl f: edgd rt wl ins fnl f and no imp* **100/1**
00-0 **6** *½* **Fire Diamond**[35] 2349 3-8-9 **60**................................. RichardKingscote 5 57
(Tom Dascombe) *chsd ldrs: rdn along over 2f out: drvn wl over 1f out: sn one pce* **20/1**
6503 **7** *shd* **Arms Around Me (IRE)**[8] 3214 4-9-4 **60**............................ TomEaves 2 60
(James Given) *in tch: hdwy 1/2-way: chsd ldrs over 2f out: sn rdn and hld whn edgd lft wl ins fnl f* **12/1**
0210 **8** *1 ¼* **Mr Cool Cash**[17] 2918 4-9-9 **68**.. PhilipPrince(3) 9 65
(Richard Guest) *sn chsng ldr: rdn wl over 1f out: drvn appr fnl f: rdr dropped whip and sn wknd* **11/2**[3]
0011 **9** *¾* **Red Charmer (IRE)**[19] 2810 6-10-0 **70**............................ PJMcDonald 7 66+
(Ann Duffield) *hld up in midfield: hdwy 2f out: rdn to chse ldrs over 1f out: hld whn n.m.r and hmpd wl ins fnl f* **7/1**
-040 **10** *2 ¾* **Munjally**[45] 2053 5-9-1 **57**... JackGarritty 8 45+
(Patrick Holmes) *t.k.h: a towards rr* **33/1**
0-50 **11** *¾* **Mr Chuckles (IRE)**[55] 1789 3-9-1 **66**............................ AndrewMullen 10 50+
(Philip Kirby) *a towards rr* **20/1**
0-00 **12** *6* **Caeser The Gaeser (IRE)**[15] 2974 4-8-13 **55**............... PhillipMakin 11 28+
(Nigel Tinkler) *a towards rr* **40/1**
005 **13** *4 ½* **Kyllini**[46] 2019 3-8-0 **51**.. CamHardie 12 10+
(Marjorie Fife) *a towards rr* **100/1**

1m 32.65s (-1.15) **Going Correction** -0.10s/f (Good)
WFA 3 from 4yo+ 9lb **13** Ran SP% **118.5**
Speed ratings (Par 103): **102,99,98,96,96 95,95,93,93,89 89,82,77**
CSF £10.43 CT £96.26 TOTE £2.40: £1.10, £2.20, £3.60; EX 13.70 Trifecta £100.30.
Owner Sheikh Hamdan bin Mohammed Al Maktoum **Bred** Darley **Trained** Middleham Moor, N Yorks

The Form Book, Raceform Ltd, Newbury, RG14 5SJ

FOCUS
Rail movement added 18yds to race distance. The first division of a modest handicap and very few got into it, with those ridden prominently enjoying a big advantage.

3479 WATCH LIVE RACING AND BET WITH RACING UK H'CAP (DIV II) 7f 100y
3:00 (3:01) (Class 5) (0-70,69) 3-Y-O+ **£3,780** (£1,131; £565; £283; £141) **Stalls** Low

Form RPR

3005 **1** **Mercury**[13] 3013 4-8-12 **56**.............(b) KevinStott(3) 10 64
(Kevin Ryan) *midfield: hdwy on outer over 2f out: rdn to ld ent fnl f: drvn out* **13/2**[3]

3000 **2** *1 1/4* **Royal Holiday (IRE)**[17] 2918 9-9-10 **68**.............(p) JacobButterfield(3) 13 73
(Marjorie Fife) *chsd ldr: led 3f out: rdn and hdd wl over 1f out: sn drvn and ev ch: kpt on fnl f* **16/1**

0-03 **3** *nk* **Totally Magic (IRE)**[25] 2655 4-9-6 **61**............. KeaganLatham 4 65
(Richard Whitaker) *trckd ldng pair: hdwy over 2f out: rdn to ld wl over 1f out: drvn and hdd ent fnl f: kpt on same pce* **15/2**

0-04 **4** *hd* **Bertha Burnett (IRE)**[29] 2525 5-8-9 **50** oh4............. JamesSullivan 11 54
(Brian Rothwell) *towards rr: hdwy on inner wl over 1f out: rdn and styd on wl fnl f: nrst fin* **33/1**

-430 **5** *1/2* **Miramonte Dancer (IRE)**[28] 2553 3-8-10 **60**.............(p) OisinMurphy 2 62+
(David C Griffiths) *towards rr: hdwy wl over 1f out: n.m.r: swtchd rt and rdn jst ins fnl f: fin wl* **5/1**[2]

4101 **6** *1* **Star Of The Stage**[41] 2153 4-9-11 **66**.............(p) AdamBeschizza 1 66
(Julia Feilden) *hld up towards rr: hdwy over 2f out: rdn to chse ldrs over 1f out: drvn and kpt on same pce fnl f* **7/2**[1]

33-0 **7** *hd* **Charava (IRE)**[17] 2918 4-9-0 **62**.............(p) PaulaMuir(7) 5 62
(Patrick Holmes) *trckd ldrs: hdwy 3f out: rdn along 2f out: kpt on same pce fnl f* **14/1**

-363 **8** *nse* **Saxon Gold (IRE)**[20] 2801 3-8-6 **56**.............(p) SamJames 8 53
(John Davies) *chsd ldrs: rdn along over 2f out: drvn wl over 1f out: sn one pce* **10/1**

3056 **9** *1 1/4* **I'm Super Too (IRE)**[19] 2810 9-8-9 **55**............. GemmaTutty(5) 3 52
(Karen Tutty) *stdd s: hld up: a towards rr* **8/1**

56-0 **10** *1/2* **Who's Shirl**[35] 2330 10-9-2 **57**............. AndrewElliott 9 53
(Chris Fairhurst) *a in rr* **20/1**

0-44 **11** *2* **Isntshesomething**[21] 2778 4-8-11 **52**............. ConnorBeasley 6 43
(Richard Guest) *chsd ldrs: rdn along over 2f out: sn drvn and wknd* **14/1**

02-0 **12** *2 3/4* **Cuppatee (IRE)**[20] 2802 3-9-5 **69**............. PJMcDonald 12 51
(Ann Duffield) *a in rr* **22/1**

0-36 **F** **Kung Hei Fat Choy (USA)**[152] 276 7-9-6 **66**.... RachelRichardson(5) 7
(Lucinda Egerton) *led: rdn along and hdd 3f out: sn crashed through rail and fell: fatally injured* **25/1**

1m 33.59s (-0.21) **Going Correction** -0.10s/f (Good)
WFA 3 from 4yo+ 9lb **13** Ran SP% **119.3**
Speed ratings (Par 103): **97,95,95,95,94 93,93,93,91,91 88,85,**
CSF £99.78 CT £828.43 TOTE £6.70: £2.60, £5.60, £2.70; EX 125.00 Trifecta £1604.80.
Owner Mrs Angie Bailey **Bred** Park Farm Racing **Trained** Hambleton, N Yorks

FOCUS
Rail movement added 18yds to race distance. This race was marred by a terrible incident inside the last 3f when the early leader \bKung Hei Fat Choy\p, who had just been headed, crashed through both sets of rails on the inside of the track. The winning time was nearly a second slower than the first division.

3480 RACING UK ANDROID APP RACINGUK.COM/MOBILE H'CAP 1m 4f 16y
3:30 (3:40) (Class 5) (0-70,70) 4-Y-O+ **£3,780** (£1,131; £565; £283; £141) **Stalls** Low

Form RPR

460U **1** **Lean On Pete (IRE)**[7] 3253 7-8-2 **51** oh1............. JamesSullivan 1 62
(Ollie Pears) *mde all: 10 l clr after 4f: stdd gallop 1/2-way: rdn clr wl over 2f out: kpt on strly* **15/2**

5554 **2** *3 3/4* **Saint Thomas (IRE)**[13] 3012 9-8-4 **53**............. JoeFanning 8 58
(John Mackie) *hld up: hdwy 3f out: rdn to chse wnr over 1f out: drvn and no imp fnl f* **4/1**[2]

1-10 **3** *1 1/4* **Major Rowan**[28] 2558 5-8-7 **56**............. SamJames 7 59+
(John Davies) *hld up and bhd: hdwy on wd outside wl over 1f out: sn rdn: kpt on fnl f* **6/1**[3]

6-46 **4** *3/4* **Multi Grain**[13] 3018 4-8-10 **59**.............(p) PJMcDonald 2 61
(Micky Hammond) *hld up in rr: hdwy over 2f out: rdn wl over 1f out: kpt on fnl f* **16/1**

0500 **5** *2 1/4* **Eeny Mac (IRE)**[104] 876 9-8-3 **52** oh6 ow1............. RoystonFfrench 5 50
(John Wainwright) *chsd wnr: rdn along wl over 2f out: drvn wl over 1f out: grad wknd* **50/1**

6-04 **6** *hd* **Aneedh**[24] 2672 6-8-11 **63**.............(p) JoeDoyle(3) 3 61
(Clive Mulhall) *hld up in tch: hdwy on inner to chse ldrs over 2f out: rdn wl over 1f out: sn drvn and wknd* **9/4**[1]

3/55 **7** *2 1/4* **Another Lincolnday**[12] 3052 5-9-4 **67**............. TomEaves 4 61
(Michael Herrington) *trckd ldng pair: effrt 3f out: rdn over 2f out: sn drvn and btn* **7/1**

2-0 **8** *16* **Deep Blue Diamond**[40] 2176 4-9-2 **70**............. NoelGarbutt(5) 6 39
(Denis Quinn) *chsd ldrs: rdn along 3f out: sn drvn and wknd* **13/2**

2m 37.0s (-2.80) **Going Correction** -0.10s/f (Good) **8** Ran SP% **110.5**
Speed ratings (Par 103): **105,102,101,101,99 99,98,87**
CSF £34.95 CT £181.77 TOTE £8.00: £2.30, £1.90, £1.50; EX 36.70 Trifecta £245.40.
Owner K C West **Bred** Mrs T Mahon **Trained** Norton, N Yorks

FOCUS
Rail movement added 18yds to race distance. A modest middle-distance handicap and a stop-start gallop very much played into the hands of the winner.

3481 JAMIE GORDON THE BIG 40 H'CAP 1m 1f 207y
4:00 (4:02) (Class 4) (0-80,75) 4-Y-O+ **£6,301** (£1,886; £943; £472; £235) **Stalls** Low

Form RPR

0045 **1** **Final**[13] 3011 4-9-4 **72**............. JoeFanning 3 81
(Mark Johnston) *in tch: hdwy wl over 2f out: rdn to chse clr ldr over 1f out: drvn and styd on fnl f to ld last 100yds* **9/4**[2]

0031 **2** *1 1/2* **Mysterial**[13] 3012 6-8-12 **73**............. GerO'Neill(7) 1 79
(Declan Carroll) *led and sn clr: pushed along 2f out: rdn over 1f out: hdd and no ex last 100yds* **6/1**[3]

0632 **3** *5* **Peterhouse (USA)**[7] 3252 4-9-7 **75**............. BenCurtis 4 72
(Jason Ward) *in tch: pushed along 1/2-way: rdn over 3f out: drvn 2f out: plugged on one pce* **6/4**[1]

2-50 **4** *1/2* **Le Deluge (FR)**[4] 3363 6-8-9 **63**.............(t) PJMcDonald 2 59
(Micky Hammond) *chsd clr ldr: rdn along wl over 2f out: drvn wl over 1f: grad wknd* **10/1**

3530 **5** *1/2* **Nonchalant**[10] 3166 5-9-6 **74**.............(v) DanielTudhope 5 69
(David O'Meara) *hld up in rr: sme hdwy on inner over 2f out: rdn wl over 1f out: n.d* **6/1**[3]

2m 4.79s (-2.21) **Going Correction** -0.10s/f (Good) **5** Ran SP% **108.4**
Speed ratings (Par 105): **104,102,98,98,98**
CSF £14.71 TOTE £2.70: £1.50, £2.00; EX 11.50 Trifecta £20.20.
Owner C H Greensit & W A Greensit **Bred** C H And W A Greensit **Trained** Middleham Moor, N Yorks

FOCUS
Rail movement added 18yds to race distance. Not a bad little handicap and certainly no shortage of early pace thanks to the runner-up.

3482 RACING UK ON SKY 432 H'CAP 1m 1f 207y
4:30 (4:38) (Class 6) (0-65,65) 3-Y-O **£2,587** (£770; £384; £192) **Stalls** Low

Form RPR

0021 **1** **French Legend**[7] 3256 3-8-11 **55** 6ex............. OisinMurphy 11 61
(Andrew Balding) *trckd ldrs: hdwy over 2f out: rdn to ld appr fnl f: drvn and kpt on wl towards fin* **5/2**[1]

0316 **2** *1/2* **Monsieur Glory**[25] 2652 3-9-6 **64**.............(v) RichardKingscote 2 70
(Tom Dascombe) *trckd ldrs: smooth hdwy on inner 2f out: effrt and nt clr run over 1f out: swtchd lft ent fnl f: sn rdn to chse wnr: drvn and kpt on towards fin* **3/1**[2]

064- **3** *1/2* **Reckless Wave (IRE)**[237] 7545 3-8-11 **55**............. PhillipMakin 1 59+
(Ed Walker) *in tch: hdwy on inner 2f out: nt clr run and swtchd markedly lft ent fnl f: sn rdn and styd on wl towards fin* **11/1**

5000 **4** *3/4* **High On Light**[13] 3015 3-8-4 **48**............. JamesSullivan 12 51
(Tim Easterby) *in tch: hdwy over 2f out: rdn over 1f out: kpt on fnl f* **16/1**

2-06 **5** *3* **Strathearn (IRE)**[29] 2538 3-9-7 **65**............. PaulMulrennan 13 62
(Michael Bell) *trckd ldr: cl up 4f out: chal over 3f out: rdn 2f out: drvn to ld briefly over 1f out: sn hdd & wknd fnl f* **12/1**

6-12 **6** *1/2* **New Abbey Angel (IRE)**[57] 1698 3-9-4 **62**............. JoeFanning 14 58
(Gay Kelleway) *t.k.h: trckd ldrs: hdwy over 2f out: rdn over 1f out: sn one pce* **15/2**

0-20 **7** *hd* **Indulgent**[13] 3015 3-8-11 **55**............. BarryMcHugh 9 51
(Tony Coyle) *hld up in rr: hdwy on inner over 2f out: rdn over 1f out: kpt on fnl f* **20/1**

55-0 **8** *3/4* **Sunlit Waters**[46] 1989 3-9-5 **63**............. PaulHanagan 7 57
(Eve Johnson Houghton) *hld up towards rr: hdwy over 2f out: rdn wl over 1f out: styd on fnl f* **6/1**[3]

0-40 **9** *2 3/4* **Wayside Magic**[26] 2615 3-8-8 **52**.............(p) ConnorBeasley 8 41
(Michael Dods) *led: jnd over 3f out: rdn over 2f out: drvn wl over 1f out: hdd jst over 1f out: sn wknd* **33/1**

6-56 **10** *5* **Chilli Jam**[10] 3141 3-9-0 **58**.............(p) ShaneGray 6 37
(Ed de Giles) *a towards rr* **10/1**

050- **11** *4 1/2* **Ingleby Erin**[256] 7084 3-8-1 **50**............. NathanEvans(5) 4 21
(Michael Easterby) *chsd ldrs: rdn along over 2f out: sn wknd* **33/1**

0504 **12** *1/2* **Citadel**[13] 3015 3-8-2 **46** oh1.............(p) CamHardie 15 16
(John Wainwright) *towards rr: effrt on outer wl over 2f out: sn rdn and hung rt: nvr a factor* **33/1**

504 **13** *11* **Rich Pursuit**[37] 2271 3-8-3 **47**.............(p) JoeyHaynes 3
(James Bethell) *dwlt: a in rr* **33/1**

2m 6.43s (-0.57) **Going Correction** -0.10s/f (Good) **13** Ran SP% **127.1**
Speed ratings (Par 97): **98,97,97,96,94 93,93,93,90,86 83,82,74**
CSF £9.92 CT £69.72 TOTE £3.40: £1.40, £2.40, £3.40; EX 13.80 Trifecta £90.30.
Owner J C Smith **Bred** Littleton Stud **Trained** Kingsclere, Hants
■ Melgate Melody (11-1) was withdrawn. Rule 4 applies to all bets struck prior to withdrawal, but not to SP bets. Deduction - 5p in the pound. New market formed.

FOCUS
Rail movement added 18yds to race distance. A moderate 3yo handicap reduced by one when Melgate Melody was withdrawn after getting under his stall and running loose. Only three of these had won before and a couple of them filled the first two places.

3483 RACING UK PROFITS ALL RETURNED TO RACING MEDIAN AUCTION MAIDEN STKS 1m 100y
5:00 (5:02) (Class 5) 3-Y-O **£3,780** (£1,131; £565; £283; £141) **Stalls** Low

Form RPR

50 **1** **Jabbaar**[20] 2790 3-9-5 0............. PaulHanagan 4 73
(Owen Burrows) *mde all: jnd and rdn 2f out: drvn ent fnl f: kpt on wl towards fin* **7/2**[2]

-604 **2** *3/4* **Brorocco**[10] 3156 3-9-5 74............. OisinMurphy 7 71+
(Andrew Balding) *s.i.s and bhd: hdwy over 2f out: rdn and edgd lft wl over 1f out: drvn and styd on wl fnl f* **5/6**[1]

6 **3** *hd* **Al Nasser Alwashik**[7] 3264 3-9-5 0............. SamJames 8 71+
(David Loughnane) *hld up towards rr: hdwy wl over 2f out: rdn over 1f out: drvn and styd on wl fnl f* **25/1**

0-46 **4** *1/2* **Reaver (IRE)**[11] 3111 3-9-5 63............. PaulMulrennan 2 70
(Eve Johnson Houghton) *trckd wnr: cl up 3f out: chal 2f out: sn rdn and ev ch tl drvn and one pce ins fnl f* **7/2**[2]

66 **5** *6* **Tell The Stars**[8] 3209 3-8-11 0............. JacobButterfield(3) 1 52
(Ollie Pears) *trckd ldng pair: effrt 2f out and sn rdn: drvn over 1f out: sn wknd* **66/1**

30-6 **6** *3 1/2* **Bigbadboy (IRE)**[13] 3014 3-9-5 52............. JamesSullivan 3 49
(Clive Mulhall) *chsd ldrs: rdn along 2f out: sn drvn and wknd* **40/1**

7 *6* **Olympus Mons (FR)** 3-9-5 0............. DanielTudhope 6 36
(David O'Meara) *a towards rr* **9/1**[3]

65 **8** *8* **Oyster Card**[25] 2667 3-9-2 0............. AlistairRawlinson(3) 5 18
(Michael Appleby) *t.k.h on outer: chsd ldrs: rdn along over 3f out: sn lost pl and bhd* **33/1**

1m 47.49s (-0.11) **Going Correction** -0.10s/f (Good) **8** Ran SP% **119.7**
Speed ratings (Par 99): **96,95,95,94,88 85,79,71**
CSF £7.05 TOTE £4.00: £1.70, £1.02, £5.50; EX 8.80 Trifecta £69.00.
Owner Hamdan Al Maktoum **Bred** Cheveley Park Stud Ltd **Trained** Lambourn, Berks

FOCUS
Rail movement added 18yds to race distance. A moderate and uncompetitive 3yo maiden and this looked an opportunity missed for the odds-on favourite.

3484 GO RACING IN YORKSHIRE FUTURE STARS APPRENTICE H'CAP 5f
5:30 (5:31) (Class 6) (0-60,60) 3-Y-O+ **£2,587** (£770; £384; £192) **Stalls** Low

Form RPR

6503 **1** **Seamster**[7] 3268 9-9-4 **56**.............(t) CameronNoble(5) 16 67
(David Loughnane) *sn trcking ldrs: hdwy 1/2-way: chsd ldr wl over 1f out: rdn to ld ent fnl f: kpt on strly* **13/2**[3]

0423 **2** *1 3/4* **Poppy In The Wind**[13] 3010 4-9-10 **60**.............(v) PaddyBradley(3) 15 65
(Alan Brown) *towards rr: hdwy on wd outside wl over 1f out: sn rdn: styd on strly fnl f* **11/2**[2]

2500 **3** *nk* **Tinsill**[13] 3009 5-8-11 **51**......(p) DavidEgan(7) 3 55
(Nigel Tinkler) *in tch: hdwy 2f out: rdn to chse ldng pair ent fnl f: sn drvn and kpt on same pce towards fin* **14/1**

50-0 **4** *1* **Zebelini (IRE)**[32] 2423 4-9-1 **53**......(b[1]) RobertDodsworth(5) 5 53
(Ollie Pears) *led and sn clr: rdn over 1f out: drvn and hdd ent fnl f: kpt on same pce* **16/1**

3200 **5** *1* **Monsieur Jimmy**[12] 3070 4-8-9 **47**......(b) GerO'Neill(5) 9 46
(Declan Carroll) *awkward s and in rr: t.k.h whn nt clr run and hmpd 2f out: sn swtchd rt: rdn over 1f out: fin strly* **14/1**

0-05 **6** *3/4* **Henry Morgan**[13] 3022 9-9-2 **52**...... DavidParkes(3) 1 46
(David Brown) *chsd ldr on inner: rdn along wl over 1f out: grad wknd fnl f* **16/1**

202 **7** *1 3/4* **Little Belter (IRE)**[19] 2808 4-9-7 **57**......(v) AdamMcNamara(3) 4 44
(Keith Dalgleish) *in tch: hdwy to chse ldrs 2f out: sn rdn and kpt on same pce* **4/1**[1]

-220 **8** *shd* **Minty Jones**[12] 3070 7-9-0 **52**......(v) JaneElliott(5) 11 41
(Michael Mullineaux) *towards rr: effrt whn nt clr run wl over 1f out: sn rdn and kpt on fnl f* **12/1**

4-20 **9** *nse* **Adiator**[58] 1676 8-9-6 **58**......(p) CliffordLee(5) 12 45
(Neville Bycroft) *stdd and swtchd markedly rt s: in rr: hdwy whn n.m.r and swtchd lft over 1f out: sn rdn and kpt on fnl f* **12/1**

0-U0 **10** *1* **Thornaby Princess**[13] 3009 5-8-12 **50**...... HarryBurns(5) 6 33
(Colin Teague) *chsd ldr: rdn along 2f out: sn drvn and wknd over 1f out* **20/1**

3005 **11** *nse* **Major Muscari (IRE)**[32] 2442 8-9-9 **59**......(p) CharlieBennett(3) 13 42
(Shaun Harris) *chsd ldrs: rdn along 2f out: sn wknd* **33/1**

-104 **12** *1 1/4* **Lady Poppy**[24] 2676 6-9-8 **60**...... KieranSchofield(5) 7 39
(Jedd O'Keeffe) *chsd ldrs: rdn along 2f out: sn drvn and wknd* **8/1**

5-00 **13** *3/4* **Kingfisher Girl**[7] 3268 3-8-9 **53**...... BenRobinson(5) 2 27
(Michael Appleby) *in tch on inner: hdwy to chse ldrs 1/2-way: rdn along 2f out: sn wknd* **33/1**

0100 **14** *1* **Harpers Ruby**[57] 1720 6-9-0 **50**...... RobJFitzpatrick(3) 8 22
(Lynn Siddall) *chsd ldrs: rdn along 1/2-way: sn wknd* **50/1**

3200 **15** *2* **Anieres Boy**[7] 3268 4-9-10 **60**......(p) AnnaHesketh(3) 10 25
(Michael Easterby) *in tch: rdn along over 3f out: sn hung rt and wknd* **8/1**

1m 3.13s (-0.37) **Going Correction** -0.025s/f (Good)
WFA 3 from 4yo+ 6lb **15** Ran SP% **124.0**
Speed ratings (Par 101): **101,98,97,96,94 93,90,90,90,88 88,86,85,83,80**
CSF £41.61 CT £510.12 TOTE £6.60: £2.10, £2.40, £5.80; EX 47.80 Trifecta £1001.40.
Owner P Bamford **Bred** D G Hardisty Bloodstock **Trained** Market Drayton, Shropshire

FOCUS
Race distance as advertised. A moderate if competitive apprentice sprint handicap to end with and although normally low draws are favoured on the sprint track here, on this occasion the pair drawn widest filled the first two places.
T/Jkpt: Part won. £10,000.00 to a £1 stake. Pool: £1,456.31 - 0.50 winning tickets. T/Plt: £31.00 to a £1 stake. Pool: £68,240.05 - 1,603.47 winning tickets. T/Qpdt: £18.80 to a £1 stake. Pool: £3,944.35 - 155.00 winning tickets. **Joe Rowntree**

[3254]BRIGHTON (L-H)
Tuesday, June 21

OFFICIAL GOING: Good to soft
Wind: Fresh, against Weather: Fine

3485 ATKINS FINANCIAL SOLUTIONS MORTGAGE AND INSURANCE NOVICE AUCTION STKS 5f 213y
2:15 (2:17) (Class 5) 2-Y-O **£2,911** (£866; £432; £216) **Stalls** Centre

Form RPR
32 **1** **Fair Power (IRE)**[5] 3315 2-8-13 0...... TomMarquand(3) 6 72
(Sylvester Kirk) *mde all: hrd rdn over 1f out: r.o wl* **5/6**[1]

55 **2** *2* **Rising Eagle**[12] 3065 2-9-2 0...... DarryllHolland 4 66
(Charles Hills) *dwlt: hld up in 6th: hdwy to chal in centre 2f out: unable qck ins fnl f* **12/1**[3]

3 *2* **Dixie Peach** 2-8-11 0...... CharlesBishop 8 55
(Eve Johnson Houghton) *hld up in rr: hdwy in centre over 1f out: swtchd ins and styd on fnl f* **14/1**

4 *nk* **Secret Potion** 2-9-2 0...... DavidProbert 2 59
(Ronald Harris) *dwlt: sn rdn along and in tch: outpcd 2f out: styd on fnl f* **20/1**

234 **5** *1 1/2* **Peachey Carnehan**[15] 2963 2-9-2 0...... FrannyNorton 1 57
(Mark Johnston) *prom: rdn 4f out: wknd over 1f out* **2/1**[2]

200 **6** *2 1/4* **Masquerade Bling (IRE)**[18] 2847 2-8-11 0...... RyanClark 3 43
(Simon Hodgson) *chsd ldrs tl outpcd 2f out* **16/1**

0 **7** *10* **Blast Of Faith (IRE)**[5] 3301 2-9-2 0...... ShaneKelly 7 18
(Richard Hughes) *chsd wnr tl wknd over 2f out* **20/1**

8 *10* **Rise Of Phoenix** 2-8-11 0...... SamHitchcott 5
(John Spearing) *s.s: sn wl bhd* **33/1**

1m 12.07s (1.87) **Going Correction** +0.30s/f (Good) **8** Ran SP% **120.6**
Speed ratings (Par 93): **99,96,93,93,91 88,74,61**
CSF £13.68 TOTE £1.80: £1.10, £2.70, £3.10; EX 13.00 Trifecta £73.20.
Owner Fairway Racing **Bred** Pitrizzia Partnership **Trained** Upper Lambourn, Berks

FOCUS
Rail dolled out slightly between the 5f & 4f marker, adding 1yd to all race distances. The ground was drying all the time and general consensus after the opener was that it was near enough good. A modest novice event, rated around the winner.

3486 HARRINGTONSLETTINGS.CO.UK H'CAP 5f 213y
2:45 (2:49) (Class 6) (0-60,57) 3-Y-O+ **£2,264** (£673; £336; £168) **Stalls** Centre

Form RPR
-000 **1** **Titus Secret**[49] 1949 4-9-0 **45**...... FergusSweeney 11 52
(Malcolm Saunders) *mid-div on outer: rdn 1/2-way: effrt and hung lft wl over 1f out: styd on to ld ins fnl f* **14/1**

4043 **2** *1/2* **Wahaab (IRE)**[14] 3004 5-9-12 **57**...... ShaneKelly 1 64
(Richard Hughes) *in tch: rdn to press ldrs on inner whn bmpd and lost footing over 1f out: rallied and r.o wl nr fin* **9/4**[1]

-000 **3** *nk* **Essaka (IRE)**[15] 2964 4-9-4 **54**...... PaddyPilley(5) 12 58
(Tony Carroll) *s.s: bhd: stdy hdwy over 2f out: prom whn edgd lft and hmpd 3 rivals over 1f out: r.o* **8/1**[2]

032 **4** *1 3/4* **Spirit Of Rosanna**[31] 2458 4-9-8 **53**......(tp) StevieDonohoe 3 52
(Steph Hollinshead) *led: rdn over 2f out: hdd ins fnl f: one pce* **9/4**[1]

-550 **5** *1* **Nelson's Pride**[5] 3320 5-8-7 **45**......(t) RhiainIngram(7) 8 41
(Roger Ingram) *towards rr: rdn over 2f out: styd on fnl f* **40/1**

5505 **6** *3/4* **Fossa**[15] 2964 6-9-0 **45**...... RyanClark 9 39
(Mark Brisbourne) *stdd s: t.k.h in rr: rdn over 2f out: nrest at fin* **14/1**

6460 **7** *1 1/4* **Burauq**[83] 1138 4-9-7 **52**......(p) FrannyNorton 10 42+
(Milton Bradley) *chsd ldrs tl squeezed and lost pl 2f out: n.d after* **20/1**

4016 **8** *hd* **Diamond Vine (IRE)**[15] 2964 8-9-8 **53**......(p) DavidProbert 5 42
(Ronald Harris) *bhd: hrd rdn 3f out: n.d* **12/1**[3]

1606 **9** *hd* **Chetan**[19] 2821 4-9-12 **57**......(tp) MartinLane 6 52
(Charlie Wallis) *prom: rdn 3f out: bdly hmpd over 1f out: nt rcvr* **8/1**[2]

6004 **10** *11* **Simply Black (IRE)**[7] 3260 5-8-13 **49**......(p) AnnStokell(5) 4 5
(Ann Stokell) *prom: rdn whn bdly hmpd over 1f out: nt rcvr* **33/1**

1m 11.3s (1.10) **Going Correction** +0.30s/f (Good)
WFA 3 from 4yo+ 7lb **10** Ran SP% **114.9**
Speed ratings (Par 101): **104,103,102,100,99 98,96,96,96,81**
CSF £44.31 CT £284.35 TOTE £13.10: £2.70, £1.20, £2.40; EX 44.20 Trifecta £449.20.
Owner M S Saunders **Bred** M S Saunders **Trained** Green Ore, Somerset
■ Stewards' Enquiry : Paddy Pilley four-day ban: careless riding (Jul 5-7,11)

FOCUS
Race distance increased by 1yd. A moderate sprint handicap and it got rather messy over 1f out, the runner-up looking an unfortunate loser. The winner may have a bit more to offer.

3487 JANES SOLICITORS H'CAP 5f 59y
3:15 (3:15) (Class 4) (0-80,80) 3-Y-O+ **£4,690** (£1,395; £697; £348) **Stalls** Centre

Form RPR
140 **1** **Bouclier (IRE)**[22] 2754 6-9-9 **80**...... GeorgeDowning(3) 4 86
(Tony Carroll) *disp modest 3rd: rdn 3f out: hdwy ent fnl f: r.o to ld on line* **2/1**[1]

5042 **2** *nse* **Bahamian Sunrise**[18] 2846 4-8-10 **69**...... GeorgeBuckell(5) 6 75
(John Gallagher) *chsd clr ldr: clsd over 1f out: led ins fnl f: kpt on u.p: hdd on line* **7/2**[3]

3241 **3** *hd* **Ginzan**[10] 3123 8-9-10 **78**...... GeorgeBaker 2 83
(Malcolm Saunders) *off the pce in last: shkn up 2f out: hdwy ent fnl f: chal fnl 50yds: r.o* **9/4**[2]

0346 **4** *1 1/2* **Monumental Man**[10] 3123 7-9-8 **76**......(p) WilliamCarson 5 76
(Michael Attwater) *led at str pce: sn 4 l clr: hrd rdn and hdd ins fnl f: no ex* **6/1**

-416 **5** *3 1/2* **Whitecrest**[16] 2931 8-9-0 **71**...... TomMarquand(3) 3 58
(John Spearing) *off the pce in 5th: rdn over 2f out: no imp over 1f out* **8/1**

00-0 **6** *5* **Storm Lightning**[8] 3217 7-9-2 **73**...... DanielMuscutt(3) 1 42
(Mark Brisbourne) *disp modest 3rd: rdn over 3f out: wknd 1f out* **12/1**

1m 3.06s (0.76) **Going Correction** +0.30s/f (Good) **6** Ran SP% **119.4**
Speed ratings (Par 105): **105,104,104,102,96 88**
CSF £10.26 TOTE £2.30: £1.30, £3.10; EX 10.10 Trifecta £44.20.
Owner M Chung **Bred** Dayton Investments Ltd **Trained** Cropthorne, Worcs

FOCUS
Race distance increased by 1yd. Ordinary handicap form and there was little between the first three. The race was run at a strong pace, though. The winner is rated close to this year's Polytrack form.

3488 GIBBONS MANNINGTON & PHIPPS LLP H'CAP 1m 1f 209y
3:45 (3:45) (Class 6) (0-65,64) 4-Y-O+ **£2,264** (£673; £336; £168) **Stalls** High

Form RPR
6314 **1** **Solveig's Song**[16] 2930 4-8-12 **55**......(p) JackMitchell 4 65
(Steve Woodman) *dwlt: sn in tch: hmpd over 4f out: led over 2f out: pushed clr ins fnl f* **4/1**[2]

6032 **2** *2 3/4* **Whip Up A Frenzy (IRE)**[10] 3142 4-8-11 **54**...... StevieDonohoe 2 59
(Richard Rowe) *led tl 1/2-way: hrd rdn over 1f out: one pce* **9/4**[1]

0460 **3** *2 1/4* **Jazri**[12] 3064 5-9-1 **58**......(b) FrannyNorton 3 59
(Milton Bradley) *s.s: bhd: effrt over 2f out: styd on u.p: nvr able to chal* **6/1**

-040 **4** *nk* **Roly Tricks**[39] 2205 5-9-7 **64**...... RyanClark 5 64
(Natalie Lloyd-Beavis) *dwlt: t.k.h in 5th: hdwy to ld 1/2-way: hdd over 2f out: wknd over 1f out* **5/1**

2600 **5** *4 1/2* **Gunner Moyne**[21] 2769 4-9-4 **61**...... GeorgeBaker 1 53
(Gary Moore) *chsd ldrs tl outpcd over 2f out* **9/2**[3]

6300 **6** *6* **Castanea**[31] 2462 4-8-2 **45**...... PaoloSirigu 7 25
(Ronald Harris) *dwlt: a towards rr: n.d whn hung lft over 1f out* **20/1**

620- **7** *11* **Par Three (IRE)**[234] 7192 5-9-5 **62**...... WilliamCarson 8 21
(Tony Carroll) *prom tl wknd over 2f out* **20/1**

2m 6.91s (3.31) **Going Correction** +0.30s/f (Good) **7** Ran SP% **109.4**
Speed ratings (Par 101): **98,95,94,93,90 85,76**
CSF £12.23 CT £46.47 TOTE £4.10: £2.70, £1.50; EX 10.50 Trifecta £51.40.
Owner Sally Woodman D Mortimer **Bred** Mrs Sally Woodman & Mr D Mortimer **Trained** East Lavant, W Sussex
■ Stewards' Enquiry : William Carson caution: careless riding

FOCUS
Race distance increased by 1yd. More moderate stuff, but the winner was good value. Straightforward form in behind.

3489 GMP ACCOUNTANTS & DAVID HAWKINS 60TH H'CAP (DIV I) 7f 214y
4:15 (4:15) (Class 6) (0-55,53) 3-Y-O+ **£2,264** (£673; £336; £168) **Stalls** Centre

Form RPR
5103 **1** **Fairy Mist (IRE)**[7] 3255 9-9-10 **53**......(b) WilliamCarson 3 59
(John Bridger) *hld up towards rr: nt clr run and swtchd outside over 1f out: str run to ld wl ins fnl f* **9/2**[3]

4340 **2** *1/2* **Lutine Charlie (IRE)**[32] 2442 9-9-6 **49**...... TomQueally 8 54
(Emma Owen) *chsd ldrs: led wl over 1f out: hrd rdn and hdd wl ins fnl f: r.o* **10/1**

30-3 **3** *nk* **Its A Sheila Thing**[27] 2590 3-8-13 **52**...... CharlesBishop 5 54
(Linda Jewell) *t.k.h in rr: hdwy 2f out: drvn to chal ins fnl f: r.o* **13/2**

-325 **4** *2 3/4* **Cadland Lad (IRE)**[12] 3070 3-8-11 **53**......(t) DannyBrock(3) 7 49
(John Ryan) *prom: lost pl over 2f out: styd on u.p fnl f* **11/4**[1]

040 **5** *1* **Ditripleseven (IRE)**[24] 2698 3-8-11 **50**...... ShaneKelly 1 44
(Richard Hughes) *disp ld tl wl over 1f out: no ex* **7/2**[2]

0036 **6** *nk* **Ocean Bentley (IRE)**[13] 3043 4-8-9 **45**...... JoshuaBryan(7) 6 40
(Tony Carroll) *disp ld tl wl over 1f out: sn hrd rdn and btn* **10/1**

0560 **7** *5* **Abertillery**[39] 2210 4-9-9 **52**......(p) DavidProbert 9 35
(Michael Blanshard) *dwlt: a towards rr: rdn and n.d fnl 2f* **7/1**

-600 **8** *12* **Sunshine Always (IRE)**[41] 2155 10-9-2 **50**...... CallumShepherd(5) 2 6
(Michael Attwater) *in tch tl wknd 2f out* **33/1**

1m 38.3s (2.30) **Going Correction** +0.30s/f (Good)
WFA 3 from 4yo+ 10lb **8** Ran SP% **114.0**
Speed ratings (Par 101): **100,99,99,96,95 95,90,78**
CSF £47.65 CT £291.64 TOTE £5.40: £1.90, £2.80, £2.30; EX 37.60 Trifecta £143.30.
Owner J J Bridger **Bred** Sandro Garavelli **Trained** Liphook, Hants

FOCUS
Race distance increased by 1yd. The first division of a lowly handicap. Straightforward form around the front pair.

3490 GMP ACCOUNTANTS & DAVID HAWKINS 60TH H'CAP (DIV II) 7f 214y
4:45 (4:47) (Class 6) (0-55,53) 3-Y-O+ **£2,264** (£673; £336; £168) **Stalls** Centre

Form RPR

60-3 **1** **Frank Bridge**[15] 2969 3-8-10 **49**.. JohnFahy 7 59+
(Eve Johnson Houghton) *hld up in rr: hdwy in centre 2f out: led 1f out: sn clr: easily* **11/2**[2]

0045 **2** *4* **Divine Touch**[15] 2969 3-8-6 **45**.. PaoloSirigu 6 46
(Robert Eddery) *cl up: jnd ldr over 3f out: one pce fnl 2f* **8/1**

0040 **3** *nk* **Altaira**[12] 3064 5-9-10 **53**.. WilliamCarson 9 55
(Tony Carroll) *cl up: rdn to press ldrs over 1f out: one pce* **12/1**

-063 **4** *3 1/2* **Lucky Leyf**[10] 3146 4-9-8 **51**.. GeorgeBaker 5 45
(Philip Hide) *t.k.h: chsd ldr: led 1/2-way: kicked on 2f out: hdd and no ex 1f out* **6/1**[3]

000 **5** *1* **Eisha Baby**[26] 2606 3-8-10 **52**..................................(p) TomMarquand(3) 4 42
(Richard Hannon) *dwlt: hld up in 6th: effrt 3f out: rdn and btn 2f out* **11/2**[2]

1022 **6** *2* **Ashford Island**[15] 2969 3-8-7 **53**..................................(p) KevinLundie(7) 3 38
(Mike Murphy) *stdd s: hld up in rr: sme hdwy on inner 2f out: wknd over 1f out* **15/8**[1]

/00- **7** *13* **Praise N Glory**[468] 225 5-9-2 **45**..................................(p) CharlesBishop 1 2
(Linda Jewell) *prom tl wknd over 2f out* **66/1**

-600 **8** *55* **Long Island**[15] 2968 3-8-7 **51**.. PaddyPilley(5) 2
(Mark Brisbourne) *led tl 1/2-way: wknd qckly: sn wl bhd and eased* **7/1**

1m 37.52s (1.52) **Going Correction** +0.30s/f (Good)
WFA 3 from 4yo+ 10lb **8** Ran SP% **112.6**
Speed ratings (Par 101): **104,100,99,96,95 93,80,25**
CSF £46.79 CT £389.92 TOTE £5.10: £1.30, £2.20, £3.50; EX 40.40 Trifecta £444.50.
Owner John Dyer **Bred** Catherine Dyer **Trained** Blewbury, Oxon
■ Stewards' Enquiry : Paddy Pilley jockey said filly ran too freely to post

FOCUS
Race distance increased by 1yd. The 3yos came to the fore in division two, with the improving winner far too good. The runner-up offers perspective.

3491 TRAIL WALKER 23RD JULY H'CAP 6f 209y
5:15 (5:15) (Class 5) (0-70,69) 3-Y-O+ **£2,911** (£866; £432; £216) **Stalls** Centre

Form RPR

0621 **1** **Soaring Spirits (IRE)**[15] 2964 6-9-6 **61**..................(b) RobertWinston 10 71
(Dean Ivory) *mde all: rdn and qcknd clr 2f out: drvn along ins fnl f: readily* **2/1**[1]

0004 **2** *1 3/4* **Pick A Little**[22] 2734 8-9-7 **69**.. MitchGodwin(7) 2 74
(Michael Blake) *pressed wnr: outpcd 2f out: kpt on u.p: jst hld 2nd* **13/2**

3102 **3** *shd* **Malaysian Boleh**[13] 3040 6-6-8 **54**..................(b) CallumShepherd(5) 8 59
(Shaun Lycett) *chsd ldrs: effrt and hung lft fr 2f out: styd on fnl f* **9/2**[3]

-044 **4** *nk* **Port Lairge**[11] 3097 6-9-7 **65**..................(v) MichaelJMMurphy(3) 6 69
(John Gallagher) *a.p: outpcd by wnr fnl 2f* **9/4**[2]

0-06 **5** *3 1/4* **Pure Soul**[57] 1701 3-9-3 **67**..................................(p) ThomasBrown 1 59
(Ismail Mohammed) *hld up in rr: effrt 2f out: wknd over 1f out* **9/1**

6000 **6** *2 3/4* **Smoothtalkinrascal (IRE)**[10] 3159 6-10-0 **69**..................(t) ShaneKelly 9 57
(Peter Crate) *t.k.h: in tch on outer tl rdn and btn over 2f out* **12/1**

1m 24.59s (1.49) **Going Correction** +0.30s/f (Good)
WFA 3 from 4yo+ 9lb **6** Ran SP% **113.3**
Speed ratings (Par 103): **103,101,100,100,96 93**
CSF £15.59 CT £51.37 TOTE £2.60: £1.30, £2.90; EX 15.30 Trifecta £51.60.
Owner Mrs Doreen Carter **Bred** Kevin & Meta Cullen **Trained** Radlett, Herts

FOCUS
Race distance increased by 1yd. Little got into this, the winner making all and the runner-up pressing him early. Straightforward form.

3492 STREAMLINE TAXIS AMATEUR RIDERS' H'CAP 1m 3f 196y
5:45 (5:45) (Class 6) (0-65,61) 4-Y-O+ **£2,183** (£677; £338; £169) **Stalls** High

Form RPR

5-43 **1** **Roy Rocket (FR)**[25] 2645 6-11-0 **61**.. MrRBirkett 6 71
(John Berry) *confidently rdn in rr: gd hdwy to ld 2f out: drvn clr over 1f out: styd on wl* **1/1**[1]

0-00 **2** *4 1/2* **Dellbuoy**[130] 354 7-10-4 **56**.. MissLDempster(5) 5 58
(Pat Phelan) *dwlt: hld up towards rr: hdwy to ld briefly over 2f out: outpcd by wnr over 1f out* **15/2**[3]

-002 **3** *4 1/2* **Flag Of Glory**[1] 3470 9-10-3 **55**..................................(b) MissMEdden(5) 3 50
(Peter Hiatt) *in tch: jnd ldrs on inner over 2f out: sn outpcd* **5/1**[2]

6-06 **4** *8* **Caerleon Kate**[25] 2634 4-9-12 **45**..................................(b) MrPMillman 4 27
(Rod Millman) *disp ld for 5f: prom tl wknd over 2f out* **5/1**[2]

566- **5** *9* **Mystical Maze**[385] 2799 5-9-10 **46**.. MrMJPKendrick(3) 8 13
(Mark Brisbourne) *chsd ldrs tl wknd over 2f out* **33/1**

0500 **6** *5* **Ron Waverly (IRE)**[17] 2899 6-9-5 **45**..................(t) MissJMOlliver(7) 2 4
(Paddy Butler) *s.s: towards rr: rdn 5f out: sn struggling* **20/1**

5650 **7** *2 3/4* **Bond Mystery**[17] 2899 4-9-7 **45**..................................(b[1]) MrWillPettis(5) 7
(Natalie Lloyd-Beavis) *prom: led 7f out tl wknd over 2f out* **14/1**

-420 **8** *22* **Estibdaad (IRE)**[18] 2872 6-10-8 **60**..................(t) MissMBryant(5) 1
(Paddy Butler) *disp ld for 5f: wknd 4f out* **16/1**

2m 37.21s (4.51) **Going Correction** +0.30s/f (Good) **8** Ran SP% **115.4**
Speed ratings (Par 101): **96,93,90,84,78 75,73,58**
CSF £9.46 CT £26.84 TOTE £1.80: £1.02, £2.10, £2.90; EX 9.40 Trifecta £30.40.
Owner McCarthy & Berry **Bred** John Berry **Trained** Newmarket, Suffolk

FOCUS
Race distance increased by 1yd. They got racing a fair way out in this lowly amateurs' handicap and that suited the winner ideally. Straightforward form on drying ground.
T/Plt: £96.80 to a £1 stake. Pool: £74,279.38 - 559.92 winning tickets. T/Qpdt: £33.40 to a £1 stake. Pool: £5,799.91 - 128.4 winning tickets. **Lee McKenzie**

3134 LEICESTER (R-H)
Tuesday, June 21

OFFICIAL GOING: Heavy
Wind: Light behind Weather: Cloudy with sunny spells

3493 LEICESTER INTERACTIVE H'CAP 1m 3f 183y
6:10 (6:12) (Class 6) (0-65,65) 3-Y-O **£2,264** (£673; £336; £168) **Stalls** Low

Form RPR

65-3 **1** **Young Tom**[8] 3215 3-8-12 56.. AndrewMullen 10 66
(Michael Appleby) *chsd ldrs: rdn over 3f out: chsd ldr over 2f out: styd on to ld wl ins fnl f* **9/1**

065 **2** *3/4* **Fishergate**[10] 3141 3-9-1 59.. AdamBeschizza 1 68
(Richard Rowe) *led 1f: led again over 9f out: rdn over 2f out: edgd rt and hdd wl ins fnl f* **20/1**

2-02 **3** *6* **Nanny Makfi**[27] 2590 3-8-6 50.. MartinDwyer 12 49
(Stuart Kittow) *chsd ldrs: wnt 2nd over 4f out tl rdn over 2f out: styd on same pce appr fnl f* **8/1**

-106 **4** *2* **Captain Peacock**[26] 2615 3-9-5 63..................................(p) JimCrowley 7 59
(William Knight) *hld up: hdwy over 3f out: sn rdn: styd on same pce fnl 2f* **4/1**[2]

0003 **5** *9* **Rosie's Vision**[10] 3141 3-8-4 48.. KieranO'Neill 13 29
(Mark Usher) *mid-div: hdwy u.p over 4f out: wknd over 2f out* **20/1**

-051 **6** *1 3/4* **Trident Tested**[19] 2825 3-9-1 59.. KierenFox 4 38
(John Best) *hld up: rdn over 3f out: nvr on terms* **12/1**

00-5 **7** *1/2* **Lady Turpin (IRE)**[13] 3015 3-8-8 52.. TonyHamilton 6 30
(Richard Fahey) *prom: rdn over 3f out: wknd 2f out* **16/1**

03-4 **8** *5* **Tyrell (IRE)**[13] 3033 3-9-0 58.. WilliamTwiston-Davies 5 28
(Alan King) *s.i.s: hld up: pushed along over 5f out: rdn over 3f out: n.d* **5/1**[3]

4435 **9** *1 3/4* **Asafoetida (IRE)**[25] 2639 3-9-6 64.. AdrianMcCarthy 2 31
(Peter Chapple-Hyam) *hld up: sme hdwy u.p 4f out: sn wknd* **25/1**

-640 **10** *44* **Lady Blanco (USA)**[13] 3042 3-8-11 60.................. EdwardGreatrex(5) 3
(Andrew Balding) *hld up: nt clr run 5f out: rdn and wknd over 3f out* **40/1**

005- **11** *11* **Monjeni**[199] 8122 3-9-4 62.. LukeMorris 9
(Sir Mark Prescott Bt) *pushed along in rr early: hdwy into mid-div over 10f out: rn green and pushed along at various stages sn after: lost pl over 5f out: bhd fnl 4f: eased* **7/2**[1]

0005 **12** *31* **Monpazier (IRE)**[19] 2829 3-8-2 46 oh1..................(v[1]) RaulDaSilva 14
(K R Burke) *pushed along to ld after 1f: hdd over 9f out: chsd ldr tl lost pl over 4f out: sn bhd and eased* **16/1**

2m 46.02s (12.12) **Going Correction** +0.95s/f (Soft) **12** Ran SP% **115.3**
Speed ratings (Par 97): **97,96,92,91,85 84,83,80,79,49 42,21**
CSF £176.98 CT £1494.93 TOTE £9.30: £2.90, £7.30, £2.00; EX 198.30 Trifecta £1025.50.
Owner Formulated Polymer Products Ltd **Bred** Executors Of N A Blyth **Trained** Oakham, Rutland

FOCUS
The meeting had to pass a morning inspection. Race distances as advertised. Jockeys involved in the opener described the ground as "hard work", "heavy" and "tacky". The first three were always prominent in this very modest handicap. The field finished strung out and the time was 17sec slower than standard. The form is taken at something like face value.

3494 LANGHAM LADIES' H'CAP (LADY AMATEUR RIDERS) 5f
6:40 (6:40) (Class 5) (0-75,73) 3-Y-O+ **£2,807** (£870; £435; £217) **Stalls** High

Form RPR

0-00 **1** **Addicted To Luck**[45] 2044 3-8-13 **62**.. MissCRobinson(5) 6 69
(Jo Hughes) *chsd clr ldr: pushed along 1/2-way: clsd to ld over 1f out: rdn and hdd ins fnl f: rallied to ld post* **11/1**

1110 **2** *shd* **Mitchum**[27] 2572 7-9-11 **68**..................................(p) MrsVDavies(5) 3 77
(Ron Barr) *s.i.s: hdwy 1/2-way: rdn to ld ins fnl f: edgd rt and hdd post* **7/2**[2]

3250 **3** *2 1/4* **Noodles Blue Boy**[26] 2622 10-10-6 **72**..................(p) MissSBrotherton 7 73
(Ollie Pears) *chsd ldrs: rdn and hung rt fr over 1f out: styd on same pce ins fnl f* **4/1**[3]

6355 **4** *2 1/2* **Ambitious Icarus**[8] 3217 7-10-7 **73**..................(e) MissJoannaMason 5 65
(Richard Guest) *in rr: pushed along 1/2-way: styd on ins fnl f: nvr nrr* **5/2**[1]

6622 **5** *2 1/4* **Bronze Beau**[10] 3136 9-9-8 **65**..................(tp) MissKMargarson(5) 1 48
(Kristin Stubbs) *led and sn clr: hdd over 1f out: wknd ins fnl f* **7/1**

-000 **6** *6* **Two Turtle Doves (IRE)**[13] 3016 10-9-2 **54** oh4...... MissMMullineaux 8 16
(Michael Mullineaux) *chsd ldrs: pushed along 1/2-way: wknd wl over 1f out* **33/1**

3-00 **7** *nk* **Red Invader (IRE)**[66] 1496 6-9-6 **63**.. MrsRWilson(5) 4 24
(Paul D'Arcy) *in rr: hdwy u.p over 1f out: wknd fnl f* **6/1**

1m 2.54s (2.54) **Going Correction** +0.625s/f (Yiel)
WFA 3 from 4yo+ 6lb **7** Ran SP% **108.9**
Speed ratings (Par 103): **104,103,100,96,92 83,82**
CSF £44.48 CT £164.57 TOTE £13.40: £5.30, £2.40; EX 54.70 Trifecta £220.20.
Owner Dalwhinnie Racing **Bred** Dalwhinnie Bloodstock **Trained** Lambourn. Berks

FOCUS
Some old foes met in this very modest sprint, including the first four from the race last year. The first two finished clear and the third helps with the level.

3495 OSBASTON NOVICE STKS (PLUS 10 RACE) 6f
7:10 (7:10) (Class 4) 2-Y-O **£4,204** (£1,251; £625; £312) **Stalls** High

Form RPR

2132 **1** **Kreb's Cycle (IRE)**[26] 2604 2-9-0 0.. GaryMahon(5) 5 77
(Richard Hannon) *w ldr: plld hrd: led over 4f out: rdn over 1f out: edgd lft ins fnl f: styd on* **5/2**[2]

50 **2** *2* **Phoenix Dawn**[12] 3058 2-9-2 0.. MartinDwyer 4 68
(Brendan Powell) *led: hdd over 4f out: chsd wnr: rdn over 2f out: styd on same pce ins fnl f: eased whn hld nr fin* **33/1**

2 **3** *1* **Good Time Ahead (IRE)**[27] 2570 2-9-2 0.. TonyHamilton 6 65
(Richard Fahey) *trckd ldrs: plld hrd: rdn over 2f out: styd on same pce fnl f* **2/1**[1]

5 **4** *2 1/4* **Bazwind (IRE)**[11] 3093 2-9-2 0.. FMBerry 7 58
(David Evans) *s.i.s: sn chsng ldrs: rdn over 2f out: edgd rt and wknd ins fnl f* **5/1**[3]

5 *1/2* **Nature Boy (IRE)** 2-9-2 0.. RobertHavlin 8 57
(Peter Chapple-Hyam) *dwlt: hdwy 1/2-way: rdn over 1f out: wknd fnl f* **5/2**[2]

1m 16.5s (3.50) **Going Correction** +0.625s/f (Yiel) **5** Ran SP% **110.1**
Speed ratings (Par 95): **101,98,97,94,93**
CSF £49.85 TOTE £3.20: £2.00, £7.80; EX 55.00 Trifecta £226.40.
Owner Middleham Park Racing CIV **Bred** Michael Fennessy **Trained** East Everleigh, Wilts

FOCUS
A fair novice stakes. The winner replicated his recent improved Chelmsford form.

3496 KING'S NORTON FILLIES' H'CAP 1m 60y
7:40 (7:40) (Class 5) (0-70,69) 3-Y-O+ **£3,234** (£962; £481; £240) **Stalls** Low

Form RPR

0454 **1** **Imperial Link**[3] 3401 4-8-4 **50** oh2..................(p) EdwardGreatrex(5) 5 59
(John O'Shea) *sn led: rdn over 1f out: edgd rt ins fnl f: styd on wl* **8/1**

3622 **2** *2 1/4* **Phoenix Beat**[19] 2824 3-9-4 **69**.. PatCosgrave 4 71
(Gay Kelleway) *led early: settled to chse ldrs: rdn to chse wnr over 1f out: no ex wl ins fnl f* **7/4**[1]

01-0 **3** *1* **Hermarna (IRE)**[24] 2701 3-9-0 **65**.. FMBerry 7 65
(Harry Dunlop) *plld hrd: trckd wnr after 1f: rdn over 2f out: lost 2nd over 1f out: styd on same pce ins fnl f* **11/2**[3]

4-30 **4** *2 1/4* **Pastoral Star**[41] 2152 3-8-11 **62**..................................(p) JimCrowley 1 57
(Hughie Morrison) *chsd ldrs: rdn over 2f out: styd on same pce fnl f* **5/2**[2]

00-0 **5** *1 ¾* **Prisom (IRE)**[34] 2372 3-9-1 **66**.. TimmyMurphy 2 57
(Gay Kelleway) *hld up: rdn over 2f out: btn fnl f* **25/1**

-060 **6** *10* **Vallance Road**[21] 2770 3-8-13 **64**........................ WilliamTwiston-Davies 3 33
(Robyn Brisland) *in rr: rdn over 2f out: sn wknd* **8/1**

1m 52.02s (6.92) **Going Correction** +0.95s/f (Soft)
WFA 3 from 4yo 10lb **6** Ran SP% **106.4**
Speed ratings (Par 100): **103,100,99,97,95 85**
CSF £20.19 CT £68.37 TOTE £9.20: £5.90, £1.10; EX 22.40 Trifecta £114.40.
Owner The Cross Racing Club **Bred** Mrs E A Bass **Trained** Elton, Gloucs

FOCUS
Very ordinary fillies' form and it proved hard to make ground. The form is rated at face value.

3497 VIS-A-VIS SYMPOSIUMS H'CAP 1m 1f 218y
8:10 (8:10) (Class 5) (0-70,69) 4-Y-0+ **£3,234** (£962; £481; £240) **Stalls** Low

Form RPR

-030 **1** **Miningrocks (FR)**[12] 3072 4-8-0 **53**.................................... PhilDennis(5) 2 59
(Declan Carroll) *mde all: set stdy pce tl qcknd over 2f out: rdn: edgd lft and flashed tail over 1f out: styd on wl* **10/1**

446 **2** *2 ¾* **Critical Speed (IRE)**[35] 2320 4-9-7 **69**................................. LukeMorris 4 70
(Sylvester Kirk) *trckd ldrs: plld hrd: rdn over 2f out: chsd wnr over 1f out: styd on same pce fnl f* **8/1**

0402 **3** *4 ½* **Sakhalin Star (IRE)**[8] 3220 5-9-3 **65**........................(e) ConnorBeasley 5 58
(Richard Guest) *hld up in tch: plld hrd: rdn over 2f out: hung rt over 1f out: styd on same pce: wnt 3rd post* **7/4**[1]

4012 **4** *nse* **Scent Of Power**[10] 3135 4-8-2 **57**.................................. GeorgeWood(7) 6 50
(Barry Leavy) *hld up: hdwy over 3f out: chsd wnr over 2f out tl rdn over 1f out: wknd ins fnl f* **7/2**[3]

320 **5** *8* **Hold Hands**[40] 2182 5-9-5 **67**.. FMBerry 1 45
(Brendan Powell) *s.i.s: hld up: rdn over 2f out: sn wknd* **11/4**[2]

0540 **6** *10* **Bognor (USA)**[8] 3220 5-9-1 **63**................................(v) AndrewMullen 7 23
(Michael Attwater) *chsd wnr tl rdn over 2f out: sn wknd* **20/1**

2m 17.88s (9.98) **Going Correction** +0.95s/f (Soft) **6** Ran SP% **110.2**
Speed ratings (Par 103): **98,95,92,92,85 77**
CSF £78.26 TOTE £14.50: £5.00, £3.30; EX 75.20 Trifecta £284.40.
Owner Mrs Sarah Bryan **Bred** M Daguzan-Garros & Rolling Hills Farm **Trained** Malton, N Yorks

FOCUS
A very modest event, and again it proved hard to make ground on the round course. The form is rated a shade negatively.

3498 BRUNTINGTHORPE H'CAP 1m 3f 183y
8:45 (8:46) (Class 6) (0-65,65) 4-Y-0+ **£2,587** (£770; £384; £192) **Stalls** Low

Form RPR

5-56 **1** **Medburn Cutler**[33] 2392 6-9-7 **65**.................................(p) JimCrowley 14 75
(Paul Henderson) *chsd ldrs: led over 2f out: rdn and hdd over 1f out: rallied to ld wl ins fnl f* **3/1**[1]

25-6 **2** *nk* **Mexican Mick**[31] 2462 7-8-1 **48**.................................... ShelleyBirkett(3) 8 58
(Peter Hiatt) *hld up: hdwy 5f out: chsd wnr over 2f out: led over 1f out: rdn and hdd wl ins fnl f* **10/1**

-444 **3** *10* **Phantom River**[18] 2860 4-9-4 **62**....................(p) WilliamTwiston-Davies 5 56
(Alan King) *hld up: hdwy over 3f out: rdn and hung rt over 1f out: wknd fnl f* **13/2**[3]

0450 **4** *¾* **Ninepointsixthree**[24] 1002 6-9-2 **65**..........................(v) CiaranMckee(5) 1 57+
(John O'Shea) *s.v.s: bhd: styd on fnl 2f: nrst fin* **12/1**

31 **5** *3 ¼* **Hydrant**[7] 3253 10-9-1 **59** 5ex... ConnorBeasley 9 46
(Richard Guest) *led 1f: chsd ldrs: rdn over 3f out: wknd over 1f out* **9/2**[2]

0006 **6** *1 ½* **Rail Dancer**[8] 3230 4-9-2 **60**.....................................(p) AdamBeschizza 12 45
(Richard Rowe) *led after 1f: rdn and hdd over 2f out: wknd fnl f* **12/1**

50 **7** *1* **Irish Thistle (IRE)**[12] 3067 9-9-2 **60**..........................(p) PaulMulrennan 2 43
(Dai Williams) *hld up: nt clr run over 5f out: hdwy over 4f out: rdn over 3f out: wknd 2f out* **16/1**

0-30 **8** *12* **Moon Over Rio (IRE)**[19] 2836 5-9-4 **62**.............................. JoeyHaynes 4 26
(Ben Haslam) *prom: rdn over 3f out: wknd 2f out* **10/1**

00 **9** *15* **Champagne Rules**[19] 2836 5-9-7 **65**.............................. PaddyAspell 10 5
(Sharon Watt) *chsd ldrs tl rdn and wknd over 2f out* **25/1**

4-04 **10** *20* **Sofias Number One (USA)**[90] 1048 8-8-2 **46** oh1......(b) KieranO'Neill 7
(Roy Bowring) *a in rr: pushed along over 8f out: bhd fnl 4f* **25/1**

5-03 **11** *6* **Shareni (IRE)**[27] 2588 7-9-1 **59**... LukeMorris 15
(Zoe Davison) *hld up: hdwy 8f out: wknd over 4f out* **50/1**

4-00 **12** *10* **High Intensity**[113] 766 4-9-5 **63**.. BenCurtis 3
(Scott Dixon) *hld up: pushed along over 7f out: wknd over 4f out* **25/1**

000 **13** *24* **The Skipper's Cat**[28] 2557 4-8-2 **46** oh1...................... AndrewMullen 13
(Michael Appleby) *mid-div: lost pl over 7f out: bhd fnl 5f* **66/1**

-043 **14** *15* **Cape Spirit (IRE)**[13] 3031 4-8-6 **55**.....................(v) EdwardGreatrex(5) 11
(Andrew Balding) *prom: rdn over 5f out: wknd over 4f out* **10/1**

2m 43.19s (9.29) **Going Correction** +0.95s/f (Soft) **14** Ran SP% **120.0**
Speed ratings (Par 101): **107,106,100,99,97 96,95,87,77,64 60,53,37,27**
CSF £31.76 CT £186.95 TOTE £3.60: £1.90, £3.70, £2.20; EX 38.80 Trifecta £304.10.
Owner Eddie Evans **Bred** Eddie Evans **Trained** Whitsbury, Hants

FOCUS
They finished well string out in this very modest handicap, the first two finishing well clear in this bad ground.

3499 SKEFFINGTON H'CAP 1m 60y
9:15 (9:15) (Class 5) (0-70,65) 3-Y-O **£3,234** (£962; £481; £240) **Stalls** Low

Form RPR

6-32 **1** **Fort Jefferson**[8] 3224 3-8-13 **62**............................. EdwardGreatrex(5) 7 82
(Andrew Balding) *hld up in tch: led over 2f out: rdn clr over 1f out: easily* **1/1**[1]

00-5 **2** *11* **Ring Of Art**[13] 3014 3-9-0 **58**.. TonyHamilton 6 55
(Richard Fahey) *hld up: hdwy over 2f out: rdn to chse wnr over 1f out: wknd fnl f* **7/1**

6-20 **3** *2 ½* **The Knave (IRE)**[30] 2506 3-9-2 **60**.. BenCurtis 3 49
(Scott Dixon) *chsd ldrs: rdn over 5f out: ev ch over 2f out: wknd over 1f out* **9/2**[2]

0-00 **4** *12* **Oceanella (IRE)**[20] 2801 3-8-6 **55**..........................(p) JordanVaughan(5) 8 17
(K R Burke) *led: hdd over 6f out: rdn and ev ch over 2f out: sn wknd* **8/1**

2320 **5** *½* **Atrayu (IRE)**[12] 3069 3-9-5 **63**.. LukeMorris 4 24
(Paul D'Arcy) *hld up: pushed along over 4f out: rdn and wknd over 2f out* **6/1**[3]

00-0 **6** *2 ½* **Virtual Song**[10] 3135 3-7-9 **46** oh1.. RPWalsh(7) 1 2
(Barry Leavy) *hld up: hdwy to ld over 3f out: hdd over 2f out: rdn and wknd over 1f out* **66/1**

5252 **7** *19* **Sea Of Uncertainty**[56] 1764 3-9-7 **65**............................ TimmyMurphy 2
(James Evans) *chsd ldr tl led over 6f out: rdn and hdd over 3f out: wknd over 2f out* **25/1**

1m 52.34s (7.24) **Going Correction** +0.95s/f (Soft) **7** Ran SP% **111.4**
Speed ratings (Par 99): **101,90,87,75,75 72,53**
CSF £8.23 CT £20.97 TOTE £2.00: £1.20, £2.30; EX 9.60 Trifecta £25.00.
Owner Kingsclere Racing Club **Bred** Kingsclere Stud **Trained** Kingsclere, Hants

FOCUS
The leaders went off quick in this very modest event, which saw a wide-margin winner. A minor best from the winner.
T/Plt: £1,676.80 to a £1 stake. Pool: £60,298.36 - 26.25 winning tickets. T/Qpdt: £125.30 to a £1 stake, Pool: £5,929.36 - 35.00 winning tickets. **Colin Roberts**

3500 - 3506a (Foreign Racing) - See Raceform Interactive

DIEPPE (R-H)
Tuesday, June 21

OFFICIAL GOING: Turf: heavy

3507a PRIX DREAM WELL (PRIX CAMILLE SAINT-SAENS) (MAIDEN) (2YO) (TURF) 5f 110y
11:10 (12:00) 2-Y-O **£7,352** (£2,941; £2,205; £1,470; £735)

RPR

1 **Dandyman Port (IRE)** 2-8-9 0.. EddyHardouin 5 86
(E J O'Neill, France) **25/1**

2 *4 ½* **Notte A Roma (IRE)**[14] 2-9-2 0.................................(b[1]) ThierryThulliez 8 78
(C Lerner, France) **23/5**[3]

3 *7* **California Tee**[39] 2-8-13 0... AntoineHamelin 7 52
(Matthieu Palussiere, France) **9/2**[2]

4 *3* **The Night Is Ours (IRE)**[16] 2933 2-8-13 0...................... ThierryJarnet 2 42
(J S Moore) *broke wl and led: hdd sn after 1/2-way: lft bhd by front two fr 2f out: wknd ins fnl f* **68/10**

5 *1 ½* **Imperial Tango (FR)**[20] 2-8-13 0.................................. UmbertoRispoli 6 37
(G Botti, France) **16/1**

6 *3* **Vagabonde (IRE)**[45] 2-8-13 0.. MaximeGuyon 3 27
(C Laffon-Parias, France) **7/10**[1]

7 *11* **Daffodil Mulligan**[31] 2457 2-8-13 0................................. LouisBeuzelin 1
(J S Moore) *outpcd in rr: reminders wl bef 1/2-way and lost tch: t.o* **26/1**

WIN (incl. 1 euro stake): 26.20. PLACES: 5.40, 2.00, 1.80. DF: 59.30. SF: 182.30
Owner Myles J Walshe **Bred** Kilnamoragh Stud **Trained** France

3121 BATH (L-H)
Wednesday, June 22

OFFICIAL GOING: Soft (good to soft in places)
Wind: Light across Weather: Overcast

3508 LORD ASHLEY MURRAY 40TH BIRTHDAY MAIDEN STKS 1m 3f 144y
6:10 (6:11) (Class 5) 3-Y-O+ **£2,911** (£866; £432; £216) **Stalls** Low

Form RPR

2 **1** **Rasmiya (IRE)**[58] 1704 3-8-9 0.. PatCosgrave 3 76
(William Haggas) *a.p: chsd ldr over 9f out: rdn over 3f out: hung lft over 2f out: styd on to ld and edgd lft wl ins fnl f* **9/4**[2]

04 **2** *1 ¾* **Vanishing Point**[20] 2816 3-8-11 0.................................... RobHornby(3) 1 78
(Andrew Balding) *sn prom: rdn and outpcd over 2f out: rallied over 1f out: r.o to go 2nd wl ins fnl f* **10/1**

2-36 **3** *2 ¼* **West Drive (IRE)**[18] 2909 3-9-0 82.................................. JackMitchell 11 76
(Roger Varian) *chsd ldr tl led over 9f out: rdn over 1f out: hdd and n.m.r wl ins fnl f: no ex* **8/13**[1]

4 *5* **Alberta (IRE)**[42] 7-10-0 0... TimmyMurphy 2 67
(Jim Best) *s.i.s: wnt prom after 1f: rdn over 3f out: styd on same pce fnl 2f* **20/1**

3 **5** *nk* **London Prize**[10] 3190 5-9-11 0.............................. GeorgeDowning(3) 10 66
(Ian Williams) *plld hrd and prom: lost pl over 4f out: rdn over 3f out: no imp fnl 2f* **7/1**[3]

60 **6** *4 ½* **Mister Showman**[20] 2816 3-9-0 0.. RyanClark 4 59
(Jonathan Portman) *chsd ldrs: lost pl over 7f out: rdn over 3f out: wknd 2f out* **80/1**

4 **7** *½* **Rue Balzac (IRE)**[35] 2368 3-9-0 0.. LiamJones 7 58
(Neil King) *s.i.s: sn pushed along in rr: nvr on terms* **33/1**

0 **8** *12* **Hepburn**[41] 2183 3-8-6 0.. TomMarquand(3) 9 34
(Ali Stronge) *hld up: effrt over 3f out: wknd over 2f out* **66/1**

3 **9** *31* **Embroidery (IRE)**[20] 2826 3-8-9 0.............................. RichardKingscote 6
(Harry Dunlop) *led: hdd over 9f out: chsd ldrs: rdn over 3f out: wknd over 2f out* **33/1**

4 **10** *¾* **Buachaillnaheirean (IRE)**[20] 2825 3-9-0 0..... WilliamTwiston-Davies 5
(Neil King) *s.i.s: wnt prom after 1f: lost pl 9f out: rdn over 4f out: wknd over 3f out* **50/1**

2m 33.2s (2.60) **Going Correction** +0.40s/f (Good)
WFA 3 from 5yo+ 14lb **10** Ran SP% **129.6**
Speed ratings (Par 103): **107,105,104,101,100 97,97,89,68,68**
CSF £25.65 TOTE £3.00: £1.10, £2.30, £1.10; EX 22.10 Trifecta £61.20.
Owner Al Shaqab Racing **Bred** C O P Hanbury **Trained** Newmarket, Suffolk

FOCUS
Race distance as advertised. William Twiston-Davies described the ground as "soft, heavy in places". Three fair types came clear in this ordinary maiden. Those down the field will prove the key to the level.

3509 FINDERS KEEPERS H'CAP 1m 3f 144y
6:40 (6:41) (Class 6) (0-60,60) 3-Y-O **£2,264** (£673; £336; £168) **Stalls** Low

Form RPR

00-0 **1** **Madame Claud**[20] 2829 3-9-1 **54**........................ WilliamTwiston-Davies 1 62
(Hughie Morrison) *s.i.s: hdwy over 9f out: rdn over 3f out: chsd ldr over 1f out: styd on to ld wl ins fnl f* **25/1**

0-42 **2** *¾* **Final Choice**[19] 2851 3-8-10 **52**..........................(p) KieranShoemark(3) 8 61
(Roger Charlton) *hld up: hdwy 3f out: shkn up and nt clr run fr over 1f out tl swtchd rt wl ins fnl f: r.o: unlucky* **7/2**[1]

00-6 **3** *1 ¾* **Primobella**[14] 3015 3-9-5 **58**... DaleSwift 2 62
(Ed McMahon) *chsd ldrs: rdn over 3f out: led over 2f out: hdd and unable qck wl ins fnl f* **14/1**

5610 **4** *3 ¼* **Rockliffe**[28] 2590 3-9-7 **60**.. RichardKingscote 16 59
(Mick Channon) *led 4f: remained w ldr: rdn and ev ch over 2f out: no ex ins fnl f* **5/1**[2]

00-0 **5** *1 1/4* **Pacharana**[26] 2653 3-9-5 **58**.................................. MartinLane 15 55
(Luca Cumani) *w ldr 2f: remained handy: rdn over 4f out: styd on same pce fnl 2f* **11/2**[3]

006 **6** *3 1/2* **Midnight Mood**[19] 2877 3-9-4 **57**.............................. TimmyMurphy 11 48
(Dominic Ffrench Davis) *prom: rdn over 3f out: wknd wl over 1f out* **25/1**

0-44 **7** *hd* **Coarse Cut (IRE)**[29] 2563 3-9-7 **60**.............................. PatCosgrave 9 51
(Eve Johnson Houghton) *prom: chsd ldr over 9f out: led over 7f out: rdn and hdd over 2f out: wknd over 1f out* **8/1**

1461 **8** *3* **Rainbow Lad (IRE)**[14] 3015 3-9-0 **56**.................... TomMarquand[(3)] 5 42
(Michael Appleby) *prom: rdn over 3f out: wknd wl over 1f out* **6/1**

-062 **9** *3/4* **Moon Over Mobay**[10] 3198 3-9-4 **60**.......................... RobHornby[(3)] 12 45
(Andrew Balding) *mid-div: lost pl over 7f out: n.d after* **6/1**

-630 **10** *4* **Ochos Rios**[13] 3063 3-9-4 **57**.................................... SteveDrowne 6 35
(David Evans) *s.i.s: sn pushed along in rr: nvr on terms* **16/1**

1604 **11** *1 1/2* **Zebedee's Son (IRE)**[20] 2828 3-8-8 **54**...............(p) RhiainIngram[(7)] 13 30
(Roger Ingram) *hld up: rdn over 3f out: a in rr* **33/1**

445 **12** *2 1/4* **Gamesters Boy**[14] 3028 3-9-5 **58**.............................. LiamJones 14 30
(Mark Brisbourne) *mid-div: sn pushed along: rdn and wknd 3f out* **25/1**

0000 **13** *1/2* **Opera Buffa (IRE)**[64] 1551 3-8-10 **52**.......................... EoinWalsh[(3)] 7 24
(Steve Flook) *s.i.s: hld up: rdn over 3f out: hung lft and wknd over 2f out* **100/1**

0-03 **14** *9* **Ocean Gale**[35] 2368 3-9-0 **53**...................................... JFEgan 10 10
(Richard Price) *hld up: rdn and wknd over 3f out* **33/1**

2m 35.84s (5.24) **Going Correction** +0.40s/f (Good) **14** Ran SP% **124.9**
Speed ratings (Par 97): **98,97,96,94,93 91,90,88,88,85 84,83,82,76**
CSF £109.76 CT £1337.70 TOTE £27.20: £7.80, £1.70, £4.70; EX 153.80 Trifecta £2399.20.
Owner Rhydian Morgan-Jones **Bred** Rhydian Morgan-Jones **Trained** East Ilsley, Berks

FOCUS
Race distance as advertised. Moderate handicap form and little doubting the favourite should have won. Improvement from the winner.

3510 WINTERFLOOD SECURITIES ETF H'CAP 5f 161y
7:10 (7:11) (Class 5) (0-70,69) 4-Y-O+ **£3,067** (£905; £453) **Stalls** Centre

Form RPR

3-05 **1** **Oeil De Tigre (FR)**[15] 3004 5-9-4 **69**.................... GeorgeDowning[(3)] 3 76
(Tony Carroll) *hld up in tch: rdn over 2f out: r.o to ld towards fin* **12/1**

6400 **2** *1/2* **Head Space (IRE)**[22] 2765 8-8-10 **65**.................(vt) JoshuaBryan[(7)] 1 70
(Brian Barr) *chsd ldrs: rdn to ld ins fnl f: hdd towards fin* **25/1**

4636 **3** *nk* **Secret Witness**[6] 3320 10-8-7 **58**.........................(b) TomMarquand[(3)] 7 62
(Ronald Harris) *hld up: hdwy and swtchd lft over 1f out: sn rdn: r.o* **8/1**

3505 **4** *1/2* **Indian Affair**[12] 3098 6-9-4 **66**..................................(vt[1]) OisinMurphy 6 69
(Milton Bradley) *a.p: chsd ldr 1/2-way: rdn to ld over 1f out: hdd ins fnl f: styd on same pce* **11/2**[2]

2210 **5** *1 3/4* **One Big Surprise**[25] 2697 4-9-3 **65**.............................. ShaneKelly 11 62
(Richard Hughes) *hld up: hdwy 2f out: rdn over 1f out: styd on same pce ins fnl f* **3/1**[1]

0660 **6** *1 1/2* **Ambitious Boy**[43] 2130 7-8-10 **63**.......................... CiaranMckee[(5)] 4 55
(John O'Shea) *s.i.s: bhd: r.o ins fnl f: nvr nrr* **16/1**

0440 **7** *hd* **Noverre To Go (IRE)**[12] 3098 10-8-9 **60**................(p) DannyBrock[(3)] 15 51
(Ronald Harris) *s.i.s: hdwy over 3f out: rdn over 1f out: no ex ins fnl f* **16/1**

640- **8** *nk* **Quiet Warrior (IRE)**[52] 1902 5-8-6 **54**.................................. JFEgan 12 44
(Tony Carroll) *hld up: shkn up over 1f out: nvr on terms* **11/2**[2]

6055 **9** *2 1/4* **Catalinas Diamond (IRE)**[19] 2845 8-8-10 **58**............(t) SteveDrowne 10 41
(Pat Murphy) *in rr: hdwy over 1f out: wknd and eased ins fnl f* **14/1**

2400 **10** *2 3/4* **Mambo Spirit (IRE)**[25] 2697 12-8-7 **58**.......................... EoinWalsh[(3)] 14 32
(Tony Newcombe) *led: rdn and hdd over 1f out: wknd fnl f* **25/1**

100 **11** *3 1/2* **Spellmaker**[25] 2697 7-8-9 **60**.............................. MichaelJMMurphy[(3)] 9 22
(Tony Newcombe) *prom: rdn and ev ch over 1f out: wknd fnl f* **16/1**

-022 **12** *8* **Jaganory (IRE)**[12] 3098 4-8-13 **61**...................................(p) PatCosgrave 5
(Christopher Mason) *prom: lft to r alone far side over 2f out: sn rdn: wknd and eased fnl f* **6/1**[3]

1m 13.11s (1.91) **Going Correction** +0.40s/f (Good) **12** Ran SP% **120.9**
Speed ratings (Par 103): **103,102,101,101,98 96,96,96,93,89 84,74**
CSF £282.10 CT £2564.42 TOTE £11.40: £3.20, £7.70, £3.00; EX 432.70 Trifecta £4301.40.
Owner A W Carroll **Bred** Jedburgh Stud & Madame Clody Norton **Trained** Cropthorne, Worcs

FOCUS
Race distance as advertised. They fanned across the track in this modest sprint, with the action unfolding down the centre. Straightforward, ordinary form.

3511 BRITISH STALLION STUDS EBF NOVICE FILLIES' STKS (PLUS 10 RACE) 5f 161y
7:40 (7:41) (Class 4) 2-Y-O **£5,175** (£1,540; £769; £384) **Stalls** Centre

Form RPR

1 **Santafiora** 2-8-11 0.................................. KieranShoemark[(3)] 8 76+
(Roger Charlton) *free to post: s.i.s: hdwy over 3f out: rdn over 2f out: r.o to ld nr fin* **20/1**

431 **2** *1* **Lexington Sky (IRE)**[22] 2764 2-9-1 0.......................... GaryMahon[(5)] 4 79
(Richard Hannon) *w ldrs: rdn and ev ch ins fnl f: unable qck nr fin* **9/2**[3]

03 **3** *shd* **Madame Bounty (IRE)**[21] 2793 2-9-0 0.................................. FMBerry 7 73
(Ed Walker) *w ldrs: led over 2f out: rdn over 1f out: hdd nr fin* **7/2**[2]

4 *1* **Singing Sands (IRE)** 2-9-0 0.. OisinMurphy 2 69+
(Ralph Beckett) *s.s: hdwy 3f out: rdn over 2f out: styd on same pce ins fnl f* **6/1**

5 *5* **Express (IRE)** 2-9-0 0.. SeanLevey 13 53
(Richard Hannon) *hld up: rdn over 2f out: styd on fr over 1f out: nt trble ldrs* **20/1**

6 *3* **Clip Art** 2-9-0 0.. TimmyMurphy 15 43
(Jamie Osborne) *s.i.s: shkn up over 1f out: nvr nrr* **33/1**

7 *nse* **Compton Poppy** 2-8-11 0.................................... GeorgeDowning[(3)] 12 43
(Tony Carroll) *sn pushed along in rr: nvr on terms* **100/1**

00 **8** *1 1/4* **Bills Delight**[64] 1543 2-9-0 0.. TimClark 14 39
(Bill Turner) *s.i.s: hld up: n.d* **100/1**

9 *1* **Incentive** 2-9-0 0... SilvestreDeSousa 5 35
(Stuart Kittow) *led 2f: rdn: hung rt and wknd over 1f out: eased* **33/1**

2 **10** *1/2* **Seed Corn**[14] 3037 2-9-0 0.. PatCosgrave 1 34
(William Haggas) *w ldrs: led over 3f out: hdd over 2f out: wknd fnl f* **11/10**[1]

11 *4* **Grand Myla (IRE)** 2-9-0 0.. FergusSweeney 10 21
(Gary Moore) *hld up: pushed along 3f out: a in rr* **16/1**

00 **12** *24* **Lilly Ballerina (IRE)**[20] 2822 2-9-0 0.. JFEgan 11
(Tony Carroll) *prom: lost pl 3f out: eased fnl 2f* **100/1**

1m 14.78s (3.58) **Going Correction** +0.40s/f (Good) **12** Ran SP% **126.6**
Speed ratings (Par 92): **92,90,90,89,82 78,78,76,75,74 69,37**
CSF £110.99 TOTE £27.70: £7.40, £1.90, £2.20; EX 183.20 Trifecta £1493.30.
Owner Axom LXIV **Bred** Highbury Stud & John Troy **Trained** Beckhampton, Wilts

FOCUS
Race distance as advertised. They came down the centre in what looked a fair fillies' event, albeit there was a surprise winner, the placed horses perhaps getting into it sooner than ideal given the conditions. The form fits with the race average.

3512 POMMERY CHAMPAGNE H'CAP 5f 11y
8:10 (8:10) (Class 4) (0-85,85) 3-Y-O **£4,690** (£1,395; £697) **Stalls** Centre

Form RPR

01-6 **1** **Kassia (IRE)**[19] 2875 3-9-7 **85**.......................... SilvestreDeSousa 6 95
(Mick Channon) *mde virtually all: rdn over 1f out: edgd lft ins fnl f: jst hld on* **5/2**[3]

2001 **2** *nk* **Emerald Loch**[9] 3218 3-8-4 **73** 6ex.....................(p) PatrickO'Donnell[(5)] 4 82
(Ralph Beckett) *a.p: chsd wnr 1/2-way: rdn over 1f out: r.o towards fin* **11/10**[1]

1-50 **3** *3* **Pine Ridge**[16] 2981 3-8-9 **73**.. RyanTate 1 71
(Clive Cox) *racd keenly: trckd wnr to 1/2-way: rdn over 1f out: no ex ins fnl f* **2/1**[2]

1m 4.32s (1.82) **Going Correction** +0.40s/f (Good) **3** Ran SP% **109.5**
Speed ratings (Par 101): **101,100,95**
CSF £5.65 TOTE £2.70; EX 4.20 Trifecta £5.70.
Owner Jon and Julia Aisbitt **Bred** Old Carhue Stud **Trained** West Ilsley, Berks

FOCUS
Race distance as advertised. Only half of the original six remained and it was an unsatisfactory race. The winner is fully entitled to rate this high on her 2yo form.

3513 BERTIE 375 GREEN MEMORIAL RACE H'CAP 5f 161y
8:40 (8:41) (Class 6) (0-60,60) 3-Y-O **£2,264** (£673; £336; £168) **Stalls** Centre

Form RPR

405 **1** **Hamish McGonagain**[13] 3069 3-9-4 **57**.........................(p) MartinLane 5 65
(Jeremy Gask) *led 1f: led again over 2f out: rdn over 1f out: edgd lft ins fnl f: r.o* **11/2**[2]

0024 **2** *nk* **Lady McGuffy (IRE)**[10] 3198 3-9-0 **53**.............................(t) ShaneKelly 3 60
(David Evans) *a.p: rdn to chse wnr over 1f out: sn ev ch: r.o* **7/1**

35-2 **3** *4* **Secret Interlude (IRE)**[149] 327 3-8-11 **55**.................. LucyKBarry[(5)] 9 49
(Jamie Osborne) *led over 4f out: hdd over 2f out: sn rdn: no ex ins fnl f* **11/1**

1-00 **4** *1 3/4* **Desirable**[13] 3062 3-9-5 **58**.. FMBerry 17 46
(Hughie Morrison) *s.i.s: hld up: hdwy u.p and hung lft fr over 1f out: nt trble ldrs* **12/1**

1103 **5** *hd* **Bushwise (IRE)**[20] 2824 3-9-7 **60**.................................(p) OisinMurphy 6 47
(Milton Bradley) *chsd ldrs: rdn over 1f out: wknd ins fnl f* **6/1**[3]

-020 **6** *3/4* **Blackdown Warrior**[32] 2458 3-8-8 **47**.......................... FergusSweeney 14 32
(Rod Millman) *w ldrs tl rdn wl over 1f out: wknd ins fnl f* **9/1**

004 **7** *nk* **Hodgkins Trust (IRE)**[11] 3127 3-8-10 **49** ow1.................. RobertTart 7 33
(Jeremy Gask) *s.i.s: in rr: rdn over 2f out: n.d* **25/1**

0345 **8** *1 1/4* **Wilspa's Magic (IRE)**[10] 3198 3-9-5 **58**.......................... GeorgeBaker 15 38
(Ron Hodges) *chsd ldrs: rdn 1/2-way: wknd fnl f* **8/1**

0005 **9** *2* **Mostashreqah**[11] 3126 3-9-7 **60**................................(tp) RoystonFfrench 12 33
(Milton Bradley) *plld hrd and prom: rdn 1/2-way: wknd over 1f out* **33/1**

502 **10** *nk* **The Lillster**[29] 2559 3-9-3 **59**.................................. GeorgeDowning[(3)] 13 31
(Tony Carroll) *s.i.s: hld up: plld hrd: rdn and wknd over 1f out* **12/1**

0600 **11** *3/4* **Lillyput (IRE)**[13] 3062 3-9-4 **57**.......................... SilvestreDeSousa 16 27
(Mick Channon) *hld up: hdwy u.p over 2f out: edgd lft and wknd fnl f* **11/4**[1]

1m 14.36s (3.16) **Going Correction** +0.40s/f (Good) **11** Ran SP% **120.5**
Speed ratings (Par 97): **94,93,88,85,85 84,84,82,79,79 78**
CSF £45.02 CT £417.56 TOTE £5.30: £2.00, £2.20, £3.80; EX 57.80 Trifecta £433.40.
Owner Jamie & Lucy Hart **Bred** Llety Farms **Trained** Stockbridge, Hants

FOCUS
Race distance as advertised. The front pair came clear in this modest sprint. Neither has the most convincing profile.

3514 HAPPY 21ST BIRTHDAY JACK INKPEN H'CAP 1m 5y
9:10 (9:13) (Class 5) (0-70,70) 4-Y-O+ **£2,911** (£866; £432; £216) **Stalls** Low

Form RPR

0441 **1** **Marcano (IRE)**[26] 2635 4-9-7 **70**...................................(t) RyanTate 12 79+
(Rod Millman) *hld up: hdwy over 1f out: rdn to ld ins fnl f: r.o wl: comf* **4/1**[2]

2060 **2** *2 1/4* **Gannicus**[13] 3061 5-9-7 **70**..(p) FMBerry 6 73
(Brendan Powell) *chsd ldrs: rdn over 2f out: ev ch ins fnl f: styd on same pce* **7/2**[1]

0141 **3** *nse* **Lady Bayside**[12] 3096 8-9-6 **69**.. GeorgeBaker 3 72
(Malcolm Saunders) *sn led: rdn over 1f out: hdd ins fnl f: styd on same pce* **5/1**[3]

0243 **4** *1 1/4* **Lord Of The Storm**[26] 2635 8-9-0 **63**...................... SilvestreDeSousa 10 63
(Michael Attwater) *w ldrs: rdn and ev ch ins fnl f: styd on same pce* **4/1**[2]

6355 **5** *1/2* **Caledonia Laird**[11] 3125 5-9-3 **66**.................................... JFEgan 14 65
(Jo Hughes) *w ldrs 2f: remained handy: rdn and ev ch over 1f out: no ex ins fnl f* **10/1**

4504 **6** *nk* **Miss Inga Sock (IRE)**[26] 2636 4-8-10 **62**..............(p) TomMarquand[(3)] 7 60
(Eve Johnson Houghton) *hld up: hdwy over 1f out: sn rdn: no ex ins fnl f* **10/1**

66-5 **7** *6* **Avon Scent**[19] 2849 6-7-9 **51** oh6..................................(p) RPWalsh[(7)] 2 35
(Christopher Mason) *hld up: racd keenly: hmpd 6f out: rdn over 3f out: wknd over 1f out* **50/1**

0030 **8** *nk* **Saint Pois (FR)**[36] 2347 5-9-2 **68**.......................... GeorgeDowning[(3)] 4 52
(Tony Carroll) *hld up in tch: rdn over 2f out: wknd over 1f out* **10/1**

-114 **9** *nk* **Jumbo Prado (USA)**[67] 1502 7-9-3 **66**...........................(b) OisinMurphy 9 49
(Daniel Mark Loughnane) *sn pushed along into mid-div: rdn over 3f out: wknd over 1f out* **14/1**

5650 **10** *2* **Red Unico (IRE)**[22] 2769 4-8-5 **61**.......................... JoshuaBryan[(7)] 15 39
(Brian Barr) *prom: racd keenly: rdn over 3f out: wknd over 1f out* **16/1**

1m 44.87s (4.07) **Going Correction** +0.425s/f (Yiel) **10** Ran SP% **120.7**
Speed ratings (Par 103): **96,93,93,92,91 91,85,85,85,83**
CSF £19.18 CT £74.56 TOTE £3.60: £2.10, £2.50, £1.90; EX 10.70 Trifecta £112.80.
Owner The Links Partnership **Bred** David Barry **Trained** Kentisbeare, Devon

FOCUS
Race distance as advertised. Modest form, although the winner did well to come from so far back. He's rated back to his best.

T/Plt: £760.10 to a £1 stake. Pool of £50848.62 - 48.83 winning tickets. T/Qpdt: £166.80 to a £1 stake. Pool of £4021.74 - 17.84 winning tickets. **Colin Roberts**

3208 CARLISLE (R-H)

Wednesday, June 22

OFFICIAL GOING: Good to firm (7.2)

Wind: Breezy, half against Weather: Overcast

3515 EDMUNDSON CABLETECH CARLISLE NOVICE AUCTION STKS 5f

2:00 (2:03) (Class 5) 2-Y-O **£3,234** (£962; £481; £240) **Stalls** Low

Form RPR

3 **1** **Alicante Dawn**[11] 3148 2-9-2 0 ConnorBeasley 2 75+
(Bryan Smart) *awkward s: in tch: hdwy and rdn 2f out: led ins fnl f: kpt on strly* **1/1**[1]

0 **2** *1* **Little Miss Lola**[9] 3208 2-8-11 0 DarryllHolland 8 66
(Alan Swinbank) *t.k.h: hld up in tch on outside: hdwy to ld over 1f out: rdn: edgd rt and hdd ins fnl f: kpt on: hld nr fin* **10/1**[3]

3 *1 1/4* **Nifty Niece (IRE)** 2-8-11 0 PJMcDonald 3 62
(Ann Duffield) *hld up in tch: pushed along 2f out: kpt on ins fnl f: nt pce to chal* **25/1**

64 **4** *2 1/4* **Traveltalk (IRE)**[25] 2675 2-9-2 0 BenCurtis 1 59
(Brian Ellison) *w ldr: rdn along over 1f out: outpcd ins fnl f* **7/2**[2]

5 *1/2* **Silk Mill Blue** 2-9-2 0 GeorgeChaloner 9 57
(Richard Whitaker) *s.i.s: rn green and outpcd in rr: rdn 1/2-way: kpt on fnl f: nvr rchd ldrs* **66/1**

0 **6** *hd* **Precious Skye (IRE)**[12] 3112 2-8-11 0 KeaganLatham 6 51
(David O'Meara) *t.k.h: mde most to over 1f out: wknd ins fnl f* **16/1**

3631 **7** *1 1/4* **Harome (IRE)**[20] 2807 2-9-9 0 SamJames 7 61
(David Loughnane) *trckd ldrs: rdn and ev ch briefly over 1f out: wknd ins fnl f* **7/2**[2]

1m 1.55s (0.75) **Going Correction** -0.175s/f (Firm) **7** Ran SP% **114.8**
Speed ratings (Par 93): **87,85,83,79,79 78,76**
CSF £12.95 TOTE £1.80: £1.30, £4.40; EX 13.00 Trifecta £117.30.
Owner B Smart **Bred** Natton House Thoroughbreds **Trained** Hambleton, N Yorks

■ Best Away was withdrawn. Price at time of withdrawal 12/1. Rule 4 applies to bets struck prior to withdrawal but not to SP bets. Deduct 5p in the pound. New market formed.

FOCUS

Race distances as advertised. Unusually the going got officially quicker overnight, from good, good to firm in places to good to firm, but the GoingStick reading went down, from 8.2 to 7.2. Clerk Of The Course Kirkland Tellwright said: "The ground has been spiked, which might account for it, but it demonstrates that they are both opinions of one sort or another." The time of the opening novice event strongly suggested quick ground and riders were complimentary afterwards. The winner is rated to his debut mark.

3516 TOTEPOOLLIVEINFO.COM EBF NOVICE STKS 5f 193y

2:30 (2:53) (Class 5) 2-Y-O **£3,234** (£962; £481; £240) **Stalls** Low

Form RPR

0 **1** **Burrishoole Abbey (IRE)**[27] 2611 2-9-2 0 DougieCostello 8 89
(K R Burke) *mde all: rdn over 1f out: kpt on strly fnl f* **3/1**[1]

2 *2 1/4* **Town Charter (USA)** 2-9-2 0 JoeFanning 11 81
(Mark Johnston) *in tch: hdwy on outside to chse wnr over 2f out: effrt and pushed along over 1f out: kpt on same pce ins fnl f* **10/3**[2]

3 *7* **Abiento (IRE)** 2-9-2 0 TonyHamilton 7 59
(Richard Fahey) *t.k.h early: trckd ldrs tl shkn up and outpcd by first two fr over 1f out* **13/2**[3]

0 **4** *3 3/4* **Regal Decree**[20] 2830 2-9-2 0 TomEaves 12 47
(Jedd O'Keeffe) *chsd clr ldng gp: pushed along 1/2-way: hdwy over 1f out: kpt on fnl f: no imp* **50/1**

5 *shd* **Ladofash** 2-9-2 0 PJMcDonald 4 47+
(Ann Duffield) *in tch: rdn and outpcd 1/2-way: rallied fnl f: nvr able to chal* **25/1**

6 *3/4* **Pepys** 2-9-2 0 ConnorBeasley 6 44
(Bryan Smart) *s.i.s and rn green in rr: effrt and drvn along over 2f out: kpt on fnl f: no imp* **18/1**

7 *1 1/4* **Four Wishes** 2-9-2 0 DavidAllan 3 40
(Tim Easterby) *missed break: bhd and outpcd: kpt on fnl f: nvr on terms* **11/1**

0 **8** *1/2* **Operational**[18] 2913 2-9-2 0 JackGarritty 2 39
(Jedd O'Keeffe) *prom: drvn and outpcd over 2f out: n.d after* **28/1**

9 *1 3/4* **Dream On Dreamer (IRE)** 2-8-11 0 PaulMulrennan 5 28
(Michael Dods) *noisy and green in paddock: s.i.s and rn green in rr: nvr on terms* **12/1**

10 *7* **Saint Equiano** 2-9-2 0 PhillipMakin 9
(Keith Dalgleish) *t.k.h: pressed wnr to over 2f out: rdn and wknd over 1f out* **3/1**[1]

11 *6* **Joyroo (IRE)** 2-9-2 0 BenCurtis 1
(Brian Ellison) *s.i.s: outpcd in rr: no ch fr 1/2-way* **33/1**

1m 12.3s (-1.40) **Going Correction** -0.175s/f (Firm) 2y crse rec **11** Ran SP% **119.9**
Speed ratings (Par 93): **102,99,89,84,84 83,81,81,78,69 61**
CSF £12.91 TOTE £3.80: £1.30, £1.60, £2.30; EX 15.30 Trifecta £42.60.
Owner Mrs M Gittins **Bred** Grange Stud **Trained** Middleham Moor, N Yorks

■ Sir Alexanderwas withdrawn. Price at time of withdrawal 33/1. Rule 4 does not apply.

FOCUS

There was a 23min delay to this novice contest after \bSir Alexander\p went down in his gate, sadly with tragic consequences. The stalls were moved forward, meaning a slightly shortened 6f, and after a frantic pace few got involved. Form to treat with some caution, although the first pair are clearly useful.

3517 BOOKIES.COM CARLISLE BELL CONSOLATION (H'CAP) 7f 173y

3:00 (3:26) (Class 4) (0-85,81) 3-Y-O+ **£6,469** (£1,925; £962; £481) **Stalls** Low

Form RPR

3000 **1** **Gurkha Friend**[12] 3115 4-9-6 **77** DavidNolan 15 87
(Karen McLintock) *mde all: sn crossed over to ins rail: rdn 2f out: kpt on wl fnl f* **11/1**

-131 **2** *1 3/4* **Qaffaal (USA)**[26] 2660 5-8-10 **72** NathanEvans(5) 13 79
(Michael Easterby) *hld up towards rr: effrt whn nt clr run and swtchd rt over 2f out: hdwy over 1f out: wnt 2nd wl ins fnl f: nt rch wnr* **8/1**[3]

5442 **3** *1/2* **Gold Flash**[5] 3344 4-9-1 **72** (b) PhillipMakin 14 77
(Keith Dalgleish) *hld up: smooth hdwy over 2f out: chsd wnr and rdn over 1f out: edgd rt and lost 2nd wl ins fnl f: no ex* **10/1**

-304 **4** *2 1/2* **Red Paladin (IRE)**[10] 3185 6-9-1 **72** (p) DougieCostello 16 71
(Kristin Stubbs) *s.v.s: bhd: rdn 3f out: hdwy over 1f out: kpt on wl fnl f: nvr able to chal* **40/1**

5000 **5** *1/2* **Eutropius (IRE)**[11] 3166 7-9-4 **75** DarryllHolland 7 72
(Alan Swinbank) *t.k.h early: hld up in tch: effrt and rdn 2f out: kpt on same pce fnl f* **14/1**

0300 **6** *nse* **Torrid**[11] 3166 5-9-7 **78** CamHardie 6 75
(Michael Easterby) *chsd ldrs: drvn along over 2f out: kpt on same pce fr over 1f out* **14/1**

5202 **7** *hd* **Pumaflor (IRE)**[10] 3185 4-9-4 **75** GeorgeChaloner 3 72
(Richard Whitaker) *trckd ldrs: effrt and wnt 2nd briefly over 1f out: rdn and outpcd fnl f* **16/1**

-460 **8** *1/2* **Chiswick Bey (IRE)**[11] 3166 8-8-13 **70** TonyHamilton 9 66
(Richard Fahey) *hld up on ins: drvn along over 2f out: hdwy over 1f out: no imp fnl f* **25/1**

6-00 **9** *1 1/4* **Homeland (IRE)**[65] 1526 4-8-11 **75** (t) AdamMcNamara(7) 17 68
(Brian Rothwell) *hld up: effrt on outside over 2f out: no imp fr over 1f out* **66/1**

3411 **10** *shd* **Just Be Lucky (IRE)**[29] 2555 4-9-9 **80** (be[1]) AndrewMullen 1 72
(Ivan Furtado) *t.k.h: in tch on ins: rdn over 2f out: wknd over 1f out* **15/2**[2]

3406 **11** *hd* **Beautiful Stranger (IRE)**[16] 2959 5-9-0 **71** (p) GrahamGibbons 5 63
(Keith Dalgleish) *hld up on ins: drvn and outpcd over 2f out: kpt on fnl f: nt pce to chal* **33/1**

-126 **12** *1/2* **Rocco's Delight**[23] 1521 4-9-8 **79** (p) BenCurtis 10 70
(Brian Ellison) *pressed ldr tl rdn and wknd over 1f out* **22/1**

-311 **13** *1/2* **Cymraeg Bounty**[16] 2959 4-9-7 **78** JoeFanning 8 67
(Iain Jardine) *t.k.h: in tch: stdy hdwy on outside over 2f out: rdn over 1f out: wknd fnl f* **3/1**[1]

-323 **14** *1 1/4* **Sovereign Bounty**[28] 2579 4-9-1 **72** JackGarritty 4 58
(Jedd O'Keeffe) *hld up in midfield: drvn along over 2f out: wknd over 1f out* **10/1**

0001 **15** *shd* **Artful Prince**[9] 3212 6-9-2 **76** 6ex (b) JoeDoyle(3) 11 62
(James Given) *hld up: rdn along over 3f out: nvr on terms* **12/1**

-040 **16** *3/4* **Buccaneers Vault (IRE)**[18] 2917 4-9-6 **77** PaulMulrennan 2 61
(Michael Dods) *midfield on ins: drvn and outpcd over 2f out: sn btn* **12/1**

1m 37.11s (-2.89) **Going Correction** -0.175s/f (Firm) **16** Ran SP% **124.1**
Speed ratings (Par 105): **107,105,104,102,101 101,101,101,99,99 99,98,98,97,97 96**
CSF £93.35 CT £631.76 TOTE £18.20: £4.60, £1.90, £2.90, £8.10; EX 177.90 Trifecta £3371.50.

Owner Don Eddy **Bred** Mrs J Imray **Trained** Ingoe, Northumberland

FOCUS

This competitive handicap was run at something of an uneven pace and once again it paid to be handy. High draws dominated and the form is rated around the placed horses.

3518 BOOKIES.COM CARLISLE BELL H'CAP 7f 173y

3:35 (4:03) (Class 4) (0-85,86) 3-Y-O+

£18,675 (£5,592; £2,796; £1,398; £699; £351) **Stalls** Low

Form RPR

0050 **1** **Edgar Balthazar**[25] 2679 4-9-5 **84** (p) PhillipMakin 6 92
(Keith Dalgleish) *hld up: effrt and pushed along on outside over 2f out: hdwy over 1f out: led ins fnl f: drvn out* **25/1**

-230 **2** *1/2* **Alejandro (IRE)**[12] 3115 7-9-5 **84** DavidNolan 4 91
(David O'Meara) *hld up in tch: rdn over 2f out: hdwy whn nt clr run briefly over 1f out: chsd wnr wl ins fnl f: kpt on fin* **14/1**

0314 **3** *3/4* **Alexandrakollontai (IRE)**[14] 3021 6-9-4 **83** (b) ConnorBeasley 16 88
(Alistair Whillans) *bhd: drvn along over 3f out: gd hdwy on outside to ld over 1f out: hdd ins fnl f: kpt on same pce* **25/1**

0001 **4** *1* **Woody Bay**[11] 3166 6-9-2 **81** JasonHart 10 84
(Mark Walford) *trckd ldr: led over 3f out to over 1f out: kpt on same pce ins fnl f* **12/1**

0-01 **5** *nse* **Ginger Jack**[39] 2257 9-9-4 **83** DavidAllan 9 86
(Garry Moss) *hld up in midfield: rdn over 2f out: hdwy over 1f out: kpt on ins fnl f* **6/1**[3]

0-00 **6** *1* **Yourartisonfire**[40] 2216 6-9-1 **85** (v) JordanVaughan(5) 13 85
(K R Burke) *hld up: rdn on outside over 2f out: kpt on fnl f: nrst fin* **28/1**

-005 **7** *nk* **Glenalmond (IRE)**[20] 2833 4-9-3 **82** (v) DougieCostello 14 82
(K R Burke) *t.k.h early: chsd ldr: led over 3f out to over 1f out: sn one pce* **16/1**

0631 **8** *nk* **Dubai Dynamo**[7] 3286 11-9-7 **86** 6ex PJMcDonald 11 86
(Ruth Carr) *s.i.s: hld up: rdn over 3f out: kpt on fnl f: nt pce to chal* **16/1**

1501 **9** *nk* **Kalk Bay (IRE)**[18] 2910 9-9-1 **85** (t) NathanEvans(5) 3 83
(Michael Easterby) *hld up: rdn whn nt clr run briefly over 2f out: hdwy over 1f out: no ex ins fnl f* **5/1**[1]

2215 **10** *1* **Jacbequick**[11] 3166 5-8-12 **82** (v) JoshDoyle(5) 1 78
(David O'Meara) *led at decent gallop to over 3f out: rdn and wknd appr fnl f* **9/1**

10-0 **11** *3 1/4* **Argaki (IRE)**[69] 1445 6-8-10 **82** CliffordLee(7) 7 71
(Keith Dalgleish) *hld up in midfield on outside: drvn and hung rt 2f out: sn outpcd* **66/1**

1333 **12** *1* **Muntadab (IRE)**[36] 2328 4-9-4 **83** JoeyHaynes 5 69
(David Loughnane) *trckd ldrs: j. path after 2f: rdn over 3f out: wknd over 1f out* **8/1**

-410 **13** *1 1/4* **Hulcolt (IRE)**[27] 2628 5-9-3 **82** GrahamGibbons 12 65
(Ivan Furtado) *prom: drvn along over 3f out: wknd over 1f out* **12/1**

0-00 **14** *2 1/2* **Santefisio**[18] 2910 10-9-5 **84** (b) JoeFanning 15 62
(Keith Dalgleish) *s.i.s: hld up: rdn along over 3f out: sn struggling* **33/1**

2-14 **15** *11* **Funding Deficit (IRE)**[35] 2361 6-9-3 **82** PaulMulrennan 17 34
(Jim Goldie) *hld up: drvn and outpcd 3f out: sn btn* **25/1**

-323 **16** *82* **Hard To Handel**[18] 2917 4-9-6 **85** DanielTudhope 8
(David O'Meara) *hld up: struggling after 3f: virtually p.u* **11/2**[2]

1m 37.02s (-2.98) **Going Correction** -0.175s/f (Firm) course record **16** Ran SP% **120.7**
Speed ratings (Par 105): **107,106,105,104,104 103,103,103,102,101 98,97,96,93,82**
CSF £320.91 CT £8917.84 TOTE £28.50: £5.10, £3.00, £6.50, £3.60; EX 411.40 Trifecta £4435.40.
Owner Middleham Park racing XXII **Bred** Natton House Thoroughbreds **Trained** Carluke, S Lanarks

■ Lavetta was withdrawn. Price at time of withdrawal 16/1. Rule 4 does not apply.

FOCUS

There was no hanging around in this age-old handicap and it suited the closers. It resulted in a new course record. Straightforward form.

3519 EBFSTALLIONS.COM "ETERNAL" FILLIES' STKS (LISTED RACE) 6f 195y

4:10 (4:28) (Class 1) 3-Y-O

£22,684 (£8,600; £4,304; £2,144; £1,076; £540) **Stalls** Low

Form RPR

0-20 **1** **Opal Tiara (IRE)**[7] 3274 3-9-0 **98** GrahamGibbons 3 100
(Mick Channon) *chsd clr ldr: smooth hdwy to ld over 1f out: rdn and kpt on strly fnl f: eased nr fin* **7/2**[3]

31 **2** *2 1/4* **Red Box**[9] 3209 3-9-0 0 LukeMorris 4 94
(Sir Mark Prescott Bt) *t.k.h early: hld up in tch: rdn along 3f out: hdwy over 1f out: chsd wnr wl ins fnl f: kpt on: no imp* **2/1**[1]

1-1 **3** ½ **Eternally**[21] 2795 3-9-0 81 RobertHavlin 5 93
(John Gosden) *prom: stdy hdwy over 2f out: effrt and chsd wnr over 1f out to wl ins fnl f: one pce* **11/4**[2]

04-0 **4** 3 **Chiringuita (USA)**[21] 2789 3-9-0 89 DanielTudhope 2 84
(James Bethell) *hld up in tch on ins: drvn along over 2f out: kpt on fnl f: nt pce to chal* **10/1**

5126 **5** 1½ **Quick N Quirky (IRE)**[18] 2907 3-9-0 80 (tp) DavidAllan 8 80
(Tim Easterby) *hld up: rdn and effrt over 2f out: no imp fr over 1f out* **9/1**

31-0 **6** 2¼ **Our Joy (IRE)**[40] 2220 3-9-0 80 [1] PaulMulrennan 6 74
(Clive Cox) *dwlt and wnt lft s: bhd: struggling 1/2-way: sme late hdwy: nvr on terms* **12/1**

1046 **7** ½ **Alyaa (IRE)**[14] 3039 3-9-0 72 TomEaves 7 73
(Conrad Allen) *t.k.h: led and sn clr: rdn over 2f out: hdd over 1f out: sn wknd* **80/1**

110- **8** 11 **Silhuette (IRE)**[277] 6514 3-9-0 88 PJMcDonald 1 43
(Ann Duffield) *plld hrd early: in tch: drvn and outpcd over 2f out: sn struggling* **20/1**

1m 24.58s (-2.52) **Going Correction** -0.175s/f (Firm) **8** Ran SP% **115.0**
Speed ratings (Par 104): **107,104,103,100,98 96,95,83**
CSF £11.00 TOTE £4.60: £1.70, £2.50, £1.10; EX 12.40 Trifecta £31.20.
Owner Qatar Racing & The Sweet Partnership **Bred** Mcb Ltd & Mrs G Hedley **Trained** West Ilsley, Berks

FOCUS
Not the strongest fillies' race for the class. It was another strongly run affair and it's straightforward form. The winner and fifth help with the level.

3520 TOTEPOOL CUMBERLAND PLATE H'CAP 1m 3f 39y
4:40 (4:55) (Class 4) (0-85,85) 3-Y-O+
£18,675 (£5,592; £2,796; £1,398; £699; £351) **Stalls** High

Form RPR

1 **1** **Sindarban (IRE)**[40] 2197 5-9-10 **85** PhillipMakin 5 96+
(Keith Dalgleish) *s.i.s: hld up: nt clr run over 2f out to wl over 1f out: swtchd lft and gd hdwy to ld ins fnl f: rdn out* **5/1**[2]

4062 **2** 1¼ **Modernism**[11] 3129 7-9-2 **84** AdamMcNamara(7) 12 91
(Richard Fahey) *hld up: rdn along over 2f out: hdwy over 1f out: chsd wnr ins fnl f: kpt on: nt pce to chal* **14/1**

3112 **3** ½ **Masterpaver**[11] 3162 5-9-3 **78** TonyHamilton 1 84
(Richard Fahey) *midfield: drvn and outpcd over 4f out: rallied and swtchd lft over 1f out: kpt on ins fnl f: nrst fin* **5/2**[1]

4504 **4** ¾ **Top Of The Glas (IRE)**[36] 2328 5-9-3 **78** BenCurtis 14 83+
(Brian Ellison) *pressed ldr: drvn to ld wl over 1f out: hdd ins fnl f: kpt on same pce* **7/1**[3]

1434 **5** 1½ **Two Jabs**[12] 3117 6-9-10 **85** AndrewMullen 9 88
(Michael Appleby) *hld up in tch: rdn and outpcd over 2f out: rallied ins fnl f: nt pce to chal* **7/1**[3]

1113 **6** 1 **Inniscastle Lad**[13] 3057 4-9-5 **80** (b) LukeMorris 2 81+
(Ed Dunlop) *led: rdn over 2f out: hdd wl over 1f out: rallied: outpcd fnl f* **16/1**

0464 **7** 1½ **Mukhayyam**[12] 3113 4-9-7 **82** (p) PaulMulrennan 8 83
(Tim Easterby) *t.k.h in midfield: gng wl whn nt clr run over 2f out to over 1f out: sn rdn and outpcd: no imp fnl f* **14/1**

2642 **8** ½ **Jolievitesse (FR)**[13] 3057 4-9-2 **77** JoeyHaynes 11 75
(K R Burke) *hld up: hdwy on outside to chse ldrs wl over 1f out: sn rdn and edgd rt: wknd fnl f* **17/2**

0541 **9** 4½ **Skiddaw Valleys**[7] 3294 4-8-9 **77** 6ex CliffordLee(7) 15 68
(Alan Swinbank) *hld up: stdy hdwy on outside to chse ldrs over 2f out: rdn: edgd rt and wknd over 1f out* **18/1**

2-50 **10** 4½ **Multellie**[42] 2163 4-9-8 **83** DavidAllan 7 66
(Tim Easterby) *t.k.h: cl up: rdn and outpcd over 2f out: wknd over 1f out* **18/1**

001 **11** 4 **Plane Song (IRE)**[8] 3263 4-9-6 **81** 6ex DarryllHolland 3 58
(Alan Swinbank) *prom: nt clr run over 2f out: rdn and wknd over 1f out* **28/1**

64-0 **12** 7 **Moshe (IRE)**[173] 6 5-8-12 **78** PhilDennis(5) 16 44
(Philip Kirby) *prom on outside: drvn and outpcd over 3f out: sn btn* **80/1**

053 **13** shd **Biff Johnson (IRE)**[5] 3347 4-9-5 **80** (b) DougieCostello 6 46
(Keith Dalgleish) *trckd ldrs: rdn and hung rt over 2f out: wknd over 1f out* **25/1**

2m 20.83s (-2.27) **Going Correction** -0.175s/f (Firm) **13** Ran SP% **119.0**
Speed ratings (Par 105): **101,100,99,99,98 97,96,95,92,89 86,81,81**
CSF £71.80 CT £217.64 TOTE £5.50: £2.00, £4.10, £1.60; EX 71.80 Trifecta £288.30.
Owner Paul & Clare Rooney **Bred** His Highness The Aga Khan's Studs S C **Trained** Carluke, S Lanarks

FOCUS
As ever this year's Plate was extremely competitive. The leaders went too hard and the principals came from near last off the home turn. There's more to come from the lightly raced winner.

3521 EBF STALLIONS BREEDING WINNERS FILLIES' H'CAP 6f 195y
5:10 (5:25) (Class 4) (0-80,78) 3-Y-O+ **£6,469** (£1,925; £962; £481) **Stalls** Low

Form RPR

4600 **1** **Maureb (IRE)**[11] 3132 4-9-4 **68** (p) BenCurtis 7 78
(Tony Coyle) *in tch: hdwy to ld appr fnl f: rdn out* **18/1**

1131 **2** 1¼ **Bajan Rebel**[14] 3020 5-8-6 **61** NathanEvans(5) 10 68
(Michael Easterby) *chsd ldr: effrt and rdn 2f out: chsd wnr appr fnl f: kpt on: hld nr fin* **8/1**

-203 **3** 1¼ **Dominannie (IRE)**[9] 3213 3-8-6 **65** NeilFarley 9 66
(Alan Swinbank) *hld up: rdn and hdwy 3f out: kpt on ins fnl f: nrst fin* **15/2**

1024 **4** ½ **Fidelma Moon (IRE)**[11] 3132 4-9-4 **73** JordanVaughan(5) 8 75
(K R Burke) *led: clr 1/2-way: rdn and hdd appr fnl f: kpt on same pce* **7/1**

0312 **5** 6 **Popsies Joy (IRE)**[9] 3213 3-8-10 **69** DuranFentiman 5 52
(Tim Easterby) *t.k.h: hld up on ins: drvn and outpcd over 2f out: no imp fr over 1f out* **9/2**[2]

-263 **6** 4½ **Hawatif (IRE)**[19] 2855 3-9-5 **78** JoeFanning 4 49+
(Mark Johnston) *chsd ldrs: rdn over 2f out: wknd wl over 1f out* **10/3**[1]

1000 **7** 3 **Siri**[12] 3111 3-8-13 **72** GrahamGibbons 3 35
(Mick Channon) *s.i.s: bhd: rdn along 1/2-way: btn and eased over 1f out* **15/2**

415 **8** 1½ **Normandie Lady**[14] 3029 3-9-4 **77** TonyHamilton 1 36
(Richard Fahey) *hld up on ins: drvn and outpcd over 2f out: n.d after* **6/1**[3]

01-0 **9** 29 **Cheeky Angel (IRE)**[46] 2049 3-8-13 **72** PaulMulrennan 12
(Michael Dods) *s.i.s: bhd: struggling after 3f: t.o* **14/1**

1m 25.6s (-1.50) **Going Correction** -0.175s/f (Firm)
WFA 3 from 4yo+ 9lb **9** Ran SP% **114.6**
Speed ratings (Par 102): **101,99,98,97,90 85,82,80,47**
CSF £152.42 CT £1182.56 TOTE £16.80: £3.90, £2.40, £2.50; EX 142.50 Trifecta £1935.60.
Owner Gap Personnel & Tony Coyle **Bred** Lynn Lodge Stud **Trained** Norton, N Yorks

FOCUS
This fillies' handicap was another race run at a frantic pace and the closers came to the fore. The form is rated around the winner.
T/Jkpt: Not won. T/Plt: £251.70 to a £1 stake. Pool of £70188.83 - 203.51 winning tickets.
T/Qpdt: £118.70 to a £1 stake. Pool of £5611.94 - 34.96 winning tickets. **Richard Young**

3030 KEMPTON (A.W) (R-H)
Wednesday, June 22

OFFICIAL GOING: Polytrack: standard
Wind: almost nil Weather: fine, cloudy

3522 RACINGUK.COM APPRENTICE H'CAP 1m (P)
6:20 (6:20) (Class 6) (0-60,60) 4-Y-O+ **£2,264** (£673; £336; £168) **Stalls** Low

Form RPR

-050 **1** **Paladin (IRE)**[42] 2153 7-9-7 **60** PaddyPilley 8 67
(Michael Blake) *a handy: tk clsr order over 3f out: upsides over 2f out: rdn to ld 2f out: kpt on wl ins fnl f* **8/1**

0104 **2** 1 **Runaiocht (IRE)**[14] 3030 6-9-4 **60** (b) DavidParkes(3) 3 65
(Paul Burgoyne) *wnt to post early: hld up in rr: impr position ent st: rdn over 2f out and kpt on ins fnl f* **5/1**[1]

1500 **3** 1¾ **Gavarnie Encore**[14] 3030 4-9-3 **56** GeorgeBuckell 4 56
(Michael Blanshard) *settled in mid-div early: pushed along fr bef 1/2-way: taken rt by rival 2f out: stdy prog fr over 1f out to take 3rd nr post* **8/1**

0324 **4** ½ **Little Indian**[11] 3146 6-9-4 **60** CharlieBennett(3) 2 59
(J R Jenkins) *settled in mid-div on inner: rdn over 2f out: tk 2nd fr over 1f out: wknd nr fin and lost two pls* **7/1**[3]

24-0 **5** nk **Deftera Lad (IRE)**[16] 2969 4-8-9 **53** SophieRalston(5) 10 51
(Pat Phelan) *chsd ldrs: t.k.h: rdn over 2f out: kpt on one pce fr over 1f out* **16/1**

-006 **6** 1 **Monna Valley**[13] 3078 4-9-7 **60** (vt[1]) AaronJones 7 56
(Stuart Williams) *hld up in mid-div: rdn 2f out: kpt on one pce fr over 1f out* **6/1**[2]

046 **7** 1 **Storm Runner (IRE)**[42] 2153 8-8-13 **57** JaneElliott(5) 11 51
(George Margarson) *settled in mid-div: swtchd to rail st: rdn over 2f out: wknd fnl f* **14/1**

00-0 **8** ½ **Glorious Dancer**[77] 1262 4-9-3 **59** PaddyBradley(3) 13 51
(Lee Carter) *hld up in rr: rdn under 3f out: nt qckn: kpt on fr 1f out: nrst fin* **14/1**

2333 **9** nk **Ertidaad (IRE)**[141] 430 4-8-12 **56** (b) GeorgeWood(5) 1 48
(Emma Owen) *settled bhd ldrs: rdn 3f out: sme prog tl wknd fr over 1f out* **9/1**

4400 **10** 4 **Bookmaker**[19] 2872 6-9-2 **60** (b) MitchGodwin(5) 14 42
(John Bridger) *led: rdn under 3f out: hdd 2f out: wknd fr over 1f out* **10/1**

0060 **11** 1¼ **Alketios (GR)**[13] 3064 5-9-4 **60** MeganNicholls(3) 5 39
(Chris Gordon) *in rr: nvr involved* **12/1**

0003 **12** 4½ **Bennelong**[36] 2326 10-9-3 **56** (b) JennyPowell 9 24
(Lee Carter) *broke wl and sn settled in mid-div: rdn over 2f out: hung rt and sn one pce: wknd fnl f* **12/1**

000- **13** 9 **Aspasius (GER)**[190] 8228 4-9-4 **57** HectorCrouch 12 4
(Gary Moore) *hld up in rr: rdn over 2f out: nvr involved* **25/1**

1m 39.97s (0.17) **Going Correction** +0.025s/f (Slow) **13** Ran SP% **123.2**
Speed ratings (Par 101): **100,99,97,96,96 95,94,93,93,89 88,83,74**
CSF £49.26 CT £341.99 TOTE £10.90: £4.00, £2.10, £3.80; EX 63.30 Trifecta £645.00.
Owner The Moonlighters **Bred** Jim McCormack **Trained** Trowbridge, Wilts

FOCUS
A moderate handicap run at an ordinary early gallop. Straightforward form.

3523 32RED H'CAP (LONDON MILE SERIES QUALIFIER) 1m (P)
6:50 (6:51) (Class 4) (0-85,85) 3-Y-O+ **£4,690** (£1,395; £697; £348) **Stalls** Low

Form RPR

-351 **1** **Bastille Day**[20] 2819 4-9-10 **81** PatDobbs 6 90
(David Elsworth) *chsd ldrs: gng wl over 2f out: rdn over 1f out and sn led: kpt on wl ins fnl f* **5/2**[1]

3444 **2** ¾ **Franco's Secret**[20] 2819 5-9-11 **82** (v) CharlesBishop 3 88
(Peter Hedger) *settled in mid-div: rdn 2f out: kpt on wl ins fnl f take 2nd nr fin* **5/1**[3]

-446 **3** ½ **Miniaturist (FR)**[13] 3079 3-8-9 **76** FrannyNorton 1 79
(Mark Johnston) *settled in rr of pack: tk clsr order over 2f out on inner: rdn 2f out: kpt on* **8/1**

61-0 **4** ¾ **Dream Of Summer (IRE)**[32] 2479 3-8-9 **76** TomQueally 5 77
(Andrew Balding) *led: rdn over 2f out: hdd over 1f out and wknd fnl f* **7/1**

-000 **5** ½ **Cornelious (IRE)**[27] 2623 4-8-9 **66** (v) AdamBeschizza 4 68
(Clifford Lines) *chsd ldr: rdn 2f out: kpt on tl wknd nr fin* **25/1**

6632 **6** 1½ **Dutch Art Dealer**[14] 3035 5-9-11 **82** (b) MartinHarley 8 80
(Paul Cole) *hld up in rr: nudged along ent st: rdn 2f out: nt qckn and sn one pce* **8/1**

2222 **7** 2½ **Ice Royal (IRE)**[20] 2818 3-9-4 **85** JamieSpencer 2 75+
(Jamie Osborne) *missed break and lost several l: grad ct up by 1/2-way: rdn over 2f out: one pce fnl f* **11/4**[2]

5-60 **8** 8 **Powderhorn (IRE)**[42] 2161 3-9-0 **81** JamesDoyle 7 52
(Mark Johnston) *in rr of pack: rdn over 2f out: nt qckn and wknd over 1f out: eased fnl f* **14/1**

1m 39.18s (-0.62) **Going Correction** +0.025s/f (Slow)
WFA 3 from 4yo+ 10lb **8** Ran SP% **117.1**
Speed ratings (Par 105): **104,103,102,102,101 100,97,89**
CSF £15.92 CT £88.05 TOTE £4.20: £1.20, £1.90, £3.10; EX 15.20 Trifecta £89.10.
Owner Lordship Stud & David Elsworth **Bred** New England Stud And Partners **Trained** Newmarket, Suffolk

FOCUS
The early gallop wasn't strong and they finished in a bit of a heap, but the winner is improving and can rate higher. The runner-up helps with the level.

3524 32RED.COM/BRITISH STALLION STUDS EBF NOVICE STKS 7f (P)
7:20 (7:20) (Class 5) 2-Y-O **£3,234** (£962; £481; £240) **Stalls** Low

Form RPR

1 **Permian (IRE)** 2-9-2 0 FrannyNorton 6 80+
(Mark Johnston) *disp ld: drvn 2f out: 1 l down on ldr over 1f out: shoved along 1f out: picked up wl fnl 110yds: led last stride* **8/1**

4 **2** nse **Aventinus (IRE)**[32] 2489 2-8-13 0 MarcMonaghan(3) 3 80
(Hugo Palmer) *mostly led: rdn over 2f out: clr ldr over 1f out: kpt on wl ins fnl f: hdd last stride* **5/2**[2]

3 2¾ **Tobrave (IRE)** 2-9-2 0 HarryBentley 1 73+
(Roger Varian) *t.k.h bhd ldrs: shkn up and pushed along under 2f out: nt qckn and kpt on under hands and heels fnl f: bttr for run* **5/1**[3]

6 **4** ½ **Outre Mer (IRE)**[22] 2757 2-9-2 0 JamesDoyle 5 71+
(John Gosden) *settled in mid-div: lost pl and rdn over 2f out: nt qckn tl kpt on wl ins fnl f: nrst fin* **5/4**[1]
05 **5** 1 ½ **Challow (IRE)**[19] 2873 2-9-2 0 JimCrowley 4 67
(Sylvester Kirk) *chsd ldrs: rdn over 2f out: sn no imp and one pce fnl f: eased nring fin* **10/1**
6 1 ½ **Shadow Warrior** 2-9-2 0 PatDobbs 2 63+
(Paul D'Arcy) *in rr: rdn 2f out: lft bhd 1f out: one pce* **50/1**
0 **7** 5 **General Allenby**[22] 2756 2-9-2 0 StevieDonohoe 7 50
(Henry Tett) *in rr: rdn over 2f out: prom on rail over 1f out: wknd qckly and eased fnl f* **100/1**
8 1 ½ **Alligator** 2-9-2 0 MartinHarley 8 46
(Ed Dunlop) *wnt lft s: in rr: rdn over 2f out: sn hld and eased fnl f* **33/1**

1m 27.26s (1.26) **Going Correction** +0.025s/f (Slow) **8** Ran SP% **115.8**
Speed ratings (Par 93): **93,92,89,89,87 85,80,78**
CSF £28.65 TOTE £9.40: £2.30, £2.00, £1.50; EX 37.40 Trifecta £155.80.
Owner Sheikh Hamdan bin Mohammed Al Maktoum **Bred** Darley **Trained** Middleham Moor, N Yorks

FOCUS
The early pace was steady and it paid to race handily. The race average helps with the level.

3525 32RED ON THE APP STORE H'CAP (LONDON MIDDLE DISTANCE SERIES QUALIFIER) 1m 3f (P)
7:50 (7:52) (Class 4) (0-85,85) 4-Y-O+ **£4,690** (£1,395; £697; £348) **Stalls** Low

Form RPR
2-23 **1** **Higher Power**[35] 2377 4-9-5 **83** TomQueally 3 91+
(James Fanshawe) *settled in mid-div: nudged along over 2f out: rdn over 1f out: led 1f out: kpt on wl ins fnl f* **7/4**[1]
2422 **2** 1 ¼ **Life Less Ordinary (IRE)**[18] 2888 4-9-5 **83** JamieSpencer 2 89
(Jamie Osborne) *in rr-div: gng wl over 2f out: rdn over 1f out: kpt on fnl f: hld 2nd post* **5/1**[2]
-021 **3** hd **Demonstration (IRE)**[13] 3057 4-9-7 **85** (p) JamesDoyle 5 91
(William Jarvis) *led: rdn 2f out: hdd 1f out: kpt on again ins fnl f: pressed for 2nd nr fin* **11/2**[3]
-035 **4** ¾ **Dolphin Village (IRE)**[26] 2663 6-9-0 **78** FrederikTylicki 10 83
(Jane Chapple-Hyam) *t.k.h in mid-div: rdn 2f out: prog ins fnl f* **10/1**
3232 **5** 3 **Taper Tantrum (IRE)**[7] 3276 4-8-12 **79** (v) LouisSteward(3) 6 79
(Michael Bell) *t.k.h chsng ldrs: rdn 2f out: kpt on tl wknd ins fnl f* **10/1**
1305 **6** ¾ **Viewpoint (IRE)**[6] 3304 7-9-3 **84** AlistairRawlinson(3) 4 82
(Michael Appleby) *in rr: shuffled along fr over 2f out to over 1f out: kpt on ins fnl f* **33/1**
-402 **7** hd **Sarsted**[35] 2377 4-9-5 **83** (b) RyanMoore 12 81
(Hughie Morrison) *chsd ldrs: rdn 2f out: one pce fr over 1f out* **8/1**
3002 **8** 4 ½ **Prendergast Hill (IRE)**[16] 2978 4-9-5 **83** JimCrowley 11 74
(Ed de Giles) *chsd ldrs: rdn over 2f out: one pce and wknd ins fnl f* **10/1**
10-0 **9** 5 **El Campeon**[30] 2549 4-8-11 **75** HarryBentley 7 58
(Simon Dow) *mid-div on outer: rdn over 2f out: wknd and eased fnl f* **50/1**
-000 **10** 4 ½ **Saoi (USA)**[41] 2176 9-9-4 **82** MartinHarley 9 60
(William Knight) *in rr: tk clsr order over 2f out: rdn and wknd qckly fnl f: eased* **20/1**
0000 **11** 4 ½ **El Tren (IRE)**[27] 2628 5-9-7 **85** (v) AdamBeschizza 8 56
(Michael Attwater) *in rr: nvr involved: eased fnl f* **100/1**

2m 18.18s (-3.72) **Going Correction** +0.025s/f (Slow) **11** Ran SP% **117.5**
Speed ratings (Par 105): **114,113,112,112,110 109,109,106,102,99 96**
CSF £9.88 CT £40.61 TOTE £2.70: £1.90, £1.50, £1.90; EX 12.10 Trifecta £58.90.
Owner Mrs Martin Armstrong **Bred** Mrs Martin Armstrong **Trained** Newmarket, Suffolk

FOCUS
Not a bad handicap, and it was run at a sound gallop. The field finished quite compressed and it's hard to rate the form higher.

3526 32RED CASINO/EBFSTALLIONS.COM NOVICE STKS (PLUS 10 RACE) 6f (P)
8:20 (8:20) (Class 4) 2-Y-O **£4,269** (£1,270; £634; £317) **Stalls** Low

Form RPR
2144 **1** **Mailshot (USA)**[25] 2669 2-9-8 0 JamesDoyle 7 86
(Mark Johnston) *sn led and set mod pce: rdn over 2f out: kpt on wl u.p ins fnl f* **10/3**[2]
53 **2** nk **Prerogative (IRE)**[22] 2757 2-9-2 0 PatDobbs 3 79
(Richard Hannon) *chsd ldrs: rdn 2f out: kpt on ins fnl f to press wnr nr fin* **11/2**[3]
3 nk **Bellevarde (IRE)** 2-8-11 0 FrederikTylicki 5 73+
(James Fanshawe) *chsd ldr: rdn 2f out: ev ch under 2f out: kpt on again nr fin* **8/1**
15 **4** 3 ¼ **Tibr (USA)**[19] 2865 2-9-8 0 RyanMoore 4 74
(Ed Dunlop) *settled in mid-div: pushed along over 2f out: no prog fr over 1f out* **8/11**[1]
5 1 ¾ **Rita's Man (IRE)** 2-9-2 0 KieranO'Neill 8 63
(Richard Hannon) *chsd ldrs: rdn over 2f out and lost pl w ldng trio: sn one pce* **33/1**
6 1 ¾ **Elementary** 2-9-2 0 WilliamCarson 6 58
(Michael Bell) *in rr: pushed along over 1f out: nt clr run under hands and heels fnl f: kpt on* **33/1**
4 **7** hd **Nicky Baby (IRE)**[30] 2543 2-9-2 0 RobertWinston 2 57
(Dean Ivory) *in rr-div: rdn over 2f out on rail: limited prog and wknd over 1f out* **33/1**

1m 13.77s (0.67) **Going Correction** +0.025s/f (Slow) **7** Ran SP% **116.3**
Speed ratings (Par 95): **96,95,95,90,88 86,85**
CSF £21.82 TOTE £4.10: £1.90, £2.50; EX 23.10 Trifecta £106.40.
Owner Sheikh Hamdan bin Mohammed Al Maktoum **Bred** Darley **Trained** Middleham Moor, N Yorks
■ Stewards' Enquiry : Pat Dobbs two-day ban: use of whip (6-7 July)

FOCUS
A decent novice, but the pace wasn't strong early and the first three maintained their advantage throughout. The form is rated around the race average.

3527 £10 FREE BET AT 32REDSPORT.COM FILLIES' H'CAP (JOCKEY CLUB GRASSROOTS SPRINT SERIES QUALIFIER) 6f (P)
8:50 (8:52) (Class 5) (0-70,68) 3-Y-O+ **£2,911** (£866; £432; £216) **Stalls** Low

Form RPR
000 **1** **Dance Band (IRE)**[18] 2904 3-8-13 **60** [1] HarryBentley 6 69+
(Roger Varian) *chsd ldrs: rdn 2f out: led 110yds out: kpt on wl nr fin* **7/1**
1304 **2** ½ **Tigserin (IRE)**[20] 2824 3-9-4 **65** JackMitchell 4 72
(Giles Bravery) *half-rrd ss: in rr: nudged along over 2f out: swtchd to outer and drvn over 1f out: str run ins fnl f: tk 2nd 100yds out and pressed wnr nr fin* **4/1**[3]
2-05 **3** 1 ¼ **Langham**[35] 2375 3-9-4 **68** JosephineGordon(3) 3 71
(Martyn Meade) *led: rdn 2f out: kpt on wl tl hdd 110yds out: lost 2nd nr fin* **7/2**[2]
44-0 **4** nk **Regal Miss**[34] 2403 4-9-6 **63** DanielMuscutt(3) 5 67
(Patrick Chamings) *chsd ldrs: upsides 2f out: rdn jst over 1f out: kpt on one pce fnl f* **12/1**
-404 **5** 1 **Angie's Girl**[16] 2980 3-9-3 **64** JohnFahy 2 63
(Clive Cox) *tk fierce hold early in mid-div: rdn on inner over 1f out: sn one pce and hld* **3/1**[1]
4206 **6** ½ **She's All Mine**[20] 2824 3-9-1 **62** PatDobbs 7 60
(Richard Hannon) *settled in mid-div: rdn 2f out: one pce ent fnl f* **14/1**
0030 **7** ¾ **Sakhee's Rose**[21] 2794 6-9-6 **60** (b) JimCrowley 9 57
(Ed McMahon) *hld up in rr: rdn and one pce fr 2f out: nvr involved* **16/1**
4612 **8** 3 ¼ **Guapo Bay**[29] 2560 3-7-12 **52** TinaSmith(7) 8 37
(Richard Hannon) *mid-div on outer: rdn 2f out: no imp and one pce fr over 1f out* **9/1**
-606 **9** ½ **Foxinthehenhouse**[28] 2585 3-9-4 **65** FrederikTylicki 1 48
(J R Jenkins) *chsd ldrs: rdn 2f out: wknd qckly fr over 1f out: eased* **16/1**

1m 13.17s (0.07) **Going Correction** +0.025s/f (Slow)
WFA 3 from 4yo+ 7lb **9** Ran SP% **115.8**
Speed ratings (Par 100): **100,99,97,97,95 95,94,89,89**
CSF £35.26 CT £115.49 TOTE £6.10: £2.30, £1.70, £3.00; EX 44.50 Trifecta £200.80.
Owner Cheveley Park Stud **Bred** Ballylinch Stud **Trained** Newmarket, Suffolk

FOCUS
A modest fillies' handicap. The winner can do better than this.

3528 RACING UK H'CAP 2m (P)
9:20 (9:22) (Class 6) (0-65,65) 4-Y-O+ **£2,264** (£673; £336; £168) **Stalls** Low

Form RPR
4200 **1** **Delagoa Bay (IRE)**[26] 2634 8-8-0 **51** ow3 MitchGodwin(7) 2 56
(Sylvester Kirk) *hld up in mid-div: impr position 3f out: drvn and clsd on ldr fr over 1f out: led ins fnl f: cosily* **12/1**
/004 **2** ¾ **Intimidator (IRE)**[14] 3041 5-8-8 **55** DanielMuscutt(3) 7 59
(Miss Joey Ellis) *chsd ldr: travelling wl over 3f out: led over 1f out: sn rdn and hdd ins fnl f: one pce nr fin* **33/1**
3632 **3** 4 ½ **Prince Of Islay (IRE)**[12] 3099 5-8-9 **53** (b) FrannyNorton 11 52
(Amanda Perrett) *chsd ldr: led over 4f out: rdn over 2f out: hdd over 1f out: one pce fnl f* **6/1**[2]
-443 **4** 3 ¾ **Madame Lafite**[12] 3099 4-9-5 **63** FrederikTylicki 13 57
(Jonathan Portman) *settled in mid-div: rdn over 2f out: kpt on under hands and heels fnl f: nrst fin* **6/1**[2]
50-0 **5** 3 ¼ **The Lampo Genie**[15] 38 4-9-5 **63** StevieDonohoe 10 53
(Johnny Farrelly) *hld up in rr: rdn over 2f out: prog past btn horses over 1f out: one pce* **25/1**
30-0 **6** nk **Ginger Fizz**[13] 3067 9-8-10 **57** (tp) JackDuern(3) 9 47
(Ben Case) *chsd ldrs: rdn along over 3f out: one pce after* **25/1**
7 2 ¼ **Harristown**[28] 6-8-11 **55** (p) JamieSpencer 5 42
(Charlie Longsdon) *hld up in rr: rdn over 3f out: bmpd over 2f out: kpt on one pce* **3/1**[1]
5040 **8** ½ **Dukes Den**[18] 2916 5-8-4 **51** (v[1]) JosephineGordon(3) 3 38
(Mark Usher) *hld up in rr: rdn over 3f out: kpt on one pce fr over 1f out: nvr involved* **6/1**[2]
-510 **9** 1 ½ **King Olav (UAE)**[125] 619 11-9-7 **65** JimCrowley 1 50
(Tony Carroll) *settled in mid-div: rdn over 3f out: sn no imp* **12/1**
5221 **10** 5 **Jezza**[54] 1831 10-9-1 **64** (bt) CallumShepherd(5) 8 43
(Victor Dartnall) *in rr: rdn over 3f out: nvr involved* **10/1**
30-4 **11** 4 ½ **Westerly**[105] 882 5-9-6 **64** KieranO'Neill 14 37
(Luke Dace) *settled in mid-div: rdn to chse ldng trio over 3f out: wknd over 1f out* **25/1**
0-63 **12** 11 **Moncarno**[14] 3041 6-9-0 **58** KierenFox 12 18
(John Best) *in rr: rdn over 3f out: sn one pce: eased: t.o* **25/1**
-450 **13** 9 **Hall Of Beauty**[13] 3067 4-8-2 **46** RyanPowell 6
(Michael Appleby) *chsd ldrs: rdn 4f out: sn lost pl and wknd ent st: t.o* **33/1**
6310 **14** 85 **Tarakkom (FR)**[31] 2501 4-9-2 **60** WilliamCarson 4
(Peter Hiatt) *led: rdn and hdd 4f out: wknd v qckly and eased fr 2f out* **7/1**[3]

3m 29.79s (-0.31) **Going Correction** +0.025s/f (Slow) **14** Ran SP% **126.1**
Speed ratings (Par 101): **101,100,98,96,94 94,93,93,92,90 87,82,77,35**
CSF £378.25 CT £2616.24 TOTE £11.70: £4.30, £10.40, £2.60; EX 685.60 Trifecta £2335.10 Part won..
Owner Homebred Racing **Bred** J Ryan **Trained** Upper Lambourn, Berks

FOCUS
An ordinary staying handicap, but it was run at a good pace. The winner is rated just above her recent form.
T/Plt: £32.80 to a £1 stake. Pool of £61159.0 - 1358.42 winning tickets. T/Qpdt: £7.30 to a £1 stake. Pool of £3972.40 - 399.60 winning tickets. **Cathal Gahan**

3192 SALISBURY (R-H)
Wednesday, June 22

OFFICIAL GOING: Soft (6.4)
Wind: mild breeze against Weather: sunny periods

3529 WHITSBURY MANOR STUD EBF STALLIONS BLAGRAVE MAIDEN STKS (PLUS 10 RACE) 6f 212y
2:10 (2:10) (Class 4) 2-Y-O **£4,528** (£1,347; £673; £336) **Stalls** Centre

Form RPR
1 **Jackhammer (IRE)** 2-9-5 0 GeorgeBaker 11 76
(William Knight) *racd stands' side: hld up: hdwy over 2f out: rdn to ld ent fnl f: r.o wl* **25/1**
2 **2** 2 ¼ **Sea Fox (IRE)**[13] 3058 2-9-5 0 FMBerry 1 70+
(David Evans) *hld up in gp of 4 far side: hdwy whn swtchd to stands' side gp over 2f out: rdn and ev ch ent fnl f: kpt on but nt pce of wnr* **5/4**[1]
4 **3** 1 **Native Prospect**[32] 2478 2-9-5 0 OisinMurphy 12 68
(Andrew Balding) *racd stands' side: trckd ldrs: rdn over 2f out: kpt on ins fnl f* **8/1**
6 **4** 1 **Star Maker**[12] 3108 2-9-5 0 JimCrowley 7 65
(Sylvester Kirk) *racd stands' side: trckd ldr: rdn over 2f out: kpt on same pce fnl f* **7/1**[3]
5 ¾ **Eolian** 2-9-5 0 MartinHarley 6 63+
(William Knight) *racd stands' side: sn pushed along towards rr: hdwy over 1f out: r.o nicely fnl f* **25/1**

0 **6** *nk* **Crucial Moment**[81] 1199 2-9-2 0 TimClark(3) 9 62
(Bill Turner) *led stands' side gp: prom overall: rdn 2f out: ev ch over 1f out: no ex fnl 120yds* **66/1**

00 **7** *3/4* **Hawridge Glory (IRE)**[15] 2997 2-9-5 0 FrederikTylicki 13 60
(Rod Millman) *racd stands' side: racd keenly in mid-div: rdn over 2f out: no imp* **66/1**

8 *1/2* **Geneva Convention (IRE)** 2-9-5 0 SeanLevey 2 59+
(Richard Hannon) *led far side gp and overall ldr: rdn over 2f out: drifted to stands' side gp over 1f out: hdd ent fnl f: no ex* **9/1**

0 **9** *2* **Buskin River (IRE)**[26] 2649 2-9-5 0 PatDobbs 3 54+
(Richard Hannon) *racd far side: trckd ldr: rdn over 2f out: drifted lft over 1f out: sn wknd* **9/2**[2]

4 **10** *6* **Limelight Lady**[52] 1895 2-9-0 0 RichardKingscote 14 33
(Harry Dunlop) *racd stands' side: trckd ldr tl rdn over 2f out: sn wknd* **40/1**

11 *4* **Dewan (IRE)** 2-9-5 0 SilvestreDeSousa 5 28+
(Mick Channon) *s.i.s: racd far side: chsd ldrs: swtchd to stands' side over 3f out: sn rdn: wknd fnl f* **12/1**

12 *15* **Sir Plato (IRE)** 2-9-5 0 RyanTate 10
(Rod Millman) *racd stands' side: sn pushed along towards rr: hdwy 3f out: wknd over 1f out* **50/1**

1m 32.27s (3.67) **Going Correction** +0.425s/f (Yiel) **12** Ran SP% **119.0**
Speed ratings (Par 95): **96,93,92,91,90 89,89,88,86,79 74,57**
CSF £55.53 TOTE £24.30: £5.60, £1.10, £3.00; EX 75.80 Trifecta £971.50.
Owner The Oil Men Partnership 1 **Bred** F Dunne **Trained** Patching, W Sussex

FOCUS
After another 1mm of rain in the morning the going remained soft, good to soft in places and the jockeys in the opener confirmed that the ground was soft. Quite a decent maiden to start and an impressive winner, but a slightly messy race as they split into two groups early with four starting off on the far side while the rest came up the nearside. The quartet who started off on the far side eventually made their way over to join the main group at various stages of the contest. This looked quite a test for these 2yos with the winning time 6.27sec outside standard. The favourite is rated a bit below his previous.

3530 INSPIRE FOUNDATION VETERANS' H'CAP 5f
2:40 (2:42) (Class 4) (0-80,75) 6-Y-O+ **£5,175** (£1,540; £769; £384) **Stalls** Low

Form RPR
13-4 **1** **Silverrica (IRE)**[11] 3123 6-9-4 **75** JosephineGordon(3) 6 81
(Malcolm Saunders) *trckd ldrs: rdn over 1f out: r.o ins fnl f: led towards fin: hld on* **11/4**[1]

0252 **2** *hd* **New Rich**[8] 3258 6-8-11 **65** (v[1]) JohnFahy 3 70
(Eve Johnson Houghton) *chsd ldrs: rdn 2f out: swtchd rt and kpt on wl fnl 75yds: snatched 2nd fnl stride: jst failed* **3/1**[2]

600 **3** *shd* **Angel Way (IRE)**[52] 1898 7-8-10 **67** MichaelJMMurphy(3) 1 72
(John Gallagher) *pressed ldr: rdn to ld narrowly ent fnl f: no ex whn hdd towards fin* **6/1**

0000 **4** *1 1/2* **Keep It Dark**[11] 3159 7-9-3 **71** MartinHarley 2 71
(William Knight) *led: rdn 2f out: narrowly hdd ent fnl f: no ex fnl 75yds* **6/1**

0205 **5** *3 3/4* **Perfect Pastime**[32] 2469 8-8-13 **67** (p) SamHitchcott 5 53
(Jim Boyle) *s.i.s: a outpcd in last pair: nvr on terms* **9/2**[3]

0553 **6** *4 1/2* **Swendab (IRE)**[12] 3098 8-8-8 **67** (v) CiaranMckee(5) 4 37
(John O'Shea) *burst stalls open but slowly away: a struggling in last pair: nvr on terms* **6/1**

1m 3.13s (2.13) **Going Correction** +0.425s/f (Yiel) **6** Ran SP% **112.7**
Speed ratings: **99,98,98,96,90 82**
CSF £11.38 TOTE £2.80: £1.60, £2.10; EX 9.40 Trifecta £51.60.
Owner Mrs Ginny Nicholas **Bred** Miss A R Byrne **Trained** Green Ore, Somerset

FOCUS
A fair sprint handicap for 6yos and upwards. All six runners came up the nearside rail and the principals finished in a bit of a heap. The form is rated around the front three.

3531 NEW FOREST FARM MACHINERY/JOHN DEERE AUCTION STKS (CONDITIONS RACE) (PLUS 10 RACE) 6f
3:10 (3:10) (Class 3) 2-Y-O **£7,115** (£2,117; £1,058; £529) **Stalls** Low

Form RPR
12 **1** **Groupie**[11] 3122 2-8-2 0 ow1 TomMarquand(3) 6 82
(Richard Hannon) *trckd ldrs: rdn to ld whn drifted lft ent fnl f: r.o: a holding on* **3/1**[2]

6311 **2** *1/2* **Mistime (IRE)**[12] 3100 2-8-3 0 FrannyNorton 4 82
(Mark Johnston) *led for 2f: rdn in cl 3rd whn short of room and snatched up ent fnl f: hld after but r.o wl whn swtchd rt: wnt 2nd towards fin* **4/5**[1]

4116 **3** *1/2* **Sayesse**[19] 2865 2-8-4 0 SilvestreDeSousa 5 78
(Mick Channon) *prom: led after 2f out: rdn and hdd whn carried lft ent fnl f: kpt on but no ex fnl 75yds* **4/1**[3]

4 *4 1/2* **Black Bubba (IRE)** 2-8-4 0 KieranO'Neill 2 65
(David Evans) *hld up bhd ldrs: rdn over 2f out: nt pce to threaten* **20/1**

03 **5** *9* **Jumping Jack (IRE)**[50] 1944 2-8-10 0 ShaneKelly 7 44
(Richard Hughes) *hld up bhd ldrs: rdn over 2f out: nvr threatened: wknd over 1f out* **33/1**

1m 18.03s (3.23) **Going Correction** +0.425s/f (Yiel) **5** Ran SP% **108.3**
Speed ratings (Par 97): **95,94,93,87,75**
CSF £5.62 TOTE £3.90: £1.90, £1.10; EX 5.90 Trifecta £8.90.
Owner Mrs J K Powell **Bred** John M Troy **Trained** East Everleigh, Wilts
■ Stewards' Enquiry : Tom Marquand caution: careless riding

FOCUS
An interesting little auction event and again they came up the stands' side. Things got a bit tight between the front three coming to the last furlong and the stewards took a look, but they allowed the result to stand. Straightforward form.

3532 WHITSBURY MANOR STUD BIBURY CUP (H'CAP) 1m 4f
3:45 (3:45) (Class 3) (0-95,87) 3-Y-O
£13,695 (£4,100; £2,050; £1,025; £512; £257) **Stalls** Low

Form RPR
-621 **1** **Marmajuke Bay**[27] 2615 3-8-9 **75** (p) SteveDrowne 4 83
(Mark Usher) *trckd ldrs: rdn to ld jst over 1f out: styd on wl fnl f* **10/1**

-221 **2** *3/4* **Rex Bell (IRE)**[9] 3235 3-9-3 **86** 6ex (p) KieranShoemark(3) 5 93
(John Gosden) *led: rdn whn edgd lft and hdd jst over 1f out: styd on gamely but hld fnl 120yds* **7/1**

6-11 **3** *1 1/4* **Master Blueyes (IRE)**[25] 2687 3-9-3 **83** WilliamTwiston-Davies 2 88
(Alan King) *hld up bhd ldrs: hdwy over 2f out: rdn to chal over 1f out: kpt on tl no ex fnl 120yds* **5/2**[1]

-521 **4** *1* **The Graduate (IRE)**[25] 2700 3-8-7 **73** OisinMurphy 6 77
(Andrew Balding) *trckd ldr: chal 3f out tl 2f out: cl up but hld whn squeezed up jst over 1f out: styd on same pce* **4/1**[2]

1-14 **5** *1* **Mainstream**[32] 2471 3-9-7 **87** RyanMoore 3 89
(Sir Michael Stoute) *dwlt: 6/7 l detached tl latched onto main gp after 3f: hdwy 3f out: sn rdn: ev ch ent fnl f tl fdd fnl 120yds* **5/2**[1]

15 **6** *4 1/2* **Combative**[34] 2413 3-9-7 **87** JimCrowley 1 82
(Amanda Perrett) *trckd ldrs: rdn 3f out: sn one pce* **11/2**[3]

2m 41.45s (3.45) **Going Correction** +0.35s/f (Good) **6** Ran SP% **114.1**
Speed ratings (Par 103): **102,101,100,100,99 96**
CSF £75.03 TOTE £13.40: £3.80, £3.40; EX 75.90 Trifecta £392.20.
Owner The Ridgeway Alchemist's **Bred** The Welldiggers Partnership **Trained** Upper Lambourn, Berks
■ Stewards' Enquiry : Kieran Shoemark four-day ban: use of whip (6-7, 11-12 Jul)

FOCUS
A decent 3yo middle-distance handicap won last year by the subsequent dual Group 1 winner Simple Verse (at 14-1!). A small field this time, but four of the six had won their most recent starts and the form should work out. The field came over to the stands' side after turning for home. The winner stepped up on his latest win.

3533 H S LESTER MEMORIAL H'CAP 1m 6f 21y
4:20 (4:21) (Class 4) (0-85,85) 4-Y-O+ **£5,175** (£1,540; £769; £384) **Stalls** Far side

Form RPR
0-51 **1** **Hatsaway (IRE)**[50] 1947 5-8-2 **66** JFEgan 6 79+
(Pat Phelan) *hld up: smooth hdwy over 4f out: led over 2f out: sn edgd lft: rdn clr over 1f out: styd on strly: comf* **20/1**

0-42 **2** *3 3/4* **Champagne Champ**[28] 2582 4-8-13 **77** FrederikTylicki 4 85
(Rod Millman) *trckd ldrs: rdn over 2f out: chal for hld 2nd over 1f out: wnt 2nd fnl strides: no ch w wnr* **8/1**[3]

3611 **3** *hd* **Touch The Sky**[11] 3161 5-9-7 **85** OisinMurphy 2 93
(David Elsworth) *led: rdn and hdd over 2f out: readily hld by wnr over 1f out: styd on but no ex whn lost 2nd fnl strides* **3/1**[2]

6-63 **4** *10* **Ivanhoe**[18] 2887 6-8-2 **66** oh1 (p) KieranO'Neill 9 61
(Michael Blanshard) *mid-div: rdn over 3f out: wnt hld 4th over 1f out: styd on same pce* **25/1**

3244 **5** *1 1/4* **Music Man (IRE)**[51] 1934 6-8-13 **77** FergusSweeney 3 70
(Laura Mongan) *mid-div: rdn 4f out: styd on same pce fnl 2f: nvr threatened to get involved* **20/1**

6 *hd* **Dell' Arca (IRE)**[46] 7-9-0 **78** (b) RyanMoore 10 71
(David Pipe) *trckd ldrs: rdn over 3f out: sn one pce* **9/4**[1]

0353 **7** *4 1/2* **Agent Gibbs**[10] 3192 4-9-5 **83** SilvestreDeSousa 8 70
(John O'Shea) *hld up: rdn 4f out: swtchd lft over 3f out: nvr any imp* **10/1**

5015 **8** *8* **Bohemian Rhapsody (IRE)**[17] 2932 7-8-12 **76** (p) FMBerry 11 53
(Brendan Powell) *hld up: hdwy over 4f out: sn rdn: nvr threatened: wknd over 1f out* **14/1**

0-45 **9** *14* **Forced Family Fun**[34] 2399 6-8-13 **77** SteveDrowne 5 36
(George Baker) *rn in snatches: towards rr: short-lived effrt over 3f out: nvr threatened: wknd 2f out* **8/1**[3]

1420 **10** *6* **Knight's Parade (IRE)**[16] 2971 6-8-11 **75** (t) JimCrowley 7 26
(Sarah Humphrey) *kpt wd 1st 3f: trckd ldr: rdn over 4f out: wknd over 2f out* **50/1**

55-2 **11** *23* **Opera Lad (IRE)**[54] 1824 4-8-10 **74** DavidProbert 1
(Andrew Balding) *w ldr tl rdn over 4f out: wknd 3f out: eased fnl 2f* **10/1**

3m 9.96s (2.56) **Going Correction** +0.35s/f (Good) **11** Ran SP% **118.2**
Speed ratings (Par 105): **106,103,103,98,97 97,94,90,82,78 65**
CSF £165.88 CT £626.56 TOTE £22.40: £5.90, £2.90, £1.50; EX 203.60 Trifecta £1042.50.
Owner P Wheatley **Bred** Grangecon Stud **Trained** Epsom, Surrey

FOCUS
This race was started by flag. A fair staying handicap run at a reasonable pace, but the conditions seemed to find out plenty of these and they finished well spread out. Again they came up the nearside rail in the straight. The winner has better back form than this.

3534 MOLSON COORS H'CAP 1m
4:50 (4:53) (Class 2) (0-100,95) 3-Y-O+
£12,450 (£3,728; £1,864; £932; £466; £234) **Stalls** Low

Form RPR
51-4 **1** **Storm Ahead (IRE)**[18] 2891 3-8-5 **82** RoystonFfrench 3 92
(Marcus Tregoning) *trckd ldrs: rdn over 2f out: led ent fnl f: r.o wl* **10/1**[3]

-124 **2** *2 3/4* **Sinfonietta (FR)**[39] 2246 4-9-9 **90** ShaneKelly 5 96
(David Menuisier) *led: rdn 2f out: hdd ent fnl f: kpt on but no ex* **5/1**[2]

1050 **3** *1/2* **Australian Queen**[19] 2869 3-8-13 **90** OisinMurphy 10 93
(David Elsworth) *hld up towards rr: rdn and stdy prog fr 2f out: swtchd rt fnl f: r.o: wnt 3rd towards fin* **14/1**

540 **4** *1/2* **Palawan**[6] 3299 3-9-4 **95** RyanMoore 9 97
(Richard Hannon) *trckd ldrs: rdn over 2f out: nt quite pce to chal: no ex fnl 100yds* **11/1**

5535 **5** *3/4* **Dance Of Fire**[32] 2484 4-9-6 **87** (p) DavidProbert 14 89
(Andrew Balding) *prom tl rdn over 2f out: kpt on same pce fnl f* **16/1**

-000 **6** *3/4* **Fire Ship**[20] 2819 7-9-4 **85** SilvestreDeSousa 6 86
(William Knight) *mid-div: bmpd over 4f out: rdn and hdwy over 2f out: one pce fnl f* **14/1**

0060 **7** *1 3/4* **The Warrior (IRE)**[21] 2796 4-9-11 **92** JimCrowley 8 89
(Amanda Perrett) *hld up towards rr: hdwy over 3f out: sn rdn: fdd ins fnl f* **33/1**

0-05 **8** *1 1/2* **Czech It Out (IRE)**[34] 2391 6-9-7 **88** PatDobbs 1 81
(Amanda Perrett) *hld up towards rr: rdn over 2f out: no imp tl styd on fnl f: n.d* **20/1**

-330 **9** *nk* **Hail Clodius (IRE)**[39] 2246 4-9-4 **85** SeanLevey 2 78
(Richard Hannon) *trckd ldr tl rdn over 2f out: wknd fnl f* **20/1**

106- **10** *4 1/2* **Welford**[285] 6274 3-9-2 **93** FrannyNorton 4 74
(Mark Johnston) *trckd ldrs: rdn over 2f out: wknd fnl f* **25/1**

0500 **11** *4* **Kinglami**[23] 2754 7-8-12 **79** FergusSweeney 12 53
(John O'Shea) *hld up: hdwy 3f out: sn rdn: wknd fnl f* **100/1**

6455 **12** *2 3/4* **Cordite (IRE)**[19] 2868 5-9-2 **83** SamHitchcott 11 51
(Jim Boyle) *mid-div: rdn 3f out: wknd over 1f out* **33/1**

1-2 **13** *10* **Next Stage**[18] 2891 3-8-11 **88** JamesDoyle 13 32
(Saeed bin Suroor) *mid-div: rdn over 2f out: nvr any imp: eased whn btn fnl f* **6/5**[1]

1m 44.98s (1.48) **Going Correction** +0.40s/f (Good)
WFA 3 from 4yo+ 10lb **13** Ran SP% **119.0**
Speed ratings (Par 109): **108,105,104,104,103 102,101,99,99,94 90,87,77**
CSF £54.52 CT £735.01 TOTE £13.40: £3.30, £1.90, £4.20; EX 77.40 Trifecta £1107.70.
Owner Guy Brook **Bred** Victor Stud And Brendan Cummins **Trained** Whitsbury, Hants

FOCUS
A warm handicap, but they bet 10-1 bar three. They appeared to go an even pace up the nearside rail. The winner built on his good reappearance.

3535 PAM ROBERTSHAW BIRTHDAY CELEBRATION EBF STALLIONS MAIDEN STKS 1m 1f 198y
5:20 (5:22) (Class 5) 3-Y-O+ **£4,204** (£1,251; £625; £312) **Stalls** Low

Form RPR
2-22 **1** **Wave Reviews**[27] 2619 3-9-0 81....................................(p) RyanMoore 11 83+
(William Haggas) *mid-div: hdwy 5f out: rdn to chal 2f out: led ent fnl f: styd on wl: rdn out* **4/6**[1]
32 **2** *2 1/4* **Gibbs Hill (GER)**[18] 2914 3-9-0 0.................................... HarryBentley 13 79+
(Roger Varian) *trckd ldrs: led 2f out: sn rdn: hdd ent fnl f: no ex* **5/2**[2]
3 *2 1/2* **Attest** 3-9-0 0.. JimCrowley 4 74
(Amanda Perrett) *mid-div: nt clr run over 3f out: hdwy over 2f out: styd on to go 3rd fnl f but nt pce of front pair* **20/1**
4-0 **4** *1* **Rehearse (IRE)**[26] 2640 3-9-0 0.. OisinMurphy 8 72
(Andrew Balding) *trckd ldr: chal over 2f out: rdn and ev ch sn after tl jst over 1f out: no ex fnl f* **50/1**
5 *1 1/2* **Coeur De Lion** 3-9-0 0.. FergusSweeney 9 69
(Alan King) *mid-div: bmpd ins 1st f: rdn 3f out: styd on but nt pce to get on terms* **40/1**
0 **6** *hd* **Royal Occassion**[34] 2414 4-9-12 0.................................. SamHitchcott 2 68
(Jim Boyle) *led: rdn and hdd 2f out: sn no ex* **66/1**
7 *1 1/2* **Dance The Dream** 3-8-9 0... MartinDwyer 7 60+
(Marcus Tregoning) *hmpd ins 1st f: towards rr: styd on past btn horses fr over 1f out: nvr on terms* **25/1**
8 *2 1/4* **Pure Innocence (IRE)** 3-8-9 0... FMBerry 6 56
(Ralph Beckett) *snatched up ins 1st f: towards rr: hdwy over 2f out: nvr threatened: wknd ins fnl f* **10/1**[3]
0- **9** *7* **Great And Small**[190] 8232 3-8-9 0.................................... DavidProbert 1 42
(Andrew Balding) *mid-div: rdn 3f out: wknd over 1f out* **16/1**
10 *4* **Silk Suit (FR)** 3-9-0 0... LemosdeSouza 10 39
(Luca Cumani) *s.i.s: hung lft fnl 2f: a towards rr* **25/1**
0 **11** *3/4* **Tractive Effort**[20] 2815 3-9-0 0... KierenFox 3 37
(Michael Attwater) *trckd ldrs: rdn over 2f out: sn wknd* **200/1**
0-5 **12** *hd* **Voices Of Kings**[172] 15 3-9-0 0............................ RoystonFfrench 12 37
(William Muir) *trckd ldrs tl rdn over 3f out: sn wknd* **80/1**

2m 13.26s (3.36) **Going Correction** +0.35s/f (Good)
WFA 3 from 4yo 12lb **12** Ran SP% **123.6**
Speed ratings (Par 103): **100,98,96,95,94 94,92,91,85,82 81,81**
CSF £2.32 TOTE £1.60: £1.02, £1.60, £5.50; EX 3.90 Trifecta £23.40.
Owner Nicholas Jones **Bred** Coln Valley Stud **Trained** Newmarket, Suffolk
FOCUS
An ordinary and uncompetitive older-horse maiden with the finish dominated by the two form horses. The form is rated around the second.
T/Plt: £106.50 to a £1 stake. Pool of £45962.28 - 314.90 winning tickets. T/Qpdt: £26.60 to a £1 stake. Pool of £2839.04 - 78.90 winning tickets. **Tim Mitchell**

3536 - 3538a (Foreign Racing) - See Raceform Interactive

2715 NAAS (L-H)
Wednesday, June 22
OFFICIAL GOING: Good to yielding

3539a CORAL.IE EUROPEAN BREEDERS FUND NAAS OAKS TRIAL (LISTED RACE) 1m 2f
7:30 (7:33) 3-Y-O
£23,860 (£7,683; £3,639; £1,617; £808; £404)

RPR
1 **Discipline**[59] 1680 3-9-0 102... PatSmullen 10 96+
(D K Weld, Ire) *trckd ldr in 2nd: travelled wl 2f out: led appr fnl f: sn rdn to assert: kpt on wl in clsng stages* **9/10**[1]
2 *1/2* **Earring (USA)**[28] 2596 3-9-0 95................................(t) SeamieHeffernan 9 95
(A P O'Brien, Ire) *sn led: strly pressed under 2f out: hdd appr fnl f: rallied wl tl no ex w wnr in clsng stages* **5/1**[2]
3 *3/4* **How High The Moon (IRE)**[10] 3202 3-9-0 94......(p) ColmO'Donoghue 2 94+
(A P O'Brien, Ire) *t.k.h to trck ldrs in 3rd: pushed along in 4th over 2f out: wnt 3rd appr fnl f: kpt on wl wout rching principals* **9/1**
4 *1/2* **Red Stars (IRE)**[73] 1369 3-9-0 93............................ DeclanMcDonogh 8 93+
(John M Oxx, Ire) *chsd ldrs in 4th: rdn in 3rd over 2f out: nt qckn in 4th appr fnl f: kpt on same pce* **12/1**
5 *1/2* **Planchart (USA)**[42] 2171 3-9-0 90... BillyLee 4 92
(Andrew Slattery, Ire) *chsd ldrs: rdn in 5th over 2f out: nt qckn over 1f out in 7th: kpt on wl again ins fnl f into 5th in clsng stages* **8/1**[3]
6 *1/2* **Santa Monica**[19] 2883 3-9-0 98... ChrisHayes 3 91+
(Charles O'Brien, Ire) *racd in rr: stmbld after 3f: prog whn swtchd to outer 2f out: wnt 5th appr fnl f: sn no imp: kpt on one pce* **16/1**
7 *1* **Siamsaiocht (IRE)**[10] 3202 3-9-0 91.........................(tp) KevinManning 5 89
(J S Bolger, Ire) *hld up: rdn towards rr 2f out: prog on inner over 1f out: no imp and wknd ins fnl 100yds* **14/1**
8 *3 3/4* **Just Joan (IRE)**[17] 2939 3-9-0 82.................................... WayneLordan 6 81
(T Stack, Ire) *racd in mid-div: pushed along and dropped towards rr 2f out: sn one pce* **33/1**
9 *12* **Californiadreaming (IRE)**[6] 3329 3-9-0 80...................(tp) AnaO'Brien 1 57
(A P O'Brien, Ire) *racd in mid-div on inner: rdn and nt qckn over 1f out: sn wknd: eased in clsng stages* **50/1**
10 *4 3/4* **Like A Star (IRE)**[77] 1280 3-9-0 0.............................. DonnachaO'Brien 7 48
(A P O'Brien, Ire) *a towards rr: rdn and dropped to rr 2f out: sn detached: eased ins fnl f* **16/1**

2m 14.3s (-1.30) **10** Ran SP% **121.4**
CSF £5.88 TOTE £2.00: £1.02, £2.20, £2.80; DF 6.20 Trifecta £11.40.
Owner K Abdullah **Bred** Juddmonte Farms Ltd **Trained** Curragh, Co Kildare
■ Stewards' Enquiry : Seamie Heffernan one-day ban: used whip above shoulder height (tbn)
FOCUS
Not the strongest of Listed races on the face of it but the first two are unexposed and could be better than this grade. Both are daughters of Dansili.

3540 - 3542a (Foreign Racing) - See Raceform Interactive

3450 CHANTILLY (R-H)
Wednesday, June 22
OFFICIAL GOING: Turf: soft; polytrack: standard

3543a PRIX DAPHNIS (GROUP 3) (3YO COLTS & GELDINGS) (TURF) 1m 1f
11:56 (12:00) 3-Y-O **£29,411** (£11,764; £8,823; £5,882; £2,941)

RPR
1 **Taareef (USA)**[38] 2283 3-8-11 0................................. IoritzMendizabal 3 108
(J-C Rouget, France) *hld up: rdn 3f out: styd on steadily and chal wl ins fnl f: got up to ld cl home* **4/1**[2]
2 *3/4* **George Patton (USA)**[38] 2283 3-8-11 0..........(p) ChristopheSoumillon 1 107
(J-C Rouget, France) *led: gng best 2f out: rdn and qcknd over 1f out: styd on but reeled in fnl f and hdd cl home: no ex* **4/5**[1]
3 *1 3/4* **Maximum Aurelius (FR)**[23] 2755 3-8-11 0........ Pierre-CharlesBoudot 2 102
(F-H Graffard, France) *trckd ldr: rdn and effrt 2f out: styd on same pce and hld in 3rd towards fin* **5/1**[3]
4 *1 1/2* **Victory Bond**[41] 2190 3-8-11 0... OlivierPeslier 4 99
(William Haggas) *midfield: rdn 3f out: hung rt u.p and styd on same pce in st: nt able to chal* **13/2**
5 *dist* **Beijing**[44] 3-8-11 0...(b) MickaelBarzalona 5
(A Fabre, France) *hld up and nvr out of last: rdn 3f out: lost tch 2f out: sn wl btn: eased: t.o* **9/1**

1m 55.48s (4.38) **5** Ran SP% **115.6**
WIN (incl. 1 euro stake): 4.10. PLACES: 1.50, 1.30. SF: 6.80.
Owner Hamdan Al Maktoum **Bred** Dixiana Farms Llc **Trained** Pau, France

3544a LA COUPE (GROUP 3) (4YO+) (TURF) 1m 2f
1:05 (12:00) 4-Y-O+ **£29,411** (£11,764; £8,823; £5,882; £2,941)

RPR
1 **Air Pilot**[52] 1909 7-8-11 0.. ChristopheSoumillon 8 115
(Ralph Beckett) *trckd ldr: clsd and rdn to chal over 1f out: led ent fnl f: styd on wl and asserted: comf* **6/4**[1]
2 *2* **Elliptique (IRE)**[111] 805 5-8-11 0....................... Pierre-CharlesBoudot 4 111+
(A Fabre, France) *hld up: last 2f out: rdn and hdwy over 1f out: styd on into 2nd fnl f but no real imp on wnr* **9/4**[2]
3 *3* **Night Wish (GER)**[45] 2075 6-8-11 0..............................(p) OlivierPeslier 5 105
(Frau S Steinberg, Germany) *led and sn wnt clr: clsd down over 1f out: rdn and hdd ent fnl f: no ex and fdd: jst hld on for 3rd* **16/1**
4 *nk* **Tamarind Cove (IRE)**[24] 2729 4-8-11 0...................... CristianDemuro 2 104+
(Josef Vana, Czech Republic) *disp early: prom in main body of field on settling: rdn over 2f out: styd on same pce u.p fnl f and jst missed 3rd: no threat to front pair* **12/1**
5 *2 1/2* **Spring Leaf (FR)**[25] 2713 4-8-8 0..................................... TheoBachelot 3 96
(S Wattel, France) *midfield: rdn 2f out: sn outpcd: n.d* **14/1**
6 *3 1/2* **Pretty Girl (ARG)**[47] 2020 4-8-8 0............................... VincentCheminaud 1 89
(M Delzangles, France) *hld up: rdn to cl over 2f out: no ex over 1f out: wknd fnl f* **4/1**[3]
7 *nk* **Free Port Lux**[73] 1375 5-9-4 0..................................... MickaelBarzalona 6 99
(F Head, France) *hld up in last: rdn to try and cl 2f out: outpcd and btn fnl f* **8/1**

2m 7.66s (2.86) **7** Ran SP% **122.1**
WIN (incl. 1 euro stake): 3.10. PLACES: 1.40, 1.40, 2.20. DF: 3.90. SF: 8.30.
Owner Lady Cobham **Bred** Lady Cobham **Trained** Kimpton, Hants

3546a PRIX DU CHEMIN ROI (CLAIMER) (3YO) (POLYTRACK) 1m
2:05 (12:00) 3-Y-O **£9,926** (£3,970; £2,977; £1,985; £992)

RPR
1 **Plougastel (ITY)**[46] 3-9-8 0.. GeraldMosse 6 82
(A Marcialis, Italy) **223/10**
2 *snk* **Super Mac (FR)**[30] 2551 3-9-5 0............................ ChristopheSoumillon 4 79
(Cedric Rossi, France) **7/2**[1]
3 *nk* **Donuts Reyor (FR)**[17] 2948 3-9-1 0.............................. PierreBazire(3) 3 77
(Y Barberot, France) **54/10**[3]
4 *nk* **Shiver In The River (FR)**[23] 3-8-13 0......................... CristianDemuro 1 72
(G Botti, France) **30/1**
5 *1* **Highland Dragon**[28] 2578 3-9-2 0.............................. IoritzMendizabal 13 72
(William Haggas) *dropped in fr wdst draw and hld up in last: stl in rr 2f out: r.o wl fnl f but nvr able to chal: nrst fin* **37/10**[2]
6 *3* **Exclusive Potion (FR)**[59] 1686 3-9-8 0......................... UmbertoRispoli 8 71
(A Giorgi, Italy) **10/1**
7 *3/4* **Zip Code (FR)**[15] 3007 3-8-8 0...................................(p) GregoryBenoist 2 56
(Robert Collet, France) **14/1**
8 *4* **Little Ghetto Boy**[37] 3-8-10 0.. HugoJourniac(6) 5 54
(J-C Rouget, France) **54/10**[3]
9 *3 1/2* **Santorina (FR)**[38] 3-8-11 0...................................(b) VincentCheminaud 7 41
(M Delzangles, France) **21/1**
10 *3/4* **Dark Redeemer**[104] 3-8-4 0...................................... AdrienMoreau(7) 11 40
(N Caullery, France) **40/1**
11 *4 1/2* **Khien Shan (FR)**[15] 3-9-6 0..........................(p) Pierre-CharlesBoudot 10 38
(J Phelippon, France) **56/10**

\n\x\x WIN (incl. 1 euro stake): 23.30. PLACES: 5.00, 1.70, 2.10. DF: 51.30. SF:
Owner Scuderia Fert Sas **Bred** Scuderia Fert Sas Di Ferrario Paolo **Trained** Italy

3545 - 3546a (Foreign Racing) - See Raceform Interactive

3282 HAMILTON (R-H)
Thursday, June 23
OFFICIAL GOING: Good (good to firm in places; 7.9)
Wind: Light, half behind Weather: Overcast

3547 SAINTS & SINNERS AMATEUR RIDERS' H'CAP (FOR THE SAINTS & SINNERS CHALLENGE CUP) 1m 5f 15y
6:00 (6:00) (Class 5) (0-70,68) 4-Y-O+ **£3,743** (£1,161; £580; £290) **Stalls** High

Form RPR
3032 **1** **Lara Carbonara (IRE)**[15] 3018 4-10-9 **66**............ MrLJMcGuinness(3) 5 76
(John Patrick Shanahan, Ire) *hld up in tch: hdwy over 3f out: led 2f out: rdn clr ins fnl f* **11/4**[2]

-160 **2** *2 ¾* **Duke Of Yorkshire**[6] 3342 6-10-2 **61**......................(b) MissEEasterby(5) 4 67
(Tim Easterby) *t.k.h: trckd ldr: led over 3f out to 2f out: plugged on same pce fnl f* **9/1**

66-0 **3** *3* **Gunner Lindley (IRE)**[22] 2656 9-10-3 **57**........................ MrTHamilton 2 59
(Stuart Coltherd) *led at ordinary gallop: rdn and hdd over 3f out: rallied: outpcd fr over 1f out* **25/1**

0105 **4** *hd* **Solid Justice (IRE)**[21] 2813 5-9-13 **53**.............................. MissCWalton 1 54
(Kenny Johnson) *prom: rdn and outpcd over 3f out: rallied and edgd lft over 2f out: edgd rt and no imp fr over 1f out* **8/1**

0045 **5** *1* **Moon Arc (IRE)**[8] 3288 4-10-1 **55**....................................(p) MrsCBartley 7 55
(Keith Dalgleish) *hld up: rdn and outpcd over 3f out: rallied and edgd rt wl over 1f out: sn no imp* **9/1**

2445 **6** *1 ¼* **Northside Prince (IRE)**[22] 2805 10-10-13 **67**.................... MrSWalker 6 65
(Alan Swinbank) *prom: rdn and outpcd over 3f out: n.d after* **5/2**[1]

-353 **7** *4 ½* **Sherman McCoy**[26] 2678 10-10-11 **65**........................ MrJohnDawson 8 56
(Marjorie Fife) *trckd ldrs: drvn and outpcd over 3f out: btn fnl 2f* **6/1**[3]

1-00 **8** *5* **La Bacouetteuse (FR)**[22] 2805 11-10-7 **68**...................(b) MrBLynn(7) 3 52
(Iain Jardine) *s.v.s: sn rcvrd and jnd gp: drvn and outpcd 1/2-way: struggling fnl 3f* **12/1**

2m 52.78s (-1.12) **Going Correction** -0.075s/f (Good) **8** Ran SP% **112.2**
Speed ratings (Par 103): **100,98,96,96,95 94,92,89**
CSF £26.40 CT £499.38 TOTE £3.30: £1.50, £2.40, £5.10; EX 26.60 Trifecta £249.00.
Owner Thistle Bloodstock Limited **Bred** Thistle Bloodstock Ltd **Trained** Kells, Co Kilkenny
■ Stewards' Enquiry : Mr L J McGuinness two-day ban: used whip above permitted level (Juyl 7,13)

FOCUS
Rail out 6yds on the loop adding 24yds to Races 1, 4 and 5. A modest amateur riders' handicap. They went an ordinary gallop on ground officially described as good, good to firm in places.

3548 HIGHLAND SPRING WATER MAIDEN STKS (£20,000 HIGHLAND SPRING WATER HAMILTON PARK SERIES QUALIFIER) 6f 6y

6:30 (6:31) (Class 5) 2-Y-O **£3,557** (£1,058; £529; £264) **Stalls** High

Form RPR

24 **1** **Montataire (IRE)**[20] 2873 2-9-5 0.......................... JoeFanning 1 83+
(Mark Johnston) *mde all: crossed to stands' rail after 1f: shkn up and qcknd over 1f out: kpt on wl fnl f: unchal* **6/4**[2]

2 **2** *2 ¼* **What's The Story**[8] 3283 2-9-5 0.......................... PhillipMakin 6 76+
(Keith Dalgleish) *trckd wnr: rdn along over 2f out: effrt over 1f out: kpt on same pce fnl f* **11/10**[1]

52 **3** *3 ¾* **Galahad**[31] 2530 2-9-5 0.......................... DavidNolan 5 65+
(Richard Fahey) *in tch: rdn over 2f out: kpt on fnl f: nt pce to chal* **16/1**

0 **4** *3 ½* **Bongrace (IRE)**[23] 2756 2-9-0 0.......................... ShaneGray 4 50
(Kevin Ryan) *trckd ldrs: pushed along and hung rt over 2f out: wknd over 1f out* **33/1**

46 **5** *1 ¼* **Indigo Beat**[26] 2670 2-9-0 0.......................... PJMcDonald 3 46
(Ann Duffield) *in tch on outside: rdn over 2f out: wknd over 1f out* **18/1**

6 *½* **Flash Of White** 2-9-5 0.......................... TadhgO'Shea 2 49
(Bryan Smart) *dwlt and wnt rt s: hld up: pushed along over 2f out: wknd over 1f out* **12/1**[3]

7 *5* **Cliff Bay (IRE)** 2-9-5 0.......................... BarryMcHugh 7 34
(Keith Dalgleish) *missed break: outpcd in rr: struggling fr 1/2-way: nvr on terms* **33/1**

1m 11.32s (-0.88) **Going Correction** -0.225s/f (Firm) **7** Ran SP% **112.3**
Speed ratings (Par 93): **96,93,88,83,81 81,74**
CSF £3.32 TOTE £2.40: £1.50, £1.30; EX 3.50 Trifecta £14.70.
Owner Sheikh Hamdan bin Mohammed Al Maktoum **Bred** Tinnakill, P Lawlor & C Beale **Trained** Middleham Moor, N Yorks

FOCUS
A fair juvenile maiden. They went a decent gallop.

3549 JORDAN ELECTRICS (S) H'CAP 5f 7y

7:00 (7:01) (Class 6) (0-60,60) 3-Y-O+ **£2,911** (£866; £432; £216) **Stalls** Centre

Form RPR

4622 **1** **Whispering Soul (IRE)**[8] 3289 3-8-9 **51**......................(b) PJMcDonald 11 59
(Ann Duffield) *in tch nr side of gp: effrt and rdn over 1f out: disp ld wl ins fnl f: led last stride* **3/1**[1]

0-03 **2** *nse* **Indastar**[19] 2919 6-9-3 **53**.......................... JoeFanning 9 63
(Michael Herrington) *cl up on nr side of gp: hdwy to ld over 1f out: sn rdn: jnd wl ins fnl f: hdd last stride* **11/2**[2]

4501 **3** *1 ½* **Very First Blade**[15] 3022 7-9-0 **50**..........................(p) RobertTart 4 54
(Michael Mullineaux) *cl up centre: effrt and ev ch over 1f out: rdn and one pce ins fnl f* **6/1**[3]

0100 **4** *nk* **Under Approval**[21] 2808 5-8-10 **51**..........................(b) GemmaTutty(5) 10 54
(Karen Tutty) *prom on nr side of gp: effrt and pushed along 2f out: kpt on ins fnl f* **10/1**

-034 **5** *2 ¼* **Pilgrims Path**[30] 2559 3-9-1 **57**..........................(p) BarryMcHugh 7 50
(Scott Dixon) *in tch centre: drvn along over 2f out: kpt on ins fnl f: nt pce to chal* **9/1**

6430 **6** *hd* **Pabusar**[8] 3289 8-8-10 **53**..........................(vt) AdamMcNamara(7) 8 48
(Micky Hammond) *missed break: bhd and outpcd: gd hdwy on far side over 1f out: kpt on fnl f: no imp* **6/1**[3]

40-6 **7** *¾* **Ya Boy Sir (IRE)**[15] 3022 9-8-10 **46**..........................(p) RoystonFfrench 13 38
(Iain Jardine) *stdd s: hld up centre: rdn and hdwy over 1f out: kpt on: no imp* **14/1**

-006 **8** *1 ½* **Sunrise Dance**[26] 2676 7-8-10 **46** oh1.......................... ShaneGray 1 32
(Kenny Johnson) *cl up on far side of gp: rdn over 2f out: wknd over 1f out* **22/1**

20-4 **9** *hd* **Studio Star**[31] 2528 4-9-0 **50**.......................... JamesSullivan 5 36
(Wilf Storey) *t.k.h to post: plld hrd in tch: rdn over 2f out: outpcd fr over 1f out* **16/1**

-500 **10** *¾* **Spring Bird**[10] 3211 7-9-10 **60**.......................... NeilFarley 3 43
(Alan Swinbank) *led centre to over 1f out: sn rdn and wknd* **18/1**

000- **11** *½* **Mandalay King (IRE)**[330] 4761 11-9-2 **55**.......................... JacobButterfield(3) 2 36
(Marjorie Fife) *cl up on far side of gp: rdn and wknd over 1f out* **33/1**

-000 **12** *3* **Alba Dawn (IRE)**[15] 3017 3-8-11 **53**..........................(p) PhillipMakin 6 21
(Keith Dalgleish) *hld up in midfield in centre: drvn and outpcd over 2f out: sn btn* **20/1**

58.88s (-1.12) **Going Correction** -0.225s/f (Firm)
WFA 3 from 4yo+ 6lb **12** Ran SP% **117.9**
Speed ratings (Par 101): **99,98,96,96,92 92,90,88,88,87 86,81**
CSF £17.91 CT £95.48 TOTE £4.00: £1.70, £2.00, £2.10; EX 19.50 Trifecta £39.80.
Owner John Dance & John Gatenby **Bred** Rossenarra Bloodstock Limited **Trained** Constable Burton, N Yorks

FOCUS
A moderate selling handicap. They went a proper gallop and three of the first four home were drawn high.

3550 THISTLE BLOODSTOCK MAIDEN STKS 1m 1f 34y

7:35 (7:37) (Class 5) 3-4-Y-O **£3,881** (£1,155; £577; £288) **Stalls** Low

Form RPR

3- **1** **Parliamentarian (IRE)**[241] 7518 3-9-3 0.......................... PhillipMakin 1 78+
(Charlie Appleby) *t.k.h: trckd ldrs on ins: effrt whn nt clr run wl briefly wl over 1f out: rdn and led wl ins fnl f: kpt on* **4/6**[1]

23 **2** *nk* **Warp Factor (IRE)**[41] 2197 3-9-3 80..........................(b[1]) ShaneGray 4 75
(John Patrick Shanahan, Ire) *led at ordinary gallop: rdn 2f out: edgd lft and hdd wl ins fnl f: kpt on* **85/40**[2]

- **3** *2 ¾* **Fivehundredmiles (IRE)** 3-9-3 0.......................... TadhgO'Shea 2 70
(John Patrick Shanahan, Ire) *trckd ldr: rdn over 2f out: kpt on same pce fnl f* **9/1**[3]

0-0 **4** *½* **Page Of Wands**[171] 40 3-8-12 0.......................... JamesSullivan 3 64
(Karen McLintock) *hld up: rdn and outpcd over 3f out: rallied and flashed tail over 1f out: kpt on fnl f: no imp* **100/1**

45 **5** *1 ½* **Eez Eh (IRE)**[6] 3343 3-9-3 0.......................... JoeFanning 6 66
(Keith Dalgleish) *t.k.h: in tch: rdn over 2f out: wknd over 1f out* **20/1**

6 *11* **Alice Thornton**[12] 4-9-9 0.......................... DavidNolan 5 40
(Martin Todhunter) *s.i.s: hld up in tch: drvn and outpcd over 2f out: sn wknd* **66/1**

1m 58.82s (-0.88) **Going Correction** -0.075s/f (Good)
WFA 3 from 4yo 11lb **6** Ran SP% **109.2**
Speed ratings (Par 103): **100,99,97,96,95 85**
CSF £2.10 TOTE £1.60: £1.10, £1.40; EX 2.20 Trifecta £3.80.
Owner Godolphin **Bred** Darley **Trained** Newmarket, Suffolk

FOCUS
Rail out 6yds on the loop adding 24yds to race distance. A fair maiden. The ground is riding a tad slower on the round course, although they went an ordinary gallop after an initial skirmish for prominent positions.

3551 EBF STALLIONS CAPTAIN J.C. STEWART FILLIES' H'CAP 1m 67y

8:05 (8:05) (Class 4) (0-80,78) 3-Y-O+ **£6,469** (£1,925; £962; £481) **Stalls** Low

Form RPR

-266 **1** **Hidden Rebel**[12] 3152 4-10-0 **78**.......................... ConnorBeasley 2 86
(Alistair Whillans) *hld up in tch: effrt and hdwy 2f out: flashed tail and led wl ins fnl f: kpt on* **5/1**[3]

-443 **2** *1* **Rosamaria (IRE)**[5] 3399 3-8-8 **68**.......................... JoeFanning 4 72
(Mark Johnston) *led at modest gallop: rdn and qcknd wl over 1f out: hdd and no ex wl ins fnl f* **5/2**[2]

21-3 **3** *1 ¾* **Sunnua (IRE)**[15] 3026 3-8-9 **76**.......................... AdamMcNamara(7) 1 76
(Richard Fahey) *trckd ldr 2f: cl up: effrt and regained 2nd over 1f out to ins fnl f: kpt on same pce* **9/4**[1]

51 **4** *5* **Ionization (IRE)**[8] 3284 3-9-3 **77** 6ex.......................... TadhgO'Shea 5 65
(John Patrick Shanahan, Ire) *in tch: hdwy to press ldr after 2f: rdn over 2f out: hung rt and lost 2nd over 1f out: sn btn* **9/4**[1]

0-30 **5** *½* **Cadmium**[53] 1884 5-9-4 **68**..........................(p) PJMcDonald 3 57
(Micky Hammond) *hld up in tch: rdn over 2f out: wknd over 1f out* **25/1**

1m 46.62s (-1.78) **Going Correction** -0.075s/f (Good)
WFA 3 from 4yo+ 10lb **5** Ran SP% **110.6**
Speed ratings (Par 102): **105,104,102,97,96**
CSF £17.78 TOTE £5.30: £2.40, £1.70; EX 18.50 Trifecta £44.30.
Owner J D Wright **Bred** D Curran **Trained** Newmill-On-Slitrig, Borders

FOCUS
Rail out 6yds on the loop adding 24yds to race distance. A fair little fillies' handicap. They went a respectable gallop.

3552 PATERSONS OF GREENOAKHILL H'CAP 5f 7y

8:40 (8:40) (Class 4) (0-80,79) 3-Y-O+ **£6,469** (£1,925; £962; £481) **Stalls** Centre

Form RPR

-365 **1** **Curtain Call**[12] 3131 3-8-9 **77**.......................... AdamMcNamara(7) 1 86+
(Richard Fahey) *pressed ldr: led over 1f out: rdn and edgd lft ins fnl f: r.o wl* **5/1**[3]

-651 **2** *1 ¼* **Imperial Legend (IRE)**[29] 2572 7-9-7 **76**.......................... PaulQuinn 4 82
(David Nicholls) *dwlt: hld up: hdwy and swtchd lft over 1f out: chsd wnr ins fnl f: kpt on: nt pce to chal* **8/1**

0034 **3** *¾* **Royal Brave (IRE)**[17] 2975 5-9-4 **73**.......................... BarryMcHugh 6 76
(Rebecca Bastiman) *trckd ldrs: effrt and rdn over 1f out: kpt on same pce wl ins fnl f* **6/1**

00-0 **4** *hd* **Foxtrot Knight**[12] 3133 4-9-10 **79**.......................... JamesSullivan 3 82+
(Ruth Carr) *trckd ldrs gng wl: shkn up and chsd wnr over 1f out to ins fnl f: no ex* **16/1**

0613 **5** *¾* **Kopton**[17] 2974 4-9-10 **79**.......................... DavidNolan 2 79
(Jo Hughes) *dwlt: hld up: rdn and hdwy on outside over 1f out: kpt on ins fnl f* **10/3**[2]

0000 **6** *¾* **Native Falls (IRE)**[9] 3265 5-9-3 **72**.......................... NeilFarley 5 69
(Alan Swinbank) *led tl rdn and hdd over 1f out: outpcd ins fnl f* **40/1**

5-00 **7** *1* **Jack Luey**[27] 2665 9-9-1 **75**..........................(b) JoshDoyle(5) 8 69
(Lawrence Mullaney) *in tch: rdn over 2f out: outpcd fr over 1f out* **14/1**

0031 **8** *5* **Apricot Sky**[7] 3326 6-9-9 **78** 6ex.......................... JoeFanning 7 68
(David Nicholls) *dwlt: t.k.h and sn prom: rdn over 1f out: wknd fnl f: eased last 100yds* **2/1**[1]

58.13s (-1.87) **Going Correction** -0.225s/f (Firm)
WFA 3 from 4yo+ 6lb **8** Ran SP% **113.5**
Speed ratings (Par 105): **105,103,101,101,100 99,97,89**
CSF £43.35 CT £244.37 TOTE £5.30: £1.90, £2.50, £1.70; EX 41.80 Trifecta £227.50.
Owner Cheveley Park Stud **Bred** Cheveley Park Stud Ltd **Trained** Musley Bank, N Yorks

FOCUS
A fairly decent sprint handicap. They went a decent gallop and the quick winning time suggested the ground had dried out to genuinely good to firm on the straight track.

3553 RACINGUK.COM H'CAP 6f 6y

9:10 (9:10) (Class 5) (0-75,75) 3-Y-O+ **£3,881** (£1,155; £577; £288) **Stalls** High

Form RPR

15 **1** **Born Innocent (IRE)**[8] 3285 3-8-7 **61**.......................... TadhgO'Shea 2 68+
(John Patrick Shanahan, Ire) *prom: effrt whn nt clr run 2f out: rallied and chsd wnr ins fnl f: kpt on to ld last stride* **7/2**[2]

0602 **2** *nse* **Cosmic Chatter**[15] 3021 6-9-13 **74**..........................(p) JamesSullivan 4 83
(Ruth Carr) *hld up: gd hdwy on outside to ld over 1f out: kpt on ins fnl f: hdd last stride* **5/1**[3]

0-06 **3** *nk* **Amood (IRE)**[12] 3168 5-9-11 **72**..........................(p) DougieCostello 5 80+
(Simon West) *t.k.h: hld up: hdwy whn nt clr run over 1f out: swtchd lft and kpt on wl u.p fnl f: jst hld* **7/1**

0020 **4** 3 ½ **Meandmyshadow**[12] 3168 8-10-0 **75**................................(b) DaleSwift 1 73
(Alan Brown) *w ldrs to over 1f out: outpcd ins fnl f* **20/1**

2206 **5** ½ **Chookie's Lass**[21] 2808 5-9-1 **62**.. JasonHart 9 58
(Keith Dalgleish) *t.k.h: cl up: led 1/2-way to over 1f out: no ex ins fnl f* **14/1**

0400 **6** 1 ¾ **Percy's Gal**[10] 3211 5-9-1 **67**... GemmaTutty(5) 3 58
(Karen Tutty) *t.k.h: prom: pushed along 2f out: wknd ins fnl f* **20/1**

5004 **7** 4 ½ **Pryers Princess**[14] 3069 4-9-0 **61**.............................. PJMcDonald 7 38
(David C Griffiths) *in tch: rdn over 2f out: wknd wl over 1f out* **9/1**

-001 **8** 2 **Royal Connoisseur (IRE)**[8] 3289 5-8-11 **65**......... AdamMcNamara(7) 6 36
(Richard Fahey) *in tch: rdn along whn bmpd repeatedly 2f out: sn wknd* **3/1**[1]

3304 **9** 2 ½ **Spowarticus**[59] 1712 7-8-11 **58**....................................(b) BarryMcHugh 8 22
(Scott Dixon) *t.k.h: led to 1/2-way: rdn and wknd over 1f out* **16/1**

0-05 **10** 4 **Lothair (IRE)**[10] 3214 7-9-4 **65**.............................. JoeFanning 10 17
(Alan Swinbank) *hld up: rdn over 2f out: wknd wl over 1f out* **9/1**

1m 10.47s (-1.73) **Going Correction** -0.225s/f (Firm)
WFA 3 from 4yo+ 7lb **10** Ran SP% **118.5**
Speed ratings (Par 103): **102,101,101,96,96 93,87,85,81,76**
CSF £21.88 CT £114.30 TOTE £5.00: £1.70, £2.00, £2.70; EX 26.20 Trifecta £150.70.
Owner Thistle Bloodstock Limited **Bred** Thistle Bloodstock Ltd **Trained** Kells, Co Kilkenny

FOCUS
A fair sprint handicap. They went a respectable gallop.
T/Plt: £26.50 to a £1 stake. Pool: £55,965.83 - 1583.94 winning units. T/Qpdt: £8.80 to a £1 stake. Pool: £6,394.96 - 535.45 winning units. **Richard Young**

3058 NEWBURY (L-H)

Thursday, June 23

OFFICIAL GOING: Good to soft (soft in places) changing to soft after race 1 (5.35)
Wind: Almost nil Weather: Overcast, drizzly, quite humid

3554 PUMP TECHNOLOGY H'CAP 7f (S)
5:35 (5:37) (Class 5) (0-75,74) 3-Y-O+ **£3,234** (£962; £481; £240) **Stalls** High

Form RPR

24-6 **1** **Kitaaby (IRE)**[14] 3062 3-9-4 **73**....................................... JimmyFortune 6 83
(Brian Meehan) *racd centre: chsd ldr: rdn to ld over 1f out: drvn out* **8/1**

04-1 **2** 1 **Tripartite (IRE)**[20] 2864 3-9-0 **69**.. MartinLane 4 76
(Jeremy Gask) *racd centre: prom: drvn to chse wnr 1f out and tried to chal: kpt on but hld nr fin* **9/2**[2]

3223 **3** 1 ¼ **Golden Wedding (IRE)**[13] 3097 4-9-11 **71**.................. CharlesBishop 7 78
(Eve Johnson Houghton) *racd centre: trckd ldrs: rdn over 2f out and sn outpcd: styd on fr over 1f out to take 3rd nr fin* **6/1**

0-52 **4** ½ **Gold Hunter (IRE)**[13] 3097 6-9-10 **73**...................... TomMarquand(3) 2 79
(Steve Flook) *racd wdst of all in centre: wl in tch: rdn 2f out: cl up over 1f out: chsd ldng pair ins fnl f: one pce and lost 3rd nr fin* **4/1**[1]

-120 **5** ¾ **Pacolita (IRE)**[27] 2655 4-9-8 **68**... PatDobbs 10 72
(Sylvester Kirk) *racd centre: t.k.h: hld up in rr: shkn up over 2f out: prog over 1f out: styd on fnl f: nrst fin but unable to chal* **20/1**

233- **6** ½ **Fast Sprite (IRE)**[185] 8324 4-9-3 **63**..................................... KierenFox 8 65
(John Best) *dwlt: t.k.h: sn trckd ldrs in centre: rdn and lost pl over 2f out: styd on again fr over 1f out* **10/1**

2040 **7** ½ **Sarmadee (IRE)**[13] 3097 4-9-7 **72**.................................. PaddyPilley(5) 9 73
(Mick Channon) *racd centre: led to over 1f out: fdd fnl f* **28/1**

-006 **8** 8 **Bold Grove**[14] 3070 4-8-9 **55** oh10.............................(p) SamHitchcott 12 34
(Edward Bevan) *s.i.s: racd towards nr side: nt on terms w centre gp fr 1/2-way: led gp over 1f out but no ch* **100/1**

00-4 **9** 2 ½ **Unnoticed**[31] 2540 4-9-6 **66**... ShaneKelly 13 39
(Luca Cumani) *stdd s: racd centre: nvr on terms: wknd over 2f out* **11/2**[3]

4-20 **10** 2 ½ **Invigorate**[33] 2459 3-8-11 **66**.. PatCosgrave 14 29
(Harry Dunlop) *racd towards nr side: nvr on terms w centre gp: no ch over 2f out* **33/1**

430- **11** ½ **Dont Have It Then**[215] 7949 5-9-5 **65**......................... StevieDonohoe 11 29
(Willie Musson) *racd towards nr side: nvr on terms w centre gp: no ch over 2f out* **25/1**

0-65 **12** 8 **With Approval (IRE)**[15] 3030 4-9-7 **67**........................... JimCrowley 15 10
(Laura Mongan) *rring in stalls: racd towards nr side: nvr on terms: t.o* **25/1**

4040 **13** 2 ¾ **Embankment**[43] 2153 7-8-13 **59**.................................. FrederikTylicki 16
(Michael Attwater) *racd towards nr side: nvr on terms: t.o* **14/1**

1m 27.88s (2.18) **Going Correction** +0.375s/f (Good)
WFA 3 from 4yo+ 9lb **13** Ran SP% **114.6**
Speed ratings (Par 103): **102,100,99,98,98 97,96,87,84,82 81,72,69**
CSF £38.51 CT £196.01 TOTE £9.00: £3.00, £1.80, £2.30; EX 63.80 Trifecta £534.60.
Owner Hamdan Al Maktoum **Bred** Joseph Broderick **Trained** Manton, Wilts

FOCUS
Rail had been moved in on the round course from the 8f to the 5f since last meeting. Race distances as advertised. The ground was changed to soft following the opener and Freddie Tylicki said: "It's soft, wet. That bit of rain has helped them get through it." A modest handicap in which they raced centre-to-near side, with the main action unfolding down the middle.

3555 WIN RACES WITH JONATHAN PORTMAN NOVICE AUCTION FILLIES' STKS (PLUS 10 RACE) 6f 8y
6:10 (6:11) (Class 4) 2-Y-O **£3,946** (£1,174; £586; £293) **Stalls** High

Form RPR

1 **Funky Footsteps (IRE)** 2-8-8 0................................. CharlesBishop 11 73
(Eve Johnson Houghton) *in tch towards rr: shkn up over 1f out and gd prog after: r.o fnl f to ld nr fin* **25/1**

2 ½ **Perfect Angel (IRE)** 2-8-12 0... DavidProbert 7 76
(Andrew Balding) *dwlt: hld up in rr: stdy prog gng wl to trck ldr over 1f out: produced to ld last 150yds: styd on but hdd nr fin* **8/1**

4 **3** 2 ¼ **Affair**[16] 2997 2-8-3 0.. CharlieBennett(5) 2 65
(Hughie Morrison) *chsd ldrs on wd outside: rdn to dispute 2nd 2f out: kpt on one pce fr over 1f out* **11/4**[2]

2 **4** hd **Stop The Wages (IRE)**[21] 2817 2-9-0 0......................... JimmyFortune 8 70
(Brian Meehan) *t.k.h: led: gng easily 2f out: pushed along over 1f out: hdd and fdd last 150yds* **9/4**[1]

0 **5** 2 ¼ **Fanfair**[26] 2696 2-8-5 0.. TomMarquand(3) 10 57
(Richard Hannon) *trckd ldrs: shkn up and cl up wl over 1f out: fdd* **8/1**

5 **6** nk **Brexit**[24] 2748 2-8-8 0.. KieranO'Neill 12 57
(Pat Phelan) *prom: chsd ldr over 2f out to over 1f out: wknd fnl f* **6/1**[3]

7 1 ½ **Three Duchesses** 2-8-12 0... WilliamCarson 5 56
(Michael Bell) *in tch in rr: pushed along 1/2-way: nvr gng pce to threaten but kpt on fnl f* **16/1**

8 nk **All About The Pace** 2-8-8 0.. JohnFahy 6 51
(Mark Usher) *dwlt: detached in last early and rn green thrght: sme prog 1/2-way: hanging and no ch over 1f out but kpt on* **25/1**

46 **9** 5 **Crystal Secret**[26] 2696 2-8-2 0 ow1.............................. MitchGodwin(7) 9 37
(John Bridger) *prom: chsd ldr 1/2-way to over 2f out: sn wknd* **33/1**

10 1 ¼ **Warba (IRE)** 2-8-10 0.. MartinDwyer 4 34
(Joseph Tuite) *chsd ldr to 1/2-way: sn btn* **33/1**

11 2 ¾ **Cautious Choice (IRE)** 2-8-5 0................................ DannyBrock(3) 13 24
(J S Moore) *pushed along in rr bef 1/2-way: nvr a factor* **66/1**

1m 16.28s (3.28) **Going Correction** +0.375s/f (Good) **11** Ran SP% **114.9**
Speed ratings (Par 92): **93,92,89,89,86 85,83,83,76,74 71**
CSF £199.72 TOTE £17.60: £4.80, £2.80, £2.40; EX 201.70 Trifecta £994.50.
Owner Mrs J E O'Halloran **Bred** Mrs J O'Halloran **Trained** Blewbury, Oxon

FOCUS
Race distance as advertised. An ordinary fillies novice, they raced in one group down the centre and a pair of newcomers, both of whom sat in rear for much of the race, came to the fore.

3556 PUMPMATIC PUMP STATIONS BY PUMP TECHNOLOGY NOVICE FILLIES' STKS (PLUS 10 RACE) 7f (S)
6:40 (6:42) (Class 4) 2-Y-O **£3,946** (£1,174; £586; £293) **Stalls** High

Form RPR

1 **Emmie (IRE)** 2-9-0 0... JimCrowley 2 81+
(Harry Dunlop) *trckd ldrs: wnt 2nd 2f out: shkn up to ld over 1f out: rdn and r.o wl fnl f* **20/1**

62 **2** 2 ¾ **Naifah (IRE)**[19] 2885 2-9-0 0.. RobertHavlin 6 74
(John Gosden) *led: shkn up 2f out: hdd and edgd rt over 1f out: nt qckn* **6/5**[1]

3 nk **Texas Katie** 2-9-0 0.. CharlesBishop 9 73+
(Mick Channon) *hung bdly lft first 100yds: hld up in rr: stl last 2f out: gd prog over 1f out: shkn up to press for 2nd ins fnl f: kpt on* **20/1**

4 3 **Dancing Elegance** 2-9-0 0...[1] WilliamCarson 3 66
(Michael Bell) *dwlt: in rr on outer of gp: shkn up over 2f out: effrt over 1f out: one pce after* **25/1**

5 nk **Darwasl** 2-9-0 0.. JimmyFortune 1 65
(Brian Meehan) *dwlt: towards rr: prog on outer of gp 2f out: one pce fr over 1f out* **12/1**[3]

6 1 ½ **Fleeting Motion** 2-9-0 0.. PatDobbs 8 61
(Richard Hannon) *dwlt: hld up in tch: shkn up and no prog 2f out: one pce and no hdwy after* **5/2**[2]

05 **7** 1 ¼ **Met By Moonlight**[21] 2822 2-9-0 0.................................. DavidProbert 10 58
(Ron Hodges) *dwlt: t.k.h and sn pressed ldr: lost 2nd 2f out: wknd* **16/1**

8 2 **Varun's Bride (IRE)** 2-9-0 0.. KieranO'Neill 4 53
(Richard Hannon) *trckd ldrs tl lost pl qckly fr 2f out* **20/1**

04 **9** nk **Jasmincita (IRE)**[15] 3024 2-9-0 0...................................... SteveDrowne 7 52
(George Baker) *hld up in tch: effrt towards nr side over 2f out: wknd qckly over 1f out* **20/1**

10 1 **Intisha (IRE)** 2-9-0 0... RyanClark 5 50
(Jonathan Portman) *in tch in rr: prog on nr side over 2f out and on terms: wknd qckly over 1f out* **33/1**

1m 32.04s (6.34) **Going Correction** +0.375s/f (Good) **10** Ran SP% **113.4**
Speed ratings (Par 92): **78,74,74,71,70 69,67,65,64,63**
CSF £40.30 TOTE £18.20: £3.70, £1.02, £3.40; EX 55.70 Trifecta £766.20.
Owner Mrs Mary-Anne Parker **Bred** Tullpark Ltd **Trained** Lambourn, Berks

FOCUS
Race distance as advertised. Racing centre-to-stands' side, as in the previous 2yo race it went to one of the newcomers, also an outsider.

3557 PEGASUS PUMPS LTD H'CAP 1m 2f 6y
7:15 (7:15) (Class 4) (0-85,85) 3-Y-O+ **£4,690** (£1,395; £697; £348) **Stalls** Centre

Form RPR

41 **1** **Huge Future**[19] 2914 3-9-2 **85**.. JamesDoyle 4 101+
(Saeed bin Suroor) *hld up in midfield: clsd and swtchd rt over 2f out: prog to ld jst over 1f out: pushed out: comf* **2/1**[1]

1240 **2** 2 **Lord Huntingdon**[35] 2393 3-8-8 **77**................................ DavidProbert 8 86
(Andrew Balding) *led: gng strly over 2f out: rdn and hdd jst over 1f out: kpt on wl and clr of rest but no match for wnr* **10/1**

10-5 **3** 3 ½ **Cosmeapolitan**[12] 3156 3-8-11 **80**.................................. MartinHarley 13 82
(Alan King) *hld up in last quartet: stdy prog fr 3f out: rdn wl over 1f out: kpt on same pce to snatch 3rd last strides* **5/1**[3]

-34 **4** hd **Alcatraz (IRE)**[20] 2868 4-9-12 **83**...............................(t) PatCosgrave 9 85
(George Baker) *pressed ldr: rdn over 2f out: lost 2nd over 1f out and outpcd after: lost 3rd last strides* **9/1**

-240 **5** nk **Squire**[14] 3061 5-9-7 **78**.. RobertHavlin 2 79
(Michael Attwater) *trckd ldrs: rdn and nt qckn over 2f out: sn outpcd: kpt on fnl f* **20/1**

5-40 **6** 1 ¾ **Starwatch**[59] 1716 9-9-4 **82**..(v) MitchGodwin(7) 7 80
(John Bridger) *t.k.h: hld up in midfield: rdn over 2f out: one pce and no imp on ldrs* **20/1**

34-5 **7** 2 ¼ **Thames Knight**[17] 2978 4-9-5 **76**....................................... MartinDwyer 5 70
(Marcus Tregoning) *cl up: lost pl fr 1/2-way: in last pair whn rdn over 2f out: no ch but plugged on again fnl f* **16/1**

0-21 **8** ½ **Prosecute (FR)**[15] 3042 3-8-8 **77**...................................... JimCrowley 3 70
(David Simcock) *s.i.s: hld up in last pair: gng bttr than sme 3f out: reminder over 1f out and limited prog: nvr involved* **4/1**[2]

2130 **9** 2 ¾ **Sheila's Buddy**[59] 1716 7-9-8 **82**............................ TomMarquand(3) 12 70
(J S Moore) *s.s: mostly in last pair: rdn wl over 2f out: no great prog* **25/1**

-046 **10** 1 **Cricklewood Green (USA)**[14] 3061 5-9-4 **75**...................... PatDobbs 6 62
(Sylvester Kirk) *t.k.h: hld up in last quartet: rdn and no prog over 2f out: wknd over 1f out* **25/1**

-003 **11** 15 **Smaih (GER)**[17] 2978 4-9-13 **84**.................................... WilliamCarson 10 44
(Jamie Osborne) *pressed ldng pair: rdn 3f out: lost pl over 2f out and sn wknd: heavily eased ins fnl f* **22/1**

2m 10.99s (2.19) **Going Correction** +0.375s/f (Good)
WFA 3 from 4yo+ 12lb **11** Ran SP% **116.5**
Speed ratings (Par 105): **106,104,101,101,101 99,98,97,95,94 82**
CSF £20.64 CT £86.92 TOTE £2.90: £1.40, £3.10, £1.90; EX 25.40 Trifecta £122.60.
Owner Godolphin **Bred** W And R Barnett Ltd **Trained** Newmarket, Suffolk

FOCUS
Race distance as advertised. A fairly ordinary handicap, but a good winner who looks set to rate much higher in time.

3558 JUNG PUMPEN & PUMP TECHNOLOGY H'CAP 1m 7y(R)
7:45 (7:48) (Class 5) (0-70,70) 3-Y-O £3,881 (£1,155; £577; £288) Stalls High

Form RPR
6-03 **1** **Bluff Crag**[41] 2212 3-9-4 **67**.... DavidProbert 7 77+
(Andrew Balding) *sn hld up towards rr: prog over 2f out: rdn over 1f out: sustained effrt to ld last 100yds: drvn out* **9/2**[2]
-141 **2** 1/2 **Here's Two**[29] 2586 3-9-7 **70**.... RobertHavlin 2 78
(Ron Hodges) *t.k.h early: hld up bhd ldrs: prog towards far side 2f out: rdn to ld over 1f out: hdd last 100yds: styd on* **6/1**[3]
4-33 **3** 4 **Bonhomie**[29] 2585 3-9-2 **65**.... JamesDoyle 10 64
(Michael Bell) *pressed ldr: led over 2f out: sn hrd rdn: hdd over 1f out: fdd ins fnl f* **6/1**[3]
1-06 **4** 1 1/4 **Sheila's Treat (IRE)**[13] 3110 3-9-4 **67**.... OisinMurphy 8 63
(Denis Coakley) *prom: rdn to chal fr over 2f out to jst over 1f out: fdd ins fnl f* **10/1**
1555 **5** 3/4 **Ruby Wednesday**[37] 2341 3-9-7 **70**.... KierenFox 11 65
(John Best) *restrained s: hld up in detached last: shkn up 3f out: prog and rdn 2f out: kpt on but no ch to be involved* **20/1**
2602 **6** 1 1/4 **Blacklister**[37] 2341 3-9-6 **69**.... CharlesBishop 5 61
(Mick Channon) *prom: chal over 2f out to over 1f out: wknd* **8/1**
2-04 **7** 2 **Kuantan**[37] 2340 3-9-3 **69**....(p) KieranShoemark(3) 1 57
(Roger Charlton) *hld up towards rr: rdn over 2f out: no great prog over 1f out* **4/1**[1]
4-00 **8** 1 3/4 **Mr Marchwood**[23] 2770 3-9-4 **67**.... JimCrowley 3 51
(Sylvester Kirk) *hld up towards rr: rdn 3f out: last and wl btn 2f out* **33/1**
5-45 **9** 2 **Protest (IRE)**[52] 1917 3-9-0 **63**.... SamHitchcott 12 42
(Sylvester Kirk) *in tch: prog towards nr side and tried to chal over 2f out: sn btn and wknd* **40/1**
0-44 **10** *shd* **Zabdi**[18] 2935 3-9-6 **69**.... PatDobbs 6 48
(Richard Hannon) *led at gd pce: hdd over 2f out: nudged along and steadily dropped away* **9/1**
000 **11** 3 1/4 **Roccor**[16] 2999 3-9-0 **66**.... TomMarquand(3) 9 38
(Richard Hannon) *hld up: prog towards nr side gng wl 3f out: rdn and wknd qckly 2f out* **14/1**

1m 41.07s (2.37) **Going Correction** +0.375s/f (Good) **11** Ran SP% **113.8**
Speed ratings (Par 99): **103,102,98,97,96 95,93,91,89,89 86**
CSF £29.86 CT £164.85 TOTE £5.70: £1.90, £1.80, £2.50; EX 28.50 Trifecta £130.30.
Owner James/Michaelson/Greenwood 1 **Bred** Mrs Fiona Denniff **Trained** Kingsclere, Hants

FOCUS
Race distance as advertised. Run on the Round Mile, it proved quite hard work late on and the front pair came a few lengths clear.

3559 LEE SAN MARINE SANITATION H'CAP 5f 34y
8:20 (8:20) (Class 5) (0-70,70) 3-Y-O+ £3,881 (£1,155; £577; £288) Stalls High

Form RPR
0125 **1** **Pharoh Jake**[7] 3316 8-9-1 **59**.... WilliamTwiston-Davies 3 67
(John Bridger) *prom: wnt 2nd 1/2-way: rdn to chal over 1f out: led ins fnl f: drvn out* **5/1**[3]
0006 **2** 1/2 **Quickaswecan**[9] 3259 5-9-8 **66**....(p) OisinMurphy 5 72
(Milton Bradley) *led: shkn up 2f out: hdd ins fnl f: kpt on u.p* **11/1**
-050 **3** 2 1/4 **Equistar**[17] 2981 3-9-6 **70**....(t) FrederikTylicki 1 66
(Jonathan Portman) *w.w: effrt 2f out: rdn to chse ldng pair over 1f out: no imp after* **3/1**[2]
0600 **4** 2 **Rocket Rob (IRE)**[12] 3159 10-9-0 **58**.... StevieDonohoe 6 49
(Willie Musson) *w.w: shkn up over 1f out: one pce and nvr a threat* **9/1**
0001 **5** 1 1/2 **Dusty Blue**[7] 3316 4-9-0 **61** 6ex.... GeorgeDowning(3) 2 47
(Tony Carroll) *dwlt: w.w: shkn up 2f out: no imp over 1f out: wknd ins fnl f* **3/1**[2]
6261 **6** 1 1/2 **Racing Angel (IRE)**[12] 3136 4-9-10 **68**.... WilliamCarson 7 48
(Mick Quinn) *pressed ldr to 1/2-way: sn rdn: wknd over 1f out* **11/4**[1]

1m 3.35s (1.95) **Going Correction** +0.375s/f (Good)
WFA 3 from 4yo+ 6lb **6** Ran SP% **111.7**
Speed ratings (Par 103): **99,98,94,91,89 86**
CSF £52.52 TOTE £5.90: £2.90, £3.40; EX 47.90 Trifecta £248.90.
Owner J J Bridger Mrs J Stamp **Bred** J J Bridger **Trained** Liphook, Hants
■ Stewards' Enquiry : William Twiston-Davies two-day ban: used whip above permitted level (Jul 7,11)

FOCUS
Race distance as advertised. Few got into this, the first two dominating from a fair way out.

3560 PUMP TECHNOLOGY APPRENTICE H'CAP 1m 3f 5y
8:50 (8:50) (Class 5) (0-70,70) 4-Y-O+ £3,234 (£962; £481; £240) Stalls Centre

Form RPR
1652 **1** **Turnbury**[10] 3230 5-8-13 **60**....(p) MeganNicholls(3) 9 68
(Nikki Evans) *trckd ldrs: stmbld 7f out: led against far rail wl over 2f out: rdn and kpt on steadily after* **8/1**
2400 **2** 1 1/2 **Saint Honore**[28] 2623 4-9-6 **67**.... PaddyBradley(3) 12 72
(Pat Phelan) *hld up wl off the pce in rr: stdy prog on outer over 3f out: rdn 2f out: kpt on to take 2nd over 1f out: unable to chal* **16/1**
5-54 **3** *hd* **Glens Wobbly**[35] 2399 8-9-10 **68**.... HectorCrouch 4 72
(Jonathan Geake) *rousted s but unable to ld: pressed ldrs: wnt 2nd briefly u.p wl over 2f out: kpt on fr over 1f out* **9/1**
3/01 **4** 2 1/4 **Eugenic**[21] 2814 5-8-4 **53**.... GeorgeWood(5) 2 53
(Rod Millman) *sn in tch in midfield: prog on outer over 3f out: chsd wnr over 2f out to over 1f out: fdd fnl f* **9/1**
3546 **5** 6 **Bushel (USA)**[16] 3002 6-9-10 **68**.... GeorgeBuckell 8 58
(Tony Newcombe) *hld up in rr and wl off the pce: rdn over 3f out: plugged on to take modest 5th fnl f: no ch* **8/1**
12-2 **6** 2 1/2 **Putaringonit (IRE)**[20] 2860 4-9-9 **70**.... DavidParkes(3) 5 56
(Jeremy Gask) *t.k.h: prom: rdn over 3f out: wknd over 2f out* **9/2**[1]
00-6 **7** 1/2 **Hallingham**[18] 2911 6-9-4 **62**....(v) JennyPowell 6 47
(Chris Gordon) *wl in rr and off the pce: rdn 4f out: nvr a factor but passed a few late on* **20/1**
2603 **8** 1/2 **Classic Mission**[18] 2930 5-9-8 **69**....(p[1]) CharlieBennett(3) 11 53
(Jonathan Portman) *sn pushed along in midfield: u.p over 3f out: no prog and wl btn 2f out* **7/1**[3]
2-20 **9** 2 1/2 **Rock Of Max**[28] 2605 4-9-6 **69**....(p) CameronNoble(5) 1 49
(Michael Bell) *pressed ldr to 4f out: wknd 3f out* **11/1**
1 **10** 3/4 **Lady Makfi (IRE)**[23] 2781 4-8-9 **58**.... CliffordLee(5) 3 37
(Johnny Farrelly) *won battle for ld: hdd & wknd wl over 2f out* **5/1**[2]
0105 **11** 22 **Fleetwood Poppy**[37] 2326 4-8-4 **51** oh3.... RhiainIngram(3) 13
(Michael Attwater) *hld up wl off the pce: effrt on outer over 3f out: wknd over 2f out: t.o* **50/1**
206 **12** 37 **Nouvelle Ere**[57] 1796 5-9-2 **60**....(t) AaronJones 7
(Tony Carroll) *chsd ldrs to 1/2-way: sn wknd qckly: t.o and virtually p.u over 1f out* **20/1**

2m 27.12s (5.92) **Going Correction** +0.375s/f (Good) **12** Ran SP% **115.3**
Speed ratings (Par 103): **93,91,91,90,85 83,83,83,81,80 64,37**
CSF £121.68 CT £1172.61 TOTE £11.00: £3.10, £4.20, £3.30; EX 155.70 Trifecta £1068.60.
Owner Dragon Racing **Bred** Tarworth Bloodstock & Genesis Green Stud **Trained** Pandy, Monmouths

FOCUS
Race distance as advertised. They were soon strung out in this apprentice handicap, not hanging around considering the conditions. They raced centre-to-far side in the straight.
T/Plt: £281.00 to a £1 stake. Pool: £57,892.71 - 150.37 winning units. T/Qpdt: £33.40 to a £1 stake. Pool: £7,881.87 - 174.50 winning units. **Jonathan Neesom**

2913 NEWCASTLE (A.W) (L-H)
Thursday, June 23

OFFICIAL GOING: Tapeta: standard
Wind: light 1/2 behind Weather: fine and sunny, very warm

3561 BETFRED TV NOVICE MEDIAN AUCTION STKS 7f 14y (Tp)
1:50 (1:53) (Class 5) 2-Y-O £3,234 (£962; £481; £240) Stalls Centre

Form RPR
4 **1** **Alcazar**[13] 3093 2-9-2 0.... JamieSpencer 9 74+
(David Simcock) *hld up in rr: hdwy 3f out: upsides over 1f out: led last 150yds: drvn rt out* **8/15**[1]
55 **2** *nk* **Major Cornwallis (IRE)**[13] 3114 2-9-2 0.... TonyHamilton 1 74
(Richard Fahey) *w ldrs: led over 1f out: hdd last 150yds: no ex clsng stages* **13/2**[3]
3 5 **Mister Belvedere** 2-9-2 0.... PaulMulrennan 2 60
(Michael Dods) *sn trcking ldrs: drvn over 2f out: kpt on one pce appr fnl f* **4/1**[2]
0 **4** 2 1/4 **Parkwarden (IRE)**[38] 2301 2-9-2 0.... JackGarritty 3 54
(Chris Grant) *w ldr: reminders 4f out: led over 2f out: hdd over 1f out: one pce* **100/1**
5 1 1/4 **Harry George (IRE)** 2-9-2 0.... BenCurtis 4 51+
(Brian Ellison) *s.i.s: sn mid-div: reminders over 3f out: outpcd over 1f out: kpt on clsng stages* **16/1**
300 **6** 3/4 **Born To Boogie**[34] 2424 2-8-11 0.... ConnorBeasley 8 44
(Chris Grant) *led tl over 2f out: wknd fnl f* **50/1**
0 **7** 10 **Zarkavon**[12] 3167 2-8-11 0.... PaddyAspell 10 17
(John Wainwright) *in rr: drvn over 3f out: lost pl 2f out: sn bhd* **100/1**
00 **8** 2 1/2 **My Girl Maisie (IRE)**[12] 3167 2-8-11 0.... JasonHart 6 10
(Richard Guest) *in rr: drvn over 2f out: sn lost pl and bhd* **33/1**
0 **9** *nk* **Flawed Diamond (FR)**[23] 2771 2-8-11 0.... DougieCostello 7
(K R Burke) *trckd ldrs: lost pl over 1f out: sn bhd* **8/1**
0 **10** 3/4 **Miss Island Ruler**[23] 2771 2-8-11 0.... TomEaves 5
(Shaun Harris) *led tl over 2f out: lost pl over 1f out: sn bhd* **100/1**

1m 27.3s (1.10) **Going Correction** -0.05s/f (Stan) **10** Ran SP% **123.4**
Speed ratings (Par 93): **91,90,84,82,80 80,68,65,65,64**
CSF £5.34 TOTE £1.40: £1.02, £2.00, £1.50; EX 5.40 Trifecta £13.20.
Owner Never Say Die Partnership **Bred** I & Mrs M Shenkin **Trained** Newmarket, Suffolk

FOCUS
There will be no speed figures at this track until there is sufficient data to calculate median times. The first three-day Northumberland Plate Festival to take place on Newcastle's new Tapeta surface started off with a modest median auction event, with few of those with previous experience (all on turf) having achieved a great deal. The winner was an exception, but he made very hard work of landing the odds.

3562 BETFRED "1400 SHOPS NATIONWIDE" NOVICE STKS (PLUS 10 RACE) 6f (Tp)
2:20 (2:23) (Class 4) 2-Y-O £4,528 (£1,347; £673; £336) Stalls Centre

Form RPR
14 **1** **Hyperfocus (IRE)**[20] 2865 2-9-2 0.... MarcMonaghan(3) 4 87
(Hugo Palmer) *trckd ldrs: led over 2f out: rdn and edgd lft over 1f out: kpt on: all out* **10/11**[1]
2 *hd* **Six Strings** 2-9-2 0.... TonyHamilton 1 83
(Richard Fahey) *dwlt: hdwy 3f out: upsides 2f out: carried lft fnl f: no ex nr fin* **9/4**[2]
40 **3** 4 **Dusker (USA)**[66] 1520 2-9-2 0.... WilliamBuick 5 71
(Mark Johnston) *chsd ldrs: drvn and swtchd lft over 2f out: one pce over 1f out* **11/2**[3]
3 **4** 3/4 **Jamacho**[38] 2301 2-9-2 0.... DaleSwift 2 69
(Brian Ellison) *led tl over 2f out: one pce over 1f out* **9/1**
5 **5** 7 **Expenditure (IRE)**[21] 2830 2-9-2 0.... JackGarritty 7 48
(Jedd O'Keeffe) *w ldr: wknd fnl 2f* **33/1**
6 *nk* **Whitby Bay** 2-8-6 0.... NathanEvans(5) 6 42
(Michael Easterby) *sn chsng ldrs: drvn over 2f out: lost pl over 1f out* **66/1**
0 **7** 4 1/2 **Pontecarlo Boy**[10] 3223 2-9-2 0.... GeorgeChaloner 8 33
(Richard Whitaker) *wnt rt s: in rr: edgd rt 2f out: sn lost pl and bhd* **100/1**

1m 12.41s (-0.09) **Going Correction** -0.05s/f (Stan) **7** Ran SP% **114.0**
Speed ratings (Par 95): **98,97,92,91,82 81,75**
CSF £3.13 TOTE £1.80: £1.20, £1.50; EX 3.90 Trifecta £8.80.
Owner MPH Racing - II **Bred** Stephanie Von Schilcher & Gavan Kinch **Trained** Newmarket, Suffolk

FOCUS
A fair novice event and another race in which the odds-on favourite was forced to work for it.

3563 BETFRED "RACING'S BIGGEST SUPPORTER" H'CAP 1m 2f 42y (Tp)
2:55 (2:55) (Class 5) (0-75,75) 4-Y-O+ £4,528 (£1,347; £673; £336) Stalls High

Form RPR
50-0 **1** **Suitor**[57] 1775 4-9-4 **72**.... BenCurtis 4 85
(Brian Ellison) *chsd ldrs: 2nd over 2f out: styd on to ld last 100yds: drvn out* **3/1**[3]
0401 **2** 1 1/2 **Briardale (IRE)**[28] 2618 4-9-7 **75**.... PJMcDonald 5 85
(James Bethell) *led: hdd and no ex last 100yds* **5/2**[1]
1-50 **3** 5 **Roman De Brut (IRE)**[131] 568 4-8-4 **58**.... LukeMorris 1 59
(Daniel Mark Loughnane) *mid-div: effrt over 3f out: 3rd 2f out: kpt on one pce* **16/1**
-026 **4** 2 1/4 **Bogardus (IRE)**[21] 2832 5-8-11 **65**.... DougieCostello 2 61
(Patrick Holmes) *stdd s: hld up in rr: effrt over 2f out: kpt on to take modest 4th clsng stages* **7/1**

-450 **5** *3/4* **The Third Man**[27] 2651 5-9-5 **73**.................................(p) PaulMulrennan 8 68
(Henry Spiller) *hld up in mid-div: hdwy and 4th 2f out: wknd fnl 150yds* **12/1**

22-0 **6** *6* **Paddy's Rock (IRE)**[28] 2618 5-8-10 **64**.............................. JackGarritty 9 48
(Lynn Siddall) *dwlt: hld up in last: kpt on fnl 2f: nvr a factor* **33/1**

5214 **7** *2* **Grand Canyon (IRE)**[8] 3294 4-9-6 **74**........................(p) DanielTudhope 7 54
(David O'Meara) *chsd ldrs: drvn over 3f out: lost pl over 1f out* **11/4**[2]

/3-5 **8** *4* **Mumford**[38] 2307 4-9-2 **70**.. DavidAllan 6 42
(Geoffrey Harker) *chsd ldr: reminders over 3f out: lost pl over 1f out* **28/1**

0-00 **9** *1/2* **Inspector Norse**[26] 2673 5-8-11 **65**...................................... JasonHart 3 36
(Tim Easterby) *chsd ldrs: drvn 5f out: lost pl over 2f out* **25/1**

2m 10.56s (0.16) **Going Correction** +0.125s/f (Slow) **9** Ran SP% **116.5**
Speed ratings (Par 103): **104,102,98,97,96 91,90,86,86**
CSF £10.83 CT £100.99 TOTE £4.90: £1.30, £1.40, £2.80; EX 14.10 Trifecta £183.60.
Owner A Barnes **Bred** Cheveley Park Stud Ltd **Trained** Norton, N Yorks

FOCUS
An ordinary handicap and the pace looked just fair.

3564 BETFRED "SUPPORTS JACK BERRY HOUSE" H'CAP 1m 2f 42y (Tp)
3:30 (3:30) (Class 6) (0-60,60) 4-Y-O+ **£3,234** (£962; £481; £240) **Stalls** High

Form RPR

5020 **1** **Almutamarred (USA)**[60] 1675 4-8-11 **55**............ PatrickO'Donnell(5) 11 67
(Kevin Morgan) *mid-div: hdwy over 2f out: led over 1f out: pushed out* **5/1**[3]

4440 **2** *1 1/2* **Kicking The Can (IRE)**[27] 2660 5-9-5 **58**.......................... LukeMorris 3 67
(David Thompson) *led 2f: chsd ldr: led over 2f out: hdd over 1f out: kpt on same pce* **9/1**

300- **3** *3 3/4* **Our Kylie (IRE)**[39] 4486 4-9-6 **59**.. BenCurtis 8 61
(Brian Ellison) *chsd ldrs: drvn over 3f out: kpt on one pce over 1f out* **10/3**[1]

3-52 **4** *1 3/4* **Exclusive Diamond**[19] 2915 4-9-3 **56**.......................... DanielTudhope 1 55
(David O'Meara) *chsd ldrs: effrt over 3f out: one pce fnl 2f* **9/2**[2]

1-00 **5** *4* **Glasgon**[19] 2915 6-8-11 **57**.. RowanScott(7) 4 48
(Ray Craggs) *prom: drvn over 3f out: chsng ldrs over 2f out: fdd appr fnl f* **14/1**

6552 **6** *1 3/4* **First Summer**[15] 3031 4-9-2 **55**.. DavidAllan 7 43
(Shaun Harris) *mid-div: chsng ldrs over 5f out: drvn over 3f out: fdd fnl 2f* **8/1**

0-53 **7** *nk* **Neuf Des Coeurs**[12] 3154 5-9-2 **60**........................(p) GarryWhillans(5) 10 47
(Iain Jardine) *mid-div: hdwy to chse ldrs over 2f out: wknd over 1f out* **16/1**

-004 **8** *1 3/4* **Gabrial's Hope (FR)**[6] 3363 7-9-2 **55**............................ FrannyNorton 12 39+
(Tracy Waggott) *s.v.s: hdwy 7f out: chsng ldrs over 2f out: sn wknd* **16/1**

5404 **9** *1/2* **Nelson's Bay**[7] 3327 7-9-3 **56**.. CamHardie 2 39
(Wilf Storey) *rr-div: drvn and hdwy 3f out: wknd over 1f out* **14/1**

3040 **10** *1* **Illustrious Prince (IRE)**[7] 3327 9-9-4 **57**.................. ConnorBeasley 6 38
(Julie Camacho) *hld up towards rr: effrt over 2f out: nvr a factor* **20/1**

00-0 **11** *4 1/2* **Exclusive Waters (IRE)**[18] 2618 6-9-7 **60**........................ RaulDaSilva 5 32+
(George Charlton) *s.v.s: bhd: sme hdwy 3f out: lost pl over 1f out* **25/1**

0405 **12** *1 1/2* **Outlaw Torn (IRE)**[19] 2915 7-9-2 **55**..............................(e) JasonHart 14 25
(Richard Guest) *racd wd: trckd ldrs: led after 2f: hdd over 2f out: wknd over 1f out: eased clsng stages* **14/1**

/0-6 **13** *5* **May's Boy**[26] 2436 8-9-3 **56**..(p) TomEaves 9 16
(James Moffatt) *in rr: drvn over 4f out: eased whn bhd clsng stages* **66/1**

00-0 **14** *14* **Spokesperson (USA)**[31] 2526 8-9-4 **57**........................(p) PaulMulrennan 13
(Fred Watson) *chsd ldrs: drvn over 3f out: lost pl 2f out: bhd whn heavily eased clsng stages* **33/1**

2m 11.53s (1.13) **Going Correction** +0.125s/f (Slow) **14** Ran SP% **123.8**
Speed ratings (Par 101): **100,98,95,94,91 89,89,88,87,86 83,82,78,66**
CSF £49.29 CT £176.44 TOTE £6.50: £2.90, £2.40, £2.20; EX 57.60 Trifecta £262.30.
Owner S P Giles **Bred** Shadwell Farm LLC **Trained** Gazeley, Suffolk

FOCUS
A moderate handicap and the winning time was around a second slower than the preceding 0-75.

3565 BETFRED SEATON DELAVAL H'CAP 1m 5y (Tp)
4:00 (4:00) (Class 2) (0-105,105) 4-Y-O+
£12,450 (£3,728; £1,864; £932; £466; £234) **Stalls** Centre

Form RPR

-003 **1** **Mothers Finest (IRE)**[19] 2890 4-8-8 **92**..............................(t) BenCurtis 1 102
(K R Burke) *hld up in rr: hdwy far side over 4f out: w ldrs 3f out: led 2f out: edgd rt: drvn rt out* **10/1**

2060 **2** *1* **Si Senor (IRE)**[82] 1195 5-8-11 **95**.. LukeMorris 8 103
(Ed Vaughan) *hld up in rr: effrt stands' side over 2f out: rdr briefly lost iron and eased for a few strides 1f out: chsd wnr fnl 150yds: styd on same pce clsng stages* **4/1**[2]

-064 **3** *6* **Home Cummins (IRE)**[12] 3152 4-8-3 **87**..................(p) PatrickMathers 7 80
(Richard Fahey) *chsd ldrs: effrt over 2f out: kpt on one pce fnl f* **6/1**

-003 **4** *1/2* **Father Bertie**[61] 1643 4-8-4 **88**................................(p) DuranFentiman 4 80
(Tim Easterby) *w ldrs: one pce appr fnl f* **14/1**

3623 **5** *1/2* **Mont Ras (IRE)**[75] 1344 9-8-10 **94**...................................... SamJames 5 85
(David Loughnane) *chsd ldrs: drvn over 2f out: wknd appr fnl f* **8/1**

0-06 **6** *5* **Baraweez (IRE)**[12] 3164 6-9-7 **105**.. DaleSwift 2 84
(Brian Ellison) *in tch: effrt 3f out: sn chsng ldrs: wknd over 1f out: eased clsng stages* **7/2**[1]

06-0 **7** *5* **Jacob Black**[28] 2628 5-8-8 **92**.. GrahamGibbons 9 59
(Keith Dalgleish) *led: hdd 2f out: wknd appr fnl f* **9/1**

000- **8** *3 1/4* **Altharoos (IRE)**[251] 7247 6-8-4 **88**.............................. ConnorBeasley 3 47
(Sally Hall) *mid-div: pushed along over 4f out: sn chsng ldrs: wknd fnl 2f* **33/1**

-503 **9** *4 1/2* **Alfred Hutchinson**[12] 3163 8-9-2 **100**........................(p) DanielTudhope 6 48
(David O'Meara) *trckd ldrs: drvn over 2f out: hung rt and lost pl over 1f out: eased clsng stages* **9/2**[3]

1m 36.9s (-1.70) **Going Correction** -0.05s/f (Stan) **9** Ran SP% **114.5**
Speed ratings (Par 109): **106,105,99,98,98 93,88,84,80**
CSF £49.37 CT £265.62 TOTE £7.10: £2.30, £1.80, £1.90; EX 39.00 Trifecta £179.00.
Owner Hubert John Strecker **Bred** Tony Doyle **Trained** Middleham Moor, N Yorks

FOCUS
A warm handicap in which the first two pulled well clear and the form looks solid.

3566 BETFRED "HOME OF GOALS GALORE" H'CAP 7f 14y (Tp)
4:35 (4:36) (Class 2) (0-105,102) 3-Y-O+
£12,450 (£3,728; £1,864; £932; £466; £234) **Stalls** Centre

Form RPR

6105 **1** **Mr Bossy Boots (IRE)**[12] 3157 5-8-12 **91**............(t) PatrickO'Donnell(5) 1 100
(Ralph Beckett) *in rr-div far side: hdwy to chse ldrs over 2f out: led 1f out: hld on clsng stages* **8/1**[3]

2-10 **2** *3/4* **Hold Tight**[47] 2027 4-9-8 **96**..[1] WilliamBuick 13 103
(Saeed bin Suroor) *hld up in mid-div: effrt toward stands' side over 2f out: chsd ldrs 1f out: kpt on to take 2nd post* **4/1**[1]

0-00 **3** *nse* **Northgate Lad (IRE)**[20] 2862 4-9-0 **88**.................................. BenCurtis 8 95
(Brian Ellison) *led: hdd 2f out: kpt on wl fnl f: no ex clsng stages* **40/1**

/050 **4** *1/2* **Lord Of The Land (IRE)**[42] 2191 5-10-0 **102**............ DanielTudhope 14 108
(David O'Meara) *trckd ldrs stands' side: effrt 2f out: kpt on same pce last 100yds* **16/1**

-205 **5** *3* **Candelisa (IRE)**[20] 2871 3-9-1 **98**.. JackGarritty 6 92
(Jedd O'Keeffe) *chsd ldrs: one pce over 1f out* **25/1**

1-22 **6** *3/4* **Certificate**[138] 486 5-9-9 **97**...(v) JackMitchell 4 92
(Roger Varian) *trckd ldrs towards far side: qcknd to ld 2f out: hdd 1f out: wknd fnl 150yds* **5/1**[2]

3350 **7** *1/2* **Georgian Bay (IRE)**[33] 2485 6-9-5 **98**...................(v) JordanVaughan(5) 9 92
(K R Burke) *in rr: hdwy over 2f out: kpt on: nvr a threat* **14/1**

6354 **8** *1/2* **Wilde Inspiration (IRE)**[21] 2833 5-9-1 **89**.................... ConnorBeasley 2 82
(Julie Camacho) *chsd ldrs: drvn 3f out: one pce over 1f out* **10/1**

000 **9** *11* **Free Code (IRE)**[5] 3419 5-9-0 **88**................................ GrahamGibbons 3 51
(David Barron) *towards rr: drvn over 3f out: lost pl 2f out* **16/1**

6-00 **10** *2 1/2* **Enlace**[35] 2391 4-9-4 **92**.. FrannyNorton 5 48
(Mark Johnston) *rr-div: brief effrt towards far side over 2f out: sn lost pl* **33/1**

0-10 **11** *2 3/4* **Lord Of The Rock (IRE)**[42] 2191 4-9-5 **93**................ PaulMulrennan 10 42
(Michael Dods) *chsd ldrs: drvn over 2f out: sn lost pl* **9/1**

01-1 **12** *hd* **Can't Change It (IRE)**[35] 2391 5-9-8 **96**......................(p) JamieSpencer 7 44+
(David Simcock) *in rr: effrt towards stands' side over 2f out: sn btn* **4/1**[1]

-046 **13** *nk* **Love Island**[13] 3116 7-8-12 **86**..................................(t) GeorgeChaloner 11 33
(Richard Whitaker) *chsd ldrs: drvn over 3f out: lost pl 2f out* **80/1**

00-4 **14** *1* **Toocoolforschool (IRE)**[68] 1491 4-10-0 **102**........(tp) DougieCostello 12 47
(K R Burke) *chsd ldrs towards stands' side: hung lft and lost pl 2f out* **25/1**

1m 24.59s (-1.61) **Going Correction** -0.05s/f (Stan)
WFA 3 from 4yo+ 9lb **14** Ran SP% **119.6**
Speed ratings (Par 109): **107,106,106,105,102 101,100,100,87,84 81,81,80,79**
CSF £37.88 CT £1262.81 TOTE £8.70: £2.90, £1.70, £7.20; EX 56.30 Trifecta £4966.00.
Owner P J Scargill & Partner **Bred** Kilfrush Stud **Trained** Kimpton, Hants
■ Stewards' Enquiry : Patrick O'Donnell seven-day ban: used whip above permitted level (Jul 7-9,11-14)

FOCUS
Another decent handicap and very competitive with five in a line across the track passing the furlong pole. The pace looked solid.

3567 BETFRED "SIX BEST ODDS RACES DAILY" H'CAP (DIV I) 7f 14y (Tp)
5:10 (5:10) (Class 5) (0-75,75) 3-Y-O **£3,881** (£1,155; £577; £288) **Stalls** Centre

Form RPR

46-6 **1** **Awesome Quality (USA)**[16] 2998 3-8-13 **67**..................... LukeMorris 2 79+
(James Tate) *sn trcking ldrs: led over 1f out: edgd rt ins fnl f: drvn rt out* **7/2**[1]

-146 **2** *3 1/2* **Wowcha (IRE)**[37] 2336 3-9-6 **74**... JasonHart 5 77
(John Quinn) *trckd ldrs: effrt 2f out: chsd wnr fnl f: no imp* **13/2**

1600 **3** *2* **Be Kool (IRE)**[12] 3130 3-9-0 **68**... BenCurtis 1 66
(Brian Ellison) *dwlt: in rr: sn pushed along in rr: hdwy over 2f out: modest 3rd 1f out: kpt on one pce* **9/2**[2]

1500 **4** *5* **Ronnie Baird**[8] 3286 3-9-7 **75**..(p) FrannyNorton 9 59
(Kristin Stubbs) *in rr: outpcd 3f out: kpt on fnl f* **12/1**

00-0 **5** *3 3/4* **Firedanser**[33] 2477 3-9-7 **75**.. TonyHamilton 4 49
(Richard Fahey) *chsd ldrs: effrt over 2f out: wknd over 1f out* **9/1**

2-41 **6** *1/2* **Ponty Royale (IRE)**[31] 2533 3-8-11 **65**............................... DavidAllan 10 38
(Tim Easterby) *dwlt: in rr: drvn over 3f out: chsng ldrs over 1f out: sn fdd* **9/2**[2]

6450 **7** *1/2* **Firesnake (IRE)**[13] 3111 3-9-4 **72**..............................(v[1]) DougieCostello 7 43
(K R Burke) *set str pce: sn clr: hdd over 1f out: sn wknd* **20/1**

6-00 **8** *5* **Jordan James (IRE)**[6] 3366 3-9-1 **69**.................................... DaleSwift 6 27
(Brian Ellison) *chsd ldrs: lost pl over 1f out* **20/1**

4-30 **9** *1* **Kirkham**[10] 3224 3-8-13 **67**.. ConnorBeasley 8 22
(Julie Camacho) *chsd ldrs: drvn over 3f out: lost pl 2f out* **5/1**[3]

1m 24.81s (-1.39) **Going Correction** -0.05s/f (Stan) **9** Ran SP% **115.8**
Speed ratings (Par 99): **105,101,98,93,88 88,87,81,80**
CSF £26.63 CT £101.53 TOTE £4.70: £1.60, £3.00, £2.00; EX 33.00 Trifecta £186.70.
Owner Sheikh Rashid Dalmook Al Maktoum **Bred** Fred W Hertrich III & John D Fielding **Trained** Newmarket, Suffolk

FOCUS
The first division of an ordinary 3yo handicap. The early pace was strong thanks to the tearaway leader and they finished well spread out.

3568 BETFRED "SIX BEST ODDS RACES DAILY" H'CAP (DIV II) 7f 14y (Tp)
5:40 (5:42) (Class 5) (0-75,75) 3-Y-O **£3,881** (£1,155; £577; £288) **Stalls** Centre

Form RPR

-066 **1** **Like No Other**[17] 2973 3-9-1 **69**.. DavidAllan 1 85+
(Les Eyre) *dwlt: sn drvn along: hdwy far side to ld 2f out: clr 1f out: edgd rt and drvn out* **16/1**

023 **2** *6* **Little Miss Kodi (IRE)**[90] 1079 3-9-5 **73**........................ FrannyNorton 10 73
(Daniel Mark Loughnane) *trckd ldrs: effrt over 2f out: kpt on to take modest 2nd last 100yds* **13/2**

5-62 **3** *1 1/2* **Strummer (IRE)**[31] 2533 3-8-13 **67**.. TomEaves 6 63
(Kevin Ryan) *w ldrs: kpt on same pce appr fnl f* **4/1**[2]

321- **4** *3/4* **Jameerah**[245] 7413 3-9-6 **74**... LukeMorris 7 68+
(James Tate) *hld up; towards rr: t.k.h: effrt over 2f out: kpt on one pce over 1f out* **11/2**[3]

-460 **5** *1 3/4* **Ancient Astronaut**[40] 2239 3-9-7 **75**.. JasonHart 2 64
(John Quinn) *trckd ldrs: t.k.h: effrt over 1f out: fdd clsng stages* **7/1**

1-00 **6** *nse* **Wilsons Ruby (IRE)**[28] 2622 3-8-11 **65**.................................[1] DaleSwift 8 54
(Brian Ellison) *dwlt: in rr: hdwy stands' side over 2f out: one pce over 1f out* **14/1**

-000 **7** *8* **Mon Beau Visage (IRE)**[22] 2802 3-9-4 **72**................(p) DanielTudhope 5 39
(David O'Meara) *hld up towards rr: hdwy over 2f out: lost pl over 1f out: eased clsng stages* **14/1**

-355 **8** *5* **Oscar Hughes (IRE)**[31] 2533 3-8-4 **58**.............................(p) CamHardie 4 12
(Julie Camacho) *trckd ldrs: drvn over 3f out: lost pl over 1f out: bhd whn eased clsng stages* **33/1**

450 **9** *27* **Total Power**[31] 2545 3-9-1 **69**...[1] BenCurtis 9
(Brian Ellison) *chsd ldrs: lost pl 2f out: sn bhd: heavily eased last 100yds: virtually p.u: t.o* **12/1**

-261 **10** *nk* **Kafoo**[23] 2770 3-8-12 **66**.. PaulMulrennan 3
(Ed Dunlop) *led: reminders over 2f out: sn hdd and lost pl: bhd whn heavily eased last 100yds: virtually p.u: t.o* **11/4**[1]

1m 25.91s (-0.29) **Going Correction** -0.05s/f (Stan) **10** Ran SP% **117.7**
Speed ratings (Par 99): **99,92,90,89,87 87,78,72,41,41**
CSF £117.40 CT £517.56 TOTE £19.30: £4.80, £2.20, £2.10; EX 164.60 Trifecta £1276.20.
Owner M Rozenbroek & J L Eyre **Bred** Whitwell Bloodstock **Trained** Catwick, N Yorks

FOCUS
The winner completely took this race apart. The time was 1.1sec slower than the first leg.
T/Jkpt: Not won. T/Plt: £27.50 to a £1 stake. Pool: £64,498.29 - 1707.02 winning units. T/Qpdt: £19.40 to a £1 stake. Pool: £5,868.24 - 222.90 winning units. **Walter Glynn**

3408 NEWMARKET (R-H)
Thursday, June 23

OFFICIAL GOING: Soft (6.2)
Wind: virtually nil Weather: light cloud and showers

3569 COUNTRYSIDE ALLIANCE NOVICE STKS (PLUS 10 RACE) 6f
2:00 (2:01) (Class 4) 2-Y-O **£4,528** (£1,347; £673; £336) **Stalls** High

Form RPR

1 **Unabated (IRE)** 2-9-2 0.. JamesDoyle 6 76+
(Marco Botti) *t.k.h: trckd ldng pair: swtchd rt 2f out: sn rdn and clsd to chal 1f out: rdr dropped whip but led ins fnl f: pushed along and kpt on fnl 100yds: jst hld on* **8/1**

5 **2** *hd* **Wahash (IRE)**[41] 2203 2-9-2 0.. FrankieDettori 2 75
(Richard Hannon) *chsd ldr: clsd and upsides over 2f out: rdn 2f out: drvn to ld 1f out: hdd ins fnl f: kpt on but a hld fnl 100yds* **8/11**[1]

3 *nse* **Mucho Applause (IRE)** 2-9-2 0.................................... DavidProbert 3 75+
(Andrew Balding) *wnt rt s and s.i.s: rn green and pushed along early: in tch in last pair: effrt and hung lft over 1f out: no imp tl styd on wl ins fnl f* **4/1**[2]

4 *1 3/4* **Glorious Rocket** 2-9-2 0.. AdamKirby 7 70
(Luca Cumani) *led: rdn 2f out: hdd 1f out: stl ev ch tl no ex 100yds out: wknd towards fin* **6/1**[3]

5 *6* **King Of Nepal** 2-9-2 0.. FergusSweeney 1 52
(Henry Candy) *hld up in tch in last pair: effrt 2f out: sn outpcd: wknd ins fnl f* **16/1**

1m 17.96s (5.46) **Going Correction** +0.575s/f (Yiel) **5** Ran SP% **109.2**
Speed ratings (Par 95): **86,85,85,83,75**
CSF £14.38 TOTE £8.80: £3.80, £1.10; EX 14.40 Trifecta £36.40.
Owner Mubarak Al Naemi **Bred** Mubarak Al Naemi **Trained** Newmarket, Suffolk

FOCUS
Far side of course used. The stalls were on the far side except over 1m4f, when they were in the centre. After 7.55mm of overnight rain the going was eased to soft. Little form to go on for this maiden which was run at an even pace.

3570 COUNTRYSIDE ALLIANCE H'CAP 1m 4f
2:30 (2:32) (Class 5) (0-75,75) 3-Y-O+ **£3,234** (£962; £481; £240) **Stalls** Centre

Form RPR

-351 **1** **Hearty (IRE)**[21] 2829 3-8-0 **61**...(p) JimmyQuinn 3 67
(Jeremy Noseda) *s.i.s: t.k.h: hld up in tch towards rr: hdwy to chse ldrs 5f out: ev ch over 2f out: rdn and edgd rt over 1f out: sustained duel w runner-up after: led wl ins fnl f: rdn out: gamely* **7/4**[1]

425 **2** *shd* **Jarir**[19] 2900 3-8-13 **74**..(b) FrankieDettori 4 79
(Richard Hannon) *chsd ldr tl 5f out: styd wl in tch: effrt to ld 2f out: rdn and sustained duel w wnr fr over 1f out: hdd wl ins fnl f: kpt on but jst hld towards fin* **11/4**[2]

0-20 **3** *2 1/4* **Sky Of Stars (IRE)**[58] 1738 3-8-9 **70**........................ SilvestreDeSousa 6 71
(William Knight) *chsd ldrs: wnt 2nd 5f out: rdn to ld 3f out tl 2f out: sltly outpcd whn short of room and swtchd lft over 1f out: edgd lft and kpt on same pce fnl f* **11/2**

1415 **4** *nk* **Dakota City**[103] 922 5-9-9 **70**....................................(v) AdamBeschizza 2 71
(Julia Feilden) *hld up in tch in rr: effrt over 2f out: drvn ent fnl f: kpt on but nvr enough pce to threaten ldrs* **11/1**

040 **5** *1 1/4* **Eastern Lady (IND)**[21] 2816 3-9-0 **75**...................... RichardKingscote 1 74
(William Knight) *hld up in tch in last pair: effrt over 2f out: drvn and stl chsng ldrs over 1f out: wknd ins fnl f* **5/1**[3]

5/0 **6** *2 1/2* **Vocaliser (IRE)**[21] 2819 4-10-0 **75**................................... PaulHanagan 7 70
(Robin Dickin) *led: rdn and hdd 3f out: struggling to qckn whn n.m.r over 1f out: wknd 1f out* **16/1**

2m 40.2s (7.30) **Going Correction** +0.575s/f (Yiel) **6** Ran SP% **109.3**
WFA 3 from 4yo+ 14lb
Speed ratings (Par 103): **98,97,96,96,95 93**
CSF £6.33 CT £17.60 TOTE £2.40: £1.50, £1.70; EX 6.50 Trifecta £18.20.
Owner Miss Yvonne Jacques **Bred** Ronan Fitzpatrick **Trained** Newmarket, Suffolk
■ Stewards' Enquiry : Jimmy Quinn caution: careless riding; two-day ban: used whip above permitted level (Jul 7,11)

FOCUS
Race distance increased by 22yds due to repositioning of the bend into the home straight. The pace was steady for this open handicap with the field racing up the centre.

3571 RACING UK DAY PASS JUST £10 H'CAP 7f
3:05 (3:06) (Class 4) (0-85,84) 3-Y-O+ **£5,175** (£1,540; £769; £384) **Stalls** High

Form RPR

2-21 **1** **Fawaareq (IRE)**[44] 2122 3-9-5 **84**...................................... PaulHanagan 5 91+
(Owen Burrows) *chsd ldrs: rdn to ld over 2f out: jnd and drvn over 1f out: forged ahd ins fnl f: styd on* **10/3**[2]

3436 **2** *1 1/2* **Cincuenta Pasos (IRE)**[18] 2934 5-10-0 **84**..................... TomQueally 13 90+
(Joseph Tuite) *hld up in tch in last quartet: hdwy u.p over 1f out: styd on ins fnl f: wnt 2nd towards fin* **8/1**

0500 **3** *3/4* **Athletic**[18] 2934 7-8-12 **75**..(v) GeorgeWood[(7)] 8 79
(Andrew Reid) *stdd s: hld up in tch in last quartet: hdwy over 2f out: rdn and ev ch over 1f out: no ex and btn 100yds out: wknd and lost 2nd towards fin* **16/1**

0001 **4** *1* **Secret Glance**[13] 3097 4-9-13 **83**................................ AdamBeschizza 11 84
(Richard Rowe) *led for 1f: chsd ldr: rdn 2f out: lost 2nd and unable qck wl over 1f out: kpt on same pce ins fnl f* **10/1**

20-0 **5** *2 3/4* **Jay Kay**[51] 1954 7-9-5 **75**... JoeyHaynes 3 69
(K R Burke) *chsd ldr tl led after 1f: rdn and hdd over 2f out: wknd fnl f* **20/1**

1-44 **6** *1/2* **Hope Cove**[54] 1865 3-9-4 **83**.. GeorgeBaker 12 73
(Ed Walker) *stdd s: hld up in tch in last quartet: hdwy and edgd lft over 1f out: no imp after* **7/2**[3]

-312 **7** *2* **Frenchman (FR)**[18] 2935 3-9-0 **79**.................................. RyanMoore 10 64
(Charles Hills) *in tch in midfield: rdn 3f out: sn struggling and lost pl 2f out: wknd over 1f out* **11/4**[1]

40-0 **8** *6* **Sarangoo**[33] 2460 8-9-4 **77**...................................... JosephineGordon[(3)] 4 49
(Malcolm Saunders) *in tch in midfield: rdn over 2f out: sn struggling: wknd over 1f out* **25/1**

301- **9** *9* **Mr Quicksilver**[178] 8381 4-9-7 **77**.........................(t) SilvestreDeSousa 9 26
(Ed Walker) *s.i.s: in tch in last quartet: effrt over 2f out: sn btn: wknd over 1f out* **14/1**

5-00 **10** *6* **Bold**[29] 2587 4-9-4 **74**..(t) FMBerry 7 7
(Stuart Williams) *chsd ldrs: struggling u.p over 2f out: lost pl and btn over 1f out: bhd and eased ins fnl f* **33/1**

1m 29.65s (3.95) **Going Correction** +0.575s/f (Yiel)
WFA 3 from 4yo+ 9lb **10** Ran SP% **116.3**
Speed ratings (Par 105): **100,98,97,96,93 92,90,83,73,66**
CSF £29.29 CT £381.73 TOTE £3.90: £1.50, £2.80, £5.10; EX 27.10 Trifecta £201.30.
Owner Hamdan Al Maktoum **Bred** Shadwell Estate Company Limited **Trained** Lambourn, Berks

FOCUS
A competitive handicap run at a steady pace. The field raced up the far rail.

3572 DISCOVERNEWMARKET.CO.UUK MAIDEN STKS 7f
3:40 (3:41) (Class 5) 3-Y-O+ **£3,881** (£1,155; £577; £288) **Stalls** High

Form RPR

45 **1** **Horrah**[16] 2999 3-9-5 0.. GeorgeBaker 9 82+
(Roger Charlton) *trckd ldrs: effrt to chal over 1f out: rdn to ld ins fnl f: styd on wl* **9/4**[2]

05 **2** *2* **Cadeaux Boxer**[13] 3104 3-9-2 0.. TimClark[(3)] 7 77
(Martin Smith) *t.k.h: chsd ldrs: effrt 2f out: drvn and pressing ldrs over 1f out: styd on same pce ins fnl f: wnt 2nd last strides* **66/1**

34 **3** *hd* **Edward Lewis**[26] 2686 3-9-5 0....................................... FrankieDettori 11 76
(John Gosden) *trckd ldr: upsides and gng wl 2f out: rdn to ld over 1f out: hdd ins fnl f: one pce after: lost 2nd last strides* **5/4**[1]

4 *1/2* **Sumou (IRE)** 3-9-5 0... PaulHanagan 3 75+
(Marcus Tregoning) *in tch in midfield: rdn and outpcd over 1f out: rallied and kpt on wl again ins fnl f* **16/1**

5 *2 1/4* **Nellie Deen (IRE)** 3-9-0 0.. SilvestreDeSousa 8 64+
(David Elsworth) *wnt rt s and s.i.s: rn green: t.k.h: hld up in rr of main gp: hdwy and edging lft over 1f out: kpt on ins fnl f: nvr trbld ldrs* **7/1**[3]

6 *1* **Walking In Rhythm (IRE)** 3-9-0 0.................................... SeanLevey 2 62
(Richard Hannon) *wnt rt s and s.i.s: hld up in tch: rdn and sme hdwy over 1f out: kpt on same pce ins fnl f* **25/1**

0 **7** *1 1/2* **Luang Prabang (IRE)**[33] 2483 3-9-0 0............................... TedDurcan 4 58
(Chris Wall) *in tch in midfield: clsd to press ldrs 2f out: sn rdn and unable qck: wknd ins fnl f* **25/1**

0 **8** *1* **Ms Arsenal**[19] 2904 4-9-6 0..................................... JosephineGordon[(3)] 6 58
(Giles Bravery) *t.k.h: led tl rdn and hdd over 1f out: wknd ins fnl f* **100/1**

9 *3/4* **Iberica Road (USA)** 3-9-2 0..................................(t) RobHornby[(3)] 12 58
(Andrew Balding) *in tch towards rr of main gp: rdn 3f out: sn outpcd: no threat to ldrs but plugged on ins fnl f* **33/1**

10 *2 3/4* **Poetic Guest** 3-9-5 0... AdamKirby 10 51
(George Margarson) *hld up in tch in midfield: rdn 2f out: sn edgd lft and outpcd: wknd fnl f* **20/1**

11 *2 3/4* **Mr Piglet** 3-9-5 0... FMBerry 14 44
(William Jarvis) *in tch in midfield: rdn 2f out: sn lost pl and wknd over 1f out* **50/1**

\- **12** *nse* **Happisburgh Man** 4-10-0 0... JimmyQuinn 13 47
(Dr Jon Scargill) *stdd s: hld up in rr of main gp: outpcd and shkn up over 2f out: wknd wl over 1f out* **100/1**

13 *14* **Sea The Waves** 3-9-5 0.. TomQueally 5 7
(Emma Owen) *wnt rt and s.i.s: sn rcvrd and in tch in midfield after 1f: lost pl over 2f out: bhd fnl f* **66/1**

14 *11* **Nelson's Victory**[46] 6-10-0 0.. FergusSweeney 1
(Gary Moore) *wnt bdly rt s and s.i.s: a detached in last: lost tch 3f out: t.o* **66/1**

1m 30.94s (5.24) **Going Correction** +0.575s/f (Yiel)
WFA 3 from 4yo+ 9lb **14** Ran SP% **117.4**
Speed ratings (Par 103): **93,90,90,89,87 86,84,83,82,79 76,76,60,47**
CSF £156.88 TOTE £3.00: £1.20, £15.00, £1.10; EX 187.40 Trifecta £398.00.
Owner Mrs H Thomson Jones **Bred** Theobalds Stud **Trained** Beckhampton, Wilts

FOCUS
Not the strongest maiden for the track but it was run at a fair pace and the winner did it well.

3573 HOME OF RACING H'CAP 5f
4:10 (4:11) (Class 2) (0-100,97) 3-Y-O+ **£12,938** (£3,850; £1,924; £962) **Stalls** High

Form RPR

0600 **1** **Green Door (IRE)**[12] 3151 5-9-9 **94**..................................(v) AdamKirby 4 106
(Robert Cowell) *chsd ldrs: effrt to ld over 1f out: styd on strly and clr ins fnl f: eased cl home* **4/1**[2]

0000 **2** *2 3/4* **Lucky Beggar (IRE)**[22] 2787 6-8-13 **84**............................. RyanMoore 9 86
(Charles Hills) *taken down early: chsd ldr: effrt and upsides ldrs over 1f out: outpcd by wnr and styd on same pce ins fnl f* **7/2**[1]

1600 **3** *3/4* **Dungannon**[110] 835 9-9-4 **92**..(b) RobHornby[(3)] 5 91
(Andrew Balding) *hld up in tch in last trio: clsd and nt clrest of runs 2f out: effrt over 1f out: kpt on u.p ins fnl f: wnt 3rd last strides* **20/1**

-601 **4** *hd* **Oh So Sassy**[20] 2863 6-9-6 **91**... GeorgeBaker 6 90
(Chris Wall) *led: rdn and hdd over 1f out: 3rd and outpcd jst ins fnl f: lost 3rd last strides* **4/1**[2]

0-00 **5** *shd* **Son Of Africa**[42] 2188 4-9-10 **95**................................... FergusSweeney 3 93
(Henry Candy) *stdd and wnt rt s: hld up in tch in rr: hdwy u.p ent fnl f: kpt on u.p: nvr trbld ldrs* **10/1**

2400 **6** *2 1/2* **Basil Berry**[103] 923 5-9-9 **97**..........................(p) JosephineGordon[(3)] 2 86
(Chris Dwyer) *stdd s: hld up in tch in rr: effrt 2f out: sn drvn and no hdwy: plugged on same pce fnl f* **9/1**

0053 **7** *1* **Plagiarism (USA)**[14] 3056 3-8-4 **81**........................ SilvestreDeSousa 7 65
(Mark Johnston) *dwlt: sn rcvrd and in tch in midfield: rdn and unable qck wl over 1f out: wknd ins fnl f* **8/1**

6434 8 1 3/4 **Waseem Faris (IRE)**[19] 2898 7-9-1 **86**.......... JamesDoyle 1 65
(Joseph Tuite) *in tch in midfield: rdn and unable qck 2f out: sn lost pl: wknd fnl f* **11/2**[3]
1m 0.88s (1.78) **Going Correction** +0.575s/f (Yiel)
WFA 3 from 4yo+ 6lb 8 Ran SP% **112.6**
Speed ratings (Par 109): **108,103,102,102,101 97,96,93**
CSF £17.80 CT £244.30 TOTE £4.50: £2.10, £1.50, £5.60; EX 19.90 Trifecta £404.30.
Owner Mrs Fitri Hay **Bred** Mrs Sue Lenehan **Trained** Six Mile Bottom, Cambs
FOCUS
A number of well-handicapped runners lined up for this contest which was run at a sound pace. It paid to race handy.

3574 WHITING & PARTNERS H'CAP 1m
4:45 (4:45) (Class 4) (0-85,84) 3-Y-O **£5,175** (£1,540; £769; £384) **Stalls** High

Form RPR
0-21 1 **Silent Attack**[22] 2790 3-9-6 **83**.......... JamesDoyle 2 96+
(Saeed bin Suroor) *racd in centre: stdd s: hld up in tch in rr: clsd to trck ldrs 2f out: rdn and qcknd to ld ins fnl f: styd on* **2/1**[1]
5140 2 2 **Fashaak (IRE)**[21] 2818 3-9-5 **82**.......... SeanLevey 5 87
(Richard Hannon) *racd in centre: chsd ldr tl led gng wl 2f out: rdn over 1f out: hdd and one pce ins fnl f* **8/1**
0-1 3 2 1/4 **Tukhoom (IRE)**[13] 3104 3-9-7 **84**.......... PaulHanagan 3 84
(Marcus Tregoning) *wnt rt s: racd in centre: chsd ldrs tl led 3f out: sn rdn and hdd 2f out: unable qck over 1f out: kpt on same pce fnl f* **7/2**[2]
3-15 4 nk **Dubai's Secret**[19] 2891 3-9-6 **83**.......... RyanMoore 7 82
(Richard Hannon) *swtchd to r on far rail after 1f: midfield overall: effrt u.p to chse ldrs over 2f out: no imp and one pce fr over 1f out* **5/1**[3]
1 5 6 **Youre Always Right (IRE)**[38] 2312 3-9-6 **83**.......... AdamKirby 8 68
(Clive Cox) *racd on far rail thrght: led: rdn and hdd 3f out: lost pl 2f out: wknd over 1f out* **10/1**
01-0 6 1 1/2 **Kummiya**[48] 1992 3-8-12 **75**.......... WilliamTwiston-Davies 4 57
(Roger Charlton) *racd in centre: stdd s: t.k.h: hld up in tch in rr: effrt 2f out: no ex and btn 1f out: sn wknd* **8/1**
160 7 3 1/4 **Prince Of Arran**[19] 2892 3-9-6 **83**..........(v) TomQueally 1 57
(Charlie Fellowes) *racd in centre: stdd and hmpd s: hld up in tch in midfield: rdn over 2f out: lost pl and bhd over 1f out: sn wknd* **10/1**
1m 44.01s (4.01) **Going Correction** +0.575s/f (Yiel) 7 Ran SP% **112.6**
Speed ratings (Par 101): **102,100,97,97,91 89,86**
CSF £18.12 CT £51.78 TOTE £2.70: £1.70, £4.90; EX 21.30 Trifecta £72.60.
Owner Godolphin **Bred** Ship Commodities **Trained** Newmarket, Suffolk
FOCUS
An open handicap run at a sound pace. The main field raced up the centre.

3575 OMEGA INGREDIENTS INNOVATIVE NATURAL FLAVOURS FILLIES' H'CAP 6f
5:20 (5:20) (Class 4) (0-85,85) 3-Y-O+ **£5,175** (£1,540; £769; £384) **Stalls** High

Form RPR
-061 1 **Guishan**[5] 3397 6-9-11 **85** 6ex.......... TimClark(3) 8 96
(Michael Appleby) *taken down early: racd towards far side: mde all: rdn 2f out: edgd rt u.p 1f out: styd on gamely u.p ins fnl f* **8/1**[3]
21-5 2 1 3/4 **Dutch Destiny**[15] 3034 3-9-3 **81**.......... RyanMoore 7 85
(William Haggas) *racd towards far side: chsd wnr: effrt 2f out: drvn and pressing wnr 1f out: kpt on same pce ins fnl f* **2/1**[1]
-522 3 2 **Pixeleen**[14] 3068 4-9-8 **82**.......... JosephineGordon(3) 6 82
(Malcolm Saunders) *taken down early: in tch in midfield: split gps tl jnd centre gp after 2f: effrt to chse ldng pair over 1f out: styd on same pce ins fnl f* **2/1**[1]
0034 4 5 **Rural Celebration**[13] 3116 5-9-10 **81**.......... JamesDoyle 3 66
(David O'Meara) *racd in centre: in tch in midfield: effrt 2f out: 4th and outpcd 1f out: wknd ins fnl f* **7/1**[2]
-235 5 3 1/4 **Exoplanet Blue**[24] 2737 4-9-0 **71**..........(p) FergusSweeney 1 46
(Henry Candy) *racd in centre: in tch in midfield: effrt 2f out: no imp over 1f out: wknd ins fnl f* **25/1**
-055 6 hd **Fever Few**[98] 969 7-8-13 **77**.......... SamuelClarke(7) 2 51
(Chris Wall) *stdd and awkward leaving stalls: a in rr: rdn 2f out: sn btn: bhd fnl f* **20/1**
-310 7 10 **Justice Angel (IRE)**[26] 2683 3-9-7 **85**.......... SilvestreDeSousa 9 27
(David Elsworth) *taken down early: racd towards far side: s.i.s: a bhd: rdn 2f out: sn btn: wl bhd and eased ins fnl f* **8/1**[3]
1m 14.77s (2.27) **Going Correction** +0.575s/f (Yiel)
WFA 3 from 4yo+ 7lb 7 Ran SP% **110.0**
Speed ratings (Par 102): **107,104,102,95,91 90,77**
CSF £22.58 CT £41.11 TOTE £8.50: £3.20, £1.70; EX 26.70 Trifecta £90.60.
Owner Brian D Cantle **Bred** B D Cantle **Trained** Oakham, Rutland
FOCUS
They went a sound pace in the conditions for this fair handicap. The front three finished clear.
T/Plt: £23.60 to a £1 stake. Pool: £61,326.50 - 1893.66 winning units. T/Qpdt: £11.70 to a £1 stake. Pool: £4,611.64 - 291.50 winning units. **Steve Payne**

3216 NOTTINGHAM (L-H)
Thursday, June 23

OFFICIAL GOING: Soft (6.2)
Wind: Nil Weather: Overcast

3576 32RED CASINO NOVICE AUCTION STKS 6f 15y
2:10 (2:12) (Class 5) 2-Y-O **£3,067** (£905; £453) **Stalls** High

Form RPR
53 1 **Mister Blue Sky (IRE)**[14] 3065 2-9-2 0.......... OisinMurphy 7 74
(Sylvester Kirk) *chsd ldr tl led 1/2-way: rdn clr and hung lft ins fnl f* **4/6**[1]
0 2 5 **Kath's Boy (IRE)**[16] 2997 2-8-13 0.......... GeorgeDowning(3) 6 59
(Tony Carroll) *prom: rdn over 2f out: chsd wnr over 1f out: edgd lft and wknd wl ins fnl f* **33/1**
3 hd **Ivor's Magic (IRE)** 2-8-4 0.......... AdamMcLean(7) 5 53
(David Elsworth) *chsd ldrs: rdn and edgd lft 2f out: styd on same pce fr over 1f out* **6/1**[3]
4164 4 1 1/4 **Nazik**[13] 3114 2-9-9 0.......... JFEgan 4 62
(David Evans) *led to 1/2-way: rdn over 1f out: edgd lft and wknd ins fnl f* **4/1**[2]
0 5 5 **Nyx**[12] 3167 2-8-8 0.......... EoinWalsh(3) 1 35
(Richard Guest) *chsd ldrs: rdn and hung lft over 2f out: wknd over 1f out* **20/1**
6 9 **Copa Beech** 2-8-11 0.......... CallumShepherd(5) 2 13
(Olly Williams) *s.i.s: sn pushed along in rr: wknd 1/2-way* **25/1**
7 9 **The Batham Boy (IRE)** 2-9-2 0.......... RobertHavlin 3
(Daniel Mark Loughnane) *s.s: outpcd* **16/1**
1m 17.81s (3.11) **Going Correction** +0.175s/f (Good) 7 Ran SP% **111.7**
Speed ratings (Par 93): **86,79,79,77,70 58,46**
CSF £31.62 TOTE £1.50: £1.10, £7.70; EX 22.30 Trifecta £99.00.
Owner Deauville Daze Partnership 1 **Bred** Shadwell Estate Company Limited **Trained** Upper Lambourn, Berks
FOCUS
Outer track used. The rail was set out 4 yards on whole track, adding approximately 12 yards to races 2, 3, 4 and 7. The going dried out to soft, having been heavy, soft in places. Not a strong race, run in conditions most are not likely to see too often again this season.

3577 £10 FREE BET AT 32RED.COM MAIDEN STKS 1m 75y
2:45 (2:45) (Class 5) 3-Y-O+ **£2,911** (£866; £432; £216) **Stalls** Centre

Form RPR
-322 1 **Perigee**[14] 3066 3-9-2 80.......... RobertHavlin 5 82+
(John Gosden) *led after 1f: pushed clr fr over 1f out* **1/4**[1]
0 2 4 **Western Way (IRE)**[9] 3264 7-9-12 0.......... JFEgan 4 75+
(Don Cantillon) *s.i.s: hld up: pushed along and hung lft fr over 3f out: hdwy over 1f out: wnt 2nd ins fnl f: no ch w wnr* **16/1**[3]
05 3 1 3/4 **Proctor**[28] 2614 3-9-2 0.......... OisinMurphy 2 69
(Stuart Kittow) *prom: rdn over 2f out: no ex fnl f* **5/1**[2]
00 4 3 **Glittering**[40] 2234 3-8-11 0.......... RyanTate 6 57
(James Eustace) *racd keenly: led 1f: racd in 2nd pl: rdn over 2f out: lost 2nd over 1f out: wknd fnl f* **33/1**
06 5 1/2 **Wallangarra**[28] 2614 3-9-2 0.......... HarryBentley 7 61
(Jeremy Gask) *hld up: rdn over 3f out: edgd lft over 1f out: n.d* **20/1**
00 6 6 **Isostatic**[22] 2790 3-8-11 0.......... SaleemGolam 3 42
(Rae Guest) *s.i.s: hld up: sme hdwy over 2f out: wknd wl over 1f out* **100/1**
00 7 2 1/2 **Keyman (IRE)**[14] 3066 3-9-2 0.......... NickyMackay 1 41
(Jeremy Gask) *chsd ldrs: rdn over 2f out: wknd wl over 1f out* **100/1**
1m 50.57s (1.57) **Going Correction** +0.175s/f (Good)
WFA 3 from 7yo 10lb 7 Ran SP% **112.2**
Speed ratings (Par 103): **99,95,93,90,89 83,81**
CSF £5.43 TOTE £1.10: £1.02, £6.90; EX 6.10 Trifecta £9.60.
Owner K Abdullah **Bred** Juddmonte Farms Ltd **Trained** Newmarket, Suffolk
FOCUS
The rail was set out 4 yards on the whole track adding approximately 12 yards to this race. The betting suggested it would be one-way traffic, and so it proved.

3578 32RED ON THE APP STORE MAIDEN STKS 1m 2f 50y
3:20 (3:24) (Class 5) 3-Y-O+ **£2,911** (£866; £432; £216) **Stalls** Low

Form RPR
2- 1 **De Veer Cliffs (IRE)**[253] 7219 3-8-9 0.......... HarryBentley 2 81+
(Martyn Meade) *chsd ldr tl over 8f out: wnt 2nd again over 5f out: led over 1f out: shkn up ins fnl f: r.o: comf* **4/6**[1]
6 2 1 1/4 **Martha McCandles**[13] 3094 5-9-2 0.......... CallumShepherd(5) 1 76
(Alan King) *hld up: hdwy over 4f out: rdn to chse wnr ins fnl f: styd on* **33/1**
-620 3 1 1/4 **Pleasure Dome**[14] 3060 3-8-9 82.......... AdrianMcCarthy 6 73
(Peter Chapple-Hyam) *sn led: rdn and hdd over 1f out: styd on same pce ins fnl f* **3/1**[2]
6-6 4 8 **Lee Bay**[11] 3190 3-9-0 0..........(b[1]) RobertHavlin 3 63
(John Gosden) *s.i.s: sn prom: lost pl over 4f out: hdwy over 2f out: sn rdn: wknd over 1f out* **6/1**[3]
5 5 **Rasmee** 3-8-11 0.......... DanielMuscutt(3) 7 54
(Marco Botti) *s.s: hld up: hdwy u.p over 2f out: sn wknd* **10/1**
6 24 **Quiet Approach** 3-9-0 0.......... RyanTate 5 8
(John Davies) *pushed along to chse ldr over 8f out tl over 5f out: sn rdn: wknd over 2f out* **33/1**
2m 18.1s (3.80) **Going Correction** +0.175s/f (Good)
WFA 3 from 5yo 12lb 6 Ran SP% **114.2**
Speed ratings (Par 103): **91,90,89,82,78 59**
CSF £27.30 TOTE £1.60: £1.10, £8.30; EX 15.90 Trifecta £44.60.
Owner Mrs Jane Newett **Bred** Epona Bloodstock Ltd **Trained** Newmarket, Suffolk
FOCUS
The rail was set out 4 yards on the whole track adding approximately 12 yards to this race. Torquay delayed the start by dropping her rider a couple of times and was eventually taken out.

3579 32REDSPORT.COM H'CAP 1m 75y
3:50 (3:50) (Class 5) (0-70,70) 3-Y-O **£2,911** (£866; £432; £216) **Stalls** Centre

Form RPR
1343 1 **Carbutt's Ridge (IRE)**[8] 3285 3-8-5 **54**..........(v) AndrewMullen 5 65
(K R Burke) *chsd ldr: shkn up to ld over 2f out: rdn over 1f out: styd on wl* **7/2**[3]
6556 2 3 **Bit Of A Quirke**[23] 2777 3-8-7 **56**.......... JFEgan 8 59
(Mark Walford) *hld up: rdn over 3f out: hdwy over 1f out: r.o to go 2nd wl ins fnl f: no ch w wnr* **5/1**
-140 3 2 1/4 **Tricky Dicky**[30] 2553 3-8-10 **59**.......... OisinMurphy 3 57
(Olly Williams) *hld up: rdn over 2f out: hdwy u.p to chse wnr over 1f out: styd on same pce ins fnl f* **5/2**[1]
340S 4 3 1/4 **Deben**[10] 3224 3-8-3 **55**.......... JoeDoyle(3) 7 46
(Kevin Ryan) *hld up in tch: racd keenly: rdn over 2f out: wknd over 1f out* **17/2**
-200 5 nk **Premier Currency (IRE)**[24] 2749 3-9-7 **70**..........(p) HarryBentley 6 60
(Mike Murphy) *led: rdn and hdd over 2f out: wknd fnl f* **3/1**[2]
4-00 6 8 **St Andrews (IRE)**[85] 1151 3-9-4 **70**..........(t) GeorgeDowning(3) 1 43
(Ian Williams) *sn pushed along to chse ldrs: rdn over 3f out: wknd over 2f out* **17/2**
1m 50.51s (1.51) **Going Correction** +0.175s/f (Good) 6 Ran SP% **113.5**
Speed ratings (Par 99): **99,96,93,90,90 82**
CSF £21.26 CT £49.96 TOTE £3.50: £1.40, £2.80; EX 13.70 Trifecta £55.20.
Owner Ontoawinner 9 & Mrs E Burke **Bred** Thomas Hassett **Trained** Middleham Moor, N Yorks
FOCUS
The rail was set out 4 yards on the whole track adding approximately 12 yards to this race. It's probably best to presume this was just a modest contest.

3580 32RED H'CAP 6f 15y
4:25 (4:25) (Class 4) (0-80,79) 3-Y-O+ **£4,851** (£1,443; £721; £360) **Stalls** High

Form RPR
-433 1 **Escalating**[12] 3168 4-9-13 **78**..........(tp) AndrewMullen 5 89
(Michael Appleby) *chsd ldrs: rdn to ld over 1f out: r.o wl* **2/1**[1]
3400 2 4 1/2 **Llewellyn**[26] 2680 8-8-11 **67**..........(b) PhilDennis(5) 6 65
(Declan Carroll) *led: rdn and hdd over 1f out: no ex ins fnl f* **16/1**

5606 **3** 1 ¾ **Heartsong (IRE)**[19] 2903 7-9-7 **75**........................ MichaelJMMurphy(3) 8 67
(John Gallagher) *hld up: hdwy over 2f out: rdn and hung lft over 1f out: styd on same pce* **8/1**

3-60 **4** ¾ **Ormskirk**[19] 2891 3-8-13 **76**..................................(p) CallumShepherd(5) 7 64+
(Brian Ellison) *stmbld s: bhd: rdn over 2f out: styd on ins fnl f: nrst fin* **7/1**

6162 **5** hd **Sir Domino (FR)**[8] 3284 4-9-7 **75**...................................(b) KevinStott(3) 2 64
(Kevin Ryan) *chsd ldrs: rdn over 1f out: no ex* **4/1**[2]

00-0 **6** 2 ½ **Boy In The Bar**[85] 1143 5-9-10 **78**.........................(b) GeorgeDowning(3) 4 60
(Ian Williams) *w ldr tl rdn over 2f out: wknd fnl f* **8/1**

01-0 **7** 3 **Times Legacy**[27] 2650 3-9-3 **75**..................................... AdrianMcCarthy 3 46
(Peter Chapple-Hyam) *s.i.s: hld up: hdwy over 2f out: rdn and wknd over 1f out: eased* **6/1**[3]

0600 **8** 8 **Clubland (IRE)**[20] 2857 7-10-0 **79**... JFEgan 1 28
(Roy Bowring) *chsd ldrs: pushed along 1/2-way: wknd over 2f out* **25/1**

1m 16.64s (1.94) **Going Correction** +0.175s/f (Good)
WFA 3 from 4yo+ 7lb **8** Ran SP% **112.1**
Speed ratings (Par 105): **94,88,85,84,84 81,77,66**
CSF £35.19 CT £209.50 TOTE £2.90: £1.30, £3.50, £2.50; EX 36.40 Trifecta £170.40.
Owner The Horse Watchers **Bred** Juddmonte Farms Ltd **Trained** Oakham, Rutland

FOCUS
This looked a fair sprint, but it appeared to fall apart around 1f out, with many not really getting into serious contention.

3581 32RED.COM H'CAP 5f 13y
5:00 (5:00) (Class 5) (0-70,70) 3-Y-O **£2,911** (£866; £432; £216) **Stalls** High

Form RPR

4220 **1** **Sir Theodore (IRE)**[21] 2834 3-9-4 **70**.......................... LouisSteward(3) 3 78+
(Richard Spencer) *mde virtually all: rdn over 1f out: edgd lft ins fnl f: r.o: comf* **3/1**[1]

5124 **2** 1 ¼ **Lady Joanna Vassa (IRE)**[5] 3423 3-8-6 **58**.................... EoinWalsh(3) 5 61
(Richard Guest) *s.i.s: sn prom: rdn to chse wnr ins fnl f: styd on* **3/1**[1]

4-00 **3** ¾ **Lady Nayef**[24] 2742 3-9-6 **69**.. JFEgan 4 69
(John Butler) *w wnr tl pushed along over 3f out: rdn over 1f out: styd on same pce ins fnl f* **7/1**

6302 **4** ½ **Sarabi**[9] 3268 3-8-13 **62**..(p) NickyMackay 1 60
(Scott Dixon) *hld up: hdwy over 1f out: sn rdn: styd on same pce ins fnl f* **5/1**[2]

5-00 **5** 3 ¾ **Manipura**[7] 3307 3-8-6 **60**...(p) NoelGarbutt(5) 6 45
(Derek Shaw) *s.i.s: pushed along in rr: nvr on terms* **25/1**

205 **6** 1 ¾ **Misu Moneypenny**[10] 3218 3-9-0 **70**.........................(p) NatalieHambling(7) 7 48
(Scott Dixon) *prom: rdn 1/2-way: wknd over 1f out* **6/1**[3]

0005 **7** 4 ½ **Men United (FR)**[5] 3423 3-8-5 **59** ow2..................(t) CallumShepherd(5) 2 21
(Roy Bowring) *chsd ldrs: rdn over 2f out: wknd and eased over 1f out* **6/1**[3]

1m 2.35s (0.85) **Going Correction** +0.175s/f (Good) **7** Ran SP% **111.6**
Speed ratings (Par 99): **100,98,96,96,90 87,80**
CSF £11.27 TOTE £3.70: £2.20, £2.10; EX 11.40 Trifecta £65.10.
Owner Rebel Racing **Bred** Kilshannig Stud **Trained** Newmarket, Suffolk

FOCUS
It paid to be reasonably handy in this modest sprint.

3582 32RED "HANDS AND HEELS" APPRENTICE SERIES H'CAP (RACING EXCELLENCE INITIATIVE) 1m 75y
5:30 (5:30) (Class 5) (0-70,70) 4-Y-O+ **£2,911** (£866; £432; £216) **Stalls** Centre

Form RPR

064 **1** **Uncle Dermot (IRE)**[33] 2460 8-9-7 **68**...................... RichardCondon(3) 1 75
(Brendan Powell) *rrd s: hdwy to chse ldr after 1f: pushed along 2f out: led ins fnl f: styd on* **6/1**

-060 **2** nk **Handheld**[42] 2174 9-8-13 **62**..(p) LiamDoran(5) 3 68
(Julia Feilden) *led: pushed along 2f out: hdd ins fnl f: kpt on* **8/1**

61-6 **3** ½ **Sublimation (IRE)**[37] 2343 6-9-0 **63**.............................. JoshuaBryan(5) 5 68
(Steve Gollings) *a.p: pushed along over 2f out: styd on* **10/3**[2]

0-03 **4** 1 ¼ **The Gay Cavalier**[17] 2965 5-9-7 **70**..........................(t) JonathanFisher(5) 7 72
(John Ryan) *s.i.s: hld up: pushed along and hdwy over 1f out: r.o: nt rch ldrs* **8/1**

3113 **5** 1 **Little Choosey**[14] 3072 6-8-6 **55**.......................(bt) LiamLewis-Salter(5) 4 55
(Roy Bowring) *s.i.s: hdwy on outer 5f out: pushed along over 2f out: no ex ins fnl f* **4/1**[3]

-002 **6** 1 ¼ **Framley Garth (IRE)**[10] 3212 4-9-6 **67**............................ PaulaMuir(3) 6 65
(Patrick Holmes) *hld up: pushed along over 2f out: styd on towards fin: nvr on terms* **3/1**[1]

3030 **7** 7 **Lendal Bridge**[37] 2329 5-8-6 **53**................................... BenRobinson(3) 2 35
(Tony Coyle) *racd keenly: trckd ldr 1f: remained handy: pushed along over 3f out: wknd over 2f out* **8/1**

1m 51.04s (2.04) **Going Correction** +0.175s/f (Good) **7** Ran SP% **115.7**
Speed ratings (Par 103): **96,95,95,93,92 91,84**
CSF £52.70 TOTE £8.10: £2.70, £5.00; EX 49.30 Trifecta £314.30.
Owner K Rhatigan **Bred** Ballyhane Stud **Trained** Upper Lambourn, Berks

FOCUS
The rail was set out 4 yards on the whole track adding approximately 12 yards to this race. There was a good finish to this, a race in which whips were carried but not allowed to be used.
T/Plt: £21.10 to a £1 stake. Pool: £42,975.89 - 1480.73 winning units. T/Qpdt: £12.40 to £1 stake. Pool: £2,935.09 - 174.15 winning units. **Colin Roberts**

3583 - 3590a (Foreign Racing) - See Raceform Interactive

[3128]CHESTER (L-H)
Friday, June 24

OFFICIAL GOING: Good to soft (good in places; 6.8)
Wind: light across Weather: fine

3591 CALDWELL CONSTRUCTION APPRENTICE H'CAP 7f 122y
6:35 (6:39) (Class 4) (0-80,79) 3-Y-O **£6,225** (£1,864; £932; £466; £233; £117) **Stalls** Low

Form RPR

3164 **1** **Viscount Barfield**[22] 2818 3-9-1 **73**.. RobHornby 7 84
(Andrew Balding) *midfield: smooth hdwy 2f out: pushed along to ld over 1f out: kpt on wl to draw clr* **7/2**[2]

-460 **2** 4 ½ **Bell Heather (IRE)**[13] 3152 3-9-0 **77**.......................... AdamMcNamara(5) 5 77
(Richard Fahey) *midfield: rdn 2f out: kpt on fnl f: wnt 2nd 75yds out* **8/1**

210 **3** 1 **Irish Optimism (IRE)**[27] 2695 3-9-5 **77**.................................. KevinStott 6 74
(John Quinn) *trckd ldng pair: rdn 2f out: chsd wnr appr fnl f: one pce: lost 2nd 75yds out* **11/2**[3]

0124 **4** ½ **Outback Blue**[13] 3130 3-9-0 **79**...(t) AledBeech(7) 9 75
(David Evans) *stdd s: hld up: rdn 2f out: kpt on: nvr threatened* **17/2**

5620 **5** 1 **Theos Lolly (IRE)**[41] 2239 3-8-9 **72**.......................... NatalieHambling(5) 8 65
(Richard Fahey) *swtchd lft jst after s: hld up in midfield on inner: rdn over 2f out: kpt on ins fnl f: nvr threatened* **14/1**

30-2 **6** 2 ¼ **Donttouchthechips (IRE)**[34] 2459 3-8-7 **67** ow1.......... GaryMahon(3) 4 56
(Nikki Evans) *pressed ldr: rdn over 2f out: wknd fnl f* **13/2**

1400 **7** 1 ¾ **Galesburg (IRE)**[13] 3155 3-9-0 **77**........................... RobJFitzpatrick(5) 2 60
(Mark Johnston) *slowly away: collided w rail after 110yds: hld up in rr: pushed along over 3f out: nvr threatened* **10/3**[1]

0460 **8** 1 ½ **Big Amigo (IRE)**[14] 3111 3-8-6 **69**................................ AnnaHesketh(5) 1 49
(Tom Dascombe) *fly leapt s: sn led: racd keenly: rdn whn hdd over 1f out: wknd* **14/1**

2360 **9** hd **Winged Dancer**[31] 2565 3-8-11 **74**.............................. MitchGodwin(5) 3 53
(Sylvester Kirk) *trckd ldng pair: rdn 2f out: wknd over 1f out* **20/1**

1m 34.09s (0.29) **Going Correction** +0.325s/f (Good) **9** Ran SP% **113.8**
Speed ratings (Par 101): **111,106,105,105,104 101,100,98,98**
CSF £31.07 CT £149.68 TOTE £3.40: £1.10, £2.90, £2.30; EX 29.20 Trifecta £116.50.
Owner David Brownlow **Bred** Rockwell Bloodstock **Trained** Kingsclere, Hants

FOCUS
A handicap for apprentices run over 13 yards further than advertised. The pace was strong, and the form is best treated with caution as the pace collapsed in the closing stages and it was run to favour the closers. The race has been rated around the runner-up.

3592 STELLAR GROUP MAIDEN FILLIES' STKS (PLUS 10 RACE) 7f 2y
7:05 (7:10) (Class 4) 2-Y-O **£6,225** (£1,864; £932; £466; £233; £117) **Stalls** Low

Form RPR

5336 **1** **Hi Milady (IRE)**[20] 2885 2-9-0 0......................................[1] FrederikTylicki 1 68
(Dominic Ffrench Davis) *led: jnd 3f out: rdn over 2f out: hdd appr fnl f: rallied to ld again post* **8/1**

3 **2** shd **Preobrajenska**[15] 3074 2-9-0 0... WilliamCarson 3 68
(Michael Bell) *trckd ldr: pressed ldr 3f out: rdn and hung rt on bnd over 2f out: led appr fnl f: sn drvn: one pce fnl 50yds and hdd post* **7/2**[2]

2 **3** 1 ½ **Conqueress (IRE)**[12] 3186 2-9-0 0............................... RichardKingscote 4 64
(Tom Dascombe) *in tch: rdn over 2f out: kpt on fnl f* **5/4**[1]

4 1 ¾ **Miss Danby (IRE)** 2-9-0 0... FrannyNorton 6 59
(Mark Johnston) *trckd ldr: rdn over 2f out: no ex ins fnl f* **4/1**[3]

0200 **5** 3 **Black Redstart**[19] 2933 2-8-7 0.............................. LiamLewis-Salter(7) 2 51+
(Alan Bailey) *rrd leaving stalls and bhd: hdwy and in tch over 3f out: rdn over 2f out: wknd ins fnl f* **33/1**

6 6 **Clenymistra (IRE)** 2-9-0 0.. AndreaAtzeni 5 35
(Marco Botti) *hld up: pushed along over 3f out: wknd and bhd fnl 2f* **13/2**

1m 30.09s (3.59) **Going Correction** +0.325s/f (Good) **6** Ran SP% **114.1**
Speed ratings (Par 92): **92,91,90,88,84 77**
CSF £36.43 TOTE £11.10: £4.40, £1.90; EX 41.80 Trifecta £90.30.
Owner N Pickett **Bred** John Webb **Trained** Lambourn, Berks

FOCUS
This was over 13 yards further than advertised, the pace was fair and it didn't look a strong event.

3593 GROSVENOR SHOPPING CENTRE/EBF BREEDERS' SERIES FILLIES' H'CAP 1m 2f 75y
7:35 (7:38) (Class 3) (0-90,86) 3-Y-O+ **£12,450** (£3,728; £1,864; £932; £466; £234) **Stalls** High

Form RPR

4-12 **1** **Sightline**[17] 3001 3-8-11 **84**... KevinStott(3) 3 93+
(Ralph Beckett) *in tch: rdn 2f out: led jst ins fnl f: kpt on wl* **13/8**[1]

21-0 **2** 1 **Sharja Queen**[54] 1888 3-9-2 **86**... AndreaAtzeni 5 93+
(Roger Varian) *midfield: sltly short of room 2f out and forced: sn pushed along and hdwy: rdn and briefly hung lft in bhd ldr ins fnl f: kpt on wl fnl 110yds* **17/2**

152 **3** hd **Mighty Lady**[20] 2900 3-8-4 **74**.. JimmyQuinn 2 80
(Robyn Brisland) *midfield: briefly n.m.r over 1f out: sn rdn: kpt on ins fnl f: edgd lft fnl 110yds* **8/1**

2-16 **4** 1 ¼ **Wholesome (USA)**[14] 3107 3-8-12 **82**............................. FrederikTylicki 1 85
(K R Burke) *dwlt: sn trckd ldr: rdn 2f out: kpt on same pce* **5/1**[3]

-304 **5** ¾ **Empress Ali (IRE)**[14] 3113 5-10-0 **86**............................. JamesSullivan 4 88
(Tom Tate) *led: hdd 11f out: trckd ldr: rdn to chal over 2f out: led again over 1f out: hdd jst ins fnl f: wknd* **9/2**[2]

50-3 **6** 2 ¼ **Lido Lady (IRE)**[77] 1314 3-8-4 **74**..................................... FrannyNorton 8 71
(Mark Johnston) *trckd ldr: led 11f out: jnd over 2f out: sn rdn: hdd over 1f out: wknd ins fnl f* **18/1**

-141 **7** nk **Island Flame (IRE)**[12] 3189 3-8-4 **74** 6ex...................... PatrickMathers 7 70
(Richard Fahey) *hld up: pushed along over 2f out: nvr threatened* **7/1**

0126 **8** 2 **Yorkindred Spirit**[9] 3276 4-8-13 **71**.......................(v) RichardKingscote 6 63
(Mark Johnston) *dwlt: hld up: rdn over 2f out: nvr threatened* **25/1**

2m 14.46s (3.26) **Going Correction** +0.325s/f (Good)
WFA 3 from 4yo+ 12lb **8** Ran SP% **116.2**
Speed ratings (Par 104): **99,98,98,97,96 94,94,92**
CSF £16.99 CT £87.70 TOTE £2.50: £1.10, £3.10, £2.50; EX 17.20 Trifecta £74.70.
Owner J H Richmond-Watson **Bred** Lawn Stud **Trained** Kimpton, Hants

FOCUS
A handicap for fillies and mares run over 14 yards further than advertised. It was run at a moderate gallop and several pulled hard. The winner continues on the up and won despite the muddling pace.

3594 GARY CORBETT CELEBRATORY CLAIMING STKS 7f 122y
8:05 (8:06) (Class 4) 4-Y-O+ **£6,225** (£1,864; £932; £466; £233; £117) **Stalls** Low

Form RPR

-401 **1** **Hillbilly Boy (IRE)**[49] 1993 6-9-7 98......................... RichardKingscote 3 95
(Tom Dascombe) *mde all: pushed along over 2f out: rdn ins fnl f: kpt on* **4/6**[1]

0220 **2** 2 ¼ **Big Time (IRE)**[14] 3115 5-9-5 88....................................(p) FrannyNorton 6 87
(David Nicholls) *racd keenly: trckd ldr: rdn 2f out: kpt on but no threat wnr* **10/3**[2]

0000 **3** 1 ¼ **Anonymous John (IRE)**[36] 2391 4-8-12 85.... WilliamTwiston-Davies 2 77
(David Evans) *trckd ldr: rdn 2f out: no ex fnl 110yds* **8/1**[3]

2035 **4** 2 ¾ **Never To Be (USA)**[14] 3097 5-8-7 65 ow3...................(t) GaryMahon(5) 1 70?
(Nikki Evans) *hld up in rr: rdn 4f out: hdwy and in tch 3f out: wknd ins fnl f* **33/1**

631 **5** 1 ¾ **Bush Beauty (IRE)**[13] 3132 5-8-4 68.......................... SophieKilloran(7) 8 65
(Eric Alston) *racd keenly: hld up: pushed along over 1f out: nvr threatened* **14/1**

1020 **6** 3 1/2 **Captain Revelation**27 2689 4-8-10 82 AnnaHesketh(5) 4 60
(Tom Dascombe) *midfield: rdn over 1f out: sn wknd* **12/1**
1m 34.53s (0.73) **Going Correction** +0.325s/f (Good) **6** Ran SP% **111.5**
Speed ratings (Par 105): **109,106,105,102,101 97**
CSF £3.06 TOTE £1.80: £1.02, £3.20; EX 3.10 Trifecta £7.20.
Owner Macguire's Bloodstock Ltd **Bred** Tipper House Stud **Trained** Malpas, Cheshire
FOCUS
A claimer run over 13 yards further than advertised in which the winner had by far the best credentials and was also able to dictate the gallop which was fair. They finished well strung out.

3595 CLOSE BROTHERS ASSET FINANCE H'CAP 7f 2y
8:40 (8:47) (Class 4) (0-85,82) 3-Y-O+
£6,225 (£1,864; £932; £466; £233; £117) **Stalls** Low

Form RPR
0001 **1** **Gabrial The Tiger (IRE)**13 3153 4-9-0 75 AdamMcNamara(7) 4 85
(Richard Fahey) *mde all: pushed along and qcknd 3 l clr over 1f out: drvn ins fnl f: reduced advantage nr fin but nvr in danger* **9/2**1
3250 **2** 1 1/2 **Ocean Sheridan (IRE)**27 2679 4-10-0 82 BenCurtis 12 88
(Michael Dods) *midfield: rdn over 2f out: hdwy to chse ldr 1f out: kpt on* **16/1**
0523 **3** 1/2 **My Target (IRE)**42 2213 5-9-9 77 WilliamTwiston-Davies 9 82+
(Michael Wigham) *hld up: hdwy on outer 2f out: rdn over 1f out: kpt on* **9/1**
0513 **4** nse **Favourite Treat (USA)**7 3344 6-9-9 77 (e) JamesSullivan 1 83+
(Ruth Carr) *dwlt: hld up in midfield: pushed along and hdwy whn bdly hmpd over 1f out: kpt on wl fnl f pushed out: unlucky nt to fin clsr* **6/1**2
0-13 **5** nk **Lil Sophella (IRE)**13 3152 7-9-13 81 JackGarritty 11 85+
(Patrick Holmes) *hld up in rr: stl lot to do 2f out: pushed along and hdwy over 1f out: swtchd lft 1f out: kpt on wl: nrst fin* **10/1**
6205 **6** 2 **Dr Red Eye**27 2677 8-8-6 67 (p) NatalieHambling(7) 7 65
(Scott Dixon) *chsd ldr: rdn over 2f out: wknd ins fnl f* **12/1**
-504 **7** shd **Fullon Clarets**38 2331 4-9-11 79 PatrickMathers 6 77
(Richard Fahey) *chsd ldrs: rdn over 2f out: outpcd over 1f out: plugged on fnl f* **15/2**
3020 **8** 9 **Clockmaker (IRE)**106 890 10-9-11 82 KevinStott(3) 3 56
(Conor Dore) *chsd ldr: rdn over 2f out: lost pl whn short of room over 1f out: wknd* **10/1**
2010 **9** 4 1/2 **Mr Christopher (IRE)**48 2028 4-9-2 70 (p) RichardKingscote 10 32
(Tom Dascombe) *hld up: rdn over 2f out: sn wknd* **25/1**
2-03 **10** 61 **Gold Trade (IRE)**17 2998 3-9-1 81 (p) MarcMonaghan(3) 5
(Hugo Palmer) *in tch: rdn over 3f out: wknd qckly 2f out and eased* **13/2**3
1m 27.98s (1.48) **Going Correction** +0.325s/f (Good)
WFA 3 from 4yo+ 9lb **10** Ran SP% **103.2**
Speed ratings (Par 105): **104,102,101,101,101 99,98,88,83,13**
CSF £62.66 CT £472.65 TOTE £4.10: £1.60, £4.20, £2.90; EX 49.50 Trifecta £239.90.
Owner Dr Marwan Koukash **Bred** Kenneth Heelan **Trained** Musley Bank, N Yorks
■ Compass Hill was withdrawn. Price at time of withdrawal 5-1. Rule 4 applies to all bets - deduct 15p in the pound.
FOCUS
A competitive handicap run over 13 yards further than advertised. The pace was strong, but the winner made all.

3596 PRINTWORKS H'CAP 1m 2f 75y
9:10 (9:16) (Class 4) (0-80,80) 3-Y-O **£6,225** (£1,864; £932; £466) **Stalls** High

Form RPR
4244 **1** **Justice Grace (IRE)**27 2694 3-9-3 76 (b1) RichardKingscote 4 82
(Ralph Beckett) *mde all: pushed along over 2f out: rdn over 2f out: kpt on wl* **9/4**3
-036 **2** 3 **Strictly Art (IRE)**38 2341 3-8-3 62 FrannyNorton 2 62
(Alan Bailey) *in tch in 3rd: pushed along over 3f out: rdn 2f out: wnt 2nd ins fnl f: kpt on but no threat wnr* **8/1**
4122 **3** 1 1/4 **Daisy Bere (FR)**18 2973 3-9-2 80 (p) JordanVaughan(5) 6 78
(K R Burke) *dwlt: hld up in tch in 4th: rdn 2f out: kpt on fnl f: nvr threatened* **7/4**1
0451 **4** 3 **Clayton Hall (IRE)**27 2694 3-9-3 76 BenCurtis 3 68
(Brian Ellison) *trckd ldr in 2nd: rdn over 2f out: wknd ins fnl f* **2/1**2
2m 14.93s (3.73) **Going Correction** +0.325s/f (Good) **4** Ran SP% **111.6**
Speed ratings (Par 101): **98,95,94,92**
CSF £16.75 TOTE £4.70; EX 19.30 Trifecta £30.90.
Owner Robert Ng **Bred** Tom Kelly **Trained** Kimpton, Hants
FOCUS
Just four runners for this handicap which was run over 14 yards further than advertised. The pace was no more than ordinary and the winner was able to dictate.
T/Plt: £112.00 to a £1 stake. Pool: £54,988.84 - 358.15 winning tickets T/Qpdt: £23.10 to a £1 stake. Pool: £4,485.67 - 143.50 winning tickets **Andrew Sheret**

3185 DONCASTER (L-H)
Friday, June 24
OFFICIAL GOING: Good to soft (good in places, 7.4)
Wind: Moderate against Weather: Cloudy with sunny periods

3597 BEST ODDS GUARANTEED AT 188BET BRITISH STALLIONS EBF FILLIES' NOVICE STKS (PLUS 10 RACE) 6f
2:10 (2:11) (Class 5) 2-Y-O **£3,881** (£1,155; £577; £288) **Stalls** High

Form RPR
1 **Asidious Alexander (IRE)** 2-9-0 0 FrankieDettori 2 86+
(Simon Crisford) *trckd ldrs: smooth hdwy 2f out: shkn up and qcknd to ld ent fnl f: readily* **9/4**1
6 **2** 1 1/2 **Hope Solo (IRE)**10 3261 2-9-0 0 DavidAllan 4 79
(Tim Easterby) *in tch: hdwy on outer to trck ldrs over 2f out: effrt to chal over 1f out: sn rdn and ev ch ins fnl f: kpt on same pce towards fin* **9/2**
33 **3** 5 **Turanga Leela**13 3122 2-9-0 0 RichardKingscote 1 64
(Tom Dascombe) *led: pushed along 2f out: jnd and rdn over 1f out: hdd and drvn ent fnl f: kpt on same pce* **4/1**3
4 1 3/4 **Temerity (IRE)** 2-9-0 0 TonyHamilton 7 59
(Richard Fahey) *trckd ldrs: pushed along: green and edgd lft 2f out: rdn and hung bdly lft over 1f out: sn one pce* **3/1**2
5 4 1/2 **Edged In Blue** 2-9-0 0 DougieCostello 3 45+
(K R Burke) *dwlt and green in rr: hdwy over 2f out: rdn over 1f out: kpt on fnl f* **18/1**
6 2 1/4 **Laureate** 2-9-0 0 JoeFanning 9 39
(Mark Johnston) *chsd ldrs: rdn along over 2f out: sn wknd* **14/1**
06 **7** 6 **Rose Berry**16 3037 2-9-0 0 FrederikTylicki 8 21
(Chris Dwyer) *chsd ldr: pushed along at 1/2-way: rdn wl over 2f out: sn wknd* **18/1**
8 hd **Sai Kung Star** 2-9-0 0 TomEaves 5 20
(Nigel Tinkler) *green and a in rr* **50/1**
1m 16.57s (2.97) **Going Correction** +0.325s/f (Good) **8** Ran SP% **113.1**
Speed ratings (Par 90): **93,91,84,82,76 73,65,64**
CSF £12.44 TOTE £3.20: £1.30, £1.60, £1.60; EX 12.80 Trifecta £34.80.
Owner Noel O'Callaghan **Bred** Martyn J McEnery **Trained** Newmarket, Suffolk
FOCUS
Drying conditions. The round course was railed out from 1m2f until the straight, adding about six yards to races five and six. Probably just a fair fillies' event, but the winner travelled well and was impressive.

3598 £25 FREE BET AT 188BET NOVICE STKS (PLUS 10 RACE) 7f
2:40 (2:40) (Class 4) 2-Y-O **£4,204** (£1,251; £625; £312) **Stalls** High

Form RPR
1 **Bahamas (IRE)** 2-8-13 0 DanielMuscutt(3) 6 83+
(Marco Botti) *in tch: hdwy on bit over 2f out: led over 1f out: rdn: green and wandered ins fnl f: kpt on wl towards fin* **16/1**
2 1/2 **Timeless Flight** 2-9-2 0 (t) WilliamBuick 1 82+
(Charlie Appleby) *hld up in rr: stdy hdwy on outer wl over 2f out: rdn to chal ent fnl f: ev ch tl no ex towards fin* **5/2**1
3 1/2 **Muzeel (IRE)** 2-9-2 0 PaulHanagan 2 81+
(Sir Michael Stoute) *trckd ldrs: pushed along and sltly outpcd over 2f out: rdn over 1f out: styd on and ch ins fnl f: no ex towards fin* **15/2**
34 **4** 3 3/4 **Our Boy (IRE)**28 2649 2-9-2 0 FMBerry 3 71
(David Evans) *prom: chsd ldr 2f out: rdn over 1f out and ev ch tl drvn and wknd fnl f* **4/1**3
5 6 **Tread Lightly** 2-9-2 0 DavidAllan 5 54
(Tim Easterby) *in rr: pushed along over 2f out: sn swtchd rt and rdn: kpt on fnl f* **33/1**
0 **6** 2 **Pillar Of Society (IRE)**15 3058 2-9-2 0 RyanMoore 8 49
(Richard Hannon) *trckd ldr: cl up 1/2-way: rdn along over 2f out: sn drvn and wknd* **7/2**2
3 **7** hd **See The City (IRE)**34 2478 2-9-2 0 JoeFanning 4 48
(Mark Johnston) *led: pushed along 3f out: rdn 2f out: drvn and hdd over 1f out: sn wknd* **4/1**3
8 1 1/2 **Break The Silence** 2-9-2 0 BenCurtis 7 44
(Scott Dixon) *in rr: green and pushed along 1/2-way: sn rdn and outpcd fnl 2f* **50/1**
1m 29.09s (2.79) **Going Correction** +0.325s/f (Good) **8** Ran SP% **113.3**
Speed ratings (Par 95): **97,96,95,91,84 82,82,80**
CSF £55.19 TOTE £19.10: £3.90, £1.20, £2.40; EX 58.80 Trifecta £598.50.
Owner C J Murfitt **Bred** Lynn Lodge Stud **Trained** Newmarket, Suffolk
FOCUS
A fair novice race with the first three posting nice debuts.

3599 188BET.CO.UK H'CAP 1m (R)
3:10 (3:10) (Class 5) (0-70,70) 3-Y-O+ **£3,881** (£1,155; £577; £288) **Stalls** Low

Form RPR
5164 **1** **Victoire De Lyphar (IRE)**6 3421 9-10-0 70 (e) JamesSullivan 4 79
(Ruth Carr) *hld up in rr: gd hdwy on outer 3f out: rdn to ld and hung lft over 1f out: rdn out* **6/1**
4023 **2** 2 1/4 **Sakhalin Star (IRE)**3 3497 5-9-9 65 (e) JoeFanning 7 69
(Richard Guest) *hld up: hdwy over 2f out: rdn to chse ldrs over 1f: drvn and kpt on same pce fnl f* **10/3**2
5-55 **3** 3 1/2 **Aberlady (USA)**24 2770 3-9-2 68 (b) RyanMoore 11 62
(Sir Michael Stoute) *trckd ldrs: hdwy 3f out: led over 2f out and sn rdn: hdd and n.m.r over 1f out: sn swtchd rt and drvn: kpt on one pce* **11/4**1
6166 **4** 2 1/2 **Call Out Loud**11 3214 4-9-8 67 (t) AlistairRawlinson(3) 2 57
(Michael Appleby) *in tch: hdwy to trck ldrs over 3f out: rdn along over 2f out: drvn wl over 1f out and sn no imp* **13/2**
0002 **5** 3/4 **Cyflymder (IRE)**13 3153 10-8-11 53 DavidAllan 3 41
(David C Griffiths) *led: pushed along 3f out: hdd and rdn over 2f out: sn drvn and one pce* **12/1**
0340 **6** 1/2 **The Firm (IRE)**27 2673 7-9-11 67 (be) DougieCostello 5 54
(Daniel Mark Loughnane) *hld up in tch: effrt on outer 3f out: rdn along over 2f out: n.d* **28/1**
-000 **7** 1 1/2 **Caeser The Gaeser (IRE)**3 3478 4-8-6 55 (p) KieranSchofield(7) 9 39
(Nigel Tinkler) *trckd ldng pair on inner: pushed along over 3f out: rdn over 2f out: sn drvn and wknd* **50/1**
4234 **8** 2 **Depth Charge (IRE)**7 3367 4-10-0 70 (vt) TonyHamilton 1 49
(Kristin Stubbs) *hld up: a in rr* **9/2**3
000- **U** **Mrs Eve (IRE)**245 7440 4-9-1 57 FMBerry 10
(Alan Bailey) *trckd ldr tl lost action and hung bdly lft home turn: sn uns rdr: fatally injured* **22/1**
1m 41.62s (1.92) **Going Correction** +0.325s/f (Good)
WFA 3 from 4yo+ 10lb **9** Ran SP% **113.0**
Speed ratings (Par 103): **103,100,97,94,94 93,92,90,**
CSF £25.21 CT £66.93 TOTE £7.00: £2.20, £1.80, £1.30; EX 27.30 Trifecta £84.80.
Owner P Newell & Mrs R Carr **Bred** Mrs Monica Hackett **Trained** Huby, N Yorks
FOCUS
A modest handicap and the form looks very ordinary.

3600 188BET H'CAP 1m (R)
3:45 (3:45) (Class 3) (0-95,90) 3-Y-O **£7,762** (£2,310; £1,154; £577) **Stalls** Low

Form RPR
613- **1** **Hornsby**358 3809 3-9-3 86 WilliamBuick 2 91+
(Charlie Appleby) *hld up in tch on inner: n.m.r and swtchd rt wl over 1f out: sn rdn: styd on to chal ins fnl f: sn drvn: led towards fin: edgd rt nr line* **3/1**2
0-60 **2** nk **Mikmak**8 3299 3-9-5 88 DougieCostello 4 92
(William Muir) *trckd ldrs: hdwy 2f out: chal over 1f out: rdn to take slt ld ent fnl f: sn drvn: hdd and no ex towards fin* **20/1**
0005 **3** 1 **Essenaitch (IRE)**34 2479 3-8-8 77 SaleemGolam 6 79
(David Evans) *hld up in rr: hdwy on outer whn sltly hmpd over 1f out: sn rdn and chsd ldng pair wl ins fnl f: keeping on whn n.m.r nr line* **20/1**
-501 **4** 1 3/4 **Haley Bop (IRE)**13 3152 3-9-6 89 JoeFanning 7 89
(Mark Johnston) *led: pushed along over 2f out: rdn wl over 1f out: drvn and hdd narrowly ent: wknd last 110yds* **9/1**
45-2 **5** 2 **Nimr**41 2237 3-9-5 88 (t) FrankieDettori 5 81
(Richard Fahey) *hld up in rr: effrt 2f out: sn rdn along on outer: drvn and no imp appr fnl f* **7/5**1

The Form Book, Raceform Ltd, Newbury, RG14 5SJ

6-10 **6** 3/4 **Red Artist**[27] 2695 3-9-2 **85** ...... MartinLane 8 77
(Simon Crisford) *trckd ldr: cl up wl over 2f out: sn rdn to chal: drvn over 1f out: grad wknd* **8/1**

6340 **7** 3/4 **Storm Rising (IRE)**[21] 2871 3-9-7 **90** ...... (b[1]) RyanMoore 1 80
(Richard Hannon) *trckd ldrs on inner: effrt wl over 2f out and sn rdn along: drvn and wknd over 1f out* **11/2**[3]

1m 43.38s (3.68) **Going Correction** +0.325s/f (Good) **7 Ran SP% 112.7**
Speed ratings (Par 103): **94,93,92,90,88 88,87**
CSF £54.09 CT £1006.14 TOTE £4.60: £2.80, £6.10; EX 64.40 Trifecta £685.60.
Owner Godolphin **Bred** Darley **Trained** Newmarket, Suffolk

FOCUS
A decent enough 3yo handicap and a likeable effort from the winner, but the time was slow and the form looks a bit muddling.

3601 WIMBLEDON BETTING AT 188BET MAIDEN FILLIES' STKS 1m 2f 60y
4:20 (4:20) (Class 5) 3-Y-O+ **£3,881** (£1,155; £577; £288) **Stalls** Low

Form RPR

3 **1** **Ruscombe**[25] 2735 3-9-0 0 ...... RyanMoore 10 79+
(Sir Michael Stoute) *trckd ldrs: effrt and nt clr run 2f out: n.m.r and swtchd rt over 1f out: drvn to chse ldng pair ins fnl f: led last 50yds: edgd lft and jst hld on* **1/2**[1]

2 nse **To Eternity** 3-9-0 0 ...... WilliamBuick 3 79+
(John Gosden) *s.i.s and green in rr: gd hdwy on outer wl over 2f out: chsd ldrs jst over 1f out: rdn and styd on strly fnl f: jst failed* **4/1**[2]

4 **3** 1 1/4 **Entsar (IRE)**[15] 3059 3-9-0 0 ...... FrankieDettori 4 77
(William Haggas) *trckd ldrs on inner: smooth hdwy to ld wl over 3f out: shkn up and qcknd 2f out: sn rdn: drvn ent fnl f: hdd and no ex last 50yds* **9/2**[3]

0-0 **4** 2 1/2 **Princess Raihana**[43] 2183 3-8-11 0 ...... DanielMuscutt(3) 7 72
(Marco Botti) *trckd ldr: cl up over 2f out: rdn wl over 1f out: ev ch tl drvn ent fnl f and kpt on same pce* **66/1**

5 1 **Gala** 3-9-0 0 ...... NickyMackay 11 70
(John Gosden) *dwlt: hdwy on outer to trck ldrs after 1f: pushed along over 2f out: rdn wl over 1f out: wknd appr fnl f* **16/1**

6 2 **Novalina (IRE)** 3-9-0 0 ...... BenCurtis 8 67
(William Haggas) *hld up: hdwy and n.m.r over 2f out: sn rdn and no imp* **12/1**

7 1 1/4 **Notion Of Beauty (USA)** 3-9-0 0 ...... DougieCostello 9 64
(K R Burke) *hld up: hdwy 3f out: rdn along 2f out: sn one pce* **33/1**

0 **8** 2 **Always Summer**[24] 2767 3-9-0 0 ...... TomQueally 6 60
(James Fanshawe) *hld up: a towards rr* **50/1**

0 **9** 4 **Social Media**[20] 2914 3-8-7 0 ...... HarryBurns(7) 5 53
(Ed Dunlop) *awkward s and t.k.h: trckd ldrs on inner: hdwy 3f out: rdn along 2f out: sn wknd* **50/1**

10 3 3/4 **Tanera Mor (IRE)** 3-9-0 0 ...... RoystonFfrench 1 46
(Alan Bailey) *led: pushed along over 4f out: hdd wl over 3f out and sn wknd* **100/1**

2m 18.09s (8.69) **Going Correction** +0.325s/f (Good) **10 Ran SP% 127.8**
Speed ratings (Par 100): **78,77,76,74,74 72,71,69,66,63**
CSF £3.41 TOTE £1.50: £1.02, £1.90, £1.50; EX 4.00 Trifecta £9.80.
Owner K Abdullah **Bred** Juddmonte Farms Ltd **Trained** Newmarket, Suffolk

FOCUS
This was run over about six yards further than advertised. A decent fillies' maiden, but a muddling pace and the winner may not have matched her debut form..

3602 EURO 2016 BETTING AT 188BET H'CAP 1m 6f 132y
4:50 (4:50) (Class 4) (0-85,82) 4-Y-O+ **£5,175** (£1,540; £769; £384) **Stalls** Low

Form RPR

0-36 **1** **Itlaaq**[14] 3118 10-8-4 **72** ...... (t) DanielleMooney(7) 3 81+
(Michael Easterby) *hld up: hdwy on bit whn n.m.r 2f out: hmpd over 1f out: sn swtchd rt to outer and rdn: qckndl wl fnl f: led towards fin* **16/1**

2526 **2** 1 **Hubertas**[20] 2897 4-9-1 **81** ...... (v[1]) CallumShepherd(5) 6 87
(John Quinn) *hld up in rr: gd hdwy on outer over 2f out: chsd ldrs over 1f out: rdn to chal ent fnl f: sn drvn and ev ch: kpt on* **5/1**[3]

-011 **3** nk **Dew Pond**[12] 3191 4-8-3 **69** ...... RachelRichardson(5) 7 75
(Tim Easterby) *trckd ldr: cl up over 4f out: led wl over 3f out: rdn wl over 1f out: drvn ent fnl f: hdd and no ex towards fin* **9/4**[1]

-321 **4** 2 **Hurry Home Poppa (IRE)**[20] 2887 6-8-9 **70** ...... RoystonFfrench 9 73
(John Mackie) *trckd ldrs: hdwy over 3f out: chsd ldrs 2f out: rdn over 1f out: drvn and kpt on same pce fnl f* **12/1**

14 **5** nk **Jam Session (IRE)**[15] 3092 4-9-6 **81** ...... PJMcDonald 4 84
(Ian Williams) *dwlt: hdwy to trck ldrs after 1f: effrt 3f out: sn chsng ldr: rdn wl over 1f out: wknd appr fnl f* **7/2**[2]

40 **6** 2 **Time Of My Life (GER)**[34] 2487 5-9-7 **82** ...... (p) JackGarritty 5 82
(Patrick Holmes) *trckd ldrs: hdwy over 3f out: rdn along over 2f out: n.m.r and drvn wl over 1f out: wknd* **12/1**

-323 **7** 1/2 **Rock On Bollinski**[23] 2805 6-8-12 **73** ...... (p) BenCurtis 2 72
(Brian Ellison) *s.i.s and in rr: sme hdwy on inner 3f out: rdn along over 2f out: n.d* **9/1**

1-63 **8** 3/4 **Zenafire**[13] 3129 7-8-7 **68** ...... (p) PaulQuinn 1 66
(Sarah Hollinshead) *trckd ldrs on inner: hdwy 3f out: rdn along 2f out: sn n.m.r: drvn and wknd over 1f out* **16/1**

-155 **9** 6 **Kuriosa (IRE)**[30] 2582 4-8-13 **77** ...... DanielMuscutt(3) 8 68
(Marco Botti) *led: pushed along and hdd wl over 3f out: sn rdn and wknd* **10/1**

3m 14.76s (7.36) **Going Correction** +0.325s/f (Good) **9 Ran SP% 115.9**
Speed ratings (Par 105): **93,92,92,91,91 90,89,89,86**
CSF £94.28 CT £253.25 TOTE £20.30: £3.90, £1.60, £1.60; EX 92.80 Trifecta £408.30.
Owner W H & Mrs J A Tinning 1 **Bred** Shadwell Estate Company Limited **Trained** Sheriff Hutton, N Yorks

FOCUS
This was run over about six yards further than advertised. The first two finishers filled the last two spots at the top of the straight. The winner may be a bit better than the bare form after a troubled run.

3603 FREE SPINS AT 188BET CASINO H'CAP (DIV I) 6f
5:20 (5:21) (Class 5) (0-70,70) 3-Y-O **£3,881** (£1,155; £577; £144; £144) **Stalls** High

Form RPR

-031 **1** **Laila Honiwillow**[24] 2777 3-8-12 **61** ...... JackGarritty 6 73+
(Jedd O'Keeffe) *cl up: led 2f out and sn rdn: drvn and edgd lft ins fnl f: kpt on wl towards fin* **3/1**[1]

064 **2** 3/4 **Portland Street (IRE)**[28] 2667 3-8-6 **55** ...... KieranO'Neill 2 64
(Bryan Smart) *prom: hdwy 2f out: chal over 1f out: sn rdn and ev ch: drvn and edgd persistently lft ins fnl f: no ex towards fin* **12/1**

0040 **3** 2 3/4 **Dalalah**[15] 3069 3-8-2 **51** oh3 ...... (v[1]) RoystonFfrench 8 51
(Richard Guest) *hld up: hdwy over 2f out: rdn over 1f out: drvn and kpt on fnl f* **28/1**

3 **4** 3 1/2 **Waseefa**[18] 2980 3-9-0 **70** ...... DavidEgan(7) 3 59
(John Butler) *dwlt and towards rr: hdwy 2f out: rdn over 1f out: kpt on fnl f: nrst fin* **7/1**[3]

40-0 **4** dht **Cape Crusader (IRE)**[61] 1673 3-8-1 **55** ...... (p) PhilDennis(5) 7 44
(Michael Dods) *hld up in tch: hdwy over 2f out: rdn and n.m.r wl over 1f out: kpt on fnl f* **50/1**

-203 **6** nk **Mister Mischief**[28] 2667 3-9-3 **66** ...... PJMcDonald 4 54
(Paul Midgley) *dwlt and in rr: hdwy wl over 1f out: sn rdn and kpt on fnl f: nrst fin* **15/2**

13 **7** 1 **Its Only Mossy (IRE)**[42] 2201 3-9-6 **69** ...... TomQueally 9 54
(Jennie Candlish) *slt ld: rdn along over 2f out: sn hdd: drvn over 1f out: sn wknd* **4/1**[2]

-106 **8** 3/4 **Undertow (IRE)**[22] 2834 3-8-9 **65** ...... CliffordLee(7) 11 47
(K R Burke) *chsd ldrs: rdn along wl over 2f out: grad wknd* **8/1**

-33P **9** 3/4 **Penny Pot Lane**[24] 2777 3-9-4 **67** ...... KeaganLatham 10 47
(Richard Whitaker) *bhd: swtchd lft 2f out and sn rdn: plugged on fnl f* **11/1**

353 **10** 3 3/4 **Excellent World (IRE)**[31] 2557 3-9-1 **64** ...... DuranFentiman 5 32
(Tony Coyle) *dwlt: sn chsng ldrs: cl up 1/2-way: rdn along and edgd lft over 2f out: sn wknd* **8/1**

0050 **11** 4 **Teversham**[9] 3280 3-8-11 **60** ...... (b) IrineuGoncalves 1 15
(Chris Dwyer) *dwlt: sn swtchd lft and racd alone towards far rail: in tch: rdn 2f out: sn wknd* **25/1**

1m 14.33s (0.73) **Going Correction** +0.325s/f (Good) **11 Ran SP% 116.8**
Speed ratings (Par 99): **108,107,103,98,98 98,96,95,94,89 84**
CSF £39.49 CT £866.44 TOTE £3.00: £1.50, £3.50, £7.00; EX 33.70 Trifecta £791.70.
Owner Caron & Paul Chapman **Bred** J P Coggan **Trained** Middleham Moor, N Yorks

FOCUS
A fair race for the grade, a couple of improvers finishing clear in a time 1.55sec quicker than the second division.

3604 FREE SPINS AT 188BET CASINO H'CAP (DIV II) 6f
5:50 (5:50) (Class 5) (0-70,70) 3-Y-O **£3,881** (£1,155; £577; £288) **Stalls** High

Form RPR

-504 **1** **King's Currency**[24] 2776 3-8-6 **55** ...... PJMcDonald 3 62
(Jedd O'Keeffe) *dwlt and in rr: hdwy 2f out: chsd ldrs over 1f out: rdn to ld jst ins fnl f: sn drvn and edgd rt: hld on wl towards fin* **5/1**[3]

0-46 **2** hd **Geoff Potts (IRE)**[18] 2974 3-9-0 **68** ...... DavidParkes(5) 5 74
(Jeremy Gask) *dwlt: t.k.h and towards rr: hdwy 2f out: rdn to chse ldrs whn nt clr run over 1f out and rdr dropped whip: styd on strly to chal jst ins fnl f: sn edgd lft and ev ch tl no ex nr fin* **7/1**

066 **3** 2 1/2 **Dark Confidant (IRE)**[21] 2854 3-8-10 **59** ...... (b[1]) RoystonFfrench 2 57
(Richard Guest) *prom: cl up 2f out: rdn over 1f out: drvn to ld briefly ent fnl f: hld whn hmpd and no ex last 110yds* **12/1**

2354 **4** 2 **Spice Mill (IRE)**[18] 2974 3-9-0 **66** ...... AlistairRawlinson(3) 4 62+
(Michael Appleby) *led: rdn along 2f out: drvn over 1f out: hdd ent fnl f: hld whn hmpd and swtchd rt last 110yds* **4/1**[2]

4-40 **5** 2 3/4 **Rebel Raiser**[21] 2864 3-8-9 **65** ...... (b) KillianHennessy(7) 1 48
(Richard Spencer) *dwlt and towards rr: gd hdwy on outer 1/2-way and sn cl up: effrt wl over 1f out and sn rdn: rdn and wknd appr fnl f* **9/1**

3412 **6** 1 3/4 **Ada Misobel (IRE)**[24] 2784 3-8-5 **54** ...... (p) KieranO'Neill 6 31
(Roy Bowring) *t.k.h: cl up: rdn along wl over 1f out: grad wknd* **10/1**

0-00 **7** 1 1/2 **Colombe Bleu**[7] 3367 3-9-0 **63** ...... DuranFentiman 7 35
(Tony Coyle) *chsd ldrs: rdn along over 2f out: sn drvn and wknd* **33/1**

-000 **8** 10 **Show Legend**[15] 3062 3-9-4 **70** ...... LouisSteward(3) 8 10
(Michael Bell) *chsd ldrs: rdn along 2f out: sn wknd* **10/1**

65-0 **9** 1 **Cautionary Note**[24] 2776 3-8-1 **57** ...... KieranSchofield(7) 9
(Nigel Tinkler) *chsd ldrs on outer: rdn along over 2f out: sn wknd* **40/1**

3532 **10** 9 **Mustn't Grumble (IRE)**[13] 3140 3-9-2 **65** ...... (p) DavidNolan 10
(Ivan Furtado) *chsd ldrs: rdn along wl over 2f out: sn wknd* **3/1**[1]

1m 15.88s (2.28) **Going Correction** +0.325s/f (Good) **10 Ran SP% 115.4**
Speed ratings (Par 99): **97,96,93,90,87 84,82,69,68,56**
CSF £39.49 CT £398.36 TOTE £5.10: £1.90, £2.60, £3.80; EX 40.40 Trifecta £459.40.
Owner Highbeck Racing **Bred** Whatton Manor Stud **Trained** Middleham Moor, N Yorks

FOCUS
The time was much slower than the first division, but still personal bests from the first two.
T/Jkpt: Not won. T/Plt: £20.90 to a £1 stake. Pool: £75,339.95 - 2,624.39 winning tickets T/Qpdt: £7.60 to a £1 stake. Pool: £6,894.72 - 667.5 winning tickets **Joe Rowntree**

3561 NEWCASTLE (A.W) (L-H)
Friday, June 24

OFFICIAL GOING: Tapeta: standard
Wind: Almost nil Weather: Overcast, heavy rain during race 5

3605 BETFRED "STILL TREBLE ODDS ON LUCKY15'S" H'CAP 1m 5y (Tp)
6:10 (6:10) (Class 4) (0-85,85) 3-Y-O+ **£5,822** (£1,732; £865; £432) **Stalls** Centre

Form RPR

1-00 **1** **Pensax Boy**[38] 2345 4-9-4 **75** ...... JimCrowley 5 86
(Ian Williams) *cl up: rdn to ld over 1f out: sn hrd pressed: hld on wl fnl f* **14/1**

4-21 **2** 1/2 **Mutamid**[22] 2821 4-9-7 **78** ...... AdamKirby 1 88
(Ismail Mohammed) *prom: hdwy and ev ch over 1f out: sn rdn: kpt on same pce wl ins fnl f* **3/1**[1]

1104 **3** 2 **Pirate's Treasure**[31] 2565 3-8-13 **80** ...... MartinHarley 3 83
(James Tate) *hld up: hdwy on outside 2f out: rdn and kpt on fnl f: nt rch first two* **8/1**

2-00 **4** 1 **Mustaqqil (IRE)**[20] 2917 4-9-7 **78** ...... (p) DanielTudhope 8 81
(David O'Meara) *hld up: hdwy to chse ldrs over 1f out: rdn and one pce ins fnl f* **33/1**

2524 **5** 1 **Rockwood**[13] 3166 5-9-2 **73** ...... (v) PaulMulrennan 13 73
(Karen McLintock) *hld up: hdwy and prom over 2f out: rdn and outpcd fnl f* **13/2**

2000 **6** 1 **Pivotman**[13] 3166 8-9-2 **78** ...... (t) NathanEvans(5) 4 76
(Michael Easterby) *hld up: pushed along over 2f out: hdwy over 1f out: no imp fnl f* **25/1**

5033 **7** 3/4 **Smokethatthunders (IRE)**[13] 3137 6-9-6 **77** ...... HarryBentley 11 73
(James Unett) *hld up bhd ldng gp: drvn and outpcd over 2f out: kpt on fnl f: no imp* **25/1**

-050 **8** 1 1/4 **Gerry The Glover (IRE)**[27] 2689 4-10-0 **85** ...... (p) DaleSwift 12 79
(Brian Ellison) *prom: drvn along over 2f out: wknd fnl f* **4/1**[2]

-343 **9** *1 ¼* **Hernando Torres**[148] 360 8-9-0 **71**.....(t) CamHardie 9 62
(Michael Easterby) *hld up: rdn over 2f out: edgd lft over 1f out: nvr able to chal* **33/1**

1005 **10** *nk* **Al Hamd (IRE)**[12] 3187 3-8-13 **80**.....(v[1]) PaulHanagan 6 68
(Ed Dunlop) *plld hrd: cl up: rdn over 2f out: wknd over 1f out* **15/2**

1-62 **11** *½* **Count Montecristo (FR)**[22] 2832 4-9-11 **82**..... TomEaves 2 71
(Kevin Ryan) *led: rdn over 2f out: hdd over 1f out: wknd fnl f* **6/1**[3]

0000 **12** *4 ½* **Border Bandit (USA)**[7] 3367 8-8-10 **67**.....(p) ConnorBeasley 7 45
(Tracy Waggott) *prom: drvn and outpcd wl over 2f out: sn btn* **80/1**

00-0 **13** *8* **Thornaby Nash**[16] 3011 5-9-5 **76**..... GrahamGibbons 10 36
(Colin Teague) *dwlt: sn in tch: rdn over 2f out: sn struggling* **100/1**

1m 38.58s (-0.02) **Going Correction** 0.0s/f (Stan)
WFA 3 from 4yo+ 10lb **13** Ran SP% **118.0**
Speed ratings (Par 105): **100,99,97,96,95 94,93,92,91,90 90,85,77**
CSF £52.59 CT £310.65 TOTE £13.90: £4.20, £1.40, £2.40; EX 67.10 Trifecta £575.90.
Owner S & A Mares **Bred** C A Cyzer **Trained** Portway, Worcs

FOCUS
There will be no speed figures at this track until there is sufficient data to calculate median times. Plenty with a profile that made them interesting for a handicap more competitive than the money might have suggested and they went a fair pace too.

3606 BETFRED GOSFORTH PARK CUP (H'CAP) 5f (Tp)
6:45 (6:45) (Class 2) (0-105,99) 3-Y-O+
£18,675 (£5,592; £2,796; £1,398; £699; £351) **Stalls** Centre

Form RPR

0111 **1** **Orion's Bow**[10] 3265 5-9-4 **91** 6ex..... BarryMcHugh 1 104+
(David Nicholls) *trckd ldrs on far side of gp: rdn to ld 1f out: kpt on wl u.p* **9/4**[1]

4112 **2** *1* **Bowson Fred**[9] 3277 4-9-5 **97**..... NathanEvans[(5)] 3 106
(Michael Easterby) *cl up far side of gp: led 1/2-way to 1f out: kpt on same pce last 100yds* **6/1**[3]

20-2 **3** *1 ¼* **Memories Galore (IRE)**[30] 2581 4-8-13 **86**..... JimCrowley 4 91
(Harry Dunlop) *prom on far side of gp: gng wl over 1f out: sn rdn: kpt on ins fnl f: nt rch first two* **14/1**

-226 **4** *½* **Soie D'Leau**[37] 2364 4-9-1 **88**..... TonyHamilton 14 91+
(Kristin Stubbs) *hld up in midfield on nr side of gp: effrt and hdwy 2f out: edgd lft and kpt on ins fnl f: no imp* **40/1**

40-0 **5** *1 ½* **El Viento (FR)**[12] 3188 8-9-4 **91**.....(v) GeorgeChaloner 7 88
(Richard Fahey) *s.i.s: bhd and outpcd in centre: hdwy over 1f out: kpt on fnl f: nvr able to chal* **50/1**

2200 **6** *1 ½* **Fast Track**[13] 3151 5-9-5 **92**.....[1] PhillipMakin 12 84
(David Barron) *hld up in centre: rdn 1/2-way: kpt on fnl f: nvr rchd ldrs* **16/1**

-020 **7** *½* **Bogart**[12] 3188 7-9-1 **88**.....(p) TomEaves 10 78
(Kevin Ryan) *prom centre: rdn over 2f out: outpcd fr over 1f out* **12/1**

3020 **8** *nk* **Patrick (IRE)**[34] 2488 4-9-5 **92**..... PaulHanagan 8 81
(Richard Fahey) *s.i.s: bhd and outpcd centre: hdwy nr side over 1f out: kpt on: nvr on terms* **8/1**

1103 **9** *¾* **Encore D'Or**[9] 3277 4-9-9 **96**.....(p) MartinHarley 5 82
(Robert Cowell) *in tch towards far side of gp: rdn over 2f out: wknd over 1f out* **9/2**[2]

310 **10** *nse* **Bosham**[91] 1066 6-9-12 **99**.....(bt) CamHardie 2 85
(Michael Easterby) *led on far side of gp to 1/2-way: rdn and wknd over 1f out* **33/1**

-601 **11** *1 ¾* **Meadway**[13] 3150 5-9-9 **96**.....(p) ConnorBeasley 11 76
(Bryan Smart) *in tch centre: drvn along 1/2-way: wknd over 1f out* **25/1**

12 *2 ¼* **Steelriver (IRE)**[90] 1090 6-9-8 **95**..... GrahamGibbons 13 67
(David Barron) *s.i.s and swtchd lft s: rdn 1/2-way: edgd lft and struggling over 1f out* **20/1**

6420 **13** *4* **Red Baron (IRE)**[13] 3151 7-9-12 **99**..... NeilFarley 9 56
(Eric Alston) *in tch centre: drvn along 1/2-way: wknd wl over 1f out* **20/1**

57.98s (-1.52) **Going Correction** 0.0s/f (Stan) **13** Ran SP% **115.3**
Speed ratings (Par 109): **112,110,108,107,105 102,102,101,100,100 97,93,87**
CSF £13.06 CT £140.24 TOTE £3.00: £1.50, £2.00, £3.40; EX 16.00 Trifecta £119.90.
Owner T J Swiers **Bred** Cheveley Park Stud Ltd **Trained** Sessay, N Yorks

FOCUS
The Gosforth Park Cup does not carry quite the money or the prestige that it used to but this was a cracking 5f handicap, full of sprinters seemingly primed for a big effort, with plenty of potential front-runners in the field to ensure a hot pace. The race has been rated around the runner-up.

3607 BETFRED RACING "FOLLOW US ON TWITTER" CLASSIFIED STKS 1m 4f 98y (Tp)
7:15 (7:15) (Class 5) 3-Y-O **£3,881** (£1,155; £577; £288) **Stalls** Low

Form RPR

513 **1** **West Coast Flyer**[21] 2859 3-9-0 74..... JimCrowley 4 83+
(David Simcock) *stdd in last pl: niggled along briefly over 4f out: bk on bridle and hdwy over 2f out: rdn to ld appr fnl f: edgd lft: r.o wl* **5/4**[1]

2524 **2** *¾* **Kings Gold (IRE)**[24] 2774 3-9-0 75.....(p) PaulMulrennan 2 81
(Michael Dods) *in tch: smooth hdwy to ld 2f out: sn rdn and edgd lft: hdd appr fnl f: rallied: one pce last 75yds* **9/1**

-365 **3** *6* **Machine Learner**[30] 2580 3-9-0 75.....(p) MartinHarley 1 71
(Michael Bell) *trckd ldrs: rdn and chsd clr ldng pair over 1f out: sn no imp* **13/2**

-332 **4** *1* **Ice Galley (IRE)**[21] 2858 3-9-0 74..... TomEaves 5 70
(Kevin Ryan) *led at modest gallop: rdn and hdd 3f out: rallied: outpcd fr over 1f out* **7/2**[2]

2433 **5** *5* **Moueenn**[30] 2580 3-8-7 75.....(p) CameronNoble[(7)] 3 62
(Roger Varian) *pressed ldr: led and rdn 3f out: hdd 2f out: sn wknd* **4/1**[3]

2m 41.11s (0.01) **Going Correction** 0.0s/f (Stan) **5** Ran SP% **110.0**
Speed ratings (Par 99): **99,98,94,93,90**
CSF £12.87 TOTE £2.00: £1.10, £3.30; EX 13.30 Trifecta £52.00.
Owner Ali Saeed **Bred** Miss K Rausing **Trained** Newmarket, Suffolk

FOCUS
Precious little between these five on either Racing Post or BHA ratings, but four of the field were still maidens and the fact that three were being tried in cheekpieces for the first time suggested they had been frustrating connections.

3608 BETFRED TV/EBF STALLIONS HOPPINGS STKS (LISTED RACE) (F&M) 1m 2f 42y (Tp)
7:45 (7:47) (Class 1) 3-Y-O+
£22,684 (£8,600; £4,304; £2,144; £1,076; £540) **Stalls** High

Form RPR

113 **1** **Nezwaah**[41] 2245 3-8-7 95..... HarryBentley 3 108+
(Roger Varian) *hld up: hdwy 3f out: led over 1f out: edgd lft and rdn clr fnl f* **3/1**[1]

-142 **2** *3* **More Mischief**[37] 2363 4-9-5 99..... JoeyHaynes 6 101
(Jedd O'Keeffe) *prom on outside: rdn and hdwy to ld over 2f out: hdd over 1f out: kpt on fnl f: nt pce of wnr* **11/2**[3]

2324 **3** *hd* **Oakley Girl**[20] 2893 4-9-5 100..... MartinHarley 7 102+
(Stuart Williams) *hld up: shkn up over 2f out: rdn and hdwy over 1f out: kpt on fnl f: nrst fin* **10/1**

2 **4** *1* **Rosental**[27] 2671 4-9-5 93..... MartinLane 10 99
(Luca Cumani) *s.i.s: hld up: rdn and edgd lft over 2f out: hdwy over 1f out: kpt on fnl f: nt pce to chal* **25/1**

41-0 **5** *nk* **Chain Of Daisies**[37] 2363 4-9-9 103..... FergusSweeney 8 102
(Henry Candy) *led at ordinary gallop: shkn up and qcknd over 3f out: hdd over 2f out: rallied: kpt on same pce fnl f* **14/1**

2-64 **6** *3* **Sound Of Freedom (IRE)**[23] 2797 4-9-5 104..... JimCrowley 11 92
(Marco Botti) *chsd ldrs: drvn along wl over 2f out: wknd over 1f out* **20/1**

11-0 **7** *½* **Intimation**[55] 1861 4-9-5 90..... TedDurcan 1 91
(Sir Michael Stoute) *hld up on ins: pushed along over 2f out: rdn and no imp fr over 1f out* **4/1**[2]

2-14 **8** *3 ½* **Secret Sense (USA)**[34] 2490 3-8-7 77..... ConnorBeasley 5 84
(Ralph Beckett) *hld up: rdn on outside over 2f out: wknd over 1f out* **16/1**

5-12 **9** *3 ½* **Tears Of The Sun**[23] 2797 5-9-5 97..... AdamKirby 9 77
(Clive Cox) *hld up: rdn and edgd lft over 2f out: btn over 1f out* **8/1**

1001 **10** *30* **Imshivalla (IRE)**[21] 2866 5-9-5 94..... PaulHanagan 4 17
(Richard Fahey) *plld hrd: in tch: rdn over 2f out: sn wknd: t.o* **28/1**

-112 **11** *3 ¼* **Sagely (IRE)**[34] 2490 3-8-7 90..... JoeFanning 2 11
(Ed Dunlop) *trckd ldrs: rdn over 2f out: wkng whn hmpd over 1f out: sn eased* **8/1**

2m 7.56s (-2.84) **Going Correction** 0.0s/f (Stan)
WFA 3 from 4yo+ 12lb **11** Ran SP% **116.3**
Speed ratings (Par 111): **111,108,108,107,107 105,104,101,99,75 72**
CSF £18.53 TOTE £4.00: £1.50, £3.50, £3.20; EX 20.80 Trifecta £129.10.
Owner Sheikh Ahmed Al Maktoum **Bred** Darley **Trained** Newmarket, Suffolk

FOCUS
The wide range of form claims typical of a fillies' Listed race, arguably the trappiest of punting propositions. But there were several improving contenders for a contest won by future Group 1 winner Covert Love last year and they went a strong pace. The race has been rated around the second and third.

3609 BETFRED "BET ON THE EUROS" MAIDEN STKS 7f 14y (Tp)
8:15 (8:17) (Class 5) 3-Y-O+ **£3,557** (£1,058; £529; £264) **Stalls** Centre

Form RPR

52 **1** **Marbooh (IRE)**[17] 2999 3-9-3 0..... PaulHanagan 1 81
(Charles Hills) *mde virtually all: rdn and hrd pressed fr over 1f out: hld on gamely cl home* **11/4**[1]

2 *shd* **Trenches (USA)** 3-9-3 0..... AdamKirby 14 81
(Charlie Appleby) *hld up nr side of gp: hdwy to dispute ld over 1f out: riidden kpt on fnl f: jst hld* **7/2**[2]

3 **3** *nk* **Run To The Hills (USA)**[30] 2578 3-9-3 0..... StevieDonohoe 4 80
(George Peckham) *dwlt: sn cl up: rdn and ev ch over 1f out: kpt on fnl f: hld nr fin* **11/4**[1]

42- **4** *1 ¼* **Regal Response (IRE)**[252] 7253 3-9-3 0..... PaulMulrennan 12 77
(Michael Dods) *t.k.h: prom: effrt and rdn 2f out: kpt on same pce wl ins fnl f* **14/1**

6- **5** *4* **Safe Voyage (IRE)**[422] 1810 3-9-3 0..... CamHardie 2 66
(John Quinn) *hld up on far side of gp: shkn up over 2f out: hdwy over 1f out: kpt on: nt gng pce to chal* **66/1**

4-6 **6** *1 ½* **Qortaaj**[10] 3267 3-9-3 0..... SamJames 5 62
(David Loughnane) *hld up: rdn over 2f out: kpt on fr over 1f out: nvr able to chal* **66/1**

34- **7** *1 ¼* **First Wheat**[242] 7516 3-8-12 0..... NathanEvans[(5)] 9 58
(Michael Easterby) *cl up: rdn and hung lft over 2f out: wknd over 1f out* **14/1**

8 *4* **Arrest Warrant** 3-9-3 0..... GrahamGibbons 6 48
(Michael Easterby) *dwlt: t.k.h and sn in tch: lost pl over 2f out: n.d after* **33/1**

04- **9** *1 ½* **Never Give In**[245] 7430 3-9-3 0..... DougieCostello 13 44
(K R Burke) *hld up: rdn and outpcd over 2f out: n.d after* **25/1**

40 **10** *11* **Table Manners**[35] 2419 4-9-4 0..... MissEmmaSayer[(3)] 8 12
(Wilf Storey) *prom: lost pl 3f out: sn struggling* **100/1**

11 *¾* **Angelical (IRE)** 3-8-12 0..... JoeFanning 10 7
(Daniel Mark Loughnane) *dwlt: hld up: rdn and edgd lft over 2f out: sn btn* **66/1**

2 **12** *6* **Eisha Flower (USA)**[9] 3293 3-8-12 0..... TonyHamilton 7
(Richard Fahey) *hld up bhd ldng gp: pushed along and struggling 3f out: sn btn* **4/1**[3]

6- **13** *3 ¾* **Wright Patterson (IRE)**[242] 7516 3-9-3 0..... JasonHart 11
(John Quinn) *t.k.h: cl up tl rdn and wknd over 2f out* **66/1**

14 *11* **Bettercallphoenix** 3-9-3 0..... DavidAllan 3
(David C Griffiths) *t.k.h: hld up in midfield on far side of gp: rdn and edgd lft over 2f out: sn wknd* **100/1**

1m 28.5s (2.30) **Going Correction** 0.0s/f (Stan)
WFA 3 from 4yo 9lb **14** Ran SP% **123.6**
Speed ratings (Par 103): **86,85,85,84,79 77,76,71,70,57 56,49,45,32**
CSF £12.47 TOTE £3.50: £1.40, £2.20, £1.40; EX 15.90 Trifecta £48.60.
Owner Hamdan Al Maktoum **Bred** Hugh O'Brien & Michael McCallan **Trained** Lambourn, Berks

FOCUS
A handful of promising 3yos and a choicely-bred newcomer stood out in a maiden less competitive than the size of the field might suggest and a race run in a torrential downpour.

3610 BETFRED "WATCH FRED'S PUSHES ON BETFRED TV" H'CAP 6f (Tp)
8:50 (8:51) (Class 5) (0-70,70) 3-Y-O+ **£4,204** (£1,251; £625; £312) **Stalls** Centre

Form RPR

000 **1** **Slingsby**[18] 2974 5-9-2 **65**.....(p) GrahamGibbons 4 75
(Michael Easterby) *mde all in centre of gp: rdn over 1f out: hrd pressed ins fnl f: hld on wl u.p towards fin* **13/2**[2]

610/ **2** *½* **More Beau (USA)**[723] 3855 5-9-3 **66**..... BarryMcHugh 2 74+
(David Nicholls) *hld up on far side of gp: hdwy over 1f out: effrt and disp ld ins fnl f: kpt on: hld cl home* **16/1**

4515 **3** *1* **Kenny The Captain (IRE)**[16] 3021 5-9-3 **66**.....(b) DuranFentiman 1 71
(Tim Easterby) *cl up on wd outside of gp: rdn along over 1f out: kpt on same pce ins fnl f* **4/1**[1]

00-0 **4** *1 ½* **Disclosure**[38] 2345 5-9-2 **65**..... DavidAllan 7 65
(Les Eyre) *t.k.h: hld up in centre: rdn and hdwy over 1f out: kpt on fnl f: nt pce to chal* **16/1**

5-00 **5** *2 ½* **Bop It**[13] 3168 7-9-1 **69**.....(v[1]) JoshDoyle[(5)] 8 61
(David O'Meara) *cl up in centre: rdn and outpcd over 1f out: plugged on last 100yds: no imp* **12/1**

04-0 **6** 1 **Barney McGrew (IRE)**[41] 2238 13-9-6 **69**.................. PaulMulrennan 11 58
(Michael Dods) *hld up centre: rdn over 2f out: hdwy over 1f out: kpt on: nt pce to chal* **25/1**

0-00 **7** nk **Tavener**[18] 2974 4-9-5 **68**.. DanielTudhope 3 56
(David O'Meara) *cl up on far side of gp: rdn along over 2f out: outpcd fnl f* **10/1**[3]

40-0 **8** 1 3/4 **Aussie Ruler (IRE)**[38] 2342 4-9-3 **66**................................. JoeFanning 5 48
(Daniel Mark Loughnane) *in tch centre: rdn over 2f out: wknd over 1f out* **10/1**[3]

-303 **9** 1 1/2 **American Hustle (IRE)**[38] 2332 4-9-2 **65**..........................(p) DaleSwift 9 42
(Brian Ellison) *sn pushed along and prom in centre: drvn over 2f out: rallied: wknd over 1f out* **4/1**[1]

0006 **10** 3/4 **Mercers Row**[9] 3284 9-9-6 **69**... DavidNolan 12 44
(Michael Herrington) *hld up towards nr side of gp: rdn and edgd lft over 2f out: nvr on terms* **50/1**

6-24 **11** 3/4 **Classic Pursuit**[38] 2342 5-9-4 **67**.................................(p) MartinHarley 14 40
(Ivan Furtado) *s.i.s: sn prom on nr side of gp: struggling over 2f out: sn btn* **13/2**[2]

2005 **12** 1/2 **Monsieur Jimmy**[3] 3484 4-8-11 **67**..............................(b) GerO'Neill(7) 13 38
(Declan Carroll) *t.k.h: hld up on nr side of gp: rdn along over 2f out: sn wknd* **20/1**

111- **13** 7 **Misu Mac**[403] 2337 6-9-4 **70**.................................... JacobButterfield(3) 10 19
(Neville Bycroft) *prom in centre: lost pl 1/2-way: sn struggling* **25/1**

1m 11.69s (-0.81) **Going Correction** 0.0s/f (Stan) **13** Ran SP% **118.7**
Speed ratings (Par 103): **105,104,103,101,97 96,95,93,91,90 89,88,79**
CSF £99.95 CT £378.96 TOTE £7.30: £2.40, £6.00, £2.00; EX 142.70 Trifecta £838.30.
Owner S Hull, B Hoggarth & Mrs C Mason **Bred** R H Mason **Trained** Sheriff Hutton, N Yorks

FOCUS
Few with a convincing profile for this judged on recent efforts and a handful of them pulled clear late on. The winner was on a good mark on his early 2015 form.

3611 BETFRED "SUPPORTS JACK BERRY HOUSE" H'CAP 5f (Tp)
9:20 (9:20) (Class 5) (0-75,78) 3-Y-O **£4,204** (£1,251; £625; £312) **Stalls** Centre

Form RPR

1552 **1** **September Issue**[18] 2981 3-9-7 **75**............................(p) DougieCostello 1 80
(Gay Kelleway) *cl up: rdn to ld over 1f out: drvn out fnl f* **11/2**[3]

1111 **2** 1 **Black Grass**[4] 3471 3-9-5 **78** 12ex................................ NathanEvans(5) 2 79
(Michael Easterby) *led: rdn: edgd rt and hdd over 1f out: rallied: one pce last 100yds* **5/6**[1]

315 **3** hd **Semana Santa**[25] 2742 3-9-4 **72**................................... GrahamGibbons 4 74+
(David Barron) *t.k.h early: trckd ldrs: rdn whn carried rt ins fnl f: kpt on ins fnl f* **7/2**[2]

3460 **4** nk **Bromley Cross (IRE)**[7] 3368 3-8-11 **65**............................(tp) DaleSwift 6 65
(Brian Ellison) *s.i.s: bhd: drvn along 1/2-way: hdwy over 1f out: kpt on: no imp* **16/1**

0635 **5** 5 **Miningggold**[11] 3210 3-8-12 **66**... DavidAllan 5 48+
(Tim Easterby) *chsd ldrs: rdn 1/2-way: keeping on same pce whn hmpd over 1f out: nt rcvr* **8/1**

59.2s (-0.30) **Going Correction** 0.0s/f (Stan) **5** Ran SP% **109.2**
Speed ratings (Par 99): **102,100,100,99,91**
CSF £10.52 TOTE £4.70: £2.40, £1.10; EX 11.20 Trifecta £23.20.
Owner Short, Moore, Buy & Kerr **Bred** Bearstone Stud Ltd **Trained** Exning, Suffolk
■ Stewards' Enquiry : Nathan Evans two-day ban: careless riding (11-12 July)

FOCUS
This revolved around whether a busy spell of racing and a double penalty would catch up with the progressive top-weight, which they did. The winner has been rated to the best of his early form.
T/Plt: £23.20 to a £1 stake. Pool: £76,301.48 - 2,398.68 winning tickets T/Qpdt: £9.00 to a £1 stake. Pool: £5,967.94 - 487.88 winning tickets **Richard Young**

3569 NEWMARKET (R-H)
Friday, June 24

OFFICIAL GOING: Soft (6.3)
Wind: light, behind Weather: bright spells and showers

3612 CELEBRATING 350 YEARS OF MAKING HISTORY H'CAP 1m
5:45 (5:45) (Class 5) (0-75,73) 3-Y-O+ **£3,234** (£962; £481; £240) **Stalls** Low

Form RPR

-212 **1** **Lord Reason**[18] 2965 4-9-13 **72**................................ SilvestreDeSousa 10 79
(John Butler) *midfield and off the pce tl clsd and in tch 1/2-way: effrt to chse ldng pair 3f out: pressing ldrs but wanting to hang lft fr over 1f out: looked hld tl stvd on ins fnl f to ld towards fin* **5/1**[3]

5-00 **2** 1/2 **Henshaw**[32] 2545 3-9-3 **72**...(b) JamesMcDonald 9 76
(Charles Hills) *racd keenly: led and clr tl 1/2-way: rdn 2f out: drvn and battled on wl 1f out tl hdd and no ex towards fin* **10/1**

6-2 **3** 1/2 **Stoked (IRE)**[36] 2402 4-9-10 **72**............................. JosephineGordon(3) 4 77
(Chris Dwyer) *taken down early: t.k.h: chsd clr ldr: clsd to trck ldr 1/2-way: rdn 2f out: pressing ldr over 1f out: no imp ins fnl f tl styd on towards fin* **6/1**

-361 **4** 2 1/4 **Honey Badger**[16] 3043 5-8-8 **58**....................................(v) AaronJones(5) 3 58
(Eugene Stanford) *dwlt: off the pce in last trio: clsd 1/2-way: effrt u.p over 2f out: 5th and in tch over 1f out: kpt on same pce ins fnl f* **9/2**[2]

02 **5** 2 **Severus (GER)**[22] 2821 6-9-13 **72**..................................... DavidProbert 1 67
(Des Donovan, Ire) *off the pce in midfield: clsd and in tch 1/2-way: effrt over 2f out: cl enough in 4th over 1f out: wknd ins fnl f* **13/2**

44-2 **6** 14 **Rocket Ronnie (IRE)**[16] 3011 6-10-0 **73**......................... GeorgeBaker 7 36
(Ed McMahon) *stdd s: hld up off the pce in last trio: clsd 1/2-way: short-lived effrt 2f out: sn btn: wl bhd and eased ins fnl f* **5/2**[1]

-020 **7** 3 **Red Cossack (CAN)**[22] 2821 5-9-12 **71**.............................(t) PatDobbs 2 27
(Paul Webber) *half-rrd and stdd leaving stalls: hld up off the pce in last trio: effrt over 2f out: no imp 2f out: sn wknd: wl bhd whn eased ins fnl f* **14/1**

00-0 **8** 1 3/4 **Kawaii**[24] 2769 4-8-9 **57**.. TimClark(3) 6 9
(Martin Smith) *chsd clr ldng pair: clsd to trck ldrs 1/2-way: rdn and lost pl over 2f out: wl bhd and eased ins fnl f* **25/1**

1m 44.9s (4.90) **Going Correction** +0.725s/f (Yiel)
WFA 3 from 4yo+ 10lb **8** Ran SP% **110.6**
Speed ratings (Par 103): **104,103,103,100,98 84,81,80**
CSF £49.51 CT £291.65 TOTE £4.90: £1.30, £3.70, £1.90; EX 45.10 Trifecta £232.00.
Owner Greenstead Hall Racing Ltd **Bred** Greenstead Hall Racing Ltd **Trained** Newmarket, Suffolk

FOCUS
The far side of the course was used. Stalls were on the stands' side except over 1m2f and 1m5f, when they were in the centre. They were strung out early in this ordinary handicap and were kicking up the turf. It still paid to race prominently and a small personal best from the winner.

3613 BRITISH STALLION STUDS EBF NOVICE FILLIES' STKS (PLUS 10 RACE) 6f
6:20 (6:20) (Class 4) 2-Y-O **£4,528** (£1,347; £673; £336) **Stalls** Low

Form RPR

1 **Spiritual Lady** 2-9-0 0.. SilvestreDeSousa 7 81+
(Philip McBride) *hld up in tch in midfield: gng wl and nt clr run briefly wl over 1f out: sn rdn and led jst over 1f out: styd on strly: eased towards fin: readily* **9/4**[1]

2 2 3/4 **Paulownia (IRE)** 2-9-0 0.. SeanLevey 5 71
(Richard Hannon) *dwlt: hld up in tch towards rr: swtchd lft and effrt wl over 1f out: 4th and cl enough 1f out: nvr gng pce of wnr but kpt on to go 2nd 100yds* **10/1**[3]

6 **3** 1 1/4 **Amathyst**[18] 2963 2-9-0 0... AndrewMullen 1 67
(Michael Appleby) *chsd ldr: rdn and ev ch wl over 1f out: hung lft and unable qck 1f out: kpt on same pce and lost 2nd 100yds out* **12/1**

4 2 1/4 **Fabric** 2-9-0 0... RyanMoore 2 60
(Richard Hannon) *t.k.h: led: rdn 2f out: hdd jst over 1f out: sn btn: wknd ins fnl f* **9/4**[1]

5 **5** 2 1/4 **Ciel Rouge**[9] 3275 2-9-0 0.. AdamBeschizza 4 54
(Charlie Wallis) *chsd ldrs: rdn 2f out: outpcd and hung rt over 1f out: wknd fnl f* **80/1**

6 9 **Tisbutadream (IRE)** 2-9-0 0... OisinMurphy 6 27
(David Elsworth) *rn green in last pair: dropped to last and detached after 2f: nvr on terms after* **5/2**[2]

7 11 **Pemberley House (IRE)** 2-9-0 0...................................... ShaneKelly 3
(Paul D'Arcy) *stdd s: t.k.h: sn in midfield: rdn over 2f out: sn lost pl: wl bhd and eased wl ins fnl f* **33/1**

1m 15.88s (3.38) **Going Correction** +0.75s/f (Yiel) **7** Ran SP% **111.1**
Speed ratings (Par 92): **107,103,101,98,95 83,69**
CSF £23.70 TOTE £2.90: £1.60, £4.30; EX 25.10 Trifecta £179.20.
Owner PMRacing **Bred** J W Mitchell **Trained** Newmarket, Suffolk

FOCUS
They went a routine pace more towards the stands' side in this novice event. Perhaps a bit below the race's usual depth, but a nice start from the well-backed and impressive winner.

3614 GOODWIN MALATESTA 10TH ANNIVERSARY H'CAP 7f
6:55 (6:55) (Class 4) (0-80,78) 3-Y-O **£5,175** (£1,540; £769; £384) **Stalls** Low

Form RPR

1-2 **1** **Sainted**[13] 3138 3-9-5 **76**.. RyanMoore 1 90+
(William Haggas) *hld up in tch in last trio: clsd to trck ldrs gng wl over 1f out: ev ch over 1f out: rdn to ld ent fnl f: styd on strly* **11/4**[2]

21 **2** 2 3/4 **Stars N Angels (IRE)**[12] 3197 3-8-13 **70** 6ex.............(p) AndrewMullen 7 76
(Michael Appleby) *w ldr: rdn and ev ch over 1f out: 3rd and unable qck 1f out: kpt on same pce after: wnt 2nd again towards fin* **10/1**

1262 **3** 3/4 **Baron Bolt**[16] 3036 3-9-5 **76**...(p) LukeMorris 5 80
(Paul Cole) *t.k.h: chsd ldrs: ev ch 2f out: rdn to ld over 1f out: sn hdd and drvn: outpcd ins fnl f: lost 2nd and wknd towards fin* **8/1**

5031 **4** 1 **Boycie**[36] 2402 3-9-4 **75**...(b) PatDobbs 3 76
(Richard Hannon) *led: rdn and hdd over 1f out: outpcd ent fnl f: kpt on same pce ins fnl f* **14/1**

2-10 **5** 1 1/4 **Kylla Instinct**[62] 1623 3-9-6 **77**.................................. SilvestreDeSousa 6 75
(Philip McBride) *in tch in midfield: clsd to chse ldrs and rdn over 1f out: no ex and btn 1f out: wknd ins fnl f* **8/1**

3-00 **6** 7 **Broughtons Vision**[17] 2998 3-8-10 **67**.............................. RobertHavlin 2 47
(Willie Musson) *hld up in tch in last trio: effrt 2f out: sn outpcd and btn: wknd fnl f* **20/1**

-352 **7** 10 **Generalship (IRE)**[15] 3062 3-9-6 **77**............................(b) JamesDoyle 10 31
(John Gosden) *hld up in tch in last trio: effrt 2f out: sn btn and wknd over 1f out: eased wl ins fnl f* **5/2**[1]

-104 **8** 39 **Mywayistheonlyway (IRE)**[15] 3079 3-9-6 **77**..................(t) SeanLevey 4
(Martyn Meade) *in tch in midfield tl lost pl 3f out: wl bhd over 1f out: eased fnl f: t.o* **6/1**[3]

1m 28.97s (3.27) **Going Correction** +0.775s/f (Yiel) **8** Ran SP% **112.3**
Speed ratings (Par 101): **112,108,108,106,105 97,86,41**
CSF £28.91 CT £194.16 TOTE £3.30: £1.40, £2.40, £2.30; EX 29.70 Trifecta £179.60.
Owner Cheveley Park Stud **Bred** Cheveley Park Stud Ltd **Trained** Newmarket, Suffolk

FOCUS
This modest 3yo handicap was run in driving rain. Straightforward form, but more to come from the winner.

3615 32RED.COM H'CAP 1m 5f
7:25 (7:28) (Class 4) (0-80,78) 3-Y-O **£5,175** (£1,540; £769; £384) **Stalls** Centre

Form RPR

2113 **1** **Regal Monarch**[20] 2909 3-9-7 **78**.............................. SilvestreDeSousa 3 91
(Mark Johnston) *travelled strly thrght: chsd ldr tl led over 3f out: shkn up and wnt clr 2f out: in n.d 1f out: styd on strly: eased towards fin: v easily* **11/8**[1]

0-40 **2** 9 **Clear Evidence**[28] 2652 3-8-5 **65**............................... TomMarquand(3) 4 64
(Michael Bell) *hld up in tch in midfield: swtchd lft and effrt 3f out: rdn to chse wnr over 2f out: outpcd over 1f out: no ch w wnr but kpt on for clr 2nd fnl f* **20/1**

3-63 **3** 3 3/4 **Free Bounty**[31] 2563 3-8-5 **62**... LukeMorris 2 55
(Philip McBride) *chsd ldrs: rdn 3f out: 3rd and outpcd u.p 2f out: wl hld but battled on to hold modest 3rd fnl f* **16/1**

6601 **4** nk **Aristocles (IRE)**[23] 2798 3-9-0 **71**.................................(p) RyanMoore 5 64
(Sir Michael Stoute) *stdd s: hld up in last pair: effrt 2f out: sn swtchd lft and drvn: sn outpcd and wl btn 1f out: battling for modest 3rd ins fnl f: plugged on* **4/1**[2]

4041 **5** nse **Muaither (IRE)**[15] 3063 3-9-2 **73**................................(b) FrankieDettori 7 66
(John Gosden) *in tch in last pair but niggled along at times: effrt and rdn 3f out: outpcd and btn wl over 1f out: no ch but battling for modest 3rd fnl f: plugged on* **4/1**[2]

5210 **6** 10 **Shoofly (IRE)**[42] 2224 3-9-6 **77**.. SeanLevey 6 55
(Martyn Meade) *in tch in midfield: hdwy to chse wnr 3f out tl over 2f out: sn struggling u.p: wknd qckly over 1f out* **13/2**[3]

4360 **7** 37 **Harlequin Rock**[16] 3042 3-8-5 **62**... JFEgan 1
(Mick Quinn) *sn led: hdd and rdn over 3f out: sn bhd: t.o and virtually p.u ins fnl f* **28/1**

2m 57.71s (13.71) **Going Correction** +0.80s/f (Soft) **7** Ran SP% **109.5**
Speed ratings (Par 101): **89,83,81,80,80 74,52**
CSF £29.30 TOTE £2.00: £1.10, £6.40; EX 25.40 Trifecta £193.30.
Owner East Layton Stud Ltd **Bred** A H Bennett **Trained** Middleham Moor, N Yorks

FOCUS
They went a sound enough pace in this fair 3yo handicap. Another step forward from the winner.

3616 EBF STALLIONS FILLIES' CONDITIONS STKS 6f
7:55 (7:56) (Class 3) 3-Y-O+ **£9,056** (£2,695; £1,346; £673) **Stalls** Low

Form RPR
0-06 **1** **Lulu The Zulu (IRE)**[13] 3163 8-8-13 98 SilvestreDeSousa 4 105
(Michael Appleby) *stdd s: chsd ldr and racd away fr rivals for 2f: led 4f out and c to stands' rail: rdn 2f out: hung lft over 1f out: hrd drvn and forged ahd ins fnl f: styd on: gamely* **9/4**[1]

50-0 **2** *1* **Golden Amber (IRE)**[73] 1394 5-8-13 98 RobertWinston 5 102
(Dean Ivory) *chsd ldng pair: effrt ent fnl 2f: swtchd rt over 1f out: kpt on u.p ins fnl f: wnt 2nd towards fin* **8/1**[3]

440- **3** *1/2* **Stroll Patrol**[258] 7117 4-8-13 0 OisinMurphy 3 100
(Ralph Beckett) *t.k.h: led for 2f: chsd ldr: rdn and ev ch whn carried lft over 1f out: no ex and btn 100yds out: wknd and lost 2nd towards fin* **9/2**[2]

1-13 **4** *7* **Mehronissa**[14] 3116 4-8-13 93 LukeMorris 2 78
(Ed Vaughan) *stdd s: t.k.h: hld up in tch in rr: effrt 2f out: no hdwy u.p ent fnl f: wknd ins fnl f* **9/4**[1]

1m 17.0s (4.50) **Going Correction** +0.825s/f (Soft) **4** Ran SP% **90.8**
Speed ratings (Par 104): **103,101,101,91**
CSF £12.02 TOTE £2.50; EX 10.70 Trifecta £20.70.

Owner The Ab Kettlebys **Bred** Hong Kong Breeders Club **Trained** Oakham, Rutland

■ Iseemist was withdrawn. Price at time of withdrawal 4-1. Rule 4 applies to all bets - deduction 20p in the pound.

FOCUS
A good-quality little fillies' conditions event and a game effort from the winner.

3617 WINNERS BINGO THETFORD H'CAP (JOCKEY CLUB GRASSROOTS FLAT MIDDLE DISTANCE SERIES QUALIFIER) 1m 2f
8:25 (8:26) (Class 4) (0-80,80) 3-Y-O+ **£5,175** (£1,540; £769; £384) **Stalls** Centre

Form RPR
0-55 **1** **Compton Mill**[23] 2791 4-9-7 73 (t) GeorgeBaker 8 81
(Hughie Morrison) *trckd ldr tl led on bit 2f out: shkn up 1f out: urged along hands and heels and a doing enough to hold chalr ins fnl f* **9/2**[2]

-655 **2** *1/2* **Cottesloe (IRE)**[139] 488 7-9-8 74 (b) JFEgan 7 81
(John Berry) *stdd s: hld up in last pair: clsd 2f out: effrt to chse wnr over 1f out: rdn and chalng ins fnl f: kpt on but a hld* **12/1**

13-4 **3** *7* **Four On Eight**[43] 2179 3-9-2 80 FrankieDettori 1 73
(Luca Cumani) *stdd s: hld up in tch in midfield: nt clr run and shuffled bk over 2f out: swtchd lft and hdwy u.p over 1f out: chsd clr ldng pair 1f out: no imp and sn outpcd* **11/10**[1]

-440 **4** *3/4* **Tyrsal (IRE)**[9] 3276 5-9-0 66 DarryllHolland 6 58
(Clifford Lines) *stdd and dropped in bhd after s: hld up in rr: clsd and swtchd lft 2f out: effrt over 1f out: no ch w ldng pair and kpt on same pce fnl f* **25/1**

-402 **5** *1 3/4* **Warofindependence (USA)**[16] 3030 4-9-9 75 (v) SeanLevey 3 63
(Alan Bailey) *hld up in tch in midfield: effrt over 2f out: 3rd and outpcd over 1f out: lost 3rd 1f out and sn wknd* **14/1**

6012 **6** *3 1/4* **Best Tamayuz**[11] 3219 5-8-13 65 LukeMorris 2 47
(Scott Dixon) *t.k.h: chsd ldrs: rdn over 2f out: drvn and lost pl over 1f out: sn wknd* **10/1**

1610 **7** *7* **Cat Royale (IRE)**[42] 2209 3-8-10 77 (p) DannyBrock(3) 4 45
(Jane Chapple-Hyam) *led tl rdn and hdd 2f out: sn outpcd and bhd 1f out: wknd fnl f* **11/2**[3]

2m 18.33s (12.83) **Going Correction** +0.85s/f (Soft)
WFA 3 from 4yo+ 12lb **7** Ran SP% **108.5**
Speed ratings (Par 105): **82,81,76,75,74 71,65**
CSF £48.65 CT £86.47 TOTE £5.40: £2.30, £5.40; EX 54.20 Trifecta £116.50.

Owner M T Bevan **Bred** M E Broughton **Trained** East Ilsley, Berks

FOCUS
It was an advantage to race on the pace in this modest handicap. The form looks ordinary outside of the winner.

3618 DISCOVERNEWMARKET.CO.UK H'CAP 5f
9:00 (9:00) (Class 4) (0-85,85) 3-Y-O+ **£5,175** (£1,540; £769; £384) **Stalls** Low

Form RPR
2612 **1** **Major Pusey**[13] 3159 4-9-5 81 MichaelJMMurphy(3) 2 92
(John Gallagher) *chsd ldrs tl led 1/2-way: rdn over 1f out: forged ahd u.p ins fnl f: styd on: rdn out* **7/1**

50 **2** *1 1/2* **Indian Tinker**[11] 3217 7-8-4 66 DannyBrock(3) 6 72
(Robert Cowell) *hld up in tch: clsd to join ldr 2f out: rdn over 1f out: drvn and no ex ins fnl f: styd on same pce fnl 100yds* **13/2**

-000 **3** *6* **It Must Be Faith**[15] 3068 6-9-9 82 (p) SilvestreDeSousa 1 66
(Michael Appleby) *dwlt: racd in last pair: effrt 2f out: hdwy u.p to chse ldng pair over 1f out: no imp: wknd ins fnl f* **5/1**[3]

2451 **4** *1/2* **Jaywalker (IRE)**[13] 3159 5-9-6 79 CharlesBishop 7 62
(Mick Channon) *w ldr tl 1/2-way: sn rdn: lost pl 2f out: wl hld 4th and plugged on same pce ins fnl f* **5/2**[2]

3123 **5** *1 1/2* **Majestic Hero (IRE)**[21] 2863 4-9-12 85 JamieSpencer 3 62
(Ronald Harris) *led tl 1/2-way: rdn and lost pl 2f out: sn btn and wknd over 1f out* **9/4**[1]

343- **6** *1* **Excellent George**[285] 6345 4-9-4 77 SeanLevey 4 51
(Stuart Williams) *racd in last pair: effrt 2f out: sn drvn and no hdwy: wknd fnl f* **8/1**

1m 3.06s (3.96) **Going Correction** +0.875s/f (Soft) **6** Ran SP% **113.0**
Speed ratings (Par 105): **103,100,91,90,87 86**
CSF £49.87 TOTE £5.70: £2.60, £3.20; EX 27.90 Trifecta £306.00.

Owner C R Marks (banbury) **Bred** C R Marks (Banbury) **Trained** Chastleton, Oxon

FOCUS
A modest sprint handicap, but the winner continues on the upgrade. There was a split opinion about the ground and the centre proved best.

T/Plt: £460.00 to a £1 stake. Pool: £48,396.37 - 76.80 winning tickets T/Qpdt: £66.20 to a £1 stake. Pool: £4,079.43 - 45.60 winning tickets **Steve Payne**

[3073]YARMOUTH (L-H)
Friday, June 24

OFFICIAL GOING: Good to soft changing to good after race 3 (3.20)
Wind: Light across Weather: Cloudy with sunny spells

3619 TRAFALGAR RESTAURANT AT GREAT YARMOUTH RACECOURSE NOVICE STKS (PLUS 10 RACE) 6f 3y
2:20 (2:22) (Class 4) 2-Y-O **£5,304** (£1,578; £788; £394) **Stalls** Centre

Form RPR
42 **1** **Final Reckoning (IRE)**[13] 3167 2-9-2 0 JamesDoyle 2 83+
(Charlie Appleby) *mde all: pushed out: comf* **2/5**[1]

2 *1 1/4* **Stanhope** 2-9-2 0 PatCosgrave 1 76
(Mick Quinn) *chsd ldrs: shkn up over 2f out: chsd wnr over 1f out: styd on* **50/1**

3 *1/2* **Via Egnatia (USA)** 2-9-2 0 RobertHavlin 4 74+
(John Gosden) *hld up: plld hrd: shkn up over 1f out: r.o ins fnl f: nt rch ldrs* **5/2**[2]

4 *6* **Law Power** 2-9-2 0 LukeMorris 3 55
(Sir Mark Prescott Bt) *chsd wnr tl shkn up over 1f out: wknd ins fnl f* **12/1**[3]

5 *3* **Time Down Under** 2-9-2 0 DarryllHolland 5 46
(Mark H Tompkins) *s.i.s: sn prom and racd keenly: shkn up over 2f out: outpcd over 1f out* **50/1**

1m 14.45s (0.05) **Going Correction** -0.025s/f (Good) **5** Ran SP% **111.6**
Speed ratings (Par 95): **98,96,95,87,83**
CSF £23.44 TOTE £1.20: £1.02, £20.80; EX 24.80 Trifecta £50.00.
Owner Godolphin **Bred** Azienda Agricola Loreto Luciani **Trained** Newmarket, Suffolk

FOCUS
Lacking in numbers but a fair juvenile novice event, run at a medium pace. The winner was dominant and may prove better than this.

3620 WEDDINGS AT GREAT YARMOUTH RACECOURSE H'CAP 1m 2f 23y
2:50 (2:50) (Class 6) (0-60,60) 4-Y-O+ **£2,587** (£770; £384; £192) **Stalls** Low

Form RPR
315 **1** **Hydrant**[3] 3498 10-9-7 60 6ex JFEgan 3 67
(Richard Guest) *chsd ldr tl led 4f out: rdn over 1f out: styd on* **9/2**[3]

5300 **2** *1 1/2* **Highlife Dancer**[15] 3072 8-9-3 56 CharlesBishop 6 60
(Mick Channon) *hld up: hdwy over 2f out: rdn over 1f out: styd on to go 2nd post* **4/1**[2]

0651 **3** *nse* **Togetherwecan (IRE)**[7] 3342 4-9-1 54 6ex (b) SilvestreDeSousa 13 58
(Mark Johnston) *s.s: pushed along in rr early: hdwy over 2f out: rdn to chse wnr over 1f out: styd on same pce ins fnl f* **9/4**[1]

0124 **4** *1 1/2* **Sexy Secret**[15] 3072 5-8-13 55 (p) SimonPearce(3) 5 57
(Lydia Pearce) *chsd ldrs: rdn over 2f out: kpt on* **9/1**

3-30 **5** *1/2* **Capelena**[149] 348 5-9-4 57 RobertHavlin 11 58
(Miss Joey Ellis) *hld up: hdwy to chse wnr over 2f out tl rdn over 1f out: no ex ins fnl f* **14/1**

/001 **6** *2 1/2* **Catharina**[20] 2901 4-9-3 56 RenatoSouza 4 52
(Dean Ivory) *plld hrd and prom: rdn over 3f out: sn outpcd: swtchd rt over 1f out: kpt on ins fnl f* **6/1**

0500 **7** *4 1/2* **Miss Buckaroo (IRE)**[15] 3072 4-8-8 47 (b) AndrewMullen 2 35
(James Given) *prom: chsd wnr over 3f out tl rdn over 2f out: hung lft and wknd over 1f out* **28/1**

6-00 **8** *2 3/4* **Smile That Smile**[28] 2645 4-9-6 59 (p) DarryllHolland 8 42
(Mark H Tompkins) *hld up: pushed along over 3f out: a in rr* **12/1**

0052 **9** *16* **Troy Boy**[16] 3041 6-8-0 46 oh1 (p) RPWalsh(7) 1
(Rebecca Bastiman) *led 6f: sn rdn: wknd over 2f out* **22/1**

0566 **10** *9* **General Tufto**[16] 3044 11-8-2 46 oh1 (b) PaddyPilley(5) 9
(Charles Smith) *dwlt: a in rr: pushed along 1/2-way: wknd over 3f out* **66/1**

2m 11.36s (0.86) **Going Correction** +0.125s/f (Good) **10** Ran SP% **116.9**
Speed ratings (Par 101): **101,99,99,98,98 96,92,90,77,70**
CSF £22.53 CT £50.81 TOTE £5.30: £1.90, £1.50, £1.40; EX 25.60 Trifecta £70.00.
Owner Mrs Alison Guest **Bred** Lord Halifax **Trained** Ingmanthorpe, W Yorks

FOCUS
A modest race run at a routine tempo. The form looks straightforward.

3621 WATERAID CHARITY H'CAP 1m 3f 104y
3:20 (3:20) (Class 4) (0-85,88) 3-Y-O+ **£5,045** (£1,501; £750; £375) **Stalls** Low

Form RPR
2-11 **1** **Red Cardinal (IRE)**[12] 3192 4-10-4 88 6ex JamieSpencer 3 103+
(David Simcock) *trckd ldr tl lft in ld 7f out: rdn and edgd lft ins fnl f: r.o* **1/1**[1]

3P/2 **2** *2 3/4* **Ruwasi**[18] 2979 5-9-12 82 PatCosgrave 2 92
(James Tate) *hld up in tch: chsd wnr over 1f out: sn rdn and ev ch: edgd lft and no ex ins fnl f* **9/2**[3]

-264 **3** *6* **Spa's Dancer (IRE)**[31] 2556 9-10-0 84 RyanTate 4 84
(James Eustace) *prom: racd keenly: lft chsng wnr 7f out: rdn over 2f out: lost 2nd over 1f out: wknd fnl f* **9/1**

55-1 **4** *15* **Space Mountain**[130] 593 3-8-3 72 SilvestreDeSousa 1 58
(Mark Johnston) *led: propped and hdd 7f out: sn lost pl and pushed along: drvn over 4f out: hung rt over 2f out: sn wknd* **5/2**[2]

2m 32.74s (4.04) **Going Correction** +0.125s/f (Good)
WFA 3 from 4yo+ 13lb **4** Ran SP% **106.8**
Speed ratings (Par 105): **90,88,83,72**
CSF £5.58 TOTE £1.80; EX 5.20 Trifecta £13.60.
Owner Walters Plant Hire Ltd **Bred** Lynch Bages Ltd **Trained** Newmarket, Suffolk

FOCUS
A small field, but decent quality for the prize money though the winner's task was made easier by the wayward fourth. The pace was modest until quickening 2f out.

3622 ASL SILVER ANNIVERSARY H'CAP 7f 3y
3:55 (3:56) (Class 3) (0-95,95) 4-Y-O **£7,561** (£2,263; £1,131; £566; £282) **Stalls** Centre

Form RPR
310- **1** **Pick Your Choice**[335] 4617 4-9-0 88 [1] PatCosgrave 7 97+
(William Haggas) *trckd ldrs: rdn over 1f out: r.o to ld nr fin* **3/1**[2]

5522 **2** *3/4* **Easy Tiger**[14] 3101 4-8-8 82 MartinDwyer 3 89
(William Muir) *led: shkn up over 1f out: rdn ins fnl f: hdd nr fin* **11/4**[1]

0030 **3** *1 1/4* **Mujassam**[13] 3163 4-9-7 95 (v) JackMitchell 5 99
(Roger Varian) *w ldr tl over 5f out: racd in 2nd: rdn over 1f out: styd on same pce wl ins fnl f* **7/1**

0-06 **4** *2 3/4* **Brazos (IRE)**[7] 3358 5-9-5 93 JamieSpencer 6 89
(James Tate) *chsd ldrs: rdn over 2f out: no ex ins fnl f* **11/4**[1]

1401 **5** 2½ **Mezmaar**[16] 3035 7-8-6 **80** .... LukeMorris 2 69
(Kevin Morgan) *s.i.s: hld up: pushed along 1/2-way: rdn over 1f out: nvr on terms* **11/2**[3]

1054 **6** 1¼ **Jammy Guest (IRE)**[48] 2032 6-8-9 **83** .... RyanPowell 1 69
(George Margarson) *hld up: racd keenly: rdn over 2f out: wknd fnl f* **25/1**

1m 24.97s (-1.63) **Going Correction** -0.025s/f (Good) **6** Ran SP% **110.1**
Speed ratings (Par 107): **108,107,105,102,99 98**
CSF £11.17 TOTE £3.60: £1.90, £1.60; EX 9.00 Trifecta £39.90.
Owner The Queen **Bred** The Queen **Trained** Newmarket, Suffolk

FOCUS
A good handicap run at a medium gallop and the winner still has some potential. The going was changed to "good" before this race.

3623 ESSEX AND SUFFOLK WATER H'CAP 1m 3y

4:30 (4:30) (Class 2) (0-105,102) 4-Y-0+ **£12,602** (£3,772; £1,886; £944) **Stalls** Centre

Form RPR

0-31 **1** **Light And Shade**[48] 2026 4-8-13 **94** .... JamieSpencer 1 100+
(James Tate) *trckd ldrs: wnt 2nd 2 out: shkn up to ld over 1f out: pushed out* **2/1**[2]

0-20 **2** *nk* **Ghalib (IRE)**[20] 2898 4-9-1 **96** .... LukeMorris 3 101
(Ed Walker) *led at stdy pce tl qcknd over 2f out: rdn and hdd over 1f out: rallied and ev ch ins fnl f: unable qck nr fin* **4/1**[3]

31-1 **3** 1¾ **Knight Owl**[55] 1861 6-8-4 **92** .... GeorgeWood(7) 6 93
(James Fanshawe) *plld hrd: w ldr tl settled into 2nd over 6f out: lost 2nd 1/2-way: rdn over 1f out: styd on same pce ins fnl f* **6/5**[1]

500 **4** 2 **Starboard**[79] 1274 7-8-4 **90** ....(p) GeorgeBuckell(5) 5 86
(David Simcock) *hld up: hdwy to chse ldr 1/2-way: lost 2nd 2f out: sn rdn: no ex ins fnl f* **10/1**

1m 40.78s (0.18) **Going Correction** -0.025s/f (Good) **4** Ran SP% **107.9**
Speed ratings (Par 109): **98,97,95,93**
CSF £9.57 TOTE £2.30; EX 7.50 Trifecta £9.10.
Owner Saeed Manana **Bred** M H And Mrs G Tourle **Trained** Newmarket, Suffolk

FOCUS
These good handicappers went a pedestrian pace until quickening over 2f out. A small personal best from the winner.

3624 ROA/RACING POST OWNERS JACKPOT H'CAP 1m 3y

5:00 (5:01) (Class 6) (0-55,54) 4-Y-0+ **£2,587** (£770; £384; £192) **Stalls** Centre

Form RPR

1261 **1** **Theydon Thunder**[7] 3354 4-8-12 **52** .... GeorgeWood(7) 2 66
(Peter Charalambous) *hld up: hdwy over 3f out: led over 2f out: rdn clr over 1f out: comf* **8/11**[1]

5054 **2** 2¾ **Big Red**[11] 3220 4-8-5 **45** .... RPWalsh(7) 11 49
(Rebecca Bastiman) *awkward s: hld up: hdwy u.p over 1f out: r.o to go 2nd nr fin: no ch w wnr* **16/1**

3603 **3** *hd* **Gulland Rock**[16] 3044 5-8-13 **53** .... LukeCarson(7) 3 56
(Anthony Carson) *chsd ldrs: led over 3f out: hdd over 2f out: sn rdn: no ex ins fnl f* **11/1**

4-56 **4** *nk* **Titan Goddess**[29] 2607 4-9-7 **54** .... TimmyMurphy 8 57
(Mike Murphy) *w ldr over 4f: rdn over 2f out: styd on same pce fnl f* **20/1**

0002 **5** 3 **Spinning Rose**[20] 2901 4-9-7 **54** .... RobertWinston 4 50
(Dean Ivory) *trckd ldrs: rdn over 2f out: no ex fnl f* **5/1**[2]

-160 **6** *nse* **Trust Me Boy**[66] 1544 8-9-0 **47** .... SamHitchcott 6 43
(John E Long) *prom: rdn over 2f out: styd on same pce fnl f* **20/1**

050 **7** 6 **Ted's Brother (IRE)**[9] 3287 8-9-6 **53** ....(b[1]) JamieSpencer 9 35
(Richard Guest) *hld up: hdwy over 2f out: rdn over 1f out: wknd fnl f* **8/1**[3]

0-00 **8** 2 **Suzi Icon**[20] 2901 4-9-5 **52** .... JFEgan 1 29
(John Butler) *led: hdd over 3f out: rdn and wknd over 1f out* **22/1**

-000 **9** 4½ **Indomitable Spirit**[63] 1596 4-9-5 **52** .... PatCosgrave 14 19
(Martin Smith) *racd alone stands' side: in tch: rdn and hung lft over 2f out: wknd over 1f out* **33/1**

00-0 **10** 14 **Born To Fly (IRE)**[13] 3146 5-9-0 **47** .... RyanTate 12
(Christine Dunnett) *hld up: wknd over 2f out* **50/1**

0000 **11** 1 **Away In May**[28] 2645 5-8-6 **46** .... MeganNicholls(7) 7
(John Spearing) *dwlt: hld up: hdwy 1/2-way: rdn and wknd over 2f out* **66/1**

1m 40.74s (0.14) **Going Correction** -0.025s/f (Good) **11** Ran SP% **120.2**
Speed ratings (Par 101): **98,95,95,94,91 91,85,83,79,65 64**
CSF £13.51 CT £87.01 TOTE £1.50: £1.10, £4.40, £3.50; EX 14.80 Trifecta £89.60.
Owner pcracing.co.uk **Bred** Mill Farm Stud **Trained** Newmarket, Suffolk

FOCUS
All the field except Indomitable Spirit (drawn closest to the stands' rail) raced in midtrack for most of the race. The pace was solid. The winner was well in and down in grade. Straightforward form in behind.

3625 TIPSTERTABLES.COM H'CAP 5f 42y

5:35 (5:37) (Class 5) (0-75,74) 3-Y-0 **£3,234** (£962; £481; £240) **Stalls** Centre

Form RPR

61-5 **1** **Olympic Runner**[16] 3038 3-9-7 **74** .... PatCosgrave 1 85+
(William Haggas) *chsd ldrs: shkn up to ld over 1f out: r.o wl* **10/3**[3]

050 **2** 3 **Gabrielle**[43] 2177 3-9-7 **74** .... JamieSpencer 2 73
(Ed Dunlop) *hld up: hdwy over 1f out: r.o to go 2nd and edgd rt ins fnl f: nt trble wnr* **8/1**

5051 **3** ¾ **Shypen**[16] 3038 3-8-13 **73** .... JaneElliott(7) 3 69
(George Margarson) *hld up: hdwy over 1f out: r.o* **9/4**[1]

66-0 **4** ½ **Archimedes (IRE)**[21] 2846 3-9-3 **70** ....(p) SamHitchcott 6 65
(Robert Cowell) *disp ld tl wnt on 1/2-way: rdn and hdd over 1f out: styd on same pce ins fnl f* **11/2**

51-6 **5** 1¾ **Sir Roger Moore (IRE)**[18] 2981 3-9-6 **73** .... JFEgan 7 61
(John Butler) *disp ld to 1/2-way: sn rdn: btn whn hmpd ins fnl f* **3/1**[2]

0-00 **6** 1½ **Clever Divya**[41] 2234 3-8-1 **57** ow2........ DannyBrock(3) 5 40
(J R Jenkins) *hld up: rdn over 1f out: wknd fnl f* **20/1**

1m 2.35s (-0.35) **Going Correction** -0.025s/f (Good) **6** Ran SP% **110.1**
Speed ratings (Par 99): **101,96,95,94,91 89**
CSF £27.39 TOTE £3.30: £1.90, £3.50; EX 26.10 Trifecta £52.90.
Owner J C Smith **Bred** Littleton Stud **Trained** Newmarket, Suffolk

FOCUS
A mid-range handicap run at a medium pace. The winner was well on top and has improved.
T/Plt: £20.10 to a £1 stake. Pool: £59,538.15 - 2,160.26 winning tickets T/Qpdt: £11.10 to a £1 stake. Pool: £3,336.65 - 221.90 winning tickets **Colin Roberts**

3626 - 3629a (Foreign Racing) - See Raceform Interactive

2920 CURRAGH (R-H)

Friday, June 24

OFFICIAL GOING: Good to yielding (good in places on round course)

3630a IRISH STALLION FARMS EUROPEAN BREEDERS FUND "RAGUSA" H'CAP (PREMIER HANDICAP) 1m 4f

7:30 (7:31) 3-Y-0+

£21,691 (£6,985; £3,308; £1,470; £735; £367)

RPR

1 **Avenante**[12] 3202 4-8-13 **90** .... GaryHalpin(5) 1 97+
(John M Oxx, Ire) *chsd ldrs: 5th 1/2-way: tk clsr order bhd ldrs in 3rd 2f out: rdn to ld ins fnl f and styd on wl to extend advantage clsng stages: won gng away* **6/1**[3]

2 2½ **Intisari (IRE)**[12] 3203 4-10-0 **100** .... ColinKeane 6 103
(G M Lyons, Ire) *towards rr early tl sn tk clsr order in mid-div: 7th 1/2-way: hdwy to chse ldrs under 2f out: rdn into 2nd wl ins fnl f and kpt on same pce: nt trble wnr* **16/1**

3 ¾ **Highly Toxic (IRE)**[12] 3203 5-9-5 **91** ....(b) DannyGrant 7 93
(Patrick J Flynn, Ire) *trckd ldrs tl sn led: 1 l clr at 1/2-way: rdn and pressed clly under 2f out: hdd ins fnl f and sn no imp on wnr u.p in 3rd: kpt on same pce* **14/1**

4 *shd* **Shadagann (IRE)**[23] 2498 6-9-0 **86** ....(b[1]) ShaneFoley 12 88
(M Halford, Ire) *s.i.s and in rr early tl impr into 9th bef 1/2-way: rdn 2f out and hdwy u.p on outer to chse ldrs wl ins fnl f: kpt on same pce in 4th clsng stages: nt trble wnr* **14/1**

5 *nk* **Princess Aloof (IRE)**[6] 3429 5-9-3 **89** ....(p) ColmO'Donoghue 8 90
(Mrs John Harrington, Ire) *broke wl to ld briefly tl sn settled bhd ldrs in 6th: rdn 2f out and no imp on ldrs u.p in 5th ins fnl f: kpt on same pce clsng stages* **11/1**

6 2½ **An Cailin Orga (IRE)**[15] 3085 3-8-4 **90** oh5........ RoryCleary 11 87
(J S Bolger, Ire) *chsd ldrs and wnt 2nd after 2f: rdn in 2nd 2f out and no ex ins fnl f where dropped to 4th: wknd clsng stages* **10/1**

7 ½ **Multiculture (IRE)**[3] 3501 4-7-11 **76** oh2........(t) KillianLeonard(7) 10 72
(John Joseph Murphy, Ire) *towards rr: 13th 1/2-way: tk clsr order out wd over 2f out: sn rdn and no imp on ldrs over 1f out: kpt on ins fnl f: nvr nrr* **16/1**

8 1 **Ringside Humour (IRE)**[12] 3203 4-8-12 **84** ....(t) KevinManning 13 79
(J S Bolger, Ire) *towards rr: 11th 1/2-way: rdn out wd over 2f out and no imp on ldrs in 9th over 1f out: kpt on one pce* **20/1**

9 *nk* **Renneti (FR)**[188] 7115 7-9-4 **90** .... ChrisHayes 3 84
(W P Mullins, Ire) *cl up early tl sn settled bhd ldrs: 4th 1/2-way: pushed along in 4th over 3f out and sn no ex u.p: lost tch fr 2f out* **5/1**[2]

10 *shd* **Ballybacka Queen (IRE)**[12] 3203 5-9-5 **98**........ DanielRedmond(7) 2 92
(P A Fahy, Ire) *cl up and settled bhd ldrs in 3rd after 2f: rdn and no ex 2f out: wknd fr over 1f out* **9/1**

11 4¼ **Elishpour (IRE)**[328] 3252 6-9-11 **97** ....[1] BillyLee 5 84
(Alan Fleming, Ire) *towards rr thrght: 12th 1/2-way: rdn and no imp over 2f out* **10/1**

12 1½ **Time To Inspire (IRE)**[331] 4769 4-9-9 **95** .... LeighRoche 4 80
(D K Weld, Ire) *hld up: 10th 1/2-way: rdn and no imp over 2f out* **10/1**

13 8 **Dawn Missile**[259] 7076 4-9-8 **94** .... PatSmullen 9 66
(William Haggas) *mid-div: 8th 1/2-way: rdn and no ex over 2f out: sn wknd: eased in rr ins fnl f* **4/1**[1]

2m 39.58s (1.08) **Going Correction** +0.325s/f (Good)
WFA 3 from 4yo+ 14lb **13** Ran SP% **126.4**
Speed ratings: **109,107,106,106,106 104,104,103,103,103 100,99,94**
CSF £104.44 CT £1321.94 TOTE £7.30: £2.50, £6.10, £4.30; DF 153.30 Trifecta £2345.20.
Owner Mrs S Grassick **Bred** John James **Trained** Currabeg, Co Kildare

FOCUS
The winner looked a consistent filly that was maybe a little bit higher in the handicap than she deserved, but she put the lie to that here.

3631 - 3632a (Foreign Racing) - See Raceform Interactive

3591 CHESTER (L-H)

Saturday, June 25

OFFICIAL GOING: Good (good to soft in places; 6.5)
Wind: light half against Weather: sunny

3633 MALIBU COCONUT CUP MAIDEN STKS (PLUS 10 RACE) 5f 16y

1:50 (1:51) (Class 4) 2-Y-0

£6,225 (£1,864; £932; £466; £233; £117) **Stalls** Low

Form RPR

2 **1** **Rosabelle**[16] 3074 2-9-0 0 .... DavidProbert 9 75
(Alan Bailey) *carried sltly rt s: swtchd lft and hld up: pushed along and gd hdwy on inner over 1f out: led 110yds out: kpt on wl* **14/1**

5 **2** 1½ **Three C'S (IRE)**[36] 2437 2-9-5 0 .... JFEgan 5 75
(David Dennis) *chsd ldrs: rdn 2f out: kpt on* **20/1**

30 **3** 1½ **Cajmere**[14] 3167 2-9-5 0 .... RichardKingscote 7 69+
(Tom Dascombe) *led narrowly: rdn whn hdd over 1f out: led again 1f out: hdd 110yds out: one pce* **5/1**[3]

345 **4** *nk* **The Nazca Lines (IRE)**[38] 2371 2-9-5 0 ....(v[1]) CamHardie 6 68
(John Quinn) *chsd ldrs: rdn 1/2-way: one pce fnl f* **12/1**

5 *shd* **Atteq** 2-9-5 0 .... GeorgeChaloner 2 68
(Richard Fahey) *dwlt: hld up: sn pushed along: hdwy on outer 1/2-way: rdn over 1f out: one pce ins fnl f* **5/2**[2]

5564 **6** 1 **Love Oasis**[30] 2611 2-9-0 0 .... FrannyNorton 4 59
(Mark Johnston) *pressed ldr: rdn to ld narrowly over 1f out: hdd 1f out: wknd fnl 110yds* **13/2**

0 **7** 1¼ **Arthurthedelegator**[5] 3472 2-9-0 0 .... NathanEvans(5) 1 60
(Oliver Greenall) *hld up in tch: rdn 2f out: one pce and nvr threatened* **25/1**

06 **8** 3¼ **Tennessee Rose (IRE)**[9] 3301 2-8-9 0........(t) AnnaHesketh(5) 3 43
(Tom Dascombe) *s.i.s: hld up: pushed along over 1f out: nvr threatened* **33/1**

9 1¼ **Albizu Campos** 2-9-5 0 .... JasonHart 10 43
(Lawrence Mullaney) *s.i.s: hld up: nvr threatened* **100/1**

20 **10** 2¾ **Megan Lily (IRE)**[27] 2718 2-9-0 0 .... JackGarritty 8 29
(Richard Fahey) *prom towards outer: rdn 1/2-way: wknd over 1f out* **9/4**[1]

1m 3.07s (2.07) **Going Correction** +0.375s/f (Good) **10** Ran SP% **116.2**
Speed ratings (Par 95): **98,95,93,92,92 90,88,83,81,77**
CSF £255.12 TOTE £12.30: £3.10, £6.10, £2.00; EX 285.00 Trifecta £3155.70 Part won..

Owner P T Tellwright **Bred** P T Tellwright **Trained** Newmarket, Suffolk

FOCUS

The running rail between the 6f and 1.5f point was moved out a further 3yds after racing on Friday. This meant the actual distance for this race was 5f 36yds (+20yds). Probably just a modest contest. Richard Kingscote and David Probert reported afterwards that they both felt it was 'good ground'. The winner is rated to have stepped up from her debut.

3634 FRANKLIN AND SONS SOFT DRINKS MAIDEN STKS 7f 122y

2:20 (2:21) (Class 4) 3-Y-O+

£6,225 (£1,864; £932; £466; £233; £117) **Stalls** Low

Form			Horse	RPR
3-25	**1**		**Dark Intention (IRE)**[35] 2490 3-8-12 73 CamHardie 5 (Lawrence Mullaney) *trckd ldng pair: rdn to ld over 1f out: sn strly pressed: kpt on wl* **4/1**[3]	76
44	**2**	*1*	**Predetermined (IRE)**[24] 2790 3-9-3 0 DavidProbert 6 (Andrew Balding) *hld up: gd hdwy on outer 3f out: pushed along to chal strly over 1f out: drvn ins fnl f: one pce fnl 110yds* **11/10**[1]	78
	3	*3/4*	**Organza**[73] 3-8-12 0 FrannyNorton 1 (Mick Channon) *s.i.s: hld up on inner: pushed along and hdwy over 1f out: angled rt to outer appr fnl f: kpt on* **7/2**[2]	71
45	**4**	*3 1/2*	**Check 'Em Tuesday (IRE)**[25] 2780 3-8-12 0 JFEgan 4 (Daniel Mark Loughnane) *midfield: rdn over 2f out: one pce and nvr threatened* **20/1**	62
-03	**5**	*4*	**Queen's Code (IRE)**[50] 1998 3-8-12 0 RichardKingscote 3 (Charles Hills) *dwlt: pushed along and sn led: racd keenly: rdn whn hdd over 1f out: wknd ins fnl f* **5/1**	52
4336	**6**	*7*	**Ten Rocks**[28] 2686 3-9-0 67 JosephineGordon(3) 7 (Lisa Williamson) *restless in stall: dwlt: midfield: rdn 3f out: wknd over 1f out* **25/1**	40
6000	**7**	*7*	**Muhtadim (IRE)**[17] 3040 4-9-8 44 (b[1]) RobJFitzpatrick(5) 8 (Charles Smith) *pressed ldr towards outer: rdn 3f out: wknd 2f out* **100/1**	24

1m 35.82s (2.02) **Going Correction** +0.375s/f (Good)
WFA 3 from 4yo 10lb **7** Ran SP% **116.1**
Speed ratings (Par 105): **104,103,102,98,94 87,80**
CSF £9.00 TOTE £5.10: £2.50, £1.10; EX 10.40 Trifecta £29.40.
Owner Ian Buckley **Bred** Desert Star Phoenix Jvc **Trained** Great Habton, N Yorks

FOCUS

The running rail between the 6f and 1.5f point was moved out a further 3yds after racing on Friday. This meant the actual distance for this race was 7f 146yds (+24yds). This contest can easily be measured through the winner's official mark.

3635 COCA COLA ZERO SUGAR H'CAP 7f 2y

2:55 (2:55) (Class 2) (0-100,93) 3-Y-O

£12,450 (£3,728; £1,864; £932; £466; £234) **Stalls** Low

Form			Horse	RPR
3104	**1**		**Arcanada (IRE)**[9] 3299 3-9-7 93 RichardKingscote 3 (Tom Dascombe) *dwlt sltly: in midfield: pushed along and hdwy over 1f out: rdn fnl f: kpt on wl: led 50yds out* **9/4**[1]	102
0-41	**2**	*1/2*	**Penwortham (IRE)**[20] 2935 3-8-8 80 GeorgeChaloner 1 (Richard Fahey) *trckd ldng pair: rdn over 1f out: led jst ins fnl f: kpt on but hdd 50yds out* **6/1**	88
-104	**3**	*2*	**Short Work**[14] 3155 3-8-9 81 (p) DavidProbert 8 (Ralph Beckett) *hld up: rdn 2f out: kpt on fnl f: wnt 3rd fnl 50yds* **20/1**	84
1-53	**4**	*1 1/4*	**Sky Ship**[14] 3130 3-8-7 82 JosephineGordon(3) 5 (Sir Michael Stoute) *hld up in rr: pushed along 3f out: rdn over 1f out: swtchd lft 1f out: kpt on: nvr threatened ldrs* **11/2**[3]	81
0422	**5**	*nk*	**Lagenda**[17] 3029 3-8-13 88 (p) JoeDoyle(3) 2 (Kevin Ryan) *pressed ldr: rdn 2f out: led appr fnl f: hdd jst ins fnl f: wknd* **9/2**[2]	86
4402	**6**	*2 1/4*	**Dawaa**[15] 3116 3-9-3 89 FrannyNorton 7 (Mark Johnston) *led narrowly: rdn 2f out: hdd appr fnl f: wknd* **9/1**	81
2221	**7**	*nk*	**Destroyer**[14] 3155 3-8-9 81 (p) SamHitchcott 4 (William Muir) *in tch: rdn over 2f out: wknd fnl f* **9/1**	73
-052	**8**	*1*	**Gallipoli (IRE)**[19] 2972 3-9-1 87 JackGarritty 6 (Richard Fahey) *hld up: rdn over 2f out: wknd fnl f* **7/1**	76

1m 27.36s (0.86) **Going Correction** +0.375s/f (Good) **8** Ran SP% **115.9**
Speed ratings (Par 105): **110,109,107,105,105 102,102,101**
CSF £16.38 CT £215.83 TOTE £3.10: £1.40, £2.40, £3.00; EX 20.30 Trifecta £288.00.
Owner The Arcanada Partnership **Bred** C J Foy **Trained** Malpas, Cheshire

FOCUS

The running rail between the 6f and 1.5f point was moved out a further 3yds after racing on Friday. This meant the actual distance for this race was 7f 26yds (+24yds). A sound effort by the winner, who was giving plenty of weight to the next four home.

3636 WOODFORD RESERVE H'CAP 1m 4f 66y

3:30 (3:30) (Class 4) (0-80,78) 3-Y-O+

£6,225 (£1,864; £932; £466; £233; £117) **Stalls** Low

Form			Horse	RPR
0-21	**1**		**Man Look**[14] 3121 4-9-13 77 DavidProbert 10 (Andrew Balding) *trckd ldr: led gng wl 2f out: pushed along over 1f out: edgd lft: styd on wl* **9/2**[1]	87
0/40	**2**	*2 3/4*	**Doesyourdogbite (IRE)**[28] 2699 4-9-8 72 (p) JackGarritty 9 (Jonjo O'Neill) *midfield: hdwy 4f out: rdn to chse ldr over 1f out: styd on but no ch w wnr* **14/1**	77
0000	**3**	*nk*	**The Character (IRE)**[16] 3057 5-9-5 69 (p) RichardKingscote 5 (Tom Dascombe) *midfield: rdn over 2f out: styd on fr over 1f out: wnt 3rd ins fnl f* **7/1**	74
3-61	**4**	*3 3/4*	**Marengo**[14] 3129 5-9-7 78 (p) JordanWilliams(7) 8 (Bernard Llewellyn) *in tch: rdn 3f out: one pce* **13/2**	77
0405	**5**	*1 1/4*	**Omotesando**[7] 3395 6-9-3 72 CharlieBennett(5) 2 (Mark Brisbourne) *hld up: rdn 3f out: plugged on: nvr threatened* **16/1**	69
1-53	**6**	*1 1/4*	**Goldslinger (FR)**[49] 2041 4-9-13 77 CamHardie 6 (Dean Ivory) *led: clr 10f out tl 4f out: rdn whn hdd 2f out: sn wknd* **15/2**	72
1322	**7**	*1*	**Distant High**[15] 3095 5-8-9 64 (p) NathanEvans(5) 7 (Richard Price) *midfield: rdn over 3f out: wknd over 1f out* **12/1**	57
0146	**8**	*1/2*	**Bayan Kasirga (IRE)**[11] 3251 6-9-3 74 NatalieHambling(7) 1 (Richard Fahey) *s.i.s: hld up: pushed along over 3f out: nvr threatened* **13/2**	67
-000	**9**	*1 1/2*	**Perrault (IRE)**[14] 3149 4-9-11 75 (p) GeorgeChaloner 3 (Richard Fahey) *hld up: pushed along over 4f out: rdn over 3f out: sn btn* **6/1**[3]	65
00-3	**10**	*7*	**Sennockian Song**[8] 3348 3-8-5 69 FrannyNorton 11 (Mark Johnston) *chsd clr ldr: pushed along and lost pl 4f out: wknd over 2f out* **11/2**[2]	48

2m 42.14s (3.64) **Going Correction** +0.375s/f (Good)
WFA 3 from 4yo+ 14lb **10** Ran SP% **119.0**
Speed ratings (Par 105): **102,100,99,97,96 95,95,94,93,89**
CSF £70.09 CT £441.64 TOTE £3.80: £1.80, £5.60, £2.90; EX 78.00 Trifecta £953.30.
Owner C C Buckley **Bred** Hunscote House Farm Stud **Trained** Kingsclere, Hants

FOCUS

The running rail between the 6f and 1.5f point was moved out a further 3yds after racing on Friday. This meant the actual distance for this race was 1m4f 104yds (+38yds). A competitive but ordinary handicap. The winner appears most progressive and won in fair style.

3637 BOTTEGA GOLD H'CAP 5f 16y

4:00 (4:00) (Class 3) (0-90,90) 3-Y-O+

£9,337 (£2,796; £1,398; £699; £349; £175) **Stalls** Low

Form			Horse	RPR
303	**1**		**Powerallied (IRE)**[14] 3131 3-8-13 83 FrannyNorton 2 (Richard Fahey) *trckd ldr: pushed along to ld 1f out: kpt on wl: comf* **7/4**[1]	93
-505	**2**	*2 1/4*	**Blithe Spirit**[21] 2895 5-9-12 90 JasonHart 5 (Eric Alston) *led: rdn whn hdd 1f out: kpt on but no ch w wnr* **9/2**[3]	94
-031	**3**	*1/2*	**Lexi's Hero (IRE)**[14] 3133 8-9-6 84 (v) GeorgeChaloner 4 (Richard Fahey) *in tch: rdn 1/2-way: kpt on* **5/1**	86
0010	**4**	*1/2*	**Confessional**[14] 3151 9-9-7 85 (e) JackGarritty 6 (Tim Easterby) *in tch: rdn 2f out: kpt on* **10/1**	85
000-	**5**	*2 1/2*	**Smart Daisy K**[204] 8106 6-9-5 83 PaulQuinn 1 (Sarah Hollinshead) *dwlt sltly: tk str hold in midfield on inner: rdn over 1f out: one pce and nvr threatened ldrs* **16/1**	74
5041	**6**	*nk*	**Snap Shots (IRE)**[30] 2613 4-9-12 90 (tp) RichardKingscote 3 (Tom Dascombe) *hld up: rdn 2f out: kpt on ins fnl f: nvr threatened* **3/1**[2]	80
61-0	**7**	*3/4*	**Red Stripes (USA)**[161] 213 4-9-6 87 JosephineGordon(3) 7 (Lisa Williamson) *chsd ldr: rdn 1/2-way: wknd over 1f out* **20/1**	75
-000	**8**	*1/2*	**Masamah (IRE)**[13] 3188 10-9-5 83 (p) CamHardie 11 (Patrick Morris) *midfield: rdn 1/2-way: wknd over 1f out* **50/1**	69
60-0	**9**	*1/2*	**Royal Acquisition**[22] 2863 6-8-7 76 CharlieBennett(5) 10 (Ivan Furtado) *s.i.s: hld up: nvr threatened* **40/1**	60

1m 1.93s (0.93) **Going Correction** +0.375s/f (Good)
WFA 3 from 4yo+ 6lb **9** Ran SP% **120.3**
Speed ratings (Par 107): **107,103,102,101,97 97,96,95,94**
CSF £10.38 CT £34.62 TOTE £2.90: £1.10, £1.40, £2.30; EX 13.40 Trifecta £38.80.
Owner Dr Marwan Koukash **Bred** John R Jeffers **Trained** Musley Bank, N Yorks

FOCUS

The running rail between the 6f and 1.5f point was moved out a further 3yds after racing on Friday. This meant the actual distance for this race was 5f 36yds (+20yds). A decent sprint run at a solid gallop and the winner had the perfect trip tracking the pace..

3638 STELLA ARTOIS H'CAP 5f 16y

4:35 (4:36) (Class 4) (0-85,85) 4-Y-O+

£6,225 (£1,864; £932; £466; £233; £117) **Stalls** Low

Form			Horse	RPR
-104	**1**		**Bondi Beach Boy**[29] 2665 7-9-4 82 RichardKingscote 2 (James Turner) *prom: rdn to ld narrowly over 1f out: kpt on wl* **4/1**[2]	89
0002	**2**	*3/4*	**Ballesteros**[14] 3133 7-9-5 83 FrannyNorton 5 (Richard Fahey) *dwlt: hld up: pushed along and hdwy into midfield 1/2-way: angled rt to outer appr fnl f: sn rdn: r.o wl: wnt 2nd towards fin* **11/4**[1]	88+
4331	**3**	*hd*	**Come On Dave (IRE)**[32] 2562 7-8-9 76 (v) JosephineGordon(3) 9 (John Butler) *trckd ldr: rdn to chal strly over 1f out: no ex towards fin* **11/1**	80
6353	**4**	*1/2*	**Secret Asset (IRE)**[14] 3123 11-8-13 77 (v) JackGarritty 1 (Lisa Williamson) *chsd ldr: rdn 1/2-way: kpt on same pce* **12/1**	79
0030	**5**	*3/4*	**Vimy Ridge**[7] 3414 4-8-13 77 (p) DavidProbert 4 (Alan Bailey) *hld up: pushed along 1/2-way: r.o fnl f: nrst fin* **7/1**	77
5166	**6**	*hd*	**Rusty Rocket (IRE)**[25] 2775 7-8-13 82 NathanEvans(5) 8 (Paul Green) *chsd ldrs on outer: rdn 1/2-way: one pce fnl f* **16/1**	81
-050	**7**	*1/2*	**Distant Past**[14] 3150 5-9-4 85 (b[1]) JoeDoyle(3) 7 (Kevin Ryan) *midfield on inner: rdn 1/2-way: one pce* **17/2**	82
0020	**8**	*shd*	**Rita's Boy (IRE)**[56] 1874 4-8-11 82 (v) CliffordLee(7) 12 (K R Burke) *dwlt: midfield on outside: rdn and outpcd 1/2-way: plugged on ins fnl f* **25/1**	79
031-	**9**	*hd*	**Invincible Ridge (IRE)**[404] 2328 8-9-7 85 NeilFarley 10 (Eric Alston) *midfield: rdn 1/2-way: no imp* **33/1**	81
1252	**10**	*hd*	**King Crimson**[13] 3193 4-9-6 84 JFEgan 3 (Mick Channon) *led: rdn whn hdd over 1f out: wknd ins fnl f* **9/2**[3]	79
1000	**11**	*3 1/4*	**Evanescent (IRE)**[7] 3414 7-8-10 77 GeorgeDowning(3) 6 (Tony Carroll) *rrd s and slowly away: sn pushed along in rr: a bhd* **16/1**	60
140-	**12**	*58*	**Gowanharry (IRE)**[255] 7223 7-9-6 84 (tp) CamHardie 11 (Michael Dods) *hld up: pushed along 1/2-way: sn wknd: eased and t.o* **33/1**	

1m 2.72s (1.72) **Going Correction** +0.375s/f (Good) **12** Ran SP% **125.4**
Speed ratings (Par 105): **101,99,99,98,97 97,96,96,95,95 90,**
CSF £16.10 CT £118.10 TOTE £5.90: £2.60, £1.70, £3.40; EX 21.80 Trifecta £259.50.
Owner G R Turner & H Turner **Bred** G R & H Turner **Trained** Norton-le-Clay, N Yorks

FOCUS

The running rail between the 6f and 1.5f point was moved out a further 3yds after racing on Friday. This meant the actual distance for this race was 5f 36yds (+20yds). This looked another decent sprint on the card, which was run at a sound pace. A small personal best from the winner.

3639 PIMMS NO.1 H'CAP 1m 7f 195y

5:10 (5:10) (Class 4) (0-85,85) 4-Y-O+

£6,225 (£1,864; £932; £466; £233; £117) **Stalls** Low

Form			Horse	RPR
-113	**1**		**Always Resolute**[7] 3409 5-8-9 73 FrannyNorton 4 (Brian Ellison) *trckd ldr on inner: pushed along 2f out: rdn to ld jst ins fnl f: styd on* **2/1**[1]	81
324-	**2**	*1 1/2*	**Diamond Joel**[247] 6310 4-9-0 78 JFEgan 1 (Mick Channon) *led: rdn over 2f out: hdd jst ins fnl f: kpt on* **8/1**	84
6466	**3**	*2 1/2*	**Communicator**[25] 2782 8-9-1 79 (v) DavidProbert 12 (Andrew Balding) *midfield: rdn 3f out: styd on fr over 1f out* **13/2**[3]	82
1046	**4**	*2 1/2*	**Newera**[14] 3129 4-9-6 84 (p) RichardKingscote 9 (Tom Dascombe) *hld up in midfield: rdn over 3f out: styd on fr over 1f out* **16/1**	84
/121	**5**	*1/2*	**Argent Knight**[50] 1987 6-9-0 81 (p) JoeDoyle(3) 11 (Christopher Kellett) *hld up: rdn 3f out: styd on fnl f: nvr threatened* **12/1**	80

5400 **6** *1* **Gabrial The Duke (IRE)**[14] 3149 6-9-2 **80**.................. GeorgeChaloner 7 77
(Richard Fahey) *dwlt: hld up: rdn over 3f out: nvr threatened: fin 7th: plcd 6th* **12/1**

3040 **7** *nse* **Spiritoftomintoul**[25] 2782 7-8-10 **77**......................(t) GeorgeDowning[(3)] 5 74
(Tony Carroll) *s.i.s: hld up: rdn 3f out: nvr threatened: fin 8th: plcd 7th* **20/1**

-000 **8** *½* **Norab (GER)**[8] 3351 5-8-6 **77**..................................(b[1]) MitchGodwin[(7)] 2 73
(Bernard Llewellyn) *in tch: rdn over 3f out: lost pl over 3f out: btn whn sltly hmpd and swtchd rt appr fnl f: fin 9th: plcd 8th* **33/1**

/505 **9** *¾* **Nabhan**[14] 3129 4-9-2 **85**... RobJFitzpatrick[(5)] 6 80
(Bernard Llewellyn) *in tch: rdn and hdwy on outer to chse ldr over 3f out: lost pl and edgd lft over 1f out: wknd fnl f: fin 10th: plcd 9th* **14/1**

022/ **10** *8* **Perspicace**[27] 7067 5-8-13 **77**..............................(p) SamHitchcott 3 62
(David Pipe) *midfield: rdn 4f out: wknd over 2f out: eased: fin 12th: plcd 11th* **4/1**[2]

110/ **D** *½* **Kelvingrove (IRE)**[50] 7210 6-9-7 **85**.................................. JackGarritty 8 83
(Jonjo O'Neill) *trckd ldr: rdn over 3f out: lost pl whn hmpd over 1f out: plugged on fnl f: fin 6th: disqualified and plcd last* **10/1**

3m 34.21s (6.21) **Going Correction** +0.375s/f (Good) **11** Ran SP% **122.5**
Speed ratings (Par 105): **99,98,97,95,95 94,94,94,94,90 95**
CSF £19.66 CT £93.90 TOTE £2.60: £1.20, £2.90, £2.90; EX 24.00 Trifecta £119.90.
Owner Market Avenue Racing Club Ltd **Bred** Jarvis Associates **Trained** Norton, N Yorks
■ Stewards' Enquiry : Jack Garritty two-day ban; careless riding (11th-12th July)

FOCUS
The running rail between the 6f and 1.5f point was moved out a further 3yds after racing on Friday. This meant the actual distance for this race was 2m 41yds (+46yds). It paid to be fairly handy in this staying contest. The winner is on a good mark on his jumps form.
T/Plt: £122.90 to a £1 stake. Pool of £76492.22 - 454.16 winning tickets. T/Qpdt: £15.20 to a £1 stake. Pool of £5067.05 - 245.66 winning tickets. **Andrew Sheret**

3597 DONCASTER (L-H)
Saturday, June 25

OFFICIAL GOING: Straight course - good (good to soft in places); round course - good to soft (good in places)
Wind: Moderate against Weather: Cloudy with showers

3640 SUN BRITISH STALLION STUDS EBF NOVICE FILLIES' STKS (PLUS 10 RACE) 7f
5:50 (5:50) (Class 5) 2-Y-O **£3,881** (£1,155; £577; £288) **Stalls** High

Form RPR

1 **Reachforthestars (IRE)** 2-9-0 0....................................... SamJames 7 76+
(David O'Meara) *trckd ldrs on outer: smooth hdwy to ld wl over 1f out: rdn: green and edgd lft ins fnl f: kpt on* **7/4**[1]

2 *¾* **See The Sea (IRE)** 2-9-0 0.. SeanLevey 1 74
(Richard Hannon) *dwlt and hld up in rr: hdwy 1/2-way: rdn along over 2f out: green and drvn over 1f out: styd on wl fnl f* **9/4**[2]

3 *1* **Lucky Esteem** 2-9-0 0.. AndrewMullen 4 71
(Mark Johnston) *t.k.h: trckd ldrs: green and pushed along to chal wl over 1f out: sn rdn and ev ch: hld whn n.m.r wl ins fnl f* **11/2**

4 *6* **Speciale Di Giorno (IRE)** 2-9-0 0................................. PaoloSirigu 3 55
(Marco Botti) *trckd ldr: cl up 1/2-way: rdn along over 2f out: grad wknd* **7/2**[3]

00 **5** *¾* **Lucky Return**[14] 3143 2-9-0 0....................................... DuranFentiman 5 53
(Des Donovan, Ire) *led: pushed along wl over 2f out: rdn and hdd wl over 1f out: sn wknd* **25/1**

0 **6** *9* **Just Heather (IRE)**[21] 2885 2-9-0 0................................ PaddyAspell 2 29
(John Wainwright) *in tch: hdwy on outer to trck ldrs 1/2-way: rdn along wl over 2f out: sn outpcd and bhd* **50/1**

1m 28.87s (2.57) **Going Correction** +0.05s/f (Good) **6** Ran SP% **110.5**
Speed ratings (Par 90): **87,86,85,78,77 67**
CSF £5.76 TOTE £2.70: £1.90, £1.40; EX 6.40 Trifecta £15.90.
Owner Geoff & Sandra Turnbull **Bred** Roundhill Stud & T Stewart **Trained** Upper Helmsley, N Yorks

FOCUS
Round course railed out from 1m2f until meeting the straight. Add 6yds to race 2 and 3 race distances. An ordinary juvenile fillies' novice contest and they went an ordinary gallop on ground officially described as good to soft, good in places on the round course and good, good to soft in places on the straight track.

3641 PJ TOWEY H'CAP 1m 4f
6:20 (6:20) (Class 5) (0-75,75) 4-Y-O+ **£3,881** (£1,155; £577; £288) **Stalls** Low

Form RPR

311 **1** **Viserion**[8] 3363 4-9-6 **74**...(p) SamJames 1 83+
(David Simcock) *hld up in rr: hdwy on inner 3f out: swtchd rt and effrt 2f out: sn rdn: chsd ldr over 1f out: drvn and styd on wl fnl f to ld last 100yds* **1/1**[1]

06-5 **2** *1 ½* **Smoky Hill (IRE)**[30] 2616 7-8-2 **56** oh1............................. JoeyHaynes 9 62
(Tony Carroll) *trckd ldng pair: hdwy to chse ldr over 3f out: led wl over 2f out: rdn clr wl over 1f out: drvn ins fnl f: hdd and no ex last 100yds* **16/1**

1 **3** *1* **Hard Toffee (IRE)**[31] 2588 5-9-2 **70**................................... PaddyAspell 8 74
(Conrad Allen) *t.k.h: hld up and bhd: hdwy on inner 3f out: swtchd rt and rdn 2f out: chsd ldng pair over 1f out: kpt on u.p fnl f: nrst fin* **12/1**

56-5 **4** *1 ¾* **Persian Breeze**[19] 2965 4-9-4 **72**.........................(p) SeanLevey 2 73
(Lucy Wadham) *in tch on inner: hdwy over 4f out: chsd ldrs 3f out and sn rdn along: drvn wl over 1f out: kpt on same pce* **8/1**[3]

0-00 **5** *7* **Captain Swift (IRE)**[23] 2836 5-9-0 **68**............................ AndrewMullen 6 58
(John Mackie) *hld up towards rr: hdwy over 3f out: rdn along over 2f out: sn btn* **8/1**[3]

0312 **6** *10* **Mysterial**[4] 3481 6-8-12 **73**.. GerO'Neill[(7)] 7 47
(Declan Carroll) *sn led: clr after 3f: rdn along 4f out: hdd wl over 2f out and sn wknd* **7/2**[2]

3-00 **7** *10* **Flying Power**[42] 2233 8-8-6 **63** ow1.......................... JacobButterfield[(3)] 5 21
(John Norton) *trckd ldr: pushed along 4f out: rdn 3f out: sn wknd* **14/1**

0000 **8** *3 ¼* **That Be Grand**[9] 3325 5-7-13 **56** oh11........................(b[1]) ShelleyBirkett[(3)] 3 9
(Shaun Harris) *trckd ldrs: hdwy 4f out: rdn along 3f out: sn drvn and wknd over 2f out* **50/1**

2m 35.81s (0.91) **Going Correction** +0.20s/f (Good) **8** Ran SP% **116.6**
Speed ratings (Par 103): **104,103,102,101,96 89,83,81**
CSF £20.95 CT £131.51 TOTE £2.00: £1.02, £4.80, £2.90; EX 21.60 Trifecta £238.30.
Owner Tick Tock Partnership **Bred** Sheikh Sultan Bin Khalifa Al Nahyan **Trained** Newmarket, Suffolk

FOCUS
Add 6yds to race distance. A fair middle-distance handicap and they went a respectable gallop, but not much depth to the form.

3642 PANELCRAFT ACCESS PANELS FILLIES' H'CAP 1m 2f 60y
6:50 (6:50) (Class 5) (0-70,68) 4-Y-O+ **£3,881** (£1,155; £577; £144; £144) **Stalls** Low

Form RPR

2250 **1** **Miss Ranger (IRE)**[11] 3251 4-8-13 **65**.................... CallumShepherd[(5)] 11 73+
(Brian Ellison) *hld up in rr: gd hdwy on outer over 2f out: rdn to chse ldng pair over 1f out: drvn and styd on strly to ld last 50yds* **4/1**[2]

-522 **2** *½* **Henpecked**[33] 2526 6-8-13 **67**... RowanScott[(7)] 9 74
(Alistair Whillans) *trckd ldng pair: hdwy wl over 2f out: rdn to chse ldr wl over 1f out: drvn and ev ch ins fnl f: kpt on same pce towards fin* **2/1**[1]

010/ **3** *¾* **Amthal (IRE)**[1701] 7169 7-9-3 **64**... SeanLevey 10 70
(Lucy Wadham) *t.k.h: trckd ldr: cl up over 4f out: led over 3f out: rdn wl over 1f out: drvn ent fnl f: hdd and no ex last 50yds* **9/1**

2-66 **4** *8* **Jersey Jewel (FR)**[30] 2616 4-9-2 **68**............................. AnnaHesketh[(5)] 2 58
(Tom Dascombe) *trckd ldrs: hdwy 3f out: rdn over 2f out: sn drvn: edgd lft and one pce* **10/1**

1025 **4** *dht* **La Havrese (FR)**[22] 2860 5-8-12 **64**................................. JoshDoyle[(5)] 1 54
(Lynn Siddall) *hld up in tch: hdwy on inner wl over 2f out and sn rdn: drvn wl over 1f out: one pce* **9/1**

-044 **6** *½* **Bertha Burnett (IRE)**[4] 3479 5-8-2 **49** oh3.................. DuranFentiman 5 38
(Brian Rothwell) *hld up and bhd: hdwy 3f out: chsd ldrs whn nt clr run 2f out: sn swtchd rt and rdn: no imp* **9/1**

0242 **7** *2 ¾* **The Dukkerer (IRE)**[16] 3072 5-9-1 **62**................................ TomEaves 3 45
(James Given) *trckd ldrs on inner: hdwy 3f out: swtchd rt and rdn 2f out: sn drvn and btn* **6/1**[3]

006- **8** *13* **Bond Starprincess**[151] 4449 4-8-2 **49** oh4........................ JoeyHaynes 6 6
(Ben Haslam) *chsd ldrs: pushed along 1/2-way: rdn wl over 3f out: sn drvn and wknd* **40/1**

0-06 **9** *29* **Secret Lightning (FR)**[10] 3291 4-9-4 **65**...................(p) AndrewMullen 7
(Michael Appleby) *led: rdn along 4f out: hdd over 3f out: wkng whn hmpd on inner wl over 2f out: sn bhd and eased* **16/1**

2m 12.5s (3.10) **Going Correction** +0.20s/f (Good) **9** Ran SP% **115.0**
Speed ratings (Par 100): **95,94,94,87,87 87,85,74,51**
CSF £12.34 CT £66.45 TOTE £4.70: £1.40, £1.40, £3.20; EX 14.00 Trifecta £98.10.
Owner Jane Greetham & Victoria Greetham **Bred** J F Tuthill **Trained** Norton, N Yorks

FOCUS
Add 6yds to race distance. A modest fillies' handicap, but they went a respectable gallop and there is probably more to come from the winner at the trip..

3643 M & G ASBESTOS REMOVAL AND SURVEYING MAIDEN STKS 6f
7:25 (7:25) (Class 5) 3-Y-O+ **£3,881** (£1,155; £577; £288) **Stalls** High

Form RPR

-040 **1** **Florenza**[12] 3213 3-9-0 72.. AndrewElliott 3 79
(Chris Fairhurst) *prom: chal wl over 1f out: sn rdn: led ins fnl f: kpt on* **12/1**

42-2 **2** *¾* **Hyland Heather (IRE)**[28] 2681 3-9-0 78.......................... TonyHamilton 4 77
(Richard Fahey) *led: rdn wl over 1f out: hdd and drvn ins fnl f: kpt on same pce* **4/1**

334 **3** *3 ¼* **Tommy G**[39] 2333 3-9-5 80.. DanielTudhope 10 71
(Jim Goldie) *swtchd lft sn after s: in tch: hdwy wl over 1f out: sn rdn: drvn and kpt on fnl f: tk 3rd on line* **3/1**[2]

\- **4** *nse* **L C Saloon** 3-9-5 0.. DavidAllan 8 71
(David C Griffiths) *cl up: rdn along wl over 1f out: drvn ent fnl f: kpt on same pce: lost 3rd on line* **50/1**

2-22 **5** *½* **Andar**[14] 3127 3-9-5 80..(p) RyanTate 6 69
(Clive Cox) *trckd ldrs: hdwy over 2f out: rdn along wl over 1f out: wknd appr fnl f* **9/4**[1]

0-03 **6** *2* **Khor Al Udaid**[18] 2999 3-9-5 77......................................(b) RobertHavlin 9 63
(John Gosden) *racd nr stands' rail: prom: pushed along and edgd lft over 2f out: rdn and hung bdly lft wl over 1f out: sn btn* **7/2**[3]

65 **7** *2* **Justice Pleasing**[7] 3400 3-9-5 0.. SamJames 11 57
(David Loughnane) *racd nr stands' rail: pushed along and edgd lft over 2f out: rdn wl over 1f out: n.d* **33/1**

06 **8** *3* **Oasis Moon**[7] 3406 3-8-7 0... GeorgiaCox[(7)] 1 42
(William Haggas) *hld up: hdwy 1/2-way: chsd ldrs 2f out: sn rdn and wknd over 1f out* **25/1**

0-00 **9** *7* **Respectability**[16] 3066 4-9-4 0............................ AlistairRawlinson[(3)] 5 22
(Ivan Furtado) *in tch on outer: rdn along 1/2-way: sn outpcd and bhd* **66/1**

000- **10** *nk* **Hannahs Lad**[182] 8355 3-9-5 0... JimmyQuinn 7 24
(Ronald Thompson) *a towards rr: rdn along over 2f out: sn outpcd* **100/1**

11 *2 ¾* **Culturehull** 3-9-0 0... JasonHart 2 10
(Les Eyre) *s.i.s and green: sn detached and a bhd* **40/1**

1m 13.18s (-0.42) **Going Correction** +0.05s/f (Good)
WFA 3 from 4yo 7lb **11** Ran SP% **119.4**
Speed ratings (Par 103): **104,103,98,98,97 95,92,88,79,78 75**
CSF £58.26 TOTE £15.40: £3.30, £1.60, £1.50; EX 85.20 Trifecta £315.40.
Owner 980 Racing **Bred** 980 Racing **Trained** Middleham, N Yorks

FOCUS
A fairly decent maiden rated around the runner-up. They went a proper gallop.

3644 BEAVER 84 H'CAP 5f 140y
7:55 (7:56) (Class 4) (0-85,84) 3-Y-O **£6,469** (£1,925; £962; £481) **Stalls** High

Form RPR

6305 **1** **Kestrel Call (IRE)**[59] 1789 3-8-10 **73**........................(t) AndrewMullen 1 80
(Michael Appleby) *t.k.h early: trckd ldr: hdwy 1/2-way: led 2f out: rdn over 1f out: drvn ent fnl f: kpt on wl towards fin* **20/1**

-031 **2** *½* **Laughton**[26] 2742 3-9-0 **77**.. ShaneGray 2 82
(Kevin Ryan) *trckd ldrs: hdwy on outer over 2f out: chal over 1f out and sn rdn: drvn and ev ch ins fnl f: no ex towards fin* **7/2**[2]

5-12 **3** *1* **Cersei**[12] 3218 3-9-0 **77**...(t) TomEaves 3 79
(David Simcock) *trckd ldrs: hdwy over 2f out: ev ch whn nt clr run over 1f out: swtchd rt and rdn ent fnl f: kpt on* **5/1**[3]

32-1 **4** *3 ¼* **Spanish City**[26] 2750 3-9-0 **77**.. AndreaAtzeni 6 68
(Roger Varian) *trckd ldng pair: hdwy 2f out: rdn over 1f out: sn drvn and ev ch tl wknd ins fnl f* **5/6**[1]

401 **5** *1 ½* **Chez Vegas**[42] 2234 3-8-12 **75**.. BenCurtis 4 61
(Scott Dixon) *slt ld: jnd and rdn along 1/2-way: hdd 2f out: grad wknd* **11/2**

1m 9.69s (0.89) **Going Correction** +0.05s/f (Good) **5** Ran SP% **113.6**
Speed ratings (Par 101): **96,95,94,89,87**
CSF £87.12 TOTE £16.70: £8.20, £2.60; EX 85.60 Trifecta £238.50.
Owner Craig Buckingham **Bred** W J Kennedy **Trained** Oakham, Rutland

FOCUS
The feature contest was a decent 3yo sprint handicap with the winner back to form. They went an ordinary gallop.

3645 JORDAN ROAD SURFACING H'CAP — 7f
8:25 (8:28) (Class 4) (0-85,85) 4-Y-O+ **£5,175** (£1,540; £769; £384) **Stalls** High

Form RPR
1506 **1** **Boots And Spurs**[70] 1478 7-8-12 **76**..........(v) BarryMcHugh 12 85
(Scott Dixon) *a.p: led wl over 1f out and sn rdn: drvn ins fnl f: kpt on gamely towards fin* **25/1**
16-6 **2** *1* **Johnny Cavagin**[83] 1215 7-9-4 **82**..........(t) JimmyQuinn 4 88
(Ronald Thompson) *dwlt and in rr: hdwy over 2f out: rdn to chse ldrs over 1f out: drvn to chal ins fnl f: ev ch tl nt qckn towards fin* **20/1**
4042 **3** *shd* **Fuwairt (IRE)**[7] 3419 4-8-13 **77**.......... SamJames 11 83
(David Loughnane) *in tch: hdwy on outer wl over 1f out: rdn to chal and hung lft ins fnl f: kpt on* **7/1**[2]
6-50 **4** *3/4* **Fray**[7] 3394 5-8-9 **73**.......... PaulMulrennan 8 77
(Jim Goldie) *dwlt and in rr: swtchd markedly lft and hdwy over 1f out: n.m.r and rdn ins fnl f: swtchd rt and kpt on wl towards fin* **25/1**
0-51 **5** *1 3/4* **Raising Sand**[19] 2980 4-9-7 **85**.......... AndreaAtzeni 1 84
(Roger Varian) *in tch: hdwy 2f out: chsd ldrs over 1f out: sn rdn and kpt on same pce fnl f* **11/2**[1]
6343 **6** *nk* **Beardwood**[7] 3419 4-9-4 **82**.......... BenCurtis 3 80
(Brian Ellison) *dwlt and towards rr: hdwy and midfield 1/2-way: rdn 2f out: styd on u.p fnl f: nrst fin* **11/2**[1]
0000 **7** *1* **Dutch Breeze**[14] 3168 5-8-9 **73**..........(p) DavidAllan 15 69
(Tim Easterby) *sn led: rdn along 2f out: sn hdd and drvn: grad wknd appr fnl f* **12/1**
3311 **8** *1 1/4* **Classic Seniority**[8] 3344 4-9-2 **83**.......... JacobButterfield(3) 5 75
(Marjorie Fife) *midfield: effrt and hdwy 2f out: sn rdn and no imp fnl f* **10/1**[3]
00-0 **9** *nse* **Zacynthus (IRE)**[7] 3419 8-9-3 **81**.......... ShaneGray 9 73
(John Balding) *towards rr: hdwy wl over 1f out: sn rdn and no imp fnl f* **33/1**
-203 **10** *nk* **Outback Ruler (IRE)**[20] 2934 4-9-7 **85**.......... RyanTate 10 76
(Clive Cox) *trckd ldrs: hdwy over 2f out: cl up and rdn wl over 1f out: drvn and wknd ent fnl f* **7/1**[2]
4053 **11** *1 3/4* **Steal The Scene (IRE)**[15] 3101 4-9-0 **78**.......... SeanLevey 7 65
(Richard Hannon) *nvr bttr than midfield* **12/1**
540 **12** *1/2* **Mount Tahan (IRE)**[15] 3115 4-9-5 **83**..........(t) DanielTudhope 14 68
(Kevin Ryan) *cl up: effrt 2f out: sn rdn and ev ch tl drvn and wknd appr fnl f* **14/1**
300 **13** *2* **Showboating (IRE)**[7] 3414 8-8-12 **83**.......... LewisEdmunds(7) 6 63
(John Balding) *racd wd: rdn along over 2f out: a towards rr* **33/1**
1664 **14** *4 1/2* **Taysh (USA)**[7] 3419 4-9-2 **83**.......... AlistairRawlinson(3) 16 51
(Michael Appleby) *chsd ldrs: rdn along over 2f out: sn drvn and wknd* **12/1**
-313 **15** *29* **Normandy Barriere (IRE)**[15] 3115 4-9-7 **85**.......... TomEaves 13
(Nigel Tinkler) *midfield: pushed along wl over 2f out: rdn wl over 1f out: sn lost pl and bhd whn eased fnl f* **7/1**[2]
02-0 **16** *12* **Red Harry (IRE)**[19] 2974 4-8-4 **68**.......... RoystonFfrench 2
(David C Griffiths) *chsd ldrs: pushed along over 2f out: rdn wl over 2f out: lost pl qckly: sn bhd and eased* **33/1**

1m 25.89s (-0.41) **Going Correction** +0.05s/f (Good) **16** Ran SP% **128.4**
Speed ratings (Par 105): **104,102,102,101,99 99,98,96,96,96 94,94,91,86,53 39**
CSF £453.21 CT £3996.44 TOTE £33.30: £5.60, £6.00, £2.40, £5.00; EX 599.00 Trifecta £3432.70 Part won..
Owner S Chappell **Bred** Miss G Abbey **Trained** Babworth, Notts

FOCUS
A decent handicap with the winner rated to his winter Southwell form. They went a proper gallop centrally.

3646 BEAVER 84 HIRE AND SALES H'CAP — 6f
8:55 (8:56) (Class 4) (0-85,85) 3-Y-O+ **£5,822** (£1,732; £865; £432) **Stalls** High

Form RPR
0504 **1** **Art Obsession (IRE)**[14] 3168 5-9-0 **74**.......... JoeDoyle(3) 11 83
(Paul Midgley) *trckd ldrs: hdwy 2f out: rdn over 1f out: drvn ins fnl f: led nr fin* **13/2**[2]
5-00 **2** *nk* **Compton Park**[11] 3265 9-9-4 **75**.......... DavidAllan 1 83
(Les Eyre) *dwlt and in rr: swtchd lft and gd hdwy wl over 1f out: rdn to chal jst ins fnl f: led last 100yds: edgd rt and hdd nr fin* **25/1**
-006 **3** *nk* **Personal Touch**[14] 3133 7-9-6 **77**.......... AndrewMullen 4 84
(Michael Appleby) *towards rr: hdwy over 2f out: chsd ldrs over 1f out: sn rdn and kpt on fnl f* **16/1**
-110 **4** *1/2* **Avenue Of Stars**[29] 2650 3-9-0 **78**..........(v[1]) DavidNolan 17 81
(Karen McLintock) *in tch on outer: hdwy and rdn whn hung bdly lft 1 1/2f out: sn drvn and kpt on fnl f* **25/1**
00-0 **5** *nk* **Gin In The Inn (IRE)**[19] 2972 3-8-13 **77**.......... TonyHamilton 7 80+
(Richard Fahey) *trckd ldrs: hdwy over 1f out: rdn and ev ch ent fnl f: drvn and hld whn hmpd nr fin* **16/1**
5034 **6** *nk* **Mishaal (IRE)**[14] 3133 6-9-10 **81**.......... BarryMcHugh 19 84
(Michael Herrington) *chsd ldrs on wd outside: hdwy over 1f out: rdn and kpt on same pce fnl f* **20/1**
2125 **7** *1/2* **Best Trip (IRE)**[15] 3115 9-9-8 **84**.......... NathanEvans(5) 12 86
(Marjorie Fife) *led and clr: rdn wl over 1f out: drvn ent fnl f: hdd & wknd last 100yds* **9/1**
-046 **8** *hd* **Tiger Jim**[39] 2331 6-9-10 **81**.......... DougieCostello 6 82+
(Jim Goldie) *towards rr: hdwy whn sltly hmpd over 1f out: rdn and kpt on fnl f* **8/1**
/0-0 **9** *hd* **Naggers (IRE)**[14] 3168 5-9-0 **71**.......... JackGarritty 2 72
(Paul Midgley) *chsd ldrs: rdn along over 1f out: drvn and wknd ins fnl f* **10/1**
0054 **10** *3/4* **Meshardal (GER)**[13] 3188 6-9-6 **77**.......... JamesSullivan 10 75+
(Ruth Carr) *hld up and bhd: hdwy 2f out: styng on whn hmpd over 1f out: no ch after* **7/1**[3]
-051 **11** *1 1/2* **Eastern Racer (IRE)**[11] 3266 4-9-13 **84**..........(p) DaleSwift 3 80+
(Brian Ellison) *midfield: rdn along 2f out: drvn whn hmpd and wknd over 1f out* **10/1**
0600 **12** *nk* **Mime Dance**[14] 3168 5-8-11 **71**.......... ShelleyBirkett(3) 5 63
(David O'Meara) *in tch: rdn along 2f out: wknd over 1f out* **33/1**
-101 **13** *2 1/4* **Pomme De Terre (IRE)**[14] 3168 4-9-13 **84**..........(b) TomEaves 13 69
(Michael Dods) *chsd ldrs: rdn along 2f out: wkng whn hmpd over 1f out* **7/1**[3]
-050 **14** *1 1/4* **Fyrecracker (IRE)**[17] 3021 5-9-0 **71**.......... ShaneGray 14 52
(Grant Tuer) *in tch: hdwy 2f out: rdn and styng on whn hmpd over 1f out: no ch after* **25/1**
0023 **15** *9* **Mass Rally (IRE)**[11] 3265 9-9-11 **82**..........(b) PaulMulrennan 9 34+
(Michael Dods) *hld up in rr: hdwy whn hmpd over 1f out: no ch after* **6/1**[1]
0006 **16** *13* **Whozthecat (IRE)**[7] 3394 9-9-1 **72**.......... JasonHart 15
(Declan Carroll) *chsd clr ldr: rdn along 2f out: wknd and hmpd over 1f out: sn bhd* **16/1**

1m 12.93s (-0.67) **Going Correction** +0.05s/f (Good)
WFA 3 from 4yo+ 7lb **16** Ran SP% **128.8**
Speed ratings (Par 105): **106,105,105,104,104 103,103,102,102,101 99,99,96,94,82 65**
CSF £174.65 CT £2645.32 TOTE £7.80: £2.30, £7.50, £4.00, £4.30; EX 277.70 Trifecta £3540.60 Part won..
Owner Pee Dee Tee Syndicate & T W Midgley **Bred** Lynch Bages Ltd & Camas Park Stud **Trained** Westow, N Yorks

FOCUS
Another decent handicap with the first three all on good marks on their best form. They went a sound gallop centrally.
T/Plt: £263.20 to a £1 stake. Pool: £62,477.46 - 173.25 winning tickets T/Qpdt: £105.20 to a £1 stake. Pool: £6,591.36 - 46.36 winning tickets **Joe Rowntree**

3401 LINGFIELD (L-H)
Saturday, June 25

OFFICIAL GOING: Polytrack: standard
Wind: Light, across Weather: Fine

3647 188BET.CO.UK EBF NOVICE STKS — 5f 6y(P)
5:40 (5:43) (Class 5) 2-Y-O **£3,881** (£1,155; £577; £288) **Stalls** High

Form RPR
216 **1** **Pretty Vacant**[11] 3247 2-9-6 0.......... JackMitchell 5 85
(Roger Varian) *trckd ldng trio: smooth prog over 1f out: led last 150yds: easily* **4/6**[1]
02 **2** *2 1/4* **Cappananty Con**[17] 3032 2-9-0 0 ow2.......... DavidParkes(5) 8 73
(Dean Ivory) *hld up towards rr fr wd draw: wd bnd 2f out: prog 1f out: shkn up and r.o to take 2nd last 75yds: no ch w wnr but shaped wl* **8/1**
3 **3** *1 1/4* **Second Nature**[22] 2847 2-9-2 0.......... TimmyMurphy 3 65
(James Tate) *prom: chsd ldr 2f out to 1f out: fdd and lost 2nd last 75yds* **7/2**[2]
0 **4** *1/2* **Goodwood Crusader (IRE)**[26] 2732 2-9-2 0.......... ShaneKelly 1 64
(Richard Hughes) *chsd ldrs: shkn up and no imp over 1f out: one pce after* **16/1**
0 **5** *1/2* **Xenon**[10] 3290 2-8-11 0.......... RyanPowell 10 57
(Sir Mark Prescott Bt) *hld up in last pair fr wdst draw: nudged along on inner over 1f out: nvr a threat but fin quite strly* **50/1**
0 **6** *nk* **Seprani**[17] 3037 2-8-11 0.......... SaleemGolam 7 56
(Mrs Ilka Gansera-Leveque) *nvr bttr than midfield: rdn and no prog 2f out: kpt on* **66/1**
0 **7** *1/2* **Roundabout Magic (IRE)**[9] 3315 2-9-2 0.......... NickyMackay 6 59
(Simon Dow) *mde most: drvn and hdd last 150yds: wknd rapidly* **33/1**
6 **8** *nk* **Mums The Word**[26] 2732 2-8-8 0.......... TomMarquand(3) 2 53
(Richard Hannon) *chsd ldr to 2f out: lost pl u.p over 1f out: wknd* **7/1**[3]
30 **9** *nk* **Big Lachie**[11] 3247 2-8-11 0.......... LucyKBarry(5) 9 57
(Jamie Osborne) *hld up in last pair fr wd draw: shkn up on outer over 1f out: no ch but kpt on fnl f* **16/1**

58.49s (-0.31) **Going Correction** -0.05s/f (Stan) **9** Ran SP% **124.0**
Speed ratings (Par 93): **100,96,94,93,92 92,91,91,90**
CSF £8.08 TOTE £1.70: £1.02, £2.70, £1.50; EX 8.40 Trifecta £16.40.
Owner Miss C A Baines **Bred** D R Botterill **Trained** Newmarket, Suffolk

FOCUS
Race run over advertised distance. An interesting enough novice stakes with a very strong favourite, who has the scope to do better.

3648 WIMBLEDON BETTING AT 188BET H'CAP — 7f 1y(P)
6:10 (6:10) (Class 6) (0-65,67) 3-Y-O+ **£2,587** (£770; £384; £192) **Stalls** Low

Form RPR
6414 **1** **Packing (IRE)**[25] 2770 3-8-13 **64**.......... LucyKBarry(5) 4 70
(Jamie Osborne) *led 2f: pressed ldr after: narrow ld again over 1f out: idled in front but fnd enough to hold on* **3/1**[2]
-100 **2** *nk* **Gunman**[26] 2749 3-9-2 **65**.......... TomMarquand(3) 6 70
(Richard Hannon) *led after 2f: rdn and hdd over 1f out: kpt on wl and pressed wnr after: jst hld* **9/2**[3]
0-66 **3** *1 1/4* **Bryght Boy**[22] 2864 3-9-3 **63**.......... AntonioFresu 1 65+
(Ed Walker) *hld up towards rr: waiting for a gap on inner 2f out: plld out wd over 1f out: styd on fnl f and tk 3rd last strides: no ch to threaten* **11/4**[1]
-043 **4** *hd* **Hardy Black (IRE)**[43] 2229 5-9-10 **61**..........(p) SaleemGolam 3 65
(Kevin Frost) *chsd ldrs in 6th: rdn and prog jst over 1f out: chsd ldng pair 100yds out: n.d and lost 3rd last strides* **9/1**
0003 **5** *1 3/4* **Whaleweigh Station**[9] 3320 5-9-12 **63**.......... LemosdeSouza 12 63
(J R Jenkins) *t.k.h: chsd ldng pair to over 2f out: sn shkn up: kpt on to take 3rd again briefly ins fnl f: one pce after* **10/1**
0-00 **6** *3/4* **Haames (IRE)**[129] 609 9-8-10 **47**.......... ShaneKelly 5 45
(Kevin Morgan) *hld up in midfield: prog on outer to chse ldng pair over 2f out: no imp 1f out: sn lost 3rd and fdd* **16/1**
-500 **7** *1/2* **Welsh Inlet (IRE)**[15] 3101 8-9-1 **55**.......... DannyBrock(3) 2 51
(John Bridger) *t.k.h early: chsd ldrs: rdn wl over 2f out: outpcd over 1f out: plugged on* **10/1**
0044 **8** *3 1/2* **Copper Cavalier**[45] 2155 5-9-1 **52**..........(b) SteveDrowne 14 39
(Michael Blanshard) *hld up in rr: shkn up and no prog over 2f out: no ch after* **12/1**
0-66 **9** *1 1/2* **Equal Point**[15] 3104 3-9-3 **63**.......... MartinHarley 8 43
(William Knight) *hld up in rr: shkn up and no rspnse over 1f out* **12/1**
560- **10** *16* **Purple Lane (IRE)**[319] 5240 5-9-4 **62**.......... JoshQuinn(7) 10 1
(Luke Dace) *mostly in last: wknd 3f out: t.o* **33/1**

1m 25.18s (0.38) **Going Correction** -0.05s/f (Stan)
WFA 3 from 4yo+ 9lb **10** Ran SP% **122.2**
Speed ratings (Par 101): **95,94,93,93,91 90,89,85,83,65**
CSF £18.04 CT £43.34 TOTE £4.20: £1.70, £1.90, £1.60; EX 22.50 Trifecta £76.60.
Owner Mr & Mrs I Barratt **Bred** Century Bloodstock **Trained** Upper Lambourn, Berks

FOCUS
Race was run over advertised distance. A competitive if lowly handicap run at a slow pace where the 3yos came to the fore.

3649 TRAK365 FILLIES' H'CAP — 7f 1y(P)
6:40 (6:40) (Class 5) (0-75,75) 3-Y-O+ **£3,234** (£962; £481; £240) **Stalls** Low

Form — RPR

5421 **1** **Make Music**^{23} 2824 3-9-5 **75** OisinMurphy 1 — 82
(Andrew Balding) *mde all: kicked on 2f out: rdn and styd on wl fnl f: unchal* **2/1**^{2}

1-55 **2** 1 ½ **Izmir (IRE)**^{16} 3062 3-9-2 **72** PatCosgrave 6 — 75
(William Haggas) *chsd wnr: rdn wl over 1f out: nt qckn and no imp fnl f: kpt on* **7/2**^{3}

1-P3 **3** 1 ¼ **Nassuvian Pearl**^{17} 3034 3-9-2 **72** AdamKirby 2 — 72
(Ralph Beckett) *tk fierce hold in 3rd: rdn to dispute 2nd over 1f out: one pce fnl f* **5/4**^{1}

6410 **4** 1 ¾ **Cliffhanger**^{8} 3357 3-9-4 **74** MartinHarley 4 — 69
(Paul Cole) *hld up in 5th: lft bhd fr 2f out: shkn up to take 4th over 1f out: nvr nr enough to threaten* **12/1**

10-6 **5** 2 ¼ **Serradura (IRE)**^{58} 1812 3-8-13 **72** TomMarquand$^{(3)}$ 5 — 61
(Charles Hills) *chsd ldrs in 4th: rdn and no rspnse wl over 1f out: wl btn after* **22/1**

000 **6** 4 ½ **Rial (IRE)**^{39} 2337 3-8-5 **68** CameronNoble$^{(7)}$ 3 — 45
(Denis Quinn) *a in last: urged along and struggling wl over 2f out* **66/1**

1m 24.52s (-0.28) **Going Correction** -0.05s/f (Stan) **6** Ran SP% **113.5**
Speed ratings (Par 100): **99,97,95,93,91 86**
CSF £9.65 TOTE £2.90: £1.50, £1.80; EX 8.60 Trifecta £13.10.
Owner Mrs I A Balding **Bred** Brook Stud Bloodstock Ltd **Trained** Kingsclere, Hants

FOCUS
Race distance as advertised. A decent 3yo fillies' handicap where the winner led throughout and the order didn't change much.

3650 RBL SURREY H'CAP — 5f 6y(P)
7:10 (7:10) (Class 5) (0-70,78) 3-Y-O+ **£2,098** (£2,098; £481; £240) **Stalls** High

Form — RPR

5444 **1** **Stormflower**^{8} 3353 3-9-0 **66** DannyBrock$^{(3)}$ 5 — 69
(John Bridger) *chsd ldr: rdn over 1f out: grad clsd fnl f: forced dead-heat last stride* **3/1**^{2}

3242 **1** dht **Red Flute**^{9} 3316 4-8-5 **51** oh2 (v) TimClark$^{(3)}$ 2 — 56
(Denis Quinn) *led: drvn over 1f out: kpt on fnl f: jnd post* **6/1**

00- **3** shd **Flying Bear (IRE)**^{206} 8072 5-10-2 **78** DavidParkes$^{(5)}$ 6 — 83+
(Jeremy Gask) *hld up in last: rdn and prog fnl f: r.o wl nr fin: jst failed* **11/4**^{1}

3455 **4** ¾ **Diamond Charlie (IRE)**^{25} 2768 8-10-2 **73** NickyMackay 3 — 75
(Simon Dow) *slowly away: hld up in 5th: shkn up over 1f out: styd on ins fnl f: nrst fin but unable to chal* **7/2**^{3}

0-55 **5** shd **Fabulous Flyer**^{11} 3260 3-7-11 **51** oh2 NoelGarbutt$^{(5)}$ 4 — 51
(Jeremy Gask) *dwlt but sn chsd ldng pair: rdn to cl fnl f: kpt on but lost pls nr fin* **16/1**

3354 **6** 3 ¼ **Fine 'n Dandy (IRE)**^{7} 3407 5-9-11 **68** AdamKirby 7 — 58
(J R Jenkins) *chsd ldng trio: shkn up over 1f out: wknd ins fnl f* **4/1**

58.54s (-0.26) **Going Correction** -0.05s/f (Stan)
WFA 3 from 4yo+ 6lb **6** Ran SP% **114.1**
Speed ratings (Par 103): **100,100,99,98,98 93**
WIN: Stormflower £2.10, Red Flute £3.20; PL: Stormflower £2.10, Red Flute 2.10. Exacta: SF&RF £11.30, RF&SF £13.10; CSF: SF&RF £10.62, RF&SF £12.37; TF: SF&RF&FB £37.40; RF&SF&FB £54.30.
Owner Mr & Mrs K Finch **Bred** R B R Burtt & D R Botterill **Trained** Liphook, Hants
Owner Tariq Al Nisf **Bred** D R Tucker **Trained** Newmarket, Suffolk

FOCUS
Race distance as advertised. A tight sprint handicap with a thrilling finish, but the form may not be reliable.

3651 PLAY CASINO AT 188BET (S) STKS — 1m 4f (P)
7:40 (7:40) (Class 6) 3-Y-O+ **£2,587** (£770; £384; £192) **Stalls** Low

Form — RPR

-200 **1** **Nutbourne Lad (IRE)**^{38} 2366 3-8-8 62 (b) OisinMurphy 1 — 62
(Amanda Perrett) *led 1f: trckd ldr: shkn up 2f out: rdn to ld 1f out: styd on* **5/1**^{3}

356- **2** 1 ¾ **Cry Fury**^{8} 4545 8-9-8 67 SaleemGolam 5 — 59
(Sophie Leech) *hld up in 4th: shkn up to chse ldng pair over 2f out: kpt on fr over 1f out to take 2nd last strides* **8/1**

-203 **3** ½ **What A Dandy (IRE)**^{18} 2996 5-9-8 67 (p) PatCosgrave 6 — 58
(Jim Boyle) *t.k.h: led after 1f: shkn up 3f out: drvn and tried to go for home on inner 2f out: hdd 1f out: one pce and lost 2nd last strides* **11/10**^{1}

3360 **4** 5 **Singular Quest**^{5} 3470 4-9-8 67 (b^{1}) MartinHarley 3 — 50
(Kevin Frost) *hld up in 5th: outpcd and shkn up over 2f out: plugged on to take 4th fnl f* **4/1**^{2}

0042 **5** 1 **Lady Fontenail**^{8} 2825 3-7-12 46 (p) PatrickO'Donnell$^{(5)}$ 2 — 44
(Neil King) *chsd ldng pair to over 2f out: steadily wknd* **8/1**

6 11 **Athou Du Nord (FR)**^{10} 6-9-5 0 (tp) TomMarquand$^{(3)}$ 4 — 31
(Ali Stronge) *a last: rdn and wknd 3f out: sn bhd* **20/1**

2m 32.4s (-0.60) **Going Correction** -0.05s/f (Stan)
WFA 3 from 4yo+ 14lb **6** Ran SP% **111.3**
Speed ratings (Par 101): **100,98,98,95,94 87**
CSF £41.04 TOTE £5.80: £2.90, £3.20; EX 34.40 Trifecta £111.30.There was no bid for the winner.
Owner Nutbourne Lad Partnership **Bred** Storeway Ltd **Trained** Pulborough, W Sussex

FOCUS
Race distance as advertised. A weak seller with little between the principals on the figures.

3652 188BET H'CAP — 1m 4f (P)
8:10 (8:10) (Class 5) (0-70,67) 3-Y-O **£3,234** (£962; £481; £240) **Stalls** Low

Form — RPR

000 **1** **Diamond Geyser (IRE)**^{33} 2541 3-9-5 **65** MartinLane 2 — 76+
(Luca Cumani) *hld up in rr: prog on wd outside over 2f out: drvn to cl and lft in 2nd 1f out: led jst ins fnl f: hrd pressed last 100yds: hld on wl* **4/1**^{2}

000 **2** nk **Zain Arion (IRE)**^{22} 2861 3-8-11 **57** StevieDonohoe 3 — 66+
(Charlie Fellowes) *hld up in rr: waiting for room over 2f out: prog on inner over 1f out: tk 2nd and str chal last 100yds: styd on but jst hld* **20/1**

3152 **3** 2 **Schoolboy Error (IRE)**^{16} 3053 3-9-2 **62** TimmyMurphy 4 — 68
(Jamie Osborne) *led 1f: trckd ldrs after: clsd on inner over 1f out: chal jst ins fnl f: nt qckn last 100yds* **8/1**

6-52 **4** ½ **All The Rage**^{9} 3318 3-9-2 **65** RosieJessop$^{(3)}$ 8 — 70
(Sir Mark Prescott Bt) *t.k.h: trckd ldr after 2f: led over 2f out gng strly: rdn over 1f out: hdd and fdd jst ins fnl f* **8/1**

10 **5** 3 ½ **Pivotal Flame (IRE)**^{85} 1185 3-9-7 **67** MartinHarley 7 — 67
(James Tate) *t.k.h: trckd ldrs: rdn over 2f out: wknd over 1f out* **10/1**

0-23 **6** hd **Gimlet**^{39} 2348 3-9-4 **67** (p) MarcMonaghan$^{(3)}$ 6 — 66
(Hugo Palmer) *in tch: rdn and struggling 4f out: nvr on terms after: plugged on* **9/1**

6-44 **7** 1 **Scarlet Pimpernel**^{28} 2700 3-9-5 **65** JimmyFortune 11 — 63
(Hughie Morrison) *hld up in last pair: rdn 3f out: no ch whn hmpd 1f out: plugged on* **17/2**

006 **8** 7 **Catskill Mountains (IRE)**^{23} 2835 3-9-5 **65** JackMitchell 5 — 51
(Roger Varian) *hld up in last pair: rdn and struggling over 3f out: sn no ch* **10/1**

33-2 **9** 2 ¾ **Signed And Sealed**^{13} 3189 3-9-7 **67** AdamKirby 9 — 49
(Mark Johnston) *led after 1f: rdn and hdd over 2f out: wknd qckly* **6/1**^{3}

00-4 **10** 50 **Trust The Man (IRE)**^{80} 1265 3-8-13 **59** NickyMackay 10
(Simon Dow) *rdn in midfield on outer 1/2-way: wknd over 4f out: sn t.o* **50/1**

5-04 **P** **Pourquoi Non (IRE)**^{21} 2900 3-9-5 **65** OisinMurphy 1
(Denis Coakley) *trckd ldrs: plld out and prog fr 2f out: clsng to chal whn broke down bdly 1f out and p.u* **7/2**^{1}

2m 30.29s (-2.71) **Going Correction** -0.05s/f (Stan) **11** Ran SP% **124.2**
Speed ratings (Par 99): **107,106,105,105,102 102,102,97,95,62**
CSF £85.83 CT £632.90 TOTE £5.40: £2.10, £6.20, £1.80; EX 119.80 Trifecta £1229.50.
Owner Leonidas Marinopoulos **Bred** Mount Coote Stud, Richard Pegum & M Bell Racing **Trained** Newmarket, Suffolk

FOCUS
Race distance as advertised. A competitive 3yo handicap which was fought out between two handicap debutants. The winner can be rated a bit better than the bare form after a wide trip.

3653 EURO 2016 BETTING AT 188BET MAIDEN AUCTION STKS — 1m 2f (P)
8:40 (8:40) (Class 6) 3-Y-O **£2,587** (£770; £384; £192) **Stalls** Low

Form — RPR

5 **1** **Petite Jack**^{23} 2826 3-8-12 0 JackMitchell 2 — 70
(Neil King) *hld up in 7th: gd prog on outer over 1f out: r.o wl fnl f to ld last strides* **33/1**

-224 **2** ½ **The Major**^{39} 2341 3-8-9 74 LouisSteward$^{(3)}$ 5 — 69
(Michael Bell) *sn chsd ldr: rdn over 2f out: clsd to chal ins fnl f: upsides nr fin: jst outpcd* **5/2**^{1}

042 **3** ½ **Pastoral Music**^{6} 3434 3-8-12 0 JimmyFortune 10 — 68
(Hughie Morrison) *led: rdn over 2f out: kpt on wl fnl f but hdd last strides* **7/2**^{2}

0- **4** nk **Reconcilliation**^{192} 8246 3-8-12 0 OisinMurphy 8 — 69
(Ed Vaughan) *stdd s: t.k.h: hld up in last pair: prog and squeezed through gap 1f out: clsng but hld whn rn out of room last 50yds* **28/1**

36 **5** ½ **Hellavashock**^{8} 3359 3-8-12 0 AdamBeschizza 3 — 67
(Giles Bravery) *chsd ldng pair: rdn over 2f out: no imp but hld on to 3rd tl one pce last 100yds* **4/1**^{3}

0-55 **6** 2 ¾ **Silhouette (IRE)**^{26} 2749 3-9-2 69 TimmyMurphy 4 — 66
(Daniel Kubler) *trckd ldrs in 5th: lost pl and pushed along on inner over 2f out: nt clr run briefly over 1f out: shkn up and one pce after* **13/2**

4500 **7** 2 ¾ **The Juggler**^{23} 2828 3-9-0 57 (v^{1}) MartinHarley 7 — 58
(William Knight) *in tch in 6th: rdn and prog on outer over 2f out: no hdwy over 1f out: sn fdd* **14/1**

00 **8** 3 ¾ **Roman Urn**^{66} 1577 3-8-9 0 DavidParkes$^{(5)}$ 9 — 51
(Brett Johnson) *stdd s: t.k.h: hld up in last pair: rdn over 2f out: sn wknd* **100/1**

2220 **9** 7 **Rain In The Face**^{29} 2640 3-9-2 74 AdamKirby 6 — 40
(Ralph Beckett) *chsd ldng trio to over 2f out: sn btn: no ch whn hmpd 1f out and eased* **7/2**^{2}

2m 6.83s (0.23) **Going Correction** -0.05s/f (Stan) **9** Ran SP% **120.4**
Speed ratings (Par 97): **97,96,96,95,95 93,91,88,82**
CSF £118.76 TOTE £30.50: £5.10, £1.40, £1.60; EX 172.90 Trifecta £1716.60.
Owner W Burn **Bred** Mrs Liz Nelson Mbe **Trained** Barbury Castle, Wiltshire

FOCUS
Race distance as advertised. A low-level maiden auction that provided a thrilling finale, but an ordinary feel to the form.
T/Plt: £127.10 to a £1 stake. Pool: £51,514.82 - 295.72 winning tickets T/Qpdt: £97.80 to a £1 stake. Pool: £3,976.50 - 30.06 winning tickets **Jonathan Neesom**

3605 NEWCASTLE (A.W) (L-H)
Saturday, June 25

OFFICIAL GOING: Tapeta: standard
Wind: Almost nil Weather: Overcast, showers

3654 BETFRED "BET ON THE EUROS" EBF NOVICE STKS (PLUS 10 RACE) — 5f (Tp)
1:55 (1:56) (Class 3) 2-Y-O **£6,301** (£1,886; £943; £472; £235) **Stalls** High

Form — RPR

2212 **1** **Poet's Society**^{21} 2908 2-9-8 0 JamesDoyle 5 — 85
(Mark Johnston) *trckd ldr: led and edgd lft over 1f out: drvn and kpt on wl fnl f* **8/13**^{1}

50 **2** ½ **Lady Cristal (IRE)**^{25} 2771 2-8-11 0 DougieCostello 10 — 72
(K R Burke) *trckd ldrs: effrt and chsd wnr over 1f out: edgd lft: kpt on ins fnl f* **20/1**

423 **3** 1 **Pulsating (IRE)**^{10} 3282 2-8-11 0 JoeyHaynes 2 — 69
(Rebecca Menzies) *in tch: effrt and rdn 2f out: kpt on fnl f: hld towards fin* **9/1**

30 **4** 3 **Champion Harbour (IRE)**^{56} 1850 2-9-2 0 TonyHamilton 6 — 63
(Richard Fahey) *in tch: effrt and rdn 2f out: styng on steadily whn hmpd 1f out: sn no imp* **8/1**^{3}

20 **5** hd **Affordability**^{23} 2822 2-9-2 0 LukeMorris 4 — 62
(Daniel Mark Loughnane) *prom: rdn along 2f out: outpcd fnl f* **16/1**

6 **6** 3 ¼ **Trick Of The Lyte (IRE)**^{22} 2852 2-9-2 0 PhillipMakin 1 — 51
(John Quinn) *taken early to post: hld up bhd ldng gp: pushed along 1/2-way: stdy hdwy over 1f out: kpt on fnl f: nvr nr ldrs* **66/1**

4 **7** 2 ½ **Seebring (IRE)**^{32} 2552 2-9-2 0 BenCurtis 8 — 42
(Brian Ellison) *sn in tch: rdn along over 2f out: wknd over 1f out* **11/1**

8 4 **Shakabula (IRE)** 2-9-2 0 DaleSwift 9 — 27
(Brian Ellison) *dwlt: sn wl bhd: nvr on terms* **40/1**

3 **9** hd **My Cherry Blossom**^{10} 3290 2-8-11 0 DavidAllan 11 — 21
(Tim Easterby) *t.k.h: led to over 1f out: sn rdn and wknd* **7/1**^{2}

10 15 **Joysunny** 2-8-11 0 JamesSullivan 3
(Michael Easterby) *s.i.s: sn wl bhd: lost tch fr 1/2-way: t.o* **50/1**
59.54s (0.04) **Going Correction** -0.025s/f (Stan) **10** Ran SP% **120.4**
Speed ratings (Par 97): **98,97,95,90,90 85,81,74,74,50**
CSF £21.11 TOTE £1.50: £1.02, £5.90, £2.60; EX 17.10 Trifecta £87.40.

Owner Sheikh Hamdan bin Mohammed Al Maktoum **Bred** Darley **Trained** Middleham Moor, N Yorks

■ Stewards' Enquiry : Dougie Costello caution; careless riding

FOCUS
There will be no speed figures at this track until there is sufficient data to calculate median times. The winner set a useful standard in this fair novice stakes.

3655 BETFRED CHIPCHASE STKS (GROUP 3) 6f (Tp)
2:30 (2:30) (Class 1) 3-Y-O+

£34,026 (£12,900; £6,456; £3,216; £1,614; £810) **Stalls** High

Form				RPR
5-53	1		**Markaz (IRE)**[49] 2030 4-9-3 110 PaulMulrennan 1 (Owen Burrows) *trckd ldrs on far side of gp: led appr fnl f: drvn out* **9/2**[2]	116
110-	2	1	**Pretend (IRE)**[390] 2783 5-9-3 112 JamesMcDonald 2 (Charlie Appleby) *t.k.h: prom: effrt and rdn over 1f out: edgd lft and chsd wnr wl ins fnl f: r.o* **9/2**[2]	113
-323	3	1 1/4	**Watchable**[13] 3195 6-9-3 110 (v) GrahamGibbons 8 (David O'Meara) *led: rdn and hdd appr fnl f: hung lft and no ex ins fnl f* **9/1**	109
1000	4	1 3/4	**Chookie Royale**[92] 1066 8-9-3 107 (p) PhillipMakin 3 (Keith Dalgleish) *w ldr: rdn over 2f out: outpcd ins fnl f* **25/1**	103
-331	5	1/2	**Mr Lupton (IRE)**[14] 3165 3-8-10 111 JamieSpencer 10 (Richard Fahey) *hld up on nr side of gp: rdn and outpcd over 2f out: r.o ins fnl f: nt gng pce to chal* **11/2**[3]	100+
2030	6	1	**Naadirr (IRE)**[13] 3195 5-9-3 108 (p) AndreaAtzeni 6 (Marco Botti) *s.i.s: hld up: rdn and effrt on far side of gp 2f out: no imp fnl f* **12/1**	98
2-04	7	1/2	**Buratino (IRE)**[28] 2692 3-8-10 116 JamesDoyle 7 (Mark Johnston) *prom: drvn along over 2f out: edgd lft and no ex over 1f out* **11/4**[1]	95
1600	8	1	**Rivellino**[49] 2027 6-9-3 102 DougieCostello 5 (K R Burke) *prom: rdn over 2f out: wknd wl over 1f out* **16/1**	94
4-20	9	2	**George Dryden (IRE)**[45] 2158 4-9-3 103 ConnorBeasley 11 (Ann Duffield) *hld up on nr side of gp: rdn and hung lft 1/2-way: sn struggling* **20/1**	87
30-0	10	1 1/4	**Polybius**[13] 3195 5-9-3 107 TedDurcan 9 (David Lanigan) *hld up: rdn along over 2f out: sn no imp: btn fnl f* **10/1**	83

1m 10.38s (-2.12) **Going Correction** -0.025s/f (Stan)
WFA 3 from 4yo+ 7lb **10** Ran SP% **119.7**
Speed ratings (Par 113): **113,111,110,107,107 105,105,103,101,99**
CSF £25.87 TOTE £5.30: £1.90, £1.80, £3.30; EX 32.80 Trifecta £249.10.

Owner Hamdan Al Maktoum **Bred** Yeomanstown Stud & Doc Bloodstock **Trained** Lambourn, Berks

FOCUS
A decent Group 3. The main action took place on the far side of the track with those drawn low dominating. A personal best from the winner.

3656 BETFRED TV H'CAP 6f (Tp)
3:05 (3:07) (Class 2) (0-100,99) 3-Y-O+

£12,450 (£3,728; £1,864; £932; £466; £234) **Stalls** High

Form				RPR
00-0	1		**Amazour (IRE)**[74] 1394 4-9-2 92 JamesDoyle 3 (Ismail Mohammed) *in tch on far side of gp: effrt and drvn along 2f out: led ins fnl f: hld on wl* **6/1**[2]	102
-000	2	nk	**Moonraker**[13] 3195 4-9-8 98 GeorgeBaker 2 (Mick Channon) *hld up on far side: hdwy and swtchd to nr side of gp over 1f out: kpt on take 2nd towards fin: jst hld* **14/1**	107
10-2	3	1 1/2	**Sir Robert Cheval**[35] 2480 5-9-8 98 JamieSpencer 10 (Robert Cowell) *cl up on far side of gp: rdn and effrt over 1f out: ev ch briefly ins fnl f: kpt on tl no ex and lost 2nd nr fin* **11/2**[1]	102
3414	4	3/4	**Magnus Maximus**[10] 3279 5-9-3 93 JimCrowley 12 (Robyn Brisland) *in tch on nr side of gp: rdn over 2f out: hdwy to chse ldrs over 1f out: edgd lft and no ex ins fnl f* **12/1**	95
4402	5	hd	**Boomerang Bob (IRE)**[10] 3279 7-9-4 94 WilliamCarson 7 (Jamie Osborne) *prom centre: drvn along 1/2-way: kpt on u.p ins fnl f* **12/1**	95
-110	6	nk	**See The Sun**[14] 3151 5-9-3 93 DavidAllan 4 (Tim Easterby) *cl up on far side of gp: led over 1f out to ins fnl f: sn no ex* **14/1**	93
00-6	7	3/4	**Ruwaiyan (USA)**[36] 2434 7-9-9 99 (p) LukeMorris 6 (James Tate) *sn pushed along in rr in centre: rdn and hdwy whn swtchd lft over 1f out: sn no imp* **9/1**	97
6-06	8	1/2	**George Bowen (IRE)**[21] 2898 4-9-7 97 TonyHamilton 5 (Richard Fahey) *prom centre: rdn over 2f out: outpcd fr over 1f out* **11/2**[1]	93
-001	9	3 3/4	**Blaine**[21] 2898 6-9-8 98 (b) BarryMcHugh 9 (David Nicholls) *in tch centre: drvn along whn nt clr run over 1f out: sn btn* **7/1**[3]	82
-1U2	10	3/4	**Mythmaker**[45] 2158 4-9-7 97 PaulMulrennan 13 (Bryan Smart) *prom in centre: pushed along over 2f out: wknd fnl f* **10/1**	79
-104	11	2	**Exchequer (IRE)**[21] 2910 5-9-5 95 ShaneGray 8 (David Brown) *taken early to post: cl up centre tl rdn and wknd over 1f out* **12/1**	70
1000	12	1	**Arctic Feeling (IRE)**[21] 2898 8-8-11 94 AdamMcNamara[(7)] 11 (Richard Fahey) *bhd and outpcd centre: struggling 1/2-way: edgd lft and sn btn* **40/1**	66
1/1-	13	2 3/4	**Captain Colby (USA)**[406] 2285 4-9-5 95 (b) TomEaves 14 (Ed Walker) *led on nr side of gp: edgd into centre 1/2-way: hdd & wknd over 1f out* **16/1**	58

1m 11.08s (-1.42) **Going Correction** -0.025s/f (Stan) **13** Ran SP% **121.4**
Speed ratings (Par 109): **108,107,105,104,104 103,102,102,97,96 93,92,88**
CSF £88.88 CT £512.73 TOTE £7.10: £2.40, £4.50, £2.30; EX 118.00 Trifecta £1564.40.

Owner Sheikh Juma Dalmook Al Maktoum **Bred** J F Tuthill **Trained** Newmarket, Suffolk

■ Merdon Castle was withdrawn. Price at time of withdrawal 40-1. Rule 4 does not apply.

FOCUS
A good handicap, although it was short on progressive types. As in the preceding Group 3 over C&D, the far side of the track was the place to be. The winner enjoyed a good trip and recorded a personal best.

3657 BETFRED NORTHUMBERLAND VASE H'CAP (CONSOLATION RACE FOR THE JOHN SMITH'S NORTHUMBERLAND PLATE) 2m 56y (Tp)
3:40 (3:40) (Class 2) 3-Y-O+

£46,687 (£13,980; £6,990; £3,495; £1,747; £877) **Stalls** Low

Form				RPR
20-1	1		**Dannyday**[58] 1802 4-9-8 91 TedDurcan 16 (Sir Michael Stoute) *hld up towards rr: stdy hdwy 3f out: effrt whn nt clr run over 1f out: plld out and styd on wl fnl f to ld nr fin* **7/2**[1]	101+
2145	2	nk	**Haines**[35] 2472 5-9-2 88 RobHornby[(3)] 20 (Andrew Balding) *hld up towards rr: stdy hdwy 3f out: rdn over 1f out: led briefly wl ins fnl f: jst hld* **25/1**	96
12/2	3	3/4	**Poyle Thomas**[42] 2249 7-9-7 90 AndreaAtzeni 9 (Ralph Beckett) *prom: smooth hdwy to ld 2f out: sn rdn: hdd and no ex wl ins fnl f* **9/1**	98
-113	4	1 1/4	**Sir Chauvelin**[28] 2685 4-9-7 90 PaulMulrennan 6 (Jim Goldie) *in tch on ins: hdwy and ev ch fr 2f out to ins fnl f: kpt on same pce* **14/1**	96
-101	5	1 1/4	**Stonecutter (IRE)**[25] 2782 5-9-5 88 PhillipMakin 14 (James Unett) *hld up in tch: rdn over 2f out: edgd lft and kpt on fr over 1f out: nrst fin* **20/1**	93
2200	6	3/4	**Royal Marskell**[44] 2194 7-9-8 91 DougieCostello 3 (Gay Kelleway) *hld up on outside: hdwy to chse ldrs 2f out: rdn and no ex ins fnl f* **33/1**	95
35/4	7	nk	**Cardinal Walter (IRE)**[44] 2194 7-9-8 91 JamesMcDonald 19 (Nicky Henderson) *hld up: hdwy on outside over 2f out: rdn over 1f out: kpt on same pce ins fnl f* **11/1**	94
16-2	8	nk	**The Cashel Man (IRE)**[44] 2194 4-9-6 89 (p) JamieSpencer 7 (David Simcock) *s.i.s: hld up: pushed along 3f out: hdwy over 1f out: kpt on fnl f: nvr able to chal* **11/2**[2]	92+
030	9	2 3/4	**Wordiness**[20] 2932 8-9-3 86 JamesDoyle 12 (David Evans) *midfield: effrt whn nt clr run briefly over 2f out: rdn and edgd lft over 1f out: sn no imp* **28/1**	86
0-00	10	3/4	**Aramist (IRE)**[55] 1880 6-9-2 85 JoeFanning 17 (Alan Swinbank) *hld up on outside: rdn whn nt clr run briefly wl over 2f out: plugged on fr over 1f out: nvr able to chal* **50/1**	84
-350	11	1/2	**Gabrial's King (IRE)**[35] 2472 7-9-2 92 AdamMcNamara[(7)] 11 (Richard Fahey) *hld up: rdn and effrt wl over 2f out: kpt on fnl f: nt pce to chal* **16/1**	90
121-	12	1 1/2	**Sea Of Heaven (IRE)**[287] 6310 4-9-3 86 LukeMorris 15 (Sir Mark Prescott Bt) *t.k.h: led: rdn and hdd 2f out: wknd appr fnl f* **13/2**[3]	82
1541	13	1	**Albahar (FR)**[37] 2392 5-9-9 92 (p) JimCrowley 18 (Chris Gordon) *dwlt: hld up: effrt on outside over 2f out: edgd lft and wknd over 1f out* **16/1**	87
-050	14	1	**Grumeti**[7] 3387 8-9-5 88 WilliamTwiston-Davies 1 (Alan King) *midfield: rdn along over 2f out: wknd over 1f out* **20/1**	82
-000	15	1 1/2	**Min Alemarat (IRE)**[15] 3117 5-9-5 88 (b[1]) DavidAllan 13 (Tim Easterby) *chsd ldng pair: drvn along 3f out: wknd over 1f out* **40/1**	80
-330	16	3 1/2	**Eton Rambler (USA)**[35] 2468 6-9-5 88 GrahamGibbons 2 (George Baker) *midfield: rdn whn nt clr run briefly 2f out: wknd over 1f out* **33/1**	76
-656	17	1	**Swaheen**[15] 3117 4-9-5 88 ConnorBeasley 10 (Julie Camacho) *chsd ldr to over 2f out: rdn and sn wknd* **50/1**	75
100-	18	hd	**Apterix (FR)**[49] 4844 6-9-5 88 BenCurtis 4 (Brian Ellison) *prom: drvn along 3f out: wknd fr 2f out* **16/1**	74
410-	19	2 1/2	**Cousin Khee**[26] 7757 9-9-6 89 GeorgeBaker 5 (Hughie Morrison) *hld up: rdn over 3f out: sn struggling* **33/1**	72
-054	20	1 3/4	**Gabrial's Star**[8] 3345 7-9-6 89 (b) TonyHamilton 8 (Richard Fahey) *hld up: rdn and outpcd over 3f out: sn wknd* **25/1**	70

3m 29.87s (-5.33) **Going Correction** 0.0s/f (Stan) course record **20** Ran SP% **129.4**
Speed ratings (Par 109): **113,112,112,111,111 110,110,110,109,108 108,107,107,106,106 104,103,103,102,101**
CSF £103.40 CT £765.80 TOTE £3.90: £1.40, £5.90, £2.80, £3.70; EX 110.10 Trifecta £1448.90.

Owner Sir Evelyn De Rothschild **Bred** Southcourt Stud **Trained** Newmarket, Suffolk
■ Stewards' Enquiry : Andrea Atzeni two-day ban; used whip in the incorrect place (11th-12th July)

FOCUS
The first running of this consolation race, and a valuable prize in its own right. It was also only the second race to be run over C&D on the Tapeta. They went an even gallop and the first two both overcame wide draws. The time was about a second quicker than that of the main event and there is more to come from the winner.

3658 JOHN SMITH'S NORTHUMBERLAND PLATE (HERITAGE H'CAP) 2m 56y (Tp)
4:15 (4:17) (Class 2) 3-Y-O+

£92,385 (£27,810; £13,905; £6,930; £3,480; £1,755) **Stalls** Low

Form				RPR
50-4	1		**Antiquarium (IRE)**[35] 2482 4-9-5 99 JamesMcDonald 3 (Charlie Appleby) *hld up in midfield: pushed along and plenty to do whn n.m.r briefly 2f out: hdwy over 1f out: qcknd to ld wl ins fnl f: styd on* **16/1**	109+
60-6	2	1 1/4	**Seamour (IRE)**[35] 2486 5-9-5 99 BenCurtis 12 (Brian Ellison) *hld up in midfield on outside: stdy hdwy over 3f out: rdn to ld over 1f out: hung lft and sn qcknd 3 l clr: hdd and no ex wl ins fnl f* **13/2**[1]	107
1-52	3	2 1/4	**Nearly Caught (IRE)**[52] 1963 6-9-8 102 GeorgeBaker 20 (Hughie Morrison) *cl up: led after 6f: rdn: blkd and hdd over 1f out: chsd wnr to ins fnl f: no ex* **16/1**	107
0-24	4	nk	**Moscato**[11] 3246 5-9-0 94 (b[1]) LukeMorris 18 (Sir Mark Prescott Bt) *prom: effrt on outside over 2f out: cl up up whn hung lft and blkd over 1f out: continued to hang lft: one pce ins fnl f* **14/1**	99
0-01	5	nk	**Saigon City**[44] 2194 6-8-12 92 TomEaves 17 (Declan Carroll) *hld up: rdn along and plenty to do over 2f out: kpt on wl fnl f: nrst fin* **20/1**	96+
11-4	6	3/4	**Gabrial The Hero (USA)**[52] 1967 7-9-1 95 (p) TonyHamilton 8 (Richard Fahey) *hld up on outside: effrt and rdn over 2f out: kpt on fr over 1f out: nt gng pce to chal* **8/1**[2]	98
0-30	7	hd	**Seismos (IRE)**[59] 1772 8-9-6 103 DanielMuscutt[(3)] 11 (Marco Botti) *hld up on ins: rdn along and plenty to do over 2f out: swtchd rt and kpt on fnl f: nrst fin* **40/1**	106
0-10	8	1 1/4	**Steve Rogers (IRE)**[52] 1967 5-9-0 94 AndreaAtzeni 4 (Roger Varian) *plld hrd: in tch: drvn along and outpcd 3f out: rallied 2f out: edgd lft and outpcd fnl f* **9/1**[3]	96

-254 **9** *nk* **Gavlar**[35] 2468 5-8-8 **93** CallumShepherd[(5)] 13 94+
(William Knight) *hld up: rdn along 3f out: sme hdwy fnl f: nvr rchd ldrs* **16/1**

11-2 **10** *¾* **Nakeeta**[52] 1967 5-9-2 **96** RoystonFfrench 9 96+
(Iain Jardine) *hld up towards rr: stdy hdwy over 2f out: rdn whn hmpd over 1f out: sn n.d* **8/1**[2]

0-21 **11** *½* **My Reward**[35] 2472 4-9-2 **96** DavidAllan 2 96
(Tim Easterby) *in tch on ins: rdn along over 2f out: wknd over 1f out* **12/1**

-110 **12** *1½* **Gang Warfare**[52] 1967 5-9-10 **104** RobertHavlin 19 102
(Simon Crisford) *stdd and swtchd lft s: hld up: rdn along wl over 2f out: nvr rchd ldrs* **14/1**

0-50 **13** *¾* **Tommy Docc (IRE)**[7] 3387 4-8-13 **93** PhillipMakin 6 90
(Keith Dalgleish) *hld up: pushed along over 2f out: no imp fr over 1f out* **25/1**

-030 **14** *2½* **Hardstone (USA)**[21] 2897 5-8-12 **92** PaulMulrennan 14 86
(Michael Dods) *led 6f: cl up: rdn 3f out: wknd over 1f out* **66/1**

0530 **15** *1* **Notarised**[8] 3340 5-9-7 **101** JoeFanning 16 94
(Mark Johnston) *prom: drvn along 3f out: hung lft and wknd over 1f out* **33/1**

-003 **16** *2¼* **Angel Gabrial (IRE)**[35] 2486 7-9-2 **103** AdamMcNamara[(7)] 5 93
(Richard Fahey) *hld up in midfield on outside: stdy hdwy and prom over 6f out: rdn and drifted lft 2f out: wknd appr fnl f* **25/1**

6/10 **17** *2¼* **No Heretic**[11] 3246 8-9-3 **97** JamieSpencer 10 84
(Nicky Henderson) *t.k.h: trckd ldrs: rdn and edgd rt over 2f out: wknd over 1f out* **16/1**

2/11 **18** *½* **Arch Villain (IRE)**[129] 614 7-9-6 **100** (b) JimCrowley 1 87
(Amanda Perrett) *in tch on ins: drvn along over 2f out: wkng whn n.m.r over 1f out* **12/1**

1100 **19** *2½* **Sunblazer (IRE)**[11] 3246 6-9-3 **97** (t) WilliamTwiston-Davies 7 81
(Kim Bailey) *hld up: rdn along 3f out: sn struggling* **40/1**

30-2 **20** *5* **Polarisation**[21] 2897 4-9-3 **97** JamesDoyle 15 75
(Charlie Appleby) *prom: drvn along over 3f out: wknd fr 2f out* **8/1**[2]

3m 30.91s (-4.29) **Going Correction** 0.0s/f (Stan) **20** Ran SP% **130.7**
Speed ratings (Par 109): **110,109,108,108,107 107,107,106,106,106 106,105,104,103,103 102,100,100,99,96**
CSF £113.99 CT £1749.26 TOTE £20.40: £3.60, £2.20, £3.10, £3.80; EX 154.30 Trifecta £2621.50.
Owner Godolphin **Bred** Darley **Trained** Newmarket, Suffolk

FOCUS
The first running of this historic handicap on Tapeta, but a quality renewal with six runners rated 100 or more, and a minimum rating of 92 required to get in. It didn't look to be that strongly run and the time was around a second slower than that of the consolation race, but the winner was strong late on and there is possibly more to come from him as a stayer. There appeared no real advantage draw-wise.

3659 BETFRED MOBILE H'CAP 1m 4f 98y (Tp)
4:50 (4:50) (Class 4) (0-80,79) 4-Y-0+ **£5,175** (£1,540; £769; £384) **Stalls** Low

Form RPR

0403 **1** **Be Perfect (USA)**[8] 3345 7-9-6 **78** (p) JamesSullivan 4 87
(Ruth Carr) *pressed ldr: led gng wl over 2f out: drvn out fnl f* **7/2**[2]

5044 **2** *¾* **Top Of The Glas (IRE)**[3] 3520 5-9-6 **78** BenCurtis 3 85
(Brian Ellison) *in tch on outside: hdwy to chse wnr over 2f out: rdn and kpt on ins fnl f* **5/2**[1]

0-44 **3** *¾* **Osaruveetil (IRE)**[29] 2659 5-9-6 **78** PhillipMakin 12 84
(David O'Meara) *hld up on outside: stdy hdwy over 3f out: rdn 2f out: kpt on ins fnl f* **4/1**[3]

1-00 **4** *2* **Sabre Rock**[45] 2163 6-9-6 **78** (t) GeorgeBaker 2 81
(Julia Feilden) *t.k.h: hld up in tch: stdy hdwy over 2f out: rdn and one pce appr fnl f* **14/1**

2644 **5** *1¾* **Victoria Pollard**[18] 2994 4-9-4 **79** (p) RobHornby[(3)] 5 79
(Andrew Balding) *hld up: stdy hdwy over 2f out: rdn over 1f out: kpt on: nvr able to chal* **6/1**

1-60 **6** *¾* **Wor Lass**[14] 3149 8-8-12 **77** AdamMcNamara[(7)] 6 76
(Susan Corbett) *s.i.s: hld up: rdn along over 3f out: kpt on fr over 1f out: nt pce to chal* **14/1**

16-0 **7** *1* **Symbolic Star (IRE)**[21] 2917 4-8-12 **75** PhilDennis[(5)] 9 72
(Barry Murtagh) *dwlt: hld up: smooth hdwy over 2f out: rdn over 1f out: wknd ins fnl f* **100/1**

10-6 **8** *9* **Card High (IRE)**[80] 1250 6-9-5 **77** (t) ShaneGray 7 60
(Wilf Storey) *hld up: rdn along over 3f out: wknd over 2f out* **33/1**

110/ **9** *2* **Soul Intent (IRE)**[630] 6930 6-9-6 **78** DaleSwift 1 58
(Brian Ellison) *prom: drvn over 3f out: wknd fr 2f out* **12/1**

5035 **10** *5* **Chilworth Bells**[7] 3403 4-9-0 **72** (p) PaulMulrennan 11 44
(Conor Dore) *in tch: hdwy to ld 1/2-way: rdn and hdd over 2f out: wknd over 1f out* **22/1**

000- **11** *21* **Hot Spice**[246] 7425 8-9-7 **79** GrahamGibbons 8 17
(Michael Easterby) *led to 1/2-way: cl up tl rdn and wknd fr 3f out: t.o* **25/1**

1230 **12** *3¼* **Weald Of Kent (USA)**[33] 2549 4-9-5 **77** (v) LukeMorris 13 10
(Michael Appleby) *prom on outside: drvn along over 3f out: wknd over 1f out* **33/1**

2m 39.86s (-1.24) **Going Correction** 0.0s/f (Stan) **12** Ran SP% **121.2**
Speed ratings (Par 105): **104,103,103,101,100 100,99,93,92,88 74,72**
CSF £12.30 CT £37.35 TOTE £4.90: £1.70, £1.40, £1.90; EX 16.60 Trifecta £66.90.
Owner The Beer Stalkers & Ruth Carr **Bred** Joseph Allen **Trained** Huby, N Yorks

FOCUS
A well-run handicap and fair form for the grade.

3660 BETFRED "FOLLOW US ON INSTAGRAM" H'CAP 1m 2f 42y (Tp)
5:25 (5:25) (Class 4) (0-85,86) 4-Y-0+ **£6,469** (£1,925; £962; £481) **Stalls** High

Form RPR

21-6 **1** **Fallen For A Star**[38] 2377 4-9-6 **84** JamieSpencer 1 97+
(Luca Cumani) *stdd s: hld up: smooth hdwy over 2f out: swtchd rt and shkn up to ld ins fnl f: pushed out: comf* **2/1**[1]

0-43 **2** *2* **Rotherwick (IRE)**[23] 2832 4-9-6 **84** (bt[1]) LukeMorris 2 89
(Paul Cole) *chsd ldrs: effrt and ev ch over 1f out to ins fnl f: kpt on: nt gng pce of wnr* **9/2**[3]

P/P- **3** *shd* **Like A Diamond (IRE)**[458] 1028 6-9-2 **80** DaleSwift 4 85
(Brian Ellison) *t.k.h: hld up in tch: stdy hdwy and led over 1f out: hdd ins fnl f: kpt on same pce* **9/1**

-231 **4** *13* **Mountain Rescue (IRE)**[40] 2296 4-9-5 **83** GeorgeBaker 6 62
(Chris Wall) *t.k.h: led: rdn over 2f out: hdd over 1f out: sn wknd* **7/2**[2]

00-0 **5** *nk* **Carthage (IRE)**[45] 2163 5-8-11 **75** PaulMulrennan 8 53
(Brian Ellison) *s.v.s: detached in last pl: sme hdwy 1/2-way: rdn and outpcd fr 3f out* **40/1**

15-0 **6** *½* **Regal Ways (IRE)**[46] 2121 4-8-10 **74** BenCurtis 5 51
(Brian Ellison) *s.i.s: hld up: hdwy on outside over 2f out: edgd lft: wknd wl over 1f out* **50/1**

02 **7** *6* **Star Of Spring (IRE)**[31] 2574 4-8-4 **68** RoystonFfrench 10 33
(Iain Jardine) *cl up: rdn wl over 2f out: sn wknd* **14/1**

1-23 **8** *1¾* **Street Artist (IRE)**[9] 3304 6-9-8 **86** JoeFanning 7 48
(David Nicholls) *w ldr to over 2f out: rdn and wknd wl over 1f out* **9/2**[3]

5-00 **9** *2¾* **El Beau (IRE)**[28] 2688 5-9-4 **82** DougieCostello 3 38
(John Quinn) *prom: drvn and outpcd over 3f out: btn fnl 2f* **22/1**

2m 9.69s (-0.71) **Going Correction** 0.0s/f (Stan) **9** Ran SP% **117.3**
Speed ratings (Par 105): **102,100,100,89,89 89,84,83,80**
CSF £11.30 CT £66.25 TOTE £3.10: £1.40, £1.70, £2.30; EX 14.10 Trifecta £175.20.
Owner Normandie Stud Ltd **Bred** Normandie Stud Ltd **Trained** Newmarket, Suffolk

FOCUS
There was a contested pace and a good gallop on in this modest handicap. The first three finished a long way clear. The winner was on a good mark on his maiden best and is bred to be better.
T/Jkpt: Not won. T/Plt: £125.50 to a £1 stake. Pool: £160,217.40 - 931.63 winning tickets T/Qpdt: £25.90 to a £1 stake. Pool: £13,026.85 - 371.16 winning tickets **Richard Young**

3612 NEWMARKET (R-H)
Saturday, June 25

OFFICIAL GOING: Soft changing to heavy after race 2 (2.45)
Wind: light breeze Weather: overcast and unsettled; 20 degrees; heavy rain by race two and intermittent thundery showers after

3661 MARGARET GIFFEN MEMORIAL NOVICE STKS (PLUS 10 RACE) 7f
2:10 (2:10) (Class 4) 2-Y-0 **£4,528** (£1,347; £673; £336) **Stalls** Low

Form RPR

1 **Taamol (IRE)** 2-9-2 0 PaulHanagan 2 89+
(Sir Michael Stoute) *pressed ldr and racd enthusiastically: drew upsides 3f out: rdn to ld 2f out: rn green but qcknd clr over 1f out: hung bdly lft after: rather impressive* **4/1**[3]

3 **2** *1½* **Devil's Bridge (IRE)**[16] 3054 2-9-2 0 PatDobbs 5 82
(Richard Hannon) *slt ld tl jnd 3f out: rdn and hdd 2f out: easily outpcd by wnr over 1f out* **5/4**[1]

3 *½* **Khalidi** 2-9-2 0 FrankieDettori 1 81
(John Gosden) *settled trcking ldrs: drvn 2f out: styd on nicely ins fnl f: no ch w wnr* **5/2**[2]

4 *6* **Hartswell** 2-9-2 0 WilliamBuick 3 65
(John Gosden) *stdd s: pressed ldrs: rdn 2f out: little rspnse and sn btn* **7/1**

5 **5** *1¼* **Mister Moosah (IRE)**[14] 3167 2-9-2 0 PJMcDonald 6 62
(Micky Hammond) *pressed ldrs: pushed along 1/2-way: btn wl over 1f out* **14/1**

1m 31.33s (5.63) **Going Correction** +1.00s/f (Soft) **5** Ran SP% **112.2**
Speed ratings (Par 95): **107,105,104,97,96**
CSF £9.73 TOTE £5.20: £2.20, £1.20; EX 10.20 Trifecta £31.30.
Owner Hamdan Al Maktoum **Bred** Derek Gibbons, Tomas Kerin & Ann Gibbons **Trained** Newmarket, Suffolk

FOCUS
Far side of course used. Stalls on stands' side except races over 1m2f and 1m4f, when they were in the centre. Genuine soft ground going into this seven-race card and the time of the opening novice stakes reflected that. This seemed a decent contest on paper and it looks like it produced a horse with a big future.

3662 TANGENT OFFICE FURNITURE SUPPORTING THE AHT FRED ARCHER STKS (LISTED RACE) 1m 4f
2:45 (2:46) (Class 1) 4-Y-0+ **£20,982** (£7,955; £3,981; £1,983; £995) **Stalls** Centre

Form RPR

1-25 **1** **Bateel (IRE)**[35] 2465 4-8-9 99 [1] WilliamBuick 6 106+
(David Simcock) *hld up last: effrt over 2f out: pushed ahd over 1f out: readily c clr* **8/11**[1]

150- **2** *2¼* **Kallisha**[237] 7667 5-8-9 94 SeanLevey 2 100
(Brendan Powell) *2nd tl led over 2f out: sn rdn: hdd over 1f out: immediately outpcd by wnr but clr of rest after* **9/1**

0010 **3** *6* **John Reel (FR)**[8] 3340 7-9-0 101 DanielTudhope 1 95
(David Evans) *led at stdy pce: hdd over 2f out: sn rdn: btn over 1f out* **13/2**[3]

003- **4** *1¾* **Havana Beat (IRE)**[274] 6712 6-9-0 105 (t) FrederikTylicki 5 93
(Rod Millman) *pressed ldrs: rdn over 3f out: struggling over 1f out* **8/1**

2515 **5** *1¼* **Sagaciously (IRE)**[24] 2797 4-8-9 95 PaulHanagan 3 86
(Ed Dunlop) *settled trcking ldrs: rdn 2f out: wknd over 1f out* **5/1**[2]

2m 43.18s (10.28) **Going Correction** +1.00s/f (Soft) **5** Ran SP% **109.0**
Speed ratings (Par 111): **105,103,99,98,97**
CSF £7.74 TOTE £1.50: £1.10, £4.30; EX 7.30 Trifecta £42.00.
Owner Al Asayl Bloodstock Ltd **Bred** Sheikh Sultan Bin Khalifa Al Nayhan **Trained** Newmarket, Suffolk

FOCUS
Add 22 yards to race distance. Conditions deteriorated during this race and the field were running into driving rain in the straight. The official going description was changed to heavy afterwards. They appeared to go a very steady pace early, but most of these were floundering in the closing stages and the time was very slow.

3663 CAMBRIDGE MAGAZINE SUPPORTING THE AHT EMPRESS STKS (LISTED RACE) (FILLIES) 6f
3:20 (3:20) (Class 1) 2-Y-0
£14,744 (£5,590; £2,797; £1,393; £699; £351) **Stalls** Low

Form RPR

22 **1** **Nations Alexander (IRE)**[17] 3024 2-9-0 0 PatDobbs 8 88
(Richard Hannon) *trckd ldrs: rdn 2f out: qckndto ld ins fnl f: sn in command* **8/1**

41 **2** *1¼* **Hellofahaste**[18] 2997 2-9-0 0 FrederikTylicki 3 84
(Rod Millman) *t.k.h: prom: rdn 2f out: led narrowly over 1f out tl hdd and outpcd by wnr ins fnl f: stuck on gamely cl home* **9/1**

1 **3** *½* **Marie Of Lyon**[14] 3167 2-9-0 0 PaulHanagan 1 83
(Richard Fahey) *prom: rdn 2f out: ev ch 1f out: nt qckn fnl 100yds* **9/4**[1]

1 **4** *½* **Shamsaya (IRE)**[24] 2800 2-9-0 0 HarryBentley 5 81
(Simon Crisford) *pressed ldrs: rdn 2f out: chal ldr 1f out: kpt on same pce ins fnl f* **13/2**[3]

315 **5** *2½* **Simmie (IRE)**[10] 3270 2-9-0 0 FrankieDettori 2 74
(Sylvester Kirk) *led: rdn 2f out: hdd over 1f out: sn btn* **13/2**[3]

1 **6** *¾* **Angel Meadow**[15] 3112 2-9-0 0 PJMcDonald 7 72
(Micky Hammond) *plld hrd in rr: rdn and effrt 2f out: btn over 1f out* **14/1**

1 **7** *3* **Somebody To Love (IRE)**[15] 3106 2-9-0 0........................ SeanLevey 6 63+
(Richard Hannon) *slowly away: t.k.h and sn in tch in rr: rdn and struggling 1/2-way* **11/4**[2]

1m 18.39s (5.89) **Going Correction** +1.00s/f (Soft) **7** Ran SP% **111.9**
Speed ratings (Par 98): **100,98,97,97,93 92,88**
CSF £71.34 TOTE £8.70: £3.80, £5.30; EX 88.00 Trifecta £326.10.
Owner Noel O'Callaghan **Bred** Oakhill Stud **Trained** East Everleigh, Wilts

FOCUS
A competitive fillies' Listed contest for juveniles was won by a runner that had already been beaten twice. Also, testing conditions wouldn't have been ideal for most of these, so this might not be the strongest form for the grade.

3664 JOHN SUNLEY MEMORIAL CRITERION STKS (GROUP 3) 7f
3:55 (3:56) (Class 1) 3-Y-O+
£34,026 (£12,900; £6,456; £3,216; £1,614; £810) **Stalls** Low

Form RPR
2-34 **1** **Breton Rock (IRE)**[28] 2691 6-9-3 112.............................. MartinHarley 4 116
(David Simcock) *visibility severely limited by torrential rain: u.p and duelled for ld fnl 2f: hdd narrowly ins fnl f: battled bk to ld nr fin* **11/4**[1]

6-60 **2** *hd* **Adaay (IRE)**[28] 2691 4-9-3 110......................................(p) FrankieDettori 1 115
(William Haggas) *visibility severely limited by torrential rain: duelled w wnr fnl 2f: drvn and led briefly ins fnl f: jst hld cl home* **17/2**

6-30 **3** *2 1/4* **Here Comes When (IRE)**[28] 2691 6-9-3 109...................... PatDobbs 6 110
(Andrew Balding) *visibility severely limited by torrential rain: rdn and chsd ldng pair vainly fnl f* **7/1**

3-13 **4** *6* **So Beloved**[28] 2691 6-9-3 113.. DanielTudhope 3 94
(David O'Meara) *visibility severely limited by torrential rain: ev ch 2f out: wknd and no ch w ldng trio fr over 1f out* **4/1**[3]

25/3 **5** *5* **Muwaary**[14] 3164 5-9-3 112.. PaulHanagan 10 81
(John Gosden) *visibility severely limited by torrential rain: taken down early: chsd ldrs: eased whn btn ins fnl f* **3/1**[2]

0240 **6** *11* **Dark Emerald (IRE)**[114] 810 6-9-3 108......................(vt) HarryBentley 5 52
(Brendan Powell) *visibility severely limited by torrential rain: no ch fnl 2f: t.o and eased over 1f out* **16/1**

33-0 **7** *2 1/4* **Birchwood (IRE)**[41] 2283 3-8-8 114................................ WilliamBuick 9 44
(Richard Fahey) *visibility severely limited by torrential rain: t.o and eased over 1f out* **10/1**

30- **8** *37* **Windfast (IRE)**[266] 6919 5-9-3 109...................................... MartinLane 7
(Brian Meehan) *visibility severely limited by torrential rain: sn floundering: t.o and eased 2f out* **33/1**

1m 29.9s (4.20) **Going Correction** +1.00s/f (Soft)
WFA 3 from 4yo+ 9lb **8** Ran SP% **112.6**
Speed ratings (Par 113): **116,115,113,106,100 88,85,43**
CSF £25.73 TOTE £3.80: £1.30, £2.70, £2.30; EX 25.00 Trifecta £148.00.
Owner John Cook **Bred** George Kent **Trained** Newmarket, Suffolk

FOCUS
Conditions were getting worse with the track under attack from thunder and lightning and, unsurprisingly, they finished well strung out here. The winner has been rated to his best.

3665 LLOYDS COMMERCIAL BANKING SUPPORTING THE AHT FILLIES' H'CAP 1m 4f
4:25 (4:29) (Class 3) (0-95,97) 3-Y-O+ **£9,056** (£2,695; £1,346; £673) **Stalls** Centre

Form RPR
113- **1** **Return Ace**[239] 7596 4-9-6 87.. FrederikTylicki 3 97+
(James Fanshawe) *settled in last pair: effrt 3f out: led gng wl 2f out: shkn up 1f out: rdn to maintain advantage fnl f* **11/4**[2]

3-21 **2** *3/4* **Stockhill Diva**[26] 2753 6-9-9 90.. PatDobbs 1 98
(Brendan Powell) *settled in last pair: effrt 3f out: pressed wnr and ev ch 2f out tl drvn drvn and jst hld fnl 75yds* **7/1**

331- **3** *6* **Bellajeu**[247] 7417 4-8-11 78.. WilliamBuick 7 76
(Ralph Beckett) *led: set stdy pce: rdn and hdd 2f out: fdd 1f out* **9/2**[3]

021 **4** *12* **Talent To Amuse (IRE)**[23] 2826 3-8-2 83......................... HarryBentley 6 62
(Roger Varian) *prom: rdn 3f out: wknd 2f out: t.o and eased* **15/8**[1]

61 **5** *18* **Haddajah (IRE)**[25] 2767 3-8-3 84...................................... JimmyQuinn 5 34
(Sir Michael Stoute) *pressed ldr after 4f: rdn 3f out: sn btn: t.o and eased over 1f out* **9/2**[3]

2m 47.12s (14.22) **Going Correction** +1.00s/f (Soft)
WFA 3 from 4yo+ 14lb **5** Ran SP% **110.3**
Speed ratings (Par 104): **92,91,87,79,67**
CSF £20.44 TOTE £3.30: £1.90, £2.70; EX 11.00 Trifecta £60.70.
Owner Helena Springfield Ltd **Bred** Altitude Bloodstock **Trained** Newmarket, Suffolk

FOCUS
Add 22 yards to race distance. Some progressive fillies on show here, but conditions were tough and the front two came a long way clear.

3666 TREASURE BEACH HOTEL SUPPORTING THE AHT H'CAP 1m 2f
5:00 (5:01) (Class 2) (0-100,100) 3-Y-O+ **£12,938** (£3,850; £1,924; £962) **Stalls** Centre

Form RPR
-505 **1** **Percy Street**[21] 2892 3-8-6 95.................................. JordanVaughan(5) 8 104
(K R Burke) *pressed ldr: pushed ahd over 1f out: styd on gamely fnl f* **11/4**[2]

21/ **2** *1 1/2* **Flight Officer**[619] 7210 5-9-7 93... WilliamBuick 4 99
(Saeed bin Suroor) *t.k.h in rr: effrt 2f out: rdn over 1f out: carried hd high: no imp on wnr fnl f but snatched 2nd* **6/4**[1]

0-04 **3** *nk* **Awake My Soul (IRE)**[45] 2157 7-9-10 96..................... DanielTudhope 9 101
(David O'Meara) *t.k.h early: hld up: rdn over 2f out: no imp tl edgd lft and kpt on wl ins fnl f: snatched 3rd* **5/1**[3]

0-22 **4** *1/2* **Gold Prince (IRE)**[22] 2866 4-9-6 92.............................. FrankieDettori 2 96
(Sylvester Kirk) *led: rdn and hdd over 1f out: kpt on one pce in 2nd after tl lost two pls cl home* **5/1**[3]

-240 **5** *4 1/2* **Chancery (USA)**[43] 2222 8-10-0 100.................................(p) PatDobbs 10 95
(David O'Meara) *last pair: rdn 3f out: sn outpcd* **20/1**

0020 **6** *shd* **Master Of Finance (IRE)**[22] 2866 5-9-11 97.............(b) FrederikTylicki 6 92
(Mark Johnston) *prom: rdn over 2f out: outpcd wl over 1f out* **12/1**

2m 20.8s (15.30) **Going Correction** +1.00s/f (Soft)
WFA 3 from 4yo+ 12lb **6** Ran SP% **112.5**
Speed ratings (Par 109): **78,76,76,76,72 72**
CSF £7.33 CT £17.47 TOTE £3.70: £2.00, £1.40; EX 8.50 Trifecta £32.60.
Owner J Henderson & Mrs E Burke **Bred** Worksop Manor Stud **Trained** Middleham Moor, N Yorks

FOCUS
Add 22 yards to race distance. A much reduced field because of the conditions, but plenty of these had soft-ground form so this was an open heat on paper. They went a sensible pace and the winner was the only 3yo in the field.

3667 BETSI GOLDEN MILE EBF STALLIONS FILLIES' H'CAP 1m
5:35 (5:37) (Class 3) (0-95,96) 3-Y-O+ **£9,056** (£2,695; £1,346; £673) **Stalls** Low

Form RPR
36-0 **1** **Little Lady Katie (IRE)**[80] 1274 4-8-8 80................ JordanVaughan(5) 4 91
(K R Burke) *pressed ldr: led over 2f out: reminders to go clr 1f out: styd on stoutly* **5/1**

1116 **2** *7* **Lucy The Painter (IRE)**[24] 2789 4-9-7 88........................ HarryBentley 3 83
(Ed de Giles) *cl up: rdn 2f out: chsd wnr after: easily outpcd 1f out* **9/2**[3]

4123 **3** *6* **Bocking End (IRE)**[15] 3107 3-8-0 77................................. RaulDaSilva 7 56
(Michael Bell) *plld hrd and chsd ldrs: rdn 2f out: little rspnse: vied for poor 3rd fnl f* **7/1**

-205 **4** *3/4* **Ghinia (IRE)**[6] 3438 5-8-10 84.................................... MeganNicholls(7) 1 63
(Pam Sly) *led: rdn and hdd over 2f out: sn btn: lost duel for poor 3rd fnl 50yds* **7/2**[2]

1-6 **5** *20* **Chastushka (IRE)**[42] 2245 3-9-5 96................................ WilliamBuick 6 27
(John Gosden) *last away: nvr impr: rdn and struggling over 3f out: t.o and eased* **11/8**[1]

1m 46.3s (6.30) **Going Correction** +1.00s/f (Soft)
WFA 3 from 4yo+ 10lb **5** Ran SP% **111.7**
Speed ratings (Par 104): **108,101,95,94,74**
CSF £26.56 TOTE £6.60: £2.50, £2.50; EX 29.30 Trifecta £115.50.
Owner Ontoawinner 5, M Hulin & Mrs E Burke **Bred** Roger K Lee **Trained** Middleham Moor, N Yorks

FOCUS
Not many of these ran their race, so this wouldn't be form to go overboard about, though a personal best from the winner..
T/Plt: £214.30 to a £1 stake. Pool: £79,405.91 - 270.47 winning tickets T/Qpdt: £125.40 to a £1 stake. Pool: £5,714.14 - 33.70 winning tickets **Iain Mackenzie**

3463 WINDSOR (R-H)
Saturday, June 25

OFFICIAL GOING: Soft (heavy in places; 5.6)
Wind: light, behind Weather: bright spells and showers

3668 SKY BET NOVICE STKS 6f
2:05 (2:06) (Class 5) 2-Y-O **£2,911** (£866; £432; £216) **Stalls** Low

Form RPR
3 **1** **On Her Toes (IRE)**[16] 3073 2-8-11 0................................ PatCosgrave 5 80+
(William Haggas) *trckd ldrs: effrt to chal 2f out: rdn to ld over 1f out: styd on wl and drew clr ins fnl f: eased towards fin* **7/4**[1]

63 **2** *2 3/4* **Racemaker**[11] 3254 2-9-2 0... OisinMurphy 7 75
(Mick Channon) *sn w ldr: led 1/2-way: rdn and hdd 2f out: chsd wnr and styd on same pce fr over 1f out* **16/1**

54 **3** *1 1/2* **Latest Quest (IRE)**[36] 2429 2-9-2 0................................... AdamKirby 6 70
(Sylvester Kirk) *in tch: clsd to trck ldrs 1/2-way: effrt and drvn to chse ldrs 2f out: outpcd and btn whn n.m.r 1f out: plugged on same pce after* **9/2**[2]

352 **4** *1 1/4* **Logi (IRE)**[15] 3093 2-9-2 0... JimmyFortune 1 66
(Richard Hannon) *led tl 1/2-way: rdn to ld again 2f out: hdd over 1f out: sn outpcd and hung lft 1f out: wknd ins fnl f* **7/4**[1]

60 **5** *1 1/2* **Moneyoryourlife**[18] 2997 2-8-13 0................................ TomMarquand(3) 3 62
(Richard Hannon) *dwlt: a in rr: rdn over 2f out: no imp and plugged on same pce fr over 1f out* **20/1**

6 *shd* **Father McKenzie** 2-9-2 0... CharlesBishop 2 61
(Mick Channon) *in tch: effrt 2f out: unable qck and btn over 1f out: wknd ins fnl f* **14/1**[3]

1m 15.8s (2.80) **Going Correction** +0.50s/f (Yiel) **6** Ran SP% **108.2**
Speed ratings (Par 93): **101,97,95,93,91 91**
CSF £28.87 TOTE £2.60: £1.80, £5.10; EX 28.30 Trifecta £71.10.
Owner Cheveley Park Stud **Bred** Knocklong House Stud **Trained** Newmarket, Suffolk

FOCUS
After a couple of substantial morning showers, conditions were soft, verging on heavy ahead of this uncompetitive opener, byt the winner was quite impressive..

3669 ANDERSON ROOFING SUPPLIES MAIDEN STKS 5f 10y
2:40 (2:41) (Class 5) 3-Y-O+ **£2,911** (£866; £432; £216) **Stalls** Low

Form RPR
2422 **1** **Dark Shot**[19] 2980 3-9-6 81... OisinMurphy 4 83
(Andrew Balding) *mde all: shkn up 2f out: asserted u.p jst over 1f out: styd on: eased towards fin: comf* **2/9**[1]

2200 **2** *6* **Silver Bid (USA)**[17] 3035 4-9-12 68................................... AdamKirby 1 63
(Alan Bailey) *hld up in tch: clsd to trck ldrs 1/2-way: hdwy and rdn to chse wnr over 1f out: sn no imp: clr 2nd but wl fnl f* **7/1**[3]

0 **3** *6* **German Whip**[7] 3406 3-9-1 0................................... HectorCrouch(5) 3 40
(Gary Moore) *hld up in tch in rr: effrt over 1f out: no ch w wnr but plugged on into modest 3rd ins fnl f* **25/1**

000- **4** *1 1/4* **Golden Rosanna**[197] 8173 3-9-1 40.............................. AdamBeschizza 6 30
(Steph Hollinshead) *chsd ldrs: sn niggled along: drvn 2f out: outpcd and wl hld 3rd jst over 1f out: wknd ins fnl f* **66/1**

3-2 **5** *12* **K'Gari Spirit**[170] 83 3-9-1 0.. NickyMackay 2
(Jeremy Gask) *w wnr tl wl over 1f out: lost 2nd and wkng whn faltered over 1f out: bhd and eased ins fnl f* **6/1**[2]

1m 2.31s (2.01) **Going Correction** +0.50s/f (Yiel)
WFA 3 from 4yo 6lb **5** Ran SP% **114.0**
Speed ratings (Par 103): **103,93,83,81,62**
CSF £2.78 TOTE £1.10: £1.02, £2.20; EX 2.00 Trifecta £11.10.
Owner J C Smith **Bred** Littleton Stud **Trained** Kingsclere, Hants

FOCUS
This proved plain sailing for the long odds-on favourite, who gained a long overdue success.

3670 SKY BET H'CAP 1m 3f 135y
3:15 (3:15) (Class 2) (0-100,96) 4-Y-O+ **£12,938** (£3,850; £1,924; £962) **Stalls** Centre

Form RPR
1-11 **1** **Desert Encounter (IRE)**[42] 2249 4-8-13 91...........[1] TomMarquand(3) 5 100+
(David Simcock) *hld up in last pair: clsd 3f out: chsd ldr over 2f out: rdn to ld over 1f out: doing little in front and edgd lft ins fnl f: a doing enough: rdn out* **11/2**

0533 **2** *3/4* **Passover**[19] 2979 5-9-2 91... OisinMurphy 9 97
(Andrew Balding) *sn led: rdn and kicked on over 2f out: hdd and drvn over 1f out: swtchd rt ins fnl f: styd on same pce fnl 100yds* **9/1**

-406 **3** 1 1/4 **English Summer**[14] 3162 9-9-0 **89**....(t) DavidNolan 2 93
(Richard Fahey) *hld up in last pair: rdn and hdwy 2f out: chsd ldng pair over 1f out: kpt on u.p ins fnl f* **20/1**

2-11 **4** 6 **Baadi**[33] 2549 4-8-13 **88**.... StevieDonohoe 6 82
(Charlie Fellowes) *chsd ldrs: rdn over 2f out: unable qck u.p and btn 4th over 1f out: wknd ins fnl f* **10/3**[1]

61-0 **5** 6 **Karraar**[21] 2897 5-9-0 **89**....(p) PatCosgrave 1 73
(William Haggas) *in tch in midfield: effrt u.p over 2f out: no imp and sn outpcd: wl btn 5th over 1f out: wknd ins fnl f* **7/2**[2]

3550 **6** 5 **Blue Surf**[21] 2897 7-9-7 **96**.... AdamKirby 4 72
(Amanda Perrett) *in tch in midfield: rdn 4f out: lost pl and bhd 2f out: sn wknd* **10/1**

2132 **7** 18 **Rideonastar (IRE)**[14] 3161 5-8-10 **85**.... FergusSweeney 8 31
(Brendan Powell) *mostly chsd ldr tl lost pl u.p over 2f out: wknd wl over 1f out: wl bhd and eased ins fnl f: t.o* **4/1**[3]

110- **8** 110 **Sweet P**[234] 7703 5-8-11 **89**.... LouisSteward[(3)] 3
(Marcus Tregoning) *chsd ldrs tl lost pl qckly over 3f out: wl bhd and virtually p.u fnl 2f: t.o* **8/1**

2m 34.0s (4.50) **Going Correction** +0.55s/f (Yiel) **8** Ran SP% **115.6**
Speed ratings (Par 109): **107,106,105,101,97 94,82,**
CSF £53.86 CT £920.02 TOTE £4.60: £1.80, £2.80, £3.10; EX 58.20 Trifecta £396.40.
Owner Abdulla Al Mansoori **Bred** Tally-Ho Stud **Trained** Newmarket, Suffolk

FOCUS
Add 28yds to race distance. A solid renewal of this handicap, in which the first three pulled well clear.

3671 SKY BET ROYAL WINDSOR SPRINT SERIES H'CAP (QUALIFIER FOR THE WINDSOR SPRINT SERIES FINAL) 6f
3:50 (3:51) (Class 2) (0-105,102) 3-Y-0+

£12,450 (£3,728; £1,864; £932; £466; £234) **Stalls** Low

Form RPR
4441 **1** **Growl**[16] 3068 4-9-5 **93**.... DavidNolan 8 105
(Richard Fahey) *hld up in tch in midfield: hdwy over 1f out: rdn to ld 1f out: edgd lft but r.o wl ins fnl f: rdn out* **15/2**[3]

-001 **2** 2 **Rio Ronaldo (IRE)**[26] 2754 4-8-13 **87**.... RobertWinston 3 92
(Mike Murphy) *stdd s: t.k.h: hld up in rr: clsd and nt clr run over 1f out: sn swtchd rt and hdwy: rdn to chse clr wnr ins fnl f: kpt on but no imp* **11/1**

133 **3** 3/4 **Sir Billy Wright (IRE)**[22] 2862 5-8-10 **87**.... PhilipPrince[(3)] 7 90
(David Evans) *taken down early: in tch in midfield: effrt 2f out: nt clr run and swtchd rt jst over 1f out: styd on u.p ins fnl f: no threat to wnr* **12/1**

0145 **4** shd **Clear Spring (IRE)**[13] 3195 8-10-0 **102**.... ShaneKelly 12 105
(John Spearing) *hld up in tch in midfield: nt clrest of runs over 1f out: squeezed through and hdwy jst ins fnl f: styd on u.p: no threat to wnr* **16/1**

3122 **5** hd **Reflektor (IRE)**[14] 3131 3-8-12 **96**.... TomMarquand[(3)] 1 96
(Tom Dascombe) *chsd ldrs: rdn over 2f out: unable qck and sltly outpcd over 1f out: rallied and kpt on again ins fnl f* **7/1**[2]

-000 **6** shd **Charles Molson**[21] 2898 5-9-5 **93**.... PatCosgrave 11 95
(Patrick Chamings) *hld up in tch towards rr: effrt over 1f out: hdwy u.p 1f out: styd on ins fnl f* **20/1**

0-20 **7** 1/2 **New Bidder**[55] 1887 5-9-2 **90**....(b) TomQueally 2 90
(David Barron) *chsd ldr: rdn and ev ch wl over 1f out: led jst over 1f out: sn hdd: lost 2nd and wknd ins fnl f* **16/1**

30-5 **8** 1 **Kickboxer (IRE)**[43] 2206 5-9-8 **99**....(p) KevinStott[(3)] 10 96
(Saeed bin Suroor) *in tch in midfield: effrt in 4th over 2f out: unable qck u.p over 1f out: wknd ins fnl f* **7/1**[2]

1220 **9** 1/2 **Roudee**[21] 2895 4-9-8 **96**.... LiamJones 6 91
(Tom Dascombe) *chsd ldrs: rdn and unable qck over 2f out: outpcd over 1f out: wknd ins fnl f* **33/1**

260- **10** 1/2 **Suzi's Connoisseur**[259] 7122 5-9-10 **98**....(v) OisinMurphy 4 92
(Stuart Williams) *hld up in tch towards rr: effrt and sme hdwy over 1f out: no imp ins fnl f: nvr trbld ldrs* **25/1**

0355 **11** 1 1/2 **Lincoln (IRE)**[14] 3163 5-8-11 **92**.... KillianHennessy[(7)] 5 81
(Mick Channon) *hld up in tch towards rr: effrt 2f out: no hdwy u.p over 1f out: nvr involved* **7/1**[2]

1423 **12** 1 **Stellarta**[22] 2875 5-8-9 **83**.... SteveDrowne 14 69
(Michael Blanshard) *hld up towards rr: effrt and swtchd rt over 1f out: no hdwy and wl hld fnl f: n.d* **25/1**

640- **13** 2 1/2 **Musical Comedy**[280] 6533 5-9-9 **97**.... JimmyFortune 9 75
(Mike Murphy) *led tl rdn and hdd over 1f out: losing pl whn sltly squeezed for room jst ins fnl f: sn wknd* **33/1**

-251 **14** 3 1/4 **Ice Lord (IRE)**[33] 2547 4-9-3 **91**.... AdamKirby 15 58
(Clive Cox) *in tch in midfield: rdn 2f out: sn drvn and btn: wknd fnl f* **3/1**[1]

1m 14.45s (1.45) **Going Correction** +0.50s/f (Yiel)
WFA 3 from 4yo+ 7lb **14** Ran SP% **120.4**
Speed ratings (Par 109): **110,107,106,106,105 105,105,103,103,102 100,99,95,91**
CSF £81.29 CT £984.64 TOTE £7.60: £2.90, £3.80, £2.90; EX 107.00 Trifecta £3050.10 Part won..
Owner Dr Marwan Koukash **Bred** Kincorth Investments Inc **Trained** Musley Bank, N Yorks

FOCUS
This was hotly contested and rates as solid soft-ground form. They went quick up front and it suited those held up.

3672 SKY BET MIDSUMMER STKS (LISTED RACE) 1m 67y
4:20 (4:22) (Class 1) 3-Y-0+

£20,982 (£7,955; £3,981; £1,983; £995; £499) **Stalls** Low

Form RPR
5465 **1** **Gabrial (IRE)**[14] 3164 7-9-4 108.... DavidNolan 4 112
(Richard Fahey) *hld up in tch in midfield: effrt over 1f out: hdwy u.p to ld jst ins fnl f: edgd lft u.p but r.o wl: rdn out* **9/2**[2]

1560 **2** 1/2 **Captain Cat (IRE)**[10] 3273 7-9-4 105.... KieranShoemark 3 111
(Roger Charlton) *hld up in tch: effrt 2f out: hdwy u.p on far rail over 1f out: chsd ldrs 1f out: short of room and squeezed through to chse wnr ins fnl f: kpt on u.p* **8/1**

1112 **3** 1 1/2 **Clotilde**[28] 2689 4-8-13 90.... PatCosgrave 6 103
(William Knight) *chsd ldrs: clsd to join ldr 3f out: rdn to ld over 2f out: drvn over 1f out: hdd jst ins fnl f: struggling to qckn and looked hld whn squeezed out and lost 2nd ins fnl f: kpt on same pce after* **10/1**

406- **4** nk **Chil The Kite**[238] 7634 7-9-4 110.... RobertWinston 1 107
(Hughie Morrison) *stdd s: hld up in rr: effrt over 1f out: styd on u.p ins fnl f: no threat to wnr* **13/2**[3]

0-05 **5** 2 1/4 **Merry Me (IRE)**[21] 2893 5-8-13 95.... OisinMurphy 8 97
(Andrew Balding) *chsd ldr tl 3f out: sn rdn: unable qck over 1f out: btn whn swtchd lft ins fnl f* **12/1**

2-22 **6** 2 1/4 **Atlantic Sun**[30] 2627 3-8-8 102.... TomQueally 7 95
(Richard Hannon) *sn led: rdn and hdd over 2f out: drvn over 1f out: stl cl up but struggling to qckn whn squeezed for room and swtchd rt jst ins fnl f: sn wknd* **10/3**[1]

0-40 **7** 1 3/4 **Johnny Barnes (IRE)**[42] 2243 4-9-4 107.... JimmyFortune 2 92
(John Gosden) *dwlt: hld up in tch in last trio: effrt 2f out: no hdwy u.p over 1f out: wl hld fnl f* **10/3**[1]

0-00 **8** 6 **Ocean Tempest**[28] 2684 7-9-4 92.... AdamKirby 5 79
(John Ryan) *in tch in midfield: rdn 4f out: lost pl over 2f out: bhd fnl f* **16/1**

1m 46.72s (2.02) **Going Correction** +0.55s/f (Yiel)
WFA 3 from 4yo+ 10lb **8** Ran SP% **111.4**
Speed ratings (Par 111): **111,110,109,108,106 104,102,96**
CSF £37.73 TOTE £5.90: £1.80, £2.90, £2.90; EX 41.70 Trifecta £286.40.
Owner Dr Marwan Koukash **Bred** B Kennedy **Trained** Musley Bank, N Yorks
■ Stewards' Enquiry : David Nolan six-day ban; careless riding (9th, 11th-15th July)

FOCUS
Add 28yds to race distance. The 13th running of this feature Listed contest. It developed into a messy race and the winner had to survive a stewards' enquiry. He has been rated to the best of his form outside of Group 1 company.

3673 PETER MILES MEMORIAL FILLIES' H'CAP 1m 67y
4:55 (4:56) (Class 5) (0-75,74) 3-Y-0+ **£2,911** (£866; £432; £216) **Stalls** Low

Form RPR
3040 **1** **Specialv (IRE)**[12] 3224 3-8-7 **63**....(p) StevieDonohoe 8 73
(Brian Ellison) *hld up in tch in midfield: hdwy to chse ldr and edgd lft over 1f out: led ins fnl f: styd on wl: rdn out* **16/1**

35-3 **2** 1 **Red Tea**[16] 3062 3-8-11 **67**.... AdamBeschizza 1 75
(Peter Hiatt) *chsd ldrs: effrt over 2f out: rdn to ld over 1f out: hdd ins fnl f: clr 2nd and styd on same pce after* **9/4**[1]

6353 **3** 4 **Summer Collection (IRE)**[29] 2644 3-8-11 **70**.... MichaelJMMurphy[(3)] 2 69
(Charles Hills) *hld up in tch in midfield: effrt 2f out: no imp over 1f out: kpt on u.p to pass btn horses ins fnl f: wnt 3rd nr fin* **15/2**

-303 **4** nk **China Girl (IND)**[22] 2872 4-9-7 **67**.... AdamKirby 5 67
(William Knight) *taken down early: hld up in tch in midfield: clsd to chse ldrs and rdn over 2f out: unable qck over 1f out: 3rd and wl hld ins fnl f: wknd wl ins fnl f and lost 3rd last strides* **4/1**[2]

36-6 **5** 2 1/2 **Up To You (USA)**[25] 2767 3-9-2 **72**.... JimmyFortune 3 64
(John Gosden) *led: rdn over 2f out: hdd over 1f out and sn outpcd: wknd ins fnl f* **8/1**

-3 **6** 4 **Lulani (IRE)**[60] 1756 4-10-0 **74**.... TomQueally 7 59
(Harry Dunlop) *chsd ldr: clsd and upsides 1/2-way: rdn over 2f out: struggling and losing pl whn short of room and swtchd rt over 1f out: sn wknd* **11/2**[3]

-335 **7** 4 1/2 **Norse Magic**[36] 2431 3-8-10 **71**.... GaryMahon[(5)] 10 44
(Sylvester Kirk) *in tch in midfield: struggling u.p over 2f out: wknd over 1f out: bhd fnl f* **6/1**

0653 **8** 2 1/2 **Dark Amber**[14] 3121 6-9-1 **66**.... JennyPowell[(5)] 9 35
(Brendan Powell) *dwlt: in tch in last pair: effrt whn sltly hmpd jst over 2f out: sn struggling: bhd fnl f* **16/1**

1m 47.1s (2.40) **Going Correction** +0.55s/f (Yiel)
WFA 3 from 4yo+ 10lb **8** Ran SP% **115.1**
Speed ratings (Par 100): **110,109,105,104,102 98,93,91**
CSF £52.69 CT £306.02 TOTE £17.80: £3.50, £1.30, £2.50; EX 61.30 Trifecta £558.40.
Owner D Gilbert, M Lawrence, A Bruce **Bred** Peter & Hugh McCutcheon **Trained** Norton, N Yorks

FOCUS
Add 28yds to race distance. Winning form was thin on the ground in this fillies' handicap and the form should be treated with caution. The first two finished clear and the winner has been rated back to her Southwell win in January.

3674 JOHN AXTEN 50TH BIRTHDAY APPRENTICE H'CAP 6f
5:30 (5:30) (Class 5) (0-70,69) 4-Y-0+ **£3,067** (£905; £453) **Stalls** Low

Form RPR
1036 **1** **Secret Look**[16] 3069 6-9-7 **64**....(p) KevinStott 11 75
(Ed McMahon) *hld up in tch in midfield: effrt to chse ldr over 1f out: drvn to ld wl ins fnl f: styd on* **9/2**[2]

6606 **2** 1/2 **Potternello (IRE)**[5] 3469 4-8-12 **60**.... KillianHennessy[(5)] 1 69
(Mick Channon) *trckd ldr tl rdn to ld over 1f out: drvn and clr w wnr ins fnl f: hdd and one pce wl ins fnl f* **7/1**

6465 **3** 3 1/4 **Honcho (IRE)**[14] 3153 4-9-5 **69**.... JonathanFisher[(7)] 3 68
(John Ryan) *dwlt: sn rcvrd and in tch in midfield: effrt and edgd lft u.p over 1f out: chsd clr ldng pair jst ins fnl f: no imp* **9/1**

5111 **4** 1 **Gilmer (IRE)**[15] 3098 5-9-6 **66**.... NoelGarbutt[(3)] 6 62
(Laura Young) *taken down early: hld up in rr: hdwy u.p and edging lft over 1f out: wnt 4th ins fnl f: no imp after: nvr trbld ldrs* **7/2**[1]

0206 **5** 1/2 **Tancred (IRE)**[11] 3258 5-9-0 **60**....(b) HectorCrouch[(3)] 4 54
(Conor Dore) *hld up in tch in rr: hdwy u.p and edging lft 1f out: styd on ins fnl f: nvr trbld ldrs* **14/1**

4340 **6** 3/4 **For Ayman**[55] 1899 5-8-10 **60**....(t) SeanMooney[(7)] 7 52
(Joseph Tuite) *in tch in midfield: effrt over 1f out: no imp 1f out: wknd ins fnl f* **12/1**

-000 **7** 2 **Firgrove Bridge (IRE)**[15] 3098 4-9-3 **60**.... MarcMonaghan 5 45
(Steph Hollinshead) *dwlt: hld up in tch in rr: effrt 2f out: sme prog over 1f out: no imp fnl f: nvr trbld ldrs* **28/1**

22 **8** 4 1/2 **Wattaboutsteve**[9] 3320 5-8-2 **50** oh1.... RhiainIngram[(5)] 10 21
(Ralph J Smith) *led tl rdn and hdd over 1f out: sn btn and wknd* **6/1**[3]

0650 **9** nk **Renounce (IRE)**[23] 2821 4-9-6 **63**....(t) KieranShoemark 2 33
(Charlie Wallis) *t.k.h: chsd ldrs: lost pl and rdn 2f out: sn wknd* **10/1**

4601 **10** 2 3/4 **Goadby**[16] 3070 5-9-4 **61**.... MichaelJMMurphy 12 22
(John Holt) *chsd ldrs: rdn and ev ch 2f out: unable qck and lost pl over 1f out: sn wknd* **8/1**

000- **11** 1 3/4 **Angelito**[241] 7555 7-9-12 **69**.... EoinWalsh 9 25
(Tony Newcombe) *in tch in midfield: rdn 2f out: no hdwy and sn struggling: wknd over 1f out* **25/1**

1m 15.16s (2.16) **Going Correction** +0.50s/f (Yiel) **11** Ran SP% **119.0**
Speed ratings (Par 103): **105,104,100,98,98 97,94,88,87,84 81**
CSF £36.65 CT £281.18 TOTE £6.20: £2.50, £2.20, £3.40; EX 33.50 Trifecta £409.30.
Owner S L Edwards **Bred** S L Edwards **Trained** Lichfield, Staffs

FOCUS
A fair race for the grade, in which the favourite was bidding for a four-timer. The winner has been rated to his April C&D win and last year's form.
T/Plt: £310.90 to a £1 stake. Pool of £62,933.01 - 147.73 winning tickets. T/Qpdt: £93.90 to a £1 stake. Pool of £4,923.89 - 38.80 winning tickets. **Steve Payne**

3675 - 3676a (Foreign Racing) - See Raceform Interactive

3626 CURRAGH (R-H)

Saturday, June 25

OFFICIAL GOING: Good to yielding

3677a DUBAI DUTY FREE MILLENIUM MILLIONAIRE CELEBRATION STKS (LISTED RACE) 1m

4:05 (4:06) 3-Y-O+

£21,691 (£6,985; £3,308; £1,470; £735; £367)

RPR

1 **Sruthan (IRE)**[48] 2067 6-9-9 106 (p) ColmO'Donoghue 1 111+
(P D Deegan, Ire) *dwlt sltly: sn chsd ldrs: 5th 1/2-way: n.m.r on inner over 2f out: sn swtchd lft and rdn in 4th over 1f out: r.o wl ins fnl f to ld cl home: won gng away* **10/1**

2 ¾ **Sovereign Debt (IRE)**[14] 3164 7-10-0 0 ChrisHayes 8 115
(David Nicholls) *cl up on outer: 3rd 1/2-way: impr on outer to ld over 2f out where edgd sltly rt: all out wl ins fnl f where strly pressed and hdd cl home* **3/1**[1]

3 nk **Hint Of A Tint (IRE)**[35] 2497 6-9-4 103 WayneLordan 5 104
(David Wachman, Ire) *on toes befhand: chsd ldrs: 4th 1/2-way: rdn into 2nd 1 1/2f out and pressed ldr ins fnl f: no imp on wnr in 3rd clsng stages: kpt on wl* **13/2**[3]

4 3 ¾ **Lily's Rainbow (IRE)**[27] 2716 4-9-7 101 LeighRoche 7 98
(Mrs Denise Foster, Ire) *cl up and sn led: jnd briefly bef 1/2-way: narrow ld at 1/2-way: pushed along into st and hdd u.p over 2f out: no imp on ldrs in 4th fr 1f out: dropped to 5th briefly ins fnl f: kpt on one pce* **20/1**

5 hd **Cougar Mountain (IRE)**[11] 3242 5-10-0 113 (tp) RyanMoore 10 105
(A P O'Brien, Ire) *w.w towards rr: 9th 1/2-way: hdwy 2f out to chse ldrs u.p in 5th 1f out: no ex in 4th briefly ins fnl f: kpt on one pce* **3/1**[1]

6 3 ¾ **Foxtrot Charlie (USA)**[16] 3084 3-9-2 102 PatSmullen 4 92
(D K Weld, Ire) *mid-div: 6th 1/2-way: tk clsr order bhd ldrs u.p fr 2f out: no ex ent fnl f and one pce after* **4/1**[2]

7 ½ **Brendan Brackan (IRE)**[48] 2067 7-9-12 103 ColinKeane 3 93
(G M Lyons, Ire) *broke wl to ld early tl sn hdd: disp briefly bef 1/2-way: cl 2nd at 1/2-way: rdn and wknd 2f out* **12/1**

8 2 **Alphonsus**[48] 2067 3-8-13 100 (p) DeclanMcDonogh 9 84
(John M Oxx, Ire) *w.w towards rr: 8th 1/2-way: tk clsr order 2f out: sn rdn and no imp on ldrs over 1f out: one pce after* **11/1**

9 1 ½ **Current State (IRE)**[16] 3084 4-9-4 84 BillyLee 11 77
(T Stack, Ire) *hld up in rr: last at 1/2-way: rdn under 2f out and no imp* **50/1**

10 ½ **Round Two (IRE)**[6] 3447 3-8-13 98 (t) KevinManning 6 79
(J S Bolger, Ire) *mid-div: 7th 1/2-way: pushed along in 7th 3f out and sn no ex u.p: wknd fnl 2f* **20/1**

1m 40.3s (-5.70) **Going Correction** -0.75s/f (Hard)
WFA 3 from 4yo+ 10lb **10** Ran SP% **119.9**
Speed ratings: **98,97,96,93,93 89,88,86,85,84**
CSF £40.49 TOTE £13.20: £3.70, £1.30, £2.20; DF 44.00 Trifecta £492.30.

Owner Robert Ng **Bred** Messrs J , R & J Hyland **Trained** The Curragh, Co Kildare

FOCUS
A pretty standard renewal and the first three pulled away. The second and third help with the standard.

3678a GAIN RAILWAY STKS (GROUP 2) 6f

4:40 (4:41) 2-Y-O

£49,889 (£16,066; £7,610; £3,382; £1,691; £845)

RPR

1 **Medicine Jack**[28] 2702 2-9-3 0 ColinKeane 3 107
(G M Lyons, Ire) *chsd ldrs: 5th 1/2-way: gng wl 2f out: sn swtchd rt and prog on outer to ld narrowly over 1f out: hdd briefly ins fnl 150yds tl rallied to sn regain advantage: kpt on wl cl home* **6/1**[2]

2 ½ **Peace Envoy (FR)**[9] 3295 2-9-3 0 RyanMoore 8 106
(A P O'Brien, Ire) *chsd ldrs: 4th 1/2-way: impr nr side to chal ent fnl f: rdn to ld briefly ins fnl 150yds where wandered sltly and sn hdd: kpt on wl wout matching wnr cl home* **7/4**[1]

3 1 ½ **Dream Of Dreams (IRE)**[29] 2649 2-9-3 0 PatSmullen 2 101
(Kevin Ryan) *s.i.s and in rr early tl sn chsd ldrs: 3rd 1/2-way: gng wl and almost on terms over 2f out: disp briefly over 1f out and rdn: no ex in 3rd wl ins fnl f: kpt on same pce* **7/4**[1]

4 ¾ **King Electric (IRE)**[14] 3169 2-9-3 0 GaryCarroll 4 99
(G M Lyons, Ire) *led tl hdd bef 1/2-way: 2nd at 1/2-way: sn lost pl and pushed along in 3rd: rdn 2f out and no imp on ldrs in 6th 1f out where swtchd rt: kpt on u.p into 4th ins fnl 75yds* **6/1**[2]

5 1 ¼ **Ready To Roc (IRE)**[35] 2494 2-9-3 0 SeamieHeffernan 7 95
(J P Murtagh, Ire) *reluctant to load: hld up: 6th 1/2-way: hdwy on outer 2f out to chse ldrs in 4th: rdn and no ex ins fnl f: one pce after* **16/1**[3]

6 ½ **Mirdif**[9] 3328 2-9-3 0 KierenFallon 1 94
(M D O'Callaghan, Ire) *cl up bhd ldr tl led bef 1/2-way: pushed along over 2f out: sn jnd and hdd u.p over 1f out: sn wknd* **16/1**[3]

7 ½ **Grand Coalition (IRE)**[11] 3243 2-9-3 0 ConnorKing 5 92
(J P Murtagh, Ire) *hld up: 7th 1/2-way: pushed along over 2f out and no ex u.p ent fnl f: kpt on one pce* **25/1**

8 ¾ **Glenamoy Lad**[2] 3583 2-9-3 0 ShaneFoley 9 90
(K J Condon, Ire) *upset in stalls briefly: sn settled in rr: last at 1/2-way: rdn under 2f out and no ex ent fnl f: kpt on one pce* **33/1**

1m 13.2s (-2.30) **Going Correction** -0.275s/f (Firm) **8** Ran SP% **119.9**
Speed ratings: **104,103,101,100,98 98,97,96**
CSF £17.85 TOTE £6.70: £2.10, £1.02, £1.30; DF 22.80 Trifecta £82.20.

Owner Sean Jones **Bred** Downfield Cottage Stud **Trained** Dunsany, Co Meath

FOCUS
An interesting Railway Stakes. The runner-up, sent off favourite, brought Royal Ascot form to the table. The winner produced a smart turn of foot down the centre of the track to score, but the field was quite compressed and the race has been rated just below its recent average.

3679a DUBAI DUTY FREE IRISH DERBY (GROUP 1) (ENTIRE COLTS & FILLIES) 1m 4f

5:20 (5:20) 3-Y-O

£628,676 (£209,558; £99,264; £44,117; £22,058; £11,029)

RPR

1 **Harzand (IRE)**[21] 2896 3-9-0 123 PatSmullen 2 121+
(D K Weld, Ire) *settled bhd ldrs in 3rd: gng wl into st and impr on outer to ld 2 1/2f out: rdn and strly pressed fr over 1f out: kpt on wl u.p ins fnl f to assert clsng stages* **4/6**[1]

2 ½ **Idaho (IRE)**[21] 2896 3-9-0 118 RyanMoore 4 120+
(A P O'Brien, Ire) *sweated up befhand: chsd ldrs: 4th 1/2-way: tk clsr order bhd ldrs after 1/2-way and wnt 2nd gng wl fr 2f out: sn rdn and almost on terms ins fnl f: kpt on wl wout matching wnr clsng stages* **11/4**[2]

3 3 ¾ **Stellar Mass (IRE)**[7] 3428 3-9-0 100 RonanWhelan 1 114
(J S Bolger, Ire) *w.w towards rr: clsr and disp 5th at 1/2-way: rdn in 4th under 2f out and clsd u.p into 3rd over 1f out: no imp on ldrs ins fnl f: kpt on same pce to jst hold 3rd* **33/1**

4 shd **Red Verdon (USA)**[21] 2896 3-9-0 105 SilvestreDeSousa 9 114
(Ed Dunlop) *settled in mid-div early: niggled along briefly in rr fr 1/2-way: hdwy on outer fr 2f out to chse ldrs in 5th over 1f out: kpt on wl in 4th ins fnl 150yds: jst failed for 3rd: nvr trbld ldrs* **10/1**[3]

5 2 ½ **Port Douglas (IRE)**[21] 2896 3-9-0 111 (tp) SeamieHeffernan 5 110
(A P O'Brien, Ire) *settled bhd ldr in 2nd: rdn in 2nd over 2f out and sn no imp on wnr u.p in 3rd: no ex in 4th ent fnl f and one pce after* **14/1**

6 1 ¾ **Moonlight Magic**[21] 2896 3-9-0 111 KevinManning 7 107
(J S Bolger, Ire) *w.w towards rr: 8th 1/2-way: tk clsr order appr st: rdn in 5th 2f out and no imp on ldrs over 1f out where n.m.r briefly and swtchd lft: one pce in 6th ins fnl f* **11/1**

7 2 **Shogun (IRE)**[21] 2896 3-9-0 109 ColmO'Donoghue 3 104
(A P O'Brien, Ire) *sweated up befhand: sn led tl hdd after 1f and settled bhd ldrs: disp 5th at 1/2-way: rdn in 6th 2f out and no imp u.p in 7th over 1f out: one pce fnl f* **33/1**

8 2 ¾ **Claudio Monteverdi (IRE)**[22] 2883 3-9-0 98 (tp) DonnachaO'Brien 6 99
(A P O'Brien, Ire) *sweated up befhand: hld up in tch: 7th 1/2-way: rdn on outer over 2f out and sn no imp on ldrs: one pce after* **50/1**

9 35 **Ebediyin (IRE)**[8] 3341 3-9-0 98 LeighRoche 8 43
(D K Weld, Ire) *s.i.s: towards rr and pushed along early tl rapid hdwy to ld after 1f: sn extended advantage and clr: reduced advantage over 4f out and hdd 2 1/2f out: sn wknd and eased* **50/1**

2m 38.05s (-0.45) **Going Correction** +0.30s/f (Good) **9** Ran SP% **120.5**
Speed ratings: **113,112,110,110,108 107,105,104,80**
CSF £2.75 TOTE £1.90: £1.02, £1.30, £6.20; DF 3.00 Trifecta £29.20.

Owner H H Aga Khan **Bred** His Highness The Aga Khan's Studs S C **Trained** Curragh, Co Kildare

FOCUS
No \bUS Army Ranger\p, ruled out by an unsatisfactory scope, but the first, third, sixth, 14th, 15th and 16th from Epsom all renewed rivalry. The ground was officially good to yielding and probably quicker than it was at Epsom. The winner had a pacemaker and \bEbediyin\p ensured it was a true test. There were no hard-luck stories.

3680a DUBAI DUTY FREE TENNIS CHAMPIONSHIP EUROPEAN BREEDERS FUND H'CAP 2m

6:00 (6:00) (60-100,97) 4-Y-O+ **£12,887** (£3,981; £1,886; £838; £314)

RPR

1 **Papa's Way (IRE)**[8] 3375 6-8-8 **79** (p) ChrisHayes 87
(P D Deegan, Ire) *mde virtually all: rdn into st and pressed clly: jnd u.p fnl 50yds: kpt on wl clsng stages to prevail on line: all out* **20/1**

2 nse **Modem**[22] 2881 6-9-3 **88** (p) ColmO'Donoghue 96
(Mrs John Harrington, Ire) *chsd ldrs: 5th 1/2-way: rdn in 4th into st and clsd u.p on outer to chal in 2nd wl ins fnl f: disp fnl 50yds tl denied on line* **12/1**

3 2 ½ **Weather Watch (IRE)**[11] 2942 6-8-7 **83** (p) TomMadden[(5)] 88
(Mrs John Harrington, Ire) *mid-div: 7th 1/2-way: pushed along in 8th into st and hdwy fr under 2f out to chse ldrs in 4th wl ins fnl f: kpt on clsng stages into nvr nrr 3rd fnl stride: nvr trbld ldrs* **16/1**

4 nse **Abraham (IRE)**[16] 3086 4-8-8 **79** DeclanMcDonogh 84
(J R Barry, Ire) *chsd ldrs: 3rd 1/2-way: rdn in 3rd into st and wnt 2nd over 2f out: no ex wl ins fnl f where dropped to 3rd: denied 3rd fnl stride* **9/1**

5 hd **Botany Bay (IRE)**[22] 2881 4-9-1 **86** RyanMoore 91
(Charles O'Brien, Ire) *in rr of mid-div early tl impr to chse ldrs after 2f: 6th at 1/2-way: rdn in 6th into st and no imp on ldrs whn swtchd lft wl ins fnl f: kpt on same pce* **7/2**[1]

6 2 ¼ **McKinley**[16] 3086 6-8-9 **80** (p) ConorHoban 83
(W P Mullins, Ire) *mid-div: 8th 1/2-way: sme hdwy 2f out: no imp on ldrs u.p in 6th wl ins fnl f: kpt on one pce* **9/1**

7 1 ½ **Three Kingdoms (IRE)**[101] 6113 7-8-11 **82** PatSmullen 83
(D K Weld, Ire) *hld up: 11th 1/2-way: rdn on outer 2f out and sme hdwy u.p 1f out: no ex and kpt on one pce under hands and heels ins fnl f* **8/1**[3]

8 1 ¼ **Asbury Boss (IRE)**[20] 2942 5-8-13 **84** (p) ShaneFoley 83
(M Halford, Ire) *trckd ldr: rdn in 2nd into st and no imp on wnr u.p in 4th under 2f out: sn wknd* **8/1**[3]

9 1 ½ **Asian Wing (IRE)**[134] 545 7-8-4 **75** (p) YNarredu 73
(John James Feane, Ire) *lost grnd s and detached in rr: stl in rr appr st: sme hdwy fr under 3f out: no imp in mod 9th 1f out: kpt on one pce* **50/1**

10 2 ½ **Synopsis**[13] 3203 4-8-10 **81** ColinKeane 76
(G M Lyons, Ire) *in rr of mid-div: 9th 1/2-way: rdn on outer over 2f out and no imp: one pce fnl 2f* **8/1**[3]

11 6 **Mandatario**[16] 3086 5-9-12 **97** (t) KevinManning 85
(J S Bolger, Ire) *towards rr thrght: 12th 1/2-way: rdn and no imp 2f out* **12/1**

12 1 **Hidden Justice (IRE)**[64] 1598 7-9-2 **90** DonnachaO'Brien[(3)] 77
(John Quinn) *towards rr: 10th 1/2-way: hdwy over 5f out to chse ldrs in 7th briefly: rdn and no ex appr st: sn dropped towards rr* **14/1**

13 nk **Don Vincenzo (IRE)**[9] 3334 7-8-5 **76** (t) RoryCleary 63
(Colin Bowe, Ire) *chsd ldrs: 4th 1/2-way: rdn in 5th over 3f out and sn no ex: wknd over 2f out* **5/1**[2]

3m 36.7s (3.70) **Going Correction** +0.30s/f (Good) **13** Ran SP% **126.9**
Speed ratings: **102,101,100,100,100 99,98,98,97,96 93,92,92**
CSF £256.24 CT £3942.18 TOTE £23.20: £5.10, £4.00, £4.60; DF 296.90 Trifecta £1351.80.

Owner Ms Rosha Lyttle **Bred** Miss Rosha Lyttle **Trained** The Curragh, Co Kildare

The Form Book, Raceform Ltd, Newbury, RG14 5SJ

FOCUS
A typically-competitive staying handicap. The winner made most. A lot of the field did not get into the race and it seemed to suit those who were ridden prominently.

3681a DUBAI DUTY FREE JUMEIRAH CREEKSIDE DASH STKS (LISTED RACE) 6f
6:30 (6:31) 3-Y-O+
£20,606 (£6,636; £3,143; £1,397; £698; £349)

RPR
1 **Toscanini (IRE)**[36] 2450 4-9-7 107 [1] ShaneFoley 9 111
(M Halford, Ire) *sn led nr side tl hdd narrowly bef 1/2-way: regained advantage over 1f out: strly pressed u.p wl ins fnl f: kpt on wl clsng stages to hold on: all out* **4/1**[2]
2 *hd* **Flight Risk (IRE)**[35] 2495 5-9-7 106 KevinManning 8 110
(J S Bolger, Ire) *chsd ldrs nr side: 6th 1/2-way: tk clsr order bhd ldrs over 1f out and rdn into 2nd fnl 150yds where strly pressed wnr: kpt on wl clsng stages: jst hld* **10/3**[1]
3 *2 1/2* **Jamesie (IRE)**[85] 1189 8-9-7 102 (t) PatSmullen 2 102+
(David Marnane, Ire) *broke wl to ld tl sn hdd: regained advantage far side bef 1/2-way: rdn and hdd over 1f out: dropped to 3rd fnl 150yds and no imp on ldrs: kpt on same pce* **8/1**
4 *3/4* **The Happy Prince (IRE)**[7] 3386 4-9-7 98 (t) RyanMoore 1 100
(A P O'Brien, Ire) *towards rr nr side: last at 1/2-way: sme hdwy 1f out where swtchd rt in 6th: r.o ins fnl 150yds into nvr threatening 4th: nvr trbld ldrs* **4/1**[2]
5 *nk* **G Force (IRE)**[265] 6972 5-9-7 109 (t) KierenFallon 7 99
(Adrian Paul Keatley, Ire) *in tch nr side: 7th 1/2-way: swtchd rt fr 2f out and sme hdwy u.p over 1f out: no ex in 4th briefly ins fnl f: kpt on same pce in 5th clsng stages* **12/1**
6 *1/2* **Bebhinn (USA)**[270] 6843 3-8-12 105 ChrisHayes 3 93+
(Kevin Prendergast, Ire) *stmbld sltly leaving stalls: trckd ldr in 2nd far side: disp 3rd at 1/2-way: rdn over 1f out and sn no ex: wknd ins fnl f* **10/1**
7 *1 1/2* **Maarek**[20] 2943 9-9-10 106 SeamieHeffernan 10 96
(Miss Evanna McCutcheon, Ire) *on toes befhand: s.i.s and in rr nr side early: 8th at 1/2-way: rdn 2f out and no imp ent fnl f: kpt on one pce* **7/1**[3]
8 *nk* **Moviesta (USA)**[45] 2159 6-9-12 106 (v[1]) WayneLordan 6 97
(Edward Lynam, Ire) *hooded to load: cl up and racd keenly early: disp 3rd nr side at 1/2-way: rdn under 2f out and no ex 1f out: wknd* **9/1**
9 *4 1/2* **Yuften**[16] 3084 5-9-7 101 ConnorKing 5 77
(J P Murtagh, Ire) *chsd ldrs nr side: 5th 1/2-way: rdn 2f out and wknd to rr 1f out* **20/1**

1m 12.15s (-3.35) **Going Correction** -0.275s/f (Firm)
WFA 3 from 4yo+ 7lb — **9** Ran SP% **118.2**
Speed ratings: **111,110,107,106,106 105,103,102,96**
CSF £18.26 TOTE £4.40: £1.40, £1.50, £2.10; DF 16.90 Trifecta £96.90.
Owner Godolphin **Bred** Darley **Trained** Doneany, Co Kildare

FOCUS
The run of ill-luck and disappointments in stakes races was finally ended by the winner in atypical fashion.

3682 - 3683a (Foreign Racing) - See Raceform Interactive

[3668]WINDSOR (R-H)
Sunday, June 26

OFFICIAL GOING: Soft (good to soft in places; 5.9)
Wind: Moderate, behind Weather: Fine but cloudy

3684 SPORTSABLE CHANGING LIVES THROUGH DISABILITY SPORT MAIDEN FILLIES' STKS 1m 67y
2:10 (2:11) (Class 4) 3-5-Y-O
£5,175 (£1,540; £769; £384) **Stalls** Low

Form — RPR
-024 **1** **Ejayteekay**[29] 2701 3-8-7 74 GeorgeWood(7) 5 81
(Hughie Morrison) *dwlt: sn trckd ldng pair: rdn over 2f out: led wl over 1f out: drvn clr and styd on wl* **2/1**[2]
0 **2** *5* **Excellent Sounds**[22] 2904 3-9-0 0 PatDobbs 6 70
(Hughie Morrison) *pressed ldr: led over 2f out to wl over 1f out: sn outpcd and btn: kpt on* **25/1**
0 **3** *2 3/4* **St Mary'S**[36] 2470 3-9-0 0 OisinMurphy 8 63
(Andrew Balding) *dwlt: hld up in last pair: pushed along in 6th and outpcd 3f out: no prog tl styd on wl fnl f to take 3rd last strides* **10/1**
00 **4** *1/2* **Encore Moi**[17] 3059 3-9-0 0 AndreaAtzeni 4 62
(Marco Botti) *chsd ldng trio: urged along fr 1/2-way: drvn to chsng clr ldng pair fnl f: no imp and lost 3rd last strides* **8/1**[3]
25 **5** *1* **Dame Judi (IRE)**[17] 3059 3-9-0 0 SilvestreDeSousa 3 60
(Simon Crisford) *led: tk field to far side but hdd over 2f out: pushed along and steadily wknd* **10/11**[1]
0-0 **6** *1 1/2* **Helfire**[6] 3464 3-8-9 0 CharlieBennett(5) 7 56
(Hughie Morrison) *hld up in midfield: pushed along in 5th over 3f out and nt on terms: no imp after* **16/1**
0 **7** *1 1/4* **Staplehurst (IRE)**[14] 3194 3-9-0 0 TimmyMurphy 1 53
(Geoffrey Deacon) *hld up: outpcd fr 1/2-way and sn in poor 7th: nudged along and n.d after but kpt on fnl f* **66/1**
8 *13* **Dance With Kate** 5-9-7 0 TimClark(3) 2 26
(Polly Gundry) *s.s and rousted to get in tch: wknd over 3f out: t.o* **100/1**

1m 48.08s (3.38) **Going Correction** +0.275s/f (Good)
WFA 3 from 5yo 10lb — **8** Ran SP% **118.1**
Speed ratings (Par 102): **94,89,86,85,84 83,82,69**
CSF £49.08 TOTE £3.00: £1.10, £5.70, £2.40; EX 60.40 Trifecta £219.50.
Owner TMBS Solutions Ltd **Bred** Pinehurst Stud **Trained** East Ilsley, Berks

FOCUS
Soft ground for this seven- race card. The inner of the straight was dolled out 10yds at 6f and 8yds at the winning line, while the top bend was dolled out 7yds from the normal inner configuration, adding 28yds to race distances of 1m-plus. As is often the case when the ground is soft here, the jockeys decided to go far side in the straight. This looked a fairly modest fillies' maiden on paper and it was won convincingly by a 74-rated runner who came here pretty exposed.

3685 SPORTSABLE #PUSHYOURSELF H'CAP 5f 10y
2:40 (2:40) (Class 3) (0-95,93) 3-Y-O
£7,439 (£2,213; £1,106; £553) **Stalls** Low

Form — RPR
204 **1** **Lady Macapa**[8] 3413 3-9-7 93 [1] SilvestreDeSousa 5 98
(William Knight) *mde virtually all: tk field to centre fr 3f out: rdn over 1f out: kpt on wl fnl f* **11/4**[3]
20-3 **2** *1* **This Is For You**[20] 2982 3-8-6 78 ow1 OisinMurphy 3 79
(Andrew Balding) *chsd wnr: drvn to chal over 1f out: kpt on fnl f but a hld* **15/8**[1]
0-22 **3** *5* **Silken Skies (IRE)**[20] 2982 3-8-9 81 TedDurcan 1 64
(Clive Cox) *trckd ldng pair: outpcd and shkn up whn swtchd lft over 1f out: n.d after* **2/1**[2]
15-0 **4** *1* **Teresar (IRE)**[44] 2218 3-9-3 89 PatDobbs 4 69
(Richard Hannon) *hld up in last: shkn up and no prog 2f out: pressed for wl btn 3rd fnl f* **7/1**

1m 0.65s (0.35) **Going Correction** +0.175s/f (Good) — **4** Ran SP% **107.3**
Speed ratings (Par 103): **104,102,94,92**
CSF £8.10 TOTE £2.60; EX 8.30 Trifecta £8.90.
Owner Fromthestables.com Racing V **Bred** Peter Winkworth **Trained** Patching, W Sussex

FOCUS
An open little handicap, but with only two of the four rated above 81 this would be weak form for a 0-95 handicap.

3686 BRITISH STALLION STUDS EBF FILLIES' CONDITIONS STKS (PLUS 10 RACE) 5f 10y
3:10 (3:11) (Class 2) 2-Y-O
£10,893 (£3,262; £1,631; £815; £407) **Stalls** Low

Form — RPR
1 **1** **Mrs Danvers**[15] 3143 2-8-12 0 RyanClark 1 88+
(Jonathan Portman) *pressed ldr: led 2f out and kpt towards nr side: shkn up over 1f out: styd on wl* **4/5**[1]
2 **2** *2 1/4* **Blue Suede (IRE)**[16] 3106 2-8-12 0 PatDobbs 2 78
(Richard Hannon) *hld up: prog on outer to chse wnr over 1f out: styd on but nvr able to threaten* **10/3**[2]
015 **3** *6* **Miss Rosina (IRE)**[18] 3037 2-8-12 0 AndreaAtzeni 3 56
(George Margarson) *led to 2f out: wknd over 1f out* **15/2**[3]
40 **4** *4* **Whiteley (IRE)**[38] 2410 2-8-12 0 SilvestreDeSousa 4 42
(Mick Channon) *sn pushed along in last: brief effrt 2f out: sn no prog and wl btn* **12/1**
01 **5** *9* **Queen Celeste (IRE)**[8] 3396 2-8-12 0 FrannyNorton 5 10
(Mark Johnston) *in tch on wd outside: wknd rapidly 2f out* **10/1**

1m 0.74s (0.44) **Going Correction** +0.175s/f (Good) — **5** Ran SP% **107.2**
Speed ratings (Par 96): **103,99,89,83,69**
CSF £3.41 TOTE £1.60: £1.10, £1.80; EX 3.70 Trifecta £7.70.
Owner Turf Club 2014 **Bred** M A Burton & Connie Hopper **Trained** Upper Lambourn, Berks

FOCUS
Not the deepest of conditions races and they finished quite well strung out, but the impresssive winner has been rated in line with the better recent winners.

3687 SPORTSABLE ALTERNATIVE TEAM BUILDING H'CAP 1m 2f 7y
3:40 (3:40) (Class 3) (0-90,88) 3-Y-O
£7,439 (£2,213; £1,106; £553) **Stalls** Centre

Form — RPR
0-02 **1** **Goodwood Zodiac (IRE)**[22] 2892 3-9-6 87 SilvestreDeSousa 1 98
(William Knight) *hld up in last pair: shkn up to cl over 2f out: led wl over 1f out: drifted lft u.p towards far side but asserted fnl f* **15/8**[1]
4-1 **2** *1 1/4* **Rockspirit (IRE)**[34] 2548 3-9-7 88 AndreaAtzeni 5 96
(Marco Botti) *mostly in last pair tl rdn and prog 3f out: chal 2f out: pressed wnr after tl one pce ins fnl f* **3/1**[2]
2-11 **3** *2 1/4* **Goldenfield (IRE)**[30] 2644 3-9-3 84 (p) GeorgeBaker 3 88
(Gary Moore) *led: tk field in centre fr 3f out: rdn over 2f out: hdd and one pce wl over 1f out* **3/1**[2]
3045 **4** *3 1/4* **Lilbourne Prince (IRE)**[16] 3102 3-8-6 73 JFEgan 4 70
(David Evans) *chsd ldr: rdn 3f out: chal 2f out: fdd over 1f out* **9/1**
2-05 **5** *1/2* **Southern Gailes (IRE)**[65] 1602 3-8-10 77 JoeyHaynes 2 73
(K R Burke) *chsd ldng pair: rdn 3f out: chal 2f out: sn btn: wknd fnl f* **11/2**[3]

2m 9.54s (0.84) **Going Correction** +0.275s/f (Good) — **5** Ran SP% **110.2**
Speed ratings (Par 103): **107,106,104,101,101**
CSF £7.75 TOTE £2.80: £1.40, £1.80; EX 6.80 Trifecta £13.60.
Owner Goodwood Racehorse Owners Group (22) Ltd **Bred** Kabansk Ltd & Rathbarry Stud **Trained** Patching, W Sussex

FOCUS
Add 28yds to race distance. A wide open little handicap with all five runners going off a single-figure price in the betting. The two highest-rated horses in the race came clear in the final furlong.

3688 SPORTSABLE VENUE HIRE H'CAP 1m 67y
4:15 (4:15) (Class 2) (0-105,104) 3-Y-O+ **£12,938** (£3,850; £1,924; £962) **Stalls** Low

Form — RPR
2-66 **1** **Kingston Kurrajong**[36] 2473 3-8-1 87 JimmyQuinn 4 92
(Andrew Balding) *trckd ldng pair: chal fr wl over 1f out: drvn and styd on wl to ld last 75yds* **7/1**
3-65 **2** *nk* **Grand Inquisitor**[50] 2027 4-9-5 95 TedDurcan 5 101
(Sir Michael Stoute) *hld up in 5th: prog 3f out: pressed ldr fr 2f out: narrow ld u.p ins fnl f: hdd last 75yds: kpt on* **9/4**[1]
4311 **3** *hd* **Felix Leiter**[15] 3163 4-9-3 100 CliffordLee(7) 2 106
(K R Burke) *led at gd pce: tk field towards far side 3f out: rdn and pressed fr 2f out: hdd ins fnl f: kpt on wl but hld last 50yds* **7/2**[2]
4006 **4** *2* **Birdman (IRE)**[27] 2744 6-10-0 104 DanielTudhope 3 105
(David O'Meara) *trckd ldng trio to 3f out: sn shkn up: outpcd fr 2f out: kpt on again fnl f* **11/2**[3]
2622 **5** *2 1/2* **Montsarrat (IRE)**[22] 2889 3-8-4 90 FrannyNorton 7 83
(Mark Johnston) *pressed ldr to 2f out: steadily wknd* **11/2**[3]
0-00 **6** *1* **Storm Rock**[57] 1871 4-9-7 97 DavidProbert 1 90
(Harry Dunlop) *hld up in 6th: clsd on ldrs over 2f out: shkn up and no rspnse wl over 1f out: sn wknd* **7/1**
/005 **7** *1 1/4* **Vercingetorix (IRE)**[8] 3391 5-8-9 85 ShaneKelly 6 75
(David Evans) *hld up in last: detached 3f out: no prog after* **16/1**

1m 44.73s (0.03) **Going Correction** +0.275s/f (Good)
WFA 3 from 4yo+ 10lb — **7** Ran SP% **114.6**
Speed ratings (Par 109): **110,109,109,107,105 104,102**
CSF £23.30 TOTE £8.10: £3.60, £1.20; EX 22.10 Trifecta £119.20.
Owner Richard Hains **Bred** Kingston Park Studs Pty Ltd **Trained** Kingsclere, Hants

FOCUS
Add 28yds to race distance. A decent little handicap which was run at what looked an even gallop and it served up a cracking three-way finish.

3689 SKY BET ROYAL WINDSOR SPRINT SERIES H'CAP (QUALIFIER FOR THE WINDSOR SPRINT SERIES FINAL) 6f
4:45 (4:47) (Class 4) (0-85,84) 3-Y-O
£6,792 (£2,021; £1,010; £505) **Stalls** Low

Form — RPR
2013 **1** **Black Bess**[16] 3111 3-9-1 78 PatCosgrave 6 85
(Jim Boyle) *chsd ldrs: rdn and prog over 1f out: chsd ldr fnl f: drvn and r.o wl to ld last 75yds* **11/2**[3]

-015 **2** ½ **Wayward Hoof**[20] 2972 3-9-4 **81** DougieCostello 9 86
(K R Burke) *w ldr: led 2f out: sn drvn: styd on but hdd and jst outpcd last 75yds* **5/1**[2]
04-4 **3** 2 **Topology**[56] 1894 3-9-2 **79** OisinMurphy 7 78
(Joseph Tuite) *hld up in last pair: rdn in last 2f out and no prog: swtchd to far rail and r.o fnl f to take 3rd last strides* **20/1**
12 **4** nk **Dynamic Girl (IRE)**[16] 3111 3-8-5 **68** ow1 JFEgan 5 66
(Brendan Powell) *trckd ldrs: tk 2nd wl over 1f out and sn chalng: fdd ins fnl f* **7/1**
-120 **5** ¾ **Ower Fly**[16] 3105 3-8-13 **83** MeganNicholls(7) 10 78
(Richard Hannon) *trckd ldrs: rdn and nt qckn wl over 1f out: one pce after* **12/1**
-041 **6** 1½ **Alizoom (IRE)**[15] 3138 3-9-5 **82** AndreaAtzeni 3 72
(Roger Varian) *hld up: in tch 2f out: rdn and effrt wl over 1f out: sn no prog: wknd fnl f* **9/2**[1]
-321 **7** 1¾ **He's My Cracker**[15] 3147 3-9-3 **80** AdamKirby 1 65
(Clive Cox) *chsd ldrs: styd alone nr side fr 1/2-way: sn rdn: nt on terms fr over 1f out* **7/1**
12-0 **8** 1¾ **Art Collection (FR)**[24] 2818 3-9-7 **84** (b) GeorgeBaker 4 63
(Gary Moore) *hld up in last pair: shkn up and in tch 2f out: hanging bdly lft and rn into trble over 1f out: wknd* **20/1**
6-54 **9** 12 **Point Of Woods**[15] 3131 3-9-5 **82** SilvestreDeSousa 8 23
(Ralph Beckett) *led to 2f out: wknd rapidly and eased: t.o* **7/1**
1m 13.56s (0.56) **Going Correction** +0.175s/f (Good) **9** Ran SP% **104.9**
Speed ratings (Par 101): **103,102,99,99,98 96,93,91,75**
CSF £27.73 CT £398.39 TOTE £6.30: £2.30, £1.70, £4.40; EX 31.80 Trifecta £584.90.
Owner The Clean Sweep Partnership **Bred** Paddock Space **Trained** Epsom, Surrey
■ Pusey's Secret was withdrawn. Price at time of withdrawal 10/1. Rule 4 applies to all bets - deduction 5p in the pound.
FOCUS
A competitive heat for the grade with several coming into this in good form.

3690 SPORTSABLE #TEAMSPORTSABLE H'CAP 1m 3f 135y
5:20 (5:20) (Class 4) (0-80,78) 4-Y-O+ **£5,453** (£1,610; £805) **Stalls** Centre

Form RPR
3552 **1** **William Hunter**[15] 3139 4-9-2 **74** WilliamTwiston-Davies 6 82
(Alan King) *trckd ldrs: rdn to ld wl over 1f out: edgd lft u.p fr over 1f out: hrd pressed nr fin: hld on* **2/1**[2]
1000 **2** hd **Bazooka (IRE)**[32] 2582 5-9-3 **75** SilvestreDeSousa 3 82
(David Flood) *hld up in last pair: rdn and prog over 2f out: chal over 1f out: sltly checked and swtchd rt jst ins fnl f: hrd drvn and styd on: jst hld* **7/1**
2-30 **3** ¾ **Clovelly Bay (IRE)**[22] 2888 5-8-9 **74** TylerSaunders(7) 1 80
(Marcus Tregoning) *dwlt: sn cl up: trckd ldrs 7f out to 5f out: lost pl over 3f out: rallied over 1f out: tk 3rd fnl f and clsd on ldng pair fin* **8/1**
0-25 **4** 2½ **Priors Brook**[34] 2549 5-9-5 **77** OisinMurphy 7 79
(Andrew Balding) *led: shkn up and hdd over 3f out: pressed ldr and upsides 2f out: fdd over 1f out* **15/8**[1]
-300 **5** 3 **Full Day**[15] 3149 5-9-6 **78** (b[1]) AdamKirby 4 75
(Brian Ellison) *urged along early to stay in tch: mostly in last pair: rdn over 3f out: no prog and btn 2f out* **6/1**[3]
-135 **6** ½ **Hound Music**[27] 2753 4-9-2 **74** FergusSweeney 5 70
(Jonathan Portman) *trckd ldr to 7f out and again 5f out: led over 3f out: hdd & wknd tamely wl over 1f out* **14/1**
2m 33.77s (4.27) **Going Correction** +0.275s/f (Good) **6** Ran SP% **112.7**
Speed ratings (Par 105): **96,95,95,93,91 91**
CSF £16.17 TOTE £2.70: £1.50, £2.70; EX 8.90 Trifecta £60.70.
Owner Incipe Partnership **Bred** Barbury Castle Stud **Trained** Barbury Castle, Wilts
FOCUS
Add 28yds to race distance. Just a run-of-the-mill affair in which the front three pulled clear.
T/Plt: £87.00 to a £1 stake. Pool: £70,500.58 - 591.5 winning units T/Qpdt: £10.30 to a £1 stake. Pool: £5,574.49 - 397.46 winning units **Jonathan Neesom**

3691 - (Foreign Racing) - See Raceform Interactive

3675 CURRAGH (R-H)
Sunday, June 26
OFFICIAL GOING: Yielding (good to yielding in places)

3692a FINLAY VOLVO INTERNATIONAL STKS (GROUP 3) 1m 2f
2:45 (2:47) 3-Y-O+ **£28,198** (£9,080; £4,301; £1,911; £955)

RPR
1 **Sir Isaac Newton**[8] 3383 4-9-9 107 RyanMoore 1 111+
(A P O'Brien, Ire) *w.w bhd ldrs: clsr in 3rd bef 1/2-way: lost pl briefly appr st: hdwy far side gng wl fr 2f out: n.m.r on inner in cl 2nd fr over 1f out: led ins fnl 100yds and kpt on wl: readily* **11/8**[1]
2 ¾ **Chemical Charge (IRE)**[22] 2924 4-9-9 105 ColinKeane 4 109
(G M Lyons, Ire) *led: over 1 l clr at 1/2-way: jnd briefly appr st: sn rdn w narrow advantage: strly pressed fr over 1f out and hdd ins fnl 100yds: no imp on wnr cl home* **6/4**[2]
3 4 **In My Pocket (IRE)**[28] 2716 4-9-9 103 DeclanMcDonogh 2 101
(John M Oxx, Ire) *settled bhd ldrs in 3rd early: 4th 1/2-way: tk clsr order bhd ldrs in 3rd appr st: rdn on outer over 1f out and sn no imp on ldrs: kpt on same pce* **8/1**
4 4¼ **Sanus Per Aquam (IRE)**[36] 2496 3-9-1 109 KevinManning 5 97+
(J S Bolger, Ire) *sn settled in rr: pushed along over 3f out: sn rdn and no imp on ldrs: kpt on one pce ins fnl f into mod 4th clsng stages* **7/1**[3]
5 ¾ **Agnes Stewart (IRE)**[618] 7240 4-9-6 104 BillyLee 3 88
(Edward Lynam, Ire) *hooded to load: settled bhd ldr in 2nd: disp briefly appr st: sn rdn in cl 2nd and no ex under 2f out: dropped to 4th over 1f out and wknd to rr clsng stages* **16/1**
2m 12.25s (2.95) **Going Correction** +0.425s/f (Yiel)
WFA 3 from 4yo 12lb **5** Ran SP% **111.6**
Speed ratings: **105,104,101,97,97**
CSF £3.82 TOTE £1.70: £1.02, £1.50; DF 3.80 Trifecta £12.70.
Owner Derrick Smith & Mrs John Magnier & Michael Tabor **Bred** Newsells Park Stud **Trained** Cashel, Co Tipperary

FOCUS
A classy contest, but the steady pace made it pretty messy - and intriguing viewing for all of that. The winner is rated to his mark.

3694a GRANGECON STUD STKS (GROUP 3) (FILLIES) 6f
3:45 (3:46) 2-Y-O
£28,198 (£9,080; £4,301; £1,911; £955; £477)

RPR
1 **Roly Poly (USA)**[11] 3270 2-9-0 0 RyanMoore 3 98
(A P O'Brien, Ire) *chsd ldrs: disp 3rd at 1/2-way: impr to chal under 2f out: rdn on terms ent fnl f and kpt on wl u.p to ld narrowly fnl 50ys* **3/1**[1]
2 nk **Seafront**[28] 2718 2-9-0 0 PatSmullen 5 97
(James Tate) *settled bhd ldr in 2nd: pushed along in 2nd under 2f out and edgd sltly rt: led narrowly under 2f out: sn strly pressed and jnd: hdd narrowly fnl 50yds and kpt on wl wout matching wnr cl home* **7/2**[2]
3 ¾ **Elusive Beauty (IRE)**[24] 2838 2-9-0 0 ShaneFoley 7 95
(K J Condon, Ire) *sn chsd ldrs: disp 3rd at 1/2-way: lost pl bhd horses 2f out and sn pushed along: u.p in 6th ent fnl f: r.o again into 3rd clsng stages: nvr trbld ldrs* **12/1**
4 ½ **Ellery Lane (IRE)**[9] 3371 2-9-0 0 ChrisHayes 6 93
(P J Prendergast, Ire) *sn led: 1 l clr at 1/2-way: rdn and hdd under 2f out: no imp bhd ldrs u.p ins fnl f: kpt on same pce* **8/1**
5 nk **Magical Fire (IRE)**[18] 3045 2-9-0 0 KierenFallon 1 92
(M D O'Callaghan, Ire) *hooded to load: hld up in tch: 5th 1/2-way: tk clsr order on outer 2f out: effrt almost on terms 1 1/2f out: no ex ins fnl f and one pce clsng stages where dropped to 5th* **4/1**[3]
6 1¾ **Spy Ring (IRE)**[28] 2718 2-9-0 0 ColinKeane 4 87
(M D O'Callaghan, Ire) *hld up towards rr: 6th 1/2-way: tk clsr order in 5th under 2f out: rdn in 4th briefly ins fnl f and no imp on ldrs: wknd clsng stages* **7/2**[2]
7 4½ **Miss Cogent (IRE)**[14] 3199 2-9-0 0 RossCoakley 9 74
(J P Murtagh, Ire) *dwlt and a in rr: rdn 1 1/2f out and no imp ent fnl f: one pce* **20/1**
1m 15.32s (-0.18) **Going Correction** -0.45s/f (Firm) **7** Ran SP% **113.0**
Speed ratings: **83,82,81,80,80 78,72**
CSF £13.39 TOTE £3.40: £1.60, £2.00; DF 9.20 Trifecta £53.70.
Owner Michael Tabor & Derrick Smith & Mrs John Magnier **Bred** Misty For Me Syndicate **Trained** Cashel, Co Tipperary
FOCUS
A solid group 3 run at a pretty decent pace. The form has been rated at the low end of the race averages.

3695a SEA THE STARS PRETTY POLLY STKS (GROUP 1) (F&M) 1m 2f
4:20 (4:22) 3-Y-O+ **£108,639** (£35,110; £16,727; £7,536; £3,860)

RPR
1 **Minding (IRE)**[23] 2869 3-8-12 120 RyanMoore 3 122+
(A P O'Brien, Ire) *cl up in 2nd early tl sn settled bhd ldrs: mod 3rd at 1/2-way: pushed along into 2nd under 2f out and styd on wl to ld ins fnl f: drvn clr clsng stages: comf* **1/5**[1]
2 4½ **Bocca Baciata (IRE)**[35] 2512 4-9-10 106 ColmO'Donoghue 5 113
(Mrs John Harrington, Ire) *led and extended advantage after 1f: 6 l clr at 1/2-way and extended ld briefly bef st: pushed along w reduced ld 2f out: sn rdn and hdd ins fnl f: no ch w wnr and kpt on same pce clsng stages* **25/1**
3 5 **Lucida (IRE)**[11] 3271 4-9-10 113 KevinManning 2 103
(J S Bolger, Ire) *hld up towards rr: last at 1/2-way: tk clsr order bhd ldrs in 4th over 2f out where rdn: sn swtchd lft and kpt on one pce into 3rd fnl 150yds: nvr trbld ldrs* **14/1**
4 ½ **Koora**[45] 2189 4-9-10 109 JamieSpencer 1 102
(Luca Cumani) *dwlt and pushed along in rr early tl prog into 2nd after 1f: mod 2nd at 1/2-way: tk clsr order into st: sn pushed along and dropped to 3rd u.p under 2f out: one pce after and dropped to 4th fnl 150yds* **8/1**[2]
5 ½ **Speedy Boarding**[28] 2727 4-9-10 107 FrederikTylicki 4 101
(James Fanshawe) *hooded to load: sn settled in rr: mod 4th at 1/2-way: tk clsr order bhd ldrs into st: rdn over 2f out and sn no imp in rr: kpt on one pce ins fnl f* **10/1**[3]
2m 9.94s (0.64) **Going Correction** +0.425s/f (Yiel)
WFA 3 from 4yo 12lb **5** Ran SP% **114.0**
Speed ratings: **114,110,106,106,105**
CSF £8.74 TOTE £1.10: £1.10, £3.80; DF 8.00 Trifecta £27.00.
Owner Derrick Smith & Mrs John Magnier & Michael Tabor **Bred** Orpendale, Chelston & Wynatt **Trained** Cashel, Co Tipperary
FOCUS
Hardly a vintage renewal, and the runner-up has been well-exposed as more of a Group 2 sort, though the winner is clearly exceptional. It was a messy race although the runner-up set a fair pace. .

3696a TOTE ROCKINGHAM H'CAP (PREMIER HANDICAP) 5f
4:55 (4:55) 3-Y-O+
£43,382 (£13,970; £6,617; £2,941; £1,470; £735)

RPR
1 **Sors (IRE)**[22] 2922 4-7-11 **82** oh7 KillianLeonard(7) 13 92
(Andrew Slattery, Ire) *prom alone nr side early: rdn bhd ldrs on stands' side of centre gp under 2f out and kpt on best u.p ins fnl f to ld ins fnl 100yds* **20/1**
2 1¾ **Kimberella**[15] 3151 6-9-5 **97** FrederikTylicki 1 101
(David Nicholls) *chsd ldrs far side gp: rdn and hdwy over 1f out: ev ch almost on terms wl ins fnl f: kpt on wl wout matching wnr clsng stages* **4/1**[1]
3 shd **Desert Law (IRE)**[15] 3151 8-9-7 **99** MartinLane 10 103
(Paul Midgley) *chsd ldrs centre gp: rdn in 5th over 1f out and clsd u.p to chal briefly wl ins fnl f: no ex in 3rd clsng stages* **8/1**
4 ½ **Ardhoomey (IRE)**[14] 3201 4-9-12 **104** ColinKeane 12 106
(G M Lyons, Ire) *led nr side pair: rdn in mid-div over 1f out and r.o wl u.p wl ins fnl f into nvr nrr 4th: nvr trbld ldrs* **5/1**[2]
5 ½ **A Few Dollars More (IRE)**[15] 3171 4-7-13 **82** oh6 TomMadden(5) 7 82
(Andrew Slattery, Ire) *chsd ldrs centre gp: rdn bef 1/2-way and no imp on ldrs u.p in 6th wl ins fnl f: kpt on same pce clsng stages* **20/1**
6 nk **Tylery Wonder (IRE)**[15] 3170 6-8-4 **82** oh1 (b) LeighRoche 4 81
(W McCreery, Ire) *prom centre gp: rdn w narrow advantage under 2f out: edgd rt u.p ins fnl f and hdd ins fnl 100yds: no ex and wknd clsng stages* **12/1**
7 1¾ **Dikta Del Mar (SPA)**[14] 3201 4-8-12 **90** (t) ShaneFoley 8 83
(T Hogan, Ire) *towards rr centre gp: pushed along bef 1/2-way and no imp u.p over 1f out: kpt on ins fnl f: nvr nrr* **25/1**

8 *nk* **Ostatnia (IRE)**[31] 2630 4-9-5 **83**....................(b) WayneLordan 5 75
(W McCreery, Ire) *chsd ldrs centre gp: rdn 1 1/2f out and sn no imp on ldrs: wknd wl ins fnl f* **7/1**[3]

9 *3/4* **Kasbah (IRE)**[15] 3170 4-9-1 **93**....................(v) ConnorKing 11 82
(J P Murtagh, Ire) *trckd ldr nr side pair: rdn under 2f out and no imp towards rr 1f out: kpt on one pce* **10/1**

10 *1 1/2* **Shepherd's Purse**[20] 2984 4-9-3 **95**.................... GaryCarroll 9 78
(Joseph G Murphy, Ire) *towards rr centre gp: pushed along bef 1/2-way and no imp ent fnl f: kpt on one pce* **14/1**

11 *1/2* **Dutch Masterpiece**[34] 2546 6-9-11 **103**....................(v) RyanMoore 6 85
(Gary Moore) *towards rr centre gp: rdn under 2f out and swtchd rt 1f out: no imp far side and one pce ins fnl f* **10/1**

12 *4 1/4* **Chiclet (IRE)**[31] 2630 5-8-13 **91**.................... PatSmullen 3 57
(Tracey Collins, Ire) *stmbld sltly after s: sn led far side gp: rdn bhd ldrs under 2f out and sn wknd: eased ins fnl f* **12/1**

13 *3 1/4* **Abstraction (IRE)**[37] 2450 6-9-10 **102**.................... SeamieHeffernan 2 57
(Miss Natalia Lupini, Ire) *cl up far side gp early: rdn bhd ldrs 2f out and wknd over 1f out* **8/1**

59.4s (-3.50) **Going Correction** -0.45s/f (Firm) 13 Ran SP% **125.0**
Speed ratings: **110,107,107,106,105 104,102,101,100,98 97,90,85**
CSF £100.50 CT £746.35 TOTE £26.60: £7.80, £1.40, £2.90; DF 171.00 Trifecta £1907.50.
Owner Men Of Forty Eight Syndicate **Bred** Brian Wallace **Trained** Thurles, Co Tipperary

FOCUS
As competitive as ever, with the honours going to a horse who had previously shown his best form at Dundalk. He saw off a strong British challenge and is rated back to his juvenile best.

3697a CORAL.IE CURRAGH CUP (GROUP 2) 1m 6f
5:25 (5:27) 3-Y-O+ **£52,058** (£16,764; £7,941; £3,529)

RPR

1 **Sword Fighter (IRE)**[9] 3341 3-8-10 101.................... SeamieHeffernan 1 106
(A P O'Brien, Ire) *mde all: over 1 l clr at 1/2-way: rdn over 2f out and pressed clly: styd on wl to assert wl ins fnl f* **11/4**[3]

2 *2* **Landofhopeandglory (IRE)**[9] 3341 3-8-10 100.................... RyanMoore 2 103+
(A P O'Brien, Ire) *w.w bhd ldrs in 3rd: tk clsr order bhd ldr on inner into st: sn n.m.r in 3rd 1 1/2f out: swtchd rt ent fnl f and sn no imp on wnr in 2nd: kpt on same pce* **15/8**[1]

3 *1 3/4* **Alveena (IRE)**[14] 3203 4-9-8 99.................... PatSmullen 4 96+
(D K Weld, Ire) *hld up bhd ldrs in rr: hdwy on outer into st and impr into 2nd over 2f out where pressed wnr clly: rdn over 1f out and sn no imp on wnr u.p in 3rd: kpt on same pce* **9/4**[2]

4 *16* **Cymro (IRE)**[9] 3340 4-9-11 104.................... RichardKingscote 3 76
(Tom Dascombe) *trckd ldr: pushed along in cl 2nd 4f out and dropped to rr over 2f out: no imp on ldrs and wknd under 2f out: eased ins fnl f* **5/1**

3m 8.37s (-1.03) **Going Correction** +0.425s/f (Yiel)
WFA 3 from 4yo 17lb 4 Ran SP% **108.9**
Speed ratings: **119,117,116,107**
CSF £8.24 TOTE £2.70; DF 4.20 Trifecta £10.70.
Owner Michael Tabor & Derrick Smith & Mrs John Magnier **Bred** Glenvale Stud **Trained** Cashel, Co Tipperary

FOCUS
A poor turn-out for this Group 3 event, with two of the four runners supplied by Aidan O'Brien, whose Bondi Beach beat Order Of St George 12 months ago to complete a hat-trick for the stable. Another one-two for Ballydoyle here and Sword Fighter continues to progress. It proved hard to make up ground.

3693 & 3698 - (Foreign Racing) - See Raceform Interactive

DORTMUND (R-H)
Sunday, June 26

OFFICIAL GOING: Turf: good to soft

3699a GROSSER PREIS DER WIRTSCHAFT (GROUP 3) (3YO+) (TURF) 1m 165y
3:40 (12:00) 3-Y-O+ **£23,529** (£8,823; £4,411; £2,205; £1,470)

RPR

1 **Potemkin (GER)**[267] 6949 5-9-5 0.................... EduardoPedroza 2 104
(A Wohler, Germany) *hld up in tch on inner: drvn to ld wl over 1f out: forged clr ins fnl f: a holding runner-up last 75yds* **3/1**[2]

2 *1 1/2* **Noor Al Hawa (FR)**[41] 2315 3-8-6 0.................... StephenHellyn 5 98
(A Wohler, Germany) *w.w in midfield between horses: rowed along and nt qckn appr 1 1/2f out: styd on u.p ins fnl f: nt pce to trble wnr* **7/2**[3]

3 *3/4* **Nacar (GER)**[29] 2711 3-8-7 0 ow1.................... AndreasSuborics 1 97
(Mario Hofer, Germany) *led: scrubbed along whn pressed more than 1/2f out: hdd wl over 1f out: kpt on at same pce* **231/10**

4 *3/4* **Pagino (GER)**[27] 2755 3-8-6 0.................... MarcLerner 8 95
(Waldemar Hickst, Germany) *cl up on outer: rdn and nt qckn 2f out: styd on at same pce fnl f* **141/10**

5 *hd* **Wild Chief (GER)**[33] 2568 5-9-3 0.................... AlexanderPietsch 6 95
(J Hirschberger, Germany) *chsd ldr: rdn and no imp appr 1 1/2f out: plugged on at one pce fr 1f out* **6/5**[1]

6 *3 1/4* **Guizot (IRE)**[56] 3-8-6 0.................... FilipMinarik 7 87
(Jean-Pierre Carvalho, Germany) *outpcd in rr early: rdn and shortlived effrt wl over 1 1/2f out: sn btn: wknd ins fnl f* **99/10**

7 *9* **Lucky Lion**[49] 2074 5-9-3 0.................... AdriedeVries 4 68
(Andreas Lowe, Germany) *w.w in fnl pair: smooth hdwy on outer 2 1/2f out: ev ch whn hrd rdn and no further imp wl over 1f out: wknd qckly* **42/10**

1m 52.94s (112.94)
WFA 3 from 4yo+ 11lb 7 Ran SP% **131.9**
WIN (incl. 10 euro stake): 40. PLACES: 23, 26, 51. SF: 149.
Owner Klaus Allofs & Stiftung Gestut Fahrhof **Bred** Siftung Gestut Fahrhof **Trained** Germany

3700a (Foreign Racing) - See Raceform Interactive

[3455] SAN SIRO (R-H)
Sunday, June 26

OFFICIAL GOING: Turf: good

3701a PREMIO PRIMI PASSI (GROUP 3) (2YO) (TURF) 6f
4:10 (12:00) 2-Y-O **£18,382** (£11,323; £6,176; £3,088)

RPR

1 **Hargeisa (USA)**[32] 2-8-8 0.................... CarloFiocchi 4 94
(Mario Hofer, Germany) *a cl up: shkn up to ld wl over 1f out: drvn clr ins fnl f: comf* **20/7**[3]

2 *2* **Biz Power (IRE)**[56] 2-8-11 0.................... SilvanoMulas 3 91
(Stefano Botti, Italy) *settled in 4th: rdn to chse ldr appr fnl f: styd on at same pce u.p* **9/4**[2]

3 *1 1/2* **Penalty (ITY)** 2-8-11 0.................... UmbertoRispoli 6 86
(Stefano Botti, Italy) *t.k.h in fnl pair: angled out and hdwy appr fnl f: styd on u.p: nt pce to get on terms* **76/100**[1]

4 *2* **Triticum Vulgare (IRE)** 2-8-11 0.................... LucaManiezzi 2 79
(F Saggiomo, Italy) *chsd ldr: cl up and ev ch 1 1/2f out: sn hrd rdn and nt qckn: grad lft bhd fnl f* **269/10**

5 *1/2* **Blu Marshall (ITY)**[56] 2-8-11 0.................... DarioVargiu 1 78
(Il Cavallo In Testa, Italy) *broke wl and led on stands' rail: hdd wl over 1f out: sn btn* **9/1**

6 *3* **Into The Wild (IRE)** 2-8-11 0.................... SalvatoreSulas 5 68
(A Peraino, Italy) *t.k.h: hld up in rr: hrd rdn and no imp ins fnl 2f: wl hld fr 1f out* **33/1**

1m 10.5s (-1.30) 6 Ran SP% **130.0**
WIN (incl. 1 euro stake): 3.86. PLACES: 2.09, 1.80. DF: 10.97.
Owner Stiftung Gestut Fahrhof **Bred** Gestut Fahrhof **Trained** Germany

3702 - 3703a (Foreign Racing) - See Raceform Interactive

[3148] MUSSELBURGH (R-H)
Monday, June 27

OFFICIAL GOING: Good (good to soft in places)
Wind: Fresh, half against Weather: Cloudy, bright

3704 RACING UK PROFITS RETURNED TO RACING APPRENTICE H'CAP 2m
6:10 (6:10) (Class 6) (0-65,61) 4-Y-O+ **£2,587** (£770; £384; £192) **Stalls** High

Form RPR

-061 **1** **Stoneham**[9] 3418 5-9-9 **58**.................... KevinStott 4 67
(Iain Jardine) *hld up in midfield: hmpd jst bef 1/2-way: hdwy 3f out: rdn to ld over 1f out: pushed clr ins fnl f* **3/1**[2]

4313 **2** *2 3/4* **Roc De Prince**[9] 3417 7-9-12 **61**....................(p) JoeDoyle 7 67
(Keith Dalgleish) *t.k.h: sn trcking ldrs on outside: led over 4f out: rdn and hdd over 1f out: kpt on ins fnl f: nt pce of wnr* **5/2**[1]

0056 **3** *1 1/2* **No Not Yet**[9] 3417 4-8-7 **45**.................... PhilDennis[(3)] 10 49
(Michael Dods) *t.k.h: trckd ldrs: rdn and hung rt over 2f out: rallied: kpt on same pce fnl f* **15/2**

-0P4 **4** *3/4* **Perennial**[9] 3418 7-9-0 **54**....................(p) RowanScott[(5)] 3 57
(Philip Kirby) *s.i.s: hld up: rdn over 2f out: effrt and swtchd lft over 1f out: edgd rt and kpt on fnl f: no imp* **10/1**

00-0 **5** *2 1/2* **Danzella**[9] 3418 4-8-7 **45**.................... NathanEvans[(3)] 5 45
(Chris Fairhurst) *hld up: effrt on ins whn short of room briefly 3f out: sn rdn: no imp fr over 1f out* **22/1**

0-40 **6** *4* **Pencaitland**[11] 3325 4-8-3 **45**.................... BenRobinson[(7)] 1 40
(Noel Wilson) *led or disp ld to over 4f out: rallied: rdn over 2f out: wknd wl over 1f out* **25/1**

-401 **7** *1* **Byronegetonefree**[23] 2916 5-8-11 **51**.................... AdamMcNamara[(5)] 8 45
(Stuart Coltherd) *prom: faltered jst bef 1/2-way: rdn and outpcd over 3f out: rallied and edgd lft over 2f out: wknd over 1f out* **13/2**[3]

0-10 **8** *1 1/4* **Van Mildert (IRE)**[11] 3325 7-8-11 **49**....................(p) JordanVaughan[(3)] 6 42
(Kenneth Slack) *hld up: hdwy on outside 3f out: sn rdn: wknd over 1f out* **7/1**

20-0 **9** *7* **Strikemaster (IRE)**[28] 2746 10-8-8 **48**....................(t) AnnaHesketh[(5)] 9 32
(Lee James) *s.i.s: hld up: pushed along over 3f out: struggling fnl 2f* **66/1**

20-0 **10** *6* **Goldan Jess (IRE)**[23] 2916 12-9-11 **60**.................... JacobButterfield 2 37
(Philip Kirby) *led or disp ld to over 4f out: rdn and wknd over 2f out* **25/1**

3m 37.64s (4.14) **Going Correction** +0.25s/f (Good) 10 Ran SP% **113.8**
Speed ratings (Par 101): **99,97,96,96,95 93,92,92,88,85**
CSF £10.11 CT £49.14 TOTE £3.80: £1.40, £2.20, £2.00; EX 12.30 Trifecta £92.80.
Owner The Dregs Of Humanity & Partner **Bred** Norman Court Stud **Trained** Carrutherstown, D'fries & G'way

FOCUS
All races on the round track were run over seven yards further than advertised. This was a low-grade apprentice handicap run at just an ordinary gallop. The form is straightforward rated around the front three.

3705 BRITISH STALLION STUDS EBF NOVICE STKS (PLUS 10 RACE) 7f 30y
6:40 (6:40) (Class 4) 2-Y-O **£4,204** (£1,251; £625; £312) **Stalls** Low

Form RPR

1 **1** **Monticello (IRE)**[17] 3108 2-9-8 0.................... JoeFanning 5 92+
(Mark Johnston) *mde all: shkn up and qcknd clr over 1f out: pushed out: readily* **5/6**[1]

03 **2** *5* **Wigan Warrior**[21] 2956 2-8-13 0.................... KevinStott[(3)] 6 72
(David Brown) *dwlt: sn chsng ldrs: pushed along 1/2-way: effrt and chsd (clr) wnr over 1f out: edgd rt: kpt on fnl f: no imp* **7/1**[3]

44 **3** *1 3/4* **Heatongrad (IRE)**[12] 3283 2-8-9 0.................... AdamMcNamara[(7)] 4 67
(Richard Fahey) *t.k.h: chsd wnr: rdn over 2f out: lost 2nd over 1f out: sn no ex* **9/4**[2]

4 *1 3/4* **Actualisation** 2-9-2 0.................... PhillipMakin 1 63
(John Quinn) *t.k.h: hld up in tch: rdn over 2f out: no imp fr wl over 1f out* **12/1**

5 **5** *1/2* **Miss Bates**[13] 3248 2-8-11 0.................... PJMcDonald 3 56
(Ann Duffield) *fly j. s: hld up: rdn along 3f out: outpcd fr 2f out* **28/1**

1m 30.29s (1.29) **Going Correction** +0.25s/f (Good) 5 Ran SP% **109.0**
Speed ratings (Par 95): **102,96,94,92,91**
CSF £7.17 TOTE £1.50: £1.10, £3.80; EX 6.90 Trifecta £9.30.
Owner Dr J Walker **Bred** Mrs C Regalado-Gonzalez **Trained** Middleham Moor, N Yorks

FOCUS
A novice event run at only a modest gallop, but an interesting winner who was again impressive.

3706 RACING WELFARE STABLE STAFF WEEK H'CAP 1m 4f 100y
7:10 (7:10) (Class 6) (0-65,65) 4-Y-O+ **£2,587** (£770; £384; £192) **Stalls** Low

Form RPR

6122 **1** **Henry Smith**[12] 3288 4-9-5 **63**....................(be) DavidAllan 3 70
(Garry Moss) *hld up in midfield: stdy hdwy over 2f out: rdn to ld over 1f out: edgd rt ins fnl f: kpt on wl* **7/2**[2]

6-03 **2** *1 1/4* **Gunner Lindley (IRE)**[4] 3547 9-8-13 **57**.................... JasonHart 9 62
(Stuart Coltherd) *chsd ldr: rdn over 2f out: pressed wnr fnl f: kpt on: hld towards fin* **25/1**

34-0 **3** *1 1/4* **Amirli (IRE)**[32] 2618 5-9-7 **65**.................... PJMcDonald 8 68
(Alistair Whillans) *prom: effrt and rdn over 2f out: ch over 1f out: one pce ins fnl f* **12/1**

005 **4** *hd* **Annigoni (IRE)**[14] 3212 4-8-6 **50**....................(p) JoeFanning 2 53
(Ruth Carr) *trckd ldrs: rdn to ld over 2f out: edgd lft: hdd over 1f out: kpt on same pce ins fnl f* **16/1**

1000 **5** *hd* **Gabrial The Terror (IRE)**[16] 3129 6-9-0 **65**.....(p) AdamMcNamara(7) 12 67
(Richard Fahey) *s.i.s: hld up: rdn along over 4f out: styd on wl fr 2f out: nt pce to chal* **12/1**

33/0 **6** *3 1/4* **Gold Show**[10] 3363 7-8-11 **58**.................... KevinStott(3) 11 55
(Grant Tuer) *hld up in midfield: hdwy and ev ch over 2f out: sn rdn: wknd ins fnl f* **20/1**

-530 **7** *1* **Neuf Des Coeurs**[4] 3564 5-8-11 **60**..............(p) GarryWhillans(5) 13 56
(Iain Jardine) *hld up: hdwy on outside to chse ldrs over 2f out: rdn: sn rdn: wknd fnl f* **14/1**

5404 **8** *4 1/2* **Thankyou Very Much**[9] 3417 6-8-7 **56**..............(p) NathanEvans(5) 4 44
(James Bethell) *hld up: rdn along over 2f out: sn no imp* **6/1**[3]

054 **9** *1/2* **Silva Samourai**[35] 2522 7-8-4 **48**.................... RaulDaSilva 10 36
(Susan Corbett) *dwlt: bhd: drvn along over 3f out: sme late hdwy: nvr on terms* **66/1**

00-1 **10** *2 3/4* **Tonto's Spirit**[16] 3154 4-8-5 **49**.................... AndrewMullen 6 32
(Kenneth Slack) *t.k.h: led: hung lft bnd after 3f: rdn and hdd over 2f out: wknd wl over 1f out* **2/1**[1]

-500 **11** *1/2* **Ronald Gee (IRE)**[23] 2911 9-9-6 **64**.................... PhillipMakin 7 46
(Jim Goldie) *hld up: stdy hdwy 3f out: rdn and wknd 2f out* **16/1**

-046 **12** *11* **Elle Dorado**[26] 2799 4-8-6 **50** ow1.................... SamJames 1 15
(David Loughnane) *prom: drvn and outpcd over 2f out: sn btn* **40/1**

13 *20* **Hubal (POL)**[22] 4-8-3 **52**....................(b[1]) PhilDennis(5) 14
(George Charlton) *chsd ldrs on outside: drvn along over 4f out: wknd over 3f out: t.o* **50/1**

/00- **14** *11* **Lipstickandpowder (IRE)**[136] 410 4-8-2 **46** oh1....... DuranFentiman 5
(Dianne Sayer) *bhd: struggling over 3f out: sn btn: t.o* **66/1**

2m 45.09s (3.09) **Going Correction** +0.25s/f (Good) **14** Ran SP% **119.7**
Speed ratings (Par 101): **99,98,97,97,97 94,94,91,90,89 88,81,68,60**
CSF £99.41 CT £958.59 TOTE £4.40: £1.30, £6.30, £3.10; EX 87.40 Trifecta £869.20.
Owner Pinnacle Duo Partnership **Bred** M Pennell **Trained** Wynyard, Stockton-On-Tees

FOCUS
A low-grade handicap run at a good gallop in which the first five finished clear. The winner remains fairly treated and continues his great run of form.

3707 RACINGUK.COM (S) STKS 5f
7:40 (7:40) (Class 5) 2-Y-O **£3,234** (£962; £481; £240) **Stalls** High

Form RPR

0 **1** **Franca Florio (IRE)**[17] 3112 2-8-4 0.................... JoeDoyle(3) 3 66+
(Kevin Ryan) *mde all: shkn up over 1f out: hung rt ins fnl f: kpt on strly* **13/8**[1]

2 *1 1/2* **Dandy Highwayman (IRE)** 2-8-9 0.............. JacobButterfield(3) 5 66
(Ollie Pears) *dwlt and sn crossed to stands' rail: sn green and outpcd: hdwy on outside over 1f out: chsd wnr ins fnl f: r.o* **6/1**[3]

05 **3** *2* **Samran Says (IRE)**[16] 3148 2-8-7 0.................... GeorgeChaloner 8 53
(Richard Fahey) *rrd s: in tch on outside: hdwy to chse wnr over 1f out to ins fnl f: no ex* **7/1**

2164 **4** *4* **Chevalier Du Lac (IRE)**[12] 3282 2-8-10 0............ AdamMcNamara(7) 4 49
(John Quinn) *trckd ldr to 1/2-way: cl up tl rdn and wknd over 1f out* **7/4**[2]

0250 **5** *15* **Poppy Pivot (IRE)**[14] 3208 2-8-7 0.................... PJMcDonald 7
(Ann Duffield) *dwlt and hmpd sn after s: sn chsng ldrs: wnt 2nd 1/2-way to over 1f out: sn wknd: lost tch ins fnl f* **14/1**

1m 2.45s (2.05) **Going Correction** +0.05s/f (Good) **5** Ran SP% **107.9**
Speed ratings (Par 93): **85,82,79,73,49**
CSF £10.92 TOTE £2.70: £2.00, £2.10; EX 12.50 Trifecta £41.90.There was no bid for the winner.
Owner FF Partners **Bred** Rathbarry Stud **Trained** Hambleton, N Yorks

FOCUS
A juvenile seller run at no more than a fair gallop in which several had problems at the start

3708 FORTICRETE H'CAP 7f 30y
8:10 (8:10) (Class 4) (0-80,79) 4-Y-O+ **£5,175** (£1,540; £769; £384) **Stalls** Low

Form RPR

2100 **1** **Slemy (IRE)**[9] 3419 5-9-6 **78**.................... JamesSullivan 9 85
(Ruth Carr) *stdd s: hld up: plenty to do 1/2-way: stdy hdwy over 2f out: rdn fnl f: kpt on strly to ld cl home* **13/2**

2613 **2** *nk* **Shamaheart (IRE)**[11] 3327 6-8-12 **73**..............(p) KevinStott(3) 5 79
(Geoffrey Harker) *hld up: stdy hdwy whn n.m.r over 2f out to over 1f out: swtchd lft and kpt on wl to take 2nd cl home: jst hld* **8/1**

1312 **3** *nse* **Bajan Rebel**[5] 3521 5-7-12 **61**.................... NathanEvans(5) 6 67+
(Michael Easterby) *led: rdn and hrd pressed fr over 2f out: kpt on wl fnl f: hdd and no ex cl home* **5/2**[1]

-023 **4** *shd* **Honeysuckle Lil (IRE)**[16] 3132 4-9-2 **74**..............(p) DavidAllan 3 80
(Tim Easterby) *chsd ldrs: drvn and ev ch over 1f out to ins fnl f: kpt on: hld cl home* **6/1**[3]

6300 **5** *1* **Ralphy Boy (IRE)**[10] 3344 7-9-2 **74**.................... PJMcDonald 1 77
(Alistair Whillans) *chsd ldr 2f: cl up: drvn over 2f out: rallied: one pce ins fnl f* **11/1**

-626 **6** *2 1/2* **Desire**[16] 3132 4-8-6 **64**....................(p) GeorgeChaloner 4 61
(Richard Fahey) *prom: rdn over 2f out: no ex whn checked 1f out: sn btn* **11/1**

123 **7** *hd* **Surewecan**[9] 3405 4-9-0 **72**.................... JoeFanning 2 68
(Mark Johnston) *cl up: wnt 2nd after 2f: ev ch over 2f out to over 1f out: wknd ins fnl f* **9/2**[2]

5650 **8** *1* **Rasaman (IRE)**[23] 2906 12-8-7 **65**.................... SamJames 11 58
(Jim Goldie) *hld up: rdn along over 2f out: outpcd fr over 1f out* **16/1**

-000 **9** *6* **Comino (IRE)**[30] 2679 5-9-4 **79**.................... JoeDoyle(3) 7 56
(Kevin Ryan) *hld up bhd ldng gp: rdn along over 2f out: sn wknd* **16/1**

1m 29.72s (0.72) **Going Correction** +0.25s/f (Good) **9** Ran SP% **113.9**
Speed ratings (Par 105): **105,104,104,104,103 100,100,99,92**
CSF £56.44 CT £163.75 TOTE £6.40: £2.20, £2.20, £1.40; EX 61.40 Trifecta £220.70.
Owner J A Swinburne **Bred** Derek Veitch **Trained** Huby, N Yorks

FOCUS
Exposed sorts in this handicap which was run at a strong pace, the winner came from last to first and only half a length covered the first four home.

3709 RACING UK NOW IN HD! H'CAP 5f
8:40 (8:40) (Class 5) (0-70,70) 3-Y-O+ **£3,234** (£962; £481; £240) **Stalls** High

Form RPR

2102 **1** **Fumbo Jumbo (IRE)**[24] 2854 3-9-6 **70**.................... DavidAllan 5 86
(Garry Moss) *mde all: shkn up and qcknd clr over 1f out: readily* **5/2**[2]

0423 **2** *4* **Flash City (ITY)**[11] 3326 8-9-12 **70**..............(b) JamesSullivan 6 74
(Ruth Carr) *stdd s: hld up: stdy hdwy over 2f out: effrt and rdn over 1f out: edgd rt and chsd wnr ins fnl f: kpt on: no imp* **4/1**[3]

5031 **3** *1* **Seamster**[6] 3484 9-9-0 **58**....................(t) SamJames 7 58
(David Loughnane) *rrd s: sn pressing ldr: drvn wl over 1f out: no ex and lost 2nd ins fnl f* **9/4**[1]

0-30 **4** *1 3/4* **Pavers Star**[13] 3268 7-8-11 **55**....................(p) JoeFanning 9 49
(Noel Wilson) *trckd ldrs: rdn over 2f out: edgd rt and outpcd fnl f* **28/1**

6430 **5** *3/4* **Bunce (IRE)**[16] 3150 8-9-5 **63**.................... PJMcDonald 2 54
(Linda Perratt) *hld up in tch: drvn along 1/2-way: no imp fr over 1f out* **25/1**

5501 **6** *1 1/4* **Searanger (USA)**[9] 3423 3-8-10 **67**.................... RowanScott(7) 1 52
(Ann Duffield) *hld up: drvn along over 2f out: sn outpcd: n.d after* **9/1**

4304 **7** *2* **Pushkin Museum (IRE)**[11] 3307 5-9-3 **68**..........(v) AdamMcNamara(7) 4 47
(Richard Fahey) *prom: drvn along over 2f out: edgd lft and wknd over 1f out* **8/1**

056 **8** *6* **Henry Morgan**[6] 3484 9-8-8 **52**.................... AndrewMullen 3 10
(David Brown) *dwlt: sn in tch on outside: struggling 1/2-way: btn over 1f out* **28/1**

1m 0.18s (-0.22) **Going Correction** +0.05s/f (Good)
WFA 3 from 5yo+ 6lb **8** Ran SP% **111.2**
Speed ratings (Par 103): **103,96,95,92,91 89,85,76**
CSF £12.05 CT £23.29 TOTE £3.10: £1.30, £1.50, £1.30; EX 11.70 Trifecta £25.40.
Owner Pinnacle Four Partnership **Bred** Tally-Ho Stud **Trained** Wynyard, Stockton-On-Tees

FOCUS
A seemingly competitive sprint for the grade with several coming into the race in good form, but a wide-margin and easy winner.

3710 WATCH RACING UK IN HD H'CAP 1m
9:10 (9:12) (Class 6) (0-65,62) 3-Y-O **£2,587** (£770; £384; £192) **Stalls** Low

Form RPR

0002 **1** **Causey Arch (IRE)**[12] 3287 3-9-5 **60**..............(p) ConnorBeasley 9 68
(Michael Dods) *pressed ldr: led over 3f out: edgd lft appr fnl f: drvn clr* **13/8**[1]

0040 **2** *2 3/4* **Toffee Apple (IRE)**[62] 1734 3-8-4 **45**.................... JoeFanning 4 46+
(Keith Dalgleish) *hld up: effrt and pushed along over 2f out: hdwy to chse (clr) wnr ins fnl f: kpt on: nt pce to chal* **6/1**[3]

00-0 **3** *1/2* **Bahrikate**[25] 2835 3-8-4 **45**.................... JamesSullivan 3 45
(Michael Herrington) *trckd ldrs: effrt and wnt 2nd over 2f out: edgd lft over 1f out: lost 2nd and no ex ins fnl f* **50/1**

406 **4** *1/2* **Yours Forever**[34] 2557 3-9-0 **58**.................... KevinStott(3) 6 57
(Kevin Ryan) *hld up towards rr: hdwy over 2f out: drvn and effrt over 1f out: kpt on same pce fnl f* **8/1**

4140 **5** *nk* **Frap**[16] 3130 3-9-0 **62**.................... AdamMcNamara(7) 1 60
(Richard Fahey) *prom: drvn along over 2f out: effrt on outside over 1f out: no imp fnl f* **3/1**[2]

054- **6** *1 3/4* **She's Golden**[265] 7020 3-9-7 **62**.................... PJMcDonald 7 56
(Ann Duffield) *s.i.s: sn wl bhd: hdwy over 2f out: kpt on fnl f: n.d* **16/1**

-640 **7** *14* **Chookie Valentine**[19] 3020 3-8-7 **48**.................... JasonHart 5 8
(Keith Dalgleish) *dwlt: hld up: drvn and outpcd 3f out: btn fnl 2f* **8/1**

0604 **8** *14* **Bazula (IRE)**[19] 3014 3-9-3 **58**....................(b) DavidAllan 8
(Tim Easterby) *t.k.h: led to over 3f out: wknd over 2f out: eased whn btn ins fnl f* **16/1**

50-0 **9** *14* **Ingleby Erin**[6] 3482 3-8-4 **50**....................(p) NathanEvans(5) 2
(Michael Easterby) *prom: rdn along over 4f out: wknd over 3f out: t.o* **25/1**

1m 42.69s (1.49) **Going Correction** +0.25s/f (Good) **9** Ran SP% **117.2**
Speed ratings (Par 97): **102,99,98,98,97 96,82,68,54**
CSF £12.19 CT £351.20 TOTE £2.90: £1.60, £1.90, £7.30; EX 13.70 Trifecta £582.10.
Owner J A Wynn-Williams & D Neale **Bred** Irish National Stud **Trained** Denton, Co Durham

FOCUS
A low-grade handicap in which they set off fast, but the pace slowed at halfway. The winner won decisively in the end.
T/Plt: £25.30 to a £1 stake. Pool: £64,683.98 - 1863.19 winning units. T/Qpdt: £11.90 to a £1 stake. Pool: £5,517.36 - 895.26 winning units. **Richard Young**

3433 PONTEFRACT (L-H)
Monday, June 27

OFFICIAL GOING: Good to firm (good in places; 8.4)
Wind: fine Weather: fresh 1/2 behind

3711 AUDREY MARTIN MEMORIAL LADIES' H'CAP (LADY AMATEUR RIDERS) 1m 2f 6y
2:00 (2:01) (Class 5) (0-75,74) 3-Y-O+ **£3,119** (£967; £483; £242) **Stalls** Low

Form RPR

4022 **1** **Belle Travers**[12] 3291 4-10-0 **74**.................... MissEmilyBullock(7) 12 85
(Richard Fahey) *swtchd lft after s: trckd ldrs: 2nd over 2f out: led over 1f out: sn clr: drvn out* **10/1**

422 **2** *4 1/2* **Obboorr**[32] 2616 7-9-12 **70**.................... MissHDukes(5) 4 72
(Tim Fitzgerald) *hld up in mid-div: hdwy on ins over 3f out: kpt on to take modest 2nd last 100yds* **11/2**[2]

0212 **3** *1 1/4* **Wotabreeze (IRE)**[25] 2831 3-9-4 **69**.................... MissSBrotherton 5 69+
(John Quinn) *mid-div: hdwy over 2f out: swtchd rt over 1f out: kpt on wl clsng stages to take modest 3rd* **3/1**[1]

0051 **4** *1 1/4* **Mustaqbal (IRE)**[10] 3366 4-10-0 **74**.................... MissSEDods(7) 11 71
(Michael Dods) *swtchd lft after s: trckd ldrs: hung lft over 1f out: kpt on clsng stages: tk modest 4th line* **12/1**

1602 **5** *hd* **Duke Of Yorkshire**[4] 3547 6-9-2 **60**..............(b) MissEEasterby(5) 13 57
(Tim Easterby) *swtchd lft after s: led: hdd over 1f out: wknd clsng stages* **16/1**

-346 **6** *2* **Qibtee (FR)**[18] 3052 6-9-6 **59**.................... MissADeniel 2 52
(Les Eyre) *dwlt: hld up in rr: hdwy over 2f out: swtchd rt over 1f out: kpt on same pce* **8/1**[3]

0-00 **7** *6* **Correggio**[16] 3166 6-10-4 **74**.................... MissBeckySmith(3) 6 55
(Micky Hammond) *mid-div: effrt over 2f out: chsng ldrs over 1f out: wknd fnl 150yds* **14/1**

2303 **8** *16* **Heart Locket**[12] 3278 4-10-7 **74**.................... MissJoannaMason 14 23
(Michael Easterby) *swtchd lft after s: w ldrs: t.k.h: lost pl over 2f out* **20/1**

246- **9** *5* **Triassic (IRE)**[240] 7630 3-8-10 **66**.................... MissEmmaBedford(5) 1 5
(Mark Johnston) *chsd ldr: lost pl over 2f out: sn bhd* **3/1**[1]

150/ **10** *1 3/4* **Attraction Ticket**[215] 7994 7-9-7 **63**..............(tp) MissETodd(3) 10
(Joanne Foster) *in rr: drvn over 4f out: bhd fnl 2f* **100/1**

-600 **11** *5* **Splash Of Verve (IRE)**[68] 1561 4-9-2 **58**.................... MissAWaugh(3) 8
(Philip Kirby) *s.s: t.k.h in rr: hdwy over 5f out: lost pl over 2f out: sn bhd* **20/1**

00-0 **P** **Kisumu**[17] 3118 4-9-12 **65** MissCWalton 9
(Micky Hammond) *in rr: hdwy on outside over 5f out: sn drvn: mid-div whn sddle slipped and p.u over 2f out* **33/1**

2m 14.72s (1.02) **Going Correction** +0.225s/f (Good)
WFA 3 from 4yo+ 12lb **12** Ran SP% **119.3**
Speed ratings (Par 103): **104,100,99,98,98 96,91,79,75,73 69,**
CSF £62.14 CT £209.84 TOTE £10.10: £3.50, £1.90, £1.40; EX 48.50 Trifecta £109.80.
Owner H J P Farr **Bred** Worksop Manor Stud **Trained** Musley Bank, N Yorks

FOCUS
A fair handicap for amateur riders. The gallop was fairly sedate initially, not really picking up until after 2f or so, and the pace held up. After rail movements the actual race distance was 1m2f 14yds.

3712 EBF STALLIONS SPINDRIFTER CONDITIONS STKS (PLUS 10 RACE) 6f
2:35 (2:37) (Class 2) 2-Y-O **£11,205** (£3,355; £1,677; £838) **Stalls** Low

Form RPR
1 **1** **Love Dreams (IRE)**[12] 3283 2-8-12 0 SilvestreDeSousa 2 93+
(Mark Johnston) *mde all: pushed along over 2f out: clr over 1f out: eased clsng stages* **8/11**[1]
20 **2** *5* **Bolt Phantom (USA)**[13] 3247 2-8-12 0 PaulMulrennan 1 76
(Ismail Mohammed) *dwlt: sn trcking ldng pair: 2nd over 2f out: kpt on same pce over 1f out: no ch w wnr* **3/1**[3]
1 **3** *½* **Scofflaw**[30] 2682 2-8-12 0 TonyHamilton 3 75
(Richard Fahey) *w wnr: drvn over 2f out: hung lft over 1f out: kpt on same pce* **11/4**[2]
402 **4** *39* **Smiley Riley (IRE)**[17] 3114 2-8-12 0 BarryMcHugh 4
(Tony Coyle) *sn outpcd and detached in last: bhd fnl 2f: heavily eased last 100yds: t.o* **50/1**

1m 17.68s (0.78) **Going Correction** +0.225s/f (Good) **4** Ran SP% **111.5**
Speed ratings (Par 99): **103,96,95,43**
CSF £3.44 TOTE £1.60; EX 3.60 Trifecta £4.80.
Owner Crone Stud Farms Ltd **Bred** John O'Connor **Trained** Middleham Moor, N Yorks

FOCUS
A really taking performance from the winner who looks ready for a higher grade. After rail movements the actual race distance was 6f 8yds.

3713 ROSE BEATTIE - A LIFETIME IN RACING H'CAP 5f
3:05 (3:06) (Class 5) (0-75,74) 3-Y-O+ **£3,234** (£962; £481; £240) **Stalls** Low

Form RPR
6522 **1** **Oriental Splendour (IRE)**[14] 3217 4-9-6 **66** JamesSullivan 10 76+
(Ruth Carr) *swtchd rt after s: hld up towards rr: hdwy and swtchd rt over 1f out: styd on wl to ld last 50yds* **15/2**
3124 **2** *1 ½* **Henley**[11] 3326 4-9-9 **69** ConnorBeasley 11 74
(Tracy Waggott) *w ldr: led 2f out: hdd and no ex last 50yds* **11/1**
6530 **3** *hd* **Groundworker (IRE)**[25] 2808 5-9-6 **66** BarryMcHugh 13 70
(Paul Midgley) *swtchd lft after s: chsd ldrs: upsides over 1f out: kpt on same pce last 50yds* **25/1**
3554 **4** *3 ½* **Ambitious Icarus**[6] 3494 7-9-12 **72** (e) RoystonFfrench 9 64
(Richard Guest) *in rr and sn drvn along: hdwy on outside over 1f out: kpt on to take modest 4th last 50yds* **12/1**
56-4 **5** *2 ¾* **Sandra's Secret (IRE)**[28] 2742 3-9-2 **68** PaulHanagan 3 48+
(Les Eyre) *mid-div: effrt and chsng ldrs over 2f out: wknd fnl f* **7/2**[1]
3240 **6** *½* **You're Cool**[119] 764 4-9-10 **70** GrahamGibbons 8 50
(John Balding) *led: hdd over 2f out: wknd fnl f* **25/1**
13-0 **7** *1* **Outrage**[51] 2040 4-9-11 **71** LukeMorris 5 47
(Daniel Kubler) *in rr: drvn over 2f out: nvr on terms* **14/1**
-426 **8** *1* **Ruby's Day**[18] 3056 7-9-11 **71** TomEaves 14 44
(David Brown) *in rr: hdwy and hung bdly lft over 1f out: n.m.r: kpt on one pce* **12/1**
-000 **9** *¾* **Aprovado (IRE)**[11] 3326 4-9-12 **72** (p) PaulMulrennan 4 42
(Michael Dods) *chsd ldrs: rdn over 2f out: lost pl over 1f out* **7/1**[3]
4332 **10** *nk* **Hit The Lights (IRE)**[11] 3322 6-9-1 **68** (v) DannielleMooney(7) 2 37
(David Nicholls) *half-rrd s: sn in mid-div: effrt on ins over 2f out: wknd over 1f out* **5/1**[2]
6000 **11** *1 ¼* **Uptight (FR)**[16] 3168 4-10-0 **74** (b) ShaneGray 1 39
(Kevin Ryan) *chsd ldrs: drvn over 2f out: lost pl over 1f out* **12/1**
1116 **12** *1* **Roy's Legacy**[11] 3307 7-9-2 **67** CharlieBennett(5) 15 28
(Shaun Harris) *stmbld s: swtchd lft after s: chsd ldrs on outer: effrt over 2f out: sn lost pl* **33/1**
5206 **13** *¾* **Daylight**[7] 3474 6-9-5 **65** (t) CamHardie 7 23
(Michael Easterby) *chsd ldrs: lost pl over 2f out: eased clsng stages* **14/1**

1m 3.71s (0.41) **Going Correction** +0.225s/f (Good)
WFA 3 from 4yo+ 6lb **13** Ran SP% **118.5**
Speed ratings (Par 103): **105,102,102,96,92 91,89,88,87,86 84,83,81**
CSF £84.82 CT £1285.04 TOTE £8.80: £2.80, £4.10, £8.70; EX 103.40 Trifecta £3974.80.
Owner M Baldam & Mrs R Carr **Bred** H R H Sultan Ahmad Shah **Trained** Huby, N Yorks

FOCUS
Just a run-of-the-mill handicap rated around the second and third, but the winner deserves credit for coming from well off the pace to collar a pair who weren't stopping, the three of them nicely clear of the rest. The actual race distance was 5f8yds.

3714 EBF STALLIONS ALAN MERCER 60TH BIRTHDAY FILLIES' H'CAP 6f
3:40 (3:43) (Class 3) (0-90,90) 3-Y-O+
£9,337 (£2,796; £1,398; £699; £349; £175) **Stalls** Low

Form RPR
0660 **1** **Gran Canaria Queen**[17] 3116 7-8-10 **77** RachelRichardson(5) 8 87
(Tim Easterby) *hld up in mid-div: hdwy on outside wl over 1f out: edgd lft and led last 100yds: drvn out* **8/1**
0061 **2** *¾* **Dutch Mist**[21] 2972 3-9-0 **83** (b) KeaganLatham 11 88
(Kevin Ryan) *swtchd lft after s: in rr: hdwy on wd outside wl over 1f out: edgd rt: kpt on to take 2nd clsng stages* **5/1**[1]
0-43 **3** *1 ¼* **Appleberry (IRE)**[14] 3218 4-8-13 **75** (p) DougieCostello 1 78
(Michael Appleby) *led: hung rt: hdd and no ex last 100yds* **16/1**
242- **4** *1 ¾* **Gale Song**[242] 7578 3-8-8 **77** LukeMorris 6 72
(Ed Walker) *dwlt: hld up towards rr: hdwy over 2f out: chsng ldrs over 1f out: kpt on same pce* **11/2**[2]
00-4 **5** *½* **Rosie's Premiere (IRE)**[24] 2875 4-9-11 **90** JackDuern(3) 4 86
(Dean Ivory) *chsd ldrs: drvn over 2f out: one pce over 1f out: kpt on towards fin* **5/1**[1]
6-06 **6** *1 ¼* **Zaina Rizeena**[14] 3213 3-8-5 **74** PaulHanagan 7 64
(Richard Fahey) *n.m.r sn after s: sn trcking ldrs: effrt over 1f out: one pce* **6/1**[3]
10-0 **7** *4* **Azhar**[44] 2237 3-9-4 **87** (p) WilliamBuick 3 64
(Saeed bin Suroor) *hmpd s: t.k.h towards rr: effrt and outpcd over 2f out: nvr a factor* **20/1**
1213 **8** *½* **Baileys Mirage (FR)**[12] 3279 5-9-9 **85** (b) SilvestreDeSousa 9 62
(Chris Dwyer) *w ldr: wkng whn n.m.r 100yds out: sn eased* **8/1**
-045 **9** *7* **Lady Clair (IRE)**[17] 3116 3-9-5 **88** JoeyHaynes 10 41
(K R Burke) *chsd ldrs: drvn over 2f out: lost pl over 1f out: heavily eased clsng stages* **12/1**

1m 17.66s (0.76) **Going Correction** +0.225s/f (Good)
WFA 3 from 4yo+ 7lb **9** Ran SP% **103.6**
Speed ratings (Par 104): **103,102,100,98,97 95,90,89,80**
CSF £38.83 CT £456.19 TOTE £8.80: £2.10, £2.10, £3.70; EX 47.80 Trifecta £451.90.
Owner The Senators **Bred** H Moszkowicz And Whitsbury Manor Stud **Trained** Great Habton, N Yorks
■ Sabrewing was withdrawn. Price at time of withdrawal 7-1. Rule 4 applies to all bets - deduction 10p in the pound.

FOCUS
A fairly useful fillies event which was well run, the leading pair both coming from off the pace and the third possibly deserving of a little extra credit after seeing things out a lot better than her fellow pacesetter. The actual race distance was 6f 8yds.

3715 WAYNE CONWAY MEMORIAL H'CAP 1m 4f 8y
4:10 (4:10) (Class 5) (0-70,70) 3-Y-O **£3,234** (£962; £481; £240) **Stalls** Low

Form RPR
5-00 **1** **Alquffaal**[16] 3160 3-9-6 **69** PaulHanagan 9 85+
(Roger Varian) *hld up towards rr: hdwy 5f out: effrt on outside over 2f out: edgd lft and led 1f out: rdn clr: readily* **9/2**
5-44 **2** *3 ½* **Zubeida**[18] 3063 3-9-5 **68** (p) SilvestreDeSousa 1 77
(Ismail Mohammed) *led: drvn over 2f out: hdd 1f out: kpt on same pce* **11/4**[1]
-323 **3** *5* **Kajaki (IRE)**[19] 3025 3-9-7 **70** (p) TomEaves 2 71
(Kevin Ryan) *sn chsng ldrs: drvn over 3f out: one pce appr fnl f* **4/1**[3]
4226 **4** *1 ½* **Adherence**[27] 2772 3-8-11 **60** BarryMcHugh 3 59
(Tony Coyle) *stdd s: hld up in rr: hdwy to chse ldrs over 3f out: rdn over 2f out: one pce* **12/1**
-526 **5** *2 ½* **Duck A L'Orange (IRE)**[18] 3063 3-9-7 **70** WilliamBuick 4 65
(Michael Bell) *trckd ldrs: drvn over 3f out: hung lft over 1f out: grad wknd* **5/1**
-415 **6** *15* **Tyrannical**[21] 2967 3-8-5 **54** LukeMorris 6 25
(Sir Mark Prescott Bt) *trckd ldr: rdn over 2f out: wknd over 1f out: eased clsng stages* **7/2**[2]
030 **7** *1 ½* **The Detainee**[25] 2815 3-9-3 **66** AdamBeschizza 8 34
(Jeremy Gask) *in rr: reminders over 5f out: lost pl over 3f out: sn bhd* **28/1**
-565 **8** *30* **Calypso Delegator (IRE)**[14] 3215 3-8-4 **53** JoeyHaynes 5
(Micky Hammond) *chsd ldrs: drvn over 5f out: lost pl over 2f out: sn wl bhd: eased whn t.o fnl f: eventually completed* **50/1**

2m 41.07s (0.27) **Going Correction** +0.225s/f (Good) **8** Ran SP% **116.8**
Speed ratings (Par 99): **108,105,102,101,99 89,88,68**
CSF £17.74 CT £53.65 TOTE £5.50: £1.70, £1.70, £1.60; EX 22.90 Trifecta £102.50.
Owner Hamdan Al Maktoum **Bred** Shadwell Estate Company Limited **Trained** Newmarket, Suffolk

FOCUS
A one-sided handicap, the easy winner much improved switched to handicaps and a longer trip. The runner-up dictated what looked no more than a modest gallop, gradually increasing the tempo in the final 4f. The actual race distance was 1m4f 16yds.

3716 WILFRED UNDERWOOD MEMORIAL CLASSIFIED STKS 6f
4:40 (4:42) (Class 5) 3-Y-O **£3,234** (£962; £481; £240) **Stalls** Low

Form RPR
2522 **1** **Highly Sprung (IRE)**[8] 3439 3-9-0 75 SilvestreDeSousa 4 81
(Mark Johnston) *n.m.r sn after s: in rr: drvn and modest 3rd over 2f out: styd on wl fnl f: led post* **10/3**[2]
3221 **2** *hd* **Rococoa (IRE)**[18] 3069 3-9-0 73 LukeMorris 1 80
(Ed Walker) *chsd ldrs: modest 2nd over 2f out: styd on fnl f: led nr fin: hdd post* **2/1**[1]
2214 **3** *½* **Geno (IRE)**[10] 3360 3-9-0 74 (b) ShaneGray 8 79
(Kevin Ryan) *swtchd lft after s: led: wnt abt 4 l clr over 2f out: hdd and no ex nr fin* **28/1**
4154 **4** *4 ½* **Van Gerwen**[21] 2972 3-9-0 74 PaulHanagan 7 64
(Les Eyre) *trckd ldrs on outer: t.k.h: outpcd and lost pl over 2f out: hdwy and edgd rt over 1f out: tk modest 4th nr fin* **10/1**[3]
21 **5** *1* **Get Up And Dance**[31] 2667 3-9-0 75 OisinMurphy 3 61
(William Haggas) *sltly hmpd s: in rr: effrt on inner over 2f out: modest 4th over 1f out: fdd clsng stages* **2/1**[1]
0-03 **6** *2 ¼* **Dark Forest**[31] 2657 3-9-0 72 DougieCostello 6 54
(Simon West) *trckd ldrs on outer: t.k.h: effrt over 2f out: wknd over 1f out* **40/1**
-525 **7** *2 ½* **King Of Swing**[41] 2337 3-9-0 74 TomEaves 5 46
(James Given) *trckd ldrs: t.k.h: effrt over 2f out: lost pl over 1f out* **14/1**
3000 **8** *12* **Heraldic (USA)**[23] 2917 3-9-0 74 WilliamBuick 2 8
(Mark Johnston) *wnt sltly rt s: chsd ldrs: lost pl over 2f out: bhd whn eased clsng stages* **25/1**

1m 17.37s (0.47) **Going Correction** +0.225s/f (Good) **8** Ran SP% **115.2**
Speed ratings (Par 99): **105,104,104,98,96 93,90,74**
CSF £10.34 TOTE £6.90: £2.30, £1.10, £5.50; EX 11.80 Trifecta £134.80.
Owner Douglas Livingston **Bred** Patrick J Moloney **Trained** Middleham Moor, N Yorks

FOCUS
Fairly useful form from the principals in this classified event. The third attempted to nick it from the front, going around 4l clear after halfway but tiring late on. The winner has been rated to his best.

3717 LES WARD MEMORIAL H'CAP 1m 4y
5:10 (5:10) (Class 4) (0-80,78) 3-Y-O+ **£5,175** (£1,540; £769; £384) **Stalls** Low

Form RPR
5000 **1** **Shouranour (IRE)**[16] 3166 6-9-6 **75** (b[1]) JoshDoyle(5) 9 84
(Alan Brown) *chsd ldrs: led 2f out: edgd rt: kpt on fnl f: jst hld on* **25/1**
-340 **2** *nk* **Trinity Star (IRE)**[16] 3166 5-9-12 **76** (p) PaulMulrennan 8 84
(Michael Dods) *in rr: effrt 3f out: styd on over 1f out: styd on wl fnl 75yds: jst hld* **15/2**
-561 **3** *½* **Hanseatic**[15] 3185 7-9-11 **75** CamHardie 1 82
(Michael Easterby) *s.i.s: sn chsng ldrs: chsd wnr over 1f out: kpt on same pce last 50yds* **3/1**[1]
0013 **4** *1 ¾* **Auspicion**[16] 3166 4-10-0 **78** AndrewElliott 7 81+
(Tom Tate) *trckd ldrs: n.m.r and lost pl over 3f out: reminders over 2f out: rallied and modest 3rd 1f out: kpt on same pce* **6/1**
5564 **5** *1 ¾* **Energia Flavio (BRZ)**[10] 3364 5-9-11 **75** PaulHanagan 5 74
(Richard Fahey) *in rr: hdwy on outer over 1f out: kpt on same pce to take 5th nr fin* **11/2**[3]

3342 **6** ½ **Sands Chorus**[11] 3324 4-10-0 **78**.. TomEaves 3 76
(James Given) *trckd ldrs: one pce appr fnl f* **9/2**[2]

6525 **7** 1 ½ **Kiwi Bay**[21] 2959 11-9-12 **76**.. TonyHamilton 12 70
(Michael Dods) *hld up in rr: hdwy 3f out: drvn and n.m.r over 1f out: nvr a factor* **28/1**

4-00 **8** 10 **Ivors Involvement (IRE)**[11] 3327 4-9-0 **64**..................(e[1]) JoeyHaynes 2 35
(Tina Jackson) *s.s: hdwy to chse ldrs over 4f out: lost pl over 1f out: sn bhd and eased* **100/1**

6022 **9** 7 **Rosy Morning (IRE)**[8] 3438 3-8-13 **73**............................ WilliamBuick 4 26
(Mark Johnston) *led: hdd and hung lft 2f out: wknd fnl f: eased and bhd clsng stages* **9/2**[2]

0000 **10** 10 **Border Bandit (USA)**[3] 3605 8-9-1 **65**..................(v[1]) DougieCostello 10
(Tracy Waggott) *chsd ldrs: effrt over 2f out: lost pl over 1f out: eased whn bhd clsng stages* **25/1**

1m 46.6s (0.70) **Going Correction** +0.225s/f (Good)
WFA 3 from 4yo+ 10lb **10** Ran SP% **114.9**
Speed ratings (Par 105): **105,104,104,102,100 100,98,88,81,71**
CSF £193.09 CT £755.03 TOTE £26.90: £7.30, £2.40, £1.40; EX 301.70 Trifecta £1486.90.
Owner David Lumley **Bred** His Highness The Aga Khan's Studs S C **Trained** Yedingham, N Yorks

FOCUS
A fair handicap, the runner-up catching the eye as he finished with a flourish, while the winner was on a good mark. The actual race distance was 1m 12yds.
T/Jkpt: Not won. T/Plt: £193.40 to a £1 stake. Pool: £81,362.31 - 307.05 winning units. T/Qpdt: £48.30 to a £1 stake. Pool: £6,788.82 - 103.80 winning units. **Walter Glynn**

3684 WINDSOR (R-H)
Monday, June 27

OFFICIAL GOING: Good to soft (6.2)
Wind: Moderate, behind Weather: Fine but cloudy

3718 ANDREW AND CHRISTOPHER WEATHERBY MEMORIAL EBF STALLIONS MEDIAN AUCTION MDN FILLIES' STKS (PLUS 10) 5f 10y
5:55 (5:57) (Class 5) 2-Y-O **£3,234** (£962; £481; £240) **Stalls** Low

Form RPR

22 **1** **Paco's Angel**[16] 3143 2-9-0 0.. ShaneKelly 3 74
(Richard Hughes) *pressed ldr: rdn to ld over 1f out: drvn out and hld on nr fin* **2/5**[1]

6 **2** nk **Cool Echo**[26] 2793 2-9-0 0.. FrederikTylicki 1 73
(J R Jenkins) *outpcd and adrift in last pair after 2f: gd prog jst over 2f out: drvn to chse wnr ins fnl f: clsd at fin: jst hld* **12/1**

3 2 ¾ **Suffragette City (IRE)** 2-8-11 0........................ TomMarquand(3) 5 63
(Richard Hannon) *dwlt: sn chsd ldrs: rdn wl over 1f out and hanging lft: outpcd sn after: kpt on to snatch 3rd last stride* **11/2**[2]

4 shd **Rosie Briar** 2-9-0 0.. DavidProbert 4 63
(Andrew Balding) *pressed ldrs: stl wl there jst over 1f out: fdd ins fnl f* **9/1**[3]

5 shd **Equimou** 2-9-0 0.. WilliamCarson 6 62
(Robert Eddery) *led: rdn and hdd over 1f out: wknd ins fnl f* **25/1**

0 **6** 8 **Kadi (IRE)**[16] 3122 2-9-0 0.. JFEgan 7 34
(Joseph Tuite) *chsd ldrs but sn pushed along: drvn over 2f out: wknd wl over 1f out* **40/1**

7 1 ¼ **Whatalove** 2-9-0 0.. TomQueally 2 29
(Martin Keighley) *slowly away: a bhd* **66/1**

1m 0.97s (0.67) **Going Correction** +0.10s/f (Good) **7** Ran SP% **112.3**
Speed ratings (Par 90): **98,97,93,92,92 80,78**
CSF £6.15 TOTE £1.30: £1.10, £4.90; EX 5.90 Trifecta £12.60.
Owner Biddestone Racing Partnership XVII **Bred** Biddestone Stud Ltd **Trained** Upper Lambourn, Berkshire

FOCUS
Inner of straight dolled out 10yds at 6f and 8yds at the winning line. Top bend dolled out 7yds from normal inner configuration, adding 28yds to race distances of 1m and over. Drying ground, with it changed to good to soft, and they came down the centre of the narrowed track in this modest maiden. The winner has been rated to her pre-race form.

3719 SPINAL RESEARCH (S) STKS 6f
6:25 (6:25) (Class 6) 3-Y-O+ **£2,264** (£673; £336; £168) **Stalls** Low

Form RPR

5-05 **1** **Magical Daze**[24] 2846 4-8-12 72.. PatDobbs 3 59
(Sylvester Kirk) *trckd ldrs: prog to cl 3rd 2f out: chsd ldr jst over 1f out: drvn and styd on to ld last strides* **6/5**[1]

5545 **2** shd **Ocean Legend (IRE)**[25] 2821 11-9-1 62..................... JoshuaBryan(7) 1 69
(Tony Carroll) *cl up: squeezed through against nr side rail to ld over 1f out: edgd lft after: kpt on u.p fnl f: hdd last strides* **6/1**[3]

445 **3** 1 ¾ **Time Medicean**[61] 1782 10-9-0 61........................ GeorgeDowning(3) 5 58
(Tony Carroll) *in tch in last pair: shkn up over 2f out: styd on take 3rd ins fnl f: nvr able to threaten* **10/1**

0530 **4** 1 ¾ **Robert The Painter (IRE)**[9] 3405 8-9-3 72....................(v) KierenFox 6 53
(Lee Carter) *pressed ldr: pushed along after 2f: lost 2nd 2f out: fdd* **9/4**[2]

3600 **5** nk **Presto Boy**[16] 3146 4-8-10 45........................ StephanieJoannides(7) 4 52
(Richard Hughes) *awkward s: t.k.h: hld up: gng strly but nt clr run over 2f out: to jst over 1f out: pushed along and no prog after* **50/1**

0-00 **6** 1 ¾ **Dismantle (IRE)**[35] 2537 3-8-5 60.. JFEgan 2 40
(Grace Harris) *led to over 1f out: imped sn after and wknd* **20/1**

1m 14.2s (1.20) **Going Correction** +0.10s/f (Good)
WFA 3 from 4yo+ 7lb **6** Ran SP% **106.3**
Speed ratings (Par 101): **96,95,93,91,90 88**
CSF £7.90 TOTE £1.90: £1.30, £2.40; EX 7.50 Trifecta £22.90.Winner was sold to Dave Penman for £5,000
Owner Timothy Pearson **Bred** The Pocock Family **Trained** Upper Lambourn, Berks
■ Stewards' Enquiry : Joshua Bryan caution: careless riding

FOCUS
Race distance as advertised. The favourite was best in at the weights and barely got it done.

3720 CRESTA RUN MAIDEN FILLIES' STKS 6f
6:55 (6:55) (Class 5) 3-4-Y-O **£2,911** (£866; £432; £216) **Stalls** Low

Form RPR

360 **1** **Nightingale Valley**[20] 2998 3-9-0 73.. TomQueally 8 78
(Stuart Kittow) *in tch: prog 1/2-way to chse ldr 2f out: rdn to ld jst over 1f out: pushed out last 100yds* **9/2**[2]

40 **2** ¾ **Poole Belle (IRE)**[24] 2877 3-9-0 0.. FergusSweeney 7 75
(Henry Candy) *w ldr: led 1/2-way: rdn 2f out: hdd jst over 1f out: styd on but safely hld* **13/2**

2063 **3** 3 ½ **Greenfyre (IRE)**[15] 3197 3-8-11 67........................ TomMarquand(3) 5 63
(Richard Hannon) *chsd ldrs: drvn over 2f out: nvr gng pce to threaten but kpt on u.p fnl f* **7/2**[1]

0 **4** 1 ½ **Atalante**[68] 1577 3-9-0 0.. DavidProbert 4 59
(Andrew Balding) *in tch: prog on outer and cl up 1/2-way: rdn 2f out: fdd fnl f* **7/2**[1]

00 **5** ¾ **Apache Myth**[33] 2578 3-9-0 0.. RyanTate 9 56
(James Eustace) *settled in last pair: pushed along fr 1/2-way: kpt on to take 5th fnl f: n.d* **8/1**

60- **6** 5 **Pintle's Image**[243] 7554 4-9-7 0.. SamHitchcott 1 42
(John Spearing) *shoved along in last after 2f: brief effrt over 2f out: nvr a factor* **33/1**

00 **7** ¾ **Archipentura**[42] 2312 4-9-7 0.. FrederikTylicki 2 40
(J R Jenkins) *dropped to rr after 2f: rdn and no prog sn after 1/2-way* **33/1**

35-0 **8** ¾ **Canford Lilli (IRE)**[83] 1246 3-9-0 74.. ShaneKelly 6 35
(Eve Johnson Houghton) *led to 1/2-way: lost 2nd and wknd 2f out* **5/1**[3]

0 **9** 8 **Cool Angel (IRE)**[40] 2375 3-9-0 0.. MartinDwyer 3 10
(William Muir) *plld hrd: cl up: squeezed out sn after 1/2-way: wknd qckly: eased and t.o fnl f* **16/1**

1m 13.53s (0.53) **Going Correction** +0.10s/f (Good)
WFA 3 from 4yo 7lb **9** Ran SP% **115.5**
Speed ratings (Par 100): **100,99,94,92,91 84,83,82,72**
CSF £33.81 TOTE £5.00: £1.70, £2.40, £1.70; EX 32.60 Trifecta £131.40.
Owner M E Harris **Bred** M Harris **Trained** Blackborough, Devon

FOCUS
Race distance as advertised. Modest maiden form with the first three always prominent.

3721 WILLIAM SHAND KYDD SHUTTLECOCK H'CAP 1m 2f 7y
7:25 (7:25) (Class 4) (0-80,80) 3-Y-O+ **£4,690** (£1,395; £697; £348) **Stalls** Centre

Form RPR

5-62 **1** **Third Rock (IRE)**[30] 2701 3-8-1 68....................(v) JosephineGordon(3) 7 78
(Sir Michael Stoute) *hld up: pushed along 3f out: prog on outer over 2f out: drvn to cl over 1f out: led last 100yds: styd on wl* **13/8**[1]

-523 **2** ¾ **Perceived**[20] 3001 4-9-2 73.. JennyPowell(5) 3 81
(Henry Candy) *trckd ldr: clsd 2f out: rdn to ld over 1f out: hdd last 100yds: styd on* **6/1**[3]

-335 **3** 2 ¼ **Choral Festival**[22] 2930 10-9-2 68.. WilliamCarson 4 72
(John Bridger) *in tch: prog to chse ldrs and rdn 2f out: kpt on one pce fr over 1f out* **10/1**

0040 **4** ½ **Polar Forest**[10] 3364 6-9-11 80..............................(e) TomMarquand(3) 8 83
(Richard Guest) *led: clr after 3f to 4f out: kicked on again 3f out: hdd over 1f out: hung lft and one pce* **10/1**

3-64 **5** ½ **Sahara (IRE)**[21] 2978 4-9-9 75.. TedDurcan 2 77
(Chris Wall) *hld up: shkn up over 2f out: nt qckn and no imp over 1f out: one pce after* **3/1**[2]

0/0- **6** nk **Defining Year (IRE)**[34] 2532 8-9-13 79........................(t) SamHitchcott 5 80
(Hugo Froud) *hld up in detached last: drvn and sme prog 2f out: nvr on terms* **66/1**

5220 **7** 10 **Robins Pearl (FR)**[39] 2415 4-9-8 74.. JimCrowley 6 55
(Harry Dunlop) *chsd ldrs tl wknd qckly 2f out* **14/1**

0005 **8** 9 **Popeswood (IRE)**[14] 3234 4-9-6 77........................ HectorCrouch(5) 1 40
(Ron Hodges) *dwlt: sn chsd ldrs: wknd rapidly over 2f out: t.o* **14/1**

2m 9.54s (0.84) **Going Correction** +0.225s/f (Good)
WFA 3 from 4yo+ 12lb **8** Ran SP% **110.4**
Speed ratings (Par 105): **105,104,102,102,101 101,93,86**
CSF £10.94 CT £66.59 TOTE £2.60: £1.70, £1.80, £2.20; EX 10.60 Trifecta £45.70.
Owner Robert Ng **Bred** Nesco II **Trained** Newmarket, Suffolk

FOCUS
Race distance increased by 28yds. Reasonable form for the level, with the winner continuing to progress.

3722 RIK EDWARDS THE PREFERENCE SHARE KING FILLIES' H'CAP 1m 3f 135y
7:55 (7:58) (Class 5) (0-70,66) 3-Y-O+ **£2,911** (£866; £432; £216) **Stalls** Centre

Form RPR

0-23 **1** **Matidia**[11] 3318 3-9-0 66.. PatDobbs 1 74
(Ralph Beckett) *mde all: rdn 2f out: hrd pressed fnl f: kpt finding and hld on gamely* **11/4**[2]

-006 **2** shd **Taurian**[20] 2994 5-9-11 63.. JimCrowley 6 71
(Ian Williams) *hld up in last: gng strly 3f out: pushed along and prog to take 2nd wl over 1f out: str chal fnl f: styd on wl but jst denied* **7/1**

560 **3** 6 **Sisania (IRE)**[25] 2815 3-8-11 66........................ DanielMuscutt(3) 4 64
(Marco Botti) *chsd ldrs: rdn over 3f out: no prog tl plugged on over 1f out to take 3rd nr fin* **12/1**

4-01 **4** ½ **Merry Dancer (IRE)**[14] 3230 4-9-9 61.. DavidProbert 2 58
(Patrick Chamings) *chsd ldrs: rdn wl over 2f out: lost 2nd wl over 1f out: fdd and lost 3rd nr fin* **9/4**[1]

054 **5** 3 ½ **Loose Ends**[54] 1962 3-8-10 62.. SaleemGolam 7 54
(David Simcock) *in tch: rdn 3f out: no imp 2f out: wknd over 1f out* **5/1**[3]

2320 **6** 1 **Mikro Polemistis (IRE)**[11] 3318 3-8-1 53....................(p) JimmyQuinn 5 43
(Brian Ellison) *t.k.h: hld up in tch: rdn over 3f out: no prog 2f out: sn wknd* **6/1**

0440 **7** 7 **Fun Money**[16] 3141 3-8-0 52 oh1.. NickyMackay 3 30
(Ed Dunlop) *t.k.h: trckd ldng pair: rdn 3f out: wknd 2f out* **16/1**

2m 32.53s (3.03) **Going Correction** +0.225s/f (Good)
WFA 3 from 4yo+ 14lb **7** Ran SP% **114.5**
Speed ratings (Par 100): **98,97,93,93,91 90,85**
CSF £22.12 TOTE £3.50: £1.50, £2.50; EX 21.80 Trifecta £134.80.
Owner J L Rowsell **Bred** Ashbrittle Stud **Trained** Kimpton, Hants
■ Stewards' Enquiry : Pat Dobbs four-day ban: used whip above permitted level (Jul 11-14)

FOCUS
Race distance increased by 28yds. The front pair came clear in what was a modest handicap and a personal best from the winner.

3723 ROUSE PARTNERS ACCOUNTANTS MAIDEN STKS 1m 67y
8:25 (8:28) (Class 5) 3-Y-O **£3,067** (£905; £453) **Stalls** Low

Form RPR

2 **1** **Most Celebrated (IRE)**[19] 3023 3-9-5 0.. JamesDoyle 5 85+
(Saeed bin Suroor) *mde all and sn had field stretched: rdn over 1f out and sn pressed: styd on wl to assert last 150yds* **4/6**[1]

2 **2** 2 ¾ **Lastmanlastround (IRE)**[135] 557 3-9-5 0.. DavidProbert 3 77
(Rae Guest) *chsd wnr: rdn wl over 2f out: clsd to chal jst over 1f out: hld last 150yds and wknd after* **5/2**[2]

3 2 **His Kyllachy (IRE)** 3-9-5 0.. PatCosgrave 7 72+
(William Haggas) *hld up in 5th and off the pce: pushed along over 3f out: styd on to take 3rd over 1f out: no threat to ldng pair* **14/1**

06 **4** 1 ½ **Street Poet (IRE)**[60] 1800 3-9-5 0.. TedDurcan 4 69
(Sir Michael Stoute) *mostly abt same pl: nvr on terms w ldrs: shkn up over 2f out: kpt on same pce* **6/1**[3]

0 **5** ½ **Jetstream Express (IRE)**[41] 2327 3-9-5 0 JimCrowley 2 68
(Simon Crisford) *chsd clr ldng pair: lft bhd over 3f out: shkn up 2f out: no imp and lost 3rd over 1f out* **8/1**

6 5 **Lord Of The North (IRE)** 3-9-5 0 JFEgan 1 63
(Gay Kelleway) *difficult to load into stall: hld up in 6th and wl off the pce: shkn up over 2f out: clsd and ch of a pl over 1f out: rn green and wknd fnl f: eased* **40/1**

7 1½ **Major Ben** 3-9-5 0 MartinDwyer 6 53
(William Muir) *a in last pair and sn wl bhd: pushed along 1/2-way: no prog* **33/1**

00 **8** 1½ **Tynecastle Park**[10] 3359 3-9-5 0 JackMitchell 8 49
(Robert Eddery) *hld up in last and sn wl bhd: pushed along 1/2-way: no prog* **40/1**

1m 45.05s (0.35) **Going Correction** +0.225s/f (Good) **8** Ran SP% **128.4**
Speed ratings (Par 99): **107,104,102,100,100 95,93,92**
CSF £3.09 TOTE £1.50: £1.02, £1.80, £2.60; EX 3.40 Trifecta £18.40.
Owner Godolphin **Bred** Aleyrion Bloodstock Ltd **Trained** Newmarket, Suffolk

FOCUS
Race distance increased by 28yds. Little got into this, the favourite having his field stretched from an early stage. A positive view should be taken of the form.

3724 OAKLEY COURT HOTEL H'CAP 1m 67y
8:55 (8:55) (Class 5) (0-70,68) 3-Y-O+ **£2,911** (£866; £432; £216) **Stalls** Low

Form RPR

0542 **1** **Shifting Star (IRE)**[14] 3234 11-10-0 **68** (vt) WilliamCarson 9 77
(John Bridger) *mistimed s but sn led: racd keenly: had most in trble fr 3f out: rdn over 1f out: styd on wl* **11/4**[2]

0-65 **2** 2¾ **Aye Aye Skipper (IRE)**[31] 2647 6-9-1 **55** (p) PatDobbs 1 58
(Ken Cunningham-Brown) *chsd ldng trio: shkn up and prog to go 2nd over 1f out: tried to cl but no imp fnl f* **17/2**

-224 **3** 3½ **Funny Oyster (IRE)**[40] 2366 3-8-6 **59** (p) TomMarquand(3) 7 52
(George Baker) *chsd wnr to over 4f out: rdn 3f out: disp 2nd again briefly over 1f out: sn one pce* **2/1**[1]

030- **4** 3 **Rajadamri**[260] 7142 3-8-13 **63** FrederikTylicki 8 49
(Rod Millman) *chsd ldrs in 5th: reminder 1/2-way: struggling to stay in tch 3f out: n.d fnl 2f* **16/1**

4-00 **5** 2½ **Fastnet Prince (IRE)**[14] 3224 3-8-10 **60** (t) JFEgan 2 40
(David Evans) *t.k.h: prom: chsd wnr over 4f out to over 1f out: wknd* **11/2**[3]

5-00 **6** ½ **Synodic (USA)**[14] 3234 4-9-11 **65** JackMitchell 4 46
(Seamus Durack) *slowly away: hld up in last: rdn over 3f out: nvr on terms* **33/1**

50-0 **7** ¾ **Wally's Wisdom**[9] 3402 4-9-2 **56** KierenFox 3 35
(Lee Carter) *hld up in last trio: rdn and struggling over 3f out* **20/1**

30-3 **8** 11 **Matilda's Law**[47] 2152 3-9-0 **64** TedDurcan 5 16
(Chris Wall) *hld up in last trio: rdn and no prog over 3f out: wl btn 2f out: heavily eased fnl f* **13/2**

1m 46.06s (1.36) **Going Correction** +0.225s/f (Good)
WFA 3 from 4yo+ 10lb **8** Ran SP% **112.8**
Speed ratings (Par 103): **102,99,95,92,90 89,89,78**
CSF £25.49 CT £55.05 TOTE £3.60: £1.10, £2.10, £2.00; EX 28.80 Trifecta £55.10.
Owner Night Shadow Syndicate **Bred** Hardys Of Kilkeel Ltd **Trained** Liphook, Hants

FOCUS
Race distance increased by 28yds. A moderate handicap, the winner making most against the stands' rail and improving his fine record in the race. He has been rated back to last year's best.
T/Plt: £15.00 to a £1 stake. Pool: £63,641.45 - 3091.35 winning units. T/Qpdt: £5.70 to a £1 stake. Pool: £6,927.15 - 895.26 winning units. **Jonathan Neesom**

3470 WOLVERHAMPTON (A.W) (L-H)
Monday, June 27

OFFICIAL GOING: Tapeta: standard
Wind: Fresh behind Weather: Cloudy with sunny spells

3725 HOMEMOVEBOX.COM H'CAP 5f 216y (Tp)
2:15 (2:17) (Class 6) (0-65,65) 3-Y-O **£2,425** (£721; £360; £180) **Stalls** Low

Form RPR

3006 **1** **Tahiti One**[10] 3353 3-8-7 **51** WilliamCarson 10 57
(Tony Carroll) *mde all: rdn over 1f out: jst hld on* **28/1**

-421 **2** hd **Jack The Laird (IRE)**[38] 2447 3-9-4 **62** (b) RobertWinston 5 67
(Dean Ivory) *pushed along and sn prom: chsd wnr over 3f out: ev ch fr over 1f out: rdn and edgd lft ins fnl f: styd on* **7/4**[1]

5400 **3** ½ **Abberley Dancer (IRE)**[25] 2824 3-9-4 **65** JosephineGordon(3) 12 69
(J S Moore) *prom: lost pl 5f out: hdwy over 1f out: r.o* **14/1**

0465 **4** ½ **Miss Phillyjinks (IRE)**[12] 3280 3-9-6 **64** (b) AdamKirby 4 66
(Paul D'Arcy) *hld up: racd keenly: hdwy over 1f out: sn rdn: styd on* **14/1**

2360 **5** 1 **Born To Finish (IRE)**[17] 3098 3-9-7 **65** (b[1]) RichardKingscote 2 64
(Jeremy Gask) *s.i.s: hld up: hdwy over 1f out: nt clr run and swtchd rt ins fnl f: nt rch ldrs* **7/2**[2]

-000 **6** 1¾ **Kodimoor (IRE)**[14] 3211 3-9-5 **63** (p) FrannyNorton 1 57
(Christopher Kellett) *hld up in tch: racd keenly: rdn over 1f out: styd on same pce fnl f* **33/1**

6512 **7** 3¾ **Ettie Hart (IRE)**[16] 3146 3-8-5 **56** KillianHennessy(7) 6 39
(Mick Channon) *prom: rdn over 1f out: wknd fnl f* **7/1**[3]

-645 **8** hd **Kingstreet Lady**[20] 3000 3-8-4 **53** PatrickO'Donnell(5) 11 35
(Richard Price) *mid-div: rdn on outer over 2f out: wknd over 1f out* **20/1**

020 **9** ¾ **The Lillster**[5] 3513 3-8-12 **59** GeorgeDowning(3) 7 39
(Tony Carroll) *s.i.s: hld up: pushed along 1/2-way: a in rr* **16/1**

-042 **10** ½ **Dream Dana (IRE)**[12] 3280 3-9-7 **65** TimmyMurphy 3 44
(Jamie Osborne) *chsd ldrs: rdn over 1f out: wknd fnl f* **16/1**

0-04 **11** 2 **Showbizzy**[16] 3136 3-9-2 **60** JamieSpencer 8 36
(Richard Fahey) *chsd wnr tl over 3f out: rdn over 2f out: hung lft over 1f out: sn wknd* **16/1**

1m 14.87s (0.37) **Going Correction** +0.025s/f (Slow) **11** Ran SP% **113.2**
Speed ratings (Par 97): **98,97,97,96,95 92,87,87,86,85 83**
CSF £66.84 CT £592.83 TOTE £33.80: £7.80, £1.10, £3.80; EX 168.00 Trifecta £2721.20 Part won..
Owner Seasons Holidays **Bred** B Hurley **Trained** Cropthorne, Worcs
■ Stewards' Enquiry : Robert Winston two-day ban: used whip above permitted level (Jul 11-12)

FOCUS
A modest 3yo handicap with thr winner looking best on the AW. They went a decent gallop on standard Tapeta.

3726 CITIBET LOGISTICS (S) STKS 5f 216y (Tp)
2:50 (2:50) (Class 6) 3-Y-O+ **£2,264** (£673; £336; £168) **Stalls** Low

Form RPR

6500 **1** **City Of Angkor Wat (IRE)**[24] 2856 6-9-8 70 (p) JamieSpencer 1 75
(Conor Dore) *chsd ldr: lost pl after 1f: hdwy 2f out: rdn to ld and hung rt ins fnl f: r.o: wnt lft towards fin: comf* **5/1**

500 **2** 1¼ **Greyfriarschorista**[81] 1291 9-9-8 79 (vt) RobertWinston 5 71
(Giles Bravery) *hld up: hdwy 2f out: rdn and edgd lft ins fnl f: styd on same pce* **9/4**[2]

6121 **3** ¾ **Layla's Hero (IRE)**[9] 3421 9-10-0 75 (b) FrannyNorton 7 77
(David Nicholls) *chsd ldrs: wnt 2nd over 2f out: led over 1f out: rdn and hdd whn hmpd ins fnl f: styd on same pce* **7/4**[1]

1100 **4** ½ **Fear Or Favour (IRE)**[16] 3123 5-10-0 79 AdamKirby 4 74
(George Scott) *chsd ldrs: wnt 2nd over 4f out tl led over 2f out: rdn and hdd over 1f out: no ex wl ins fnl f* **9/2**[3]

0500 **5** 2¾ **Diatomic (IRE)**[14] 3210 4-9-8 58 RichardKingscote 6 59
(Tom Dascombe) *led 1f: chsd ldrs: nt clr run and lost pl over 2f out: sn rdn: no ex fnl f* **25/1**

0-56 **6** 39 **Misleading**[59] 1832 4-8-11 70 (b[1]) CallumShepherd(5) 2
(Lee Carter) *s.i.s: sn pushed along: rcvrd to ld 5f out: rdn and hdd over 2f out: eased wl over 1f out* **20/1**

1m 15.12s (0.62) **Going Correction** +0.025s/f (Slow) **6** Ran SP% **110.6**
Speed ratings (Par 101): **96,94,93,92,89 37**
.Layla's Hero was bought by Mr Roger Teal for £6000\n\x\x
Owner Mrs Louise Marsh **Bred** T Jones **Trained** Hubbert's Bridge, Lincs

FOCUS
A fair seller with the winner clearly on top late on. They went a respectable gallop.

3727 PROCESSING CENTRE MEDIAN AUCTION MAIDEN STKS 1m 4f 50y (Tp)
3:20 (3:20) (Class 6) 3-4-Y-O **£2,264** (£673; £336; £168) **Stalls** Low

Form RPR

23-3 **1** **Alyssa**[25] 2815 3-8-9 74 RichardKingscote 1 73+
(Ralph Beckett) *pushed along to chse ldrs: shkn up over 2f out: carried rt ins fnl f: styd on to ld nr fin* **6/5**[1]

-436 **2** ¾ **Stetchworth Park**[45] 2224 3-9-0 78 JamieSpencer 2 77
(Michael Bell) *chsd ldr tl led over 1f out: rdn and hung rt ins fnl f: hdd nr fin* **5/2**[2]

2 **3** 7 **Swashbuckle**[33] 2589 3-8-7 0 JoshuaBryan(7) 5 66
(Andrew Balding) *chsd ldrs: pushed along over 3f out: outpcd fnl 2f* **12/1**

42 **4** ½ **Zanjabeel**[27] 2774 3-9-0 0 (t) RobertHavlin 4 65
(Simon Crisford) *led at stdy pce tl qcknd over 2f out: rdn and hdd over 1f out: wknd wl ins fnl f* **11/4**[3]

0-6 **5** 5 **Regal Gait (IRE)**[26] 2790 3-9-0 0 HarryBentley 3 57
(Simon Dow) *hld up: rdn over 3f out: sme hdwy wl over 1f out: wknd fnl f* **33/1**

2m 38.91s (-1.89) **Going Correction** +0.025s/f (Slow) **5** Ran SP% **111.3**
Speed ratings (Par 101): **107,106,101,101,98**
CSF £4.57 TOTE £1.70: £1.10, £2.50; EX 4.00 Trifecta £19.30.
Owner Miss K Rausing **Bred** Miss K Rausing **Trained** Kimpton, Hants
■ Stewards' Enquiry : Jamie Spencer caution: careless riding

FOCUS
A fair little middle-distance maiden. They went a respectable gallop at best and the winner has the scope to rate higher than this.

3728 RACING WELFARE STABLE STAFF WEEK H'CAP 1m 4f 50y (Tp)
3:55 (3:55) (Class 4) (0-80,77) 3-Y-O **£4,851** (£1,443; £721; £360) **Stalls** Low

Form RPR

63 **1** **White Shaheen**[17] 3110 3-9-7 **77** MartinDwyer 8 87+
(William Muir) *chsd ldr tl led and qcknd 3f out: shkn up and clr over 1f out: edgd rt ins fnl f: styd on* **4/1**[2]

0-52 **2** 2¼ **Nucky Thompson**[24] 2859 3-9-0 **73** LouisSteward(3) 5 78
(Richard Spencer) *a.p: chsd wnr over 2f out: rdn over 1f out: edgd lft ins fnl f: no imp* **8/1**

-660 **3** ¾ **Ride The Lightning**[23] 2900 3-9-3 **73** JimmyFortune 6 77
(Brian Meehan) *hld up: racd keenly: hdwy 2f out: rdn over 1f out: edgd lft ins fnl f: r.o: nt rch ldrs* **10/1**

0-26 **4** 7 **De Aguilar (USA)**[62] 1739 3-9-5 **75** (p) JamieSpencer 3 68
(Roger Charlton) *hld up: rdn over 2f out: styd on ins fnl f: nvr nrr* **16/1**

-143 **5** ½ **Jive Time**[19] 3042 3-9-6 **76** AdamKirby 1 68
(James Tate) *chsd ldrs: rdn over 2f out: styd on same pce fr over 1f out* **6/1**[3]

1105 **6** 2 **Recognition (IRE)**[11] 3306 3-9-0 **70** AndreaAtzeni 2 59
(Roger Varian) *hld up: rdn over 2f out: n.d* **6/1**[3]

2-44 **7** ¾ **Hammer Gun (USA)**[24] 2859 3-9-2 **72** (b[1]) TedDurcan 7 59
(Sir Michael Stoute) *s.s: hld up: rdn over 2f out: a in rr* **10/1**

1-35 **8** 2¾ **City Of Ideas**[39] 2411 3-9-4 **74** RobertHavlin 4 57
(John Gosden) *led at stdy pce: pushed along and hdd 3f out: wknd over 1f out* **2/1**[1]

2m 39.26s (-1.54) **Going Correction** +0.025s/f (Slow) **8** Ran SP% **117.1**
Speed ratings (Par 101): **106,104,104,99,99 97,97,95**
CSF £36.56 CT £301.03 TOTE £4.80: £1.60, £3.00, £2.80; EX 36.00 Trifecta £303.40.
Owner Syed Pervez Hussain **Bred** Meon Valley Stud **Trained** Lambourn, Berks

FOCUS
A fair 3yo middle-distance handicap. Once again they went a respectable gallop at best and the pace held up quite well.

3729 13-TEN.COM APPRENTICE CLAIMING STKS 7f 32y (Tp)
4:25 (4:25) (Class 6) 4-Y-O+ **£2,264** (£673; £336; £168) **Stalls** High

Form RPR

0026 **1** **The Tichborne (IRE)**[24] 2849 8-8-9 68 (v) KevinLundie(3) 4 71
(Roger Teal) *chsd ldrs: wnt 2nd over 2f out: led over 1f out: rdn and edgd lft ins fnl f: styd on* **5/1**[3]

24-2 **2** 1 **Great Fun**[42] 2309 5-9-5 79 JordanUys(5) 3 80
(Brian Meehan) *hld up in tch: rdn over 1f out: chsd wnr and edgd lft ins fnl f: r.o* **5/6**[1]

260 **3** 2½ **Top Offer**[10] 3366 7-9-0 67 (p) GeorgeWood(3) 5 66
(Patrick Morris) *hld up: hdwy over 1f out: rdn and edgd lft ins fnl f: styd on same pce* **9/2**[2]

6-06 **4** 1½ **King Torus (IRE)**[21] 2977 8-9-4 79 (b) CallumShepherd 7 64
(Lee Carter) *w ldr tl led over 2f out: rdn and hdd over 1f out: edgd rt and no ex ins fnl f* **7/1**

5460 **5** 6 **Salvado (IRE)**[7] 3469 6-8-9 44 RhiainIngram(3) 1 43
(Tony Carroll) *prom: rdn over 2f out: wknd over 1f out* **50/1**
40-0 **6** 3 1/4 **Gotasinggotadance**[13] 3258 4-8-5 40 NoelGarbutt 2 28
(Philip Hide) *s.i.s: hld up: rdn over 2f out: sn wknd* **100/1**
1200 **7** 4 **Afkar (IRE)**[23] 2918 8-9-6 68 (b) PatrickO'Donnell 6 33
(Mandy Rowland) *led: rdn and hdd over 2f out: wknd over 1f out* **12/1**
1m 29.47s (0.67) **Going Correction** +0.025s/f (Slow) **7** Ran SP% **112.5**
Speed ratings (Par 101): **97,95,93,91,84 80,76**
CSF £9.26 TOTE £7.30: £3.00, £1.10; EX 9.70 Trifecta £30.30.Great Fun was bought by Mr Michael Blake for £10,000; The Tichborne was bought by Mr Matt Watkinson for £4,000
Owner Roger Teal **Bred** Ms Alyson Flower And Chris Simpson **Trained** Great Shefford, Berks

FOCUS
A fair apprentices' claimer and the form looks straightforward. The two horses who contested the lead faded out of contention.

3730 EBF STALLIONS HAPPY 10TH BIRTHDAY CITIPOST MAIL MAIDEN STKS 7f 32y (Tp)
4:55 (4:57) (Class 5) 2-Y-O **£3,234** (£962; £481; £240) **Stalls** High

Form RPR
1 **Euginio (IRE)** 2-9-5 0 SeanLevey 3 78+
(Richard Hannon) *edgd lft s: chsd ldr tl led over 2f out: rdn and edgd lft over 1f out: styd on* **10/1**
0 **2** 1 **Hurricane Rush (IRE)**[18] 3058 2-9-5 0 JamesMcDonald 2 76+
(Charles Hills) *s.i.s and hmpd s: hld up: hdwy over 2f out: shkn up over 1f out: r.o: nt rch wnr* **6/4**[1]
3 3/4 **The Amber Fort (USA)** 2-9-5 0 RobertHavlin 1 74+
(John Gosden) *sn prom: rdn to chse wnr over 1f out: styd on* **7/1**[3]
5 **4** 2 1/4 **Harbour Master**[21] 2976 2-9-5 0 JamieSpencer 4 69
(Jamie Osborne) *trckd ldrs: shkn up over 1f out: edgd lft and styd on same pce ins fnl f* **4/1**[2]
0 **5** 1/2 **Sufrah (USA)**[18] 3058 2-9-5 0 JimmyFortune 8 67
(Brian Meehan) *prom: rdn: edgd rt and outpcd over 2f out: styd on ins fnl f* **4/1**[2]
5 dht **Roaring Character (IRE)** 2-9-5 0 LiamJones 5 67
(Tom Dascombe) *led: rdn and hdd over 2f out: wknd wl ins fnl f* **40/1**
7 4 1/2 **Oxford Blu** 2-9-5 0 RyanPowell 6 56
(Sir Mark Prescott Bt) *s.i.s: pushed along in rr: nvr nrr* **50/1**
44 **8** shd **Charlie Beer Punt (IRE)**[19] 3008 2-9-5 0 RichardKingscote 10 56
(Tom Dascombe) *hld up: rdn 1/2-way: nvr on terms* **20/1**
9 3 3/4 **Mukallaf (IRE)** 2-9-5 0 AndreaAtzeni 9 47
(Roger Varian) *mid-div: pushed along over 2f out: sn wknd* **10/1**
10 2 3/4 **Gog Elles (IRE)** 2-9-0 0 KieranO'Neill 7 35
(J S Moore) *s.i.s: towards rr: sme hdwy u.p 3f out: wknd 2f out* **50/1**
1m 30.08s (1.28) **Going Correction** +0.025s/f (Slow) **10** Ran SP% **121.8**
Speed ratings (Par 93): **93,91,91,88,87 87,82,82,78,75**
CSF £26.09 TOTE £9.30: £2.20, £1.40, £2.30; EX 26.80 Trifecta £179.60.
Owner Saleh Al Homaizi & Imad Al Sagar **Bred** Arkle Bloodstock **Trained** East Everleigh, Wilts

FOCUS
An ordinary juvenile maiden in terms of form in the book, but some interesting newcomers on show. They went a respectable gallop.

3731 CITIPOSTMAIL.CO.UK H'CAP (DIV I) 1m 141y (Tp)
5:25 (5:26) (Class 6) (0-60,60) 3-Y-O+ **£2,425** (£721; £360; £180) **Stalls** Low

Form RPR
5033 **1** **Miss Lillie**[34] 2566 5-9-13 59 (p) RobertWinston 4 65
(Roger Teal) *mid-div: hdwy over 2f out: r.o to ld nr fin* **9/2**[2]
-020 **2** nk **Gladys Cooper (IRE)**[18] 3080 3-9-0 57 AntonioFresu 6 61
(Ed Walker) *led over 7f out: rdn over 2f out: hdd over 1f out: r.o* **16/1**
0501 **3** hd **Paladin (IRE)**[5] 3522 7-10-0 60 MartinLane 7 65
(Michael Blake) *chsd ldrs: rdn over 2f out: led over 1f out: hdd nr fin* **11/8**[1]
3550 **4** 2 **Natalia**[27] 2778 7-8-11 46 oh1 (p) RobHornby(3) 8 47
(Sarah Hollinshead) *hld up: hdwy over 1f out: r.o: nt rch ldrs* **25/1**
00-0 **5** 1 1/2 **Always A Dream**[49] 2108 3-8-10 60 SamuelClarke(7) 2 57
(Chris Wall) *chsd ldrs: pushed along over 2f out: styd on same pce fnl f* **8/1**[3]
2206 **6** 2 3/4 **Dreaming Again**[32] 2610 6-9-2 48 KieranO'Neill 3 40
(Jimmy Fox) *mid-div: rdn over 2f out: hdwy over 1f out: styd on same pce fnl f* **16/1**
4051 **7** nse **Ventura Falcon (IRE)**[11] 3319 3-9-0 57 SeanLevey 9 48
(Richard Hannon) *prom: chsd ldr over 5f out: rdn over 2f out: wknd ins fnl f* **12/1**
6260 **8** hd **Pipers Piping (IRE)**[38] 2448 10-9-5 51 AdamKirby 11 42
(Mandy Rowland) *hld up: rdn over 2f out: nvr on terms* **25/1**
0062 **9** 1/2 **Schottische**[10] 3354 6-9-1 54 (p) LiamLewis-Salter(7) 1 44
(Alan Bailey) *hld up: rdn and edgd lft over 1f out: nvr trbld ldrs* **16/1**
000- **10** 5 **Inwithachance (IRE)**[230] 7785 3-7-12 46 NoelGarbutt(5) 10 25
(Daniel Mark Loughnane) *s.i.s: in rr and drvn along 1/2-way: n.d* **50/1**
-540 **11** 1 **Carlovian**[36] 2506 3-8-12 55 FrannyNorton 5 32
(Christopher Kellett) *led 1f: chsd ldrs: rdn over 2f out: wknd fnl f* **10/1**
44-0 **12** 3 3/4 **Magician Coutinho**[7] 3474 4-9-11 57 [1] DanielTudhope 12 27
(David O'Meara) *s.i.s: hld up: rdn over 3f out: wknd over 2f out* **8/1**[3]
1m 50.98s (0.88) **Going Correction** +0.025s/f (Slow)
WFA 3 from 4yo+ 11lb **12** Ran SP% **126.6**
Speed ratings (Par 101): **97,96,96,94,93 91,90,90,90,85 85,81**
CSF £78.34 CT £153.95 TOTE £6.70: £2.00, £5.30, £1.40; EX 80.30 Trifecta £323.50.
Owner The Rat Racers **Bred** Newsells Park Stud & Cannon Bloodstock **Trained** Great Shefford, Berks

FOCUS
The first division of a moderate handicap. They went a modest gallop.

3732 CITIPOSTMAIL.CO.UK H'CAP (DIV II) 1m 141y (Tp)
6:00 (6:00) (Class 6) (0-60,60) 3-Y-O+ **£2,425** (£721; £360; £180) **Stalls** Low

Form RPR
0023 **1** **Filament Of Gold (USA)**[7] 3476 5-9-4 55 (p) GaryMahon(5) 10 64
(Roy Brotherton) *chsd ldrs: led wl over 1f out: sn rdn: edgd rt ins fnl f: styd on* **4/1**[2]
-003 **2** 3/4 **Pacific Salt (IRE)**[11] 3319 3-8-10 56 KieranShoemark(3) 4 62
(Roger Charlton) *hld up in tch: racd keenly: rdn over 2f out: hung lft over 1f out: styd on* **7/2**[1]
-500 **3** 3 **Alans Pride (IRE)**[13] 3262 4-9-11 57 (p) SeanLevey 3 58
(Michael Dods) *chsd ldr tl led 2f out: sn rdn and hdd: edgd rt and no ex ins fnl f* **10/1**
0641 **4** 1/2 **Admirable Art (IRE)**[43] 2285 6-9-7 53 AdamKirby 1 53
(Tony Carroll) *hld up in tch: rdn over 1f out: edgd rt ins fnl f: styd on same pce* **8/1**

6000 **5** 1/2 **Heat Storm (IRE)**[25] 2814 5-8-11 46 oh1 (t) RobHornby(3) 6 45
(James Unett) *hld up: hdwy u.p over 1f out: hung rt and styd on same pce fnl f* **50/1**
0-30 **6** 3 1/2 **Henry Grace (IRE)**[32] 2609 5-9-5 51 (b) KieranO'Neill 2 43
(Jimmy Fox) *prom: rdn over 3f out: wknd fnl f* **20/1**
-540 **7** shd **Judicial Enquiry**[31] 2652 3-9-2 59 (p) RichardKingscote 11 49
(Ed Walker) *sn led: rdn and hdd 2f out: wknd fnl f* **9/2**[3]
00-0 **8** 1/2 **Gaelic Angel (IRE)**[36] 2505 3-9-3 60 WilliamTwiston-Davies 5 49
(Michael Scudamore) *s.i.s: hld up: rdn over 2f out: nt trble ldrs* **16/1**
062 **9** 6 **Orlando Rogue (IRE)**[7] 3474 4-10-0 60 (p) JamieSpencer 7 38
(Conor Dore) *hld up: rdn and wknd over 1f out* **4/1**[2]
645 **10** 1 **Pensax Lady (IRE)**[126] 675 3-9-1 58 RobertWinston 9 33
(Daniel Mark Loughnane) *s.i.s: hld up: rdn over 2f out: wknd over 1f out* **14/1**
1m 50.61s (0.51) **Going Correction** +0.025s/f (Slow)
WFA 3 from 4yo+ 11lb **10** Ran SP% **119.9**
Speed ratings (Par 101): **98,97,94,94,93 90,90,90,84,83**
CSF £19.03 CT £135.68 TOTE £6.00: £2.50, £1.30, £3.30; EX 24.20 Trifecta £160.50.
Owner M A Geobey **Bred** Darley **Trained** Elmley Castle, Worcs

FOCUS
The second division of a moderate handicap. They went a respectable gallop, at best, and the winning time was only marginally quicker. A small step up from the winner on recent efforts.
T/Plt: £50.00 to a £1 stake. Pool: £67,704.12 - 987.50 winning units. T/Qpdt: £11.60 to a £1 stake. Pool: £6,202.91 - 392.84 winning units. **Colin Roberts**

LE CROISE-LAROCHE
Monday, June 27

OFFICIAL GOING: Turf: very soft

3733a PRIX PAUL-NOEL DELAHOUTRE (CLAIMER) (4YO+) (GENTLEMEN RIDERS) (TURF) 2m
1:05 (12:00) 4-Y-O+ **£5,514** (£2,205; £1,654; £1,102; £551)

RPR
1 **Roskilly (IRE)**[59] 1846 5-10-12 0 MrEMonfort 3 47
(P Monfort, France) **7/2**[2]
2 3/4 **Garinsha (FR)**[35] 9-9-12 0 (b) MrGonzagueCottreau(4) 7 36
(T Lemarie, France) **39/1**
3 shd **Demoiselledavignon (FR)**[59] 1846 5-10-2 0 MrTeddyWindrif(7) 1 43
(D Windrif, France) **19/5**[3]
4 nk **Solmen (FR)**[59] 1846 8-10-13 0 MrJean-PhilippeBoisgontier 5 47
(M Krebs, France) **19/5**[3]
5 hd **Ercolano (FR)**[5] 4-10-6 0 MrFlorentGuy 10 40
(F-X De Chevigny, France) **114/10**
6 2 1/2 **Helmsman (IRE)**[24] 2850 4-10-9 0 ow7 (p) MrFTett(7) 6 47
(J S Moore) *stmbld s: sn ldng: pushed along to maintain narrow ld fr 3f out: hdd 2f out: sn btn: wknd fnl f* **14/5**[1]
7 3/4 **Shotgun (FR)**[23] 4-10-10 0 MrHugoBoutin(7) 8 47
(C Boutin, France) **116/10**
8 9 **Marendinio (FR)**[176] 11-9-13 0 MrDamienArtu(7) 4 26
(D De Waele, France) **30/1**
9 9 **La Mere Beaude (FR)**[255] 5-10-2 0 (p) MrKevinBraye 9 12
(S Jesus, France) **100/1**
10 8 **Flers (GER)**[176] 7-10-0 0 ow1 KieranBraem(7) 2 8
(Ecurie Fievez, France) **17/1**
11 20 **Good Friend (GER)**[257] 6-9-13 0 (p) MrAdrienDesespringalle(7) 11
(Mme M-C Chaalon, France) **97/1**
Owner Gerard L Ferron **Bred** Gigginstown House Stud **Trained** France
PARI-MUTUEL (all including 1 euro stake): WIN 4.50; PLACE 1.90, 7.30, 2.20;DF 99.80; SF 169.90

3485 BRIGHTON (L-H)
Tuesday, June 28

OFFICIAL GOING: Good
Wind: Fresh, half against Weather: Fine early, rain from race 6

3734 CASH OUT AT BET365 H'CAP (DIV I) 5f 213y
2:15 (2:15) (Class 6) (0-55,55) 3-Y-O+ **£2,587** (£770; £384; £192) **Stalls** Low

Form RPR
2353 **1** **Assertive Agent**[33] 2609 6-9-4 52 DavidProbert 1 61
(Tony Carroll) *towards rr: hdwy 2f out: led over 1f out: hld on wl whn chal ins fnl f* **6/1**[3]
0001 **2** 1/2 **Titus Secret**[7] 3486 4-9-3 51 6ex FergusSweeney 3 58
(Malcolm Saunders) *s.s: bhd: gd hdwy in centre 2f out: hung lft: str chal fnl f: r.o* **11/4**[1]
3-00 **3** 2 1/2 **Cooperess**[16] 3198 3-8-11 52 (bt[1]) KieranO'Neill 5 50+
(Ali Stronge) *in tch on inner: led 2f out tl over 1f out: one pce ins fnl f* **25/1**
00-0 **4** 2 **Mendacious Harpy (IRE)**[90] 1147 5-9-7 55 SteveDrowne 9 49
(George Baker) *dwlt: towards rr: hdwy and n.m.r 2f out: hrd rdn over 1f out: styd on* **16/1**
0000 **5** shd **Pacohontas**[12] 3319 3-8-12 53 ow1 RobertWinston 4 44+
(Dean Ivory) *rdn early: prom tl one pce appr fnl f* **11/1**
0563 **6** 1 3/4 **Canford Belle**[22] 2964 3-9-0 55 JimCrowley 10 41
(Amanda Perrett) *towards rr: effrt in centre 2f out: styd on same pce* **9/2**[2]
0-06 **7** 1 **Any Guest (IRE)**[19] 3080 3-8-11 52 (p) RyanPowell 2 35
(George Margarson) *dwlt: towards rr: hdwy over 2f out: wknd over 1f out* **9/2**[2]
-000 **8** 2 1/2 **Steel City Boy (IRE)**[31] 2676 13-8-7 46 oh1 CharlieBennett(5) 8 23+
(Shaun Harris) *led tl wknd 2f out* **50/1**
4600 **9** 1 **Burauq**[7] 3486 4-9-4 52 (p) OisinMurphy 7 26+
(Milton Bradley) *chsd ldrs tl outpcd and short of room 2f out* **10/1**
4235 **10** 3 **Arizona Snow**[36] 2537 4-9-3 54 (p) TomMarquand(3) 11 19+
(Ronald Harris) *chsd ldrs on outer tl outpcd and squeezed out wl over 1f out* **17/2**
000- **11** 2 1/2 **Sweet Piccolo**[266] 7002 6-8-9 46 oh1 JosephineGordon(3) 12 4
(Paddy Butler) *a bhd* **100/1**
0660 **12** 1 1/2 **Barnsdale**[17] 3140 3-7-12 46 oh1 (p) MeganEllingworth(7) 6 +
(John Holt) *prom tl wknd 2f out* **100/1**
1m 10.53s (0.33) **Going Correction** +0.125s/f (Good)
WFA 3 from 4yo+ 7lb **12** Ran SP% **118.9**
Speed ratings (Par 101): **102,101,98,95,95 92,91,88,86,82 79,77**
CSF £22.60 CT £391.00 TOTE £7.20: £2.50, £1.60, £5.70; EX 33.00 Trifecta £477.80.
Owner Wedgewood Estates **Bred** Miss Liza Judd **Trained** Cropthorne, Worcs

The Form Book, Raceform Ltd, Newbury, RG14 5SJ

FOCUS
Rail dolled-out between the 4.5f and 2.5f marker, adding 3 yards to race distances. Division one of a weak sprint, the front pair came from behind and drew away late on. The time was almost a second faster than division two.

3735 CASH OUT AT BET365 H'CAP (DIV II) 5f 213y
2:45 (2:51) (Class 6) (0-55,55) 3-Y-O+ **£2,587** (£770; £384; £192) **Stalls** Low

Form RPR
-666 **1** **Curious Fox**[13] 3280 3-9-0 **55** DavidProbert 2 64
(Anthony Carson) *dwlt: sn chsng ldrs: led over 1f out: rdn out* **14/1**

0003 **2** 1 ¼ **Essaka (IRE)**[7] 3486 4-9-1 **54** PaddyPilley[(5)] 10 61+
(Tony Carroll) *s.s: t.k.h in rr: gd hdwy in centre 2f out: hung lft fnl f: r.o: a hld* **2/1**[1]

3 **3** 1 ¼ **Minminwin (IRE)**[35] 2560 3-8-5 **46** oh1 LukeMorris 9 47
(Gay Kelleway) *mid-div: rdn over 2f out: styd on wl fnl f* **9/2**[2]

1203 **4** hd **Tasaaboq**[20] 3040 5-9-3 **54** (t) JosephineGordon[(3)] 12 57
(Phil McEntee) *t.k.h: sn in tch on outer: hrd rdn and hung lft over 1f out: styd on same pce* **7/1**[3]

0463 **5** 2 ½ **Kenstone (FR)**[8] 3473 3-8-6 **47** (p) MartinDwyer 6 40
(David Dennis) *prom tl no ex appr fnl f* **8/1**

5505 **6** ½ **Nelson's Pride**[7] 3486 5-8-5 **46** oh1 (t) RhiainIngram[(7)] 8 40
(Roger Ingram) *towards rr: effrt in centre over 2f out: nvr able to chal* **25/1**

00-0 **7** ½ **Interchoice Star**[12] 3320 11-8-12 **46** oh1 (p) FergusSweeney 7 38
(Ray Peacock) *chsd ldrs: led 2f out tl over 1f out: wknd fnl f* **33/1**

5400 **8** 1 **Frangarry (IRE)**[20] 3016 4-9-5 **53** (b[1]) DarryllHolland 3 45
(Alan Bailey) *s.i.s: towards rr: hdwy 2f out: in tch whn hung lft and bmpd jst ins fnl f: eased whn btn* **10/1**

00-0 **9** 1 ½ **Overstone Lass (IRE)**[22] 2969 4-8-12 **46** oh1 (b[1]) KieranO'Neill 1 34
(John Spearing) *led tl 2f out: wknd over 1f out* **66/1**

1420 **10** 2 ¾ **Compton Prince**[14] 3259 7-9-4 **52** (b) OisinMurphy 5 28
(Milton Bradley) *mid-div: lost pl 3f out: sme hdwy and styng on whn n.m.r jst ins fnl f* **10/1**

0-30 **11** 14 **Heathfield Park (IRE)**[104] 952 3-9-0 **55** FrederikTylicki 4
(William Stone) *in tch tl wknd over 2f out* **33/1**

0-00 **12** shd **Stylish Minerva**[21] 3003 3-8-11 **52** (b[1]) SeanLevey 11
(Richard Hannon) *bhd: modest effrt in centre over 2f out: sn wknd* **14/1**

1m 11.5s (1.30) **Going Correction** +0.125s/f (Good)
WFA 3 from 4yo+ 7lb **12 Ran SP% 117.9**
Speed ratings (Par 101): **96,94,92,92,89 88,87,86,84,80 62,61**
CSF £40.88 CT £156.01 TOTE £14.40: £4.00, £1.60, £1.70; EX 55.40 Trifecta £307.40.
Owner Carson, Francis, Ghauri & Percy **Bred** Minster Stud **Trained** Newmarket, Suffolk

FOCUS
Race distance increased by 3 yards. The time of this was almost a second slower than division one.

3736 BET365 MAIDEN STKS 1m 1f 209y
3:15 (3:17) (Class 5) 3-Y-O **£2,911** (£866; £432; £216) **Stalls** High

Form RPR
34 **1** **Fashion Parade**[33] 2614 3-9-0 0 DavidProbert 6 81
(Charles Hills) *t.k.h: in tch: effrt over 2f out: styd on to ld fnl strides* **8/1**

66 **2** hd **Henry Croft**[17] 3160 3-9-5 0 RobertHavlin 4 85
(John Gosden) *trckd ldr: rdn to ld 1f out: kpt on u.p: hdd fnl strides* **9/2**[2]

222 **3** 4 **Hepplewhite**[36] 2548 3-9-2 84 (t) TomMarquand[(3)] 7 77
(Robert Eddery) *mde most tl 1f out: no ex* **7/4**[1]

0-5 **4** 1 **The Otmoor Poet**[15] 3235 3-9-5 0 FergusSweeney 9 75+
(Alan King) *towards rr: hdwy 2f out: styd on fnl f* **16/1**

0 **5** 2 ¾ **Intercepted**[23] 2929 3-9-5 0 GeorgeBaker 1 69+
(David Lanigan) *hld up and bhd: pushed along and styd on fnl 2f: nvr nrr* **16/1**

0032 **6** 1 ½ **Glance My Way (IRE)**[32] 2652 3-9-5 71 SeanLevey 10 66
(Richard Hannon) *hld up in midfield: rdn over 2f out: edgd lft 1f out: styd on same pce* **11/2**[3]

60 **7** nk **Madame Chow (IRE)**[17] 3160 3-9-0 0 OisinMurphy 2 60
(Ralph Beckett) *t.k.h: prom tl outpcd fnl 2f* **20/1**

0 **8** 1 **Sycara (IRE)**[19] 3059 3-9-0 0 JimCrowley 12 59
(Jeremy Noseda) *hld up: hdwy 2f out: drvn to chse ldrs over 1f out: no ex fnl f* **33/1**

0 **9** ½ **Ex Lover**[15] 3235 3-9-5 0 AndreaAtzeni 8 62
(Roger Varian) *in tch: wnt prom over 2f out: hrd rdn and wknd over 1f out* **6/1**

0-0 **10** ¾ **Cockney Boy**[46] 2207 3-9-5 0 MichaelJMMurphy 3 61
(John Gallagher) *t.k.h in rr: rdn 3f out: n.d* **66/1**

11 1 ¾ **Snug** 3-9-0 0 MartinDwyer 11 52
(Jane Chapple-Hyam) *rdn 1/2-way: a towards rr* **66/1**

12 46 **Mandela (IRE)** 3-9-5 0 SteveDrowne 5
(Seamus Mullins) *chsd ldrs tl wknd 3f out: bhd and eased over 1f out* **100/1**

2m 4.98s (1.38) **Going Correction** +0.125s/f (Good) **12 Ran SP% 118.8**
Speed ratings (Par 99): **99,98,95,94,92 91,91,90,90,89 88,51**
CSF £42.69 TOTE £9.40: £3.00, £1.60, £1.20; EX 49.30 Trifecta £218.80.
Owner Abdulla Al Khalifa **Bred** Sheikh Abdulla Bin Isa Al-Khalifa **Trained** Lambourn, Berks

FOCUS
Race distance increased by 3 yards. An ordinary maiden, with the 84-rated third not worthy of his mark, but the first two are both improving.

3737 BET365.COM H'CAP 1m 1f 209y
3:45 (3:46) (Class 6) (0-55,61) 4-Y-O+ **£2,587** (£770; £384; £192) **Stalls** High

Form RPR
500 **1** **Frantical**[20] 3043 4-8-13 **50** (b[1]) GeorgeDowning[(3)] 12 61
(Tony Carroll) *dwlt: t.k.h: sn chsng ldrs: led ins fnl f: drvn out* **14/1**

3141 **2** hd **Solveig's Song**[7] 3488 4-9-8 **61** 6ex (p) MeganNicholls[(5)] 5 72
(Steve Woodman) *mid-div on outer: hdwy over 2f out: led wl over 1f out tl ins fnl f: hung lft: r.o* **5/2**[1]

5006 **3** 10 **Fitzwilliam**[10] 3401 4-8-8 **49** KillianHennessy[(7)] 11 41
(Mick Channon) *in tch: effrt over 2f out: wnt 3rd over 1f out: no ex* **11/1**

00-6 **4** 1 ¾ **Lady Hare (IRE)**[32] 2646 4-9-2 **55** DavidParkes[(5)] 2 44
(Ken Cunningham-Brown) *mid-div: rdn and lost pl 4f out: sme hdwy on inner over 2f out: no imp* **25/1**

0322 **5** ½ **Whip Up A Frenzy (IRE)**[7] 3488 4-8-13 **54** (p) GeorgeWood[(7)] 10 42+
(Richard Rowe) *led for 2f: pressed ldr: led 4f out tl wknd wl over 1f out* **11/4**[2]

5651 **6** 2 ¼ **Megalala (IRE)**[10] 3401 15-9-0 **53** AaronJones[(5)] 3 36+
(John Bridger) *prom: led after 2f tl 4f out: wknd 2f out* **9/1**

/0-0 **7** 1 ½ **Master Dancer**[174] 62 5-9-7 **55** DavidProbert 8 36
(Tim Vaughan) *dwlt: towards rr: rdn 3f out: n.d* **6/1**[3]

0460 **8** 2 **Standing Strong (IRE)**[10] 3401 8-8-12 **46** oh1 (p) LukeMorris 1 23
(Zoe Davison) *towards rr: rdn 3f out: nvr trbld ldrs* **66/1**

000- **9** 1 ¼ **My Mistress (IRE)**[44] 7814 4-8-9 **46** JosephineGordon[(3)] 4 20
(Phil McEntee) *mid-div: rdn over 2f out: sn outpcd* **33/1**

0660 **10** 9 **Little Flo**[63] 1748 5-8-12 **46** (t) JFEgan 9
(William Stone) *prom tl wknd over 2f out* **25/1**

6000 **11** 7 **Occult**[76] 1413 4-9-6 **54** JimCrowley 13
(Simon Dow) *dwlt: a bhd* **12/1**

2m 3.45s (-0.15) **Going Correction** +0.125s/f (Good) **11 Ran SP% 114.3**
Speed ratings (Par 101): **105,104,96,95,95 93,92,90,89,82 76**
CSF £46.31 CT £409.84 TOTE £15.30: £3.80, £1.60, £3.10; EX 64.60 Trifecta £640.50.
Owner A W Carroll **Bred** L J Vaessen **Trained** Cropthorne, Worcs
■ Secret Shot was withdrawn. Price at time of withdrawal 66/1. Rule 4 does not apply.

FOCUS
Race distance increased by 3 yards. The front pair came a long way clear in this moderate handicap. The winner was capable of earning RPRs in the high 60s last year.

3738 BET365 H'CAP 1m 3f 196y
4:15 (4:17) (Class 5) (0-70,69) 3-Y-O+ **£2,911** (£866; £432; £216) **Stalls** High

Form RPR
-431 **1** **Roy Rocket (FR)**[7] 3492 6-9-12 **67** 6ex JFEgan 2 79
(John Berry) *hld up in rr: hdwy in centre and wnt 6 l 2nd 2f out: styd on u.p to ld fnl strides* **3/1**[2]

-042 **2** hd **Palisade**[15] 3215 3-8-5 **60** (v) LukeMorris 5 72
(Sir Mark Prescott Bt) *chsd ldr: led 3f out: kicked 6 l clr 2f out: hrd rdn fnl f: ct fnl strides* **5/2**[1]

0-00 **3** 15 **Sixties Love**[21] 2994 5-10-0 **69** JimCrowley 3 57
(Simon Dow) *hld up in 5th: wnt 3rd in centre 2f out: no imp* **16/1**

2126 **4** ½ **Hint Of Grey (IRE)**[12] 3318 3-8-0 **62** GeorgeWood[(7)] 4 49
(Don Cantillon) *t.k.h: chsd ldrs tl hrd rdn and wknd 2f out* **10/3**[3]

012 **5** 22 **Ifan (IRE)**[50] 2086 8-9-5 **60** (p) DavidProbert 7 12
(Tim Vaughan) *broke wl: led tl 3f out: sn wknd* **15/2**

065 **6** 6 **Cliff Edge (IRE)**[26] 2835 3-8-10 **65** AndreaAtzeni 1 7
(Roger Varian) *chsd ldrs: rdn 5f out: wknd over 3f out* **11/2**

2m 33.57s (0.87) **Going Correction** +0.125s/f (Good)
WFA 3 from 5yo+ 14lb **6 Ran SP% 109.7**
Speed ratings (Par 103): **102,101,91,91,76 72**
CSF £10.38 TOTE £3.60: £1.50, £2.40; EX 9.00 Trifecta £83.70.
Owner McCarthy & Berry **Bred** John Berry **Trained** Newmarket, Suffolk

FOCUS
Race distance increased by 3 yards. Another race in which two dominated, the market leaders pulling 15l clear.

3739 CASINO AT BET365 H'CAP 7f 214y
4:45 (4:46) (Class 6) (0-65,65) 4-Y-O+ **£2,911** (£866; £432; £216) **Stalls** Low

Form RPR
1334 **1** **Duke Of North (IRE)**[21] 3004 4-9-0 **65** RhiainIngram[(7)] 6 72
(Jim Boyle) *chsd ldrs: led over 1f out: pushed out* **6/1**[3]

-404 **2** ½ **Bloodsweatandtears**[70] 1546 8-9-1 **59** FrederikTylicki 7 65
(William Knight) *hld up in rr: hdwy in centre 2f out: r.o to press wnr fnl 100yds: jst hld* **5/1**[2]

5461 **3** shd **Castle Talbot (IRE)**[14] 3258 4-9-3 **61** ShaneKelly 9 67
(Richard Hughes) *t.k.h towards rr: cajoled along and hdwy over 1f out: r.o fnl f* **11/4**[1]

3524 **4** 1 ½ **Knight Of The Air**[14] 3258 4-9-5 **63** GeorgeBaker 8 65
(Mick Channon) *t.k.h in midfield: promising hdwy on inner over 1f out: unable qck ins fnl f* **5/1**[2]

2455 **5** nk **Limerick Lord (IRE)**[32] 2646 4-8-12 **59** (p) ShelleyBirkett[(3)] 3 60
(Julia Feilden) *led at gd pce: 7 l clr 1/2-way: hdd over 1f out: no ex fnl f* **14/1**

1515 **6** nse **Hawk Moth (IRE)**[14] 3258 8-9-5 **63** (p) LukeMorris 1 64
(John Spearing) *towards rr: hdwy over 1f out: styng on at fin* **11/1**

0330 **7** 4 ½ **Sylvette**[97] 1047 4-8-13 **57** AndreaAtzeni 5 47
(Roger Varian) *prom tl wknd over 1f out* **10/1**

00-0 **8** ¾ **Just Isla**[12] 3314 6-8-13 **57** (p) DavidProbert 11 46
(Michael Blanshard) *in tch: effrt over 2f out: wknd over 1f out* **25/1**

000- **9** 9 **Perfect Orange**[260] 7164 4-9-1 **59** JimCrowley 2 26
(Lucy Wadham) *prom tl wknd wl over 1f out: eased* **10/1**

000- **10** 24 **Zamastar**[256] 7255 5-8-7 **56** ow1 JennyPowell[(5)] 4
(Brendan Powell) *a bhd: eased fnl 2f* **14/1**

1m 36.53s (0.53) **Going Correction** +0.125s/f (Good) **10 Ran SP% 118.0**
Speed ratings (Par 101): **102,101,101,99,99 99,95,94,85,61**
CSF £36.57 CT £102.08 TOTE £6.40: £2.30, £1.80, £1.90; EX 44.20 Trifecta £173.50.
Owner The Paddock Space Partnership **Bred** Kenilworth Partnership **Trained** Epsom, Surrey

FOCUS
Race distance increased by 3 yards. A modest handicap, but the form looks straightforward for the grade with the gallop a good one.

3740 POKER AT BET365 H'CAP 6f 209y
5:15 (5:15) (Class 5) (0-70,70) 3-Y-O **£2,911** (£866; £432; £216) **Stalls** Low

Form RPR
1505 **1** **False Id**[11] 3353 3-9-2 **65** (t) AndreaAtzeni 8 71+
(Robert Eddery) *t.k.h in rr: hdwy in centre over 1f out: r.o to ld fnl stride* **10/1**[3]

1-40 **2** shd **Marcle (IRE)**[29] 2749 3-8-11 **63** RobHornby[(3)] 6 68
(Ed de Giles) *led: kpt on u.p fnl f: ct fnl stride* **10/1**[3]

0061 **3** nk **Bay Of St Malo (IRE)**[22] 2968 3-9-7 **70** KieranO'Neill 5 74
(Richard Hannon) *in tch: rdn to join ldr 1f out: str chal fnl f: r.o* **4/1**[1]

-050 **4** 2 ¼ **Claymore (IRE)**[25] 2864 3-9-6 **69** (p) GeorgeBaker 9 67
(David Lanigan) *plld hrd in rr: rdn and r.o fnl 2f: nrest at fin* **4/1**[1]

-320 **5** nk **Naziba (IRE)**[50] 2106 3-9-1 **64** ShaneKelly 2 61
(David Menuisier) *towards rr: hdwy and in tch 2f out: kpt on fnl f* **10/1**[3]

-006 **6** ¾ **Star Jeanie**[21] 3000 3-9-1 **64** SeanLevey 4 59
(Richard Hannon) *mid-div: rdn 2f out: styd on same pce* **20/1**

4403 **7** ½ **Nidnod**[16] 3198 3-8-1 **53** ow1 DannyBrock[(3)] 3 47
(John Bridger) *chsd ldr: chal in centre 2f out: no ex over 1f out* **12/1**

-006 **8** 1 ¾ **Boutan**[34] 2586 3-9-1 **64** SteveDrowne 11 53
(George Baker) *t.k.h in rr: rdn and n.d fnl 2f* **16/1**

4065 **9** 2 ¼ **Angelic Guest (IRE)**[22] 2968 3-9-2 **65** LukeMorris 10 48
(Mick Channon) *in tch on outer: wknd 2f out* **10/1**[3]

0-01 **10** nse **R Bar Open (FR)**[21] 3003 3-9-2 **65** RobertWinston 1 48
(Dean Ivory) *in tch on inner: rdn over 2f out: wknd 1f out* **9/2**[2]

0450 **11** 7 **Boom Junior**[90] 1141 3-7-13 **51** oh6 JosephineGordon[(3)] 7 15
(Tony Carroll) *prom tl wknd over 2f out* **33/1**

1m 24.19s (1.09) **Going Correction** +0.125s/f (Good) **11 Ran SP% 115.8**
Speed ratings (Par 99): **98,97,97,94,94 93,93,91,88,88 80**
CSF £104.33 CT £469.14 TOTE £11.90: £3.50, £2.70, £1.80; EX 121.60 Trifecta £1101.80.

Owner Edwin Phillips & Mrs Pamela Aitken **Bred** N E Poole And George Thornton **Trained** Newmarket, Suffolk

FOCUS

Race distance increased by 3 yards. Several had their chance in what was an open handicap. The winner was well on top late and may build on this now.

3741 BINGO AT BET365 H'CAP 5f 59y

5:45 (5:45) (Class 5) (0-70,69) 3-Y-O+ **£2,911** (£866; £432; £216) **Stalls** Low

Form RPR

4400 **1** **Noverre To Go (IRE)**[6] 3510 10-9-3 **60**........................(p) DavidProbert 3 67
(Ronald Harris) *in tch: effrt 2f out: r.o wl to ld nr fin* **15/2**

0422 **2** 1/2 **Bahamian Sunrise**[7] 3487 4-9-12 **69**..................(p) MichaelJMMurphy 2 74
(John Gallagher) *led: kpt on u.p fnl 2f: hdd nr fin* **7/4**[1]

3-51 **3** shd **Hepworth Marble (IRE)**[12] 3320 3-9-5 **68**...................... GeorgeBaker 9 71
(Gary Moore) *pressed ldr: str chal fnl f: r.o* **11/4**[2]

125 **4** 2 **Secret Millionaire (IRE)**[50] 2088 9-9-0 **62**............(p) CharlieBennett(5) 6 60
(Shaun Harris) *hld up in 5th: hdwy on inner 2f out: one pce fnl f* **12/1**

4004 **5** 1 **Showtime Star**[14] 3259 6-9-11 **68**...................................... LukeMorris 5 62
(Gay Kelleway) *hld up in 6th: effrt and swtchd rt wl over 1f out: no imp* **4/1**[3]

0036 **6** 1 1/4 **Spray Tan**[25] 2845 6-8-0 **50**...(b) GeorgeWood(7) 8 40
(Tony Carroll) *s.i.s: outpcd* **16/1**

-220 **7** 2 1/2 **Excellent Aim**[73] 1496 9-9-1 **65**... JaneElliott(7) 1 46
(George Margarson) *prom tl wknd wl over 1f out* **25/1**

1m 3.22s (0.92) **Going Correction** +0.125s/f (Good)
WFA 3 from 4yo+ 6lb **7** Ran SP% **112.2**
Speed ratings (Par 103): **97,96,96,92,91 89,85**
CSF £20.31 CT £44.81 TOTE £7.90: £3.70, £1.50; EX 19.80 Trifecta £84.50.
Owner Robert & Nina Bailey **Bred** Gestut Gorlsdorf **Trained** Earlswood, Monmouths

FOCUS

Race distance increased by 3 yards. A modest sprint with the winner showing his best form since November.

T/Jkpt: Not won. T/Plt: £13.30 to a £1 stake. Pool of £87900.27 - 4800.03 winning tickets.
T/Qpdt: £6.20 to a £1 stake. Pool of £7505.18 - 893.30 winning tickets. **Lee McKenzie**

3093 CHEPSTOW (L-H)

Tuesday, June 28

OFFICIAL GOING: Soft

Wind: moderate half against Weather: drizzle, heavy shower race 3

3742 BRAINS BEER/EBF NOVICE STKS 6f 16y

6:10 (6:10) (Class 5) 2-Y-O **£3,234** (£962; £481; £240) **Stalls** Centre

Form RPR

3 **1** **Hedging (IRE)**[18] 3093 2-9-2 0.. JohnFahy 4 70+
(Eve Johnson Houghton) *s.i.s: in tch towards rr: rdn and hdwy 1/2-way: styd on to ld fnl 75yds: cosily* **7/4**[1]

54 **2** 1/2 **Bazwind (IRE)**[7] 3495 2-9-2 0.. SaleemGolam 6 68
(David Evans) *chsd ldrs: rdn 2f out: ev ch ins fnl f: hld nr fin* **7/1**

1644 **3** 3/4 **Nazik**[5] 3576 2-8-13 0... PaddyBradley(7) 7 69
(David Evans) *cl up: rdn over 2f out: led narrowly over 1f out tl unable qck fnl 75yds* **6/1**[3]

40 **4** 3/4 **Restore (IRE)**[25] 2847 2-8-11 0....................................... GaryMahon(5) 2 63
(Richard Hannon) *trckd ldrs: rdn over 2f out: disp ld over 1f out tl wandered jst ins fnl f: kpt on same pce* **12/1**

0 **5** 1 3/4 **Wentwell Yesterday (IRE)**[47] 2180 2-9-2 0................ WilliamCarson 3 58
(Jamie Osborne) *in tch: rdn over 2f out: clsd over 1f out: wknd fnl f* **14/1**

0 **6** 5 **Zebby Sizz (IRE)**[16] 3196 2-9-2 0... PatDobbs 9 43
(Richard Hannon) *led tl rdn and hdd over 2f out: wknd over 1f out* **9/2**[2]

5 **7** 6 **Altiko Tommy (IRE)**[50] 2082 2-9-2 0.................................. PatCosgrave 8 25
(George Baker) *chsd ldrs: rdn 1/2-way: n.m.r 2f out: sn wknd* **25/1**

8 2 **Stag Party (IRE)** 2-8-11 0....................................... EdwardGreatrex(5) 5 19
(Andrew Balding) *s.i.s: rn green and sn wl bhd: modest hdwy fnl f* **7/1**

9 shd **Viola Park** 2-8-11 0... JordanNason(5) 1 18
(Ronald Harris) *s.i.s: hung lft and a outpcd* **66/1**

1m 16.51s (4.51) **Going Correction** +0.475s/f (Yiel) **9** Ran SP% **113.5**
Speed ratings (Par 93): **88,87,86,85,83 76,68,65,65**
CSF £14.23 TOTE £2.40: £1.10, £2.00, £1.90; EX 13.80 Trifecta £36.40.
Owner The Picnic Partnership **Bred** Old Carhue & Graeng Bloodstock **Trained** Blewbury, Oxon

FOCUS

A fair juvenile novice contest. They went a respectable gallop on the soft ground with the winner on top late on.

3743 EQUESTRIAN SURFACES LTD H'CAP 6f 16y

6:40 (6:41) (Class 6) (0-65,65) 3-Y-O+ **£2,264** (£673; £336; £168) **Stalls** Centre

Form RPR

6136 **1** **Satchville Flyer**[14] 3255 5-8-9 **49**........................... KieranShoemark(3) 6 67
(David Evans) *chsd one other in centre: led overall wl over 1f out: rdn and veered lft fnl f: r.o strly: eased nr fin* **14/1**

-531 **2** 6 **Consistant**[22] 2974 8-9-10 **64**.. EoinWalsh(3) 8 63
(Brian Baugh) *prom stands' side: rdn 2f out: wnt 2nd 1f out: kpt on: no ch w wnr* **10/1**

20-0 **3** hd **Jacksonfire**[39] 2442 4-8-10 **48** oh1 ow1...........................(p) RobertTart 2 45
(Michael Mullineaux) *chsd ldr in gp of 4 far side: relegated to last in gp over 3f out: rdn and hdwy 2f out: r.o wl fnl f to dispute 2nd: no ch w wnr* **80/1**

62-4 **4** nk **Don't Blame Me**[173] 77 3-9-7 **65**.. JohnFahy 13 61
(Clive Cox) *chsd ldrs stands' side: led gp over 3f out tl rdn 2f out: r.o same pce fnl f* **12/1**

1244 **5** 1/2 **Camdora (IRE)**[103] 969 4-9-10 **61**.................................. TimmyMurphy 5 57
(Jamie Osborne) *led gp of 4 far side tl 1/2-way: rdn 2f out: one pce fnl f* **20/1**

0160 **6** 1/2 **Diamond Vine (IRE)**[7] 3486 8-9-2 **53**..........................(p) MartinHarley 12 48
(Ronald Harris) *towards rr stands' side: rdn over 2f out: styd on u.p fnl f* **33/1**

6330 **7** 1/2 **Divine Call**[25] 2846 9-10-0 **65**...(v) FrannyNorton 3 58
(Milton Bradley) *chsd ldrs in gp of 4 far side: swtchd rt to join main gp over 2f out: kpt on same pce* **20/1**

6363 **8** nk **Secret Witness**[6] 3510 10-9-3 **57**..........................(b) DanielMuscutt(3) 14 49
(Ronald Harris) *towards rr stands' side: rdn 2f out: r.o fnl f* **8/1**[3]

0423 **9** 3/4 **Mrs Warren**[14] 3258 6-9-8 **59**.. PatCosgrave 17 49
(George Baker) *prom stands' side: rdn over 2f out: one pce* **7/1**[2]

0060 **10** 1 3/4 **Bold Grove**[5] 3554 4-8-9 **46** oh1.................................(p) SamHitchcott 10 31
(Edward Bevan) *dwlt: towards rr stands' side: hdwy 1/2-way: rdn 2f out: wknd fnl f* **11/1**

0432 **11** nk **Wahaab (IRE)**[7] 3486 5-9-6 **57**... PatDobbs 9 41
(Richard Hughes) *wnt to post early: t.k.h: chsd ldrs stands' side: rdn over 2f out: wknd over 1f out* **13/8**[1]

0000 **12** 3 1/4 **Steel Rain**[38] 2458 8-8-4 **46** oh1................................ EdwardGreatrex(5) 7 20
(Nikki Evans) *led pair in centre and overall: rdn over 2f out: hdd wl over 1f out: grad wknd* **25/1**

00-0 **13** 3/4 **Euroquip Boy (IRE)**[36] 2542 9-8-12 **54**......................... NoelGarbutt(5) 1 26
(Michael Scudamore) *s.i.s: last in gp of 4 far side: hdwy to ld gp 1/2-way: sn rdn: wknd over 1f out* **20/1**

0-00 **14** 10 **Orbit The Moon (IRE)**[25] 2849 8-9-7 **58**................(bt) StevieDonohoe 11
(Grace Harris) *led stands' side gp and cl up overall: lost ld of gp over 3f out: sn rdn: bhd fnl 2f* **50/1**

1m 13.88s (1.88) **Going Correction** +0.475s/f (Yiel)
WFA 3 from 4yo+ 7lb **14** Ran SP% **117.8**
Speed ratings (Par 101): **106,98,97,97,96 96,95,94,93,91 91,86,85,72**
CSF £131.72 CT £10351.61 TOTE £16.50: £4.50, £3.00, £15.70; EX 236.30 Trifecta £3613.70 Part won..
Owner Anthony Cooke **Bred** Newsells Park Stud **Trained** Pandy, Monmouths

FOCUS

A modest handicap. They went a decent gallop and the winner was capable at this level last year, so this was no fluke.

3744 MERRY MILLERS AND WYE VALLEY GROUP MEDIAN AUCTION MAIDEN STKS 7f 16y

7:10 (7:12) (Class 6) 3-4-Y-O **£2,264** (£673; £336; £168) **Stalls** Centre

Form RPR

1 **Donnelly's Rainbow (IRE)** 3-9-5 0.............................. BarryMcHugh 5 70+
(Rebecca Bastiman) *t.k.h: bhd ldrs: pushed along to ld over 1f out: rdn and r.o wl fnl f: eased nr fin* **12/1**

- **2** 1 1/2 **Spinners Ball (IRE)** 3-9-2 0.. TomMarquand(3) 2 64+
(Sylvester Kirk) *towards rr: rdn and hdwy over 2f out: stl only 5th 1f out: r.o to go 2nd 75yds out but hld by wnr* **3/1**[2]

3 1 **Booborowie (IRE)** 3-9-5 0.. AdamBeschizza 4 62
(Jeremy Gask) *led to 4f out: rdn over 2f out: outpcd by ldng pair over 1f out: kpt on ins fnl f* **12/1**

6-00 **4** 1 1/2 **Golden Cape**[127] 679 3-9-0 50.. RobertTart 9 53
(Michael Mullineaux) *towards rr: rdn 3f out: no prog tl styd on wl fnl f* **25/1**

P3-0 **5** nk **Cause And Effect (IRE)**[21] 2998 3-9-5 0............................. PatDobbs 1 57
(Ralph Beckett) *cl up: led 4f out tl over 2f out: wknd over 1f out* **4/6**[1]

-660 **6** 1 1/4 **Equal Point**[3] 3648 3-9-0 63....................................[1] EdwardGreatrex(5) 6 54
(William Knight) *cl up: led narrowly over 2f out tl hdd over 1f out: sn edgd lft u.p: wknd and lost four pls fnl 75yds* **7/1**[3]

7 18 **Paca Punch** 3-9-0 0.. WilliamTwiston-Davies 8 4
(Michael Blanshard) *s.i.s: towards rr: rdn over 3f out: wknd and lost tch over 2f out* **25/1**

5-0 **8** 43 **Beyond The Edge**[25] 2848 4-9-9 0................................... StevieDonohoe 3
(Christopher Mason) *t.k.h: chsd ldrs tl wknd qckly 1/2-way: lost tch over 2f out: eased fnl f: t.o* **66/1**

1m 28.56s (5.36) **Going Correction** +0.475s/f (Yiel)
WFA 3 from 4yo 9lb **8** Ran SP% **122.1**
Speed ratings (Par 101): **88,86,85,83,83 81,61,11**
CSF £50.63 TOTE £16.20: £2.90, £1.30, £3.40; EX 82.60 Trifecta £402.00.
Owner Bastiman, Dorman & Dorman **Bred** Airlie Stud **Trained** Cowthorpe, N Yorks

FOCUS

A modest maiden. They went a sensible gallop on the soft surface, but the form is hard to pin down.

3745 FUSELAND RENEWABLES H'CAP 1m 14y

7:40 (7:40) (Class 5) (0-75,75) 3-Y-O+ **£2,911** (£866; £432; £216) **Stalls** Centre

Form RPR

00-0 **1** **Lorelina**[19] 3062 3-8-0 **62**.. EdwardGreatrex(5) 5 70
(Andrew Balding) *trckd ldr: rdn 2f out: led appr fnl f: r.o* **25/1**

3160 **2** 2 **Finelcity (GER)**[24] 2892 3-9-2 **73**....................................(b) PatCosgrave 8 76
(Harry Dunlop) *led: rdn 2f out: hdd appr fnl f: edgd rt and no ex fnl 100yds* **5/1**[3]

006 **3** 3/4 **Champagne Bob**[15] 3220 4-8-10 **62**........................ PatrickO'Donnell(5) 3 66
(Richard Price) *t.k.h: chsd ldrs: rdn and edgd lft over 2f out: one pce fnl f* **22/1**

2-12 **4** 2 **Feed The Goater (FR)**[11] 3357 3-9-3 **74**............................. PatDobbs 7 71
(Richard Hannon) *trckd ldrs: rdn over 2f out: one pce* **7/4**[2]

2-41 **5** 3 **Weather Front (USA)**[11] 3367 3-9-4 **75**......................... MartinHarley 2 65+
(James Tate) *hld up in last: rdn over 2f out: one pce and no real imp* **13/8**[1]

04-0 **6** nk **Paco Pat**[48] 2152 3-8-2 **62**.. TomMarquand(3) 4 51
(Richard Hannon) *chsd ldrs: rdn 3f out: one pce fnl 2f* **16/1**

0-00 **7** 1 3/4 **Monsieur Valentine**[36] 2542 4-8-8 **58**...................... GeorgeDowning(3) 1 45
(Tony Carroll) *hld up: rdn and sme hdwy over 2f out: wknd fnl f* **33/1**

1m 39.1s (2.90) **Going Correction** +0.475s/f (Yiel)
WFA 3 from 4yo 10lb **7** Ran SP% **108.1**
Speed ratings (Par 103): **104,102,101,99,96 95,94**
CSF £128.21 CT £2497.01 TOTE £22.00: £6.70, £2.50; EX 147.30 Trifecta £926.80.
Owner Tim Wixted & Tony Anderson **Bred** Tony Anderson & Tim Wixted **Trained** Kingsclere, Hants

FOCUS

A fair handicap. They went a respectable gallop and the winner had disappointed since her debut win, but was back to form here.

3746 BRAINS BEER H'CAP 2m 49y

8:10 (8:10) (Class 5) (0-75,75) 4-Y-O+ **£2,911** (£866; £432; £216) **Stalls** Low

Form RPR

-561 **1** **Medburn Cutler**[7] 3498 6-9-3 **71** 6ex...........................(p) FrannyNorton 9 82+
(Paul Henderson) *trckd ldr: shkn up to ld 2f out: styd on strly* **13/8**[1]

-304 **2** 3 **Fitzwilly**[17] 3161 6-9-7 **75**.. JFEgan 7 80
(Mick Channon) *led: rdn 4f out: hdd 2f out: sn no ch w wnr but kpt on to hold 2nd* **13/2**[2]

2141 **3** 3/4 **Urban Space**[18] 3099 10-8-3 **60**.......................................(t) TimClark(3) 4 64+
(John Flint) *mid-div: rdn and sltly outpcd over 3f out: swtchd rt over 2f out: styd on ins fnl f: tk 3rd nr fin* **13/2**[2]

6203 **4** 1/2 **Horseguardsparade**[15] 3221 5-9-0 **68**.........(p) WilliamTwiston-Davies 1 71
(Nigel Twiston-Davies) *s.i.s: hld up: racd wd in bk st tl c over and impr into midfield 1/2-way: chsd ldng pair 3f out: no further imp: lost 3rd nr fin* **16/1**

2-43 **5** 1 1/2 **Our Folly**[13] 2338 8-8-11 **65**..(t) MartinDwyer 3 66
(Stuart Kittow) *t.k.h early: chsd ldrs: rdn and lost pl 4f out: styd on fnl 2f* **13/2**[2]

460- **6** 3 **Kleitomachos (IRE)**[26] 7597 8-9-2 **70**.......................(tp[1]) TimmyMurphy 5 68
(Stuart Kittow) *chsd ldrs: rdn over 2f out: wknd over 1f out* **16/1**

6442 **7** ½ **Riptide**[9] 3437 10-8-6 **65**.......... EdwardGreatrex(5) 13 62
(Michael Scudamore) *hld up: rdn over 3f out: one pce and no real imp* **9/1**

0- **8** 1¼ **Willem (FR)**[7] 5781 6-8-10 **67**..........(p) TomMarquand(3) 10 63
(David Pipe) *racd keenly: hld up towards rr: rdn and hdwy 3f out: wknd appr fnl f* **20/1**

2210 **9** 29 **Jezza**[6] 3528 10-8-7 **64**..........(bt) KieranShoemark(3) 2 25
(Victor Dartnall) *trckd ldng pair: rdn over 3f out: qckly lost pl: eased whn no ch fnl f: t.o* **8/1**[3]

4/6- **10** ½ **Bilidn**[488] 689 8-9-1 **74**.......... NoelGarbutt(5) 12 34
(Laura Young) *a in rr: rdn 7f out: lost tch 4f out: t.o* **80/1**

3m 52.09s (13.19) **Going Correction** +0.65s/f (Yiel) **10** Ran SP% **117.0**
Speed ratings (Par 103): **93,91,91,90,90 88,88,87,73,73**
CSF £12.40 CT £55.78 TOTE £2.80: £1.30, £2.30, £2.40; EX 14.40 Trifecta £94.40.

Owner Eddie Evans **Bred** Eddie Evans **Trained** Whitsbury, Hants

FOCUS
A fair staying handicap. They went a sensible gallop on the soft surface with the first two dominating throughout and a step forward from the winner.

3747 FUSELAND ELECTRICAL AND MECHANICAL SERVICES H'CAP 1m 4f 23y
8:40 (8:40) (Class 6) (0-60,60) 4-Y-O+ **£2,264** (£673; £336; £168) **Stalls** Low

Form RPR

1-00 **1** **Bernisdale**[34] 1450 8-9-0 **56**.......... DanielMuscutt(3) 8 62
(John Flint) *chsd ldrs: wnt 2nd 6f out: led narrowly over 2f out: hld on gamely u.p fnl f* **14/1**

3642 **2** shd **Ring Eye (IRE)**[19] 3052 8-8-10 **54**.......... EdwardGreatrex(5) 14 60
(John O'Shea) *chsd ldrs: chal over 2f out: rdn over 1f out: ev ch fnl f: jst hld* **5/2**[2]

6260 **3** 1¾ **Invincible Wish (IRE)**[28] 2781 4-9-3 **59**.......... EoinWalsh(3) 10 62
(Trevor Wall) *s.s: in rr: hdwy 5f out: rdn 3f out: swtchd rt over 1f out: styd on to go 3rd post* **22/1**

3050 **4** hd **Doctor Kehoe**[19] 3072 4-9-0 **56**..........(vt) PhilipPrince(3) 12 59
(David Evans) *mid-div: hdwy over 5f out: rdn 3f out: wnt 3rd 2f out: sn edgd rt: kpt on: lost 3rd post* **15/2**[3]

5-62 **5** 2¼ **Mexican Mick**[7] 3498 7-8-6 **48**.......... ShelleyBirkett(3) 4 48
(Peter Hiatt) *towards rr: dropped to last over 4f out: sn rdn: hdwy on ins 3f out: one pce fnl 2f* **5/4**[1]

056- **6** 6 **Welsh Rebel**[214] 8014 4-8-13 **52**.......... JFEgan 2 43
(Nikki Evans) *t.k.h: chsd ldrs: rdn 4f out: wknd 2f out* **25/1**

650- **7** 4 **Honour Promise (IRE)**[245] 7543 4-9-0 **53**..(p) WilliamTwiston-Davies 11 38
(Bernard Llewellyn) *trckd ldr: led after 4f: rdn 4f out: hdd over 2f out: wknd over 1f out* **12/1**

4/2- **8** ¾ **Thundering Home**[49] 594 9-9-1 **54**..........(t) PatDobbs 9 37
(Richard Mitchell) *hld up: rdn 3f out: wknd 2f out* **16/1**

40/ **9** 19 **Petit Ecuyer (FR)**[56] 651 10-8-4 **48**.......... NoelGarbutt(5) 5 3
(Dai Williams) *mid-div tl rdn and wknd over 4f out: t.o* **66/1**

6-60 **10** 4 **Miss Mittens**[24] 2901 4-8-7 **46** oh1.......... JohnFahy 1
(Geoffrey Deacon) *led 4f: styd prom tl wknd over 3f out: t.o* **66/1**

2m 48.76s (9.76) **Going Correction** +0.65s/f (Yiel) **10** Ran SP% **116.2**
Speed ratings (Par 101): **93,92,91,91,90 86,83,82,70,67**
CSF £47.89 CT £785.61 TOTE £16.90: £3.30, £1.80, £5.30; EX 64.70 Trifecta £514.90.

Owner Roderick James **Bred** Evelyn Duchess Of Sutherland **Trained** Kenfig Hill, Bridgend

FOCUS
A moderate middle-distance handicap. They went a sensible gallop under testing conditions and the winner proved very game. The form is very straightforward for the level.

3748 ALL WEATHER RIDING SURFACES FROM EQUESTRIAN SURFACES H'CAP 1m 2f 36y
9:10 (9:11) (Class 6) (0-65,65) 4-Y-O+ **£2,264** (£673; £336; £168) **Stalls** Low

Form RPR

0000 **1** **Indian Chief (IRE)**[26] 2836 6-9-7 **65**.......... BarryMcHugh 6 77
(Rebecca Bastiman) *hld up: hdwy 5f out: wnt 2nd gng wl 3f out: led 2f out: sn drew clr: easily* **5/1**[3]

36-0 **2** 6 **Approaching Star (FR)**[26] 1049 5-7-11 **46**.......... NoelGarbutt(5) 8 44
(Dai Burchell) *cl up: led after 2f: rdn over 2f out: sn hdd: kpt on same pce and no ch w easy wnr* **16/1**

3002 **3** 1¼ **Highlife Dancer**[4] 3620 8-8-12 **56**.......... CharlesBishop 5 52
(Mick Channon) *led 2f: styd prom: lost 2nd 3f out: kpt on same pce u.p* **10/3**[1]

0031 **4** 1¾ **Dovil's Duel (IRE)**[48] 2144 5-9-4 **65**.......... EoinWalsh(3) 3 58
(Tony Newcombe) *dwlt: hld up: hdwy in centre of trck 4f out: rdn over 2f out: one pce appr fnl f* **7/2**[2]

3122 **5** ½ **Innoko (FR)**[18] 3095 6-9-2 **63**.......... GeorgeDowning(3) 10 55
(Tony Carroll) *mid-div: lost pl over 5f out: clsd again over 3f out: one pce fnl 2f* **6/1**

4-35 **6** 3¼ **Edge (IRE)**[39] 2448 5-8-5 **49**..........(b) JimmyQuinn 11 35
(Bernard Llewellyn) *s.i.s: towards rr: hdwy over 3f out: disp hld 3rd over 1f out tl wknd ins fnl f* **12/1**

3040 **7** 11 **Subordinate (GER)**[21] 2996 7-9-7 **65**..........(vt[1]) TimmyMurphy 1 31
(Emma Lavelle) *prom: wnt 2nd after 4f: c over to stands' side home turn over 4f out: sn rdn and lost pl: no ch fnl 2f* **9/1**

2536 **8** 29 **Coup De Vent**[18] 3096 5-8-3 **52** ow1..........(be) PatrickO'Donnell(5) 4
(John O'Shea) *hld up: rdn over 4f out: wknd over 3f out: bhd fnl 2f: t.o* **25/1**

0-00 **9** 2½ **Kaaber (USA)**[25] 2849 5-8-3 **47**..........(b) RyanPowell 2
(Roy Brotherton) *chsd ldrs tl wknd over 3f out: bhd fnl 2f: t.o* **66/1**

245- **10** 1¾ **Prim And Proper**[292] 6237 5-9-4 **65**..........(p) DanielMuscutt(3) 9
(John Flint) *chsd ldrs: rdn over 3f out: wknd qckly: bhd fnl 2f: t.o* **8/1**

2m 16.44s (5.84) **Going Correction** +0.65s/f (Yiel) **10** Ran SP% **116.3**
Speed ratings (Par 101): **102,97,96,94,94 91,83,59,57,56**
CSF £81.04 CT £304.89 TOTE £5.10: £1.70, £4.50, £1.40; EX 92.40 Trifecta £335.50.

Owner Castle Construction (NE) Ltd **Bred** Paget Bloodstock **Trained** Cowthorpe, N Yorks

FOCUS
A modest handicap and the winner, who was rated as high as 90 last year, hacked up. They went a respectable gallop.

T/Plt: £1,313.10 to a £1 stake. Pool of £79133.56 - 43.99 winning tickets. T/Qpdt: £140.10 to a £1 stake. Pool of £8068.96 - 42.60 winning tickets. **Richard Lowther**

[3547] HAMILTON (R-H)
Tuesday, June 28

OFFICIAL GOING: Good to firm (good in places; 8.5)
Wind: Light, half behind Weather: Overcast, raining from race 5 (4.00)

3749 HIGHLAND SPRING WATER AVON GORGE NOVICE AUCTION STKS (£20,000 HIGHLAND SPRING SERIES QUALIFIER) 6f 6y
2:00 (2:01) (Class 5) 2-Y-O **£3,557** (£1,058; £529; £264) **Stalls** High

Form RPR

0 **1** **Baileys Showgirl (FR)**[12] 3301 2-8-11 0.......... JoeFanning 1 77
(Mark Johnston) *pressed ldr: rdn over 2f out: led over 1f out: drvn clr ins fnl f* **15/2**[3]

2 **2** 3 **Princeofthequeen (USA)**[15] 3222 2-9-2 0.......... DanielTudhope 6 73
(David O'Meara) *t.k.h: trckd ldrs: effrt and drvn along wl over 1f out: chsd wnr ins fnl f: kpt on: no imp* **3/1**[2]

3 **3** hd **Alfie's Angel (IRE)**[15] 3208 2-9-2 0.......... PaulMulrennan 3 72
(Bryan Smart) *led: edgd rt over 3f out: rdn and hdd over 1f out: kpt on same pce ins fnl f* **1/1**[1]

4 **4** 8 **Harbour Lightning**[14] 3261 2-8-11 0.......... PJMcDonald 4 43
(Ann Duffield) *dwlt: t.k.h and sn prom on outside: effrt and rdn over 1f out: hung rt and sn wknd* **8/1**

0 **5** nk **Our Boy John (IRE)**[15] 3208 2-9-2 0.......... TonyHamilton 5 48
(Richard Fahey) *t.k.h: trckd ldrs: drvn and outpcd over 2f out: sn n.d* **14/1**

00 **6** 4 **Kazanan (IRE)**[15] 3223 2-8-11 0.......... ConnorBeasley 2 31
(Michael Dods) *hld up on outside: pushed along and effrt on outside over 2f out: wknd wl over 1f out* **100/1**

7 1½ **Elmwood** 2-9-2 0.......... DougieCostello 7 31
(Andrew Slattery, Ire) *t.k.h: hld up: rdn and outpcd over 2f out: btn over 1f out* **25/1**

1m 12.43s (0.23) **Going Correction** -0.05s/f (Good) **7** Ran SP% **109.4**
Speed ratings (Par 93): **96,92,91,81,80 75,73**
CSF £27.58 TOTE £9.00: £3.20, £1.40; EX 29.30 Trifecta £45.60.

Owner G R Bailey Ltd (Baileys Horse Feeds) **Bred** Ecurie Des Monceaux **Trained** Middleham Moor, N Yorks

FOCUS
The ground had dried out a little and was now good to firm, good in places. The rail on the loop was out by 6 yards, adding around 24 yards to the distances of races 2 and 3. A few of these in this ordinary novice auction event had already shown ability and the first three pulled right away. Joe Fanning said that it was good ground. The placed horses have been rated to their opening marks.

3750 FERNIEGAIR H'CAP 1m 67y
2:30 (2:31) (Class 6) (0-60,60) 3-Y-O+ **£2,911** (£866; £432; £216) **Stalls** Low

Form RPR

-503 **1** **Whitkirk**[15] 3224 3-8-12 **54**.......... JoeyHaynes 1 65+
(Jedd O'Keeffe) *in tch on ins: hdwy over 2f out: led over 1f out: rdn clr fnl f* **5/2**[2]

-006 **2** 4 **Intensified (IRE)**[22] 2958 5-9-0 **46** oh1..........(b[1]) JamesSullivan 11 48
(Ruth Carr) *hld up: hdwy over 2f out: sn rdn: chsd (clr) wnr ins fnl f: no imp* **20/1**

6444 **3** ½ **Incurs Four Faults**[13] 3287 5-9-3 **49**.......... JasonHart 6 50
(Keith Dalgleish) *hld up: stdy hdwy over 3f out: kpt on ins fnl f: nrst fin* **9/1**

31 **4** 1¾ **Jocks Wa Hae (IRE)**[13] 3287 3-9-0 **56**..........(p) JoeFanning 10 51+
(John Patrick Shanahan, Ire) *in tch on outside: lost pl after 2f: sn pushed along: rdn and effrt on outside over 2f out: kpt on fnl f: no imp* **2/1**[1]

400- **5** 1¾ **Taopix**[283] 6527 4-9-7 **53**.......... DavidNolan 5 46
(Karen McLintock) *hld up: rdn and outpcd over 3f out: rallied fnl f: nvr able to chal* **22/1**

3060 **6** ½ **Gone With The Wind (GER)**[11] 3367 5-10-0 **60**........(t) AndrewMullen 7 52
(Rebecca Bastiman) *s.i.s: hld up: stdy hdwy over 3f out: sn rdn: outpcd over 1f out* **16/1**

-034 **7** ¾ **Riponian**[20] 3020 6-9-2 **48**.......... TonyHamilton 3 38
(Susan Corbett) *led: clr over 4f out: hdd over 1f out: wknd fnl f* **6/1**[3]

004 **8** 4 **Beadlam (IRE)**[14] 3249 3-8-13 **55**.......... SamJames 2 34
(David Loughnane) *chsd ldrs: wnt 2nd over 4f out to over 2f out: rdn and wknd over 1f out* **33/1**

5606 **9** 6 **Opt Out**[11] 3344 6-10-0 **60**..........(p) PaulMulrennan 4 27
(Alistair Whillans) *prom: rdn along over 2f out: hung rt and wknd wl over 1f out* **12/1**

3-60 **10** 22 **Tseo**[24] 2899 4-9-9 **55**.......... TomEaves 9
(David Brown) *in tch on outside: struggling over 3f out: sn wknd: t.o* **66/1**

4000 **11** 7 **Coolcalmcollected (IRE)**[19] 3078 4-9-9 **55**..........(p) PJMcDonald 8
(Andrew Crook) *chsd ldr to over 4f out: sn rdn and struggling: t.o* **50/1**

1m 47.56s (-0.84) **Going Correction** -0.05s/f (Good)
WFA 3 from 4yo+ 10lb **11** Ran SP% **115.3**
Speed ratings (Par 101): **102,98,97,95,94 93,92,88,82,60 53**
CSF £57.17 CT £398.31 TOTE £3.20: £1.30, £5.00, £2.40; EX 58.00 Trifecta £578.20.

Owner T S Ingham **Bred** Whatton Manor Stud **Trained** Middleham Moor, N Yorks

FOCUS
Rail movement added around 24 yards to race distance. A moderate handicap in which few came into it in much form, but the pace was good and the draw may have played its part too. A personal best from the winner.

3751 RACING WELFARE STABLE STAFF WEEK H'CAP 1m 4f 14y
3:00 (3:00) (Class 5) (0-75,73) 3-Y-O+ **£3,881** (£1,155; £577; £288) **Stalls** Low

Form RPR

40-1 **1** **Sharjah (IRE)**[25] 2882 6-9-11 **70**..........(b) TonyHamilton 6 78
(Andrew Slattery, Ire) *t.k.h: mde all at modest gallop: rdn 2f out: kpt on strly fnl f: unchal* **10/1**

-615 **2** 1½ **Hillgrove Angel (IRE)**[17] 3149 4-9-12 **71**.......... DanielTudhope 5 76
(Iain Jardine) *prom: effrt and rdn over 2f out: chsd wnr over 1f out: kpt on fnl f: nt pce to chal* **8/1**

44-2 **3** hd **Long Call**[20] 3042 3-9-0 **73**.......... MartinLane 3 78
(Charlie Appleby) *t.k.h early: trckd ldrs: rdn and outpcd over 2f out: rallied and disp 2nd pl over 1f out: kpt on ins fnl f* **2/1**[1]

3162 **4** ½ **Monsieur Glory**[7] 3482 3-8-5 **64**..........(p) PJMcDonald 4 68+
(Tom Dascombe) *hld up: drvn along over 2f out: no imp tl styd on fnl f: nt pce to chal* **9/2**[3]

2061 **5** 1½ **The Kid**[25] 2853 5-10-0 **73**..........(p) DougieCostello 2 74
(John Quinn) *hld up in tch on ins: rdn over 2f out: no imp fr over 1f out* **20/1**

5012 **6** 2¾ **San Quentin (IRE)**[26] 2813 5-9-8 **72**.............................(p) JoshDoyle[(5)] 1 69
(David Loughnane) *hld up in last pl: stdy hdwy on outside over 3f out: rdn over 2f out: wknd over 1f out* **8/1**

0321 **7** ¾ **Lara Carbonara (IRE)**[5] 3547 4-9-13 **72** 6ex..................... JoeFanning 7 68
(John Patrick Shanahan, Ire) *t.k.h: chsd wnr: rdn over 2f out: lost 2nd over 1f out: wknd ins fnl f* **4/1**[2]

0-54 **R** **Clear Spell (IRE)**[10] 3395 5-9-3 **69**................................ RowanScott[(7)] 8
(Alistair Whillans) *ref to r* **25/1**

2m 40.01s (1.41) **Going Correction** -0.05s/f (Good)
WFA 3 from 4yo+ 14lb **8** Ran SP% **111.4**
Speed ratings (Par 103): **93,92,91,91,90 88,88,**
CSF £81.68 CT £219.83 TOTE £12.80: £2.90, £2.40, £1.20; EX 87.10 Trifecta £480.30.

Owner Mrs S Slattery **Bred** John Connaughton **Trained** Thurles, Co Tipperary

FOCUS
Rail movement added around 24yds to race distance. An ordinary handicap run at a stop-start gallop and a finely judged ride by the winning jockey. The field was reduced by one when Clear Spell firmly planted himself as the gates opened. The winner has been rated to his better Irish form last year.

3752 EBF STALLIONS SOBA CONDITIONS STKS 5f 7y
3:30 (3:30) (Class 3) 3-Y-0+ **£9,960** (£2,982; £1,491; £745) **Stalls** Centre

Form RPR

2000 **1** **Monsieur Joe (IRE)**[17] 3151 9-9-4 104.............................. MartinLane 4 111
(Paul Midgley) *pressed ldr: pushed along 2f out: drvn to ld ins fnl f: kpt on strly* **11/2**[2]

0000 **2** ¾ **Move In Time**[14] 3244 8-9-4 107.................................(v) DanielTudhope 2 108
(David O'Meara) *led: rdn over 1f out: hdd ins fnl f: kpt on same pce towards fin* **5/4**[1]

4041 **3** ¾ **Line Of Reason (IRE)**[14] 3250 6-9-4 106..................... PaulMulrennan 3 106
(Paul Midgley) *dwlt: t.k.h: trckd ldrs: rdn and sltly outpcd over 1f out: kpt on ins fnl f* **5/4**[1]

400- **4** 3¼ **Muhadathat**[302] 5952 3-8-7 95.. JoeFanning 1 87
(Mark Johnston) *chsd ldrs: pushed along over 2f out: wknd fnl f* **22/1**[3]

58.63s (-1.37) **Going Correction** -0.05s/f (Good)
WFA 3 from 6yo+ 6lb **4** Ran SP% **108.6**
Speed ratings (Par 107): **108,106,105,100**
CSF £12.92 TOTE £6.40; EX 14.10 Trifecta £17.70.

Owner Taylor's Bloodstock Ltd **Bred** Nicola And Eleanor Kent **Trained** Westow, N Yorks

FOCUS
An interesting conditions sprint in which the quartet came up the middle. Paul Midgley was doubly represented and took the prize, but not with the one most people would have expected. The winner has been rated to last year's best.

3753 TOTEPOOL CHATELHERAULT PALACE H'CAP 6f 6y
4:00 (4:00) (Class 4) (0-80,80) 3-Y-0+ **£6,469** (£1,925; £962; £481) **Stalls** High

Form RPR

0-33 **1** **Spirit Of Zeb (IRE)**[20] 3021 4-9-2 **75**..................... AdamMcNamara[(7)] 6 85
(Richard Fahey) *pressed ldr: led over 1f out: sn hrd pressed: hld on gamely ins fnl f* **11/2**[3]

151 **2** shd **Born Innocent (IRE)**[5] 3553 3-8-8 **67** 6ex......................... JoeFanning 3 75
(John Patrick Shanahan, Ire) *cl up: chal over 1f out: sn rdn: kpt on fnl f: jst hld* **9/4**[1]

6022 **3** 1¾ **Cosmic Chatter**[5] 3553 6-9-8 **74**.................................(p) JamesSullivan 9 77
(Ruth Carr) *hld up in tch: effrt and rdn over 1f out: kpt on ins fnl f: nt rch first two* **11/2**[3]

-064 **4** ½ **Dark Defender**[10] 3394 3-9-5 **78**...................................(v[1]) PhillipMakin 2 78
(Keith Dalgleish) *t.k.h: hld up: rdn and effrt over 1f out: kpt on ins fnl f* **5/1**[2]

2330 **5** 1 **Barkston Ash**[45] 2259 8-10-0 **80**.......................................(p) JasonHart 7 78
(Eric Alston) *hld up in tch: effrt and hdwy on outside over 1f out: outpcd ins fnl f* **10/1**

5040 **6** 2½ **Sunraider (IRE)**[20] 3021 9-9-6 **72**.. MartinLane 4 61
(Paul Midgley) *dwlt: sn pushed along in rr: struggling 1/2-way: sme late hdwy: nvr on terms* **12/1**

0-52 **7** ¾ **Tikthebox (IRE)**[46] 2200 3-9-7 **80**... TomEaves 5 64
(David Brown) *led tl rdn and hdd over 1f out: sn wknd* **20/1**

32-1 **8** 2 **Birkdale (IRE)**[26] 2809 3-9-4 **77**.................................. DanielTudhope 10 54
(David O'Meara) *hld up in tch: drvn and outpcd over 2f out: n.d after* **8/1**

4-00 **9** 5 **Baltic Raider (IRE)**[31] 2695 3-9-3 **76**........................... PaulMulrennan 1 35
(Michael Dods) *dwlt and wnt rt s: bhd: rdn over 2f out: wknd wl over 1f out* **33/1**

1m 11.04s (-1.16) **Going Correction** -0.05s/f (Good)
WFA 3 from 4yo+ 7lb **9** Ran SP% **113.8**
Speed ratings (Par 105): **105,104,102,101,100 97,96,93,86**
CSF £17.97 CT £70.90 TOTE £6.00: £1.90, £1.50, £2.50; EX 21.70 Trifecta £90.90.

Owner IMEJ Racing **Bred** Tally-Ho Stud **Trained** Musley Bank, N Yorks

FOCUS
Not a bad sprint handicap and the field raced more towards the nearside. A turf perssonal best from the winner.

3754 RACINGUK.COM MAIDEN STKS 6f 6y
4:30 (4:36) (Class 5) 3-Y-0+ **£3,881** (£1,155; £577) **Stalls** High

Form RPR

4-22 **1** **David's Duchess (IRE)**[15] 3209 3-9-0 75....................... TonyHamilton 6 73+
(Richard Fahey) *mde all: qcknd clr on bridle fr over 1f out: canter* **1/3**[1]

455 **2** 2½ **Lucky Violet (IRE)**[14] 3264 4-9-7 0............................. RoystonFfrench 3 59
(Iain Jardine) *t.k.h early: chsd wnr: rdn over 1f out: plugged on fnl f: no ch w easy wnr* **14/1**[3]

2036 **3** 9 **Mister Mischief**[4] 3603 3-9-5 66.................................(p) PaulMulrennan 4 33
(Paul Midgley) *t.k.h: trckd ldrs: shkn up and edgd rt over 2f out: wknd over 1f out: eased whn btn ins fnl f* **3/1**[2]

1m 12.88s (0.68) **Going Correction** -0.05s/f (Good)
WFA 3 from 4yo 7lb **3** Ran SP% **106.7**
Speed ratings (Par 103): **93,89,77**
CSF £4.83 TOTE £1.10; EX 4.40 Trifecta £3.40.

Owner Crown Select **Bred** J Cullinan **Trained** Musley Bank, N Yorks

■ Silently was withdrawn. Price at time of withdrawal 20/1. Rule 4 does not apply.

FOCUS
As uncompetitive a maiden as you are ever likely to see, reduced by one when the newcomer Silently was withdrawn after getting into a state and breaking out through the back of her stall. The race has been rated around the runner-up.

3755 HIGH DEFINITION RACING UK H'CAP 5f 7y
5:00 (5:08) (Class 6) (0-65,65) 3-Y-0+ **£2,911** (£866; £432; £216) **Stalls** Centre

Form RPR

6225 **1** **Bronze Beau**[7] 3494 9-10-0 **65**...(tp) ShaneGray 8 72
(Kristin Stubbs) *mde all: shkn up over 1f out: hrd pressed ins fnl f: pushed out* **15/2**

2065 **2** ½ **Chookie's Lass**[5] 3553 5-9-11 **62**.. JasonHart 5 67
(Keith Dalgleish) *cl up: rdn and ev ch over 1f out: edgd lft ins fnl f: kpt on: hld nr fin* **6/1**

0445 **3** 2½ **Tribesman**[14] 3265 3-9-6 **63**...(p) DanielTudhope 2 57
(Marjorie Fife) *in tch on outside: rdn over 2f out: kpt on ins fnl f: nt rch first two* **7/2**[2]

2020 **4** ¾ **Little Belter (IRE)**[7] 3484 4-9-6 **57**...................................(p) JoeFanning 7 51
(Keith Dalgleish) *prom: effrt and rdn over 1f out: no ex ins fnl f* **11/2**[3]

0-00 **5** hd **Slim Chance (IRE)**[15] 3211 7-9-7 **58**................................ AndrewElliott 1 51
(Simon West) *taken early to post: rrd and lost grnd s: bhd on outside: rdn and hdwy 1/2-way: no imp fnl f* **10/1**

0012 **6** 1 **Fuel Injection**[20] 3022 5-9-0 **51**.................................. PaulMulrennan 10 40
(Paul Midgley) *in tch nr side of gp: rdn over 2f out: outpcd over 1f out* **11/2**[3]

232 **7** 3 **Lady Wootton**[20] 3017 3-9-3 **60**.......................................(b) PhillipMakin 6 36
(Keith Dalgleish) *chsd ldrs tl rdn and wknd over 1f out* **3/1**[1]

0556 **8** 1 **Mystical King**[36] 2523 6-8-9 **46** oh1...........................(p) AndrewMullen 9 21
(Linda Perratt) *awkward s: bhd and outpcd: nvr on terms* **80/1**

0000 **9** 11 **It's Time For Bed**[20] 3022 4-8-9 **46** oh1......................... JamesSullivan 4
(Linda Perratt) *sn bhd: struggling bef 1/2-way: lost tch fr over 1f out* **100/1**

59.41s (-0.59) **Going Correction** -0.05s/f (Good)
WFA 3 from 4yo+ 6lb **9** Ran SP% **115.4**
Speed ratings (Par 101): **102,101,97,96,95 94,89,87,70**
CSF £51.81 CT £187.52 TOTE £8.40: £2.30, £2.10, £1.60; EX 49.20 Trifecta £236.30.

Owner D Arundale **Bred** Meon Valley Stud **Trained** Norton, N Yorks

FOCUS
A moderate sprint handicap with several of these finding it difficult to win.
T/Plt: £165.40 to a £1 stake. Pool of £60092.48 - 265.10 winning tickets. T/Qpdt: £25.60 to a £1 stake. Pool of £4908.64 - 141.40 winning tickets. **Richard Young**

3756 - 3762a (Foreign Racing) - See Raceform Interactive

3335 SAINT-CLOUD (L-H)
Tuesday, June 28

OFFICIAL GOING: Turf: good

3763a PRIX DE NOISY-LE-ROI (CLAIMER) (2YO) (TURF) 7f
1:20 (1:20) 2-Y-O **£9,926** (£3,970; £2,977; £1,985; £992)

RPR

1 **Erica Bing**[21] 3006 2-9-3 0.. MaximeGuyon 11 78
(Jo Hughes) *led: rdn and jnd 2f out: wnt on again over 1f out: kpt on gamely fnl f and a jst doing enough* **14/5**[2]

2 ½ **Frozen Queen (IRE)**[19] 3091 2-8-8 0....................... IoritzMendizabal 12 68
(D Windrif, France) **16/1**

3 1¾ **Jenychope (FR)**[12] 2-8-11 0.............................. ChristopheSoumillon 10 66
(D Windrif, France) **13/5**[1]

4 1½ **Countess Allegro (FR)**[12] 2-8-8 0.............................. GregoryBenoist 1 59
(M Boutin, France) **43/5**

5 ¾ **Cholpon Ata (FR)**[12] 2-8-8 0.................................... MickaelBarzalona 5 57
(Mme P Butel, France) **18/1**

6 2 **Jantine (FR)**[21] 2-8-8 0.. PierreBazire[(3)] 3 55
(Mme M Bollack-Badel, France) **55/1**

7 hd **Chiquit Indian (FR)** 2-9-1 0...................................... SebastienMaillot 2 58
(E Caroux, France) **59/1**

8 1¼ **Macho Falcon (FR)** 2-8-11 0.. ThierryJarnet 14 51
(J-P Lopez, France) **29/1**

9 3½ **Last Paradise (IRE)**[11] 3361 2-8-8 0.............................. ThierryThulliez 13 38
(Harry Dunlop) *prom on outer: rdn and effrt 2f out: no ex over 1f out: wknd* **9/1**

10 2½ **Ilovetoboogie (FR)** 2-8-11 0.. TheoBachelot 6 34
(S Wattel, France) **12/1**

11 3 **Freeze Fly (IRE)**[26] 2844 2-8-8 0.................................. CristianDemuro 8 23
(J-V Toux, France) **21/1**

12 2 **Miss Bombay (IRE)** 2-8-11 0.. UmbertoRispoli 7 21
(A Giorgi, Italy) **13/2**[3]

13 2½ **Zing (FR)**[6] 2-9-1 0... RonanThomas 4 18
(Robert Collet, France) **41/1**

1m 30.74s (-1.46) **13** Ran SP% **120.4**
WIN (incl. 1 euro stake): 3.80. PLACES: 1.60, 3.80, 1.50. DF: 31.10. SF: 57.20.
Owner Richard Kent & Jo Hughes **Bred** Mickley Stud & Sue Shone **Trained** Lambourn, Berks

3764a PRIX DE BAILLY (CLAIMER) (3YO) (TURF) 7f
2:20 (2:20) 3-Y-O **£8,455** (£3,382; £2,536; £1,691; £845)

RPR

1 **Rip Van Suzy (IRE)**[21] 3007 3-8-11 0............................ MaximeGuyon 6 72
(Jo Hughes) *in tch: rdn to chal 2f out: led ent fnl f: r.o strly and asserted: readily* **36/5**[3]

2 2 **Passeport (IRE)**[57] 3-8-13 0 ow2....................... ChristopheSoumillon 11 69
(Z Koplik, Czech Republic) **56/1**

3 ½ **Basse Reine (FR)**[33] 3-9-1 0...................................... AntoineHamelin 10 69
(M Figge, Germany) **13/1**

4 nk **Sing Something**[19] 3-9-1 0...(b) TheoBachelot 12 68
(P Monfort, France) **89/10**

5 1 **Lily Paramount (FR)**[164] 3-8-11 0...................(p) Pierre-CharlesBoudot 5 62
(J C Napoli, France) **20/1**

6 ½ **Kenshaba (FR)**[50] 2117 3-9-1 0................................ StephanePasquier 9 64
(N Clement, France) **2/1**[1]

7 ½ **Take A Look (FR)**[252] 3-9-1 0.. PierreBazire[(3)] 4 66
(Gianluca Bietolini, Italy) **19/1**

8 nk **Insolito (FR)**[19] 3-8-11 0... UmbertoRispoli 1 58
(A Bonin, France) **36/1**

9 ½ **Mesonera (FR)**[19] 3-9-1 0..(p) FabriceVeron 3 61
(J Parize, France) **20/1**

10 *snk* **Secretariatus (FR)**[48] 3-9-1 0 GeraldMosse 8 60
(V Luka Jr, Czech Republic) **65/1**
11 *shd* **Marchia Rosay (FR)**[16] 3-8-11 0 ThomasMessina 2 56
(P Monfort, France) **62/1**
12 *½* **Diva Bere (FR)**[23] 3-9-2 0 EddyHardouin 7 60
(E Wianny, France) **21/1**
13 *2½* **Rigel Star (IRE)**[17] 3-9-4 0 VincentCheminaud 13 55
(M Delzangles, France) **54/10**[2]
1m 29.35s (-2.85) **13** Ran SP% **105.0**
WIN (incl. 1 euro stake): 8.20. PLACES: 2.80, 2.80. 3.90. DF: 14.90. SF: 39.90.
Owner R P Phillips **Bred** Diomed Bloodstock Ltd **Trained** Lambourn. Berks

[3508] BATH (L-H)
Wednesday, June 29

OFFICIAL GOING: Soft (5.3)
Wind: quite strong, against Weather: rain becoming heavier (poor visibility last 3 races)

3765 DJ & P H'CAP (BATH SUMMER STAYERS' SERIES QUALIFIER) 1m 3f 144y
6:00 (6:03) (Class 6) (0-60,60) 3-Y-O **£2,264** (£673; £336; £168) **Stalls** Low

Form RPR
-422 **1** **Final Choice**[7] 3509 3-8-10 **52** (p) KieranShoemark(3) 14 61
(Roger Charlton) *s.i.s: sn mid-div: smooth hdwy over 2f out: rdn to ld ent fnl f: briefly drifted lft: styd on* **1/2**[1]
0-03 **2** *2½* **Bob's Boy**[11] 3401 3-8-13 **52** (p) JackMitchell 6 56
(Jose Santos) *led: rdn and hdd ent fnl f: styd on but sn hld by wnr* **9/1**[2]
0030 **3** *3¼* **Sixties Idol**[20] 3063 3-9-1 **54** CharlesBishop 3 53
(Mick Channon) *hld up towards rr: hdwy 2f out: sn rdn: styd on wl fnl f: snatched 3rd fnl strides* **16/1**
0-06 **4** *½* **Iballisticvin**[44] 2294 3-8-7 **46** oh1 SamHitchcott 5 44
(Gary Moore) *mid-div: hdwy 2f out: sn rdn: chsd ldng pair briefly fnl 100yds: lost 3rd fnl strides* **20/1**
400- **5** *nse* **Lilly Bonbon (IRE)**[201] 8177 3-9-5 **58** GeorgeBaker 8 56
(Gary Moore) *hld up towards rr: rdn and hdwy 2f out: styd on fnl f but nt pce to get on terms: nrly snatched 4th* **16/1**
-006 **6** *nk* **Desert Tango**[35] 2590 3-8-7 **49** JosephineGordon(3) 12 46
(Jonathan Portman) *racd keenly: prom: rdn and ev ch 2f out: no ex fnl f* **12/1**[3]
06-6 **7** *1¾* **Little Salamanca**[172] 122 3-9-2 **55** AdamKirby 7 50
(Clive Cox) *in tch: rdn over 4f out: wknd ins fnl f* **14/1**
0-00 **8** *7* **Russian Rascal**[26] 2851 3-8-7 **46** MartinLane 1 29
(Stuart Kittow) *racd keenly: trckd ldrs tl rdn over 3f out: wknd over 2f out* **66/1**
60-0 **9** *3½* **Rod Of Iron**[18] 3160 3-8-9 **51** DanielMuscutt(3) 4 29
(Michael Madgwick) *s.i.s: sn mid-div: rdn over 3f out: wknd over 2f out* **33/1**
-000 **10** *2¼* **Charlie Parker (IRE)**[32] 2700 3-8-7 **46** oh1 (p) JFEgan 2 20
(Dominic Ffrench Davis) *a towards rr* **80/1**
00-0 **11** *3½* **Boychick (IRE)**[18] 3141 3-9-2 **55** (b) LukeMorris 15 24
(Ed Walker) *trckd ldrs: rdn over 3f out: wknd jst over 2f out* **16/1**
2m 39.51s (8.91) **Going Correction** +0.80s/f (Soft) **11** Ran SP% **119.1**
Speed ratings (Par 97): **102,100,98,97,97 97,96,91,89,87 85**
CSF £5.54 CT £40.00 TOTE £1.50: £1.10, £2.20, £4.40; EX 7.00 Trifecta £35.40.
Owner The Queen **Bred** The Queen **Trained** Beckhampton, Wilts
FOCUS
Race distances as advertised. The ground has eased further, with Sam Hitchcott describing it as "soft". Few got into this and it was straightforward for the favourite.

3766 HITACHI RAILWAY "RESTRICTED" H'CAP 1m 2f 46y
6:30 (6:31) (Class 4) (0-80,80) 3-Y-O+ **£5,175** (£1,540; £769; £384) **Stalls** Low

Form RPR
4202 **1** **Icebuster**[32] 2699 8-9-11 **77** AdamKirby 7 86
(Rod Millman) *mde all: 5 l clr 5f out: styd on strly to draw further clr fnl f: rdn out* **6/1**[3]
4505 **2** *7* **Loading (IRE)**[12] 3355 3-8-13 **77** SeanLevey 4 72
(Richard Hannon) *trckd ldrs: rdn to chse wnr wl over 2f out: styd on but nt pce to get on terms* **6/1**[3]
25-2 **3** *2¼* **Chantecler**[42] 2369 5-9-4 **70** TomQueally 1 61
(Neil Mulholland) *racd keenly: hld up in last pair: hdwy into 3rd 3f out: sn rdn: styd on same pce fnl 2f* **8/1**
5253 **4** *1* **Peak Storm**[18] 3124 7-9-11 **77** LukeMorris 8 66
(John O'Shea) *hld up in tch: rdn over 2f out: styd on but nt pce to threaten* **10/1**
2304 **5** *1½* **Mister Musicmaster**[18] 3124 7-10-0 **80** (p) GeorgeBaker 2 66
(Ron Hodges) *hld up last: hdwy over 2f out: sn rdn: styd on same pce fnl f* **17/2**
-554 **6** *13* **Banham (USA)**[19] 3110 3-8-8 **72** (b) DavidProbert 3 32
(Roger Charlton) *trckd ldrs: rdn 3f out: wknd 2f out* **2/1**[1]
130- **7** *1¾* **Gold Merlion (IRE)**[290] 6364 3-8-12 **76** FrannyNorton 6 32
(Mark Johnston) *pressed wnr for 3f: trckd wnr tl rdn 3f out: wknd 2f out* **5/1**[2]
2m 17.54s (6.54) **Going Correction** +0.80s/f (Soft)
WFA 3 from 5yo+ 12lb **7** Ran SP% **109.3**
Speed ratings (Par 105): **105,99,97,96,95 85,83**
CSF £37.38 CT £262.91 TOTE £6.20: £2.40, £3.50; EX 43.70 Trifecta £188.20.
Owner The Links Partnership **Bred** Cheveley Park Stud Ltd **Trained** Kentisbeare, Devon
FOCUS
Rrace distance as advertised. Little got into this, with the enterprisingly ridden winner making all. He earned his best rating since missing last year.

3767 EY H'CAP 2m 1f 34y
7:00 (7:00) (Class 5) (0-70,70) 4-Y-O+ **£2,911** (£866; £432; £216) **Stalls** Centre

Form RPR
544 **1** **Princess Roania (IRE)**[31] 1499 5-8-8 **64** (tp) JoshuaBryan(7) 7 77
(Peter Bowen) *squeezed up s: hld up: smooth hdwy on outer over 3f out: led jst over 2f out: rdn clr ent fnl f: edgd rt: readily* **3/1**[1]
4611 **2** *6* **Cosette (IRE)**[49] 2149 5-9-5 **68** (p) WilliamTwiston-Davies 5 73
(Bernard Llewellyn) *trckd ldr: rdn to ld v briefly over 2f out: styd on but sn hld by wnr* **4/1**[2]
/3-5 **3** *7* **Argot**[22] 583 5-9-3 **66** AdamKirby 2 63
(Charlie Longsdon) *led: rdn and hdd over 2f out: sn one pce* **15/2**
0444 **4** *½* **Agreement (IRE)**[19] 3099 6-8-10 **59** (b) LukeMorris 8 56
(Nikki Evans) *chsd ldrs: squeezed up 3f out but sn outpcd: styd on to regain wl hld 4th fnl f* **8/1**
0-20 **5** *½* **Snowy Dawn**[41] 2392 6-9-7 **70** RoystonFfrench 1 66
(Steph Hollinshead) *trckd ldr tl rdn wl over 2f out: sn hld: no ex fnl f* **4/1**[2]
-335 **6** *2½* **Deepsand (IRE)**[17] 3191 7-8-13 **62** (tp) CharlesBishop 6 55
(Ali Stronge) *squeezed up s: hld up: hdwy over 6f out: rdn to chse ldng pair over 2f out: nvr threatened: wknd ins fnl f* **11/2**[3]
44-0 **7** *24* **Royal Battalion**[29] 1854 5-9-6 **69** (p) GeorgeBaker 4 36
(Gary Moore) *in tch: rdn 4f out: wknd over 2f out* **10/1**
-605 **8** *12* **Comedy House**[52] 950 8-8-4 **53** (p) KieranO'Neill 3 7
(Michael Madgwick) *in tch: struggling 4f out: wknd over 2f out* **50/1**
4m 4.25s (12.35) **Going Correction** +0.80s/f (Soft) **8** Ran SP% **114.3**
Speed ratings (Par 103): **102,99,95,95,95 94,82,77**
CSF £15.07 CT £80.52 TOTE £4.60: £2.50, £1.50, £2.50; EX 18.40 Trifecta £144.30.
Owner Mrs Tania Stepney **Bred** Mrs Karen McLoughney **Trained** Little Newcastle, Pembrokes
FOCUS
Race distance as advertised. The two mares dominated this moderate staying handicap and a biggish step from the winner.

3768 KELSTON CUP H'CAP 1m 5f 22y
7:30 (7:30) (Class 3) (0-90,84) 3-Y-O **£9,703** (£2,887; £1,443; £721) **Stalls** High

Form RPR
4323 **1** **Emperor Napoleon**[39] 2471 3-9-0 **77** OisinMurphy 6 91+
(Andrew Balding) *mde all: drew clr whn shkn up over 1f out: unchal: eased towards fin* **7/2**[3]
-421 **2** *4½* **St Michel**[13] 3306 3-8-13 **76** LukeMorris 2 82
(Sir Mark Prescott Bt) *trckd ldrs: hdwy to chse wnr over 2f out: sn rdn: styd on but nt pce to get on terms* **6/4**[1]
-310 **3** *2* **Blakeney Point**[25] 2909 3-8-10 **73** DavidProbert 5 75
(Roger Charlton) *last but wl in tch: pushed along at times: rdn over 2f out: wnt 3rd sn after: styd on same pce fnl f* **7/1**
-032 **4** *2¾* **Rainbow Dreamer**[39] 2471 3-9-7 **84** WilliamTwiston-Davies 3 83
(Alan King) *trckd ldrs: rdn over 2f out: sn one pce* **3/1**[2]
1021 **5** *6* **Snan (IRE)**[21] 3025 3-9-2 **79** (b[1]) SeanLevey 4 68
(Richard Hannon) *trckd ldr tl drvn 3f out: sn one pce and hld: fdd ins fnl f* **7/1**
3m 1.66s (9.66) **Going Correction** +0.80s/f (Soft) **5** Ran SP% **112.2**
Speed ratings (Par 103): **102,99,98,96,92**
CSF £9.44 TOTE £3.50: £1.40, £3.60; EX 8.80 Trifecta £31.70.
Owner The Napoleon Partnership **Bred** Trinity Park Stud **Trained** Kingsclere, Hants
FOCUS
Race distance as advertised. A fair handicap and another all-the-way winner who was value for extra and has a progressive profile.

3769 EXCELLO LAW MAIDEN STKS (PLUS 10 RACE) 1m 5y
8:00 (8:00) (Class 4) 3-Y-O **£7,762** (£2,310; £1,154; £577) **Stalls** Low

Form RPR
0- **1** **Cloudberry**[250] 7431 3-9-5 0 GeorgeBaker 9 80
(Roger Charlton) *trckd ldr: rdn to ld ent fnl f: jst hld on* **9/4**[2]
2 *nse* **Toulson** 3-9-5 0 CharlesBishop 8 79
(Eve Johnson Houghton) *trckd ldrs: rdn 2f out: str run fnl 100yds: jst failed* **40/1**
3 *2¾* **Amaany** 3-9-0 0 MichaelJMMurphy 2 68
(Charles Hills) *mid-div: rdn over 2f out: hdwy over 1f out: r.o wl to go 3rd ins fnl f* **16/1**
00 **4** *1¼* **Perpetual Change (IRE)**[37] 2541 3-9-5 0 AdamKirby 13 70
(Clive Cox) *mid-div: hdwy 2f out: sn rdn: kpt on ins fnl f: wnt 4th towards fin* **25/1**
32 **5** *¾* **Burguillos**[26] 2861 3-9-5 0 WilliamTwiston-Davies 3 68
(Alan King) *trckd ldr: led over 2f out: sn rdn: hdd ent fnl f: fdd* **11/10**[1]
64 **6** *2¾* **The Invisible Dog (IRE)**[22] 2998 3-9-5 0 SeanLevey 4 62
(Richard Hannon) *led: rdn and hdd over 2f out: wknd fnl f* **5/1**[3]
0- **7** *6* **Dream Journey (IRE)**[232] 7788 3-9-0 0 LukeMorris 5 43
(Charles Hills) *little slowly away: sn mid-div: rdn wl over 2f out: nvr any imp* **50/1**
8 *5* **Buckle Street** 3-9-5 0 TomQueally 11 37
(Mary Hambro) *towards rr of midfield: rdn 3f out: no imp* **100/1**
4- **9** *1¼* **Colour Play (USA)**[329] 4999 3-9-0 0 FrannyNorton 1 29
(Mark Johnston) *stmbld leaving stalls: a towards rr* **16/1**
00 **10** *5* **Willyegolassiego**[30] 2750 3-9-0 0 SamHitchcott 6 17
(Neil Mulholland) *mid-div: rdn 3f out: wknd 2f out* **200/1**
00 **11** *¾* **Dream Free**[22] 2999 3-9-5 0 MartinLane 12 21
(David Lanigan) *s.i.s: a towards rr* **33/1**
0 **12** *1¼* **Monologue (IRE)**[9] 3464 3-9-5 0 RyanClark 10 18
(Simon Hodgson) *dwlt bdly: bhd: effrt 3f out: wknd 2f out* **200/1**
13 *55* **Brooke's Point** 3-9-5 0 WilliamCarson 7
(Neil Mulholland) *s.i.s: a bhd: lost tch 3f out* **80/1**
1m 48.87s (8.07) **Going Correction** +0.80s/f (Soft) **13** Ran SP% **121.2**
Speed ratings (Par 101): **91,90,88,86,86 83,77,72,71,66 65,64,9**
CSF £100.95 TOTE £3.60: £1.40, £6.80, £3.00; EX 116.90 Trifecta £3895.20.
Owner Lady Rothschild **Bred** Carwell Equities Ltd **Trained** Beckhampton, Wilts
FOCUS
Race distance as advertised. This may not have taken much winning with the favourite disappointing, but the winner improved on his sole 2yo run.

3770 ARC RACING SYNDICATES NOVICE AUCTION STKS 5f 11y
8:30 (8:37) (Class 6) 2-Y-O **£2,264** (£673; £336; £168) **Stalls** Centre

Form RPR
1 **Springbourne** 2-8-10 0 SamHitchcott 8 79+
(Sylvester Kirk) *chsd ldrs: led 2f out: clr ent fnl f: readily* **18/1**[3]
03 **2** *6* **Irish Melody (IRE)**[23] 2963 2-8-12 0 (p) JFEgan 2 60
(Bill Turner) *prom: rdn over 2f out: wnt 2nd over 1f out: kpt on but nt pce of wnr* **8/1**[2]
5 **3** *¾* **Marquee Club**[25] 2902 2-8-10 0 WilliamCarson 5 55
(Jamie Osborne) *prom: led briefly over 2f out: sn rdn: kpt on same pce fnl f* **8/1**[2]
3 **4** *3¾* **Dixie Peach**[8] 3485 2-8-5 0 JohnFahy 7 37
(Eve Johnson Houghton) *led: rdn and hdd over 2f out: sn one pce* **7/2**[1]
0 **5** *3¾* **Legendoire (IRE)**[26] 2873 2-9-0 0 MichaelJMMurphy 10 32
(John Gallagher) *chsd ldrs: rdn over 2f out: wknd fnl f* **40/1**
6 *2½* **Decruz (IRE)** 2-8-11 0 SeanLevey 1 20
(Richard Hannon) *little slowly away: chsd ldrs tl outpcd over 2f out* **7/2**[1]
1m 6.74s (4.24) **Going Correction** +0.925s/f (Soft) **6** Ran SP% **74.4**
Speed ratings (Par 91): **103,93,92,86,80 76**
CSF £65.71 TOTE £13.60: £5.60, £2.10; EX 70.60 Trifecta £334.40.
Owner Ansells Of Watford **Bred** Bolton Grange **Trained** Upper Lambourn, Berks

■ Kody Ridge (15-8f) and Seaview (16-1) were withdrawn. Rule 4 applies to all bets - deduction 30p in the pound.

FOCUS

Race distance as advertised. Not much of this was seen, with visibility poor. Two were withdrawn in the moments before the race, including the favourite, but the winner was well on top for a decisive success.

3771 RACING WELFARE STABLE STAFF WEEK H'CAP (BATH SUMMER SPRINT SERIES QUALIFIER) 5f 161y

9:00 (9:00) (Class 5) (0-75,75) 3-Y-O+ **£3,067** (£905; £453) **Stalls** Centre

Form RPR

1423 **1** **Showmethewayavrilo**[18] 3126 3-8-11 **68**............ JosephineGordon(3) 2 75
(Malcolm Saunders) *mde all: kpt on gamely fnl f: rdn out* **7/2**[1]

0-05 **2** *1* **Vincentti (IRE)**[44] 2290 6-9-10 **71**.................... OisinMurphy 5 76
(Ronald Harris) *broke open stalls: trckd ldrs: hdwy u.p wl over 1f out: chsd wnr fnl 170yds: a being hld* **5/1**[3]

514 **3** *2* **Fantasy Justifier (IRE)**[32] 2680 5-9-11 **72**................. RoystonFfrench 1 70
(Ronald Harris) *trckd ldr: ev ch 2f out: sn rdn: kpt on same pce* **6/1**

4645 **4** *½* **Midnight Rider (IRE)**[18] 3123 8-9-8 **74**.................. JordanVaughan(5) 4 70
(Rod Millman) *trckd ldrs: rdn wl over 1f: nt pce to mount chal* **4/1**[2]

2060 **5** *4 ½* **Willsy**[9] 3465 3-9-7 **75**.. FrannyNorton 3 53
(Mick Channon) *trckd ldrs: rdn over 2f out: wknd fnl f* **5/1**[3]

1621 **6** *3* **Posh Bounty**[49] 2146 5-9-10 **71**.. JFEgan 7 40
(Joseph Tuite) *trckd ldrs: rdn over 2f out: wknd ent fnl f* **7/2**[1]

1m 16.15s (4.95) **Going Correction** +0.925s/f (Soft)
WFA 3 from 5yo+ 7lb **6** Ran SP% **112.1**
Speed ratings (Par 103): **104,102,100,99,93 89**
CSF £20.85 CT £98.91 TOTE £3.40: £2.30, £2.70; EX 16.90 Trifecta £106.70.
Owner Pat Hancock & Eric Jones **Bred** Eric Jones, Pat Hancock **Trained** Green Ore, Somerset
■ Stewards' Enquiry : Oisin Murphy two-day ban: used whip above the permitted level (Jul 13-14)

FOCUS

Race distance as advertised. It paid to race up with the pace in this modest sprint.
T/Plt: £523.60. Pool: £67,540.98. 94.16 winning tickets. T/Qpdt: £156.00 Pool: £6,648.79. 31.52 winning tickets. **Tim Mitchell**

2852 CATTERICK (L-H)

Wednesday, June 29

OFFICIAL GOING: Good to soft (soft in places) changing to soft after 2.00 (race 1)

Wind: Light, behind changing to fresh, across after 3.30 Weather: Heavy rain then squally showers

3772 EBFSTALLIONS.COM NOVICE MEDIAN AUCTION STKS 5f 212y

2:00 (2:00) (Class 5) 2-Y-O **£3,234** (£962; £481; £240) **Stalls** Low

Form RPR

5210 **1** **Rusumaat (IRE)**[15] 3243 2-9-9 0.. JoeFanning 5 91+
(Mark Johnston) *trckd ldr: led wl over 2f out: sn pushed clr: readily* **10/11**[1]

02 **2** *4 ½* **Notalot (IRE)**[16] 3216 2-9-2 0......................................(v) PaulMulrennan 6 68
(Michael Bell) *hld up towards rr: hdwy on outer wl over 2f out: rdn wl over 1f out: kpt on fnl f: no ch w wnr* **22/1**

63 **3** *2 ¼* **Suitcase 'N' Taxi**[16] 3222 2-9-2 0.. DavidAllan 7 61
(Tim Easterby) *midfield: hdwy over 2f out: rdn wl over 1f out: kpt on fnl f* **9/1**[3]

00 **4** *1 ½* **Doctor Dynamite (IRE)**[16] 3208 2-9-2 0......................... AndrewElliott 1 56
(Tim Easterby) *slt ld: pushed along 1/2-way: sn hdd and rdn: drvn wl over 1f out: grad wknd* **66/1**

5 *¾* **Whigwham** 2-8-11 0.. TonyHamilton 9 49
(Richard Fahey) *sltly hmpd s and towards rr: hdwy 2f out: rdn over 1f out: kpt on fnl f: nrst fin* **16/1**

6 *¾* **Zebedee Star** 2-8-11 0... PhillipMakin 8 47
(Keith Dalgleish) *bhd tl sme late hdwy* **28/1**

43 **7** *1 ¼* **Major Jumbo**[37] 2530 2-9-2 0.. TomEaves 12 48
(Kevin Ryan) *wnt lft s: chsd ldng pair: hdwy over 2f out: rdn wl over 1f out: wknd appr fnl f* **11/1**

62 **8** *½* **London Grammar (IRE)**[11] 3416 2-8-11 0......................... CamHardie 4 42
(John Quinn) *towards rr: hdwy 1/2-way: in tch over 2f out: sn rdn and wknd* **12/1**

2 **9** *½* **Peach Pavlova (IRE)**[15] 3261 2-8-11 0......................... PJMcDonald 11 40
(Ann Duffield) *hmpd s: a towards rr* **7/2**[2]

6 **10** *3 ¼* **Babouska**[13] 3321 2-8-11 0.. GrahamGibbons 2 30
(Michael Easterby) *chsd ldrs: rdn along bef 1/2-way: sn wknd* **50/1**

0 **11** *8* **I Call The Shots**[44] 2301 2-8-13 0............................. JacobButterfield(3) 3 11
(Ollie Pears) *chsd ldng pair: rdn along wl over 2f out: sn wknd* **66/1**

1m 16.66s (3.06) **Going Correction** +0.325s/f (Good) **11** Ran SP% **119.3**
Speed ratings (Par 93): **92,86,83,81,80 79,77,76,76,71 61**
CSF £31.63 TOTE £1.90: £1.10, £5.30, £1.90; EX 28.80 Trifecta £158.10.
Owner Hamdan Al Maktoum **Bred** J C Bloodstock **Trained** Middleham Moor, N Yorks

FOCUS

Following 20mm of rain the previous day and 5mm of rain on race day, the going had eased to good to soft, soft in places (GoingStick: 8.1), but after riding in the opener, Joe Fanning, Paul Mulrennan and Tom Eaves all called the ground 'very soft', and the official description was changed to soft. This novice race proved pretty uncompetitive and they stayed far side in the straight.

3773 WIMBLEDON BETTING AT 188BET H'CAP 5f

2:30 (2:32) (Class 6) (0-65,60) 3-Y-O **£2,587** (£770; £384; £192) **Stalls** Low

Form RPR

062- **1** **Rio Deva (IRE)**[276] 6782 3-9-3 **56**................................... PhillipMakin 11 64
(Keith Dalgleish) *mde all: rdn over 1f out: kpt on wl* **11/2**

-400 **2** *½* **Someone Exciting**[12] 3367 3-8-11 **50**......................... PatrickMathers 10 56
(David Thompson) *chsd ldrs on outer: hdwy 1/2-way and sn cl up: rdn wl over 1f out: drvn and kpt on fnl f* **9/1**

-054 **3** *2* **Tarnend Lass**[12] 3368 3-8-11 **50**....................................(bt[1]) DavidAllan 7 49
(Tim Easterby) *cl up on inner: effrt to chal wl over 1f out: sn rdn and ev ch ent fnl f: sn drvn and kpt on same pce* **3/1**[2]

063 **4** *½* **Noah Amor (IRE)**[14] 3293 3-9-7 **60**................................. BarryMcHugh 9 57
(David Nicholls) *t.k.h early: trckd wnr: effrt 2f out and sn rdn: drvn and wknd ent fnl f* **15/8**[1]

2625 **5** *hd* **La Asomada**[36] 2559 3-9-6 **59**.................................... GrahamGibbons 8 55
(David Barron) *trckd ldrs: pushed along over 2f out: rdn wl over 1f out: one pce* **5/1**[3]

1m 0.96s (1.16) **Going Correction** +0.25s/f (Good) **5** Ran SP% **101.8**
Speed ratings (Par 97): **100,99,96,95,94**
CSF £39.40 TOTE £4.90: £1.90, £3.90; EX 44.80 Trifecta £135.70.
Owner D R Tucker **Bred** Michael Staunton **Trained** Carluke, S Lanarks
■ Another Desperado was withdrawn. Price at time of withdrawal 12-1. Rule 4 applies to all bets - deduction 5p in the pound.

FOCUS

A moderate sprint badly cut up by non-runners and the pace held up.

3774 EURO 2016 BETTING AT 188BET H'CAP 1m 3f 214y

3:00 (3:00) (Class 6) (0-65,65) 4-Y-O+ **£3,234** (£962; £481; £240) **Stalls** Low

Form RPR

-534 **1** **Fillydelphia (IRE)**[18] 3154 5-8-5 **54**..................... RachelRichardson(5) 11 61
(Patrick Holmes) *hld up: hdwy and in tch 1/2-way: trckd ldrs 3f out: wd st: rdn to chal over 1f out: styd on wl to ld ins fnl f* **13/2**[3]

3530 **2** *nk* **Sherman McCoy**[6] 3547 10-9-4 **65**............................... JacobButterfield(3) 5 71
(Marjorie Fife) *trckd ldrs on inner: pushed along and sltly outpcd towards inner over 2f out: rdn to chse ldrs wl over 1f out: drvn and ev ch ins fnl f: kpt on* **4/1**[1]

3253 **3** *2 ¼* **Percys Princess**[30] 2738 5-9-3 **61**.. AndrewMullen 7 63
(Michael Appleby) *trckd ldr: led 3f out: wd st: rdn wl over 1f out: drvn and hdd ins fnl f: kpt on same pce* **4/1**[1]

0006 **4** *¾* **Whitchurch**[12] 3342 4-8-8 **52**.. PJMcDonald 9 53
(Philip Kirby) *hld up in rr: stdy hdwy over 4f out: chsd ldrs over 2f out: rdn and ev ch appr fnl f: sn drvn and kpt on same pce* **11/1**

2445 **5** *½* **San Cassiano (IRE)**[13] 3325 9-9-4 **62**..........................(p) JamesSullivan 1 62
(Ruth Carr) *midfield: pushed along 5f out: rdn along and lost pl 4f out: wd st to stands' rail: drvn and hdwy to chse ldrs over 1f out: no imp fnl f* **4/1**[1]

64-0 **6** *2 ¾* **Arriella**[14] 3287 4-8-2 **46** oh1.. PatrickMathers 4 42
(John Davies) *pushed along s and towards rr: hdwy over 2f out: sn rdn and n.d* **40/1**

02-5 **7** *shd* **Bright Applause**[27] 2836 8-9-5 **63**.................................. BarryMcHugh 3 59
(Tracy Waggott) *trckd ldrs: hdwy 4f out: rdn to chse ldrs over 2f out: drvn wl over 1f out: grad wknd* **11/2**[2]

0566 **8** *2 ¼* **Ullswater (IRE)**[14] 3288 8-8-2 **51**...............................(tp) PhilDennis(5) 2 43
(Philip Kirby) *a towards rr* **11/1**

06-0 **9** *½* **Zruda**[40] 2419 5-7-13 **48** oh1 ow2.................................. NathanEvans(5) 6 39
(David Thompson) *prom: rdn along 4f out: sn wknd* **25/1**

6-00 **10** *43* **Belle Peinture (FR)**[20] 3072 5-8-2 **46** oh1.....................(b) CamHardie 12
(Alan Lockwood) *prom: rdn along over 3f out: drvn wl over 2f out: sn wknd and bhd whn eased over 1f out* **40/1**

/000 **11** *2 ½* **Private Dancer**[30] 2746 5-8-3 **47**.................................. DuranFentiman 15
(Ron Barr) *led: rdn along 4f out: hdd 3f out: sn wknd and bhd* **28/1**

2m 43.46s (4.56) **Going Correction** +0.325s/f (Good) **11** Ran SP% **117.6**
Speed ratings (Par 101): **97,96,95,94,94 92,92,91,90,62 60**
CSF £31.59 CT £117.74 TOTE £7.30: £2.60, £2.00, £1.80; EX 44.50 Trifecta £168.00.
Owner FPR Syndicate 7 **Bred** D J G Murray Smith **Trained** Middleham, N Yorks

FOCUS

A modest affair in which there was something of a scrap for the early lead. The form is straightforward.

3775 £25 FREE BET AT 188BET H'CAP 7f

3:30 (3:31) (Class 4) (0-80,80) 3-Y-O **£6,469** (£1,925; £962; £481) **Stalls** Low

Form RPR

223 **1** **Brockholes**[16] 3209 3-8-10 **69**.. PJMcDonald 10 80
(Ann Duffield) *trckd ldng pair: wd st towards stands' rail: led 2f out: rdn clr over 1f out: kpt on strly* **6/1**

6-01 **2** *3 ½* **Invermere**[26] 2855 3-9-3 **76**.. TonyHamilton 8 78
(Richard Fahey) *trckd ldrs: hdwy and wd st: rdn 2f out: drvn and kpt on fnl f* **5/2**[1]

1315 **3** *1 ½* **Ordinal**[14] 3292 3-9-1 **74**.. JoeFanning 6 72
(Mark Johnston) *trckd ldr: hdwy and wd st: cl up 2f out and sn rdn: drvn ent fnl f and kpt on same pce* **11/2**[3]

1265 **4** *2 ½* **Quick N Quirky (IRE)**[7] 3519 3-9-7 **80**............................(tp) DavidAllan 3 72
(Tim Easterby) *dwlt and in rr: wd st to stands' rail and hdwy 2f out: sn rdn: kpt on fnl f* **7/2**[2]

03-6 **5** *½* **Auxiliary**[37] 2532 3-9-4 **77**... DavidNolan 7 67
(Patrick Holmes) *a towards rr* **16/1**

1-20 **6** *1* **Captain Dion**[32] 2695 3-9-3 **76**.. TomEaves 4 64
(Kevin Ryan) *led: pushed along 3f out: rdn and hdd 2f out: sn drvn and grad wknd* **7/1**

4500 **7** *2 ¼* **Firesnake (IRE)**[6] 3567 3-8-6 **72**.................................(v) CliffordLee(7) 1 54
(K R Burke) *chsd ldrs on inner: rdn along wl over 2f out: sn drvn and wknd* **20/1**

4506 **8** *20* **He's A Dreamer (IRE)**[23] 2972 3-9-3 **76**............................ PhillipMakin 2 6
(David O'Meara) *in tch: sme hdwy 3f out: rdn along over 2f out: sn wknd* **10/1**

1m 27.83s (0.83) **Going Correction** +0.325s/f (Good) **8** Ran SP% **112.7**
Speed ratings (Par 101): **108,104,102,99,98 97,95,72**
CSF £20.76 CT £86.16 TOTE £6.70: £1.80, £1.30, £1.90; EX 21.40 Trifecta £69.00.
Owner David W Armstrong **Bred** Highfield Farm Llp **Trained** Constable Burton, N Yorks

FOCUS

A fair handicap and an easy winner who can rate higher.

3776 188BET.CO.UK H'CAP (DIV I) 5f 212y

4:00 (4:00) (Class 6) (0-65,65) 3-Y-O+ **£2,587** (£770; £384; £192) **Stalls** Low

Form RPR

5463 **1** **Danish Duke (IRE)**[20] 3070 5-9-7 **58**..........................(p) JamesSullivan 6 68
(Ruth Carr) *trckd ldrs on outer: wd st to stands' rail: led 2f out: pushed clr over 1f out: readily* **3/1**[2]

52-5 **2** *2 ½* **El Principe**[26] 2864 3-9-2 **60**... DavidAllan 7 60
(Les Eyre) *slt ld 2f: cl up on inner: effrt 2f out: sn rdn and ev ch: drvn over 1f out and kpt on same pce* **2/1**[1]

0-00 **3** *1* **Indego Blues**[53] 2053 7-8-11 **55**..........................(p) DanielleMooney(7) 10 54
(David Nicholls) *in tch on outer: wd st to stands' rail and hdwy 2f out: rdn to chse ldng pair over 1f out: drvn and kpt on fnl f* **13/2**

0234 **4** *1 ½* **Mrs Biggs**[16] 3214 4-9-13 **64**... DanielTudhope 4 58+
(Declan Carroll) *towards rr: hdwy over 2f out: sn rdn and kpt on fnl f* **4/1**[3]

500- **5** *¾* **Cosmic Dust**[257] 7253 3-8-7 **51**.................................. GeorgeChaloner 1 41+
(Richard Whitaker) *in rr: hdwy on inner 2f out and sn rdn: drvn to chse ldrs over 1f out: sn no imp* **33/1**

0005 **6** *1* **Hashtag Frenzy**[14] 3289 3-8-2 **46** oh1..........................(p) RaulDaSilva 11 33
(Rebecca Menzies) *cl up: slt ld after 2f: wd st: rdn and hdd 2f out: sn drvn and grad wknd* **12/1**

1000 **7** *nk* **Harpers Ruby**[8] 3484 6-8-13 **50**.. AndrewElliott 3 38
(Lynn Siddall) *chsd ldrs: rdn along wl over 2f out: sn drvn and wknd over 1f out* **50/1**

55-0 **8** *3 ¾* **Perfectly Fair**[25] 2886 3-9-5 **63**.................................. DuranFentiman 5 38
(Simon West) *dwlt: a in rr* **50/1**

04-0 **9** *1 ¾* **Tan Arabiq**[32] 2674 3-9-4 **65**.................................. AlistairRawlinson(3) 2 34
(Michael Appleby) *a in rr* **16/1**

4306 **10** *4 ½* **Pabusar**[6] 3549 8-9-0 **51**..(vt) PJMcDonald 12 9
(Micky Hammond) *chsd ldrs: rdn along 1/2-way: sn wknd* **16/1**

1m 15.24s (1.64) **Going Correction** +0.325s/f (Good)
WFA 3 from 4yo+ 7lb **10** Ran SP% **118.0**
Speed ratings (Par 101): **102,98,97,95,94 93,92,87,85,79**
CSF £9.44 CT £35.11 TOTE £3.70: £1.20, £1.20, £2.10; EX 9.90 Trifecta £54.00.
Owner Michael Hill **Bred** Dean Harron & Ciaran Conroy **Trained** Huby, N Yorks

FOCUS
Moderate sprinting form. Once again they came stands' side in the straight and the winner very much had the run of things.

3777 188BET.CO.UK H'CAP (DIV II) 5f 212y
4:30 (4:30) (Class 6) (0-65,64) 3-Y-O+ **£2,587** (£770; £384; £192) **Stalls** Low

Form RPR

0000 **1** **Bold Spirit**[23] 2974 5-9-6 **56**..(bt) DanielTudhope 9 63
(Declan Carroll) *cl up on outer: led over 3f out and wd to stands' rail home turn: rdn along wl over 1f out: hdd ins fnl f: drvn and rallied to ld nr line* **11/1**

-000 **2** *nk* **Betty Boo (IRE)**[40] 2423 6-8-2 **45**....................................... RPWalsh(7) 11 51
(Shaun Harris) *in tch: hdwy and wd st: cl up 2f out: rdn to ld jst ins fnl f: edgd lft last 75yds: hdd nr line* **14/1**

0234 **3** *1* **Atreus**[18] 3153 4-9-2 **57**..(p) NathanEvans(5) 6 60
(Michael Easterby) *led: hdd over 3f out: cl up and wd st: rdn along 2f out and ev ch tl drvn ent fnl f and kpt on same pce* **5/2**[2]

-000 **4** *3* **Kingfisher Girl**[8] 3484 3-8-7 **50**....................................... AndrewMullen 8 42
(Michael Appleby) *chsd ldrs: rdn along wl over 1f out: drvn and wknd appr fnl f* **25/1**

4522 **5** *2 ½* **Exotic Guest**[16] 3210 6-10-0 **64**..................................(p) JamesSullivan 1 51+
(Ruth Carr) *hmpd s and bhd: hdwy on inner wl over 1f out and sn rdn: drvn and no imp fnl f* **7/4**[1]

-U00 **6** *nk* **Thornaby Princess**[8] 3484 5-9-0 **50**................................ DavidAllan 12 36+
(Colin Teague) *bhd: wd st and hdwy 2f out: rdn wl over 1f out: kpt on fnl f* **22/1**

0-00 **7** *2 ¾* **Solar Spirit (IRE)**[32] 2680 11-9-9 **59**................................ JoeFanning 7 36+
(Tracy Waggott) *dwlt and in rr: sme hdwy over 2f out: sn rdn and n.d* **8/1**[3]

4404 **8** *4 ½* **Jess**[21] 3017 3-9-7 **64**..(b[1]) ShaneGray 4 26
(Kevin Ryan) *wnt lft s: chsd ldng pair: rdn along over 2f out: sn drvn and wknd* **8/1**[3]

-400 **9** *nk* **Tallulah Fleur**[20] 3070 3-8-2 **45**.......................................(p) CamHardie 3 6
(Ann Duffield) *hmpd s: chsd ldrs on inner: rdn along over 2f out: sn wknd* **20/1**

1m 15.85s (2.25) **Going Correction** +0.325s/f (Good)
WFA 3 from 4yo+ 7lb **9** Ran SP% **115.1**
Speed ratings (Par 101): **98,97,96,92,88 88,84,78,78**
CSF £144.26 CT £510.65 TOTE £9.10: £2.70, £4.20, £1.70; EX 112.20 Trifecta £977.80.
Owner Mrs Sarah Bryan **Bred** The Queen **Trained** Malton, N Yorks

FOCUS
Another moderate sprint and the slower of the two divisions by 0.61sec.

3778 188BET H'CAP 1m 5f 175y
5:00 (5:00) (Class 5) (0-75,71) 3-Y-O **£3,234** (£962; £481; £240) **Stalls** Low

Form RPR

1-34 **1** **Purple Magic**[15] 3251 3-9-4 **71**.................................... LouisSteward(3) 5 80
(Michael Bell) *trckd ldng pair: hdwy and wd st: chal over 1f out: rdn to ld appr fnl f: drvn out* **11/2**

2-20 **2** *5* **Argyle (IRE)**[41] 2411 3-9-6 **70**.. MartinDwyer 3 72
(William Muir) *hld up in rr: hdwy over 4f out and sn niggled along: wd st to stands' rail and rdn to ld 2f out: drvn and hdd appr fnl f: kpt on same pce* **7/2**[2]

1122 **3** *4* **Scarpeta (FR)**[13] 3306 3-9-5 **69**.. JoeFanning 4 65
(Mark Johnston) *trckd ldr: hdwy and cl up over 4f out: led wl over 3f out: wd st: rdn and hdd 2f out: sn drvn and kpt on same pce* **11/8**[1]

-544 **4** *2 ¼* **Becky The Thatcher**[13] 3323 3-8-13 **63**........................ PJMcDonald 1 56
(Micky Hammond) *in tch: hdwy over 3f out: rdn 2f out: sn drvn and btn* **12/1**

0-41 **5** *78* **Dusky Raider (IRE)**[29] 2772 3-8-13 **63**........................ PaulMulrennan 2
(Michael Dods) *led: rdn along over 4f out: hdd wl over 3f out and sn wknd* **4/1**[3]

3m 10.27s (6.67) **Going Correction** +0.325s/f (Good) **5** Ran SP% **107.4**
Speed ratings (Par 99): **93,90,87,86,42**
CSF £23.00 TOTE £7.00: £2.30, £2.00; EX 22.20 Trifecta £33.30.
Owner Lady Bamford **Bred** Lady Bamford **Trained** Newmarket, Suffolk

FOCUS
This was run at a true pace and proved a genuine test of stamina in the conditions. The winner improved for the longer trip and the race has been rated around the runner-up.

3779 FREE SPINS AT 188BET CASINO H'CAP 5f
5:30 (5:30) (Class 6) (0-65,65) 4-Y-O+ **£3,234** (£962; £481; £240) **Stalls** Low

Form RPR

0313 **1** **Seamster**[2] 3709 9-8-7 **58**...(t) CameronNoble(7) 6 73
(David Loughnane) *cl up: led 1/2-way: rdn clr over 1f out: kpt on strly* **11/8**[1]

6250 **2** *4 ½* **Compton River**[12] 3368 4-8-7 **51**.................................. ConnorBeasley 2 50
(Bryan Smart) *hld up: hdwy 2f out: rdn over 1f out: drvn to chse wnr ins fnl f: no imp* **4/1**[2]

1554 **3** *2 ¾* **Perfect Words (IRE)**[15] 3268 6-9-1 **62**...................... JacobButterfield(3) 3 51
(Marjorie Fife) *chsd ldrs: rdn along wl over 1f out: drvn and kpt on same pce fnl f* **11/2**[3]

6200 **4** *nk* **Lorimer's Lot (IRE)**[15] 3268 5-8-6 **50**.........................(p) DuranFentiman 9 38
(Mark Walford) *slt ld: hdd 1/2-way: rdn wl over 1f out: sn drvn and wknd appr fnl f* **7/1**

3236 **5** *¾* **See Vermont**[21] 3009 8-9-0 **65**..(p) RPWalsh(7) 10 50
(Rebecca Bastiman) *dwlt: sn chsng ldrs: rdn 2f out: drvn over 1f out: sn wknd* **8/1**

1450 **6** *5* **Windforpower (IRE)**[21] 3010 6-9-5 **63**............................(p) JoeFanning 5 30
(Tracy Waggott) *chsd ldrs: rdn along 2f out: sn wknd and eased fnl f* **15/2**

1m 0.69s (0.89) **Going Correction** +0.25s/f (Good) **6** Ran SP% **112.9**
Speed ratings (Par 101): **102,94,90,89,88 80**
CSF £7.17 CT £21.76 TOTE £2.20: £1.50, £2.00; EX 7.60 Trifecta £33.10.
Owner Bamford and Fell **Bred** D G Hardisty Bloodstock **Trained** Market Drayton, Shropshire

FOCUS
This proved very straightforward for the in-form winner, but it may be dangerous to take the form too literally.

T/Jkpt: £31,336.50 to a £1 stake. Pool: £31,336.50 - 1 winning unit T/Plt: £96.60 to a £1 stake. Pool: £60,996.81. 460.87 winning tickets. T/Qpdt: £7.20 to a £1 stake. Pool: £5,555.56. 565.34 winning tickets. **Joe Rowntree**

3522 KEMPTON (A.W) (R-H)
Wednesday, June 29

OFFICIAL GOING: Polytrack: standard
Wind: Fresh, half behind Weather: Overcast, cool

3780 RACING WELFARE STABLE STAFF WEEK APPRENTICE H'CAP 6f (P)
6:10 (6:10) (Class 5) (0-75,75) 4-Y-O+ **£2,911** (£866; £432; £108; £108) **Stalls** Low

Form RPR

0014 **1** **Eljaddaaf (IRE)**[27] 2821 5-9-3 **71**............................. CharlesEddery(3) 10 78
(Dean Ivory) *in tch in midfield: rdn 2f out: prog over 1f out: r.o best of many fast finers to ld last 50yds* **5/1**[1]

1250 **2** *nk* **Picket Line**[26] 2846 4-9-9 **74**.. PaddyPilley 4 80
(Geoffrey Deacon) *wnt lft s: chsd clr ldng pair: rdn 2f out: clsd w plenty of others ins fnl f: tk 2nd last strides but jst outpcd* **6/1**[3]

3406 **3** *½* **For Ayman**[4] 3674 5-8-4 **60**..(t) SeanMooney(5) 6 64
(Joseph Tuite) *s.i.s and impeded s: hld up in last: gd prog on inner fr 2f out: styd on wl to take 3rd last strides but jst outpcd* **9/1**

4624 **4** *hd* **Only Ten Per Cent (IRE)**[42] 2380 8-8-8 **62**.............. CharlieBennett(3) 5 66
(J R Jenkins) *impeded s: towards rr: prog over 2f out: rdn and clsd w others to chal last 50yds: jst outpcd* **25/1**

5000 **4** *dht* **Major Valentine**[47] 2201 4-9-3 **68**................................ EdwardGreatrex 9 72
(John O'Shea) *pressed ldr and clr of rest: led 2f out: rdn and hrd pressed after: hdd and swamped by several rivals last 50yds* **16/1**

3213 **6** *hd* **Desert Strike**[11] 3407 10-9-10 **75**...............................(p) HectorCrouch 2 78
(Conor Dore) *led to 2f out: styd pressing ldr: upsides wl ins fnl f: swamped last 50yds* **8/1**

0606 **7** *nse* **Doctor Parkes**[44] 2309 10-9-9 **74**.. AaronJones 7 77
(Stuart Williams) *hld up in last trio: rdn and no prog jst over 2f out: gd hdwy on outer jst over 1f out: styd on wl w others and jst missed out in bunched fin* **8/1**

102 **8** *nse* **Believe It (IRE)**[29] 2769 4-8-7 **63**.............................. NicolaCurrie(5) 3 66+
(Richard Hughes) *chsd ldrs: lost pl and pushed along 2f out: styd on wl fnl f: gng on at fin* **11/2**[2]

3005 **9** *6* **Ripinto (IRE)**[29] 2765 4-9-1 **69**.................................(v) RhiainIngram(3) 1 53
(Jim Boyle) *trckd ldrs: pushed along 2f out: lost pl over 1f out: wknd* **15/2**

62-3 **10** *1* **Costa Filey**[18] 3159 5-8-13 **67**.................................... MeganNicholls(3) 8 47
(Ed Vaughan) *rrd s: chsd ldrs: rdn 2f out: wknd over 1f out* **8/1**

0065 **11** *3* **Temple Road (IRE)**[13] 3307 8-8-12 **66**.....................(bt) GeorgeWood(3) 11 37
(Milton Bradley) *hld up in rr: pushed along and no prog 2f out: no ch after* **40/1**

1m 12.18s (-0.92) **Going Correction** 0.0s/f (Stan) **11** Ran SP% **113.6**
Speed ratings (Par 103): **106,105,104,104,104 104,104,104,96,94 90**
CSF £33.23 CT £264.80 TOTE £5.20: £2.00, £2.50, £2.90; EX 37.00 Trifecta £302.70.
Owner Wentdale Ltd & Mrs L A Ivory **Bred** Shadwell Estate Company Limited **Trained** Radlett, Herts

FOCUS
Just a fair apprentice handicap. They went a solid pace, which only collapsed inside the final furlong and led to a bunched finish. The winner continues to progress.

3781 £10 FREE BET AT 32REDSPORT.COM MAIDEN FILLIES' STKS 1m 4f (P)
6:40 (6:42) (Class 5) 3-Y-O+ **£2,911** (£866; £432; £216) **Stalls** Centre

Form RPR

5 **1** **Taqaareed (IRE)**[68] 1609 3-9-0 0.................................... PaulHanagan 2 88+
(John Gosden) *mde all: stretched clr jst over 2f out: rdn over 1f out: styd on wl* **10/11**[1]

30- **2** *7* **Tuolumne Meadows**[249] 7467 3-9-0 0........................... MartinHarley 11 74
(Paul Cole) *hld up in 8th: urged along and prog on outer 3f out: racd sltly awkwardly 2f out but maintained hdwy to take 2nd jst ins fnl f: no ch w wnr* **20/1**

4 **3** *¾* **Mazalto (IRE)**[29] 2767 3-9-0 0.. JamesDoyle 9 73+
(Hugo Palmer) *trckd ldng trio: rdn and nt qckn wl over 2f out and sn outpcd: styd on again to take 3rd last strides* **7/1**[3]

03 **4** *½* **Queen Of The Stars**[21] 3028 3-9-0 0.............................. PatCosgrave 6 72
(William Haggas) *slowly away and also impeded s: rousted to rcvr and sn trckd ldng pair: chsd wnr wl over 2f out but sn outpcd: lost 2nd jst ins fnl f and lost 3rd last strides* **7/2**[2]

00-3 **5** *1 ¾* **Great Thoughts (IRE)**[34] 2619 3-9-0 72....................... JamieSpencer 5 69
(David Simcock) *trckd wnr to wl over 2f out: sn outpcd: one pce after* **9/1**

0 **6** *1* **Contingency**[16] 3235 3-9-0 0.. JimCrowley 3 68
(Stuart Williams) *trckd ldrs in 5th: rdn and effrt over 2f out but sn outpcd: fdd* **100/1**

5 **7** *2* **Notice (IRE)**[19] 3094 3-9-0 0.. SaleemGolam 4 65
(David Simcock) *settled in last quartet: pushed along over 2f out: reminder over 1f out: no ch but kpt on nr fin* **33/1**

50 **8** *nse* **Tangba**[17] 3194 3-9-0 0.. AndreaAtzeni 8 65
(Roger Varian) *sn hld up in 6th: shkn up and outpcd over 2f out: n.d after* **12/1**

00 **9** *nk* **Lily Trotter**[19] 3094 3-9-0 0... PatDobbs 7 64
(Ralph Beckett) *settled in 7th: pushed along and outpcd wl over 2f out: no prog after* **50/1**

10 *3 ¼* **Shift On Sheila** 3-8-11 0... TimClark(3) 12 59
(Pam Sly) *slowly away: mostly in last pair: shkn up and lft bhd fr 3f out* **100/1**

11 *1* **Kitty For Me** 3-9-0 0.. DougieCostello 1 57
(William Muir) *a in last quartet: shkn up and lft bhd fr 3f out* **50/1**

0 **12** *1* **Three Loves (IRE)**[48] 2182 3-8-11 0.............................. RobHornby(3) 10 56
(Andrew Balding) *dwlt: a in last pair: pushed along and lft bhd fr 3f out* **100/1**

2m 32.98s (-1.52) **Going Correction** 0.0s/f (Stan) **12** Ran SP% **119.4**
Speed ratings (Par 100): **105,100,99,99,98 97,96,96,96,93 93,92**
CSF £27.29 TOTE £1.80: £1.20, £4.50, £2.10; EX 25.00 Trifecta £104.20.
Owner Hamdan Al Maktoum **Bred** Shadwell Estate Company Limited **Trained** Newmarket, Suffolk

FOCUS
Not a great deal of depth to this fillies' maiden, but the winner did it really well.

3782 BRITISH STALLION STUDS EBF NOVICE FILLIES' STKS (PLUS 10 RACE) 7f (P)
7:10 (7:10) (Class 5) 2-Y-O **£3,234** (£962; £481; £240) **Stalls** Low

Form RPR

1 **1** **Urban Fox**[20] 3074 2-9-7 0 MartinHarley 4 79
(James Tate) *mostly in 2nd pl tl led and swvd rt jst over 2f out: shkn up over 1f out: stl looked green but in command after: pushed out* **5/2**[2]

1 **2** 1 ½ **Miss Sugars**[16] 3222 2-9-4 0 JamieSpencer 5 72
(David Simcock) *in tch: chsd ldng pair wl over 2f out: drvn to take 2nd over 1f out: kpt on but no imp on wnr* **9/1**

3 nk **Elas Ruby** 2-9-0 0 RobertHavlin 1 67
(John Gosden) *slowly away: settled in last: pushed along firmly fr over 2f out: styd on to take 3rd nr fin and clsd on runner-up* **10/1**

4 ½ **Double Spin** 2-9-0 0 FrankieDettori 6 66
(John Gosden) *dwlt: t.k.h and rapid prog to ld over 5f out: hdd and impeded jst over 2f out: pushed along and one pce after* **3/1**[3]

4 **5** 2 ¼ **Pacofilha**[63] 1793 2-8-11 0 TomMarquand(3) 2 60
(Paul Cole) *pushed along in last pair over 4f out: effrt over 2f out but sn outpcd: plugged on fr over 1f out* **12/1**

1 **6** 3 ¼ **Fancy Day (IRE)**[10] 3433 2-9-7 0 JamesDoyle 3 58
(Mark Johnston) *led to over 5f out: sn nudged along: lost pl and struggling fr 3f out: steadily wknd* **9/4**[1]

1m 27.0s (1.00) **Going Correction** 0.0s/f (Stan) **6** Ran SP% **111.1**
Speed ratings (Par 90): **94,92,91,91,88 85**
CSF £23.42 TOTE £2.80: £1.30, £2.60; EX 24.60 Trifecta £121.90.
Owner Saeed Manana **Bred** Mascalls Stud **Trained** Newmarket, Suffolk

FOCUS
Three maiden fillies and three penalised winners faced each other in this decent novice race.

3783 32RED CASINO H'CAP (LONDON MILE SERIES QUALIFIER) 1m (P)
7:40 (7:40) (Class 4) (0-85,85) 3-Y-O+ **£4,690** (£1,395; £697; £348) **Stalls** Low

Form RPR

1000 **1** **Abareeq**[17] 3187 3-9-4 **85** PaulHanagan 7 92
(Mark Johnston) *trckd ldng trio: prog to 3rd wl over 1f out: drvn and clsd to ld 100yds out: styd on on* **8/1**

3300 **2** ½ **Hail Clodius (IRE)**[7] 3534 4-10-0 **85** PatDobbs 2 93
(Richard Hannon) *trckd ldng pair: wnt 2nd 2f out: drvn to ld over 1f out: kpt on but hdd and hld last 100yds* **6/1**[3]

4-00 **3** nse **Cloud Seven**[47] 2214 4-9-9 **80** TedDurcan 10 88+
(Chris Wall) *stdd fr wd draw and hld up in last quartet: gd prog on inner fr 2f out: drvn to chal fnl f: styd on but jst hld* **15/2**

0335 **4** 1 ½ **Major Crispies**[13] 3303 5-10-0 **85** RyanTate 6 89
(James Eustace) *trckd ldrs in 5th: pushed along to take 4th jst over 1f out: shkn up and styd on same pce after: nvr chal* **11/2**[2]

4442 **5** 2 **Franco's Secret**[7] 3523 5-9-11 **82** (v) DarryllHolland 9 81+
(Peter Hedger) *stdd s: hld up in last: shkn up over 2f out: styd on fr over 1f out to take 5th nr fin: to much to do* **4/1**[1]

0046 **6** ½ **Air Of York (IRE)**[18] 3124 4-9-7 **78** ShaneKelly 4 76
(David Evans) *hld up in midfield: prog on inner over 1f out: rdn and wknd ins fnl f* **25/1**

-100 **7** 1 ½ **Telegram**[41] 2393 3-9-1 **85** TomMarquand(3) 11 78
(Richard Hannon) *hld up in 8th: drvn over 2f out: no prog but kpt on fr over 1f out* **14/1**

3014 **8** 1 **Exalted (IRE)**[21] 3035 5-9-2 **73** (t) JimCrowley 5 65
(William Knight) *t.k.h: trckd ldr: led wl over 2f out: hdd over 1f out: wknd qckly fnl f* **8/1**

-320 **9** nse **Quality Song (USA)**[41] 2399 4-9-8 **79** JamieSpencer 3 71+
(Richard Hughes) *hld up and sn racd on outer in last quartet: rdn over 2f out and no prog: kpt on fnl f* **6/1**[3]

2300 **10** 1 ¼ **Freddy With A Y (IRE)**[71] 1546 6-9-1 **72** JimmyQuinn 8 61
(Paul Burgoyne) *chsd ldrs in 6th: shkn up 2f out: n.m.r briefly sn after: no hdwy over 1f out: wknd fnl f* **66/1**

1000 **11** 2 ½ **St Patrick's Day (IRE)**[44] 2313 4-9-11 **82** FrederikTylicki 12 65
(J R Jenkins) *hld up in last quartet: rdn and no prog wl over 2f out* **66/1**

1000 **12** hd **Harry Holland**[20] 3061 4-9-8 **79** [1] DougieCostello 1 62
(William Muir) *led to wl over 2f out: sn wknd* **25/1**

1m 39.42s (-0.38) **Going Correction** 0.0s/f (Stan)
WFA 3 from 4yo+ 10lb **12** Ran SP% **115.3**
Speed ratings (Par 105): **101,100,100,98,96 96,94,93,93,92 90,89**
CSF £52.32 CT £380.10 TOTE £8.60: £2.30, £2.70, £2.30; EX 92.20 Trifecta £661.30.
Owner Hamdan Al Maktoum **Bred** Shadwell Estate Company Limited **Trained** Middleham Moor, N Yorks

FOCUS
An above-average handicap which in 2014 was taken by Tenor and last year by Mutawathea who both now possess three-figure ratings. It looked wide open and the winner showed a good attitude.

3784 32RED ON THE APP STORE H'CAP 2m (P)
8:10 (8:11) (Class 3) (0-90,88) 4-Y-O+
£7,158 (£2,143; £1,071; £535; £267; £134) **Stalls** Low

Form RPR

-013 **1** **Royal Reef (IRE)**[27] 2820 4-8-4 **71** JimmyQuinn 4 77+
(William Knight) *flashed tail on occasions: trckd ldr: led after 4f to 7f out: led again 5f out: kicked clr wl over 2f out: drvn over 1f out: ld dwindled fnl f but a holding on* **8/1**

-504 **2** ½ **Percy Veer**[24] 2932 4-9-4 **85** PatDobbs 10 90
(Sylvester Kirk) *prom: trckd ldr 10f out to 7f out: rdn wl over 2f out: chsd clr wnr jst over 1f out: kpt on and grad clsd but nvr able to get there* **5/1**[2]

60-0 **3** 1 **Air Squadron**[32] 2699 6-8-11 **78** RichardKingscote 3 82+
(Ralph Beckett) *hld up in midfield: dropped to rr sn after 1/2-way and lot to do once wnr kicked clr wl over 2f out: styd on wl fr over 1f out to take 3rd last strides* **15/2**[3]

5602 **4** nk **Cotton Club (IRE)**[24] 2932 5-8-11 **85** GeorgeWood(7) 1 88
(Rod Millman) *hld up in rr: rdn once wnr kicked for home wl over 2f out: prog over 1f out: kpt on and pressed for a pl nr fin* **5/1**[2]

2412 **5** shd **Zakatal**[29] 2782 10-9-1 **82** MartinHarley 2 85
(Rebecca Menzies) *hld up in last pair: rapid prog to ld 7f out: hdd 5f out: outpcd by wnr over 2f out: lost 2nd jst over 1f out: one pce* **14/1**

0-15 **6** nk **Planetoid (IRE)**[29] 2782 8-9-1 **82** (b) TimmyMurphy 9 85
(Jim Best) *wl plcd early: steadily drifted to rr: shkn up and prog on inner fr 2f out: pressed for a pl ins fnl f: one pce nr fin* **33/1**

2000 **7** shd **Shades Of Silver**[11] 3387 6-9-6 **87** PatCosgrave 7 90
(Ed de Giles) *hld up in midfield: rdn once wnr kicked for home wl over 2f out: kpt on fr over 1f out: pressed for a pl nr fin* **11/1**

4-03 **8** 2 ¼ **King Calypso**[24] 2932 5-8-11 **83** EdwardGreatrex(5) 6 83
(Denis Coakley) *hld up: plenty to do once wnr kicked for home wl over 2f out: drvn and sme prog on outer wl over 1f out: no hdwy fnl f* **9/2**[1]

-001 **9** 9 **Saborido (USA)**[22] 2995 10-8-5 **77** HectorCrouch(5) 8 66
(Amanda Perrett) *led 4f: styd prom: urged along 5f out: wknd qckly over 2f out* **25/1**

6-22 **10** 1 ½ **Glan Y Gors (IRE)**[152] 385 4-9-7 **88** JamieSpencer 5 76
(David Simcock) *stdd s: hld up in last pair: stl there whn effrt and hmpd 2f out: no ch after and wknd* **9/2**[1]

3m 29.75s (-0.35) **Going Correction** 0.0s/f (Stan) **10** Ran SP% **114.4**
Speed ratings (Par 107): **100,99,99,99,99 98,98,97,93,92**
CSF £46.80 CT £313.38 TOTE £9.40: £2.20, £2.10, £3.10; EX 64.00 Trifecta £524.60.
Owner W J Knight **Bred** Herbertstown House Stud **Trained** Patching, W Sussex

FOCUS
A competitive staying handicap, but it proved pretty tactical with a stop/start gallop.

3785 32RED H'CAP 1m 4f (P)
8:40 (8:41) (Class 3) (0-95,92) 4-Y-O+
£7,158 (£2,143; £1,071; £535; £267; £134) **Stalls** Centre

Form RPR

30-0 **1** **Elysian Fields (GR)**[40] 2433 5-9-4 **89** JimCrowley 3 96
(Amanda Perrett) *led: rdn clr over 2f out: c bk to rivals fnl f: hdd 100yds out: keeping on wl but hld whn lft in ld post* **11/1**

5242 **2** nse **Sbraase**[20] 3077 5-8-12 **83** MartinHarley 6 91+
(James Tate) *hld up in last: gng easily wl over 1f out: rapid prog through rivals to take 2nd jst ins fnl f and clsd on wnr: urged into narrow ld 100yds out: narrow but decisive ld whn appeared to be eased last strides: hdd post* **5/1**[3]

0-00 **3** 1 ¼ **Shell Bay (USA)**[25] 2897 4-9-3 **88** PatDobbs 10 93
(Richard Hannon) *hld up in midfield: rdn and prog 2f out to chse wnr over 1f out: clsd but lost 2nd jst ins fnl f: kpt on same pce* **20/1**

1-20 **4** 1 ¼ **Winter House**[30] 2744 4-9-6 **91** (v[1]) JamesDoyle 9 94
(Saeed bin Suroor) *trckd wnr after 2f: rdn and outpcd over 2f out: lost 2nd over 1f out: one pce after* **9/4**[1]

-032 **5** 1 ½ **Steppe Daughter (IRE)**[23] 2966 5-8-4 **80** EdwardGreatrex(5) 1 81
(Denis Coakley) *hld up in last pair: effrt on inner 2f out: no great prog fr over 1f out* **14/1**

3P-0 **6** ½ **London Citizen (USA)**[42] 2377 6-9-1 **86** TedDurcan 7 86
(Chris Wall) *trckd wnr 2f: styd handy: rdn over 2f out: fnd nil and btn over 1f out* **12/1**

221- **7** 2 **Pecking Order (IRE)**[277] 6764 4-9-2 **87** FrederikTylicki 4 84
(James Fanshawe) *hld up in midfield: rdn over 2f out and outpcd: no hdwy over 1f out: wknd ins fnl f* **11/4**[2]

6604 **8** nk **Sennockian Star**[13] 3304 6-9-2 **87** (v) RichardKingscote 2 83
(Mark Johnston) *urged along to try to ld but couldn't: prom: rdn 3f out: steadily wknd fr 2f out* **10/1**

2m 32.23s (-2.27) **Going Correction** 0.0s/f (Stan) **8** Ran SP% **110.6**
Speed ratings (Par 107): **107,106,106,105,104 103,102,102**
CSF £60.66 CT £1039.06 TOTE £8.30: £2.80, £1.90, £4.50; EX 60.40 Trifecta £485.90.
Owner Mrs Alexandra J Chandris **Bred** Queensway S A **Trained** Pulborough, W Sussex

FOCUS
This had the look of a decent race and it played host to a tight finish. The winner was given a good ride, but may have been fortunate.

3786 32RED.COM H'CAP (JOCKEY CLUB GRASSROOTS FLAT SPRINT SERIES QUALIFIER) 6f (P)
9:10 (9:10) (Class 5) (0-70,69) 3-Y-O **£2,911** (£866; £432; £216) **Stalls** Low

Form RPR

-462 **1** **Geoff Potts (IRE)**[5] 3604 3-9-6 **68** RichardKingscote 8 72+
(Jeremy Gask) *pressed ldr after 1f: rdn to chal and pressed new ldr over 1f out: drvn ahd last 150yds: hld on wl* **7/4**[1]

0242 **2** nk **Lady McGuffy (IRE)**[7] 3513 3-8-5 **53** (t) AdamBeschizza 6 56
(David Evans) *chsd ldrs: rdn 2f out: clsd over 1f out: tk 2nd last 100yds: pressed wnr after: jst hld* **8/1**[3]

26-0 **3** ¾ **Song Of Paradise**[43] 2337 3-9-6 **68** TedDurcan 4 69
(Chris Wall) *dwlt: in tch: prog on inner 2f out: drvn and styd on to take 3rd nr fin: unable to chal* **20/1**

5636 **4** ¾ **Canford Belle**[1] 3734 3-8-4 **57** ow2 HectorCrouch(5) 1 56
(Amanda Perrett) *prom: rdn to cl 2f out: drvn ahd over 1f out: hdd and fdd last 150yds* **4/1**[2]

0506 **5** 1 **Le Manege Enchante (IRE)**[14] 3280 3-8-5 **58** (p) NoelGarbutt(5) 2 53
(Derek Shaw) *dwlt: hld up in last pair: rdn over 2f out: styd on fr over 1f out: nrst fin but n.d* **20/1**

02-0 **6** hd **Burningfivers (IRE)**[21] 3036 3-9-4 **69** TomMarquand(3) 3 64
(Joseph Tuite) *mostly in midfield: rdn and no prog 2f out: styd on ins fnl f: no ch* **10/1**

1-00 **7** hd **Pop Culture**[35] 2586 3-8-12 **63** DannyBrock(3) 5 57
(Jonathan Portman) *led: drvn and hdd over 1f out: wknd fnl f* **33/1**

0-00 **8** 2 **Keiba (IRE)**[33] 2642 3-9-0 **62** ShaneKelly 7 50
(Gary Moore) *hld up in last: pushed along 2f out: passed a few late on: nvr involved* **33/1**

653 **9** nk **Inner Knowing (IRE)**[16] 3210 3-9-0 **62** (p) DougieCostello 11 49
(K R Burke) *spd fr wd draw and prom: wknd over 1f out* **16/1**

3-00 **10** 1 **Arlecchino's Rock**[20] 3062 3-9-4 **66** SteveDrowne 9 50
(Mark Usher) *awkward s: racd wd: nvr beyond midfield: wknd over 1f out* **10/1**

3306 **11** 4 **Ginger Joe**[29] 2770 3-9-1 **66** (t) KieranShoemark(3) 10 37
(David Brown) *chsd ldr 1f: sn lost pl and struggling: last and wkng over 1f out* **14/1**

1m 13.6s (0.50) **Going Correction** 0.0s/f (Stan) **11** Ran SP% **113.6**
Speed ratings (Par 99): **96,95,94,93,92 92,91,89,88,87 82**
CSF £14.45 CT £202.10 TOTE £2.60: £1.60, £2.60, £4.40; EX 16.30 Trifecta £310.00.
Owner Jamie & Lucy Hart **Bred** Hyde Park Stud **Trained** Stockbridge, Hants

FOCUS
A modest race and the first two looked well in on previous week's runs.
T/Plt: £247.30 to a £1 stake. Pool: £70,188.26. 207.11 winning tickets. T/Qpdt: 68.60 to a £1 stake. Pool: £5,602.92. 60.40 winning tickets. **Jonathan Neesom**

3787 - 3795a (Foreign Racing) - See Raceform Interactive

2755 MAISONS-LAFFITTE (R-H)

Wednesday, June 29

OFFICIAL GOING: Turf: good

3796a PRIX DE RIS-ORANGIS (GROUP 3) (3YO+) (TURF) 6f (S)

2:55 (12:00) 3-Y-O+ **£29,411** (£11,764; £8,823; £5,882; £2,941)

RPR

1 **Damila (FR)**[24] 2943 3-8-5 0 CristianDemuro 4 106
(H-A Pantall, France) *midfield: clsd 1/2-way: rdn to chal 2f out: led over 1f out: r.o: jst prevailed* **16/1**

2 shd **Love Spirit**[25] 2927 6-9-1 0 Pierre-CharlesBoudot 2 111+
(J Baudron, France) *sn led on rail: rdn and strly pressed 2f out: hdd over 1f out: r.o and battle bk gamely fnl f: jst denied* **9/4**[1]

3 2 1/2 **Pupa Di Saronno (FR)**[20] 3090 5-8-11 0 FabriceVeron 5 99
(H-A Pantall, France) *trckd ldr: rdn and effrt over 2f out: outpcd by front pair fnl f: kpt on and jst up for 3rd fnl strides* **16/1**

4 hd **Finsbury Square (IRE)**[24] 2943 4-9-5 0 (b) ChristopheSoumillon 8 106
(F Chappet, France) *midfield: shuffled bk to rr over 1f out: sn rdn: kpt on wout threatening fnl f: jst missed 3rd* **3/1**[2]

5 snk **Ross Castle (IRE)**[14] 3269 3-8-13 0 EddyHardouin 1 105
(Matthieu Palussiere, France) *hld up: rdn in last 2f out: kpt on fnl f but nvr able to chal* **12/1**

6 nse **Plusquemavie (IRE)**[38] 2518 5-9-5 0 (b) GianpasqualeFois 7 106
(V Fazio, Italy) *hld up: rdn over 2f out: effrt to chse ldrs over 1f out: outpcd fnl f and lost multiple pls cl home* **9/2**[3]

7 3/4 **Catcall (FR)**[24] 2943 7-9-1 0 OlivierPeslier 3 99
(P Sogorb, France) *trckd ldr: rdn and effrt 2f out: no ex fnl f: wknd* **3/1**[2]

8 14 **Gammarth (FR)**[64] 1769 8-9-5 0 (b) MickaelBarzalona 6 59
(J Phelippon, France) *hld up: rdn 1/2-way: dropped to last fnl f: eased whn btn: t.o* **14/1**

1m 10.5s (-2.90)
WFA 3 from 4yo+ 7lb **8** Ran SP% **125.1**
WIN (incl. 1 euro stake): 15.40. PLACES: 3.50, 1.80, 3.50. DF: 22.70. SF: 64.80.
Owner Pierre Pasquiou **Bred** P Pasquiou **Trained** France

3797 - (Foreign Racing) - See Raceform Interactive

2892 EPSOM (L-H)

Thursday, June 30

OFFICIAL GOING: Good to soft (soft in places; 6.2)

Wind: Moderate, across Weather: Fine but cloudy

3798 VOLTA DATA CENTRES COLOCATION H'CAP 1m 4f 10y

6:10 (6:13) (Class 5) (0-75,75) 4-Y-O+ **£3,234** (£962; £481; £240) **Stalls** Centre

Form RPR

-511 1 **Hatsaway (IRE)**[8] 3533 5-9-4 **72** 6ex JFEgan 9 85
(Pat Phelan) *trckd ldr w field sn spread out: led ent st: shkn up 2f out: styd on wl drew away fnl f* **13/8**[1]

0543 2 5 **Brandon Castle**[73] 1531 4-9-7 **75** OisinMurphy 7 82
(Andrew Balding) *hld up off the pce in 5th: prog to 4th st and chsd wnr wl over 2f out: tried to cl over 1f out: no imp fnl f* **4/1**[2]

132- 3 12 **Mr Fickle (IRE)**[187] 7140 7-9-5 **73** GeorgeBaker 4 59
(Gary Moore) *hld up in last and long way adrift: 7th st: prog to take modest 3rd over 1f out: kpt on but no ch w ldng pair* **11/1**

-002 4 9 **Dellbuoy**[9] 3492 7-7-9 **56** SophieRalston[(7)] 2 27
(Pat Phelan) *chsd ldrs early: sn lost pl: dropped to last st and long way adrift: kpt on again to take remote 4th fnl strides* **16/1**

6021 5 nk **Vale Of Iron (IRE)**[12] 3403 4-9-7 **75** KierenFox 3 46
(John Best) *chsd ldng pair: wnt 2nd briefly 3f out: sn lft bhd by ldng pair: steadily wknd* **10/1**

2310 6 3 **Prayer Time**[27] 1675 4-8-8 **62** (p[1]) JoeyHaynes 6 28
(Mark H Tompkins) *nvr on terms: pushed along 1/2-way: 6th and off the pce st: no prog* **40/1**

016- 7 6 **Duke Of Sonning**[242] 6638 4-9-3 **71** JimCrowley 8 28
(Alan King) *chsd ldrs: dropped to 5th and pushed along st: sn struggling* **11/2**[3]

-421 8 16 **Onorina (IRE)**[42] 2400 4-9-0 **68** SamHitchcott 1
(Jim Boyle) *led at str pce and sn had field strung out: hdd & wknd ent st: t.o* **8/1**

560/ 9 3 1/2 **First Avenue**[26] 3453 11-9-1 **74** MeganNicholls[(5)] 5
(Laura Mongan) *hld up: a wl off the pce: 7th: st: sn rdn and wknd: t.o* **20/1**

2m 45.57s (6.67) **Going Correction** +0.60s/f (Yiel) **9** Ran SP% **115.1**
Speed ratings (Par 103): **101,97,89,83,83 81,77,66,64**
CSF £7.89 CT £52.18 TOTE £2.20: £1.30, £1.60, £2.20; EX 8.80 Trifecta £66.80.
Owner P Wheatley **Bred** Grangecon Stud **Trained** Epsom, Surrey

FOCUS

Race run over 12 yards further than advertised. A modest handicap in which they finished at wide margins on easy ground. After the first John Egan said: "Slow side of good. I thought it would be softer," while "It's dead and hard work" was Sam Hitchcott's verdict. The winner continued his resurgence and is back to his old best.

3799 BRITISH STALLION STUDS EBF NOVICE MEDIAN AUCTION STKS 7f

6:45 (6:49) (Class 5) 2-Y-O **£3,881** (£1,155; £577; £288) **Stalls** Low

Form RPR

223 1 **Tap Tap Boom**[20] 3100 2-9-2 0 SteveDrowne 2 76
(George Baker) *mde all: shkn up over 1f out: styd on wl* **4/1**[2]

5 2 1 1/4 **Manolito De Madrid (GER)**[20] 3108 2-9-2 0 OisinMurphy 9 73+
(Andrew Balding) *trckd wnr: tried to chal fr over 2f out but hanging lft rest of way and nvr able to seriously threaten* **1/1**[1]

3 2 3/4 **Novoman (IRE)** 2-9-2 0 PatCosgrave 4 65+
(William Haggas) *slowly away: sn rcvrd and 5th st: prog to chse ldng pair wl over 1f out and looked a threat: one pce sn after* **7/1**

05 4 2 **Zamadance**[22] 3032 2-9-2 0 JimCrowley 1 60
(Sylvester Kirk) *trckd ldrs: 4th st: chsd ldng pair 3f out to wl over 1f out: no ex* **25/1**

5 5 1/2 **Metronomic (IRE)**[12] 3408 2-9-2 0 KieranO'Neill 5 58
(Richard Hannon) *t.k.h: trckd ldng pair to 3f out: styd in tch: fdd over 1f out* **9/2**[3]

0 6 2 1/4 **Dewan (IRE)**[8] 3529 2-9-2 0 CharlesBishop 3 52
(Mick Channon) *a abt same pl: nt on terms w ldrs in st: no prog 2f out* **20/1**

7 9 **Too Many Shots** 2-9-2 0 KierenFox 8 28
(John Best) *a in rr: 8th st: bhd over 2f out* **33/1**

00 8 1 **Myredbush (IRE)**[24] 2963 2-8-11 0 NickyMackay 10 20
(Simon Dow) *a in rr: 7th st: bhd over 2f out* **66/1**

9 7 **Don't You Think** 2-9-2 0 ShaneKelly 11 6
(Richard Hughes) *slowly away: mostly in last: bhd fr 3f out: t.o* **25/1**

1m 26.94s (3.64) **Going Correction** +0.60s/f (Yiel) **9** Ran SP% **117.6**
Speed ratings (Par 93): **103,101,98,96,95 93,82,81,73**
CSF £8.12 TOTE £4.30: £1.10, £2.00, £1.90; EX 10.30 Trifecta £30.00.
Owner Steve & Jolene De'Lemos **Bred** London Thoroughbred Services Ltd **Trained** Manton, Wilts

FOCUS

Race run over 6 yards further than advertised. Just fair novice form with the winner enjoying the run of things.

3800 TOTEQUADPOT RACES 3,4,5 AND 6 H'CAP 6f

7:15 (7:16) (Class 3) (0-95,94) 3-Y-O+ **£7,439** (£2,213; £1,106; £553) **Stalls** High

Form RPR

-212 1 **Shanghai Glory (IRE)**[12] 3414 3-9-5 **92** MichaelJMMurphy 4 96
(Charles Hills) *chsd ldr: shkn up over 2f out: looked hld over 1f out: styd on wl fnl f to ld last strides* **2/1**[1]

0250 2 nk **Iseemist (IRE)**[26] 2898 5-10-0 **94** JoeyHaynes 1 99
(John Gallagher) *led: shkn up 2f out: 2 l ahd whn edgd rt over 1f out: wilted and hdd last strides* **7/2**[3]

-100 3 nk **Khelman (IRE)**[12] 3419 6-9-5 **85** GeorgeChaloner 3 89
(Richard Fahey) *chsd ldng pair: urged along wl over 2f out: grad clsd on inner fnl f: nvr quite able to chal* **10/1**

4331 4 2 3/4 **Escalating**[7] 3580 4-9-4 **84** 6ex (tp) AndrewMullen 5 79
(Michael Appleby) *hld up in last: shkn up 2f out: tk 4th over 1f out: nvr on terms* **9/4**[2]

/605 5 1 1/4 **Shamshon (IRE)**[15] 3277 5-10-0 **94** GeorgeBaker 7 85
(Jamie Osborne) *racd in 4th: pushed along and no prog 2f out: dropped to last over 1f out: btn after* **7/1**

1m 11.88s (2.48) **Going Correction** +0.60s/f (Yiel)
WFA 3 from 4yo+ 7lb **5** Ran SP% **107.9**
Speed ratings (Par 107): **107,106,106,102,100**
CSF £8.85 TOTE £3.00: £1.80, £1.90; EX 10.40 Trifecta £35.30.
Owner Kangyu Int Racing (HK) Ltd & F Ma **Bred** Owenstown Stud **Trained** Lambourn, Berks

FOCUS

A decent handicap, run over 4yds further than advertised. The winner was on top late and continues to progress.

3801 TOTETRIFECTA PICK THE 1,2,3 H'CAP (JOCKEY CLUB GRASSROOTS FLAT MIDDLE DISTANCE SERIES QUALIFIER) 1m 2f 18y

7:50 (7:51) (Class 4) (0-80,80) 3-Y-O+ **£4,690** (£1,395; £697; £348) **Stalls** Low

Form RPR

-313 1 **Grapevine (IRE)**[38] 2538 3-9-0 **78** MichaelJMMurphy 1 91
(Charles Hills) *t.k.h and restrained to last after 3f: quick prog 3f out to ld jst over 2f out: shot clr: rdn out* **11/10**[1]

6030 2 10 **Firestorm (GER)**[12] 3403 5-9-7 **73** GeorgeBaker 7 68
(Michael Attwater) *pressed ldr: led 1/2-way: rdn and hdd jst over 1f out: kpt on but no ch w wnr after* **9/2**[3]

0221 3 2 **Melendez (USA)**[79] 1400 3-9-1 **79** WilliamCarson 2 70
(Jamie Osborne) *hld up in tch: 4th st: effrt and cl up over 2f out: sn easily outpcd by wnr* **7/1**

25-4 4 2 1/2 **Yensir**[71] 1570 3-9-1 **79** JFEgan 5 66
(Pat Phelan) *in tch: pushed along over 4f out: 3rd st: sn dropped to last and struggling: plugged on* **4/1**[2]

4-60 5 1 **Bahamian C**[45] 2296 5-9-6 **72** GeorgeChaloner 6 57
(Richard Fahey) *led to 1/2-way: sn urged along: 2nd striaght: racd awkwardly over 2f out: sn btn* **8/1**

2m 14.89s (5.19) **Going Correction** +0.60s/f (Yiel)
WFA 3 from 4yo+ 12lb **5** Ran SP% **109.4**
Speed ratings (Par 105): **103,95,93,91,90**
CSF £6.26 TOTE £1.90: £1.40, £2.30; EX 7.20 Trifecta £21.20.
Owner Mrs J K Powell **Bred** Colman O'Flynn Jnr **Trained** Lambourn, Berks

FOCUS

Race run over 12yds further than advertised. This modest handicap proved easy pickings for the favourite with doubts over the others and it's hard to know how much he needed to improve. They raced away from the inside rail in the home straight.

3802 TOTEEXACTA PICK THE 1ST AND 2ND H'CAP 1m 114y

8:20 (8:22) (Class 5) (0-75,75) 4-Y-O+ **£3,234** (£962; £481; £240) **Stalls** Low

Form RPR

2403 1 **Zaria**[20] 3096 5-7-11 **58** (p) HollieDoyle[(7)] 1 66
(Richard Price) *chsd ldng trio: clr of rest fr 1/2-way: rdn over 2f out and no imp: kpt changing legs and picked up wl fnl f: r.o to ld last 75yds* **8/1**

-130 2 3/4 **Double Czech (IRE)**[20] 3097 5-9-3 **71** GeorgeBaker 7 77
(Patrick Chamings) *taken steadily to post: won battle for ld and set gd pce: narrowly hdd 3f out to 2f out: fought off persistent rival over 1f out: hdd and no ex last 75yds* **5/1**[3]

641 3 2 1/4 **Uncle Dermot (IRE)**[7] 3582 8-9-0 **68** JFEgan 6 69
(Brendan Powell) *taken down early: tried to ld but had to chse ldr: chal fr 1/2-way: narrow ld 3f out to 2f out: btn off over 1f out: fdd and lost 2nd ins fnl f* **7/2**[1]

4212 4 2 **First Experience**[18] 3197 5-9-3 **71** (p) KierenFox 8 67
(Lee Carter) *chsd ldng pair: rdn over 2f out: no imp and lost 3rd over 1f out: fdd ins fnl f* **8/1**

50-0 5 3/4 **Topamichi**[46] 212 6-9-5 **73** DarryllHolland 3 68
(Mark H Tompkins) *pushed along early in 5th: outpcd by ldrs fr 1/2-way and wl off the pce st: styd on fr over 1f out: nrst fin* **20/1**

0402 6 hd **Barren Brook**[36] 2588 9-9-0 **68** OisinMurphy 4 62
(Laura Mongan) *taken down early: hld up in 7th: wl off the pce fr 1/2-way: styd on fr over 1f out: no ch to threaten* **12/1**

6444 7 3/4 **Little Lord Nelson**[13] 3354 4-8-3 **62** (tp) AaronJones[(5)] 2 54
(Stuart Williams) *hld up in 6th: wl off the pce fr 1/2-way: effrt on outer 3f out but no prog: styd on fr over 1f out: no ch* **6/1**

1-56 8 4 **Nosey Barker (IRE)**[23] 2996 4-9-7 **75** (p) KieranO'Neill 5 58
(Richard Hannon) *hld up in last: wl off the pce fr 1/2-way: nvr a factor* **10/1**

6020 **9** 2 **Live Dangerously**[17] 3234 6-9-1 **69** .... WilliamCarson 9 48
(John Bridger) *taken down early: hld up in 8th: wl off the pce fr 1/2-way: rdn and no prog 3f out: bhd after* **9/2**[2]

1m 48.91s (2.81) **Going Correction** +0.60s/f (Yiel) **9** Ran SP% **115.1**
Speed ratings (Par 103): **111,110,108,106,105 105,105,101,99**
CSF £47.53 CT £167.47 TOTE £8.70: £2.50, £1.70, £1.70; EX 62.40 Trifecta £282.00.
Owner Mrs K Oseman **Bred** Exors Of The Late J R Good **Trained** Ullingswick, H'fords

FOCUS
Race run over 12yds further than advertised. There were nine runners in this moderate handicap, but only the first four ever counted and it was a small personal best from the winner.

3803 TOTEPOOL CHIP AND PIN BETTING H'CAP 7f
8:50 (8:52) (Class 4) (0-85,85) 3-Y-O+ **£4,690** (£1,395; £697; £348) **Stalls** Low

Form RPR
1404 **1** **Fingal's Cave (IRE)**[17] 3233 4-9-10 **81** .... CharlesBishop 4 89+
(Mick Channon) *slowly away: towards rr early: hdwy and 8th st: prog on outer over 2f out to ld over 1f out: hung lft after: hld on nr fin* **6/1**[3]

551 **2** nk **Harlequin Striker (IRE)**[17] 3234 4-9-12 **83** .... RobertWinston 3 90+
(Dean Ivory) *chsd ldrs: 6th st: rdn and swtchd rt over 2f out: n.m.r over 1f out: r.o wl to take 2nd ins fnl f: clsd on wnr but hld nr fin* **7/2**[1]

-035 **3** ¾ **Fast Dancer (IRE)**[19] 3133 4-9-11 **82** .... JFEgan 10 87
(Joseph Tuite) *towards rr: 9th and pushed along st: eased towards outer over 2f out: drvn and r.o fr over 1f out to take 3rd nr fin* **12/1**

-001 **4** 1 ¼ **Hidden Treasures**[19] 3137 3-8-6 **72** .... GeorgeChaloner 9 71
(Richard Fahey) *chsd ldrs: 5th st: clsd to chal 2f out: fdd fnl f* **14/1**

6112 **5** 1 **Flying Fantasy**[19] 3137 4-9-1 **77** .... AaronJones(5) 8 76
(Stuart Williams) *chsd ldrs: 7th st: nt qckn over 2f out: kpt on same pce fr over 1f out* **9/1**

3060 **6** ½ **Majestic Myles (IRE)**[36] 2579 8-9-7 **85** .... PaddyBradley(7) 1 83
(Lee Carter) *led to wl over 2f out: shkn up and steadily lost pl: one pce over 1f out* **25/1**

-410 **7** 4 **Arlecchino's Leap**[25] 2934 4-9-10 **81** ....(p) MichaelJMMurphy 12 68
(Mark Usher) *wl in rr: 12th st: modest late prog: nvr a factor* **12/1**

-600 **8** hd **Aqua Ardens (GER)**[25] 2934 8-9-13 **84** ....(t) SteveDrowne 7 71
(George Baker) *towards rr: 10th st: shkn up over 2f out: nvr really figured* **10/1**

0-22 **9** ¾ **Doctor Bong**[23] 3004 4-9-2 **73** ....(p) OisinMurphy 5 58
(Andrew Balding) *chsd ldr to 3f out: sn lost pl and btn* **5/1**[2]

0000 **10** hd **Field Game**[13] 3358 4-9-5 **76** ....(t) JimCrowley 2 60
(Hughie Morrison) *trckd ldrs: 4th st: chal and upsides over 2f out: wknd qckly over 1f out* **8/1**

2222 **11** 1 **Straits Of Malacca**[12] 3405 5-8-13 **70** ....(p) NickyMackay 6 52
(Simon Dow) *t.k.h: pressed ldng pair: led wl over 2f out to over 1f out: wknd rapidly* **25/1**

6312 **12** 8 **Good Luck Charm**[41] 2430 7-9-5 **76** ....(b) GeorgeBaker 13 37
(Gary Moore) *dwlt: a wl in rr: 11th st: no prog over 2f out: eased over 1f out* **14/1**

1-60 **13** 11 **Musical Taste**[71] 1571 3-8-6 **72** .... LiamJones 14
(Pat Phelan) *dwlt: a last and sn t.o* **40/1**

1m 26.34s (3.04) **Going Correction** +0.60s/f (Yiel)
WFA 3 from 4yo+ 9lb **13** Ran SP% **122.2**
Speed ratings (Par 105): **106,105,104,103,102 101,97,96,96,95 94,85,72**
CSF £27.33 CT £260.87 TOTE £6.30: £2.00, £2.20, £4.00; EX 28.70 Trifecta £365.50.
Owner The Motley Cru I **Bred** Rathasker Stud **Trained** West Ilsley, Berks

FOCUS
Race run over 6yds further than advertised. A competitive handicap run at a sound gallop.
T/Plt: £9.20 to a £1 stake. Pool: £70,949.16 - 5598.48 winning units. T/Qpdt: £8.40 to a £1 stake. Pool: £4,761.11 - 417.30 winning units. **Jonathan Neesom**

3395 HAYDOCK (L-H)
Thursday, June 30

OFFICIAL GOING: Soft (6.3)
Wind: light 1/2 against Weather: overcast, light rain race 7 (5.00)

3804 RITEC 35TH ANNIVERSARY H'CAP 1m 2f 95y
2:00 (2:00) (Class 5) (0-70,68) 3-Y-O+ **£2,911** (£866; £432; £216) **Stalls** Centre

Form RPR
6033 **1** **Raven Banner (IRE)**[21] 3053 3-8-11 **63** .... GrahamGibbons 1 71
(Daniel Mark Loughnane) *trckd ldrs: t.k.h: 3rd over 2f out: led appr fnl f: drvn rt out* **3/1**[1]

0-50 **2** 1 ¼ **Lopito De Vega (IRE)**[22] 3011 4-9-9 **63** .... DavidAllan 6 68
(David C Griffiths) *trckd ldrs: 2nd over 3f out: upsides over 1f out: kpt on same pce last 100yds* **6/1**[3]

2542 **3** ¾ **British Embassy (IRE)**[13] 3363 4-10-0 **68** .... SamJames 7 72
(David Loughnane) *led: t.k.h: clr after 2f: drvn over 2f out: hdd appr fnl f: rallied and n.m.r on inner 100yds out: kpt on same pce* **5/1**[2]

4003 **4** ½ **Stoneboat Bill**[17] 3220 4-9-9 **63** ....(b[1]) DanielTudhope 5 66
(Declan Carroll) *hld up in rr: t.k.h: hdwy over 3f out: trckd ldrs over 2f out: kpt on same pce fnl f* **3/1**[1]

600 **5** ¾ **Shrubland**[21] 3066 3-8-7 **59** ....(b[1]) JamesSullivan 4 61
(Ed Walker) *hld up in rr: hdwy over 3f out: keeping one pce whn n.m.r clsng stages* **7/1**

-000 **6** 2 ¾ **We'll Shake Hands (FR)**[38] 2526 5-9-11 **65** ....(v) BenCurtis 3 61
(K R Burke) *hld up in rr: drvn over 3f out: one pce: nvr a threat* **7/1**

0005 **7** 1 ½ **First Sargeant**[16] 3253 6-9-4 **58** ....(p) CamHardie 8 51
(Lawrence Mullaney) *chsd clr ldr: drvn over 3f out: lost pl over 1f out* **16/1**

2m 16.41s (0.91) **Going Correction** -0.025s/f (Good)
WFA 3 from 4yo+ 12lb **7** Ran SP% **111.8**
Speed ratings (Par 103): **95,94,93,93,92 90,89**
CSF £20.36 CT £84.23 TOTE £4.10: £1.90, £2.60; EX 24.00 Trifecta £131.00.
Owner David Slater **Bred** F Dunne **Trained** Baldwin's Gate, Staffs

FOCUS
Following 17mm of rain the previous day, the going was given as soft (GoingStick: 6.3). The wind was light, half against. All races were run on the Inner Home Straight. Race distance reduced by 5yds. A modest affair run at a good gallop with the winner building on her handicap debut at this track.

3805 PILKINGTON GLASS EBF STALLIONS NOVICE STKS (PLUS 10 RACE) 6f
2:30 (2:32) (Class 4) 2-Y-O **£4,269** (£1,270; £634; £317) **Stalls** Centre

Form RPR
31 **1** **Miss Infinity (IRE)**[12] 3388 2-9-3 0 .... JoeFanning 1 86
(Mark Johnston) *mde all: drvn over 1f out: kpt on wl fnl 150yds* **11/4**[2]

240 **2** 1 ¼ **Leontes**[16] 3247 2-9-2 0 .... DavidProbert 6 81
(Andrew Balding) *chsd ldrs: drvn over 2f out: kpt on same pce fnl f: tk 2nd nr fin* **3/1**[3]

3 nk **Mjjack (IRE)** 2-9-2 0 .... DougieCostello 3 80+
(K R Burke) *s.i.s: sn chsng ldrs: drvn over 2f out: kpt on fnl f* **25/1**

2 **4** 3 **Winning Ways (IRE)**[10] 3463 2-9-2 0 .... BenCurtis 2 71
(William Haggas) *trckd ldrs: effrt over 1f out: edgd rt and wknd fnl 100yds* **11/8**[1]

3 **5** hd **Bengal Lancer**[18] 3196 2-9-2 0 .... StevieDonohoe 4 71
(Ian Williams) *chsd ldrs: drvn over 2f out: one pce over 1f out* **10/1**

6 1 ¼ **Golden Apollo** 2-9-2 0 .... DavidAllan 5 67
(Tim Easterby) *gave problems loading: sn midfield: drvn over 2f out: kpt on fnl f* **50/1**

66 **7** 6 **Sheila's Return**[51] 2119 2-8-11 0 .... PaulMulrennan 8 44
(Bryan Smart) *mid-div: effrt over 2f out: sn chsng ldrs: lost pl over 1f out* **33/1**

8 10 **Heaven's Rock (IRE)** 2-9-2 0 .... RichardKingscote 7 19
(Tom Dascombe) *wnt rt s and s.i.s: reminders: hung lft and lost pl over 2f out: sn bhd* **20/1**

9 9 **Shadow Of Hercules (IRE)** 2-9-2 0 .... RobertTart 9
(Michael Mullineaux) *dwlt and wnt rt s: a last: wl outpcd and bhd over 3f out* **100/1**

1m 16.78s (2.98) **Going Correction** +0.525s/f (Yiel) **9** Ran SP% **117.4**
Speed ratings (Par 95): **101,99,98,94,94 93,85,71,59**
CSF £11.09 TOTE £3.30: £1.10, £1.60, £5.60; EX 11.60 Trifecta £114.80.
Owner Mrs Jane Newett **Bred** Desert Star Phoenix Jvc **Trained** Middleham Moor, N Yorks

FOCUS
A decent novice and a good performance from the winner whose previous win is working out.

3806 FLOAT GLASS INDUSTRIES H'CAP 5f
3:00 (3:00) (Class 5) (0-70,76) 3-Y-O **£2,911** (£866; £432; £216) **Stalls** Centre

Form RPR
-135 **1** **Show Palace**[16] 3268 3-8-13 **62** .... JoeFanning 5 71+
(Jennie Candlish) *dwlt: t.k.h: hdwy to trck ldrs over 2f out: hung lft and led last 100yds: drvn out* **11/4**[2]

-001 **2** nk **Rose Eclair**[13] 3368 3-9-2 **65** ....(b) DavidAllan 3 73
(Tim Easterby) *n.m.r s: sn chsng ldrs: n.m.r and swtchd rt over 1f out: styd on to take 2nd nr fin* **7/1**

1242 **3** nk **Lady Joanna Vassa (IRE)**[7] 3581 3-8-9 **58** .... ConnorBeasley 1 65
(Richard Guest) *led 1f: w ldr: led over 1f out: hdd and no ex last 100yds* **7/2**[3]

5613 **4** 5 **Twentysvnthlancers**[12] 3420 3-9-5 **68** .... DougieCostello 7 57
(Paul Midgley) *w ldr: led after 1f: hdd over 1f out: wknd fnl 150yds* **10/1**

2201 **5** ½ **Sir Theodore (IRE)**[7] 3581 3-9-10 **76** 6ex .... LouisSteward(3) 2 63
(Richard Spencer) *w ldrs: edgd lft over 1f out: wknd fnl 150yds* **2/1**[1]

-423 **6** 2 **Spirit Glance**[115] 858 3-9-3 **66** .... PaulMulrennan 4 46
(Tim Easterby) *wnt lft s: chsd ldrs: drvn over 2f out: lost pl over 1f out* **12/1**

1m 3.4s (2.60) **Going Correction** +0.525s/f (Yiel) **6** Ran SP% **111.5**
Speed ratings (Par 99): **100,99,99,91,90 87**
CSF £21.19 TOTE £3.50: £1.90, £3.80; EX 19.70 Trifecta £73.10.
Owner P and Mrs G A Clarke **Bred** M C Humby **Trained** Basford Green, Staffs

FOCUS
A modest 3yo handicap with the favourite disappointing. There was a three-way battle for the lead here and that set things up nicely for the first two, who were ridden more patiently.

3807 DISTINCTION DOORS NXT-GEN H'CAP 7f
3:30 (3:31) (Class 5) (0-75,75) 3-Y-O+ **£3,234** (£962; £481; £240) **Stalls** Low

Form RPR
0506 **1** **Janaab (IRE)**[14] 3327 6-8-12 **64** ....(t) RachelRichardson(5) 3 73
(Tim Easterby) *towards rr: hdwy on outside over 2f out: styd on to ld towards fin* **17/2**

1444 **2** nk **Chaplin Bay (IRE)**[15] 3284 4-9-10 **71** .... JamesSullivan 10 79
(Ruth Carr) *hld up in rr: smooth hdwy on outer over 2f out: led appr fnl f: hdd and no ex towards fin* **11/2**[3]

0661 **3** 1 ½ **Like No Other**[7] 3568 3-9-0 **70** 6ex .... DavidAllan 6 71
(Les Eyre) *s.i.s: in rr: nt clr run over 2f out tl swtchd rt over 1f out: styd on to take 3rd clsng stages* **7/2**[2]

0-60 **4** ¾ **Niqnaaqpaadiwaaq**[44] 2345 4-9-3 **64** .... NeilFarley 4 66+
(Eric Alston) *hood removed v late: sn mid-div: nt clr run 2f out: kpt on fnl f* **10/1**

0-52 **5** ¾ **Celtic Sixpence (IRE)**[19] 3132 8-9-6 **67** .... RobertTart 8 67
(Nick Kent) *trckd ldrs: led briefly wl over 1f out: fdd fnl 75yds* **17/2**

4256 **6** hd **Viva Verglas (IRE)**[17] 3211 5-9-4 **65** .... GrahamGibbons 9 65
(Daniel Mark Loughnane) *swtchd lft after s: hld up in rr: t.k.h: hdwy over 2f out: nt clr run: kpt on fnl f* **25/1**

-306 **7** nk **Sophisticated Heir (IRE)**[24] 2960 6-10-0 **75** ....(b) SamJames 1 74
(David Loughnane) *chsd ldrs: nt clr run on ins over 1f out: one pce* **7/1**

U055 **8** 4 ½ **Musaaid (IRE)**[14] 3327 4-9-7 **73** .... NathanEvans(5) 5 60
(Michael Easterby) *chsd ldrs on outer: drvn over 2f out: wknd over 1f out* **3/1**[1]

4406 **9** ¾ **Peak Hill**[22] 3029 3-9-1 **71** .... PaulMulrennan 11 53
(David Evans) *chsd ldr: led over 4f out: hdd wl over 1f out: sn wknd* **14/1**

304- **10** 5 **Dear Bruin (IRE)**[297] 6157 4-9-10 **71** .... StevieDonohoe 2 43
(David W Drinkwater) *led tl over 4f out: drvn over 3f out: lost pl 2f out* **33/1**

1m 29.74s (-0.96) **Going Correction** -0.025s/f (Good)
WFA 3 from 4yo+ 9lb **10** Ran SP% **118.7**
Speed ratings (Par 103): **104,103,101,101,100 100,99,94,93,87**
CSF £55.77 CT £203.73 TOTE £9.20: £2.10, £1.80, £2.60; EX 56.30 Trifecta £296.10.
Owner Numac Engineering Ltd **Bred** Ballylinch Stud **Trained** Great Habton, N Yorks

FOCUS
Race distance reduced by 5yds. A well-run handicap in which the first three were in the last four places early on. The winner has slipped to a good mark and this was still 5lb off last year's best.

3808 TUFFX GLASS EBF STALLIONS NOVICE STKS (PLUS 10 RACE) 7f
4:00 (4:00) (Class 4) 2-Y-O **£4,269** (£1,270; £634; £317) **Stalls** Low

Form RPR
5 **1** **Bacchus**[21] 3058 2-9-2 0 .... RichardKingscote 4 81
(Brian Meehan) *trckd ldrs: hung lft and led appr fnl f: sn wnt clr: eased towards fin* **6/4**[2]

2 **2** 2 ½ **Bear Valley (IRE)**[16] 3248 2-9-2 0 .... JoeFanning 2 73
(Mark Johnston) *led: drvn over 2f out: hdd appr fnl f: kpt on same pce* **11/8**[1]

0 **3** ¾ **Klaremount (IRE)**[15] 3283 2-9-2 0 .... DougieCostello 5 71
(K R Burke) *w ldr: drvn over 2f out: one pce whn sltly hmpd appr fnl f* **20/1**

4 nk **Lester Kris (IRE)** 2-9-2 0 GrahamGibbons 7 70+
(Richard Hannon) *stmbld sltly s: in rr: shkn up over 4f out: drvn over 2f out: kpt on towards fin* **7/1**[3]

4 **5** 10 **Black Bubba (IRE)**[8] 3531 2-9-2 0 PaulMulrennan 1 45
(David Evans) *t.k.h: trckd ldrs: drvn over 2f out: lost pl over 1f out: bhd whn eased clsng stages* **11/1**

0 **6** 8 **Permanent**[21] 3058 2-9-2 0 TimmyMurphy 6 25
(Daniel Kubler) *hld up in rr: effrt over 2f out: sn lost pl and bhd* **25/1**

1m 30.71s (0.01) **Going Correction** -0.025s/f (Good) **6** Ran SP% **111.5**
Speed ratings (Par 95): **98,95,94,93,82 73**
CSF £3.85 TOTE £2.30: £1.10, £1.30; EX 4.30 Trifecta £26.30.
Owner G P M Morland,D J Erwin,John G S Woodman **Bred** D J Erwin Bloodstock **Trained** Manton, Wilts

FOCUS
Race distance reduced by 5yds. The winner put up a good performance in this novice contest.

3809 BOHLE 20TH ANNIVERSARY H'CAP 1m 6f
4:30 (4:30) (Class 3) (0-95,84) 3-Y-O **£7,781** (£2,330; £1,165) **Stalls** Low

Form RPR
-232 **1** **Injam (IRE)**[14] 3323 3-9-1 **77** PaulMulrennan 3 87
(Jedd O'Keeffe) *w ldr: led after 4f: pushed along over 6f out: styd on wl and abt 4 l clr 1f out: kpt up to work* **5/4**[1]

1140 **2** 6 **Project Bluebook (FR)**[26] 2909 3-9-0 **76** JasonHart 4 80
(John Quinn) *trckd ldng pair: 2nd 8f out: sn upsides: reminders over 3f out: one pce fnl 2f: heavily eased clsng stages* **15/8**[2]

0-52 **3** 18 **Kaatskill Nap (FR)**[41] 2440 3-9-7 **83** DavidNolan 1 68
(David Menuisier) *drvn away fr stalls to ld: hdd after 4f: drvn 6f out: outpcd over 4f out: lost tch over 2f out: heavily eased clsng stages* **11/4**[3]

3m 2.04s (0.04) **Going Correction** -0.025s/f (Good) **3** Ran SP% **105.9**
Speed ratings (Par 103): **98,94,84**
CSF £3.71 TOTE £2.10; EX 2.90 Trifecta £3.70.
Owner Miss S Long **Bred** John M Weld **Trained** Middleham Moor, N Yorks

FOCUS
Race distance reduced by 5yds. Just the three runners, but they went a good gallop and this was a proper test at the distance.

3810 SUPALITE TILED ROOF FILLIES' H'CAP 1m
5:00 (5:05) (Class 5) (0-75,75) 3-Y-O+ **£2,911** (£866; £432; £216) **Stalls** Low

Form RPR
3235 **1** **My Lucille (IRE)**[17] 3209 3-8-10 **67** DavidAllan 5 72
(Tim Easterby) *mde all: drvn over 2f out: fnd ex clsng stages* **12/1**

532 **2** 1 1/2 **Sonnet (IRE)**[16] 3249 3-8-9 **66** RichardKingscote 4 68
(Charles Hills) *hld up towards rr: effrt over 3f out: upsides over 1f out: no ex clsng stages* **5/2**[2]

315 **3** nk **Bush Beauty (IRE)**[6] 3594 5-9-0 **68** SophieKilloran(7) 7 71+
(Eric Alston) *hld up in rr: t.k.h: hdwy on ins over 3f out: nt clr run fr over 2f out: nt rcvr* **9/2**[3]

66-3 **4** 1 1/2 **Cacica**[24] 2968 3-8-11 **68** StevieDonohoe 1 66
(George Scott) *slowl into stride: sn chsng ldrs: drvn over 3f out: kpt on fnl f* **13/2**

53-5 **5** 3 3/4 **Triathlon (USA)**[39] 2505 3-9-3 **74** DanielTudhope 3 63
(Sir Michael Stoute) *trckd ldrs: 2nd over 6f out: upsides over 2f out: rdn over 1f out: sn wknd: wl btn whn eased clsng stages* **15/8**[1]

1m 44.87s (1.17) **Going Correction** -0.025s/f (Good)
WFA 3 from 5yo+ 10lb **5** Ran SP% **102.6**
Speed ratings (Par 100): **93,91,91,89,85**
CSF £35.83 TOTE £9.40: £3.90, £1.60; EX 31.80 Trifecta £140.40.
Owner M J Macleod **Bred** Knockainey Stud **Trained** Great Habton, N Yorks
■ Sister Dude was withdrawn. Price at time of withdrawal 11-1. Rule 4 applies to all bets - deduction 5p in the pound.

FOCUS
Race distance reduced by 5yds. An ordinary handicap, run in a downpour, and the race was controlled from the front by the winner.
T/Plt: £53.20 to a £1 stake. Pool: £62,883.60 - 862.68 winning units. T/Qpdt: £10.30 to a £1 stake. Pool: £4,012.95 - 285.85 winning units. **Walter Glynn**

3554 NEWBURY (L-H)
Thursday, June 30

OFFICIAL GOING: Good to soft (soft in places; 5.9)
Wind: quite strong half against Weather: cloudy

3811 DONNINGTON GROVE HOTEL & FAIRFIELD RESIDENTIAL APPRENTICE H'CAP 5f 34y
5:55 (5:55) (Class 5) (0-70,67) 3-Y-O+ **£2,911** (£866; £432; £216) **Stalls** High

Form RPR
0062 **1** **Quickaswecan**[7] 3559 5-9-10 **63** (p) EdwardGreatrex 7 75
(Milton Bradley) *mde all: r.o strly fnl f: readily* **9/2**[2]

-003 **2** 3 1/4 **Diminutive (IRE)**[38] 2537 4-8-10 **49** (p) HectorCrouch 4 50
(Grace Harris) *s.i.s: in last pair: rdn and hdwy fr 2f out: chsd wnr wl ins fnl f: nvr any threat* **16/1**

1251 **3** 1 **Pharoh Jake**[7] 3559 8-9-11 **64** 6ex AaronJones 5 62
(John Bridger) *chsd ldrs: rdn over 2f out: disp 2nd over 1f out: kpt on same pce fnl f* **5/1**[3]

1600 **4** nk **Sir Geoffrey (IRE)**[14] 3326 10-8-10 **54** (b) NatalieHambling(5) 8 50
(Scott Dixon) *chsd wnr: rdn over 2f out: no ex whn lost 2nd ins fnl f* **16/1**

2422 **5** 1 **Lady McGuffy (IRE)**[1] 3786 3-8-3 **53** (t) AledBeech(5) 1 44
(David Evans) *s.i.s: last: hdwy over 2f out: sn rdn: nt pce to get on terms: fdd fnl 120yds* **15/8**[1]

003 **6** hd **Angel Way (IRE)**[8] 3530 7-9-11 **67** RhiainIngram(3) 2 59
(John Gallagher) *chsd ldrs: rdn over 2f out: fdd fnl f* **9/2**[2]

0543 **7** 6 **Putemintheboot (IRE)**[19] 3140 3-7-10 **48** (t) DavidEgan(7) 3 17
(David Evans) *chsd ldrs tl outpcd 1/2-way: wknd ins fnl f* **9/1**

0-00 **8** 3 1/4 **Rubheira**[24] 2964 4-8-6 **48** oh3 (b) DavidParkes(3) 6 8
(Paul Burgoyne) *short of room leaving stalls: sn chsng ldrs: outpcd over 2f out: wknd fnl f* **50/1**

1m 3.58s (2.18) **Going Correction** +0.375s/f (Good)
WFA 3 from 4yo+ 6lb **8** Ran SP% **111.5**
Speed ratings (Par 103): **97,91,90,89,88 87,78,73**
CSF £67.33 CT £363.24 TOTE £3.10: £1.20, £3.90, £1.80; EX 61.40 Trifecta £412.10.
Owner E A Hayward **Bred** Mrs R D Peacock **Trained** Sedbury, Gloucs

FOCUS
The rail had been moved out since the last meeting around the 7f & 5f bends. The 1m4f and 1m2f races were 13yds longer. Eddie Greatrex described the ground as "soft", although after the second race Pat Dobbs said: "It's not too bad; good to soft." A moderate apprentice sprint that was dominated by the winner.

3812 CHRISTIAN MARNER EBF NOVICE FILLIES' STKS (PLUS 10 RACE) 6f 8y
6:25 (6:28) (Class 4) 2-Y-O **£4,851** (£1,443; £721; £360) **Stalls** High

Form RPR
5 **1** **Poet's Princess**[18] 3196 2-9-0 0 AdamKirby 10 80
(Hughie Morrison) *led after 1f: rdn over 1f out: r.o strly to assert ins fnl f: readily* **8/1**[3]

2 4 1/2 **Coral Sea** 2-9-0 0 DavidProbert 5 67
(Charles Hills) *racd freely: led for 1f: upsides wnr: rdn and ev ch over 1f out: no ex ins fnl f* **8/1**[3]

3 1/2 **Company** 2-9-0 0 PatDobbs 8 65
(Richard Hannon) *mid-div: rdn and hdwy fr 2f out: kpt on ins fnl f: clsng qckly on runner-up towards fin* **4/1**[1]

4 1/2 **Sky Ballerina** 2-9-0 0 JimmyFortune 11 66
(Simon Crisford) *dwlt: towards rr: swtchd lft and stdy hdwy fr 2f out: kpt on ins fnl f wout ever threatening: wnt 4th cl home* **8/1**[3]

5 1/2 **Dusty Berry** 2-9-0 0 JohnFahy 9 62
(Eve Johnson Houghton) *mid-div: rdn over 2f out: kpt on ins fnl f but nt pce to get on terms* **16/1**

0 **6** nk **Sukiwarrior (IRE)**[40] 2467 2-9-0 0 MartinHarley 6 61
(Charles Hills) *in tch: chal for hld 4th over 1f out: one pce fnl f* **33/1**

7 3 **Iconic Belle** 2-9-0 0 PaulHanagan 7 52
(Mick Channon) *s.i.s: sn mid-div: outpcd over 2f out: no threat after* **16/1**

8 2 1/2 **In The Spotlight (IRE)** 2-9-0 0 RyanMoore 2 45
(Richard Hughes) *s.i.s: mid-div after 2f: short of room 2f out: sn rdn: no further imp* **4/1**[1]

9 1 **Angel Of Darkness** 2-9-0 0 WilliamBuick 3 42
(Charles Hills) *s.i.s: a towards rr* **5/1**[2]

10 nk **Cheeky Fox** 2-8-7 0 TylerSaunders(7) 1 41+
(Marcus Tregoning) *awkwardly away: sn towards rr: nvr a factor* **33/1**

11 1 1/2 **Diva Power (IRE)** 2-9-0 0 RoystonFfrench 4 36
(Marcus Tregoning) *wnt lft s: chsd ldrs: rdn over 2f out: wknd ent fnl f* **25/1**

12 20 **Ashazuri** 2-8-9 0 CharlieBennett(5) 12
(Jonathan Portman) *chsd ldrs: rdn wl over 2f out: wknd wl over 1f out* **18/1**

1m 16.53s (3.53) **Going Correction** +0.375s/f (Good) **12** Ran SP% **116.8**
Speed ratings (Par 92): **91,85,84,83,83 82,78,75,73,73 71,44**
CSF £68.16 TOTE £9.30: £2.50, £2.80, £2.70; EX 60.10 Trifecta £448.90.
Owner Paul Brocklehurst **Bred** Jointsense Limited **Trained** East Ilsley, Berks

FOCUS
Race distance as advertised. Little got into this, with them soon being strung out racing against the stands' rail. The first two home were the front pair throughout and quite a taking performance from the winner.

3813 RONALD PHILLIPS NOVICE STKS (PLUS 10 RACE) (C&G) 6f 8y
7:00 (7:02) (Class 4) 2-Y-O **£5,175** (£1,540; £769; £384) **Stalls** High

Form RPR
2 **1** **Mutawatheb (IRE)**[27] 2873 2-9-0 0 PaulHanagan 5 85+
(Richard Hannon) *a.p: shkn up to ld over 1f out: r.o wl* **11/8**[1]

2 1 **Tis Marvellous** 2-9-0 0 (t) AdamKirby 7 80+
(Clive Cox) *trckd ldrs: nt clrest of runs fr over 2f out tl ent fnl f: r.o wl: wnt 2nd towards fin: nvr threatening wnr* **14/1**

2 **3** nk **Salouen (IRE)**[18] 3196 2-9-0 0 PatDobbs 1 79
(Sylvester Kirk) *led after 1f: rdn and hdd over 1f out: kpt on but no ex whn lost 2nd towards fin* **3/1**[2]

4 nk **Monoshka (IRE)** 2-9-0 0 RyanMoore 2 78
(Richard Hannon) *chsd ldrs: rdn 2f out: kpt on but nt pce to chal fnl f* **20/1**

6 **5** hd **Angel Down**[23] 2997 2-9-0 0 MartinHarley 8 78
(Henry Candy) *led for 1f: rdn over 2f out: kpt on same pce* **22/1**

6 3 **Glorious Artist (IRE)** 2-9-0 0 DavidProbert 4 69
(Charles Hills) *nvr bttr than mid-div* **50/1**

60 **7** 1/2 **Devilish Guest (IRE)**[20] 3093 2-8-7 0 KillianHennessy(7) 3 67
(Mick Channon) *towards rr of mid-div: rdn 2f out: sme late prog: nt pce to get involved* **66/1**

8 1 **Singula** 2-9-0 0 WilliamTwiston-Davies 9 64
(Alan King) *s.i.s: towards rr of midfield: sme late prog: nvr trbld ldrs* **25/1**

3 **9** 3/4 **Mutawakked (IRE)**[20] 3106 2-9-0 0 JimmyFortune 10 62
(Brian Meehan) *trckd ldrs: rdn 2f out: wknd ent fnl f* **7/1**[3]

10 nk **Good Craic** 2-9-0 0 WilliamBuick 11 61
(John Gosden) *mid-div: effrt over 2f out: wknd fnl f* **10/1**

11 nk **Wearethepeople** 2-9-0 0 MartinDwyer 12 60
(William Muir) *a towards rr* **25/1**

12 3/4 **Curve Ball (IRE)** 2-8-11 0 TomMarquand(3) 6 58
(Richard Hughes) *mid-div: rdn over 2f out: no imp: fdd fnl 120yds* **40/1**

13 5 **Makemerichjohn (IRE)** 2-9-0 0 BenCurtis 13 43
(David Evans) *sn outpcd: a towards rr* **66/1**

64 **14** 9 **Control Centre (IRE)**[22] 3032 2-8-9 0 GaryMahon(5) 14 16
(Richard Hannon) *sn outpcd: a towards rr* **66/1**

1m 15.39s (2.39) **Going Correction** +0.375s/f (Good) **14** Ran SP% **121.0**
Speed ratings (Par 95): **99,97,97,96,96 92,91,90,89,89 88,87,81,69**
CSF £21.17 TOTE £2.30: £1.20, £4.00, £1.60; EX 22.20 Trifecta £109.50.
Owner Hamdan Al Maktoum **Bred** Rosetown Bloodstock **Trained** East Everleigh, Wilts

FOCUS
Race distance as advertised. Racing more down the centre this time, there were four in a line behind the winner as they hit the line and it's likely this was an ordinary event.

3814 PELICAN H'CAP 1m 4f 5y
7:30 (7:32) (Class 4) (0-85,85) 3-Y-O **£4,690** (£1,395; £697; £348) **Stalls** Centre

Form RPR
2346 **1** **Scarlet Dragon**[26] 2892 3-8-12 **79** TomMarquand(3) 6 88
(Eve Johnson Houghton) *hld up bhd ldrs: hdwy 5f out: led over 2f out: sn rdn: 1 l up ent fnl f: jst hld on* **7/1**

1 **2** hd **Corinthian**[41] 2440 3-9-7 **85** AndreaAtzeni 5 93+
(Roger Varian) *rousted along whn slowly away: trckd ldrs after 1f: drvn whn outpcd in 5th over 2f out: swtchd rt over 1f out: hdwy ent fnl f: styd on wl: jst failed* **7/2**[2]

-534 **3** 1 **Yangtze**[26] 2909 3-8-10 **74** RyanMoore 4 80
(Sir Michael Stoute) *trckd ldrs: rdn to chse wnr wl over 1f out: edgd lft fnl 120yds: no ex cl home* **6/5**[1]

4250 **4** *5* **Juste Pour Nous**[14] 3300 3-9-4 **82**.................... AdamKirby 3 80
(Mark Johnston) *trckd wnr: rdn over 2f out: lost 2nd wl over 1f out: fdd ins fnl f* **6/1**[3]

5322 **5** *1 1/2* **Skeaping**[10] 3465 3-9-2 **80**.................... PatDobbs 7 76
(Richard Hannon) *hld up bhd ldrs: rdn over 3f out: nt pce to get involved: wknd fnl f* **8/1**

5330 **6** *9* **Magnum (IRE)**[13] 3341 3-9-2 **80**....................(b) WilliamBuick 2 61
(Brian Meehan) *led: rdn and hdd over 2f out: wknd over 1f out* **16/1**

2m 40.34s (4.84) **Going Correction** +0.375s/f (Good) **6** Ran SP% **111.5**
Speed ratings (Par 101): **98,97,97,93,92 86**
CSF £30.82 TOTE £9.50: £3.30, £3.10; EX 40.20 Trifecta £91.60.
Owner W H Ponsonby **Bred** Usk Valley Stud **Trained** Blewbury, Oxon
■ Stewards' Enquiry : Andrea Atzeni four-day ban: used whip above permitted level (Jul 14-17)

FOCUS
Race distance increased by 13yds. This had the look of quite a good handicap beforehand and the front three came clear, with the winner finding improvement for the step up in trip.

3815 COOLMORE STUD EBF FILLIES' H'CAP — 6f 8y
8:05 (8:07) (Class 4) (0-85,84) 3-Y-O+ **£6,469** (£1,925; £962; £481) **Stalls** High

Form RPR

45-3 **1** **Silver Rainbow (IRE)**[26] 2903 4-10-0 **84**.................... WilliamBuick 2 99
(Charles Hills) *a.p: led jst over 2f out: sn rdn: kpt on wl and a holding on fnl f* **5/1**

-036 **2** *1/2* **Spring Fling**[18] 3188 5-9-13 **83**.................... MartinHarley 1 96
(Henry Candy) *hld up: snatched up whn nt clr run wl over 1f out: hdwy ent fnl f: r.o wl: a being hld fnl 75yds* **2/1**[1]

2413 **3** *3 1/2* **Ginzan**[9] 3487 8-9-8 **78**.................... FergusSweeney 3 80
(Malcolm Saunders) *wnt sltly rt s: trckd ldrs: rdn over 2f out: kpt on but nt pce to chal* **12/1**

-211 **4** *1/2* **Very Honest (IRE)**[20] 3105 3-9-7 **84**.................... MartinDwyer 4 82
(Brett Johnson) *hmpd s: cl up: rdn to chse wnr over 1f out: kpt on same pce fnl f* **9/2**[3]

1244 **5** *2 1/4* **Elusive Ellen (IRE)**[26] 2903 6-9-8 **78**.................... RyanMoore 5 71
(Brendan Powell) *hmpd s: hld up: rdn 2f out: nt pce to get involved* **7/2**[2]

216- **6** *1/2* **Little Voice (USA)**[321] 5336 3-9-5 **82**.................... AndreaAtzeni 8 71
(Charles Hills) *trckd ldr: rdn and ev ch over 1f out: wknd fnl f* **16/1**

020 **7** *2 1/4* **Perfect Alchemy (IRE)**[28] 2821 5-9-8 **78**.................... AdamKirby 6 62
(Patrick Chamings) *cl up: swtchd lft for short-lived effrt over 1f out: sn wknd* **25/1**

613 **8** *nse* **Pink Martini (IRE)**[113] 881 3-8-5 **75**.................... SeanMooney(7) 7 57
(Joseph Tuite) *led: rdn and hdd jst over 2f out: wknd over 1f out* **33/1**

1m 14.88s (1.88) **Going Correction** +0.375s/f (Good)
WFA 3 from 4yo+ 7lb **8** Ran SP% **110.8**
Speed ratings (Par 102): **102,101,96,96,93 92,89,89**
CSF £14.41 CT £103.37 TOTE £5.80: £1.90, £1.10, £3.40; EX 14.80 Trifecta £67.70.
Owner R J Tufft **Bred** Austin Curran **Trained** Lambourn, Berks

FOCUS
Race distance as advertised. The front pair came clear in what was a fair fillies' handicap and the winner was up a length or so on her 3yo form.

3816 DENFORD STUD H'CAP — 1m (S)
8:35 (8:35) (Class 5) (0-75,75) 3-Y-O **£3,234** (£962; £481; £240) **Stalls** High

Form RPR

-321 **1** **Fort Jefferson**[9] 3499 3-9-3 **71** 6ex.................... DavidProbert 5 80+
(Andrew Balding) *hld up in tch: hdwy over 2f out: chsd ldr over 1f out: sn rdn: r.o wl fnl 80yds: led fnl stride* **4/5**[1]

R105 **2** *shd* **Beleave**[20] 3111 3-9-2 **70**.................... RoystonFfrench 4 78
(Luke Dace) *awkwardly away: last: hdwy over 2f out: rdn to ld over 1f out: edgd rt: kpt on: hdd fnl stride* **14/1**

6413 **3** *7* **Betsalottie**[17] 3236 3-8-5 **62**.................... DannyBrock(3) 3 54
(John Bridger) *led: rdn 2f out: hdd sn after: kpt on same pce fnl f* **7/1**[3]

060- **4** *3/4* **The Greedy Boy**[300] 6051 3-8-5 **59**.................... MartinDwyer 8 49
(Mick Channon) *hld up in tch: rdn over 2f out: kpt on fnl f but nt pce to get involved* **50/1**

3431 **5** *hd* **Carbutt's Ridge (IRE)**[7] 3579 3-8-7 **61** 6ex....................(v) BenCurtis 6 51
(K R Burke) *trckd ldrs: rdn over 2f out: kpt on same pce fr over 1f out* **9/2**[2]

306 **6** *1 3/4* **Bond Trader**[23] 2999 3-9-4 **72**.................... JohnFahy 10 58
(Clive Cox) *hld up: rdn over 3f out: nvr threatened* **12/1**

000- **7** *3 1/2* **Totally Committed**[253] 7395 3-9-1 **69**.................... AdamKirby 1 47
(Clive Cox) *trckd ldrs: rdn and ev ch briefly 2f out: wknd fnl f* **8/1**

5-00 **8** *13* **Art Echo**[42] 2412 3-9-7 **75**.................... RyanClark 7 23
(Jonathan Portman) *trckd ldrs: rdn over 3f out: wknd 2f out* **33/1**

1m 41.7s (2.00) **Going Correction** +0.375s/f (Good) **8** Ran SP% **116.6**
Speed ratings (Par 99): **105,104,97,97,96 95,91,78**
CSF £14.98 CT £52.74 TOTE £1.70: £1.10, £3.70, £1.60; EX 12.90 Trifecta £44.10.
Owner Kingsclere Racing Club **Bred** Kingsclere Stud **Trained** Kingsclere, Hants

FOCUS
Race distance as advertised. The front pair came right away in this modest handicap, the odds-on favourite grabbing what looked an unlikely victory. He has been rated close to his Leicester figure.

3817 PANCREATIC CANCER UK H'CAP — 1m 2f 6y
9:10 (9:10) (Class 5) (0-70,70) 4-Y-O+ **£3,234** (£962; £481; £240) **Stalls** Centre

Form RPR

5415 **1** **Loving Your Work**[34] 2645 5-9-1 **64**.................... PatDobbs 7 72
(Ken Cunningham-Brown) *hld up: hdwy 3f out: str run ent fnl f: led fnl 120yds: kpt on strly* **9/2**[2]

2451 **2** *1* **Pike Corner Cross (IRE)**[36] 2577 4-9-3 **66**.................... AndreaAtzeni 2 72
(Ed de Giles) *hld up in last pair: hdwy 2f out: r.o wl ent fnl f: wnt 2nd cl home: a being hld by wnr* **7/2**[1]

-543 **3** *nk* **Glens Wobbly**[7] 3560 8-9-0 **68**.................... HectorCrouch(5) 8 73
(Jonathan Geake) *led: rdn over 2f out: hld on gamely tl hdd fnl 120yds: no ex whn lost 2nd cl home* **5/1**[3]

4462 **4** *2 1/4* **Critical Speed (IRE)**[9] 3497 4-9-3 **69**.................... TomMarquand(3) 9 70
(Sylvester Kirk) *trckd ldrs: rdn and ev ch 2f out: kpt on same pce fnl f* **7/1**

2604 **5** *1/2* **Ravenous**[12] 3403 5-9-7 **70**.................... RoystonFfrench 6 70
(Luke Dace) *in tch: hdwy 3f out: rdn 2f out: styd on same pce fnl f* **15/2**

0/25 **6** *1* **Officer Drivel (IRE)**[48] 2205 5-9-5 **68**....................(v) TimmyMurphy 3 66
(Jim Best) *racd keenly: trckd ldrs: rdn and ev ch 2f out: wknd ins fnl f* **10/1**

6215 **7** *4 1/2* **Pink Ribbon (IRE)**[17] 3230 4-8-10 **64**....................(p) EdwardGreatrex(5) 1 53
(Sylvester Kirk) *trckd ldr: rdn wl over 2f out: wknd ent fnl f* **8/1**

2032 **8** *5* **Pearly Prince**[23] 2996 4-9-7 **70**.................... AdamKirby 5 49
(Peter Hedger) *hld up last: hdwy 3f out: sn rdn: nvr threatened: wknd ent fnl f* **7/1**

2m 11.69s (2.89) **Going Correction** +0.375s/f (Good) **8** Ran SP% **114.0**
Speed ratings (Par 103): **103,102,101,100,99 98,95,91**
CSF £20.52 CT £80.58 TOTE £5.20: £2.00, £1.50, £1.90; EX 20.30 Trifecta £164.70.
Owner Danebury Racing Stables **Bred** Dukes Stud & Overbury Stallions Ltd **Trained** Danebury, Hants

FOCUS
Race distance increased by 13yds. Modest form, although there was a good gallop on. The winner has a good record here and is rated close to his 3yo form.
T/Plt: £35.70 to a £1 stake. Pool: £60,934.95 - 1244.49 winning units. T/Qpdt: £7.00 to a £1 stake. Pool: £5,746.31 - 605.36 winning units. **Tim Mitchell**

3619 YARMOUTH (L-H)
Thursday, June 30

OFFICIAL GOING: Good to firm (good in places; 7.7)
Wind: light breeze Weather: hot and sunny; 22 degrees

3818 BRITISH STALLION STUDS EBF NOVICE STKS (PLUS 10 RACE) (DIV I) — 6f 3y
1:50 (1:50) (Class 4) 2-Y-O **£4,657** (£1,386; £692; £346) **Stalls** Centre

Form RPR

3 **1** **Nobly Born**[13] 3356 2-9-2 0.................... FrankieDettori 1 82
(John Gosden) *racd keenly: travelled wl pressing ldrs: rdn over 1f out: led fnl 120yds: sn in clr command: quite impressive* **4/6**[1]

5 **2** *1 3/4* **Kamra (USA)**[29] 2786 2-9-2 0....................(v[1]) JamieSpencer 9 74
(Jeremy Noseda) *cl up: rdn 2f out: styd on wl ins fnl f: snatched 2nd but no match for wnr* **9/1**[3]

3 *shd* **Keyser Soze (IRE)** 2-9-2 0.................... HarryBentley 10 74+
(Richard Spencer) *dwlt: bhd: rdn and hdwy and weaved through fnl f: fin stoutly and nrly snatched 2nd* **20/1**

241 **4** *hd* **Jacquard (IRE)**[10] 3472 2-9-8 0.................... JamesDoyle 4 79
(Mark Johnston) *led: rdn 2f out: hdd fnl 120yds: kpt on wl but lost two pls nr fin* **5/1**[2]

5 *hd* **Bassmah** 2-8-11 0.................... ThomasBrown 8 68+
(Ismail Mohammed) *plld hrd: chsd ldrs: rdn 2f out: n.m.r over 1f out: fin strly fnl 100yds: promising* **100/1**

6 *hd* **Colonel Frank** 2-9-2 0.................... LukeMorris 5 72+
(Ed Walker) *edgd rt s: pressed ldrs: rdn and outpcd 2f out: rallied wl and kpt on in driving fin for placings fnl 100yds* **40/1**

7 *3/4* **Seyasah (IRE)** 2-8-11 0.................... TedDurcan 7 65
(Chris Wall) *n.m.r after s: chsd ldrs over 4f: rdn and nt qckn over 1f out* **33/1**

8 *1 1/2* **Twiggy** 2-8-11 0.................... FrederikTylicki 6 60
(Jane Chapple-Hyam) *racd keenly: pressed ldr: rdn 1/2-way: lost pl 2f out* **20/1**

9 *1/2* **Ripper Street (IRE)** 2-9-2 0.................... SilvestreDeSousa 3 63
(Ed Dunlop) *t.k.h: chsd ldrs tl 1/2-way: rdn and sn btn* **22/1**

10 *2 3/4* **Victory Angel (IRE)** 2-9-2 0.................... AndreaAtzeni 11 55
(Roger Varian) *towards rr: rdn 2f out: sn btn* **14/1**

1m 13.73s (-0.67) **Going Correction** -0.175s/f (Firm) **10** Ran SP% **113.6**
Speed ratings (Par 95): **97,94,94,94,94 93,92,90,90,86**
CSF £5.94 TOTE £1.60: £1.02, £2.90, £5.50; EX 9.90 Trifecta £90.10.
Owner Cheveley Park Stud **Bred** Cheveley Park Stud Ltd **Trained** Newmarket, Suffolk

FOCUS
Despite 1mm of rain overnight the ground had dried out a little from previously forecast and was now good to firm, good in places (from good, good to firm in places). Quite an interesting novice event to start, and the hot favourite did it nicely, while there were some eye-catching performances in behind. James Doyle said of the ground: "It's the fast side of good", while Frankie Dettori said: "It's quick."

3819 BRITISH STALLION STUDS EBF NOVICE STKS (PLUS 10 RACE) (DIV II) — 6f 3y
2:20 (2:20) (Class 4) 2-Y-O **£4,657** (£1,386; £692; £346) **Stalls** Centre

Form RPR

1 **Mubtasim (IRE)** 2-9-2 0.................... PatCosgrave 10 89+
(William Haggas) *cl up: shkn up over 2f out: rdn to ld 1f out: kpt on strly* **7/2**[3]

2 *2* **Jumira Bridge** 2-9-2 0.................... AndreaAtzeni 1 82+
(Roger Varian) *chsd ldrs: rdn and effrt over 1f out: wnt 2nd 120yds out: a hld by wnr after* **9/4**[1]

1243 **3** *3/4* **Boater (IRE)**[26] 2908 2-9-3 0.................... JamesDoyle 7 81
(Mark Johnston) *led: rdn 2f out: hdd 1f out: edgd lft: lost 2nd fnl 120yds* **11/4**[2]

4 *1* **Marilyn** 2-8-11 0.................... TedDurcan 4 72+
(Chris Wall) *bhd: gd hdwy over 1f out: fin wl to snatch 4th but n.d to ldrs* **28/1**

3 **5** *hd* **Kodiac Khan (IRE)**[35] 2604 2-9-2 0.................... FrankieDettori 9 76
(Hugo Palmer) *prom: rdn 2f out: 4th and btn whn impeded ins fnl f* **4/1**

6 **6** *3* **Spun Gold**[21] 3065 2-9-2 0.................... MartinLane 5 66+
(Luca Cumani) *midfield and rn green: pushed along and btn 2f out* **40/1**

0 **7** *3 1/2* **Alligator**[8] 3524 2-9-2 0.................... SilvestreDeSousa 2 55
(Ed Dunlop) *towards rr: rdn and btn over 2f out* **40/1**

0 **8** *nk* **Juanito Chico (IRE)**[34] 2648 2-9-2 0.................... TomQueally 6 54
(William Jarvis) *missed break: plld hrd and sn rcvrd to go prom: drvn and lost pl wl over 1f out* **33/1**

9 *16* **Single Estate** 2-9-2 0....................[1] LukeMorris 3
(Sir Mark Prescott Bt) *s.s: drvn and racing awkwardly in poor last: t.o 1/2-way* **40/1**

1m 12.5s (-1.90) **Going Correction** -0.175s/f (Firm) **9** Ran SP% **113.4**
Speed ratings (Par 95): **105,102,101,100,99 95,91,90,69**
CSF £11.06 TOTE £4.20: £1.30, £1.60, £1.10; EX 14.60 Trifecta £30.10.
Owner Sheikh Rashid Dalmook Al Maktoum **Bred** Mrs Natasha Drennan **Trained** Newmarket, Suffolk
■ Stewards' Enquiry : James Doyle caution: careless riding

FOCUS
This didn't look as strong as the first division, but winners should still emerge from it.

3820 AKS SKIPS OF NORWICH (S) STKS — 6f 3y
2:50 (2:50) (Class 6) 2-Y-O **£2,264** (£673; £336; £168) **Stalls** Centre

Form RPR

052 **1** **Benidiction (IRE)**[22] 3008 2-8-9 0.................... PJMcDonald 2 62+
(Ann Duffield) *pressed ldr: rdn to ld over 1f out: urged clr ins fnl f* **4/6**[1]

05 **2** *5* **Chotto (IRE)**[47] 2235 2-8-9 0.................... JamieSpencer 4 46
(George Scott) *led: rdn and hdd over 1f out: no ch w wnr after* **2/1**[2]

3 *3 1/4* **Birchfield Lady** 2-8-9 0.................... PaoloSirigu 3 36
(Robert Eddery) *lost 4 l s: wnt 3rd 1/2-way: rdn 2f out: mod 3rd 1f out* **8/1**[3]

00 **4** *6* **Fair Skies (IRE)**[10] 3472 2-9-0 0 LemosdeSouza 1 21
(Ivan Furtado) *t.k.h: sn j. path: cl up: rdn over 2f out: btn wl over 1f out* **33/1**

000 **5** *9* **Lilly Ballerina (IRE)**[8] 3511 2-8-9 0 LukeMorris 5
(Tony Carroll) *lost 3 l s: rdn 1/2-way: t.o fnl 2f* **50/1**

1m 14.02s (-0.38) **Going Correction** -0.175s/f (Firm) **5** Ran SP% **109.3**
Speed ratings (Par 91): **95,88,84,76,64**
CSF £2.18 TOTE £1.50: £1.10, £2.00; EX 2.50 Trifecta £3.30.
Owner John Dance **Bred** Barnane Stud **Trained** Constable Burton, N Yorks

FOCUS
A poor seller and not a race to dwell on.

3821 RACING WELFARE STABLE STAFF H'CAP 7f 3y
3:20 (3:20) (Class 5) (0-75,75) 3-Y-O+ **£2,911** (£866; £432; £216) **Stalls** Centre

Form RPR
4-04 **1** **Gothic Empire (IRE)**[36] 2579 4-9-11 **75** DanielMuscutt(3) 3 94
(James Fanshawe) *towards rr early: effrt 3f out: led gng best over 1f out: rdn and sn drew rt away* **6/1**[3]

10-4 **2** *8* **Palenville (IRE)**[20] 3111 3-9-5 **75** RobertHavlin 1 70
(Simon Crisford) *2nd or 3rd tl led 2f out: sn rdn: hdd over 1f out: immediately outpcd by wnr* **7/2**[2]

1221 **3** *1 1/4* **Johnny B Goode (IRE)**[21] 3078 4-9-4 **65** SilvestreDeSousa 9 60
(Chris Dwyer) *taken down early: plld hrd: cl up: rdn and lost pl over 2f out: rallied and styd on u.p ins fnl f to snatch 3rd* **13/2**

0304 **4** *3/4* **Great Expectations**[19] 3144 8-9-6 **67** (vt) FrederikTylicki 7 60
(J R Jenkins) *midfield: rdn 3f out: no real imp fnl 2f: wnt poor 3rd briefly ins fnl f* **40/1**

-65 **5** *1 1/2* **Ace Master**[38] 2540 8-9-10 **74** (b) AlistairRawlinson(3) 2 63
(Roy Bowring) *led: drvn and hdd 2f out: little rspnse: lost two pls fnl f* **25/1**

6-61 **6** *1 1/4* **Awesome Quality (USA)**[7] 3567 3-9-3 **73** 6ex LukeMorris 10 56
(James Tate) *midfield: drvn 1/2-way: btn 2f out* **2/1**[1]

2124 **7** *1 3/4* **Semra (USA)**[22] 3034 3-9-5 **75** JamesDoyle 4 53
(Marco Botti) *t.k.h: prom: rdn 3f out: wknd 2f out* **12/1**

4400 **8** *5* **Makhfar (IRE)**[21] 3078 5-8-4 **56** PatrickO'Donnell(5) 5 24
(Kevin Morgan) *slowly away: rdn and prog to chse ldrs 1/2-way: fdd over 2f out: eased and t.o* **20/1**

342 **9** *nk* **Snappy Guest**[36] 2577 4-9-8 **72** (p) NathanAlison(3) 8 40
(George Margarson) *bhd: rdn and struggling over 2f out: eased and t.o* **9/1**

1m 24.55s (-2.05) **Going Correction** -0.175s/f (Firm)
WFA 3 from 4yo+ 9lb **9** Ran SP% **111.9**
Speed ratings (Par 103): **104,94,93,92,90 89,87,81,81**
CSF £25.75 CT £138.91 TOTE £6.60: £1.90, £1.70, £1.60; EX 28.00 Trifecta £166.90.
Owner Global First Racing & Bloodstock **Bred** Michael O'Mahony **Trained** Newmarket, Suffolk

FOCUS
An ordinary handicap taken apart by the winner who may now be living up to early promise.

3822 JENNINGS BET H'CAP 5f 42y
3:50 (3:50) (Class 6) (0-60,58) 3-Y-O+ **£2,264** (£673; £336; £168) **Stalls** Centre

Form RPR
0000 **1** **Willow Spring**[22] 3040 4-8-6 **45** NoelGarbutt(5) 11 55
(Conrad Allen) *taken down early: reluctant to go down: trckd ldrs: rdn to go 2nd 2f out and sn clr of rest: clsd grad fnl f: ct ldr fnl stride* **40/1**

4000 **2** *shd* **Frangarry (IRE)**[2] 3735 4-9-5 **53** (b) DarryllHolland 12 63
(Alan Bailey) *led: only one on bridle 2f out: drew clr w wnr 1f out: pushed along and carried hd awkwardly fnl 100yds: pipped on post* **13/2**

4304 **3** *5* **Commanche**[24] 2964 7-9-9 **57** (b) SilvestreDeSousa 10 49
(Chris Dwyer) *completely outpcd and drvn in rr: styd on over 1f out: tk 3rd nr fin* **3/1**[1]

3-45 **4** *1/2* **Westbourne Grove (USA)**[31] 2750 3-9-2 **56** JamieSpencer 4 44
(John Butler) *taken down early: lost 6 l s: completely outpcd for over 3f: drvn and passed faders ins fnl f* **5/1**[3]

3340 **5** *1/2* **Give Us A Belle (IRE)**[14] 3307 7-9-3 **54** (bt) DannyBrock(3) 2 42
(Christine Dunnett) *prom: drvn 2f out: sn lost tch w ldng pair: lost two pls fnl 100yds* **10/1**

00-3 **6** *3/4* **Poplar**[15] 3280 3-9-4 **58** LukeMorris 3 42
(Robyn Brisland) *midfield: rdn 2f out: sn btn* **7/2**[2]

4600 **7** *1/2* **Blue Bounty**[14] 3316 5-8-10 **51** (p) GeorgiaDobie(7) 7 35
(Mark H Tompkins) *prom tl rdn over 2f out: sn btn* **8/1**

400- **8** *2* **Pass The Moon (IRE)**[290] 6390 3-9-1 **58** SimonPearce(3) 1 33
(Lydia Pearce) *immediately drvn: a outpcd in midfield* **33/1**

2246 **9** *1* **Imjin River (IRE)**[16] 3260 9-8-11 **45** (tp) MartinLane 6 18
(William Stone) *cl up tl drvn and lost pl tamely over 2f out* **22/1**

600 **10** *3 1/4* **Piazza San Pietro**[36] 2584 10-9-6 **54** RobertHavlin 8 15
(Zoe Davison) *toiling after 2f* **20/1**

0-00 **11** *1 1/4* **Delysdream**[22] 3040 4-8-11 **45** (t) AdamBeschizza 9
(Christine Dunnett) *toiling after 2f* **80/1**

660 **12** *4* **Single Summit**[141] 513 4-8-11 **45** (v) FrederikTylicki 5
(J R Jenkins) *prom tl hrd drvn and fdd qckly 2f out: t.o* **25/1**

1m 1.66s (-1.04) **Going Correction** -0.175s/f (Firm)
WFA 3 from 4yo+ 6lb **12** Ran SP% **117.0**
Speed ratings (Par 101): **101,100,92,92,91 90,89,86,84,79 77,70**
CSF £264.45 CT £850.29 TOTE £63.50: £11.60, £2.10, £1.60; EX 513.70 Trifecta £6883.00 Part won..
Owner John C Davies **Bred** Kirtlington Stud Ltd **Trained** Newmarket, Suffolk

FOCUS
A moderate sprint handicap in which the pair who raced closest to the stands' rail pulled a long way clear of the rest. The race has been rated around the runner-up.

3823 NORWICH AIRPORT H'CAP 1m 3y
4:20 (4:24) (Class 5) (0-70,70) 3-Y-O+ **£3,234** (£962; £481; £240) **Stalls** Centre

Form RPR
-263 **1** **Mithqaal (USA)**[27] 2864 3-9-1 **67** SilvestreDeSousa 8 76
(Owen Burrows) *chsd ldrs centre: effrt 2f out: rdn over 1f out: styd on to ld fnl 75yds: all out* **5/2**[1]

54- **2** *nk* **Hollywood Road (IRE)**[201] 8204 3-9-3 **69** FrankieDettori 11 77
(Don Cantillon) *midfield in centre gp: rdn over 2f out: clsd ins fnl f: kpt on wl but jst hld* **7/2**[2]

0-41 **3** *nk* **Four Poets**[41] 2428 3-9-4 **70** JamieSpencer 6 77
(David Simcock) *chsd ldrs far side: drvn to ld over 1f out: hdd and no ex fnl 75yds* **6/1**[3]

-450 **4** *1 3/4* **Anastazia**[22] 3038 4-9-12 **68** JamesDoyle 13 73
(Paul D'Arcy) *racd stands' gp: rdn and effrt over 1f out: hld fnl 100yds* **25/1**

-012 **5** *5* **He's My Boy (IRE)**[34] 2646 5-9-7 **70** GeorgeWood(7) 3 64
(James Fanshawe) *last away: sn rcvrd to chse ldrs far side: led 2f out: hdd over 1f out: sn wknd* **17/2**

25-0 **6** *nk* **Party Thyme**[48] 2212 3-8-13 **65** TedDurcan 1 56
(Chris Wall) *chsd ldrs far side: effrt 2f out: rdn and btn over 1f out* **25/1**

43-6 **7** *1 1/4* **Forest Lakes (IRE)**[42] 2415 3-8-12 **69** CallumShepherd(5) 12 57
(George Scott) *sn bhd: n.d fnl 2f* **33/1**

-163 **8** *1/2* **Roxie Lot**[13] 3354 4-9-7 **66** RobHornby(3) 10 55
(Pam Sly) *midfield: rdn and btn over 2f out* **20/1**

3040 **9** *nk* **World Record (IRE)**[13] 3354 6-9-6 **62** MartinLane 4 50
(Mick Quinn) *led far side: rdn and hdd 2f out: sn lost pl* **33/1**

4-02 **10** *3/4* **Port Paradise**[21] 3080 3-8-10 **62** TomQueally 5 47
(William Jarvis) *prom far side: rdn 3f out: btn 2f out* **12/1**

0606 **11** *3/4* **Tommy's Secret**[13] 3354 6-9-7 **68** PaddyPilley(5) 14 53
(Jane Chapple-Hyam) *midfield stands' gp: rdn and btn 2f out* **22/1**

0- **12** *5* **Caribbean Spring (IRE)**[257] 7302 3-8-6 **65** JaneElliott(7) 15 36
(George Margarson) *led stands' gp but nt overall: rdn 3f out: btn 2f out* **50/1**

420- **13** *9* **Amazing Charm**[277] 6780 4-9-13 **69** LukeMorris 7 22
(James Tate) *hooded in parade ring: prom in centre: rdn 3f out: fnd nil: eased fnl 2f: t.o* **12/1**

0240 **14** *2 1/4* **Shining Romeo**[13] 3354 4-9-7 **66** (p[1]) TimClark(3) 9 14
(Denis Quinn) *shkn up 1/2-way: sn btn: eased and t.o* **33/1**

/040 **15** *15* **Rising Rainbow**[22] 3012 5-8-9 **51** oh6 (p[1]) RaulDaSilva 2
(Ivan Furtado) *pressed ldr far side: drvn 3f out: sn struggling: t.o and eased* **150/1**

1m 38.18s (-2.42) **Going Correction** -0.175s/f (Firm)
WFA 3 from 4yo+ 10lb **15** Ran SP% **119.2**
Speed ratings (Par 103): **105,104,104,102,97 97,96,95,95,94 93,88,79,77,62**
CSF £9.07 CT £48.12 TOTE £3.40: £1.80, £2.80, £2.40; EX 16.30 Trifecta £64.90.
Owner Hamdan Al Maktoum **Bred** Extern Developments Ltd **Trained** Lambourn, Berks

FOCUS
A modest handicap with not that much covering the first four home, the quartet pulling clear. The game winner was building on his possibly unlucky Doncaster run.

3824 MOULTON NURSERY OF ACLE H'CAP 1m 1f 21y
4:50 (4:52) (Class 4) (0-80,80) 3-Y-O **£5,045** (£1,501; £750; £375) **Stalls** Low

Form RPR
-404 **1** **Shahbar**[21] 3077 3-9-7 **80** (b[1]) FrankieDettori 9 92+
(Marco Botti) *settled towards rr and gng wl: smooth prog 3f out: led wl over 1f out: sn in command: eased fnl 100yds* **9/1**

5-25 **2** *1 3/4* **Cote D'Azur**[33] 2674 3-8-12 **71** LukeMorris 5 79
(Sir Mark Prescott Bt) *hld up last tl home turn: effrt on far rails and rdn over 2f out: racd awkwardly: w wnr wl over 1f out but no match for him fnl f* **11/2**[3]

3-50 **3** *1 1/2* **Absolute Zero (IRE)**[26] 2891 3-9-1 **74** HarryBentley 3 78
(Roger Varian) *racd keenly in 2nd or 3rd: clsd on clr ldr 3f out: rdn and ev ch 2f out: nt qckn 1f out* **7/1**

50-3 **4** *nk* **Melabi (IRE)**[21] 3079 3-8-11 **77** GeorgiaCox(7) 6 80
(William Haggas) *stdd s: keen in rr: rdn and effrt 2f out: disp wl hld 3rd fnl f* **7/2**[1]

1-10 **5** *2* **Cajoled (FR)**[42] 2394 3-9-6 **79** (t) TedDurcan 8 78
(George Scott) *bhd: stl last and too much to do 3f out: rdn 2f out: styng on wl ins fnl f* **13/2**

0-41 **6** *2 1/2* **Lord Kelvin (IRE)**[16] 3252 3-9-3 **76** JamieSpencer 4 70
(Charles Hills) *led 1f: t.k.h chsng clr ldr: clsd on him but lost 2nd 3f out: rdn 2f out: sn btn* **5/1**[2]

0006 **7** *1* **Western Prince**[13] 3355 3-8-11 **70** RobertHavlin 1 62
(John Gosden) *dwlt but led after 1f: 7 l clr home turn: rdn and hdd wl over 1f out: dropped out immediately: eased fnl f* **16/1**

4-20 **8** *3 1/4* **Wafi Star (IRE)**[31] 2749 3-8-13 **72** SilvestreDeSousa 7 57
(Simon Crisford) *plld hrd and chsd ldrs: rdn over 3f out: little rspnse and sn btn: eased fnl f* **8/1**

1420 **9** *2 3/4* **Ilzam (IRE)**[52] 2099 3-9-4 **77** (t) JamesDoyle 2 56
(Marco Botti) *taken down early: chsd ldrs: rdn over 3f out: sn btn: t.o* **14/1**

1m 53.77s (-2.03) **Going Correction** -0.175s/f (Firm) **9** Ran SP% **113.8**
Speed ratings (Par 101): **102,100,99,98,97 94,93,91,88**
CSF £56.85 CT £367.95 TOTE £8.90: £3.00, £2.00, £2.10; EX 66.70 Trifecta £584.70.
Owner Al Shaqab Racing **Bred** Widden Stud Australia Pty Ltd **Trained** Newmarket, Suffolk

FOCUS
A fair 3yo handicap. The bulk of the field tended to ignore the clear leader.

3825 FOLLOW GREAT YARMOUTH RACECOURSE ON TWITTER "HANDS AND HEELS" SERIES APPRENTICE H'CAP 1m 3f 104y
5:25 (5:25) (Class 6) (0-65,65) 4-Y-O+ **£2,264** (£673; £336; £168) **Stalls** Low

Form RPR
6-52 **1** **Smoky Hill (IRE)**[5] 3641 7-8-11 **55** JoshuaBryan(5) 2 68
(Tony Carroll) *patiently rdn in last tl effrt 4f out: led wl over 2f out: sn pushed clr and unassailable* **5/4**[1]

0445 **2** *10* **Theydon Bois**[21] 3076 4-9-2 **55** (p) HarryBurns 3 53
(Peter Charalambous) *led: hdd 7f out: drvn 3f out: in vain pursuit of wnr fnl 2f* **8/1**

3523 **3** *2 1/2* **Hope You Dance (FR)**[14] 3302 4-9-9 **65** (p) CliffordLee(3) 1 58
(David Simcock) *in tch tl dropped bk last and rdn 4f out: no ch w ldng pair fnl 2f* **11/4**[2]

4223 **4** *shd* **What A Party (IRE)**[21] 3076 4-9-4 **57** (v) GeorgeWood 4 50
(Gay Kelleway) *handy tl rdn 4f out: plodded on whn no ch fnl 2f* **9/2**[3]

-165 **5** *1* **Master Of Song**[21] 3072 9-9-0 **58** (p) LiamLewis-Salter(5) 5 49
(Roy Bowring) *t.k.h: 2nd tl led 7f out: rdn 3f out: hdd wl over 2f out: plugged on w no ch after* **10/1**

2m 29.66s (0.96) **Going Correction** -0.175s/f (Firm) **5** Ran SP% **109.5**
Speed ratings (Par 101): **89,81,79,79,79**
CSF £11.47 TOTE £1.80: £1.60, £3.50; EX 10.10 Trifecta £26.30.
Owner Millen & Cooke **Bred** Ballylinch Stud **Trained** Cropthorne, Worcs

■ Stewards' Enquiry : George Wood seven-day ban: used whip contrary to race conditions (Jul 14,15,17-20,22)

FOCUS
A moderate apprentice handicap, run at an ordinary pace, and the well-treated winner bolted up.
T/Plt: £10.60 to a £1 stake. Pool: £63,385.67 - 4331.40 winning units. T/Qpdt: £4.90 to a £1 stake. Pool: £5,576.82 - 826.60 winning units. **Iain Mackenzie**

3826- 3837a (Foreign Racing) - See Raceform Interactive

3477 BEVERLEY (R-H)

Friday, July 1

OFFICIAL GOING: Good (good to soft in places) changing to soft (good to soft in places) after race 1 (6.15)

Wind: moderate 1/2 against Weather: changeable, heavy showers

3838 ICE AND EASY FROZEN ALCOHOLIC SLUSHIES (S) STKS — 7f 100y

6:15 (6:15) (Class 6) 3-Y-0+ **£2,587** (£770; £384; £192) **Stalls** Low

Form — RPR

024 **1** **Corroyer (IRE)**[27] 2914 3-8-10 73 JasonHart 10 — 73
(John Quinn) *trckd ldrs: effrt and swtchd lft over 1f out: sn chsng ldr: led last 100yds: drvn out* **11/4**[2]

4430 **2** *2* **Talent Scout (IRE)**[18] 3214 10-8-13 65 GemmaTutty(5) 9 — 71
(Karen Tutty) *swtchd lft after s: led: hdd and no ex last 100yds* **4/1**[3]

0-63 **3** *5* **Lady Nahema (IRE)**[31] 2777 3-8-5 64 PJMcDonald 3 — 52
(Ann Duffield) *sn trcking ldrs: t.k.h: effrt over 2f out: kpt on same pce to take modest 3rd towards fin* **9/4**[1]

00-0 **4** *1 1/4* **Shadowtime**[23] 3011 11-9-4 62 BarryMcHugh 8 — 57
(Tracy Waggott) *t.k.h in rr: hdwy to trck ldrs 5f out: kpt on one pce over 1f out* **10/1**

-260 **5** *1 1/2* **Andaz**[20] 3153 3-8-5 67 (e1) CamHardie 7 — 45
(Marjorie Fife) *hld up in rr: effrt on outer over 2f out: kpt on: nvr a threat* **16/1**

0500 **6** *nk* **Jersey Roy**[13] 3421 3-8-10 60 TonyHamilton 1 — 49
(Richard Fahey) *stdd s: hld up towards rr: hdwy over 4f out: edgd rt over 1f out: one pce* **10/1**

4-46 **7** *nk* **Cranberry Park (IRE)**[44] 2360 3-8-5 52 (v1) JamesSullivan 4 — 44
(Brian Ellison) *sn trcking ldrs: t.k.h: wknd fnl f* **14/1**

5-40 **8** *1 1/4* **Piccacard**[11] 3473 3-7-12 49 (p) MitchGodwin(7) 6 — 41
(Michael Appleby) *in rr: effrt on outside over 2f out: nvr a factor* **40/1**

3064 **9** *2 1/4* **Mr Lucas (IRE)**[32] 2741 3-8-10 45 (v) JoeFanning 11 — 40
(Peter Niven) *hld up in rr: sme hdwy over 2f out: wknd over 1f out* **28/1**

0356 **10** *16* **Alpha Tauri (USA)**[67] 1712 10-9-4 38 GrahamGibbons 5 — 6
(Charles Smith) *chsd ldr: lost pl over 1f out: eased fnl 100yds* **100/1**

1m 34.9s (1.10) **Going Correction** +0.225s/f (Good)
WFA 3 from 4yo+ 8lb — **10** Ran SP% **115.0**
Speed ratings (Par 101): **102,99,94,92,90 90,90,88,86,67**
CSF £13.87 TOTE £5.10: £2.10, £1.50, £1.20; EX 16.40 Trifecta £30.20.The winner was bought in for £4,200.
Owner Mrs S Quinn **Bred** Scea Des Prairies **Trained** Settrington, N Yorks

FOCUS
The going was good, good to soft in places. A modest seller run at a sound pace with the winner holding a much better profile than the rest. The race has been rated around the runner-up.

3839 JACKSON'S YORKSHIRE CHAMPION BREAD EBF NOVICE STKS (PLUS 10 RACE) — 5f

6:45 (6:45) (Class 4) 2-Y-0 **£5,040** (£1,508; £754; £377; £188) **Stalls** Low

Form — RPR

1 **Naples Bay** 2-9-2 0 CamHardie 8 — 74
(John Quinn) *dwlt: t.k.h in rr: swtchd rt after 1f: hdwy on outer over 2f out: edgd rt and styd on fnl f: led post* **10/1**

2 *nse* **Whirl Me Round** 2-8-13 0 JoeDoyle(3) 5 — 74
(Kevin Ryan) *trckd ldrs: effrt over 1f out: led last 150yds: hdd post* **12/1**

03 **3** *2 1/2* **Clear As A Bell (IRE)**[42] 2424 2-8-11 0 DuranFentiman 1 — 60
(Tim Easterby) *in rr: outpcd and pushed along over 2f out: hdwy over 1f out: kpt on: tk 3rd clsng stages* **16/1**

501 **4** *1 1/4* **Ventura Secret (IRE)**[20] 3148 2-9-9 0 DavidAllan 9 — 67
(Tim Easterby) *trckd ldr: t.k.h: effrt over 1f out: kpt on same pce* **3/1**[3]

323 **5** *hd* **Dubai Knights (IRE)**[16] 3283 2-9-2 0 PJMcDonald 6 — 60
(Ann Duffield) *led: drvn over 1f out: hdd last 150yds: fdd clsng stages* **5/2**[2]

6 *1 3/4* **Indie Rock** 2-8-11 0 JoeFanning 3 — 48
(Mark Johnston) *chsd ldrs on inner: drvn and nt clr run 2f out: wknd fnl 75yds* **2/1**[1]

06 **7** *13* **Mr Enthusiastic**[38] 2552 2-9-2 0 BarryMcHugh 7 — 7
(Noel Wilson) *t.k.h: sn trcking ldrs: hung lft over 2f out: lost pl over 1f out* **28/1**

1m 5.18s (1.68) **Going Correction** +0.325s/f (Good) — **7** Ran SP% **113.0**
Speed ratings (Par 96): **99,98,94,92,92 89,69**
CSF £112.89 TOTE £11.50: £4.00, £3.70; EX 80.80 Trifecta £1198.10.
Owner D Ward **Bred** Tirnaskea Stud **Trained** Settrington, N Yorks
■ Stewards' Enquiry : Joe Doyle four-day ban; used whip above permitted level (15th-18th July)

FOCUS
The going was eased to soft, good to soft in places prior to the this race. They went a sound pace for this fair contest which was dominated by two promising newcomers.

3840 AUNT BESSIE'S H'CAP — 7f 100y

7:15 (7:15) (Class 4) (0-80,81) 3-Y-0+ **£5,040** (£1,508; £754; £377; £188) **Stalls** Low

Form — RPR

033 **1** **Spryt (IRE)**[19] 3185 4-9-12 78 (v) DanielTudhope 5 — 87
(David O'Meara) *mde all: drvn over 1f out: kpt on wl: unchal* **9/1**

6402 **2** *2* **Relight My Fire**[10] 3478 6-9-0 66 (p) DavidAllan 1 — 70
(Tim Easterby) *trckd wnr: effrt over 2f out: kpt on same pce fnl f* **11/2**[2]

500 **3** *3/4* **Purple Rock (IRE)**[21] 3115 4-9-5 76 (t) NathanEvans(5) 3 — 78
(Michael Easterby) *dwlt: mid-div: drvn over 3f out: chsng ldrs 2f out: kpt on same pce to take 3rd last 100yds* **14/1**

1641 **4** *1* **Viscount Barfield**[7] 3591 3-8-13 73 DavidProbert 9 — 70
(Andrew Balding) *wnt lft s: hld up in last: effrt over 3f out: kpt on fnl f: tk 4th last 75yds: nvr a threat* **4/6**[1]

0001 **5** *3 3/4* **Shouranour (IRE)**[4] 3717 6-9-10 81 6ex (b) JoshDoyle(5) 2 — 71
(Alan Brown) *chsd ldrs: drvn over 2f out: wknd last 150yds* **6/1**[3]

1641 **6** *5* **Victoire De Lyphar (IRE)**[7] 3599 9-9-10 76 6ex (e) JamesSullivan 6 — 54
(Ruth Carr) *t.k.h in mid-div: effrt over 3f out: hung lft over 2f out: sn lost pl: b.b.v* **10/1**

1m 34.33s (0.53) **Going Correction** +0.225s/f (Good)
WFA 3 from 4yo+ 8lb — **6** Ran SP% **115.4**
Speed ratings (Par 105): **105,102,101,100,96 90**
CSF £57.34 CT £692.68 TOTE £8.50: £3.20, £1.80; EX 50.30 Trifecta £316.20.
Owner N D Crummack & D Lumley **Bred** Moyglare Stud Farm Ltd **Trained** Upper Helmsley, N Yorks

FOCUS
Four withdrawals took some of the interest out of this handicap, which was run at a sound pace in the conditions and the first two dominated throughout.

3841 HODGSON SEALANTS H'CAP — 1m 100y

7:45 (7:45) (Class 5) (0-75,74) 3-Y-0 **£3,780** (£1,131; £565; £283; £141) **Stalls** Low

Form — RPR

-225 **1** **Thaqaffa (IRE)**[26] 2935 3-9-7 74 RoystonFfrench 2 — 83
(Marcus Tregoning) *trckd ldrs: t.k.h: def 2nd over 3f out: shkn up to ld over 1f out: drvn clr last 150yds* **13/8**[1]

642 **2** *3 1/4* **Dasheen**[13] 3400 3-9-2 69 JoeFanning 5 — 71
(Mark Johnston) *in rr: sn pushed along: hdwy over 5f out: chsng ldrs over 2f out: 2nd 1f out: kpt on one pce* **10/3**[2]

5005 **3** *6* **Taking Libertys**[25] 2973 3-9-7 74 TomEaves 3 — 63
(Kevin Ryan) *led: drvn over 3f out: hdd over 1f out: edgd lft and wknd fnl f* **11/2**

60 **4** *2* **Albert Boy (IRE)**[14] 3355 3-9-3 70 DaleSwift 4 — 55
(Scott Dixon) *chsd ldrs: drvn over 3f out: wknd appr fnl f* **15/2**

4-40 **5** *4* **Sayedaati Saadati (IRE)**[36] 2619 3-8-11 64 GrahamGibbons 1 — 41
(David Simcock) *trckd ldrs: t.k.h: drvn over 2f out: lost pl over 1f out* **7/2**[3]

1m 49.96s (2.36) **Going Correction** +0.225s/f (Good) — **5** Ran SP% **110.5**
Speed ratings (Par 100): **97,93,87,85,81**
CSF £7.31 TOTE £2.30: £2.10, £1.70; EX 7.00 Trifecta £27.90.
Owner Hamdan Al Maktoum **Bred** Incense Partnership **Trained** Whitsbury, Hants

FOCUS
They went a solid pace for this interesting handicap, with the winner building on his Goodwood run.

3842 STEVE FENWICK (REGY) MEMORIAL BEVERLEY MIDDLE DISTANCE SERIES H'CAP — 1m 4f 16y

8:15 (8:15) (Class 6) (0-60,60) 3-Y-0+ **£2,587** (£770; £384; £192) **Stalls** Low

Form — RPR

5542 **1** **Saint Thomas (IRE)**[10] 3480 9-9-2 53 JoeFanning 12 — 60
(John Mackie) *trckd ldrs: led over 2f out: jnd last 75yds: all out* **10/3**[2]

0050 **2** *nse* **First Sargeant**[1] 3804 6-9-7 58 (p) CamHardie 2 — 65
(Lawrence Mullaney) *in rr: reminders over 6f out: hdwy over 2f out: chsng ldrs over 1f out: 2nd last 100yds: sn upsides: jst denied* **6/1**

43-3 **3** *1 1/2* **Maple Stirrup (IRE)**[177] 71 4-8-11 55 PaulaMuir(7) 11 — 60
(Patrick Holmes) *chsd ldrs: drvn over 3f out: 2nd over 1f out: edgd lft and kpt on same pce* **14/1**

-353 **4** *1 3/4* **Cool Music (IRE)**[27] 2915 6-9-6 57 PJMcDonald 6 — 59
(Antony Brittain) *in rr: hdwy over 3f out: chsng ldrs over 1f out: kpt on one pce* **4/1**[3]

0040 **5** *6* **Gabrial's Hope (FR)**[8] 3564 7-9-3 54 ConnorBeasley 10 — 47
(Tracy Waggott) *s.s: hld up in last: hdwy on outer over 2f out: wnt rt over 1f out: sn wknd* **12/1**

00-0 **6** *9* **Sigurd (GER)**[38] 2558 4-9-4 55 (p) TomEaves 1 — 35+
(Kevin Ryan) *w ldr 2f: trckd ldr: upsides over 4f out: led over 3f out: hdd over 2f out: grad wknd* **16/1**

00-1 **7** *24* **The Blue Banana (IRE)**[23] 3018 7-9-3 54 PaddyAspell 7
(Grant Tuer) *s.s: hdwy 9f out: drvn over 4f out: lost pl over 2f out: sn bhd: eased clsng stages* **8/1**

60U1 **8** *11* **Lean On Pete (IRE)**[10] 3480 7-9-5 56 6ex JamesSullivan 3 — +
(Ollie Pears) *led: clr after 2f: jnd over 4f out: lost pl over 2f out: sn bhd: t.o whn heavily eased fnl f* **3/1**[1]

2m 42.7s (2.90) **Going Correction** +0.225s/f (Good) — **8** Ran SP% **113.7**
Speed ratings (Par 101): **99,98,97,96,92 86,70,63**
CSF £23.33 CT £243.30 TOTE £4.00: £1.60, £2.00, £3.30; EX 24.00 Trifecta £221.10.
Owner P Riley **Bred** S Coughlan **Trained** Church Broughton , Derbys

FOCUS
They went a strong early gallop for this modest handicap.

3843 FERGUSON FAWSITT ARMS H'CAP — 5f

8:45 (8:46) (Class 6) (0-60,64) 3-Y-0+ **£2,587** (£770; £384; £192) **Stalls** Low

Form — RPR

4232 **1** **Poppy In The Wind**[10] 3484 4-9-10 60 (v) DaleSwift 16 — 69
(Alan Brown) *sn drvn along in mid-div: hdwy over 1f out: styd on to ld nr fin* **15/2**[2]

3131 **2** *nk* **Seamster**[2] 3779 9-9-7 64 6ex (t) CameronNoble(7) 3 — 72
(David Loughnane) *w ldr: led over 2f out: hdd and no ex nr fin* **6/4**[1]

-005 **3** *3/4* **Slim Chance (IRE)**[3] 3755 7-9-8 58 JasonHart 10 — 63
(Simon West) *led to post: chsd ldrs: hung rt and kpt on same pce last 75yds* **12/1**

-406 **4** *1 1/4* **The Armed Man**[14] 3368 3-9-5 60 AndrewElliott 2 — 59
(Chris Fairhurst) *chsd ldrs: drvn and outpcd over 2f out: kpt on fnl f: tk 4th nr fin* **9/1**[3]

6004 **5** *hd* **Rocket Rob (IRE)**[8] 3559 10-9-8 58 TonyHamilton 12 — 58
(Willie Musson) *swtchd rt after s: in rr: hdwy over 1f out* **20/1**

5003 **6** *nse* **Tinsill**[10] 3484 5-9-1 51 (p) TomEaves 5 — 53
(Nigel Tinkler) *chsd ldrs: swtchd lft appr fnl f: kpt on same pce* **9/1**[3]

500- **7** *nk* **Culloden**[185] 8388 4-8-11 52 CharlieBennett(5) 7 — 51
(Shaun Harris) *led tl over 2f out: one pce fnl f* **28/1**

0-20 **8** *1 3/4* **Kinloch Pride**[14] 3368 4-9-2 52 (p) JoeFanning 8 — 45
(Noel Wilson) *chsd ldrs: fdd over 1f out* **10/1**

2212 **9** *1/2* **Fortinbrass (IRE)**[22] 3070 6-9-3 60 LewisEdmunds(7) 9 — 51
(John Balding) *mid-div: drvn over 2f out: wknd over 1f out* **12/1**

2556 **10** *hd* **Lizzy's Dream**[23] 3040 8-9-3 53 BarryMcHugh 17 — 43
(Rebecca Bastiman) *wnt lft s: in rr: kpt on fnl 2f: nvr a factor* **33/1**

004- **11** *1* **Clouded Gold**[213] 8066 4-8-12 51 AlistairRawlinson(3) 4 — 37
(Michael Appleby) *in rr: nvr a factor* **20/1**

3565 **12** *1/2* **Lucky Mark (IRE)**[85] 1299 7-9-0 53 (p) JoeDoyle(3) 13 — 38
(John Balding) *half-rrd s: in rr: sme hdwy over 1f out: nvr on terms* **25/1**

-600 **13** *3/4* **Armelle (FR)**[55] 2053 5-9-0 57 NatalieHambling(7) 14 — 39
(Scott Dixon) *chsd ldrs: lost pl over 1f out* **16/1**

1004 **14** *4* **Under Approval**[8] 3549 5-8-10 51 (b) GemmaTutty(5) 11 — 19
(Karen Tutty) *mid-div: lost pl over 2f out: sn bhd* **25/1**

1m 4.78s (1.28) **Going Correction** +0.325s/f (Good)
WFA 3 from 4yo+ 5lb — **14** Ran SP% **125.7**
Speed ratings (Par 101): **102,101,100,98,98 97,97,94,93,93 91,91,89,83**
CSF £18.04 CT £150.60 TOTE £8.40: £2.20, £1.30, £4.90; EX 25.90 Trifecta £223.90.
Owner Mrs M Doherty & Mrs W A D Craven **Bred** P Balding **Trained** Yedingham, N Yorks

FOCUS
A modest concluding contest featuring a form reversal.
T/Plt: £577.20 to a £1 stake. Pool: £45,762.00 - 79.27 winning tickets T/Qpdt: £16.20 to a £1 stake. Pool: £4,497.00 - 271.26 winning tickets **Walter Glynn**

[3640]DONCASTER (L-H)

Friday, July 1

OFFICIAL GOING: Soft (good to soft in places) changing to soft after race 1 (2.00)

Wind: Moderate against Weather: Cloudy with showers

3844 YOU MEDICALS H'CAP — 1m 4f

2:00 (2:00) (Class 5) (0-70,70) 4-Y-O+ **£3,881** (£1,155; £577; £288) **Stalls** Low

Form RPR

-041 **1** **Duke Of Diamonds**[22] 3067 4-8-12 **64**...................... ShelleyBirkett(3) 10 75+
(Julia Feilden) *trckd ldr: led wl over 2f out: rdn wl over 1f out: drvn and kpt on wl fnl f* **8/1**

4-63 **2** *1 ½* **Arrowtown**[29] 2836 4-9-2 **70**.. NathanEvans(5) 3 78
(Michael Easterby) *t.k.h early: trckd ldrs: hdwy over 2f out: rdn to chse wnr over 1f out: drvn and kpt on same pce fnl f* **11/4**[2]

-604 **3** *2 ¼* **Storm Check**[40] 2507 4-7-13 **55**.................................... HollieDoyle(7) 11 59
(Andrew Crook) *hld up in rr: hdwy on outer 4f out: chsd ldrs 2f out: sn rdn and edgd persistently lft: drvn and kpt no imp fnl f* **12/1**

-005 **4** *1* **Captain Swift (IRE)**[6] 3641 5-9-5 **68**................................. JoeFanning 5 70
(John Mackie) *hld up in rr: hdwy over 3f out: chsd ldrs and swtchd lft wl over 1f out: sn rdn and chsd ldng pair: drvn and kpt on same pce fnl f* **12/1**

13 **5** *5* **Hard Toffee (IRE)**[6] 3641 5-9-7 **70**.................................... RyanMoore 7 64
(Conrad Allen) *in tch: hdwy to trck ldrs over 3f out: pushed along over 2f out: sn rdn and wknd over 1f out* **2/1**[1]

3212 **6** *1* **Chauvelin**[15] 3325 5-8-2 **51** oh1..................................(b) PatrickMathers 2 44
(Richard Guest) *trckd ldrs: effrt over 3f out: rdn along 2f out: sn drvn and grad wknd* **10/1**

1113 **7** *15* **Bamako Du Chatelet (FR)**[28] 2876 5-9-4 **67**...............(p) JamesDoyle 4 36
(Ian Williams) *hld up towards rr: effrt and sme hdwy 4f out: rdn along over 3f out: sn outpcd* **9/2**[3]

05-0 **8** *1 ¼* **In Vino Veritas (IRE)**[19] 3191 5-8-7 **56**........................... AndrewElliott 9 23
(Lynn Siddall) *led: pushed along 4f out: rdn 3f out: sn hdd & wknd* **33/1**

00-0 **9** *50* **Fledermaus (IRE)**[16] 3294 6-8-6 **55**............................(t) JamesSullivan 1
(Tina Jackson) *trckd ldrs on inner: pushed along over 4f out: rdn wl over 3f out: sn wknd and bhd whn eased over 1f out* **66/1**

2m 40.82s (5.92) **Going Correction** +0.625s/f (Yiel) **9** Ran SP% **118.2**
Speed ratings (Par 103): **105,104,102,101,98 97,87,87,53**
CSF £31.07 CT £270.20 TOTE £9.80: £2.40, £1.90, £3.40; EX 33.80 Trifecta £429.80.

Owner Carol Bushnell & Partners **Bred** Barry Walters Farms **Trained** Exning, Suffolk

FOCUS
The round course was railed out from the 1m2f point until the round joins the straight, adding about 6yds to the first three races. Due to 3.6mm of overnight rain the going was downgraded to soft all over. There was something of an uneven pace on in this modest handicap. The in-form winner looks like rating higher again.

3845 NORMANDIE STUD MAIDEN STKS — 1m 4f

2:30 (2:30) (Class 5) 3-Y-O+ **£3,881** (£1,155; £577; £288) **Stalls** Low

Form RPR

62 **1** **Marmelo**[29] 2815 3-9-1 0.. PJMcDonald 10 93
(Hughie Morrison) *in tch: smooth hdwy over 3f out: led over 2f out: rdn clr over 1f out: styd on strly* **4/1**[2]

06 **2** *10* **Lord Napier (IRE)**[56] 2000 3-9-1 0................................(b[1]) RobertTart 13 77
(John Gosden) *hld up towards rr: hdwy on wd outside 3f out: chsd ldrs and rdn wl over 1f out: drvn and kpt on fnl f: no ch w wnr* **33/1**

62 **3** *1* **Cape Cova (IRE)**[14] 3359 3-9-1 0................................ FrankieDettori 11 76
(John Gosden) *hld up in midfield: hdwy over 3f out and sn pushed along: rdn 2f out: styd on to chse wnr over 1f out: sn drvn and kpt on same pce* **4/1**[2]

2 **4** *½* **Endless Acres (IRE)**[18] 3235 3-9-1 0......................... StevieDonohoe 15 75
(Charlie Fellowes) *hld up in rr: hdwy wl over 2f out: rdn wl over 1f out: styd on appr fnl f* **16/1**

0- **5** *1 ¼* **Toola Boola**[246] 3961 6-9-9 0... JackGarritty 14 68
(Jedd O'Keeffe) *in rr: hdwy over 4f out: rdn wl over 2f out: drvn wl over 1f out and plugged on one pce* **66/1**

35 **6** *1 ¾* **London Prize**[9] 3508 5-9-11 0.................................. GeorgeDowning(3) 1 70
(Ian Williams) *hld up and bhd: hdwy over 3f out: pushed along wl over 2f out: plugged on appr fnl f* **28/1**

422 **7** *3 ¾* **Withhold**[19] 3190 3-9-1 80... RyanMoore 6 64
(Charles Hills) *trckd ldng pair: hdwy 3f out: rdn along over 2f out: drvn and hung lft over 1f out: sn wknd* **11/4**[1]

3 **8** *shd* **Tobouggaloo**[21] 3094 5-9-9 0.. MartinLane 8 59
(Stuart Kittow) *towards rr: sme hdwy on inner 3f out: in tch and rdn along 2f out: sn drvn and wknd* **12/1**[3]

4 **9** *1* **Stanley**[20] 3160 3-9-1 0... AdamKirby 12 62
(Luca Cumani) *trckd ldrs: hdwy 3f out and sn cl up: rdn along over 2f out: drvn wl over 1f out and sn wknd* **11/4**[1]

3 **10** *10* **Ceyhan**[74] 1529 4-10-0 0.. PatCosgrave 3 46
(Joseph Tuite) *t.k.h: trckd ldrs on inner: hdwy and cl up over 3f out: rdn along over 2f out: wkng whn sltly hmpd over 1f out* **20/1**

11 *2 ¾* **Southern Strife**[478] 5-10-0 0... CamHardie 4 42
(Tim Easterby) *chsd clr ldr: tk clsr order 4f out: rdn along 3f out: wknd over 2f out* **66/1**

0/0 **12** *1 ¼* **Not Another Bill**[62] 1873 5-10-0 0...................................... DavidAllan 2 40
(Chris Wall) *midfield: rdn along 5f out: sn wknd* **100/1**

0 **13** *7* **Pray For Paris**[32] 2735 3-8-10 0.................................. PaulMulrennan 5 24
(Martyn Meade) *led and sn clr: pushed along 4f out: rdn over 3f out: hdd wl over 2f out and sn wknd* **50/1**

2m 41.93s (7.03) **Going Correction** +0.625s/f (Yiel)
WFA 3 from 4yo+ 13lb **13** Ran SP% **124.0**
Speed ratings (Par 103): **101,94,93,93,92 91,88,88,88,81 79,78,74**
CSF £139.39 TOTE £4.90: £1.60, £8.70, £1.90; EX 157.50 Trifecta £1386.60.

Owner The Fairy Story Partnership **Bred** Deepwood Farm Stud **Trained** East Ilsley, Berks

FOCUS
The winner was impressive and this maiden ought to prove a fair source of future winners. Race distance increased by 6yds.

3846 CHESTERFIELD ESTATES EBF STALLIONS BREEDING WINNERS FILLIES' H'CAP — 1m 4f

3:05 (3:06) (Class 4) (0-85,85) 3-Y-O+ **£6,469** (£1,925; £962; £481) **Stalls** Low

Form RPR

61 **1** **Dubka**[21] 3094 3-8-9 **79**... RyanMoore 2 91+
(Sir Michael Stoute) *trckd ldng pair: hdwy to trck ldr over 5f out: cl up over 3f out: led wl over 2f out: edgd rt and clr over 1f out: readily* **5/6**[1]

-231 **2** *4 ½* **Shafafya**[16] 3291 3-9-1 **85**.. PaulMulrennan 5 90
(Ed Dunlop) *hld up in rr: hdwy 3f out: effrt to chse wnr 2f out: sn rdn and swtchd lft over 1f out: drvn and no imp fnl f* **3/1**[2]

1-65 **3** *8* **Mediation**[16] 3278 4-9-9 **80**.. HarryBentley 1 72
(Roger Varian) *trckd ldr: hdwy and cl up over 3f out: rdn along over 2f out: drvn wl over 1f out and sn one pce* **6/1**[3]

-100 **4** *4* **Mirsaalah**[43] 2394 3-8-11 **81**... DavidAllan 4 67
(James Tate) *set stdy pce: pushed along 4f out and sn jnd: rdn and hdd wl over 2f out: sn drvn and wknd* **13/2**

2m 40.37s (5.47) **Going Correction** +0.625s/f (Yiel)
WFA 3 from 4yo 13lb **4** Ran SP% **107.2**
Speed ratings (Par 102): **106,103,97,95**
CSF £3.50 TOTE £1.60; EX 4.00 Trifecta £5.60.

Owner Sir Evelyn De Rothschild **Bred** Southcourt Stud **Trained** Newmarket, Suffolk

FOCUS
This was a fair fillies' handicap and should prove straightforward form. Race distance increased by 6yds.

3847 BETFAIR STABLE STAFF WEEK FILLIES' H'CAP — 5f

3:35 (3:37) (Class 4) (0-80,79) 3-Y-O+ **£5,175** (£1,540; £769; £384) **Stalls** High

Form RPR

3024 **1** **Sarabi**[8] 3581 3-8-7 **65**...(p) BenCurtis 6 73
(Scott Dixon) *mde most: rdn wl over 1f out: kpt on wl fnl f* **5/1**

0402 **2** *1 ¼* **Fruit Salad**[13] 3397 3-8-5 **68**... NathanEvans(5) 2 71
(James Bethell) *trckd ldrs: hdwy on outer 1/2-way and sn cl up: rdn over 1f out: drvn and kpt on same pce fnl f* **5/2**[1]

3-14 **3** *hd* **Futoon (IRE)**[13] 3397 3-9-4 **76**... RyanMoore 5 78
(Kevin Ryan) *trckd ldrs: hdwy over 2f out: rdn over 1f out: drvn to chse wnr ins fnl f: no imp towards fin* **10/3**[2]

6116 **4** *1 ½* **Saved My Bacon (IRE)**[30] 2787 5-9-9 **79**............ JosephineGordon(3) 4 78
(Chris Dwyer) *trckd ldrs: hdwy 1/2-way: rdn to chal over 1f out: ev ch tl drvn ent fnl f and kpt on same pce* **9/1**

6160 **5** *nk* **Crombay (IRE)**[13] 3397 3-9-0 **72**.. DavidAllan 8 68
(Tim Easterby) *chsd ldrs: hdwy over 2f out: rdn over 1f out: drvn and one pce fnl f* **8/1**

11-0 **6** *3* **Misu Mac**[7] 3610 6-9-0 **70**.. JacobButterfield(3) 1 57
(Neville Bycroft) *prom: pushed along 1/2-way: sn lost pl and bhd* **25/1**

4-14 **7** *2 ¾* **Evangelical**[18] 3218 3-9-6 **78**... TonyHamilton 3 53
(Richard Fahey) *chsd ldrs: rdn along 2f out: wkng whn stmbld over 1f out and sn in rr* **9/2**[3]

1m 2.98s (2.48) **Going Correction** +0.625s/f (Yiel)
WFA 3 from 4yo+ 5lb **7** Ran SP% **111.5**
Speed ratings (Par 102): **105,103,102,100,99 95,90**
CSF £16.98 CT £45.31 TOTE £6.90: £3.60, £1.40; EX 19.60 Trifecta £95.20.

Owner Paul J Dixon & Yvonne Lowe **Bred** Horizon Bloodstock Limited **Trained** Babworth, Notts

FOCUS
A modest fillies' sprint handicap and a clear step up from the winner on recent runs.

3848 BETFAIR STABLE STAFF WEEK CLASSIFIED STKS — 7f

4:10 (4:10) (Class 3) 4-Y-O+ **£7,762** (£2,310; £1,154; £577) **Stalls** High

Form RPR

5322 **1** **George Cinq**[19] 3188 6-9-3 89... JamesDoyle 5 95
(George Scott) *trckd ldrs: smooth hdwy over 1f out: shkn up to ld jst appr fnl f: rdn out* **13/8**[1]

-001 **2** *nk* **Pastoral Player**[21] 3101 9-8-12 88........................ CharlieBennett(5) 2 94
(Hughie Morrison) *t.k.h: trckd ldrs on outer: hdwy wl over 1f out: rdn to chal ent fnl f: sn drvn and kpt on wl towards fin* **9/2**

-620 **3** *1 ¾* **Jack's Revenge (IRE)**[28] 2868 8-9-3 88.......................(bt) PatCosgrave 9 89
(George Baker) *hld up in rr: rdn along and outpcd over 2f out: swtchd rt over 1f out: styd on u.p fnl f: nrst fin* **4/1**[3]

5440 **4** *½* **Bint Dandy (IRE)**[16] 3271 5-8-11 87..................(b) JosephineGordon(3) 1 85
(Chris Dwyer) *chsd ldr: effrt 2f out: sn rdn and kpt on same pce fnl f* **3/1**[2]

550- **5** *2 ½* **Sakhee's Return**[225] 7898 4-9-3 87.................................. DuranFentiman 6 82
(Tim Easterby) *slt ld at stdy pce: rdn and qckn jst over 2f out: drvn and hdd appr fnl f: sn wknd* **10/1**

1m 29.95s (3.65) **Going Correction** +0.625s/f (Yiel) **5** Ran SP% **110.4**
Speed ratings (Par 107): **104,103,101,101,98**
CSF £9.25 TOTE £2.00: £1.10, £2.00; EX 8.60 Trifecta £18.60.

Owner Breen, Bryan, Humphreys & Randle **Bred** Oakhill Stud **Trained** Newmarket, Suffolk

FOCUS
There was a fair pace on in this good-quality conditions event. The first two have been rated to form.

3849 BARCLAYS SUPPORTING RACING WELFARE CLAIMING STKS — 1m (S)

4:40 (4:40) (Class 5) 4-Y-O+ **£3,234** (£962; £481; £240) **Stalls** High

Form RPR

006 **1** **Yourartisonfire**[9] 3518 6-9-0 85.............................(v) JordanVaughan(5) 1 86
(K R Burke) *trckd ldrs: hdwy over 2f out: rdn to ld over 1f out: styd on* **15/8**[1]

3005 **2** *1 ½* **Our Boy Jack (IRE)**[13] 3421 7-8-13 77...................... GeorgeChaloner 6 77
(Richard Fahey) *trckd ldrs: hdwy 2f out: rdn over 1f out: drvn to chse wnr ins fnl f: no imp* **7/1**

0130 **3** *1 ¾* **Anton Chigurh**[13] 3398 7-8-8 70.................................. AnnaHesketh(5) 2 73
(Tom Dascombe) *trckd ldrs: hdwy to ld wl over 2f out: rdn along and hdd over 1f out: drvn and kpt on same pce fnl f* **12/1**

5100 **4** *6* **Samsonite (IRE)**[15] 3327 4-8-9 60.. KevinStott 4 55
(Tony Coyle) *hld up and bhd: hdwy over 2f out: rdn wl over 1f out: plugged on: n.d* **22/1**

-340 **5** *3 ½* **Baltic Brave (IRE)**[22] 3061 5-9-11 84...............................(t) RyanMoore 5 63
(Hughie Morrison) *hld up towards rr: sme hdwy over 2f out: sn rdn and nvr a factor* **5/2**[2]

635- **6** *1* **Conry (IRE)**[324] 5261 10-8-13 68.................................. StevieDonohoe 3 49
(Ian Williams) *a towards rr* **33/1**

0-62 **7** *5* **Balducci**[13] 3421 9-8-11 83 ....(b) SamJames 8 35
(David Loughnane) *cl up: led after 3f: rdn along and hdd wl over 2f out: sn wknd* **4/1**[3]
4-00 **8** *76* **Walk Like A Giant**[16] 3294 5-8-10 68 ....(b[1]) PaulMulrennan 7
(Julia Brooke) *slt ld 3f: rdn along over 3f out: sn wknd and wl bhd fnl 2f* **33/1**
1m 46.86s (7.56) **Going Correction** +0.85s/f (Soft) **8** Ran SP% **113.8**
Speed ratings (Par 103): **96,94,92,86,83 82,77,1**
CSF £15.30 TOTE £2.40: £1.20, £2.60, £2.60; EX 16.50 Trifecta £110.80.
Owner J O'Shea, W Rooney & Ontoawinner **Bred** J A And Mrs M A Knox **Trained** Middleham Moor, N Yorks

FOCUS
The rain arrived again prior to this fair claimer. Only the principals mattered from 2f out and a race to rate cautiously.

3850 RACING WELFARE THE HELPING HAND MAIDEN FILLIES' STKS 7f
5:15 (5:19) (Class 5) 3-Y-O+ **£3,881** (£1,155; £577; £288) **Stalls** High

Form RPR
0-23 **1** **Delve (IRE)**[28] 2877 3-9-0 87 .... RyanMoore 7 88+
(Sir Michael Stoute) *trckd ldrs: led over 3f out: pushed clr over 1f out: kpt on strly* **5/6**[1]
2 *5* **Hilldale** 3-9-0 0 .... PaulMulrennan 1 72+
(Michael Dods) *dwlt and towards rr: hdwy over 2f out: rdn and styd on fnl f: no ch w wnr* **14/1**
0 **3** *1 1/4* **Wonderful Life (IRE)**[50] 2177 3-9-0 0 .... HarryBentley 9 69
(Richard Spencer) *towards rr: hdwy wl over 2f out: rdn to chse wnr wl over 1f out: drvn and kpt on same pce appr fnl f* **8/1**
0 **4** *10* **Corella (IRE)**[22] 3059 3-9-0 0 .... AdamKirby 11 43
(Clive Cox) *t.k.h early: trckd ldrs: pushed along wl over 2f out: rdn wl over 1f out: sn one pce* **16/1**
2 **5** *1* **Al Hawraa**[23] 3014 3-9-0 0 .... KevinStott 5 40
(Kevin Ryan) *prom: rdn along wl over 2f out: sn wknd* **13/2**[3]
6 *1 3/4* **Soundstrings** 3-9-0 0 .... PatCosgrave 6 36+
(William Haggas) *trckd ldrs: pushed along over 2f out: rdn: green and edgd rt wl over 1f out: wknd* **5/2**[2]
0-00 **7** *6* **Fool's Dream**[56] 2019 3-9-0 44 .... SamJames 8 20
(Bryan Smart) *nvr bttr than midfield* **66/1**
00 **8** *hd* **Bravadora (IRE)**[47] 2271 3-9-0 0 ....[1] DaleSwift 2 19
(Scott Dixon) *led: rdn along 1/2-way: sn hdd & wknd* **100/1**
- **9** *11* **Cytringan** 3-8-11 0 .... SimonPearce(3) 10
(Lydia Pearce) *dwlt: a in rr* **50/1**
0-00 **10** *3* **Euro Mac**[31] 2773 4-9-5 45 .... JacobButterfield(3) 3
(Neville Bycroft) *chsd ldrs: rdn along 1/2-way: sn lost pl and bhd* **80/1**
1m 31.41s (5.11) **Going Correction** +0.85s/f (Soft)
WFA 3 from 4yo 8lb **10** Ran SP% **125.8**
Speed ratings (Par 100): **104,98,96,85,84 82,75,75,62,59**
CSF £18.17 TOTE £1.80: £1.10, £3.70, £2.90; EX 16.10 Trifecta £74.00.
Owner James Wigan **Bred** London Thoroughbred Services Ltd **Trained** Newmarket, Suffolk

FOCUS
An uncompetitive fillies' maiden, rated around the odds-on winner.
T/Plt: £60.30 to a £1 stake. Pool: £76,551.05 - 925.45 winning tickets T/Qpdt: £9.30 to a £1 stake. Pool: £6,300.21 - 498.04 winning tickets **Joe Rowntree**

3804 HAYDOCK (L-H)
Friday, July 1

OFFICIAL GOING: Heavy (6.0)
Wind: Moderate, half against Weather: heavy showers prior to racing

3851 BETFRED "WIN TICKETS ON OUR FACEBOOK" APPRENTICE TRAINING SERIES H'CAP 5f
6:30 (6:30) (Class 5) (0-75,75) 3-Y-O+ **£2,911** (£866; £432; £216) **Stalls** Centre

Form RPR
242 **1** **Orient Class**[15] 3326 5-9-4 67 .... AdamMcNamara(2) 5 75
(Paul Midgley) *chsd ldrs: led over 1f out: edgd lft ins fnl f: kpt on wl* **2/1**[1]
3320 **2** *1* **Hit The Lights (IRE)**[4] 3713 6-9-3 68 .... DanielleMooney(4) 6 72
(David Nicholls) *a.p: rdn over 1f out: kpt on ins fnl f: a hld* **9/2**
0033 **3** *6* **Toni's A Star**[13] 3397 4-8-13 62 .... GeorgiaCox(2) 4 44
(Tony Carroll) *chsd ldrs: effrt to ld 2f out: edgd lft and hdd over 1f out: btn fnl f* **3/1**[3]
546 **4** *3/4* **Bahango (IRE)**[17] 3268 4-8-8 57 ....(p) RowanScott(2) 1 37
(Patrick Morris) *led: hdd 2f out: wknd fnl f* **12/1**
0034 **5** *11* **Musharrif**[18] 3217 4-9-10 75 .... GerO'Neill(4) 2 15
(Declan Carroll) *in rr: u.p 1/2-way: wl bhd over 1f out* **11/4**[2]
1m 4.06s (3.26) **Going Correction** +0.775s/f (Yiel)
WFA 3 from 4yo+ 5lb **5** Ran SP% **110.9**
Speed ratings (Par 103): **104,102,92,91,74**
CSF £11.29 TOTE £2.80: £2.60, £1.80; EX 12.70 Trifecta £24.30.
Owner F Brady,A Williams,P Lindley,S Wibberley **Bred** Frank Brady **Trained** Westow, N Yorks

FOCUS
There had been plenty of rain and the going was given as heavy (GoingStick: 6.0). All races were run over the Inner Home Straight. A modest sprint with the winner taking a small step up on recent form.

3852 BETFRED "LOOKING FORWARD TO JESS GLYNNE" NURSERY H'CAP 6f
7:00 (7:01) (Class 5) 2-Y-O **£3,234** (£962; £481; £240) **Stalls** Centre

Form RPR
024 **1** **Tawny Port**[27] 2913 2-8-9 63 .... DougieCostello 1 71
(James Given) *in tch: effrt over 2f out: led over 1f out: rdn out and styd on* **4/1**[3]
016 **2** *1 3/4* **Letmestopyouthere (IRE)**[58] 1965 2-9-4 75 .... TomMarquand(3) 6 78
(David Evans) *in rr: rdn over 2f out: hdwy over 1f out to chse wnr: hung lft ins fnl f: no imp* **3/1**[2]
445 **3** *2 3/4* **Tagur (IRE)**[16] 3283 2-9-1 69 .... ShaneGray 4 64
(Kevin Ryan) *hld up: outpcd 1/2-way: sme hdwy 1f out: kpt on ins fnl f: nt pce to trble front two* **11/2**
244 **4** *hd* **Sidewinder (IRE)**[22] 3054 2-9-5 73 ....(p) RichardKingscote 2 67
(Tom Dascombe) *led for 2f: remained prom: rdn and ev ch over 1f out: kpt on same pce ins fnl f* **5/2**[1]
4444 **5** *1/2* **Bonnie Arlene (IRE)**[19] 3186 2-8-9 63 .... FrannyNorton 3 55
(Mark Johnston) *chsd ldrs: rdn and lost pl 2f out: outpcd over 1f out: plugged on towards fin but n.d* **13/2**
534 **6** *1 1/2* **Trois Bon Amis (IRE)**[18] 3223 2-8-13 67 .... AndrewMullen 7 55
(Tim Easterby) *prom: j. path early on: led after 2f: rdn 2f out: hdd over 1f out: wknd ins fnl f* **14/1**
1m 19.07s (5.27) **Going Correction** +0.775s/f (Yiel) **6** Ran SP% **109.0**
Speed ratings (Par 94): **95,92,89,88,88 86**
CSF £15.31 TOTE £4.80: £2.00, £3.40; EX 18.00 Trifecta £48.70.
Owner Tawny Port Ptners & Lovely Bubbly Racing **Bred** Mrs D O'Brien **Trained** Willoughton, Lincs

FOCUS
The leaders went off pretty fast given the conditions and the first three were the ones held up early. The form is taken at face value.

3853 BETFRED "NEW LADIES DAY 6TH AUGUST" H'CAP 1m 2f 95y
7:30 (7:30) (Class 4) (0-80,78) 3-Y-O **£5,175** (£1,540; £769; £384) **Stalls** Centre

Form RPR
45-3 **1** **Jaameh (IRE)**[14] 3343 3-9-4 75 .... FrannyNorton 4 81+
(Mark Johnston) *chsd ldr: rdn whn hmpd and carried rt over 1f out: r.o gamely to ld towards fin* **5/1**[3]
2152 **2** *nk* **Town's History (USA)**[22] 3079 3-9-7 78 .... JamesDoyle 2 83+
(Saeed bin Suroor) *hld up in rr: hdwy gng wl 2f out: led over 1f out: sn rdn: hdd towards fin* **13/8**[1]
-623 **3** *1 1/2* **Torremar (FR)**[14] 3365 3-9-1 72 .... KeaganLatham 8 74
(Kevin Ryan) *hld up: rdn over 2f out: hdwy over 1f out: kpt on ins fnl f: no imp on front two* **4/1**[2]
533 **4** *3/4* **Just Hiss**[59] 1953 3-9-4 75 .... AndrewMullen 1 76
(Tim Easterby) *chsd ldrs: rdn and edgd rt over 1f out: nt qckn ins fnl f: kpt on same pce* **6/1**
4304 **5** *hd* **Perceysvivace**[14] 3365 3-8-5 62 ....(p) PatrickMathers 6 62
(Richard Fahey) *led: pushed along over 2f out: rdn and edgd rt whn hdd over 1f out: kpt on same pce ins fnl f* **9/1**
-034 **6** *5* **Shadow Spirit**[22] 3071 3-9-0 74 .... TomMarquand(3) 5 65
(James Eustace) *chsd ldrs tl rdn and wknd over 1f out* **8/1**
2m 19.93s (4.43) **Going Correction** +0.55s/f (Yiel) **6** Ran SP% **110.2**
Speed ratings (Par 102): **104,103,102,101,101 97**
CSF £13.09 CT £31.98 TOTE £6.10: £2.00, £2.20; EX 11.60 Trifecta £75.10.
Owner Hamdan Al Maktoum **Bred** Peter & Hugh McCutcheon **Trained** Middleham Moor, N Yorks

FOCUS
Race distance reduced by 5yds. The early gallop wasn't that strong and they finished quite well bunched. The winner was taking a biggish step up from his maiden form.

3854 LONGINES IRISH CHAMPIONS WEEKEND EBF MAIDEN STKS (PLUS 10 RACE) 7f
8:00 (8:01) (Class 4) 2-Y-O **£4,269** (£1,270; £634; £317) **Stalls** Low

Form RPR
4 **1** **Londinium**[13] 3408 2-9-5 0 .... JamesDoyle 2 76
(Mark Johnston) *chsd ldrs: rdn over 1f out: led fnl 110yds: hld on wl nr fin* **15/8**[1]
2 *nk* **Tommy Taylor (USA)** 2-9-5 0 .... ShaneGray 8 75+
(Kevin Ryan) *midfield: rdn and lost pl over 4f out: outpcd after: hung lft and hdwy over 1f out: tk 2nd fnl 50yds and r.o* **9/2**[2]
3 *1* **Navarone (IRE)** 2-9-5 0 .... DavidNolan 3 73+
(Richard Fahey) *midfield: hdwy over 3f out: led 2f out: rn green and jinked lft ins fnl f: hdd fnl 110yds: no ex nr fin* **5/1**[3]
6 **4** *nk* **Ok By Me (IRE)**[35] 2648 2-9-0 0 .... JFEgan 9 67
(David Evans) *midfield: rdn 2f out: hdwy over 1f out: chsd ldrs ins fnl f: styd on u.p: nt quite pce of ldrs* **5/1**[3]
0 **5** *3 1/2* **Hugging The Rails (IRE)**[35] 2649 2-9-5 0 .... AndrewMullen 4 63
(Tim Easterby) *chsd ldrs: rdn over 1f out: kpt on same pce fnl 100yds* **18/1**
6 *3/4* **Withnell** 2-9-5 0 .... BenCurtis 1 61
(Brian Ellison) *midfield: rdn and outpcd over 2f out: styd on ins fnl f nt get to ldrs* **16/1**
40 **7** *1/2* **Servo (IRE)**[18] 3223 2-9-5 0 .... NeilFarley 11 60
(Alan Swinbank) *racd keenly: hld up: rdn over 2f out: edgd lft over 1f out: nvr a threat* **33/1**
0 **8** *1/2* **Baker Street**[21] 3108 2-9-5 0 .... RichardKingscote 6 59+
(Tom Dascombe) *led: rdn and hdd 2f out: wknd ins fnl f* **7/1**
6 **9** *1 1/2* **Bahkit (IRE)**[13] 3416 2-9-2 0 .... TomMarquand(3) 5 55+
(Alan Swinbank) *chsd ldrs: rdn over 2f out: wknd over 1f out* **33/1**
10 *30* **Bobbys Helmet (IRE)** 2-9-5 0 .... DougieCostello 10
(David C Griffiths) *missed break: in rr: lft bhd 3f out: eased whn wl btn ins fnl f* **16/1**
1m 34.69s (3.99) **Going Correction** +0.55s/f (Yiel) **10** Ran SP% **121.7**
Speed ratings (Par 96): **99,98,97,97,93 92,91,91,89,55**
CSF £10.75 TOTE £2.70: £1.60, £1.60, £1.80; EX 12.30 Trifecta £36.10.
Owner Sheikh Hamdan bin Mohammed Al Maktoum **Bred** Darley **Trained** Middleham Moor, N Yorks

FOCUS
Race distance reduced by 5yds. A fair maiden, but a compressed finish on the bad ground.

3855 BETFRED "THANKS OUR STAFF HERE TONIGHT" H'CAP 1m
8:30 (8:30) (Class 3) (0-95,94) 3-Y-O+ **£8,086** (£2,406; £1,202; £601) **Stalls** Low

Form RPR
4000 **1** **Silvery Moon (IRE)**[22] 3055 9-9-1 86 .... RachelRichardson(5) 2 95
(Tim Easterby) *hld up: hdwy 5f out: rdn and wnt 2nd over 2f out: styd on to ld fnl 100yds: kpt on cl home* **7/1**
5355 **2** *1* **Dance Of Fire**[9] 3534 4-9-4 87 .... RobHornby(3) 4 94
(Andrew Balding) *hld up in rr: hdwy over 2f out: styd on to take 2nd towards fin: nt quite get to wnr* **4/1**[2]
1111 **3** *1/2* **Ice Slice (IRE)**[34] 2689 5-9-11 91 .... RyanTate 8 97
(James Eustace) *led: rdn over 1f out: hdd fnl 100yds: no ex nr fin* **3/1**[1]
1201 **4** *9* **Chosen Character (IRE)**[13] 3398 8-8-13 79 ....(vt) RichardKingscote 1 64
(Tom Dascombe) *chsd ldr tl rdn over 2f out: wknd over 1f out* **5/1**[3]
504 **5** *1* **Indy (IRE)**[15] 3324 5-9-1 88 .... RowanScott(7) 5 71
(David Barron) *hld up: pushed along and outpcd over 3f out: edgd lft u.p over 1f out: plugged on but no threat fnl f* **8/1**
6235 **6** *hd* **Mont Ras (IRE)**[8] 3565 9-10-0 94 .... SamJames 3 76
(David Loughnane) *chsd ldrs: rdn 3f out: wknd over 1f out* **14/1**
-501 **7** *6* **Zealous (IRE)**[19] 3187 3-8-9 84 ow1 .... DarryllHolland 7 50
(Alan Swinbank) *prom: rdn 3f out: lost pl and wknd 2f out* **3/1**[1]
1m 46.49s (2.79) **Going Correction** +0.55s/f (Yiel)
WFA 3 from 4yo+ 9lb **7** Ran SP% **116.9**
Speed ratings (Par 107): **108,107,106,97,96 96,90**
CSF £36.16 CT £103.15 TOTE £7.40: £3.20, £2.30; EX 40.00 Trifecta £124.90.
Owner C H Stevens **Bred** Colin Kennedy **Trained** Great Habton, N Yorks

FOCUS
Race distance reduced by 5yds. An open handicap with the winner rated back to his best.

3856 BETFRED "VISIT OUR SHOPS ON-COURSE" MAIDEN STKS 1m
9:00 (9:02) (Class 5) 3-Y-0+ **£2,911** (£866; £432; £216) **Stalls** Low

Form RPR

33 **1** **Throckley**[30] 2804 5-9-9 0 TomMarquand(3) 5 84
(John Davies) *midfield: hdwy over 3f out: c through between horses to ld fnl 150yds: r.o* **11/2**[3]

6- **2** 1 ¾ **Confident Kid**[336] 4831 3-9-3 0 JamesDoyle 1 78
(Saeed bin Suroor) *led: rdn ins fnl f: hdd fnl 150yds: hld towards fin* **7/4**[1]

-002 **3** 1 ¼ **La Celebs Ville (IRE)**[13] 3399 3-8-12 69 RichardKingscote 3 70
(Tom Dascombe) *prom: rdn over 2f out: ev ch over 1f out: no ex towards fin* **2/1**[2]

63 **4** 2 **Al Nasser Alwashik**[10] 3483 3-9-3 0 SamJames 9 70
(David Loughnane) *trckd ldrs: ev ch 2f out: rdn and hung lft over 1f out: no ex fnl 150yds* **9/1**

5 6 **Eastern Shore (IRE)** 3-9-3 0 DougieCostello 2 57
(K R Burke) *trckd ldrs: rdn 2f out: wknd over 1f out* **22/1**

6 6 **Agha Des Mottes (FR)**[210] 6-9-12 0 DavidNolan 4 45
(Ian Williams) *s.i.s: hld up: pushed along over 3f out: outpcd 2f out: wl btn* **33/1**

6-0 **7** ½ **Frozon**[62] 1849 3-9-3 0 BenCurtis 11 42+
(Brian Ellison) *racd keenly: hld up: lft bhd over 1f out* **20/1**

0- **8** ¾ **Ravelin (USA)**[244] 7628 3-8-12 0 FrannyNorton 6 35
(Charles Hills) *prom tl rdn and wknd over 1f out* **20/1**

9 shd **Go George Go (IRE)** 3-9-3 0 DarryllHolland 8 40
(Alan Swinbank) *midfield: lost pl 4f out: outpcd after* **14/1**

0 **10** 15 **Declined**[69] 1622 4-9-12 0 ShaneGray 7 7
(David C Griffiths) *in rr: lft wl bhd over 2f out: eased whn btn ins fnl f* **22/1**

1m 48.41s (4.71) **Going Correction** +0.55s/f (Yiel)
WFA 3 from 4yo+ 9lb **10** Ran SP% **122.9**
Speed ratings (Par 103): **98,96,95,93,87 81,80,79,79,64**
CSF £15.25 TOTE £6.90: £1.70, £1.20, £1.40; EX 18.40 Trifecta £47.10.
Owner The Maroon Stud **Bred** The Maroon Stud **Trained** Piercebridge, Durham

FOCUS
Race distance reduced by 5yds. A modest maiden with an ordinary standard set by the third.
T/Plt: £51.50 to a £1 stake. Pool: £47,097.00 - 914.28 winning tickets T/Qpdt: £11.80 to a £1 stake. Pool: £3,979.00 - 355.70 winning tickets **Darren Owen**

3155 SANDOWN (R-H)
Friday, July 1

OFFICIAL GOING: Sprint course: soft (good to soft in places); round course: good to soft (good in places)
Wind: Moderate, against Weather: Overcast becoming brighter

3857 RACING WELFARE STABLE STAFF "PALACEGATE TOUCH" H'CAP 5f 6y
2:20 (2:21) (Class 3) (0-95,95) 3-Y-0+
£7,470 (£2,236; £1,118; £559; £279; £140) **Stalls** Low

Form RPR

1163 **1** **Ladweb**[19] 3193 6-8-9 **78** MichaelJMMurphy 2 87
(John Gallagher) *lw: pressed ldr over 3f out: led 2f out and sn kicked 2 l clr: hrd pressed last 100yds: hld on wl* **7/2**[2]

100- **2** ½ **Union Rose**[251] 7461 4-9-12 **95** (p) MartinHarley 8 102
(Ronald Harris) *racd wd: in tch: rdn and prog to chse wnr over 1f out: clsd to chal last 100yds: styd on but no imp nr fin* **25/1**

5-00 **3** 2 ¾ **Sahreej (IRE)**[13] 3393 3-8-13 **87** PaulHanagan 3 82
(Charles Hills) *s.i.s: sn in midfield: rdn and prog to take 3rd over 1f out: kpt on but no imp on ldng pair* **6/1**[3]

3-0 **4** 1 ½ **Exceed The Limit**[49] 3-9-4 **92** (p) JamieSpencer 7 82
(Robert Cowell) *tall: hld up in last pair: shkn up 2f out: prog to take 4th ins fnl f: n.d* **7/1**

00-5 **5** 1 **Newton's Law (IRE)**[19] 3193 5-8-3 **79** (t) JordanUys(7) 5 67
(Brian Meehan) *s.i.s: pushed along in last pair 1/2-way: no prog tl kpt on fnl f* **8/1**

110- **6** nk **Threave**[266] 7091 8-9-5 **88** GeorgeBaker 6 75
(Laura Mongan) *racd towards outer: chsd ldrs: pushed along and lost pl 2f out: sn btn* **12/1**

6016 **7** 2 ¾ **Stake Acclaim (IRE)**[62] 1857 4-9-6 **89** (p) RobertWinston 1 66
(Dean Ivory) *chsd ldr to over 3f out: styd handy tl wknd over 1f out* **15/8**[1]

000- **8** 3 ¼ **Elysian Flyer (IRE)**[188] 8356 4-9-12 **95** ShaneKelly 4 61
(Richard Hughes) *led and crossed to far rail: hdd 2f out: wknd qckly over 1f out* **16/1**

1m 3.44s (1.84) **Going Correction** +0.575s/f (Yiel)
WFA 3 from 4yo+ 5lb **8** Ran SP% **112.3**
Speed ratings (Par 107): **108,107,102,100,98 98,93,88**
CSF £77.84 CT £507.47 TOTE £4.70: £1.50, £4.50, £2.30; EX 84.80 Trifecta £723.60.
Owner The Juniper Racing Club & Andrew Bell **Bred** Adweb Ltd **Trained** Chastleton, Oxon

FOCUS
The ground had dried out a little from previously forecast and was now soft, good to soft in places on the 5f course and good to soft, good in places on the round course. Rail out from 1m1f to winning post, adding 30yds to race distances on the round course. A decent sprint handicap to start, but several of these had a question mark over their current well-being and a few were returning from absences and/or making their debut for new stables. The first two pulled well clear and the winner's effort fits in with past form.

3858 RACINGUK/DAYPASS DRAGON STKS (LISTED RACE) 5f 6y
2:50 (2:50) (Class 1) 2-Y-0
£14,744 (£5,590; £2,797; £1,393; £699; £351) **Stalls** Low

Form RPR

1222 **1** **The Last Lion (IRE)**[15] 3295 2-9-2 0 FrannyNorton 8 101+
(Mark Johnston) *pressed ldrs on outer: led 2f out and sn clr: rdn out fnl f but nvr in any danger* **10/11**[1]

2 **2** 2 **Smokey Lane (IRE)**[13] 3388 2-9-2 0 ShaneKelly 4 94
(David Evans) *athletic: rdn in last trio bef 1/2-way: prog and swtchd lft to outer over 1f out: drvn to take 2nd jst ins fnl f: styd on but unable to threaten* **20/1**

30 **3** 2 ¾ **Just An Idea (IRE)**[17] 3247 2-9-2 0 MartinHarley 2 84
(Harry Dunlop) *w ldr: led fr 1/2-way to 2f out: chsd clr wnr after tl jst ins fnl f: one pce* **12/1**

2161 **4** 1 ½ **Pretty Vacant**[6] 3647 2-9-2 0 AndreaAtzeni 1 79
(Roger Varian) *narrow ldr against far rail to 1/2-way: rdn 2f out: sn outpcd* **9/4**[2]

3331 **5** 1 ¾ **El Torito (IRE)**[18] 3231 2-9-2 0 SamHitchcott 6 72
(Jim Boyle) *w'like: leggy: a in last trio: rdn and no prog 1/2-way: no ch whn sltly impeded over 1f out* **33/1**

553 **6** 1 ¼ **Await The Storm (IRE)**[15] 3321 2-9-2 0 (v[1]) JimmyFortune 7 68
(Brian Meehan) *pushed along in last pair by 1/2-way: no prog and nvr a factor* **50/1**

1100 **7** 8 **Stormy Clouds (IRE)**[16] 3270 2-8-11 0 SeanLevey 3 34
(Richard Hannon) *w ldrs to 2f out: wknd rapidly: t.o* **8/1**[3]

1m 4.2s (2.60) **Going Correction** +0.575s/f (Yiel) **7** Ran SP% **111.6**
Speed ratings (Par 102): **102,98,94,92,89 87,74**
CSF £22.17 TOTE £1.60: £1.10, £7.70; EX 18.50 Trifecta £80.30.
Owner John Brown & Megan Dennis **Bred** Barronstown Stud And Mrs T Stack **Trained** Middleham Moor, N Yorks

FOCUS
Probably not the most competitive of Listed events and class eventually told. Nine of the last ten winners of this contest had won at least once before and that trend continued.

3859 LONGINES IRISH CHAMPIONS WEEKEND EBF MAIDEN STKS 7f 16y
3:25 (3:25) (Class 5) 2-Y-0 **£3,881** (£1,155; £577; £288) **Stalls** Low

Form RPR

1 **Larchmont Lad (IRE)** 2-9-5 0 SeanLevey 12 86+
(Richard Hannon) *athletic: chsd ldrs on outer: rdn and prog over 2f out: led over 1f out: drew clr fnl f* **8/1**[3]

2 3 ¼ **Maths Prize** 2-9-5 0 GeorgeBaker 7 78+
(Roger Charlton) *lengthy: lw: hld up and sn in last pair: pushed along over 2f out: gd prog on outer over 1f out: r.o to take 2nd nr fin: no ch to threaten wnr* **9/2**[2]

3 ½ **Plant Pot Power (IRE)** 2-9-5 0 PatDobbs 3 76
(Richard Hannon) *tall: str: lw: trckd ldng trio: smooth prog to ld 2f out: shkn up and hdd over 1f out: nt qckn and sn outpcd: lost 2nd nr fin* **8/1**[3]

4 1 ¾ **Naval Warfare (IRE)** 2-9-5 0 WilliamBuick 6 72+
(Andrew Balding) *str: lw: chsd ldrs: pushed along 3f out: styd on same pce fr 2f out to take 4th ins fnl f: n.d* **7/2**[1]

5 ½ **Western Duke (IRE)** 2-9-5 0 JohnFahy 9 70
(Ralph Beckett) *tall: bit bkwd: towards rr on outer: shkn up over 2f out: prog over 1f out to chse ldrs: one pce fnl f* **8/1**[3]

36 **6** hd **Oceanus (IRE)**[34] 2682 2-9-5 0 AndreaAtzeni 5 70
(Ed Dunlop) *t.k.h: trckd ldng pair: rdn and tried to cl 2f out: one pce fr over 1f out* **9/2**[2]

7 1 ¼ **Glendun (USA)** 2-9-5 0 JimmyFortune 2 67
(Brian Meehan) *w'like: leggy: a in midfield: shkn up and no imp on ldrs over 2f out: n.d after* **14/1**

8 hd **City Dreamer (IRE)** 2-9-5 0 FergusSweeney 10 66
(Alan King) *leggy: cls cpld: dwlt: mostly in last pair: pushed along over 2f out: kpt on and reminder 1f out: nvr nrr: nt disgracd* **14/1**

9 hd **Onomatopoeia** 2-9-0 0 RobertHavlin 11 61
(Roger Ingram) *lengthy: str: led: clr 1/2-way: hdd & wknd 2f out* **50/1**

10 ½ **Arborist (IRE)** 2-9-5 0 PaulHanagan 8 64
(Sylvester Kirk) *athletic: hld up towards rr: pushed along 3f out: no prog* **12/1**

11 7 **Junoesque** 2-9-0 0 MichaelJMMurphy 4 41
(John Gallagher) *w'like: leggy: dwlt: a in last trio: shkn up and no prog 3f out: bhd over 1f out* **25/1**

12 1 ¾ **Rakematiz** 2-9-2 0 DannyBrock(3) 1 42
(Brett Johnson) *str: chsd ldr: rdn 3f out: lost 2nd and wknd rapidly jst over 2f out* **33/1**

1m 33.25s (3.75) **Going Correction** +0.50s/f (Yiel) **12** Ran SP% **121.7**
Speed ratings (Par 94): **98,94,93,91,91 90,89,89,89,88 80,78**
CSF £44.46 TOTE £9.50: £2.80, £2.00, £2.70; EX 55.40 Trifecta £399.40.
Owner Michael Geoghegan **Bred** Domenico Fonzo **Trained** East Everleigh, Wilts

FOCUS
Rail movement added 30yds to race distance. An interesting maiden with only one of these having seen the racecourse before. Unsurprisingly a few caught the eye, including the winner.

3860 AMBANT GALA STKS (LISTED RACE) 1m 2f 7y
4:00 (4:00) (Class 1) 3-Y-0+ **£20,982** (£7,955; £3,981; £1,983; £995) **Stalls** Low

Form RPR

-326 **1** **Ayrad (IRE)**[26] 2947 5-9-5 109 (p) AndreaAtzeni 5 109
(Roger Charlton) *lw: mde virtually all: set mod pce tl kicked for home over 2f out: jnd wl over 1f out: drvn and asserted again last 100yds* **5/4**[1]

-650 **2** ¾ **Spark Plug (IRE)**[16] 3273 5-9-5 102 (p) SeanLevey 3 107
(Brian Meehan) *mostly in cl 4th tl prog to go 2nd 2f out: sn jnd wnr: gd battle after tl nt qckn last 100yds* **7/2**[3]

-100 **3** ¾ **Gm Hopkins**[16] 3273 5-9-8 112 RobertHavlin 2 109
(John Gosden) *lw: trckd ldng pair after 2f: urged along and nt qckn whn pce lifted over 2f out: styd on ins fnl f but nvr able to chal* **9/4**[2]

-400 **4** 1 ¼ **Dessertoflife (IRE)**[15] 3297 3-8-3 99 FrannyNorton 4 98
(Mark Johnston) *pressed ldr to 2f out: one pce u.p after* **10/1**

606- **5** 3 ¼ **Jelly Monger (IRE)**[207] 8139 4-9-0 90 JimCrowley 6 92
(Dominic Ffrench Davis) *broke wl but restrained into last: rdn and outpcd whn pce lifted over 2f out: nvr on terms after* **33/1**

2m 14.6s (4.10) **Going Correction** +0.50s/f (Yiel)
WFA 3 from 4yo+ 11lb **5** Ran SP% **109.5**
Speed ratings (Par 111): **103,102,101,100,98**
CSF £5.92 TOTE £2.00: £1.20, £1.90; EX 5.70 Trifecta £12.10.
Owner Saleh Al Homaizi & Imad Al Sagar **Bred** Gerrardstown House Stud **Trained** Beckhampton, Wilts

FOCUS
Rail movement added 30yds to race distance. Not the most competitive of Listed events and a dawdling early gallop meant this became tactical, but the winner was given a well-judged ride.

3861 PAY FOR RACINGUK VIA PHONE BILL H'CAP 1m 2f 7y
4:30 (4:32) (Class 3) (0-95,92) 3-Y-0+
£7,470 (£2,236; £1,118; £559; £279; £140) **Stalls** Low

Form RPR

1-00 **1** **Zamperini (IRE)**[21] 3109 4-9-6 **84** JimCrowley 4 93+
(Mike Murphy) *trckd ldrs in 5th: pushed along and waiting for room over 2f out: prog over 1f out: drvn to chse ldr ins fnl f: r.o wl to ld post* **10/1**

3-06 **2** nse **Scrutinise**[41] 2468 4-10-0 **92** AndreaAtzeni 11 101
(Ed Dunlop) *trckd ldng trio: prog on outer to ld jst over 1f out: drvn and r.o fnl f: hdd post* **14/1**

2152 **3** 2 **Both Sides**[21] 3110 3-8-1 **81** EdwardGreatrex(5) 2 89+
(Andrew Balding) *lw: trckd ldng pair: trapped on inner fr over 2f out and twice hmpd whn trying for a gap: in the clr last 150yds and r.o to take 3rd fnl strides* **9/4**[1]

6502 **4** ½ **Fiftyshadesfreed (IRE)**[21] 3109 5-9-7 **85**..................(p) JimmyFortune 1 89
(George Baker) *slowly away: hld up in last pair: rdn and prog fr 2f out: styd on to take 4th last strides: no ch* **12/1**

00-1 **5** nk **Primogeniture (IRE)**[15] 3304 5-9-12 **90**..................... TimmyMurphy 12 93
(Mary Hambro) *trckd ldr: shkn up to ld briefly over 1f out: outpcd fnl f* **20/1**

3031 **6** 1½ **Altarsheed (IRE)**[21] 3102 3-8-13 **88**................................ PaulHanagan 8 88+
(Richard Hannon) *hld up in last trio: shkn up 2f out: sme late hdwy but nvr a real factor* **4/1**[2]

1220 **7** 1 **Whinging Willie (IRE)**[27] 2897 7-9-0 **83**................. HectorCrouch(5) 10 81
(Gary Moore) *t.k.h: hld up in last pair: shkn up on outer over 2f out: no prog and btn over 1f out: one pce* **25/1**

1-51 **8** nse **Oasis Spear**[25] 2978 4-9-10 **88**... GeorgeBaker 6 86
(Chris Wall) *lw: led: rdn over 2f out: hdd over 1f out: fdd* **9/2**[3]

210- **9** nk **Royal Toast (IRE)**[282] 6649 4-9-8 **86**................................... PatDobbs 5 84
(Richard Hannon) *dwlt: hld up in rr: shkn up wl over 1f out: no real prog and nvr involved* **12/1**

1/00 **10** ½ **Pasaka Boy**[28] 2866 6-9-6 **87**... DannyBrock(3) 7 84
(Jonathan Portman) *chsd ldrs in 6th: rdn wl over 2f out: no prog and btn over 1f out: fdd fnl f* **16/1**

2m 14.23s (3.73) **Going Correction** +0.50s/f (Yiel)
WFA 3 from 4yo+ 11lb **10** Ran SP% **114.6**
Speed ratings (Par 107): **105,104,103,102,102 101,100,100,100,100**
CSF £137.88 CT £425.19 TOTE £12.90: £2.80, £4.10, £1.30; EX 166.00 Trifecta £862.50.
Owner Robert E Tillett **Bred** Maurice Craig **Trained** Westoning, Beds

FOCUS
Rail movement added 30yds to race distance. A competitive handicap, but again the pace was modest and, as a result, there wasn't a great deal of room to play with up the home straight.

3862 PAY AND WATCH RACINGUK VIA MOBILE H'CAP 1m 6f
5:05 (5:06) (Class 4) (0-85,85) 3-Y-O+ **£5,175** (£1,540; £769; £384) **Stalls** Low

Form RPR

5214 **1** **The Graduate (IRE)**[9] 3532 3-8-1 **73**................................ JimmyQuinn 2 83+
(Andrew Balding) *trckd ldng pair: led over 2f out: rdn clr 1f out: styd on strly* **11/4**[1]

0611 **2** 2¼ **Jacob Cats**[13] 3409 7-9-12 **83**.......................................(v) AndreaAtzeni 8 90
(William Knight) *stdd s: hld up in last: shkn up wl over 2f out: drvn and prog wl over 1f out: chsd wnr ins fnl f: r.o but no real imp* **10/1**

4-11 **3** 2¾ **The New Pharaoh (IRE)**[20] 3139 5-9-5 **76**...................... GeorgeBaker 9 79
(Chris Wall) *t.k.h: hld up in midfield: clsd over 2f out and disp 2nd sn after: cajoled along and one pce fr jst over 1f out* **5/1**[3]

51-2 **4** ½ **Faithful Mount**[19] 3192 7-9-13 **84**...................................... WilliamBuick 6 86
(Ian Williams) *lw: hld up in tch: prog on outer to chse wnr 2f out: sn no imp and btn: fdd ins fnl f* **9/2**[2]

-422 **5** hd **Champagne Champ**[9] 3533 4-9-6 **77**............................ FrederikTylicki 1 79
(Rod Millman) *led 3f: chsd ldr: urged along and fnd nil 3f out: lost pl and btn 2f out: kpt on nr fin* **9/2**[2]

0-64 **6** 1 **Spice Fair**[14] 3351 9-9-11 **82**.. JimmyFortune 7 83
(Mark Usher) *stdd s: hld up in last pair: shkn up wl over 2f out: no great prog* **16/1**

2331 **7** ½ **Be My Sea (IRE)**[29] 2820 5-9-8 **79**................................ WilliamCarson 3 79
(Tony Carroll) *trckd ldrs: shkn up over 3f out: stl wl in tch over 1f out: fdd* **12/1**

6-23 **8** 17 **Desdichado**[20] 3161 4-9-9 **80**.. JamieSpencer 4 56
(Ralph Beckett) *awkward s and shkn up early: prog to ld after 3f: hdd & wknd over 2f out: t.o* **15/2**

3m 9.08s (4.58) **Going Correction** +0.50s/f (Yiel)
WFA 3 from 4yo+ 15lb **8** Ran SP% **114.1**
Speed ratings (Par 105): **106,104,103,102,102 102,101,92**
CSF £31.31 CT £130.19 TOTE £3.80: £1.40, £2.20, £1.70; EX 30.90 Trifecta £119.80.
Owner Mick and Janice Mariscotti **Bred** Daniel Chassagneux **Trained** Kingsclere, Hants

FOCUS
Rail movement added 30yds to race distance. A fair staying handicap, but not the severest test at the distance. The field came up the centre on reaching the straight.
T/Plt: £44.00 to a £1 stake. Pool: £82,609.20 - 1,369.37 winning tickets T/Qpdt: £12.80 to a £1 stake. Pool: £6,848.94 - 394.96 winning tickets **Jonathan Neesom**

3863 - 3870a (Foreign Racing) - See Raceform Interactive

CLAIREFONTAINE (R-H)
Friday, July 1

OFFICIAL GOING: Turf: soft

3871a PRIX DES POIRIERS (MAIDEN) (2YO COLTS & GELDINGS) (TURF) 7f
3:15 (12:00) 2-Y-O **£9,191** (£3,676; £2,757; £1,838; £919)

RPR

1 **Pazeer (FR)**[23] 2-9-2 0... ChristopheSoumillon 16 86
(J-C Rouget, France) **9/5**[1]

2 4 **King Of Spades (FR)**[21] 3100 2-9-2 0............................. AlexisBadel 13 76
(Mick Channon) *trckd ldr: rdn and effrt 3f out: kpt on wl for 2nd but no ch w wnr who racd alone against nr side rail in st* **7/2**[2]

3 ¾ **L'Ami Cagnois (FR)**[14] 2-9-2 0...................................... EddyHardouin 9 74
(S Jesus, France) **11/1**

4 nk **Phoceen (FR)**[14] 2-9-2 0.. Pierre-CharlesBoudot 7 73
(F Chappet, France) **9/1**[3]

5 nk **Real Value (FR)** 2-8-13 0.. MickaelForest 12 69
(Mario Hofer, Germany) **59/1**

6 snk **Earl (FR)** 2-8-10 0.. HugoJourniac(6) 11 72
(J-C Rouget, France) **10/1**

7 1¼ **Tornibush (IRE)** 2-8-13 0.. FranckBlondel 2 66
(P Decouz, France) **15/1**

8 shd **Something Brewing (FR)** 2-8-13 0........................... AntoineHamelin 4 66
(Matthieu Palussiere, France) **35/1**

9 1½ **Puelo (FR)** 2-9-2 0.. GeraldMosse 5 65
(A De Royer-Dupre, France) **15/1**

10 3 **Ermontois (FR)** 2-9-2 0.. MaximeGuyon 14 57
(L Viel, France) **29/1**

11 3 **Mister Art (IRE)**[24] 2-9-2 0... StephanePasquier 3 49
(Matthieu Palussiere, France) **11/1**

12 2½ **Volare Alto** 2-8-13 0... LouisBeuzelin 8 40
(Miss V Haigh, France) **117/1**

13 1¼ **Diboy (FR)**[9] 2-9-2 0.. FabriceVeron 6 39
(Matthieu Palussiere, France) **37/1**

14 ½ **Sowgay (FR)**[33] 2724 2-9-2 0.......................................(b) AdrienFouassier 1 38
(C Plisson, France) **97/1**

15 hd **American Song (FR)**[15] 2-9-2 0................................(p) RichardJuteau 10 38
(C Plisson, France) **89/1**

16 3 **Petard (FR)** 2-8-13 0.. MickaelBarzalona 15 27
(F Doumen, France) **43/1**

1m 27.7s (87.70) **16** Ran SP% **121.9**
PARI-MUTUEL (all including 1 euro stake): WIN 2.80; PLACE 1.60, 1.80, 2.50; DF 5.80; SF 10.00.
Owner H H Aga Khan **Bred** Haras De S.A. Aga Khan Scea **Trained** Pau, France

3838 BEVERLEY (R-H)
Saturday, July 2

OFFICIAL GOING: Good to soft (soft in places)
Wind: Fresh against Weather: Cloudy & blustery

3872 AWARD-WINNING COACHMAN CARAVANS MAIDEN AUCTION STKS 7f 100y
1:50 (1:51) (Class 5) 2-Y-O **£3,780** (£1,131; £565; £283; £141) **Stalls** Low

Form RPR

03 **1** **Muirsheen Durkin**[11] 3477 2-9-0 0..................................(p) LiamJones 4 75
(Tom Dascombe) *trckd ldr: hdwy to ld over 2f out: rdn clr appr fnl f: kpt on wl* **5/1**[3]

552 **2** 2¾ **Major Cornwallis (IRE)**[9] 3561 2-8-11 0.............. AdamMcNamara(5) 3 70
(Richard Fahey) *trckd ldng pair: hdwy 2f out: rdn over 1f out: drvn and kpt on same pce fnl f* **15/8**[1]

423 **3** ½ **Bridal March**[14] 3404 2-8-10 0... FrannyNorton 1 63
(Mark Johnston) *led: pushed along 3f out: rdn and hdd over 2f out: drvn and kpt on fnl f* **5/2**[2]

0 **4** nk **Sir Viktor (IRE)**[75] 1520 2-9-3 0.. BenCurtis 7 69
(K R Burke) *in tch: hdwy on outer 1 1/2f out: rdn to chse ldrs ent fnl f: sn drvn and kpt on same pce* **8/1**

0 **5** ½ **Dream On Dreamer (IRE)**[10] 3516 2-8-12 0.............. ConnorBeasley 5 63
(Michael Dods) *in tch: effrt wl over 2f out and sn pushed along: hdwy over 1f out: sn rdn and kpt on fnl f: nrst fin* **20/1**

6 1 **Micolys (FR)** 2-8-11 0.. PJMcDonald 9 60+
(K R Burke) *wnt lft s and bhd: hdwy 2f out: rdn and kpt on fnl f: nrst fin* **25/1**

05 **7** ¾ **Our Charlie Brown**[48] 2264 2-9-2 0.................................... JasonHart 8 63
(Tim Easterby) *hld up: a towards rr* **25/1**

30 **8** ½ **He's A Toff (IRE)**[19] 3208 2-9-3 0.............................(b[1]) AndrewMullen 2 63
(Tim Easterby) *dwlt: a in rr* **14/1**

0 **9** 1¾ **Georgio (GER)**[14] 3404 2-9-3 0....................................... PhillipMakin 6 59
(Andrew Balding) *t.k.h: chsd ldrs on outer: pushed along wl over 2f out: rdn wl over 1f out: sn wknd* **14/1**

1m 36.22s (2.42) **Going Correction** +0.275s/f (Good) **9** Ran SP% **116.9**
Speed ratings (Par 94): **97,93,93,92,92 91,90,89,87**
CSF £14.60 TOTE £5.50: £1.30, £1.20, £1.20; EX 18.20 Trifecta £43.80.
Owner The Roaring Twenties **Bred** Lady Bamford **Trained** Malpas, Cheshire

FOCUS
A run-of-the-mill 2yo maiden in which the pace held up, rated around the placed horses.

3873 BRITISH STALLION STUDS LEISURE FURNISHINGS EBF MAIDEN STKS (DIV I) 5f
2:25 (2:27) (Class 5) 2-Y-O **£3,780** (£1,131; £565; £283; £141) **Stalls** Low

Form RPR

1 **Fields Of Song (IRE)** 2-9-0 0... ShaneGray 8 70+
(Kevin Ryan) *hmpd s: in tch: trckd ldrs 2f out: hdwy to ld jst ins fnl f and sn rdn: hld on wl towards fin* **5/1**[3]

0 **2** hd **Sheepscar Lad (IRE)**[19] 3222 2-9-5 0............................. AndrewMullen 1 72
(Nigel Tinkler) *dwlt: sn in tch: hdwy wl over 1f out: rdn to chal and edgd lft ins fnl f: sn drvn and ev ch tl no ex nr fin* **40/1**

2 **3** 4 **Climax**[17] 3290 2-9-0 0.. FrannyNorton 6 55
(Mark Johnston) *cl up: slt ld after 2f: rdn wl over 1f out: drvn and hdd whn hmpd jst ins fnl f: swtchd rt and kpt on same pce after* **6/4**[1]

0 **4** ¾ **Not Now Nadia (IRE)**[26] 2970 2-9-0 0........................ ConnorBeasley 4 50
(Michael Dods) *trckd ldrs: effrt over 1f out: sn rdn and kpt on same pce fnl f* **11/1**

2 **5** nk **Liquid (IRE)**[21] 3148 2-9-5 0.. PJMcDonald 9 54
(David Barron) *trckd ldrs on outer: effrt wl over 1f out: sn rdn and one pce fnl f* **13/8**[2]

60 **6** 1 **Geego**[28] 2913 2-9-0 0.. AdamMcNamara(5) 2 51
(Richard Fahey) *in rr: sn rdn along and outpcd: styd on appr fnl f: nrst fin* **20/1**

50 **7** ½ **Breaking Free**[47] 2301 2-9-5 0.. CamHardie 7 49
(John Quinn) *hmpd s and bhd tl styd on appr fnl f* **16/1**

8 ½ **Rebounded** 2-9-5 0.. NeilFarley 5 47
(Declan Carroll) *qckly away and slt ld 2f: cl up: rdn and ev ch over 1f out: wknd ins fnl f* **25/1**

1m 6.03s (2.53) **Going Correction** +0.325s/f (Good) **8** Ran SP% **120.0**
Speed ratings (Par 94): **92,91,85,84,83 82,81,80**
CSF £183.16 TOTE £6.40: £2.00, £10.40, £1.10; EX 244.40 Trifecta £966.10.
Owner Sheikh Juma Dalmook Al Maktoum **Bred** Ballyreddin Stud **Trained** Hambleton, N Yorks

FOCUS
This modest 2yo maiden saw a pair come nicely clear at the finish.

3874 BRITISH STALLION STUDS LEISURE FURNISHINGS EBF MAIDEN STKS (DIV II) 5f
3:00 (3:01) (Class 5) 2-Y-O **£3,780** (£1,131; £565; £283; £141) **Stalls** Low

Form RPR

3 **1** **Clef**[21] 3134 2-9-0 0.. GeorgeChaloner 1 72
(Richard Fahey) *trckd ldrs: rdn and hdwy over 1f out: drvn to chal ins fnl f: kpt on wl to ld nr fin* **3/1**[2]

2 nk **Lonely The Brave (IRE)** 2-9-5 0................................... FrannyNorton 9 76
(Mark Johnston) *cl up: led 1 1/2f out: sn rdn: drvn ent fnl f: hdd and no ex towards fin* **11/8**[1]

3 1 **Jeany (IRE)** 2-9-0 0.. ConnorBeasley 8 67
(Bryan Smart) *chsd ldrs: rdn along wl over 1f out: drvn and kpt on fnl f* **9/1**[3]

66 **4** 3½ **Trick Of The Lyte (IRE)**[7] 3654 2-9-5 0.............................. JasonHart 5 60
(John Quinn) *wnt rt s: chsd ldrs on inner: rdn along wl over 1f out: kpt on one pce* **20/1**

The Form Book, Raceform Ltd, Newbury, RG14 5SJ

6 **5** 1 3/4 **African Grey**[19] 3222 2-9-5 0.....(e[1]) SamJames 2 53
(David Barron) *wnt lft s: t.k.h and slt ld: rdn along and hdd 1 1/2f out: sn wknd* **3/1**[2]

6 1 1/4 **Gold Patch (IRE)** 2-9-5 0..... JamesSullivan 4 51+
(Michael Easterby) *hmpd s: a towards rr* **20/1**

7 2 1/4 **Magic Journey (IRE)** 2-9-5 0..... CamHardie 3 41
(John Quinn) *hmpd s: a in rr* **14/1**

1m 6.57s (3.07) **Going Correction** +0.325s/f (Good) **7** Ran SP% **118.3**
Speed ratings (Par 94): **88,87,85,80,77 75,71**
CSF £7.95 TOTE £3.70: £1.70, £1.20; EX 7.20 Trifecta £36.50.
Owner Cheveley Park Stud **Bred** Cheveley Park Stud Ltd **Trained** Musley Bank, N Yorks

FOCUS
The second division of the modest sprint 2yo maiden. It was run in a time around half a second slower than the first.

3875 COACHMAN CARAVANS QUALITY H'CAP 5f
3:35 (3:36) (Class 4) (0-85,85) 3-Y-O **£7,561** (£2,263; £1,131; £566; £282) **Stalls** Low

Form RPR

-400 **1** **My Name Is Rio (IRE)**[14] 3419 6-9-12 **85**..... ConnorBeasley 12 95
(Michael Dods) *in rr: hdwy and nt clr run over 1f out: squeezed through ins fnl f: led last 100yds* **5/1**[2]

3000 **2** 1 **Mappin Time (IRE)**[21] 3168 8-9-2 **75**.....(b) AndrewMullen 8 81
(Tim Easterby) *towards rr: gd hdwy wl over 1f out: n.m.r over 1f out: rdn to chal ent fnl f: sn drvn and ev ch: no ex towards fin* **16/1**

-164 **3** hd **Something Lucky (IRE)**[69] 1666 4-9-6 **79**.....(p) RoystonFfrench 2 84
(Kristin Stubbs) *towards rr: gd hdwy on inner wl over 1f out: rdn to chal ent fnl f: ev ch tl drvn and no ex towards fin* **16/1**

0350 **4** 1/2 **Singeur (IRE)**[21] 3168 9-9-4 **77**..... BarryMcHugh 14 80
(Rebecca Bastiman) *towards rr: hdwy on wd outside over 1f out: rdn to chse ldrs and edgd rt ins fnl f: kpt on* **14/1**

0310 **5** 1/2 **Apricot Sky**[9] 3552 6-8-11 **77**..... DanielleMooney(7) 1 78+
(David Nicholls) *trckd ldrs: hdwy and cl up wl over 1f out: rdn to ld ent fnl f: drvn and hdd last 100yds: kpt on same pce towards fin* **8/1**

0060 **6** nk **Whozthecat (IRE)**[7] 3646 9-8-11 **70**.....(t) JasonHart 6 70
(Declan Carroll) *in rr: hdwy on inner over 1f out: rdn and styd on fnl f: nrst fin* **12/1**

6512 **7** 3 1/4 **Imperial Legend (IRE)**[9] 3552 7-9-4 **77**..... FrannyNorton 10 66
(David Nicholls) *chsd ldrs: rdn along over 1f out: grad wknd* **7/1**[3]

2043 **8** hd **One Boy (IRE)**[19] 3217 5-8-10 **74**.....(p) AdamMcNamara(5) 4 62
(Richard Fahey) *trckd ldr: effrt and ev ch over 1f out: rdn and n.m.r ent fnl f: sn wknd* **3/1**[1]

000 **9** 1 **Jack Luey**[9] 3552 9-8-13 **72**.....(b) CamHardie 5 56
(Lawrence Mullaney) *chsd ldrs: rdn along wl over 1f out: sn drvn and wknd* **8/1**

100 **10** 3/4 **Bosham**[8] 3606 6-9-10 **83**.....(bt) JamesSullivan 9 65
(Michael Easterby) *led: rdn wl over 1f out: hdd and drvn ent fnl f: sn wknd* **16/1**

2114 **11** 5 **Eleuthera**[86] 1291 4-9-7 **80**..... ShaneGray 13 44
(Kevin Ryan) *t.k.h: in tch: pushed along 1/2-way: sn rdn and wknd* **8/1**

0600 **12** 6 **Master Bond**[23] 3056 7-9-5 **78**.....(v) SamJames 16 20
(David O'Meara) *chsd ldrs on outer: rdn along 2f out: sn drvn and wknd* **14/1**

1m 4.34s (0.84) **Going Correction** +0.325s/f (Good) **12** Ran SP% **126.2**
Speed ratings (Par 105): **106,104,104,103,102 102,96,96,94,93 85,76**
CSF £88.18 CT £1242.14 TOTE £6.70: £3.00, £6.00, £4.70; EX 106.70 Trifecta £1899.30.
Owner K Kirkup & Mrs T Galletley **Bred** Anthony J Keane **Trained** Denton, Co Durham

FOCUS
They went a frantic pace in this fair sprint handicap and it suited the closers.

3876 C.G.I. H'CAP 1m 100y
4:10 (4:10) (Class 5) (0-70,70) 3-Y-O+ **£5,040** (£1,508; £566; £566; £188) **Stalls** Low

Form RPR

5423 **1** **British Embassy (IRE)**[2] 3804 4-9-12 **68**..... SamJames 2 74
(David Loughnane) *mde all: rdn wl over 1f out: drvn and edgd lft ins fnl f: hld on wl towards fin* **9/4**[1]

3535 **2** nk **Jintshi**[18] 3252 3-9-5 **70**.....(b[1]) FrannyNorton 3 73
(Mark Johnston) *trckd wnr: chal wl over 1f out and sn rdn: drvn and ev ch whn edgd lft ins fnl f: kpt on* **11/4**[2]

1652 **3** 1/2 **John Caesar (IRE)**[18] 3253 5-9-8 **64**.....(t) BarryMcHugh 5 68
(Rebecca Bastiman) *in tch: hdwy over 2f out: trckd ldrs over 1f out: effrt to chal and swtchd rt ins fnl f: sn rdn and kpt on* **6/1**

6636 **3** dht **The King's Steed**[19] 3236 3-9-3 **68**..... ShaneGray 9 70+
(Ralph Beckett) *hld up: hdwy 2f out: n.m.r over 1f out: swtchd rt and rdn ins fnl f: fin strly* **5/1**[3]

6426 **5** shd **Stun Gun**[20] 3185 6-8-13 **55**.....(p) GeorgeChaloner 4 59
(Derek Shaw) *chsd ldrs: rdn wl over 1f out: drvn and kpt on same pce fnl f* **20/1**

10-0 **6** 1 **Jan De Heem**[15] 3363 6-9-3 **59**.....(p) BenCurtis 7 60
(Tina Jackson) *rrd s: sn pushed along and detached in rr: rdn and hdwy on wd outside 2f out: kpt on fnl f: nrst fin* **25/1**

0102 **7** 1 **The Wee Barra (IRE)**[15] 3342 4-8-13 **62**.....(p) LewisEdmunds(7) 6 61
(Kevin Ryan) *chsd ldng pair: rdn along 2f out: drvn over 1f out: wknd fnl f* **10/1**

3406 **8** 1/2 **The Firm (IRE)**[8] 3599 7-9-9 **65**.....(be) DaleSwift 1 63
(Daniel Mark Loughnane) *chsd ldrs: hdwy over 2f out: rdn wl over 1f out: drvn appr fnl f: sn wknd* **16/1**

0020 **9** 12 **Last Wish (IRE)**[23] 3072 5-8-10 **52**.....(b) ConnorBeasley 8 22
(Richard Guest) *a bhd* **16/1**

1m 49.16s (1.56) **Going Correction** +0.275s/f (Good)
WFA 3 from 4yo+ 9lb **9** Ran SP% **117.9**
Speed ratings (Par 103): **103,102,102,102,102 101,100,99,87**
PL: John Caesar £0.90, Jintshi: £1.70, The King's Steed £0.80, EX: £9.60; CSF: £8.72; TRICAST: BE/J/JC £16.16, BE/J/KS £13.91; TRIFECTA: BE/J/JC £20.40, BE/J/KS £18.10; TOTE £2.90.
Owner R G Fell **Bred** Corduff Stud Ltd & T J Rooney **Trained** Market Drayton, Shropshire
■ Stewards' Enquiry : Sam James two-day ban (16-17 July): used whip above permitted level

FOCUS
An ordinary handicap, rated around the fifth and a small personal best from the winner.

3877 ELTHERINGTON H'CAP 7f 100y
4:45 (4:46) (Class 5) (0-70,69) 3-Y-O **£3,780** (£1,131; £565; £283; £141) **Stalls** Low

Form RPR

4300 **1** **Ravenhoe (IRE)**[18] 3266 3-9-6 **68**..... FrannyNorton 7 74
(Mark Johnston) *mde all: rdn over 1f out: drvn ins fnl f: kpt on wl towards fin* **11/1**

2440 **2** 1 **Dark Command**[19] 3224 3-8-12 **60**.....(p) ConnorBeasley 9 64+
(Michael Dods) *hld up towards rr: hdwy wl over 1f out: rdn ins fnl f: styd on wl towards fin* **4/1**[2]

1560 **3** 3/4 **Arcane Dancer (IRE)**[15] 3366 3-8-12 **60**.....(p) GeorgeChaloner 8 62
(Lawrence Mullaney) *trckd ldrs: hdwy and cl up 2f out: rdn wl over 1f out: drvn and ev ch ent fnl f: kpt on same pce towards fin* **12/1**

3125 **4** nk **Popsies Joy (IRE)**[10] 3521 3-9-7 **69**..... JasonHart 2 70+
(Tim Easterby) *hld up in tch: hdwy 2f out: rdn over 1f out: drvn and kpt on same pce fnl f* **3/1**[1]

365 **5** hd **Olympic Duel (IRE)**[26] 2980 3-8-12 **60**..... AndrewMullen 1 60
(Peter Hiatt) *trckd ldrs on inner: hdwy over 2f out: rdn over 1f out: drvn and kpt on same pce fnl f* **10/1**

3424 **6** 1/2 **Weld Al Khawaneej (IRE)**[17] 3285 3-9-2 **64**..... ShaneGray 5 63
(Kevin Ryan) *chsd ldrs: rdn along wl over 1f out: drvn and hld whn n.m.r wl ins fnl f* **6/1**[3]

46-3 **7** 2 1/4 **My Two Scoops**[21] 3153 3-9-6 **68**..... PJMcDonald 6 62
(Ann Duffield) *hld up in tch: swtchd lft to outer and effrt 2f out: sn rdn: drvn appr fnl f and no imp* **3/1**[1]

6-60 **8** nk **King Oswald (USA)**[46] 2341 3-9-3 **65**..... BenCurtis 3 58
(James Unett) *a in rr* **20/1**

0040 **U** **Beadlam (IRE)**[4] 3750 3-8-7 **55**..... SamJames 4
(David Loughnane) *a towards rr: stmbld and uns rdr over 2f out* **25/1**

1m 35.35s (1.55) **Going Correction** +0.275s/f (Good) **9** Ran SP% **118.0**
Speed ratings (Par 100): **102,100,100,99,99 98,96,95,**
CSF £55.92 CT £433.67 TOTE £11.70: £2.90, £1.60, £3.60; EX 73.00 Trifecta £603.40.
Owner J David Abell **Bred** Miss Linda Lyons **Trained** Middleham Moor, N Yorks

FOCUS
This moderate 3yo handicap looked wide open. They went a solid early pace and the third sets the level.

3878 POWERPART FILLIES' H'CAP 1m 1f 207y
5:20 (5:23) (Class 5) (0-70,70) 3-Y-O **£3,780** (£1,131; £565; £283; £141) **Stalls** Low

Form RPR

-665 **1** **Lime And Lemon (IRE)**[37] 2615 3-8-13 **67**..... AdamMcNamara(5) 8 75
(Philip McBride) *trckd ldrs: hdwy over 2f out: rdn to ld over 1f out: drvn ins fnl f: hld on gamely towards fin* **3/1**[1]

-500 **2** hd **Dora's Field (IRE)**[31] 2795 3-9-6 **69**..... FrannyNorton 1 76
(Ed Dunlop) *hld up in tch: hdwy over 2f out: rdn over 1f out: drvn ent fnl f: kpt on wl towards fin* **4/1**[3]

4-00 **3** 2 **Mystikana**[23] 3063 3-8-12 **61**.....(b) RoystonFfrench 4 64
(Marcus Tregoning) *trckd ldng pair: hdwy 2f out: sn cl up: rdn and ev ch ent fnl f: sn drvn: kpt on same pce towards fin* **9/2**

5134 **4** 1/2 **Livella Fella (IRE)**[17] 3286 3-9-7 **70**..... ConnorBeasley 7 72
(Keith Dalgleish) *trckd ldr: hdwy to ld wl over 2f out: rdn and hdd over 1f out: sn drvn and kpt on same pce* **7/2**[2]

0-03 **5** 8 **Sunshineandbubbles**[44] 2405 3-9-0 **63**..... DaleSwift 9 49
(Daniel Mark Loughnane) *hld up in rr: hdwy over 2f out: rdn wl over 1f out: sn drvn and n.d* **20/1**

0-30 **6** 5 **Shine**[22] 3094 3-9-1 **64**..... PJMcDonald 2 40
(Jonathan Portman) *chsd ldrs: pushed along 1/2-way: rdn wl over 2f out: sn outpcd* **12/1**

2-40 **7** 13 **Chelabella**[38] 2574 3-9-4 **67**.....(b[1]) JackMitchell 3 17
(Michael Bell) *led: rdn along 3f out: sn hdd & wknd 2f out* **11/1**

0-60 **8** 7 **Tiga Tuan (FR)**[54] 2108 3-9-3 **66**..... ShaneGray 5
(Kevin Ryan) *in tch: hdwy to chse ldrs and wd st: rdn along over 2f out: sn wknd* **7/1**

2m 8.55s (1.55) **Going Correction** +0.275s/f (Good) **8** Ran SP% **118.7**
Speed ratings (Par 97): **104,103,102,101,95 91,81,75**
CSF £15.94 CT £53.90 TOTE £4.20: £1.70, £1.80, £1.90; EX 15.70 Trifecta £96.20.
Owner Qatar Racing Limited **Bred** Vimal And Gillian Khosla **Trained** Newmarket, Suffolk

FOCUS
A moderate fillies' handicap, but it seems fair form for the grade with the winner on a fair mark on her maiden form.

3879 THETFORD MAIDEN STKS 5f
5:50 (5:51) (Class 5) 3-Y-O+ **£3,780** (£1,131; £565; £283; £141) **Stalls** Low

Form RPR

2 **1** **Acclaim The Nation (IRE)**[46] 2333 3-9-5 0..... JasonHart 3 68+
(Eric Alston) *cl up: led 1/2-way: rdn appr fnl f: kpt on strly* **2/1**[2]

653 **2** 1 1/4 **Enjoy Life (IRE)**[18] 3267 3-9-0 62..... ShaneGray 4 58
(Kevin Ryan) *trckd ldrs: hdwy to chse wnr over 1f out: rdn to chal ent fnl f: sn drvn and no imp towards fin* **9/2**[3]

0000 **3** 4 1/2 **Muhtadim (IRE)**[7] 3634 4-9-3 44.....(b) BenRobinson(7) 8 49
(Charles Smith) *racd wd: slt ld to 1/2-way: cl up: rdn wl over 1f out and sn edgd rt: kpt on same pce after* **50/1**

2-22 **4** 1 1/4 **Hyland Heather (IRE)**[7] 3643 3-8-9 78..... AdamMcNamara(5) 2 38
(Richard Fahey) *trckd ldrs: effrt 2f out: sn rdn and btn over 1f out* **10/11**[1]

0 **5** 5 **Lovin' Spoonful**[36] 2667 3-9-0 0..... ConnorBeasley 1 20
(Bryan Smart) *dwlt: a in rr* **14/1**

000- **6** 11 **Compton Mews**[259] 7284 3-9-0 0..... FrannyNorton 5
(Les Eyre) *chsd ldrs: rdn along 1/2-way: sn outpcd and bhd* **28/1**

1m 6.29s (2.79) **Going Correction** +0.325s/f (Good)
WFA 3 from 4yo+ 5lb **6** Ran SP% **116.0**
Speed ratings (Par 103): **90,88,80,78,70 53**
CSF £11.96 TOTE £3.00: £1.30, £2.00; EX 14.60 Trifecta £116.90.
Owner Con Harrington **Bred** Con Harrington **Trained** Longton, Lancs

FOCUS
The first pair dominated the finish of this weak sprint maiden, with the time slow and the favourite disappointing.
T/Plt: £66.10 to a £1 stake. Pool of £65956.40 - 727.99 winning tickets. T/Qpdt: £30.30 to a £1 stake. Pool of £4065.19 - 99.14 winning tickets. **Joe Rowntree**

3515 CARLISLE (R-H)
Saturday, July 2

OFFICIAL GOING: Good to soft (good in places last 4f) changing to good to soft after race 2 (6.35)
Wind: Fresh, half against Weather: Overcast

3880 ATKINS WHITEHAVEN APPRENTICE H'CAP 5f 193y
6:05 (6:05) (Class 5) (0-75,74) 4-Y-O+ **£2,911** (£866; £432; £216) **Stalls** Low

Form RPR

0000 **1** **Free Zone**[14] 3419 7-9-12 **74**.....(v) JoshDoyle 5 86
(David O'Meara) *trckd ldrs: edgd rt sn after s: rdn to ld over 1f out: drew clr ins fnl f* **9/1**

0-01 **2** 3 **Bondi Beach Babe**[29] 2856 6-9-3 **70**........................(p) MitchGodwin[(5)] 1 72
(James Turner) *cl up: rdn: edgd lft and ev ch over 1f out: kpt on fnl f: nt gng pce of wnr* **11/2**[3]

5506 **3** hd **Cliff (IRE)**[18] 3262 6-8-11 **64**..................................(p) KieranSchofield[(5)] 8 66
(Nigel Tinkler) *sn pushed along in rr: drvn 1/2-way: hdwy over 1f out: kpt on fnl f: nrst fin* **5/1**[2]

3002 **4** 1 1/4 **Mallymkun**[19] 3211 4-9-1 **63**.. JordanVaughan 9 61
(K R Burke) *in tch on outside: rdn and outpcd over 2f out: rallied fnl f: nvr able to chal* **5/1**[2]

4631 **5** 1 3/4 **Spirit Of Wedza (IRE)**[19] 3210 4-9-2 **67**....................(p) RowanScott[(3)] 2 59
(Julie Camacho) *led after 1f: rdn and hdd over 1f out: wknd fnl f* **3/1**[1]

6063 **6** 1 3/4 **Cool Strutter (IRE)**[36] 2643 4-9-4 **66**...........................(b) GemmaTutty 4 53
(Karen Tutty) *n.m.r sn after s: chsd ldng gp: pushed along over 2f out: edgd rt and wknd over 1f out* **14/1**

4-00 **7** 6 **Circuitous**[28] 2906 8-8-8 **59**......................................(p) SophieKilloran[(3)] 6 26
(Keith Dalgleish) *s.i.s: bhd and outpcd: nvr on terms* **14/1**

4002 **8** 2 1/4 **Llewellyn**[9] 3580 8-9-5 **67**..(b) PhilDennis 7 27
(Declan Carroll) *t.k.h: led 1f: cl up tl rdn and wknd wl over 1f out* **10/1**

0655 **9** 1 1/4 **Gold Beau (FR)**[19] 3211 6-9-1 **63**..................................(v) NathanEvans 3 19
(Kristin Stubbs) *n.m.r sn after s: sn rdn along in rr: struggling 1/2-way: nvr on terms* **11/1**

1m 15.13s (1.43) **Going Correction** +0.425s/f (Yiel) **9** Ran SP% **114.5**
Speed ratings (Par 103): **107,103,102,101,98 96,88,85,83**
CSF £57.22 CT £277.81 TOTE £8.60: £2.30, £1.50, £2.10; EX 57.80 Trifecta £637.60.
Owner Fromthestables.com Racing McBride McKay **Bred** Richard Levin **Trained** Upper Helmsley, N Yorks

FOCUS
The rail was moved out 2yds on the old stable bend and in the home straight, adding 5yds to races 4, 5 and 7. The official going had eased slightly before racing to good to soft. A fair apprentice handicap in which the pace was strong and the winner took advantage of his reduced mark.

3881 STORY CONTRACTING NOVICE MEDIAN AUCTION STKS 5f
6:35 (6:37) (Class 5) 2-Y-O **£2,911** (£866; £432; £216) **Stalls** Low

Form RPR

142 **1** **Cuppacoffee (IRE)**[17] 3282 2-9-5 0.............................. RowanScott[(7)] 7 84
(Ann Duffield) *pressed ldr: led over 1f out: rdn and drew clr w runner-up fnl f: kpt on wl* **7/4**[1]

2 3/4 **Perfect Symphony (IRE)** 2-9-5 0...................................... KevinStott 9 74
(Kevin Ryan) *trckd ldrs: effrt and chsd wnr over 1f out: drew clr of rest ins fnl f: hld towards fin: improve* **25/1**

006 **3** 6 **Roys Dream**[32] 2771 2-9-0 0... PaddyAspell 5 48
(Kristin Stubbs) *hld up: drvn along over 2f out: hdwy on outside over 1f out: chsd clr ldng pair ins fnl f: no imp* **22/1**

4 nk **Reckless Serenade (IRE)** 2-9-0 0................................ PhillipMakin 4 47
(Keith Dalgleish) *towards rr: rdn along 1/2-way: hdwy on wd outside over 1f out: kpt on fnl f: no imp* **10/1**

666 **5** 1 1/4 **Zebedee Cat (IRE)**[17] 3283 2-9-5 0............................ DougieCostello 1 47
(Iain Jardine) *trckd ldrs: rdn along 2f out: wknd ins fnl f* **18/1**

40 **6** 1 3/4 **Coco La Belle (IRE)**[18] 3261 2-9-0 0................................ DavidAllan 10 36
(Tim Easterby) *in tch on outside: rdn along over 2f out: outpcd fr over 1f out* **50/1**

425 **7** 1 1/2 **Vaux (IRE)**[39] 2552 2-9-0 0.....................................(p) JordanVaughan[(5)] 3 35
(Ben Haslam) *dwlt: sn in tch: rdn over 2f out: wknd over 1f out* **8/1**

02 **8** 1 3/4 **Little Miss Lola**[10] 3515 2-9-0 0.................................... DarryllHolland 2 24
(Alan Swinbank) *t.k.h: led to over 1f out: wknd fnl f* **7/1**[3]

9 1/2 **Right Action** 2-9-5 0.. TonyHamilton 8 27
(Richard Fahey) *green in preliminaries: missed break: bhd: pushed along after 2f: nvr on terms* **16/1**

10 6 **Impassioned** 2-9-0 0.. LukeMorris 6
(Sir Mark Prescott Bt) *sn drvn along in rr: struggling over 3f out: btn whn hung rt over 1f out* **11/4**[2]

1m 3.4s (2.60) **Going Correction** +0.425s/f (Yiel) **10** Ran SP% **117.0**
Speed ratings (Par 94): **96,94,85,84,82 79,77,74,73,64**
CSF £54.63 TOTE £2.90: £1.50, £6.70, £6.00; EX 51.10 Trifecta £732.00.
Owner A Starkie, C A Gledhill & B Craig **Bred** Mrs Brid Cosgrove **Trained** Constable Burton, N Yorks

FOCUS
Little depth to a fair novice event and the two principals came clear.

3882 CLEANEVENT GROUP H'CAP 5f
7:05 (7:05) (Class 5) (0-70,68) 3-Y-O+ **£2,911** (£866; £432; £216) **Stalls** Low

Form RPR

0004 **1** **Lydiate Lady**[19] 3211 4-8-10 **52**..................................... PaulMulrennan 1 61
(Paul Green) *trckd ldrs: shkn up to ld ins fnl f: pushed out towards fin* **7/2**[2]

5356 **2** 1 1/4 **Ryedale Rio (IRE)**[17] 3293 3-8-13 **60**.................................. DavidAllan 5 63
(Tim Easterby) *plld hrd early: hld up: hdwy on outside over 1f out: chsd wnr ins fnl f: kpt on: hld nr fin* **8/1**

0006 **3** 1 1/4 **Native Falls (IRE)**[9] 3552 5-9-12 **68**.............................. DarryllHolland 4 68
(Alan Swinbank) *led: rdn 2f out: hdd ins fnl f: kpt on same pce* **7/1**

-521 **4** 3/4 **Burtonwood**[24] 3010 4-9-5 **68**.. RowanScott[(7)] 7 65
(Julie Camacho) *trckd ldrs on outside: wnt 2nd over 2f out: rdn and ev ch over 1f out to ins fnl f: kpt on same pce* **7/4**[1]

0060 **5** 4 **Tom Sawyer**[26] 2975 8-9-11 **67**....................................(b) TonyHamilton 3 50
(Julie Camacho) *in tch: drvn along and outpcd over 2f out: n.d after* **11/1**

320 **6** 2 1/4 **Lady Wootton**[4] 3755 3-8-13 **60**....................................(v[1]) DougieCostello 6 33
(Keith Dalgleish) *dwlt: sn chsng ldr: rdn and lost 2nd over 2f out: struggling whn edgd lft over 1f out* **4/1**[3]

1m 4.39s (3.59) **Going Correction** +0.425s/f (Yiel)
WFA 3 from 4yo+ 5lb **6** Ran SP% **110.5**
Speed ratings (Par 103): **88,86,84,82,76 72**
CSF £28.90 TOTE £3.70: £2.10, £4.00; EX 30.90 Trifecta £116.70.
Owner The Scotch Piper (lydiate) **Bred** Catridge Farm Stud **Trained** Lydiate, Merseyside

FOCUS
Only a modest handicap and they went a sensible pace, so the form is not entirely convincing.

3883 STORY CONTRACTING H'CAP 1m 1f
7:35 (7:35) (Class 5) (0-70,70) 4-Y-O+ **£2,911** (£866; £432; £216) **Stalls** Low

Form RPR

0343 **1** **Save The Bees**[19] 3212 8-8-12 **68**..................................(b) GerO'Neill[(7)] 7 77
(Declan Carroll) *mde all: sn 4 l clr: rdn over 1f out: hld on wl fnl f* **7/2**[2]

4266 **2** nk **Freight Train (IRE)**[23] 3077 4-9-7 **70**.........................(p) PaulMulrennan 3 78
(Mark Johnston) *chsd wnr: clr of rest and rdn over 2f out: edgd lft over 1f out: kpt on fnl f: jst hld* **7/1**

045 **3** 7 **Lostock Hall (IRE)**[24] 3012 4-8-12 **66**..................... JordanVaughan[(5)] 9 59
(K R Burke) *chsd ldng pair: rdn and outpcd over 2f out: kpt on fnl f: no ch w first two* **3/1**[1]

0026 **4** 6 **Framley Garth (IRE)**[9] 3582 4-9-2 **70**................. RachelRichardson[(5)] 4 51
(Patrick Holmes) *hld up in tch: rdn along over 2f out: no imp over 1f out* **8/1**

0-04 **5** 1/2 **Judicious**[19] 3212 9-8-7 **56**.. DavidAllan 1 36
(Geoffrey Harker) *hld up in tch: rdn and edgd rt over 2f out: outpcd over 1f out* **7/1**

3432 **6** 3/4 **Ferdy (IRE)**[19] 3214 7-8-9 **58**... KevinStott 5 36
(Paul Green) *dwlt: hld up: drvn along over 2f out: no imp fr over 1f out* **9/2**[3]

0606 **7** 19 **Tectonic (IRE)**[19] 3212 7-9-0 **63**....................................(p) PhillipMakin 10
(Keith Dalgleish) *stdd s: t.k.h in rr: rdn and outpcd over 2f out: sn btn: lost tch and eased fnl f* **10/1**

2m 0.2s (2.60) **Going Correction** +0.425s/f (Yiel) **7** Ran SP% **110.6**
Speed ratings (Par 103): **105,104,98,93,92 92,75**
CSF £25.79 CT £76.02 TOTE £4.40: £2.20, £3.30; EX 17.00 Trifecta £153.70.
Owner Steve Ryan **Bred** S P Ryan **Trained** Malton, N Yorks

FOCUS
Rail movement added 5yds to race distance. A fair handicap in which the front two were first and second throughout and the winner stepped up on this year's form.

3884 LLOYD MOTOR GROUP H'CAP 7f 173y
8:05 (8:05) (Class 4) (0-85,87) 3-Y-O+ **£5,175** (£1,540; £769; £384) **Stalls** Low

Form RPR

6354 **1** **Breakable**[28] 2890 5-9-5 **81**.................................... RachelRichardson[(5)] 4 89
(Tim Easterby) *in tch: hdwy over 1f out: led ins fnl f: pushed out* **9/1**

6142 **2** 1 3/4 **Archie's Advice**[17] 3286 5-9-3 **74**...................................... PhillipMakin 3 78+
(Keith Dalgleish) *hld up in tch on ins: rdn over 2f out: swtchd lft and hdwy over 1f out: kpt on to take 2nd cl home: nt rch wnr* **11/4**[1]

02 **3** nse **Dawn Mirage**[61] 1924 4-9-5 **76**.....................................(p) TonyHamilton 9 80
(Richard Fahey) *dwlt: hld up bhd ldng gp: rdn over 2f out: edgd rt over 1f out: kpt on ins fnl f* **11/2**

0-54 **4** hd **Dark Ocean (IRE)**[75] 1526 6-9-11 **82**.................................. CamHardie 1 86
(Jedd O'Keeffe) *trckd ldrs: effrt and rdn over 1f out: one pce wl ins fnl f* **8/1**

0001 **5** hd **Gurkha Friend**[10] 3517 4-9-13 **84**...................................... DavidNolan 2 87
(Karen McLintock) *led: rdn 2f out: hdd ins fnl f: no ex and lost three pls towards fin* **3/1**[2]

3-05 **6** 8 **Eqleem**[24] 3026 3-9-4 **84**... PaulMulrennan 8 67
(Mark Johnston) *trckd ldrs on outside: rdn over 2f out: lost pl over 1f out* **4/1**[3]

031- **7** 3/4 **Strong Man**[354] 4230 8-9-6 **82**...................................... NathanEvans[(5)] 6 65
(Michael Easterby) *pressed ldr: rdn over 2f out: wknd over 1f out* **28/1**

3044 **8** 5 **Red Paladin (IRE)**[10] 3517 6-9-0 **71**........................(p) DougieCostello 5 42
(Kristin Stubbs) *s.s: bhd: struggling over 2f out: sn btn* **18/1**

1m 42.18s (2.18) **Going Correction** +0.425s/f (Yiel)
WFA 3 from 4yo+ 9lb **8** Ran SP% **116.9**
Speed ratings (Par 105): **106,104,104,104,103 95,95,90**
CSF £34.85 CT £153.59 TOTE £8.40: £2.40, £1.70, £2.10; EX 36.10 Trifecta £258.90.
Owner Ryedale Partners No 9 **Bred** Habton Farms **Trained** Great Habton, N Yorks

FOCUS
Rail movement added 5yds to race distance. A useful handicap, but they finished in a heap behind the winner who was recording a small personal best.

3885 LLOYD LTD H'CAP 6f 195y
8:35 (8:35) (Class 4) (0-85,83) 3-Y-O **£5,175** (£1,540; £769; £384) **Stalls** Low

Form RPR

0606 **1** **Explosive Power (IRE)**[21] 3130 3-9-2 **83**............... JordanVaughan[(5)] 7 89
(K R Burke) *trckd ldrs: drvn along over 2f out: rallied over 1f out: led ins fnl f: hld on wl* **7/2**[3]

-600 **2** nk **Forever A Lady (IRE)**[21] 3152 3-8-10 **72**..................... DougieCostello 3 77
(Keith Dalgleish) *trckd ldrs: effrt and swtchd rt over 1f out: ev ch ins fnl f: kpt on: hld nr fin* **22/1**

3-04 **3** hd **Reputation (IRE)**[29] 2871 3-9-6 **82**................................... CamHardie 8 86
(John Quinn) *bhd: drvn and outpcd over 3f out: gd hdwy on outside to ld over 1f out: hdd ins fnl f: no ex nr fin* **3/1**[2]

-221 **4** 6 **Heir To A Throne (FR)**[35] 2686 3-9-7 **83**............................ KevinStott 6 71
(Kevin Ryan) *t.k.h: led: edgd lft and hdd over 1f out: edgd rt and sn wknd* **11/4**[1]

4432 **5** 1/2 **Rosamaria (IRE)**[9] 3551 3-8-7 **69**.................................. PaulMulrennan 5 56
(Mark Johnston) *pressed ldr: rdn over 2f out: wknd over 1f out* **5/1**

-504 **6** 1/2 **Holy Grail (IRE)**[20] 3187 3-9-5 **81**....................................... LukeMorris 2 66
(Simon West) *dwlt: t.k.h in tch: rdn over 2f out: sn wknd* **9/1**

-416 **7** 15 **Ponty Royale (IRE)**[9] 3567 3-8-3 **65**............................ DuranFentiman 4 10
(Tim Easterby) *dwlt: hld up: struggling over 2f out: lost tch fr over 1f out* **10/1**

1m 30.36s (3.26) **Going Correction** +0.425s/f (Yiel) **7** Ran SP% **114.0**
Speed ratings (Par 102): **98,97,97,90,90 89,72**
CSF £68.51 CT £255.41 TOTE £4.40: £1.70, £6.70; EX 75.60 Trifecta £361.50.
Owner Market Avenue Racing Club & P Garvey **Bred** Georgestown Stud **Trained** Middleham Moor, N Yorks

FOCUS
A useful and competitive 3yo handicap with the first three pulling clear. A small personal best from the winner.

3886 ANDERSONS (DENTON HOLME) SAWMILLS CARLISLE MAIDEN STKS 1m 3f 39y
9:05 (9:07) (Class 5) 3-Y-O+ **£2,911** (£866; £432; £216) **Stalls** High

Form RPR

042 **1** **Vanishing Point**[10] 3508 3-9-2 80.. LukeMorris 4 75+
(Andrew Balding) *in tch: pushed along fr 1/2-way: effrt whn nt clr run over 2f out to over 1f out: swtchd lft and hdwy to ld ins fnl f: edgd rt: drvn out* **1/1**[1]

2 1/2 **Autumn Surprise (IRE)** 3-8-11 0... DavidAllan 3 66+
(Tim Easterby) *s.i.s: hld up: pushed along over 4f out: hdwy and bk on bridle over 2f out: led briefly ent fnl f: rn green: kpt on: hld nr fin: bttr for r* **16/1**[3]

65 **3** 1 3/4 **Steely Rock**[15] 3362 3-9-2 0.. PaulMulrennan 6 68
(Mark Johnston) *towards rr: rdn along and outpcd over 4f out: rallied wl over 1f out: kpt on ins fnl f: nrst fin* **16/1**[3]

06 **4** 1 1/4 **Ya Jammeel**[15] 3343 3-9-2 0... DavidNolan 9 66
(Richard Fahey) *trckd ldrs: pushed along over 3f out: hdwy to ld wl over 1f out: edgd lft and hdd ent fnl f: sn one pce* **8/1**[2]

6505 **5** 8 **Shulammite Man (IRE)**[46] 2348 3-9-2 47..................... DarryllHolland 7 52
(Alan Swinbank) *in tch: rdn and outpcd over 3f out: no imp fr 2f out* **50/1**

0 **6** *6* **Adrakhan (FR)**[28] 2914 5-9-11 0 MissEmmaSayer(3) 8 41
(Wilf Storey) *prom: led over 2f out to wl over 1f out: sn rdn and wknd* **100/1**

04 **7** *½* **You'll Do**[15] 3343 3-8-11 0 GarryWhillans(5) 10 40
(Maurice Barnes) *led to over 2f out: rdn and wknd over 1f out* **20/1**

00 **8** *1¼* **My Brown Eyed Girl**[46] 2327 3-8-11 0 RaulDaSilva 11 33
(Susan Corbett) *bhd: drvn and outpcd over 4f out: sn struggling* **50/1**

3 **9** *15* **Chiron (IRE)**[54] 2094 7-10-0 0 DougieCostello 2 11
(Keith Dalgleish) *chsd ldrs tl rdn and wknd fr over 2f out* **33/1**

2m 33.2s (10.10) **Going Correction** +0.425s/f (Yiel)
WFA 3 from 5yo+ 12lb 9 Ran SP% **85.5**
Speed ratings (Par 103): **80,79,78,77,71 67,66,66,55**
CSF £6.75 TOTE £1.30: £1.02, £2.80, £3.00; EX 9.30 Trifecta £51.10.
Owner Castle Down Racing **Bred** Meon Valley Stud **Trained** Kingsclere, Hants
■ Desert Way was withdrawn. Price at time of withdrawal 6/4. Rule 4 applies to all bets - deduct 40p in the pound.

FOCUS
Rail movement added 5yds to race distance. Just an ordinary maiden which was weakened even further when Desert Way refused to enter the stalls. There is probably more to come from the winner, though.
T/Plt: £522.50 to a £1 stake. Pool of £54448.03 - 76.06 winning tickets. T/Qpdt: £87.30 to a £1 stake. Pool of £5153.61 - 43.68 winning tickets. **Richard Young**

3851 HAYDOCK (L-H)
Saturday, July 2

OFFICIAL GOING: Soft (heavy in places; 6.5)
Wind: fresh 1/2 against Weather: changeable at first but mainly fine and sunny, heavy shower race 5 (4.00)

3887 BET365 H'CAP 1m 2f 95y
1:45 (1:46) (Class 3) (0-95,92) 3-Y-O **£12,938** (£3,850; £1,924; £962) **Stalls** Centre

Form RPR

5-00 **1** **Wall Of Fire (IRE)**[16] 3299 3-9-3 **88** (b) JamesDoyle 4 96
(Hugo Palmer) *racd in last: effrt over 3f out: 3rd appr fnl f: styd on wl to ld last 75yds* **4/1**[2]

-101 **2** *2¼* **Threat Assessed (IRE)**[21] 3156 3-9-1 **86** JohnFahy 6 90
(Clive Cox) *trckd ldrs: t.k.h: 2nd over 2f out: sn upsides: drvn and hung lft over 1f out: led briefly last 100yds: kpt on same pce* **11/8**[1]

0-40 **3** *nk* **Champagne City**[28] 2892 3-9-7 **92** PaulMulrennan 2 95
(Mark Johnston) *led: qcknd pce over 3f out: jnd and crowded over 1f out: hdd and no ex last 100yds* **7/1**

5-10 **4** *3* **Navajo War Dance**[16] 3300 3-9-1 **86** DougieCostello 5 84
(K R Burke) *sn trcking ldrs: drvn over 3f out: swtchd rt 2f out: kpt on one pce to take modest 4th 1f out* **4/1**[2]

1-30 **5** *2½* **Dark Devil (IRE)**[28] 2892 3-9-1 **86** TonyHamilton 3 79
(Richard Fahey) *trckd ldr: drvn 3f out: hung lft: wknd appr fnl f* **11/2**[3]

2m 20.42s (4.92) **Going Correction** +0.375s/f (Good) 5 Ran SP% **110.0**
Speed ratings (Par 104): **95,93,92,90,88**
CSF £9.99 TOTE £5.50: £2.40, £1.40; EX 9.50 Trifecta £37.70.
Owner Carmichael Jennings **Bred** B V Sangster **Trained** Newmarket, Suffolk

FOCUS
All races run on Stands' Side Home Straight. Allowing for rail movements, distances were amended as follows; Races 1, 2 & 3 +43 yards. A fair opener, in which three of the five runners were down in grade after finishing unplaced at Royal Ascot. It was very steadily run and the form should be treated with caution. The race has been rated around the runner-up.

3888 BET365 LANCASHIRE OAKS (GROUP 2) (F&M) 1m 3f 200y
2:15 (2:15) (Class 1) 3-Y-O+
£52,740 (£19,995; £10,006; £4,984; £2,501; £1,255) **Stalls** Centre

Form RPR

011- **1** **Endless Time (IRE)**[258] 7321 4-9-5 107 JamesDoyle 5 111
(Charlie Appleby) *trckd ldrs: effrt over 3f out: edgd rt 2f out: styd on wl fnl f: led last 50yds* **11/4**[1]

352 **2** *½* **Furia Cruzada (CHI)**[17] 3271 5-9-5 110 JimmyFortune 6 110
(John Gosden) *hld up in last: hdwy over 1f out: styd on to take 2nd nr fin* **11/2**[3]

20-1 **3** *½* **Loving Things**[13] 3436 4-9-5 102 MartinLane 1 109
(Luca Cumani) *led: pushed along over 3f out: jnd over 1f out: hdd and no ex last 50yds* **4/1**[2]

10-0 **4** *¾* **Nightflower (IRE)**[34] 2723 4-9-5 111 FrederikTylicki 8 108
(P Schiergen, Germany) *hld up: hdwy on ins 4f out: sn w ldrs: kpt on same pce last 100yds* **4/1**[2]

5/1 **5** *nse* **Lady Of Camelot (IRE)**[33] 2735 4-9-5 93 RobertHavlin 4 108
(John Gosden) *trckd ldr: chal 3f out: upsides over 1f out: kpt on same pce last 100yds* **6/1**

1-13 **6** *4½* **Carnachy (IRE)**[49] 2241 4-9-5 103 JamieSpencer 9 101
(David Simcock) *s.i.s: hdwy to trck ldrs after 2f: drvn and n.m.r over 1f out: wknd last 150yds: eased clsng stages* **11/2**[3]

2m 40.21s (6.41) **Going Correction** +0.375s/f (Good)
WFA 3 from 4yo+ 13lb 6 Ran SP% **111.7**
Speed ratings (Par 115): **93,92,92,91,91 88**
CSF £17.82 TOTE £3.40: £2.00, £2.50; EX 17.30 Trifecta £52.70.
Owner Godolphin **Bred** Mabaki Investments **Trained** Newmarket, Suffolk

FOCUS
This was a casualty of four non-runners but still featured some very talented fillies. They went very steadily and, as a consequence, the first five home finished in a heap and the first three have been rated to their marks. Rail movements added 43 yards to the race distance.

3889 BET365 OLD NEWTON CUP (HERITAGE H'CAP) 1m 3f 200y
2:50 (2:50) (Class 2) 4-Y-O+
£62,250 (£18,640; £9,320; £4,660; £2,330; £1,170) **Stalls** Centre

Form RPR

1152 **1** **Tawdeea**[24] 3027 4-9-3 **95** DanielTudhope 2 106+
(David O'Meara) *mid-div: hdwy 4f out: drvn and styd on fnl 2f: led last 100yds: kpt on wl* **8/1**

-224 **2** *1½* **Gold Prince (IRE)**[7] 3666 4-8-13 **91** LukeMorris 10 100
(Sylvester Kirk) *trckd ldrs: 2nd over 1f out: styd on same pce last 100yds* **25/1**

-111 **3** *2¼* **Desert Encounter (IRE)**[7] 3670 4-9-4 **96** JamieSpencer 3 101+
(David Simcock) *hld up in rr: n.m.r over 2f out: swtchd rt and gd hdwy over 1f out: fin wl to take 3rd in clsng stages* **4/1**[1]

2641 **4** *1½* **Snoano**[21] 3162 4-8-11 **94** RachelRichardson(5) 19 97
(Tim Easterby) *s.i.s: sn trcking ldrs: 2nd gng wl over 2f out: sn led: hdd and kpt on same pce last 100yds* **12/1**

60/0 **5** *¾* **Penglai Pavilion (USA)**[18] 3246 6-9-2 **94** JamesDoyle 14 96
(Charlie Appleby) *chsd ldrs: drvn over 3f out: kpt on one pce appr fnl f* **9/1**

-103 **6** *hd* **Dance King**[13] 3435 6-8-11 **89** (tp) DavidAllan 6 90
(Tim Easterby) *hld up in rr: hdwy over 2f out: kpt on wl: nt rch ldrs* **25/1**

60/0 **7** *1¼* **Stars Over The Sea (USA)**[28] 2897 5-8-11 **89** JimmyFortune 18 88
(Mark Johnston) *led after 1f: hdd 2f out: one pce* **33/1**

212- **8** *1* **Revision (FR)**[236] 7779 4-8-9 **87** KierenFox 1 85
(John Best) *in rr: hdwy on ins over 4f out: chsng ldrs over 2f out* **14/1**

5300 **9** *hd* **Notarised**[7] 3658 5-9-8 **100** RobertHavlin 9 98
(Mark Johnston) *chsd ldrs: drvn over 2f out: one pce* **20/1**

03-4 **10** *1* **Havana Beat (IRE)**[7] 3662 6-9-8 **100** FrederikTylicki 17 96
(Rod Millman) *mid-div: hdwy 4f out: one pce fnl 2f* **33/1**

4-25 **11** *nk* **Duretto**[28] 2897 4-9-2 **94** JimCrowley 12 89
(Andrew Balding) *rr-div: pushed along over 3f out: kpt on fnl 2f: nvr a factor* **6/1**[2]

-014 **12** *3¾* **First Sitting**[15] 3340 5-9-10 **102** GeorgeBaker 7 91
(Chris Wall) *hld up in rr: hdwy 4f out: wknd over 1f out* **8/1**

-650 **13** *½* **Windshear**[15] 3340 5-9-7 **99** SeanLevey 16 88
(Richard Hannon) *mid-div: sme hdwy over 3f out: wknd over 1f out* **33/1**

0-21 **14** *1* **Green Light**[28] 2897 5-9-2 **94** (v) MartinHarley 5 81
(Ralph Beckett) *stdd s: hld up in rr: sme hdwy and swtchd lft over 2f out: sn wknd* **7/1**[3]

1002 **15** *2* **Watersmeet**[42] 2482 5-9-7 **99** PaulMulrennan 13 83
(Mark Johnston) *led 1f: chsd ldrs: wknd over 1f out* **20/1**

-130 **16** *5* **Barwick**[28] 2897 8-8-12 **90** SteveDrowne 11 66
(George Baker) *s.i.s: sme hdwy 4f out: lost pl over 2f out* **20/1**

02 **17** *18* **Paddys Motorbike (IRE)**[62] 1885 4-9-0 **92** ShaneKelly 15 39
(David Evans) *towards rr: sme hdwy on outer 3f out: sn hung rt and lost pl: bhd whn eased fnl 100yds* **25/1**

2m 35.25s (1.45) **Going Correction** +0.375s/f (Good) 17 Ran SP% **128.0**
Speed ratings (Par 109): **110,109,107,106,106 105,105,104,104,103 103,100,100,99,98 95,83**
CSF £204.17 CT £929.53 TOTE £8.10: £2.40, £4.90, £1.60, £3.30; EX 217.80 Trifecta £1345.40.
Owner Middleham Park Racing LXVI **Bred** Shadwell Estate Company Limited **Trained** Upper Helmsley, N Yorks
■ Stewards' Enquiry : Luke Morris two-day ban (16-17 July): used whip above shoulder height

FOCUS
A typically competitive renewal of this historic handicap. They went a good clip throughout and form looks particularly strong with the winner continuing to improve. Rail movement added 43 yards to the race distance.

3890 CASH OUT AT BET365 H'CAP 6f
3:25 (3:26) (Class 2) (0-100,99) 3-Y-O+ **£12,938** (£3,850; £1,924; £962) **Stalls** Centre

Form RPR

5600 **1** **Hoof It**[20] 3188 9-8-13 **91** NathanEvans(5) 6 100
(Michael Easterby) *w ldr: led after 1f: drvn appr fnl f: jst hld on* **15/2**

-200 **2** *hd* **New Bidder**[7] 3671 5-9-3 **90** GrahamGibbons 10 98
(David Barron) *hld up in mid-div: effrt over 2f out: chsd wnr fnl 150yds: gng on at fin: jst hld* **13/2**

4041 **3** *1¾* **Intense Style (IRE)**[20] 3188 4-9-4 **91** DavidAllan 4 93
(Les Eyre) *trckd ldrs: effrt over 1f out: kpt on same pce last 100yds* **5/1**[3]

4-00 **4** *½* **Tatlisu (IRE)**[52] 2158 6-9-12 **99** TonyHamilton 7 100
(Richard Fahey) *hld up towards rr: effrt 2f out: kpt on fnl f* **14/1**

112- **5** *2¾* **Shady McCoy (USA)**[274] 6891 6-9-0 **87** JamesDoyle 3 79
(Ian Williams) *hld up in rr: nt clr run over 2f out: hdwy over 1f out: fdd fnl 150yds* **9/2**[2]

0-02 **6** *¾* **Cornwallville (IRE)**[15] 3346 4-9-6 **98** JoshDoyle(5) 2 88
(David Loughnane) *w ldrs towards far side: upsides over 2f out: wknd fnl 150yds* **6/1**

2500 **7** *1¼* **Take The Helm**[49] 2251 3-8-2 **88** JordanUys(7) 8 73
(Brian Meehan) *chsd ldrs: drvn over 2f out: wknd over 1f out* **16/1**

1225 **8** *2* **Reflektor (IRE)**[7] 3671 3-9-3 **96** LukeMorris 5 74
(Tom Dascombe) *led 1f: chsd ldrs: drvn over 2f out: wknd fnl f* **3/1**[1]

0-40 **9** *8* **Zanetto**[28] 2898 6-9-8 **95** DougieCostello 9 49
(John Quinn) *trckd ldrs towards stands' side: t.k.h: lost pl over 1f out: bhd whn eased clsng stages* **25/1**

1m 16.45s (2.65) **Going Correction** +0.675s/f (Yiel)
WFA 3 from 4yo+ 6lb 9 Ran SP% **115.6**
Speed ratings (Par 109): **109,108,106,105,102 101,99,96,86**
CSF £55.45 CT £270.48 TOTE £8.50: £2.70, £2.00, £1.80; EX 57.70 Trifecta £288.70.
Owner A Chandler & L Westwood **Bred** Bond Thoroughbred Corporation **Trained** Sheriff Hutton, N Yorks

FOCUS
A decent sprint handicap, with the top two in the field both rated within 2lb of the ceiling of 100. The winner has been rated to his best in the past year.

3891 BET365 CONDITIONS STKS 6f
4:00 (4:04) (Class 2) 3-Y-O+ **£12,450** (£3,728; £1,864; £932) **Stalls** Centre

Form RPR

4533 **1** **Glen Moss (IRE)**[14] 3386 7-8-11 102 PaulMulrennan 2 109
(Michael Dods) *mde all: shkn up over 1f out: pushed out: readily* **2/1**[2]

0240 **2** *2¼* **Coulsty (IRE)**[14] 3386 5-8-11 106 (b) SeanLevey 3 102
(Richard Hannon) *chsd ldrs: 2nd and drvn over 2f out: edgd lft and regained 2nd last 75yds: no imp* **6/4**[1]

0-40 **3** *1¾* **Ninjago**[14] 3386 6-8-11 101 MartinLane 5 96
(Paul Midgley) *hld up: trckd ldrs: effrt and chsd wnr over 1f out: kpt on same pce last 100yds* **6/1**[3]

-064 **4** *4½* **Another Wise Kid (IRE)**[18] 3250 8-8-11 97 DougieCostello 1 82
(Paul Midgley) *chsd wnr: drvn over 2f out: wknd fnl f* **16/1**

1m 16.51s (2.71) **Going Correction** +0.675s/f (Yiel) 4 Ran SP% **93.5**
Speed ratings (Par 109): **108,105,102,96**
CSF £3.90 TOTE £2.30; EX 3.30 Trifecta £6.00.
Owner Ritchie Fiddes **Bred** Rathbarry Stud **Trained** Denton, Co Durham
■ Clear Spring was withdrawn. Price at time of withdrawal 4/1. Rule 4 applies to all bets - deduct 20p in the pound.

FOCUS
The winner proved much the best in this informative conditions event. The first three had all run in the Wokingham.

3892 BET365.COM H'CAP 6f
4:35 (4:35) (Class 4) (0-80,80) 3-Y-O+ **£6,469** (£1,925; £962; £481) **Stalls** Centre

Form RPR
206 **1** **Dandyleekie (IRE)**[14] 3414 4-9-11 **79**........................ DanielTudhope 12 89
(David O'Meara) *mid-div: hdwy over 2f out: 2nd over 1f out: drvn to ld last 175yds: kpt on* **7/2**[1]
2-10 **2** 1¾ **By Rights**[14] 3397 5-8-11 **70**.. PaddyPilley[(5)] 9 74
(Tony Carroll) *led: hdd and no ex last 175yds* **33/1**
2234 **3** *hd* **Manatee Bay**[18] 3266 6-9-9 **77**..(v) PaulQuinn 4 80
(David Nicholls) *wnt rt andbmpd s: in rr and drvn along: hdwy over 2f out: kpt on to take 3rd last 75yds* **12/1**
3-24 **4** 1½ **Foresight (FR)**[40] 2544 3-9-6 **80**..................................... JamieSpencer 3 77
(David Simcock) *swtchd rt s: mid-div: effrt over 2f out: chsng ldrs over 1f out: kpt on one pce* **4/1**[2]
3305 **5** ¾ **Barkston Ash**[4] 3753 8-9-12 **80**.................................(p) PatrickMathers 8 76
(Eric Alston) *s.i.s: in rr and sn drvn along: kpt on fnl 2f* **10/1**
143 **6** 7 **Fantasy Justifier (IRE)**[3] 3771 5-9-4 **72**....................... GeorgeBaker 15 45
(Ronald Harris) *racd alone stands' side: chsd ldrs: upsides over 3f out: wknd over 1f out* **8/1**[3]
0005 **7** 1½ **Piazon**[21] 3137 5-9-7 **75**... PaulMulrennan 7 44
(Kevin Ryan) *wnt lft s: chsd ldrs: drvn over 2f out: wknd over 1f out* **10/1**
2060 **8** 1¾ **Daylight**[5] 3713 6-8-11 **65**...(t) KeaganLatham 5 28
(Michael Easterby) *hmpd s: mid-div: drvn over 2f out: lost pl over 1f out* **40/1**
0000 **9** ½ **Evanescent (IRE)**[7] 3638 7-9-9 **77**.......................... GrahamGibbons 10 38
(Tony Carroll) *chsd ldrs: drvn over 2f out: lost pl over 1f out* **20/1**
0630 **10** 1¾ **Casterbridge**[46] 2346 4-9-6 **79**.......................... RachelRichardson[(5)] 11 35
(Eric Alston) *rrd s: in rr: sme hdwy towards stands' side over 3f out: lost pl 2f out* **8/1**[3]
-250 **11** 7 **Dominate**[57] 2016 6-9-11 **79**..(v) JamesDoyle 13 12
(George Scott) *hld up in mid-div: effrt over 2f out: lost pl and eased fnl 175yds* **10/1**
5153 **12** 16 **Kenny The Captain (IRE)**[8] 3610 5-9-4 **72**.............(b) DuranFentiman 2
(Tim Easterby) *rrd bdly s: v.s.a: eventually set off detached in last* **8/1**[3]

1m 16.72s (2.92) **Going Correction** +0.675s/f (Yiel)
WFA 3 from 4yo+ 6lb **12** Ran SP% **120.7**
Speed ratings (Par 105): **107,104,104,102,101 92,90,87,87,84 75,54**
CSF £130.54 CT £1291.07 TOTE £5.20: £2.40, £9.20, £3.10; EX 196.40 Trifecta £4827.40.
Owner Gallop Racing **Bred** Morgan Kavanagh **Trained** Upper Helmsley, N Yorks
■ Stewards' Enquiry : James Doyle jockey said the gelding lost action. The Veterinary Officer reported that a post-race examination of the gelding failed to reveal any abnormalities.
Paul Quinn jockey said the gelding anticipated the start and reared as the stalls opened.
Rachel Richardson jockey said the gelding reared as the stalls opened and was slowly away.

FOCUS
Another hotly contested handicap. Many of these probably weren't at their best on this surface, however. The winner has been rated back to his Irish best.

3893 CASINO AT BET365.COM H'CAP 5f
5:10 (5:10) (Class 4) (0-85,82) 3-Y-O **£6,469** (£1,925; £962; £481) **Stalls** Centre

Form RPR
2322 **1** **Just Glamorous (IRE)**[14] 3407 3-8-9 **70**........................... ShaneKelly 5 82
(Ronald Harris) *racd stands' side: mde all: clr over 1f out: edgd lft: drvn out* **4/1**[3]
6-32 **2** 2¾ **Rantan (IRE)**[31] 2802 3-9-7 **82**..................................... GrahamGibbons 1 84
(David Barron) *carried lft s: racd towards centre: brought towards stands;' side over 3f out: drvn over 2f out: chsd wnr appr fnl f: no imp* **9/4**[1]
-341 **3** 1½ **Rose Marmara**[14] 3394 3-9-5 **80**.. DavidNolan 3 77
(Richard Fahey) *wnt lft s: racd towards centre: brought towards stands' side over 3f out: wnt 3rd appr fnl f: kpt on same pce* **3/1**[2]
0211 **4** 2½ **East Street Revue**[15] 3360 3-9-1 **76**........................(b) DuranFentiman 4 64
(Tim Easterby) *racd towards centre: brought to stands' side after 150yds: outpcd and drvn over 2f out: wnt modest 4th last 100yds: nvr a threat* **9/4**[1]
-610 **5** 1½ **Dodgy Bob**[31] 2802 3-9-7 **82**......................................(b[1]) KeaganLatham 2 64
(Kevin Ryan) *carried lft s: racd towards centre: chsd wnr: brought stands' side over 3f out: wknd fnl 150yds* **11/1**

1m 2.84s (2.04) **Going Correction** +0.675s/f (Yiel) **5** Ran SP% **114.9**
Speed ratings (Par 102): **110,105,103,99,96**
CSF £13.98 TOTE £5.50: £2.50, £1.40; EX 15.90 Trifecta £34.30.
Owner Robert & Nina Bailey **Bred** Glamorous Air Partnership **Trained** Earlswood, Monmouths

FOCUS
A tight little handicap on paper was turned into a procession with the winner recording a personal best.
T/Plt: £159.40 to a £1 stake. Pool of £129023.64 - 590.75 winning tickets. T/Qpdt: £42.70 to a £1 stake. Pool of £8271.73 - 143.10 winning tickets. **Walter Glynn**

3493 LEICESTER (R-H)
Saturday, July 2

OFFICIAL GOING: Soft (4.9)
Wind: light, half behind Weather: bright spells

3894 EBF STALLIONS/MEDICAL PIPED GASES LTD FILLIES' H'CAP 1m 1f 218y
2:05 (2:05) (Class 4) (0-80,79) 3-Y-O **£7,561** (£2,263; £1,131; £566; £282) **Stalls** Low

Form RPR
5042 **1** **Motdaw**[15] 3352 3-9-2 **78**.. JFEgan 4 90
(Mick Channon) *hld up in tch in 5th: clsd to chse ldrs over 3f out: rdn to ld over 2f out: clr over 1f out: r.o strly and drew wl clr 1f out: eased towards fin: easily* **9/4**[1]
5-12 **2** 10 **Kath's Legacy**[36] 2666 3-8-11 **73**... RyanTate 6 65
(Ben De Haan) *in tch in 4th: clsd to chse ldr over 3f out: chsd wnr but outpcd u.p over 1f out: no ch w wnr but battled on to hold 2nd ins fnl f* **9/4**[1]
566 **3** *shd* **East Coast Lady (IRE)**[14] 3410 4-9-5 **70**....................... PatCosgrave 7 62
(William Stone) *v.s.a: t.k.h: hld up in rr: clsd and in tch after 2f out: effrt ent fnl 2f: no ch w wnr but battling for 2nd 1f out: kpt on* **14/1**
336 **4** 3¾ **Taffeta Lady**[20] 3194 3-9-0 **79**.............................(p) JosephineGordon[(3)] 3 63
(Lucy Wadham) *chsd ldrs: rdn over 3f out: outpcd u.p and btn over 1f out: wknd fnl f* **3/1**[2]
50-5 **5** 1¾ **Trulee Scrumptious**[21] 3132 7-8-2 **60**.......................(v) GeorgeWood[(7)] 5 41
(Peter Charalambous) *led tl rdn and hdd over 2f out: unable qck and btn over 1f out: wknd fnl f* **9/1**[3]
2-46 **6** 44 **Combe Hay (FR)**[51] 2178 3-8-10 **72**................................... TomQueally 1
(Henry Spiller) *chsd ldr: hung rt 4f out: sn lost pl: last and lost tch 2f out: eased ins fnl f: t.o* **10/1**

2m 12.23s (4.33) **Going Correction** +0.725s/f (Yiel)
WFA 3 from 4yo+ 11lb **6** Ran SP% **112.3**
Speed ratings (Par 102): **111,103,102,99,98 63**
CSF £7.53 TOTE £3.10: £1.70, £1.60; EX 8.60 Trifecta £40.40.
Owner Derek And Jean Clee **Bred** D D & Mrs J P Clee **Trained** West Ilsley, Berks

FOCUS
The ground had dried out a little and was now soft all over (from soft, heavy in places). A fair fillies' handicap to start, but they finished spread out all over Leicestershire.

3895 H.A.C. PIPELINE SUPPLIES LTD H'CAP 7f
2:40 (2:40) (Class 3) (0-95,94) 3-Y-O **£12,602** (£3,772; £1,886; £944; £470) **Stalls** High

Form RPR
-002 **1** **Dream Walker (FR)**[14] 3398 7-8-11 **77**........................(t) StevieDonohoe 2 88
(Brian Ellison) *hld up in rr: effrt jst over 2f out: chsd ldrs and drvn over 1f out: hdwy and chsd wnr ins fnl f: r.o to ld fnl 50yds: sn in command: eased cl home* **9/1**
5061 **2** 1 **Boots And Spurs**[7] 3645 7-8-11 **80**....................(v) JosephineGordon[(3)] 3 88
(Scott Dixon) *in tch in midfield: clsd to chse ldrs and rdn over 2f out: led wl over 1f out: sn drvn and clr jst ins fnl f: hdd and no ex fnl 50yds* **5/1**[2]
103 **3** 1¾ **Toboggan's Fire**[18] 3252 3-7-8 **75**.................................. DavidEgan[(7)] 5 75
(Ann Duffield) *in tch in midfield: effrt u.p jst over 2f out: 5th and drvn over 1f out: kpt on u.p to go 3rd ins fnl f* **11/1**
2113 **4** 2½ **Dilgura**[42] 2460 6-9-1 **84**.. MatthewCosham[(3)] 4 81
(Stuart Kittow) *chsd ldrs: effrt over 2f out: drvn to chse ldrs over 1f out: no ex 1f out: wknd fnl 100yds* **7/2**[1]
0121 **5** 4½ **Welliesinthewater (IRE)**[29] 2862 6-8-12 **83**............(v) NoelGarbutt[(5)] 10 68
(Derek Shaw) *chsd ldrs: wnt 2nd 3f out tl unable qck and lost pl wl over 1f out: wknd fnl f* **10/1**
4362 **6** 2¾ **Cincuenta Pasos (IRE)**[9] 3571 5-9-5 **85**.......................(p) TomQueally 1 76
(Joseph Tuite) *hld up in tch: clsd but wanting to hang rt over 2f out: rdn and ev ch wl over 1f out: hung rt and unable qck 1f out: sn btn: eased ins fnl f* **7/2**[1]
501- **7** 7 **Kakatosi**[298] 6185 9-9-8 **88**.. TedDurcan 9 48
(Mike Murphy) *stdd s: hld up in rr: effrt over 2f out: no hdwy: n.d* **20/1**
0-05 **8** ¾ **Jay Kay**[9] 3571 7-8-9 **75** oh1... JoeyHaynes 11 33
(K R Burke) *led: rdn and hdd wl over 1f out: sn dropped out: bhd fnl f* **10/1**
3310 **9** 1¼ **Arnold Lane (IRE)**[15] 3358 7-9-7 **94**....................... KillianHennessy[(7)] 7 49
(Mick Channon) *chsd ldr tl 3f out: sn u.p and lost pl: bhd fnl f* **14/1**
-140 **10** 8 **Bahama Moon (IRE)**[28] 2910 4-9-6 **86**............................ PatCosgrave 8 20
(David Barron) *hld up towards rr: swtchd lft after 1f: rdn over 2f out: sn btn: wl bhd fnl f* **7/1**[3]

1m 26.28s (0.08) **Going Correction** +0.30s/f (Good)
WFA 3 from 4yo+ 8lb **10** Ran SP% **121.6**
Speed ratings (Par 107): **111,109,107,105,99 96,88,87,86,77**
CSF £55.97 CT £514.66 TOTE £9.90: £2.60, £1.90, £3.90; EX 57.80 Trifecta £985.80.
Owner Keith Brown **Bred** John Berry **Trained** Norton, N Yorks

FOCUS
A warm and competitive handicap run at a solid pace in the conditions. The field split into two early with the main group racing more towards the centre while four came nearside, but that quartet appeared to be at a disadvantage. After this race Pat Cosgrave said: "It's horrible ground", while Tom Queally said: "It's tacky."

3896 H.A.C. GROUP OF COMPANIES H'CAP 1m 60y
3:15 (3:16) (Class 6) (0-65,65) 3-Y-O+ **£3,234** (£962; £481; £240) **Stalls** Low

Form RPR
4541 **1** **Imperial Link**[11] 3496 4-8-13 **55**.............................(p) EdwardGreatrex[(5)] 9 63
(John O'Shea) *mde all: rdn ent fnl 2f: styd on u.p to forge ahd over 1f out: styd on wl* **5/1**[2]
-065 **2** 3¼ **Strathearn (IRE)**[11] 3482 3-9-0 **63**..........................(p) LouisSteward[(3)] 10 62
(Michael Bell) *chsd ldrs: rdn over 2f out: styd on u.p to chse ldr over 1f out: no ex and plugged on same pce ins fnl f* **6/1**[3]
000 **3** ½ **Smile That Smile**[8] 3620 4-9-6 **57**...................................(b[1]) JoeyHaynes 13 57
(Mark H Tompkins) *stdd and dropped in bhd after s: hld up in last trio: hdwy on inner 3f out: drvn to chse ldrs 2f out: 3rd and kpt in same pce ins fnl f* **20/1**
2611 **4** 2¾ **Theydon Thunder**[8] 3624 4-9-3 **61**.............................. GeorgeWood[(7)] 1 55
(Peter Charalambous) *hld up in tch in midfield: 5th and rdn 3f out: swtchd lft over 2f out: edging lft and no imp over 1f out* **6/4**[1]
0-06 **5** ½ **L'Es Fremantle (FR)**[40] 2537 5-8-6 **46** oh1........... MatthewCosham[(3)] 4 39
(Michael Chapman) *in tch in midfield: rdn over 4f out: outpcd u.p over 2f out: rallied and styd on to pass btn horses ins fnl f: no threat to ldrs* **80/1**
4-00 **6** *shd* **Monopoli**[91] 1202 7-8-10 **52**.. LanceBetts[(5)] 6 44
(Ivan Furtado) *hld up in last trio: rdn jst over 2f out: no imp tl hdwy 1f out: kpt on to pass btn horses ins fnl f: nvr trbld ldrs* **8/1**
4126 **7** 1¾ **Ada Misobel (IRE)**[8] 3604 3-8-8 **54**..(p) JFEgan 5 41
(Roy Bowring) *t.k.h: chsd ldrs: rdn over 2f out: 5th and no ex u.p over 1f out: wknd ins fnl f* **14/1**
340 **8** ¾ **Playful Dude (USA)**[36] 2640 3-9-5 **65**............................... HarryBentley 7 50
(Peter Chapple-Hyam) *t.k.h: hld up in midfield: drvn and no hdwy 2f out: wl hld and plugged on same pce after* **10/1**
063 **9** 2¾ **Letbygonesbeicons**[33] 2741 3-9-1 **61**.............................. TomQueally 12 40
(Ann Duffield) *t.k.h: chsd wnr: rdn and lost 2nd over 1f out: sn btn: wknd fnl f* **12/1**
0452 **10** 7 **Divine Touch**[11] 3490 3-8-0 **46** oh1....................................... PaoloSirigu 8 9
(Robert Eddery) *awkward leaving stalls and s.i.s: hld up in rr: effrt over 2f out: no hdwy: bhd fnl f* **14/1**

1m 50.48s (5.38) **Going Correction** +0.725s/f (Yiel)
WFA 3 from 4yo+ 9lb **10** Ran SP% **118.2**
Speed ratings (Par 101): **102,98,98,95,95 94,93,92,89,82**
CSF £35.65 CT £435.95 TOTE £6.40: £2.10, £2.00, £4.10; EX 43.20 Trifecta £1779.70.
Owner The Cross Racing Club **Bred** Mrs E A Bass **Trained** Elton, Gloucs
■ Pepper was withdrawn. Price at time of withdrawal 40/1. Rule 4 does not apply.
■ Stewards' Enquiry : Louis Steward two-day ban (16-17 July): used whip above permitted level

FOCUS
A moderate handicap.

3897 TAP'N'SHOWER.COM (S) STKS 6f
3:50 (3:51) (Class 6) 2-Y-O **£2,587** (£770; £384; £192) **Stalls** High

Form RPR

0 **1** **Luduamf (IRE)**[19] 3232 2-8-5 0 .... HollieDoyle(7) 2 58+
(Richard Hannon) *pressed ldr tl 1/2-way: styd handy: ev ch over 1f out: rdn to ld ent fnl f: edgd lft 1f out: styd on and steadily drew clr fnl f* **5/1**[2]

2 3 ¼ **Yorkshire Star (IRE)** 2-8-7 0 .... HectorCrouch(5) 3 48
(Bill Turner) *dropped to last pair after 1f: rn green: pushed along and outpcd 4f out: rdn over 2f out: hdwy jst over 1f out: kpt on ins fnl f and snatched 2nd on post: no threat to wnr* **5/1**[2]

04 **3** nse **Elements Legacy**[15] 3361 2-8-12 0 .... (v) JoeyHaynes 7 48
(K R Burke) *pressed ldr: upsides 1/2-way: rdn jst over 2f out: stl ev ch but finding little u.p and edgd rt ent fnl f: easily outpcd by wnr fnl 150yds: lost 2nd on post* **7/1**[3]

0 **4** 1 ½ **Jackman**[32] 2757 2-8-9 0 .... (p) GeorgeDowning(3) 6 45
(Tony Carroll) *rn green: sn dropped to rr and hanging: outpcd 4f out: rdn over 2f out: clsd and nt clr run whn swtchd rt ent fnl f: styd on same pce ins fnl f* **20/1**

3 **5** ¾ **Birchfield Lady**[2] 3820 2-8-7 0 .... PaoloSirigu 5 36
(Robert Eddery) *hung rt thrght: in tch in midfield: styd on same pce fr over 1f out* **10/1**

0 **6** 3 ¼ **Rise Of Phoenix**[11] 3485 2-8-7 0 .... WilliamCarson 4 27+
(John Spearing) *led: rdn over 2f out: hdd wl over 1f out: edgd lft and hdd jst over 1f out: losing pl whn short of room ent fnl f: sn wknd* **18/1**

4054 **7** 13 **Cosmic Beau (IRE)**[19] 3232 2-8-12 0 .... (t) FergusSweeney 1
(Tom Dascombe) *stdd s: hld up in tch in midfield: effrt to chal 2f out: rdn to ld over 1f out: edgd lft and hdd ent fnl f: sn lost pl and eased ins fnl f* **10/11**[1]

1m 17.38s (4.38) **Going Correction** +0.30s/f (Good) **7** Ran SP% **117.3**
Speed ratings (Par 92): **82,77,77,75,74 70,52**
CSF £31.09 TOTE £6.90: £3.10, £1.70; EX 33.40 Trifecta £220.00.The winner was bought in 7,500gns.
Owner R Hannon **Bred** J & J Waldron **Trained** East Everleigh, Wilts

FOCUS
A moderate 2yo seller, especially with the hot favourite running so poorly.

3898 H.A.C. MEDICAL GAS TRAINING AND SERVICE LTD FILLIES' H'CAP 6f
4:25 (4:28) (Class 5) (0-70,68) 3-Y-O+ **£4,528** (£1,347; £673; £336) **Stalls** High

Form RPR

324 **1** **Spirit Of Rosanna**[11] 3486 4-8-10 **52** .... (tp) AdamBeschizza 4 61
(Steph Hollinshead) *mde all: rdn 2f out: forged ahd u.p 1f out: pressed again ins fnl f: hld on gamely towards fin* **5/1**[2]

6062 **2** ½ **Potternello (IRE)**[7] 3674 4-9-7 **63** .... JFEgan 8 70
(Mick Channon) *in tch in midfield: effrt to chse ldrs over 1f out: wnt 2nd and pressing wnr ins fnl f: ev ch fnl 100yds: kpt on but hld towards fin* **3/1**[1]

0265 **3** 2 ½ **Beau Mistral (IRE)**[14] 3397 7-8-11 **56** .... GeorgeDowning(3) 7 55
(Tony Carroll) *hld up in tch in last pair: effrt 2f out: hdwy u.p 1f out: kpt on ins fnl f: wnt 3rd last strides: no threat to ldng pair* **14/1**

6300 **4** nk **Refuse Colette (IRE)**[24] 3038 7-9-12 **68** .... WilliamCarson 2 66
(Mick Quinn) *w ldr: rdn and ev ch ent fnl 2f: no ex u.p 1f out: lost 2nd ins fnl f: wknd towards fin and lost 2nd last strides* **10/1**

5-35 **5** 1 **Full Of Promise**[13] 3439 3-9-1 **63** .... JackGarritty 5 57
(Richard Fahey) *in tch in last trio: effrt over 2f out: styd on same pce ins fnl f* **7/1**[3]

-001 **6** 1 ½ **Addicted To Luck**[11] 3494 3-9-1 **66** .... JosephineGordon(3) 1 55
(Jo Hughes) *chsd ldrs: rdn 2f out: unable qck and btn 1f out: wknd ins fnl f* **3/1**[1]

644 **7** 4 **Fly True**[32] 2780 3-8-12 **65** .... HectorCrouch(5) 3 42
(Jeremy Gask) *stdd s: hld up in tch in last pair: effrt 2f out: sn rdn and no hdwy: wknd fnl f* **7/1**[3]

1060 **8** 8 **Undertow (IRE)**[8] 3603 3-9-3 **65** .... JoeyHaynes 6 16
(K R Burke) *in tch in midfield: rdn 2f out: sn lost pl: bhd and eased ins fnl f* **10/1**

1m 14.22s (1.22) **Going Correction** +0.30s/f (Good)
WFA 3 from 4yo+ 6lb **8** Ran SP% **116.5**
Speed ratings (Par 100): **103,102,99,98,97 95,89,79**
CSF £20.85 CT £199.44 TOTE £6.30: £1.70, £1.40, £4.30; EX 19.60 Trifecta £183.50.
Owner J Holcombe **Bred** Redmyre Bloodstock & Tweenhills Stud **Trained** Upper Longdon, Staffs
■ Stewards' Enquiry : Adam Beschizza four-day ban (16-19 July): used whip above permitted level

FOCUS
An ordinary fillies' handicap and not many got into it. Those that started off racing more towards the nearside soon joined the others up the centre.

3899 EBF BREEDERS HOPE AGAINST CANCER RATING RELATED MAIDEN STKS 7f
5:00 (5:01) (Class 5) 3-Y-O **£4,528** (£1,347; £673; £336) **Stalls** High

Form RPR

22-3 **1** **Prying Pandora (FR)**[43] 2419 3-9-0 75 .... JackGarritty 4 84+
(Richard Fahey) *mde all: stl cruising 2f out: nudged along and readily asserted over 1f out: eased wl ins fnl f: v easily* **11/4**[3]

2-52 **2** 4 ½ **Hillside Dream (IRE)**[24] 3038 3-8-11 75 .... EoinWalsh(3) 1 69
(James Tate) *hld up in tch in last pair: clsd to chse ldrs 2f out: rdn to chse clr wnr jst over 1f out: no imp* **9/4**[2]

5232 **3** 7 **Compas Scoobie**[21] 3145 3-9-0 74 .... HarryBentley 6 51
(Roger Varian) *t.k.h: hld up in tch in last: hdwy to chse wnr 1/2-way: rdn and little rspnse 2f out: 3rd and btn jst over 1f out: wknd* **15/8**[1]

55-5 **4** 10 **Blue Moon Rising (IRE)**[28] 2904 3-9-0 74 .... WilliamTwiston-Davies 3 25
(Michael Bell) *chsd ldrs: rdn over 2f out: sn lost pl and btn: wl bhd fnl f* **13/2**

2-06 **5** 29 **Cancan Katy**[47] 2303 3-9-0 74 .... FergusSweeney 2
(Tom Dascombe) *chsd ldr tl 1/2-way: sn rdn and lost pl: t.o over 1f out* **14/1**

1m 28.46s (2.26) **Going Correction** +0.30s/f (Good) **5** Ran SP% **112.2**
Speed ratings (Par 100): **99,93,85,74,41**
CSF £9.54 TOTE £3.30: £1.60, £1.70; EX 8.80 Trifecta £14.50.
Owner Middleham Park Racing X **Bred** Francis Montauban **Trained** Musley Bank, N Yorks

FOCUS
One gelding against four fillies in this modest rating related maiden and just 1lb covered the five runners on official ratings, but it proved to be one-way traffic.

3900 H.A.C. TECHNICAL GAS SERVICES LTD H'CAP 5f
5:30 (5:30) (Class 5) (0-70,75) 3-Y-O **£4,528** (£1,347; £673; £336) **Stalls** High

Form RPR

2423 **1** **Lady Joanna Vassa (IRE)**[2] 3806 3-8-9 **58** .... MichaelJMMurphy 6 65
(Richard Guest) *mde all: rdn and hung rt over 1f out: stl gng rt ins fnl f out a doing enough: styd on* **5/4**[1]

-005 **2** ¾ **Manipura**[9] 3581 3-8-1 **55** .... (p) NoelGarbutt(5) 4 58
(Derek Shaw) *dwlt: hld up in tch in rr: swtchd rt and hdwy to chse ldrs 1/2-way: rdn to chse wnr over 1f out: flashed tail u.p and one pce ins fnl f* **14/1**

35-4 **3** 3 **Andalusite**[19] 3209 3-8-10 **59** .... RobertHavlin 2 51
(Ed McMahon) *chsd wnr: rdn 2f out: 3rd and btn jst over 1f out: wknd ins fnl f* **3/1**[3]

0-60 **4** 1 ¼ **Guilded Rock**[26] 2980 3-8-6 **58** .... MatthewCosham(3) 5 46
(Stuart Kittow) *in tch tl rdn and outpcd 1/2-way: no real imp after: keeping on but no ch w ldrs whn hung rt ins fnl f* **8/1**

6541 **5** 4 **David's Beauty (IRE)**[21] 3140 3-8-5 **57** .... EoinWalsh(3) 3 30
(Brian Baugh) *chsd ldrs tl outpcd u.p 2f out: wl hld and sltly hmpd jst ins fnl f: wknd* **5/2**[2]

1m 2.09s (2.09) **Going Correction** +0.30s/f (Good) **5** Ran SP% **115.8**
Speed ratings (Par 100): **95,93,89,87,80**
CSF £19.44 TOTE £2.00: £1.10, £7.10; EX 19.60 Trifecta £48.60.
Owner www.primelawns.co.uk **Bred** Tom Radley **Trained** Ingmanthorpe, W Yorks
■ Stewards' Enquiry : Matthew Cosham jockey said the gelding ran green

FOCUS
Just a modest 3yo sprint handicap to end with.
T/Plt: £203.20 to a £1 stake. Pool of £57068.56 - 205.0 winning tickets. T/Qpdt: £33.20 to a £1 stake. Pool of £4513.56 - 100.52 winning tickets. **Steve Payne**

3576 NOTTINGHAM (L-H)
Saturday, July 2

OFFICIAL GOING: Soft
Wind: Fresh across Weather: Showers

3901 GENTING CASINO NOTTINGHAM LADY AMATEUR RIDERS' H'CAP 1m 2f 50y
5:45 (5:45) (Class 6) (0-65,71) 4-Y-O+ **£2,183** (£677; £338; £169) **Stalls** Low

Form RPR

0001 **1** **Indian Chief (IRE)**[4] 3748 6-10-13 **71** 6ex .... MissSBrotherton 5 83
(Rebecca Bastiman) *hld up: racd keenly: hdwy 1/2-way: led over 2f out: c readily clr fr over 1f out: easily* **1/1**[1]

0023 **2** 7 **Flag Of Glory**[11] 3492 9-9-3 **53** oh1 .... (b) MissMEdden(5) 2 50
(Peter Hiatt) *prom: lost pl over 8f out: hdwy on outer to go 2nd over 1f out: no ch w wnr* **14/1**

0 **3** 4 ½ **Operateur (IRE)**[73] 1561 8-9-8 **55** .... MissBeckySmith(3) 6 45
(Ben Haslam) *hld up: hdwy over 1f out: styd on to go 3rd wl ins fnl f: nvr nrr* **40/1**

6212 **4** 1 ¾ **Engai (GER)**[28] 2899 10-10-0 **63** .... MissPBridgwater(5) 7 50
(David Bridgwater) *chsd ldrs: pushed along over 2f out: wknd over 1f out* **16/1**

3151 **5** shd **Hydrant**[8] 3620 10-10-7 **65** .... MissJoannaMason 4 52
(Richard Guest) *chsd ldrs: led over 8f out: hdd over 2f out: wknd over 1f out* **8/1**

6025 **6** 2 ¼ **Duke Of Yorkshire**[5] 3711 6-9-13 **62** .... (p) MissEEasterby(5) 9 45
(Tim Easterby) *led: hdd over 8f out: chsd ldr: pushed along over 2f out: wknd over 1f out* **8/1**

1-63 **7** 9 **Sublimation (IRE)**[9] 3582 6-10-5 **63** .... MissGAndrews 8 30
(Steve Gollings) *chsd ldrs: pushed along over 2f out: sn wknd* **5/1**[2]

6513 **8** 16 **Togetherwecan (IRE)**[8] 3620 4-9-8 **57** .... (b) MissEmmaBedford(5) 1
(Mark Johnston) *s.s: a in rr: wknd over 3f out* **15/2**[3]

2m 22.25s (7.95) **Going Correction** +0.80s/f (Soft) **8** Ran SP% **115.6**
Speed ratings (Par 101): **100,94,90,89,89 87,80,67**
CSF £17.76 CT £355.70 TOTE £1.80: £1.10, £4.10, £9.40; EX 16.60 Trifecta £280.70.
Owner Castle Construction (NE) Ltd **Bred** Paget Bloodstock **Trained** Cowthorpe, N Yorks

FOCUS
Following 14mm of rain between Monday and Thursday, and 5mm on Friday evening, the going was given as soft (GoingStick: 5.8). The outer track was in use. The rail was out 6yds on the home bend and 4yds on the stands' bend. Race distance increased by 18yds. This proved plain sailing for the favourite.

3902 GO CASINO EXPERIENCE MAIDEN AUCTION FILLIES' STKS (PLUS 10 RACE) 5f 13y
6:15 (6:15) (Class 5) 2-Y-O **£2,911** (£866; £432; £216) **Stalls** High

Form RPR

4020 **1** **Mightaswellsmile**[18] 3261 2-8-3 0 .... JoeDoyle(3) 6 68
(James Given) *w ldr: rdn to ld wl ins fnl f: edgd rt: styd on* **2/1**[1]

2 1 **Quiet Moment (IRE)** 2-8-10 0 .... JoeyHaynes 1 68+
(Ben Haslam) *sn pushed along towards rr: hdwy 1/2-way: sn edgd lft: styd on to go 2nd wl ins fnl f* **25/1**

5 **3** ¾ **Pranceleya (IRE)**[16] 3301 2-9-0 0 .... LiamJones 9 70
(Marco Botti) *awkward leaving stalls: sn prom: rdn over 1f out: styd on* **12/1**

333 **4** nk **Turanga Leela**[8] 3597 2-8-6 0 .... WilliamCarson 10 61
(Tom Dascombe) *led: shkn up and hdd wl ins fnl f: no ex towards fin* **2/1**[1]

0 **5** 1 **Biologist (IRE)**[28] 2902 2-9-0 0 .... (v[1]) PatCosgrave 4 65
(William Haggas) *pushed along towards rr early: running on whn nt clr run and swtchd lft wl ins fnl f: n.m.r and eased nr fin* **8/1**[3]

6 4 **Jakastar (IRE)** 2-8-10 0 .... KieranO'Neill 5 47
(Richard Hannon) *s.s: outpcd: swtchd lft over 1f out: nvr nrr* **9/2**[2]

7 2 ¼ **Amy Gardner** 2-8-6 0 .... JamesSullivan 2 35
(James Given) *s.i.s: rdn over 1f out: a in rr* **25/1**

0 **8** ½ **Cosmic Sky**[49] 2254 2-9-0 0 .... AndrewElliott 3 41
(Tim Easterby) *chsd ldrs: pushed along 1/2-way: wknd over 1f out* **20/1**

1m 4.92s (3.42) **Going Correction** +0.80s/f (Soft) **8** Ran SP% **116.1**
Speed ratings (Par 91): **104,102,101,100,99 92,89,88**
CSF £62.13 TOTE £3.10: £1.30, £3.90, £2.60; EX 56.50 Trifecta £761.50.
Owner Tim Bostwick **Bred** Highclere Stud **Trained** Willoughton, Lincs

FOCUS
An ordinary maiden.

3903 CATHERINE AND DAVID DURIC RETIREMENT H'CAP 1m 6f 15y
6:45 (6:45) (Class 5) (0-70,70) 4-Y-O+ **£2,911** (£866; £432; £216) **Stalls** Low

Form RPR
4043 **1** **Arthurs Secret**[14] 3418 6-9-2 **65**....................(v) PatCosgrave 9 75
(John Quinn) *s.i.s: rcvrd to chse ldr after 1f: led over 2f out: rdn over 1f out: styd on* **4/1**[2]
4054 **2** 1 ¼ **Nolecce**[33] 2738 9-7-9 **51**.................... HollieDoyle[(7)] 7 59
(Tony Forbes) *s.i.s: hld up: hdwy over 3f out: chsd wnr over 2f out: rdn over 1f out: kpt on* **10/1**
-634 **3** 2 ¾ **Ivanhoe**[10] 3533 6-9-2 **65**....................(p) KieranO'Neill 2 69
(Michael Blanshard) *chsd ldrs: rdn over 2f out: styd on same pce fnl f* **4/1**[2]
1034 **4** 3 ½ **Frosty The Snowman (IRE)**[23] 3067 5-8-7 **56**.......... JamesSullivan 1 55
(Ruth Carr) *hld up: pushed along over 6f out: sme hdwy over 1f out: no ex ins fnl f* **9/2**[3]
50-0 **5** 1 ¾ **Enchanted Moment**[39] 2564 4-9-1 **64**....................(p) HarryBentley 5 61
(Chris Wall) *hld up: hdwy over 2f out: rdn and wknd over 1f out* **10/1**
3214 **6** 3 **Hurry Home Poppa (IRE)**[8] 3602 6-9-7 **70**.................... TomEaves 8 62
(John Mackie) *chsd ldrs: rdn over 2f out: wknd fnl f* **3/1**[1]
0643 **7** 18 **King Of Paradise (IRE)**[24] 3018 7-9-1 **64**.................... NeilFarley 6 31
(Eric Alston) *led: racd keenly: hdd & wknd over 2f out* **8/1**
3m 18.66s (11.66) **Going Correction** +0.80s/f (Soft) 7 Ran SP% **112.5**
Speed ratings (Par 103): **98,97,95,93,92 91,80**
CSF £40.46 CT £167.53 TOTE £3.90: £2.40, £4.30; EX 45.00 Trifecta £212.50.
Owner David Scott and Co (Pattern Makers) Ltd **Bred** Howard Barton Stud **Trained** Settrington, N Yorks

FOCUS
Race distance increased by 30yds. A modest staying handicap run at an uneven tempo and they were well bunched early in the straight before the pace picked up.

3904 BLACKJACK ACES JACKPOT CLASSIFIED STKS 1m 2f 50y
7:15 (7:15) (Class 5) 3-Y-O **£3,067** (£905; £453) **Stalls** Low

Form RPR
303 **1** **Pointel (FR)**[19] 3235 3-9-0 75.................... FrederikTylicki 4 80+
(James Fanshawe) *chsd ldr: rdn over 2f out: led ins fnl f: styd on: edgd lft nr fin* **11/10**[1]
4155 **2** 1 ¼ **Tap The Honey**[15] 3365 3-9-0 75....................(p) JoeyHaynes 3 77
(K R Burke) *led at stdy pce tl qckng over 3f out: rdn over 1f out: hdd ins fnl f: styng on same pce whn hmpd towards fin* **5/1**[3]
5242 **3** 1 ¾ **Kings Gold (IRE)**[8] 3607 3-9-0 72....................(p) TomEaves 2 74
(Michael Dods) *s.i.s: sn prom: rdn over 2f out: sn outpcd: styd on ins fnl f* **5/1**[3]
0 **4** ½ **Saga Sprint (IRE)**[15] 3341 3-8-11 75.................... TomMarquand[(3)] 5 73
(J R Jenkins) *chsd ldrs: rdn over 3f out: outpcd over 2f out: hung lft and r.o ins fnl f* **16/1**
65-0 **5** 7 **Rubensian**[19] 3235 3-9-0 70.................... JamieSpencer 6 62
(David Simcock) *hld up: hdwy over 2f out: sn rdn: wknd ins fnl f* **7/2**[2]
2m 27.16s (12.86) **Going Correction** +0.80s/f (Soft) 5 Ran SP% **109.1**
Speed ratings (Par 100): **80,79,77,77,71**
CSF £6.83 TOTE £2.10: £1.40, £2.00; EX 6.10 Trifecta £18.20.
Owner Swinburn, Godfrey & French **Bred** Franklin Finance S A **Trained** Newmarket, Suffolk

FOCUS
Race distance increased by 18yds. This was steadily run and it paid to be on the pace.

3905 GENTING CASINO AMERICAN ROULETTE H'CAP (JOCKEY CLUB GRASSROOTS MIDDLE DISTANCE SERIES QUALIFIER) 1m 2f 50y
7:45 (7:45) (Class 4) (0-80,80) 3-Y-O+ **£4,851** (£1,082; £1,082; £360) **Stalls** Low

Form RPR
0436 **1** **Lord Franklin**[23] 3057 7-9-11 **77**.................... NeilFarley 3 83
(Eric Alston) *chsd ldr 1f: remained handy: wnt 2nd again 3f out: rdn over 1f out: styd on gamely u.p to ld post* **13/2**
5105 **2** nse **Freewheel (IRE)**[15] 3347 6-9-9 **78**.................... TomMarquand[(3)] 6 84
(Garry Moss) *led: rdn over 1f out: styd on gamely: hdd post* **4/1**[2]
0210 **2** dht **Bigger And Better**[24] 3033 3-8-4 **67**.................... KieranO'Neill 5 73
(Richard Hannon) *hld up in tch: shkn up over 3f out: rdn and swtchd lft over 1f out: edgd lft ins fnl f: sn hrd rdn and ev ch: styd on gamely* **9/2**[3]
3111 **4** 2 ¾ **Viserion**[7] 3641 4-9-8 **79**....................(p) GeorgeBuckell[(5)] 7 80
(David Simcock) *sn prom: rdn over 1f out: styd on same pce ins fnl f* **5/2**[1]
-654 **5** 3 ¾ **Collodi (GER)**[23] 3064 7-9-0 **66**.................... JimmyQuinn 2 60
(David Bridgwater) *s.s: hld up: hdwy over 2f out: sn rdn: wknd fnl f* **22/1**
0404 **6** 8 **Polar Forest**[5] 3721 6-10-0 **80**....................(e) RoystonFfrench 1 58
(Richard Guest) *plld hrd and prom: stdd and lost pl after 1f: hdwy over 2f out: sn rdn: wknd over 1f out* **5/1**
1056 **7** 6 **Farham (USA)**[13] 3435 4-9-4 **70**.................... JackGarritty 4 37
(Richard Fahey) *chsd ldr after 1f: rdn and lost 2nd 3f out: sn wknd* **8/1**
2m 20.99s (6.69) **Going Correction** +0.80s/f (Soft)
WFA 3 from 4yo+ 11lb 7 Ran SP% **112.2**
Speed ratings (Par 105): **105,104,104,102,99 93,88**
WIN: £9.20. Lord Franklin; PL:Lord Franklin: £3.90, Freewheel £1.40, Bigger And Better £0.90 EX: LF/F £18.10, LF/BB £18.80; CSF: LF/F £15.60, F/BB £17.05; TRIFECTA: LF/F/B £127.80, LF/B/F £97.60..
Owner Whitehills Racing Syndicate **Bred** Tony Ferguson & Liam Ferguson **Trained** Longton, Lancs
■ Stewards' Enquiry : Neil Farley two-day ban (16-17 July): used whip above permitted level
Kieran O'Neill two-day ban (16-17 July): used whip above permitted level

FOCUS
Race distance increased by 18yds. There was a tight finish to this fair handicap.

3906 NK MOTORS H'CAP 1m 2f 50y
8:15 (8:15) (Class 5) (0-70,70) 3-Y-O **£2,911** (£866; £432; £216) **Stalls** Low

Form RPR
46-0 **1** **Ravens Quest**[50] 2209 3-9-7 **70**.................... RobertWinston 6 84+
(Hughie Morrison) *mde all: shkn up over 1f out: styd on wl: eased nr fin* **9/4**[1]
650 **2** 2 ¼ **Patent**[31] 2790 3-8-11 **63**.................... TomMarquand[(3)] 4 69
(Richard Hannon) *hld up: hdwy over 3f out: chsd wnr over 1f out: styd on same pce* **5/1**[3]
4606 **3** 6 **Henry The Explorer (CAN)**[15] 3357 3-9-5 **68**.................... JFEgan 1 63
(Jo Hughes) *hdwy to go prom 8f out: chsd wnr 3f out tl rdn over 1f out: wknd fnl f* **14/1**
6026 **4** 7 **Blacklister**[9] 3558 3-9-5 **68**.................... GeorgeBaker 2 49
(Mick Channon) *dwlt: hld up: hdwy over 2f out: sn rdn and hung lft: wknd over 1f out* **5/1**[3]
-443 **5** 4 ½ **Corpus Chorister (FR)**[15] 3355 3-9-4 **67**.................... ShaneKelly 5 40
(David Menuisier) *pushed along to chse wnr: rdn and lost 2nd 3f out: wknd over 2f out* **4/1**[2]
-600 **6** 1 ¾ **Pivotal Dream (IRE)**[38] 2590 3-7-11 **51** oh2.................... NoelGarbutt[(5)] 8 20
(Mark Brisbourne) *sn chsng ldrs: rdn over 3f out: wknd 2f out* **33/1**
0010 **7** 22 **Captain Gerald**[26] 2967 3-8-3 **55**....................(p) JosephineGordon[(3)] 7
(John Ryan) *prom: lost pl after 2f: rdn over 6f out: wknd over 3f out* **14/1**
0-06 **8** nk **Touch Of Color**[35] 2701 3-9-1 **64**....................(p) RyanTate 3
(Clive Cox) *chsd ldrs: rdn over 4f out: wknd over 2f out* **16/1**
3205 **9** 21 **Atrayu (IRE)**[11] 3499 3-8-10 **62**.................... DannyBrock[(3)] 9
(Paul D'Arcy) *hld up: hung lft and wknd over 3f out* **20/1**
2m 23.36s (9.06) **Going Correction** +0.80s/f (Soft) 9 Ran SP% **111.0**
Speed ratings (Par 100): **95,93,88,82,79 77,60,59,43**
CSF £12.64 CT £117.91 TOTE £2.50: £1.10, £1.30, £3.90; EX 14.30 Trifecta £123.40.
Owner The Fairy Story Partnership **Bred** Deepwood Farm Stud **Trained** East Ilsley, Berks

FOCUS
Race distance increased by 18yds. They finished well strung out in this modest handicap.

3907 GENTING CASINO NOTTINGHAM AT CORNERHOUSE H'CAP 6f 15y
8:45 (8:45) (Class 5) (0-75,73) 3-Y-O+ **£2,911** (£866; £432; £216) **Stalls** High

Form RPR
6512 **1** **Giant Spark**[24] 3016 4-9-9 **70**.................... JackGarritty 5 86+
(Paul Midgley) *racd centre: w ldr tl led overall over 1f out: r.o wl: comf: 1st of 6 in gp* **9/4**[1]
/43- **2** 2 ¼ **Magical Effect (IRE)**[317] 5560 4-9-12 **73**.................... JamesSullivan 6 81
(Ruth Carr) *racd centre: s.i.s: hld up: hdwy to chse wnr over 1f out: no imp ins fnl f: 2nd of 6 in gp* **20/1**
6032 **3** 2 ¾ **Regal Parade**[15] 3349 12-9-6 **70**....................(t) KieranShoemark[(3)] 9 69
(Charlie Wallis) *racd stands' side: chsd ldr: edgd lft over 2f out: led his gp over 1f out: sn rdn: no ex ins fnl f: 1st of 3 in gp* **7/2**[2]
5544 **4** 1 **Ambitious Icarus**[5] 3713 7-9-10 **71**....................(e) RoystonFfrench 3 67
(Richard Guest) *racd centre: hld up in tch: rdn over 1f out: wknd fnl f: 3rd of 6 in gp* **8/1**
4653 **5** 3 ½ **Honcho (IRE)**[7] 3674 4-9-4 **68**.................... DannyBrock[(3)] 1 53
(John Ryan) *racd centre: chsd ldrs: rdn 1/2-way: wknd over 1f out: 4th of 6 in gp* **8/1**
0400 **6** 4 ½ **Sarmadee (IRE)**[9] 3554 4-9-8 **69**.................... GeorgeBaker 4 39
(Mick Channon) *overall ldr in centre: rdn: hung lft an hdd over 1f out: sn wknd: 5th of 6 in gp* **5/1**[3]
3544 **7** hd **Spice Mill (IRE)**[8] 3604 3-8-11 **64**.................... AndrewMullen 2 33
(Michael Appleby) *racd centre: sn pushed and in tch: rdn over 2f out: wknd over 1f out: last of 6 in gp* **6/1**
3-06 **8** 14 **Bushephalus (IRE)**[18] 3266 4-9-9 **70**....................(b[1]) RobertWinston 7
(Ivan Furtado) *s.i.s: racd stands' side: hld up: a in rr: wknd 1/2-way: 2nd of 3 in gp* **16/1**
0-06 **9** hd **Storm Lightning**[11] 3487 7-9-5 **69**.................... DanielMuscutt[(3)] 8
(Mark Brisbourne) *led stands' side trio: rdn: hung lft and hdd over 1f out: sn wknd: last of 3 in gp* **40/1**
1m 19.1s (4.40) **Going Correction** +0.80s/f (Soft)
WFA 3 from 4yo+ 6lb 9 Ran SP% **119.2**
Speed ratings (Par 103): **102,99,95,94,89 83,83,64,64**
CSF £53.37 CT £161.05 TOTE £3.60: £1.50, £3.40, £2.40; EX 26.80 Trifecta £127.20.
Owner Frank Brady **Bred** Frank Brady **Trained** Westow, N Yorks

FOCUS
A routine sprint, but it was won by an improving 4yo.
T/Plt: £79.90 to a £1 stake. Pool of £54386.80 - 496.31 winning tickets. T/Qpdt: £35.10 to a £1 stake. Pool of £4748.60 - 99.85 winning tickets. **Colin Roberts**

3857 SANDOWN (R-H)
Saturday, July 2

OFFICIAL GOING: Sprint course: soft (good to soft in places); round course: good to soft changing to soft on all courses after race 1 (1.25)
Wind: Moderate, against Weather: Early showers then fine

3908 CORAL.CO.UK H'CAP 7f 16y
1:25 (1:26) (Class 3) (0-90,90) 3-Y-O
£7,470 (£2,236; £1,118; £559; £279; £140) **Stalls** Low

Form RPR
1321 **1** **Sir Roderic (IRE)**[12] 3465 3-9-1 **84**.................... AndreaAtzeni 2 95
(Rod Millman) *trckd ldrs in 5th: pushed along and prog 2f out: led 1f out: rdn out and styd on wl* **4/1**[1]
5-24 **2** 1 ½ **Silk Cravat**[29] 2861 3-8-12 **81**....................[1] FrankieDettori 6 88
(Simon Crisford) *t.k.h: led after 1f and sn stretched field: brought field to centre in st: jnd 2f out: hdd 1f out: kpt on* **5/1**[2]
5302 **3** ¾ **London Protocol (FR)**[21] 3155 3-8-11 **87**.................... CliffordLee[(7)] 4 92
(K R Burke) *led 1f: chsd ldr after: chal and upsides fr 2f out to 1f out: one pce* **8/1**[3]
-216 **4** 1 **Bernie's Boy**[99] 1071 3-8-11 **80**.................... OisinMurphy 11 82
(Andrew Balding) *hld up in 7th: shkn up over 2f out: styd on fr over 1f out: nrst fin but n.d* **14/1**
1016 **5** hd **Brilliant Vanguard (IRE)**[17] 3292 3-8-13 **82**.................... TomEaves 7 84
(Kevin Ryan) *hld up in 8th: urged along 3f out: sme prog fr over 1f out: kpt on but no ch* **25/1**
-230 **6** nk **Monteverdi (FR)**[16] 3299 3-9-7 **90**.................... RyanMoore 5 91
(Jamie Osborne) *hld up in 6th: shkn up over 2f out: one pce and nvr able to threaten* **4/1**[1]
3001 **7** ¾ **Another Boy**[22] 3111 3-8-4 **78**....................(p) PatrickO'Donnell[(5)] 1 77
(Ralph Beckett) *trckd ldng pair: rdn over 2f out: lost pl over 1f out and fdd* **12/1**
2210 **8** 1 ½ **Destroyer**[7] 3635 3-8-12 **81**....................(p) MartinDwyer 9 76
(William Muir) *t.k.h: hld up in last and wl off the pce: rdn wl over 2f out: no great prog* **14/1**
2-02 **9** ½ **Albernathy**[24] 3026 3-9-4 **87**.................... WilliamBuick 10 81
(Charlie Appleby) *trckd ldng trio: shkn up over 2f out: lost pl and btn over 1f out* **4/1**[1]
1m 31.18s (1.68) **Going Correction** +0.375s/f (Good) 9 Ran SP% **112.6**
Speed ratings (Par 104): **105,103,102,101,101 100,99,98,97**
CSF £23.19 CT £149.71 TOTE £4.90: £1.60, £1.90, £2.30; EX 23.60 Trifecta £174.80.
Owner The Links Partnership **Bred** Thomas G Cooke **Trained** Kentisbeare, Devon

FOCUS
Round course rail out from 1m1f to entrance to home straight, adding 14yds to all round course distances. There was a heavy shower before racing and jockeys were unanimous in calling the ground 'soft', which it was changed to officially following this opener. A useful handicap, with the runner-up having them stretched from an early stage, and they came towards the centre in the straight. The winner was taking another step forward.

3909 CORAL CHARGE (REGISTERED AS THE SPRINT STKS) (GROUP 3) 5f 6y
2:00 (2:01) (Class 1) 3-Y-O+

£36,861 (£13,975; £6,994; £3,484; £1,748; £877) **Stalls** Low

Form RPR
-122 **1** **Brando**[14] 3386 4-9-3 107 TomEaves 8 114+
(Kevin Ryan) *w ldr: led 1/2-way: clr over 1f out and stl cantering: rdn ins fnl f: jst hld on* **2/1**[1]
0001 **2** *shd* **Monsieur Joe (IRE)**[4] 3752 9-9-3 104 AdamKirby 5 113
(Paul Midgley) *shoved along in midfield over 3f out: prog 2f out: drvn to chse wnr jst over 1f out: styd on really wl nr fin: jst failed* **8/1**[2]
0/01 **3** *5* **Jane's Memory (IRE)**[42] 2474 4-9-0 101 FrankieDettori 9 92
(Rae Guest) *chsd ldrs: rdn 2f out: kpt on to take 3rd fnl f: no threat to ldng pair* **12/1**[3]
3200 **4** *1 1/4* **Taexali (IRE)**[21] 3165 3-8-12 94 SamHitchcott 3 89+
(John Patrick Shanahan, Ire) *pushed along and sn dropped to last pair: stl there whn nt clr run over 1f out and swtchd to outer: r.o last 150yds to take 4th nr fin* **50/1**
-401 **5** *3/4* **Spirit Quartz (IRE)**[20] 3201 8-9-3 108 (p) PatSmullen 10 88
(Robert Cowell) *prom: rdn to chse wnr 2f out to jst over 1f out: fdd ins fnl f* **8/1**[2]
-004 **6** *1 1/4* **Iffranesia (FR)**[27] 2943 6-9-0 100 OisinMurphy 11 80
(Robert Cowell) *hld up fr wd draw: effrt on outer 2f out: no hdwy fnl f* **33/1**
1632 **7** *1/2* **Willytheconqueror (IRE)**[21] 3158 3-8-12 104 MartinDwyer 4 80
(William Muir) *racd against rail but forced to chse ldrs: rdn 2f out: steadily lft bhd* **8/1**[2]
-310 **8** *nk* **Log Out Island (IRE)**[15] 3338 3-8-12 110 WilliamBuick 12 78
(Richard Hannon) *racd on outer in midfield: lost pl 1/2-way and sn in rr: effrt again over 1f out: modest late hdwy* **8/1**[2]
0000 **9** *2* **Humidor (IRE)**[14] 3386 9-9-3 100 TomMarquand 1 73
(George Baker) *dwlt: mostly in last pair on inner: nvr a factor* **33/1**
05-4 **10** *3/4* **Soapy Aitken**[21] 3158 3-8-12 98 (b[1]) RyanMoore 7 69
(Clive Cox) *hld up and impeded after 150yds: rdn and struggling 2f out: no prog* **16/1**
2133 **11** *2 3/4* **Duke Of Firenze**[21] 3151 7-9-3 99 AndreaAtzeni 2 61
(David C Griffiths) *nvr on terms w ldrs: struggling fr 2f out* **8/1**[2]
1200 **12** *4* **Lancelot Du Lac (ITY)**[18] 3244 6-9-3 106 RobertWinston 6 46
(Dean Ivory) *led to 1/2-way: wknd rapidly over 1f out: eased* **12/1**[3]

1m 3.28s (1.68) **Going Correction** +0.675s/f (Yiel)
WFA 3 from 4yo+ 5lb **12** Ran SP% **118.0**
Speed ratings (Par 113): **113,112,104,102,101 99,98,98,95,93 89,83**
CSF £17.63 TOTE £2.90: £1.30, £3.00, £3.60; EX 20.60 Trifecta £268.00.
Owner Mrs Angie Bailey **Bred** Car Colston Hall Stud **Trained** Hambleton, N Yorks

FOCUS
Race distance as advertised. Little got into this and the first pair finished clear. The winner is probably better than the bare form.

3910 CORAL CHALLENGE (H'CAP) 1m 14y
2:35 (2:35) (Class 2) 3-Y-O+

£43,113 (£12,978; £6,489; £3,234; £1,624; £819) **Stalls** Low

Form RPR
5034 **1** **Secret Art (IRE)**[21] 3157 6-8-5 **91** MartinDwyer 4 100
(William Knight) *trckd ldrs: clsd fr 2f out and racd nrest to far side: drvn to ld last 150yds: styd on wl* **16/1**
-250 **2** *1 1/2* **Donncha (IRE)**[17] 3273 5-8-11 **100** TomMarquand(3) 3 106+
(Robert Eddery) *slowly away: hld up in last pair: rdn over 2f out: prog over 1f out and racd nrest to far side: styd on wl to take 2nd nr fin* **7/1**[3]
4055 **3** *1/2* **Highland Colori (IRE)**[15] 3358 8-8-6 **92** (v) DavidProbert 8 96
(Andrew Balding) *led 2f: led again wl over 2f out in centre: sn drvn: edgd lft: hdd and no ex last 150yds* **25/1**
3-40 **4** *nk* **Melvin The Grate (IRE)**[29] 2868 6-8-6 **92** ow2 OisinMurphy 1 96
(Andrew Balding) *dwlt: sn in midfield: prog towards far side 2f out: clsd 1f out: styd on same pce after* **14/1**
4130 **5** *nk* **King's Pavilion (IRE)**[16] 3299 3-8-0 **95** oh2 (p) NickyMackay 2 96
(Mark Johnston) *prom: rdn over 2f out: disp 2nd over 1f out: one pce after and drifted lft fnl f* **20/1**
35-6 **6** *1/2* **White Lake**[70] 1637 4-9-3 **103** AndreaAtzeni 15 105+
(Roger Varian) *stdd s fr wd draw and hld up in last: rdn and prog over 2f out: tried to cl on ldrs 1f out: one pce last 100yds* **11/1**
0120 **7** *3/4* **You're Fired (IRE)**[21] 3164 5-9-1 **108** CliffordLee(7) 6 108
(K R Burke) *in tch in midfield: rdn and no prog over 2f out: kpt on fr over 1f out: nvr gng pce to threaten* **14/1**
3030 **8** *nk* **What About Carlo (FR)**[14] 3383 5-8-13 **99** RyanMoore 11 98
(Eve Johnson Houghton) *nvr beyond midfield: rdn and no prog over 2f out: kpt on fnl f* **8/1**
500/ **9** *1/2* **Quixote (GER)**[89] 6-8-11 **97** PatDobbs 5 95
(Tony Carroll) *hld up wl in rr: rdn and no prog over 2f out: kpt on ins fnl f: nrst fin* **66/1**
0310 **10** *hd* **Secret Brief (IRE)**[17] 3273 4-9-4 **104** JamesMcDonald 12 102
(Charlie Appleby) *chsd ldrs: lost pl u.p fr 2f out* **10/1**
0006 **11** *shd* **Fire Ship**[10] 3534 7-8-0 **86** oh3 (v[1]) JimmyQuinn 14 84
(William Knight) *spd fr wd draw and led after 2f: brought field to centre in st: hdd wl over 2f out: wknd over 1f out* **16/1**
-401 **12** *1/2* **Chevallier**[37] 2628 4-8-2 **88** KieranO'Neill 10 84
(K R Burke) *t.k.h: chsd ldng pair: rdn over 2f out: stl disputing 2nd over 1f out: wknd* **16/1**
2-06 **13** *3* **Best Of Times**[14] 3383 4-9-5 **105** WilliamBuick 13 95
(Saeed bin Suroor) *in tch in midfield: brought towards nr side fr over 2f out and sn struggling* **11/2**[2]
-301 **14** *nse* **Mutamakkin (USA)**[21] 3157 4-8-10 **96** PaulHanagan 7 85
(Sir Michael Stoute) *chsd ldrs: brought to r against nr side rail over 2f out: sn btn* **7/2**[1]
-052 **15** *6* **Whitman**[14] 3389 3-8-0 **95** oh1 JoeFanning 9 69
(Mark Johnston) *n.m.r after 1f: nvr bttr than midfield: wknd over 2f out* **20/1**

1m 44.09s (0.79) **Going Correction** +0.375s/f (Good)
WFA 3 from 4yo+ 9lb **15** Ran SP% **124.5**
Speed ratings (Par 109): **111,109,109,108,108 107,107,106,106,106 106,105,102,102,96**
CSF £122.14 CT £2829.89 TOTE £21.00: £5.30, £2.60, £6.00; EX 178.40 Trifecta £3018.20.
Owner Art Of Racing **Bred** Grange Stud **Trained** Patching, W Sussex

FOCUS
Race distance increased by 14yds. Run at a decent gallop, they were spread centre-to-stands' side in the straight with plenty having their chance. The winner has been rated to his past AW best and a length personal best on turf.

3911 CORAL DISTAFF (LISTED RACE) (FILLIES) 1m 14y
3:10 (3:10) (Class 1) 3-Y-O

£20,982 (£7,955; £3,981; £1,983; £995; £499) **Stalls** Low

Form RPR
2360 **1** **Light Up Our World (IRE)**[17] 3274 3-9-0 98 PatDobbs 6 102
(Richard Hannon) *mde all: tk field to centre in st: shkn up over 2f out: pressed and rdn over 1f out: styd on stoutly* **20/1**
21 **2** *1 1/4* **Wilamina (IRE)**[14] 3412 3-9-0 89 ColmO'Donoghue 5 99
(Martyn Meade) *cl up: chsd wnr wl over 1f out: drvn and kpt on but no imp ins fnl f* **3/1**[2]
20-3 **3** *1 1/2* **Sharaakah (IRE)**[17] 3274 3-9-0 97 JoeFanning 10 96
(Ed Dunlop) *t.k.h early: hld up bhd ldrs: rdn 2f out: chsd ldng pair over 1f out: styd on same pce* **9/2**[3]
3-13 **4** *1* **Snow Moon**[23] 3060 3-9-0 94 FrankieDettori 8 93
(John Gosden) *hld up in last trio: rdn and prog fr 2f out: tk 4th fnl f: edgd rt and nt qckn after* **11/4**[1]
-520 **5** *2 1/4* **Make Fast**[17] 3274 3-9-0 98 RyanMoore 3 88
(Andrew Balding) *trckd wnr: rdn and lost 2nd wl over 1f out: steadily wknd* **11/2**
20-0 **6** *2 1/2* **Alamode**[17] 3274 3-9-0 100 (p) MartinDwyer 1 82
(Marcus Tregoning) *t.k.h: hld up bhd ldrs: shkn up over 2f out: no prog over 1f out: wknd* **20/1**
0503 **7** *1* **Australian Queen**[10] 3534 3-9-0 90 OisinMurphy 4 80
(David Elsworth) *hld up in last trio: shkn up over 2f out: no prog and sn btn* **10/1**
0241 **8** *1/2* **Ejayteekay**[6] 3684 3-9-0 74 RobertWinston 9 79
(Hughie Morrison) *dwlt: hld up in last: effrt over 2f out: sn no prog: wknd over 1f out* **33/1**
30-2 **9** *4 1/2* **Raaqy (IRE)**[66] 1771 3-9-0 94 PaulHanagan 7 69
(Owen Burrows) *t.k.h: disp 2nd pl to jst over 2f out: sn wknd* **11/1**

1m 45.5s (2.20) **Going Correction** +0.375s/f (Good) **9** Ran SP% **115.1**
Speed ratings (Par 105): **104,102,101,100,98 95,94,94,89**
CSF £77.62 TOTE £20.70: £5.10, £1.80, £1.40; EX 102.60 Trifecta £630.10.
Owner D Boocock **Bred** D Boocock **Trained** East Everleigh, Wilts

FOCUS
Race distance increased by 14yds. No great gallop on here and the winner, under a fine ride, made all. She has been rated as achieving a length personal best, in line with her better 2yo form. They again came up the middle in the straight.

3912 CORAL-ECLIPSE (BRITISH CHAMPIONS SERIES) (GROUP 1) 1m 2f 7y
3:45 (3:48) (Class 1) 3-Y-O+

£297,727 (£112,875; £56,490; £28,140; £14,122; £7,087) **Stalls** Low

Form RPR
1-11 **1** **Hawkbill (USA)**[16] 3296 3-8-10 110 WilliamBuick 3 123
(Charlie Appleby) *trckd ldr: led over 2f out to 2f out: sn drvn: led again narrowly over 1f out: battled on wl and a holding runner-up nr fin* **6/1**[2]
12 **2** *1/2* **The Gurkha (IRE)**[18] 3245 3-8-10 120 (t) RyanMoore 7 122
(A P O'Brien, Ire) *trckd ldrs: quick move to ld 2f out: sn rdn and hdd over 1f out: pressed wnr after but nt qckn fnl f and hld nr fin* **4/6**[1]
10-1 **3** *1 3/4* **Time Test**[37] 2626 4-9-7 121 PatSmullen 1 119
(Roger Charlton) *trckd ldrs: chal over 2f out: nt qckn and hld in 3rd fr wl over 1f out: styd on last 150yds* **6/1**[2]
60-2 **4** *2 1/4* **Countermeasure**[30] 2819 4-9-7 81 PatDobbs 5 114?
(Roger Charlton) *led: shkn up and hdd over 2f out: sn outpcd but kpt on* **150/1**
-151 **5** *3/4* **My Dream Boat (IRE)**[17] 3272 4-9-7 122 AdamKirby 2 113
(Clive Cox) *hld up in 6th: rdn over 2f out: one pce and nvr threatened ldrs* **6/1**[2]
2223 **6** *5* **Western Hymn**[17] 3272 5-9-7 115 FrankieDettori 4 103
(John Gosden) *hld up in last w hd to one side: rdn and no rspnse wl over 2f out: eased whn no ch fnl f* **12/1**[3]
40 **7** *18* **Bravery (IRE)**[13] 3447 3-8-10 103 ColmO'Donoghue 6 67
(A P O'Brien, Ire) *plld hrd and sn hld up in 5th: wknd qckly over 2f out: t.o* **33/1**

2m 10.71s (0.21) **Going Correction** +0.375s/f (Good)
WFA 3 from 4yo+ 11lb **7** Ran SP% **114.1**
Speed ratings (Par 117): **114,113,112,110,109 105,91**
CSF £10.40 TOTE £6.10: £3.10, £1.10; EX 12.60 Trifecta £38.10.
Owner Godolphin **Bred** Helen K Groves Revokable Trust **Trained** Newmarket, Suffolk

FOCUS
Race distance increased by 14yds. A race that often provides the first major clash of the generations, the pacemaker ensured it wasn't run at a crawl although they hardly went blazing off, and they came centre-field in the straight. The two fancied 3yos came to the fore, with it going to a highly progressive winner, although there's little doubt neither of the leading older contenders were at their best. The pacemaker finished closer than he was entitled to, so not sure this is conclusive, but the winner is on the up.

3913 CORAL MARATHON (REGISTERED AS THE ESHER STKS) (LISTED RACE) 2m 78y
4:20 (4:23) (Class 1) 4-Y-O+

£20,982 (£7,955; £3,981; £1,983; £995; £499) **Stalls** Centre

Form RPR
1265 **1** **Sandro Botticelli (IRE)**[14] 3387 4-9-0 107 (p) FrankieDettori 3 110
(John Ryan) *cl up: rdn whn ldr wnt for home over 2f out: tk 2nd wl over 1f out: drvn and styd on to ld last 50yds: jst hld on* **8/1**[3]
5-21 **2** *shd* **She Is No Lady**[17] 3278 4-8-9 95 AndreaAtzeni 8 105
(Ralph Beckett) *hld up in midfield: prog over 2f out: disp 2nd over 1f out: clsd to chal fnl f: tk 2nd last strides: jst failed* **9/1**
-523 **3** *1/2* **Nearly Caught (IRE)**[7] 3658 6-9-0 105 WilliamBuick 5 109
(Hughie Morrison) *led 1f: trckd ldng pair: brought wd and quick move to ld wl over 2f out and sent for home: drvn over 1f out: kpt on but hdd last 50yds* **14/1**
4-10 **4** *3/4* **Pallasator**[16] 3298 7-9-5 112 OisinMurphy 10 114+
(Sir Mark Prescott Bt) *taken down early: hld up in last trio: gd prog over 2f out to chse ldng trio over 1f out: nt clr run sn after and lost momentum: styd on again nr fin* **4/1**[1]
0-10 **5** *1 1/4* **Astronereus (IRE)**[14] 3384 5-9-5 111 PatDobbs 6 113+
(Amanda Perrett) *hld up in midfield: effrt whn nt clr run over 2f out to over 1f out: styd on fnl f: nrst fin but unable to chal* **12/1**

3-44 **6** *nse* **Oriental Fox (GER)**[14] 3387 8-9-0 106.................... JoeFanning 12 107
(Mark Johnston) *hld up in midfield: prog on outer jst over 2f out: chsd ldrs 1f out: one pce after* **4/1**[1]

060- **7** *9* **Vent De Force**[293] 6363 5-9-0 108.................... RobertWinston 7 96
(Hughie Morrison) *hld up towards rr: rdn wl over 2f out: sn lft bhd by ldrs* **10/1**

1130 **8** *½* **Mirsaale**[18] 3246 6-9-0 97....................(p) PatSmullen 2 95
(Keith Dalgleish) *t.k.h: hld up in midfield: rdn and no prog over 2f out: eased fnl f* **25/1**

4652 **9** *hd* **Cayirli (FR)**[14] 3387 4-9-0 102.................... TimmyMurphy 4 95
(Seamus Durack) *pressed ldr after 1f: led 4f out and styd on inner in st: hdd wl over 2f out: sn wknd* **12/1**

30-0 **10** *¾* **Fun Mac (GER)**[16] 3298 5-9-0 105....................(t) RyanMoore 1 94
(Hughie Morrison) *hld up towards rr: rdn and no prog wl over 2f out: sn btn* **6/1**[2]

2/00 **11** *2 ¼* **Slowfoot (GER)**[56] 2037 8-9-0 93....................(v[1]) SamHitchcott 11 92?
(Jim Best) *slowly away: hld up in last pair: no prog over 2f out: no ch after* **66/1**

2130 **12** *1* **Noble Gift**[14] 3383 6-9-0 104.................... CallumShepherd 15 90
(William Knight) *taken down early: led after 1f to 4f out: styd chsng ldrs tl wknd rapidly wl over 1f out* **25/1**

2-00 **13** *7* **Amber Flush**[31] 1772 7-8-9 0.................... TimClark 14 77
(Martin Smith) *dwlt: a in last pair: lost tch 4f out: bhd after* **100/1**

-623 **14** *13* **Ballynanty (IRE)**[99] 1067 4-9-0 102....................(t) DonnachaO'Brien 13 66
(Andrew Balding) *chsd ldrs: drvn 3f out: wknd rapidly over 2f out: t.o* **20/1**

3m 44.25s (5.55) **Going Correction** +0.375s/f (Good) **14** Ran SP% **121.5**
Speed ratings (Par 111): **101,100,100,100,99 99,95,94,94,94 93,92,89,82**
CSF £75.02 TOTE £8.30: £2.80, £3.00, £4.00; EX 93.90 Trifecta £1002.40.
Owner Graham Smith-Bernal & Alan Dee **Bred** Ask For The Moon Syndicate **Trained** Newmarket, Suffolk

FOCUS
Race distance increased by 14yds. A bigger field than is often the case and it looked very competitive. They went a fair pace and it proved a good test at the distance, so although there was little between the first six, the form makes sense.

3914 DOWNLOAD THE CORAL APP H'CAP — 1m 2f 7y
4:55 (4:56) (Class 4) (0-85,83) 3-Y-O **£6,469** (£1,925; £962; £481) **Stalls** Low

Form RPR

322 **1** **Gibbs Hill (GER)**[10] 3535 3-9-3 **79**.................... AndreaAtzeni 9 88+
(Roger Varian) *hld up in tch: prog on outer over 2f out: led over 1f out: sn idled and rdn: jnd ins fnl f: drvn and hld on wl* **3/1**[1]

31 **2** *shd* **White Shaheen**[5] 3728 3-9-7 **83** 6ex.................... MartinDwyer 13 91
(William Muir) *trckd ldrs: led 2f out: rdn and hdd over 1f out: rallied to join wnr ins fnl f: jst pipped* **7/2**[2]

0-04 **3** *1 ½* **Imari Kid (IRE)**[22] 3104 3-8-6 **68**.................... SamHitchcott 10 73
(Gary Moore) *t.k.h: hld up in last: rdn over 2f out: prog u.p over 1f out: styd on to take 3rd last 100yds* **25/1**

4210 **4** *1* **High Draw (FR)**[21] 3156 3-9-0 **83**.................... CliffordLee(7) 4 86
(K R Burke) *t.k.h: pressed ldr after 2f: led 1/2-way: hdd 2f out: one pce after* **12/1**

5561 **5** *¾* **Kesselring**[15] 3348 3-9-4 **80**.................... PatDobbs 1 82
(Richard Hannon) *pushed up to chse ldrs: rdn over 2f out and nt qckn: safely hld after but kpt on ins fnl f* **6/1**[3]

5-1 **6** *hd* **Natural Scenery**[15] 3359 3-9-5 **81**.................... WilliamBuick 3 82
(Saeed bin Suroor) *hld up towards rr: effrt towards inner over 2f out: chsd ldrs over 1f out: no prog after* **3/1**[1]

5145 **7** *1* **Visage Blanc**[36] 2638 3-9-0 **76**.................... CharlesBishop 6 75
(Mick Channon) *chsd ldr 2f: rdn over 2f out and sn outpcd: kpt on again nr fin* **16/1**

105 **8** *3 ¾* **Fisher Green (IRE)**[40] 2532 3-9-2 **78**.................... PaulHanagan 7 70
(Michael Dods) *in tch: dropped to last pair over 4f out: struggling 3f out: n.d after* **16/1**

3600 **9** *1 ¾* **Winged Dancer**[8] 3591 3-8-8 **70**.................... OisinMurphy 11 58
(Sylvester Kirk) *led to 1/2-way: pressed ldr to over 2f out: sn wknd* **50/1**

-421 **10** *1* **Dot Green (IRE)**[17] 3281 3-9-4 **80**.................... AdamKirby 2 66
(Mark H Tompkins) *hld up in tch: stdy prog over 2f out to trck ldrs wl over 1f out: sn rdn: fnd nil and wknd qckly fnl f* **12/1**

2m 13.87s (3.37) **Going Correction** +0.375s/f (Good) **10** Ran SP% **119.5**
Speed ratings (Par 102): **101,100,99,98,98 98,97,94,92,92**
CSF £13.94 CT £223.61 TOTE £3.80: £1.50, £1.60, £6.80; EX 16.40 Trifecta £241.70.
Owner Paul Smith **Bred** Gestut Gorlsdorf **Trained** Newmarket, Suffolk
■ Stewards' Enquiry : Andrea Atzeni four-day ban (18-21 July): used whip above permitted level

FOCUS
Race distance increased by 14yds. No great gallop on here, but probably a fair little race that should produce winners and it has been rated similar to recent years.
T/Jkpt: Not won. T/Plt: £481.00 to a £1 stake. Pool: £144,266.00 - 299.92 winning tickets T/Qpdt: £105.10 to a £1 stake. Pool: £11,386.00 - 108.32 winning tickets **Jonathan Neesom**

3915 - (Foreign Racing) - See Raceform Interactive

HAMBURG (R-H)
Saturday, July 2

OFFICIAL GOING: Turf: soft to heavy

3916a FRANZ-GUNTHER VON GAERTNER GEDACHTNISRENNEN (HAMBURGER STUTENMEILE) (GROUP 3) (3YO+ FILLIES & MARES) — 1m
3:30 (12:00) 3-Y-O+ **£23,529** (£8,823; £4,411; £2,205; £1,470)

RPR

1 **Shy Witch (GER)**[27] 2949 3-8-7 0.................... IanFerguson 10 106
(H-J Groschel, Germany) *towards rr of midfield: rdn and gd hdwy to claim nrside rail 2f out: led over 1f out: awkward hd carriage whn clr fnl f: rdn out* **7/2**[3]

2 *2 ¼* **Nymeria (GER)**[37] 2633 4-9-2 0.................... AndreasSuborics 9 103
(Waldemar Hickst, Germany) *towards rr: rdn and gd hdwy fr 2 1/2f out: ev ch over 1f out: kpt on wl: nt pce of wnr* **27/10**[1]

3 *1 ½* **Schutzenpost (GER)**[13] 4-9-0 0.................... AlexanderPietsch 2 98
(J Hirschberger, Germany) *led: rdn over 2f out: hdd over 1f out: kpt on gamely fnl f to hold 3rd* **94/10**

4 *shd* **Toinette (IRE)**[38] 2602 3-8-7 0.................... FabriceVeron 7 97
(H-A Pantall, France) *trckd ldrs: rdn and outpcd over 2f out: squeezed out and dropped to rr 2f out: styd on wl fnl f* **41/10**

5 *shd* **Blumenfee (GER)**[63] 3-8-7 0.................... MichaelCadeddu 3 97
(J Hirschberger, Germany) *midfield: effrt 2f out: kpt on same pce* **29/1**

6 *2 ¼* **Rosebay (GER)**[13] 5-9-2 0.................... AdriedeVries 6 94
(Markus Klug, Germany) *trckd ldrs: drvn and unable qck 2f out: wknd steadily fnl f* **58/10**

7 *1 ½* **Walun (GER)**[27] 2949 3-8-7 0.................... DanielePorcu 11 88
(P Schiergen, Germany) *chsd ldrs: drvn and outpcd 3f out: plugged on* **23/1**

8 *2 ¾* **Excilly**[17] 3271 4-9-2 0.................... RichardKingscote 8 84
(Tom Dascombe) *in rr: rdn and sme hdwy 2f out: wknd 1f out* **33/10**[2]

9 *shd* **La Merced (GER)**[27] 2949 3-8-7 0.................... FilipMinarik 1 82
(P Schiergen, Germany) *midfield: drvn and sme hdwy 3f out: short of room under 2f out: sn wknd* **187/10**

1m 45.64s (105.64)
WFA 3 from 4yo+ 9lb **9** Ran SP% **129.0**
WIN (incl. 10 euro stake): 45. PLACES: 14, 14, 20. SF: 132.
Owner Frau K Schwerdtfeger **Bred** Frau Karin Schwerdtfeger **Trained** Germany

3380 LES LANDES
Friday, July 1

OFFICIAL GOING: Good
Wind: Fresh, half behind towards stand Weather: Cool and cloudy

3917a LA VERTE RUE H'CAP — 1m 1f
8:15 (8:15) 3-Y-O+ **£1,780** (£640; £380)

RPR

1 **Grey Panel (FR)**[14] 8-8-13 0.................... TimClark 3 43
(T Le Brocq, Jersey) *trckd ldr: led wl over 2f out: rdn clr* **5/2**[2]

2 *5* **City Ground (USA)**[22] 3064 9-10-12 0.................... MissSBrotherton 5 59
(Michael Appleby) *t.k.h: trckd ldrs: briefly outpcd over 2f out: 5th and c stands' side st: rallied to take 2nd fnl strides* **1/1**[1]

3 *½* **Chapeau Bleu (IRE)**[14] 3380 4-10-0 0.................... MarkQuinlan 2 46
(Mrs C Gilbert, Jersey) *hld up: hdwy fr 3f out: 2nd into st but unable to go w wnr: lost 2nd fnl strides* **12/1**

4 *nk* **Jackpot**[14] 3380 6-9-3 0....................(p) MissCRobinson 10 34
(Brendan Powell) *hld up in rr: shkn up and kpt on wl past btn rivals in st: nrest at fin* **15/2**[3]

5 *4* **Brown Velvet**[14] 4-9-12 0.................... PhilipPrince 9 35
(K Kukk, Jersey) *hld up: hdwy fr over 2f out: wnt 4th into st: one pce* **8/1**

6 *8* **Engaging Smile**[14] 3381 4-10-1 0.................... RichardCondon 6 21
(J Moon, Jersey) *led: rdn and hdd wl over 2f out: sn wknd* **10/1**

7 *4* **Rainbow Charlie**[14] 5-8-5 0 oh19....................(p) AliceMills 8
(Mrs A Corson, Jersey) *hld up: nvr able to chal* **33/1**

8 *3* **Larch (IRE)**[14] 4-9-4 0.................... JemmaMarshall 1
(Mrs A Malzard, Jersey) *unruly in preliminaries: 6th into st: nvr able to chal* **10/1**

9 *½* **Frankki M**[32] 2955 6-8-5 0 oh18....................(v) NoraLooby 4
(Mrs A Corson, Jersey) *hld up: nvr able to chal* **33/1**

10 *½* **Rebel Woman**[341] 10-8-7 0 oh20 ow2....................(p) MissMHooper 7
(Mrs A Corson, Jersey) *prom: wnt 2nd 6f out tl wknd 4f out* **33/1**

Owner The Le Brocq Boys **Bred** John Berry **Trained** Jersey

3918a "BUILDING A BETTER WORKING WORLD" H'CAP — 1m 4f
8:50 (8:50) 3-Y-O+ **£1,780** (£640; £380)

RPR

1 **Mr Opulence**[14] 3381 7-8-5 0 oh1.................... TimClark 2 42
(T Le Brocq, Jersey) *disp ld: led 5f out: reminders over 3f out: drvn out* **5/2**[2]

2 *1 ½* **Zarliman (IRE)**[57] 1413 6-8-10 0....................(p) AmyBaker 9 45
(Neil Mulholland) *t.k.h: hld up: rdn fr over 3f out: 4th into st: ev ch 1f out: no ex* **11/4**[3]

3 *2* **Aussie Lyrics (FR)**[32] 2952 6-10-1 0.................... MarkQuinlan 3 60
(Mrs C Gilbert, Jersey) *trckd ldrs: 5th into st: kpt on one pce* **4/1**

4 *½* **Black Night (IRE)**[14] 4-10-12 0.................... RichardCondon 5 71
(J Moon, Jersey) *trckd ldrs: 5th into st: kpt on one pce* **5/2**[2]

5 *shd* **King Kenny**[14] 3381 11-8-5 0 oh8.................... NoraLooby 6 35
(Mrs A Corson, Jersey) *trckd ldrs: 3rd into st and ev ch: one pce* **9/1**

6 *½* **Bowl Imperior**[14] 3381 4-9-3 0.................... JemmaMarshall 8 47
(Mrs A Malzard, Jersey) *hld up in rr: outpcd fr over 3f out: nvr nrr* **12/1**

7 *½* **Major Maximus**[47] 9-8-8 0.................... AliceMills 1 37
(Mrs C Gilbert, Jersey) *hld up: outpcd fr over 3f out: n.d* **9/4**[1]

8 *1 ½* **Spring Overture**[14] 3381 4-8-5 0 oh20.................... MissCRobinson 4 31
(Brendan Powell) *hld up: briefly rdn on turn over 7f out: outpcd fr over 3f out* **12/1**

9 *10* **Lady Petrus**[32] 2955 11-8-9 0 oh31 ow4....................(p) PhilipPrince 7 19
(K Kukk, Jersey) *disp ld: rdn and hdd 5f out: wknd rapidly* **20/1**

Owner S M Smith **Bred** Miss Victoria Haigh **Trained** Jersey

3388 AYR (L-H)
Sunday, July 3

OFFICIAL GOING: Good to soft (soft in places; 7.3)
Wind: Fresh, against Weather: Overcast

3919 TOTEQUADPOT INSURE YOUR LAST FOUR EBF MAIDEN STKS — 1m 2f
2:25 (2:28) (Class 5) 3-Y-O+ **£3,881** (£1,155; £577; £288) **Stalls** High

Form RPR

4 **1** **The Begum**[51] 2208 3-8-12 0.................... PhillipMakin 7 79
(Ralph Beckett) *dwlt: sn led: qcknd clr 3f out: shkn up over 1f out: easily* **8/11**[1]

2 *10* **Street Of Dreams** 3-9-3 0.................... JoeFanning 1 69
(Saeed bin Suroor) *early ldr: chsd wnr: rdn and hung lft over 2f out: sn no imp: btn fnl f* **6/5**[2]

00 **3** *18* **Ginger Charlie**[82] 1400 3-9-3 0.................... JamesSullivan 3 28
(Ruth Carr) *t.k.h early: chsd ldrs: drvn and outpcd over 3f out: sn wknd* **12/1**

/0P- **4** *7* **Piper Bill**[393] 2953 5-10-0 0.................... PaulMulrennan 2 14
(Jim Goldie) *t.k.h: prom tl rdn and wknd over 3f out* **50/1**[3]

2m 17.7s (5.70) **Going Correction** +0.40s/f (Good)
WFA 3 from 5yo 11lb **4** Ran SP% **107.3**
Speed ratings (Par 103): **93,85,70,65**
CSF £1.82 TOTE £1.60; EX 1.60 Trifecta £3.70.
Owner Rhydian Morgan-Jones **Bred** Juddmonte Farms Ltd **Trained** Kimpton, Hants

■ Ajman Prince was withdrawn. Price at time of withdrawal 25-1. Rule 4 does not apply

FOCUS

Due to rail movement the first five races were extended 21yds. This proved a lively betting heat and the winner looks very useful.

3920 TOTEQUADPOT FOUR PLACES IN FOUR RACES H'CAP 1m 2f

2:55 (2:55) (Class 4) (0-85,85) 3-Y-O+ **£5,498** (£1,636; £817; £408) **Stalls** High

Form RPR

6624 **1** **Innocent Touch (IRE)**[16] 3347 5-10-0 **85** TonyHamilton 3 93
(Richard Fahey) *dwlt: hld up in tch: effrt over 1f out: edgd lft and rdn to ld last 25yds: kpt on wl* **11/2**[3]

0000 **2** *nk* **Buonarroti (IRE)**[29] 2897 5-9-9 **80** (b[1]) DanielTudhope 5 87+
(Declan Carroll) *missed break: hld up: hdwy over 1f out: rdn and pressed wnr last 30yds: kpt on: jst hld* **7/2**[1]

4024 **3** *½* **Gworn**[15] 3391 6-9-9 **80** ConnorBeasley 6 86
(R Mike Smith) *t.k.h: hld up: effrt and hdwy over 1f out: kpt on ins fnl f: hld towards fin* **5/1**[2]

0530 **4** *hd* **Biff Johnson (IRE)**[11] 3520 4-9-9 **80** (b) PhillipMakin 8 85
(Keith Dalgleish) *trckd ldrs: smooth hdwy to ld over 1f out: sn rdn: hdd and no ex last 25yds* **11/1**

-300 **5** *3* **Picture Painter (IRE)**[29] 2909 3-8-2 **70** JamesSullivan 10 69
(Jim Goldie) *hld up: effrt and rdn on outside 2f out: no imp fnl f* **16/1**

020 **6** *nk* **Star Of Spring (IRE)**[8] 3660 4-8-11 **68** RoystonFfrench 9 67
(Iain Jardine) *trckd ldr: rdn and ev ch over 1f out: wknd ins fnl f* **12/1**

0-06 **7** *1 ¼* **Arantes**[16] 3347 5-8-13 **70** (p) PJMcDonald 4 66
(R Mike Smith) *hld up in tch: rdn over 2f out: edgd lft and wknd over 1f out* **28/1**

5222 **8** *1* **Henpecked**[8] 3642 6-8-4 **68** RowanScott(7) 1 62
(Alistair Whillans) *trckd ldrs: rdn over 2f out: wknd fnl f* **7/2**[1]

0300 **9** *5* **Cyril**[36] 2688 4-9-9 **80** (p) ShaneGray 7 64
(Kevin Ryan) *led: rdn over 2f out: hdd over 1f out: sn wknd* **11/1**

2m 14.43s (2.43) **Going Correction** +0.40s/f (Good)
WFA 3 from 4yo+ 11lb **9** Ran SP% **110.2**
Speed ratings (Par 105): **106,105,105,105,102 102,101,100,96**
CSF £23.21 CT £94.68 TOTE £5.60: £1.80, £1.90, £2.00; EX 23.60 Trifecta £79.80.
Owner Nicholas Wrigley & Kevin Hart **Bred** B Kennedy **Trained** Musley Bank, N Yorks

FOCUS

Rail movement added 21yds to race distance. This fair handicap proved messy in the home straight and there was a tight four-way finish.

3921 TOTEQUADPOT RACES 3, 4, 5 AND 6 H'CAP 1m 2f

3:30 (3:31) (Class 6) (0-60,60) 3-Y-O+ **£2,587** (£770; £384; £192) **Stalls** High

Form RPR

0004 **1** **High On Light**[12] 3482 3-8-3 **48** CamHardie 3 58+
(Tim Easterby) *t.k.h: hld up in midfield: smooth hdwy to ld over 1f out: pushed out fnl f: comf* **9/2**[2]

055- **2** *1 ½* **Highfield Lass**[251] 7519 5-8-12 **46** oh1 ConnorBeasley 9 50
(Michael Dods) *hld up: hdwy on wd outside over 2f out: chsd wnr and rdn over 1f out: kpt on ins fnl f: nt pce to chal* **15/2**

-006 **3** *¾* **Galilee Chapel (IRE)**[18] 3287 7-8-12 **46** oh1 (b) BarryMcHugh 4 49
(Alistair Whillans) *t.k.h: hld up: shkn up and hdwy over 2f out: rdn and edgd rt over 1f out: kpt on ins fnl f: nrst fin* **16/1**

-000 **4** *1 ½* **Kerry Icon**[25] 3015 3-8-2 **47** oh1 ow1 [1] JoeFanning 1 47
(Iain Jardine) *t.k.h: prom: rdn over 2f out: edgd rt over 1f out: kpt on same pce* **9/1**

0301 **5** *hd* **Miningrocks (FR)**[12] 3497 4-9-5 **58** PhilDennis(5) 6 58
(Declan Carroll) *led: jnd after 2f: rdn and hdd over 1f out: sn one pce* **13/2**[3]

0453 **6** *1 ¾* **Question Of Faith**[27] 2962 5-9-0 **48** ow1 DavidNolan 11 45
(Martin Todhunter) *s.i.s: hld up: rdn and hung lft over 2f out: hdwy over 1f out: kpt on: nvr able to chal* **14/1**

0350 **7** *nk* **Bushtiger (IRE)**[25] 3020 4-8-12 **46** oh1 JamesSullivan 7 42
(Ruth Carr) *hld up: rdn over 2f out: hdwy over 1f out: no imp* **12/1**

005- **8** *3* **Latin Rebel (IRE)**[146] 7059 9-9-7 **55** (b) PaulMulrennan 2 46
(Jim Goldie) *hld up: stdy hdwy over 2f out: rdn over 1f out: sn no imp* **16/1**

5500 **9** *¾* **Ryan The Giant**[18] 3287 3-8-1 **46** oh1 (p) RaulDaSilva 8 35
(Keith Dalgleish) *prom: rdn and lost pl over 2f out: n.d after* **25/1**

6633 **10** *½* **L'Apogee**[18] 3287 3-9-1 **60** TonyHamilton 5 49
(Richard Fahey) *hld up in midfield on outside: lost pl and struggling over 2f out: sn n.d* **7/2**[1]

0-66 **11** *1 ¼* **Jubilee Song**[41] 2525 4-8-12 **46** oh1 (b) GeorgeChaloner 12 32
(Richard Whitaker) *midfield: hdwy to chse ldrs after 2f: rdn over 2f out: wknd wl over 1f out* **40/1**

0400 **12** *½* **Al Furat (USA)**[39] 2573 8-8-12 **46** oh1 (p) DavidAllan 13 31
(Ron Barr) *s.i.s: hld up: rdn along over 2f out: sn btn* **40/1**

6-65 **13** *1 ½* **Judith Gardenier**[27] 2958 4-8-12 **46** oh1 DougieCostello 14 29
(Iain Jardine) *prom: hdwy to join ldr after 2f: rdn over 2f out: wknd wl over 1f out* **25/1**

4-20 **14** *nk* **Drinks For Losers (IRE)**[18] 3287 5-8-9 **46** JoeDoyle(3) 10 28
(Linda Perratt) *in tch on outside: rdn and effrt over 2f out: sn wknd* **16/1**

2m 15.17s (3.17) **Going Correction** +0.40s/f (Good)
WFA 3 from 4yo+ 11lb **14** Ran SP% **120.1**
Speed ratings (Par 101): **103,101,101,100,99 98,98,95,95,94 93,93,92,91**
CSF £36.75 CT £499.85 TOTE £6.10: £2.20, £2.00, £6.60; EX 45.40 Trifecta £664.20.
Owner Habton Farms **Bred** Highclere Stud **Trained** Great Habton, N Yorks

FOCUS

Rail movement added 21yds to race distance. There was a sound pace on in this weak handicap. Straightforward enough form.

3922 TOTEQUADPOT AVAILABLE ON ALL UK MEETINGS H'CAP 1m

4:00 (4:01) (Class 5) (0-75,74) 3-Y-O+ **£3,557** (£1,058; £529; £264) **Stalls** High

Form RPR

4060 **1** **Beautiful Stranger (IRE)**[11] 3517 5-9-9 **69** (p) TomQueally 6 78+
(Keith Dalgleish) *hld up: hdwy on outside to ld over 1f out: rdn and idled ins fnl f: kpt on* **9/1**

550 **2** *1* **Dark Crystal**[27] 2960 5-9-0 **60** PJMcDonald 2 66+
(Linda Perratt) *in tch: effrt whn n.m.r over 2f out and over 1f out: kpt on fnl f to take 2nd cl home* **18/1**

2232 **3** *shd* **Eastern Dragon (IRE)**[17] 3327 6-9-11 **71** RoystonFfrench 1 76
(Iain Jardine) *trckd ldrs: effrt and ev ch over 1f out: sn chsng ldr: kpt on fnl f: lost 2nd cl home* **9/4**[1]

-504 **4** *¾* **Fray**[8] 3645 5-9-12 **72** PaulMulrennan 8 76+
(Jim Goldie) *hld up: shkn up over 2f out: effrt and swtchd lft wl over 1f out: styng on whn nt clr run ins fnl f: kpt on fin* **7/2**[2]

-000 **5** *nk* **Haymarket**[18] 3286 7-9-6 **66** ConnorBeasley 7 69
(R Mike Smith) *cl up: led and rdn 3f out: hdd over 1f out: kpt on same pce ins fnl f* **28/1**

1060 **6** *½* **Ellaal**[20] 3214 7-9-7 **67** JamesSullivan 10 69
(Ruth Carr) *chsd ldrs: rdn and effrt 2f out: kpt on same pce ins fnl f* **16/1**

0514 **7** *nk* **Mustaqbal (IRE)**[6] 3711 4-9-9 **74** (p) PhilDennis(5) 5 75
(Michael Dods) *dwlt: hld up: hdwy over 2f out: rdn and ev ch over 1f out: outpcd ins fnl f* **4/1**[3]

-000 **8** *¾* **Zeshov (IRE)**[33] 2773 5-9-6 **66** BarryMcHugh 12 69+
(Rebecca Bastiman) *hld up: rdn over 2f out: hdwy whn repeatedly denied room ins fnl f: nt rcvr* **12/1**

0002 **9** *2 ¾* **Royal Holiday (IRE)**[12] 3479 9-9-6 **69** (p) JacobButterfield(3) 3 62
(Marjorie Fife) *led to 3f out: drvn and wknd over 1f out* **11/1**

0-00 **10** *53* **Gun Case**[18] 3286 4-9-10 **70** TomEaves 9
(Alistair Whillans) *hld up: rdn and struggling fr 1/2-way: sn lost tch: t.o* **50/1**

1m 47.3s (3.50) **Going Correction** +0.40s/f (Good) **10** Ran SP% **115.6**
Speed ratings (Par 103): **98,97,96,96,95 95,95,94,91,38**
CSF £155.58 CT £488.74 TOTE £11.00: £2.60, £3.90, £1.40; EX 114.50 Trifecta £728.50.
Owner Weldspec Glasgow Limited **Bred** D Veitch & B Douglas **Trained** Carluke, S Lanarks

FOCUS

Rail movement added 21yds to race distance. A modest, but competitive handicap. They went a solid pace.

3923 TOTEPOOL SUPPORTING SCOTTISH RACING H'CAP 1m

4:35 (4:36) (Class 3) (0-95,91) 3-Y-O+ **£9,056** (£2,695; £1,346; £673) **Stalls** High

Form RPR

23-3 **1** **Pintura**[41] 2527 9-9-13 **90** (b) PhillipMakin 2 98
(Alistair Whillans) *trckd ldrs: rdn to ld over 1f out: sn hrd pressed: edgd lft u.p ins fnl f: hld on wl* **10/1**

6000 **2** *nse* **Two For Two (IRE)**[15] 3390 8-10-0 **91** DavidNolan 10 99
(David Loughnane) *t.k.h early: hld up in tch: hdwy to chal over 1f out: sn rdn: kpt on fnl f: jst hld* **13/2**

12 **3** *nk* **Nicholas T**[15] 3391 4-9-1 **78** DanielTudhope 7 85+
(Jim Goldie) *reluctant to enter stalls: dwlt: hld up: effrt and swtchd rt wl over 1f out: drvn and kpt on strly fnl f: jst hld* **3/1**[1]

1016 **4** *¾* **Spring Offensive (IRE)**[30] 2868 4-9-8 **90** AdamMcNamara(5) 1 95
(Richard Fahey) *trckd ldrs: rdn whn n.m.r briefly wl over 1f out: kpt on ins fnl f* **7/2**[2]

0034 **5** *1 ¾* **Father Bertie**[10] 3565 4-9-11 **88** (tp) DavidAllan 6 89
(Tim Easterby) *trckd ldr: led over 2f out to over 1f out: kpt on same pce fnl f* **6/1**[3]

6310 **6** *hd* **Dubai Dynamo**[11] 3518 11-9-7 **84** PJMcDonald 4 85
(Ruth Carr) *hld up: rdn over 3f out: hdwy over 1f out: kpt on fnl f: nrst fin* **14/1**

0005 **7** *2* **Ingleby Angel (IRE)**[16] 3364 7-9-11 **88** RoystonFfrench 11 84
(Colin Teague) *hld up on outside: rdn over 2f out: no imp fr over 1f out* **66/1**

5100 **8** *1 ¾* **Finn Class (IRE)**[24] 3055 5-9-13 **90** TomEaves 8 82
(Michael Dods) *hld up: rdn along over 2f out: outpcd over 1f out* **12/1**

06-0 **9** *5* **Invoke (IRE)**[51] 2223 5-9-10 **87** TomQueally 5 68
(Keith Dalgleish) *led to over 2f out: rdn and wknd over 1f out* **28/1**

3-01 **10** *¾* **Le Chat D'Or**[41] 2527 8-9-9 **86** (bt) PaulMulrennan 3 65
(Michael Dods) *dwlt: hld up: rdn over 2f out: sn no imp: btn over 1f out* **7/1**

1m 45.92s (2.12) **Going Correction** +0.40s/f (Good) **10** Ran SP% **115.7**
Speed ratings (Par 107): **105,104,104,103,102 101,99,98,93,92**
CSF £72.98 CT £250.08 TOTE £11.00: £2.80, £2.50, £1.50; EX 76.10 Trifecta £620.10.
Owner Michael Beaumont **Bred** Dulverton Equine **Trained** Newmill-On-Slitrig, Borders

FOCUS

Rail movement added 21yds to race distance. The feature was run at a fair pace and it served up a cracking finish.

3924 TOTEPOOL BETTING ON ALL UK RACING H'CAP 6f

5:10 (5:14) (Class 5) (0-75,75) 3-Y-O+ **£3,557** (£1,058; £529; £264) **Stalls** High

Form RPR

0013 **1** **Inexes**[18] 3284 4-9-9 **72** (p) PhillipMakin 6 80+
(Marjorie Fife) *dwlt: t.k.h in rr: nt clr run fr over 2f out: squeezed through and qcknd to ld ins fnl f: edgd lft: comf* **11/2**[2]

4452 **2** *½* **Vallarta (IRE)**[15] 3394 6-9-9 **72** JamesSullivan 5 78
(Ruth Carr) *cl up: led over 1f out to ins fnl f: kpt on: hld nr fin* **7/2**[1]

6411 **3** *¾* **In My Place**[20] 3211 3-8-11 **71** (p) AdamMcNamara(5) 9 75+
(Richard Fahey) *t.k.h: trckd ldrs: effrt whn nt clr run over 2f out to over 1f out: keeping on whn n.m.r cl home* **7/2**[1]

2224 **4** *hd* **Keene's Pointe**[20] 3210 6-9-1 **64** TonyHamilton 10 67
(Kristin Stubbs) *prom: nt clr run over 2f out to over 1f out: rdn and kpt on ins fnl f: nt pce to chal* **9/1**

-403 **5** *hd* **Blue Sonic**[41] 2524 6-9-4 **67** PJMcDonald 7 69+
(Linda Perratt) *hld up: effrt whn nt clr run over 1f out: swtchd rt and kpt on fnl f: nrst fin* **14/1**

2060 **6** *1* **Go Go Green (IRE)**[22] 3150 10-9-7 **70** DanielTudhope 3 69
(Jim Goldie) *dwlt: sn in tch: effrt and ev ch over 1f out to ins fnl f: no ex last 75yds* **15/2**

660 **7** *2 ¼* **Be Bop Tango (FR)**[36] 2693 3-9-0 **69** (p) DougieCostello 2 60
(K R Burke) *trckd ldrs: rdn along over 1f out: wknd ins fnl f* **16/1**

-400 **8** *nk* **Clergyman**[22] 3150 4-9-11 **74** BarryMcHugh 4 65
(Rebecca Bastiman) *midfield on outside: rdn and hdwy to chse ldrs over 1f out: one pce whn bmpd twice ins fnl f: wknd* **12/1**

000- **9** *shd* **Centre Haafhd**[241] 3222 5-8-11 **60** PaulMulrennan 1 51
(Jim Goldie) *hld up: rdn along over 2f out: no imp fr over 1f out* **33/1**

0-20 **10** *1 ¼* **Master Mirasol (IRE)**[57] 2049 3-9-6 **75** (p) TomEaves 8 61
(Kevin Ryan) *led: rdn and hdd over 1f out: wknd fnl f* **7/1**[3]

1m 15.69s (3.29) **Going Correction** +0.65s/f (Yiel)
WFA 3 from 4yo+ 6lb **10** Ran SP% **117.3**
Speed ratings (Par 103): **104,103,102,102,101 100,97,97,96,95**
CSF £25.24 CT £77.67 TOTE £7.20: £2.50, £1.60, £1.60; EX 33.20 Trifecta £135.80.
Owner 21st Century Racing **Bred** Meon Valley Stud **Trained** Stillington, N Yorks

■ Stewards' Enquiry : Barry McHugh four-day ban; careless riding (17th-20th July)
Dougie Costello two-day ban; careless riding (17th-18th July)

FOCUS
Not a bad sprint for the grade. It proved a rough race.

3925 MYTOTEPOOL.COM AMATEUR RIDERS' H'CAP 5f
5:40 (5:44) (Class 6) (0-65,68) 4-Y-0+ **£2,495** (£774; £386; £193) **Stalls** High

Form RPR
5543 **1** **Perfect Words (IRE)**[4] 3779 6-10-11 **62**.............(p) MissBeckySmith[(3)] 4 68
(Marjorie Fife) *in tch: hdwy to ld appr fnl f: hld on wl cl home* **9/2**[3]
0066 **2** *shd* **Reflation**[25] 3016 4-9-11 **52**...........................(p) MissCADods[(7)] 9 58
(Michael Dods) *trckd ldrs: effrt and pushed along over 1f out: hdwy to press wnr ins fnl f: kpt on: jst hld* **13/2**
0550 **3** *1* **Penny Royale**[19] 3268 4-10-9 **62**.............................(p) MissEEasterby[(5)] 2 64
(Tim Easterby) *in tch on wd outside: effrt and ev ch over 1f out: kpt on same pce ins fnl f* **9/4**[1]
-R0 **4** *hd* **A J Cook (IRE)**[44] 2423 6-9-11 **50**.................................. MrsVDavies[(5)] 5 51
(Ron Barr) *dwlt: sn in tch: hdwy and ev ch over 1f out: kpt on same pce ins fnl f* **16/1**
50-0 **5** *shd* **Red Forever**[175] 136 5-9-9 **46**............................ MissHelenCuthbert[(3)] 3 47
(Thomas Cuthbert) *cl up: effrt and ev ch over 1f out: nt qckn ins fnl f* **11/1**
254 **6** *2 1/4* **Secret Millionaire (IRE)**[5] 3741 9-11-0 **62**.................(p) MrsCBartley 10 55
(Shaun Harris) *cl up: led 2f out to appr fnl f: sn outpcd* **6/1**
0000 **7** *1/2* **Takahiro**[29] 2906 4-9-6 **45**...(t) MrBJames[(5)] 8 36
(Linda Perratt) *dwlt: bhd: outpcd 1/2-way: sme hdwy over 1f out: nvr rchd ldrs* **40/1**
5560 **8** *5* **Mystical King**[5] 3755 6-9-11 **45**.........................(p) MissJoannaMason 11 18
(Linda Perratt) *uns rdr bef s: bhd and sn struggling: nvr on terms* **25/1**
2251 **9** *1 3/4* **Bronze Beau**[5] 3755 9-10-13 **68** 6ex............(tp) MrBenjaminStephens[(7)] 7 35
(Kristin Stubbs) *led: edgd lft and hdd 2f out: sn wknd* **7/2**[2]
1m 2.81s (3.41) **Going Correction** +0.65s/f (Yiel) **9** Ran SP% **119.3**
Speed ratings (Par 101): **98,97,96,95,95 92,91,83,80**
CSF £35.05 CT £83.94 TOTE £5.80: £1.80, £2.20, £1.40; EX 33.10 Trifecta £151.70.
Owner Green Lane **Bred** Rathasker Stud **Trained** Stillington, N Yorks
FOCUS
A weak sprint for amateurs riders.
T/Jkpt: Not won. T/Plt: £69.90 to a £1 stake. Pool: £104,207.54 - 1,087.35 winning tickets
T/Qpdt: £29.30 to a £1 stake. Pool: £8,039.67 - 202.50 winning tickets **Richard Young**

3926 - 3933a (Foreign Racing) - See Raceform Interactive

3916 HAMBURG (R-H)
Sunday, July 3
OFFICIAL GOING: Turf: soft to heavy

3934a WWW.PFERDEWETTEN.DE - GROSSER HANSA-PREIS (GROUP 2) (3YO+) (TURF) 1m 4f
3:45 (12:00) 3-Y-0+ **£29,411** (£11,397; £5,882; £2,941; £1,838)

RPR
1 **Protectionist (GER)**[28] 6-9-6 0.................................. EduardoPedroza 3 119+
(A Wohler, Germany) *settled in midfield: clsd fr 2f out: rdn and led in centre of trck 1 1/2f out: drvn clr fnl f: a in control* **7/5**[1]
2 *3 1/4* **Iquitos (GER)**[35] 2723 4-9-6 0...................................... IanFerguson 1 114
(H-J Groschel, Germany) *w.w in rr: stdy hdwy over 2 1/2f out: rdn to chse ldr appr fnl f: styd on u.p: no ch w wnr* **11/5**[2]
3 *4* **Guignol (GER)**[28] 2947 4-9-6 0...................................... FilipMinarik 7 108
(Jean-Pierre Carvalho, Germany) *chsd ldng pair: rdn and nt qckn 2f out: kpt on at one pce: no match for front two* **47/10**[3]
4 *1 1/4* **Techno Queen (IRE)**[38] 5-9-3 0...................................... AdriedeVries 2 103
(T Potters, Germany) *bmpd leaving stalls: w.w in fnl pair: rdn and no immediate imp 2 1/2f out: c stands' side into st: styd on u.p fr 1 1/2f out: nvr in contention* **87/10**
5 *4 1/4* **Eric (GER)**[35] 2723 5-9-6 0.. AlexanderPietsch 4 99+
(C Von Der Recke, Germany) *racd alone in midfield on inner: styd on inner rail turning for home and led 2f out: hdd 1 1/2f out: sn wknd* **35/1**
6 *4* **Sirius (GER)**[56] 2075 5-9-6 0.......................................(b) StephenHellyn 6 92
(Andreas Lowe, Germany) *hld up in midfield: rdn and unable to get on terms wl over 2f out: wl hld fnl 1 1/2f* **66/10**
7 *3* **Fair Mountain (GER)**[35] 2723 4-9-6 0.............................. JozefBojko 5 88
(A Wohler, Germany) *chsd ldr: c wdst of all into st: rdn and nt qckn on stands' rail fr 2f out: sn wknd* **156/10**
8 *21* **Vif Monsieur (GER)**[56] 2075 6-9-6 0.............................. KoenClijmans 8 54
(Mario Hofer, Germany) *led main body abt five horse widths off rail: hdd whn c wd into st 2f out: wknd over 1 1/2f out* **128/10**
2m 47.29s (12.74)
WFA 3 from 4yo+ 13lb **8** Ran SP% **130.0**
WIN (incl. 10 euro stake): 24. PLACES: 13, 13, 15. SF: 93.
Owner Australian Bloodstock Stable **Bred** Dr Christoph Berglar **Trained** Germany

3763 SAINT-CLOUD (L-H)
Sunday, July 3
OFFICIAL GOING: Turf: good

3935a PRIX DE MALLERET (GROUP 2) (3YO FILLIES) (TURF) 1m 4f
1:55 (12:00) 3-Y-0 **£54,485** (£21,029; £10,036; £6,691; £3,345)

RPR
1 **Al Wathna**[28] 2944 3-8-11 0.. GregoryBenoist 7 102
(J-C Rouget, France) *w.w in midfield on outer: nudged along and clsd wl over 2 1/2f out: led appr 2f out: edgd rt 1 1/2f out: drvn out fnl f* **4/5**[1]
2 *snk* **Impressionist (IRE)**[20] 3241 3-8-11 0............... Pierre-CharlesBoudot 3 102+
(A Fabre, France) *settled in fnl pair: rdn and hdwy 2 1/2f out: styd on to chal outside two rivals over 1f out: r.o u.p: a jst hld by wnr* **7/2**[2]
3 *hd* **Do Re Mi Fa Sol (FR)**[21] 3-8-11 0.................................. FranckBlondel 2 101+
(P Decouz, France) *w.w in rr: last and rdn on outer 2f out: styd on fr wl over 1f out: r.o fnl f: nvr quite on terms* **14/1**
4 *1/2* **Mango Tango (FR)**[35] 2726 3-8-11 0.............................. LouisBeuzelin 4 101+
(P Bary, France) *w.w in midfield: rdn and chsd ldr 1 1/2f out: nt clr run and angled out wl over 1f out: styd on wl u.p fnl f: nvr on terms* **7/1**[3]
5 *1/2* **Fee Du Hazard (FR)**[19] 3-8-11 0.. JulienAuge 5 100
(C Ferland, France) *led: set mod gallop: qcknd tempo more than 3f out: sn rdn and hdd appr 2f out: rallied gamely and cl 2nd 1f out: kpt on same pce ins fnl f* **17/2**

6 *1 1/4* **Gambissara (FR)**[35] 2730 3-8-11 0.............................. BertrandFlandrin 1 98
(Lennart Hammer-Hansen, Germany) *t.k.h: restrained bhd ldr on inner: rdn and nt qckn 1 1/2f out: grad lft bhd fnl f* **18/1**
7 *1 1/2* **Jollify (IRE)**[28] 2944 3-8-11 0...................................... MickaelBarzalona 6 95
(A Fabre, France) *broke awkwardly: sn cl up on outer: rdn and lost pl appr 2f out: wl hld fr over 1f out: nt given a hrd time last 100yds* **10/1**
2m 39.38s (-1.02) **7** Ran SP% **121.8**
WIN (incl. 1 euro stake): 1.90. PLACES: 1.10, 1.40, 1.90. DF: 4.50. SF: 5.90.
Owner Al Shaqab Racing **Bred** Petra Bloodstock Agency Ltd **Trained** Pau, France
FOCUS
A bunch finish and the winning time was over ten seconds slower than the Grand Prix de Saint-Cloud.

3936a GRAND PRIX DE SAINT-CLOUD (GROUP 1) (4YO+) (TURF) 1m 4f
3:15 (12:00) 4-Y-0+ **£168,058** (£67,235; £33,617; £16,794; £8,411)

RPR
1 **Silverwave (FR)**[40] 2568 4-9-2 0...................................... MaximeGuyon 3 118
(P Bary, France) *settled in midfield: clsd to chse ldrs fr 1/2-way: rdn to chal 1 1/2f out: styd on u.p to ld 1f out: drvn out: readily* **14/1**
2 *1 1/4* **Erupt (IRE)**[40] 2568 4-9-2 0...................................... StephanePasquier 6 116+
(F-H Graffard, France) *w.w in fnl trio: rdn 2f out: hdwy appr 1 1/2f out: styd on wl fnl f: wnt 2nd cl home: nvr trbld wnr* **18/1**
3 *nk* **Siljan's Saga (FR)**[35] 2727 6-8-13 0.................... Pierre-CharlesBoudot 9 113+
(J-P Gauvin, France) *hld up in fnl trio: hdwy over 2f out: chsd ldng trio fr 1 1/2f out: styd on fnl f: nt pce to chal* **18/1**
4 *hd* **Manatee**[35] 2725 5-9-2 0.. MickaelBarzalona 2 115+
(A Fabre, France) *w.w towards rr: 2nd last: angled out and rdn 2f out: styd on u.p fr ins fnl 1 1/2f: clsng thrght fnl f: nt pce to chal* **25/1**
5 *nk* **Garlingari (FR)**[28] 2947 5-9-2 0................................(p) ThierryThulliez 11 115
(Mme C Barande-Barbe, France) *a cl up on outer: shkn up to ld wl over 2 1/2f out: kicked for home ins fnl 2f: hdd 1f out: kpt on at same pce* **18/1**
6 *nk* **One Foot In Heaven (IRE)**[28] 2947 4-9-2 0.................. OlivierPeslier 4 114
(A De Royer-Dupre, France) *tk v t.k.h: hld up in fnl trio: hdwy on inner 2 1/2f out: cl 7th and n.m.r 2f out: rdn and styd on appr fnl f: nt pce to get on terms* **7/2**[2]
7 *nse* **Vazirabad (FR)**[35] 2725 4-9-2 0.......................... ChristopheSoumillon 7 114
(A De Royer-Dupre, France) *w.w in midfield: gd hdwy fnl bnd wl over 2 1/2f out: 2 l 3rd whn hrd rdn 1 1/2f out but no imp: kpt on at one pce fnl f* **1/1**[1]
8 *1 1/4* **Harlem**[28] 2947 4-9-2 0.. VincentCheminaud 1 112
(A Fabre, France) *nudged along early to chse ldrs: sn settled in midfield: rdn along 3f out but no immediate rspnse: plugged on at same pce fr 1 1/2f out: unable to muster pce to get involved* **10/1**
9 *hd* **Eagle Top**[50] 2241 5-9-2 0.. FrankieDettori 10 112
(John Gosden) *settled in midfield: rdn and angled out 2f fr home: no real imp and jst kpt on at one pce* **15/2**[3]
10 *5 1/2* **Dylan Mouth (IRE)**[35] 2728 5-9-2 0.............................. CristianDemuro 5 103
(Marco Botti) *led: hdd after 2f: remained cl up on inner: rdn and lost pl 1 1/2f out: wl hld whn eased ins fnl f* **18/1**
11 *12* **Alamgiyr (IRE)**[36] 2706 4-9-2 0..(p) AlexisBadel 8 84
(A De Royer-Dupre, France) *trckd ldr on outer: led after 2f: rdn 3f out: hdd wl over 2 1/2f out: sn wknd* **80/1**
2m 29.2s (-11.20) **11** Ran SP% **125.9**
WIN (incl. 1 euro stake): 10.30. PLACES: 3.30, 5.70, 4.00. DF: 56.70. SF: 145.10.
Owner Hspirit **Bred** Mlle M-L Collet, J Collet & Mme M Collet **Trained** Chantilly, France
FOCUS
This Group 1 contest has been won by some genuine top-notch performers in recent years, not least the dual Arc winner Treve who beat Flintshire last year. This season's renewal didn't look quite up to that standard, but it may have unearthed a genuine Arc contender for the home team. The pacemaker set a reasonable gallop without by any means going mad.

3376 DEAUVILLE (R-H)
Saturday, July 2
OFFICIAL GOING: Turf: good to soft; polytrack: standard

3937a PRIX DU BOIS (GROUP 3) (2YO) (TURF) 5f
12:20 (12:00) 2-Y-0 **£29,411** (£11,764; £8,823; £5,882; £2,941)

RPR
1 **Cosachope (FR)**[21] 3182 2-8-8 0...................................... MaximeGuyon 3 101
(P Sogorb, France) *prom: drvn 2f out: led 1f out: r.o wl: drvn out* **12/1**
2 *nk* **Fixette (IRE)**[21] 3182 2-8-8 0...................................... GregoryBenoist 4 100
(F-H Graffard, France) *towards rr: rdn and hdwy fr 2f out: r.o wl fnl f: nt quite able to chal wnr* **6/1**[3]
3 *hd* **Sans Equivoque (GER)**[21] 3182 2-8-8 0.............................. ThierryJarnet 5 99
(D Guillemin, France) *dwlt: in rr: rdn and hdwy on outer fr 2f out: ev ch ins fnl f: no ex cl home* **9/2**[2]
4 *1 1/4* **Vega Sicilia (FR)**[38] 2599 2-8-8 0...................................... TheoBachelot 1 95
(Y Barberot, France) *trckd ldrs: drvn 2f out: kpt on wl but nt gng pce to chal* **6/1**[3]
5 *shd* **Rapacity Alexander (IRE)**[21] 3182 2-8-8 0.................... GeraldMosse 2 94
(David Evans) *led: rdn 2f out: hdd 1f out: wknd steadily fnl f* **4/5**[1]
6 *4* **Stratton Street (USA)**[15] 3378 2-8-11 0.................... MickaelBarzalona 6 85
(A Fabre, France) *midfield: rdn and outpcd 2f out: hmpd 1f out: sn btn* **11/1**
58.77s (1.27) **6** Ran SP% **118.3**
WIN (incl. 1 euro stake): 8.90. PLACES: 5.20, 3.70. SF: 48.70.
Owner Guy Pariente **Bred** A Chopard **Trained** France

3938a PRIX DE LA PORTE MAILLOT (GROUP 3) (3YO+) (TURF) 7f
12:50 (12:00) 3-Y-0+ **£29,411** (£11,764; £8,823; £5,882; £2,941)

RPR
1 **Jimmy Two Times (FR)**[23] 3089 3-8-7 0.................. VincentCheminaud 2 112+
(A Fabre, France) *towards rr: rdn and gd hdwy fr 2f out: led 1f out: sn in command: pushed out* **9/4**[2]
2 *1* **Jallota**[21] 3164 5-9-1 0.. OlivierPeslier 6 112
(Charles Hills) *trckd ldr: rdn to ld over 2f out: sn drvn: hdd 1f out: kpt on wl but nt gng pce of wnr* **4/1**[3]
3 *2* **Caointiorn (FR)**[38] 2603 5-8-11 0...................................... TheoBachelot 5 103
(S Wattel, France) *dwlt: in rr: rdn and hdwy fr 2f out: kpt on wl fnl f but nvr any ch w wnr* **16/1**
4 *1 3/4* **Okana**[23] 3089 3-8-4 0.. MaximeGuyon 1 96
(C Laffon-Parias, France) *midfield: effrt 2f out: wknd 1f out* **14/1**

5 1 **Steip Amach (IRE)**[55] 2067 4-9-1 0 GregoryBenoist 3 99
(D Smaga, France) *trckd ldrs: drvn and unable qck 2f out: wknd ins fnl f* **4/1**[3]

6 3 **Moon Trouble (IRE)**[21] 3183 3-8-7 0 MickaelBarzalona 4 88
(F Head, France) *led: rdn and hdd over 2f out: wknd over 1f out* **7/4**[1]

1m 23.19s (-5.11)
WFA 3 from 4yo+ 8lb **6** Ran SP% **119.7**
WIN (incl. 1 euro stake): 3.10. PLACES:1.90, 2.70. SF: 15.00.
Owner Scea Haras De Saint Pair **Bred** F Teboul & J Boniche **Trained** Chantilly, France

3919 AYR (L-H)
Monday, July 4

OFFICIAL GOING: Good to soft (soft in places) changing to soft (good to soft in places) after race 1 (1.45) changing to soft after race 5 (3.50)
Wind: Almost nil Weather: Overcast, raining

3939 RACING UK NOW IN HD! EBF MAIDEN STKS 6f
1:45 (1:47) (Class 5) 2-Y-O **£3,234** (£962; £481; £240) **Stalls** Centre

Form RPR

2 **1** **Town Charter (USA)**[12] 3516 2-9-0 0 JoeFanning 10 87+
(Mark Johnston) *mde all: shkn up: edgd lft and drew clr fr over 1f out: pricked ears ins fnl f: readily* **1/1**[1]

2 4 ½ **Midaawi (IRE)** 2-9-0 0 ShaneGray 7 73+
(Kevin Ryan) *dwlt: in tch: hdwy over 3f out: shkn up and outpcd over 1f out: rallied to chse (clr) wnr ins fnl f: kpt on: improve* **13/2**[3]

40 **3** 1 ½ **Bear Essentials (IRE)**[18] 3321 2-9-0 0 DanielTudhope 3 68
(David O'Meara) *chsd ldrs on far side of gp: drvn along over 2f out: kpt on same pce fnl f* **11/1**

22 **4** ½ **Carson City**[23] 3128 2-9-0 0 TonyHamilton 9 67
(Richard Fahey) *t.k.h: chsd wnr: rdn along 2f out: edgd rt and outpcd ins fnl f* **2/1**[2]

04 **5** 5 **Foxy Boy**[16] 3416 2-9-0 0 ConnorBeasley 6 52
(Michael Dods) *stdd s: hld up: hdwy over 2f out: rdn and wknd over 1f out* **25/1**

6 2 **No Luck Penny** 2-8-9 0 BarryMcHugh 5 41
(Noel Wilson) *missed break: hld up: rdn over 2f out: sn wknd* **80/1**

0 **7** nk **Cliff Bay (IRE)**[11] 3548 2-9-0 0 DougieCostello 2 45
(Keith Dalgleish) *hld up: effrt over 2f out: wknd over 1f out* **66/1**

0 **8** 2 ½ **Shake And Bakes**[19] 3283 2-9-0 0 TomEaves 8 37
(Marjorie Fife) *plld hrd: in tch tl rdn and wknd 2f out* **100/1**

1m 13.75s (1.35) **Going Correction** +0.15s/f (Good) **8** Ran SP% **112.6**
Speed ratings (Par 94): **97,91,89,88,81 79,78,75**
CSF £8.03 TOTE £1.90: £1.10, £1.90, £2.90; EX 7.60 Trifecta £34.70.
Owner Sheikh Hamdan bin Mohammed Al Maktoum **Bred** Darley **Trained** Middleham Moor, N Yorks
■ Scots Sonnet was withdrawn. Price at time of withdrawal 33/1.Rule 4 does not apply.

FOCUS
Race 3 54yds extra; races 4,6 & 7 27yds extra; remainder as advertised. Stands' side rail in 5m. This didn't look a bad 2yo maiden and yet the winner took it apart.

3940 RACING UK DAY PASS JUST £10 H'CAP (DIV I) 6f
2:15 (2:18) (Class 6) (0-60,64) 3-Y-O+ **£2,587** (£770; £384; £192) **Stalls** Centre

Form RPR

4631 **1** **Danish Duke (IRE)**[5] 3776 5-10-0 64 6ex (p) JamesSullivan 3 72
(Ruth Carr) *t.k.h: prom: nt clr run fr over 2f out tl swtchd rt over 1f out: rdn and kpt on strly fnl f: led cl home* **6/5**[1]

162- **2** nk **Declamation (IRE)**[219] 8035 6-9-5 55 TomEaves 7 60
(Alistair Whillans) *hld up: smooth hdwy to ld appr fnl f: rdn and edgd rt last 100yds: hdd cl home* **10/1**

66-0 **3** ¾ **Spirit Of Zebedee (IRE)**[71] 1670 3-8-11 53 (p) DougieCostello 2 55
(John Quinn) *trckd ldrs: rdn along 2f out: chsd wnr 1f out to last 25yds: no ex* **8/1**

-403 **4** 2 ¼ **Secret City (IRE)**[19] 3289 10-9-8 58 (b) DanielTudhope 9 54
(Rebecca Bastiman) *cl up: rdn along over 2f out: rallied: outpcd ins fnl f* **11/2**[3]

0060 **5** 5 **Sunrise Dance**[11] 3549 7-8-10 46 oh1 KevinStott 5 27
(Kenny Johnson) *led: rdn and hdd appr fnl f: sn wknd* **28/1**

00-0 **6** 1 **Our Place In Loule**[49] 2302 3-8-13 55 BarryMcHugh 8 32
(Noel Wilson) *chsd ldrs: rdn over 2f out: outpcd whn n.m.r briefly appr fnl f: sn btn* **40/1**

-003 **7** 2 ½ **Indego Blues**[5] 3776 7-9-5 55 (p) PaulQuinn 11 26
(David Nicholls) *bmpd s: t.k.h and sn cl up: rdn over 2f out: wknd over 1f out* **10/3**[2]

6000 **8** 28 **Final Spring (IRE)**[23] 3153 3-8-3 48 oh1 ow2 JoeDoyle(3) 10
(Jim Goldie) *dwlt and wnt rt s: bhd: struggling over 2f out: sn lost tch: t.o* **100/1**

1m 14.83s (2.43) **Going Correction** +0.425s/f (Yiel)
WFA 3 from 4yo+ 6lb **8** Ran SP% **111.0**
Speed ratings (Par 101): **100,99,98,95,88 87,84,46**
CSF £13.68 CT £63.65 TOTE £2.10: £1.10, £2.60, £2.60; EX 13.00 Trifecta £62.20.
Owner Michael Hill **Bred** Dean Harron & Ciaran Conroy **Trained** Huby, N Yorks

FOCUS
Heavy rain fell prior to this moderate sprint handicap. The principals came clear towards the stands' side. This could be rated a little higher.

3941 RACING UK DAY PASS JUST £10 H'CAP (DIV II) 6f
2:45 (2:45) (Class 6) (0-60,60) 3-Y-O+ **£2,587** (£770; £384; £192) **Stalls** Centre

Form RPR

0015 **1** **Hab Reeh**[26] 3016 8-9-2 52 (p) JamesSullivan 5 62
(Ruth Carr) *pressed ldr: rdn to ld ins fnl f: kpt on wl* **4/1**[2]

4200 **2** 1 ¼ **Goninodaethat**[17] 3344 8-9-6 56 PaulMulrennan 6 62
(Jim Goldie) *t.k.h: led: rdn over 1f out: hdd ins fnl f: kpt on same pce* **4/1**[2]

5-64 **3** ½ **Ss Vega**[19] 3293 3-8-8 50 JoeyHaynes 3 54
(James Bethell) *in tch: rdn over 2f out: rallied over 1f out: kpt on ins fnl f* **5/1**

0-40 **4** 2 ½ **Studio Star**[11] 3549 4-8-12 48 CamHardie 8 45
(Wilf Storey) *prom: drvn along over 2f out: one pce appr fnl f* **25/1**

0400 **5** 1 ½ **Munjally**[13] 3478 5-9-5 55 (v) DavidNolan 9 48
(Patrick Holmes) *bhd and early reminders: drvn along over 3f out: kpt on fnl f: nvr able to chal* **9/2**[3]

0000 **6** nk **Takahiro**[1] 3925 4-8-10 46 oh1 (tp) GeorgeChaloner 1 38
(Linda Perratt) *in tch: drvn along over 2f out: wknd over 1f out* **40/1**

0200 **7** 1 **Ay Up Audrey**[17] 3368 5-8-6 49 RPWalsh(7) 4 38
(Rebecca Bastiman) *dwlt: t.k.h: hld up in tch: pushed along over 2f out: wknd over 1f out* **25/1**

0663 **8** 7 **Dark Confidant (IRE)**[10] 3604 3-9-3 59 (b) ConnorBeasley 11 26
(Richard Guest) *wnt rt s: hld up: drvn along over 2f out: sn wknd* **3/1**[1]

0000 **9** 1 ¼ **Kylla**[16] 3423 3-8-4 46 oh1 RaulDaSilva 10 9
(Shaun Harris) *bhd: struggling over 2f out: sn btn* **100/1**

1m 14.98s (2.58) **Going Correction** +0.425s/f (Yiel)
WFA 3 from 4yo+ 6lb **9** Ran SP% **111.0**
Speed ratings (Par 101): **99,97,96,93,91 90,89,80,78**
CSF £18.79 CT £76.48 TOTE £4.50: £1.70, £1.60, £1.90; EX 21.30 Trifecta £92.40.
Owner Grange Park Racing IX & Mrs B Taylor **Bred** The Anglo Irish Choral Society **Trained** Huby, N Yorks

FOCUS
There was no hanging about in this second division of the 6f handicap yet the leaders were not for catching. It was marginally slower than the first. The winner is in his best form for years.

3942 FOLLOW @RACING_UK ON TWITTER H'CAP 1m 5f 13y
3:15 (3:15) (Class 5) (0-75,74) 4-Y-O+ **£3,234** (£962; £481; £240) **Stalls** Low

Form RPR

0-23 **1** **Ingleby Hollow**[32] 2813 4-9-0 67 (p) DanielTudhope 4 78
(David O'Meara) *chsd ldr: smooth hdwy to ld over 2f out: rdn clr and edgd lft over 1f out: kpt on wl* **9/4**[1]

0045 **2** 3 ¼ **Love Marmalade (IRE)**[17] 3345 6-9-1 68 CamHardie 2 73
(Alistair Whillans) *hld up in tch: rdn and outpcd over 3f out: rallied to chse (clr) wnr ins fnl f: no imp* **13/2**

-004 **3** ½ **Chebsey Beau**[30] 2888 6-9-1 73 AdamMcNamara(5) 1 77
(John Quinn) *chsd ldrs: drvn and outpcd over 3f out: rallied to chse (clr) wnr over 1f out to ins fnl f: no ex* **7/2**[2]

5410 **4** 8 **Skiddaw Valleys**[12] 3520 4-9-7 74 TonyHamilton 7 66
(Alan Swinbank) *prom: rdn 3f out: wknd wl over 1f out* **5/1**[3]

15 **5** 1 **An Fear Ciuin (IRE)**[32] 2820 5-8-12 72 (v) CallumRodriguez(7) 8 63
(Richard Ford) *led at decent gallop: clr fr 1/2-way tl hdd over 2f out: wknd over 1f out* **10/1**

0-04 **6** 7 **Onda District (IRE)**[31] 2876 4-9-5 72 DougieCostello 3 52
(Richard Ford) *hld up: drvn and struggling 4f out: sn btn* **25/1**

/550 **7** hd **Another Lincolnday**[13] 3480 5-8-11 64 TomEaves 6 44
(Michael Herrington) *dwlt: hld up: struggling over 4f out: sn btn* **14/1**

500- **8** 35 **Jonny Delta**[100] 6049 9-9-2 69 PaulMulrennan 5
(Jim Goldie) *hld up: pushed along over 5f out: sn struggling: t.o* **7/1**

3m 1.01s (7.01) **Going Correction** +0.65s/f (Yiel) **8** Ran SP% **115.1**
Speed ratings (Par 103): **104,102,101,96,96 91,91,70**
CSF £17.60 CT £49.56 TOTE £3.00: £1.30, £1.70, £1.40; EX 17.50 Trifecta £59.50.
Owner Dave Scott & The Fallen Angels **Bred** Dave Scott **Trained** Upper Helmsley, N Yorks

FOCUS
Race distance increased by 54yds. They were strung out early in this modest staying handicap, courtesy of An Fear Ciuin. Form to treat with a degree of caution, rated around the runner-up and third close to recent marks.

3943 RACINGUK.COM H'CAP 1m 1f 20y
3:50 (3:50) (Class 6) (0-60,66) 3-Y-O+ **£2,587** (£770; £384; £192) **Stalls** Low

Form RPR

0021 **1** **Causey Arch (IRE)**[7] 3710 3-9-10 66 6ex (p) ConnorBeasley 7 75
(Michael Dods) *mde all: rdn over 1f out: kpt on gamely fnl f: edgd rt cl home* **7/4**[1]

0402 **2** 1 **Toffee Apple (IRE)**[7] 3710 3-8-4 46 oh1 JoeFanning 6 53
(Keith Dalgleish) *a cl up: effrt and wnt 2nd over 2f out: ev ch ent fnl f: kpt on: hld nr fin* **4/1**[2]

0542 **3** 5 **Big Red**[10] 3624 4-8-7 46 oh1 RPWalsh(7) 8 44
(Rebecca Bastiman) *t.k.h: hld up: rdn on outside over 2f out: hdwy to chse clr ldng pair over 1f out: no imp and drifted rt ins fnl f* **8/1**

6060 **4** 1 ¾ **Opt Out**[6] 3750 6-10-0 60 (v[1]) CamHardie 1 55
(Alistair Whillans) *hld up: drvn along over 2f out: hdwy over 1f out: no imp fr over 1f out* **16/1**

3430 **5** hd **Music Hall (FR)**[41] 981 6-9-0 46 PaulMulrennan 10 40
(Shaun Harris) *hld up in tch: stdy hdwy over 2f out: wknd over 1f out* **25/1**

4050 **6** 3 ¼ **Outlaw Torn (IRE)**[11] 3564 7-9-7 53 (e) DougieCostello 5 41
(Richard Guest) *cl up tl rdn and wknd wl over 1f out* **16/1**

0660 **7** hd **Call Me Crockett (IRE)**[14] 3476 4-9-2 55 (p) JamieGormley(7) 2 42
(Iain Jardine) *hld up: pushed along over 2f out: nvr on terms* **22/1**

0054 **8** 3 ¾ **Almuhalab**[17] 3366 5-10-0 60 JamesSullivan 9 40
(Ruth Carr) *dwlt: sn in tch on outside: hdwy to chse wnr over 4f out to over 2f out: sn rdn: wknd over 1f out* **9/2**[3]

00 **9** ½ **Let Right Be Done**[30] 2906 4-9-12 58 GeorgeChaloner 3 37
(Linda Perratt) *in tch: drvn along over 2f out: wknd wl over 1f out* **10/1**

2m 5.12s (7.62) **Going Correction** +0.925s/f (Soft)
WFA 3 from 4yo+ 10lb **9** Ran SP% **114.7**
Speed ratings (Par 101): **103,102,97,96,95 93,92,89,89**
CSF £8.49 CT £42.98 TOTE £2.60: £1.30, £1.40, £2.60; EX 8.80 Trifecta £25.30.
Owner J A Wynn-Williams & D Neale **Bred** Irish National Stud **Trained** Denton, Co Durham

FOCUS
Race distance increased by 27yds. It paid to race handily in this moderate handicap and the first pair came well clear. The winner is improving.

3944 RACING UK PROFITS RETURNED TO RACING H'CAP 5f
4:25 (4:26) (Class 3) (0-90,91) 3-Y-O+ **£7,762** (£2,310; £1,154; £577) **Stalls** Centre

Form RPR

0644 **1** **Dark Defender**[6] 3753 3-8-11 78 (v) JoeFanning 1 88
(Keith Dalgleish) *in tch on outside: effrt and hdwy over 1f out: led ins fnl f: kpt on strly* **10/3**[2]

2466 **2** 2 **Classy Anne**[16] 3393 6-9-0 76 PaulMulrennan 5 81
(Jim Goldie) *prom: rdn along over 2f out: chsd wnr ins fnl f: kpt on: no imp* **9/2**[3]

0160 **3** ¾ **Soul Brother (IRE)**[38] 2665 5-9-6 82 (b) JackGarritty 2 84
(Tim Easterby) *led: rdn over 1f out: hdd ins fnl f: kpt on same pce* **12/1**

4001 **4** nse **My Name Is Rio (IRE)**[2] 3875 6-10-1 91 6ex (p) ConnorBeasley 6 93
(Michael Dods) *hld up in tch: rdn along over 2f out: kpt on fnl f: no imp* **11/4**[1]

0200 **5** 2 ¼ **Rita's Boy (IRE)**[9] 3638 4-9-5 81 (v) DougieCostello 3 75
(K R Burke) *missed break: sn pushed along and cl up: rdn over 2f out: wknd ins fnl f* **10/1**

0606 **6** hd **Go Go Green (IRE)**[1] 3924 10-8-5 70 JoeDoyle(3) 4 63
(Jim Goldie) *hld up in tch: drvn along over 2f out: no imp fr over 1f out* **12/1**

0221 **7** ½ **Lexington Place**[16] 3393 6-9-12 88 JamesSullivan 7 80
(Ruth Carr) *stdd s: hld up: rdn along over 1f out: sn n.d* **13/2**

4035 **8** 1 3/4 **Blue Sonic**[1] 3924 6-8-7 **69** oh2 .... CamHardie 8 54
(Linda Perratt) *sn towards rr: drvn along over 2f out: wknd over 1f out* **20/1**

1m 0.64s (1.24) **Going Correction** +0.425s/f (Yiel)
WFA 3 from 4yo+ 5lb **8** Ran SP% **110.5**
Speed ratings (Par 107): **107,103,102,102,98 98,97,95**
CSF £17.39 CT £148.55 TOTE £3.60: £1.30, £1.90, £3.10; EX 18.60 Trifecta £170.00.
Owner Prestige Thoroughbred Racing **Bred** Mrs C J Walker **Trained** Carluke, S Lanarks

FOCUS
The feature sprint handicap was another race where it paid to race handily. The winner had slipped to a good mark on his early 2yo form.

3945 RACINGUK.COM/HD H'CAP 7f 50y
4:55 (4:57) (Class 4) (0-85,82) 3-Y-O+ £5,498 (£1,636; £817; £408) Stalls High

Form RPR
3110 **1** **Cymraeg Bounty**[12] 3517 4-9-10 **78** .... DavidNolan 8 93+
(Iain Jardine) *t.k.h early: mde all: shkn up and clr over 1f out: unchal* **13/2**
340 **2** 2 3/4 **Sophie P**[17] 3343 3-8-7 **69** .... ConnorBeasley 12 71
(R Mike Smith) *prom: rdn along over 3f out: rallied over 1f out: chsd (clr) wnr ins fnl f: kpt on: no imp* **25/1**
2103 **3** 1 3/4 **Irish Optimism (IRE)**[10] 3591 3-9-1 **77** .... CamHardie 10 74
(John Quinn) *in tch: drvn and outpcd over 3f out: rallied over 1f out: kpt on fnl f: nt gng pce to chal* **10/1**
5134 **4** 2 1/2 **Favourite Treat (USA)**[10] 3595 6-9-10 **78** ....(e) JamesSullivan 3 72+
(Ruth Carr) *hld up in midfield: rdn over 2f out: hdwy to chse wnr over 1f out to ins fnl f: no ex* **12/1**
4150 **5** 1/2 **Mystic Miraaj**[24] 3115 4-9-12 **80** ....(b) JackGarritty 11 72
(Tim Easterby) *chsd wnr: rdn over 2f out: hung lft and wknd over 1f out* **10/1**
0423 **6** 1 **Fuwairt (IRE)**[9] 3645 4-9-10 **78** .... KevinStott 5 68
(David Loughnane) *hld up: drvn along 3f out: hdwy over 1f out: sn no imp* **5/1**[2]
-050 **7** 1/2 **Green Howard**[24] 3115 8-10-0 **82** .... BarryMcHugh 1 70
(Rebecca Bastiman) *hld up: rdn along over 2f out: nvr able to chal* **6/1**[3]
0230 **8** 5 **Mass Rally (IRE)**[9] 3646 9-10-0 **82** ....(b) PaulMulrennan 4 57
(Michael Dods) *hld up: rdn and hdwy over 2f out: edgd lft and wknd over 1f out* **12/1**
0050 **9** 12 **Glenalmond (IRE)**[12] 3518 4-9-13 **81** ....(v) DougieCostello 7 25
(K R Burke) *midfield: drvn and struggling over 3f out: sn lost tch* **15/2**
4431 **10** 13 **Shadow Game**[13] 3478 3-8-13 **75** .... JoeFanning 2
(Mark Johnston) *chsd ldrs tl rdn and wknd over 3f out: t.o* **7/2**[1]

1m 38.67s (5.27) **Going Correction** +0.925s/f (Soft)
WFA 3 from 4yo+ 8lb **10** Ran SP% **115.7**
Speed ratings (Par 105): **106,102,100,98,97 96,95,90,76,61**
CSF £151.17 CT £1117.33 TOTE £7.20: £2.20, £6.40, £2.90; EX 208.90 Trifecta £1483.70.
Owner M Andrews **Bred** Richard Evans **Trained** Carrutherstown, D'fries & G'way

FOCUS
Race distance increased by 27yds. Little got into this modest handicap, the impressive winner making all.

3946 RACING UK APPRENTICE H'CAP 7f 50y
5:30 (5:31) (Class 6) (0-65,65) 3-Y-O+ £2,587 (£770; £384; £192) Stalls High

Form RPR
06-0 **1** **Madam Mai Tai**[26] 3044 4-8-6 **46** oh1 .... RowanScott(3) 10 52
(Rebecca Bastiman) *s.i.s: bhd: rdn along 3f out: hdwy over 1f out: edgd lft and kpt on wl fnl f to ld towards fin* **33/1**
40 **2** 1/2 **Dolphin Rock**[21] 3220 9-9-6 **62** ....(b) CallumRodriguez(5) 1 67
(Richard Ford) *led: rdn over 2f out: kpt on fnl f: hdd and no ex towards fin* **6/1**
6-02 **3** 1 3/4 **Gypsy Major**[26] 3043 4-9-1 **55** ....(b) RobJFitzpatrick(3) 4 56
(Garry Moss) *t.k.h: in tch: effrt over 2f out: hdwy and hung lft over 1f out: kpt on same pce ins fnl f* **7/2**[2]
-455 **4** 3 1/2 **Fine Example**[41] 2553 3-8-13 **58** .... JoeDoyle 5 47
(Kevin Ryan) *t.k.h: prom: rdn and outpcd 2f out: rallied fnl f: no imp* **3/1**[1]
0000 **5** 6 **Tiger's Home**[26] 3020 6-9-5 **56** .... KevinStott 3 33
(Iain Jardine) *trckd ldr: rdn over 2f out: wknd ins fnl f* **9/1**
-540 **6** 3 1/4 **Stormy Art (IRE)**[21] 3224 3-8-12 **57** .... PhilDennis 2 23
(Michael Dods) *t.k.h: trckd ldrs: rdn over 2f out: wknd over 1f out* **5/1**[3]
000- **7** 8 **Wootton Vale (IRE)**[284] 6682 3-8-2 **50** .... SophieKilloran(3) 7
(Richard Fahey) *hld up in tch: lost grnd after 3f: sn struggling: n.d after* **17/2**
55-0 **8** 9 **Jessie Allan (IRE)**[26] 3016 5-8-9 **46** oh1 ....(v[1]) ShelleyBirkett 6
(Jim Goldie) *bhd: struggling 1/2-way: nvr on terms* **50/1**
0000 **9** 11 **Inshaa**[21] 3212 4-9-11 **65** .... AdamMcNamara(3) 12
(Michael Herrington) *prom on outside: struggling over 3f out: sn btn: eased whn no ch over 1f out* **7/1**

1m 40.52s (7.12) **Going Correction** +0.925s/f (Soft)
WFA 3 from 4yo+ 8lb **9** Ran SP% **116.1**
Speed ratings (Par 101): **96,95,93,89,82 78,69,59,46**
CSF £220.45 CT £892.33 TOTE £26.60: £7.60, £2.10, £1.50; EX 314.60 Trifecta £1445.30.
Owner Ms M Austerfield **Bred** Whitsbury Manor Stud & Trickledown Stud **Trained** Cowthorpe, N Yorks
■ Stewards' Enquiry : Rowan Scott four-day ban: use of whip (18 -21 Jul)

FOCUS
Race distance increased by 27yds. In contrast to the previous race, over the same trip, the winner came from well off the pace, causing a bit of a surprise. The runner-up set the pace with conditions to suit, helps the level, with the winner a slight improver.
T/Plt: £14.50 to a £1 stake. Pool of £69141.76 - 3477.12 winning tickets. T/Qpdt: £5.80 to a £1 stake. Pool of £6872.09 - 867.84 winning tickets. **Richard Young**

3321 RIPON (R-H)
Monday, July 4

OFFICIAL GOING: Good (8.1)
Wind: light 1/2 behind Weather: showers

3947 KIRKGATE MAIDEN AUCTION FILLIES' STKS (PLUS 10 RACE) 6f
6:45 (6:47) (Class 5) 2-Y-O £2,911 (£866; £432; £216) Stalls High

Form RPR
5 **1** **Seduce Me**[20] 3261 2-9-0 0 .... JoeyHaynes 8 84+
(K R Burke) *w ldr: led over 3f out: drvn clr appr fnl f* **7/2**[2]
43 **2** 6 **La Casa Tarifa (IRE)**[32] 2807 2-9-0 0 .... FrannyNorton 5 66
(Mark Johnston) *w ldrs: 2nd over 2f out: kpt on same pce over 1f out* **9/2**[3]
0 **3** 3 3/4 **Lucy's Law (IRE)**[18] 3321 2-9-0 0 .... AndrewElliott 9 55
(Tom Tate) *mid-div: swtchd rt over 4f out: hdwy and swtchd rt over 1f out: kpt on: tk modest 3rd in clsng stages* **100/1**
42 **4** shd **Local Artist (IRE)**[21] 3208 2-9-0 0 .... JasonHart 13 54
(John Quinn) *led tl over 3f out: fdd over 1f out* **5/2**[1]
5 **5** 1/2 **Party Nights**[25] 3073 2-9-0 0 .... PatCosgrave 4 53+
(Luca Cumani) *mid-div: edgd lft over 2f out: kpt on fnl f: gng on at fin* **7/2**[2]
6 1 3/4 **Sadieroseclifford (IRE)** 2-8-11 0 .... SimonPearce(3) 2 48
(Lydia Pearce) *wnt rt s: mid-div: hdwy over 2f out: one pce over 1f out* **50/1**
7 1 1/4 **Myllachy** 2-9-0 0 .... DavidAllan 10 44
(Tim Easterby) *mid-div: n.m.r on inner and swtchd rt over 2f out: kpt on fnl f* **16/1**
0 **8** 1 **Beau Strata (IRE)**[15] 3433 2-9-0 0 .... AndrewMullen 12 41
(Clive Mulhall) *led to post: w ldrs: drvn over 2f out: lost pl over 1f out* **66/1**
9 2 **Dyna Might** 2-8-7 0 .... RobertDodsworth(7) 11 35
(Ollie Pears) *s.i.s: outpcd and in rr: sme hdwy over 1f out: nvr a factor* **50/1**
5 **10** 1/2 **Spanish Beauty**[18] 3321 2-8-11 0 .... JacobButterfield(3) 7 33
(Ollie Pears) *s.v.s: detached in last: sme hdwy over 1f out: nvr on terms* **40/1**
0 **11** 1 1/2 **Tael O' Gold**[19] 3290 2-9-0 0 .... RoystonFfrench 3 29
(Iain Jardine) *chsd ldrs: drvn over 2f out: lost pl over 1f out* **12/1**
0 **12** 2 3/4 **Whisper A Word (IRE)**[35] 2739 2-9-0 0 .... DuranFentiman 6 21
(Tim Easterby) *dwlt: in rr and sn drvn along* **25/1**
00 **13** 3 3/4 **Miss Island Ruler**[11] 3561 2-8-11 0 .... TimClark(3) 1 9
(Shaun Harris) *mid-div: hdwy on outside over 2f out: lost pl over 1f out* **200/1**

1m 12.96s (-0.04) **Going Correction** +0.025s/f (Good) **13** Ran SP% **118.0**
Speed ratings (Par 91): **101,93,88,87,87 84,83,81,79,78 76,72,67**
CSF £18.83 TOTE £4.70: £2.10, £1.90, £12.40; EX 20.70 Trifecta £3319.50.
Owner Ontoawinner, R Mckeown & E Burke **Bred** Jeremy Green And Sons **Trained** Middleham Moor, N Yorks

FOCUS
Not the strongest maiden but it was run at a sound pace and the winner did it well. The runner-up is rated to form with not a great deal of depth behind.

3948 CULTURAL AMBASSADOR ASHLEY THOMASON 50TH BIRTHDAY H'CAP 6f
7:15 (7:15) (Class 5) (0-70,70) 3-Y-O £3,234 (£962; £481; £240) Stalls High

Form RPR
0642 **1** **Portland Street (IRE)**[10] 3603 3-8-10 **59** .... KieranO'Neill 1 68+
(Bryan Smart) *chsd ldrs on outside: effrt over 2f out: styd on fnl f: led nr fin* **3/1**[1]
3020 **2** hd **Dance Alone**[28] 2974 3-9-4 **67** .... ShaneGray 9 75
(Kevin Ryan) *led: edgd rt fnl 75yds: hdd and no ex nr fin* **14/1**
6-05 **3** 1 3/4 **Dyllan (IRE)**[17] 3368 3-9-6 **69** .... JasonHart 4 71
(Ruth Carr) *chsd ldrs: kpt on same pce fnl f* **13/2**[3]
5232 **4** 3/4 **Kingthistle**[17] 3368 3-9-2 **70** .... NathanEvans(5) 2 70
(Michael Easterby) *chsd ldrs: kpt on same pce appr fnl f* **7/1**
0245 **5** 1 3/4 **Silver Sands (IRE)**[16] 3422 3-9-3 **66** ....(p) DavidAllan 5 60
(Tim Easterby) *chsd ldrs: effrt over 2f out: one pce over 1f out* **11/2**[2]
220 **6** 1/2 **Bad Girl Caoimhe (IRE)**[21] 3213 3-9-7 **70** .... BenCurtis 3 63+
(Brian Ellison) *rr-div: hdwy on outside over 2f out: one pce over 1f out* **11/2**[2]
4-60 **7** 2 **Indian Pursuit (IRE)**[58] 2049 3-9-7 **70** .... TomEaves 7 56
(John Quinn) *trckd ldrs: effrt over 2f out: wknd over 1f out* **20/1**
2-00 **8** 1 **Cuppatee (IRE)**[13] 3479 3-9-4 **67** .... PJMcDonald 10 50
(Ann Duffield) *hmpd s: sn chsng ldrs: lost pl over 4f out: hdwy whn nt clr run and swtchd lft 1f out* **25/1**
4-66 **9** nk **Qortaaj**[10] 3609 3-9-2 **68** .... EdwardGreatrex(3) 8 61
(David Loughnane) *wnt lft s: in rr: hdwy on ins whn nt clr run and swtchd rt over 1f out: hmpd 1f out: nt rcvr* **10/1**
0-33 **10** 1 1/2 **Chip Or Pellet**[16] 3423 3-8-3 **52** oh4 ow1 .... AndrewMullen 6 29
(Nigel Tinkler) *dwlt: sn chsng ldrs: edgd lft 1f out: sn wknd* **11/1**

1m 13.07s (0.07) **Going Correction** +0.025s/f (Good) **10** Ran SP% **114.3**
Speed ratings (Par 100): **100,99,97,96,94 93,90,89,89,87**
CSF £47.05 CT £259.90 TOTE £4.40: £1.40, £3.60, £2.60; EX 51.70 Trifecta £207.80.
Owner Michael Moses & Terry Moses **Bred** Ballylinch Stud **Trained** Hambleton, N Yorks
■ Stewards' Enquiry : Kieran O'Neill four-day ban: use of whip (18-21 Jul)
Edward Greatrex caution: careless riding

FOCUS
The pace was sound for this open contest. The winner is unexposed and the runner-up has been rated close to his best.

3949 SANLAM PRIVATE WEALTH AND GUESTS H'CAP 1m 4f 10y
7:45 (7:45) (Class 4) (0-80,80) 3-Y-O £5,175 (£1,540; £769; £384) Stalls Centre

Form RPR
5321 **1** **Knights Table**[17] 3343 3-9-6 **79** .... DavidAllan 5 91+
(James Tate) *trckd ldr: upsides on bit over 3f out: shkn up to ld over 1f out: drew clr fnl 150yds: eased towards fin* **15/8**[1]
0166 **2** 3 1/2 **Michael's Mount**[24] 3103 3-8-13 **72** .... PatCosgrave 2 76
(Ed Dunlop) *hld up in rr: hdwy over 4f out: chsng ldrs over 2f out: wnt 2nd 1f out: no imp* **4/1**[3]
6406 **3** 4 1/2 **Heavensfield**[18] 3306 3-9-0 **73** ow1 .... DarryllHolland 3 70
(Mark H Tompkins) *hld up towards rr: t.k.h: hdwy 8f out: drvn over 3f out: kpt on same pce and 3rd last 50yds* **10/1**
-012 **4** 1 **Arcamist**[25] 3071 3-9-4 **77** .... MichaelJMMurphy 6 72
(Charles Hills) *t.k.h: led: clr over 8f out tl over 4f out: hdd over 1f out: wknd fnl 75yds* **8/1**
2-14 **5** 2 **Street Duel (USA)**[89] 1260 3-9-7 **80** .... FrannyNorton 4 72
(Mark Johnston) *trckd ldrs: upsides over 3f out: drvn over 2f out: fdd over 1f out* **5/2**[2]
-300 **6** 1/2 **Lady Canford (IRE)**[17] 3366 3-8-3 **62** .... JoeyHaynes 1 53
(James Bethell) *hld up in last: effrt over 3f out: chsng ldrs over 2f out: fdd over 1f out* **18/1**

2m 39.41s (2.71) **Going Correction** +0.15s/f (Good) **6** Ran SP% **108.8**
Speed ratings (Par 102): **96,93,90,90,88 88**
CSF £9.04 TOTE £2.70: £1.10, £2.20; EX 9.20 Trifecta £53.50.
Owner Saeed Manana **Bred** Ashbrittle Stud **Trained** Newmarket, Suffolk

FOCUS
Rail on bend from back straight to home straight dolled out 5yds adding 10yds to race distance. They went an honest pace for this fair handicap. Improved form from the winner and this race could prove a bit better than rated.

3950 WILMOT-SMITH MEMORIAL H'CAP — 1m 1f 170y
8:15 (8:15) (Class 3) (0-90,90) 3-Y-O+ **£7,762** (£2,310; £1,154; £577) **Stalls** Low

Form — RPR

6225 **1** **Montsarrat (IRE)**[8] 3688 3-9-3 **90**.................... FrannyNorton 3 — 99+
(Mark Johnston) *mde all: shkn up over 3f out: edgd lft over 2f out: styd on to forge clr fnl 150yds: readily* **10/3**[1]

6320 **2** *1 ¾* **Salmon Sushi**[44] 2487 5-9-6 **82**.................... DavidAllan 2 — 85
(Tim Easterby) *stdd s: hld up in last: effrt 3f out: sn chsng ldrs: kpt on fnl f: tk 2nd last 50yds* **5/1**

3513 **3** *1* **Corton Lad**[16] 3391 6-9-11 **87**....................(tp) PhillipMakin 1 — 88
(Keith Dalgleish) *trckd ldrs: drvn over 3f out: edgd lft and kpt on one pce over 1f out* **11/2**

4640 **4** *3* **Mukhayyam**[12] 3520 4-9-1 **82**....................(p) RachelRichardson(5) 5 — 77
(Tim Easterby) *hld up towards rr: t.k.h: hdwy to chse ldrs over 3f out: one pce over 1f out* **4/1**[3]

5314 **5** *nk* **Carnageo (FR)**[26] 3026 3-8-4 **77**.................... PatrickMathers 6 — 71
(Richard Fahey) *chsd ldrs: drvn 3f out: one pce fnl 2f* **7/2**[2]

3210 **6** *15* **Dutch Uncle**[31] 2868 4-9-11 **87**.................... PatCosgrave 4 — 50
(Ed Dunlop) *w wnr: t.k.h: drvn 3f out: edgd lft 2f out: sn wknd: heavily eased fnl f: struck into* **6/1**

2m 5.1s (-0.30) **Going Correction** +0.15s/f (Good)
WFA 3 from 4yo+ 11lb — **6** Ran SP% **111.6**
Speed ratings (Par 107): **107,105,104,102,102 90**
CSF £19.71 CT £85.48 TOTE £4.00: £2.10, £2.00; EX 22.30 Trifecta £80.60.
Owner Sheikh Hamdan bin Mohammed Al Maktoum **Bred** Agricola Del Parco **Trained** Middleham Moor, N Yorks

FOCUS
Rail on bend from back straight to home straight dolled out 5yds adding 10yds to race distance. A competitive handicap run at a steady pace and an improved winner.

3951 SIS TRADING SERVICES MAIDEN STKS — 1m
8:45 (8:45) (Class 5) 3-Y-O+ **£2,911** (£866; £432; £216) **Stalls** Low

Form — RPR

05 **1** **Shargiah (IRE)**[16] 3412 3-9-3 0.................... HarryBentley 5 — 80+
(Roger Varian) *chsd ldrs: effrt 3f out: styd on to ld last 150yds: drvn rt out* **5/1**[3]

23 **2** *1* **Imperial Focus (IRE)**[20] 3264 3-9-3 0.................... RoystonFfrench 3 — 77
(Simon Waugh) *led: qcknd pce over 3f out: hdd and no ex last 150yds* **7/1**

344- **3** *nse* **Wrapped**[272] 7013 3-8-12 77.................... PatCosgrave 1 — 72
(William Haggas) *trckd ldr: shkn up and upsides over 2f out: wandered and kpt on same pce fnl f* **13/5**[2]

3- **4** *2* **Tegara**[282] 6756 3-8-12 0.................... TomQueally 6 — 67
(James Fanshawe) *trckd ldrs: shkn up and upsides over 2f out: kpt on same pce fnl f* **11/10**[1]

00 **5** *1 ¼* **Sante (IRE)**[44] 2470 3-8-12 0.................... MichaelJMMurphy 7 — 64
(Charles Hills) *dwlt: hld up towards rr: hdwy to chse ldrs over 2f out: kpt on one pce fnl f* **25/1**

0 **6** *10* **Hightime Girl**[32] 2835 3-8-9 0....................(t) EdwardGreatrex(3) 2 — 40
(David Loughnane) *mid-div: hdwy 5f out: chsng ldrs over 2f out: lost pl over 1f out* **66/1**

00- **7** *25* **Rob's Legacy**[255] 7423 3-9-3 0.................... BenCurtis 4
(Shaun Harris) *s.i.s: hld up detached in last: lost pl over 3f out: sn bhd: t.o* **150/1**

1m 41.81s (0.41) **Going Correction** +0.15s/f (Good) — **7** Ran SP% **110.6**
Speed ratings (Par 103): **103,102,101,99,98 88,63**
CSF £35.28 TOTE £6.90: £3.10, £1.80; EX 33.90 Trifecta £68.10.
Owner Saif Ali **Bred** Rabbah Bloodstock Limited **Trained** Newmarket, Suffolk

FOCUS
Rail on bend from back straight to home straight dolled out 5yds adding 10yds to race distance. A fair maiden run at an even tempo. This is rated around the second, with the third close to last year's debut run.

3952 CHILDRENS FESTIVAL CIRCUS HERE 1ST AUGUST H'CAP — 1m
9:15 (9:15) (Class 5) (0-70,74) 3-Y-O+ **£3,234** (£962; £481; £240) **Stalls** Low

Form — RPR

6000 **1** **Furiant**[19] 3284 3-9-5 **70**.................... FrannyNorton 11 — 74
(Mark Johnston) *trckd ldr: upsides over 4f out: styd on fnl f: led post* **28/1**

0-05 **2** *shd* **Midlight**[46] 2409 4-8-13 **55**....................(t) GeorgeChaloner 5 — 61
(Richard Whitaker) *led: t.k.h: kpt on wl fnl 2f: hdd post* **12/1**

442 **3** *nk* **Yulong Xiongba (IRE)**[17] 3367 4-9-9 **65**.................... ConnorBeasley 12 — 70
(Julie Camacho) *sn chsng ldrs: kpt on fnl f: no ex nr fin* **8/1**

2563 **4** *¾* **Newmarket Warrior (IRE)**[17] 3366 5-9-12 **68**.........(p) RoystonFfrench 4 — 71
(Iain Jardine) *trckd ldrs on inner: effrt over 1f out: kpt on same pce last 100yds* **13/2**[2]

4202 **5** *1 ½* **Cabal**[17] 3366 9-9-12 **68**....................(v) DavidAllan 6 — 68
(Geoffrey Harker) *chsd ldrs: drvn over 2f out: one pce over 1f out* **12/1**

5546 **6** *1 ¾* **The Magic Pencil (IRE)**[48] 2327 3-9-3 **68**.................... TomEaves 3 — 61
(Kevin Ryan) *sn chsng ldrs: reminders over 3f out: nt clr run over 2f out: one pce fnl 2f* **7/1**[3]

2100 **7** *nse* **Mr Cool Cash**[13] 3478 4-9-9 **68**....................(t) JacobButterfield(3) 1 — 63+
(Richard Guest) *mid-div: nt clr run over 2f out: kpt on fnl f: nvr a threat* **8/1**

3335 **8** *1 ¾* **Mango Chutney**[21] 3224 3-8-8 **59**.................... AndrewMullen 9 — 48
(John Davies) *s.i.s: in rr: sme hdwy over 2f out: kpt on: nvr a factor* **13/2**[2]

-011 **9** *nk* **Barwah (USA)**[26] 3013 5-9-3 **59**.................... JackGarritty 13 — 49+
(Peter Niven) *hld up in rr: nt clr run over 2f out tl swtchd lft over 1f out: kpt on: nvr a factor* **8/1**

0-00 **10** *1* **Fazza**[17] 3367 9-9-2 **58**.................... PaddyAspell 2 — 46
(Grant Tuer) *towards rr: hdwy on inner over 3f out: nt clr run 2f out: nvr a factor* **28/1**

0446 **11** *1* **Bertha Burnett (IRE)**[9] 3642 5-8-9 **51** oh1.................... JamesSullivan 10 — 37
(Brian Rothwell) *in rr: sme hdwy on outside over 2f out: nvr on terms* **40/1**

4231 **12** *2 ¾* **British Embassy (IRE)**[2] 3876 4-10-1 **74** 6ex......... EdwardGreatrex(3) 7 — 53
(David Loughnane) *led to post: trckd ldrs: t.k.h: drvn over 2f out: lost pl over 1f out: bhd whn eased in clsng stages* **5/1**[1]

-305 **13** *6* **Cadmium**[11] 3551 5-9-9 **65**....................(p) PJMcDonald 8 — 30
(Micky Hammond) *in rr: drvn over 4f out: hung rt over 1f out: sn bhd* **25/1**

1m 41.53s (0.13) **Going Correction** +0.15s/f (Good)
WFA 3 from 4yo+ 9lb — **13** Ran SP% **117.7**
Speed ratings (Par 103): **105,104,104,103,102 100,100,98,98,97 96,93,87**
CSF £319.37 CT £3035.56 TOTE £20.30: £6.40, £3.70, £3.10; EX 287.80 Trifecta £2824.20.
Owner Sheikh Hamdan bin Mohammed Al Maktoum **Bred** F Krief, Riviera Equine & Haras Etreham **Trained** Middleham Moor, N Yorks

FOCUS
Rail on bend from back straight to home straight dolled out 5yds adding 10yds to race distance. An open contest run at a steady pace. It paid to race handy. This has been rated around the third.
T/Plt: £1218.80 to a £1 stake. Pool of £80296.74 - 48.09 winning units. T/Qpdt: £178.30 to a £1 stake. Pool of £6508.14 - 27.00 winning units. **Walter Glynn**

3718 WINDSOR (R-H)
Monday, July 4

OFFICIAL GOING: Good to firm
Wind: Fresh, behind Weather: Overcast

3953 LOVE TRAVEL, LOVE TRAILFINDERS APPRENTICE H'CAP — 6f
6:05 (6:06) (Class 6) (0-65,65) 4-Y-O+ **£2,264** (£673; £336; £168) **Stalls** Low

Form — RPR

-004 **1** **Etienne Gerard**[25] 3070 4-9-3 **63**....................(p) DavidEgan(7) 1 — 72
(Nigel Tinkler) *racd towards nr side: prom: rdn 2f out: led over 1f out: styd on wl* **7/1**[2]

0-03 **2** *1 ¾* **Malvia**[23] 3136 4-9-5 **58**....................(b) GeorgeDowning 7 — 61
(Ian Williams) *dwlt: hld up in rr: prog 1/2-way: rdn 2f out: styd on to take 2nd ins fnl f: unable to chal* **14/1**

0300 **3** *1 ¼* **Hipz (IRE)**[34] 2765 5-9-6 **64**.................... MeganNicholls(5) 4 — 63
(Laura Mongan) *mostly chsd ldr: rdn to ld 2f out: hdd and one pce over 1f out: lost 2nd ins fnl f* **11/1**

0-00 **4** *1 ¾* **Aussie Ruler (IRE)**[10] 3610 4-9-10 **63**..............(b[1]) JosephineGordon 15 — 57
(Daniel Mark Loughnane) *racd on outer: chsd ldrs: rdn 2f out: kpt on fr over 1f out: n.d* **8/1**[3]

0006 **5** *½* **Smoothtalkinrascal (IRE)**[13] 3491 6-9-9 **65**.........(t) HectorCrouch(3) 10 — 57
(Peter Crate) *hld up wl in rr: rdn over 2f out: styd on fr over 1f out: nvr able to threaten* **10/1**

2055 **6** *shd* **Perfect Pastime**[12] 3530 8-9-7 **65**....................(p) PaddyBradley(5) 9 — 57
(Jim Boyle) *prom: rdn and stl wl there over 1f out: fdd* **14/1**

4-05 **7** *1 ½* **Deftera Lad (IRE)**[12] 3522 4-8-5 **49**.................... HollieDoyle(5) 11 — 36
(Natalie Lloyd-Beavis) *chsd ldrs: lost pl and struggling 1/2-way: sn no ch: plugged on fnl f* **8/1**[3]

2350 **8** *hd* **Arizona Snow**[6] 3734 4-8-12 **54**....................(p) JordanNason(3) 3 — 40
(Ronald Harris) *hld up towards rr: prog 1/2-way: rdn 2f out: one pce after* **33/1**

0622 **9** *1 ¼* **Potternello (IRE)**[2] 3898 4-9-5 **63**.................... KillianHennessy(5) 5 — 45
(Mick Channon) *prom: rdn and lost pl over 1f out: sn wknd* **5/2**[1]

100- **10** *3 ¼* **Named Asset**[296] 6297 4-8-13 **57**.................... GeorgeWood(5) 12 — 29
(Martin Bosley) *hld up and racd on outer: struggling fr 2f out* **20/1**

4003 **11** *2 ¼* **Noble Deed**[20] 3259 6-9-9 **65**.................... CallumShepherd(3) 13 — 30
(Michael Attwater) *awkward s: racd on wd outside: a in rr: no ch over 1f out* **8/1**[3]

00-0 **12** *1* **Rich Harvest (USA)**[14] 3469 11-8-7 **46** oh1..............(p) TomMarquand 2 — 8
(Ray Peacock) *led against nr side rail: hdd & wknd qckly 2f out* **100/1**

360- **13** *½* **Kylies Wild Card**[255] 7441 4-8-9 **48**.................... RobHornby 6 — 8
(Simon Hodgson) *prom tl wknd u.p over 2f out* **33/1**

1m 11.87s (-1.13) **Going Correction** -0.10s/f (Good) — **13** Ran SP% **116.8**
Speed ratings (Par 101): **103,100,99,96,96 95,93,93,91,87 84,83,82**
CSF £95.08 CT £1101.01 TOTE £6.00: £1.70, £3.30, £3.40; EX 53.50 Trifecta £424.60.
Owner welovewhitby.com **Bred** R Biggs **Trained** Langton, N Yorks
■ The first winner for David Egan, son of jockey John Egan.
■ Al's Memory was withdrawn. Price at time of withdrawal 10/1. Rule 4 applies to all bets struck prior to withdrawal but no to SP bets. Deduct 5p in the pound. New market formed.

FOCUS
Top bend dolled out 10yds from normal inner configuration adding 33yds to race distances 1m plus. The ground was on the quick side, a view backed up by those who rode in the opener. A pretty moderate sprint, the winner came relatively near the stands' rail in the straight, whereas most of the field ended up down the centre. This has been rated around the winner back to his best.

3954 SKY BET BRITISH STALLION STUDS EBF MAIDEN STKS — 6f
6:35 (6:40) (Class 5) 2-Y-O **£3,234** (£962; £481; £240) **Stalls** Low

Form — RPR

2 **1** **Kodiline (IRE)**[31] 2847 2-9-5 0.................... AdamKirby 9 — 82
(Clive Cox) *mde all against nr side: rdn over 1f out: hrd pressed fnl f: styd on wl* **13/8**[1]

2 *nk* **Majeste** 2-9-5 0.................... SeanLevey 2 — 81+
(Richard Hannon) *cl up: rdn to chse wnr over 1f out: str chal fnl f: styd on but jst hld* **9/2**[3]

3 *2 ½* **Best Solution (IRE)** 2-9-5 0.................... JamesDoyle 12 — 73+
(Saeed bin Suroor) *dwlt: sn in midfield: prog over 2f out: tk 3rd fnl f: one pce after* **9/2**[3]

4 **4** *2 ¼* **Law Power**[10] 3619 2-9-5 0.................... LukeMorris 8 — 66
(Sir Mark Prescott Bt) *chsd ldrs: rdn 2f out: kpt on same pce fr over 1f out* **25/1**

5 *1* **He's A Lad (IRE)** 2-9-5 0.................... DavidProbert 7 — 63+
(Andrew Balding) *mostly in midfield: drvn 2f out: kpt on fr over 1f out: n.d* **20/1**

6 *nk* **Redgrave (IRE)** 2-9-5 0.................... AndreaAtzeni 3 — 62
(Charles Hills) *prom: chsd wnr over 2f out to over 1f out: wknd fnl f* **4/1**[2]

6 **7** *½* **Father McKenzie**[9] 3668 2-9-5 0.................... CharlesBishop 14 — 60
(Mick Channon) *chsd ldrs: rdn 2f out: fdd fr over 1f out* **50/1**

8 *4 ½* **Seaview** 2-9-0 0.................... RenatoSouza 4 — 41
(Dean Ivory) *towards rr: modest late prog but nvr a factor* **66/1**

9 *½* **Sir Dancealot (IRE)** 2-9-5 0.................... JimCrowley 13 — 44+
(David Elsworth) *s.s: rn green and wl off the pce in rr: kpt on fnl 2f: nvr a factor* **33/1**

0 **10** *2* **Surfina**[34] 2764 2-9-0 0.................... RobertWinston 10 — 33
(Dean Ivory) *chsd ldrs tl wknd 2f out* **50/1**

11 *2* **Ninety Years Young** 2-9-5 0.................... ShaneKelly 11 — 31
(David Elsworth) *a off the pce towards rr: no prog fnl 2f* **33/1**

12 *4 ½* **Secret Agent** 2-9-5 0.................... MartinDwyer 6 — 17
(William Muir) *s.s: rn green and shoved along in rr: nvr a factor* **20/1**

13 *½* **Gala Celebration (IRE)** 2-9-5 0.................... MartinLane 16 — 15
(John Gallagher) *racd on outer: chsd wnr to over 2f out: wknd rapidly* **40/1**

14 *8* **Dragon Dream (IRE)** 2-8-7 0.................... RhiainIngram(7) 1
(Roger Ingram) *dwlt: rn green and sn wl bhd: sltly hmpd after 2f: t.o* **100/1**

F **Paddy A (IRE)** 2-9-2 0 LouisSteward(3) 5
(Philip McBride) *dwlt: wl in rr whn fell after 2f* **50/1**

1m 11.94s (-1.06) **Going Correction** -0.10s/f (Good) **15** Ran SP% **124.5**
Speed ratings (Par 94): **103,102,99,96,94 94,93,87,87,84 81,75,75,64,**
CSF £8.15 TOTE £2.60: £1.40, £2.20, £2.10; EX 12.30 Trifecta £48.80.
Owner Martin McHale **Bred** Miss Aoife Boland **Trained** Lambourn, Berks

FOCUS
Race distance as advertised. Little got into this, with the right horses dominating, and it was probably a fair maiden with there being a few performances of note. It's been rated around the winner to his debut form.

3955 TRAILFINDERS FOR ALL YOUR TRAVEL NEEDS CLAIMING STKS 1m 2f 7y
7:05 (7:05) (Class 5) 3-Y-O **£2,911** (£866; £432; £216) **Stalls** Centre

Form RPR
5-54 **1** **Fool To Cry (IRE)**49 2291 3-9-0 76 AndreaAtzeni 4 68+
(Roger Varian) *hld up in 4th: coaxed along over 2f out: led over 1f out: rdn out and styd on fnl f* **8/13**1

1650 **2** 1 ¾ **Clive Clifton (IRE)**54 2152 3-8-13 64 (v) ShaneKelly 2 63
(David Evans) *dwlt and stdd s: hld up in last: clsd jst over 2f out: drvn and styd on to take 2nd jst ins fnl f: no imp on wnr* **11/1**

-304 **3** 1 ¼ **Pastoral Star**13 3496 3-8-9 60 CharlieBennett(5) 1 62
(Hughie Morrison) *led: drvn for home over 3f out: hdd and one pce over 1f out* **8/1**

2250 **4** 1 ¼ **Divine Joy**34 2783 3-8-9 69 LukeMorris 3 54
(Marco Botti) *chsd ldr: urged along over 3f out: stl on terms u.p 2f out: fdd jst over 1f out* **6/1**2

4064 **5** 8 **Yours Forever**7 3710 3-8-12 58 RobertWinston 5 41
(Kevin Ryan) *chsd ldng pair: rdn to try to chal jst over 2f out: wknd qckly over 1f out* **15/2**3

2m 11.01s (2.31) **Going Correction** -0.025s/f (Good) **5** Ran SP% **107.4**
Speed ratings (Par 100): **89,87,86,85,79**
CSF £7.63 TOTE £1.40: £1.10, £2.90; EX 6.60 Trifecta £31.20.Fool To Cry was claimed by N Mulholland for £12000.
Owner J Shack **Bred** Rathasker Stud **Trained** Newmarket, Suffolk

FOCUS
Race distance increased by 33yds. A stop-start gallop but that didn't prevent the favourite from scoring in what was a pretty weak claimer. The winner didn't have to run to his best, with the level set around the second and third.

3956 SKY BET WINDSOR SPRINT SERIES H'CAP (A QUALFIER FOR THE WINDSOR SPRINT SERIES FINAL) 5f 10y
7:35 (7:36) (Class 3) (0-95,95) 3-Y-O+ **£7,439** (£2,213; £1,106; £553) **Stalls** Low

Form RPR
0335 **1** **Bashiba (IRE)**25 3056 5-8-9 **78** (t) AndreaAtzeni 12 86
(Nigel Tinkler) *trckd ldrs: drvn over 1f out: led ins fnl f: hrd pressed nr fin: jst hld on* **15/2**3

0-04 **2** hd **Foxtrot Knight**11 3552 4-8-9 **78** LukeMorris 10 85
(Ruth Carr) *chsd ldrs in 7th: prog on outer over 1f out: drvn to chal last 100yds: jst failed* **5/1**2

1-30 **3** shd **Bapak Asmara (IRE)**47 2364 4-8-11 **80** RobertWinston 14 87
(Kevin Ryan) *led: drvn 2f out: clung on to the ld tl ins fnl f: kpt on wl nr fin: jst hld* **12/1**

2404 **4** ½ **Long Awaited (IRE)**18 3322 8-8-6 **78** (b) JosephineGordon(3) 5 83
(Conor Dore) *chsd ldrs: rdn 2f out: fnd room and drvn fnl f: styd on and nrst fin* **33/1**

250 **5** ½ **Pensax Lad (IRE)**33 2787 5-8-7 **76** TomMarquand 8 79
(Ronald Harris) *t.k.h: n.m.r after 100yds: chsd ldrs: drvn over 1f out: styd on but nvr quite able to chal in driving fin* **14/1**

5104 **6** nse **Equally Fast**25 3056 4-9-0 **83** (b) MartinDwyer 11 86+
(William Muir) *s.s: off the pce in last pair: prog on outer 2f out: hanging lft but clsd on ldrs 1f out: one pce last 100yds* **14/1**

20-0 **7** 1 ¼ **Nocturn**35 2754 7-8-13 **82** (p) DavidProbert 9 80
(Ronald Harris) *pressed ldr tl jst over 1f out: one pce and lost pls fnl f* **16/1**

40-0 **8** hd **Musical Comedy**9 3671 5-9-12 **95** JamesDoyle 1 93+
(Mike Murphy) *slowly away: off the pce in last trio: rdn and tried to cl fr over 1f out: kpt on but unable to threaten* **14/1**

6121 **9** shd **Major Pusey**10 3618 4-9-2 **85** MartinLane 7 82
(John Gallagher) *pressed ldng pair to over 1f out: one pce after* **5/1**2

333 **10** hd **Sir Billy Wright (IRE)**9 3671 5-9-4 **87** AdamKirby 3 84
(David Evans) *in tch in 8th: rdn 2f out: swtchd to nr side rail over 1f out: kpt on but nvr gng pce to threaten* **7/2**1

0-10 **11** 6 **Marmalady (IRE)**31 2875 6-9-3 **86** TedDurcan 2 61
(Robert Cowell) *a in last trio: wknd 2f out: bhd fnl f* **8/1**

58.79s (-1.51) **Going Correction** -0.10s/f (Good) **11** Ran SP% **114.9**
Speed ratings (Par 107): **108,107,107,106,105 105,103,103,103,103 93**
CSF £43.77 CT £348.93 TOTE £8.30: £2.50, £1.60, £4.30; EX 32.40 Trifecta £520.60.
Owner M Webb **Bred** John T Heffernan & Grainne Dooley **Trained** Langton, N Yorks

FOCUS
Race distance as advertised. A competitive sprint and the main action unfolded centre-track. A minor pb from the winner, with the second close to his best and the third also posting a small pb.

3957 SKY BET H'CAP 1m 67y
8:05 (8:05) (Class 4) (0-85,84) 3-Y-O+ **£4,690** (£1,395; £697; £348) **Stalls** Low

Form RPR
-231 **1** **Quebee**35 2749 3-9-4 **83** AdamKirby 5 89+
(Clive Cox) *trckd ldng trio: clsd over 2f out: rdn to ld over 1f out: kpt on fnl f: drvn out* **15/8**1

2210 **2** ¾ **Banish (USA)**30 2892 3-9-5 **84** (tp) JamesDoyle 7 88+
(Hugo Palmer) *s.s: mostly in 6th: pushed along over 3f out whn ldrs kicked for home and a lot to do: no prog tl r.o fnl f to take 2nd last 75yds: nt rch wnr* **12/1**

-410 **3** ½ **Philadelphia (IRE)**53 2179 3-9-1 **80** AndreaAtzeni 3 83+
(Roger Varian) *v.s.a in ragged s: mostly in last: lot to do 3f out and urged along: no prog tl styd on fnl f: nrst fin* **5/1**3

-435 **4** ¾ **Hot Mustard**23 3124 6-9-4 **74** MartinDwyer 6 77
(William Muir) *anticipated s but couldn't ld: trckd ldr: rdn to ld wl over 2f out: hdd over 1f out: fdd nr fin* **11/1**

512 **5** ½ **Harlequin Striker (IRE)**4 3803 4-9-13 **83** RobertWinston 1 85
(Dean Ivory) *chsd ldng pair: rdn over 2f out: tried to cl over 1f out: one pce u.p* **9/4**2

-002 **6** 2 **Henshaw**10 3612 3-8-10 **75** (b) DavidProbert 2 70
(Charles Hills) *led: kicked for home over 3f out but sn pressed: hdd wl over 2f out: fdd jst over 1f out* **8/1**

3- **7** 7 **Camakasi (IRE)**105 5778 5-9-12 **82** (tp) JimCrowley 4 62
(Ali Stronge) *s.s: a in last trio: rdn 3f out: no prog* **25/1**

1m 44.85s (0.15) **Going Correction** -0.025s/f (Good)
WFA 3 from 4yo+ 9lb **7** Ran SP% **113.2**
Speed ratings (Par 105): **98,97,96,96,95 93,86**
CSF £24.50 CT £97.03 TOTE £2.60: £1.50, £3.90; EX 22.20 Trifecta £87.60.
Owner Martin A Collins **Bred** M A Collins **Trained** Lambourn, Berks

FOCUS
Race distance increased by 33yds. A fair handicap but both the second and third have claims to being unfortunate as it was a ragged start and the winner got first run.

3958 IMAGEDIRECT EVERYTHING YOUR OFFICE NEEDS MAIDEN FILLIES' STKS 1m 67y
8:35 (8:37) (Class 5) 3-4-Y-O **£2,911** (£866; £432; £216) **Stalls** Low

Form RPR
6-22 **1** **Laugh Aloud**16 3412 3-9-0 81 (t) JamesDoyle 13 89+
(John Gosden) *mde all: easily drew rt away fr over 1f out* **4/11**1

0 **2** 7 **Jantina**59 2009 3-9-0 0 TedDurcan 5 68
(Sir Michael Stoute) *chsd ldrs: reminders sn after 1/2-way: prog and rdn 2f out: kpt on to take modest 2nd ins fnl f* **6/1**2

3 2 **Poyle Emily** 3-9-0 0 PatDobbs 12 63
(Ralph Beckett) *forced to r wd early but sn chsd wnr: clr of rest 3f out: easily lft bhd wl over 1f out: lost 2nd ins fnl f* **15/2**3

50 **4** hd **Heart Of Oak**16 3412 3-9-0 0 StevieDonohoe 1 63
(George Peckham) *prom: shkn up wl over 2f out: easily lft bhd fr over 1f out* **20/1**

00 **5** ¾ **Tasteofexcellence (IRE)**27 2999 3-8-7 0 RhiainIngram(7) 7 61
(Roger Ingram) *hld up in last and wl off the pce: gd prog and reminders fr 2f out: pushed along and no hdwy fnl f: nt disgracd* **66/1**

0-0 **6** 1 ½ **Limonata (IRE)**25 3059 3-9-0 0 MartinHarley 3 60+
(Henry Candy) *hld up in midfield: pushed along and sme prog to join chsng gp 2f out: stl pushed along and fdd fnl f* **10/1**

7 2 ¼ **Occasional Dream (IRE)** 3-9-0 0 JFEgan 4 52
(Joseph Tuite) *slowly away: wl in rr: pushed along fr 3f out: kpt on steadily fr over 1f out* **25/1**

6 **8** 1 **Just For Show (IRE)**17 3350 3-8-11 0 JosephineGordon(3) 2 50
(Shaun Lycett) *racd in midfield: vigorously rdn 1/2-way: nvr on terms after: kpt on* **100/1**

0-0 **9** 7 **Lisala (FR)**17 3359 3-9-0 0 LukeMorris 11 33
(George Peckham) *chsd ldrs: rdn and hung rt 2f out: sn wknd qckly* **25/1**

00 **10** ¾ **Dancing Rainbow (GR)**29 2929 3-8-9 0 HectorCrouch(5) 6 31
(Amanda Perrett) *a in rr: shkn up and no prog 3f out* **80/1**

00 **11** 3 ½ **Hepburn**12 3508 3-9-0 0 TomMarquand 9 23
(Ali Stronge) *chsd ldrs tl rdn and wknd 3f out* **100/1**

12 ¾ **Flying Sakhee** 3-9-0 0 WilliamCarson 8 21
(John Bridger) *hung lft bhd 6f out to 5f out: effrt on outer 3f out: hanging lft and wknd over 2f out* **66/1**

13 2 **Winterton** 3-9-0 0 (t) KierenFox 10 16
(Christine Dunnett) *slowly away: a wl in rr* **80/1**

1m 43.12s (-1.58) **Going Correction** -0.025s/f (Good) **13** Ran SP% **128.3**
Speed ratings (Par 100): **106,99,97,96,96 94,92,91,84,83 80,79,77**
CSF £3.23 TOTE £1.30: £1.10, £2.10, £2.40; EX 4.40 Trifecta £13.10.
Owner Godolphin **Bred** Darley **Trained** Newmarket, Suffolk

FOCUS
Race distance increased by 33yds. No depth to this and the favourite won as she pleased. The winner was impressive and the level is set around the fourth, fifth and sixth.

3959 TRAILFINDERS WORLDWIDE CRUISE HOLIDAYS H'CAP 1m 2f 7y
9:05 (9:06) (Class 5) (0-75,72) 3-Y-O+ **£2,911** (£866; £432; £216) **Stalls** Centre

Form RPR
-421 **1** **Athlon (IRE)**21 3236 3-9-3 **72** GeorgeBaker 4 83+
(David Lanigan) *trckd ldrs: waiting for a gap over 2f out: pushed into ld over 1f out: in n.d after: comf* **11/8**1

0-04 **2** 1 ½ **Guns Of Leros (USA)**26 3042 3-9-2 **71** AdamKirby 1 77
(Gary Moore) *led: rdn wl over 2f out: hdd over 1f out: kpt on but no ch w wnr* **13/2**

56-4 **3** 1 ¾ **Maroc**21 3235 3-9-3 **72** (t) LukeMorris 6 75
(Paul Cole) *t.k.h: pressed ldr: drvn wl over 2f out: lost 2nd over 1f out: hanging lft and nt qckn after* **8/1**

0626 **4** shd **Deluxe**28 2965 4-9-3 **61** JFEgan 2 63
(Pat Phelan) *hld up in last: cl up 2f out but stl last: reminders to dispute 3rd fnl f: nvr really involved* **33/1**

03 **5** 1 ¼ **Cosmic Storm**48 2320 3-9-1 **70** PatDobbs 8 70
(Ralph Beckett) *stmbld s: rcvrd and sn in tch: rdn over 2f out and on terms: fdd fnl f* **7/2**2

0021 **6** ¾ **Sporty Yankee (USA)**14 3468 3-8-5 **67** CliffordLee(7) 7 65
(K R Burke) *in tch: rdn on outer and in tch over 2f out: fnd little and btn over 1f out* **9/2**3

2m 7.45s (-1.25) **Going Correction** -0.025s/f (Good)
WFA 3 from 4yo+ 11lb **6** Ran SP% **109.9**
Speed ratings (Par 103): **104,102,101,101,100 99**
CSF £10.42 CT £46.29 TOTE £2.00: £1.50, £2.70; EX 10.50 Trifecta £39.60.
Owner The Athlon Partnership **Bred** Thomas Maher **Trained** Newmarket, Suffolk

FOCUS
Race distance increased by 33yds. No great pace on and the field was bunched on straightening but the short-price favourite still proved much the best.
T/Plt: £33.50 to a £1 stake. Pool of £82096.28 - 1786.28 winning tickets. T/Qpdt: £8.10 to a £1 stake. Pool of £7615.05 - 688.76 winning tickets. **Jonathan Neesom**

3960 - 3969a (Foreign Racing) - See Raceform Interactive

3734 BRIGHTON (L-H)
Tuesday, July 5

OFFICIAL GOING: Good (good to firm in places; 8.5)
Wind: light, across Weather: mainly sunny

3970 JOHN SMITH'S RACEDAY 3RD AUGUST (S) H'CAP 5f 213y
5:40 (5:43) (Class 6) (0-60,60) 3-Y-O+ **£2,264** (£673; £336; £168) **Stalls** Centre

Form RPR
4-00 **1** **Indus Valley (IRE)**63 1949 9-9-2 **52** (v) KierenFox 7 59
(Lee Carter) *hld up in midfield: rdn and hdwy over 1f out: chal jst ins fnl f: sustained duel w runner up after: styd on u.p to ld cl home* **9/1**

453 **2** nk **Time Medicean**8 3719 10-9-7 **60** GeorgeDowning(3) 9 66
(Tony Carroll) *hld up in last quartet: rdn and gd hdwy over 1f out: rdn to chal 1f out: sn led: sustained duel w wnr after: hdd and no ex last strides* **6/1**3

5006 **3** 3/4 **Indie Music**[28] 3003 3-8-11 **56**................................ EdwardGreatrex(3) 13 59
(Sylvester Kirk) *midfield but sn pushed along: dropped to last trio and rdn after 1f out: hdwy u.p 1f out: styd on wl to go 3rd 75yds out: nt quite rch ldng pair* **13/2**

-003 **4** 1 3/4 **Cooperess**[7] 3734 3-8-10 **52**..(bt) KieranO'Neill 4 49
(Ali Stronge) *chsd ldng pair: effrt 2f out: hdwy u.p to chal over 1f out: led 1f out: sn hdd and unable qck: wknd fnl 75yds* **11/2**[2]

0055 **5** 2 **Strictly Carter**[18] 3360 3-9-2 **58**.......................................(p) AdamKirby 3 49+
(Alan Bailey) *broke v fast: led: rdn wl over 1f out: hdd 1f out: no ex: wknd fnl 100yds* **7/1**

2205 **6** nse **Generalyse**[21] 3259 7-9-7 **57**..(b) MartinHarley 11 48
(Anabel K Murphy) *in tch in midfield: effrt and drifting lft over 1f out: stl edging lft but sme hdwy 1f out: kpt on same pce ins fnl f* **15/2**

-640 **7** 3 3/4 **Edith Weston**[133] 688 3-8-0 **46** oh1 ow1...................(p) AaronJones(5) 1 25
(Robert Cowell) *chsd ldr: rdn 2f out: unable qck u.p over 1f out: wknd ins fnl f* **20/1**

4605 **8** 1 **Salvado (IRE)**[8] 3729 6-8-10 **46** oh1.............................. WilliamCarson 2 22
(Tony Carroll) *taken down early and led to post: hld up in tch in midfield: effrt over 2f out: sn drvn and no hdwy over 1f out: wknd ins fnl f* **16/1**

-000 **9** 3/4 **Sakhastic**[26] 3080 3-7-12 **46** oh1 ow1......................... MitchGodwin(7) 12 20
(Christine Dunnett) *sn in last pair: rdn over 2f out: sme modest late hdwy: nvr trbld ldrs* **100/1**

5-23 **10** nse **Secret Interlude (IRE)**[13] 3513 3-8-8 **55**....................... LucyKBarry(5) 6 28
(Jamie Osborne) *in tch in midfield: effrt over 1f out: nt clrest of runs ent fnl f: sn btn: wknd ins fnl f* **5/1**[1]

0260 **11** 2 3/4 **Jolly Red Jeanz (IRE)**[115] 919 5-9-3 **53**..................... CharlesBishop 8 18
(Anabel K Murphy) *in tch in midfield: rdn 2f out: no prog and sn btn: wknd ins fnl f* **16/1**

00-0 **12** 1 **Praise N Glory**[14] 3490 5-8-10 **46** oh1.......................(b[1]) TomMarquand 5 8
(Linda Jewell) *dwlt: sn pushed along: a in rr: nvr on terms* **100/1**

4-06 **13** 3 **Hurricane Alert**[36] 2953 4-9-3 **58**.............................. HectorCrouch(5) 10 10
(Natalie Lloyd-Beavis) *taken down early: chsd ldng trio tl lost pl 2f out: sn dropped out: bhd ins fnl f* **50/1**

1m 10.62s (0.42) **Going Correction** +0.075s/f (Good)
WFA 3 from 4yo+ 6lb **13** Ran SP% **114.4**
Speed ratings (Par 101): **100,99,98,96,93 93,88,87,86,86 82,81,77**
CSF £58.33 CT £388.71 TOTE £11.20: £3.40, £2.00, £1.90; EX 78.30 Trifecta £1286.50.There was no bid for the winner.
Owner Clear Racing **Bred** P Morris & B McKenna **Trained** Epsom, Surrey

FOCUS
There was only 1mm of rain the previous day, and the ground, which had been watered around the 4f bend, was given as good, good to firm in places (GoingStick: 8.5). The rail was dolled out between the 4 1/2f point and the 2 1/2f marker, adding 8yds to each race distance. This was run at a good gallop and the first three came from off the pace.

3971 SUPPORTERS OF RONALD MCDONALD HOUSE BRIGHTON MAIDEN STKS 6f 209y
6:10 (6:10) (Class 5) 2-Y-O **£2,911** (£866; £432; £216) **Stalls** Centre

Form RPR

6 **1** **Majoris (IRE)**[39] 2649 2-9-5 0...(t) JimCrowley 7 77+
(Hugo Palmer) *dwlt: hld up in tch in last trio: effrt over 1f out: hdwy u.p ent fnl f: led 75yds out: rn green in front but kpt on and in command towards fin* **5/6**[1]

6 **2** 3/4 **Fortune Of War**[18] 3356 2-9-5 0...................................... PatCosgrave 6 74
(Jane Chapple-Hyam) *chsd ldrs: swtchd rt 2f out: rdn to ld over 1f out: drvn 1f out: hdd 75yds out: kpt on but a hld* **12/1**

6 **3** 2 **Mutahaady (IRE)**[64] 1915 2-9-5 0..................................... SeanLevey 10 69
(Richard Hannon) *in tch in midfield: effrt over 1f out: rdn ent fnl f: hdwy ins fnl f: wnt 3rd wl ins fnl f: kpt on wout threatening ldrs* **5/1**[2]

00 **4** 1 3/4 **Brise De Mer (FR)**[32] 2873 2-9-5 0................................. SteveDrowne 5 64
(George Baker) *dwlt and bustled along leaving stalls: sn rcvrd and chsd ldng trio: effrt 2f out: unable qck u.p ent fnl f: wknd fnl f* **66/1**

632 **5** 1 **Racemaker**[10] 3668 2-9-5 0... CharlesBishop 3 61
(Mick Channon) *w ldr tl over 1f out: unable qck u.p 1f out: wknd ins fnl f* **7/1**

3 **6** 1/2 **Plato's Kode (IRE)**[15] 3463 2-9-5 0................................... ShaneKelly 1 60
(Seamus Durack) *t.k.h: led: rdn wl over 1f out: unable qck ent fnl f: wknd ins fnl f* **16/1**

5 **7** 1 3/4 **Eolian**[13] 3529 2-9-5 0... MartinHarley 2 59+
(William Knight) *s.i.s: in tch in last pair: effrt over 1f out: sme prog but nt threatening ldrs whn squeezed for room 100yds: nvr much room after and eased towards fin* **6/1**[3]

0 **8** 1 3/4 **Quothquan (FR)**[15] 3463 2-8-12 0................................ GeorgeWood(7) 8 50
(Michael Madgwick) *in tch in midfield: swtchd lft and effrt wl over 1f out: no imp: losing pl whn short of room 100yds out* **100/1**

05 **9** hd **Wentwell Yesterday (IRE)**[7] 3742 2-9-5 0.................. WilliamCarson 9 50
(Jamie Osborne) *stdd bk to rr after s: t.k.h: pushed along 2f out: keeping on same pce whn swtchd rt arnd field ins fnl f: nvr trbld ldrs* **33/1**

1m 24.12s (1.02) **Going Correction** +0.075s/f (Good) **9** Ran SP% **117.0**
Speed ratings (Par 94): **97,96,93,91,90 90,88,86,85**
CSF £13.10 TOTE £1.70: £1.10, £2.90, £2.20; EX 11.60 Trifecta £39.20.
Owner Al Asayl Bloodstock Ltd **Bred** Al Asayl Bloodstock Ltd **Trained** Newmarket, Suffolk

FOCUS
Race distance increased by 8yds. A fair maiden and the level is fluid for now.

3972 ROC SOLUTIONS - OFFICIAL ELECTRICAL & SECURITY PARTNER H'CAP 1m 3f 196y
6:40 (6:40) (Class 4) (0-80,80) 4-Y-O+ **£4,690** (£1,395; £697; £348) **Stalls** High

Form RPR

-051 **1** **Nigel**[29] 2965 4-9-7 **80**... ShaneKelly 1 88
(Richard Hughes) *mde all: rdn over 1f out: reminders 1f out: pushed along hands and heels and a holding chalr fnl 75yds: styd on* **7/2**[2]

020 **2** nk **Rose Above**[17] 3409 4-8-12 **74**................................. EdwardGreatrex(3) 5 81
(Andrew Balding) *hld up in tch in midfield: shkn up and effrt to chse wnr over 1f out: sn drvn and chalng ins fnl f: styd on but a hld* **16/1**

0005 **3** 2 1/2 **Lungarno Palace (USA)**[25] 3117 5-9-5 **78**............ MichaelJMMurphy 7 81
(John Gallagher) *chsd wnr tl over 2f out: sn drvn: sltly outpcd and lost pl over 1f out: styd on again ins fnl f: no threat to ldng pair* **5/1**[3]

6221 **4** 3/4 **Yankee Mail (FR)**[21] 3257 4-8-13 **72**................................ PatCosgrave 3 74
(Gay Kelleway) *stdd s: hld up in tch in midfield: effrt 2f out: unable qck u.p ent fnl f: styd on same pce ins fnl f* **8/1**

236- **5** nk **Every Instinct (IRE)**[197] 8327 4-9-3 **76**............................. JimCrowley 6 77
(David Simcock) *hld up in tch in last pair: effrt and nt clrest of runs over 1f out: styd on same pce u.p ins fnl f* **6/1**

4311 **6** 2 1/4 **Roy Rocket (FR)**[7] 3738 6-9-0 **73** 6ex.. JFEgan 2 71
(John Berry) *stdd after s: hld up in rr: clsd and wl in tch 3f out: swtchd rt and effrt 2f out: no imp over 1f out: btn whn swtchd lft jst ins fnl f* **9/4**[1]

-221 **7** 3 **Longside**[27] 3041 4-8-13 **72**.. ThomasBrown 4 65
(James Eustace) *chsd ldrs tl wnt 2nd over 2f out: drifted lft u.p and lost pl over 1f out: wknd fnl f* **10/1**

2m 34.44s (1.74) **Going Correction** +0.075s/f (Good) **7** Ran SP% **110.0**
Speed ratings (Par 105): **97,96,95,94,94 92,90**
CSF £49.78 CT £258.36 TOTE £4.90: £2.50, £3.30; EX 32.20 Trifecta £203.00.
Owner Normandie Stud Ltd **Bred** Normandie Stud Ltd **Trained** Upper Lambourn, Berkshire

FOCUS
Race distance increased by 8yds. This handicap was dominated from the front by the winner. A small pb from the second.

3973 FROSTS LADIES DAY 4TH AUGUST H'CAP 7f 214y
7:10 (7:11) (Class 6) (0-55,56) 3-Y-O+ **£2,264** (£673; £336; £168) **Stalls** Centre

Form RPR

6414 **1** **Admirable Art (IRE)**[8] 3732 6-9-2 **50**...............................(p) AdamKirby 7 60
(Tony Carroll) *mde all: rdn and kicked clr over 1f out: being clsd down fnl 100yds but nvr gng to get ct: rdn out* **4/1**[2]

5050 **2** 1 **African Showgirl**[28] 3003 3-8-12 **55**................................ SteveDrowne 8 61
(George Baker) *hld up in last quartet: hdwy and switching lft over 1f out: chsd clr wnr 100yds: styd on wl but nvr getting to wnr* **25/1**

-640 **3** nk **Patanjali (IRE)**[32] 2851 3-8-11 **54**................................. CharlesBishop 11 60
(Eve Johnson Houghton) *hld up in tch in midfield: effrt over 1f out: nt clr run and swtchd rt 1f out: styd on strly ins fnl f: nt rch ldrs* **6/1**[3]

000 **4** 1 1/4 **Purple Party (IRE)**[29] 2980 3-7-12 **46** oh1.................. NoelGarbutt(5) 14 48
(Gary Moore) *in tch in midfield: swtchd rt and drvn over 1f out: kpt on ins fnl f: nvr enough pce to threaten wnr* **50/1**

54-0 **5** 3/4 **Decisive (IRE)**[26] 3078 4-9-6 **54**..................................... WilliamCarson 4 56
(Anthony Carson) *chsd ldrs: wnt 2nd and effrt 2f out: sn hung lft and unable qck: lost 2nd and wknd fnl 100yds* **8/1**

001 **6** 1/2 **Frantical**[7] 3737 4-9-5 **56** 6ex.................................(b) GeorgeDowning(3) 5 57
(Tony Carroll) *s.i.s: sn bustled along and rcvrd to r in midfield: swtchd lft and effrt u.p 2f out: styd on same pce ins fnl f* **5/2**[1]

2224 **7** nk **Tax Reform (IRE)**[36] 2954 6-8-5 **46** oh1.....................(b) HollieDoyle(7) 10 46
(Natalie Lloyd-Beavis) *chsd ldng trio: effrt over 1f out: edgd lft and fnd little for press ent fnl f: wknd ins fnl f* **25/1**

4520 **8** 1/2 **Divine Touch**[3] 3896 3-8-3 **46** oh1.............................. TomMarquand 3 43
(Robert Eddery) *in tch in midfield: effrt 2f out: sn drvn and unable qck over 1f out: wknd fnl f* **16/1**

3402 **9** 1 1/4 **Lutine Charlie (IRE)**[14] 3489 9-9-3 **51**............................. TomQueally 12 47
(Emma Owen) *chsd wnr tl 2f out: lost pl u.p and n.m.r ent fnl f: wknd ins fnl f* **7/1**

60-6 **10** nk **Fenner Hill Neasa (IRE)**[160] 345 3-8-6 **49**............................. JFEgan 1 42
(Pat Phelan) *stdd s: t.k.h: hld up in rr: sme hdwy and swtchd rt over 1f out: no real imp ins fnl f: nvr trbld ldrs* **25/1**

0030 **11** 1 1/4 **Ron's Ballad**[29] 2967 3-8-3 **46** oh1................................. KieranO'Neill 6 36
(Michael Madgwick) *stdd after s: hld up in tch in last quartet: effrt towards inner 2f out: swtchd rt and no hdwy ent fnl f: wknd ins fnl f* **25/1**

12 9 **Duke Of Dance (IRE)**[40] 5936 6-8-12 **46** oh1.......... AdamBeschizza 15 17
(Denis Quinn) *in tch in midfield: rdn and unable qck 2f out: sn lost pl and btn: wknd fnl f* **66/1**

005 **13** 1 3/4 **Vivre La Reve**[34] 2799 4-9-6 **54**.. PatCosgrave 2 21
(James Unett) *in tch in midfield: rdn 2f out: no rspnse and losing pl qckly over 1f out: fdd fnl f* **16/1**

50-0 **14** 2 3/4 **Whistler Mountain**[39] 2635 4-9-4 **55**...................(t) EdwardGreatrex(3) 9 15
(Brian Barr) *a towards rr: rdn wl over 2f out: no prog: wknd over 1f out: bhd and eased wl ins fnl f* **33/1**

1m 36.11s (0.11) **Going Correction** +0.075s/f (Good)
WFA 3 from 4yo+ 9lb **14** Ran SP% **120.0**
Speed ratings (Par 101): **102,101,100,99,98 98,97,97,96,95 94,85,83,81**
CSF £107.16 CT £606.16 TOTE £4.90: £1.80, £4.90, £2.60; EX 81.80 Trifecta £2951.80.
Owner D Morgan **Bred** Longview Stud & Bloodstock Ltd **Trained** Cropthorne, Worcs

FOCUS
Race distance increased by 8yds. A moderate heat, but a good performance from the winner.

3974 CHECKATRADE RACEDAY 5TH AUGUST FILLIES' H'CAP 6f 209y
7:40 (7:40) (Class 5) (0-70,70) 3-Y-O+ **£2,911** (£866; £432; £216) **Stalls** Centre

Form RPR

1205 **1** **Pacolita (IRE)**[12] 3554 4-9-7 **66**.............................. EdwardGreatrex(3) 8 76+
(Sylvester Kirk) *hld up in tch: nt clr run and boxed in jst over 2f out tl gap opened 1f out: qcknd u.p to ld 75yds out: r.o wl* **5/2**[1]

2105 **2** 1 1/2 **One Big Surprise**[13] 3510 4-9-8 **64**.................................... ShaneKelly 1 69
(Richard Hughes) *hld up in tch in midfield: swtchd rt and clsd to trck ldrs over 2f out: rdn to ld over 1f out: hdd and outpcd by wnr fnl 75yds* **4/1**[2]

-605 **3** hd **Feeling Easy (IRE)**[18] 3349 4-9-9 **65**............................. TomMarquand 6 69
(Robert Eddery) *hld up in tch in last trio: effrt 2f out: hdwy to chse ldrs 1f out: hung lft and kpt on same pce ins fnl f* **12/1**

602 **4** 1 1/4 **Pyla (IRE)**[26] 3078 4-9-9 **65**.. LemosdeSouza 4 68
(Denis Quinn) *hld up in tch in midfield: swtchd lft and clsd 2f out: rdn and ev ch jst over 1f out: sddle slipped and rdr unable to offer maximum assistance ins fnl f: wknd fnl 75yds* **5/1**[3]

-050 **5** 3 **Lolita**[27] 3038 4-10-0 **70**.. JimCrowley 7 63
(J R Jenkins) *hld up in last pair: swtchd lft and effrt over 1f out: no imp ins fnl f: nvr trbld ldrs* **16/1**

064- **6** 2 **Many Dreams (IRE)**[190] 8377 3-9-4 **68**.......................... SteveDrowne 2 52
(Mark Usher) *chsd ldrs: unable qck u.p over 1f out: wknd ins fnl f* **7/1**

3-42 **7** hd **Plauseabella**[25] 3096 5-9-5 **61**..(p) TomQueally 3 48
(Stuart Kittow) *led: rdn and hdd over 1f out: no ex and wknd ins fnl f* **6/1**

4402 **8** 8 **Silver Springs (IRE)**[15] 3473 3-9-1 **65**.............................. AdamKirby 5 27
(David Evans) *sn w ldr: rdn and unable qck wl over 1f out: lost pl and bhd 1f out: sn wknd* **12/1**

1m 23.06s (-0.04) **Going Correction** +0.075s/f (Good)
WFA 3 from 4yo+ 8lb **8** Ran SP% **113.3**
Speed ratings (Par 100): **103,101,101,99,96 93,93,84**
CSF £12.19 CT £97.81 TOTE £3.00: £1.40, £2.10, £3.80; EX 13.20 Trifecta £173.00.
Owner G Dolan & P Wheatley **Bred** Ms Clara O'Reilly **Trained** Upper Lambourn, Berks

FOCUS
Race distance increased by 8yds. There was a fair pace on here, and the three who were in the front rank early ended up dropping out to finish in the last three places. The runner-up is rated close to form.

3975 FORD SUMMER FESTIVAL RUN 16TH JULY H'CAP 6f 209y
8:10 (8:10) (Class 6) (0-60,60) 3-Y-O **£2,264** (£673; £336; £168) **Stalls** Centre

Form RPR

0-31 **1** **Frank Bridge**[14] 3490 3-9-4 **57**.. JohnFahy 11 66+
(Eve Johnson Houghton) *hld up in tch in midfield: str run u.p but gng lft fr over 1f out: led 1f out: asserting whn hmpd runner-up ins fnl f: in command after: eased towards fin* **5/2**[1]

6044 **2** 1 ¾ **Harmony Bay (IRE)**[28] 3003 3-9-3 **59**..................... EdwardGreatrex(3) 3 61
(Sylvester Kirk) *chsd ldrs: effrt to chal over 1f out: ev ch 1f out: jst beginning to get outpcd by wnr whn squeezed for room and snatched up ins fnl f: styd on same pce after* **4/1**[2]

2405 **3** 2 **Espoir**[24] 3146 3-8-11 **50**..(v) ShaneKelly 1 45
(David Evans) *stdd after s: hld up in tch towards rr: hdwy on inner over 2f out: effrt over 1f out: wnt 3rd ins fnl f: kpt on but no threat to wnr* **14/1**

5120 **4** 1 ¼ **Ettie Hart (IRE)**[8] 3725 3-9-3 **56**...................................... CharlesBishop 9 48
(Mick Channon) *led: rdn wl over 1f out: hdd 1f out: sn outpcd: wknd ins fnl f* **11/2**[3]

00-0 **5** ½ **Just Fred (IRE)**[49] 2325 3-9-2 **55**....................................... TomQueally 5 45
(Denis Coakley) *hld up in tch in midfield: effrt and unable qck over 1f out: trying to rally whn nt clr run ins fnl f: swtchd lft and kpt on towards fin: no ch w wnr* **20/1**

0-60 **6** ½ **Baz's Boy**[35] 2784 3-8-2 **46** oh1.. NoelGarbutt(5) 4 35
(John Flint) *chsd ldr tl unable qck and lost pl u.p over 1f out: wknd ins fnl f* **22/1**

4454 **7** 3 ¼ **Aksum**[29] 2968 3-8-3 **49**..(p) GeorgeWood(7) 10 29
(Michael Bell) *chsd ldng trio: unable qck u.p and btn over 1f out: wknd ins fnl f* **11/2**[3]

0010 **8** 1 ¼ **Let There Be Light**[50] 2293 3-9-7 **60**.................................. AdamKirby 6 37
(Gay Kelleway) *dwlt: hld up in tch towards rr: effrt u.p wl over 1f out: no hdwy: wknd ins fnl f* **15/2**

0040 **9** nse **Hodgkins Trust (IRE)**[13] 3513 3-8-7 **46**.................. AdamBeschizza 12 23
(Jeremy Gask) *dwlt: hld up in tch in rr: rdn over 2f out: no imp and outpcd over 1f out: wknd fnl f* **33/1**

5506 **10** 4 **Secret Sonnet**[31] 2905 3-8-12 **51**...................................... MartinHarley 8 17
(Stuart Williams) *hld up in tch in rr: effrt u.p ent fnl 2f: no hdwy: wknd over 1f out* **25/1**

0566 **11** 6 **No Body's Fool**[19] 3317 3-8-7 **46** oh1.............................. KieranO'Neill 7
(Michael Madgwick) *hld up in tch towards rr: no hdwy u.p over 1f out: sn wknd* **100/1**

1m 23.95s (0.85) **Going Correction** +0.075s/f (Good) **11** Ran SP% **114.7**
Speed ratings (Par 98): **98,96,93,92,91 91,87,86,85,81 74**
CSF £10.99 CT £115.19 TOTE £2.70: £1.30, £1.90, £3.10; EX 11.90 Trifecta £121.10.
Owner John Dyer **Bred** Catherine Dyer **Trained** Blewbury, Oxon

FOCUS
Race distance increased by 8yds. An ordinary handicap, but the winner is improving.

3976 FROSTS4CARS.CO.UK LADIES DAY H'CAP 5f 213y
8:40 (8:40) (Class 5) (0-75,75) 3-Y-O **£2,911** (£866; £432; £216) **Stalls** Centre

Form RPR

33-0 **1** **Fang**[27] 3029 3-9-7 **75**..(t) SeanLevey 5 82
(Brian Meehan) *mde all: forged ahd u.p 1f out: styd on wl: rdn out* **11/4**[2]

40-0 **2** 2 ½ **Chandresh**[46] 2435 3-8-6 **60**.. KieranO'Neill 7 59
(Robert Cowell) *chsd wnr thrght: rdn wl over 1f out: unable qck ent fnl f: wl hld by wnr but hld on to 2nd ins fnl f* **16/1**

6000 **3** ¾ **Sweet Temptation (IRE)**[33] 2824 3-8-13 **67**.................. MartinHarley 6 64
(Stuart Williams) *hld up in tch in last pair: swtchd rt and effrt 2f out: kpt on u.p ins fnl f: wnt 3rd towards fin: no threat to wnr* **9/1**

56-0 **4** nk **Peter Park**[25] 3111 3-9-3 **71**... AdamKirby 3 67
(Clive Cox) *dwlt: t.k.h: hld up in tch in last pair: clsd and nt clr run 2f out: gap opened and rdn jst over 1f out: styd on same pce: wnt 4th cl home* **11/4**[2]

2033 **5** nk **Verne Castle**[24] 3127 3-8-11 **68**..............................[1] EdwardGreatrex(3) 1 63
(Andrew Balding) *t.k.h: chsd ldrs: effrt u.p ent fnl f: unable qck over 1f out: wknd ins fnl f: lost 2 pls towards fin* **5/2**[1]

4-00 **6** 6 **The Burnham Mare (IRE)**[27] 3036 3-8-3 **64**..............(p) HollieDoyle(7) 2 39
(J S Moore) *in tch in midfield: unable qck u.p over 1f out: wknd ins fnl f* **7/1**[3]

1m 10.5s (0.30) **Going Correction** +0.075s/f (Good) **6** Ran SP% **110.3**
Speed ratings (Par 100): **101,97,96,96,95 87**
CSF £39.03 TOTE £3.00: £1.80, £2.70; EX 41.20 Trifecta £331.30.
Owner Lady Rothschild **Bred** Kincorth Investments Inc **Trained** Manton, Wilts

FOCUS
Race distance increased by 8yds. The early pace wasn't strong in this sprint handicap, and the winner was always best placed. The winner has been rated in line with his early 2yo form.
T/Plt: £77.70 to a £1 stake. Pool: £77,618.29 T/Qpdt: £21.90 to a £1 stake. Pool: £8,134.07
Steve Payne

3711 PONTEFRACT (L-H)
Tuesday, July 5

OFFICIAL GOING: Good (8.2)
Wind: Strong behind Weather: Fine and blustery

3977 DIANNE NURSERY H'CAP 6f
2:10 (2:10) (Class 4) 2-Y-O **£4,528** (£1,347; £673; £336) **Stalls** Low

Form RPR

31 **1** **On Her Toes (IRE)**[10] 3668 2-9-6 **78**.............................. FrankieDettori 3 83
(William Haggas) *trckd ldng pair: pushed along 2f out: rdn over 1f out: led ins fnl f: kpt on* **10/11**[1]

532 **2** ¾ **Prerogative (IRE)**[13] 3526 2-9-7 **79**...................................... PatDobbs 5 81
(Richard Hannon) *trckd ldr: hdwy to ld wl over 1f out: sn rdn: drvn and hdd ins fnl f: kpt on* **9/4**[2]

424 **3** 6 **Katebird (IRE)**[24] 3148 2-8-5 **63**.. FrannyNorton 1 47
(Mark Johnston) *led: pushed along over 2f out: rdn and hdd wl over 1f out: grad wknd* **5/1**[3]

6146 **4** 7 **Springwood (IRE)**[38] 2669 2-9-2 **74**.............................. TonyHamilton 4 37
(Richard Fahey) *in rr: pushed along 1/2-way: rdn over 2f out: sn outpcd* **12/1**

1m 18.67s (1.77) **Going Correction** +0.35s/f (Good) **4** Ran SP% **107.5**
Speed ratings (Par 96): **102,101,93,83**
CSF £3.16 TOTE £1.60; EX 2.90 Trifecta £4.20.
Owner Cheveley Park Stud **Bred** Knocklong House Stud **Trained** Newmarket, Suffolk

FOCUS
The rail was dolled out 15ft from the 6f bend to the winning post, adding approximately 8yds to all races. Both Frankie Dettori and Franny Norton agreed the ground was 'good'. The big two in the market dominated this nursery, the four runners finishing in market order.

3978 CAREHOMECLAIMS IS BACK H'CAP 5f
2:40 (2:43) (Class 5) (0-75,75) 3-Y-O **£3,234** (£962; £481; £240) **Stalls** Low

Form RPR

-533 **1** **Wilde Extravagance (IRE)**[43] 2534 3-8-10 **67**............... JoeDoyle(3) 11 74
(Julie Camacho) *dwlt and towards rr: hdwy on outer wl over 1f out: sn rdn and edgd lft ins fnl f: styd on strly to ld last 75yds* **9/1**

3153 **2** ½ **Mr Orange (IRE)**[16] 3439 3-8-7 **61**....................................(p) CamHardie 7 66
(Paul Midgley) *trckd ldrs: hdwy on inner whn n.m.r ent fnl f: sn rdn and styd on wl towards fin* **4/1**[2]

0-00 **3** ¾ **Market Choice (IRE)**[17] 3420 3-9-7 **75**........................ PaulMulrennan 4 78
(Michael Dods) *hld up in rr: hdwy on outer over 1f out: sltly hmpd and swtchd rt ins fnl f: rdn and styd on wl towards fin* **8/1**

2663 **4** 1 ¼ **Emerald Asset (IRE)**[18] 3368 3-8-4 **58**......................... JamesSullivan 6 56
(Paul Midgley) *in rr: hdwy wl over 1f out: rdn to chse ldrs whn n.m.r ins fnl f: swtchd rt and kpt on wl towards fin* **9/1**

400 **5** nk **New Road Side**[17] 3420 3-9-4 **72**..............................(v[1]) BarryMcHugh 1 69
(Tony Coyle) *led: rdn clr wl over 1f out: drvn ent fnl f: hdd and no ex last 75yds* **10/1**

3153 **6** nk **Semana Santa**[11] 3611 3-9-4 **72**................................... GrahamGibbons 3 68
(David Barron) *prom: rdn to chse clr ldr wl over 1f out: drvn ins fnl f: wknd last 75yds* **3/1**[1]

-006 **7** 1 ¾ **Gowanless**[17] 3420 3-9-2 **70**.......................................(p) ConnorBeasley 9 60
(Michael Dods) *dwlt and sn pushed along to chse ldrs: rdn along 2f out: drvn over 1f out: wknd fnl f* **12/1**

31-6 **8** 1 ¼ **Consulting**[18] 3360 3-9-6 **74**... HarryBentley 8 59
(Martyn Meade) *in tch: pushed along over 2f out: sn rdn and wknd* **11/2**[3]

0-00 **9** 3 ½ **French**[16] 3439 3-9-0 **68**...(p) DanielTudhope 12 40
(Antony Brittain) *prom on outer: rdn along 2f out: drvn over 1f out: sn wknd* **14/1**

1m 5.25s (1.95) **Going Correction** +0.35s/f (Good) **9** Ran SP% **114.9**
Speed ratings (Par 100): **98,97,96,94,93 93,90,88,82**
CSF £44.71 CT £305.35 TOTE £9.40: £2.70, £1.70, £2.60; EX 28.90 Trifecta £386.40.
Owner Judy & Richard Peck **Bred** Miss M McWey **Trained** Norton, N Yorks

FOCUS
Race distance increased by 8yds. The pace collapsed in this modest sprint and the closers were very much favoured. A pb from the winner, with the second helping to set the standard.

3979 WEATHERBYS GSB PIPALONG STKS (LISTED RACE) (F&M) 1m 4y
3:10 (3:10) (Class 1) 4-Y-O+
£22,684 (£8,600; £4,304; £2,144; £1,076; £540) **Stalls** Low

Form RPR

6-10 **1** **Spirit Raiser (IRE)**[20] 3273 5-9-0 102............................ FrederikTylicki 1 97
(James Fanshawe) *trckd ldng pair on inner: swtchd rt and hdwy over 1f out: rdn to ld ent fnl f: sn jnd and drvn: rdr dropped whip towards fin: kpt on gamely* **2/1**[1]

-330 **2** ½ **Black Cherry**[20] 3271 4-9-0 103.. PatDobbs 9 96
(Richard Hannon) *midfield: gd hdwy 2f out: chsd wnr ent fnl f: sn rdn to chal and ev ch tl drvn and no ex towards fin* **9/2**[2]

-135 **3** 1 ½ **Lil Sophella (IRE)**[11] 3595 7-9-0 81................................ JackGarritty 11 92
(Patrick Holmes) *in rr: hdwy on inner over 1f out: sn rdn and kpt on wl fnl f* **50/1**

4211 **4** nk **Esteemable**[16] 3438 4-9-0 83... DanielMuscutt 8 92
(James Fanshawe) *in tch: hdwy wl over 1f out: sn rdn and styd on fnl f* **20/1**

1162 **5** hd **Lucy The Painter (IRE)**[10] 3667 4-9-0 88...................... HarryBentley 3 91
(Ed de Giles) *trckd ldrs: hdwy over 1f out: rdn and ch ent fnl f: sn drvn and n.m.r: kpt on same pce* **20/1**

5620 **6** 5 **Lady Marl**[101] 1093 5-9-0 84.. PaulMulrennan 10 80
(Gary Moore) *towards rr: hdwy wl over 1f out: n.m.r and swtchd lft ent fnl f: sn rdn and no imp* **50/1**

4016 **7** 1 ½ **Loaves And Fishes**[31] 2893 4-9-0 94...........................[1] DanielTudhope 2 76
(David O'Meara) *led: rdn along wl over 1f out: hdd and drvn ent fnl f: grad wknd* **14/1**

0031 **8** ½ **Mothers Finest (IRE)**[12] 3565 4-9-0 102............................(t) BenCurtis 6 75
(K R Burke) *towards rr: effrt and wd st: sn rdn and n.d* **12/1**

-055 **9** ¾ **Merry Me (IRE)**[10] 3672 5-9-0 95.................................... DavidProbert 4 73
(Andrew Balding) *cl up: rdn 2f out: sn drvn and wknd* **9/1**

0-61 **10** 3 ½ **Gratzie**[24] 3124 5-9-0 95.. GrahamGibbons 12 65
(Mick Channon) *dwlt: a in rr* **16/1**

1123 **11** 2 **Clotilde**[10] 3672 4-9-0 100.. RichardKingscote 7 61
(William Knight) *trckd ldng pair on outer: cl up 3f out: sn rdn along and wknd wl over 1f out* **6/1**[3]

35-3 **12** ½ **Alfajer**[102] 1065 4-9-0 97..(b) AndreaAtzeni 13 59
(Marco Botti) *midfield: effrt and sme hdwy wl over 2f out: sn rdn and btn* **16/1**

-254 **13** 50 **Brandybend (IRE)**[26] 3088 4-9-0 97.................................. JamesDoyle 5
(Marco Botti) *chsd ldrs: rdn along wl over 2f out: sn wknd* **20/1**

1m 45.93s (0.03) **Going Correction** +0.35s/f (Good) **13** Ran SP% **120.1**
Speed ratings (Par 111): **113,112,111,110,110 105,104,103,102,99 97,96,46**
CSF £9.36 TOTE £3.20: £1.60, £1.70, £11.60; EX 14.80 Trifecta £561.80.
Owner Lord Vestey **Bred** Stowell Park Stud **Trained** Newmarket, Suffolk

FOCUS
Race distance increased by 8yds. An ordinary fillies' Listed race, with the third to sixth all rated in the 80s, but the market leaders finished one-two without having to be at their best.

3980 KING RICHARD III (H'CAP) 6f
3:40 (3:41) (Class 3) (0-90,90) 3-Y-O+ **£7,762** (£2,310; £1,154; £577) **Stalls** Low

Form RPR

6-62 **1** **Johnny Cavagin**[10] 3645 7-9-5 **83**.................................(t) JimmyQuinn 5 93
(Ronald Thompson) *in tch: hdwy on inner over 1f out: swtchd rt and rdn ent fnl f: drvn to ld last 75yds: kpt on wl towards fin* **10/1**

4442 **2** ½ **Chaplin Bay (IRE)**[5] 3807 4-8-7 **71**................................. JamesSullivan 8 79
(Ruth Carr) *dwlt and towards rr: hdwy on outer wl over 1f out: sn rdn: drvn and edgd lft ins fnl f: sn ev ch: no ex towards fin* **6/1**[2]

11 **3** shd **Agree (IRE)**[38] 2693 3-9-2 **86**... BenCurtis 10 93+
(Brian Ellison) *hld up: gd hdwy on outer wl over 1f out: rdn ent fnl f: drvn and ev ch whn n.m.r last 100yds: kpt on* **11/4**[1]

111 **4** ½ **Final Venture**[27] 3021 4-9-7 **85**... NeilFarley 9 91+
(Alan Swinbank) *led: clr 2f out: rdn overc1f out: drvn ent fnl f: hdd and no ex last 75yds* **10/1**

The Form Book, Raceform Ltd, Newbury, RG14 5SJ

0006 **5** 1 1/2 **Ballymore Castle (IRE)**[45] 2476 4-9-3 **86**........(p) AdamMcNamara(5) 12 87
(Richard Fahey) *bhd: rdn along over 2f out: hdwy on inner over 1f out: styd on wl fnl f: nrst fin* **14/1**

30-0 **6** 2 1/4 **Fendale**[23] 3188 4-9-12 **90**.......... PaulMulrennan 3 84
(Michael Dods) *midfield: rdn along wl over 1f out: kpt on fnl f: nrst fin* **10/1**

2502 **7** 1 **Ocean Sheridan (IRE)**[11] 3595 4-9-5 **83**.......... ConnorBeasley 2 74
(Michael Dods) *trckd ldrs: hdwy over 2f out: rdn to chse ldr over 1f out: drvn and kpt on same pce fnl f* **17/2**[3]

0063 **8** 2 **Personal Touch**[10] 3646 7-9-0 **78**.......... AndrewMullen 14 62
(Michael Appleby) *trckd ldrs: rdn along 2f out: sn drvn and grad wknd* **25/1**

0-01 **9** 1 **Monarch Maid**[28] 3004 5-8-6 **73**.......... ShelleyBirkett(3) 4 54
(Peter Hiatt) *cl up: rdn along 2f out: drvn over 1f out: wknd fnl f* **25/1**

6265 **10** *hd* **Handsome Dude**[23] 3188 4-9-10 **88**..........(b) GrahamGibbons 1 69
(David Barron) *a towards rr* **10/1**

-002 **11** *hd* **Compton Park**[10] 3646 9-9-0 **78**.......... DavidAllan 7 58
(Les Eyre) *in tch: hdwy over 2f out: rdn to chse ldrs over 1f out: drvn and wknd fnl f* **14/1**

0406 **12** 3/4 **Sunraider (IRE)**[7] 3753 9-8-8 **72**.......... BarryMcHugh 13 50
(Paul Midgley) *a towards rr* **25/1**

1-00 **13** 14 **Majdool (IRE)**[24] 3155 3-9-6 **90**.......... PaulHanagan 11 22
(Roger Varian) *trckd ldrs: pushed along over 2f out: sn rdn and wknd wl over 1f out* **20/1**

1m 17.85s (0.95) **Going Correction** +0.35s/f (Good)
WFA 3 from 4yo+ 6lb **13** Ran SP% **117.5**
Speed ratings (Par 107): **107,106,106,105,103 100,99,96,95,94 94,93,75**
CSF £64.18 CT £209.80 TOTE £11.90: £3.80, £2.40, £1.50; EX 76.20 Trifecta £448.00.
Owner A Bell **Bred** A Bell **Trained** Stainforth, S Yorks

FOCUS
Race distance increased by 8yds. Plenty of pace on in what was a good sprint and the closers were favoured. The winner is rated back to his best.

3981 SOLUTIONS 4 CLEANING MAIDEN STKS 1m 2f 6y
4:10 (4:11) (Class 5) 3-Y-O+ **£3,234** (£962; £481; £240) **Stalls** Low

Form RPR

23 **1** **Trainnah**[23] 3194 3-8-12 0.......... FrankieDettori 7 81+
(William Haggas) *trckd ldr: effrt on outer over 2f out: rdn wl over 1f out: drvn to chse ldr ins fnl f: styd on to ld last 100yds* **8/15**[1]

05 **2** 1/2 **Brief Visit**[23] 3194 3-8-12 0.......... DavidProbert 1 78
(Andrew Balding) *in tch: hdwy to trck ldrs 7f out: effrt on inner 2f out and sn led: rdn over 1f out: drvn and hdd last 100yds: no ex* **5/1**[3]

3 4 1/2 **Different Journey** 3-9-3 0.......... JamesDoyle 4 74
(Saeed bin Suroor) *led: pushed along over 2f out: rdn and hdd wl over 1f out: drvn and kpt on same pce appr fnl f* **4/1**[2]

0-0 **4** 1 1/2 **Sautter**[32] 2861 3-9-3 0.......... AndreaAtzeni 2 71
(Peter Chapple-Hyam) *chsd ldrs: rdn along wl over 2f out: sn one pce* **14/1**

04 **5** 1/2 **Fastnet Blast (IRE)**[60] 2000 3-9-3 0.......... HarryBentley 6 70
(Ed Walker) *in rr: hdwy over 3f out: rdn along wl over 2f out: sn drvn and one pce* **14/1**

4 **6** 42 **Dawn Flight (IRE)**[18] 3362 3-9-3 0.......... PJMcDonald 3
(John Davies) *trckd ldng pair: pushed along 1/2-way: sn lost pl and bhd whn eased fnl 2f* **20/1**

6 **7** 26 **Snappydresser**[18] 3362 3-8-12 0.......... ConnorBeasley 8
(Tracy Waggott) *a in rr: bhd whn eased fnl 2f* **50/1**

2m 16.77s (3.07) **Going Correction** +0.35s/f (Good) **7** Ran SP% **122.0**
Speed ratings (Par 103): **101,100,97,95,95 61,41**
CSF £4.38 TOTE £1.40: £1.10, £2.60; EX 4.00 Trifecta £9.60.
Owner Al Shaqab Racing **Bred** Stetchworth & Middle Park Studs Ltd **Trained** Newmarket, Suffolk

FOCUS
Race distance increased by 8yds. Two useful fillies pulled clear late in what was a fair maiden.

3982 PONTEFRACT SQUASH & LEISURE CLUB H'CAP 1m 4y
4:40 (4:41) (Class 5) (0-70,70) 3-Y-O **£3,234** (£962; £481; £240) **Stalls** Low

Form RPR

6205 **1** **Theos Lolly (IRE)**[11] 3591 3-9-7 **70**.......... DavidNolan 2 77
(Richard Fahey) *trckd ldrs: hdwy over 2f out: rdn over 1f out: led ins fnl f and edgd lft: drvn out* **6/1**[2]

5562 **2** 1 1/2 **Bit Of A Quirke**[12] 3579 3-8-8 **57**.......... JasonHart 1 61
(Mark Walford) *trckd ldrs on inner: hdwy wl over 1f out: sn rdn and styd on fnl f* **7/1**

2033 **3** 3/4 **Dominannie (IRE)**[13] 3521 3-9-1 **64**.......... NeilFarley 6 66
(Alan Swinbank) *hld up: hdwy on wd outside wl over 1f out: rdn and kpt on wl fnl f* **7/1**

4246 **4** *nk* **Weld Al Khawaneej (IRE)**[3] 3877 3-8-12 **64**..........(p) JoeDoyle(3) 4 66+
(Kevin Ryan) *trckd ldrs: effrt over 1f out: rdn and nt clr run ins fnl f: kpt on same pce* **5/1**[1]

-443 **5** 1 **The Excel Queen (IRE)**[21] 3249 3-8-10 **59**.......... BarryMcHugh 8 58
(Tony Coyle) *led: hdd over 4f out: cl up: rdn and ev ch over 1f out: sn drvn and grad wknd fnl f* **25/1**

5006 **6** 1 3/4 **Allfredandnobell (IRE)**[34] 2801 3-8-6 **55**.......... PJMcDonald 14 50+
(Micky Hammond) *hld up and bhd: hdwy on inner 2f out: kpt on fnl f: nrst fin* **25/1**

5031 **7** 1 1/2 **Whitkirk**[7] 3750 3-8-12 **61** 6ex.......... JoeyHaynes 12 52+
(Jedd O'Keeffe) *trckd ldrs: effrt 2f out and sn rdn: drvn appr fnl f and no imp* **5/1**[1]

10-5 **8** 1 3/4 **Executor**[69] 1777 3-9-4 **70**.......... KieranShoemark(3) 3 57
(Roger Charlton) *trckd ldr: led over 4f out: rdn along 2f out: drvn and hdd jst ins fnl f: sn wknd* **13/2**[3]

6-54 **9** 1 1/2 **Ballyer Rallyer (IRE)**[21] 3267 3-9-4 **67**.......... DaleSwift 9 51
(Daniel Mark Loughnane) *dwlt: a towards rr* **33/1**

364 **10** 10 **Wasseem (IRE)**[21] 3264 3-9-4 **67**..........(tp) AndreaAtzeni 10 28
(Simon Crisford) *dwlt: a towards rr* **8/1**

260- **11** 3/4 **Guanabara Bay (IRE)**[271] 7054 3-9-6 **69**.......... PaulMulrennan 5 28
(Martyn Meade) *chsd ldrs: rdn along over 2f out: sn wknd* **14/1**

00-0 **12** 16 **Blue Jay (FR)**[50] 2307 3-8-2 **51** oh1.......... JimmyQuinn 11
(Ronald Thompson) *a in rr* **40/1**

1m 49.69s (3.79) **Going Correction** +0.35s/f (Good) **12** Ran SP% **116.8**
Speed ratings (Par 100): **95,93,92,92,91 89,88,86,84,74 74,58**
CSF £45.00 CT £306.19 TOTE £6.00: £2.20, £2.70, £2.70; EX 54.50 Trifecta £413.00.
Owner M J Macleod **Bred** Mrs Claire Doyle **Trained** Musley Bank, N Yorks

FOCUS
Race distance increased by 8yds. The low-drawn runners came to the fore in what was a modest handicap. The winner has been rated close to his best 2yo form.

3983 PONTEFRACT SPORTS & EDUCATION FOUNDATION APPRENTICE H'CAP 1m 2f 6y
5:10 (5:10) (Class 5) (0-75,74) 3-Y-O+ **£3,234** (£962; £481; £240) **Stalls** Low

Form RPR

13-3 **1** **Azzir (IRE)**[17] 3395 4-9-7 **74**.......... CliffordLee(7) 8 83
(K R Burke) *in tch on inner: smooth hdwy to trck ldrs over 2f out: rdn to ld ent fnl f: sn drvn and kpt on wl* **8/1**

2501 **2** 1 **Miss Ranger (IRE)**[10] 3642 4-9-5 **68**.......... CallumShepherd(3) 12 75+
(Brian Ellison) *hld up in rr: hdwy on outer 3f out: rdn wl over 1f out: styd on strly fnl f* **16/1**

-525 **3** 1/2 **Stardrifter**[26] 3057 4-9-8 **73**.......... AdamMcNamara(5) 4 79
(Richard Fahey) *trckd ldr: effrt wl over 1f out: sn rdn and ev ch tl drvn and kpt on same pce ins fnl f* **9/4**[1]

110 **4** 4 1/2 **Red Charmer (IRE)**[14] 3478 6-9-5 **70**.......... RowanScott(5) 1 67
(Ann Duffield) *trckd ldr on inner: hdwy to ld 2f out: sn rdn: drvn and hdd ent fnl f: grad wknd* **6/1**[3]

3466 **5** *nse* **Qibtee (FR)**[8] 3711 6-8-6 **59**.......... BenRobinson(7) 10 56
(Les Eyre) *towards rr: pushed along 3f out: hdwy wl over 1f out: sn rdn and kpt on fnl f* **33/1**

0126 **6** 3/4 **San Quentin (IRE)**[7] 3751 5-9-9 **72**..........(p) JoshDoyle(3) 9 67
(David Loughnane) *hld up in rr: hdwy 2f out: rdn and kpt on fnl f* **20/1**

0006 **7** 3/4 **Tafahom (IRE)**[38] 2673 4-9-2 **65**..........(p) NathanEvans(3) 5 59
(Michael Easterby) *chsd ldrs: rdn along 2f out: sn one pce* **12/1**

1-60 **8** 2 **Heaven Scent**[22] 3215 3-7-12 **62**..........(p) DavidEgan(7) 2 52
(Ann Duffield) *led: sddle slipped after 2f: hdd 2f out and sn wknd* **16/1**

00-5 **9** 2 **Age Of Elegance (IRE)**[75] 1588 4-9-6 **73**.......... CameronNoble(7) 11 59
(David Loughnane) *dwlt: a towards rr* **14/1**

0-36 **10** 4 1/2 **Lido Lady (IRE)**[11] 3593 3-8-9 **71**.......... RobJFitzpatrick(5) 6 48
(Mark Johnston) *trckd ldrs: pushed along over 2f out: sn rdn and hld whn nt clr run over 1f out: wknd after* **9/1**

0341 **11** 1 3/4 **Palmerston**[22] 3224 3-9-1 **72**.......... AlistairRawlinson 7 45
(Michael Appleby) *trckd ldrs on outer: pushed along wl over 2f out: rdn wl over 1f out and sn wknd* **5/1**[2]

2m 17.33s (3.63) **Going Correction** +0.35s/f (Good)
WFA 3 from 4yo+ 11lb **11** Ran SP% **116.7**
Speed ratings (Par 103): **99,98,97,94,94 93,92,91,89,86 84**
CSF £127.17 CT £383.85 TOTE £9.20: £2.60, £3.60, £1.60; EX 60.80 Trifecta £220.70.
Owner Mohamed Alhameli & Partners **Bred** Sean Madigan **Trained** Middleham Moor, N Yorks

FOCUS
Race distance increased by 8yds. The front three came clear in what was a modest apprentice handicap run at an ordinary gallop. It's been rated around the third.
T/Plt: £44.10 to a £1 stake. Pool: £78,583.87 - 1,299.26 winning units. T/Qpdt: £9.60 to a £1 stake. Pool: £7,424.29 - 570.69 winning units. **Joe Rowntree**

3725 WOLVERHAMPTON (A.W) (L-H)
Tuesday, July 5

OFFICIAL GOING: Tapeta: standard
Wind: Fresh across Weather: Sunny spells

3984 FOLLOW @ATTHERACES ON TWITTER H'CAP 5f 216y (Tp)
2:25 (2:25) (Class 6) (0-60,60) 3-Y-O+ **£2,264** (£673; £336; £168) **Stalls** Low

Form RPR

-006 **1** **Langley Vale**[18] 3349 7-9-10 **60**..........(v[1]) FergusSweeney 4 67
(Roger Teal) *sn pushed along and prom: rdn over 1f out: hung rt ins fnl f: r.o to ld post* **5/1**[2]

3136 **2** *nk* **Dream Ally (IRE)**[69] 1794 6-9-4 **54**..........(be) DarryllHolland 3 60
(John Weymes) *chsd ldr tl led wl over 1f out: sn rdn: hdd post* **12/1**

2034 **3** 1 1/4 **Tasaaboq**[7] 3735 5-9-4 **57**..........(t) JosephineGordon(3) 6 59
(Phil McEntee) *hld up: hdwy over 2f out: rdn over 1f out: styd on same pce towards fin* **9/2**[1]

2321 **4** 3/4 **Wedgewood Estates**[27] 3040 5-9-6 **56**.......... LukeMorris 9 59
(Tony Carroll) *s.s: hld up: hdwy: nt clr run and swtchd rt over 1f out: sn rdn: r.o: nt rch ldrs* **5/1**[2]

2000 **5** 1 **Whipphound**[22] 3211 8-9-4 **54**.......... TomEaves 5 51
(Ruth Carr) *a.p: shkn up over 1f out: styng on same pce whn nt clr run ins fnl f* **20/1**

5403 **6** 3/4 **Bogsnog (IRE)**[27] 3016 6-9-4 **54**.......... JoeFanning 10 49
(Kristin Stubbs) *chsd ldrs: rdn over 2f out: no ex ins fnl f* **5/1**[2]

4200 **7** 2 1/4 **Compton Prince**[7] 3735 7-9-10 **60**..........(b) RoystonFfrench 7 48
(Milton Bradley) *mid-div: pushed along over 3f out: effrt and nt clr run over 1f out: no ex ins fnl f* **16/1**

0300 **8** *hd* **Sakhee's Rose**[13] 3527 6-9-8 **58**..........(b) GeorgeBaker 12 46
(Ed McMahon) *s.i.s: hld up: nvr nrr* **8/1**[3]

0440 **9** 1/2 **Copper Cavalier**[10] 3648 5-9-2 **52**..........(b) RobertHavlin 8 38
(Michael Blanshard) *mid-div: rdn over 2f out: wknd over 1f out* **14/1**

-065 **10** 2 **Verus Delicia (IRE)**[15] 3474 7-9-5 **55**.......... StevieDonohoe 11 35
(Daniel Mark Loughnane) *hld up: pushed along 1/2-way: nvr on terms* **12/1**

0040 **11** 2 1/4 **Pryers Princess**[12] 3553 4-9-9 **59**.......... MartinDwyer 1 32
(David C Griffiths) *s.s: sn pushed along and a in rr* **14/1**

06-6 **12** 4 1/2 **Knockamany Bends (IRE)**[27] 3010 6-9-2 **52**..........(p) PaddyAspell 2 12
(John Wainwright) *led: rdn and hdd wl over 1f out: wknd fnl f* **25/1**

1m 14.72s (0.22) **Going Correction** +0.10s/f (Slow) **12** Ran SP% **122.5**
Speed ratings (Par 101): **102,101,99,98,97 96,93,93,92,90 87,81**
CSF £66.25 CT £296.58 TOTE £6.10: £2.20, £4.00, £2.30; EX 86.90 Trifecta £356.90.
Owner Mrs Muriel Forward & Dr G C Forward **Bred** Miss Brooke Sanders **Trained** Great Shefford, Berks

FOCUS
Low-grade sprint handicap form.

3985 CITY OF GEMS ENJOYWOLVERHAMPTON.COM CLASSIFIED CLAIMING STKS 5f 216y (Tp)
2:55 (2:55) (Class 5) 3-Y-O+ **£2,911** (£866; £432; £216) **Stalls** Low

Form RPR

0361 **1** **Secret Look**[10] 3674 6-9-8 68..........(p) MartinDwyer 5 73
(Ed McMahon) *a.p: rdn over 2f out: r.o to ld wl ins fnl f* **11/2**[3]

5001 **2** *nk* **City Of Angkor Wat (IRE)**[8] 3726 6-9-3 70....(p) JosephineGordon(3) 10 70
(Conor Dore) *chsd ldr: led over 1f out: rdn and hdd wl ins fnl f: r.o* **7/2**[2]

4002 **3** 3/4 **Head Space (IRE)**[13] 3510 8-8-11 66..........(vt) JoshuaBryan(7) 4 66
(Brian Barr) *hld up: hdwy over 1f out: r.o* **8/1**

0504 **4** ¾ **Claymore (IRE)**^{7} 3740 3-9-6 69 (p) GeorgeBaker 7 71
(David Lanigan) *s.i.s: hld up: shkn up over 1f out: rdn: hung lft and r.o ins fnl f: nt rch ldrs* **5/2**^{1}

4040 **5** ½ **Jess**^{6} 3777 3-9-6 64 (p) TomEaves 3 69
(Kevin Ryan) *chsd ldrs: rdn over 1f out: styd on same pce ins fnl f* **25/1**

3366 **6** 2¼ **Ten Rocks**^{10} 3634 3-8-8 67 MartinLane 6 51
(Lisa Williamson) *sn pushed along to ld: rdn and hdd over 1f out: no ex ins fnl f: eased nr fin* **25/1**

1023 **7** ¾ **Malaysian Boleh**^{14} 3491 6-9-4 67 (b) LukeMorris 2 53
(Shaun Lycett) *mid-div: rdn over 2f out: no ex fnl f* **7/1**

4565 **8** 6 **Thee And Me (IRE)**^{15} 3473 3-8-6 66 RoystonFfrench 9 28
(Mike Murphy) *hld up: rdn over 2f out: a in rr* **13/2**

0560 **9** 9 **National Service (USA)**^{41} 2571 5-9-4 63 (tp) TimmyMurphy 11 8
(Rebecca Menzies) *s.s: hld up: rdn over 2f out: sn wknd and eased* **14/1**

1m 14.59s (0.09) **Going Correction** +0.10s/f (Slow)
WFA 3 from 5yo+ 6lb **9** Ran SP% **117.5**
Speed ratings (Par 103): **103,102,101,100,99 96,95,87,75**
CSF £25.57 TOTE £6.80: £2.30, £1.50, £3.00; EX 30.90 Trifecta £182.00.
Owner S L Edwards **Bred** S L Edwards **Trained** Lichfield, Staffs

FOCUS
A moderate event run in a slightly slower time than the opening Class 6 handicap.

3986 VISIT ATTHERACES.COM MAIDEN AUCTION STKS 7f 32y (Tp)
3:25 (3:25) (Class 6) 2-Y-O **£2,264** (£673; £336; £168) **Stalls** High

Form RPR

0 **1** **Woodukheleyfit**^{28} 2997 2-9-3 0 GeorgeBaker 7 70
(Sylvester Kirk) *chsd ldr tl led 2f out: rdn and hung rt ins fnl f: styd on: fin 1st: disqualified and plcd 2nd* **6/1**^{2}

222 **2** hd **Bayston Hill**^{17} 3404 2-9-3 0 LukeMorris 4 70
(Mark Usher) *prom: pushed along over 2f out: rdn over 1f out: carried rt ins fnl f: r.o: fin 2nd: plcd 1st* **2/1**^{1}

3 1 **Salieri (FR)** 2-9-3 0 WilliamTwiston-Davies 6 68
(Alan King) *s.i.s: hld up: hdwy over 1f out: nt clr run wl ins fnl f: r.o to go 3rd nr fin* **8/1**^{3}

05 **4** 1¼ **If I Say So**^{17} 3404 2-9-0 0 JosephineGordon$^{(3)}$ 2 64
(J S Moore) *plld hrd and prom: rdn over 1f out: styd on same pce ins fnl f* **8/1**^{3}

5 **5** ¾ **Roaring Character (IRE)**^{8} 3730 2-9-3 0 LiamJones 1 63
(Tom Dascombe) *pushed along in rr: effrt over 1f out: nt trble ldrs* **2/1**^{1}

0 **6** 2½ **All About The Pace**^{12} 3555 2-8-12 0 RobertHavlin 5 52
(Mark Usher) *s.i.s: hld up: rdn and hung lft over 1f out: nvr on terms* **14/1**

6 **7** 5 **Warleggan (FR)**^{81} 1454 2-9-3 0 (b^{1}) FergusSweeney 3 44
(Eve Johnson Houghton) *led: rdn and hdd 2f out: wknd fnl f* **16/1**

1m 31.13s (2.33) **Going Correction** +0.10s/f (Slow) **7** Ran SP% **115.7**
Speed ratings (Par 92): **90,89,88,87,86 83,77**
CSF £15.29 TOTE £2.20: £1.10, £3.40; EX 19.60 Trifecta £53.80.
Owner Lady O'Brien **Bred** Worksop Manor Stud **Trained** Upper Lambourn, Berks

FOCUS
Ordinary form. The first three ended up towards the stands' rail and the first past the post was thrown out by the stewards.

3987 AT THE RACES APP ON ANDROID H'CAP (DIV I) 7f 32y (Tp)
3:55 (3:59) (Class 6) (0-60,60) 3-Y-O+ **£2,264** (£673; £336; £168) **Stalls** High

Form RPR

0434 **1** **Hardy Black (IRE)**^{10} 3648 5-9-12 **60** (p) LukeMorris 1 68
(Kevin Frost) *prom: lost pl 6f out: hdwy 1/2-way: rdn and swtchd rt over 2f out: chsd ldr over 1f out: led and hung lft ins fnl f: styd on* **11/4**^{1}

3201 **2** ¾ **Illusive Force (IRE)**^{15} 3474 4-9-11 **59** (v) MartinLane 7 65
(Derek Shaw) *hld up: hdwy u.p over 1f out: r.o* **4/1**^{2}

5056 **3** ¾ **Fossa**^{14} 3486 6-8-12 **51** CharlieBennett$^{(5)}$ 5 56
(Mark Brisbourne) *s.i.s: hld up: hmpd over 2f out: hdwy over 1f out: r.o: nt rch ldrs* **14/1**

0-00 **4** ½ **The Resdev Way**^{34} 2801 3-8-5 **47** PaulQuinn 9 47
(Richard Whitaker) *hld up: rdn over 1f out: r.o ins fnl f: nvr nrr* **10/1**

0-50 **5** ½ **Steel Stockholder**^{49} 2329 10-9-9 **57** WilliamTwiston-Davies 3 59
(Antony Brittain) *chsd ldrs: led over 3f out: rdn over 1f out: hdd ins fnl f: styd on same pce* **14/1**

0-00 **6** 2½ **Prince Of Time**^{48} 2365 4-8-12 **53** CallumRodriguez$^{(7)}$ 8 49
(Richard Ford) *s.i.s: hld up: hdwy 2f out: rdn over 1f out: styd on same pce fnl f* **25/1**

00-0 **7** ¾ **Windmills Girl**^{42} 2559 3-8-8 **55** DavidParkes$^{(5)}$ 6 46
(Jeremy Gask) *prom: racd keenly: lost pl 6f out: rdn over 2f out: no imp fr over 1f out* **16/1**

0-10 **8** 2¼ **Tulip Dress**^{26} 3080 3-9-1 **60** DannyBrock$^{(3)}$ 11 45
(Anthony Carson) *chsd ldrs: rdn over 2f out: wknd ins fnl f* **12/1**

6004 **9** 2¼ **Dandys Perier (IRE)**^{15} 3474 5-9-3 **56** JordanNason$^{(5)}$ 2 39
(Ronald Harris) *led: hmpd over 6f out: sn hdd: remained handy: rdn over 2f out: wknd fnl f* **8/1**

4635 **10** 5 **Kenstone (FR)**^{7} 3735 3-8-10 **52** (p) MartinDwyer 4 20
(David Dennis) *jnd ldr 6f out tl led wl over 3f out: sn hdd: wknd over 1f out* **9/2**^{3}

0050 **11** 6 **Mostashreqah**^{13} 3513 3-9-0 **56** (tp) JoeFanning 10 9
(Milton Bradley) *hld up: rdn over 2f out: sn wknd* **16/1**

-000 **12** 2½ **Respectability**^{10} 3643 4-8-12 **46** oh1 (p) StevieDonohoe 12
(Ivan Furtado) *w ldr: led 6f out tl wl over 3f out: sn rdn: wknd wl over 1f out* **33/1**

1m 30.82s (2.02) **Going Correction** +0.10s/f (Slow)
WFA 3 from 4yo+ 8lb **12** Ran SP% **124.6**
Speed ratings (Par 101): **92,91,90,89,89 86,85,82,80,74 67,64**
CSF £13.97 CT £139.89 TOTE £3.40: £1.50, £1.90, £4.60; EX 12.90 Trifecta £86.60.
Owner Blue Grey Chevron Racing **Bred** A M V Nicoll **Trained** Market Drayton, Shropshire

FOCUS
This was fast and furious, but the slower division by 1.41 sec. The winner is rated back to last year's level.

3988 AT THE RACES APP ON ANDROID H'CAP (DIV II) 7f 32y (Tp)
4:25 (4:27) (Class 6) (0-60,60) 3-Y-O+ **£2,264** (£673; £336; £168) **Stalls** High

Form RPR

6033 **1** **Gulland Rock**^{11} 3624 5-9-4 **55** DannyBrock$^{(3)}$ 9 64
(Anthony Carson) *chsd ldr: led 4f out: rdn clr fnl 2f* **6/1**

6500 **2** 3¼ **Red Unico (IRE)**^{13} 3514 4-9-3 **58** JoshuaBryan$^{(7)}$ 4 59
(Brian Barr) *prom: rdn to go 2nd over 1f out: styd on: no ch w wnr* **11/1**

3020 **3** 2¼ **Grey Destiny**^{31} 2918 6-9-12 **60** WilliamTwiston-Davies 5 56
(Antony Brittain) *s.i.s: hld up: rdn over 1f out: r.o to go 3rd nr fin* **10/1**

0050 **4** 1¼ **Major Muscari (IRE)**^{14} 3484 8-9-3 **56** (p) CharlieBennett$^{(5)}$ 6 48
(Shaun Harris) *hld up: hdwy u.p over 1f out: edgd lft and styd on same pce ins fnl f* **20/1**

4040 **5** ¾ **Red Chatterbox (IRE)**^{33} 2834 3-8-4 **49** JosephineGordon$^{(3)}$ 2 37
(Scott Dixon) *led 3f: chsd wnr tl rdn and wknd over 1f out* **33/1**

-450 **6** 1 **Protest (IRE)**^{12} 3558 3-9-4 **60** LukeMorris 10 45+
(Sylvester Kirk) *s.i.s: hld up: rdn over 2f out: nvr nrr* **11/2**^{3}

0066 **7** shd **Rising Sunshine (IRE)**^{19} 3319 3-8-13 **55** JoeFanning 8 40+
(Richard Hannon) *hld up: hdwy over 1f out: wknd ins fnl f* **13/2**

-634 **8** 4½ **Constable Clouds (USA)**^{19} 3319 3-9-1 **57** (v) RyanMoore 11 31+
(Gary Moore) *prom: rdn over 2f out: wknd fnl f* **7/2**^{1}

5400 **9** ½ **Carlovian**^{8} 3731 3-8-13 **55** RobertHavlin 7 28
(Christopher Kellett) *hld up: racd keenly: rdn over 2f out: wknd over 1f out* **33/1**

00-0 **10** 2 **Tsarglas**^{59} 2047 5-8-12 **46** oh1 (p) RoystonFfrench 3 17
(Colin Teague) *chsd ldrs tl rdn and wknd over 2f out* **80/1**

-512 **11** 6 **Moi Aussie**^{28} 3003 3-9-4 **60** MartinDwyer 1 13
(Ed McMahon) *hld up: plld hrd: rdn and wknd over 2f out* **4/1**^{2}

1m 29.41s (0.61) **Going Correction** +0.10s/f (Slow)
WFA 3 from 4yo+ 8lb **11** Ran SP% **114.5**
Speed ratings (Par 101): **100,96,93,92,91 90,90,85,84,82 75**
CSF £65.24 CT £656.63 TOTE £6.30: £2.00, £3.70, £3.00; EX 76.00 Trifecta £565.30.
Owner W H Carson **Bred** Whitsbury Manor Stud **Trained** Newmarket, Suffolk

FOCUS
This was the quicker division by 1.41 sec. The winning jockey pinched it, and a number of these were just never seen with a chance.

3989 NEAL WOOD SEVENTH ANNIVERSARY MEMORIAL H'CAP 7f 32y (Tp)
4:55 (4:57) (Class 5) (0-75,75) 3-Y-O+ **£3,234** (£962; £481; £240) **Stalls** High

Form RPR

1- **1** **Certified (IRE)**^{243} 7716 3-9-6 **75** LukeMorris 2 84+
(James Tate) *hld up: hdwy over 2f out: rdn to ld ins fnl f: edgd rt: drvn out* **5/2**^{2}

603 **2** 3 **Top Offer**^{8} 3729 7-9-6 **67** (p) TimmyMurphy 1 71
(Patrick Morris) *hld up: hdwy 2f out: rdn ins fnl f: styd on same pce* **25/1**

6-53 **3** hd **Avalanche Express**^{27} 3035 4-9-10 **71** MartinDwyer 4 74+
(William Muir) *hld up in tch: nt clr run and swtchd rt over 1f out: r.o to go 3rd nr fin* **9/4**^{1}

200 **4** ½ **Light From Mars**^{41} 2579 11-10-0 **75** TomEaves 6 77
(Ronald Harris) *chsd ldrs: led 1f out: sn rdn and hdd: styd on same pce* **12/1**

3-00 **5** ¾ **Outrage**^{8} 3713 4-9-10 **71** GeorgeBaker 7 71
(Daniel Kubler) *chsd ldrs: rdn and n.m.r over 1f out: styd on same pce fnl f* **20/1**

05 **6** ½ **Caledonia Duchess**^{60} 2004 3-8-10 **65** (p) RobertHavlin 10 61
(Jo Hughes) *prom: chsd ldr over 5f out: rdn to ld over 1f out: hdd 1f out: no ex* **25/1**

0100 **7** 1¼ **Mr Christopher (IRE)**^{11} 3595 4-9-8 **74** (p) AnnaHesketh$^{(5)}$ 5 69
(Tom Dascombe) *hld up: rdn over 2f out: nt trble ldrs* **10/1**

6060 **8** ½ **Chetan**^{14} 3486 4-9-6 **67** (tp) MartinLane 8 61
(Charlie Wallis) *s.s: rdn over 2f out: hung lft over 1f out: nvr nrr* **25/1**

0010 **9** 1½ **Shamlan (IRE)**^{73} 1652 4-9-10 **71** (tp) StevieDonohoe 11 61
(Kevin Frost) *s.i.s: hld up: nvr on terms* **25/1**

3536 **10** 1½ **For Shia And Lula (IRE)**^{35} 2769 7-9-1 **62** (p) JoeFanning 12 48
(Daniel Mark Loughnane) *sn led: rdn and hdd over 1f out: wknd fnl f* **9/1**^{3}

620 **11** 1½ **Orlando Rogue (IRE)**^{8} 3732 4-8-13 **63** (p) JosephineGordon$^{(3)}$ 3 45
(Conor Dore) *hld up: nt clr run over 2f out: n.d* **12/1**

62-5 **12** 7 **Arcanista (IRE)**^{56} 2128 3-8-8 **63** FergusSweeney 9 23
(Richard Hughes) *s.i.s: hld up: rdn over 2f out: sn wknd* **16/1**

1m 28.99s (0.19) **Going Correction** +0.10s/f (Slow)
WFA 3 from 4yo+ 8lb **12** Ran SP% **119.8**
Speed ratings (Par 103): **102,98,98,97,96 96,94,94,92,90 89,81**
CSF £73.20 CT £156.48 TOTE £3.60: £1.60, £7.10, £1.40; EX 81.90 Trifecta £313.60.
Owner Saeed Manana **Bred** Rabbah Bloodstock Limited **Trained** Newmarket, Suffolk

FOCUS
The quickest of the C&D times. A step up from the unexposed winner, with the runner-up the key to the level.

3990 FOLLOW AT THE RACES ON INSTAGRAM MAIDEN FILLIES' STKS 1m 1f 103y (Tp)
5:25 (5:27) (Class 5) 3-4-Y-O **£3,234** (£962; £481; £240) **Stalls** Low

Form RPR

42- **1** **Colonial Classic (FR)**^{270} 7077 3-9-0 0 RobertHavlin 12 90+
(John Gosden) *a.p: chsd ldr over 6f out: led wl over 1f out: r.o: comf* **9/2**^{3}

3-25 **2** 2½ **September Stars (IRE)**^{47} 2394 3-9-0 80 MartinLane 8 85
(Ralph Beckett) *plld hrd: trckd ldr 3f: remained handy: rdn over 1f out: styd on same pce ins fnl f* **11/4**^{2}

30 **3** nse **Cape Peninsular**^{60} 1989 3-9-0 0 LukeMorris 7 85
(James Tate) *chsd ldrs: rdn over 2f out: edgd lft fr over 1f out: styd on same pce ins fnl f* **10/1**

4-2 **4** 2¾ **Statuesque**^{23} 3194 3-9-0 0 RyanMoore 10 79
(Sir Michael Stoute) *led at stdy pce tl qcknd over 2f out: rdn and hdd over 1f out: no ex ins fnl f* **1/1**^{1}

-33 **5** nse **Ecureuil (IRE)**^{18} 3350 3-8-11 0 MarcMonaghan$^{(3)}$ 2 79
(Hugo Palmer) *a.p: rdn over 1f out: styd on same pce fnl f* **10/1**

04 **6** 3½ **Sleeplessinseattle**^{18} 3350 3-9-0 0 JoeFanning 5 72
(James Fanshawe) *hld up: hdwy over 2f out: wknd ins fnl f* **16/1**

00 **7** 8 **Fire Jet (IRE)**^{44} 2505 3-9-0 0 RoystonFfrench 6 55
(John Mackie) *s.i.s: pushed along in rr early: rdn over 3f out: wknd over 2f out* **100/1**

60 **8** hd **Astrosecret**^{18} 3359 3-9-0 0 DarryllHolland 1 54
(Mark H Tompkins) *mid-div: rdn over 2f out: sn wknd* **66/1**

0- **9** 4 **Permaisuri (IRE)**^{250} 7585 3-9-0 0 TomEaves 9 46
(Kevin Ryan) *s.i.s: hld up: wknd over 2f out* **100/1**

00 **10** 1¼ **Social Media**^{11} 3601 3-8-7 0 HarryBurns$^{(7)}$ 4 43
(Ed Dunlop) *hld up: a in rr: wknd over 2f out* **100/1**

0 **11** shd **Snug**^{7} 3736 3-8-11 0 DannyBrock$^{(3)}$ 3 43
(Jane Chapple-Hyam) *s.i.s: pushed along in rr early: rdn and wknd over 2f out* **100/1**

12 22 **Freesia (IRE)** 3-9-0 0 ^{1} PaoloSirigu 11
(Marco Botti) *s.i.s: sn pushed along in rr: rdn and wknd over 3f out* **50/1**

2m 1.43s (0.63) **Going Correction** +0.10s/f (Slow) **12** Ran SP% **126.3**
Speed ratings (Par 100): **101,98,98,96,96 93,86,85,82,81 81,61**
CSF £18.69 TOTE £6.30: £2.00, £1.30, £3.90; EX 21.60 Trifecta £135.20.
Owner Merry Fox Stud Limited **Bred** Merry Fox Stud **Trained** Newmarket, Suffolk

The Form Book, Raceform Ltd, Newbury, RG14 5SJ

FOCUS
This fillies' maiden ought to produce a few winners. The pace was only steady. A pb from the winner, with the second close to form.

3991 AT THE RACES VIRGIN 535 H'CAP — 1m 4f 50y (Tp)
5:55 (5:55) (Class 5) (0-75,75) 3-Y-O+ — **£2,911** (£866; £432; £216) **Stalls** Low

Form — RPR

1-23 **1** **Mayasa (IRE)**[31] 2900 3-9-1 **75**......(b) RobertHavlin 4 83
(James Tate) *led: hdd over 10f out: chsd ldr tl led again over 4f out: pushed clr over 2f out: rdn over 1f out: jst hld on* **15/2**

315 **2** *nk* **Isharah (USA)**[19] 3323 3-9-0 **74**...... JoeFanning 3 81
(Mark Johnston) *hld up: hdwy over 2f out: rdn to chse wnr over 1f out: edgd lft: r.o: nt quite get there* **9/4**[1]

055 **3** *1 1/4* **Marshall Aid (IRE)**[23] 3190 3-8-5 **68**......(t) JosephineGordon[(3)] 8 74+
(Hugo Palmer) *hld up: hdwy over 1f out: r.o to go 3rd wl ins fnl f: nt rch ldrs* **13/2**[3]

2106 **4** *3 1/4* **Shoofly (IRE)**[11] 3615 3-9-1 **75**...... FergusSweeney 11 75
(Martyn Meade) *hld up: hdwy over 4f out: rdn over 2f out: no ex ins fnl f* **7/1**

05-0 **5** *2 3/4* **Monjeni**[14] 3493 3-8-0 **60**......(v[1]) LukeMorris 10 56
(Sir Mark Prescott Bt) *plld hrd and prom: chsd wnr over 3f out tl rdn over 1f out: wknd fnl f* **10/1**

0042 **6** *5* **New Street (IRE)**[17] 3403 5-9-12 **73**......(v) WilliamTwiston-Davies 9 61
(Jim Best) *dwlt: hld up: sme hdwy over 1f out: sn wknd* **16/1**

-654 **7** *4* **Forgiving Flower**[26] 3053 3-8-3 **63**...... RoystonFfrench 5 44
(K R Burke) *hld up: rdn over 3f out: wknd wl over 1f out* **12/1**

-644 **8** *2 1/4* **Pinstripe**[18] 3348 3-8-6 **66**...... MartinLane 1 44
(Luca Cumani) *chsd ldrs: rdn over 4f out: wknd 2f out* **10/3**[2]

43/0 **9** *44* **Amantius**[17] 3403 7-9-2 **63**......(b) StevieDonohoe 2
(Johnny Farrelly) *hld up: rdn and wknd over 3f out* **50/1**

2300 **10** *20* **Weald Of Kent (USA)**[10] 3659 4-10-0 **75**......(v) LiamJones 6
(Michael Appleby) *pushed along to ld over 10f out: rdn and hdd over 4f out: wknd wl over 3f out* **50/1**

2m 38.9s (-1.90) **Going Correction** +0.10s/f (Slow)
WFA 3 from 4yo+ 13lb — **10** Ran SP% **118.0**
Speed ratings (Par 103): **110,109,108,106,104 101,98,97,68,54**
CSF £25.02 CT £117.92 TOTE £6.30: £2.30, £1.20, £2.50; EX 23.10 Trifecta £202.00.
Owner Sheikh Rashid Dalmook Al Maktoum **Bred** Tom McDonald **Trained** Newmarket, Suffolk

FOCUS
The 3yos dominated this ordinary handicap. The 1-2-3 are all improving but the level is fluid.
T/Jkpt: Not won. T/Plt: £60.80 to a £1 stake. Pool: £76,818.35 - 921.04 winning units. T/Qpdt: £11.00 to a £1 stake. Pool: £6,876.78 - 460.78 winning units. **Colin Roberts**

3934 HAMBURG (R-H)
Tuesday, July 5

OFFICIAL GOING: Turf: heavy

3992a SPARKASSE HOLSTEIN-CUP (HAMBURGER FLIEGER TROPHY) (GROUP 3) (3YO+) (TURF) — 6f
6:00 (12:00) 3-Y-O+ — **£23,529** (£8,823; £4,411; £2,205; £1,470)

RPR

1 **Schang (GER)**[30] 3-8-10 0...... FedericoBossa 2 112
(P Vovcenko, Germany) *trckd ldr: chal gng strly and led 2f out: rdn over 1f out: r.o strly and drew clr fnl f: readily* **63/10**

2 *3 1/4* **Fly First**[37] 2722 7-9-0 0...... AndreasHelfenbein 1 101
(Ferdinand J Leve, Germany) *midfield: rdn and effrt early in st: ev ch over 1f out: kpt on wout matching wnr fnl f* **11/1**

3 *1 1/4* **Mc Queen (FR)**[40] 2633 4-9-0 0...... StephenHellyn 6 97
(Yasmin Almenrader, Germany) *hld up: rdn in rr into st: kpt on fnl f and wnt 3rd cl home: nvr able to chal* **22/5**[2]

4 *1/2* **Daring Match (GER)**[37] 2722 5-9-2 0...... AlexanderPietsch 4 97
(J Hirschberger, Germany) *midfield on inner: rdn and effrt early in st: ev ch over 1f out: no ex fnl f: fdd and lost 3rd cl home* **6/1**[3]

5 *2 1/4* **Easy Road**[16] 6-9-2 0...... NelsonDeSouza 3 90
(Cathrine Erichsen, Norway) *midfield: rdn into st: outpcd fnl 2f* **19/10**[1]

6 *3* **Birthday Prince (GER)**[33] 8-9-0 0......(p) EduardoPedroza 7 79
(Frau Erika Mader, Germany) *hld up: rdn into st: outpcd and btn fnl f* **9/1**

7 *2 3/4* **Flashy Approach**[37] 2722 6-9-0 0...... KoenClijmans 8 70
(P Bradik, Germany) *midfield on outer: rdn and dropped to rr into st: sn btn* **23/1**

8 *7 1/2* **Ambiance (IRE)**[44] 5-9-0 0...... IanFerguson 10 46
(Katharina Stenefeldt, Sweden) *led: rdn and hdd 2f out: qckly btn: wknd: eased fnl f* **13/1**

9 *1 3/4* **Volatile (SWE)**[63] 4-9-0 0......(b) KevinStott 12 40
(Jessica Long, Sweden) *trckd ldr: rdn and brieft effrt into st: sn no ex and btn: wknd: dropped to last fnl f* **9/1**

1m 17.42s (4.73)
WFA 3 from 4yo+ 6lb — **9** Ran SP% **120.6**
WIN (incl. 10 euro stake): 73. PLACES: 24, 28, 18. SF: 653.
Owner Stall Biancolino **Bred** A Jorres **Trained** Germany

3765 BATH (L-H)
Wednesday, July 6

OFFICIAL GOING: Good
Wind: slight breeze Weather: overcast

3993 FENWICK 50 H'CAP — 5f 161y
6:00 (6:03) (Class 6) (0-55,58) 3-Y-O+ — **£2,264** (£673; £336; £168) **Stalls** Centre

Form — RPR

0012 **1** **Titus Secret**[8] 3734 4-9-1 **49**...... FergusSweeney 4 66+
(Malcolm Saunders) *trckd ldrs: travelling strly whn upsides ldr 2f out: shkn up to ld ent fnl f: qcknd clr: easily* **2/1**[1]

1043 **2** *3 3/4* **Blistering Dancer (IRE)**[16] 3469 6-9-2 **50**...... AdamKirby 7 55
(Tony Carroll) *led: rdn whn jnd 2f out: hdd ent fnl f: kpt on but sn outpcd by wnr* **5/1**[2]

0-04 **3** *1 1/4* **Mendacious Harpy (IRE)**[8] 3734 5-9-7 **55**...... SteveDrowne 10 56
(George Baker) *towards rr: hdwy over 1f out: sn rdn: r.o fnl f: wnt 3rd fnl 120yds* **16/1**

12-0 **4** *3/4* **Virile (IRE)**[25] 3171 5-9-6 **54**......(b) RobertWinston 15 52
(S Donohoe, Ire) *mid-div: hdwy over 2f out: sn rdn: kpt on same pce fnl f* **8/1**

40-0 **5** *2* **The Wee Chief (IRE)**[91] 1261 10-9-3 **54**...... TimClark[(3)] 3 46
(Jimmy Fox) *s.i.s: towards rr: hdwy but nt clr run over 1f out and jst ins fnl f: r.o fnl 120yds but no ch* **25/1**

6000 **6** *1/2* **Lillyput (IRE)**[14] 3513 3-9-1 **55**...... RonanWhelan 2 44
(Mick Channon) *mid-div: rdn and hdwy over 2f out: kpt on same pce fnl f* **16/1**

6000 **7** *2 1/4* **Buraug**[8] 3734 4-8-13 **50**......(b) EdwardGreatrex[(3)] 14 33
(Milton Bradley) *prom: rdn and ev ch 2f out: sn hld: fdd fnl f* **33/1**

6004 **8** *2 1/4* **Pursuit Of Time**[49] 2373 3-8-10 **50**......(p) TimmyMurphy 1 24
(Neil Mulholland) *mid-div: rdn over 2f out: fdd fnl f* **20/1**

3531 **9** *1/2* **Assertive Agent**[8] 3734 6-9-10 **58** 6ex...... DavidProbert 6 32
(Tony Carroll) *unsettled stalls: s.i.s: sn pushed along towards rr: sme hdwy u.p 2f out: nvr threatened: fdd fnl f* **7/1**[3]

5343 **10** *3/4* **Cerulean Silk**[106] 1026 6-8-6 **47**...... GeorgeWood[(7)] 5 18
(Tony Carroll) *a towards rr* **25/1**

0045 **11** *nk* **Multi Quest**[28] 3040 4-9-2 **50**......(v) MartinLane 11 20
(John E Long) *mid-div: rdn over 2f out: wknd ent fnl f* **10/1**

0600 **12** *1/2* **Top Cop**[33] 2845 7-9-0 **48**......(p) RaulDaSilva 17 17
(Ronald Harris) *prom: rdn over 2f out: wknd over 1f out* **20/1**

0366 **13** *21* **Spray Tan**[8] 3741 6-8-13 **50**......(b) GeorgeDowning[(3)] 13
(Tony Carroll) *racd keenly on outer in mid-div: effrt over 2f out: wknd over 1f out: eased* **20/1**

1m 11.13s (-0.07) **Going Correction** +0.025s/f (Good)
WFA 3 from 4yo+ 6lb — **13** Ran SP% **119.4**
Speed ratings (Par 101): **101,96,94,93,90 90,87,84,83,82 81,81,53**
CSF £9.55 CT £128.14 TOTE £2.60: £1.10, £2.00, £6.40; EX 14.50 Trifecta £180.90.
Owner M S Saunders **Bred** M S Saunders **Trained** Green Ore, Somerset

FOCUS
Distances as advertised. This was a weak handicap and best rated around the placed horses.

3994 CREST NICHOLSON BATH RIVERSIDE H'CAP (BATH SUMMER SPRINT SERIES QUALIFIER) — 5f 11y
6:30 (6:31) (Class 6) (0-65,62) 3-Y-O+ — **£2,587** (£770; £384; £192) **Stalls** Centre

Form — RPR

004- **1** **Go Amber Go**[223] 7995 4-8-3 **46**...... GeorgeWood[(7)] 13 61
(Rod Millman) *chsd ldrs: rdn 2f out: led fnl 120yds: r.o wl* **25/1**

4212 **2** *2 3/4* **Jack The Laird (IRE)**[9] 3725 3-9-7 **62**......(b) RobertWinston 17 65
(Dean Ivory) *s.i.s: towards rr: hdwy over 1f out: briefly checked ent fnl f: r.o wl to go 2nd cl home* **9/2**[1]

0-61 **3** *hd* **Captain Ryan**[33] 2845 5-9-11 **61**...... TimmyMurphy 10 65
(Geoffrey Deacon) *chsd ldrs: rdn 2f out: kpt on ins fnl f: wnt 3rd cl home* **11/2**[3]

555 **4** *hd* **Fabulous Flyer**[11] 3650 3-8-8 **49**...... MartinLane 6 51
(Jeremy Gask) *chsd ldr: rdn 2f out: nt quite pce to chal: no ex cl home* **20/1**

003 **5** *shd* **Go Charlie**[22] 3260 5-8-11 **47**...... LemosdeSouza 8 50
(Lisa Williamson) *taken to s early: s.i.s: towards rr: travelling wl but nt clr run fr 2f out tl ent fnl f: r.o wl but too much to do* **25/1**

-210 **6** *1* **Lucky Clover**[36] 2785 5-9-9 **62**...... JosephineGordon[(3)] 5 62
(Malcolm Saunders) *trckd ldrs: rdn 2f out: kpt on same pce fnl f* **5/1**[2]

6106 **7** *3/4* **Your Gifted (IRE)**[36] 2785 9-9-8 **58**......(v) RaulDaSilva 12 55
(Lisa Williamson) *led: rdn over 1f out: hdd fnl 120yds: no ex* **33/1**

234 **8** *nk* **Kiringa**[32] 2905 3-8-10 **51**......(p) FergusSweeney 4 45
(Robert Cowell) *a in mid-div* **16/1**

66-5 **9** *nse* **The Special One (IRE)**[51] 2288 3-9-5 **60**...... AdamKirby 3 58
(Clive Cox) *mid-div: drvn 2f out: keeping on in cl 6th whn nt clr run fnl 75yds: no ch after* **10/1**

6500 **10** *shd* **Renounce (IRE)**[11] 3674 4-9-10 **60**......(tp) AdamBeschizza 15 58
(Charlie Wallis) *a in mid-div* **16/1**

0015 **11** *3/4* **Dusty Blue**[13] 3559 4-9-8 **61**......(t) EoinWalsh[(3)] 2 61
(Tony Carroll) *racd keenly in mid-div: rdn 2f out: keeping on at same pce but hld whn squeezed up ins fnl f* **16/1**

003 **12** *hd* **Agerzam**[20] 3317 6-9-10 **60**......(b) DavidProbert 11 55
(Ronald Harris) *towards rr: rdn 2f out: sn hung lft: styng on at same pce but hld whn short of room ins fnl f* **12/1**

-600 **13** *1* **Tally's Song**[33] 2848 3-7-11 **45**...... RPWalsh[(7)] 7 31
(Grace Harris) *s.i.s: a towards rr* **100/1**

0550 **14** *hd* **Catalinas Diamond (IRE)**[14] 3510 8-9-7 **57**......(t) SteveDrowne 1 45
(Pat Murphy) *a towards rr* **16/1**

16/0 **15** *3/4* **Molly Jones**[29] 3004 7-9-4 **57**...... TimClark[(3)] 18 42
(Matthew Salaman) *towards rr: hdwy into midfield 2f out: sn rdn: wknd fnl f* **25/1**

4-44 **16** *2 3/4* **Sabato (IRE)**[56] 2143 3-9-1 **59**......(t) RobHornby[(3)] 16 32
(Fergal O'Brien) *mid-div: rdn over 2f out: wknd over 1f out* **8/1**

2235 **17** *3 3/4* **Hot Stuff**[45] 2503 3-9-4 **62**...... GeorgeDowning[(3)] 9 22
(Tony Carroll) *fly-leapt leaving stalls: mid-div: rdn over 2f out: wknd over 1f out* **16/1**

1m 3.06s (0.56) **Going Correction** +0.025s/f (Good)
WFA 3 from 4yo+ 5lb — **17** Ran SP% **127.8**
Speed ratings (Par 101): **96,91,91,90,90 89,88,87,87,87 86,85,84,83,82 78,72**
CSF £131.86 CT £743.59 TOTE £33.40: £7.90, £1.80, £1.90, £5.90; EX 280.30 Trifecta £2622.90.
Owner AJ & CS Bricknell-Webb **Bred** Percys (north Harrow) Ltd **Trained** Kentisbeare, Devon

FOCUS
Another weak sprint handicap, but it's fair enough form for the grade. The likes of the third help pin the level.

3995 BLAYTHWAYT PLATE H'CAP — 5f 11y
7:00 (7:00) (Class 4) (0-80,80) 3-Y-O+ — **£8,086** (£2,406; £1,202; £601) **Stalls** Centre

Form — RPR

1-35 **1** **Go On Go On Go On**[26] 3105 3-9-6 **79**...... AdamKirby 4 87
(Clive Cox) *chsd ldrs: rdn 2f out: led ent fnl f: edgd sltly lft cl home: kpt on wl* **9/2**[1]

6-02 **2** *3/4* **Free To Love**[25] 3123 4-9-7 **75**...... SteveDrowne 10 82
(Charles Hills) *trckd ldr: rdn to ld narrowly over 1f out: hdd ent fnl f: kpt on but hld whn edgd sltly rt cl home* **5/1**[2]

4514 **3** *nk* **Jaywalker (IRE)**[12] 3618 5-9-11 **79**...... RonanWhelan 1 85
(Mick Channon) *chsd ldrs: rdn ent fnl f: keeping on in cl 3rd whn squeezed up nring fin* **9/2**[1]

1-15 **4** *1* **Summer Chorus**[144] 559 3-9-6 **79**...... DavidProbert 2 79+
(Andrew Balding) *in last pair: rdn over 2f out: hdwy ent fnl f: kpt on but nt pce to get on terms* **7/1**[3]

00-0 **5** *2* **Angelito**[11] 3674 7-8-9 **66** EoinWalsh(3) 7 61
(Tony Newcombe) *in last pair: rdn 2f out: no imp tl r.o fnl 120yds* **33/1**

20-4 **6** *shd* **Ejbaar**[25] 3159 4-9-8 **76** FergusSweeney 5 71
(Robert Cowell) *in last pair: rdn and drifted lft fr over 1f out: kpt on fnl f* **9/2**[1]

-002 **7** *nse* **Emjayem**[31] 2931 6-9-7 **78** GeorgeDowning(3) 6 73
(Ed McMahon) *racd keenly in mid-div: effrt 2f out: kpt on same pce fnl f* **10/1**

3-41 **8** *3/4* **Silverrica (IRE)**[14] 3530 6-9-6 **77** JosephineGordon(3) 3 69
(Malcolm Saunders) *mid-div: rdn over 2f out: sn one pce* **7/1**[3]

5015 **9** *2* **Powerful Wind (IRE)**[31] 2931 7-9-9 **77** AdamBeschizza 9 62
(Charlie Wallis) *led: rdn and hdd over 1f out: wknd fnl f* **25/1**

2640 **10** *9* **Burning Thread (IRE)**[23] 3233 9-9-9 **80** (b) EdwardGreatrex(3) 8 32
(David Elsworth) *mid-div: rdn over 2f out: wknd over 1f out* **20/1**

1m 1.88s (-0.62) **Going Correction** +0.025s/f (Good)
WFA 3 from 4yo+ 5lb **10** Ran SP% **116.9**
Speed ratings (Par 105): **105,103,103,101,98 98,98,97,93,79**
CSF £26.34 CT £110.07 TOTE £5.00: £1.80, £1.60, £2.00; EX 31.20 Trifecta £135.90.
Owner Paul & Clare Rooney **Bred** Richard Kent & Robert Percival **Trained** Lambourn, Berks

FOCUS
A modest sprint handicap, rated around the second and third, with the unexposed winner improving on her AW form.

3996 PPC PRINTERS CONSERVATIVE MAIDEN STKS 1m 5y
7:30 (7:30) (Class 4) 3-Y-O+ **£7,762** (£2,310; £1,154; £577) **Stalls** Low

Form RPR

4 **1** **Justice Smart (IRE)**[60] 2039 3-9-5 0 AdamKirby 9 85+
(Sir Michael Stoute) *mid-div: hdwy over 2f out: led over 1f out: kpt on wl: comf* **4/1**[2]

6020 **2** *2 1/4* **Cape Banjo (USA)**[26] 3110 3-9-0 77 PatrickO'Donnell(5) 7 78
(Ralph Beckett) *mid-div: hdwy whn nt clr run and swtchd rt over 1f out: r.o fnl f: snatched 2nd cl home* **7/1**

6-20 **3** *hd* **Corked (IRE)**[55] 2183 3-8-11 75 MarcMonaghan(3) 11 72
(Hugo Palmer) *trckd ldrs: rdn to ld over 2f out: hdd over 1f out: sn hld by wnr: no ex whn lost 2nd cl home* **9/2**[3]

3 **4** *4 1/2* **Mubajal**[18] 3411 3-9-5 0 DaneO'Neill 5 66
(Owen Burrows) *trckd ldrs: hung lft u.p 2f out: sn one pce* **10/11**[1]

43 **5** *6* **Hilltop Ranger (IRE)**[25] 3145 3-9-0 0 SteveDrowne 1 47
(Daniel Kubler) *racd keenly: sn led: rdn and hdd over 2f out: kpt on tl fdd fnl f* **16/1**

0 **6** *6* **Skiff**[16] 3464 4-9-9 0 JennyPowell(5) 4 40
(Brendan Powell) *trckd ldr: rdn 3f out: wknd jst over 1f out* **50/1**

7 *1/2* **Race Time (USA)** 3-9-0 0 (p) TimmyMurphy 6 31
(Seamus Durack) *mid-div: effrt over 2f out: wknd jst over 1f out* **33/1**

0/4- **8** *2 1/4* **No No Cardinal (IRE)**[321] 1840 7-9-7 33 RPWalsh(7) 3 33
(Mark Gillard) *hld up towards rr: hdwy into midfield u.p over 2f out: wknd over 1f out* **100/1**

0 **9** *1/2* **Dance With Kate**[10] 3684 5-9-6 0 TimClark(3) 12 27
(Polly Gundry) *slowly away: a towards rr* **100/1**

00 **10** *3 1/2* **Signal Hill (IRE)**[29] 2999 3-9-5 0 DavidProbert 10 21
(Andrew Balding) *hld up towards rr: hdwy on outer into midfield over 2f out: wknd over 1f out* **33/1**

00- **11** *3 1/4* **Love In The Dark**[280] 6865 3-8-11 0 EdwardGreatrex(3) 8 9
(Nikki Evans) *hung rt on bnd over 4f out: a towards rr* **100/1**

12 *18* **Moayadd (USA)** 4-10-0 0 FergusSweeney 2
(Neil Mulholland) *a bhd* **33/1**

1m 42.52s (1.72) **Going Correction** +0.15s/f (Good)
WFA 3 from 4yo+ 9lb **12** Ran SP% **122.7**
Speed ratings (Par 105): **97,94,94,90,84 78,77,75,74,71 68,50**
CSF £32.31 TOTE £5.60: £1.60, £2.40, £2.00; EX 33.10 Trifecta £84.90.
Owner Robert Ng **Bred** Deerpark Stud **Trained** Newmarket, Suffolk

FOCUS
Straightforward maiden form rated around the second and third.

3997 IES 25TH ANNIVERSARY H'CAP 1m 2f 46y
8:00 (8:00) (Class 6) (0-60,60) 3-Y-O+ **£2,264** (£673; £336; £168) **Stalls** Low

Form RPR

632 **1** **Zephyros (GER)**[22] 3255 5-9-6 **59** GeorgeWood(7) 11 68
(David Bridgwater) *mid-div: racing keenly whn hdwy on outer over 4f out: led over 2f out: sn rdn: jst hld on* **8/1**

-506 **2** *nse* **Monday Club**[33] 2851 3-8-9 **55** JosephineGordon(3) 4 64
(Dominic Ffrench Davis) *trckd ldrs: rdn over 2f out: styd on wl ins fnl f: jst failed* **8/1**

6400 **3** *1 1/4* **Lady Blanco (USA)**[15] 3493 3-9-1 **58** DavidProbert 6 65
(Andrew Balding) *racd keenly: trckd ldrs: rdn and ev ch fr over 2f out tl no ex fnl 120yds: lost 2nd towards fin* **16/1**

0-51 **4** *1 3/4* **Desert Cross**[33] 2851 3-8-13 **56** WilliamCarson 10 59
(Jonjo O'Neill) *trckd ldrs tl lost pl after 3f: mid-div: rdn and hdwy fr over 2f out: styd on fnl f but nvr gng pce to get bk on terms* **7/1**[3]

66-0 **5** *3 1/2* **Nona Blu**[37] 2734 4-10-0 **60** (p) AdamKirby 9 57
(Michael Wigham) *mid-div: rdn and hdwy over 2f out: styd on but nt pce to get involved* **16/1**

-030 **6** *hd* **Azure Amour (IRE)**[27] 3064 4-9-9 **55** RobertWinston 15 51
(Rod Millman) *mid-div on outer: rdn over 2f out: nvr any imp* **5/1**[1]

0023 **7** *1/2* **Highlife Dancer**[8] 3748 8-9-11 **57** RonanWhelan 16 52
(Mick Channon) *trckd ldr: rdn wl over 2f out: wknd ent fnl f* **6/1**[2]

4000 **8** *1 1/4* **Kay Sera**[29] 3002 8-9-9 **58** EoinWalsh(3) 3 51
(Tony Newcombe) *s.i.s: towards rr: rdn over 2f out: styd on fnl f: nvr trbld ldrs* **14/1**

420 **9** *nk* **Tamujin (IRE)**[50] 2323 8-9-1 **50** (p) RobHornby(3) 5 42
(Ken Cunningham-Brown) *nvr bttr than mid-div* **12/1**

1004 **10** *2 1/2* **Ferryview Place**[32] 2899 7-8-10 **49** (p) LukeCatton(7) 14 37
(Ian Williams) *v awkward s: a towards rr* **11/1**

6-22 **11** *hd* **The Bay Bandit**[50] 2323 9-9-5 **54** (p) EdwardGreatrex(3) 1 41
(Neil Mulholland) *mid-div: rdn over 2f out: nvr threatened: wknd fnl f* **6/1**[2]

-605 **12** *1 1/2* **Zeteah**[28] 3044 6-9-2 **48** MartinLane 2 32
(Tony Carroll) *racd keenly: a towards rr* **25/1**

24-0 **13** *3 1/2* **Lettuce Snow (IRE)**[18] 3401 4-9-4 **50** TimmyMurphy 13 28
(Geoffrey Deacon) *racd keenly: in tch: rdn over 2f out: wknd fnl f* **40/1**

20-0 **14** *3* **Par Three (IRE)**[15] 3488 5-9-9 **60** CiaranMckee(5) 12 32
(Tony Carroll) *towards rr of midfield: rdn over 2f out: wknd over 1f out* **50/1**

060 **15** *7* **Nouvelle Ere**[13] 3560 5-9-9 **58** (t) GeorgeDowning(3) 8 28
(Tony Carroll) *led: rdn and hdd over 2f out: sn wknd* **25/1**

2m 12.16s (1.16) **Going Correction** +0.15s/f (Good)
WFA 3 from 4yo+ 11lb **15** Ran SP% **126.5**
Speed ratings (Par 101): **101,100,99,98,95 95,95,94,93,91 91,90,87,85,84**
CSF £71.61 CT £1030.18 TOTE £7.40: £2.80, £4.70, £3.20; EX 93.10 Trifecta £2215.00 Part won..
Owner MMG Racing **Bred** Chr Bruer U A Tiedtke **Trained** Icomb, Gloucs

FOCUS
It doesn't come much more open than this moderate handicap. There was a fair pace on and the form makes sense.

3998 HAPPY BIRTHDAY ROGER LEWIS H'CAP 1m 3f 144y
8:30 (8:32) (Class 6) (0-65,65) 3-Y-O **£2,587** (£770; £384; £192) **Stalls** Low

Form RPR

3-40 **1** **Tyrell (IRE)**[15] 3493 3-8-10 **54** (b[1]) FergusSweeney 2 64
(Alan King) *sn led: rdn clr over 2f out: styd on wl* **8/1**

0-02 **2** *1 1/2* **Pongo Twistleton**[39] 2700 3-9-0 **58** WilliamCarson 9 66
(Jonjo O'Neill) *trckd ldrs: rdn to chse wnr over 2f out: styd on fnl f but a being hld* **11/4**[1]

4-00 **3** *1 1/2* **Fandango (GER)**[28] 3033 3-9-4 **62** RobertWinston 1 67
(Jeremy Gask) *hld up bhd: rdn and stdy prog over 2f out: swtchd rt over 1f out: drifted lft but styd on fnl f: wnt 3rd fnl 100yds* **12/1**

6103 **4** *1 1/2* **Harry's Endeavour**[39] 2700 3-9-4 **62** (p) TimmyMurphy 13 65
(Daniel Kubler) *s.i.s: sn mid-div: rdn and hdwy over 2f out: chal for 2nd over 1f out: styd on same pce fnl f* **7/1**[3]

5502 **5** *1 1/4* **Skylark Lady (IRE)**[19] 1297 3-9-3 **61** AdamKirby 14 62
(Michael Wigham) *hld up towards rr: hdwy on outer over 3f out: sn rdn: chal for 2nd over 2f out tl fdd ent fnl f* **10/1**

0405 **6** *hd* **Dltripleseven (IRE)**[15] 3489 3-8-2 **49** JosephineGordon(3) 12 49
(Richard Hughes) *mid-div: rdn over 2f out: styd on same pce* **20/1**

0-63 **7** *3 1/2* **Primobella**[14] 3509 3-8-13 **60** GeorgeDowning(3) 5 55
(Ed McMahon) *in tch: rdn wl over 2f out: wknd ent fnl f* **4/1**[2]

-160 **8** *1 1/2* **Elocution**[27] 3063 3-8-11 **58** EdwardGreatrex(3) 10 50
(Denis Coakley) *hld up towards rr: sme minor late hdwy: nvr any threat* **7/1**[3]

-626 **9** *1* **Le Tissier**[48] 2411 3-9-3 **64** RobHornby(3) 4 55
(Michael Attwater) *trckd ldrs: rdn over 2f out: wknd over 1f out* **16/1**

605- **10** *4 1/2* **Karens Star**[205] 8225 3-9-2 **60** AdamBeschizza 6 44
(Steph Hollinshead) *mid-div: hdwy 3f out: rdn 2f out: wknd ent fnl f* **33/1**

-506 **11** *11* **Royal Mahogany (IRE)**[28] 3042 3-9-6 **64** MartinLane 15 30
(Luca Cumani) *a towards rr* **10/1**

00-6 **12** *9* **Sir Renos Santi**[68] 1835 3-8-2 **46** oh1 (v[1]) RyanPowell 7
(Ian Williams) *prom tl rdn 3f out: sn btn* **66/1**

0-65 **13** *4 1/2* **Provoking (USA)**[35] 2798 3-9-6 **64** [1] SteveDrowne 8 8
(David Evans) *mid-div: rdn over 2f out: sn wknd* **33/1**

2m 32.21s (1.61) **Going Correction** +0.15s/f (Good) **13** Ran SP% **126.7**
Speed ratings (Par 98): **100,99,98,97,96 96,93,92,92,89 81,75,72**
CSF £31.16 CT £280.57 TOTE £11.00: £3.40, £2.00, £5.30; EX 47.10 Trifecta £907.90.
Owner Apple Tree Stud **Bred** Gigginstown House Stud **Trained** Barbury Castle, Wilts

FOCUS
An ordinary 3yo handicap, run at an ordinary pace and the form makes some sense.

3999 BRANDON TRUST H'CAP (BATH SUMMER STAYERS' SERIES QUALIFIER) 1m 5f 22y
9:00 (9:00) (Class 6) (0-60,60) 4-Y-O+ **£2,587** (£770; £384; £192) **Stalls** High

Form RPR

-001 **1** **Blue Top**[33] 2850 7-8-6 **50** (v) NoelGarbutt(5) 3 60
(Dai Burchell) *chsd ldrs: chsd clr ldr in clr 2nd over 9f out: led over 3f out: sn rdn: sn in command: styd on wl* **7/1**

31 **2** *4* **Ballyfarsoon (IRE)**[34] 2813 5-9-1 **54** (v) AdamKirby 2 58
(Ian Williams) *mid-div: rdn 4f out: chsd ldng pair over 2f out: styd on to go 2nd ent fnl f but a hld* **7/2**[1]

1413 **3** *1 3/4* **Urban Space**[8] 3746 10-9-4 **60** (t) TimClark(3) 1 62+
(John Flint) *in tch in chsng gp: rdn and stdy prog fr 2f out: styd on wl to go 3rd fnl f: nvr on terms* **9/2**[2]

50 **4** *3 1/4* **Surprise Us**[28] 3031 9-8-0 **46** oh1 (p) RPWalsh(7) 8 43
(Mark Gillard) *led: sn clr: rdn and hdd over 3f out: kpt chsng wnr tl ent fnl f: no ex* **25/1**

1562 **5** *nk* **Captain George (IRE)**[40] 2634 5-9-5 **58** (p) SteveDrowne 9 55
(Michael Blake) *mid-div of chsng gp: rdn wl over 2f out: styd on same pce* **6/1**[3]

000- **6** *2 1/4* **Moon Trip**[163] 5548 7-8-8 **50** JosephineGordon(3) 6 44
(Geoffrey Deacon) *trckd ldr in clr 2nd tl over 9f out: rdn over 3f out: wknd over 1f out* **14/1**

420/ **7** *shd* **Bishop Wulstan (IRE)**[87] 6193 5-9-0 **60** (v) JoshuaBryan(7) 11 54
(Peter Bowen) *mid-div of chsng gp: rdn wl over 2f out: nvr any imp* **6/1**[3]

00/0 **8** *1 1/2* **Magnus Romeo**[18] 3402 5-9-5 **58** (t) TimmyMurphy 4 50
(Johnny Farrelly) *chsd clr ldrs: rdn 3f out: wknd over 1f out* **50/1**

0-60 **9** *3 1/2* **Hallingham**[13] 3560 6-9-6 **59** (b) FergusSweeney 13 46
(Chris Gordon) *pushed along in rr early: rdn 3f out: nvr any threat* **16/1**

0016 **10** *1 3/4* **Catharina**[12] 3620 4-9-3 **56** RobertWinston 10 40
(Dean Ivory) *a towards rr* **7/1**

0-00 **11** *2 3/4* **Sakhra**[23] 3221 5-8-7 **46** oh1 WilliamCarson 12 26
(Mark Brisbourne) *mid-div of chsng gp: rdn wl over 2f out: sn btn* **33/1**

6-05 **12** *nk* **Lineman**[27] 3067 6-9-3 **59** (v) GeorgeDowning(3) 14 39
(Sarah Hollinshead) *a towards rr* **10/1**

2m 54.85s (2.85) **Going Correction** +0.15s/f (Good) **12** Ran SP% **124.4**
Speed ratings (Par 101): **97,94,93,91,91 89,89,88,86,85 83,83**
CSF £32.87 CT £128.31 TOTE £9.20: £3.10, £1.50, £2.20; EX 47.30 Trifecta £237.80.
Owner B M G Group **Bred** Mrs Joan M Langmead **Trained** Briery Hill, Blaenau Gwent

FOCUS
An unsatisfactory affair with two clear leaders ignored by the chasing pack and it's form to treat with caution.

T/Jkpt: Not won. T/Plt: £159.30 to a £1 stake. Pool of £62068.64 - 284.43 winning tickets.
T/Qpdt: £52.10 to a £1 stake. Pool of £6409.10 - 91.02 winning tickets. **Tim Mitchell**

3772 CATTERICK (L-H)

Wednesday, July 6

OFFICIAL GOING: Good (8.5)

Wind: Moderate across Weather: Cloudy

4000 WIMBLEDON BETTING AT 188BET CLAIMING STKS 5f

2:20 (2:21) (Class 6) 2-Y-O **£2,264** (£673; £336; £168) **Stalls** Low

Form RPR

625 **1** **Eva Gore**[21] 3282 2-9-2 0 DanielTudhope 6 64
(David O'Meara) *cl up: rdn to ld over 1f out: rdn out* **15/8**[2]

2233 **2** ½ **Decadent Times (IRE)**[45] 2500 2-9-0 0 LiamJones 3 60
(Tom Dascombe) *slt ld: rdn along and hdd over 1f out: sn drvn and kpt on* **13/8**[1]

06 **3** 2½ **Precious Skye (IRE)**[14] 3515 2-8-13 0 KeaganLatham 1 50
(David O'Meara) *stmbld s: sn swtchd rt and trckd ldrs: hdwy 2f out: rdn over 1f out: kpt on same pce fnl f* **9/1**

00 **4** 1 **Ey Up**[34] 2830 2-8-7 0 PJMcDonald 4 41
(Paul Midgley) *chsd ldrs: rdn along wl over 1f out: drvn and one pce fnl f* **28/1**

0 **5** 1¼ **Joysunny**[11] 3654 2-8-9 0 CamHardie 7 38
(Michael Easterby) *cl up: rdn along wl over 1f out: wknd appr fnl f* **25/1**

565 **6** 1¾ **Tough To Bear**[28] 3008 2-8-7 0 JacobButterfield(3) 2 33
(Ollie Pears) *in tch: pushed along 1/2-way: hdwy to chse ldrs wl over 1f out and sn rdn: drvn and btn appr fnl f* **12/1**

03 **7** ½ **Forster Square (IRE)**[18] 3396 2-9-7 0 TonyHamilton 5 42
(Richard Fahey) *chsd ldrs: rdn along 2f out: sn wknd* **7/1**[3]

1m 1.64s (1.84) **Going Correction** +0.175s/f (Good) 7 Ran SP% **110.4**

Speed ratings (Par 92): **92,91,87,85,83 80,80**

CSF £4.88 TOTE £2.40: £1.20, £1.20; EX 5.50 Trifecta £20.60.Decadent Times was claimed by Marjorie Fife for £8000.

Owner Nick Bradley Racing (Inagh River) **Bred** Glebe Farm Stud **Trained** Upper Helmsley, N Yorks

FOCUS

It was dry overnight and the going was given as good (GoingStick: 8.5). Jockeys who rode in the first described it as 'good' or on the 'soft side of good.' All distances as advertised. A modest claimer, but a small step up from the winner.

4001 EURO 2016 BETTING AT 188BET MEDIAN AUCTION MAIDEN STKS 1m 3f 214y

2:50 (2:51) (Class 5) 3-4-Y-O **£2,911** (£866; £432; £216) **Stalls** Low

Form RPR

4362 **1** **Stetchworth Park**[9] 3727 3-8-12 78 (p) LouisSteward(3) 6 78+
(Michael Bell) *trckd ldrs: smooth hdwy on inner over 2f out: nt clr run over 1f out: sn swtchd rt to outer and rdn to chse ldr ins fnl f: drvn and styd on wl to ld nr fin* **8/11**[1]

23 **2** hd **Swashbuckle**[9] 3727 3-9-1 0 PhillipMakin 8 76
(Andrew Balding) *in tch: hdwy on outer to trck ldrs 5f out: effrt on outer 2f out: led over 1f out and sn rdn: clr and drvn ins fnl f: hdd and no ex nr fin* **5/1**[2]

00 **3** 5 **Disquotational**[24] 3194 3-8-10 0 GrahamGibbons 7 63
(David Simcock) *trckd ldrs: hdwy over 3f out: pushed along 2f out: rdn wl over 1f out: drvn and kpt on one pce fnl f* **13/2**[3]

4 hd **La Salesse (FR)** 3-8-10 0 JoeFanning 1 63
(Mark Johnston) *trckd ldr: hdwy to ld over 2f out: rdn wl over 1f out: sn hdd and grad wknd* **5/1**[2]

6-00 **5** 11 **Invincible Bond**[16] 3475 3-8-12 42 JoeDoyle(3) 10 50?
(Simon Waugh) *led: pushed along over 3f out: rdn and hdd over 2f out: sn wknd* **200/1**

0- **6** 4½ **Lord Aslan (IRE)**[238] 7792 3-9-1 0 RoystonFfrench 9 43
(Andrew Balding) *rdn along s and a in rr* **28/1**

00-0 **7** 6 **Wisteria**[18] 3421 4-9-4 40 (t) GarryWhillans(5) 2 28
(Susan Corbett) *in tch: rdn along over 5f out: sn outpcd* **200/1**

8 5 **Lord Of The Valley** 3-9-1 0 PaulMulrennan 5 25
(Mark Johnston) *s.i.s: a in rr* **14/1**

00-0 **9** hd **Miss Mozaico**[37] 2741 3-8-10 27 GeorgeChaloner 3 20
(Richard Whitaker) *in tch: rdn along 7f out: lost pl 1/2-way and sn bhd* **200/1**

0 **10** 73 **Olympus Mons (FR)**[15] 3483 3-9-1 0 DanielTudhope 4
(David O'Meara) *t.k.h: chsd ldng pair: cl up after 3f: riedden along 1/2-way: sn lost pl and bhd* **33/1**

2m 39.19s (0.29) **Going Correction** -0.05s/f (Good)

WFA 3 from 4yo 13lb 10 Ran SP% **119.1**

Speed ratings (Par 103): **97,96,93,93,86 83,79,75,75,26**

CSF £4.93 TOTE £1.60: £1.10, £1.60, £2.10; EX 6.60 Trifecta £17.80.

Owner W J and T C O Gredley **Bred** Litex Commerce **Trained** Newmarket, Suffolk

FOCUS

An ordinary maiden.

4002 NEWMARKET JULY MEETING AT 188BET NURSERY H'CAP 5f 212y

3:20 (3:20) (Class 4) 2-Y-O **£4,204** (£1,251; £625; £312) **Stalls** Low

Form RPR

3232 **1** **Springforth**[19] 3361 2-8-8 61 TonyHamilton 1 65
(Richard Fahey) *trckd ldng pair: swtchd rt and hdwy wl over 1f out: rdn to take slt ld ent fnl f: sn drvn and kpt on wl towards fin* **10/3**[2]

3454 **2** ½ **The Nazca Lines (IRE)**[11] 3633 2-9-7 74 (b[1]) CamHardie 2 76
(John Quinn) *led: pushed along 2f out: jnd and rdn over 1f out: hdd narrowly ent fnl f: sn drvn and no ex towards fin* **10/3**[2]

506 **3** 2 **Yes You (IRE)**[34] 2830 2-7-12 56 NathanEvans(5) 5 52
(James Given) *cl up: rdn along 2f out: drvn over 1f out: kpt on same pce* **4/1**[3]

505 **4** 2¼ **Shadow Wing (IRE)**[21] 3290 2-8-13 66 PJMcDonald 4 55
(Tom Dascombe) *hld up: hdwy 2f out: sn rdn and no imp appr fnl f* **4/1**[3]

022 **5** 7 **Hope Against Hope (IRE)**[37] 2739 2-9-2 69 JoeFanning 3 37
(Mark Johnston) *trckd ldng pair: effrt 2f out: sn rdn and wknd* **3/1**[1]

1m 14.46s (0.86) **Going Correction** -0.05s/f (Good) 5 Ran SP% **111.2**

Speed ratings (Par 96): **92,91,88,85,76**

CSF £14.66 TOTE £3.50: £1.30, £2.00; EX 11.80 Trifecta £45.00.

Owner Mrs H Steel **Bred** Mrs H Steel **Trained** Musley Bank, N Yorks

FOCUS

With all five runners priced between 3-1 and 4-1, this was a competitive heat. A small step up from the winner.

4003 188BET H'CAP 7f

3:50 (3:50) (Class 5) (0-75,75) 3-Y-O **£2,911** (£866; £432; £216) **Stalls** Low

Form RPR

2623 **1** **Baron Bolt**[12] 3614 3-9-7 75 (p) PJMcDonald 5 88+
(Paul Cole) *hld up towards rr: gd hdwy wl over 1f out: rdn to chal jst over 1f out: led last 120yds: kpt on strly* **9/4**[1]

0505 **2** 2½ **Novinophobia**[19] 3344 3-8-12 66 TonyHamilton 2 72
(Richard Fahey) *trckd ldrs: hdwy to chse ldr over 1f out: rdn to ld briefly ent fnl f: sn drvn: hdd and no ex last 120yds* **4/1**[3]

-000 **3** shd **Baby Ballerina**[37] 2742 3-8-9 63 (b[1]) BenCurtis 3 69
(Brian Ellison) *hld up in rr: hdwy on wd outside wl over 1f out: rdn to chse ldrs ent fnl f: sn drvn and kpt on same pce* **16/1**

1403 **4** 1¾ **Tricky Dicky**[13] 3579 3-8-4 58 DuranFentiman 8 60
(Olly Williams) *dwlt: t.k.h and sn chsng ldrs on outer: hdwy to ld 3f out: rdn along 2f out: drvn and hdd over 1f out: wknd fnl f* **10/1**

560 **5** 2¼ **The Lynch Man**[23] 3224 3-8-12 66 (p) CamHardie 7 61
(John Quinn) *chsd ldrs: rdn along 2f out: sn drvn and no imp* **12/1**

000 **6** nk **Galesburg (IRE)**[12] 3591 3-9-7 75 JoeFanning 1 69
(Mark Johnston) *hld up towards rr: pushed along wl over 2f out: sn rdn and no hdwy* **3/1**[2]

3640 **7** ¾ **Kadooment Day (IRE)**[22] 3262 3-8-5 64 (p) JordanVaughan(5) 10 56
(K R Burke) *cl up: rdn along wl over 2f out: sn drvn and wknd wl over 1f out* **22/1**

3-45 **8** 7 **Joyful Day (IRE)**[22] 3267 3-8-11 65 GrahamGibbons 6 38
(Robert Cowell) *led: hdd 3f out and sn rdn along: drvn 2f out and sn wknd* **9/1**

1m 26.24s (-0.76) **Going Correction** -0.05s/f (Good) 8 Ran SP% **112.8**

Speed ratings (Par 100): **102,99,99,97,94 94,93,85**

CSF £11.10 CT £110.42 TOTE £2.80: £1.50, £1.60, £3.30; EX 11.20 Trifecta £84.70.

Owner Asprey Wright Meyrick PJL Racing Wilcock **Bred** J A And M A Knox **Trained** Whatcombe, Oxon

FOCUS

Not a bad little handicap.

4004 188BET.CO.UK H'CAP (FOR THE TURMERIC CHALLENGE TROPHY) 1m 7f 177y

4:20 (4:21) (Class 4) (0-85,83) 3-Y-O+ **£6,469** (£1,925; £962; £481) **Stalls** Low

Form RPR

0113 **1** **Dew Pond**[12] 3602 4-8-13 73 RachelRichardson(5) 6 80+
(Tim Easterby) *hld up in tch: smooth hdwy 3f out: sn trcking ldrs: led appr fnl f: styd on* **15/8**[2]

4-00 **2** 1½ **Moshe (IRE)**[14] 3520 5-9-7 76 PJMcDonald 1 81
(Philip Kirby) *led: pushed along 3f out: rdn 2f out: drvn and hdd appr fnl f: kpt on wl* **14/1**

1-01 **3** 2 **Dominada (IRE)**[40] 2659 4-9-9 83 CallumShepherd(5) 3 86
(Brian Ellison) *trckd ldrs: effrt on inner over 2f out: rdn over 1f out: ev ch tl drvn and kpt on same pce fnl f* **6/4**[1]

5140 **4** nk **Jan Smuts (IRE)**[25] 3149 8-8-12 72 (tp) NathanEvans(5) 4 74
(Wilf Storey) *hld up in rr: pushed along and outpcd over 3f out: rdn and hdwy wl over 1f out: drvn and kpt on same pce fnl f* **8/1**

5302 **5** 1¼ **Sherman McCoy**[7] 3774 10-8-6 64 oh2 JacobButterfield(3) 2 65
(Marjorie Fife) *trckd ldr: cl up over 2f out and sn rdn: drvn and wknd over 1f out* **5/1**[3]

3m 31.23s (-0.77) **Going Correction** -0.05s/f (Good)

WFA 3 from 4yo+ 19lb 5 Ran SP% **109.2**

Speed ratings (Par 105): **99,98,97,97,96**

CSF £23.25 TOTE £2.50: £1.20, £3.40; EX 19.70 Trifecta £39.60.

Owner Ashfield Caravan Park **Bred** Pollards Stables **Trained** Great Habton, N Yorks

FOCUS

This staying handicap was run at a good gallop. A small step up from the winner.

4005 £25 FREE BET AT 188BET H'CAP (DIV I) 7f

4:50 (4:51) (Class 6) (0-65,65) 3-Y-O+ **£2,264** (£673; £336; £168) **Stalls** Low

Form RPR

1 **Mister Royal (IRE)**[326] 5402 5-8-9 46 oh1 BenCurtis 10 59+
(Brian Ellison) *in tch: hdwy 3f out: chal 2f out: rdn to ld over 1 1/2f out: drvn and kpt on wl fnl f* **4/1**[2]

0444 **2** 1½ **Tanawar (IRE)**[22] 3262 6-9-12 63 (b) JamesSullivan 14 70
(Ruth Carr) *hld up: smooth hdwy on outer 3f out: wd st: effrt to chal over 1f out: sn rdn and ev ch ins fnl f: drvn and kpt on same pce last 100yds* **5/1**[3]

000- **3** 1¾ **Lord Rob**[246] 7674 5-8-10 47 PatrickMathers 15 49
(David Thompson) *towards rr: hdwy over 2f out: rdn wl over 1f out: styd on strly appr fnl f: nrst fin* **100/1**

4005 **4** 2 **Munjally**[2] 3941 5-9-4 55 (v) DavidNolan 3 52
(Patrick Holmes) *hld up towards rr: hdwy on inner 2f out: rdn over 1f out: styd on wl fnl f: nrst fin* **16/1**

2056 **5** 1½ **Dr Red Eye**[12] 3595 8-10-0 65 (p) DanielTudhope 5 58
(Scott Dixon) *led: rdn along over 2f out: hdd and drvn 1 1/2f out: grad wknd* **9/4**[1]

2343 **6** ¾ **Atreus**[7] 3777 4-9-1 57 (p) NathanEvans(5) 11 48
(Michael Easterby) *towards rr: hdwy wl over 1f out: sn rdn and kpt on fnl f: nrst fin* **4/1**[2]

/05- **7** 1 **No Refund (IRE)**[401] 2769 5-9-3 54 SamJames 12 43
(David Loughnane) *dwlt and towards rr: hdwy wl over 1f out: sn rdn and kpt on fnl f* **28/1**

6010 **8** ¾ **Goadby**[11] 3674 5-9-10 61 RoystonFfrench 2 47
(John Holt) *chsd ldrs on inner: rdn along 2f out: sn drvn and wknd over 1f out* **20/1**

00-5 **9** 2½ **Cosmic Dust**[7] 3776 3-8-6 51 GeorgeChaloner 7 27
(Richard Whitaker) *trckd ldrs: hdwy to chse ldr 3f out: rdn along 2f out: drvn and wknd over 1f out* **33/1**

-400 **10** 3¾ **Rise Up Singing**[28] 3010 3-8-1 46 oh1 AndrewMullen 6 12
(Colin Teague) *chsd ldr: rdn along wl over 2f out: sn wknd* **125/1**

0200 **11** hd **Pyroclastic (IRE)**[91] 1261 4-9-9 60 JoeFanning 9 29
(Nick Kent) *chsd ldrs: rdn along 2f out: sn wknd* **25/1**

0633 **12** 5 **Jebel Tara**[23] 3211 11-9-12 63 (bt) DaleSwift 1 18
(Alan Brown) *a towards rr* **12/1**

4610 **13** 2¼ **Ciaras Cookie (IRE)**[16] 3474 4-8-10 52 CallumShepherd(5) 13 1
(Mandy Rowland) *in tch: rdn along 3f out: sn wknd* **100/1**

/0-0 **P** **Luvlylynnthomas**[19] 3366 4-8-9 **46** oh1 PJMcDonald 4
(Micky Hammond) *s.i.s and a detached: t.o whn lost action and p.u bef 1/2-way* **125/1**

1m 26.2s (-0.80) **Going Correction** -0.05s/f (Good)
WFA 3 from 4yo+ 8lb **14** Ran SP% **119.6**
Speed ratings (Par 101): **102,100,98,96,94 93,92,91,88,84 84,78,75,**
CSF £22.75 CT £1729.76 TOTE £4.90: £1.80, £2.00, £19.10; EX 30.40 Trifecta £2860.90.
Owner Mrs J O'Sullivan **Bred** Michael Feeney **Trained** Norton, N Yorks

FOCUS
A moderate affair, but a decent gamble was landed. The second helps set the level but this could be a bit higher.

4006 £25 FREE BET AT 188BET H'CAP (DIV II) 7f
5:20 (5:20) (Class 6) (0-65,65) 3-Y-O+ **£2,264** (£673; £336; £168) **Stalls** Low

Form RPR

40S4 **1** **Deben**[13] 3579 3-8-5 **53** JoeDoyle(3) 1 61
(Kevin Ryan) *trckd ldrs on inner: hdwy 2f out: effrt and swtchd rt off rail over 1f out: sn rdn: styd on to ld wl ins fnl f* **10/1**

-200 **2** 1 1/4 **Adiator**[15] 3484 8-8-12 **56** (p) CliffordLee(7) 7 63
(Neville Bycroft) *hld up towards rr: hdwy on wd outside 2f out: rdn over 1f out: edgd lft and chal ins fnl f: kpt on* **18/1**

033 **3** 1 **Totally Magic (IRE)**[15] 3479 4-9-10 **61** KeaganLatham 3 65
(Richard Whitaker) *trckd ldrs: hdwy to chse clr ldr wl over 1f out: sn rdn and bmpd: drvn and ev ch ins fnl f: kpt on* **4/1**[1]

6004 **4** nk **Cascading Stars (IRE)**[26] 3096 4-9-11 **62** GrahamGibbons 11 65
(Daniel Mark Loughnane) *led: rdn clr 2f out: drvn over 1f out: hdd wl ins fnl f: no ex* **10/1**

0345 **5** 3/4 **Saltarello (IRE)**[19] 3367 4-9-7 **58** (p) SamJames 6 59
(Marjorie Fife) *midfield: hdwy on outer over 2f out: rdn to chse ldrs over 1f out: drvn and kpt on fnl f* **5/1**[3]

004 **6** nk **Longroom**[32] 2906 4-9-2 **53** BarryMcHugh 2 53
(Noel Wilson) *hld up: hdwy 2f out: rdn over 1f out: kpt on fnl f* **9/1**

4006 **7** 1 **Percy's Gal**[13] 3553 5-9-9 **65** GemmaTutty(5) 4 63
(Karen Tutty) *towards rr: hdwy on inner wl over 1f out: sn rdn and kpt on fnl f* **12/1**

3560 **8** 2 **Alpha Tauri (USA)**[5] 3838 10-8-2 **46** oh1 BenRobinson(7) 5 38
(Charles Smith) *chsd ldrs: rdn wl over 1f out: sn drvn and no imp* **66/1**

0345 **9** 1 **Pilgrims Path**[13] 3549 3-8-10 **55** (p) BenCurtis 14 41
(Scott Dixon) *chsd ldr: rdn along 3f out: drvn over 2f out and sn wknd* **14/1**

046- **10** shd **Good Move (IRE)**[279] 6875 4-8-9 **46** oh1 (b) JamesSullivan 12 35
(Brian Rothwell) *chsd ldrs: rdn along 2f out: wknd over 1f out* **100/1**

0-06 **11** 1 3/4 **A Boy Named Sue**[23] 3224 3-7-12 **48** NathanEvans(5) 8 29+
(Peter Niven) *a towards rr* **9/2**[2]

00-0 **12** 1 1/4 **Savannah Star**[53] 2234 3-7-8 **46** oh1 LiamLewis-Salter(7) 10 24
(Nick Kent) *a in rr* **100/1**

/440 **13** 15 **Douglas Bank (IRE)**[19] 3368 4-9-9 **63** AlistairRawlinson(3) 9 4
(Roy Bowring) *a in rr* **33/1**

-000 **U** **White Flag**[28] 3013 5-8-12 **54** RachelRichardson(5) 13
(Tim Easterby) *stmbld and uns rdr s* **10/1**

1m 27.3s (0.30) **Going Correction** -0.05s/f (Good)
WFA 3 from 4yo+ 8lb **14** Ran SP% **118.2**
Speed ratings (Par 101): **96,94,93,93,92 91,90,88,87,87 85,83,66,**
CSF £172.36 CT £866.33 TOTE £9.70: £2.70, £5.90, £1.60; EX 191.30 Trifecta £713.10.
Owner Jon Beard **Bred** Mocca Syndicate **Trained** Hambleton, N Yorks
■ Stewards' Enquiry : Joe Doyle four-day ban: careless riding (20-24 Jul)

FOCUS
The slower of the two divisions by 1.10sec. The second is a good guide to the level.

4007 MOBILE BETTING AT 188BET H'CAP 5f 212y
5:50 (5:50) (Class 5) (0-75,74) 3-Y-O **£2,911** (£866; £432; £216) **Stalls** Low

Form RPR

34-0 **1** **First Wheat**[12] 3609 3-8-11 **69** NathanEvans(5) 10 76
(Michael Easterby) *in rr: swtchd rt and hdwy wl over 1f out: rdn ent fnl f: styd on wl to ld nr line* **6/1**[3]

0012 **2** hd **Rose Eclair**[6] 3806 3-8-12 **65** (b) DavidAllan 3 71
(Tim Easterby) *in tch: hdwy on outer 2f out: rdn over 1f out: styd on wl to ld towards fin: hdd and no ex nr line* **3/1**[2]

0050 **3** 1 **Men United (FR)**[13] 3581 3-8-2 **55** (t) RoystonFfrench 5 57
(Roy Bowring) *chsd ldrs: hdwy to chse clr ldr wl over 1f out: drvn ent fnl f: kpt on* **28/1**

2143 **4** 1/2 **Geno (IRE)**[9] 3716 3-9-4 **74** (b) JoeDoyle(3) 2 74
(Kevin Ryan) *led: pushed clr 2f out: rdn ent fnl f: sn drvn: hdd and no ex towards fin* **1/1**[1]

240- **5** 2 1/4 **Bahamian Bird**[277] 6922 3-8-9 **62** TonyHamilton 8 54
(Richard Fahey) *in rr: hdwy on wd outside 2f out: rdn to chse ldrs over 1f out: drvn and one pce fnl f* **10/1**

010 **6** 9 **I T Guru**[37] 2741 3-8-6 **59** (t) BarryMcHugh 9 19
(Noel Wilson) *chsd ldr: rdn along 2f out: drvn and wknd over 1f out* **33/1**

-500 **7** 6 **Mr Chuckles (IRE)**[15] 3478 3-8-11 **64** AndrewMullen 1 2
(Philip Kirby) *chsd ldng pair: rdn along 2f out: sn drvn and wknd over 1f out* **12/1**

1m 13.4s (-0.20) **Going Correction** -0.05s/f (Good) **7** Ran SP% **112.5**
Speed ratings (Par 100): **99,98,97,96,93 81,73**
CSF £23.48 CT £460.48 TOTE £7.00: £2.80, £3.20; EX 27.90 Trifecta £134.40.
Owner Mrs C E Mason **Bred** R H Mason **Trained** Sheriff Hutton, N Yorks

FOCUS
The favourite set a strong pace in this sprint handicap and there was a clear pb from the winner.
T/Plt: £37.30 to a £1 stake. Pool of £39415.73 - 770.3 winning tickets. T/Qpdt: £25.40 to a £1 stake. Pool of £2947.87 - 85.84 winning tickets. **Joe Rowntree**

3780 KEMPTON (A.W) (R-H)
Wednesday, July 6

OFFICIAL GOING: Polytrack: standard
Wind: nil Weather: Fine

4008 32RED ON THE APP STORE APPRENTICE H'CAP 7f (P)
5:45 (5:47) (Class 5) (0-70,69) 4-Y-O+ **£2,911** (£866; £432; £216) **Stalls** Low

Form RPR

2-00 **1** **Dunnscotia**[19] 3349 4-9-5 **65** (t) GeorgiaCox(3) 4 75
(Paul Webber) *walked to post: missed break and in rr: shkn up and gd prog up inner over 2f out: rdn wl over 1f out: led jst over 1f out: pushed out wl ins fnl f* **14/1**

-650 **2** 2 **With Approval (IRE)**[13] 3554 4-9-5 **65** MeganNicholls(3) 9 70
(Laura Mongan) *rring in stalls: fly-leaped s: pushed along and sn settled bhd ldr: rdn 2f out: kpt on* **20/1**

0042 **3** 1 1/2 **Pick A Little**[15] 3491 8-9-7 **69** MitchGodwin(5) 7 70
(Michael Blake) *wnt to post early: led: rdn 2f out: hdd jst over 1f out: kpt on* **8/1**[3]

123 **4** shd **Capolavoro (FR)**[19] 3349 5-9-10 **67** AaronJones 6 68
(Robert Cowell) *racd in 5th: t.k.h: rdn 2f out: kpt on one pce ins fnl f* **2/1**[1]

0000 **5** nk **Dukes Meadow**[36] 2769 5-9-2 **62** (b[1]) RhiainIngram(3) 10 62
(Roger Ingram) *racd in 4th: shkn up over 2f out: kpt on one pce fnl f* **14/1**

-624 **6** 3/4 **George Baker (IRE)**[40] 2646 9-9-10 **67** HectorCrouch 3 65
(George Baker) *settled in mid-div: rdn over 2f out: no imp fnl f* **10/1**

4063 **7** hd **For Ayman**[7] 3780 5-8-10 **58** SeanMooney(5) 1 55
(Joseph Tuite) *in rr: pushed along 2f out: n.m.r: shkn up over 1f out: nt qckn* **5/1**[2]

5100 **8** shd **Victor's Bet (SPA)**[27] 3064 7-9-12 **69** GaryMahon 5 66
(Ralph J Smith) *mostly in last quartet on outer: pushed along ent st: no imp fr over 1f out* **9/1**

3244 **9** 1/2 **Little Indian**[14] 3522 6-9-0 **60** CharlieBennett(3) 2 56
(J R Jenkins) *in rr and t.k.h: stl in rr over 2f out: sn rdn: no imp fnl f* **9/1**

2000 **10** 1 3/4 **Nasri**[28] 3035 10-9-3 **63** DavidParkes(3) 8 54
(Emma Owen) *racd in 3rd: rdn under 3f out: wknd fr over 1f out* **33/1**

1m 26.34s (0.34) **Going Correction** +0.025s/f (Slow) **10** Ran SP% **111.2**
Speed ratings (Par 103): **99,96,95,94,94 93,93,93,92,90**
CSF £247.90 CT £2390.65 TOTE £17.30: £5.30, £6.50, £2.90; EX 292.30 Trifecta £6746.40 Part won..
Owner Mrs P Scott-Dunn **Bred** Patricia Ann Scott-Dunn **Trained** Mollington, Oxon

FOCUS
This open handicap, confined to apprentice riders, was run at a steady pace.

4009 CELTIC CONTRACTORS H'CAP 1m (P)
6:15 (6:16) (Class 6) (0-65,65) 3-Y-O+ **£2,264** (£673; £336; £168) **Stalls** Low

Form RPR

-464 **1** **Reaver (IRE)**[15] 3483 3-9-4 **65** CharlesBishop 9 74+
(Eve Johnson Houghton) *settled in rr: stl in rr over 2f out: gd prog 2f out: rdn over 1f out to chse clr ldrs: str run ins fnl f to ld nr fin* **8/1**[3]

0005 **2** 3/4 **Cornelious (IRE)**[14] 3523 4-9-11 **63** (v) DarryllHolland 14 72
(Clifford Lines) *sn led: nudged along over 2f out: rdn over 1f out: kpt on gamely tl hdd nr fin* **11/1**

50-2 **3** 1 **Dheyaa (IRE)**[51] 2294 3-9-4 **65** RobertHavlin 2 70
(Owen Burrows) *chsd ldr on inner: ev ch 2f out: sn rdn and no rspnse: kpt on same pce fnl f* **3/1**[1]

0400 **4** 3 1/2 **Embankment**[13] 3554 7-9-5 **57** FrederikTylicki 5 55
(Michael Attwater) *racd in 8th: in last quartet ent st: rdn along wl over 2f out: swtchd to inner 2f out: sme prog fnl f* **16/1**

5013 **5** hd **Paladin (IRE)**[9] 3731 7-9-13 **65** LukeMorris 4 63
(Michael Blake) *t.k.h: settled bhd ldrs: rdn over 2f out: wknd fnl f* **5/1**[2]

4654 **6** shd **Miss Phillyjinks (IRE)**[9] 3725 3-9-3 **64** (b) OisinMurphy 6 59+
(Paul D'Arcy) *missed break and in rr: stl last over 2f out: swtchd to outer: no imp tl kpt on ins fnl f: nrst fin* **20/1**

0000 **7** 3/4 **Rock Palm (IRE)**[27] 3059 3-9-4 **65** GeorgeBaker 7 59
(Brendan Powell) *settled in mid-div: shkn up over 2f out: checked 2f out: shuffled along after: nvr involved* **25/1**

1-25 **8** 1/2 **Bahamian Boy**[29] 3003 3-8-11 **63** CharlieBennett(5) 13 55
(Hughie Morrison) *in rr: stl in last trio whn shkn up over 2f out: styd on passed btn horses fnl f* **14/1**

5003 **9** nk **Gavarnie Encore**[14] 3522 4-9-4 **56** KieranO'Neill 1 50
(Michael Blanshard) *racd in 5th: pushed along 1/2-way: rdn over 3f out: kpt on one pce tl wknd ins fnl f* **20/1**

3605 **10** 1 **Born To Finish (IRE)**[9] 3725 3-9-4 **65** RichardKingscote 12 54
(Jeremy Gask) *racd in mid-div on outer: rdn over 2f out: sn lft bhd and wknd fnl f* **9/1**

1042 **11** 3/4 **Runaiocht (IRE)**[14] 3522 6-9-10 **62** (b) JimmyQuinn 11 52
(Paul Burgoyne) *racing in 7th: pushed along ent st: 5th 2f out: wknd ins fnl f* **14/1**

0-00 **12** hd **Glorious Dancer**[14] 3522 4-8-12 **57** PaddyBradley(7) 10 46
(Lee Carter) *in rr: rdn on inner over 2f out: sn no imp* **9/1**

3330 **13** 15 **Ertidaad (IRE)**[14] 3522 4-9-3 **55** (v) JoeyHaynes 3 8
(Emma Owen) *in rr: rdn to hold pl over 3f out: lft bhd over 2f out: eased fnl f* **25/1**

1m 39.69s (-0.11) **Going Correction** +0.025s/f (Slow)
WFA 3 from 4yo+ 9lb **13** Ran SP% **117.5**
Speed ratings (Par 101): **101,100,99,95,95 95,94,94,93,92 92,91,76**
CSF £85.98 CT £332.45 TOTE £9.50: £3.60, £3.60, £1.80; EX 122.30 Trifecta £573.20.
Owner Anthony Pye-Jeary **Bred** Kildaragh Stud **Trained** Blewbury, Oxon

FOCUS
A fair contest for the grade run at a sound pace. The front three finished clear.

4010 32RED.COM H'CAP (LONDON MILE SERIES QUALIFIER) 1m (P)
6:45 (6:47) (Class 4) (0-80,80) 3-Y-O **£4,690** (£1,395; £697; £348) **Stalls** Low

Form RPR

3520 **1** **Generalship (IRE)**[12] 3614 3-9-5 **78** (b) JamesDoyle 14 89+
(John Gosden) *broke wl and led: mde all after: styd wd tl c over to rail 5f out: shkn up 2f out: rdn out ins fnl f: easily* **14/1**

1-12 **2** 3 **North Creek**[91] 1267 3-9-5 **78** TedDurcan 2 82
(Chris Wall) *broke wl: restrained into 7th on rail: shkn up 2f out: kpt on wl to take 2nd ins fnl f: no ch w wnr* **6/1**[3]

4510 **3** nk **Wimpole Hall**[18] 3415 3-9-7 **80** CharlesBishop 7 83
(William Jarvis) *settled in 8th on outer: rdn over 2f out: kpt on wl ins fnl f to take 3rd nr fin* **12/1**

21-3 **4** 1/2 **Rock Steady (IRE)**[16] 3465 3-9-6 **79** GeorgeBaker 10 81+
(Roger Charlton) *in rr: in last quartet 2f out: sn rdn: picked up wl ins fnl f: to take 4th nr fin* **5/2**[1]

-425 **5** hd **Rebel Lightning (IRE)**[39] 2694 3-9-3 **76** (p) WilliamTwiston-Davies 11 78
(Richard Spencer) *chsd ldrs: rdn in 2nd over 2f out: kpt on tl wknd wl ins fnl f* **16/1**

6-20 **6** 1/2 **Ocean Ready (USA)**[32] 2907 3-8-12 **71** LukeMorris 5 71+
(Sir Mark Prescott Bt) *slow to stride: in rr: nudged along in mid-div: lost pl ent st: rdn in rr: picked up fnl f: nvr nred* **11/1**

2601 **7** nk **Zain Emperor (IRE)**[27] 3079 3-9-6 **79** (v) StevieDonohoe 12 79
(Charlie Fellowes) *racd in mid-div on over: rdn over 2f out: no imp fr over 1f out* **5/1**[2]

3100 **8** 1/2 **Rosenborg Rider (IRE)**[24] 3187 3-9-2 **75** RichardKingscote 13 73
(Ralph Beckett) *styd wd w wnr tl c across 5f out: styd prom: rdn over 2f out: stl there over 1f out: no ex fnl f and lost numerous pls* **11/1**

0314 **9** 1 ¼ **Boycie**[12] 3614 3-8-9 **75**....................(b) HollieDoyle(7) 9 70
(Richard Hannon) *in rr: rdn over 2f out: no ex fnl f* **33/1**

20-0 **10** 1 ¼ **Able Jack**[91] 1270 3-9-6 **79**.................... OisinMurphy 8 71
(Andrew Balding) *slow to gather stride: in rr: rdn over 2f out: sn no imp* **25/1**

3-00 **11** ½ **Fatherly Friend (USA)**[60] 2029 3-8-13 **72**.................... JoeyHaynes 3 63
(K R Burke) *racd in 4th: rdn over 2f out: sn wknd* **20/1**

-160 **12** *nk* **Papou Tony**[51] 2299 3-8-13 **72**.................... JimCrowley 6 63
(George Baker) *racd in 5th: rdn over 2f out: wknd ins fnl f* **25/1**

3-55 **13** ¾ **See You When (IRE)**[18] 3411 3-9-6 **79**.................... TomMarquand 4 68
(Richard Hannon) *s.i.s: in rr: rdn over 2f out: nvr involved* **20/1**

1m 38.47s (-1.33) **Going Correction** +0.025s/f (Slow) **13** Ran SP% **116.6**
Speed ratings (Par 102): **107,104,103,103,103 102,102,101,100,99 98,98,97**
CSF £86.32 CT £1081.02 TOTE £14.20: £4.10, £2.10, £3.10; EX 79.10 Trifecta £1080.70.
Owner Godolphin **Bred** Rabbah Bloodstock Limited **Trained** Newmarket, Suffolk

FOCUS
The pace was strong for this competitive handicap.

4011 32RED/IRISH STALLION FARMS EBF MAIDEN FILLIES' STKS (PLUS 10 RACE) 6f (P)

7:15 (7:17) (Class 5) 2-Y-O **£3,234** (£962; £481; £240) **Stalls** Low

Form RPR

26 **1** **Rajar**[20] 3315 2-9-0 0.................... KieranO'Neill 12 77
(Richard Hannon) *t.k.h early in 3rd: rdn 2f out: kpt on wl to ld 110yds out: rdn out* **14/1**

4 **2** 2 **Singing Sands (IRE)**[14] 3511 2-9-0 0.................... OisinMurphy 3 71
(Ralph Beckett) *chsd ldr: rdn and led over 1f out: kpt on wl tl hdd 110yds* **15/8**[2]

3 ½ **Queensbrydge** 2-9-0 0.................... WilliamTwiston-Davies 6 70
(Robyn Brisland) *racd in 4th: rdn out wd 2f out: kpt on wl ins fnl f to take 3rd 100yds out* **33/1**

22 **4** 2 **Blue Suede (IRE)**[10] 3686 2-9-0 0.................... TomMarquand 7 64
(Richard Hannon) *led: rdn 2f out: hdd over 1f out: one pce fnl f: lost 3rd 110yds out* **13/8**[1]

5 ¾ **Imperial City (USA)** 2-9-0 0.................... JimCrowley 4 61+
(Charles Hills) *bmpd s and in rr: in rr: nudges along over 2f out: hands and heels fr over 1f out* **14/1**

6 *hd* **Aryeh (IRE)** 2-9-0 0.................... JamesDoyle 9 61+
(Hugo Palmer) *in rr: rdn over 2f out on inner: no imp fr over 1f out: hands and heels fnl f* **10/1**

7 2 ¼ **Storm Cry** 2-9-0 0.................... FrannyNorton 5 54
(Mark Johnston) *in rr: rdn 2f out: nt qckn over 1f out: one pce* **6/1**[3]

04 **8** *nk* **Wakened (IRE)**[25] 3134 2-9-0 0.................... RichardKingscote 2 53
(Tom Dascombe) *in rr: rdn over 2f out: nvr involved* **16/1**

03 **9** 3 **Swan Serenade**[32] 2902 2-9-0 0.................... LukeMorris 1 44
(Jonathan Portman) *racd in 4th on rail: rdn 2f out: wknd fr 1f out: eased fnl f* **50/1**

10 3 **Tallulah Rocks** 2-8-11 0.................... DannyBrock(3) 10 35
(Jonathan Portman) *missed break and wl in rr: rdn over 2f out: nvr involved: eased fnl f* **50/1**

11 2 ¼ **Take This Waltz** 2-8-9 0.................... HectorCrouch(5) 8 28
(Bill Turner) *in rr: rdn over 2f out: no imp fr over 1f out: eased ins fnl f* **100/1**

1m 13.52s (0.42) **Going Correction** +0.025s/f (Slow) **11** Ran SP% **123.3**
Speed ratings (Par 91): **98,95,94,92,91 90,87,87,83,79 76**
CSF £42.31 TOTE £19.20: £4.20, £1.30, £6.90; EX 64.20 Trifecta £2020.30.
Owner Robin Blunt & Partners **Bred** Robin Blunt **Trained** East Everleigh, Wilts

FOCUS
An interesting maiden. It was run at a sound pace and the winner did it well, showing improved form, although the level is fluid.

4012 LEONARD CURTIS H'CAP 2m (P)

7:45 (7:47) (Class 5) (0-75,75) 4-Y-O+ **£2,911** (£866; £432; £216) **Stalls** Low

Form RPR

2-04 **1** **Mister Bob (GER)**[36] 2782 7-9-0 **68**....................(p) TedDurcan 8 74
(James Bethell) *hld up in rr: shkn up ent st: rdn in 7th jst over 2f out: kpt on wl ins fnl f to ld last strides* **10/1**

-000 **2** *nk* **Arty Campbell (IRE)**[36] 2782 6-9-7 **75**.................... StevieDonohoe 7 80
(Bernard Llewellyn) *racd in 4th: kicked on and led over 4f out: rdn and hrd pressed fr over 1f out: hdd last strides* **7/1**[3]

2445 **3** ½ **Music Man (IRE)**[14] 3533 6-9-7 **75**.................... GeorgeBaker 3 79
(Laura Mongan) *racd in 3rd: rdn 3f out: pressed ldr on inner ent fnl f: stl ev ch wl ins fnl f: wknd in last strides* **9/4**[1]

3-01 **4** *nk* **Voice Control (IRE)**[20] 3302 4-9-4 **72**.................... KierenFox 9 76
(Laura Mongan) *hld up in rr: shkn up over 2f out: rdn in 7th 2f out: kpt on one pce: nvr nrr* **8/1**

4632 **5** ½ **Starcrossed**[33] 2850 4-8-13 **67**....................(b) ShaneKelly 6 70
(Eve Johnson Houghton) *wnt lft s: sn pushed up to ld: hdd 4f out but remained prom: 2nd over 2f out whn taken to outer: sn rdn: kpt on one pce fr over 1f out* **7/1**[3]

2122 **6** 2 **Hurricane Volta (IRE)**[32] 2887 5-8-13 **67**....................(p) CharlesBishop 1 68
(Peter Hedger) *settled in 6th: rdn 2f out: stl there over 1f out: wknd ins fnl f* **5/1**[2]

2001 **7** ½ **Delagoa Bay (IRE)**[14] 3528 8-7-9 **56** oh1.................... MitchGodwin(7) 2 56
(Sylvester Kirk) *bked into stalls: racd in rr on rail: rdn over 2f out: stl there on inner over 1f out: wknd ins fnl f* **14/1**

2200 **8** 7 **Golly Miss Molly**[26] 3099 5-8-12 **66**....................(b) LukeMorris 4 58
(Jeremy Gask) *racd in 5th: rdn over 2f out: lft bhd fr over 1f out: no ex and wknd* **16/1**

20/6 **9** 4 **Secure Cloud (IRE)**[42] 2582 5-9-4 **72**.................... WilliamTwiston-Davies 5 59
(Lawney Hill) *chsd ldr tl 3rd 4f out: rdn 3f out: c wd and racd awkward: no ex fr over 1f out* **10/1**

0-00 **10** 1 ½ **Kashgar**[36] 2782 7-8-11 **72**....................(t) WilliamCox(7) 10 57
(Bernard Llewellyn) *c across fr wd drawn to settle in rr: lost pl and last over 3f out: no imp st* **66/1**

3m 32.41s (2.31) **Going Correction** +0.025s/f (Slow) **10** Ran SP% **115.8**
Speed ratings (Par 103): **95,94,94,94,94 93,92,89,87,86**
CSF £77.62 CT £214.25 TOTE £9.60: £3.20, £2.60, £1.10; EX 84.00 Trifecta £442.60.
Owner Robert Gibbons **Bred** Newsells Park Stud Ltd **Trained** Middleham Moor, N Yorks

FOCUS
A steadily run handicap.

4013 BYRNE GROUP H'CAP (LONDON MIDDLE DISTANCE SERIES QUALIFIER) 1m 3f (P)

8:15 (8:16) (Class 4) (0-80,80) 3-Y-O+ **£4,690** (£1,395; £697; £348) **Stalls** Low

Form RPR

1040 **1** **Kelvin Hall**[23] 3215 3-8-1 **65**.................... FrannyNorton 1 71
(Mark Johnston) *settled in 3rd on inner: shkn up 2f out: sn rdn and kpt on wl to press runner-up ins fnl f: led last stride* **20/1**

3120 **2** *nse* **Carry Me Home**[54] 2209 3-9-1 **79**.................... MichaelJMMurphy 8 85
(Charles Hills) *chsd ldr: shkn up and led 2f out: pressed by wnr fr 1f out: kpt on wl ins fnl f tl hdd fnl stride* **5/1**[3]

0354 **3** 1 ½ **Dolphin Village (IRE)**[14] 3525 6-9-12 **78**.................... LukeMorris 3 81
(Jane Chapple-Hyam) *racd in 4th: shkn up over 2f out: swtchd out wd sn after: kpt on wl ins fnl f* **5/2**[1]

41-4 **4** 1 **Trevisani (IRE)**[22] 3263 4-9-12 **78**....................(b) GeorgeBaker 4 80
(David Lanigan) *settled in 8th: taken wd st: kpt on under hands and heels ins fnl f: nvr nrr* **3/1**[2]

6420 **5** 1 **Jolievitesse (FR)**[14] 3520 4-9-11 **77**.................... JoeyHaynes 7 77
(K R Burke) *racd in 6th: rdn along over 3f out: kpt on one pce ins fnl f* **5/1**[3]

51 **6** ¾ **Petite Jack**[11] 3653 3-8-12 **76**.................... JackMitchell 5 75
(Neil King) *racd in 7th on rail: rdn over 2f out: one pce fr over 1f out* **9/1**

5406 **7** 1 ½ **Biotic**[30] 2978 5-10-0 **80**.................... FrederikTylicki 6 76
(Rod Millman) *settled in 5th: rdn over 1f out: 3rd ent fnl f: wknd ins fnl f* **7/1**

4404 **8** 2 ¾ **Tyrsal (IRE)**[12] 3617 5-8-12 **64**.................... DarryllHolland 9 55
(Clifford Lines) *s.i.s: in rr: rdn over 2f out: swtchd to rail: no imp sn after* **33/1**

4200 **9** 2 ½ **Estibdaad (IRE)**[15] 3492 6-9-3 **69**....................(t) WilliamTwiston-Davies 2 56
(Paddy Butler) *led: rdn 3f out: hdd 2f out: wknd qckly over 1f out* **50/1**

2m 21.36s (-0.54) **Going Correction** +0.025s/f (Slow)
WFA 3 from 4yo+ 12lb **9** Ran SP% **119.1**
Speed ratings (Par 105): **102,101,100,100,99 98,97,95,93**
CSF £118.70 CT £346.76 TOTE £22.30: £3.60, £1.50, £1.60; EX 96.80 Trifecta £790.90.
Owner Kingsley Park 4 - Ready To Run **Bred** Clive Dennett **Trained** Middleham Moor, N Yorks

FOCUS
They went a honest pace for this fair handicap.

4014 32RED CASINO H'CAP 6f (P)

8:45 (8:45) (Class 4) (0-80,80) 3-Y-O+ **£4,690** (£1,395; £697; £348) **Stalls** Low

Form RPR

5312 **1** **Lightning Charlie**[25] 3144 4-9-11 **79**.................... JimCrowley 3 89
(Amanda Perrett) *settled in 4th: shkn up 2f out: sn rdn on outer and led 1f out: kpt on wl to hold off runner-up ins fnl f: on top nring fin* **9/4**[1]

365- **2** ¾ **Gung Ho Jack**[333] 5151 7-9-3 **71**.................... KierenFox 4 78
(John Best) *racd in 4th on rail: upsides and rdn over 1f out: kpt on wl to press wnr ins fnl f: hld nring fin* **20/1**

4300 **3** 2 **Dominium (USA)**[33] 2846 9-9-4 **77**....................(b) DavidParkes(5) 5 78
(Jeremy Gask) *settled in 8th: swtchd wd and niggled along over 2f out: rdn 2f out: kpt on ins fnl f to take 3rd fnl stride* **11/1**[3]

256 **4** *nse* **Under Siege (IRE)**[63] 1958 4-9-9 **77**....................(p) FrederikTylicki 10 77
(David Simcock) *chsd ldr: upsides and rdn 2f out: kpt on tl wknd ins fnl f: lost 3rd fnl stride* **9/2**[2]

-346 **5** 2 **Adham (IRE)**[30] 2982 3-9-6 **80**.................... LukeMorris 7 73
(James Tate) *racd in 6th: rdn over 2f out: stdy prog under drvn fr over 1f out* **14/1**

2136 **6** 2 ¼ **Desert Strike**[7] 3780 10-9-2 **75**....................(p) HectorCrouch(5) 9 62
(Conor Dore) *led: rdn over 2f out: kpt on tl hdd 1f out: sn wknd* **12/1**

30-0 **7** ¾ **Dont Have It Then**[13] 3554 5-9-0 **68**.................... StevieDonohoe 2 52
(Willie Musson) *in rr: rdn over 2f out: nvr involved* **20/1**

1006 **8** *nk* **The Big Lad**[26] 3101 4-9-9 **77**.................... ShaneKelly 6 60
(Richard Hughes) *racd in rr: rdn 2f out: sn no imp fnl f* **9/2**[2]

0230 **9** ¾ **Lucky Di**[46] 2469 6-9-6 **74**.................... CharlesBishop 8 55
(Peter Hedger) *hld up in rr: rdn wl over 2f out: nvr involved* **25/1**

1-15 **10** 1 **Dutch Golden Age (IRE)**[174] 169 4-9-9 **77**.................... GeorgeBaker 11 55
(Gary Moore) *s.s and hld up in rr: shuffled along on rail 2f out: no imp and eased fnl f* **12/1**

5000 **11** 9 **Multitask**[42] 2584 6-9-0 **68**.................... WilliamTwiston-Davies 1 17
(Gary Moore) *racd in 3rd: stl prom 2f out: rdn and wknd qckly fr over 1f out: eased fnl f* **14/1**

1m 12.56s (-0.54) **Going Correction** +0.025s/f (Slow)
WFA 3 from 4yo+ 6lb **11** Ran SP% **117.6**
Speed ratings (Par 105): **104,103,100,100,97 94,93,93,92,90 78**
CSF £55.82 CT £421.22 TOTE £2.90: £1.40, £5.00, £3.60; EX 60.70 Trifecta £912.30.
Owner Lightning Charlie Partnership **Bred** J A E Hobby **Trained** Pulborough, W Sussex

FOCUS
They went a decent pace for this fair handicap.
T/Plt: £659.30 to a £1 stake. Pool of £48432.69 - 53.62 winning tickets. T/Qpdt: £28.10 to a £1 stake. Pool of £5650.92 - 148.80 winning tickets. **Cathal Gahan**

3647 LINGFIELD (L-H)

Wednesday, July 6

OFFICIAL GOING: Turf course - good (good to firm in places); all-weather - polytrack: standard
Wind: Almost nil Weather: Fine, warm

4015 188BET.CO.UK NURSERY H'CAP 5f

2:00 (2:00) (Class 5) 2-Y-O **£3,234** (£962; £481; £240) **Stalls** Centre

Form RPR

004 **1** **Maazel (IRE)**[27] 3065 2-8-12 **66**.................... AndreaAtzeni 9 70+
(Roger Varian) *dwlt: hld up in last pair: prog 2f out: rdn to chse ldr ins fnl f: drvn and styd on wl to ld last strides* **11/4**[1]

503 **2** *hd* **Little Nosegay (IRE)**[31] 2933 2-8-4 **58**.................... JFEgan 3 60
(David Evans) *t.k.h: w ldr: led 2f out: drvn fnl f: hdd last strides* **16/1**

552 **3** 1 ¼ **Rising Eagle**[15] 3485 2-8-13 **67**.................... LukeMorris 1 65
(Charles Hills) *s.i.s: towards rr: pushed along 1/2-way: prog jst over 1f out: styd on to take 3rd nr fin* **5/1**

4235 **4** ¾ **Tiggaliscious (IRE)**[40] 2637 2-9-7 **75**.................... TomMarquand 6 70
(Richard Hannon) *trckd ldng pair: rdn to try to chal over 1f out: one pce fnl f* **4/1**[3]

265 **5** *1* **Trust The Indian**[23] 3232 2-7-7 **54** oh2 (p) DavidEgan(7) 5 45
(Bill Turner) *mostly in rr: pushed along and struggling fr 1/2-way: kpt on fnl f: n.d* **25/1**

500 **6** *nk* **Battle Of Wits (IRE)**[29] 2997 2-7-7 **54** oh2 HollieDoyle(7) 4 44
(J S Moore) *chsd ldrs on outer: rdn 2f out: fdd jst over 1f out* **25/1**

022 **7** *hd* **Cappananty Con**[11] 3647 2-9-6 **74** RobertWinston 7 64
(Dean Ivory) *led against nr side rail: hdd 2f out: hanging lft and wknd fnl f* **3/1**[2]

462 **8** *nk* **Valley Lodge**[18] 3396 2-8-13 **67** AdamBeschizza 8 56
(Julia Feilden) *sn pushed along to chse ldrs: nvr gng pce to make prog* **10/1**

0046 **9** *1/2* **Patrouille De Nuit (IRE)**[23] 3232 2-8-3 **57** KieranO'Neill 2 44
(J S Moore) *dwlt: racd on outer in last pair: shkn up and no prog over 1f out* **16/1**

58.82s (0.62) **Going Correction** +0.025s/f (Good) **9** Ran SP% **116.9**
Speed ratings (Par 94): **96,95,93,92,90 90,90,89,88**
CSF £48.23 CT £208.85 TOTE £3.70: £1.40, £4.20, £1.90; EX 47.20 Trifecta £201.30.
Owner The Maazel Partnership **Bred** Myles Haughney **Trained** Newmarket, Suffolk

FOCUS
Straight remains dolled in 4yds on the stands rail. A modest nursery and the favourite did well to win. The field finished compressed.

4016 188BET MAIDEN AUCTION STKS 6f
2:30 (2:30) (Class 5) 2-Y-O **£3,234** (£962; £481; £240) **Stalls** Centre

Form RPR

22 **1** **Sea Fox (IRE)**[14] 3529 2-9-3 0 AdamKirby 9 78
(David Evans) *racd against nr side rail: mde all: rdn over 1f out: styd on wl fnl f* **4/7**[1]

2 *1* **Grey Britain** 2-9-3 0 JackMitchell 8 75+
(John Ryan) *racd against rail: trckd ldrs: effrt to chse wnr jst over 1f out: styd on but no imp last 100yds* **14/1**

2 **3** *2 3/4* **Quick Thought (IRE)**[20] 3301 2-8-12 0 JimmyQuinn 2 62
(Dr Jon Scargill) *rrd s: t.k.h: racd against rail and hld up in rr: prog over 1f out: shkn up and kpt on to take 3rd nr fin* **7/1**[3]

5 **4** *nk* **What A Boy**[37] 2747 2-9-0 0 RichardKingscote 6 63
(Ralph Beckett) *w wnr to 2f out: lost 2nd and one pce jst over 1f out* **7/2**[2]

55 **5** *1 1/4* **Roman Legion (IRE)**[30] 2963 2-9-0 0 RobertWinston 1 59
(Dean Ivory) *hld up in last of main gp and off the pce: clsd over 2f out: pushed along and sme prog over 1f out: no hdwy fnl f: possible improver* **12/1**

0 **6** *nse* **Tullinahoo (IRE)**[37] 2747 2-9-3 0 OisinMurphy 5 62
(Denis Coakley) *t.k.h: cl up: tried to press ldrs on outer 2f out: fdd fnl f* **20/1**

55 **7** *shd* **Ciel Rouge**[12] 3613 2-8-6 0 AdamBeschizza 3 51
(Charlie Wallis) *hld up in rr: effrt on wd outside over 2f out: fdd over 1f out* **25/1**

40 **8** *1* **A Sure Welcome**[34] 2822 2-8-11 0 TomMarquand 7 53
(John Spearing) *w ldng pair 2f out: chsd them after tl wknd over 1f out* **33/1**

9 *36* **Maysonri** 2-8-11 0 KieranO'Neill 10
(Mark Hoad) *dwlt: rn v green and sn t.o* **100/1**

1m 11.52s (0.32) **Going Correction** +0.025s/f (Good) **9** Ran SP% **125.3**
Speed ratings (Par 94): **98,96,93,92,90 90,90,89,41**
CSF £12.29 TOTE £1.40: £1.02, £4.70, £2.20; EX 13.30 Trifecta £67.40.
Owner Eric Griffiths & P D Evans **Bred** Tally-Ho Stud **Trained** Pandy, Monmouths

FOCUS
Little got into this modest maiden, with the rail runners dominating. The form is likely to prove fluid.

4017 FREE SPINS AT 188BET CASINO MEDIAN AUCTION MAIDEN STKS 7f
3:00 (3:00) (Class 6) 3-4-Y-O **£2,587** (£770; £384; £192) **Stalls** High

Form RPR

1 **Wild Dancer** 3-8-8 0 HectorCrouch(5) 12 73+
(Patrick Chamings) *racd against nr side rail: mde all: shkn up and drew clr fr over 1f out: r.o wl* **20/1**

3-00 **2** *5* **Arctic Flower (IRE)**[42] 2586 3-8-10 49 DannyBrock(3) 10 60
(John Bridger) *chsd wnr: only danger fr over 2f out: outpcd over 1f out: kpt on* **20/1**

66 **3** *2 1/4* **Shongololo (IRE)**[16] 3464 3-9-4 0 OisinMurphy 5 58
(Andrew Balding) *chsd ldng pair: no imp whn shkn up over 2f out: kpt on one pce after* **5/1**[3]

00- **4** *3 1/4* **Fantasy Queen**[299] 6276 3-8-13 0 CharlesBishop 8 44
(Eve Johnson Houghton) *hld up against nr side rail: outpcd fr 3f out: shkn up and kpt on fr over 1f out: n.d: possible improver* **10/1**

6 **5** *3/4* **Walking In Rhythm (IRE)**[13] 3572 3-8-13 0 TomMarquand 3 42
(Richard Hannon) *pushed along in 6th by 1/2-way and nt on terms: no real prog after* **9/5**[1]

0- **6** *2 1/2* **Noneedtotellme (IRE)**[359] 4208 3-8-13 0 SamHitchcott 2 35
(James Unett) *chsd ldng pair on outer to 3f out: steadily wknd* **66/1**

0-0 **7** *nse* **Fire Empress**[16] 3475 3-8-13 0 AdamBeschizza 11 35
(James Unett) *dwlt: chsd ldrs against rail: rdn over 2f out: no prog and wknd sn after* **100/1**

8 *1 1/4* **Thecornishcavalier (IRE)** 3-9-4 0 RyanPowell 4 37+
(John Ryan) *slowly away: t.k.h and hld up in last pair: grad edgd towards outer fr 1/2-way: nvr involved* **25/1**

9 *nk* **Onesie (IRE)** 3-9-4 0 AndreaAtzeni 1 36
(Marco Botti) *slowly away: a in rr on outer: brief effrt over 2f out: sn no prog* **8/1**

00- **10** *13* **Drawn To Be A Lady**[236] 7824 3-8-13 0 LukeMorris 7
(Michael Attwater) *hld up in rr: shkn up and no prog 3f out: sn no ch: t.o* **33/1**

11 *96* **Late Starter (IRE)** 3-9-4 0 JamesDoyle 6
(Hugo Palmer) *a in rr: wknd over 2f out: t.o whn virtually p.u fnl f: dismntd after fin* **7/1**

05 **P** **Royal Hero**[16] 3464 3-9-4 0 GeorgeBaker 9
(Amanda Perrett) *a in rr: no ch whn wknd rapidly 2f out: t.o whn p.u and dismntd nr fin* **7/2**[2]

1m 23.0s (-0.30) **Going Correction** +0.025s/f (Good) **12** Ran SP% **126.1**
Speed ratings (Par 101): **102,96,93,90,89 86,86,84,84,69 ,**
CSF £360.85 TOTE £33.30: £6.40, £3.70, £1.80; EX 327.40 Trifecta £3224.90.
Owner The Foxford House Partnership **Bred** Wheelers Land Stud **Trained** Baughurst, Hants

FOCUS
A weak maiden, with the market leaders disappointing and a seemingly unfancied newcomer, who had the benefit of the rail, being chased home by a 49-rated runner. They finished strung out.

4018 MOBILE BETTING AT 188BET FILLIES' H'CAP 1m 4f (P)
3:30 (3:30) (Class 5) (0-70,70) 3-Y-O+ **£3,234** (£962; £481; £240) **Stalls** Low

Form RPR

306 **1** **Mischief Maisy (IRE)**[30] 2967 3-8-0 **55** oh3 JimmyQuinn 3 62
(Amanda Perrett) *trckd ldng trio: drvn and prog to ld 3f out: hrd pressed fr over 1f out: kpt on fnl f: jst hld on* **10/1**

000 **2** *nk* **Cliff Face (IRE)**[61] 2009 3-8-3 **58** KieranO'Neill 1 67+
(Ed Dunlop) *trckd ldng pair: lost pl whn others mde effrts fr 3f out: 5th whn nt clr run on inner 2f out: swtchd to outer jst over 1f out: str run fnl f: gaining fast at fin* **8/1**

0062 **3** *1* **Taurian**[9] 3722 5-9-7 **63** JamesDoyle 2 68
(Ian Williams) *settled in 5th: shkn up and prog wl over 2f out: drvn to chse ldng pair over 1f out and cl enough: styd on one pce fnl f* **3/1**[2]

-524 **4** *1/2* **All The Rage**[11] 3652 3-8-10 **65** LukeMorris 7 69
(Sir Mark Prescott Bt) *hld up in 6th: smooth prog to trck wnr over 2f out: drvn and fnd nil over 1f out: lost 2 pls nr fin* **5/4**[1]

-430 **5** *5* **Evidence (FR)**[79] 1542 3-9-1 **70** SamHitchcott 5 66
(Harry Dunlop) *led to 3f out: wknd on inner over 1f out* **20/1**

40-0 **6** *4* **Unsuspected Girl (IRE)**[24] 3198 3-7-9 **55** oh1 NoelGarbutt(5) 6 45
(David Simcock) *dwlt: hld up in last pair: outpcd and pushed along 3f out: no prog after: nvr involved* **25/1**

22/5 **7** *4* **Jazzy Lady (IRE)**[16] 3470 5-10-0 **70** (p) WilliamTwiston-Davies 4 50
(Jim Best) *frequently pushed along in last pair: bhd fr over 2f out* **25/1**

5-00 **8** *1 3/4* **Sunlit Waters**[15] 3482 3-8-6 **61** TomMarquand 8 41
(Eve Johnson Houghton) *trckd ldr to 3f out: wknd rapidly over 2f out* **6/1**[3]

2m 31.69s (-1.31) **Going Correction** 0.0s/f (Stan)
WFA 3 from 5yo 13lb **8** Ran SP% **116.4**
Speed ratings (Par 100): **104,103,103,102,99 96,92,92**
CSF £83.91 CT £298.37 TOTE £13.20: £3.10, £3.30, £1.30; EX 71.80 Trifecta £519.90.
Owner Cotton, Conway **Bred** J K Thoroughbreds **Trained** Pulborough, W Sussex

FOCUS
A tight finish to an ordinary fillies' handicap, muddling form.

4019 BARRY FEATHERSTONE 70TH BIRTHDAY CELEBRATORY H'CAP 1m 7f 169y(P)
4:00 (4:01) (Class 6) (0-60,60) 4-Y-O+ **£2,587** (£770; £384; £192) **Stalls** Low

Form RPR

6050 **1** **Lily Edge**[18] 3402 7-8-4 **46** oh1 (v) DannyBrock(3) 12 54+
(John Bridger) *hld up in midfield: rdn and prog on outer 3f out: led wl over 1f out: sn drvn clr: styd on wl* **14/1**

/002 **2** *3 3/4* **Hier Encore (FR)**[23] 3221 4-9-3 **56** GeorgeBaker 13 60
(David Menuisier) *prom: rdn to chal jst over 2f out: sn outpcd by wnr: kpt on to take 2nd nr fin* **5/1**[3]

00-0 **3** *1/2* **Willshebetrying**[71] 1748 5-8-7 **46** oh1 (v) SamHitchcott 9 49
(Jim Best) *led after 1f: drvn and hdd wl over 1f out: one pce and lost 2nd nr fin* **20/1**

0-05 **4** *1 3/4* **Lucky Diva**[26] 3099 9-8-7 **51** (p) HectorCrouch(5) 4 52
(Bill Turner) *hld up in midfield: gng wl enough on inner but waiting for a gap over 2f out: rdn over 1f out: kpt on to take 4th fnl f: n.d* **8/1**

306F **5** *2 1/4* **Machiavelian Storm (IRE)**[23] 3230 4-8-7 **46** oh1 KieranO'Neill 5 44
(Richard Mitchell) *led 1f: trckd ldng pair: nt clr run briefly over 2f out: fdd over 1f out* **33/1**

5025 **6** *shd* **Rosie Royale (IRE)**[18] 3409 4-9-7 **60** OisinMurphy 6 58
(Roger Teal) *chsd ldr after 1f to jst over 2f out: sn wknd* **5/1**[3]

50/0 **7** *1 1/4* **Double Dealites**[69] 1807 6-8-7 **46** KierenFox 7 42
(Jamie Poulton) *a in midfield: rdn and no imp on ldrs 3f out: one pce* **14/1**

2050 **8** *3/4* **Danglydontask**[20] 3302 5-9-5 **58** LukeMorris 1 54
(David Arbuthnot) *dwlt: t.k.h and hld up: drvn on outer wl over 3f out: plugged on fr over 1f out: no ch* **9/2**[2]

5/00 **9** *2 1/2* **Aramadyh**[18] 3402 5-9-6 **59** WilliamTwiston-Davies 10 52
(Jim Best) *stdd s: hld up in last pair: taken to wd outside over 3f out and rdn: modest prog over 2f out: sn no hdwy* **25/1**

135- **10** *2 1/4* **My Anchor**[7] 3545 5-8-8 **52** (bt[1]) MeganNicholls(5) 2 42
(Charlie Mann) *dwlt: nvr gng wl in rr: lost tch over 3f out* **10/1**

-436 **11** *4* **Lucky Dottie**[40] 2645 5-8-12 **51** JFEgan 8 36
(Pat Phelan) *hld up in last pair: pushed along 4f out: no prog u.p 3f out: sn wknd* **4/1**[1]

6454 **12** *1* **Investissement**[35] 2792 10-8-8 **47** (tp) TomMarquand 3 31
(Paddy Butler) *hld up towards rr: rdn and no prog over 3f out: sn wknd* **10/1**

3m 27.55s (1.85) **Going Correction** 0.0s/f (Stan) **12** Ran SP% **125.7**
Speed ratings (Par 101): **95,93,92,92,90 90,90,89,88,87 85,84**
CSF £85.84 CT £1447.21 TOTE £20.90: £6.00, £2.80, £10.70; EX 107.80 Trifecta £2752.20.
Owner J J Bridger **Bred** W J Wyatt **Trained** Liphook, Hants

FOCUS
Lowly handicap form, there was no great gallop on and the winner was kicked at the right time for a ready victory. The winner will still be well treated in the short term.

4020 NEWMARKET JULY MEETING BETTING AT 188BET (S) STKS 1m 2f (P)
4:30 (4:30) (Class 6) 3-Y-O+ **£2,587** (£770; £384; £192) **Stalls** Low

Form RPR

4026 **1** **Barren Brook**[6] 3802 9-9-4 68 GeorgeBaker 5 71
(Laura Mongan) *hld up in 5th: smooth prog on inner over 2f out: pushed into ld over 1f out: edgd rt and idled after: drvn out* **11/4**[2]

6060 **2** *1* **Captain Felix**[28] 3030 4-9-9 72 TomMarquand 1 74
(George Scott) *led: rdn over 2f out: hdd over 1f out: edgd rt fnl f: one pce* **2/1**[1]

5406 **3** *4* **Bognor (USA)**[15] 3497 5-9-4 77 LukeMorris 6 62
(Michael Attwater) *trckd ldng pair: drvn to chal on outer over 2f out but fnd nil and sn btn in 4th: tk modest 3rd again nr fin* **6/1**[3]

-064 **4** *3/4* **King Torus (IRE)**[9] 3729 8-9-9 79 (v) AmirQuinn 2 65
(Lee Carter) *trckd ldr: rdn over 2f out: fdd over 1f out* **8/1**

0141 **5** *3 1/4* **Jamhoori**[57] 1174 8-10-5 76 (v) WilliamTwiston-Davies 4 69
(Jim Best) *trckd ldng trio to over 2f out: sn drvn and wknd* **11/4**[2]

6/0- **6** *55* **Sutton Sid**[59] 341 6-8-13 50 (v) CiaranMckee(5) 3
(Paddy Butler) *s.s: rousted to catch up after 3f: sn lost tch again and t.o* **66/1**

2m 6.78s (0.18) **Going Correction** 0.0s/f (Stan) **6** Ran SP% **113.6**
Speed ratings (Par 101): **99,98,95,94,91 47**
CSF £8.88 TOTE £3.20: £1.70, £1.50; EX 9.40 Trifecta £39.50.There was no bid for the winner.
Owner Mrs L J Mongan **Bred** David Allan **Trained** Epsom, Surrey

FOCUS
The front pair came clear in a seller run at an ordinary gallop. The winner has the scope to rate a bit higher again on this evidence.

4021 £25 FREE BET AT 188BET H'CAP 1m 2f (P)
5:00 (5:01) (Class 6) (0-60,60) 3-Y-O **£2,587** (£770; £384; £192) **Stalls** Low

Form RPR
0422 **1** **Palisade**[8] 3738 3-9-7 **60**...(b[1]) LukeMorris 8 74
(Sir Mark Prescott Bt) *trckd ldr after 2f and t.k.h: urged into ld jst over 2f out: lugging lft but drvn clr over 1f out: eased last 75yds* **4/7**[1]
-605 **2** 6 **Alzebarh (IRE)**[20] 3319 3-8-13 **52**... TomQueally 2 53
(James Fanshawe) *led 1f: mostly trckd ldng pair after: rdn and nt qckn over 2f out: kpt on to win battle for modest 2nd fnl f* **7/1**[2]
0100 **3** shd **Captain Gerald**[4] 3906 3-9-2 **55**...(p) RyanPowell 7 55
(John Ryan) *led after 1f: drvn and hdd jst over 2f out: sn no ch w wnr: lost 2nd fnl f: kpt on* **20/1**
30-1 **4** ½ **Whitstable Pearl (IRE)**[125] 794 3-9-0 **53**... KierenFox 11 52
(John Best) *hld up on outer: outpcd in 7th wl over 2f out: prog and reminders to take modest 4th over 1f out: pushed along and clsd on plcd horses nr fin* **10/1**
54 **5** 3¾ **Becca Campbell (IRE)**[30] 2967 3-9-0 **53**...(p) TomMarquand 3 45
(Eve Johnson Houghton) *in tch: rdn wl over 2f out: outpcd sn after: n.d* **8/1**[3]
64-6 **6** 3½ **Rock Icon**[55] 2184 3-8-7 **46** oh1... NickyMackay 1 32
(Patrick Chamings) *hld up in rr: pushed along and outpcd on inner over 2f out: nvr a factor* **33/1**
015 **7** 1¾ **Lady Rocka**[22] 3256 3-9-5 **58**...(b) JimCrowley 4 40
(Amanda Perrett) *t.k.h: hld up in tch: rdn and wknd over 2f out* **10/1**
0005 **8** 8 **Eisha Baby**[15] 3490 3-8-5 **51**...(p) HollieDoyle(7) 5 18
(Richard Hannon) *mostly in last and nvr gng wl: lost tch over 3f out: sn bhd* **25/1**
0-50 **9** 8 **Voices Of Kings**[14] 3535 3-8-13 **52**... MartinDwyer 9 4
(William Muir) *t.k.h on outer: jnd ldng pair 7f out to 5f out: drvn and wknd over 3f out: t.o* **20/1**

2m 6.05s (-0.55) **Going Correction** 0.0s/f (Stan) **9** Ran SP% **121.8**
Speed ratings (Par 98): **102,97,97,96,93 90,89,83,76**
CSF £5.21 CT £47.20 TOTE £1.50: £1.10, £2.10, £5.30; EX 7.30 Trifecta £74.50.
Owner Cheveley Park Stud **Bred** Cheveley Park Stud Ltd **Trained** Newmarket, Suffolk

FOCUS
A moderate handicap run at a steady gallop and the favourite was much too strong. The winner was thrown in but this was still probably a minor step up.
T/Plt: £688.80 to a £1 stake. Pool of £49522.49 - 52.48 winning tickets. T/Qpdt: £155.50 to a £1 stake. Pool of £3993.40 - 19.0 winning tickets. **Jonathan Neesom**

3818 YARMOUTH (L-H)
Wednesday, July 6

OFFICIAL GOING: Good to firm (good in places; 7.8)
Wind: light, across Weather: bright spells

4022 FIRST FURNISHINGS OF GORLESTON MAIDEN AUCTION STKS 5f 42y
2:10 (2:11) (Class 5) 2-Y-O **£2,975** (£885; £442; £221) **Stalls** Centre

Form RPR
6 **1** **Nile Empress**[71] 1741 2-8-13 0... JamesMcDonald 11 77
(Hugo Palmer) *trckd ldrs tl wnt 2nd over 3f out: effrt to ld 1f out: in command and r.o wl ins fnl f* **5/1**[3]
2 1¾ **Lightning North** 2-8-8 0... TomEaves 8 66
(James Tate) *stdd s: hld up in tch: hdwy and travelling wl over 1f out: chsd ldrs and swtchd lft 1f out: chsd wnr 100yds out: kpt on* **15/2**
3 **3** 1½ **Ivor's Magic (IRE)**[13] 3576 2-8-1 0... AdamMcLean(7) 12 60+
(David Elsworth) *in tch in midfield: n.m.r and swtchd rt over 1f out: styd on strly u.p ins fnl f: wnt 3rd cl home* **9/1**
322 **4** ½ **Kody Ridge (IRE)**[32] 2902 2-9-4 0... DougieCostello 10 69
(David Dennis) *dwlt: sn rcvrd and in tch in midfield: effrt over 1f out: 4th and unable qck 1f out: styd on same pce after* **11/4**[1]
53 **5** ½ **Marquee Club**[7] 3770 2-8-13 0... WilliamCarson 6 62
(Jamie Osborne) *led: rdn and wanting to hang lft over 1f out: hdd 1f out: no ex: wknd fnl 100yds: lost 2 pls cl home* **22/1**
0 **6** 3 **Champagne Queen**[32] 2902 2-8-13 0...(t) MartinHarley 5 51
(Rae Guest) *hld up in tch in last trio: effrt over 1f out: styd on to pass btn horses ins fnl f: nvr trbld ldrs* **18/1**
05 **7** ½ **Waves (IRE)**[29] 2997 2-8-13 0... PatCosgrave 4 49
(Eve Johnson Houghton) *chsd ldrs: rdn and unable qck over 1f out: sn struggling: wknd ins fnl f* **28/1**
8 nk **Highland Lotus** 2-8-8 0... PaulHanagan 1 43
(William Haggas) *in tch in midfield: rdn 1/2-way: outpcd and btn over 1f out: wl hld and plugged on same pce fnl f* **6/1**
9 2¾ **Prancelina (IRE)** 2-8-1 0... JaneElliott(7) 3 33
(Phil McEntee) *chsd ldr tl over 3f out: hung lft and lost pl over 1f out: bhd ins fnl f* **66/1**
10 ½ **Happy Queen** 2-8-13 0... JamieSpencer 2 36
(George Margarson) *awkward leaving stalls and s.i.s: hld up in tch in rr: effrt swtchd rt over 1f out: sn nt clr run and swtchd bk lft: no hdwy: bhd ins fnl f* **4/1**[2]

1m 1.69s (-1.01) **Going Correction** -0.30s/f (Firm) **10** Ran SP% **113.9**
Speed ratings (Par 94): **96,93,90,90,89 84,83,83,78,77**
CSF £40.34 TOTE £5.90: £2.10, £2.70, £2.80; EX 44.70 Trifecta £324.50.
Owner Mr And Mrs A E Pakenham **Bred** Mr & Mrs A E Pakenham **Trained** Newmarket, Suffolk

FOCUS
The going remained good to firm, good in places after just 1mm of rain since the previous day. An ordinary maiden auction to start with and the runners came up the middle. The winner did it well, though, and a couple behind caught the eye. After the race Paul Hanagan said of the ground: "It's good to firm", while William Carson said: "It's fast."

4023 GREAT YARMOUTH MERCURY H'CAP 1m 6f 17y
2:40 (2:41) (Class 5) (0-75,74) 4-Y-O+ **£2,911** (£866; £432; £216) **Stalls** High

Form RPR
1412 **1** **Sandy Cove**[25] 3121 5-9-0 **67**... RyanTate 3 73
(James Eustace) *hld up in tch in midfield: effrt to chse ldr over 2f out: drvn to press wnr 1f out: led ins fnl f: styd on wl: rdn out* **8/1**[3]
0414 **2** 1 **Safira Menina**[25] 3139 4-8-10 **70**... NatalieHambling(7) 5 74
(Martin Smith) *hld up in tch in rr: hdwy on outer over 3f out: led over 2f out: rdn over 1f out: hdd and styd on same pce ins fnl f* **25/1**
5441 **3** nk **Princess Roania (IRE)**[7] 3767 5-8-10 **70** 6ex...(tp) JoshuaBryan(7) 1 74
(Peter Bowen) *hld up in tch: clsd to chse ldrs 3f out: rdn wl over 1f out: kpt on same pce ins fnl f* **1/1**[1]
4200 **4** hd **Knight's Parade (IRE)**[14] 3533 6-9-5 **72**...(t) DougieCostello 9 76
(Sarah Humphrey) *chsd ldrs: pushed along and clsd to press ldrs 4f out: rdn to ld 3f out: sn hdd: kpt on same pce u.p ins fnl f* **50/1**
-602 **5** nk **The Ducking Stool**[24] 3191 9-8-13 **69**... ShelleyBirkett(3) 6 72
(Julia Feilden) *chsd ldr tl 12f out: styd prom rdn 3f out: kpt on same pce ins fnl f* **9/1**
2-44 **6** 1¾ **Kristjano (GER)**[18] 3409 4-9-1 **68**...(p) MartinHarley 4 68
(Chris Wall) *chsd ldrs: wnt 2nd 12f out tl unable qck u.p 3f out: hld and styd on same pce fr over 1f out* **7/2**[2]
5343 **7** 1½ **Vedani (IRE)**[20] 3325 7-7-9 **55** oh1... SophieKilloran(7) 8 53
(Tony Carroll) *led: rdn and hdd 3f out: lost pl u.p 2f out: hld and kpt on same pce after* **10/1**
534 **8** 5 **Oratorio's Joy (IRE)**[29] 3002 6-9-1 **68**... WilliamCarson 7 58
(Jamie Osborne) *in tch in midfield: rdn 4f out: unable qck u.p: lost pl and bhd 1f out: wknd* **14/1**

3m 4.16s (-3.44) **Going Correction** -0.125s/f (Firm) **8** Ran SP% **114.9**
Speed ratings (Par 103): **104,103,103,103,102 101,101,98**
CSF £173.87 CT £367.37 TOTE £7.20: £1.80, £4.10, £1.40; EX 108.90 Trifecta £545.80.
Owner Blue Peter Racing 12 **Bred** D J And Mrs Deer **Trained** Newmarket, Suffolk

FOCUS
A muddling staying handicap rated cautiously. They went steadily, with all eight runners in a line across the track coming to the last 3f.

4024 LADIES NIGHT AT GREAT YARMOUTH RACECOURSE (S) STKS 1m 3f 104y
3:10 (3:10) (Class 6) 3-4-Y-O **£2,264** (£673; £336; £168) **Stalls** Low

Form RPR
440 **1** **Coarse Cut (IRE)**[14] 3509 3-8-5 58...(p) PaulHanagan 2 55
(Eve Johnson Houghton) *led tl over 3f out: rdn and sltly outpcd over 2f out: chsd wnr over 1f out: chalng 1f out: styd on to ld nr fin* **5/6**[1]
0544 **2** nk **Dalavand (IRE)**[22] 3256 3-8-5 57... WilliamCarson 5 55
(Jamie Osborne) *chsd ldr tl led over 3f out: rdn over 2f out: drvn 1f out: hdd and no ex nr fin* **13/8**[2]
00-0 **3** ¾ **My Mistress (IRE)**[8] 3737 4-8-12 46... DougieCostello 3 48
(Phil McEntee) *hld up in tch in last pair: clsd to trck ldrs over 2f out: effrt over 1f out: hung lft 1f out: styd on same pce ins fnl f* **25/1**
3-P0 **4** hd **Duc De Seville (IRE)**[23] 3230 4-8-12 50...(b) AnnaHesketh(5) 1 53
(Michael Chapman) *chsd ldrs: rdn 3f out: drvn and hdwy 2f out: pressing ldrs 1f out: styd on same pce ins fnl f* **33/1**
0366 **5** 8 **Ocean Bentley (IRE)**[15] 3489 4-8-10 43... JoshuaBryan(7) 6 40
(Tony Carroll) *stdd and wnt rt leaving stalls: hld up in rr: effrt over 2f out: no imp: wknd over 1f out* **16/1**[3]
0050 **6** 5 **Monpazier (IRE)**[15] 3493 3-7-12 37...(tp) SophieKilloran(7) 4 32
(K R Burke) *t.k.h: hld up wl in tch: clsd to press ldrs 5f out: chsd ldr 3f out tl rdn and lost pl over 1f out: wknd fnl f* **25/1**

2m 33.19s (4.49) **Going Correction** -0.125s/f (Firm)
WFA 3 from 4yo 12lb **6** Ran SP% **109.2**
Speed ratings (Par 101): **78,77,77,77,71 67**
CSF £2.18 TOTE £1.70: £1.10, £1.30; EX 2.40 Trifecta £9.80.The winner bought in 4,800gns.
Owner Equi ex Incertis Partners **Bred** M E Wates **Trained** Blewbury, Oxon

FOCUS
A bad seller, with the six runners officially rated between 37 and 58.

4025 WELL BALANCED LEDGER AT J&H SIMPSON FILLIES' H'CAP 1m 2f 23y
3:40 (3:40) (Class 5) (0-70,70) 3-Y-O+ **£2,911** (£866; £432; £216) **Stalls** Low

Form RPR
1260 **1** **Yorkindred Spirit**[12] 3593 4-10-0 **70**...(v) FrannyNorton 2 77
(Mark Johnston) *hld up in tch: hdwy 3f out: rdn to chse ldrs over 1f out: styd on to chal ins fnl f: kpt on u.p to ld 50yds out: rdn out* **9/1**
-150 **2** ½ **Wings Of Esteem (IRE)**[35] 2795 3-9-0 **67**... DougieCostello 6 73
(K R Burke) *chsd ldr: clsd and upsides 4f out: rdn to ld over 1f out: hrd pressed and drvn jst ins fnl f: hdd and styd on same pce fnl 50yds* **11/2**[3]
05 **3** 2 **Princesse Eva (FR)**[16] 3475 3-8-12 **68**... DanielMuscutt(3) 5 70
(James Fanshawe) *hld up in tch in midfield: effrt to chse ldrs 2f out: sn u.p: styd on same pce ins fnl f* **13/2**
222 **4** 2 **Phoenix Beat**[15] 3496 3-9-2 **69**... FrankieDettori 1 67
(Gay Kelleway) *led: rdn and hdd over 1f out: no ex u.p 1f out: wknd fnl 100yds* **2/1**[1]
0352 **5** ½ **Refulgence (FR)**[58] 2108 3-8-11 **64**... MartinHarley 8 61
(Marco Botti) *t.k.h: hld up in tch in last pair: pushed along 3f out: 6th and no imp over 1f out: kpt on but no threat to ldrs ins fnl f* **8/1**
000 **6** ½ **Rowlestonerendezvu**[29] 2998 3-8-5 **58**... PaulHanagan 7 54
(Tony Carroll) *hld up in tch in midfield: effrt over 2f out: no imp u.p over 1f out: styd on same pce ins fnl f* **9/2**[2]
4060 **7** 11 **Mops Angel**[16] 3474 5-8-8 **55**...(p) AdamMcNamara(5) 4 29
(Michael Appleby) *dwlt: t.k.h and sn rcvrd to chse ldrs: rdn over 2f out: sn struggling: bhd fnl f* **20/1**
06-0 **8** 83 **Dark Avenue**[40] 2652 3-9-1 **68**... JamieSpencer 3
(William Knight) *stdd s: hld up in tch in rr: effrt 3f out: no hdwy and sn eased: t.o* **14/1**

2m 8.07s (-2.43) **Going Correction** -0.125s/f (Firm)
WFA 3 from 4yo+ 11lb **8** Ran SP% **112.8**
Speed ratings (Par 100): **104,103,102,100,100 99,90,24**
CSF £55.84 CT £343.83 TOTE £7.90: £2.00, £1.80, £2.80; EX 70.90 Trifecta £284.50.
Owner Paul Robert York **Bred** Ed's Stud Ltd **Trained** Middleham Moor, N Yorks

FOCUS
A modest fillies' handicap run at an ordinary pace. The 3yos looked strong in this, but it turned out to be one for the older brigade. They came up the centre in the straight. This has been rated around the first and second.

4026 GROSVENOR CASINO AT GREAT YARMOUTH H'CAP 1m 1f 21y
4:10 (4:11) (Class 3) (0-90,89) 3-Y-O- **£7,561** (£2,263; £1,131; £424; £424) **Stalls** Low

Form RPR
44-0 **1** **Heisman (IRE)**[27] 3055 5-9-10 **85**...(p) PatCosgrave 2 92
(George Baker) *chsd ldrs: effrt over 1f out: drvn to chal 1f out: led ins fnl f: hld on wl u.p* **6/1**[2]
4003 **2** ½ **Bold Prediction (IRE)**[20] 3303 6-9-9 **89**... AdamMcNamara(5) 5 95
(Ed Walker) *led tl 7f out: styd w ldr: rdn and ev ch fr 2f out: kpt on: unable qck wl ins fnl f* **16/1**
2050 **3** nk **Emerald (ITY)**[20] 3304 4-9-9 **87**...(b[1]) DanielMuscutt(3) 7 92
(Marco Botti) *hld up in tch in last pair: clsd and n.m.r over 1f out: gap opened and rdn to press ldrs 1f out: ev ch ins fnl f: unable qck wl ins fnl f* **11/1**

-156 **4** ½ **Haalan**[49] 2363 4-9-12 **87** .... MartinHarley 1 91
(James Tate) *w ldr tl led 7f out: rdn 2f out: drvn ent fnl f: hdd ins fnl f: styd on same pce fnl 75yds* **9/1**

5-00 **4** *dht* **Laurence**[26] 3113 4-9-10 **85** .... JamesMcDonald 6 89+
(Luca Cumani) *hld up in tch in midfield: trying to cl but nvr enough room fr over 1f out tl small gap opened: rdn and styd on nr fin* **13/2**[3]

2403 **6** *nk* **Solo Hunter**[26] 3109 5-10-0 **89** ....(b) FrankieDettori 3 93
(Martyn Meade) *dwlt: sn rcvrd and hld up in tch in midfield: rdn over 2f out: styd on to press ldrs ins fnl f: no ex and one pce wl ins fnl f* **13/2**[3]

01/4 **7** *1* **Heatstroke (IRE)**[41] 2628 4-9-12 **87** .... JamieSpencer 8 89
(Charles Hills) *t.k.h: hld up in tch in last pair: effrt over 1f out: sn drvn: styd on same pce ins fnl f* **7/4**[1]

-034 **8** *2¼* **What Say You (IRE)**[27] 3055 4-9-10 **85** .... DougieCostello 4 81
(K R Burke) *chsd ldng trio: rdn ent fnl 2f out: unable qck and lost pl over 1f out: hld and styd on same pce ins fnl f* **8/1**

0010 **9** *1½* **Artful Prince**[14] 3517 6-8-13 **74** ....(b) TomEaves 9 67
(James Given) *hld up wl in tch in last trio: effrt 2f out: sn outpcd and dropped to last over 1f out: styd on same pce ins fnl f* **40/1**

1m 53.82s (-1.98) **Going Correction** -0.125s/f (Firm) **9** Ran SP% **115.1**
Speed ratings (Par 107): **103,102,102,101,101 101,100,98,97**
CSF £94.84 CT £1026.96 TOTE £6.30: £2.10, £3.90, £3.80; EX 79.30 Trifecta £2148.00.
Owner Michael H Watt **Bred** Keatly Overseas Ltd **Trained** Manton, Wilts

FOCUS
A decent handicap, but they didn't go a great pace and they finished in a bit of a heap. Again they came up the middle. The winner has been rated close to last year's form.

4027 VAUXHALL HOLIDAY PARK MEDIAN AUCTION MAIDEN STKS 1m 3y
4:40 (4:40) (Class 5) 3-Y-O **£3,622** (£1,078; £538; £269) **Stalls** Centre

Form RPR

1 **Esprit De Tauber (IRE)** 3-9-0 0 .... PaulHanagan 5 74+
(Don Cantillon) *hld up in tch in last pair: clsd and travelling wl 2f out: pushed along and qcknd to ld 1f out: r.o wl: pushed out* **16/1**[3]

0 **2** *1* **Best Laid Plans**[70] 1798 3-9-0 0 .... MartinHarley 6 71
(James Tate) *hld up wl in tch in midfield: effrt to chse ldrs over 1f out: rdn 1f out: chsd wnr ins fnl f: styd on but a hld* **20/1**

33 **3** *2* **Crystallographer (IRE)**[16] 3475 3-9-0 0 .... JamesMcDonald 3 66
(David Lanigan) *t.k.h: chsd ldrs tl wnt 2nd 1/2-way: rdn and little rspnse over 1f out: styd on same pce ins fnl f* **9/4**[2]

562 **4** *1* **Warrior Prince**[22] 3264 3-9-5 77 .... FrankieDettori 4 69
(Ed Dunlop) *led: rdn over 1f out: hdd over 1f out: hdd and unable qck over 1f out: outpcd ins fnl f* **8/13**[1]

0 **5** *2¾* **Gomez**[18] 3412 3-9-5 0 .... SaleemGolam 1 62
(Rae Guest) *hld up in tch in midfield: rdn 2f out: outpcd and btn over 1f out: wl hld and kpt on same pce ins fnl f* **33/1**

0-4 **6** *19* **Cool Silk Girl**[65] 1920 3-9-0 0 .... TomEaves 7 14
(James Given) *chsd ldr tl 1/2-way: lost pl u.p over 2f out: lost tch over 1f out: eased wl ins fnl f* **33/1**

7 *31* **Zam I Am** 3-9-5 0 ....[1] DougieCostello 2
(Christine Dunnett) *stdd s: hld up in last pair: rdn 3f out: sn btn: t.o and eased ins fnl f* **66/1**

1m 37.39s (-3.21) **Going Correction** -0.30s/f (Firm) **7** Ran SP% **110.7**
Speed ratings (Par 100): **104,103,101,100,97 78,47**
CSF £211.02 TOTE £12.80: £5.00, £7.80; EX 113.30 Trifecta £414.70.
Owner Mrs Catherine Reed **Bred** Camas Park Stud **Trained** Newmarket, Suffolk

FOCUS
Very little depth to this 3yo maiden and it has been rated around the third. They raced more centre-to-nearside this time.

4028 HUGH CRANE OF ACLE H'CAP 1m 3y
5:10 (5:10) (Class 4) (0-80,80) 3-Y-O+ **£4,690** (£1,395; £697; £348) **Stalls** Centre

Form RPR

3200 **1** **Brigliadoro (IRE)**[26] 3115 5-9-9 **80** .... AdamMcNamara(5) 4 94
(Philip McBride) *hld up in tch in midfield: clsd to ld on bit over 1f out: rdn and readily qckd clr ins fnl f: comf* **11/2**[3]

113 **2** *3½* **Mukaabra**[18] 3410 3-9-5 **80** .... MartinHarley 3 84
(James Tate) *chsd ldrs: effrt to chal 2f out: chsd wnr over 1f out: easily brushed aside jst ins fnl f: styd on same pce after* **13/8**[1]

21-2 **3** *4½* **Coherent (IRE)**[84] 1411 3-9-2 **77** .... JamieSpencer 8 71
(William Haggas) *t.k.h: chsd ldr: rdn and ev ch jst over 2f out tl outpcd and btn over 1f out: 3rd and wkng whn hung lft ins fnl f* **5/2**[2]

12-0 **4** *2¾* **Harry Champion**[33] 2871 3-9-3 **78** .... JamesMcDonald 7 65
(Hugo Palmer) *led: rdn ent fnl 2f: hdd over 1f out and sn btn: wkng whn wandered jst ins fnl f* **12/1**

0-50 **5** *4* **Salvo**[35] 2795 3-9-4 **79** .... FrankieDettori 2 57
(Charlie Fellowes) *hld up in tch in last pair: effrt 2f out: sn btn: wknd over 1f out* **8/1**

2-64 **6** *1* **Ataman (IRE)**[27] 3061 4-9-11 **77** ....[1] DougieCostello 5 55
(Chris Wall) *stdd after s: hld up in tch in rr: effrt ent fnl 2f: sn btn: wknd over 1f out* **9/1**

1m 37.08s (-3.52) **Going Correction** -0.30s/f (Firm)
WFA 3 from 4yo+ 9lb **6** Ran SP% **110.9**
Speed ratings (Par 105): **105,101,97,94,90 89**
CSF £14.56 CT £25.81 TOTE £5.70: £2.90, £1.40; EX 21.90 Trifecta £56.80.
Owner Serafino Agodino **Bred** D Naughton, Zubieta & Javier Salmean **Trained** Newmarket, Suffolk

FOCUS
A fair handicap to end with and another race where the 3yos looked particularly strong, but again they found an experienced older rival much too good. The winner has been rated close to his AW form, with the level set around the second.
T/Plt: £2,345.70 to a £1 stake. Pool of £45308.77 - 14.10 winning tickets. T/Qpdt: £586.00 to a £1 stake. Pool of £4672.63 - 5.90 winning tickets. **Steve Payne**

4029 - 4030a (Foreign Racing) - See Raceform Interactive

3992 HAMBURG (R-H)
Wednesday, July 6

OFFICIAL GOING: Turf: heavy

4031a LANGER HAMBURGER (LISTED RACE) (4YO+) (TURF) 2m
7:25 (12:00) 4-Y-O+ **£10,294** (£4,779; £2,205; £1,102)

RPR

1 **Rock Of Romance (IRE)**[20] 6-8-9 0 .... EduardoPedroza 3 104+
(A Wohler, Germany) **16/5**[3]

2 *9½* **Summershine (IRE)** 5-8-6 0 .... BayarsaikhanGanbat 6 91
(Frau Anna Schleusner-Fruhriep, Germany) **20/1**

3 *6* **Damour (GER)**[46] 4-8-8 0 .... MartinSeidl 7 86
(Markus Klug, Germany) **67/10**

4 *4* **Amour De Nuit (IRE)**[18] 3387 4-9-0 0 .... DennisSchiergen 4 88
(Sir Mark Prescott Bt) **8/5**[1]

5 *2¾* **Iraklion (GER)**[31] 4-8-9 0 .... FilipMinarik 1 80
(Christian Sprengel, Germany) **29/10**[2]

6 *49* **Empoli (GER)**[31] 6-8-10 0 ow1 .... AdriedeVries 2 27
(P Schiergen, Germany) **56/10**

3m 52.98s (232.98) **6** Ran SP% **120.8**
WIN (incl. 10 euro stake): 42. PLACES: 28, 53. SF: 346.
Owner Hans-Georg Stihl **Bred** Brendan Corbett **Trained** Germany

3880 CARLISLE (R-H)
Thursday, July 7

OFFICIAL GOING: Good to soft (6.9) changing to good to soft (good in places) after race 1 (2.00)
Wind: Light, half against Weather: Overcast

4032 APOLLOBET HOME OF CASHBACK OFFERS H'CAP 5f
2:00 (2:00) (Class 4) (0-85,84) 3-Y-O+ **£5,175** (£1,540; £769; £384) **Stalls** Low

Form RPR

0104 **1** **Confessional**[12] 3637 9-9-10 **84** ....(e) JackGarritty 7 94
(Tim Easterby) *hld up: effrt and plld out over 1f out: hung rt and qcknd to ld ins fnl f: pushed clr* **7/2**[2]

1625 **2** *2¼* **Sir Domino (FR)**[14] 3580 4-9-2 **76** ....(p) TomEaves 3 77
(Kevin Ryan) *rrd s: sn trcking ldrs: pushed along 2f out: effrt whn carried rt ent fnl f: sn chsng wnr: kpt on: no imp* **15/2**

-046 **3** *shd* **Desert Ace (IRE)**[41] 2665 5-9-7 **81** ....(p) DanielTudhope 1 82
(Iain Jardine) *in tch: effrt and rdn over 1f out: checked briefly ins fnl f: sn disputing 2nd pl: kpt on: hld nr fin* **9/4**[1]

1666 **4** *1¼* **Rusty Rocket (IRE)**[12] 3638 7-9-7 **81** .... PJMcDonald 5 77
(Paul Green) *prom: lost pl over 4f out: rallied whn nt clr run over 1f out: kpt on ins fnl f: nt pce to chal* **6/1**

2520 **5** *½* **King Crimson**[12] 3638 4-9-10 **84** .... LukeMorris 6 78
(Mick Channon) *led at decent gallop: rdn 2f out: hdd ins fnl f: kpt on same pce* **4/1**[3]

/0-0 **6** *1¾* **Star Citizen**[20] 3346 4-9-5 **79** .... JasonHart 4 67
(Fred Watson) *hld up on ins: rdn over 2f out: hdwy whn nt clr run over 1f out: kpt on fnl f: no imp* **28/1**

000- **7** *2¼* **Astrophysics**[208] 8200 4-9-8 **82** .... PaddyAspell 8 62
(Lynn Siddall) *dwlt: hld up on outside: hdwy over 2f out: lost pl and struggling appr fnl f* **40/1**

02-0 **8** *7* **Ayresome Angel**[55] 2218 3-9-3 **82** .... TonyHamilton 2 35
(Bryan Smart) *chsd ldr: rdn along 2f out: one pce whn hmpd ent fnl f: sn lost pl and eased* **16/1**

1m 1.66s (0.86) **Going Correction** +0.225s/f (Good)
WFA 3 from 4yo+ 5lb **8** Ran SP% **110.8**
Speed ratings (Par 105): **102,98,98,96,95 92,89,77**
CSF £27.76 CT £67.11 TOTE £4.30: £1.60, £2.20, £1.10; EX 22.70 Trifecta £107.70.
Owner Bearstone Stud Limited **Bred** Bearstone Stud Ltd **Trained** Great Habton, N Yorks

FOCUS
The race was run over the advertised distance. The going had dried out overnight to good to soft. A moderate sprint handicap where they seemed to a fairly good clip. The winner's best form since last September.

4033 APOLLOBET HOME OF CASHBACK OFFERS H'CAP 1m 6f 32y
2:30 (2:30) (Class 5) (0-70,70) 3-Y-O **£2,911** (£866; £432; £216) **Stalls** Low

Form RPR

5-41 **1** **Silva Eclipse**[24] 3215 3-9-7 **70** .... JackGarritty 1 81+
(Jedd O'Keeffe) *t.k.h: trckd ldrs: effrt whn nt clr run over 3f out to over 2f out: swtchd rt and rdn to ld over 1f out: drvn and kpt on wl fnl f* **11/4**[1]

0-55 **2** *nk* **Mystique Heights**[29] 3033 3-8-8 **57** .... LukeMorris 4 67
(Sir Mark Prescott Bt) *dwlt and bmpd s: hld up on ins: drvn along over 4f out: rallied u.p 3f out: edgd rt and hdwy to chse wnr ins fnl f: kpt on u.p* **10/3**[2]

00-3 **3** *1* **Transpennine Star**[68] 1873 3-8-13 **62** .... BarryMcHugh 8 71
(Michael Dods) *hld up in tch: hdwy and cl up after 4f: rdn and pressed ldr 3f out to 2f out: kpt on ins fnl f* **33/1**

-402 **4** *9* **Clear Evidence**[13] 3615 3-8-12 **64** .... LouisSteward(3) 5 61
(Michael Bell) *cl up: led over 3f out: rdn and hdd over 1f out: wknd ins fnl f: eased last 75yds* **9/2**

-1U4 **5** *10* **Sattelac**[24] 3215 3-9-2 **65** .... PhillipMakin 6 49
(Keith Dalgleish) *plld hrd early: stdd in rr: hdwy on outside whn hung lft over 3f out: hung lft and wknd 2f out* **12/1**

5-31 **6** *11* **Young Tom**[16] 3493 3-9-1 **64** .... AndrewMullen 7 34
(Michael Appleby) *prom: effrt and drvn along over 3f out: wknd 2f out* **7/2**[3]

6104 **7** *7* **Rockliffe**[15] 3509 3-8-11 **60** .... TomEaves 3 21
(Mick Channon) *led at modest gallop: rdn and hdd over 3f out: lost tch fr 2f out* **10/1**

3m 11.86s (4.36) **Going Correction** +0.325s/f (Good) **7** Ran SP% **109.9**
Speed ratings (Par 100): **100,99,99,94,88 82,78**
CSF £11.10 CT £216.03 TOTE £2.90: £1.90, £2.00; EX 10.60 Trifecta £174.10.
Owner Geoff & Sandra Turnbull **Bred** R F Broad **Trained** Middleham Moor, N Yorks

FOCUS
Race was run over 24yds further than advertised. An interesting long distance 3yo handicap where the winner just held on under a good ride. The first three were clear and the form may prove better than rated.

4034 STALLIONS BREEDING WINNERS EBF FILLIES' H'CAP 5f 193y
3:00 (3:00) (Class 4) (0-80,79) 3-Y-O+ **£6,469** (£1,925; £962; £481) **Stalls** Low

Form RPR

0012 **1** **Emerald Loch**[15] 3512 3-9-2 **75** ....(p) GrahamGibbons 1 83
(Ralph Beckett) *pressed ldr: shkn up 2f out: led appr fnl f: drvn and hld on wl towards fin* **10/3**[2]

6002 **2** *½* **Forever A Lady (IRE)**[5] 3885 3-8-13 **72** .... PhillipMakin 3 78
(Keith Dalgleish) *bhd: rdn along over 2f out: hdwy over 1f out: chsd wnr wl ins fnl f: kpt on fin* **2/1**[1]

0204 **3** *¾* **Meandmyshadow**[14] 3553 8-9-2 **74** ....(b) JoshDoyle(5) 5 79
(Alan Brown) *led: rdn and hdd appr fnl f: rallied: lost 2nd and no ex wl ins fnl f* **12/1**

0344 **4** *2* **Rural Celebration**[14] 3575 5-9-12 **79** ....(v[1]) DanielTudhope 2 77
(David O'Meara) *prom: n.m.r after 1f: effrt and pushed along 2f out: no ex ins fnl f: eased cl home* **9/2**[3]

-240 **5** ¾ **Flowing Clarets**[22] 3292 3-9-4 **77** .... TonyHamilton 6 72
(Richard Fahey) *hld up bhd ldng gp: effrt on outside over 2f out: hung rt: kpt on fnl f: no imp* **13/2**

-433 **6** 2¼ **Appleberry (IRE)**[10] 3714 4-9-3 **75** ....(p) AdamMcNamara(5) 4 64
(Michael Appleby) *chsd ldr: rdn and hung rt 2f out: wknd ins fnl f* **11/2**

1m 14.2s (0.50) **Going Correction** +0.225s/f (Good)
WFA 3 from 4yo+ 6lb 6 Ran SP% **111.0**
Speed ratings (Par 102): **105,104,103,100,99 96**
CSF £10.19 TOTE £3.40: £1.50, £1.80; EX 12.30 Trifecta £69.60.
Owner J C Smith **Bred** Littleton Stud **Trained** Kimpton, Hants

FOCUS
The race distance was as advertised. The feature race was a decent-looking fillies handicap that was truly run and it produced a good finish. The form is rated around the third.

4035 BREEDERS BACKING RACING EBF MAIDEN STKS 7f 173y
3:35 (3:35) (Class 5) 3-4-Y-O **£3,881** (£1,155; £577; £288) **Stalls** Low

Form RPR

0-3 **1** **Fidaawy**[34] 2861 3-9-3 0 .... DanielTudhope 1 87+
(Sir Michael Stoute) *t.k.h: stdd in tch: stdy hdwy 2f out: shkn up to ld ins fnl f: readily* **1/3**[1]

3 **2** 2 **Organza**[12] 3634 3-8-12 70 .... FrannyNorton 5 76
(Mick Channon) *cl up: led gng wl over 2f out: rdn and hdd ins fnl f: no ch w ready wnr* **4/1**[2]

32 **3** 16 **Hilary J**[19] 3422 3-8-12 0 .... PJMcDonald 2 38
(Ann Duffield) *plld hrd: prom: wnt 2nd over 2f out to over 1f out: sn wknd* **7/1**[3]

0 **4** 14 **Hellracer**[20] 3362 3-9-3 0 .... TonyHamilton 4 9
(Bryan Smart) *led to over 2f out: hung rt and wknd wl over 1f out* **50/1**

5 2½ **The Cheese Gang**[26] 4-9-7 0 ....[1] GarryWhillans(5) 3
(Susan Corbett) *chsd ldrs: rdn over 3f out: hung lft and wknd over 2f out* **100/1**

1m 41.71s (1.71) **Going Correction** +0.325s/f (Good)
WFA 3 from 4yo 9lb 5 Ran SP% **110.5**
Speed ratings (Par 103): **104,102,86,72,69**
CSF £2.08 TOTE £1.20: £1.10, £2.00; EX 2.20 Trifecta £2.70.
Owner Hamdan Al Maktoum **Bred** Shadwell Estate Company Limited **Trained** Newmarket, Suffolk

FOCUS
The race was run over 6yds further than advertised. An uncompetitive maiden which resulted in a bloodless victory for the red-hot favourite. The first two improved.

4036 APOLLOBET WEEKLY GOLF REFUNDS H'CAP 7f 173y
4:05 (4:06) (Class 5) (0-75,75) 3-Y-O **£2,911** (£866; £432; £216) **Stalls** Low

Form RPR

105- **1** **Yorkee Mo Sabee (IRE)**[250] 7637 3-9-7 **75** .... FrannyNorton 6 83+
(Mark Johnston) *t.k.h early: mde all: clr after 2f to over 3f out: qcknd over 2f out: rdn out: unchal* **7/2**[1]

400 **2** 3 **Muroor**[24] 3224 3-9-0 **68** ow1 .... DanielTudhope 4 69
(David O'Meara) *t.k.h: in tch: effrt and pushed along 2f out: edgd rt: kpt on to take 2nd towards fin: nt rch wnr* **5/1**[3]

-623 **3** 1 **Strummer (IRE)**[14] 3568 3-8-13 **67** .... TomEaves 5 66+
(Kevin Ryan) *stdd in tch: effrt and hdwy to chse (clr) wnr over 1f out: one pce ins fnl f: lost 2nd towards fin* **4/1**[2]

3430 **4** 3 **The Name's Paver**[34] 2864 3-8-13 **67** .... BarryMcHugh 1 58
(Noel Wilson) *chsd wnr to over 1f out: sn rdn and wknd* **17/2**

1-0 **5** 2¼ **Bronte Flyer**[61] 2029 3-9-7 **75** .... PJMcDonald 3 61
(Ann Duffield) *t.k.h: hld up in tch: rdn over 2f out: wknd over 1f out* **7/2**[1]

324- **6** 4½ **Catastrophe**[240] 7785 3-9-5 **73** .... JasonHart 2 48
(John Quinn) *t.k.h: prom: rdn along over 2f out: wknd wl over 1f out* **4/1**[2]

1m 42.03s (2.03) **Going Correction** +0.325s/f (Good) 6 Ran SP% **111.6**
Speed ratings (Par 100): **102,99,98,95,92 88**
CSF £20.70 TOTE £4.50: £2.10, £2.50; EX 20.60 Trifecta £79.10.
Owner Paul Robert York **Bred** Corduff Stud Ltd **Trained** Middleham Moor, N Yorks

FOCUS
The race was run over 6yds further than advertised. An open 3yo handicap where the pacesetter stayed on well to win. It would be no surprise to see him better this.

4037 APOLLOBET BET ON LOTTERIES MAIDEN FILLIES' STKS (PLUS 10 RACE) 6f 195y
4:40 (4:40) (Class 5) 2-Y-O **£2,911** (£866; £432; £216) **Stalls** Low

Form RPR

0 **1** **Riviere Argentee (FR)**[29] 3024 2-9-0 0 .... BenCurtis 7 74
(K R Burke) *cl up on outside: rdn to ld 1f out: kpt on wl fnl f* **22/1**

6 **2** ½ **Laureate**[13] 3597 2-9-0 0 .... FrannyNorton 1 73
(Mark Johnston) *cl up: led after 1f: rdn and hdd 1f out: rallied and ev ch fnl f: kpt on: hld nr fin* **14/1**

4000 **3** 2 **Melesina (IRE)**[20] 3336 2-9-0 0 .... TonyHamilton 3 68
(Richard Fahey) *trckd ldrs: drvn along over 2f out: no imp tl kpt on ins fnl f: nt rch first two* **4/6**[1]

2 **4** nk **Miss Sheridan (IRE)**[18] 3433 2-9-0 0 .... GrahamGibbons 2 67
(Michael Easterby) *led 1f: pressed ldr and t.k.h: rdn and ev ch fr 2f out to ent fnl f: sn no ex* **7/2**[2]

04 **5** 2¼ **Bongrace (IRE)**[14] 3548 2-9-0 0 .... KevinStott 9 61
(Kevin Ryan) *hld up bhd ldng gp: rdn along over 2f out: hung rt over 1f out: kpt on fnl f: no imp* **12/1**[3]

0 **6** 5 **Lil's Affair (IRE)**[37] 2771 2-9-0 0 .... TomEaves 5 48
(Bryan Smart) *hld up in tch: hdwy and prom over 2f out: rdn and wknd over 1f out* **33/1**

7 2¾ **Our Lois (IRE)** 2-9-0 0 .... PhillipMakin 6 41
(Keith Dalgleish) *s.i.s: bhd: drvn and outpcd over 3f out: n.d after* **16/1**

8 3½ **Dreamorchid (IRE)** 2-9-0 0 .... JasonHart 8 32
(Tim Easterby) *s.i.s: hld up: pushed along and outpcd over 3f out: n.d after* **25/1**

9 2¼ **Davinci Dawn** 2-9-0 0 .... PJMcDonald 4 26
(Ann Duffield) *t.k.h: hld up in tch: drvn and outpcd over 2f out: sn wknd* **16/1**

1m 31.19s (4.09) **Going Correction** +0.325s/f (Good) 9 Ran SP% **119.5**
Speed ratings (Par 91): **89,88,86,85,83 77,74,70,67**
CSF £295.51 TOTE £19.90: £4.10, £3.80, £1.10; EX 209.00 Trifecta £975.50.
Owner Global Racing Club & Mrs E Burke **Bred** San Gabriel Inv Inc & R Geringer **Trained** Middleham Moor, N Yorks

FOCUS
The race was run over 6yds further than advertised. A fillies' maiden run at a fairly sedate pace that might be a decent standard.

4038 APOLLOBET DAILY RACING REFUNDS H'CAP 1m 1f
5:15 (5:15) (Class 5) (0-70,77) 3-Y-O+ **£2,911** (£866; £432; £216) **Stalls** Low

Form RPR

2662 **1** **Freight Train (IRE)**[5] 3883 4-10-0 **70** ....(p) FrannyNorton 9 82
(Mark Johnston) *trckd ldrs: wnt 2nd 4f out: led gng wl over 2f out: shkn up and clr over 1f out: kpt on wl: unchal* **9/4**[2]

-055 **2** 4 **Weapon Of Choice (IRE)**[36] 2526 8-9-8 **67** .....(tp) MissEmmaSayer(3) 2 71
(Dianne Sayer) *in tch: rdn and hdwy to chse wnr over 1f out: kpt on fnl f: nt pce to chal* **16/1**

6060 **3** 1 **Tectonic (IRE)**[5] 3883 7-9-7 **63** ....(v) PhillipMakin 1 65
(Keith Dalgleish) *t.k.h: hld up in tch: effrt and edgd rt over 1f out: kpt on ins fnl f* **25/1**

5133 **4** 1¼ **Ghostly Arc (IRE)**[29] 3012 4-9-6 **62** .... BarryMcHugh 6 61
(Noel Wilson) *led: rdn and hdd over 2f out: lost 2nd and no ex over 1f out* **7/1**[3]

2-06 **5** 1¼ **Paddy's Rock (IRE)**[14] 3563 5-9-6 **62** .... JackGarritty 3 59
(Lynn Siddall) *hld up in tch: hdwy on outside over 3f out: rdn and no imp over 1f out* **14/1**

0-40 **6** 6 **Remember Rocky**[31] 2959 7-9-9 **65** ....(p) TomEaves 4 49
(Lucy Normile) *chsd ldr to 4f out: rdn and wknd over 1f out* **28/1**

0000 **7** ½ **Moccasin (FR)**[31] 2958 7-8-12 **54** ....(v) PJMcDonald 10 37
(Geoffrey Harker) *hld up in tch: effrt and pushed along over 3f out: wknd over 1f out* **16/1**

0011 **8** 3 **Indian Chief (IRE)**[5] 3901 6-10-2 **77** 12ex .... AdamMcNamara(5) 8 54
(Rebecca Bastiman) *s.i.s: t.k.h in rr: rdn over 2f out: edgd lft and sn wknd* **11/8**[1]

40-0 **9** 20 **Edas**[42] 2616 14-8-9 **51** oh4 .... AndrewMullen 7
(Thomas Cuthbert) *hld up: drvn and struggling 3f out: sn wknd: t.o* **100/1**

431- **10** 1¾ **Wolf Heart (IRE)**[368] 3932 8-8-9 **51** oh3 .... KevinStott 5
(Lucy Normile) *hld up in midfield: pushed along fr 1/2-way: drvn on outside over 3f out: wknd over 2f out: t.o* **33/1**

1m 59.22s (1.62) **Going Correction** +0.325s/f (Good) 10 Ran SP% **115.0**
Speed ratings (Par 103): **105,101,100,99,98 93,92,89,72,70**
CSF £35.41 CT £732.28 TOTE £3.20: £1.40, £3.50, £4.20; EX 43.00 Trifecta £518.00.
Owner M B Spence **Bred** Rozelle Bloodstock **Trained** Middleham Moor, N Yorks

FOCUS
The race was run over 12yds further than advertised. A moderate handicap lacking depth but run at a good pace. The winner is rated back to his 3yo form.
T/Plt: £16.80 to a £1 stake. Pool: £33,180.18. 1,435.20 winning tickets. T/Qpdt: £6.00 to a £1 stake. Pool: £2,684.80. 329.80 winning tickets. **Richard Young**

3844 DONCASTER (L-H)
Thursday, July 7

OFFICIAL GOING: Good (good to firm in places; 7.0)
Wind: Moderate, against Weather: Cloudy

4039 WE-FIT! WORKSOP'S INSULATED CONSERVATORY ROOFING SYSTEMS H'CAP 5f
2:20 (2:20) (Class 5) (0-75,73) 3-Y-O+ **£3,881** (£1,155; £577; £288) **Stalls** Low

Form RPR

4232 **1** **Flash City (ITY)**[10] 3709 8-9-9 **70** .... JamesSullivan 8 78
(Ruth Carr) *hld up in rr: hdwy 2f out: chsd ldrs whn n.m.r over 1f out: rdn to chal and n.m.r ins fnl f: drvn and kpt on to ld nr line* **7/2**[1]

1312 **2** shd **Seamster**[6] 3843 9-8-13 **67** 6ex ....(t) CameronNoble(7) 4 74
(David Loughnane) *trckd ldrs: hdwy 2f out: led over 1f out: jnd and rdn ins fnl f: sn drvn and edgd rt: hdd and no ex nr line* **4/1**[2]

1010 **3** 1¾ **Razin' Hell**[48] 2416 5-9-6 **67** ....(v) MartinHarley 5 68
(John Balding) *trckd ldrs: hdwy wl over 1f out: rdn to chal ins fnl f: sn drvn and edgd lft: kpt on same pce* **16/1**

5303 **4** 2 **Groundworker (IRE)**[10] 3713 5-9-5 **66** .... PaulMulrennan 9 60
(Paul Midgley) *prom: rdn along wl over 1f out: drvn and kpt on same pce fnl f* **4/1**[2]

012 **5** ½ **Dutch Archer**[17] 3471 3-9-4 **70** .... RichardKingscote 7 60
(Jeremy Gask) *hld up in rr: hdwy wl over 1f out: rdn and kpt on fnl f: nrst fin* **9/1**

0-41 **6** nk **Rainbow Orse**[24] 3217 4-9-7 **73** ....(p) AaronJones(5) 2 64
(Robert Cowell) *cl up: led 2f out: rdn and hdd over 1f out: grad wknd* **5/1**[3]

00-4 **7** shd **Loumarin (IRE)**[178] 146 4-8-9 **59** .... AlistairRawlinson(3) 3 49
(Michael Appleby) *trckd ldrs: rdn along over 2f out: grad wknd* **12/1**

1601 **8** 1 **Coiste Bodhar (IRE)**[23] 3268 5-8-11 **65** .... NatalieHambling(7) 6 52
(Scott Dixon) *sn led: rdn along and hdd 2f out: sn drvn and wknd* **12/1**

4165 **9** nk **Whitecrest**[16] 3487 8-9-9 **70** .... WilliamTwiston-Davies 10 56
(John Spearing) *chsd ldrs on outer: cl up 1/2-way: rdn along 2f out: sn wknd* **20/1**

59.75s (-0.75) **Going Correction** -0.05s/f (Good)
WFA 3 from 4yo+ 5lb 9 Ran SP% **114.9**
Speed ratings (Par 103): **104,103,101,97,97 96,96,94,94**
CSF £17.42 CT £195.80 TOTE £4.70: £1.30, £2.70, £3.90; EX 20.90 Trifecta £298.90.
Owner S R Jackson **Bred** G Riccioni Et Al **Trained** Huby, N Yorks

FOCUS
The ground had dried out quite a bit from previously forecast and was now good, good to firm in places (from good to soft, good in places). Rail on round course railed out from 1m2f to where it meets the straight, adding about 9yds to races 6 and 7. A modest sprint handicap in which they raced up the middle and it produced a tight finish. The winning rider said of the ground: "It's mainly good, but just a bit on the quick side. It will be good on the round course." The winner's best form since late last year.

4040 PATRICK MILES - MEEHAN IRISH STALLION FARMS EBF MAIDEN STKS 6f
2:50 (2:50) (Class 5) 2-Y-O **£3,881** (£1,155; £577; £288) **Stalls** Low

Form RPR

62 **1** **Waqaas**[41] 2649 2-9-5 0 .... DaneO'Neill 2 86+
(Charles Hills) *mde all: qcknd clr 2f out: readily* **8/15**[1]

0 **2** 2¼ **Used To Be**[27] 3112 2-9-5 0 .... JoeyHaynes 6 75
(K R Burke) *trckd ldrs: hdwy 2f out: sn rdn: styd on wl fnl f: no ch w wnr* **10/1**[3]

3 1½ **Double Touch** 2-9-5 0 .... DavidNolan 9 71+
(Richard Fahey) *hld up towards rr: hdwy over 2f out: chsd ldrs and swtchd lft over 1f out: sn rdn and kpt on fnl f* **10/1**[3]

4 **4** *nk* **Act Of Freedom (IRE)**[17] [3463] 2-9-5 0 HarryBentley 10 70
(Charlie Appleby) *cl up on outer: pushed along over 2f out: rdn wl over 1f out: kpt on same pce appr fnl f* **7/2**[2]

5 *3 ¼* **Third Order (IRE)** 2-9-5 0 FrederikTylicki 11 60
(K R Burke) *in tch on outer: green and pushed along 1/2-way: rdn wl over 2f out: kpt on fnl f* **18/1**

6 *nk* **George Reme (IRE)** 2-9-5 0 CamHardie 5 59
(John Quinn) *chsd ldrs: rdn 2f out: sltly hmpd over 1f out: one pce after* **20/1**

0 **7** *1 ½* **Can Can Dream**[22] [3290] 2-9-0 0 PaulMulrennan 1 50
(Olly Williams) *trckd ldrs: rdn along over 2f out: sn wknd* **100/1**

8 *1* **Chalieb** 2-9-0 0 WilliamTwiston-Davies 4 47
(Nigel Tinkler) *dwlt: a towards rr* **50/1**

9 *shd* **Knight Destroyer (IRE)** 2-9-5 0 WilliamCarson 8 52
(Jonjo O'Neill) *dwlt: a towards rr* **50/1**

0 **10** *½* **Reinstorm**[28] [3054] 2-9-5 0 GeorgeChaloner 7 50
(Richard Fahey) *chsd wnr: rdn along over 2f out: sn wknd* **33/1**

11 *1 ¾* **Out Of Order (IRE)** 2-9-5 0 JamesSullivan 3 45
(Tim Easterby) *t.k.h early: chsd ldrs: pushed along 1/2-way: sn rdn and wknd* **20/1**

1m 14.03s (0.43) **Going Correction** +0.10s/f (Good) **11** Ran SP% **128.3**
Speed ratings (Par 94): **101,98,96,95,91 90,88,87,86 84**
CSF £7.95 TOTE £1.40: £1.02, £3.30, £2.90; EX 7.20 Trifecta £50.80.
Owner Hamdan Al Maktoum **Bred** The Red Mischief Partnership **Trained** Lambourn, Berks

FOCUS
A maiden lacking depth, with the pair that had already shown ability dominating the market, and the hot favourite could hardly have done it any easier. They went over to race against the far rail this time.

4041 YORKSHIRE TILE COMPANY MAIDEN STKS 6f
3:25 (3:26) (Class 5) 3-Y-O+ **£3,881** (£1,155; £577; £288) **Stalls** Low

Form RPR

343 **1** **Edward Lewis**[14] [3572] 3-9-5 82 NickyMackay 5 85+
(John Gosden) *trckd ldr: hdwy to ld 2f out: rdn over 1f out: kpt on strly* **9/4**[2]

02 **2** *1 ½* **Excellent Sounds**[11] [3684] 3-9-0 0 FrederikTylicki 8 74
(Hughie Morrison) *trckd ldrs: hdwy over 2f out: rdn wl over 1f out: kpt on fnl f* **11/1**

33- **3** *hd* **Tanasoq (IRE)**[237] [7835] 3-9-5 0 DaneO'Neill 12 79
(Owen Burrows) *trckd ldrs: hdwy to chse wnr wl over 1f out and sn rdn: drvn and kpt on same pce fnl f* **2/1**[1]

4 **4** *2* **Noble Act**[44] [2561] 3-9-0 0 TedDurcan 1 67+
(Rae Guest) *t.k.h: hld up in tch: swtchd rt and hdwy wl over 1f out: kpt on fnl f: nrst fin* **25/1**

0 **5** *1 ¼* **Sea The Waves**[14] [3572] 3-9-5 0 JoeyHaynes 9 68
(Emma Owen) *chsd ldrs: pushed along 1/2-way: rdn 2f out: kpt on u.p fnl f* **200/1**

3 **6** *1 ½* **Dreaming Lady (IRE)**[111] [984] 3-9-0 0 MartinHarley 2 58
(James Tate) *chsd ldrs: rdn along 2f out: grad wknd* **9/2**[3]

6-5 **7** *shd* **Safe Voyage (IRE)**[13] [3609] 3-9-5 0 PaulMulrennan 14 63+
(John Quinn) *dwlt and in rr: hdwy wl over 1f out: kpt on fnl f* **11/1**

0-0 **8** *¾* **Fleeting Dream (IRE)**[23] [3267] 3-9-0 0 RichardKingscote 3 56
(William Haggas) *led: rdn along and hdd 2f out: sn wknd* **20/1**

9 *nk* **African Trader (USA)** 3-9-5 0 (t) DaleSwift 7 60
(Daniel Mark Loughnane) *dwlt and in rr tl sme late hdwy* **66/1**

0 **10** *nk* **Arrest Warrant**[13] [3609] 3-9-0 0 NathanEvans[(5)] 4 59
(Michael Easterby) *t.k.h: hld up towards rr: sme late hdwy* **40/1**

3 **11** *2* **Gift From God**[26] [3147] 3-9-0 0 DavidParkes[(5)] 11 52
(Hugo Froud) *t.k.h: hld up towards rr: hdwy on wd outside and in tch 1/2-way: rdn along over 2f out and sn wknd* **25/1**

6-0 **12** *2 ½* **Wright Patterson (IRE)**[13] [3609] 3-9-5 0 CamHardie 10 44
(John Quinn) *chsd ldrs: rdn along wl over 2f out: sn wknd* **80/1**

13 *12* **Mrs Frosty (IRE)** 3-9-0 0 JamesSullivan 13
(Clive Mulhall) *s.i.s: a bhd* **150/1**

1m 13.81s (0.21) **Going Correction** +0.10s/f (Good) **13** Ran SP% **117.7**
Speed ratings (Par 103): **102,100,99,97,95 93,93,92,91,91 88,85,69**
CSF £24.81 TOTE £3.40: £1.60, £2.20, £1.50; EX 21.50 Trifecta £82.90.
Owner C J Murfitt **Bred** Pantile Stud **Trained** Newmarket, Suffolk

FOCUS
This maiden was won by the high-class sprinters Muthmir in 2014 and Strath Burn last year. The majority of those that had already shown ability in this field had done so over longer trips, including the winner and second. Again they went far side. Juat an ordinary maiden, with a pb from the winner.

4042 PPM BARNSLEY FILLIES' H'CAP 1m (R)
3:55 (3:56) (Class 4) (0-85,84) 3-Y-O+ **£5,822** (£1,732; £865; £432) **Stalls** Low

Form RPR

42-1 **1** **Pirouette**[51] [2341] 3-8-5 75 CharlieBennett[(5)] 3 86+
(Hughie Morrison) *trckd ldrs on inner: smooth hdwy 2f out: nt clr run and swtchd rt over 1f out: rdn and styd on wl to ld last 75yds* **9/4**[2]

12 **2** *1 ¾* **Pure Art**[36] [2795] 3-9-2 81 RichardKingscote 5 87+
(Ralph Beckett) *trckd ldr: effrt over 2f out: rdn to chal whn rdr dropped reins appr fnl f: sn rcvrd and drvn to ld ins fnl f: hdd and no ex last 75yds* **11/8**[1]

4-21 **3** *¾* **Jawaayiz**[23] [3249] 3-8-10 75 DaneO'Neill 7 79
(Simon Crisford) *led: pushed along wl over 2f out: rdn wl over 1f out: drvn: n.m.r and hdd ins fnl f: kpt on* **7/1**

-035 **4** *2 ½* **Ninetta (IRE)**[22] [3291] 3-8-12 84 RowanScott[(7)] 4 82
(Ann Duffield) *t.k.h: trckd ldrs: hdwy 3f out: rdn along wl over 1f out: sn drvn and no imp* **20/1**

1620 **5** *hd* **Push Me (IRE)**[26] [3152] 9-9-4 81 JamieGormley[(7)] 1 81
(Iain Jardine) *hld up in rr: hdwy on inner 3f out: rdn along and sltly outpcd 2f out: kpt on fnl f* **25/1**

5-23 **6** *nk* **Volition (IRE)**[28] [3059] 3-9-1 80 TedDurcan 6 77
(Sir Michael Stoute) *hld up in rr: hdwy on outer over 2f out: rdn and edgd rt over 1f out: sn drvn and btn* **6/1**[3]

1m 39.7s **Going Correction** +0.15s/f (Good)
WFA 3 from 4yo+ 9lb **6** Ran SP% **108.3**
Speed ratings (Par 102): **106,104,103,101,100 100**
CSF £5.27 TOTE £3.00: £1.40, £1.40; EX 6.60 Trifecta £17.00.
Owner The End-R-Ways Partnership & Partners **Bred** The Lavington Stud **Trained** East Ilsley, Berks

FOCUS
A fair fillies' handicap with a 9yo taking on five 3yos. Although they seemed to go an even pace, it suited those ridden handily. The winner is progressing and the third helps with the level.

4043 BETHANY AND FAYE MANTERFIELD FILLIES' H'CAP 7f
4:30 (4:31) (Class 5) (0-75,75) 3-Y-O+ **£3,881** (£1,155; £577; £288) **Stalls** Low

Form RPR

3105 **1** **Bint Arcano (FR)**[24] [3213] 3-8-12 70 JacobButterfield[(3)] 3 77
(Julie Camacho) *trckd ldrs: hdwy 2f out: led appr fnl f: sn rdn and kpt on strly* **5/1**

1462 **2** *2* **Wowcha (IRE)**[14] [3567] 3-9-6 75 RichardKingscote 4 77
(John Quinn) *cl up: slt ld wl over 1f out: sn rdn and hdd appr fnl f: drvn and kpt on same pce fnl f* **2/1**[1]

6-00 **3** *nse* **Who's Shirl**[16] [3479] 10-8-9 56 AndrewElliott 10 61
(Chris Fairhurst) *in rr: sn outpcd and detached after 2f: hdwy on wd outside 2f out: rdn over 1f out: styd on and ch ins fnl f: kpt on same pce towards fin* **16/1**

1-00 **4** *2 ¾* **Cheeky Angel (IRE)**[15] [3521] 3-9-0 69 PaulMulrennan 9 63
(Michael Dods) *trckd ldrs: rdn along and sltly outpcd over 2f out: kpt on fnl f* **25/1**

3123 **5** *1* **Bajan Rebel**[10] [3708] 5-8-11 63 NathanEvans[(5)] 2 58
(Michael Easterby) *slt ld: rdn along and hdd wl over 1f out: grad wknd* **4/1**[3]

10-0 **6** *5* **Alpine Dream (IRE)**[40] [2674] 3-8-11 66 JamesSullivan 5 44
(Tim Easterby) *trckd ldrs: rdn along 2f out: sn drvn and wknd* **25/1**

-P33 **7** *3* **Nassuvian Pearl**[12] [3649] 3-9-3 72 FrederikTylicki 7 42
(Ralph Beckett) *dwlt: sn cl up: disp ld 2f out: sn rdn and wknd* **11/4**[2]

04-0 **8** *22* **Dear Bruin (IRE)**[7] [3807] 4-9-3 71 PaddyBradley[(7)] 6
(David W Drinkwater) *cl up on outer: pushed along 1/2-way: rdn 3f out: sn wknd* **33/1**

1m 26.17s (-0.13) **Going Correction** +0.10s/f (Good)
WFA 3 from 4yo+ 8lb **8** Ran SP% **113.2**
Speed ratings (Par 100): **104,101,101,98,97 91,88,63**
CSF £14.97 CT £146.34 TOTE £6.30: £1.80, £1.10, £4.30; EX 19.30 Trifecta £138.10.
Owner G B Turnbull Ltd **Bred** Rabbah Bloodstock Limited **Trained** Norton, N Yorks

FOCUS
A lesser fillies' handicap than the preceding race, but run at a fair pace thanks to a disputed lead. The form is rated around the second.

4044 YOUDAN TROPHY INTERNATIONAL FOOTBALL TOURNAMENT SHEFFIELD H'CAP 1m 4f
5:05 (5:05) (Class 4) (0-85,83) 3-Y-O+ **£5,175** (£1,540; £769; £384) **Stalls** Low

Form RPR

P/22 **1** **Ruwasi**[13] [3621] 5-9-13 82 MartinHarley 4 92+
(James Tate) *hld up in rr: hdwy on bit on inner over 2f out: led over 1f out: rdn ins fnl f: kpt on strly* **2/1**[2]

154 **2** *1 ¼* **Sam Missile (IRE)**[27] [3102] 3-9-1 83 FrederikTylicki 7 90
(James Fanshawe) *hld up in rr: hdwy over 2f out: n.m.r and swtchd rt over 1f out: sn rdn: chsd wnr and edgd lft jst ins fnl f: sn drvn and no imp* **6/5**[1]

-500 **3** *¾* **Multellie**[15] [3520] 4-9-12 81 JamesSullivan 5 87
(Tim Easterby) *trckd ldr: cl up 3f out: rdn along to ld briefly 1 1/2f out: sn hdd and drvn: kpt on same pce fnl f* **12/1**

210 **4** *3* **Tamayuz Magic (IRE)**[27] [3118] 5-9-5 79 (b) NathanEvans[(5)] 6 80
(Michael Easterby) *t.k.h: trckd ldrs: pushed along wl over 2f out: rdn wl over 1f out: sn drvn and one pce* **10/1**

44-1 **5** *1* **Snow Prince**[34] [2858] 5-9-1 77 (p) PaddyBradley[(7)] 2 77
(Steve Gollings) *set stdy pce: pushed along and qcknd 3f out: sn rdn: drvn and hdd 1 1/2f out: sn wknd* **8/1**[3]

0-00 **6** *8* **Cloud Monkey (IRE)**[23] [3263] 6-9-6 75 DavidNolan 1 62
(Martin Todhunter) *trckd ldng pair on inner: cl up 4f out: pushed along wl over 2f out: sn rdn and wknd* **28/1**

2m 35.64s (0.74) **Going Correction** +0.15s/f (Good)
WFA 3 from 4yo+ 13lb **6** Ran SP% **110.1**
Speed ratings (Par 105): **103,102,101,99,99 93**
CSF £4.55 CT £16.19 TOTE £2.90: £1.90, £1.20; EX 5.10 Trifecta £17.80.
Owner Saeed Manana **Bred** Highbury Terrace Owners Club **Trained** Newmarket, Suffolk

FOCUS
Rail movement added about 9yds to race distance. A fair handicap though a lopsided betting market. The pace looked ordinary but the first two came from the rear. The winner was close to his 3yo form.

4045 CARROLL, GRACE AND RADCLIFFE, SUNSHINE H'CAP (FOR AMATEUR RIDERS) 2m 110y
5:40 (5:40) (Class 5) (0-70,70) 4-Y-O+ **£3,743** (£1,161; £580; £290) **Stalls** Low

Form RPR

6454 **1** **Rosette**[25] [3190] 4-10-3 59 MrSWalker 5 64+
(Alan Swinbank) *hld up: hdwy over 3f out: chsd ldrs over 1f out and sn rdn: drvn ins fnl f: styd on wl to ld on line* **9/2**[2]

0-42 **2** *nse* **Sinbad The Sailor**[51] [1450] 11-10-3 62 (tp) MrJamesKing[(3)] 11 67
(George Baker) *in tch: hdwy on outer 6f out: trckd ldng pair 4f out: cl up 3f out: led 2f out: sn rdn and hdd over 1f out: drvn and styd on to ld last 50yds: hdd on line* **5/1**[3]

5-55 **3** *hd* **Bowdler's Magic**[18] [2916] 9-10-3 64 MrHHunt[(5)] 3 68
(David Thompson) *trckd ldrs: hdwy 3f out: rdn to ld over 1f out: sn drvn and edgd lft: hdd and no ex last 50yds* **14/1**

0253 **4** *1 ¼* **Medieval Bishop (IRE)**[26] [3139] 7-9-8 55 (p) MissPBridgwater[(5)] 1 58
(Tony Forbes) *trckd ldr: cl up over 5f out: disp ld 3f out: sn rdn and ev ch tl drvn and wknd appr fnl f* **14/1**

6020 **5** *2 ½* **Nashville (IRE)**[31] [2971] 7-10-1 57 MissCWalton 10 57
(Andrew Crook) *hld up towards rr: hdwy on outer over 3f out: rdn to chse ldrs wl over 1f out: sn drvn and kpt on same pce* **14/1**

225/ **6** *1 ¼* **Nafaath (IRE)**[26] [6514] 10-10-9 70 MissAMcCain[(5)] 6 68
(Donald McCain) *hld up and bhd: hdwy 3f out: rdn 2f out: no imp fnl f* **10/1**

0P44 **7** *shd* **Perennial**[10] [3704] 7-9-9 54 (p) MissJWalton[(3)] 8 52
(Philip Kirby) *in tch: pushed along and lost pl over 6f out: hdwy 3f out: rdn to chal 2f out: wknd appr fnl f* **16/1**

6010 **8** *shd* **Desktop**[28] [3067] 4-9-13 60 MrMEnnis[(5)] 7 58
(Antony Brittain) *led: jnd 4f out and sn rdn along: drvn and hdd 2f out: grad wknd* **10/1**

0501 **9** *11* **Balmusette**[19] [3417] 7-9-12 57 MissETodd[(3)] 9 42
(Keith Reveley) *trckd ldrs: effrt on inner over 3f out: rdn along wl over 2f out: sn drvn and wknd* **5/2**[1]

143- **10** *18* **Cavalieri (IRE)**[199] [8328] 6-10-3 62 (p) KaineWood[(3)] 4 25
(Philip Kirby) *midfield: hdwy and in tch 7f out: rdn along over 3f out: sn wknd* **14/1**

00-0 **11** 4½ **Madrasa (IRE)**[183] 71 8-9-8 **53**.........................(b) MissBeckySmith[(3)] 2 11
(Tony Forbes) *trckd ldrs on inner: rdn along over 5f out: sn wknd* **40/1**
3m 41.05s (0.65) **Going Correction** +0.15s/f (Good) **11** Ran SP% **116.6**
Speed ratings (Par 103): **104,103,103,103,102 101,101,101,96,87 85**
CSF £27.05 CT £292.60 TOTE £5.40: £1.40, £2.80, £3.00; EX 20.70 Trifecta £243.20.
Owner Guy Reed Racing **Bred** G Reed **Trained** Melsonby, N Yorks

FOCUS
Rail movement added about 9yds to race distance. A modest amateur riders' event run at just a fair pace, but a thrilling finish. The form makes sense.
T/Plt: £7.90 to a £1 stake. Pool: £47,035.49. 4,323.19 winning tickets. T/Qpdt: £2.90 to a £1 stake. Pool: £4,037.69. 1,013.83 winning tickets. **Joe Rowntree**

[3798]EPSOM (L-H)
Thursday, July 7

OFFICIAL GOING: Good (good to firm in places) (7.5)
Wind: Light, across Weather: Fine

4046 TADWORTH H'CAP 1m 2f 18y
6:10 (6:14) (Class 5) (0-75,74) 3-Y-O **£3,234** (£962; £481; £240) **Stalls** Low

Form RPR
6013 **1** **Sixties Groove (IRE)**[17] 3468 3-9-4 **71**..........................(p) JimCrowley 2 88+
(Jeremy Noseda) *nudged along in detached last early: gd prog on outer over 2f out: led over 1f out: hung lft but sn drew rt away: easily* **13/8**[1]
4214 **2** 7 **Panko (IRE)**[25] 3189 3-9-2 **69**.................................. MichaelJMMurphy 6 75+
(Ed de Giles) *trckd ldng pair: led over 2f out: rdn and hdd over 1f out: kpt on but no ch w wnr* **7/1**[3]
-610 **3** 3¼ **Pack It In (IRE)**[50] 2366 3-9-5 **72**...............................(b) DarryllHolland 8 69
(Brian Meehan) *trckd ldrs: cl 5th st: rdn over 2f out and sn wl outpcd: modest 3rd fr over 1f out* **10/1**
00-5 **4** nk **Mamoo**[20] 3357 3-8-7 **60**.. MartinLane 4 56
(Mike Murphy) *s.i.s: in tch: 6th st: rdn and no prog wl over 2f out: kpt on fnl f to press for 3rd nr fin* **10/1**
2522 **5** 1½ **Red Hot Chilly (IRE)**[64] 1961 3-9-7 **74**.................................... JFEgan 1 67
(Joseph Tuite) *led after 2f: rdn and hdd over 2f out: sn btn* **10/1**
3-00 **6** 2 **Cautious Optimism**[31] 2981 3-9-2 **72**..........................[1] RobHornby[(3)] 5 61
(William Muir) *led 2f: pressed ldr after: rdn and fnd nil over 2f out: sn wknd* **20/1**
5352 **7** nse **Jintshi**[5] 3876 3-9-3 **70**..(v[1]) RoystonFfrench 7 59
(Mark Johnston) *t.k.h: trckd ldrs: cl 4th st: rdn and wknd over 2f out* **7/2**[2]
-320 **8** 4½ **Brave Archibald (IRE)**[33] 2900 3-9-5 **72**........................ TomMarquand 3 52
(Paul Cole) *hld up in 7th: rdn and wknd 3f out: sn bhd* **7/1**[3]
2m 9.68s (-0.02) **Going Correction** +0.175s/f (Good) **8** Ran SP% **117.4**
Speed ratings (Par 100): **107,101,98,98,97 95,95,92**
CSF £14.23 CT £88.73 TOTE £2.60: £1.10, £2.80, £3.40; EX 14.40 Trifecta £102.10.
Owner Mrs Susan Roy **Bred** Minch Bloodstock **Trained** Newmarket, Suffolk

FOCUS
Rail out from 1m2f to winning post, adding 27yds to race distance. This was competitive enough for the grade.

4047 BRITISH STALLION STUDS EBF MAIDEN STKS 6f
6:40 (6:40) (Class 5) 2-Y-O **£3,881** (£1,155; £577; £288) **Stalls** High

Form RPR
322 **1** **Zamjar**[21] 3321 2-9-5 0.. JimCrowley 2 80
(Ed Dunlop) *pressed ldr: urged into narrow ld over 1f out: edgd lft ins fnl f: rdn and asserted last 100yds* **6/5**[1]
52 **2** 2½ **Three C'S (IRE)**[12] 3633 2-9-5 0.. JFEgan 7 73
(David Dennis) *led: hrd pressed fr over 2f out: hdd over 1f out: kpt on wl to press wnr tl sltly intimidated and no ex last 100yds* **3/1**[2]
00 **3** 6 **The Big Short**[25] 3196 2-9-5 0.................................. MichaelJMMurphy 6 55+
(Charles Hills) *plld hrd: chsd ldng pair: ill at ease on trck fr over 2f out and lft bhd: eased nr fin* **7/1**
4 nk **Neptunes Secret** 2-9-5 0.. SamHitchcott 1 54
(Sylvester Kirk) *dwlt: chsd ldng trio: shkn up and outpcd fr over 2f out: kpt on nr fin and nrly snatched 3rd* **11/1**
36 **5** 2½ **Book Of Poetry (IRE)**[50] 2358 2-9-5 0............................ RoystonFfrench 5 46
(Mark Johnston) *dwlt: racd in last: shkn up and struggling 3f out: sn no ch* **5/1**[3]
5 **6** 4½ **Time Down Under**[13] 3619 2-9-5 0................................. DarryllHolland 3 33
(Mark H Tompkins) *racd in 5th: rdn and wknd over 2f out* **33/1**
1m 11.08s (1.68) **Going Correction** +0.175s/f (Good) **6** Ran SP% **110.9**
Speed ratings (Par 94): **95,91,83,83,79 73**
CSF £4.83 TOTE £1.90: £1.20, £1.70; EX 3.90 Trifecta £10.30.
Owner Abdullah Saeed Al Naboodah **Bred** Manor Farm Stud (rutland) **Trained** Newmarket, Suffolk

FOCUS
Rail out from 1m2f to winning post, adding 16yds to race distance. A fair maiden run at a sound pace. The front two finished clear.

4048 TPA GOING THE EXTRA FURLONG H'CAP 1m 114y
7:10 (7:10) (Class 4) (0-85,85) 3-Y-O+ **£5,175** (£1,540; £769; £384) **Stalls** Low

Form RPR
3511 **1** **Bastille Day**[15] 3523 4-10-0 **85**.. DarryllHolland 4 95+
(David Elsworth) *hld up in 5th: stdy prog on outer over 2f out: rdn to ld 1f out: hld on wl* **7/2**[2]
-523 **2** nk **The Salmon Man**[24] 3234 4-9-1 **72**...................................... JimCrowley 1 81+
(Brendan Powell) *hld up in 6th: pushed along and waiting for room over 2f out: clsd over 1f out: squeezed through to chse wnr last 100yds: styd on but jst hld* **11/4**[1]
3002 **3** 1 **Hail Cladius (IRE)**[8] 3783 4-9-12 **83**.............................. TomMarquand 8 90
(Richard Hannon) *hld up in 4th: prog to trck ldr jst over 2f out: sn chalng: drvn and upsides 1f out: kpt on same pce* **7/2**[2]
4550 **4** 3¼ **Cordite (IRE)**[15] 3534 5-9-10 **81**....................................... SamHitchcott 2 81
(Jim Boyle) *t.k.h: trckd ldng pair: rdn 3f out: styd in tch tl fdd over 1f out* **9/1**[3]
1-04 **5** ½ **Dream Of Summer (IRE)**[15] 3523 3-8-8 **75**........................ MartinLane 3 72
(Andrew Balding) *led: hrd pressed fr 2f out: hdd & wknd 1f out* **7/2**[2]
5006 **6** 9 **Forceful Appeal (USA)**[78] 1576 8-9-8 **79**................................ JFEgan 5 57
(Simon Dow) *hld up in last: rdn and no prog wl over 2f out: sn wknd* **20/1**
-600 **7** ½ **Powderhorn (IRE)**[15] 3523 3-8-10 **77**......................... RoystonFfrench 6 53
(Mark Johnston) *chsd ldr to jst over 2f out: wknd qckly* **16/1**
1m 46.26s (0.16) **Going Correction** +0.175s/f (Good)
WFA 3 from 4yo+ 10lb **7** Ran SP% **114.0**
Speed ratings (Par 105): **106,105,104,101,101 93,93**
CSF £13.48 CT £34.91 TOTE £4.00: £1.80, £1.80; EX 12.40 Trifecta £20.20.
Owner Lordship Stud & David Elsworth **Bred** New England Stud And Partners **Trained** Newmarket, Suffolk

FOCUS
Rail out from 1m2f to winning post, adding 27yds to race distance. This interesting handicap was run at a decent pace. The first two are on the up.

4049 TOWERGATE INSURING THE WIN LADIES' DERBY H'CAP (FOR LADY AMATEUR RIDERS) 1m 4f 10y
7:45 (7:45) (Class 4) (0-80,80) 4-Y-O+ **£4,991** (£1,548; £773; £387) **Stalls** Centre

Form RPR
0-03 **1** **Tapis Libre**[26] 3162 8-10-9 **79**..............................(p) MissJoannaMason 5 87
(Jacqueline Coward) *mde all: shkn up over 2f out: kpt on wl and in command fr over 1f out* **5/2**[1]
1415 **2** 1¼ **Sureness (IRE)**[20] 3352 6-10-5 **80**.........................(t) MissCRobinson[(5)] 1 85
(Charlie Mann) *dwlt: trckd ldrs: cl 4th st: shkn up to chse wnr wl over 1f out: kpt on but nvr able to chal* **5/1**[3]
0-63 **3** 1½ **Sunday Royal (FR)**[47] 2463 4-10-0 **73**.......................... MissPFuller[(3)] 4 76
(Harry Dunlop) *sn chsd wnr: shkn up and lost 2nd wl over 1f out: one pce after* **5/1**[3]
310/ **4** nse **Zamoyski**[482] 8327 6-10-4 **77**......................................(p) MissAWaugh[(3)] 8 80
(Steve Gollings) *awkward s: prom: cl 3rd st: shkn up over 2f out: kpt on one pce fr over 1f out* **12/1**
1231 **5** 2½ **My Lord**[31] 2977 8-9-11 **72**.. MissMBryant[(5)] 2 71
(Paddy Butler) *slowly away: detached early: last tl wnt 7th over 4f out: brought wd in st: pushed along and kpt on but nvr gng pce to threaten* **20/1**
310- **6** ½ **Syncopate**[232] 7893 7-10-10 **80**...................................... MissGAndrews 7 78
(Pam Sly) *in tch: cl 6th st: rdn and no imp on ldrs fr over 2f out* **7/1**
4002 **7** 2¼ **Saint Honore**[14] 3560 4-9-11 **67**................................ MissSBrotherton 3 61
(Pat Phelan) *trckd ldrs: 5th st: no prog and lost pl over 2f out: n.d after* **4/1**[2]
1460 **8** ½ **Bayan Kasirga (IRE)**[12] 3636 6-9-12 **73**.............. MissEmilyBullock[(5)] 6 66
(Richard Fahey) *dwlt: a in rr: last st: no prog fnl 2f* **8/1**
2m 43.62s (4.72) **Going Correction** +0.175s/f (Good) **8** Ran SP% **118.0**
Speed ratings (Par 105): **91,90,89,89,87 87,85,85**
CSF £15.85 CT £58.86 TOTE £3.40: £1.30, £1.90, £1.70; EX 17.70 Trifecta £81.30.
Owner Mrs Susan E Mason **Bred** Sedgecroft Stud **Trained** Dalby, North Yorks

FOCUS
Rail out from 1m2f to winning post, adding 27yds to race distance. A fair handicap, confined to lady amateur riders, run at a steady pace. The winner is rated back to last year's level.

4050 LANDLORD INVESTMENT SHOW H'CAP 1m 2f 18y
8:20 (8:20) (Class 5) (0-75,74) 4-Y-O+ **£3,234** (£962; £481; £240) **Stalls** Low

Form RPR
4-50 **1** **Thames Knight**[14] 3557 4-9-7 **74**................................ RoystonFfrench 3 80+
(Marcus Tregoning) *led 1f: trckd ldrs: 3rd st: rdn 2f out: c between rivals to ld 1f out: jnd 100yds out: fnd ex* **11/4**[1]
-034 **2** nk **The Gay Cavalier**[14] 3582 5-9-2 **69**............................(t) JackMitchell 2 74
(John Ryan) *s.i.s: hld up in last: prog on outer over 2f out: clsd to take 2nd ins fnl f and sn jnd wnr: nt qckn last strides* **5/1**
0-05 **3** 2¾ **Topamichi**[7] 3802 6-9-6 **73**.. DarryllHolland 5 73
(Mark H Tompkins) *hld up: t.k.h and quick prog to trck ldr 7f out: rdn to chal and upsides 2f out to 1f out: fdd* **13/2**
-016 **4** nk **Fearless Lad (IRE)**[19] 3402 6-8-8 **61**.................................. KierenFox 1 60
(John Best) *hld up in tch: 5th st: shkn up and no prog over 2f out: kpt on ins fnl f: nrly tk 3rd* **7/1**
1440 **5** ¾ **Celtic Ava (IRE)**[24] 3230 4-8-6 **59**... JFEgan 6 56
(Pat Phelan) *hld up in tch: 6th st: shkn up and prog fr 3f out: chal and upsides 2f out to 1f out: wknd* **4/1**[3]
05- **6** 1¼ **Zarawi (IRE)**[30] 4298 5-8-11 **64**............................. MichaelJMMurphy 7 59
(John Gallagher) *trckd ldrs: 4th st: rdn 3f out: lost pl over 2f out: hanging and no prog after* **14/1**
0302 **7** nk **Firestorm (GER)**[7] 3801 5-9-6 **73**.. JoeFanning 8 67
(Michael Attwater) *led after 1f: jnd 2f out: hdd & wknd 1f out* **7/2**[2]
2m 12.56s (2.86) **Going Correction** +0.175s/f (Good) **7** Ran SP% **118.1**
Speed ratings (Par 103): **95,94,92,92,91 90,90**
CSF £17.75 CT £82.66 TOTE £3.50: £1.60, £2.80; EX 17.90 Trifecta £91.00.
Owner R C C Villers **Bred** Mr & Mrs A E Pakenham **Trained** Whitsbury, Hants

FOCUS
Rail out from 1m2f to winning post, adding 27yds to race distance. The pace was steady for this open handicap. There was not a great deal of depth to the race.

4051 LEADING START TO FINISH H'CAP 6f
8:50 (8:50) (Class 4) (0-85,85) 3-Y-O+ **£5,175** (£1,540; £769; £384) **Stalls** High

Form RPR
3263 **1** **Upstaging**[24] 3233 4-9-4 **77**...(b) TomMarquand 7 85
(Paul Cole) *prom: wnt 2nd st: rdn 2f out: clsd and drvn ahd last 150yds: styd on wl* **7/2**[1]
6-00 **2** 1 **Morache Music**[20] 3358 8-9-9 **85**............................. DanielMuscutt[(3)] 4 90
(Patrick Chamings) *chsd ldrs: 4th st: rdn 2f out: styd on wl last 150yds to take 2nd nr fin* **9/1**
4213 **3** nk **Pettochside**[32] 2931 7-8-9 **75**....................................... MitchGodwin[(7)] 8 79
(John Bridger) *led: rdn 2f out: hdd 150yds out: no ex and lost 2nd nr fin* **7/2**[1]
2220 **4** shd **Straits Of Malacca**[7] 3803 5-8-11 **70**.................................(p) JFEgan 9 74
(Simon Dow) *dwlt: t.k.h: hld up bhd ldrs: stmbld 4f out: 5th st: effrt over 2f out: nt qckn over 1f out: styd on ins fnl f to press for a pl last 100yds* **14/1**
0-05 **5** 2½ **Bahamian Heights**[28] 3068 5-9-7 **80**.................................. JimCrowley 10 76
(Robert Cowell) *s.v.s: hld up in last: effrt on outer over 2f out: kpt on one pce and nvr able to rch ldrs* **8/1**
3-05 **6** hd **Force (IRE)**[26] 3130 3-9-1 **80**................................... MichaelJMMurphy 2 74
(Charles Hills) *dwlt: hld up: 7th st: no prog over 2f out and sn dropped to last: kpt on again nr fin* **6/1**[3]
0530 **7** hd **Plagiarism (USA)**[14] 3573 3-9-2 **81**.. JoeFanning 6 75
(Mark Johnston) *chsd ldr tl st: styd disputing 2nd pl to 2f out: fdd over 1f out* **8/1**
2-00 **8** 1 **Art Collection (FR)**[11] 3689 3-9-0 **84**.......................(b) HectorCrouch[(5)] 3 75
(Gary Moore) *a in rr: no prog over 2f out: hanging and wl hld after* **16/1**
0644 **9** 1 **Swiss Cross**[21] 3320 9-8-4 **66** oh2......................(bt) JosephineGordon[(3)] 1 54
(Phil McEntee) *hld up: 6th st: shkn up and no imp 2f out: fdd over 1f out* **5/1**[2]
1m 10.63s (1.23) **Going Correction** +0.175s/f (Good)
WFA 3 from 4yo+ 6lb **9** Ran SP% **120.2**
Speed ratings (Par 105): **98,96,96,96,92 92,92,90,89**
CSF £37.70 CT £120.75 TOTE £4.40: £1.60, £3.30, £1.20; EX 35.60 Trifecta £193.30.
Owner H R H Sultan Ahmad Shah **Bred** Glebe Stud **Trained** Whatcombe, Oxon

FOCUS
Rail out from 1m2f to winning post, adding 16yds to race distance. A competitive handicap run at a sound pace. The winner is rated to a better view of his previous efforts from this sort of mark.

T/Plt: £15.90 to a £1 stake. Pool: £59,351.81. 2,715.22 winning tickets. T/Qpdt: £7.30 to a £1 stake. Pool: £4,575.74. 462.30 winning tickets. **Jonathan Neesom**

3811 NEWBURY (L-H)
Thursday, July 7

OFFICIAL GOING: Good to firm
Wind: light breeze, across Weather: overcast

4052 SODOTSO.COM GENTLEMEN AMATEUR RIDERS' H'CAP 1m 2f 6y
6:00 (6:00) (Class 5) (0-70,70) 3-Y-O+ **£3,119** (£967; £483; £242) **Stalls** Low

Form RPR

-053 **1** **Silver Alliance**[28] 3064 8-10-9 **65**....................(b) MrRBirkett 5 73
(Julia Feilden) *hld up bhd ldrs: hdwy over 2f out: sn rdn: r.o wl fnl f: led fnl 75yds* **10/3**[2]

2205 **2** *nk* **Thecornishbarron (IRE)**[28] 3077 4-10-11 **70**........ MrShaneQuinlan(3) 1 77
(John Ryan) *trckd ldr: chal 4f out: rdn to ld jst over 2f out: kpt on: hdd fnl 75yds* **11/2**

-521 **3** *1* **Smoky Hill (IRE)**[7] 3825 7-10-2 **58**.................... MrAlexEdwards 2 63
(Tony Carroll) *in tch: hdwy 3f out: rdn 2f out: kpt on wl to go cl 3rd fnl 120yds* **15/8**[1]

0-40 **4** *¾* **Westerly**[15] 3528 5-9-11 **58**.................... MrJDoe(5) 4 62
(Luke Dace) *led: rdn 3f out: hdd jst over 2f out: kpt on chsng ldr tl no ex fnl 120yds* **12/1**

406- **5** *2 ¼* **Unison (IRE)**[18] 7347 6-10-9 **68**.................... RobertHawker(3) 8 67
(Jeremy Scott) *racd keenly: trckd ldrs: effrt over 2f out: kpt on but nt pce to mount chal* **9/2**[3]

0-00 **6** *5* **Royal Etiquette (IRE)**[28] 3072 9-9-11 **56**...........(vt) MrAlexFerguson(3) 6 45
(Lawney Hill) *s.i.s: sn trcking ldrs: effrt 3f out: wknd over 1f out* **25/1**

4126 **7** *3 ¼* **Cahar Fad (IRE)**[122] 862 4-9-8 **57**....................(bt) MrSHawkins(7) 7 40
(Steph Hollinshead) *stdd s: effrt over 3f out: nvr threatened: wknd 2f out* **12/1**

2m 15.5s (6.70) **Going Correction** -0.025s/f (Good) **7** Ran SP% **110.7**
Speed ratings (Par 103): **72,71,70,70,68 64,61**
CSF £20.32 CT £40.33 TOTE £3.40: £2.00, £2.90; EX 20.10 Trifecta £57.50.
Owner In It To Win Partnership **Bred** Peter Harris **Trained** Exning, Suffolk

FOCUS
The going was given as good to firm (no GoingStick reading avaliable). The rail had been moved out on the back straight to give a fresh line. The 8f bend had been moved out 10yds to give an extra 14yds. The 5f bend had been set 5yds out. Race distance increased by 19yds. This modest event was run at a steady early gallop and they finished in a bit of a heap. The winner fpouns something on the form of his latest effort.

4053 MIRAGE SIGNS MAIDEN AUCTION STKS 6f 8y
6:30 (6:32) (Class 5) 2-Y-O **£3,234** (£962; £481; £240) **Stalls** Centre

Form RPR

322 **1** **Mr Hobbs**[17] 3472 2-8-5 0.................... EdwardGreatrex(3) 1 80
(Sylvester Kirk) *led: rdn and hdd over 1f out: rallied fnl 120yds: led fnl stride* **15/8**[1]

2 *nse* **Phijee** 2-8-7 0.................... DannyBrock(3) 13 82+
(William Muir) *s.i.s and hmpd: towards rr: smooth hdwy fr over 2f out: led over 1f out: sn rdn: kpt on: hdd fnl stride* **7/1**[3]

3 *3 ½* **Golden Eye** 2-7-13 0.................... MitchGodwin(7) 9 67
(Sylvester Kirk) *trckd ldrs: rdn over 1f out: kpt on but nt pce of front pair* **33/1**

0 **4** *shd* **Glory Of Paris (IRE)**[17] 3463 2-8-10 0.................... RyanTate 4 71
(Rod Millman) *mid-div: hdwy 2f out: sn rdn: kpt on fnl f but nt pce to get on terms* **33/1**

322 **5** *2* **Northern Thunder (IRE)**[42] 2611 2-8-13 0.................... PatCosgrave 15 68
(Richard Hannon) *trckd ldrs: rdn 2f out: kpt on same pce* **3/1**[2]

6 *¾* **Moi Moi Moi (IRE)** 2-8-6 0.................... JordanUys(7) 5 66
(Brian Meehan) *trckd ldrs tl rdn over 2f out: one pce fnl f* **10/1**

7 *¾* **Equal Rights** 2-8-8 0.................... AdamBeschizza 8 59
(Eve Johnson Houghton) *mid-div: rdn over 2f out: sn one pce* **16/1**

30 **8** *1 ¼* **Kings Heart (IRE)**[38] 2748 2-8-10 0.................... SteveDrowne 12 57
(Mark Usher) *awkward leaving stalls: towards rr: sme late prog: nvr trbld ldrs* **25/1**

00 **9** *¾* **Alligator**[7] 3819 2-8-3 0.................... GeorgeWood(7) 2 55
(Ed Dunlop) *mid-div: rdn over 2f out: fdd fnl f* **50/1**

10 *1 ¾* **Lord Cooper** 2-8-8 0....................(t) LemosdeSouza 7 47
(Jose Santos) *hld up towards rr: hdwy over 2f out: sn rdn: nvr threatened: fdd fnl f* **66/1**

0 **11** *1 ¾* **Charlie Victor**[43] 2583 2-8-8 0.................... JohnFahy 10 42
(Clive Cox) *trckd ldrs: rdn over 2f out: wknd over 1f out* **12/1**

12 *shd* **Lightoller (IRE)** 2-8-10 0.................... RonanWhelan 14 44
(Mick Channon) *mid-div: rdn over 2f out: wknd over 1f out* **25/1**

13 *shd* **Bismarck The Flyer (IRE)** 2-8-13 0.................... KieranO'Neill 3 46
(Richard Hannon) *mid-div tl wknd 2f out* **14/1**

14 *2 ¼* **Hisar (IRE)** 2-8-13 0.................... TadhgO'Shea 6 40
(Ronald Harris) *slowly away: rn green: a last* **25/1**

1m 12.97s (-0.03) **Going Correction** -0.025s/f (Good) **14** Ran SP% **122.5**
Speed ratings (Par 94): **99,98,94,94,91 90,89,87,86,84 82,82,81,78**
CSF £14.54 TOTE £2.60: £1.20, £2.60, £9.50; EX 17.50 Trifecta £370.60.
Owner Ciara Murphy & Partner **Bred** Card Bloodstock **Trained** Upper Lambourn, Berks

FOCUS
No more than a fair maiden.

4054 JOHNSONS STALBRIDGE LINEN SERVICES MAIDEN AUCTION FILLIES' STKS (PLUS 10 RACE) 6f 8y
7:00 (7:07) (Class 5) 2-Y-O **£3,234** (£962; £481; £240) **Stalls** Centre

Form RPR

20 **1** **Madam Dancealot (IRE)**[22] 3270 2-8-6 0.................... MartinDwyer 11 80
(Joseph Tuite) *trckd ldr: led ent fnl f: r.o wl: readily* **10/3**[3]

3 **2** *2 ¾* **Ariena (IRE)**[30] 2997 2-8-6 0.................... JohnFahy 1 72
(Clive Cox) *trckd ldrs: led over 2f out: rdn and hdd ent fnl f: no ex fnl 120yds* **11/4**[1]

0 **3** *1 ¼* **Three Duchesses**[14] 3555 2-8-8 0.................... WilliamCarson 7 70+
(Michael Bell) *mid-div: hdwy over 2f out: rdn over 1f out: kpt on wl to go 3rd ins fnl f* **50/1**

4 *½* **Kiruna Peak (IRE)** 2-8-8 0.................... RonanWhelan 13 69+
(Mick Channon) *hld up towards rr: nt clr run whn swtchd rt 2f out: r.o strly fnl f: wnt 4th nring fin: improve*

5 *¾* **Wind In Her Sails (IRE)** 2-8-3 0.................... GeorgeWood(7) 9 68
(Giles Bravery) *in tch: hdwy over 2f out: rdn and ev ch over 1f out: no ex ins fnl f* **16/1**

24 **6** *1 ¼* **Stop The Wages (IRE)**[14] 3555 2-8-3 0.................... JordanUys(7) 15 65
(Brian Meehan) *racd keenly: trckd ldrs: rdn and hung lft over 1f out: no ex fnl f* **7/1**

7 *¾* **Madeleine Bond** 2-8-8 0.................... DavidProbert 8 60
(Henry Candy) *towards rr: hdwy over 2f out: kpt on fnl f but nt pce to get on terms* **20/1**

8 *4* **Aureana** 2-8-6 0.................... OisinMurphy 3 46
(Ralph Beckett) *wnt rt s: towards rr: hdwy into midfield over 3f out: sn rdn: no further imp* **3/1**[2]

05 **9** *2 ¾* **Fanfair**[14] 3555 2-8-6 0.................... KieranO'Neill 12 38
(Richard Hannon) *rdn over 2f out: nvr bttr than mid-div* **28/1**

10 *5* **Kokanee Creek** 2-8-8 0.................... RyanTate 6 25
(Mark Usher) *s.i.s: a towards rr* **100/1**

11 *3 ¼* **Raze Aqlaam** 2-8-6 0.................... AdamBeschizza 4 13
(Giles Bravery) *slowly away and hmpd s: a towards rr* **100/1**

12 *2* **Miss Anticipation (IRE)** 2-8-13 0.................... JamesDoyle 5 14
(Roger Charlton) *wnt lft s: led tl over 2f out: wknd over 1f out* **10/1**

13 *1 ¼* **Miss Mayson** 2-8-10 0.................... RobertWinston 14 8
(Roger Teal) *s.i.s: towards rr: midfield 3f out: sn rdn: wknd jst over 1f out* **40/1**

14 *2 ¼* **Miss Salt** 2-8-3 0.................... DannyBrock(3) 2
(Dominic Ffrench Davis) *chsd ldrs tl wknd 2f out* **66/1**

34 **15** *15* **Dixie Peach**[8] 3770 2-8-3 0.................... EdwardGreatrex(3) 10
(Eve Johnson Houghton) *chsd ldrs tl wknd 2f out* **33/1**

1m 12.54s (-0.46) **Going Correction** -0.025s/f (Good) **15** Ran SP% **124.2**
Speed ratings (Par 91): **102,98,96,96,95 93,92,87,83,76 72,69,68,65,45**
CSF £12.28 TOTE £3.80: £1.50, £1.80, £7.30; EX 14.50 Trifecta £415.20.
Owner Mrs Olivia Hoare **Bred** Tally-Ho Stud **Trained** Lambourn, Berks

FOCUS
This fillies' maiden was run in a time 0.43sec faster than the colts managed in the previous maiden on the card.

4055 RELYON CLEANING NEWBURY H'CAP 1m 7y(R)
7:30 (7:39) (Class 4) (0-85,83) 3-Y-O+ **£6,469** (£1,925; £962; £481) **Stalls** Low

Form RPR

-154 **1** **Dubai's Secret**[14] 3574 3-9-5 **83**.................... KieranO'Neill 8 88
(Richard Hannon) *trckd ldrs: rdn to chal jst over 2f out: led ent fnl f: edgd rt: jst hld on* **10/1**

24-0 **2** *nse* **Laidback Romeo (IRE)**[26] 3157 4-10-0 **83**.................... RyanTate 12 92+
(Clive Cox) *wnt rt s: hld up: nt clr run fr 2f out tl swtchd rt jst over 1f out: rdn and r.o strly fnl f: jst failed* **9/1**

3224 **3** *¾* **Torch**[20] 3355 3-9-2 **80**.................... JamesDoyle 6 83
(Richard Hannon) *trckd ldrs: rdn 2f out: edgd lft but kpt on ins fnl f: wnt 3rd fnl 75yds* **8/1**

521 **4** *½* **Marbooh (IRE)**[13] 3609 3-9-2 **80**.................... AndreaAtzeni 3 82+
(Charles Hills) *disp ld tl def advantage over 2f out: rdn and hdd ent fnl f: no ex fnl 120yds* **9/2**[1]

1010 **5** *nk* **Jack Of Diamonds (IRE)**[28] 3061 7-9-11 **80**.................... RobertWinston 4 83
(Roger Teal) *trckd ldrs: rdn 2f out: kpt on ins fnl f* **14/1**

1-00 **6** *hd* **Jim Dandy**[27] 3110 3-9-0 **78**.................... WilliamTwiston-Davies 11 79
(Alan King) *hld up: hdwy 3f out: sn rdn: kpt on ins fnl f* **16/1**

-033 **7** *1* **Jimenez (IRE)**[28] 3066 3-8-12 **76**.................... OisinMurphy 5 74
(Brian Meehan) *disp ld tl rdn and narrowly hdd over 2f out: edgd lft and no ex ins fnl f* **7/1**

6-23 **8** *hd* **Loaded (IRE)**[40] 2686 3-9-4 **82**.................... DavidProbert 10 80+
(Andrew Balding) *mid-div: rdn over 2f out: no imp tl kpt on ins fnl f* **6/1**[3]

4411 **9** *½* **Marcano (IRE)**[15] 3514 4-9-7 **76**....................(t) GeorgeBaker 1 75+
(Rod Millman) *hld up: denied clr run fr 2f out and could nvr get involved* **11/2**[2]

0-65 **10** *4* **Welsh Gem**[41] 2636 4-9-3 **72**.................... JohnFahy 9 62
(Clive Cox) *mid-div on outer: rdn 3f out: wknd ent fnl f* **40/1**

5-06 **11** *1 ¼* **Plymouth Sound**[55] 2214 4-9-12 **81**....................(p) PatCosgrave 2 68
(Eve Johnson Houghton) *mid-div: rdn 3f out: wknd ent fnl f* **14/1**

510- **12** *1* **Inn The Bull (GER)**[270] 7142 3-9-2 **80**.................... FergusSweeney 7 62
(Alan King) *mid-div: rdn wl over 2f out: wknd ent fnl f* **20/1**

1m 37.96s (-0.74) **Going Correction** -0.025s/f (Good)
WFA 3 from 4yo+ 9lb **12** Ran SP% **117.0**
Speed ratings (Par 105): **102,101,101,100,100 100,99,99,98,94 93,92**
CSF £95.71 CT £771.80 TOTE £10.80: £3.20, £2.20, £2.70; EX 103.90 Trifecta £270.20.
Owner Saeed Manana **Bred** Mrs T A Foreman **Trained** East Everleigh, Wilts

FOCUS
Race distance increased by 5yds. This was steadily run early on and developed into a bit of a dash for home. They were bunched at the finish. A length pb from the winner.

4056 COMPTON BEAUCHAMP ESTATES LTD MAIDEN STKS 1m 2f 6y
8:05 (8:08) (Class 5) 3-Y-O **£3,234** (£962; £481; £240) **Stalls** Low

Form RPR

3 **1** **Frontiersman**[32] 2929 3-9-5 0.................... JamesDoyle 5 93+
(Charlie Appleby) *trckd ldrs: briefly pushed along 4f out: led over 2f out: in command fnl f: pushed out* **5/4**[2]

052 **2** *1 ½* **Makzeem**[26] 3160 3-9-5 83.................... GeorgeBaker 3 90+
(Roger Charlton) *trckd ldrs: rdn over 1f out: hanging lft whn chsng wnr ent fnl f: kpt on but a being hld* **11/10**[1]

0 **3** *1* **Dance The Dream**[15] 3535 3-8-7 0.................... TylerSaunders(7) 14 83
(Marcus Tregoning) *trckd ldrs: ev ch 2f out: sn rdn: kpt on same pce fnl f* **50/1**

3 **4** *8* **Torquay**[62] 2000 3-9-0 0.................... KieranO'Neill 1 67
(Harry Dunlop) *mid-div: hdwy over 2f out: wnt 4th over 1f out: styd on but nt pce to get on terms* **16/1**[3]

6 **5** *1 ½* **Novalina (IRE)**[13] 3601 3-9-0 0.................... PatCosgrave 8 64
(William Haggas) *mid-div: rdn over 2f out: styd on fnl f but nvr trbld ldrs* **25/1**

4 **6** *½* **Daily News**[29] 3028 3-9-5 0.................... AndreaAtzeni 10 68
(Roger Varian) *trckd ldrs: rdn over 2f out: sn one pce* **25/1**

7 *1* **Enmeshing** 3-9-5 0.................... TomQueally 6 66+
(James Fanshawe) *s.i.s: towards rr: hdwy 4f out: hung lft and one pce fnl 2f* **25/1**

8 *2* **Want The Fairytale** 3-9-0 0.................... JohnFahy 13 57
(Clive Cox) *s.i.s: bhd: struggling 4f out: nvr gng pce to get involved* **66/1**

0-0 **9** *½* **Sirdaal (USA)**[26] 3160 3-9-5 0.................... DavidProbert 7 61
(Owen Burrows) *sn led: rdn and hdd over 2f out: wknd over 1f out* **100/1**

5 **10** *nk* **Coeur De Lion**[15] 3535 3-9-5 0.................... FergusSweeney 9 60
(Alan King) *mid-div tl wknd 2f out* **25/1**

00 **11** *6* **Staplehurst (IRE)**[11] 3684 3-9-0 0.................... TimmyMurphy 2 43
(Geoffrey Deacon) *mid-div tl wknd 2f out* **100/1**

0 **12** *10* **Al Haffanah (IRE)**[71] 1798 3-9-0 0 OisinMurphy 11 23
(Richard Hannon) *slowly away: struggling 4f out: a towards rr* **50/1**
2m 7.13s (-1.67) **Going Correction** -0.025s/f (Good) **12** Ran SP% **120.7**
Speed ratings (Par 100): **105,103,103,96,95 95,94,92,92,91 87,79**
CSF £2.69 TOTE £2.30: £1.40, £1.02, £11.30; EX 3.00 Trifecta £70.80.

Owner Godolphin **Bred** Stanley Estate And Stud Co **Trained** Newmarket, Suffolk

■ Angrywhitepyjamas was withdrawn. Rule 4 does not apply.

FOCUS
Race distance increased by 19yds. The market had this as a two-horse race and, together with the third, they finished well clear of the rest. The winner has more to offer.

4057 DONNINGTON GROVE VETERINARY SURGERY H'CAP 1m 5f 61y
8:40 (8:40) (Class 5) (0-75,75) 3-Y-O+ **£3,234** (£962; £481; £240) **Stalls** Low

Form RPR
3503 **1** **Niceonecenturion**[28] 3063 3-8-10 **71** MartinDwyer 14 83+
(William Knight) *s.i.s: towards rr: hdwy 4f out: chal ins fnl f: styd on strly to ld fnl 75yds: rdn out* **4/1**[2]

0001 **2** *½* **Diamond Geyser (IRE)**[12] 3652 3-8-10 **71** AndreaAtzeni 10 82+
(Luca Cumani) *mid-div: hdwy fr 4f out: rdn to ld wl over 1f out: no ex whn hdd fnl 75yds* **1/1**[1]

0 **3** *4* **Brittleton**[49] 2392 4-10-0 **75** (b) JamesDoyle 6 80
(Harry Dunlop) *trckd ldrs: rdn to ld over 2f out: hdd wl over 1f out: styd on but no ex fnl f* **14/1**

50-0 **4** *nk* **Fix Up Look Sharp**[69] 1826 5-9-1 **62** CharlesBishop 5 67
(Jamie Poulton) *hld up: rdn 3f out: hdwy whn swtchd lft over 2f out: wnt 4th ent fnl f: styd on same pce* **50/1**

402 **5** *½* **Doesyourdogbite (IRE)**[12] 3636 4-9-12 **73** (p) GeorgeBaker 15 77
(Jonjo O'Neill) *mid-div: rdn and hdwy 2f out: styd on same pce fnl f* **8/1**[3]

10P- **6** *3½* **Meetings Man (IRE)**[273] 7064 9-9-13 **74** (p) PatCosgrave 8 73
(Ali Stronge) *mid-div: hdwy over 2f out: sn rdn: one pce fnl f* **50/1**

6565 **7** *2* **Gloryette**[23] 3251 3-8-10 **71** OisinMurphy 13 67
(Ed Dunlop) *trckd ldrs: rdn wl over 2f out: ch sn after: fdd fnl f* **10/1**

6521 **8** *4½* **Turnbury**[14] 3560 5-8-12 **64** (p) MeganNicholls(5) 4 53
(Nikki Evans) *disp ld tl clr ldr over 4f out: rdn and hdd over 2f out: wknd fnl f* **16/1**

5/06 **9** *6* **Vocaliser (IRE)**[14] 3570 4-9-9 **70** [1] WilliamTwiston-Davies 12 50
(Robin Dickin) *a towards rr* **25/1**

0-30 **10** *22* **Le Rock (IRE)**[68] 1852 4-9-10 **71** DavidProbert 3 18
(J S Moore) *disp ld tl rdn over 4f out: wknd 2f out: eased* **22/1**

/2-0 **11** *17* **Thundering Home**[9] 3747 9-8-2 **56** oh2 (t) GeorgeWood(7) 2
(Richard Mitchell) *s.i.s: sn mid-div: rdn over 3f out: wknd 2f out: eased* **33/1**

2m 50.19s (-1.81) **Going Correction** -0.025s/f (Good)
WFA 3 from 4yo+ 14lb **11** Ran SP% **117.8**
Speed ratings (Par 103): **104,103,101,101,100 98,97,94,90,77 66**
CSF £7.91 CT £49.11 TOTE £4.60: £1.80, £1.10, £2.90; EX 8.80 Trifecta £71.20.

Owner The Expendables **Bred** Meon Valley Stud **Trained** Patching, W Sussex

FOCUS
Race distance increased by 19yds. With the two leaders taking each other on, this was run at a sound gallop. The first two both progresed again.

4058 PREMIER FOOD COURTS H'CAP 7f (S)
9:10 (9:16) (Class 5) (0-75,75) 3-Y-O+ **£3,234** (£962; £481; £240) **Stalls** Centre

Form RPR
2233 **1** **Golden Wedding (IRE)**[14] 3554 4-9-10 **71** RobertWinston 3 79
(Eve Johnson Houghton) *trckd ldrs: rdn 2f out: kpt on wl fnl f: led fnl 100yds* **3/1**[1]

6013 **2** *nk* **Exceeding Power**[28] 3061 5-9-3 **71** GeorgeWood(7) 5 78
(Martin Bosley) *trckd ldr: rdn to chal over 1f out: narrow ld jst ins fnl f: hdd fnl 100yds: kpt on* **7/2**[2]

500 **3** *½* **Oat Couture**[28] 3070 4-9-1 **62** PatCosgrave 4 68
(Henry Candy) *led main gp in centre: overall chsd clr ldr: rdn to ld over 1f out: narrowly hdd jst ins fnl f: kpt on but no ex fnl 120yds* **20/1**

106 **4** *1½* **Summersault (IRE)**[34] 2846 5-9-5 **66** GeorgeBaker 12 68
(Jamie Osborne) *racd keenly: mid-div: hdwy 2f out: sn rdn: kpt on same pce fnl f* **13/2**

5000 **5** *¾* **Danecase**[41] 2650 3-9-6 **75** FergusSweeney 7 72
(David Dennis) *hld up: hdwy 2f out: sn rdn to chse ldrs: kpt on same pce fnl f* **8/1**

0000 **6** *2* **Siri**[15] 3521 3-9-3 **72** CharlesBishop 8 63
(Mick Channon) *hld up: rdn 2f out: r.o fnl f: nvr trbld ldrs* **16/1**

13-0 **7** *½* **Jan Steen (IRE)**[34] 2846 3-9-4 **73** OisinMurphy 6 63
(Denis Coakley) *mid-div: rdn 2f out: kpt on but nt pce to get on terms fnl f* **20/1**

4-06 **8** *1* **Captain Marmalade (IRE)**[24] 3233 4-9-7 **68** KieranO'Neill 2 58
(Jimmy Fox) *mid-div: rdn 2f out: nt pce to get involved* **33/1**

0200 **9** *2¾* **Live Dangerously**[7] 3802 6-9-7 **68** WilliamCarson 13 51
(John Bridger) *racd alone on stands' side: sn in clr ld: rdn and hdd over 1f out: sn wknd* **25/1**

40-0 **10** *1¼* **Meroula (FR)**[62] 2004 3-8-7 **65** EdwardGreatrex(3) 1 42
(Harry Dunlop) *trckd ldrs: rdn over 2f out: sn wknd* **50/1**

3-24 **11** *4* **Daring Day**[19] 3406 3-8-13 **68** AndreaAtzeni 11 34
(George Peckham) *a towards rr* **11/2**[3]

1m 25.18s (-0.52) **Going Correction** -0.025s/f (Good)
WFA 3 from 4yo+ 8lb **11** Ran SP% **111.2**
Speed ratings (Par 103): **101,100,100,98,97 95,94,93,90,88 84**
CSF £11.05 CT £149.12 TOTE £3.80: £1.40, £1.60, £5.80; EX 13.20 Trifecta £194.50.

Owner Mrs R F Johnson Houghton **Bred** Mrs R F Johnson Houghton **Trained** Blewbury, Oxon

■ Severus was withdrawn. Price at time of withdrawal 12-1. Rule 4 applies to all bets - deduction 5p in the pound.

FOCUS
A modest handicap, but it was fairly competitive.

T/Plt: £37.40 to a £1 stake. Pool: £60,338.36. 1,175.13 winning tickets. T/Qpdt: £6.60 to a £1 stake. Pool: £6,368.38. 710.99 winning tickets. **Tim Mitchell**

3661 NEWMARKET (R-H)
Thursday, July 7

OFFICIAL GOING: Good to firm (good in places) (stands' side 8.2, centre 8.0, far side 8.1)
Wind: light, half behind Weather: light cloud and bright spells

4059 BAHRAIN TROPHY (GROUP 3) 1m 5f
2:10 (2:15) (Class 1) 3-Y-O
£56,710 (£21,500; £10,760; £5,360; £2,690; £1,350) **Stalls** Centre

Form RPR
344 **1** **Housesofparliament (IRE)**[20] 3337 3-9-1 107 (t) RyanMoore 2 108
(A P O'Brien, Ire) *swtg: hld up in tch in midfield: effrt to chal over 2f out: drvn to ld over 1f out: styd on to forge ahd fnl 100yds: rdn out* **9/2**[3]

5-42 **2** *1½* **Platitude**[21] 3300 3-9-1 103 FrankieDettori 4 106
(Sir Michael Stoute) *chsd ldng pair: effrt to chal over 2f out: rdn to ld over 1f out: hdd over 1f out: stl ev ch tl no ex and one pce fnl 100yds* **7/2**[2]

-303 **3** *shd* **Harrison**[21] 3300 3-9-1 93 AndreaAtzeni 5 106
(Mick Channon) *chsd ldng trio: effrt to chal over 2f out: sn drvn: stl ev ch tl no ex ins fnl f: styd on same pce fnl 100yds* **14/1**

2112 **4** *nk* **Harbour Law**[20] 3341 3-9-1 102 GeorgeBaker 9 105
(Laura Mongan) *lw: chsd ldr: rdn to ld wl over 2f out: sn hdd but stl ev ch tl no ex ins fnl f: styd on same pce fnl 100yds* **10/1**

6-11 **5** *1¾* **Shabeeb (USA)**[33] 2889 3-9-1 100 PaulHanagan 7 103
(Roger Varian) *lengthy: hld up in tch in midfield: effrt to chal over 2f out: sn drvn: unable qck u.p over 1f out: 5th and kpt on same pce ins fnl f* **5/1**

0-01 **6** *nk* **Goldmember**[54] 2260 3-9-1 89 OisinMurphy 6 102
(David Simcock) *taken down early: stdd s: hld up in tch: effrt over 2f out: unable qck u.p: hld and kpt on same pce fr over 1f out* **25/1**

1526 **7** *4* **Gunnery (FR)**[20] 3341 3-9-1 98 JamieSpencer 8 96
(Peter Chapple-Hyam) *stdd s: hld up in tch in last pair: effrt to chse ldrs over 2f out: hung lft and no hdwy over 1f out: wknd and btn whn drifted bk rt ins fnl f* **25/1**

-222 **8** *11* **Prize Money**[21] 3296 3-9-1 107 JamesDoyle 3 80
(Saeed bin Suroor) *stdd s: t.k.h: hld up in tch in last pair: short-lived effrt over 2f out: no imp and wknd over 1f out* **9/4**[1]

4246 **9** *nk* **Race Day (IRE)**[21] 3296 3-9-1 98 MartinLane 1 79
(Saeed bin Suroor) *racd keenly: led: rdn and hdd wl over 2f out: sn lost pl: wknd over 1f out* **33/1**

2m 44.39s (0.39) **Going Correction** -0.15s/f (Firm) **9** Ran SP% **114.2**
Speed ratings (Par 110): **92,91,91,90,89 89,87,80,80**
CSF £19.93 TOTE £5.10: £1.60, £1.70, £4.00; EX 19.80 Trifecta £195.20.

Owner Derrick Smith & Mrs John Magnier & Michael Tabor **Bred** Smithfield Inc **Trained** Cashel, Co Tipperary

FOCUS
Stands' side course used. Stalls on far side except 1m4f and 1m5f, centre. Race distances as advertised. Dry overnight, the ground had been watered but was still on the fast side, with Frankie Dettori describing it as "beautiful". GoingStick readings were as follows: Stands' side 8.2, centre 8.0 and far side 8.1. No great gallop on early, with the pace only really increasing over 4f out. The form, however, looks fairly solid for the level, with the winner and fourth having run well in Group 2 and Listed events respectively at Royal Ascot and the second and third filling the same places in a good edition of the King George V handicap at the same meeting. The form seems sound enough.

4060 ARQANA JULY STKS (GROUP 2) (C&G) 6f
2:40 (2:42) (Class 1) 2-Y-O
£45,368 (£17,200; £8,608; £4,288; £2,152; £1,080) **Stalls** High

Form RPR
1122 **1** **Mehmas (IRE)**[23] 3243 2-9-0 0 FrankieDettori 8 111
(Richard Hannon) *lw: trckd ldng pair: rdn and hdwy to ld jst over 1f out: drvn and styd on wl ins fnl f: rdn out* **11/4**[1]

2 *½* **Intelligence Cross (USA)**[12] 3675 2-9-0 0 (t) RyanMoore 5 110
(A P O'Brien, Ire) *tall: stdd s: hld up in tch in rr: clsd 2f out: swtchd rt and hdwy u.p jst over 1f out: chsd wnr wl ins fnl f: styd on wl u.p: nvr quite getting to wnr* **7/1**

1 **3** *1* **Broken Stones (IRE)**[47] 2489 2-9-0 0 JamieSpencer 6 107
(Kevin Ryan) *tall: scope: hld up in tch in last trio: pushed along over 2f out: hdwy u.p over 1f out: chsd wnr ent fnl f: styd on same pce and lost 2nd wl ins fnl f* **8/1**

13 **4** *shd* **Silver Line (IRE)**[21] 3295 2-9-0 0 JamesDoyle 9 106
(Saeed bin Suroor) *hld up in tch in midfield: effrt 2f out: drvn to chse ldrs ent fnl f: styd on same pce fnl 150yds* **6/1**[3]

21 **5** *2½* **Medici Banchiere**[45] 2530 2-9-0 0 DougieCostello 3 99
(K R Burke) *lw: hld up in tch in midfield: swtchd rt and effrt ent fnl f: styd on steadily u.p ins fnl f: no threat to ldrs* **25/1**

41 **6** *shd* **Barrington (IRE)**[45] 2543 2-9-0 0 AndreaAtzeni 4 98
(Charles Hills) *tall: athletic: racd keenly: w ldr: rdn wl over 1f out: unable qck u.p ent fnl f: hung lft and btn jst ins fnl f: wknd fnl 100yds* **16/1**

13 **7** *1½* **Bohemian Flame (IRE)**[42] 2624 2-9-0 0 DavidProbert 2 94
(Andrew Balding) *lengthy: tall: hld up in tch in last pair: effrt 2f out: drvn and no imp over 1f out: kpt on ins fnl f: nvr threatened ldrs* **33/1**

110 **8** *1¼* **Yalta (IRE)**[23] 3243 2-9-0 0 JamesMcDonald 7 93
(Mark Johnston) *led: rdn wl over 1f out: hdd jst over 1f out: sn outpcd and losing pl whn squeezed for room and hmpd jst ins fnl f: wknd* **7/1**

11 **9** *nk* **Ardad (IRE)**[23] 3247 2-9-0 0 RobertHavlin 1 89
(John Gosden) *trckd ldng trio: rdn over 1f out: no rspnse and sn lost pl: wknd ins fnl f* **7/2**[2]

1m 10.92s (-1.58) **Going Correction** -0.15s/f (Firm) **9** Ran SP% **112.0**
Speed ratings (Par 106): **104,103,102,101,98 98,96,94,94**
CSF £21.46 TOTE £3.10: £1.30, £2.10, £2.40; EX 19.40 Trifecta £96.00.

Owner Al Shaqab Racing **Bred** Epona Bloodstock Ltd **Trained** East Everleigh, Wilts

FOCUS
A year ago this went to subsequent dual Group 1 scorer Shalaa. This looked a decent edition of this historic race, but they finished compressed and it's been rated an average renewal. They went a decent initial gallop and the time was half a second outside the standard.

4061 PRINCESS OF WALES'S ARQANA RACING CLUB STKS (GROUP 2) 1m 4f
3:15 (3:17) (Class 1) 3-Y-O+
£56,710 (£21,500; £10,760; £5,360; £2,690; £1,350) **Stalls** Centre

Form RPR
5-23 **1** **Big Orange**[68] 1863 5-9-2 114 (p) JamesMcDonald 5 119
(Michael Bell) *mde all: rdn 2f out: 2 l clr 1f out: styd on strly fnl f: nvr seriously chal: rdn out* **8/1**

36-4 **2** 2 1/2 **The Grey Gatsby (IRE)**[22] 3272 5-9-2 122 .... JamieSpencer 4 115
(Kevin Ryan) *stdd after s: hld up in 6th: clsd and nt clr run over 1f out: sn swtchd rt and hdwy to chse ldrs 1f out: styd on u.p to go 2nd wl ins fnl f: nvr threatening wnr* **11/4**[1]

3-10 **3** 1/2 **Exospheric**[19] 3384 4-9-5 119 .... RyanMoore 6 117
(Sir Michael Stoute) *t.k.h: hld up in 3rd: effrt to chse wnr 2f out: sn drvn: no imp and styd on same pce ins fnl f: lost 2nd wl ins fnl f* **4/1**[2]

2-14 **4** 3 1/2 **Battersea**[126] 811 5-9-2 104 .... AndreaAtzeni 1 109
(Roger Varian) *taken down early: stdd after s: hld up in tch in rr: effrt 2f out: kpt on to pass btn rivals ins fnl f: no threat to wnr* **16/1**

0-35 **5** 1/2 **Second Step (IRE)**[33] 2894 5-9-2 111 .... FrankieDettori 7 108
(Luca Cumani) *lw: sn chsng wnr: rdn 3f out: lost 2nd 2f out and unable qck u.p over 1f out: wknd ins fnl f* **9/2**[3]

0-12 **6** 3/4 **Elite Army**[20] 3340 5-9-2 109 .... JamesDoyle 3 107
(Saeed bin Suroor) *hld up in tch in 4th: effrt 2f out: sn drvn and unable qck: wknd ins fnl f* **4/1**[2]

13-4 **7** 6 **Muntazah**[56] 2190 3-8-3 105 .... PaulHanagan 2 97
(Owen Burrows) *swtg: stdd after s: t.k.h: hld up in 5th: effrt 2f out: unable ton qckn and lost pl over 1f out: wknd fnl f* **15/2**

2m 29.93s (-2.97) **Going Correction** -0.15s/f (Firm)
WFA 3 from 4yo+ 13lb **7** Ran SP% **113.6**
Speed ratings (Par 115): **103,101,101,98,98 97,93**
CSF £29.87 TOTE £8.90: £3.30, £1.70; EX 34.50 Trifecta £168.20.
Owner W J and T C O Gredley **Bred** Stetchworth & Middle Park Studs **Trained** Newmarket, Suffolk

FOCUS
Race distance as advertised. A good edition of this Group 2 prize. They raced in single file at an ordinary gallop for much of the contest, the pace really lifting over 4f out, and Big Orange made all for back-to-back wins in the race. He's been rated aas running a small pb, and could be worth more at face value.

4062 BETFRED MOBILE HERITAGE H'CAP 6f
3:45 (3:48) (Class 2) (0-105,101) 3-Y-O
£62,250 (£18,640; £9,320; £4,660; £2,330; £1,170) **Stalls** High

Form RPR

-112 **1** **Dancing Star**[26] 3165 3-9-2 **96** .... DavidProbert 3 108
(Andrew Balding) *lw: wl in tch in midfield: effrt to chse ldrs over 1f out: r.o wl u.p ins fnl f: led wl ins fnl f: rdn out* **7/1**[2]

5-05 **2** 3/4 **Priceless**[47] 2474 3-9-1 **95** .... AdamKirby 19 104
(Clive Cox) *taken down early: chsd ldr after 1f: rdn to ld 2f out: drvn over 1f out: hdd wl ins fnl f: styd on same pce after* **25/1**

51-3 **3** 3/4 **Bounce**[38] 2736 3-8-10 **90** .... FergusSweeney 9 97
(Henry Candy) *lw: chsd ldrs: effrt to chse ldr over 1f out: drvn and ev ch 1f out: unable qck ins fnl f: styd on same pce fnl 75yds* **8/1**[3]

041- **4** hd **Projection**[281] 6869 3-9-5 **99** .... GeorgeBaker 11 105+
(Roger Charlton) *taken down early: stdd after s: hld up towards rr: clsng and switching rt over 1f out: rdn and hdwy ins fnl f: styd on strly fnl 100yds: nt rch ldrs* **14/1**

-602 **5** nse **Mont Kiara (FR)**[19] 3413 3-8-9 **89** .... JamieSpencer 17 95+
(Kevin Ryan) *taken down early: stdd after s: hld up in rr: clsd 2f out: hdwy over 1f out: swtchd lft and effrt 1f out: styd on wl ins fnl f: nt rch ldrs* **33/1**

1-61 **6** nk **Taneen (USA)**[38] 2736 3-9-7 **101** .... PaulHanagan 14 106
(Roger Varian) *lw: hld up wl in tch in midfield: hdwy and rdn to chse ldrs 2f out: unable qck u.p 1f out: styd on same pce ins fnl f* **11/2**[1]

30-1 **7** 3/4 **Show Stealer**[54] 2251 3-8-12 **92** .... MartinDwyer 15 95
(Rae Guest) *lw: hld up in tch in midfield: effrt u.p over 1f out: sme hdwy 1f out: kpt on ins fnl f: nvr quite enough pce to rch ldrs* **10/1**

1-61 **8** 3/4 **Flying Pursuit**[22] 3292 3-8-10 **90** .... DavidAllan 20 90
(Tim Easterby) *in tch in midfield: effrt u.p over 1f out: drvn 1f out: styd on same pce and no imp ins fnl f* **25/1**

2350 **9** shd **Scrutineer (IRE)**[22] 3269 3-9-6 **100** .... OisinMurphy 7 100
(Mick Channon) *in tch in midfield: effrt and nt clrest of runs over 1f out: drvn and unable qck 1f out: kpt on same pce ins fnl f* **25/1**

5211 **10** 1/2 **Gunmetal (IRE)**[19] 3415 3-8-8 **88** .... MichaelJMMurphy 4 86
(Charles Hills) *lw: hld up in tch in midfield: effrt over 1f out: sme hdwy but wanting to hang lft 1f out: stl edging lft but kpt on ins fnl f: no threat to ldrs* **11/1**

-304 **11** 3/4 **Venturous (IRE)**[26] 3165 3-9-3 **97** .... JamesMcDonald 1 95+
(Charlie Appleby) *lw: hld up towards rr: effrt and nt clr run over 1f out: swtchd lft 1f out: kpt on ins fnl f: nvr trbld ldrs* **12/1**

0101 **12** 2 1/2 **Sign Of The Kodiac (IRE)**[19] 3413 3-8-12 **95** .... JoeDoyle(3) 8 83
(James Given) *led for 1f: chsd ldrs after tl unable qck and lost pl over 1f out: wknd ins fnl f* **25/1**

10-0 **13** nse **Strong Challenge (IRE)**[47] 2466 3-8-12 **92** .... JamesDoyle 5 80
(Saeed bin Suroor) *taken down early: dwlt: hld up towards rr: nt clr run wl over 1f out: swtchd lft and hdwy jst over 1f out: no ch w ldrs and eased wl ins fnl f* **16/1**

-445 **14** hd **Dhahmaan (IRE)**[26] 3158 3-9-6 **100** .... ColmO'Donoghue 16 87
(Marco Botti) *hld up in tch towards rr: effrt and hdwy over 1f out: edging lft and no hdwy 1f out: wknd ins fnl f* **25/1**

-040 **15** nk **Riflescope (IRE)**[26] 3165 3-8-13 **93** .... JoeFanning 10 79
(Mark Johnston) *hld up in tch in rr: nt clr run 2f out: effrt and no hdwy over 1f out: wknd ins fnl f* **20/1**

-420 **16** 1 1/4 **Madrinho (IRE)**[26] 3165 3-8-11 **91** .... PatDobbs 18 73
(Richard Hannon) *t.k.h: hld up in tch in midfield: effrt over 1f out: carried sltly lft and no hdwy 1f out: wknd ins fnl f* **33/1**

1-20 **17** nk **Light Music**[22] 3269 3-9-4 **98** .... RyanMoore 2 79
(William Haggas) *stdd s: hld up in rr: effrt 2f out: rdn and no imp over 1f out: bhd ins fnl f* **10/1**

1235 **18** 3/4 **Kadrizzi (FR)**[26] 3165 3-9-6 **100** .... RobertWinston 12 79
(Dean Ivory) *in tch in midfield: shuffled bk to rr and rdn wl over 1f out: no hdwy: btn and eased ins fnl f* **25/1**

1311 **19** 2 **A Momentofmadness**[25] 3193 3-8-11 **91** .... AndreaAtzeni 6 63
(Charles Hills) *t.k.h and nvr settled: led after 1f tl hdd 2f out: sn dropped out: bhd and eased ins fnl f* **16/1**

-556 **20** 9 **King Of Rooks**[19] 3413 3-9-7 **101** .... FrankieDettori 13 45
(Richard Hannon) *in tch in midfield: rdn 2f out: sn lost pl: bhd 1f out: eased ins fnl f* **25/1**

1m 10.51s (-1.99) **Going Correction** -0.15s/f (Firm) **20** Ran SP% **129.2**
Speed ratings (Par 106): **107,106,105,104,104 104,103,102,102,101 100,97,97,96,96 94,94,93,90,78**
CSF £179.45 CT £1485.60 TOTE £7.20: £2.10, £5.50, £2.50, £3.60; EX 227.30 Trifecta £4219.30.
Owner J C Smith **Bred** Littleton Stud **Trained** Kingsclere, Hants

FOCUS
Traditionally one of the hottest races of its type, this produced an Abbaye winner, Total Gallery, in 2009, and last year's scorer Magical Memory has been placed at the top level. They were spread out across the track, the winner racing near the stands' side, and there didn't seem to be any track bias. The first three home were fillies. The form has been rated slightly positively in line with the race standard.

4063 BRITISH STALLION STUDS EBF MAIDEN FILLIES' STKS (PLUS 10 RACE) (DIV I) 6f
4:20 (4:26) (Class 4) 2-Y-O
£6,469 (£1,443; £1,443; £481) **Stalls** High

Form RPR

6 **1** **Hawana (USA)**[35] 2817 2-9-0 0 .... JamesDoyle 4 76
(John Gosden) *mde all: rdn and fnd ex ent fnl f: in command and styd on wl fnl f: rdn out* **4/1**[2]

2 2 **Manama (IRE)** 2-9-0 0 .... JamesMcDonald 9 70+
(Charlie Appleby) *athletic: in tch in midfield: effrt and hdwy to chse ldrs jst over 1f out: kpt on ins fnl f but no imp on wnr* **7/1**

3 **2** dht **Texas Katie**[14] 3556 2-9-0 0 .... CharlesBishop 11 70
(Mick Channon) *leggy: taken down early: chsd ldrs: rdn to chse wnr over 1f out: unable qck w wnr ent fnl f: styd on same pce fnl 150yds* **8/1**

4 1 **Magical Dreamer (IRE)** 2-9-0 0 .... TomQueally 6 66+
(James Fanshawe) *str: lengthy: lw: s.i.s: in tch towards rr: effrt and swtchd lft wl over 1f out: hdwy and flashing tail jst ins fnl f: kpt on steadily wout threatening wnr* **5/1**[3]

5 shd **The Lacemaker** 2-9-0 0 .... JoeFanning 1 66+
(Ed Dunlop) *athletic: s.i.s: hld up in tch in rr: rdn and effrt jst over 1f out: kpt on steadily ins fnl f: no threat to wnr* **50/1**

6 1 3/4 **Copper Baked (FR)** 2-9-0 0 .... DougieCostello 8 60+
(K R Burke) *tall: chsd ldr tl unable qck u.p and lost pl over 1f out: wknd ins fnl f* **25/1**

7 1/2 **Believable** 2-9-0 0 .... RyanMoore 2 59+
(Sir Michael Stoute) *str: lw: hld up in tch in midfield: effrt and no imp over 1f out: kpt on same pce ins fnl f: nvr threatened ldrs* **5/2**[1]

8 1/2 **Arwa (IRE)** 2-9-0 0 .... AndreaAtzeni 10 57+
(Charles Hills) *str: lw: hld up in tch in midfield: rdn and hdwy over 1f out: 4th and no imp 1f out: wknd ins fnl f* **14/1**

9 1 **Snow Squaw** 2-9-0 0 .... JamieSpencer 3 56+
(David Elsworth) *tall: s.i.s: hld up in tch in rr: effrt over 1f out: edging lft and no real imp 1f out: btn whn nt clr run ins fnl f: eased wl ins fnl f* **11/2**

10 3/4 **Instigation** 2-9-0 0 .... AdamKirby 12 52
(Ed Dunlop) *unf: scope: in tch in midfield: effrt u.p over 1f out: no imp and btn 1f out: wknd ins fnl f* **50/1**

11 nk **Sun Angel (IRE)** 2-9-0 0 .... OisinMurphy 5 51
(Henry Candy) *str: lw: hld up in tch in midfield: effrt over 1f out: sn hung lft and no hdwy: wknd fnl f* **20/1**

1m 13.04s (0.54) **Going Correction** -0.15s/f (Firm) **11** Ran SP% **123.4**
Speed ratings (Par 93): **90,87,87,86,85 83,82,82,80,79 79**
WIN: 5.40; PL: Hawana 1.90, Manama 2.50, Texas Katie 2.50; EX: H-M 15.50, H-TK 16.90; CSF: H-M 16.38, H-TK 18.32; TRIFECTA: H-M-TK 100.30, H-TK-M 102.80.
Owner Abdulla Al Mansoori **Bred** Indian Creek **Trained** Newmarket, Suffolk

■ Oh So Terrible was withdrawn. Price at time of withdrawal 5-1. Rule 4 applies only to bets struck prior to withdrawal - deduction 15p in the pound. New market formed.

FOCUS
The first division of a maiden that can throw a smart filly, and those with experience came to the fore. The time, however, was 0.80secs slower than the second leg. The form is rated in line with the race average.

4064 BRITISH STALLION STUDS EBF MAIDEN FILLIES' STKS (PLUS 10 RACE) (DIV II) 6f
4:55 (4:55) (Class 4) 2-Y-O
£6,469 (£1,925; £962; £481) **Stalls** High

Form RPR

1 **Easy Victory** 2-9-0 0 .... JamesDoyle 11 82+
(Saeed bin Suroor) *lw: sn chsng ldr: clsd and upsides over 1f out: rdn and qcknd to ld jst ins fnl f: sn in command and r.o wl: comf* **11/2**[3]

3 **2** 2 **Tropical Rock**[62] 1988 2-9-0 0 .... DavidProbert 4 76
(Ralph Beckett) *in tch in midfield: effrt over 1f out: kpt on ins fnl f to go 2nd towards fin: no threat to wnr* **11/4**[2]

0 **3** 3/4 **Grand Myla (IRE)**[15] 3511 2-9-0 0 .... ShaneKelly 5 73
(Gary Moore) *neat: racd keenly: led: rdn jst over 1f out: hdd ins fnl f: sn outpcd and by wnr and kpt on same pce after: lost 2nd towards fin* **66/1**

4 nk **Island In The Sky (IRE)** 2-9-0 0 .... OisinMurphy 8 72+
(David Simcock) *str: in tch in midfield: hdwy to chse ldrs over 1f out: sn rdn and edgd lft: kpt on same pce ins fnl f* **20/1**

5 shd **Glitter Girl** 2-9-0 0 .... RyanMoore 6 72+
(William Haggas) *unf: in tch in midfield: effrt over 1f out: kpt on ins fnl f: no threat to wnr* **10/1**

3 **6** nk **Suffragette City (IRE)**[10] 3718 2-9-0 0 .... PatDobbs 10 71
(Richard Hannon) *leggy: t.k.h: chsd ldrs: grad stdd bk into last pair over 4f out: effrt but wanting to hang lft and nt clr run over 1f out: kpt on wl ins fnl f: no threat to wnr* **14/1**

7 hd **Bouquet De Flores (USA)** 2-9-0 0 .... JamesMcDonald 9 70+
(Charlie Appleby) *str: lw: s.i.s: hld up in tch: effrt over 1f out: rdn and styd on same pce ins fnl f: no threat to wnr* **10/11**[1]

8 7 **Mythical Spirit (IRE)** 2-9-0 0 .... DavidAllan 7 48
(James Tate) *leggy: athletic: in tch in last quartet: rdn over 1f out: sn outpcd: wknd fnl f* **50/1**

9 7 **Marwa** 2-9-0 0 .... AdamKirby 2 26
(Ed Dunlop) *lengthy: bit bkwd: in tch in rr: swtchd rt and effrt ent fnl 2f: sn outpcd and wl btn 1f out: bhd and eased wl ins fnl f* **25/1**

0 **10** 8 **Cadela Rica**[28] 3073 2-9-0 0 .... DougieCostello 3
(Gay Kelleway) *tall: chsd ldrs tl 2f out: sn pl: wl bhd and eased wl ins fnl f* **100/1**

1m 12.24s (-0.26) **Going Correction** -0.15s/f (Firm) **10** Ran SP% **123.2**
Speed ratings (Par 93): **95,92,91,90,90 90,90,80,71,60**
CSF £21.63 TOTE £6.90: £2.30, £1.20, £12.70; EX 22.80 Trifecta £826.10.
Owner Godolphin **Bred** Cliveden Stud Ltd **Trained** Newmarket, Suffolk

FOCUS
This has produced some smart fillies over the years. Lumiere won a division a year ago before taking the Cheveley Park Stakes (and the previous race on this card) and earlier winners Certify and Fantasia were first and second respectively in the Fillies' Mile. This was the quicker division by 0.8sec and was won by a very bright prospect.

4065 PLUSVITAL SIR HENRY CECIL STKS (FORMERLY THE STUBBS STAKES) (LISTED RACE) 1m
5:30 (5:31) (Class 1) 3-Y-O

£22,684 (£8,600; £4,304; £2,144; £1,076; £540) **Stalls** High

Form RPR

21-0 **1** **Lumiere**[67] 1888 3-8-12 116 .... JoeFanning 2 113+
(Mark Johnston) *travelled strly: trckd ldrs tl clsd to ld jst over 2f out: shkn up and asserted ent fnl f: r.o strly and drew wl clr fnl 150yds: comf* **3/1**[1]

-054 **2** *6* **Cymric (USA)**[23] 3245 3-9-3 109 .... JamesDoyle 11 104
(John Gosden) *racd on far rail thrght: chsd ldrs: chsd wnr 2f out: sn rdn: unable qck w wnr 1f out: wknd ins fnl f but a holding 2nd* **7/1**

51 **3** *1* **Manaboo (USA)**[34] 2877 3-8-12 89 .... JamesMcDonald 3 96
(Charlie Appleby) *hld up in tch in midfield: effrt over 1f out: rdn to go 3rd ins fnl f: kpt on same pce: no ch w wnr* **6/1**[2]

-550 **4** *hd* **Kentuckyconnection (USA)**[56] 2190 3-9-3 108 ....(p) ConnorBeasley 4 101
(Bryan Smart) *stdd after s and t.k.h early: in tch in midfield: effrt over 1f out: wnt 3rd but no threat to wnr 1f out: kpt on same pce u.p after* **12/1**

-226 **5** *2 1/4* **Atlantic Sun**[12] 3672 3-9-3 102 .... PatDobbs 5 96
(Richard Hannon) *in tch in midfield: hdwy to go cl 3rd 2f out: sn rdn and unable qck: lost 3rd and wandered 1f out: wknd* **7/1**

53-4 **6** *2* **Mohab**[86] 1393 3-9-3 98 .... JamieSpencer 7 91+
(Kevin Ryan) *stdd s: hld up in rr: effrt wl over 1f out: sn rdn and no hdwy: wknd fnl f* **14/1**

4 **7** *2* **General Macarthur (USA)**[26] 3175 3-9-3 92 ....(t) RyanMoore 1 87
(A P O'Brien, Ire) *stdd and dropped in bhd after s: short-lived effrt over 1f out: sn btn and wknd fnl f* **8/1**

1060 **8** *1 3/4* **Sea Of Flames**[21] 3299 3-9-6 98 .... ShaneKelly 9 86
(David Elsworth) *t.k.h: chsd ldr tl led after 2f: grad edgd over to far rail: hdd and rdn jst over 2f out: lost pl and wl btn over 1f out: wknd fnl f* **25/1**

14- **9** *nk* **Final Frontier (IRE)**[298] 6362 3-9-3 108 ....(p) ColmO'Donoghue 8 82
(Mrs John Harrington, Ire) *str: hld up towards rr: effrt 2f out: sn rdn and no hdwy: wknd fnl f* **11/1**

21- **10** *6* **Estidraak (IRE)**[246] 7701 3-9-3 93 .... PaulHanagan 10 68
(Sir Michael Stoute) *tall: lengthy: swtg: t.k.h: led for 2f: chsd ldr tl over 2f out: sn lost pl and bhd 2f out: wknd over 1f out: eased ins fnl f* **13/2**[3]

1m 35.74s (-4.26) **Going Correction** -0.15s/f (Firm) **10** Ran SP% **115.3**
Speed ratings (Par 108): **115,109,108,107,105 103,101,99,99,93**
CSF £23.57 TOTE £3.00: £1.60, £2.70, £2.30; EX 25.20 Trifecta £173.80.
Owner Sheikh Hamdan bin Mohammed Al Maktoum **Bred** Darley **Trained** Middleham Moor, N Yorks

FOCUS
A strong Listed race, with the second and fourth boasting good runs in Group 1 company this season, and it was hard not to be impressed with the back-to-form winner. The runner-up raced alone on the far rail for much of it, before being joined by the outsider of the field, but there appeared no advantage. Lumiere is rated back to her best.

4066 ROBINSONS MERCEDES-BENZ H'CAP 5f
6:05 (6:05) (Class 3) (0-90,90) 3-Y-O+ **£9,703** (£2,887; £1,443; £721) **Stalls** High

Form RPR

2264 **1** **Soie D'Leau**[13] 3606 4-9-10 88 .... JoeFanning 2 97
(Kristin Stubbs) *chsd ldr: upsides 1/2-way tl rdn to ld over 1f out: styd on wl to assert ins fnl f: rdn out* **9/2**[1]

0600 **2** *1 1/2* **Primrose Valley**[104] 1065 4-9-9 90 ....(b) DanielMuscutt(3) 10 94
(Ed Vaughan) *wnt rt s: chsd ldrs: effrt to chal over 1f out: drvn 1f out: no ex and outpcd by wnr fnl 100yds* **6/1**[3]

5104 **3** *nse* **Top Boy**[36] 2787 6-8-10 79 ....(v) NoelGarbutt(5) 7 82
(Derek Shaw) *stdd after s: t.k.h: hld up in tch: hdwy u.p jst over 1f out: styd on ins fnl f* **8/1**

0416 **4** *1/2* **Snap Shots (IRE)**[12] 3637 4-9-7 90 ....(tp) AnnaHesketh(5) 9 92
(Tom Dascombe) *sltly hmpd and swtchd lft sn after s: hld up in tch: rdn and hdwy to chse ldrs over 1f out: styd on same pce ins fnl f* **8/1**

023 **5** *hd* **Diamond Lady**[54] 2253 5-9-5 83 .... PaulHanagan 1 84
(William Stone) *in tch in midfield: clsd to press ldrs 1/2-way: rdn over 1f out: unable qck and styd on same pce ins fnl f* **8/1**

0305 **6** *3/4* **Vimy Ridge**[12] 3638 4-8-10 77 ....(p) JosephineGordon(3) 4 75
(Alan Bailey) *dwlt: hld up in tch: effrt and hdwy u.p over 1f out: kpt on same pce and no imp ins fnl f* **6/1**[3]

0-45 **7** *nk* **Rosie's Premiere (IRE)**[10] 3714 4-9-9 90 .... JackDuern(3) 8 87
(Dean Ivory) *dwlt and sltly hmpd leaving stalls: hld up in tch towards rr: n.m.r over 1f out: effrt 1f out: styd on same pce ins fnl f* **8/1**

0500 **8** *1* **Normal Equilibrium**[22] 3277 6-9-6 84 .... AdamKirby 3 78
(Robert Cowell) *led: rdn and hdd over 1f out: sn unable qck and btn 1f out: wknd ins fnl f* **5/1**[2]

430 **9** *1/2* **Sandfrankskipsgo**[33] 2895 7-9-7 85 .... ShaneKelly 6 77
(Peter Crate) *stdd after s: t.k.h: hld up in tch in midfield: effrt over 1f out: sn lost pl: bhd whn swtchd rt ins fnl f* **12/1**

58.19s (-0.91) **Going Correction** -0.15s/f (Firm)
WFA 3 from 4yo+ 5lb **9** Ran SP% **115.6**
Speed ratings (Par 107): **101,98,98,97,97 96,95,94,93**
CSF £31.43 CT £210.85 TOTE £5.30: £1.90, £2.20, £2.50; EX 34.50 Trifecta £275.40.
Owner F A T J Partnership **Bred** Mrs M Lingwood **Trained** Norton, N Yorks

FOCUS
Just a fair sprint handicap, lacking progressive sorts. A small pb from the winner.
T/Jkpt: Not won. T/Plt: £147.10 to a £1 stake. Pool: £119,394.38. 592.31 winning tickets. T/Qpdt: £29.60 to a £1 stake. Pool: £9,718.65. 242.78 winning tickets. **Steve Payne**

4067 - 4069a (Foreign Racing) - See Raceform Interactive

[3583]LEOPARDSTOWN (L-H)
Thursday, July 7

OFFICIAL GOING: Good

4070a IRISH STALLION FARMS EUROPEAN BREEDERS FUND "NASRULLAH" H'CAP (PREMIER HANDICAP) 1m 2f
7:20 (7:20) 3-Y-O+

£43,382 (£13,970; £6,617; £2,941; £1,102; £1,102)

RPR

1 **Qatari Hunter (IRE)**[13] 3631 3-8-9 96 .... KevinManning 6 103+
(J S Bolger, Ire) *racd towards rr: prog on outer over 1f out: wnt 6th 1f out: styd on strly to ld cl home* **2/1**[1]

2 *hd* **Tennessee Wildcat (IRE)**[28] 3084 6-9-10 100 .... ColinKeane 3 107
(G M Lyons, Ire) *racd in mid-div: gd prog under 2f out: led ent fnl f: styd on wl: hdd cl home* **12/1**

3 *2* **Castle Guest (IRE)**[26] 2708 7-8-13 89 ....(t) ShaneFoley 5 92
(M Halford, Ire) *trckd early ldr in 2nd: sn 3rd: rdn 2f out: briefly wnt 2nd appr fnl f: sn dropped to 3rd: kpt on same pce: no ex w ldng pair clsng stages* **20/1**

4 *nk* **Erik The Red (FR)**[45] 2527 4-9-7 97 .... ShaneGray 4 99
(Kevin Ryan) *chsd ldrs in 4th: rdn and nt qckn in 6th under 2f out: styd on wl again ins fnl f into 4th fnl 50yds: nvr on terms* **7/2**[2]

5 *1* **Le Vagabond (FR)**[51] 2356 4-8-5 88 .... KillianLeonard(7) 7 88
(E J O'Grady, Ire) *hld up: prog on inner under 2f out: swtchd rt ent fnl f: styd on wl to dead-heat for 5th clsng stages* **8/1**

5 *dht* **Pullman Brown (USA)**[14] 3587 4-8-7 88 ....(t) DonaghO'Connor(5) 1 88
(David Marnane, Ire) *racd in mid-div: 6th 4f out: prog on inner over 1f out whn n.m.r: 8th 1f out: swtchd rt and kpt on wl clsng stages to dead-heat for 5th* **16/1**

7 *shd* **I'll Be Your Clown (IRE)**[9] 3760 5-8-5 81 ....(b) ChrisHayes 10 81
(A Oliver, Ire) *trckd ldr in cl 3rd: sn 2nd: rdn over 2f out: nt qckn in 4th whn squeezed for room 1f out: kpt on same pce* **10/1**

8 *nk* **Stronger Than Me (IRE)**[11] 3698 8-8-13 89 .... WayneLordan 8 88
(W T Farrell, Ire) *racd in rr: kpt on wl fr over 1f out: nvr nrr* **16/1**

9 *shd* **Maudlin Magdalen (IRE)**[12] 3676 6-8-5 88 .... RobbieDolan(7) 9 87
(Donal Kinsella, Ire) *led: strly pressed ent fnl f and sn hdd: wknd* **16/1**

10 *2 1/2* **Ashraf (IRE)**[18] 3447 4-9-12 102 .... PatSmullen 2 96
(D K Weld, Ire) *settled off ldrs in 5th: clsr on inner in 4th under 2f out: nt qckn ins fnl f: wknd and eased clsng stages* **7/1**[3]

2m 7.58s (-0.62) **Going Correction** +0.075s/f (Good)
WFA 3 from 4yo+ 11lb **10** Ran SP% **118.4**
Speed ratings: **105,104,103,103,102 102,102,101,101,99**
CSF £28.66 CT £383.88 TOTE £2.70: £1.02, £3.00, £5.00; DF 33.00 Trifecta £320.60.
Owner Mubarak Al Naemi **Bred** Inis Boffin Syndicate **Trained** Coolcullen, Co Carlow

FOCUS
A four-timer for the winner whose improvement shows no sign of abating with the trainer hopeful that he might have another of these in him. This was also a pb from the second.

4071 - 4073a (Foreign Racing) - See Raceform Interactive

[3871]CLAIREFONTAINE (R-H)
Thursday, July 7

OFFICIAL GOING: Turf: good

4074a PRIX DES COSMOS (CLAIMER) (4YO+) (TURF) 1m 1f
2:05 (12:00) 4-Y-O+ **£8,455** (£3,382; £2,536; £1,691; £845)

RPR

1 **Wireless (FR)**[35] 5-9-4 0 .... TheoBachelot 9 92
(V Luka Jr, Czech Republic) **18/5**[1]

2 *3* **Motabaary (IRE)** 6-9-5 0 ....(b) EddyHardouin 2 87
(Werner Glanz, Germany) **11/1**

3 *2* **Lugana (GER)**[20] 4-9-1 0 .... MaximeGuyon 5 79
(Mme Pia Brandt, France) **41/10**[2]

4 *1* **Freud (FR)**[36] 2806 6-8-11 0 .... AdrienFouassier 8 72
(Ian Williams) *dwlt and hld up: rdn in last into st: styd on u.p fnl 2f and tk n.d 4th post* **27/1**

5 *nse* **Skaters Waltz (IRE)**[67] 5-9-5 0 ....(b) ThierryJarnet 7 80
(D Prod'Homme, France) **43/10**[3]

6 *3/4* **Menardais (FR)**[20] 3376 7-9-2 0 .... UmbertoRispoli 1 76
(T Castanheira, France) **13/2**

7 *2 1/2* **Mount Isa (IRE)**[18] 4-9-1 0 ....(p) MickaelBarzalona 6 69
(Mme Pia Brandt, France) **9/1**

8 *6* **Arvios**[36] 4-8-8 0 .... DamienMorin(8) 4 58
(C Laffon-Parias, France) **63/10**

9 *10* **Monte Fanum (ITY)**[66] 6-8-11 0 .... CristianDemuro 3 32
(Gianluca Bietolini, Italy) **84/10**

WIN (incl. 1 euro stake): 4.60. PLACES: 1.70, 3.10, 1.80. DF: 43.40. SF: 70.90
Owner Leram **Bred** Scea Haras De Manneville **Trained** Czech Republic

[3382]ASCOT (R-H)
Friday, July 8

OFFICIAL GOING: Good to firm (good in places on round course; str 8.6, rnd 7.8)
Wind: Almost nil Weather: Fine but cloudy, warm

4075 HELICAL BAR EBF STALLIONS MAIDEN STKS (PLUS 10 RACE) 6f
2:30 (2:30) (Class 3) 2-Y-O **£9,056** (£2,695; £1,346; £673) **Stalls** High

Form RPR

1 **Seven Heavens** 2-9-5 0 .... RobertHavlin 1 87+
(John Gosden) *dwlt and wnt rt s: sn trckd ldrs in centre: prog to ld overall wl over 1f out: sn clr: drifted lft fnl f: rdn out* **5/4**[1]

2 *1* **Lockheed** 2-9-5 0 .... PatCosgrave 14 84+
(William Haggas) *hld up in last of nr side trio: led gp jst over 1f out: tk 2nd overall ins fnl f: r.o wl but nt rch wnr* **11/4**[2]

3 *3* **Malcolm The Pug (IRE)** 2-9-5 0 .... KieranO'Neill 9 74+
(Richard Hannon) *trckd ldr in centre: effrt to chal 2f out but sn outpcd by wnr: one pce and lost 2nd ins fnl f* **40/1**

4 **4** 3/4 **Thammin**[38] 2757 2-9-5 0 DaneO'Neill 13 72+
(Owen Burrows) *dwlt: led nr side trio and on terms to over 2f out: lost gp ld over 1f out: one pce* **10/1**

00 **5** 1 **Juanito Chico (IRE)**[8] 3819 2-9-5 0 CharlesBishop 12 69
(William Jarvis) *hld up in rr in centre: pushed along over 2f out: n.d but kpt on quite wl fr over 1f out* **100/1**

6 nse **Solomon's Bay (IRE)** 2-9-5 0 TedDurcan 10 69
(Roger Varian) *trckd ldrs in centre: pushed along over 2f out: sn outpcd: kpt on steadily fr over 1f out* **20/1**

7 1 **Sea Shack** 2-9-5 0 LukeMorris 5 65
(William Knight) *toward rr in centre: shkn up wl over 2f out: no ch but kpt on fr over 1f out* **50/1**

4 **8** 1 1/4 **Monoshka (IRE)**[8] 3813 2-9-5 0 TomMarquand 2 61
(Richard Hannon) *dwlt: rcvrd to chse ldrs in centre: outpcd over 2f out: n.d after* **11/2**[3]

5 **9** 3 1/4 **Dangerous Ends**[24] 3254 2-9-2 0 DannyBrock(3) 11 51
(Brett Johnson) *w ldr in nr side trio to 2f out: wknd over 1f out* **33/1**

10 5 **Graphite Storm** 2-9-5 0 AdamKirby 6 35
(Clive Cox) *dwlt: in rr in centre: rdn over 2f out: no prog and sn btn* **14/1**

00 **11** nk **Buskin River (IRE)**[16] 3529 2-9-5 0 JimmyFortune 3 34
(Richard Hannon) *led gp in centre to wl over 1f out: wknd qckly* **33/1**

12 3 3/4 **Jacob's Dream** 2-9-5 0 FergusSweeney 4 22
(Gary Moore) *dwlt: a in rr in centre: bhd fnl 2f* **50/1**

1m 15.87s (1.37) **Going Correction** +0.05s/f (Good) **12** Ran SP% **118.3**
Speed ratings (Par 98): **92,90,86,85,84 84,82,81,76,70 69,64**
CSF £4.30 TOTE £2.20: £1.10, £1.70, £6.50; EX 5.80 Trifecta £105.30.
Owner K Abdullah **Bred** Cheveley Park Stud Ltd **Trained** Newmarket, Suffolk

FOCUS
A highly informative maiden and yet another juvenile winner for first season sire, Frankel. They raced in two groups, the runner-up likely inconvenienced by racing in the smallest group of three. The first two are both likely to do better next time.

4076 KNIGHTS NURSERY H'CAP 6f
3:00 (3:01) (Class 3) 2-Y-O **£7,762** (£2,310; £1,154; £577) **Stalls** High

Form RPR

241 **1** **Montataire (IRE)**[15] 3548 2-8-8 **78** GeraldMosse 8 83
(Mark Johnston) *mde all: shkn up over 1f out and gng best: rdn out fnl f: a in command* **15/8**[1]

531 **2** 1/2 **Mister Blue Sky (IRE)**[15] 3576 2-8-2 **72** LukeMorris 3 75
(Sylvester Kirk) *wnt rt s: hld up in rr: prog and rdn 2f out: tk 2nd ins fnl f: styd on but a hld* **8/1**

055 **3** nk **Challow (IRE)**[16] 3524 2-8-0 **70** KieranO'Neill 5 72
(Sylvester Kirk) *trckd ldrs: rdn 2f out: styd on fr over 1f out to take 3rd wl ins fnl f: nrst fin* **16/1**

1163 **4** nk **Sayesse**[16] 3531 2-8-9 **79** CharlesBishop 7 80
(Mick Channon) *hld up in last trio: rdn 2f out: styd on fr over 1f out: nrst fin and almost snatched 3rd* **20/1**

131 **5** 1 **Afandem (IRE)**[24] 3254 2-9-4 **91** MarcMonaghan(3) 6 89
(Hugo Palmer) *t.k.h: prom: chsd wnr 1/2-way: rdn 2f out: hung rt 1f out: lost 2nd and nt qckn ins fnl f* **5/2**[2]

410 **6** 1 3/4 **Nibras Bounty (IRE)**[24] 3243 2-8-12 **82** DaneO'Neill 1 75
(Richard Hannon) *in tch in rr: rdn over 2f out: kpt on fr over 1f out but nvr gng pce to chal* **10/1**

253 **7** 2 **Juan Horsepower**[22] 3315 2-7-12 **75** HollieDoyle(7) 9 61
(Richard Hannon) *trckd wnr to 1/2-way: sn shkn up: kpt in tch tl fdd over 1f out* **6/1**[3]

416 **8** 5 **Reign On**[28] 3100 2-8-6 **76** (b[1]) JohnFahy 2 46
(Ralph Beckett) *squeezed out s: in tch in rr to 2f out wknd* **22/1**

1m 15.15s (0.65) **Going Correction** +0.05s/f (Good) **8** Ran SP% **112.8**
Speed ratings (Par 98): **97,96,95,95,94 91,89,82**
CSF £17.23 CT £182.03 TOTE £2.90: £1.40, £1.30, £4.90; EX 11.00 Trifecta £133.00.
Owner Sheikh Hamdan bin Mohammed Al Maktoum **Bred** Tinnakill, P Lawlor & C Beale **Trained** Middleham Moor, N Yorks

FOCUS
The market proved a key guide to this fair nursery. The winner built on his previous victory.

4077 CLOSE BROTHERS PROPERTY FINANCE H'CAP 1m 6f
3:35 (3:36) (Class 3) (0-95,94) 3-Y-O+ **£9,703** (£2,887; £1,443; £721) **Stalls** Low

Form RPR

3-40 **1** **Oceane (FR)**[27] 3162 4-9-4 **84** (p) FergusSweeney 6 92
(Alan King) *wl in tch: rdn over 2f out: clsd on ldrs over 1f out: styd on wl to ld last 75yds* **8/1**

-100 **2** 1/2 **Steve Rogers (IRE)**[13] 3658 5-10-0 **94** HarryBentley 8 101
(Roger Varian) *trckd ldng pair: rdn to chal 2f out: upsides ins fnl f: jst outpcd last 75yds* **6/1**[2]

326/ **3** hd **Cool Macavity (IRE)**[48] 7407 8-9-5 **85** DougieCostello 13 91
(Nicky Henderson) *wl in tch: clsd on ldrs 2f out: drvn to take narrow ld over 1f out: kpt on but hdd last 75yds* **20/1**

1123 **4** shd **Masterpaver**[16] 3520 5-8-13 **79** JimmyFortune 11 85
(Richard Fahey) *trckd ldr: led 2f out but immediately chal on all sides: hdd over 1f out: styd pressing ldrs: jst outpcd last 100yds* **3/1**[1]

10-0 **5** 1 **All Talk N No Do (IRE)**[21] 3351 5-10-0 **94** (tp) GeorgeBaker 7 98
(Seamus Durack) *dwlt: sn prom: lost pl sltly 5f out: renewed effrt to chal 2f out: stl ch 1f out: fdd last 100yds* **10/1**

00- **6** 1/2 **Noble Silk**[202] 8308 7-9-8 **91** (v) JosephineGordon(3) 10 95
(Lucy Wadham) *dwlt: hld up in last trio in slowly run event: gd prog on outer wl over 1f out: r.o wl nr fin: no ch to threaten* **7/1**[3]

60-0 **7** shd **Continuum**[68] 1893 7-9-10 **90** (v[1]) TedDurcan 4 94
(Peter Hedger) *s.s: hld up in last in slowly run event: gd prog on inner fr 2f out: r.o wl nr fin: no ch to threaten* **9/1**

20-0 **8** 1/2 **Dawn Missile**[14] 3630 4-9-10 **90** [1] PatCosgrave 2 93
(William Haggas) *mostly in midfield: drvn and no imp on ldrs over 2f out: kpt on fnl f: n.d* **8/1**

1521 **9** hd **Knight Music**[32] 2966 4-9-5 **85** RobertHavlin 12 88
(Michael Attwater) *trckd ldrs: drvn to chal 2f out: nt qckn and lost pl over 1f out: one pce after* **12/1**

300 **10** nk **Wordiness**[13] 3657 8-9-0 **85** NoelGarbutt(5) 9 87
(David Evans) *towards rr: rdn wl over 2f out: no imp on ldrs: kpt on* **16/1**

0300 **11** 3 1/4 **Hardstone (USA)**[13] 3658 5-9-10 **90** ShaneKelly 14 88
(Michael Dods) *led at modest pce: drvn and hdd 2f out: wknd fnl f: eased nr fin* **25/1**

4/0 **12** hd **Chartbreaker (FR)**[24] 3246 5-9-5 **85** SamHitchcott 3 82
(Chris Gordon) *chsd ldrs: rdn over 3f out and sn lost pl: no ch over 1f out* **66/1**

-156 **13** 3/4 **Planetoid (IRE)**[9] 3784 8-9-2 **82** (b) MartinDwyer 1 78
(Jim Best) *hld up in last trio: shkn up and no prog over 2f out* **33/1**

3m 13.09s (12.09) **Going Correction** +0.225s/f (Good) **13** Ran SP% **119.7**
Speed ratings (Par 107): **74,73,73,73,72 72,72,72,72,72 70,70,69**
CSF £53.49 CT £941.61 TOTE £10.60: £3.20, £1.80, £5.30; EX 55.90 Trifecta £1113.50.
Owner McNeill Family **Bred** S C E A Haras De Manneville **Trained** Barbury Castle, Wilts

FOCUS
A hotly contested staying handicap, which served up a thrilling finish with only 3 1/2l covering the first ten home. They went very steadily early on and it paid to be handy. The form is taken at face value, bit this isn't a race to be confident about.

4078 CUSHMAN & WAKEFIELD EBF BREEDERS' SERIES FILLIES' H'CAP (FOR THE JOHN TRAVERS MEMORIAL TROPHY) 1m 4f
4:10 (4:11) (Class 3) (0-95,95) 3-Y-O+ **£12,938** (£3,850; £1,924; £962) **Stalls** Low

Form RPR

2-06 **1** **California (IRE)**[37] 2797 4-9-11 **92** RobertHavlin 6 100
(John Gosden) *trckd ldr: shkn up over 2f out: clsd over 1f out: rdn to ld jst ins fnl f: styd on wl* **17/2**

-211 **2** 1 1/4 **Peloponnese (FR)**[21] 3352 3-8-10 **90** (v) TedDurcan 10 96
(Sir Michael Stoute) *trckd ldrs: lost pl sltly fr 4f out: rdn over 2f out: prog over 1f out: styd on to take 2nd last strides: unable to chal* **2/1**[1]

64- **3** nk **Lovely Story (IRE)**[252] 5-9-9 **90** GeorgeBaker 4 96
(Seamus Durack) *led: brought field to centre in st: shkn up 2f out: drvn and hdd jst ins fnl f: one pce and lost 2nd last strides* **33/1**

1112 **4** nk **Indira**[41] 2685 5-9-6 **90** JosephineGordon(3) 5 95
(John Berry) *pressed ldrs: rdn and tried to chal 2f out: nt qckn over 1f out: one pce after* **8/1**[3]

0421 **5** 2 1/4 **Motdaw**[6] 3894 3-8-4 **84** 6ex MartinDwyer 3 85
(Mick Channon) *hld up in last pair: prog on inner 2f out: edgd lft and no imp on ldrs fnl f* **8/1**[3]

2-43 **6** nk **Perestroika**[30] 3027 4-9-7 **88** DaneO'Neill 7 89
(Henry Candy) *hld up in rr: rdn over 2f out: nt qckn and wl hld after: kpt on nr fin* **9/1**

-212 **7** 1 **Saumur**[31] 2994 4-8-10 **77** PatCosgrave 1 76
(Denis Coakley) *pushed along early: sn prom: cl up jst over 2f out: wknd over 1f out* **14/1**

31- **8** 1/2 **Bess Of Hardwick**[280] 6900 4-9-6 **87** AdamKirby 2 86
(Luca Cumani) *hld up in midfield: shkn up over 2f out: nt qckn and wl btn over 1f out* **3/1**[2]

2300 **9** 1 1/2 **Intense Tango**[27] 3162 5-9-4 **85** (t) DougieCostello 8 81
(K R Burke) *prog into midfield on outer after 4f: rdn over 2f out: wknd wl over 1f out* **20/1**

00-0 **10** 5 **Forte**[37] 2797 4-10-0 **95** ShaneKelly 9 83
(David O'Meara) *v awkward s and slowly away: a last: rdn and looked reluctant 2f out: bhd after* **50/1**

2m 32.68s (0.18) **Going Correction** +0.225s/f (Good)
WFA 3 from 4yo+ 13lb **10** Ran SP% **117.4**
Speed ratings (Par 104): **108,107,106,106,105 105,104,104,103,99**
CSF £25.63 CT £551.53 TOTE £9.70: £3.00, £1.50, £6.70; EX 28.90 Trifecta £567.30.
Owner Denford Stud **Bred** Epona Bloodstock Ltd And P A Byrne **Trained** Newmarket, Suffolk

FOCUS
Five of these had either won or finished second on their previous outing and it represents solid form for the grade. It's rated around the fourth.

4079 LONG HARBOUR H'CAP 6f
4:40 (4:44) (Class 3) (0-90,90) 3-Y-O+ **£9,703** (£2,887; £1,443; £721) **Stalls** High

Form RPR

6643 **1** **Misterioso (IRE)**[20] 3414 4-9-6 **84** GeorgeBaker 18 94
(Jamie Osborne) *dwlt: hld up in last: stl there whn swtchd sharply lft over 1f out: str run on nr side of gp fnl f to ld last 75yds* **7/1**[2]

4501 **2** 1/2 **Merhoob (IRE)**[20] 3405 4-9-5 **83** RyanPowell 14 91
(John Ryan) *dwlt: hld up in rr: shkn up and threaded through rivals fr 2f out: r.o wl to take 2nd last strides: jst outpcd by wnr* **25/1**

0264 **3** nk **Flowers On Venus (IRE)**[29] 3068 4-9-8 **86** ShaneKelly 3 93
(David Evans) *in tch in midfield: pushed along over 2f out: gd prog over 1f out: drvn to ld briefly 100yds out: outpcd nr fin* **11/1**

2-30 **4** 1 1/2 **Vibrant Chords**[37] 2788 3-9-4 **88** HarryBentley 5 89
(Henry Candy) *trckd ldrs: prog on far side of gp to ld jst over 1f out: hdd and outpcd last 100yds* **9/1**

0012 **5** 1/2 **Rio Ronaldo (IRE)**[13] 3671 4-9-10 **88** RobertWinston 9 89
(Mike Murphy) *dwlt: hld up in rr: nt clr run fr over 2f out to jst over 1f out: r.o fnl f: too late to pose a threat* **8/1**[3]

14 **6** 1 1/4 **Mustallib (IRE)**[41] 2693 3-8-13 **83** DaneO'Neill 4 79
(Charles Hills) *prom: trckd ldr 1/2-way: led wl over 1f out to jst over 1f out: fdd* **5/1**[1]

0002 **7** 3/4 **Valley Of Fire**[27] 3163 4-9-10 **88** (p) PatCosgrave 12 82
(William Haggas) *in tch in midfield: rdn and no prog over 2f out: styd on fnl f: n.d* **11/1**

3466 **8** 1 **Yeeoow (IRE)**[44] 2581 7-9-4 **82** DougieCostello 7 73
(K R Burke) *hld up in midfield: shkn up and nt qckn 2f out: n.d after: kpt on ins fnl f* **25/1**

3130 **9** 1/2 **Normandy Barriere (IRE)**[13] 3645 4-9-7 **85** JimmyFortune 19 74
(Nigel Tinkler) *wl in rr: rdn and no prog over 2f out: kpt on fnl f: no ch* **10/1**

2650 **10** 3/4 **Handsome Dude**[3] 3980 4-9-7 **88** (b) RobHornby(3) 10 75
(David Barron) *led to wl over 1f out: wknd fnl f* **25/1**

-206 **11** 1/2 **Francisco**[23] 3279 4-9-9 **87** TomMarquand 6 72
(Richard Hannon) *chsd ldr to 1/2-way: lost pl and wl btn over 2f out: plugged on nr fin* **25/1**

2-00 **12** hd **Racquet**[55] 2239 3-8-11 **81** KieranO'Neill 1 65
(Richard Hannon) *hld up towards rr: pushed along over 2f out: nt clr run briefly sn after: no real prog* **66/1**

1-03 **13** 1/2 **Little Palaver**[29] 3068 4-9-10 **88** AdamKirby 11 71
(Clive Cox) *pressed ldrs: rdn 2f out: wknd jst over 1f out* **16/1**

0055 **14** 1/2 **Captain Bob (IRE)**[20] 3414 5-8-12 **76** FergusSweeney 15 58
(Robert Cowell) *trckd ldrs: rdn and tried to mount a chal 2f out: wknd over 1f out* **10/1**

-500 **15** 2 1/2 **Barnet Fair**[27] 3150 8-9-6 **84** KierenFox 8 58
(David Nicholls) *taken down early: t.k.h: hld up in rr: hrd rdn and no prog 2f out* **10/1**

-040 **16** 4 1/2 **Cartmell Cleave**[29] 3068 4-9-10 **88** TedDurcan 16 47
(Stuart Kittow) *a towards rr: rdn and struggling 2f out* **14/1**

-006 **17** hd **Fast Act (IRE)**[21] 3346 4-9-9 **87** KeaganLatham 13 46
(Kevin Ryan) *hld up in rr: shkn up and no prog 2f out: wl btn after* **66/1**

5351 **18** *8* **Young John (IRE)**[18] 3466 3-9-2 **86**................................ MartinDwyer 2 18
(Richard Fahey) *prom: urged along 1/2-way: wknd 2f out: eased and t.o* **20/1**

1m 13.67s (-0.83) **Going Correction** +0.05s/f (Good)
WFA 3 from 4yo+ 6lb **18** Ran SP% **129.9**
Speed ratings (Par 107): **107,106,105,103,103 101,100,99,98,97 96,96,96,95,92 86,85,75**
CSF £185.02 CT £1997.34 TOTE £8.60: £2.50, £7.10, £3.30, £3.40; EX 232.90 Trifecta £2128.20.
Owner Mrs E Solomentseva **Bred** Eyrefield Lodge Stud **Trained** Upper Lambourn, Berks
■ Extrasolar was withdrawn. Price at time of withdrawal 50-1. Rule 4 does not apply

FOCUS
A devilishly competitive sprint handicap. They went hard early and the winner came from last.

4080 JLL H'CAP 1m (R)
5:15 (5:17) (Class 3) (0-90,89) 3-Y-O **£9,703** (£2,887; £1,443; £721) **Stalls** Low

Form RPR

13-0 **1** **Bobby Wheeler (IRE)**[77] 1603 3-9-5 **87**........................... AdamKirby 10 96
(Clive Cox) *mde all: set gd pce and racd wd first 2f: shkn up 2f out: in command whn hung lft u.p ins fnl f: hld on* **16/1**

-163 **2** *3/4* **War Story (IRE)**[27] 3155 3-9-4 **86**.. ShaneKelly 6 93
(Luca Cumani) *trckd ldrs: shkn up and prog over 2f out: chsd wnr over 1f out: styd on and clsd gap nr fin but a hld* **9/2**[3]

12-0 **3** *1 1/4* **Shwaimsa (IRE)**[21] 3358 3-9-6 **88**.................................. TomMarquand 3 92
(Richard Hannon) *trckd ldng pair: shkn up to dispute 2nd pl 2f out to over 1f out: nt qckn and nvr able to chal after: kpt on* **16/1**

0-13 **4** *1 1/4* **Tukhoom (IRE)**[15] 3574 3-9-2 **84**... DaneO'Neill 4 85
(Marcus Tregoning) *hld up in midfield: shkn up over 2f out: kpt on same pce fr over 1f out: no ch* **2/1**[1]

1-5 **5** *1* **Vincent's Forever**[87] 1393 3-9-3 **85**................................. NickyMackay 8 84
(John Gosden) *dwlt: hld up in last: shkn up over 2f out: brief effrt over 1f out: no prog after* **10/1**

5014 **6** *1 1/2* **Haley Bop (IRE)**[14] 3600 3-9-7 **89**................................... GeraldMosse 2 84
(Mark Johnston) *chsd wnr: shkn up over 2f out: lost 2nd wl over 1f out: wknd* **7/1**

0053 **7** *1/2* **Essenaitch (IRE)**[14] 3600 3-8-9 **77**................................. SaleemGolam 9 71
(David Evans) *t.k.h: hld up in last pair: rdn and no real prog 2f out* **14/1**

2-15 **8** *5* **Symbolic**[55] 2237 3-9-4 **86**... RobertHavlin 1 69
(John Gosden) *trckd ldng pair: shkn up over 2f out: sn wknd qckly* **10/3**[2]

1m 42.08s (1.38) **Going Correction** +0.225s/f (Good) **8** Ran SP% **114.6**
Speed ratings (Par 104): **102,101,100,98,97 96,95,90**
CSF £86.43 CT £1199.85 TOTE £12.50: £2.10, £1.90, £2.80; EX 119.00 Trifecta £1125.50.
Owner Peter Ridgers **Bred** Glenvale Stud **Trained** Lambourn, Berks

FOCUS
This featured some unexposed handicappers. The second to fifth were within a length of their expected marks.

4081 SAVILLS APPRENTICE H'CAP 1m (S)
5:50 (5:51) (Class 4) (0-85,85) 4-Y-O+ **£6,469** (£1,925; £962; £481) **Stalls** High

Form RPR

5/0- **1** **Bluegrass Blues (IRE)**[511] 556 6-9-4 **80**................. HectorCrouch(3) 8 90
(Heather Main) *dwlt: hld up in last pair: prog jst over 2f out and nt clr run briefly sn after: led over 1f out: drvn and hrd pressed fnl f: hld on wl* **33/1**

01-0 **2** *nk* **Mr Quicksilver**[15] 3571 4-9-2 **75**..............................(t) ThomasBrown 14 84
(Ed Walker) *hld up in last pair: rapid prog on nr side fr 2f out to take 2nd fnl f: sn chalng: nt qckn 100yds out: kpt on again nr fin* **22/1**

4600 **3** *1 1/4* **Chiswick Bey (IRE)**[16] 3517 8-8-9 **68**..................................... TimClark 4 74
(Richard Fahey) *hld up in rr: stdy prog over 2f out: chal over 1f out: styd on but outpcd by ldng pair fnl f* **20/1**

3330 **4** *3 1/2* **Muntadab (IRE)**[16] 3518 4-9-3 **83**.............................. CameronNoble(7) 5 81
(David Loughnane) *cl up: rdn to ld 2f out: hdd and fnd little over 1f out: wl hld in 4th fnl f* **6/1**[2]

2321 **5** *3/4* **Van Huysen (IRE)**[23] 3276 4-8-11 **70**....................... JosephineGordon 12 66
(Dominic Ffrench Davis) *led or disp to 2f out: steadily fdd* **13/2**[3]

344 **6** *3/4* **Alcatraz (IRE)**[15] 3557 4-9-9 **82**................................(tp) TomMarquand 10 77
(George Baker) *wl in tch in midfield: rdn over 2f out: no prog and wl hld over 1f out* **5/1**[1]

-236 **7** *1/2* **Mezzotint (IRE)**[25] 3234 7-8-13 **77**.............................. PaddyBradley(5) 9 70
(Lee Carter) *trckd ldrs: pushed along whn n.m.r 2f out and lost pl: no ch after but kpt on fnl f* **16/1**

1154 **8** *1 1/4* **Berkeley Vale**[28] 3109 5-8-13 **77**................................(v) KevinLundie(5) 15 67
(Roger Teal) *w ldrs: chal and hung bdly rt 2f out: continued to hang and steadily wknd* **12/1**

-200 **8** *dht* **Goring (GER)**[33] 2934 4-9-10 **83**................................... KieranShoemark 2 73
(Eve Johnson Houghton) *racd towards far side: wl on terms w ldrs to 2f out: fdd* **16/1**

2324 **10** *1* **Ttainted Love**[25] 3234 4-8-12 **78**................................(p) SamuelClarke(7) 7 66
(Chris Wall) *hld up in tch: nt clr run over 2f out: dropped towards rr and no ch after* **7/1**

0460 **11** *5* **Cricklewood Green (USA)**[15] 3557 5-9-1 **74**......... AlistairRawlinson 3 51
(Sylvester Kirk) *in tch to over 2f out: sn wknd* **12/1**

00-0 **12** *4 1/2* **Extremity (IRE)**[28] 3109 5-9-12 **85**................................ MarcMonaghan 13 51
(Hugo Palmer) *disp ld to 3f out: wknd qckly u.p* **8/1**

0564 **13** *24* **Isis Blue**[26] 3192 6-8-8 **67**..(p) DannyBrock 1
(Rod Millman) *t.k.h: in tch on outer of gp: wknd rapidly over 2f out: t.o* **20/1**

1m 42.94s (2.14) **Going Correction** +0.05s/f (Good) **13** Ran SP% **111.9**
Speed ratings (Par 105): **91,90,89,85,85 84,83,82,82,81 76,72,48**
CSF £548.66 CT £12453.44 TOTE £24.60: £10.80, £6.60, £7.80; EX 994.20 Trifecta £6065.60.
Owner Marcus Scott Russell & Sam Thomasson **Bred** Yeomanstown Stud **Trained** Kingston Lisle, Oxon

FOCUS
The first three pulled clear in this competitive finale. It was strongly run and benefited those held up.

T/Plt: £152.60 to a £1 stake. Pool: £82,683.62 - 395.46 winning tickets T/Qpdt: £108.70 to a £1 stake. Pool: £5,156.98 - 35.10 winning tickets **Jonathan Neesom**

3742 CHEPSTOW (L-H)
Friday, July 8

OFFICIAL GOING: Good (good to firm in back straight; 7.5)
Wind: slight half against Weather: sunny spells

4082 N-ERGY CELEBRATING 9 YEARS OF SUCCESS APPRENTICE H'CAP (RACING EXCELLENCE INITIATIVE) 1m 4f 23y
6:05 (6:05) (Class 5) (0-70,67) 4-Y-O+ **£3,234** (£962; £481; £240) **Stalls** Low

Form RPR

-300 **1** **Petrify**[35] 2850 6-8-4 **48** oh2....................................(tp) MitchGodwin(3) 11 57
(Bernard Llewellyn) *s.s: in rr: t.k.h and hdwy to go prom after 3f: led over 3f out: rdn over 2f out: styd on wl* **16/1**

0430 **2** *2 1/2* **Cape Spirit (IRE)**[17] 3498 4-8-7 **53**...........................(v) JoshuaBryan(5) 5 58
(Andrew Balding) *trckd ldrs: rdn 3f out: chsd wnr 1f out: styd on same pce* **7/1**

2225 **3** *1/2* **Flutterbee**[36] 2814 4-9-5 **65**..(p) AledBeech(5) 2 69
(George Baker) *t.k.h: a.p: rdn to chse wnr 2f out: lost 2nd 1f out: one pce* **13/2**[3]

6422 **4** *1/2* **Ring Eye (IRE)**[10] 3747 8-8-13 **54**.................................. MeganNicholls 1 57
(John O'Shea) *hld up towards rr: stdy hdwy on outside 3f out: rdn 2f out: one pce* **3/1**[2]

100/ **5** *3/4* **Tamarillo Grove (IRE)**[7] 7053 9-9-5 **60**......................(t) SophieKilloran 6 62
(Sophie Leech) *hld up in rr: rdn over 2f out: no imp tl styd on wl fnl f: nrst fin* **14/1**

2603 **6** *nk* **Invincible Wish (IRE)**[10] 3747 4-9-4 **59**.................... KillianHennessy 10 61
(Trevor Wall) *s.s: t.k.h: in rr tl hdwy 1/2-way: chsd ldrs 4f out: rdn 3f out: no ex fnl f* **12/1**

0623 **7** *1/2* **Taurian**[2] 4018 5-9-8 **63**.. RhiainIngram 4 64
(Ian Williams) *led and set stdy pce tl hdd after 5f: styd prom: rdn over 2f out: wknd fnl f* **2/1**[1]

650- **8** *3/4* **Sweet World**[22] 5550 12-8-1 **49**.. WilliamCox(7) 9 49
(Bernard Llewellyn) *mid-div: rdn and outpcd 3f out: styd on fnl f* **50/1**

-220 **9** *4* **Start Seven**[31] 3002 4-9-7 **67**.. SeanMooney(5) 8 60
(Joseph Tuite) *hld up: rdn over 3f out: a towards rr* **25/1**

50-0 **10** *15* **Honour Promise (IRE)**[10] 3747 4-8-9 **53**.....................(p) JoshQuinn(3) 3 22
(Bernard Llewellyn) *t.k.h: trckd ldr tl led after 5f: hdd over 3f out: sn wknd: eased 1f out* **25/1**

2m 39.95s (0.95) **Going Correction** -0.125s/f (Firm) **10** Ran SP% **114.1**
Speed ratings (Par 103): **91,89,89,88,88 87,87,87,84,74**
CSF £118.45 CT £808.79 TOTE £19.00: £4.70, £2.40, £1.80; EX 182.40 Trifecta £1186.60.
Owner B J Llewellyn **Bred** Fittocks Stud **Trained** Fochriw, Caerphilly

FOCUS
The ground had dried out to good (good to firm in the back straight) and no changes to race distances for the opener, a moderate handicap in which they went a slow gallop.

4083 WELCOME TO WORLD TYMEO/EBF STALLIONS NOVICE STKS (PLUS 10 RACE) 5f 16y
6:35 (6:36) (Class 4) 2-Y-O **£5,175** (£1,540; £769; £384) **Stalls** Centre

Form RPR

1 **Nayyar** 2-8-11 0.. CallumShepherd(5) 6 80+
(Charles Hills) *s.i.s: sn in tch: shkn up 2f out: led appr fnl f: r.o wl* **9/2**[2]

4 **2** *2 1/4* **Sheila's Palace**[25] 3231 2-8-11 0... JohnFahy 8 66
(J S Moore) *led: shkn up 2f out: hdd appr fnl f: hld by wnr after but kpt on to hold 2nd* **20/1**

3 *hd* **Dixie's Double** 2-8-6 0.. PaddyPilley(5) 2 66
(Daniel Kubler) *prom: chsd ldr after 1f: rdn 2f out: sn lost 2nd: keeping on whn n.m.r cl home* **25/1**

5 **4** *hd* **Night Law**[50] 2410 2-8-8 0... EdwardGreatrex(3) 3 65
(Andrew Balding) *s.i.s: t.k.h towards rr: hdwy 1/2-way: rdn over 1f out: unable qck fnl f* **4/7**[1]

5 *8* **Trotter** 2-9-2 0.. WilliamCarson 1 41
(Stuart Kittow) *sn outpcd and rdn along in rr: r.o fnl f: nvr nr ldrs* **20/1**

0226 **6** *1 3/4* **Davarde (IRE)**[26] 3196 2-9-2 0... SteveDrowne 5 35
(David Evans) *chsd ldr 1f: styd prom: rdn 1/2-way: wknd over 1f out* **6/1**[3]

7 *6* **Pentito Rap (USA)** 2-9-2 0.. LukeMorris 7 13
(Sir Mark Prescott Bt) *rn green: bustled along to chse ldrs: lost pl 1/2-way: bhd fnl 2f* **14/1**

59.22s (-0.08) **Going Correction** -0.125s/f (Firm) **7** Ran SP% **116.2**
Speed ratings (Par 96): **95,91,91,90,77 75,65**
CSF £82.56 TOTE £5.50: £2.50, £7.30; EX 61.60 Trifecta £864.80.
Owner Abdulla Al Khalifa **Bred** Sheikh Abdulla Bin Isa Al Khalifa **Trained** Lambourn, Berks

FOCUS
A fair novice stakes, though the withdrawal of the favourite took away some of the shine. They went a good pace and the time was just 1.22sec outside of the standard. A nice start from the winner, the form rated cautiously.

4084 HUSKINS NEWLYWED CHALLENGE H'CAP 5f 16y
7:05 (7:06) (Class 5) (0-70,67) 3-Y-O+ **£3,234** (£962; £481; £240) **Stalls** Centre

Form RPR

1114 **1** **Gilmer (IRE)**[13] 3674 5-9-6 **66**... NoelGarbutt(5) 7 77
(Laura Young) *wnt to post early: towards rr and sn pushed along to stay in tch: hdwy over 1f out: rdn to ld 100yds out: r.o* **4/1**[3]

5536 **2** *1* **Swendab (IRE)**[16] 3530 8-9-7 **67**.........................(b) CiaranMckee(5) 8 74
(John O'Shea) *pushed along: w ldr: rdn to ld 1f out: hdd and unable qck fnl 100yds* **14/1**

1361 **3** *2* **Satchville Flyer**[10] 3743 5-8-9 **55** 6ex...................... CallumShepherd(5) 6 55
(David Evans) *chsd ldrs: rdn after 2f: kpt on same pce fnl f: nvr able to chal* **13/8**[1]

0621 **4** *1 3/4* **Quickaswecan**[8] 3811 5-9-9 **67**.........................(p) EdwardGreatrex(3) 5 61
(Milton Bradley) *led narrowly: rdn over 1f out: sn hdd: no ex ins fnl f* **3/1**[2]

0220 **5** *nk* **Jaganory (IRE)**[16] 3510 4-9-6 **61**..(p) LukeMorris 4 53
(Christopher Mason) *mid-div: sn rdn along to stay in tch w ldrs: hung lft over 1f out: kpt on same pce fnl f* **9/1**

6000 **6** *3/4* **Tally's Song**[2] 3994 3-7-9 **48** oh3.. RPWalsh(7) 3 36
(Grace Harris) *chsd ldrs: rdn 2f out: sn carried lft: grad wknd* **50/1**

606 **7** *8* **Ambitious Boy**[16] 3510 7-9-6 **61**.. TimmyMurphy 2 22
(John O'Shea) *wnt lft leaving stalls and v.s.a: a bhd* **15/2**

58.87s (-0.43) **Going Correction** -0.125s/f (Firm)
WFA 3 from 4yo+ 5lb **7** Ran SP% **113.5**
Speed ratings (Par 103): **98,96,93,90,89 88,75**
CSF £53.98 CT £124.03 TOTE £4.90: £2.40, £3.80; EX 50.30 Trifecta £173.00.
Owner Total Plumbing Supporters Club **Bred** Darley **Trained** Broomfield, Somerset

FOCUS
An average sprint handicap and they probably went too fast, setting things up for the patiently ridden winner.

4085 N-ERGY UNLOCKING POTENTIAL AND TRANSFORMING LIVES H'CAP 6f 16y
7:35 (7:35) (Class 5) (0-70,70) 3-Y-O **£3,234** (£962; £481; £240) **Stalls** Centre

Form RPR
5-40 **1** **Joules**[59] 2141 3-9-7 **70**.....(t) TimmyMurphy 4 78
(Natalie Lloyd-Beavis) *mid-div: clsd to trck ldrs 1/2-way: rdn over 1f out: r.o to ld cl home* **8/1**[3]
0612 **2** *nk* **Caitie (IRE)**[21] 3353 3-9-6 **69**.....(t) LukeMorris 5 76
(Paul Cole) *s.i.s: in tch towards rr: hdwy 1/2-way: sn rdn: led narrowly ins fnl f: hdd cl home* **11/4**[2]
-000 **3** *2* **Swanton Blue (IRE)**[57] 2185 3-9-1 **69**..... CallumShepherd[(5)] 3 70
(Ed de Giles) *led: rdn over 1f out: hdd ins fnl f: no ex towards fin* **14/1**
0000 **4** *3* **Roccor**[15] 3558 3-9-2 **65**..... KieranO'Neill 9 56
(Richard Hannon) *hld up in rr: nudged along after 2f: rdn and hdwy 2f out: kpt on fnl f: nvr able to chal* **8/1**[3]
4003 **5** *1 3/4* **Abberley Dancer (IRE)**[11] 3725 3-9-2 **65**..... JohnFahy 2 51
(J S Moore) *hld up in rr: shuffled along over 2f out: hdwy over 1f out: rdn and kpt on fnl f: nvr nr ldrs* **8/1**[3]
-440 **6** *1 3/4* **Zabdi**[15] 3558 3-8-12 **68**..... HollieDoyle[(7)] 1 48
(Richard Hannon) *trckd ldrs tl rdn and lost 2nd over 2f out: wknd over 1f out* **5/2**[1]
-604 **7** *5* **Guilded Rock**[6] 3900 3-8-9 **58**..... WilliamCarson 6 22
(Stuart Kittow) *chsd ldrs: rdn 2f out: wknd appr fnl f* **16/1**
6-55 **8** *1/2* **Master Pekan**[130] 763 3-7-12 **54** oh6 ow3..... MitchGodwin[(7)] 10 17
(Roy Brotherton) *chsd ldrs: rdn 3f out: wknd over 1f out* **66/1**
4506 **9** *3 1/2* **Tim The Taxi**[27] 3126 3-8-0 **54**..... NoelGarbutt[(5)] 7 5
(David Evans) *s.i.s: towards rr: rdn 1/2-way: no imp: wknd over 1f out* **25/1**
1035 **10** *3 1/4* **Bushwise (IRE)**[16] 3513 3-8-6 **58**.....(p) EdwardGreatrex[(3)] 8
(Milton Bradley) *mid-div: rdn 1/2-way: wknd 2f out* **11/1**

1m 10.54s (-1.46) **Going Correction** -0.125s/f (Firm) **10 Ran SP% 114.8**
Speed ratings (Par 100): **104,103,100,96,94 92,85,84,80,75**
CSF £29.76 CT £306.44 TOTE £8.20: £2.20, £1.50, £4.40; EX 37.50 Trifecta £287.80.
Owner Parsonage Racing Partnership **Bred** Norelands & Hugo Lascelles **Trained** East Garston, Berks

FOCUS
A modest sprint handicap in which the highest rated runners dominated in a tight finish.

4086 BILL TURNER MEMORIAL H'CAP 7f 16y
8:05 (8:06) (Class 4) (0-85,85) 3-Y-O+ **£5,498** (£1,636; £817; £408) **Stalls** Centre

Form RPR
-150 **1** **Lyfka**[20] 3405 4-9-12 **83**.....(tp) LukeMorris 8 91
(Paul Cole) *towards rr: rdn and hdwy 3f out: hung lft over 1f out: r.o u.p to ld fnl 50yds* **20/1**
-446 **2** *1/2* **Hope Cove**[15] 3571 3-9-4 **83**.....(p) PatCosgrave 5 86
(Ed Walker) *a.p: rdn to ld 2f out: sn edgd rt u.p: hdd and unable qck fnl 50yds* **7/2**[1]
6454 **3** *nk* **Midnight Rider (IRE)**[9] 3771 8-8-12 **74**.....(b[1]) AliceMills[(5)] 3 79
(Rod Millman) *t.k.h: mid-div: rdn 1/2-way: r.o wl fnl f: clsng nr fin* **10/1**
2534 **4** *2 1/4* **Peak Storm**[9] 3766 7-9-6 **77**.....(p) TimmyMurphy 6 76
(John O'Shea) *chsd ldrs: rdn 1/2-way: sn sltly outpcd: styd on fnl f* **12/1**
6326 **5** *1/2* **Dutch Art Dealer**[16] 3523 5-9-11 **82**.....(p) WilliamCarson 4 80
(Paul Cole) *hld up: pushed along 1/2-way: swtchd rt over 1f out: sn hmpd: r.o wl fnl f: gng on fin* **7/1**[3]
215 **6** *shd* **Catalan (IRE)**[27] 3152 3-8-11 **76**..... RobertWinston 7 71
(Hughie Morrison) *led: rdn and hdd 2f out: stl cl 3rd whn n.m.r 1f out: nt rcvr* **7/2**[1]
5000 **7** *hd* **Kinglami**[16] 3534 7-8-13 **75**.....(p) CiaranMckee[(5)] 2 72
(John O'Shea) *hld up: pushed along 1/2-way: rdn 2f out: n.m.r ins fnl f: r.o towards fin* **20/1**
412- **8** *2* **Guiding Light (IRE)**[344] 4778 4-9-11 **85**..... EdwardGreatrex[(3)] 1 77
(Andrew Balding) *mid-div: rdn over 2f out: unable to chal: wknd fnl f* **8/1**
-163 **9** *2 3/4* **Irish Eclare (IRE)**[36] 2818 3-8-13 **78**..... SteveDrowne 10 59
(Charles Hills) *chsd ldrs: rdn over 2f out: wknd 1f out* **11/2**[2]
0-00 **10** *nse* **Sarangoo**[15] 3571 8-8-11 **75**.....(p) RhiainIngram[(7)] 9 59
(Malcolm Saunders) *chsd ldrs: rdn over 2f out: wknd over 1f out* **22/1**

1m 22.14s (-1.06) **Going Correction** -0.125s/f (Firm)
WFA 3 from 4yo+ 8lb **10 Ran SP% 114.1**
Speed ratings (Par 105): **101,100,100,97,96 96,96,94,91,91**
CSF £85.01 CT £777.68 TOTE £18.00: £5.20, £1.50, £3.60; EX 96.20 Trifecta £765.60.
Owner A H Robinson **Bred** A H & C E Robinson **Trained** Whatcombe, Oxon

FOCUS
Not much solid form on show for this fair handicap, but several interesting 3yos gave it some substance and there were some noteworthy efforts behind the winner.

4087 N-ERGY PROUD SUPPORTERS OF OFFENDER REFORM FILLIES' H'CAP 1m 14y
8:35 (8:38) (Class 5) (0-75,73) 3-Y-O+ **£3,234** (£962; £481; £240) **Stalls** Centre

Form RPR
0613 **1** **Bay Of St Malo (IRE)**[10] 3740 3-9-0 **70**..... KieranO'Neill 2 78
(Richard Hannon) *t.k.h in rr: hdwy over 2f out: chsd ldr over 1f out: chal ins fnl f: led cl home* **9/2**[3]
-552 **2** *hd* **Izmir (IRE)**[13] 3649 3-9-3 **73**..... PatCosgrave 4 80
(William Haggas) *trckd ldrs: led over 1f out: jnd and edgd lft ins fnl f: r.o: hdd cl home* **2/1**[1]
5411 **3** *3* **Imperial Link**[6] 3896 4-8-11 **61** 6ex.....(p) EdwardGreatrex[(3)] 6 63
(John O'Shea) *led tl rdn and hdd over 1f out: lost 2nd 1f out: one pce* **9/1**
1413 **4** *1 1/4* **Lady Bayside**[16] 3514 8-9-5 **69**..... JosephineGordon[(3)] 5 68
(Malcolm Saunders) *reluctant to enter stalls: chsd ldr over 6f: sn rdn: no ex fnl f* **9/2**[3]
2224 **5** *2* **Gleaming Girl**[26] 3197 4-9-2 **70**.....[1] SophieKilloran[(7)] 1 65
(David Simcock) *wnt to post early: s.i.s: hld up: rdn over 2f out: no real imp* **8/1**
3-64 **6** *3* **Just Fab (IRE)**[50] 2405 3-8-9 **65**..... SteveDrowne 3 51
(Ali Stronge) *in tch: rdn 1/2-way: no imp* **20/1**
3-04 **7** *1 1/4* **Mercifilly (FR)**[21] 3357 3-8-10 **66**..... LukeMorris 7 49
(Ed Walker) *s.i.s: trckd ldrs: rdn 3f out: wknd 2f out* **4/1**[2]

1m 34.37s (-1.83) **Going Correction** -0.125s/f (Firm)
WFA 3 from 4yo+ 9lb **7 Ran SP% 115.6**
Speed ratings (Par 100): **104,103,100,99,97 94,93**
CSF £14.28 TOTE £5.30: £3.20, £1.40; EX 16.40 Trifecta £106.50.
Owner Coriolan Partnership **Bred** T Purcell & K Purcell **Trained** East Everleigh, Wilts

FOCUS
A tight handicap featuring several in-form individuals. They went a fair pace and the favourite was just denied in a bobbing finish.

4088 N-ERGY MAKING A DIFFERENCE H'CAP 1m 14y
9:05 (9:07) (Class 5) (0-70,70) 3-Y-O+ **£3,234** (£962; £481; £240) **Stalls** Centre

Form RPR
2406 **1** **Diamonds A Dancing**[27] 3125 6-8-7 **54**.....(be) CiaranMckee[(5)] 2 64
(John O'Shea) *chsd ldrs: led 3f out: sn rdn: narrowly hdd over 1f out: rallied to ld last strides* **20/1**
1-24 **2** *shd* **Wakame (IRE)**[17] 3478 3-8-10 **61**..... KieranO'Neill 10 69
(Ed de Giles) *t.k.h: cl up: sltly hmpd after 1f: rdn 3f out: led narrowly over 1f out: hdd last strides* **9/2**[2]
-556 **3** *nk* **Silhouette (IRE)**[13] 3653 3-9-4 **69**..... TimmyMurphy 12 76
(Daniel Kubler) *hld up towards rr: hdwy 3f out: rdn over 1f out: ev ch fnl f: jst hld* **8/1**[3]
-413 **4** *nk* **Four Poets**[8] 3823 3-9-5 **70**..... PatCosgrave 6 77
(David Simcock) *hld up in rr: hdwy 3f out: swtchd rt over 2f out: sn rdn: ev ch ins fnl f: unable qck nr fin* **5/4**[1]
0600 **5** *8* **Bold Grove**[10] 3743 4-8-2 **51** oh6.....(p) RPWalsh[(7)] 5 41
(Edward Bevan) *t.k.h: chsd ldrs: hmpd and stmbld after 1f: rdn 2f out: wknd 1f out* **25/1**
6-02 **6** *2* **Approaching Star (FR)**[10] 3748 5-8-4 **51** oh5..... NoelGarbutt[(5)] 7 37
(Dai Burchell) *in tch: rdn over 3f out: sn outpcd: styd on fnl f* **14/1**
321- **7** *2 1/2* **Seven Clans (IRE)**[212] 8151 4-9-10 **66**..... WilliamCarson 1 46
(Neil Mulholland) *prom: rdn 3f out: wknd 2f out* **10/1**
00/0 **8** *1 1/2* **Whitstable Native**[37] 2448 8-8-6 **51** oh4.....(t) EdwardGreatrex[(3)] 11 27
(Sophie Leech) *towards rr: hdwy to chse ldrs 1/2-way: rdn over 2f out: wknd over 1f out* **50/1**
0001 **9** *6* **Zebs Lad (IRE)**[27] 3146 4-8-13 **60**.....(p) MeganNicholls[(5)] 13 23
(Nikki Evans) *led: veered lft after 1f: hdd 3f out: edgd rt and wknd over 1f out* **16/1**
050- **10** *1 1/4* **General Brook (IRE)**[17] 6237 6-9-6 **62**..... LukeMorris 9 22
(John O'Shea) *s.s: wnt lft to r alone on ins rail over 3f out: a bhd* **20/1**
016 **11** *64* **Henryhudsonbridge (USA)**[28] 3097 4-9-4 **63**.....(b) RobHornby[(3)] 4
(Edward Bevan) *chsd ldrs: rdn 3f out: sn wknd: t.o* **9/1**

1m 34.43s (-1.77) **Going Correction** -0.125s/f (Firm)
WFA 3 from 4yo+ 9lb **11 Ran SP% 120.7**
Speed ratings (Par 103): **103,102,102,102,94 92,89,88,82,81 17**
CSF £106.73 CT £823.67 TOTE £40.30: £4.00, £2.00, £2.80; EX 165.50 TRIFECTA Not won..
Owner The Cross Racing Club **Bred** Lady Caffyn-Parsons **Trained** Elton, Gloucs
■ Stewards' Enquiry : Megan Nicholls caution; careless riding

FOCUS
A modest finale in which they went a decent gallop, and it produced another close finish. The first four came clear and the form should stand up.
T/Plt: £4,779.00 to a £1 stake. Pool: £68,739.12 - 10.50 winning tickets T/Qpdt: £46.50 to a £1 stake. Pool: £9,324.16 - 148.10 winning tickets **Richard Lowther**

3633 CHESTER (L-H)
Friday, July 8

OFFICIAL GOING: Good (good to soft in places; 6.7)
Wind: moderate 1/2 against Weather: fine

4089 EUROGOLD GROUP H'CAP (FOR LADY AMATEUR RIDERS) 7f 122y
6:20 (6:20) (Class 4) (0-80,76) 4-Y-O+
£5,996 (£1,873; £936; £468; £234; £118) **Stalls** Low

Form RPR
-000 **1** **Echo Of Lightning**[24] 3252 6-9-11 **71**.....(p) MissLWilson[(5)] 2 79
(Brian Ellison) *trckd ldrs: drvn over 2f out: styd on to ld last 75yds* **9/2**[2]
00 **2** *1 1/4* **Baltic Prince (IRE)**[30] 3013 6-9-10 **65**..... MissCWalton 6 70
(Tony Carroll) *led: jnd over 3f out: hdd and no ex last 75yds* **18/1**
1664 **3** *hd* **Call Out Loud**[14] 3599 4-9-11 **66**.....(p) MissSBrotherton 10 71
(Michael Appleby) *trckd ldrs: t.k.h: upsides over 3f out: hung lft over 1f out: kpt on same pce last 75yds* **12/1**
0123 **4** *nk* **Curzon Line**[21] 3367 7-9-13 **68**..... MissJoannaMason 9 72+
(Michael Easterby) *mid-div: hdwy on outer over 1f out: styd on to take 4th nr line* **4/1**[1]
0606 **5** *3/4* **Ellaal**[5] 3922 7-9-12 **67**..... MissBeckySmith 4 69
(Ruth Carr) *chsd ldrs: drvn over 2f out: one pce over 1f out* **12/1**
230 **6** *1/2* **Surewecan**[11] 3708 4-9-12 **72**..... MissEmmaBedford[(5)] 5 73
(Mark Johnston) *mid-div: effrt over 2f out: kpt on over 1f out: nt trble ldrs* **10/1**
0005 **7** *3/4* **Character Onesie (IRE)**[20] 3398 4-9-10 **70**.....(p) MissFMcSharry[(5)] 3 69
(Richard Fahey) *in rr: hdwy over 1f out: kpt on: nt rch ldrs* **5/1**[3]
-605 **8** *2 3/4* **Order Of Service**[26] 3185 6-10-7 **76**..... MrsCBartley 7 68
(Shaun Harris) *s.s: in rr: hdwy over 1f out: nvr on terms* **20/1**
2605 **9** *1 1/4* **Royal Normandy**[28] 3101 4-9-8 **68**.....(b) MissPBridgwater[(5)] 11 57
(Andrew Balding) *mid-div: effrt over 2f out: wknd fnl f* **20/1**
5003 **10** *2 3/4* **Athletic**[15] 3571 7-10-5 **74**.....(v) MissGAndrews 1 56
(Andrew Reid) *s.i.s: hld up in rr: effrt over 2f out: nvr on terms* **4/1**[1]
1102 **11** *10* **Mitchum**[17] 3494 7-9-11 **71**.....(p) MrsVDavies[(5)] 8 28
(Ron Barr) *half-rrd s: mid-div: lost pl over 2f out: bhd fnl f* **25/1**

1m 37.56s (3.76) **Going Correction** +0.575s/f (Yiel) **11 Ran SP% 118.0**
Speed ratings (Par 105): **104,102,102,101 101,100,97,96,93 83**
CSF £79.28 CT £930.05 TOTE £6.80: £3.20, £3.50, £2.70; EX 87.80 Trifecta £1849.50.
Owner Victoria Greetham & Emily Beasley **Bred** Gracelands Stud **Trained** Norton, N Yorks
■ Stewards' Enquiry : Miss L Wilson two-day ban; used whip in the incorrect place (tba)

FOCUS
There was 2mm of overnight rain and the going was given as good, good to soft in places (GoingStick: 6.7). The rail between between the 6f and 1 1/2f point had been moved out by 6yds. Race distance increased by 37yds. Few got into this amateur riders' race, with the front three dominating throughout.

4090 STELLA ARTOIS NURSERY H'CAP 7f 2y
6:50 (6:51) (Class 4) 2-Y-O **£6,225** (£1,864; £932; £466) **Stalls** Low

Form RPR
14 **1** **Aardwolf (USA)**[21] 3356 2-9-5 **82**..... FrannyNorton 5 91+
(Mark Johnston) *half-rrd s: led: qcknd pce 3f out: drvn clr last 150yds: eased towards fin* **4/5**[1]
603 **2** *5* **Coverham (IRE)**[20] 3416 2-7-7 **63** oh1..... DavidEgan[(7)] 4 58
(James Bethell) *hld up in last: effrt over 2f out: chsd wnr over 1f out: no imp* **10/1**

1543 **3** 2 1/4 **Cullingworth (IRE)**[20] 3388 2-9-0 **82**...................... AdamMcNamara(5) 2 71
(Richard Fahey) *trckd ldrs: t.k.h: effrt over 2f out: edgd lft: one pce* **9/4**[2]
3361 **4** 18 **Hi Milady (IRE)**[14] 3592 2-8-9 **72**...................................... DavidProbert 1 12
(Dominic Ffrench Davis) *awkward s: trckd ldrs: t.k.h: drvn over 2f out: wkng whn hmpd and lost pl wl over 1f out: bhd whn heavily eased last 50yds* **6/1**[3]
1m 30.14s (3.64) **Going Correction** +0.575s/f (Yiel) **4** Ran SP% **109.7**
Speed ratings (Par 96): **102,96,93,73**
CSF £8.87 TOTE £1.90; EX 7.50 Trifecta £14.30.
Owner Sheikh Hamdan bin Mohammed Al Maktoum **Bred** Darley **Trained** Middleham Moor, N Yorks

FOCUS
Race distance increased by 37yds. This had little depth and proved a simple task for the favourite.

4091 EDMUNDSON ELECTRICAL/EBF CONDITIONS STKS (PLUS 10 RACE) 5f 16y
7:20 (7:21) (Class 2) 2-Y-O **£12,450** (£3,728; £1,864; £932) **Stalls** Low

Form RPR
10 **1** **Big Time Baby (IRE)**[22] 3295 2-8-12 0..................(t) RichardKingscote 2 94
(Tom Dascombe) *wnt rt s: trckd ldr: effrt over 2f out: qcknd to ld last 150yds: pushed out* **10/11**[1]
121 **2** 1 3/4 **Groupie**[16] 3531 2-8-12 0.. DavidProbert 3 88
(Richard Hannon) *dwlt: sn trcking ldrs: styd on to take 2nd clsng stages* **7/1**
10 **3** 1 1/4 **Plata O Plomo**[22] 3295 2-9-1 0.. BarryMcHugh 1 86
(Tony Coyle) *led to post: led: hdd last 150yds: fdd clsng stages* **7/2**[3]
3210 **4** 2 **Camargue**[23] 3270 2-8-10 0.. FrannyNorton 4 74
(Mark Johnston) *trckd ldrs: effrt over 2f out: lost pl over 1f out* **3/1**[2]
1m 3.21s (2.21) **Going Correction** +0.575s/f (Yiel) **4** Ran SP% **112.1**
Speed ratings (Par 100): **105,102,100,97**
CSF £7.79 TOTE £1.50; EX 5.90 Trifecta £17.00.
Owner Jones & Owen Promotions Ltd **Bred** Paul & Billy McEnery **Trained** Malpas, Cheshire

FOCUS
Race distance increased by 30yds. This was a well-run conditions race and the form is rated a shade positively.

4092 STELLA CIDRE H'CAP 1m 2f 75y
7:50 (7:50) (Class 4) (0-85,84) 3-Y-O **£6,225** (£1,864; £932; £466) **Stalls** High

Form RPR
31 **1** **Al Neksh**[30] 3023 3-9-7 **84**.. BenCurtis 5 89+
(William Haggas) *hld up: t.k.h: hdwy to trck ldng pair over 5f out: effrt and edgd rt appr fnl f: styd on to ld post* **15/8**[2]
2441 **2** nse **Justice Grace (IRE)**[14] 3596 3-9-5 **82**..................(b) RichardKingscote 1 86
(Ralph Beckett) *led: qcknd pce over 2f out: rdn over 1f out: edgd lft and hdd post* **3/1**[3]
-331 **3** 1 3/4 **Real Dominion (USA)**[44] 2580 3-9-5 **82**.......................... DavidProbert 4 83
(Andrew Balding) *trckd ldr: t.k.h: effrt over 2f out: kpt on same pce fnl f* **6/1**
3131 **4** 2 1/2 **Grapevine (IRE)**[8] 3801 3-9-7 **84** 6ex...................... MichaelJMMurphy 3 80
(Charles Hills) *trckd ldrs: t.k.h: effrt over 2f out: one pce over 1f out* **7/4**[1]
2m 19.19s (7.99) **Going Correction** +0.575s/f (Yiel) **4** Ran SP% **110.4**
Speed ratings (Par 102): **91,90,89,87**
CSF £7.76 TOTE £4.10; EX 8.70 Trifecta £17.10.
Owner Al Shaqab Racing **Bred** The Pocock Family **Trained** Newmarket, Suffolk

FOCUS
Race distance increased by 39yds. This was run at a crawl early on and the winner did well to come from behind and get up.

4093 MERSEYRAIL DAY H'CAP 5f 16y
8:20 (8:20) (Class 4) (0-80,80) 3-Y-O
£6,225 (£1,864; £932; £466; £233; £117) **Stalls** Low

Form RPR
6532 **1** **Midnight Malibu (IRE)**[20] 3420 3-9-3 **76**...................... JamesSullivan 2 83
(Tim Easterby) *led 1f: trckd ldr: effrt over 2f out: led 1f out: drvn rt out* **11/4**[2]
0312 **2** 3/4 **Laughton**[13] 3644 3-9-5 **78**.. ShaneGray 6 82+
(Kevin Ryan) *dwlt: in rr: hdwy over 2f out: styd on fnl 150yds: tk 2nd clsng stages* **4/1**[3]
0-32 **3** nk **This Is For You**[12] 3685 3-9-4 **77**................................ DavidProbert 1 80
(Andrew Balding) *t.k.h: led after 1f: hdd 1f out: kpt on same pce* **5/4**[1]
130 **4** 1 1/2 **Pink Martini (IRE)**[8] 3815 3-9-2 **75**................................ TomQueally 3 73
(Joseph Tuite) *trckd ldrs: one pce over 1f out* **22/1**
2120 **5** hd **First Bombardment**[20] 3420 3-8-13 **77**.................. AdamMcNamara(5) 4 74
(David O'Meara) *trckd ldrs: drvn 2f out: kpt on fnl 100yds* **9/1**
-510 **6** 3 **Belledesert**[41] 2693 3-9-4 **77**.. RoystonFfrench 7 63
(Steph Hollinshead) *in rr: drvn 3f out: sn reminders: nvr a factor* **11/1**
1m 3.47s (2.47) **Going Correction** +0.575s/f (Yiel) **6** Ran SP% **113.8**
Speed ratings (Par 102): **103,101,101,98,98 93**
CSF £14.38 CT £19.05 TOTE £2.40: £1.30, £2.10; EX 14.80 Trifecta £26.40.
Owner D A West **Bred** Kabansk Ltd & Rathbarry Stud **Trained** Great Habton, N Yorks

FOCUS
Race distance increased by 30yds. Not for the first time on the card, it paid to race handily.

4094 RUSSIAN STANDARD H'CAP 7f 2y
8:50 (8:51) (Class 4) (0-80,80) 3-Y-O+
£6,225 (£1,864; £932; £466; £233; £117) **Stalls** Low

Form RPR
0011 **1** **Gabrial The Tiger (IRE)**[14] 3595 4-9-7 **80**........... AdamMcNamara(5) 10 94
(Richard Fahey) *led after 1f: drvn clr over 1f out: styd on wl* **13/2**
4422 **2** 3 **Chaplin Bay (IRE)**[3] 3980 4-9-3 **71**................................ JamesSullivan 3 76
(Ruth Carr) *dwlt: in rr: hdwy on outside over 1f out: styd on to take 2nd clsng stages* **2/1**[1]
5233 **3** 1 **My Target (IRE)**[14] 3595 5-9-9 **77**.................................. PaulMulrennan 7 80
(Michael Wigham) *hld up towards rr: nt clr run over 2f out tl swtchd rt over 1f out: styd on to take 3rd clsng stages* **7/2**[2]
3606 **4** 1 **Queen Aggie (IRE)**[20] 3398 6-9-1 **72**...................... GeorgeDowning(3) 2 72
(Tony Carroll) *hld up in mid-div: t.k.h: effrt over 1f out: kpt on* **16/1**
2636 **5** 1/2 **Hawatif (IRE)**[16] 3521 3-9-2 **78**.................................... FrannyNorton 9 74+
(Mark Johnston) *s.i.s: detached in last: kpt on over 1f out: nvr a factor* **11/1**
00-4 **6** nse **Intensical (IRE)**[20] 3398 5-9-9 **77**.................................... RaulDaSilva 1 76
(Ivan Furtado) *chsd ldrs: one pce over 1f out* **9/2**[3]
3005 **7** shd **Ralphy Boy (IRE)**[11] 3708 7-9-6 **74**.............................. ConnorBeasley 6 72
(Alistair Whillans) *chsd ldrs: effrt over 2f out: one pce fnl 2f* **14/1**
0206 **8** 7 **Captain Revelation**[14] 3594 4-9-12 **80**.................. RichardKingscote 12 59
(Tom Dascombe) *led 1f: chsd wnr drvn over 2f out: lost pl appr fnl f: bhd whn eased clsng stages* **25/1**
0435 **9** 1 **Know Your Name**[23] 3286 5-9-5 **73**.. NeilFarley 8 50
(Eric Alston) *chsd ldrs: effrt over 2f out: wknd over 1f out* **25/1**
0200 **10** 1 **Clockmaker (IRE)**[14] 3595 10-9-12 **80**.............................. TomQueally 4 54
(Conor Dore) *mid-div: effrt on outer over 2f out: lost pl over 1f out: sn bhd* **16/1**
1m 30.11s (3.61) **Going Correction** +0.575s/f (Yiel)
WFA 3 from 4yo+ 8lb **10** Ran SP% **121.5**
Speed ratings (Par 105): **102,98,97,96,95 95,95,87,86,85**
CSF £20.76 CT £55.40 TOTE £5.80: £2.00, £1.80, £2.60; EX 24.30 Trifecta £72.00.
Owner Dr Marwan Koukash **Bred** Kenneth Heelan **Trained** Musley Bank, N Yorks

FOCUS
Race distance increased by 37yds. Once again the pace held up, the winner making every yard.

4095 HASHTAG AT ROSIES H'CAP 1m 4f 66y
9:20 (9:20) (Class 3) (0-90,90) 3-Y-O+
£7,781 (£2,330; £1,165; £582; £291; £146) **Stalls** Low

Form RPR
-000 **1** **Mistiroc**[27] 3162 5-9-12 **88**...(v1) BenCurtis 9 93
(John Quinn) *led 1f: trckd ldrs: upsides over 3f out: styd on to ld towards fin* **9/1**
0464 **2** 1/2 **Newera**[13] 3639 4-9-8 **84**..(p) RichardKingscote 1 88
(Tom Dascombe) *led after 1f: qcknd pce over 2f out: hdd and no ex clsng stages* **5/1**[3]
0622 **3** 3/4 **Modernism**[16] 3520 7-9-10 **86**.. FrannyNorton 2 89
(Richard Fahey) *trckd ldrs: drvn over 2f out: kpt on same pce to take 3rd clsng stages* **7/2**[2]
240- **4** 3/4 **Energia Fox (BRZ)**[302] 6245 6-9-7 **83**............................ BarryMcHugh 3 85
(Richard Fahey) *hld up in mid-div: hdwy on ins over 2f out: kpt on same pce fnl f* **15/2**
4063 **5** 3/4 **English Summer**[13] 3670 9-9-8 **89**......................(t) AdamMcNamara(5) 4 89
(Richard Fahey) *chsd ldrs: drvn over 2f out: kpt on one pce over 1f out* **5/1**[3]
-614 **6** 3 1/4 **Marengo**[13] 3636 5-8-11 **78**......................................(p) GeorgeBuckell(5) 5 73
(Bernard Llewellyn) *t.k.h in rr: hdwy after 5f: chsng ldrs over 5f out: drvn 3f out: one pce whn rdr dropped whip 100yds out* **18/1**
0-00 **7** nse **Hernandoshideaway**[58] 2157 4-10-0 **90**...................... PaulMulrennan 7 85
(Michael Dods) *stdd s: t.k.h in rr: sme hdwy over 1f out: nvr a factor* **14/1**
-211 **8** 6 **Man Look**[13] 3636 4-9-9 **85**.. DavidProbert 6 71+
(Andrew Balding) *s.s: hld up in rr: t.k.h: hdwy on outside to trck ldrs after 4f: upsides over 3f out: wknd over 1f out* **11/4**[1]
0-00 **9** 3 1/4 **Brigadoon**[28] 3118 9-9-1 **77**.. TomQueally 8 57
(Michael Appleby) *mid-div: t.k.h: drvn over 4f out: lost pl over 2f out* **33/1**
2m 46.2s (7.70) **Going Correction** +0.575s/f (Yiel) **9** Ran SP% **118.9**
Speed ratings (Par 107): **97,96,96,95,95 93,92,88,86**
CSF £55.12 CT £191.68 TOTE £10.70: £2.60, £1.80, £1.70; EX 58.60 Trifecta £523.50.
Owner Drew & Ailsa Russell **Bred** Jethro Bloodstock **Trained** Settrington, N Yorks

FOCUS
Race distance increased by 58yds. Another race run at a steady gallop, and the first two shared those positions throughout.
T/Plt: £133.10 to a £1 stake. Pool: £59,438.50 - 325.98 winning tickets T/Qpdt: £20.40 to a £1 stake. Pool: £4,947.12 - 178.70 winning tickets **Walter Glynn**

3704 MUSSELBURGH (R-H)
Friday, July 8

OFFICIAL GOING: Good (good to soft in places; 6.5)
Wind: Fresh, half against Weather: Cloudy, bright

4096 EPPERSTON H'CAP 5f
2:10 (2:10) (Class 6) (0-60,60) 3-Y-O+ **£3,234** (£962; £481; £240) **Stalls** High

Form RPR
00-0 **1** **Culloden**[7] 3843 4-8-11 **52**.. CharlieBennett(5) 7 57
(Shaun Harris) *mde all against stands' rail: rdn over 1f out: kpt on strly fnl f* **4/1**[3]
U006 **2** 2 1/4 **Thornaby Princess**[9] 3777 5-8-7 **48**......................(p) AnnaHesketh(5) 9 45
(Colin Teague) *t.k.h: chsd wnr thrght: effrt and rdn over 1f out: kpt on same pce ins fnl f* **12/1**
506- **3** nk **Cheeni**[335] 5138 4-8-7 **46** oh1.. JoeDoyle(3) 8 42
(Jim Goldie) *dwlt: bhd and outpcd: hdwy over 1f out: edgd rt and kpt on fnl f: nrst fin* **33/1**
6000 **4** 1 **Caymus**[24] 3268 3-9-0 **55** ow2...(t1) DaleSwift 11 45
(Tracy Waggott) *dwlt: hld up in tch: hdwy and swtchd rt over 1f out: kpt on same pce ins fnl f* **25/1**
0-60 **5** 6 **Ya Boy Sir (IRE)**[15] 3549 9-8-10 **46** oh1......................(p) AndrewMullen 5 17
(Iain Jardine) *s.i.s: hld up bhd ldng gp: rdn over 2f out: wknd over 1f out* **12/1**
0204 **6** 6 **Little Belter (IRE)**[10] 3755 4-9-6 **56**..............................(p) PhillipMakin 6 5
(Keith Dalgleish) *chsd ldrs tl rdn and wknd appr fnl f* **5/2**[2]
0000 **7** 2 1/2 **It's Time For Bed**[10] 3755 4-8-10 **46** oh1........................ DuranFentiman 12
(Linda Perratt) *trckd ldrs: rdn 1/2-way: wknd over 1f out* **80/1**
3562 **8** 5 **Ryedale Rio (IRE)**[6] 3882 3-9-5 **60**...................................... DavidAllan 4
(Tim Easterby) *hld up on outside: drvn along 1/2-way: wknd wl over 1f out* **13/8**[1]
1m 1.82s (1.42) **Going Correction** +0.375s/f (Good)
WFA 3 from 4yo+ 5lb **8** Ran SP% **110.1**
Speed ratings (Par 101): **103,99,98,97,87 78,74,66**
CSF £44.74 CT £1278.18 TOTE £5.40: £2.20, £1.90, £5.70; EX 51.10 Trifecta £1921.40 Part won..
Owner Burflex (Scaffolding) Ltd **Bred** Burton Agnes Stud Co Ltd **Trained** Carburton, Notts

FOCUS
The going was good, good to soft in places. The bottom bend was out 2yds adding 7yds to the races at 7f and further. They went a fair pace in this modest handicap and the first four pulled clear. Weakish form for the grade.

4097 MUSSELBURGH SILVER ARROW MAIDEN STKS 7f 30y
2:50 (2:50) (Class 5) 2-Y-O **£3,234** (£962; £481; £240) **Stalls** Low

Form RPR
1 **Syphax (USA)** 2-9-5 0.. TomEaves 7 74+
(Kevin Ryan) *noisy and green in paddock: missed break: hld up: hdwy on outside over 2f out: led ins fnl f: pushed out* **2/1**[2]

3 **2** *3/4* **Lucky Esteem**[13] 3640 2-9-0 0.. PhillipMakin 3 67
(Mark Johnston) *led: rdn and hrd pressed fr 2f out: hdd ins fnl f: kpt on towards fin* **11/10**[1]

6 **3** *1/2* **Elementary**[16] 3526 2-9-2 0.................................. DonnachaO'Brien(3) 1 71
(Michael Bell) *t.k.h early: trckd ldr: nt clr run briefly over 2f out: effrt and ev ch over 1f out to ins fnl f: kpt on same pce* **9/2**[3]

4 *5* **Peny Arcade** 2-9-0 0.. AndrewMullen 6 53
(Alistair Whillans) *trckd ldrs: drvn along over 2f out: wknd over 1f out* **33/1**

0 **5** *2* **Bajan Spice (IRE)**[20] 3416 2-8-7 0.............................. RowanScott(7) 5 48
(Ann Duffield) *green and unruly in paddock: chsd ldrs: drvn along over 2f out: wknd over 1f out* **40/1**

6 *hd* **Halawain (USA)** 2-9-5 0.. CamHardie 2 52
(John Quinn) *dwlt: t.k.h in tch: nt clr run over 2f out: swtchd lft wl over 1f out: sn btn* **7/1**

1m 31.66s (2.66) **Going Correction** +0.375s/f (Good) **6** Ran SP% **117.0**
Speed ratings (Par 94): **99,98,97,91,89 89**
CSF £4.85 TOTE £4.00: £2.40, £1.30; EX 6.30 Trifecta £13.60.
Owner K&J Bloodstock Ltd **Bred** Pin Oak Stud LLC **Trained** Hambleton, N Yorks

FOCUS
Rce distance increased by 7 yards. They went a good pace and the three market leaders finished clear of the rest in this maiden. A good effort from the winner.

4098 MUSSELBURGH BI-CENTENARY CUP FILLIES' H'CAP 1m 208y
3:25 (3:27) (Class 5) (0-70,70) 3-Y-O **£5,175** (£1,540; £769; £384) **Stalls** Low

Form RPR

1344 **1** **Livella Fella (IRE)**[6] 3878 3-9-7 **70**.................................... PhillipMakin 3 72
(Keith Dalgleish) *mde all: set slow pce: rdn: edgd lft and hrd pressed over 1f out: hld on gamely ins fnl f* **11/4**[2]

0-04 **2** *hd* **Page Of Wands**[15] 3550 3-9-0 **63**.. DavidNolan 1 64
(Karen McLintock) *trckd ldrs: rdn over 2f out: flashed tail repeatedly fr over 1f out: pressed wnr last 100yds: kpt on: jst hld* **16/1**

0-63 **3** *1/2* **Forecaster**[44] 2576 3-9-0 **66**.................................. DonnachaO'Brien(3) 5 66
(Michael Bell) *dwlt: sn trcking wnr: rdn and ev ch over 1f out: kpt on same pce last 75yds* **6/5**[1]

0004 **4** *2 1/2* **Kerry Icon**[5] 3921 3-8-2 **51** oh6.. AndrewMullen 2 46
(Iain Jardine) *t.k.h: hld up in tch: effrt and rdn over 2f out: hdwy over 1f out: outpcd ins fnl f* **9/1**

0331 **5** *3 3/4* **Raven Banner (IRE)**[8] 3804 3-9-6 **69** 6ex.............................. DaleSwift 4 55
(Daniel Mark Loughnane) *hld up in tch: effrt and pushed along on outside over 2f out: wknd over 1f out* **7/2**[3]

1m 54.84s (0.94) **Going Correction** +0.375s/f (Good) **5** Ran SP% **110.2**
Speed ratings (Par 97): **110,109,109,107,103**
CSF £35.82 TOTE £3.30: £1.50, £5.00; EX 31.70 Trifecta £77.00.
Owner Middleham Park Racing Xxiii **Bred** Manister House Stud **Trained** Carluke, S Lanarks

FOCUS
Race distance increased by 7 yards. This was tactical and there was a tight three-way finish.

4099 MUSSELBURGH RIDING OF THE MARCHES H'CAP 1m 4f 100y
3:55 (3:56) (Class 6) (0-65,69) 4-Y-O+ **£3,234** (£962; £481; £240) **Stalls** Low

Form RPR

1221 **1** **Henry Smith**[11] 3706 4-9-6 **69** 6ex.......................(b) RobJFitzpatrick(5) 10 79+
(Garry Moss) *dwlt and wnt sharply rt s: hld up: smooth hdwy on outside to ld over 2f out: sn pushed clr: idled ins fnl f: kpt on* **11/4**[1]

4-03 **2** *1/2* **Amirli (IRE)**[11] 3706 5-9-7 **65**..(p) CamHardie 2 72
(Alistair Whillans) *t.k.h early: trckd ldrs: rdn and outpcd over 2f out: rallied to chse wnr 1f out: kpt on fin* **9/2**[2]

5300 **3** *1* **Neuf Des Coeurs**[11] 3706 5-8-9 **58**..........................(p) GarryWhillans(5) 5 64
(Iain Jardine) *hld up in last pl: hdwy on outside over 2f out: rdn and kpt on ins fnl f: nt pce to chal* **12/1**

0264 **4** *3* **Bogardus (IRE)**[15] 3563 5-9-5 **63**.. DavidNolan 12 64
(Patrick Holmes) *led at modest gallop: rdn and hdd over 2f out: rallied: lost 2nd and outpcd 1f out* **7/1**

0666 **5** *1 3/4* **New Colours**[27] 3154 5-8-2 **46** oh1..............................(p) AndrewMullen 6 44
(Linda Perratt) *t.k.h in midfield: drvn and outpcd over 3f out: rallied over 1f out: nvr able to chal* **33/1**

600- **6** *3/4* **Ronaldinho (IRE)**[8] 5777 6-8-13 **57**....................................(t) TomEaves 8 54
(Dianne Sayer) *prom: drvn along fr 5f out: rallied: outpcd fr 2f out* **20/1**

4005 **7** *1/2* **Chorus of Lies**[20] 3418 4-9-2 **60**.. DaleSwift 13 56
(Tracy Waggott) *chsd ldrs: wnt 2nd briefly over 2f out: outpcd over 1f out* **16/1**

0540 **8** *3/4* **Silva Samourai**[11] 3706 7-8-4 **48**................................. DuranFentiman 9 43
(Susan Corbett) *bmpd s: hld up on outside: hdwy and prom over 4f out: rdn over 2f out: edgd rt and wknd over 1f out* **66/1**

2126 **9** *1/2* **Chauvelin**[7] 3844 5-8-6 **50**...(b) AndrewElliott 1 44
(Richard Guest) *plld hrd: hld up: pushed along over 3f out: no imp whn nt clr run briefly over 1f out: sn btn* **11/2**[3]

6-0 **10** *2* **Big McIntosh (IRE)**[44] 2582 4-8-9 **60**........................ JonathanFisher(7) 7 51
(John Ryan) *chsd ldr to over 2f out: wknd over 1f out* **12/1**

0-06 **11** *1/2* **Cassandane (IRE)**[39] 2086 4-8-4 **53**.......................... CharlieBennett(5) 4 43
(Shaun Harris) *dwlt: hld up: drvn along over 3f out: btn fnl 2f* **50/1**

-405 **12** *6* **Merchant Of Dubai**[32] 2962 11-9-1 **62**.............................. JoeDoyle(3) 3 42
(Jim Goldie) *in tch on ins: drvn over 3f out: wknd over 2f out* **9/1**

2m 47.38s (5.38) **Going Correction** +0.375s/f (Good) **12** Ran SP% **115.2**
Speed ratings (Par 101): **97,96,96,94,92 92,92,91,91,89 89,85**
CSF £13.46 CT £125.74 TOTE £4.60: £2.00, £2.60, £2.70; EX 15.30 Trifecta £133.90.
Owner Pinnacle Duo Partnership **Bred** M Pennell **Trained** Wynyard, Stockton-On-Tees

FOCUS
Race distance increased by 7 yards. The well-backed favourite looked value for more than the winning margin in this handicap. Straightforward form in behind.

4100 MUSSELBURGH LINKS, THE OLD COURSE H'CAP 5f
4:25 (4:25) (Class 4) (0-80,78) 3-Y-O+ **£6,469** (£1,925; £962; £481) **Stalls** High

Form RPR

4662 **1** **Classy Anne**[4] 3944 6-9-7 **76**..(p) JoeDoyle(3) 13 85
(Jim Goldie) *hld up on ins: nt clr run fr 1/2-way: weaved through and gd hdwy to ld wl ins fnl f: kpt on strly* **11/2**[2]

1242 **2** *1* **Henley**[11] 3711 4-9-3 **69**.. DaleSwift 10 71
(Tracy Waggott) *trckd ldrs: n.m.r 1/2-way: effrt whn nt clr run over 1f out: kpt on wl fnl f to take 2nd last stride* **7/1**

4054 **3** *shd* **Pearl Acclaim (IRE)**[27] 3150 6-9-12 **78**..............................(p) TomEaves 6 83
(David Nicholls) *trckd ldrs: led gng wl over 1f out: sn rdn: hdd wl ins fnl f: kpt on* **13/2**[3]

1021 **4** *nse* **Fumbo Jumbo (IRE)**[11] 3709 3-9-5 **76** 6ex........................ DavidAllan 9 78+
(Garry Moss) *prom: nt clr run fr 1/2-way: swtchd rt and hdwy ins fnl f: kpt on: nrst fin* **11/10**[1]

4305 **5** *nse* **Bunce (IRE)**[11] 3709 8-8-11 **63**.. AndrewMullen 11 67+
(Linda Perratt) *bhd and sn pushed along: hdwy whn nt clr run fr over 1f out to ins fnl f: kpt on wl towards fin* **50/1**

5120 **6** *1 1/4* **Imperial Legend (IRE)**[6] 3875 7-9-11 **77**.............................. PaulQuinn 1 77
(David Nicholls) *bhd and sn pushed along: hdwy on outside to chse ldrs over 1f out: no ex ins fnl f* **16/1**

0366 **7** *1/2* **Salvatore Fury (IRE)**[30] 3021 6-8-12 **64**........................(p) PhillipMakin 3 62
(Keith Dalgleish) *hld up: hdwy to press ldrs over 1f out: rdn and no ex ins fnl f* **12/1**

600/ **8** *shd* **Storm Trooper (IRE)**[640] 7017 5-8-6 **65**................. DanielleMooney(7) 5 63
(David Nicholls) *trckd ldrs: nt clr run over 2f out to over 1f out: wknd ins fnl f* **50/1**

6535 **9** *5* **Honcho (IRE)**[6] 3907 4-8-9 **68**.................................... JonathanFisher(7) 4 48
(John Ryan) *missed break: bhd and outpcd: nvr on terms* **22/1**

-004 **10** *2* **Captain Dunne (IRE)**[38] 2775 11-9-11 **77**..................... DuranFentiman 2 49
(Tim Easterby) *w ldrs: led 1/2-way to over 1f out: wknd ins fnl f* **20/1**

105- **11** *2 1/4* **I'll Be Good**[286] 6747 7-9-9 **75**.. CamHardie 8 39
(John David Riches) *led to 1/2-way: rdn and wknd over 1f out* **22/1**

1m 1.59s (1.19) **Going Correction** +0.375s/f (Good)
WFA 3 from 4yo+ 5lb **11** Ran SP% **119.8**
Speed ratings (Par 105): **105,103,103,103,103 101,100,100,92,88 85**
CSF £41.49 CT £262.62 TOTE £6.20: £2.40, £2.30, £2.30; EX 52.20 Trifecta £292.70.
Owner Johnnie Delta Racing **Bred** Jonayro Investments **Trained** Uplawmoor, E Renfrews

FOCUS
Race distance increased by 7 yards. They raced centre to stands' side in this sprint handicap and there were some hard-luck stories.

4101 MUSSELBURGH FAIR DAY ASSOCIATION H'CAP 2m
4:55 (4:56) (Class 4) (0-80,80) 4-Y-O+ **£6,469** (£1,925; £962; £481) **Stalls** High

Form RPR

/235 **1** **Frederic**[23] 3294 5-8-10 **69**.. TomEaves 8 76
(Micky Hammond) *hld up in tch: hdwy whn nt clr run over 2f out: rdn to ld ins fnl f: hld on wl* **10/1**

-105 **2** *shd* **Maoi Chinn Tire (IRE)**[25] 3221 9-9-0 **73**..............................(p) DavidNolan 1 79
(Jennie Candlish) *cl up: rdn over 2f out: led 1f out to ins fnl f: rallied: jst hld* **12/1**

6043 **3** *1 3/4* **Giant Redwood (IRE)**[19] 3437 4-9-1 **77**............(p) DonnachaO'Brien(3) 4 81
(Michael Bell) *led at ordinary gallop: rdn over 2f out: hdd 1f out: kpt on same pce* **9/2**[2]

5322 **4** *1 1/4* **Aldreth**[27] 3149 5-8-11 **70**..(p) CamHardie 3 72
(Michael Easterby) *prom: stdy hdwy over 2f out: rdn over 1f out: kpt on same pce fnl f* **5/2**[1]

1404 **5** *1 1/4* **Jan Smuts (IRE)**[2] 4004 8-8-10 **72**............................(tp) ShelleyBirkett(3) 6 73
(Wilf Storey) *hld up: rdn over 2f out: hdwy over 1f out: no imp fnl f* **15/2**

0132 **6** *1 3/4* **Kiwayu**[20] 3417 7-8-10 **69**..(p) AndrewMullen 2 68
(Philip Kirby) *prom: drvn along over 2f out: sn outpcd: no imp fr over 1f out* **13/2**

-606 **7** *2 1/4* **Wor Lass**[13] 3659 8-8-12 **76**.. AnnaHesketh(5) 7 72
(Susan Corbett) *dwlt: hld up: rdn over 3f out: nvr on terms* **18/1**

-102 **7** *dht* **Braes Of Lochalsh**[21] 3345 5-9-1 **77**.................................. JoeDoyle(3) 10 73
(Jim Goldie) *racd wd 4f: cl up: rdn over 2f out: sn lost pl* **5/1**[3]

-000 **9** *2 3/4* **La Bacouetteuse (FR)**[15] 3547 11-8-9 **68**..........................(b) DavidAllan 5 61
(Iain Jardine) *hld up: drvn and outpcd over 2f out: n.d after* **20/1**

3m 37.48s (3.98) **Going Correction** +0.375s/f (Good) **9** Ran SP% **115.3**
Speed ratings (Par 105): **105,104,104,103,102 101,100,100,99**
CSF £121.55 CT £617.53 TOTE £6.40: £2.00, £2.50, £2.00; EX 117.60 Trifecta £362.20.
Owner Paul & Clare Rooney **Bred** Fittocks Stud **Trained** Middleham, N Yorks

FOCUS
They went a steady pace and there was a tight finish in this fair staying handicap.

4102 ADAM NISH 50 YEARS SERVICE H'CAP 7f 30y
5:30 (5:30) (Class 5) (0-70,69) 3-Y-O+ **£3,234** (£962; £481; £240) **Stalls** Low

Form RPR

6500 **1** **Rasaman (IRE)**[11] 3708 12-9-7 **65**.. JoeDoyle(3) 7 71
(Jim Goldie) *rrd s: hld up: shkn up and hdwy over 1f out: kpt on wl fnl f to ld cl home* **16/1**

-000 **2** *shd* **Circuitous**[6] 3880 8-9-4 **59**...(v) TomEaves 12 65
(Keith Dalgleish) *led: rdn 2f out: kpt on fnl f: hdd cl home* **25/1**

-023 **3** *2 1/4* **Gypsy Major**[4] 3946 4-9-0 **55**..(b) DavidAllan 9 55
(Garry Moss) *trckd ldr: effrt and rdn over 2f out: kpt on same pce ins fnl f* **11/4**[1]

1000 **4** *1 1/2* **Mr Cool Cash**[4] 3952 4-9-10 **68**...........................(t) DonnachaO'Brien(3) 6 64
(Richard Guest) *prom: rdn over 2f out: kpt on same pce fnl f* **4/1**[3]

3-00 **5** *nse* **Charava (IRE)**[17] 3479 4-9-5 **60**.....................................(v[1]) DavidNolan 10 59
(Patrick Holmes) *plld hrd: hld up: hdwy and prom over 1f out: keeping on whn short of room and blkd ins fnl f* **10/1**

454 **6** *2* **Check 'Em Tuesday (IRE)**[13] 3634 3-9-2 **65**........................ DaleSwift 5 52
(Daniel Mark Loughnane) *bhd: pushed along 1/2-way: hdwy over 1f out: nvr able to chal* **16/1**

02 **7** *shd* **Dark Crystal**[5] 3922 5-9-5 **60**.. AndrewMullen 2 58
(Linda Perratt) *t.k.h: hld up in midfield: rdn over 2f out: hdwy over 1f out: one pce whn bdly hmpd ins fnl f: nt rcvr* **7/1**

3100 **8** *4 1/2* **Faintly (USA)**[20] 3394 5-9-13 **68**... CamHardie 3 46
(Ruth Carr) *hld up in midfield: rdn over 2f out: drifted lft and wknd wl over 1f out* **16/1**

6422 **9** *2 3/4* **Dasheen**[7] 3841 3-9-6 **69**... PhillipMakin 8 36
(Mark Johnston) *chsd ldrs: drvn and outpcd over 3f out: btn fnl 2f* **10/3**[2]

0000 **10** *3 3/4* **Marmarus**[30] 3040 5-8-4 **52**.. DanielleMooney(7) 4 12
(David Nicholls) *dwlt: t.k.h in rr: hdwy to chse ldrs 1/2-way: rdn and wknd over 2f out* **50/1**

1m 31.0s (2.00) **Going Correction** +0.375s/f (Good)
WFA 3 from 4yo+ 8lb **10** Ran SP% **114.8**
Speed ratings (Par 103): **103,102,100,98,98 96,96,91,87,83**
CSF £346.25 CT £1431.21 TOTE £12.50: £2.00, £2.30, £2.00; EX 178.30 Trifecta £5510.80 Part won..
Owner J S Goldie **Bred** Rasana Partnership **Trained** Uplawmoor, E Renfrews

FOCUS
Race distance increased by 7 yards. There was an exciting finish in this minor handicap and a 12yo swooped late.

T/Plt: £276.30 to a £1 stake. Pool: £26,705.87 - 70.55 winning tickets T/Qpdt: £45.30 to a £1 stake. Pool: £4,060.12 - 66.20 winning tickets **Richard Young**

[4059]NEWMARKET (R-H)

Friday, July 8

OFFICIAL GOING: Good to firm (overall 8.0, stands' side 8.2, centre 8.0, far side 8.1)

Wind: light, half behind Weather: overcast turning bright after race 2

4103 WEATHERBYS EBF STALLIONS MAIDEN STKS (PLUS 10 RACE) 7f

2:05 (2:05) (Class 4) 2-Y-O **£6,469** (£1,925; £962; £481) **Stalls** Low

Form				RPR
	1		**Dubai Hero (FR)** 2-9-0 0 JamesDoyle 6 (Saeed bin Suroor) *squeezed out leaving stalls: hld up in tch in last trio: smooth hdwy over 1f out: led over 1f out: sn rn green and hung rt: r.o wl ins fnl f* **11/1**	88+
	2	1 ½	**D'bai (IRE)** 2-9-0 0 JamesMcDonald 2 (Charlie Appleby) *hld up in tch in last trio: effrt over 1f out: rdn and hdwy ins fnl f: styd on strly fnl 100yds: wnt 2nd last strides* **9/2**[3]	84+
62	3	nk	**Hyde Park**[20] 3408 2-9-0 0 FrankieDettori 1 (John Gosden) *hld up in tch in midfield: effrt over 1f out: sn chsng wnr: kpt on but no imp ins fnl f: lost 2nd last strides* **11/4**[1]	83
3	4	1	**Khalidi**[13] 3661 2-9-0 0 RyanMoore 3 (John Gosden) *chsd ldrs: rdn over 1f out: unable qck whn sltly impeded and swtchd lft 1f out: styd on same pce ins fnl f* **7/2**[2]	80
	5	¾	**Mr Tyrrell (IRE)** 2-9-0 0 PatDobbs 10 (Richard Hannon) *chsd ldr: rdn and edgd lft wl over 1f out: unable qck ent fnl f: styd on same pce after* **10/1**	78
23	6	1 ¾	**Evergate**[38] 2756 2-9-0 0 JimCrowley 11 (Hugo Palmer) *t.k.h: led: rdn and hdd over 1f out: no ex u.p 1f out: wknd ins fnl f* **13/2**	74
	7	hd	**Fujaira Bridge (IRE)** 2-9-0 0 AndreaAtzeni 9 (Roger Varian) *t.k.h: hld up in tch in midfield: effrt and squeezed for room over 1f out: unable qck and sltly impeded ent fnl f: wknd ins fnl f* **8/1**	75+
	8	1 ¾	**Gilgamesh** 2-9-0 0 JamieSpencer 4 (George Scott) *stdd s: hld up in tch in last trio: pushed along over 1f out: kpt on same pce ins fnl f: nvr trbld ldrs* **33/1**	68
	9	2 ½	**Amlad (IRE)** 2-9-0 0 JoeFanning 5 (Ed Dunlop) *in tch in midfield: rdn 2f out: sn outpcd and btn whn swtchd lft 1f out: wknd ins fnl f* **33/1**	62
	10	½	**Mungo Madness** 2-9-0 0 AdamBeschizza 7 (Julia Feilden) *stdd and wnt rt s: t.k.h: hld up in tch in midfield: rdn over 1f out: sn outpcd u.p: wknd fnl f* **100/1**	60
	11	8	**Chaparrachik (IRE)** 2-9-0 0 OisinMurphy 8 (Amanda Perrett) *hld up in tch in midfield: lost pl and rdn 2f out: bhd 1f out: wknd* **33/1**	39

1m 24.72s (-0.98) **Going Correction** -0.225s/f (Firm) **11 Ran SP% 118.8**

Speed ratings (Par 96): **96,94,93,92,91 89,89,87,84,84 75**

CSF £59.36 TOTE £12.90: £3.20, £1.90, £1.40; EX 56.90 Trifecta £404.10.

Owner Godolphin **Bred** S C E A Haras De Saint Pair **Trained** Newmarket, Suffolk

FOCUS

Stands'-side track used and all race distances as advertised. Stalls on stands' side except 1m2f, centre. The ground had dried out overnight with the 'good in places' removed, so it was good to firm all over (GoingStick: far side and centre 8.4, stands' side 8.6). The winning rider in the opener said of the conditions: "It's quick ground, quite similar to yesterday really." This opening maiden has been won by some decent performers over the years, including the subsequent Group 1 winner Rio De La Plata and the Group winners Soul City, Elusive Pimpernel and Native Khan during the past ten runnings. There should be plenty of winners coming out of this year's renewal, which resulted in a 1-2 for Godolphin. They came up the centre and the winning time was 1.72sec outside standard. The form is rated around the good race average and the third and fourth home.

4104 JOHN BANKS INFINITI CAMBRIDGE H'CAP 1m

2:40 (2:40) (Class 3) (0-90,90) 3-Y-O+ **£12,938** (£3,850; £1,924; £962) **Stalls** Low

Form				RPR
-211	1		**Fawaareq (IRE)**[15] 3571 3-9-4 89 PaulHanagan 7 (Owen Burrows) *t.k.h: hld up in tch in midfield: effrt to chal and hung lft over 1f out: sustained effrt to ld wl ins fnl f: rdn out* **7/1**[3]	95
1-04	2	nk	**Ifwecan**[21] 3358 5-10-0 90 FrankieDettori 6 (Martin Smith) *led for 1f: styd chsng ldr tl rdn to wl over 1f out: drvn over 1f out: battled on wl tl hdd wl ins fnl f: kpt on but a jst hld after* **20/1**	97
-462	3	¾	**Archie (IRE)**[29] 3055 4-9-12 88 OisinMurphy 10 (Clive Cox) *taken down early: racd towards far side thrght: t.k.h: chsd ldrs overall: rdn to chse ldng pair over 1f out: drvn pressing ldrs 1f out: kpt on same pce ins fnl f* **16/1**	93
-001	4	½	**Pensax Boy**[14] 3605 4-9-4 80 JimCrowley 4 (Ian Williams) *chsd ldrs: effrt and drifted lft u.p over 1f out: styd on same pce ins fnl f* **25/1**	84
3-0	5	¾	**Mediciman**[50] 2412 3-8-7 78 MickaelBarzalona 2 (Henry Candy) *hld up in tch in midfield: effrt over 1f out: hung lft 1f out: kpt on u.p fnl 100yds: nt rch ldrs* **9/1**	78
41	6	1 ¼	**Clear Water (IRE)**[48] 2483 3-9-5 90 JamesDoyle 3 (Saeed bin Suroor) *in tch towards rr: rdn and hdwy wl over 1f out: chsd ldrs 1f out: hung lft and nt clrest of run ins fnl f: wknd towards fin* **15/2**	86
30-2	7	2 ¼	**Weld Al Emarat**[29] 3061 4-9-10 86 RyanMoore 12 (Simon Crisford) *racd towards far side thrght: nt that wl away but sn rcvrd to ld after 1f: hdd and rdn wl over 1f out: no ex u.p over 1f out: btn and eased wl ins fnl f* **6/1**[2]	78
0600	8	nk	**The Warrior (IRE)**[16] 3534 4-9-13 89 PatDobbs 5 (Amanda Perrett) *hld up in tch towards rr: effrt 2f out: sme hdwy u.p over 1f out: no imp 1f out: wknd ins fnl f* **33/1**	80
61-5	9	2 ¾	**Column**[76] 1623 3-9-4 89 FrederikTylicki 11 (James Fanshawe) *racd towards far side thrght: hld up towards rr overall: rdn 2f out: no imp and wl hld 1f out* **7/1**[3]	71
12	10	7	**Blair House (IRE)**[34] 2907 3-9-5 90 JamesMcDonald 9 (Charlie Appleby) *racd towards far side thrght: dwlt: sn rcvrd and chsd ldrs overall: rdn over 1f out: sn lost pl and btn: wknd fnl f* **5/2**[1]	53
P030	P		**Passing Star**[22] 3303 5-9-10 86 AndreaAtzeni 8 (Charles Hills) *in tch in midfield: rdn 2f out: sn lost pl: bhd whn p.u and dismntd ins fnl f* **28/1**	
0501	P		**Edgar Balthazar**[16] 3518 4-9-12 88 (p) JoeFanning 1 (Keith Dalgleish) *dwlt: hld up in tch in rr: effrt over 1f out: no imp whn faltered and lost action 1f out: sn eased: p.u and dismntd ins fnl f* **25/1**	

1m 36.79s (-3.21) **Going Correction** -0.225s/f (Firm)

WFA 3 from 4yo+ 9lb **12 Ran SP% 114.3**

Speed ratings (Par 107): **107,106,105,105,104 103,101,100,98,91 ,**

CSF £141.02 CT £2138.72 TOTE £7.90: £2.60, £4.10, £4.50; EX 128.50 Trifecta £1068.40.

Owner Hamdan Al Maktoum **Bred** Shadwell Estate Company Limited **Trained** Lambourn, Berks

FOCUS

A warm handicap which became something of a war of attrition with a couple of the market leaders disappointing and two horses pulled up. The field split into two early with the larger group coming centre-to-nearside while four raced more towards the far side, but the whole field ended the race towards the far rail. The winning time was only just over half a second outside standard. The winner is on the upgrade.

4105 PRICE BAILEY EBF STALLIONS FILLIES' H'CAP 7f

3:10 (3:11) (Class 2) (0-100,99) 3-Y-O

£15,562 (£4,660; £2,330; £1,165; £582; £292) **Stalls** Low

Form				RPR
-130	1		**Mise En Rose (USA)**[23] 3274 3-9-1 93 JamesMcDonald 13 (Charlie Appleby) *trckd ldr: clsd and upsides travelling strly 2f out: pushed into ld over 1f out: qcknd and in command 1f out: r.o wl: quite comf* **13/2**	104
1-13	2	1 ¼	**Eternally**[16] 3519 3-8-9 87 JimCrowley 7 (John Gosden) *t.k.h: chsd ldrs: swtchd lft and effrt over 1f out: chsd wnr and rt 1f out: r.o u.p for clr 2nd but nvr gng pce to chal wnr* **4/1**[2]	95
4-04	3	1 ¾	**Chiringuita (USA)**[16] 3519 3-8-7 85 MickaelBarzalona 12 (James Bethell) *stdd s: t.k.h: wl in tch in midfield: effrt over 1f out: 3rd and styd on same pce u.p ins fnl f* **14/1**	88
6500	4	1 ½	**Rebel Surge (IRE)**[23] 3274 3-8-12 90 WilliamTwiston-Davies 11 (Richard Spencer) *hld up in tch in last quarter: rdn and hdwy over 1f out: 4th and styd on same pce u.p ins fnl f* **25/1**	89
1	5	hd	**Permission**[20] 3411 3-8-9 90 DanielMuscutt[(3)] 4 (James Fanshawe) *stdd s: t.k.h: hld up in tch in last quartet: effrt over 1f out: swtchd rt ent fnl f: styd on u.p ins fnl f: no threat to ldrs* **6/1**[3]	89+
626-	6	½	**Aqua Libre**[251] 7631 3-8-8 86 OisinMurphy 10 (Philip McBride) *awkward leaving stalls and s.i.s: hld up in tch in rr: hdwy u.p ent fnl f: styd on same pce after: nvr trbld ldrs* **25/1**	83
5-61	7	hd	**Al Shahaniya (IRE)**[25] 3213 3-8-5 83 JimmyQuinn 1 (John Quinn) *hld up in cl 5th: rdn to chse ldrs over 1f out: unable qck 1f out: outpcd ins fnl f* **14/1**	80
0-20	8	hd	**Aljuljalah (USA)**[23] 3274 3-9-7 99 AndreaAtzeni 5 (Roger Varian) *chsd ldrs: effrt u.p to chse wnr over 1f out tl 1f out: outpcd ins fnl f* **8/1**	95
3-32	9	1 ¾	**Aristocratic**[49] 2431 3-8-2 80 oh1 JoeFanning 6 (Sir Michael Stoute) *t.k.h: hld up in tch in midfield: rdn and unable qck over 1f out: wknd ins fnl f* **7/2**[1]	72
110-	10	¾	**Drifting Spirit (IRE)**[273] 7073 3-8-12 90 FrederikTylicki 8 (Richard Fahey) *hld up in tch in midfield: effrt and no imp over 1f out: btn 1f out: wl hld and plugged on same pce ins fnl f* **14/1**	80
-520	11	6	**Alsaaden**[27] 3130 3-8-8 86 PaulHanagan 3 (Richard Hannon) *hld up in tch in last quartet: effrt over 1f out: no imp whn sltly hmpd ent fnl f: sn btn: no ch whn eased ins fnl f* **22/1**	59
-340	12	1 ¾	**Quality Time (IRE)**[23] 3274 3-9-3 95 [1] JamesDoyle 2 (Saeed bin Suroor) *led: jnd and rdn 2f out: hdd over 1f out and sn lost pl: bhd and eased ins fnl f* **12/1**	64

1m 23.51s (-2.19) **Going Correction** -0.225s/f (Firm) **12 Ran SP% 120.7**

Speed ratings (Par 103): **103,101,99,97,97 97,96,96,94,93 86,84**

CSF £32.44 CT £361.59 TOTE £5.40: £1.70, £2.20, £5.60; EX 36.70 Trifecta £465.40.

Owner Godolphin **Bred** Hinkle Farms **Trained** Newmarket, Suffolk

FOCUS

This good-quality fillies' handicap turned into something of a dash nearing the two-furlong marker and racing handily was again a must. A clear pb from the winner.

4106 DUCHESS OF CAMBRIDGE STKS (SPONSORED BY IMAGINE CRUISING) (THE CHERRY HINTON) (GROUP 2) (FILLIES) 6f

3:45 (3:45) (Class 1) 2-Y-O

£45,368 (£17,200; £8,608; £4,288; £2,152; £1,080) **Stalls** Low

Form				RPR
401	1		**Roly Poly (USA)**[12] 3694 2-9-0 0 RyanMoore 7 (A P O'Brien, Ire) *w ldr: rdn and ev ch over 1f out: wandered lft u.p 1f out: drvn to ld 100yds out: styd on: drvn out* **6/1**[3]	105
55	2	½	**Magical Fire (IRE)**[12] 3694 2-9-0 0 ColmO'Donoghue 10 (M D O'Callaghan, Ire) *hld up wl in tch in midfield: effrt to press ldrs jst over 1f out: ev ch ins fnl f: kpt on u.p: wnt 2nd nr fin* **33/1**	103+
221	3	hd	**Nations Alexander (IRE)**[13] 3663 2-9-0 0 PatDobbs 8 (Richard Hannon) *pressed ldng pair: rdn and ev ch over 1f out: kpt on u.p: unable qck towards fin* **16/1**	103
16	4	shd	**Kilmah**[21] 3336 2-9-0 0 JoeFanning 4 (Mark Johnston) *sn led: rdn over 1f out: edgd lft 1f out: hdd 100yds out: styd on same pce u.p after* **6/1**[3]	102
1232	5	2	**Seafront**[12] 3694 2-9-0 0 JamieSpencer 6 (James Tate) *hld up wl in tch in midfield: effrt 2f out: rdn and unable qck over 1f out: styd on same pce ins fnl f* **14/1**	96
12	6	nk	**Bletchley**[21] 3336 2-9-0 0 OisinMurphy 3 (Ralph Beckett) *t.k.h: hld up in tch in midfield: clsd to chse ldrs 2f out: rdn and unable qck over 1f out: hld and styd on same pce ins fnl f* **9/4**[1]	95
1	7	nk	**Asidious Alexander (IRE)**[14] 3597 2-9-0 0 FrankieDettori 9 (Simon Crisford) *stdd bk into midfield after s: hld up in tch: effrt over 1f out: no imp: hld and styd on same pce ins fnl f* **8/1**	94
10	8	1 ¼	**Somebody To Love (IRE)**[13] 3663 2-9-0 0 AndreaAtzeni 2 (Richard Hannon) *s.i.s: hld up in tch in rr: effrt wl over 1f out: no imp and drifting lft ent fnl f: no ch but kpt on steadily ins fnl f* **16/1**	90
1	9	1 ¼	**Nasimi**[43] 2612 2-9-0 0 JamesDoyle 5 (Charlie Appleby) *stdd bk towards rr after 1f: in tch: effrt 2f out: sn rdn and no imp: wl hld and styd on same pce fnl f* **9/2**[2]	86
1	10	7	**Soul Silver (IRE)**[29] 3073 2-9-0 0 JimCrowley 1 (David Simcock) *restless in stalls: hld up in tch in last pair: effrt 2f out: sn rdn and no hdwy: wknd fnl f* **16/1**	64

1m 10.72s (-1.78) **Going Correction** -0.225s/f (Firm) **10 Ran SP% 115.9**

Speed ratings (Par 107): **102,101,101,100,98 97,97,95,94,84**

CSF £176.99 TOTE £7.10: £2.00, £9.50, £4.40; EX 161.20 Trifecta £1241.70.

Owner Michael Tabor & Derrick Smith & Mrs John Magnier **Bred** Misty For Me Syndicate **Trained** Cashel, Co Tipperary

FOCUS
Only one previous Group race winner in this season's renewal, but several of these had smart form coming into the race including a Listed winner and the second and sixth from the Albany. The race also featured three fillies who had been successful in their only previous starts. However, it was a Group 3 contest at the Curragh a couple of weeks earlier that proved the key, with the 1-2-5 from that contest finishing 1-5-2 here. Those that raced up with the pace appeared to hold the advantage, but with barely a length covering the first four home the form doesn't anything out of this world, especially with a couple of the fancied contenders running below par. Just an ordinary renewal.

4107 TATTERSALLS 250TH YEAR FALMOUTH STKS (BRITISH CHAMPIONS SERIES) (GROUP 1) (F&M) 1m
4:15 (4:18) (Class 1) 3-Y-O+

£113,420 (£43,000; £21,520; £10,720; £5,380; £2,700) **Stalls** Low

Form RPR
3303 **1** **Alice Springs (IRE)**21 3339 3-8-12 111 RyanMoore 4 116
(A P O'Brien, Ire) *trckd ldng pair: effrt wl over 1f out: rdn to ld ent fnl f: drifting rt but asserting ins fnl f: r.o strly: rdn out* **5/2**2

-116 **2** 2 1/4 **Very Special (IRE)**104 1106 4-9-7 114 JamesMcDonald 5 113
(Saeed bin Suroor) *led: rdn and hdd 2f out: styd pressing ldrs tl unable qck ent fnl f: chsd clr wnr ins fnl f: kpt on same pce after* **16/1**

2-13 **3** nse **Always Smile (IRE)**23 3271 4-9-7 110 JamesDoyle 8 113
(Saeed bin Suroor) *in tch in midfield: rdn ent fnl 2f: outpcd u.p over 1f out: rallied to go 3rd ins fnl f: kpt on and battling for 2nd fnl 75yds: no threat to wnr* **8/1**

-420 **4** 1 1/2 **Irish Rookie (IRE)**27 3178 4-9-7 106 ColmO'Donoghue 1 109
(Martyn Meade) *pressed ldr: rdn to ld 2f out: hdd and unable qck ent fnl f: lost 2nd and btn ins fnl f: wknd towards fin* **50/1**

0-16 **5** 1 **Ashadihan**21 3339 3-8-12 106 JamieSpencer 3 105
(Kevin Ryan) *stdd after s: in tch in rr: rdn ent fnl 2f: drvn and drifted lft over 1f out: no imp and styd on same pce ins fnl f* **33/1**

0-11 **6** 1/2 **Usherette (IRE)**23 3271 4-9-7 119 MickaelBarzalona 2 106
(A Fabre, France) *stdd bk after s: hld up in tch in last pair: effrt wl over 1f out: no imp over 1f out: wl hld and styd on same pce ins fnl f* **11/10**1

0-36 **7** shd **Amazing Maria (IRE)**24 3242 5-9-7 115 OlivierPeslier 7 105
(David O'Meara) *hld up in tch in midfield: effrt 2f out: no imp over 1f out: wl hld and styd on same pce ins fnl f* **7/1**3

1m 34.42s (-5.58) **Going Correction** -0.225s/f (Firm) course record
WFA 3 from 4yo+ 9lb **7 Ran SP% 110.6**
Speed ratings (Par 117): **118,115,115,114,113 112,112**
CSF £36.88 CT £262.96 TOTE £3.10: £1.70, £4.20; EX 40.10 Trifecta £133.00.
Owner Mrs John Magnier & Michael Tabor & Derrick Smith **Bred** Lynch - Bages & Longfield Stud **Trained** Cashel, Co Tipperary

FOCUS
This looked up to scratch on paper, but the favourite didn't run her race. There was a sound pace on, resulting in a course record time, but once again on the day it was an advantage to race handily and the form should be treated with a degree of caution. An improved effort from Alice Springs, with the next two close to form.

4108 BET365 H'CAP 1m 2f
4:45 (4:50) (Class 2) (0-105,95) 3-Y-O

£43,575 (£13,048; £6,524; £3,262; £1,631; £819) **Stalls** Centre

Form RPR
6506 **1** **Ode To Evening**27 3157 3-9-5 93 JamesMcDonald 13 104
(Mark Johnston) *chsd ldr tl 3f out: styd chsng ldrs: rdn to ld and wandered jst over 1f out: hld on wl fnl 100yds: pushed out* **25/1**

-421 **2** 1/2 **Autocratic**27 3160 3-8-13 87 RyanMoore 12 97
(Sir Michael Stoute) *chsd ldrs: effrt over 1f out: drvn to chse ldr 1f out: styd on and pressing wnr 100yds out: r.o but a hld* **9/2**2

-156 **3** 2 **Dwight D**64 1974 3-8-10 84 (p) JamieSpencer 10 90+
(William Haggas) *stdd s: hld up in rr: clsd and looking for gap 2f out: rdn and hdwy over 1f out: chsd ldrs 1f out: wnt 3rd ins fnl f: styd on: no threat to ldrs* **14/1**

-153 **4** 1 1/4 **Wild Hacked (USA)**27 3156 3-8-7 84 DanielMuscutt(3) 5 88
(Marco Botti) *chsd ldrs: clsd and upsides ldr 3f out: rdn to ld over 1f out: hdd and no ex 1f out: styd on same pce ins fnl f* **11/1**

-221 **5** 1/2 **Banksea**19 3435 3-9-6 94 AndreaAtzeni 9 97
(Luca Cumani) *t.k.h early: hld up in tch in midfield: effrt u.p to chse ldrs over 1f out: no ex 1f out: styd on same pce ins fnl f* **4/1**1

06-0 **6** 1/2 **Welford**16 3534 3-9-2 90 JoeFanning 14 92
(Mark Johnston) *stdd and dropped in bhd after s: hld up in tch in last quartet: effrt and hdwy u.p over 1f out: no imp and kpt on same pce fnl f* **20/1**

0610 **7** 1 **Bathos (IRE)**34 2892 3-9-1 89 JamesDoyle 7 89
(Mark Johnston) *chsd ldrs: rdn and swtchd rt over 1f out: drvn and no imp ent fnl f: styd on same pce after* **14/1**

1353 **8** 3/4 **High Grounds (IRE)**34 2892 3-9-7 95 OisinMurphy 1 93
(Charles Hills) *t.k.h early: hld up in tch towards rr: effrt and sme hdwy over 1f out: no imp and styd on same pce ins fnl f* **6/1**3

2-30 **9** 1 1/2 **Zodiakos (IRE)**22 3299 3-9-1 89 PatDobbs 2 84
(Hugo Palmer) *led: jnd 3f out: rdn and hdd over 1f out: no ex and btn 1f out: wknd ins fnl f* **8/1**

1340 **10** 1 1/4 **Biodynamic (IRE)**34 2896 3-9-6 94 FrederikTylicki 3 87
(K R Burke) *hld up in tch in midfield: effrt whn short of room and hmpd over 1f out: nt rcvr and no imp after: wl hld ins fnl f* **14/1**

-220 **11** 2 **Midhmaar**22 3300 3-9-2 90 PaulHanagan 11 79
(Owen Burrows) *hld up in tch in last quartet: effrt over 1f out: sn rdn and no hdwy: wknd ins fnl f* **12/1**

5511 **12** 2 1/2 **Euchen Glen**21 3347 3-8-11 85 JFEgan 8 69
(Jim Goldie) *hld up in tch in midfield: effrt 2f out: no hdwy u.p over 1f out: wknd fnl f* **14/1**

5-20 **13** 8 **Cartago**34 2892 3-9-6 94 FrankieDettori 6 62
(John Gosden) *t.k.h early: hld up in tch in midfield: effrt whn short of room and hmpd over 1f out: dropped to rr and wl hld after: eased ins fnl f* **9/1**

2m 1.97s (-3.53) **Going Correction** -0.225s/f (Firm) **13 Ran SP% 124.9**
Speed ratings (Par 106): **105,104,103,102,101 101,100,99,98,97 96,94,87**
CSF £140.33 CT £1698.24 TOTE £56.90: £8.20, £1.90, £6.90; EX 260.90 Trifecta £7273.50 Part won..
Owner Sheikh Hamdan bin Mohammed Al Maktoum **Bred** Darley **Trained** Middleham Moor, N Yorks

FOCUS
A competitive 3yo handicap, though possibly not quite the class of previous runnings with the top weight 10lb below the race ceiling. This was another contest where it was an advantage to be handy and remarkably trainer Mark Johnston took it for the fourth successive year. The winner is rated back to his reappearance form on the AW.

4109 PEGASUS GROUP TOWN & COUNTRY PLANNING H'CAP (SILVER BUNBURY CUP) 7f
5:20 (5:20) (Class 2) 3-Y-O+

£18,675 (£5,592; £2,796; £1,398; £699; £351) **Stalls** Low

Form RPR
116 **1** **Swift Approval (IRE)**34 2910 4-9-4 92 (p) FrederikTylicki 10 100
(Kevin Ryan) *mde all: rdn over 1f out: drvn and hrd pressed 1f out: styd on gamely and a holding rival ins fnl f: rdn out* **7/1**3

60-0 **2** 3/4 **Suzi's Connoisseur**13 3671 5-9-10 98 (vt) OisinMurphy 11 104
(Stuart Williams) *chsd wnr thrght: effrt wl over 1f out: drvn and ev ch 1f out: kpt on u.p but a jst hld* **12/1**

-024 **3** 1 1/4 **Withernsea (IRE)**27 3163 5-9-9 97 PaulHanagan 1 100+
(Richard Fahey) *hld up in tch in last quartet: effrt over 1f out: no imp tl styd on wl fnl 100yds: snatched 3rd last strides* **6/1**2

5012 **4** nk **Plucky Dip**35 2862 5-8-13 87 FrankieDettori 2 89
(John Ryan) *hld up in tch in midfield: effrt 2f out: hdwy u.p to chse ldrs: kpt on same pce ins fnl f* **8/1**

6203 **5** nse **Jack's Revenge (IRE)**7 3848 8-9-0 88 (bt) JoeFanning 5 90
(George Baker) *hld up in tch in last quartet: rdn and hdwy over 1f out: kpt on ins fnl f wout ever threatening ldng pair* **12/1**

-102 **6** hd **Hold Tight**15 3566 4-9-8 96 JamesDoyle 7 97
(Saeed bin Suroor) *chsd ldng trio: effrt in 3rd over 1f out: unable qck 1f out: styd on same pce ins fnl f: lost 3 pls cl hone* **11/4**1

-350 **7** 1 **Outer Space**29 3055 5-9-1 89 PatDobbs 14 87
(Jamie Osborne) *stdd and dropped in bhd after s: rdn and hdwy over 1f out: styd on same pce ins fnl f* **14/1**

2-13 **8** 2 **Muir Lodge**46 2547 5-9-5 93 (t) JimCrowley 6 86
(George Baker) *stdd s: hld up in last pair: hdwy over 1f out: sn rdn and no imp 1f out: wknd ins fnl f* **8/1**

-000 **9** 6 **Enlace**15 3566 4-9-4 92 (b1) JamesMcDonald 4 69
(Mark Johnston) *dwlt: nudged and rcvrd to chse ldrs after 1f: lost pl and rdn 2f out: sn wl btn: eased wl ins fnl f* **14/1**

0-10 **10** 4 **Fieldsman (USA)**35 2868 4-9-3 91 WilliamTwiston-Davies 3 57
(George Scott) *in tch in midfield: rdn 3f out: lost pl over 1f out: bhd and eased wl ins fnl f* **8/1**

1m 22.91s (-2.79) **Going Correction** -0.225s/f (Firm)
WFA 3 from 4yo+ 8lb **10 Ran SP% 115.5**
Speed ratings (Par 109): **106,105,103,103,103 103,101,99,92,88**
CSF £86.55 CT £545.98 TOTE £8.10: £2.40, £4.00, £2.20; EX 99.80 Trifecta £609.60.
Owner Middleham Park Racing XLIX **Bred** Mrs Jean Brennan **Trained** Hambleton, N Yorks

FOCUS
This was blown wide open by the withdrawal of Librisa Breeze. They went steadily early on and yet again the pace bias towards prominent racers came firmly into play. A length pb from the winner.
T/Jkpt: Not won. T/Plt: £4,871.50 to a £1 stake. Pool: £152,553.40 - 22.86 winning tickets
T/Qpdt: £157.70 to a £1 stake. Pool: £11,280.10 - 52.90 winning tickets **Steve Payne**

3162 YORK (L-H)
Friday, July 8

OFFICIAL GOING: Good (good to firm in places; overall 7.1; home straight: far side 7.1, centre 7.2, stands' side 7.0)
Wind: Strong across Weather: Cloudy with sunny periods, blustery

4110 COOPERS MARQUEES IRISH STALLION FARMS EBF MAIDEN STKS (PLUS 10 RACE) 5f 89y
1:50 (1:51) (Class 3) 2-Y-O **£7,115** (£2,117; £1,058; £529) **Stalls** High

Form RPR
22 **1** **Naafer**38 2764 2-9-0 0 MartinHarley 7 88+
(William Haggas) *trckd ldrs: hdwy over 2f out: led wl over 1f out: rdn ins fnl f: kpt on wl* **6/5**1

2 1 **Fashion Queen** 2-9-0 0 DanielTudhope 8 85+
(David O'Meara) *hld up: hdwy over 2f out: swtchd lft and effrt wl over 1f out: rdn to chse wnr ent fnl f: sn ev ch: no ex towards fin* **5/2**2

3 4 1/2 **Golden Easter (USA)** 2-9-0 0 1 ShaneGray 4 69+
(Kevin Ryan) *trckd ldrs: pushed along and sltly outpcd 2f out: styd on fnl f* **16/1**

6 **4** 1 1/4 **Indie Rock**7 3839 2-9-0 0 FrannyNorton 2 65
(Mark Johnston) *cl up: chal 2f out: sn rdn and wknd ent fnl f* **7/1**3

65 **5** 1 **Emerald Secret (IRE)**28 3112 2-9-0 0 PaulMulrennan 3 61
(Paul Midgley) *sn led: rdn along over 2f out: hdd wl over 1f out: grad wknd* **25/1**

4 **6** 1 3/4 **Rubiesnpearls**28 3112 2-9-0 0 TonyHamilton 5 55
(Richard Fahey) *a towards rr* **8/1**

0 **7** 2 3/4 **Yorkshire Bounty**53 2301 2-9-5 0 GeorgeChaloner 1 50
(Richard Fahey) *wnt lft s: chsd ldrs on outer: rdn along over 2f out: sn wknd* **50/1**

5 **8** 22 **Scuzeme**70 1840 2-9-5 0 GrahamGibbons 6
(David Barron) *towards rr: hdwy nr stands' rail to trck ldrs after 1f: cl up 1/2-way: rdn 2f out: sn wknd* **14/1**

1m 5.06s (0.96) **Going Correction** 0.0s/f (Good) **8 Ran SP% 116.0**
Speed ratings (Par 98): **92,90,83,81,79 76,72,37**
CSF £4.34 TOTE £2.00: £1.02, £1.60, £4.00; EX 5.20 Trifecta £36.60.
Owner Hamdan Al Maktoum **Bred** Shadwell Estate Company Limited **Trained** Newmarket, Suffolk

FOCUS
All race dsitances as advertised. Following 7.5mm of overnight rain the official going had eased slightly to good, good to firm in places. They went a good pace in the opening maiden but it was won in a time 2.86sec over Racing Post standard and, though the cross wind did not help, that was an early sign that the ground may not be that quick. The form is rated a shade positively.

4111 GARBUTT + ELLIOTT STKS (NURSERY H'CAP) 5f
2:20 (2:20) (Class 3) 2-Y-O **£7,439** (£2,213; £1,106; £553) **Stalls** High

Form RPR
133 **1** **Rainbow Mist (IRE)**41 2669 2-9-3 84 PJMcDonald 1 95+
(Ann Duffield) *hld up towards rr: hdwy over 2f out: trckd ldrs over 1f out: rdn to ld jst ins fnl f: styd on strly* **7/2**1

10 **2** 2 1/4 **Tahoo (IRE)**34 2908 2-8-11 78 JoeyHaynes 6 81
(K R Burke) *trckd ldrs: hdwy and cl up wl over 1f out: rdn to ld ent fnl f: sn jnd and hdd: drvn and kpt on same pce* **12/1**

2312 **3** 2 1/2 **Merry Banter**[36] 2807 2-8-4 **71** .... LiamJones 4 65
(Paul Midgley) *led: rdn along wl over 1f put: drvn and hdd ent fnl f: kpt on same pce* **6/1**

0410 **4** 1/2 **Vona (IRE)**[23] 3270 2-9-7 **88** .... JackGarritty 5 80
(Richard Fahey) *chsd ldr: cl up 1/2-way: rdn along wl over 1f out: grad wknd* **13/2**

5114 **5** 4 **Lawless Louis**[34] 2908 2-9-3 **84** .... DanielTudhope 2 62
(David O'Meara) *chsd ldrs: rdn along 2f out: sn drvn and btn* **4/1**[2]

21 **6** 1 1/4 **Rosebride**[23] 3290 2-8-10 **77** .... TonyHamilton 7 50
(Richard Fahey) *chsd ldrs: rdn along 2f out: sn drvn and wknd* **9/2**[3]

10 **7** 5 **Katrine (IRE)**[23] 3270 2-8-9 **76** .... FrannyNorton 3 31
(Mark Johnston) *slowly away and in rr: pushed along bef 1/2-way: rdn 2f out: nvr a factor* **5/1**

59.31s (0.01) **Going Correction** 0.0s/f (Good) **7** Ran SP% **112.4**
Speed ratings (Par 98): **99,95,91,90,84 82,74**
CSF £42.62 TOTE £5.00: £2.70, £6.60; EX 42.70 Trifecta £231.10.
Owner Craig Buckingham **Bred** Skymarc Farm **Trained** Constable Burton, N Yorks

FOCUS
A useful, open-looking nursery, in which all seven runners were making their handicap debuts, and an impressive winner. He came from a very strong race at Beverley.

4112 188BET.CO.UK STKS (H'CAP) 5f
2:55 (2:56) (Class 3) (0-95,94) 3-Y-O+ **£11,644** (£3,465; £1,731; £865) **Stalls** Centre

Form RPR

-153 **1** **Alpha Delphini**[42] 2665 5-9-1 **83** .... ConnorBeasley 2 94
(Bryan Smart) *hld up: hdwy over 2f out: chsd ldrs over 1f out: rdn ins fnl f: styd on strly to ld nr fin* **8/1**[3]

004 **2** hd **Gamesome (FR)**[21] 3346 5-9-11 **93** .... PaulMulrennan 7 103
(Paul Midgley) *trckd ldrs: smooth hdwy to chal jst ins fnl f and sn rdn: led last 100yds: drvn: hdd and nt qckn towards fin* **10/1**

-032 **3** 3/4 **Thesme**[27] 3151 4-9-7 **94** .... RachelRichardson(5) 14 101
(Nigel Tinkler) *led: pushed along wl over 1f out: rdn ent fnl f: sn jnd and drvn: hdd and no ex last 50yds* **9/2**[1]

/1-0 **4** 1/2 **Captain Colby (USA)**[13] 3656 4-9-11 **93** ....(b) AntonioFresu 9 98+
(Ed Walker) *hld up: hdwy wl over 1f out: rdn and styng on whn n.m.r and swtchd rt ins fnl f: kpt on: nrst fin* **16/1**

-005 **5** 1 1/4 **Lathom**[20] 3413 3-9-5 **92** .... DanielTudhope 6 91
(David O'Meara) *hld up: hdwy wl over 1f out: rdn to chse ldrs and swtchd lft ins fnl f: kpt on: nrst fin* **9/1**

0000 **6** 1/2 **Arctic Feeling (IRE)**[13] 3656 8-9-10 **92** .... PatrickMathers 10 91
(Richard Fahey) *in rr: pushed along bef 1/2-way: rdn 2f out: styd on strly appr fnl f: nrst fin* **33/1**

6126 **7** 1/2 **Brother Tiger**[23] 3277 7-9-10 **92** .... GrahamGibbons 5 89
(David C Griffiths) *prom: cl up 2f out: rdn over 1f out: drvn and wknd fnl f* **33/1**

2321 **8** 1 1/4 **Celebration**[27] 3131 3-9-0 **87** ....(p) JackGarritty 13 77
(Richard Fahey) *in tch: hdwy to chse ldrs 2f out: rdn over 1f out: drvn and no imp fnl f* **9/1**

0002 **9** hd **Seve**[47] 2504 4-9-9 **91** ....(t) MartinHarley 11 83
(Tom Dascombe) *prom: rdn along wl over 1f out: drvn and wknd fnl f* **20/1**

4013 **10** 1 3/4 **Fredricka**[20] 3393 5-9-3 **85** .... JasonHart 4 70
(David Barron) *dwlt and in rr: hdwy 2f out: sn rdn and kpt on fnl f* **14/1**

1041 **11** 3/4 **Bondi Beach Boy**[13] 3638 7-9-3 **85** ....(p) GeorgeChaloner 15 68
(James Turner) *chsd ldrs: rdn along 2f out: sn drvn and wknd* **16/1**

4000 **12** nse **Related**[48] 2488 6-9-10 **92** ....(v) MartinLane 16 75
(Paul Midgley) *chsd ldrs: rdn along 2f out: sn drvn and wknd* **25/1**

3405 **13** 1/2 **Silvanus (IRE)**[20] 3393 11-9-8 **90** .... TomQueally 19 71
(Paul Midgley) *a towards rr* **33/1**

0200 **14** nk **Bogart**[14] 3606 7-9-5 **87** ....(p) KevinStott 3 67
(Kevin Ryan) *chsd ldrs: rdn along 1/2-way: sn lost pl and bhd* **7/1**[2]

2264 **15** 3/4 **El Astronaute (IRE)**[20] 3393 3-8-8 **88** .... GeorgeWood(7) 17 63
(John Quinn) *a towards rr* **14/1**

504 **16** 1 **Excessable**[20] 3420 3-8-8 **81** ....(e[1]) PJMcDonald 12 52
(Tim Easterby) *a towards rr* **16/1**

1334 **17** 1 1/2 **Paddy Power (IRE)**[23] 3292 3-9-0 **87** ....(p) TonyHamilton 1 53
(Richard Fahey) *chsd ldrs on outer: rdn along 2f out: sn wknd* **10/1**

2245 **18** 1 3/4 **Krystallite**[105] 1070 3-8-9 **82** .... BarryMcHugh 8 42
(Scott Dixon) *chsd ldr: rdn along wl over 1f out: drvn appr fnl f: sn wknd* **50/1**

000 **19** 9 **Bosham**[6] 3875 6-8-10 **83** ....(bt) NathanEvans(5) 18 12
(Michael Easterby) *in tch: rdn along 1/2-way: sn outpcd and bhd whn eased fnl f* **33/1**

58.23s (-1.07) **Going Correction** 0.0s/f (Good)
WFA 3 from 4yo+ 5lb **19** Ran SP% **133.3**
Speed ratings (Par 107): **108,107,106,105,103 102,102,100,99,96 95,95,94,94,93 91,89,86,72**
CSF £85.94 CT £431.36 TOTE £8.50: £2.60, £3.60, £1.60, £5.90; EX 102.20 Trifecta £539.20.
Owner The Alpha Delphini Partnership **Bred** Mrs B A Matthews **Trained** Hambleton, N Yorks

FOCUS
A typically competitive big-field sprint handicap for the track, in which they went a good pace, and there was a tight finish. Solid form.

4113 RAYLOR'S - 70 YEARS IN YORK STKS (H'CAP) 1m 2f 88y
3:30 (3:30) (Class 4) (0-85,85) 3-Y-O+ **£7,439** (£2,213; £1,106; £553) **Stalls** Low

Form RPR

421 **1** **Istanbul Bey**[21] 3362 3-8-12 **80** .... BenCurtis 2 95+
(William Haggas) *t.k.h: trckd ldrs: smooth hdwy on inner over 2f out: led 1 1/2f out: rdn and clr whn hung bdly rt ent fnl f: styd on strly* **3/1**[1]

0006 **2** 5 **Novelty Seeker (USA)**[28] 3113 7-9-9 **80** .... GrahamGibbons 11 85
(Michael Easterby) *trckd ldrs: hdwy on outer 3f out: chal wl over 1f out: sn rdn and ev ch: drvn and kpt on fnl f: no ch w wnr* **14/1**

0014 **3** 1 **Woody Bay**[16] 3518 6-9-10 **81** .... JasonHart 10 84
(Mark Walford) *sn led: pushed along 3f out: rdn 2f out: hdd 1 1/2f out: sn drvn and kpt on same pce* **12/1**

1-04 **4** 3/4 **Optima Petamus**[25] 3219 4-9-7 **78** ....(p) JackGarritty 4 80
(Patrick Holmes) *in tch: hdwy wl over 2f out: sn rdn and chsd ldrs over 1f out: drvn and kpt on same pce fnl f* **40/1**

654- **5** 2 **Siren's Cove**[205] 8256 4-9-5 **76** .... TonyHamilton 3 74
(Richard Fahey) *midfield: hdwy over 3f out: rdn along 2f out: chsd ldrs ins fnl f: no impresiion* **20/1**

050 **6** 1 **Warfare**[58] 2163 7-9-5 **76** .... BarryMcHugh 13 72
(Tim Fitzgerald) *prom: trckd ldr 1/2-way: rdn along wl over 2f out: drvn wl over 1f out: grad wknd* **33/1**

5613 **7** 1 **Hanseatic**[11] 3717 7-8-13 **75** .... NathanEvans(5) 8 69
(Michael Easterby) *hld up towards rr: hdwy wl over 2f out: sn rdn and plugged on fnl f: n.d* **15/2**

0610 **8** 1 **Normandy Knight**[27] 3166 4-9-4 **75** .... PatrickMathers 14 67
(Richard Fahey) *hld up towards rr: hdwy wl over 2f out: rdn wl over 1f out: plugged on fnl f: n.d* **25/1**

3104 **9** 2 1/2 **Flyboy (IRE)**[20] 3389 3-9-0 **82** .... DanielTudhope 5 69
(David O'Meara) *hld up in rr: hdwy 3f out: rdn to chse ldrs 2f out: sn drvn and wknd* **5/1**[3]

341 **10** 2 3/4 **Berlusca (IRE)**[41] 2688 7-9-9 **85** ....[1] JoshDoyle(5) 12 66
(David O'Meara) *a towards rr* **16/1**

-055 **11** 1 3/4 **Intiwin (IRE)**[29] 3055 4-9-8 **79** .... GeorgeChaloner 9 57
(Richard Fahey) *trckd ldr: pushed along 3f out: rdn over 2f out: sn drvn and wknd* **14/1**

0006 **12** nse **Pivotman**[14] 3605 8-8-6 **68** .... PhilDennis(5) 6 45
(Michael Easterby) *hld up: a in rr* **50/1**

3430 **13** 3 1/4 **Hernando Torres**[14] 3605 8-9-0 **71** .... KevinStott 7 42
(Michael Easterby) *hld up: a towards rr* **33/1**

2-1 **14** 11 **De Veer Cliffs (IRE)**[15] 3578 3-9-0 **82** .... PaulMulrennan 1 31
(Martyn Meade) *trckd ldrs: effrt on inner 3f out: rdn along over 2f out: sn wknd* **4/1**[2]

2m 12.35s (-0.15) **Going Correction** +0.15s/f (Good)
WFA 3 from 4yo+ 11lb **14** Ran SP% **119.2**
Speed ratings (Par 105): **106,102,101,100,99 98,97,96,94,92 91,90,88,79**
CSF £42.93 CT £451.91 TOTE £4.00: £1.80, £4.80, £3.50; EX 46.60 Trifecta £1351.10.
Owner Simon Munir & Isaac Souede **Bred** Arbib Bloodstock Partnership **Trained** Newmarket, Suffolk

FOCUS
A decent handicap, but not the strongest for the grade, and they went a steady pace. The form is rated around the runner-up.

4114 188BET SUMMER STKS (GROUP 3) (F&M) 6f
4:00 (4:00) (Class 1) 3-Y-O+
£34,026 (£12,900; £6,456; £3,216; £1,614; £810) **Stalls** Centre

Form RPR

6124 **1** **Ridge Ranger (IRE)**[20] 3392 5-9-4 103 .... JasonHart 1 111
(Eric Alston) *qckly away: mde all: rdn appr fnl f: kpt on strly towards fin* **9/1**

-340 **2** 1 3/4 **Besharah (IRE)**[21] 3339 3-8-12 110 ....(p) GrahamGibbons 4 104
(William Haggas) *trckd ldrs: hdwy wl over 1f out: rdn to chse wnr ent fnl f: drvn and no imp last 100yds* **11/4**[2]

1-54 **3** 1 1/4 **La Rioja**[21] 3338 3-8-12 108 .... MartinHarley 8 100
(Henry Candy) *hld up in rr: hdwy wl over 2f out: chsd ldrs over 1f out: sn rdn: drvn and kpt on same pce fnl f* **10/3**[3]

4061 **4** 2 1/2 **Divine (IRE)**[34] 2923 5-9-6 108 .... RonanWhelan 2 95
(Mick Channon) *trckd ldng pair: hdwy to chse wnr wl over 1f out: sn rdn: drvn appr fnl f: grad wknd* **13/2**

0-10 **5** hd **Spangled**[23] 3271 4-9-4 100 .... PaulMulrennan 6 93
(Roger Varian) *dwlt and swtchd lft s: hld up: hdwy on outer to chse ldrs over 2f out: rdn along wl over 1f out: sn drvn and one pce* **8/1**

45-1 **6** hd **Mayfair Lady**[28] 3116 3-8-12 107 .... JackGarritty 3 91
(Richard Fahey) *chsd wnr: cl up 1/2-way: rdn along 2f out: sn wknd* **5/2**[1]

0-02 **7** 4 **Golden Amber (IRE)**[14] 3616 5-9-4 98 .... PJMcDonald 7 79
(Dean Ivory) *a in rr* **33/1**

1m 10.01s (-1.89) **Going Correction** 0.0s/f (Good)
WFA 3 from 4yo+ 6lb **7** Ran SP% **115.7**
Speed ratings (Par 113): **112,109,108,104,104 104,98**
CSF £34.80 TOTE £12.20: £4.90, £1.90; EX 48.70 Trifecta £247.40.
Owner Con Harrington **Bred** Con Harrington **Trained** Longton, Lancs

FOCUS
A competitive Group 3, albeit not the strongest for the level, and the pace was fast throughout. A clear pb from Ridge Ranger at face value, but there has to be some doubt.

4115 GROCERYAID CHAIRMAN'S CHARITY CUP (H'CAP) 1m 4f
4:30 (4:30) (Class 2) (0-100,99) 3-Y-O+
£12,450 (£3,728; £1,864; £932; £466; £234) **Stalls** Centre

Form RPR

2400 **1** **Yorkidding**[27] 3162 4-9-0 **85** .... PJMcDonald 3 93
(Mark Johnston) *trckd ldrs: pushed along 3f out: rdn and sltly outpcd 2f out: hdwy and swtchd lft ent fnl f: styd on to ld last 100yds: drvn out* **9/1**

-542 **2** 1/2 **Forgotten Hero (IRE)**[28] 3113 7-9-8 **93** ....(t) MichaelJMMurphy 5 100
(Kim Bailey) *hld up and bhd: stdy hdwy on outer fr wl over 2f out: rdn to chse ldrs ent fnl f: sn drvn and kpt on wl towards fin* **9/1**

-130 **3** 1/2 **Top Tug (IRE)**[21] 3340 5-10-0 **99** .... MartinHarley 4 105
(Alan King) *trckd ldrs: hdwy over 2f out: rdn to ld 1 1/2f out: drvn ent fnl f: hdd and no ex last 100yds* **11/2**[3]

-121 **4** 1 1/4 **Central Square (IRE)**[20] 3391 4-9-11 **96** .... PaulMulrennan 6 100
(Roger Varian) *trckd ldrs: hdwy over 3f out: cl up 2f out: rdn over 1f out and ev ch tl drvn ins fnl f and kpt on same pce* **7/4**[1]

-340 **5** 3 **Pinzolo**[20] 3387 5-10-0 **99** .... MartinLane 2 98
(Charlie Appleby) *led 1f: trckd ldr: cl up 3f out: rdn along 2f out: drvn and wknd over 1f out* **11/1**

161- **6** 1 3/4 **Argus (IRE)**[258] 7462 4-9-7 **92** .... GrahamGibbons 7 89+
(Ralph Beckett) *trckd ldng pair: hdwy and cl up 3f out: led briefly 2f out: sn rdn and hdd: drvn and ev ch ent fnl f: wknd* **9/2**[2]

1600 **7** 2 **Hit The Jackpot (IRE)**[19] 3436 7-9-12 **97** .... DanielTudhope 9 90
(David O'Meara) *hld up towards rr: sme hdwy 3f out: rdn along 2f out: n.d* **10/1**

-040 **8** 7 **Sellingallthetime (IRE)**[27] 3129 5-8-6 **82** ow1 ......(p) GeorgeBuckell(5) 1 64
(Michael Appleby) *towards rr: effrt and sme hdwy 3f out: sn rdn and outpcd fnl 2f* **18/1**

4420 **9** 6 **Croquembouche (IRE)**[28] 3109 7-9-3 **88** .... ShaneGray 8 61
(Ed de Giles) *tardy s and sn rdn along to ld after 1f: pushed along 3f out: rdn over 2f out: sn hdd and drvn: wknd over 1f out* **18/1**

2m 32.29s (-0.91) **Going Correction** +0.15s/f (Good) **9** Ran SP% **117.9**
Speed ratings (Par 109): **109,108,108,107,105 104,103,98,94**
CSF £88.32 CT £492.93 TOTE £10.20: £2.10, £2.80, £1.90; EX 82.70 Trifecta £633.60.
Owner Paul Robert York **Bred** Bluehills Racing Limited **Trained** Middleham Moor, N Yorks

■ Stewards' Enquiry : Michael J M Murphy four-day ban; used whip above permitted level (22nd, 24th-26th July)

FOCUS

A decent handicap but they went an ordinary gallop and this is muddling form. The winner is rated to her C&D run in May.

4116 ACTURIS APPRENTICE STKS (H'CAP) 7f

5:05 (5:05) (Class 3) (0-95,93) 3-Y-O **£7,439** (£2,213; £1,106; £553) **Stalls** Low

Form RPR

4026 **1** **Dawaa**[13] 3635 3-9-8 **89** LouisSteward 6 94
(Mark Johnston) *led 2f: cl up: rdn to ld again whn hung rt over 1f out: drvn ins fnl f: hld on gamely* **5/1**[2]

-500 **2** *shd* **Twin Sails**[27] 3165 3-9-12 **93** (b[1]) JackDuern 9 98
(Dean Ivory) *trckd ldrs: hdwy on outer and cl up 1/2-way: rdn to chal over 1f out: drvn ins fnl f: ev ch: jst hld* **10/1**

2654 **3** *nk* **Quick N Quirky (IRE)**[9] 3775 3-8-9 **79** (tp) JoshDoyle(3) 4 83
(Tim Easterby) *hld up: hdwy on outer wl over 1f out: rdn to chse ldng pair ins fnl f: drvn and styd on wl towards fin* **8/1**

4354 **4** *1 ¼* **Ice Age (IRE)**[18] 3466 3-8-7 **77** AaronJones(3) 7 78
(Eve Johnson Houghton) *trckd ldrs: effrt 2f out and sn rdn along: drvn and kpt on same pce fnl f* **9/1**

13-4 **5** *2* **Company Asset (IRE)**[25] 3213 3-8-13 **80** KevinStott 5 75
(Kevin Ryan) *hld up towards rr: effrt and sme hdwy over 2f out: sn rdn and no imp fnl f* **13/2**[3]

3023 **6** *nk* **London Protocol (FR)**[6] 3908 3-8-13 **87** (p) CliffordLee(7) 8 84
(K R Burke) *t.k.h: cl up: led after 2f: rdn along 2f out: sn hdd: drvn and hld whn hmpd over 1f out: wknd after* **5/2**[1]

1-50 **7** *¾* **Tawdheef (IRE)**[27] 3165 3-9-3 **89** (p) GeorgeWood(5) 3 81
(Simon Crisford) *hld up: a towards rr* **5/1**[2]

-010 **8** *5* **Back To Bond**[34] 2907 3-8-4 **74** PhilDennis(3) 2 53
(Richard Fahey) *trckd ldrs on inner: pushed along wl over 2f out: sn rdn and wknd* **20/1**

51-0 **9** *1* **Easy Code**[62] 2029 3-8-10 **82** GeorgiaCox(5) 1 58
(William Haggas) *a in rr* **14/1**

1m 25.22s (-0.08) **Going Correction** +0.125s/f (Good) **9** Ran SP% **116.9**

Speed ratings (Par 104): **105,104,104,103,100 100,99,93,92**

CSF £54.40 CT £398.79 TOTE £5.40: £1.80, £3.80, £2.50; EX 72.00 Trifecta £376.30.

Owner Hamdan Al Maktoum **Bred** Shadwell Estate Company Limited **Trained** Middleham Moor, N Yorks

FOCUS

A useful apprentice handicap and a head-bobbing finish.

T/Plt: £573.30 to a £1 stake. Pool: £99,419.31 - 126.58 winning tickets T/Qpdt: £116.00 to a £1 stake. Pool: £7,348.43 - 46.85 winning tickets **Joe Rowntree**

4117 - 4123a (Foreign Racing) - See Raceform Interactive

4029 DEAUVILLE (R-H)

Friday, July 8

OFFICIAL GOING: Turf: good; polytrack: standard

4124a PRIX DE LA SOURCE (MAIDEN) (2YO) (POLYTRACK) 6f 110y

1:05 (1:05) 2-Y-O **£9,191** (£3,676; £2,757; £1,838; £919)

RPR

1 **Team Of Teams (USA)**[26] 2-8-13 0 ChristopheSoumillon 5 80
(J-C Rouget, France) **9/5**[1]

2 *3 ½* **Dolokhov**[24] 3243 2-9-2 0 (b) TonyPiccone 10 73
(J S Moore) *worked across fr wdst draw and sn disputing: rdn 2f out: hdd aproaching fnl f: lft bhd by wnr but kpt on for wl hld 2nd* **9/1**

3 *1 ½* **Imperial Tango (FR)**[17] 3507 2-8-13 0 UmbertoRispoli 9 66
(G Botti, France) **21/1**

4 *1 ½* **Thrust Home (IRE)**[20] 2-8-13 0 (b) MaximeGuyon 2 62
(Y Durepaire, France) **16/5**[2]

5 *3 ½* **Maiandra (FR)**[31] 2-8-13 0 AntoineWerle 4 52
(T Lemer, France) **47/10**[3]

6 *snk* **Swanning Around (IRE)** 2-8-13 0 AntoineHamelin 7 52
(Matthieu Palussiere, France) **15/1**

7 *2 ½* **So Hoity Toity**[53] 2-8-13 0 CristianDemuro 8 45
(E J O'Neill, France) **32/5**

8 *8* **Carlton Choice (IRE)** 2-8-13 0 (p) AdrienFouassier 3 22
(Louis Baudron, France) **28/1**

9 *1 ¼* **Sunday Winner (FR)**[56] 2-9-2 0 (p) StephanePasquier 1 22
(Y Gourraud, France) **17/1**

WIN (incl. 1 euro stake): 2.80. PLACES: 1.60, 3.20, 5.10. DF: 12.30. SF: 18.30

Owner Joseph Allen **Bred** Joseph Allen Llc **Trained** Pau, France

4075 ASCOT (R-H)

Saturday, July 9

OFFICIAL GOING: Good to firm (good in places on round course)

Wind: Fresh, against Weather: Fine but cloudy

4125 KELLY GROUP MAIDEN AUCTION STKS (PLUS 10 RACE) (DIV I) 7f

2:10 (2:11) (Class 4) 2-Y-O **£6,469** (£1,925; £962; £481) **Stalls** High

Form RPR

0 **1** **Geneva Convention (IRE)**[17] 3529 2-9-3 0 KieranO'Neill 5 81+
(Richard Hannon) *mde all against nr side rail: shkn up and clr over 1f out: edgd rt ins fnl f: styd on wl* **3/1**[2]

2 *2 ¾* **Ray's The Money (IRE)** 2-9-3 0 WilliamCarson 1 74+
(Michael Bell) *hld up in 6th: prog and swtchd to outer 2f out: shkn up and styd on to take 2nd last 100yds: no threat to wnr* **4/1**[3]

3 **3** *1 ½* **Pantera Negra (IRE)**[27] 3186 2-8-12 0 PatCosgrave 10 65
(Ed Dunlop) *trckd ldng pair: chsd wnr wl over 1f out: hanging rt whn rdn and no imp: lost 2nd last 100yds* **11/4**[1]

06 **4** *¾* **Dewan (IRE)**[9] 3799 2-9-3 0 RonanWhelan 4 68
(Mick Channon) *chsd wnr: pushed along 3f out: lost 2nd wl over 1f out: one pce after* **33/1**

5 *5* **Masterofdiscovery** 2-9-3 0 GeraldMosse 3 54
(Clive Cox) *dwlt: rn green in 7th and wl off the pce: shkn up 3f out: nvr on terms but kpt on fr over 1f out* **8/1**

6 *3 ½* **Pass The Cristal (IRE)** 2-9-3 0 MartinDwyer 6 45
(William Muir) *t.k.h: trckd ldng trio: pushed along 3f out: wknd wl over 1f out* **16/1**

7 *9* **Northdown** 2-9-3 0 GeorgeBaker 2 20
(David Lanigan) *s.s: mostly in last and a bhd* **8/1**

8 *3 ¼* **Ravenoak (IRE)** 2-9-3 0 GrahamGibbons 7 11
(Tom Dascombe) *slowly away: in tch in 5th tl wknd qckly over 2f out* **7/1**

1m 30.12s (2.52) **Going Correction** +0.25s/f (Good) **8** Ran SP% **115.2**

Speed ratings (Par 96): **95,91,90,89,83 79,69,65**

CSF £15.62 TOTE £3.80: £1.40, £1.50, £1.40; EX 14.50 Trifecta £78.60.

Owner Mrs J K Powell, W Drew and Partner **Bred** Stonecross Stud **Trained** East Everleigh, Wilts

FOCUS

The going remained good to firm, good in places on the round course and the jockeys in the opener agreed that the ground was still on the quick side. Rail on round course out around 3yds from innermost position from the 1m4f start, increasing to 9yds out on the bend into the straight. Rail then finishes as a cutaway in the home straight. Race distances on the round course increased by varying degrees as a consequence. An ordinary maiden to start by Ascot standards and, with the early pace a pedestrian one, those that raced prominently were favoured. The fourth is likely to be they key to this form.

4126 TOTESCOOP6 HERITAGE H'CAP 5f

2:45 (2:46) (Class 2) 3-Y-O+

£62,250 (£18,640; £9,320; £4,660; £2,330; £1,170) **Stalls** High

Form RPR

6601 **1** **Royal Birth**[24] 3277 5-8-5 **92** (t) AaronJones(5) 14 100
(Stuart Williams) *dwlt: hld up nr side gng wl: prog on outer of gp over 1f out: r.o wl fnl f to ld last strides* **8/1**[1]

00-6 **2** *hd* **Robot Boy (IRE)**[28] 3151 6-8-13 **95** GrahamGibbons 13 102
(David Barron) *led nr side gp and racd against rail: drvn over 1f out: kpt on wl but hdd last strides* **8/1**[1]

0-13 **3** *nk* **Lexington Abbey**[48] 2504 5-8-13 **95** PatSmullen 11 101
(Kevin Ryan) *hld up in rr of nr side gp: effrt on outer whn impeded 2f out: prog over 1f out: r.o wl nr fin: jst hld* **12/1**[3]

0000 **4** *hd* **Jack Dexter**[21] 3386 7-9-2 **101** JoeDoyle(3) 2 106
(Jim Goldie) *hld up in rr of centre gp: prog over 1f out: drvn and r.o to ld gp last strides: jst hld* **20/1**

00-2 **5** *nse* **Union Rose**[8] 3857 4-9-1 **97** (p) DavidProbert 17 102
(Ronald Harris) *w ldrs nr side: drifted rt into centre fr 2f out: styd on fnl f: jst hld* **20/1**

1122 **6** *nk* **Bowson Fred**[15] 3606 4-9-4 **100** KieranO'Neill 9 104
(Michael Easterby) *led centre gp: drvn and hrd pressed fnl f: kpt on but hdd last strides* **20/1**

2-20 **7** *hd* **Maljaa**[35] 2895 4-9-10 **106** (b) DaneO'Neill 7 109
(Roger Varian) *hld up in tch in centre: prog wl over 1f out to chal fnl f: one pce last 100yds* **16/1**

6000 **8** *½* **Stepper Point**[21] 3386 7-9-4 **100** (p) MartinDwyer 18 102
(William Muir) *w ldr nr side tl jst ins fnl f: fdd last 100yds* **14/1**

2133 **9** *1* **Dougan**[57] 2206 4-8-11 **93** SteveDrowne 3 91
(David Evans) *hld up in tch in centre: rdn 2f out: kpt on wl but nvr quite pce to chal* **9/1**[2]

6400 **10** *shd* **Boom The Groom (IRE)**[21] 3386 5-9-3 **99** WilliamCarson 4 97
(Tony Carroll) *taken down early: prom in centre: chsd ldr 2f out: tried to chal fnl f: hld whn squeezed out last 75yds and eased* **14/1**

0002 **11** *nk* **Moonraker**[14] 3656 4-9-5 **101** GeorgeBaker 10 97
(Mick Channon) *prom in centre: rdn 2f out: lost pl over 1f out: wl hld after* **8/1**[1]

0053 **12** *½* **Desert Law (IRE)**[13] 3696 8-9-3 **99** MartinLane 19 94
(Paul Midgley) *chsd nr side ldrs: rdn and no imp over 1f out: fdd ins fnl f* **8/1**[1]

4611 **12** *dht* **Hoofalong**[28] 3151 6-8-13 **100** (b) NathanEvans(5) 16 95
(Michael Easterby) *s.i.s: towards rr nr side: drvn 2f out: kpt on but nvr gng pce to threaten* **8/1**[1]

1330 **14** *1* **Duke Of Firenze**[7] 3909 7-9-3 **99** JimmyFortune 1 90
(David C Griffiths) *dwlt and wnt rt s: hld up in centre gp: prog over 1f out: tried to cl ins fnl f: fdd last 100yds* **16/1**

0200 **15** *2* **Patrick (IRE)**[15] 3606 4-8-9 **91** (p) TedDurcan 20 75
(Richard Fahey) *chsd nr side ldrs tl wknd over 1f out* **22/1**

2610 **16** *nk* **Harry Hurricane**[35] 2895 4-9-2 **98** PatCosgrave 15 81
(George Baker) *stmbld s: chsd nr side ldrs tl wknd over 1f out* **16/1**

00-0 **17** *4 ½* **Secretinthepark**[28] 3151 6-8-10 **92** (p) TomMarquand 6 59
(Robert Cowell) *chsd ldr in centre to 2f out: wknd qckly* **20/1**

-005 **18** *6* **Foxy Forever (IRE)**[25] 3250 6-8-13 **95** (b) StevieDonohoe 5 40
(Michael Wigham) *v awkward s and lost many l: a bhd in centre* **25/1**

1m 0.32s (-0.18) **Going Correction** +0.25s/f (Good)

WFA 3 from 4yo+ 5lb **18** Ran SP% **131.5**

Speed ratings (Par 109): **111,110,110,109,109 109,109,108,106,106 105,105,105,103,100 99,92,83**

CSF £65.18 CT £797.82 TOTE £9.50: £3.00, £2.70, £3.10, £6.40; EX 86.60 Trifecta £1418.40.

Owner The Morley Family **Bred** Old Mill Stud & S Williams & J Parry **Trained** Newmarket, Suffolk

FOCUS

A red-hot sprint handicap and unsurprisingly they split into two groups. The first three came from the group that raced nearside, but there was so little covering the principals at the line that any advantage they enjoyed was minimal. A turf best from the winner.

4127 FRED COWLEY MBE MEMORIAL SUMMER MILE STKS (GROUP 2) 1m (R)

3:15 (3:19) (Class 1) 4-Y-O+

£68,052 (£25,800; £12,912; £6,432; £3,228; £1,620) **Stalls** Low

Form RPR

23-1 **1** **Mutakayyef**[28] 3164 5-9-1 112 DaneO'Neill 7 119+
(William Haggas) *trckd ldrs: shkn up and clsd on outer over 2f out: led over 1f out: r.o wl and in command fnl f* **7/2**[1]

5-20 **2** *2 ¼* **Dutch Connection**[56] 2243 4-9-1 115 GeorgeBaker 9 114
(Charles Hills) *stdd s: hld up in 9th: prog on inner over 2f out: rdn to try to chal jst over 1f out: chsd wnr after but readily hld* **5/1**[3]

4651 **3** *shd* **Gabrial (IRE)**[14] 3672 7-9-1 108 JimmyFortune 4 114
(Richard Fahey) *hld up in tch: rdn 2f out: prog over 1f out on outer: styd on fnl f to press for 2nd last strides* **25/1**

3403 **4** *1 ¼* **Custom Cut (IRE)**[36] 2867 7-9-1 114 RonanWhelan 8 111
(David O'Meara) *led 1f: trckd ldr: led again briefly wl over 1f out: one pce after* **12/1**

/10- **5** *shd* **Richard Pankhurst**[234] 7891 4-9-1 114 NickyMackay 2 111
(John Gosden) *t.k.h: hld up in 8th: clsd on ldrs fr 2f out and looking for a gap: kpt on same pce fnl f* **16/1**

0-00 **6** *¾* **Kodi Bear (IRE)**[25] 3242 4-9-1 115 GeraldMosse 5 109
(Clive Cox) *trckd ldng pair: rdn to try to chal jst over 2f out: nt qckn over 1f out: one pce after* **9/2**[2]

0220 **7** *1 ¾* **Convey**[24] 3273 4-9-1 113 PatSmullen 3 105
(Sir Michael Stoute) *hld up in 7th: clsd on ldrs 2f out: rdn and no rspnse over 1f out: hld whn short of room ins fnl f* **6/1**

-154 **8** *nk* **Toormore (IRE)**[25] 3242 5-9-4 116 TomMarquand 6 107
(Richard Hannon) *led after 1f to wl over 1f out: fdd* **9/2**[2]

6-10 **9** *1 ½* **Blond Me (IRE)**[24] 3271 4-8-12 107 DavidProbert 1 98
(Andrew Balding) *rel to r: ct up after 3f: rdn and no prog over 2f out* **16/1**

3525 **10** *12* **Battle Of Marathon (USA)**[24] 3273 4-9-1 110 (p) PatCosgrave 10 73
(John Ryan) *prom tl wknd rapidly over 2f out: t.o* **16/1**

1m 40.88s (0.18) **Going Correction** +0.25s/f (Good) **10** Ran SP% **118.7**
Speed ratings (Par 115): **109,106,106,105,105 104,102,102,101,89**
CSF £21.36 TOTE £4.40: £2.00, £1.90, £3.20; EX 18.00 Trifecta £256.80.
Owner Hamdan Al Maktoum **Bred** Cheveley Park Stud Ltd **Trained** Newmarket, Suffolk

FOCUS
Rail movement added 10yds to race distance. A decent renewal of this Group 2 contest, but the pace was ordinary with the result that eight of the ten runners were still within a length or so of each other coming to the last furlong. The third looks the key to the form.

4128 KELLY GROUP MAIDEN AUCTION STKS (PLUS 10 RACE) (DIV II) 7f
3:50 (3:53) (Class 4) 2-Y-O **£6,469** (£1,925; £962; £481) **Stalls** High

Form RPR

2 **1** **Paulownia (IRE)**[15] 3613 2-8-12 0 DaneO'Neill 5 78+
(Richard Hannon) *trckd ldng trio: clsd to ld over 1f out: shkn up and styd on wl* **11/4**[2]

2 *1 ¾* **Good Omen** 2-9-3 0 PatCosgrave 8 78+
(William Haggas) *trckd ldrs in 5th: effrt 2f out: shkn up and prog to take 2nd ins fnl f: no imp on wnr* **15/8**[1]

0 **3** *½* **Drochaid**[39] 2756 2-9-3 0 DavidProbert 1 77
(Andrew Balding) *pressed ldr: narrow ld 2f out to over 2f out: styd on same pce u.p* **12/1**

4 *2 ¼* **Shipping Forecast** 2-9-3 0 JimmyFortune 2 71
(Brian Meehan) *dwlt: sn in tch: effrt on outer 2f out: ch of a pl 1f out: fdd last 100yds* **12/1**

5 *½* **Forgivethenforget** 2-9-3 0 TedDurcan 4 70+
(Ismail Mohammed) *hld up towards rr: pushed along and outpcd over 2f out: kpt on ins fnl f* **14/1**

0 **6** *nk* **Poetic Force (IRE)**[30] 3058 2-9-3 0 MartinLane 10 69
(Jonathan Portman) *trckd ldng pair to jst over 2f out: fdd over 1f out* **50/1**

7 *nk* **Syncopation (IRE)** 2-9-3 0 PatSmullen 7 68
(Sylvester Kirk) *dwlt: hld up in rr: outpcd and rn green over 2f out: pushed along and kpt on fnl f* **9/1**

2530 **8** *4* **Juan Horsepower**[1] 4076 2-9-3 0 KieranO'Neill 9 57
(Richard Hannon) *led to 2f out: wknd qckly over 1f out* **6/1**[3]

9 *¾* **Epsom Secret** 2-8-12 0[1] WilliamCarson 3 50
(Pat Phelan) *s.s: t.k.h: hld up in last: rn green and wknd 2f out* **33/1**

10 *7* **Getgo** 2-9-3 0 GeorgeBaker 6 36
(David Lanigan) *a in rr: bhd fnl 2f* **12/1**

1m 30.43s (2.83) **Going Correction** +0.25s/f (Good) **10** Ran SP% **120.4**
Speed ratings (Par 96): **93,91,90,87,87 86,86,82,81,73**
CSF £8.62 TOTE £3.50: £1.60, £1.20, £3.30; EX 8.10 Trifecta £94.80.
Owner Knockainey **Bred** Woodcote Stud Ltd **Trained** East Everleigh, Wilts

FOCUS
As in the first division they went steady early and the winning time was 0.31sec slower than the first leg. The winner looks the type to improve again.

4129 PLAYBOY CLUB LONDON H'CAP 1m 2f
4:25 (4:28) (Class 3) (0-95,95) 3-Y-O+ **£9,703** (£2,887; £1,443; £721) **Stalls** Low

Form RPR

113- **1** **Move Up**[273] 7116 3-9-2 94 WilliamCarson 5 104
(Saeed bin Suroor) *chsd ldrs: prog over 3f out: rdn over 2f out: chsd ldr over 1f out: str chal fnl f: led last strides* **13/2**[3]

1-61 **2** *shd* **Gershwin**[47] 2538 3-9-1 93 GeorgeBaker 9 103+
(David Lanigan) *prom: trckd ldr over 3f out: led 2f out gng easily: shkn up over 1f out: styd on ins fnl f: hdd last strides* **6/5**[1]

6040 **3** *2 ¼* **Sennockian Star**[10] 3785 6-9-4 85 (v) GeraldMosse 3 91
(Mark Johnston) *cl up: lost pl sltly over 3f out: rdn over 2f out: prog over 1f out: styd on to take 3rd ins fnl f* **8/1**

4-65 **4** *¾* **Mustaaqeem (USA)**[56] 2246 4-9-5 86 DaneO'Neill 13 90
(Sir Michael Stoute) *t.k.h to post: sweating: reluctant to enter stalls: led after 1f and racd freely: hdd 2f out: one pce u.p after* **7/2**[2]

-415 **5** *1 ½* **Nayel (IRE)**[28] 3162 4-9-8 89 (b[1]) PatCosgrave 4 90
(Richard Hannon) *led 1f: chsd ldr to over 3f out: rdn and cl up jst over 2f out: fdd over 1f out* **8/1**

0050 **6** *2 ¾* **Vercingetorix (IRE)**[13] 3688 5-9-1 82 GrahamGibbons 7 78
(David Evans) *dwlt: hld up in last pair: pushed along 3f out: modest late prog and shkn up fnl f: nvr involved* **33/1**

562 **7** *hd* **Buckland Beau**[38] 2791 5-8-13 80 StevieDonohoe 6 75
(Charlie Fellowes) *hld up towards rr: rdn wl over 2f out: no real prog after* **25/1**

00-0 **8** *3 ¾* **Faithful Creek (IRE)**[22] 3340 4-9-11 92 (t) JimmyFortune 10 80
(Brian Meehan) *chsd ldrs: rdn and lost pl on outer over 2f out: steadily wknd* **20/1**

003 **9** *½* **Purple Rock (IRE)**[8] 3840 4-8-4 76 oh1 (t) NathanEvans(5) 1 63
(Michael Easterby) *hld up towards rr: no prog u.p over 2f out* **33/1**

00-0 **10** *4 ½* **The Rectifier (USA)**[28] 3157 9-10-0 95 (t) TimmyMurphy 2 73
(Seamus Durack) *hld up in last pair: shkn up and no prog over 2f out: sn wknd* **50/1**

2m 7.69s (0.29) **Going Correction** +0.25s/f (Good)
WFA 3 from 4yo+ 11lb **10** Ran SP% **119.7**
Speed ratings (Par 107): **108,107,106,105,104 102,101,98,98,94**
CSF £14.42 CT £67.13 TOTE £6.90: £2.20, £1.10, £2.80; EX 17.40 Trifecta £154.60.
Owner Godolphin **Bred** The Lavington Stud **Trained** Newmarket, Suffolk
■ Stewards' Enquiry : William Carson two-day ban: use of whip (24-25 Jul)

FOCUS
Rail movement added 13yds to race distance. A decent handicap and they seemed to go a good pace, but even so you had to be handy. The finish was fought out between the two remaining 3yos, of whom we should be hearing plenty more. The form is rated on the positive side.

4130 TRANT ENGINEERING FILLIES' H'CAP 1m (S)
5:00 (5:02) (Class 3) (0-90,88) 3-Y-O+ **£12,938** (£3,850; £1,924; £962) **Stalls** High

Form RPR

-131 **1** **Singyoursong (IRE)**[31] 3039 3-8-6 75 KieranO'Neill 7 82+
(David Simcock) *stdd s: trckd ldng pair and t.k.h: prog to ld jst over 1f out: drvn and styd on wl* **10/3**[2]

0-00 **2** *1 ¼* **Gypsy Eyes (IRE)**[24] 3274 3-9-5 88 GeorgeBaker 5 92+
(Charles Hills) *stdd s: hld up in last: rdn over 2f out: styd on fr over 1f out to take 2nd last 75yds: unable to chal* **11/2**

-311 **3** *½* **Desert Haze**[29] 3107 3-8-13 82 PatSmullen 8 85
(Ralph Beckett) *led: hld together 2f out: hdd and rdn over 1f out: nt qckn and hld after: lost 2nd last 75yds* **2/1**[1]

-310 **4** *1 ¾* **Golden Glimmer (IRE)**[42] 2695 3-9-1 84 PatCosgrave 4 83
(Tom Dascombe) *trckd ldng trio: rdn jst over 2f out: cl enough but nt qckn over 1f out: fdd fnl f* **10/1**

0-33 **5** *nk* **Margaret's Mission (IRE)**[21] 3390 5-9-9 86 JoeDoyle(3) 6 86
(Jim Goldie) *hld up in 5th: shkn up 2f out: no prog and btn 1f out: one pce* **4/1**[3]

6-01 **6** *1 ¼* **Aghaany**[30] 3059 3-8-13 82 DaneO'Neill 1 77
(Roger Varian) *trckd ldr: rdn 2f out: sn lost 2nd and wknd* **8/1**

1m 42.69s (1.89) **Going Correction** +0.25s/f (Good)
WFA 3 from 4yo+ 9lb **6** Ran SP% **112.0**
Speed ratings (Par 104): **100,98,98,96,96 94**
CSF £21.29 CT £44.04 TOTE £3.90: £1.90, £2.90; EX 21.60 Trifecta £82.00.
Owner Saeed Jaber **Bred** Rabbah Bloodstock Limited **Trained** Newmarket, Suffolk

FOCUS
A decent fillies' handicap featuring some progressive 3yos, but the pace was modest and it developed into something of a 2f sprint. The winner is on the upgrade.

4131 JOHNNY BRETT H'CAP 1m 4f
5:35 (5:35) (Class 2) (0-105,99) 3-Y-O
£31,125 (£9,320; £4,660; £2,330; £1,165; £585) **Stalls** Low

Form RPR

1012 **1** **Manjaam (IRE)**[21] 3428 3-8-12 90 PatSmullen 4 98
(Ed Dunlop) *trckd ldr: rdn to ld 2f out: hrd pressed after: hld on wl nr fin* **6/1**

-111 **2** *hd* **Shabbah (IRE)**[29] 3110 3-8-9 87 TedDurcan 8 94
(Sir Michael Stoute) *led: drvn and hdd 2f out: fought on wl and pressed wnr hrd fnl f: jst hld* **9/4**[1]

2-01 **3** *hd* **Dal Harraild**[35] 2909 3-9-3 95 PatCosgrave 10 102+
(William Haggas) *hld up in last: nt clr run briefly over 2f out: gd prog over 1f out: tk 3rd last 100yds and clsd on ldng pair fin: too much to do* **5/1**[3]

2-31 **4** *1 ½* **High Shields (IRE)**[34] 2929 3-8-11 89 DaneO'Neill 2 93
(Roger Charlton) *trckd ldng trio: chsd ldng pair 3f out: rdn and cl enough wl over 1f out: nt qckn and lost 3rd last 100yds* **9/2**[2]

4004 **5** *1 ¼* **Dessertoflife (IRE)**[8] 3860 3-9-7 99 GeraldMosse 3 101
(Mark Johnston) *dwlt: t.k.h and sn in 5th: rdn to chse ldng trio 2f out: nt qckn over 1f out: fdd ins fnl f* **25/1**

1-56 **6** *nse* **Paris Protocol**[23] 3300 3-8-13 91 JimmyFortune 6 93
(Richard Hannon) *hld up in 9th: rdn and no prog over 2f out: kpt on fr over 1f out: nvr gng pce to threaten* **7/1**

2630 **7** *2 ¾* **Second Serve (IRE)**[23] 3300 3-8-4 82 WilliamCarson 7 80
(Mark Johnston) *t.k.h: hld up in 6th: rdn and no prog over 2f out: wl btn after* **20/1**

-221 **8** *2* **Wave Reviews**[17] 3535 3-8-7 85 (p) GrahamGibbons 5 80
(William Haggas) *t.k.h: hld up in 7th: rdn and no prog over 2f out: brief effrt over 1f out: wknd fnl f* **7/1**

-021 **9** *1 ½* **Chelsea's Boy (IRE)**[29] 3103 3-8-0 78 NickyMackay 1 70
(Clive Cox) *trckd ldng pair to 3f out: sn wknd 2f out* **20/1**

2m 34.29s (1.79) **Going Correction** +0.25s/f (Good) **9** Ran SP% **118.3**
Speed ratings (Par 106): **104,103,103,102,101 101,100,98,97**
CSF £19.87 CT £74.28 TOTE £6.90: £1.90, £1.70, £1.90; EX 16.30 Trifecta £87.00.
Owner Mohammed Jaber **Bred** Ballylinch Stud **Trained** Newmarket, Suffolk
■ Stewards' Enquiry : Ted Durcan two-day ban: use of whip (24-25 Jul)

FOCUS
Rail movement added 13yds to race distance. Won by the subsequent Group-race winner Dartmouth last year, this was a decent 3yo handicap, albeit one in which the top weight was 6lb below the race ceiling and a few of the main players had to prove themselves at the trip. They only went an ordinary pace and a few were inclined to take a grip. The first two held those positions throughout, but this is still a race to view positively.

4132 GL EVENTS OWEN BROWN H'CAP 7f
6:05 (6:07) (Class 4) (0-85,85) 3-Y-O+ **£8,086** (£2,406; £1,202; £601) **Stalls** High

Form RPR

-603 **1** **Experto Crede (IRE)**[21] 3415 3-9-1 80 GeorgeBaker 3 87+
(Ed Walker) *trckd ldng pair: wnt 2nd over 2f out: led over 1f out gng wl: shkn up and styd on wl fnl f: readily* **5/2**[2]

2552 **2** *1 ¼* **Dutch Law**[22] 3358 4-9-13 84 PatSmullen 8 91
(Hughie Morrison) *hld up in 6th: nt clr run over 2f out to over 1f out: squeezed through and chsd wnr ins fnl f: r.o but no ch to chal* **15/8**[1]

066 **3** *1 ¾* **Corporal Maddox**[21] 3405 9-9-6 77 (p) RonanWhelan 5 79
(Ronald Harris) *awkward s: hld up in 7th: prog on outer 2f out: drvn to chse wnr briefly jst ins fnl f: one pce after* **20/1**

2220 **4** *nk* **Ice Royal (IRE)**[17] 3523 3-9-6 85 WilliamCarson 7 83
(Jamie Osborne) *s.v.s: detached in last tl after 1/2-way: swtchd to outer and prog over 1f out: drvn to take 4th ins fnl f: styd on but no ch* **9/1**

6000 **5** *1 ½* **Aqua Ardens (GER)**[9] 3803 8-9-11 82 (t) PatCosgrave 2 79
(George Baker) *trckd ldrs in 5th: rdn and nt qckn 2f out: n.d over 1f out: kpt on* **20/1**

-500 **6** *2* **Redvers (IRE)**[35] 2910 8-9-7 78 GrahamGibbons 1 70
(Noel Wilson) *chsd ldr to over 2f out: wknd jst over 1f out* **25/1**

3120 **7** *nse* **Frenchman (FR)**[16] 3571 3-9-0 79 DaneO'Neill 4 68
(Charles Hills) *awkward s but led at gd clip: hdd over 1f out: sn wknd* **7/2**[3]

140 **8** *2* **Funding Deficit (IRE)**[17] 3518 6-9-8 82 JoeDoyle(3) 9 68
(Jim Goldie) *trckd ldng trio: n.m.r over 2f out and sn lost pl: hmpd over 1f out and dropped to last: no ch after* **16/1**

1m 28.97s (1.37) **Going Correction** +0.25s/f (Good)
WFA 3 from 4yo+ 8lb **8** Ran SP% **114.8**
Speed ratings (Par 105): **102,100,98,98,96 94,94,91**
CSF £7.38 CT £71.64 TOTE £3.10: £1.30, £1.30, £4.60; EX 8.50 Trifecta £69.70.
Owner P K Siu **Bred** Rabbah Bloodstock Limited **Trained** Upper Lambourn, Berks

FOCUS
A fair handicap, but another steadily run contest and a rather messy race. The winner did it nicely, though, and the second ran as well as ever.

T/Plt: £41.70 to a £1 stake. Pool: £115,162.05 - 2015.12 winning units. T/Qpdt: £10.20 to a £1 stake. Pool: £7,747.80 - 559.17 winning units. **Jonathan Neesom**

4089 CHESTER (L-H)

Saturday, July 9

OFFICIAL GOING: Soft (5.8)

Wind: fresh 1/2 behind Weather: mainly fine but overcast and breezy

4133 STELLA ARTOIS/EBF STALLIONS MAIDEN STKS (PLUS 10 RACE) 5f 16y

2:00 (2:00) (Class 4) 2-Y-O

£6,225 (£1,864; £932; £466; £233; £117) **Stalls** Low

Form RPR

62 **1** **Hope Solo (IRE)**[15] 3597 2-9-0 0 DavidAllan 8 79
(Tim Easterby) *trckd ldrs: led over 1f out: kpt on wl* **4/1**[3]

234 **2** 1 3/4 **Full Intention**[25] 3247 2-9-5 0 RichardKingscote 9 78+
(Tom Dascombe) *trckd ldrs: chsd wnr over 1f out: kpt on same pce last 100yds* **10/11**[1]

6 **3** 4 1/2 **Nautical Haven**[28] 3167 2-9-5 0 GrahamLee 7 62
(Kevin Ryan) *mid-div: hdwy on outer over 2f out: kpt on to take modest 3rd last 100yds* **7/2**[2]

0 **4** 4 **Albizu Campos**[14] 3633 2-9-5 0 JasonHart 6 47
(Lawrence Mullaney) *mid-div: effrt over 2f out: kpt on to take modest 4th clsng stages* **66/1**

00 **5** 1/2 **Arthurthedelegator**[14] 3633 2-9-5 0 KevinStott 2 45
(Oliver Greenall) *chsd ldr: led briefly wl over 1f out: sn wknd* **20/1**

0 **6** 5 **Rebel Heart**[98] 1203 2-9-0 0 DarryllHolland 4 22
(Bill Turner) *mid-div: outpcd and lost pl over 3f out: sn bhd* **20/1**

7 1 3/4 **Tess Graham** 2-9-0 0 PatrickMathers 3 16
(Sarah Hollinshead) *dwlt: a outpcd and in rr* **28/1**

056 **8** nk **Redrosezorro**[28] 3128 2-9-5 0 (b) NeilFarley 1 20
(Eric Alston) *led: hdd wl over 1f out: sn wknd* **12/1**

1m 3.71s (2.71) **Going Correction** +0.525s/f (Yiel) **8 Ran SP% 116.8**

Speed ratings (Par 96): **99,96,89,82,81 73,71,70**

CSF £7.93 TOTE £4.00: £1.30, £1.10, £1.10; EX 11.40 Trifecta £29.90.

Owner Clipper Logistics **Bred** Old Long Hill Ballinteskin Stud Ltd **Trained** Great Habton, N Yorks

FOCUS

Following 11mm of rain since 8am the going had eased to soft (GoingStick: 5.8). The running rail had been moved back to the very inside after racing the previous evening, and all race distances were as advertised. The first two in this maiden already had useful form in the book, and they overcame their wide draws to finish well clear of the rest. The form could rate higher than initial suspicions.

4134 CSP AUDIO VISUAL H'CAP 6f 18y

2:30 (2:31) (Class 4) (0-80,80) 3-Y-O

£6,225 (£1,864; £932; £466; £233; £117) **Stalls** Low

Form RPR

0601 **1** **Roll On Rory**[20] 3439 3-9-0 73 (v[1]) JFEgan 3 83
(Jason Ward) *w ldr: led over 1f out: fnd ex clsng stages* **5/1**

13 **2** 1/2 **Tarboosh**[31] 3029 3-9-6 79 WilliamTwiston-Davies 7 88
(William Haggas) *dwlt: hdwy on ins to trck ldrs over 4f out: 3rd over 2f out: jnd wnr appr fnl f: no ex clsng stages* **3/1**[1]

10-4 **3** 2 3/4 **Symposium**[50] 2446 3-9-4 77 RichardKingscote 4 77
(William Haggas) *chsd ldrs: lost pl over 4f out: hdwy and nt clr run over 2f out: kpt on to take modest 3rd last 75yds* **5/1**

4605 **4** 1 1/2 **Ancient Astronaut**[16] 3568 3-9-0 73 [1] JasonHart 8 68
(John Quinn) *in rr: effrt over 2f out: kpt on fnl f* **10/1**

-031 **5** nk **Operative**[21] 3422 3-9-4 80 JosephineGordon[(3)] 6 74
(Ed de Giles) *in rr: drvn over 3f out: hdwy over 2f out: kpt on one pce over 1f out* **4/1**[3]

241 **6** 3 **Evenlode (IRE)**[35] 2886 3-9-2 75 DavidAllan 1 60
(David Barron) *led: hdd over 1f out: wknd fnl f* **7/2**[2]

32-2 **7** 13 **Ballylare**[21] 3406 3-9-2 75 KierenFox 9 18
(John Best) *chsd ldrs: lost pl 2f out: sn bhd: eased clsng stages* **16/1**

1m 16.57s (2.77) **Going Correction** +0.575s/f (Yiel) **7 Ran SP% 115.5**

Speed ratings (Par 102): **104,103,99,97,97 93,75**

CSF £20.81 CT £78.77 TOTE £7.00: £4.20, £1.30; EX 30.50 Trifecta £215.40.

Owner P Adams, P Clarke, T Wickins, J Sutton **Bred** Stuart Matheson **Trained** Middleham, N Yorks

FOCUS

A competitive handicap. A small pb from the winner.

4135 CORBETTSPORTS CITY PLATE (LISTED RACE) 7f 2y

3:05 (3:05) (Class 1) 3-Y-O+

£22,684 (£8,600; £4,304; £2,144; £1,076; £540) **Stalls** Low

Form RPR

3-00 **1** **Birchwood (IRE)**[14] 3664 3-8-8 110 (v[1]) PatrickMathers 1 110
(Richard Fahey) *trckd ldrs: t.k.h: nt clr run over 1f out: styd on to ld last 75yds* **7/1**

5422 **2** 1 **Sovereign Debt (IRE)**[14] 3677 7-9-2 113 DarryllHolland 4 114+
(David Nicholls) *mid-div: hdwy over 2f out: sn chsng ldrs: nt clr run and swtchd rt 100yds out: styd on wl to take 2nd last 50yds* **2/1**[1]

3333 **3** 2 1/4 **Jamesie (IRE)**[14] 3681 8-9-2 102 (t) SamHitchcott 2 105
(David Marnane, Ire) *led: hdd last 75yds: no ex* **12/1**

4104 **4** nk **Kelinni (IRE)**[23] 3332 8-9-2 107 (p) ShaneGray 11 104
(Kevin Ryan) *hld up towards rr: effrt over 2f out: styd on fnl f: tk 4th nr fin* **20/1**

-215 **5** shd **Yattwee (USA)**[23] 3299 3-8-8 100 KevinStott 9 101
(Saeed bin Suroor) *swtchd lft after s: sn w ldr: edgd rt fnl f: one pce* **4/1**[3]

-303 **6** 4 1/2 **Here Comes When (IRE)**[14] 3664 6-9-2 108 FrannyNorton 8 92
(Andrew Balding) *t.k.h: trckd ldrs: upsides over 2f out: wknd fnl f* **11/4**[2]

2660 **7** 3 3/4 **Tupi (IRE)**[21] 3386 4-9-2 107 JFEgan 6 83
(Richard Hannon) *in rr: effrt over 2f out: nvr on terms* **12/1**

40-3 **8** 22 **Stroll Patrol**[15] 3616 4-8-11 98 GrahamLee 5 20
(Ralph Beckett) *mid-div: t.k.h: drvn over 2f out: sn lost pl: bhd whn eased clsng stages* **20/1**

1m 28.73s (2.23) **Going Correction** +0.625s/f (Yiel)

WFA 3 from 4yo+ 8lb **8 Ran SP% 117.4**

Speed ratings (Par 111): **112,110,108,107,107 102,98,73**

CSF £22.07 TOTE £7.30: £1.50, £1.20, £2.70; EX 18.80 Trifecta £236.60.

Owner Godolphin **Bred** Marathon Bloodstock **Trained** Musley Bank, N Yorks

FOCUS

A bit of a tactical affair. Richard Fahey has now won this Listed prize in four of the last six years. The form is rated around the third and the winner was possibly lucky.

4136 TECHNICAL DEMOLITION SERVICES LTD H'CAP 6f 18y

3:35 (3:36) (Class 2) (0-105,102) 3-Y-O+

£15,562 (£4,660; £2,330; £1,165; £582; £292) **Stalls** Low

Form RPR

-004 **1** **Right Touch**[70] 1856 6-9-5 95 PatrickMathers 7 106
(Richard Fahey) *in rr: hdwy over 2f out: swtchd rt over 1f out: styd on wl to ld last 50yds* **7/1**

3242 **2** 3/4 **Kimberella**[13] 3696 6-9-7 97 FrannyNorton 8 105
(David Nicholls) *trckd ldrs: upsides over 1f out: led last 150yds: hdd and no ex last 50yds* **4/1**[1]

3560 **3** 1 1/4 **Poyle Vinnie**[21] 3386 6-9-9 102 AlistairRawlinson[(3)] 5 106+
(Michael Appleby) *trckd ldrs: nt clr run 2f out: kpt on to take 3rd nr fin* **8/1**

0100 **4** nk **Calder Prince (IRE)**[24] 3269 3-9-3 99 LiamJones 6 101
(Tom Dascombe) *s.i.s: sn mid-div: chsng ldrs over 1f out: sn swtchd rt kpt on to take 4th nr fin* **20/1**

1106 **5** 3/4 **See The Sun**[14] 3656 5-9-2 92 DavidAllan 12 93
(Tim Easterby) *w ldr: led over 1f out: hdd last 150yds: kpt on same pce* **16/1**

5020 **6** 1/2 **Shared Equity**[21] 3386 5-9-10 100 GrahamLee 11 99+
(Jedd O'Keeffe) *towards rr: hdwy over 1f out: kpt on wl last 150yds* **11/2**[2]

2200 **7** nse **Roudee**[14] 3671 4-9-0 95 AnnaHesketh[(5)] 2 94
(Tom Dascombe) *mid-div: t.k.h: effrt over 2f out: kpt on fnl f* **6/1**[3]

0210 **8** nk **Secret Hint**[28] 3163 5-9-1 91 JimmyQuinn 1 89
(Andrew Balding) *trckd ldrs on inner: hmpd over 1f out: edgd rt and one pce fnl f* **4/1**[1]

3-00 **9** 1 1/4 **Ashpan Sam**[21] 3386 7-9-7 97 DarryllHolland 3 91
(David W Drinkwater) *led: hdd over 1f out: wknd fnl f* **12/1**

50-2 **10** 8 **Go Far**[50] 2434 6-9-4 97 (v) JosephineGordon[(3)] 9 65
(Alan Bailey) *in rr: effrt on outside over 2f out: sn bhd* **14/1**

1m 16.92s (3.12) **Going Correction** +0.675s/f (Yiel)

WFA 3 from 4yo+ 6lb **10 Ran SP% 118.3**

Speed ratings (Par 109): **106,105,103,102,101 101,101,100,99,88**

CSF £35.70 CT £233.29 TOTE £7.80: £2.80, £1.90, £2.70; EX 40.60 Trifecta £326.90.

Owner Nicholas Wrigley & Kevin Hart **Bred** The Athenians **Trained** Musley Bank, N Yorks

FOCUS

A good sprint handicap in which they went a decent gallop. A small pb from the winner.

4137 RAYMOND & KATHLEEN CORBETT MEMORIAL H'CAP 1m 6f 91y

4:10 (4:10) (Class 3) (0-90,83) 3-Y-O

£15,562 (£4,660; £2,330; £1,165; £582; £292) **Stalls** Low

Form RPR

-153 **1** **Hereawi**[42] 2687 3-9-2 78 GrahamLee 1 88
(Ralph Beckett) *mde all: qcknd pce over 3f out: styd on wl: readily* **9/4**[1]

1223 **2** 2 3/4 **Scarpeta (FR)**[10] 3778 3-8-7 69 FrannyNorton 5 75
(Mark Johnston) *trckd ldrs: drvn over 2f out: kpt on to take 2nd last 75yds: no imp* **8/1**

-113 **3** nk **Master Blueyes (IRE)**[17] 3532 3-9-7 83 WilliamTwiston-Davies 2 89
(Alan King) *trckd ldrs: effrt over 2f out: chsd wnr over 1f out: kpt on same pce* **5/2**[2]

1402 **4** 2 **Project Bluebook (FR)**[9] 3809 3-9-0 76 JasonHart 4 79
(John Quinn) *hld up wl in tch: hdwy on inner over 2f out: one pce* **8/1**

3653 **5** 3/4 **Monaco Rose**[23] 3306 3-8-4 66 PatrickMathers 3 68
(Richard Fahey) *hld up wl in tch: effrt over 2f out: one pce* **10/1**

2141 **6** 12 **The Graduate (IRE)**[8] 3862 3-9-4 80 JimmyQuinn 6 67
(Andrew Balding) *hld up wl in tch: racd wd: hdwy to trck ldrs after 6f: drvn 3f out: lost pl over 1f out: bhd whn eased clsng stages* **7/2**[3]

3m 17.68s (10.68) **Going Correction** +0.725s/f (Yiel) **6 Ran SP% 112.9**

Speed ratings (Par 104): **98,96,96,95,94 87**

CSF £20.41 TOTE £2.90: £1.50, £2.60; EX 19.70 Trifecta £80.30.

Owner J H Richmond-Watson **Bred** Lawn Stud **Trained** Kimpton, Hants

FOCUS

This staying handicap was dominated from the front by the winner. He reversed recent course form with the third.

4138 MANOR CAR HIRE H'CAP 1m 2f 75y

4:45 (4:46) (Class 4) (0-80,81) 4-Y-O+

£6,225 (£1,864; £932; £466; £233; £117) **Stalls** High

Form RPR

5352 **1** **Eurystheus (IRE)**[28] 3166 7-9-4 77 (tp) JimmyQuinn 8 86
(Michael Appleby) *trckd ldrs: effrt over 2f out: led over 1f out: drvn out: readily* **7/1**

6552 **2** 1 3/4 **Cottesloe (IRE)**[15] 3617 7-9-3 76 (b) JFEgan 12 81
(John Berry) *in rr: pushed along after 3f: hdwy 3f out: chsd wnr fnl 150yds: no imp* **8/1**

022 **3** nse **Berrahri (IRE)**[43] 2651 5-9-2 75 KierenFox 1 80
(John Best) *trckd ldrs: pushed along 5f out: upsides over 1f out: kpt on same pce* **7/2**[1]

4055 **4** 2 3/4 **Omotesando**[14] 3636 6-8-6 70 CharlieBennett[(5)] 5 70
(Mark Brisbourne) *in rr: drvn over 4f out: hdwy 3f out: styd on one pce fnl f* **20/1**

0003 **5** 2 **The Character (IRE)**[14] 3636 5-8-10 69 (p) LiamJones 3 65
(Tom Dascombe) *led: drvn over 4f out: hdd over 1f out: edgd rt: grad wknd* **7/1**

1123 **6** 16 **Bakht A Rawan (IRE)**[26] 3219 4-9-4 77 WilliamTwiston-Davies 10 42
(Stuart Kittow) *hld up towards rr: hdwy over 6f out: drvn 4f out: lost pl over 1f out: bhd whn n.m.r on inner and sn swtchd rt: eased clsng stages* **7/1**

3431 **7** 3 3/4 **Save The Bees**[7] 3883 8-8-7 73 (b) GerO'Neill[(7)] 9 31
(Declan Carroll) *chsd ldr: upsides over 4f out: wknd over 1f out: bhd whn heavily eased last 100yds* **8/1**

-254 **8** 39 **Priors Brook**[13] 3690 5-9-3 76 (p) FrannyNorton 11
(Andrew Balding) *sn chsng ldrs: drvn over 4f out: lost pl over 2f out: heavily eased over 1f out: eventually completed: t.o* **6/1**[3]

0221 **9** 20 **Belle Travers**[12] 3711 4-9-8 81 PatrickMathers 4
(Richard Fahey) *sn chsng ldrs: lost pl over 2f out: sn bhd: virtually p.u over 1f out: eventually completed: t.o* **11/2**[2]

2m 18.04s (6.84) **Going Correction** +0.775s/f (Yiel) **9 Ran SP% 116.4**

Speed ratings (Par 105): **103,101,101,99,97 84,81,50,34**

CSF £62.01 CT £230.34 TOTE £9.10: £4.00, £3.00, £1.10; EX 67.50 Trifecta £307.20.

Owner Midest Partnership **Bred** Calley House Uk **Trained** Oakham, Rutland

FOCUS
This was run at a good gallop and it paid to be held up. The form is rated around the first three.

4139 JUNE ROBERTS MEMORIAL APPRENTICE H'CAP 7f 122y
5:15 (5:15) (Class 4) (0-80,80) 3-Y-O
£6,225 (£1,864; £932; £466; £233; £117) **Stalls** Low

Form RPR
1-33 **1** **Sunnua (IRE)**[16] 3551 3-9-8 **76** KevinStott 9 83
(Richard Fahey) *rr-div: hdwy over 3f out: led appr fnl f: drvn out* **12/1**
-055 **2** ¾ **Worlds His Oyster**[21] 3415 3-9-9 **77** CallumShepherd 2 81
(John Quinn) *trckd ldrs: upsides appr fnl f: kpt on same pce last 50yds* **11/2**[3]
1210 **3** ¾ **Nouvelli Dancer (IRE)**[56] 2239 3-9-6 **74** AlistairRawlinson 1 78+
(Ivan Furtado) *trckd ldrs: nt clr run and dropped bk over 1f out: styd on fnl 150yds: tk 3rd nr fin* **20/1**
4211 **4** nk **Make Music**[14] 3649 3-9-5 **80** JoshuaBryan(7) 6 81
(Andrew Balding) *w ldr: led over 5f out: edgd rt and hdd appr fnl f: kpt on same pce last 100yds* **3/1**[1]
0023 **5** ½ **La Celebs Ville (IRE)**[8] 3856 3-8-12 **69** (p) AnnaHesketh(3) 8 69
(Tom Dascombe) *s.i.s: swtchd lft after s: in rr: hdwy over 2f out: kpt on same pce fnl f* **12/1**
5-13 **6** ½ **Easter Mate (IRE)**[35] 2891 3-9-5 **80** (p) DavidEgan(7) 7 79
(Ralph Beckett) *rr-div: hdwy over 3f out: edgd rt and kpt on one pce fnl f* **4/1**[2]
4602 **7** 3 **Bell Heather (IRE)**[15] 3591 3-9-9 **77** LouisSteward 3 68
(Richard Fahey) *trckd ldrs: wkng whn n.m.r 150yds out* **4/1**[2]
1244 **8** shd **Outback Blue**[15] 3591 3-9-4 **79** (t) AledBeech(7) 5 70
(David Evans) *in rr: sme hdwy on inner over 1f out: wknd fnl 150yds* **8/1**
-036 **9** 7 **Dark Forest**[12] 3716 3-8-13 **72** SophieKilloran(5) 4 46
(Simon West) *led tl over 5f out: lost pl 2f out: bhd whn eased clsng stages* **16/1**

1m 39.25s (5.45) **Going Correction** +0.825s/f (Soft) **9** Ran SP% **117.5**
Speed ratings (Par 102): **105,104,103,103,102 102,99,99,92**
CSF £77.82 CT £1332.78 TOTE £10.70: £3.00, £2.30, £2.40; EX 104.50 Trifecta £3106.50 Part won..
Owner Mrs Clodagh Mitchell **Bred** J Waldron & W R Muir **Trained** Musley Bank, N Yorks

FOCUS
A pretty competitive handicap. The form makes some sense.
T/Plt: £22.90 to a £1 stake. Pool: £68,241.66 - 2169.96 winning units. T/Qpdt: £9.60 to a £1 stake. Pool: £3,989.13 - 306.356 winning units. **Walter Glynn**

3749 HAMILTON (R-H)
Saturday, July 9

OFFICIAL GOING: Good to soft (5.8)
Wind: Breezy, half behind Weather: Overcast, raining during race 7 (9.15)

4140 HIGHLAND SPRING MAIDEN AUCTION STKS (PLUS 10 RACE) (£20,000 HIGHLAND SPRING WATER SERIES QUAL) 5f 7y
6:15 (6:18) (Class 4) 2-Y-O
£4,528 (£1,347; £673; £336) **Stalls** High

Form RPR
4 **1** **Reckless Serenade (IRE)**[7] 3881 2-8-10 0 ConnorBeasley 1 67
(Keith Dalgleish) *mde all: sn crossed to stands' rail: rdn 2f out: kpt on wl fnl f* **3/1**[2]
U **2** ¾ **Baie D'Amour (FR)**[94] 1284 2-8-10 0 JoeyHaynes 4 64
(K R Burke) *trckd ldrs on outside: rdn and wnt 2nd over 1f out: kpt on fnl f: hld nr fin* **6/5**[1]
05 **3** 1½ **Our Boy John (IRE)**[11] 3749 2-8-13 0 KeaganLatham 5 62
(Richard Fahey) *prom: rdn and outpcd over 2f out: rallied fnl f: kpt on: nt pce to chal* **12/1**
4 1¾ **Western Presence** 2-8-13 0 BarryMcHugh 7 56
(Richard Fahey) *colty in preliminaries: chsd wnr to over 1f out: drvn and one pce fnl f* **9/2**[3]
5 9 **Bruny Island (IRE)** 2-9-2 0 RoystonFfrench 3 26
(Mark Johnston) *reluctant to enter stalls: chsd ldrs: drvn over 2f out: wknd over 1f out* **13/2**
6 10 **Kirkby's Phantom** 2-8-2 0 PhilDennis(5) 6
(John David Riches) *missed break: bhd and a outpcd* **50/1**

1m 1.76s (1.76) **Going Correction** +0.10s/f (Good) **6** Ran SP% **111.6**
Speed ratings (Par 96): **89,87,85,82,68 52**
CSF £6.93 TOTE £3.80: £1.70, £1.40; EX 8.80 Trifecta £41.70.
Owner Weldspec Glasgow Limited **Bred** Tally-Ho Stud **Trained** Carluke, S Lanarks

FOCUS
All distances as advertised. A routine juvenile maiden dominated by the prominent runners.

4141 SAS "THE POWER TO KNOW" H'CAP 5f 7y
6:45 (6:45) (Class 6) (0-65,61) 3-Y-O
£2,911 (£866; £432; £216) **Stalls** High

Form RPR
62-1 **1** **Rio Deva (IRE)**[10] 3773 3-9-7 **61** ConnorBeasley 4 66
(Keith Dalgleish) *mde all: rdn and hrd pressed fr over 1f out: hld on gamely fnl f* **2/1**[1]
5-00 **2** nk **Lady Elizabeth (IRE)**[21] 3423 3-9-0 **54** (p) BarryMcHugh 1 58
(Scott Dixon) *disp ld thrght: drvn along 2f out: kpt on wl fnl f: hld towards fin* **14/1**
0543 **3** 1¼ **Tarnend Lass**[10] 3773 3-8-10 **50** (tp) JamesSullivan 2 49
(Tim Easterby) *trckd ldrs: effrt and plld out over 1f out: drvn and ev ch ins fnl f: no ex last 50yds* **3/1**[3]
55 **4** 4 **North Spirit (IRE)**[36] 2854 3-9-0 **59** JoshDoyle(5) 3 44
(David O'Meara) *w ldrs to 2f out: sn rdn: edgd rt and wknd ent fnl f* **9/4**[2]
-000 **5** 1½ **Sophistica (IRE)**[21] 3423 3-9-1 **55** RoystonFfrench 5 35
(Iain Jardine) *t.k.h: prom: rdn and hung rt 2f out: sn wknd* **7/1**

1m 1.07s (1.07) **Going Correction** +0.10s/f (Good) **5** Ran SP% **108.3**
Speed ratings (Par 98): **95,94,92,86,83**
CSF £24.88 TOTE £2.30: £1.60, £4.60; EX 22.30 Trifecta £38.90.
Owner D R Tucker **Bred** Michael Staunton **Trained** Carluke, S Lanarks

FOCUS
A moderate handicap, with only the winner coming into it in top form.

4142 SUNDAY MAIL H'CAP 6f 6y
7:15 (7:16) (Class 5) (0-75,80) 3-Y-O+
£3,881 (£1,155; £577; £288) **Stalls** Centre

Form RPR
0001 **1** **Free Zone**[7] 3880 7-9-13 **80** (v) JoshDoyle(5) 2 92
(David O'Meara) *chsd centre ldr: rdn to ld over 1f out: pushed clr fnl f: comf* **11/4**[2]
0131 **2** 2¼ **Inexes**[6] 3924 4-10-2 **78** 6ex SamJames 3 83
(Marjorie Fife) *dwlt: in tch centre: drvn 2f out: hdwy to chse (clr) wnr ins fnl f: no imp* **9/4**[1]
3040 **3** 2 **Spowarticus**[16] 3553 7-8-8 **56** (v) DavidAllan 1 54
(Scott Dixon) *led and overall ldr centre: rdn over 2f out: edgd rt and hdd over 1f out: lost 2nd and wknd ins fnl f* **12/1**
6266 **4** 6 **Desire**[12] 3708 4-9-0 **62** (p) KeaganLatham 6 41
(Richard Fahey) *chsd stands' side ldr: drvn along over 2f out: led that trio over 1f out: no ch w centre ldrs* **15/2**
2244 **5** 2½ **Keene's Pointe**[6] 3924 6-9-2 **64** ConnorBeasley 7 35
(Kristin Stubbs) *dwlt: sn pushed along bhd stands' side ldrs: drvn and outpcd 1/2-way: n.d after* **7/2**[3]
620- **6** 2¾ **Economic Crisis (IRE)**[256] 7525 7-9-9 **71** JamesSullivan 5 33
(John David Riches) *led stands' side trio: already struggling whn lost ld in that gp over 1f out: edgd rt and wknd* **8/1**

1m 11.88s (-0.32) **Going Correction** +0.10s/f (Good) **6** Ran SP% **110.2**
Speed ratings (Par 103): **106,103,100,92,89 85**
CSF £9.00 TOTE £3.20: £1.70, £1.70; EX 6.00 Trifecta £62.80.
Owner J A Osborne **Bred** Richard Levin **Trained** Upper Helmsley, N Yorks

FOCUS
The first three all raced in the centre of the track early on, with the other three on the stands' rail. While the first two home were probably the best on the day anyway, it did appear to give them an extra advantage.

4143 RACINGUK.COM H'CAP 1m 3f 14y
7:45 (7:45) (Class 5) (0-75,74) 3-Y-O+
£5,175 (£1,540; £769; £384) **Stalls** Low

Form RPR
5310 **1** **Oriental Tiger**[22] 3363 5-9-10 **70** JamesSullivan 1 81
(Iain Jardine) *t.k.h early: hld up in last pl: stdy hdwy 3f out: swtchd rt and led over 1f out: pushed out ins fnl f* **8/1**[3]
3152 **2** 2½ **Isharah (USA)**[4] 3991 3-9-2 **74** RoystonFfrench 5 81
(Mark Johnston) *dwlt: sn chsng ldrs: rdn over 3f out: rallied over 2f out: effrt and ev ch over 1f out: kpt on same pce ins fnl f* **11/8**[1]
0502 **3** 2¼ **First Sargeant**[8] 3842 6-9-0 **60** (p) DavidAllan 8 63
(Lawrence Mullaney) *hld up: rdn and hdwy over 2f out: edgd rt and kpt on fnl f: nt rch ldrs* **8/1**[3]
2103 **4** 2¼ **Kip**[25] 3251 4-9-12 **72** SamJames 7 71
(David O'Meara) *chsd ldr: clr of rest over 3f out: led over 2f out to over 1f out: wknd ins fnl f* **8/1**[3]
53-4 **5** 6 **Siege Of Boston (IRE)**[28] 3174 3-8-12 **70** (t) ConnorBeasley 2 59
(Gordon Elliott, Ire) *in tch: rdn along over 3f out: shortlived effrt whn hung rt wl over 1f out: sn wknd* **5/2**[2]
6000 **6** 12 **Splash Of Verve (IRE)**[12] 3711 4-8-9 **55** JoeyHaynes 4 24
(Philip Kirby) *led: clr w one other over 3f out: hdd over 2f out: sn wknd* **28/1**
2500 **7** 7 **Ralphy Lad (IRE)**[63] 2051 5-10-0 **74** NeilFarley 6 31
(Alan Swinbank) *in tch: drvn and outpcd wl over 3f out: sn btn* **18/1**

2m 25.52s (-0.08) **Going Correction** +0.10s/f (Good)
WFA 3 from 4yo+ 12lb **7** Ran SP% **112.7**
Speed ratings (Par 103): **104,102,100,98,94 85,80**
CSF £18.96 CT £91.52 TOTE £8.50: £3.70, £1.30; EX 17.20 Trifecta £85.10.
Owner A Barclay **Bred** James Thom And Sons **Trained** Carrutherstown, D'fries & G'way

FOCUS
In this mid-range handicap, a searching gallop played into the hands of the patiently ridden winner.

4144 HAMILTON ADVERTISER H'CAP 1m 67y
8:15 (8:15) (Class 6) (0-60,58) 3-Y-O+
£2,911 (£866; £432; £216) **Stalls** Low

Form RPR
4022 **1** **Toffee Apple (IRE)**[5] 3943 3-8-4 **45** JoeyHaynes 1 60+
(Keith Dalgleish) *trckd ldrs: led gng wl over 2f out: shkn up and qcknd clr over 1f out: eased nr fin: readily* **7/4**[1]
1222 **2** 8 **Affectionate Lady (IRE)**[53] 2329 5-9-7 **58** (b) PhilDennis(5) 2 55
(Keith Reveley) *in tch: drvn along over 2f out: rallied to chse (clr) wnr ins fnl f: no imp* **7/1**
6600 **3** hd **Call Me Crockett (IRE)**[5] 3943 4-9-2 **55** (p) JamieGormley(7) 5 52
(Iain Jardine) *prom: outpcd and hung rt over 2f out: drvn and kpt on fnl f: nt pce to chal* **28/1**
0062 **4** ¾ **Intensified (IRE)**[11] 3750 5-9-1 **47** (b) JamesSullivan 8 42
(Ruth Carr) *hld up: rdn along and plld out over 2f out: kpt on fnl f: n.d* **10/1**
3455 **5** 2½ **Saltarello (IRE)**[3] 4006 4-9-12 **58** (p) SamJames 3 47
(Marjorie Fife) *led tl rdn and hdd over 2f out: edgd lft over 1f out: outpcd fnl f* **5/1**[2]
0045 **6** 1 **Mr Sundowner (USA)**[22] 3363 4-9-11 **57** (t) DavidAllan 4 44
(Wilf Storey) *chsd ldr: drvn along over 2f out: wknd ins fnl f* **5/1**[2]
500 **7** 2 **Ted's Brother (IRE)**[15] 3624 8-9-4 **50** (b) ConnorBeasley 7 33
(Richard Guest) *missed break: t.k.h: hld up: stdy hdwy 3f out: sn pushed along: wknd fnl f* **16/1**
5144 **8** hd **Joyful Star**[22] 3344 6-9-11 **57** BarryMcHugh 6 39
(Fred Watson) *hld up: drvn and outpcd 3f out: nvr on terms* **13/2**[3]

1m 48.2s (-0.20) **Going Correction** +0.10s/f (Good)
WFA 3 from 4yo+ 9lb **8** Ran SP% **114.0**
Speed ratings (Par 101): **105,97,96,96,93 92,90,90**
CSF £14.53 CT £249.63 TOTE £2.70: £1.40, £2.00, £3.40; EX 12.70 Trifecta £237.10.
Owner Ronnie Docherty **Bred** Ms Sinead Maher **Trained** Carluke, S Lanarks

FOCUS
In an otherwise unremarkable race, run at an ordinary pace, the improving winner was far too good at the weights.

4145 RACING UK ON SKY 432 FILLIES' H'CAP 1m 67y
8:45 (8:46) (Class 5) (0-75,76) 3-Y-O+
£3,881 (£1,155; £577; £288) **Stalls** Low

Form RPR
2351 **1** **My Lucille (IRE)**[9] 3810 3-9-1 **71** DavidAllan 2 80+
(Tim Easterby) *led to over 4f out: pressed ldr: led gng wl 2f out: shkn up and sn clr: easily* **3/1**[2]
0220 **2** 2½ **Rosy Morning (IRE)**[12] 3717 3-9-4 **74** RoystonFfrench 5 76
(Mark Johnston) *s.i.s: sn prom: rdn over 3f out: rallied over 2f out: edgd lft over 1f out: chsd (clr) wnr ins fnl f: no imp* **10/1**
0244 **3** shd **Fidelma Moon (IRE)**[17] 3521 4-9-4 **72** CliffordLee(7) 7 76
(K R Burke) *plld hrd: hdwy to press wnr after 2f: led over 4f out: edgd lft and hdd 2f out: one pce whn lost 2nd ins fnl f* **5/1**[3]
0333 **4** 4 **Dominannie (IRE)**[4] 3982 3-8-8 **64** NeilFarley 4 57
(Alan Swinbank) *t.k.h: hld up: stdy hdwy whn nt clr run and swtchd lft over 2f out: sn shkn up and hung lft: wknd over 1f out* **7/4**[1]

4423 **5** *3* **Ingleby Spring (IRE)**[37] 2810 4-9-1 **62**.......................... BarryMcHugh 3 50
(Richard Fahey) *chsd wnr 2f: cl up: drvn along over 2f out: wknd over 1f out* **7/1**

-210 **6** *3/4* **Lincoln Rocks**[20] 3438 3-9-5 **75**.. SamJames 6 59
(David O'Meara) *hld up in tch: drvn and outpcd wl over 2f out: sn btn* **9/1**

1m 49.21s (0.81) **Going Correction** +0.10s/f (Good)
WFA 3 from 4yo 9lb **6 Ran SP% 109.6**
Speed ratings (Par 100): **99,96,96,92,89 88**
CSF £29.22 TOTE £3.90: £1.60, £3.30; EX 28.50 Trifecta £135.60.
Owner M J Macleod **Bred** Knockainey Stud **Trained** Great Habton, N Yorks

FOCUS
In a race run at a decent gallop, the winner was the most progressive.

4146 BILL & DAVID MCHARG H'CAP — 1m 1f 34y
9:15 (9:15) (Class 6) (0-65,63) 3-Y-O+ **£2,911** (£866; £432; £216) **Stalls** Low

Form RPR

0-50 **1** **Lady Turpin (IRE)**[18] 3493 3-8-5 **50** ow1........................ BarryMcHugh 7 55
(Richard Fahey) *chsd clr ldr: stdy hdwy over 2f out: shkn up to ld over 1f out: edgd lft ins fnl f: rdn out* **3/1**[3]

-30 **2** *1/2* **Lady Fandango (IRE)**[159] 420 4-10-0 **63**........................ SamJames 6 68
(Gordon Elliott, Ire) *in tch: rdn over 2f out: hdwy over 1f out: chsd wnr ins fnl f: clsng at fin* **9/4**[1]

0603 **3** *3 3/4* **Tectonic (IRE)**[2] 4038 7-9-10 **59**.................................(v) ConnorBeasley 1 57
(Keith Dalgleish) *t.k.h: trckd ldrs: stdy hdwy over 2f out: shkn up and chsd ldrs over 1f out: wknd ins fnl f* **5/2**[2]

0506 **4** *3 3/4* **Outlaw Torn (IRE)**[5] 3943 7-9-4 **53**..........................(e) RoystonFfrench 5 44
(Richard Guest) *led: clr after 2f: rdn and hdd over 1f out: wknd ins fnl f* **4/1**

0000 **5** *14* **Private Dancer**[10] 3774 5-8-10 **45**....................................... DavidAllan 3 9
(Ron Barr) *plld hrd: hld up: rdn and struggling over 3f out: sn btn* **20/1**

46-0 **6** *1 1/2* **Breton Blues**[31] 3014 6-9-6 **55**.................................(be[1]) JamesSullivan 2 16
(Fred Watson) *s.i.s: hld up: struggling 3f out: btn fnl 2f* **25/1**

2m 0.65s (0.95) **Going Correction** +0.10s/f (Good)
WFA 3 from 4yo+ 10lb **6 Ran SP% 112.9**
Speed ratings (Par 101): **99,98,95,91,79 78**
CSF £10.33 TOTE £4.40: £2.00, £2.30; EX 15.50 Trifecta £41.70.
Owner UK Racing Syndicate **Bred** Michael Kelly **Trained** Musley Bank, N Yorks

FOCUS
A low-grade event, with few of them in any kind of form and the winner never having previously finished in the first four.
T/Plt: £16.20 to a £1 stake. Pool: £49, 346.69 - 2218.47 winning units. T/Qpdt: £7.90 to a £1 stake. Pool: £4,276.71 - 400.60 winning units. **Richard Young**

4103 NEWMARKET (R-H)
Saturday, July 9

OFFICIAL GOING: Good to firm (8.2; stands' side 8.4:, centre: 8.3, far side: 8.1)
Wind: light, half behind Weather: overcast

4147 ROSSDALES EBF STALLIONS MAIDEN FILLIES' STKS (PLUS 10 RACE) — 7f
2:15 (2:15) (Class 4) 2-Y-O **£6,469** (£1,925; £962; £481) **Stalls** Low

Form RPR

1 **Dabyah (IRE)** 2-9-0 0... FrankieDettori 8 92+
(John Gosden) *str: lw: trckd ldrs: effrt and qcknd to ld over 1f out: jst over 2 l clr ins fnl f: in command and pushed out after: eased towards fin* **3/1**[1]

2 *1/2* **Amabilis** 2-9-0 0.. RyanMoore 4 90+
(Ralph Beckett) *tall: lengthy: t.k.h early: chsd ldr after 1f out: rdn to chal over 1f out: chsng wnr nt matching her pce ent fnl f: rallied and keeping on again fnl 100yds* **9/2**[3]

5 **3** *6* **Dubara**[30] 3074 2-9-0 0.. AdamKirby 10 73
(Luca Cumani) *athletic: led: rdn and hdd over 1f out: sn outpcd and btn 3rd 1f out: no ch w ldng pair but kpt on for clr 3rd ins fnl f* **4/1**[2]

4 *4* **Pichola Dance (IRE)** 2-9-0 0.. HarryBentley 7 63
(Roger Varian) *w'like: in tch: effrt 2f out: sn outpcd: no ch w ldrs and kpt on same pce ins fnl f* **10/1**

5 *nk* **Carol (IRE)** 2-9-0 0.. OisinMurphy 2 62
(Ed Dunlop) *leggy: in tch towards rr: pushed along over 2f out: outpcd over 1f out: no ch w ldrs and kpt on same pce ins fnl f* **14/1**

6 *1/2* **Sasini** 2-9-0 0... JamesDoyle 6 60
(Charles Hills) *str: lw: hld up in tch towards rr: effrt ent fnl 2f: rdn and outpcd over 1f out: no ch w ldrs and kpt on same pce ins fnl f* **13/2**

7 *1/2* **Whispered Promise (IRE)** 2-9-0 0....................... MichaelJMMurphy 9 59
(Charles Hills) *athletic: wnt lft s: hld up in tch towards rr: effrt ent fnl 2f: outpcd and wl hld over 1f out: pluged on same pce ins fnl f* **25/1**

8 *2* **Excellent Sunset (IRE)** 2-9-0 0.. TomQueally 1 54
(David Lanigan) *in tch towards rr: effrt and hdwy jst over 2f out: outpcd by ldrs and hung lft over 1f out: wknd ins fnl f* **14/1**

0 **9** *2* **Varun's Bride (IRE)**[16] 3556 2-9-0 0...................................... PatDobbs 3 48
(Richard Hannon) *leggy: chsd ldr for 1f: styd chsng ldrs: rdn jst over 2f out: sn lost pl and wl btn whn hung lft jst over 1f out: wknd fnl f* **25/1**

10 *4* **Mary Anne Evans** 2-9-0 0... RobertHavlin 5 38
(John Gosden) *unf: s.i.s: rn green in rr: sltly hmpd 1/2-way: outpcd 2f out: wl bhd fnl f* **10/1**

1m 25.22s (-0.48) **Going Correction** +0.05s/f (Good) **10 Ran SP% 115.7**
Speed ratings (Par 93): **104,103,96,92,91 91,90,88,85,81**
CSF £16.17 TOTE £3.00: £1.60, £1.50, £1.70; EX 13.80 Trifecta £29.60.
Owner Abdullah Saeed Al Naboodah **Bred** Rabbah Bloodstock Limited **Trained** Newmarket, Suffolk

FOCUS
Race distances as advertised. Stalls on far side except 1m4f, centre. The track was watered overnight. After the first Frankie Dettori said: "It's good to firm, fast," while Robert Havlin's take was: "It rides slower than it walks." This was one of the hottest maidens of last year with Ballydoyle, subsequent winner of the Prix Marcel Boussac, beating Nemoralia who has been placed three times at the top level. Eight of the ten runners won next time out. The first winner of this race, Winters Moon in 2014, was third in the Fillies' Mile. This edition looks well worth following. It proved difficult to make ground from off the pace and the first two finished clear.

4148 SPA AT BEDFORD LODGE HOTEL NURSERY H'CAP — 7f
2:50 (2:50) (Class 2) 2-Y-O **£12,938** (£3,850; £1,924; £962) **Stalls** Low

Form RPR

413 **1** **Pleaseletmewin (IRE)**[21] 3408 2-9-7 **85**............................ RyanMoore 8 93
(Ralph Beckett) *lw: chsd ldr: rdn over 2f out: drvn to ld ent fnl f: battled on wl u.p: edgd rt towards fin: gamely* **4/1**[2]

51 **2** *1/2* **Bacchus**[9] 3808 2-9-3 **81**.. FrankieDettori 1 88
(Brian Meehan) *tall: lw: in tch towards rr: clsd to press ldrs over 2f out: drvn and ev ch ent fnl f: r.o u.p but a jst hld: bmpd towards fin* **4/1**[2]

3112 **3** *1 1/2* **Mistime (IRE)**[17] 3531 2-9-3 **81**.. JoeFanning 9 84
(Mark Johnston) *chsd ldrs: effrt 2f out: nt clr run and swtchd lft ent fnl f: styd on same pce u.p fnl 150yds* **13/2**

1321 **4** *1 1/4* **Kreb's Cycle (IRE)**[18] 3495 2-9-6 **84**.................................... PatDobbs 4 83
(Richard Hannon) *lw: stdd s: hld up in tch in rr: clsd to trck ldrs 2f out: nt clr run: swtchd lft and effrt and ent fnl f: styd on same pce ins fnl f* **10/1**

231 **5** *2* **Spiritous (USA)**[22] 3356 2-9-4 **82**..................................(p) JamesDoyle 10 76
(John Gosden) *str: racd away fr main gp towards far side: racd freely: led: hung rt and hdd over 1f out: sn btn: wknd ins fnl f* **11/4**[1]

31 **6** *5* **High Acclaim (USA)**[23] 3315 2-9-2 **80**............................. OisinMurphy 3 60
(Roger Teal) *leggy: hld up in tch: clsd to press ldrs and travelling wl over 2f out: rdn 2f out: unable qck and sn outpcd: wknd fnl f* **9/2**[3]

604 **7** *10* **Ingleby Mackenzie**[29] 3108 2-8-10 **74**........................... CharlesBishop 6 27
(Mick Channon) *in tch in midfield: rdn 3f out: sn struggling and lost pl: bhd 2f out: wknd over 1f out* **25/1**

01 **8** *1 1/4* **Quandary Peak**[21] 3404 2-8-0 **64** oh2................................ DannyBrock 7 14
(J S Moore) *leggy: in tch: clsd to chse ldrs over 3f out: rdn ent 2f out: sn struggling and lost pl: bhd and wknd over 1f out* **50/1**

1m 25.74s (0.04) **Going Correction** +0.05s/f (Good) **8 Ran SP% 113.1**
Speed ratings (Par 100): **101,100,98,97,95 89,77,76**
CSF £19.90 CT £99.99 TOTE £4.70: £2.00, £1.60, £1.80; EX 22.00 Trifecta £96.90.
Owner R Roberts **Bred** Ballykilbride Stud **Trained** Kimpton, Hants

FOCUS
Decent nursery form. Last year's winner First Selection went on to win a Group 3. The form is rated slightly on the positive side.

4149 BET365 MILE (H'CAP) — 1m
3:25 (3:26) (Class 2) (0-100,99) 3-Y-O
£18,675 (£5,592; £2,796; £1,398; £699; £351) **Stalls** Low

Form RPR

21-4 **1** **Von Blucher (IRE)**[78] 1603 3-8-8 **86**...............................(t) RobertHavlin 2 95+
(John Gosden) *hld up in tch: clsd to trck ldrs and travelling wl over 1f out: shkn up and qcknd to ld over 1f out: hung lft u.p 1f out: r.o wl ins fnl f* **7/1**

-211 **2** *1 1/4* **Silent Attack**[16] 3574 3-9-0 **92**... JamesDoyle 5 97+
(Saeed bin Suroor) *str: lengthy: stdd s: hld up in tch in rr: hdwy 2f out: clsd to chse ldrs and swtchd lft over 1f out: styd on u.p ins fnl f: wnt 2nd last strides* **5/2**[2]

13-1 **3** *shd* **Hornsby**[15] 3600 3-8-12 **90**.. HarryBentley 7 94
(Charlie Appleby) *str: lw: hld up wl in tch in midfield: hdwy over 2f out: drvn over 1f out: chsd wnr ins fnl f: kpt on but no imp fnl 50yds: lost 2nd last strides* **5/1**[3]

1-10 **4** *1 1/4* **Manson**[23] 3299 3-9-2 **94**... RyanMoore 10 95+
(Dominic Ffrench Davis) *hld up in tch: effrt over 2f out: drvn to chse ldr 1f out: styd on same pce after and lost 2 pls ins fnl f* **2/1**[1]

41-5 **5** *1/2* **Perkunas (IRE)**[133] 756 3-9-7 **99**.................................... FrankieDettori 9 99
(Brian Meehan) *in tch: rdn and hdwy to ld over 2f out: drvn and hdd over 1f out: wknd ins fnl f* **14/1**

404 **6** *7* **Palawan**[17] 3534 3-9-2 **94**.. PatDobbs 4 77
(Richard Hannon) *t.k.h: hld up in tch in midfield: hdwy to chse ldrs after 2f: rdn over 2f out: lost pl and bhd over 1f out: wknd fnl f* **12/1**

0520 **7** *2* **Whitman**[7] 3910 3-9-2 **94**.. JoeFanning 3 72
(Mark Johnston) *led for 2f: styd wl in tch: effrt u.p to press ldrs over 2f out: lost pl over 1f out: wknd fnl f* **12/1**

052 **8** *2 1/2* **Cadeaux Boxer**[16] 3572 3-7-13 **82**..................................... NoelGarbutt(5) 6 54
(Martin Smith) *swtg: t.k.h: hdwy to ld after 2f: rdn and hdd over 2f out: dropped out and bhd over 1f out: wknd fnl f* **40/1**

1m 37.69s (-2.31) **Going Correction** +0.05s/f (Good) **8 Ran SP% 115.6**
Speed ratings (Par 106): **113,111,111,110,109 102,100,98**
CSF £25.19 CT £97.29 TOTE £7.10: £1.60, £1.30, £1.90; EX 27.30 Trifecta £109.20.
Owner Ms Rachel D S Hood **Bred** George Kent **Trained** Newmarket, Suffolk

FOCUS
A good-quality handicap. The early pace was steady, with a few of them racing keenly, but did increase and the right horses came to the fore. The level is set around the fifth.

4150 BET365 SUPERLATIVE STKS (GROUP 2) — 7f
4:00 (4:01) (Class 1) 2-Y-O
£45,368 (£17,200; £8,608; £4,288; £2,152; £1,080) **Stalls** Low

Form RPR

1 **1** **Boynton (USA)**[36] 2873 2-9-1 0... AdamKirby 10 114
(Charlie Appleby) *tall: str: t.k.h early: hld up in tch towards rr: rdn and gd hdwy to ld over 2f out: drvn and wnt clr w wnr over 1f out: hdd ins fnl f: sn led again: styd on wl* **7/1**[3]

2 *3/4* **War Decree (USA)**[36] 2878 2-9-1 0...................................... RyanMoore 8 112
(A P O'Brien, Ire) *tall: athletic: lw: trckd ldrs: effrt to chal 2f out: wnt clr w wnr over 1f out: led and edgd lft ins fnl f: edgd bk rt u.p and sn hdd: no ex and one pce towards fin* **1/1**[1]

4134 **3** *5* **Mr Scaramanga**[21] 3382 2-9-1 0.. PatDobbs 7 98
(Richard Hannon) *t.k.h early: hld up in tch: effrt whn nt clr run and hmpd 2f out: hdwy u.p to chse clr ldng pair 1f out: kpt on but no imp after* **16/1**

13 **4** *3/4* **Cunco (IRE)**[21] 3382 2-9-1 0.. RobertHavlin 1 96
(John Gosden) *pressed ldrs: rdn and ev ch over 2f out: outpcd u.p and btn over 1f out: wl hld 4th and kpt on same pce ins fnl f* **7/2**[2]

1 **5** *1 1/2* **White Tower (IRE)**[23] 3321 2-9-1 0...................................... JoeFanning 9 92
(Mark Johnston) *str: chsd ldr: rdn to ld wl over 2f out: sn hdd: outpcd u.p over 1f out: wl hld 5th and plugged on same pce fnl f* **20/1**

3110 **6** *6* **Monks Stand (USA)**[25] 3243 2-9-1 0.............................(v[1]) TomQueally 2 76
(Jeremy Noseda) *stdd s: t.k.h: hld up in tch in rr: and hdwy to chse ldrs over 2f out: hung lft and outpcd over 1f out: sn wknd* **25/1**

1 **7** *1 3/4* **Bin Battuta**[33] 2976 2-9-1 0... JamesDoyle 6 71
(Saeed bin Suroor) *cmpt: stdd s: hld up in tch in rr: effrt whn nt clr run and hmpd 2f out: swtchd rt and tried to rcvr over 1f out: no hdwy and wl btn fnl f* **8/1**

512 **8** *nk* **Spirit Of Sarwan (IRE)**[18] 3477 2-9-1 0......................... AdamBeschizza 5 71
(Julia Feilden) *led tl rdn and hdd wl over 2f out: lost pl and bhd over 1f out: wknd fnl f* **100/1**

141 **9** *5* **Hyperfocus (IRE)**[16] 3562 2-9-1 0...................................... FrankieDettori 4 57
(Hugo Palmer) *t.k.h: hld up in tch towards rr: effrt 2f out: no reponse: sn wknd and wl bhd ins fnl f* **14/1**

1m 24.86s (-0.84) **Going Correction** +0.05s/f (Good) **9 Ran SP% 118.0**
Speed ratings (Par 106): **106,105,99,98,96 90,88,87,81**
CSF £14.52 TOTE £7.80: £2.20, £1.10, £4.70; EX 18.50 Trifecta £188.50.
Owner Godolphin **Bred** Twin Creeks Farm **Trained** Newmarket, Suffolk

FOCUS
Olympic Glory, successful in 2012, was the last winner who went on to Group 1 glory. The first two, both winners of their only start, pulled five lengths clear in what looked a good edition of this event. It has been rated the joint-best renewal in the last ten years. The third looks the key to the form.

4151 DARLEY JULY CUP (BRITISH CHAMPIONS SERIES AND GLOBAL SPRINT CHALLENGE) (GROUP 1) 6f

4:35 (4:37) (Class 1) 3-Y-O+

£302,689 (£114,756; £57,431; £28,609; £14,357; £7,205) **Stalls** Low

Form RPR

12-4 **1** **Limato (IRE)**[56] 2243 4-9-6 119.. HarryBentley 16 125
(Henry Candy) *hld up wl in tch in midfield: clsd to trck ldrs 2f out: rdn to ld over 1f out: sn qcknd and clr whn wnt bdly rt ins fnl f: r.o wl: impressive* **9/2**[1]

-225 **2** *2* **Suedois (FR)**[21] 3385 5-9-6 113.. RobertHavlin 9 118
(David O'Meara) *lw: wl in tch in midfield: clsd to press ldrs over 2f out: rdn and ev ch over 1f out: outpcd by wnr in 2nd 1f out: styd on same pce after* **25/1**

-111 **3** *hd* **Quiet Reflection**[22] 3338 3-8-11 117............................. DougieCostello 7 113
(K R Burke) *hld up wl in tch in midfield: effrt to chse ldrs over 1f out: battling for 2nd but outpcd by wnr 1f out: kpt on* **7/1**[3]

-111 **4** *1 1/4* **Profitable (IRE)**[25] 3244 4-9-6 117.................................... AdamKirby 13 113
(Clive Cox) *hld up wl in tch in midfield: edgd lft and hdwy u.p over 1f out: edgd rt 1f out: styd on same pce u.p ins fnl f* **11/1**

0123 **5** *nk* **Washington DC (IRE)**[22] 3338 3-9-0 111..................(t) WayneLordan 18 111
(A P O'Brien, Ire) *hld up in tch in midfield: hdwy 2f out: carried sltly lft and drvn to chse ldrs over 1f out: outpcd 1f out: styd on same pce ins fnl f* **25/1**

10-4 **6** *1/2* **Eastern Impact (IRE)**[59] 2159 5-9-6 112.......................... JackGarritty 6 110
(Richard Fahey) *led for 2f: styd prom: rdn and ev ch wl over 1f out: sn drvn and outpcd by wnr 1f out: styd on same pce ins fnl f* **25/1**

-114 **7** *nk* **Magical Memory (IRE)**[21] 3385 4-9-6 114.................... FrankieDettori 10 109
(Charles Hills) *stdd bk after s: hld up in tch in midfield: effrt whn nt clr run over 1f out: swtchd lft 1f out: kpt on ins fnl f: no threat to wnr* **5/1**[2]

300 **8** *nk* **Sole Power**[70] 1862 9-9-6 112.. ChrisHayes 15 111+
(Edward Lynam, Ire) *stdd and dropped in after s: hld up in tch towards rr: clsd and travelling whn 2f out: nt clr run over 1f out: swtchd lft and hmpd 1f out: styd on ins fnl f: no threat to wnr* **33/1**

3-32 **9** *1/2* **Danzeno**[27] 3195 5-9-6 113.. AndrewMullen 3 107
(Michael Appleby) *stdd s: hld up in tch towards rr: hdwy 2f out: rdn over 1f out: kpt on ins fnl f: nvr trbld ldrs* **20/1**

3003 **10** *1/2* **Goken (FR)**[25] 3244 4-9-6 111... TomEaves 1 105+
(Kevin Ryan) *stdd s: hld up in tch in rr: clsd but nt clr run wl over 1f out tl ins fnl f: nvr trbld ldrs* **33/1**

5-00 **11** *hd* **Mongolian Saturday (USA)**[25] 3244 6-9-6 115................ PatDobbs 12 105
(Enebish Ganbat, U.S.A) *lw: taken down early and ponied to s: t.k.h: midfield early: hdwy to ld after 2f: rdn and hdd over 1f out: no ex: wknd ins fnl f* **50/1**

1-00 **12** *1* **Air Force Blue (USA)**[49] 2496 3-9-0 118.......................... RyanMoore 8 100+
(A P O'Brien, Ire) *stdd s: hld up in tch in rr: clsd 2f out: nt clr run over 1f out: nvr enough room after and nvr able to cl: eased wl ins fnl f* **8/1**

-022 **13** *nk* **Cotai Glory**[25] 3244 4-9-6 114.................................. MichaelJMMurphy 5 100
(Charles Hills) *taken down early: in tch in midfield: clsd to chse ldrs 2f out: no ex u.p ent fnl f: wknd ins fnl f* **33/1**

2-51 **14** *shd* **Twilight Son**[21] 3385 4-9-6 117....................................... MartinHarley 2 100
(Henry Candy) *hld up in tch towards rr: clsd 2f out: rdn and unable qck jst over 1f out: wknd ins fnl f* **7/1**[3]

2424 **15** *3* **Jungle Cat (IRE)**[25] 3244 4-9-6 112................................ JamesDoyle 11 91
(Charlie Appleby) *lw: chsd ldrs: rdn wl over 1f out: unable qck and lost pl over 1f out: wknd ins fnl f* **16/1**

-151 **16** *hd* **Don't Touch**[27] 3195 4-9-6 114...................................... TonyHamilton 14 90
(Richard Fahey) *chsd ldrs: rdn and unable qck and btn over 1f out: wknd ins fnl f* **16/1**

-335 **17** *6* **Waady (IRE)**[25] 3244 4-9-6 110...................................... PaulHanagan 4 71
(John Gosden) *swtg: t.k.h: hld up towards rr: hdwy over 2f out: sn u.p: wknd over 1f out: bhd and eased wl ins fnl f* **25/1**

0-3 **18** *10* **Arod (IRE)**[73] 1774 5-9-6 118.. OisinMurphy 17 39
(Peter Chapple-Hyam) *chsd ldrs: rdn and lost pl 2f out: sn bhd: eased ins fnl f* **16/1**

1m 9.97s (-2.53) **Going Correction** +0.05s/f (Good)
WFA 3 from 4yo+ 6lb **18** Ran SP% **127.9**
Speed ratings (Par 117): **118,115,115,113,113 112,111,111,110,110 109,108,108,108,104 103,95,82**
CSF £127.13 CT £832.07 TOTE £5.90: £2.50, £8.20, £2.70; EX 140.40 Trifecta £1170.10.
Owner Paul G Jacobs **Bred** Seamus Phelan **Trained** Kingston Warren, Oxon
■ Stewards' Enquiry : Adam Kirby two-day ban: careless riding (24-25 Jul)

FOCUS
A deep edition of the race. It had looked wide-open but the well backed favourite ran out a deeply impressive winner on this return to sprinting, being value for more than the 2l winning margin after hanging right late. With the Commonwealth Cup and King's Stand winners in third and fourth respectively there's every reason to believe this is solid form. Limato is rated marginally the best winner in the last ten years, with a small pb from Suedois and Quiet Reflection to her Ascot form.

4152 BET365 BUNBURY CUP (HERITAGE H'CAP) 7f

5:10 (5:10) (Class 2) 3-Y-O+

£74,700 (£22,368; £11,184; £5,592; £2,796; £1,404) **Stalls** Low

Form RPR

3603 **1** **Golden Steps (FR)**[42] 2684 5-9-0 99............................ FrankieDettori 14 107
(Marco Botti) *taken down early: hld up in tch: effrt and rdn to chal over 1f out: led jst ins fnl f: r.o wl: rdn out* **7/1**[1]

0002 **2** *3/4* **Heaven's Guest (IRE)**[49] 2485 6-9-5 104......................... JackGarritty 1 110
(Richard Fahey) *hld up in tch in midfield: swtchd rt and effrt over 1f out: r.o wl u.p fnl 100yds: wnt 2nd last strides* **9/1**[3]

5320 **3** *nk* **Mutawathea**[21] 3386 5-9-3 102...................................(p) RobertHavlin 9 107
(Simon Crisford) *lw: led: rdn and hrd pressed over 1f out: hdd ins fnl f: styd on same pce u.p after: lost 2nd last strides* **9/1**[3]

4411 **4** *shd* **Growl**[14] 3671 4-9-0 99 6ex.. TonyHamilton 5 104
(Richard Fahey) *hld up wl in tch in midfield: effrt 2f out: swtchd rt and drvn over 1f out: styd on u.p fnl 100yds* **8/1**[2]

4510 **5** *1/2* **Flash Fire (IRE)**[21] 3386 4-9-10 109................................. JamesDoyle 12 113
(Charlie Appleby) *wl in tch in midfield: effrt 2f out: drvn and ev ch over 1f out: unable qck jst onside fnl f: styd on same pce fnl 100yds* **10/1**

3-00 **6** *hd* **Farlow (IRE)**[86] 1441 8-9-1 100... TomEaves 18 103+
(Richard Fahey) *hld up in tch towards rr: effrt and swtchd lft over 1f out: styd on u.p ins fnl f: nt rch ldrs* **40/1**

0450 **7** *1/2* **Dinkum Diamond (IRE)**[21] 3386 8-8-12 102.............. HectorCrouch(5) 4 104
(Henry Candy) *hld up in tch in midfield: rdn and hdwy over 1f out: chsd ldrs and drvn 1f out: styd on same pce fnl 150yds* **22/1**

-100 **8** *1/2* **Accession (IRE)**[21] 3386 7-8-12 100...................... DanielMuscutt(3) 19 100
(Charlie Fellowes) *lw: chsd ldrs: rdn and ev ch over 1f out: unable qck u.p 1f out: outpcd fnl 100yds* **25/1**

0-35 **9** *nk* **Buckstay (IRE)**[21] 3386 6-9-3 109.........................(p) GeorgeWood(7) 20 109
(Peter Chapple-Hyam) *hld up in tch towards rr: clsd 2f out: rdn ent fnl f: drvn and styd on same pce ins fnl f* **7/1**[1]

0020 **10** *1* **Emell**[24] 3273 6-9-2 101...(b) PatDobbs 2 98
(Richard Hannon) *hld up in tch in midfield: effrt over 1f out: no imp tl styd on steadily ins fnl f: nvr threatened ldrs* **20/1**

006 **11** *hd* **Bossy Guest (IRE)**[24] 3273 4-9-5 104......................... CharlesBishop 11 100
(Mick Channon) *sn dropped to detached last and nt travelling wl: rdn 2f out: hdwy 1f out: styd on wl ins fnl f: nvr trbld ldrs* **11/1**

2000 **12** *shd* **Majestic Moon (IRE)**[21] 3386 6-9-1 100......................... TomQueally 13 96
(John Gallagher) *pressed ldr: rdn and ev ch over 2f out tl no ex ent fnl f: wknd ins fnl f* **25/1**

000- **13** *nk* **Tanzeel (IRE)**[280] 6919 5-9-2 101.................................... PaulHanagan 3 96
(Charles Hills) *s.i.s: hld up in tch towards rr: swtchd rt and effrt 2f out: no real imp: styd on same pce fnl f* **16/1**

5040 **14** *2* **B Fifty Two (IRE)**[21] 3386 7-9-1 100..................... MichaelJMMurphy 10 90
(Charles Hills) *s.i.s: hld up in tch towards rr: effrt over 1f out: no imp u.p 1f out: nvr trbld ldrs* **33/1**

0540 **15** *6* **Glory Awaits (IRE)**[24] 3273 6-9-0 99............................(b) MartinHarley 8 73
(David Simcock) *lw: pressed ldrs: rdn over 2f out: lost pl wl over 1f out: wknd fnl f* **8/1**[2]

141/ **P** **Glorious Empire (IRE)**[427] 5-9-1 100.............................. RyanMoore 17
(Ed Walker) *swtg: hld up wl in tch in midfield: eased over 2f out: sn lost tch: p.u and dismntd ins fnl f: burst blood vessel* **12/1**

1m 23.99s (-1.71) **Going Correction** +0.05s/f (Good) **16** Ran SP% **120.4**
Speed ratings (Par 109): **111,110,109,109,109 108,108,107,107,106 106,105,105,103,96**
CSF £60.68 CT £604.29 TOTE £6.90: £2.40, £2.20, £3.20, £2.20; EX 60.90 Trifecta £848.50.
Owner M A A Al-Mannai **Bred** T Jeffroy, B Jeffroy Et Al **Trained** Newmarket, Suffolk

FOCUS
Another competitive renewal of this historic handicap. Royal Ascot form was well represented, seven of these having run in the Wokingham, and the first four in the Victoria Cup met again. Only around 3l covered the first nine home. Solid form, the winner rated to his best.

4153 LONGINES IRISH CHAMPIONS WEEKEND H'CAP 1m 4f

5:45 (5:46) (Class 3) (0-90,91) 3-Y-O+ **£9,703** (£2,887; £1,443; £721) **Stalls** Centre

Form RPR

1-52 **1** **Gold Faith (IRE)**[45] 2580 3-8-4 79.................................... HarryBentley 5 89
(Ralph Beckett) *lw: stdd s: hld up in tch in last pair: clsd and travelling wl 4f out: rdn to ld ent fnl f: r.o wl: readily* **6/1**[3]

4-12 **2** *2 1/4* **Rockspirit (IRE)**[13] 3687 3-9-2 91...................................... RyanMoore 4 97
(Marco Botti) *chsd ldr: clsd to press ldr 3f out: rdn and ev ch 2f out: edgd lft and unable qck ent fnl f: kpt on same pce after* **11/4**[1]

104- **3** *nk* **Al**[255] 7564 4-9-6 82.. AdamKirby 7 88
(Luca Cumani) *chsd ldrs: pushed along and clsd to press ldr 3f out: ev ch after tl unable qck and carried lft ent fnl f: styd on same pce after* **9/2**[2]

1-21 **4** *3/4* **Lord George (IRE)**[30] 3077 3-9-0 89.................................. TomQueally 2 94
(James Fanshawe) *lw: hld up in last trio: clsd on ldr over 3f out: rdn to chse ldrs over 1f out: styd on same pce ins fnl f* **11/4**[1]

2422 **5** *3/4* **Sbraase**[10] 3785 5-9-10 86.. MartinHarley 6 90
(James Tate) *stdd and dropped in bhd after s: hld up in rr: clsd over 3f out: wl in tch and nt clr run 2f out tl ent fnl f: sn rdn and styd on same pce after* **9/1**

-116 **6** *2 1/4* **Cape Of Glory (IRE)**[66] 1971 3-8-12 87........................(b[1]) RobertHavlin 3 87
(James Tate) *sn led: clr 8f out tl 3f: no ex u.p and carried lft ent fnl f: wknd ins fnl f* **25/1**

223 **7** *8* **Hepplewhite**[11] 3736 3-8-7 82... PaoloSirigu 1 69
(Robert Eddery) *midfield: effrt to chse ldrs 3f out: lost pl and btn over 1f out: wknd fnl f* **18/1**

511 **8** *19* **Another Go (IRE)**[87] 1411 3-8-12 87.............................. TonyHamilton 8 44
(Alan Swinbank) *w'like: str: in tch in midfield: lost pl and bhd whn drvn over 2f out: no rspnse and lost tch over 1f out: wl bhd and eased ins fnl f: t.o* **12/1**

2m 32.05s (-0.85) **Going Correction** +0.05s/f (Good)
WFA 3 from 4yo+ 13lb **8** Ran SP% **112.6**
Speed ratings (Par 107): **104,102,102,101,101 99,94,81**
CSF £22.16 CT £80.20 TOTE £5.60: £1.60, £1.60, £2.10; EX 27.50 Trifecta £146.40.
Owner Sutong Pan **Bred** Mrs Fiona McStay **Trained** Kimpton, Hants

FOCUS
A useful handicap, the 3yos predictably dominated with the winner scoring with something in hand. The pace was ordinary.
T/Plt: £29.00 to a £1 stake. Pool: £183,666.77 - 4622.12 winning units. T/Qpdt: £9.80 to a £1 stake. Pool: £14,012.17 - 1055.50 winning units. **Steve Payne**

3529 SALISBURY (R-H)
Saturday, July 9

OFFICIAL GOING: Good to firm (8.6)
Wind: light breeze against Weather: overcast

4154 BATHWICK TYRES BRITISH STALLION STUDS EBF MAIDEN STKS (PLUS 10 RACE) 6f 212y

6:00 (6:04) (Class 4) 2-Y-O **£4,528** (£1,347; £673; £336) **Stalls** Low

Form RPR

22 **1** **Isomer (USA)**[21] 3382 2-9-5 0... DavidProbert 3 81+
(Andrew Balding) *mid-div: hdwy 2f out: sddle sn slipped: hdwy to ld jst ins fnl f: r.o wl* **1/5**[1]

2 *2* **Harmonise** 2-8-9 0.. PaddyPilley(5) 6 67
(Mick Channon) *mid-div: rdn and hdwy 2f out: led briefly ent fnl f: kpt on same pce* **14/1**

3 *1 1/4* **Helmsdale** 2-8-9 0.. GaryMahon(5) 7 63+
(Richard Hannon) *hld up: outpcd 2f out: r.o wl ent fnl f: nvr trbld ldrs* **12/1**

5 **4** *hd* **Herm (IRE)**[29] 3100 2-9-2 0.. KieranShoemark(3) 1 68
(David Evans) *hld up: rdn over 2f out: no imp tl r.o fnl f* **10/1**[3]

4 **5** *1* **Himself**[33] 2976 2-9-5 0... TomMarquand 2 65
(Richard Hannon) *trckd ldrs: rdn to ld over 1f out: hdd ent fnl f: no ex* **9/2**[2]

6 **6** *1 3/4* **Opening Time**[21] 3408 2-9-5 0 SteveDrowne 8 60
(Richard Hannon) *trckd ldrs: rdn 2f out: wknd ins fnl f* **10/1**[3]
0 **7** *2 3/4* **Dravid**[74] 1736 2-9-5 0 RyanTate 12 53
(Rod Millman) *led tl rdn and hdd over 1f out: wknd fnl f* **33/1**
00 **8** *3 1/2* **General Allenby**[17] 3524 2-9-5 0 StevieDonohoe 10 43
(Henry Tett) *chsd ldr: rdn over 2f out: wknd fnl f* **100/1**
9 *9* **Hollow Crown** 2-8-11 0 RobHornby(3) 4 14
(Denis Coakley) *s.i.s: a towards rr* **50/1**

1m 28.73s (0.13) **Going Correction** -0.075s/f (Good) **9** Ran SP% **139.9**
Speed ratings (Par 96): **96,93,92,92,90 88,85,81,71**
CSF £8.96 TOTE £1.20: £1.02, £4.40, £3.10; EX 10.90 Trifecta £60.30.
Owner Mrs Fitri Hay **Bred** Mrs Fitriani Hay **Trained** Kingsclere, Hants

FOCUS
A decent juvenile maiden. They went a respectable gallop on good to firm ground.

4155 OAKWOODS H'CAP 6f
6:30 (6:32) (Class 5) (0-75,75) 3-Y-O+ **£3,234** (£962; £481; £240) **Stalls** Low

Form RPR
311 **1** **Inclination (IRE)**[28] 3126 3-9-2 **71** RyanTate 1 79
(Clive Cox) *mid-div: hdwy over 2f out: led ent fnl f: r.o: rdn out* **2/1**[1]
5-25 **2** *3/4* **Jack Nevison**[31] 3036 3-9-3 **72** TimmyMurphy 11 77
(Henry Candy) *mid-div: rdn and hdwy over 1f out: kpt on ins fnl f but a being hld* **10/1**
1160 **3** *1* **Englishwoman**[119] 924 3-9-3 **75** KieranShoemark(3) 3 77
(David Evans) *led: rdn 3f out: hdd ent fnl f: no ex* **33/1**
5054 **4** *hd* **Indian Affair**[17] 3510 6-9-0 **66** (vt) GeorgeDowning(3) 14 68
(Milton Bradley) *mid-div: rdn over 2f out: no imp* **14/1**
046 **5** *1 1/4* **Babyfact**[42] 2697 5-8-11 **60** MartinDwyer 4 58
(Malcolm Saunders) *trckd ldrs: rdn over 2f out: kpt on same pce* **8/1**[3]
3-05 **6** *3/4* **Storm Melody**[33] 2982 3-9-4 **73** SteveDrowne 12 68
(Jonjo O'Neill) *towards rr: rdn 2f out: kpt on fnl f but nvr gng pce to get involved* **16/1**
0021 **7** *1 3/4* **Mad Endeavour**[22] 3349 5-9-1 **64** MartinLane 10 54
(Stuart Kittow) *trckd ldrs: rdn over 2f out: fdd ins fnl f* **7/2**[2]
4006 **8** *1/2* **Sarmadee (IRE)**[7] 3907 4-8-13 **67** PaddyPilley(5) 9 56
(Mick Channon) *slowly away: towards rr: hung lft u.p 2f out: nvr threatened ldrs* **14/1**
4234 **9** *3/4* **Jayjinski (IRE)**[40] 2750 3-9-6 **75** TomMarquand 8 60
(Richard Hannon) *mid-div: rdn 3f out: wknd jst over 1f out* **9/1**
1400 **10** *1/2* **Harwoods Star (IRE)**[51] 2396 6-9-4 **67** (v) SaleemGolam 2 52
(John Butler) *a towards rr* **33/1**
3300 **11** *3/4* **Divine Call**[11] 3743 9-8-10 **62** (v) RobHornby(3) 7 44
(Milton Bradley) *a towards rr* **25/1**

1m 13.95s (-0.85) **Going Correction** -0.075s/f (Good)
WFA 3 from 4yo+ 6lb **11** Ran SP% **114.7**
Speed ratings (Par 103): **102,101,99,99,97 96,94,93,92,92 91**
CSF £21.98 CT £496.22 TOTE £2.70: £1.30, £2.50, £4.90; EX 21.20 Trifecta £283.00.
Owner James M Egan **Bred** Corduff Stud & T J Rooney **Trained** Lambourn, Berks

FOCUS
A fair handicap. They went a decent gallop from the far side to the centre of the track.

4156 CARA GLASS MAIDEN STKS 6f 212y
7:00 (7:04) (Class 5) 3-Y-O+ **£3,557** (£1,058; £529; £264) **Stalls** Low

Form RPR
23- **1** **You're Hired**[260] 7431 3-9-2 0 KieranShoemark(3) 2 84+
(Amanda Perrett) *mid-div: swtchd lft and hdwy fr jst over 2f out: r.o wl fnl f: led cl home* **6/4**[1]
2 *nk* **Khairaat (IRE)** 3-9-5 0 StevieDonohoe 12 83+
(Sir Michael Stoute) *s.i.s: towards rr: rdn and gd hdwy over 1f out: led jst ins fnl f: kpt on but no ex whn hdd cl home* **2/1**[2]
2-03 **3** *3/4* **Menai (IRE)**[71] 1837 3-9-5 77 SteveDrowne 9 81
(Charles Hills) *led: rdn and hdd jst ins fnl f: no ex fnl 100yds* **11/2**
0- **4** *4 1/2* **Hereward The Wake**[213] 8153 3-9-5 0 JackMitchell 10 69
(Sylvester Kirk) *trckd ldr: rdn 3f out: kpt on same pce* **50/1**
3 **5** *4* **Land Of Dubai (IRE)**[36] 2848 3-9-0 0 RyanTate 8 53
(Clive Cox) *mid-div: rdn wl over 2f out: sn one pce* **5/1**[3]
0 **6** *1* **Iberica Road (USA)**[16] 3572 3-9-2 0 (t) RobHornby(3) 7 55
(Andrew Balding) *a mid-div* **25/1**
06 **7** *3 1/2* **Staffa (IRE)**[36] 2848 3-9-0 0 TomMarquand 4 41
(Denis Coakley) *towards rr: sme late prog: nvr trbld ldrs* **40/1**
00 **8** *4 1/2* **Mybrotherjohnny**[19] 3464 5-9-13 0 TimmyMurphy 11 37
(Jamie Poulton) *mid-div: rdn over 2f out: wknd over 1f out* **66/1**
00 **9** *shd* **Monologue (IRE)**[10] 3769 3-9-5 0 RyanClark 13 33
(Simon Hodgson) *trckd ldr: rdn 3f out: wknd over 1f out* **100/1**
0 **10** *3/4* **Brooke's Point**[10] 3769 3-9-2 0 GeorgeDowning(3) 6 31
(Neil Mulholland) *towards rr of midfield: rdn over 2f out: no imp* **100/1**
05-0 **11** *1/2* **Sun In His Eyes**[159] 423 4-9-8 30 MeganNicholls(5) 3 33
(Ed de Giles) *trckd ldrs: rdn over 2f out: sn wknd* **100/1**
-000 **12** *2 1/4* **Links Bar Marbella (IRE)**[28] 3146 3-9-0 44 (b) GaryMahon(5) 5 24
(Eric Wheeler) *mid-div: rdn 3f out: wknd 2f out* **125/1**
13 *15* **Scarlet Not Blue** 4-9-13 0 DavidProbert 1
(Matthew Salaman) *a towards rr* **33/1**

1m 27.54s (-1.06) **Going Correction** -0.075s/f (Good)
WFA 3 from 4yo+ 8lb **13** Ran SP% **121.8**
Speed ratings (Par 103): **103,102,101,96,92 90,86,81,81,80 80,77,60**
CSF £4.55 TOTE £2.50: £1.10, £1.50, £2.00; EX 5.70 Trifecta £18.80.
Owner George Materna **Bred** Cheveley Park Stud Ltd **Trained** Pulborough, W Sussex

FOCUS
A fair maiden. They went a decent gallop.

4157 RODNEY BOULT MEMORIAL H'CAP 1m
7:30 (7:33) (Class 4) (0-80,79) 3-Y-O+ **£5,453** (£1,610; £805) **Stalls** Low

Form RPR
56-3 **1** **Alnashama**[64] 2010 4-9-10 **75** TomMarquand 4 82
(Charles Hills) *trckd ldrs: rdn over 2f out: str run ins fnl f: led fnl stride* **9/2**[2]
0-40 **2** *nse* **Big Chill (IRE)**[21] 3405 4-9-3 **75** MitchGodwin(7) 12 82
(Patrick Chamings) *a.p: rdn to ld over 1f out: kpt on: hdd fnl stride* **25/1**
-561 **3** *nk* **Wind In My Sails**[28] 3125 4-9-7 **75** RobHornby(3) 6 81
(Ed de Giles) *hld up: hdwy over 2f out: rdn over 1f out: ev ch ins fnl f: kpt on but no ex cl home* **8/1**
2403 **4** *1* **Handytalk (IRE)**[19] 3466 3-9-4 **78** JackMitchell 7 80
(Rod Millman) *mid-div: hdwy over 1f out: sn rdn: kpt on same pce* **9/1**
3065 **5** *1/2* **Justice Lass (IRE)**[21] 3410 3-9-1 **75** TimmyMurphy 10 75
(David Elsworth) *mid-div: hdwy over 3f out: ev ch whn rdn wl over 1f out: kpt on same pce fnl f* **7/1**[3]

0602 **6** *1/2* **Gannicus**[17] 3514 5-9-5 **70** (p) MartinDwyer 5 71
(Brendan Powell) *mid-div: hdwy over 3f out: rdn over 2f out: kpt on same pce fnl f* **9/1**
0454 **7** *1* **Lilbourne Prince (IRE)**[13] 3687 3-8-9 **72** ow1[1] KieranShoemark(3) 8 70
(David Evans) *towards rr: hdwy over 3f out: rdn over 2f out: one pce fnl f* **10/1**
362 **8** *3/4* **Major Assault**[19] 3464 3-9-1 **75** RyanTate 13 70
(Clive Cox) *towards rr: sme late prog: nvr trbld ldrs* **8/1**
6530 **9** *3* **Dark Amber**[14] 3673 6-8-9 **65** JennyPowell(5) 1 55
(Brendan Powell) *s.i.s: a towards rr* **33/1**
-421 **10** *3 3/4* **Shadad (IRE)**[19] 3475 3-9-3 **77** MartinLane 2 56
(Ralph Beckett) *led: rdn and hdd over 1f out: sn wknd* **11/4**[1]
3045 **11** *1 1/2* **Mister Musicmaster**[10] 3766 7-10-0 **79** SteveDrowne 3 56
(Ron Hodges) *trckd ldrs: rdn 2f out: wknd ent fnl f* **28/1**

1m 42.29s (-1.21) **Going Correction** -0.075s/f (Good)
WFA 3 from 4yo+ 9lb **11** Ran SP% **118.9**
Speed ratings (Par 105): **103,102,102,101,101 100,99,98,95,92 90**
CSF £115.36 CT £899.66 TOTE £5.40: £2.00, £7.40, £2.60; EX 129.40 Trifecta £792.80.
Owner Hamdan Al Maktoum **Bred** Shadwell Estate Company Limited **Trained** Lambourn, Berks

FOCUS
A fairly decent handicap. They went a modest gallop.

4158 BATHWICK TYRES H'CAP 1m 4f
8:00 (8:00) (Class 5) (0-75,75) 3-Y-O+ **£3,234** (£962; £481; £240) **Stalls** Low

Form RPR
2-60 **1** **Sunny Future (IRE)**[42] 2699 10-9-11 **72** MartinDwyer 7 79
(Malcolm Saunders) *hld up: hdwy over 4f out: rdn to ld over 1f out: styd on wl whn strly pressed fnl f: asserting nr fin* **16/1**
0154 **2** *1/2* **Sark (IRE)**[29] 3103 3-8-11 **74** KieranShoemark(3) 5 80
(David Evans) *mid-div: hdwy 2f out: sn rdn: ev ch ent fnl f: no ex cl home* **9/4**[1]
3143 **3** *1 1/2* **Speculator**[32] 3002 4-9-7 **68** JimmyFortune 9 72
(David Menuisier) *mid-div: rdn and hdwy over 1f out: styd on fnl f but nvr a threat: wnt 3rd towards fin* **5/1**[3]
25-5 **4** *2* **Flambeuse**[166] 329 5-9-11 **72** DavidProbert 6 77+
(Harry Dunlop) *trckd ldrs: led 3f out: rdn and hdd over 1f out: styng on in v cl 3rd but hld whn squeezed up towards fin: costing her 3rd pl* **6/1**
34-1 **5** *2 3/4* **Shalimah (IRE)**[29] 3095 4-9-12 **73** (v) RyanTate 3 69
(Clive Cox) *towards rr: struggling 4f out: styd on past btn horses fnl 2f: nvr any threat* **9/2**[2]
-436 **6** *nk* **Clever Bob (IRE)**[19] 3468 3-8-11 **71** StevieDonohoe 8 67
(Joseph Tuite) *trckd ldrs: rdn over 2f out: wknd fnl f* **10/1**
0631 **7** *15* **Tatawu (IRE)**[58] 2174 4-9-5 **66** WilliamCarson 4 38
(Peter Hiatt) *led for 1f: trckd ldr: rdn to ld briefly over 3f out: wknd 2f out* **8/1**
3220 **8** *3 3/4* **Distant High**[14] 3636 5-9-3 **64** (p) TomMarquand 2 30
(Richard Price) *trckd ldrs: rdn over 3f out: wknd over 2f out* **25/1**
2-00 **9** *7* **Yamllik**[26] 3234 4-9-7 **75** (t) MitchGodwin(7) 1 30
(Brian Barr) *led after 1f: rdn and hdd over 3f out: sn btn* **25/1**

2m 35.8s (-2.20) **Going Correction** -0.075s/f (Good)
WFA 3 from 4yo+ 13lb **9** Ran SP% **113.7**
Speed ratings (Par 103): **104,103,102,101,99 99,89,86,82**
CSF £51.43 CT £211.17 TOTE £10.90: £3.20, £1.50, £1.80; EX 66.70 Trifecta £286.90.
Owner M S Stanga **Bred** Mrs G Stanga **Trained** Green Ore, Somerset
■ Stewards' Enquiry : Martin Dwyer two-day ban: careless riding (TBC)

FOCUS
An ordinary middle-distance handicap. They went a muddling gallop.

4159 PARTY CONTINUES AT THE CHAPEL NIGHTCLUB H'CAP 1m 1f 198y
8:30 (8:30) (Class 6) (0-60,60) 3-Y-O **£2,587** (£770; £384; £192) **Stalls** Low

Form RPR
0066 **1** **Midnight Mood**[17] 3509 3-9-3 **56** TimmyMurphy 9 63
(Dominic Ffrench Davis) *in tch: rdn over 2f out: hdwy over 1f out: led fnl 100yds: r.o wl* **16/1**
3435 **2** *1/2* **Multigifted**[23] 3318 3-9-3 **56** RyanTate 7 62
(Michael Madgwick) *trckd ldr: led after 3f: rdn over 2f out: hdd fnl 100yds: kpt on but no ex* **10/1**
03 **3** *1 1/2* **Princess Zoffany (IRE)**[33] 2967 3-8-9 **48** KieranO'Neill 2 51
(Jimmy Fox) *hld up: rdn over 3f out: no imp whn sed to drift lft over 2f out: styd on fr over 1f out: fin clst to stands' side rails: wnt 3rd towards fin* **9/1**
4021 **4** *3/4* **Frivolous Prince (IRE)**[28] 3141 3-8-10 **52** (vt) KieranShoemark(3) 5 54
(David Evans) *hld up: rdn and hdwy over 1f out: styd on same pce fnl f* **9/2**[2]
0035 **5** *2* **Rosie's Vision**[18] 3493 3-8-8 **47** SteveDrowne 10 45
(Mark Usher) *trckd ldrs: rdn over 2f out: kpt on same pce* **14/1**
0544 **6** *1 1/4* **Red Rose Riot (IRE)**[28] 3141 3-9-1 **54** JimmyFortune 11 51
(David Menuisier) *sn mid-div: hdwy over 3f out: rdn to chse ldrs over 2f out: one pce fnl f* **6/1**
0660 **7** *1/2* **Rising Sunshine (IRE)**[4] 3988 3-8-11 **55** MeganNicholls(5) 3 50
(Richard Hannon) *mid-div: rdn over 3f out: one pce fnl 2f* **11/2**[3]
6-00 **8** *1 1/2* **Calliope**[31] 3033 3-9-7 **60** DavidProbert 1 52
(Andrew Balding) *led for 3f: trckd ldr: rdn over 2f out: wknd fnl f* **8/1**
052 **9** *5* **Lazizah**[25] 3256 3-9-2 **55** WilliamCarson 4 37
(Marcus Tregoning) *trckd ldrs: rdn over 2f out: nt pce to get on terms: wknd fnl f* **7/2**[1]
-030 **10** *14* **Ocean Gale**[17] 3509 3-8-12 **51** TomMarquand 6 7
(Richard Price) *s.i.s: drvn 4f out: a towards rr* **25/1**

2m 9.65s (-0.25) **Going Correction** -0.075s/f (Good) **10** Ran SP% **116.7**
Speed ratings (Par 98): **98,97,96,95,94 93,92,91,87,76**
CSF £165.99 CT £1536.92 TOTE £19.10: £4.40, £3.30, £3.10; EX 265.60 Trifecta £2093.00.
Owner Miss A Jones **Bred** B & B Equine Limited **Trained** Lambourn, Berks

FOCUS
A modest 3yo handicap. They went a respectable gallop at best.

4160 EBF STALLIONS BREEDING WINNERS LADIES' EVENING FILLIES' H'CAP 1m 1f 198y
9:00 (9:01) (Class 3) (0-95,88) 3-Y-O+ **£9,056** (£2,695; £1,346; £673) **Stalls** Low

Form RPR
1-02 **1** **Sharja Queen**[15] 3593 3-9-3 **88** JackMitchell 1 106+
(Roger Varian) *trckd ldrs: led 2f out: qcknd clr: quite impressive* **11/4**[1]
1450 **2** *6* **Visage Blanc**[7] 3914 3-8-4 **75** RyanTate 3 78
(Mick Channon) *in tch: rdn and hdwy over 2f out: styd on to go 2nd ins fnl f but nvr any ch w wnr* **11/2**[3]

1-6 **3** 1 1/2 **Zaakhir (IRE)**[51] 2394 3-8-12 **83**.............................. SteveDrowne 7 83
(Charles Hills) *led: rdn and hdd 2f out: sn outpcd by wnr: no ex whn lost 2nd ins fnl f* **9/1**

4-23 **4** 2 3/4 **Malmoosa (IRE)**[43] 2638 3-8-11 **82**.............................. MartinDwyer 5 77
(Brian Meehan) *trckd ldr: rdn and ev ch briefly 2f out: kpt on same pce* **4/1**[2]

43-1 **5** 4 **Pure Fantasy**[30] 3071 3-8-7 **78**.............................. DavidProbert 2 65
(Roger Charlton) *in tch: pushed along over 4f out: rdn over 3f out: nvr threatened: wknd ent fnl f* **11/4**[1]

1-4 **6** shd **Somethingthrilling**[68] 1932 4-9-11 **85**.............................. WilliamCarson 6 71
(David Elsworth) *slowly away: in last pair but in tch: hdwy over 3f out: effrt over 2f out: wknd over 1f out* **14/1**

0234 **7** hd **La Superba (IRE)**[22] 3352 4-9-12 **86**..............................(p) TomMarquand 4 72
(David Elsworth) *slowly away: in last pair but in tch: effrt over 3f out: nvr threatened: wknd over 1f out* **12/1**

2m 6.28s (-3.62) **Going Correction** -0.075s/f (Good)
WFA 3 from 4yo 11lb **7** Ran SP% **113.1**
Speed ratings (Par 104): **111,106,105,102,99 99,99**
CSF £17.84 TOTE £3.30: £1.80, £3.30; EX 16.90 Trifecta £106.20.
Owner Sheikh Mohammed Obaid Al Maktoum **Bred** Darley **Trained** Newmarket, Suffolk

FOCUS
The feature contest was a decent fillies' handicap. They went a respectable gallop.
T/Plt: £122.60 to a £1 stake. Pool: £60,490.16 - 360.04 winning units. T/Qpdt: £58.00 to a £1 stake. Pool: £5,298.92 - 67.50 winning units. **Tim Mitchell**

4110 YORK (L-H)

Saturday, July 9

OFFICIAL GOING: Good (good to soft in places; 7.3)
Wind: Moderate half behind Weather: Grey cloud and showers

4161 JOHN SMITH'S MEDIAN AUCTION MAIDEN STKS (PLUS 10 RACE) 6f

1:55 (1:56) (Class 3) 2-Y-O **£7,439** (£2,213; £1,106; £553) **Stalls** High

Form RPR

2 **1** **Timeless Flight**[15] 3598 2-9-5 0..............................(t) JamesMcDonald 3 84
(Charlie Appleby) *cl up: led wl over 1f out: rdn clr jst ins fnl f: kpt on* **3/1**[1]

2 3/4 **Lucky Mistake (IRE)** 2-9-5 0.............................. JimCrowley 12 82+
(Richard Fahey) *hld up: hdwy over 2f out: rdn over 1f out: chsd wnr ins fnl f: edgd lft and kpt on* **12/1**

3 1/2 **Horroob** 2-9-5 0.............................. AndreaAtzeni 5 80+
(Roger Varian) *dwlt and towards rr: hdwy 1/2-way: pushed along and green 2f out: rdn and chsd ldrs appr fnl f: kpt on wl towards fin* **9/1**

3 **4** nk **Starlight Romance (IRE)**[28] 3167 2-9-0 0.............................. GeorgeChaloner 7 74
(Richard Fahey) *prom: pushed along and outpcd 1/2-way: rdn 2f out: styd on fnl f* **8/1**

5 1/2 **Hemingway (IRE)** 2-9-5 0.............................. PaulMulrennan 6 78+
(Kevin Ryan) *led: rdn along 2f out: hdd over 1f out: grad wknd* **7/1**[3]

6 nk **Battered** 2-9-5 0.............................. BenCurtis 1 77+
(William Haggas) *dwlt and in rr: t.k.h and sn in tch on outer: chsd ldrs 2f out: sn rdn and green: no imp fnl f* **6/1**[2]

4 **7** 2 **Man About Town (IRE)**[52] 2358 2-9-5 0.............................. FrederikTylicki 9 71
(K R Burke) *prom: rdn along wl over 1f out: wknd appr fnl f* **20/1**

8 hd **Come On Percy** 2-9-0 0.............................. AdamMcNamara(5) 11 70
(Richard Fahey) *in rr: pushed along 1/2-way: rdn 2f out: kpt on fnl f* **25/1**

2 **9** 3 1/2 **Dundunah (USA)**[29] 3112 2-9-0 0.............................. DanielTudhope 8 55
(David O'Meara) *cl up: rdn along wl over 2f out: sn wknd* **3/1**[1]

10 1/2 **Mr Strutter (IRE)** 2-9-5 0.............................. CamHardie 2 58
(John Quinn) *prom: rdn 2f out: sn rdn and wknd* **66/1**

11 nk **Northern Eclipse** 2-9-5 0.............................. PhillipMakin 10 57
(David O'Meara) *dwlt: a towards rr* **40/1**

12 13 **Inlawed** 2-9-5 0.............................. LukeMorris 4 18
(Ed Walker) *towards rr: rdn along and lost tch over 2f out: bhd and eased fnl f* **25/1**

1m 11.78s (-0.12) **Going Correction** -0.275s/f (Firm) **12** Ran SP% **122.0**
Speed ratings (Par 98): **89,88,87,86,86 85,83,82,78,77 77,59**
CSF £41.64 TOTE £3.40: £1.40, £4.20, £3.30; EX 48.90 Trifecta £232.30.
Owner Godolphin **Bred** Kassala Limited **Trained** Newmarket, Suffolk

FOCUS
Rail alignment on home bend to provide fresh ground, reducing Races 2,4 & 5 by 32yds and race 3 by 30yds. Following an intermittent spell of rain during the morning, the official going description was changed to good, good to soft in places prior to racing. This looked a decent maiden, in which the winner had the best form on offer, and the form is worth keeping an eye on.

4162 JOHN SMITH'S STAYERS' STKS (H'CAP) 2m 88y

2:25 (2:26) (Class 3) (0-95,95) 4-Y-O+ **£9,703** (£2,887; £1,443; £721) **Stalls** Low

Form RPR

1-20 **1** **Magic Circle (IRE)**[21] 3387 4-9-2 **90**.............................. JimCrowley 1 102+
(Ralph Beckett) *trckd ldrs on inner: hdwy over 2f out: led wl over 1f out: rdn clr appr fnl f: styd on strly* **7/2**[1]

4345 **2** 2 1/4 **Two Jabs**[17] 3520 6-8-11 **85**.............................. LukeMorris 6 91
(Michael Appleby) *trckd ldrs: hdwy 3f out: rdn along wl over 1f out: drvn to chse wnr appr fnl f: kpt on same pce* **7/1**

0-63 **3** 1 1/2 **Vive Ma Fille (GER)**[49] 2472 4-9-7 **95**.............................. PJMcDonald 5 99
(Mark Johnston) *trckd ldr: led 10f out: pushed along 3f out: rdn over 2f out: hdd wl over 1f out: sn drvn and kpt on same pce* **11/1**

1-20 **4** 3/4 **Nakeeta**[14] 3658 5-9-7 **95**.............................. RoystonFfrench 9 98
(Iain Jardine) *hld up in midfield: hdwy over 3f out: n.m.r and swtchd lft wl over 1f out and sn rdn: chsd ldrs and drvn ent fnl f: kpt on same pce* **9/2**[2]

0/10 **5** 2 **Galizzi (USA)**[25] 3246 5-9-7 **95**..............................(t) JamesMcDonald 4 96
(Charlie Appleby) *trckd ldr: hld 10f out: chsd ldr: rdn and cl up over 2f out: drvn over 1f out and grad wknd* **11/2**[3]

5-22 **6** shd **Monotype (IRE)**[22] 3351 4-9-3 **91**.............................. AndreaAtzeni 3 92
(Roger Varian) *trckd ldrs: effrt and cl up over 3f out: rdn over 2f out: drvn wl over 1f out and grad wknd* **7/2**[1]

32-3 **7** hd **Corona Borealis**[51] 2406 5-8-11 **85**.............................. PaulMulrennan 2 86
(Martin Todhunter) *in tch: effrt and sme hdwy over 3f out: rdn along over 2f out: sn btn* **16/1**

3500 **8** 2 1/2 **Gabrial's King (IRE)**[14] 3657 7-8-11 **90**.............................. AdamMcNamara(5) 11 88
(Richard Fahey) *trckd ldrs on outer: effrt over 3f out: rdn along wl over 2f out: sn drvn and wknd* **14/1**

-000 **9** 3/4 **Aramist (IRE)**[14] 3657 6-8-9 **83**.............................. ShaneKelly 8 80
(Alan Swinbank) *a in rr* **25/1**

030/ **10** 3 1/4 **Great Fighter**[216] 4217 6-8-9 **83**.............................. BenCurtis 7 76
(Jim Goldie) *a in rr* **40/1**

3m 33.74s (-0.76) **Going Correction** -0.225s/f (Firm) **10** Ran SP% **117.7**
Speed ratings (Par 107): **92,90,90,89,88 88,88,87,86,85**
CSF £28.79 CT £246.80 TOTE £4.60: £1.80, £2.70, £2.70; EX 33.10 Trifecta £322.30.
Owner Mr and Mrs David Aykroyd **Bred** Mr & Mrs David Aykroyd **Trained** Kimpton, Hants

FOCUS
Race distance reduced by 32yds. A competitive, high class staying handicap in which the pace was steady, and a decisive winner. He was value for extra.

4163 JOHN SMITH'S RACING STKS (H'CAP) 1m

3:00 (3:02) (Class 2) (0-105,103) 3-Y-O+

£15,562 (£4,660; £2,330; £1,165; £582; £292) **Stalls** Low

Form RPR

0643 **1** **Home Cummins (IRE)**[16] 3565 4-8-12 **87**..............................(p) PaulMulrennan 6 96
(Richard Fahey) *trckd ldrs: pushed along 2f out: rdn to chal over 1f out: drvn ins fnl f: kpt on gamely to ld nr fin* **20/1**

3-45 **2** nk **Celestial Path (IRE)**[36] 2867 4-9-13 **102**..............................(p) LukeMorris 17 110
(Sir Mark Prescott Bt) *stdd and swtchd markedly lft s: hld up in rr: stdy hdwy on inner over 2f out: chsd ldrs over 1f out: rdn to take slt ld ent fnl f: drvn last 100yds: hdd and no ex nr fin* **12/1**

6-63 **3** 1/2 **One Word More (IRE)**[58] 2191 6-9-5 **99**.............................. RachelRichardson(5) 7 106
(Tim Easterby) *hld up in rr: hdwy towards outer over 2f out: sn swtchd rt and rdn to chse ldrs over 1f out: drvn and edgd lft jst ins fnl f: kpt on wl towards fin* **6/1**[1]

0010 **4** 2 1/2 **Imshivalla (IRE)**[15] 3608 5-8-13 **93**.............................. AdamMcNamara(5) 5 94
(Richard Fahey) *hld up: hdwy on inner over 2f out: rdn to chse ldrs over 1f out: drvn and kpt on fnl f* **18/1**

0612 **5** shd **Boots And Spurs**[7] 3895 7-8-9 **84** oh2..............................(v) BenCurtis 13 85
(Scott Dixon) *trckd ldng pair: hdwy over 3f out: rdn to ld over 2f out: drvn over 1f out: hdd ent fnl f: kpt on wl u.p* **16/1**

2330 **6** 3/4 **Swift Emperor (IRE)**[21] 3390 4-9-1 **90**.............................. FrederikTylicki 11 89
(David Barron) *in tch: hdwy over 2f out: chsd ldrs wl over 1f out and sn rdn: drvn and kpt on same pce fnl f* **9/1**[3]

-066 **7** nk **Baraweez (IRE)**[16] 3565 6-10-0 **103**.............................. DaleSwift 3 101
(Brian Ellison) *hld up in rr: hdwy wl over 2f out: rdn wl over 1f out: styd on fnl f: nrst fin* **11/1**

2221 **8** hd **Gabrial's Kaka (IRE)**[21] 3390 6-9-7 **96**.............................. GeorgeChaloner 10 94
(Richard Fahey) *hld up in rr: hdwy over 2f out: swtchd lft and rdn wl over 1f out: kpt on fnl f* **6/1**[1]

6143 **9** 1 1/2 **Miss Van Gogh**[36] 2868 4-9-0 **89**.............................. JimCrowley 16 84
(Richard Fahey) *midfield: hdwy on outer to chse ldrs over 2f out: rdn wl over 1f out: grad wknd* **12/1**

1305 **10** 2 1/4 **King's Pavilion (IRE)**[7] 3910 3-8-9 **93**..............................(p) PJMcDonald 8 80
(Mark Johnston) *towards rr: rdn along over 2f out: n.d* **9/1**[3]

2356 **11** hd **Mont Ras (IRE)**[8] 3855 9-9-3 **92**.............................. SamJames 15 81
(David Loughnane) *led: rdn along 3f out: hdd over 2f out and sn wknd* **33/1**

00-0 **12** 3/4 **Firmdecisions (IRE)**[56] 2247 6-9-3 **92**.............................. RobertWinston 4 79
(Dean Ivory) *trckd ldr: cl up 1/2-way: effrt over 2f out: rdn wl over 1f out: wknd appr fnl f* **25/1**

3020 **13** 1 1/4 **Off Art**[21] 3390 6-9-5 **94**..............................(p) CamHardie 2 78
(Tim Easterby) *in tch: hdwy to chse ldrs over 2f out: rdn along wl over 1f out: sn drvn and wknd* **16/1**

0-10 **14** 1 1/4 **Early Morning (IRE)**[24] 3273 5-9-9 **98**.............................. PhillipMakin 14 79
(Harry Dunlop) *dwlt: hdwy into midfield 1/2-way: effrt on outer wl over 2f out: sn rdn and wknd* **7/1**[2]

-202 **15** 6 **Ghalib (IRE)**[15] 3623 4-9-7 **96**.............................. AndreaAtzeni 9 64
(Ed Walker) *dwlt: a in rr* **9/1**[3]

1m 35.1s (-3.90) **Going Correction** -0.225s/f (Firm) course record
WFA 3 from 4yo+ 9lb **15** Ran SP% **123.4**
Speed ratings (Par 109): **110,109,109,106,106 105,105,105,103,101 101,100,99,98,92**
CSF £242.65 CT £1677.22 TOTE £20.00: £5.60, £4.20, £2.40; EX 230.90 Trifecta £4509.60 Part won..
Owner Mrs H Steel **Bred** Yeguada De Milagro Sa **Trained** Musley Bank, N Yorks

FOCUS
Race distance reduced by 30yds. The pace appeared honest in this decent handicap and the front three drew clear in a new course record time. A length best from the winner.

4164 JOHN SMITH'S SILVER CUP STKS (LISTED RACE) 1m 6f

3:40 (3:40) (Class 1) 3-Y-O+

£22,684 (£8,600; £4,304; £2,144; £1,076; £540) **Stalls** Low

Form RPR

0-00 **1** **Pamona (IRE)**[38] 2797 4-9-1 95..............................(v) JimCrowley 2 104
(Ralph Beckett) *trckd ldrs: smooth hdwy over 2f out: led 1 1/2f out: rdn ent fnl f and styd on strly* **25/1**

1113 **2** 2 **Barsanti (IRE)**[20] 3436 4-9-6 105.............................. AndreaAtzeni 5 106
(Roger Varian) *trckd ldng pair: hdwy over 3f out: led wl over 2f out: rdn and hdd 1 1/2f out: sn drvn and kpt on* **5/1**[2]

00-2 **3** 2 **Quest For More (IRE)**[49] 2486 6-9-6 109..............................(b) PhillipMakin 7 103
(Roger Charlton) *trckd ldrs: hdwy over 3f out: cl up over 2f out: rdn wl over 1f out: drvn and kpt on same pce appr fnl f* **2/1**[1]

1/0- **4** 1/2 **Francis Of Assisi (IRE)**[92] 707 6-9-6 105.............................. JamesMcDonald 8 103
(Charlie Appleby) *hld up: hdwy over 4f out: chsd ldrs 2f out: sn rdn: drvn and kpt on same pce appr fnl f* **12/1**

151 **5** 1 **Shrewd**[29] 3117 6-9-6 96.............................. KevinManning 11 101
(Iain Jardine) *hld up in rr: hdwy over 2f out: sn rdn: swtchd lft and drvn over 1f out: kpt on: nrst fin* **11/1**

1134 **6** 3/4 **Sir Chauvelin**[14] 3657 4-9-6 91.............................. PaulMulrennan 3 100
(Jim Goldie) *in tch: hdwy 4f out: rdn along wl over 2f out: sn drvn and no imp* **25/1**

4420 **7** nse **Suegioo (FR)**[23] 3298 7-9-6 108..............................(p) GeorgeChaloner 1 100
(Richard Fahey) *dwlt and reminders s: a towards rr* **15/2**

21-6 **8** hd **Mr Singh**[49] 2465 4-9-6 108..............................(b[1]) RobertTart 6 100
(John Gosden) *sn led: rdn along 3f out: hdd wl over 2f out: cl up tl drvn wl over 1f out and sn wknd* **7/1**

0-62 **9** 1 **Seamour (IRE)**[14] 3658 5-9-6 103.............................. BenCurtis 9 99
(Brian Ellison) *hld up towards rr: hdwy on outer 3f out: effrt to chse ldrs over 2f out: rdn wl over 1f out: sn btn* **11/2**[3]

50 **10** 23 **The Minch (IRE)**[21] 3387 5-9-6 0.............................. DanielTudhope 4 66
(Jim Goldie) *cl up: pushed along over 4f out: rdn over 3f out: sn lost pl: bhd and eased fnl 2f* **20/1**

2m 57.91s (-2.29) **Going Correction** -0.225s/f (Firm) **10** Ran SP% **118.1**
Speed ratings (Par 111): **97,95,94,94,93 93,93,93,92,79**
CSF £144.51 TOTE £40.30: £7.40, £2.00, £1.30; EX 214.60 Trifecta £3815.30 Part won..

Owner Highclere Thoroughbred Racing (Albany) **Bred** Diomed Bloodstock Ltd **Trained** Kimpton, Hants

FOCUS

Race distance reduced by 32yds. A well-contested Listed event, in which they went an ordinary gallop and a return to form for the big-priced winner. The form is set around the fifth.

4165 57TH JOHN SMITH'S CUP (HERITAGE H'CAP) 1m 2f 88y

4:15 (4:16) (Class 2) 3-Y-O+

£124,500 (£37,280; £18,640; £9,320; £4,660; £2,340) **Stalls** Low

Form RPR

6-25 **1** **Educate**[21] 3383 7-9-8 **108** ThomasBrown 14 116
(Ismail Mohammed) *trckd ldrs: hdwy and cl up over 2f out: led wl over 1f out: rdn ent fnl f: drvn and kpt on wl towards fin* **18/1**

-541 **2** ½ **Elbereth**[38] 2797 5-8-9 **98** EdwardGreatrex(3) 6 105
(Andrew Balding) *in tch on inner: hdwy wl over 2f out: chsd ldrs over 1f out: sn rdn: styd on wl fnl f* **16/1**

3050 **3** ½ **Earth Drummer (IRE)**[24] 3273 6-8-12 **98** ShaneKelly 2 104
(David Loughnane) *hld up towards rr: hdwy over 2f out: rdn over 1f out: styd on wl fnl f* **20/1**

614- **4** *nse* **Gold Trail (IRE)**[322] 5626 5-9-1 **101** JamesMcDonald 22 107
(Charlie Appleby) *trckd ldrs: hdwy on outer 3f out: cl up 2f out: rdn to chal over 1f out: drvn ins fnl f and ev ch tl no ex last 100yds* **12/1**[3]

34-0 **5** 1 ½ **Basem**[24] 3273 5-9-5 **110** (p) AdamMcNamara(5) 18 113
(Saeed bin Suroor) *hld up towards rr: hdwy over 2f out: rdn over 1f out: kpt on fnl f* **22/1**

5060 **6** ½ **Fire Fighting (IRE)**[21] 3383 5-9-4 **104** (b) LukeMorris 8 106+
(Mark Johnston) *in rr and hmpd early stages: hdwy 2f out: sn rdn: styd on wl fnl f* **20/1**

0214 **7** ½ **Azraff (IRE)**[24] 3273 4-8-13 **99** AndreaAtzeni 20 100
(Marco Botti) *midfield: hdwy on outer 3f out: chsd ldrs wl over 1f out: sn rdn: kpt on same pce fnl f* **12/1**[3]

-612 **8** ½ **Oasis Fantasy (IRE)**[57] 2222 5-8-12 **98** (b) KevinManning 17 98+
(Ed Dunlop) *stdd and swtchd lft s: hld up in rr: hdwy 2f out: sn rdn: kpt on fnl f* **12/1**[3]

1521 **9** ¾ **Tawdeea**[7] 3889 4-9-0 **100** 5ex DanielTudhope 5 98+
(David O'Meara) *hld up towards rr: hdwy 2f out: rdn over 1f out: drvn and kpt on fnl f* **6/1**[1]

0300 **10** ½ **What About Carlo (FR)**[7] 3910 5-9-0 **100** JohnFahy 3 97+
(Eve Johnson Houghton) *nvr bttr than midfield* **25/1**

605 **11** ½ **Belgian Bill**[142] 625 8-9-2 **102** RobertWinston 16 98
(George Baker) *prom: trckd ldr after 3f: led 3f out: rdn along over 2f out: hdd wl over 1f out: sn drvn and grad wknd* **25/1**

4-10 **12** ¾ **Carry On Deryck**[24] 3273 4-9-6 **106** PaulMulrennan 13 101+
(Saeed bin Suroor) *hld up towards rr: hdwy 2f out: swtchd rt and rdn over 1f out: n.d* **8/1**[2]

5113 **13** ½ **Revolutionist (IRE)**[21] 3383 4-9-5 **105** PJMcDonald 21 99
(Mark Johnston) *sn led: rdn along and hdd 3f out: drvn over 2f out: sn wknd* **8/1**[2]

-660 **14** 1 ¼ **Top Notch Tonto (IRE)**[28] 3164 6-9-3 **103** DaleSwift 19 94
(Brian Ellison) *dwlt: a in rr* **20/1**

066/ **15** ¾ **Mijhaar**[231] 7012 8-9-0 **100** PhillipMakin 1 90
(David O'Meara) *prom: rdn along wl over 3f out: sn wknd* **25/1**

-604 **16** ¾ **Arthenus**[21] 3383 4-9-0 **100** (v[1]) FrederikTylicki 10 88
(James Fanshawe) *dwlt and hmpd early stages: a towards rr* **6/1**[1]

3000 **17** 1 ¼ **Balty Boys (IRE)**[24] 3273 7-9-5 **105** (v[1]) BenCurtis 7 91
(Brian Ellison) *trckd ldrs: hdwy on inner 3f out: rdn over 2f out: sn drvn and wknd* **25/1**

3110 **18** 6 **Our Channel (USA)**[78] 1604 5-8-10 **103** (p) GeorgiaCox(7) 9 77
(William Haggas) *in tch: rdn along 3f out: sn drvn and wknd* **20/1**

0064 **19** 6 **Birdman (IRE)**[13] 3688 6-9-1 **104** ShelleyBirkett(3) 15 66
(David O'Meara) *hmpd early stages: a in rr* **20/1**

2m 7.34s (-5.16) **Going Correction** -0.225s/f (Firm) **19** Ran SP% **128.6**

Speed ratings (Par 109): **111,110,110,110,108 108,108,107,107,106 106,105,105,104,103 103,102,97,92**

CSF £245.20 CT £5692.27 TOTE £23.30: £5.00, £3.60, £4.80, £3.80; EX 446.50 Trifecta £4912.90 Part won..

Owner Sultan Ali **Bred** Lady Legard **Trained** Newmarket, Suffolk

FOCUS

Race distance reduced by 32yds. A strong renewal of the most valuable middle-distance handicap in Britain, in which they went an ordinary gallop and it developed into a 3f sprint. Solid form, the winner back to his old best.

4166 JOHN SMITH'S CITY WALLS STKS (LISTED RACE) 5f

4:50 (4:51) (Class 1) 3-Y-O+

£22,684 (£8,600; £4,304; £2,144; £1,076; £540) **Stalls** Centre

Form RPR

-251 **1** **Marsha (IRE)**[21] 3392 3-8-9 104 LukeMorris 5 114
(Sir Mark Prescott Bt) *dwlt and hld up in rr: smooth hdwy 1/2-way: swtchd rt to trck ldrs 2f out: rdn to chse ldr ins fnl f: drvn and kpt on wl to ld nr fin* **5/1**[2]

5-11 **2** *nk* **Easton Angel (IRE)**[28] 3158 3-8-9 109 PaulMulrennan 8 113
(Michael Dods) *trckd ldrs: hdwy to ld ent fnl f: sn rdn: jnd and drvn last 100yds: hdd and no ex nr fin* **11/2**[3]

-350 **3** ¾ **Muthmir (IRE)**[49] 2475 6-9-1 114 AndreaAtzeni 11 113
(William Haggas) *hld up in rr: hdwy wl over 1f out: sn rdn: styd on wl fnl f* **4/1**[1]

0012 **4** 1 **Monsieur Joe (IRE)**[7] 3909 9-9-1 109 PJMcDonald 7 110
(Paul Midgley) *chsd ldng pair: rdn along wl over 1f out: n.m.r and swtchd lft ent fnl f: sn drvn and kpt on* **8/1**

0461 **5** 1 ½ **Caspian Prince (IRE)**[35] 2895 7-9-1 109 (t) RobertWinston 2 104
(Dean Ivory) *cl up on outer: led 2f out and sn rdn: drvn and edgd rt appr fnl f: sn hdd & wknd* **9/1**

6162 **6** *nk* **Kachy**[22] 3338 3-8-10 112 RichardKingscote 9 101
(Tom Dascombe) *sn led: rdn along and hdd 2f out: sn drvn and wknd appr fnl f* **5/1**[2]

10-2 **7** 2 ¾ **Pretend (IRE)**[14] 3655 5-9-1 112 JamesMcDonald 10 93
(Charlie Appleby) *in tch: pushed along over 2f out: sn rdn and n.d* **8/1**

0-00 **8** 4 **Out Do**[25] 3244 7-9-1 108 (v) DanielTudhope 1 79
(David O'Meara) *a towards rr* **10/1**

-001 **9** 2 ½ **Outback Traveller (IRE)**[21] 3386 5-9-1 109 ShaneKelly 13 70
(Robert Cowell) *chsd ldrs 2f: sn lost pl and bhd* **10/1**

56.35s (-2.95) **Going Correction** -0.275s/f (Firm)

WFA 3 from 5yo+ 5lb **9** Ran SP% **119.1**

Speed ratings (Par 111): **112,111,110,108,106 105,101,95,91**

CSF £33.77 TOTE £5.60: £1.80, £2.10, £1.80; EX 29.90 Trifecta £157.60.

Owner Elite Racing Club **Bred** Elite Racing Club **Trained** Newmarket, Suffolk

FOCUS

A good-quality Listed sprint and they went a proper pace, with a couple of progressive 3yo fillies ultimately coming to the fore. The fourth gives substance to the form.

4167 JOHN SMITH'S STKS (NURSERY H'CAP) 6f

5:20 (5:20) (Class 2) 2-Y-O **£9,703** (£2,887; £1,443; £721) **Stalls** High

Form RPR

01 **1** **Franca Florio (IRE)**[12] 3707 2-8-2 **66** LukeMorris 5 70
(Kevin Ryan) *mde all: rdn and edgd rt wl over 1f out: drvn and hung rt ins fnl f: hld on wl towards fin* **9/2**[3]

352 **2** ½ **In First Place**[26] 3223 2-8-11 **75** PaulMulrennan 8 78
(Richard Fahey) *hld up in rr: hdwy over 2f out: rdn to chse ldng pair over 1f out: drvn ins fnl f: kpt on wl towards fin* **7/2**[2]

16 **3** ½ **Tailor's Row (USA)**[35] 2913 2-9-1 **79** JamesMcDonald 6 80
(Mark Johnston) *trckd ldrs: hdwy 2f out: rdn to chse wnr over 1f out: drvn to chal on stands' rail and ev ch whn n.m.r ins fnl f: kpt on same pce towards fin* **9/2**[3]

04 **4** 2 ½ **Bourbonisto**[37] 2807 2-8-6 **70** CamHardie 1 64
(Ben Haslam) *dwlt and in rr: hdwy on outer 1/2-way: chsd ldrs and rdn 2f out: drvn over 1f out: no imp fnl f* **14/1**

304 **5** 1 **Champion Harbour (IRE)**[14] 3654 2-8-5 **69** GeorgeChaloner 7 60
(Richard Fahey) *chsd ldrs: rdn along 2f out: sn drvn and no imp* **8/1**

601 **6** ½ **Allux Boy (IRE)**[21] 3416 2-8-0 **69** ow1 RachelRichardson(5) 9 58
(Nigel Tinkler) *cl up: rdn along 2f out: wknd over 1f out* **10/1**

10 **7** 7 **Fayez (IRE)**[25] 3247 2-9-6 **84** DanielTudhope 10 52
(David O'Meara) *racd cl to stands' rail: cl up: rdn along 2f out: sn wknd and bhd whn eased fnl f* **5/2**[1]

1m 11.7s (-0.20) **Going Correction** -0.275s/f (Firm) **7** Ran SP% **114.0**

Speed ratings (Par 100): **90,89,88,85,84 83,74**

CSF £20.45 CT £73.86 TOTE £4.50: £2.30, £2.30; EX 21.30 Trifecta £79.30.

Owner FF Partners **Bred** Rathbarry Stud **Trained** Hambleton, N Yorks

FOCUS

Not a bad nursery and the winner made just about all the running.

T/Jkpt: Not won. T/Plt: £448.90 to a £1 stake. Pool: £182,150.89 - 296.18 winning tickets T/Qpdt: £58.40 to a £1 stake. Pool: £13,725.86 - 173.88 winning tickets **Joe Rowntree**

4168 - 4170a (Foreign Racing) - See Raceform Interactive

3831 TIPPERARY (L-H)

Saturday, July 9

OFFICIAL GOING: Yielding (good in places on jumps course)

4171a EXCELEBRATION TIPPERARY STKS (LISTED RACE) 5f

3:45 (3:46) 2-Y-O

£20,606 (£6,636; £3,143; £1,397; £698; £349)

RPR

1 **Yulong Baobei (IRE)**[25] 3247 2-8-12 0 ShaneFoley 10 104+
(M Halford, Ire) *mde all: sn tacked over: gng wl w narrow advantage nr side fr 1/2-way: rdn clr ins fnl f and styd on wl: comf* **11/10**[1]

2 3 ¾ **Swish (IRE)**[10] 3789 2-8-12 0 NGMcCullagh 9 91
(John James Feane, Ire) *hld up bhd ldrs: pushed along nr side fr 1/2-way and rdn into 2nd ins fnl f where no imp on easy wnr: kpt on same pce* **33/1**

3 3 **Mirdif**[14] 3678 2-9-3 0 ColinKeane 6 85
(M D O'Callaghan, Ire) *on toes befhand: chsd ldrs: 4th 1/2-way: rdn under 2f out and no imp on easy wnr u.p in 3rd 1f out: kpt on same pce* **9/2**[2]

4 1 ½ **Confrontational (IRE)**[21] 3424 2-9-3 0 GaryCarroll 11 80
(John Joseph Murphy, Ire) *hld up: pushed along fr 2f out and sme hdwy bhd ldrs over 1f out where n.m.r between horses: kpt on ins fnl f to snatch 4th cl home* **6/1**

5 *shd* **Fasuba (IRE)**[14] 3675 2-9-3 0 ConnorKing 8 79
(T Stack, Ire) *hld up in tch: rdn far side under 2f out and sme hdwy u.p into mod 4th ins fnl f: no imp on easy wnr wl ins fnl f and denied 4th cl home* **25/1**

6 *nk* **Ambiguity (IRE)**[25] 3247 2-9-3 0[1] DonnachaO'Brien 12 78
(Joseph Patrick O'Brien, Ire) *hld up towards rr: rdn 2f out and sme late hdwy u.p ins fnl f: nrst fin* **11/2**[3]

7 ¾ **Grecian Divine (IRE)**[75] 1729 2-8-12 0 GaryHalpin 1 70+
(Denis Gerard Hogan, Ire) *sltly awkward s: sn chsd ldrs far side: pushed along fr 1/2-way and no imp on easy wnr u.p disputing 4th ent fnl f: wknd ins fnl f* **16/1**

8 *nk* **Miss Cogent (IRE)**[13] 3694 2-8-12 0 RossCoakley 4 69+
(J P Murtagh, Ire) *cl up: pushed along in 2nd after 1/2-way and sn no ex u.p: wknd over 1f out* **20/1**

9 1 ½ **Madam Bounska (IRE)**[9] 3826 2-8-12 0 LeighRoche 7 64
(Mrs Denise Foster, Ire) *trckd ldr early: 3rd 1/2-way: rdn 2f out and sn no ex: wknd fnl f* **20/1**

10 5 ½ **Lyin Eyes**[17] 3536 2-8-12 0 DeclanMcDonogh 5 44+
(Charles O'Brien, Ire) *a bhd: pushed along in rr fr 1/2-way and no imp trailing over 1f out* **14/1**

11 3 ½ **Hyzenthlay (IRE)**[41] 2718 2-8-12 0 AnaO'Brien 3 31+
(Joseph Patrick O'Brien, Ire) *ponied to s: chsd ldrs: rdn 2f out and sn no ex: wknd fnl f* **25/1**

59.4s (0.40) **11** Ran SP% **128.2**

CSF £63.68 TOTE £1.90: £1.02, £9.20, £1.70; DF 74.10.

Owner Zhang Yuesheng **Bred** Tom & Alex Frost **Trained** Doneany, Co Kildare

FOCUS

An explosive performance from the winner, a real sprinter and one to be excited about, even if opportunities for her in the remainder of the year are extremely limited.

4172 - (Foreign Racing) - See Raceform Interactive

3915 BELMONT PARK (L-H)

Saturday, July 9

OFFICIAL GOING: Dirt: fast; turf: firm

4173a BELMONT DERBY INVITATIONAL STKS (GRADE 1) (3YO) (TURF) 1m 2f (T)

9:38 (12:00) 3-Y-O

£455,782 (£156,462; £85,034; £57,823; £34,013; £23,809)

RPR

1 **Deauville (IRE)**[35] 2896 3-8-10 0 JamieSpencer 13 110
(A P O'Brien, Ire) **63/10**[3]

2	nk	**Highland Sky (USA)**35 3-8-10 0....(b) LuisSaez 4 (Barclay Tagg, U.S.A) **67/10**	110+
3	1 1/4	**Beach Patrol (USA)**34 3-8-10 0....(b) JavierCastellano 9 (Chad C Brown, U.S.A) **83/10**	107
4	hd	**Camelot Kitten (USA)**35 3-8-10 0....(b) IradOrtizJr 6 (Chad C Brown, U.S.A) **5/1**2	107
5	1/2	**Surgical Strike (USA)**42 3-8-10 0....(b) JoseLOrtiz 5 (Ben Colebrook, U.S.A) **245/10**	106
6	nse	**Long Island Sound (USA)**23 3296 3-8-10 0.... ColmO'Donoghue 7 (A P O'Brien, Ire) **51/20**1	106
7	nse	**Applicator (USA)**42 3-8-10 0.... LeonelReyes 3 (Mikhail Yanakov, U.S.A) **115/1**	105
8	nse	**Ralis (USA)**20 3-8-10 0.... MarioGutierrez 2 (Doug O'Neill, U.S.A) **205/10**	105+
9	nse	**Humphrey Bogart (IRE)**22 3337 3-8-10 0.... SeanLevey 10 (Richard Hannon) **189/10**	105+
10	3/4	**Airoforce (USA)**34 3-8-10 0....(b) JulienRLeparoux 8 (Mark Casse, Canada) **93/10**	104+
11	1 1/4	**Aquaphobia (USA)**17 3-8-10 0.... JoeBravo 11 (Arnaud Delacour, U.S.A) **39/1**	101+
12	1 1/2	**Toughest 'Ombre (USA)**35 3-8-10 0.... ManuelFranco 1 (Thomas Albertrani, U.S.A) **60/1**	98
13	1 1/2	**Call Provision (USA)**35 3-8-10 0.... JohnRVelazquez 12 (Chad C Brown, U.S.A) **96/10**	95+

2m 0.51s (-0.78) **13** Ran SP% **120.0**
PARI-MUTUEL (all including 2 usd stake): WIN 14.60; PLACE (1-2) 8.60, 6.90; SHOW (1-2-3) 5.80, 4.40, 6.40; SF 134.50.
Owner Mrs F Hay/M Tabor/Mrs J Magnier/D Smith **Bred** Mrs F H Hay **Trained** Cashel, Co Tipperary

4174a BELMONT OAKS INVITATIONAL STKS (GRADE 1) (3YO FILLIES) (TURF) 1m 2f (T)

10:46 (12:00) 3-Y-O
£363,945 (£125,850; £68,027; £44,217; £27,210; £20,408)

			RPR
1		**Catch A Glimpse (USA)**34 3-8-9 0.... FlorentGeroux 12 (Mark Casse, Canada) **17/5**2	112
2	1/2	**Time And Motion (USA)**34 3-8-9 0.... JohnRVelazquez 4 (James J Toner, U.S.A) **42/10**3	111+
3	3 3/4	**Coolmore (IRE)**20 3452 3-8-9 0.... JamieSpencer 13 (A P O'Brien, Ire) **16/1**	104
4	1 1/2	**Pricedtoperfection (USA)**35 3-8-9 0.... IradOrtizJr 3 (Chad C Brown, U.S.A) **37/1**	101
5	1 1/4	**Harmonize (USA)**34 3-8-9 0....(b1) JuniorAlvarado 6 (William Mott, U.S.A) **105/10**	98
6	nk	**Auntie Joy (USA)**20 3-8-9 0.... BrianJosephHernandezJr 8 (Brendan P Walsh, U.S.A) **37/1**	97
7	3/4	**Last Waltz (IRE)**34 3-8-9 0....(b) ManuelFranco 9 (Chad C Brown, U.S.A) **37/1**	96
8	hd	**Noble Beauty (USA)**20 3-8-9 0.... JavierCastellano 5 (Chad C Brown, U.S.A) **174/10**	96+
9	1 1/2	**Decked Out (USA)**20 3-8-9 0.... KentJDesormeaux 2 (J Keith Desormeaux, U.S.A) **117/10**	93
10	nk	**Magnanime**54 2316 3-8-9 0.... JulienRLeparoux 11 (F Chappet, France) **26/1**	92+
11	1/2	**Secure Access (USA)**37 3-8-9 0.... JoseLOrtiz 1 (Claude McGaughey III, U.S.A) **94/1**	91+
12	6 3/4	**Land Over Sea (USA)**50 3-8-9 0.... MarioGutierrez 10 (Doug O'Neill, U.S.A) **26/1**	77+
13	4 1/4	**Ballydoyle (IRE)**20 3452 3-8-9 0.... ColmO'Donoghue 7 (A P O'Brien, Ire) **2/1**1	69+

1m 59.87s (-1.42) **13** Ran SP% **119.5**
PARI-MUTUEL (all including 2 usd stake): WIN 8.80; PLACE (1-2) 5.30, 5.00; SHOW (1-2-3) 4.10, 4.30, 11.40; SF 45.80.
Owner Gary Barber, Michael James Ambler & Windways Farm **Bred** Branch Equine LLC **Trained** North America

4031 HAMBURG (R-H)

Saturday, July 9

OFFICIAL GOING: Turf: heavy

4175a NUTAN-RENNEN (HAMBURGER STUTEN-PREIS) (GROUP 3) (3YO FILLIES) (TURF) 1m 3f

2:20 (12:00) 3-Y-O **£23,529** (£8,823; £4,411; £2,205; £1,470)

			RPR
1		**Near England (IRE)**34 2949 3-9-2 0.... AndreasHelfenbein 2 (Markus Klug, Germany) *trckd ldr: rdn to ld appr st: styd on wl* **107/10**	101
2	1	**Son Macia (GER)**41 2730 3-9-2 0.... FilipMinarik 5 (Andreas Lowe, Germany) *in tch: rdn into st: styd on and wnt 2nd fnl f: nt quite pce of wnr* **9/2**	99
3	4 1/4	**She's Gina (GER)**20 3-9-2 0.... MaximPecheur 8 (Markus Klug, Germany) *led: rdn and hdd appr st: no ex and dropped to 3rd fnl f* **132/10**	91
4	7	**Night Music (GER)**27 3207 3-9-2 0.... EduardoPedroza 4 (A Wohler, Germany) *hld up: rdn bef st: no imp and btn fnl 2f* **13/5**2	79
5	1 3/4	**Kasalla (GER)**27 3207 3-9-2 0.... AdriedeVries 7 (Markus Klug, Germany) *midfield: rdn bef st: no imp and btn fnl 2f* **21/10**1	76
6	6	**Olala (GER)**23 3297 3-9-2 0.... AntoineHamelin 1 (M Figge, Germany) *hld up: rdn bef st: no imp and btn fnl 2f* **39/10**3	65
7	43	**Dhaba (GER)**34 2949 3-9-2 0.... MartinSeidl 3 (Markus Klug, Germany) *hld up: rdn in rr and toiling appr st: eased whn btn: t.o* **78/10**	
8	83	**Kashmar (GER)**21 3-9-2 0.... MichaelCadeddu 6 (Henk Grewe, Germany) *in tch: lost pl 1/2-way: sn detached in last: tailed rt off* **196/10**	

2m 43.61s (18.91) **8** Ran SP% **130.4**
WIN (to 10 euro stake): 117. PLACES: 29, 18, 31. SF: 495.
Owner Gestut Wittekindshof **Bred** Gestut Wittekindshof **Trained** Germany

4176a (Foreign Racing) - See Raceform Interactive

3543 CHANTILLY (R-H)

Sunday, July 10

OFFICIAL GOING: Turf: good; polytrack: standard

4183a PRIX DU BOIS DES BOULEAUX (CLAIMER) (2YO COLTS & GELDINGS) (POLYTRACK) 7f

1:05 (12:00) 2-Y-O **£6,985** (£2,794; £2,095; £1,397; £698)

			RPR
1		**Barbarigo (IRE)** 2-8-13 0.... PierreBazire(5) 2 (G Botti, France) **12/5**2	67+
2	3	**Nudge Nudge**31 3075 2-8-11 0.... HugoJourniac(4) 7 (J S Moore) *led: rdn over 2f out: hdd ins fnl 2f: rallied gamely u.p fr over 1f out: no ch w easy wnr* **6/4**1	54
3	1 1/2	**Rinky Dink Dawn (IRE)**22 3404 2-9-1 0.... IoritzMendizabal 1 (J S Moore) *hld up in 3rd: cl up and ev ch whn rdn 2f out: styd on at same pce fnl f: clr of rest* **63/10**	50
4	7	**Zing (FR)**12 3763 2-9-1 0.... RonanThomas 5 (Robert Collet, France) **13/1**	31
5	1	**Silver City (FR)** 2-9-4 0.... CristianDemuro 6 (A Giorgi, Italy) **56/10**3	31
6	6	**El Pampa King (FR)** 2-9-1 0.... AurelienLemaitre 3 (J-V Toux, France) **17/1**	12
7	6 1/2	**Salut Fripouille (FR)**39 2-9-4 0.... EddyHardouin 4 (S Jesus, France) **9/1**	

WIN (incl. 1 euro stake): 3.40. PLACES: 1.40, 1.50. SF: 7.80
Owner Eledy Srl **Bred** Eledy Srl **Trained** France

4184a PRIX CHLOE (GROUP 3) (3YO FILLIES) (TURF) 1m 1f

2:45 (12:00) 3-Y-O **£29,411** (£11,764; £8,823; £5,882; £2,941)

			RPR
1		**War Flag (USA)**39 3-8-11 0.... ChristopheSoumillon 9 (J-C Rouget, France) *w.w in rr: angled out and gd hdwy over 2f out: styd on wl to ld fnl 130yds: wl on top cl home* **17/2**	107+
2	3/4	**Chartreuse (IRE)**17 3590 3-8-11 0.... ThierryJarnet 10 (F Head, France) *sn chsng ldrs on outer: rdn and qcknd to ld wl over 1f out: styd on u.p: hdd fnl 130yds: no ex* **7/2**2	105
3	1 1/4	**Magnolea (IRE)**36 2928 3-8-11 0.... IoritzMendizabal 1 (J-C Rouget, France) *t.k.h: hld up in midfield on inner: rdn to chse ldrs 2f out: n.m.r 1 1/2f out: styd on same pce fnl f* **28/1**	102
4	nse	**Tickle Me Blue (GER)**43 2710 3-8-11 0.... OlivierPeslier 4 (Markus Klug, Germany) *w.w in fnl trio: tk clsr order 2f out: rdn and nt clr run 1 1/2f out: stdd and angled out ins fnl f: styd on u.p: nvr plcd to chal* **18/1**	102
5	shd	**Fireglow**23 3339 3-8-11 0.... JamesDoyle 7 (Mark Johnston) *trckd ldr: rdn to ld wl over 1 1/2f out: hdd appr fnl f: kpt on at one pce* **7/2**2	102
6	6	**Maquette (USA)**30 3-8-11 0.... VincentCheminaud 6 (A Fabre, France) *led: qcknd tempo 1/2-way: hdd wl over 1 1/2f out: wknd fnl f* **7/4**1	89
7	10	**Monaco Show (FR)**35 2949 3-8-11 0.... MaximeGuyon 8 (A Wohler, Germany) *w.w in fnl trio: rdn and no imp appr 1 1/2f out: lost tch appr fnl f* **16/1**	68
8	2 1/2	**Besotted (IRE)**35 2945 3-8-11 0.... Pierre-CharlesBoudot 5 (P Sogorb, France) *settled in midfield: j. path and stmbld after 3 1/2f: sn rcvrd to regain pl in midfield: rdn and wknd under 2f out: bhd whn eased fnl f* **9/2**3	65

1m 48.68s (-2.42) **8** Ran SP% **124.1**
WIN (incl. 1 euro stake): 6.80. PLACES: 2.30, 2.00, 3.70. DF: 13.10. SF: 32.10.
Owner Joseph Allen **Bred** Joseph Allen **Trained** Pau, France

FOCUS
This race was delayed after two contenders had to be withdrawn at the start.

4185a PRIX JEAN PRAT (GROUP 1) (3YO COLTS & FILLIES) (TURF) 1m

3:15 (12:00) 3-Y-O **£168,058** (£67,235; £33,617; £16,794; £8,411)

			RPR
1		**Zelzal (FR)**29 3183 3-9-2 0.... GregoryBenoist 5 (J-C Rouget, France) *tk a str hold: hld up in midfield: gd hdwy over 1 1/2f out: led 1f out: r.o under hands and heels fnl f* **7/4**2	122+
2	2	**Stormy Antarctic**71 1864 3-9-2 0.... GeorgeBaker 8 (Ed Walker) *a cl up: chsd ldr 1 1/2f out: styd on u.p fnl f: nt match w wnr* **11/1**	116
3	snk	**Spectre (FR)**56 2282 3-8-13 0.... Pierre-CharlesBoudot 4 (M Munch, Germany) *chsd ldrs early: sn settled in midfield: smooth prog to cl over 2f out: led appr 1 1/2f out: hdd 1f out: kpt on at same pce* **18/1**	113
4	1 3/4	**Nemoralia (USA)**23 3339 3-8-13 0.... FrankieDettori 9 (Jeremy Noseda) *w.w in fnl pair on outer: hdwy 1 1/2f out: styd on at same pce fnl f: nvr on terms* **11/10**1	109
5	2	**Degas (GER)**29 3183 3-9-2 0.... ChristopheSoumillon 6 (Markus Klug, Germany) *w.w towards rr: sme mod prog over 1f out: nvr in contention* **9/1**3	107
6	2 1/2	**Alignement**22 3-9-2 0.... MaximeGuyon 7 (C Laffon-Parias, France) *w.w in fnl pair: rdn and no imp wl over 1 1/2f out: nvr figured* **40/1**	102
7	3/4	**First Selection (SPA)**26 3245 3-9-2 0.... JimCrowley 3 (Simon Crisford) *tk a t.k.h: disp ld on outer: sn led: pressed thrght: hdd appr 1 1/2f out: dropped away appr fnl f* **20/1**	100
8	1 1/2	**Zonderland**45 2627 3-9-2 0.... GeraldMosse 1 (Clive Cox) *t.k.h: hld up in tch: cl 3rd and ev ch on inner 1 1/2f out: sn rdn and btn: wknd ins fnl f* **12/1**	97
9	dist	**Positive Vibration (IRE)**56 2282 3-8-13 0.... IoritzMendizabal 2 (J-C Rouget, France) *disp ld on inner: sn hdd but pressed ldr: losing pl whn hmpd 2f out: sn wknd: eased ins fnl f* **200/1**	

1m 34.48s (-3.52) **9** Ran SP% **123.0**
WIN (incl. 1 euro stake): 2.50 (Zelzal coupled with positive Vibration). PLACES: 1.50, 3.10, 2.70. DF: 6.60. SF: 23.40.
Owner Al Shaqab Racing **Bred** Viktor Timoshenko **Trained** Pau, France

FOCUS
The progressive winner was in a different league and is beginning to look like quite a high-class colt.

[4175]HAMBURG (R-H)

Sunday, July 10

OFFICIAL GOING: Turf: heavy

4186a IDEE 147 DEUTSCHES DERBY (GROUP 1) (3YO) (TURF) 1m 4f

4:10 (12:00) 3-Y-O **£286,764** (£95,588; £57,352; £28,676; £9,558)

RPR

1 **Isfahan (GER)**[49] 2517 3-9-2 0 DarioVargiu 11 113
(A Wohler, Germany) *settled in midfield: stdy hdwy 3f out: led under 2f out: r.o gamely u.p fnl f* **158/10**

2 *hd* **Savoir Vivre (IRE)**[21] 3453 3-9-2 0 FrederikTylicki 3 113
(Jean-Pierre Carvalho, Germany) *hld up towards rr: hdwy 3f out: 8th and hrd rdn fr 2f out: r.o u.p fnl f: jst failed* **217/10**

3 *nk* **Dschingis Secret (GER)**[21] 3453 3-9-2 0 MartinSeidl 19 112
(Markus Klug, Germany) *racd in midfield on outer: cl up fr 1/2-way: rdn to chse ldr into fnl f: styd on wl u.p* **93/10**

4 *1 ¾* **Wai Key Star (GER)**[43] 2711 3-9-2 0 EduardoPedroza 6 109
(A Wohler, Germany) *tk a t.k.h: hld up in midfield: clsd to chse ldng gp 2f out: cl 3rd and styng on ent fnl f: run petered out last 80yds* **5/1**[2]

5 *6 ½* **Bora Rock (IRE)**[21] 3453 3-9-2 0 FilipMinarik 9 99
(P Schiergen, Germany) *settled in midfield: clsd to chse ldr 2 1/2f out: rdn and ev ch 2f out: wknd fnl f* **70/1**

6 *7* **Our Last Summer (IRE)**[14] 3-9-2 0 RobertHavlin 2 88
(Niels Petersen, Norway) *chsd ldr: rdn and wknd fr 2f out* **31/1**

7 *4 ¼* **Berghain (IRE)**[21] 3453 3-9-2 0 AlexanderPietsch 4 81
(J Hirschberger, Germany) *towards rr: hdwy into midfield after 1/2-way: hrd rdn 2f out but no further imp: wl hld fnl 2f* **181/10**

8 *2 ½* **Boscaccio (GER)**[21] 3453 3-9-2 0 DennisSchiergen 12 77
(Christian Sprengel, Germany) *w.w in midfield: rdn and short-lived effrt 2f out: sn btn* **2/1**[1]

9 *¾* **Buzzy (GER)**[8] 3-9-2 0 MilosMilojevic 10 76
(Guido Forster, Germany) *hld up in midfield: rdn and no imp 3f out: styd on at same pce fr 1 1/2f out: nvr in contention* **57/1**

10 *hd* **Nimrod (IRE)**[43] 2711 3-9-2 0 MrVinzenzSchiergen 1 75
(P Schiergen, Germany) *prom: lost pl 2 1/2f out: sn wl btn* **46/1**

11 *2* **El Loco (GER)**[21] 3453 3-9-2 0 AdriedeVries 14 72
(Markus Klug, Germany) *led: 2 l clr and rdn along 2 1/2f out: hdd under 2f out: sn wknd* **105/10**

12 *¾* **Zanini (GER)**[14] 3-9-2 0 (b) BayarsaikhanGanbat 8 71
(K Demme, Germany) *w.w in midfield on outer: clsd to chse ldr 3f out: grad dropped away fr over 1 1/2f out* **149/1**

13 *1 ½* **Rosenhill (IRE)**[29] 3-9-2 0 Eva-MariaZwingelstein 7 69
(Gerald Geisler, Germany) *settled in rr: rdn and short-lived effrt 2 1/2f out: sn btn and nvr a factor* **97/1**

14 *4 ½* **Noble House (GER)**[43] 2711 3-9-2 0 MartinHarley 5 61
(Mario Hofer, Germany) *towards rr: hrd rdn and no imp 2 1/2f out: sn btn: nvr a factor* **51/1**

15 *6* **Larry (FR)**[28] 3-9-2 0 MichaelCadeddu 13 52
(U Stech, Germany) *cl up: outpcd and scrubbed along 2 1/2f out: wknd ins fnl 1 1/2f* **84/10**

16 *14* **Landin (GER)**[14] 3-9-2 0 (b) DanielePorcu 18 29
(P Schiergen, Germany) *prom on outer: lost pl after 1/2-way: wl bhd fnl 2f* **62/1**

17 *½* **Licinius (GER)**[14] 3-9-2 0 StephenHellyn 17 29
(Yasmin Almenrader, Germany) *towards rr: rdn and no hdwy 3f out: bhd fnl 2f* **80/1**

18 *1 ¼* **Landofhopeandglory (IRE)**[14] 3697 3-9-2 0 RyanMoore 15 27
(A P O'Brien, Ire) *cl up on outer: lost pl fr over 3 1/2f out: rdn and wknd fnl 2f: t.o* **58/10**[3]

19 *10* **Parthenius (GER)**[77] 1689 3-9-2 0 AndreasSuborics 16
(Mario Hofer, Germany) *w.w towards rr of midfield: struggling sn after 1/2-way: t.o* **204/10**

2m 45.97s (11.42) **19** Ran SP% **128.8**

WIN (incl. 10 euro stake): 168. PLACES: 46, 67, 31. SF: 2,645.

Owner Darius Racing **Bred** Rennstall Wohler **Trained** Germany

FOCUS

The ground was 'like glue' according to several of the riders.

LE TOUQUET (L-H)

Sunday, July 10

OFFICIAL GOING: Turf: good

4187a PRIX LA BRASSERIE "LE MATISSE" LE TOUQUET (MAIDEN) (2YO) (TURF) 6f 110y

2:00 (12:00) 2-Y-O **£4,411** (£1,764; £1,323; £882; £441)

RPR

1 **Alfa Manifesto (FR)** 2-8-13 0 LudovicBoisseau(3) 1
(Matthieu Palussiere, France)

2 *nk* **Something Brewing (FR)**[9] 3871 2-9-2 0 JeromeClaudic 9
(Matthieu Palussiere, France)

3 *4* **Candyco** 2-8-13 0 MorganDelalande 6
(F-H Graffard, France)

4 *¾* **La Sarenne (FR)** 2-8-13 0 LouisBeuzelin 5
(P Bary, France)

5 *snk* **Say It Loud (FR)** 2-8-11 0 YohannBourgois 7
(R Rohne, Germany)

6 *1 ¼* **Nadeschda (FR)** 2-8-8 0 StefanieHofer 3
(Mario Hofer, Germany)

7 *1 ¼* **Nova Negrita (FR)**[64] 2-8-13 0 WilliamsSaraiva 2
(Henk Grewe, Germany)

8 *2 ½* **Plethon (GER)** 2-8-11 0 MiguelLopez 8
(S Smrczek, Germany)

9 *4 ½* **Girlofinkandstars (IRE)**[48] 2536 2-8-13 0 (b[1]) SaleemGolam 4
(Rae Guest) *w.w towards rr: rdn and no imp wl over 1 1/2f out: sn btn*

10 *16* **Harmonika (FR)** 2-8-0 0 IvanLoutte(8) 10
(F Vermeulen, France)

WIN (incl. 1 euro stake): 4.90 (coupled with Something Brewing). PLACES: 2.80, 5.60, 5.30

Bred F Aimez, Mlle L Collet Vidal & Mlle C Collet Vidal **Trained** France **Owner** Mrs Theresa Marnane

[3939]AYR (L-H)

Monday, July 11

OFFICIAL GOING: Soft (good to soft in places; 7.1)

Wind: Fresh, half against Weather: Overcast, dry

4188 LONGINES IRISH CHAMPIONS WEEKEND EBF MAIDEN STKS (PLUS 10 RACE) 7f 50y

2:00 (2:00) (Class 4) 2-Y-O **£4,269** (£1,270; £634; £317) **Stalls** High

Form RPR

52 1 **Heir Of Excitement (IRE)**[35] 2956 2-9-5 0 ShaneGray 6 77
(Kevin Ryan) *t.k.h early: pressed ldr: led over 2f out: rdn over 1f out: kpt on wl fnl f* **12/1**

3 2 *½* **Mister Belvedere**[18] 3561 2-9-5 0 PaulMulrennan 1 76
(Michael Dods) *trckd ldrs: rdn over 2f out: rallied to chse wnr ins fnl f: kpt on fin* **9/1**

4 3 *hd* **Actualisation**[14] 3705 2-9-5 0 JasonHart 7 75
(John Quinn) *prom on outside: drvn and outpcd over 2f out: rallied fnl f: kpt on: hld nr fin* **25/1**

42 4 *3 ½* **Aventinus (IRE)**[19] 3524 2-9-5 0 GrahamGibbons 2 67
(Hugo Palmer) *t.k.h early: led: rdn and hdd over 2f out: rallied: wknd ins fnl f* **5/4**[1]

4 5 *1* **Steel Helmet (IRE)**[20] 3477 2-9-5 0 BenCurtis 4 64
(Brian Ellison) *hld up in tch on ins: pushed along over 2f out: hdwy and swtchd rt over 1f out: kpt on: no imp* **16/1**

00 6 *2* **Eldorado Creek (IRE)**[23] 3382 2-9-5 0 TonyHamilton 8 59
(Richard Fahey) *t.k.h: hld up in tch: smooth hdwy over 2f out: rdn and hung lft over 1f out: wknd ins fnl f* **3/1**[2]

00 7 *1 ½* **Cliff Bay (IRE)**[7] 3939 2-9-5 0 PhillipMakin 3 55
(Keith Dalgleish) *s.i.s: hld up: stdy hdwy over 2f out: shkn up and hung lft wl over 1f out: sn btn* **100/1**

8 *¾* **Somnambulist** 2-9-5 0 TomQueally 5 53+
(Keith Dalgleish) *missed break: hld up: rdn over 2f out: sn wknd* **25/1**

9 *11* **Alexander M (IRE)** 2-9-5 0 JoeFanning 9 26
(Mark Johnston) *s.i.s: hld up on outside: struggling whn hung lft over 2f out: sn wknd* **6/1**[3]

1m 39.44s (6.04) **Going Correction** +0.625s/f (Yiel) **9** Ran SP% **116.0**

Speed ratings (Par 96): **90,89,89,85,84 81,80,79,66**

CSF £111.92 TOTE £12.90: £3.10, £2.90, £5.60; EX 84.90 Trifecta £3447.10 Part won..

Owner STS Racing Limited **Bred** Mr And Mrs P & S Martin **Trained** Hambleton, N Yorks

FOCUS

Races 1, 2, 3, and 6 extended by 12yds, and race 7 by 24yds. They went an honest pace in this modest maiden and the principals came clear at the finish. The form is rated around the race average.

4189 RACING UK HD H'CAP 1m

2:30 (2:31) (Class 5) (0-75,75) 3-Y-O+ **£3,557** (£1,058; £529; £264) **Stalls** Low

Form RPR

2323 1 **Eastern Dragon (IRE)**[8] 3922 6-9-4 **71** GarryWhillans(5) 3 81
(Iain Jardine) *trckd ldrs: hdwy over 2f out: led over 1f out: rdn clr fnl f* **2/1**[1]

50 2 *5* **Jay Kay**[9] 3895 7-9-10 **72** JoeyHaynes 6 71
(K R Burke) *led: rdn and hdd over 1f out: kpt on same pce* **5/2**[2]

-060 3 *1 ¼* **Arantes**[8] 3920 5-9-8 **70** (p) ConnorBeasley 4 66
(R Mike Smith) *trckd ldr to over 2f out: drvn and one pce fr over 1f out* **8/1**

-100 4 *4* **Haidees Reflection**[35] 2960 6-9-2 **64** PaulMulrennan 2 50
(Jim Goldie) *hld up in tch: outpcd over 3f out: plugged on fnl f: nvr able to chal* **8/1**

0601 5 *½* **Beautiful Stranger (IRE)**[8] 3922 5-9-13 **75** 6ex (p) TomQueally 5 60
(Keith Dalgleish) *s.i.s: in tch on outside: rdn over 2f out: wknd over 1f out* **7/2**[3]

-000 6 *3 ½* **Gun Case**[8] 3922 4-9-8 **70** PhillipMakin 1 47
(Alistair Whillans) *bhd: drvn and outpcd over 3f out: btn fnl 2f* **28/1**

1m 48.83s (5.03) **Going Correction** +0.725s/f (Yiel) **6** Ran SP% **109.8**

Speed ratings (Par 103): **103,98,96,92,92 88**

CSF £6.90 TOTE £2.60: £1.60, £1.90; EX 6.90 Trifecta £37.30.

Owner George Brian Davidson **Bred** James Mahon **Trained** Carrutherstown, D'fries & G'way

FOCUS

Race extended by 12 yards. This looked competitive for the class, but it proved one-way traffic for the winner. He's rated to his old best.

4190 HIGH DEFINITION RACING UK H'CAP 1m 2f

3:00 (3:00) (Class 5) (0-75,75) 3-Y-O+ **£3,557** (£1,058; £529; £264) **Stalls** Low

Form RPR

6-03 1 **Royal Regent**[54] 2362 4-9-5 **71** JoeDoyle(3) 1 81
(Lucy Normile) *mde all: set stdy pce: rdn over 1f out: qcknd clr fnl f: readily* **7/2**[2]

5245 2 *3* **Rockwood**[17] 3605 5-9-9 **72** (v) GrahamLee 7 76
(Karen McLintock) *t.k.h: in tch: hdwy to press wnr over 1f out: sn rdn: kpt on same pce fnl f* **6/1**

3-31 3 *1 ¼* **Azzir (IRE)**[6] 3983 4-9-4 **74** CliffordLee(7) 4 76
(K R Burke) *trckd wnr to over 4f out: cl up: rdn and outpcd over 1f out: kpt on ins fnl f* **11/8**[1]

1422 4 *2 ½* **Archie's Advice**[9] 3884 5-9-11 **74** JasonHart 6 71
(Keith Dalgleish) *t.k.h: hld up: rdn along over 1f out: no imp fnl f* **9/2**[3]

6-00 5 *½* **Symbolic Star (IRE)**[16] 3659 4-9-7 **75** PhilDennis(5) 5 71
(Barry Murtagh) *t.k.h: hld up in tch: nt clr run briefly over 1f out: sn rdn and no imp* **25/1**

0313 6 *4 ½* **Testa Rossa (IRE)**[24] 3342 6-9-2 **65** (b[1]) PaulMulrennan 2 52
(Jim Goldie) *trckd ldrs: wnt 2nd over 4f out: rdn over 1f out: sn wknd* **10/1**

2m 21.37s (9.37) **Going Correction** +0.725s/f (Yiel) **6** Ran SP% **109.7**

Speed ratings (Par 103): **91,88,87,85,85 81**

CSF £22.82 TOTE £4.70: £2.20, £2.90; EX 22.50 Trifecta £58.60.

Owner Steve Dick **Bred** Steve Dick **Trained** Duncrievie, Perth & Kinross

FOCUS

Race extended by 12 yards. This was run at a stop-start pace and the winner dictated matters. The race is rated around the runner-up to his turf form.

4191 RACING UK'S PROFITS RETURNED TO RACING H'CAP 6f

3:30 (3:30) (Class 5) (0-75,73) 3-Y-O+ **£3,881** (£1,155; £577; £288) **Stalls** Low

Form RPR

0-00 1 **Naggers (IRE)**[16] 3646 5-9-8 **69** PaulMulrennan 3 79+
(Paul Midgley) *hld up: hdwy 2f out: led 1f out: rdn and hung lft ins fnl f: kpt on wl* **5/2**[1]

2002 **2** 1 ¼ **Goninodaethat**[7] 3941 8-8-6 **56**.. JoeDoyle(3) 7 62
(Jim Goldie) *led: rdn and hdd 1f out: kpt on ins fnl f* **9/1**

1- **3** 1 ½ **Balance**[269] 7244 3-9-6 **73**.. TonyHamilton 5 73
(Richard Fahey) *t.k.h early: in tch: stdy hdwy over 2f out: rdn wl over 1f out: one pce fnl f* **9/2**[3]

4 3 ½ **Haqeeba (IRE)**[8] 3929 3-8-5 **65**..................................(t) KillianLeonard(7) 8 54
(Liam Lennon, Ire) *wnt rt s: hld up: pushed along over 2f out: edgd lft and no imp over 1f out* **3/1**[2]

0606 **5** 2 ¾ **Whozthecat (IRE)**[9] 3875 9-9-9 **70**....................................(t) JasonHart 6 51
(Declan Carroll) *cl up: rdn over 2f out: wknd over 1f out* **9/1**

-105 **6** 5 **Off The Scale (IRE)**[23] 3394 4-9-10 **71**................................ BenCurtis 1 36
(Brian Ellison) *hld up on far side of gp: rdn over 2f out: sn wknd* **6/1**

100- **7** 4 ½ **Rock Canyon (IRE)**[286] 6830 7-9-4 **65**....................... GeorgeChaloner 4 16
(Linda Perratt) *trckd ldrs: rdn over 2f out: wknd wl over 1f out* **50/1**

1530 **8** 13 **Kenny The Captain (IRE)**[9] 3892 5-9-11 **72**............(b) DuranFentiman 9
(Tim Easterby) *virtually ref to r: t.o whn consented to jump off* **11/1**

1m 15.55s (3.15) **Going Correction** +0.625s/f (Yiel)
WFA 3 from 4yo+ 6lb **8** Ran SP% **116.3**
Speed ratings (Par 103): **104,102,100,95,92 85,79,62**
CSF £26.38 CT £97.71 TOTE £3.30: £1.60, £3.30, £1.30; EX 27.30 Trifecta £160.90.
Owner Taylor's Bloodstock Ltd **Bred** Azienda Agricola Rosati Colarieti **Trained** Westow, N Yorks

FOCUS
There was a solid pace on in this modest sprint handicap and the form is straightforward. The winner is rated back to his 3yo form.

4192 RACING UK DAY PASS JUST £10 H'CAP 5f
4:00 (4:00) (Class 6) (0-65,67) 3-Y-O+ **£2,911** (£866; £432; £216) **Stalls** Low

Form RPR

0340 **1** **Star Cracker (IRE)**[30] 3150 4-9-12 **64**.......................(p) PaulMulrennan 1 74
(Jim Goldie) *mde all: rdn over 1f out: drew clr ins fnl f* **11/4**[2]

4453 **2** 2 ¼ **Tribesman**[13] 3755 3-9-4 **61**..(p) CamHardie 2 61
(Marjorie Fife) *disp ld: rdn over 2f out: kpt on same pce ins fnl f* **10/3**

0662 **3** hd **Reflation**[8] 3925 4-8-9 **52**..(p) PhilDennis(5) 7 53
(Michael Dods) *t.k.h: hld up: rdn 2f out: kpt on ins fnl f: nt gng pce to chal* **5/2**[1]

6634 **4** 2 **Emerald Asset (IRE)**[6] 3978 3-9-1 **58**................................ GrahamLee 5 50
(Paul Midgley) *in tch: rdn over 2f out: hdwy over 1f out: no ex ins fnl f* **3/1**[3]

0006 **5** 1 **Takahiro**[7] 3941 4-8-7 **45**..(t) GeorgeChaloner 6 35
(Linda Perratt) *dwlt: sn pushed along and hdwy to chse ldrs after 2f: sn drvn along: wknd ins fnl f* **25/1**

5600 **6** 6 **Mystical King**[8] 3925 6-8-4 **45**..(p) JoeDoyle(3) 4 14
(Linda Perratt) *in tch: rdn and outpcd over 2f out: sn btn* **33/1**

0605 **7** 3 **Sunrise Dance**[7] 3940 7-8-0 **45**....................... RobertDodsworth(7) 8
(Kenny Johnson) *prom: rdn along and wknd 2f out* **25/1**

1m 2.6s (3.20) **Going Correction** +0.625s/f (Yiel)
WFA 3 from 4yo+ 5lb **7** Ran SP% **114.0**
Speed ratings (Par 101): **99,95,95,91,90 80,75**
CSF £12.15 CT £24.55 TOTE £3.60: £2.00, £1.90; EX 13.80 Trifecta £40.50.
Owner The Vital Sparks **Bred** James Mc Claren **Trained** Uplawmoor, E Renfrews

FOCUS
A weak sprint handicap in which the main action developed near the far rail. The winner is rated to his best but there are doubts.

4193 PAY FOR RACING UK VIA PHONE BILL H'CAP 7f 50y
4:30 (4:30) (Class 4) (0-85,84) 3-Y-O+ **£5,822** (£1,732; £865; £432) **Stalls** High

Form RPR

50-5 **1** **Royal Duchess**[78] 1663 6-8-11 **70**...................................... JoeDoyle(3) 3 79
(Lucy Normile) *hld up: stdy hdwy over 2f out: rdn to ld ins fnl f: kpt on wl* **12/1**

0603 **2** ¾ **Moonlightnavigator (USA)**[23] 3398 4-9-7 **77**............ DougieCostello 5 84
(John Quinn) *hld up: effrt and drvn over 1f out: kpt on to chse wnr last 30yds: r.o* **11/2**[3]

0510 **3** 1 **Eastern Racer (IRE)**[16] 3646 4-10-0 **84**............................(p) BenCurtis 6 88
(Brian Ellison) *in tch: effrt and swtchd lft over 2f out: hdwy and ev ch briefly ent fnl f: kpt on same pce towards fin* **17/2**

402 **4** ½ **Sophie P**[7] 3945 3-8-5 **69**.. ConnorBeasley 7 69
(R Mike Smith) *t.k.h early: trckd ldrs: hdwy to ld over 2f out: hdd ins fnl f: kpt on same pce* **9/2**[1]

1104 **5** ½ **Avenue Of Stars**[16] 3646 3-9-1 **79**....................................(p) GrahamLee 4 77
(Karen McLintock) *led 1f: pressed ldr: ev ch over 2f out to over 1f out: outpcd ins fnl f* **11/1**

0460 **6** 1 **Tiger Jim**[16] 3646 6-9-11 **81**.. PaulMulrennan 1 80
(Jim Goldie) *hld up: shkn up and hdwy over 2f out: rdn and no imp fr over 1f out* **5/1**[2]

3110 **7** ½ **Classic Seniority**[16] 3645 4-9-10 **83**....................... JacobButterfield(3) 9 81
(Marjorie Fife) *hld up in tch on outside: effrt over 2f out: no imp over 1f out* **12/1**

5040 **8** 1 ¾ **Fullon Clarets**[17] 3595 4-9-3 **78**...........................(p) AdamMcNamara(5) 2 71
(Richard Fahey) *t.k.h: led after 1f: hdd over 2f out: wknd over 1f out* **5/1**[2]

4423 **9** 7 **Gold Flash**[19] 3517 4-9-4 **74**..(b) PhillipMakin 8 49
(Keith Dalgleish) *hld up: rdn over 2f out: edgd lft: sn btn* **6/1**

1m 36.89s (3.49) **Going Correction** +0.625s/f (Yiel)
WFA 3 from 4yo+ 8lb **9** Ran SP% **115.4**
Speed ratings (Par 105): **105,104,103,102,101 100,100,98,90**
CSF £76.43 CT £598.00 TOTE £16.90: £4.20, £2.30, £2.80; EX 108.70 Trifecta £1274.90.
Owner Steve Dick **Bred** Steve Dick **Trained** Duncrievie, Perth & Kinross
■ Stewards' Enquiry : Ben Curtis two-day ban (25-26 July): careless riding

FOCUS
Race extended by 12 yards. This fair handicap was run at a decent pace and the form should work out. The winner recorded a small pb.

4194 PAY AND WATCH RACING UK VIA MOBILE APPRENTICE H'CAP 1m 5f 13y
5:00 (5:00) (Class 6) (0-65,65) 4-Y-O+ **£2,587** (£770; £384; £192) **Stalls** Low

Form RPR

3132 **1** **Roc De Prince**[14] 3704 7-9-6 **62**....................................(v) CliffordLee(3) 5 69
(Keith Dalgleish) *mde all: rdn over 2f out: kpt on strly fnl f* **9/2**[2]

2 2 ½ **Bell Of The Ball (IRE)**[29] 4281 6-9-1 **54**..................... KillianLeonard 4 58
(Liam Lennon, Ire) *prom: hdwy to press wnr over 2f out: sn rdn: kpt on fnl f: nt pce to chal* **6/1**

4536 **3** ¾ **Question Of Faith**[8] 3921 5-8-3 **47**................................ BenRobinson(5) 6 49
(Martin Todhunter) *hld up in midfield: swtchd lft and hdwy over 2f out: sn rdn: kpt on ins fnl f* **15/2**

5532 **4** 2 ½ **Cape Hideaway**[23] 3418 4-9-6 **59**....................................(p) RowanScott 3 58
(Mark Walford) *chsd ldr: effrt whn nt clr run briefly and lost 2nd pl over 2f out: rallied: kpt on same pce fnl f* **11/4**[1]

-343 **5** 6 **Hero's Story**[26] 3288 6-8-9 **55**................................(p) LewisEdmunds(7) 9 46
(Jim Goldie) *hld up: stdy hdwy 3f out: rdn and outpcd 2f out: sn no imp* **7/1**

0005 **6** 6 **Gabrial The Terror (IRE)**[14] 3706 6-9-12 **65**.........(p) AdamMcNamara 1 47
(Richard Fahey) *hld up: drvn along wl over 2f out: sn wknd* **11/2**[3]

40-0 **7** 3 ¾ **Crakehall Lad (IRE)**[22] 731 5-8-8 **52**..............................(p) PaulaMuir(5) 2 29
(Andrew Crook) *midfield: drvn along and outpcd over 2f out: sn btn* **20/1**

6-0 **8** 24 **Papagayo (IRE)**[37] 2916 4-8-12 **56**.................................... GerO'Neill(5) 8
(Barry Murtagh) *t.k.h: trckd ldrs: edgd lft and outpcd over 2f out: sn btn* **14/1**

4-00 **9** 29 **Lightning Steps**[26] 3288 4-8-3 **47**......................... RobertDodsworth(5) 7
(Declan Carroll) *bhd: struggling 1/2-way: lost tch 4f out: t.o* **33/1**

3m 6.8s (12.80) **Going Correction** +0.725s/f (Yiel) **9** Ran SP% **113.2**
Speed ratings (Par 101): **89,87,87,85,81 78,75,61,43**
CSF £30.92 CT £195.72 TOTE £5.20: £1.70, £2.10, £2.70; EX 32.40 Trifecta £186.30.
Owner Ken McGarrity **Bred** Mrs James Wigan & London TB Services Ltd **Trained** Carluke, S Lanarks

FOCUS
Race extended by 24 yards. They were strung out early in this moderate handicap, confined to apprentice riders. The form makes sense.
T/Plt: £804.50 to a £1 stake. Pool: £69,997.57 - 63.51 winning tickets T/Qpdt: £45.80 to a £1 stake. Pool: £8,619.70 - 139.07 winning tickets **Richard Young**

3301 CHELMSFORD (A.W) (L-H)
Monday, July 11

OFFICIAL GOING: Polytrack: standard
Wind: medium, across Weather: bright spells and cloud, breezy

4195 GREENE KING IPA FILLIES' NOVICE STKS (PLUS 10 RACE) 5f (P)
2:15 (2:18) (Class 4) 2-Y-O **£5,822** (£1,732; £865; £432) **Stalls** Low

Form RPR

5 **1** **Equimou**[14] 3718 2-9-0 0.. AndreaAtzeni 4 83
(Robert Eddery) *chsd ldr: rdn and effrt to ld ent fnl f: r.o strly: readily* **8/1**[3]

1620 **2** 4 **Gerrard's Fur Coat**[30] 3128 2-9-3 0......................... RichardKingscote 1 72
(Tom Dascombe) *led: rdn over 1f out: sn hdd: outpcd by wnr but hld on for 2nd wl ins fnl f* **9/1**

21 **3** nk **Rosabelle**[16] 3633 2-9-6 0.. DavidProbert 2 74
(Alan Bailey) *chsd ldng pair: effrt jst over 1f out: no ch w wnr and styd on same pce ins fnl f* **15/8**[2]

2433 **4** ½ **Boater (IRE)**[11] 3819 2-9-6 0... FrannyNorton 5 72+
(Mark Johnston) *rrd as stalls opened and v.s.a: bhd: styd on u.p fr over 1f out: no ch w wnr* **1/1**[1]

05 **5** 1 ¾ **Xenon**[16] 3647 2-9-0 0... LukeMorris 3 59
(Sir Mark Prescott Bt) *dwlt: sn rcvrd and in tch in midfield: rdn and unable qck over 1f out: wl hld and plugged on same pce fnl f* **8/1**[3]

06 **6** 2 **Seprani**[16] 3647 2-9-0 0... SaleemGolam 7 52
(Mrs Ilka Gansera-Leveque) *in tch: rdn and btn over 1f out: sn wknd* **50/1**

000 **7** 11 **Bills Delight**[19] 3511 2-8-9 0.................................... HectorCrouch(5) 8 13
(Bill Turner) *a towards rr: lost tch over 1f out* **100/1**

8 28 **Penuche** 2-8-9 0... NoelGarbutt(5) 6
(Derek Shaw) *s.i.s: rn green and sn outpcd: hung rt bnd 3f out: t.o* **100/1**

59.34s (-0.86) **Going Correction** 0.0s/f (Stan) **8** Ran SP% **120.9**
Speed ratings (Par 93): **105,98,98,97,94 91,73,28**
CSF £78.97 TOTE £9.80: £2.40, £3.10, £1.30; EX 94.80 Trifecta £227.60.
Owner Edwin S Phillips **Bred** Stratford Place Stud & Minster Stud **Trained** Newmarket, Suffolk

FOCUS
A nice performance from the winner, even allowing for the favourite throwing her race away at the start. It's doubtful the bare form is worth more.

4196 TOTEJACKPOT NOVICE STKS (PLUS 10 RACE) 5f (P)
2:45 (2:45) (Class 4) 2-Y-O **£5,822** (£1,732; £865; £432) **Stalls** Low

Form RPR

2 **1** **Lonely The Brave (IRE)**[9] 3874 2-9-2 0......................... FrannyNorton 2 83+
(Mark Johnston) *chsd ldr: clsd to press ldr 2f out: rdn to ld 1f out: styd on wl* **8/11**[1]

10 **2** 2 **Prince Of Cool**[25] 3295 2-9-8 0... TomEaves 6 80
(James Given) *led and sn clr: pressed 2f out: rdn over 1f out: hdd 1f out: styd on same pce after* **2/1**[2]

30 **3** 4 ½ **Makman (IRE)**[89] 1422 2-9-2 0.. PaulHanagan 4 58
(Ed Dunlop) *wnt rt s: in tch in 3rd: swtchd rt and pressed ldrs wl over 1f out: sn rdn and outpcd: wknd fnl f* **5/1**[3]

4 10 **The Lady Hysteria (IRE)** 2-8-11 0................................[1] DannyBrock 3 17
(Phil McEntee) *in tch in rr: rdn 1/2-way: outpcd and btn over 1f out: sn wknd* **50/1**

59.94s (-0.26) **Going Correction** 0.0s/f (Stan) **4** Ran SP% **109.9**
Speed ratings (Par 96): **101,97,90,74**
CSF £2.52 TOTE £1.50; EX 2.30 Trifecta £2.90.
Owner Acorn Partnership, S Counsell & O Pawle **Bred** T Radley **Trained** Middleham Moor, N Yorks

FOCUS
The leader set a good gallop and the form looks sound. The winner should rate higher.

4197 TOTETRIFECTA H'CAP 1m 5f 66y(P)
3:15 (3:15) (Class 6) (0-65,65) 4-Y-O+ **£3,234** (£962; £481; £240) **Stalls** Low

Form RPR

10 **1** **Lady Makfi (IRE)**[18] 3560 4-9-0 **58**................................. StevieDonohoe 4 72+
(Johnny Farrelly) *hld up in tch: trckd ldrs 4f out: rdn to ld and hung lft over 1f out: sn clr: eased wl ins fnl f* **9/2**[3]

5300 **2** 10 **Awesome Rock (IRE)**[33] 3031 7-8-2 **46** oh1.................... KieranO'Neill 1 43
(Roger Ingram) *chsd ldng pair: wnt 2nd 4f out: jnd ldr travelling wl over 2f out: rdn to ld wl over 1f out: immediately outpcd and wl btn 1f out: plugged on* **16/1**

0042 **3** 7 **Intimidator (IRE)**[19] 3528 5-8-10 **57**........................... DanielMuscutt(3) 6 44
(Miss Joey Ellis) *in tch in midfield: wnt 3rd 4f out: rdn and outpcd 2f out: no ch after: wnt modest 3rd over 1f out* **9/4**[1]

3120 **4** 5 **Lorelei**[50] 2502 4-9-0 **61**.. RobHornby(3) 2 41
(William Muir) *hld up in tch in last pair: effrt in 5th over 3f out: sn struggling: no ch over 1f out: wnt modest 4th ins fnl f* **11/4**[2]

14/5 **5** 8 **Barnacle**[33] 3031 7-8-2 **46** oh1.......................................(vt) JamesSullivan 5 15
(Emma Owen) *led: rdn and hdd wl over 1f out: sn btn and fdd over 1f out* **8/1**

4504 **6** 4 **Ninepointsixthree**[20] 3498 6-9-2 **65**............................(p) CiaranMckee(5) 3 28
(John O'Shea) *wnt rt s: s.i.s and rdn along in rr for 3f: hdwy to chse ldrs 8f out tl lost pl qckly u.p 4f out: sn wl bhd* **7/1**

03-0 **7** *54* **Ledbury (IRE)**[182] 138 4-9-7 **65**..(p) AmirQuinn 7
(Lee Carter) *chsd ldr tl 4f out: sn dropped out u.p and bhd: t.o* **10/1**
2m 53.49s (-0.11) **Going Correction** 0.0s/f (Stan) **7** Ran SP% **114.2**
Speed ratings (Par 101): **99,92,88,85,80 78,44**
CSF £67.76 TOTE £5.40: £2.40, £5.10; EX 67.90 Trifecta £295.50.
Owner The Lansdowners **Bred** Coleman Bloodstock Limited **Trained** Enmore, Somerset
FOCUS
The gallop picked up a fair way from home and they finished well strung out. The winner built on her good Wolverhampton win.

4198 TOTEEXACTA H'CAP 5f (P)
3:45 (3:45) (Class 3) (0-90,90) 3-Y-O+ **£9,056** (£2,695; £1,346; £673) **Stalls** Low

Form RPR
6055 **1** **Shamshon (IRE)**[11] 3800 5-9-12 **90**................................ JamieSpencer 6 102
(Jamie Osborne) *stdd s: hld up in last trio: hdwy jst over 1f out: rdn to ld 100yds out: sn in command: eased towards fin* **7/2**[1]
-042 **2** *1 ¼* **Foxtrot Knight**[7] 3956 4-9-0 **78**.................................... JamesSullivan 11 85+
(Ruth Carr) *midfield: effrt and c wd bnd 2f out: hdwy u.p 1f out wnt 2nd wl ins fnl f: styd on* **6/1**[2]
3464 **3** *1 ¼* **Monumental Man**[20] 3487 7-8-10 **74**........................(p) AdamBeschizza 2 77
(Michael Attwater) *t.k.h: trckd ldrs: effrt jst over 1f out: wnt between rivals ins fnl f: styd on u.p to go 3rd towards fin* **7/1**[3]
2450 **4** *nk* **Krystallite**[3] 4112 3-8-13 **82**.. KieranO'Neill 5 81
(Scott Dixon) *w ldr tl led 2f out: sn drvn: hdd and no ex fnl 100yds* **10/1**
1262 **5** *nse* **Welease Bwian (IRE)**[40] 2787 7-8-7 **78**....................(v) MillyNaseb[(7)] 10 79+
(Stuart Williams) *dwlt: racd in last pair: swtchd rt and effrt over 1f out: styd on wl fnl 100yds no threat to ldrs* **8/1**
0454 **6** *½* **Dynamo Walt (IRE)**[26] 3277 5-8-8 **77**........................(v) NoelGarbutt[(5)] 8 76
(Derek Shaw) *chsd ldrs on outer: effrt over 1f out: styd on same pce ins fnl f* **6/1**[2]
1-00 **7** *1 ¾* **Red Stripes (USA)**[16] 3637 4-9-7 **85**................................ PaulHanagan 1 78
(Lisa Williamson) *led: hdd 2f out: sn rdn and stl ev ch tl wknd ins fnl f* **8/1**
336 **8** *2* **Oriental Relation (IRE)**[35] 2975 5-9-3 **81**........................(b) TomEaves 9 67
(James Given) *midfield and stuck wd tl swtchd lft to inner 3f out: sn rdn: wknd ins fnl f* **14/1**
-214 **9** *5* **Shackled N Drawn (USA)**[41] 2768 4-9-1 **79**............... CharlesBishop 4 47
(Peter Hedger) *t.k.h: trckd ldrs: rdn and unable qck over 1f out: wknd fnl f* **7/1**[3]
0-31 **10** *¾* **Ada Lovelace**[25] 3307 6-8-5 **76**..................................(p) RhiainIngram[(7)] 7 41
(John Gallagher) *sn dropped towards rr and nvr gng wl: no hdwy u.p over 1f out: bhd fnl f* **14/1**
59.17s (-1.03) **Going Correction** 0.0s/f (Stan)
WFA 3 from 4yo+ 5lb **10** Ran SP% **120.4**
Speed ratings (Par 107): **107,105,103,102,102 101,98,95,87,86**
CSF £25.06 CT £146.44 TOTE £4.20: £1.80, £1.50, £2.90; EX 29.60 Trifecta £124.30.
Owner Michael Buckley **Bred** Stonethorn Stud Farms Ltd **Trained** Upper Lambourn, Berks
FOCUS
They went a good gallop here, and that suited the hold-up horses. The form is rated aorund the runner-up.

4199 TOTEQUADPOT H'CAP 1m (P)
4:15 (4:17) (Class 4) (0-85,83) 3-Y-O+ **£6,469** (£1,925; £962; £481) **Stalls** Low

Form RPR
2-1 **1** **War Glory (IRE)**[182] 145 3-9-4 **82**................................ TomMarquand 6 91
(Richard Hannon) *prom in main gp: clsd to ld 2f out: sn rdn: r.o wl and in command ins fnl f: quite comf* **11/4**[1]
-415 **2** *2* **Weather Front (USA)**[13] 3745 3-8-11 **75**............................ DavidAllan 2 79
(James Tate) *dwlt: towards rr: clsd 3f out: rdn and effrt to chse ldrs over 1f out: kpt on u.p ins fnl f: wnt 2nd cl home* **4/1**[3]
3130 **3** *nk* **Hakam (USA)**[38] 2862 4-9-12 **81**.................................... PaulHanagan 1 86
(Charles Hills) *chsd clr ldr: clsd and handy 3rd 2f out: sn rdn to chse wnr but nt matching his pce: styd on same pce ins fnl f: lost 2nd cl home* **5/1**
006 **4** *1 ½* **Craftsmanship (FR)**[25] 3303 5-9-13 **82**.......................... AndreaAtzeni 8 83
(Robert Eddery) *towards rr: pushed along 5f out: reminder over 3f out: drvn and sme hdwy over 1f out: 4th and kpt on same pce ins fnl f* **4/1**[3]
0030 **5** *6* **Smaih (GER)**[18] 3557 4-10-0 **83**.................................... JamieSpencer 5 70
(Jamie Osborne) *hld up in rr: clsd 3f out: rdn and unable qck over 1f out: wknd fnl f* **16/1**
-004 **6** *½* **Mustaqqil (IRE)**[17] 3605 4-9-8 **77**................................(p) HarryBentley 7 63
(David O'Meara) *midfield: clsd and in tch 3f out: rdn and unable qck over 1f out: wknd fnl f* **16/1**
4463 **7** *21* **Miniaturist (FR)**[19] 3523 3-8-12 **76**........................(b[1]) RichardKingscote 3 9
(Mark Johnston) *racd freely: led and sn clr: hdd 2f out: sn rdn and btn: bhd and eased ins fnl f* **7/2**[2]
1m 39.63s (-0.27) **Going Correction** 0.0s/f (Stan)
WFA 3 from 4yo+ 9lb **7** Ran SP% **117.3**
Speed ratings (Par 105): **101,99,98,97,91 90,69**
CSF £14.70 CT £52.34 TOTE £3.80: £2.10, £2.40; EX 15.00 Trifecta £52.80.
Owner Mohamed Saeed Al Shahi **Bred** Pier House Stud **Trained** East Everleigh, Wilts
FOCUS
A fair handicap run at an ordinary pace. The form is rated around the third.

4200 TOTEPOOLLIVEINFO.COM H'CAP 1m (P)
4:45 (4:48) (Class 6) (0-65,65) 4-Y-O+ **£3,234** (£962; £481; £240) **Stalls** Low

Form RPR
2434 **1** **Lord Of The Storm**[19] 3514 8-9-5 **63**................................ KierenFox 4 70
(Michael Attwater) *chsd ldrs: effrt 2f out: rdn to ld over 1f out: hrd pressed ins fnl f: kpt on: jst hld on* **7/2**[1]
0300 **2** *nse* **Saint Pois (FR)**[19] 3514 5-9-4 **65**........................(p) GeorgeDowning[(3)] 10 72
(Tony Carroll) *chsd ldrs: effrt 2f out: drvn to go 3rd over 1f out: chsd wnr 1f out: str chal ins fnl f: r.o wl u.p: jst failed* **6/1**[3]
5216 **3** *2* **Rustique**[24] 3367 4-9-4 **62**.. ThomasBrown 8 64
(Ed Walker) *hld up in midfield: effrt wl over 1f out: hdwy u.p 1f out: styd on ins fnl f* **7/2**[1]
-305 **4** *1 ¼* **Capelena**[17] 3620 5-8-9 **56**.. DanielMuscutt[(3)] 9 55
(Miss Joey Ellis) *chsd ldr: rdn and ev ch 2f out: 3rd and unable qck 1f out: wknd ins fnl f* **8/1**
00-0 **5** *nk* **Zamastar**[13] 3739 5-8-11 **55**..(p) JackMitchell 12 53
(Brendan Powell) *stdd s: hld up in rr: clsd and c wd bnd 2f out: styd on steadily ins fnl f: nvr trbld ldrs* **33/1**
-004 **6** *4 ½* **Chella Thriller (SPA)**[23] 3402 7-9-3 **61**........................ AdamBeschizza 7 49
(Ralph J Smith) *hld up in tch towards rr: effrt ent fnl 2f: no imp u.p over 1f out: wknd ins fnl f* **16/1**
3300 **7** *½* **Sylvette**[13] 3739 4-8-12 **56**..(bt) AndreaAtzeni 1 42
(Roger Varian) *sn led: rdn and hdd over 1f out: sn outpcd and btn: wknd fnl f* **9/2**[2]
0025 **8** *3 ¼* **Cyflymder (IRE)**[17] 3599 10-8-8 **52**................................ DavidAllan 5 31
(David C Griffiths) *hld up in tch towards rr: effrt on inner wl over 1f out: no hdwy: wknd fnl f* **12/1**
4000 **9** *3 ¼* **Marmalad (IRE)**[32] 3078 4-9-5 **63**................................ PaulHanagan 3 34
(Shaun Lycett) *in tch in midfield: rdn over 3f out: lost pl and wl btn over 1f out: sn wknd* **7/1**
-000 **10** *32* **Delysdream**[11] 3822 4-8-2 **46** oh1....................................[1] DannyBrock 11
(Christine Dunnett) *dwlt: a towards rr: lost tch 2f out: t.o* **50/1**
1m 40.39s (0.49) **Going Correction** 0.0s/f (Stan) **10** Ran SP% **119.0**
Speed ratings (Par 101): **96,95,93,92,92 87,87,84,80,48**
CSF £25.37 CT £81.76 TOTE £4.30: £1.60, £2.50, £1.70; EX 31.50 Trifecta £100.90.
Owner Mrs M S Teversham **Bred** Mrs Monica Teversham **Trained** Epsom, Surrey
FOCUS
An ordinary handicap. Straightforward form, rated around the second and third.

4201 GREENE KING H'CAP 1m 2f (P)
5:15 (5:17) (Class 5) (0-70,70) 4-Y-O+ **£5,175** (£1,540; £769; £384) **Stalls** Low

Form RPR
3511 **1** **Vastly (USA)**[21] 3476 7-9-4 **67**..(t) SaleemGolam 3 73
(Sophie Leech) *trckd ldrs: swtchd rt and effrt over 1f out: hdwy u.p to ld ins fnl f: hld on wl towards fin* **9/2**[3]
3511 **2** *nk* **Choral Clan (IRE)**[23] 3402 5-9-5 **68**................................ JackMitchell 6 73
(Philip Mitchell) *hld up in tch in last pair: effrt wd wl over 1f out: hdwy 1f out: str chal fnl 100yds: r.o but hld towards fin* **10/3**[2]
-560 **3** *¾* **Nosey Barker (IRE)**[11] 3802 4-9-5 **68**........................(p) KieranO'Neill 2 72
(Richard Hannon) *dwlt: sn rcvrd and in tch in midfield: effrt and swtchd rt over 1f out: kpt on u.p ins fnl f* **6/1**
0350 **4** *nse* **Chilworth Bells**[16] 3659 4-9-4 **70**........................(p) JosephineGordon[(3)] 1 74
(Conor Dore) *led: jnd and rdn over 2f out: hdd ins fnl f: no ex and styd on same pce after* **12/1**
516 **5** *½* **Lady Lunchalot (USA)**[30] 3142 6-9-4 **67**........................(p) KierenFox 7 70
(Laura Mongan) *trckd ldng trio: effrt over 1f out: styd on same pce u.p ins fnl f* **8/1**
3504 **6** *1* **Two In The Pink (IRE)**[25] 3314 6-8-13 **62**.................. AdamBeschizza 8 63
(Ralph J Smith) *chsd ldr: rdn and ev ch over 2f out tl no ex jst ins fnl f: wknd fnl 100yds* **20/1**
6223 **6** *dht* **Weardiditallgorong**[30] 3142 4-8-4 **56**........................(b) RobHornby[(3)] 5 57
(Des Donovan, Ire) *in tch in rr: clsd over 2f out: nt clrest of runs and swtchd rt ins fnl f: styd on u.p towards fin* **8/1**
/0-1 **8** *3 ¼* **Song And Dance Man**[30] 3142 6-9-7 **70**............................ DannyBrock 4 64
(Jane Chapple-Hyam) *hld up in tch: clsd over 2f out: effrt over 1f out: unable qck u.p over 1f out: wknd ins fnl f* **3/1**[1]
2m 8.61s (0.01) **Going Correction** 0.0s/f (Stan) **8** Ran SP% **115.2**
Speed ratings (Par 103): **98,97,97,97,96 95,95,93**
CSF £20.08 CT £90.17 TOTE £4.90: £1.50, £1.30, £2.20; EX 12.20 Trifecta £106.50.
Owner Out Of Bounds Racing Club **Bred** Juddmonte Farms Inc **Trained** Elton, Gloucs
FOCUS
They finished in a bit of a heap in this modest handicap. The winner is getting back to his old best.
T/Jkpt: £29,171.80 to a £1 stake. Pool: £43,758.00 - 1.50 winning tickets T/Plt: £288.20 to a £1 stake. Pool: £73,436.06 - 186.00 winning tickets T/Qpdt: £55.40 to a £1 stake. Pool: £7,952.66 - 106.16 winning tickets **Steve Payne**

3953 WINDSOR (R-H)
Monday, July 11

OFFICIAL GOING: Good to firm
Wind: Fresh, behind Weather: Fine but cloudy, becoming sunny

4202 ENGHOUSE APPRENTICE H'CAP 6f
6:00 (6:05) (Class 6) (0-60,66) 3-Y-O+ **£2,264** (£673; £336; £168) **Stalls** Low

Form RPR
0-06 **1** **Helfire**[15] 3684 3-9-0 **58**.. CharlieBennett[(2)] 14 68
(Hughie Morrison) *taken down early: in tch in midfield: pushed along 1/2-way: prog on outer 2f out: drvn and styd on to ld last 75yds* **14/1**
0032 **2** *¾* **Essaka (IRE)**[13] 3735 4-9-3 **55**.. GeorgiaCox[(2)] 4 64
(Tony Carroll) *cl up: prog to ld wl over 1f out: edgd lft fnl f: hdd last 75yds* **7/1**[2]
45-4 **3** *½* **Showdaisy**[157] 460 3-8-12 **58**.. JoshuaBryan[(4)] 5 65
(Andrew Balding) *taken down early: s.i.s: sn chsd ldrs: rdn and clsd to chal 1f out: edgd lft and styd on same pce* **12/1**
6240 **4** *1* **Intimately**[30] 3146 3-8-4 **50**.. MitchGodwin[(4)] 3 54
(Jonathan Portman) *in tch: urged along and prog fr 2f out: chal 1f out: keeping on but hld whn squeezed out last 75yds* **25/1**
0432 **5** *3* **Blistering Dancer (IRE)**[5] 3993 6-8-12 **50**............ MeganNicholls[(2)] 15 46
(Tony Carroll) *w ldrs to 2f out: wknd fnl f* **9/2**[1]
660- **6** *1 ¾* **Uncle Rufus (IRE)**[280] 6989 5-8-10 **46** oh1........................ NoelGarbutt 13 36
(Patrick Chamings) *towards rr: prog on wd outside 2f out: no real hdwy fnl f* **33/1**
0206 **7** *nk* **Blackdown Warrior**[19] 3513 3-8-2 **46**............................ GeorgeWood[(2)] 8 34
(Rod Millman) *s.i.s: pushed along in rr and nvr gng the pce: kpt on fnl f* **14/1**
0000 **8** *1 ¾* **Firgrove Bridge (IRE)**[16] 3674 4-9-5 **57**........................ AnnaHesketh[(2)] 7 41
(Steph Hollinshead) *taken down early: wl in rr: rdn and no prog 2f out: kpt on fnl f: n.d* **20/1**
1505 **9** *3* **Cuban Queen (USA)**[25] 3320 3-8-7 **51**........................ DavidParkes[(2)] 16 25
(Jeremy Gask) *chsd ldrs to 1/2-way: lost pl 2f out: sn struggling* **25/1**
060/ **10** *hd* **Portrush Storm**[1011] 6995 11-8-10 **46** oh1.......................... JordanVaughan 2 21
(Ray Peacock) *mostly chsd ldr to over 2f out: sn wknd* **100/1**
-005 **11** *½* **Fastnet Prince (IRE)**[14] 3724 3-9-0 **58**........................(t) CharlesEddery[(2)] 6 30
(David Evans) *outpcd and dropped to last pair 1/2-way: nvr on terms after* **10/1**[3]
60-0 **12** *nk* **Dark Phantom (IRE)**[166] 341 5-8-8 **46** oh1.............. RhiainIngram[(2)] 12 18
(Geoffrey Deacon) *prom to 2f out: wknd qckly* **25/1**
35-0 **13** *1* **Suitsus**[25] 3320 5-9-8 **60**.. HollieDoyle[(2)] 1 29
(Geoffrey Deacon) *led to wl over 1f out: wkng whn virtually p.u ins fnl f* **14/1**
1m 12.09s (-0.91) **Going Correction** -0.475s/f (Firm)
WFA 3 from 4yo+ 6lb **13** Ran SP% **87.7**
Speed ratings (Par 101): **87,86,85,84,80 77,77,74,70,70 70,69,68**
CSF £56.89 CT £556.11 TOTE £9.40: £3.50, £1.90, £3.20; EX 57.50 Trifecta £1065.80 Part won..
Owner Deborah Collett & M J Watson **Bred** M J Watson **Trained** East Ilsley, Berks
■ Hardy Black, Kaaber and Wahaab were withdrawn. Prices at time of withdrawal 6-1, 66-1 & 6-1 respectively. Rule 4 applies to all bets - deduction 20p in the pound.

FOCUS
Race distance as advertised. The course had received some showers and the ground was riding loose on top but remained decent underneath. A moderate handicap, there was a delay after one got loose and two others had to be withdrawn after getting worked up. They avoided the stands' rail in the straight.

4203 EBF STALLIONS MAIDEN STKS — 6f
6:30 (6:33) (Class 5) 2-Y-O **£3,234** (£962; £481; £240) **Stalls** Low

Form RPR

2 **1** **Tis Marvellous**[11] 3813 2-9-5 0 ....(t) AdamKirby 5 95+
(Clive Cox) *mde all: easily drew rt away fr 2f out* **4/9**[1]

2 *8* **Silent Assassin (IRE)** 2-9-5 0 .... JimCrowley 3 71
(Ed Walker) *mostly chsd wnr: lft bhd and pushed along fr 2f out: kpt on* **7/1**[3]

06 **3** *nk* **Sans Souci Bay**[31] 3106 2-8-12 0 .... TinaSmith(7) 1 70
(Richard Hannon) *prom: pushed along to dispute 2nd fr 2f out: no ch w wnr but kpt on* **50/1**

3 **4** *2 1/2* **Mucho Applause (IRE)**[18] 3569 2-9-5 0 .... DavidProbert 4 63
(Andrew Balding) *chsd ldrs: rdn and outpcd 2f out: hung lft after jockey dropped whip over 1f out: one pce* **7/2**[2]

00 **5** *1* **White Chin (IRE)**[31] 3106 2-9-5 0 .... LiamJones 7 60
(Tom Dascombe) *plld hrd: hld up: effrt on wd outside over 2f out: kpt on but no ch* **50/1**

0 **6** *3/4* **Saxagogo**[32] 3074 2-9-0 0 .... RyanTate 2 52
(George Scott) *chsd ldrs: shkn up and outpcd fr 2f out* **25/1**

7 *6* **Log Off (IRE)** 2-9-0 0 .... RoystonFfrench 9 34
(David Evans) *intimidated by rival after 2f and lost momentum: struggling fr 1/2-way* **50/1**

5 **8** *1/2* **Rita's Man (IRE)**[19] 3526 2-9-0 0 .... GaryMahon(5) 8 44
(Richard Hannon) *s.i.s: rcvrd and prom after 2f: losing pl whn hmpd over 1f out: wknd qckly* **12/1**

4 **9** *2 1/4* **Gentleman Giles (IRE)**[21] 3472 2-9-5 0 .... GeorgeBaker 6 31
(Jamie Osborne) *stdd s: hld up in detached last: nudged into remote 8th briefly over 1f out: nvr involved* **16/1**

1m 11.0s (-2.00) **Going Correction** -0.475s/f (Firm) **9** Ran SP% **127.3**
Speed ratings (Par 94): **94,83,82,79,78 77,69,68,65**
CSF £5.35 TOTE £1.40: £1.02, £2.50, £11.90; EX 6.00 Trifecta £122.10.
Owner Miss J Deadman & S Barrow **Bred** Crossfields Bloodstock Ltd **Trained** Lambourn, Berks

FOCUS
Race distance as advertised. Doubtful this was anything other than an ordinary maiden and he did race against the rail when others were wider out on the track, but still a taking win for the favourite, who could be good.

4204 CBS OFFICE INTERIORS 30TH ANNIVERSARY CELEBRATION (S) STKS — 1m 2f 7y
7:00 (7:00) (Class 5) 3-4-Y-O **£2,911** (£866; £432; £216) **Stalls** Centre

Form RPR

4-06 **1** **Paco Pat**[13] 3745 3-8-5 60 .... GaryMahon(5) 3 59
(Richard Hannon) *trckd ldr 2f: styd cl up: rdn and quick move to ld 3f out and sent for home: edgd lft u.p over 1f out: drvn out and kpt on* **7/2**[3]

6502 **2** *1 3/4* **Clive Clifton (IRE)**[7] 3955 3-9-0 64 ....(v) RoystonFfrench 1 59
(David Evans) *dwlt: hld up in last: hrd rdn and prog over 2f out but wnr already gone: tk 2nd over 1f out: styd on but nvr able to chal* **10/3**[2]

-522 **3** *2 3/4* **Brasted (IRE)**[145] 616 4-9-7 75 ....(t) TomMarquand 5 50
(Paul Cole) *t.k.h: hld up in tch: outpcd and nt qckn whn wnr wnt for home 3f out: drvn and kpt on one pce after* **1/1**[1]

0440 **4** *nk* **Bazzat (IRE)**[33] 3033 3-8-10 44 ....(p) RyanPowell 6 49
(John Ryan) *led to 3f out: sn outpcd: one pce u.p fnl 2f* **20/1**

-030 **5** *9* **Spring Overture**[10] 3918 4-8-11 21 .... JennyPowell(5) 4 31
(Brendan Powell) *trckd ldr after 2f: chal jst over 3f out but sn outpcd by wnr: lost 2nd over 1f out: wknd and eased* **66/1**

063 **6** *10* **Masqueraded (USA)**[39] 2825 3-8-10 59 .... DavidProbert 2 11
(Gay Kelleway) *in tch tl wknd qckly over 2f out: t.o* **12/1**

2m 7.95s (-0.75) **Going Correction** -0.175s/f (Firm)
WFA 3 from 4yo 11lb **6** Ran SP% **109.2**
Speed ratings (Par 103): **96,94,92,92,84 76**
CSF £14.59 TOTE £4.50: £2.40, £2.30; EX 14.60 Trifecta £24.30.The winner was sold to Michael Blake for £7,600. Brasted was claimed by Mr L. A. Carter for £7,000
Owner The Calvera Partnership No 2 **Bred** John James **Trained** East Everleigh, Wilts

FOCUS
Race distance increased by 33yds. No great gallop on here and the winner was given a good ride. They headed centre-field in the straight. Not really form to place much faith in.

4205 BRITISH STALLION STUDS EBF MAIDEN STKS — 5f 10y
7:30 (7:31) (Class 5) 2-Y-O **£3,234** (£962; £481; £240) **Stalls** Low

Form RPR

4 **1** **Kyllang Rock (IRE)**[33] 3037 2-9-5 0 .... AndreaAtzeni 5 84+
(James Tate) *hld up: smooth prog on outer 2f out: pushed into ld 1f out: quite readily* **15/8**[1]

2 *3/4* **Mr Pocket (IRE)** 2-9-5 0 .... GeorgeBaker 1 80
(Paul Cole) *prom: chal and upsides over 1f out: edgd lft but chsd wnr fnl f: styd on but a hld* **5/1**[2]

4 **3** *nk* **Fabric**[17] 3613 2-9-0 0 .... JimCrowley 6 74
(Richard Hannon) *sn prom: led briefly jst over 1f out: cl up but hld whn hanging lft and nt clr run nr fin: kpt on* **15/8**[1]

4 *3* **Grey Galleon (USA)** 2-9-5 0 .... AdamKirby 7 68+
(Clive Cox) *s.s: rcvrd and in tch after 2f: chsd ldrs 2f out: hanging lft and rn green over 1f out: no hdwy after: shaped quite wl* **11/2**[3]

00 **5** *4 1/2* **Roundabout Magic (IRE)**[16] 3647 2-9-5 0 .... NickyMackay 2 52
(Simon Dow) *gd spd to ld and sn clr but hanging lft: hung lft over 1f out: sn hdd & wknd* **50/1**

5 **6** *2* **Express (IRE)**[19] 3511 2-9-0 0 .... TomMarquand 3 40
(Richard Hannon) *prom to 2f out: sn wknd* **20/1**

7 *2 1/4* **Delfie Lane** 2-9-5 0 .... JamieSpencer 8 37
(Richard Hughes) *s.s: outpcd and a wl bhd* **25/1**

8 *5* **Dandy Flame (IRE)** 2-9-5 0 .... RenatoSouza 4 19
(Jose Santos) *chsd ldrs but rn green: reminders and wknd rapidly over 2f out* **100/1**

58.9s (-1.40) **Going Correction** -0.475s/f (Firm) **8** Ran SP% **113.2**
Speed ratings (Par 94): **92,90,90,85,78 75,71,63**
CSF £11.49 TOTE £2.80: £1.10, £1.70, £1.10; EX 10.00 Trifecta £23.90.
Owner Sheikh Juma Dalmook Al Maktoum **Bred** Old Carhue & Graeng Bloodstock **Trained** Newmarket, Suffolk

FOCUS
Race distance as advertised. Probably a fair little maiden, they headed centre-field and the winner did it nicely. HE took a nice step forward.

4206 ENGHOUSE INTERACTIVE UK FILLIES' H'CAP — 1m 67y
8:00 (8:00) (Class 4) (0-80,78) 3-Y-O+ **£4,690** (£1,395; £697; £348) **Stalls** Low

Form RPR

1-53 **1** **Crowning Glory (FR)**[41] 2783 3-8-10 **69** .... JimCrowley 1 75
(Ralph Beckett) *trckd ldr in wl spced field: rdn to ld over 1f out: kpt on and hld on nr fin* **9/2**[2]

2051 **2** *nk* **Pacolita (IRE)**[6] 3974 4-9-8 **72** 6ex .... TomMarquand 2 79
(Sylvester Kirk) *trckd ldng trio: clsd over 2f out: rdn to take 3rd over 1f out: drvn and wnt 2nd last 100yds: styd on and gaining nr fin* **6/1**[3]

2146 **3** *3/4* **Intermittent**[40] 2795 3-9-5 **78** .... GeorgeBaker 4 81
(Roger Charlton) *pushed up to ld: set gd pce and stretched field: rdn 2f out and hanging sltly lft: hdd over 1f out: styd on but lost 2nd last 100yds* **15/8**[1]

633 **4** *2* **Stosur (IRE)**[27] 3257 5-9-10 **74** ....(p) AdamKirby 9 74
(Gay Kelleway) *chsd ldng pair: rdn over 3f out: lost 3rd but in tch over 1f out: no ex* **12/1**

0-05 **5** *1 3/4* **Simply Me**[33] 3023 3-8-3 **62** .... KieranO'Neill 7 56
(Tom Dascombe) *hld up in last trio: shkn up over 3f out: kpt on to take 5th over 2f out but nt on terms: no imp ldrs after* **16/1**

0-04 **6** *1 1/4* **Princess Raihana**[17] 3601 3-9-2 **75** .... AndreaAtzeni 3 66
(Marco Botti) *hld up in 6th: rdn 3f out: no prog* **12/1**

0232 **7** *nk* **Carpe Diem Lady (IRE)**[35] 2968 3-8-11 **70** .... RyanTate 6 60+
(Clive Cox) *awkward s: hld up in last pair: pushed along in last over 2f out: plugged on but nvr really involved* **9/2**[2]

2-30 **8** *3 1/2* **Indigo**[40] 2795 3-8-3 **65** .... JosephineGordon(3) 8 47
(Mark Usher) *awkward s: hld up in last: effrt and rdn 3f out: sme hdwy 2f out: wknd jst over 1f out* **14/1**

-116 **9** *13* **Frivolous Lady (IRE)**[30] 3135 3-8-5 **64** ....(v) RoystonFfrench 5 15
(David Evans) *chsd ldng quartet to over 2f out: wknd rapidly: t.o* **66/1**

1m 42.32s (-2.38) **Going Correction** -0.175s/f (Firm)
WFA 3 from 4yo+ 9lb **9** Ran SP% **114.9**
Speed ratings (Par 102): **104,103,102,100,99 97,97,94,81**
CSF £31.45 CT £66.82 TOTE £5.50: £1.70, £2.20, £1.40; EX 31.60 Trifecta £96.90.
Owner The Eclipse Partnership **Bred** Car Colston Hall Stud **Trained** Kimpton, Hants

FOCUS
Race distance increased by 33yds. No hanging around here and it was a good test at the trip. Fairly sound form for the leve, but few got involved.

4207 PATTONAIR H'CAP — 1m 3f 135y
8:30 (8:30) (Class 4) (0-85,84) 3-Y-O **£4,690** (£1,395; £697; £348) **Stalls** Centre

Form RPR

-144 **1** **Against The Odds**[45] 2638 3-9-5 **82** .... JimCrowley 2 90
(Paul Cole) *trckd clr ldr: clsd 5f out: rdn to chal over 2f out: chsd new ldr sn after: kpt on wl to ld 1f out: drvn out* **2/1**[2]

0-53 **2** *1* **Cosmeapolitan**[18] 3557 3-9-2 **79** .... FergusSweeney 4 85
(Alan King) *hld up in 3rd: clsd 4f out: rdn to ld 2f out: hdd and nt qckn 1f out: kpt on* **7/2**[3]

52-3 **3** *3* **Mytimehascome**[60] 2183 3-9-1 **78** ....[1] AndreaAtzeni 6 80
(Roger Varian) *hld up in last: asked to qckn over 2f out but couldn't: no imp on ldng pair fr over 1f out* **11/8**[1]

5-43 **4** *1 1/2* **Sepal (USA)**[35] 2973 3-8-13 **76** .... TomMarquand 1 75
(Charles Hills) *led: set modest pce early but then t.k.h and clr: c bk to rivals over 4f out: tried to kick on 3f out: hdd and one pce 2f out* **15/2**

2m 29.45s (-0.05) **Going Correction** -0.175s/f (Firm) **4** Ran SP% **109.4**
Speed ratings (Par 102): **93,92,90,89**
CSF £8.95 TOTE £2.90; EX 9.40 Trifecta £22.80.
Owner A D Spence **Bred** Mrs P M Ignarski **Trained** Whatcombe, Oxon

FOCUS
Race distance increased by 33yds. Two of the original six came out and not form to get carried away with, as it was a messy race. Still a likeable winner, though.

4208 CBS LTD H'CAP — 1m 2f 7y
9:00 (9:00) (Class 4) (0-85,85) 4-Y-O+ **£4,690** (£1,395; £697; £348) **Stalls** Centre

Form RPR

0020 **1** **Prendergast Hill (IRE)**[19] 3525 4-9-4 **82** ....(p) JimCrowley 4 90
(Ed de Giles) *trckd ldng trio and clr of rest: prog to ld 2f out and racd in centre: drvn over 1f out: hld on* **4/1**[2]

-432 **2** *3/4* **Rotherwick (IRE)**[16] 3660 4-9-6 **84** ....(bt) TomMarquand 6 90
(Paul Cole) *hld up off the pce in rr gp: rdn 4f out: prog over 2f out: clsd to take 2nd ins fnl f: nt quite rch wnr* **7/2**[1]

2325 **3** *nk* **Taper Tantrum (IRE)**[19] 3525 4-9-5 **83** ....(v) JamieSpencer 8 88
(Michael Bell) *led: taken wd after 2f and hdd: taken to far side in st: nrly on terms fnl 2f and in 2nd pl tl ins fnl f: kpt on* **6/1**

000/ **4** *1 1/2* **See The Rock (IRE)**[83] 6-9-7 **85** .... GeorgeBaker 3 87
(Jonjo O'Neill) *awkward paddock and to post: hld up wl off the pce in rr gp: stdy prog 3f out: tried to cl on ldrs over 1f out: rdn and nt qckn* **20/1**

33-0 **5** *1 3/4* **River Dart (IRE)**[31] 3109 4-9-4 **82** ....(b[1]) RoystonFfrench 1 81
(Marcus Tregoning) *trckd ldng pair and clr in gp of four: rdn over 2f out: fdd over 1f out* **11/2**[3]

330- **6** *3 1/2* **Rahmah (IRE)**[217] 8141 4-8-11 **75** .... TimmyMurphy 10 67
(Geoffrey Deacon) *hld up off the pce in rr gp: pushed along fr over 2f out: kpt on but nvr involved* **50/1**

2021 **7** *3/4* **Icebuster**[12] 3766 8-9-6 **84** .... FrederikTylicki 7 74
(Rod Millman) *led after 2f and maintained str pce: hdd & wknd 2f out* **11/2**[3]

/0-6 **8** *4 1/2* **Defining Year (IRE)**[14] 3721 8-8-13 **77** ....(t) KieranO'Neill 2 58
(Hugo Froud) *hld up in last and wl off the pce: rdn and no prog wl over 3f out: modest hdwy fnl f* **28/1**

9 *1* **Manny Owens (IRE)**[288] 6794 4-9-4 **82** ....(t) FergusSweeney 9 61
(Jonjo O'Neill) *hld up off the pce in rr gp: rdn and no prog over 3f out: pushed along and modest hdwy 2f out: wknd fnl f* **20/1**

600 **10** *3 3/4* **Charlie Bear**[25] 3303 4-9-5 **83** .... AdamKirby 5 55
(Jamie Osborne) *stdd s: hld up wl off the pce in rr gp: hrd rdn wl over 3f out: no prog and sn btn* **15/2**

2m 5.66s (-3.04) **Going Correction** -0.175s/f (Firm) **10** Ran SP% **114.0**
Speed ratings (Par 105): **105,104,104,102,101 98,98,94,93,90**
CSF £17.01 CT £81.74 TOTE £5.20: £2.00, £1.60, £1.70; EX 18.90 Trifecta £102.60.
Owner Gwyn & Samantha Powell **Bred** Barouche Stud Ireland Ltd **Trained** Ledbury, H'fords

FOCUS
Race distance increased by 33yds. They went flying off in this fair handicap, the field soon being strung out, and they headed centre-field in the straight, with the exception of the third who went far side. Straightforward form.

T/Plt: £82.40 to a £1 stake. Pool: £92,462.39 - 818.53 winning tickets T/Qpdt: £27.70 to a £1 stake. Pool: £7,205.20 - 191.98 winning tickets **Jonathan Neesom**

3984 WOLVERHAMPTON (A.W) (L-H)

Monday, July 11

OFFICIAL GOING: Tapeta: standard

Wind: Strong behind Weather: Overcast

4209 FOLLOW @ATTHERACES ON TWITTER MAIDEN AUCTION STKS 5f 216y (Tp)

6:10 (6:11) (Class 5) 2-Y-O **£2,911** (£866; £432; £216) **Stalls** Low

Form				RPR
0	1		**My Dear Baby (IRE)**[30] 3143 2-8-8 0 OisinMurphy 6 (Robert Cowell) *sn chsng ldr: led wl over 1f out: edgd rt and rdn clr ins fnl f* **15/2**	78+
4233	2	4	**Pulsating (IRE)**[16] 3654 2-8-8 0 PJMcDonald 2 (Rebecca Menzies) *hld up: hdwy and nt clr run over 1f out: r.o to go 2nd wl ins fnl f: no ch w wnr* **9/4**[1]	66
3	3	1 ¼	**Golden Eye**[4] 4053 2-8-8 0 EdwardGreatrex(3) 7 (Sylvester Kirk) *prom: rdn over 2f out: styd on same pce fnl f* **7/2**[3]	65
	4	½	**Cape Falcone** 2-8-10 0 LukeMorris 5 (James Tate) *s.i.s: hdwy 5f out: rdn over 1f out: no ex ins fnl f* **12/1**	63
	5	3	**Geophony (IRE)** 2-9-3 0 FrannyNorton 4 (Mark Johnston) *chsd ldrs: pushed along over 3f out: wknd ins fnl f* **13/2**	62
6	6	1 ½	**Aberdonian**[21] 3472 2-8-13 0 RobertTart 3 (Jeremy Gask) *prom: lost pl 5f out: pushed along over 3f out: nvr on terms after* **50/1**	52
22	7	¾	**Princeofthequeen (USA)**[13] 3749 2-9-3 0 DanielTudhope 8 (David O'Meara) *led: rdn and hdd wl over 1f out: edgd lft and wknd ins fnl f* **10/3**[2]	54
	8	2	**Swallow Street (IRE)** 2-9-1 0 WilliamCarson 1 (Jamie Osborne) *s.i.s: hld up: pushed along over 2f out: sme hdwy over 1f out: hmpd and eased ins fnl f* **33/1**	52+

1m 14.53s (0.03) **Going Correction** -0.025s/f (Stan) **8** Ran SP% **113.8**

Speed ratings (Par 94): **98,92,91,90,86 84,83,80**

CSF £24.53 TOTE £9.50: £1.90, £1.10, £1.50; EX 43.90 Trifecta £195.80.

Owner Jaber Abdullah **Bred** Kildaragh Stud **Trained** Six Mile Bottom, Cambs

FOCUS

A fair juvenile maiden. They went a respectable gallop on standard Tapeta and the winner left her debut way behind.

4210 JOIN THE BLACK COUNTRY CHAMBER OF COMMERCE H'CAP 1m 5f 194y (Tp)

6:40 (6:42) (Class 6) (0-60,59) 3-Y-O **£2,264** (£673; £336; £168) **Stalls** Low

Form				RPR
-056	1		**Street Outlaw (IRE)**[48] 2563 3-9-7 **59** (p) AndrewMullen 6 (Daniel Mark Loughnane) *hld up: hdwy over 2f out: rdn to ld wl ins fnl f: styd on: edgd lft towards fin* **17/2**	67
6003	2	1 ¾	**Chestnut Storm (IRE)**[33] 3015 3-9-3 **55** PatCosgrave 3 (Ed Dunlop) *hld up: hdwy and nt clr run over 3f out: rdn and ev ch ins fnl f: styd on same pce* **2/1**[1]	60
5000	3	nk	**Ryan The Giant**[8] 3921 3-8-7 **45** (p) RaulDaSilva 8 (Keith Dalgleish) *chsd ldr tl led over 4f out: rdn over 2f out: hung rt over 1f out: hdd and unable qck wl ins fnl f* **9/1**	50
6-02	4	1	**Denmead**[70] 1918 3-9-7 **59** ShaneKelly 7 (John Butler) *hld up: hdwy over 6f out: chsd ldr over 4f out: rdn and ev ch whn carried rt over 1f out: styd on same pce ins fnl f* **13/2**[3]	63
-533	5	3	**Regal Galaxy**[83] 1553 3-8-12 **50** DarryllHolland 1 (Mark H Tompkins) *chsd ldrs: rdn over 1f out: edgd lft and wknd ins fnl f* **16/1**	49
-003	6	3 ¾	**Britannia Boy**[46] 2608 3-8-7 **45** (p) WilliamCarson 4 (Mark Usher) *hld up in tch: lost pl over 4f out: hdwy over 1f out: wknd fnl f* **16/1**	39
0303	7	5	**Sixties Idol**[12] 3765 3-9-2 **54** CharlesBishop 10 (Mick Channon) *chsd ldrs: rdn over 2f out: wknd over 1f out* **6/1**[2]	41
0-00	8	4 ½	**Miss Marina Bay**[41] 2772 3-9-0 **52** (b[1]) LukeMorris 2 (Sir Mark Prescott Bt) *sn drvn along and flashed tail in rr: rdn over 3f out: wknd over 2f out* **9/1**	33
4450	9	10	**Gamesters Boy**[19] 3509 3-9-3 **55** RyanClark 9 (Mark Brisbourne) *hld up: hdwy over 5f out: rdn over 3f out: wknd over 1f out* **18/1**	22
-000	10	18	**Russian Rascal**[12] 3765 3-8-7 **45** MichaelJMMurphy 5 (Stuart Kittow) *led: rdn and hdd over 4f out: wknd over 2f out* **33/1**	
300	11	24	**Belle Of Seville**[49] 2548 3-8-11 **49** (tp) OisinMurphy 11 (Dominic Ffrench Davis) *sn pushed along in rr: bhd fnl 6f* **20/1**	

3m 5.25s (0.45) **Going Correction** -0.025s/f (Stan) **11** Ran SP% **116.2**

Speed ratings (Par 98): **97,96,95,95,93 91,88,85,80,69 56**

CSF £25.42 CT £161.28 TOTE £10.50: £3.40, £1.50, £2.30; EX 43.50 Trifecta £305.90.

Owner The Wild West Outlaws **Bred** Jim Halligan **Trained** Baldwin's Gate, Staffs

■ Stewards' Enquiry : Raul Da Silva two-day ban (25-26 Jul): careless riding

FOCUS

A moderate 3yo staying handicap. They went an ordinary gallop until the tempo increased down the back the final time. Recent winners of this have often been well ahead of their marks, but it remains to be seen if Street Outlaw is.

4211 VISIT ATTHERACES.COM H'CAP 5f 216y (Tp)

7:10 (7:10) (Class 4) (0-80,79) 3-Y-O+ **£4,690** (£1,395; £697; £348) **Stalls** Low

Form				RPR
555	1		**Rich Again (IRE)**[30] 3168 7-9-7 **74** (b) TedDurcan 7 (James Bethell) *hld up: swtchd lft and hdwy 1f out: rdn to ld towards fin* **7/2**[3]	82
3153	2	nk	**Ordinal**[12] 3775 3-8-13 **72** FrannyNorton 9 (Mark Johnston) *a.p: chsd ldr over 3f out: rdn and edgd rt wl over 1f out: led 1f out: hdd towards fin* **3/1**[2]	78
1623	3	½	**Kyllukey**[23] 3394 3-9-6 **79** MichaelJMMurphy 8 (Charles Hills) *hld up: hdwy on outer over 2f out: rdn over 1f out: styd on* **9/1**	83
1220	4	hd	**Available (IRE)**[23] 3394 7-9-8 **75** (tp) AndrewMullen 1 (John Mackie) *led: rdn and hdd 1f out: kpt on* **20/1**	80
3135	5	1	**Rocket Power**[39] 2818 3-9-6 **79** LukeMorris 4 (James Tate) *prom: rdn and nt clr run over 1f out: edgd lft and styd on same pce ins fnl f* **9/4**[1]	80
6060	6	1 ¾	**Doctor Parkes**[12] 3780 10-9-2 **74** AaronJones(5) 3 (Stuart Williams) *prom: nt clr run and lost pl over 2f out: rallied over 1f out: styd on same pce ins fnl f* **14/1**	70
0345	7	½	**Musharrif**[10] 3851 4-9-8 **75** BarryMcHugh 5 (Declan Carroll) *hld up: hdwy up over 1f out: sn rdn: no ex ins fnl f* **25/1**	69
1110	8	4 ½	**Point North (IRE)**[46] 2613 9-9-9 **76** (b) DanielTudhope 2 (John Balding) *s.i.s: hld up: shkn up over 1f out: nvr on terms* **16/1**	56
0466	9	hd	**Air Of York (IRE)**[12] 3783 4-9-10 **77** JFEgan 6 (David Evans) *chsd ldr tl rdn over 3f out: remained handy tl wknd and eased fnl f* **12/1**	56

1m 13.51s (-0.99) **Going Correction** -0.025s/f (Stan)

WFA 3 from 4yo+ 6lb **9** Ran SP% **116.8**

Speed ratings (Par 105): **105,104,103,103,102 100,99,93,93**

CSF £14.65 CT £84.71 TOTE £4.70: £1.80, £1.70, £2.20; EX 17.10 Trifecta £119.40.

Owner Richard T Vickers **Bred** Mrs Sandra Maye **Trained** Middleham Moor, N Yorks

FOCUS

The feature contest was a fair sprint handicap. They went a decent gallop and the winner is rated to form.

4212 UNIVERSITY OF WOLVERHAMPTON RACING CLASSIFIED CLAIMING STKS 1m 4f 50y (Tp)

7:40 (7:40) (Class 6) 3-Y-O+ **£2,264** (£673; £336; £168) **Stalls** Low

Form				RPR
1331	1		**Yasir (USA)**[21] 3470 8-8-10 60 SophieKilloran(7) 1 (Sophie Leech) *hld up: hdwy on outer to ld 2f out: rdn clr over 1f out: eased towards fin* **1/1**[1]	64+
5442	2	1 ½	**Dalavand (IRE)**[5] 4024 3-8-6 57 WilliamCarson 6 (Jamie Osborne) *hld up: nt clr run over 2f out: hdwy over 1f out: sn rdn and hung lft: wnt 2nd wl ins fnl f: styd on* **7/2**[3]	60
0-55	3	1 ½	**Little Orchid**[68] 1962 3-8-1 52 ShelleyBirkett(3) 7 (Julia Feilden) *trckd ldrs: rdn to chse wnr over 1f out tl no ex ins fnl f* **33/1**	55
-530	4	3 ¾	**El Massivo (IRE)**[48] 2558 6-9-2 57 CallumShepherd(5) 8 (Harriet Bethell) *chsd ldrs tl led 5f out: hdd over 3f out: led again over 2f out: sn rdn and hdd: wknd fnl f* **12/1**	53
0000	5	7	**Pao De Acuca (IRE)**[21] 3470 4-8-13 55 (bt) SeanMooney(7) 3 (Jose Santos) *chsd ldr 7f: rdn and wknd over 2f out* **25/1**	41
-543	6	2 ¾	**Wharane (FR)**[24] 1918 3-8-7 59 (p) LukeMorris 5 (Ian Williams) *led: stdd pce over 6f out: hdd 5f out: drvn to ld again over 3f out: hdd over 2f out: wknd over 1f out* **3/1**[2]	37

2m 40.96s (0.16) **Going Correction** -0.025s/f (Stan)

WFA 3 from 4yo+ 13lb **6** Ran SP% **111.7**

Speed ratings (Par 101): **98,97,96,93,88 87**

CSF £4.77 TOTE £1.90: £1.10, £1.90; EX 4.50 Trifecta £50.50.Yasir was claimed by Mr Conor Dore for £5,000.

Owner Mike Harris Racing Club **Bred** Shadwell Farm LLC **Trained** Elton, Gloucs

FOCUS

A moderate claimer. The respectable gallop steadied in the back straight. The winner was well in on these terms.

4213 WATCH TODAY'S REPLAYS ON THE ATR APP MEDIAN AUCTION MAIDEN STKS 1m 1f 103y (Tp)

8:10 (8:10) (Class 6) 3-4-Y-O **£2,264** (£673; £336; £168) **Stalls** Low

Form				RPR
3	1		**Angrywhitepyjamas (IRE)**[23] 3400 3-9-3 0 MartinDwyer 9 (William Muir) *s.i.s: plld hrd and rcvrd to go 2nd after 1f: shkn up to ld wl over 1f out: styd on wl* **9/1**	80
2336	2	¾	**California Lad**[30] 3145 3-9-3 76 LukeMorris 7 (Harry Dunlop) *trckd ldrs: plld hrd: rdn over 1f out: ev ch ins fnl f: styd on* **15/2**[3]	78
6042	3	1	**Brorocco**[20] 3483 3-9-3 74 OisinMurphy 3 (Andrew Balding) *s.i.s: hld up: plld hrd: hdwy over 3f out: rdn over 1f out: styd on same pce wl ins fnl f* **2/1**[2]	76
-2	4	2 ½	**Spinners Ball (IRE)**[13] 3744 3-9-0 0 EdwardGreatrex(3) 2 (Sylvester Kirk) *prom: rdn over 2f out: styd on same pce fnl f* **14/1**	71
-422	5	4	**Van Dyke**[21] 3475 3-9-3 75 (p) PJMcDonald 5 (Hughie Morrison) *led: rdn and hdd wl over 1f out: wknd ins fnl f* **11/8**[1]	64
	6	10	**Pc Dixon** 3-9-3 0 CharlesBishop 6 (Mick Channon) *s.i.s: rn green and hung rt almost thrght: rdn over 3f out: wknd over 2f out* **10/1**	45
06	7	½	**Gold Return (IRE)**[21] 3475 3-8-12 0 ShaneKelly 8 (David Lanigan) *s.i.s: hld up: plld hrd: shkn up over 2f out: sn wknd* **50/1**	39
0	8	11	**Paca Punch**[13] 3744 3-8-12 0 AndrewMullen 4 (Michael Blanshard) *hmpd after 1f: hld up: rdn and wknd over 2f out* **100/1**	18

1m 59.18s (-1.62) **Going Correction** -0.025s/f (Stan) **8** Ran SP% **115.9**

Speed ratings (Par 101): **106,105,104,102,98 89,89,79**

CSF £74.71 TOTE £8.00: £1.90, £2.00, £1.30; EX 60.50 Trifecta £230.80.

Owner O'Mulloy, Collenette, Clark **Bred** J & J Waldron **Trained** Lambourn, Berks

FOCUS

An ordinary maiden. They went a respectable gallop and the form is rated around the runner-up.

4214 AT THE RACES SKY 415 H'CAP 1m 141y (Tp)

8:40 (8:41) (Class 6) (0-60,60) 3-Y-O+ **£2,264** (£673; £336; £168) **Stalls** Low

Form				RPR
4000	1		**Anneani (IRE)**[33] 3020 4-9-2 **48** JFEgan 6 (David Evans) *pushed along in rr early: hdwy over 2f out: led 1f out: rdn out* **12/1**	58
0-02	2	2 ¾	**Sparring Queen (USA)**[25] 3319 3-9-3 **59** OisinMurphy 4 (Ralph Beckett) *a.p: chsd ldr over 4f out: ev ch over 2f out: sn rdn: styd on same pce ins fnl f* **2/1**[1]	62
5003	3	½	**Alans Pride (IRE)**[14] 3732 4-9-9 **55** (tp) ShaneKelly 12 (Michael Dods) *chsd ldr tl led over 6f out: rdn over 2f out: hdd 1f out: styd on same pce* **11/1**	58
0202	4	1	**Gladys Cooper (IRE)**[14] 3731 3-9-3 **59** LukeMorris 7 (Ed Walker) *plld hrd and prom: lost pl over 6f out: hdwy 3f out: rdn over 1f out: styd on same pce fnl f* **4/1**[2]	59
-600	5	2	**King Oswald (USA)**[9] 3877 3-9-4 **60** PatCosgrave 2 (James Unett) *led: hdd over 6f out: remained handy: rdn and ev ch over 1f out: wknd wl ins fnl f* **14/1**	56
2-34	6	1 ¼	**Overlord**[75] 1796 4-9-11 **57** AndrewMullen 9 (Mark Rimell) *hld up: pushed along and hdwy over 2f out: wknd ins fnl f* **11/2**[3]	51
00-0	7	shd	**Kantara Castle (IRE)**[32] 3072 5-9-2 **48** (tp) FrannyNorton 10 (John Mackie) *hld up: nt clr run over 2f out: nvr trbld ldrs* **14/1**	42
3216	8	4 ½	**Mount Cheiron (USA)**[52] 2448 5-8-13 **52** (v) CallumRodriguez(7) 1 (Richard Ford) *chsd ldrs tl wknd over 1f out* **18/1**	39
-503	9	2 ¼	**Roman De Brut (IRE)**[18] 3563 4-9-11 **57** (p) DaleSwift 11 (Daniel Mark Loughnane) *hld up: hdwy on outer over 6f out: rdn over 2f out: wknd over 1f out* **7/1**	37

0-00 **10** *10* **Tsarglas**[6] 3988 5-9-9 **46** oh1 (p) AnnaHesketh(5) 3 5
(Colin Teague) *prom: lost pl 7f out: wknd over 2f out* **100/1**

0-03 **11** *20* **Just Five (IRE)**[75] 1791 10-9-0 **46** (v) DarryllHolland 13
(John Weymes) *hld up: mid-div: hdwy on outer over 6f out: wknd 3f out* **33/1**

0560 **12** *30* **Chapess**[41] 2784 3-8-7 **52** (v1) EdwardGreatrex(3) 8
(Philip McBride) *s.s: outpcd* **66/1**

1m 49.47s (-0.63) **Going Correction** -0.025s/f (Stan)
WFA 3 from 4yo+ 10lb **12** Ran SP% **121.3**
Speed ratings (Par 101): **101,98,98,97,95 94,94,90,88,79 61,34**
CSF £36.89 CT £293.77 TOTE £14.30: £3.40, £1.40, £2.80; EX 52.50 Trifecta £629.80.
Owner Mike Nolan **Bred** Peter & Sarah Fortune **Trained** Pandy, Monmouths
■ Stewards' Enquiry : Anna Hesketh jockey said the gelding had a breathing problem
Pat Cosgrave four-day ban (25-26 & 28-29 July): improper riding
Edward Greatrex jockey said the filly was never travelling

FOCUS
A moderate handicap run at a respectable gallop. A pb from the winner.

4215 DOWNLOAD THE AT THE RACES APP H'CAP 7f 32y (Tp)

9:10 (9:11) (Class 5) (0-75,75) 3-Y-O **£3,234** (£962; £481; £240) **Stalls** High

Form RPR

-105 **1** **Kylla Instinct**[17] 3614 3-9-7 **75** DanielTudhope 7 79
(Philip McBride) *hld up in tch: chsd ldr wl over 1f out: sn rdn: looking hld whn lft in ld wl ins fnl f* **11/4**[2]

1-65 **2** *1 1/4* **Sir Roger Moore (IRE)**[17] 3625 3-9-4 **72** JFEgan 5 73
(John Butler) *hld up: plld hrd: rdn and r.o ins fnl f: nt rch wnr* **17/2**

6-00 **3** *hd* **So Much Fun (IRE)**[24] 3357 3-8-9 **70** (p) DavidEgan(7) 8 70
(Ismail Mohammed) *hld up: hdwy over 2f out: rdn over 1f out: styd on same pce ins fnl f* **28/1**

232 **4** *1 1/2* **Little Miss Kodi (IRE)**[18] 3568 3-9-6 **74** LukeMorris 10 70
(Daniel Mark Loughnane) *hld up: rdn over 2f out: r.o ins fnl f: nvr nrr* **8/1**[3]

0404 **5** *1 1/2* **Custard The Dragon**[23] 3399 3-8-13 **67** FrannyNorton 6 59
(John Mackie) *chsd ldrs: rdn over 1f out: styd on same pce fnl f* **10/1**

4600 **6** *2 1/4* **Big Amigo (IRE)**[17] 3591 3-8-13 **67** (v) RichardKingscote 2 53
(Tom Dascombe) *chsd ldrs: nt clr run over 2f out: rdn over 1f out: hung lft and wknd fnl f* **8/1**[3]

-650 **7** *1 1/2* **Cleverconversation (IRE)**[33] 3039 3-9-5 **73** DarryllHolland 9 55
(Jane Chapple-Hyam) *led 6f out: flashed tail almost thrght: hdd over 2f out: wknd over 1f out* **10/1**

50-6 **8** *1/2* **Cliffmeena (IRE)**[35] 2980 3-8-2 **59** EdwardGreatrex(3) 1 40
(Alex Hales) *s.i.s: hld up: nvr on terms* **80/1**

0-32 **9** *1 1/4* **Malakky (IRE)**[27] 3267 3-9-6 **74** (t) DaneO'Neill 4 81
(Brian Meehan) *led 1f: chsd ldr tl led over 2f out: rdn and looked in command whn broke down ins fnl f: sn eased and hdd: fatally injured* **2/1**[1]

1m 29.71s (0.91) **Going Correction** -0.025s/f (Stan) **9** Ran SP% **115.6**
Speed ratings (Par 100): **93,91,91,89,87 85,83,83,81**
CSF £26.55 CT £538.04 TOTE £4.10: £1.30, £3.10, £6.10; EX 28.50 Trifecta £352.50.
Owner PMRacing **Bred** Whatton Manor Stud **Trained** Newmarket, Suffolk
■ Stewards' Enquiry : Edward Greatrex jockey said the filly was never travelling.

FOCUS
A modest handicap lacking depth, and a lucky winner. They went a modest gallop.
T/Plt: £25.20 to a £1 stake. Pool: £79,546.63 - 2,295.67 winning tickets T/Qpdt: £8.90 to a £1 stake. Pool: £7,800.78 - 645.89 winning tickets **Colin Roberts**

4216 - 4217a (Foreign Racing) - See Raceform Interactive

2350 KILLARNEY (L-H)

Monday, July 11

OFFICIAL GOING: Flat course - yielding; hurdle course - good

4218a IRISH STALLION FARMS EUROPEAN BREEDERS FUND CAIRN ROUGE STKS (LISTED RACE) 1m 25y

6:50 (6:50) 3-Y-O+

£23,860 (£7,683; £3,639; £1,617; £808; £404)

RPR

1 **Creggs Pipes (IRE)**[50] 2511 4-9-9 94 DeclanMcDonogh 6 102
(Andrew Slattery, Ire) *mde all: over 1 l clr at 1/2-way: rdn over 2f out and strly pressed wl ins fnl f: kpt on wl clsng stages to hold on* **11/4**[2]

2 *nk* **Assume (IRE)**[43] 2716 4-9-9 100 WayneLordan 9 101+
(David Wachman, Ire) *mid-div: 9th 1/2-way: gd hdwy on outer fr under 2f out into 2nd ent fnl f: sn rdn and pressed wnr: kpt on wl wout matching wnr cl home* **10/1**

3 *2 1/4* **Duchess Andorra (IRE)**[16] 3676 5-9-9 86 (b) NGMcCullagh 5 96+
(J P Murtagh, Ire) *chsd ldrs: 2nd 1/2-way: rdn under 3f out and u.p in 5th over 1f out: kpt on again into 3rd clsng stages: nvr trbld ldrs* **20/1**

4 *1/2* **Midnight Crossing (IRE)**[18] 3584 3-9-0 87 (b) ColinKeane 8 93+
(Edward Lynam, Ire) *hld up towards rr: 12th 1/2-way: rdn on outer over 2f out and r.o u.p fr over 1f out into nvr nrr 4th clsng stages: nrst fin* **8/1**[3]

5 *1/2* **Colour Blue (IRE)**[16] 3682 5-9-9 92 GaryCarroll 3 94
(W McCreery, Ire) *chsd ldrs: 6th 1/2-way: rdn under 3f out and no imp on ldrs u.p over 1f out: kpt on one pce ins fnl f* **12/1**

6 *nk* **Gussy Goose (IRE)**[43] 2716 4-9-9 92 (p) LeighRoche 2 93+
(David Wachman, Ire) *mid-div: 8th 1/2-way: rdn 3f out and n.m.r bhd horses under 2f out where checked briefly: sn swtchd lft in 8th and nt clr run briefly 1f out: kpt on between horses wl ins fnl f: nvr nrr* **50/1**

7 *nk* **Earring (USA)**[19] 3539 3-9-0 97 (t) SeamieHeffernan 4 90
(A P O'Brien, Ire) *chsd ldrs: 5th 1/2-way: tk clsr order bhd ldrs over 2f out and rdn in 4th: n.m.r on inner ent fnl f and no imp on wnr: one pce clsng stages* **2/1**[1]

8 *1/2* **Emergent**[64] 2068 3-9-0 90 (v1) PatSmullen 10 89
(D K Weld, Ire) *chsd ldrs: 7th 1/2-way: rdn over 2f out and no ex in 6th briefly ent fnl f: one pce after* **12/1**

9 *3/4* **Orcia (IRE)**[32] 3084 4-9-9 94 ShaneFoley 1 89
(M Halford, Ire) *cl up bhd ldr early: 3rd 1/2-way: rdn in 2nd over 2f out and no imp on wnr over 1f out: sn wknd* **8/1**[3]

10 *hd* **Just Joan (IRE)**[19] 3539 3-9-0 83 ConnorKing 11 87
(T Stack, Ire) *hld up: 10th 1/2-way: rdn under 3f out and no imp: one pce fnl 2f* **33/1**

11 *nk* **Flirt (IRE)**[67] 1981 3-9-0 80 (p) ChrisHayes 13 86
(David Wachman, Ire) *mid-div early tl tk clsr order in 4th bef 1/2-way: rdn over 2f out and sn no ex: wknd and eased fr under 2f out* **66/1**

12 *nk* **Brosnan (IRE)**[7] 3964 4-9-9 79 (p) RonanWhelan 7 87
(J F Levins, Ire) *hld up: 11th 1/2-way: rdn and no imp over 2f out: one pce after* **40/1**

13 *6* **Californiadreaming (IRE)**[8] 3931 3-9-0 79 (tp) AnaO'Brien 12 72
(A P O'Brien, Ire) *a bhd: rdn and no imp in rr over 2f out* **50/1**

1m 42.56s (-7.84)
WFA 3 from 4yo+ 9lb **13** Ran SP% **122.3**
CSF £29.52 TOTE £3.70: £1.20, £3.10, £5.80; DF 34.00 Trifecta £625.00.
Owner Delphi Six Syndicate **Bred** John Hayes **Trained** Thurles, Co Tipperary

FOCUS
This was a well-up-scratch renewal. There were some unexposed 3yos pitched in against some proven older fillies who had cut their teeth in handicaps and it was one of the latter brigade that came out on top. The runner-up traded very short in-running. The gallop was generous throughout but the winner still managed to make all.

4219 - (Foreign Racing) - See Raceform Interactive

3683 COMPIEGNE (L-H)

Monday, July 11

OFFICIAL GOING: Turf: good to soft

4220a PRIX DE REMY (CLAIMER) (3YO) (TURF) 1m

2:25 (12:00) 3-Y-O **£6,985** (£2,794; £2,095; £1,397; £698)

RPR

1 **Supersonic Dreamer (IRE)** 3-9-4 0 AntoineHamelin 8 71
(Matthieu Palussiere, France) **111/10**

2 *snk* **Rip Van Suzy (IRE)**[13] 3764 3-9-5 0 MaximeGuyon 5 72
(Jo Hughes) *broke wl: settled bhd ldrs after 1f: angled out and chsd ldng pair fr 2 1/2f out: led ins fnl 1 1/2f: sn hrd rdn and styd on: hdd fnl 25yds: no ex* **8/5**[1]

3 *snk* **Ihaveadream (POL)** 3-8-8 0 AurelienLemaitre 13 61
(W Mongil, Germany) **143/10**

4 *snk* **Des Annees Folles (FR)**[9] 3-9-1 0 MickaelBarzalona 3 67
(P Adda, France) **29/10**[2]

5 *1 3/4* **Stateofthenation (IRE)**[352] 3-8-11 0 EddyHardouin 1 59
(Matthieu Palussiere, France) **29/1**

6 *3/4* **Marchia Rosay (FR)**[13] 3764 3-9-1 0 AlexandreRoussel 4 62
(P Monfort, France) **62/1**

7 *snk* **Insolito (FR)**[13] 3764 3-9-1 0 (p) UmbertoRispoli 2 61
(A Bonin, France) **143/10**

8 *nk* **Rainmaker (FR)** 3-9-1 0 MickaelBerto 9 61
(R Rohne, Germany) **79/10**[3]

9 *3* **Play It Again Tom (FR)**[14] 3-8-8 0 (b) JeremieCatineau(3) 12 50
(Mlle K Hoste, Belgium) **89/1**

10 *7* **Stormy Angel (FR)** 3-9-4 0 GlenBraem 6 41
(Andrew Hollinshead, France) **49/1**

11 *1 1/2* **Maua (IRE)** 3-8-8 0 AndreasSuborics 11 27
(Waldemar Hickst, Germany) **91/10**

12 *7* **Stormy Dance (FR)**[185] 3-9-4 0 CristianDemuro 7 21
(A Giorgi, Italy) **171/10**

WIN (incl. 1 euro stake): 8.60 (coupled with Stateofthenation). PLACES: 3.70, 1.40, 3.80. DF: 15.50, SF: 49.20
Owner Mrs Theresa Marnane **Bred** Ecurie Des Monceaux **Trained** France

3993 BATH (L-H)

Tuesday, July 12

OFFICIAL GOING: Good to firm (8.8)
Wind: strong breeze partially against Weather: cloudy with sunny periods

4221 ABOVE & BEYOND NURSERY H'CAP 5f 11y

2:00 (2:00) (Class 5) 2-Y-O **£4,528** (£1,347; £673; £336) **Stalls** Centre

Form RPR

5032 **1** **Little Nosegay (IRE)**[6] 4015 2-8-8 **58** JFEgan 2 59
(David Evans) *slowly away: sn pushed into ld: kpt on gamely fnl f: rdn out* **10/3**[1]

300 **2** *3/4* **Big Lachie**[17] 3647 2-9-6 **70** WilliamCarson 6 68
(Jamie Osborne) *hld up: swtchd to centre and hdwy fr 2f out: hung lft whn pushed along sn after: rdn ins fnl f: wnt 2nd fnl 120yds: a being hld* **9/2**[3]

205 **3** *2 1/4* **Affordability**[17] 3654 2-9-5 **69** SteveDrowne 4 59
(Daniel Mark Loughnane) *chsd ldrs: rdn over 2f out: kpt on ins fnl f: snatched 3rd cl home* **7/1**

563 **4** *nk* **George Ravenscar**[29] 3231 2-8-6 **56** HarryBentley 3 45
(Ed Vaughan) *chsd wnr: rdn 2f out: lost 2nd fnl 120yds: no ex whn lost 3rd fnl strides* **9/2**[3]

5646 **5** *2 3/4* **Love Oasis**[17] 3633 2-9-7 **71** FrannyNorton 1 50
(Mark Johnston) *chsd wnr tl rdn over 1f out: no ex fnl 100yds* **7/2**[2]

0460 **6** *2 3/4* **Patrouille De Nuit (IRE)**[6] 4015 2-8-7 **57** (b1) DannyBrock 5 26
(J S Moore) *in tch: rdn 2f out: wknd ins fnl f* **14/1**

032 **7** *5* **Irish Melody (IRE)**[13] 3770 2-9-0 **69** (p) HectorCrouch(5) 7 20
(Bill Turner) *in tch: effrt over 2f out: wknd ent fnl f* **8/1**

1m 3.32s (0.82) **Going Correction** +0.025s/f (Good) **7** Ran SP% **111.9**
Speed ratings (Par 94): **94,92,89,88,84 79,71**
CSF £17.74 TOTE £2.90: £1.50, £3.30; EX 19.80 Trifecta £108.70.
Owner David Berry **Bred** Mrs Amanda McCreery **Trained** Pandy, Monmouths

FOCUS
John Egan described the ground as "good, quick". A modest nursery with the winner making a lot of the running. She more than replicated her improved nursery run.

4222 HALL'S DISMANTLING AND REMOVAL LTD FILLIES' H'CAP 5f 161y

2:30 (2:30) (Class 5) (0-75,75) 3-Y-O+ **£4,204** (£1,251; £625; £312) **Stalls** Centre

Form RPR

-130 **1** **Staintondale Lass (IRE)**[37] 2935 3-9-3 **72** HarryBentley 1 87+
(Ed Vaughan) *hld up in last pair but wl in tch: nt clr run and squeezed through gap ent fnl f: sn led: r.o strly: readily* **11/1**

-133 **2** *3 1/4* **Nag's Wag (IRE)**[46] 2642 3-9-2 **71** PatCosgrave 3 75
(George Baker) *trckd ldrs: rdn over 2f out: chalng for 2nd whn bmpd ent fnl f: kpt on but nt pce of wnr fnl 120yds* **5/1**[3]

-006 **3** *3/4* **Quick March**[32] 3105 3-9-5 **74** GeorgeBaker 6 76
(Roger Charlton) *hld up in last but wl in tch: hdwy over 2f out: chalng for 2nd whn bmpd ent fnl f: kpt on same pce fnl 120yds* **4/1**[2]

-022 **4** *1/2* **Free To Love**[6] 3995 4-9-12 **75** SteveDrowne 5 76
(Charles Hills) *led: rdn over 1f out: hdd ins fnl f: no ex* **11/8**[1]

4-04 **5** 3/4 **Regal Miss**[20] 3527 4-8-11 **63** ..... DanielMuscutt(3) 2 61
(Patrick Chamings) *trckd ldrs: rdn 2f out: kpt on same pce fnl f* **14/1**

-513 **6** 3 **Hepworth Marble (IRE)**[14] 3741 3-9-0 **69** ..... FergusSweeney 7 57
(Gary Moore) *w ldr: rdn and ev ch fr 2f out tl fdd ins fnl f* **17/2**

0434 **7** 3/4 **Glastonberry**[32] 3098 8-9-6 **69** ..... (p) TimmyMurphy 4 55
(Geoffrey Deacon) *cl up: rdn 2f out: wknd ent fnl f* **14/1**

1m 11.16s (-0.04) **Going Correction** +0.025s/f (Good)
WFA 3 from 4yo+ 6lb **7** Ran SP% **111.0**
Speed ratings (Par 100): **101,96,95,95,94 90,89**
CSF £60.39 TOTE £15.20: £5.70, £2.80; EX 59.90 Trifecta £213.30.
Owner A M Pickering **Bred** Ringfort Stud **Trained** Newmarket, Suffolk
■ Stewards' Enquiry : Harry Bentley caution; careless riding

FOCUS
Ordinary sprinting form, with the favourite below par. The first three came from the rear.

4223 DRIBUILD LTD H'CAP 5f 161y
3:05 (3:06) (Class 3) (0-95,87) 3-Y-O **£8,409** (£2,502; £1,250; £625) **Stalls** Centre

Form RPR

1-61 **1** **Kassia (IRE)**[20] 3512 3-9-7 **87** ..... GeorgeBaker 2 97+
(Mick Channon) *trckd ldrs: nt clr run briefly jst over 1f out: led ins fnl f: r.o wl to assert nring fin* **5/1**[2]

3111 **2** 1 1/4 **Papa Luigi (IRE)**[34] 3036 3-9-2 **87** ..... GaryMahon(5) 7 93
(Richard Hannon) *trckd ldrs: rdn and edgd sltly lft over 1f out: led briefly jst ins fnl f: kpt on but no ex nring fin* **9/4**[1]

310- **3** 1 **Southern Belle (IRE)**[277] 7072 3-9-3 **83** ..... FergusSweeney 3 86
(Robert Cowell) *little slowly away: in last but wl in tch: rdn 2f out: kpt on ins fnl f: wnt 3rd cl home* **7/1**[3]

4221 **4** 1 **Dark Shot**[17] 3669 3-9-1 **81** ..... DavidProbert 1 80
(Andrew Balding) *led: rdn over 1f out: hdd jst ins fnl f: no ex* **9/4**[1]

-100 **5** 1 1/4 **Florencio**[68] 1977 3-9-2 **82** ..... MartinDwyer 4 77
(William Muir) *cl up: pushed along 3f out: sn rdn: wknd fnl f* **8/1**

-223 **6** hd **Silken Skies (IRE)**[16] 3685 3-9-1 **81** ..... AdamKirby 6 76
(Clive Cox) *pressed ldr: rdn over 2f out: wknd fnl f* **8/1**

1m 10.63s (-0.57) **Going Correction** +0.025s/f (Good) **6** Ran SP% **112.9**
Speed ratings (Par 104): **104,102,101,99,98 97**
CSF £16.88 TOTE £5.80: £3.20, £1.70; EX 16.40 Trifecta £78.90.
Owner Jon and Julia Aisbitt **Bred** Old Carhue Stud **Trained** West Ilsley, Berks

FOCUS
Quite a good handicap, with two in-form progressive types beating an unexposed class-dropper. The form is rated slightly positively.

4224 BIRD IN HAND SALTFORD H'CAP (BATH SUMMER SPRINT SERIES QUALIFIER) 5f 11y
3:40 (3:40) (Class 5) (0-75,75) 3-Y-O+ **£4,204** (£1,251; £625; £312) **Stalls** Centre

Form RPR

441 **1** **Rosealee (IRE)**[24] 3407 3-9-6 **74** ..... AdamBeschizza 10 77
(Jeremy Gask) *chsd ldr: rdn for str chal over 1f out: tk narrow ld fnl 75yds: jst hld on* **5/1**[3]

402- **2** shd **Go Nani Go**[258] 7546 10-9-12 **75** ..... PatCosgrave 8 80
(Ed de Giles) *hld up: swtchd to centre over 2f out: hdwy sn after: rdn over 1f out: kpt on wl fnl 120yds: jst failed* **22/1**

0251 **3** nse **Pucon**[38] 2905 7-9-11 **74** ..... (p) AdamKirby 9 79
(Roger Teal) *led: rdn whn strly pressed fr 2f out: hdd narrowly fnl 75yds: kpt on: lost 2nd fnl strides* **6/1**

0335 **4** nk **Verne Castle**[7] 3976 3-9-0 **68** ..... DavidProbert 7 70
(Andrew Balding) *mid-div: hdwy over 2f out: sn rdn: kpt on ins fnl f* **4/1**[2]

0503 **5** nk **Equistar**[19] 3559 3-9-0 **68** ..... (t) FrederikTylicki 3 69
(Jonathan Portman) *chsd ldr: rdn 2f out: swtchd lft ins fnl f: kpt on but nt quite pce to mount chal* **6/1**

4231 **6** 1 **Showmethewayavrilo**[13] 3771 3-9-4 **72** ..... MartinDwyer 4 69+
(Malcolm Saunders) *trckd ldrs: outpcd over 2f out: hdwy whn nt clr run over 1f out: kpt on same pce fnl 100yds* **7/2**[1]

-160 **7** 1 **Aragon Knight**[24] 3407 3-8-13 **72** ..... [1] HectorCrouch(5) 2 65
(Heather Main) *s.i.s: sn mid-div: rdn over 2f out: nt pce to get on terms* **12/1**

5500 **8** 1/2 **Catalinas Diamond (IRE)**[6] 3994 8-8-9 **58** ow1 ..... (t) SteveDrowne 1 52
(Pat Murphy) *s.i.s: pushed along in last pair: hdwy 2f out: nvr threatened: wknd fnl f* **16/1**

0014 **9** 8 **Entertaining Ben**[22] 3471 3-9-3 **74** ..... (p) RobHornby(3) 5 37
(William Muir) *chsd ldr: rdn over 2f out: wknd jst over 1f out* **9/1**

1m 2.36s (-0.14) **Going Correction** +0.025s/f (Good)
WFA 3 from 7yo+ 5lb **9** Ran SP% **115.4**
Speed ratings (Par 103): **102,101,101,101,100 99,97,96,84**
CSF £104.60 CT £527.59 TOTE £4.50: £1.40, £4.90, £2.00; EX 75.20 Trifecta £142.00.
Owner The Sutton Veny Syndicate **Bred** Mrs Sandra McCarthy **Trained** Stockbridge, Hants

FOCUS
A modest sprint, with little separating the first five, and it went to one of the 3yos. The form is rated around the third.

4225 DRIBUILD GROUP H'CAP (BATH SUMMER STAYERS' SERIES QUALIFIER) 1m 3f 144y
4:10 (4:10) (Class 6) (0-60,60) 3-Y-O+ **£3,881** (£1,155; £577; £288) **Stalls** Low

Form RPR

-006 **1** **Diletta Tommasa (IRE)**[25] 3363 6-9-7 **60** ..... (p) PaddyBradley(7) 2 65
(Daniel Mark Loughnane) *stdd s: in last: hdwy 2f out: sn rdn: styd on to ld fnl 120yds: drvn out* **4/1**[2]

0504 **2** nk **Doctor Kehoe**[14] 3747 4-9-10 **56** ..... (vt) ShaneKelly 4 61
(David Evans) *s.i.s: towards rr: hdwy over 2f out: rdn and ev ch whn carried sltly rt ent fnl f: hld cl home* **3/1**[1]

4200 **3** 1/2 **Tamujin (IRE)**[6] 3997 8-9-4 **50** ..... (p) PatCosgrave 1 54
(Ken Cunningham-Brown) *in tch: hdwy over 2f out: rdn and ev ch whn drifted rt ent fnl f: no ex fnl 75yds* **8/1**

326- **4** 2 1/2 **Captain Oats (IRE)**[314] 5988 13-9-2 **53** ..... RachealKneller(5) 3 53
(Pam Ford) *hld up: hdwy over 2f out: rdn to chse ldrs over 1f out: kpt on but nt pce to mount chal* **16/1**

00-0 **5** 1 **Inwithachance (IRE)**[15] 3731 3-8-1 **46** oh1 ..... (p) DannyBrock 9 44
(Daniel Mark Loughnane) *trckd ldrs: rdn to ld 2f out: kpt on u.p tl hdd fnl 120yds: no ex* **33/1**

504 **6** 1/2 **Surprise Us**[6] 3999 9-8-7 **46** oh1 ..... (p) LiamLewis-Salter(7) 7 43
(Mark Gillard) *led: rdn and hdd 2f out: kpt on w ev ch tl no ex fnl 120yds* **11/1**

120- **7** 15 **Hermosa Vaquera (IRE)**[65] 7230 6-9-6 **57** ..... (p) HectorCrouch(5) 5 30
(Gary Moore) *trckd ldr: rdn over 2f out: sn wknd* **5/1**[3]

31-0 **8** 5 **Lady D's Rock (IRE)**[177] 232 4-9-5 **51** ..... (t) AdamKirby 6 16
(Clive Cox) *trckd ldrs: rdn over 2f out: sn wknd* **5/1**[3]

006 **9** 1 3/4 **Isostatic**[19] 3577 3-7-12 **46** oh1 ..... NoelGarbutt(3) 8 9
(Rae Guest) *s.i.s: in tch: rdn 3f out: sn wknd* **8/1**

2m 31.9s (1.30) **Going Correction** 0.0s/f (Good)
WFA 3 from 4yo+ 13lb **9** Ran SP% **117.7**
Speed ratings (Par 101): **95,94,94,92,92 91,81,78,77**
CSF £16.80 CT £92.27 TOTE £5.60: £1.50, £1.50, £2.40; EX 19.30 Trifecta £131.80.
Owner J T Stimpson **Bred** Ms Sheila Lavery **Trained** Baldwin's Gate, Staffs

FOCUS
Very moderate form, with the race setting up for the closers, and the runner-up was a little unfortunate not to win.

4226 C&I SOUTHWEST LTD H'CAP 1m 5f 22y
4:45 (4:45) (Class 6) (0-65,65) 3-Y-O+ **£3,881** (£1,155; £577; £288) **Stalls** High

Form RPR

-001 **1** **Bernisdale**[14] 3747 8-9-6 **60** ..... DanielMuscutt(3) 4 65
(John Flint) *stmbld leaving stalls: chsd ldrs: chsd clr ldr 3f out: steadily clsd: led ins fnl f: styd on wl* **8/1**

0-64 **2** 1 3/4 **Lady Hare (IRE)**[14] 3737 4-8-11 **53** ..... DavidParkes(5) 1 55
(Ken Cunningham-Brown) *racd keenly: led: sn clr: 5 l clr 3f out: rdn jst over 2f out: hdd ins fnl f: no ex* **20/1**

-005 **3** 4 **Racing Knight (IRE)**[31] 3142 4-9-9 **60** ..... SteveDrowne 2 57
(David Evans) *in tch: rdn 3f out: wnt 3rd jst over 1f out: nvr threatened: styd on same pce* **7/1**[3]

1034 **4** 3 1/2 **Harry's Endeavour**[6] 3998 3-8-11 **62** ..... (p) ThomasBrown 3 54
(Daniel Kubler) *slowly away: sn pushed along in last: drvn and stdy prog fr over 2f out: wnt hld 4th ent fnl f: nvr trbld ldrs* **6/4**[1]

0-0 **5** 2 **Druot**[76] 1796 4-10-0 **65** ..... ShaneKelly 8 54
(Richard Hughes) *chsd ldr: rdn 3f out: drifted rt whn hld over 1f out: fdd fnl f* **16/1**

312 **6** 10 **Ballyfarsoon (IRE)**[6] 3999 5-9-3 **54** ..... (b) AdamKirby 7 28
(Ian Williams) *hld up in last pair: rdn on outer over 4f out: nvr threatened: wknd fnl f* **3/1**[2]

45- **7** 19 **Ice Konig (FR)**[21] 5955 7-8-4 **46** oh1 ..... MeganNicholls(5) 6
(Jimmy Frost) *chsd ldrs: rdn over 3f out: sn btn* **11/1**

5550 **8** 11 **Missandei**[102] 1182 4-8-13 **50** ..... (t) AdamBeschizza 5
(Steph Hollinshead) *in tch: rdn over 3f out: sn btn* **14/1**

2m 51.47s (-0.53) **Going Correction** 0.0s/f (Good)
WFA 3 from 4yo+ 14lb **8** Ran SP% **114.3**
Speed ratings (Par 101): **101,99,97,95,94 87,76,69**
CSF £145.35 CT £1169.43 TOTE £7.00: £1.80, £5.20, £2.00; EX 153.10 Trifecta £1287.80.
Owner Roderick James **Bred** Evelyn Duchess Of Sutherland **Trained** Kenfig Hill, Bridgend

FOCUS
A lowly handicap and few got into it, with the runner-up soon establishing a clear lead and having them strung out. The form is unlikely to be worth more than this.
T/Plt: £421.60 to a £1 stake. Pool of £73020.83 - 126.43 winning tickets. T/Qpdt: £40.40 to a £1 stake. Pool of £7990.31 - 146.32 winning tickets. **Tim Mitchell**

3872 BEVERLEY (R-H)
Tuesday, July 12

OFFICIAL GOING: Good (7.5)
Wind: Fresh against Weather: Cloudy with sunny periods

4227 RACING UK MAIDEN AUCTION STKS 5f
2:20 (2:20) (Class 5) 2-Y-O **£3,780** (£1,131; £565; £283; £141) **Stalls** Low

Form RPR

2 **1** **Dandy Highwayman (IRE)**[15] 3707 2-8-6 0 ..... JacobButterfield(3) 8 76
(Ollie Pears) *mde all: rdn over 1f out: green and edgd lft ins fnl f: kpt on wl towards fin* **7/1**[2]

2 **2** 1 **Perfect Symphony (IRE)**[10] 3881 2-8-13 0 ..... KevinStott 10 76
(Kevin Ryan) *cl up: effrt wl over 1f out and sn chal: rdn over 1f out: drvn and carried sltly lft ins fnl f: kpt on same pce towards fin* **10/11**[1]

44 **3** 2 1/4 **Harbour Lightning**[14] 3749 2-8-6 0 ..... PJMcDonald 4 61
(Ann Duffield) *trckd ldrs: hdwy to chse ldng pair over 1f out: sn rdn and kpt on same pce* **12/1**

6 **4** 4 1/2 **Flash Of White**[19] 3548 2-9-2 0 ..... PaulMulrennan 6 57
(Bryan Smart) *dwlt and swtchd rt s: towards rr: hdwy on inner wl over 1f out: sn pushed and kpt on wl fnl f* **12/1**

04 **5** hd **Regal Decree**[20] 3516 2-8-11 0 ..... JackGarritty 14 49+
(Jedd O'Keeffe) *t.k.h: towards rr: hdwy on outer wl over 1f out: rdn and kpt on fnl f* **66/1**

55 **6** 3/4 **Expenditure (IRE)**[19] 3562 2-9-2 0 ..... GrahamLee 7 54+
(Jedd O'Keeffe) *towards rr: hdwy over 1f out: n.m.r ent fnl f: styd on wl towards fin* **66/1**

B0 **7** hd **Gabridan (IRE)**[34] 3024 2-8-11 0 ..... TonyHamilton 1 46
(Richard Fahey) *in tch: rdn along on inner wl over 1f out: sn no imp* **20/1**

63 **8** 1/2 **Mary Brady**[29] 3223 2-8-11 0 ..... SamJames 9 44
(David O'Meara) *cl up: rdn along over 2f out: wknd over 1f out* **9/1**[3]

0 **9** 2 **Myllachy**[8] 3947 2-8-3 0 ..... RachelRichardson(3) 13 32
(Tim Easterby) *a in rr* **25/1**

10 3/4 **Dusty Bin** 2-9-2 0 ..... TomEaves 11 39+
(Kevin Ryan) *a in rr* **16/1**

5 **11** 1 **Snookered (IRE)**[24] 3416 2-8-11 0 ..... GeorgeChaloner 3 30
(Richard Fahey) *dwlt: a in rr* **28/1**

00 **12** 1 **Ray Donovan (IRE)**[56] 2344 2-9-2 0 ..... DanielTudhope 2 32+
(David O'Meara) *t.k.h: in tch: pushed along 2f out: sn rdn and wknd* **16/1**

13 1/2 **Flying Hope (IRE)** 2-8-6 0 ..... AndrewMullen 12 20
(Nigel Tinkler) *t.k.h: chsd ldrs: rdn along wl over 1f out: wknd fnl f* **66/1**

1m 3.32s (-0.18) **Going Correction** -0.125s/f (Firm) **13** Ran SP% **118.6**
Speed ratings (Par 94): **96,94,90,83,83 82,81,80,77,76 74,73,72**
CSF £12.79 TOTE £7.40: £2.30, £1.10, £3.90; EX 17.60 Trifecta £89.30.
Owner Ontoawinner & Ollie Pears **Bred** Michael M Byrne **Trained** Norton, N Yorks

FOCUS
The going was good (GoingStick: 7.5) and the rail was at its widest alignment. From halfway this maiden only really concerned the first two in the market. Straightforward form.

4228 MALCOLM GREENSLADE DONCASTER LVA STALWART MEMORIAL H'CAP (DIV I) 5f
2:50 (2:50) (Class 6) (0-60,60) 3-Y-O+ **£2,587** (£770; £384; £192) **Stalls** Low

Form RPR

2502 **1** **Compton River**[13] 3779 4-9-1 **51** ..... PaulMulrennan 6 58
(Bryan Smart) *trckd ldrs: hdwy on outer and cl up wl over 1f out: rdn to take slt ld ent fnl f: drvn and kpt on wl towards fin* **7/2**[2]

0036 **2** ½ **Tinsill**[11] 3843 5-9-0 **50**....(p) AndrewMullen 10 55
(Nigel Tinkler) *in tch: pushed along 1/2-way: rdn 2f out: styd on ent fnl f: sn drvn and fin strly* **6/1**[3]

2200 **3** *nk* **Minty Jones**[21] 3484 7-9-0 **50**....(v) RobertTart 8 54
(Michael Mullineaux) *in tch: hdwy wl over 1f out: sn rdn: styd on wl fnl f* **6/1**[3]

0053 **4** *nk* **Slim Chance (IRE)**[11] 3843 7-9-9 **59**....(p) JasonHart 4 62
(Simon West) *slt ld gng wl: pushed along over 1f out: rdn and hdd ent fnl f: sn drvn and kpt on same pce towards fin* **3/1**[1]

0056 **5** 1 **Hashtag Frenzy**[13] 3776 3-8-5 **46** oh1....(p) RaulDaSilva 1 43
(Rebecca Menzies) *cl up: rdn along wl over 1f out: drvn ent fnl f: one pce* **13/2**

-404 **6** 1 **Studio Star**[8] 3941 4-8-12 **48**.... CamHardie 9 44
(Wilf Storey) *towards rr: rdn along over 2f out: styd on u.p fnl f* **20/1**

50-0 **7** 1 ½ **Horsforth**[39] 2856 4-9-10 **60**....(v) BarryMcHugh 2 50
(Tony Coyle) *trckd ldrs on inner: smooth hdwy and cl up over 1f out: sn rdn and ev ch: drvn and wknd ins fnl f* **13/2**

0006 **8** 1 **Kodimoor (IRE)**[15] 3725 3-9-5 **60**....(p) DougieCostello 5 45
(Christopher Kellett) *chsd ldrs: rdn along wl over 1f out: no hdwy* **16/1**

00-0 **9** 4 ½ **Mandalay King (IRE)**[19] 3549 11-8-13 **52**....(p) JacobButterfield[(3)] 7 23
(Marjorie Fife) *dwlt: a in rr* **33/1**

\- **10** 8 **Shadow Of The Day**[330] 5459 9-8-10 **46** oh1....(bt) JamesSullivan 3
(Lee James) *dwlt: a in rr* **50/1**

1m 3.08s (-0.42) **Going Correction** -0.125s/f (Firm)
WFA 3 from 4yo+ 5lb **10** Ran SP% **118.0**
Speed ratings (Par 101): **98,97,96,96,94 93,90,89,81,69**
CSF £24.73 CT £123.56 TOTE £5.90: £1.60, £2.10, £2.20; EX 22.40 Trifecta £71.60.
Owner The Smart Inagh River Partnership **Bred** Glebe Farm Stud **Trained** Hambleton, N Yorks

FOCUS
Moderate sprinting form, possibly worth slightly more.

4229 MALCOLM GREENSLADE DONCASTER LVA STALWART MEMORIAL H'CAP (DIV II) 5f
3:25 (3:25) (Class 6) (0-60,60) 3-Y-0+ **£2,587** (£770; £384; £192) **Stalls** Low

Form RPR

0634 **1** **Noah Amor (IRE)**[13] 3773 3-9-3 **58**.... BarryMcHugh 8 67
(David Nicholls) *trckd ldrs: hdwy 2f out: led over 1f out: sn rdn: edgd lft ins fnl f: drvn out* **9/2**[3]

-600 **2** 1 ¾ **Classic Flyer**[26] 3307 4-9-10 **60**....(b[1]) DanielTudhope 5 65
(David O'Meara) *hld up in tch: hdwy wl over 1f out: rdn to chse wnr and swtchd rt ins fnl f: sn drvn and no imp towards fin* **7/2**[1]

06-0 **3** ¾ **Euxton**[66] 2053 4-9-1 **56**.... JordanNason[(5)] 1 58
(Lawrence Mullaney) *towards rr: hdwy on inner 2f out: swtchd lft wl over 1f out and sn rdn: styd on wl fnl f* **4/1**[2]

0000 **4** 4 ½ **George Bailey (IRE)**[34] 3009 4-9-0 **50**.... TomEaves 7 36
(Suzzanne France) *towards rr: rdn along wl over 1f out: kpt on fnl f* **20/1**

0000 **5** 1 ¼ **Steel City Boy (IRE)**[14] 3734 13-8-3 **46** oh1.... RPWalsh[(7)] 9 27
(Shaun Harris) *a towards rr* **66/1**

0-50 **6** 1 ½ **Midnight Robbery**[24] 3423 3-9-0 **55**.... PaulMulrennan 4 29
(Bryan Smart) *t.k.h: cl up: disp ld 1/2-way: rdn wl over 1f out: sn wknd* **11/2**

0-04 **7** ¾ **Zebelini (IRE)**[21] 3484 4-8-8 **51**....(b) RobertDodsworth[(7)] 3 24
(Ollie Pears) *slt ld: pushed along 2f out: sn rdn and hdd over 1f out: grad wknd* **9/2**[3]

-054 **8** 8 **Nefetari**[34] 3009 3-8-5 **46** oh1....(p) JimmyQuinn 2
(Alan Brown) *chsd ldng pair on inner: rdn along wl over 1f out: sn wknd* **9/1**

-040 **9** 1 ½ **Showbizzy**[15] 3725 3-9-2 **57**....(p) TonyHamilton 6
(Richard Fahey) *prom: effrt 2f out and cl up: sn rdn and wknd over 1f out* **14/1**

1m 2.69s (-0.81) **Going Correction** -0.125s/f (Firm)
WFA 3 from 4yo+ 5lb **9** Ran SP% **116.9**
Speed ratings (Par 101): **101,98,97,89,87 85,84,71,69**
CSF £20.94 CT £68.81 TOTE £5.90: £1.90, £1.70, £1.70; EX 18.70 Trifecta £94.30.
Owner Middleham Park Racing Xiv **Bred** Mrs Claire Doyle **Trained** Sessay, N Yorks

FOCUS
There was a disputed gallop here and that set things up for those in behind. It was the quicker of the two divisions by 0.39sec. The winner took advantage of a good mark.

4230 131ST YEAR OF THE WATT MEMORIAL H'CAP 2m 35y
4:00 (4:00) (Class 4) (0-85,85) 3-Y-0+
£6,225 (£1,864; £932; £466; £233; £117) **Stalls** Low

Form RPR

212 **1** **St Michel**[13] 3768 3-8-0 **76**.... RyanPowell 2 92+
(Sir Mark Prescott Bt) *trckd ldrs: hdwy to ld wl over 2f out: pushed clr wl over 1f out: easily* **8/15**[1]

-632 **2** 7 **Arrowtown**[11] 3844 4-9-2 **73**.... GrahamGibbons 4 81+
(Michael Easterby) *trckd ldng pair on inner: hdwy over 3f out: swtchd lft over 2f out and sn chsng wnr: rdn wl over 1f out: sn drvn and no imp* **7/1**[2]

0540 **3** 1 ¼ **Gabrial's Star**[17] 3657 7-9-9 **85**....(b) AdamMcNamara[(5)] 7 90
(Richard Fahey) *t.k.h: hld up: hdwy over 3f out: rdn to chse ldrs wl over 1f out: sn drvn and kpt on one pce* **12/1**[3]

3005 **4** ½ **Full Day**[16] 3690 5-9-6 **77**....(p) BenCurtis 5 81
(Brian Ellison) *trckd ldr: hdwy and cl up 3f out: sn rdn along: drvn wl over 1f out: kpt on one pce* **16/1**

530- **5** 1 ¼ **Awaywiththegreys (IRE)**[114] 6082 9-9-7 **85**....(p) JoshuaBryan[(7)] 1 87
(Peter Bowen) *dwlt: hld up in tch: effrt over 3f out: rdn along over 2f out: sn drvn and n.d* **14/1**

-003 **6** ¾ **Daghash**[36] 2971 7-9-5 **76**.... BarryMcHugh 8 78
(Stuart Kittow) *hld up in rr: effrt and sme hdwy over 3f out: rdn along over 2f out: n.d* **12/1**[3]

-230 **7** 31 **Street Artist (IRE)**[17] 3660 6-10-0 **85**.... JoeFanning 6 49
(David Nicholls) *set stdy pce: pushed along over 3f out: hdd wl over 2f out and sn wknd* **20/1**

3m 33.5s (-6.30) **Going Correction** -0.25s/f (Firm)
WFA 3 from 4yo+ 19lb **7** Ran SP% **110.4**
Speed ratings (Par 105): **105,101,100,100,100 99,84**
CSF £4.32 CT £18.52 TOTE £1.50: £1.10, £3.60; EX 4.80 Trifecta £18.00.
Owner J L C Pearce **Bred** J L C Pearce **Trained** Newmarket, Suffolk

FOCUS
This proved pretty uncompetitive, the winner taking full advantage of a generous weight-for-age allowance, and from a runner-up who herself looks nicely ahead of her mark. The first two were both eased slightly.

4231 RACING UK IN GLORIOUS HD H'CAP 7f 100y
4:30 (4:31) (Class 5) (0-75,74) 3-Y-0+ **£3,780** (£1,131; £565; £283; £141) **Stalls** Low

Form RPR

3230 **1** **Sovereign Bounty**[20] 3517 4-9-11 **72**.... GrahamLee 1 80
(Jedd O'Keeffe) *trckd ldrs: hdwy over 2f out: rdn ent fnl f: styd on wl to ld last 50yds* **9/2**[3]

6132 **2** ¾ **Shamaheart (IRE)**[15] 3708 6-9-13 **74**....(p) PaulMulrennan 8 80
(Geoffrey Harker) *hld up in rr: hdwy whn n.m.r room and swtchd lft over 1f out: swtchd rt and rdn ins fnl f: styd on strly towards fin* **9/1**

4022 **3** ¾ **Relight My Fire**[11] 3840 6-9-7 **68**....(p) DavidAllan 6 72
(Tim Easterby) *trckd ldrs: hdwy over 3f out: chsd ldr wl over 2f out: rdn over 1f out: drvn to chal ins fnl f: ev ch tl no ex last 50yds* **4/1**[2]

3060 **4** 1 ¼ **Sophisticated Heir (IRE)**[12] 3807 6-9-13 **74**....(b) SamJames 4 75
(David Loughnane) *led and sn clr: rdn over 1f out: drvn ins fnl f: hdd & wknd last 50yds* **8/1**

6613 **5** 2 **Like No Other**[12] 3807 3-9-3 **72**.... JasonHart 7 65
(Les Eyre) *chsd ldrs: rdn along wl over 1f out: sn drvn and no imp fnl f* **10/1**

1312 **6** *shd* **Qaffaal (USA)**[20] 3517 5-9-13 **74**.... GrahamGibbons 2 70
(Michael Easterby) *in tch: effrt and sme hdwy wl over 2f out: sn rdn along and n.d* **11/4**[1]

4442 **7** ½ **Tanawar (IRE)**[6] 4005 6-9-2 **63**....(b) JamesSullivan 9 57
(Ruth Carr) *hld up towards rr: effrt whn n.m.r and swtchd lft to outer wl over 1f out: sn rdn and n.d* **11/2**

4302 **8** ¾ **Talent Scout (IRE)**[11] 3838 10-9-1 **67**.... GemmaTutty[(5)] 5 60
(Karen Tutty) *chsd clr ldr: tk clsr order over 3f out: rdn along over 2f out: wknd wl over 1f out* **20/1**

5-00 **9** 4 ½ **Perfectly Fair**[13] 3776 3-8-5 **60**....[1] DuranFentiman 3 38
(Simon West) *dwlt and bmpd s: a in rr* **80/1**

1m 31.41s (-2.39) **Going Correction** -0.25s/f (Firm)
WFA 3 from 4yo+ 8lb **9** Ran SP% **116.4**
Speed ratings (Par 103): **103,102,101,99,97 97,96,96,90**
CSF £44.81 CT £176.72 TOTE £5.40: £1.60, £2.60, £1.70; EX 49.50 Trifecta £276.90.
Owner Caron & Paul Chapman **Bred** West Dereham Abbey Stud **Trained** Middleham Moor, N Yorks

FOCUS
A fair handicap run at a good pace. The first two ran pbs.

4232 IRISHBIGRACETRENDS.COM H'CAP 1m 100y
5:05 (5:05) (Class 4) (0-80,78) 3-Y-0+ **£5,040** (£1,508; £754; £377; £188) **Stalls** Low

Form RPR

0451 **1** **Final**[21] 3481 4-9-12 **76**.... JoeFanning 1 83+
(Mark Johnston) *hld up in tch: hdwy on outer over 2f out: rdn over 1f out: drvn to chse ldr and edgd rt ins fnl f: kpt on wl to ld nr fin* **11/4**[2]

6121 **2** *nk* **Planetaria (IRE)**[27] 3285 3-9-2 **75**.... DavidAllan 5 79
(Garry Moss) *led: rdn along and qcknd 2f out: drvn ins fnl f: hdd and no ex nr fin* **15/8**[1]

-000 **3** 2 **Homeland (IRE)**[20] 3517 4-9-9 **73**.... JamesSullivan 4 74
(Brian Rothwell) *trckd ldng pair on inner: hdwy over 2f out: swtchd lft and rdn wl over 1f out: kpt on same pce fnl f* **25/1**

104 **4** *hd* **Dutch Artist (IRE)**[34] 3011 4-10-0 **78**.... DanielTudhope 6 80
(David O'Meara) *trckd ldr: pushed along over 2f out: rdn wl over 1f out: drvn and nt myuch room jst ins fnl f: kpt on same pce* **7/2**[3]

22-1 **5** 1 ¾ **Billy Bond**[180] 179 4-9-9 **73**....(v) TonyHamilton 7 70
(Richard Fahey) *trckd ldrs: rdn along over 2f out: sn drvn and wknd over 1f out* **16/1**

5061 **6** ¾ **Janaab (IRE)**[12] 3807 6-9-2 **69**....(t) RachelRichardson[(3)] 3 64
(Tim Easterby) *hld up: hdwy over 2f out: rdn along wl over 1f out: drvn and no imp ent fnl f* **9/1**

4-26 **7** 1 ¾ **Rocket Ronnie (IRE)**[18] 3612 6-9-9 **73**.... DaleSwift 2 64
(Ed McMahon) *stdd s and hld up: hdwy on inner wl over 1f out: sn rdn and n.d* **8/1**

1m 46.35s (-1.25) **Going Correction** -0.25s/f (Firm)
WFA 3 from 4yo+ 9lb **7** Ran SP% **114.5**
Speed ratings (Par 105): **96,95,93,93,91 91,89**
CSF £8.37 TOTE £3.50: £1.70, £1.90; EX 10.30 Trifecta £100.90.
Owner C H Greensit & W A Greensit **Bred** C H And W A Greensit **Trained** Middleham Moor, N Yorks

FOCUS
Bar the winner, this was not a race in which the positions changed much. The third may limit the form.

4233 RACING UK ON SKY 432 H'CAP 1m 1f 207y
5:35 (5:36) (Class 6) (0-65,64) 3-Y-O **£2,587** (£770; £384; £192) **Stalls** Low

Form RPR

0221 **1** **Toffee Apple (IRE)**[3] 4144 3-8-8 **51** 6ex.... JoeyHaynes 1 57
(Keith Dalgleish) *trckd ldrs: hdwy 2f out: rdn to chse ldr over 1f out: drvn ins fnl f: styd on wl to ld towards fin* **1/1**[1]

3-20 **2** 1 **Signed And Sealed**[17] 3652 3-9-7 **64**.... JoeFanning 6 68
(Mark Johnston) *led: rdn wl over 1f out: drvn ins fnl f: hdd and no ex towards fin* **6/1**[3]

0041 **3** 1 ¾ **High On Light**[9] 3921 3-8-11 **54** 6ex.... DavidAllan 10 55
(Tim Easterby) *hld up towards rr: hdwy over 2f out: rdn and n.m.r over 1f out: drvn and kpt on fnl f* **3/1**[2]

4506 **4** 1 ½ **Canny Style**[27] 3289 3-8-13 **56**.... TomEaves 7 54
(Kevin Ryan) *hld up in rr: hdwy over 2f out: n.m.r and swtchd rt to inner over 1f out: sn rdn: kpt on fnl f* **20/1**

0040 **5** ½ **Jon H The Lawman (IRE)**[34] 3015 3-8-2 **45**.... JimmyQuinn 5 42
(Ronald Thompson) *in tch: hdwy to chse ldrs wl over 2f out: rdn wl over 1f out: drvn over 1f out: kpt on same pce* **33/1**

4456 **6** 1 **Rubis**[48] 2576 3-8-12 **55**.... TonyHamilton 4 50
(Richard Fahey) *in tch: pushed along wl over 2f out: rdn wl over 1f out: kpt on same pce* **12/1**

0-00 **7** 3 ¾ **File Of Facts (IRE)**[87] 1486 3-9-2 **59**....(vt[1]) RichardKingscote 2 47
(Tom Dascombe) *prom: rdn along on inner over 2f out: wkng whn n.m.r and hmpd over 1f out* **25/1**

-600 **8** *nk* **Heaven Scent**[7] 3983 3-8-12 **62**....(p) RowanScott[(7)] 9 49
(Ann Duffield) *chsd ldr: rdn along over 2f out: sn drvn and wknd* **20/1**

00-0 **9** *68* **Incus**[49] 2557 3-8-2 **45**.......... RyanPowell 8
(Ed de Giles) *a in rr: rdn along 4f out: sn outpcd and bhd whn eased fnl 2f* **28/1**

2m 5.04s (-1.96) **Going Correction** -0.25s/f (Firm) **9** Ran SP% **116.7**
Speed ratings (Par 98): **97,96,94,93,93 92,89,89,34**
CSF £6.86 CT £14.38 TOTE £2.00: £1.02, £2.30, £1.20; EX 7.80 Trifecta £15.30.
Owner Ronnie Docherty **Bred** Ms Sinead Maher **Trained** Carluke, S Lanarks

FOCUS
A moderate affair but sound enough form for the level. The winner was well in.

4234 DOROTHY LAIRD MEMORIAL TROPHY (PRO-AM LADIES RIDERS' H'CAP) 1m 1f 207y
6:05 (6:11) (Class 6) (0-65,65) 4-Y-O+ **£2,587** (£770; £384; £192) **Stalls** Low

Form RPR

4455 **1** **San Cassiano (IRE)**[13] 3774 9-10-2 **60**..........(b) MissSBrotherton 7 67
(Ruth Carr) *chsd ldr: led 1/2-way: clr over 3f out: rdn over 1f out: jst hld on* **7/2**[1]

4060 **2** *hd* **Attain**[25] 3354 7-9-12 **56**.......... ShelleyBirkett 14 63
(Julia Feilden) *hld up in rr: hdwy over 2f out: chsd ldrs and n.m.r over 1f out: sn swtchd lft and rdn: styd on to chse wnr ins fnl f: fin strly: jst failed* **9/1**

0560 **3** *2* **I'm Super Too (IRE)**[21] 3479 9-9-10 **54**.......... GemmaTutty 13 57
(Karen Tutty) *hld up in midfield: hdwy on inner 3f out: chsd ldrs wl over 1f out: sn rdn: drvn and kpt on same pce fnl f* **12/1**

-664 **4** *hd* **Jersey Jewel (FR)**[17] 3642 4-10-2 **65**.......... MissCAGreenway(5) 2 67
(Tom Dascombe) *prom: hdwy to chse wnr over 2f out: rdn wl over 1f out: drvn and kpt on same pce fnl f* **10/1**

506/ **5** *1 3/4* **Pevensey (IRE)**[65] 2892 14-10-2 **60**.......... MissCWalton 8 59
(Jacqueline Coward) *bhd: hdwy over 2f out: rdn wl over 1f out: styd on fnl f: nrst fin* **28/1**

-065 **6** *3/4* **L'Es Fremantle (FR)**[10] 3896 5-9-2 **46** oh1.......... AliceMills 3 44
(Michael Chapman) *in tch: hdwy to chse ldng pair 1/2-way: rdn to chse wnr 3f out: sn rdn: drvn wl over 1f out: grad wknd* **80/1**

3140 **7** *2 1/4* **Celtic Artisan (IRE)**[33] 982 5-9-10 **54**..........(bt) DanielleMooney 12 47
(Rebecca Menzies) *in tch: pushed along over 3f out: sn rdn and outpcd wl over 2f out: styd on u.p appr fnl f* **25/1**

0232 **8** *2* **Sakhalin Star (IRE)**[18] 3599 5-10-7 **65**..........(e) MissJoannaMason 15 55
(Richard Guest) *hld up towards rr: hdwy on wd outside wl over 2f out: sn rdn along and n.d* **5/1**[2]

2124 **9** *1/2* **Engai (GER)**[10] 3901 10-9-11 **60**.......... MissPBridgwater(5) 6 49
(David Bridgwater) *towards rr tl sme late hdwy* **5/1**[2]

2000 **10** *2 1/2* **Rainford Glory (IRE)**[26] 3325 6-9-6 **55**..........(p) MissHDukes(5) 4 39
(Tim Fitzgerald) *in tch: hdwy to chse ldrs over 3f out: rdn along over 2f out: sn drvn and no imp* **12/1**

-000 **11** *nk* **Belle Peinture (FR)**[13] 3774 5-8-11 **46** oh1.....(b) MissEmilyBullock(5) 11 29
(Alan Lockwood) *a towards rr* **80/1**

5660 **12** *8* **General Tufto**[18] 3620 11-9-2 **46** oh1..........(b) JennyPowell 5 14
(Charles Smith) *a towards rr* **100/1**

2600 **13** *hd* **Pipers Piping (IRE)**[15] 3731 10-9-5 **49**.......... EvaMoscrop 9 17
(Mandy Rowland) *chsd ldrs: rdn along wl over 2f out: sn drvn and wknd* **28/1**

3104 **14** *3 1/2* **Dark Diamond (IRE)**[9] 3118 6-10-4 **62**..........(b) AnnaHesketh 1 23
(Michael Chapman) *led: hdd 1/2-way: chsd wnr: rdn along over 3f out: drvn wl over 2f out and sn wknd* **6/1**[3]

2m 4.97s (-2.03) **Going Correction** -0.25s/f (Firm) **14** Ran SP% **118.5**
Speed ratings (Par 101): **98,97,96,96,94 94,92,90,90,88 88,81,81,78**
CSF £33.41 CT £345.62 TOTE £4.60: £1.70, £3.50, £4.10; EX 33.70 Trifecta £720.80.
Owner S Jackson, L Shaw, Mrs R Carr **Bred** Peter Savill **Trained** Huby, N Yorks

FOCUS
This was a well-run handicap.
T/Jkpt: £10,0000 to a £1 stake. Pool of £10,000 - 1 winning unit. T/Plt: £8.70 to a £1 stake. Pool of £68959.17 - 5723.80 winning tickets. T/Qpdt: £4.90 to a £1 stake. Pool of £5733.02 - 849.84 winning tickets. **Joe Rowntree**

3261 THIRSK (L-H)
Tuesday, July 12

OFFICIAL GOING: Good (good to firm in places; 8.3)
Wind: light 1/2 behind Weather: overcast

4235 STUART PAILOR MEMORIAL APPRENTICE MAIDEN STKS 1m
6:10 (6:16) (Class 5) 3-Y-O+ **£3,234** (£962; £481; £240) **Stalls** Low

Form RPR

03 **1** **St Mary'S**[16] 3684 3-9-0 0.......... EdwardGreatrex 9 79
(Andrew Balding) *trckd ldrs: 2nd over 2f out: carried lft last 150yds: styd on to ld post* **16/1**

52-5 **2** *shd* **Ballet Concerto**[92] 1386 3-9-5 86.......... KevinStott 6 84
(Sir Michael Stoute) *led: drvn over 2f out: hung bdly rt 150yds out: hdd post* **1/1**[1]

3 *5* **La Contessa (IRE)** 3-8-9 0.......... AdamMcNamara(5) 3 67+
(Richard Fahey) *dwlt in rr: hdwy and wnt lft 2f out: kpt on to take modest 3rd nr fin* **12/1**

323 **4** *3/4* **Sehayli (IRE)**[34] 3014 3-9-0 81.......... GeorgiaCox(5) 11 70
(William Haggas) *stmbld s: sn trcking ldrs on outer: 3rd over 1f out: kpt on one pce* **3/1**[2]

4-0 **5** *nse* **Colour Play (USA)**[13] 3769 3-9-0 0.......... LouisSteward 5 65
(Mark Johnston) *in rr: hdwy over 2f out: styd on fnl f* **25/1**

6 *2* **Percy Verence** 3-9-2 0.......... JordanVaughan(3) 7 65
(K R Burke) *towards rr: hdwy over 2f out: chsng ldrs over 1f out: one pce* **33/1**

06 **7** *3/4* **Hightime Girl**[8] 3951 3-8-7 0..........(t) CameronNoble(7) 10 58
(David Loughnane) *wnt rt s: in rr: drvn 4f out: hung rt and kpt on fnl 2f: nvr a factor* **150/1**

602- **8** *3 1/4* **Frankster (FR)**[267] 7337 3-9-2 77..........[1] CallumShepherd(3) 4 56
(Micky Hammond) *t.k.h: trckd ldr: wknd over 1f out* **9/1**

02 **9** *2 1/2* **Western Way (IRE)**[19] 3577 7-9-7 0.......... DavidEgan(7) 13 52+
(Don Cantillon) *s.i.s: swtchd lft after s: in rr: hdwy on outer over 2f out: hung lft: nvr a factor* **8/1**[3]

0 **10** *1 3/4* **Culturehull**[17] 3643 3-8-7 0.......... CliffordLee(7) 8 40
(Les Eyre) *chsd ldrs: drvn 3f out: lost pl over 1f out* **150/1**

06 **11** *2 1/2* **Adrakhan (FR)**[10] 3886 5-10-0 0.......... MissEmmaSayer 12 41
(Wilf Storey) *mid-div on outer: drvn 3f out: wknd 2f out* **200/1**

00 **12** *3/4* **Percy's Endeavour**[38] 2914 3-8-11 0.......... PhilDennis(3) 1 33
(Mark Walford) *s.i.s: sn in mid-div: lost pl 2f out* **125/1**

0-0 **13** *3 1/4* **Lady Chara**[28] 3249 3-9-0 0.......... JacobButterfield 2 25
(Ann Duffield) *mid-div: lost pl over 2f out* **100/1**

1m 42.5s (2.40) **Going Correction** +0.125s/f (Good)
WFA 3 from 5yo+ 9lb **13** Ran SP% **120.1**
Speed ratings (Par 103): **93,92,87,87,87 85,84,81,78,76 74,73,70**
CSF £32.61 TOTE £20.10: £4.60, £1.10, £3.30; EX 47.50 Trifecta £362.10.
Owner Kingsclere Racing Club **Bred** Kingsclere Stud **Trained** Kingsclere, Hants
■ Stewards' Enquiry : Kevin Stott caution; careless riding

FOCUS
Home bend dolled out by approximately 6yds, adding approximately 20yds to the standard distances for all races of 7f and upwards. The apprentices riding in the opener generally reckoned the ground was good. It paid to be handy in this uncompetitive maiden and the first pair drew well clear. The winner was a big improver but the time was ordinary.

4236 OPEN GOLF BETTING AT 188BET (S) STKS 5f
6:40 (6:42) (Class 6) 3-5-Y-O **£2,587** (£770; £384; £192) **Stalls** High

Form RPR

530 **1** **Jaarih (IRE)**[24] 3407 4-9-11 72..........(p) PaulMulrennan 4 72
(Conor Dore) *carried sltly rt s: trckd ldrs: t.k.h: effrt over 1f out: led last 100yds: kpt rt up to work towards fin* **1/1**[1]

4125 **2** *nk* **Roaring Rory**[34] 3009 3-9-3 67..........(p) JacobButterfield(3) 3 69
(Ollie Pears) *wnt sltly rt s: led: hdd last 100yds: rallied nr fin: jst hld* **5/2**[2]

5441 **3** *2 3/4* **Birrafun (IRE)**[111] 1045 3-9-1 56.......... PJMcDonald 2 54
(Ann Duffield) *w ldr: drvn over 1f out: edgd lft: kpt on one pce* **17/2**

00 **4** *nk* **Camanche Grey (IRE)**[78] 1709 5-9-5 56.......... GrahamLee 1 54
(Ben Haslam) *chsd ldrs: drvn over 2f out: one pce over 1f out* **7/1**[3]

0106 **5** *shd* **I T Guru**[6] 4007 3-9-6 59..........(t) BarryMcHugh 6 58
(Noel Wilson) *sltly hmpd s: in rr: hdwy over 2f out: chsng ldrs over 1f out: one pce* **14/1**

63- **6** *25* **Milu Mac**[347] 4840 5-9-0 0.......... DuranFentiman 5
(Neville Bycroft) *hood removed v late: s.s: detached in last: t.o fnl 2f* **33/1**

58.64s (-0.96) **Going Correction** -0.20s/f (Firm)
WFA 3 from 4yo+ 5lb **6** Ran SP% **111.2**
Speed ratings (Par 101): **99,98,94,93,93 53**
CSF £3.58 TOTE £1.60: £1.20, £1.50; EX 4.10 Trifecta £11.10.There was no bid for the winner.
Owner Chris Marsh **Bred** Dean Harron & Ciaran Conroy **Trained** Hubbert's Bridge, Lincs
■ Stewards' Enquiry : Jacob Butterfield caution; careless riding

FOCUS
A typically moderate seller. The winner didn't need to run right to his best.

4237 WEATHERBYS HAMILTON H'CAP 1m 4f
7:10 (7:11) (Class 5) (0-75,73) 3-Y-O+ **£3,234** (£962; £481; £240) **Stalls** High

Form RPR

0-05 **1** **Carthage (IRE)**[17] 3660 5-9-10 **73**.......... BenCurtis 3 79
(Brian Ellison) *dwlt: in rr: effrt over 3f out: chsng ldrs 2f out: led appr fnl f: edgd lft and kpt on towards fin* **7/1**

-000 **2** *nk* **Correggio**[15] 3711 6-9-7 **70**.......... JackGarritty 1 75
(Micky Hammond) *trckd ldrs: t.k.h: hmpd bnd after 3f: effrt over 3f out: chsng ldrs over 1f out: crowded and no ex nr fin* **9/1**

236 **3** *1 1/4* **Comanche Chieftain (CAN)**[53] 2445 4-9-4 **67**..........(p) AndrewMullen 6 71
(Michael Appleby) *led: hdd over 1f out: one pce whn bdly hmpd in clsng stages* **8/1**

0615 **4** *nk* **The Kid**[14] 3751 5-9-10 **73**..........(p) DougieCostello 5 76
(John Quinn) *hld up: effrt on ins over 3f out: n.m.r over 1f out: kpt on same pce* **6/1**[3]

-313 **5** *2 1/2* **Tourtiere**[27] 3294 8-8-12 **68**.......... HollieDoyle(7) 7 67
(Andrew Crook) *trckd ldr: led briefly over 1f out: fdd last 150yds* **11/4**[2]

6255 **6** *3/4* **Medina Sidonia (IRE)**[32] 3118 4-9-6 **72**..........(p) RachelRichardson(3) 4 69
(Tim Easterby) *chsd ldrs: one pce whn nt clr run appr fnl f: one pce* **2/1**[1]

0-0P **7** *1 1/2* **Kisumu**[15] 3711 4-9-2 **65**.......... PJMcDonald 2 60
(Micky Hammond) *s.i.s: in rr: hdwy over 8f out: chsng ldrs 2f out: fdd fnl f* **20/1**

2m 37.74s (1.54) **Going Correction** +0.125s/f (Good) **7** Ran SP% **112.7**
Speed ratings (Par 103): **99,98,97,97,96 95,94**
CSF £63.61 TOTE £7.10: £3.10, £5.30; EX 79.10 Trifecta £647.50.
Owner David Foster **Bred** Pitrizzia Partnership **Trained** Norton, N Yorks

FOCUS
Race run over 20 yards further than advertised. This modest handicap saw a messy finish due to an uneven pace. It's rated around the third.

4238 £25 FREE BET AT 188BET MAIDEN STKS 5f
7:40 (7:41) (Class 5) 3-4-Y-O **£3,234** (£962; £481; £240) **Stalls** High

Form RPR

-4 **1** **L C Saloon**[17] 3643 3-9-5 0.......... DavidAllan 1 78+
(David C Griffiths) *swtchd rt s: chsd ldr: led over 1f out: kpt on wl* **9/2**[2]

22-2 **2** *1 1/4* **Sirajiah (IRE)**[39] 2848 3-9-0 75.......... BenCurtis 11 68
(William Haggas) *led: hdd over 1f out: kpt on same pce* **5/6**[1]

0 **3** *1 1/2* **Shesthedream (IRE)**[38] 2886 3-9-0 0.......... DanielTudhope 9 63
(David O'Meara) *chsd ldrs: kpt on same pce fnl f* **16/1**

0 **4** *3/4* **Website**[46] 2667 4-9-10 75.......... JoeFanning 10 67
(Robert Cowell) *in rr and sn pushed along: hdwy over 1f out: styng on at fin* **14/1**[3]

63 **5** *1 1/2* **Princess Momoka**[38] 2886 3-9-0 0.......... JackMitchell 8 55+
(Roger Varian) *n.m.r sn after s: in rr: hdwy over 1f out: kpt on* **9/2**[2]

0 **6** *nk* **Vale Of Flight (IRE)**[38] 2886 3-9-0 0.......... GrahamLee 7 54+
(Rae Guest) *in rr: kpt on fnl 2f: nvr a factor* **22/1**

0-06 **7** *hd* **Our Place In Loule**[8] 3940 3-9-5 55.......... PatrickMathers 4 58
(Noel Wilson) *mid-div: drvn over 2f out: one pce* **100/1**

-660 **8** *1 3/4* **Qortaaj**[8] 3948 3-9-5 68.......... SamJames 2 52
(David Loughnane) *prom on outside: drvn and lost pl over 2f out: kpt on in clsng stages* **20/1**

3-25 **9** *1 1/2* **K'Gari Spirit**[17] 3669 3-9-0 0.......... NickyMackay 12 41
(Jeremy Gask) *chsd ldrs: lost pl over 1f out* **25/1**

00 **10** *3* **Lord Bopper (IRE)**[28] 3267 3-9-0 0.......... RobJFitzpatrick(5) 3 36
(Ben Haslam) *chsd ldrs on outside: drvn over 2f out: hung lft and sn lost pl* **125/1**

00-0 **11** *1/2* **Sunnyhills Belford**[34] 3014 3-9-0 45..........(b[1]) BarryMcHugh 6 29
(Noel Wilson) *mid-div: lost pl over 1f out: eased* **150/1**

58.19s (-1.41) **Going Correction** -0.20s/f (Firm)
WFA 3 from 4yo 5lb **11** Ran SP% **118.9**
Speed ratings (Par 103): **103,101,98,97,95 94,94,91,89,84 83**
CSF £8.32 TOTE £5.60: £1.80, £1.10, £4.50; EX 11.80 Trifecta £84.60.
Owner Clark Industrial Services Partnership **Bred** Usk Valley Stud **Trained** Bawtry, S Yorks

FOCUS
This wasn't a bad sprint maiden, with pbs from the winner and third.

4239 ANDERSON BARROWCLIFF CHARTERED ACCOUNTANTS H'CAP 2m
8:10 (8:10) (Class 5) (0-70,73) 4-Y-O+ **£3,234** (£962; £481; £240) **Stalls** Centre

Form RPR

-231 **1** **Ingleby Hollow**[8] 3942 4-9-10 **73** 6ex..........................(p) DanielTudhope 5 81
(David O'Meara) *racd wd early: led after 3f: sn stdd pce: increased gallop over 3f out: shkn up over 1f out: edgd lft: drvn out* **2/1**[1]

2022 **2** *1 1/2* **Wishing Well**[27] 3294 4-9-4 **67**.......................... PJMcDonald 3 72
(Micky Hammond) *hld up in rr: effrt over 3f out: chsd wnr over 1f out: swtchd rt 100yds out: kpt on same pce* **7/1**

06-6 **3** *shd* **Rocktherunway (IRE)**[79] 1665 7-9-7 **70**..................(p) ConnorBeasley 7 75
(Michael Dods) *hld up towards rr: hdwy over 7f out: chsng ldrs over 3f out: kpt on same pce fnl f* **7/2**[2]

0-26 **4** *4* **Exclusive Contract (IRE)**[43] 2745 5-8-10 **62**......... JacobButterfield(3) 1 62
(Ollie Pears) *sn hld up in rr: hdwy over 7f out: chsng ldrs over 5f out: chsd wnr over 3f out: fdd fnl f* **13/2**

1113 **5** *7* **Moonshine Ridge (IRE)**[78] 1711 5-9-7 **70**......................... JoeFanning 6 62
(Alan Swinbank) *dwlt: hld up in rr: effrt over 3f out: wknd wl over 1f out* **5/1**[3]

53-4 **6** *1 1/4* **Oliver's Gold**[16] 3325 8-8-2 **51** oh3..............................(p) DuranFentiman 2 41
(Mark Walford) *sn led: hdd after 3f: drvn over 3f out: lost pl over 1f out* **8/1**

430- **7** *14* **Rayadour (IRE)**[230] 7527 7-8-9 **58** ow2.............................. TomEaves 4 31
(Micky Hammond) *led early: chsd ldrs: drvn over 3f out: lost plaxce 2f out: eased whn bhd* **40/1**

3m 32.73s (4.43) **Going Correction** +0.125s/f (Good) **7** Ran SP% **111.6**
Speed ratings (Par 103): **93,92,92,90,86 86,79**
CSF £15.80 TOTE £2.60: £2.10, £3.50; EX 15.10 Trifecta £50.70.
Owner Dave Scott & The Fallen Angels **Bred** Dave Scott **Trained** Upper Helmsley, N Yorks

FOCUS
Race run over 20 yards further than advertised. They went a routine pace in this ordinary staying handicap, the winner dictating. The second ran to form.

4240 WEATHERBYS HAMILTON FILLIES' H'CAP 7f
8:40 (8:43) (Class 5) (0-70,68) 3-Y-O+ **£3,234** (£962; £481; £240) **Stalls** Low

Form RPR

2025 **1** **Cabal**[8] 3952 9-10-0 **68**...(v) DavidAllan 12 77
(Geoffrey Harker) *hld up towards rr: hdwy on outer over 2f out: styd on fnl f: led last 50yds* **17/2**

-343 **2** *1 1/4* **Courier**[28] 3262 4-9-9 **66**.. JacobButterfield(3) 9 72
(Marjorie Fife) *chsd ldrs: led over 1f out: hdd and no ex last 50yds* **5/1**[2]

1003 **3** *1 1/4* **Make On Madam (IRE)**[21] 3478 4-9-10 **64**.................. PaulMulrennan 1 67
(Les Eyre) *chsd ldrs: drvn over 2f out: kpt on same pce fnl 150yds* **8/1**

-005 **4** *1/2* **Lozah**[21] 3478 3-8-8 **56**...(tp) SamJames 10 54
(David Loughnane) *wnt rt s: in rr: hdwy on outside over 2f out: edgd lft and kpt on fnl f* **10/1**

3310 **5** *shd* **Colourfilly**[31] 3132 4-10-0 **68**...................................(p) RichardKingscote 5 69
(Tom Dascombe) *wnt rt s: chsd ldrs: effrt over 2f out: kpt on same pce over 1f out* **4/1**[1]

2344 **6** *3/4* **Mrs Biggs**[13] 3776 4-9-9 **63**..(t) DanielTudhope 11 62
(Declan Carroll) *hmpd s: in rr: hdwy over 2f out: one pce over 1f out* **13/2**[3]

40 **7** *3/4* **Isntshesomething**[21] 3479 4-8-11 **51**................................ JoeFanning 7 48
(Richard Guest) *trckd ldrs: effrt over 2f out: one pce over 1f out* **18/1**

2002 **8** *1 3/4* **Adiator**[6] 4006 8-8-9 **56**...(p) CliffordLee(7) 4 48
(Neville Bycroft) *in rr: hdwy over 2f out: one pce over 1f out* **17/2**

054- **9** *1* **Sugar Town**[231] 7969 6-8-9 **49**... TomEaves 8 39
(Peter Niven) *led: hdd over 1f out: wknd fnl 150yds* **14/1**

3530 **10** *4 1/2* **Excellent World (IRE)**[18] 3603 3-9-0 **62**........................ BarryMcHugh 2 36
(Tony Coyle) *t.k.h in rr: hdwy over 2f out: edgd rt over 1f out: wknd fnl 150yds: heavily eased towards fin* **14/1**

6260 **11** *2* **Comparinka**[33] 3069 3-8-5 **53**....................................(p) PatrickMathers 6 22
(Scott Dixon) *1/2 rrd and hmpd s: hdwy into mid-div over 4f out: lost pl over 1f out* **20/1**

0-03 **12** *6* **Rosie Hall (IRE)**[180] 175 6-8-9 **49** oh4..................(v[1]) RoystonFfrench 3 5
(John Wainwright) *mid-div: drvn over 3f out: lost pl 2f out: sn bhd* **80/1**

1m 27.38s (0.18) **Going Correction** +0.125s/f (Good)
WFA 3 from 4yo+ 8lb **12** Ran SP% **115.8**
Speed ratings (Par 100): **103,101,100,99,99 98,97,95,94,89 87,80**
CSF £49.42 CT £361.26 TOTE £7.70: £2.30, £2.40, £2.40; EX 62.40 Trifecta £287.30.
Owner Phil Harker & Dave Buist **Bred** Cheveley Park Stud Ltd **Trained** Thirkleby, N Yorks

FOCUS
Race run over 20 yards further than advertised. A wide-open looking fillies' handicap. They went a decent pace and the winner is rated back to her best.

4241 FREE SPINS AT 188BET CASINO H'CAP 1m
9:10 (9:10) (Class 5) (0-75,75) 3-Y-O **£3,234** (£962; £481; £240) **Stalls** Low

Form RPR

4-00 **1** **Tan Arabiq**[13] 3776 3-8-8 **62**.. AndrewMullen 6 66
(Michael Appleby) *trckd ldrs: t.k.h: drvn over 3f out: led over 1f out: hld on in clsng stages* **80/1**

-236 **2** *3/4* **Deansgate (IRE)**[28] 3252 3-9-4 **72**......................................(e) JoeDoyle 8 74
(Julie Camacho) *t.k.h on outer: hld up: hdwy over 3f out: styd on fnl f: jst hld* **8/1**[3]

634 **3** *shd* **Al Nasser Alwashik**[11] 3856 3-9-4 **72**................................ SamJames 7 74
(David Loughnane) *mid-div: effrt 3f out: chsng ldrs over 1f out: kpt on wl fnl 150yds: jst hld* **12/1**

0211 **4** *1/2* **Causey Arch (IRE)**[8] 3943 3-9-4 **72** 6ex....................(p) ConnorBeasley 1 73
(Michael Dods) *led after 1f: hdd over 1f out: kpt on same pce last 100yds* **11/4**[2]

5004 **5** *1/2* **Ronnie Baird**[19] 3567 3-9-5 **73**.......................................(b) TonyHamilton 5 72
(Kristin Stubbs) *s.i.s: hld up in rr: hdwy and swtchd rt over 1f out: styd on wl* **16/1**

3-65 **6** *hd* **Auxiliary**[13] 3775 3-9-7 **75**...(p) JackGarritty 4 74
(Patrick Holmes) *mid-div: nt clr run and swtchd rt over 1f out: kpt on same pce* **16/1**

-000 **7** *1 1/4* **Quoteline Direct**[29] 3224 3-9-0 **68**....................................... PJMcDonald 2 64
(Micky Hammond) *dwlt: in rr: hdwy over 2f out: nt clr run 1f out: kpt on same pce* **14/1**

-031 **8** *1/2* **Bluff Crag**[19] 3558 3-9-2 **73**.. EdwardGreatrex(3) 3 68
(Andrew Balding) *trckd ldrs: nt clr run on ins over 1f out: one pce* **13/8**[1]

4636 **9** *4* **Young Christian**[38] 2891 3-9-4 **72**.................................. JamesSullivan 9 57
(Tom Tate) *led 1f: chsd ldr: upsides over 2f out: wknd appr fnl f* **9/1**

1m 42.28s (2.18) **Going Correction** +0.125s/f (Good) **9** Ran SP% **113.2**
Speed ratings (Par 100): **94,93,93,92,92 91,90,90,86**
CSF £618.07 CT £8038.82 TOTE £58.00: £14.10, £2.10, £3.30; EX 351.60 Trifecta £2702.10 Part won..
Owner Sarnian Racing **Bred** Michael Appleby **Trained** Oakham, Rutland

FOCUS
Race run over 20 yards further than advertised. A modest 3yo handicap, run at a sound pace but they finished compressed and there are doubts.
T/Plt: £145.70 to a £1 stake. Pool of £58222.01 - 291.27 winning tickets. T/Qpdt: £70.50 to a £1 stake. Pool of £4641.06 - 48.69 winning tickets. **Walter Glynn**

4242 -4245a (Foreign Racing) - See Raceform Interactive

2381 DUNDALK (A.W) (L-H)
Tuesday, July 12

OFFICIAL GOING: Polytrack: standard

4246a MARSHES H'CAP 5f (P)
4:20 (4:23) 3-Y-O+ **£11,305** (£3,492; £1,654; £735; £275)

RPR

1 **Chiclet (IRE)**[16] 3696 5-9-4 **90**..[1] PatSmullen 5 103
(Tracey Collins, Ire) *mde all: gng wl over 1 l clr 2f out: extended advantage and rdn ins fnl f: styd on wl: comf* **7/2**[1]

2 *2 3/4* **Primo Uomo (IRE)**[12] 3828 4-7-11 **76** oh2...............(t) KillianLeonard(7) 6 79
(Gerard O'Leary, Ire) *chsd ldrs: gng wl under 2f out: rdn into 2nd ins fnl f and no imp on easy wnr: kpt on same pce* **11/1**

3 *nk* **Go Kart (IRE)**[12] 3828 3-8-3 **85**.................................... TomMadden(5) 11 85
(P J Prendergast, Ire) *settled bhd ldrs: tk clsr order on outer under 2f out: no imp on easy wnr u.p in 3rd wl ins fnl f: kpt on same pce* **16/1**

4 *hd* **Gentlemen**[27] 3279 5-9-7 **96**.................................... JosephineGordon(3) 9 97+
(Phil McEntee) *towards rr: pushed along fr 1/2-way and rdn under 2f out: r.o between horses fr over 1f out into nvr threatening 4th wl ins fnl f: nt trble easy wnr* **11/2**[2]

5 *nk* **Russian Soul (IRE)**[2] 4177 8-9-10 **103**..............(p) ConorMcGovern(7) 10 103+
(M Halford, Ire) *hld up: n.m.r briefly 1 1/2f out: sn rdn in 10th and kpt on u.p ins fnl f into nvr nrr 5th: nt trble easy wnr* **7/1**

6 *1/2* **Ostatnia (IRE)**[16] 3696 4-8-10 **82**.........................(v) DeclanMcDonogh 13 80+
(W McCreery, Ire) *towards rr: last 2f out: rdn and r.o fr over 1f out: nrst fin* **9/1**

7 *hd* **Golden Pearl**[40] 2839 3-8-11 **88**.. ShaneFoley 12 84+
(M Halford, Ire) *hld up: rdn in 12th 1 1/2f out and sme late hdwy u.p ins fnl f: nvr nrr* **14/1**

8 *1 1/4* **Blood Moon**[31] 3170 3-9-3 **94**..(b) ColinKeane 3 85
(G M Lyons, Ire) *chsd ldrs: rdn into 2nd briefly over 1f out: sn no ex and wknd qckly ins fnl f* **13/2**[3]

9 *nk* **Faineog (IRE)**[8] 3962 5-8-9 **81**... DannyGrant 1 73
(Mrs A M O'Shea, Ire) *chsd ldrs: pushed along in 4th fr 1/2-way and no imp on easy wnr far side ent fnl f: wknd ins fnl f* **33/1**

10 *1 1/4* **My Good Brother (IRE)**[38] 2922 7-8-4 **76** oh4..............(v) RoryCleary 2 64
(T G McCourt, Ire) *chsd ldrs and wnt 2nd bef 1/2-way: rdn in 2nd under 2f out and no imp on easy wnr 1 1/2f out: sn wknd* **25/1**

11 *nk* **Togoville (IRE)**[18] 3628 6-10-0 **100**................................(b) GaryCarroll 7 86
(Georgios Pakidis, Ire) *cl up in 2nd early tl dropped to 3rd bef 1/2-way: rdn fr 1/2-way and sn no ex: wknd over 1f out* **16/1**

12 *1 3/4* **Dikta Del Mar (SPA)**[16] 3696 4-9-0 **86**...........................(t) ChrisHayes 4 66
(T Hogan, Ire) *hld up: 9th bef 1/2-way: tk clsr order under 2f out: n.m.r and eased briefly ent fnl f: no imp after and wknd wl ins fnl f* **8/1**

13 *4 3/4* **Prince Connoisseur (IRE)**[24] 3425 5-8-4 **76** oh7......(b) NGMcCullagh 8 39
(John James Feane, Ire) *in tch: 5th bef 1/2-way: rdn and wknd qckly fr after 1/2-way* **25/1**

58.85s (58.85)
WFA 3 from 4yo+ 5lb **13** Ran SP% **121.9**
CSF £43.26 CT £577.12 TOTE £3.80: £1.60, £3.70, £4.70; DF 52.90 Trifecta £1366.50.
Owner Mrs A J Donnelly **Bred** Churchland Stud **Trained** The Curragh, Co Kildare

FOCUS
The winner had shown her prowess here before, but this was a career best performance by some margin. THE second and third are rated to par.

4247 - 4249a (Foreign Racing) - See Raceform Interactive

4216 KILLARNEY (L-H)
Tuesday, July 12

OFFICIAL GOING: Flat course - yielding (yielding to soft in places) ; nh course - good (good to yielding in places)

4250a CELTIC STEPS THE SHOW AT KILLARNEY RACECOURSE RATED RACE 1m 25y
6:20 (6:20) 3-Y-O+ **£7,687** (£2,375; £1,125; £500)

RPR

1 **Ruler Of France**[1] 4217 5-9-4 80.....................................(b) LeighRoche 1 86
(P Twomey, Ire) *led and sn clr: 15 l advantage 1/2-way: advantage reduced under 2f out: pressed in clsng stages: all out to hold on* **11/2**[3]

2 *shd* **Mr Right (IRE)**[19] 3587 4-9-7 88...................................... RonanWhelan 3 89+
(J F Levins, Ire) *hld up in mod 3rd: rdn to cl under 2f out: wnt 2nd 1f out: styd on wl to press ldr cl home: jst failed* **8/13**[1]

3 *2 3/4* **Reckless Lad (IRE)**[55] 2386 6-9-5 86.........................(tp) WayneLordan 4 81+
(Patrick Martin, Ire) *racd in rr: stl plenty to do 2f out: kpt on wl ins fnl f into 3rd cl home: nrst fin* **4/1**[2]

4 *1/2* **Hat Alnasar (IRE)**[17] 3676 4-9-2 93.....................(t) RobertSmithers(10) 2 87
(M Halford, Ire) *chsd clr ldr in 2nd: rdn over 3f out to take clsr order: dropped to 3rd 1f out: no ex fnl 100yds and dropped to 4th cl home* **6/1**

1m 44.54s (-5.86)
WFA 3 from 4yo+ 9lb **4** Ran SP% **111.6**
CSF £9.94 TOTE £5.20; DF 8.90 Trifecta £23.30.
Owner P Twomey **Bred** T J Cooper **Trained** Cashel, Co Tipperary

FOCUS
The late withdrawal of morning favourite \bGeneral Macarthur\p erased plenty of the intrigue from this. The winner got an enterprising ride from Leigh Roche who pinched a huge lead.

4251 - 4252a (Foreign Racing) - See Raceform Interactive

1907 HANOVER (L-H)
Tuesday, July 12

OFFICIAL GOING: Turf: good

4253a MAXIOS TROPHY (EX HAMBURG TROPHY) (GROUP 3) (3YO+) (TURF) 1m 2f
3:30 (12:00) 3-Y-O+ **£23,529** (£8,823; £4,411; £2,205; £1,470)

RPR
1 **Articus (FR)**[44] 2723 4-9-2 0 MarcLerner 8 109
(Waldemar Hickst, Germany) *w.w in midfield on outer: gd hdwy on outside over 2f out: led gp of two along stands' rail and sustained run: led fnl 100yds: drvn out: readily* **19/10**[2]
2 ½ **Quasillo (GER)**[422] 2315 4-9-0 0 EduardoPedroza 9 106
(A Wohler, Germany) *hld up in fnl trio: hdwy on outer over 2f out: chsd eventual wnr along stands' rail: r.o u.p fnl f: a jst hld* **4/5**[1]
3 1¼ **Incantator (GER)**[51] 4-9-4 0 JozefBojko 2 108
(A Wohler, Germany) *led: hdd after 3f and chsd ldr: rdn to chal over 1 1/2f out: led appr fnl f: styd on wl u.p: hdd 100yds out: no ex: led home gp of 7 on ins rail* **94/10**[3]
4 nk **Not So Sleepy**[24] 3383 4-9-2 0 AndreasSuborics 7 105
(Hughie Morrison) *half-rrd as gates opened: towards rr early: rushed up on outer to ld after 3f: sn 4 l clr: rdn whn pressed 1 1/2f out: rallied u.p: hdd appr 1f out: kpt on same pce* **183/10**
5 1 **Devastar (GER)**[44] 2723 4-9-0 0 AdriedeVries 6 101
(Markus Klug, Germany) *settled cl up: rdn to chse ldrs 1 1/2f out: kpt on at same pce fnl f* **94/10**[3]
6 1¾ **Palang (USA)**[23] 4-9-2 0 MichaelCadeddu 1 99
(Andreas Lowe, Germany) *w.w in midfield on inner: rdn and no real imp 2f out: kpt on at one pce fnl f* **167/10**
7 ½ **Rogue Runner (GER)**[23] 3455 4-9-2 0 DennisSchiergen 4 98
(P Schiergen, Germany) *w.w towards rr: outpcd and scrubbed along 5f out: hrd rdn and dropped to last 2f out: styd on again ins fnl f: nvr involved* **30/1**
8 1 **Vif Monsieur (GER)**[9] 3934 6-9-4 0 (p) KoenClijmans 3 98
(Mario Hofer, Germany) *sweated up: plld hrd and hld up in fnl pair: rdn and no imp over 2f out: plugged on at one pce: nvr in contention* **28/1**
9 nk **Anna Mia (GER)**[47] 4-8-10 0 FilipMinarik 5 90
(Melanie Sauer, Germany) *settled in tch: pushed along to hold pl 3f out: short-lived effrt 2f out: wknd fnl f* **123/10**

2m 6.66s (126.66) 9 Ran SP% **134.3**
WIN (incl. 10 euro stake): 29. PLACES: 10, 10, 11. SF: 67.
Owner Dr Christoph Berglar **Bred** C Berglar **Trained** Germany

4000 CATTERICK (L-H)
Wednesday, July 13

OFFICIAL GOING: Good to firm (9.1)
Wind: Moderate, against Weather: Cloudy with sunny periods

4254 BRITISH STALLION STUDS EBF FILLIES' NOVICE STKS (PLUS 10 RACE) 5f
2:05 (2:05) (Class 5) 2-Y-O **£3,234** (£962; £481; £240) **Stalls** Low

Form RPR
13 1 **Queen Kindly**[26] 3336 2-9-7 0 JamieSpencer 1 96+
(Richard Fahey) *trckd ldrs: hdwy on bit 2f out: led ent fnl f: v easily* **1/16**[1]
3 2 3½ **Jeany (IRE)**[11] 3874 2-9-0 0 JoeFanning 4 66
(Bryan Smart) *chsd ldr: rdn along 2f out: sn drvn: kpt on fnl f to take 2nd nr fin* **6/1**[2]
40 3 ¾ **Yorkshiredebut (IRE)**[33] 3112 2-9-0 0 PaulMulrennan 2 63
(Paul Midgley) *led: rdn along wl over 1f out: sn jnd: hdd ent fnl f: sn drvn and wknd: lost 2nd nr fin* **50/1**
3 4 7 **Nifty Niece (IRE)**[21] 3515 2-9-0 0 PJMcDonald 7 38
(Ann Duffield) *in tch: pushed along 1/2-way: sn rdn along and outpcd* **11/1**[3]
5 16 **Violet Mist (IRE)** 2-8-9 0 RobJFitzpatrick(5) 6
(Ben Haslam) *in tch early: green and pushed along bef 1/2-way: sn outpcd and bhd* **33/1**

59.39s (-0.41) **Going Correction** -0.225s/f (Firm) 5 Ran SP% **121.6**
Speed ratings (Par 91): **94,88,87,76,50**
CSF £1.74 TOTE £1.10: £1.10, £1.40; EX 1.60 Trifecta £10.30.
Owner Jaber Abdullah **Bred** Rabbah Bloodstock Limited **Trained** Musley Bank, N Yorks

FOCUS
The bend turning into home was straight dolled out 2yds increasing distances for races of 6f and over by 6yds. They went a frantic pace in this uncompetitive novice contest. The winner didn't need to replicate her Ascot form.

4255 ST TERESA'S HOSPICE H'CAP (QUALIFIER FOR THE 2016 CATTERICK TWELVE FURLONG SERIES FINAL) 1m 3f 214y
2:40 (2:40) (Class 5) (0-70,69) 3-Y-O **£3,881** (£1,155; £577; £288) **Stalls** Low

Form RPR
2123 1 **Wotabreeze (IRE)**[16] 3711 3-9-2 **69** AdamMcNamara(5) 8 79+
(John Quinn) *hld up in rr: swtchd wd and gd hdwy 2f out: rdn to ld jst ins fnl f: sn clr: pushed out* **9/4**[1]
5444 2 3 **Becky The Thatcher**[14] 3778 3-8-13 **61** PJMcDonald 6 65
(Micky Hammond) *trckd ldrs: pushed along over 2f out: rdn and sltly outpcd wl over 1f out: sn swtchd rt and rdn: styd on wl fnl f* **6/1**
2264 3 nk **Adherence**[16] 3715 3-8-11 **59** BarryMcHugh 5 62
(Tony Coyle) *led: pushed along wl over 2f out: sn jnd and rdn: drvn and hdd jst ins fnl f: kpt on same pce* **7/1**
4332 4 nk **Falcon's Fire (IRE)**[35] 3015 3-8-7 **55** JasonHart 7 58
(Keith Dalgleish) *hld up towards rr: hdwy over 2f out: rdn wl over 1f out: kpt on fnl f* **5/1**[3]
4610 5 1½ **Rainbow Lad (IRE)**[21] 3509 3-8-8 **56** BenCurtis 1 57
(Michael Appleby) *trckd ldrs: hdwy on inner 3f out: sn cl up: chal wl over 1f out: sn rdn and ev ch: drvn ins fnl f: kpt on same pce* **3/1**[2]
5055 6 ¾ **Shulammite Man (IRE)**[11] 3886 3-8-4 **52** JoeFanning 9 51
(Alan Swinbank) *trckd ldng pair: cl up 1/2-way: rdn along 2f out: drvn and n.m.r over 1f out: sn one pce* **16/1**
5-00 7 ¾ **Top Of The Rocks (FR)**[88] 1484 3-8-12 **60** (vt[1]) GrahamGibbons 3 58
(Tom Dascombe) *in tch: hdwy and cl up on outer after 3f: pushed along 4f out: rdn wl over 2f out: drvn whn n.m.r over 1f out: sn btn* **20/1**
0-30 8 6 **Kazoey**[58] 2308 3-8-2 **50** oh5 DuranFentiman 2 39
(Chris Fairhurst) *towards rr: pushed along wl over 3f out: rdn wl over 2f out: sn outpcd and bhd* **100/1**

2m 36.48s (-2.42) **Going Correction** -0.275s/f (Firm) **8** Ran SP% **110.9**
Speed ratings (Par 100): **97,95,94,94,93 93,92,88**
CSF £15.20 CT £75.66 TOTE £2.70: £1.10, £2.00, £2.30; EX 19.10 Trifecta £90.50.
Owner The New Century Partnership **Bred** Triermore Stud **Trained** Settrington, N Yorks

FOCUS
A weak handicap, run at a fair enough pace. The form seems sound.

4256 OPEN GOLF BETTING AT 188BET H'CAP 5f
3:15 (3:15) (Class 5) (0-75,72) 3-Y-O **£3,234** (£962; £481; £240) **Stalls** Low

Form RPR
005 1 **New Road Side**[8] 3978 3-9-7 **72** (v) BarryMcHugh 6 79
(Tony Coyle) *mde all: rdn clr wl over 1f out: drvn ins fnl f: sn edgd rt and jst hld on* **6/1**
6-45 2 hd **Sandra's Secret (IRE)**[16] 3713 3-9-1 **66** JasonHart 1 72
(Les Eyre) *trckd ldr: effrt wl over 1f out and sn rdn: drvn ins fnl f: styd on strly towards fin* **5/1**[3]
4050 3 2¼ **Danzeb (IRE)**[30] 3211 3-8-8 **66** (p) RowanScott(7) 8 64
(Ann Duffield) *hld up in tch: hdwy on outer wl over 1f out: rdn ent fnl f: kpt on same pce* **12/1**
4246 4 2¼ **Socialites Red**[32] 3131 3-9-6 **71** BenCurtis 3 61
(Scott Dixon) *chsd ldrs: rdn along wl over 1f out: drvn and one pce fnl f* **11/4**[1]
1605 5 hd **Crombay (IRE)**[12] 3847 3-9-6 **71** DavidAllan 5 60
(Tim Easterby) *chsd ldrs: hdwy 2f out: rdn over 1f out: drvn and wknd fnl f* **11/2**
650 6 3¼ **Justice Pleasing**[18] 3643 3-9-1 **66** SamJames 7 43
(David Loughnane) *a towards rr* **14/1**
4-45 7 4½ **Majestic Girl (IRE)**[23] 3471 3-8-7 **58** JoeFanning 2 19
(Robert Cowell) *dwlt: a towards rr* **20/1**
6134 8 6 **Twentysvnthlancers**[13] 3806 3-9-2 **67** GrahamLee 4 7
(Paul Midgley) *chsd ldrs: rdn along wl over 1f out: sn drvn and wknd* **9/2**[2]

59.73s (-0.07) **Going Correction** -0.225s/f (Firm) **8** Ran SP% **110.3**
Speed ratings (Par 100): **91,90,87,83,83 77,70,61**
CSF £33.31 CT £329.29 TOTE £7.30: £2.80, £1.90, £4.60; EX 31.40 Trifecta £498.80.
Owner Morecool Racing & Partner **Bred** Highclere Stud **Trained** Norton, N Yorks

FOCUS
This moderate sprint handicap saw many taken out of their comfort zone. The winner made all and is rated close to form.

4257 £25 FREE BET AT 188BET (S) STKS 5f 212y
3:50 (3:50) (Class 6) 3-Y-O+ **£2,264** (£673; £336; £168) **Stalls** Low

Form RPR
0200 1 **The Lillster**[16] 3725 3-8-3 56 FrannyNorton 1 66
(Tony Carroll) *cl up on inner: led 1/2-way: rdn wl over 1f out: drvn ins fnl f: kpt on wl towards fin* **7/1**
-616 2 1 **Smart Mover (IRE)**[25] 3421 3-8-9 74 TomEaves 7 69
(John Quinn) *trckd ldng pair: hdwy to chse wnr over 1f out: rdn and edgd lft ins fnl f: sn drvn and no imp* **2/1**[2]
-633 3 3½ **Lady Nahema (IRE)**[12] 3838 3-7-10 63 DavidEgan(7) 3 52
(Ann Duffield) *hld up in tch: hdwy 2f out: sn rdn: drvn and no imp fnl f* **15/8**[1]
5431 4 ½ **Perfect Words (IRE)**[10] 3925 6-9-3 60 (p) JacobButterfield(3) 4 62
(Marjorie Fife) *slt ld: hdd 1/2-way: rdn along 2f out: drvn over 1f out: sn one pce* **4/1**[3]
-630 5 3¼ **Charlie's Approval (IRE)**[43] 2778 4-8-4 48 (b) RobJFitzpatrick(5) 8 41
(Ben Haslam) *wnt rt s: in tch: rdn along 1/2-way: wd and slipped home turn: sn drvn and n.d* **22/1**
-055 6 1¾ **Grenade**[54] 2425 4-8-7 44 PaulaMuir(7) 2 40
(Patrick Holmes) *chsd ldrs: rdn along 1/2-way: wknd over 2f out* **66/1**
2000 7 99 **Ay Up Audrey**[9] 3941 5-8-9 49 JamesSullivan 5
(Rebecca Bastiman) *in rr: lost action and sn detached 1/2-way: virtually p.u 2f out* **25/1**

1m 12.0s (-1.60) **Going Correction** -0.275s/f (Firm)
WFA 3 from 4yo+ 6lb 7 Ran SP% **110.3**
Speed ratings (Par 101): **99,97,93,92,88 85,**
CSF £19.90 TOTE £7.30: £2.90, £1.40; EX 20.50 Trifecta £55.40.There was no bid for the winner.
Owner Paul Downing **Bred** Lady Juliet Tadgell **Trained** Cropthorne, Worcs

FOCUS
This weak seller was run at a brisk pace and few landed a blow. The fourth is a fair guide with the winner rated to last year's best.

4258 WORLD MATCHPLAY DARTS AT 188BET MEDIAN AUCTION MAIDEN STKS 7f
4:25 (4:26) (Class 6) 3-5-Y-O **£2,587** (£770; £384; £192) **Stalls** Low

Form RPR
263 1 **Coronation Day**[25] 3422 3-9-0 74 DavidAllan 10 71+
(James Tate) *trckd ldr: led wl over 2f out: rdn clr appr fnl f: kpt on strly* **10/11**[1]
-540 2 2½ **Ballyer Rallyer (IRE)**[8] 3982 3-9-5 67 GrahamGibbons 4 66
(Daniel Mark Loughnane) *trckd ldng pair: hdwy over 2f out: rdn to chse wnr over 1f out: drvn and no imp fnl f* **11/2**[3]
3 1½ **Captain Peaky** 3-9-5 0 JackGarritty 9 62
(Patrick Holmes) *in tch: hdwy on outer 2f out: rdn over 1f out: styd on wl fnl f* **28/1**
50 4 hd **Coquine**[29] 3249 3-9-0 0 DanielTudhope 8 57
(David O'Meara) *trckd ldng pair: hdwy 2f out: rdn over 1f out: drvn and kpt on same pce fnl f* **40/1**
400- 5 4½ **Swiss Lait**[221] 8119 5-9-1 49 PaulaMuir(7) 1 48
(Patrick Holmes) *dwlt and bhd: hdwy on outer over 2f out: sn rdn: kpt on fnl f* **33/1**
-400 6 nk **Piccacard**[12] 3838 3-9-0 49 (p) AndrewMullen 5 44
(Michael Appleby) *chsd ldrs: rdn along over 2f out: drvn wl over 1f out: sn wknd* **25/1**
46-0 7 4 **Triassic (IRE)**[16] 3711 3-9-5 64 JoeFanning 7 38
(Mark Johnston) *led: pushed along 3f out: sn hdd: rdn over 2f out and sn btn* **11/4**[2]
8 1¼ **Lukoutoldmakezebak** 3-9-0 0 NathanEvans(5) 6 35
(James Bethell) *dwlt: a towards rr* **20/1**
40 9 5 **A Fitting Finale**[30] 3209 3-9-0 0 TomEaves 3 16
(Kevin Ryan) *a towards rr* **14/1**

00 **10** 2 **Declined**[12] 3856 4-9-13 0.......... ShaneGray 11 19
(David C Griffiths) *a towards rr* **125/1**

1m 25.71s (-1.29) **Going Correction** -0.275s/f (Firm)
WFA 3 from 4yo+ 8lb **10** Ran SP% **119.3**
Speed ratings (Par 101): **96,93,91,91,86 85,81,79,74,71**
CSF £6.13 TOTE £1.70: £1.02, £1.60, £7.80; EX 7.60 Trifecta £87.60.
Owner James Tate Racing Limited **Bred** Whitsbury Manor Stud **Trained** Newmarket, Suffolk

FOCUS
A very ordinary maiden and the form makes sense. YThe winner was value for a bit extra.

4259 MARGARET AND TED THOMPSON MEMORIAL H'CAP 5f 212y
5:00 (5:00) (Class 4) (0-85,85) 3-Y-O+ **£6,469** (£1,925; £962; £481) **Stalls** Low

Form RPR

1250 **1** **Best Trip (IRE)**[18] 3646 9-9-11 **84**.......... SamJames 1 91
(Marjorie Fife) *mde all: rdn clr over 1f out: kpt on strly* **6/1**[2]

-331 **2** 1 **Spirit Of Zeb (IRE)**[15] 3753 4-9-2 **80**.......... AdamMcNamara[(5)] 10 84
(Richard Fahey) *a chsng wnr: rdn wl over 1f out: drvn fnl f: no imp towards fin* **17/2**

2231 **3** 1¼ **Brockholes**[14] 3775 3-8-11 **76**.......... PJMcDonald 8 75
(Ann Duffield) *trckd ldrs: hdwy to chse ldng pair 1/2-way: rdn wl over 1f out: drvn ins fnl f: kpt on same pce* **6/1**[2]

0346 **4** shd **Mishaal (IRE)**[18] 3646 6-9-7 **80**.......... PaulMulrennan 5 79
(Michael Herrington) *hmpd s: t.k.h and sn chsng ldrs: hdwy 2f out: rdn over 1f out: drvn and kpt on same pce fnl f* **9/1**

110- **5** nk **Ustinov**[266] 7390 4-9-12 **85**.......... DanielTudhope 9 84+
(David O'Meara) *in rr: hdwy over 1f out: swtchd rt and rdn ins fnl f: fin strly* **10/1**

2343 **6** 1¼ **Manatee Bay**[11] 3892 6-9-4 **77**..........(v) FrannyNorton 6 72
(David Nicholls) *wnt lft s: towards rr: hdwy wl over 1f out: sn rdn and kpt on fnl f* **6/1**[2]

-006 **7** ½ **Be Bold**[40] 2857 4-9-1 **74**.......... BarryMcHugh 2 67
(Rebecca Bastiman) *hld up: hdwy over 2f out: rdn to chse ldrs over 1f out: drvn and one pce fnl f* **50/1**

0540 **8** 1 **Meshardal (GER)**[18] 3646 6-9-4 **77**.......... JamesSullivan 7 67
(Ruth Carr) *towards rr: hdwy on wd outside 2f out: rdn over 1f out: sn drvn and n.d* **7/2**[1]

0 **9** ¾ **Steelriver (IRE)**[19] 3606 6-9-11 **84**.......... GrahamGibbons 3 71
(David Barron) *a towards rr* **16/1**

3000 **10** shd **The Hooded Claw (IRE)**[32] 3133 5-9-3 **76**..........(p) DavidAllan 4 63
(Tim Easterby) *chsd ldrs on inner: rdn along over 2f out: drvn wl over 1f out: sn wknd* **8/1**[3]

1m 11.13s (-2.47) **Going Correction** -0.275s/f (Firm)
WFA 3 from 4yo+ 6lb **10** Ran SP% **113.7**
Speed ratings (Par 105): **105,103,102,101,101 99,99,97,96,96**
CSF £54.58 CT £325.33 TOTE £6.50: £2.80, £2.50, £2.00; EX 60.80 Trifecta £165.50.
Owner Mrs Jo McHugh **Bred** Limetree Stud **Trained** Stillington, N Yorks

FOCUS
The feature handicap was run at a solid pace and the leaders were not for catching. Solid form, the winner close to his old best.

4260 BETFAIR AMATEUR RIDERS' H'CAP 1m 3f 214y
5:30 (5:30) (Class 6) (0-65,63) 4-Y-O+ **£2,183** (£677; £338; £169) **Stalls** Low

Form RPR

0256 **1** **Duke Of Yorkshire**[11] 3901 6-11-5 **61**..........(p) MissEEasterby 8 68
(Tim Easterby) *rdr lost iron s: sn rcvrd and mde all: pushed along 2f out: rdn over 1f out: kpt on wl towards fin* **5/1**[1]

1260 **2** 1 **Chauvelin**[5] 4099 5-10-8 **50**..........(b) MrTGreenwood 13 55
(Richard Guest) *stdd s and hld up in rr: gd hdwy over 3f out: trckd ldrs over 2f out: swtchd rt and rdn over 1f out: chsd ldng pair and drvn ins fnl f: sn edgd lft and kpt on* **6/1**[2]

-300 **3** nk **Graceful Act**[57] 2330 8-10-3 **45**..........(p) MissKatyLyons 7 50
(Ron Barr) *a.p: chsd wnr over 2f out: sn rdn: drvn whn sltly hmpd ins fnl f: kpt on* **16/1**

1324 **4** 3 **Toboggan's Gift**[44] 1399 4-10-10 **52**.......... RobertHogg 5 52
(Ann Duffield) *trckd ldrs: effrt over 2f out: rdn wl over 1f out: drvn and no imp fnl f* **5/1**[1]

5346 **5** 1 **Merchant Of Medici**[27] 3325 9-11-7 **63**.......... MrJoeWright 6 61
(Micky Hammond) *in tch: hdwy on outer over 2f out: rdn wl over 1f out: kpt on fnl f* **17/2**

00-0 **6** 2 **Christmas Light**[29] 3253 9-10-6 **48**.......... MissEmilyBullock 1 43
(Alan Lockwood) *hld up in rr: hdwy on inner 2f out: sn rdn: plugged on fnl f* **16/1**

5504 **7** 2½ **Natalia**[16] 3731 7-10-0 **45**..........(p) DrMVoikhansky[(3)] 11 36
(Sarah Hollinshead) *nvr bttr than midfield* **16/1**

-005 **8** 3 **Glasgon**[20] 3564 6-10-13 **55**.......... MissAMcCain 12 41
(Ray Craggs) *chsd ldrs: rdn along wl over 2f out: grad wknd* **14/1**

4000 **9** shd **Al Furat (USA)**[10] 3921 8-10-3 **45**..........(p) MissCAGreenway 4 31
(Ron Barr) *a towards rr* **28/1**

5130 **10** 2 **Togetherwecan (IRE)**[11] 3901 4-11-0 **56**..........(b) MissEmmaBedford 3 39
(Mark Johnston) *hld up in rr: rapid hdwy on outer 5f out: chsd ldng pair over 3f out: rdn along over 2f out: sn wknd* **8/1**[3]

2-20 **11** shd **Applejack Lad**[57] 2329 5-11-3 **59**..........(tp) MrMEnnis 2 42
(Michael Smith) *a towards rr* **8/1**[3]

000- **12** 9 **Come On Lulu**[389] 3414 5-10-3 **45**.......... MrJPearce 9 13
(David Thompson) *a towards rr* **66/1**

600 **13** 99 **Thiepval**[107] 1123 4-10-3 **45**.......... MissPBridgwater 10
(Jason Ward) *t.k.h: chsd ldrs: rdn along over 4f out: sn lost pl and bhd* **16/1**

2m 38.23s (-0.67) **Going Correction** -0.275s/f (Firm) **13** Ran SP% **115.5**
Speed ratings (Par 101): **91,90,90,88,87 86,84,82,82,81 81,75,9**
CSF £32.51 CT £446.46 TOTE £5.20: £2.10, £1.60, £7.00; EX 36.10 Trifecta £711.60.
Owner Habton Farms **Bred** Redhill Bloodstock & Tweenhills Stud **Trained** Great Habton, N Yorks

FOCUS
This moderate handicap, confined to amateur riders that had not won more than three races under rules, looked wide open. Once again it paid to be handy. The winner has been afforded slight improvement.

T/Plt: £17.90 to a £1 stake. Pool: £47,064.88. 1,915.63 winning tickets. T/Qpdt: £13.40 to a £1 stake. Pool: £4,151.85. 228.92 winning tickets. **Joe Rowntree**

4015 LINGFIELD (L-H)
Wednesday, July 13

OFFICIAL GOING: Turf course - good to firm (good in places); aw course - polytrack: standard
Wind: Fresh, variable Weather: Cloudy, rain race 6

4261 OPEN GOLF BETTING AT 188BET EBF MAIDEN FILLIES' STKS (PLUS 10 RACE) 6f
1:50 (1:53) (Class 5) 2-Y-O **£3,881** (£1,155; £577; £288) **Stalls** Centre

Form RPR

4 **1** **Jumping Around (IRE)**[34] 3074 2-9-0 0.......... PatCosgrave 12 76+
(William Haggas) *trckd ldrs: squeezed through over 1f out: led ins fnl f: sn clr* **9/4**[2]

40 **2** 4 **Bobby Vee**[25] 3404 2-9-0 0.......... RobertWinston 8 63
(Dean Ivory) *prom: rdn over 2f out: unable qck fnl f* **20/1**

3 1¼ **Tadkhirah** 2-9-0 0.......... DaneO'Neill 7 59+
(William Haggas) *dwlt: sn in tch: rdn to chse ldrs 2f out: styd on same pce fnl f* **6/1**[3]

5 **4** nk **Highland Dream (IRE)**[32] 3143 2-9-0 0.......... AdamKirby 11 58
(Clive Cox) *t.k.h: led on stands' rail: hrd rdn 2f out: hdd and no ex ins fnl f* **16/1**

5 ½ **Solitary Sister (IRE)** 2-8-11 0.......... LouisSteward[(3)] 10 56+
(Richard Spencer) *s.s: bhd tl hdwy far side 2f out: styd on fnl f* **16/1**

0 **6** hd **Booshbash (IRE)**[29] 3261 2-9-0 0.......... TomMarquand 13 56
(Ed Dunlop) *t.k.h: in tch: outpcd over 2f out: styd on fnl f* **50/1**

44 **7** ¾ **Giennah (IRE)**[32] 3122 2-8-7 0..........[1] JordanUys[(7)] 14 53
(Brian Meehan) *mid-div: rdn 3f out: no imp* **7/1**

6 **8** nk **Jakastar (IRE)**[11] 3902 2-9-0 0.......... SeanLevey 4 52
(Richard Hannon) *chsd ldrs tl wknd over 1f out* **16/1**

9 nk **Beautiful Escape (USA)** 2-9-0 0.......... WilliamCarson 9 51+
(Saeed bin Suroor) *s.s: bhd: shkn up and wnt lft 2f out: nvr able to chal* **7/4**[1]

5 **10** 8 **Miss Reignier**[43] 2764 2-9-0 0.......... DavidProbert 5 26
(Michael Blanshard) *t.k.h: prom tl wknd 2f out* **50/1**

11 2¾ **Handful (IRE)** 2-9-0 0.......... WilliamTwiston-Davies 3 17
(Roger Charlton) *s.s: a bhd* **20/1**

12 nk **Amberine** 2-9-0 0.......... FergusSweeney 1 16
(Malcolm Saunders) *mid-div tl wknd over 2f out* **66/1**

1m 11.69s (0.49) **Going Correction** +0.025s/f (Good) **12** Ran SP% **126.5**
Speed ratings (Par 91): **97,91,90,89,88 88,87,87,86,76 72,72**
CSF £56.60 TOTE £4.30: £1.90, £6.00, £1.40; EX 49.90 Trifecta £239.90.
Owner Sheikh Rashid Dalmook Al Maktoum **Bred** Michael O'Mahony **Trained** Newmarket, Suffolk

FOCUS
An ordinary maiden but hard not to be taken with the winner. The bare form behind looks very ordinary.

4262 £25 FREE BET AT 188BET H'CAP 6f
2:25 (2:26) (Class 6) (0-65,65) 3-Y-O **£2,587** (£770; £384; £192) **Stalls** Centre

Form RPR

0-21 **1** **Jumeirah Star (USA)**[50] 2560 3-9-1 **62** ow1..........(v) SladeO'Hara[(3)] 8 70
(Robert Cowell) *sn crossed to stands' rail: mde all: rdn 2f out: jst hld on* **8/1**

4254 **2** nk **Sciarra**[28] 3280 3-9-6 **64**.......... OisinMurphy 13 71
(Michael Bell) *broke wl: sn in midfield: hrd rdn and hdwy over 1f out: r.o wl fnl f: clsng at fin* **6/1**[2]

4045 **3** 1¾ **Angie's Girl**[21] 3527 3-9-4 **62**.......... AdamKirby 12 63
(Clive Cox) *dwlt: t.k.h: sn in tch: drvn to chse wnr over 1f out tl ins fnl f: kpt on* **7/2**[1]

051 **4** 2½ **Hamish McGonagain**[21] 3513 3-9-5 **63**..........(p) DaneO'Neill 7 56
(Jeremy Gask) *dwlt: bhd: hdwy and hung lft 2f out: styd on same pce* **6/1**[2]

-000 **5** shd **Arlecchino's Rock**[14] 3786 3-9-7 **65**.......... DavidProbert 5 58
(Mark Usher) *chsd ldrs tl one pce appr fnl f* **7/1**[3]

5-50 **6** 2¼ **Secretfact**[53] 2458 3-7-9 **46**.......... HollieDoyle[(7)] 10 31
(Malcolm Saunders) *bhd: rdn 3f out: sme hdwy over 1f out: nvr rchd ldrs* **12/1**

-000 **7** nse **Pop Culture**[14] 3786 3-9-2 **60**.......... DannyBrock 6 45
(Jonathan Portman) *prom: rdn 3f out: btn wl over 1f out* **14/1**

6450 **8** 1½ **Kingstreet Lady**[16] 3725 3-8-7 **51**.......... LukeMorris 3 32+
(Richard Price) *towards rr: effrt and hmpd 2f out: nvr able to chal* **25/1**

0100 **9** shd **Let There Be Light**[8] 3975 3-9-2 **60**.......... JimCrowley 9 40+
(Gay Kelleway) *towards rr: sme hdwy and n.m.r 2f out: no ex over 1f out* **16/1**

0-30 **10** 1½ **Ormering**[31] 3198 3-8-3 **47**..........(p) KieranO'Neill 11 22
(Roger Teal) *outpcd after 2f: sn bhd* **28/1**

6661 **11** 1¾ **Curious Fox**[15] 3735 3-9-1 **59**.......... WilliamCarson 4 29+
(Anthony Carson) *in tch tl wknd 2f out* **7/1**[3]

4030 **12** 6 **Nidnod**[15] 3740 3-7-13 **50**.......... MitchGodwin[(7)] 2 1+
(John Bridger) *chsd ldrs: wknd over 2f out: bhd and eased fnl f* **10/1**

1m 10.84s (-0.36) **Going Correction** +0.025s/f (Good) **12** Ran SP% **123.5**
Speed ratings (Par 98): **103,102,100,96,96 93,93,91,91,89 87,79**
CSF £57.90 CT £207.36 TOTE £10.20: £2.80, £2.00, £1.60; EX 45.50 Trifecta £99.10.
Owner Khalifa Dasmal & Partner **Bred** Circular Road Breeders **Trained** Six Mile Bottom, Cambs

FOCUS
The three racing nearest the stands' rail dominated this moderate handicap.

4263 PAUL KELLEWAY MEMORIAL CLASSIFIED STKS 7f 140y
3:00 (3:00) (Class 3) 3-Y-O+ **£7,246** (£2,168; £1,084; £542; £270) **Stalls** Centre

Form RPR

312 **1** **Red Box**[21] 3519 3-8-9 88.......... LukeMorris 2 90+
(Sir Mark Prescott Bt) *chsd ldr: led and edgd rt over 1f out: hrd rdn and hung lft fnl f: drvn out* **7/2**[2]

121- **2** ½ **Afjaan (IRE)**[240] 7874 4-9-7 89.......... PatCosgrave 1 92
(William Haggas) *off the pce in 6th: hdwy over 1f out: clsd on wnr fnl f: jst hld* **15/8**[1]

5-10 **3** nk **Taurean Star (IRE)**[27] 3299 3-8-9 89.......... LouisSteward[(3)] 5 89+
(Michael Bell) *hld up in 4th: effrt over 2f out: r.o fnl f* **4/1**[3]

6000 **4** nse **The Warrior (IRE)**[5] 4104 4-9-7 89..........(b) JimCrowley 7 91
(Amanda Perrett) *led: hdd and sltly hmpd over 1f out: kpt on u.p* **12/1**

3550 **5** 1¼ **Lincoln (IRE)**[18] 3671 5-9-7 90.......... GeorgeBaker 3 88
(Mick Channon) *hld up in rr: hdwy and hrd rdn over 1f out: r.o* **8/1**

-041 **6** hd **Gothic Empire (IRE)**[13] 3821 4-9-4 87.......... DanielMuscutt[(3)] 6 88
(James Fanshawe) *chsd ldrs: rdn 2f out: one pce fnl f* **6/1**

0320 **7** 1 1/4 **Yeah Baby Yeah (IRE)**28 3274 3-8-9 88 DavidProbert 4 79
(Gay Kelleway) *broke wl: t.k.h: sn stdd bk to 5th: rdn over 2f out: no ex fnl f* **25/1**

1m 31.01s (-1.29) **Going Correction** +0.025s/f (Good)
WFA 3 from 4yo+ 9lb **7** Ran SP% **113.9**
Speed ratings (Par 107): **107,106,106,106,104 104,103**
CSF £10.43 TOTE £3.80: £1.60, £1.40; EX 8.30 Trifecta £32.30.
Owner Cheveley Park Stud **Bred** Cheveley Park Stud Ltd **Trained** Newmarket, Suffolk

FOCUS
Racing near enough in single file along the stands' rail for much of the race, the winner was well placed and held on despite drifting centre-track late on. The fourth is the key to the level.

4264 188BET.CO.UK H'CAP 5f
3:35 (3:35) (Class 6) (0-60,60) 3-Y-O+ **£2,587** (£770; £384; £192) **Stalls** Centre

Form RPR
2031 **1** **John Joiner**23 3469 4-9-5 **55** AdamKirby 10 62
(Peter Hedger) *mid-div: hdwy 2f out: led ins fnl f: drvn out* **3/1**2
465 **2** 1/2 **Babyfact**4 4155 5-9-10 **60** GeorgeBaker 2 65
(Malcolm Saunders) *hld up towards rr: hdwy 2f out: r.o wl fnl f* **11/4**1
0-05 **3** *shd* **The Wee Chief (IRE)**7 3993 10-9-4 **54** KieranO'Neill 6 59
(Jimmy Fox) *dwlt: bhd: gd hdwy over 1f out: fin wl* **14/1**
0050 **4** 1 1/4 **Deer Song**23 3469 3-8-11 **52** DannyBrock 9 50
(John Bridger) *chsd ldr: led 2f out tl ins fnl f: one pce* **25/1**
4554 **5** *shd* **Diamond Charlie (IRE)**18 3650 8-9-8 **58** (p) JimCrowley 4 58
(Simon Dow) *dwlt: towards rr: hdwy 2f out: one pce fnl f* **5/1**3
0001 **6** 2 1/4 **Willow Spring**13 3822 4-8-11 **50** NoelGarbutt(3) 8 42
(Conrad Allen) *prom tl outpcd fnl 2f* **14/1**
3405 **7** 3/4 **Give Us A Belle (IRE)**13 3822 7-8-12 **53** (bt) PaddyPilley(5) 14 42
(Christine Dunnett) *bhd and drvn along: styd on fnl f* **7/1**
060 **8** 1 3/4 **Hurricane Alert**8 3970 4-9-3 **58** HectorCrouch(5) 5 41
(Natalie Lloyd-Beavis) *prom tl wknd jst over 1f out* **50/1**
-000 **9** *nse* **Rubheira**13 3811 4-8-6 **47** oh1 ow1 (b) DavidParkes(5) 12 30
(Paul Burgoyne) *dwlt: nvr trbld ldrs* **66/1**
000- **10** 1 1/4 **Purple Belle**245 7795 3-7-12 **46** oh1 MitchGodwin(7) 3 22
(Jimmy Fox) *sn outpcd* **66/1**
645- **11** 1/2 **Touch The Clouds**214 8196 5-9-1 **51** (b) PaddyAspell 7 27
(William Stone) *sn chsng ldrs: wknd wl over 1f out* **20/1**
2421 **12** *shd* **Red Flute**18 3650 4-8-13 **52** (v) TimClark(3) 13 28
(Denis Quinn) *led tl 2f out: wknd over 1f out* **8/1**
0400 **13** *30* **Johnny Splash (IRE)**23 3474 7-9-7 **57** (b) RobertWinston 11 +
(Roger Teal) *chsd ldrs: wnt lame and rdr tried to pull up 2f out: wl bhd and eased fnl f* **12/1**

58.19s (-0.01) **Going Correction** +0.025s/f (Good)
WFA 3 from 4yo+ 5lb **13** Ran SP% **126.5**
Speed ratings (Par 101): **101,100,100,98,97 94,93,90,90,88 87,87,39**
CSF £11.98 CT £108.34 TOTE £3.10: £1.70, £1.30, £5.80; EX 11.80 Trifecta £153.10.
Owner Mrs S Lynch & A Lomax **Bred** Mrs J McMahon **Trained** Hook, Hampshire

FOCUS
No hanging around here and the draw had no effect, with the main action unfolding centre-field and the runner-up racing furthest from the stands' rail throughout. Low-grade form.

4265 WORLD MATCHPLAY DARTS AT 188BET MAIDEN STKS 1m 4f (P)
4:10 (4:10) (Class 5) 3-4-Y-O **£3,234** (£962; £481; £240) **Stalls** Low

Form RPR
623 **1** **Cape Cova (IRE)**12 3845 3-9-1 83 TomQueally 6 83+
(John Gosden) *trckd ldr: led 2f out: rdn clr over 1f out: pushed out* **2/1**1
24 **2** 1 1/4 **Endless Acres (IRE)**12 3845 3-9-1 0 StevieDonohoe 5 80
(Charlie Fellowes) *cajoled along early: towards rr: rdn 3f out: hdwy over 1f out: fin wl* **7/2**3
3 1 1/2 **Ardamir (FR)**119 4-10-0 0 WilliamTwiston-Davies 8 78
(Alan King) *stdd in rr s: gd hdwy on outer 3f out: one pce appr fnl f* **12/1**
0323 **4** 1 1/4 **Lexington Law (IRE)**26 3359 3-9-1 82 KieranO'Neill 2 76
(Richard Hannon) *led tl 2f out: wknd 1f out* **11/4**2
34 **5** 1 3/4 **Torquay**6 4056 3-8-10 0 SamHitchcott 3 68
(Harry Dunlop) *hld up towards rr: hdwy on inner over 1f out: no ex fnl f* **12/1**
00 **6** *1* **Always Summer**19 3601 3-8-7 0 DanielMuscutt(3) 1 67
(James Fanshawe) *trckd ldrs and gng wl: rdn 2f out: wknd over 1f out* **33/1**
2 **7** *3* **Potters Lady Jane**27 3305 4-9-9 0 LukeMorris 9 62
(Lucy Wadham) *in tch: rdn 3f out: wknd over 1f out* **12/1**
0- **8** *19* **McCools Gold**259 7560 3-9-1 0 1 RobertWinston 7 36
(Eve Johnson Houghton) *prom on outer tl wknd 3f out* **40/1**
9 *15* **Divine Prince (GR)** 3-9-1 0 JimCrowley 4 12
(Amanda Perrett) *mid-div: rdn along after 4f: wknd qckly over 4f out: sn t.o* **16/1**

2m 34.46s (1.46) **Going Correction** +0.275s/f (Slow)
WFA 3 from 4yo 13lb **9** Ran SP% **116.6**
Speed ratings (Par 103): **106,105,104,103,102 101,99,86,76**
CSF £9.28 TOTE £2.70: £1.20, £1.60, £2.40; EX 12.60 Trifecta £77.30.
Owner Mohamed Obaida **Bred** Basil Brindley **Trained** Newmarket, Suffolk

FOCUS
A fair maiden run at a steady gallop and the winner was always well placed. The form makes sense, with the winner progressing.

4266 BEST ODDS GUARANTEED AT 188BET H'CAP 1m 7f 169y(P)
4:40 (4:41) (Class 5) (0-75,75) 3-Y-O+ **£3,234** (£962; £481; £240) **Stalls** Low

Form RPR
-300 **1** **Le Rock (IRE)**6 4057 4-9-5 **71** DannyBrock 1 77
(J S Moore) *chsd clr ldr: clsd 1/2-way: drew level 2f out: drvn to ld ins fnl f* **10/1**
3420 **2** 1 3/4 **Tempuran**27 3302 7-9-4 **70** OisinMurphy 5 74
(David Bridgwater) *led: sn 12 l clr: breather and c bk 1/2-way: jnd by wnr 2f out: hdd and no ex ins fnl f* **6/1**3
051- **3** *nk* **Rainbow Pride (IRE)**272 7240 4-9-2 **68** LukeMorris 3 72
(Sir Mark Prescott Bt) *t.k.h: hld up off the pce: wnt 3rd and in tch 5f out: effrt over 2f out: r.o fnl f* **7/4**1
3042 **4** 3/4 **Fitzwilly**15 3746 6-9-9 **75** GeorgeBaker 4 78
(Mick Channon) *hld up off the pce: rdn over 2f out: styd on fnl f* **3/1**2
2100 **5** *6* **Fern Owl**49 2582 4-9-7 **73** JimCrowley 2 69
(Hughie Morrison) *hld up off the pce: hdwy and in tch 5f out: rdn over 2f out: sn outpcd* **3/1**2

3m 31.53s (5.83) **Going Correction** +0.275s/f (Slow) **5** Ran SP% **109.7**
Speed ratings (Par 103): **96,95,94,94,91**
CSF £61.54 TOTE £13.20: £5.30, £2.30; EX 65.50 Trifecta £133.90.
Owner G V March & J S Moore **Bred** Haras Du Mont Dit Mont **Trained** Upper Lambourn, Berks

FOCUS
Run in the pouring rain, the first two home were in the front pair throughout, with them going a good gallop initially as the runner-up went clear. The form is a bit unconvincing.

4267 188BET ROA/RACING POST OWNERS JACKPOT H'CAP 1m 2f (P)
5:15 (5:16) (Class 6) (0-60,60) 3-Y-O+ **£2,587** (£770; £384; £192) **Stalls** Low

Form RPR
64-3 **1** **Reckless Wave (IRE)**22 3482 3-8-13 **57** LukeMorris 14 63
(Ed Walker) *towards rr: drvn along 5f out: gd hdwy over 1f out: str run to ld fnl strides* **3/1**1
6516 **2** 1/2 **Megalala (IRE)**15 3737 15-8-13 **53** MitchGodwin(7) 5 58
(John Bridger) *broke wl: led: kpt on gamely fnl f: jst ct* **16/1**
6005 **3** *nk* **Gunner Moyne**22 3488 4-9-13 **60** FergusSweeney 4 64
(Gary Moore) *in tch: effrt over 2f out: styd on fnl f* **14/1**
0025 **4** 1 3/4 **Spinning Rose**19 3624 4-9-7 **54** RobertWinston 8 55
(Dean Ivory) *chsd ldrs: effrt over 2f out: one pce fnl f* **10/1**
-035 **5** 1 3/4 **Sunshineandbubbles**11 3878 3-8-13 **60** (p) GeorgeDowning(3) 7 58
(Daniel Mark Loughnane) *mid-div on inner: hdwy over 1f out: styd on same pce* **33/1**
0426 **6** *nse* **Buzz Lightyere**29 3256 3-9-2 **60** JimCrowley 12 58
(Michael Attwater) *prom: rdn 3f out: no ex fnl f* **8/1**3
0055 **7** *hd* **Power Up**25 3402 5-9-6 **58** CharlieBennett(5) 2 55
(Jane Chapple-Hyam) *mid-div: effrt 3f out: styd on fnl f* **10/1**
60-0 **8** 1/2 **Purple Lane (IRE)**18 3648 5-9-5 **59** (t) JoshQuinn(7) 13 55+
(Luke Dace) *bhd tl r.o fnl 2f* **50/1**
0-33 **9** 2 1/2 **Its A Sheila Thing**22 3489 3-8-9 **53** WilliamCarson 11 45
(Linda Jewell) *towards rr: sme hdwy over 1f out: nvr able to chal* **16/1**
-126 **10** 2 1/4 **New Abbey Angel (IRE)**22 3482 3-9-2 **60** DavidProbert 10 47
(Gay Kelleway) *mid-div on outer: no imp fnl 3f* **9/2**2
00-0 **11** 1/2 **Summerling (IRE)**25 3401 5-8-10 **46** (b1) EoinWalsh(3) 9 32
(Phil McEntee) *a towards rr* **33/1**
000 **12** *nk* **Roman Urn**18 3653 3-8-6 **55** ow1 (v1) DavidParkes(5) 1 41
(Brett Johnson) *prom tl wknd over 1f out* **33/1**
5025 **13** *6* **Gabster (IRE)**26 3348 3-9-2 **60** OisinMurphy 6 34
(Amanda Perrett) *chsd ldrs: outpcd 3f out: btn whn rn wd into st* **3/1**1

2m 8.97s (2.37) **Going Correction** +0.275s/f (Slow)
WFA 3 from 4yo+ 11lb **13** Ran SP% **126.7**
Speed ratings (Par 101): **101,100,100,98,97 97,97,96,94,93 92,92,87**
CSF £58.58 CT £617.44 TOTE £3.70: £1.20, £5.20, £4.40; EX 55.10 Trifecta £1061.50.
Owner Mrs T Walker **Bred** John Connaughton **Trained** Upper Lambourn, Berks
■ Stewards' Enquiry : Jim Crowley two-day ban; careless riding (28-29th July)

FOCUS
Moderate form but the winner came from a long way back and can rate higher. Megalala is rated to his best 2015 form.
T/Jkpt: Not won. T/Plt: £117.70 to a £1 stake. Pool: 60,691.40. 376.42 winning tickets. T/Qpdt: £29.10 to a £1 stake. Pool: £6,111.03. 155.37 winning tickets. **Lee McKenzie**

3908 SANDOWN (R-H)
Wednesday, July 13

OFFICIAL GOING: Good (good to soft in places)
Wind: Moderate, against Weather: heavy shower before racing; overcast becoming fair

4268 XL CATLIN H'CAP 5f 6y
6:05 (6:06) (Class 4) (0-85,84) 3-Y-O **£4,690** (£1,395; £697; £348) **Stalls** High

Form RPR
3221 **1** **Just Glamorous (IRE)**11 3893 3-9-0 **77** MartinHarley 1 93
(Ronald Harris) *mde all and sn clr: cantering and wl ahd 1/2-way: rdn out fnl f and maintained ld* **5/4**1
-000 **2** *10* **Art Collection (FR)**6 4051 3-9-5 **82** AdamKirby 2 62
(Gary Moore) *lw: bdly outpcd in last pair: styd on u.p fr 2f out to take remote 2nd ins fnl f* **7/1**
-540 **3** 1 1/2 **Point Of Woods**17 3689 3-9-2 **79** SeanLevey 4 54
(Ralph Beckett) *chsd clr wnr: rdn and no imp over 2f out: lost remote 2nd ins fnl f* **5/1**3
4441 **4** *9* **Stormflower**18 3650 3-8-2 **68** ow1 EdwardGreatrex(3) 8 10
(John Bridger) *racd wd in 3rd pl but long way bhd wnr: rdn 1/2-way: lost 3rd over 1f out: wknd* **6/1**
1005 **5** *11* **Florencio**1 4223 3-9-5 **82** (t) MartinDwyer 3
(William Muir) *s.i.s: bdly outpcd in last pair: a wl bhd* **7/2**2

1m 1.57s (-0.03) **Going Correction** +0.05s/f (Good) **5** Ran SP% **110.1**
Speed ratings (Par 102): **102,86,83,69,51**
CSF £10.42 TOTE £1.80: £1.10, £3.10; EX 8.20 Trifecta £30.30.
Owner Robert & Nina Bailey **Bred** Glamorous Air Partnership **Trained** Earlswood, Monmouths

FOCUS
Race distances as advertised. Four withdrawals took some interest out of this handicap but it was run at a sound pace and the winner could not have been more impressive. The time was decent too.

4269 ROR - RETRAINING OF RACEHORSES H'CAP 7f 16y
6:35 (6:38) (Class 5) (0-70,71) 3-Y-O **£3,234** (£962; £481; £240) **Stalls** Low

Form RPR
0034 **1** **Cooperess**8 3970 3-8-3 **52** (bt) KieranO'Neill 3 61
(Ali Stronge) *trckd ldrs: prog 2f out: rdn to ld jst over 1f out: drvn and kpt on wl* **33/1**
-663 **2** 1 1/2 **Bryght Boy**18 3648 3-9-0 **63** FrederikTylicki 4 68
(Ed Walker) *lw: trckd ldr: rdn to ld 2f out: hdd jst over 1f out: kpt on but no imp on wnr last 100yds* **7/2**1
0442 **3** *hd* **Harmony Bay (IRE)**8 3975 3-8-7 **59** EdwardGreatrex(3) 11 63+
(Sylvester Kirk) *t.k.h: hld up in last trio: prog on wd outside jst over 2f out: tk 3rd jst ins fnl f: styd on and nrly snatched 2nd* **8/1**3
-621 **4** 1 1/2 **You're A Goat**153 533 3-9-0 **63** WilliamTwiston-Davies 5 63+
(Gary Moore) *hld up wl in rr: rdn and threaded through rivals fr over 2f out: tk 4th ins fnl f: nvr able to chal* **25/1**
0-10 **5** *2* **Ebbisham (IRE)**61 2212 3-9-2 **65** PatCosgrave 16 60
(Jim Boyle) *lw: hld up wl in rr: prog 2f out: kpt on to take 5th wl ins fnl f: n.d* **14/1**
4641 **6** 1 1/2 **Reaver (IRE)**7 4009 3-9-8 **71** 6ex CharlesBishop 9 63+
(Eve Johnson Houghton) *lw: hld up wl in rr: prog into midfield 2f out: nvr clrest of runs and one pce fr over 1f out: eased nr fin* **9/2**2
1321 **7** *shd* **Broughtons Fancy**23 3473 3-9-7 **70** TomMarquand 14 61
(Andrew Reid) *trckd ldrs: rdn to chal 2f out: fnd little and wknd fnl f* **12/1**

0-45 **8** ¾ **Sexton Blake (IRE)**[25] 3406 3-8-13 **67**........................ HectorCrouch(5) 2 56
(Gary Moore) *pressed ldrs: tried to chal on inner 2f out: wknd jst over 1f out* **20/1**

0060 **9** 1½ **Attitude Rocks**[34] 3062 3-8-11 **60**....................................(b[1]) RyanTate 10 45
(Clive Cox) *dwlt and stdd s: hld up in last: reminder 3f out: stl last wl over 1f out: passed a few late on: nvr involved* **20/1**

4506 **10** nk **Protest (IRE)**[8] 3988 3-8-11 **60**............................... MartinDwyer 7 44
(Sylvester Kirk) *t.k.h: hld up in midfield: prog on inner to chse ldrs 2f out: wknd jst over 1f out* **20/1**

2005 **11** ¾ **Premier Currency (IRE)**[20] 3579 3-9-5 **68**.....................(p) TomQueally 1 50
(Mike Murphy) *led to 2f out: wknd qckly jst over 1f out* **14/1**

402 **12** 1 **Marcle (IRE)**[15] 3740 3-8-13 **65**...................................... RobHornby(3) 13 44
(Ed de Giles) *chsd ldrs: lost pl 2f out: steadily wknd* **9/1**

31-0 **13** 1¾ **Tesoro (IRE)**[35] 3036 3-9-4 **67**................................... MartinHarley 15 41
(Dean Ivory) *t.k.h: hld up towards rr: effrt 3f out: nt clr run over 2f out: wknd over 1f out* **25/1**

64-4 **14** 6 **Magic Strike (IRE)**[47] 2642 3-9-4 **67**.................................. AdamKirby 6 25
(Clive Cox) *chsd ldrs: rdn and wknd fr over 2f out* **8/1**[3]

4043 **15** 12 **Russian Ranger (IRE)**[58] 2293 3-8-13 **62**.......................(p) RyanClark 12
(Jonathan Portman) *nvr bttr than midfield: struggling over 3f out: sn wknd: eased over 1f out: t.o* **33/1**

1m 31.84s (2.34) **Going Correction** +0.325s/f (Good) **15** Ran SP% **121.5**
Speed ratings (Par 100): **99,97,97,95,93 91,91,90,88,88 87,86,84,77,63**
CSF £135.86 CT £1076.80 TOTE £38.80: £10.80, £1.40, £3.20; EX 231.20 Trifecta £2467.00.
Owner Tim Dykes **Bred** Norman Court Stud & Mike Channon B/S Ltd **Trained** Eastbury, Berks

FOCUS
The pace was sound for this open handicap. Modest form for thr track, few of these progressive.

4270 RORSOURCEAHORSE.ORG.UK MAIDEN AUCTION STKS 7f 16y
7:05 (7:10) (Class 5) 2-Y-O **£3,234** (£962; £481; £240) **Stalls** Low

Form RPR

1 **Balgair** 2-8-13 ⁰.. FrederikTylicki 9 78+
(Jonathan Portman) *leggy: free to post: in tch in midfield: prog over 2f out: led over 1f out and sn swept clr: in n.d fnl f: rdn out* **20/1**

2 2 **Fields Of Fortune** 2-8-11 ⁰.. TomMarquand 10 71+
(Richard Hannon) *leggy: athletic: lw: s.s: rn green in last quartet: shoved along and sme prog over 2f out: picked up over 1f out: r.o wl to take 2nd last 100yds* **6/1**[2]

3 2¾ **Count Calabash (IRE)** 2-9-3 ⁰.......................................[1] LukeMorris 2 69
(Paul Cole) *str: wnt lft s: in tch in midfield: shkn up 3f out: prog and rdn 2f out: styd on wl fnl f to snatch 3rd last stride* **14/1**

4 shd **Pitch High (IRE)** 2-8-10 ⁰.................................. ShelleyBirkett(3) 8 65
(Julia Feilden) *w'like: in tch in midfield: prog on outer over 2f out: tried to chal over 1f out but sn outpcd: chsd wnr ins fnl f: kpt on but lost 2 pls last 100yds* **25/1**

02 **5** nk **Born To Please**[30] 3232 2-8-6 ⁰....................................... KieranO'Neill 5 57
(Mark Usher) *w'like: led: hdd and outpcd over 1f out: lost pls ins fnl f* **6/1**[2]

6 1¾ **Accidental Agent** 2-8-13 ⁰... CharlesBishop 6 59
(Eve Johnson Houghton) *str: lw: dwlt: wl in rr: urged along on inner over 2f out and sme prog: one pce fr over 1f out* **7/1**[3]

0 **7** 1 **Stag Party (IRE)**[15] 3742 2-8-12 ⁰......................... EdwardGreatrex(3) 14 59
(Andrew Balding) *rn green and sn pushed along in midfield: dropped to rr and urged along over 2f out: kpt on quite wl fr over 1f out* **20/1**

8 4 **Daring Guest (IRE)** 2-9-3 ⁰... TomQueally 11 50
(George Margarson) *str: t.k.h: chsd ldr to jst over 2f out: sn wknd* **50/1**

9 nk **Viking Hoard (IRE)** 2-9-3 ⁰.. MartinHarley 4 49
(Harry Dunlop) *leggy: dwlt and hmpd s: mostly in last quartet: shkn up and kpt on fr over 1f out* **20/1**

10 ¾ **Poetic Voice** 2-9-1 ⁰.. AdamKirby 7 45
(Ralph Beckett) *athletic: lw: trckd ldrs: shkn up and no prog over 2f out: wknd over 1f out* **10/3**[1]

11 ½ **Kozier (GER)** 2-9-3 ⁰...................................... WilliamTwiston-Davies 15 46
(Alan King) *cmpt: dwlt: a wl in rr: nvr a factor* **16/1**

12 2 **Harbour Town** 2-8-13 ⁰... JimCrowley 3 36
(Harry Dunlop) *w'like: in tch in midfield: pushed along and no prog over 2f out: wknd over 1f out* **10/1**

44 **13** 6 **Cj Parker**[28] 3275 2-8-12 ⁰.. PatCosgrave 16 19
(Jim Boyle) *leggy: t.k.h: pressed ldrs tl rdn and wknd wl over 2f out* **10/1**

14 10 **Desidero (SPA)** 2-8-8 ⁰... RyanTate 12
(Pat Phelan) *str: s.v.s: a bhd in last trio: t.o* **33/1**

15 1¼ **Ultimat Power (IRE)** 2-8-13 ⁰.. RyanClark 13
(Mark Hoad) *w'like: bit bkwd: a in rr: struggling 3f out: t.o* **66/1**

054 **16** 35 **If I Say So**[8] 3986 2-8-11 ⁰.. DannyBrock 1
(J S Moore) *chsd ldrs: wknd rapidly 3f out: t.o whn virtually p.u over 1f out* **20/1**

1m 33.1s (3.60) **Going Correction** +0.325s/f (Good) **16** Ran SP% **124.2**
Speed ratings (Par 94): **92,89,86,86,86 84,82,78,78,77 76,74,67,56,54 14**
CSF £127.43 TOTE £24.70: £7.50, £2.40, £4.50; EX 239.00 Trifecta £855.60.
Owner J T Habershon-Butcher **Bred** G Doyle & Lord Margadale **Trained** Upper Lambourn, Berks

FOCUS
Those with experience had shown little and it was unsurprisingly dominated by two newcomers. Probably relatively ordinary form by Sandown's standards.

4271 SKY BET PROUD TO SUPPORT ROR H'CAP 1m 14y
7:40 (7:41) (Class 3) (0-90,91) 3-Y-O+ **£7,439** (£2,213; £1,106; £553) **Stalls** Low

Form RPR

3211 **1** **Sir Roderic (IRE)**[11] 3908 3-9-5 **90**................................ FrederikTylicki 3 95+
(Rod Millman) *hld up in 4th: boxed in over 2f out: swtchd out wd and prog over 1f out: shkn up to ld 1f out: styd on wl* **11/8**[1]

41 **2** 1 **El Hayem (IRE)**[40] 2861 3-9-3 **88**....................................... PatCosgrave 1 89+
(Sir Michael Stoute) *lw: trckd ldng pair: rdn to chal on inner wl over 1f out: chsd wnr ins fnl f: styd on but a hld* **7/4**[2]

0-00 **3** ¾ **Directorship**[48] 2628 10-9-9 **90**................................. HectorCrouch(5) 6 91
(Patrick Chamings) *led at modest pce: narrowly hdd over 2f out: kpt pressing and stl ch 1f out: styd on same pce* **8/1**

451 **4** 1¾ **Horrah**[20] 3572 3-9-1 **86**....................................... WilliamTwiston-Davies 4 81
(Roger Charlton) *hld up in last: prog on outer over 2f out: narrow ld over 1f out to 1f out: fdd ins fnl f* **11/2**[3]

2-10 **5** 25 **Honiara**[38] 2948 3-9-2 **87**.. LukeMorris 5 22
(Paul Cole) *t.k.h: pressed ldr: narrow ld over 2f out to over 1f out: sn btn and wknd: heavily eased and t.o* **16/1**

1m 49.42s (6.12) **Going Correction** +0.325s/f (Good)
WFA 3 from 4yo+ 9lb **5** Ran SP% **110.8**
Speed ratings (Par 107): **82,81,80,78,53**
CSF £4.10 TOTE £2.30: £1.40, £1.70; EX 4.30 Trifecta £14.90.
Owner The Links Partnership **Bred** Thomas G Cooke **Trained** Kentisbeare, Devon

FOCUS
They went a steady pace for this fair handicap. The form is rated a bit cautiously.

4272 CAPPAGH LIFE AFTER RACING H'CAP 1m 2f 7y
8:10 (8:11) (Class 4) (0-80,78) 3-Y-O **£4,690** (£1,395; £697; £348) **Stalls** Low

Form RPR

053 **1** **Proctor**[20] 3577 3-9-1 **72**... OisinMurphy 1 83
(Stuart Kittow) *lw: trckd ldng pair: clsd to ld over 2f out: rdn clr over 1f out: styd on wl* **6/1**[3]

4-45 **2** 4½ **Scottish Summit (IRE)**[41] 2816 3-9-2 **73**.......................... PatCosgrave 8 75
(Sir Michael Stoute) *lw: hld up in 5th: shkn up and prog over 2f out: drvn to chse wnr over 1f out: no imp: jst hung on for 2nd* **10/3**[2]

0-34 **3** nk **Melabi (IRE)**[13] 3824 3-9-6 **77**.. GeorgeBaker 11 78
(William Haggas) *slowly away and lost 6 l: hld up in detached last: cajoled along fr 3f out: prog 2f out but looked awkward: styd on fnl f and nrly snatched 2nd* **15/8**[1]

-000 **4** 1 **Marshal Dan Troop (IRE)**[34] 3079 3-9-2 **73**.................... DavidProbert 6 72
(Peter Chapple-Hyam) *trckd ldr: chal over 2f out: chsd wnr to over 1f out: outpcd but kpt on again nr fin* **14/1**

5052 **5** nk **Loading (IRE)**[14] 3766 3-9-6 **77**... SeanLevey 2 76
(Richard Hannon) *hld up in 4th: shkn up over 2f out: disp 2nd over 1f out: no ex* **6/1**[3]

3306 **6** 8 **Magnum (IRE)**[13] 3814 3-9-7 **78**....................................(p) MartinDwyer 7 61
(Brian Meehan) *hld up in 6th: rdn and no prog 3f out: toiling after* **8/1**

42-3 **7** ½ **Bretoncelles (FR)**[43] 2767 3-9-5 **76**................................. MartinHarley 5 58
(Harry Dunlop) *led at decent pce and stretched field: hdd over 2f out: wknd qckly over 1f out* **10/1**

2m 13.25s (2.75) **Going Correction** +0.325s/f (Good) **7** Ran SP% **113.3**
Speed ratings (Par 102): **102,98,98,97,97 90,90**
CSF £25.73 CT £51.07 TOTE £7.10: £4.00, £1.40; EX 30.50 Trifecta £82.20.
Owner Qatar Racing Limited **Bred** Qatar Bloodstock Ltd **Trained** Blackborough, Devon

FOCUS
Plenty of unexposed runners in this handicap which was run at a sound pace. A clear pb from the winner.

4273 ROR NEW CAREERS FOR FORMER RACEHORSES H'CAP 1m 6f
8:40 (8:40) (Class 5) (0-70,68) 3-Y-O **£3,234** (£962; £481; £240) **Stalls** Low

Form RPR

-552 **1** **Mystique Heights**[6] 4033 3-8-10 **57**...................................... LukeMorris 3 65
(Sir Mark Prescott Bt) *trckd ldng pair: rousted along 3f out: clsd grad and drvn to ld 1f out: hung lft ins fnl f: kpt on* **8/11**[1]

1064 **2** ¾ **Captain Peacock**[22] 3493 3-9-2 **63**...............................(v[1]) JimCrowley 5 70
(William Knight) *trckd ldr: led jst over 2f out: hung bdly lft after: hdd 1f out: kpt on even though ended against nr side rail: jst hld* **5/1**[3]

-401 **3** ¾ **Tyrell (IRE)**[7] 3998 3-8-13 **60** 6ex...............................(b) FergusSweeney 4 66
(Alan King) *t.k.h: trckd ldng trio: rdn and nt qckn over 2f out: wl hld over 1f out: kpt on wl nr fin* **7/2**[2]

0516 **4** 2¼ **Trident Tested**[22] 3493 3-8-11 **58**.. KierenFox 2 61
(John Best) *led: rdn and hdd jst over 2f out: steadily fdd over 1f out* **25/1**

0-50 **5** 1 **Permera**[27] 3318 3-8-8 **55**... HarryBentley 8 57
(Mark H Tompkins) *hld up in last pair: rdn to cl on ldrs over 2f out: fdd over 1f out* **12/1**

6-04 **6** 1 **Centuro (USA)**[47] 2639 3-9-2 **63**...................................(tp) TimmyMurphy 7 63
(Jonjo O'Neill) *hld up in last pair: shkn up and no prog 3f out: detached in last 2f out: plugged on* **20/1**

3m 14.72s (10.22) **Going Correction** +0.325s/f (Good) **6** Ran SP% **113.1**
Speed ratings (Par 100): **83,82,82,80,80 79**
CSF £4.98 CT £7.75 TOTE £1.70: £1.10, £2.10; EX 4.50 Trifecta £14.60.
Owner G C Woodall **Bred** Brightwalton Stud **Trained** Newmarket, Suffolk

FOCUS
An uncompetitive handicap run at an honest pace. The fourth looks the key to the form.
T/Plt: £45.10 to a £1 stake. Pool: £62,153.63. 1,005.30 winning tickets. T/Qpdt: £17.90 to a £1 stake. Pool: £5,977.92. 246.67 winning tickets. **Jonathan Neesom**

4022 YARMOUTH (L-H)
Wednesday, July 13

OFFICIAL GOING: Good to firm (good in back straight; 7.6)
Wind: Light, behind Weather: light cloud

4274 BAZUKA BRITISH STALLION STUDS EBF MAIDEN STKS (PLUS 10 RACE) 7f 3y
5:45 (5:45) (Class 4) 2-Y-O **£4,657** (£1,386; £692; £346) **Stalls** Centre

Form RPR

3 **1** **Ronald R (IRE)**[34] 3058 2-9-5 ⁰... JamieSpencer 7 85
(Michael Bell) *hld up in tch in last pair: pushed along and hdwy 2f out: rdn to ld over 1f out: rn green and edgd lft ins fnl f: styd on wl and forged ahd fnl 100yds* **11/2**[3]

2 **2** 1¼ **Jumira Bridge**[13] 3819 2-9-5 ⁰... AndreaAtzeni 6 82
(Roger Varian) *travelled wl: hld up in tch in 4th: clsd to join ldrs on bit over 1f out: rdn ent fnl f: unable qck and btn 100yds out: wknd towards fin* **5/2**[2]

3 ½ **Ultimate Avenue (IRE)** 2-9-5 ⁰.. TedDurcan 5 80
(Ed Walker) *stdd after s: hld up in tch: effrt to chse ldrs 2f out: swtchd lft over 1f out: kpt on same pce ins fnl f* **18/1**

2 **4** nk **Celestial Spheres (IRE)**[33] 3108 2-9-5 ⁰................. JamesMcDonald 1 79
(Charlie Appleby) *sn led: rdn and hdd over 1f out: unable qck 1f out: styd on same pce ins fnl f* **5/2**[2]

3 **5** 3½ **Muzeel (IRE)**[19] 3598 2-9-5 ⁰... PaulHanagan 3 70
(Sir Michael Stoute) *t.k.h: chsd ldr tl unable qck over 1f out: outpcd and btn 1f out: plugged on same pce ins fnl f* **9/4**[1]

06 **6** 8 **Crucial Moment**[21] 3529 2-8-12 ⁰................................ GeorgeWood(7) 2 48
(Bill Turner) *chsd ldng pair tl lost pl and rdn ent fnl 2f: wknd over 1f out* **80/1**

0 **7** 9 **Single Estate**[13] 3819 2-9-5 ⁰.. RyanPowell 4 24
(Sir Mark Prescott Bt) *in tch in rr: pushed along 4f out: rdn and struggling over 2f out: lost tch 2f out* **200/1**

1m 24.84s (-1.76) **Going Correction** -0.225s/f (Firm) **7** Ran SP% **110.3**
Speed ratings (Par 96): **101,99,99,98,94 85,75**
CSF £18.22 TOTE £5.90: £3.10, £1.70; EX 13.70 Trifecta £150.60.
Owner W J and T C O Gredley **Bred** M Morrissey **Trained** Newmarket, Suffolk

FOCUS
Despite 12mm of overnight rain, a drying day meant the going was given officially as good to firm, good in the back straight. After the first, Andrea Atzeni concurred that it was on the fast side of good. The opener had the look of a strong maiden with some powerful stables represented. The winner built on his debut effort.

4275 AEROPAK H'CAP — 1m 1f 21y
6:15 (6:16) (Class 6) (0-55,55) 3-Y-O — **£2,264** (£673; £336; £168) **Stalls** Low

Form — RPR

6403 **1** **Patanjali (IRE)**[8] 3973 3-9-6 **54**.....[1] JohnFahy 8 — 61
(Eve Johnson Houghton) *hld up in tch in last trio: hdwy over 2f out: rdn to chse ldr over 1f out: styd on u.p to ld 100yds out: gng away at fin* **4/1**[2]

-232 **2** 1 ¼ **Go On Gal (IRE)**[48] 2608 3-9-2 **50**..... AdamBeschizza 13 — 55
(Julia Feilden) *t.k.h: chsd ldrs: effrt in 3rd 2f out: rdn to ld over 1f out: sn drvn: hdd 100yds out: one pce after* **5/1**[3]

0-06 **3** 2 **Unsuspected Girl (IRE)**[7] 4018 3-9-1 **54**..... GeorgeBuckell(5) 12 — 55
(David Simcock) *dwlt: hld up in tch in last trio: clsd and nt clr run over 2f out: swtchd rt and hdwy u.p over 1f out: wnt 3rd 1f out: kpt on* **16/1**

00-0 **4** 3 ½ **Rosecomb (IRE)**[184] 148 3-9-4 **52**..... JamieSpencer 3 — 46
(Michael Bell) *s.i.s: hld up in tch in rr: effrt wl over 1f out: hdwy u.p ent fnl f: kpt on same pce and no threat to ldrs ins fnl f* **16/1**

-400 **5** ½ **Wayside Magic**[22] 3482 3-9-2 **50**.....(p) ConnorBeasley 9 — 43
(Michael Dods) *w ldr: rdn and ev ch 2f out tl unable qck over 1f out: wknd ins fnl f* **14/1**

0-00 **6** 3 **Blue Jay (FR)**[8] 3982 3-9-2 **50**.....(t) JimmyQuinn 2 — 37
(Ronald Thompson) *hld up in tch in midfield: effrt 3f out: unable qck and outpcd 2f out: wknd over 1f out* **100/1**

-004 **7** hd **Oceanella (IRE)**[22] 3499 3-9-5 **53**..... JoeyHaynes 1 — 39
(K R Burke) *rdn along leaving stalls: sn prom: rdn over 4f out: struggling u.p over 2f out: wknd over 1f out* **11/1**

-004 **8** 2 **Golden Cape**[15] 3744 3-9-7 **55**..... RobertTart 10 — 37
(Michael Mullineaux) *in tch in midfield: rdn over 3f out: struggling u.p over 2f out: wknd over 1f out* **25/1**

-032 **9** 3 ½ **Bob's Boy**[14] 3765 3-9-7 **55**.....(p) JackMitchell 6 — 30
(Jose Santos) *sn rdn along to ld: rdn 3f out: hdd over 1f out: sn btn: wknd fnl f* **10/3**[1]

060 **10** 2 **Oasis Moon**[18] 3643 3-9-3 **51**..... AndreaAtzeni 7 — 22
(William Haggas) *in tch in midfield: rdn over 2f out: no rspnse and sn struggling: wknd over 1f out* **11/2**

0-00 **11** 4 ½ **Boychick (IRE)**[14] 3765 3-9-4 **52**.....(b) PaulHanagan 14 — 14
(Ed Walker) *chsd ldrs: c to centre over 4f out: rdn 3f out: lost pl and btn 2f out: bhd and eased ins fnl f* **12/1**

1m 56.01s (0.21) **Going Correction** -0.075s/f (Good) — **11** Ran SP% **114.4**
Speed ratings (Par 98): **96,94,93,90,89 86,86,84,81,80 76**
CSF £23.62 CT £285.70 TOTE £4.90: £1.30, £1.90, £5.30; EX 25.10 Trifecta £370.60.
Owner Ms Kathy Phillips **Bred** Endeavour Bloodstock **Trained** Blewbury, Oxon

FOCUS
A poor handicap with very little solid form on display. Straightforward to assess.

4276 DIOMED DEVELOPMENT H'CAP — 1m 2f 23y
6:45 (6:45) (Class 2) (0-100,100) 3-Y£12,286 (£3,677; £1,838; £920; £458) **Stalls** Low

Form — RPR

-000 **1** **Majeed**[160] 455 6-9-11 **97**..... AndreaAtzeni 5 — 106
(David Simcock) *hld up in tch in last pair: swtchd rt 2f out: sn rdn and gd hdwy to chse ldr ent fnl f: led ins fnl f: sn in command and pushed out towards fin* **8/1**

162- **2** 1 ½ **New Year's Night (IRE)**[431] 2064 5-9-7 **93**..... JamesMcDonald 7 — 99
(Charlie Appleby) *chsd ldr: upsides 4f out: rdn to ld over 2f out: drvn and hdd ins fnl f: styd on same pce after* **9/1**

1002 **3** 1 ¼ **Darshini**[24] 3435 4-9-4 **90**..... TedDurcan 2 — 94
(Sir Michael Stoute) *hld up in tch in midfield: effrt ent fnl 2f: drvn to chse ldrs over 1f out: styd on same pce ins fnl f* **6/1**[3]

1-61 **4** ¾ **Fallen For A Star**[18] 3660 4-9-5 **91**..... JamieSpencer 3 — 93
(Luca Cumani) *taken down early: stdd s: hld up in tch: effrt and swtchd rt over 2f out: hdwy to chse ldr over 1f out tl ent fnl f: no ex and styd on same pce ins fnl f* **3/1**[2]

0213 **5** 10 **Demonstration (IRE)**[21] 3525 4-8-3 **82**.....(p) GeorgeWood(7) 6 — 64
(William Jarvis) *led: jnd 4f out: rdn and hdd over 2f out: lost pl and btn over 1f out: wknd fnl f* **8/1**

0-05 **6** ½ **Niceofyoutotellme**[48] 2626 7-10-0 **100**..... JohnFahy 4 — 81
(Ralph Beckett) *stdd s: t.k.h: hld up in tch in rr: gd hdwy to join ldrs 4f out: rdn over 2f out: sn lost pl: bhd and wknd over 1f out* **10/1**

20-0 **7** 18 **Spanish Squeeze (IRE)**[63] 2157 4-9-12 **98**..... PaulHanagan 1 — 43
(Hugo Palmer) *trckd ldrs: effrt on inner wl over 2f out: no imp and struggling 2f out: sn wknd: bhd and eased ins fnl f* **9/4**[1]

2m 8.17s (-2.33) **Going Correction** -0.075s/f (Good) — **7** Ran SP% **111.4**
Speed ratings (Par 109): **106,104,103,103,95 94,80**
CSF £70.70 TOTE £9.50: £4.10, £3.60; EX 77.70 Trifecta £260.80.
Owner Khalifa Dasmal **Bred** Newsells Park Stud & Strategic B'Stock **Trained** Newmarket, Suffolk

FOCUS
An intriguing contest which, on paper at least, looked like a decent handicap. However, they got racing a long way from home and the last to make their challenge ran out the winner.

4277 FREEDERM H'CAP — 1m 3f 104y
7:20 (7:21) (Class 5) (0-70,72) 3-Y-O+ — **£2,911** (£866; £432; £216) **Stalls** Low

Form — RPR

0002 **1** **Zain Arion (IRE)**[18] 3652 3-8-9 **63**..... AndreaAtzeni 5 — 70
(Charlie Fellowes) *t.k.h: chsd ldr tl led after 2f: mde rest: rdn and fnd ex over 1f out: styd on and a doing enough ins fnl f* **7/2**[3]

4221 **2** 1 ¾ **Palisade**[7] 4021 3-9-4 **72** 6ex.....(v) RyanPowell 3 — 76
(Sir Mark Prescott Bt) *stdd s: t.k.h: hld up in tch in last pair: effrt 2f out: rdn to chse ldr over 1f out: drvn and styd on same pce ins fnl f* **2/1**[1]

0334 **3** ½ **Dream Factory (IRE)**[27] 3306 3-9-2 **70**.....(b[1]) LiamJones 4 — 73
(Marco Botti) *t.k.h: reluctant ldr for 2f: chsd ldr for 7f out: styd handy: rdn to chse wnr again 2f out tl over 1f out: styd on same pce after* **9/1**

4154 **4** 1 ¼ **Dakota City**[20] 3570 5-9-13 **69**.....(v) AdamBeschizza 1 — 70
(Julia Feilden) *stdd s: hld up in tch in rr: effrt over 1f out: 4th and styd on same pce ins fnl f* **12/1**

6002 **5** 4 **Knight Commander**[23] 3468 3-9-2 **70**..... JamieSpencer 6 — 64
(William Knight) *hld up wl in tch in 4th: clsd 3f out: rdn and unable qck over 1f out: wknd ins fnl f* **5/2**[2]

0201 **6** ½ **Almutamarred (USA)**[20] 3564 4-9-6 **62**..... ShaneKelly 2 — 56
(Kevin Morgan) *t.k.h: trckd ldrs tl wnt 2nd 7f out tl 2f out: sn rdn and lost pl: wknd fnl f* **10/1**

2m 35.48s (6.78) **Going Correction** -0.075s/f (Good)
WFA 3 from 4yo+ 12lb — **6** Ran SP% **110.9**
Speed ratings (Par 103): **72,70,70,69,66 66**
CSF £10.67 TOTE £5.00: £2.60, £1.40; EX 11.40 Trifecta £61.20.
Owner Asaad Al Banwan **Bred** Lynch Bages & Camas Park Stud **Trained** Newmarket, Suffolk

FOCUS
The 3yos held sway in this modest handicap but it was, on the whole, an unsatisfactory affair. They crawled through the first half of the race and didn't exactly go much quicker after until they sprinted for home, with the long-time leader outpointing them. The form isn't cast-iron.

4278 4HEAD H'CAP — 6f 3y
7:50 (7:50) (Class 6) (0-60,59) 3-Y-O+ — **£2,264** (£673; £336; £168) **Stalls** Centre

Form — RPR

44-0 **1** **Vincenzo Coccotti (USA)**[46] 2697 4-9-8 **57**..... ShaneKelly 4 — 66
(Ken Cunningham-Brown) *stdd s: t.k.h: hld up in tch in midfield: hdwy 2f out: pushed into ld 1f out: edgd lft u.p ins fnl f: pushed out and jst doing enough towards fin* **14/1**

0600 **2** nk **Chetan**[8] 3989 4-9-7 **56**.....(tp) AdamBeschizza 6 — 64
(Charlie Wallis) *taken down early: led for 2f: w ldr after: drvn to ld over 1f out: hdd 1f out: rallied u.p ins fnl f: kpt on* **11/1**

0450 **3** ½ **Multi Quest**[7] 3993 4-9-1 **50**.....(b) RyanPowell 11 — 56
(John E Long) *w ldrs tl led after 2f: rdn 2f out: hdd over 1f out: stl ev ch ins fnl f: unable qck and one pce fnl 100yds* **20/1**

0343 **4** 2 ¾ **Tasaaboq**[8] 3984 5-9-2 **54**.....(t) JosephineGordon(3) 13 — 52
(Phil McEntee) *hld up in tch towards rr: hdwy to chse ldrs and drvn over 1f out: hung lft and no imp ins fnl f* **8/1**

00-2 **5** ¾ **Reinforced**[43] 2776 3-9-3 **58**..... ConnorBeasley 2 — 52
(Michael Dods) *wl in tch in midfield: clsd to chse ldrs and rdn 2f out: unable qck u.p over 1f out: wknd ins fnl f* **3/1**[1]

-100 **6** nk **Tulip Dress**[8] 3987 3-9-4 **59**..... PaulHanagan 1 — 52
(Anthony Carson) *stdd after s: hld up in tch: effrt over 2f out: drvn and no hdwy over 1f out: wknd ins fnl f* **14/1**

4-04 **7** hd **Mc Diamond (IRE)**[40] 2845 4-9-2 **58**..... GeorgeWood(7) 12 — 52
(Michael Mullineaux) *hld up in tch in midfield: effrt over 2f out: no imp over 1f out: hld and keeping on same pce whn carried lft ins fnl f* **25/1**

0066 **8** 1 **Monna Valley**[21] 3522 4-9-5 **59**.....(bt[1]) AaronJones(5) 5 — 49
(Stuart Williams) *in tch in last quartet: effrt 2f out: edgd lft and no hdwy over 1f out: wl hld and plugged on same pce ins fnl f* **15/2**[3]

-454 **9** 1 ½ **Westbourne Grove (USA)**[13] 3822 3-9-1 **56**..... JamieSpencer 10 — 41
(John Butler) *taken down early: stdd s: hld up in rr: swtchd rt and effrt 2f out: no real imp tl styd on to pass btn horses ins fnl f: nvr trbld ldrs* **9/1**

6600 **10** nk **Single Summit**[13] 3822 4-8-10 **45**.....(v) JFEgan 8 — 30
(J R Jenkins) *hld up in tch: effrt 2f out: no imp: wl hld and plugged on same pce ins fnl f* **100/1**

3043 **11** hd **Commanche**[13] 3822 7-9-7 **56**.....(b) AndreaAtzeni 7 — 40
(Chris Dwyer) *in tch in midfield: rdn over 2f out: no rspnse and lost pl wl over 1f out: wl hld and plugged on same pce ins fnl f* **7/1**[2]

060- **12** 2 ½ **Plantation (IRE)**[261] 7517 3-9-0 **55**.....(p) TedDurcan 9 — 30
(Robert Cowell) *t.k.h: hld up in tch in midfield: effrt over 2f out: sn struggling and lost pl over 1f out: wknd fnl f* **20/1**

0035 **13** 3 ¾ **Whaleweigh Station**[18] 3648 5-9-7 **56**..... LemosdeSouza 3 — 20
(J R Jenkins) *restless in stalls: chsd ldrs tl lost pl over 2f out: bhd ins fnl f* **17/2**

1m 12.73s (-1.67) **Going Correction** -0.225s/f (Firm)
WFA 3 from 4yo+ 6lb — **13** Ran SP% **116.9**
Speed ratings (Par 101): **102,101,100,97,96 95,95,94,92,91 91,88,83**
CSF £149.33 CT £3155.37 TOTE £16.20: £3.70, £3.60, £6.20; EX 165.90 Trifecta £2518.00.
Owner David Henery **Bred** Gainesway Thoroughbreds Ltd Et Al **Trained** Danebury, Hants

■ Stewards' Enquiry : Shane Kelly Trainer said regarding the apparent improvement in form that the gelding had benefitted from its previous run after a long break
Paul Hanagan two-day ban; excessive use of whip (28-29th July)

FOCUS
The field shunned the rails and went up the middle. Moderate fare and not form to dwell upon. The winner and the third are the keys to the form.

4279 OTEX H'CAP — 1m 3y
8:20 (8:21) (Class 6) (0-65,64) 3-Y-O — **£2,264** (£673; £336; £168) **Stalls** Centre

Form — RPR

-044 **1** **Fol O'Yasmine**[34] 3080 3-9-3 **60**.....(p) AndreaAtzeni 3 — 69
(William Haggas) *trckd ldng pair: effrt over 1f out: hdwy u.p to ld ins fnl f: r.o wl* **11/4**[1]

5-06 **2** 1 ¼ **Party Thyme**[13] 3823 3-9-5 **62**..... TedDurcan 6 — 67
(Chris Wall) *chsd ldr: rdn to ld over 1f out: drvn and hdd ins fnl f: styd on same pce after* **8/1**

3600 **3** nk **Harlequin Rock**[19] 3615 3-9-3 **60**..... JFEgan 4 — 64
(Mick Quinn) *stdd after s: t.k.h: hld up in last pair: effrt over 1f out: styd on wl u.p fnl 100yds: no threat to wnr* **14/1**

-311 **4** ½ **Frank Bridge**[8] 3975 3-9-6 **63** 6ex..... JohnFahy 1 — 66
(Eve Johnson Houghton) *stdd after s: hld up in tch in last pair: effrt 2f out: drvn to chse ldrs over 1f out: styd on same pce u.p ins fnl f* **7/2**[3]

6-65 **5** nk **Pina**[51] 2545 3-9-5 **62**..... JamieSpencer 2 — 64
(Roger Charlton) *tk keen hld: hld up in tch in midfield: effrt 2f out: pressing ldrs but unable qck 1f out: styd on same pce ins fnl f* **10/3**[2]

505 **6** 1 ½ **Tamara Love (IRE)**[41] 2824 3-9-0 **57**.....(t) AdamBeschizza 5 — 56
(Stuart Williams) *awkward leaving stalls and s.i.s: t.k.h: in tch in midfield: effrt but unable qck over 1f out: r.o same pce fnl f* **33/1**

4-00 **7** 1 ¼ **Lee's Hall (IRE)**[74] 1860 3-9-7 **64**..... ShaneKelly 9 — 60
(Murty McGrath) *t.k.h: hld up in tch in midfield: rdn and unable qck over 1f out: lost pl 1f out: bhd and one pce after* **10/1**

3254 **8** 1 ¼ **Cadland Lad (IRE)**[22] 3489 3-8-6 **52**.....(t) JosephineGordon(3) 7 — 45
(John Ryan) *racd keenly: led: rdn and hdd over 1f out: sn outpcd: wknd ins fnl f* **9/1**

1m 41.69s (1.09) **Going Correction** -0.225s/f (Firm) — **8** Ran SP% **111.8**
Speed ratings (Par 98): **85,83,83,82,82 81,79,78**
CSF £24.13 CT £253.44 TOTE £4.20: £1.40, £2.10, £3.50; EX 24.20 Trifecta £220.20.
Owner Saleh Al Homaizi & Imad Al Sagar **Bred** Saleh Al Homaizi & Imad Al Sagar **Trained** Newmarket, Suffolk

FOCUS
A modest handicap which didn't take much winning. Spread right across the course with 2f to run, there were no excuses for the also-rans. The form is rated around the placed horses.

4280 IBULEVE H'CAP 5f 42y
8:50 (8:50) (Class 5) (0-70,69) 3-Y-O **£2,911** (£866; £432; £216) **Stalls** Centre

Form RPR

4232 **1** **Justice Lady (IRE)**[26] 3360 3-9-1 **63** ShaneKelly 8 72+
(David Elsworth) *stdd s: t.k.h: hld up in tch in rr: clsd to trck ldrs over 1f out: swtchd rt and effrt ent fnl f: pushed into ld ins fnl f: r.o wl: pushed out* **9/4**[1]

2122 **2** *1 ¼* **Jack The Laird (IRE)**[7] 3994 3-9-1 **63** (b) PaulHanagan 6 67
(Dean Ivory) *chsd ldr tl 1/2-way: styd prom: rdn and ev ch over 1f out: kpt on u.p: wnt 2nd but nt matching pce of wnr wl ins fnl f* **11/4**[3]

6-04 **3** *nk* **Archimedes (IRE)**[19] 3625 3-9-6 **68** (v[1]) JamieSpencer 7 71
(Robert Cowell) *swtchd rt after s: chsd ldrs tl wnt 2nd 1/2-way: rdn to ld over 1f out: hdd ins fnl f: r.o same pce after* **5/2**[2]

-003 **4** *1* **Lady Nayef**[20] 3581 3-9-7 **69** (v[1]) JFEgan 5 68
(John Butler) *sn bustled along to ld: c to stands' rail after 1f: rdn and hdd over 1f out: no ex and outpcd ins fnl f* **17/2**

3660 **5** *1 ¼* **Justice Rock**[23] 3473 3-8-0 **55** GeorgeWood(7) 1 50
(Phil McEntee) *in tch: effrt but unable qck over 1f out: wknd ins fnl f* **25/1**

-053 **6** *7* **Langham**[21] 3527 3-9-3 **68** JosephineGordon(3) 4 37
(Martyn Meade) *in tch in last pair: rdn and struggling 1/2-way: wknd and bhd over 1f out* **8/1**

1m 1.74s (-0.96) **Going Correction** -0.225s/f (Firm) **6** Ran SP% **111.5**
Speed ratings (Par 100): **98,96,95,93,91 80**
CSF £8.64 CT £14.77 TOTE £3.20: £1.80, £2.30; EX 8.30 Trifecta £23.20.
Owner Robert Ng **Bred** Miss Audrey F Thompson **Trained** Newmarket, Suffolk

FOCUS
A run-of-the-mill handicap, but there were a few who could prove better than their current rating so form to be positive about. The race is rated around the runner-up.
T/Plt: Part won. £39,448.80 to a £1 stake. Pool: £54,039.54. 0.50 winning tickets. T/Qpdt: £2,019.10 to a £1 stake. Pool: £6,330.35. 2.32 winning tickets. **Steve Payne**

4281 - 4286a (Foreign Racing) - See Raceform Interactive

[4082]CHEPSTOW (L-H)
Thursday, July 14

OFFICIAL GOING: Good to firm (good in places on straight course; firm in places on back straight; 7.8)
Wind: sunny spells Weather: light across

4287 COVEA INSURANCE MEDIAN AUCTION MAIDEN STKS 6f 16y
2:10 (2:11) (Class 6) 2-Y-O **£2,587** (£770; £384; £192) **Stalls** Centre

Form RPR

1 **Parsnip (IRE)** 2-9-0 0 WilliamCarson 5 76+
(Michael Bell) *wore a hood in parade ring: hld up in mid-div: rdn and hdwy 2f out: led ins fnl f: pushed out* **15/2**

542 **2** *2 ¾* **Bazwind (IRE)**[16] 3742 2-9-5 0 JFEgan 16 72
(David Evans) *chsd ldrs: pushed along 1/2-way: wnt 2nd 100yds out: kpt on: hld by wnr* **11/2**[3]

3 *1 ¼* **Coronation Cottage** 2-9-0 0 RyanTate 11 63
(Malcolm Saunders) *a.p: rdn to ld 2f out: edgd rt and hdd ins fnl f: no ex and lost 2nd 100yds out* **33/1**

60 **4** *½* **Father McKenzie**[10] 3954 2-9-5 0 CharlesBishop 9 66
(Mick Channon) *chsd ldrs: rdn over 2f out: kpt on same pce fnl f* **25/1**

0 **5** *shd* **Incentive**[22] 3511 2-9-0 0 TomQueally 2 61
(Stuart Kittow) *t.k.h in mid-div: rdn and hdwy 2f out: nudged along and kpt on wl fnl f* **100/1**

0 **6** *hd* **Singula**[14] 3813 2-9-5 0 FergusSweeney 17 65
(Alan King) *hld up in mid-div: hdwy 1/2-way: rdn 2f out: sn ev ch: unable qck fnl f* **11/4**[1]

7 *½* **Seafarer (IRE)** 2-8-12 0 TylerSaunders(7) 13 66+
(Marcus Tregoning) *dwlt: in rr: pushed along and hdwy 1/2-way: r.o wl fnl f* **33/1**

8 *1 ¼* **Drop Kick Murphi (IRE)** 2-9-5 0 SteveDrowne 12 60
(George Baker) *a in mid-div: styd on fnl f: nvr able to chal* **16/1**

9 *shd* **Mission Authorized (IRE)**[15] 3789 2-9-0 0 LeighRoche 10 55
(Adrian Paul Keatley, Ire) *chsd ldrs: rdn 1/2-way: sltly outpcd 2f out: wknd fnl f* **8/1**

4 **10** *½* **Secret Potion**[23] 3485 2-9-5 0 ShaneKelly 14 58
(Ronald Harris) *cl up: led over 3f out to 2f out: wknd 1f out* **20/1**

06 **11** *6* **Zebby Sizz (IRE)**[16] 3742 2-9-5 0 TomMarquand 8 39
(Richard Hannon) *led over 2f: styd prom: rdn 2f out: wknd 1f out* **16/1**

0 **12** *1 ¾* **Oxford Blu**[17] 3730 2-9-5 0 LukeMorris 6 33
(Sir Mark Prescott Bt) *s.i.s: a towards rr* **33/1**

13 *shd* **Zymyran** 2-9-5 0 JimCrowley 3 33
(David Simcock) *s.i.s: rdn 2f out: a towards rr* **9/2**[2]

5 **14** *1 ¼* **Dusty Berry**[14] 3812 2-9-0 0 JohnFahy 4 24
(Eve Johnson Houghton) *mid-div tl dropped to rr 1/2-way: no ch after* **12/1**

15 *4* **Precious Equity (FR)** 2-8-7 0 RPWalsh(7) 1 11
(David Menuisier) *a towards rr* **66/1**

40 **16** *9* **Limelight Lady**[22] 3529 2-9-0 0 SamHitchcott 7
(Harry Dunlop) *chsd ldrs tl lost pl after 2f: bhd fnl 2f* **66/1**

1m 11.81s (-0.19) **Going Correction** -0.275s/f (Firm) **16** Ran SP% **124.0**
Speed ratings (Par 92): **90,86,84,84,83 83,82,81,81,80 72,70,70,68,63 51**
CSF £45.92 TOTE £8.30: £2.40, £1.80, £9.70; EX 54.40 Trifecta £2277.40 Part won..
Owner Lady Bamford **Bred** Mrs M Fox **Trained** Newmarket, Suffolk

FOCUS
Race distance as advertised. An ordinary maiden, with the form horse Leontes a non-runner, but a likeable effort from the winner.

4288 GLAMORGAN FEDERATION WOMEN'S INSTITUTE H'CAP 1m 14y
2:40 (2:41) (Class 5) (0-75,75) 3-Y-O+ **£3,881** (£1,155; £577; £288) **Stalls** Centre

Form RPR

-124 **1** **Feed The Goater (FR)**[16] 3745 3-9-4 **74** TomMarquand 3 81
(Richard Hannon) *hld up in tch: rdn and hdwy 2f out: r.o to ld fnl 75yds: jst hld on* **9/2**[2]

54-2 **2** *nse* **Hollywood Road (IRE)**[14] 3823 3-9-2 **72** (p) JimCrowley 4 79
(Don Cantillon) *t.k.h: a.p: rdn to ld appr fnl f: hdd 75yds out: r.o: jst hld* **2/1**[1]

0-44 **3** *1* **Hardington**[31] 3236 3-8-13 **69** FergusSweeney 11 74
(Alan King) *hld up bhd ldrs: rdn 2f out: ev ch ins fnl f: no ex towards fin* **5/1**[3]

30-4 **4** *2* **Rajadamri**[17] 3724 3-8-4 **60** RyanTate 8 60
(Rod Millman) *chsd ldrs: rdn 2f out: styd on fnl f* **33/1**

60-5 **5** *1 ¼* **Fast And Hot (IRE)**[189] 85 3-8-4 **60** KieranO'Neill 2 57
(Richard Hannon) *cl up: rdn over 3f out: carried sltly lft 2f out: styd on same pce fnl f* **22/1**

00- **6** *1 ¾* **An Duine Uasal (IRE)**[15] 3792 3-8-11 **67** (b) LeighRoche 1 60
(Adrian Paul Keatley, Ire) *prom: rdn 3f out: led 2f out tl hdd appr fnl f: edgd rt and sn wknd* **14/1**

521 **7** *¾* **Saint Helena (IRE)**[41] 2849 8-9-9 **70** (b) TomQueally 5 63
(Mark Gillard) *s.i.s: in rr: drvn over 3f out: hdwy 2f out: one pce fnl f* **11/1**

6240 **8** *2 ½* **Molten Lava (IRE)**[42] 2827 4-10-0 **75** (b) LukeMorris 7 63
(Paul Cole) *wnt to post early: t.k.h in mid-div: hdwy after 3f: rdn over 2f out: sn wknd* **10/1**

-120 **9** *¾* **Beauty Night**[52] 2545 3-9-3 **73** JohnFahy 10 57
(Clive Cox) *narrow ld tl rdn and hdd 2f out: wknd fnl f* **10/1**

45-0 **10** *3 ¼* **Prim And Proper**[16] 3748 5-9-0 **64** (p) NoelGarbutt(3) 9 43
(John Flint) *t.k.h: cl up: rdn over 2f out: wknd over 1f out* **25/1**

1360 **11** *2 ¾* **Karnage (IRE)**[39] 2930 4-9-11 **72** (b) TimmyMurphy 6 44
(Daniel Kubler) *t.k.h: cl up tl wknd over 2f out* **33/1**

1m 34.43s (-1.77) **Going Correction** -0.275s/f (Firm)
WFA 3 from 4yo+ 9lb **11** Ran SP% **115.4**
Speed ratings (Par 103): **97,96,95,93,92 90,90,87,86,83 80**
CSF £12.95 CT £45.67 TOTE £4.60: £1.70, £1.20, £2.20; EX 13.80 Trifecta £53.20.
Owner Middleham Park Racing LXXI **Bred** Haras Du Mezeray **Trained** East Everleigh, Wilts

FOCUS
Race distance as advertised. A pretty modest handicap but the right horses came to the fore. The form is rated around them.

4289 CHEPSTOW PLANT INTERNATIONAL H'CAP (DIV I) 7f 16y
3:15 (3:19) (Class 6) (0-55,59) 3-Y-O+ **£2,587** (£770; £384; £192) **Stalls** Centre

Form RPR

-050 **1** **Carcharias (IRE)**[28] 3319 3-8-6 **48** JohnFahy 10 55
(Ed de Giles) *led tl over 3f out: styd cl up: rdn over 1f out: led wl ins fnl f: sn clr* **12/1**

0331 **2** *2* **Gulland Rock**[9] 3988 5-9-4 **59** 6ex LukeCarson(7) 12 65
(Anthony Carson) *chsd ldrs: rdn 3f out: led over 1f out: jockey only able to push as sadlle slipped: hdd and no ex wl ins fnl f* **5/1**[1]

1204 **3** *1* **Ettie Hart (IRE)**[9] 3975 3-8-6 **55** KillianHennessy(7) 1 54
(Mick Channon) *prom: rdn 2f out: kpt on fnl f* **9/1**

6120 **4** *½* **Guapo Bay**[22] 3527 3-8-3 **52** (b) TinaSmith(7) 9 50
(Richard Hannon) *chsd ldrs: rdn to ld over 3f out: edgd rt over 2f out: hdd and veered lft over 1f out: one pce* **14/1**

233U **5** *nse* **Wild Flower (IRE)**[38] 2969 4-9-2 **50** KieranO'Neill 7 51
(Jimmy Fox) *towards rr: hdwy 1/2-way: rdn over 3f out: one pce fnl 2f* **6/1**[2]

6005 **6** *1 ¾* **Bold Grove**[6] 4088 4-8-9 **46** oh1 (p) NathanAlison(3) 3 45+
(Edward Bevan) *walked to s: wnt rt s and v.s.a: bhd: stl last 2f out: hdwy whn nt clr run over 1f out: styd on fnl f* **8/1**[3]

2336 **7** *nk* **Israfel**[38] 2969 3-8-11 **53** WilliamCarson 6 45
(Jamie Osborne) *mid-div: rdn over 2f out: one pce ins fnl f* **12/1**

2240 **8** *nk* **Tax Reform (IRE)**[9] 3973 6-8-9 **46** oh1 (b) EoinWalsh(3) 11 40
(Natalie Lloyd-Beavis) *s.s: t.k.h in rr: hdwy 1/2-way: rdn 3f out: nt run on appr fnl f* **25/1**

43-4 **9** *½* **The Reel Way (GR)**[38] 2969 5-8-7 **48** MitchGodwin(7) 16 41
(Patrick Chamings) *mid-div: rdn over 2f out: one pce: b.b.v* **8/1**[3]

-050 **10** *nk* **Outlaw Kate (IRE)**[42] 2810 4-8-12 **46** oh1 (p) RobertTart 2 38
(Michael Mullineaux) *towards rr tl styd on and modest hdwy fnl f* **33/1**

0040 **11** *½* **Dandys Perier (IRE)**[9] 3987 5-9-6 **54** DavidProbert 15 45
(Ronald Harris) *cl up: rdn over 2f out: wknd over 1f out* **8/1**[3]

06/0 **12** *¾* **Captain Devious**[86] 1556 5-8-5 **46** oh1 RPWalsh(7) 14 35
(Grace Harris) *chsd ldrs: rdn over 3f out: wknd 2f out* **100/1**

6646 **13** *¾* **Wishing Tree**[26] 3423 3-8-8 **55** CallumShepherd(5) 13 39
(Brian Ellison) *chsd ldrs: rdn 1/2-way: grad wknd fnl 2f* **6/1**[2]

5000 **14** *14* **Flashy King (IRE)**[28] 3317 3-7-11 **46** oh1 (t) SophieKilloran(7) 4
(Joseph Tuite) *drvn 1/2-way: a in rr* **66/1**

60-6 **15** *1 ½* **Pintle's Image**[17] 3720 4-9-0 **48** LukeMorris 5
(John Spearing) *mid-div tl rdn and dropped to rr after 3f: no ch after* **25/1**

1m 22.59s (-0.61) **Going Correction** -0.275s/f (Firm)
WFA 3 from 4yo+ 8lb **15** Ran SP% **123.7**
Speed ratings (Par 101): **92,89,88,88,87 85,85,85,84,84 83,82,82,66,64**
CSF £69.92 CT £597.84 TOTE £16.10: £5.20, £1.30, £4.20; EX 124.00 Trifecta £1705.40.
Owner Boardman, Golder, Sercombe & Viall I **Bred** Mrs Helen Walsh **Trained** Ledbury, H'fords

FOCUS
Race distance as advertised. The first division of a moderate handicap, the favourite got worked up in the stalls and the sixth did remarkably well considering he was awkward exiting the stalls and then went badly right, losing many lengths.

4290 CHEPSTOW PLANT INTERNATIONAL H'CAP (DIV II) 7f 16y
3:45 (3:48) (Class 6) (0-55,55) 3-Y-O+ **£2,587** (£770; £384; £192) **Stalls** Centre

Form RPR

-000 **1** **Prince Of Cardamom (IRE)**[33] 3125 4-9-1 **49** (p) FergusSweeney 15 55
(Jonathan Geake) *chsd ldrs: rdn over 2f out: r.o u.p to ld last stride* **20/1**

5-04 **2** *shd* **Poor Duke (IRE)**[27] 3342 6-8-12 **46** RobertTart 13 52
(Michael Mullineaux) *chsd ldrs: rdn to chal 2f out: led over 1f out: hdd last stride* **7/1**[3]

-043 **3** *1* **Mendacious Harpy (IRE)**[8] 3993 5-9-6 **54** SteveDrowne 1 57
(George Baker) *mid-div: hdwy over 2f out: chsd ldrs over 1f out: repeatedly flashed tail and kpt on same pce fnl f* **5/1**[1]

0306 **4** *¾* **Concur (IRE)**[32] 3198 3-8-6 **48** RyanTate 10 46
(Rod Millman) *chsd ldr tl led 1/2-way: rdn and hdd over 1f out: lost 2nd ins fnl f: no ex towards fin* **13/2**[2]

0-00 **5** *3 ½* **Euroquip Boy (IRE)**[16] 3743 9-9-0 **51** NoelGarbutt(3) 8 43
(Michael Scudamore) *prom: chsd ldr 3f out: rdn and ev ch 2f out: wknd ins fnl f* **16/1**

0563 **6** *3* **Fossa**[9] 3987 6-8-12 **46** oh1 RyanClark 14 29
(Mark Brisbourne) *mid-div: rdn over 2f out: styd on same pce fnl f* **8/1**

7 *5* **Buzz Boy (ITY)**[26] 3426 3-8-7 **49** (b[1]) LeighRoche 4 16
(Adrian Paul Keatley, Ire) *towards rr: rdn 1/2-way: modest late hdwy* **5/1**[1]

6-50 **8** *½* **Avon Scent**[22] 3514 6-8-5 **46** oh1 (p) RPWalsh(7) 2 15
(Christopher Mason) *towards rr: rdn 1/2-way: plugged on past btn rivals fnl f* **20/1**

6000 **9** *½* **Top Cop**[8] 3993 7-9-0 **48** (p) DavidProbert 5 15
(Ronald Harris) *a in mid-div: wknd over 1f out* **12/1**

3665 **10** *nk* **Ocean Bentley (IRE)**[8] 4024 4-8-12 **46** oh1 JimCrowley 7 12
(Tony Carroll) *mid-div: wknd over 2f out* **14/1**

000/ **11** 4½ **Saxony**[709] 5005 5-8-12 **46** oh1 WilliamCarson 12
(Matthew Salaman) *t.k.h: led to 1/2-way: lost 2nd 3f out: rdn and wknd over 1f out* **66/1**

0-05 **12** 2¼ **Just Fred (IRE)**[9] 3975 3-8-13 **55** TomQueally 9
(Denis Coakley) *s.i.s: a in rr* **13/2**[2]

00-0 **13** 9 **Dramatic Voice**[57] 2368 3-8-4 **46** oh1 KieranO'Neill 11
(Paul Cole) *chsd ldrs to 1/2-way: sn wknd* **25/1**

0-00 **14** 31 **Overstone Lass (IRE)**[16] 3735 4-8-12 **46** oh1 (b) ShaneKelly 3
(John Spearing) *mid-div: wknd 1/2-way: sn bhd: eased over 1f out: t.o* **50/1**

1m 22.07s (-1.13) **Going Correction** -0.275s/f (Firm)
WFA 3 from 4yo+ 8lb **14** Ran SP% **120.7**
Speed ratings (Par 101): **95,94,93,92,88 85,79,79,78,78 73,70,60,24**
CSF £148.02 CT £848.58 TOTE £26.90: £10.00, £2.70, £1.80; EX 266.90 Trifecta £2615.20 Part won..
Owner Mrs P D Gulliver **Bred** Kildaragh Stud **Trained** East Kennett, Wilts

FOCUS
Race distance as advertised. This was run in a time 0.52secs quicker than the first leg.

4291 CASTLE BINGO MANAGERS CHOICE H'CAP 6f 16y
4:15 (4:17) (Class 4) (0-80,80) 3-Y-O+ **£6,469** (£1,925; £962; £481) **Stalls** Centre

Form RPR

-505 **1** **Sydney Ruffdiamond**[31] 3233 4-9-12 **80** ShaneKelly 1 89
(Richard Hughes) *led pair on far side and overall ldr: rdn over 2f out: r.o wl* **11/1**

-010 **2** 1¼ **Monarch Maid**[9] 3980 5-9-5 **73** WilliamCarson 9 78
(Peter Hiatt) *led gp of 8 on nr side: cl up: r.o u.p fnl f: clsng on wnr on far side towards fin but a hld* **16/1**

1141 **3** 1 **Gilmer (IRE)**[6] 4084 5-9-1 **72** 6ex NoelGarbutt[(3)] 6 74+
(Laura Young) *wnt to post early: towards rr in gp of 8 nr side: rdn along 1/2-way: hdwy over 1f out: kpt on ins fnl f: unable to chal* **9/2**[1]

-152 **4** 2 **Mo Henry**[27] 3369 4-8-9 **63** (v) LeighRoche 8 58
(Adrian Paul Keatley, Ire) *racd in gp of 8 nr side: chsd ldrs: rdn 2f out: wknd fnl f* **6/1**[2]

4660 **5** 1 **Air Of York (IRE)**[3] 4211 4-9-2 **77** (v[1]) MitchGodwin[(7)] 11 69
(David Evans) *racd in gp of 8 nr side: chsd ldrs: rdn ins fnl 2f: wknd fnl f* **20/1**

1213 **6** ½ **Layla's Hero (IRE)**[17] 3726 9-9-10 **78** (b) JimCrowley 2 69
(Roger Teal) *chsd wnr in pair far side: one pce and no ch fnl 2f* **11/1**

0544 **7** hd **Indian Affair**[5] 4155 6-8-12 **66** (vt) RoystonFfrench 7 56
(Milton Bradley) *racd in gp of 8 nr side: chsd ldrs: rdn 2f out: wknd over 1f out* **8/1**[3]

4133 **8** 1¾ **Ginzan**[14] 3815 8-9-11 **79** FergusSweeney 3 63
(Malcolm Saunders) *chsd ldr in gp of 3 in centre: led gp wl over 1f out but no imp on wnr far side: wknd ins fnl f* **10/1**

6406 **9** shd **Brazen Spirit**[37] 3004 4-9-4 **72** (v) LukeMorris 10 56
(Clive Cox) *racd in gp of 8 nr side: chsd ldrs: pushed along 1/2-way: wknd over 2f out* **25/1**

3000 **10** 1¼ **Divine Call**[5] 4155 9-8-8 **62** (v) TomMarquand 13 42
(Milton Bradley) *racd in gp of 8 nr side: a bhd* **25/1**

4505 **11** 2 **Jacob's Pillow**[28] 3326 5-8-11 **68** NathanAlison[(3)] 4 42
(Rebecca Bastiman) *wnt to post early: led gp of 3 in centre: prom overall: hdd in gp over 1f out: wknd and eased whn no ch ins fnl f* **8/1**[3]

3601 **12** 1¼ **Nightingale Valley**[17] 3720 3-9-5 **79** TomQueally 5 48
(Stuart Kittow) *racd in gp of 3 centre: chsd ldrs tl wknd wl over 1f out* **12/1**

-052 **13** 2 **Vincentti (IRE)**[15] 3771 6-9-4 **72** DavidProbert 12 35
(Ronald Harris) *s.s: racd in gp of 8 nr side: a in rr* **8/1**[3]

1m 9.57s (-2.43) **Going Correction** -0.275s/f (Firm)
WFA 3 from 4yo+ 6lb **13** Ran SP% **117.6**
Speed ratings (Par 105): **105,103,102,99,98 97,97,94,94,92 90,88,85**
CSF £167.62 CT £940.05 TOTE £12.40: £4.40, £5.20, £1.60; EX 195.60 Trifecta £4433.30 Part won..
Owner Gallagher Equine Ltd **Bred** Cavendish Inv Ltd & Mr & Mrs B W Hills **Trained** Upper Lambourn, Berkshire

FOCUS
Race distance as advertised. A fair handicap with the winner coming home far side. He's rated back to his 3yo form.

4292 DRIBUILD DASH H'CAP (ROUND 3 OF THE CHEPSTOW SPRINT SERIES) 5f 16y
4:50 (4:51) (Class 6) (0-55,55) 3-Y-O+ **£2,587** (£770; £384; £192) **Stalls** Centre

Form RPR

4456 **1** **Quantum Dot (IRE)**[28] 3316 5-9-2 **50** (b) JimCrowley 3 62
(Ed de Giles) *mde all on far side: clr whn rdn over 1f out: r.o strly* **8/1**

04-1 **2** 2¾ **Go Amber Go**[8] 3994 4-9-4 **52** 6ex RyanTate 11 54
(Rod Millman) *chsd wnr thrght: one pce and no imp fnl f* **11/4**[1]

5560 **3** 2 **Lizzy's Dream**[13] 3843 8-9-3 **51** TomQueally 8 46
(Rebecca Bastiman) *chsd ldrs: rdn over 1f out: one pce* **16/1**

5013 **4** hd **Very First Blade**[21] 3549 7-9-2 **50** (p) RobertTart 1 44
(Michael Mullineaux) *hld up: hdwy over 1f out: r.o ins fnl f* **12/1**

2-04 **5** hd **Virile (IRE)**[8] 3993 5-9-6 **54** (b) ShaneKelly 7 47
(Sylvester Kirk) *s.s: towards rr: hdwy over 1f out: r.o ins fnl f* **9/2**[2]

0006 **6** 2¼ **Tally's Song**[6] 4084 3-8-0 **46** oh1 RPWalsh[(7)] 12 29
(Grace Harris) *chsd ldrs: rdn and no imp over 1f out: wknd fnl f* **66/1**

035 **7** 1 **Go Charlie**[8] 3994 5-8-13 **47** LemosdeSouza 14 29+
(Lisa Williamson) *wnt to post early: s.s and in rr in gp of 4 nr side: hdwy to ld gp over 1f out: no ch w far side* **14/1**

0311 **8** ½ **Triple Dream**[44] 2765 11-9-4 **52** LukeMorris 2 32
(Milton Bradley) *mid-div: rdn and no imp over 1f out: wknd fnl f* **8/1**

0000 **9** 1¾ **Buraug**[8] 3993 4-9-0 **48** (v[1]) KieranO'Neill 15 22+
(Milton Bradley) *prom in gp of 4 nr side: led gp over 2f out tl rdn over 1f out: no imp on far side: wknd fnl f* **25/1**

0650 **10** 1 **Temple Road (IRE)**[15] 3780 8-9-2 **50** (vt[1]) FergusSweeney 5 20
(Milton Bradley) *a towards rr* **22/1**

-606 **11** nk **Baz's Boy**[9] 3975 3-8-4 **46** oh1 NoelGarbutt[(3)] 10 13
(John Flint) *mid-div: pushed along 1/2-way: nvr on terms* **14/1**

00-3 **12** 4½ **Mo Wonder**[36] 3046 3-8-11 **50** (p) LeighRoche 13 +
(Adrian Paul Keatley, Ire) *prom in gp of 4 nr side but but nvr on terms w far side: rdn 1/2-way: wknd 2f out* **7/1**[3]

-006 **13** ¾ **Dismantle (IRE)**[17] 3719 3-9-2 **55** JFEgan 16 3+
(Grace Harris) *chsd ldr in gp of 4 nr side but nvr on terms overall: wknd 2f out* **33/1**

40-0 **14** 1¼ **Indian Tim**[41] 2845 4-8-12 **46** oh1 TomMarquand 6
(Milton Bradley) *mid-div: rdn over 3f out: sn lost pl and bhd* **50/1**

58.24s (-1.06) **Going Correction** -0.275s/f (Firm)
WFA 3 from 4yo+ 5lb **14** Ran SP% **121.1**
Speed ratings (Par 101): **97,92,89,89,88 85,83,82,79,78 77,70,69,67**
CSF £28.94 CT £368.87 TOTE £9.60: £3.80, £1.10, £4.40; EX 40.80 Trifecta £397.20.
Owner Mrs Yvonne Fleet **Bred** R N Auld **Trained** Ledbury, H'fords

FOCUS
Race distance as advertised. Little got into this sprint, with the winner making all against the far rail.

4293 CAVENDISH MAINE RECRUITMENT H'CAP 1m 2f 36y
5:25 (5:25) (Class 5) (0-70,70) 3-Y-O+ **£3,881** (£1,155; £577; £288) **Stalls** Low

Form RPR

2142 **1** **Panko (IRE)**[7] 4046 3-9-2 **69** JimCrowley 1 80+
(Ed de Giles) *chsd ldr: led 2f out: rdn and r.o strly fnl f* **5/4**[1]

5012 **2** 2½ **Miss Ranger (IRE)**[9] 3983 4-9-7 **68** CallumShepherd[(5)] 3 73+
(Brian Ellison) *t.k.h in 4th: impr a pl after 4f: rdn 2f out: sn no ch w wnr but r.o fnl f to go 2nd post* **5/2**[2]

0-01 **3** nse **Senza Una Donna**[33] 3135 3-8-12 **70** (t) CharlieBennett[(5)] 6 75
(Hughie Morrison) *hld up in last pair: rdn and clsd over 2f out: wnt 2nd over 1f out: no imp on wnr fnl f: ct for 2nd post* **3/1**[3]

0000 **4** 4½ **Living Leader**[34] 3097 7-9-7 **63** (tp) JFEgan 8 59
(Grace Harris) *hld up in last pair: rdn over 3f out: styd on same pce fnl 2f* **33/1**

5-00 **5** ½ **Who'sthedaddy**[160] 463 4-9-8 **64** [1] TimmyMurphy 5 59
(Daniel Kubler) *led and set stdy pce: rdn and hdd 2f out: wknd appr fnl f* **16/1**

4603 **6** 4 **Jazri**[23] 3488 5-9-1 **57** (v[1]) LukeMorris 2 44
(Milton Bradley) *chsd ldrs: rdn 2f out: sn wknd* **14/1**

2m 11.13s (0.53) **Going Correction** -0.075s/f (Good)
WFA 3 from 4yo+ 11lb **6** Ran SP% **113.5**
Speed ratings (Par 103): **94,92,91,88,87 84**
CSF £4.74 CT £6.84 TOTE £2.50: £1.60, £1.40; EX 6.60 Trifecta £10.10.
Owner Simon Treacher **Bred** Jennifer & Evelyn Cullen **Trained** Ledbury, H'fords

FOCUS
Race distance as advertised. Not a terribly strong handicap and no surprise to see one of the 3yos emerge on top. IT was steadily run and isn't form to take too literally.

4294 MARSTON'S PLC APPRENTICE H'CAP 1m 4f 23y
5:55 (5:56) (Class 6) (0-65,65) 4-Y-O+ **£2,587** (£770; £384; £192) **Stalls** Low

Form RPR

3001 **1** **Petrify**[6] 4082 6-8-1 **52** 6ex (tp) MitchGodwin[(7)] 1 59+
(Bernard Llewellyn) *dwlt and lost 8 l: clsd and in tch after 3f: rdn and hdwy on ins 3f out: wnt 2nd wl over 1f out: led ent fnl f: styd on wl* **10/3**[1]

20-5 **2** 1¼ **Grams And Ounces**[25] 2850 9-8-13 **60** (t) NoelGarbutt[(3)] 7 65
(Grace Harris) *chsd ldrs: led over 3f out: rdn 2f out: hdd ent fnl f: kpt on: no ex towards fin* **10/1**

-625 **3** 4 **Mexican Mick**[16] 3747 7-8-8 **55** AaronJones[(3)] 6 54
(Peter Hiatt) *chsd ldrs tl lost pl 1/2-way: last and drvn along over 3f out: hdwy on outer fnl 2f: wnt 3rd 1f out: no imp on ldng pair* **5/1**[3]

2200 **4** ¾ **Distant High**[5] 4158 5-9-1 **64** (p) CharlieBennett[(5)] 2 61
(Richard Price) *hld up in mid-div: rdn 3f out: styd on same pce fnl 2f* **8/1**

0230 **5** 2¼ **Highlife Dancer**[8] 3997 8-8-8 **57** KillianHennessy[(5)] 10 51
(Mick Channon) *led tl rdn and hdd over 3f out: lost 2nd 2f out: one pce* **6/1**

1355 **6** 3¼ **Kawartha**[37] 2995 4-9-7 **65** TomMarquand 9 54
(Robert Stephens) *chsd ldr tl relegated to 3rd over 3f out: sn rdn: wknd appr fnl f* **5/1**[3]

4443 **7** 9 **Phantom River**[23] 3498 4-9-1 **62** (p) CallumShepherd[(3)] 5 36
(Alan King) *hld up: hdwy 5f out: rdn over 2f out: wknd over 1f out* **7/2**[2]

2m 37.7s (-1.30) **Going Correction** -0.075s/f (Good) **7** Ran SP% **113.1**
Speed ratings (Par 101): **101,100,97,97,95 93,87**
CSF £35.00 CT £162.83 TOTE £3.90: £2.50, £4.80; EX 33.30 Trifecta £92.20.
Owner B J Llewellyn **Bred** Fittocks Stud **Trained** Fochriw, Caerphilly

FOCUS
Race distance as advertised. A moderate handicap, although the first two pulled clear and the winner did exceptionally well considering he walked out the gate, losing several lengths.
T/Jkpt: Not won. T/Plt: £193.70 to a £1 stake. Pool: £119,489.96 - 450.20 winning tickets. T/Qpdt: £16.60 to a £1 stake. Pool: £6,038.59 - 268.77 winning tickets. **Richard Lowther**

4039 DONCASTER (L-H)
Thursday, July 14

OFFICIAL GOING: Good to firm (good in places; 8.3)
Wind: Moderate against Weather: Fine & dry

4295 SOLUTIONS 4 CLEANING APPRENTICE H'CAP 5f
6:00 (6:00) (Class 5) (0-70,70) 3-Y-O+ **£3,234** (£962; £481; £240) **Stalls** Centre

Form RPR

3122 **1** **Seamster**[7] 4039 9-9-7 **68** (t) CameronNoble[(5)] 8 77
(David Loughnane) *trckd ldrs: effrt over 1f out: rdn to chal ins fnl f: kpt on wl to ld nr line* **9/4**[1]

2406 **2** nse **You're Cool**[17] 3713 4-9-7 **68** LewisEdmunds[(5)] 4 76
(John Balding) *cl up: led wl over 1f out and sn rdn: drvn ins fnl f: hdd nr line* **25/1**

0-3 **3** 1¼ **Flying Bear (IRE)**[19] 3650 5-10-0 **70** DavidParkes 5 74
(Jeremy Gask) *trckd ldrs: hdwy 2f out: rdn over 1f out: kpt on fnl f* **7/2**[2]

-012 **4** ¾ **Bondi Beach Babe**[12] 3880 6-9-11 **70** (p) HarryBurns[(3)] 7 71
(James Turner) *in rr: hdwy over 2f out: rdn over 1f out: kpt on wl fnl f* **6/1**[3]

2503 **5** hd **Noodles Blue Boy**[23] 3494 10-9-9 **70** (p) RobertDodsworth[(5)] 11 70
(Ollie Pears) *wnt rt s: chsd ldrs on outer: slt ld over 3f out: rdn along and hdd over 1f out: drvn: edgd rt and no ex fnl f* **20/1**

4260 **6** ¾ **Ruby's Day**[17] 3713 7-9-9 **70** TomDonoghue[(5)] 10 67
(David Brown) *towards rr: hdwy 2f out: rdn over 1f out: kpt on fnl f* **12/1**

3202 **7** nk **Hit The Lights (IRE)**[13] 3851 6-9-8 **67** (v) DanielleMooney[(3)] 1 63
(David Nicholls) *cl up: rdn along 2f out: wknd over 1f out* **11/1**

6004 **8** ½ **Sir Geoffrey (IRE)**[14] 3811 10-8-7 **52** (b) NatalieHambling[(3)] 9 47
(Scott Dixon) *led: hdd over 3f out: cl up: rdn wl over 1f out: wknd appr fnl f* **20/1**

2365 **9** ¾ **See Vermont**[15] 3779 8-9-5 **64** (p) CallumRodriguez[(3)] 6 56
(Rebecca Bastiman) *a towards rr* **16/1**

4222 **10** 1¼ **Bahamian Sunrise**[16] 3741 4-9-9 **70** (p) LauraCoughlan[(5)] 2 57
(John Gallagher) *dwlt: sn chsng ldrs on outer: rdn along 2f out: grad wknd* **8/1**

1160 **11** 3 ½ **Roy's Legacy**[17] 3713 7-9-5 **66**.. DavidEgan(5) 3 41
(Shaun Harris) *in tch: rdn along 2f out: sn drvn and wknd over 1f out* **25/1**

59.6s (-0.90) **Going Correction** -0.40s/f (Firm) **11** Ran SP% **117.5**
Speed ratings (Par 103): **91,90,88,87,87 86,85,84,83,81 76**
CSF £70.50 CT £192.76 TOTE £2.90: £1.20, £8.60, £1.70; EX 64.70 Trifecta £747.60.
Owner Bamford and Fell **Bred** D G Hardisty Bloodstock **Trained** Market Drayton, Shropshire

FOCUS
The ground had dried out and was good to firm, good in places. This was a sprint run at a strong pace. This takes the winner to the level of his winter AW form.

4296 FRENCHGATE FASHION FILLIES' NURSERY H'CAP 6f
6:35 (6:35) (Class 4) 2-Y-O **£4,528** (£1,347; £673; £336) **Stalls** Centre

Form RPR

31 **1** **Clef**[12] 3874 2-8-11 **69**.. PaulHanagan 1 73
(Richard Fahey) *trckd ldrs: cl up 1/2-way: chal wl over 1f out and sn rdn: drvn ins fnl f: kpt on gamely to ld nr fin* **5/1**

12 **2** *hd* **Miss Sugars**[15] 3782 2-8-13 **71**.. JamieSpencer 8 74
(David Simcock) *hld up: hdwy wl over 1f out: swtchd rt and effrt to chal jst ins fnl f: sn rdn and ev ch: drvn: green and hung lft last 75yds: kpt on* **7/2**[2]

1 **3** *hd* **Appointed**[56] 2404 2-9-7 **79**.. DavidAllan 2 82
(Tim Easterby) *cl up: led over 2f out: rdn wl over 1f out: drvn ins fnl f: hdd and hmpd last 50yds: kpt on* **15/8**[1]

1 **4** 1 ½ **Funky Footsteps (IRE)**[21] 3555 2-9-3 **75**.......................... CharlesBishop 3 73
(Eve Johnson Houghton) *dwlt: hld up in rr: hdwy over 2f out: chsd ldrs over 1f out: sn rdn and kpt on same pce fnl f* **5/1**

063 **5** 1 **Roys Dream**[12] 3881 2-8-5 **63**.. ShaneGray 5 58
(Kristin Stubbs) *led: rdn along 1/2-way: hdd over 2f out: grad wknd* **22/1**

253 **6** 3 ½ **Four Dragons**[33] 3128 2-8-7 **65**.. BenCurtis 7 50
(Tom Dascombe) *t.k.h: chsd ldrs: rdn along 2f out: sn wknd* **9/2**[3]

1m 13.39s (-0.21) **Going Correction** -0.40s/f (Firm) **6** Ran SP% **112.9**
Speed ratings (Par 93): **85,84,84,82,81 76**
CSF £22.83 CT £43.36 TOTE £6.00: £2.60, £2.20; EX 16.10 Trifecta £45.70.
Owner Cheveley Park Stud **Bred** Cheveley Park Stud Ltd **Trained** Musley Bank, N Yorks

FOCUS
Just an ordinary gallop to this fillies' nursery in which only two heads covered the first three home and the bare form may not prove totally reliable.

4297 TRENT FURNACE NOVICE STKS (PLUS 10 RACE) 6f
7:05 (7:06) (Class 4) 2-Y-O **£4,528** (£1,347; £673; £336) **Stalls** Centre

Form RPR

1 **1** **Blue Point (IRE)**[35] 3065 2-9-8 0.. JamesMcDonald 2 110+
(Charlie Appleby) *trckd ldr: led after 2f out: qcknd clr on bridle wl over 1f out: impressive* **30/100**[1]

14 **2** 11 **Shamsaya (IRE)**[19] 3663 2-9-3 0.. RobertHavlin 8 68
(Simon Crisford) *led 2f: trckd wnr: rdn along 2f out: kpt on same pce* **9/2**[2]

00 **3** ¾ **Asfaar (IRE)**[34] 3093 2-9-2 0.. PaulHanagan 6 64
(Brian Meehan) *chsd ldrs: rdn along over 2f out: sn drvn and kpt on same pce* **40/1**

4 4 ½ **Election Day** 2-9-2 0.. FrannyNorton 7 50
(Mark Johnston) *chsd ldrs: rdn along 2f out: sn wknd* **7/1**[3]

5 4 ½ **Thorndyke** 2-9-2 0.. ShaneGray 1 36
(Kevin Ryan) *chsd ldrs: rdn along over 2f out: sn outpcd* **33/1**

6 3 ½ **Dandy Place (IRE)** 2-9-2 0.. DavidAllan 5 24+
(Tim Easterby) *s.i.s: a bhd* **50/1**

1m 11.75s (-1.85) **Going Correction** -0.40s/f (Firm) **6** Ran SP% **114.9**
Speed ratings (Par 96): **96,81,80,74,68 63**
CSF £2.21 TOTE £1.30: £1.10, £1.50; EX 2.30 Trifecta £10.80.
Owner Godolphin **Bred** Oak Lodge Bloodstock **Trained** Newmarket, Suffolk

FOCUS
Just a small field and a long odds-on favourite but a most impressive winner. The form is rated just a shade negatively but the winner looks a proper Group horse.

4298 RICHARD PENCOTT MEMORIAL BRITISH STALLION STUDS EBF MAIDEN FILLIES' STKS (PLUS 10 RACE) 7f
7:35 (7:37) (Class 5) 2-Y-O **£3,881** (£1,155; £577; £288) **Stalls** Centre

Form RPR

1 **San Sebastiana** 2-9-0 0.. DougieCostello 11 78
(K R Burke) *towards rr: hdwy over 2f out: swtchd lft and rdn over 1f out: styd on strly fnl f to ld last 50yds* **50/1**

622 **2** ½ **Naifah (IRE)**[21] 3556 2-9-0 0.. RobertHavlin 3 77
(John Gosden) *sn trcking ldrs: hdwy to ld 2f out: rdn over 1f out: hdd narrowly ins fnl f: sn drvn and rallied to ld again last 100yds: hdd and no ex last 50yds* **2/1**[1]

3 1 ¼ **Vanity Queen** 2-9-0 0.. JamieSpencer 6 75+
(Luca Cumani) *dwlt and in rr: stdy hdwy on outer over 2f out: chal over 1f out: rdn to take slt ld jst ins fnl f: hdd and no ex last 100yds* **16/1**

4 2 **Aimez La Vie (IRE)** 2-9-0 0.. GeorgeChaloner 8 71+
(Richard Fahey) *t.k.h: sn trcking ldrs: n.m.r and swtchd rt whn stmbld bdly and lost pl over 1f out: sn swtchd lft and rdn: styd on wl fnl f* **25/1**

5 **5** ½ **Bassmah**[14] 3818 2-9-0 0.. PaulMulrennan 2 67
(Ismail Mohammed) *rrd s and dwlt: t.k.h: hdwy to chse ldrs 2f out: rdn over 1f out: kpt on same pce* **4/1**[3]

2 **6** *nse* **See The Sea (IRE)**[19] 3640 2-9-0 0.. SeanLevey 9 67
(Richard Hannon) *hld up in tch: hdwy over 2f out: rdn and kpt on fnl f* **3/1**[2]

33 **7** 1 ¾ **Ivor's Magic (IRE)**[8] 4022 2-8-7 0.. AdamMcLean(7) 12 62
(David Elsworth) *chsd ldrs: rdn along 2f out: grad wknd* **16/1**

8 1 ¼ **Silver Gleam (IRE)** 2-9-0 0.. DavidAllan 13 59
(Tim Easterby) *dwlt and t.k.h in rr: tl sme late hdwy* **66/1**

0 **9** *nk* **Hazy Manor (IRE)**[36] 3024 2-9-0 0.. BenCurtis 10 58
(Tom Dascombe) *cl up: rdn along 2f out: drvn and wknd over 1f out* **100/1**

10 ½ **Vista Steppe** 2-9-0 0.. MartinHarley 14 56
(David Simcock) *a towards rr* **16/1**

00 **11** 1 ¼ **Flawed Diamond (FR)**[21] 3561 2-8-9 0.......................... JordanVaughan(5) 7 53
(K R Burke) *prom: rdn along 2f out: sn drvn and wknd* **25/1**

12 *hd* **Savannah Moon (IRE)** 2-9-0 0.. ShaneGray 15 53
(Kevin Ryan) *led: rdn along over 2f out: sn hdd & wknd* **14/1**

5 **13** 2 ¾ **Darwasi**[21] 3556 2-9-0 0.. PaulHanagan 16 45
(Brian Meehan) *midfield on outer: pushed along wl over 2f out: sn rdn and outpcd* **8/1**

0 **14** 4 ½ **Sai Kung Star**[20] 3597 2-8-11 0.......................... RachelRichardson(3) 5 33
(Nigel Tinkler) *in tch: rdn along 3f out: sn wknd* **100/1**

1m 27.45s (1.15) **Going Correction** -0.40s/f (Firm) **14** Ran SP% **126.9**
Speed ratings (Par 91): **77,76,75,72,72 72,70,68,68,67 66,66,62,57**
CSF £154.86 TOTE £64.00: £14.60, £1.10, £4.30; EX 389.10 Trifecta £4447.60 Part won..
Owner Tim Dykes & Mrs E Burke **Bred** D Boocock **Trained** Middleham Moor, N Yorks

FOCUS
Quite an interesting fillies' maiden though the pace was ordinary. The initial level of the form is fluid.

4299 TERRY BELLAS MEMORIAL H'CAP 7f
8:10 (8:13) (Class 3) (0-90,90) 3-Y-O+ **£7,762** (£2,310; £1,154; £577) **Stalls** Centre

Form RPR

-064 **1** **Brazos (IRE)**[20] 3622 5-9-13 **89**.. (b) MartinHarley 16 98
(James Tate) *trckd ldng pair: chsd ldr after 2f: led 2f out: rdn over 1f out: drvn ins fnl f: jst hld on* **8/1**[2]

-060 **2** *nse* **Regal Dan (IRE)**[34] 3115 6-9-5 **84**.......................... ShelleyBirkett(3) 11 93
(David O'Meara) *hld up towards rr: hdwy over 2f out: swtchd lft over 1f out: rdn to chal ins fnl f: sn drvn and ev ch: jst failed* **8/1**[2]

01-0 **3** 1 ½ **Rex Imperator**[34] 3115 7-10-0 **90**.. (p) RobertHavlin 8 95
(David O'Meara) *trckd ldrs: effrt 2f out and sn rdn: styd on fnl f* **20/1**

4-20 **4** ½ **Commodore (IRE)**[61] 2246 4-9-10 **86**.. SteveDrowne 13 90+
(George Baker) *hld up towards rr: hdwy over 2f out: swtchd rt and rdn over 1f out: styd on fnl f* **25/1**

0345 **5** *nk* **Father Bertie**[11] 3923 4-9-12 **88**.. (tp) DavidAllan 2 91
(Tim Easterby) *prom: rdn along over 2f out: drvn over 1f out: kpt on u.p fnl f* **10/1**

4236 **6** *nse* **Fuwairt (IRE)**[10] 3945 4-9-2 **78**.. SamJames 4 81
(David Loughnane) *in tch: pushed along and hdwy 2f out: rdn over 1f out: styd on fnl f* **8/1**[2]

2440 **7** *shd* **Bertiewhittle**[27] 3358 8-9-9 **88**.......................... RachelRichardson(3) 14 90
(David Barron) *towards rr: hdwy 2f out and sn pushed along: n.m.r and swtchd rt over 1f out: kpt on wl fnl f* **12/1**

-000 **8** ¾ **Hawkeyethenoo (IRE)**[27] 3346 10-9-7 **83**.. JoeDoyle 7 83
(Jim Goldie) *towards rr: hdwy on outer wl over 1f out: sn rdn and kpt on fnl f* **20/1**

1001 **9** 1 ¼ **Slemy (IRE)**[17] 3708 5-9-4 **80**.. JamesSullivan 18 77
(Ruth Carr) *hld up in rr: sme hdwy 2f out: sn rdn and no imp* **9/1**[3]

0-06 **10** 2 ¾ **Fendale**[9] 3980 4-10-0 **90**.. PaulMulrennan 10 80
(Michael Dods) *trckd ldrs: effrt over 2f out and sn pushed along: rdn wl over 1f out: grad wknd* **8/1**[2]

000 **11** *nk* **Showboating (IRE)**[19] 3645 8-9-3 **79**.. JamieSpencer 9 68
(John Balding) *hld up: a towards rr* **25/1**

-621 **12** 1 ¾ **Johnny Cavagin**[9] 3980 7-9-13 **89** 6ex.. (t) JimmyQuinn 1 73
(Ronald Thompson) *plld hrd: chsd ldrs: rdn along over 2f out: sn btn* **7/1**[1]

0-00 **13** *nse* **Zacynthus (IRE)**[19] 3645 8-9-2 **78**.. BenCurtis 12 62
(John Balding) *a in rr* **25/1**

0014 **14** *hd* **Hidden Treasures**[14] 3803 3-8-2 **72**.. PatrickMathers 5 52
(Richard Fahey) *a towards rr* **14/1**

5-15 **15** 1 ¾ **Zaeem**[186] 134 7-9-9 **90**.. (p) LanceBetts(5) 17 69
(Ivan Furtado) *sn led and clr: rdn along and hdd 2f out: sn wknd* **33/1**

0004 **16** 23 **Chookie Royale**[19] 3655 8-10-0 **90**.. (p) PhillipMakin 3 7
(Keith Dalgleish) *chsd ldrs: rdn along over 3f out: wknd wl over 2f out: bhd and eased over 1f out* **8/1**[2]

1m 24.88s (-1.42) **Going Correction** -0.40s/f (Firm)
WFA 3 from 4yo+ 8lb **16** Ran SP% **125.5**
Speed ratings (Par 107): **92,91,90,89,89 89,89,88,86,83 83,81,81,81,79 52**
CSF £65.48 CT £1316.12 TOTE £8.60: £2.40, £3.40, £5.90, £6.10; EX 103.50 Trifecta £2221.90.
Owner Saeed Manana **Bred** John O'Kelly Bloodstock Services **Trained** Newmarket, Suffolk

FOCUS
A competitive 7f handicap run at a fair clip and the form should work out.

4300 YESSS ELECTRICAL H'CAP 1m 2f 60y
8:40 (8:40) (Class 4) (0-85,85) 4-Y-O+ **£5,175** (£1,540; £769; £384) **Stalls** Low

Form RPR

2-45 **1** **Shakopee**[45] 2752 4-9-7 **85**.. JamieSpencer 2 98+
(Luca Cumani) *in tch: hdwy on outer over 2f out: led over 1f out and sn rdn clr: styd on* **3/1**[2]

-303 **2** 1 ¾ **Goodwood Mirage (IRE)**[35] 3077 6-9-4 **85**.......................... LouisSteward(3) 7 93+
(Michael Bell) *trckd ldrs: gng wl whn nt clr run wl over 1f out: sn swtchd rt and rdn to chse wnr ent fnl f: kpt on* **8/1**

3202 **3** 1 ¾ **Salmon Sushi**[10] 3950 5-9-4 **82**.. DavidAllan 1 86
(Tim Easterby) *hld up in rr: hdwy 3f out: rdn to chse ldrs wl over 1f out: drvn and kpt on fnl f* **6/1**

2314 **4** 2 ¼ **Mountain Rescue (IRE)**[19] 3660 4-9-4 **82**.......................... JamesMcDonald 10 82
(Chris Wall) *t.k.h: prom: effrt over 2f out: rdn along wl over 1f out: sn drvn and one pce* **11/2**[3]

0403 **5** 4 **Sennockian Star**[5] 4129 6-9-7 **85**.. (v) FrannyNorton 3 77
(Mark Johnston) *led: hdd 1/2-way: cl up on inner and rdn along 3f out: sn btn* **15/8**[1]

-560 **6** 2 **Illusive (IRE)**[45] 2752 5-9-7 **85**.. (b) GrahamGibbons 9 73
(George Scott) *trckd ldrs: hdwy to ld 1/2-way: rdn along wl over 2f out: drvn 2f out: sn hdd & wknd* **14/1**

5-06 **6** *dht* **Regal Ways (IRE)**[19] 3660 4-8-8 **72**.. BenCurtis 4 60
(Brian Ellison) *towards rr: rdn along wl over 2f out: n.d* **40/1**

-000 **8** 2 **El Beau (IRE)**[19] 3660 5-9-1 **79**.. CamHardie 8 63
(John Quinn) *chsd ldrs: rdn along 3f out: drvn over 2f out and sn wknd* **25/1**

2m 9.05s (-0.35) **Going Correction** +0.10s/f (Good) **8** Ran SP% **113.5**
Speed ratings (Par 105): **105,103,102,100,97 95,95,94**
CSF £26.66 CT £133.93 TOTE £3.70: £1.30, £2.50, £2.50; EX 26.90 Trifecta £117.80.
Owner Kangyu International Racing (HK) Limited **Bred** Fittocks Stud **Trained** Newmarket, Suffolk

FOCUS
Race distance increased by 9 yards. Just an ordinary gallop to this handicap in which the first two were the clear picks. Probably decent form for the grade.

4301 EQUESTRIAN SURFACES LTD H'CAP 1m 2f 60y
9:10 (9:11) (Class 5) (0-70,70) 3-Y-O **£3,881** (£1,155; £577; £288) **Stalls** Low

Form RPR

00-1 **1** **Mia Tesoro (IRE)**[35] 3080 3-9-0 **63**.. StevieDonohoe 7 67
(Charlie Fellowes) *trckd ldng pair: hdwy over 2f out: rdn to ld jst over 1f out: drvn out* **5/6**[1]

065 **2** *nk* **Wallangarra**[21] 3577 3-9-1 **64**.. AdamBeschizza 5 67
(Jeremy Gask) *led: jnd and pushed along 3f out: rdn wl over 1f out: hdd appr fnl f: sn drvn: rallied gamely last 100yds: kpt on* **9/2**[3]

5650 **3** 1 ¾ **Calypso Delegator (IRE)**[17] 3715 3-8-2 **51** oh1.......................... JimmyQuinn 2 51
(Micky Hammond) *trckd ldr: hdwy 3f out and sn chal: rdn 2f out: drvn and ev ch appr fnl f: kpt on same pce last 150yds* **12/1**

6-34 **4** *1* **Cacica**[14] 3810 3-9-3 **66**....................(p) WilliamTwiston-Davies 3 63
(George Scott) *hld up in rr: hdwy wl over 2f out: rdn over 1f out: drvn and no imp fnl f* **9/4**[2]
2m 16.26s (6.86) **Going Correction** +0.10s/f (Good) **4** Ran SP% **111.2**
Speed ratings (Par 100): **76,75,74,73**
CSF £5.15 TOTE £1.80; EX 5.00 Trifecta £22.60.
Owner Deron Pearson **Bred** D Pearson **Trained** Newmarket, Suffolk
FOCUS
Race distance increased by 9 yards. Just an ordinary gallop to this handicap and the form is unlikely to be strong. The first two recorded pbs.
T/Plt: £115.70 to a £1 stake. Pool: £80,325.97 - 506.68 winning tickets. T/Qpdt: £31.00 to a £1 stake. Pool: £7,933.58 - 189.11 winning tickets. **Joe Rowntree**

4046 EPSOM (L-H)
Thursday, July 14

OFFICIAL GOING: Good
Wind: Light, across Weather: Fine

4302 JEM ROBINSON APPRENTICE H'CAP 1m 114y
6:10 (6:12) (Class 5) (0-75,70) 4-Y-0+ £3,881 (£1,155; £577; £288) Stalls Low

Form RPR
0134 **1** **Wordismybond**[33] 3142 7-9-0 **65**.................. StephenCummins(7) 1 72
(Richard Hughes) *mde all: pushed along 2f out: wl in command 1f out: comf* **6/1**[3]
031 **2** *1* **Zaria**[14] 3802 5-8-13 **62**..........................(p) HollieDoyle(5) 4 67
(Richard Price) *chsd wnr: rdn 2f out: kpt on but nvr able to chal* **9/2**[2]
1412 **3** *¾* **Solveig's Song**[16] 3737 4-9-9 **67**...................(p) EdwardGreatrex 9 70+
(Steve Woodman) *chsd ldrs: 5th and pushed along st: rdn over 2f out: kpt on to take 3rd ins fnl f* **7/1**
3341 **4** *1 ¼* **Duke Of North (IRE)**[16] 3739 4-9-4 **67**............... RhiainIngram(5) 3 67
(Jim Boyle) *trckd ldng pair: cl up on inner 2f out: nt qckn over 1f out: one pce* **4/1**[1]
1000 **5** *¾* **Victor's Bet (SPA)**[8] 4008 7-9-11 **69**................ GeorgeDowning 8 68
(Ralph J Smith) *dwlt: hld up: last st: effrt whn nt clr run 2f out: hanging lft but kpt on fr over 1f out* **7/1**
13-0 **6** *¾* **Dubai Light**[30] 2872 5-9-7 **68**....................... HectorCrouch(3) 5 65
(Gary Moore) *hld up in 7th: effrt whn nt clr run over 2f out: no hdwy over 1f out: plugged on* **8/1**
0005 **7** *1* **Dukes Meadow**[8] 4008 5-9-4 **62**..................(b) MarcMonaghan 10 57
(Roger Ingram) *awkward s: hld up: 8th st: effrt on outer over 2f out: sn no prog: wl btn fnl f* **14/1**
5000 **8** *1 ¾* **Welsh Inlet (IRE)**[19] 3648 8-9-6 **64**.................... DannyBrock 6 55
(John Bridger) *in tch: 6th st: sn rdn: wknd wl over 1f out* **33/1**
2052 **9** *nk* **Thecornishbarron (IRE)**[7] 4052 4-9-5 **70**........... JonathanFisher(7) 2 60
(John Ryan) *dwlt: sn trckd ldrs: 4th st: pushed along and no prog 2f out: wknd over 1f out* **9/2**[2]
1m 48.98s (2.88) **Going Correction** +0.10s/f (Good) **9** Ran SP% **116.4**
Speed ratings (Par 103): **91,90,89,88,87 87,86,84,84**
CSF £33.43 CT £195.61 TOTE £7.20: £2.80, £1.20, £2.50; EX 42.10 Trifecta £195.10.
Owner T W Wellard & Partners **Bred** Henry And Mrs Rosemary Moszkowicz **Trained** Upper Lambourn, Berkshire
■ The first winner for Stephen Cummins.
FOCUS
Race distances as advertised. A run-of-the-mill apprentice event which was steadily run, the winner very much enjoying the run of it from the front under a well-judged ride. The winner is rated back to her Brighton May form.

4303 KINGSWOOD H'CAP 1m 4f 10y
6:45 (6:51) (Class 5) (0-75,75) 3-Y-0+ £3,881 (£1,155; £577; £288) Stalls Centre

Form RPR
3-31 **1** **Alyssa**[17] 3727 3-9-1 **75**.......................... SilvestreDeSousa 7 91
(Ralph Beckett) *trckd ldrs: wnt 2nd st: led 3f out: pushed along 2f out: drew rt away over 1f out* **1/2**[1]
3653 **2** *10* **Machine Learner**[20] 3607 3-8-10 **73**...............(v[1]) EdwardGreatrex(3) 3 73
(Michael Bell) *hld up in tch: 4th st: prog to chse wnr wl over 2f out and sn only danger: drew wl clr of rest but easily lft bhd fr over 1f out* **9/2**[2]
0024 **3** *23* **Dellbuoy**[14] 3798 7-8-2 **56** oh1.................. SophieRalston(7) 6 19
(Pat Phelan) *hld up: detached 1/2-way: 6th st: kpt on to take poor 4th over 2f out: tk remote 3rd ins fnl f* **16/1**
52 **4** *4* **Fishergate**[23] 3493 3-8-5 **65**...........................(b[1]) RyanPowell 1 22
(Richard Rowe) *pushed up to ld then r freely: hdd 3f out and sn wknd qckly: lost remote 3rd ins fnl f* **10/1**[3]
5465 **5** *18* **Bushel (USA)**[21] 3560 6-9-2 **66**........................(p) EoinWalsh(3) 2
(Tony Newcombe) *chsd ldrs: rdn 5f out: 5th and struggling st: t.o* **14/1**
500/ **6** *6* **John Biscuit (IRE)**[58] 7976 8-9-8 **74**.................. DannyBurton(5) 5
(Jo Davis) *hld up: rdn and lost tch 1/2-way: last and t.o st* **33/1**
-003 **7** *1* **Sixties Love**[16] 3738 5-9-6 **67**....................... MichaelJMMurphy 4
(Simon Dow) *chsd ldr tl ent st: sn wknd rapidly: t.o* **20/1**
2m 39.4s (0.50) **Going Correction** +0.10s/f (Good)
WFA 3 from 5yo+ 13lb **7** Ran SP% **114.2**
Speed ratings (Par 103): **102,95,80,77,65 61,60**
CSF £3.10 TOTE £1.30: £1.10, £2.30; EX 3.30 Trifecta £15.30.
Owner Miss K Rausing **Bred** Miss K Rausing **Trained** Kimpton, Hants
FOCUS
A race which fell apart after the leaders went hard but the winner is clearly progressive. There wasn't much depth to this.

4304 IRISH STALLION FARMS EBF MAIDEN STKS 7f
7:15 (7:16) (Class 5) 2-Y-0 £3,881 (£1,155; £577; £288) Stalls Low

Form RPR
22 **1** **Bear Valley (IRE)**[14] 3808 2-9-5 0.................. SilvestreDeSousa 3 83
(Mark Johnston) *mde all: shkn up over 2f out: drvn and styd on wl fr over 1f out* **15/8**[1]
02 **2** *2* **Hurricane Rush (IRE)**[17] 3730 2-9-5 0.............. MichaelJMMurphy 5 78
(Charles Hills) *t.k.h and sn hld up in 5th: rdn and prog to chse ldng pair wl over 1f out: nvr able to threaten wnr but kpt on to snatch 2nd last stride* **15/8**[1]
3 **3** *nse* **Navarone (IRE)**[13] 3854 2-9-5 0.................... TonyHamilton 1 78
(Richard Fahey) *trckd ldrs: 4th st: prog to chse wnr over 2f out: rdn and no imp after: kpt on but lost 2nd last stride* **9/4**[2]
460 **4** *8* **Crystal Secret**[21] 3555 2-9-0 0.......................... DannyBrock 6 51
(John Bridger) *chsd wnr to jst over 3f out: wknd 2f out* **66/1**
0 **5** *3 ¾* **Dragon Dream (IRE)**[10] 3954 2-8-7 0................ RhiainIngram(7) 2 41
(Roger Ingram) *mostly in last: nvr a factor and no prog over 2f out* **100/1**

34 **6** *¾* **Zaatar (IRE)**[50] 2583 2-8-9 0........................ PaddyPilley(5) 7 39
(Mick Channon) *t.k.h: trckd ldng pair 5f out: wnt 2nd jst over 3f out to over 2f out: wknd qckly* **14/1**[3]
1m 25.75s (2.45) **Going Correction** +0.10s/f (Good) **6** Ran SP% **109.5**
Speed ratings (Par 94): **90,87,87,78,74 73**
CSF £5.39 TOTE £2.70: £1.40, £1.90; EX 5.80 Trifecta £6.80.
Owner Sheikh Hamdan bin Mohammed Al Maktoum **Bred** Darley **Trained** Middleham Moor, N Yorks
FOCUS
Fairly useful form from the first three who came well clear. The winner dictated his own terms.

4305 TATTENHAM CORNER CLAIMING STKS 7f
7:50 (7:50) (Class 5) 3-Y-0+ £3,234 (£962; £481; £240) Stalls Low

Form RPR
2202 **1** **Big Time (IRE)**[20] 3594 5-9-13 88.................(v) RoystonFfrench 2 96
(David Nicholls) *mde all: pushed along over 1f out: drew wl clr fnl f* **6/4**[1]
3100 **2** *7* **Arnold Lane (IRE)**[12] 3895 7-9-13 92.............. SilvestreDeSousa 3 77
(Mick Channon) *chsd wnr: rdn over 2f out: hld on for 2nd but readily lft bhd over 1f out* **2/1**[2]
0005 **3** *¾* **Aqua Ardens (GER)**[5] 4132 8-9-8 82....................(t) PatCosgrave 1 70
(George Baker) *chsd ldng pair: shkn up over 2f out and chal for 2nd sn after: one pce and no ch w wnr* **3/1**[3]
300- **4** *6* **Take A Note**[286] 6892 7-9-8 88......................(v) HectorCrouch(5) 4 59
(Patrick Chamings) *t.k.h: hld up in tch: 4th st: shkn up and no prog over 2f out: wl btn over 1f out* **8/1**
4063 **5** *2 ½* **Bognor (USA)**[8] 4020 5-8-10 60.................... EdwardGreatrex(3) 5 38
(Michael Attwater) *cl up on outer tl lost grnd qckly over 4f out: last and bhd st: no prog* **33/1**
1m 23.35s (0.05) **Going Correction** +0.10s/f (Good) **5** Ran SP% **112.4**
Speed ratings (Par 103): **103,95,94,87,84**
CSF £4.95 TOTE £2.30: £1.02, £3.60; EX 5.50 Trifecta £7.50.Big Time was claimed by K. A. Ryan for £20,000.
Owner Mrs C C Regalado-Gonzalez **Bred** Highfort Stud **Trained** Sessay, N Yorks
FOCUS
A useful effort from the winner who dominated throughout. The form is rated around the second.

4306 ARTHUR BUDGETT MEMORIAL H'CAP 7f
8:20 (8:20) (Class 4) (0-85,85) 3-Y-0+ £5,822 (£1,732; £865; £432) Stalls Low

Form RPR
0131 **1** **Black Bess**[18] 3689 3-9-4 **83**........................... PatCosgrave 6 88
(Jim Boyle) *trckd ldr after 2f: led 2f out: drvn and hrd pressed fr over 1f out: hld on wl* **8/1**
-524 **2** *¾* **Gold Hunter (IRE)**[21] 3554 6-9-2 **73**..................... TedDurcan 8 78
(Steve Flook) *dwlt: in rr: prog and 5th st: rdn over 2f out: chsd ldng pair and chal fnl f: kpt on and snatched 2nd last stride* **7/1**
0353 **3** *nse* **Fast Dancer (IRE)**[14] 3803 4-9-11 **82**........................ JFEgan 4 87
(Joseph Tuite) *trckd ldrs: 3rd st: rdn to chse wnr over 1f out and sn chalng: edgd lft ins fnl f: jst hld and lost 2nd last stride* **6/1**[3]
4041 **4** *½* **Fingal's Cave (IRE)**[14] 3803 4-9-13 **84**............ SilvestreDeSousa 3 88
(Mick Channon) *t.k.h: hld up in rr: 7th st: nt clr run briefly 2f out: prog and drvn over 1f out: tk 4th ins fnl f: clsd on ldrs but too late to chal* **7/2**[2]
0010 **5** *3 ¼* **Another Boy**[12] 3908 3-8-13 **78**........................(p) JimCrowley 1 70
(Ralph Beckett) *in tch: 6th st: rdn 2f out: nt qckn and no imp over 1f out: fdd fnl f* **7/1**
2030 **6** *2* **Outback Ruler (IRE)**[19] 3645 4-10-0 **85**...............(p) JohnFahy 7 74
(Clive Cox) *in tch in rr: last st: shkn up and no prog over 2f out* **14/1**
-412 **7** *1 ¾* **Penwortham (IRE)**[19] 3635 3-9-5 **84**.................. TonyHamilton 2 66
(Richard Fahey) *led to 2f out: nt handling trck and wknd over 1f out* **5/2**[1]
2202 **8** *3* **Rosy Morning (IRE)**[5] 4145 3-8-9 **74**............... MichaelJMMurphy 5 48
(Mark Johnston) *trckd ldr 2f: 4th st: sn hrd rdn: wknd and hanging 2f out* **12/1**
1m 23.66s (0.36) **Going Correction** +0.10s/f (Good)
WFA 3 from 4yo+ 8lb **8** Ran SP% **115.5**
Speed ratings (Par 105): **101,100,100,99,95 93,91,88**
CSF £62.85 CT £364.26 TOTE £9.10: £2.20, £2.90, £1.70; EX 90.50 Trifecta £440.40.
Owner The Clean Sweep Partnership **Bred** Paddock Space **Trained** Epsom, Surrey
FOCUS
A fairly useful handicap. The second and third set the standard.

4307 MOLSON COORS H'CAP 1m 2f 18y
8:50 (8:50) (Class 4) (0-80,79) 3-Y-0+ £5,175 (£1,540; £769; £384) Stalls Low

Form RPR
0342 **1** **The Gay Cavalier**[7] 4050 5-9-4 **69**...................(t) JackMitchell 8 78
(John Ryan) *slowly away: mostly in last tl prog and 6th st: hdwy on outer 2f out: drvn and clsd to ld last 150yds: styd on wl* **6/1**[3]
2-13 **2** *1 ½* **Inke (IRE)**[24] 3467 4-10-0 **79**........................(p) PatCosgrave 5 85
(Jim Boyle) *hld up in tch: 5th st: prog on outer over 2f out: led over 1f out to last 150yds: kpt on* **8/1**
023 **3** *5* **Dawn Mirage**[12] 3884 4-9-11 **76**..................... TonyHamilton 7 72
(Richard Fahey) *chsd ldr: rdn over 2f out: lost 2nd over 1f out: fdd* **4/1**[2]
2405 **4** *2* **Squire**[21] 3557 5-9-11 **76**.............................. JimCrowley 6 68
(Michael Attwater) *hld up: nt handle downhill and last st: nvr on terms after but kpt on fnl 2f to take 4th nr fin* **7/2**[1]
2121 **5** *1* **Lord Reason**[20] 3612 4-9-11 **76**.................... SilvestreDeSousa 1 66
(John Butler) *led: drvn 2f out: hdd & wknd over 1f out* **7/2**[1]
-416 **6** *1* **Lord Kelvin (IRE)**[14] 3824 3-8-13 **75**...........(b[1]) MichaelJMMurphy 4 63
(Charles Hills) *trckd ldrs: 4th st: rdn and nt qckn over 2f out: wl hld after: fdd* **6/1**[3]
5-44 **7** *4* **Yensir**[14] 3801 3-9-1 **77**..................................(v[1]) JFEgan 3 57
(Pat Phelan) *rousted after s then tk fierce hold: trckd ldrs: 3rd st: wknd 2f out* **10/1**
5600 **8** *shd* **Prince Of Paris**[37] 3002 4-8-9 **67**.................(t) RhiainIngram(7) 2 47
(Roger Ingram) *hld up in rr: 7th st: pushed along and no prog over 2f out: nvr involved* **16/1**
2m 12.02s (2.32) **Going Correction** +0.10s/f (Good)
WFA 3 from 4yo+ 11lb **8** Ran SP% **119.1**
Speed ratings (Par 105): **94,92,88,87,86 85,82,82**
CSF £54.80 CT £217.93 TOTE £7.30: £2.30, £2.30, £1.60; EX 62.80 Trifecta £174.70.
Owner The Gay Cavaliers Partnership **Bred** Philip Newton **Trained** Newmarket, Suffolk
FOCUS
A fair handicap. The gallop looked pretty sedate in the first half of the race but the leading pair both came from well off the pace. The form can't be rated much higher than this.
T/Plt: £52.50 to a £1 stake. Pool: £59,976.08 - 833.93 winning tickets. T/Qpdt: £19.30 to a £1 stake. Pool: £4,411.60 - 168.60 winning tickets. **Jonathan Neesom**

The Form Book, Raceform Ltd, Newbury, RG14 5SJ

[4140]HAMILTON (R-H)

Thursday, July 14

OFFICIAL GOING: Good (good to soft in places; 7.8)

Wind: Breezy, half behind Weather: Cloudy, bright

4308 IRISH STALLION FARMS EBF MAIDEN STKS (PLUS 10 RACE) (£20,000 HIGHLAND SPRING WATER QUALIFIER) 5f 7y

2:00 (2:01) (Class 4) 2-Y-O **£4,269** (£1,270; £634; £317) **Stalls** High

Form RPR

2 **1** **Whirl Me Round**[13] 3839 2-9-5 0 JoeDoyle 5 75+
(Kevin Ryan) *trckd ldrs gng wl: shkn up to ld ent fnl f: qcknd clr: readily* **30/100**[1]

2 2 ¼ **Wild Acclaim (IRE)** 2-9-5 0 PJMcDonald 7 64+
(Ann Duffield) *dwlt: sn pushed along in last pl: hdwy over 1f out: chsd wnr ins fnl f: kpt on: no imp* **10/1**[3]

3 2 ½ **Sky Gypsy** 2-9-0 0 TomEaves 3 50
(David Brown) *pressed ldr: led over 1f out to ent fnl f: sn outpcd* **6/1**[2]

650 **4** 1 ¾ **Chickenfortea (IRE)**[33] 3128 2-9-5 0 NeilFarley 4 49
(Eric Alston) *taken early to post: led to over 1f out: sn rdn and btn* **28/1**

5 5 **El Hombre** 2-9-5 0 JoeFanning 1 34
(Keith Dalgleish) *dwlt: sn prom on outside: rdn and edgd rt wl over 1f out: sn wknd* **14/1**

1m 1.97s (1.97) **Going Correction** +0.275s/f (Good) **5** Ran SP% **110.4**
Speed ratings (Par 96): **95,91,87,84,76**
CSF £4.27 TOTE £1.10: £1.02, £3.90; EX 4.00 Trifecta £9.30.
Owner Guy Reed Racing **Bred** Copgrove Hall Stud **Trained** Hambleton, N Yorks

FOCUS
Loop rail in innermost position, all distances as advertised. The going was good, good to soft in places. A weakly contested maiden and the short-priced favourite made no mistake.

4309 WATCH RACING UK IN HD H'CAP 5f 7y

2:30 (2:31) (Class 6) (0-60,60) 3-Y-O+ **£2,911** (£866; £432; £216) **Stalls** High

Form RPR

6002 **1** **Classic Flyer**[2] 4229 4-9-7 **60** (b) DanielTudhope 4 70
(David O'Meara) *cl up on outside: led over 1f out: rdn out fnl f* **9/4**[1]

0362 **2** 2 **Tinsill**[2] 4228 5-8-11 **50** (p) JoeFanning 8 53
(Nigel Tinkler) *prom: rdn over 2f out: rallied and ev ch over 1f out: one pce ins fnl f* **9/4**[1]

0534 **3** ¾ **Slim Chance (IRE)**[2] 4228 7-9-6 **59** (p) JasonHart 3 59
(Simon West) *taken early to post: rrd s: hld up: stdy hdwy 1/2-way: rdn and kpt on fnl f: no imp* **9/2**[2]

1003 **4** 1 ¾ **Gaelic Wizard (IRE)**[28] 3322 8-9-2 **60** (v) GemmaTutty(5) 6 54
(Karen Tutty) *t.k.h: trckd ldrs: rdn 2f out: edgd rt: kpt on same pce fnl f* **6/1**[3]

00-5 **5** 3 ½ **Duncan Of Scotland (IRE)**[26] 3426 3-8-11 **55** (b) JoeyHaynes 2 34
(Lee Smyth, Ire) *dwlt: sn prom on outside: drvn over 2f out: wknd over 1f out* **12/1**

560 **6** 2 ¾ **Henry Morgan**[17] 3709 9-8-9 **48** TomEaves 1 19
(David Brown) *led to over 1f out: sn rdn and wknd* **16/1**

00-0 **7** 12 **Bannock Town**[36] 3022 5-8-2 **46** oh1 (p) NathanEvans(5) 5
(Linda Perratt) *bhd: drvn along after 2f: lost tch wl over 1f out* **100/1**

1m 1.19s (1.19) **Going Correction** +0.275s/f (Good)
WFA 3 from 4yo+ 5lb **7** Ran SP% **108.6**
Speed ratings (Par 101): **101,97,96,93,88 83,64**
CSF £6.42 CT £16.43 TOTE £3.20: £1.90, £1.90; EX 6.70 Trifecta £22.80.
Owner The Classic Strollers Partnership **Bred** Pippa Bloodstock **Trained** Upper Helmsley, N Yorks

FOCUS
A modest sprint handicap. The second and third are rated just below their recent form.

4310 RACING UK CLUB DAY HERE TODAY MEDIAN AUCTION MAIDEN STKS 6f 6y

3:05 (3:08) (Class 6) 3-5-Y-O **£2,911** (£866; £432; £216) **Stalls** Centre

Form RPR

5-06 **1** **Bay Mirage (IRE)**[38] 2957 3-9-5 72 (p) TomEaves 4 66
(Kevin Ryan) *mde all: rdn over 1f out: edgd rt ins fnl f: kpt on wl* **2/1**[1]

00-0 **2** 2 ½ **Gabbys Lad (IRE)**[31] 3209 3-9-0 40 NeilFarley 1 53
(Eric Alston) *t.k.h early: trckd ldrs: rdn 2f out: chsd wnr ins fnl f: kpt on* **16/1**[3]

-200 **3** 1 **Run Rio Run (IRE)**[26] 3422 3-9-5 65 ConnorBeasley 6 55
(Michael Dods) *plld hrd: chsd wnr: rdn 2f out: no ex and lost 2nd ins fnl f* **2/1**[1]

5 **4** 17 **Dalness Express**[90] 1451 3-9-0 0 CiaranMckee(5) 3 4
(John O'Shea) *s.v.s: hdwy and prom 1/2-way: drvn and wknd fr 2f out: t.o* **7/1**[2]

1m 14.53s (2.33) **Going Correction** +0.275s/f (Good)
WFA 3 from 4yo 6lb **4** Ran SP% **85.0**
Speed ratings (Par 101): **95,91,90,67**
CSF £14.97 TOTE £1.80: £1.90; EX 16.40 Trifecta £22.30.
Owner NAD Partnership **Bred** David John Brown **Trained** Hambleton, N Yorks
■ Any Joy was withdrawn. Price at time of withdrawal 11-4. Rule 4 applies to all bets - deduction 25p in the pound.

FOCUS
A weak maiden and this isn't form to get carried away with. It's been rated negatively.

4311 CONUNDRUM HR CONSULTING H'CAP 1m 5f 15y

3:35 (3:37) (Class 4) (0-85,84) 3-Y-O+ **£6,469** (£1,925; £962; £481) **Stalls** High

Form RPR

406 **1** **Time Of My Life (GER)**[20] 3602 5-9-10 **80** (p) DanielTudhope 7 88
(Patrick Holmes) *hld up: rdn over 2f out: hdwy and plld out wl over 1f out: led ins fnl f: kpt on wl* **8/1**

-251 **2** ½ **Lord Yeats**[28] 3323 3-8-13 **83** JackGarritty 5 90
(Jedd O'Keeffe) *pressed ldr: led and rdn over 2f out: hung lft and hdd ins fnl f: kpt on: hld nr fin* **5/4**[1]

3210 **3** 3 ½ **Lara Carbonara (IRE)**[16] 3751 4-9-1 **71** TadhgO'Shea 8 73
(John Patrick Shanahan, Ire) *trckd ldrs: effrt and drvn along over 2f out: kpt on same pce fnl f* **20/1**

3530 **4** nk **Agent Gibbs**[22] 3533 4-9-10 **80** (p) JoeFanning 3 82
(John O'Shea) *led: rdn and hdd over 2f out: rallied: outpcd fnl f* **8/1**

1-24 **5** 1 ¾ **Faithful Mount**[13] 3862 7-10-0 **84** PJMcDonald 1 83
(Ian Williams) *hld up in tch: hdwy to chse ldrs over 3f out: rdn whn n.m.r briefly and edgd rt over 2f out: wknd fnl f* **3/1**[2]

00-0 **6** 3 ¾ **Hot Spice**[19] 3659 8-9-2 **77** NathanEvans(5) 6 70
(Michael Easterby) *hld up: outpcd 3f out: sme late hdwy: nvr nrr* **66/1**

4031 **7** 5 **Be Perfect (USA)**[19] 3659 7-9-12 **82** (p) JamesSullivan 2 68
(Ruth Carr) *t.k.h early: hld up in tch: effrt and rdn on outside over 2f out: wknd over 1f out* **6/1**[3]

2m 50.53s (-3.37) **Going Correction** -0.125s/f (Firm)
WFA 3 from 4yo+ 14lb **7** Ran SP% **112.2**
Speed ratings (Par 105): **105,104,102,102,101 98,95**
CSF £17.83 CT £193.34 TOTE £10.00: £4.60, £1.10; EX 21.40 Trifecta £320.80.
Owner Mrs C M Clarke **Bred** Gestut Karlshof **Trained** Middleham, N Yorks

FOCUS
A useful handicap and they went a decent pace. The winner is rated back to his seasonal debut form.

4312 RACING UK NOW AVAILABLE £10 PER DAY H'CAP 1m 1f 34y

4:05 (4:06) (Class 4) (0-85,85) 3-Y-O+ **£6,469** (£1,925; £962; £481) **Stalls** Low

Form RPR

-342 **1** **Robinnielly (IRE)**[60] 2269 3-8-13 **80** PhillipMakin 3 92
(Keith Dalgleish) *early ldr: trckd ldrs: effrt and angled lft over 2f out: shkn up and qcknd to ld over 1f out: edgd rt: pushed clr* **15/8**[1]

2150 **2** 3 ¼ **Jacbequick**[22] 3518 5-9-6 **82** (v) JoshDoyle(5) 4 88
(David O'Meara) *sn led and set ordinary gallop: rdn and hdd over 1f out: kpt on fnl f: nt pce of wnr* **9/2**[3]

260 **3** 1 ½ **Terhaal (IRE)**[33] 3166 4-9-6 **77** DanielTudhope 2 80
(David O'Meara) *hld up in last pl: effrt whn hmpd over 2f out: sn rdn: rallied over 1f out: kpt on: no imp* **3/1**[2]

53-2 **4** 1 ½ **Carbon Dating (IRE)**[36] 3019 4-9-5 **76** TadhgO'Shea 6 76
(John Patrick Shanahan, Ire) *cl up: wnt 2nd after 2f: effrt and rdn over 2f out: one pce fr over 1f out* **9/2**[3]

-346 **5** 1 ¾ **Templier (IRE)**[41] 2859 3-8-5 **72** (b) JoeFanning 1 67
(Mark Johnston) *t.k.h: hld up in tch: stdy hdwy over 2f out: rdn over 1f out: wknd fnl f* **8/1**

2000 **6** 1 ½ **Spes Nostra**[26] 3391 8-9-9 **85** (b) GarryWhillans(5) 5 78
(Iain Jardine) *prom: rdn over 2f out: hung rt and wknd wl over 1f out* **20/1**

1m 59.45s (-0.25) **Going Correction** -0.125s/f (Firm)
WFA 3 from 4yo+ 10lb **6** Ran SP% **112.0**
Speed ratings (Par 105): **96,93,91,90,88 87**
CSF £10.63 TOTE £2.50: £1.80, £2.00; EX 8.80 Trifecta £21.80.
Owner Prestige Thoroughbred Racing **Bred** Kellsgrange Stud **Trained** Carluke, S Lanarks

FOCUS
They went a steady pace in this useful handicap and it turned into a 3f sprint. A pb from the winner with the second close to form.

4313 FAIR FRIDAY RACENIGHT TOMORROW MAIDEN AUCTION STKS 1m 67y

4:40 (4:41) (Class 5) 3-Y-O **£3,881** (£1,155; £577; £288) **Stalls** Low

Form RPR

3 **1** **Archippos**[38] 2957 3-9-5 0 PJMcDonald 1 79
(Philip Kirby) *in tch: effrt and plld out over 2f out: rdn and chsd clr ldr over 1f out: led wl ins fnl f: pushed out* **9/2**[3]

3223 **2** 1 ¾ **Haraz (IRE)**[26] 3389 3-9-5 79 DanielTudhope 7 76
(David O'Meara) *t.k.h: led: shkn up and clr over 2f out: rdn over 1f out: hdd and no ex whn checked wl ins fnl f* **11/8**[1]

25 **3** 2 ¾ **Al Hawraa**[13] 3850 3-9-0 0 KevinStott 6 64
(Kevin Ryan) *hld up: hdwy against far rail over 2f out: rdn over 1f out: no imp fnl f* **17/2**

4 **4** 5 **Aislabie (FR)**[43] 2804 3-9-5 0 JasonHart 4 58
(Mark Walford) *t.k.h early: prom: drvn along over 3f out: edgd rt and no imp fr 2f out* **6/1**

5 1 **Black Agnes (IRE)**[13] 3864 3-9-0 0 JoeyHaynes 5 50
(Lee Smyth, Ire) *t.k.h: hdwy to press ldr after 2f: rdn along over 3f out: wknd over 1f out* **22/1**

00- **6** 18 **Lawman's Justice (IRE)**[314] 6065 3-9-5 0 ConnorBeasley 2 14
(Michael Dods) *missed break: bhd: pushed along 1/2-way: drvn and wknd 3f out: t.o* **22/1**

7 shd **Zamindo** 3-9-5 0 JoeFanning 3 14
(Mark Johnston) *dwlt: t.k.h and chsd ldr 2f: rdn over 3f out: wknd over 2f out: eased whn no ch over 1f out* **4/1**[2]

1m 49.02s (0.62) **Going Correction** -0.125s/f (Firm) **7** Ran SP% **113.8**
Speed ratings (Par 100): **91,89,86,81,80 62,62**
CSF £11.02 TOTE £6.00: £2.50, £1.20; EX 13.10 Trifecta £65.90.
Owner The Well Oiled Partnership **Bred** Mrs K E Collie **Trained** East Appleton, N Yorks

FOCUS
Only an ordinary maiden, but the unexposed winner did it nicely. The time was ordinary.

4314 RACING UK PROFITS RETURNED TO RACING H'CAP 1m 67y

5:15 (5:16) (Class 6) (0-60,60) 3-Y-O+ **£2,911** (£866; £432; £216) **Stalls** Low

Form RPR

0063 **1** **Galilee Chapel (IRE)**[11] 3921 7-8-7 **46** oh1 (b) JoshDoyle(5) 6 52
(Alistair Whillans) *hld up on ins: rdn and hdwy over 2f out: drvn to ld ins fnl f: kpt on wl* **7/1**[3]

6033 **2** ½ **Tectonic (IRE)**[5] 4146 7-9-11 **59** (v) JoeFanning 3 64
(Keith Dalgleish) *t.k.h: hld up: effrt on outside over 1f out: rdn and wnt 2nd wl ins fnl f: kpt on* **6/1**[2]

0054 **3** nk **Munjally**[8] 4005 5-9-7 **55** (v) JackGarritty 1 59
(Patrick Holmes) *in tch: effrt and swtchd lft over 2f out: rdn and led briefly ins fnl f: kpt on: hld towards fin* **9/1**

53-2 **4** ¾ **Penelope Pitstop**[16] 3761 4-8-13 **47** GrahamLee 7 49
(Lee Smyth, Ire) *trckd ldrs: effrt and rdn 2f out: kpt on same pce last 100yds* **10/1**

-650 **5** 5 **Judith Gardenier**[11] 3921 4-8-12 **46** oh1 JasonHart 10 37
(Iain Jardine) *hld up: rdn over 2f out: rallied over 1f out: kpt on: nvr able to chal* **28/1**

55-2 **6** 1 **Highfield Lass**[11] 3921 5-8-12 **46** oh1 ConnorBeasley 2 35
(Michael Dods) *trckd ldrs: rdn and ev ch over 2f out to over 1f out: wknd ins fnl f* **7/2**[1]

314 **7** 1 ½ **Jocks Wa Hae (IRE)**[16] 3750 3-8-13 **56** TadhgO'Shea 13 39
(John Patrick Shanahan, Ire) *s.i.s: sn rushed up on outside and prom: rdn over 4f out: hdwy to ld over 2f out: hung rt over 1f out: hdd ins fnl f: wknd* **7/2**[1]

0-40 **8** 2 ½ **Prairie Impulse**[29] 3289 3-8-10 **60** RowanScott(7) 4 38
(Ann Duffield) *hld up in midfield: rdn whn nt clr run briefly over 2f out: btn over 1f out* **28/1**

4440 **9** 1 ¾ **Frightened Rabbit (USA)**[25] 2233 4-9-7 **60** GarryWhillans(5) 11 35
(Susan Corbett) *hld up: drvn and outpcd over 2f out: n.d after* **50/1**

3500 **10** ¾ **Bushtiger (IRE)**[11] 3921 4-8-12 **46** oh1 TomEaves 14 20
(Ruth Carr) *prom tl rdn and wknd fr 2f out* **28/1**

560- **11** 1 ¾ **Scruffy McGuffy**[280] 7054 3-9-3 **60** PJMcDonald 12 28
(Ann Duffield) *led to over 2f out: sn rdn and wknd* **25/1**

0005 **12** *7* **Tiger's Home**[10] 3946 6-9-3 **56** ShirleyTeasdale(5) 8 10
(Iain Jardine) *hld up in midfield on outside: rdn along over 2f out: sn wknd* **22/1**

0051 **13** *3 1/2* **Mercury**[23] 3479 4-9-12 **60** (b) KevinStott 9 6
(Kevin Ryan) *dwlt: hld up: drvn along 3f out: sn btn* **9/1**

1m 49.3s (0.90) **Going Correction** -0.125s/f (Firm)
WFA 3 from 4yo+ 9lb **13** Ran SP% **120.8**
Speed ratings (Par 101): **90,89,89,88,83 82,80,78,76,75 74,67,63**
CSF £45.15 CT £303.18 TOTE £8.80: £3.10, £2.30, £3.10; EX 65.30 Trifecta £689.40.
Owner A C Whillans **Bred** Tally-Ho Stud **Trained** Newmill-On-Slitrig, Borders

FOCUS
A modest, open-looking handicap, in which they went a good pace. The winner didn't need to replicate his best.
T/Plt: £5.60 to a £1 stake. Pool: £36,970.39 - 4,758.12 winning tickets. T/Qpdt: £4.10 to a £1 stake. Pool: £2,607.96 - 469.86 winning tickets. **Richard Young**

3894 LEICESTER (R-H)
Thursday, July 14

OFFICIAL GOING: Good
Wind: Light behind Weather: Cloudy with sunny spells

4315 COLD OVERTON NURSERY H'CAP 7f
1:50 (1:50) (Class 5) 2-Y-O **£2,911** (£866; £432; £216) **Stalls** High

Form RPR

040 **1** **Global Revival (IRE)**[40] 2913 2-9-4 **69** SilvestreDeSousa 8 75
(Ed Dunlop) *s.i.s: sn pushed along in rr: hdwy and hung rt over 1f out: r.o to ld wl ins fnl f* **7/2**[3]

31 **2** *1 1/4* **Hedging (IRE)**[16] 3742 2-9-6 **71** DaneO'Neill 3 74
(Eve Johnson Houghton) *hld up: hdwy over 2f out: led over 1f out: rdn and hdd wl ins fnl f* **2/1**[1]

523 **3** *hd* **Galahad**[21] 3548 2-8-11 **62** PaulHanagan 5 65
(Richard Fahey) *hld up: pushed along over 2f out: swtchd lft over 1f out: hung rt and r.o ins fnl f* **10/3**[2]

6446 **4** *3 1/2* **Princess Way (IRE)**[33] 3122 2-8-8 **59** AndrewMullen 4 52
(David Evans) *led: rdn and hdd over 1f out: no ex ins fnl f* **25/1**

606 **5** *3* **Geego**[12] 3873 2-8-8 **59** BarryMcHugh 2 43
(Richard Fahey) *chsd ldrs: drvn and outpcd over 2f out: n.d whn hung rt over 1f out* **20/1**

404 **6** *1* **Restore (IRE)**[16] 3742 2-9-0 **65** SeanLevey 6 47
(Richard Hannon) *plld hrd: w ldr 2f: remained handy: rdn over 2f out: hmpd over 1f out: wknd fnl f* **7/1**

5425 **7** *3 3/4* **Vinnievanbaileys**[49] 2604 2-9-7 **72** DavidAllan 7 44
(Chris Dwyer) *s.i.s: sn chsng ldrs: rdn over 2f out: hung rt over 1f out: wknd fnl f* **10/1**

550 **8** *3 1/4* **Apple Scruffs (IRE)**[26] 3404 2-9-1 **66** AdamBeschizza 1 29
(Michael Attwater) *plld hrd and prom: jnd ldr 5f out: rdn over 2f out: wknd over 1f out* **33/1**

1m 26.32s (0.12) **Going Correction** 0.0s/f (Good) **8** Ran SP% **111.8**
Speed ratings (Par 94): **99,97,97,93,89 88,84,80**
CSF £10.33 CT £23.61 TOTE £4.30: £1.70, £1.10, £1.90; EX 11.40 Trifecta £35.40.
Owner Dr Johnny Hon **Bred** John Cullinan **Trained** Newmarket, Suffolk

FOCUS
A fair nursery handicap. They went a respectable gallop, at best, on good ground.

4316 GAULBY (S) STKS 7f
2:20 (2:21) (Class 6) 3-Y-O **£2,587** (£770; £384; £192) **Stalls** High

Form RPR

0060 **1** **Boutan**[16] 3740 3-9-0 60 (p) PatCosgrave 9 68
(George Baker) *mde all and hung rt thrght: racd alone tl jnd main gp over 4f out: rdn over 1f out: styd on* **5/1**[3]

0340 **2** *3 1/2* **Mecca's Missus (IRE)**[29] 3285 3-9-0 59 (p) PaulMulrennan 3 59
(Michael Dods) *w ldrs: rdn and ev ch over 1f out: hung rt and no ex ins fnl f* **9/4**[1]

5045 **3** *1 3/4* **Smirnova (IRE)**[80] 1725 3-8-7 64 DanielMuscutt(3) 8 50
(Marco Botti) *chsd ldrs: rdn 1/2-way: outpcd over 2f out: styd on ins fnl f* **11/2**

206 **4** *1 1/2* **Last Star Falling (IRE)**[38] 2968 3-8-10 65 (p) SilvestreDeSousa 4 46
(Henry Spiller) *w wnr tl rdn over 2f out: hung rt over 1f out: no ex* **11/4**[2]

6000 **5** *2* **Long Island**[23] 3490 3-8-10 48 DavidAllan 5 40
(Mark Brisbourne) *sn pushed along in rr: rdn 1/2-way: styd on ins fnl f: nvr nrr* **25/1**

0000 **6** *5* **Links Bar Marbella (IRE)**[5] 4156 3-9-1 44 [1] FrannyNorton 2 32
(Eric Wheeler) *s.i.s: sn pushed along and a in rr* **100/1**

00-0 **7** *1 1/4* **Fast Operator (IRE)**[42] 2835 3-8-10 55 AndrewMullen 6 24
(Nigel Tinkler) *prom: rdn over 4f out: wknd 1/2-way* **14/1**

0226 **8** *2 3/4* **Ashford Island**[23] 3490 3-9-5 52 (p) HarryBentley 1 25
(Mike Murphy) *prom tl rdn and wknd 1/2-way* **8/1**

0000 **9** *2 1/2* **Sakhastic**[9] 3970 3-9-1 43 (v) AdamBeschizza 7 14
(Christine Dunnett) *hood removed late: s.i.s: sn outpcd* **100/1**

1m 25.74s (-0.46) **Going Correction** 0.0s/f (Good) **9** Ran SP% **113.1**
Speed ratings (Par 98): **102,98,96,94,92 86,84,81,78**
CSF £16.19 TOTE £6.10: £2.30, £1.02, £2.10; EX 18.80 Trifecta £91.70.The winner was bought in for 7,000.00gns.
Owner Seaton Partnership **Bred** Seaton Partnership **Trained** Manton, Wilts

FOCUS
A modest 3yo seller. They went a respectable gallop.

4317 GATELEY PLC H'CAP 1m 60y
2:50 (2:52) (Class 4) (0-80,80) 3-Y-O+ **£4,851** (£1,443; £721; £360) **Stalls** Low

Form RPR

1 **1** **Miss Carbonia (IRE)**[33] 3145 3-9-2 **77** ThomasBrown 7 85
(Ismail Mohammed) *hld up: hdwy over 2f out: led over 1f out: sn edgd rt: rdn out* **3/1**[3]

41 **2** *nk* **On The Bill (IRE)**[50] 2578 3-9-3 **78** SilvestreDeSousa 5 85
(Ed Dunlop) *s.i.s: hld up: rdn over 2f out: hdwy over 1f out: chsd wnr ins fnl f: r.o* **5/2**[2]

0000 **3** *3 1/2* **Rock Palm (IRE)**[8] 4009 3-8-4 **65** JimmyQuinn 2 64
(Brendan Powell) *sn pushed along to ld: qcknd over 3f out: rdn and hdd over 1f out: no ex ins fnl f* **16/1**

4354 **4** *1/2* **Hot Mustard**[10] 3957 6-9-8 **74** MartinDwyer 4 74
(William Muir) *plld hrd and prom: rdn over 2f out: styd on same pce fnl f* **7/1**

4236 **5** *4* **Aleko**[36] 3026 3-9-3 **78** JamesDoyle 1 66
(Mark Johnston) *chsd ldr: rdn over 3f out: lost 2nd over 2f out: wknd fnl f* **7/4**[1]

1m 45.47s (0.37) **Going Correction** -0.125s/f (Firm)
WFA 3 from 5yo+ 9lb **5** Ran SP% **108.3**
Speed ratings (Par 105): **93,92,89,88,84**
CSF £10.46 TOTE £3.80: £1.80, £1.50; EX 8.20 Trifecta £27.60.
Owner Sheikh Juma Dalmook Al Maktoum **Bred** Mrs Elizabeth O'Leary **Trained** Newmarket, Suffolk

FOCUS
A fair handicap. They went a respectable gallop at best.

4318 EBF STALLIONS BREEDING WINNERS FILLIES' H'CAP 7f
3:25 (3:25) (Class 4) (0-85,84) 3-Y-O+ **£6,301** (£1,886; £707; £707; £235) **Stalls** High

Form RPR

5352 **1** **Subtle Knife**[25] 3448 7-9-9 **82** JosephineGordon(3) 6 90
(Giles Bravery) *chsd ldrs: rdn over 2f out: hung rt over 1f out: nt clr run and swtchd lft ins fnl f: r.o to ld nr fin* **11/1**

6365 **2** *3/4* **Hawatif (IRE)**[6] 4094 3-9-0 **78** FrannyNorton 4 81
(Mark Johnston) *led: rdn over 1f out: hdd nr fin* **10/3**[2]

0234 **3** *2* **Honeysuckle Lil (IRE)**[17] 3708 4-9-5 **75** (p) DavidAllan 3 76
(Tim Easterby) *chsd ldr to 1/2-way: wnt 2nd again over 2f out: rdn and ev ch over 1f out: no ex wl ins fnl f* **6/1**[3]

-506 **3** *dht* **Doubly Motivated (IRE)**[26] 3389 3-9-5 **83** JamesDoyle 2 81
(Charles Hills) *hld up: hdwy 2f out: rdn over 1f out: styd on same pce ins fnl f* **9/1**

2-31 **5** *nk* **Prying Pandora (FR)**[12] 3899 3-9-4 **82** PaulHanagan 8 79
(Richard Fahey) *sn chsng ldrs: rdn over 1f out: styd on same pce ins fnl f* **2/1**[1]

3656 **6** *1* **Blue Geranium (IRE)**[36] 3038 3-8-9 **73** RobertHavlin 5 67
(John Gosden) *plld hrd and prom: swtchd lft to r alone 5f out: sn edging rt: rdn over 2f out: kpt on* **9/1**

3143 **7** *3/4* **Alexandrakollontai (IRE)**[22] 3518 6-10-0 **84** (b) DougieCostello 1 79
(Alistair Whillans) *s.i.s: hld up: rdn over 2f out: nvr on terms* **7/1**

1m 25.27s (-0.93) **Going Correction** 0.0s/f (Good)
WFA 3 from 4yo+ 8lb **7** Ran SP% **111.5**
Speed ratings (Par 102): **105,104,101,101,101 100,99**
TC: SK/H/DM 170.45, SK/H/HL119.36; TF: SK/H/DM 224.60, SK/H/HL 132.70 CSF £45.08 TOTE £9.50: £3.60, £2.00; EX 34.20.
Owner D B Clark **Bred** Mrs F Bravery **Trained** Newmarket, Suffolk

FOCUS
A decent fillies' handicap. They went a respectable gallop.

4319 BREEDERS BACKING RACING EBF MAIDEN STKS 1m 1f 218y
3:55 (3:55) (Class 5) 3-Y-O **£3,881** (£1,155; £577; £288) **Stalls** Low

Form RPR

4-3 **1** **Great Order (USA)**[26] 3412 3-9-5 0 JamesDoyle 8 89+
(Saeed bin Suroor) *w ldr tl led over 6f out: shkn up over 2f out: rdn out* **11/10**[1]

0-22 **2** *1 1/2* **Stratum**[39] 2929 3-9-5 83 RobertHavlin 10 86
(John Gosden) *a.p: chsd wnr over 5f out: rdn over 1f out: edgd rt: styd on* **7/4**[2]

5 **3** *4 1/2* **Sir Valentine (GER)**[33] 3160 3-9-5 0 WilliamTwiston-Davies 4 77
(Alan King) *hld up: pushed along and hdwy over 2f out: wnt 3rd over 1f out: nt trble ldrs* **7/1**[3]

4 *3 3/4* **Vernatti** 3-8-11 0 RobHornby(3) 7 65
(Pam Sly) *s.i.s: hld up: nt clr run over 2f out: rdn and hung lft over 1f out: styd on ins fnl f: nvr nrr* **50/1**

0 **5** *1 1/2* **Stamford Raffles**[26] 3411 3-9-5 0 HarryBentley 5 67
(Stuart Williams) *plld hrd and prom: rdn and wknd over 1f out* **66/1**

0 **6** *1 3/4* **Pure Innocence (IRE)**[22] 3535 3-9-0 0 SeanLevey 1 58
(Ralph Beckett) *led: hdd over 6f out: remained handy: rdn over 2f out: wknd over 1f out* **14/1**

0 **7** *2* **Shift On Sheila**[15] 3781 3-8-9 0 MeganNicholls(5) 9 54
(Pam Sly) *hld up: hdwy over 5f out: rdn and wknd over 1f out* **80/1**

-04 **8** *24* **Gatillo**[24] 3464 3-9-5 0 JimmyQuinn 2 11
(George Margarson) *prom: rdn over 3f out: wknd 2f out* **50/1**

9 *10* **Foible** 3-9-5 0 NickyMackay 3
(John Gosden) *s.i.s: rn green and outpcd* **12/1**

0 **10** *16* **Out Of The Ashes**[35] 3066 3-9-5 0 PaulMulrennan 6
(Philip McBride) *hld up: rdn over 4f out: wknd 3f out* **100/1**

2m 6.57s (-1.33) **Going Correction** -0.125s/f (Firm) **10** Ran SP% **118.5**
Speed ratings (Par 100): **100,98,95,92,91 89,88,68,60,48**
CSF £3.21 TOTE £1.90: £1.02, £1.30, £2.10; EX 3.50 Trifecta £12.40.
Owner Godolphin **Bred** Darley **Trained** Newmarket, Suffolk

FOCUS
A decent 3yo maiden. They went a respectable gallop.

4320 KUBE EXHIBITION CENTRE H'CAP 1m 3f 183y
4:25 (4:25) (Class 6) (0-65,63) 4-Y-O+ **£2,587** (£770; £384; £192) **Stalls** Low

Form RPR

5421 **1** **Saint Thomas (IRE)**[13] 3842 9-9-0 **56** FrannyNorton 3 64
(John Mackie) *a.p: jnd ldrs over 2f out: rdn to ld ins fnl f: styd on* **11/4**[1]

4452 **2** *1* **Theydon Bois**[14] 3825 4-8-10 **55** (p) RosieJessop(3) 5 61
(Peter Charalambous) *chsd ldrs: rdn and hung rt over 2f out: led over 1f out: hdd ins fnl f: unable qck towards fin* **10/1**

0034 **3** *1 3/4* **Stoneboat Bill**[14] 3804 4-9-0 **63** GerO'Neill(7) 2 67
(Declan Carroll) *hld up: racd keenly: hdwy over 3f out: rdn and edgd rt over 1f out: no ex wl ins fnl f: eased nr fin* **7/2**[2]

-604 **4** *3 1/2* **County Wexford (IRE)**[49] 2605 5-9-0 **59** (t) DanielMuscutt(3) 8 57
(Miss Joey Ellis) *led: rdn over 2f out: hdd over 1f out: no ex ins fnl f* **4/1**[3]

2533 **5** *2 1/2* **Percys Princess**[15] 3774 5-9-5 **61** AndrewMullen 1 55
(Michael Appleby) *racd keenly: trckd ldr tl over 7f out: remained handy: wnt 2nd again 4f out tl rdn over 2f out: wknd fnl f* **5/1**

-000 **6** *6* **Sakhra**[8] 3999 5-8-3 **45** JimmyQuinn 4 29
(Mark Brisbourne) *hld up: rdn over 3f out: wknd over 1f out* **25/1**

0-05 **7** *11* **Grand Proposal**[26] 3401 4-8-4 **46** (p[1]) PatrickMathers 7 13
(Mike Murphy) *hld up: rdn and wknd over 3f out* **14/1**

-000 **8** *40* **Flying Power**[19] 3641 8-9-0 **59** (v[1]) JacobButterfield(3) 6
(John Norton) *chsd ldrs: wnt 2nd over 7f out tl rdn 4f out: sn wknd* **10/1**

2m 33.08s (-0.82) **Going Correction** -0.125s/f (Firm) **8** Ran SP% **114.3**
Speed ratings (Par 101): **97,96,95,92,91 87,79,53**
CSF £31.07 CT £97.74 TOTE £3.40: £1.90, £2.80, £1.20; EX 30.30 Trifecta £144.20.
Owner P Riley **Bred** S Coughlan **Trained** Church Broughton , Derbys

FOCUS
A modest middle-distance handicap. They went a respectable gallop.

4321 SUTTON APPRENTICE H'CAP — 6f
5:00 (5:03) (Class 6) (0-65,65) 3-Y-O+ **£2,587** (£770; £384; £192) **Stalls** High

Form RPR

2056 **1** **Generalyse**[9] 3970 7-9-3 **57**.....(b) JoshuaBryan(3) 5 66
(Anabel K Murphy) *led: rdn and hdd over 1f out: styd on to ld nr fin* **7/1**

0330 **2** 1 3/4 **First Excel**[35] 3069 4-9-4 **55**.....(b) KevinLundie 2 59
(Roy Bowring) *chsd ldr tl led over 1f out: sn rdn: hdd nr fin* **13/2**[3]

3613 **3** 3/4 **Satchville Flyer**[6] 4084 5-9-5 **59**..... AledBeech(3) 6 61
(David Evans) *plld hrd and prom: rdn over 1f out: edgd lft ins fnl f: r.o* **9/2**[1]

0-04 **4** 1/2 **Disclosure**[20] 3610 5-9-11 **65**..... CliffordLee(3) 1 65
(Les Eyre) *hld up: hdwy over 2f out: rdn over 1f out: styd on same pce wl ins fnl f* **11/2**[2]

002R **5** 1 **Teetotal (IRE)**[29] 3289 6-9-4 **58**..... KieranSchofield(3) 7 55
(Nigel Tinkler) *s.i.s: hld up: rdn over 2f out: styd on fr over 1f out: nvr nrr* **10/1**

3044 **6** nse **Great Expectations**[14] 3821 8-10-0 **65**.....(vt) GeorgiaCox 8 62
(J R Jenkins) *hld up: swtchd rt and hdwy over 1f out: nt trble ldrs* **12/1**

5312 **7** 1 1/2 **Consistant**[16] 3743 8-9-13 **64**..... AdamMcNamara 10 56
(Brian Baugh) *chsd ldrs: rdn over 1f out: no ex ins fnl f* **9/2**[1]

6004 **8** 2 **Clon Rocket (IRE)**[25] 3439 3-9-3 **65**..... MeganEllingworth(5) 11 50
(John Holt) *prom: rdn over 2f out: styd on same pce fr over 1f out* **11/1**

5600 **9** 4 1/2 **Alpha Tauri (USA)**[8] 4006 10-8-6 **46** oh1..... BenRobinson(3) 9 19
(Charles Smith) *plld hrd and prom: rdn and wknd over 1f out* **66/1**

-440 **10** 2 3/4 **Sabato (IRE)**[8] 3994 3-9-2 **59**..... MeganNicholls 3 23
(Fergal O'Brien) *s.i.s: hld up: wknd 2f out* **16/1**

5060 **11** 9 **Secret Sonnet**[9] 3975 3-8-5 **51**.....(t) MillyNaseb(3) 4
(Stuart Williams) *s.i.s: pushed along over 4f out: sn lost tch* **33/1**

1m 12.67s (-0.33) **Going Correction** 0.0s/f (Good)
WFA 3 from 4yo+ 6lb **11** Ran SP% **113.0**
Speed ratings (Par 101): **102,99,98,98,96 96,94,91,85,82 70**
CSF £49.87 CT £226.23 TOTE £8.80: £2.90, £2.70, £1.20; EX 55.90 Trifecta £321.20.
Owner Aiden Murphy & All The Kings Horses **Bred** Mrs D Vaughan **Trained** Wilmcote, Warwicks
■ Tilsworth Micky was withdrawn. Price at time of withdrawal 40-1. Rule 4 does not apply.

FOCUS
A modest apprentice riders' handicap. They went a respectable gallop.
T/Plt: £28.30 to a £1 stake. Pool: £58,838.44 - 1,513.51 winning tickets. T/Qpdt: £17.90 to a £1 stake. Pool: £3,790.76 - 156.50 winning tickets. **Colin Roberts**

4322 - 4325a (Foreign Racing) - See Raceform Interactive

4067 LEOPARDSTOWN (L-H)
Thursday, July 14

OFFICIAL GOING: Good to firm

4326a ICON MELD STKS (GROUP 3) — 1m 1f
8:00 (8:00) 3-Y-O+
£27,330 (£8,801; £4,169; £1,852; £926; £463)

RPR

1 **Decorated Knight**[41] 2867 4-9-9 109..... GeorgeBaker 9 112
(Roger Charlton) *hld up in 6th tl prog whn swtchd to outer under 2f out: rapid hdwy to press ldr in 2nd appr fnl f: sn led and qcknd clr: comf* **9/4**[2]

2 2 **Portage (IRE)**[29] 3273 4-9-9 111..... JamesDoyle 1 108
(M Halford, Ire) *sn led: rdn and pressed 1f out: sn hdd and nt qckn w wnr: kpt on same pce* **5/6**[1]

3 2 1/4 **Adool (IRE)**[42] 2843 3-8-11 0..... PatSmullen 10 100+
(D K Weld, Ire) *racd in rr: swtchd wd and prog under 2f out: styd on wl into 3rd ins fnl 100yds: nt trble principals* **16/1**

4 1 1/4 **General Macarthur (USA)**[7] 4065 3-9-0 0.....(t) SeamieHeffernan 4 101
(A P O'Brien, Ire) *chsd ldrs in 3rd: rdn and nt qckn 1f out: kpt on same pce and dropped to 4th ins fnl 100yds* **20/1**

5 1/2 **Tennessee Wildcat (IRE)**[7] 4070 6-9-9 102..... ColinKeane 8 100
(G M Lyons, Ire) *hld up: bit short of room over 1f out: rdn in 6th: kpt on same pce into 5th ins fnl f: nvr on terms* **8/1**[3]

6 1 3/4 **Elleval (IRE)**[14] 3832 6-9-9 105.....(p) ColmO'Donoghue 5 96
(David Marnane, Ire) *racd in mid-div: 4th at 1/2-way: briefly wnt 3rd over 1f out: nt qckn ins fnl f: wknd* **25/1**

7 2 1/4 **Captain Joy (IRE)**[72] 1957 7-9-9 106..... ChrisHayes 6 91
(Tracey Collins, Ire) *led: sn hdd and trckd ldr in 2nd: rdn and wknd appr fnl f* **25/1**

1m 55.93s (1.83)
WFA 3 from 4yo+ 10lb **7** Ran SP% **114.8**
CSF £4.41 TOTE £3.00: £1.50, £1.02; DF 3.90 Trifecta £21.30.
Owner Saleh Al Homaizi & Imad Al Sagar **Bred** Saleh Al Homaizi & Imad Al Sagar **Trained** Beckhampton, Wilts

FOCUS
A pretty taking performance from a consistent horse in a contest that seemed to suit him well.

4327 - 4328a (Foreign Racing) - See Raceform Interactive

OVREVOLL (R-H)
Thursday, July 14

OFFICIAL GOING: Turf: good

4329a SUBARU OSLO CUP (GROUP 3) (3YO+) (TURF) — 1m 4f
7:35 (12:00) 3-Y-O+ **£23,006** (£11,503; £5,521; £3,680; £2,300)

RPR

1 **Hurricane Red (IRE)**[39] 6-9-6 0..... JacobJohansen 2 103
(Lennart Reuterskiold Jr, Sweden) **17/10**[1]

2 2 3/4 **Bokan (FR)**[295] 4-9-4 0..... Jan-ErikNeuroth 6 97
(Wido Neuroth, Norway) **31/5**

3 1/2 **Quarterback (GER)**[27] 3340 4-9-4 0.....(p) CarlosLopez 8 96
(Rune Haugen) **51/10**

4 2 3/4 **Jumeirah (DEN)**[357] 8-9-4 0..... OliverWilson 9 91
(Lone Bager, Denmark) **231/10**

5 1/2 **Eye In The Sky (IRE)**[133] 811 5-9-6 0..... ShaneKarlsson 4 93
(Niels Petersen, Norway) **39/10**[2]

6 2 1/4 **Khyber (FR)**[326] 4-9-4 0..... NikolajStott 1 87
(Wido Neuroth, Norway) **237/10**

7 4 1/4 **Matauri (IRE)**[298] 6576 5-9-4 0..... NelsonDeSouza 3 80
(Niels Petersen, Norway) **19/2**

8 1 1/4 **Jubilance (IRE)**[25] 3449 7-9-4 0..... ManuelSantos 7 78
(Bent Olsen, Denmark) **54/1**

9 2 1/4 **Bank Of Burden (USA)**[298] 6576 9-9-6 0..... Per-AndersGraberg 5 77
(Niels Petersen, Norway) **22/5**[3]

2m 35.5s (1.40) **9** Ran SP% **125.8**
.
Owner Stall Zada **Bred** Grangemore Stud **Trained** Sweden

3935 SAINT-CLOUD (L-H)
Thursday, July 14

OFFICIAL GOING: Turf: good to soft

4330a PRIX DES BLANCS MANTEAUX (CONDITIONS) (2YO) (TURF) — 7f
4:50 (12:00) 2-Y-O **£12,500** (£5,000; £3,750; £2,500; £1,250)

RPR

1 **Icalo (FR)**[26] 2-9-0 0..... FabriceVeron 1 90
(H-A Pantall, France) **6/4**[1]

2 snk **Admiralty Arch**[26] 3382 2-9-0 0..... MickaelBarzalona 6 90
(Richard Hannon) *settled in fnl trio: shkn up and hdwy on outer 2f out: rdn and qcknd to ld narrowly wl over 1f out: r.o under driving: hdd 60yds out: no ex* **23/5**[3]

3 2 1/2 **Sunderia (FR)**[22] 2-8-6 0..... AnthonyCrastus 5 75
(Mme S Allouche, France) **13/1**

4 1/2 **Spirit De Cerisy (FR)**[36] 2-9-0 0..... AntoineHamelin 4 82
(Matthieu Palussiere, France) **9/1**

5 1 **Nofoemaypass (FR)**[43] 2-9-0 0..... AlexisBadel 2 80
(H-F Devin, France) **4/1**[2]

6 8 **Holy Makfi**[13] 2-8-10 0..... StephanePasquier 3 56
(Y Gourraud, France) **58/10**

7 10 **Merci Patron (FR)**[33] 3182 2-8-9 0..... IoritzMendizabal 7 30
(N Caullery, France) **17/2**

1m 25.47s (-6.73) **7** Ran SP% **120.2**
WIN (incl. 1 euro stake): 2.50. PLACES: 1.80, 2.40. SF: 11.70.
Owner Sandro V Gianella **Bred** Appapays Racing Club **Trained** France

4331a PRIX DE THIBERVILLE (LISTED RACE) (3YO FILLIES) (TURF) — 1m 4f
5:20 (12:00) 3-Y-O **£20,220** (£8,088; £6,066; £4,044; £2,022)

RPR

1 **Golden Valentine (FR)**[25] 3450 3-9-2 0..... AurelienLemaitre 8 94
(F Head, France) **9/10**[1]

2 nk **Last Tango Inparis**[61] 2245 3-8-11 0..... FrederikTylicki 6 88
(Hughie Morrison) *trckd ldr on outer: rdn to ld 2f out: hrd pressed and dug in 1 1/2f out: virtually jnd and rallied 1f out: styd on wl u.p: hdd cl home* **241/10**

3 snk **Gargotiere (FR)**[46] 2726 3-8-11 0..... AlexisBadel 5 88
(H-F Devin, France) **54/10**[2]

4 1 1/2 **Alakhana (FR)**[31] 3241 3-8-11 0..... MaximeGuyon 2 86
(F Head, France) **76/10**

5 1 1/2 **Golden Gazelle (IRE)**[31] 3-8-11 0..... Pierre-CharlesBoudot 3 83
(A Fabre, France) **67/10**[3]

6 1/2 **Dimaniya (FR)**[66] 2115 3-8-11 0..... ChristopheSoumillon 1 82
(A De Royer-Dupre, France) **77/10**

7 1/2 **Praskovia (IRE)**[17] 3-8-11 0..... MickaelBarzalona 4 82
(A Fabre, France) *led: hdd 2f out: responded u.p: outpcd over 1f out: wknd fnl f* **14/1**

8 1 1/2 **Chilli Spice (IRE)**[24] 3-8-11 0..... FranckBlondel 7 79
(F-H Graffard, France) **33/1**

2m 32.14s (-8.26) **8** Ran SP% **118.0**
WIN (incl. 1 euro stake): 1.90. PLACES: 1.20, 3.90, 1.60. DF: 25.60. SF: 47.30.
Owner LNJ Foxwoods **Bred** Foxwood Stables **Trained** France

4332a JUDDMONTE GRAND PRIX DE PARIS (GROUP 1) (3YO COLTS & FILLIES) (TURF) — 1m 4f
6:35 (12:00) 3-Y-O **£252,088** (£100,852; £50,426; £25,191; £12,617)

RPR

1 **Helene Charisma (FR)**[31] 3240 3-9-2 0..... CristianDemuro 4 116
(Mme Pia Brandt, France) *hld up in tch on inner: shkn up to ld 2f out: r.o u.p fnl f: a holding chalrs* **33/1**

2 1 1/4 **Red Verdon (USA)**[19] 3679 3-9-2 0..... VincentCheminaud 5 114
(Ed Dunlop) *w.w in fnl pair: hdwy on outer wl over 2f out: sn hrd rdn: styd on to go 2nd 1f out: chsd wnr fnl f: nt pce to chal* **5/1**[2]

3 nk **Cloth Of Stars (IRE)**[40] 2896 3-9-2 0..... Pierre-CharlesBoudot 1 114
(A Fabre, France) *w.w in share of 5th on inner: smooth hdwy and n.m.r 2f out: sn chsng ldrs: styd on u.p fnl f: run flattened out fnl 75yds* **5/1**[2]

4 1 **Mekhtaal**[39] 2946 3-9-2 0..... GregoryBenoist 2 112
(J-C Rouget, France) *chsd ldrs: outpcd and scrubbed along 3f out: hrd rdn 2f out: styd on fr wl over 1f out: clsng in 4th whn squeezed out and snatched up 130yds out: nt rcvr* **13/8**[1]

5 snk **Talismanic**[39] 2946 3-9-2 0..... MickaelBarzalona 8 112
(A Fabre, France) *settled in share of 5th on outer: rdn 2 1/2f out: no imp tl kpt on u.p ins fnl f: nt pce to get on terms* **7/1**[3]

6 nse **Maniaco**[51] 2567 3-9-2 0..... MaximeGuyon 6 112
(A Fabre, France) *dwlt: w.w in fnl pair: hrd rdn and no immediate responce 2f out: styd on fr 1 1/2f out: nrest at fin* **12/1**

7 8 **Spring Master**[25] 3450 3-9-2 0..... OlivierPeslier 3 99
(P Bary, France) *chsd ldng pair: plld way to front bef 1/2-way but sn hdd: rdn to chal outside two rivals 2f out: sn btn* **10/1**

8 3 **Beacon Rock (IRE)**[27] 3337 3-9-2 0.....(b[1]) RyanMoore 9 94
(A P O'Brien, Ire) *led: t.k.h: hdd briefly bef 1/2-way: qckly regained ld: wandered between horses 2 1/2f out: rdn and hdd 2f out: sn wknd* **5/1**[2]

2m 29.56s (-10.84) **8** Ran SP% **120.3**
WIN (incl. 1 euro stake): 18.90. PLACES: 3.60, 2.30, 2.40. DF: 67.40. SF: 106.60.
Owner Gerard Augustin-Normand **Bred** Franklin Finance S.A. **Trained** France

FOCUS
An interesting renewal of a long-established contest usually run at Longchamp, in which early pace looked sound if unspectacular and quickened up off the final bend. The winner wasn't the easiest to find before the off, but the second appeared to run somewhere near his best. A bunch finish, and a pb from Mont Ormel.

4333a PRIX MAURICE DE NIEUIL (GROUP 2) (4YO+) (TURF) 1m 6f
7:50 (12:00) 4-Y-0+ **£54,485** (£21,029; £10,036; £6,691; £3,345)

RPR
1 **Candarliya (FR)**[46] 2727 4-8-10 0 ow1 ChristopheSoumillon 2 113+
(A De Royer-Dupre, France) *settled in 4th: shkn up to remain in tch over 2 1/2f out: rdn to ld wl over 1f out: drvn clr fnl f: comf* **10/11**[1]
2 2 **Launched (IRE)**[26] 3432 4-8-13 0 StephanePasquier 5 113
(P Bary, France) *trckd ldr on outer: drvn to ld 2f out: hdd wl over 1f out: readily outpcd by eventual wnr: hld on wl for 2nd* **6/1**[3]
3 snk **Now We Can**[34] 7-8-13 0 Pierre-CharlesBoudot 3 113+
(N Clement, France) *w.w in 5th: rdn and styd on fr 1 1/2f out: nrest at fin* **17/2**
4 2 **Meandre (FR)**[39] 8-8-13 0 FabriceVeron 6 110+
(A Savujev, Czech Republic) *t.k.h: hld up in rr: rdn and no real imp 2f out: styd on wl ins fnl f: nvr nrr* **12/1**
5 2 **Walzertakt (GER)**[46] 2725 7-8-13 0 MaximeGuyon 1 107
(Jean-Pierre Carvalho, Germany) *led early: hdd after 1 1/2f: trckd ldr on inner: outpcd and scrubbed along wl over 3f out: rallied u.p to chal 2f out: sn btn* **18/1**
6 2 **Mille Et Mille**[28] 3298 6-8-13 0 ThierryThulliez 4 105
(C Lerner, France) *led after 1 1/2f: qcknd tempo 3f out: sn labouring and hdd 2f out: grad lft bhd* **5/2**[2]
3m 4.79s (-7.41) 6 Ran SP% **118.7**
WIN (incl. 1 euro stake): 2.00. PLACES: 1.40, 2.30. SF: 8.90.
Owner H H Aga Khan **Bred** Haras De Son Altesse L'Aga Khan **Trained** Chantilly, France

4334 - (Foreign Racing) - See Raceform Interactive

4308 HAMILTON (R-H)
Friday, July 15

OFFICIAL GOING: Good to soft (soft in places) changing to soft after race 2 (6.40)
Wind: Fairly strong, half behind Weather: Overcast, raining

4335 RACINGUK.COM APPRENTICE H'CAP 1m 67y
6:05 (6:05) (Class 5) (0-70,75) 4-Y-0+ **£3,881** (£1,155; £577; £288) **Stalls** Low

Form RPR
0264 1 **Framley Garth (IRE)**[13] 3883 4-8-13 69 PaulaMuir(8) 7 77
(Patrick Holmes) *t.k.h: hld up in tch: rdn and outpcd over 2f out: rallied and swtchd lft over 1f out: led ins fnl f: rdn out* **18/1**
402 2 2 1/4 **Dolphin Rock**[11] 3946 9-8-8 62 (b) CallumRodriguez(6) 3 65
(Richard Ford) *dwlt: hdwy to chse ldr after 1f: led over 2f out: sn rdn: hdd ins fnl f: kpt on same pce* **7/1**[3]
4423 3 nk **Yulong Xiongba (IRE)**[11] 3952 4-9-3 65 JoshDoyle 6 67
(Julie Camacho) *t.k.h: trckd ldrs: effrt and rdn 2f out: ev ch briefly ins fnl f: no ex towards fin* **5/2**[2]
4113 4 2 1/4 **Imperial Link**[7] 4087 4-9-0 62 (p) NathanEvans 2 59
(John O'Shea) *led to over 2f out: rallied: wknd ins fnl f* **15/2**
5634 5 3 **Newmarket Warrior (IRE)**[11] 3952 5-9-6 68 (p) AdamMcNamara 1 58
(Iain Jardine) *hld up in tch: stdy hdwy 3f out: rdn and wknd over 1f out* **15/8**[1]
6015 6 3 1/2 **Beautiful Stranger (IRE)**[4] 4189 5-9-10 75 6ex (p) PatrickVaughan(3) 5 57
(Keith Dalgleish) *t.k.h: hld up: rdn and outpcd over 3f out: n.d after* **15/2**
3050 7 3/4 **Cadmium**[11] 3952 5-9-0 65 (v[1]) RobJFitzpatrick(3) 4 45
(Micky Hammond) *in tch: effrt over 2f out: wknd over 1f out* **20/1**
1m 52.14s (3.74) **Going Correction** +0.35s/f (Good) 7 Ran SP% **109.4**
Speed ratings (Par 103): **95,92,92,90,87 83,82**
CSF £123.06 TOTE £19.40: £9.40, £3.40; EX 154.00 Trifecta £984.80.
Owner FPR Yorkshire Syndicate **Bred** G Morrin **Trained** Middleham, N Yorks

FOCUS
Race distances as advertised. The ground had softened significantly after plenty of rain on the day of racing. Most of these handicappers had shown their form of late and despite the size of the field this was quite competitive as apprentice races go. A surprise pb from the winner.

4336 BRITISH STALLION STUDS EBF MAIDEN STKS (PLUS 10 RACE) (A £20,000 HIGHLAND SPRING WATER QUALIFIER) 6f 6y
6:40 (6:41) (Class 4) 2-Y-O **£4,269** (£1,270; £634; £317) **Stalls** High

Form RPR
2402 1 **Leontes**[15] 3805 2-9-5 0 PJMcDonald 11 83
(Andrew Balding) *cl up: drvn and ev ch over 1f out: led ins fnl f: hld on gamely* **6/4**[1]
22 2 shd **What's The Story**[22] 3548 2-9-5 0 JoeFanning 3 83
(Keith Dalgleish) *t.k.h: w ldr: led over 2f out: rdn: edgd lft and hdd ins fnl f: rallied: jst hld* **13/8**[2]
3 4 1/2 **Lualiwa** 2-9-5 0 ShaneGray 2 69+
(Kevin Ryan) *s.i.s: sn pushed along in rr: hdwy over 1f out: kpt on fnl f: nt pce to chal* **14/1**
4 1/2 **Robben Rainbow** 2-9-5 0 GrahamGibbons 7 68
(David Barron) *t.k.h: trckd ldrs: effrt and ev ch over 1f out: wknd ins fnl f* **9/1**[3]
5 2 **Royal Cosmic** 2-8-9 0 AdamMcNamara(5) 9 57
(Richard Fahey) *s.i.s: chsd clr ldng gp: outpcd 1/2-way: kpt on fnl f: nvr able to chal* **18/1**
0 6 2 1/4 **Jock Talk (IRE)**[51] 2570 2-9-5 0 TadhgO'Shea 1 55
(John Patrick Shanahan, Ire) *dwlt: bhd: hdwy over 3f out: rdn and wknd over 1f out* **28/1**
55 7 1/2 **Metronomic (IRE)**[15] 3799 2-9-5 0 SeanLevey 10 53
(Richard Hannon) *led to over 2f out: rdn and wknd over 1f out* **10/1**
1m 14.62s (2.42) **Going Correction** +0.475s/f (Yiel) 7 Ran SP% **112.6**
Speed ratings (Par 96): **102,101,95,95,92 89,88**
CSF £4.04 TOTE £2.30: £1.10, £1.50; EX 4.10 Trifecta £22.50.
Owner David Brownlow **Bred** D J Weston **Trained** Kingsclere, Hants

FOCUS
A couple of these had run well enough beforehand to show themselves likely future maiden winners and they pulled clear from two newcomers.

4337 JOHN SMITH'S EXTRA SMOOTH H'CAP 6f 6y
7:10 (7:10) (Class 5) (0-70,70) 3-Y-O+ **£3,881** (£1,155; £577; £288) **Stalls** Centre

Form RPR
0010 1 **Royal Connoisseur (IRE)**[22] 3553 5-9-7 68 AdamMcNamara(5) 4 78
(Richard Fahey) *mde all: drvn along over 1f out: drew clr ins fnl f* **7/2**[3]
10/2 2 3 **More Beau (USA)**[21] 3610 5-9-13 69 BarryMcHugh 2 69
(David Nicholls) *t.k.h: trckd ldrs: wnt 2nd over 2f out: sn rdn: kpt on same pce fnl f* **11/8**[1]
-032 3 1 3/4 **Malvia**[11] 3953 4-9-2 58 (b) PJMcDonald 3 53
(Ian Williams) *missed break: t.k.h in tch: effrt and rdn over 1f out: carried hd awkwardly: sn no ex* **5/2**[2]
-500 4 3 3/4 **Magical Lasso (IRE)**[53] 2533 3-9-2 64 PhillipMakin 6 46
(Keith Dalgleish) *pressed ldr to over 2f out: rdn and wknd over 1f* **6/1**
1m 15.37s (3.17) **Going Correction** +0.475s/f (Yiel)
WFA 3 from 4yo+ 6lb 4 Ran SP% **107.2**
Speed ratings (Par 103): **97,93,90,85**
CSF £8.64 TOTE £3.80; EX 9.70 Trifecta £22.40.
Owner S & G Clayton, A Blower **Bred** Mrs Sheila Morrissey **Trained** Musley Bank, N Yorks

FOCUS
The ground was changed officially to soft before this race. A small field, and with the second and third probably not at their best the bare form is far from strong. The winner does have better back form.

4338 JOHN SMITH'S SCOTTISH STEWARDS' CUP H'CAP 6f 6y
7:40 (7:42) (Class 2) (0-105,100) 3-Y-O+
£21,165 (£6,337; £3,168; £1,584; £792; £397) **Stalls** Centre

Form RPR
1111 1 **Orion's Bow**[21] 3606 5-9-11 97 BarryMcHugh 11 111+
(David Nicholls) *cl up stands' side gp: led gng wl over 1f out: edgd lft ins fnl f: rdn clr: 1st of 6 in gp* **13/2**[1]
6001 2 3 1/4 **Hoof It**[13] 3890 9-9-4 95 NathanEvans(5) 14 99
(Michael Easterby) *led and overall ldr stands' side: rdn and hdd over 1f out: kpt on fnl f: no ch w wnr: 2nd of 6 in gp* **14/1**
0413 3 1/2 **Intense Style (IRE)**[13] 3890 4-9-5 91 DavidAllan 15 93
(Les Eyre) *trckd stands' side ldrs: rdn over 2f out: hung rt over 1f out: kpt on same pce fnl f: 3rd of 6 in gp* **10/1**
-061 4 1 1/4 **Lulu The Zulu (IRE)**[21] 3616 8-10-0 100 OisinMurphy 2 98
(Michael Appleby) *cl up centre gp: rdn and led that gp over 1f out: kpt on fnl f: no ch w stands' side ldrs: 1st of 8 in gp* **12/1**
-026 5 hd **Cornwallville (IRE)**[13] 3890 4-9-12 98 (v[1]) PJMcDonald 7 95
(David Loughnane) *bhd centre: rdn and edgd lft over 2f out: kpt on wl fnl f: nvr able to chal: 2nd of 8 in gp* **25/1**
0014 6 2 1/2 **My Name Is Rio (IRE)**[11] 3944 6-9-3 89 ConnorBeasley 9 78
(Michael Dods) *dwlt: sn in tch centre: rdn over 2f out: wknd over 1f out: 3rd of 8 in gp* **16/1**
10-3 7 1 **Nameitwhatyoulike**[83] 1644 7-9-13 99 JoeFanning 8 85
(Bryan Smart) *led centre gp to over 1f out: sn rdn and wknd: 4th of 8 in gp* **9/1**
-004 8 1 **Tatlisu (IRE)**[13] 3890 6-9-7 98 AdamMcNamara(5) 6 81
(Richard Fahey) *dwlt: bhd centre: rdn over 2f out: hdwy over 1f out: kpt on fnl f: nvr able to chal: 5th of 8 in gp* **7/1**[2]
0-10 9 nk **Munfallet (IRE)**[72] 1958 5-9-1 87 SeanLevey 16 69
(David Brown) *cl up stands' side: drvn along and hung rt 2f out: sn wknd: 4th of 6 in gp* **14/1**
2004 10 3 **Taexali (IRE)**[13] 3909 3-9-2 94 TadhgO'Shea 10 65
(John Patrick Shanahan, Ire) *prom centre: rdn 1/2-way: hung rt and wknd 2f out: 6th of 8 in gp* **16/1**
0-01 11 1 **Amazour (IRE)**[20] 3656 4-9-10 96 MartinLane 4 65
(Ismail Mohammed) *cl up centre: rdn along over 2f out: wknd wl over 1f out: 7th of 8 in gp* **8/1**
0010 12 3/4 **Blaine**[20] 3656 6-9-12 98 (b) DougieCostello 13 65
(David Nicholls) *dwlt: bhd stands' side: drvn along over 2f out: nvr on terms: 5th of 6 in gp* **11/1**
2002 13 nk **New Bidder**[13] 3890 5-9-7 93 GrahamGibbons 1 59
(David Barron) *sn towards rr in centre: drvn along over 2f out: btn over 1f out: last of 8 in gp* **11/1**
46-1 14 9 **Mickey (IRE)**[45] 2780 3-8-9 87 (t) RichardKingscote 12 23
(Tom Dascombe) *prom stands' side: rdn and hung rt over 2f out: sn wknd: last of 6 in gp* **15/2**[3]
1m 13.59s (1.39) **Going Correction** +0.475s/f (Yiel)
WFA 3 from 4yo+ 6lb 14 Ran SP% **121.1**
Speed ratings (Par 109): **109,104,104,102,102 98,97,96,95,91 90,89,88,76**
CSF £96.67 CT £915.51 TOTE £4.70: £1.90, £5.30, £4.30; EX 60.70 Trifecta £1437.30.
Owner T J Swiers **Bred** Cheveley Park Stud Ltd **Trained** Sessay, N Yorks

FOCUS
This is invariably an ultra-competitive handicap and it attracted a field full of sprinters primed for a big run, with none in the line-up safe to discount at the weights. Though several ultimately failed to give their running that should not detract from the performance of the winner, who was highly impressive. The form is set around the second and third.

4339 EBF STALLIONS GLASGOW STKS (LISTED RACE) 1m 3f 14y
8:15 (8:15) (Class 1) 3-Y-O
£23,818 (£9,030; £4,519; £2,251; £1,129; £567) **Stalls** High

Form RPR
1060 1 **Ventura Storm (IRE)**[40] 2946 3-9-9 101 SeanLevey 6 102
(Richard Hannon) *trckd ldrs: smooth hdwy to ld over 2f out: sn rdn: kpt on gamely u.p ins fnl f* **8/1**
-330 2 1 1/4 **Ormito (GER)**[28] 3341 3-9-5 98 OisinMurphy 1 96
(Andrew Balding) *hld up in tch: rdn and hdwy over 2f out: chsd wnr wl ins fnl f: kpt on: nt pce to chal* **9/2**[2]
2251 3 2 1/4 **Montsarrat (IRE)**[11] 3950 3-9-5 88 JoeFanning 2 92
(Mark Johnston) *led at ordinary gallop: rdn and hdd over 2f out: rallied and ev ch tl over 1f out: no ex ins fnl f* **15/2**
-160 4 1 1/2 **Carrington (FR)**[29] 3299 3-9-5 90 [1] MartinLane 3 90
(Charlie Appleby) *s.s: hld up: rdn and hdwy on outside 3f out: no imp over 1f out* **18/1**
232 5 1 **Warp Factor (IRE)**[22] 3550 3-9-5 79 TadhgO'Shea 7 88?
(John Patrick Shanahan, Ire) *cl up: rdn and ev ch over 2f out to over 1f out: wknd ins fnl f* **50/1**

5051 **6** 1 **Percy Street**[20] 3666 3-9-5 98 .... DougieCostello 4 86
(K R Burke) *t.k.h: trckd ldrs: rdn over 2f out: edgd rt and wknd over 1f out* **11/2**[3]

1- **7** 9 **Wajeez (IRE)**[254] 7707 3-9-5 95 .... RichardKingscote 8 71
(John Gosden) *hld up: rdn over 3f out: shortlived effrt over 2f out: hung rt and wknd wl over 1f out* **11/10**[1]

2m 26.98s (1.38) **Going Correction** +0.35s/f (Good) **7** Ran SP% **111.3**
Speed ratings (Par 108): **108,107,105,104,103 102,96**
CSF £41.06 TOTE £9.60: £4.10, £1.90; EX 44.50 Trifecta £179.80.
Owner Middleham Park Racing LXXII **Bred** Laurence Kennedy **Trained** East Everleigh, Wilts

FOCUS
This has become a decent springboard for progressive three-year-olds since it was switched from a Derby trial to a mid-July event, with three of the five winners going on to land a Group race - Hunter's Light and Postponed both scored in Group 1 company. They went just a sensible gallop, with the pace increasing from three furlongs out, and it was not easy making up ground in these conditions. Probably a pretty ordinary renewal.

4340 JORDAN ELECTRICS H'CAP — 1m 3f 14y
8:45 (8:45) (Class 5) (0-70,75) 3-Y-O+ **£3,881** (£1,155; £577; £288) **Stalls** High

Form RPR

3324 **1** **Falcon's Fire (IRE)**[2] 4255 3-8-1 55 .... JoeFanning 2 66+
(Keith Dalgleish) *trckd ldrs: hdwy to ld over 2f out: clr whn edgd lft ins fnl f: pushed out* **3/1**[3]

-442 **2** 2 3/4 **Zubeida**[18] 3715 3-9-2 70 ....(p) MartinLane 4 75+
(Ismail Mohammed) *t.k.h: trckd ldr: chal over 3f out tl outpcd over 2f out: rallied to chse (clr) wnr ins fnl f: kpt on: no imp* **9/4**[2]

4665 **3** 1/2 **Qibtee (FR)**[10] 3983 6-9-1 57 .... DavidAllan 3 61
(Les Eyre) *hld up in tch: rdn and hdwy over 2f out: edgd rt over 1f out: kpt on same pce ins fnl f* **9/1**

1231 **4** 1 **Wotabreeze (IRE)**[2] 4255 3-9-2 75 6ex........ AdamMcNamara(5) 5 77
(John Quinn) *prom: rdn over 3f out: hdwy and ev ch over 2f out: sn rdn: kpt on same pce ins fnl f* **2/1**[1]

0064 **5** 2 1/2 **Whitchurch**[16] 3774 4-8-9 51 .... PJMcDonald 6 49
(Philip Kirby) *hld up: drvn and outpcd over 3f out: no imp fr 2f out* **9/1**

-005 **6** shd **Invincible Bond**[9] 4001 3-7-12 57 oh9 ow3........ NathanEvans(5) 1 55
(Simon Waugh) *led to over 2f out: sn drvn along: wknd wl over 1f out* **25/1**

2m 30.9s (5.30) **Going Correction** +0.35s/f (Good)
WFA 3 from 4yo+ 12lb **6** Ran SP% **112.9**
Speed ratings (Par 103): **94,92,91,90,89 89**
CSF £10.33 TOTE £4.40: £1.60, £2.00; EX 10.00 Trifecta £34.60.
Owner Ronnie Docherty **Bred** Patrick Headon **Trained** Carluke, S Lanarks

FOCUS
Just a fair pace for this handicap which was run in heavy rain. The winner reversed recent Catterick form with the favourite.

4341 JOHN SMITH'S H'CAP — 1m 1f 34y
9:15 (9:16) (Class 5) (0-70,70) 3-Y-O+ **£3,881** (£1,155; £577; £288) **Stalls** Low

Form RPR

2220 **1** **Henpecked**[12] 3920 6-9-7 68 ....(p) GarryWhillans(5) 4 75
(Alistair Whillans) *stdd in tch: drvn along over 2f out: rallied over 1f out: led ins fnl f: edgd lft: kpt on* **11/2**

4443 **2** nk **Incurs Four Faults**[17] 3750 5-8-9 51 oh2........(p) JoeFanning 1 57
(Keith Dalgleish) *t.k.h: in tch: hdwy on outside to ld over 2f out: rdn and hdd ins fnl f: rallied: kpt on fin* **11/2**

406 **3** 3 1/4 **So Celebre (GER)**[29] 3323 3-9-4 70 .... PJMcDonald 5 68
(Ian Williams) *led: rdn and hdd over 2f out: rallied: kpt on same pce fnl f* **7/2**[2]

0332 **4** 1 3/4 **Tectonic (IRE)**[1] 4314 7-9-3 59 ....(v) PhillipMakin 7 55
(Keith Dalgleish) *s.i.s: t.k.h: hld up in tch: effrt and swtchd lft over 1f out: kpt on fnl f: no imp* **9/2**[3]

-605 **5** 2 1/4 **Bahamian C**[15] 3801 5-9-9 70 ....(t) AdamMcNamara(5) 6 61
(Richard Fahey) *dwlt: sn trcking ldr: rdn and ev ch over 3f out to over 2f out: rdn and wknd over 1f out* **8/1**

-111 **6** 5 **Therthaar**[45] 2784 3-9-2 68 .... MartinLane 3 47
(Ismail Mohammed) *t.k.h: trckd ldrs: ev ch over 3f out to over 2f out: rdn and wknd over 1f out* **9/4**[1]

2m 4.47s (4.77) **Going Correction** +0.35s/f (Good)
WFA 3 from 5yo+ 10lb **6** Ran SP% **113.1**
Speed ratings (Par 103): **92,91,88,87,85 80**
CSF £34.98 TOTE £6.20: £2.80, £2.40; EX 41.40 Trifecta £142.00.
Owner Eildon Hill Racing **Bred** T Hirschfeld **Trained** Newmill-On-Slitrig, Borders

FOCUS
Few obviously progressive or unexposed sorts in this handicap, which was quite a test in these conditions with heavy rain continuing to fall, and they were all still in contention 2f out. A minor pb from the winner.
T/Plt: £1,244.20 to a £1 stake. Pool: £53,230.61 - 31.23 winning tickets T/Qpdt: £160.10 to a £1 stake. Pool: £5,764.67 - 26.64 winning tickets **Richard Young**

3887 HAYDOCK (L-H)
Friday, July 15

OFFICIAL GOING: Soft (7.0)
Wind: Light, variable Weather: Overcast

4342 APOLLOBET CASHBACK IF 2ND H'CAP — 1m 2f 95y
2:10 (2:10) (Class 5) (0-75,78) 3-Y-O **£3,234** (£962; £481; £240) **Stalls** Centre

Form RPR

0326 **1** **Glance My Way (IRE)**[17] 3736 3-9-3 71 .... KieranO'Neill 4 81
(Richard Hannon) *in rr: niggled along at times: hdwy over 3f out: rdn over 2f out: styd on to ld jst over 1f out: kpt on ins fnl f* **7/1**

5334 **2** 3/4 **Just Hiss**[14] 3853 3-9-6 74 .... JasonHart 6 82
(Tim Easterby) *racd keenly: a.p: travelling wl 3f out: rdn to chal 2f out: led briefly over 1f out: kpt on ins fnl f: hld towards fin* **9/2**[3]

2423 **3** 3 1/4 **Kings Gold (IRE)**[13] 3904 3-9-4 72 ....(p) PaulMulrennan 5 74
(Michael Dods) *led: rdn over 2f out: hdd over 1f out: kpt on same pce fnl 150yds* **7/1**

6233 **4** 7 **Torremar (FR)**[14] 3853 3-9-4 72 .... KeaganLatham 8 61
(Kevin Ryan) *prom: lost pl over 3f out: u.p after: plugged on but n.d ins fnl f* **7/2**[2]

6005 **5** 2 1/4 **Shrubland**[15] 3804 3-8-5 59 ....(b) CamHardie 1 43
(Ed Walker) *s.i.s: hld up: hdwy 4f out: pushed along over 3f out: rdn whn chsng ldrs over 2f out: no imp: wknd 1f out* **12/1**

463 **6** shd **Touchdown Banwell (USA)**[30] 3281 3-9-4 72 .... OisinMurphy 2 56
(Andrew Balding) *racd keenly: hld up in tch: pushed along over 3f out: sn btn* **10/1**

0111 **7** 6 **Caponova (IRE)**[27] 3395 3-9-7 75 .... RichardKingscote 3 48
(Tom Dascombe) *racd keenly: hld up: hdwy after 2f: wnt prom 6f out: c wd ent st over 4f out: rdn whn carried hd to one side and lost pl over 3f out: wknd over 2f out: eased whn wl btn ins fnl f* **2/1**[1]

2m 16.08s (0.58) **Going Correction** +0.075s/f (Good) **7** Ran SP% **115.5**
Speed ratings (Par 100): **100,99,96,91,89 89,84**
CSF £38.90 CT £230.35 TOTE £8.40: £3.10, £3.40; EX 40.90 Trifecta £312.00.
Owner Brian Dolan **Bred** D J Maher **Trained** East Everleigh, Wilts

FOCUS
All races were run over the inner home straight. Allowing for rail movement, approximate race distances were: 5f 6f 7f 218yds 1m 2f 93yds 1m 5f 218yds. This modest 3yo handicap was predictably hard work and two came clear. The winner is rated back to a better view of his 2yo form.

4343 APOLLOBET DAILY RACING REFUNDS EBF NOVICE STKS (PLUS 10 RACE) — 6f
2:40 (2:40) (Class 4) 2-Y-O **£4,269** (£1,270; £634; £317) **Stalls** High

Form RPR

1 **1** **South Seas (IRE)**[25] 3463 2-9-8 0 .... OisinMurphy 2 89
(Andrew Balding) *prom: led 2f out: drew away ins fnl f: kpt on wl* **1/5**[1]

3 **2** 2 3/4 **Abiento (IRE)**[23] 3516 2-9-2 0 .... TonyHamilton 5 75
(Richard Fahey) *racd keenly: prom: effrt under 2f out: wnt 2nd 1f out: no imp on wnr ins fnl f* **40/1**

1 **3** 1 1/2 **Naples Bay**[14] 3839 2-9-8 0 .... CamHardie 4 76
(John Quinn) *hld up: pushed along 2f out: kpt on ins fnl f to take 3rd towards fin* **14/1**[3]

3 **4** nk **Mjjack (IRE)**[15] 3805 2-9-2 0 .... DougieCostello 3 69
(K R Burke) *racd keenly: hld up bhd ldrs: rdn and nt qckn 2f out: kpt on same pce ins fnl f: nvr able to chal* **5/1**[2]

14 **5** 4 **Fiery Character (IRE)**[72] 1965 2-9-3 0 .... RichardKingscote 1 58
(Tom Dascombe) *sweating: led: hdd 2f out: wknd ins fnl f: eased whn wl btn towards fin* **14/1**[3]

1m 17.06s (3.26) **Going Correction** +0.40s/f (Good) **5** Ran SP% **115.8**
Speed ratings (Par 96): **94,90,88,87,82**
CSF £14.44 TOTE £1.20: £1.10, £10.00; EX 13.10 Trifecta £55.10.
Owner Qatar Racing Limited **Bred** Stonepark Farms **Trained** Kingsclere, Hants

FOCUS
They went a fair pace in this novice event and the third is the best guide. The winner wasn't as impressive this time.

4344 HAYBURN ROCK FINANCIAL PLANNING LTD H'CAP — 6f
3:15 (3:16) (Class 4) (0-85,84) 3-Y-O **£5,175** (£1,540; £769; £384) **Stalls** High

Form RPR

1-52 **1** **Dutch Destiny**[22] 3575 3-9-6 83 .... PatCosgrave 1 95+
(William Haggas) *prom: led over 2f out: kpt on wl and in command fnl 100yds* **11/4**[1]

-322 **2** 2 **Rantan (IRE)**[13] 3893 3-9-5 82 .... GrahamGibbons 4 87
(David Barron) *midfield: rdn over 2f out: hdwy to take 2nd over 1f out: edgd lft u.p ins fnl f: no imp on wnr fnl 100yds* **6/1**[3]

-225 **3** 2 1/4 **Andar**[20] 3643 3-9-1 78 ....(p) RichardKingscote 5 76
(Clive Cox) *bmpd s: pushed along early to chse ldrs: rdn over 2f out: kpt on same pce fnl 100yds* **9/1**

0002 **4** 3/4 **English Hero**[25] 3466 3-8-13 76 .... GrahamLee 6 72
(John Mackie) *bmpd s: midfield: pushed along 1/2-way: rdn to chse ldrs 1f out: one pce fnl 100yds* **16/1**

442 **5** 1 1/4 **Predetermined (IRE)**[20] 3634 3-8-13 76 .... OisinMurphy 3 68
(Andrew Balding) *prom: pushed along 1/2-way: rdn over 1f out: wknd ent fnl f* **4/1**[2]

3232 **6** 2 1/2 **Bossipop**[30] 3292 3-9-7 84 ....(p) JasonHart 7 68
(Tim Easterby) *bmpd s: racd keenly: hld up: rdn over 2f out: effrt over 1f out: no imp: wknd and eased fnl 100yds* **4/1**[2]

3343 **7** nk **Tommy G**[20] 3643 3-9-3 80 .... PaulMulrennan 8 63
(Jim Goldie) *hld up in rr: u.p and lft bhd over 1f out* **16/1**

0-05 **8** 1 **Gin In The Inn (IRE)**[20] 3646 3-8-13 76 .... TonyHamilton 2 55
(Richard Fahey) *led: hdd over 2f out: wknd over 1f out* **9/1**

1m 15.76s (1.96) **Going Correction** +0.40s/f (Good) **8** Ran SP% **112.7**
Speed ratings (Par 102): **102,99,96,95,93 90,89,88**
CSF £18.98 CT £128.40 TOTE £3.50: £1.50, £2.20, £2.90; EX 16.00 Trifecta £95.80.
Owner Cheveley Park Stud **Bred** Cheveley Park Stud Ltd **Trained** Newmarket, Suffolk

FOCUS
This looked a competitive 3yo sprint handicap. Straightforward form, with a biggish step up from the winner.

4345 APOLLOBET HOME OF CASHBACK OFFERS H'CAP — 5f
3:50 (3:50) (Class 4) (0-80,80) 3-Y-O+ **£5,175** (£1,540; £769; £384) **Stalls** High

Form RPR

6000 **1** **Adam's Ale**[31] 3265 7-9-6 77 .... RachelRichardson(3) 1 87
(Mark Walford) *hld up: rdn 2f out: hdwy over 1f out: styd on to ld fnl 75yds: in control cl home* **4/1**[2]

2421 **2** 1 **Orient Class**[14] 3851 5-9-2 70 .... GrahamLee 5 76
(Paul Midgley) *chsd ldrs: rdn to ld ins fnl f: hdd fnl 75yds: no ex nr fin* **7/2**[1]

6300 **3** 1 1/4 **Casterbridge**[13] 3892 4-9-10 78 .... JasonHart 6 80
(Eric Alston) *sed awkwardly: hld up in rr: rdn and hdwy over 1f out: chsng ldrs whn n.m.r and checked abt 150yds out: styd on towards fin* **13/2**

1043 **4** 1/2 **Top Boy**[8] 4066 6-9-11 79 ....(v) TonyHamilton 7 79
(Derek Shaw) *in rr: hdwy whn swtchd lft over 1f out: sn chsng ldrs: swtchd rt whn nt clr run ins fnl f: kpt on u.p towards fin* **6/1**

505 **5** shd **Pensax Lad (IRE)**[11] 3956 5-9-5 76 .... GeorgeDowning(3) 2 75
(Ronald Harris) *prom: led 2f out: rdn over 1f out: hdd ins fnl f: stl ev ch u.p 110yds out: no ex towards fin* **11/2**[3]

4044 **6** 6 **Long Awaited (IRE)**[11] 3956 8-9-10 78 ....(b) PaulMulrennan 4 56
(Conor Dore) *hld up in tch: effrt to chse ldrs over 1f out: wknd fnl 150yds* **10/1**

1140 **7** 1 1/2 **Eleuthera**[13] 3875 4-9-8 76 .... PatCosgrave 3 48
(Kevin Ryan) *led: hdd 2f out: rdn and wknd over 1f out* **8/1**

2210 **8** 7 **Elusivity (IRE)**[45] 2768 8-9-12 80 ....(p) CamHardie 8 27
(Conor Dore) *prom: pushed along over 2f out: wknd under 2f out* **11/1**

1m 3.01s (2.21) **Going Correction** +0.40s/f (Good) **8** Ran SP% **113.8**
Speed ratings (Par 105): **98,96,94,93,93 83,81,70**
CSF £18.21 CT £88.15 TOTE £5.00: £1.50, £2.20, £2.70; EX 20.10 Trifecta £115.80.
Owner Mrs M Hills **Bred** Mrs M J Hills **Trained** Sherriff Hutton, N Yorks

FOCUS
An open-looking sprint handicap, rated around the runner-up to his old best.

4346 BROWN SHIPLEY H'CAP 1m 6f
4:25 (4:25) (Class 4) (0-85,84) 3-Y-O **£5,175** (£1,540; £769; £384) **Stalls** Low

Form RPR
0215 **1** **Snan (IRE)**[16] 3768 3-9-2 **79**........(b) TomQueally 3 87+
(Richard Hannon) *chsd ldr after nrly 2f: pushed along 5f out: moved upsides and helped increase pce 4f out: led over 3f out: rdn over 1f out: styd on wl fnl f* **11/2**[3]
0324 **2** 2 ¼ **Rainbow Dreamer**[16] 3768 3-9-7 **84**........ WilliamTwiston-Davies 1 89+
(Alan King) *dwlt: sn rcvrd to ld: pressed and increased pce 4f out: hdd over 3f out: swtchd rt over 1f out: edgd lft u.p whn unable to go w wnr ins fnl f: no imp after* **15/8**[1]
3233 **3** ¾ **Kajaki (IRE)**[18] 3715 3-8-7 **70**........(p) KieranO'Neill 2 73
(Kevin Ryan) *led early: chsd ldrs after: pushed along over 3f out: sn outpcd: rdn over 2f out: kpt on u.p ins fnl f: clsd on runner-up nr fin* **10/3**[2]
5131 **4** 15 **West Coast Flyer**[21] 3607 3-9-1 **78**........ OisinMurphy 4 73
(David Simcock) *hld up in rr: pushed along over 3f out: sn outpcd: rdn over 2f out: eased whn btn 1f out* **15/8**[1]
3m 9.71s (7.71) **Going Correction** +0.075s/f (Good) **4** Ran SP% **108.0**
Speed ratings (Par 102): **80,78,78,69**
CSF £15.79 TOTE £4.10; EX 16.90 Trifecta £34.60.
Owner Al Shaqab Racing **Bred** Slow Sand Syndicate **Trained** East Everleigh, Wilts

FOCUS
This was unsurprisingly tactical and the going played a big part. The winner reversed Bath form with the second.

4347 APOLLOBET BET ON LOTTERIES MAIDEN STKS 1m
4:55 (4:57) (Class 5) 3-Y-O+ **£2,911** (£866; £432; £216) **Stalls** Low

Form RPR
5-22 **1** **Fastnet Tempest (IRE)**[44] 2804 3-9-3 84........(p) PatCosgrave 6 87+
(William Haggas) *mde all: rdn over 1f out: kpt on wl fnl f: drvn out* **5/6**[1]
4 **2** 1 ¾ **Sumou (IRE)**[22] 3572 3-9-0 0........ LouisSteward(3) 2 82+
(Marcus Tregoning) *chsd wnr: pushed along 3f out: effrt over 2f out: sn edgd lft: nt qckn over 1f out: edgd rt and rallied ins fnl f: no imp fnl 75yds* **9/2**[3]
2 **3** 2 ¼ **Toulson**[16] 3769 3-9-3 0........ TomQueally 4 77
(Eve Johnson Houghton) *dwlt: wnt prom after 2f: rdn over 2f out: nt qckn over 1f out: no ex fnl 75yds* **3/1**[2]
3 **4** 2 ¼ **Booborowie (IRE)**[17] 3744 3-9-3 0........ AdamBeschizza 1 72
(Jeremy Gask) *hld up in midfield: rdn over 2f out: no imp over 1f out: one pce ins fnl f* **22/1**
62 **5** ½ **Martha McCandles**[22] 3578 5-9-7 0........ WilliamTwiston-Davies 5 68
(Alan King) *hld up: rdn over 2f out: no imp over 1f out: one pce ins fnl f* **12/1**
6 7 **Jonofark (IRE)** 3-9-3 0........ PaddyAspell 3 55
(Brian Rothwell) *s.s: in rr: struggling over 2f out: nvr a threat* **66/1**
54- **7** 1 **Executive Bay**[328] 5628 3-8-12 0........ AnnaHesketh(5) 7 52
(Tom Dascombe) *racd keenly: prom: dropped to trck ldrs after 2f: lost pl 4f out: n.d after* **22/1**
1m 48.51s (4.81) **Going Correction** +0.075s/f (Good)
WFA 3 from 5yo 9lb **7** Ran SP% **115.6**
Speed ratings (Par 103): **78,76,74,71,71 64,63**
CSF £5.10 TOTE £1.90: £1.20, £1.90; EX 5.50 Trifecta £11.10.
Owner O T I Racing & Partner **Bred** Rockhart Trading Ltd **Trained** Newmarket, Suffolk

FOCUS
A fair maiden on pre-race figures that saw a slow-motion finish. The first three are likely to rate higher.

4348 APOLLOBET HAYDOCK PARK APPRENTICE TRAINING SERIES H'CAP (RACING EXCELLENCE INITIATIVE) 1m
5:25 (5:28) (Class 5) (0-75,73) 4-Y-O+ **£2,911** (£866; £432; £216) **Stalls** Low

Form RPR
65 **1** **Italian Beauty (IRE)**[70] 2015 4-9-8 **69**........ CallumShepherd 2 76
(Brian Ellison) *bustled along early to dispute ld: pushed along and hdd over 3f out: rdn and upsides chalng over 2f out: led narrowly ins fnl f: kpt on towards fin* **5/1**
153 **2** ½ **Bush Beauty (IRE)**[15] 3810 5-9-4 **68**........ SophieKilloran(3) 3 74
(Eric Alston) *racd keenly: chsd ldrs: upsides over 3f out: led over 2f out and pressed: rdn over 1f out: hdd narrowly ins fnl f: hld nr fin* **9/4**[1]
4060 **3** 1 ¾ **The Firm (IRE)**[13] 3876 7-8-13 **63**........(be) CharlieBennett(3) 5 65
(Daniel Mark Loughnane) *hld up: rdn over 2f out: sme hdwy to chse ldng duo over 1f out: styd on towards fin wout rching ldrs* **10/1**
5645 **4** 2 ½ **Energia Flavio (BRZ)**[18] 3717 6-9-12 **73**........ PhilDennis 4 69
(Richard Fahey) *disp ld: def advantage over 3f out: rdn and hdd over 2f out: one pce 1f out* **5/2**[2]
1303 **5** 1 **Anton Chigurh**[14] 3849 7-9-8 **72**........ AnnaHesketh(3) 6 66
(Tom Dascombe) *hld up: rdn over 2f out: hung lft and no imp over 1f out: one pce after* **9/2**[3]
45-0 **6** 6 **Moonadee (IRE)**[56] 2441 4-9-9 **70**........(t) PaddyPilley 1 50
(Daniel Mark Loughnane) *s.s: in rr: struggling over 2f out: nvr a threat* **10/1**
1m 46.16s (2.46) **Going Correction** +0.075s/f (Good) **6** Ran SP% **112.4**
Speed ratings (Par 103): **90,89,87,85,84 78**
CSF £16.71 TOTE £6.10: £2.60, £1.40; EX 16.80 Trifecta £80.00.
Owner L S Keys & Kristian Strangeway **Bred** Ms Ellen O'Neill **Trained** Norton, N Yorks

FOCUS
Another handidcap, confined to apprentice riders, which took some getting.
T/Plt: £127.50 to a £1 stake. Pool: £54,536.80 - 312.04 winning units T/Qpdt: £33.90 to a £1 stake. Pool: £4,697.52 - 102.53 winning units **Darren Owen**

4052 NEWBURY (L-H)
Friday, July 15

OFFICIAL GOING: Good to firm (7.4)
Wind: Moderate, half against Weather: Overcast, drizzly

4349 HIGHCLERE THOROUGHBRED RACING EBF STALLIONS MAIDEN STKS (PLUS 10 RACE) 7f (S)
2:00 (2:01) (Class 4) 2-Y-O **£6,469** (£1,925; £962; £481) **Stalls** Centre

Form RPR
1 **Escobar (IRE)** 2-9-5 0........ JamesMcDonald 2 88+
(Hugo Palmer) *dwlt: racd centre thrght: sn in tch: prog to trck ldrs over 2f out: rdn to ld jst over 1f out: styd on wl* **16/1**
32 **2** 2 **Devil's Bridge (IRE)**[20] 3661 2-9-5 0........ PatDobbs 1 83
(Richard Hannon) *racd centre thrght: mde most: rdn and hdd jst over 1f out: one pce* **4/1**[2]
3 ½ **Red Ensign (IRE)** 2-9-5 0........ HarryBentley 9 82+
(Simon Crisford) *dwlt: racd towards nr side early: sn in tch: prog to trck ldrs over 2f out: shkn up and kpt on to take 3rd fnl f: shaped wl* **25/1**
4 **4** 2 ½ **Asaas (USA)**[36] 3058 2-9-5 0........ RyanMoore 4 75
(Roger Varian) *racd centre thrght: pressed ldr: stl wl there 2f out: fdd fnl f* **5/2**[1]
5 **5** ¾ **Thaaqib**[28] 3356 2-9-5 0........ PaulHanagan 6 73
(Charles Hills) *racd nr side early: prom: stl wl there 2f out: fdd fnl f* **11/2**[3]
5 **6** ½ **Mr Tyrrell (IRE)**[7] 4103 2-9-5 0........ TomMarquand 3 72
(Richard Hannon) *racd centre thrght: chsd ldrs: rdn 2f out: one pce and no imp fnl f* **9/1**
7 ¾ **Go On Mayson** 2-9-5 0........ ShaneKelly 13 70+
(David Evans) *wl in rr: shkn up over 2f out: kpt on steadily fr over 1f out: nvr nrr* **66/1**
8 nse **Never Surrender (IRE)** 2-9-5 0........ SteveDrowne 11 69
(Charles Hills) *racd towards nr side early: trckd ldrs: cl up over 2f out: fdd over 1f out* **66/1**
23 **9** ½ **Salouen (IRE)**[15] 3813 2-9-2 0........ EdwardGreatrex(3) 7 68
(Sylvester Kirk) *racd towards nr side early: in tch: shkn up over 2f out: no hdwy over 1f out* **6/1**
10 2 ¼ **Jewel House** 2-9-5 0........ FrankieDettori 12 62
(John Gosden) *racd towards nr side early: a towards rr: pushed along and no significant prog over 1f out* **7/1**
5 **11** 2 **King Of Nepal**[22] 3569 2-9-5 0........ AdamKirby 10 57
(Henry Candy) *racd towards nr side early: w ldrs tl wknd qckly 2f out* **40/1**
12 3 ¼ **I'Vegotthepower (IRE)** 2-9-5 0........ MartinDwyer 5 48
(Brian Meehan) *racd centre thrght: chsd ldrs to 1/2-way: sn lost pl: bhd 2f out* **66/1**
0 **13** 6 **Makemerichjohn (IRE)**[15] 3813 2-9-5 0........ SamHitchcott 14 32
(David Evans) *racd towards nr side early: led gp 3f: sn lost pl: bhd over 1f out* **125/1**
14 31 **Sixties Symphony** 2-9-0 0........ DavidProbert 8
(Michael Blanshard) *rn green and sn struggling: t.o* **100/1**
1m 26.6s (0.90) **Going Correction** +0.075s/f (Good) **14** Ran SP% **119.2**
Speed ratings (Par 96): **97,94,94,91,90 89,89,88,88,85 83,79,72,37**
CSF £77.01 TOTE £24.30: £6.30, £1.80, £8.50; EX 118.60 Trifecta £1945.80.
Owner Westward Bloodstock Limited **Bred** Peter Evans **Trained** Newmarket, Suffolk

FOCUS
Some starts have been moved at this track following remeasuring, so some races will not have speed figures until there is sufficient data to calculate updated median times. There was 8mm of water put on the straight 6f the previous Saturday, 8mm on the whole course on Tuesday and another 8mm on the whole course on Wednesday, but after this opener the jockeys said the ground was quick. This was probably a decent 2yo maiden, with promising newcomers in 1st and 3rd, and the 2nd, 4th, 5th and 6th having already shown a fair level of ability. They raced up the middle and those towards the far side of the group had the edge.

4350 BET365 EBF STALLIONS MAIDEN FILLIES' STKS (PLUS 10 RACE) 6f 8y
2:30 (2:31) (Class 4) 2-Y-O **£6,469** (£1,925; £962; £481) **Stalls** Centre

Form RPR
5 **1** **Tiburtina (IRE)**[43] 2817 2-8-11 0........ EdwardGreatrex(3) 8 75
(Sylvester Kirk) *pressed ldrs: rdn 2f out: chal jst over 1f out: led last 100yds: kpt on wl* **16/1**
2 ½ **Spinnaker Bay (IRE)** 2-8-11 0........ AnnaJones(3) 1 73
(William Jarvis) *w ldr: led over 2f out: shkn up over 1f out: hdd last 100yds: nt qckn and edgd lft nr fin* **25/1**
3 ¾ **Beck And Call** 2-9-0 0........ FergusSweeney 4 71
(Henry Candy) *in tch: trckd ldrs over 2f out gng wl: pushed along over 1f out: styd on to take 3rd nr fin: promising* **20/1**
32 **4** ½ **Texas Katie**[8] 4063 2-9-0 0........ CharlesBishop 2 69
(Mick Channon) *t.k.h: trckd ldrs: chal over 1f out: upsides ins fnl f: nt qckn last 100yds: lost 3rd and short of room nr fin* **7/2**[2]
5 hd **Sparkle** 2-9-0 0........ DavidProbert 14 69
(Ed Dunlop) *dwlt: rn green in rr: shkn up over 2f out: kpt on steadily fr over 1f out: shaped w promise* **12/1**
6 hd **Heavenly Angel** 2-9-0 0........ PatDobbs 3 68
(Richard Hannon) *dwlt: in tch in rr: pushed along 2f out: tried to cl on ldrs 1f out: one pce last 100yds* **10/1**
0 **7** nk **Intisha (IRE)**[22] 3556 2-9-0 0........ RyanTate 6 67
(Jonathan Portman) *in tch: shkn up and rn green fr 2f out: kpt on but nvr able to chal* **66/1**
8 hd **Joyful Dream (IRE)** 2-9-0 0........ DannyBrock 5 67
(J S Moore) *rn green in rr: swtchd lft over 2f out: shkn up over 1f out: nvr a threat but kpt on ins fnl f* **100/1**
9 1 **Foxcatcher** 2-9-0 0........ AdamKirby 9 63
(Clive Cox) *pressed ldrs: wl on terms and shkn up 2f out: rn green and wknd over 1f out* **5/1**[3]
10 ¾ **Partitia** 2-9-0 0........ RyanMoore 12 61
(Sir Michael Stoute) *hld up in rr: pushed along over 1f out: no prog* **5/2**[1]
053 **11** 9 **Royal Melody**[38] 2990 2-8-9 0........ HectorCrouch(5) 11 32
(Heather Main) *mde most to jst over 2f out: rn green and wknd qckly* **66/1**
12 7 **Faith In Me (IRE)** 2-9-0 0........ FrankieDettori 13 10
(Simon Crisford) *in tch to over 2f out: sn bhd* **5/1**[3]
1m 14.22s (1.22) **Going Correction** +0.075s/f (Good) **12** Ran SP% **119.4**
Speed ratings (Par 93): **94,93,92,91,91 91,90,90,89,88 76,66**
CSF £365.13 TOTE £20.20: £4.50, £7.40, £5.90; EX 424.80 Trifecta £4179.70 Part won..
Owner The Kathryn Stud **Bred** The Kathryn Stud **Trained** Upper Lambourn, Berks

FOCUS
The three shortest-priced newcomers didn't feature, finishing 9th, 10th and 12th, and the first eight were covered by under 3l, so the bare form can surely only be fair. It's hard to believe it can be worth much more.

4351 UPHAM BREWERY FILLIES' H'CAP 1m 5f 61y
3:05 (3:05) (Class 3) (0-95,89) 3-Y-O **£16,172** (£4,812; £2,405; £1,202) **Stalls** Low

Form RPR
-341 **1** **Purple Magic**[16] 3778 3-8-6 **77**........ EdwardGreatrex(3) 2 86+
(Michael Bell) *mde all: rdn 3f out: responded wl and drew clr over 1f out: styd on wl* **7/1**
5-24 **2** 1 ½ **Engage (IRE)**[48] 2687 3-9-3 **85**........ PatDobbs 4 92+
(Sir Michael Stoute) *dwlt: hld up in last pair: gng bttr than most over 2f out: tried to make prog 2f out but nvr clrest of passages: rdn and styd on to take 2nd nr fin: no ch to chal* **7/2**[3]

31 **3** *hd* **Ruscombe**[21] 3601 3-9-6 **88** RyanMoore 3 93
(Sir Michael Stoute) *trckd ldng trio after 3f: rdn to chse wnr wl over 1f out: no imp after: lost 2nd nr fin* **11/4**[1]

0214 **4** *3* **Talent To Amuse (IRE)**[20] 3665 3-9-1 **83** HarryBentley 5 84
(Roger Varian) *chsd ldng trio 3f: rdn over 3f out and sn dropped to last: plugged on again over 1f out* **16/1**

-210 **5** *1* **Girling (IRE)**[28] 3341 3-9-7 **89** FrankieDettori 6 88
(Ralph Beckett) *trckd ldng pair: rdn 3f out: nt qckn over 2f out: fdd over 1f out* **3/1**[2]

-310 **6** *3/4* **Daphne**[28] 3341 3-9-2 **84** JamesMcDonald 7 82
(William Haggas) *s.i.s: hld up in last pair: effrt on outer over 2f out: sn rdn and nt qckn: fdd over 1f out* **10/1**

1341 **7** *1* **Genuine Approval (IRE)**[31] 3251 3-9-3 **85** DannyBrock 1 82
(Jonathan Portman) *chsd wnr: rdn and tried to chal over 2f out: lost 2nd and wknd wl over 1f out* **9/1**

2m 50.46s (-1.54) **Going Correction** +0.05s/f (Good) 7 Ran SP% **111.4**
Speed ratings (Par 101): **106,105,104,103,102 102,101**
CSF £29.90 TOTE £8.40: £3.70, £2.20; EX 33.00 Trifecta £135.20.
Owner Lady Bamford **Bred** Lady Bamford **Trained** Newmarket, Suffolk

FOCUS
Race run over 19 yards further than advertised. The winner got her own way in front and some of those in behind can do better. The time was decent.

4352 TKP SURFACING ROSE BOWL STKS (LISTED RACE) 6f 8y
3:40 (3:41) (Class 1) 2-Y-O
£14,461 (£5,482; £2,743; £1,366; £685; £344) **Stalls** Centre

Form RPR

10 **1** **Mokarris (USA)**[31] 3243 2-9-0 0 PaulHanagan 3 106+
(Simon Crisford) *hld up: smooth prog to trck ldr 2f: led over 1f out: pushed clr: comf* **9/4**[1]

31 **2** *2 3/4* **Nobly Born**[15] 3818 2-9-0 0 FrankieDettori 8 94
(John Gosden) *hld up in last: rdn and prog jst over 2f out: chsd ldng pair over 1f out: styd on to take 2nd nr fin* **5/1**[3]

21 **3** *nk* **Kodiline (IRE)**[11] 3954 2-9-0 0 AdamKirby 2 93
(Clive Cox) *w ldr: led 1/2-way: rdn and hdd over 1f out: no ch w wnr after: lost 2nd nr fin* **8/1**

154 **4** *1 1/2* **Tibr (USA)**[23] 3526 2-9-0 0 JamesMcDonald 7 88
(Ed Dunlop) *settled in last pair: rdn over 2f out: kpt on u.p fr over 1f out: tk 4th last strides* **16/1**

311 **5** *hd* **Miss Infinity (IRE)**[15] 3805 2-8-9 0 FrannyNorton 9 83
(Mark Johnston) *led to 1/2-way: rdn 2f out: fdd over 1f out* **4/1**[2]

22 **6** *4* **Smokey Lane (IRE)**[14] 3858 2-9-0 0 ShaneKelly 6 75
(David Evans) *t.k.h: trckd ldrs: rdn 2f out: wknd over 1f out* **16/1**

1216 **7** *1/2* **Legendary Lunch (IRE)**[29] 3295 2-9-3 0 RyanMoore 5 76
(Richard Hannon) *trckd ldrs: rdn 2f out: sn wknd* **11/2**

61 **8** *3* **Farleigh Mac**[33] 3196 2-9-0 0 DavidProbert 4 64
(Andrew Balding) *prom: disp 2nd jst over 2f out: sn rdn and wknd qckly* **12/1**

1m 12.2s (-0.80) **Going Correction** +0.075s/f (Good) 8 Ran SP% **113.4**
Speed ratings (Par 102): **108,104,103,101,101 96,95,91**
CSF £13.39 TOTE £3.40: £1.70, £2.10, £2.40; EX 14.20 Trifecta £86.00.
Owner Hamdan Al Maktoum **Bred** St Elias Stables LLC **Trained** Newmarket, Suffolk

FOCUS
Four of these were keen early so the initial gallop probably wasn't fast, but it soon picked up. Not a bad Listed race and the winner is smart. The third is perhaps the key to the form.

4353 COMPTON BEAUCHAMP ESTATES LTD SILVER BAR H'CAP 2m 2f
4:15 (4:16) (Class 2) (0-100,95) 3-Y-O+ **£16,172** (£4,812; £2,405; £1,202) **Stalls** Low

Form RPR

-411 **1** **Sweet Selection**[34] 3149 4-9-1 **82** RyanMoore 2 94+
(Hughie Morrison) *hld up off the pce: prog 3f out: drvn 2f out: clsd on ldng pair over 1f out: led last 150yds: styd on wl* **3/1**[1]

21-0 **2** *1 3/4* **Sea Of Heaven (IRE)**[20] 3657 4-9-5 **86** LukeMorris 9 96+
(Sir Mark Prescott Bt) *t.k.h: hld up off the pce: prog and hung lft over 3f out: led over 2f out: hrd rdn and hdd last 150yds: hanging lft and no ex* **5/1**[2]

0-05 **3** *3* **Montaly**[31] 3246 5-9-13 **94** DavidProbert 5 101
(Andrew Balding) *hld up off the pce in last pair: prog over 3f out: trckd ldr over 2f out gng strly: rdn and fnd nil over 1f out: lost 2nd fnl f* **5/1**[2]

0-03 **4** *3 1/4* **Air Squadron**[16] 3784 6-8-12 **79** ShaneKelly 7 82
(Ralph Beckett) *hld up off the pce in rr: pushed along 1/2-way: prog u.p 3f out: tk 4th over 1f out: one pce after* **15/2**[3]

5042 **5** *1 1/4* **Percy Veer**[16] 3784 4-9-5 **86** PatDobbs 8 88
(Sylvester Kirk) *hld up off the pce in 5th: lost pl over 3f out: nt clr run tl over 2f out: one pce u.p after and no imp on ldrs* **10/1**

10-4 **6** *10* **Leah Freya (IRE)**[86] 1568 5-9-2 **90** PaddyBradley[(7)] 4 81
(Pat Phelan) *hld up off the pce in last pair: rdn and sme prog on outer over 2f out: no hdwy and wl btn over 1f out* **25/1**

0/0- **7** *2 1/4* **Royal Irish Hussar (IRE)**[323] 3252 6-9-9 **90** JamesMcDonald 11 79
(Nicky Henderson) *t.k.h: trckd ldng pair and clr of rest: rdn to dispute 2nd briefly 3f out: sn wknd* **20/1**

0433 **8** *1* **Giant Redwood (IRE)**[7] 4101 4-8-7 **77** (p) EdwardGreatrex[(3)] 6 64
(Michael Bell) *trckd ldr: rdn 5f out: lost 2nd and wknd 3f out* **14/1**

-000 **9** *5* **See And Be Seen**[26] 3437 6-8-2 **76** oh3 (p) MitchGodwin[(7)] 10 58
(Sylvester Kirk) *hld up off the pce in 4th: rdn whn sltly impeded over 3f out: sn wknd* **20/1**

-633 **10** *7* **Vive Ma Fille (GER)**[6] 4162 4-10-0 **95** FrankieDettori 3 69
(Mark Johnston) *led at decent pce: tried to go for home 4f out: hdd & wknd over 2f out: eased* **5/1**[2]

3m 55.59s (235.59) **10** Ran SP% **115.9**
CSF £17.01 CT £72.32 TOTE £3.30: £1.30, £2.00, £2.50; EX 19.70 Trifecta £109.90.
Owner Paul Brocklehurst **Bred** S A Douch **Trained** East Ilsley, Berks

FOCUS
Race run over 19 yards further than advertised. A decent staying handicap and the field were soon strung out, with the early 1-2-3 finishing 10-8-7. The winner probably has more to offer.

4354 R & M ELECTRICAL GROUP H'CAP 7f (S)
4:45 (4:47) (Class 5) (0-75,75) 3-Y-O+ **£3,234** (£962; £481; £240) **Stalls** Centre

Form RPR

3-34 **1** **Hitman**[39] 2981 3-9-5 **74** SamHitchcott 3 80
(William Muir) *s.i.s: pushed along in last pair after 2f: rdn and prog 2f out: styd on wl to ld ins fnl f: drvn out* **11/4**[1]

3120 **2** *3/4* **Good Luck Charm**[15] 3803 7-9-9 **75** (b) HectorCrouch[(5)] 4 82
(Gary Moore) *t.k.h: hld up in last pair: smooth prog to ld over 1f out: hung rt to nr side rail and hdd ins fnl f: nt qckn* **9/1**

0444 **3** *1 1/2* **Port Lairge**[24] 3491 6-8-12 **64** (v) GeorgeBuckell[(5)] 1 67
(John Gallagher) *mde most: rdn 2f out: hdd and one pce over 1f out* **7/1**[3]

0063 **4** *hd* **Champagne Bob**[17] 3745 4-8-10 **60** EdwardGreatrex[(3)] 2 62
(Richard Price) *cl up: rdn 2f out: one pce fr over 1f out* **9/1**

124 **5** *2 1/4* **Dynamic Girl (IRE)**[19] 3689 3-8-12 **67** RichardMullen 7 60
(Brendan Powell) *t.k.h: trckd ldrs: moved up to chal jst over 2f out: rdn over 1f out: sn fdd* **11/4**[1]

0605 **6** *nk* **Willsy**[16] 3771 3-9-5 **74** CharlesBishop 6 67
(Mick Channon) *trckd ldrs: tried to chal wl over 1f out: wknd fnl f* **14/1**

4060 **7** *3* **Peak Hill**[15] 3807 3-9-0 **69** (v[1]) AdamKirby 5 53
(David Evans) *mostly trckd ldr to 2f out: wknd over 1f out* **9/2**[2]

1m 26.08s (0.38) **Going Correction** +0.075s/f (Good)
WFA 3 from 4yo+ 8lb 7 Ran SP% **110.7**
Speed ratings (Par 103): **100,99,97,97,94 94,90**
CSF £26.33 TOTE £3.80: £2.40, £2.70; EX 23.00 Trifecta £134.50.
Owner Carmel Stud **Bred** Carmel Stud **Trained** Lambourn, Berks

FOCUS
Not many with appealing profiles in this 0-75. The first two came from the rear.

4355 OAKLEY COACHBUILDERS APPRENTICE H'CAP 6f 8y
5:15 (5:17) (Class 5) (0-75,75) 4-Y-O+ **£3,234** (£962; £481; £240) **Stalls** Centre

Form RPR

0000 **1** **Field Game**[15] 3803 4-9-6 **74** (t) CameronNoble[(5)] 5 84
(Hughie Morrison) *hld up in last: prog 2f out: rdn to ld 1f out: styd on wl* **11/2**[3]

2133 **2** *1 3/4* **Pettochside**[8] 4051 7-9-12 **75** MitchGodwin 7 79
(John Bridger) *led: rdn 2f out: hdd 1f out: kpt on same pce* **5/1**[2]

6-11 **3** *1/2* **Pandar**[67] 2088 7-9-10 **73** CliffordLee 3 75
(Patrick Chamings) *hld up in tch: rdn 2f out: prog to take 3rd fnl f: styd on but unable to chal* **3/1**[1]

0023 **4** *1 1/2* **Head Space (IRE)**[10] 3985 8-8-12 **66** (vt) JoshuaBryan[(5)] 9 64
(Brian Barr) *trckd ldrs: rdn 2f out: lost pl over 1f out: one pce after* **8/1**

0004 **5** *nk* **Major Valentine**[16] 3780 4-8-8 **62** AledBeech[(5)] 6 59
(John O'Shea) *t.k.h: pressed ldr to over 1f out: fdd* **8/1**

020 **6** *shd* **Believe It (IRE)**[16] 3780 4-8-7 **63** NicolaCurrie[(7)] 4 59
(Richard Hughes) *in tch: effrt over 2f out: no imp on ldrs over 1f out: fdd ins fnl f* **8/1**

3003 **7** *1 1/2* **Hipz (IRE)**[11] 3953 5-8-10 **64** SophieRalston[(5)] 1 56
(Laura Mongan) *in tch towards rr: rdn and tried to cl on ldrs 2f out: no prog over 1f out: fdd* **11/1**

6063 **8** *3/4* **Heartsong (IRE)**[22] 3580 7-9-3 **73** LauraCoughlan[(7)] 8 62
(John Gallagher) *trckd ldrs: rdn 2f out: wknd over 1f out* **16/1**

0556 **U** **Fever Few**[22] 3575 7-9-8 **74** SamuelClarke[(3)] 2
(Chris Wall) *virtually ref to r then uns rdr leaving stalls* **11/1**

1m 13.1s (0.10) **Going Correction** +0.075s/f (Good) 9 Ran SP% **112.9**
Speed ratings (Par 103): **102,99,99,97,96 96,94,93,**
CSF £32.31 CT £97.06 TOTE £7.50: £2.10, £1.60, £1.60; EX 33.80 Trifecta £150.10.
Owner Lord Carnarvon **Bred** Earl Of Carnarvon **Trained** East Ilsley, Berks

FOCUS
All of these are capable on their day so not bad form. It was sound run.
T/Jkpt: Not Won. T/Plt: £2,291.70 to a £1 stake. Pool: £81,624.55 - 26.0 winning units T/Qpdt: £23.00 to a £1 stake. Pool: £7,592.14 - 243.96 winning units **Jonathan Neesom**

4147 NEWMARKET (R-H)
Friday, July 15

OFFICIAL GOING: Good to firm
Wind: light breeze Weather: overcast and dull; becoming sunny later; 18 degrees

4356 32RED.COM FILLIES' H'CAP (JOCKEY CLUB GRASSROOTS FLAT MIDDLE DISTANCE SERIES QUALIFIER) 1m 2f
5:40 (5:40) (Class 4) (0-75,74) 3-Y-O+ **£3,234** (£962; £481; £240) **Stalls** Centre

Form RPR

346 **1** **Cold Fusion (IRE)**[133] 814 3-8-4 **64** JosephineGordon[(3)] 6 76
(Ed Vaughan) *chsd clr ldr: rdn 2f out: clsd qckly over 1f out and sn led and drew rt away* **16/1**

0-55 **2** *5* **Trulee Scrumptious**[13] 3894 7-8-11 **57** (v) JimmyQuinn 4 59
(Peter Charalambous) *led and sn had field strung out: 6 l clr 4f out: rdn 2f out: kpt on gamely tl hdd ins fnl f: immediately outpcd by wnr* **8/1**[3]

20-3 **3** *2 3/4* **Heartstone (IRE)**[59] 2321 3-9-2 **73** SilvestreDeSousa 5 70
(Charles Hills) *s.s: keen early: midfield: drvn and n.d to ldrs fnl 3f* **5/2**[2]

1-5 **4** *1/2* **Danilovna (IRE)**[57] 2415 3-9-3 **74** GeorgeBaker 7 73
(David Lanigan) *chsd ldrs but off pce: drvn and edgd rt over 2f out: sn no imp and hanging lft* **7/4**[1]

2214 **5** *1 1/2* **Yankee Mail (FR)**[10] 3972 4-9-12 **72** HayleyTurner 3 65
(Gay Kelleway) *stdd s: bhd: rdn 4f out: struggling over 2f out* **8/1**[3]

1356 **6** *15* **Hound Music**[19] 3690 4-9-12 **72** JamesDoyle 1 35
(Jonathan Portman) *hanging rt: racd in 3rd pl: rdn 4f out: lost pl over 2f out: t.o and eased ins fnl f* **12/1**

5663 **7** *44* **East Coast Lady (IRE)**[13] 3894 4-9-10 **70** JamieSpencer 2
(William Stone) *rrd after leaving stalls and nvr in tch after: rdn 3f out: eased and t.o fnl 2f* **10/1**

2m 6.33s (0.83) **Going Correction** +0.225s/f (Good)
WFA 3 from 4yo+ 11lb 7 Ran SP% **109.8**
Speed ratings (Par 102): **105,101,98,98,97 85,50**
CSF £122.62 CT £403.36 TOTE £12.70: £4.50, £2.20; EX 162.40 Trifecta £358.30.
Owner J Bryan & Partner **Bred** Cora Srl **Trained** Newmarket, Suffolk

FOCUS
Far-side course used. Stalls far side except 1m2f, centre. Race 1 distance increased by 15 yards. An unsatisfactory event. The runner-up enjoyed an uncontested lead, and while the winner and the sixth kept tabs on the pacesetter, the other four were held up some way off the pace and never looked like becoming seriously involved. Not easy to assess, the winner not an obvious improver on AW form.

4357 COLCHESTER CANCER CENTRE CAMPAIGN MAIDEN FILLIES' STKS (PLUS 10 RACE) 7f
6:15 (6:15) (Class 5) 2-Y-O **£3,881** (£1,155; £577; £288) **Stalls** High

Form RPR

1 **Grecian Light (IRE)** 2-9-0 0 JamesMcDonald 5 80+
(Charlie Appleby) *racd enthusiastically: settled towards rr: rdn and effrt 2f out: rn green briefly: led 1f out: kpt on strly* **7/2**[3]

2 *1/2* **Voice Of Truth (IRE)** 2-9-0 0 JamesDoyle 3 79+
(Saeed bin Suroor) *hld up last: smooth prog on outer 2f out: led briefly over 1f out: sn drvn: a jst hld after but kpt on wl* **7/4**[1]

3 *3* **Blending** 2-9-0 0 .... FrankieDettori 2 67+
(John Gosden) *trckd ldrs: rdn and ev ch over 1f out: kpt on nicely in wl hld 3rd fnl f* **2/1**[2]

4 *6* **Midnight Vixen** 2-9-0 0 .... RyanMoore 1 50
(Sir Michael Stoute) *prom: rdn 3f out: ev ch over 1f out: rn green and sn wknd* **15/2**

0 5 *½* **Masterfilly (IRE)**[55] 2467 2-9-0 0 .... AntonioFresu 4 49
(Ed Walker) *led at stdy pce: drven 2f out: hdd over 1f out: sn btn* **20/1**

6 6 *2¾* **Clenymistra (IRE)**[21] 3592 2-9-0 0 .... HayleyTurner 6 41
(Marco Botti) *prom: rdn 3f out: last and btn over 1f out* **25/1**

1m 28.17s (2.47) **Going Correction** -0.075s/f (Good) 6 Ran SP% **112.3**
Speed ratings (Par 91): **82,81,78,71,70 67**
CSF £10.09 TOTE £4.60: £2.20, £1.30; EX 9.60 Trifecta £23.50.
Owner Godolphin **Bred** Stilvi Compania Financiera Sa **Trained** Newmarket, Suffolk

FOCUS
The ground was officially amended to Good to firm all round prior to this maiden, which was won by subsequent Fillies' Mile winner Rainbow View in 2008. Godolphin had a 1-2, taking the tally of their various stables to six wins in the last seven runnings. The pace was steady but the first three all look nice prospects who can leave the bare form behind.

4358 NGK SPARK PLUGS H'CAP 1m
6:50 (6:50) (Class 4) (0-85,85) 3-Y-O **£5,175** (£1,540; £769; £384) **Stalls** High

Form RPR

1-62 1 **Rostova (USA)**[27] 3410 3-9-7 **85** .... RyanMoore 3 94+
(Sir Michael Stoute) *bhd: drvn 2f out: clsd over 1f out: led u.p fnl 100yds: hung on gamely* **6/4**[1]

-131 2 *shd* **George William**[37] 3029 3-9-7 **85** .... TomMarquand 7 93
(Richard Hannon) *taken down early: cl up: rdn 2f out: led over 1f out tl hdd 100yds out: kpt on but jst hld* **11/2**[2]

5046 3 *2¼* **Holy Grail (IRE)**[13] 3885 3-8-12 **79** .... JosephineGordon(3) 6 82
(Simon West) *2nd tl led 1/2-way: rdn and hdd over 1f out: nt qckn after* **25/1**

3001 4 *1½* **Ravenhoe (IRE)**[13] 3877 3-8-8 **72** .... SilvestreDeSousa 2 71
(Mark Johnston) *cl up: rdn 2f out: hld in 4th fnl f* **10/1**

6-34 5 *2¾* **Calvados Spirit**[27] 3412 3-8-13 **77** .... MartinDwyer 4 70
(William Muir) *hld up: effrt and drvn 2f out: sn hanging lft: btn 1f out* **11/2**[2]

-210 6 *9* **Prosecute (FR)**[22] 3557 3-8-13 **77** ....[1] JamieSpencer 1 48
(David Simcock) *last mostly: rdn 3f out: racd awkwardly and sn fnd nil: eased fnl f* **6/1**[3]

4410 7 *25* **Heart Of Lions (USA)**[41] 2891 3-9-5 **83** .... JamesDoyle 5
(John Gosden) *led tl 1/2-way: drvn and fdd 2f out: sn eased and t.o* **13/2**

1m 38.43s (-1.57) **Going Correction** -0.075s/f (Good) 7 Ran SP% **111.3**
Speed ratings (Par 102): **104,103,101,100,97 88,63**
CSF £9.46 TOTE £2.10: £1.40, £2.90; EX 7.40 Trifecta £79.10.
Owner K Abdullah **Bred** Juddmonte Farms Inc **Trained** Newmarket, Suffolk

FOCUS
This fair handicap was run at a reasonable gallop. The form is rated around the third.

4359 BRITISH STALLION STUDS EBF CONDITIONS STKS 5f
7:20 (7:20) (Class 3) 3-Y-O+ **£9,056** (£2,695; £1,346; £673) **Stalls** High

Form RPR

0124 1 **Monsieur Joe (IRE)**[6] 4166 9-9-6 109 .... LukeMorris 1 112
(Paul Midgley) *racd enthusiastically: 2nd of centre pair: drvn 2f out: chal 1f out: styd on wl to ld fnl 75yds* **7/2**[1]

/000 2 *¾* **Hay Chewed (IRE)**[31] 3244 5-8-6 97 .... SilvestreDeSousa 7 95
(Conrad Allen) *led: drvn 2f out: kpt on gamely tl hdd and no ex fnl 75yds* **11/2**[3]

6320 3 *1* **Willytheconqueror (IRE)**[13] 3909 3-8-11 104 .... MartinDwyer 6 100
(William Muir) *towards rr: rdn and bdly outpcd 2f out: rallied ins fnl f and kpt on strly* **10/1**

-140 4 *½* **Steady Pace**[30] 3269 3-9-1 107 ....(p) JamesDoyle 8 102
(Saeed bin Suroor) *cl up: drvn after 2f: nt qckn 1f out* **7/1**

3-04 5 *nse* **Exceed The Limit**[14] 3857 3-8-11 90 ....(p) TomMarquand 4 98
(Robert Cowell) *sn pushed along: chsd ldrs: rdn over 1f out: nt qckn after* **25/1**

3-23 6 *1* **Ornate**[34] 3158 3-8-11 108 .... RyanMoore 2 94
(William Haggas) *plld hrd: led centre pair but nt overall: drvn 2f out: no ex over 1f out* **7/2**[1]

0413 7 *½* **Line Of Reason (IRE)**[17] 3752 6-9-6 106 .... PaulHanagan 5 98
(Paul Midgley) *chsd ldrs: rdn 2f out: nvr gng wl enough: nt qckn fnl f* **9/2**[2]

-050 8 *3* **Kingsgate Native (IRE)**[33] 3195 11-8-11 103 .... JamieSpencer 3 79
(Robert Cowell) *last away and pushed along: rdn 2f out: nvr gng fast enough to get involved: eased ins fnl f* **10/1**

58.22s (-0.88) **Going Correction** -0.075s/f (Good)
WFA 3 from 5yo+ 5lb 8 Ran SP% **112.5**
Speed ratings (Par 107): **104,102,101,100,100 98,97,93**
CSF £22.16 TOTE £4.50: £1.70, £2.10, £2.50; EX 28.80 Trifecta £368.70.
Owner Taylor's Bloodstock Ltd **Bred** Nicola And Eleanor Kent **Trained** Westow, N Yorks

FOCUS
A good conditions sprint. Two of them, including the winner, raced down the centre of the track, with the other half-dozen positioned close to the far rail. The time was only 0.72sec outside standard. The form is rated around the winner.

4360 DISCOVERNEWMARKET.CO.UK H'CAP (A JOCKEY CLUB GRASSROOTS FLAT SPRINT SERIES QUALIFIER) 6f
7:50 (7:50) (Class 4) (0-80,80) 3-Y-O+ **£5,175** (£1,540; £769; £384) **Stalls** High

Form RPR

43-6 1 **Excellent George**[21] 3618 4-9-6 **77** ....(t) AaronJones(5) 4 89
(Stuart Williams) *prom: drvn to ld over 1f out: kpt on wl* **20/1**

-063 2 *1½* **Amood (IRE)**[22] 3553 5-9-8 **74** ....(p) JamieSpencer 3 81
(Simon West) *bhd: rdn and racing awkwardly over 2f out: gd hdwy fnl f: passed two rivals cl home but nt rch wnr* **9/2**[2]

2212 3 *nk* **Rococoa (IRE)**[18] 3716 3-9-4 **76** .... LukeMorris 12 81
(Ed Walker) *prom: rdn 2f out: ev ch 1f out: nt qckn fnl 100yds and jst lost 2nd* **7/2**[1]

41 4 *nk* **Bahamian Dollar**[46] 2740 3-9-5 **80** .... EoinWalsh(3) 8 84
(James Tate) *cl up and t.k.h: rdn over 1f out: nt qckn fnl 100yds and jst lost 3rd* **8/1**

4-00 5 *2* **Rio's Cliffs**[32] 3213 3-9-4 **76** .... HarryBentley 6 74
(Martyn Meade) *chsd ldrs: rdn 2f out: one pce fnl f* **20/1**

2213 6 *nk* **Johnny B Goode (IRE)**[15] 3821 4-8-13 **65** .... SilvestreDeSousa 2 63
(Chris Dwyer) *taken down early: chsd ldrs: drvn 2f out: nt qckn 1f out* **9/1**

0015 7 *nse* **Crew Cut (IRE)**[30] 3279 8-9-7 **80** .... MillyNaseb(7) 11 78
(Stuart Williams) *bhd: pushed along 1/2-way: effrt over 1f out: plugged on ins fnl f* **9/1**

-124 8 *3½* **Until Midnight (IRE)**[69] 2028 6-9-0 **73** .... DavidEgan(7) 9 60
(Eugene Stanford) *pressed ldrs: rdn 4f out: wknd 1f out* **8/1**

0001 9 *1¼* **Syrian Pearl**[27] 3414 5-9-13 **79** .... TedDurcan 5 62
(Chris Wall) *bhd: rdn 1/2-way: sn btn: eased ins fnl f* **11/2**[3]

2002 10 *8* **Silver Bid (USA)**[20] 3669 4-9-2 **68** .... ShaneKelly 10 25
(Alan Bailey) *mounted outside paddock and on his toes: led: drvn and hdd over 2f out: fdd qckly and sn eased* **33/1**

0-50 11 *2¼* **Royal Mezyan (IRE)**[46] 2754 5-9-13 **79** .... GeorgeBaker 7 29
(Henry Spiller) *prom and t.k.h: drvn to ld over 2f out tl over 1f out: sn struggling: eased and t.o fnl f* **14/1**

1m 12.05s (-0.45) **Going Correction** -0.075s/f (Good)
WFA 3 from 4yo+ 6lb 11 Ran SP% **117.1**
Speed ratings (Par 105): **100,98,97,97,94 94,94,89,87,77 74**
CSF £105.25 CT £406.46 TOTE £16.80: £4.80, £1.70, £2.10; EX 158.10 TRIFECTA Not won..
Owner D A Shekells **Bred** Old Mill Stud & S Williams & J Parry **Trained** Newmarket, Suffolk

FOCUS
Ordinary sprint handicap form. The winner belatedly confirmed his early 3yo level.

4361 SCWS FIFTIETH ANNIVERSARY MAIDEN FILLIES' STKS 1m
8:25 (8:27) (Class 5) 3-Y-O+ **£3,881** (£1,155; £577; £288) **Stalls** High

Form RPR

2 1 **Dazzling Rose**[146] 654 3-9-0 0 .... FrankieDettori 6 89+
(John Gosden) *racd freely: taken to far side and led after 2f: rdn and clr w runner-up over 1f out: sn outpcd her: styd on stoutly for ready success* **9/2**[3]

4 2 *3½* **Labyrinth (IRE)**[51] 2578 3-9-0 0 .... RyanMoore 2 80+
(Sir Michael Stoute) *2nd of centre pair: rdn to pass that ldr 2f out: chsd wnr wl over 1f out: nvr making any imp but wl clr of rest* **9/4**[1]

3-0 3 *6* **Courtsider**[59] 2321 4-9-9 0 .... GeorgeBaker 12 68
(Lucy Wadham) *bhd: drvn and styd on fr over 1f out: snatched modest 3rd* **40/1**

4 *nk* **Paper Faces (USA)** 3-9-0 0 .... HarryBentley 9 65
(Roger Varian) *a abt same pl: drvn 2f out: outpcd by ldng pair over 1f out: lost mod 3rd cl home* **25/1**

3- 5 *2* **Nawkhatha (USA)**[289] 6866 3-9-0 0 .... JimmyFortune 8 60
(Brian Meehan) *chsd ldrs: rdn 2f out: btn over 1f out* **8/1**

65 6 *1¼* **Walking In Rhythm (IRE)**[9] 4017 3-9-0 0 .... SilvestreDeSousa 4 57
(Richard Hannon) *led centre pair but nt overall: racing awkwardly whn passed by centre rival 2f out: drvn and btn over 1f out* **25/1**

00 7 *1¼* **Tenerezza (IRE)**[33] 3194 3-9-0 0 .... ShaneKelly 11 54
(David Lanigan) *midfield: rdn and lost tch w ldrs over 2f out* **33/1**

3- 8 *4½* **Tranquil Time**[337] 5303 3-9-0 0 ....[1] LukeMorris 3 43
(James Tate) *chsd ldrs 5f: sn rdn: dwlt: t.o* **25/1**

9 *1¼* **Garter (IRE)** 3-9-0 0 .... JamesMcDonald 7 40
(Charles Hills) *bhd: shkn up 1/2-way: sn btn: t.o* **16/1**

10 *hd* **Sistine Chapel** 3-9-0 0 .... TedDurcan 14 40
(Brian Meehan) *struggling in rr: t.o* **25/1**

3 11 *¾* **Amaany**[16] 3769 3-9-0 0 .... PaulHanagan 10 38
(Charles Hills) *prom: rdn and fdd over 2f out: t.o* **4/1**[2]

0 12 *6* **Winterton**[11] 3958 3-9-0 0 .... KierenFox 13 24
(Christine Dunnett) *led 2f: prom tl drvn 3f out: wknd 2f out: t.o* **100/1**

13 *1¼* **Al Markhiya (IRE)** 3-9-0 0 .... TomMarquand 1 21
(Richard Hannon) *dwlt: nvr on terms: t.o fnl 2f* **7/1**

66 14 *4½* **On The Clock**[165] 423 3-8-11 0 .... TimClark(3) 5 10
(Denis Quinn) *plld hrd in rr: t.o over 2f out* **100/1**

1m 38.92s (-1.08) **Going Correction** -0.075s/f (Good)
WFA 3 from 4yo 9lb 14 Ran SP% **121.2**
Speed ratings (Par 100): **102,98,92,92,90 88,87,83,81,81 81,75,73,69**
CSF £13.88 TOTE £5.30: £1.80, £1.40, £9.80; EX 13.50 Trifecta £459.90.
Owner Newsells Park Stud **Bred** Newsells Park Stud **Trained** Newmarket, Suffolk

FOCUS
Probably a modest race behind the first two, who raced wide apart. They finished clear.

4362 MARITIME CARGO SERVICES H'CAP 7f
8:55 (8:56) (Class 5) (0-75,74) 4-Y-O+ **£3,234** (£962; £481; £240) **Stalls** High

Form RPR

011 1 **Robero**[31] 3262 4-9-4 **71** .... BenCurtis 7 81+
(Brian Ellison) *racd enthusiastically: mde all: rdn over 1f out: edgd clr fnl 100yds* **2/1**[1]

6440 2 *2* **Swiss Cross**[8] 4051 9-8-8 **64** ....(t) JosephineGordon(3) 1 68
(Phil McEntee) *plld hrd in rr: effrt 3f out: rdn and r.o ins fnl f to snatch 2nd: nt rch wnr* **33/1**

0125 3 *shd* **He's My Boy (IRE)**[15] 3823 5-9-2 **69** .... HayleyTurner 10 73
(James Fanshawe) *cl up: pressed wnr over 2f out: ev ch 1f out: nt qckn and pipped for 2nd* **10/1**

33-6 4 *1¼* **Fast Sprite (IRE)**[22] 3554 4-8-9 **62** .... KierenFox 8 62+
(John Best) *prom: rdn 3f out: sn bdly outpcd: rallied fnl f: kpt on but too much to do* **8/1**

5242 5 *½* **Gold Hunter (IRE)**[1] 4306 6-8-13 **73** .... JoshuaBryan(7) 5 72
(Steve Flook) *rrd leaving stalls and lost abt 8 l: hdwy 2f out: rdn 1f out: no real imp after* **6/1**[3]

-000 6 *1¾* **My Dad Syd (USA)**[53] 2547 4-9-6 **73** .... HarryBentley 3 67
(Ian Williams) *hld up in rr: effrt over 2f out: no imp over 1f out* **16/1**

0116 7 *½* **Upavon**[36] 3068 6-9-7 **74** ....(t) MartinHarley 4 67
(Stuart Williams) *cl up and tk v t.k.h: rdn 2f out: kpt on tl no ex 1f out* **8/1**

4504 8 *hd* **Anastazia**[15] 3823 4-9-0 **67** ....(p) ShaneKelly 6 59
(Paul D'Arcy) *chsd ldrs: rdn over 2f out: sn btn* **14/1**

6-23 9 *16* **Stoked (IRE)**[21] 3612 4-9-6 **73** .... SilvestreDeSousa 9 22
(Chris Dwyer) *w ldr: rdn over 2f out: sn lost pl: t.o and virtually p.u ins fnl f* **11/2**[2]

6114 10 *29* **Theydon Thunder**[13] 3896 4-8-7 **60** .... LukeMorris 2
(Peter Charalambous) *mounted pre-parade ring: racd freely in midfield: lost pl over 2f out: t.o and virtually p.u fnl f* **12/1**

1m 26.09s (0.39) **Going Correction** -0.075s/f (Good) 10 Ran SP% **117.5**
Speed ratings (Par 103): **94,91,91,90,89 87,87,86,68,35**
CSF £82.65 CT £566.34 TOTE £3.10: £1.40, £6.90, £2.10; EX 69.10 Trifecta £936.70.
Owner Alan Zheng **Bred** Mrs P C Burton & R J Lampard **Trained** Norton, N Yorks

FOCUS
Modest handicap form. The form is rated around the second.
T/Plt: £225.90 to a £1 stake. Pool: £60,629.82 - 195.91 winning tickets T/Qpdt: £8.70 to a £1 stake. Pool: £7,310.94 - 617.31 winning tickets **Iain Mackenzie**

3901 NOTTINGHAM (L-H)

Friday, July 15

OFFICIAL GOING: Good (good to soft in places; 7.6)

Wind: Light against Weather: Overcast

4363 IRISH STALLION FARMS EBF MAIDEN STKS — 6f 15y

1:50 (1:52) (Class 5) 2-Y-O — **£3,234** (£962; £481; £240) **Stalls** Centre

Form — RPR

33 **1** **Second Nature**[20] 3647 2-9-5 0 .... MartinHarley 11 — 80
(James Tate) *mde all: rdn along wl over 1f out: drvn ins fnl f: kpt on gamely towards fin* **16/1**

3 **2** ½ **Bellevarde (IRE)**[23] 3526 2-9-0 0 .... FrederikTylicki 4 — 74
(James Fanshawe) *trckd ldrs: hdwy on outer 2f out: rdn to chal ins fnl f: ev ch tl drvn and no ex nr fin* **7/2**[3]

3 *nk* **Parfait (IRE)** 2-9-5 0 .... JamesDoyle 12 — 78+
(John Gosden) *wnt rt s: sn trcking ldrs: hdwy and cl up 1/2-way: chal 2f out: rdn and green over 1f out: kpt on wl towards fin* **5/2**[2]

422 **4** *4* **Tafaakhor (IRE)**[36] 3065 2-9-5 0 .... JimCrowley 5 — 66
(Richard Hannon) *cl up: pushed along 1/2-way: rdn over 2f out: drvn wl over 1f out: wknd* **1/1**[1]

5 *1 ¾* **Nibras Again** 2-9-5 0 .... ThomasBrown 1 — 60
(Ismail Mohammed) *towards rr: hdwy wl over 2f out: rdn to chse ldrs over 1f out: no imp fnl f* **40/1**

6 *1* **Lanjano** 2-9-5 0 .... KevinStott 7 — 57
(Kevin Ryan) *trckd ldrs: effrt over 2f out: rdn along wl over 1f out: sn wknd* **50/1**

5 **7** *7* **Elegantly Bound (IRE)**[50] 2617 2-9-5 0 .... TomEaves 9 — 36
(James Given) *prom: rdn along wl over 2f out: sn wknd* **16/1**

8 *1 ¾* **Thenewsfromspain (IRE)** 2-9-5 0 ....[1] AndrewMullen 3 — 31
(Ollie Pears) *s.i.s: a in rr* **150/1**

0 **9** *¾* **Pentito Rap (USA)**[7] 4083 2-9-5 0 .... RyanPowell 2 — 29
(Sir Mark Prescott Bt) *wnt rt s: a in rr* **100/1**

0 **10** *1* **On Show (IRE)**[49] 2648 2-9-5 0 .... TedDurcan 6 — 26
(David Brown) *midfield: rdn along 1/2-way: sn outpcd* **100/1**

1m 15.96s (1.26) **Going Correction** +0.125s/f (Good) — **10** Ran SP% **119.6**

Speed ratings (Par 94): **96,95,94,89,87 85,76,74,73,71**

CSF £73.19 TOTE £18.50: £4.30, £1.60, £2.20; EX 85.00 Trifecta £233.20.

Owner Sheikh Rashid Dalmook Al Maktoum **Bred** Maywood Stud **Trained** Newmarket, Suffolk

FOCUS

Outer course used, and race distances as advertised. Few could be seriously fancied in this fair juvenile event. The first three pulled nicely clear.

4364 BDN CONSTRUCTION NURSERY H'CAP — 6f 15y

2:20 (2:20) (Class 5) 2-Y-O — **£2,911** (£866; £432; £216) **Stalls** Centre

Form — RPR

0241 **1** **Tawny Port**[14] 3852 2-9-0 **69** .... TomEaves 1 — 71
(James Given) *wnt lft s and in rr: swtchd rt to outer over 2f out: chsd ldrs wl over 1f out and sn rdn: drvn to chal ins fnl f: kpt on u.p to ld nr line* **1/1**[1]

000 **2** *shd* **Kilbaha Lady (IRE)**[55] 2489 2-8-2 **57** .... AndrewMullen 6 — 59
(Nigel Tinkler) *trckd ldng pair: hdwy 2f out: sn chsng ldr: rdn to ld ins fnl f: sn drvn: hdd and no ex nr line* **14/1**

500 **3** *2* **Breaking Free**[13] 3873 2-8-4 **59** .... JimmyQuinn 2 — 55
(John Quinn) *chsd ldrs: hdwy 2f out and sn rdn: drvn and kpt on fnl f* **10/1**

214 **4** *2 ¾* **Melaniemillie**[30] 3290 2-9-4 **76** .... JacobButterfield(3) 5 — 63
(Ollie Pears) *sn led: rdn jst over 1f out: edgd lft and rdr dropped reins ins fnl f: sn hdd: hung lft and wknd* **9/2**[3]

16 **5** *1 ½* **Fancy Day (IRE)**[16] 3782 2-9-2 **76** .... RossCoakley(5) 3 — 59
(Mark Johnston) *in tch: rdn along over 2f out: sn outpcd* **7/2**[2]

4024 **6** *1 ½* **Smiley Riley (IRE)**[18] 3712 2-9-1 **70** .... DuranFentiman 4 — 48
(Tony Coyle) *trckd ldr: pushed along wl over 2f out: sn rdn and wknd* **20/1**

1m 16.81s (2.11) **Going Correction** +0.125s/f (Good) — **6** Ran SP% **110.9**

Speed ratings (Par 94): **90,89,87,83,81 79**

CSF £16.22 TOTE £2.00: £1.40, £5.10; EX 14.20 Trifecta £64.40.

Owner Tawny Port Ptners & Lovely Bubbly Racing **Bred** Mrs D O'Brien **Trained** Willoughton, Lincs

FOCUS

The market proved a good guide to this nursery. The winner pretty much replicated his previous nursery win.

4365 JIM TAYLOR MEMORIAL H'CAP — 6f 15y

2:55 (2:56) (Class 5) (0-70,76) 3-Y-O — **£2,911** (£866; £432; £216) **Stalls** Centre

Form — RPR

5065 **1** **Le Manege Enchante (IRE)**[16] 3786 3-8-5 **57** ....(p) NoelGarbutt(3) 2 — 65
(Derek Shaw) *in tch: hdwy 1/2-way: sn chsng ldrs: rdn to chal whn hung lft 1 1/2f out: drvn and edgd lft ins fnl f: kpt on wl to ld nr fin* **40/1**

6122 **2** *shd* **Caitie (IRE)**[7] 4085 3-9-6 **69** ....(t) MartinHarley 7 — 76
(Paul Cole) *in tch: hdwy wl over 2f out: rdn to ld over 1f out: drvn ins fnl f: hdd and no ex towards fin* **5/2**[1]

5543 **3** *2* **Iceaxe**[28] 3353 3-9-1 **64** .... RoystonFfrench 9 — 64
(John Holt) *cl up: slt ld 1/2-way: rdn 2f out: hdd over 1f out: drvn and kpt on same pce fnl f* **6/1**

0503 **4** *1* **Men United (FR)**[9] 4007 3-8-6 **55** ....(t) JimmyQuinn 4 — 52
(Roy Bowring) *qckly away and wnt lft s: led and sn swtchd lft to r wd: hdd 1/2-way and cl up: rdn and ev ch whn bmpd 1 1/2f out: sn drvn and kpt on same pce fnl f* **20/1**

34 **5** *1 ½* **Waseefa**[21] 3603 3-9-5 **68** .... JFEgan 6 — 60
(John Butler) *chsd ldrs: cl up 1/2-way: rdn along over 2f out: sn drvn and grad wknd* **15/2**

0403 **6** *3* **Dalalah**[21] 3603 3-8-2 **51** oh3 ....(v) AndrewMullen 5 — 34
(Richard Guest) *wnt rt s: a towards rr* **16/1**

5041 **7** *2* **King's Currency**[21] 3604 3-8-10 **59** .... JackGarritty 1 — 35
(Jedd O'Keeffe) *dwlt: a in rr* **11/2**[3]

6500 **8** *4 ½* **Jazz Legend (USA)**[46] 2742 3-9-3 **66** ....(b) TomEaves 10 — 28
(James Given) *racd towards stands' rail: prom: rdn and ev ch 2f out: sn drvn and wknd* **40/1**

-401 **9** *1 ¼* **Joules**[7] 4085 3-9-6 **76** 6ex ....(t) JordanWilliams(7) 8 — 34
(Natalie Lloyd-Beavis) *in tch: rdn along over 2f out: sn wknd* **3/1**[2]

-000 **10** *1* **Art Echo**[15] 3816 3-9-7 **70** ....(b[1]) RyanClark 3 — 25
(Jonathan Portman) *chsd ldrs: rdn along wl over 2f out: sn wknd* **22/1**

1m 16.21s (1.51) **Going Correction** +0.125s/f (Good) — **10** Ran SP% **114.9**

Speed ratings (Par 100): **94,93,91,89,87 83,81,75,73,72**

CSF £133.07 CT £725.65 TOTE £39.30: £10.50, £1.80, £2.20; EX 204.90 Trifecta £1889.40.

Owner Nigel Franklin **Bred** Tally-Ho Stud **Trained** Sproxton, Leics

FOCUS

A moderate sprint handicap, which was run at a strong pace on rain-softened ground. It produced a slow-motion finish. The shock winner is rated back to his 2yo turf form.

4366 BDN BLACK DOG LONG RUN HOME H'CAP — 6f 15y

3:30 (3:31) (Class 3) (0-95,95) 3-Y-O+ — **£7,762** (£2,310; £1,154; £577) **Stalls** Centre

Form — RPR

2540 **1** **Solar Flair**[28] 3358 4-9-7 **90** ....[1] JimCrowley 8 — 100
(William Knight) *cl up: led wl over 1f out: rdn ent fnl f: drvn and edgd lft last 100yds: kpt on wl towards fin* **5/1**[2]

-000 **2** *1* **Grandad's World (IRE)**[44] 2803 4-9-3 **86** .... JackGarritty 5 — 93
(Richard Fahey) *prom: cl up 1/2-way: rdn and ev ch over 1f out: drvn ins fnl f: kpt on* **14/1**

330 **3** *¾* **Sir Billy Wright (IRE)**[11] 3956 5-9-4 **87** .... JFEgan 2 — 91
(David Evans) *t.k.h: hld up in tch: hdwy 2f out: rdn and ev ch ins fnl f: drvn and nt qckn towards fin* **8/1**

4313 **4** *nk* **Duke Cosimo**[28] 3346 6-9-0 **83** .... TomEaves 11 — 86+
(Michael Herrington) *hld up in rr: hdwy wl over 1f out: swtchd rt and rdn ins fnl f: styd on wl towards fin* **6/1**[3]

-320 **5** *nse* **Shipyard (USA)**[34] 3150 7-9-7 **90** .... BenCurtis 9 — 93
(Michael Appleby) *trckd ldrs: cl up over 2f out: rdn over 1f out: drvn ins fnl f: kpt on same pce* **9/2**[1]

-005 **6** *½* **Son Of Africa**[22] 3573 4-9-12 **95** .... MartinHarley 6 — 97
(Henry Candy) *dwlt: t.k.h and sn chsng ldrs: rdn along over 1f out: kpt on same pce fnl f* **8/1**

0-10 **7** *nse* **Tangerine Trees**[34] 3151 11-9-5 **88** ....(v) AndrewMullen 7 — 90
(Michael Appleby) *led: rdn along and hdd wl over 1f out: sn drvn and grad wknd* **16/1**

0006 **8** *shd* **Charles Molson**[20] 3671 5-9-10 **93** .... ThomasBrown 4 — 94
(Patrick Chamings) *hld up in rr: hdwy 2f out: effrt and nt clr run ent fnl f: sn rdn and no imp* **17/2**

31-0 **9** *¾* **Invincible Ridge (IRE)**[20] 3638 8-9-0 **83** .... NeilFarley 3 — 82
(Eric Alston) *racd wd: prom: rdn along 2f out: sn drvn and wknd* **28/1**

4660 **10** *4 ½* **Yeeoow (IRE)**[7] 4079 7-8-13 **82** .... JoeyHaynes 10 — 66
(K R Burke) *chsd ldrs: rdn along 2f out: sn drvn and wknd* **15/2**

400- **11** *4 ½* **Willbeme**[307] 6312 8-9-3 **89** .... JacobButterfield(3) 12 — 59
(Neville Bycroft) *racd wd: prom: rdn along 1/2-way: sn outpcd and bhd fnl 2f* **20/1**

1m 14.4s (-0.30) **Going Correction** +0.125s/f (Good) — **11** Ran SP% **114.4**

Speed ratings (Par 107): **107,105,104,104,104 103,103,103,102,96 90**

CSF £70.77 CT £559.76 TOTE £5.20: £1.90, £4.10, £2.70; EX 69.90 Trifecta £621.00.

Owner Art Of Racing & The Kimber Family **Bred** Farmers Hill Stud **Trained** Patching, W Sussex

FOCUS

A competitive sprint handicap. It was steadily run and only really developed from halfway. Sound form.

4367 BDN MORE THAN A BUILDING COMPANY MAIDEN FILLIES' STKS (PLUS 10 RACE) — 1m 2f 50y

4:05 (4:08) (Class 5) 3-Y-O — **£2,911** (£866; £432; £216) **Stalls** Low

Form — RPR

02- **1** **Very Dashing**[266] 7422 3-9-0 0 .... FrederikTylicki 7 — 84+
(Luca Cumani) *trckd ldrs: hdwy 1/2-way: led wl over 1f out: sn rdn clr: readily* **10/1**

2 **2** *1* **To Eternity**[21] 3601 3-9-0 0 .... RobertHavlin 9 — 82+
(John Gosden) *hld up in midfield: hdwy 4f out: pushed along over 2f out: rdn to chse wnr ent fnl f: styd on* **13/8**[1]

3 *2 ½* **Blue Jean Baby** 3-9-0 0 .... MartinHarley 4 — 77
(George Scott) *dwlt: sn in tch: hdwy to trck ldrs over 3f out: rdn to chse ldng pair 2f out: drvn and kpt on same pce fnl f* **50/1**

0 **4** *1* **Straw Hat (IRE)**[70] 1989 3-9-0 0 .... BenCurtis 14 — 75
(William Haggas) *cl up: led wl over 3f out: rdn along over 2f out: hdd wl over 1f out: sn drvn and kpt on one pce fnl f* **9/2**[3]

4-0 **5** *7* **Iona Island**[84] 1608 3-9-0 0 .... MichaelJMMurphy 12 — 62
(Charles Hills) *towards rr: hdwy 6f out and sn in tch: pushed along to chse ldrs over 2f out: rdn wl over 1f out: no imp* **33/1**

0- **6** *nk* **Fiftyshadesofpink (IRE)**[228] 8048 3-9-0 0 .... JackMitchell 1 — 61
(Hugo Palmer) *led: rdn along 4f out: sn hdd: drvn wl over 2f out and sn wknd* **33/1**

7 *1 ½* **Maqam (IRE)** 3-9-0 0 .... JimCrowley 10 — 58
(Richard Hannon) *dwlt and towards rr: hdwy 3f out: rdn along over 2f out: n.d* **20/1**

22- **8** *1* **Honorina**[345] 5014 3-9-0 0 .... TedDurcan 8 — 56
(Sir Michael Stoute) *hld up in midfield: hdwy 4f out: rdn along over 2f out: sn btn* **9/4**[2]

0 **9** *¾* **Want The Fairytale**[8] 4056 3-9-0 0 .... JohnFahy 13 — 55
(Clive Cox) *a towards rr* **80/1**

06 **10** *¾* **Contingency**[16] 3781 3-9-0 0 .... RoystonFfrench 5 — 54
(Stuart Williams) *chsd ldrs on inner: rdn along over 3f out: drvn over 2f out: sn wknd* **100/1**

00-6 **11** *2 ¼* **Mooizo (IRE)**[189] 96 3-9-0 38 .... AdrianMcCarthy 11 — 49
(Peter Chapple-Hyam) *a towards rr* **150/1**

12 *4* **Iconic Sky** 3-9-0 0 .... ThomasBrown 15 — 42
(Lucy Wadham) *a towards rr* **50/1**

06 **13** *6* **Alaskan Breeze (IRE)**[36] 3059 3-9-0 0 .... JimmyFortune 6 — 30
(Brian Meehan) *chsd ldrs: rdn along 3f out: sn wknd* **50/1**

-0 **14** *31* **The Black Cygnet**[67] 2098 3-8-7 0 .... RPWalsh(7) 2
(David Menuisier) *s.i.s: a outpcd in rr: bhd fnl 3f* **125/1**

2m 10.92s (-3.38) **Going Correction** -0.35s/f (Firm) — **14** Ran SP% **116.3**

Speed ratings (Par 97): **99,98,96,95,89 89,88,87,86,86 84,81,76,51**

CSF £24.66 TOTE £11.60: £2.50, £1.40, £8.10; EX 32.80 Trifecta £695.30.

Owner Helena Springfield Ltd **Bred** Meon Valley Stud **Trained** Newmarket, Suffolk

FOCUS

An informative fillies' maiden. Four came clear and the first two home look above average.

4368 BDN A NAME YOU CAN TRUST H'CAP — 1m 75y

4:35 (4:36) (Class 4) (0-85,85) 3-Y-O+ — **£4,787** (£1,424; £711; £355) **Stalls** Centre

Form — RPR

5-12 **1** **Poet's Beauty (IRE)**[49] 2654 3-9-0 **80** ....(p) ThomasBrown 1 — 87+
(Ismail Mohammed) *set stdy pce: qcknd over 2f out: rdn clr over 1f out: kpt on strly* **6/4**[1]

4110 **2** *1 ¾* **Marcano (IRE)**[8] 4055 4-9-5 **76** ....(t) FrederikTylicki 2 — 79
(Rod Millman) *hld up: hdwy 3f out: rdn over 1f out: drvn and kpt on to chse wnr ent fnl f: sn no imp* **3/1**[2]

4-06 **3** *1* **Tournament**[51] 2579 5-9-7 **78** ....(t) MartinHarley 6 — 79
(Seamus Durack) *trckd ldng pair: hdwy 2f out: sn chsng wnr: rdn over 1f out: drvn and kpt on same pce fnl f* **8/1**

0261 **4** ½ **Abushamah (IRE)**[28] 3364 5-10-0 **85** .... JamesSullivan 5 85
(Ruth Carr) *sn trcking wnr: cl up over 3f out: rdn along 2f out: drvn over 1f out: one pce fnl f* **4/1**[3]

1306 **5** 2 **Intrude**[29] 3304 4-9-11 **82** .... SaleemGolam 3 77
(David Simcock) *hld up: hdwy 2f out: rdn and edgd lft over 1f out: sn drvn and no imp fnl f* **15/2**

1m 51.4s (2.40) **Going Correction** -0.35s/f (Firm)
WFA 3 from 4yo+ 9lb **5** Ran SP% **107.9**
Speed ratings (Par 105): **74,72,71,70,68**
CSF £5.91 TOTE £2.20: £1.10, £1.90; EX 5.80 Trifecta £21.90.
Owner Dr Ali Ridha **Bred** Rabbah Bloodstock Limited **Trained** Newmarket, Suffolk

FOCUS
This proved easy pickings for the progressive favourite, who got an easy lead. The runner-up is rated to his recent form.

4369 RACINGUK.COM H'CAP (DIV I) 1m 75y
5:05 (5:05) (Class 6) (0-65,65) 3-Y-O+ **£2,385** (£704; £352) **Stalls** Centre

Form RPR

-242 **1** **Wakame (IRE)**[7] 4088 3-9-1 **61** .... JimCrowley 8 71
(Ed de Giles) *prom: led wl over 1f out and sn rdn: drvn ins fnl f: hld on gamely towards fin* **7/4**[2]

1 **2** *nse* **Mister Royal (IRE)**[9] 4005 5-9-0 **51** 6ex .... BenCurtis 9 63
(Brian Ellison) *trckd ldrs: hdwy on outer over 2f out: rdn to chse wnr over 1f out: chal ins fnl f: ev ch tl drvn and no ex nr fin* **5/4**[1]

-604 **3** 4½ **Niqnaaqpaadiwaaq**[15] 3807 4-9-12 **63** .... NeilFarley 3 64
(Eric Alston) *led 2f: cl up: led again 3f out: pushed along 2f out and sn hdd: sn rdn and kpt on same pce appr fnl f* **13/2**[3]

5656 **4** ½ **Earthwindorfire**[58] 2369 5-10-0 **65** .... TimmyMurphy 2 65
(Geoffrey Deacon) *trckd ldrs: hdwy 2f out: rdn over 1f out: sn drvn and one pce* **20/1**

262 **5** 2¼ **Almanack**[90] 1498 6-9-8 **62** .... (t) NathanAlison(3) 6 56
(Daniel Mark Loughnane) *hld up: effrt and sme hdwy 2f out: sn rdn and no imp* **20/1**

0-00 **6** *hd* **Savannah Star**[9] 4006 3-7-7 **46** oh1 .... RPWalsh(7) 7 38
(Nick Kent) *towards rr: sme hdwy on outer over 2f out: sn rdn and n.d* **40/1**

6-01 **7** 3 **Madam Mai Tai**[11] 3946 4-8-2 **46** oh1 .... RowanScott(7) 10 33
(Rebecca Bastiman) *hld up in rr: hdwy wl over 2f out: sn rdn along: drvn wl over 1f out: sn btn* **12/1**

6000 **8** 16 **Pipers Piping (IRE)**[3] 4234 10-8-12 **49** .... (v) RyanPowell 4
(Mandy Rowland) *dwlt: rapid hdwy to ld after 2f: rdn along over 3f out: sn hdd & wknd* **33/1**

1m 45.96s (-3.04) **Going Correction** -0.35s/f (Firm)
WFA 3 from 4yo+ 9lb **8** Ran SP% **116.7**
Speed ratings (Par 101): **101,100,96,95,93 93,90,74**
CSF £4.17 CT £9.92 TOTE £2.50: £1.10, £1.30, £2.30; EX 4.80 Trifecta £11.30.
Owner Simon Treacher **Bred** Tally-Ho Stud **Trained** Ledbury, H'fords

FOCUS
This looked by far the strongest of the two divisions and provided a good finish between two progressive types, who pulled clear.

4370 RACINGUK.COM H'CAP (DIV II) 1m 75y
5:35 (5:37) (Class 6) (0-65,63) 3-Y-O+ **£2,385** (£704; £352) **Stalls** Centre

Form RPR

00-0 **1** **Wootton Vale (IRE)**[11] 3946 3-8-6 **50** .... RaulDaSilva 3 54
(Richard Fahey) *trckd ldrs on inner: swtchd rt and hdwy over 2f out: rdn to chal over 1f out: drvn to take slt ld jst ins fnl f: kpt on gamely towards fin* **20/1**

6-00 **2** *shd* **Frozon**[14] 3856 3-9-1 **59** .... BenCurtis 6 63
(Brian Ellison) *t.k.h: chsd ldr: led after 2f: rdn along over 2f out: jnd and drvn over 1f out: hung lft and hdd jst ins fnl f: sn rallied gamely and ev ch: jst hld* **4/1**[3]

0404 **3** 1¾ **Roly Tricks**[24] 3488 5-10-0 **63** .... RyanClark 7 65
(Natalie Lloyd-Beavis) *hld up: hdwy on outer over 2f out: rdn to chal over 1f out: ev ch tl drvn ins fnl f and kpt on same pce* **9/2**

-105 **4** 1½ **Blushes (FR)**[51] 2576 3-8-11 **62** .... HarryBurns(7) 5 58
(Ed Dunlop) *hld up towards rr: hdwy over 2f out: rdn wl over 1f out: kpt on fnl f* **10/3**[1]

3655 **5** ½ **Olympic Duel (IRE)**[13] 3877 3-9-2 **60** .... WilliamCarson 8 55
(Peter Hiatt) *in tch: pushed along 3f out: rdn over 2f out: sn drvn and kpt on one pce* **7/2**[2]

4400 **6** 4½ **Douglas Bank (IRE)**[9] 4006 4-9-11 **63** .... (bt) AlistairRawlinson(3) 4 49
(Roy Bowring) *a in rr* **25/1**

54-6 **7** *hd* **She's Golden**[18] 3710 3-9-2 **60** .... KevinStott 1 44
(Ann Duffield) *led 2f: cl up: rdn along over 2f out: sn drvn and wknd over 1f out* **8/1**

04-0 **8** ½ **Clouded Gold**[14] 3843 4-9-0 **49** .... AndrewMullen 9 34
(Michael Appleby) *t.k.h: chsd ldng pair: rdn along wl over 2f out: sn wknd* **11/1**

1m 47.01s (-1.99) **Going Correction** -0.35s/f (Firm)
WFA 3 from 4yo+ 9lb **8** Ran SP% **111.5**
Speed ratings (Par 101): **95,94,93,91,91 86,86,85**
CSF £93.43 CT £428.83 TOTE £22.80: £5.20, £1.50, £2.00; EX 54.40 Trifecta £723.80.
Owner John Nicholls Ltd/David Kilburn **Bred** Corrin Stud **Trained** Musley Bank, N Yorks

FOCUS
A weak handicap, fought out by two horses with little previous form. It's rated around the third.
T/Plt: £122.50 to a £1 stake. Pool: £50,796.4 - 302.7 winning units T/Qpdt: £17.10 to a £1 stake. Pool: £5,233.11 - 225.3 winning units **Joe Rowntree**

3977 PONTEFRACT (L-H)
Friday, July 15

OFFICIAL GOING: Good to firm (good in places) changing to good after race 2 (7.00)
Wind: moderate 1/2 benhind Weather: Fine

4371 COUNTRYWIDE FREIGHT MAIDEN AUCTION STKS (PLUS 10 RACE) 6f
6:30 (6:31) (Class 4) 2-Y-O **£4,528** (£1,347; £673; £336) **Stalls** Low

Form RPR

1 **Belle Meade (IRE)** 2-8-10 0 .... TonyHamilton 14 84+
(Richard Fahey) *trckd ldrs: 2nd over 1f out: led last 150yds: pushed out: eased nr fin* **11/1**

0 **2** 1¾ **Right Action**[13] 3881 2-8-13 0 .... JackGarritty 8 81
(Richard Fahey) *chsd ldr: led over 1f out: hdd and no ex last 150yds* **14/1**

35 **3** 9 **Bengal Lancer**[15] 3805 2-8-8 0 .... GeorgeDowning(3) 9 52
(Ian Williams) *chsd ldrs: kpt on same pce over 1f out: modest 3rd post* **3/1**[1]

30 **4** *hd* **Snuggy (IRE)**[31] 3261 2-8-8 0 .... RoystonFfrench 5 48
(David Barron) *chsd ldrs: one pce fnl 2f* **10/1**

5 3 **Canford Bay (IRE)** 2-9-4 0 .... PaulMulrennan 12 49
(Michael Dods) *hld up in rr: hdwy and edgd rt over 1f out: kpt on* **13/2**[2]

6 1 **Grinty (IRE)** 2-8-13 0 .... GrahamLee 2 41+
(Michael Dods) *in rr: hdwy 2f out: keeping on at fin* **25/1**

5 **7** *nk* **Silk Mill Blue**[23] 3515 2-8-13 0 .... GeorgeChaloner 13 40
(Richard Whitaker) *s.i.s: in rr: hdwy 2f out: hung rt 1f out: kpt on* **33/1**

5 **8** 2½ **Oceanic (IRE)**[27] 3388 2-9-1 0 .... JasonHart 3 35
(John Quinn) *led: hdd over 1f out: wknd qckly last 150yds* **9/1**[3]

9 4 **Faulkwood** 2-9-4 0 .... JoeyHaynes 1 26
(K R Burke) *in rr-div: sme hdwy over 1f out: nvr on terms* **3/1**[1]

10 3 **Rag Tatter** 2-8-13 0 .... TomEaves 15 12
(Kevin Ryan) *swtchd lft after s: in rr-div: sme hdwy and wnt rt over 1f out: nvr a factor* **20/1**

0 **11** *nk* **Magic Journey (IRE)**[13] 3874 2-8-13 0 .... CamHardie 11 11
(John Quinn) *s.i.s: sn mid-div: nvr a factor* **66/1**

40 **12** 2 **Vatican Hill (IRE)**[41] 2913 2-9-4 0 .... PatrickMathers 6 10
(Richard Fahey) *mid-div: lost pl over 2f out* **25/1**

13 1¼ **Sheriff Garrett (IRE)** 2-9-1 0 .... DuranFentiman 4 3
(Tim Easterby) *s.i.s: a towards rr* **25/1**

6 **14** 20 **Copa Beech**[22] 3576 2-8-10 0 .... RachelRichardson(3) 7
(Olly Williams) *chsd ldrs: lost pl over 2f out: sn bhd: eased clsng stages: t.o* **80/1**

1m 18.3s (1.40) **Going Correction** +0.175s/f (Good) **14** Ran SP% **119.4**
Speed ratings (Par 96): **97,94,82,82,78 77,76,73,68,64 63,60,59,32**
CSF £142.48 TOTE £10.60: £3.80, £4.20, £2.00; EX 128.50 Trifecta £480.80.
Owner Merchants and Missionaries **Bred** E O'Gorman **Trained** Musley Bank, N Yorks

FOCUS
Rail dolled out 15ft from the 6f bend to the winning post, adding 8yds to all races. After only 2mm of rain prior to racing the official going remained good to firm, good in places. Not many got into this fair maiden, with Richard Fahey responsible for the first two home.

4372 TOTEPOOL SUPPORTS JACK BERRY HOUSE MAIDEN AUCTION STKS (PLUS 10 RACE) 1m 4f 8y
7:00 (7:01) (Class 4) 3-Y-O **£5,175** (£1,540; £769; £384) **Stalls** Low

Form RPR

0-40 **1** **Icefall (IRE)**[63] 2224 3-9-5 70 .... JasonHart 6 83
(Tim Easterby) *trckd ldrs: shkn up 6f out: led over 2f out: idled and drvn rt out nr fin* **16/1**

0-4 **2** ½ **Reconcilliation**[20] 3653 3-9-5 0 .... GrahamLee 1 82
(Ed Vaughan) *s.s: hld up towards rr: smooth hdwy 3f out: chsd wnr 2f out: rallied clsng stages: jst hld* **9/2**[3]

5265 **3** 27 **Duck A L'Orange (IRE)**[18] 3715 3-9-5 69 .... (p) DanielTudhope 5 39
(Michael Bell) *led: hdd over 2f out: sn wl outpcd* **4/1**[2]

3444 **4** 3¾ **Proven Point (IRE)**[30] 3281 3-9-5 72 .... (p) PaulMulrennan 7 33
(Tony Coyle) *hld up in rr: shkn up 6f out: effrt 3f out: sn wknd* **7/1**

3 **5** 13 **Waiting For Richie**[26] 3434 3-9-5 0 .... JamesSullivan 8 12
(Tom Tate) *towards rr: hdwy 4f out: sn drvn: lost pl over 2f out* **11/2**

644- **6** 4½ **Wynford (IRE)**[212] 8246 3-9-2 73 .... RobHornby(3) 4
(Andrew Balding) *trckd ldrs: drvn and lost pl over 2f out* **5/1**

4 **7** 8 **La Salesse (FR)**[9] 4001 3-9-0 0 .... FrannyNorton 3
(Mark Johnston) *chsd ldrs: drvn over 5f out: lost pl 3f out: sn bhd* **10/3**[1]

2m 42.28s (1.48) **Going Correction** +0.175s/f (Good) **7** Ran SP% **111.7**
Speed ratings (Par 102): **102,101,83,81,72 69,64**
CSF £81.49 TOTE £18.00: £7.30, £2.30; EX 95.60 Trifecta £342.10.
Owner Ryedale Partners No 10 **Bred** Victor Stud Bloodstock Ltd **Trained** Great Habton, N Yorks

FOCUS
Race run over 8 yards further than advertised. Ordinary maiden form and the two principals pulled well clear of the rest. THe winner is rated back to a better view of his 2yo best.

4373 BETFRED SUPPORTS JACK BERRY HOUSE H'CAP 5f
7:30 (7:36) (Class 3) (0-95,93) 3-Y-O+
£9,337 (£2,796; £1,398; £699; £349; £175) **Stalls** Low

Form RPR

114 **1** **Final Venture**[10] 3980 4-9-6 **87** .... NeilFarley 8 104+
(Alan Swinbank) *led: shkn up over 1f out: sn wnt clr: eased towards fin* **6/1**[3]

0042 **2** 6 **Gamesome (FR)**[7] 4112 5-9-12 **93** .... TomQueally 3 88
(Paul Midgley) *mid-div: hdwy over 2f out: n.m.r and swtchd rt over 1f out: 2nd last 150yds: no ch w wnr* **5/2**[1]

0-02 **3** 1½ **Dragon King (IRE)**[27] 3393 4-9-8 **89** .... PaulMulrennan 1 79
(Michael Dods) *trckd ldrs: 3rd appr fnl f: kpt on same pce* **10/3**[2]

2210 **4** *nk* **Lexington Place**[11] 3944 6-9-7 **88** .... JamesSullivan 2 77+
(Ruth Carr) *s.i.s: hld up in rr: effrt over 2f out: n.m.r over 1f out: edgd rt and kpt on fnl f: tk 4th nr fin* **9/1**

1041 **5** 1¼ **Confessional**[8] 4032 9-9-9 **90** 6ex .... (e) JackGarritty 6 74
(Tim Easterby) *mid-div: drvn over 2f out: n.m.r over 1f out: kpt on one pce* **12/1**

0-05 **6** *nk* **El Viento (FR)**[21] 3606 8-9-8 **89** .... (v) TonyHamilton 7 72
(Richard Fahey) *in rr: sn drvn along: sme hdwy whn nt clr run and swtchd rt 1f out: nvr a factor* **25/1**

0020 **7** *hd* **Seve**[7] 4112 4-9-10 **91** .... (t) LiamJones 5 74
(Tom Dascombe) *mid-div: sn drvn along: hdwy and swtchd outside 2f out: nvr a factor* **25/1**

0410 **8** 1½ **Bondi Beach Boy**[7] 4112 7-9-4 **85** .... (p) GeorgeChaloner 9 62
(James Turner) *chsd ldrs: sltly hmpd over 1f out: wknd last 150yds* **16/1**

4050 **9** *nk* **Silvanus (IRE)**[7] 4112 11-9-9 **90** .... GrahamLee 11 66
(Paul Midgley) *swtchd lft after s: hld up in rr: hdwy over 2f out: wknd fnl f* **16/1**

6215 **10** 3¾ **Stanghow**[34] 3150 4-9-1 **82** .... DanielTudhope 4 45
(Antony Brittain) *chsd ldrs: lost pl and hmpd 100yds out: sn eased* **17/2**

1m 3.98s (0.68) **Going Correction** +0.175s/f (Good) **10** Ran SP% **113.6**
Speed ratings (Par 107): **101,91,89,88,86 86,85,83,82,76**
CSF £20.73 CT £58.32 TOTE £7.60: £2.40, £1.10, £1.60; EX 25.30 Trifecta £87.00.
Owner Brian Valentine **Bred** Newsells Park Stud **Trained** Melsonby, N Yorks

The Form Book, Raceform Ltd, Newbury, RG14 5SJ

FOCUS
Race run over 8 yards further than advertised. A very useful sprint handicap, in which the winner was dominant from the front. It's hard to know how literally to take this.

4374 COLSTROPE CUP H'CAP — 1m 4y
8:05 (8:05) (Class 3) (0-95,95) 3-Y-O+ **£7,762** (£2,310; £1,154; £577) **Stalls** Low

Form RPR

0015 **1** **Gurkha Friend**[13] 3884 4-9-3 **84**.......................... GrahamLee 7 91
(Karen McLintock) *led: pushed along over 2f out: hdd narrowly appr fnl f: led again last 150yds: drvn rt out* **7/1**

0164 **2** ½ **Spring Offensive (IRE)**[12] 3923 4-9-9 **90**.................... TonyHamilton 4 96
(Richard Fahey) *trckd ldrs: effrt and swtchd lft over 1f out: styd on to take 2nd last 50yds: no ex* **7/2**[2]

2251 **3** nk **Thaqaffa (IRE)**[14] 3841 3-8-5 **81**.......................... RoystonFfrench 5 84
(Marcus Tregoning) *trckd wnr: t.k.h: effrt over 2f out: led narrowly appr fnl f: hdd and no ex last 150yds* **3/1**[1]

0001 **4** 2¼ **Silvery Moon (IRE)**[14] 3855 9-9-5 **89**.................. RachelRichardson(3) 1 89
(Tim Easterby) *hld up in mid-div: effrt over 2f out: kpt on one pce over 1f out* **4/1**[3]

00-0 **5** 2½ **Altharoos (IRE)**[22] 3565 6-9-7 **88**.......................... JoeyHaynes 6 82
(Sally Hall) *dwlt: in rr: effrt over 2f out: one pce* **25/1**

3402 **6** hd **Trinity Star (IRE)**[18] 3717 5-8-11 **78**.....................(p) PaulMulrennan 3 72
(Michael Dods) *sn trcking ldrs: effrt over 2f out: hung lft and one pce over 1f out* **3/1**[1]

030- **7** 1½ **Holiday Magic (IRE)**[331] 5525 5-10-0 **95**.................. JamesSullivan 8 85
(Michael Easterby) *swtchd lft after s: hld up in rr: effrt over 2f out: nvr a factor* **25/1**

1m 49.68s (3.78) **Going Correction** +0.175s/f (Good)
WFA 3 from 4yo+ 9lb — 7 Ran SP% **112.4**
Speed ratings (Par 107): **88,87,87,84,82 82,80**
CSF £30.49 CT £88.25 TOTE £8.90: £4.70, £2.80; EX 24.80 Trifecta £170.30.
Owner Don Eddy **Bred** Mrs J Imray **Trained** Ingoe, Northumberland

FOCUS
Race run over 8 yards further than advertised. A useful handicap run at an ordinary pace. The form is rated around the runner-up.

4375 INJURED JOCKEYS FUND MAIDEN H'CAP — 1m 2f 6y
8:35 (8:40) (Class 5) (0-70,65) 3-Y-O+ **£3,234** (£962; £481; £240) **Stalls** Low

Form RPR

323- **1** **Intrigue**[295] 6671 4-9-11 **62**..............................(b) TomQueally 3 69
(Daniel Kubler) *s.i.s: in last and sn pushed along: hdwy over 2f out: 2nd over 1f out: styd on to ld nr fin* **16/1**

-202 **2** nk **Signed And Sealed**[3] 4233 3-9-2 **64**.......................... FrannyNorton 5 70+
(Mark Johnston) *led: pushed clr over 2f out: abt 6 l clr over 1f out: drvn fnl f: grad wknd: ct nr fin* **5/4**[1]

0066 **3** 1¾ **Allfredandnobell (IRE)**[10] 3982 3-8-7 **55**.................... JoeyHaynes 2 57
(Micky Hammond) *in rr: drvn over 4f out: hdwy over 2f out: 3rd last 75yds: kpt on* **7/1**[3]

3045 **4** 2¼ **Perceysvivace**[14] 3853 3-8-12 **60**.......................... TonyHamilton 1 58
(Richard Fahey) *trckd ldrs: drvn over 3f out: chsd ldr 2f out: wknd fnl 100yds* **11/4**[2]

5-42 **5** 10 **Inflexiball**[54] 2507 4-9-8 **59**.......................... GrahamLee 4 37
(John Mackie) *trckd ldrs: rdn and lost pl over 2f out: sn bhd* **8/1**

-200 **6** 11 **Indulgent**[24] 3482 3-8-5 **53**.......................... DuranFentiman 8 9
(Tony Coyle) *trckd ldrs: lost pl over 2f out: sn bhd* **25/1**

450 **7** 1¼ **Hidden Gem**[51] 2578 3-9-3 **65**.......................... PaulMulrennan 7 18
(Ed Walker) *trckd ldrs: drvn over 4f out: lost pl 2f out: sn bhd* **12/1**

00-5 **8** 1 **Taopix**[17] 3750 4-8-13 **50**.......................... JamesSullivan 6
(Karen McLintock) *mid-div: drvn over 5f out: lost pl over 2f out: sn bhd: eased clsng stages* **20/1**

2m 18.46s (4.76) **Going Correction** +0.175s/f (Good)
WFA 3 from 4yo 11lb — 8 Ran SP% **116.9**
Speed ratings (Par 103): **87,86,85,83,75 66,65,64**
CSF £37.53 CT £165.43 TOTE £11.50: £2.40, £1.10, £2.00; EX 32.10 Trifecta £233.00.
Owner Mr & Mrs G Middlebrook **Bred** Mr & Mrs G Middlebrook **Trained** Lambourn, Berks

FOCUS
Race run over 8 yards further than advertised. Just a modest maiden handicap. The runner-up got an uncontested lead.

4376 JACK BERRY HOUSE H'CAP — 6f
9:05 (9:08) (Class 5) (0-75,75) 3-Y-O+ **£3,234** (£962; £481; £240) **Stalls** Low

Form RPR

1532 **1** **Mr Orange (IRE)**[10] 3978 3-8-6 **61**..............................(p) CamHardie 3 73
(Paul Midgley) *trckd ldrs: effrt 2f out: styd on to ld last 150yds* **3/1**[2]

0311 **2** 1 **Laila Honiwillow**[21] 3603 3-8-12 **67**.......................... JackGarritty 1 76
(Jedd O'Keeffe) *led: hdd briefly over 1f out: hdd and no ex last 150yds* **6/4**[1]

4522 **3** 1½ **Vallarta (IRE)**[12] 3924 6-9-9 **72**.......................... JamesSullivan 7 77
(Ruth Carr) *hld up in rr: t.k.h: effrt and n.m.r wl over 1f out: kpt on same pce to take 3rd clsng stages* **11/2**[3]

0500 **4** ¾ **Fyrecracker (IRE)**[20] 3646 5-9-8 **71**.......................... TomEaves 9 74
(Grant Tuer) *w ldr: led narrowly over 1f out: sn hdd: kpt on same pce* **16/1**

02R5 **5** 1 **Teetotal (IRE)**[1] 4321 6-8-2 **58**.......................... KieranSchofield(7) 5 58
(Nigel Tinkler) *slowly away: in last: hdwy over 2f out: edgd rt over 1f out: one pce* **15/2**

-401 **6** ¾ **Round The Island**[43] 2834 3-8-8 **63**..............................(p) PaulQuinn 4 59
(Richard Whitaker) *s.i.s: sn chsng ldrs: drvn over 2f out: hung lft over 1f out: one pce* **8/1**

0060 **7** 10 **Mercers Row**[21] 3610 9-9-7 **70**.......................... TonyHamilton 8 35
(Michael Herrington) *trckd ldrs: t.k.h: qeakened last 150yds: heavily eased clsng stages* **28/1**

1m 20.18s (3.28) **Going Correction** +0.175s/f (Good)
WFA 3 from 4yo+ 6lb — 7 Ran SP% **112.6**
Speed ratings (Par 103): **85,83,81,80,79 78,65**
CSF £7.64 CT £21.37 TOTE £3.80: £2.10, £1.30; EX 8.70 Trifecta £33.10.
Owner J Blackburn & A Turton **Bred** Rathbarry Stud **Trained** Westow, N Yorks

FOCUS
Race run over 8 yards further than advertised. A fair handicap, in which the pace was good, and a couple of in-form 3yos came to the fore. Both improved again.
T/Plt: £63.10 to a £1 stake. Pool: £60,793.27 - 702.79 winning tickets T/Qpdt: £8.80 to a £1 stake. Pool: £5,031.70 - 420.94 winning tickets **Walter Glynn**

4342 HAYDOCK (L-H)
Saturday, July 16

OFFICIAL GOING: Soft (heavy in places; 6.3)
Wind: light 1/2 against Weather: Fine and sunny

4377 APOLLOBET CASHBACK IF 2ND H'CAP — 1m 2f 95y
6:30 (6:30) (Class 5) (0-75,75) 4-Y-O+ **£2,911** (£866; £432; £216) **Stalls** Centre

Form RPR

-502 **1** **Lopito De Vega (IRE)**[16] 3804 4-8-10 **64**.................. GrahamGibbons 5 70
(David C Griffiths) *trckd ldr: effrt over 3f out: led over 2f out: hdd last 150yds: rallied and hung lft to ld again nr fin* **4/1**[2]

-065 **2** ¾ **Paddy's Rock (IRE)**[9] 4038 5-8-6 **60**.......................... AndrewElliott 6 64
(Lynn Siddall) *hld up detached in last: hdwy in centre over 3f out: upsides over 1f out: led last 150yds: hdd and no ex nr fin* **12/1**

-046 **3** ½ **Onda District (IRE)**[12] 3942 4-8-8 **69**.................. CallumRodriguez(7) 4 72
(Richard Ford) *s.i.s: sn mid-div: hdwy toward centre to trck ldrs over 3f out: upsides over 1f out: kpt on clsng stages* **16/1**

0126 **4** 1 **Best Tamayuz**[22] 3617 5-8-11 **65**.......................... BenCurtis 3 66
(Scott Dixon) *led: clr after 2f: hdd over 2f out: rallied fnl f: kpt on same pce* **11/1**

0554 **5** 1¾ **Omotesando**[7] 4138 6-8-9 **68**.......................... CharlieBennett(5) 8 66
(Mark Brisbourne) *trckd ldrs: upsides over 2f out: one pce fnl furiong* **6/1**[3]

0035 **6** 2¼ **The Character (IRE)**[7] 4138 5-9-0 **68**..................(p) RichardKingscote 1 61
(Tom Dascombe) *mid-div: pushed along over 3f out: one pce* **11/4**[1]

4512 **7** 2 **Pike Corner Cross (IRE)**[16] 3817 4-8-10 **67**.................. RobHornby(3) 7 57
(Ed de Giles) *hld up in rr: effrt 3f out: nvr a factor* **11/4**[1]

-005 **8** 4 **Symbolic Star (IRE)**[5] 4190 4-9-2 **75**.......................... PhilDennis(5) 2 57
(Barry Murtagh) *hld up in rr: hdwy to chse ldrs over 2f out: lost pl over 1f out* **20/1**

2m 19.63s (4.13) **Going Correction** +0.45s/f (Yiel) — 8 Ran SP% **114.3**
Speed ratings (Par 103): **101,100,100,99,97 96,94,91**
CSF £49.86 CT £688.82 TOTE £5.50: £2.20, £2.60, £4.70; EX 58.20 Trifecta £902.40.
Owner D Poulton & N Hildred **Bred** Mrs C Regalado-Gonzalez **Trained** Bawtry, S Yorks

FOCUS
All races run over the inside home straight. Allowing for rail movement on the bends, approximate race distances were: 5f 6f 218yds 7f 218yds 1m 2f 93yds 1m 5f 218yds. This modest handicap was run at a decent pace and they came stands' side off the home turn. A minor pb from the winner.

4378 APOLLOBET HOME OF CASHBACK OFFERS FILLIES' H'CAP — 5f
7:00 (7:00) (Class 5) (0-70,68) 3-Y-O+ **£2,911** (£866; £432; £216) **Stalls** High

Form RPR

241 **1** **Spirit Of Rosanna**[14] 3898 4-8-12 **56**....................(tp) RoystonFfrench 8 64
(Steph Hollinshead) *chsd ldr: led 2f out: drvn out* **4/1**[1]

0041 **2** ½ **Lydiate Lady**[14] 3882 4-8-12 **56**.......................... FrannyNorton 1 62
(Paul Green) *trckd ldrs: nt clr run 2f out: 2nd 1f out: kpt on same pce last 75yds* **5/1**[3]

0122 **3** ½ **Rose Eclair**[10] 4007 3-9-6 **68**..............................(b) DuranFentiman 9 71
(Tim Easterby) *dwlt: sn midfield stands' side: nt clr run over 1f out: styd on fnl 100yds: tk 3rd cl home* **9/2**[2]

6532 **4** ¾ **Enjoy Life (IRE)**[14] 3879 3-9-0 **62**.......................... ShaneGray 3 63
(Kevin Ryan) *edgd rt s: mid-div: effrt over 2f out: kpt on same pce fnl f* **5/1**[3]

6220 **5** hd **Potternello (IRE)**[12] 3953 4-9-9 **67**.......................... CharlesBishop 7 68
(Mick Channon) *in rr: nt clr run over 1f out: kpt on fnl 150yds* **11/2**

5230 **6** ¾ **Taffetta**[67] 2120 4-9-7 **65**..............................(p) BarryMcHugh 5 63
(Tony Coyle) *bmpd s: hdwy to chse ldrs over 2f out: kpt on same pce fnl f: fdd clsng stages* **15/2**

056 **7** 1¾ **Misu Moneypenny**[23] 3581 3-9-5 **67**.......................... BenCurtis 2 58
(Scott Dixon) *led: hdd 2f out: wknd appr fnl f* **16/1**

0006 **8** 5 **Two Turtle Doves (IRE)**[25] 3494 10-8-10 **54** oh4.............. RobertTart 6 28
(Michael Mullineaux) *outpcd in last: hdwy over 2f out: swtchd lft over 1f out: sn wknd* **25/1**

1060 **9** 1¾ **Your Gifted (IRE)**[10] 3994 9-8-12 **56**..............................(v) RaulDaSilva 4 24
(Lisa Williamson) *wnt rt s: sn mid-div: hdwy over 2f out: wknd fnl f* **16/1**

1m 4.22s (3.42) **Going Correction** +0.45s/f (Yiel)
WFA 3 from 4yo+ 4lb — 9 Ran SP% **114.3**
Speed ratings (Par 100): **90,89,88,87,86 85,82,74,72**
CSF £23.76 CT £92.76 TOTE £5.20: £1.60, £2.30, £1.30; EX 26.80 Trifecta £117.20.
Owner J Holcombe **Bred** Redmyre Bloodstock & Tweenhills Stud **Trained** Upper Longdon, Staffs

FOCUS
This fillies' sprint was competitive for the class. The first pair were always handy. Another pb from the winner, with the runner-up and third close to their recent form.

4379 BRITISH STALLION STUDS EBF NOVICE STKS (PLUS 10 RACE) — 7f
7:35 (7:35) (Class 4) 2-Y-O **£4,269** (£1,270; £634; £317) **Stalls** Low

Form RPR

1 **Star Of Rory (IRE)** 2-9-2 0.......................... RichardKingscote 4 75+
(Tom Dascombe) *dwlt: outpcd and pushed along: hdwy over 3f out: chsng ldrs and nt clr run over 1f out: swtchd lft: styd on to ld post* **16/1**

032 **2** nse **Wigan Warrior**[19] 3705 2-9-2 0.......................... JamieSpencer 3 75
(David Brown) *trckd ldrs: effrt and upsides over 2f out: led narrowly last 150yds: hdd post* **7/1**

41 **3** 1 **Londinium**[15] 3854 2-9-8 0.......................... FrannyNorton 1 78
(Mark Johnston) *led over 1f: trckd ldr: led over 2f out: hdd last 75yds: kpt on same pce* **3/1**[3]

34 **4** ½ **Jamacho**[23] 3562 2-9-2 0.......................... BenCurtis 2 71
(Brian Ellison) *w ldr: led over 5f out: hdd over 2f out: kpt on same pce fnl f* **14/1**

4 **5** 1½ **Lester Kris (IRE)**[16] 3808 2-9-2 0.......................... GrahamGibbons 5 67
(Richard Hannon) *wnt lft s: chsd ldrs: kpt on same pce over 1f out* **5/2**[2]

6 2¾ **Bay Of Poets (IRE)** 2-9-2 0.......................... PhillipMakin 6 61
(Charlie Appleby) *hld up in rr: smooth hdwy over 3f out: upsides over 2f out: wknd fnl f* **15/8**[1]

1m 33.73s (3.03) **Going Correction** +0.45s/f (Yiel) — 6 Ran SP% **113.4**
Speed ratings (Par 96): **100,99,98,98,96 93**
CSF £117.36 TOTE £10.10: £4.70, £3.00; EX 47.40 Trifecta £358.10.
Owner D R Passant & Hefin Williams **Bred** Kilcarn Stud **Trained** Malpas, Cheshire
■ Stewards' Enquiry : Franny Norton two-day ban; used whip in wrong place (31st Jul-1st Aug)

FOCUS
They went a respectable pace in this open novice event and yet again they came stands' side. They finished in a heap, and the second, third and fourth have all been rated as improvers.

4380 BILL ROTHWELL MEMORIAL CONDITIONS STKS 7f
8:05 (8:05) (Class 3) 3-Y-O+ **£8,086** (£2,406; £1,202) **Stalls** Low

Form RPR
0142 **1** **Jallota**[14] 3938 5-9-1 110 JamieSpencer 4 109+
(Charles Hills) *mde all: wnt clr appr fnl f: v easily* **1/3**[1]

3060 **2** 4 1/2 **Sirius Prospect (USA)**[58] 2391 8-9-1 97 (p) RobertWinston 5 94
(Dean Ivory) *trckd other pair: rdn to chse ldr 1f out: no ch w wnr* **7/2**[2]

05-0 **3** 2 1/2 **No Education**[118] 1024 3-9-2 105 DougieCostello 2 93
(Jo Hughes) *t.k.h: trckd wnr: drvn over 2f out: wknd fnl f* **8/1**[3]

1m 32.72s (2.02) **Going Correction** +0.45s/f (Yiel)
WFA 3 from 4yo+ 7lb 3 Ran SP% **108.4**
Speed ratings (Par 107): **106,100,98**
CSF £1.87 TOTE £1.20; EX 1.80 Trifecta £1.80.
Owner Mrs Fitri Hay **Bred** Barry Walters **Trained** Lambourn, Berks

FOCUS
This was hit by non-runners and it was a cakewalk for the winner. The winner has been rated close to form.

4381 GPW RECRUITMENT H'CAP 1m 6f
8:35 (8:35) (Class 4) (0-80,77) 4-Y-O+ **£5,175** (£1,540; £769; £384) **Stalls** Low

Form RPR
6/60 **1** **Lexi's Boy (IRE)**[40] 2971 8-9-7 77 (tp) DavidNolan 11 90
(Donald McCain) *prom: hdwy to ld over 3f out: kpt on fnl f: hld on nr fin* **20/1**

53-1 **2** hd **Jack Bear**[33] 3221 5-9-3 73 JamieSpencer 8 85
(Harry Whittington) *stdd s: hld up bhd in last: hdwy 6f out: chsd wnr over 2f out: drvn upsides over 1f out: no ex towards fin* **6/4**[1]

5432 **3** 7 **Brandon Castle**[16] 3798 4-9-5 75 DougieCostello 7 78
(Simon West) *hld up in rr: hdwy 8f out: chsng ldrs over 4f out: 3rd 2f out: kpt on same pce* **10/1**[3]

-002 **4** 2 1/2 **Moshe (IRE)**[10] 4004 5-9-6 76 PJMcDonald 2 76
(Philip Kirby) *mid-div: hdwy to trck ldrs over 7f out: drvn over 2f out: 4th and one pce 1f out* **14/1**

3230 **5** 2 1/2 **Rock On Bollinski**[22] 3602 6-9-2 72 (p) BenCurtis 1 69
(Brian Ellison) *s.i.s: reluctant and reminders after s: sn bhd: hdwy 7f out: outpcd and lost pl over 3f out: kpt on fnl 2f* **9/1**[2]

1020 **6** 1/2 **Braes Of Lochalsh**[8] 4101 5-9-6 76 DanielTudhope 10 72
(Jim Goldie) *stdd s: hld up in rr: sme hdwy 6f out: effrt over 3f out: kpt on one pce: nvr a factor* **10/1**[3]

-361 **7** 2 1/2 **Itlaaq**[22] 3602 10-9-0 77 (t) DanielleMooney[(7)] 5 70
(Michael Easterby) *mid-div: hdwy over 3f out: chsng ldrs over 2f out: wknd over 1f out* **10/1**[3]

0150 **8** 3/4 **Bohemian Rhapsody (IRE)**[24] 3533 7-9-5 75 (p) RichardKingscote 12 67
(Brendan Powell) *chsd ldrs: effrt over 3f out: wknd fnl 2f* **10/1**[3]

-630 **9** 3 3/4 **Zenafire**[22] 3602 7-8-12 68 (p) PatrickMathers 9 55
(Sarah Hollinshead) *mid-div: effrt over 3f out: wknd fnl 2f* **16/1**

311/ **10** 1 1/2 **Atalanta Bay (IRE)**[645] 7072 6-8-11 67 RoystonFfrench 6 52
(Marcus Tregoning) *chsd ldrs: drvn 4f out: lost pl over 1f out* **16/1**

-536 **11** 16 **Goldslinger (FR)**[21] 3636 4-9-5 75 RobertWinston 3 39
(Dean Ivory) *trckd ldrs: t.k.h: pushed along 7f out: lost pl over 2f out: sn eased and wl bhd* **10/1**[3]

33-5 **12** 17 **Slipper Satin (IRE)**[42] 2912 6-8-11 67 (tp) JasonHart 4 9
(Simon West) *led: hdd over 3f out: lost pl 2f out: sn heavily eased and wl bhd* **33/1**

3m 7.09s (5.09) **Going Correction** +0.45s/f (Yiel) 12 Ran SP% **121.6**
Speed ratings (Par 105): **103,102,98,97,96 95,94,93,91,90 81,72**
CSF £51.48 CT £350.19 TOTE £19.60: £4.90, £1.20, £3.00; EX 74.50 Trifecta £2344.20.
Owner T G Leslie **Bred** R S Cockerill (farms) Ltd & Peter Dodd **Trained** Cholmondeley, Cheshire

FOCUS
The first pair came a long way clear in this modest staying handicap. The level is a bit fluid, but the third has been rated close to his recent form.

4382 RACING UNION H'CAP 1m
9:05 (9:05) (Class 5) (0-75,74) 3-Y-O **£2,911** (£866; £432; £216) **Stalls** Low

Form RPR
0264 **1** **Blacklister**[14] 3906 3-9-0 67 CharlesBishop 6 73
(Mick Channon) *led: drvn over 2f out: kpt on fnl f: all out* **8/1**

0235 **2** shd **La Celebs Ville (IRE)**[7] 4139 3-9-2 69 (p) RichardKingscote 1 75
(Tom Dascombe) *trckd ldrs: styd far side over 4f out and racd alone: drvn 3f out: kpt on wl fnl f: jst failed* **3/1**[1]

1 **3** 3/4 **Tomahawk Kid**[28] 3400 3-9-0 70 GeorgeDowning[(3)] 5 74
(Ian Williams) *s.i.s: hdwy over 3f out: chsng ldrs over 2f out: edgd lft fnl f: kpt on same pce last 75yds* **4/1**[3]

1602 **4** 1 3/4 **Finelcity (GER)**[18] 3745 3-9-6 73 (b) DougieCostello 2 73
(Harry Dunlop) *trckd ldr: drvn along over 2f out: kpt on one pce* **7/2**[2]

0401 **5** 3/4 **Specialv (IRE)**[21] 3673 3-9-3 70 (p) StevieDonohoe 4 69
(Brian Ellison) *hld up in rr: hdwy over 3f out: chsng ldrs over 1f out: edgd lft and styd on fnl 150yds* **7/2**[2]

1405 **6** 4 1/2 **Frap**[19] 3710 3-8-7 60 FrannyNorton 8 48
(Richard Fahey) *in rr: effrt over 3f out: lost pl 2f out* **6/1**

600- **7** 22 **Mr Conundrum**[287] 6938 3-8-3 56 oh3 ow1 PatrickMathers 7
(Lynn Siddall) *mid-div: effrt over 3f out: lost pl 2f out: bhd whn heavily eased last 100yds* **33/1**

1m 46.54s (2.84) **Going Correction** +0.45s/f (Yiel) 7 Ran SP% **117.8**
Speed ratings (Par 100): **103,102,102,100,99 95,73**
CSF £33.64 CT £113.00 TOTE £8.50: £3.10, £2.50; EX 31.70 Trifecta £172.70.
Owner Box 41 Racing **Bred** Aston House Stud **Trained** West Ilsley, Berks

FOCUS
An ordinary 3yo handicap, run at a solid early pace. The winner has been rated close to his recent best, with a small pb from the runner-up.

T/Plt: £372.30 to a £1 stake. Pool: £60,259.01 - 118.15 winning units T/Qpdt: £32.90 to a £1 stake. Pool: £5,215.34 - 117.17 winning units **Walter Glynn**

4261 LINGFIELD (L-H)
Saturday, July 16

OFFICIAL GOING: Good to firm (8.1)
Wind: nil Weather: Fine, sunny

4383 WORLD MATCHPLAY DARTS AT 188BET H'CAP 1m 2f
5:35 (5:35) (Class 5) (0-75,75) 4-Y-O+ **£3,408** (£1,006; £503) **Stalls** Low

Form RPR
-312 **1** **Ickymasho**[32] 3257 4-9-10 75 FrederikTylicki 6 85
(Jonathan Portman) *sn led: mde all after: shkn up over 2f out: press and rdn 2f out: kpt on wl ins fnl f: on top at fin* **9/4**[1]

6321 **2** 1 1/4 **Zephyros (GER)**[10] 3997 5-8-4 62 GeorgeWood[(7)] 3 69
(David Bridgwater) *hld up in 7th: tk clsr order out wd on bnd: nudged into cl up 2nd 2f out: sn rdn and chsd wnr fnl f: hld fr over 110yds out* **3/1**[2]

2150 **3** 3 1/2 **Pink Ribbon (IRE)**[16] 3817 4-8-13 64 (p) SeanLevey 5 64
(Sylvester Kirk) *chsd wnr: shkn up 3f out: sn rdn: kpt on one pce after* **7/1**

6026 **4** 1 3/4 **Gannicus**[7] 4157 5-9-5 70 (tp) MartinDwyer 8 67
(Brendan Powell) *settled in 5th: rdn 3f out: sn no imp: one pce fnl f* **9/2**[3]

422/ **5** 1/2 **Little Buxted (USA)**[63] 7831 6-9-7 72 TimmyMurphy 4 68
(Jim Best) *racd in 4th: rdn 3f out: kpt on again wl ins fnl f* **33/1**

2315 **6** 1 3/4 **My Lord**[9] 4049 8-9-7 72 WilliamCarson 1 64
(Paddy Butler) *settled in 6th: t.k.h on bnd into st: rdn over 2f out: wknd ins fnl f* **20/1**

245 **7** 1 3/4 **I'm Harry**[37] 3064 7-9-3 68 (vt) SteveDrowne 7 57
(George Baker) *missed break and racd in rr: rdn 3f out: no imp: nvr involved* **10/1**

2-26 **8** 2 **Putaringonit (IRE)**[23] 3560 4-9-0 70 HectorCrouch[(5)] 2 55
(Jeremy Gask) *racd in 3rd: rdn 3f out on rail: losing grnd 2f out: wknd fnl f* **7/1**

2m 9.95s (-0.55) **Going Correction** +0.05s/f (Good) 8 Ran SP% **115.7**
Speed ratings (Par 103): **104,103,100,98,98 97,95,94**
CSF £9.24 CT £39.56 TOTE £2.60: £1.10, £1.20, £2.30; EX 9.30 Trifecta £50.40.
Owner C R Lambourne, M Forbes, D Losse **Bred** Allseasons Bloodstock **Trained** Upper Lambourn, Berks

FOCUS
A fair handicap, in which the winner was allowed an uncontested lead. The winner has been rated to her May AW win.

4384 NEIL FALCONERS 80TH BIRTHDAY CELEBRATION MAIDEN STKS 1m 3f 106y
6:10 (6:10) (Class 5) 3-Y-O+ **£3,234** (£962; £481; £240) **Stalls** High

Form RPR
240- **1** **Great Glen**[393] 3346 4-10-0 97 OisinMurphy 6 85+
(Ralph Beckett) *broke wl and sn led: hdd after 2f: chsd ldr after: shkn up and led 2f out: rdn over 1f out: sn clr: eased cl home* **4/7**[1]

502 **2** 3 **Beauty Sleep (IRE)**[29] 3350 3-8-12 77 MartinHarley 5 75
(William Haggas) *settled in 5th and rn in snatches: shkn up over 2f out: no imp fr over 1f out tl wl ins fnl f: fnd stride and styd on strly fr over 110yds out to take 2nd post* **7/2**[2]

4 **3** shd **Alberta (IRE)**[24] 3508 7-10-0 0 TimmyMurphy 3 80
(Jim Best) *settled in 6th: rdn over 2f out: tk 2nd over 1f out: one pce ins fnl f: lost 2nd post* **14/1**

522 **4** 4 1/2 **Mahfooz (IRE)**[59] 2368 3-9-3 80 MichaelJMMurphy 1 72
(Charles Hills) *chsd ldr tl led after 2f: rdn over 2f out: hdd 2f out: no ex over 1f out: wknd fnl f* **9/2**[3]

0-6 **5** 20 **Lord Aslan (IRE)**[10] 4001 3-8-10 0 WilliamCox[(7)] 4 39
(Andrew Balding) *settled in 4th: rdn 3f out: sn no imp: wknd and eased fr over 1f out* **50/1**

06 **6** 1/2 **Skiff**[10] 3996 4-9-9 0 JennyPowell[(5)] 9 39
(Brendan Powell) *settled in 7th: rdn over 3f out: lft bhd fr 2f out: one pce and eased fnl f* **50/1**

0 **7** 72 **Beauchamp Pasha**[44] 2816 3-9-3 0 WilliamCarson 7
(Harry Dunlop) *s.s: pushed up into in 3rd on outer: rdn 6f out: last over 3f out: eased wl over 1f out: t.o* **50/1**

2m 31.42s (-0.08) **Going Correction** +0.05s/f (Good)
WFA 3 from 4yo+ 11lb 7 Ran SP% **116.6**
Speed ratings (Par 103): **102,99,99,96,81 81,29**
CSF £3.07 TOTE £1.50: £1.40, £1.70; EX 3.10 Trifecta £12.80.
Owner J H Richmond-Watson **Bred** Lawn Stud **Trained** Kimpton, Hants

FOCUS
An ordinary maiden and the short-priced favourite made no mistake. The third is the key to the level.

4385 CONSULTUS CARE & NURSING CHARITY H'CAP 1m 6f
6:40 (6:41) (Class 6) (0-65,65) 3-Y-O+ **£2,587** (£770; £384; £192) **Stalls** Low

Form RPR
4056 **1** **Dltripleseven (IRE)**[10] 3998 3-7-12 52 oh2 ow1 JosephineGordon[(3)] 6 58+
(Richard Hughes) *rrd bhd stalls and uns rdr: briefly got loose: fractious in stalls after: broke wl and settled in 4th: gng wl 3f out: shkn up over 2f out: led over 1f out: sn in command and pushed out hands and heels ins fnl f* **13/2**

0/00 **2** 3 1/4 **Double Dealites**[10] 4019 6-8-9 46 oh1 KierenFox 7 47
(Jamie Poulton) *hld up in rr: reminders hdwy: pushed along 6f out: hld together on bnd w plenty to do: rdn along over 3f out: 4th over 1f out: styd on to take 2nd wl ins fnl f* **25/1**

6323 **3** 3/4 **Prince Of Islay (IRE)**[24] 3528 5-9-2 53 (v[1]) JimCrowley 4 53
(Amanda Perrett) *settled in 2nd: rdn over 3f out: led over 2f out: hdd over 1f out: kpt on one pce fnl f: lost 2nd wl ins fnl f* **3/1**[2]

600 **4** 1 3/4 **Madame Chow (IRE)**[18] 3736 3-8-13 64 (p) OisinMurphy 1 62+
(Ralph Beckett) *settled in 7th: ct bhd wkng horses turning into st: gd prog in st: kpt on one pce fr 1f out* **5/1**[3]

-063 **5** 4 1/2 **Stonecoldsoba**[67] 2126 3-8-7 58 JFEgan 3 50
(David Evans) *led: rdn and hdd wl over 2f out: briefly hung lft into rival sn after: wknd fr over 1f out* **2/1**[1]

050 **6** 1 1/4 **Alcanar (USA)**[45] 2790 3-9-0 65 WilliamCarson 8 55
(Michael Bell) *settled in 4th: rdn over 3f out: briefly hmpd by rival over 2f out: kpt on one pce fr 2f out: wknd fnl f* **7/1**

1050 **7** 18 **Fleetwood Poppy**[23] 3560 4-8-11 48 FrederikTylicki 2 15
(Michael Attwater) *settled in sixth: n.m.r on bnd: rdn over 3f out: sn hld* **25/1**

0-40 **8** 1 3/4 **Ragdollianna**[27] 2634 12-9-1 52 ShaneKelly 5 17
(Mark Hoad) *settled in 5th: rdn along over 4f out: sn lft bhd and no imp st* **25/1**

606 **9** *15* **Mister Showman**[24] 3508 3-8-12 **63**.................................... RyanClark 9 8
(Jonathan Portman) *racd in 3rd: nt handle bnds: rdn along 6f out: sn btn and weakend st* **16/1**

3m 11.67s (1.67) **Going Correction** +0.05s/f (Good)
WFA 3 from 4yo+ 14lb **9** Ran SP% **118.3**
Speed ratings (Par 101): **97,95,94,93,91 90,80,79,70**
CSF £155.34 CT £580.56 TOTE £9.00: £2.50, £7.00, £1.60; EX 166.20 Trifecta £800.00.
Owner Advantage Chemicals Holdings Ltd **Bred** Advantage Chemicals Holdings Ltd **Trained** Upper Lambourn, Berkshire

FOCUS
It paid to race prominently in this modest staying handicap. The third is among those who help set the level.

4386 FREE SPINS AT 188BET CASINO NURSERY H'CAP 6f
7:15 (7:15) (Class 5) 2-Y-O **£3,234** (£962; £481; £240) **Stalls** Centre

Form RPR

404 **1** **Whiteley (IRE)**[20] 3686 2-8-10 **63**.. JFEgan 7 67
(Mick Channon) *broke wl and settled under restraint in cl up 2nd one off rail: rdn and led 2f out: pressed over 1f out: kpt on and on top wl ins fnl f* **12/1**

5422 **2** *3/4* **Bazwind (IRE)**[2] 4287 2-8-13 **69**............................. KieranShoemark[(3)] 3 71
(David Evans) *racd in 3rd on outer: shkn up and upsides over 2f out: rdn 2f out: kpt on tl hld by wnr wl ins fnl f* **7/4**[1]

430 **3** *1 1/4* **Speed Freak**[32] 3261 2-9-7 **74**...(p) OisinMurphy 6 72
(Ralph Beckett) *sed awkwardly but got rail and sn led: rdn and hdd 2f out: sn hld and one pce ins fnl f* **3/1**[3]

5006 **4** *1/2* **Battle Of Wits (IRE)**[10] 4015 2-7-12 **54** oh1 ow1[1] JosephineGordon[(3)] 2 50
(J S Moore) *in rr on outer: rdn 2f out: upsides on outer over 1f out: wknd out of contention ins fnl f* **20/1**

050 **5** *1 1/4* **Wentwell Yesterday (IRE)**[11] 3971 2-8-8 **61**................ WilliamCarson 4 53
(Jamie Osborne) *t.k.h in 4th: rdn 2f out: no imp after* **10/1**

043 **6** *7* **At The Beach**[30] 3301 2-9-1 **68**.. SeanLevey 5 38
(Richard Hannon) *in rr: rdn and no imp fr 2f out* **5/2**[2]

1m 12.12s (0.92) **Going Correction** +0.05s/f (Good) **6** Ran SP% **111.5**
Speed ratings (Par 94): **95,94,92,91,90 80**
CSF £33.12 TOTE £12.20: £4.00, £1.40; EX 43.10 Trifecta £174.50.
Owner Peter Taplin & Susan Bunney **Bred** Yeomanstown Stud **Trained** West Ilsley, Berks

FOCUS
A fair nursery and the first three home were up there throughout.

4387 188BET EBF MAIDEN STKS 7f
7:50 (7:50) (Class 5) 2-Y-O **£3,881** (£1,155; £577; £288) **Stalls** Centre

Form RPR

34 **1** **Rebel De Lope**[28] 3388 2-9-5 0............................... MichaelJMMurphy 3 85+
(Charles Hills) *a.p on outside: gng wl and led jst over 2f out: stl travelling best over 1f out: rdn and scooted clr fnl f: easily* **2/1**[2]

2 *8* **Migyaas (USA)** 2-9-5 0.. WilliamCarson 1 63+
(Saeed bin Suroor) *s.s: in rr on rail: rdn 3f out: swtchd to centre over 1f out: kpt on one pce fnl f: tk 2nd 110yds out* **11/4**[3]

00 **3** *1 1/4* **Georgio (GER)**[14] 3872 2-8-12 0...................................... WilliamCox[(7)] 4 60
(Andrew Balding) *t.k.h bhd ldrs: led over 3f out: hdd jst over 2f out: kpt on one pce over 1f out: lost 3rd 110yds out* **25/1**

4 *3* **Contrast (IRE)** 2-9-5 0.. SeanLevey 6 52
(Richard Hannon) *broke wl and led tl hdd and dropped to rr-div over 5f out: rdn and no imp fr over 2f out* **13/8**[1]

5 *3* **Newport Place (IRE)** 2-9-0 0.. LucyKBarry[(5)] 5 44
(Jamie Osborne) *pressed ldr tl led over 5f out: hdd over 3f out: rdn and hdd 2f out: sn hld and one pce* **25/1**

0 **6** *8* **In The Spotlight (IRE)**[16] 3812 2-9-0 0.............................. ShaneKelly 7 17
(Richard Hughes) *tk fierce hold bhd ldrs: upsides on rail 3f out: shkn up over 2f out: sn wknd and hld fr over 1f out* **8/1**

1m 24.46s (1.16) **Going Correction** +0.05s/f (Good) **6** Ran SP% **116.9**
Speed ratings (Par 94): **95,85,84,81,77 68**
CSF £8.45 TOTE £2.90: £1.50, £1.90; EX 9.40 Trifecta £77.20.
Owner P K Siu **Bred** Azienda Agricola Antonio Celli **Trained** Lambourn, Berks

FOCUS
An interesting maiden featuring a couple of well-bred newcomers from major yards, but it was one-way traffic for the twice-raced winner. The third may hold the key to the level.

4388 188BET.CO.UK H'CAP 7f
8:20 (8:22) (Class 6) (0-65,65) 3-Y-O+ **£2,587** (£770; £384; £192) **Stalls** Centre

Form RPR

6024 **1** **Pyla (IRE)**[11] 3974 4-10-0 **65**.....................................(p[1]) LemosdeSouza 10 74
(Denis Quinn) *settled cl up in mid-div: shkn up over 2f out: led over 1f out: idling ins fnl f tl kpt on again whn pressed by runner-up: edgd sltly lft cl home but a holding on* **7/2**[2]

4613 **2** *nk* **Castle Talbot (IRE)**[18] 3739 4-9-11 **62**.............................(p) ShaneKelly 6 70
(Richard Hughes) *settled in mid-div: rdn 2f out: prog over 1f out to chse wnr: press wnr ins fnl f: carried sltly lft nr fin: hld* **11/4**[1]

000 **3** *3 1/4* **Infiniti (IRE)**[28] 3411 3-8-12 **56**.. SaleemGolam 7 52
(Rae Guest) *in rr: rdn over 2f out: kpt on wl fr over 1f out: tk 3rd ins fnl f* **20/1**

5244 **4** *1 1/4* **Knight Of The Air**[18] 3739 4-9-11 **62**.. JFEgan 4 58
(Mick Channon) *racd in 3rd early: rdn 2f out: kpt on tl wknd and lost 3rd ins fnl f* **6/1**

0350 **5** *1* **Whaleweigh Station**[3] 4278 5-8-12 **56**...................(p) GeorgeWood[(7)] 11 49
(J R Jenkins) *t.k.h in rr: rdn over 2f out: kpt on ins fnl f* **5/1**[3]

-002 **6** *5* **Arctic Flower (IRE)**[10] 4017 3-9-2 **60**................................ DannyBrock 5 37
(John Bridger) *chsd ldr: rdn 2f out: briefly led 2f out: hdd sn after and wknd ins fnl f* **16/1**

5156 **7** *3/4* **Hawk Moth (IRE)**[18] 3739 8-9-12 **63**.........................(p) TomMarquand 12 41
(John Spearing) *settled nr rr on rail: rdn over 3f out: mod hdwy after* **8/1**

2-50 **8** *nk* **Arcanista (IRE)**[11] 3989 3-8-12 **63**........................ StephenCummins[(7)] 9 37
(Richard Hughes) *s.s: pushed up wdst of all to lay prom 1/2-way: stl there 2f out: no ex fr over 1f out: wknd fnl f* **25/1**

20-5 **9** *3 3/4* **Royal Caper**[37] 3078 6-9-4 **58**.. DanielMuscutt[(3)] 3 25
(Miss Joey Ellis) *settled in mid-div bhd ldrs: rdn over 2f out: wknd fnl f* **14/1**

0-00 **10** *2 1/4* **Born To Fly (IRE)**[22] 3624 5-8-9 **46** oh1.............................(b) KierenFox 2 7
(Christine Dunnett) *in rr: a bhd* **50/1**

0634 **11** *2* **Lucky Leyf**[25] 3490 4-8-12 **49**.. SeanLevey 1 4
(Philip Hide) *led: rdn over 2f out: hdd 2f out: wknd qckly fr over 1f out* **25/1**

0014 **12** *4* **The Happy Hammer (IRE)**[54] 2542 10-9-0 **51**............ WilliamCarson 8
(Eugene Stanford) *a in rr: reminders in rr 1/2-way: nvr involved* **10/1**

1m 23.22s (-0.08) **Going Correction** +0.05s/f (Good)
WFA 3 from 4yo+ 7lb **12** Ran SP% **127.0**
Speed ratings (Par 101): **102,101,97,96,95 89,88,88,84,81 79,74**
CSF £14.04 CT £179.71 TOTE £4.50: £1.50, £1.80, £5.00; EX 17.30 Trifecta £276.70.
Owner Miss Amy Murphy **Bred** Stuart Weld **Trained** Newmarket, Suffolk
■ Stewards' Enquiry : Lemos de Souza caution; careless riding

FOCUS
A modest handicap which was fought out by a couple of in-form rivals. The race could be rated higher, but the winner has already been afforded a 2lb pb as it stands.

4389 £25 FREE BET AT 188BET AMATEUR RIDERS' H'CAP 6f
8:50 (8:52) (Class 6) (0-65,65) 3-Y-O+ **£2,634** (£810; £405) **Stalls** Centre

Form RPR

1052 **1** **One Big Surprise**[11] 3974 4-11-0 **65**..................................... MrSWalker 6 73
(Richard Hughes) *hld up bhd ldr on rail: shkn up 2f out: squeezed through gap gng wl over 1f out: nudged into ld 110yds out: cosily* **11/10**[1]

4555 **2** *3/4* **Limerick Lord (IRE)**[18] 3739 4-10-7 **58**..............................(p) MrRBirkett 3 64
(Julia Feilden) *pressed ldr: rdn and led 2f out: kpt on wl tl hdd 110yds out* **6/1**[2]

0045 **3** *1 3/4* **Showtime Star**[18] 3741 6-11-0 **65**............................. MissSBrotherton 5 65
(Gay Kelleway) *sn led: shkn up and hdd 2f out: rdn over 1f out: kpt on one pce* **13/2**[3]

5046 **4** *1* **Miss Inga Sock (IRE)**[24] 3514 4-10-3 **61**.............(p) MissJSpinkova[(7)] 4 58
(Eve Johnson Houghton) *settled bhd ldrs: rdn and briefly threatened over 1f out: sn hld and one pce nr fin* **8/1**

2000 **5** *3/4* **Compton Prince**[11] 3984 7-9-6 **50**................................(b) MrJCJones[(7)] 9 44
(Milton Bradley) *broke wl and marginal ldr tl restrained into rr: rdn 2f out: sme prog fr over 1f out: nrst fin* **25/1**

1031 **6** *1/2* **Fairy Mist (IRE)**[25] 3489 9-9-12 **56**................(b) MissTannyaBagoban[(7)] 7 49
(John Bridger) *in rr on rail: drifted to centre wl over 1f out: kpt on wl ins fnl f* **12/1**

2230 **7** *3* **Krazy Paving**[37] 3070 4-10-2 **53**.............................(b) MissJoannaMason 8 36
(Anabel K Murphy) *in rr: rdn over 3f out: nvr involved* **16/1**

6150 **8** *14* **Monsieur Jamie**[100] 1298 8-10-7 **65**...................................(v) MrSSayers[(7)] 2 3
(J R Jenkins) *prom: rdn over 2f out: sn lft bhd: wknd fnl f* **33/1**

6133 **9** *13* **Satchville Flyer**[2] 4321 5-10-3 **59**............................ MissEMacKenzie[(5)] 1
(David Evans) *t.k.h to post: racd out wd: rdn over 3f out: wknd qckly after: t.o* **6/1**[2]

1m 12.48s (1.28) **Going Correction** +0.05s/f (Good) **9** Ran SP% **121.0**
Speed ratings (Par 101): **93,92,89,88,87 86,82,64,46**
CSF £8.70 CT £32.65 TOTE £2.20: £1.10, £2.30, £2.40; EX 9.90 Trifecta £40.50.
Owner Withyslade **Bred** Withyslade **Trained** Upper Lambourn, Berkshire

FOCUS
Just a modest handicap for amateur riders.
T/Plt: £24.80 to a £1 stake. Pool: £57,565.69 - 1692.33 winning units T/Qpdt: £13.20 to a £1 stake. Pool: £5,747.53 - 322.15 winning units **Cathal Gahan**

4349 NEWBURY (L-H)
Saturday, July 16

OFFICIAL GOING: Good to firm (7.4)
Wind: light, half against Weather: mainly sunny, light cloud

4390 BATHWICK TYRES MAIDEN STKS (PLUS 10 RACE) (C&G) 6f 8y
2:00 (2:01) (Class 4) 2-Y-O **£4,690** (£1,395; £697; £348) **Stalls** Centre

Form RPR

2 **1** **Majeste**[12] 3954 2-9-0 0.. SeanLevey 6 85+
(Richard Hannon) *stdd after s: t.k.h: hld up in tch in midfield: effrt over 1f out: hdwy u.p to chse ldr 100yds out: led fnl 50yds: styd on wl and gng away at fin* **7/2**[2]

2 **2** *2* **Hathiq (IRE)**[29] 3356 2-9-0 0.. PaulHanagan 8 79
(Owen Burrows) *t.k.h: hld up in tch in midfield: clsd to trck ldrs over 3f out: rdn to ld over 1f out: drvn ins fnl f: hdd 50yds out: sn btn and wknd towards fin* **11/8**[1]

3 *hd* **Serengeti Sky (USA)** 2-9-0 0...(t) JamesDoyle 3 78
(Charlie Appleby) *trckd ldrs: effrt over 1f out: unable qck ent fnl f: kpt on towards fin* **5/1**[3]

6 **4** *shd* **Glorious Artist (IRE)**[16] 3813 2-9-0 0..................... MichaelJMMurphy 5 78
(Charles Hills) *chsd ldr: clsd and upsides over 3f out: rdn and ev ch wl over 1f out tl unable qck jst ins fnl f: lost 2nd and hung lft 100yds out: one pce after* **16/1**

3 **5** *3/4* **Via Egnatia (USA)**[22] 3619 2-9-0 0................................. RobertHavlin 4 75+
(John Gosden) *stdd s: t.k.h: hld up in tch in rr: clsd over 2f out: effrt over 1f out: kpt on same pce ins fnl f* **7/1**

3 **6** *2* **Malcolm The Pug (IRE)**[8] 4075 2-9-0 0............................... PatDobbs 1 69
(Richard Hannon) *led and clr tl over 3f out: hdd over 1f out: sn rdn and hung bdly lft: wknd ins fnl f* **8/1**

7 *6* **Intimate Art (IRE)** 2-9-0 0... DavidProbert 7 50
(Andrew Balding) *hld up in tch in last pair: effrt ent fnl 2f: sn struggling and outpcd over 1f out: wknd fnl f* **25/1**

8 *9* **Henry Did It (IRE)** 2-9-0 0.. JFEgan 2 21
(Tony Carroll) *in tch in midfield: rdn and lost pl 1/2-way: bhd over 1f out* **40/1**

1m 13.1s (0.10) **Going Correction** +0.05s/f (Good) **8** Ran SP% **116.8**
Speed ratings (Par 96): **101,98,98,97,96 94,86,74**
CSF £8.91 TOTE £4.60: £1.60, £1.10, £2.20; EX 11.00 Trifecta £38.90.
Owner Mohamed Saeed Al Shahi **Bred** Marston Stud **Trained** East Everleigh, Wilts

FOCUS
There had been only light drizzle in the past 24 hours and the jockeys said the ground was again quick. The rail from the 8f to the 5f on the round course had been moved in by three yards from the meeting the previous day. There were some useful colts with decent connections in this opening maiden - the first three came into this with Group-race entries - but a few of the main players were keen and/or awkward so the bare form probably isn't as good as it might have been.

4391 BATHWICK TYRES EBF BREEDERS' SERIES FILLIES' H'CAP 1m (S)
2:30 (2:33) (Class 2) (0-100,95) 3-Y-O+
£18,675 (£5,592; £2,796; £1,398; £699; £351) **Stalls** Centre

Form RPR

-211 **1** **Golden Stunner (IRE)**[28] 3410 3-8-13 **88**.............................. JimCrowley 7 98+
(Ralph Beckett) *wnt lft s: chsd ldr tl rdn to ld over 2f out: wnt lft and idling in front 1f out: fnd ex to hold off chalr whn pressed wl ins fnl f: rdn out* **3/1**[2]

15-0 **2** ½ **Bahaarah (IRE)**[77] 1867 3-9-4 **93** SeanLevey 1 101
(Richard Hannon) *stdd s: t.k.h: hld up in tch in last pair: clsd 2f out: effrt to chse wnr and swtchd lft ent fnl f: styd on and str chal wl ins fnl f: hld towards fin* **12/1**

2-03 **3** 2 **Shwaimsa (IRE)**[8] 4080 3-8-13 **88** PatDobbs 2 91
(Richard Hannon) *t.k.h: hld up in tch in midfield: effrt over 2f out: drvn over 1f out: styd on ins fnl f to go 3rd fnl 50yds: nvr enough pce to rch ldrs* **7/1**

2661 **4** ¾ **Hidden Rebel**[23] 3551 4-9-0 **81** ConnorBeasley 8 84
(Alistair Whillans) *t.k.h: hld up in tch in midfield: effrt to press wnr over 2f out: unable qck and flashed tail u.p jst over 1f out: styd on same pce ins fnl f: lost 3rd fnl 50yds* **11/1**

-610 **5** 2¼ **Gratzie**[11] 3979 5-10-0 **95** GeorgeBaker 6 93
(Mick Channon) *stdd s: t.k.h: hld up in tch in last pair: effrt 2f out: sn rdn: styd on same pce and no imp fnl f* **12/1**

06-5 **6** nk **Jelly Monger (IRE)**[15] 3860 4-9-9 **90** JamesDoyle 4 87
(Dominic Ffrench Davis) *led: rdn and hdd over 2f out: sn outpcd u.p: wl hld and plugged on same pce ins fnl f* **25/1**

1311 **7** nse **Singyoursong (IRE)**[7] 4130 3-8-6 **81** KieranO'Neill 3 76
(David Simcock) *stdd s: t.k.h: hld up in tch in last trio: effrt ent fnl 2f: no imp and drifted lft 1f out: wl hld and plugged on same pce after* **11/4**[1]

2-31 **8** 2¼ **Alyday**[29] 3350 3-8-4 **82** JosephineGordon(3) 5 72
(Sir Michael Stoute) *chsd ldrs: rdn over 2f out: lost pl u.p over 1f out: wknd fnl f* **4/1**[3]

1m 38.34s (-1.36) **Going Correction** +0.05s/f (Good)
WFA 3 from 4yo+ 8lb **8** Ran SP% **111.7**
Speed ratings (Par 96): **108,107,105,104,102 102,102,99**
CSF £36.23 CT £228.18 TOTE £3.60: £1.60, £3.20, £1.90; EX 35.50 Trifecta £262.40.
Owner Sutong Pan **Bred** Fergus Cousins **Trained** Kimpton, Hants

FOCUS
A decent fillies' handicap. The third has been rated close to her latest.

4392 BET365 STKS (REGISTERED AS THE STEVENTON STAKES) (LISTED RACE) 1m 2f 6y

3:00 (3:03) (Class 1) 3-Y-O+

£20,982 (£7,955; £3,981; £1,983; £995; £499) **Stalls** Low

Form RPR

51-3 **1** **Scottish (IRE)**[51] 2626 4-9-4 113 JamesDoyle 3 116+
(Charlie Appleby) *sn led and mde rest: travelling best 2f out: rdn and readily wnt 2 l clr ent fnl f: r.o wl: comf* **10/11**[1]

1/00 **2** 1¾ **Berkshire (IRE)**[29] 3377 5-9-4 107 (b[1]) JimCrowley 6 111
(Paul Cole) *stdd s: t.k.h: hld up in 6th: clsd and nt clr run 2f out: sn swtchd rt and rdn: hdwy 1f out: styd on u.p to chse wnr wl ins fnl f: kpt on for clr 2nd but no ch w wnr* **16/1**

240- **3** 1½ **Trip To Paris (IRE)**[230] 8042 5-9-4 116 GrahamLee 8 108
(Ed Dunlop) *chsd ldrs tl wnt 2nd 5f out: rdn over 2f out: unable qck w wnr over 1f out: styd on same pce after: lost 2nd wl ins fnl f* **12/1**

1003 **4** ½ **Gm Hopkins**[15] 3860 5-9-7 112 RobertHavlin 4 110
(John Gosden) *t.k.h: chsd wnr tl 5f out: styd handy: effrt wl over 1f out: styd on same pce and no imp ins fnl f* **13/2**[2]

6502 **5** 2½ **Spark Plug (IRE)**[15] 3860 5-9-4 104 (p) SeanLevey 2 102
(Brian Meehan) *taken down early: hld up in tch in midfield: rdn and hdwy ent fnl 2f: unable qck over 1f out: wknd ins fnl f* **15/2**[3]

4346 **6** hd **Master Carpenter (IRE)**[42] 2894 5-9-4 110 FrederikTylicki 1 102
(Rod Millman) *in tch in midfield: clsd to chse ldrs 4f out: rdn ent fnl 2f: unable qck over 1f out: wknd ins fnl f* **15/2**[3]

06-4 **7** shd **Chil The Kite**[21] 3672 7-9-4 108 GeorgeBaker 7 101
(Hughie Morrison) *stdd s: t.k.h: hld up in tch in rr: clsd 3f out: effrt wl over 1f out: sn no imp: wknd ins fnl f* **8/1**

2m 7.23s (-1.57) **Going Correction** -0.025s/f (Good) **7** Ran SP% **113.9**
Speed ratings (Par 111): **105,103,102,102,100 99,99**
CSF £17.69 TOTE £1.80: £1.70, £4.00; EX 15.90 Trifecta £94.40.
Owner Godolphin **Bred** Knocktoran Stud **Trained** Newmarket, Suffolk

FOCUS
This was run over 13 yards further than advertised. With question marks over most of the others, the winner stood out on form, hence his short price, and was allowed a totally uncontested lead, so this probably isn't form to be strong on. The winner has been rated to form.

4393 BET365 HACKWOOD STKS (GROUP 3) 6f 8y

3:35 (3:36) (Class 1) 3-Y-O+

£34,026 (£12,900; £6,456; £3,216; £1,614; £810) **Stalls** Centre

Form RPR

4-10 **1** **The Tin Man**[28] 3385 4-9-4 114 TomQueally 3 117+
(James Fanshawe) *stdd s: hld up in rr: clsd and nt clr run over 1f out: hdwy ent fnl f: nudged along and qcknd to ld ins fnl f: a doing enough under tender handling in front: comf* **11/4**[1]

0614 **2** hd **Divine (IRE)**[8] 4114 5-9-4 108 FrederikTylicki 6 114
(Mick Channon) *s.i.s: hld up in tch in last quartet: hdwy 2f out: clsd and nt clr run jst over 1f out: sn swtchd rt and hdwy to chse wnr fnl 100yds: clsng on wnr at fin but a hld* **20/1**

-530 **3** 1¾ **Raucous**[31] 3269 3-8-13 102 (t) JimCrowley 4 107
(William Haggas) *hld up in tch in midfield: effrt 2f out: drvn ent fnl f: led jst ins fnl f: sn hdd and styd on same pce fnl 100yds* **20/1**

4650 **4** 1¼ **Aeolus**[32] 3244 5-9-4 108 GeorgeBaker 2 104
(Ed Walker) *stdd and dropped in bhd after s: hld up in tch in last quartet: hdwy 2f out: rdn to press ldrs ent fnl f: no ex ins fnl f: outpcd fnl 100yds* **10/1**

0504 **5** ½ **Lord Of The Land (IRE)**[23] 3566 5-9-4 102 (v[1]) DanielTudhope 9 103
(David O'Meara) *chsd ldr tl rdn to ld jst over 2f out: drvn over 1f out: hdd jst ins fnl f: sn outpcd: wknd wl ins fnl f* **20/1**

11/4 **6** nk **Charming Thought**[34] 3195 4-9-4 116 (t) JamesDoyle 10 102
(Charlie Appleby) *chsd ldrs: effrt 2f out: drvn and unable qck ent fnl f: wknd ins fnl f* **5/1**[2]

-136 **7** nk **Aclaim (IRE)**[35] 3165 3-8-13 97 (t) GrahamLee 11 100
(Martyn Meade) *hld up in tch in midfield: effrt wl over 1f out: keeping on same pce whn nt clr run and swtchd lft ins fnl f: kpt on but no threat to ldrs after* **33/1**

-040 **8** shd **Buratino (IRE)**[21] 3655 3-8-13 112 RobertHavlin 7 100
(Mark Johnston) *wl in tch in midfield: rdn ent fnl 2f: drvn and unable qck 1f out: wknd ins fnl f* **11/1**

3-14 **9** 1 **Ibn Malik (IRE)**[31] 3269 3-8-13 109 PaulHanagan 8 96
(Charles Hills) *t.k.h: chsd ldrs: rdn ent fnl 2f: unable qck and btn: wknd and wl hld whn eased towards fin* **5/1**[2]

6-05 **10** 2¾ **Illuminate (IRE)**[29] 3338 3-8-10 110 PatDobbs 13 85
(Richard Hannon) *hld up in tch in midfield: effrt wl over 1f out: sn rdn and no imp: wknd ins fnl f* **12/1**

3315 **11** 8 **Mr Lupton (IRE)**[21] 3655 3-8-13 111 JamieSpencer 5 62
(Richard Fahey) *stdd and swtchd rt after s: hld up in tch in last quartet: effrt 2f out: sn swtchd rt and no hdwy u.p over 1f out: wknd fnl f* **8/1**[3]

3233 **12** 4½ **Watchable**[21] 3655 6-9-4 109 (b) LukeMorris 12 49
(David O'Meara) *racd freely: led tl rdn and hdd over 1f out: sn lost pl: bhd 1f out: wknd and eased wl ins fnl f* **16/1**

1m 11.61s (-1.39) **Going Correction** +0.05s/f (Good)
WFA 3 from 4yo+ 5lb **12** Ran SP% **119.3**
Speed ratings (Par 113): **111,110,108,106,106 105,105,105,103,100 89,83**
CSF £67.65 TOTE £3.50: £1.40, £6.20, £7.60; EX 58.30 Trifecta £516.10.
Owner Fred Archer Racing - Ormonde **Bred** Mrs Elizabeth Grundy **Trained** Newmarket, Suffolk

FOCUS
A quality Group 3 and they went hard enough, with the first four finishers being held up early - the winner came from last. The winner didn't need to improve to win.

4394 WEATHERBYS SUPER SPRINT 5f 34y

4:10 (4:12) (Class 2) 2-Y-O

£122,925 (£52,275; £24,600; £14,750; £9,825; £7,375) **Stalls** Centre

Form RPR

11 **1** **Mrs Danvers**[20] 3686 2-8-0 0 LukeMorris 13 89+
(Jonathan Portman) *stdd and wnt rt s: hld up wl in tch: clsd to chse ldr jst over 2f out: rdn to ld over 1f out: clr and edgd rt jst ins fnl f: r.o wl: rdn out* **9/2**[1]

1000 **2** 1¼ **Stormy Clouds (IRE)**[15] 3858 2-8-4 0 (b[1]) KieranO'Neill 16 88+
(Richard Hannon) *hmpd s: hld up towards rr: effrt 2f out: hdwy over 1f out: styd on wl u.p ins fnl f: chsd wnr wl ins fnl f: kpt on but nvr a threat to wnr* **20/1**

2123 **3** 1¼ **Clem Fandango (FR)**[31] 3270 2-8-0 0 AndrewMullen 8 80+
(Keith Dalgleish) *hld up in tch in midfield: effrt 2f out: rdn and hdwy to chse ldrs ent fnl f: chsd wnr ins fnl f: styd on but no imp: lost 2nd wl ins fnl f* **9/2**[1]

424 **4** nse **Diable D'Or (IRE)**[34] 3196 2-8-5 0 EdwardGreatrex 12 84
(Eve Johnson Houghton) *led: rdn and hung rt over 1f out: sn hdd and unable qck: styd on same pce and lost 2 pls ins fnl f* **50/1**

1 **5** ¾ **Spiritual Lady**[22] 3613 2-8-0 0 CamHardie 18 77
(Philip McBride) *hmpd s: hld up wl in tch: effrt over 1f out: styd on same pce ins fnl f* **6/1**[2]

421 **6** ½ **Super Julius**[35] 3128 2-8-13 0 ShaneKelly 2 88
(Eve Johnson Houghton) *chsd ldrs: unable qck u.p over 1f out: styd on same pce ins fnl f* **14/1**

0162 **7** nk **Letmestopyouthere (IRE)**[15] 3852 2-8-10 0 SamJames 15 84
(David Evans) *hld up in midfield: hdwy u.p over 1f out: kpt on ins fnl f: no threat to wnr* **50/1**

3155 **8** 1 **Simmie (IRE)**[21] 3663 2-8-0 0 JimmyQuinn 5 70
(Sylvester Kirk) *midfield: effrt 2f out: drvn over 1f out: kpt on same pce and no imp fnl f* **16/1**

2 **9** ¾ **Six Strings**[23] 3562 2-9-0 0 TonyHamilton 6 81
(Richard Fahey) *hld up in midfield: effrt 2f out: unable qck and no imp over 1f out: hld and styd on same pce fnl f* **12/1**

0220 **10** 1 **Cappananty Con**[10] 4015 2-8-8 0 RobertHavlin 11 72
(Dean Ivory) *hld up in tch in midfield: effrt 2f out: drvn and no hdwy over 1f out: hld and styd on same pce ins fnl f* **100/1**

6202 **11** ½ **Dolokhov**[8] 4124 2-8-3 0 (b) JosephineGordon 1 65
(J S Moore) *midfield: effrt 2f out: sme hdwy u.p over 1f out: sn no imp: wknd ins fnl f* **66/1**

1 **12** nse **Lady In Question (IRE)**[32] 3261 2-8-5 0 PaulHanagan 3 67
(Richard Fahey) *in tch in midfield: effrt and unable qck 1f out: wknd ins fnl f* **10/1**

230 **13** nk **Perfect Madge (IRE)**[29] 3336 2-8-12 0 (p) JamieSpencer 22 73
(Kevin Ryan) *hld up in rr: effrt 2f out: sme hdwy u.p over 1f out: no imp fnl f: nvr trbld ldrs* **25/1**

314 **14** 3¼ **Boundsy (IRE)**[33] 3208 2-8-6 0 SamHitchcott 4 58
(Richard Fahey) *chsd ldr tl jst over 2f out: sn losing pl and short of room: wknd fnl f* **50/1**

2 **15** nk **Lucky Mistake (IRE)**[7] 4161 2-8-4 0 ConnorBeasley 9 52
(Richard Fahey) *in tch in midfield: rdn and lost pl ent fnl 2f: wl btn over 1f out: wknd fnl f* **8/1**[3]

3522 **16** ½ **In First Place**[7] 4167 2-8-11 0 GrahamLee 20 57
(Richard Fahey) *in tch in midfield: rdn jst over 2f out: no rspnse and lost pl over 1f out: wknd fnl f* **33/1**

621 **17** 2¾ **Hope Solo (IRE)**[7] 4133 2-8-2 0 JamesSullivan 17 38
(Tim Easterby) *hmpd s: midfield but nvr on terms w ldrs: rdn 2f out: drvn and no hdwy over 1f out: wknd fnl f* **16/1**

23 **18** nse **Good Time Ahead (IRE)**[25] 3495 2-8-8 0 JFEgan 14 44+
(Richard Fahey) *hmpd s: hld up in midfield: lost pl qckly ent fnl 2f: wl btn over 1f out* **25/1**

224 **19** nk **Carson City**[12] 3939 2-8-13 0 PatrickMathers 24 48+
(Richard Fahey) *a towards rr: effrt but stl plenty to do whn swtchd lft fr over 1f out: no prog: n.d* **66/1**

321 **20** 1¾ **Fair Power (IRE)**[25] 3485 2-8-8 0 DavidProbert 25 37
(Sylvester Kirk) *nvr bttr than midfield: effrt 2f out: sn hung lft and btn: wknd over 1f out* **33/1**

2160 **21** 2½ **Copper Knight (IRE)**[32] 3247 2-9-0 0 (b) JamesDoyle 21 40
(Hugo Palmer) *midfield: rdn over 1f out: no rspnse and sn btn: wknd and wl bhd whn eased wl ins fnl f* **25/1**

5014 **22** 1¾ **Ventura Secret (IRE)**[15] 3839 2-8-10 0 JimCrowley 19 40
(Tim Easterby) *midfield: rdn and unable qck over 1f out: sn btn and heavily eased ins fnl f* **66/1**

210 **23** 2 **Mister Sunshine (IRE)**[34] 3196 2-8-3 0 RyanTate 23 9
(Clive Cox) *a in rr: hung lft and lost tch over 1f out* **33/1**

1m 1.19s (-0.21) **Going Correction** +0.05s/f (Good) **23** Ran SP% **133.4**
Speed ratings (Par 100): **103,101,99,98,97 96,96,94,93,92 91,91,90,85,85 84,79,79,79,76 72,69,66**
CSF £101.57 TOTE £5.30: £2.40, £4.30, £2.30; EX 121.40 Trifecta £689.70.
Owner Turf Club 2014 **Bred** M A Burton & Connie Hopper **Trained** Upper Lambourn, Berks

The Form Book, Raceform Ltd, Newbury, RG14 5SJ

FOCUS
A typically huge field but not much got into it and middle to stands' side was the place to be. A minor pb from the runner-up.

4395 BET365 H'CAP 7f (S)
4:45 (4:47) (Class 2) (0-110,107) 3-Y-O+£16,172 (£4,812; £2,405; £1,202) Stalls Centre

Form RPR
4050 1 **Boomshackerlacker (IRE)**[31] 3273 6-9-0 **97**............ FergusSweeney 7 104
(George Baker) *hld up in tch in midfield: clsd and swtchd lft jst over 1f out: hdwy u.p to chal 100yds out: led fnl 50yds: r.o: rdn out* **9/1**
2406 2 *nk* **Dark Emerald (IRE)**[21] 3664 6-9-9 **106**......................(vt) RichardMullen 5 112
(Brendan Powell) *trckd ldrs: swtchd rt and effrt 2f out: wnt 2nd over 1f out: clsd u.p to chal jst ins fnl f: led 75yds out: sn hdd: r.o but hld towards fin* **7/1**[3]
30-0 3 *1 1/4* **Windfast (IRE)**[21] 3664 5-9-3 **107**.............................. JordanUys[(7)] 6 110
(Brian Meehan) *t.k.h: led: rdn wl over 1f out: hrd pressed and drvn 1f out: edgd lft and hdd 75yds out: no ex: edgd lft and outpcd wl ins fnl f* **20/1**
-150 4 *1/2* **C Note (IRE)**[31] 3269 3-8-9 **99**.. DavidProbert 1 97
(Martyn Meade) *t.k.h: trckd ldrs: effrt ent fnl 2f: sn drvn: clsd to press ldrs jst ins fnl f: unable qck and one pce fnl 100yds: squeezed for room nr fin* **4/1**[2]
00/0 5 *nk* **Quixote (GER)**[14] 3910 6-8-13 **95**............................ PatDobbs 4 96
(Tony Carroll) *stdd and dropped in bhd after s: hld up in rr: rdn ent fnl 2f: outpcd over 1f out: rallied ins fnl f: styd on strly fnl 100yds* **25/1**
2150 6 *hd* **Pure Diamond**[31] 3274 3-8-13 **103**............................ JamesDoyle 9 100
(Saeed bin Suroor) *stdd s: hld up in tch: clsd 1/2-way: effrt u.p to chse ldrs over 1f out: unable qck 1f out: wknd fnl 100yds* **10/1**
15-2 7 *shd* **Dragon Mall (USA)**[63] 2250 3-8-12 **102**......................... JamieSpencer 8 101
(David Simcock) *stdd and sltly hmpd leaving stall: sn swtchd rt and hld up in last trio: rdn and hdwy over 1f out: drvn and pressed ldrs 1f out: no ex ins fnl f: hld and eased towards fin* **2/1**[1]
0-60 8 *2 3/4* **Ruwaiyan (USA)**[21] 3656 7-9-0 **97**...............................(p) GrahamLee 3 89
(James Tate) *t.k.h: hld up in tch in midfield: effrt over 1f out: unable qck 1f out: wknd ins fnl f: b.b.v* **8/1**
-004 9 *1 1/2* **Room Key**[45] 2796 4-8-10 **93**...............................(v[1]) EdwardGreatrex[(3)] 2 84
(Eve Johnson Houghton) *t.k.h: chsd ldr: rdn and ev ch 2f out: sn drvn and lost pl: bhd whn short of room jst ins fnl f: sn wknd* **8/1**
1m 24.93s (-0.77) **Going Correction** +0.05s/f (Good)
WFA 3 from 4yo+ 7lb **9** Ran SP% **115.8**
Speed ratings (Par 109): **106,105,104,103,103 103,102,99,98**
CSF £70.43 CT £1229.79 TOTE £9.00: £2.10, £2.50, £4.70; EX 71.30 Trifecta £406.00.
Owner PJL Racing **Bred** Miss Elaine Marie Smith **Trained** Manton, Wilts

FOCUS
Some old favourites in here, but a lack of well-handicapped runners. The runner-up has been rated to form.

4396 GRUNDON RECYCLING H'CAP 1m 2f 6y
5:15 (5:15) (Class 3) (0-95,91) 3-Y-O+
£7,470 (£2,236; £1,118; £559; £279; £140) Stalls Low

Form RPR
0/00 1 **Stars Over The Sea (USA)**[14] 3889 5-9-10 **87**............. GeorgeBaker 4 99
(Mark Johnston) *mde all: rdn and fnd ex over 1f out: in command and styd on strly ins fnl f: comf* **5/1**
-112 2 *3* **Dommersen (IRE)**[35] 3156 3-9-4 **91**............................ RobertHavlin 1 97
(John Gosden) *hld up in tch in 4th: swtchd rt 3f out: sn rdn: hdwy to chse wnr over 1f out: no imp and one pce fnl f* **5/2**[2]
3-00 3 *2* **Ladurelli (IRE)**[30] 3304 4-9-6 **83**.. LukeMorris 6 85
(Paul Cole) *hld up in tch in 5th: effrt on inner 2f out: drvn in 3rd 1f out: styd on same pce and no imp after* **12/1**
-435 4 *1 1/2* **Danehill Kodiac (IRE)**[30] 3300 3-8-13 **86**........................... PatDobbs 3 85
(Richard Hannon) *chsd on inner: rdn to cl ent fnl 2f: unable qck over 1f out: 4th and btn whn wandered rt 1f out: one pce after* **4/1**[3]
21 5 *2 1/4* **Most Celebrated (IRE)**[19] 3723 3-8-11 **84**...................... JamesDoyle 5 79
(Saeed bin Suroor) *racd in 3rd: effrt ent fnl 2f: no ex u.p over 1f out: wknd ins fnl f* **2/1**[1]
10-0 6 *16* **Senrima (IRE)**[42] 2897 4-9-9 **86**................................. JimmyFortune 7 49
(Brian Meehan) *stdd s: hld up in last: effrt over 2f out: sn btn: wl bhd over 1f out* **20/1**
2m 5.35s (-3.45) **Going Correction** -0.025s/f (Good)
WFA 3 from 4yo+ 10lb **6** Ran SP% **111.0**
Speed ratings (Par 107): **112,109,108,106,105 92**
CSF £17.47 TOTE £5.70: £2.10, £1.80; EX 19.50 Trifecta £129.50.
Owner R S Brookhouse **Bred** W S Farish & Watership Down Stud **Trained** Middleham Moor, N Yorks

FOCUS
This was run over 13 yards further than advertised. A muddling race, the winner allowed to set a pace to suit. The winner has been rated back to his 3yo form, with the runner-up to a small pb and the third to his AW latest.
T/Plt: £268.30 to a £1 stake. Pool: £129,411.57 - 352.1 winning units T/Qpdt: £102.40 to a £1 stake. Pool: £10,027.27 - 72.44 winning units **Steve Payne**

4356 NEWMARKET (R-H)
Saturday, July 16

OFFICIAL GOING: Good to firm (7.6)
Wind: Fresh across Weather: Sunny spells

4397 LETTERGOLD MAIDEN AUCTION FILLIES' STKS (PLUS 10 RACE) 7f
2:10 (2:11) (Class 5) 2-Y-O £3,881 (£1,155; £577; £288) Stalls Low

Form RPR
4 1 **Kiruna Peak (IRE)**[9] 4054 2-8-8 0.................................. OisinMurphy 5 71
(Mick Channon) *chsd ldrs: pushed along 1/2-way: rdn to chse ldr over 1f out: styd on u.p to ld wl ins fnl f* **5/2**[1]
23 2 *shd* **Conqueress (IRE)**[22] 3592 2-8-10 0............................... MartinHarley 6 73
(Tom Dascombe) *w ldr tl led 1/2-way: rdn over 1f out: hdd wl ins fnl f: styd on* **6/1**[3]
3 *1 1/4* **Jive Talking (IRE)** 2-8-13 0...................................... JamesMcDonald 7 73
(Michael Bell) *hld up: hdwy 1/2-way: rdn over 1f out: styd on* **10/3**[2]
4 *hd* **Starlite Sienna (IRE)** 2-8-11 0................................... GeorgeChaloner 8 70
(Richard Fahey) *chsd ldrs: rdn over 1f out: kpt on* **8/1**
36 5 *3 3/4* **Ocean Temptress**[64] 2211 2-8-8 0.......................................[1] DannyBrock 2 57
(John Ryan) *s.i.s: hdwy over 5f out: jnd ldr 1/2-way: rdn over 2f out: no ex fnl f* **22/1**
23 6 *1 1/4* **Quick Thought (IRE)**[10] 4016 2-8-10 0......................... WilliamCarson 9 56
(Dr Jon Scargill) *led towards centre to 1/2-way: remained handy: rdn over 1f out: wknd ins fnl f* **12/1**
7 *1 1/4* **Carducci** 2-8-11 0.. TomMarquand 10 53
(Richard Hannon) *s.i.s: outpcd: styd on ins fnl f: nvr nrr* **7/1**
8 *3 3/4* **Silver Chimes** 2-8-7 0.. MartinDwyer 4 39
(William Knight) *sn outpcd* **16/1**
9 *1 3/4* **Bianca Minola (FR)** 2-8-0 0.. RPWalsh[(7)] 3 34
(David Menuisier) *s.i.s: outpcd: bhd whn hung lft over 2f out* **25/1**
4 10 *1/2* **Speciale Di Giorno (IRE)**[21] 3640 2-8-10 0.................. DarryllHolland 11 36
(Marco Botti) *sn pushed along in rr: wknd 1/2-way* **16/1**
0 11 *37* **Tigerfish (IRE)**[54] 2535 2-8-6 0.................................... NickyMackay 1
(William Stone) *plld hrd and prom: rdn and wknd over 2f out* **50/1**
1m 26.0s (0.30) **Going Correction** -0.075s/f (Good) **11** Ran SP% **119.2**
Speed ratings (Par 91): **95,94,93,93,88 87,86,81,79,79 36**
CSF £17.65 TOTE £3.50: £1.20, £1.80, £2.00; EX 13.90 Trifecta £27.20.
Owner M Channon **Bred** Kildaragh Stud **Trained** West Ilsley, Berks

FOCUS
Far side course in use. Satlls on far side except 1m2f and 1m4f, centre. The re-positioning of the bend into the home straight increased the distance of the 1m2f and 1m4f races by 15yds. The ground had been watered, but "fast" and "firm" were the descriptions given by Oisin Murphy and Martin Dwyer respectively. An ordinary maiden and it proved quite a grind for these 2yos. A nice step forward from the winner, but the fifth offers some perspective in what appeared to be a pretty ordinary race for the track.

4398 EBF BREEDERS' SERIES FILLIES' H'CAP 6f
2:40 (2:44) (Class 3) (0-95,93) 3-Y-O+ £12,938 (£3,850; £1,924; £962) Stalls Low

Form RPR
5-31 1 **Silver Rainbow (IRE)**[16] 3815 4-9-9 **90**..................... JamesMcDonald 7 106
(Charles Hills) *a.p: rdn over 1f out: r.o to ld wl ins fnl f: sn clr* **4/1**[1]
-221 2 *2 3/4* **David's Duchess (IRE)**[18] 3754 3-8-3 **75**....................... NickyMackay 3 81
(Richard Fahey) *chsd ldrs: led over 1f out: rdn: hdd and unable qck wl ins fnl f* **8/1**
0611 3 *3/4* **Guishan**[23] 3575 6-9-7 **91**.. TimClark[(3)] 2 96
(Michael Appleby) *led: rdn and hdd over 1f out: no ex wl ins fnl f* **13/2**[2]
4230 4 *1* **Stellarta**[21] 3671 5-9-2 **83**... AdamKirby 15 84+
(Michael Blanshard) *hld up: hdwy u.p and hung lft over 1f out: nt rch ldrs* **12/1**
-143 5 *1/2* **Futoon (IRE)**[15] 3847 3-8-4 **76**.. JoeFanning 14 75
(Kevin Ryan) *chsd ldrs: rdn over 1f out: styd on same pce ins fnl f* **16/1**
0401 6 *3/4* **Florenza**[21] 3643 3-8-7 **79**.. AndrewElliott 1 75
(Chris Fairhurst) *prom: rdn over 2f out: sn hung lft: styd on same pce fr over 1f out* **16/1**
0-35 7 *1/2* **Mustique (IRE)**[32] 3266 3-8-7 **79**................................ GeorgeChaloner 6 74
(Richard Fahey) *hld up: pushed along and hdwy 1/2-way: rdn over 1f out: styd on same pce fnl f* **14/1**
040- 8 *3/4* **Spiraea**[252] 7755 6-8-12 **79**... TomMarquand 8 72
(Andrew Reid) *mid-div: hdwy over 1f out: sn rdn: no ex ins fnl f* **33/1**
1-00 9 *3 1/4* **Veena (FR)**[45] 2789 3-8-8 **80**.. WilliamCarson 9 62
(David Simcock) *s.i.s: rdn and swtchd rt over 1f out: nvr on terms* **14/1**
6601 10 *nk* **Gran Canaria Queen**[19] 3714 7-8-13 **83**.......... RachelRichardson[(3)] 4 65
(Tim Easterby) *dwlt: rdn 1/2-way: a in rr* **8/1**
024- 11 *3 3/4* **Welsh Rose**[245] 7861 3-8-0 **75**..................................... NoelGarbutt[(3)] 11 44
(William Muir) *prom: rdn over 1f out: wknd fnl f* **25/1**
-062 12 *1 1/2* **Calypso Choir**[36] 3105 3-8-11 **83**................................... MartinDwyer 10 47
(Sylvester Kirk) *plld hrd: w ldrs: rdn over 1f out: wknd fnl f* **7/1**[3]
-000 13 *3/4* **Souville**[56] 2474 5-8-11 **85**.. SamuelClarke[(7)] 12 48
(Chris Wall) *plld hrd and prom: rdn over 2f out: wknd over 1f out* **16/1**
6-0P 14 *3/4* **Queen's Pearl (IRE)**[36] 3116 4-9-11 **92**......................... HarryBentley 13 52
(Roger Varian) *hld up: rdn 1/2-way: wknd over 1f out* **10/1**
1m 10.72s (-1.78) **Going Correction** -0.075s/f (Good)
WFA 3 from 4yo+ 5lb **14** Ran SP% **122.6**
Speed ratings (Par 104): **108,104,103,102,101 100,99,98,94,93 88,86,85,84**
CSF £35.45 CT £210.60 TOTE £4.60: £1.80, £2.50, £2.90; EX 40.30 Trifecta £105.80.
Owner R J Tufft **Bred** Austin Curran **Trained** Lambourn, Berks

FOCUS
A useful handicap, the right horses coming to the fore. The third helps set the standard.

4399 NEXUS INFRASTRUCTURE H'CAP 1m
3:15 (3:16) (Class 2) (0-105,102) 3-Y-O+
£28,012 (£8,388; £4,194; £2,097; £1,048; £526) Stalls Low

Form RPR
0532 1 **Franklin D (USA)**[35] 3157 4-9-4 **96**......................(v) JamesMcDonald 12 112
(Michael Bell) *chsd ldrs: led over 2f out: rdn clr fnl f: easily* **7/2**[1]
-500 2 *6* **Hors De Combat**[31] 3273 5-9-10 **102**.............................. OisinMurphy 10 104
(James Fanshawe) *hld up in tch: rdn over 1f out: chsd wnr ins fnl f: no imp* **13/2**[3]
-042 3 *1 1/2* **Ifwecan**[8] 4104 5-9-0 **92**... PatCosgrave 8 91
(Martin Smith) *chsd ldrs: rdn over 1f out: styd on same pce fnl f* **7/1**
2-12 4 *shd* **Firmament**[30] 3303 4-8-10 **91**................................. ShelleyBirkett[(3)] 7 89
(David O'Meara) *hld up: hdwy over 2f out: rdn over 1f out: styd on same pce* **17/2**
2515 5 *hd* **Pactolus (IRE)**[112] 1089 5-8-5 **88**..............................(t) AaronJones[(5)] 11 86
(Stuart Williams) *hld up: hdwy over 3f out: rdn over 1f out: styd on same pce fnl f* **28/1**
0-00 6 *nk* **Miracle Of Medinah**[49] 2684 5-9-1 **93**.............................. DaneO'Neill 4 90
(Mark Usher) *s.i.s: hld up: hdwy over 2f out: sn rdn: no ex ins fnl f* **12/1**
6100 7 *5* **Bathos (IRE)**[8] 4108 3-8-3 **89**.. NickyMackay 5 73
(Mark Johnston) *prom: rdn over 2f out: wknd fnl f* **10/1**
5210 8 *3 1/4* **Al Khan (IRE)**[49] 2684 7-9-0 **92**...................................... HarryBentley 3 70
(Kevin Ryan) *prom: rdn over 2f out: wknd over 1f out* **20/1**
-652 9 *1* **Grand Inquisitor**[20] 3688 4-9-3 **95**...................................(p) TedDurcan 2 71
(Sir Michael Stoute) *hld up: rdn over 2f out: wknd fnl f* **9/2**[2]
2106 10 *2 1/4* **Dutch Uncle**[12] 3950 4-8-9 **87**...................................(p) TomMarquand 13 58
(Ed Dunlop) *hld up: hdwy over 3f out: rdn and wknd over 1f out* **20/1**
4460 11 *1/2* **Solar Deity (IRE)**[31] 3273 7-9-3 **95**...............................(p) MartinHarley 1 65
(Jane Chapple-Hyam) *hld up: rdn over 2f out: a in rr* **25/1**
0400 12 *1* **Riflescope (IRE)**[9] 4062 3-8-5 **91**.................................... JoeFanning 9 56
(Mark Johnston) *chsd ldrs tl rdn and wknd over 1f out* **14/1**
0/6- 13 *30* **Stomachion (IRE)**[444] 1799 6-9-3 **95**............................... AdamKirby 6
(John Butler) *led over 5f: sn wknd* **33/1**
1m 36.47s (-3.53) **Going Correction** -0.075s/f (Good)
WFA 3 from 4yo+ 8lb **13** Ran SP% **120.0**
Speed ratings (Par 109): **114,108,106,106,106 105,100,97,96,94 93,92,62**
CSF £23.89 CT £154.71 TOTE £3.40: £1.70, £2.60, £2.30; EX 25.50 Trifecta £103.00.
Owner W J and T C O Gredley **Bred** Grapestock LLC **Trained** Newmarket, Suffolk

FOCUS
What had looked quite an open handicap was taken apart by the favourite. The fourth and fifth have been rated as running turf personal bests.

4400 NEWSELLS PARK STUD STKS (REGISTERED AS THE APHRODITE STAKES) (LISTED RACE) (F&M) 1m 4f
3:50 (3:51) (Class 1) 3-Y-O+

£20,982 (£7,955; £3,981; £1,983; £995; £499) **Stalls** Centre

Form RPR

-014 **1** **Forever Popular (USA)**[31] 3278 4-9-2 84......................(p) DaneO'Neill 6 105
(William Haggas) *hld up: hdwy over 2f out: chsd ldr over 1f out: sn rdn: led wl ins fnl f: styd on* **16/1**

-344 **2** ¾ **Twitch (IRE)**[34] 3202 4-9-2 97..................................(p) JamesMcDonald 8 104
(Hugo Palmer) *led 1f: chsd ldr tl led again over 3f out: rdn over 1f out: hdd wl ins fnl f: styd on* **15/2**

5-63 **3** 7 **Miss Marjurie (IRE)**[49] 2690 6-9-2 108.......................... OisinMurphy 10 95
(Denis Coakley) *hld up: pushed along over 3f out: hdwy over 2f out: rdn and edgd rt over 1f out: wknd wl ins fnl f* **5/1[3]**

-212 **4** 2 ¼ **Stockhill Diva**[21] 3665 6-9-2 93.. TedDurcan 3 89
(Brendan Powell) *hld up: hdwy over 2f out: rdn over 1f out: wknd ins fnl f* **11/1**

001 **5** 2 ½ **Tioga Pass**[57] 2433 5-9-2 97..(p) MartinHarley 7 85
(Paul Cole) *s.i.s: hld up: bhd and pushed along 4f out: hdwy u.p over 1f out: wknd ins fnl f* **16/1**

-646 **6** 2 ¼ **Sound Of Freedom (IRE)**[22] 3608 4-9-2 98..................... AdamKirby 9 82
(Marco Botti) *prom: racd keenly: rdn over 3f out: wknd over 1f out* **11/1**

-215 **7** 1 ¼ **Shall We (IRE)**[30] 3297 3-8-4 105....................................... JoeFanning 2 80+
(Sir Michael Stoute) *chsd ldrs tl rdn and wknd over 1f out* **3/1[2]**

6401 **8** nk **Edge Of Reason**[30] 3318 3-8-4 75................................ AntonioFresu 11 79
(Ed Walker) *s.i.s: rcvrd to ld after 1f: hdd over 3f out: rdn and wknd over 1f out* **50/1**

51 **9** ¾ **Taqaareed (IRE)**[17] 3781 3-8-4 92............................... TomMarquand 4 78+
(John Gosden) *trckd ldrs: plld hrd: rdn over 2f out: wknd over 1f out* **5/2[1]**

2m 39.92s (7.02) **Going Correction** +0.05s/f (Good)
WFA 3 from 4yo+ 12lb **9** Ran SP% **112.4**
Speed ratings (Par 111): **78,77,72,71,69 68,67,67,66**
CSF £125.99 TOTE £21.30: £4.50, £2.00, £1.60; EX 163.50 Trifecta £965.30.
Owner Lael Stable **Bred** Mr And Mrs M Roy Jackson **Trained** Newmarket, Suffolk

FOCUS
Race distance increased by 15yds. No great gallop on here and the market leaders disappointed. The front pair came clear but the winner was rated just 84 coming into the race. A clear pb from the winner.

4401 GREENALL'S GIN MAIDEN STKS 7f
4:25 (4:32) (Class 5) 3-Y-O+ **£3,881** (£1,155; £577; £288) **Stalls** Low

Form RPR

2 **1** **Trenches (USA)**[22] 3609 3-9-5 0............................... JamesMcDonald 8 83+
(Charlie Appleby) *w ldrs: led wl over 1f out: rdn and edgd lft ins fnl f: jst hld on* **15/8[1]**

4- **2** hd **In The City**[344] 5115 3-9-5 0... PatCosgrave 11 82+
(William Haggas) *hld up: hdwy over 2f out: rdn to chse wnr ins fnl f: r.o* **15/8[1]**

6 **3** 1 ¼ **Lord Of The North (IRE)**[19] 3723 3-9-5 0..................... DarryllHolland 1 79
(Gay Kelleway) *hld up: hdwy over 1f out: sn rdn: r.o* **66/1**

55- **4** 1 ¼ **Masarzain (IRE)**[330] 5585 3-9-5 0................................ DaneO'Neill 14 75
(Owen Burrows) *chsd ldrs: rdn and swtchd lft over 1f out: styd on same pce ins fnl f* **14/1[3]**

00 **5** 2 **Where Next**[39] 2998 3-9-5 0... HayleyTurner 7 70
(Henry Candy) *prom: rdn and hung lft over 1f out: no ex ins fnl f* **66/1**

00 **6** 3 ¼ **Luang Prabang (IRE)**[23] 3572 3-9-0 0.......................... HarryBentley 16 56
(Chris Wall) *mid-div: hdwy over 1f out: sn rdn: no ex fnl f* **66/1**

03 **7** ¾ **German Whip**[21] 3669 3-9-5 0....................................... DougieCostello 3 59
(Gary Moore) *mid-div: shkn up over 2f out: nt trble ldrs* **66/1**

8 1 ¼ **Manshood (IRE)** 3-9-5 0..(b[1]) OisinMurphy 13 56
(William Haggas) *w ldrs: led 1/2-way: hdd wl over 1f out: hung lft and wknd wl ins fnl f* **14/1[3]**

3 **9** 2 **Song Of Namibia (IRE)**[38] 3023 5-9-12 0........................ TedDurcan 4 53
(Sir Michael Stoute) *led to 1/2-way: rdn over 1f out: wknd fnl f* **4/1[2]**

05 **10** ½ **Gomez**[10] 4027 3-9-5 0... SaleemGolam 5 49
(Rae Guest) *hld up: rdn over 2f out: hung lft and wknd over 1f out* **66/1**

53 **11** 2 ¼ **Ramblow**[96] 1383 3-8-7 0.. GeorgiaCox(7) 9 38
(William Haggas) *hld up: rdn over 2f out: wknd over 1f out* **40/1**

B **12** 7 **Squire Hockey**[28] 3406 3-9-5 0.................................. StevieDonohoe 12 24
(Gary Moore) *mid-div: lost pl over 4f out: wknd over 2f out* **100/1**

0 **13** 2 ¾ **Poetic Guest**[23] 3572 3-9-5 0... AdamKirby 10 17
(George Margarson) *prom: shkn up over 2f out: wknd over 1f out* **80/1**

0 **14** 1 ¼ **Mr Piglet**[23] 3572 3-9-5 0... JoeFanning 2 13
(William Jarvis) *hld up: wknd wl over 1f out* **14/1**

-0 **15** 16 **Happisburgh Man**[23] 3572 4-9-12 0.............................. NickyMackay 6
(Dr Jon Scargill) *got loose on the way to post: s.i.s: hung rt and looked rel to r: sn wl bhd* **80/1**

1m 25.28s (-0.42) **Going Correction** -0.075s/f (Good)
WFA 3 from 4yo+ 7lb **15** Ran SP% **118.7**
Speed ratings (Par 103): **99,98,97,95,93 89,89,87,85,84 82,74,71,69,51**
CSF £4.72 TOTE £3.00: £1.40, £1.50, £9.00; EX 6.00 Trifecta £234.70.
Owner Godolphin **Bred** Dorothy A Matz **Trained** Newmarket, Suffolk
■ Sunset Dream was withdrawn. Price at time of withdrawal 25/1. Rule 4 does not apply

FOCUS
Just a fair maiden. It's been rated around the first two.

4402 PRICE BAILEY CHARTERED ACCOUNTANTS H'CAP 7f
4:55 (4:59) (Class 3) (0-90,88) 3-Y-O+ **£7,762** (£2,310; £1,154; £577) **Stalls** Low

Form RPR

5522 **1** **Dutch Law**[7] 4132 4-9-11 85... OisinMurphy 3 92+
(Hughie Morrison) *s.i.s and pushed along early in rr: shkn up 1/2-way: swtchd rt over 1f out: rdn and hdwy sn after: r.o to ld nr fin* **11/4[1]**

000 **2** nse **Free Code (IRE)**[23] 3566 5-9-13 87............................... HarryBentley 5 93
(David Barron) *disp ld 2f: remained handy: rdn and ev ch fr over 1f out: r.o* **14/1**

2306 **3** nk **Surewecan**[8] 4089 4-8-12 72... JoeFanning 8 77
(Mark Johnston) *chsd ldrs: rdn to ld over 1f out: hdd nr fin* **14/1**

0020 **4** 2 ¼ **Valley Of Fire**[8] 4079 4-10-0 88.................................. PatCosgrave 2 87
(William Haggas) *chsd ldrs: rdn over 2f out: styd on same pce ins fnl f* **7/1**

0030 **5** ½ **Athletic**[8] 4089 7-9-0 74...(v) TomMarquand 4 72
(Andrew Reid) *hld up: hdwy over 1f out: sn rdn: styd on same pce ins fnl f* **9/1**

-245 **6** ½ **Arab Poet**[35] 3155 3-9-5 86... StevieDonohoe 6 79
(Sir Michael Stoute) *hld up in tch: plld hrd: rdn over 1f out: styd on same pce ins fnl f* **5/1[3]**

-043 **7** 1 ¾ **Reputation (IRE)**[14] 3885 3-9-2 83........................(v[1]) JamesMcDonald 7 72
(John Quinn) *disp ld tl wnt on 5f out: rdn and hdd over 1f out: no ex whn n.m.r ins fnl f* **4/1[2]**

0124 **8** 23 **Plucky Dip**[8] 4109 5-9-11 85... AdamKirby 1 44
(John Ryan) *hld up: racd keenly: hdwy 1/2-way: rdn over 2f out: wknd and eased fnl f* **7/1**

1m 25.25s (-0.45) **Going Correction** -0.075s/f (Good)
WFA 3 from 4yo+ 7lb **8** Ran SP% **111.7**
Speed ratings (Par 107): **99,98,98,96,95 94,92,66**
CSF £40.36 CT £448.21 TOTE £2.90: £1.20, £3.70, £4.20; EX 44.20 Trifecta £591.40.
Owner Raymond Tooth **Bred** Raymond Clive Tooth **Trained** East Ilsley, Berks

FOCUS
This competitive-looking handicap turned into a sprint nearing the two-furlong pole. The second and third have been rated to form.

4403 GREENALL'S GIN H'CAP 1m 2f
5:30 (5:30) (Class 3) (0-90,88) 3-Y-O **£7,762** (£2,310; £1,154; £577) **Stalls** Centre

Form RPR

-123 **1** **Shaan (IRE)**[58] 2412 3-9-5 88....................................... TomMarquand 4 97
(Richard Hannon) *mde all: set stdy pce tl qcknd over 3f out: rdn over 1f out: styd on* **12/1**

1 **2** 1 ¼ **Lusory**[51] 2614 3-9-3 86...(t) JamesMcDonald 5 92
(Charlie Appleby) *a.p: rdn and edgd rt over 1f out: sn rdn: styd on same pce wl ins fnl f* **5/4[1]**

-145 **3** nse **Mainstream**[24] 3532 3-9-4 87....................................... StevieDonohoe 3 93
(Sir Michael Stoute) *s.i.s: hld up: hdwy over 1f out: rdn and edgd lft ins fnl f: carried hd high: styd on same pce* **7/1**

2-11 **4** 2 ¼ **Muzdawaj**[29] 3365 3-9-2 85... DaneO'Neill 1 87
(William Haggas) *chsd ldrs: rdn and hung lft over 1f out: styd on same pce ins fnl f* **11/4[2]**

01 **5** 5 **Staunch**[37] 3066 3-9-4 87.. AdamKirby 6 82
(Clive Cox) *chsd ldr: rdn over 2f out: nt clr run over 1f out: wknd ins fnl f* **9/2[3]**

2m 7.96s (2.46) **Going Correction** +0.05s/f (Good) **5** Ran SP% **109.5**
Speed ratings (Par 104): **92,91,90,89,85**
CSF £27.58 TOTE £12.60: £4.00, £1.30; EX 30.90 Trifecta £115.20.
Owner Al Shaqab Racing **Bred** J F Tuthill **Trained** East Everleigh, Wilts

FOCUS
Race distance increased by 15yds. This good-quality 3yo handicap was a tactical affair. The third may not be straightforward but has been rated to the better view of his form for now.
T/Jkpt: Not Won. T/Plt: £39.40 to a £1 stake. Pool: £105,160.13 - 1947.83 winning tickets
T/Qpdt: £19.90 to a £1 stake. Pool: £6,470.02 - 239.8 winning tickets **Colin Roberts**

3947 RIPON (R-H)
Saturday, July 16

OFFICIAL GOING: Good (good to firm in places; 8.4)
Wind: Fresh half behind Weather: Sunny periods and blustery

4404 DOBSONS GASKETS (S) STKS 6f
2:05 (2:08) (Class 6) 2-Y-O **£3,234** (£962; £481; £240) **Stalls** High

Form RPR

6325 **1** **Racemaker**[11] 3971 2-9-0 0... CharlesBishop 1 65
(Mick Channon) *trckd ldrs: cl up 1/2-way: chal over 1f out: sn rdn: led ent fnl f: sn drvn and edgd lft: kpt on wl towards fin* **5/4[1]**

406 **2** ½ **Coco La Belle (IRE)**[14] 3881 2-8-9 0................................[1] DavidAllan 2 59
(Tim Easterby) *sn led: jnd and rdn over 1f out: hdd narrowly ent fnl f: sn drvn and ev ch tl no ex last 100yds* **9/1**

205 **3** 7 **Playful Trickster (IRE)**[51] 2612 2-8-9 0.......................... BenCurtis 3 38
(Tom Dascombe) *in tch on outer: effrt over 2f out: rdn over 1f out: drvn and kpt on fnl f* **7/1[3]**

034 **4** ¾ **Jester Spirit (IRE)**[28] 3396 2-9-0 0..................................(p) LiamJones 8 40
(Tom Dascombe) *in tch: pushed along 1/2-way and sn chsng ldrs: rdn over 1f out: drvn and one pce fnl f* **16/1**

0 **5** 1 **Amy Gardner**[14] 3902 2-8-9 0.. JackGarritty 4 32
(James Given) *chsd ldrs: rdn along wl over 2f out: sn one pce* **16/1**

3006 **6** ¾ **Born To Boogie**[23] 3561 2-8-9 0..................................... BarryMcHugh 9 30
(Chris Grant) *chsd ldrs on inner: rdn along 1/2-way: sn drvn and wknd* **14/1**

063 **7** ¾ **Precious Skye (IRE)**[10] 4000 2-8-9 0.......................... KeaganLatham 7 28
(David O'Meara) *chsd ldrs: rdn along wl over 1f out: sn drvn and wknd* **8/1**

2 **8** 9 **Yorkshire Star (IRE)**[14] 3897 2-8-9 0.......................... NathanEvans(5) 6 6
(Bill Turner) *chsd ldrs: rdn along and lost pl bef 1/2-way: sn bhd* **6/1[2]**

9 10 **Anshika (IRE)** 2-8-2 0.. RobertDodsworth(7) 5
(Ollie Pears) *green: sn rdn along and outpcd in rr: bhd fr 1/2-way* **25/1**

1m 12.33s (-0.67) **Going Correction** -0.15s/f (Firm) **9** Ran SP% **114.6**
Speed ratings (Par 92): **98,97,88,87,85 84,83,71,58**
CSF £13.25 TOTE £2.10: £1.10, £2.80, £2.10; EX 13.30 Trifecta £43.10.
Owner M Channon **Bred** R W K Lewis **Trained** West Ilsley, Berks

FOCUS
After riding in the opener Jack Garritty and Charles Bishop called the ground good to firm, while Liam Jones said it was "good, quick ground". A modest event in which the first two finished a long way clear. They and the third home came from the three lowest stalls.

4405 BRITISH STALLION STUDS EBF MAIDEN STKS (PLUS 10 RACE) 5f
2:35 (2:37) (Class 4) 2-Y-O **£5,175** (£1,540; £769; £384) **Stalls** High

Form RPR

4542 **1** **The Nazca Lines (IRE)**[10] 4002 2-9-5 0.......................(v) JasonHart 4 79
(John Quinn) *led: pushed along and hdd over 2f out: rdn to ld again over 1f out: drvn ins fnl f: kpt on wl towards fin* **5/1[3]**

033 **2** nk **Madame Bounty (IRE)**[24] 3511 2-9-0 0......................... PhillipMakin 9 73
(Ed Walker) *trckd ldng pair: hdwy over 1f out: rdn to chal ins fnl f: ev ch tl drvn and nt qckn towards fin* **15/8[1]**

5 **3** 1 ¾ **Whigwham**[17] 3772 2-9-0 0... BarryMcHugh 3 67
(Richard Fahey) *trckd ldrs: hdwy over 1f out: sn rdn: kpt on same pce fnl f* **12/1**

23 **4** *1* **Climax**[14] 3873 2-9-0 0 FrannyNorton 10 63
(Mark Johnston) *cl up on stands' rail: led wl over 2f out: rdn and hdd over 1f out: sn drvn and kpt on same pce* **7/2**[2]
02 **5** *5* **Sheepscar Lad (IRE)**[14] 3873 2-9-5 0 RoystonFfrench 2 50
(Nigel Tinkler) *dwlt and towards rr: hdwy over 2f out: sn rdn and n.d* **15/2**
6 *3 1/4* **Wilderswood (IRE)** 2-9-5 0 PJMcDonald 5 38
(Ann Duffield) *chsd ldrs: rdn along 2f out: sn wknd* **11/1**
00 **7** *3/4* **Cosmic Sky**[14] 3902 2-9-0 0 DavidAllan 7 31
(Tim Easterby) *rrd s: midfield: rdn along over 2f out: nvr a factor* **22/1**
65 **8** *hd* **African Grey**[14] 3874 2-9-5 0 (e) GrahamGibbons 6 35
(David Barron) *dwlt: a in rr* **25/1**
0 **9** *1/2* **Lightoller (IRE)**[9] 4053 2-9-5 0 CharlesBishop 8 33
(Mick Channon) *a towards rr* **25/1**
00 **10** *4 1/2* **Operational**[24] 3516 2-9-5 0 JackGarritty 1 17
(Jedd O'Keeffe) *a towards rr* **50/1**

58.65s (-1.35) **Going Correction** -0.15s/f (Firm) **10** Ran SP% **115.5**
Speed ratings (Par 96): **104,103,100,99,91 85,84,84,83,76**
CSF £13.99 TOTE £5.20: £1.30, £1.10, £5.00; EX 17.10 Trifecta £234.70.
Owner Ross Harmon **Bred** Rathasker Stud **Trained** Settrington, N Yorks

FOCUS
William Haggas has won this maiden in recent seasons with the smart pair Rosdhu Queen and Ornate, but this looked a modest race. It has been rated around the winner and runner-up.

4406 SKY BET GO-RACING-IN-YORKSHIRE SUMMER FESTIVAL H'CAP 1m 1f 170y
3:10 (3:10) (Class 4) (0-85,81) 3-Y-O- **£6,931** (£2,074; £1,037; £519; £258) **Stalls** Low

Form RPR
1522 **1** **Town's History (USA)**[15] 3853 3-9-4 **81** MartinLane 3 89+
(Saeed bin Suroor) *trckd ldrs: hdwy over 2f out: swtchd rt: rdn along and squeezed through on inner wl over 1f out: sn rdn: chal ent fnl f: drvn and kpt on to ld last 100yds* **9/4**[1]
2504 **2** *hd* **Juste Pour Nous**[16] 3814 3-8-12 **80** RossCoakley(5) 7 87
(Mark Johnston) *hld up and bhd: gd hdwy on wd outside wl over 2f out: rdn to take slt ld jst over 1f out: sn drvn: edgd rt ins fnl f: hdd last 100yds: kpt on* **9/2**[3]
3145 **3** *2* **Carnageo (FR)**[12] 3950 3-8-12 **75** JackGarritty 2 78
(Richard Fahey) *trckd ldrs: hdwy over 3f out: led over 2f out: sn rdn: hdd and drvn jst over 1f out: kpt on same pce ins fnl f* **7/2**[2]
33-5 **4** *2 3/4* **Zabeel Star (IRE)**[51] 2620 4-9-5 **77** AdamMcNamara(5) 4 74
(Graeme McPherson) *hld up: hdwy over 3f out: chsd ldrs over 2f out: sn rdn and ev ch: drvn and wknd over 1f out* **18/1**
6621 **5** *9* **Freight Train (IRE)**[9] 4038 4-9-10 **77** (p) FrannyNorton 6 56
(Mark Johnston) *led 4f: cl up: rdn and ev ch over 2f out: sn drvn and wknd appr fnl f* **6/1**
0143 **6** *3* **Gulf Of Poets**[30] 3324 4-9-4 **76** NathanEvans(5) 5 49
(Michael Easterby) *cl up on inner: led after 4f: rdn along and hdd over 2f out: sn drvn and grad wknd* **9/1**
5304 **7** *1 3/4* **Biff Johnson (IRE)**[13] 3920 4-9-6 **80** (b) CliffordLee(7) 1 49
(Keith Dalgleish) *trckd ldrs on inner: hdwy over 3f out: cl up over 2f out: sn rdn and cl up whn sltly hmpd wl over 1f: sn wknd* **8/1**

2m 3.39s (-2.01) **Going Correction** -0.15s/f (Firm)
WFA 3 from 4yo 10lb **7** Ran SP% **111.8**
Speed ratings (Par 105): **102,101,100,98,90 88,87**
CSF £12.00 CT £32.64 TOTE £2.20: £1.20, £5.10; EX 14.50 Trifecta £30.30.
Owner Godolphin **Bred** Darley **Trained** Newmarket, Suffolk

FOCUS
The rail on the bend from the back straight to the home straight was dolled out by 5 yards, adding 10 yards to all races on the round course. A fair handicap but something of a messy race, in which there was a contested lead. The runner-up has been rated to the best view of his form.

4407 RIPON BELL-RINGER H'CAP 1m 4f 10y
3:45 (3:45) (Class 2) (0-100,100) 3-Y-O+
£15,562 (£4,660; £2,330; £1,165; £582; £292) **Stalls** Low

Form RPR
2000 **1** **Soldier In Action (FR)**[29] 3341 3-8-6 **90** FrannyNorton 4 98
(Mark Johnston) *mde all: pushed along wl over 2f out: rdn wl over 1f out: drvn and kpt on strly fnl f* **4/1**[2]
6414 **2** *1 1/4* **Snoano**[14] 3889 4-9-8 **94** DavidAllan 2 100
(Tim Easterby) *in tch: hdwy to trck ldrs over 3f out: effrt 2f out: rdn to chse wnr over 1f out: drvn and ev ch ent fnl f: kpt on same pce towards fin* **4/1**[2]
-031 **3** *1/2* **Tapis Libre**[9] 4049 8-8-6 **83** NathanEvans(5) 1 88
(Jacqueline Coward) *trckd ldrs on inner: effrt 2f out: rdn over 1f out: drvn ent fnl f: kpt on* **20/1**
-300 **4** *nk* **Blue Hussar (IRE)**[35] 3162 5-8-8 **85** (p) CallumShepherd(5) 10 90
(Micky Hammond) *hld up towards rr: gd hdwy on wd outside over 2f out: rdn to chal jst over 1f out and ev ch: drvn and edgd rt ins fnl f: kpt on* **20/1**
1036 **5** *1* **Dance King**[14] 3889 6-9-2 **88** (tp) JasonHart 14 91
(Tim Easterby) *stdd and swtchd rt s: towards rr: hdwy 3f out: rdn wl over 1f out: styd on wl fnl f: nrst fin* **14/1**
-016 **6** *3/4* **Odeon**[29] 3345 5-8-9 **81** JackGarritty 15 83
(James Given) *midfield: gd hdwy on outer to trck wnr after 4f: rdn along over 2f out: drvn over 1f out: grad wknd* **33/1**
6223 **7** *nk* **Modernism**[8] 4095 7-9-0 **86** BarryMcHugh 13 87
(Richard Fahey) *hld up and bhd: hdwy on inner over 2f out: pushed along wl over 1f out: sn n.m.r: rdn and kpt on fnl f: nrst fin* **20/1**
11 **8** *1* **Sindarban (IRE)**[24] 3520 5-9-5 **91** PhillipMakin 11 91
(Keith Dalgleish) *trckd ldrs: smooth hdwy on outer over 3f out and sn cl up: pushed along 2f out: sn rdn: drvn over 1f out: sn edgd lft and wknd* **11/4**[1]
6-06 **9** *4 1/2* **Welford**[8] 4108 3-8-5 **89** LiamJones 7 82
(Mark Johnston) *trckd wnr: cl up over 4f out: rdn along wl over 2f out: drvn over 1f out: grad wknd* **11/1**[3]
5133 **10** *1/2* **Corton Lad**[12] 3950 6-9-1 **87** (tp) JoeyHaynes 3 79
(Keith Dalgleish) *trckd ldrs: pushed along 3f out: rdn 2f out: sn drvn and wknd* **25/1**
20 **11** *1* **Paddys Motorbike (IRE)**[14] 3889 4-9-6 **92** GrahamGibbons 9 82
(David Evans) *chsd ldrs: rdn along over 3f out: sn wknd* **25/1**
2405 **12** *1* **Chancery (USA)**[21] 3666 8-9-12 **98** (vt[1]) DavidNolan 6 87
(David O'Meara) *a towards rr* **25/1**
2406 **13** *4* **Burano (IRE)**[28] 3391 7-8-9 **86** JoshDoyle(5) 12 68
(David O'Meara) *hld up towards rr: effrt and sme hdwy on outer over 3f out: rdn along over 2f out: sn wknd* **16/1**
3-00 **14** *9* **Fattsota**[47] 2744 8-9-7 **100** PatrickVaughan(7) 8 68
(David O'Meara) *a towards rr* **25/1**

2m 33.96s (-2.74) **Going Correction** -0.15s/f (Firm)
WFA 3 from 4yo+ 12lb **14** Ran SP% **120.2**
Speed ratings (Par 109): **103,102,101,101,100 100,100,99,96,96 95,94,92,86**
CSF £17.30 CT £291.62 TOTE £5.00: £2.10, £1.50, £8.60; EX 24.60 Trifecta £355.90.
Owner A D Spence **Bred** Randolf Peters **Trained** Middleham Moor, N Yorks

FOCUS
Race run over 10 yards further than advertised. The second running of this as an all-aged handicap, and a competitive event. The form should prove sound. It's been rated around the second and third.

4408 VW VAN CENTRE (WEST YORKSHIRE) H'CAP 1m
4:20 (4:20) (Class 4) (0-85,85) 3-Y-O **£6,931** (£2,074; £1,037; £519; £258) **Stalls** Low

Form RPR
-100 **1** **Huntlaw**[42] 2907 3-8-10 **75** FrannyNorton 2 84
(Mark Johnston) *t.k.h: mde most: rdn wl over 1f out: drvn ins fnl f: styd on strly* **9/2**[1]
3106 **2** *1 3/4* **Dubai Dynamo**[13] 3923 11-9-13 **84** PJMcDonald 1 91
(Ruth Carr) *hld up in tch: hdwy 2f out: swtchd lft and rdn over 1f out: chsd wnr ins fnl f: sn drvn and no imp towards fin* **9/2**[1]
3634 **3** *1 3/4* **Simply Shining (IRE)**[27] 3438 6-9-2 **78** AdamMcNamara(5) 6 81
(Richard Fahey) *t.k.h: disp ld early: cl up: effrt to chal over 2f out: sn rdn and ev ch tl drvn ent fnl f and kpt on same pce* **5/1**[2]
3230 **4** *1 1/4* **Hard To Handel**[24] 3518 4-10-0 **85** PhillipMakin 7 85
(David O'Meara) *hld up towards rr: hdwy on wd outside over 2f out: rdn to chal over 1f out: drvn and kpt on same pce fnl f* **7/1**[3]
41 **5** *1/2* **Lawyer (IRE)**[30] 3327 5-9-2 **73** GrahamGibbons 9 72
(David Barron) *trckd ldng pair: hdwy 3f out: rdn along over 2f out: drvn over 1f out: sn wknd* **5/1**[2]
0015 **6** *1* **Shouranour (IRE)**[15] 3840 6-9-2 **78** (b) JoshDoyle(5) 5 75
(Alan Brown) *trckd ldrs: effrt over 2f out: rdn along on inner wl over 1f out: drvn and wknd appr fnl f* **8/1**
0500 **7** *3 3/4* **Green Howard**[12] 3945 8-9-9 **80** (b[1]) BarryMcHugh 8 68
(Rebecca Bastiman) *hld up: a towards rr* **12/1**
5105 **8** *6* **Nonno Giulio (IRE)**[28] 3419 5-9-7 **78** DavidNolan 4 52
(David Loughnane) *trckd ldng pair on inner: effrt over 2f out: rdn and n.m.r wl over 1f out: wknd appr fnl f* **15/2**

1m 39.19s (-2.21) **Going Correction** -0.15s/f (Firm)
WFA 3 from 4yo+ 8lb **8** Ran SP% **112.8**
Speed ratings (Par 105): **105,103,101,100,99 98,95,89**
CSF £23.98 CT £103.89 TOTE £4.30: £1.70, £2.40, £1.10; EX 26.10 Trifecta £84.40.
Owner Duke Of Roxburghe **Bred** Floors Farming **Trained** Middleham Moor, N Yorks

FOCUS
Race run over 10 yards further than advertised. They went a solid gallop in this fair handicap. The runner-up has been rated slightly up on his recent form, with the third close to form.

4409 F. B. TAYLOR 50TH ANNIVERSARY CUP (H'CAP) 1m 4f 10y
4:50 (4:50) (Class 4) (0-80,87) 3-Y-O+ **£6,301** (£1,886; £943; £472; £235) **Stalls** Low

Form RPR
3211 **1** **Knights Table**[12] 3949 3-9-9 **87** DavidAllan 8 97+
(James Tate) *trckd ldrs: effrt 2f out: swtchd lft over 1f out: sn rdn and qcknd to ld ent fnl f: sn clr* **11/8**[1]
5-31 **2** *2* **Jaameh (IRE)**[15] 3853 3-9-1 **79** FrannyNorton 5 86
(Mark Johnston) *trckd ldrs: cl up after 4f: led 2f out: sn rdn and edgd rt: hdd and drvn ent fnl f: kpt on same pce* **11/4**[2]
2051 **3** *2 1/2* **Theos Lolly (IRE)**[11] 3982 3-8-12 **76** JackGarritty 3 79
(Richard Fahey) *trckd ldrs: pushed along over 2f out: rdn over 1f out: styd on fnl f* **7/1**
-443 **4** *1 3/4* **Osaruveetil (IRE)**[21] 3659 5-9-13 **79** DavidNolan 1 79
(David O'Meara) *set stdy pce: rdn and qcknd wl over 2f out: hdd 2f out and sn drvn: kpt on one pce* **6/1**[3]
0-50 **5** *2 1/4* **Age Of Elegance (IRE)**[11] 3983 4-9-6 **72** JoeyHaynes 2 69
(David Loughnane) *dwlt and towards rr: hdwy on outer to trck ldrs after 4f: effrt over 2f out: sn rdn: drvn wl over 1f out: sn wknd* **20/1**
3130 **6** *4* **Russian Royale**[20] 3117 6-9-9 **75** PJMcDonald 4 65
(Micky Hammond) *hld up towards rr: effrt over 3f out: rdn along 2f out: no hdwy* **22/1**
12-0 **7** *1 1/4* **Dhaular Dhar (IRE)**[35] 3162 14-9-2 **75** LewisEdmunds(7) 7 63
(Jim Goldie) *hld up: a in rr* **33/1**
0631 **8** *16* **Pertuis (IRE)**[30] 3325 10-8-6 **63** (p) CallumShepherd(5) 6 26
(Micky Hammond) *hld up in rr: hdwy on outer 3f out: rdn to chse ldrs 2f out: sn drvn and outpcd over 1f out: bhd and eased fnl f* **16/1**

2m 35.28s (-1.42) **Going Correction** -0.15s/f (Firm)
WFA 3 from 4yo+ 12lb **8** Ran SP% **113.5**
Speed ratings (Par 105): **98,96,95,93,92 89,88,78**
CSF £4.96 CT £17.66 TOTE £2.00: £1.20, £1.10, £2.50; EX 5.20 Trifecta £14.20.
Owner Saeed Manana **Bred** Ashbrittle Stud **Trained** Newmarket, Suffolk

FOCUS
Race run over 10 yards further than advertised. This was a good race for the grade, featuring four last-time-out winners. The pace was fairly steady until it lifted in the last half-mile. It's been rated around the front-running fourth to his turf form.

4410 SIS ON-DEMAND RACING GAMES MAIDEN H'CAP 6f
5:20 (5:21) (Class 5) (0-70,70) 3-Y-O+ **£3,234** (£962; £481; £240) **Stalls** High

Form RPR
6-03 **1** **Spirit Of Zebedee (IRE)**[12] 3940 3-8-5 **54** ow1 (p) PJMcDonald 10 62
(John Quinn) *prom: cl up 2f out: rdn to ld ent fnl f: sn drvn and kpt on wl towards fin* **13/2**[3]
2455 **2** *3/4* **Silver Sands (IRE)**[12] 3948 3-9-1 **64** (p) DavidAllan 11 69
(Tim Easterby) *prom on stands' rail: hdwy to ld wl over 1f out: hdd ent fnl f: sn drvn and ev ch tl no ex last 50yds* **9/2**[2]
-200 **3** *2 1/2* **Kinloch Pride**[15] 3843 4-8-7 **51** (p) NeilFarley 8 49
(Noel Wilson) *chsd ldrs: hdwy 1/2-way: cl up 2f out: sn rdn and ev ch tl drvn and kpt on same pce fnl f* **16/1**
-004 **4** *1 3/4* **The Resdev Way**[11] 3987 3-8-0 **54** oh5 ow3 NathanEvans(5) 12 45
(Richard Whitaker) *in tch: hdwy over 2f out: rdn wl over 1f out: kpt on fnl f* **8/1**
0202 **5** *1* **Dance Alone**[12] 3948 3-9-0 **70** LewisEdmunds(7) 6 58
(Kevin Ryan) *trckd ldrs: hdwy and cl up over 2f out: sn rdn and ev ch tl drvn and wknd over 1f out* **9/4**[1]
60-0 **6** *shd* **Guanabara Bay (IRE)**[11] 3982 3-9-4 **67** PhillipMakin 13 55
(Martyn Meade) *bhd: hdwy 2f out: sn rdn and kpt on fnl f* **10/1**
5-00 **7** *8* **Cautionary Note**[22] 3604 3-7-12 **54** ow1 (p) KieranSchofield(7) 1 16
(Nigel Tinkler) *chsd ldrs on wd outside: rdn along over 2f out: sn drvn and grad wknd* **33/1**

0-50 **8** *1* **Cosmic Dust**[10] 4005 3-8-2 **51** oh6 PaulQuinn 5 10
(Richard Whitaker) *chsd ldrs: swtchd lft and rdn wl over 2f out: sn wknd* **22/1**
6040 **9** *5* **Bazula (IRE)**[19] 3710 3-8-9 **58** (b) MartinLane 9
(Tim Easterby) *led: rdn along over 2f out: sn hdd & wknd* **25/1**
0-06 **10** *24* **Sea Of Green**[42] 2919 4-8-9 **53** JackGarritty 7
(Jim Goldie) *a towards rr* **12/1**
6630 **11** *16* **Dark Confidant (IRE)**[12] 3941 3-8-4 **58** (b) CallumShepherd(5) 4
(Richard Guest) *in tch towards outer: rdn along 1/2-way: sddle slipped and sn bhd* **16/1**
2046 **12** *dist* **Little Belter (IRE)**[8] 4096 4-8-9 **53** (p) JoeyHaynes 3
(Keith Dalgleish) *rrd s: virtually ref to r* **11/1**

1m 11.35s (-1.65) **Going Correction** -0.15s/f (Firm)
WFA 3 from 4yo 5lb **12** Ran SP% **121.4**
Speed ratings (Par 103): **105,104,100,98,97 96,86,84,78,46 24,**
CSF £35.95 CT £461.31 TOTE £6.60: £1.70, £1.50, £5.50; EX 35.60 Trifecta £480.40.
Owner Malcolm Walker **Bred** N Hartery **Trained** Settrington, N Yorks

FOCUS
A very modest event in which the runners had contested 120 races between them without success. The first two home both raced on the stands' rail from their high draws. A pb from the winner, with the runner-up rated to form.
T/Plt: £11.10 to a £1 stake. Pool: £57,863.11 - 3795.36 winning units T/Qpdt: £7.20 to a £1 stake. Pool: £3,923.96 - 399.6 winning units **Joe Rowntree**

4411 - 4412a (Foreign Racing) - See Raceform Interactive

3691 CURRAGH (R-H)
Saturday, July 16

OFFICIAL GOING: Round course - good; straight course - good to yielding

4413a KILFRUSH STUD SAPPHIRE STKS (GROUP 2) 5f
4:05 (4:06) 3-Y-O+

£52,058 (£16,764; £7,941; £3,529; £1,764; £882)

RPR

1 **Mecca's Angel (IRE)**[32] 3244 5-9-4 118 PaulMulrennan 1 120+
(Michael Dods) *sn cl-up in 2nd: led narrowly over 2f out: rdn ent fnl f and sn wnt clr: r.o strly cl home: comf* **5/4**[1]
2 *3* **Brando**[14] 3909 4-9-7 110 TomEaves 5 112
(Kevin Ryan) *sn chsd ldrs in 3rd: rdn to chal over 1f out but nt qckn w wnr: kpt on same pce u.p to go 2nd 50yds out: no ch w wnr* **9/4**[2]
3 *½* **Gracious John (IRE)**[49] 2692 3-9-3 106 DeclanMcDonogh 3 109
(David Evans) *sn led narrowly: hdd over 2f out: sn rdn to chse wnr but no imp u.p ins fnl f and dropped to 3rd 50yds out* **20/1**
4 *¾* **Sole Power**[7] 4151 9-9-7 112 PatSmullen 4 108
(Edward Lynam, Ire) *hld up in rr: pushed along 1 1/2f out and sme hdwy between horses ins fnl f to go 4th cl home but nvr nr to chal* **4/1**[3]
5 *¾* **Ardhoomey (IRE)**[20] 3696 4-9-7 104 ColinKeane 6 105
(G M Lyons, Ire) *chsd ldrs: cl 4th 1/2-way: pushed along to chal 2f out: no ex u.p fr 1f out and dropped to 5th cl home* **10/1**
6 *1 ¼* **G Force (IRE)**[21] 3681 5-9-7 108 (t) ChrisHayes 2 100
(Adrian Paul Keatley, Ire) *hld up in 5th: pushed along under 2f out: sn no imp on principals and one pce ins fnl f: dropped to 6th cl home* **18/1**

58.61s (-4.29) **Going Correction** -0.625s/f (Hard)
WFA 3 from 4yo+ 4lb **6** Ran SP% **114.3**
Speed ratings: **109,104,103,102,101 99**
CSF £4.43 TOTE £2.10: £1.02, £1.40; DF 4.30 Trifecta £29.20.
Owner David T J Metcalfe **Bred** Yeomanstown Stud & Doc Bloodstock **Trained** Denton, Co Durham

FOCUS
An impressive return to form for the winner after her poor effort at Ascot and she may well have re-established herself as the best of the 5f sprinters. A clash between her at her best and Limato at his best might be seen yet. Mecca's Angel is rated close to her best.

4414a JEBEL ALI RACECOURSE & STABLES ANGLESEY STKS (GROUP 3) 6f 63y
4:40 (4:41) 2-Y-O

£28,198 (£9,080; £4,301; £1,911; £955; £477)

RPR

1 **Peace Envoy (FR)**[21] 3678 2-9-3 106 RyanMoore 5 109
(A P O'Brien, Ire) *chsd ldrs in 4th: gng wl ent fnl f and swtchd to nr side to chal: sn rdn and qcknd to ld 125yds out: r.o wl* **3/1**[2]
2 *1 ¾* **Psychedelic Funk**[32] 3243 2-9-3 0 ColinKeane 1 104
(G M Lyons, Ire) *chsd ldrs in 3rd: pushed along to chal under 2f out: r.o u.p to dispute ld jst ins fnl f: hdd 125yds out and sn no ex* **9/10**[1]
3 *½* **Mirdif**[7] 4171 2-9-3 91 PatSmullen 6 102
(M D O'Callaghan, Ire) *sn trckd ldr in 2nd: rdn to chal under 2f out: led narrowly ent fnl f: jnd jst ins fnl f: no ex u.p and hdd 125yds out: sn one pce in 3rd* **25/1**
4 *¾* **Radio Silence (USA)**[9] 4067 2-9-3 0 KevinManning 3 100
(J S Bolger, Ire) *hld up towards rr: 5th 1/2-way: pushed along 2f out and wnt 4th u.p ent fnl f: sn no ex and kpt on same pce* **7/2**[3]
5 *3 ¾* **Ready To Roc (IRE)**[21] 3678 2-9-3 95 FrankieDettori 2 89
(J P Murtagh, Ire) *hld up in rr: 6th 1/2-way: pushed along 2f out and sn no imp on principals: kpt on same pce to go 5th cl home* **18/1**
6 *nk* **Ambiguity (IRE)**[7] 4171 2-9-3 91 (tp) DonnachaO'Brien 4 88
(Joseph Patrick O'Brien, Ire) *sn led narrowly: rdn whn pressed for ld under 2f out: hdd ent fnl f and sn no ex u.p: wknd to 6th cl home* **50/1**

1m 17.13s (-1.97) **Going Correction** -0.625s/f (Hard) **6** Ran SP% **110.9**
Speed ratings: **88,85,85,84,79 78**
CSF £5.93 TOTE £3.50: £1.40, £1.02; DF 5.90 Trifecta £26.70.
Owner Mrs John Magnier & Michael Tabor & Derrick Smith **Bred** Team Hogdala A B **Trained** Cashel, Co Tipperary

FOCUS
A decent performance from the winner, winning his third race over hurdles and that might be construed as a bonus.

4415a EVOKE.IE SCURRY H'CAP (PREMIER HANDICAP) 6f 63y
5:10 (5:14) 3-Y-O+

£43,382 (£13,970; £6,617; £2,941; £1,470; £735)

RPR

1 **Perfect Pasture**[42] 2898 6-9-8 **99** (v) PaulMulrennan 14 112
(Michael Easterby) *chsd ldrs on nr side: wnt 3rd over 2f out: sn rdn and r.o wl u.p to ld jst ins fnl f: kpt on strly* **16/1**
2 *2* **Master Speaker (IRE)**[56] 2493 6-8-13 **90** (bt) ColmO'Donoghue 19 97
(Martin Hassett, Ire) *hld up towards rr on nr side: rdn 2f out and hdwy u.p to go 2nd 100yds out: hld cl home* **12/1**
3 *2 ½* **Distant Past**[21] 3638 5-8-6 **83** (p) LeighRoche 5 82
(Kevin Ryan) *chsd ldrs in centre: wnt 2nd over 2f out: rdn to ld 1 1/2f out: kpt on wl u.p but hdd jst ins fnl f: sn no ex and dropped to 3rd 100yds out* **33/1**
4 *½* **In Salutem**[22] 3628 6-9-7 **98** (t) ShaneFoley 7 95
(K J Condon, Ire) *sn chsd ldrs: rdn 2f out and nt qckn w principals but r.o wl u.p to go 4th cl home* **11/1**
5 *hd* **Captain Power (IRE)**[22] 3628 4-8-5 **85** RobbieDowney(3) 16 81
(Edward Lynam, Ire) *mid-div: rdn 2f out and sme hdwy u.p between horses ent fnl f: kpt on wl to go 5th cl home* **12/1**
6 *½* **Peticoatgovernment (IRE)**[34] 3200 3-8-6 **88** WayneLordan 18 82
(W McCreery, Ire) *chsd ldrs on nr side: rdn 2f out and nt qckn w principals but kpt on wl u.p to go 6th cl home* **20/1**
7 *½* **Penny Pepper (IRE)**[21] 3682 4-8-10 **87** ChrisHayes 6 80
(Kevin Prendergast, Ire) *chsd ldrs in centre: rdn 2f out and kpt on wl u.p but no ex ins fnl f* **12/1**
8 *nk* **Fast In The Wind (IRE)**[6] 4177 5-7-13 **81** 5ex oh3.. (t) TomMadden(5) 10 73
(P D Deegan, Ire) *mid-div: pushed along over 2f out and sme prog ent fnl f but nvr nr to chal* **25/1**
9 *1 ¼* **The Happy Prince (IRE)**[21] 3681 4-9-9 **100** (t) RyanMoore 2 88
(A P O'Brien, Ire) *mid-div in centre of crse: rdn 2f out and no ex ent fnl f: kpt on same pce* **8/1**[2]
10 *½* **Sors (IRE)**[20] 3696 4-8-5 **89** KillianLeonard(7) 1 76
(Andrew Slattery, Ire) *led and sn clr in centre: reduced advantage 1/2-way: hdd 1 1/2f out: no ex u.p and wknd* **16/1**
11 *1 ½* **Downforce (IRE)**[56] 2493 4-9-2 **93** BillyLee 12 75
(W McCreery, Ire) *mid-div: rdn 2f out and sn no imp: one pce* **9/2**[1]
12 *¾* **Spring Loaded (IRE)**[28] 3386 4-9-9 **100** PatSmullen 9 79
(Paul D'Arcy) *chsd ldrs in centre: rdn and no imp fr 2f out* **8/1**[2]
13 *shd* **Kibaar**[35] 3150 4-8-8 **85** TomEaves 13 64
(Kevin Ryan) *chsd ldrs on nr side: disp 3rd u.p 1 1/2f out but sn no ex and wknd* **20/1**
14 *nk* **George Bowen (IRE)**[21] 3656 4-9-5 **96** DeclanMcDonogh 3 74
(Richard Fahey) *mid-div in centre: rdn over 2f out and sn no ex: wknd ent fnl f* **9/1**[3]
15 *1 ½* **Shepherd's Purse**[20] 3696 4-9-4 **95** GaryCarroll 11 68
(Joseph G Murphy, Ire) *a towards rr: rdn over 2f out and no imp* **33/1**
16 *½* **Captain Cullen (IRE)**[6] 4177 7-8-13 **90** KevinManning 17 62
(Joseph Anthony Murray, Ire) *hld up towards rr: wnt for gap between horses 3f out but squeezed on outer and short of room: sn rdn and no imp fr 2f out* **12/1**
17 *2* **Fairway To Heaven (IRE)**[207] 8342 7-8-4 **81** oh1 (p) RoryCleary 4 46
(Michael Wigham) *dwlt and slowly away: in rr: nvr in contention* **33/1**
18 *2* **Moviesta (USA)**[21] 3681 6-9-5 **103** OisinOrr(7) 15 62
(Edward Lynam, Ire) *in rr of mid-div: rdn fr 2f out and no imp* **18/1**
19 *6 ½* **Your Pal Tal**[8] 4120 6-8-4 **81** oh6 (p) SilvestreDeSousa 8 19
(J F Levins, Ire) *sn chsd ldrs: pushed along fr 1/2-way and no ex: wknd and eased* **25/1**

1m 15.17s (-3.93) **Going Correction** -0.625s/f (Hard)
WFA 3 from 4yo+ 5lb **19** Ran SP% **132.6**
Speed ratings: **101,98,95,94,94 93,92,92,90,90 88,87,86,86,84 83,81,78,69**
CSF £192.43 CT £6319.01 TOTE £20.00: £4.40, £3.40, £9.20, £3.00; DF 242.90 Trifecta £2402.00.
Owner S Hull, S Hollings & D Swales **Bred** Mrs Jean Turpin **Trained** Sheriff Hutton, N Yorks

FOCUS
A race that was turned into a bit of a procession in the end by the easy winner, as British sprint handicappers again dominated one of these valuable Irish handicaps.

4416a DARLEY IRISH OAKS (GROUP 1) (FILLIES) 1m 4f
5:45 (5:54) 3-Y-O

£167,647 (£55,882; £26,470; £11,764; £5,882; £2,941)

RPR

1 **Seventh Heaven (IRE)**[43] 2869 3-9-0 98 SeamieHeffernan 9 115+
(A P O'Brien, Ire) *hld up towards rr: 10th 1/2-way: pushed along 3f out and gd prog on inner into st: sn swtchd lft and hdwy between horses 2f out where carried sltly lft by rival: rdn to ld 200yds out and sn asserted* **14/1**
2 *2 ¾* **Architecture (IRE)**[30] 3297 3-9-0 113 FrankieDettori 3 110
(Hugo Palmer) *mid-div: 6th 1/2-way: pushed along over 2f out and sn wnt 4th: pushed sltly lft by rival 2f out: rdn to ld 1 1/2f out: kpt on wl u.p but hdd 200yds out and no ex* **6/1**[2]
3 *1 ¼* **Harlequeen**[43] 2869 3-9-0 102 SilvestreDeSousa 2 108
(Mick Channon) *mid-div: 7th 1/2-way: pushed along to chal over 2f out and sn short of room bhd horses: fnd room ent fnl f and r.o u.p to go 3rd but hld cl home* **14/1**
4 *4* **Turret Rocks (IRE)**[43] 2869 3-9-0 108 [1] KevinManning 4 101
(J S Bolger, Ire) *t.k.h early: chsd ldrs: sn settled in 3rd: pushed along to chal over 2f out and sn wnt 2nd: wnt sltly lft u.p 2f out: kpt on but no ex in 4th ins fnl f* **14/1**
5 *½* **Somehow (IRE)**[43] 2869 3-9-0 98 [1] DonnachaO'Brien 6 100
(A P O'Brien, Ire) *in rr of mid-div: 8th 1/2-way: pushed along 3f out and sme prog to chse ldrs: carried sltly lft 2f out: sn rdn and no ex: kpt on same pce* **14/1**
6 *5* **An Cailin Orga (IRE)**[22] 3630 3-9-0 85 RonanWhelan 12 92
(J S Bolger, Ire) *in rr: 11th 1/2-way: rdn under 3f out and sme hdwy u.p: kpt on steadily to go modest 6th ins fnl f but nvr nr to chal* **80/1**
7 *4 ¼* **Even Song (IRE)**[30] 3297 3-9-0 110 RyanMoore 7 86
(A P O'Brien, Ire) *hld up towards rr: 9th 1/2-way: pushed along 3f out: taken to outer in st over 2f out and sn no imp u.p: one pce* **4/5**[1]
8 *hd* **Red Stars (IRE)**[12] 3964 3-9-0 103 DeclanMcDonogh 11 85
(John M Oxx, Ire) *cl-up: sn trckd ldr in 2nd: rdn to chal 3f out but sn no ex and wknd in st* **33/1**
9 *1* **We Are Ninety (IRE)**[30] 3297 3-9-0 104 PatSmullen 8 84
(Hugo Palmer) *chsd ldrs: 5th 1/2-way: pushed along 3f out and no imp u.p 2f out: wknd* **25/1**
10 *1 ¾* **Pretty Perfect (IRE)**[34] 3202 3-9-0 105 ColmO'Donoghue 10 81
(A P O'Brien, Ire) *sn led: pushed along over 2f out whn chal: hdd 1 1/2f out: sn no ex and eased ins fnl f* **9/1**[3]
11 *75* **Ajman Princess (IRE)**[30] 3297 3-9-0 107 AndreaAtzeni 5
(Roger Varian) *chsd ldrs: 4th 1/2-way: pushed along fr 4f out and sn no ex: wknd qckly and eased: t.o* **14/1**

2m 34.53s (-3.97) **Going Correction** -0.325s/f (Firm) **11** Ran SP% **121.2**
Speed ratings: **100,98,97,94,94 91,88,88,87,86 36**
CSF £97.49 CT £1224.01 TOTE £16.80: £4.30, £1.80, £3.60; DF 114.60 Trifecta £1579.90.

Owner Derrick Smith & Mrs John Magnier & Michael Tabor **Bred** La Traviata Syndicate **Trained** Cashel, Co Tipperary

FOCUS

A very disappointing display from the favourite, but the stable had some able substitutes and one of them came up trumps. Seventh Heaven progressed and the next two are rated to their Epsom form.

4417a BOODLES LADIES DERBY H'CAP 1m 4f

6:20 (6:22) 4-Y-O+ **£13,566** (£4,191; £1,985; £882; £330)

RPR

1 **Zeftan (IRE)**[13] 3932 7-9-0 **70** MissHMooney[(7)] 4 86+
(Adrian Paul Keatley, Ire) *hld up in rr: 9th 1/2-way: gng wl over 2f out and sn smooth hdwy on outer to cruise into ld 1 1/2f out: kpt up to work ins fnl f: easily* **14/1**

2 9 **Udogo**[9] 4072 5-9-7 **75** MissSO'Brien[(5)] 6 77
(Joseph Patrick O'Brien, Ire) *chsd ldrs: wnt 2nd after 3f: dropped to cl 3rd 4f out: gng wl and prog to ld 3f out: sn rdn and r.o wl: hdd 1 1/2f out and sn no ch w wnr* **4/1**[2]

3 nk **Modem**[21] 3680 6-10-8 **90** (p) MissKHarrington[(5)] 9 91
(Mrs John Harrington, Ire) *mid-div: wnt 4th 4f out: rdn 2 1/2f out and kpt on steadily u.p but no ch w wnr* **4/1**[2]

4 1 ½ **Rossvoss**[15] 3870 8-9-7 **70** oh3 (bt) MsKWalsh 3 69
(T M Walsh, Ire) *hld up towards rr: 7th 1/2-way: rdn 2 1/2f out and prog into 5th: wnt 3rd 1 1/2f out: sn no ex u.p and dropped to 4th ins fnl f* **8/1**

5 2 ¾ **Whats The Plot (IRE)**[25] 3505 4-9-4 **70** oh4 MissJMMangan[(3)] 7 64
(A L T Moore, Ire) *hld up in rr: 8th 1/2-way: rdn under 3f out and kpt on steadily u.p on outer to go modest 5th ent fnl f* **8/1**

6 5 **Suitor**[23] 3563 4-10-2 **79** MsNCarberry 10 65
(Brian Ellison) *settled in mid-div: 5th 4f out: sn pushed along and no imp u.p fr over 2f out: no ex* **11/4**[1]

7 2 ½ **Moonmeister (IRE)**[45] 2498 5-9-12 **82** MissABO'Connor[(7)] 8 64
(John F Davison, Ire) *chsd ldrs: hdwy to go 2nd 4f out: rdn over 2f out and sn no ex: wknd* **25/1**

8 17 **Highly Toxic (IRE)**[22] 3630 5-10-7 **91** (b) MsLO'Neill[(7)] 5 46
(Patrick J Flynn, Ire) *cl-up: led after 1f: pushed along over 3f out and hdd: sn no ex and wknd* **7/1**[3]

9 1 **Moojaned (IRE)**[34] 3192 5-9-12 **82** KatherineGlenister[(7)] 1 36
(David Evans) *sn led: hdd after 1f: dropped to 3rd after 3f: rdn 3f out and sn no ex u.p: wknd* **16/1**

2m 38.29s (-0.21) **Going Correction** -0.325s/f (Firm) **9** Ran SP% **117.8**
Speed ratings: **87,81,80,79,77 74,72,61,60**
CSF £70.71 CT £273.41 TOTE £16.50: £3.20, £1.90, £1.20; DF 81.50 Trifecta £376.80.
Owner Adrian Paul Keatley **Bred** His Highness The Aga Khan's Studs S C **Trained** Friarstown, Co. Kildare

FOCUS

Ordinary fare by it's nature but the winner won this like a group horse in a handicap

4418 - 4420a (Foreign Racing) - See Raceform Interactive

1957 JAGERSRO (R-H)

Saturday, July 16

OFFICIAL GOING: Dirt: standard

4421a ZAWAWI CUP (GROUP 3) (3YO+) (DIRT) 6f (D)

7:50 (12:00) 3-Y-O+

£48,231 (£16,077; £8,038; £4,823; £1,607; £1,607)

RPR

1 **Giftorm (USA)**[27] 6-9-6 0 KevinStott 7 101
(Fredrik Reuterskiold, Sweden) **4/1**[2]

2 3 **Let'sgoforit (IRE)**[74] 8-9-6 0 OliverWilson 3 91
(Bodil Hallencreutz, Sweden) **83/100**[1]

3 3 **Over The Ocean (USA)**[27] 6-9-6 0 (b) Per-AndersGraberg 5 82
(Niels Petersen, Norway) **79/10**

4 1 ¼ **Spykes Bay (USA)**[282] 7-9-6 0 JacobJohansen 6 78
(Vanja Sandrup, Sweden) **41/5**

5 2 **Saving Kenny (IRE)**[27] 6-9-6 0 EduardoPedroza 1 71
(Roy Arne Kvisla, Sweden) **77/10**[3]

5 dht **Hall Of Fame (SWE)**[247] 4-9-6 0 ElioneChaves 8 71
(Dina Danekilde, Sweden) **117/10**

7 4 **Hills And Dales (IRE)**[283] 7034 4-9-6 0 ShaneKarlsson 4 59
(Hans-Inge Larsen, Sweden) **26/1**

8 dist **Varlo (SAF)** 4-9-6 0 CarlosLopez 2
(Lars Kelp, Denmark) **174/10**

1m 11.38s (71.38) **8** Ran SP% **125.3**
PARI-MUTUEL (all including 1sek stake): WIN 5.02; PLACE 1.64, 1.27, 1.97; SF 13.35.
Owner Mr Ascot **Bred** Janavar Thoroughbreds Llc **Trained** Sweden

4422 - (Foreign Racing) - See Raceform Interactive

3416 REDCAR (L-H)

Sunday, July 17

OFFICIAL GOING: Good to firm (9.3)

Wind: fresh half behind Weather: Sunny

4423 RACINGUK.COM BRITISH STALLION STUDS EBF MAIDEN STKS 7f

1:55 (1:55) (Class 5) 2-Y-O **£3,234** (£962; £481; £240) **Stalls** Centre

Form RPR

1 **Andok (IRE)** 2-9-5 0 TonyHamilton 1 83+
(Richard Fahey) *hld up in midfield: pushed along and hdwy over 2f out: bk on bit and trcking ldrs over 1f out: forced way through gap appr fnl f: led jst ins fnl f: kpt on wl pushed out* **5/1**[3]

2 2 ¼ **Kings Gift (IRE)** 2-9-5 0 PaulMulrennan 8 73+
(Michael Dods) *midfield: pushed along and hdwy over 1f out: rdn to chse ldr appr fnl f: kpt on* **4/1**[2]

05 3 1 ¼ **Quantum Field (USA)**[43] 2885 2-9-0 0 OisinMurphy 4 65
(David Brown) *led: rdn 2f out: hdd jst ins fnl f: one pce* **25/1**

4 ½ **Sofia's Rock (FR)** 2-9-5 0 FrannyNorton 10 69+
(Mark Johnston) *trckd ldr: rdn to chal over 1f out: no ex ins fnl f* **13/8**[1]

05 5 2 ½ **Hugging The Rails (IRE)**[16] 3854 2-9-5 0 AndrewMullen 5 62
(Tim Easterby) *midfield: pushed along over 2f out: one pce* **33/1**

55 6 nk **Mister Moosah (IRE)**[22] 3661 2-9-5 0 PJMcDonald 12 61
(Micky Hammond) *in tch: rdn and hdwy to chal over 1f out: wknd ins fnl f* **14/1**

7 1 ½ **Sunday Prospect (FR)** 2-9-5 0 JoeFanning 6 57
(K R Burke) *midfield: pushed along 2f out: nvr threatened* **16/1**

8 ¾ **Hellomoto** 2-9-5 0 TomEaves 9 55
(Kevin Ryan) *dwlt: hld up: pushed along and sme hdwy 2f out: wknd ins fnl f* **25/1**

0 9 1 **Mr Strutter (IRE)**[8] 4161 2-9-5 0 CamHardie 2 52
(John Quinn) *racd keenly: trckd ldr: rdn over 2f out: wknd over 1f out* **50/1**

6 10 3 **Withnell**[16] 3854 2-9-5 0 BenCurtis 7 44
(Brian Ellison) *hld up: rdn over 2f out: nvr threatened* **18/1**

11 ½ **Final Chapter** 2-9-5 0 DavidAllan 13 43
(Tim Easterby) *dwlt: sn midfield racing keenly: pushed along over 2f out: wknd over 1f out* **25/1**

12 2 ½ **Backinanger** 2-9-5 0 ShaneGray 11 36
(Kevin Ryan) *a towards rr* **33/1**

1m 25.05s (0.55) **Going Correction** -0.05s/f (Good) **12** Ran SP% **112.0**
Speed ratings (Par 94): **94,91,90,89,86 86,84,83,82,79 78,75**
CSF £21.66 TOTE £5.90: £1.60, £1.70, £5.90; EX 28.20 Trifecta £619.20.
Owner N O'Keeffe **Bred** Leslie Laverty **Trained** Musley Bank, N Yorks

FOCUS

There was 4mm of water applied to the whole track on Thursday, Friday and Saturday, and the ground was given as good to firm. The 1st, 2nd, and 4th were newcomers from decent stables and prominent in the market, and although the 3rd had shown only limited form, she's a nicely bred filly who got the run of the race in front, and they were clear of the others, so probably a fair maiden.

4424 WATCH RACING UK TODAY JUST £10 H'CAP (DIV I) 1m 1f

2:30 (2:33) (Class 6) (0-60,60) 3-Y-O+ **£2,587** (£770; £384; £192) **Stalls** Low

Form RPR

504 1 **Le Deluge (FR)**[26] 3481 6-9-12 **60** (t) PJMcDonald 14 73
(Micky Hammond) *midfield: hdwy 3f out: rdn to ld over 1f out: kpt on wl* **8/1**

-524 2 5 **Exclusive Diamond**[24] 3564 4-9-3 **56** JoshDoyle[(5)] 10 59
(David O'Meara) *trckd ldrs: rdn over 2f out: one pce* **5/1**[2]

6330 3 1 ½ **L'Apogee**[14] 3921 3-9-2 **59** (p) TonyHamilton 4 57
(Richard Fahey) *trckd ldrs: rdn to ld over 2f out: hdd over 1f out: no ex ins fnl f* **6/1**[3]

0000 4 nk **Kopassus (IRE)**[41] 2974 4-9-0 **53** JordanNason[(5)] 8 52
(Lawrence Mullaney) *prom: rdn over 2f out: sn one pce* **16/1**

1004 5 nk **Samsonite (IRE)**[16] 3849 4-9-12 **60** BarryMcHugh 5 58
(Tony Coyle) *midfield: rdn 3f out: one pce and nvr threatened* **16/1**

4555 6 nk **Highway Robber**[30] 3366 3-8-1 **51** HollieDoyle[(7)] 7 47
(Wilf Storey) *midfield: rdn over 2f out: one pce and one pce and nvr threatened* **14/1**

0000 7 ¾ **Thello**[39] 3013 4-9-2 **50** JasonHart 3 47
(Nigel Tinkler) *in tch on inner: pushed along over 2f out: persistently short of room ins fnl f* **9/1**

6-60 8 ½ **Mariners Moon (IRE)**[23] 609 5-9-6 **54** (tp) JackGarritty 6 49
(Patrick Holmes) *led: rdn whn hdd over 2f out: sn wknd* **28/1**

5000 9 shd **Ted's Brother (IRE)**[8] 4144 8-8-13 **47** (b) ConnorBeasley 13 42
(Richard Guest) *swtchd lft s: hld up in rr: rdn 3f out: nvr threatened* **33/1**

2605 10 ½ **Andaz**[16] 3838 3-9-3 **60** (e) CamHardie 12 53
(Marjorie Fife) *hld up in midfield: rdn and sme hdwy towards outer over 2f out: wknd ins fnl f* **25/1**

000 11 2 ½ **Lobster Cocktail (IRE)**[29] 3412 3-8-13 **56** AntonioFresu 1 43
(Ed Walker) *midfield towards inner: rdn over 3f out: angled rt towards outer over 2f out: nvr threatened* **4/1**[1]

0600 12 1 ½ **Playboy Bay**[30] 3366 4-9-2 **50** (v) AndrewMullen 2 35
(Ron Barr) *hld up: nvr threatened* **80/1**

5423 13 4 ½ **Big Red**[13] 3943 4-8-12 **46** oh1 PaulMulrennan 9 22
(Rebecca Bastiman) *hld up: nvr threatened* **8/1**

1m 51.88s (-1.12) **Going Correction** -0.05s/f (Good)
WFA 3 from 4yo+ 9lb **13** Ran SP% **113.1**
Speed ratings (Par 101): **102,97,96,95,95 95,94,94,94,93 91,90,86**
CSF £43.54 CT £264.66 TOTE £7.80: £2.90, £1.70, £2.70; EX 43.90 Trifecta £196.30.
Owner The Rat Pack Racing Club **Bred** J F Gribomont **Trained** Middleham, N Yorks

FOCUS

The winner took advantage of a handy mark, recording a time 0.53sec quicker than the second division, but the next three home in this are now 0-33 combined. The winner has been rated to the best of his domestic form in recent years, but it's been rated as very ordinary form in behind, with the field compressed.

4425 WATCH RACING UK TODAY JUST £10 H'CAP (DIV II) 1m 1f

3:00 (3:11) (Class 6) (0-60,60) 3-Y-O+ **£2,587** (£770; £384; £192) **Stalls** Low

Form RPR

-633 1 **Ronya (IRE)**[30] 3363 5-9-8 **56** RoystonFfrench 7 63
(Tracy Waggott) *mde all: rdn over 2f out: kpt on: all out* **3/1**[1]

0002 2 shd **Grandest**[41] 2958 5-9-8 **56** BenCurtis 12 63
(Brian Ellison) *hld up in midfield: rdn and hdwy over 2f out: styd on wl fnl f* **4/1**[3]

1400 3 1 ½ **Celtic Artisan (IRE)**[5] 4234 5-9-6 **54** (bt) OisinMurphy 5 58
(Rebecca Menzies) *chsd ldr: rdn over 2f out: kpt on* **11/1**

-133 4 1 ½ **Charles De Mille**[51] 2661 8-9-12 **60** GrahamLee 3 60
(Jedd O'Keeffe) *trckd ldrs: rdn 3f out: one pce* **7/2**[2]

00-3 5 1 **Lord Rob**[11] 4005 5-8-12 **46** oh1 PatrickMathers 6 44
(David Thompson) *trckd ldrs: rdn over 2f out: no ex ins fnl f* **9/1**

400 6 1 ¾ **Table Manners**[23] 3609 4-9-1 **56** HollieDoyle[(7)] 1 51
(Wilf Storey) *midfield: rdn 3f out: one pce and nvr threatened* **33/1**

650- 7 1 ¼ **War Girl (USA)**[316] 6105 4-9-2 **50** GrahamGibbons 11 42
(David Barron) *in tch: rdn over 2f out: wknd ins fnl f* **25/1**

0040 8 3 **Oceanella (IRE)**[4] 4275 3-8-5 **53** (tp) JordanVaughan[(5)] 8 38
(K R Burke) *hld up: rdn 4f out: nvr threatened* **14/1**

5064 9 5 **Outlaw Torn (IRE)**[8] 4146 7-9-3 **51** (e) ConnorBeasley 15 26
(Richard Guest) *midfield: rdn over 3f out: wknd over 1f out* **14/1**

2-00 10 6 **Canford Kilbey (IRE)**[100] 1325 3-8-4 **52** NathanEvans[(5)] 14 14
(Michael Easterby) *in tch: rdn 3f out: wknd over 1f out* **33/1**

405- 11 nk **Desert Chief**[257] 7674 4-9-0 **48** (p) PaulQuinn 9 10
(Richard Whitaker) *s.i.s: a towards rr* **66/1**

0000 12 6 **Moccasin (FR)**[10] 4038 7-9-3 **51** (p) DavidAllan 13
(Geoffrey Harker) *s.i.s: a towards rr* **12/1**

036/ 13 1 ½ **Tawan**[68] 5336 5-8-13 **47** JamesSullivan 10
(Brian Rothwell) *hld up: rdn over 3f out: sn wknd* **66/1**

1m 52.41s (-0.59) **Going Correction** -0.05s/f (Good)
WFA 3 from 4yo+ 9lb **13** Ran SP% **119.3**
Speed ratings (Par 101): **100,99,98,97,96 94,93,91,86,81 80,75,74**
CSF £14.17 CT £119.90 TOTE £4.10: £1.50, £1.60, £2.70; EX 18.40 Trifecta £124.60.
Owner David Tate **Bred** P F Headon **Trained** Spennymoor, Co Durham

■ Kyllini was withdrawn. Price at time of withdrawal 100/1. Rule 4 does not apply.

■ Stewards' Enquiry : Ben Curtis two-day ban; used whip above the permitted level (31st July-1 Aug)
Hollie Doyle caution; careless riding

FOCUS
Kyllini got loose before being withdrawn and others proved hard to load, delaying the start for more than 11 minutes. The winner was given just enough rope in front. It's been rated around the third.

4426 HIGH DEFINITION ON RACING UK H'CAP 5f
3:35 (3:40) (Class 5) (0-70,70) 3-Y-O **£3,234** (£962; £481; £240) **Stalls** Centre

Form RPR
-053 **1** **Dyllan (IRE)**[13] **3948** 3-9-6 **69**.. JamesSullivan 2 76
(Ruth Carr) *hld up in tch: pushed along and hdwy 2f out: rdn to chal ent fnl f: kpt on: led towards fin* **9/4**[1]
3012 **2** *nk* **Bond Bombshell**[29] **3423** 3-8-13 **67**................................ JoshDoyle(5) 6 73
(David O'Meara) *led narrowly: rdn 2f out: wandered ins fnl f: one pce: hdd towards fin* **7/2**[2]
340 **3** *½* **Kiringa**[11] **3994** 3-8-2 **51** oh2..[1] DannyBrock 7 55
(Robert Cowell) *chsd ldrs: rdn 1/2-way: kpt on* **9/1**
-430 **4** *1 ½* **Sunnyside Bob (IRE)**[28] **3439** 3-9-0 **70**.................. PatrickVaughan(7) 5 69
(David O'Meara) *prom: rdn and lost pl 1/2-way: kpt on ins fnl f* **15/2**
-000 **5** *nk* **Cautionary Note**[1] **4410** 3-7-13 **55** ow2................(p) KieranSchofield(7) 4 53
(Nigel Tinkler) *dwlt: hld up in tch: rdn 2f out: nvr threatened* **22/1**
1252 **6** *½* **Roaring Rory**[5] **4236** 3-9-1 **67**..............................(p) JacobButterfield(3) 1 63
(Ollie Pears) *pressed ldr: rdn 1/2-way: hung rt over 1f out: wknd fnl f* **9/2**[3]
330 **7** *1 ½* **Chip Or Pellet**[13] **3948** 3-8-2 **51** oh4...........................(p) AndrewMullen 8 42
(Nigel Tinkler) *dwlt: hld up: nvr threatened* **12/1**
6-00 **8** *1 ¾* **Irish Cailin (IRE)**[44] **2854** 3-8-6 **55**................................ BarryMcHugh 3 39
(Paul Midgley) *prom: rdn 1/2-way: hung lft over 1f out: wknd fnl f* **18/1**
58.28s (-0.32) **Going Correction** -0.05s/f (Good) **8** Ran SP% **110.2**
Speed ratings (Par 100): **100,99,98,96,95 95,92,89**
CSF £9.26 CT £52.50 TOTE £3.10: £1.30, £1.50, £1.70; EX 10.30 Trifecta £41.30.
Owner RHD & Ruth Carr **Bred** Ciara Eglington **Trained** Huby, N Yorks

FOCUS
A modest sprint handicap. Straightforward form with the first three rated close to their marks.

4427 RACING UK PROFITS RETURNED TO RACING CLASSIFIED CLAIMING STKS 1m 2f
4:10 (4:10) (Class 6) 3-Y-O+ **£2,587** (£770; £384; £192) **Stalls** Low

Form RPR
0602 **1** **Captain Felix**[11] **4020** 4-9-1 72..................................... GrahamGibbons 1 71
(George Scott) *trckd ldr: pushed along to ld over 2f out: rdn over 1f out: edgd rt appr fnl f: kpt on* **3/1**[2]
5250 **2** *½* **Kiwi Bay**[20] **3717** 11-9-6 74.. PaulMulrennan 6 75
(Michael Dods) *hld up: rdn over 2f out: hdwy to chse ldr appr fnl f: kpt on* **3/1**[2]
0052 **3** *3* **Our Boy Jack (IRE)**[16] **3849** 7-9-0 75.................... AdamMcNamara(5) 4 68
(Richard Fahey) *in tch: rdn 3f out: one pce* **7/2**[3]
0604 **4** *1 ¾* **Sophisticated Heir (IRE)**[5] **4231** 6-9-2 74...................(b) OisinMurphy 2 62
(David Loughnane) *in tch: rdn and hdwy to chal 2f out: wknd fnl f* **9/4**[1]
0050 **5** *nk* **Chorus of Lies**[9] **4099** 4-9-4 57..(p) DaleSwift 7 63
(Tracy Waggott) *led: rdn whn hdd 3f out: sn outpcd: plugged on fnl f* **25/1**
0405 **6** *4* **Gabrial's Hope (FR)**[16] **3842** 7-8-13 52........................ ConnorBeasley 5 51
(Tracy Waggott) *hld up: nvr threatened* **25/1**
2m 4.53s (-2.57) **Going Correction** -0.05s/f (Good)
WFA 3 from 4yo+ 10lb **6** Ran SP% **110.7**
Speed ratings (Par 101): **108,107,105,103,103 100**
CSF £12.01 TOTE £3.20: £1.80, £1.90; EX 12.80 Trifecta £36.10.Sophisticated Heir was claimed by M. Herrington for £6000.
Owner Matt Bartram **Bred** Matt Bartram **Trained** Newmarket, Suffolk

FOCUS
Not form to be strong on. It's been rated around the principals to their base recent form.

4428 SKY BET GO-RACING-IN-YORKSHIRE SUMMER FESTIVAL H'CAP 6f
4:45 (4:45) (Class 4) (0-85,85) 3-Y-O+ **£6,469** (£1,925; £962; £481) **Stalls** Centre

Form RPR
0630 **1** **Red Tycoon (IRE)**[36] **3168** 4-9-5 **78**........................ GrahamGibbons 8 88
(David Barron) *hld up: pushed along and gd hdwy over 1f out: swtchd rt ent fnl f: rdn to ld 110yds out: kpt on wl* **14/1**
4160 **2** *1 ½* **Explain**[38] **3068** 4-9-10 **83**.. JamesSullivan 1 88
(Ruth Carr) *midfield: rdn and hdwy over 1f out: kpt on* **7/1**[2]
5030 **3** *hd* **Mississippi**[37] **3115** 7-9-6 **79**... GrahamLee 9 84
(Paul Midgley) *hld up: rdn over 1f out: r.o wl fnl f* **8/1**
0020 **4** *½* **Compton Park**[12] **3980** 9-9-5 **78**.. DavidAllan 4 81
(Les Eyre) *led: rdn over 1f out: hdd 110yds out: no ex* **16/1**
0060 **5** *nse* **Highland Acclaim (IRE)**[35] **3188** 5-9-11 **84**...................... DavidNolan 3 87
(David O'Meara) *trckd ldrs: rdn 2f out: one pce* **15/2**[3]
0011 **6** *½* **Free Zone**[8] **4142** 7-9-7 **85**...(v) JoshDoyle(5) 10 86
(David O'Meara) *prom: rdn over 2f out: no ex fnl f* **4/1**[1]
0002 **7** *2* **Mappin Time (IRE)**[15] **3875** 8-8-13 **75**.............(b) RachelRichardson(3) 2 70
(Tim Easterby) *prom: rdn 2f out: wknd fnl f* **9/1**
0430 **8** *nk* **One Boy (IRE)**[15] **3875** 5-9-0 **73**...................................(v[1]) TonyHamilton 5 67
(Richard Fahey) *chsd ldrs: rdn over 2f out: wknd fnl f* **16/1**
0463 **9** *shd* **Desert Ace (IRE)**[10] **4032** 5-9-3 **81**................................(p) PhilDennis(5) 7 75
(Iain Jardine) *hld up: briefly short of room over 1f out: rdn appr fnl f: no imp* **9/1**
060- **10** *1* **Augusta Ada**[384] **3716** 5-9-2 **75**...................................... PaulMulrennan 12 65
(Bryan Smart) *midfield: rdn 2f out: no imp* **40/1**
0460 **11** *1* **Love Island**[24] **3566** 7-9-11 **84**.. GeorgeChaloner 6 71
(Richard Whitaker) *chsd ldrs: rdn over 2f out: wknd fnl f* **16/1**
06 **12** *1 ½* **Savannah Beau**[29] **3397** 4-9-4 **77**.. TomEaves 14 59
(Marjorie Fife) *slowly away: hld up: rdn over 1f out: nvr threatened* **12/1**
400 **13** *2* **Funding Deficit (IRE)**[8] **4132** 6-9-7 **80**............................ OisinMurphy 13 56
(Jim Goldie) *slowly away: hld up: nvr threatened* **28/1**
4-04 **14** *4 ½* **Questo**[29] **3422** 4-8-9 **68**.. RoystonFfrench 11 30
(Tracy Waggott) *chsd ldrs: rdn over 2f out: wknd over 1f out* **25/1**
1m 10.42s (-1.38) **Going Correction** -0.05s/f (Good) **14** Ran SP% **117.1**
Speed ratings (Par 105): **107,105,104,104,104 103,100,100,100,98 97,95,92,86**
CSF £104.02 CT £870.73 TOTE £16.10: £4.50, £2.70, £3.40; EX 124.30 Trifecta £1272.10.
Owner Lets Be Lucky Racing 4 **Bred** Redpender Stud Ltd **Trained** Maunby, N Yorks

FOCUS
A fair sprint handicap. The winner has been rated back to his best, with the runner-up close to form.

4429 REDCAR CRICKET CLUB FILLIES' H'CAP 1m
5:20 (5:22) (Class 5) (0-75,74) 3-Y-O+ **£3,234** (£962; £481; £240) **Stalls** Centre

Form RPR
-360 **1** **Lido Lady (IRE)**[12] **3983** 3-9-0 **68**.. JoeFanning 2 75
(Mark Johnston) *in tch: rdn over 2f out: hdwy to chal over 1f out: led ins fnl f: kpt on* **5/1**[3]
2103 **2** *½* **Nouvelli Dancer (IRE)**[8] **4139** 3-9-6 **74**........................... OisinMurphy 8 80
(Ivan Furtado) *trckd ldr: rdn to ld over 1f out: hdd ins fnl f: one pce* **9/2**[2]
-600 **3** *1 ¾* **Tiga Tuan (FR)**[15] **3878** 3-8-9 **63**.. GrahamLee 7 65
(Kevin Ryan) *led: rdn 3f out: hdd over 1f out: plugged on* **14/1**
0251 **4** *1* **Cabal**[5] **4240** 9-9-13 **73** 6ex...(v) DavidAllan 1 75
(Geoffrey Harker) *s.i.s: hld up: rdn over 2f out: sme hdwy over 1f out: one pce fnl f* **7/2**[1]
0110 **5** *½* **Barwah (USA)**[13] **3952** 5-8-13 **59**.. JackGarritty 6 59
(Peter Niven) *hld up: rdn over 2f out: one pce and nvr threatened* **9/2**[2]
600- **6** *5* **Lilozza (IRE)**[265] **7516** 3-8-1 **55** oh1 ow3............. RachelRichardson(3) 4 45
(Tim Easterby) *dwlt: hld up: racd keenly: rdn over 2f out: wknd fnl f* **20/1**
-004 **7** *9* **Cheeky Angel (IRE)**[10] **4043** 3-8-12 **66**.......................(p) PaulMulrennan 5 32
(Michael Dods) *chsd ldr: rdn 4f out: wknd over 1f out* **7/1**
1m 36.15s (-0.45) **Going Correction** -0.05s/f (Good)
WFA 3 from 4yo+ 8lb **7** Ran SP% **99.2**
Speed ratings (Par 100): **100,99,97,96,96 91,82**
CSF £20.40 CT £183.75 TOTE £6.10: £2.80, £2.00; EX 24.20 Trifecta £170.90.
Owner Kingsley Park 3 - Originals **Bred** Barronstown Stud **Trained** Middleham Moor, N Yorks
■ Gleaming Girl was withdrawn. Price at time of withdrawal 6/1. Rule 4 applies to all bets - deduct 10p in the pound.

FOCUS
Gleaming Girl went down in the stalls, but seemed to get out unscathed and briefly ran loose. She was withdrawn ahead of what was just a modest fillies' handicap. The third has been rated close to her maiden form.

4430 GO RACING IN YORKSHIRE FUTURE STARS APPRENTICE H'CAP 1m 6f 19y
5:50 (5:51) (Class 5) (0-70,79) 4-Y-O+ **£3,234** (£962; £481; £240) **Stalls** Low

Form RPR
040 **1** **Midnight Warrior**[35] **3191** 6-8-10 **54**................................... RowanScott 1 60
(Ron Barr) *trckd ldr: rdn over 2f out: led 1f out: styd on wl* **8/1**
2311 **2** *¾* **Ingleby Hollow**[5] **4239** 4-10-4 **79** 6ex.....................(p) PatrickVaughan(3) 4 84
(David O'Meara) *sn led: rdn over 2f out: hdd 1f out: kpt on but a jst hld* **13/8**[1]
43-0 **3** *3 ¼* **Cavalieri (IRE)**[10] **4045** 6-9-2 **60**.. HollieDoyle 2 60
(Philip Kirby) *midfield: rdn and sme hdwy over 2f out: one pce fr over 1f out* **12/1**
1326 **4** *nk* **Kiwayu**[9] **4101** 7-9-11 **69**..(p) AdamMcNamara 5 69
(Philip Kirby) *hld up: rdn and hdwy 3f out: one pce fr over 1f out* **9/4**[2]
2660 **5** *2* **Next Edition (IRE)**[37] **3118** 8-9-3 **64**............................(p) HarryBurns(3) 6 61
(Philip Kirby) *midfield: rdn and sme hdwy over 2f out: wknd ins fnl f* **7/1**[3]
-540 **6** *shd* **Celtic Power**[36] **3149** 4-9-0 **65**...................................... LewisEdmunds(7) 8 62
(Jim Goldie) *hld up: pushed along over 2f out: nvr threatened* **16/1**
6-00 **7** *6* **Zruda**[18] **3774** 5-8-7 **51** oh6.. AnnaHesketh 3 40
(David Thompson) *in tch: pushed along and lost pl 3f out: wknd over 1f out* **80/1**
0-05 **8** *6* **Danzella**[20] **3704** 4-8-2 **51** oh6.. PaulaMuir(5) 7 31
(Chris Fairhurst) *racd keenly in midfield: rdn over 3f out: hung rt over 2f out: sn wknd* **16/1**
3m 4.63s (-0.07) **Going Correction** -0.05s/f (Good) **8** Ran SP% **113.2**
Speed ratings (Par 103): **98,97,95,95,94 94,90,87**
CSF £21.00 CT £156.47 TOTE £7.80: £1.60, £1.20, £3.00; EX 24.80 Trifecta £195.80.
Owner K Trimble **Bred** Tarworth Bloodstock Investments Ltd **Trained** Seamer, N Yorks
■ Stewards' Enquiry : Patrick Vaughan two-day ban; used whip above the permitted level (31st July-1st Aug)

FOCUS
Few got into this, with the runner-up was allowed to dominate, closely pursued by the winner. Another pb from the runner-up.
T/Jkpt: Not won. T/Plt: £178.80 to a £1 stake. Pool of £70972.10 - 289.74 winning tickets.
T/Qpdt: £46.60 to a £1 stake. Pool of £6316.21 - 100.14 winning tickets. **Andrew Sheret**

4431 - 4432a (Foreign Racing) - See Raceform Interactive

4411 CURRAGH (R-H)
Sunday, July 17

OFFICIAL GOING: Good (good to yielding in places on straight course)

4433a FRIARSTOWN STUD MINSTREL STKS (GROUP 2) 7f
3:05 (3:07) 3-Y-O+
£52,058 (£16,764; £7,941; £3,529; £1,764; £882)

RPR
1 **Gordon Lord Byron (IRE)**[17] **3832** 8-9-9 107........................... BillyLee 6 116
(T Hogan, Ire) *chsd ldr in 2nd: clsr to press ldr whn carried lft ent fnl f: kpt on wl to ld fnl 100yds: styd on wl* **16/1**
2 *½* **Sovereign Debt (IRE)**[8] **4135** 7-9-9 113............................. ChrisHayes 2 115+
(David Nicholls) *racd in mid-div: rdn in 5th 2f out: gd prog into 3rd ins fnl f: kpt on wl into 2nd fnl 50yds: nt rch wnr* **7/2**[1]
3 *1 ¼* **Toscanini (IRE)**[22] **3681** 4-9-9 109...................................... JamesDoyle 4 111
(M Halford, Ire) *led: rdn over 2f out and hung lft: again edgd lft ins fnl f where hdd: no ex clsng stages and jst hld on for 3rd* **8/1**
4 *hd* **Adaay (IRE)**[22] **3664** 4-9-9 111..(p) PaulHanagan 8 111
(William Haggas) *racd in mid-div: rdn in 6th over 2f out: kpt on wl on far side into 4th ins fnl f: jst hld for 3rd* **4/1**[2]
5 *1 ¼* **Flight Risk (IRE)**[22] **3681** 5-9-9 108............................ KevinManning 9 107+
(J S Bolger, Ire) *settled off ldrs in 4th: rdn over 2f out: no imp whn hmpd in 4th ins fnl f and dropped to 5th: kpt on same pce* **7/1**
6 *2 ½* **Cheikeljack (FR)**[30] **3338** 3-9-2 110.................................. FrankieDettori 1 98
(H-A Pantall, France) *chsd ldrs in 3rd: rdn over 2f out: nt qckn ent fnl f in 5th: wknd* **5/1**[3]
7 *2* **Dick Whittington (IRE)**[31] **3332** 4-9-9 108.......................... RyanMoore 7 95
(A P O'Brien, Ire) *racd towards rr: rdn in 7th over 2f out: no imp ent fnl f* **7/2**[1]
8 *6 ½* **Alphonsus**[22] **3677** 3-9-2 99................................... DeclanMcDonogh 5 75
(John M Oxx, Ire) *sn in rr: detached after 2f: nvr a factor: kpt on one pce fnl f* **40/1**

9 3 **Final Frontier (IRE)**[10] 4065 3-9-2 106..................(p) ColmO'Donoghue 3 67
(Mrs John Harrington, Ire) *hld up: rdn in 8th over 2f out: sn wknd* **25/1**

1m 23.3s (-7.50) **Going Correction** -0.85s/f (Hard)
WFA 3 from 4yo+ 7lb 9 Ran SP% **116.9**
Speed ratings: **108,107,106,105,104 101,99,91,88**
CSF £72.36 TOTE £24.40: £3.30, £1.02, £2.60; DF 115.10 Trifecta £1577.30.
Owner Dr Cyrus Poonawalla & Morgan J Cahalan **Bred** Roland H Alder **Trained** Nenagh, Co Tipperary

FOCUS
A serious return to form from the winner, really putting his head down and battling despite some considerable interference, and it was a return to close to his very best. The second and third are solid markers.

4435a KILBOY ESTATE STKS (GROUP 2) (F&M) 1m 1f
4:15 (4:15) 3-Y-O+
£49,889 (£16,066; £7,610; £3,382; £1,691; £845)

RPR

1 **Bocca Baciata (IRE)**[21] 3695 4-9-9 111.................. ColmO'Donoghue 2 105+
(Mrs John Harrington, Ire) *racd in mid-div: travelled wl to chse ldrs 2f out: rdn into 3rd appr fnl f: styd on wl to ld cl home* **4/1**[2]

2 ½ **Earring (USA)**[6] 4218 3-9-0 97..................................(t) SeamieHeffernan 8 103
(A P O'Brien, Ire) *chsd ldrs in 3rd: sn trckd ldr in 2nd: rdn to ld narrowly under 2f out: kpt on wl fnl f: hdd cl home* **12/1**

3 shd **Hawksmoor (IRE)**[42] 2949 3-9-3 106.........................(b) FrankieDettori 12 106
(Hugo Palmer) *sn led: strly pressed over 2f out and narrowly hdd: rallied wl: dropped to 3rd cl home* **11/2**[3]

4 ¾ **Epsom Icon**[43] 2893 3-9-0 105.................................. SilvestreDeSousa 7 101
(Mick Channon) *racd in mid-div: clsr to chse ldrs in 5th 1f out: kpt on wl into 4th fnl 100yds: nrst fin* **7/1**

5 1 **Devonshire (IRE)**[32] 3271 4-9-12 109.............................. JamesDoyle 1 103
(W McCreery, Ire) *chsd ldrs in 4th: clsr in 3rd 3f out: rdn and nt qckn ent fnl f in 4th: no ex in 5th fnl 100yds* **8/1**

6 hd **Best In The World (IRE)**[35] 3202 3-9-0 96...................... RyanMoore 6 99
(A P O'Brien, Ire) *hld up: bit clsr on inner 3f out: sn swtchd lft: kpt on wl ins fnl f into 6th cl home: nrst fin* **9/1**

7 nse **Santa Monica**[25] 3539 3-9-0 97.............................. DeclanMcDonogh 11 99
(Charles O'Brien, Ire) *racd in rr: swtchd lft to outer 2f out: styd on strly ins fnl f into 7th cl home: nrst fin* **33/1**

8 nk **Kind Of Magic (IRE)**[70] 2068 3-9-0 96.................... EmmetMcNamara 9 98
(A P O'Brien, Ire) *racd towards rr: last under 2f out: kpt on wl on far side ins fnl f: nvr nrr* **33/1**

9 ½ **Duchess Andorra (IRE)**[6] 4218 5-9-9 90..................(b) NGMcCullagh 4 98
(J P Murtagh, Ire) *trckd ldr early in 2nd: sn 3rd: rdn and nt qckn under 2f out: kpt on one pce fnl f* **50/1**

10 4½ **Lady Of Dubai**[66] 2189 4-9-9 109...................................... HarryBentley 5 88
(Roger Varian) *sn chsd ldrs: rdn over 2f out: no imp appr fnl f: wknd and eased in clsng stages* **8/1**

11 nk **Tanaza (IRE)**[30] 3339 3-9-0 105... PatSmullen 13 87
(D K Weld, Ire) *racd in mid-div: prog on outer over 2f out: sn rdn and no imp over 1f out: eased ins fnl f* **7/2**[1]

12 7 **Kyllachy Queen (IRE)**[37] 3119 4-9-9 102....................... ChrisHayes 14 73
(Marco Botti) *hld up: pushed along over 3f out: no imp under 2f out and dropped to rr: no ex: eased fnl f* **33/1**

1m 54.38s (-0.52) **Going Correction** -0.05s/f (Good)
WFA 3 from 4yo+ 9lb 12 Ran SP% **120.8**
Speed ratings: **100,99,99,98,97 97,97,97,96,92 92,86**
CSF £50.84 TOTE £4.50: £1.60, £3.80, £1.80; DF 57.10 Trifecta £406.70.
Owner Flaxman Stables Ireland Ltd **Bred** Citadel Stud **Trained** Moone, Co Kildare

FOCUS
A Group 2 event which was suitably competitive, with plenty of strength-in-depth.

4434 - 4437a (Foreign Racing) - See Raceform Interactive

[2949]DUSSELDORF (R-H)
Sunday, July 17

OFFICIAL GOING: Turf: good

4438a AENGEVELT MEILEN TROPHY (GROUP 2) (3YO+) (TURF) 1m
4:00 (12:00) 3-Y-O+ **£29,411** (£11,397; £5,882; £2,941; £1,838)

RPR

1 **Kaspersky (IRE)**[49] 2729 5-9-2 0.................................. UmbertoRispoli 5 110
(Endo Botti, Italy) *chsd ldr: shkn up to chal over 2f out: rdn and led appr 1 1/2f out: r.o u.p fr 1f out: asserted fnl 50yds* **21/10**[2]

2 1 **Pas De Deux (GER)**[28] 3451 6-9-2 0................................. IanFerguson 6 108
(Yasmin Almenrader, Germany) *w.w in midfield: chsd ldng pair over 1 1/2f out: sustained chal to ldr fnl f: no ex fnl 50yds* **8/5**[1]

3 hd **Drummer (GER)**[31] 4-9-2 0.................................. AndraschStarke 3 107+
(P Schiergen, Germany) *w.w one fr last: rdn and hdwy on outer wl over 1 1/2f out: styd on fnl f: nt pce to chal* **63/10**

4 2 **Diplomat (GER)**[28] 3449 5-9-5 0................................ AndreasSuborics 4 106
(Mario Hofer, Germany) *cl up on inner: outpcd and rdn wl over 1 1/2f out: kpt on again fnl f: nvr on terms* **56/10**

5 shd **Wildpark (GER)**[52] 2633 5-9-2 0......................................(b) FilipMinarik 7 102
(Melanie Sauer, Germany) *led: rdn whn pressed 2f out: hdd appr 1 1/2f out: grad dropped away fnl f* **3/1**[3]

6 1¾ **Felician (GER)**[28] 3455 8-9-2 0.............................. AndreasHelfenbein 2 98
(Ferdinand J Leve, Germany) *settled in rr: rdn wl over 1 1/2f out: styd on fr over 1f out: nvr in contention: eased fnl 50yds* **106/10**

1m 34.98s (-6.18)
WFA 3 from 4yo+ 8lb 6 Ran SP% **133.2**
WIN (incl. 10 euro stake): 31. PLACES: 14, 14. SF: 49.
Owner Allevamento La Nuova Sbarra **Bred** Allevamento La Nuova Sbarra **Trained** Italy

[3967]MAISONS-LAFFITTE (R-H)
Sunday, July 17

OFFICIAL GOING: Turf: good

4439a PRIX EUGENE ADAM (GRAND PRIX DE MAISONS-LAFFITTE) (GROUP 2) (3YO) (STRAIGHT) (TURF) 1m 2f (S)
2:50 (12:00) 3-Y-O **£54,485** (£21,029; £10,036; £6,691; £3,345)

RPR

1 **Heshem (IRE)**[80] 1823 3-8-11 0.................................. GregoryBenoist 1 114+
(C Ferland, France) *cl up on outer of stands' side gp: 4th of eight stands' side whn shkn up appr 2f out: gd prog to ld 1 1/2f out: drvn and r.o fnl f: readily* **15/2**

2 ¾ **Ultra (IRE)**[287] 6968 3-8-11 0...................................... MickaelBarzalona 8 112
(A Fabre, France) *t.k.h: hld up 5th of eight in stands' side gp: tk clsr order over 2f out: followed eventual wnr fr 1 1/2f out: r.o u.p: a jst hld* **11/10**[1]

3 3 **Spectroscope (USA)**[19] 3-8-11 0...................... Pierre-CharlesBoudot 3 106
(A Fabre, France) *w.w towards rr of stands' side gp: styd on fr 2f out: chsd ldrs 1 1/2f out: kpt on same pce fnl f: readily outpcd by front two* **7/1**[3]

4 1¾ **Raseed**[42] 2946 3-8-11 0... AurelienLemaitre 4 103
(F Head, France) *trckd ldng pair on stands' side: rdn to chal 2f out: led appr 1 1/2f out but sn hdd: one pce fnl f* **11/2**[2]

5 1¼ **Craven's Legend (IRE)**[63] 3-8-11 0.................. VincentCheminaud 10 100+
(A Fabre, France) *chsd clr ldr on far side: clsd 2 1/2f out: led far side u.p 1 1/2f out: styd on u.p: wl hld by stands' side gp* **17/2**

6 1¼ **Kidmenever (IRE)**[35] 3-8-11 0.................................. CristianDemuro 6 98
(F Vermeulen, France) *w.w in rr of stands' side gp: prog wl over 1 1/2f out: kpt on at same pce fnl f: nvr in contention* **14/1**

7 nk **Lamarck**[36] 3-8-11 0.. OlivierPeslier 7 97
(M G Mintchev, Germany) *led gp of eight on stands' side: hdd appr 1 1/2f out: sn btn and grad dropped away* **40/1**

8 5 **Bueller (USA)**[46] 3-8-11 0... JeffersonSmith 2 87
(A Fabre, France) *hld up towards rr of stands' side gp: rdn and shortlived effrt over 2f out: sn btn* **28/1**

9 6 **Golden Bridge (FR)**[42] 2946 3-8-11 0......................... DavidMorisson 5 75
(C Gourdain, France) *chsd ldr on stands' rail: rdn and nt qckn appr 2f out: sn wknd* **10/1**

10 6 **Viserano (FR)**[105] 1230 3-8-11 0......................... ChristopheSoumillon 9 63+
(D Prod'Homme, France) *led pair on far rail: clr 1/2-way: rdn and labouring wl over 2f out: sn hdd: wknd qckly* **10/1**

2m 0.3s (-2.10) 10 Ran SP% **128.5**
WIN (incl. 1 euro stake): 8.20. PLACES: 2.30, 1.70, 2.20. DF: 12.60. SF: 27.90.
Owner Al Shaqab Racing **Bred** Yeguada De Milagro Sa **Trained** France

FOCUS
This was run over the straight mile due to flood damagae on the round course, and it resulted in a messy race. They split into two groups, with the fifth and the tenth, who was a long way clear at one stage, racing isolating on the far rail. The form fits the race averages.

4440a (Foreign Racing) - See Raceform Interactive

4441a PRIX MESSIDOR (GROUP 3) (3YO+) (STRAIGHT) (TURF) 1m (S)
3:50 (12:00) 3-Y-O+ **£29,411** (£11,764; £8,823; £5,882; £2,941)

RPR

1 **Vadamos (FR)**[54] 2568 5-9-7 0............................... VincentCheminaud 1 121+
(A Fabre, France) *w.w in 3rd: angled out and rdn to chal over 1f out: qcknd to ld ins fnl f: drvn clr: comf* **15/8**[2]

2 3 **Mr Owen (USA)**[32] 3273 4-9-1 0....................................... OlivierPeslier 5 108
(F Rohaut, France) *trckd ldr: rdn to ld on outer appr 1f out: hdd ent fnl f: readily outpcd by wnr: hld on for 2nd* **17/2**

3 snk **Territories (IRE)**[28] 3451 4-9-1 0............................. MickaelBarzalona 4 108+
(A Fabre, France) *w.w in rr of single file field: hdwy 1 1/2f out: styd on ins fnl f: jst missed 2nd and nvr on terms w wnr* **7/2**[3]

4 snk **Shutterbug (FR)**[22] 3683 4-9-1 0.............................(b) AntoineHamelin 3 107
(M Figge, Germany) *led: pushed along and qcknd tempo over 2f out: hdd appr 1f out: kpt on at same pce* **18/1**

5 1¾ **Dariyan (FR)**[54] 2568 4-9-10 0.............................. ChristopheSoumillon 2 112
(A De Royer-Dupre, France) *settled in 4th: rdn and shortlived effrt 1 1/2f out: sn btn* **5/4**[1]

1m 35.1s (-7.20) 5 Ran SP% **117.2**
WIN (incl. 1 euro stake): 3.20. PLACES: 1.60, 2.40. SF: 12.10.
Owner Scea Haras De Saint Pair **Bred** Scea Haras De Saint Pair **Trained** Chantilly, France

[4188]AYR (L-H)
Monday, July 18

OFFICIAL GOING: Good to soft (soft in places; 7.2)
Wind: Breezy, half against Weather: Overcast, warm

4442 GEORGE & RONA DONE WORKING RACE MAIDEN AUCTION FILLIES' STKS (PLUS 10 RACE) 7f 50y
1:55 (1:56) (Class 5) 2-Y-O **£3,881** (£1,155; £577; £288) **Stalls** Low

Form RPR

6 1 **Micolys (FR)**[16] 3872 2-8-10 0... BenCurtis 1 63+
(K R Burke) *trckd ldrs: rdn to chal whn leant on by runner-up over 1f out: led and hung rt ins fnl f: rdn out* **3/1**[2]

05 2 nk **Dream On Dreamer (IRE)**[16] 3872 2-8-11 0............... PaulMulrennan 2 63
(Michael Dods) *s.i.s: sn led: rdn and jnd whn hung lft over 1f out: hdd ins fnl f: carried rt towards fin: kpt on* **7/1**[3]

620 3 3¼ **London Grammar (IRE)**[19] 3772 2-8-12 0..............[1] CamHardie 4 56
(John Quinn) *t.k.h: hld up in tch: rdn and outpcd over 2f out: rallied fnl f: kpt on: nt rch first two* **8/1**

0 4 ½ **Our Lois (IRE)**[11] 4037 2-8-9 0... JasonHart 6 52+
(Keith Dalgleish) *s.i.s: bhd: drvn and outpcd 3f out: kpt on fnl f: n.d* **25/1**

545 5 1 **Serenity Dove**[27] 3477 2-8-12 0...................................... DougieCostello 5 52
(K R Burke) *t.k.h: hld up in tch: rdn and outpcd over 2f out: rallied over 1f out: no imp fnl f* **16/1**

03 6 9 **Three Duchesses**[11] 4054 2-8-12 0.................................... JoeFanning 3 30
(Michael Bell) *early ldr: trckd ldr to over 3f out: drvn and hung lft over 2f out: wknd over 1f out* **1/1**[1]

1m 35.89s (2.49) **Going Correction** +0.325s/f (Good) 6 Ran SP% **108.3**
Speed ratings (Par 91): **98,97,93,93,92 81**
CSF £21.61 TOTE £3.20: £2.10, £3.20; EX 23.50 Trifecta £85.30.
Owner Hambleton Racing Ltd Trio & E Burke **Bred** S C E A Haras Du Grand Lys Et Al **Trained** Middleham Moor, N Yorks

FOCUS
The straight course could not be used at this fixture. There had been 3mm of rain in the past 24 hours and the going was given as good to soft, soft in places, although the track was at its innermost line to provide fresh ground (distances were as advertised) and it was a drying day. This looked a modest fillies' maiden and it was hard enough work for the 2yos. Very ordinary form.

4443 POLYFLOR H'CAP — 7f 50y
2:30 (2:30) (Class 4) (0-85,85) 3-Y-O+ **£5,822** (£1,732; £865; £432) **Stalls** High

Form — RPR

0022 **1** — **Forever A Lady (IRE)**[11] 4034 3-8-10 **74** .... JoeFanning 3 — 79
(Keith Dalgleish) *mde all at ordinary gallop: rdn over 1f out: hld on wl fnl f* **9/2**[3]

6032 **2** ½ **Moonlightnavigator (USA)**[7] 4193 4-9-6 **77** .... DougieCostello 4 — 84
(John Quinn) *trckd ldrs: rdn over 2f out: hdwy and edgd rt over 1f out: chsd wnr ins fnl f: clsng at fin* **7/2**[2]

4606 **3** nk **Tiger Jim**[7] 4193 6-9-10 **81** .... PaulMulrennan 8 — 87
(Jim Goldie) *t.k.h: hld up: pushed along over 2f out: hdwy on outside over 1f out: kpt on wl fnl f: nrst fin* **7/1**

6643 **4** 1½ **Call Out Loud**[10] 4089 4-8-10 **67** .... (p) AndrewMullen 7 — 69
(Michael Appleby) *t.k.h early: pressed wnr: rdn and ev ch over 2f out to over 1f out: edgd lft: no ex and lost 2 pls ins fnl f* **12/1**

6-00 **5** nse **Invoke (IRE)**[15] 3923 5-10-0 **85** .... ConnorBeasley 1 — 87
(Keith Dalgleish) *hld up in tch: effrt whn nt clr run briefly over 1f out: swtchd lft and sn rdn: no imp fnl f* **16/1**

061 **6** ½ **Dandyleekie (IRE)**[16] 3892 4-9-11 **82** .... DanielTudhope 9 — 83
(David O'Meara) *in tch: stdy hdwy over 2f out: rdn over 1f out: outpcd ins fnl f* **10/3**[1]

0-51 **7** 2¾ **Royal Duchess**[7] 4193 6-9-0 **76** 6ex .... AdamMcNamara(5) 5 — 70
(Lucy Normile) *taken early to post: hld up in last pl: rdn and effrt over 2f out: no imp over 1f out: btn fnl f* **11/2**

1260 **8** 1 **Rocco's Delight**[26] 3517 4-9-7 **78** .... (p) BenCurtis 6 — 69
(Brian Ellison) *t.k.h: prom: drvn along over 2f out: wknd over 1f out* **9/1**

1m 35.27s (1.87) **Going Correction** +0.325s/f (Good)
WFA 3 from 4yo+ 7lb — **8** Ran SP% **114.9**
Speed ratings (Par 105): **102,101,101,99,99 98,95,94**
CSF £20.77 CT £108.76 TOTE £3.40: £1.60, £1.40, £1.90; EX 19.50 Trifecta £119.10.
Owner Ken McGarrity **Bred** Mick McGinn **Trained** Carluke, S Lanarks

FOCUS
The winner got a well-judged front-running ride. The runner-up is rated to his C&D latest.

4444 RACING UK DAY PASS JUST £10 H'CAP (DIV I) — 7f 50y
3:05 (3:06) (Class 6) (0-65,64) 3-Y-O+ **£2,587** (£770; £384; £192) **Stalls** High

Form — RPR

020 **1** — **Dark Crystal**[10] 4102 5-9-10 **60** .... DavidNolan 5 — 70
(Linda Perratt) *in tch: stdy hdwy over 2f out: rdn and chsd wnr appr fnl f: kpt on u.p to ld last stride* **5/1**[3]

4402 **2** nse **Dark Command**[16] 3877 3-9-5 **62** .... (p) ConnorBeasley 7 — 69
(Michael Dods) *trckd ldrs gng wl: smooth hdwy to ld over 1f out: sn rdn and edgd lft: kpt on fnl f: hdd last stride* **5/2**[1]

1520 **3** 5 **Emblaze**[56] 2528 4-9-3 **58** .... PhilDennis(5) 4 — 56
(Bryan Smart) *trckd ldrs: rdn and ev ch over 2f out to over 1f out: outpcd by first two ins fnl f* **12/1**

0340 **4** ½ **Riponian**[20] 3750 6-8-7 **48** .... (t) NathanEvans(5) 8 — 44
(Susan Corbett) *led at decent gallop: rdn and hdd over 1f out: kpt on same pce fnl f* **8/1**

-643 **5** 3 **Ss Vega**[14] 3941 3-8-6 **49** .... JoeyHaynes 2 — 35+
(James Bethell) *hld up: pushed along and outpcd 1/2-way: rallied over 1f out: kpt on fnl f: nvr able to chal* **10/3**[2]

-200 **6** 1 **Drinks For Losers (IRE)**[15] 3921 5-8-9 **45** .... AndrewMullen 10 — 32
(Linda Perratt) *s.i.s: hld up: rdn along over 2f out: sme hdwy over 1f out: nvr rchd ldrs* **16/1**

016- **7** 1¼ **Straight Arrow**[17] 3867 4-9-7 **64** .... (t) RobbieDolan(7) 3 — 48
(Noel C Kelly, Ire) *s.i.s: bhd: drvn along over 2f out: sn no imp* **16/1**

000- **8** shd **Icy Blue**[299] 6656 8-9-1 **51** .... GeorgeChaloner 9 — 34
(Richard Whitaker) *s.i.s: hld up: rdn along and effrt on outside over 2f out: no further imp over 1f out: btn fnl f* **25/1**

00-0 **9** 13 **Centre Haafhd**[15] 3924 5-9-7 **57** .... PaulMulrennan 1 — 8
(Jim Goldie) *s.i.s: hld up in midfield on ins: rdn over 2f out: sn wknd* **25/1**

4-50 **10** nk **Amy Blair**[37] 3153 3-8-7 **50** .... JoeFanning 6
(Keith Dalgleish) *t.k.h: trckd ldr: drvn over 2f out: sn wknd* **9/1**

1m 35.11s (1.71) **Going Correction** +0.325s/f (Good)
WFA 3 from 4yo+ 7lb — **10** Ran SP% **116.6**
Speed ratings (Par 101): **103,102,97,96,93 92,90,90,75,75**
CSF £17.86 CT £139.22 TOTE £6.10: £1.90, £1.40, £2.70; EX 21.10 Trifecta £110.10.
Owner Nil Sine Labore Partnership **Bred** R Biggs **Trained** East Kilbride, S Lanarks

FOCUS
A moderate handicap where pace held up well. The winner is rated back to last year's level.

4445 RACING UK DAY PASS JUST £10 H'CAP (DIV II) — 7f 50y
3:40 (3:40) (Class 6) (0-65,63) 3-Y-O+ **£2,587** (£770; £384; £192) **Stalls** High

Form — RPR

-005 **1** — **Charava (IRE)**[10] 4102 4-9-10 **59** .... (v) DanielTudhope 2 — 65
(Patrick Holmes) *t.k.h: hld up: stdy hdwy and edging lft fr over 2f out: rdn to ld ins fnl f: jst hld on* **10/3**[2]

6043 **2** nse **Niqnaaqpaadiwaaq**[3] 4369 4-10-0 **63** .... NeilFarley 6 — 69
(Eric Alston) *led: rdn over 2f out: hdd ins fnl f: rallied: jst failed* **11/4**[1]

-355 **3** 2¾ **Full Of Promise**[16] 3898 3-9-1 **62** .... AdamMcNamara(5) 5 — 58
(Richard Fahey) *prom: drvn along over 2f out: kpt on u.p fnl f: nt rch first two* **8/1**

2-52 **4** nse **El Principe**[19] 3776 3-9-4 **60** .... JasonHart 7 — 56
(Les Eyre) *t.k.h: pressed ldr to over 1f out: drvn and kpt on same pce ins fnl f* **4/1**[3]

2222 **5** 2 **Affectionate Lady (IRE)**[9] 4144 5-9-3 **57** .... (b) PhilDennis(5) 4 — 51
(Keith Reveley) *s.i.s: sn rdn in rr: drvn over 2f out: kpt on fnl f: nvr able to chal* **9/2**

0-04 **6** ¾ **Cape Crusader (IRE)**[24] 3603 3-8-11 **53** .... ConnorBeasley 3 — 42
(Michael Dods) *trckd ldrs: effrt and drvn along over 2f out: wknd ins fnl f* **16/1**

-660 **7** ¾ **Jubilee Song**[15] 3921 4-8-10 **45** .... (b) GeorgeChaloner 9 — 35
(Richard Whitaker) *prom: drvn along over 2f out: wknd wl over 1f out* **66/1**

0-61 **8** 2½ **Lady Cordie**[61] 2360 4-9-0 **49** .... PaulMulrennan 1 — 33
(Jim Goldie) *s.i.s: t.k.h: hld up on ins: struggling over 2f out: sn btn* **16/1**

0065 **9** 1 **Takahiro**[7] 4192 4-8-10 **45** .... (tp) AndrewMullen 8 — 26
(Linda Perratt) *s.i.s: hld up: drvn along wl over 2f out: sn btn* **50/1**

1m 35.46s (2.06) **Going Correction** +0.325s/f (Good)
WFA 3 from 4yo+ 7lb — **9** Ran SP% **114.3**
Speed ratings (Par 101): **101,100,97,97,95 94,93,90,89**
CSF £12.77 CT £66.44 TOTE £4.50: £1.50, £1.40, £2.40; EX 13.90 Trifecta £76.40.
Owner Oakfield Racing **Bred** Mike Hyde **Trained** Middleham, N Yorks

FOCUS
The second division of a moderate handicap. The winner is rated near last year's best.

4446 WATCH RACING UK IN HD H'CAP — 1m 1f 20y
4:10 (4:10) (Class 5) (0-75,77) 3-Y-O+ **£3,557** (£1,058; £529; £264) **Stalls** Low

Form — RPR

4224 **1** — **Archie's Advice**[7] 4190 5-9-13 **74** .... JasonHart 3 — 83
(Keith Dalgleish) *t.k.h: prom: rdn to ld 1f out: edgd lft: kpt on wl fnl f* **4/1**[3]

5044 **2** 1½ **Fray**[15] 3922 5-9-11 **72** .... PaulMulrennan 2 — 78
(Jim Goldie) *hld up in last pl: stdy hdwy whn nt clr run over 2f out to over 1f out: plld out and chsd wnr ins fnl f: kpt on: nt pce to chal* **5/1**

3231 **3** 1¾ **Eastern Dragon (IRE)**[7] 4189 6-9-11 **77** 6ex .... GarryWhillans(5) 1 — 79
(Iain Jardine) *trckd ldrs: drvn along over 2f out: n.m.r briefly over 1f out: kpt on same pce ins fnl f* **10/3**[1]

6612 **4** 1 **Mujazif (IRE)**[30] 3395 6-10-0 **75** .... (p) AndrewMullen 4 — 75
(Michael Appleby) *s.i.s: hld up in tch on outside: rdn 3f out: hdwy and edgd lft over 1f out: no imp fnl f* **7/2**[2]

0053 **5** 2¼ **Taking Libertys**[17] 3841 3-9-1 **71** .... (b[1]) DanielTudhope 5 — 65
(Kevin Ryan) *led: rdn over 2f out: hdd 1f out: wknd last 100yds* **7/1**

0540 **6** 6 **Almuhalab**[14] 3943 5-8-12 **59** .... JackGarritty 6 — 41
(Ruth Carr) *pressed ldr tl rdn: edgd lft and wknd fr 2f out* **10/1**

005 **7** 2 **Haymarket**[15] 3922 7-9-4 **65** .... ConnorBeasley 7 — 42
(R Mike Smith) *trckd ldrs on outside: drvn along over 2f out: wknd wl over 1f out* **12/1**

3-60 **8** shd **Spirit Of The Sea (IRE)**[181] 251 4-8-9 **56** .... GeorgeChaloner 9 — 33
(Richard Whitaker) *s.i.s: hld up: drvn along 3f out: btn fnl 2f* **40/1**

2m 1.4s (3.90) **Going Correction** +0.325s/f (Good)
WFA 3 from 4yo+ 9lb — **8** Ran SP% **113.7**
Speed ratings (Par 103): **95,93,92,91,89 83,82,82**
CSF £23.97 CT £72.56 TOTE £5.20: £1.90, £1.10, £1.50; EX 22.20 Trifecta £110.90.
Owner A R M Galbraith **Bred** G L S Partnership **Trained** Carluke, S Lanarks

FOCUS
A modest handicap and they didn't look to go that quick. The winner looks back to his best.

4447 HIGH DEFINITION RACING UK APPRENTICE H'CAP — 1m 5f 13y
4:40 (4:40) (Class 6) (0-65,65) 3-Y-O+ **£2,587** (£770; £384; £192) **Stalls** Low

Form — RPR

044- **1** — **Thackeray**[120] 8269 9-8-4 **46** oh1 .... PaulaMuir(5) 4 — 52
(Chris Fairhurst) *hld up in last pl: hdwy on outside over 2f out: led ins fnl f: rdn and kpt on wl* **28/1**

3241 **2** nk **Falcon's Fire (IRE)**[3] 4340 3-8-8 **61** 6ex .... CliffordLee(3) 5 — 67
(Keith Dalgleish) *pressed ldr: rdn to ld over 2f out: hdd ins fnl f: kpt on: hld nr fin* **2/1**[2]

0-33 **3** shd **Transpennine Star**[11] 4033 3-9-1 **65** .... AdamMcNamara 6 — 70
(Michael Dods) *led: rn wd bnd after nrly 2f: rdn and hdd over 2f out: rallied and sn ev ch: kpt on ins fnl f: hld towards fin* **5/4**[1]

60 **4** 4½ **Shumaker (IRE)**[20] 3761 4-8-4 **46** .... RobbieDolan(5) 1 — 45
(Noel C Kelly, Ire) *hld up in tch: drvn and outpcd over 2f out: edgd lft over 1f out: kpt on fnl f: nt pce to chal* **8/1**

05-0 **5** ½ **Latin Rebel (IRE)**[15] 3921 9-8-8 **52** .... (p) LewisEdmunds(7) 2 — 50
(Jim Goldie) *in tch: stdy hdwy over 2f out: rdn over 1f out: outpcd fnl f* **16/1**

0401 **6** 10 **Kelvin Hall**[12] 4013 3-9-0 **64** .... GeorgiaCox 3 — 47
(Mark Johnston) *chsd ldrs: drvn along over 2f out: sn wknd* **13/2**[3]

3m 1.59s (7.59) **Going Correction** +0.325s/f (Good)
WFA 3 from 4yo+ 13lb — **6** Ran SP% **111.6**
Speed ratings (Par 101): **90,89,89,86,86 80**
CSF £83.04 TOTE £27.70: £9.70, £1.30; EX 59.10 Trifecta £377.70.
Owner Mrs C A Arnold **Bred** Mrs R D Peacock **Trained** Middleham, N Yorks

FOCUS
The second and third gave each other no peace up front and the winner came from last. He was entitled to win on last year's form.

4448 RACING UK GLASGOW FAIR H'CAP — 1m
5:10 (5:12) (Class 2) (0-100,97) 3-Y-O+
£15,562 (£4,660; £2,330; £1,165; £582; £292) **Stalls** Low

Form — RPR

0021 **1** — **Dream Walker (FR)**[16] 3895 7-8-13 **82** .... (t) BenCurtis 8 — 93
(Brian Ellison) *prom on outside: smooth hdwy to ld over 2f out: rdn and edgd lft over 1f out: kpt on strly fnl f* **15/2**[3]

-010 **2** 1¾ **Le Chat D'Or**[15] 3923 8-9-3 **86** .... (bt) PaulMulrennan 9 — 93
(Michael Dods) *dwlt: hld up: effrt whn nt clr run over 2f out to over 1f out: gd hdwy to chse wnr ins fnl f: kpt on* **33/1**

0460 **3** 1¾ **Fort Bastion (IRE)**[30] 3390 7-9-11 **94** .... (b) DanielTudhope 13 — 97
(David O'Meara) *dwlt: hld up: hdwy on outside over 2f out: chsd wnr briefly ins fnl f: kpt on same pce* **9/1**

0243 **4** 1¾ **Gworn**[15] 3920 6-8-11 **80** .... (p) JoeyHaynes 1 — 79
(R Mike Smith) *hld up in tch on ins: effrt and rdn over 2f out: kpt on same pce fnl f* **16/1**

02 **5** ½ **Mikmak**[24] 3600 3-8-13 **90** .... AndrewMullen 14 — 86
(William Muir) *hld up: hdwy on outside to chse wnr over 1f out to ins fnl f: sn no ex* **12/1**

1210 **6** ½ **Dolphin Vista (IRE)**[37] 3157 3-9-4 **95** .... JackGarritty 11 — 90
(Richard Fahey) *midfield on outside: rdn over 2f out: hdwy over 1f out: sn no imp* **15/2**[3]

1-20 **7** ¾ **Another Touch**[58] 2473 3-9-2 **93** .... DavidNolan 3 — 86
(Richard Fahey) *trckd ldrs: nt clr run over 2f out to over 1f out: sn rdn and one pce* **8/1**

1000 **8** 1½ **Finn Class (IRE)**[15] 3923 5-9-6 **89** .... ConnorBeasley 10 — 80
(Michael Dods) *chsd ldr 2f: prom: nt clr run briefly over 2f out: sn rdn: outpcd appr fnl f* **18/1**

123 **9** 4 **Nicholas T**[15] 3923 4-8-11 **80** .... JasonHart 6 — 62
(Jim Goldie) *t.k.h: led to over 2f out: rdn and wknd over 1f out* **6/1**[2]

0-10 **10** 1¼ **Keystroke**[107] 1195 4-9-13 **96** .... JoeFanning 2 — 75
(Jeremy Noseda) *hld up: effrt whn nt clr run over 2f out to over 1f out: sn rdn and no imp* **9/2**[1]

0320 **11** ¾ **Lat Hawill (IRE)**[30] 3390 5-9-7 **97** .... CliffordLee(7) 4 — 75
(Keith Dalgleish) *prom: nt clr run briefly over 2f out: sn rdn and wknd* **20/1**

3-31 **12** ½ **Pintura**[15] 3923 9-9-9 **92**....................(b) CamHardie 12 69
(Alistair Whillans) *hld up towards rr: drvn along over 2f out: wknd wl over 1f out* **20/1**

52-5 **13** 5 **Lord Ben Stack (IRE)**[104] 1245 4-9-12 **95**.................. DougieCostello 5 60
(K R Burke) *prom: hdwy to press ldr after 2f: rdn over 3f out: wkng whn hmpd over 1f out* **17/2**

1m 44.07s (0.27) **Going Correction** +0.325s/f (Good)
WFA 3 from 4yo+ 8lb **13** Ran SP% **118.9**
Speed ratings (Par 109): **111,109,107,105,105 104,104,102,98,97 96,96,91**
CSF £238.79 CT £2257.87 TOTE £7.60: £2.60, £10.20, £3.70; EX 184.00 Trifecta £4867.10.
Owner Keith Brown **Bred** John Berry **Trained** Norton, N Yorks

FOCUS
A decent handicap run at a sound pace. The winner looks back to something like his best.

4449 RACING UK HD H'CAP 1m
5:40 (5:41) (Class 6) (0-65,65) 3-Y-O+ **£2,911** (£866; £432; £216) **Stalls** Low

Form RPR

605 **1** **The Lynch Man**[12] 4003 3-9-6 **65**....................(v[1]) CamHardie 6 71
(John Quinn) *t.k.h: prom: wnt 2nd over 2f out: sn rdn: kpt on wl fnl f to ld towards fin* **8/1**

4005 **2** nk **Wayside Magic**[5] 4275 3-8-5 **50**....................(p) ConnorBeasley 1 55
(Michael Dods) *led: rdn over 2f out: kpt on u.p fnl f: hdd and no ex towards fin* **9/1**

-406 **3** 1¾ **Remember Rocky**[11] 4038 7-9-7 **63**....................(b[1]) AdamMcNamara[(5)] 2 66
(Lucy Normile) *chsd ldrs: drvn and outpcd over 3f out: rallied over 1f out: kpt on ins fnl f* **15/2**[3]

2211 **4** hd **Toffee Apple (IRE)**[6] 4233 3-9-1 **60** 6ex.................... JoeyHaynes 8 61
(Keith Dalgleish) *hld up in tch: effrt and rdn over 2f out: kpt on ins fnl f: no imp* **1/1**[1]

333 **5** shd **Totally Magic (IRE)**[12] 4006 4-9-10 **61**....................(p) KeaganLatham 5 64
(Richard Whitaker) *hld up: hdwy on outside over 2f out: chsd ldrs over 1f out: no ex ins fnl f* **5/1**[2]

4046 **6** 11 **Studio Star**[6] 4228 4-8-4 **46**.................... NathanEvans[(5)] 3 23
(Wilf Storey) *s.i.s: bhd: drvn along over 2f out: sn btn* **20/1**

1004 **7** 30 **Haidees Reflection**[7] 4189 6-9-13 **64**....................(p) PaulMulrennan 4
(Jim Goldie) *t.k.h early: pressed ldr: drvn and lost pl over 2f out: sn struggling: eased whn no ch fnl f* **10/1**

1m 46.73s (2.93) **Going Correction** +0.325s/f (Good)
WFA 3 from 4yo+ 8lb **7** Ran SP% **113.4**
Speed ratings (Par 101): **98,97,95,95,95 84,54**
CSF £73.25 CT £560.31 TOTE £8.80: £3.30, £5.50; EX 97.90 Trifecta £500.30.
Owner Bob McMillan **Bred** M C Humby **Trained** Settrington, N Yorks

FOCUS
It proved hard to make up ground in this moderate handicap. The fourth helps with the level.
T/Jkpt: Not won. T/Plt: £66.90 to a £1 stake. Pool of £73019.22 - 795.75 winning tickets. T/Qpdt: £10.60 to a £1 stake. Pool of £8259.14 - 572.85 winning tickets. **Richard Young**

4227 BEVERLEY (R-H)
Monday, July 18

OFFICIAL GOING: Good to firm (8.2)
Wind: Light against Weather: Fine & dry

4450 RIO RIO CARNIVAL NIGHT MAIDEN H'CAP 2m 35y
5:35 (5:35) (Class 6) (0-65,60) 3-Y-O **£2,587** (£770; £384; £192) **Stalls** Low

Form RPR

0-64 **1** **Hazely**[48] 2772 3-8-8 **47**.................... PJMcDonald 3 55
(James Bethell) *trckd ldng pair: effrt and nt clr run over 1f out: sn swtchd lft and rdn ent fnl f: styd on wl to ld last 100yds* **9/2**[3]

5-05 **2** 1¼ **Monjeni**[13] 3991 3-9-7 **60**....................(v) LukeMorris 2 66
(Sir Mark Prescott Bt) *plld hrd early: hld up in rr: pushed along 5f out: hdwy on bit to trck ldrs over 2f out: effrt over 1f out: sn rdn to ld ent fnl f: sn drvn: carried hd high and hung rt: hdd and no ex last 100yds* **13/8**[2]

0032 **3** 1½ **Chestnut Storm (IRE)**[7] 4210 3-9-2 **55**.................... SilvestreDeSousa 5 60
(Ed Dunlop) *trckd ldr: cl up 4f out: led over 2f out and sn rdn: drvn and hdd ent fnl f: kpt on wl u.p tl hmpd on inner ent fnl 100yds: nt rcvr* **11/10**[1]

00-0 **4** 14 **Rob's Legacy**[14] 3951 3-8-1 **45**.................... CharlieBennett[(5)] 4 32
(Shaun Harris) *t.k.h early: trckd ldrs: pushed along 4f out: rdn over 2f out: sn drvn and wknd* **50/1**

5040 **5** 9 **Citadel**[8] 3482 3-8-6 **45**....................(b[1]) RoystonFfrench 1 21
(John Wainwright) *set stdy pce: pushed along and qcknd over 4f out: rdn along 3f out: hdd over 2f out: sn drvn and wknd* **20/1**

3m 36.42s (-3.38) **Going Correction** -0.375s/f (Firm) **5** Ran SP% **110.6**
Speed ratings (Par 98): **93,92,91,84,80**
CSF £12.37 TOTE £6.80: £2.20, £1.30; EX 11.80 Trifecta £17.00.
Owner Clarendon Thoroughbred Racing **Bred** Whitley Stud **Trained** Middleham Moor, N Yorks

FOCUS
An ordinary staying event but the third is a reasonable yardstick and the winner should continue to go the right way. The gallop looked pretty sedate until past halfway. After rail movement the actual race distance was 2m23yds.

4451 RACING AGAIN NEXT TUESDAY MAIDEN FILLIES' STKS (PLUS 10 RACE) 5f
6:05 (6:09) (Class 5) 2-Y-O **£3,780** (£1,131; £565; £283; £141) **Stalls** Low

Form RPR

1 **The Wagon Wheel (IRE)** 2-9-0 0.................... TonyHamilton 3 73+
(Richard Fahey) *trckd ldng pair: pushed along over 2f out: rdn to ld appr fnl f: sn drvn and kpt on wl towards fin* **11/10**[1]

24 **2** ¾ **Broadhaven Honey (IRE)**[47] 2793 2-9-0 0.................... GrahamLee 2 70
(Ed McMahon) *trckd ldr: hdwy and cl up over 1f out: rdn to chal ins fnl f: ev ch tl drvn and no ex towards fin* **3/1**[2]

0 **3** 1½ **Frozen Kiss**[65] 2254 2-9-0 0.................... SamJames 4 65
(Bryan Smart) *chsd ldrs: rdn and hdwy over 1f out: kpt on fnl f* **16/1**

4 nk **Mere Brow** 2-9-0 0.................... PJMcDonald 8 64+
(Ann Duffield) *midfield: pushed along 2f out: rdn over 1f out: kpt on fnl f* **25/1**

5 1¼ **Street Jazz** 2-9-0 0.................... TomEaves 12 59+
(James Given) *in tch on wd outside: pushed along 2f out: rdn over 1f out: kpt on fnl f* **25/1**

6 ½ **Bloomin Lovely (IRE)** 2-9-0 0.................... SilvestreDeSousa 9 58
(John Quinn) *towards rr: hdwy 2f out: styd on fnl f: nrst fin* **5/1**[3]

033 **7** 1 **Clear As A Bell (IRE)**[17] 3839 2-9-0 0.................... DuranFentiman 6 54
(Tim Easterby) *chsd ldrs: rdn along wl over 1f out: no imp* **9/1**

0 **8** 4 **Flying Hope (IRE)**[6] 4227 2-9-0 0.................... RoystonFfrench 10 40+
(Nigel Tinkler) *qckly away and set str pce: rdn wl over 1f out: hdd and drvn appr fnl f: sn wknd* **80/1**

00 **9** 1¾ **Beau Strata (IRE)**[14] 3947 2-9-0 0.................... JamesSullivan 5 33
(Clive Mulhall) *a towards rr* **100/1**

0 **10** 1 **Dreamorchid (IRE)**[11] 4037 2-9-0 0.................... DavidAllan 1 30
(Tim Easterby) *a towards rr* **40/1**

11 13 **Henrietta's Dream** 2-9-0 0.................... PaddyAspell 11
(John Wainwright) *green sn outpcd and detached in rr* **100/1**

12 6 **Piccolino** 2-8-9 0.................... JordanVaughan[(5)] 7
(John David Riches) *unruly in preliminaries: green: sn rdn along and outpcd: detached bef 1/2-way* **80/1**

1m 2.1s (-1.40) **Going Correction** -0.325s/f (Firm) **12** Ran SP% **119.7**
Speed ratings (Par 91): **98,96,94,93,91 91,89,83,80,78 57,48**
CSF £4.19 TOTE £2.10: £1.10, £1.70, £5.40; EX 5.60 Trifecta £33.60.
Owner T Proctor **Bred** Rathbarry Stud & Abbeylands Farm **Trained** Musley Bank, N Yorks

FOCUS
A fair fillies' maiden, the winner overcoming greenness to justify strong support on debut. A few of the other newcomers showed promise and are likely to improve for this initial experience. The form is rated around the runner-up.

4452 JAIMIE KERR MEMORIAL H'CAP 5f
6:35 (6:35) (Class 5) (0-75,75) 3-Y-O+ **£3,780** (£1,131; £565; £283; £141) **Stalls** Low

Form RPR

30/0 **1** **Ziggy Lee**[48] 2775 10-9-12 **75**.................... RichardKingscote 1 83
(Lawrence Mullaney) *trckd ldrs on inner: hdwy over 1f out: swtchd lft and rdn to chal ins fnl f: led last 75yds: drvn out* **12/1**

5221 **2** nk **Oriental Splendour (IRE)**[21] 3713 4-9-8 **71**.................... JamesSullivan 12 78+
(Ruth Carr) *towards rr: gd hdwy on outer over 1f out: rdn and edgd rt ins fnl f: fin strly* **5/1**[2]

6001 **3** ¾ **Maureb (IRE)**[26] 3521 4-9-10 **73**....................(p) DuranFentiman 3 77
(Tony Coyle) *hld up towards rr: hdwy on inner over 1f out: n.m.r ins fnl f: swtchd lft and squeezed through last 100yds: kpt on* **11/1**

0001 **4** nk **Eternitys Gate**[42] 2975 5-9-11 **74**.................... SilvestreDeSousa 6 77
(Ivan Furtado) *led 1f: cl up: rdn wl over 1f out and ev ch: drvn ins fnl f and kpt on towards fin* **3/1**[1]

3034 **5** shd **Groundworker (IRE)**[11] 4039 5-9-3 **66**.................... GrahamLee 7 69
(Paul Midgley) *sn in tch: hdwy to chse ldrs 2f out: rdn over 1f out: styd on fnl f: n.m.r towards fin* **9/1**

0-60 **6** ½ **Innocently (IRE)**[42] 2975 5-8-13 **67**.................... JoshDoyle[(5)] 5 68
(David O'Meara) *cl up on inner: rdn to ld wl over 1f out: drvn ent fnl f: hdd and no ex last 75yds* **10/1**

4506 **7** ¾ **Windforpower (IRE)**[19] 3779 6-8-13 **62**....................(p) DaleSwift 4 60
(Tracy Waggott) *chsd ldrs: rdn over 1f out: drvn ins fnl f: hld whn n.m.r towards fin* **33/1**

5214 **8** 1 **Burtonwood**[16] 3882 4-8-12 **68**....................(p) KieranSchofield[(7)] 14 63
(Julie Camacho) *midfield: hdwy wl over 1f out: sn rdn and no imp fnl f* **20/1**

3040 **9** shd **Pushkin Museum (IRE)**[21] 3709 5-9-3 **66**....................(p) FrannyNorton 2 60
(Richard Fahey) *chsd ldrs: rdn along wl over 1f out: drvn and wknd appr fnl f* **10/1**

6065 **10** nk **Whozthecat (IRE)**[7] 4191 9-9-7 **70**....................(b) DavidAllan 13 63
(Declan Carroll) *dwlt: a in rr* **9/1**

4250 **11** 1 **Flicka's Boy**[42] 2975 4-9-8 **71**....................(b[1]) BarryMcHugh 8 61
(Tony Coyle) *chsd ldrs: rdn along wl over 1f out: sn drvn and wknd* **8/1**[3]

2510 **12** 1½ **Bronze Beau**[15] 3925 9-9-5 **68**....................(tp) ShaneGray 9 52
(Kristin Stubbs) *cl up: led after 1f: rdn along 2f out: sn hdd: drvn and wknd over 1f out* **28/1**

1m 2.06s (-1.44) **Going Correction** -0.325s/f (Firm) **12** Ran SP% **118.1**
Speed ratings (Par 103): **98,97,96,95,95 94,93,92,91,91 89,87**
CSF £69.24 CT £703.85 TOTE £10.80: £3.50, £1.80, £4.00; EX 52.20 Trifecta £317.00.
Owner Rothmere Racing Limited **Bred** Ian Allan **Trained** Great Habton, N Yorks

FOCUS
A fair sprint with some in-form horses coming to the fore, the second and third both shaping well. The winner retains most of his ability.

4453 RICHARD AND CAROL HUDSON H'CAP 7f 100y
7:05 (7:05) (Class 4) (0-85,83) 3-Y-O+ **£6,301** (£1,886; £707; £707; £235) **Stalls** Low

Form RPR

1502 **1** **Jacbequick**[4] 4312 5-9-8 **82**....................(v) JoshDoyle[(5)] 3 95
(David O'Meara) *dwlt and in rr: hdwy on outer over 2f out: chsd ldrs over 1f out: rdn to ld jst ins fnl f: rdr dropped whip 100yds out: kpt on: sn clr* **4/1**[1]

0001 **2** 4 **Abareeq**[19] 3783 3-9-1 **77**.................... FrannyNorton 8 77
(Mark Johnston) *in tch: rdn along over 2f out and sn outpcd: styd on strly u.p on outer fnl f: tk 2nd nr line* **6/1**[3]

-012 **3** hd **Invermere**[19] 3775 3-9-0 **76**.................... TonyHamilton 6 75
(Richard Fahey) *chsd ldng pair: hdwy over 2f out: rdn wl over 1f out: drvn and kpt on same pce fnl f* **5/1**[2]

0223 **3** dht **Relight My Fire**[6] 4231 6-8-10 **68**....................(p) RachelRichardson[(3)] 4 70
(Tim Easterby) *chsd ldrs: rdn along 2f out: styd on u.p fnl f* **5/1**[2]

4100 **5** nk **Hulcolt (IRE)**[26] 3518 5-9-13 **82**.................... SilvestreDeSousa 2 83
(Ivan Furtado) *chsd clr ldr: rdn along 2f out: drvn over 1f out: kpt on u.p fnl f* **4/1**[1]

331 **6** ½ **Spryt (IRE)**[17] 3840 4-10-0 **83**....................(v) GrahamGibbons 1 83
(David O'Meara) *set str pce and sn clr: rdn along over 1f out: drvn and hdd jst ins fnl f: kpt on same pce* **4/1**[1]

1344 **7** 16 **Favourite Treat (USA)**[14] 3945 6-9-9 **78**....................(e) JamesSullivan 7 38
(Ruth Carr) *stmbld s: a in rr* **14/1**

1m 30.34s (-3.46) **Going Correction** -0.375s/f (Firm)
WFA 3 from 4yo+ 7lb **7** Ran SP% **114.3**
Speed ratings (Par 105): **104,99,99,99,98 98,80**
WIN: £2.90 Jacbequick; PL: £1.90 Jacbequick, £3.20 Abareeq; EXACTA: £31.90; CSF: 28.03; TRIFECTA: J/A/T £57.50, J/A/R £74.00..
Owner Cherry Garth Racing **Bred** Russ Wake **Trained** Upper Helmsley, N Yorks

FOCUS
After rail movement the actual race distance was 7f 123yds. A pretty useful effort from the winner who benefited from being held up in a race run at strong pace courtesy of his stablemate.

4454 SKY BET GO-RACING-IN-YORKSHIRE SUMMER FESTIVAL H'CAP 7f 100y
7:40 (7:40) (Class 6) (0-65,65) 3-Y-O+ **£2,587** (£770; £384; £192) **Stalls** Low

Form RPR

0326 **1** **City Of Night (IRE)**[31] 3366 4-9-4 **60**....................(e) JoshDoyle[(5)] 8 67
(Julie Camacho) *hld up towards rr: gd hdwy on outer over 2f out: rdn to ld over 1f out: drvn clr ins fnl f: kpt on* **7/1**[3]

1000 **2** ½ **Faintly (USA)**[10] 4102 5-10-0 **65**................................(b[1]) JamesSullivan 5 72
(Ruth Carr) *hld up towards rr: hdwy on inner 2f out: nt clr run and swtchd lft ent fnl f: rdn and fin strly* **20/1**

2464 **3** 1 ¾ **Weld Al Khawaneej (IRE)**[13] 3982 3-9-5 **63**...................(p) TomEaves 6 61
(Kevin Ryan) *hld up in rr: hdwy on outer wl over 1f out: sn rdn and styd on wl fnl f* **7/1**[3]

0-04 **4** ¾ **Shadowtime**[17] 3838 11-9-9 **60**.. DaleSwift 10 61
(Tracy Waggott) *hld up towards rr: hdwy 2f out: rdn over 1f out: styd on wl towards fin* **16/1**

0033 **5** 1 ½ **Make On Madam (IRE)**[6] 4240 4-9-13 **64**.......................... DavidAllan 9 60
(Les Eyre) *hld up: hdwy wl over 1f out: rdn and kpt on fnl f* **5/1**[2]

0020 **6** ¾ **Adiator**[6] 4240 8-9-7 **58**....................................(p) SilvestreDeSousa 4 52+
(Neville Bycroft) *trckd ldr: cl up 3f out: rdn 2f out and ev ch tl drvn and wknd appr fnl f* **10/1**

0233 **7** shd **Gypsy Major**[10] 4102 4-8-12 **54**..........................(v[1]) RobJFitzpatrick(5) 13 48+
(Garry Moss) *trckd ldrs: hdwy on outer to chse ldng pair over 2f out: led wl over 1f out and sn rdn: drvn and hdd appr fnl f: grad wknd* **9/1**

-340 **8** ½ **Mowhoob**[31] 3363 6-9-1 **52**.......................................(p) RoystonFfrench 11 44
(David Nicholls) *dwlt and bhd: hdwy wl over 1f out: kpt on fnl f: n.d* **12/1**

0636 **9** 1 ¼ **Cool Strutter (IRE)**[16] 3880 4-9-9 **65**.......................(b) GemmaTutty(5) 3 58+
(Karen Tutty) *trckd ldrs: hdwy wl over 2f out: effrt and n.m.r over 1f out: sn rdn and nt clr run ins fnl f: no imp after* **25/1**

0000 **10** 1 **Zeshov (IRE)**[15] 3922 5-10-0 **65**.................................. BarryMcHugh 2 65+
(Rebecca Bastiman) *hld up in midfield: stdy hdwy on inner to trck ldrs 2f out: effrt and nt clr run over 1f out: nt rcvr* **5/1**[2]

5603 **11** nse **Arcane Dancer (IRE)**[16] 3877 3-9-3 **61**................(p) RichardKingscote 1 53+
(Lawrence Mullaney) *trckd ldrs: hdwy 3f out: cl up and rdn over 2f out: drvn and n.m.r ent fnl f: one pce after* **4/1**[1]

0-00 **12** ½ **Anushka Noo Noo**[63] 2306 3-8-13 **60**.............(b[1]) JacobButterfield(3) 12 42+
(Ollie Pears) *sn led: rdn along wl over 2f out: drvn and hdd wl over 1f out: wknd* **50/1**

6550 **13** nk **Gold Beau (FR)**[16] 3880 6-9-11 **62**..................................(p) ShaneGray 7 47+
(Kristin Stubbs) *chsd ldrs: rdn along 2f out: sn drvn and wknd over 1f out* **33/1**

1m 31.91s (-1.89) **Going Correction** -0.375s/f (Firm)
WFA 3 from 4yo+ 7lb **13** Ran SP% **124.5**
Speed ratings (Par 101): **95,94,92,91,89 89,88,88,86,85 85,85,84**
CSF £147.98 CT £1036.33 TOTE £8.50: £2.90, £5.00, £2.10; EX 170.60 Trifecta £1044.50.
Owner Miss Julie Camacho **Bred** Select Bloodstock **Trained** Norton, N Yorks

FOCUS

After rail movement the actual race distance was 7f 123yds. A run-of-the-mill contest. Typical of many big-field events here there were a few hard-luck stories, the runner-up doing particularly well to get as close as he did while a few others were repeatedly blocked in their runs. The pace was good.

4455 GEORGE KILBURN MEMORIAL H'CAP 1m 1f 207y

8:10 (8:11) (Class 5) (0-75,74) 3-Y-O+ **£3,780** (£1,131; £565; £283; £141) **Stalls** Low

Form RPR

1624 **1** **Monsieur Glory**[20] 3751 3-8-11 **67**........................(v) RichardKingscote 8 76
(Tom Dascombe) *chsd ldng pair: led after 2f: rdn wl over 1f out: drvn ins fnl f: kpt on strly* **4/1**[2]

0005 **2** 1 **Eutropius (IRE)**[26] 3517 7-9-13 **73**........................... SilvestreDeSousa 3 80
(Alan Swinbank) *trckd ldrs: hdwy over 3f out: rdn over 1f out: chsd wnr ins fnl f: sn drvn and kpt on* **2/1**[1]

0-06 **3** 2 ½ **Jan De Heem**[16] 3876 6-8-13 **59**.......................................(p) TomEaves 2 61
(Tina Jackson) *hld up: hdwy wl over 2f out: effrt and n.m.r over 1f out: sn rdn and styd on fnl f* **12/1**

-616 **4** hd **King Of The Celts (IRE)**[40] 3012 8-9-6 **69**.......... RachelRichardson(3) 1 71
(Tim Easterby) *trckd ldrs: effrt over 2f out: rdn along wl over 1f out: drvn and no imp fnl f* **9/1**

0560 **5** ½ **Farham (USA)**[16] 3905 4-9-9 **69**..................................(p) TonyHamilton 6 70
(Richard Fahey) *in rr: hdwy over 2f out: rdn and n.m.r over 1f out: styd on wl fnl f: nrst fin* **14/1**

2601 **6** 2 ¼ **Yorkindred Spirit**[12] 4025 4-9-13 **73**.........................(v) FrannyNorton 12 69
(Mark Johnston) *hld up in rr: hdwy over 2f out: swtchd lft to outer and rdn wl over 1f out: kpt on same pce* **8/1**[3]

5305 **7** 4 **Nonchalant**[27] 3481 5-9-12 **72**...................................(v) GrahamGibbons 4 60
(David O'Meara) *led 2f: prom: chsd wnr over 4f out: rdn along over 2f out: drvn wl over 1f out: grad wknd* **16/1**

1034 **8** nk **Kip**[9] 4143 4-9-6 **71**.. JoshDoyle(5) 5 59
(David O'Meara) *hld up: hdwy over 3f out: rdn along on outer to chse ldrs 2f out: sn drvn and wknd* **8/1**[3]

330- **9** nk **Best Boy**[279] 7181 4-9-5 **65**..(t) DavidAllan 7 52
(David C Griffiths) *a in rr* **14/1**

3126 **10** 1 ¾ **Mysterial**[23] 3641 6-9-7 **74**.. GerO'Neill(7) 9 57
(Declan Carroll) *prom: rdn along on inner over 2f out: drvn wl over 1f out: sn wknd* **14/1**

3300 **11** 3 ¾ **Dunquin (IRE)**[51] 2672 4-9-9 **69**..................................... PJMcDonald 10 45
(John Mackie) *in tch: effrt on outer over 3f out: rdn along wl over 2f out: sn wknd* **25/1**

2m 2.7s (-4.30) **Going Correction** -0.375s/f (Firm)
WFA 3 from 4yo+ 10lb **11** Ran SP% **123.0**
Speed ratings (Par 103): **102,101,99,99,98 96,93,93,93,91 88**
CSF £13.00 CT £92.44 TOTE £4.90: £1.80, £1.60, £3.90; EX 15.70 Trifecta £111.40.
Owner Kangyu Int Racing (HK) Ltd & F Ma **Bred** Crossfields Bloodstock Ltd **Trained** Malpas, Cheshire

FOCUS

After rail movement the actual race distance was 1m 2f 10yds.A fair handicap. The gallop initially looked quite strong but there's a chance the winner steadied things towards the end of the back straight, nothing really threatening to land a serious blow from off the pace. The winner is rated back to form.

4456 RACING UK H'CAP 1m 1f 207y

8:40 (8:43) (Class 6) (0-55,55) 3-Y-O+ **£2,587** (£770; £384; £192) **Stalls** Low

Form RPR

4056 **1** **Gabrial's Hope (FR)**[1] 4427 7-9-7 **52**.................................. DaleSwift 3 58
(Tracy Waggott) *dwlt and in rr: hdwy towards inner over 2f out: nt clr run and swtchd lft ent fnl f: sn rdn and forced way through ins fnl100yds: led nr fin* **14/1**

5245 **2** nk **Indian Giver**[33] 3287 8-9-5 **55**...............................(p) JordanVaughan(5) 7 60
(John David Riches) *trckd ldrs: hdwy wl over 2f out: rdn over 1f out: sn chal and ev ch: drvn ins fnl f and kpt on towards fin* **13/2**[3]

135 **3** shd **Little Choosey**[25] 3582 6-9-7 **55**.........................(tp) AlistairRawlinson(3) 5 60
(Roy Bowring) *trckd ldng pair: hdwy to ld over 2f out: rdn wl over 1f out: drvn ent fnl f: hdd and no ex towards fin* **8/1**

-045 **4** nk **Judicious**[16] 3883 9-9-9 **54**..(p) DavidAllan 6 59
(Geoffrey Harker) *hld up in midfield: hdwy wl over 2f out: chsd ldrs over 1f out and sn rdn: drvn to chal ins fnl f: ev ch tl no ex towards fin* **5/1**[1]

-006 **5** 1 **Monopoli**[16] 3896 7-9-0 **50**...(p) LanceBetts(5) 14 53
(Ivan Furtado) *chsd ldr: cl up over 2f out: rdn wl over 1f out: sn chal: drvn and cl up whn bmpd ins fnl 100yds: one pce after* **11/1**

0460 **6** ¾ **Elle Dorado**[21] 3706 4-9-1 **46**.......................................(v[1]) PJMcDonald 8 47
(David Loughnane) *towards rr: hdwy 2f out: rdn over 1f out: drvn and styd on wl fnl f: nrst fin* **25/1**

0624 **7** nk **Intensified (IRE)**[9] 4144 5-9-1 **46**................................(b) JamesSullivan 4 47
(Ruth Carr) *trckd ldrs: hdwy over 2f out: swtchd rt and rdn over 1f out: drvn ins fnl f and kpt on same pce* **17/2**

0-00 **8** 1 **Kantara Castle (IRE)**[7] 4214 5-9-3 **48**.........................(tp) FrannyNorton 1 47
(John Mackie) *towards rr: hdwy over 2f out: rdn wl over 1f out: kpt on fnl f* **6/1**[2]

5603 **9** 2 ¼ **I'm Super Too (IRE)**[6] 4234 9-9-4 **54**.......................... GemmaTutty(5) 16 49
(Karen Tutty) *towards rr: sme hdwy 2f out: sn rdn along and n.d* **7/1**

0-00 **10** ½ **Fledermaus (IRE)**[17] 3844 6-9-5 **50**..................................(t) TomEaves 9 44
(Tina Jackson) *towards rr: hdwy on inner over 2f out: rdn along wl over 1f out: n.d* **50/1**

6003 **11** ¾ **Call Me Crockett (IRE)**[9] 4144 4-9-0 **52**.............(p) JamieGormley(7) 10 44
(Iain Jardine) *midfield: hdwy over 2f out: rdn wl over 1f out: wkng whn n.m.r ent fnl f* **12/1**

-532 **12** 8 **Elle Rebelle**[180] 255 6-9-7 **52**................................. SilvestreDeSousa 17 29
(Mark Brisbourne) *in tch: pushed along 3f out: rdn 2f out: sn drvn and wknd* **14/1**

-000 **13** 1 ½ **Lightning Steps**[7] 4194 4-9-2 **47**.............................(b[1]) GrahamGibbons 2 21
(Declan Carroll) *led: rdn along 3f out: hdd over 2f out: sn drvn and wknd* **25/1**

660- **14** 3 ½ **Yawail**[297] 6715 5-9-4 **49**...(p) BarryMcHugh 15 17
(Brian Rothwell) *midfield: effrt wl over 2f out: sn rdn along and wknd* **40/1**

1260 **15** 21 **Cahar Fad (IRE)**[11] 4052 4-9-9 **54**.........................(bt) RoystonFfrench 13
(Steph Hollinshead) *t.k.h: hld up in midfield: effrt and sme hdwy over 2f out: sn rdn and wknd: bhd whn eased appr fnl f* **20/1**

2m 4.07s (-2.93) **Going Correction** -0.375s/f (Firm) **15** Ran SP% **124.6**
Speed ratings (Par 101): **96,95,95,95,94 94,93,93,91,90 90,83,82,79,63**
CSF £99.61 CT £801.54 TOTE £16.60: £5.50, £2.40, £2.80; EX 114.10 Trifecta £2126.50.
Owner David Tate **Bred** Mrs G Forien & G Forien **Trained** Spennymoor, Co Durham
■ Stewards' Enquiry : Dale Swift Caution: Careless riding.

FOCUS

After rail movement the actual race distance was 1m 2f 10yds. A blanket finish to this low-grade handicap which was run at a good pace. Not really a race to be taking a horse forward from.
T/Plt: £153.60 to a £1 stake. Pool of £60167.80 - 285.80 winning tickets. T/Qpdt: £61.00 to a £1 stake. Pool of £6346.95 - 76.90 winning tickets. **Joe Rowntree**

4202 WINDSOR (R-H)

Monday, July 18

OFFICIAL GOING: Good to firm (good in places)

Wind: Almost nil Weather: Sunny, hot

4457 BRITISH STALLION STUDS EBF MAIDEN FILLIES' STKS (PLUS 10 RACE) 6f

5:45 (5:45) (Class 4) 2-Y-O **£4,269** (£1,270; £634; £317) **Stalls** Low

Form RPR

32 **1** **Tropical Rock**[11] 4064 2-9-0 0.. JimCrowley 9 77
(Ralph Beckett) *mde virtually all: shkn up to assert over 1f out: hrd pressed ins fnl f: drvn out* **2/9**[1]

60 **2** ¾ **Mums The Word**[23] 3647 2-8-9 0............................ MeganNicholls(5) 1 75
(Richard Hannon) *chsd ldrs: pushed along and prog to take 2nd over 1f out: chal ins fnl f: no imp last 50yds* **12/1**

3 3 ½ **Moonlit Show** 2-9-0 0.. StevieDonohoe 4 63
(Charlie Fellowes) *chsd ldrs: shkn up to dispute 2nd briefly over 1f out: outpcd fnl f* **10/1**[3]

4 2 ½ **Miss Laila (IRE)** 2-9-0 0... ShaneKelly 7 55+
(Richard Hughes) *pressed wnr and clr of rest 1/2-way: lost 2nd and wknd over 1f out* **7/1**[2]

060 **5** nk **Tennessee Rose (IRE)**[23] 3633 2-9-0 0............................ LiamJones 8 54
(Tom Dascombe) *racd on outer: nvr bttr than midfield: n.d fnl 2f: plugged on* **25/1**

6 1 **Topmeup** 2-8-11 0.. EdwardGreatrex(3) 3 51
(Stuart Edmunds) *racd on outer: nvr bttr than midfield: n.d fnl 2f* **20/1**

7 1 **Sweet Pursuit** 2-9-0 0.. FrederikTylicki 2 48
(Rod Millman) *dwlt: struggling in last trio by 1/2-way: nvr on terms: kpt on* **14/1**

6 **8** 1 ¼ **Ablaze**[48] 2764 2-9-0 0.. KierenFox 5 44
(Laura Mongan) *mostly in last trio and struggling by 1/2-way* **50/1**

9 ½ **Lemon Drop** 2-9-0 0.. PatCosgrave 6 42
(Jim Boyle) *dwlt: outpcd and wl bhd in last: nvr a factor but kpt on fnl f* **22/1**

0 **10** 16 **Whatalove**[21] 3718 2-9-0 0.. TomQueally 10
(Martin Keighley) *chsd ldrs to wl over 1f out: wknd v rapidly: t.o* **150/1**

1m 12.52s (-0.48) **Going Correction** -0.10s/f (Good) **10** Ran SP% **133.4**
Speed ratings (Par 93): **99,98,93,90,89 88,86,85,84,63**
CSF £5.88 TOTE £1.30: £1.02, £3.50, £2.80; EX 7.60 Trifecta £33.70.
Owner J C Smith **Bred** Littleton Stud **Trained** Kimpton, Hants

FOCUS

Inner of straight is at normal inner configuration, making the straight maximum width. Top bend dolled out 10yds from normal inner configuration, adding 33yds to race distances of 1m-plus. An uncompetitive opener. The first pair wee clear at the finish. The winner is rated just below her latest form.

4458 SKY BET MAIDEN STKS 1m 2f 7y

6:15 (6:16) (Class 5) 3-4-Y-O **£2,911** (£866; £432; £216) **Stalls** Centre

Form RPR

0522 **1** **Makzeem**[11] 4056 3-9-4 85... GeorgeBaker 12 88+
(Roger Charlton) *mde all: drew clr effrtlessly fr over 2f out: eased fnl f* **1/2**[1]

0- **2** 2 **Blaze Of Hearts (IRE)**[269] 7423 3-9-4 0........................ RobertWinston 3 76
(Dean Ivory) *in tch: pushed along and effrt to chse wnr wl over 2f out: sn lft bhd: kpt on* **66/1**

22- **3** 2 ½ **Nonios (IRE)**[227] 8108 4-10-0 0.. JamieSpencer 5 71
(David Simcock) *hld up in midfield: outpcd fr 3f out: swtchd lft 2f out: shkn up and styd on to take 3rd fnl f* **9/2**[2]

00 **4** 3 ¾ **Faction**[37] 3160 3-9-4 0 OisinMurphy 13 63
(Andrew Balding) *prom: disp 2nd pl 3f out: steadily fdd fr 2f out* **40/1**

3- **5** *nk* **Cap Canaille (USA)**[244] 7878 3-9-4 0 JimmyFortune 8 62
(Jeremy Noseda) *chsd wnr to wl over 2f out: steadily wknd* **8/1**[3]

0- **6** ½ **Vermeulen**[289] 6924 3-9-4 0 RobertHavlin 10 61+
(John Gosden) *hld up towards rr: pushed along and kpt on steadily fr over 2f out: should do bttr* **9/2**[2]

0- **7** *6* **Fast Play (IRE)**[427] 2343 4-9-9 0 ShaneKelly 2 44
(Richard Hughes) *hld up in last trio: pushed along and kpt on fr 2f out: nvr involved but nt disgracd* **80/1**

06 **8** *7* **Royal Occassion**[26] 3535 4-10-0 0 SamHitchcott 6 35
(Jim Boyle) *dwlt: hld up in rr: rapid prog on wd outside bnd over 6f out to over 4f out: wknd 3f out* **100/1**

0 **9** *4* **Moayadd (USA)**[12] 3996 4-10-0 0 FergusSweeney 7 27
(Neil Mulholland) *dwlt: mostly in last trio: u.p sn after 1/2-way: wl btn after* **150/1**

05 **10** ½ **Stamford Raffles**[4] 4319 3-9-4 0 PatCosgrave 11 26
(Stuart Williams) *in tch in midfield: hanging lft fr 4f out: shkn up and wknd over 2f out: heavily eased over 1f out* **50/1**

11 *shd* **Brahma** 3-9-4 0 AdamKirby 1 26
(Hughie Morrison) *dwlt: a in last trio: nvr a factor* **25/1**

12 2 ½ **Rebel Woods (FR)** 3-9-4 0 TimmyMurphy 9 21
(Geoffrey Deacon) *chsd ldrs to 1/2-way: wknd qckly* **100/1**

2m 5.82s (-2.88) **Going Correction** -0.10s/f (Good)
WFA 3 from 4yo 10lb **12** Ran SP% **127.8**
Speed ratings (Par 103): **107,105,103,100,100 99,94,89,86,85 85,83**
CSF £80.80 TOTE £1.60: £1.10, £16.80, £1.70; EX 59.60 Trifecta £255.60.
Owner D J Deer **Bred** D J And Mrs Deer **Trained** Beckhampton, Wilts

FOCUS
Add 33 yards to race distance. Another uncompetitive maiden. It was run at an uneven pace but the time compared well with the following handicap. The winner was value for extra.

4459 SKY BET H'CAP 1m 2f 7y
6:45 (6:45) (Class 5) (0-75,75) 3-Y-O+ **£2,911** (£866; £432; £216) **Stalls** Centre

Form RPR

503 **1** **Absolute Zero (IRE)**[18] 3824 3-9-3 **74** HarryBentley 7 87
(Roger Varian) *mde all: shkn up and sent for home wl over 2f out: drvn over 1f out: styd on wl* **9/4**[1]

6063 **2** 1 ¾ **Henry The Explorer (CAN)**[16] 3906 3-8-7 **67** JosephineGordon(3) 4 76
(Jo Hughes) *mostly chsd wnr: rdn over 2f out: tried to chal over 1f out: styd on but no imp ins fnl f* **5/1**[3]

0426 **3** *6* **New Street (IRE)**[13] 3991 5-9-12 **73** (v) TimmyMurphy 6 70
(Jim Best) *t.k.h: trckd ldng pair: disp 2nd pl 5f out to over 2f out: wknd over 1f out: hld on for 3rd* **22/1**

066- **4** *nk* **Mr Rock (IRE)**[245] 7876 5-9-5 **66** SteveDrowne 3 62
(George Baker) *t.k.h: hld up in midfield: shkn up and nt qckn over 2f out: kpt on fnl f and nrly tk 3rd* **7/1**

004 **5** ½ **Perpetual Change (IRE)**[19] 3769 3-9-0 **71** AdamKirby 5 66
(Clive Cox) *t.k.h: trckd ldng trio: rdn 3f out: no imp 2f out: wknd over 1f out* **7/2**[2]

0261 **6** 1 ½ **Barren Brook**[12] 4020 9-9-9 **70** GeorgeBaker 2 62
(Laura Mongan) *s.v.s: t.k.h: hld up in detached last: stl there over 2f out: shuffled along and reminder over 1f out: passed a few late on: nvr involved* **10/1**

3455 **7** 2 ¼ **Top Diktat**[53] 2623 8-9-11 **72** FergusSweeney 8 59
(Gary Moore) *hld up in midfield: shkn up and no prog wl over 2f out: n.d after* **12/1**

405 **8** *3* **Celtic Ava (IRE)**[11] 4050 4-8-10 **57** JFEgan 9 38
(Pat Phelan) *s.i.s: hld up in last trio: effrt on outer over 2f out: sn no prog: wknd over 1f out* **14/1**

1415 **9** 4 ½ **Jamhoori**[12] 4020 8-10-0 **75** TomQueally 1 47
(Jim Best) *mostly in last trio: rdn and no prog on outer 3f out: wl btn after* **33/1**

2m 7.98s (-0.72) **Going Correction** -0.10s/f (Good)
WFA 3 from 4yo+ 10lb **9** Ran SP% **112.9**
Speed ratings (Par 103): **98,96,91,91,91 89,88,85,82**
CSF £13.23 CT £189.07 TOTE £2.00: £1.80, £1.70, £4.50; EX 13.20 Trifecta £209.80.
Owner J Collins, C Fahy & S Piper **Bred** Mighty Universe Ltd **Trained** Newmarket, Suffolk

FOCUS
Add 33 yards to race distance. The first pair were up there throughout this ordinary handicap, and finished clear. The time was modest.

4460 SKY BET TOP PRICE EVERY FAVOURITE H'CAP 6f
7:15 (7:15) (Class 4) (0-85,84) 3-Y-O+ **£4,690** (£1,395; £697; £348) **Stalls** Low

Form RPR

3544 **1** **Ice Age (IRE)**[10] 4116 3-8-13 **76** RobertWinston 4 82
(Eve Johnson Houghton) *pressed ldr: rdn to chal wl over 1f out: narrow ld ins fnl f: drvn out* **4/1**[2]

5223 **2** *nk* **Pixeleen**[25] 3575 4-9-10 **82** OisinMurphy 3 88
(Malcolm Saunders) *led: rdn and hrd pressed wl over 1f out: narrowly hdd ins fnl f: kpt on* **13/8**[1]

3121 **3** *nk* **Lightning Charlie**[12] 4014 4-9-12 **84** JimCrowley 1 89
(Amanda Perrett) *trckd ldng pair: plld out over 1f out: drvn to chal ins fnl f: nt qckn last 100yds* **9/2**[3]

0003 **4** *3* **Anonymous John (IRE)**[24] 3594 4-9-10 **82** AdamKirby 2 77
(David Evans) *hld up in last pair: plld out and reminder over 1f out: pushed along after and kpt on but no imp on ldng trio* **9/2**[3]

-340 **5** *8* **Quite A Story**[45] 2846 4-8-11 **69** DavidProbert 5 39
(Patrick Chamings) *dwlt: hld up in last pair: rdn and no prog 2f out: sn wknd* **10/1**

11-5 **6** 1 ¾ **Parkour (IRE)**[83] 1763 3-9-6 **83** (b[1]) JimmyQuinn 6 46
(Marco Botti) *s.i.s: hld up bhd ldng pair: shkn up over 2f out: wknd qckly over 1f out* **10/1**

1m 11.4s (-1.60) **Going Correction** -0.10s/f (Good)
WFA 3 from 4yo 5lb **6** Ran SP% **112.6**
Speed ratings (Par 105): **106,105,105,101,90 88**
CSF £11.05 TOTE £5.70: £2.50, £1.20; EX 11.10 Trifecta £48.70.
Owner Eden Racing III **Bred** Piercetown Stud **Trained** Blewbury, Oxon

FOCUS
A tight little sprint handicap which saw a bunched three-way finish. A small pb from the winner with the second to form.

4461 SKY BET WINDSOR SPRINT SERIES H'CAP (A QUALIFIER FOR THE WINDSOR SPRINT SERIES FINAL) 5f 10y
7:50 (7:56) (Class 3) (0-90,90) 3-Y-O+ **£7,439** (£2,213; £1,106; £553) **Stalls** Low

Form RPR

-351 **1** **Go On Go On Go On**[12] 3995 3-9-0 **82** AdamKirby 5 95+
(Clive Cox) *in tch bhd ldrs: prog 2f out: pushed into ld jst over 1f out: edgd lft but sn clr: readily* **5/2**[1]

6014 **2** 2 ¼ **Oh So Sassy**[25] 3573 6-9-12 **90** GeorgeBaker 8 96
(Chris Wall) *racd towards far side: wl on terms: narrow ld wl over 1f out to jst over 1f out: one pce* **9/2**[2]

1235 **3** ¾ **Majestic Hero (IRE)**[24] 3618 4-9-7 **85** DavidProbert 6 88
(Ronald Harris) *racd towards far side: wl on terms: pressed ldr wl over 1f out to jst over 1f out: one pce* **12/1**

-450 **4** *nk* **Rosie's Premiere (IRE)**[11] 4066 4-9-10 **88** RobertWinston 9 90
(Dean Ivory) *towards rr: rdn over 2f out: styd on fnl f: nvr able to threaten* **6/1**[3]

0422 **5** 1 ¼ **Foxtrot Knight**[7] 4198 4-9-1 **79** JimCrowley 12 77
(Ruth Carr) *chsd ldrs: in tch 2f out: rdn and nt qckn over 1f out: no prog after* **5/2**[1]

0-60 **6** ½ **Noble Asset**[36] 3193 5-8-11 **78** EdwardGreatrex(3) 2 74
(Milton Bradley) *led: briefly lft clr 1/2-way: taken down centre after: hdd wl over 1f out: wknd fnl f* **28/1**

00-0 **7** 1 ½ **Elysian Flyer (IRE)**[17] 3857 4-9-12 **90** ShaneKelly 11 81
(Richard Hughes) *s.s: a in rr and nvr able to regain grnd* **25/1**

6400 **8** ½ **Burning Thread (IRE)**[12] 3995 9-8-6 **77** (b) AdamMcLean(7) 1 66
(David Elsworth) *dwlt: a struggling to go the pce: nvr on terms* **33/1**

0-00 **9** *20* **Nocturn**[14] 3956 7-9-2 **80** (p) OisinMurphy 10
(Ronald Harris) *sn outpcd and bhd: t.o* **12/1**

/00- **P** **Pal Of The Cat**[221] 8170 6-8-8 **72** (tp) JimmyQuinn 4
(Michael Attwater) *w ldr tl broke down 1/2-way: uns rdr sn after* **40/1**

58.86s (-1.44) **Going Correction** -0.10s/f (Good)
WFA 3 from 4yo+ 4lb **10** Ran SP% **117.7**
Speed ratings (Par 107): **107,103,102,101,99 98,96,95,63,**
CSF £13.54 CT £114.16 TOTE £3.00: £1.40, £1.80, £2.90; EX 16.60 Trifecta £75.30.
Owner Paul & Clare Rooney **Bred** Richard Kent & Robert Percival **Trained** Lambourn, Berks
■ Equally Fast was withdrawn. Price at time of withdrawal 12/1. Rule 4 applies to bets struck prior to withdrawal but not to SP bets - deduct 5p in the pound. New market formed.

FOCUS
This looked competitive, but it proved a messy sprint handicap and there was a difference of opinion as to the best ground. This is rated around the runner-up, with another pb from the winner.

4462 EBF STALLIONS BREEDING WINNERS FILLIES' H'CAP 1m 3f 135y
8:20 (8:20) (Class 4) (0-80,80) 3-Y-O+ **£6,630** (£1,973; £986; £493) **Stalls** Centre

Form RPR

341 **1** **Fashion Parade**[20] 3736 3-9-2 **80** DavidProbert 4 86+
(Charles Hills) *led after 3f at mod pce: pushed along and hdd over 3f out: led again over 2f out: drvn and clr over 1f out: kpt on wl* **5/2**[2]

4142 **2** 2 ¼ **Safira Menina**[12] 4023 4-8-13 **72** NatalieHambling(7) 5 74
(Martin Smith) *s.s: hld up in last: prog on outer over 2f out: rdn to take 2nd fnl f: no imp on wnr* **10/1**

0-35 **3** ½ **Great Thoughts (IRE)**[19] 3781 3-8-9 **73** ow1 JamieSpencer 3 74
(David Simcock) *hld up in 5th: shkn up and no prog over 2f out: drvn jst over 1f out: styd on to take 3rd last strides* **5/1**

1550 **4** *nk* **Kuriosa (IRE)**[24] 3602 4-9-6 **75** DanielMuscutt(3) 1 76
(Marco Botti) *t.k.h: trckd ldng pair: rdn and effrt over 2f out: nt qckn over 1f out: one pce after* **12/1**

5-33 **5** ½ **All My Love (IRE)**[84] 1717 4-9-7 **76** RobHornby(3) 6 76
(Pam Sly) *trckd ldng trio: effrt to dispute 2nd pl 2f out to jst over 1f out: no ex* **9/2**[3]

5002 **6** 3 ½ **Dora's Field (IRE)**[16] 3878 3-8-8 **72** HarryBentley 7 66
(Ed Dunlop) *led at mod pce 3f: pressed ldr: led again over 3f out to over 2f out: lost 2nd and wknd jst over 1f out* **9/4**[1]

2m 32.95s (3.45) **Going Correction** -0.10s/f (Good)
WFA 3 from 4yo 12lb **6** Ran SP% **111.0**
Speed ratings (Par 102): **84,82,82,81,81 79**
CSF £25.34 TOTE £2.80: £1.10, £6.70; EX 22.20 Trifecta £75.20.
Owner Abdulla Al Khalifa **Bred** Sheikh Abdulla Bin Isa Al-Khalifa **Trained** Lambourn, Berks

FOCUS
Add 33 yards to race distance. There was a tight finish to this fillies' handicap, due to an ordinary pace, but the form looks fair enough. The winner can probably do better.

4463 OAKLEY COURT HOTEL H'CAP 1m 67y
8:50 (8:50) (Class 5) (0-75,74) 3-Y-O+ **£2,911** (£866; £432; £216) **Stalls** Low

Form RPR

50 **1** **Bunbury**[35] 3234 4-9-13 **73** ShaneKelly 1 82
(Richard Hughes) *trckd ldng trio: prog to ld wl over 1f out: pressed jst ins fnl f: drvn and r.o wl after* **15/8**[1]

0005 **2** *2* **Dana's Present**[77] 1916 7-9-6 **66** PatCosgrave 7 71
(Tom Dascombe) *t.k.h: hld up in last pair: stl there 2f out: gd prog over 1f out to chse wnr jst ins fnl f and sn chalng: one pce last 100yds* **10/1**

-003 **3** 1 ¼ **Golden Isles (IRE)**[39] 3080 3-8-2 **59** JosephineGordon(3) 2 59
(J S Moore) *chsd ldng pair: pushed along over 3f out: nvr gng pce to chal but kpt on fr over 1f out* **7/1**

420 **4** *nk* **Snappy Guest**[18] 3821 4-9-12 **72** TomQueally 4 73
(George Margarson) *hld up in last: rdn and prog on outer over 1f out: styd on same pce ins fnl f* **12/1**

5421 **5** 1 ¼ **Shifting Star (IRE)**[21] 3724 11-9-13 **73** (vt) WilliamCarson 8 71
(John Bridger) *led at gd pce: rdn and hdd wl over 1f out: wknd* **6/1**[3]

-064 **6** *2* **Sheila's Treat (IRE)**[25] 3558 3-8-12 **66** OisinMurphy 3 58
(Denis Coakley) *in tch bhd ldrs: effrt on outer over 2f out: nt qckn over 1f out: wknd fnl f* **9/2**[2]

21-0 **7** 3 ¼ **Seven Clans (IRE)**[10] 4088 4-9-2 **65** LouisSteward(3) 5 51
(Neil Mulholland) *in tch: rdn and tried to make prog on outer over 2f out: wknd over 1f out* **16/1**

6035 **8** *3* **Woofie (IRE)**[46] 2827 4-9-11 **71** (p) GeorgeBaker 9 50
(Laura Mongan) *chsd ldr to over 2f out: wknd wl over 1f out* **7/1**

1m 43.76s (-0.94) **Going Correction** -0.10s/f (Good)
WFA 3 from 4yo+ 8lb **8** Ran SP% **114.9**
Speed ratings (Par 103): **100,98,96,96,95 93,89,86**
CSF £22.26 CT £109.60 TOTE £2.10: £1.20, £3.10, £2.30; EX 24.90 Trifecta £173.50.
Owner The Villains **Bred** Juddmonte Farms Ltd **Trained** Upper Lambourn, Berkshire

FOCUS
Add 33 yards to race distance. This modest handicap was run at a solid pace and the placed horses set the level. There wasn't much depth to this.
T/Plt: £20.90 to a £1 stake. Pool of £80688.79 - 2809.91 winning tickets. T/Qpdt: £17.60 to a £1 stake. Pool of £7383.98 - 310.22 winning tickets. **Jonathan Neesom**

4464 - 4470a (Foreign Racing) - See Raceform Interactive

4285 CHANTILLY (R-H)
Monday, July 18

OFFICIAL GOING: Turf: good

4471a PRIX DU BOIS DU LUDE (CLAIMER) (2YO) (TURF) 7f
3:55 (12:00) 2-Y-O **£9,926** (£3,970; £2,977; £1,985; £992)

RPR
1 **Kambura (FR)** 2-8-11 0 ... Jean-BernardEyquem 9 71
(K Borgel, France) **41/5**
2 *1 1/4* **Jenychope (FR)**[20] 3763 2-8-13 0 ow2 ... ChristopheSoumillon 3 70
(D Windrif, France) **37/10**[2]
3 *nk* **Swanning Around (IRE)**[10] 4124 2-8-11 0 ... AntoineHamelin 10 67
(Matthieu Palussiere, France) **10/1**
4 *nk* **Frozen Queen (IRE)**[8] 2-8-8 0 ... IoritzMendizabal 2 63
(D Windrif, France) **33/10**[1]
5 *4* **Le Phantom**[81] 1820 2-9-1 0 ... Pierre-CharlesBoudot 12 60
(E J O'Neill, France) **23/5**[3]
6 *2 1/2* **Rinky Dink Dawn (IRE)**[8] 4183 2-8-11 0 ... TonyPiccone 4 49
(J S Moore) *wnt lft s: sn led and swtchd ins to rail: kicked for home over 2 1/2f out: hdd ent fnl 2f: wknd fnl f* **13/1**
7 *3 1/2* **Cholpon Ata (FR)**[20] 3763 2-8-8 0 ... MickaelBarzalona 8 36
(Mme P Butel, France) **24/1**
8 *3 1/2* **Cima Jelois (FR)**[18] 2-8-11 0 ...(b) AnthonyCrastus 1 30
(Robert Collet, France) **9/1**
9 *1 1/2* **Sunday Winner (FR)**[10] 4124 2-8-11 0 ...(p) HugoJourniac(4) 5 30
(Y Gourraud, France) **33/1**
10 *5 1/2* **Diboy (FR)**[17] 3871 2-9-1 0 ...(b) EddyHardouin 7 15
(Matthieu Palussiere, France) **27/1**
11 *9* **Heavens Stream (FR)**[12] 2-8-11 0 ...(b) MaximeGuyon 6
(Y Gourraud, France) **43/5**

1m 26.42s (0.32) **11** Ran SP% **120.4**
WIN (incl. 1 euro stake): 9.20. PLACES: 2.70, 1.90, 2.80. DF: 26.60. SF: 68.30.
Owner Jacques Piasco **Bred** Mme G Forien & G Forien **Trained** France

4195 CHELMSFORD (A.W) (L-H)
Tuesday, July 19

OFFICIAL GOING: Polytrack: standard
Wind: light, across Weather: sunny and hot

4472 HANNAH BLOWERS MEMORIAL APPRENTICE H'CAP 5f (P)
5:50 (5:50) (Class 6) (0-60,57) 3-Y-O+ **£3,234** (£962; £481; £240) **Stalls** Low

Form RPR
0-01 **1** **Culloden**[11] 4096 4-9-8 **57** ... CharlieBennett(3) 6 63
(Shaun Harris) *mde all: clr after 2f out: rdn over 1f out: styd on wl and a holding rival ins fnl f: rdn out* **4/1**[3]
5-43 **2** *3/4* **Andalusite**[17] 3900 3-9-7 **57** ... AaronJones 4 59
(Ed McMahon) *chsd ldr: effrt over 1f out: drvn and pressing wnr ins fnl f: styd on u.p but a hld by wnr* **5/1**
3434 **3** *2 1/2* **Tasaaboq**[6] 4278 5-9-6 **57** ...(t) JaneElliott(5) 5 51
(Phil McEntee) *dwlt and dropped in bhd after s: hld up in last pair: clsd and nt clr run over 1f out: swtchd rt 1f out: styd on wl ins fnl f: nt rch ldrs* **5/1**
235- **4** *2 1/4* **Ryan Style (IRE)**[302] 6579 10-9-7 **53** ...(p) PaddyPilley 2 39
(Lisa Williamson) *midfield: hdwy on outer and rdn 2f out: chsd ldrs but no imp 1f out: styd on same pce ins fnl f* **14/1**
0350 **5** *1/2* **Go Charlie**[5] 4292 5-8-12 **47** ... DavidParkes(3) 7 31
(Lisa Williamson) *taken down early: stdd and dropped in bhd after s: hld up in last pair: hdwy over 1f out: chsd ldrs but no imp 1f out: styd on same pce ins fnl f* **9/1**
0052 **6** *1 1/4* **Manipura**[17] 3900 3-9-2 **55** ...(p) PaddyBradley(3) 1 34
(Derek Shaw) *midfield: effrt 2f out: no imp u.p over 1f out: wknd ins fnl f* **3/1**[1]
20 **7** *1 1/4* **Wattaboutsteve**[24] 3674 5-9-3 **49** ... HectorCrouch 3 24
(Ralph J Smith) *t.k.h: chsd ldrs: nt clr run and swtchd rt over 1f out: sn rdn and no imp: wknd ins fnl f* **7/2**[2]

1m 0.96s (0.76) **Going Correction** +0.05s/f (Slow)
WFA 3 from 4yo+ 4lb **7** Ran SP% **117.2**
Speed ratings (Par 101): **95,93,89,86,85 83,81**
CSF £25.10 TOTE £4.90: £1.90, £2.80; EX 23.40 Trifecta £75.60.
Owner Burflex (Scaffolding) Ltd **Bred** Burton Agnes Stud Co Ltd **Trained** Carburton, Notts

FOCUS
A moderate event in which the winner dominated throughout at a medium sprint tempo. He built on his recent win.

4473 FOLLOW US ON TWITTER @TOTEPOOL MAIDEN STKS (PLUS 10 RACE) 6f (P)
6:20 (6:21) (Class 4) 2-Y-O **£6,469** (£1,925; £962; £481) **Stalls** Centre

Form RPR
3 **1** **Maakaasib**[41] 3037 2-9-5 0 ... RobertHavlin 2 82+
(Simon Crisford) *mde all: rdn over 1f out: drvn and clr 1f out: styd on strly* **11/10**[1]
604 **2** *3 3/4* **Father McKenzie**[5] 4287 2-9-5 0 ... SilvestreDeSousa 8 71
(Mick Channon) *chsd ldrs tl hdwy to chse wnr 4f out: rdn 2f out: outpcd by wnr 1f out: styd on same pce for clr 2nd ins fnl f* **12/1**
44 **3** *3 1/4* **Law Power**[15] 3954 2-9-5 0 ... LukeMorris 1 61
(Sir Mark Prescott Bt) *chsd ldrs: wnt 3rd over 3f out: drvn jst over 2f out: outpcd and btn over 1f out: wknd ins fnl f* **5/1**[3]
5 **4** *hd* **Thomas Cranmer (USA)**[33] 3315 2-9-5 0 ... FrannyNorton 10 61+
(Mark Johnston) *dwlt: midfield: hdwy into 4th and rdn ent fnl 2f: no imp and styd on same pce fr over 1f out* **9/4**[2]
0 **5** *1/2* **Ripper Street (IRE)**[19] 3818 2-9-5 0 ... RichardKingscote 3 59+
(Ed Dunlop) *s.i.s: hld up off the pce in last pair: hdwy and swtchd lft over 1f out: pushed along and styd on steadily ins fnl f: nvr trbld ldrs* **16/1**

6 **6** *3 3/4* **Precious Plum**[48] 2786 2-9-0 0 ... LemosdeSouza 4 43+
(Chris Dwyer) *hld up in midfield: clsd over 2f out: swtchd rt and rdn over 1f out: no imp after: nvr trbld ldrs* **50/1**
0 **7** *2 1/2* **Bismarck The Flyer (IRE)**[12] 4053 2-9-5 0 ... PatDobbs 7 40
(Richard Hannon) *s.i.s: off the pce in last: no hdwy u.p over 1f out: n.d* **20/1**
8 *5* **Desert Sport (USA)** 2-9-5 0 ... TedDurcan 9 25
(Robert Cowell) *off the pce towards rr: rdn 2f out: no imp: wl bhd and eased wl ins fnl f* **25/1**
9 *7* **Erissimus Maximus (FR)** 2-9-5 0 ... IrineuGoncalves 6
(Chris Dwyer) *t.k.h and rn green: chsd ldr for 2f: steadily lost pl: bhd over 1f out: eased ins fnl f* **66/1**

1m 14.04s (0.34) **Going Correction** +0.05s/f (Slow) **9** Ran SP% **120.7**
Speed ratings (Par 96): **99,94,89,89,88 83,80,73,64**
CSF £16.96 TOTE £2.20: £1.10, £2.30, £2.10; EX 14.70 Trifecta £34.70.
Owner Abdulla Al Mansoori **Bred** Newsells Park Stud **Trained** Newmarket, Suffolk

FOCUS
In a maiden run at a good gallop, the winner outclassed his rivals. The form has been given some credit.

4474 TOTEEXACTA H'CAP 7f (P)
6:50 (6:50) (Class 4) (0-85,85) 3-Y-O+ **£6,469** (£1,925; £962; £481) **Stalls** Low

Form RPR
2366 **1** **Fuwairt (IRE)**[5] 4299 4-9-0 **78** ... CameronNoble(7) 6 88+
(David Loughnane) *hld up in tch in last trio: clsd to go 4th and swtchd rt over 1f out: pushed along and str run to ld wl ins fnl f: sn in command* **7/1**[3]
-052 **2** *1 1/4* **Dollar Reward**[31] 3415 3-9-3 **81** ... TedDurcan 8 85
(Sir Michael Stoute) *dwlt: sn rcvrd to chse ldng pair and dropped in: effrt 2f out: stl cl enough in 3rd 1f out: drvn ins fnl f: chsd wnr and one pce fnl 50yds* **11/4**[2]
0530 **3** *1* **Steal The Scene (IRE)**[24] 3645 4-9-9 **85** ... MeganNicholls(5) 7 89
(Richard Hannon) *dwlt: sn rcvrd to press ldr tl led 5f out: rdn over 1f out: drvn ins fnl f: hdd and no ex wl ins fnl f* **14/1**
-212 **4** *hd* **Mutamid**[25] 3605 4-9-11 **82** ... SilvestreDeSousa 1 86
(Ismail Mohammed) *led tl 5f out: styd w ldr: rdn over 1f out: drvn 1f out: no ex and btn wl ins fnl f* **9/4**[1]
0546 **5** *7* **Jammy Guest (IRE)**[25] 3622 6-9-12 **83** ... AdamKirby 2 68
(George Margarson) *stdd s: hld up in tch in last trio: effrt and swtchd rt 2f out: wnt 5th but no imp over 1f out: wl hld fnl f* **14/1**
2516 **6** *6* **Foie Gras**[45] 2918 6-8-6 **66** ... AnnaJones(3) 4 35
(Chris Dwyer) *hld up in tch in last trio: dropped to last and rdn over 2f out: wknd over 1f out* **33/1**
1-1 **7** *3* **Certified (IRE)**[14] 3989 3-9-5 **83** ... LukeMorris 3 41
(James Tate) *chsd ldrs: rdn wl over 2f out: sn btn and lost pl: wl bhd fnl f* **11/4**[2]
4100 **8** *1 1/2* **Street Force (USA)**[33] 3303 5-9-10 **84** ...(b) AlistairRawlinson(3) 5 41
(Michael Appleby) *dwlt and pushed along leaving stalls: sn rcvrd and in tch in midfield: lost pl and drvn over 1f out: sn wknd* **28/1**

1m 26.68s (-0.52) **Going Correction** +0.05s/f (Slow)
WFA 3 from 4yo+ 7lb **8** Ran SP% **116.3**
Speed ratings (Par 105): **104,102,101,101,93 86,82,81**
CSF £27.12 CT £233.73 TOTE £10.10: £3.10, £1.30, £3.50; EX 37.00 Trifecta £393.10.
Owner Binns, Bamford, Corless & Fell **Bred** Tommy Burns **Trained** Market Drayton, Shropshire

FOCUS
A decent handicap in which the two leaders took one another on and set it up for two stronger finishers.

4475 TOTEQUADPOT H'CAP 6f (P)
7:20 (7:21) (Class 3) (0-90,89) 3-Y-O+ **£9,703** (£2,887; £1,443; £721) **Stalls** Low

Form RPR
564 **1** **Under Siege (IRE)**[13] 4014 4-8-13 **76** ...(t) PatDobbs 6 85
(Stuart Williams) *chsd ldr tl led after 1f: mde rest: rdn and fnd ex over 1f out: styd on fnl f: rdn out* **7/1**[3]
1-16 **2** *3/4* **Happy Call**[46] 2871 3-8-12 **85** ...(v) AaronJones(5) 4 91
(Simon Crisford) *t.k.h: hld up in tch in midfield: hdwy to chse wnr 3f out: rdn and unable qck w wnr over 1f out: kpt on ins fnl f: nvr quite getting bk to wnr* **9/4**[1]
2625 **3** *1 1/4* **Welease Bwian (IRE)**[8] 4198 7-8-8 **78** ... MillyNaseb(7) 2 81
(Stuart Williams) *hld up in tch in midfield: rdn and hdwy on inner over 1f out: chsd ldng pair 1f out: styd on same pce ins fnl f* **12/1**
6431 **4** *nk* **Misterioso (IRE)**[11] 4079 4-9-12 **89** ... AdamKirby 8 91
(Jamie Osborne) *hld up in rr: swtchd rt and effrt over 1f out: hdwy ins fnl f: styd on wl fnl 100yds: nt rch ldrs* **5/2**[2]
-100 **5** *3/4* **Gambit**[52] 2694 3-9-6 **88** ... RichardKingscote 7 86
(Tom Dascombe) *hld up in tch in last pair: effrt jst over 2f out: hdwy over 1f out: keeping on whn n.m.r jst ins fnl f: styd on fnl 100yds: no threat to ldrs* **12/1**
4643 **6** *1 1/2* **Monumental Man**[8] 4198 7-8-11 **74** ...(p) LukeMorris 1 68
(Michael Attwater) *broke wl to ld but restrained and hdd 5f out: chsd ldr tl 3f out: rdn over 1f out: drvn and unable qck whn drifted rt 1f out: wknd ins fnl f* **12/1**
2130 **7** *hd* **Baileys Mirage (FR)**[22] 3714 5-9-8 **85** ... SilvestreDeSousa 3 79
(Chris Dwyer) *in tch in midfield: effrt 2f out: unable qck u.p over 1f out: wknd ins fnl f* **7/1**[3]
2060 **8** *6* **Francisco**[11] 4079 4-9-1 **85** ... MitchGodwin(7) 5 60
(Richard Hannon) *chsd ldrs: rdn over 2f out: sn struggling and lost pl over 1f out: bhd ins fnl f* **14/1**

1m 12.91s (-0.79) **Going Correction** +0.05s/f (Slow)
WFA 3 from 4yo+ 5lb **8** Ran SP% **114.1**
Speed ratings (Par 107): **107,106,104,103,102 100,100,92**
CSF £23.06 CT £188.45 TOTE £7.70: £2.40, £1.10, £2.50; EX 27.10 Trifecta £200.00.
Owner Happy Valley Racing & Breeding Limited **Bred** Irish National Stud **Trained** Newmarket, Suffolk

FOCUS
The pace was modest for a competitive 6f sprint, playing into the hands of the winner. He's rated back to form for his new yard.

4476 TOTETRIFECTA H'CAP 1m 2f (P)
7:50 (7:52) (Class 4) (0-80,80) 3-Y-O+ **£6,469** (£1,925; £962; £481) **Stalls** Low

Form RPR
-252 **1** **Cote D'Azur**[19] 3824 3-8-11 **73** ... LukeMorris 2 85
(Sir Mark Prescott Bt) *broke wl: restrained and hld up in midfield: nt clr run on inner over 2f out: gap opened and effrt over 1f out: qcknd to ld 1f out: sn in command and r.o strly: readily* **13/8**[1]

-145 **2** 3 3/4 **Street Duel (USA)**[15] 3949 3-9-4 **80**..........................(b[1]) FrannyNorton 8 84
(Mark Johnston) *wnt rt s and slowly away: hld up in last trio: hdwy into midfield 1/2-way: rdn to chse ldr 2f out: drvn over 1f out: wnt 2nd and edgd lft jst ins fnl f: r.o same pce after* **4/1**[2]

2213 **3** 1/2 **Melendez (USA)**[19] 3801 3-9-3 **79**................................ WilliamCarson 7 82
(Jamie Osborne) *hld up in tch in last trio: swtchd rt and effrt wl over 1f out: hdwy 1f out: styd on ins fnl f: wnt 3rd towards fin: no ch w wnr* **25/1**

-505 **4** nse **Age Of Elegance (IRE)**[3] 4409 4-9-6 **72**................. SilvestreDeSousa 1 75
(David Loughnane) *hld up in tch in rr: clsd and nt clr run whn swtchd rt over 1f out: hdwy 1f out: styd on u.p ins fnl f: wnt 4th cl home: no ch w wnr* **5/1**[3]

2161 **5** nk **Frozen Force (IRE)**[45] 2900 3-9-3 **79**.................................. PatDobbs 5 81
(Amanda Perrett) *hld up in tch in midfield: effrt u.p and unable qck over 1f out: no ch w wnr but kpt on ins fnl f* **5/1**[3]

-303 **6** hd **Clovelly Bay (IRE)**[23] 3690 5-9-8 **74**............................... HayleyTurner 4 76
(Marcus Tregoning) *racd keenly: led: rdn over 1f out: hdd 1f out and sn outpcd: 3rd and btn whn pushed rt jst ins fnl f: kpt on same pce: lost 3 pls towards fin* **6/1**

4025 **7** 9 **Warofindependence (USA)**[25] 3617 4-9-9 **75**............(v) RobertHavlin 3 59
(Alan Bailey) *chsd ldrs: rdn over 2f out: lost pl and btn over 1f out: wknd fnl f* **16/1**

3000 **8** 8 **Weald Of Kent (USA)**[14] 3991 4-9-5 **74**............(v) AlistairRawlinson(3) 6 42
(Michael Appleby) *bustled along early: hdwy to press ldr after 1f: rdn 3f out: lost 2nd 2f out and sn dropped out: wl bhd ins fnl f* **66/1**

2m 7.35s (-1.25) **Going Correction** +0.05s/f (Slow)
WFA 3 from 4yo+ 10lb **8** Ran SP% **116.9**
Speed ratings (Par 105): **107,104,103,103,103 103,95,89**
CSF £8.52 CT £115.73 TOTE £2.30: £1.40, £1.70, £1.90; EX 9.20 Trifecta £85.50.
Owner Neil Greig **Bred** W N Greig **Trained** Newmarket, Suffolk

FOCUS
A middle-rank handicap, run at a modest tempo until it quickened 4f out. The form seems sound.

4477 TOTESWINGER MAIDEN STKS 1m (P)
8:20 (8:22) (Class 4) 3-Y-O+ **£6,469** (£1,925; £962; £481) **Stalls** Low

Form RPR

40 **1** **Egyptian (USA)**[46] 2861 3-9-5 0.. AdamKirby 1 87
(Jeremy Noseda) *mde all: rdn and wnt clr jst over 2f out: rn green and hung rt over 1f out: edgd bk lft u.p ins fnl f: styd on wl* **7/1**[3]

33 **2** 4 1/2 **Run To The Hills (USA)**[25] 3609 3-9-5 0................ SilvestreDeSousa 2 77
(George Peckham) *t.k.h: trck ldrs: rdn to chse clr wnr 2f out: sme hdwy on inner over 1f out: no imp 1f out: wknd ins fnl f* **15/8**[2]

06 **3** 3 **Mary Beale (IRE)**[106] 1235 3-9-0 0................................ FrannyNorton 6 65
(Mark Johnston) *rn green: hld up in midfield and stuck wd: dropped in after 2f and racd in 6th: rdn over 2f out: sn outpcd: styd on to pass btn horses to go modest 3rd 1f out: kpt on: no ch w wnr* **14/1**

00 **4** 9 **Poetic Guest**[3] 4401 3-9-5 0.. RyanPowell 4 49
(George Margarson) *chsd ldrs: rdn over 2f out: sn outpcd: wknd over 1f out* **66/1**

0-2 **5** 1 1/4 **Eskandari (IRE)**[190] 145 3-9-5 0.................................... RobertHavlin 3 47
(Simon Crisford) *bustled along leaving stalls: sn chsng ldr: rdn over 2f out: sn hung rt and lost pl: wknd over 1f out* **4/5**[1]

06-0 **6** 9 **New Revive**[81] 1826 4-9-10 47.................................... DanielMuscutt(3) 7 28
(Patrick Chamings) *stdd s: t.k.h: hld up in midfield: rdn over 2f out: sn outpcd: wknd over 1f out* **100/1**

0 **7** 45 **Thenobleprankster (IRE)**[29] 3464 7-9-13 0..................... LukeMorris 5
(Emma Owen) *sn in rr: rdn over 3f out: lost tch 2f out: sn eased: t.o* **200/1**

1m 38.35s (-1.55) **Going Correction** +0.05s/f (Slow)
WFA 3 from 4yo+ 8lb **7** Ran SP% **112.5**
Speed ratings (Par 105): **109,104,101,92,91 82,37**
CSF £19.97 TOTE £8.80: £2.70, £1.30; EX 22.80 Trifecta £114.00.
Owner Sanford Robertson & Kathryn Nikkel **Bred** Kathryn Nikkel & Sanford Robertson **Trained** Newmarket, Suffolk

FOCUS
The runner-up had previously set a fair standard for maiden company. This was the best time on the card and the winner was dominant even allowing for the favourite disappointing.

4478 TOTEPOOLLIVEINFO.COM H'CAP 2m (P)
8:50 (8:52) (Class 6) (0-65,65) 4-Y-O+ **£3,234** (£962; £481; £240) **Stalls** Low

Form RPR

101 **1** **Lady Makfi (IRE)**[8] 4197 4-9-6 **64** 6ex......................... StevieDonohoe 7 74+
(Johnny Farrelly) *stdd s: hld up in tch: clsd on inner over 3f out: rdn to ld over 1f out: r.o strly and clr ins fnl f: eased towards fin: comf* **4/5**[1]

-323 **2** 4 **Thomas Blossom (IRE)**[78] 882 6-9-7 **65**...................(t) AdamKirby 4 67
(Ali Stronge) *hld up in tch: chsd ldrs 10f out: wnt 2nd 3f out: rdn and ev ch 2f out: 2nd but outpcd by wnr 1f out: kpt on same pce after* **7/1**[3]

5100 **3** 3/4 **King Olav (UAE)**[27] 3528 11-9-2 **63**...................... GeorgeDowning(3) 5 64
(Tony Carroll) *hld up in tch: hdwy on outer 5f out: rdn to chse ldrs 3f out: ev ch 2f out tl outpcd by wnr over 1f out: 3rd and kpt on same pce fnl f* **20/1**

0606 **4** 1 1/4 **Kirkman (IRE)**[91] 1550 5-8-6 **50**.................................... WilliamCarson 2 50
(Peter Hiatt) *racd keenly: led: rdn and pressed 2f out: hdd over 1f out: sn outpcd and btn: plugged on same pce fnl f* **33/1**

-503 **5** 7 **La Fritillaire**[40] 3067 4-8-6 **50**... FrannyNorton 6 41
(James Given) *hld up in tch: effrt in 5th over 2f out: no imp and wl btn over 1f out* **8/1**

0400 **6** 51 **Dukes Den**[27] 3528 5-8-5 **49**................................(p) SilvestreDeSousa 3
(Mark Usher) *chsd ldrs tl 10f out: styd in tch tl dropped to rr 5f out: rdn 4f out: lost tch and eased 2f out: t.o* **5/1**[2]

0P30 **7** 8 **Apollo Eleven (IRE)**[45] 2916 7-9-4 **62**.............................(p) LukeMorris 1
(Michael Appleby) *chsd ldr tl 3f out: sn dropped out: t.o and eased over 1f out: fin lame* **8/1**

3m 32.76s (2.76) **Going Correction** +0.05s/f (Slow) **7** Ran SP% **114.6**
Speed ratings (Par 101): **95,93,92,92,88 63,59**
CSF £7.22 TOTE £1.70: £1.40, £2.10; EX 7.00 Trifecta £45.60.
Owner The Lansdowners **Bred** Coleman Bloodstock Limited **Trained** Enmore, Somerset

FOCUS
A moderate stayers' event, with an improving winner, run at an undemanding gallop. The form is rated around the second and third.

T/Plt: £60.50 to a £1 stake. Pool: £60,644.50 - 731.28 winning tickets. T/Qpdt: £15.30 to a £1 stake. Pool: £8,298.90 - 400.96 winning tickets. **Steve Payne**

FFOS LAS (L-H)
Tuesday, July 19

OFFICIAL GOING: Good (good to soft in places; 7.3)
Wind: fresh, mainly behind Weather: fine and warm

4479 TOTEQUADPOT FOUR PLACES IN FOUR RACES MAIDEN STKS (PLUS 10 RACE) 7f 80y(R)
2:00 (2:01) (Class 4) 2-Y-O **£4,204** (£1,251; £625; £312) **Stalls** Low

Form RPR

2 **1** **Maths Prize**[18] 3859 2-9-5 0.. GeorgeBaker 3 78
(Roger Charlton) *s.i.s: sn trcking ldrs: shkn up over 1f out: sn chal: led ins fnl f: pushed out* **5/4**[1]

4 **2** 1/2 **Naval Warfare (IRE)**[18] 3859 2-9-5 0............................... OisinMurphy 7 77
(Andrew Balding) *led: rdn 2f out: sn pressed: hdd ins fnl f: kpt on* **11/4**[3]

5322 **3** 1 1/4 **Prerogative (IRE)**[14] 3977 2-9-5 0..................................... SeanLevey 6 74
(Richard Hannon) *trckd ldr: rdn 2f out: sn ev ch: no ex fnl 100yds* **5/2**[2]

4 7 **Peace And Plenty** 2-9-5 0.. MartinDwyer 5 56
(William Muir) *hld up: shkn up over 2f out: sn outpcd by ldrs: kpt on to take modest 4th ins fnl f* **16/1**

00 **5** 1/2 **Dravid**[10] 4154 2-9-5 0... FrederikTylicki 8 55
(Rod Millman) *hld up: hdwy 3f out: sn outpcd by ldrs: lost modest 4th ins fnl f* **66/1**

6 1 1/4 **Fausto** 2-9-5 0... LiamJones 1 52
(Tom Dascombe) *s.i.s: hld up: rdn over 3f out: one pce fnl 2f* **25/1**

00 **7** shd **Blast Of Faith (IRE)**[28] 3485 2-9-5 0.................................. ShaneKelly 4 52
(Richard Hughes) *chsd ldrs: rdn 3f out: sn outpcd and dropped to rr: no ch fnl 2f* **100/1**

1m 33.21s (0.21) **Going Correction** -0.075s/f (Good) **7** Ran SP% **111.9**
Speed ratings (Par 96): **95,94,93,85,84 83,82**
CSF £4.73 TOTE £2.30: £1.10, £1.90; EX 4.80 Trifecta £8.10.
Owner The Queen **Bred** The Queen **Trained** Beckhampton, Wilts

FOCUS
A fair juvenile maiden. They went a respectable gallop, at best, on ground officially described as good, good to soft in places on a hot, sunny afternoon with a tailwind in the home straight. The first three home finished clear, having reportedly stood out from the remainder of the field in the preliminaries. The first two came from the same Sandown race.

4480 TOTEQUADPOT INSURE YOUR LAST FOUR/ EBF MAIDEN STKS 7f 80y(R)
2:30 (2:31) (Class 5) 3-Y-O+ **£4,528** (£1,347; £673; £336) **Stalls** Low

Form RPR

-230 **1** **Loaded (IRE)**[12] 4055 3-9-5 81... OisinMurphy 3 83
(Andrew Balding) *wnt to post early: trckd ldr: rdn wl over 2f out: chal over 1f out: led jst ins fnl f: hld on u.p* **15/8**[2]

646 **2** hd **The Invisible Dog (IRE)**[20] 3769 3-9-5 78............................ SeanLevey 6 82
(Richard Hannon) *t.k.h: chsd ldrs: rdn over 2f out: r.o wl fnl f: wnt 2nd 100yds out: jst failed* **11/2**[3]

325 **3** 2 **Burguillos**[20] 3769 3-9-5 82.............................. WilliamTwiston-Davies 9 77
(Alan King) *led: rdn over 2f out: jnd over 1f out: hdd jst ins fnl f: no ex and sn lost 2nd* **6/4**[1]

5044 **4** 5 **Claymore (IRE)**[14] 3985 3-9-5 69..............................(p) StevieDonohoe 1 64
(Bernard Llewellyn) *trckd ldng pair: rdn over 2f out: lost 3rd over 1f out: wknd fnl f and jst hld 4th* **28/1**

0-0 **5** nse **Aurora Gray**[40] 3059 3-9-0 0.. FrederikTylicki 4 59
(Hughie Morrison) *hld up towards rr: rdn over 2f out: kpt on same pce and nvr any ch w ldrs* **25/1**

30 **6** hd **Irrevocable (IRE)**[46] 2877 3-9-0 0.................................... DaneO'Neill 5 58
(Roger Charlton) *s.i.s: in rr: sme hdwy 3f out: rdn 2f out: one pce and no further imp* **9/1**

0 **7** 2 1/4 **Occasional Dream (IRE)**[15] 3958 3-8-7 0............... SeanMooney(7) 11 53
(Joseph Tuite) *s.i.s: sn in mid-div: rdn 3f out: grad wknd fnl 2f* **50/1**

8 13 **Enduring Power (IRE)** 3-9-5 0... GeorgeBaker 2 24
(Brendan Powell) *t.k.h: shkn up over 2f out: a in rr* **20/1**

0- **9** 9 **Not My Way (IRE)**[312] 6290 3-8-9 0............................. CiaranMckee(5) 8
(John O'Shea) *rdn 3f out: a towards rr* **100/1**

1m 31.11s (-1.89) **Going Correction** -0.075s/f (Good) **9** Ran SP% **115.2**
Speed ratings (Par 103): **107,106,104,98,98 98,95,81,70**
CSF £11.74 TOTE £2.50: £1.10, £2.10, £1.10; EX 15.30 Trifecta £34.10.
Owner Mr & Mrs R M Gorell **Bred** Ms Alice Fitzgerald **Trained** Kingsclere, Hants

FOCUS
A decent maiden for the track. They went a respectable gallop and the right horses filled the first three places, with a break to the fourth. The first two ran pbs.

4481 TOTEQUADPOT RACES 3, 4, 5 AND 6 H'CAP 7f 80y(R)
3:00 (3:04) (Class 4) (0-85,85) 3-Y-O+ **£4,851** (£1,443; £721; £360) **Stalls** Low

Form RPR

-515 **1** **Raising Sand**[24] 3645 4-9-13 **84**.. GeorgeBaker 4 93
(Jamie Osborne) *hld up in last: hdwy on outside 2f out: rdn and carried rt ins fnl f: led last 75yds: on top nr fin* **3/1**[2]

6605 **2** 1 **Air Of York (IRE)**[5] 4291 4-9-1 **77**................................. GaryMahon(5) 2 83
(David Evans) *broke wl: chsd ldrs: rdn to ld 2f out: edgd rt u.p ins fnl f: hdd last 75yds: hld nr fin* **14/1**

4543 **3** 1 1/2 **Midnight Rider (IRE)**[11] 4086 8-8-12 **74**.......................(b) AliceMills(5) 1 76
(Rod Millman) *hld up: rdn 3f out: bmpd over 2f out: swtchd lft over 1f out: r.o fnl f* **8/1**

12-0 **4** 3 **Guiding Light (IRE)**[11] 4086 4-10-0 **85**............................ OisinMurphy 5 79
(Andrew Balding) *led 1f: trckd ldr: rdn over 2f out: sn ev ch: wkng whn n.m.r appr fnl f* **10/1**

4-43 **5** 3/4 **Topology**[23] 3689 3-9-1 **79**.. ShaneKelly 3 68
(Joseph Tuite) *hld up: rdn and clsd over 2f out: one pce appr fnl f* **9/2**[3]

2100 **6** 7 **Destroyer**[17] 3908 3-9-3 **81**... MartinDwyer 7 52
(William Muir) *t.k.h: chsd ldrs: rdn whn bmpd: hmpd and dropped to rr jst over 2f out: no ch after* **11/2**

05-1 **7** 3 **Yorkee Mo Sabee (IRE)**[12] 4036 3-9-3 **81**......................... DaneO'Neill 6 51
(Mark Johnston) *s.i.s: racd keenly and led after 1f: rdn over 2f out: sn hdd: wknd qckly: eased fnl f* **5/2**[1]

1m 30.51s (-2.49) **Going Correction** -0.075s/f (Good)
WFA 3 from 4yo+ 7lb **7** Ran SP% **114.0**
Speed ratings (Par 105): **111,109,108,104,103 95,92**
CSF £41.74 TOTE £4.30: £2.40, £6.60; EX 51.70 Trifecta £281.80.
Owner Nick Bradley Racing 22 & Partner **Bred** Meon Valley Stud **Trained** Upper Lambourn, Berks

FOCUS
The feature contest was a decent handicap. They went an honest gallop, but the strength of the form is questionable, as not many ran their races. It's been rated around the second.

4482 TOTEQUADPOT AVAILABLE ON ALL UK MEETINGS (S) STKS 1m 2f (R)
3:30 (3:32) (Class 6) 3-4-Y-O **£2,264** (£673; £336; £168) **Stalls** Low

Form RPR

3043 **1** **Pastoral Star**[15] 3955 3-8-2 60.................................. EdwardGreatrex[(3)] 2 67
(Hughie Morrison) *mde all: rdn and c over into centre of trck 3f out: pressed over 1f out: styd on* **9/4**[3]

2253 **2** 1 1/2 **Flutterbee**[11] 4082 4-9-5 65..(p) SteveDrowne 6 68
(George Baker) *trckd ldrs: c centre in st: rdn to chse wnr 3f out: ev ch briefly over 1f out: sn one pce* **7/4**[1]

-006 **3** 7 **Cautious Optimism**[12] 4046 3-8-10 70............................ MartinDwyer 5 56
(William Muir) *trckd wnr: c centre in st: rdn and lost 2nd 3f out: nt run on: btn in 3rd over 1f out* **15/8**[2]

0-00 **4** 14 **Honour Promise (IRE)**[11] 4082 4-9-1 50......(t) WilliamTwiston-Davies 8 24
(Bernard Llewellyn) *hld up in last pair: drvn over 4f out: c centre in st: bhd fnl 3f* **20/1**

3006 **5** 17 **Castanea**[28] 3488 4-9-6 42...(tp) OisinMurphy 7
(Ronald Harris) *s.s: a in rr: racd alone on far rail in st: bhd fnl 3f: t.o* **33/1**

2m 9.88s (0.48) **Going Correction** -0.075s/f (Good)
WFA 3 from 4yo 10lb **5** Ran SP% **109.6**
Speed ratings (Par 101): **95,93,88,77,63**
CSF £6.54 TOTE £3.70: £1.50, £1.20; EX 6.20 Trifecta £10.40.The winner was bought in for 7,000gns.

Owner G Swire & Mr & Mrs R Lloyd & R Wright **Bred** Whatton Manor Stud **Trained** East Ilsley, Berks

FOCUS
A modest seller. They went an honest gallop, but this is not a race that will live long in the memory.

4483 TOTEPOOLLIVEINFO.COM H'CAP 1m 6f (R)
4:00 (4:02) (Class 5) (0-70,70) 4-Y-O+ **£3,234** (£962; £481; £240) **Stalls** High

Form RPR

4133 **1** **Urban Space**[13] 3999 10-8-11 60...................................(t) OisinMurphy 4 68
(John Flint) *chsd ldrs: c centre st: rdn over 3f out: 3rd ent fnl f: r.o u.p to ld last strides* **8/1**

4631 **2** hd **Blenheim Warrior**[42] 3002 4-9-6 69.................................... ShaneKelly 5 76
(Richard Hughes) *led: drvn over 3f out: reduced ld ent fnl f: hdd last strides* **6/4**[1]

6343 **3** 1 1/4 **Ivanhoe**[17] 3903 6-9-1 64.. DaneO'Neill 1 69
(Michael Blanshard) *mid-div: hdwy over 3f out: chsd ldr over 2f out: lost 2nd and no ex fnl 75yds* **13/2**[3]

-000 **4** 1/2 **Kashgar**[13] 4012 7-9-4 67.. StevieDonohoe 10 71
(Bernard Llewellyn) *hld up: hdwy 5f out: c stands' side st: styd on u.p fnl 2f: clsng nr fin* **11/1**

6112 **5** shd **Cosette (IRE)**[20] 3767 5-9-5 68......................(p) WilliamTwiston-Davies 2 72
(Bernard Llewellyn) *a.p: chsd ldr over 4f out and c centre: lost 2nd over 2f out: one pce ins fnl f* **5/1**[2]

2/ **6** 8 **Zarzal (IRE)**[16] 569 8-9-4 67... SamHitchcott 6 60
(Evan Williams) *hld up in last: styd on ins in st: rdn and sme hdwy over 3f out: sn no imp* **28/1**

20/0 **7** 11 **Bishop Wulstan (IRE)**[13] 3999 5-8-3 59 ow2.........(tp) JoshuaBryan[(7)] 3 37
(Peter Bowen) *chsd ldrs tl lost pl 6f out: rdn 4f out: bhd fnl 3f* **20/1**

56-6 **8** nk **Welsh Rebel**[21] 3747 4-7-13 51 oh1............................... NoelGarbutt[(3)] 8 28
(Nikki Evans) *trckd wnr: rdn over 4f out: sn lost 2nd and c centre: wknd 3f out* **66/1**

16-0 **9** 1/2 **Duke Of Sonning**[19] 3798 4-9-7 70............................ FergusSweeney 7 46
(Alan King) *hld up: drvn over 4f out: wknd 3f out* **7/1**

3m 3.35s (-0.45) **Going Correction** -0.075s/f (Good) **9** Ran SP% **111.6**
Speed ratings (Par 103): **98,97,97,96,96 92,85,85,85**
CSF £19.37 CT £81.60 TOTE £7.80: £2.30, £1.30, £1.70; EX 22.50 Trifecta £107.90.

Owner J L Flint **Bred** Winterbeck Manor Stud **Trained** Kenfig Hill, Bridgend

FOCUS
A modest staying handicap. They went a decent gallop and the right horses came to the fore. The winner found a bit on recent form.

4484 @TOTEPOOL FOLLOW US ON TWITTER H'CAP 5f
4:30 (4:34) (Class 6) (0-60,60) 3-Y-O+ **£2,264** (£673; £336; £168) **Stalls** Centre

Form RPR

4-12 **1** **Go Amber Go**[5] 4292 4-9-4 54... FrederikTylicki 1 61
(Rod Millman) *broke wl: mde all: rdn over 1f out: hld on wl towards fin* **1/1**[1]

0030 **2** nk **Agerzam**[13] 3994 6-9-10 60...(p) OisinMurphy 7 66
(Ronald Harris) *mid-div: hdwy to chse wnr 2f out: kpt on u.p fnl f: hld towards fin* **8/1**

4225 **3** 1/2 **Lady McGuffy (IRE)**[19] 3811 3-9-4 58..............................(t) ShaneKelly 6 62
(David Evans) *hld up: nt clr run over 2f out: swtchd lft and rdn over 1f out: r.o fnl f* **6/1**[3]

0-00 **4** 2 **Indian Tim**[5] 4292 4-8-7 46 oh1................................. EdwardGreatrex[(3)] 9 43
(Milton Bradley) *wnt to post early: chsd ldrs: rdn 2f out: sn one pce* **50/1**

2205 **5** 1 **Jaganory (IRE)**[11] 4084 4-9-5 60...................................(p) GaryMahon[(5)] 8 53
(Christopher Mason) *chsd ldrs: rdn 2f out: wknd ent fnl f* **11/2**[2]

0032 **6** shd **Diminutive (IRE)**[19] 3811 4-8-10 49............................(p) NoelGarbutt[(3)] 4 42
(Grace Harris) *s.i.s: hld up: clsd 1/2-way: rdn whn nt clr run 2f out tl over 1f out: r.o fnl f* **9/1**

045/ **7** 2 3/4 **Ignight**[670] 6488 5-8-7 46 oh1... TimClark[(3)] 2 29
(Matthew Salaman) *chsd ldrs: rdn 2f out: wknd over 1f out* **33/1**

6050 **8** 2 **Speightowns Kid (USA)**[85] 1712 8-9-2 57.................(v[1]) AnnStokell[(5)] 5 33
(Ann Stokell) *s.i.s: a in rr* **20/1**

0-00 **9** 7 **Rich Harvest (USA)**[15] 3953 11-8-10 46 oh1..........(tp) FergusSweeney 3
(Ray Peacock) *walked most of way to s: chsd wnr 2f: shkn up and wknd qckly: eased fnl f* **100/1**

57.53s (-0.77) **Going Correction** -0.075s/f (Good)
WFA 3 from 4yo+ 4lb **9** Ran SP% **111.4**
Speed ratings (Par 101): **105,104,103,100,98 98,94,91,79**
CSF £8.85 CT £31.05 TOTE £2.10: £1.10, £2.40, £2.50; EX 9.60 Trifecta £30.00.

Owner AJ & CS Bricknell-Webb **Bred** Percys (north Harrow) Ltd **Trained** Kentisbeare, Devon

FOCUS
A moderate sprint handicap. The in-form winner dominated at a decent tempo from start to finish and the quick time suggests the straight track was riding faster than the round course. Straightforward form.

4485 COLLECT TOTEPOOL WINNINGS AT BETFRED SHOPS H'CAP 6f
5:00 (5:01) (Class 5) (0-70,68) 3-Y-O+ **£3,234** (£962; £481; £240) **Stalls** Centre

Form RPR

0250 **1** **King Of Spin**[80] 1847 3-9-7 68..(t) MartinDwyer 9 75+
(William Muir) *chsd ldrs: rdn 2f out: r.o u.p to ld fnl 75yds* **8/1**

-005 **2** 3/4 **Outrage**[14] 3989 4-9-12 68... DaneO'Neill 2 74+
(Daniel Kubler) *led: rdn 2f out: edgd rt u.p fnl f: hdd and no ex fnl 75yds* **7/1**[3]

5440 **3** 2 1/4 **Indian Affair**[5] 4291 6-9-7 66.................................(bt) EdwardGreatrex[(3)] 7 65
(Milton Bradley) *mid-div: rdn 1/2-way: styd on fnl f: wnt 3rd post* **7/2**[2]

4-00 **4** shd **Dear Bruin (IRE)**[12] 4043 4-9-11 67................. WilliamTwiston-Davies 3 65
(David W Drinkwater) *cl up: rdn and ev ch over 2f out: one pce fnl f: lost 3rd post* **25/1**

1064 **5** 1 1/4 **Summersault (IRE)**[12] 4058 5-9-9 65............................... GeorgeBaker 6 59+
(Jamie Osborne) *hld up in rr: rdn over 2f out: clsd over 1f out: hung lft and styd on ins fnl f: nvr able to chal* **11/8**[1]

2-06 **6** nk **Burningfivers (IRE)**[20] 3786 3-9-7 68.............................. OisinMurphy 1 61
(Joseph Tuite) *mid-div: rdn 1/2-way: one pce fnl 2f* **7/1**[3]

4001 **7** 1 **Noverre To Go (IRE)**[21] 3741 10-9-7 63.........................(p) ShaneKelly 8 53
(Ronald Harris) *chsd ldrs: rdn and ev ch over 2f out: wknd 1f out* **14/1**

-060 **8** 16 **Amenable (IRE)**[79] 1899 9-8-9 54.....................................(p) TimClark[(3)] 5
(Ann Stokell) *sn chsd along and a in rr: wknd over 2f out: t.o* **40/1**

1m 9.74s (-0.26) **Going Correction** -0.075s/f (Good)
WFA 3 from 4yo+ 5lb **8** Ran SP% **113.4**
Speed ratings (Par 103): **98,97,94,93,92 91,90,69**
CSF £61.10 CT £233.76 TOTE £7.40: £2.00, £2.30, £1.50; EX 59.60 Trifecta £276.50.
Owner Muir Racing Partnership - Nottingham **Bred** Cheveley Park Stud Ltd **Trained** Lambourn, Berks

FOCUS
A modest handicap, the winner not obviously progressive. They went a respectable gallop spread centrally and an improving 3yo made the most of his 5lb weight-for-age allowance.
T/Jkpt: £4,898.40 to a £1 stake. Pool: £26,941.50 - 5.5 winning tickets. T/Plt: £9.40 to a £1 stake. Pool: £77,403.38 - 5,963.50 winning tickets. T/Qpdt: £7.50 to a £1 stake. Pool: £4,868.56 - 478.20 winning tickets **Richard Lowther**

4096 MUSSELBURGH (R-H)
Tuesday, July 19

OFFICIAL GOING: Good to firm (7.6) (watered)
Wind: Fresh, across Weather: Cloudy, warm

4486 ROA/RACING POST OWNERS JACKPOT H'CAP 1m 1f
2:15 (2:16) (Class 6) (0-65,64) 4-Y-O+ **£2,587** (£770; £384; £192) **Stalls** Low

Form RPR

0254 **1** **La Havrese (FR)**[24] 3642 5-9-0 62..................................... JoshDoyle[(5)] 7 68
(Lynn Siddall) *hld up: rdn and edgd rt over 2f out: hdwy to ld over 1f out: kpt on wl fnl f* **9/1**

4552 **2** 1/2 **Lucky Violet (IRE)**[21] 3754 4-9-7 64............................ RoystonFfrench 9 69
(Iain Jardine) *reluctant to enter stalls: sn stdd towards rr: rdn over 2f out: hdwy to chse wnr ins fnl f: clsng at fin* **11/1**

1020 **3** 2 1/2 **The Wee Barra (IRE)**[17] 3876 4-9-5 62..........................(p) GrahamLee 8 62
(Kevin Ryan) *pressed ldr: rdn over 2f out: ev ch briefly over 1f out: sn chsng wnr: lost 2nd and no ex ins fnl f* **7/1**[3]

0456 **4** 1 1/4 **Mr Sundowner (USA)**[10] 4144 4-8-9 55....................(t) ShelleyBirkett[(3)] 1 53
(Wilf Storey) *prom: effrt whn nt clr run briefly over 2f out: sn rdn: kpt on same pce fnl f* **17/2**

0033 **5** 1 1/4 **Alans Pride (IRE)**[8] 4214 4-8-12 55..........................(bt) ConnorBeasley 2 50
(Michael Dods) *t.k.h: led to over 1f out: sn rdn and wknd* **4/1**[2]

4432 **6** 1 1/4 **Incurs Four Faults**[4] 4341 5-8-6 49.................................(p) JoeFanning 4 42
(Keith Dalgleish) *t.k.h: cl up on outside: rdn over 2f out: wknd fnl f* **5/2**[1]

6523 **7** 9 **John Caesar (IRE)**[17] 3876 5-9-7 64........................(tp) PaulMulrennan 3 39
(Rebecca Bastiman) *t.k.h: in tch: rdn over 2f out: wknd wl over 1f out* **4/1**[2]

5-00 **8** 9 **Jessie Allan (IRE)**[15] 3946 5-8-4 47 ow2................................ JoeDoyle 5 4
(Jim Goldie) *hld up: drvn and outpcd over 2f out: sn btn* **80/1**

1m 51.19s (-2.71) **Going Correction** -0.20s/f (Firm) **8** Ran SP% **111.2**
Speed ratings (Par 101): **104,103,101,100,99 98,90,82**
CSF £95.22 CT £532.90 TOTE £9.90: £2.30, £2.50, £2.40; EX 81.80 Trifecta £283.70.
Owner Jimmy Kay **Bred** S C A Elevage De La Croix De Place **Trained** Colton, N Yorks

FOCUS
A warm and sunny day, and the watered ground was given as good to firm (GoingStick: 7.6). The rail on the bottom bend was out 2yds, adding 7yds to races 1, 2, 4, 5 and 6. A modest handicap run at a good pace. The second is the key to the form.

4487 RACING WELFARE MAIDEN AUCTION STKS 7f 30y
2:45 (2:45) (Class 5) 2-Y-O **£2,726** (£805; £402) **Stalls** Low

Form RPR

045 **1** **Bongrace (IRE)**[12] 4037 2-8-9 0... KevinStott 2 70
(Kevin Ryan) *t.k.h early: pressed ldr: led over 2f out: rdn and edgd lft over 1f out: hld on wl fnl f* **11/1**

4233 **2** 1 **Bridal March**[17] 3872 2-8-8 0.. JoeFanning 3 66
(Mark Johnston) *led at modest gallop: rdn and hdd over 2f out: rallied and ev ch over 1f out to ins fnl f: kpt on: hld nr fin* **15/8**[2]

6 **3** 1/2 **Copper Baked (FR)**[12] 4063 2-8-9 0..................................... BenCurtis 1 66
(K R Burke) *dwlt: t.k.h and sn trcking ldrs: rdn and outpcd over 2f out: kpt on fnl f: nrst fin* **10/11**[1]

4 nk **Showtime Lady (IRE)** 2-8-11 0...................................... PaulMulrennan 5 67+
(Mark Johnston) *s.i.s: rn green bhd ldng pair: effrt and ev ch over 2f out to over 1f out: no ex ins fnl f* **8/1**[3]

1m 28.69s (-0.31) **Going Correction** -0.20s/f (Firm) **4** Ran SP% **106.6**
Speed ratings (Par 94): **93,91,91,90**
CSF £30.39 TOTE £11.20; EX 24.10 Trifecta £48.20.
Owner Bongrace Partners **Bred** Mrs Celine Collins **Trained** Hambleton, N Yorks

FOCUS
Race distance increased by 7yds. Effectively a fillies' maiden, this was run at a steady early gallop and they finished in a bit of a heap. The winner has improved run to run.

4488 ARTHUR MCKAY H'CAP 5f
3:15 (3:16) (Class 4) (0-80,80) 3-Y-O+ **£5,175** (£1,540; £769; £384) **Stalls** High

Form RPR

20-6 **1** **Economic Crisis (IRE)**[10] 4142 7-8-10 **69**................. NathanEvans[(5)] 6 79
(John David Riches) *trckd ldrs: wnt 2nd 1/2-way: rdn to ld ins fnl f: kpt on wl* **16/1**

621 **2** 2 1/2 **Pea Shooter**[63] 2346 7-9-11 **79**.. BenCurtis 8 80
(Brian Ellison) *prom: rdn along 2f out: kpt on to take 2nd nr fin: nt rch wnr* **4/1**[1]

-040 **3** *hd* **Lydia's Place**[31] 3420 3-9-8 **80**.................................... ConnorBeasley 10 79
(Richard Guest) *led: rdn over 1f out: edgd rt and hdd ins fnl f: r.o same pce: lost 2nd nr fin* **6/1**[3]

3351 **4** *1* **Bashiba (IRE)**[15] 3956 5-9-12 **80**....................................(t) GrahamLee 11 77
(Nigel Tinkler) *prom: effrt and drvn along wl over 1f out: edgd rt: kpt on ins fnl f* **9/2**[2]

0343 **5** 1/2 **Royal Brave (IRE)**[26] 3552 5-9-5 **73**...........................(p) BarryMcHugh 3 68
(Rebecca Bastiman) *hld up in midfield: drvn along over 2f out: kpt on fnl f: no imp* **6/1**[3]

0652 **6** 1/2 **Chookie's Lass**[21] 3755 5-8-9 **63**.. JasonHart 9 56
(Keith Dalgleish) *pressed ldr to 1/2-way: sn rdn along: one pce fr over 1f out* **8/1**

-005 **7** *hd* **Farkle Minkus**[56] 2554 3-9-4 **76**...................................(p) JoeFanning 2 67
(Keith Dalgleish) *hld up in tch on outside: effrt and pushed along 2f out: outpcd fnl f* **9/1**

6066 **8** 3/4 **Go Go Green (IRE)**[15] 3944 10-9-0 **68**................................. JoeDoyle 4 58
(Jim Goldie) *dwlt: hld up: rdn along wl over 1f out: sn no imp* **12/1**

0350 **9** 3/4 **Blue Sonic**[15] 3944 6-8-13 **67**....................................... DougieCostello 7 54
(Linda Perratt) *dwlt: bhd: rdn over 2f out: edgd rt and no imp over 1f out* **25/1**

3055 **10** 4 1/2 **Bunce (IRE)**[11] 4100 8-8-9 **63**.. PJMcDonald 1 34
(Linda Perratt) *hld up: rdn along 1/2-way: sn no imp: btn fnl f* **12/1**

00-0 **11** *5* **Rock Canyon (IRE)**[8] 4191 7-8-11 **65**............................... GeorgeChaloner 5 18
(Linda Perratt) *bhd: drvn along over 2f out: btn over 1f out* **66/1**

58.1s (-2.30) **Going Correction** -0.25s/f (Firm)
WFA 3 from 4yo+ 4lb **11** Ran SP% **114.5**
Speed ratings (Par 105): **108,104,103,102,101 100,100,98,97,90 82**
CSF £76.97 CT £436.10 TOTE £22.00: £4.80, £1.60, £2.80; EX 110.30 Trifecta £549.90.
Owner William Burns & Alan Berry **Bred** Philip Hore Jnr **Trained** Pilling, Lancashire

FOCUS
A competitive sprint handicap on paper, but the winner scooted clear in the closing stages. There's a case for rating this a pb.

4489 RACING UK NOW IN HD! H'CAP 1m 4f 100y
3:45 (3:45) (Class 6) (0-60,59) 4-Y-O+ **£2,587** (£770; £384; £192) **Stalls** Low

Form RPR

00-3 **1** **Our Kylie (IRE)**[26] 3564 4-9-0 **59**................................. BenRobinson[(7)] 5 67
(Brian Ellison) *prom: pushed along after 4f: drvn and outpcd over 3f out: rallied to chse ldrs whn nt clr run briefly and swtchd lft appr fnl f: edgd lft: kpt on wl to ld cl home* **3/1**[1]

4050 **2** *hd* **Merchant Of Dubai**[11] 4099 11-9-7 **59**.............................. PaulMulrennan 6 67
(Jim Goldie) *chsd clr ldr: clsd over 2f out: rdn to ld over 1f out: kpt on fnl f: hdd cl home* **22/1**

3003 **3** 1 1/2 **Neuf Des Coeurs**[11] 4099 5-9-1 **58**........................(p) GarryWhillans[(5)] 10 64
(Iain Jardine) *hld up: rdn over 3f out: hdwy to chse ldrs over 1f out: kpt on same pce ins fnl f* **6/1**[3]

6/0- **4** 1/2 **Sohcahtoa (IRE)**[336] 5496 10-8-7 **45**.................................(p) JoeDoyle 11 50
(Julia Brooke) *hld up: rdn over 4f out: hdwy and edgd rt over 2f out: kpt on ins fnl f: no imp* **12/1**

-003 **5** 1 1/4 **Morocco**[35] 3253 7-8-13 **51**...(e) DougieCostello 1 53+
(Karen Tutty) *led and sn wl clr: rdn and hdd over 1f out: outpcd ins fnl f* **25/1**

2602 **6** 3/4 **Chauvelin**[6] 4260 5-8-11 **49**..(b) ConnorBeasley 8 50
(Richard Guest) *hld up: rdn along over 3f out: hdwy over 2f out: no imp over 1f out* **4/1**[2]

0054 **7** *4* **Annigoni (IRE)**[22] 3706 4-8-12 **50**..................................(b[1]) JoeFanning 7 46
(Ruth Carr) *t.k.h: hld up in tch: stdy hdwy over 5f out: rdn over 2f out: wknd over 1f out* **4/1**[2]

464 **8** *10* **Multi Grain**[28] 3480 4-9-5 **57**...(p) PJMcDonald 9 36
(Micky Hammond) *dwlt: bhd and sn pushed along: struggling over 4f out: nvr on terms* **10/1**

6665 **9** *6* **New Colours**[11] 4099 5-8-7 **45**...................................(p) GeorgeChaloner 4 14
(Linda Perratt) *dwlt: hld up in midfield: struggling over 4f out: sn wknd* **18/1**

0-00 **10** *48* **Wisteria**[13] 4001 4-8-7 **45**..(t) RaulDaSilva 2
(Susan Corbett) *chsd ldrs tl hung lft and wknd over 2f out: eased whn no ch: t.o* **125/1**

2m 42.2s (0.20) **Going Correction** -0.20s/f (Firm) **10** Ran SP% **110.3**
Speed ratings (Par 101): **91,90,89,89,88 88,85,78,74,42**
CSF £70.19 CT £348.94 TOTE £4.20: £1.50, £3.40, £2.30; EX 59.20 Trifecta £159.20.
Owner Morecool & Cool Racing **Bred** Lynn Lodge Stud **Trained** Norton, N Yorks

FOCUS
Race distance increased by 7yds. The leader set a scorching pace in this handicap.

4490 RACINGUK.COM/HD H'CAP 7f 30y
4:15 (4:15) (Class 5) (0-70,66) 3-Y-O+ **£3,234** (£962; £481; £240) **Stalls** Low

Form RPR

5052 **1** **Novinophobia**[13] 4003 3-9-7 **66**.. JackGarritty 8 73
(Richard Fahey) *mde all at ordinary gallop: rdn over 1f out: edgd lft ins fnl f: hld on wl* **2/1**[1]

6065 **2** *hd* **Ellaal**[11] 4089 7-10-0 **66**.. JoeFanning 6 75
(Ruth Carr) *pressed wnr: effrt and rdn over 1f out: kpt on fnl f: jst hld* **9/2**[3]

0S41 **3** 2 3/4 **Deben**[13] 4006 3-8-13 **58**... JoeDoyle 2 57
(Kevin Ryan) *hld up in tch: stdy hdwy to chse ldrs over 1f out: sn rdn and edgd rt: one pce fnl f* **7/2**[2]

0002 **4** *5* **Circuitous**[11] 4102 8-9-8 **60**...(v) GrahamLee 1 48
(Keith Dalgleish) *trckd ldrs: rdn over 2f out: edgd rt: wknd over 1f out* **7/1**

3030 **5** *nse* **American Hustle (IRE)**[25] 3610 4-9-12 **64**........................... BenCurtis 7 52
(Brian Ellison) *t.k.h: hld up in tch: rdn over 2f out: edgd rt and wknd 1f out* **7/2**[2]

1m 27.96s (-1.04) **Going Correction** -0.20s/f (Firm)
WFA 3 from 4yo+ 7lb **5** Ran SP% **108.5**
Speed ratings (Par 103): **97,96,93,87,87**
CSF £10.77 TOTE £3.10: £1.30, £2.80; EX 10.20 Trifecta £27.20.
Owner P Timmins & A Rhodes Haulage **Bred** Whitsbury Manor Stud **Trained** Musley Bank, N Yorks

FOCUS
Race distance increased by 7yds. This was dominated from the front by the winner. The form is rated around the second.

4491 REAL WATER H'CAP 2m
4:45 (4:45) (Class 4) (0-80,78) 4-Y-O+ **£5,175** (£1,540; £769; £384) **Stalls** High

Form RPR

6152 **1** **Hillgrove Angel (IRE)**[21] 3751 4-9-0 **71**............................ DavidNolan 6 79
(Iain Jardine) *hld up in tch: stdy hdwy to ld over 2f out: rdn and edgd rt over 1f out: rdn out fnl f* **11/2**

1131 **2** 3/4 **Always Resolute**[24] 3639 5-9-0 **78**........................... BenRobinson[(7)] 7 85
(Brian Ellison) *t.k.h: trckd ldr 3f: cl up: effrt and ev ch briefly over 2f out: sn chsng wnr: kpt on u.p ins fnl f* **15/8**[1]

2351 **3** *2* **Frederic**[11] 4101 5-9-1 **72**... PJMcDonald 3 77
(Micky Hammond) *racd wout nr-fore shoe: in tch: effrt whn nt clr run over 2f out to over 1f out: rdn and kpt on ins fnl f* **5/1**[3]

4045 **4** *5* **Jan Smuts (IRE)**[11] 4101 8-8-10 **70**.........................(t) ShelleyBirkett[(3)] 4 69
(Wilf Storey) *hld up: rdn and hdwy over 2f out: rdn and no imp fr over 1f out* **20/1**

1321 **5** 1 1/4 **Roc De Prince**[8] 4194 7-8-5 **62**...(v) JoeFanning 1 59
(Keith Dalgleish) *led at ordinary gallop: rdn and hdd over 2f out: wknd over 1f out* **3/1**[2]

00-0 **6** 4 1/2 **Jonny Delta**[15] 3942 9-8-8 **65**.. JoeDoyle 2 57
(Jim Goldie) *s.i.s: hld up: rdn over 2f out: sn outpcd: btn over 1f out* **14/1**

0603 **7** 1/2 **Arantes**[8] 4189 5-8-11 **68**..(p) ConnorBeasley 5 59
(R Mike Smith) *cl up: wnt 2nd after 3f to over 2f out: sn ev ch briefly: wknd over 1f out* **16/1**

3m 27.19s (-6.31) **Going Correction** -0.20s/f (Firm) **7** Ran SP% **109.1**
Speed ratings (Par 105): **107,106,105,103,102 100,100**
CSF £14.75 TOTE £4.80: £2.30, £1.80; EX 14.90 Trifecta £44.30.
Owner JAB **Bred** Carrigbeg Stud Co Ltd **Trained** Carrutherstown, D'fries & G'way

FOCUS
Race distance increased by 7yds. A fair staying contest, and the first three finished nicely clear. A small pb from the winner.

4492 BIG PARTNERSHIP H'CAP 5f
5:15 (5:22) (Class 6) (0-60,59) 3-Y-O+ **£2,587** (£770; £384; £192) **Stalls** Low

Form RPR

0040 **1** **Under Approval**[18] 3843 5-8-9 **49**...............................(b) GemmaTutty[(5)] 9 55
(Karen Tutty) *dwlt: sn in tch: effrt and rdn over 1f out: led ins fnl f: hld on wl cl home* **12/1**

-030 **2** *shd* **Spoken Words**[55] 2571 7-8-10 **45**............................(p) PatrickMathers 10 51
(John David Riches) *trckd ldrs: rdn along 1/2-way: kpt on wl fnl f: jst hld* **25/1**

2004 **3** *shd* **Lorimer's Lot (IRE)**[20] 3779 5-9-0 **49**................................(p) JasonHart 7 54
(Mark Walford) *led: rdn along over 1f out: hdd ins fnl f: rallied: hld cl home* **11/2**[2]

0062 **4** 1 1/4 **Thornaby Princess**[11] 4096 5-8-7 **47**........................(p) AnnaHesketh[(5)] 8 48
(Colin Teague) *trckd ldrs: effrt and rdn over 1f out: edgd lft ins fnl f: kpt on same pce last 100yds* **12/1**

5603 **5** 3/4 **Lizzy's Dream**[5] 4292 8-9-2 **51**.. PaulMulrennan 11 52
(Rebecca Bastiman) *in tch: effrt whn nt clr run fr 1/2-way to ins fnl f: rdn and kpt on same pce* **5/2**[1]

1040 **6** 3 1/4 **Lady Poppy**[28] 3484 6-9-10 **59**.. GrahamLee 4 45
(Jedd O'Keeffe) *bhd and outpcd: sme hdwy over 1f out: kpt on: nvr able to chal* **6/1**[3]

0126 **7** *2* **Fuel Injection**[21] 3755 5-9-2 **51**.. JackGarritty 1 30
(Paul Midgley) *cl up on outside: drvn along over 2f out: wknd appr fnl f* **7/1**

06-3 **8** 1 1/2 **Cheeni**[11] 4096 4-8-10 **45**... JoeDoyle 6 19
(Jim Goldie) *walked to s: bhd and outpcd: nvr on terms* **10/1**

00-6 **9** 3/4 **Compton Mews**[17] 3879 3-8-6 **45**.. RaulDaSilva 3 15
(Les Eyre) *bhd and outpcd: drvn and hung rt 1/2-way: sn btn* **50/1**

0000 **10** 2 1/2 **Majestic Manannan (IRE)**[41] 3010 7-9-5 **54**.................... JoeFanning 2 16
(David Nicholls) *dwlt: sn midfield on outside: drvn along over 2f out: wknd over 1f out* **11/2**[2]

59.48s (-0.92) **Going Correction** -0.25s/f (Firm)
WFA 3 from 4yo+ 4lb **10** Ran SP% **116.4**
Speed ratings (Par 101): **97,96,96,94,93 88,85,82,81,77**
CSF £269.04 CT £1833.28 TOTE £14.70: £3.80, £5.30, £2.20; EX 372.80 Trifecta £9087.30 Part won..
Owner Grange Park Racing (Tutty Trio) **Bred** Mickley Stud **Trained** Osmotherley, N Yorks

FOCUS
There was a tight finish to this lowly sprint handicap.The winner is rated near her Catterick form.
T/Plt: £869.60 to a £1 stake. Pool: £63,982.53 - 53.71 winning tickets. T/Qpdt: £11.70 to a £1 stake. Pool: £7,068.91 - 445.80 winning tickets. **Richard Young**

4363 NOTTINGHAM (L-H)
Tuesday, July 19

OFFICIAL GOING: Good to firm (8.0) (watered)
Wind: Virtually nil Weather: Fine & dry

4493 RACINGUK.COM RACING EXCELLENCE APPRENTICE TRAINING SERIES H'CAP 1m 2f 50y
5:40 (5:43) (Class 6) (0-65,63) 4-Y-O+ **£2,264** (£673; £336; £168) **Stalls** Low

Form RPR

0006 **1** **We'll Shake Hands (FR)**[19] 3804 5-9-8 **62**..................... CliffordLee[(3)] 1 70
(K R Burke) *slt ld on inner: hdd over 3f out: cl up: led again 1 1/2f out: sn rdn and kpt on wl* **5/2**[1]

0602 **2** 1 3/4 **Handheld**[26] 3582 9-9-5 **63**...(p) LiamDoran[(7)] 4 68
(Julia Feilden) *trckd ldrs: effrt and n.m.r over 1f out: sn swtchd lft and rdn: chsd wnr ins fnl f: no imp* **7/2**[3]

2420 **3** 1/2 **The Dukkerer (IRE)**[24] 3642 5-9-11 **62**............................ AdamMcNamara 3 66
(James Given) *cl up: slt ld over 3f out: rdn along and hdd 1 1/2f out: kpt on same pce* **3/1**[2]

66-5 **4** *1* **Mystical Maze**[28] 3492 5-8-3 **45**.. DavidEgan[(5)] 8 47
(Mark Brisbourne) *in rr: pushed along 4f out: rdn wl over 2f out: kpt on u.p fnl f* **50/1**

5023 **5** 1 1/4 **First Sargeant**[10] 4143 6-9-9 **60**.......................................(p) HollieDoyle 9 59
(Lawrence Mullaney) *cl up: pushed along and lost pl over 4f out: hdwy to chse ldrs wl over 2f out: sn rdn and one pce* **4/1**

-005 **6** *nk* **Free One (IRE)**[29] 3476 4-9-11 **62**....(b) KevinLundie 6 61
(Ivan Furtado) *cl up on outer: pushed along 3f out: rdn 2f out: grad wknd* **14/1**

00-6 **7** *20* **Suni Dancer**[187] 175 5-8-13 **50**.... GeorgiaCox 2 11
(Tony Carroll) *dwlt: hdwy and in tch after 2f: pushed along to chse ldrs over 4f out: rdn along over 3f out: sn wknd* **16/1**

0-00 **8** *18* **Par Three (IRE)**[13] 3997 5-9-7 **58**.... RhiainIngram 7
(Tony Carroll) *sn outpcd and bhd fr 1/2-way* **33/1**

2m 11.29s (-3.01) **Going Correction** -0.425s/f (Firm) **8** Ran SP% **113.2**
Speed ratings (Par 101): **95,93,93,92,91 91,75,60**
CSF £11.28 CT £25.98 TOTE £2.90: £1.10, £1.90, £1.60; EX 12.40 Trifecta £36.10.
Owner Market Avenue Racing Club & Mrs E Burke **Bred** Eric Puerari **Trained** Middleham Moor, N Yorks

FOCUS
Outer course used. Rail set out 2yds on the home bend, adding 6yds to Races 1,5,6 & 7. There had been 18mm of water applied to the track over the previous two days and the going was good to firm. A modest handicap. The winner was well treated on last year's form.

4494 BRITISH STALLION STUDS EBF MAIDEN STKS 5f 13y
6:10 (6:11) (Class 5) 2-Y-O **£3,234** (£962; £481; £240) **Stalls** Centre

Form RPR

52 **1** **Kamra (USA)**[19] 3818 2-9-5 0....(v) JimCrowley 6 80
(Jeremy Noseda) *prom: hdwy to chal over 1f out: rdn and edgd lft ent fnl f: styd on to ld towards fin* **13/8**[1]

246 **2** *1/2* **Stop The Wages (IRE)**[12] 4054 2-8-7 0.... JordanUys(7) 5 73
(Brian Meehan) *cl up: rdn to ld over 1f out: sn edgd lft: drvn and edgd rt ins fnl f: hdd towards fin* **5/1**[3]

64 **3** *2* **Indie Rock**[11] 4110 2-9-0 0.... AndrewMullen 1 66
(Mark Johnston) *sn led: pushed along 2f out: rdn and hdd over 1f out: kpt on same pce* **8/1**

2 **4** *2 1/4* **Lightning North**[13] 4022 2-9-0 0.... MartinHarley 4 58
(James Tate) *hmpd and awkward s: sn trcking ldrs: effrt 2f out: sn rdn and no imp fnl f* **2/1**[2]

5 *4* **One Too Many (IRE)** 2-8-11 0.... KieranShoemark(3) 3 44
(David Brown) *dwlt: green: sn outpcd and a bhd* **25/1**

6 *9* **Sir Harry Collins (IRE)** 2-9-5 0.... HarryBentley 2 16
(Richard Spencer) *wnt rt s: prom: pushed along 1/2-way: rdn 2f out: grad wknd* **12/1**

59.99s (-1.51) **Going Correction** -0.425s/f (Firm) **6** Ran SP% **110.7**
Speed ratings (Par 94): **95,94,91,87,81 66**
CSF £9.92 TOTE £2.40: £1.60, £2.30; EX 9.10 Trifecta £37.50.
Owner Mrs Susan Roy & Charles Pigram **Bred** Randall Hartley & Dean DeRenzo **Trained** Newmarket, Suffolk

FOCUS
A fair maiden, in which the pace was ordinary. The winner's latest form is working out well.

4495 SHERWOODS RESTAURANT H'CAP 5f 13y
6:40 (6:41) (Class 5) (0-75,74) 3-Y-O+ **£2,911** (£866; £432; £216) **Stalls** Centre

Form RPR

360 **1** **Oriental Relation (IRE)**[8] 4198 5-9-4 **68**....(b) TomEaves 3 76
(James Given) *mde all: rdn wl over 1f out: drvn ent fnl f: kpt on gamely towards fin* **6/1**[3]

6000 **2** *1/2* **Master Bond**[17] 3875 7-9-10 **74**.... DanielTudhope 4 80
(David O'Meara) *bmpd s: hld up in rr: hdwy wl over 1f out: rdn to chal ent fnl f: sn drvn and ev ch tl no ex towards fin* **4/1**[2]

0-40 **3** *2 3/4* **Loumarin (IRE)**[12] 4039 4-8-10 **60** oh3.... AndrewMullen 7 56
(Michael Appleby) *chsd ldng pair on outer: cl up 2f out: rdn over 1f out: drvn and kpt on same pce fnl f* **8/1**

2606 **4** *nse* **Ruby's Day**[5] 4295 7-8-13 **70**.... TomDonoghue(7) 1 66
(David Brown) *chsd ldrs on outer: cl up 1/2-way: rdn 2f out: sn hung bdly lft to far rail: kpt on same pce* **7/1**

2601 **5** *2 3/4* **Sleepy Blue Ocean**[118] 1046 10-9-5 **69**....(p) RobertWinston 6 55
(John Balding) *cl up: rdn wl over 1f out: wknd fnl f* **8/1**

0-00 **6** *nk* **Royal Acquisition**[24] 3637 6-9-5 **72**.... JosephineGordon(3) 2 57
(Ivan Furtado) *chsd ldrs: rdn along 2f out: sn drvn and wknd* **10/1**

1650 **7** *3/4* **Whitecrest**[12] 4039 8-9-5 **69**.... MartinHarley 8 51
(John Spearing) *in tch: rdn along on outer wl over 1f out: n.d* **12/1**

1351 **8** *1/2* **Show Palace**[19] 3806 3-8-12 **66**.... TomQueally 5 46
(Jennie Candlish) *wnt rt s: t.k.h: chsd ldrs: rdn along 2f out: sn btn* **11/4**[1]

58.74s (-2.76) **Going Correction** -0.425s/f (Firm)
WFA 3 from 4yo+ 4lb **8** Ran SP% **112.5**
Speed ratings (Par 103): **105,104,99,99,95 94,93,92**
CSF £29.15 CT £193.25 TOTE £6.70: £1.50, £2.40, £2.80; EX 24.80 Trifecta £271.50.
Owner The Cool Silk Partnership **Bred** Brendan Laffan & Michael McCormick **Trained** Willoughton, Lincs

FOCUS
A fair handicap run at an even pace and not many got into it. The winner is rated back to his past turf form.

4496 RACING UK PROFITS RETURNED TO RACING H'CAP 6f 15y
7:10 (7:10) (Class 4) (0-80,80) 3-Y-O+ **£4,851** (£1,443; £721; £360) **Stalls** Centre

Form RPR

6-21 **1** **Darma (IRE)**[48] 2794 4-9-6 **77**.... JosephineGordon(3) 3 86
(Martyn Meade) *led 1f: cl up: led again 2f out: rdn over 1f out: drvn ins fnl f: kpt on wl towards fin* **6/1**

43-2 **2** *hd* **Magical Effect (IRE)**[17] 3907 4-9-6 **74**.... JamesSullivan 6 82
(Ruth Carr) *t.k.h and stdd s: hld up in rr: hdwy on wd outside over 2f out: chal ent fnl f: ev ch tl nt qckn nr fin* **9/2**[2]

655 **3** *1 3/4* **Ace Master**[19] 3821 8-9-4 **72**....(b) JimmyQuinn 11 75
(Roy Bowring) *prom: cl up 1/2-way: rdn 2f out: drvn and edgd lft ins fnl f: kpt on same pce* **20/1**

-051 **4** *1/2* **Magical Daze**[22] 3719 4-9-4 **72**.... AndrewMullen 12 73
(John Mackie) *in tch on outer: hdwy 2f out: sn rdn: drvn and kpt on fnl f* **25/1**

154 **5** *1* **Summer Chorus**[13] 3995 3-9-6 **79**.... DavidProbert 5 76
(Andrew Balding) *trckd ldrs: hdwy over 2f out: rdn over 1f out: drvn and one pce fnl f* **5/1**[3]

6315 **6** *4* **Spirit Of Wedza (IRE)**[17] 3880 4-8-10 **67**....(p) JacobButterfield(3) 8 52
(Julie Camacho) *chsd ldrs: rdn along and lost pl 1/2-way: hdwy wl over 1f out: kpt on fnl f* **8/1**

221- **7** *1/2* **Yosemite**[282] 7141 3-9-4 **77**.... TonyHamilton 9 59
(Richard Fahey) *chsd ldrs: rdn along over 2f out: sn wknd* **8/1**

0003 **8** *2 1/4* **It Must Be Faith**[25] 3618 6-9-11 **79**.... TomQueally 2 55
(Michael Appleby) *cl up: led after 1f: hdd 2f out: sn rdn and wknd over 1f out* **10/1**

6000 **9** *2* **Clubland (IRE)**[26] 3580 7-9-1 **76**.... KevinLundie(7) 4 46
(Roy Bowring) *in tch: hdwy to chse ldrs over 3f out: rdn along wl over 2f out: sn wknd* **33/1**

0315 **10** *3/4* **Operative**[10] 4134 3-9-7 **80**.... JimCrowley 10 46
(Ed de Giles) *chsd ldrs: rdn along over 2f out: sn drvn and wknd* **4/1**[1]

1m 11.7s (-3.00) **Going Correction** -0.425s/f (Firm)
WFA 3 from 4yo+ 5lb **10** Ran SP% **112.0**
Speed ratings (Par 105): **103,102,100,99,98 93,92,89,86,85**
CSF £30.90 CT £512.95 TOTE £6.70: £2.30, £1.90, £5.50; EX 23.00 Trifecta £647.60.
Owner David Caddy **Bred** Di Lualdi Lucia & C **Trained** Newmarket, Suffolk

■ Stewards' Enquiry : Josephine Gordon Two-day bane; using whip in incorrect place (2nd-3rd August)

Jim Crowley Trainer said gelding was unsuited by the undulating track, and also that he intends to experiment with headgear on the gelding's next outing.

FOCUS
A competitive sprint handicap and solid form. The winner built on her previous C&D win.

4497 NOTTINGHAM RACECOURSE AND CONFERENCE CENTRE H'CAP 1m 75y
7:40 (7:40) (Class 4) (0-80,78) 3-Y-O+ **£4,851** (£1,443; £721; £360) **Stalls** Low

Form RPR

1-06 **1** **Kummiya**[26] 3574 3-8-10 **71** ow1.... KieranShoemark(3) 2 79+
(Roger Charlton) *hld up: hdwy 4f out: cl up 2f out: rdn to ld over 1f out: drvn and kpt on wl fnl f* **2/1**[2]

1322 **2** *1 1/2* **Shamaheart (IRE)**[7] 4231 6-9-10 **74**....(p) DavidAllan 6 80+
(Geoffrey Harker) *hld up in rr: hdwy 4f out: cl up 2f out: rdn to chal over 1f out: drvn and ev ch ins fnl f: kpt on same pce towards fin* **7/4**[1]

2340 **3** *1 1/2* **Depth Charge (IRE)**[25] 3599 4-9-6 **70**....(vt) TonyHamilton 5 72
(Kristin Stubbs) *hld up in rr: hdwy 4f out: chsd ldrs 2f out: sn rdn and cl up on inner: drvn and kpt on same pce fnl f* **6/1**[3]

1120 **4** *nk* **Mr Red Clubs (IRE)**[48] 2791 7-9-10 **74**....(p) AndrewMullen 3 76
(Michael Appleby) *trckd ldr: hdwy and cl up 4f out: led over 2f out: rdn and hdd jst over 1f out: sn drvn and kpt on same pce* **8/1**

0000 **5** *7* **St Patrick's Day (IRE)**[20] 3783 4-9-11 **75**....(v) TomEaves 7 60
(J R Jenkins) *chsd ldng pair: hdwy 4f out: cl up 3f out and sn rdn: drvn 2f out and sn wknd* **20/1**

2000 **6** *4* **Clockmaker (IRE)**[11] 4094 10-9-11 **75**.... MartinHarley 1 50
(Conor Dore) *led: rdn along over 3f out: drvn and hdd jst over 2f out: sn wknd* **14/1**

1m 44.08s (-4.92) **Going Correction** -0.425s/f (Firm)
WFA 3 from 4yo+ 8lb **6** Ran SP% **106.5**
Speed ratings (Par 105): **107,105,104,103,96 92**
CSF £5.21 TOTE £3.00: £1.80, £1.30; EX 5.70 Trifecta £16.00.
Owner A E Oppenheimer **Bred** Hascombe And Valiant Studs **Trained** Beckhampton, Wilts

FOCUS
Distance increased by 6yds. Little depth to this fair handicap, in which the two market leaders came to the fore. The form is rated around the second.

4498 RACING UK IN GLORIOUS HD H'CAP 1m 75y
8:10 (8:12) (Class 6) (0-60,60) 3-Y-O+ **£2,264** (£673; £336; £168) **Stalls** Low

Form RPR

-000 **1** **Bling King**[32] 3367 7-9-10 **58**....(p) DavidAllan 7 66
(Geoffrey Harker) *hld up towards rr: gd hdwy on inner over 3f out: trckd ldrs 2f out: rdn to ld jst over 1f out: drvn out* **7/1**[2]

1260 **2** *3/4* **Ada Misobel (IRE)**[17] 3896 3-8-4 **53**....(p) KevinLundie(7) 10 57
(Roy Bowring) *hld up towards rr: hdwy over 4f out: chsd ldrs and nt clr run over 1f out: swtchd lft to inner and rdn ent fnl f: styd on strly towards fin* **33/1**

002 **3** *1* **Rosie Crowe (IRE)**[41] 3044 4-8-11 **48**....(v) JosephineGordon(3) 17 52
(Shaun Harris) *led 1 1/2f: cl up: led again wl over 3f out: rdn and hdd wl over 2f out: drvn over 1f out: kpt on u.p fnl f* **25/1**

600- **4** *3/4* **Zlatan (IRE)**[277] 7249 3-9-1 **60**.... RobHornby(3) 4 60
(Ed de Giles) *trckd ldrs: hdwy to ld wl over 2f out: rdn and hdd over 1f out: sn drvn and kpt on same pce fnl f* **8/1**[3]

650 **5** *nk* **Oyster Card**[28] 3483 3-8-10 **52**.... AndrewMullen 13 51+
(Michael Appleby) *dwlt and in rr: hdwy on inner 3f out: rdn to chse ldrs on inner 2f out: drvn and styd on fnl f: nrst fin* **50/1**

00-0 **6** *3/4* **Ahraam (IRE)**[172] 376 3-9-1 **57**.... MartinHarley 1 54
(Harry Whittington) *in tch: hdwy 3f out: rdn to chse ldrs 2f out: sn drvn and no imp appr fnl f* **16/1**

0124 **7** *1 3/4* **Scent Of Power**[28] 3497 4-9-9 **57**.... PatCosgrave 11 52
(Barry Leavy) *in tch: hdwy to chse ldrs over 2f out and sn rdn: drvn over 1f out: no imp* **16/1**

-564 **8** *1 1/4* **Titan Goddess**[25] 3624 4-9-5 **53**.... DavidProbert 14 45
(Mike Murphy) *towards rr: hdwy on outer wl over 2f out: sn rdn and kpt on fnl f* **14/1**

00 **9** *3 3/4* **Isntshesomething**[7] 4240 4-9-3 **51**....(p) HarryBentley 16 34
(Richard Guest) *chsd ldng pair: rdn along 3f out: drvn 2f out: grad wknd* **33/1**

-600 **10** *1* **Mariners Moon (IRE)**[2] 4424 5-9-3 **54**....(tp) RachelRichardson(3) 5 35
(Patrick Holmes) *cl up: led after 1 1/2f: rdn along 4f out: sn hdd & wknd over 2f out* **25/1**

5653 **11** *nk* **Cool Beans**[103] 1295 4-9-2 **50**....(p) JimmyQuinn 15 30
(Roy Bowring) *chsd ldrs on outer: rdn along 3f out: grad wknd* **25/1**

-250 **12** *3/4* **Bahamian Boy**[13] 4009 3-8-13 **55**.... JimCrowley 9 31
(Hughie Morrison) *dwlt: a towards rr* **8/1**[3]

-002 **13** *1 3/4* **Frozon**[4] 4370 3-9-3 **59**.... TomEaves 2 31+
(Brian Ellison) *chsd ldrs: rdn along 3f out: drvn over 2f out and sn wknd* **9/2**[1]

4265 **14** *1 1/4* **Stun Gun**[17] 3876 6-9-7 **55**....(p) TonyHamilton 3 26
(Derek Shaw) *a towards rr* **10/1**

0-00 **15** *1* **Sirdaal (USA)**[12] 4056 3-9-2 **58**.... PaulHanagan 8 25
(Owen Burrows) *midfield: pushed along 3f out: rdn wl over 2f out: sn wknd* **9/2**[1]

1m 44.76s (-4.24) **Going Correction** -0.425s/f (Firm)
WFA 3 from 4yo+ 8lb **15** Ran SP% **118.0**
Speed ratings (Par 101): **104,103,102,101,101 100,98,97,93,92 92,91,89,88,87**
CSF £231.98 CT £5473.63 TOTE £9.90: £2.90, £8.30, £5.10; EX 248.60 TRIFECTA Not won..
Owner P I Harker **Bred** Whitsbury Manor Stud And Mrs M E Slade **Trained** Thirkleby, N Yorks

FOCUS
Distance increased by 6yds. Only a moderate handicap. The second and third set a very straightforward level.

4499 COLWICK CUP FAMILY FUN-DAY 12TH AUGUST H'CAP 1m 6f 15y
8:40 (8:41) (Class 6) (0-60,58) 4-Y-0+ **£2,264** (£673; £336; £168) **Stalls** Low

Form RPR
0542 **1** **Nolecce**[17] 3903 9-8-13 **53**................................ RobHornby(3) 6 61
(Tony Forbes) *mde all: rdn along wl over 2f out: drvn over 1f out: kpt on strly* **7/1**
4302 **2** 3 ¼ **Cape Spirit (IRE)**[11] 4082 4-9-4 **55**........................(v) DavidProbert 3 59
(Andrew Balding) *hld up towards rr: hdwy on outer over 3f out: chsd ldrs wl over 1f out and sn rdn: drvn and kpt on same pce fnl f* **6/1**
-050 **3** shd **Lineman**[13] 3999 6-9-6 **57**........................(b) PatCosgrave 2 61
(Sarah Hollinshead) *trckd ldng pair: hdwy 3f out: rdn to chse wnr wl over 1f out: sn drvn and kpt on same pce* **16/1**
21/4 **4** 1 ¾ **Sleepy Haven (IRE)**[34] 3288 6-9-7 **58**........................(p) TomQueally 10 59
(Jennie Candlish) *hld up in rr: hdwy on wd outside 3f out: rdn wl over 1f out: no imp fnl f* **3/1**[1]
5-44 **5** 1 ½ **Magnolia Ridge (IRE)**[16] 673 6-8-7 **47**..........(p) RachelRichardson(3) 4 46
(Mark Walford) *trckd ldrs: hdwy over 3f out: rdn along over 2f out: sn drvn and btn* **6/1**
0344 **6** 9 **Frosty The Snowman (IRE)**[17] 3903 5-9-4 **55**............ JamesSullivan 8 43
(Ruth Carr) *trckd ldrs: pushed along 5f out: rdn 4f out: drvn 3f out: sn btn* **5/1**[3]
0-42 **7** 2 ¾ **Impeccability**[40] 3067 6-8-10 **47**........................(p) RoystonFfrench 5 31
(John Mackie) *trckd wnr: pushed along over 3f out: rdn over 2f out: sn drvn and wknd* **12/1**
6043 **P** **Storm Check**[18] 3844 4-9-4 **55**................................ NeilFarley 1
(Andrew Crook) *hld up towards rr: hdwy on inner over 3f out: rdn to chse ldrs on inner 2f out: cl up whn lost action and p.u wl over 1f out: fatally injured* **9/2**[2]

3m 6.72s (-0.28) **Going Correction** -0.425s/f (Firm) **8** Ran SP% **114.5**
Speed ratings (Par 101): **83,81,81,80,79 74,72,**
CSF £48.31 CT £647.94 TOTE £9.00: £2.50, £2.30, £2.00; EX 57.90 Trifecta £474.00.
Owner Tony Forbes **Bred** Hedsor Stud **Trained** Stramshall, Staffs

FOCUS
Distance increased by 6yds. An all-the-way winner in this moderate staying handicap. Perhaps not a race to take too literally.
T/Plt: £139.50 to a £1 stake. Pool: £60,500.86 - 316.46 winning tickets. T/Qpdt: £72.10 to a £1 stake. Pool: £4,435.24 - 45.50 winning tickets. **Joe Rowntree**

4221 BATH (L-H)
Wednesday, July 20

OFFICIAL GOING: Firm (10.0)
Wind: Fresh, half against; against from race 6 Weather: Fine, some cloud

4500 DESIGN WORKS GROUP H'CAP 1m 2f 46y
2:10 (2:10) (Class 6) (0-60,60) 3-Y-0 **£2,911** (£866; £432; £216) **Stalls** Low

Form RPR
4003 **1** **Lady Blanco (USA)**[14] 3997 3-9-5 **58**................................ DavidProbert 8 70
(Andrew Balding) *hld up in tch: smooth hdwy to ld wl over 1f out: drvn clr fnl f* **5/1**[3]
-514 **2** 2 ½ **Desert Cross**[14] 3997 3-9-3 **56**................................ MartinHarley 6 63
(Jonjo O'Neill) *chsd ldr: led briefly 2f out: unable qck fnl f* **5/1**[3]
6300 **3** 3 ¾ **Ochos Rios**[28] 3509 3-9-2 **55**................................ AdamKirby 7 55
(David Evans) *dwlt: hld up in 6th: hrd rdn and hdwy in centre 2f out: one pce appr fnl f* **7/1**
4523 **4** 2 ½ **Masterson (IRE)**[10] 3256 3-9-7 **60**........................(v[1]) SilvestreDeSousa 4 55
(Mick Channon) *led: rdn and hdd 2f out: wknd over 1f out* **2/1**[1]
5062 **5** 1 ¾ **Monday Club**[14] 3997 3-9-1 **57**........................ JosephineGordon(3) 5 49
(Dominic Ffrench Davis) *a abt same pl: rdn and no imp fnl 2f* **4/1**[2]
-500 **6** 8 **Voices Of Kings**[14] 4021 3-8-9 **48**................................ MartinDwyer 3 25
(William Muir) *sn bhd* **25/1**
0-00 **7** 8 **Turaathy (IRE)**[43] 3003 3-9-1 **57**................................ EoinWalsh(3) 2 19
(Tony Newcombe) *s.s: a bhd* **25/1**
3-00 **8** 13 **Daybreak Lady**[86] 1725 3-9-5 **58**................................ PatCosgrave 1
(Jo Hughes) *chsd ldrs: rdn 4f out: sn wknd* **25/1**

2m 7.89s (-3.11) **Going Correction** +0.05s/f (Good) **8** Ran SP% **110.7**
Speed ratings (Par 98): **109,107,104,102,100 94,87,77**
CSF £27.76 CT £165.03 TOTE £4.50: £1.50, £1.80, £2.30; EX 33.70 Trifecta £203.70.
Owner Mrs Fitri Hay **Bred** Fitriani Hay **Trained** Kingsclere, Hants

FOCUS
There were changes to some official distances on the card, as 10 yds needs adding to races that use the bottom bend into the home straight. This was a fairly competitive contest to start things off at a modest level. The winner's previous form here has been working out.

4501 CONTRACT FURNITURE GROUP FILLIES' H'CAP 1m 3f 144y
2:40 (2:40) (Class 3) (0-90,84) 3-Y-0 **£7,246** (£2,168; £1,084; £542; £270) **Stalls** Low

Form RPR
51 **1** **Dawn Horizons**[38] 3190 3-9-0 **82**................................ PatCosgrave 6 89+
(William Haggas) *trckd ldr: led 2f out: rdn out* **4/5**[1]
0325 **2** 1 ½ **Steppe Daughter (IRE)**[21] 3785 5-9-10 **80**..................... DavidProbert 5 85
(Denis Coakley) *chsd ldng pair: chal 2f out: kpt on same pce fnl f* **11/2**[3]
-550 **3** 1 **Miss Minuty**[43] 3001 4-9-4 **77**........................ JosephineGordon(3) 2 80
(Alexandra Dunn) *t.k.h in rr: hdwy on inner 2f out: hrd rdn: styd on same pce* **33/1**
4-13 **4** 2 ¼ **Cartier (IRE)**[51] 2753 4-9-9 **79**................................ MartinHarley 3 79
(David Simcock) *dwlt: hld up in 4th: rdn and no hdwy fnl 2f* **4/1**[2]
6206 **5** ¾ **Lady Marl**[15] 3979 5-9-9 **84**................................ HectorCrouch(5) 4 82
(Gary Moore) *s.s: t.k.h in rr: effrt over 2f out: btn over 1f out* **9/1**
26-4 **6** 2 ½ **Northern Meeting (IRE)**[30] 2753 6-9-5 **75**..................(p) AdamKirby 7 69
(Robert Stephens) *led and set modest pce: rdn and qcknd over 3f out: hdd & wknd 2f out* **14/1**

2m 30.64s (0.04) **Going Correction** +0.05s/f (Good)
WFA 3 from 4yo+ 12lb **6** Ran SP% **110.5**
Speed ratings (Par 104): **101,100,99,97,97 95**
CSF £5.47 TOTE £1.70: £1.20, £2.00; EX 4.80 Trifecta £58.80.
Owner A E Oppenheimer **Bred** Hascombe And Valiant Studs **Trained** Newmarket, Suffolk

FOCUS
Add 10 yards to race distance. A decent middle-distance race confined to fillies and mares, albeit modest form for the grade. . The least-exposed runner headed the betting and showed a good attitude to win.

4502 VISION COMMERCIAL KITCHENS H'CAP 5f 11y
3:10 (3:10) (Class 5) (0-75,74) 3-Y-0 **£3,557** (£1,058; £529; £264) **Stalls** Centre

Form RPR
-503 **1** **Pine Ridge**[28] 3512 3-9-4 **71**................................ AdamKirby 2 79
(Clive Cox) *prom on inner: led ins fnl f: drvn out* **3/1**[1]
1160 **2** ¾ **Powerful Dream (IRE)**[63] 2373 3-9-1 **68**..................... MartinHarley 7 73
(Ronald Harris) *led: hrd rdn and hdd ins fnl f: kpt on* **20/1**
0003 **3** 1 ¼ **Swanton Blue (IRE)**[12] 4085 3-9-1 **68**..................... PatCosgrave 3 69
(Ed de Giles) *dwlt: bhd: hdwy over 1f out: r.o* **6/1**[3]
1-60 **4** ½ **Consulting**[15] 3978 3-9-5 **72**........................ SilvestreDeSousa 1 71
(Martyn Meade) *broke on terms: sn outpcd in rr: hrd rdn and hdwy over 1f out: styd on* **13/2**
2316 **5** ¾ **Showmethewayavrilo**[8] 4224 3-9-2 **72**.............. JosephineGordon(3) 8 68
(Malcolm Saunders) *prom on outer: one pce appr fnl f* **7/2**[2]
3354 **6** 4 **Verne Castle**[8] 4224 3-9-1 **68**................................ DavidProbert 6 50
(Andrew Balding) *prom tl wknd over 1f out* **7/2**[2]
0140 **7** 2 ½ **Entertaining Ben**[8] 4224 3-9-7 **74**........................(p) MartinDwyer 4 47
(William Muir) *in tch: effrt over 2f out: wknd over 1f out* **25/1**
304 **8** 2 ¼ **Pink Martini (IRE)**[12] 4093 3-8-10 **70**..................... SeanMooney(7) 5 35
(Joseph Tuite) *chsd ldrs tl 1/2-way* **12/1**

1m 2.01s (-0.49) **Going Correction** +0.05s/f (Good) **8** Ran SP% **113.4**
Speed ratings (Par 100): **105,103,101,101,99 93,89,85**
CSF £60.92 CT £338.93 TOTE £3.70: £1.50, £5.70, £1.50; EX 45.20 Trifecta £357.80.
Owner Wood Hall Stud Limited **Bred** Wood Hall Stud **Trained** Lambourn, Berks

FOCUS
Most of these were in reasonable heart heading into this, so the form ought to be sound for the grade. The runner-up is the key.

4503 IRISH STALLION FARMS/DESIGN WORKS GROUP EBF NOVICE STKS (PLUS 10 RACE) 5f 11y
3:40 (3:40) (Class 4) 2-Y-0 **£4,528** (£1,347; £673; £336) **Stalls** Centre

Form RPR
216 **1** **Barroche (IRE)**[35] 3270 2-9-3 0................................ AdamKirby 3 84
(Clive Cox) *t.k.h: trckd ldr: slt ld over 3f out: hld on wl fnl f: pushed out nr fin* **4/5**[1]
2104 **2** hd **Camargue**[12] 4091 2-9-3 0........................ SilvestreDeSousa 4 83
(Mark Johnston) *led for over 1f: w wnr after: drvn and kpt on wl fnl f: jst hld* **5/2**[2]
2 **3** 1 ½ **Coral Sea**[20] 3812 2-8-11 0................................ DavidProbert 5 72
(Charles Hills) *prom: effrt and hung lft fr over 1f out: kpt on* **6/1**[3]
10 **4** 1 ½ **Quench Dolly**[35] 3270 2-9-0 0........................ MichaelJMMurphy 1 69
(John Gallagher) *s.s: sn in tch: rdn 2f out: one pce* **11/1**
40 **5** 9 **Gentleman Giles (IRE)**[9] 4203 2-9-2 0..................... TimmyMurphy 6 39
(Jamie Osborne) *bdly outpcd: sn wl bhd* **100/1**

1m 2.79s (0.29) **Going Correction** +0.05s/f (Good) **5** Ran SP% **107.7**
Speed ratings (Par 96): **99,98,96,93,79**
CSF £2.85 TOTE £1.70: £1.10, £1.80; EX 3.00 Trifecta £4.90.
Owner Wood Hall Stud Limited **Bred** T Kenny & P Byrne **Trained** Lambourn, Berks

FOCUS
Only three of these made any obvious appeal, so it was no great surprise when two of them dominated the outcome. The form is rated around the runner-up.

4504 ARCADIS H'CAP (DIV I) 1m 5y
4:10 (4:10) (Class 6) (0-55,55) 3-Y-0+ **£2,911** (£866; £432; £216) **Stalls** Low

Form RPR
/4-0 **1** **No No Cardinal (IRE)**[14] 3996 7-8-9 **46** oh1................ NoelGarbutt(3) 1 51
(Mark Gillard) *s.s: hld up in 6th: hdwy 2f out: drvn to dispute ld fnl f: jst prevailed* **25/1**
4-66 **2** nse **Rock Icon**[14] 4021 3-8-4 **46** oh1................................ JimmyQuinn 6 49
(Patrick Chamings) *in tch: led 2f out: jnd by wnr fnl f: kpt on wl: jst denied* **7/1**
0-00 **3** 2 ¼ **Just Isla**[22] 3739 6-9-4 **55**........................(b) DanielMuscutt(3) 3 55
(John Flint) *chsd ldrs: chal 2f out: no ex ins fnl f* **7/2**[2]
0000 **4** ½ **Opera Buffa (IRE)**[28] 3509 3-8-6 **48**..................(tp) SilvestreDeSousa 8 44
(Steve Flook) *chsd ldr: led 3f out tl 2f out: one pce* **12/1**
-356 **5** shd **Edge (IRE)**[22] 3748 5-9-0 **48**........................(b) DavidProbert 9 46
(Bernard Llewellyn) *missed break and lost 10 l: hld up and bhd: hdwy over 1f out: nvr rchd ldrs* **3/1**[1]
6500 **6** 5 **Bond Mystery**[29] 3492 4-8-7 **46** oh1........................(b) HectorCrouch(5) 10 32
(Natalie Lloyd-Beavis) *s.i.s: outpcd in rr: hrd rdn over 3f out: n.d* **14/1**
4053 **7** ½ **Espoir**[15] 3975 3-8-6 **48**........................(v) SamHitchcott 2 31
(David Evans) *prom tl outpcd fnl 2f* **9/2**[3]
5355 **8** 4 **Jonnie Skull (IRE)**[33] 3354 10-8-9 **46**..............(vt) JosephineGordon(3) 4 21
(Phil McEntee) *led tl 3f out: wknd over 2f out* **6/1**
4-00 **9** 10 **Lettuce Snow (IRE)**[14] 3997 4-8-12 **46**..................(p) TimmyMurphy 7
(Geoffrey Deacon) *hld up towards rr: effrt in centre over 2f out: sn wknd* **12/1**

1m 41.15s (0.35) **Going Correction** +0.05s/f (Good)
WFA 3 from 4yo+ 8lb **9** Ran SP% **118.1**
Speed ratings (Par 101): **100,99,97,97,97 92,91,87,77**
CSF £193.39 CT £781.59 TOTE £26.50: £7.30, £2.10, £1.30; EX 451.60.
Owner T J C Seegar **Bred** Mrs Eleanor Hadden **Trained** Holwell, Dorset
■ Stewards' Enquiry : Noel Garbutt two-day ban: used whip above permitted level (Aug 3-4)

FOCUS
Add 10 yards to race distance. The first division of a moderate handicap, run in a quicker time than the second, produced a shock winner. A very weak race.

4505 ARCADIS H'CAP (DIV II) 1m 5y
4:40 (4:40) (Class 6) (0-55,54) 3-Y-0+ **£2,911** (£866; £432; £216) **Stalls** Low

Form RPR
0040 **1** **Nifty Kier**[33] 3354 7-8-9 **45**........................ JosephineGordon(3) 1 52
(Phil McEntee) *led for 1f: chsd ldr: led again 2f out: hung lft 1f out: comf* **7/1**
4020 **2** 1 ¾ **Lutine Charlie (IRE)**[15] 3973 9-9-4 **51**..................(p) AdamKirby 4 54
(Emma Owen) *prom: kpt on u.p fnl 2f: wnt 2nd fnl 30yds* **6/1**[2]
000/ **3** ¾ **Lady Cavallo**[1153] 2637 6-8-12 **45**................................ MartinHarley 3 46
(Neil Mulholland) *led after 1f and wnt gd gallop: hdd 2f out: kpt on same pce: lost 2nd fnl 30yds* **12/1**
000 **4** 5 **Wassail**[45] 2929 3-7-13 **47**........................[1] MitchGodwin(7) 8 34
(Ed de Giles) *outpcd and sn wl bhd: nrest at fin* **6/1**[2]

0005 **5** *1* **Long Island**[6] 4316 3-8-4 **48** .... NoelGarbutt(3) 5 33
(Mark Brisbourne) *towards rr: effrt 3f out: no hdwy fnl 2f* **25/1**
3360 **6** *3¼* **Israfel**[6] 4289 3-8-12 **53** .... TimmyMurphy 9 30
(Jamie Osborne) *outpcd and sn wl bhd: modest late hdwy* **13/2**[3]
60-4 **7** *6* **The Greedy Boy**[20] 3816 3-8-13 **54** .... SilvestreDeSousa 6 22
(Mick Channon) *in tch: rdn over 3f out: wknd over 2f out* **11/8**[1]
-450 **8** *5* **Play The Blues (IRE)**[105] 1263 9-8-12 **48** ....(t) EoinWalsh(3) 2
(Henry Tett) *stdd s: plld hrd and sn chsng ldrs: hrd rdn and wknd 2f out* **25/1**

1m 41.85s (1.05) **Going Correction** +0.05s/f (Good)
WFA 3 from 5yo+ 8lb **8** Ran SP% **111.9**
Speed ratings (Par 101): **96,94,93,88,87 84,78,73**
CSF £46.12 CT £489.55 TOTE £6.90: £2.00, £1.70, £5.90; EX 45.70 Trifecta £331.50.
Owner Mrs Rebecca McEntee **Bred** Mrs S H Jones **Trained** Newmarket, Suffolk

FOCUS
Add 10 yards to race distance. The early gallop seemed quick but it resulted in a slower time than the first division of this moderate handicap. The winner is rated to the level he showed when winning this last year.

4506 D5 ARCHITECTS H'CAP (BATH SUMMER SPRINT SERIES QUALIFIER) 5f 161y
5:10 (5:11) (Class 6) (0-65,64) 3-Y-O+ **£2,587** (£770; £384; £192) **Stalls** Centre

Form RPR
652 **1** **Babyfact**[7] 4264 5-9-3 **58** .... JosephineGordon(3) 1 68
(Malcolm Saunders) *prom: led 2f out: pushed out* **15/8**[1]
-506 **2** *1¼* **Secretfact**[7] 4262 3-8-3 **46** .... JimmyQuinn 5 51
(Malcolm Saunders) *in tch: drvn to chse wnr fnl f: a hld* **28/1**
060 **3** *3¾* **Ambitious Boy**[12] 4084 7-9-4 **61** .... CiaranMckee(5) 2 55
(John O'Shea) *s.s: bhd: rdn and hdwy over 1f out: styd on* **25/1**
-613 **4** *1½* **Captain Ryan**[14] 3994 5-9-9 **61** .... TimmyMurphy 7 50
(Geoffrey Deacon) *led for 2f: prom tl wknd fnl f* **15/2**
0045 **5** *2¾* **Major Valentine**[5] 4355 4-9-10 **62** .... MartinHarley 8 41
(John O'Shea) *chsd ldr: led over 3f out tl 2f out: wknd over 1f out* **4/1**[3]
0650 **6** *7* **Verus Delicia (IRE)**[15] 3984 7-9-8 **60** .... MichaelJMMurphy 3 16
(Daniel Mark Loughnane) *chsd ldrs tl wknd 2f out* **20/1**
0501 **7** *8* **Carcharias (IRE)**[6] 4289 3-8-11 **54** 6ex .... SilvestreDeSousa 6
(Ed de Giles) *s.s: towards rr: rdn 3f out: eased whn wl btn over 1f out* **2/1**[2]

1m 11.5s (0.30) **Going Correction** +0.05s/f (Good)
WFA 3 from 4yo+ 5lb **7** Ran SP% **111.9**
Speed ratings (Par 101): **100,98,93,91,87 78,67**
CSF £52.80 CT £978.82 TOTE £2.50: £1.30, £7.10; EX 40.50 Trifecta £315.90.
Owner Mrs Ginny Nicholas **Bred** M S Saunders And Chris Scott **Trained** Green Ore, Somerset

FOCUS
An ordinary sprint at a mainly modest level. The winner is rated to her previous best.

4507 MJ CHURCH 40TH ANNIVERSARY H'CAP (BATH SUMMER STAYERS' SERIES QUALIFIER) 1m 5f 22y
5:45 (5:45) (Class 6) (0-65,65) 4-Y-O+ **£2,911** (£866; £432; £216) **Stalls** High

Form RPR
-060 **1** **Rum Swizzle**[41] 3064 4-9-4 **62** .... AdamKirby 5 70
(Harry Dunlop) *stdd in rr s: rdn and hdwy in centre over 2f out: led over 1f out: all out* **8/1**
5340 **2** *shd* **Oratorio's Joy (IRE)**[14] 4023 6-9-7 **65** .... TimmyMurphy 2 73
(Jamie Osborne) *chsd ldrs: drvn to chal fnl 2f: kpt on wl* **5/1**[3]
0011 **3** *5* **Bernisdale**[8] 4226 8-9-4 **65** 6ex .... DanielMuscutt(3) 1 66
(John Flint) *t.k.h: trckd ldr: led briefly over 2f out: one pce* **11/8**[1]
0306 **4** *¾* **Azure Amour (IRE)**[14] 3997 4-8-10 **54** .... SilvestreDeSousa 4 54
(Rod Millman) *led tl over 2f out: hrd rdn: sn outpcd* **3/1**[2]
-054 **5** *nk* **Lucky Diva**[14] 4019 9-8-6 **50** ....(p) JimmyQuinn 7 49
(Bill Turner) *dwlt: hld up in 4th: rdn and no imp fnl 2f* **15/2**
/-00 **6** *38* **Karl Marx (IRE)**[29] 2850 6-7-13 **46** oh1 ....(b) NoelGarbutt(3) 3
(Mark Gillard) *on and off the bridle in 5th: drvn along over 4f out: sn wl bhd* **25/1**

2m 55.24s (3.24) **Going Correction** +0.05s/f (Good) **6** Ran SP% **110.5**
Speed ratings (Par 101): **92,91,88,88,88 64**
CSF £44.69 TOTE £5.40: £4.20, £2.90; EX 56.50 Trifecta £86.40.
Owner The Nigel Bennett Partnership **Bred** Granham Farm And P Hearson Bloodstock **Trained** Lambourn, Berks
■ Stewards' Enquiry : Adam Kirby four-day ban: used whip above permitted level (Aug 3-6)

FOCUS
Add 10 yards to race distance. Just a modest staying event, and straightforward form.
T/Plt: £107.70 to a £1 stake. Pool: £65,716.54 - 445.02 winning units. T/Qpdt: £46.20 to a £1 stake. Pool: £5,977.43 - 95.60 winning units. **Lee McKenzie**

4254 CATTERICK (L-H)
Wednesday, July 20

OFFICIAL GOING: Good to firm (9.4)
Wind: light 1/2 against Weather: overcast, humid

4508 BRITISH STALLION STUDS EBF NOVICE STKS 5f 212y
2:00 (2:03) (Class 5) 2-Y-O **£3,234** (£962; £481; £240) **Stalls** Low

Form RPR
2414 **1** **Jacquard (IRE)**[20] 3818 2-9-12 0 .... FrannyNorton 2 85
(Mark Johnston) *mde all: pushed along over 2f out: drew clr 1f out: eased towards fin* **4/9**[1]
2 *¾* **The Stalking Moon (IRE)** 2-9-0 0 .... JasonHart 6 69+
(John Quinn) *trckd ldrs: drvn over 2f out: styd on to chse wnr 1f out: no real imp* **12/1**[3]
2332 **3** *3¾* **Pulsating (IRE)**[9] 4209 2-9-0 0 .... PJMcDonald 1 57
(Rebecca Menzies) *trckd ldrs: 2nd over 2f out: kpt on one pce appr fnl f* **3/1**[2]
4 *7* **Jorvik Prince** 2-9-5 0 .... ShaneGray 5 41
(Karen Tutty) *dwlt: in rr: sme hdwy 2f out: sn outpcd tk modest 4th clsng stages* **200/1**
6 **5** *1¾* **Gold Patch (IRE)**[18] 3874 2-9-0 0 .... NathanEvans(5) 4 35
(Michael Easterby) *trckd ldrs: drvn over 2f out: lost pl over 1f out* **33/1**
6 *3¼* **I Don't Believe It** 2-9-5 0 .... TomEaves 3 26
(Micky Hammond) *dwlt: in rr: lost pl over 1f out: sn bhd* **25/1**

1m 13.39s (-0.21) **Going Correction** -0.175s/f (Firm) **6** Ran SP% **109.2**
Speed ratings (Par 94): **94,93,88,78,76 72**
CSF £6.52 TOTE £1.40: £1.10, £4.70; EX 6.00 Trifecta £10.40.
Owner Sheikh Hamdan bin Mohammed Al Maktoum **Bred** Darley **Trained** Middleham Moor, N Yorks

FOCUS
Rail movements increased the race distance by 6 yards and jockeys in the first reckoned the ground was good rather than the official good to firm. Those with form set a fair standard in this juvenile novice stakes and the favourite dominated.

4509 RADIO YORKSHIRE (S) STKS 7f
2:30 (2:30) (Class 6) 2-Y-O **£2,264** (£673; £336; £168) **Stalls** Low

Form RPR
3251 **1** **Racemaker**[4] 4404 2-9-3 0 .... CharlesBishop 4 66+
(Mick Channon) *led 1f: trckd ldr: led over 2f out: drvn out* **1/1**[1]
6203 **2** *1* **London Grammar (IRE)**[2] 4442 2-8-6 0 .... CamHardie 2 52
(John Quinn) *trckd ldrs: effrt over 2f out: chsd wnr fnl f: kpt on same pce last 75yds* **2/1**[2]
05 **3** *6* **Generous Times**[33] 3361 2-8-6 0 .... ConnorBeasley 5 36
(Chris Grant) *t.k.h: led after 1f: hung rt bnd over 3f out: hdd over 2f out: wknd fnl f* **66/1**
531 **4** *½* **Areyoutheway (IRE)**[33] 3361 2-9-3 0 ....(v) FrannyNorton 3 45
(Tom Dascombe) *chsd ldrs: drvn over 2f out: lost pl over 1f out* **9/2**[3]
5600 **5** *2½* **Sheppard's Gift**[40] 3114 2-8-3 0 ....(e[1]) RachelRichardson(3) 1 27
(Tim Easterby) *hld up in last: sme hdwy over 2f out: lost pl over 1f out* **22/1**

1m 27.77s (0.77) **Going Correction** -0.175s/f (Firm) **5** Ran SP% **107.4**
Speed ratings (Par 92): **88,86,80,79,76**
CSF £3.03 TOTE £1.70: £1.10, £1.60; EX 3.20 Trifecta £61.50.Racemaker was bought for £10,000 by Andy Crook; London Grammar was the subject of a friendly claim of £7,000
Owner M Channon **Bred** R W K Lewis **Trained** West Ilsley, Berks

FOCUS
Rail movements increased the race distance by 6 yards. Varying levels of previous form amongst the runners in this juvenile seller. Mick Channon had won it twice in the last ten years and was again responsible for the winner. The time and grade point to caution over the form.

4510 SUMMER FESTIVAL SUPPORTING JACK BERRY HOUSE NURSERY H'CAP 7f
3:00 (3:02) (Class 5) 2-Y-O **£3,234** (£962; £481; £240) **Stalls** Low

Form RPR
413 **1** **Teofonic (IRE)**[35] 3275 2-9-7 **81** .... FrannyNorton 4 90+
(Mark Johnston) *sn chsng ldrs: effrt over 2f out: swtchd ins over 1f out: styd on to ld last 150yds: forged clr* **6/4**[1]
064 **2** *3½* **Dewan (IRE)**[11] 4125 2-8-8 **68** .... GrahamGibbons 1 68
(Mick Channon) *led: drvn over 2f out: hdd last 150yds: kpt on same pce: eased whn wl hld clsng stages* **5/2**[3]
6032 **3** *1½* **Coverham (IRE)**[12] 4090 2-8-1 **61** .... JamesSullivan 5 56
(James Bethell) *trckd ldr: effrt over 2f out: hung lft and one pce fnl f* **9/4**[2]
250 **4** *7* **Vaux (IRE)**[18] 3881 2-8-12 **72** .... JoeyHaynes 2 48
(Ben Haslam) *stdd s: t.k.h: drvn over 2f out: wknd appr fnl f: eased clsng stages* **10/1**

1m 26.28s (-0.72) **Going Correction** -0.175s/f (Firm) **4** Ran SP% **108.4**
Speed ratings (Par 94): **97,93,91,83**
CSF £5.51 TOTE £2.30; EX 5.50 Trifecta £5.40.
Owner Kingsley Park 5 **Bred** Floors Farming And Dominic Burke **Trained** Middleham Moor, N Yorks

FOCUS
Rail movements increased the race distance by 6 yards. A fair nursery run 1.49 secs faster than the preceding seller. Mark Johnston had won this race twice in recent seasons and added to his score. The winner is progresssing now.

4511 AUGUST 12TH IS LADIES' EVENING CLAIMING STKS 7f
3:30 (3:31) (Class 6) 3-4-Y-O **£2,264** (£673; £336; £168) **Stalls** Low

Form
4110 **1** **Just Be Lucky (IRE)**[28] 3517 4-9-8 80 ....(p) PaulMulrennan 5 77+
(Conor Dore) *narrow ldr: hdd appr fnl f: edgd rt and rallied: led again fnl strides* **4/5**[1]
6162 **2** *hd* **Smart Mover (IRE)**[7] 4257 3-8-3 74 .... CamHardie 3 62+
(John Quinn) *in last pair: hdwy over 3f out: chsng ldr over 2f out: led narrowly appr fnl f: hdd fnl strides* **11/8**[2]
0556 **3** *9* **Grenade**[7] 4257 4-8-5 44 .... PaulaMuir(7) 2 42
(Patrick Holmes) *in last pair: drvn and outpcd over 3f out: tk modest 3rd 1f out* **33/1**
543 **4** *8* **Freeze A Crowd (IRE)**[86] 1710 3-8-1 42 ow1 ....(t) JoeyHaynes 1 13
(Ben Haslam) *w wnr: drvn over 3f out: wknd over 1f out* **16/1**[3]

1m 25.56s (-1.44) **Going Correction** -0.175s/f (Firm)
WFA 3 from 4yo 7lb **4** Ran SP% **106.5**
Speed ratings (Par 101): **101,100,90,81**
CSF £2.08 TOTE £1.60; EX 1.90 Trifecta £5.70.
Owner Mrs Louise Marsh **Bred** Degner Limited **Trained** Hubbert's Bridge, Lincs

FOCUS
Rail movements increased the race distance by 6 yards. Mixed levels of ability in this claimer, which was run 0.72 secs faster than the quicker of the two earlier juvenile races over the trip. It looked a match on paper and produced a terrific finish between the pair. The third helps dictate the level.

4512 5TH REGIMENT ROYAL ARTILLERY H'CAP (DIV I) 5f 212y
4:00 (4:01) (Class 6) (0-60,66) 3-Y-O+ **£2,587** (£770; £384; £192) **Stalls** Low

Form RPR
4034 **1** **Tricky Dicky**[14] 4003 3-8-12 **56** .... DuranFentiman 6 65
(Olly Williams) *chsd ldr: styd on to ld last 150yds* **4/1**[2]
0040 **2** *1* **Sir Geoffrey (IRE)**[6] 4295 10-8-13 **52** ....(b) BenCurtis 3 59
(Scott Dixon) *led: hdd and no ex last 150yds* **7/1**
5006 **3** *3* **Kyllach Me (IRE)**[47] 2856 4-9-6 **59** ....(p) PaulMulrennan 4 56
(Bryan Smart) *trckd ldrs: effrt over 2f out: kpt on same pce over 1f out* **5/1**[3]
0021 **4** *2* **Classic Flyer**[6] 4309 4-9-13 **66** 6ex ....(v) DanielTudhope 10 57+
(David O'Meara) *towards rr on outer: drvn over 2f out: kpt on appr fnl f: nvr a threat* **3/1**[1]
6255 **5** *¾* **La Asomada**[21] 3773 3-9-0 **58** .... GrahamGibbons 8 45
(David Barron) *chsd ldrs: one pce over 1f out* **12/1**
5-50 **6** *shd* **Grandad Chunk (IRE)**[127] 936 5-9-1 **54** .... PatrickMathers 9 42+
(Colin Teague) *dwlt: in rr: hdwy over 1f out: nvr a factor* **66/1**
3060 **7** *1½* **Pabusar**[21] 3776 8-8-9 **48** ....(tp) PJMcDonald 1 31+
(Micky Hammond) *in rr: drvn over 3f out: kpt on fnl 2f: nvr on terms* **16/1**
4413 **8** *2* **Birrafun (IRE)**[8] 4236 3-8-5 **56** .... DavidEgan(7) 2 32
(Ann Duffield) *chsd ldrs: drvn over 2f out: wknd over 1f out: sddle slipped and eased nr fin* **10/1**
0565 **9** *1¼* **Hashtag Frenzy**[8] 4228 3-8-2 **46** oh1 ....(p) RaulDaSilva 5 18+
(Rebecca Menzies) *a in rr* **9/1**

5620 **10** *9* **Ryedale Rio (IRE)**[12] 4096 3-9-2 **60**.................................... JasonHart 7
(Tim Easterby) *s.i.s: in rr: sme hdwy on inner over 1f out: lost pl over 1f out: eased whn bhd clsng stages* **16/1**

1m 12.28s (-1.32) **Going Correction** -0.175s/f (Firm)
WFA 3 from 4yo+ 5lb **10** Ran SP% **114.2**
Speed ratings (Par 101): **101,99,95,93,92 91,89,87,85,73**
CSF £31.47 CT £141.57 TOTE £5.90: £2.10, £1.60, £2.50; EX 35.90 Trifecta £162.20.
Owner Eight Gents and a Lady **Bred** Onslow, Stratton & Parry **Trained** Market Rasen, Lincs

FOCUS
Rail movements increased the race distance by 6 yards. The first division of this moderate sprint handicap was run 1.11secs faster than the opening juvenile contest and very few got into it, the pace really holding up.

4513 5TH REGIMENT ROYAL ARTILLERY H'CAP (DIV II) 5f 212y
4:30 (4:31) (Class 6) (0-60,59) 3-Y-O+ **£2,587** (£770; £384; £192) **Stalls** Low

Form RPR
-031 **1** **Spirit Of Zebedee (IRE)**[4] 4410 3-9-2 **59** 6ex..............(p) PJMcDonald 7 67
(John Quinn) *w ldr: led narrowly over 2f out: fnd ex nr fin* **6/4**[1]
4036 **2** *½* **Bogsnog (IRE)**[15] 3984 6-9-0 **52**..................................... TonyHamilton 2 59
(Kristin Stubbs) *led: hdd narrowly over 2f out: remained upsides: no ex clsng stages* **11/2**[2]
4034 **3** *2* **Secret City (IRE)**[16] 3940 10-9-4 **56**..........................(b) DanielTudhope 4 57
(Rebecca Bastiman) *chsd ldrs: drvn over 2f out: edgd rt over 1f out: kpt on same pce to take 3rd clsng stages* **8/1**[3]
0005 **4** *¾* **Whipphound**[15] 3984 8-9-0 **52**....................................(p) JamesSullivan 6 51
(Ruth Carr) *chsd ldrs: kpt on same pce over 1f out* **9/1**
430 **5** *4* **Intense Starlet (IRE)**[36] 3262 5-9-3 **55**.............................. CamHardie 9 41
(Marjorie Fife) *mid-div on outer: drvn and lost pl over 3f out: kpt on fnl 2f: nvr a factor* **11/1**
0-00 **6** *hd* **Amis Reunis**[170] 418 7-8-10 **48**.. TomEaves 3 33
(Colin Teague) *rrd s: in rr: hdwy over 3f out: chsng ldrs over 2f out: one pce* **50/1**
0643 **7** *¾* **Prigsnov Dancer (IRE)**[47] 2856 11-9-7 **59**.................. PaulMulrennan 5 42
(John Balding) *mid-div: effrt over 2f out: wknd over 1f out* **10/1**
6221 **8** *½* **Whispering Soul (IRE)**[27] 3549 3-8-13 **56**............(b) GrahamGibbons 8 36
(Brian Baugh) *chsd ldrs: effrt over 2f out: wknd over 1f out* **9/1**
-334 **9** *14* **Whispering Wolf**[35] 3289 3-8-1 **51**....................... RobertDodsworth(7) 1
(Suzzanne France) *in last and sn drvn along: wl bhd fnl 3f* **16/1**

1m 12.4s (-1.20) **Going Correction** -0.175s/f (Firm)
WFA 3 from 5yo+ 5lb **9** Ran SP% **111.8**
Speed ratings (Par 101): **101,100,97,96,91 91,90,89,70**
CSF £9.12 CT £47.31 TOTE £2.30: £1.10, £2.40, £1.90; EX 9.90 Trifecta £41.80.
Owner Malcolm Walker **Bred** N Hartery **Trained** Settrington, N Yorks

FOCUS
Rail movements increased the race distance by 6 yards. The second leg of this moderate sprint looked slightly weaker and was run 0.12 secs slower than the first. Again it paid to race prominently. The winner didn't need to improve to take this.

4514 SKY BET GO-RACING-IN-YORKSHIRE SUMMER FESTIVAL H'CAP 5f
5:00 (5:03) (Class 4) (0-85,90) 3-Y-O+ **£6,469** (£1,925; £962; £481) **Stalls** Low

Form RPR
3504 **1** **Singeur (IRE)**[18] 3875 9-9-5 **77**..................................... DanielTudhope 4 88
(Rebecca Bastiman) *towards rr: hdwy in centre over 2f out: styd on wl to ld last 100yds* **11/2**[2]
4630 **2** *2* **Desert Ace (IRE)**[3] 4428 5-9-4 **81**...............................(p) PhilDennis(5) 13 85+
(Iain Jardine) *sn chsng ldrs: sddle slipped over 1f out: chsd wnr last 100yds: uns rdr sn after post* **9/1**[3]
0543 **3** *nk* **Pearl Acclaim (IRE)**[12] 4100 6-9-6 **78**........................(v) FrannyNorton 10 81
(David Nicholls) *trckd ldrs on inner: led wl over 1f out: hdd and no ex last 100yds* **5/1**[1]
2321 **4** *1* **Flash City (ITY)**[13] 4039 8-9-2 **74**.................................... JamesSullivan 1 73
(Ruth Carr) *towards rr: hdwy 2f out: styd on fnl f* **11/2**[2]
0620 **5** *3 ½* **Crosse Fire**[77] 1958 4-9-3 **75**..(p) DaleSwift 12 62
(Scott Dixon) *rr-div: kpt on fnl 2f: edgd lft last 100yds: nvr a factor* **50/1**
6664 **6** *1* **Rusty Rocket (IRE)**[13] 4032 7-9-9 **81**.............................. PJMcDonald 3 64
(Paul Green) *mid-div: drvn over 2f out: nvr a threat* **12/1**
-130 **7** *nse* **Money Team (IRE)**[131] 901 5-9-7 **79**........................ GrahamGibbons 8 62
(David Barron) *in rr: hdwy in centre over 1f out: nvr a factor* **11/1**
2-00 **8** *hd* **Ayresome Angel**[13] 4032 3-9-4 **80**............................... PaulMulrennan 7 61
(Bryan Smart) *s.i.s: in rr: hdwy on outer over 1f out: nvr on terms* **40/1**
2501 **9** *shd* **Best Trip (IRE)**[7] 4259 9-10-1 **90** 6ex.................... JacobButterfield(3) 11 72
(Marjorie Fife) *prom: drvn and outpcd over 2f out: lost pl over 1f out* **9/1**[3]
000 **10** *¾* **Bosham**[12] 4112 6-9-0 **77**..(bt) NathanEvans(5) 5 56
(Michael Easterby) *chsd ldrs: lost pl over 1f out* **22/1**
0040 **11** *shd* **Captain Dunne (IRE)**[12] 4100 11-9-1 **76**............ RachelRichardson(3) 6 55
(Tim Easterby) *chsd ldrs: lost pl over 1f out* **12/1**
5205 **12** *2 ¾* **King Crimson**[13] 4032 4-9-11 **83**.................................... CharlesBishop 9 52
(Mick Channon) *chsd ldrs on outside: lost pl over 1f out: bhd whn eased clsng stages* **14/1**
0060 **13** *7* **Fast Act (IRE)**[12] 4079 4-9-11 **83**.......................................(b[1]) TomEaves 2 27
(Kevin Ryan) *led: hdd over 1f out: sn wknd and bhd: eased nr fin* **10/1**

58.31s (-1.49) **Going Correction** -0.175s/f (Firm)
WFA 3 from 4yo+ 4lb **13** Ran SP% **115.7**
Speed ratings (Par 105): **104,100,100,98,93 91,91,91,90,89 89,85,74**
CSF £51.62 CT £271.62 TOTE £5.60: £1.60, £4.40, £1.90; EX 62.40 Trifecta £327.30.
Owner Ms M Austerfield **Bred** Patrick Cassidy **Trained** Cowthorpe, N Yorks

FOCUS
Rail movements increased the race distance by 6 yards. The feature race and a decent sprint handicap, with the time just a fraction outside the Racing Post standard. The winner is rated to the balance of his form from the past year.

4515 CATTERICKBRIDGE.CO.UK APPRENTICE TRAINING SERIES H'CAP (PART OF THE RACING EXCELLENCE INITIATIVE) 1m 3f 214y
5:30 (5:30) (Class 6) (0-65,63) 4-Y-O+ **£2,587** (£770; £384; £192) **Stalls** Low

Form RPR
0645 **1** **Whitchurch**[5] 4340 4-8-11 **51**.. HarryBurns(3) 7 58
(Philip Kirby) *hld up towards rr: hdwy over 3f out: chsng ldrs over 2f out: led over 1f out: drvn out* **3/1**[3]
6-56 **2** *½* **Rockabilly Riot (IRE)**[21] 2558 6-9-8 **59**.................(p) AdamMcNamara 1 65
(Martin Todhunter) *trckd ldrs: t.k.h: upsides over 1f out: no ex clsng stages* **5/2**[2]
3465 **3** *3 ¼* **Merchant Of Medici**[7] 4260 9-9-7 **63**........................ CameronNoble(5) 4 64
(Micky Hammond) *trckd ldrs: 2nd over 2f out: edgd rt and one pce fnl f* **9/4**[1]
0006 **4** *5* **Splash Of Verve (IRE)**[11] 4143 4-8-12 **52**............. DanielleMooney(3) 3 45
(Philip Kirby) *led: hdd over 1f out: sn wknd* **8/1**

55-0 **5** *½* **Keep Up (GER)**[10] 3418 4-8-3 **45**..................................... DavidEgan(5) 6 37
(Philip Kirby) *in rr: sn pushed along: nvr a factor* **17/2**
06-0 **6** *25* **Bond Starprincess**[25] 3642 4-8-8 **45**.....................(b[1]) MeganNicholls 8
(Ben Haslam) *chsd ldrs: lost pl over 7f out: hdwy over 3f out: lost pl over 2f out: bhd whn eased fnl f: t.o* **28/1**

2m 38.29s (-0.61) **Going Correction** -0.175s/f (Firm) **6** Ran SP% **109.4**
Speed ratings (Par 101): **95,94,92,89,88 72**
CSF £10.33 CT £16.71 TOTE £4.50: £3.70, £1.10; EX 14.10 Trifecta £34.60.
Owner The Turf N' Surf Racing Partnership **Bred** D R Tucker **Trained** East Appleton, N Yorks

FOCUS
Rail movements increased the race distance by 6 yards. A moderate apprentices' handicap which was weakened further by the absence of two previous course winners. The runner-up looks a good guide.
T/Plt: £41.50 to a £1 stake. Pool: £44,371.51 - 780.18 winning units. T/Qpdt: £22.40 to a £1 stake. Pool: £3,304.41 - 108.80 winning units. **Walter Glynn**

4315 LEICESTER (R-H)
Wednesday, July 20

OFFICIAL GOING: Good to firm (7.1)
Wind: Almost nil Weather: Fine

4516 BETFAIR AMATEUR H'CAP (FOR NOVICE AMATEUR RIDERS) 7f
5:40 (5:41) (Class 6) (0-60,56) 4-Y-O+ **£2,495** (£774; £386; £193) **Stalls** High

Form RPR
000U **1** **White Flag**[14] 4006 5-11-5 **54**....................................... MissEEasterby 10 62
(Tim Easterby) *hld up: swtchd rt over 2f out: rdn and hdwy over 1f out: styd on to ld nr fin* **17/2**
05-0 **2** *hd* **No Refund (IRE)**[14] 4005 5-11-1 **50**................................ MrJoeWright 1 57
(David Loughnane) *a.p: chsd ldr over 4f out: led over 2f out: rdn and wandered over 1f out: hdd nr fin* **4/1**[2]
0000 **3** *¾* **Caeser The Gaeser (IRE)**[26] 3599 4-11-3 **52**............(p) MrJAndrews 11 57
(Nigel Tinkler) *s.i.s: hld up: hdwy u.p over 1f out: r.o: nt rch ldrs* **12/1**
0433 **4** *1 ½* **Mendacious Harpy (IRE)**[6] 4290 5-11-2 **54**............(p) AmeliaGlass(3) 6 55
(George Baker) *chsd ldrs: rdn over 1f out: styd on same pce ins fnl f* **5/2**[1]
6206 **5** *¾* **Stanlow**[42] 3020 6-10-13 **48**..(v) MrHFNugent 2 47
(Michael Mullineaux) *mid-div: pushed along 1/2-way: hdwy u.p over 2f out: styd on same pce ins fnl f* **15/2**[3]
5040 **6** *hd* **Natalia**[7] 4260 7-10-7 **45**..(p) DrMVoikhansky(3) 9 44
(Sarah Hollinshead) *prom: pushed along 1/2-way: rdn over 1f out: styd on same pce ins fnl f* **10/1**
5400 **7** *4 ½* **Cadeaux Pearl**[47] 2872 8-11-2 **51**...................................... MrKLocking 4 38
(Scott Dixon) *led: rdn and hdd over 2f out: wknd fnl f* **8/1**
2-30 **8** *1 ¾* **Officer In Command (USA)**[180] 294 10-10-10 **45**(vt) MissCBanham 5 27
(Alan Bailey) *s.i.s: sn pushed along: nt trble ldrs* **20/1**
-006 **9** *3 ¾* **Prince Of Time**[15] 3987 4-10-12 **50**.............. MrJordanSwarbrick(3) 7 22
(Richard Ford) *mid-div: hdwy 1/2-way: rdn and wknd over 1f out* **16/1**
0140 **10** *9* **My Time**[104] 1295 7-10-13 **48**..............................(be) MissPBridgwater 12
(Michael Mullineaux) *s.i.s: in rr: swtchd rt over 4f out: rdn over 2f out: sn wknd* **50/1**
560- **P** **Shavaughn**[10] 1263 4-11-6 **55**....................................(b[1]) MrJamesKing 3
(Alexandra Dunn) *chsd ldr tl pushed along over 4f out: sn lost pl: p.u and dismouted over 2f out* **33/1**

1m 24.71s (-1.49) **Going Correction** -0.125s/f (Firm) **11** Ran SP% **114.3**
Speed ratings (Par 101): **103,102,101,100,99 99,93,91,87,77**
CSF £40.46 CT £418.35 TOTE £9.60: £2.90, £1.90, £4.00; EX 46.70 Trifecta £334.70.
Owner W A Robinson **Bred** Exors Of The Late T E Pocock **Trained** Great Habton, N Yorks

FOCUS
Following a warm and dry night the ground was changed to good to firm. Not much to dwell on in a moderate handicap. The gallop was sound.

4517 MOLYNEUX H'CAP 6f
6:10 (6:11) (Class 5) (0-70,70) 3-Y-O **£2,911** (£866; £432; £216) **Stalls** High

Form RPR
6-04 **1** **Peter Park**[15] 3976 3-8-13 **69**... WilliamCox(7) 5 74
(Clive Cox) *hld up: hdwy over 1f out: rdn to ld ins fnl f: jst hld on* **9/1**[3]
6600 **2** *hd* **Qortaaj**[8] 4238 3-9-3 **66**.. SamJames 7 71
(David Loughnane) *hld up: hdwy over 1f out: hung rt ins fnl f: r.o* **12/1**
-056 **3** *1 ½* **Storm Melody**[11] 4155 3-9-7 **70**.....................................(p) SteveDrowne 6 70
(Jonjo O'Neill) *plld hrd and prom: led over 1f out: rdn and hdd ins fnl f: styd on* **7/1**[2]
-000 **4** *3 ¼* **Perfectly Fair**[8] 4231 3-8-4 **60**....................................... HollieDoyle(7) 4 50
(Simon West) *s.i.s: hdwy over 4f out: rdn over 1f out: no ex ins fnl f* **66/1**
00 **5** *1 ½* **Indian Pursuit (IRE)**[16] 3948 3-9-4 **67**........................... DougieCostello 8 52
(John Quinn) *prom: racd keenly: rdn over 1f out: styd on same pce* **16/1**
0360 **6** *½* **Dark Forest**[11] 4139 3-9-0 **70**................................ SophieKilloran(7) 9 53
(Simon West) *chsd ldrs: led 1/2-way: rdn and hdd over 1f out: wknd ins fnl f* **12/1**
0620 **7** *1 ¾* **Take Charge**[35] 3293 3-9-0 **70**................................ TomDonoghue(7) 10 48
(David Brown) *chsd ldrs: rdn over 1f out: wknd ins fnl f* **16/1**
2542 **8** *2* **Sciarra**[7] 4262 3-8-12 **64**.. LouisSteward(3) 1 35
(Michael Bell) *sn pushed along and prom: rdn and wknd over 1f out* **13/8**[1]
6-03 **9** *hd* **Song Of Paradise**[21] 3786 3-9-2 **65**.................................. TedDurcan 12 36
(Chris Wall) *hld up: rdn over 2f out: nvr on terms* **20/1**
0-02 **10** *2 ¾* **Chandresh**[15] 3976 3-8-11 **60** ow1.. PatDobbs 3 22
(Robert Cowell) *led: hdd over 3f out: rdn whn n.m.r over 2f out: wknd over 1f out* **9/1**[3]
4236 **11** *4 ½* **Spirit Glance**[20] 3806 3-9-3 **66**... LiamJones 11 13
(Tim Easterby) *mid-div: rdn 1/2-way: lost pl over 2f out* **11/1**

1m 11.81s (-1.19) **Going Correction** -0.125s/f (Firm) **11** Ran SP% **112.3**
Speed ratings (Par 100): **102,101,99,95,93 92,90,87,87,83 77**
CSF £106.85 CT £795.59 TOTE £7.20: £1.90, £4.60, £1.90; EX 131.00 Trifecta £477.90.
Owner Mrs T L Cox **Bred** D E And Mrs J Cash **Trained** Lambourn, Berks

FOCUS
A modest handicap which took less winning than had seemed likely given the market leader disappointed. The gallop was sound and the first three finished clear. The winer is rated to his 2yo form.

4518 MEDBOURNE (S) STKS 1m 60y
6:40 (6:40) (Class 6) 3-Y-O **£2,587** (£770; £384; £192) **Stalls** Low

Form RPR
-020 **1** **Port Paradise**[20] 3823 3-8-6 62 ow3........................... SamuelClarke(7) 3 65+
(William Jarvis) *hld up in tch: rdn to chse ldr over 1f out: styd on to ld wl ins fnl f* **9/4**[1]

0601 **2** 2 1/2 **Boutan**[6] 4316 3-8-13 60........(p) SteveDrowne 1 59
(George Baker) *led: rdn over 1f out: hdd and unable qck wl ins fnl f* **9/4**[1]
636 **3** 3 1/4 **Masqueraded (USA)**[9] 4204 3-9-4 59........(v) DougieCostello 8 56
(Gay Kelleway) *chsd ldr: rdn over 3f out: lost 2nd over 1f out: no ex ins fnl f* **25/1**
4406 **4** 1/2 **Zabdi**[12] 4085 3-8-11 66 ow1........ PatDobbs 4 48
(Richard Hannon) *hld up: hdwy over 2f out: rdn and nt clr run over 1f out: styd on same pce fnl f* **3/1**[2]
0-06 **5** 6 **Virtual Song**[29] 3499 3-8-2 36........ TimClark(3) 6 28
(Barry Leavy) *hld up: outpcd over 3f out: hdwy and nt clr run over 1f out: nvr on terms* **125/1**
2540 **6** 4 1/2 **Cadland Lad (IRE)**[7] 4279 3-8-10 52........(t) StevieDonohoe 2 22
(John Ryan) *chsd ldrs: rdn over 2f out: wknd over 1f out* **16/1**
00-U **7** shd **Big Larry (IRE)**[42] 3014 3-8-3 49........ KieranSchofield(7) 5 22
(Nigel Tinkler) *prom: racd keenly: rdn over 3f out: wknd wl over 1f out* **40/1**
0155 **8** 15 **Adventure Zone (IRE)**[154] 613 3-8-7 66........(p) HollieDoyle(7) 7
(Richard Hannon) *hld up: rdn over 3f out: sn wknd* **7/1**[3]
1m 44.14s (-0.96) **Going Correction** -0.125s/f (Firm) **8** Ran SP% **112.0**
Speed ratings (Par 98): **99,96,93,92,86 82,82,67**
CSF £7.09 TOTE £3.30: £1.80, £1.02, £5.90; EX 7.50 Trifecta £104.40.
Owner William Jarvis **Bred** C R Withers **Trained** Newmarket, Suffolk

FOCUS
A low-grade seller in which the gallop was an ordinary one. The winner made the most of a drop in class.

4519 THISTLETON GAP H'CAP 7f
7:15 (7:15) (Class 4) (0-80,80) 3-Y-O+ **£4,851** (£1,443; £721; £360) **Stalls** High

Form RPR
4-61 **1** **Kitaaby (IRE)**[27] 3554 3-9-2 **77**........ PaulHanagan 6 86
(Brian Meehan) *mde all: rdn over 1f out: edgd rt ins fnl f: r.o* **13/8**[1]
60-0 **2** 2 **Le Roi Du Temps (USA)**[46] 2891 3-9-2 **77**........(p) DavidAllan 4 80
(Ivan Furtado) *chsd ldrs: rdn over 2f out: styd on same pce ins fnl f* **4/1**[3]
5600 **3** 1 **Kingsley Klarion (IRE)**[35] 3277 3-9-3 **78**........ LiamJones 2 78
(Mark Johnston) *w wnr: rdn over 2f out: ev ch over 1f out: no ex ins fnl f* **17/2**
-550 **4** 3/4 **See You When (IRE)**[14] 4010 3-9-2 **77**........ PatDobbs 1 75
(Richard Hannon) *hld up: hdwy over 1f out: sn rdn: styd on same pce ins fnl f* **15/2**
4100 **5** hd **Arlecchino's Leap**[20] 3803 4-9-12 **80**........(p) DougieCostello 3 81
(Mark Usher) *hld up: hdwy 1/2-way: rdn over 1f out: styd on same pce* **14/1**
23-5 **6** 5 **Song Of Norway**[68] 2213 5-9-9 **77**........ TedDurcan 5 64
(Chris Wall) *trckd ldrs: rdn and hung rt over 1f out: wknd fnl f* **10/3**[2]
1m 24.37s (-1.83) **Going Correction** -0.125s/f (Firm)
WFA 3 from 4yo+ 7lb **6** Ran SP% **110.1**
Speed ratings (Par 105): **105,102,101,100,100 94**
CSF £8.01 TOTE £2.00: £1.40, £2.60; EX 8.00 Trifecta £32.20.
Owner Hamdan Al Maktoum **Bred** Joseph Broderick **Trained** Manton, Wilts

FOCUS
A fair handicap but one in which not many arrived in top form. The gallop was an ordinary one, the winner having an easy lead.

4520 TOM CRIBB H'CAP 1m 3f 183y
7:45 (7:46) (Class 4) (0-85,85) 4-Y-O+ **£4,851** (£1,443; £721; £360) **Stalls** Low

Form RPR
4333 **1** **Eager Beaver**[33] 3352 4-8-11 **75**........ MartinDwyer 3 82
(William Muir) *led over 10f out: shkn up and qcknd over 3f out: rdn over 1f out: styd on gamely* **7/2**[3]
6404 **2** 3/4 **Mukhayyam**[16] 3950 4-9-2 **80**........ DavidAllan 1 85
(Tim Easterby) *a.p: chsd wnr over 3f out: rdn over 1f out: styd on* **7/4**[1]
2006 **3** 6 **Royal Marskell**[25] 3657 7-9-6 **84**........ DougieCostello 2 79
(Gay Kelleway) *led: hdd over 10f out: racd keenly and trckd wnr tl pushed along over 3f out: rdn over 1f out: no ex fnl f: eased nr fin* **11/2**
10-0 **4** 12 **Royal Toast (IRE)**[19] 3861 4-9-7 **85**........ PatDobbs 4 61
(Richard Hannon) *w ldr tl over 10f out: disp 2nd tl over 5f out: rdn over 3f out: wknd over 2f out* **9/4**[2]
3-0 **5** 41 **Camakasi (IRE)**[16] 3957 5-9-2 **80**........(tp) PaulHanagan 5
(Ali Stronge) *s.s: a in rr: rdn and wknd over 3f out* **20/1**
2m 30.36s (-3.54) **Going Correction** -0.125s/f (Firm) **5** Ran SP% **109.5**
Speed ratings (Par 105): **106,105,101,93,66**
CSF £9.96 TOTE £4.90: £2.20, £1.70; EX 9.10 Trifecta £22.90.
Owner M J Caddy **Bred** Horizon Bloodstock Limited **Trained** Lambourn, Berks

FOCUS
Exposed performers in a useful handicap and it's unlikely the winner improved. An ordinary gallop increased in the last 3f.

4521 BREEDERS BACKING RACING EBF MAIDEN STKS 5f
8:15 (8:16) (Class 5) 3-Y-O+ **£3,881** (£1,155; £577; £288) **Stalls** High

Form RPR
5035 **1** **Equistar**[8] 4224 3-9-5 68........(t) MartinLane 2 73
(Jonathan Portman) *led 3f: sn rdn: rallied to ld nr fin* **5/2**[1]
03 **2** nk **Shesthedream (IRE)**[8] 4238 3-9-0 0........ DanielTudhope 3 67
(David O'Meara) *plld hrd and prom: led 2f out: rdn ins fnl f: hdd nr fin* **7/2**[2]
44 **3** nk **Noble Act**[13] 4041 3-9-0 0........ TedDurcan 6 66
(Rae Guest) *trckd ldrs: rdn over 1f out: edgd rt ins fnl f: r.o* **7/2**[2]
-203 **4** 1 1/2 **Sacred Harp**[33] 3360 3-9-0 59........(t) PatDobbs 5 61
(Stuart Williams) *chsd ldrs: rdn over 1f out: edgd rt ins fnl f: styd on same pce* **12/1**
5 1 1/4 **By The Law** 3-9-5 0........ DavidAllan 1 62
(Tim Easterby) *prom: pushed along 1/2-way: rdn over 1f out: nt clr run and no ex ins fnl f* **20/1**
4304 **6** 1 **Sunnyside Bob (IRE)**[3] 4426 3-9-0 70........[1] JoshDoyle(5) 8 58
(David O'Meara) *prom: rdn 1/2-way: edgd rt over 1f out: no ex fnl f* **4/1**[3]
7 1 1/4 **Notoursortdear** 4-9-4 0........ CharlesBishop 7 49
(John Gallagher) *s.i.s: sn pushed along in rr: rdn over 1f out: wknd ins fnl f* **66/1**
0P- **8** nk **Bigmouth Strikes (IRE)**[376] 4086 3-8-12 0........ RPWalsh(7) 4 52
(David Menuisier) *hld up: plld hrd: rdn over 1f out: wknd ins fnl f* **20/1**
59.86s (-0.14) **Going Correction** -0.125s/f (Firm)
WFA 3 from 4yo 4lb **8** Ran SP% **111.7**
Speed ratings (Par 103): **96,95,95,92,90 89,87,86**
CSF £10.76 TOTE £4.10: £1.50, £1.60, £1.10; EX 11.60 Trifecta £43.60.
Owner Mascalls Stud **Bred** Mascalls Stud **Trained** Upper Lambourn, Berks

FOCUS
A modest maiden and one in which the pace was just fair. The winner's best form this year.

4522 MELTON MOWBRAY H'CAP 1m 1f 218y
8:50 (8:50) (Class 5) (0-70,70) 3-Y-O **£3,234** (£962; £481; £240) **Stalls** Low

Form RPR
3200 **1** **Brave Archibald (IRE)**[13] 4046 3-9-7 **70**........(b[1]) DanielTudhope 4 75
(Paul Cole) *sn chsng ldr: rdn over 1f out: r.o to ld wl ins fnl f* **15/2**
6130 **2** 1 **Spinning Pearl (IRE)**[53] 2700 3-8-13 **62**........ CharlesBishop 5 65
(Eve Johnson Houghton) *led at stdy pce tl qcknd 3f out: rdn and hdd wl ins fnl f* **20/1**
6502 **3** 3/4 **Patent**[18] 3906 3-9-2 **65**........ PatDobbs 2 67
(Richard Hannon) *chsd ldrs: rdn over 2f out: styd on* **7/4**[1]
-501 **4** 1/2 **Lady Turpin (IRE)**[11] 4146 3-8-4 **53**........ PaulHanagan 6 54
(Richard Fahey) *hld up: hdwy over 2f out: nt clr run over 1f out: styd on* **6/1**[3]
35-4 **5** hd **Possible Future**[110] 1185 3-9-6 **69**........ ThomasBrown 7 69
(Ismail Mohammed) *a.p: rdn over 2f out: kpt on* **11/4**[2]
0413 **6** 1 **High On Light**[8] 4233 3-8-5 **54**........ CamHardie 1 52
(Tim Easterby) *hld up: rdn over 2f out: nt clr run over 1f out: styd on ins fnl f: nt trble ldrs* **6/1**[3]
05-0 **7** 1 **Karens Star**[14] 3998 3-8-9 **58**........ AdamBeschizza 8 54
(Steph Hollinshead) *hld up: hdwy over 2f out: sn rdn: wknd fnl f* **33/1**
2m 9.88s (1.98) **Going Correction** -0.125s/f (Firm) **7** Ran SP% **111.1**
Speed ratings (Par 100): **87,86,85,85,85 84,83**
CSF £122.79 CT £363.95 TOTE £9.10: £3.60, £9.50; EX 77.50 Trifecta £255.50.
Owner PJL Racing Wright Asprey Meyrick Wilcock **Bred** Peter J Magnier **Trained** Whatcombe, Oxon

FOCUS
A modest handicap in which the ordinary gallop which only increased passing the 3f pole suited those right up with the pace. The first six finished in a heap and the time was slow.
T/Plt: £111.20 to a £1 stake. Pool: £60,362.76 - 396.20 winning units. T/Qpdt: £5.40 to a £1 stake. Pool: £7,854.13 - 1066.48 winning units. **Colin Roberts**

4383 LINGFIELD (L-H)
Wednesday, July 20

OFFICIAL GOING: Polytrack: standard
Wind: fresh, behind Weather: Sunny

4523 MOBILE BETTING AT 188BET MAIDEN AUCTION STKS (DIV I) 7f 1y(P)
1:50 (1:51) (Class 6) 2-Y-O **£2,587** (£770; £384; £192) **Stalls** Low

Form RPR
0 **1** **Northdown**[11] 4125 2-9-3 0........ GeorgeBaker 1 76
(David Lanigan) *settled handy in 3rd bhd ldr: shkn up over 1f out: rdn ins fnl f: kpt on wl to ld nr fin* **7/1**
5 **2** 1/2 **Geophony (IRE)**[9] 4209 2-9-5 0........ JoeFanning 8 77
(Mark Johnston) *disp ld early: pressed ldr over 2f out: rdn 2f out: led 1f out: kpt on wl tl hdd nr fin* **4/1**[3]
3 1/2 **Miss Icon** 2-8-6 0........ NickyMackay 3 63
(Patrick Chamings) *taken bk leaving stalls and settled in 7th: stl nr last whn prog out wd over 2f out: rdn 2f out: kpt on strly fnl f: nrst fin* **20/1**
01 **4** nse **Woodukheleyfit**[15] 3986 2-8-8 0........ EdwardGreatrex(3) 6 68
(Sylvester Kirk) *settled in 5th bhd ldrs: rdn and lost pl fr 2f out: kpt on again ins fnl f* **5/4**[1]
0 **5** 1 **Famous Dynasty (IRE)**[43] 2997 2-8-13 0........ HarryBentley 2 67
(Michael Blanshard) *settled in 6th on rail: rdn 2f out: ev ch jst over 1f out: no imp fnl f: wknd nr fin* **25/1**
04 **6** nk **Winning Bid**[32] 3404 2-8-13 0........ LukeMorris 4 66
(Harry Dunlop) *led: rdn 2f out: hdd 1f out: wknd ins fnl f* **7/2**[2]
7 10 **Let's Be Happy (IRE)** 2-9-0 0........ ShaneKelly 9 40
(Richard Hughes) *rousted along out wd leaving stalls: sn bhd ldrs in 4th: shkn up and rdn 3f out: lft bhd over 1f out: hands and heels fnl f* **14/1**
0 **8** 3 1/2 **Desidero (SPA)**[7] 4270 2-8-10 0........ RyanTate 7 27
(Pat Phelan) *missed break: rdn along early: a bhd* **66/1**
1m 27.54s (2.74) **Going Correction** +0.25s/f (Slow) **8** Ran SP% **115.9**
Speed ratings (Par 92): **94,93,92,92,91 91,79,75**
CSF £34.82 TOTE £6.20: £3.10, £2.00, £5.00; EX 41.20 Trifecta £388.10.
Owner Kevin Scott & Craig Scott **Bred** R W Russell **Trained** Newmarket, Suffolk

FOCUS
Standard going on the Polytrack on another sunny day where the runners experienced a slight tail wind in the home straight. A field of eight went to post for this juvenile maiden in which there looked to be little strength in depth. A compressed finish.

4524 MOBILE BETTING AT 188BET MAIDEN AUCTION STKS (DIV II) 7f 1y(P)
2:20 (2:21) (Class 6) 2-Y-O **£2,587** (£770; £384; £192) **Stalls** Low

Form RPR
543 **1** **Latest Quest (IRE)**[25] 3668 2-9-0 0........ EdwardGreatrex(3) 8 74
(Sylvester Kirk) *quick away and sn pressed ldr: led over 5f out: rdn 2f out: kpt on wl to hold off runner-up nring fin* **2/1**[2]
3 **2** 3/4 **Salieri (FR)**[15] 3986 2-8-13 0........ WilliamTwiston-Davies 6 68
(Alan King) *racd freely on outer and sn prom in 3rd: rdn along 2f out: kpt on fr 1f out: clsd on ldr nring fin* **7/4**[1]
0 **3** 6 **Epsom Secret**[11] 4128 2-8-6 0........ WilliamCarson 1 45
(Pat Phelan) *settled in 4th: rdn over 2f out: sn lft bhd: one pce fnl f* **8/1**
56 **4** 1 1/2 **Brexit**[27] 3555 2-8-8 0........ JFEgan 4 43
(Pat Phelan) *t.k.h early in 5th: rdn over 2f out: sme prog fr over 1f out* **8/1**
5 4 1/2 **Makkadangdang** 2-9-2 0........ RobHornby(3) 5 42
(Andrew Balding) *racd in 7th: pushed along over 2f out: a bhd* **7/1**[3]
6600 **6** nse **Hot N Sassy (IRE)**[37] 3232 2-8-6 0........(b[1]) DannyBrock 2 28
(J S Moore) *broke wl and led tl hdd over 5f out: remained bhd ldr: rdn over 2f out: no ex fr over 1f out: wknd fnl f* **25/1**
04 **7** 10 **Jackman**[18] 3897 2-8-10 0........(p) GeorgeDowning(3) 9 8
(Tony Carroll) *s.s: rdn along early in detached last: nvr gng pce* **33/1**
0 **8** 7 **Raze Aqlaam**[13] 4054 2-8-7 0 ow1........ AdamBeschizza 7
(Giles Bravery) *s.s: a bhd* **33/1**
1m 27.58s (2.78) **Going Correction** +0.25s/f (Slow) **8** Ran SP% **114.1**
Speed ratings (Par 92): **94,93,86,84,79 79,67,59**
CSF £5.75 TOTE £3.30: £1.60, £1.20, £1.70; EX 6.30 Trifecta £32.70.
Owner R Gander **Bred** Jerry Murphy **Trained** Upper Lambourn, Berks

The Form Book, Raceform Ltd, Newbury, RG14 5SJ

FOCUS
The second division of the juvenile maiden was run at a good gallop throughout which resulted in very few of them getting involved. The first two showed improved form in pulling clear.

4525 £25 FREE BET AT 188BET FILLIES' H'CAP 6f 1y(P)
2:50 (2:51) (Class 5) (0-70,69) 3-Y-O+ **£3,234** (£962; £481; £240) **Stalls** Low

Form RPR
-333 **1** **Lajatico**[42] 3038 3-9-7 **69**.. HarryBentley 7 85+
(Ed Vaughan) *s.s but sn ct up: t.k.h on outer in 5th: stl prom whn sddle slipped 2f out: led over 1f out: sn clr and hung rt ins fnl f: cosily* **11/4**[1]
3042 **2** 3 ½ **Tigserin (IRE)**[28] 3527 3-9-6 **68**.. JackMitchell 4 73
(Giles Bravery) *t.k.h in 8th: rdn and prog 2f out: kpt on to take 2nd 1f out: no ch w wnr* **3/1**[2]
-061 **3** 1 ½ **Helfire**[9] 4202 3-8-5 **58**.. CharlieBennett[(5)] 1 58+
(Hughie Morrison) *wnt to post early: in rr and sn pushed along to hold pl: stl in rr 4f out: sltly hmpd 3f out: stl in rr over 1f out: gd prog wl ins fnl f: nrst fin* **7/2**[3]
-315 **4** 1 ½ **Belle Mare Plage**[48] 2823 3-9-1 **63**.. OisinMurphy 9 58
(Stuart Williams) *s.s: settled on outer in 8th: tk clsr order over 3f out: shkn up over 2f out: sn rdn and kpt on one pce* **16/1**
-344 **5** shd **Foxford**[30] 3469 5-8-12 **55**.. JoeFanning 6 51
(Patrick Chamings) *settled in 2nd: led 3f out: rdn 2f out: hdd over 1f out: wknd fnl f* **8/1**
-006 **6** 1 **The Burnham Mare (IRE)**[15] 3976 3-9-4 **66**.................(p) DannyBrock 5 58
(J S Moore) *s.s: in rr: sme prog on outer over 2f out whn rdn: no ex over 1f out* **20/1**
3000 **7** 1 ¾ **Serendib's Glory (IRE)**[41] 3080 3-8-9 **57**.................. AdamBeschizza 2 43
(Julia Feilden) *settled in 6th on rail: rdn over 2f out: no imp fr 1f out: wknd fnl f* **50/1**
4020 **8** 3 ¾ **Silver Springs (IRE)**[15] 3974 3-9-3 **65**.................................... JFEgan 3 39
(David Evans) *racd in 3rd: rdn along 3f out: ev ch 1f out on inner: sn hld and wknd fnl f* **16/1**
5136 **P** **Hepworth Marble (IRE)**[8] 4222 3-9-7 **69**......................... GeorgeBaker 8
(Gary Moore) *led tl broke down 3f out: sn p.u: fatally injured* **7/1**

1m 13.12s (1.22) **Going Correction** +0.25s/f (Slow)
WFA 3 from 5yo 5lb **9** Ran SP% **116.0**
Speed ratings (Par 100): **101,96,94,92,92 90,88,83,**
CSF £11.24 CT £29.00 TOTE £3.40: £1.10, £1.80, £1.80; EX 12.70 Trifecta £36.50.
Owner D A Thorpe **Bred** Meon Valley Stud **Trained** Newmarket, Suffolk

FOCUS
Plenty went on in this fair handicap with a couple of the runners finding themselves short of room following the tragic incident which resulted in \bHepworth Marble\p losing her life. Improved from from the winner.

4526 188BET CLAIMING STKS 6f 1y(P)
3:20 (3:21) (Class 6) 2-Y-O **£2,587** (£770; £384; £192) **Stalls** Low

Form RPR
3334 **1** **Turanga Leela**[18] 3902 2-8-10 0.................................. RichardKingscote 4 73
(Tom Dascombe) *a handy in 2nd: gng wl over 2f out: prog to chse down ldr 2f out: shkn up and led over 1f out: sn clr: easily* **4/6**[1]
60 **2** 6 **Warleggan (FR)**[15] 3986 2-8-8 0..(b) JohnFahy 1 47
(Eve Johnson Houghton) *led: 3 l ld 1/2-way: rdn 2f out: hdd over 1f out: stuck on wl to hold 2nd* **14/1**
0 **3** 1 ½ **Swallow Street (IRE)**[9] 4209 2-9-6 0.............................. WilliamCarson 7 54
(Jamie Osborne) *settled in 3rd on outer: rdn along 3f out: struggling 2f out: no imp st* **7/1**[3]
2655 **4** hd **Trust The Indian**[14] 4015 2-8-13 0..................................(p) LukeMorris 9 46
(Bill Turner) *racd in 5th: rdn over 2f out: no imp on ldrs st* **16/1**
0 **5** 1 **Cautious Choice (IRE)**[27] 3555 2-8-8 0.......................... DannyBrock 5 38
(J S Moore) *settled in 6th: rdn over 2f out: no imp st: one pce fr over 1f out* **25/1**
35 **6** 7 **Birchfield Lady**[18] 3897 2-8-6 0.. PaoloSirigu 3 14
(Robert Eddery) *settled in 4th: rdn along over 2f out: wknd over 1f out* **20/1**
7 10 **Tisnowornever (IRE)** 2-8-7 0.. RyanPowell 2
(J S Moore) *s.s: rdn along early: a bhd* **25/1**
6251 **U** **Eva Gore**[14] 4000 2-8-7 0.. JoshDoyle[(5)] 6
(David O'Meara) *fly-leapt at s and uns rdr* **3/1**[2]

1m 14.45s (2.55) **Going Correction** +0.25s/f (Slow) **8** Ran SP% **122.5**
Speed ratings (Par 92): **93,85,83,82,81 72,58,**
.Turanga Leela was claimed by Ian Williams for £10,000; Warleggan was claimed by\n\x\x Linda Perratt for £300\n\x\x
Owner Chasemore Farm **Bred** Chasemore Farm **Trained** Malpas, Cheshire

FOCUS
All the money was for one horse in this claimer and although it proved right, her task was made a little easier than would have been expected after \bEva Gora\p unseated her rider leaving the stalls. The winner's best form yet.

4527 188BET.CO.UK (S) H'CAP 1m 2f (P)
3:50 (3:52) (Class 6) (0-65,65) 3-Y-O+ **£2,264** (£673; £336; £168) **Stalls** Low

Form RPR
0254 **1** **Spinning Rose**[7] 4267 4-9-2 **53**.................................(b[1]) RobertWinston 7 65
(Dean Ivory) *broke wl and led tl hld up bhd ldrs after 2f: trckd ldr on inner gng wl over 2f out: rdn 2f out: led 1f out: kpt on wl tl pressed nr fin: jst hld on* **5/1**[1]
5030 **2** hd **Roman De Brut (IRE)**[9] 4214 4-9-1 **57**...................... PaddyBradley[(5)] 6 69
(Daniel Mark Loughnane) *settled in 7th: stl gng wl 3f out: prog over 2f out: rdn over 1f out: kpt on wl ins fnl f: jst hld* **8/1**[3]
60-0 **3** 5 **Santadelacruze**[32] 3402 7-9-4 **55**..................................(b) ShaneKelly 12 58
(Mark Hoad) *settled bhd ldrs: rdn 2f out: kpt on same pce fr over 1f out: one pce fnl f* **20/1**
2033 **4** ½ **What A Dandy (IRE)**[25] 3651 5-9-7 **65**.....................(p) RhiainIngram[(7)] 5 67
(Jim Boyle) *led after 2f: niggled along 1/2-way: rdn 2f out: hdd 1f out: one pce after* **5/1**[1]
0214 **5** 1 **Frivolous Prince (IRE)**[11] 4159 3-8-5 **52**..............................(vt) JFEgan 2 52
(David Evans) *in rr: prog on outside 4f out: rdn 3f out: kpt on one pce* **6/1**[2]
4422 **6** ½ **Dalavand (IRE)**[9] 4212 3-8-10 **57**.................................. WilliamCarson 1 56
(Jamie Osborne) *in rr: rdn jst over 2f out: prog passed btn horses fnl f* **6/1**[2]
0501 **7** 3 ¼ **Lily Edge**[14] 4019 7-9-1 **52**..(v) DannyBrock 9 45
(John Bridger) *racd in cl up 3rd: shkn up over 3f out: sn rdn and wknd fr over 1f out* **10/1**
0160 **8** ½ **Catharina**[14] 3999 4-9-3 **54**.. RenatoSouza 8 46
(Dean Ivory) *settled in mid-div: rdn along 3f out: sltly hmpd and lost pl bnd: dropped to rr-div: no imp after* **25/1**
3535 **9** 2 ¼ **Lions Charge (USA)**[61] 2445 9-9-11 **62**......................(vt) GeorgeBaker 11 49
(Richard Hawker) *pressed ldr in 2nd: rdn along 2f out: wknd qckly sn after* **10/1**
0036 **10** 4 ½ **Britannia Boy**[9] 4210 3-8-0 **47** oh2..................................(p) RyanPowell 4 26
(Mark Usher) *racd in mid-div: rdn along over 2f out: sn lft bhd and wknd* **16/1**
5400 **11** 10 **Judicial Enquiry**[23] 3732 3-8-10 **57**..............................(v[1]) LukeMorris 10 17
(Ed Walker) *settled in mid-div on outer: rdn wl over 4f out: wknd sn after* **8/1**[3]

2m 10.17s (3.57) **Going Correction** +0.25s/f (Slow)
WFA 3 from 4yo+ 10lb **11** Ran SP% **116.8**
Speed ratings (Par 101): **95,94,90,90,89 89,86,86,84,80 72**
CSF £44.44 CT £738.67 TOTE £5.90: £2.20, £3.40, £7.00; EX 61.40 Trifecta £1169.30.Dalavand was bought by Mrs L. J. Mongan for £5,000
Owner John Waterfall, Richard & Ian R Gethin **Bred** Darley **Trained** Radlett, Herts

FOCUS
Those held up in this weak handicap proved at a disadvantage and two came clear inside the final furlong. The form is rated a shade positively.

4528 FREE SPINS AT 188BET CASINO H'CAP 7f 1y(P)
4:20 (4:22) (Class 5) (0-70,70) 3-Y-O+ **£3,234** (£962; £481; £240) **Stalls** Low

Form RPR
022 **1** **Excellent Sounds**[13] 4041 3-9-7 **70**.................................... JimCrowley 4 80+
(Hughie Morrison) *settled in 4th bhd ldrs on rail: effrt on inner 2f out: led over 1f out: sn in control: easily* **11/4**[1]
-001 **2** 2 ½ **Dunnscotia**[14] 4008 4-9-7 **70**...(t[1]) GeorgiaCox[(7)] 1 76
(Paul Webber) *in rr: stl plenty to do 1/2-way: rdn along 3f out: kpt on wl to take 2nd 1f out: no ch w wnr* **9/2**[3]
-060 **3** ¾ **Bushephalus (IRE)**[18] 3907 4-9-11 **67**............................ OisinMurphy 9 71
(Ivan Furtado) *racd in 6th: rdn along 2f out: kpt on wl on outer to take 3rd wl ins fnl f* **25/1**
1016 **4** ½ **Star Of The Stage**[29] 3479 4-10-0 **70**........................(p) AdamBeschizza 6 73
(Julia Feilden) *racd in 5th: rdn 2f out: kpt on one pce* **6/1**
0052 **5** shd **Cornelious (IRE)**[14] 4009 4-9-10 **66**............................(v) DarryllHolland 7 68
(Clifford Lines) *pressed ldr: rdn 2f out: lost 2nd 1f out and wknd ins fnl f* **3/1**[2]
51-5 **6** 2 ¼ **Luath**[188] 182 3-9-0 **63**... NickyMackay 3 56
(Jeremy Gask) *a bhd: outpcd 1/2-way: rdn on inner over 2f out: no imp* **25/1**
0-50 **7** ¾ **Executor**[15] 3982 3-9-4 **67**.. GeorgeBaker 8 58
(Roger Charlton) *t.k.h on outer pressing ldrs in 3rd: rdn 2f out: wknd qckly fnl f* **6/1**
2243 **8** 3 ¾ **Kristoff (IRE)**[154] 610 3-7-11 **53**................................ RhiainIngram[(7)] 11 34
(Jim Boyle) *led: rdn over 2f out: hdd over 1f out: wknd qckly fnl f* **25/1**
6200 **9** 14 **Orlando Rogue (IRE)**[15] 3989 4-9-6 **62**.........................(p) DaneO'Neill 5 8
(Conor Dore) *a in rr* **33/1**

1m 25.9s (1.10) **Going Correction** +0.25s/f (Slow)
WFA 3 from 4yo 7lb **9** Ran SP% **112.9**
Speed ratings (Par 103): **103,100,99,98,98 96,95,90,74**
CSF £14.23 CT £248.33 TOTE £5.70: £1.40, £1.50, £5.00; EX 14.00 Trifecta £129.10.
Owner Helena Springfield Ltd **Bred** Meon Valley Stud **Trained** East Ilsley, Berks

FOCUS
A fair handicap featuring a cluster of runners with decent recent form. The pace and time were sound.

4529 BEST ODDS GUARANTEED AT 188BET H'CAP 5f 6y(P)
4:50 (4:51) (Class 6) (0-65,64) 3-Y-O+ **£2,587** (£770; £384; £192) **Stalls** High

Form RPR
2326 **1** **Frank The Barber (IRE)**[145] 733 4-9-4 **56**..............(t) AdamBeschizza 4 62
(Steph Hollinshead) *mde all: rdn over 1f out: pressed nr fin: hld on* **8/1**
2513 **2** hd **Pharoh Jake**[20] 3811 8-9-10 **62**.. WilliamCarson 7 67
(John Bridger) *t.k.h early: settled in 2nd pressing wnr: rdn over 1f out: stuck on wl to press wnr: jst hld* **7/1**[3]
0504 **3** 1 **Deer Song**[7] 4264 3-9-1 **57**... DannyBrock 2 58
(John Bridger) *settled in 3rd on inner: rdn wl over 1f out: kpt on one pce fnl f* **5/1**[2]
6500 **4** ½ **Temple Road (IRE)**[6] 4292 8-9-12 **64**..........................(bt) GeorgeBaker 5 64+
(Milton Bradley) *settled in last tl rdn and prog over 1f out: no imp ins fnl f* **7/2**[1]
0351 **5** 1 **Our Lord**[36] 3260 4-9-9 **61**... LukeMorris 6 57
(Bill Turner) *settled in 4th: rdn 2f out: kpt on one pce ins fnl f* **7/2**[1]
2U35 **6** 1 ½ **Quality Art (USA)**[30] 3469 8-9-7 **62**.............................. RobHornby[(3)] 1 53
(Simon Hodgson) *racd in 5th: rdn over 1f out: sn hld* **5/1**[2]
5650 **7** nk **Eland Ally**[36] 3260 8-9-5 **57**..(p) OisinMurphy 3 47
(Anabel K Murphy) *settled in 6th: niggled along at 1/2-way: rdn over 1f out: sn hld* **8/1**

1m 0.5s (1.70) **Going Correction** +0.25s/f (Slow)
WFA 3 from 4yo+ 4lb **7** Ran SP% **112.5**
Speed ratings (Par 101): **96,95,94,93,91 89,88**
CSF £59.14 TOTE £8.40: £4.20, £3.80; EX 30.90 Trifecta £519.10.
Owner Debbie Hodson **Bred** Tally-Ho Stud **Trained** Upper Longdon, Staffs

FOCUS
Plenty of C&D form among these seasoned sprinters who are not hiding much from the handicapper. The pace held ip and the runner-upis a good guide.

4530 188BET HORSE RACING CHARTER H'CAP 1m 4f (P)
5:20 (5:21) (Class 5) (0-75,75) 3-Y-O **£3,234** (£962; £481; £240) **Stalls** Low

Form RPR
-003 **1** **Mystikana**[18] 3878 3-8-7 **61**...(b) DannyBrock 5 72
(Marcus Tregoning) *racd in 2nd: pressed ldr over 3f out: sn shkn up and led: kicked 6 l clr jst over 2f out: stride shortening 1f out but in command and nudged out ins fnl f: eased last strides* **4/1**[2]
0-54 **2** 4 **The Otmoor Poet**[22] 3736 3-9-7 **75**.............................. FergusSweeney 3 79
(Alan King) *settled in 4th: rdn 3f out: kpt on best of remainder fr over 1f out: no ch w wnr: pushed out hands and heels ins fnl f* **3/1**[1]
0423 **3** 12 **Pastoral Music**[25] 3653 3-9-5 **73**.................................... JimmyFortune 4 58
(Hughie Morrison) *racd in 5th: rdn 3f out: sn hld* **9/2**[3]
-203 **4** ¾ **Sky Of Stars (IRE)**[27] 3570 3-9-4 **72**.................(v[1]) RichardKingscote 2 56
(William Knight) *sn led: rdn and hdd 3f out: sn lft bhd: wknd fr 1f out* **3/1**[1]
036 **5** 10 **Tom's Rock (IRE)**[32] 3411 3-9-4 **72**.......................... TomQueally 6 40
(John Butler) *s.s: in rr off pce: clsr 1/2-way: rdn over 3f out: no imp and wknd fnl f: t.o* **16/1**

6-43 **6** *20* **Maroc**[16] 3959 3-9-4 **72**..(t) LukeMorris 1 8
(Paul Cole) *led early tl settled bhd ldrs on rail: niggled along over 4f out: rdn over 3f out: sn wknd: eased fnl f: t.o* **9/2**[3]

2m 34.86s (1.86) **Going Correction** +0.25s/f (Slow) **6** Ran SP% **112.2**
Speed ratings (Par 100): **103,100,92,91,85 71**
CSF £16.32 TOTE £4.40: £2.80, £1.90; EX 16.70 Trifecta £91.60.
Owner Mrs Victoria Brown **Bred** Chasemore Farm **Trained** Whitsbury, Hants
■ Stewards' Enquiry : Danny Brock two-day ban: used whip when clearly winning (Aug 3-4)

FOCUS
A fair handicap but no previous winners among the six who contested it. A sizeable pb from the winner.
T/Jkpt: £6,666.60. Pool: £10,000.00 - 1.50 winning units. T/Plt: £69.80 to a £1 stake. Pool: £66,236.35 - 692.64 winning units. T/Qpdt: £13.00 to a £1 stake. Pool: £6,947.17 - 395.10 winning units. **Cathal Gahan**

4268 SANDOWN (R-H)

Wednesday, July 20

OFFICIAL GOING: Good to firm (str 7.7; rnd 7.9)
Wind: Moderate, against Weather: Sunny, 30 degrees

4531 HAMPTON COURT APPRENTICE H'CAP (JOCKEY CLUB GRASSROOTS FLAT MIDDLE DISTANCE SERIES QUALIFIER) 1m 2f 7y
6:00 (6:00) (Class 5) (0-70,70) 4-Y-O+ **£3,234** (£962; £481; £240) **Stalls** Low

Form RPR
0602 **1** **Attain**[8] 4234 7-8-5 **56**.. LiamDoran(7) 2 64
(Julia Feilden) *trckd ldr: led 2f out gng wl: pushed along over 1f out: styd on wl and in command fnl f* **4/1**[1]
0314 **2** *2* **Dovil's Duel (IRE)**[22] 3748 5-9-7 **65**........................ JordanVaughan 9 69
(Tony Newcombe) *s.i.s and hld up in last: smooth prog over 2f out and short of room briefly: shkn up to dispute 2nd jst over 1f out: styd on but no imp on wnr ins fnl f* **9/1**[3]
6310 **3** *nk* **Tatawu (IRE)**[11] 4158 4-9-8 **66**.. AaronJones 10 69
(Peter Hiatt) *cl up in 3rd: rdn to chal 2f out: chsd wnr after: styd on but lost 2nd ins fnl f* **9/1**[3]
4123 **4** *1 1/2* **Solveig's Song**[6] 4302 4-9-9 **67**........................(p) EdwardGreatrex 7 67
(Steve Woodman) *trckd ldrs: rdn over 2f out: nvr gng pce to chal: kpt on same pce u.p fr over 1f out* **4/1**[1]
3133 **5** *1 1/4* **Tommys Geal**[37] 3230 4-9-6 **64**................................ CallumShepherd 6 62
(Michael Madgwick) *in tch in midfield: drvn over 2f out: kpt on same pce fr over 1f out: n.d* **14/1**
5603 **6** *1* **Nosey Barker (IRE)**[9] 4201 4-9-12 **70**....................(p) TomMarquand 8 66
(Richard Hannon) *chsd ldrs: urged along 4f out: nvr able to threaten: one pce* **7/1**[2]
5600 **7** *shd* **Abertillery**[16] 3489 4-8-7 **51** oh1.. GeorgeBuckell 4 47
(Michael Blanshard) *led: rdn and hdd 2f out: steadily fdd* **33/1**
3504 **8** *1/2* **Chilworth Bells**[9] 4201 4-9-12 **70**........................(p) PaddyPilley 5 65
(Conor Dore) *mostly in last quartet: rdn and no prog over 3f out: no ch fnl 2f* **12/1**
0005 **9** *hd* **Victor's Bet (SPA)**[6] 4302 7-9-11 **69**.................... KieranShoemark 11 63
(Ralph J Smith) *dropped in fr wd draw and hld up in last quartet: rdn on outer over 2f out: no prog* **10/1**
6264 **10** *1* **Deluxe**[16] 3959 4-9-3 **61**.. PaddyBradley 1 53
(Pat Phelan) *hld up in last pair: rdn and no prog on outer over 2f out* **7/1**[2]
030- **11** *3* **Dream Ruler**[276] 7308 5-9-9 **67**....................................(t) DavidParkes 3 53
(Jeremy Gask) *chsd ldrs: rdn and lost pl over 2f out: wknd over 1f out* **16/1**

2m 11.75s (1.25) **Going Correction** +0.15s/f (Good) **11** Ran SP% **117.3**
Speed ratings (Par 103): **101,99,99,97,96 96,96,95,95,94 92**
CSF £40.50 CT £308.27 TOTE £3.80: £1.30, £3.20, £3.40; EX 40.10 Trifecta £357.20.
Owner Newmarket Equine Tours Racing Club **Bred** Millsec Limited **Trained** Exning, Suffolk

FOCUS
The rail on the round course was out from the mile point to the cutaway two and a half furlongs from home, adding 24 yards to the distance of all races on the round course. Paddy Pilley described the going as being "on the quick side of good", while Callum Shepherd said that it was "good to firm, but not rattling." Paddy Bradley added that there was "no sting" to the going. There was a headwind in the straight. The opener was a just a modest handicap, run in a time 6.45 outside standard. The winner is rated similar to his Beverley form.

4532 THAMES DITTON H'CAP 1m 14y
6:30 (6:30) (Class 4) (0-85,85) 3-Y-O+ **£4,690** (£1,395; £697; £348) **Stalls** Low

Form RPR
2204 **1** **Ice Royal (IRE)**[11] 4132 3-9-5 **84**................................ JamieSpencer 3 90
(Jamie Osborne) *hld up in 5th: cajoled along and clsd qckly fr over 1f out: edgd lft but led jst ins fnl f: drvn to assert last 100yds* **5/1**
0023 **2** *1/2* **Hail Clodius (IRE)**[13] 4048 4-9-12 **83**........................ SeanLevey 6 90
(Richard Hannon) *trckd ldr after 3f: shkn up over 2f out: trying to chal whn nudged by wnr 1f out: styd on but a hld last 100yds* **10/3**[2]
2164 **3** *1 1/2* **Bernie's Boy**[18] 3908 3-9-1 **80**.. OisinMurphy 4 82
(Andrew Balding) *led: shkn up over 2f out: pressed over 1f out: drvn and hdd jst ins fnl f: one pce* **3/1**[1]
0004 **4** *1 1/2* **The Warrior (IRE)**[7] 4263 4-10-0 **85**....................(b) JimCrowley 2 86
(Amanda Perrett) *hld up in 4th: tried to cl on ldrs over 1f out: nt qckn and hld after: wknd last 100yds* **9/2**[3]
5504 **5** *2 3/4* **Cordite (IRE)**[13] 4048 5-9-9 **80**.. PatCosgrave 1 74
(Jim Boyle) *trckd ldr 3f: racd in 3rd after: reminders 2f out: no rspnse and wknd jst over 1f out* **12/1**
0105 **6** *5* **Jack Of Diamonds (IRE)**[13] 4055 7-9-8 **79**.................... GeorgeBaker 5 61
(Roger Teal) *hld up in detached last: shkn up and no prog 2f out: bhd fnl f* **9/2**[3]

1m 42.52s (-0.78) **Going Correction** +0.15s/f (Good)
WFA 3 from 4yo+ 8lb **6** Ran SP% **108.8**
Speed ratings (Par 105): **109,108,107,105,102 97**
CSF £20.42 TOTE £7.20: £3.20, £2.20; EX 22.90 Trifecta £50.80.
Owner A Taylor **Bred** Corrin Stud **Trained** Upper Lambourn, Berks

FOCUS
Race run over 24 yards further than advertised. The third set a reasonable gallop in what looked an ordinary race for the grade and track. The form is rated around the second.

4533 BRITISH STALLION STUDS EBF MAIDEN STKS 7f 16y
7:05 (7:07) (Class 5) 2-Y-O **£3,881** (£1,155; £577; £288) **Stalls** Low

Form RPR
1 **Best Of Days** 2-9-5 0.. JimCrowley 1 93+
(Hugo Palmer) *dwlt: hld up towards rr: stylish prog on outer over 2f out: pushed into ld over 1f out: stretched clr impressively* **3/1**[2]
52 **2** *6* **Wahash (IRE)**[27] 3569 2-9-5 0.. FrankieDettori 7 75
(Richard Hannon) *led: shook off nrest chalrs 2f out: hdd and totally outpcd over 1f out: kpt on* **9/2**[3]
3 *2* **Sir Nigel Gresley (USA)** 2-9-5 0................................ FergusSweeney 3 70
(Alan King) *hld up in rr: prog over 2f out: shkn up and styd on to take 3rd last 75yds: no threat* **50/1**
4 *nk* **Procurator (IRE)** 2-9-5 0.. SeanLevey 8 69
(Richard Hannon) *trckd ldrs: shkn up and tried to chal 2f out: sn outpcd: plugged on* **6/1**
0 **5** *1* **Arborist (IRE)**[19] 3859 2-9-5 0.. DaneO'Neill 10 66
(Sylvester Kirk) *in tch in midfield: shkn up over 2f out: kpt on same pce fr over 1f out: n.d* **16/1**
6 *1* **Leader's Legacy (USA)** 2-9-5 0................................ JamesDoyle 6 63
(Saeed bin Suroor) *rn sltly green: chsd ldrs: effrt to go 2nd briefly 2f out: sn outpcd and btn* **11/4**[1]
43 **7** *1 3/4* **Native Prospect**[28] 3529 2-9-5 0.. OisinMurphy 9 59
(Andrew Balding) *prom: chsd ldr 3f out to 2f out: fdd* **8/1**
0 **8** *8* **Amlad (IRE)**[12] 4103 2-9-5 0.. TomMarquand 2 37
(Ed Dunlop) *a wl in rr: bhd fnl 2f in last pair* **20/1**
0 **9** *11* **Don't You Think**[20] 3799 2-9-5 0.. ShaneKelly 4 7
(Richard Hughes) *reluctant to enter stall: in tch: shkn up over 2f out: wknd v rapidly over 1f out: t.o* **66/1**
10 *6* **Netley Abbey** 2-9-5 0.. PatCosgrave 11
(Harry Dunlop) *dwlt: a in rr: bhd fnl 2f: t.o* **50/1**
11 *6* **Poet's Charm (IRE)** 2-9-5 0.. RobertHavlin 13
(Simon Crisford) *chsd ldr to 3f out: wkng whn squeezed out over 2f out: dropped away rapidly: t.o* **12/1**

1m 29.58s (0.08) **Going Correction** +0.15s/f (Good) **11** Ran SP% **119.0**
Speed ratings (Par 94): **105,98,95,95,94 93,91,82,69,62 55**
CSF £16.78 TOTE £4.60: £1.60, £1.70, £10.60; EX 19.60 Trifecta £801.00.
Owner G Schoeningh **Bred** G Schoeningh **Trained** Newmarket, Suffolk

FOCUS
Race run over 24 yards further than advertised. Cymric beat Massaat in this maiden 12 months ago, and this year's winner is another bright prospect. The runner-up helps with the level.

4534 MOLESEY H'CAP 7f 16y
7:35 (7:36) (Class 3) (0-90,90) 3-Y-O+ **£7,439** (£2,213; £1,106; £553) **Stalls** Low

Form RPR
3500 **1** **Outer Space**[12] 4109 5-9-11 **87**.. JamieSpencer 5 94
(Jamie Osborne) *restrained s and hld up in last: gng wl 2f out: cajoled along and prog over 1f out: brought between rivals fnl f: drvn to ld last 75yds and edgd sltly lft nr fin* **5/1**[2]
6135 **2** *nk* **Koptoon**[27] 3552 4-9-2 **78**.. JamesDoyle 9 84
(Jo Hughes) *trckd ldrs: rdn to chal over 1f out: led ins fnl f: hdd and edgd sltly rt last 75yds* **5/1**[2]
0146 **3** *nk* **Haley Bop (IRE)**[12] 4080 3-9-5 **88**.. JoeFanning 7 90
(Mark Johnston) *trckd ldr: rdn to take narrow ld over 1f out: hdd ins fnl f: styd on but hld whn short of room nr fin* **7/1**
3533 **4** *1/2* **Fast Dancer (IRE)**[6] 4306 4-9-6 **82**.. JFEgan 4 86
(Joseph Tuite) *hld up in last pair: rdn 2f out: limited prog tl styd on fnl f to take 4th last stride* **4/1**[1]
-106 **5** *nse* **Red Artist**[26] 3600 3-9-1 **84**..(v1) RobertHavlin 3 85
(Simon Crisford) *trckd ldrs: rdn to chal over 1f out: upsides ins fnl f: fdd nr fin* **13/2**
-056 **6** *hd* **Force (IRE)**[13] 4051 3-8-6 **78**................................ EdwardGreatrex(3) 6 78
(Charles Hills) *hld up in tch: rdn 2f out: nt qckn over 1f out and struggling in last trio: r.o again last 100yds: gaining at fin* **10/1**
0-00 **7** *1 1/4* **Firmdecisions (IRE)**[11] 4163 6-10-0 **90**........................ RobertWinston 8 90
(Dean Ivory) *t.k.h: led: hd quite high whn encouraged along 2f out: hdd over 1f out: wknd ins fnl f* **10/1**
1412 **8** *shd* **Here's Two**[27] 3558 3-8-6 **75**.. LukeMorris 2 72
(Ron Hodges) *t.k.h: trckd ldrs: nt qckn and lost pl over 1f out: no ch after: kpt on nr fin* **11/2**[3]

1m 30.36s (0.86) **Going Correction** +0.15s/f (Good)
WFA 3 from 4yo+ 7lb **8** Ran SP% **112.7**
Speed ratings (Par 107): **101,100,100,99,99 99,98,97**
CSF £29.20 CT £173.98 TOTE £6.40: £2.30, £2.10, £2.00; EX 40.30 Trifecta £277.00.
Owner Tony Taylor & Patrick Gage **Bred** Catridge Farm Stud & B & H Jellett **Trained** Upper Lambourn, Berks

FOCUS
Race run over 24 yards further than advertised. They finished in a heap, the whole field separated by under three lengths, and this isn't solid form. The winner is rated to his old turf best.

4535 RAYNES PARK H'CAP 1m 6f
8:05 (8:05) (Class 4) (0-85,85) 4-Y-O+ **£4,690** (£1,395; £697; £348) **Stalls** Low

Form RPR
4222 **1** **Life Less Ordinary (IRE)**[28] 3525 4-9-6 **84**.................... JamieSpencer 2 90
(Jamie Osborne) *hld up in last: slipstreamed rivals over 1f out: stl only 4th but on bridle jst ins fnl f: urged along and r.o wl to ld last strides* **7/2**[2]
4/00 **2** *nk* **Chartbreaker (FR)**[12] 4077 5-9-2 **80**................................ DaneO'Neill 3 85
(Chris Gordon) *led: rdn over 2f out: fought off rivals who looked to be gng bttr: hdd last strides* **20/1**
5521 **3** *1 1/2* **William Hunter**[24] 3690 4-8-13 **77**.................... WilliamTwiston-Davies 5 80
(Alan King) *hld up in 5th: cruised up to take 2nd over 1f out and sn chalng: rdn and fnd little fnl f: dropped to 3rd last 75yds* **7/1**
6113 **4** *2 3/4* **Touch The Sky**[28] 3533 5-9-7 **85**.. OisinMurphy 6 84
(David Elsworth) *t.k.h: cl up: trckd ldr jst over 2f out and sn chalng: lost 2nd over 1f out: fdd ins fnl f* **6/4**[1]
6024 **5** *nk* **Cotton Club (IRE)**[21] 3784 5-9-0 **78**.. RyanTate 4 77
(Rod Millman) *trckd ldrs: rdn over 2f out: no prog over 1f out: wl btn after: one pce* **13/2**
0-16 **6** *4* **Atalan**[32] 3409 4-8-8 **72**.. JimCrowley 1 65
(Hughie Morrison) *tried to match strides w ldr but sn settled in 2nd: rdn and lost pl 2f out: wknd* **9/2**[3]

3m 5.99s (1.49) **Going Correction** +0.15s/f (Good) **6** Ran SP% **111.0**
Speed ratings (Par 105): **101,100,99,98,98 95**
CSF £57.64 TOTE £4.70: £2.00, £5.30; EX 63.00 Trifecta £223.90.
Owner Michael Buckley & Mrs Karima Burman **Bred** Aidan Sexton **Trained** Upper Lambourn, Berks

The Form Book, Raceform Ltd, Newbury, RG14 5SJ

FOCUS
Race run over 24 yards further than advertised. They didn't go a great gallop in this fair staying handicap. The winner could have more to offer.

4536 LEATHERHEAD H'CAP 5f 6y
8:40 (8:42) (Class 4) (0-80,80) 3-Y-O+ **£4,690** (£1,395; £697; £348) **Stalls** High

Form RPR

3534 **1** **Secret Asset (IRE)**[25] 3638 11-9-9 **77**.............................(v) LukeMorris 2 86
(Lisa Williamson) *cl up against rail: quick and decisive move to ld over 1f out and sn clr: rdn out* **8/1**[3]

5143 **2** *2¼* **Jaywalker (IRE)**[14] 3995 5-9-11 **79**.................................. GeorgeBaker 4 80
(Mick Channon) *trckd ldr: shkn up to chal wl over 1f out but sn outpcd by wnr: kpt on but no imp fnl f* **10/11**[1]

16-6 **3** *3* **Little Voice (USA)**[20] 3815 3-9-5 **80**........................ EdwardGreatrex(3) 8 69
(Charles Hills) *mostly in 6th tl prog on outer 2f out: tried to cl over 1f out but sn outpcd* **7/1**[2]

0446 **4** *½* **Long Awaited (IRE)**[5] 4345 8-9-7 **78**.................. JosephineGordon(3) 5 66
(Conor Dore) *in tch: pushed along 1/2-way: outpcd over 1f out: kpt on* **8/1**[3]

3-31 **5** *2½* **Clumber Street**[34] 3317 5-9-6 **74**..[1] KierenFox 1 53
(Lee Carter) *led against rail to over 1f out: wknd fnl f* **14/1**

0-55 **6** *1¾* **Newton's Law (IRE)**[19] 3857 5-9-1 **76**..........................(t) JordanUys(7) 7 49
(Brian Meehan) *taken steadily to post: awkward s and slowly away: mostly in last and nvr a factor* **7/1**[2]

3060 **7** *hd* **Ask The Guru**[34] 3316 6-8-7 **61**......................................(p) JimmyQuinn 6 33
(Michael Attwater) *cl up on outer to 1/2-way: sn lost pl and struggling* **16/1**

1m 1.58s (-0.02) **Going Correction** +0.125s/f (Good)
WFA 3 from 4yo+ 4lb **7** Ran SP% **112.2**
Speed ratings (Par 105): **105,101,96,95,91 89,88**
CSF £15.18 CT £53.72 TOTE £5.60: £3.50, £1.10; EX 11.00 Trifecta £36.70.
Owner Simon&JeanettePierpoint/Dave&WendyHughes **Bred** Mrs C Hartery **Trained** Saighton, Cheshire

FOCUS
An ordinary sprint handicap lacking depth. The form is rated a bit cautiously.
T/Plt: £282.50 to a £1 stake. Pool: £63,029.21 - 162.83 winning units. T/Qpdt: £36.80 to a £1 stake. Pool: £7,377.95 - 148.34 winning units. **Jonathan Neesom**

4537 - 4539a (Foreign Racing) - See Raceform Interactive

3926 NAAS (L-H)
Wednesday, July 20

OFFICIAL GOING: Good (good to firm in places)

4540a YEOMANSTOWN STUD DARK ANGEL EUROPEAN BREEDERS FUND STKS (LISTED) 6f
7:25 (7:27) 3-Y-O+
£26,029 (£8,382; £3,970; £1,764; £882; £441)

RPR

1 **Fort Del Oro (IRE)**[46] 2923 4-9-8 105...................................... BillyLee 2 104
(Edward Lynam, Ire) *hld up on far side: travelled wl to press ldr under 2f out: led over 1f out and sn pushed clr: kpt on wl clsng stages* **10/11**[1]

2 *¾* **Buying Trouble (USA)**[32] 3392 3-9-0 92................ DeclanMcDonogh 1 98+
(David Evans) *racd towards rr: prog on far side over 1f out: 4th ent fnl f: styd on strly into 2nd fnl 100yds where swtchd rt: kpt on wl cl home* **10/1**

3 *½* **Most Beautiful**[10] 4178 3-9-0 105............................... WayneLordan 10 96
(David Wachman, Ire) *hld up towards outer: tk quite t.k.h: travelled wl into 2nd over 1f out: rdn and no imp in 3rd fnl 100yds: kpt on same pce clsng stages* **3/1**[2]

4 *1¾* **Lady Mega (IRE)**[32] 3425 5-9-5 85............................... RobbieDowney 4 91
(Edward Lynam, Ire) *rrd on leaving stalls: hld up in mid-div: travelled wl in bhd ldrs 1/2-way: wnt 5th ent fnl f: kpt on wl into 4th clsng stages: nvr nrr* **16/1**

5 *½* **Vitello**[17] 3928 3-9-1 98 ow1.. JamesMcDonald 5 89
(M Halford, Ire) *chsd ldrs towards far side: on terms 1/2-way and led under 2f out: hdd over 1f out: no ex and wknd ins fnl f* **7/1**[3]

6 *hd* **Byzantium**[46] 2923 4-9-5 96....................................... ColmO'Donoghue 6 89
(Edward Lynam, Ire) *led tl jnd 1/2-way and sn hdd: nt qckn appr fnl f: kpt on one pce* **16/1**

7 *nk* **Anonymous Lady (IRE)**[26] 3628 4-9-5 85..................(bt) ShaneFoley 3 88
(Adrian Paul Keatley, Ire) *racd towards rr: prog and swtchd to outer over 1f out: kpt on wl fnl f: nvr nrr* **33/1**

8 *6½* **Juliette Fair (IRE)**[66] 2272 3-9-0 99...............................(b) PatSmullen 7 66
(D K Weld, Ire) *pressed ldr in 2nd: on terms 1/2-way: rdn and nt qckn over 1f out: wknd qckly and eased fnl f* **14/1**

9 *2¾* **Fainleog (IRE)**[8] 4246 5-9-5 79.. AdrianO'Shea 9 59
(Mrs A M O'Shea, Ire) *pressed ldrs in 3rd towards outer: rdn 1/2-way: wknd over 1f out* **100/1**

10 *5½* **Californiadreaming (IRE)**[9] 4218 3-9-0 77..................(tp) AnaO'Brien 8 40
(A P O'Brien, Ire) *hld up: rdn and nt qckn over 1f out: sn dropped to rr and eased* **66/1**

1m 10.58s (-2.62)
WFA 3 from 4yo+ 5lb **10** Ran SP% **122.8**
CSF £12.87 TOTE £1.70: £1.02, £3.50, £1.80; DF 11.80 Trifecta £33.90.
Owner Ballylinch Stud **Bred** Ballylinch Stud **Trained** Dunshaughlin, Co Meath

FOCUS
An up-to-scratch renewal with the first and third home rated 105. The winner was backed into odds-on favouritism and was always doing enough inside the final furlong. The fourth and seventh help set the standard.

4541 - 4543a (Foreign Racing) - See Raceform Interactive

4295 DONCASTER (L-H)
Thursday, July 21

OFFICIAL GOING: Good to firm (8.7)
Wind: Light against Weather: Fine & dry

4544 OWLERTON GREYHOUND STADIUM H'CAP 6f
5:50 (5:51) (Class 5) (0-70,70) 4-Y-O+ **£3,881** (£1,155; £577; £288) **Stalls** High

Form RPR

4060 **1** **Sunraider (IRE)**[16] 3980 9-9-6 **69**...................................... GrahamLee 8 78
(Paul Midgley) *in rr and sn pushed along: hdwy wl over 1f out: rdn and str ent fnl f: led towards fin* **10/1**

0103 **2** *nk* **Razin' Hell**[14] 4039 5-9-4 **67**..(v) DanielTudhope 6 75
(John Balding) *t.k.h: trckd ldrs: hdwy over 2f out: chal over 1f out: rdn to ld ent fnl f: sn hung rt and drvn: hdd and no ex towards fin* **9/1**

1221 **3** *¾* **Seamster**[7] 4295 9-9-0 **70**......................................(t) CameronNoble(7) 10 76
(David Loughnane) *trckd ldrs on outer: hdwy 2f out: rdn along wl over 1f out: kpt on u.p fnl f* **7/2**[1]

0050 **4** *1¼* **Ypres**[54] 2680 7-8-13 **62**.. JFEgan 7 64
(Jason Ward) *in tch: pushed along 1/2-way: hdwy to chse ldrs wl over 1f out: sn rdn: drvn and kpt on same pce fnl f* **25/1**

3330 **5** *nse* **Picks Pinta**[38] 3210 5-8-11 **65**...............................(p) JordanVaughan(5) 13 66
(John David Riches) *prom: rdn along wl over 1f out: drvn and kpt on same pce fnl f* **8/1**[3]

2321 **6** *½* **Poppy In The Wind**[20] 3843 4-9-1 **64**..................................(v) DaleSwift 2 64
(Alan Brown) *towards rr: pushed along 1/2-way: gd hdwy on outer 2f out: rdn to chal over 1f out: drvn and edgd lft ent fnl f: kpt on same pce* **6/1**[2]

6311 **7** *2* **Danish Duke (IRE)**[17] 3940 5-9-5 **68**................................(p) TomEaves 1 61
(Ruth Carr) *trckd ldrs: hdwy over 2f out: chsd ldrs wl over 1f out: rdn appr fnl f and grad wknd* **9/1**

2445 **8** *nk* **Keene's Pointe**[12] 4142 6-9-0 **63**.. JoeFanning 12 56
(Kristin Stubbs) *towards rr: hdwy wl over 1f out: kpt on fnl f* **16/1**

130- **9** *nk* **Balliol**[217] 8263 4-9-2 **70**.. JordanNason(5) 3 62
(Ronald Harris) *prom: led over 3f out: rdn wl over 1f out: edgd lft and hdd ent fnl f: wknd* **16/1**

-044 **10** *5* **Disclosure**[7] 4321 5-9-2 **65**.. DavidAllan 4 41
(Les Eyre) *a towards rr* **6/1**[2]

0000 **11** *2* **Aprovado (IRE)**[24] 3713 4-9-6 **69**.............................(p) PaulMulrennan 11 38
(Michael Dods) *prom: rdn along over 2f out: sn wknd* **12/1**

100- **12** *12* **Hugie Boy (IRE)**[391] 3592 4-9-3 **66**....................................(p) BenCurtis 5
(Scott Dixon) *led: hdd over 3f out: sn rdn along and wknd* **33/1**

1m 11.8s (-1.80) **Going Correction** -0.125s/f (Firm) **12** Ran SP% **117.2**
Speed ratings (Par 103): **107,106,105,103,103 103,100,100,99,93 90,74**
CSF £95.93 CT £381.71 TOTE £11.80: £3.70, £2.80, £1.50; EX 114.20 Trifecta £714.90.
Owner David Mann **Bred** Lodge Park Stud **Trained** Westow, N Yorks

FOCUS
The ground was officially good to firm and it was described as quick by jockeys riding in the opener. The presence of three last-time-out winners and last year's winner of the race gave this handicap a competitive edge for a 51-70. The winner is rated back to form.

4545 SAINT GOBAIN WEBER MAIDEN STKS (PLUS 10 RACE) 7f
6:20 (6:23) (Class 4) 2-Y-O **£4,528** (£1,347; £673; £336) **Stalls** High

Form RPR

1 **Samharry** 2-9-5 0.. PaulHanagan 2 81+
(John Gosden) *trckd ldrs: hdwy on outer to ld 2f out: rdn clr and edgd rt over 1f out: styd on wl* **11/4**[2]

2 *1½* **Total Star** 2-9-5 0.. DanielTudhope 10 76
(Luca Cumani) *hld up: hdwy: trckd ldrs wl over 2f out: rdn along over 1f out: styd on to chse wnr ins fnl f: kpt on* **14/1**

3 *2* **Portledge (IRE)** 2-9-5 0.. PJMcDonald 3 71
(James Bethell) *in tch: pushed along and outpcd 3f out: hdwy wl over 1f out: n.m.r ent fnl f: sn swtchd rt and rdn: kpt on wl towards fin* **50/1**

4 *nk* **Accento** 2-9-2 0.. MarcMonaghan(3) 6 70
(Hugo Palmer) *in tch: swtchd lft to outer and hdwy wl over 1f out: rdn to chse ldrs and edgd rt jst over 1f out: kpt on same pce* **7/2**[3]

0 **5** *shd* **Heaven's Rock (IRE)**[21] 3805 2-9-5 0..........................(t) RichardKingscote 5 69
(Tom Dascombe) *prom: cl up 1/2-way: rdn along wl over 1f out: drvn and edgd sltly lft appr fnl f: sn drvn and kpt on same pce* **33/1**

6 *2¼* **Stevie Brown** 2-9-5 0.. PhillipMakin 4 63
(David Brown) *dwlt and towards rr: pushed along and outpcd 3f out: rdn over 2f out: kpt on fnl f* **50/1**

7 *1* **Yarmouk (FR)** 2-9-5 0.. TonyHamilton 1 61
(Richard Fahey) *t.k.h: hld up in rr: hdwy over 2f out: chsd ldrs and green whn n.m.r and hmpd appr fnl f: nt rcvr* **7/2**[3]

8 *1¾* **Trooper's Gold** 2-9-5 0.. TomEaves 7 56
(Kevin Ryan) *towards rr: hdwy to trck ldrs over 4f out: pushed along over 2f out: sn rdn and grad wknd* **25/1**

9 *1¾* **Amherst Rock** 2-9-5 0.. JamesMcDonald 9 51+
(Charlie Appleby) *unruly in stalls: t.k.h: chsd ldng pair and led after 2f: rdn along over 2f out: sn hdd and wkng whn n.m.r wl over 1f out: eased after* **9/4**[1]

0 **10** *4½* **Shadow Of Hercules (IRE)**[21] 3805 2-9-5 0.................... RobertTart 11 39
(Michael Mullineaux) *slt ld 2f: prom: rdn along 1/2-way: sn wkd* **100/1**

1m 26.58s (0.28) **Going Correction** -0.125s/f (Firm) **10** Ran SP% **120.2**
Speed ratings (Par 96): **93,91,89,88,88 85,84,82,80,75**
CSF £39.06 TOTE £3.00: £1.20, £3.50, £10.90; EX 36.50 Trifecta £1148.80.
Owner Hamdan Al Maktoum **Bred** Carmel Stud **Trained** Newmarket, Suffolk
■ Stewards' Enquiry : Marc Monaghan three-day ban: careless riding (Aug 4-6)

FOCUS
Nothing to get excited about among the pair with experience but several of the newcomers had attractive profiles on paper and the chances are there were some decent two-year-olds in the field. A nice start from the winner.

4546 ESQUIRES WHEATLEY RETAIL PARK MAIDEN STKS 7f
6:50 (6:55) (Class 5) 3-Y-O+ **£3,234** (£962; £481; £240) **Stalls** High

Form RPR

2202 **1** **Raven's Corner (IRE)**[33] 3411 3-9-5 83........................ NickyMackay 7 87
(John Gosden) *mde all: rdn wl over 1f out: kpt on strly fnl f* **2/1**[1]

0 **2** *3* **Zwayyan**[33] 3412 3-9-5 0.. PaulHanagan 3 79
(William Haggas) *sn trcking ldrs: hdwy over 2f out: sn chsng wnr: rdn wl over 1f out: drvn and no imp fnl f* **3/1**[2]

2 **3** *1½* **Hilldale**[20] 3850 3-9-0 0.. PaulMulrennan 11 70
(Michael Dods) *trckd ldng pair: hdwy to chse wnr 3f out: rdn along 2f out: drvn over 1f out: kpt on same pce* **4/1**[3]

4 *nk* **Aldrin (FR)** 3-9-5 0..(t) JamesMcDonald 5 74
(Charlie Appleby) *trckd ldrs: hdwy 3f out: rdn along wl over 1f out: drvn ent fnl f: kpt on same pce* **11/2**

0 **5** *5* **Southern Strife**[20] 3845 5-9-12 0.. CamHardie 10 64
(Tim Easterby) *towards rr: pushed along bef 1/2-way: rdn wl over 2f out: plugged on fnl 2f* **66/1**

6 *1* **The Big Day (IRE)**[106] 1277 3-8-7 0........................ KieranSchofield(7) 9 53
(Nigel Tinkler) *chsd ldrs: pushed along 4f out: rdn 3f out: drvn and plugged on one pce fnl 2f* **100/1**

03 **7** *6* **Wonderful Life (IRE)**[20] 3850 3-9-0 0.............................. HarryBentley 2 37
(Richard Spencer) *in tch on outer: hdwy to chse ldrs 3f out: rdn along over 2f out: sn drvn and wknd* **6/1**

0 **8** *2* **Angelical (IRE)**[27] 3609 3-9-0 0.................................. GrahamGibbons 1 31
(Daniel Mark Loughnane) *cl up: rdn along 3f out: sn drvn and wknd* **100/1**

9 1 1/2 **Old China** 3-9-5 0 SamJames 6 32
(John Davies) *dwlt: a bhd* **66/1**

0-0 **10** 1 **Sharp Jack**[192] 145 3-9-5 0 (t) RichardKingscote 4 29
(Tom Dascombe) *a towards rr* **33/1**

5-00 **11** 9 **Sun In His Eyes**[12] 4156 4-9-7 30 CallumShepherd(5) 8 8
(Ed de Giles) *chsd ldrs: rdn along 1/2-way: sn wknd* **100/1**

1m 24.95s (-1.35) **Going Correction** -0.125s/f (Firm)
WFA 3 from 4yo+ 7lb **11** Ran SP% **116.9**
Speed ratings (Par 103): **102,98,96,96,90 89,82,80,78,77 67**
CSF £7.99 TOTE £2.80: £1.02, £2.20, £2.20; EX 9.10 Trifecta £32.10.
Owner Godolphin **Bred** Rabbah Bloodstock Limited **Trained** Newmarket, Suffolk

FOCUS
Just a handful of the previously-raced contenders had shown themselves anything like future maiden winners and the first four pulled clear. The winner set a good standard.

4547 SKY BET GO-RACING-IN-YORKSHIRE SUMMER FESTIVAL H'CAP 6f
7:25 (7:25) (Class 4) (0-80,80) 3-Y-O **£5,175** (£1,540; £769; £384) **Stalls** High

Form RPR

22-1 **1** **Gravity Flow (IRE)**[33] 3406 3-9-4 **77** JamesMcDonald 3 91+
(William Haggas) *trckd ldrs: hdwy over 2f out: rdn to ld wl over 1f out: drvn and kpt on wl fnl f* **7/4**[1]

6011 **2** 1 1/2 **Roll On Rory**[12] 4134 3-9-5 **78** (v) JFEgan 2 86
(Jason Ward) *led: rdn along over 2f out: hdd wl over 1f out: drvn and edgd lft fnl f: kpt on same pce* **11/4**[2]

-224 **3** 1 **Hyland Heather (IRE)**[19] 3879 3-9-0 **78** AdamMcNamara(5) 4 83
(Richard Fahey) *in tch: hdwy to chse ldrs 1/2-way: rdn along and outpcd wl over 2f out: drvn and kpt on appr fnl f* **14/1**

5106 **4** 1/2 **Bellesedert**[13] 4093 3-9-2 **75** RoystonFfrench 1 78
(Steph Hollinshead) *trckd ldrs: cl up 1/2-way: rdn along 2f out: sn drvn and kpt on same pce* **22/1**

2545 **5** 2 1/4 **Sir Dudley (IRE)**[33] 3420 3-9-3 **76** (b) TomEaves 9 72
(James Given) *in tch: rdn along 3f out: wknd over 2f out* **9/1**

-003 **6** 1/2 **Market Choice (IRE)**[16] 3978 3-9-2 **75** PaulMulrennan 8 70
(Michael Dods) *t.k.h: chsd ldrs: rdn along over 2f out: sn wknd* **5/1**[3]

1 **7** 1/2 **Top Of The Bank**[88] 1673 3-9-7 **80** (p) GrahamLee 5 73
(Kevin Ryan) *trckd ldrs gng wl: effrt over 2f out: sn rdn and btn* **12/1**

-520 **8** 3 1/2 **Tikthebox (IRE)**[23] 3753 3-9-6 **79** PhillipMakin 6 61
(David Brown) *t.k.h: prom: rdn along 1/2-way: sn wknd* **16/1**

1m 11.27s (-2.33) **Going Correction** -0.125s/f (Firm) **8** Ran SP% **114.3**
Speed ratings (Par 102): **110,108,106,106,103 102,101,97**
CSF £6.57 CT £47.30 TOTE £2.00: £1.10, £1.50, £3.10; EX 7.40 Trifecta £55.10.
Owner Sheikh Juma Dalmook Al Maktoum **Bred** Eimear Mulhern & Abbeville Stud **Trained** Newmarket, Suffolk

FOCUS
Plenty of these had something to prove judged on recent efforts but that should not temper enthusiasm for a progressive winner. Pace held up.

4548 EBF BRITISH STALLION STUDS FILLIES' H'CAP 7f
7:55 (7:55) (Class 3) (0-90,85) 3-Y-O+ **£9,703** (£2,887; £1,443; £721) **Stalls** High

Form RPR

3652 **1** **Hawatif (IRE)**[7] 4318 3-9-0 **78** JoeFanning 2 84
(Mark Johnston) *trckd ldng pair: hdwy over 2f out: rdn to ld 1 1/2f out: drvn and kpt on wl fnl f* **9/4**[1]

3-45 **2** 1 **Company Asset (IRE)**[13] 4116 3-9-0 **78** GrahamLee 6 81
(Kevin Ryan) *trckd ldrs: hdwy over 2f out: swtchd lft and rdn ent fnl f: sn drvn and kpt on* **7/2**

6543 **3** 3/4 **Quick N Quirky (IRE)**[13] 4116 3-9-3 **81** (tp) DavidAllan 3 82
(Tim Easterby) *set stdy pce: pushed along and qcknd over 2f out: rdn and hdd 1 1/2f out: sn drvn: kpt on same pce fnl f* **11/4**[2]

6030 **4** 1/2 **Penny Dreadful**[48] 2875 4-9-1 **72** DaleSwift 1 75
(Scott Dixon) *t.k.h: trckd ldr: pushed 2f out: sn rdn: drvn over 1f out: kpt on same pce* **16/1**

26-6 **5** 1/2 **Aqua Libre**[13] 4105 3-9-7 **85** DanielTudhope 4 84
(Philip McBride) *hld up in rr: hdwy 2f out: rdn and edgd lft over 1f out: kpt on towards fin* **3/1**[3]

1m 25.26s (-1.04) **Going Correction** -0.125s/f (Firm)
WFA 3 from 4yo 7lb **5** Ran SP% **110.5**
Speed ratings (Par 104): **100,98,98,97,96**
CSF £10.41 TOTE £3.40: £1.60, £1.90; EX 12.30 Trifecta £18.90.
Owner Abdulla Al Mansoori **Bred** T Whitehead **Trained** Middleham Moor, N Yorks

FOCUS
This fillies' handicap was dramatically weakened by the withdrawal of three major fancies and the remaining quintet did not go a great pace either. Ordinary form which makes sense.

4549 SHEFFIELD'S TOP NIGHT AT OWLERTON H'CAP 1m 2f 60y
8:25 (8:26) (Class 5) (0-75,74) 3-Y-O **£3,881** (£1,155; £577; £288) **Stalls** Low

Form RPR

5-40 **1** **Airton**[35] 3323 3-8-11 **64** PJMcDonald 2 71
(James Bethell) *hld up in tch: hdwy over 2f out: rdn to ld ent fnl f: sn drvn and kpt on wl* **7/1**

35 **2** 2 1/4 **Cosmic Storm**[17] 3959 3-9-3 **70** RichardKingscote 4 73
(Ralph Beckett) *trckd ldrs: smooth hdwy over 3f out: cl up over 2f out: led wl over 1f out and sn rdn: hdd ent fnl f: sn drvn and kpt on same pce* **3/1**[2]

1410 **3** 1/2 **Island Flame (IRE)**[27] 3593 3-9-2 **74** AdamMcNamara(5) 1 76
(Richard Fahey) *hld up in tch: effrt 2f out and sn rdn: drvn and kpt on wl fnl f* **7/2**[3]

-100 **4** shd **Ban Shoof**[76] 1994 3-9-7 **74** (p) ThomasBrown 5 75
(Ismail Mohammed) *chsd clr ldr: hdwy 3f out: cl up 2f out: sn rdn and ev ch: drvn and kpt on same pce fnl f* **7/1**

0045 **5** 3/4 **Ronnie Baird**[9] 4241 3-9-6 **73** (b) TonyHamilton 3 73
(Kristin Stubbs) *hld up in rr: effrt and pushed along over 2f out: rdn wl over 1f out: kpt on fnl f* **25/1**

501 **6** 3 **Jabbaar**[30] 3483 3-9-7 **74** PaulHanagan 7 68+
(Owen Burrows) *trckd ldng pair: chsd clr ldr 1/2-way: led wl over 2f out: sn rdn: hdd wl over 1f out: sn wknd* **11/4**[1]

1-40 **7** 3 1/2 **Sunscape (IRE)**[44] 3001 3-9-0 **72** CharlieBennett(5) 6 59+
(Hughie Morrison) *led and sn clr: pushed along 3f out: sn rdn and hdd: drvn wl over 1f out and sn wknd* **8/1**

2m 9.59s (0.19) **Going Correction** -0.075s/f (Good) **7** Ran SP% **113.8**
Speed ratings (Par 100): **96,94,93,93,93 90,87**
CSF £27.99 TOTE £8.30: £4.20, £2.30; EX 31.30 Trifecta £152.30.
Owner Clarendon Thoroughbred Racing **Bred** Clive Dennett **Trained** Middleham Moor, N Yorks

FOCUS
They went a good gallop in this three-year-old handicap, which was run over an extra nine yards due to rail movement, and the finish was dominated by those who came from off the pace. The winner's rated back to his 2yo form.

4550 EQUESTRIAN SURFACES LTD H'CAP 1m 6f 132y
9:00 (9:00) (Class 4) (0-80,78) 4-Y-O+ **£5,175** (£1,540; £769; £384) **Stalls** Low

Form RPR

03 **1** **Brittleton**[14] 4057 4-9-4 **75** (b) JamesMcDonald 7 82
(Harry Dunlop) *hld up in rr: stdy hdwy on outer over 3f out: cl up 2f out: chal over 1f out: rdn to ld ent fnl f: kpt on strly* **3/1**[2]

10/0 **2** 1 3/4 **Soul Intent (IRE)**[26] 3659 6-9-4 **75** BenCurtis 1 79
(Brian Ellison) *trckd ldr: hdwy 3f out: cl up over 2f out: rdn to ld wl over 1f out: hdd and drvn ent fnl f: kpt on* **9/1**

0120 **3** nk **Bertie Moon**[40] 3129 6-8-11 **75** (p) CliffordLee(7) 2 79
(Lydia Pearce) *led: pushed along over 3f out: rdn over 2f out: hdd wl over 1f out: sn drvn and kpt on same pce fnl f* **9/1**

6154 **4** 1/2 **The Kid**[9] 4237 5-9-2 **73** (p) CamHardie 5 76
(John Quinn) *trckd ldrs: hdwy 3f out: effrt 2f out and sn rdn: drvn appr fnl f: kpt on same pce* **6/1**

0053 **5** nk **Lungarno Palace (USA)**[16] 3972 5-9-7 **78** (p) MichaelJMMurphy 6 81
(John Gallagher) *hld up towards rr: hdwy 4f out: rdn along and sltly outpcd 2f out: drvn and kpt on fnl f* **9/2**[3]

1220 **6** 3/4 **Hallstatt (IRE)**[32] 3437 10-8-9 **66** (t) JoeFanning 3 68
(John Mackie) *trckd ldng pair on inner: hdwy 4f out: cl up 3f out: rdn 2f out: sn drvn and wknd ent fnl f* **14/1**

2-34 **7** 1/2 **Carpe Vita (IRE)**[50] 2805 4-9-1 **72** DanielTudhope 4 73
(David O'Meara) *hld up towards rr: hdwy 4f out: rdn along outpcd 2f out: sn drvn: kpt on fnl f* **11/4**[1]

3m 14.19s (6.79) **Going Correction** -0.075s/f (Good) **7** Ran SP% **110.8**
Speed ratings (Par 105): **78,77,76,76,76 76,75**
CSF £27.42 TOTE £3.90: £2.20, £5.00; EX 28.00 Trifecta £123.30.
Owner Sirphilipwroughton&mrsjamesblythcurrie **Bred** Dr A Gillespie **Trained** Lambourn, Berks

FOCUS
More of these had been heading down the handicap than up it and this contest, which was run over an extra nine yards due to rail movement, was not ultra competitive. Rather muddling form.
T/Jkpt: Not won. T/Plt: £83.30 to a £1 stake. Pool of £77153.55 - 676.05 winning tickets. T/Qpdt: £8.20 to a £1 stake. Pool of £8165.57 - 734.68 winning tickets. **Joe Rowntree**

4390 NEWBURY (L-H)
Thursday, July 21

OFFICIAL GOING: Good to firm
Wind: Moderate, across towards stands Weather: Overcast, warm

4551 VISIT NEWBURY AMATEUR RIDERS' H'CAP 1m 5f 61y
5:35 (5:37) (Class 5) (0-70,70) 3-Y-O+ **£3,119** (£967; £483; £242) **Stalls** Centre

Form RPR

4210 **1** **Onorina (IRE)**[21] 3798 4-10-12 **68** MrSWalker 7 74
(Jim Boyle) *hld up off the pce in 5th: hdwy on bit to ld 2f out: rdn and hld on wl nr fin* **2/1**[1]

6025 **2** 1/2 **The Ducking Stool**[15] 4023 9-10-13 **69** MrRBirkett 4 74
(Julia Feilden) *hld up off the pce in 4th: rdn 4f out: drvn to chse wnr fnl 2f: clsd fnl f: jst hld* **3/1**[3]

25/6 **3** 3 1/4 **Nafaath (IRE)**[14] 4045 10-10-7 **68** (p) MissAMcCain(5) 6 68
(Donald McCain) *chsd clr ldr: clsd and ch 2f out: one pce* **9/1**

-006 **4** 6 **Royal Etiquette (IRE)**[14] 4052 9-9-6 **53** (tp) MsVLPendleton(5) 5 44
(Lawney Hill) *s.s: bhd: shkn up and sme hdwy over 1f out: n.d* **25/1**

6030 **5** 6 **Classic Mission**[28] 3560 5-10-10 **69** (b) MrJHarding(3) 2 51
(Jonathan Portman) *sn led: 12 l clr after 4f: wknd and hdd 2f out* **10/1**

1130 **6** 3 **Bamako Du Chatelet (FR)**[20] 3844 5-10-11 **67** (p) MissSBrotherton 3 45
(Ian Williams) *hld up off the pce in 3rd: effrt and hrd rdn over 3f out: wknd over 2f out* **11/4**[2]

2m 54.95s (2.95) **Going Correction** +0.075s/f (Good) **6** Ran SP% **107.9**
Speed ratings (Par 103): **93,92,90,87,83 81**
CSF £7.54 CT £34.11 TOTE £2.10: £1.40, £2.70; EX 8.10 Trifecta £34.00.
Owner Sir David Prosser **Bred** J Hanly, T Stewart & A Stroud **Trained** Epsom, Surrey

FOCUS
The rail from the 1m to the 5f on the round course had been moved out to give fresh ground, thus 1m2f was 28yds longer and 1m5f also 28yds. The chasing pack ignored the clear front-runner \bClassic Mission\p n this amateur riders' handicap, and the form looks fair, rated around the second.

4552 BATHWICK TYRES IRISH STALLION FARMS EBF MAIDEN STKS (PLUS 10 RACE) 6f 8y
6:05 (6:07) (Class 4) 2-Y-O **£4,269** (£1,270; £634; £317) **Stalls** High

Form RPR

30 **1** **Mutawakked (IRE)**[21] 3813 2-9-5 0 DaneO'Neill 1 84
(Brian Meehan) *mde all: hld on gamely fnl f* **9/1**

3 **2** nk **Deningy**[85] 1770 2-9-5 0 [1] JamesDoyle 3 83
(Charlie Appleby) *pressed wnr: str chal fnl f: kpt on wl: jst hld* **5/6**[1]

3 2 1/2 **Prazeres** 2-9-5 0 JimCrowley 2 75+
(William Haggas) *chsd ldrs: rdn over 2f out: styd on fnl f* **20/1**

4 3 1/4 **Warrior's Spirit (IRE)** 2-9-5 0 SeanLevey 8 65
(Richard Hannon) *t.k.h: prom tl outpcd appr fnl f* **7/2**[2]

0 **5** 1 3/4 **Sfumato**[42] 3058 2-9-5 0 GeorgeBaker 7 59+
(Roger Charlton) *t.k.h in rr: shkn up and hdwy over 1f out: nvr rchd ldrs* **6/1**[3]

6 1 1/2 **Feel The Vibes** 2-9-5 0 PatDobbs 6 54
(Richard Hannon) *a abt same pl: n.d fnl 2f* **25/1**

7 3 1/4 **Hidden Stash** 2-9-5 0 OisinMurphy 4 44
(Andrew Balding) *rn green: a in rr* **33/1**

8 4 1/2 **Glorious Power (IRE)** 2-9-5 0 SilvestreDeSousa 5 29
(Charles Hills) *t.k.h in 5th: rn green: hung lft and wknd 2f out* **16/1**

1m 13.55s (0.55) **Going Correction** +0.15s/f (Good) **8** Ran SP% **118.5**
Speed ratings (Par 96): **102,101,98,93,91 89,85,79**
CSF £17.38 TOTE £10.60: £2.50, £1.02, £5.50; EX 22.90 Trifecta £216.50.
Owner Hamdan Al Maktoum **Bred** Pat Beirne **Trained** Manton, Wilts

The Form Book, Raceform Ltd, Newbury, RG14 5SJ

FOCUS
It paid to be handy in this fair 2yo maiden. Afterwards George Baker said it was "good to firm, but safe" while Jim Crowley added "nice ground - pretty quick." This was in keeping with the winner's debut.

4553 INDZINE NURSERY H'CAP — 6f 8y
6:35 (6:36) (Class 5) 2-Y-O — **£3,881** (£1,155; £577; £288) **Stalls** High

Form — RPR

261 **1** **Rajar**[15] 4011 2-9-1 **77** ... SeanLevey 8 — 84+
(Richard Hannon) *t.k.h: trckd ldr: led wl over 1f out: rdn out* **15/2**

2315 **2** ½ **Spiritous (USA)**[12] 4148 2-9-7 **83** ... (p) JamesDoyle 1 — 88
(John Gosden) *led tl wl over 1f out: kpt on u.p* **9/4**[1]

316 **3** *nk* **High Acclaim (USA)**[12] 4148 2-9-3 **83** ... FergusSweeney 3 — 83
(Roger Teal) *in tch: drvn to press ldrs fnl f: kpt on* **8/1**

005 **4** 2 **Juanito Chico (IRE)**[13] 4075 2-8-9 **71** ... CharlesBishop 5 — 69
(William Jarvis) *stdd s: missed break: plld hrd in rr: rdn and styd on wl fnl 2f* **16/1**

3002 **5** *shd* **Big Lachie**[9] 4221 2-8-6 **68** ... WilliamCarson 9 — 65
(Jamie Osborne) *stdd s: dwlt: plld hrd in rr: rdn and hdwy over 1f out: styd on same pce fnl f* **11/1**

650 **6** 1½ **Spin Top**[48] 2847 2-8-4 **66** ... TomMarquand 2 — 59
(Joseph Tuite) *prom tl outpcd appr fnl f* **50/1**

5523 **7** 6 **Rising Eagle**[15] 4015 2-8-5 **67** ... LukeMorris 4 — 40
(Charles Hills) *stdd s: dwlt: t.k.h in 6th: rdn and wknd 2f out* **10/1**

1634 **8** 1¼ **Sayesse**[13] 4076 2-9-4 **80** ... SilvestreDeSousa 7 — 49
(Mick Channon) *chsd ldrs tl wknd over 1f out* **7/1**[3]

312 **9** ¾ **Hedging (IRE)**[7] 4315 2-8-9 **71** ... JohnFahy 6 — 38
(Eve Johnson Houghton) *t.k.h towards rr: effrt on stands' rail whn nt clr run over 1f out: n.d after* **7/2**[2]

1m 15.0s (2.00) **Going Correction** +0.15s/f (Good) — 9 Ran SP% **113.6**
Speed ratings (Par 94): **92,91,90,88,88 86,78,76,75**
CSF £24.32 CT £140.22 TOTE £8.80: £2.70, £1.10, £3.20; EX 27.80 Trifecta £169.70.
Owner Robin Blunt & Partners **Bred** Robin Blunt **Trained** East Everleigh, Wilts

FOCUS
This looked a fair nursery and they went a sound pace down the middle. The winner is progressing.

4554 DAISY'S DREAM H'CAP — 1m 2f 6y
7:10 (7:10) (Class 4) (0-85,84) 3-Y-O — **£6,469** (£1,925; £962; £481) **Stalls** Centre

Form — RPR

3461 **1** **Scarlet Dragon**[21] 3814 3-9-7 **84** ... JimCrowley 1 — 97
(Eve Johnson Houghton) *travelled wl in 3rd: led 2f out: rdn and qcknd clr over 1f out: comf* **15/8**[1]

3301 **2** 4½ **Bedrock**[33] 3399 3-9-5 **82** ... (p) SilvestreDeSousa 7 — 86
(William Haggas) *led: hrd rdn and hdd 2f out: sn outpcd by wnr* **5/2**[2]

1-55 **3** 1 **Vincent's Forever**[13] 4080 3-9-6 **83** ... RobertHavlin 4 — 85
(John Gosden) *stdd in rr s: hdwy in centre 3f out: one pce appr fnl f* **5/1**[3]

-006 **4** *nk* **Jim Dandy**[14] 4055 3-9-0 **77** ... WilliamTwiston-Davies 3 — 78
(Alan King) *hld up in 5th: outpcd over 2f out: kpt on fnl f* **13/2**

6103 **5** 2 **Pack It In (IRE)**[14] 4046 3-8-8 **71** ... (b) MartinDwyer 8 — 68
(Brian Meehan) *t.k.h: chsd ldr tl 2f out: wknd over 1f out* **12/1**

-040 **6** ½ **Not Touch**[55] 2654 3-8-8 **71** ... TomMarquand 5 — 67
(Richard Hannon) *hld up in 4th: rdn and btn 2f out* **12/1**

2m 7.6s (-1.20) **Going Correction** +0.075s/f (Good) — 6 Ran SP% **108.7**
Speed ratings (Par 102): **107,103,102,102,100 100**
CSF £6.28 CT £15.68 TOTE £3.00: £2.10, £1.10; EX 6.10 Trifecta £19.10.
Owner W H Ponsonby **Bred** Usk Valley Stud **Trained** Blewbury, Oxon

FOCUS
Add 28 yards to race distance. Not a bad handicap. It was run at an uneven pace and the runner-up rates the benchmark. The winner built on his latest effort.

4555 SOUTH DOWNS WATER CONDITIONS STKS — 1m 2f 6y
7:40 (7:40) (Class 4) 3-Y-O+ — **£5,175** (£1,540; £769) **Stalls** Centre

Form — RPR

0 **1** **Red Napoleon (USA)**[40] 3164 4-10-0 0 ... OisinMurphy 3 — 85+
(Ralph Beckett) *stdd s: hld up in 3rd: rdn to ld over 1f out: drvn out* **2/7**[1]

3421 **2** ½ **The Gay Cavalier**[7] 4307 5-9-5 71 ... (t) JosephineGordon(3) 2 — 78
(John Ryan) *chsd clr ldr: led ent st tl over 1f out: rallied wl* **11/4**[2]

0 **3** 99 **Thecornishcavalier (IRE)**[15] 4017 3-8-5 0 ... JonathanFisher(7) 1
(John Ryan) *plld hrd: led: 7 l clr after 3f: wnt wd and hdd ent st: sn t.o* **33/1**[3]

2m 8.09s (-0.71) **Going Correction** +0.075s/f (Good)
WFA 3 from 4yo+ 10lb — 3 Ran SP% **107.4**
Speed ratings (Par 105): **105,104,25**
CSF £1.38 TOTE £1.30; EX 1.30 Trifecta £1.20.
Owner Mrs Ralph Beckett **Bred** Cali Holan **Trained** Kimpton, Hants

FOCUS
Add 28 yards to race distance. A poor turnout and a messy race. Suspect form.

4556 PARKWAY SHOPPING NEWBURY FILLIES' H'CAP — 1m (S)
8:10 (8:10) (Class 4) (0-85,85) 3-Y-O+ — **£4,690** (£1,395; £697; £348) **Stalls** High

Form — RPR

0-66 **1** **Peru**[69] 2220 3-9-2 **81** ... JamesDoyle 7 — 90
(Hugo Palmer) *chsd ldrs: led 2f out: rdn out* **4/1**[3]

1-10 **2** 1½ **Bright Flash**[68] 2236 4-9-11 **85** ... KieranShoemark(3) 6 — 92
(David Brown) *led tl 2f out: kpt on u.p* **14/1**

6131 **3** 2¾ **Bay Of St Malo (IRE)**[13] 4087 3-8-11 **76** ... SeanLevey 5 — 74
(Richard Hannon) *hld up: hdwy 2f out: one pce appr fnl f* **8/1**

1132 **4** 5 **Mukaabra**[15] 4028 3-9-1 **80** ... MartinHarley 2 — 66
(James Tate) *chsd ldr tl over 2f out: wknd over 1f out* **6/4**[1]

0-65 **5** 1¾ **Serradura (IRE)**[26] 3649 3-8-4 **69** ... SilvestreDeSousa 3 — 51
(Charles Hills) *t.k.h: chsd ldrs tl wknd 2f out* **16/1**

10-2 **6** 2¼ **Giveaway Glance**[41] 3107 3-9-0 **79** ... FergusSweeney 1 — 56
(Alan King) *stdd s: hld up in rr: effrt in centre 3f out: wknd wl over 1f out* **3/1**[2]

1m 40.53s (0.83) **Going Correction** +0.15s/f (Good)
WFA 3 from 4yo 8lb — 6 Ran SP% **108.7**
Speed ratings (Par 102): **101,99,96,91,90 87**
CSF £48.35 TOTE £4.60: £2.80, £3.00; EX 52.10 Trifecta £151.70.
Owner W J and T C O Gredley **Bred** Langton Stud **Trained** Newmarket, Suffolk

FOCUS
There was a muddling pace on in this fillies' handicap and two dominated the finish. An understandable pb from the winner.

4557 LODGE HOTEL AT NEWBURY RACECOURSE H'CAP — 7f (S)
8:45 (8:46) (Class 5) (0-75,75) 3-Y-O+ — **£3,234** (£962; £481; £240) **Stalls** High

Form — RPR

0005 **1** **Danecase**[14] 4058 3-9-5 **73** ... FergusSweeney 7 — 76+
(David Dennis) *hld up in rr: hdwy to ld 1f out: all out* **5/1**[2]

2331 **2** *shd* **Golden Wedding (IRE)**[14] 4058 4-9-12 **73** ... RobertWinston 3 — 79+
(Eve Johnson Houghton) *chsd ldrs: drvn level ins fnl f: r.o* **11/8**[1]

3-00 **3** 1 **Jan Steen (IRE)**[14] 4058 3-9-2 **70** ... OisinMurphy 8 — 70
(Denis Coakley) *hld up in 5th: rdn over 2f out: styd on fnl f* **10/1**[3]

0000 **4** ¾ **Firgrove Bridge (IRE)**[10] 4202 4-8-7 **57** ... (p) JosephineGordon(3) 5 — 58
(Steph Hollinshead) *dwlt: sn prom: led after 2f tl 1f out: kpt on same pce* **40/1**

62-5 **5** ½ **Poet's Song (IRE)**[54] 2698 3-9-7 **75** ... MartinDwyer 2 — 72
(Marcus Tregoning) *chsd ldrs: hrd rdn over 1f out: kpt on same pce* **5/1**[2]

003 **6** 1¾ **Oat Couture**[14] 4058 4-9-2 **63** ... DaneO'Neill 6 — 58
(Henry Candy) *dwlt: hld up in rr: rdn 2f out: no imp* **5/1**[2]

0050 **7** 9 **Popeswood (IRE)**[24] 3721 4-9-9 **75** ... HectorCrouch(5) 4 — 46
(Ron Hodges) *led for 2f: prom tl wknd over 2f out* **16/1**

1m 27.41s (1.71) **Going Correction** +0.15s/f (Good)
WFA 3 from 4yo 7lb — 7 Ran SP% **109.5**
Speed ratings (Par 103): **96,95,94,93,93 91,81**
CSF £11.24 CT £57.57 TOTE £5.40: £2.20, £1.20; EX 12.20 Trifecta £75.90.
Owner Favourites Racing (Syndication) Ltd 6 **Bred** D D & Mrs J P Clee **Trained** Hanley Swan, Worcestershire

FOCUS
This was a tactical affair but the form makes sense, the winner just reversing C&D form with the runner-up.
T/Plt: £16.90 to a £1 stake. Pool of £42993.72 - 1852.46 winning tickets. T/Qpdt: £10.40 to a £1 stake. Pool of £3751.12 - 266.16 winning tickets. **Lee McKenzie**

4531 SANDOWN (R-H)
Thursday, July 21

OFFICIAL GOING: Good to firm
Wind: Almost nil Weather: Fine but cloudy, warm

4558 IRISH STALLION FARMS EBF MAIDEN FILLIES' STKS (PLUS 10 RACE) — 5f 6y
2:00 (2:00) (Class 5) 2-Y-O — **£3,881** (£1,155; £577; £288) **Stalls** Low

Form — RPR

54 **1** **Night Law**[13] 4083 2-9-0 0 ... DavidProbert 6 — 76
(Andrew Balding) *fast away: mde virtually all and racd against far rail: shkn up 2f out: kpt on wl u.p fnl f to fend off rivals* **9/1**[3]

02 **2** *nk* **Her Terms**[44] 2990 2-9-0 0 ... SilvestreDeSousa 2 — 75
(William Haggas) *trckd ldng pair: chal on outer 2f out: drvn over 1f out: styd on but a hld: tk 2nd last strides* **10/11**[1]

224 **3** *shd* **Blue Suede (IRE)**[15] 4011 2-9-0 0 ... PatDobbs 9 — 75
(Richard Hannon) *t.k.h: w wnr: gng best 2f out: shkn up over 1f out: nt qckn fnl f and lost 2nd last strides* **7/2**[2]

05 **4** 3 **Halinka (IRE)**[40] 3122 2-9-0 0 ... FrederikTylicki 5 — 64+
(Roger Varian) *in tch: prog to chse ldng trio 2f out: pushed along and no imp fr over 1f out* **20/1**

5 1¼ **Dashing Poet** 2-9-0 0 ... LukeMorris 7 — 59+
(Jeremy Gask) *dwlt: mostly in last pair: pushed along 1/2-way: kpt on fnl f: n.d* **33/1**

00 **6** *nse* **Zumran**[85] 1783 2-9-0 0 ... JimCrowley 8 — 59
(Hugo Palmer) *chsd ldrs on outer: rdn 2f out: fdd over 1f out* **10/1**

7 1¼ **Heart Of Gold** 2-9-0 0 ... MartinDwyer 4 — 55
(William Muir) *slowly away: mostly in last: pushed along 2f out: nvr in it but kpt on fnl f: bttr for experience* **25/1**

8 2 **Darkroom Angel** 2-9-0 0 ... AdamKirby 3 — 47
(Clive Cox) *a towards rr: shkn up 2f out: no prog* **12/1**

6 **9** ½ **Newz Watch**[42] 3074 2-9-0 0 ... WilliamCarson 1 — 46
(Mick Quinn) *chsd ldrs against far rail: wknd over 1f out* **50/1**

1m 1.47s (-0.13) **Going Correction** -0.175s/f (Firm) — 9 Ran SP% **114.9**
Speed ratings (Par 91): **94,93,93,88,86 86,84,81,80**
CSF £17.02 TOTE £9.00: £1.80, £1.10, £1.70; EX 27.30 Trifecta £84.90.
Owner George Strawbridge **Bred** George Strawbridge **Trained** Kingsclere, Hants

FOCUS
There was watering after the previous day's racing, with 2.5mm applied to the home straight, back straight and sprint course. The sprint course rail was 4 yards in from the far side. An interesting enough fillies' maiden with the winner possibly favoured by racing against the rail. The bare form can't be worth much higher.

4559 CLAREMONT H'CAP — 1m 6f
2:30 (2:31) (Class 3) (0-90,90) 3-Y-O — **£7,439** (£2,213; £1,106; £553) **Stalls** Low

Form — RPR

3-1 **1** **Parliamentarian (IRE)**[28] 3550 3-9-0 **83** ... JamesDoyle 2 — 92
(Charlie Appleby) *in tch: pushed along in last pl over 4f out: effrt u.p on outer over 2f out: chsd ldr over 1f out: clsng to chal whn hmpd sn after: rallied fnl f to ld last stride* **7/1**

2121 **2** *shd* **St Michel**[9] 4230 3-8-13 **82** 6ex ... LukeMorris 5 — 90
(Sir Mark Prescott Bt) *plld way through to ld after 2f: rdn over 2f out: hung lft u.p over 1f out: kpt on fnl f: hdd last stride* **8/13**[1]

3621 **3** 2¼ **Stetchworth Park**[15] 4001 3-8-9 **78** ... (p) DavidProbert 1 — 83
(Michael Bell) *trckd ldr 2f: styd wl in tch: rdn to chse ldr 2f out to over 1f out: kpt on same pce fnl f* **11/2**[2]

0-00 **4** 10 **Ocean Jive**[35] 3300 3-9-0 **90** ... JordanUys(7) 3 — 81
(Brian Meehan) *plld way through to trckd ldr after 3f: lost 2nd over 4f out: wknd u.p 2f out* **20/1**

1332 **5** 6 **October Storm**[43] 3025 3-8-8 **77** ... SilvestreDeSousa 4 — 65
(Mick Channon) *led 2f: styd cl up: chsd ldr over 4f out to 2f out: sn wknd: eased fnl f* **6/1**[3]

3m 2.38s (-2.12) **Going Correction** +0.025s/f (Good) — 5 Ran SP% **108.9**
Speed ratings (Par 104): **107,106,105,99,96**
CSF £11.76 TOTE £6.00: £2.40, £1.30; EX 11.70 Trifecta £38.90.
Owner Godolphin **Bred** Darley **Trained** Newmarket, Suffolk
■ Stewards' Enquiry : James Doyle two-day ban: used whip above permitted level (Aug 4-5)

FOCUS
The round course rail was out from 1m to the false rail at 2.5 furlong mark - adding 24 yards to all round course distances. A decent staying handicap for 3yos with the favourite nailed late on. The form is rated around the runner-up.

4560 LONGINES IRISH CHAMPIONS WEEKEND EBF STALLIONS STAR STKS (LISTED RACE) (FILLIES) 7f 16y
3:05 (3:05) (Class 1) 2-Y-O
£17,013 (£6,450; £3,228; £1,608; £807; £405) **Stalls** Low

Form RPR
311 **1** **On Her Toes (IRE)**[16] 3977 2-9-0 0 .... FrankieDettori 8 98+
(William Haggas) *trckd ldr: shkn up to ld jst over 2f out: pressed after but asserted fnl f: rdn out* **5/2**[1]
1 **2** ¾ **Calare (IRE)**[39] 3186 2-9-0 0 .... JamesDoyle 6 96
(Charlie Appleby) *shoved along to get gng early and in last pair: rdn and prog 2f out: styd on to take 2nd last 100yds: a readily hld by wnr* **5/2**[1]
110 **3** nk **Grizzel (IRE)**[34] 3336 2-9-0 0 .... PatDobbs 5 96
(Richard Hannon) *hld up in tch: nt clr run 3f out to 2f out: prog on outer over 1f out: styd on to press for 2nd nr fin* **4/1**[2]
11 **4** ¾ **Urban Fox**[22] 3782 2-9-0 0 .... MartinHarley 3 93
(James Tate) *hld up: nudged by rival 3f out: prog on outer after to take 2nd 2f out and pressed wnr: hld 1f out: lost 2nd and one pce last 100yds* **4/1**[2]
510 **5** 2 ½ **High On Love (IRE)**[34] 3336 2-9-0 0 .... StevieDonohoe 4 86
(Charlie Fellowes) *trckd ldrs: rdn over 2f out: dropped to last and wl btn over 1f out: kpt on again nr fin* **25/1**
412 **6** ½ **Hellofahaste**[26] 3663 2-9-0 0 .... FrederikTylicki 2 85
(Rod Millman) *led to jst over 2f out: fdd over 1f out* **9/1**[3]

1m 31.86s (2.36) **Going Correction** +0.025s/f (Good) **6** Ran SP% **111.0**
Speed ratings (Par 99): **87,86,85,84,82 81**
CSF £8.66 TOTE £2.70: £1.50, £2.40; EX 9.10 Trifecta £22.50.
Owner Cheveley Park Stud **Bred** Knocklong House Stud **Trained** Newmarket, Suffolk
FOCUS
Round course rail out from 1m to the false rail at 2.5 furlong mark - adding 24 yards to all round course distances. Probably just ordinary form for the grade, rated around the progressive winner.

4561 EBM-PAPST H'CAP 1m 2f 7y
3:40 (3:40) (Class 4) (0-85,85) 3-Y-O+ **£4,690** (£1,395; £697; £348) **Stalls** Low

Form RPR
3032 **1** **Goodwood Mirage (IRE)**[7] 4300 6-10-0 **85** .... FrankieDettori 6 93
(Michael Bell) *trckd ldng pair: shkn up and clsd to ld over 1f out: hrd pressed ins fnl f: hld on wl nr fin* **11/2**
3412 **2** hd **Paling**[41] 3102 3-8-12 **79** .... WilliamTwiston-Davies 7 86
(Roger Charlton) *awkward and stdd s: hld up in 7th and off a str pce: gng easily 3f out: pushed along and prog 2f out: chsd wnr 1f out: str chal last 150yds: styd on but jst hld* **3/1**[2]
5-16 **3** 1 ¼ **Natural Scenery**[19] 3914 3-9-0 **81** .... JamesDoyle 8 86
(Saeed bin Suroor) *hld up off the pce in 6th: shkn up on outer wl over 2f out: prog and clsd on ldrs jst over 1f out: styd on same pce fnl f* **9/2**[3]
-551 **4** shd **Compton Mill**[27] 3617 4-9-6 **77** .... (t) GeorgeBaker 3 82
(Hughie Morrison) *trckd ldng trio: rdn and tried to cl on inner fr 2f out: styd on same pce fnl f* **12/1**
4200 **5** 1 **Croquembouche (IRE)**[13] 4115 7-9-11 **85** .... JosephineGordon[(3)] 5 88
(Ed de Giles) *rousted to ld: set str pce but pressed: rdn over 2f out: hdd over 1f out: fdd fnl f* **16/1**
1515 **6** 1 ½ **Daisy Boy (IRE)**[84] 1802 5-9-6 **82** .... (t) AaronJones[(5)] 1 82
(Stuart Williams) *pressed ldr at str pce: rdn over 2f out: lost 2nd over 1f out: steadily wknd* **20/1**
7 nk **Stanley (GER)**[60] 5-9-4 **75** .... AdamKirby 2 74
(Jonjo O'Neill) *restrained after s: hld up in last and off str pce: reminders fr 2f out: no significant prog and nvr involved* **33/1**
5042 **8** 1 ¾ **Juste Pour Nous**[5] 4406 3-8-13 **80** .... FrannyNorton 4 76
(Mark Johnston) *hld up off the pce in 5th: shkn up and no prog 3f out: wl btn over 1f out: wknd* **9/4**[1]

2m 8.38s (-2.12) **Going Correction** +0.025s/f (Good)
WFA 3 from 4yo+ 10lb **8** Ran SP% **110.6**
Speed ratings (Par 105): **109,108,107,107,106 105,105,104**
CSF £20.86 CT £75.28 TOTE £5.50: £1.90, £1.40, £1.50; EX 20.80 Trifecta £80.60.
Owner Lady Bamford & Alice Bamford **Bred** Mrs Chris Harrington **Trained** Newmarket, Suffolk
FOCUS
Round course rail out from 1m to the false rail at 2.5 furlong mark - adding 24 yards to all round course distances. A well-run handicap, in which there seemed to be no excuses for any of those beaten. The winner backed up his latest Doncaster form.

4562 GOOD LUCK RUPERT TREVELYAN H'CAP 1m 14y
4:10 (4:10) (Class 5) (0-75,75) 3-Y-O **£3,234** (£962; £481; £240) **Stalls** Low

Form RPR
0330 **1** **Jimenez (IRE)**[14] 4055 3-9-7 **75** .... (p) JimmyFortune 2 84
(Brian Meehan) *trckd ldrs: rdn over 1f out: clsd against rail to ld last 150yds: drvn out* **11/2**[3]
-045 **2** 1 ¼ **Dream Of Summer (IRE)**[14] 4048 3-9-5 **73** .... DavidProbert 10 79
(Andrew Balding) *t.k.h: trckd ldr: led jst over 2f out: drvn over 1f out: hdd last 150yds: one pce* **9/2**[1]
0341 **3** 1 **Cooperess**[8] 4269 3-7-13 **56** 6ex .... (bt) JosephineGordon[(3)] 8 60
(Ali Stronge) *hld up bhd ldrs: rdn to go cl up 2f out: styd on one pce u.p fr over 1f out* **9/2**[1]
5563 **4** nk **Silhouette (IRE)**[13] 4088 3-9-3 **71** .... TimmyMurphy 1 74+
(Daniel Kubler) *hld up in 7th: shkn up on outer over 2f out: no significant prog tl styd on fr over 1f out to take 4th nr fin* **8/1**
0-60 **5** 1 ¼ **Free Passage**[34] 3357 3-8-9 **63** .... FergusSweeney 7 63
(Henry Candy) *t.k.h: hld up in midfield: rdn and nt qckn over 2f out: nvr on terms after: kpt on ins fnl f* **7/1**
0001 **6** nk **Furiant**[17] 3952 3-9-4 **72** .... FrannyNorton 6 71
(Mark Johnston) *led: shkn up and hdd jst over 2f out: styd cl up tl fdd ins fnl f* **5/1**[2]
4352 **7** nk **Multigifted**[12] 4159 3-8-5 **59** .... RyanTate 9 58
(Michael Madgwick) *t.k.h: sn prom: rdn over 2f out: sn lost pl: n.d over 1f out* **16/1**
4150 **8** ½ **Aldair**[59] 2545 3-9-3 **71** .... PatDobbs 3 69
(Richard Hannon) *hld up in 8th: pushed along fr over 2f out: no real prog and nvr involved* **13/2**
0-54 **9** 7 **Graceful Lady**[179] 325 3-8-6 **60** .... WilliamCarson 4 42
(Robert Eddery) *dwlt: a in last: bhd fnl 2f* **25/1**

1m 43.59s (0.29) **Going Correction** +0.025s/f (Good) **9** Ran SP% **115.1**
Speed ratings (Par 100): **99,97,96,96,95 94,94,94,87**
CSF £30.35 CT £121.23 TOTE £6.80: £1.60, £2.00, £1.80; EX 38.80 Trifecta £169.80.
Owner Manton Thoroughbreds **Bred** Rathbarry Stud **Trained** Manton, Wilts
FOCUS
Round course rail out from 1m to the false rail at 2.5 furlong mark - adding 24 yards to all round course distances. A moderate 3yo handicap run at an honest pace. It lacked progressive types.

4563 LUBRICATORS H'CAP 7f 16y
4:45 (4:45) (Class 5) (0-75,75) 3-Y-O+ **£3,234** (£962; £481; £240) **Stalls** Low

Form RPR
0-00 **1** **Able Jack**[15] 4010 3-9-7 **75** .... (v[1]) DavidProbert 1 85
(Andrew Balding) *trckd ldng pair: clsd fr 2f out: drvn to ld 1f out: styd on wl* **7/1**[2]
4-12 **2** 1 ¼ **Tripartite (IRE)**[28] 3554 3-9-3 **71** .... LukeMorris 3 78
(Jeremy Gask) *trckd ldr: rdn 2f out and sn dropped to 3rd: renewed effrt to chal 1f out: styd on but readily hld last 150yds* **1/1**[1]
-000 **3** 3 **Sarangoo**[13] 4086 8-9-10 **74** .... JosephineGordon[(3)] 4 76
(Malcolm Saunders) *t.k.h: led at gd pce and stretched field: rdn 2f out: hdd 1f out: wl hld after but clr in 3rd* **16/1**
64-6 **4** 2 **Many Dreams (IRE)**[16] 3974 3-8-12 **66** .... SteveDrowne 8 60
(Mark Usher) *hld up off the pce in 7th: prog 2f out: tk 4th 1f out but nt on terms: one pce* **12/1**
0-56 **5** 4 ½ **Heart Of An Angel**[55] 2653 3-8-13 **70** .... LouisSteward[(3)] 6 51
(Philip McBride) *hld up in 5th: clsd 3f out: rdn and lft bhd 2f out: no ch after* **8/1**[3]
051 **6** shd **False Id**[23] 3740 3-9-0 **68** .... (t) WilliamCarson 5 49
(Robert Eddery) *chsd ldng trio: rdn over 2f out: steadily wknd and no ch over 1f out* **7/1**[2]
0060 **7** ½ **The Big Lad**[15] 4014 4-10-0 **75** .... ShaneKelly 2 58
(Richard Hughes) *hld up in 6th: shkn up over 2f out: lft wl bhd over 1f out: kpt on nr fin* **8/1**[3]
-600 **8** 7 **Musical Taste**[21] 3803 3-8-13 **67** .... TimmyMurphy 7 28
(Pat Phelan) *hld up in last: shkn up and no prog over 2f out: wl bhd fnl f* **33/1**

1m 29.4s (-0.10) **Going Correction** +0.025s/f (Good)
WFA 3 from 4yo+ 7lb **8** Ran SP% **113.7**
Speed ratings (Par 103): **101,99,96,93,88 88,88,80**
CSF £14.26 CT £109.04 TOTE £6.30: £1.70, £1.10, £4.20; EX 16.80 Trifecta £162.70.
Owner Happy Valley Racing & Breeding Limited **Bred** Usk Valley Stud **Trained** Kingsclere, Hants
FOCUS
Round course rail out from 1m to the false rail at 2.5 furlong mark - adding 24 yards to all round course distances. A modest finale with favourite backers denied by a revitalised winner. The pace held up and the winner improved.
T/Plt: £7.10 to a £1 stake. Pool of £62705.13 - 6360.78 winning tickets. T/Qpdt: £5.60 to a £1 stake. Pool of £5022.53- 655.46 winning tickets. **Jonathan Neesom**

4274 YARMOUTH (L-H)
Thursday, July 21

OFFICIAL GOING: Good to firm
Wind: Fresh behind Weather: Fine

4564 D O'KANE FINANCIAL SERVICES MAIDEN AUCTION STKS (PLUS 10 RACE) 6f 3y
2:10 (2:11) (Class 4) 2-Y-O **£4,657** (£1,386; £692; £346) **Stalls** Centre

Form RPR
53 **1** **Pranceleya (IRE)**[19] 3902 2-8-13 0 .... LiamJones 9 75
(Marco Botti) *wnt rt s: sn prom: chsd ldr 2f out: sn rdn and edgd lft: led wl ins fnl f: jst hld on* **10/3**[2]
2 **2** shd **Grey Britain**[15] 4016 2-9-4 0 .... JackMitchell 2 80
(John Ryan) *prom: pushed along over 3f out: sn outpcd: hdwy u.p over 1f out: r.o* **7/4**[1]
04 **3** 1 ¾ **Sir Viktor (IRE)**[19] 3872 2-9-0 0 .... (v[1]) DougieCostello 4 70
(K R Burke) *led: clr over 3f out tl rdn and edgd lft over 1f out: hdd and no ex wl ins fnl f* **11/2**[3]
4 1 ½ **Ejabah (IRE)** 2-8-13 0 .... TedDurcan 7 64
(Chris Wall) *hld up: shkn up over 2f out: r.o ins fnl f: nvr nrr* **9/1**
4 **5** 1 **Cape Falcone**[10] 4209 2-8-13 0 .... PatCosgrave 1 61
(James Tate) *prom: rdn over 1f out: styd on same pce fnl f* **11/2**[3]
6 4 ½ **Oakley Pride (IRE)** 2-8-11 0 .... AdrianMcCarthy 6 45
(Gay Kelleway) *chsd ldrs: rdn over 2f out: wknd fnl f* **28/1**
6 **7** 6 **Sadieroseclifford (IRE)**[17] 3947 2-8-3 0 .... TimClark[(3)] 5 20
(Denis Quinn) *chsd ldr tl rdn over 2f out: wknd over 1f out* **25/1**
503 **8** 4 **Secret Ballerina**[66] 2289 2-8-6 0 .... AdamBeschizza 8 8
(Julia Feilden) *s.i.s: sn pushed along in rr: rdn and wknd over 2f out* **28/1**

1m 11.16s (-3.24) **Going Correction** -0.775s/f (Hard) **8** Ran SP% **111.0**
Speed ratings (Par 96): **90,89,87,85,84 78,70,64**
CSF £8.91 TOTE £5.20: £1.60, £1.20, £1.50; EX 10.10 Trifecta £39.50.
Owner Isa Al-Khalifa **Bred** Tally-Ho Stud **Trained** Newmarket, Suffolk
FOCUS
Plenty of previous winners of this have gone on to be at least useful types, so this could be above-average form. The winner may not quite have needed to replicate her latest effort.

4565 YARMOUTH AND CAISTER GOLF PRO SHOP MAIDEN FILLIES' STKS 6f 3y
2:40 (2:41) (Class 5) 3-4-Y-O **£3,622** (£1,078; £538; £269) **Stalls** Centre

Form RPR
42-4 **1** **Gale Song**[24] 3714 3-9-0 77 .... DougieCostello 6 79+
(Ed Walker) *led: hdd over 4f out: led again over 2f out: rdn and hung lft ins fnl f: r.o* **10/11**[1]
6 **2** ½ **Soundstrings**[20] 3850 3-9-0 0 .... PatCosgrave 2 77+
(William Haggas) *trckd ldrs: racd keenly: chsd wnr over 1f out: rdn and ev ch whn edgd lft ins fnl f: r.o* **6/4**[2]
04 **3** 2 ½ **Atalante**[24] 3720 3-9-0 0 .... TedDurcan 1 69
(Andrew Balding) *hld up: racd keenly: hdwy over 2f out: rdn ins fnl f: styd on same pce* **8/1**[3]
4 4 **Pearly Queen** 3-8-11 0 ....[1] JackDuern[(3)] 7 57
(Dean Ivory) *prom: outpcd over 3f out: n.d after: nt clr run over 1f out* **20/1**
0 **5** 3 ½ **Rebel Sky**[56] 2606 3-9-0 0 .... TomQueally 8 45
(J R Jenkins) *s.i.s: sn prom: rdn over 2f out: wknd over 1f out* **66/1**
-0 **6** 2 ¼ **Cytringan**[20] 3850 3-8-11 0 .... SimonPearce[(3)] 3 38
(Lydia Pearce) *plld hrd and prom: stdd and lost pl after 1f: nvr on terms afterwards* **100/1**

The Form Book, Raceform Ltd, Newbury, RG14 5SJ

00 **7** *3* **Ms Arsenal**[28] 3572 4-8-12 0 GeorgeWood(7) 4 30
(Giles Bravery) *racd keenly: prom: led over 4f out: rdn and hdd over 2f out: wknd over 1f out* **50/1**

1m 10.3s (-4.10) **Going Correction** -0.775s/f (Hard)
WFA 3 from 4yo 5lb **7** Ran SP% **112.7**
Speed ratings (Par 100): **96,95,92,86,82 79,75**
CSF £2.39 TOTE £1.80: £1.10, £1.90; EX 2.70 Trifecta £5.50.
Owner Lordship Stud **Bred** Michael E Wates **Trained** Upper Lambourn, Berks

FOCUS
Two of these stood out in the betting and they battled it out in the latter stages. The time was relatively good.

4566 BURLINGTON PALM HOTEL AT GREAT YARMOUTH H'CAP 1m 3f 104y
3:15 (3:15) (Class 5) (0-70,70) 3-Y-O+ **£2,911** (£866; £432; £216) **Stalls** Low

Form RPR

1244 **1** **Sexy Secret**[27] 3620 5-8-9 **54** (p) SimonPearce(3) 1 58
(Lydia Pearce) *mde all: set stdy pce tl rdn: qcknd and jnd over 3f out: styd on gamely u.p* **7/1**

6-33 **2** *nk* **Kaisan**[149] 687 3-9-3 **70** (p) JamieSpencer 6 73
(Michael Bell) *trckd wnr tl wnt upsides over 3f out: rdn and ev ch ins fnl f: nt qckn towards fin* **13/8**[1]

-063 **3** *nk* **Unsuspected Girl (IRE)**[8] 4275 3-7-7 **53** oh1 SophieKilloran(7) 2 56
(David Simcock) *s.s: hdwy and nt clr run fr over 2f out: r.o* **7/2**[3]

1544 **4** *nk* **Dakota City**[8] 4277 5-9-13 **69** (v) AdamBeschizza 5 72
(Julia Feilden) *chsd ldrs: nt clr run fr over 1f out tl swtchd rt wl ins fnl f: r.o* **5/2**[2]

160- **5** *1 1/2* **Kirtling**[295] 6871 5-9-7 **63** (t) MartinLane 3 63
(Andi Brown) *s.i.s: hld up: hdwy over 3f out: rdn over 1f out: styd on same pce ins fnl f* **14/1**

2m 34.14s (5.44) **Going Correction** +0.025s/f (Good)
WFA 3 from 5yo 11lb **5** Ran SP% **108.1**
Speed ratings (Par 103): **81,80,80,80,79**
CSF £18.21 TOTE £5.00: £2.60, £1.60; EX 20.70 Trifecta £56.30.
Owner Personal Racehorse Owners 1 **Bred** W G H Barrons **Trained** Newmarket, Suffolk

FOCUS
This remained a tight handicap even after likely favourite Zain Arion came out. The form is not worth a great deal, however, as the early pace was really slow and the time was 10.64 seconds slower than Racing Post standard.

4567 GREENE KING FESTIVAL IN SEPTEMBER H'CAP 1m 2f 23y
3:50 (3:51) (Class 6) (0-60,58) 3-Y-O+ **£2,264** (£673; £336; £168) **Stalls** Low

Form RPR

0-05 **1** **Pacharana**[29] 3509 3-9-3 **57** JamieSpencer 11 66+
(Luca Cumani) *hld up: hdwy over 2f out: led and edgd lft fr over 1f out: drvn out* **1/1**[1]

000- **2** *1 1/2* **Hope Is High**[220] 8225 3-8-5 **45** AdamBeschizza 9 50+
(John Berry) *hld up: hdwy over 1f out: r.o to go 2nd wl ins fnl f: nt rch wnr* **14/1**

-346 **3** *1 1/4* **Overlord**[10] 4214 4-9-13 **57** AndrewMullen 6 60
(Mark Rimell) *hld up in tch: tk clsr order over 2f out: rdn and ev ch over 1f out: carried lft: styd on same pce ins fnl f* **6/1**[2]

0-03 **4** *3/4* **My Mistress (IRE)**[15] 4024 4-8-13 **50** GeorgeWood(7) 3 53
(Phil McEntee) *prom: nt clr run over 2f out: rdn and hmpd over 1f: styd on* **20/1**

0000 **5** *1/2* **Kay Sera**[15] 3997 8-9-8 **55** EoinWalsh(3) 10 56
(Tony Newcombe) *s.i.s: sn chsng ldrs: led over 2f out: rdn and hdd over 1f out: carried lft: no ex ins fnl f* **7/1**

50-0 **6** *6* **Royal Mighty**[49] 2829 3-8-8 **48** DannyBrock 4 40
(Jane Chapple-Hyam) *racd keenly in 2nd pl tl led over 3f out: rdn and hdd over 2f out: hmpd over 1f out: wknd ins fnl f* **20/1**

4404 **7** *2 3/4* **Bazzat (IRE)**[10] 4204 3-8-5 **45** (p) RyanPowell 8 29
(John Ryan) *broke wl: n.m.r and lost pl after 1f: effrt over 2f out: wknd over 1f out* **13/2**[3]

00-0 **8** *2 1/4* **Victoriously**[63] 2397 4-9-7 **54** (tp) NoelGarbutt(3) 7 34
(Andi Brown) *hld up: rdn over 2f out: wknd wl over 1f out* **66/1**

6600 **9** *5* **Little Flo**[23] 3737 5-9-1 **45** (t) DougieCostello 1 15
(William Stone) *sn led: rdn and hdd over 3f out: n.m.r over 2f out: sn wknd* **40/1**

003 **10** *1* **Ginger Charlie**[18] 3919 3-8-5 **45** JamesSullivan 5 13
(Ruth Carr) *prom: rdn over 3f out: edgd lft over 2f out: wknd over 1f out* **25/1**

2m 8.65s (-1.85) **Going Correction** +0.025s/f (Good)
WFA 3 from 4yo+ 10lb **10** Ran SP% **114.1**
Speed ratings (Par 101): **108,106,105,105,104 100,97,96,92,91**
CSF £14.92 CT £59.36 TOTE £1.90: £1.02, £3.90, £2.40; EX 17.40 Trifecta £91.20.
Owner S Stuckey **Bred** Stuart Stuckey **Trained** Newmarket, Suffolk

FOCUS
A really weak race, in which the market leader was all the rage in the betting. The winner can go in again.

4568 MOULTON NURSERIES OF ACLE H'CAP 1m 1f 21y
4:25 (4:29) (Class 5) (0-75,75) 3-Y-O+ **£2,911** (£866; £432; £216) **Stalls** Low

Form RPR

0520 **1** **Thecornishbarron (IRE)**[7] 4302 4-9-8 **72** JackMitchell 5 80
(John Ryan) *mde all: rdn over 1f out: styd on: eased nr fin* **13/2**[3]

645 **2** *1/2* **Sahara (IRE)**[24] 3721 4-9-10 **74** TedDurcan 2 81+
(Chris Wall) *hld up: rdn over 2f out: r.o to go 2nd wl ins fnl f: nt rch wnr* **9/4**[2]

1435 **3** *2 3/4* **Jive Time**[24] 3728 3-9-2 **75** PatCosgrave 1 75
(James Tate) *chsd ldrs: rdn over 3f out: wnt 2nd 2f out tl styd on same pce wl ins fnl f* **2/1**[1]

20-0 **4** *1* **Amazing Charm**[21] 3823 4-9-0 **67** [1] EoinWalsh(3) 4 66
(James Tate) *s.i.s: hld up: shkn up and hung lft over 2f out: styd on ins fnl f: nvr nrr* **20/1**

0100 **5** *1* **Artful Prince**[15] 4026 6-9-4 **73** (b) NathanEvans(5) 7 69
(James Given) *chsd wnr tl rdn 2f out: nt run on* **7/1**

05 **6** *1 3/4* **Toga Tiger (IRE)**[55] 2662 9-9-10 **74** LiamJones 6 67
(Kevin Frost) *hld up: hdwy over 3f out: rdn over 2f out: wknd fnl f* **10/1**

0005 **7** *4 1/2* **U S Navy Seal (USA)**[36] 3276 4-9-10 **74** TomQueally 3 57
(J R Jenkins) *prom: rdn over 2f out: wknd over 1f out* **16/1**

1m 55.2s (-0.60) **Going Correction** +0.025s/f (Good)
WFA 3 from 4yo+ 9lb **7** Ran SP% **109.7**
Speed ratings (Par 103): **103,102,100,99,98 96,92**
CSF £19.76 TOTE £6.00: £2.00, £1.90; EX 24.70 Trifecta £73.00.
Owner C Letcher & J Ryan **Bred** Ms Geraldine Regan **Trained** Newmarket, Suffolk

FOCUS
This looked a fair handicap but the slow early tempo meant the winner could set a pace to suit and do enough to hold on. Therefore, this isn't form to trust. The winner rates a small pb.

4569 HAVEN SEASHORE HOLIDAY PARK H'CAP 6f 3y
4:55 (4:56) (Class 4) (0-85,85) 3-Y-O+ **£4,690** (£1,395; £697; £348) **Stalls** Centre

Form RPR

3-01 **1** **Fang**[16] 3976 3-9-2 **80** (t) JamieSpencer 2 86
(William Jarvis) *mde all: brought the field over to the stands' side over 4f out: shkn up over 1f out: r.o: comf* **6/1**[3]

0065 **2** *1/2* **Ballymore Castle (IRE)**[16] 3980 4-9-12 **85** (p) JackGarritty 5 91+
(Richard Fahey) *hld up: swtchd lft and hdwy over 1f out: rdn to go 2nd wl ins fnl f: nt rch wnr* **3/1**[2]

-055 **3** *1/2* **Bahamian Heights**[14] 4051 5-8-12 **78** [1] GeorgeWood(7) 1 82
(Robert Cowell) *a.p: chsd wnr over 1f out: sn rdn: styd on* **9/1**

0223 **4** *nk* **Cosmic Chatter**[23] 3753 6-9-3 **76** (p) JamesSullivan 6 79
(Ruth Carr) *chsd wnr tl rdn over 1f out: styng on whn nt clr run wl ins fnl f* **11/1**

4462 **5** *4 1/2* **Hope Cove**[13] 4086 3-9-6 **84** (p) AntonioFresu 3 72
(Ed Walker) *chsd ldrs: rdn over 1f out: styd on same pce* **13/2**

132 **6** *3 1/4* **Tarboosh**[12] 4134 3-9-4 **82** (p) PatCosgrave 4 59
(William Haggas) *hld up: rdn over 1f out: wknd ins fnl f* **6/4**[1]

1m 10.45s (-3.95) **Going Correction** -0.775s/f (Hard)
WFA 3 from 4yo+ 5lb **6** Ran SP% **111.0**
Speed ratings (Par 105): **95,94,93,93,87 82**
CSF £23.58 TOTE £5.70: £2.50, £1.70; EX 23.60 Trifecta £135.50.
Owner David Batten **Bred** Kincorth Investments Inc **Trained** Newmarket, Suffolk

FOCUS
Probably a decent race for the level, and it was taken by one of the 3yos in the line-up. The whole field shifted right coming out of the stalls and made for the stands' rail.

4570 DRIFTERS FISH AND CHIPS ALL EVENTS H'CAP 6f 3y
5:25 (5:25) (Class 6) (0-60,60) 3-Y-O+ **£2,264** (£673; £336; £168) **Stalls** Centre

Form RPR

6002 **1** **Chetan**[8] 4278 4-9-6 **56** (tp) AdamBeschizza 3 68
(Charlie Wallis) *racd centre: led that gp: edgd rt over 2f out: rdn to ld overall 1f out: r.o: 1st of 4 in gp* **11/4**[2]

0561 **2** *1* **Generalyse**[7] 4321 7-8-12 **55** (b) JoshuaBryan(7) 8 64
(Anabel K Murphy) *overall ldr stands' side: rdn and hdd 1f out: styd on same pce wl ins fnl f: 1st of 4 in gp* **2/1**[1]

1006 **3** *2* **Tulip Dress**[8] 4278 3-9-4 **59** JamieSpencer 7 60
(Anthony Carson) *racd stands' side: hld up: hdwy over 1f out: rdn: nt clr run and swtchd lft ins fnl f: styd on same pce: 2nd of 4 in gp* **8/1**

4000 **4** *1 1/2* **Mambo Spirit (IRE)**[29] 3510 12-9-3 **56** EoinWalsh(3) 2 54
(Tony Newcombe) *racd centre: hld up: swtchd stands' side over 4f out: hdwy over 1f out: styd on same pce ins fnl f: 3rd of 4 in gp* **13/2**

6605 **5** *1/2* **Justice Rock**[8] 4280 3-8-7 **55** GeorgeWood(7) 9 50
(Phil McEntee) *w ldr stands' side tl rdn wl over 1f out: no ex fnl f: last of 4 in gp* **18/1**

0-0 **6** *3* **Caribbean Spring (IRE)**[21] 3823 3-8-12 **60** JaneElliott(7) 6 45
(George Margarson) *racd centre: chsd ldrs: rdn over 2f out: wknd over 1f out: 2nd of 4 in gp* **11/1**

0151 **7** *1 1/4* **Hab Reeh**[17] 3941 8-9-5 **55** (p) JamesSullivan 5 37
(Ruth Carr) *racd centre: prom: rdn over 2f out: wknd over 1f out: 3rd of 4 in gp* **6/1**[3]

000 **8** *shd* **Cecile Royale**[37] 3267 3-7-12 **46** oh1 MillyNaseb(7) 1 27
(Stuart Williams) *racd centre: sn pushed along in rr: rdn over 2f out: wknd over 1f out: last of 4 in gp* **33/1**

1m 11.59s (-2.81) **Going Correction** -0.775s/f (Hard)
WFA 3 from 4yo+ 5lb **8** Ran SP% **115.3**
Speed ratings (Par 101): **87,85,83,81,80 76,74,74**
CSF £8.76 CT £37.53 TOTE £3.40: £1.80, £1.10, £2.00; EX 8.80 Trifecta £49.30.
Owner Roger & Val Miles, Tony Stamp **Bred** Andrew W Robson **Trained** Ardleigh, Essex

FOCUS
The field split early but the race took shape down the stands' rail in the final stages. Those who remained reasonably central made little impression. This rates a slightly better effort from the winner.
T/Plt: £15.60 to a £1 stake. Pool of £48824.0 - 2279.78 winning tickets. T/Qpdt: £19.50 to a £1 stake. Pool of £3767.24 - 142.84 winning tickets. **Colin Roberts**

4571 - 4572a (Foreign Racing) - See Raceform Interactive

4322 LEOPARDSTOWN (L-H)
Thursday, July 21

OFFICIAL GOING: Good to firm

4573a JOCKEY CLUB OF TURKEY SILVER FLASH STKS (GROUP 3) 7f
7:00 (7:01) 2-Y-O
£26,029 (£8,382; £3,970; £1,764; £882; £441)

RPR

1 **Promise To Be True (IRE)**[21] 3831 2-9-0 0 RyanMoore 2 105+
(A P O'Brien, Ire) *hld up: 5th at 1/2-way: niggled along over 2f out: qcknd wl between horses ent fnl f to ld fnl 150yds: styd on wl: comf* **4/6**[1]

2 *1 1/4* **Take A Deep Breath**[18] 3926 2-9-0 0 PatSmullen 1 102
(M D O'Callaghan, Ire) *chsd ldrs in 3rd: pushed along in 4th over 2f out: styd on wl to ld 1f out: sn hdd: kpt on wl* **5/1**[2]

3 *nse* **Intricately (IRE)**[32] 3440 2-9-0 0 DonnachaO'Brien 3 101
(Joseph Patrick O'Brien, Ire) *hld up: 4th at 1/2-way: clsr in 3rd over 2f out: rdn in 4th over 1f out: kpt on same pce into 3rd fnl 100yds* **7/1**[3]

4 *2* **Drumfad Bay (IRE)**[29] 3536 2-9-0 0 ColmO'Donoghue 5 96
(Mrs John Harrington, Ire) *sn chsd ldr in 2nd: pressed ldr home turn and led under 2f out: hdd 1f out: no ex and dropped to 4th fnl 100yds* **20/1**

5 *hd* **Brooklyn's Rose (IRE)**[14] 4067 2-9-0 0 ColinKeane 4 96
(G M Lyons, Ire) *racd in rr: pushed along over 2f out: kpt on wl on outer fnl f into 5th ins fnl 100yds: nvr nrr* **20/1**

6 *3 1/2* **Oh Grace (IRE)**[34] 3336 2-9-0 99 (p) KevinManning 7 86
(J S Bolger, Ire) *led: strly pressed home turn and hdd under 2f out: wknd appr fnl f* **7/1**[3]

1m 28.83s (0.13) **6** Ran SP% **111.2**
CSF £4.28 TOTE £1.50: £1.02, £2.20; DF 4.60 Trifecta £9.50.
Owner Mrs John Magnier & Michael Tabor & Derrick Smith **Bred** Orpendale, Chelston & Wynatt **Trained** Cashel, Co Tipperary

FOCUS
This looked a fascinating renewal. The entire field had won their maidens. The gallop was good and the odds-on favourite did what she had to do. You sense we have not seen the best of her yet. Those in behind the winner will dictate the long-term level of the race.

4574a JAPAN RACING ASSOCIATION TYROS STKS (GROUP 3) 7f
7:35 (7:37) 2-Y-O

£26,029 (£8,382; £3,970; £1,764; £882; £441)

RPR

1 **Churchill (IRE)**[33] 3382 2-9-3 0 .... RyanMoore 1 106+
(A P O'Brien, Ire) *chsd ldrs in 3rd on inner: momentarily short of room under 2f out: sn chsd ldr in 2nd: led ent fnl f and sn strly pressed: kpt on wl in clsng stages* **2/5**[1]

2 *nk* **Alexios Komnenos (IRE)**[25] 3691 2-9-3 0 .... WayneLordan 3 105+
(T Stack, Ire) *racd in rr: c wd under 2f out: styd on strly to press ldr in 2nd ins fnl f: wandered and edgd lft ins fnl 100yds: hld cl home* **8/1**[3]

3 *2* **Currency Converter (USA)**[42] 3082 2-9-3 0 .... PatSmullen 5 100
(D K Weld, Ire) *chsd ldrs towards outer: rdn in 3rd whn sltly hmpd 2f out: dropped to 4th 1f out: rallied wl into 3rd whn hmpd ins fnl 100yds: no ex w principals cl home* **7/1**[2]

4 *nk* **King Electric (IRE)**[26] 3678 2-9-3 100 .... ColinKeane 6 99
(G M Lyons, Ire) *trckd ldr in 2nd: led under 2f out: strly pressed and hdd 1f out: no ex in 4th fnl 100yds* **8/1**[3]

5 *2 ¼* **Ready To Roc (IRE)**[5] 4414 2-9-3 94 .... ConnorKing 4 93
(J P Murtagh, Ire) *hld up: 5th 3f out: rdn over 2f out: nt qckn ent fnl f: sn one pce* **33/1**

6 *8* **Eagle Spirit (IRE)**[10] 4216 2-9-3 90 .... DonnachaO'Brien 2 71
(Joseph Patrick O'Brien, Ire) *led tl hdd under 2f out: wknd over 1f out* **28/1**

1m 28.37s (-0.33) **6** Ran SP% **112.5**
CSF £4.47 TOTE £1.20: £1.02, £3.70; DF 4.60 Trifecta £11.80.
Owner Michael Tabor & Derrick Smith & Mrs John Magnier **Bred** Liberty Bloodstock **Trained** Cashel, Co Tipperary

FOCUS
Aidan O'Brien had won the last two runnings of this with Gleneagles and Deauville, and completed the hat-trick here with a colt who now finds himself heading the betting for both the 2016 Epsom Derby and 2,000 Guineas. The form makes sense.

4575 - 4577a (Foreign Racing) - See Raceform Interactive

4124 DEAUVILLE (R-H)
Thursday, July 21

OFFICIAL GOING: Turf: good; polytrack: standard

4578a PRIX DU CARROUSEL (LISTED RACE) (4YO+) (TURF) 1m 7f
2:25 (12:00) 4-Y-O+ **£19,117** (£7,647; £5,735; £3,823; £1,911)

RPR

1 **Nearly Caught (IRE)**[19] 3913 6-8-11 0 .... UmbertoRispoli 3 107+
(Hughie Morrison) *mde all: broke wl and led: pressed after 1/2-way: qcknd tempo fr 2 1/2f out: kicked for home wl over 1 1/2f out: sn clr: v comf* **39/10**[2]

2 *5* **Minotaur (IRE)**[29] 3545 4-8-11 0 .... StephanePasquier 6 101
(N Clement, France) **6/4**[1]

3 *½* **Polar Eyes**[15] 4030 5-8-8 0 .... MickaelBarzalona 7 97
(Mme Pia Brandt, France) **22/1**

4 *¾* **Sassella (IRE)**[53] 2727 4-8-11 0 .... MaximeGuyon 8 99
(A Fabre, France) **47/10**[3]

5 *nk* **Slatina (IRE)**[35] 4-8-8 0 .... TheoBachelot 4 96
(S Wattel, France) **71/10**

6 *¾* **Kloud Gate (FR)**[29] 3545 4-8-11 0 .... CristianDemuro 2 98
(Gianluca Bietolini, Italy) **84/10**

7 *½* **Novano (GER)**[53] 2728 4-9-4 0 .... AndreasSuborics 1 105
(Waldemar Hickst, Germany) **15/1**

8 *12* **Zemindari (FR)**[29] 3545 4-8-11 0 .... Pierre-CharlesBoudot 5 83
(H-F Devin, France) **11/1**

3m 13.26s (-5.84) **8** Ran SP% **119.9**
WIN (incl. 1 euro stake): 4.90. PLACES: 1.80, 1.20, 3.80. DF: 5.10. SF: 11.20.
Owner A N Solomons **Bred** Irish National Stud **Trained** East Ilsley, Berks

4125 ASCOT (R-H)
Friday, July 22

OFFICIAL GOING: Good to firm (good in places on round course)
Wind: Almost nil Weather: Cloudy, humid

4579 JOHN GUEST BRITISH STALLION STUDS EBF MAIDEN FILLIES' STKS (PLUS 10 RACE) 7f
1:50 (1:52) (Class 4) 2-Y-O **£6,469** (£1,925; £962; £481) **Stalls** Centre

Form RPR

1 **Kazimiera** 2-9-0 0 .... JamesDoyle 3 77+
(Charlie Appleby) *trckd ldr: led over 2f out: shkn up and pressed over 1f out: styd on wl and in command fnl f* **6/4**[1]

2 *2* **Soldier's Girl (IRE)** 2-9-0 0 .... PatDobbs 7 72+
(Richard Hannon) *dwlt: hld up in tch: prog to chse ldng pair over 1f out: shkn up and styd on to take 2nd last stride* **8/1**

0 3 *hd* **Snow Squaw**[15] 4063 2-9-0 0 .... JamieSpencer 2 71+
(David Elsworth) *cl up: chsd wnr wl over 1f out and sn chalng: looked hld whn rdr dropped whip ins fnl f: lost 2nd last strides* **11/2**[3]

4 *1 ¼* **Horseplay** 2-9-0 0 .... DavidProbert 4 68+
(Andrew Balding) *hld up in rr but wl in tch: effrt jst over 2f out: kpt on one pce fr over 1f out* **14/1**

0 5 *1 ¼* **Junoesque**[21] 3859 2-8-9 0 .... GeorgeBuckell(5) 6 64
(John Gallagher) *led to over 2f out: steadily wknd over 1f out* **66/1**

6 *4* **Sitaarah** 2-9-0 0 .... PaulHanagan 1 53
(Simon Crisford) *dwlt: hld up in tch: pushed along 3f out: no prog and wl btn over 1f out* **11/4**[2]

64 7 *5* **Ok By Me (IRE)**[21] 3854 2-9-0 0 .... JFEgan 5 40
(David Evans) *in tch: pushed along 3f out and no prog: wknd over 1f out: eased* **11/1**

1m 29.29s (1.69) **Going Correction** +0.075s/f (Good) **7** Ran SP% **109.7**
Speed ratings (Par 93): **93,90,90,89,87 83,77**
CSF £13.13 TOTE £2.10: £1.40, £3.00; EX 8.80 Trifecta £43.80.
Owner Godolphin **Bred** Darley **Trained** Newmarket, Suffolk

FOCUS
Running rail positioned so course is as its widest configuration. All race distances as advertised. This was probably a fair 2yo fillies' maiden.

4580 ANDERS FOUNDATION EBF STALLIONS CROCKER BULTEEL MAIDEN STKS (PLUS 10 RACE) 6f
2:20 (2:21) (Class 2) 2-Y-O

£12,450 (£3,728; £1,864; £932; £466; £234) **Stalls** Centre

Form RPR

1 **Eqtiraan (IRE)** 2-9-0 0 .... PaulHanagan 2 88+
(Richard Hannon) *rn green: mde virtually all: rdn and edgd rt fr 2f out: asserted u.p ins fnl f: pushed out last 75yds* **5/2**[1]

2 *1 ¼* **Rivet (IRE)** 2-9-0 0 .... RyanMoore 3 82+
(William Haggas) *dwlt: hld up in last: pushed along over 2f out: prog over 1f out: rdn to take 2nd last 100yds: r.o but nt rch wnr* **10/3**[3]

3 *½* **Calibration (IRE)** 2-9-0 0 .... HarryBentley 4 81
(Martyn Meade) *trckd ldrs: pushed along over 2f out: shkn up and effrt over 1f out: styd on to press for 2nd last 100yds* **6/1**

4 *1 ¼* **Well Done (IRE)** 2-9-0 0 ....[1] SilvestreDeSousa 1 77
(Simon Crisford) *cl up: trckd wnr over 2f out and sn chalng: intimidated over 1f out: hld whn impeded ins fnl f: fdd* **3/1**[2]

5 *4 ½* **Galactic Prince** 2-9-0 0 .... DavidProbert 5 64
(Andrew Balding) *sltly impeded s: wl in tch: shkn up over 2f out: wknd wl over 1f out* **8/1**

6 *20* **Star Of The East (IRE)** 2-9-0 0 .... JamesDoyle 6 4
(Mark Johnston) *swvd rt s: pressed wnr to over 2f out: wknd rapidly: t.o* **12/1**

1m 15.1s (0.60) **Going Correction** +0.075s/f (Good) **6** Ran SP% **109.7**
Speed ratings (Par 100): **99,97,96,95,89 62**
CSF £10.54 TOTE £3.30: £1.60, £2.50; EX 11.30 Trifecta £51.40.
Owner Hamdan Al Maktoum **Bred** Victor Stud Bloodstock & Brendan Cummins **Trained** East Everleigh, Wilts

FOCUS
This ought to prove an above-average 2yo maiden. It's been rated around the race average.

4581 JOHN GUEST BROWN JACK STKS (H'CAP) 2m
2:55 (2:55) (Class 2) (0-100,95) 3-Y-O+

£18,675 (£5,592; £2,796; £1,398; £699; £351) **Stalls** Low

Form RPR

1-02 1 **Sea Of Heaven (IRE)**[7] 4353 4-9-5 **86** .... LukeMorris 11 96
(Sir Mark Prescott Bt) *hld up towards rr: 8th 3f out: shkn up and prog on outer over 2f out: drvn to take narrow ld jst over 1f out: styd on and gained upper hand nr fin* **9/4**[1]

-204 2 *½* **Nakeeta**[13] 4162 5-10-0 **95** .... RoystonFfrench 7 104
(Iain Jardine) *t.k.h: trckd ldrs: gng strly 3f out: prog to take 2nd wl over 1f out: chal and w wnr sn after: gd battle tl no ex last 75yds* **8/1**

4006 3 *2* **Monaleen (IRE)**[33] 3436 5-9-9 **90** .... JamieSpencer 8 96
(Ian Williams) *stdd s: hld up in last: stl there whn pce lifted 4f out: prog on outer over 2f out: styd on to take 3rd last strides: no ch to threaten* **33/1**

0000 4 *½* **See And Be Seen**[7] 4353 6-8-9 **76** oh3 ....(p) MartinDwyer 6 81
(Sylvester Kirk) *t.k.h: hld up in midfield: prog and rdn over 2f out: chsd ldrs over 1f out: kpt on same pce* **66/1**

/105 5 *nk* **Galizzi (USA)**[13] 4162 5-9-13 **94** ....(t) JamesDoyle 2 99
(Charlie Appleby) *trckd ldr: led over 2f out and committed for home: hdd jst over 1f out: one pce* **11/2**[3]

0-6 6 *1 ½* **Noble Silk**[14] 4077 7-9-7 **91** ....(v) JosephineGordon(3) 3 96+
(Lucy Wadham) *rousted along early to rch midfield: effrt whn nt clr run over 2f out and again wl over 1f out: kpt on but nvr able to threaten ldrs* **5/1**[2]

00-1 7 *8* **Boite (IRE)**[35] 3351 6-10-0 **95** .... MartinLane 12 89
(Warren Greatrex) *s.s: prog to trck ldng pair after 4f: drvn over 2f out: wknd qckly over 1f out* **8/1**

0-00 8 *2 ¾* **Continuum**[14] 4077 7-9-9 **90** ....(v) TedDurcan 5 80
(Peter Hedger) *hld up: lost pl and in last pair 1/2-way: struggling over 3f out: no prog after* **10/1**

102 9 *¾* **Sisyphus**[56] 2659 4-8-13 **80** .... AndrewMullen 1 69
(Ollie Pears) *sn trckd ldng pair: rdn wl over 2f out: wknd qckly wl over 1f out* **25/1**

1260 10 *40* **Seaside Sizzler**[34] 3387 9-9-7 **88** .... SilvestreDeSousa 9 29
(William Knight) *a towards rr: nt gng wl fr 1/2-way: wknd 4f out: t.o and eased over 1f out* **12/1**

0-05 11 *¾* **All Talk N No Do (IRE)**[14] 4077 5-9-13 **94** ....(tp) GeorgeBaker 10 35
(Seamus Durack) *led to over 2f out: wknd rapidly: t.o and eased fnl f* **14/1**

3m 28.11s (-0.89) **Going Correction** +0.075s/f (Good) **11** Ran SP% **116.8**
Speed ratings (Par 109): **105,104,103,103,103 102,98,97,96,76 76**
CSF £20.30 CT £468.97 TOTE £3.00: £1.40, £2.80, £7.60; EX 19.90 Trifecta £500.70.
Owner Lady Bamford **Bred** Lady Bamford **Trained** Newmarket, Suffolk
■ Stewards' Enquiry : Royston Ffrench two-day ban; used whip above the permitted level (5th-6th Aug)

FOCUS
A good-quality staying handicap, run at a routine pace. The winner has been rated similar to his Newbury second.

4582 CARRAIG INSURANCE EBF STALLIONS BREEDING WINNERS VALIANT STKS (LISTED RACE) (F&M) 1m (R)
3:30 (3:31) (Class 1) 3-Y-O+

£31,190 (£11,825; £5,918; £2,948; £1,479; £742) **Stalls** Low

Form RPR

3121 1 *shd* **Red Box**[9] 4263 3-8-7 88 .... LukeMorris 9 105
(Sir Mark Prescott Bt) *awkward s: hld up in last: gd prog wl over 1f out: plld out and r.o wl fnl f to take 2nd last strides: jst failed: fin 2nd: awrdd the r* **14/1**

4204 2 *nk* **Irish Rookie (IRE)**[14] 4107 4-9-1 107 .... RyanMoore 3 108+
(Martyn Meade) *hld up in 7th: gd prog jst over 2f out to chse ldr over 1f out: clsng to chal whn squeezed for room 100yds out: kpt on but nt rcvr and lost 2nd last strides: fin 3rd: plcd 2nd* **7/4**[1]

-351 3 **Namhroodah (IRE)**[35] 3358 4-9-1 99 .... JamieSpencer 8 107
(James Tate) *wl away fr wd draw: mde all and stretched field: drvn clr 2f out: hrd pressed whn edgd rt 100yds out: jst hld on: fin 1st: disqualified and plcd 3rd* **6/1**[3]

-311 4 *2 ¼* **Light And Shade**[28] 3623 4-9-1 96 .... MartinHarley 1 101
(James Tate) *chsd ldrs in 5th: rdn to dispute 3rd briefly wl over 1f out: kpt on same pce after and n.d* **14/1**

1-40 **5** 1 1/2 **Mix And Mingle (IRE)**[82] 1888 3-8-7 104 TedDurcan 5 96
(Chris Wall) *hld up in 8th: sme prog on outer over 2f out: disp 4th ins fnl f but no ch: one pce after* **3/1**[2]

3302 **6** 1 1/4 **Black Cherry**[17] 3979 4-9-1 102 PatDobbs 6 95
(Richard Hannon) *hld up in 6th: shkn up and no prog over 2f out: no ch after* **13/2**

-231 **7** 1 1/2 **Delve (IRE)**[21] 3850 3-8-7 87 RichardKingscote 4 89
(Sir Michael Stoute) *chsd ldr to over 1f out: wknd qckly* **20/1**

440- **8** hd **Muffri'Ha (IRE)**[286] 7117 4-9-1 100 PatCosgrave 7 91
(William Haggas) *t.k.h: chsd ldng trio to 2f out: sn wknd* **25/1**

0-20 **9** 3 **Raaqy (IRE)**[20] 3911 3-8-7 94 [1] PaulHanagan 2 82
(Owen Burrows) *chsd ldng pair to over 2f out: wknd* **40/1**

1m 39.09s (-1.61) **Going Correction** +0.075s/f (Good)
WFA 3 from 4yo 8lb **9** Ran SP% **113.4**
Speed ratings (Par 111): **110,110,111,108,106 105,104,103,100**
CSF £37.51 TOTE £11.50: £2.60, £1.20, £1.70; EX 37.30 Trifecta £271.60.
Owner Cheveley Park Stud **Bred** Cheveley Park Stud Ltd **Trained** Newmarket, Suffolk
■ Stewards' Enquiry : Jamie Spencer three-day ban; careless riding (5th-7th Aug)

FOCUS
They went a solid early pace in this fillies' Listed event and there was late drama. The third has been rated close to her Falmouth Stakes form.

4583 JOHN GUEST H'CAP 1m 4f
4:05 (4:05) (Class 2) (0-100,96) 3-Y-O+
£18,675 (£5,592; £2,796; £1,398; £699; £351) **Stalls** Low

Form RPR

4001 **1** **Yorkidding**[14] 4115 4-9-6 88 RichardKingscote 7 97
(Mark Johnston) *hld up in 4th: clsd over 2f out: rdn to ld over 1f out: sn jnd: edgd lft but styd on wl to assert last 100yds* **13/2**[3]

1234 **2** 3/4 **Masterpaver**[14] 4077 5-8-12 80 JamieSpencer 4 88
(Richard Fahey) *hld up in 5th: clsd on wd outside over 2f out: jnd wnr over 1f out: styd on but jst hld last 100yds* **6/1**[2]

3405 **3** 5 **Pinzolo**[14] 4115 5-10-0 96 [1] JamesDoyle 3 96
(Charlie Appleby) *led: rdn over 2f out: hdd over 1f out: readily outpcd* **7/1**

433 **4** nk **Plutocracy (IRE)**[62] 2482 6-9-9 91 GeorgeBaker 6 91
(Gary Moore) *hld up in last: effrt jst over 2f out: one pce and no ch w ldng pair over 1f out* **6/1**[2]

-420 **5** 9 **Zand (IRE)**[55] 2685 6-9-4 86 JoeFanning 1 71
(Mark Johnston) *t.k.h: trckd ldng pair to jst over 2f out: wknd qckly* **25/1**

33-1 **6** 8 **Bermondsey**[42] 3109 4-9-10 92 RyanMoore 2 73
(Luca Cumani) *t.k.h in 2nd: jnd ldr 6f out to 3f out: rdn and wknd qckly over 2f out: eased* **10/11**[1]

2m 29.99s (-2.51) **Going Correction** +0.075s/f (Good) **6** Ran SP% **110.6**
Speed ratings (Par 109): **111,110,107,106,100 95**
CSF £41.98 TOTE £6.50: £3.00, £2.30; EX 37.90 Trifecta £110.40.
Owner Paul Robert York **Bred** Bluehills Racing Limited **Trained** Middleham Moor, N Yorks

FOCUS
This fair handicap was run to suit the closers. It's been rated around the winner and third.

4584 SIS LIVE H'CAP 5f
4:35 (4:36) (Class 2) 3-Y-O+
£28,012 (£8,388; £4,194; £2,097; £1,048; £526) **Stalls** Centre

Form RPR

1531 **1** **Alpha Delphini**[14] 4112 5-8-3 88 ConnorBeasley 12 102
(Bryan Smart) *chsd ldng pair in centre: drvn to go 2nd wl over 1f out and sn chalng: w ldr fnl f: won on the nod* **8/1**

141 **2** shd **Final Venture**[7] 4373 4-8-8 93 6ex NeilFarley 16 107
(Alan Swinbank) *overall ldr in centre: drvn and jnd over 1f out: styd on wl but pipped on the post* **9/2**[1]

6011 **3** 3 1/4 **Royal Birth**[13] 4126 5-8-5 95 (t) AaronJones[(5)] 5 97
(Stuart Williams) *towards rr in centre: prog 2f out: styd on fnl f to take 3rd but no ch w ldng pair* **11/2**[2]

0551 **4** shd **Shamshon (IRE)**[11] 4198 5-8-11 96 6ex JamieSpencer 7 98
(Jamie Osborne) *hld up and sn outpcd in centre: stl wl in rr 2f out: gd prog jst over 1f out: r.o and nrly snatched 3rd* **10/1**

0125 **5** 1/2 **Rio Ronaldo (IRE)**[14] 4079 4-8-3 88 LukeMorris 6 88
(Mike Murphy) *dwlt: hld up in rr in centre: shkn up 2f out: prog jst over 1f out: r.o to press for a pl nr fin but no ch* **9/1**

-066 **6** 3/4 **Medicean Man**[38] 3244 10-9-7 106 (tp) RichardKingscote 15 103
(Jeremy Gask) *dwlt: chsd ldrs in centre: hrd rdn 2f out: one pce and nvr able to threaten* **9/1**

0-62 **7** nk **Robot Boy (IRE)**[13] 4126 6-8-12 97 GrahamGibbons 8 93
(David Barron) *in tch in centre: effrt 2f out: one pce and nvr able to threaten* **7/1**[3]

0530 **8** 1/2 **Desert Law (IRE)**[13] 4126 8-9-0 99 MartinLane 9 94
(Paul Midgley) *chsd overall ldr in centre to wl over 1f out: fdd fnl f* **16/1**

1466 **9** 3 **Taajub (IRE)**[40] 3193 9-8-0 85 oh3 NickyMackay 1 69
(Peter Crate) *racd in trio towards far side to 1/2-way: nvr on terms: no ch whn jnd centre gp* **50/1**

0000 **10** 6 **Stepper Point**[13] 4126 7-9-0 99 (p) MartinDwyer 4 61
(William Muir) *racd in far side trio: nvr on terms and no ch sn after 1/2-way* **16/1**

0-00 **11** 1 1/2 **Musical Comedy**[18] 3956 5-8-8 93 DavidProbert 3 50
(Mike Murphy) *racd in far side trio: nvr on terms and no ch sn after 1/2-way* **50/1**

0050 **12** 3/4 **Foxy Forever (IRE)**[13] 4126 6-8-10 95 (b) SamHitchcott 13 49
(Michael Wigham) *nvr bttr than midfield in centre: wknd wl over 1f out* **33/1**

4615 **13** 3 **Caspian Prince (IRE)**[13] 4166 7-9-10 109 (t) RobertWinston 17 52
(Dean Ivory) *racd alone towards nr side: nvr on terms: no ch over 1f out* **14/1**

4200 **14** 1 1/2 **Red Baron (IRE)**[28] 3606 7-9-0 99 (p) JasonHart 10 37
(Eric Alston) *racd centre: nvr bttr than midfield: no prog 2f out: wl btn over 1f out* **40/1**

6002 **15** 8 **Primrose Valley**[15] 4066 4-8-2 90 (b) JosephineGordon[(3)] 11
(Ed Vaughan) *s.v.s: a wl bhd* **10/1**

58.5s (-2.00) **Going Correction** +0.075s/f (Good)
WFA 3 from 4yo+ 4lb **15** Ran SP% **123.1**
Speed ratings (Par 109): **119,118,113,113,112 111,111,110,105,95 93,92,87,85,72**
CSF £43.61 CT £225.84 TOTE £9.40: £3.60, £2.00, £1.90; EX 52.20 Trifecta £312.70.
Owner The Alpha Delphini Partnership **Bred** Mrs B A Matthews **Trained** Hambleton, N Yorks

FOCUS
The first four home in this decent sprint handicap were last-time-out winners. Strong form. The third has been rated a bit off his C&D latest win.

4585 INVESTEC OCTOBER CLUB CHARITY FILLIES' H'CAP 5f
5:05 (5:05) (Class 4) (0-85,85) 3-Y-O+ **£6,469** (£1,925; £962; £481) **Stalls** Centre

Form RPR

5321 **1** **Midnight Malibu (IRE)**[14] 4093 3-9-2 79 GrahamGibbons 3 86
(Tim Easterby) *mde virtually all: rdn wl over 1f out: hld on wl fnl f* **11/2**[2]

30-1 **2** nk **Cosmopolitan Girl (IRE)**[41] 3127 3-8-13 76 MartinHarley 1 82
(Robert Cowell) *racd on outer: pressed wnr: rdn to chal over 1f out: styd on but hld last 100yds* **6/1**[3]

-110 **3** nk **Coto (IRE)**[34] 3392 4-8-11 75 PaddyBradley[(5)] 2 81
(M J Tynan, Ire) *racd on wd outside: trckd ldrs: rdn to chal jst over 1f out: styd on but hld ins fnl f* **11/1**

411 **4** 3/4 **Rosealee (IRE)**[10] 4224 3-8-12 80 6ex DavidParkes[(5)] 13 82+
(Jeremy Gask) *towards rr: rdn and prog to take 4th fnl f: styd on but nvr quite able to chal* **12/1**

-045 **5** 1 3/4 **Princess Tansy**[34] 3407 4-9-0 73 DavidProbert 5 70
(Gay Kelleway) *w ldrs tl nt qckn over 1f out: one pce fnl f* **33/1**

1-51 **6** 1/2 **Olympic Runner**[28] 3625 3-9-5 82 PatCosgrave 8 76
(William Haggas) *chsd ldrs: rdn and no imp wl over 1f out: one pce after* **5/2**[1]

0130 **7** 1/2 **Fredricka**[14] 4112 5-9-12 85 JasonHart 9 78
(David Barron) *stdd s: hld up wl in rr: rdn 2f out: kpt on one pce: n.d* **10/1**

/0-0 **8** nk **Immediate**[51] 2787 4-9-12 85 PatDobbs 12 77
(Robert Cowell) *dwlt: wl in rr: rdn 2f out: kpt on but nvr gng pce to threaten* **18/1**

1603 **9** 1 3/4 **Englishwoman**[13] 4155 3-8-12 75 SamHitchcott 6 60
(David Evans) *pressed ldrs to 2f out: lost pl u.p* **16/1**

-100 **10** 2 1/2 **Marmalady (IRE)**[18] 3956 6-9-12 85 RichardKingscote 4 62
(Robert Cowell) *trckd ldrs on outer: shkn up and hanging wl over 1f out: sn wknd* **12/1**

-310 **11** 11 **Ada Lovelace**[11] 4198 6-8-10 76 (p) RhiainIngram[(7)] 11 13
(John Gallagher) *pressed ldrs tl wknd rapidly over 1f out: eased and t.o* **40/1**

30 **12** 10 **Lady Kyllar**[81] 1929 4-9-10 83 JamieSpencer 10
(George Margarson) *hld up in last: shkn up and no rspnse over 1f out: sn eased and t.o* **8/1**

1m 0.32s (-0.18) **Going Correction** +0.075s/f (Good)
WFA 3 from 4yo+ 4lb **12** Ran SP% **118.7**
Speed ratings (Par 102): **104,103,103,101,99 98,97,96,94,90 72,56**
CSF £38.57 CT £282.32 TOTE £6.20: £2.00, £2.20, £4.00; EX 33.70 Trifecta £372.00.
Owner D A West **Bred** Kabansk Ltd & Rathbarry Stud **Trained** Great Habton, N Yorks

FOCUS
A fair sprint handicap for fillies. Those racing handily dominated. Another step forward from the winner, with the third the key to the level.
T/Plt: £56.90 to a £1 stake. Pool: £64,346.00 - 1,130.28 winning tickets T/Qpdt: £20.40 to a £1 stake. Pool: £5,134.00 - 251.48 winning tickets **Jonathan Neesom**

4287 CHEPSTOW (L-H)
Friday, July 22

OFFICIAL GOING: Good to firm (8.9)
Wind: almost nil Weather: fine

4586 BRAINS BEER MAIDEN AUCTION FILLIES' STKS (PLUS 10 RACE) 6f 16y
5:50 (5:51) (Class 5) 2-Y-O **£3,234** (£962; £481; £240) **Stalls** Centre

Form RPR

32 **1** **Ariena (IRE)**[15] 4054 2-9-0 0 JohnFahy 5 81+
(Clive Cox) *hld up: hdwy over 2f out: shkn up to ld over 1f out: sn pushed clr: eased towards fin* **1/1**[1]

2 4 1/2 **Quick Artist (IRE)** 2-9-0 0 TimmyMurphy 6 62
(Simon Crisford) *in rr: outpcd and detached after 2f: pushed along over 2f out: stl last 1f out: r.o wl to go 2nd wl ins fnl f* **8/1**

0 **3** 1 **Highland Lotus**[16] 4022 2-9-0 0 WilliamTwiston-Davies 7 59
(William Haggas) *chsd ldrs: rdn and unable qck over 2f out: kpt on to go 3rd nr fin* **11/1**

200 **4** 1/2 **Megan Lily (IRE)**[27] 3633 2-8-7 0 NatalieHambling[(7)] 1 57
(Richard Fahey) *awkward s: rcvrd to ld after 100yds: jnd over 2f out: sn rdn: hdd over 1f out: no ch w wnr: lost 2 pls wl ins fnl f* **4/1**[2]

6 **5** 1/2 **Rita's Girl**[37] 3282 2-9-0 0 FrederikTylicki 8 56
(K R Burke) *chsd ldrs: rdn and sltly outpcd over 2f out: kpt on same pce fnl f* **13/2**[3]

0 **6** nk **Joyful Dream (IRE)**[7] 4350 2-9-0 0 DannyBrock 4 55
(J S Moore) *mid-div: rdn over 2f out: kpt on same pce* **12/1**

0 **7** 7 **Miss Mayson**[15] 4054 2-8-7 0 KevinLundie[(7)] 2 34
(Roger Teal) *led 100yds: trckd ldr: chal over 2f out tl wknd over 1f out* **66/1**

1m 10.81s (-1.19) **Going Correction** -0.225s/f (Firm) **7** Ran SP% **112.0**
Speed ratings (Par 91): **98,92,90,90,89 88,79**
CSF £9.47 TOTE £1.70: £1.30, £3.40; EX 8.00 Trifecta £45.20.
Owner Ms Diane Williams **Bred** Mrs Diane Williams **Trained** Lambourn, Berks

FOCUS
After a dry day, the going was good to firm all over. A modest maiden auction to open proceedings, run at what appeared an overly strong pace.

4587 RUM BAR CHEPSTOW FILLIES' H'CAP 7f 16y
6:20 (6:20) (Class 5) (0-70,70) 3-Y-O+ **£3,234** (£962; £481; £240) **Stalls** Centre

Form RPR

00-4 **1** **Fantasy Queen**[16] 4017 3-8-6 55 JohnFahy 6 60
(Eve Johnson Houghton) *hld up in a detached last: rdn and hdwy over 2f out: wnt 3rd ent fnl f: r.o wl to ld post* **9/1**

300- **2** shd **Polymnia**[269] 7534 3-9-1 64 KieranO'Neill 1 68+
(Richard Hannon) *s.s: t.k.h and sn in mid-div: hdwy 3f out: rdn to ld over 1f out: wandered u.p: hung rt towards fin: hdd post* **6/1**[3]

6530 **3** nk **Inner Knowing (IRE)**[23] 3786 3-8-11 60 (b[1]) FrederikTylicki 3 63
(K R Burke) *led and racd freely: rdn over 2f out: hdd over 1f out: nt run on fnl f but stl clsng on ldr nr fin: lost 2nd last strides* **7/2**[2]

4240 **4** 3 3/4 **Zebedee's Girl (IRE)**[126] 979 3-8-8 62 GaryMahon[(5)] 8 55
(David Evans) *chsd ldrs: rdn over 2f out: styd on same pce* **9/1**

4546 **5** 3 3/4 **Check 'Em Tuesday (IRE)**[14] 4102 3-9-0 63 TimmyMurphy 5 46
(Daniel Mark Loughnane) *mid-div: rdn over 2f out: one pce and no imp* **10/1**

0006 **6** ¾ **Siri**[15] 4058 3-9-7 **70**.......... CharlesBishop 4 51
(Mick Channon) *chsd ldrs: lost 2nd over 2f out: wknd fnl f* **11/4**[1]

0505 **7** 11 **Lolita**[17] 3974 4-9-12 **68**.......... (p) TomQueally 7 22
(J R Jenkins) *chsd ldrs: rdn over 2f out: wknd over 1f out* **7/1**

3-60 **8** 13 **Forest Lakes (IRE)**[22] 3823 3-9-3 **66**.......... (b[1]) WilliamTwiston-Davies 2
(George Scott) *s.s: t.k.h in rr: hdwy and prom after 2f: rdn and wknd qckly over 2f out: eased over 1f out: t.o* **8/1**

1m 21.99s (-1.21) **Going Correction** -0.225s/f (Firm)
WFA 3 from 4yo 7lb **8** Ran SP% **115.9**
Speed ratings (Par 100): **97,96,96,92,87 87,74,59**
CSF £62.42 CT £229.26 TOTE £10.10: £2.70, £1.90, £1.10; EX 58.90 Trifecta £280.40.

Owner Mrs Zara Campbell-Harris **Bred** Mrs Z C Campbell-Harris **Trained** Blewbury, Oxon

FOCUS
A weak race, even by fillies' handicap standards, and the complexion changed dramatically in the final 100 yards.

4588 HOTSPRING HOT TUBS H'CAP — 7f 16y
6:50 (6:50) (Class 5) (0-75,79) 3-Y-O **£3,234** (£962; £481; £240) **Stalls** Centre

Form RPR

3140 **1** **Boycie**[16] 4010 3-9-7 **73**.......... (b) KieranO'Neill 2 76
(Richard Hannon) *t.k.h: trckd ldng pair: rdn over 2f out: stl 3rd 1f out: r.o u.p to ld fnl 50yds* **6/4**[1]

1 **2** 1 **Wild Dancer**[16] 4017 3-9-2 **73**.......... HectorCrouch(5) 5 73
(Patrick Chamings) *trckd ldr: rdn to ld over 1f out and sn edgd rt to stands' rail: hdd and unable qck fnl 50yds* **13/8**[2]

0-26 **3** 1¾ **Donttouchthechips (IRE)**[28] 3591 3-8-12 **67**.......... EdwardGreatrex(3) 1 62
(Nikki Evans) *led and racd keenly: rdn over 2f out: hdd over 1f out: one pce after: lost 2nd ins fnl f* **9/2**[3]

1663 **4** 8 **Sunbaked (IRE)**[87] 1764 3-8-9 **61**.......... (p) JohnFahy 4 35
(Eve Johnson Houghton) *hld up in last but wl in tch: rdn over 2f out: qckly outpcd: no ch fnl f* **7/1**

1m 22.89s (-0.31) **Going Correction** -0.225s/f (Firm) **4** Ran SP% **108.8**
Speed ratings (Par 100): **92,90,88,79**
CSF £4.29 TOTE £2.40; EX 4.30 Trifecta £6.60.

Owner Mrs V Hubbard & K T Ivory **Bred** Highclere Stud **Trained** East Everleigh, Wilts

FOCUS
Another uncompetitive handicap, with the runner-up trading at 1.01 in running before being picked off late. The winner has been rated to form, with the third fitting based on his C&D maiden form.

4589 COUNTY MARQUEES H'CAP — 1m 14y
7:20 (7:20) (Class 5) (0-70,70) 3-Y-O+ **£3,234** (£962; £481; £240) **Stalls** Centre

Form RPR

4061 **1** **Diamonds A Dancing**[14] 4088 6-8-11 **58**.......... (be) CiaranMckee(5) 3 66
(John O'Shea) *a.p: drvn over 2f out: chal over 1f out: led fnl 100yds: rdn out* **8/1**

4540 **2** ½ **Lilbourne Prince (IRE)**[13] 4157 3-9-1 **70**.......... GaryMahon(5) 4 75
(David Evans) *disp ld: rdn over 2f out: narrowly hdd ent fnl f: r.o u.p: jst hld* **4/1**[2]

1341 **3** ¾ **Wordismybond**[8] 4302 7-9-2 **65**.......... StephenCummins(7) 5 70
(Richard Hughes) *disp ld: rdn over 1f out: led ent fnl f: r.o u.p: hdd and unable qck fnl 100yds* **3/1**[1]

0331 **4** 4 **Miss Lillie**[25] 3731 5-9-6 **62**.......... (p) FrederikTylicki 2 58
(Roger Teal) *wnt to post early: hld up bhd ldrs: rdn over 2f out: one pce and nvr able to chal* **8/1**

231 **5** 3½ **Stormbound (IRE)**[86] 1780 7-9-11 **67**.......... (b) LukeMorris 7 55
(Paul Cole) *s.i.s: in rr: rdn 1/2-way: kpt on same pce and no real imp* **3/1**[1]

-420 **6** 2¼ **Plauseabella**[17] 3974 5-9-5 **61**.......... (p) TimmyMurphy 6 44
(Stuart Kittow) *t.k.h: trckd ldrs: shkn up 2f out: wknd appr fnl f* **6/1**[3]

0354 **7** 54 **Never To Be (USA)**[28] 3594 5-9-6 **65**.......... (t) EdwardGreatrex(3) 1
(Nikki Evans) *towards rr: rdn and no imp 1/2-way: bhd fnl 2f: virtually p.u: t.o* **14/1**

1m 33.1s (-3.10) **Going Correction** -0.225s/f (Firm)
WFA 3 from 5yo+ 8lb **7** Ran SP% **113.2**
Speed ratings (Par 103): **106,105,104,100,97 95,41**
CSF £38.87 TOTE £9.40: £3.90, £2.00; EX 35.20 Trifecta £335.40.

Owner The Cross Racing Club **Bred** Lady Caffyn-Parsons **Trained** Elton, Gloucs

■ Stewards' Enquiry : Gary Mahon four-day ban; excessive use of whip (5th-8th Aug)

FOCUS
The field came down the stands' rail for the first time this evening and, in another good finish, the winner followed up his C&D success a fortnight ago. The runner-up has been rated close to form.

4590 DRIBUILD DASH (ROUND 4 OF THE CHEPSTOW SPRINT SERIES H'CAP) — 5f 16y
7:50 (7:51) (Class 5) (0-70,69) 3-Y-O+ **£3,234** (£962; £481; £240) **Stalls** Centre

Form RPR

3546 **1** **Fine 'n Dandy (IRE)**[27] 3650 5-9-8 **65**.......... (t) TomQueally 3 73
(J R Jenkins) *cl up tl led after 1f: rdn over 1f out: 3 l clr ent fnl f: r.o wl* **9/1**

0234 **2** 1½ **Head Space (IRE)**[7] 4355 8-9-2 **66**.......... JoshuaBryan(7) 6 69
(Brian Barr) *hld up in last: rdn and hdwy over 1f out: r.o to go 2nd 100yds out: clsng on wnr after but a being hld* **5/2**[2]

4561 **3** 2 **Quantum Dot (IRE)**[8] 4292 5-8-13 **56** 6ex.......... (b) JohnFahy 2 51
(Ed de Giles) *led 1f: trckd wnr: swtchd rt over 2f out: sn rdn: edgd rt and unable qck ins fnl f: lost 2nd 100yds out* **11/10**[1]

00-4 **4** 1¾ **Golden Rosanna**[27] 3669 3-8-3 **50** oh5.......... LukeMorris 5 38
(Steph Hollinshead) *chsd ldrs: rdn over 2f out: sn hmpd: one pce after* **25/1**

-550 **5** shd **Master Pekan**[14] 4085 3-7-13 **53** oh5 ow3.......... MitchGodwin(7) 4 41
(Roy Brotherton) *chsd ldrs: rdn over 2f out: sn edgd rt: swtchd lft over 1f out: one pce and no imp* **33/1**

5362 **6** ¾ **Swendab (IRE)**[14] 4084 8-9-7 **69**.......... (b) CiaranMckee(5) 1 55
(John O'Shea) *sed awkwardly and chsd along fr s: in tch in 5th tl relegated to last over 1f out: nvr nr to chal* **5/1**[3]

58.35s (-0.95) **Going Correction** -0.225s/f (Firm)
WFA 3 from 5yo+ 4lb **6** Ran SP% **109.6**
Speed ratings (Par 103): **98,95,92,89,89 88**
CSF £30.23 TOTE £11.70: £4.40, £1.80; EX 29.20 Trifecta £69.60.

Owner Ms Aurelija Juskaite **Bred** G Flannery Developments **Trained** Royston, Herts

FOCUS
A small field but some in-form sorts on show and the all-the-way winner showed excellent speed. The runner-up has been rated close to his recent form.

4591 PLATINUM ANNIVERSARY H'CAP — 2m 49y
8:20 (8:20) (Class 6) (0-60,58) 3-Y-O+ **£2,587** (£770; £384; £192) **Stalls** Low

Form RPR

4224 **1** **Ring Eye (IRE)**[14] 4082 8-9-9 **56**.......... EdwardGreatrex(3) 3 64
(John O'Shea) *hld up in last: hdwy gng wl on outer 4f out: led on bit wl over 1f out: rdn out fnl f and styd on wl* **15/8**[1]

-000 **2** 3 **Miss Marina Bay**[11] 4210 3-8-5 **52**.......... LukeMorris 7 56
(Sir Mark Prescott Bt) *led: hung rt 1st f: flashed tail thrght and rn in snatches: drvn 4f out: hdd wl over 1f out: jinked 1f out: eased whn hld towards fin* **4/1**[2]

-666 **3** 5 **Taste The Wine (IRE)**[12] 3099 10-9-5 **56**.......... JordanWilliams(7) 2 54
(Bernard Llewellyn) *chsd ldrs: hdwy into 2nd 6f out: rdn and lost 2nd over 2f out: sn outpcd by ldrs: regained 3rd nr fin* **8/1**

-220 **4** ¾ **Fuzzy Logic (IRE)**[21] 3099 7-9-6 **50**.......... (b) StevieDonohoe 1 48
(Bernard Llewellyn) *hld up: hdwy after 4f: rdn 4f out: styd on same pce: in hld 3rd 1f out tl nr fin* **5/1**

0/6- **5** 8 **Mollyow (IRE)**[12] 497 8-9-0 **47**.......... (p) NoelGarbutt(3) 6 35
(Dai Burchell) *chsd ldrs tl lost pl 1/2-way: rdn 4f out: wknd 2f out* **8/1**

4444 **6** 2 **Agreement (IRE)**[23] 3767 6-9-9 **58**.......... (b) HectorCrouch(5) 4 44
(Nikki Evans) *mainly trckd ldr tl lost 2nd 6f out: rdn over 3f out: sn outpcd: no ch fnl 2f* **9/2**[3]

3m 33.61s (-5.29) **Going Correction** -0.225s/f (Firm)
WFA 3 from 4yo+ 17lb **6** Ran SP% **111.9**
Speed ratings (Par 101): **104,102,100,99,95 94**
CSF £9.48 TOTE £2.50: £1.70, £1.70; EX 11.10 Trifecta £76.80.
Owner Gary C Roberts **Bred** Derek O'Hara **Trained** Elton, Gloucs

FOCUS
A low-grade staying handicap produced an easy winner but it was more memorable for Luke Morris's heroics in getting Miss Marina Bay home in second place. The winner has been rated close to last year's form.

4592 BRAINS BEER H'CAP — 1m 4f 23y
8:55 (8:56) (Class 6) (0-65,66) 3-Y-O+ **£2,587** (£770; £384; £192) **Stalls** Low

Form RPR

1331 **1** **Urban Space**[3] 4483 10-9-10 **66** 6ex.......... (t) HectorCrouch(5) 4 73
(John Flint) *racd in 3rd: 8 l off ldng pair after 4f: rdn and clsd 4f out: chal wl over 2f out: r.o u.p in duel: won on nod* **5/2**[2]

0011 **2** nse **Petrify**[8] 4294 6-8-9 **53**.......... (tp) MitchGodwin(7) 6 60
(Bernard Llewellyn) *s.s: hld up in last: clsd 4f out: swtchd rt and led 3f out: sn jnd: r.o u.p in duel: lost on nod* **2/1**[1]

00/5 **3** 5 **Tamarillo Grove (IRE)**[14] 4082 9-9-9 **60**.......... (t) SaleemGolam 7 59
(Sophie Leech) *hld up: rdn 4f out: wnt 3rd 2f out: one pce and no imp on ldng pair* **13/2**

-026 **4** 9 **Approaching Star (FR)**[14] 4088 5-8-7 **47**.......... (p) NoelGarbutt(3) 1 32
(Dai Burchell) *disp ld: 8 l clr of rest after 4f tl reduced advantage 5f out: hdd 3f out: wknd wl over 1f out* **14/1**

0-52 **5** ½ **Grams And Ounces**[8] 4294 9-9-2 **60**.......... (t) JoshuaBryan(7) 2 44
(Grace Harris) *disp ld: 8 l clr of rest after 4f tl reduced advantage 5f out: hdd 3f out: sn wknd* **11/4**[3]

2m 34.86s (-4.14) **Going Correction** -0.225s/f (Firm) **5** Ran SP% **108.6**
Speed ratings (Par 101): **104,103,100,94,94**
CSF £7.67 TOTE £3.40: £1.70, £1.60; EX 8.10 Trifecta £19.90.
Owner J L Flint **Bred** Winterbeck Manor Stud **Trained** Kenfig Hill, Bridgend

FOCUS
Low-grade fare but it was run at a strong pace and produced a cracking finish between two in-form runners.

T/Plt: £306.20 to a £1 stake. Pool: £46,204.48 - 110.15 winning units. T/Qpdt: £66.90 to a £1 stake. Pool: £3,935.76 - 43.50 winning units. **Richard Lowther**

4397 NEWMARKET (R-H)
Friday, July 22

OFFICIAL GOING: Good to firm (7.7)
Wind: Light across Weather: Cloud clearing to leave a fine evening

4593 32RED.COM H'CAP — 1m
5:40 (5:40) (Class 5) (0-75,77) 3-Y-O+ **£3,234** (£962; £481; £240) **Stalls** High

Form RPR

5-32 **1** **Red Tea**[27] 3673 3-9-3 **72**.......... AdamBeschizza 1 82
(Peter Hiatt) *plld hrd and prom: led at stdy pce over 6f out: qcknd over 3f out: rdn over 1f out: r.o wl: comf* **7/2**[2]

1 **2** 2½ **Misty Lord (IRE)**[182] 298 3-9-3 **75**.......... (t) DanielMuscutt(3) 2 79+
(Marco Botti) *s.i.s: hld up: hdwy and edgd lft fr over 1f out: rdn to go 2nd ins fnl f: nt trble wnr* **9/2**[3]

2631 **3** ¾ **Mithqaal (USA)**[22] 3823 3-9-2 **71**.......... DaneO'Neill 5 73
(Owen Burrows) *led at stdy pce tl hdd over 6f out: rdn and edgd lft over 1f out* **9/4**[1]

2-04 **4** ½ **Harry Champion**[16] 4028 3-9-6 **75**.......... JamesMcDonald 8 76
(Hugo Palmer) *hld up: shkn up over 1f out: r.o ins fnl f: nt trble ldrs* **13/2**

4402 **5** 2¼ **Swiss Cross**[7] 4362 9-9-2 **63**.......... (t) AdamKirby 10 61
(Phil McEntee) *prom: chsd wnr over 3f out: rdn and ev ch over 2f out: wknd wl ins fnl f* **14/1**

5300 **6** hd **Dark Amber**[13] 4157 6-9-2 **63**.......... RichardMullen 3 60
(Brendan Powell) *hld up: pushed along over 2f out: r.o towards fin: nvr nrr* **33/1**

6100 **7** 1¼ **Normandy Knight**[14] 4113 4-9-13 **74**.......... PatrickMathers 9 68
(Richard Fahey) *hld up: hdwy u.p 2f out: wkng whn n.m.r wl ins fnl f* **8/1**

0-20 **8** 3¾ **Performer**[101] 1392 3-9-1 **70**.......... SeanLevey 4 53
(Richard Hannon) *edgd rt s: plld hrd and prom: shkn up over 1f out: sn wknd* **16/1**

1m 42.1s (2.10) **Going Correction** -0.05s/f (Good)
WFA 3 from 4yo+ 8lb **8** Ran SP% **111.1**
Speed ratings (Par 103): **87,84,83,83,81 80,79,75**
CSF £18.45 CT £40.37 TOTE £4.50: £1.10, £2.70, £1.10; EX 14.50 Trifecta £42.80.
Owner Ken Read Shelley Tucker Jimmy Cooper **Bred** Sheikh Hamdan Bin Maktoum Al Maktoum **Trained** Hook Norton, Oxon

The Form Book, Raceform Ltd, Newbury, RG14 5SJ

FOCUS
Stands' side used. Stalls far side except 1m4f, centre. The watered ground (10mm applied on Monday and a further 10mm applied on Thursday) was given as good to firm (GoingStick: 7.7). They went no gallop early on here, several refused to settle, and it developed into a sprint. The level is a bit fluid, with the fourth rated as running a turf pb.

4594 ADNAMS GHOST SHIP MEDIAN AUCTION MAIDEN STKS (PLUS 10 RACE) 6f
6:10 (6:13) (Class 4) 2-Y-O **£3,946** (£1,174; £586; £293) **Stalls** High

Form RPR

1 **Fly At Dawn (USA)** 2-9-5 0 .....[1] JamesDoyle 1 83
(Charlie Appleby) *mde virtually all: rdn and edgd lft over 1f out: styd on* **11/4**[2]

54 **2** *1* **Harbour Master**[25] 3730 2-9-0 0 ..... LucyKBarry(5) 8 79
(Jamie Osborne) *a.p: shkn up over 1f out: rdn: nt clr run and swtchd rt ins fnl f: r.o to go 2nd post* **25/1**

2 **3** *shd* **Stanhope**[28] 3619 2-9-5 0 ..... AdamKirby 10 79
(Mick Quinn) *a.p: rdn over 2f out: chsd wnr over 1f out: sn ev ch: no ex towards fin* **7/1**

3 **4** *2¾* **Keyser Soze (IRE)**[22] 3818 2-9-5 0 ..... FrankieDettori 6 70
(Richard Spencer) *hld up in tch: rdn and edgd lft over 1f out: nt clr run and no ex ins fnl f* **15/8**[1]

5 *¾* **Whip Nae Nae (IRE)** 2-9-5 0 ..... SeanLevey 7 68
(Richard Hannon) *prom: shkn up over 1f out: styd on same pce fnl f* **14/1**

6 *nk* **Chaplin (FR)** 2-9-5 0 ..... ShaneKelly 3 67+
(Richard Hughes) *hld up: pushed along and hdwy over 1f out: styd on same pce ins fnl f* **66/1**

7 *4* **Still Waiting** 2-9-5 0 ..... JamesMcDonald 9 54
(William Jarvis) *w wnr tl shkn up 2f out: wknd fnl f* **20/1**

0 **8** *1½* **Fire Brigade**[42] 3100 2-9-5 0 ..... HarryBentley 4 49
(Michael Bell) *hld up: wknd over 1f out* **6/1**[3]

9 *1¾* **Under Control (IRE)** 2-9-5 0 ..... SilvestreDeSousa 5 44
(William Haggas) *s.i.s: hld up: plld hrd: wknd over 1f out* **9/1**

10 *1¾* **Oh It's Saucepot** 2-9-0 0 ..... RichardMullen 2 33
(Chris Wall) *s.i.s: sn pushed along in rr: wknd 2f out* **66/1**

1m 12.97s (0.47) **Going Correction** -0.05s/f (Good) **10** Ran SP% **116.5**
Speed ratings (Par 96): **94,92,92,88,87 87,82,80,77,75**
CSF £74.00 TOTE £3.60: £1.50, £6.90, £2.60; EX 81.10 Trifecta £510.70.
Owner Godolphin **Bred** Darley **Trained** Newmarket, Suffolk
■ Stewards' Enquiry : Lucy K Barry £290 fine; received an incoming call when the phone had been outside the designated area

FOCUS
Just a fair maiden. The level is fluid, but the third helps with the opening level, along with the race average.

4595 HOME OF HORSERACING NURSERY H'CAP 7f
6:40 (6:40) (Class 4) 2-Y-O **£4,528** (£1,347; £673; £336) **Stalls** High

Form RPR

2411 **1** **Montataire (IRE)**[14] 4076 2-9-7 **82** ..... JamesDoyle 6 91+
(Mark Johnston) *mde all: rdn over 1f out: r.o wl* **4/9**[1]

01 **2** *3¼* **Luduamf (IRE)**[20] 3897 2-7-7 **62** ..... HollieDoyle(7) 4 61
(Richard Hannon) *jnd wnr after 1f tl pushed along over 3f out: lost 2nd over 2f out: rdn and edgd lft over 1f out: wnt 2nd again ins fnl f: styd on same pce* **12/1**

5120 **3** *2½* **Spirit Of Sarwan (IRE)**[13] 4150 2-9-0 **76** ..... AdamBeschizza 3 68
(Julia Feilden) *hld up: hdwy u.p and edgd rt over 1f out: no ex ins fnl f* **5/1**[2]

3045 **4** *½* **Champion Harbour (IRE)**[13] 4167 2-8-5 **67** ..... PatrickMathers 1 58
(Richard Fahey) *hld up: hdwy 1/2-way: chsd wnr over 2f out: sn rdn: no ex ins fnl f* **8/1**[3]

502 **5** *5* **Phoenix Dawn**[31] 3495 2-8-10 **72** ..... RichardMullen 7 49
(Brendan Powell) *w wnr 1f: chsd ldrs: rdn 1/2-way: wknd over 1f out* **14/1**

1m 24.83s (-0.87) **Going Correction** -0.05s/f (Good) **5** Ran SP% **111.4**
Speed ratings (Par 96): **102,98,95,94,89**
CSF £7.09 TOTE £1.40: £1.10, £3.80; EX 6.10 Trifecta £14.90.
Owner Sheikh Hamdan bin Mohammed Al Maktoum **Bred** Tinnakill, P Lawlor & C Beale **Trained** Middleham Moor, N Yorks

FOCUS
This proved straightforward for the odds-on favourite.

4596 MARITIME CARGO SERVICES FILLIES' H'CAP (LONDON MILE SERIES QUALIFIER) 1m
7:10 (7:12) (Class 5) (0-70,70) 3-Y-O+ **£3,234** (£962; £481; £240) **Stalls** High

Form RPR

-552 **1** **Trulee Scrumptious**[7] 4356 7-9-1 **57** .....(v) JimmyQuinn 1 69
(Peter Charalambous) *swtchd to r alone on stands' side sn after s: mde all: clr over 5f out: rdn and hung lft over 1f out: styd on gamely* **6/1**[3]

2320 **2** *1* **Carpe Diem Lady (IRE)**[11] 4206 3-9-6 **70** ..... AdamKirby 6 78
(Clive Cox) *pushed along to ld main gp: rdn and hung rt fr over 2f out: clsd on wnr over 1f out: styd on u.p* **9/2**[2]

0441 **3** *5* **Fol O'Yasmine**[9] 4279 3-9-2 **66** 6ex .....(p) JamesMcDonald 5 63
(William Haggas) *chsd ldr: rdn and edgd rt over 1f out: wknd wl ins fnl f* **11/4**[1]

224 **4** *3¼* **Phoenix Beat**[16] 4025 3-9-5 **69** ..... FrankieDettori 12 58
(Gay Kelleway) *chsd ldrs: rdn over 3f out: hung rt and wknd ins fnl f* **9/2**[2]

0004 **5** *1¼* **Roccor**[14] 4085 3-8-13 **63** ..... SeanLevey 4 49
(Richard Hannon) *hld up: rdn over 2f out: nvr on terms* **12/1**

5-54 **6** *¾* **Blue Moon Rising (IRE)**[20] 3899 3-8-13 **70** ..... LuluStanford(7) 8 54
(Michael Bell) *hld up: plld hrd: rdn over 2f out: wknd fnl f* **16/1**

0510 **7** *1½* **Elegant Annie**[36] 3319 3-8-3 **58** ..... CharlieBennett(5) 11 39
(Jonathan Portman) *prom: rdn over 2f out: wknd over 1f out* **10/1**

1630 **8** *1* **Roxie Lot**[22] 3823 4-9-6 **65** ..... RobHornby(3) 3 46
(Pam Sly) *chsd ldrs: rdn over 2f out: wknd over 1f out* **12/1**

040 **9** *9* **Broughtons Mystery**[46] 2967 3-8-2 **52** ..... RyanPowell 13 10
(Willie Musson) *sn pushed along in rr: rdn over 3f out: wknd wl over 1f out* **50/1**

4206 **10** *7* **Primrose Brown**[113] 1158 5-9-9 **65** ..... SilvestreDeSousa 2 9
(Conrad Allen) *hld up: sme hdwy u.p over 1f out: sn wknd and eased* **20/1**

1m 38.38s (-1.62) **Going Correction** -0.05s/f (Good)
WFA 3 from 4yo+ 8lb **10** Ran SP% **114.4**
Speed ratings (Par 100): **106,105,100,96,95 94,93,92,83,76**
CSF £32.49 CT £93.23 TOTE £6.10: £1.80, £1.80, £1.40; EX 34.10 Trifecta £88.40.
Owner pcracing.co.uk **Bred** Dxb Bloodstock Ltd **Trained** Newmarket, Suffolk

FOCUS
This was a well-run handicap and the form looks sound. The winner has been rated in line with her best fast-ground form.

4597 STORTFORD INTERIORS SILVER JUBILEE MAIDEN STKS 1m 4f
7:40 (7:42) (Class 5) 3-4-Y-O **£3,881** (£1,155; £577; £288) **Stalls** Centre

Form RPR

1 **Crimean Tatar (TUR)** 3-9-2 0 ..... JamesMcDonald 2 96+
(Hugo Palmer) *s.i.s: sn prom: chsd ldr 7f out: led 3f out: rdn clr fr over 1f out: easily* **6/4**[1]

43 **2** *7* **Mazalto (IRE)**[23] 3781 3-8-11 0 ..... JFEgan 8 77
(Pat Phelan) *hld up: hdwy over 2f out: rdn to chse wnr over 1f out: sn hung lft and styd on same pce* **14/1**

353 **3** *5* **Golden Reign (IRE)**[36] 3305 3-8-11 76 .....(p) SilvestreDeSousa 5 69
(William Haggas) *chsd ldrs: pushed along over 4f out: rdn over 2f out: wknd fnl f* **3/1**[3]

4-0 **4** *4½* **Satish**[100] 1426 3-9-2 0 .....(b[1]) FrankieDettori 1 67
(John Gosden) *led: hdd 3f out: rdn over 1f out: sn wknd* **5/2**[2]

46 **5** *18* **Daily News**[15] 4056 3-9-2 0 ..... HarryBentley 7 38
(Roger Varian) *hld up: pushed along over 7f out: hdwy over 4f out: rdn and wknd 2f out* **12/1**

0500 **6** *39* **King Julien (IRE)**[35] 3341 3-8-9 58 ..... LuluStanford(7) 3
(John Ryan) *chsd ldr over 4f: wknd over 5f out* **33/1**

2m 28.94s (-3.96) **Going Correction** -0.125s/f (Firm) **6** Ran SP% **110.9**
Speed ratings (Par 103): **108,103,100,97,85 59**
CSF £22.55 TOTE £2.00: £1.20, £5.70; EX 18.80 Trifecta £57.20.
Owner V I Araci **Bred** Vefa Ibrahim Araci **Trained** Newmarket, Suffolk

FOCUS
This was run at an honest gallop and they finished well strung out. The runner-up has been rated in line with her promising efforts for her previous yard.

4598 RACING UK HD H'CAP 1m 4f
8:10 (8:12) (Class 3) (0-95,89) 3-Y-O+ **£7,762** (£2,310; £1,154) **Stalls** Centre

Form RPR

/221 **1** **Ruwasi**[15] 4044 5-9-12 **87** ..... MartinHarley 3 97+
(James Tate) *hld up: hdwy to ld over 1f out: qcknd clr: easily* **9/4**[2]

1131 **2** *3½* **Regal Monarch**[28] 3615 3-8-12 **85** ..... JoeFanning 2 88
(Mark Johnston) *chsd ldr tl led over 2f out: rdn and hdd over 1f out: sn outpcd* **5/6**[1]

4155 **3** *19* **Nayel (IRE)**[13] 4129 4-10-0 **89** .....(b) SeanLevey 1 62
(Richard Hannon) *led at stdy pce: qcknd over 3f out: rdn and hdd over 2f out: wknd and eased over 1f out* **3/1**[3]

2m 30.68s (-2.22) **Going Correction** -0.125s/f (Firm)
WFA 3 from 4yo+ 12lb **3** Ran SP% **110.3**
Speed ratings (Par 107): **102,99,87**
CSF £4.69 TOTE £3.10; EX 4.30 Trifecta £3.20.
Owner Saeed Manana **Bred** Highbury Terrace Owners Club **Trained** Newmarket, Suffolk

FOCUS
The winner was impressive, but the early pace hadn't been strong and the winning time was 1.74sec slower than the preceding maiden. The runner-up has been rated a bit off his best.

4599 NEWMARKETRACECOURSES.CO.UK H'CAP 7f
8:45 (8:45) (Class 4) (0-85,85) 3-Y-O+ **£5,175** (£1,540; £769; £384) **Stalls** High

Form RPR

2141 **1** **Battlement**[44] 3034 3-9-2 **80** .....(p) JamesDoyle 4 86+
(Roger Charlton) *trckd ldr tl led over 2f out: rdn and edgd rt ins fnl f: r.o* **6/4**[1]

3405 **2** *½* **Baltic Brave (IRE)**[21] 3849 5-9-7 **83** .....(t) CharlieBennett(5) 3 90
(Hughie Morrison) *hld up: hdwy 2f out: rdn to chse wnr ins fnl f: r.o* **6/1**

1240 **3** *3½* **Plucky Dip**[6] 4402 5-10-0 **85** ..... FrankieDettori 5 83
(John Ryan) *hld up in tch: rdn over 2f out: chsd wnr over 1f out tl no ex ins fnl f* **4/1**[3]

-316 **4** *¾* **Inland Sea (USA)**[51] 2788 3-9-7 **85** ..... SeanLevey 2 78
(Richard Hannon) *led: racd keenly: hdd over 2f out: rdn over 1f out: styd on same pce fnl f* **6/1**

0051 **5** *7* **Kestrel Dot Com**[60] 2540 4-9-5 **76** ..... SilvestreDeSousa 1 53
(Chris Dwyer) *plld hrd and prom: rdn over 2f out: wknd ins fnl f* **10/3**[2]

1m 25.74s (0.04) **Going Correction** -0.05s/f (Good)
WFA 3 from 4yo+ 7lb **5** Ran SP% **111.7**
Speed ratings (Par 105): **97,96,92,91,83**
CSF £11.00 TOTE £2.10: £1.30, £2.80; EX 12.40 Trifecta £40.00.
Owner K Abdullah **Bred** Juddmonte Farms Ltd **Trained** Beckhampton, Wilts

FOCUS
Not a bad handicap, and it was won by an improving filly.
T/Plt: £39.50 to a £1 stake. Pool: £53,668.99 - 989.91 winning units. T/Qpdt: £10.00 to a £1 stake. Pool: £4,496.53 - 332.62 winning units. **Colin Roberts**

4235 THIRSK (L-H)
Friday, July 22

OFFICIAL GOING: Good to firm (8.9)
Wind: Breezy, half against Weather: Cloudy, sunny spells, warm

4600 SKYBET GO RACING IN YORKSHIRE SUMMER FESTIVAL (S) H'CAP 7f
2:00 (2:03) (Class 6) (0-65,62) 3-Y-O **£2,587** (£770; £384; £192) **Stalls** Low

Form RPR

3350 **1** **Mango Chutney**[18] 3952 3-9-3 **58** .....(p) PhillipMakin 1 64
(John Davies) *prom: effrt over 2f out: led over 1f out: edgd lft ins fnl f: rdn out* **9/2**[2]

0054 **2** *1* **Lozah**[10] 4240 3-9-1 **56** .....(tp) SamJames 3 59
(David Loughnane) *hld up in midfield: rdn over 2f out: hdwy over 1f out: chsd wnr ins fnl f: r.o* **6/1**

-060 **3** *hd* **A Boy Named Sue**[16] 4006 3-8-2 **48** ..... NathanEvans(5) 12 51
(Peter Niven) *t.k.h: hld up: rdn and hdwy 2f out: kpt on ins fnl f* **11/1**

3402 **4** *1¾* **Mecca's Missus (IRE)**[8] 4316 3-9-4 **59** .....(p) PaulMulrennan 6 57
(Michael Dods) *t.k.h: led: rdn over 2f out: hdd over 1f out: outpcd ins fnl f* **7/2**[1]

2043 **5** *hd* **Ettie Hart (IRE)**[8] 4289 3-9-0 **55** ..... FrannyNorton 9 52
(Mick Channon) *t.k.h: pressed ldr: rdn over 2f out: kpt on same pce appr fnl f* **5/1**[3]

6050 **6** *shd* **Andaz**[5] 4424 3-9-5 **60** .....(e) CamHardie 11 57
(Marjorie Fife) *mounted on crse and taken early to post: s.i.s: bhd: rdn over 2f out: kpt on fnl f: nvr able to chal* **20/1**

3060 **7** 1/2 **Ginger Joe**[23] 3786 3-9-4 **62** .... KieranShoemark(3) 10 58
(David Brown) *hld up in midfield: hdwy on outside over 2f out: rdn and no ex over 1f out* **16/1**

5406 **8** 3/4 **Stormy Art (IRE)**[18] 3946 3-8-12 **53** .... TomEaves 13 47
(Michael Dods) *hld up: rdn along over 2f out: nvr able to chal* **11/1**

0400 **9** 1/2 **Bazula (IRE)**[6] 4410 3-9-0 **58** ....(b) RachelRichardson(3) 2 51
(Tim Easterby) *trckd ldrs: effrt whn nt clr run over 1f out: sn rdn: outpcd fnl f* **33/1**

0220 **10** 11 **Mr Potter**[43] 3080 3-9-3 **58** ....(e) BenCurtis 4 21
(Richard Guest) *rn wout off-hind shoe: dwlt: sn in tch: rdn over 3f out: wknd over 2f out: eased whn btn fnl f* **8/1**

1m 27.16s (-0.04) **Going Correction** -0.075s/f (Good) **10** Ran SP% **112.7**
Speed ratings (Par 98): **97,95,95,93,93 93,92,91,91,78**
CSF £30.53 CT £283.61 TOTE £3.80: £1.10, £2.30, £4.20; EX 39.10 Trifecta £351.50.There was no bid for the winner
Owner P Taylor **Bred** P Taylor **Trained** Piercebridge, Durham

FOCUS
The sixth meeting of the 2016 Go Racing In Yorkshire Summer Festival. The going was officially described as Good to firm, though clerk of the course James Sanderson reported that conditions would be "on the easy side of that in places". The rail on the home bend had been moved out and resulted in Races 1, 4 and 6 being run over an additional 20 yards. A very ordinary opener. Those close up help set the straightforward level.

4601 THE EBFSTALLIONS.COM MAIDEN STKS 5f
2:30 (2:31) (Class 5) 2-Y-O **£3,234** (£962; £481; £240) **Stalls** High

Form RPR

2 **1** **Fashion Queen**[14] 4110 2-9-0 0 .... DanielTudhope 2 78+
(David O'Meara) *cl up on outside: led gng wl over 1f out: shkn up and kpt on wl fnl f: comf* **4/6**[1]

35 **2** 1 1/4 **Kodiac Khan (IRE)**[22] 3819 2-9-2 0 .... MarcMonaghan(3) 10 76
(Hugo Palmer) *prom: rdn along over 2f out: effrt and edgd lft over 1f out: chsd wnr ins fnl f: kpt on* **9/2**[3]

2 **3** 1 1/4 **Mama Africa (IRE)**[90] 1641 2-9-0 0 .... PhillipMakin 13 66
(David Barron) *cl up: ev ch over 2f out to over 1f out: rdn and kpt on same pce ins fnl f* **7/2**[2]

0 **4** 1/2 **Lou's Diamond**[71] 2193 2-8-9 0 .... NathanEvans(5) 12 64
(Michael Easterby) *led tl rdn and hdd over 1f out: outpcd ins fnl f* **50/1**

5 5 **Vocalisation (IRE)** 2-9-0 0 .... BenCurtis 9 46
(John Weymes) *cl up: rdn over 2f out: wknd over 1f out* **100/1**

6 1 1/2 **Tranquil Daze (IRE)** 2-9-2 0 .... KieranShoemark(3) 8 46
(David Brown) *midfield: drvn along over 2f out: edgd lft and wknd over 1f out* **28/1**

7 shd **Darvie** 2-9-5 0 .... SamJames 11 45
(David Barron) *dwlt: bhd tl hdwy over 1f out: nvr able to chal* **66/1**

00 **8** 3/4 **Myllachy**[10] 4227 2-8-11 0 .... RachelRichardson(3) 4 38
(Tim Easterby) *dwlt: towards rr: rdn over 2f out: edgd lft and kpt on fr over 1f out: n.d* **80/1**

6 **9** 1/2 **Whitby Bay**[29] 3562 2-9-0 0 .... CamHardie 5 36
(Michael Easterby) *towards rr: drvn along 1/2-way: btn over 1f out* **100/1**

10 1 1/4 **Cheerful Character (IRE)** 2-9-0 0 .... TonyHamilton 7 31
(Richard Fahey) *midfield: pushed along 1/2-way: hung lft and wknd over 1f out* **12/1**

00 **11** 1 1/2 **On Show (IRE)**[7] 4363 2-8-12 0 .... TomDonoghue(7) 1 31
(David Brown) *s.i.s: bhd and sn outpcd: nvr on terms* **200/1**

12 1/2 **Hot Hannah** 2-9-0 0 .... PaulMulrennan 3 24
(Michael Dods) *s.i.s: a outpcd and bhd* **25/1**

58.6s (-1.00) **Going Correction** -0.20s/f (Firm) **12** Ran SP% **122.5**
Speed ratings (Par 94): **100,98,96,95,87 84,84,83,82,80 78,77**
CSF £4.18 TOTE £1.40: £1.02, £1.70, £1.50; EX 4.40 Trifecta £10.00.
Owner Clipper Logistics **Bred** Bolton Grange **Trained** Upper Helmsley, N Yorks

FOCUS
An uncompetitive maiden, in which the favourite set a clear standard. The top three in the market filled the first three places.

4602 RACINGUK.COM/HD NURSERY H'CAP 6f
3:05 (3:05) (Class 3) 2-Y-O **£6,469** (£1,925; £962; £481) **Stalls** High

Form RPR

31 **1** **Alicante Dawn**[30] 3515 2-9-7 **76** .... PaulMulrennan 6 89+
(Bryan Smart) *mde all: rdn over 1f out: drew clr fnl f: readily* **7/2**[1]

0002 **2** 4 **Kilbaha Lady (IRE)**[7] 4364 2-8-0 **58** ow1 .... RachelRichardson(3) 5 58
(Nigel Tinkler) *dwlt: t.k.h: hld up: rdn along 2f out: swtchd rt 1f out: kpt on to take 2nd nr fin: nt pce of wnr* **10/1**

502 **3** 1/2 **Lady Cristal (IRE)**[27] 3654 2-9-5 **74** .... DougieCostello 3 73
(K R Burke) *t.k.h: trckd ldrs: rdn and wnt 2nd over 1f out: kpt on same pce fnl f: lost 2nd nr fin* **9/1**

455 **4** 3/4 **Kahrab (IRE)**[51] 2800 2-8-13 **68** .... FrannyNorton 7 64
(Mark Johnston) *dwlt: sn trcking ldrs: rdn over 2f out: kpt on same pce fnl f* **17/2**

330 **5** nk **Percy Toplis**[78] 1976 2-8-12 **67** .... ShaneGray 4 62
(Kevin Ryan) *dwlt: hld up in tch: rdn and edgd lft over 1f out: sn no imp* **12/1**

633 **6** nk **Suitcase 'N' Taxi**[23] 3772 2-8-12 **67** .... DavidAllan 9 61
(Tim Easterby) *hld up bhd ldng gp: rdn over 2f out: hdwy and drifted lft over 1f out: no ex ins fnl f* **6/1**[3]

2321 **7** 1 3/4 **Springforth**[16] 4002 2-8-11 **66** .... TonyHamilton 2 55
(Richard Fahey) *pressed wnr: rdn over 2f out: lost 2nd over 1f out: wknd ins fnl f* **11/2**[2]

403 **8** 2 1/4 **Bear Essentials (IRE)**[18] 3939 2-9-1 **70** .... DanielTudhope 8 51
(David O'Meara) *hld up: rdn and struggling over 2f out: sn btn* **11/2**[2]

503 **9** 3 1/4 **Mulwith (IRE)**[50] 2830 2-8-10 **65** .... JamesSullivan 10 36
(David Barron) *hld up: rdn over 2f out: sn struggling: btn over 1f out* **10/1**

1m 11.02s (-1.68) **Going Correction** -0.20s/f (Firm) **9** Ran SP% **113.7**
Speed ratings (Par 98): **103,97,97,96,95 95,92,89,85**
CSF £38.72 CT £288.24 TOTE £4.70: £1.40, £2.20, £3.20; EX 31.40 Trifecta £126.80.
Owner B Smart **Bred** Natton House Thoroughbreds **Trained** Hambleton, N Yorks

FOCUS
An informative race, in which seven of the nine runners were making their handicap debuts. The winner proved in a different league. The runner-up has been rated close to her latest form.

4603 BRITISH STALLION STUDS EBF MAIDEN FILLIES' STKS (PLUS 10 RACE) 7f
3:40 (3:40) (Class 4) 2-Y-O **£4,269** (£1,270; £634; £317) **Stalls** Low

Form RPR

5 **1** **Glitter Girl**[15] 4064 2-9-0 0 .... BenCurtis 11 83+
(William Haggas) *trckd ldrs on outside: rdn to ld over 1f out: kpt on strly fnl f* **5/4**[1]

0 **2** 1 1/4 **Iconic Belle**[22] 3812 2-9-0 0 .... PaulMulrennan 9 78
(Mick Channon) *s.i.s: hld up: hdwy on outside over 2f out: edgd lft and kpt on ins fnl f: tk 2nd last stride* **33/1**

34 **3** shd **Starlight Romance (IRE)**[13] 4161 2-9-0 0 .... TonyHamilton 6 77
(Richard Fahey) *chsd ldrs: rdn along over 2f out: rallied and chsd wnr over 1f out: hung lft ins fnl f: kpt on: ct for 2nd last stride* **2/1**[2]

24 **4** 5 **Miss Sheridan (IRE)**[15] 4037 2-9-0 0 .... CamHardie 7 64
(Michael Easterby) *led at ordinary gallop: rdn and hdd over 1f out: outpcd fnl f* **25/1**

25 **5** 1/2 **Conistone**[52] 2779 2-9-0 0 .... GrahamLee 2 63
(James Bethell) *hld up in tch: rdn along over 2f out: no imp fr over 1f out* **16/1**

6 1 1/4 **Mistress Viz (IRE)** 2-9-0 0 .... PJMcDonald 5 59
(John Mackie) *s.i.s: rn green in rr: sme hdwy over 1f out: nvr rchd ldrs* **100/1**

7 2 1/4 **Poppy May (IRE)** 2-9-0 0 .... TomEaves 10 53
(James Given) *in tch: effrt and rdn over 2f out: wknd appr fnl f* **50/1**

4 **8** 1 **Dancing Elegance**[29] 3556 2-9-0 0 .... WilliamCarson 3 50
(Michael Bell) *s.i.s: hdwy into midfield after 2f: rdn and outpcd over 2f out: n.d after* **16/1**

9 nk **Tomorrowcomes (IRE)** 2-9-0 0 .... DavidNolan 4 50
(Richard Fahey) *hld up: pushed along 3f out: nvr able to chal* **14/1**

4 **10** 3 3/4 **Miss Danby (IRE)**[28] 3592 2-9-0 0 .... FrannyNorton 1 42
(Mark Johnston) *cl up: rdn along over 2f out: wknd over 1f out* **11/1**[3]

11 1 1/2 **Shannah Bint Eric** 2-9-0 0 .... KevinStott 8 35
(Kevin Ryan) *dwlt: hld up on outside: hung rt bnd ent st: rdn and edgd lft over 2f out: sn btn* **40/1**

1m 27.7s (0.50) **Going Correction** -0.075s/f (Good) **11** Ran SP% **116.7**
Speed ratings (Par 93): **94,92,92,86,86 84,82,81,80,76 74**
CSF £58.90 TOTE £2.10: £1.10, £9.90, £1.20; EX 44.20 Trifecta £162.00.
Owner Cheveley Park Stud **Bred** Cheveley Park Stud Ltd **Trained** Newmarket, Suffolk

FOCUS
Rail movements added 20 yards to this race distance. The betting suggested this was little more than a match. The third has been rated close to her mark.

4604 JW 4X4 NORTHALLERTON FILLIES' H'CAP 6f
4:15 (4:15) (Class 5) (0-70,70) 3-Y-O+ **£3,234** (£962; £481; £240) **Stalls** High

Form RPR

323 **1** **Hilary J**[15] 4035 3-9-7 **70** .... PJMcDonald 8 78
(Ann Duffield) *taken early to post: mde virtually all: hrd pressed fr over 1f out: kpt on gamely last 75yds* **4/1**[2]

3432 **2** 3/4 **Courier**[10] 4240 4-9-5 **66** ....(p) JacobButterfield(3) 2 73
(Marjorie Fife) *w ldrs: str chal fr over 1f out to ins fnl f: kpt on: hld nr fin* **2/1**[1]

4160 **3** 3/4 **Ponty Royale (IRE)**[20] 3885 3-9-0 **63** .... DavidAllan 1 67
(Tim Easterby) *dwlt: hld up in tch on outside: effrt and edgd lft over 1f out: kpt on same pce ins fnl f* **5/1**[3]

40-5 **4** 1 1/2 **Bahamian Bird**[16] 4007 3-8-11 **60** .... TonyHamilton 5 59
(Richard Fahey) *hld up: rdn over 2f out: hdwy over 1f out: kpt on ins fnl f* **5/1**[3]

0060 **5** shd **Percy's Gal**[16] 4006 5-9-0 **63** .... GemmaTutty(5) 7 62
(Karen Tutty) *taken early to post: hld up: rdn and hdwy over 1f out: no imp fnl f* **6/1**

6050 **6** 13 **Sunrise Dance**[11] 4192 7-8-7 **51** oh6 .... JoeyHaynes 4 9
(Kenny Johnson) *w ldrs: rdn over 2f out: wknd over 1f out* **66/1**

-040 **7** 11 **Arize (IRE)**[52] 2777 3-9-2 **65** .... TomEaves 6
(David Brown) *cl up: rdn over 2f out: wknd wl over 1f out: eased whn btn ins fnl f* **12/1**

1m 10.42s (-2.28) **Going Correction** -0.20s/f (Firm)
WFA 3 from 4yo+ 5lb **7** Ran SP% **110.1**
Speed ratings (Par 100): **107,106,105,103,102 85,70**
CSF £11.48 CT £36.12 TOTE £4.90: £2.40, £1.30; EX 12.10 Trifecta £56.10.
Owner E & R Stott **Bred** Bumble Bloodstock Ltd **Trained** Constable Burton, N Yorks

FOCUS
A moderate fillies' only handicap. The runner-up has been rated to her latest form for now.

4605 LADIES' DAY SATURDAY 3RD SEPTEMBER BOOK NOW H'CAP 7f
4:45 (4:48) (Class 4) (0-80,79) 3-Y-O **£4,851** (£1,443; £721; £360) **Stalls** Low

Form RPR

153 **1** **Briyouni (FR)**[35] 3357 3-9-4 **76** .... KevinStott 2 86+
(Kevin Ryan) *chsd clr ldr: stdy hdwy 3f out: shkn up to ld over 1f out: pushed along and idled ins fnl f: kpt on* **5/2**[1]

5250 **2** 1/2 **King Of Swing**[25] 3716 3-9-2 **74** ....(b[1]) TomEaves 3 80
(James Given) *t.k.h: led and clr to over 2f out: rdn and hdd over 1f out: rallied: kpt on fnl f: hld nr fin* **11/1**

42-4 **3** 7 **Regal Response (IRE)**[28] 3609 3-9-3 **75** ....(p) PaulMulrennan 8 62
(Michael Dods) *chsd ldrs: effrt whn rdr dropped whip over 2f out: edgd lft and outpcd over 1f out: kpt on fnl f: no ch w first two* **10/3**[2]

0200 **4** nk **Atholblair Boy (IRE)**[33] 3439 3-9-1 **73** .... TonyHamilton 7 59
(Nigel Tinkler) *hld up: pushed along over 2f out: edgd lft over 1f out: sn no imp* **33/1**

1051 **5** 1 1/4 **Bint Arcano (FR)**[15] 4043 3-9-0 **75** .... JacobButterfield(3) 6 58
(Julie Camacho) *in tch: hdwy over 2f out: sn rdn: outpcd fnl f* **9/2**[3]

1 **6** 1 1/4 **Donnelly's Rainbow (IRE)**[24] 3744 3-9-2 **74** .... BarryMcHugh 5 54
(Rebecca Bastiman) *missed break: hld up: shkn up over 2f out: no imp fr over 1f out* **12/1**

1m 26.09s (-1.11) **Going Correction** -0.075s/f (Good) **6** Ran SP% **88.8**
Speed ratings (Par 102): **103,102,94,94,92 91**
CSF £17.26 CT £36.53 TOTE £2.70: £1.20, £4.60; EX 18.40 Trifecta £48.30.
Owner Matt & Lauren Morgan **Bred** S C E A Elevage De La Croix De Place **Trained** Hambleton, N Yorks

■ Il Piccolo Grande was withdrawn. Price at time of withdrawal 3-1. Rule 4 applies to all bets - deduction 25p in the pound.

FOCUS
Rail movements added 20 yards to the race distance. The late withdrawal of Il Piccolo Grande meant this was not as competitive as previously advertised. The first two pulled clear. The runner-up is the key to the form and has been rated to the better view of his 6f form here in May.

4606 RACING EXCELLENCE "HANDS AND HEELS" APPRENTICE H'CAP 5f
5:15 (5:15) (Class 6) (0-65,65) 3-Y-O+ **£2,587** (£770; £384; £192) **Stalls** High

Form RPR

5503 **1** **Penny Royale**[19] 3925 4-9-6 **62** ....(p) HannahWorrall(5) 5 69
(Tim Easterby) *w ldr: shkn up to ld over 1f out: hrd pressed fnl f: kpt on wl* **7/2**[1]

3622 **2** 1/2 **Tinsill**[8] 4309 5-8-10 **50**....(p) DavidEgan(3) 1 55
(Nigel Tinkler) *trckd ldrs: pushed along 1/2-way: effrt and ev ch ins fnl f: kpt on: hld nr fin* **9/2**[3]

-000 **3** *hd* **Tavener**[28] 3610 4-10-0 **65**.... PatrickVaughan 4 69
(David O'Meara) *prom: pushed along 1/2-way: effrt and ev ch briefly ins fnl f: kpt on same pce towards fin* **7/2**[1]

0034 **4** 2 1/2 **Gaelic Wizard (IRE)**[8] 4309 8-9-6 **60**....(v) PaulaMuir(3) 3 55
(Karen Tutty) *dwlt: bhd and sn outpcd: hdwy over 1f out: kpt on fnl f: nvr able to chal* **5/1**

0002 **5** 2 **Frangarry (IRE)**[22] 3822 4-9-2 **58**....(b) LiamLewis-Salter(5) 2 46
(Alan Bailey) *led: rdn and hdd over 1f out: wknd ins fnl f* **4/1**[2]

-060 **6** 11 **Storm Lightning**[20] 3907 7-10-0 **65**.... BeckyBrisbourne 6 13
(Mark Brisbourne) *sn wl bhd: no ch fr 1/2-way: t.o* **7/1**

58.68s (-0.92) **Going Correction** -0.20s/f (Firm) **6** Ran SP% **111.8**
Speed ratings (Par 101): **99,98,97,93,90 73**
CSF £19.10 CT £56.66 TOTE £4.90: £3.10, £1.60; EX 15.60 Trifecta £49.30.
Owner C H Stevens **Bred** Habton Farms **Trained** Great Habton, N Yorks

FOCUS
This was strongly run and few got involved. The winner has been rated to the best of this year's form.
T/Plt: £24.30 to a £1 stake. Pool: £55,350.37 - 1,662.04 winning tickets T/Qpdt: £5.40 to a £1 stake. Pool: £3,979.79 - 538.60 winning tickets **Richard Young**

4161 YORK (L-H)
Friday, July 22

OFFICIAL GOING: Good to firm (7.4)
Wind: Light behind Weather: Cloudy with sunny periods

4607 THINK AS ONE APPRENTICE STKS (H'CAP) 1m 208y
6:00 (6:03) (Class 4) (0-80,79) 3-Y-O **£6,469** (£1,925; £962; £481) **Stalls** Low

Form RPR

2521 **1** **Cote D'Azur**[3] 4476 3-9-7 **79** 6ex.... ManuelFernandes(5) 7 90+
(Sir Mark Prescott Bt) *stdd s and hld up in rr: smooth hdwy on inner 3f out: trckd ldrs wl over 1f out: rdn to ld ent fnl f: readily* **9/4**[1]

1-36 **2** 1 1/4 **Shufoog**[48] 2900 3-9-1 **71**.... GeorgiaCox(3) 4 76
(William Haggas) *trckd ldrs: hdwy over 3f out: cl up 2f out: rdn to ld 1 1/2f out: drvn and hdd ent fnl f: kpt on* **7/2**[2]

6343 **3** 1 1/4 **Al Nasser Alwashik**[10] 4241 3-9-0 **72**.... CameronNoble(5) 8 74
(David Loughnane) *hld up in rr: hdwy on wd outside wl over 2f out: rdn over 1f out: kpt on fnl f: nrst fin* **9/1**

4 1/2 **Khabaray (IRE)**[33] 3446 3-8-13 **71**.... CliffordLee(5) 9 72
(David O'Meara) *trckd ldng pair: hdwy and cl up 3f out: led wl over 2f out: rdn and hdd 1 1/2f out: kpt on same pce* **12/1**

-200 **5** 8 **Cryptic (IRE)**[43] 3079 3-9-0 **72**.... GabrieleMalune(5) 11 56
(Luca Cumani) *led: rdn along over 3f out: hdd wl over 2f out: sn wknd* **14/1**

4514 **6** 5 **Clayton Hall (IRE)**[28] 3596 3-9-9 **76**.... CallumShepherd 6 49
(Brian Ellison) *t.k.h: trckd ldrs: hdwy 4f out: rdn along 2f out: sn drvn and wknd* **8/1**[3]

0100 **7** 3 **Back To Bond**[14] 4116 3-9-4 **71**.... AdamMcNamara 5 37
(Richard Fahey) *chsd ldrs: rdn along over 3f out: sn outpcd and bhd* **22/1**

24-6 **8** 3/4 **Catastrophe**[15] 4036 3-9-5 **72**.... NathanEvans 2 36
(John Quinn) *trckd ldr: cl up 1/2-way: rdn along over 3f out: sn wknd* **20/1**

6363 **9** 4 1/2 **The King's Steed**[20] 3876 3-8-8 **68**.... LaurenSteade(7) 3 22
(Micky Hammond) *in tch: rdn along 4f out: sn outpcd and bhd* **16/1**

1m 50.24s (-1.76) **Going Correction** -0.225s/f (Firm) **9** Ran SP% **103.5**
Speed ratings (Par 102): **98,96,95,95,88 83,81,80,76**
CSF £7.94 CT £40.11 TOTE £2.70: £1.40, £1.30, £2.50; EX 7.20 Trifecta £43.50.
Owner Neil Greig **Bred** W N Greig **Trained** Newmarket, Suffolk
■ Haraz was withdrawn. ptice at tim eof withdrawal 13-2. Rule 4 applies to all bets - deduction 10p in the pound.

FOCUS
A competitive handicap run over 25 yards shorter than advertised. The pace wasn't strong but the winner came from last to first and scored in fine style. The runner-up is unexposed and has been rated as improving on her Lingfield latest, while the fourth has been rated to the better view of his Irish form on his debut for David O'Meara.

4608 PREMIER DESIGN & PRINT STKS (H'CAP) 6f
6:30 (6:34) (Class 4) (0-80,80) 4-Y-O+ **£6,469** (£1,925; £962; £481) **Stalls** Centre

Form RPR

2204 **1** **Available (IRE)**[11] 4211 7-9-4 **77**....(tp) FrannyNorton 5 86
(John Mackie) *cl up towards far side: hdwy to ld wl over 1f out: sn rdn: drvn ins fnl f: kpt on wl towards fin* **16/1**

-005 **2** *hd* **Bop It**[28] 3610 7-8-8 **67**....(e) BenCurtis 6 75
(David O'Meara) *in tch towards far side: hdwy over 2f out: rdn over 1f out: styd on strly fnl f* **16/1**

5004 **3** 1 1/4 **Fyrecracker (IRE)**[7] 4376 5-8-12 **71**.... TomEaves 8 76+
(Grant Tuer) *hld up in tch towards far side: hdwy 2f out: sn chsng ldrs: rdn ins fnl f: styng on whn n.m.r towards fin* **14/1**

2300 **4** *hd* **Mass Rally (IRE)**[18] 3945 9-9-7 **80**....(b) PaulMulrennan 14 83+
(Michael Dods) *towards rr: hdwy wl over 1f out: sn rdn and styd on wl fnl f* **14/1**

2043 **5** *hd* **Meandmyshadow**[15] 4034 8-9-1 **74**....(b) DaleSwift 7 77
(Alan Brown) *racd towards far side: led: rdn along 2f out: sn hdd and drvn: wkng whn n.m.r towards fin* **25/1**

663 **6** 2 1/4 **Corporal Maddox**[13] 4132 9-9-3 **76**....(p) OisinMurphy 10 72
(Ronald Harris) *towards rr far side: rdn and hdwy 2f out: drvn over 1f out: kpt on fnl f* **20/1**

0650 **7** 1 1/4 **Whozthecat (IRE)**[4] 4452 9-8-11 **70**....(b) PJMcDonald 13 62
(Declan Carroll) *racd towards stands' side: prom: rdn along 2f out: drvn over 1f out: grad wknd* **20/1**

-006 **8** 1 1/4 **Signore Piccolo**[38] 3265 5-9-4 **77**.... DanielTudhope 15 65
(David O'Meara) *in tch towards stands' side: rdn along 2f out: sn no imp* **10/1**

0001 **9** *hd* **Field Game**[7] 4355 4-9-1 **74**....(t) JimCrowley 9 61
(Hughie Morrison) *in tch towards far side: rdn along over 2f out: n.d* **7/2**[1]

0204 **10** 3/4 **Compton Park**[5] 4428 9-9-5 **78**.... DavidAllan 20 62
(Les Eyre) *towards rr stands' side: swtchd lft and rdn 2f out: sme late hdwy* **14/1**

4030 **11** 1/2 **Mon Brav**[41] 3168 9-8-7 **73**.... BenRobinson(7) 4 56
(Brian Ellison) *towards rr far side tl sme late hdwy* **8/1**[3]

5041 **12** *nk* **Art Obsession (IRE)**[27] 3646 5-9-4 **77**.... DougieCostello 2 59
(Paul Midgley) *in tch far side: rdn along over 2f out: sn wknd* **7/1**[2]

3105 **13** 2 1/2 **Apricot Sky**[20] 3875 6-9-4 **77**.... TonyHamilton 11 51
(David Nicholls) *chsd ldrs towards far side: rdn along wl over 1f out: wknd ent fnl f* **12/1**

2020 **14** *nk* **Hit The Lights (IRE)**[8] 4295 6-8-1 **67**.... DanielleMooney(7) 18 40
(David Nicholls) *wnt lft s: racd towards stands' side: chsd ldrs: rdn along 2f out: sn wknd* **33/1**

4000 **15** 2 3/4 **Clergyman**[19] 3924 4-8-12 **71**.... BarryMcHugh 16 35
(Rebecca Bastiman) *dwlt and hmpd s: a towards rr stands' side* **50/1**

1643 **16** 1 1/4 **Something Lucky (IRE)**[20] 3875 4-9-6 **79**....(p) ShaneGray 3 39
(Kristin Stubbs) *a in rr far side* **20/1**

1312 **17** *nk* **Inexes**[13] 4142 4-9-4 **77**....(p) PhillipMakin 12 36
(Marjorie Fife) *a in rr* **9/1**

0001 **18** 1 1/4 **Slingsby**[28] 3610 5-8-11 **70**....(p) CamHardie 19 25
(Michael Easterby) *racd nr stands' rail: chsd ldrs: rdn along over 2f out: sn wknd* **28/1**

00-0 **19** 1/2 **Astrophysics**[15] 4032 4-9-4 **77**.... PaddyAspell 17 31
(Lynn Siddall) *sltly hmpd s: racd towards stands' rail and sn chsng ldrs: rdn along 2f out: sn wknd* **50/1**

1m 9.57s (-2.33) **Going Correction** -0.225s/f (Firm) **19** Ran SP% **132.8**
Speed ratings (Par 105): **106,105,104,103,103 100,98,97,96,95 94,91,91,87 85,85,83,83**
CSF £243.30 CT £3689.78 TOTE £19.60: £4.00, £4.10, £3.60, £4.10; EX 334.20 Trifecta £1938.90.
Owner Derbyshire Racing V **Bred** Carrigbeg Stud & David Powell **Trained** Church Broughton , Derbys

FOCUS
A competitive 6f handicap though most were exposed sorts. Initially they split into two groups thought they joined together in the closing stages but the low drawn horses held the call. A small pb from the winner, with the runner-up close to last year's form.

4609 BEST ONE MEDIAN AUCTION MAIDEN STKS (PLUS 10 RACE) 7f
7:00 (7:03) (Class 4) 2-Y-O **£6,469** (£1,925; £962; £481) **Stalls** Low

Form RPR

2 **1** **Tommy Taylor (USA)**[21] 3854 2-9-5 0.... TomEaves 5 85
(Kevin Ryan) *sn trcking ldr: hdwy and cl up over 4f out: led 1/2-way: rdn wl over 1f out: kpt on wl towards fin* **3/1**[2]

2 1/2 **Star Archer** 2-9-5 0.... JimCrowley 1 84+
(Hugo Palmer) *trckd ldrs: hdwy on inner over 2f out: rdn to chse wnr 1f out: sn drvn and kpt on wl towards fin* **6/4**[1]

02 **3** 3 1/4 **Used To Be**[15] 4040 2-9-5 0.... DougieCostello 9 75
(K R Burke) *trckd ldng pair: hdwy wl over 2f out: rdn to chal wl over 1f out: drvn and kpt on same pce fnl f* **6/1**[3]

4 *shd* **Honourable** 2-9-0 0.... TonyHamilton 10 70+
(Richard Fahey) *towards rr: hdwy on outer over 3f out: chsd ldrs 2f out: sn rdn and kpt on fnl f* **15/2**

50 **5** 5 **Oceanic (IRE)**[7] 4371 2-9-5 0.... CamHardie 6 61
(John Quinn) *led: pushed along and hdd 1/2-way: rdn wl over 2f out: grad wknd* **22/1**

00 **6** 2 1/4 **Pontecarlo Boy**[29] 3562 2-9-5 0.... GeorgeChaloner 8 55
(Richard Whitaker) *chsd ldrs: rdn along 3f out: sn wknd* **100/1**

7 *nk* **Bollin Ted** 2-9-5 0.... DavidAllan 3 54
(Tim Easterby) *a towards rr* **25/1**

63 **8** 1 1/4 **Mutahaady (IRE)**[17] 3971 2-9-5 0.... TomMarquand 4 51
(Richard Hannon) *dwlt: a in rr* **6/1**[3]

00 **9** 1 **Reinstorm**[15] 4040 2-9-5 0.... DavidNolan 2 48
(Richard Fahey) *a towards rr* **25/1**

1m 24.62s (-0.68) **Going Correction** -0.225s/f (Firm) **9** Ran SP% **118.4**
Speed ratings (Par 96): **94,93,89,89,83 81,80,79,78**
CSF £7.83 TOTE £3.80: £1.40, £1.20, £1.90; EX 8.30 Trifecta £25.60.
Owner Mrs Angie Bailey **Bred** Dr John A Chandler **Trained** Hambleton, N Yorks

FOCUS
Potentially an interesting juvenile event though spoiled to a degree by a slow early gallop. Even so the first two were clear and the third and fourth were clear of the others and the front four are all worth bearing in mind in the next few weeks. The third has been rated to his mark.

4610 BRITISH STALLION STUDS EBF LYRIC FILLIES' STKS (LISTED RACE) 1m 2f 88y
7:30 (7:32) (Class 1) 3-Y-O+
£22,684 (£8,600; £4,304; £2,144; £1,076; £540) **Stalls** Low

Form RPR

0-15 **1** **Diploma**[37] 3274 3-8-8 **100**.... TedDurcan 5 113+
(Sir Michael Stoute) *trckd ldrs: smooth hdwy on outer 3f out: led 2f out: rdn clr and edgd lft over 1f out: readily* **9/4**[1]

4205 **2** 3 1/4 **Fireglow**[12] 4184 3-8-8 **110**.... FrannyNorton 6 104
(Mark Johnston) *chsd clr ldr: tk clsr order over 3f out: cl up 2f out: sn rdn: drvn to chse wnr fnl f: sn no imp* **9/4**[1]

0-01 **3** 2 **Pandora (IRE)**[42] 3113 4-9-4 **99**.... PhillipMakin 2 100
(David O'Meara) *s.i.s and lost several l s: hld up in rr: hdwy over 3f out: rdn along 2f out: drvn and kpt on same pce fnl f: tk 3rd nr line* **9/2**[2]

1020 **4** *hd* **Beauly**[36] 3297 3-8-8 **98**.... PaulMulrennan 8 100
(Charles Hills) *hld up towards rr: hdwy over 3f out: rdn along to chse ldrs 2f out: sn drvn and kpt on same pce: lost 3rd nr line* **10/1**[3]

3243 **5** 2 **Oakley Girl**[28] 3608 4-9-4 **100**.... OisinMurphy 4 96
(Stuart Williams) *trckd ldrs: hdwy 4f out: rdn along and cl up 2f out: sn drvn and grad wknd* **10/1**[3]

2-60 **6** 10 **Lustrous**[33] 3436 5-9-4 **101**.... DanielTudhope 3 76
(David O'Meara) *led and sn clr: pushed along over 3f out: rdn over 2f out: sn hdd & wknd* **12/1**

24 **7** 2 1/2 **Rosental**[28] 3608 4-9-4 **97**.... JimCrowley 1 71
(Luca Cumani) *chsesd ldrs on inner: rdn along over 3f out: wknd wl over 2f out* **12/1**

2m 7.52s (-4.98) **Going Correction** -0.225s/f (Firm)
WFA 3 from 4yo+ 10lb **7** Ran SP% **113.3**
Speed ratings (Par 108): **110,107,105,105,104 96,94**
CSF £7.03 TOTE £3.00: £2.10, £1.90; EX 6.50 Trifecta £12.70.
Owner The Queen **Bred** The Queen **Trained** Newmarket, Suffolk

FOCUS
Race run over 25 yards shorter than advertised. A rather stop-start gallop to this fillies' Listed event, but an impressive display by the winner. The runner-up has yet to match her Guineas figure and this rates similar to the best of the rest of her form. The fourth has been rated close to form.

4611 NOVUS STKS (H'CAP) 1m
8:00 (8:02) (Class 3) (0-90,90) 3-Y-O+ **£8,086** (£2,406; £1,202; £601) **Stalls** Low

Form RPR

4012 **1** **Briardale (IRE)**[29] 3563 4-9-2 **78** TedDurcan 5 88
(James Bethell) *t.k.h early: hld up in rr: stdy hdwy on inner over 3f out: swtchd rt and trckd ldrs 2f out: swtchd rt to outer and rdn over 1f out: drvn ins fnl f: styd on wl to ld nr fin* **8/1**[3]

3304 **2** *hd* **Muntadab (IRE)**[14] 4081 4-9-6 **82** PJMcDonald 1 91
(David Loughnane) *trckd ldrs on inner: smooth hdwy 2f out: rdn to ld ent fnl f: sn drvn: hdd and no ex nr fin* **9/2**[1]

2020 **3** *3 1/2* **Pumaflor (IRE)**[30] 3517 4-9-1 **77** GeorgeChaloner 6 78
(Richard Whitaker) *slt ld: rdn along over 2f out: drvn wl over 1f out: hdd ent fnl f: kpt on same pce* **16/1**

030 **4** *1/2* **Purple Rock (IRE)**[13] 4129 4-8-8 **75** (t) NathanEvans(5) 3 75
(Michael Easterby) *in tch on inner: hdwy to chse ldrs over 3f out: rdn along over 2f out: drvn wl over 1f out: kpt on u.p fnl f* **12/1**

2302 **5** *nse* **Alejandro (IRE)**[30] 3518 7-9-11 **87** DavidNolan 13 87
(David O'Meara) *trckd ldrs: hdwy and cl up on outer 1/2-way: rdn along over 2f out: drvn wl over 1f out: kpt on same pce fnl f* **9/2**[1]

0050 **6** *nse* **Ingleby Angel (IRE)**[19] 3923 7-9-9 **85** TomEaves 2 85
(Colin Teague) *towards rr: hdwy over 2f out and sn rdn: drvn and styd on fnl f: nrst fin* **16/1**

0156 **7** *hd* **Shouranour (IRE)**[6] 4408 6-8-11 **78** (b) JoshDoyle(5) 14 77
(Alan Brown) *cl up: disp ld fr 1/2-way: rdn over 2f out: drvn and ev ch over 1f out: wknd fnl f* **25/1**

3560 **8** *nk* **Mont Ras (IRE)**[13] 4163 9-9-7 **90** CameronNoble(7) 4 88
(David Loughnane) *towards rr: hdwy on outer over 2f out: rdn wl over 1f out: styd on wl fnl f* **12/1**

1505 **9** *1* **Mystic Miraaj**[18] 3945 4-9-2 **78** (b) DavidAllan 15 74
(Tim Easterby) *dwlt and swtchd lft s: in rr tl sme late hdwy* **10/1**

232 **10** *3/4* **Imperial Focus (IRE)**[18] 3951 3-8-9 **79** JackGarritty 11 71
(Simon Waugh) *chsd ldrs: rdn along 3f out: drvn over 2f out: grad wknd* **12/1**

5253 **11** *nk* **Stardrifter**[17] 3983 4-8-12 **74** TonyHamilton 10 68
(Richard Fahey) *hld up: effrt and sme hdwy on outer 3f out: rdn along over 2f out: sn btn* **7/1**[2]

0143 **12** *shd* **Woody Bay**[14] 4113 6-9-5 **81** DougieCostello 7 74
(Mark Walford) *hld up: hdwy and in tch over 3f out: rdn along wl over 2f out: sn drvn and wknd* **7/1**[2]

-620 **13** *1 1/2* **Balducci**[21] 3849 9-9-5 **81** (v) SamJames 8 71
(David Loughnane) *a in rr* **20/1**

1m 36.96s (-2.04) **Going Correction** -0.225s/f (Firm)
WFA 3 from 4yo+ 8lb **13** Ran SP% **125.0**
Speed ratings (Par 107): **101,100,97,96,96 96,96,96,95,94 94,94,92**
CSF £45.95 CT £585.51 TOTE £8.50: £2.40, £2.30, £6.80; EX 60.00 Trifecta £1414.90.
Owner J Carrick&Clarendon Thoroughbred Racing **Bred** Rabbah Bloodstock Limited **Trained** Middleham Moor, N Yorks

FOCUS
Race run over 23 yards shorter than advertised. No more than a fair gallop to this handicap in which the first two finished clear. A pb from the winner, and a lesser pb from the runner-up.

4612 SKY BET GO-RACING-IN-YORKSHIRE SUMMER FESTIVAL STKS (H'CAP) 5f 89y
8:30 (8:33) (Class 4) (0-85,84) 3-Y-O **£6,469** (£1,925; £962; £481) **Stalls** Centre

Form RPR

2211 **1** **Just Glamorous (IRE)**[9] 4268 3-9-6 **83** 6ex OisinMurphy 2 97
(Ronald Harris) *qckly away and sn clr: rdn over 1f out: drvn ins fnl f: hld on gamely towards fin* **11/4**[1]

2114 **2** *nk* **East Street Revue**[20] 3893 3-8-13 **76** (b) DuranFentiman 4 89
(Tim Easterby) *prom: rdn along and hdwy wl over 1f out: drvn ins fnl f: styd on wl towards fin: jst hld* **8/1**[3]

-452 **3** *3/4* **Sandra's Secret (IRE)**[9] 4256 3-8-3 **66** FrannyNorton 9 76
(Les Eyre) *chsd wnr: rdn along and hdwy 2f out: drvn ins fnl f: kpt on towards fin* **11/1**

0214 **4** *nk* **Fumbo Jumbo (IRE)**[14] 4100 3-9-4 **81** DavidAllan 10 90
(Garry Moss) *chsd ldrs: rdn along over 2f out: drvn over 1f out: kpt on fnl f* **8/1**[3]

1434 **5** *3* **Geno (IRE)**[16] 4007 3-8-12 **75** (b) ShaneGray 6 73
(Kevin Ryan) *in tch: rdn along 2f out: drvn over 1f out: no imp* **8/1**[3]

214 **6** *1/2* **Discreet Hero (IRE)**[53] 2751 3-9-7 **84** (t) JimCrowley 1 80
(Simon Crisford) *towards rr: hdwy 2f out: sn rdn and n.d* **4/1**[2]

3413 **7** *1/2* **Rose Marmara**[20] 3893 3-9-3 **80** (t) JamesSullivan 12 75
(Brian Rothwell) *hmpd s and bhd: hdwy wl over 1f out: rdn and kpt on wl fnl f* **20/1**

4621 **8** *nk* **Geoff Potts (IRE)**[23] 3786 3-8-10 **73** RobertTart 5 66
(Jeremy Gask) *towards rr: sme hdwy 2f out: sn rdn and n.d* **12/1**

2324 **9** *nk* **Kingthistle**[18] 3948 3-8-7 **70** CamHardie 8 62
(Michael Easterby) *a towards rr* **25/1**

4532 **10** *3 1/2* **Tribesman**[11] 4192 3-8-2 **65** oh4 (b[1]) JoeyHaynes 3 45
(Marjorie Fife) *a in rr* **33/1**

1112 **11** *hd* **Black Grass**[28] 3611 3-8-10 **78** NathanEvans(5) 11 57
(Michael Easterby) *wnt rt s: chsd ldrs on outer: rdn along 2f out: sn wknd* **10/1**

1205 **12** *5* **First Bombardment**[14] 4093 3-8-13 **76** DanielTudhope 13 37
(David O'Meara) *wnt lft s: chsd ldrs on wd outside: rdn 2f out: sn wknd* **20/1**

1m 2.21s (-1.89) **Going Correction** -0.225s/f (Firm) **12** Ran SP% **121.4**
Speed ratings (Par 102): **106,105,104,103,99 98,97,96,96,90 90,82**
CSF £24.40 CT £220.09 TOTE £3.40: £1.60, £3.50, £3.30; EX 28.60 Trifecta £369.10.
Owner Robert & Nina Bailey **Bred** Glamorous Air Partnership **Trained** Earlswood, Monmouths

FOCUS
A strongly-run 5f handicap for three-year-olds in which few got involved, the draw didn't appear to play a significant role and the first four were clear. The second, third and fourth have been rated close to their marks.

T/Jkpt: Not won. T/Plt: £65.60 to a £1 stake. Pool: £94,176.83 - 1047.62 winning units. T/Qpdt: £9.50 to a £1 stake. Pool: £6,446.59 - 500.40 winning units. **Joe Rowntree**

4613 - 4619a (Foreign Racing) - See Raceform Interactive

4471 CHANTILLY (R-H)
Friday, July 22

OFFICIAL GOING: Turf: good

4620a PRIX ROLAND DE CHAMBURE (LISTED RACE) (2YO) (TURF) 7f
1:45 (1:45) 2-Y-O **£20,220** (£8,088; £6,066; £4,044; £2,022)

RPR

1 **Baileys Showgirl (FR)**[24] 3749 2-8-13 0 IoritzMendizabal 4 95
(Mark Johnston) *hld up: rdn to cl 2f out: reeled in ldr and led over 1f out: shade awkward u.p but r.o wl fnl f: asserted* **4/1**[2]

2 *2* **Red Onion**[35] 3378 2-9-2 0 ThierryThulliez 1 93
(C Lerner, France) **11/10**[1]

3 *nk* **Real Value (FR)**[21] 3871 2-9-2 0 EddyHardouin 2 92
(Mario Hofer, Germany) **13/1**

4 *4* **Platon**[58] 2601 2-9-2 0 AurelienLemaitre 3 82
(G E Mikhalides, France) **41/10**[3]

5 *hd* **Fashion Queen (GER)** 2-8-13 0 CristianDemuro 5 78
(Frau C Barsig, Germany) **87/10**

6 *2* **Madame Mistral (FR)**[19] 2-8-13 0 AntoineHamelin 7 73
(Matthieu Palussiere, France) **17/1**

7 *2* **Try Please (FR)** 2-9-2 0 (p) Pierre-CharlesBoudot 6 71
(Louis Baudron, France) **89/10**

1m 27.76s (1.66) **7** Ran SP% **120.3**
WIN (incl. 1 euro stake); 5.00. PLACES: 2.10, 1.40. SF: 11.80..
Owner G R Bailey Ltd (Baileys Horse Feeds) **Bred** Ecurie Des Monceaux **Trained** Middleham Moor, N Yorks

4621 - (Foreign Racing) - See Raceform Interactive

4579 ASCOT (R-H)
Saturday, July 23

OFFICIAL GOING: Good to firm (good in places on round course; stands' side 9.2, centre 8.9, farside 8.8; round 8.0)
Wind: Almost nil Weather: Fine, very warm

4622 WOOLDRIDGE GROUP PAT EDDERY STKS (FORMERLY KNOWN AS THE WINKFIELD STAKES) (LISTED RACE) 7f
2:10 (2:11) (Class 1) 2-Y-O
£17,013 (£6,450; £3,228; £1,608; £807; £405) **Stalls** Centre

Form RPR

01 **1** **Apex King (IRE)**[35] 3408 2-9-3 0 AndreaAtzeni 3 97
(Ed Dunlop) *cmpt: in tch: rdn wl over 2f out: clsd over 1f out: styd on ins fnl f to ld last strides* **12/1**

11 **2** *nk* **Monticello (IRE)**[26] 3705 2-9-3 0 JoeFanning 8 96+
(Mark Johnston) *unf: led to 3f out: pressed ldr after: drvn to ld again 1f out: kpt on u.p: hdd last strides* **9/2**[3]

15 **3** *hd* **Frankuus (IRE)**[35] 3382 2-9-3 0 RichardKingscote 5 96
(Mark Johnston) *lw: trckd ldrs: lost pl 3f out and sn rdn: rallied jst over 1f out: kpt on to take 3rd last stride* **11/2**

21 **4** *shd* **Mutawatheb (IRE)**[23] 3813 2-9-3 0 DaneO'Neill 7 95
(Richard Hannon) *athletic: trckd ldrs: lost pl and pushed along sn after 1/2-way: renewed effrt 2f out: clsd to chal ins fnl f: no ex last 75yds* **4/1**[2]

1 **5** *1/2* **Bahamas (IRE)**[29] 3598 2-9-3 0 RyanMoore 6 94
(Marco Botti) *q str: in tch towards rr: rdn wl over 2f out: clsd on ldrs over 1f out: kpt on but nvr quite pce to chal* **8/1**

41 **6** *1/2* **Alcazar**[30] 3561 2-9-3 0 JamieSpencer 4 93
(David Simcock) *w'like: nt over-big: awkward s: hld up in detached last: tried to cl on ldrs over 2f out: no imp over 1f out: swtchd lft ins fnl f and styd on nr fin* **25/1**

1 **7** *2* **Dubai Hero (FR)**[15] 4103 2-9-3 0 JamesDoyle 2 88+
(Saeed bin Suroor) *sn trckd ldr: led 3f out: drvn and hdd 1f out: wknd* **9/4**[1]

522 **8** *13* **King Of Spades (FR)**[22] 3871 2-9-3 0 SilvestreDeSousa 9 54
(Mick Channon) *struggling in rr sn after 1/2-way: t.o* **40/1**

01 **9** *3 1/4* **Burrishoole Abbey (IRE)**[31] 3516 2-9-3 0 DougieCostello 1 45+
(K R Burke) *w'like: dwlt: hld up: smooth prog to trck ldrs 1/2-way: wknd rapidly wl over 2f out: t.o* **20/1**

1m 27.07s (-0.53) **Going Correction** 0.0s/f (Good) **9** Ran SP% **114.2**
Speed ratings (Par 102): **103,102,102,102,101 101,98,84,80**
CSF £63.01 TOTE £13.60: £3.60, £1.90, £1.90; EX 74.50 Trifecta £368.20.
Owner Mohammed Jaber **Bred** Dr W O'Brien **Trained** Newmarket, Suffolk
■ Stewards' Enquiry : Dane O'Neill 11-day ban: used whip above permitted level (6-16 Aug)

FOCUS
The running rail was positioned so the course was as its widest configuration, but all race distances were as advertised. Raven's Pass, Toronado and Kodi Bear are probably the most recognisable names to have landed this in the past decade, so today's winner might be a potential star. The pace looked decent throughout, and it produced a thrilling outcome plus a proper test.

4623 PRINCESS MARGARET JUDDMONTE STKS (GROUP 3) (FILLIES) 6f
2:45 (2:46) (Class 1) 2-Y-O
£28,355 (£10,750; £5,380; £2,680; £1,345; £675) **Stalls** Centre

Form RPR

1 **1** **Fair Eva**[45] 3024 2-9-0 0 FrankieDettori 13 111+
(Roger Charlton) *athletic: lw: hld up: smooth prog 1/2-way: led and edgd rt briefly over 1f out: drew clr fnl f: impressive* **4/6**[1]

164 **2** *4* **Kilmah**[15] 4106 2-9-0 0 JoeFanning 9 98
(Mark Johnston) *lw: trckd ldng pair: clsd to chal 2f out: sltly impeded over 1f out: easily outpcd by wnr fnl f* **12/1**[3]

10 **3** *3/4* **Dainty Dandy (IRE)**[36] 3336 2-9-0 0 OlivierPeslier 6 96
(Paul Cole) *w ldr: led after 2f to over 1f out: sn easily outpcd* **25/1**

31 **4** *1 1/4* **Tallulah Rose**[42] 3122 2-9-0 0 SteveDrowne 12 92
(George Baker) *wl in rr: rdn over 2f out: prog over 1f out: rchd 4th ins fnl f: one pce after* **40/1**

13 **5** *1 1/4* **Marie Of Lyon**[28] 3663 2-9-0 0 JamieSpencer 2 88
(Richard Fahey) *mostly in midfield: rdn over 2f out: no imp on ldrs over 1f out: one pce after* **20/1**

6 *1/2* **How (IRE)**[20] 3926 2-9-0 0 RyanMoore 1 87
(A P O'Brien, Ire) *q str: stmbld s and slowly away: prog fr rr 1/2-way: rdn wl over 1f out: no hdwy after* **8/1**[2]

201 **7** *nk* **Madam Dancealot (IRE)**[16] 4054 2-9-0 0 OisinMurphy 10 86
(Joseph Tuite) *rdn in midfield sn after 1/2-way: nvr on terms after: one pce* **25/1**

10 **8** *hd* **Nasimi**[15] 4106 2-9-0 0 JamesDoyle 8 85
(Charlie Appleby) *swtg: lost midfield pl rapidly over 3f out and sn in last: no ch after: plugged on fnl f* **20/1**

114 **9** *1 3/4* **Kocollada (IRE)**[38] 3270 2-9-0 0 TonyHamilton 3 80
(Richard Fahey) *rdn towards rr sn after 1/2-way: nvr a factor* **16/1**

51 **10** *1* **Seduce Me**[19] 3947 2-9-0 0 JoeyHaynes 7 78
(K R Burke) *cmpt: chsd ldrs to 1/2-way: wknd 2f out* **25/1**

51 **11** *2 1/4* **Poet's Princess**[23] 3812 2-9-0 0 JimCrowley 4 70
(Hughie Morrison) *neat: racd freely: led 2f: chsd ldr to over 2f out: wknd qckly* **50/1**

10 **12** *2 3/4* **Kachess**[38] 3270 2-9-0 0[1] RichardKingscote 11 62
(Tom Dascombe) *in tch to 1/2-way: wknd over 2f out* **25/1**

1m 12.54s (-1.96) **Going Correction** 0.0s/f (Good) **12** Ran SP% **114.0**
Speed ratings (Par 101): **113,107,106,105,103 102,102,102,99,98 95,91**
CSF £6.33 TOTE £1.40: £1.10, £2.80, £7.00; EX 10.80 Trifecta £96.40.
Owner K Abdullah **Bred** Juddmonte Farms Ltd **Trained** Beckhampton, Wilts

FOCUS
This looked a decent edition of this Group 3, although the withdrawal at the start of Duchess Of Cambridge runner-up Magical Fire weakened it a little. The third and eleventh home disputed the running, racing towards the far side and a little way apart from the main bulk of the field. The time was quick, marginally inside standard and just 0.08sec outside Henrythenaviagtor's 2yo track record. The impressive winner has been rated to a level good enough to win four of the last ten 1000 Guineas, and the opening level looks sensible rated around the runner-up and a few down the field.

4624 WOODFORD RESERVE H'CAP 1m (S)
3:20 (3:22) (Class 2) 3-Y-O
£28,012 (£8,388; £4,194; £2,097; £1,048; £526) **Stalls** Centre

Form RPR

-210 **1** **Mustashry**[37] 3299 3-9-4 **95** DaneO'Neill 15 105
(Sir Michael Stoute) *lw: trckd ldrs: rdn to cl fr 2f out: led 1f out towards nr side: drvn out and hld on wl* **8/1**

2-11 **2** *nk* **Pirouette**[16] 4042 3-8-3 **80** KieranO'Neill 5 89+
(Hughie Morrison) *hld up in midfield: waiting for room briefly over 2f out: prog wl over 1f out towards far side: drvn to chal ins fnl f: styd on but jst hld* **7/1**

1-10 **3** *1* **Folkswood**[37] 3299 3-9-7 **98** JamesDoyle 1 104
(Charlie Appleby) *hld up in last trio: prog fr 3f out: drvn and tried to chal fnl f: styd on same pce* **9/2**[2]

661 **4** *1* **Kingston Kurrajong**[27] 3688 3-8-12 **89** JimmyQuinn 13 93
(Andrew Balding) *racd freely: led: rdn 2f out: hdd and one pce 1f out* **25/1**

-103 **5** *nk* **Taurean Star (IRE)**[10] 4263 3-8-12 **89** JamieSpencer 6 92+
(Michael Bell) *stdd s: hld up in last: shkn up 2f out: sme prog whn short of room briefly 1f out: styd on to take 5th nr fin: too much to do* **13/2**[3]

1-55 **6** *1/2* **Perkunas (IRE)**[14] 4149 3-9-7 **98** JimmyFortune 2 100
(Brian Meehan) *lw: hld up in midfield: prog over 2f out to chal jst over 1f out: one pce u.p* **25/1**

1-41 **7** *nse* **Von Blucher (IRE)**[14] 4149 3-9-2 **93** (t) RyanMoore 12 95
(John Gosden) *lw: hld up in midfield: pushed along whn swtchd lft 2f out: rdn and no imp on ldrs over 1f out: one pce* **3/1**[1]

1110 **8** *1/2* **Oh This Is Us (IRE)**[37] 3299 3-9-1 **92** PatDobbs 9 93
(Richard Hannon) *towards rr: shkn up over 2f out: kpt on fr over 1f out: nvr gng pce to threaten* **16/1**

412 **9** *nk* **El Hayem (IRE)**[10] 4271 3-8-13 **90** FrankieDettori 11 90
(Sir Michael Stoute) *chsd ldng pair tl lost pl wl over 1f out: n.d after* **10/1**

2226 **10** *1 3/4* **Lazzam**[119] 1103 3-9-4 **95** (b) AndreaAtzeni 3 91
(Marco Botti) *dwlt: hld up in last pair: rdn and tried to make prog 2f out: swtchd rt to far side of gp 1f out: no hdwy after* **50/1**

-300 **11** *2* **Zodiakos (IRE)**[15] 4108 3-8-7 **87** JosephineGordon[(3)] 10 78
(Hugo Palmer) *swtg: chsd ldr: rdn 3f out: lost 2nd and wknd qckly over 1f out* **9/1**

3-46 **12** *1/2* **Mohab**[16] 4065 3-9-7 **98** SilvestreDeSousa 4 88
(Kevin Ryan) *trckd ldrs: rdn and on terms 2f out: sing to weaken whn short of room jst ins fnl f: eased* **33/1**

-104 **13** *10* **Manson**[14] 4149 3-9-3 **94** JimCrowley 14 60
(Dominic Ffrench Davis) *t.k.h: hld up towards rr: wknd over 2f out: t.o* **14/1**

1m 39.85s (-0.95) **Going Correction** 0.0s/f (Good) **13** Ran SP% **124.4**
Speed ratings (Par 106): **104,103,102,101,101 100,100,100,100,98 96,95,85**
CSF £63.59 CT £300.79 TOTE £9.60: £3.00, £2.80, £2.40; EX 89.40 Trifecta £439.20.
Owner Hamdan Al Maktoum **Bred** Shadwell Estate Company Limited **Trained** Newmarket, Suffolk
■ Stewards' Enquiry : Jimmy Fortune caution: careless riding
Kieran O'Neill 16 day ban: used whip above permitted level (12-22 Aug; 5 days deferred until 3 Oct)
Dane O'Neill four-day ban: used whip above permitted level (20-23 Aug)

FOCUS
Generally this handicap has gone the way of an at least very useful handicapper, but it has also fallen to subsequent Group performers like Rave (now known as Military Attack in Hong Kong) and Chil The Kite. Portage, successful in 2015, won the Royal Hunt Cup this year. This year's winner has lots of scope for improvement. The form might prove better than rated but the sixth limits things for the time being.

4625 GIGASET INTERNATIONAL STKS (HERITAGE H'CAP) 7f
3:55 (3:56) (Class 2) 3-Y-O+
£93,375 (£27,960; £13,980; £6,990; £3,495; £1,755) **Stalls** Centre

Form RPR

2-12 **1** **Librisa Breeze**[38] 3273 4-9-1 **100** RobertWinston 14 112+
(Dean Ivory) *hld up last of centre gp: stdy prog over 2f out gng easily: rdn to ld ins fnl f: r.o wl: v readily* **4/1**[1]

24-0 **2** *1 1/2* **Squats (IRE)**[77] 2027 4-8-6 **98** GeorgiaCox[(7)] 22 106
(William Haggas) *dwlt: hld up in rr in centre: gd prog over 2f out to ld gp over 1f out: hdd and outpcd ins fnl f: styd on* **20/1**

-303 **3** *nk* **Scottish Glen**[36] 3358 10-8-4 **94** HectorCrouch[(5)] 2 101
(Patrick Chamings) *hld up far side: prog over 2f out: drvn and r.o to ld gp ins fnl f: no ch w wnr* **33/1**

5105 **4** *3/4* **Flash Fire (IRE)**[14] 4152 4-9-10 **109** JamesDoyle 6 114
(Charlie Appleby) *trckd ldrs far side: prog to ld gp 2f out to ins fnl f: styd on same pce* **12/1**

5561 **5** *hd* **Nuno Tristan (USA)**[35] 3419 4-8-8 **93** JamieSpencer 4 100+
(Richard Fahey) *lw: hld up in rr far side: waiting for room 2f out: nt clr run over 1f out and swtchd rt: gd prog fnl f: r.o wl nr fin* **14/1**

5505 **6** *1 1/4* **Lincoln (IRE)**[10] 4263 5-8-5 **90** SamHitchcott 9 91
(Mick Channon) *dwlt: in rr far side: rdn over 2f out: prog over 1f out: pressed ldrs in gp fnl f: kpt on but nt pce to chal* **16/1**

0243 **7** *1/2* **Withernsea (IRE)**[15] 4109 5-8-12 **97** TonyHamilton 25 97
(Richard Fahey) *trckd rival nr side: led pair over 1f out and drifted rt after: styd on but unable to threaten* **20/1**

3203 **8** *1 1/4* **Mutawathea**[14] 4152 5-8-10 **102** (p) GeorgeWood[(7)] 15 98
(Simon Crisford) *prom in centre: rdn to chal 2f out: fdd fnl f* **10/1**[3]

-100 **8** *dht* **Fanciful Angel (IRE)**[50] 2867 4-9-8 **107**[1] FrankieDettori 12 103
(Marco Botti) *towards rr far side: rdn over 2f out: kpt on fr over 1f out: nt pce to threaten* **16/1**

0641 **10** *1* **Brazos (IRE)**[9] 4299 5-8-7 **92** 3ex (b) AndreaAtzeni 21 86
(James Tate) *lw: chsd ldrs in centre: rdn over 2f out: outpcd and no ch over 1f out: kpt on again nr fin* **10/1**[3]

0004 **11** *nk* **Jack Dexter**[14] 4126 7-9-2 **101** DougieCostello 1 94
(Jim Goldie) *dwlt: hld up in rr far side: rdn and sme prog fr 2f out: nvr gng pce to rch ldrs* **20/1**

5200 **12** *2* **Whitman**[14] 4149 3-8-2 **94** JimmyQuinn 7 78
(Mark Johnston) *w ldrs far side to 2f out: wknd over 1f out* **50/1**

0-02 **13** *1/2* **Suzi's Connoisseur**[15] 4109 5-8-12 **97** (vt) OisinMurphy 11 83
(Stuart Williams) *trckd ldrs far side: shkn up 2f out: wknd jst over 1f out* **12/1**

5/14 **14** *1/2* **Cape Icon**[37] 3303 5-8-2 **87** RyanTate 26 72
(Clive Cox) *lw: led nr side pair and wl on terms: hdd and fdd over 1f out* **14/1**

0040 **15** *1* **Room Key**[7] 4395 4-8-8 **93** JohnFahy 17 75
(Eve Johnson Houghton) *nvr beyond midfield in centre: rdn and no prog over 2f out* **50/1**

0022 **16** *shd* **Heaven's Guest (IRE)**[14] 4152 6-9-0 **104** AdamMcNamara[(5)] 16 86
(Richard Fahey) *prom in centre: led gp over 2f out to over 1f out: wknd* **8/1**[2]

/0-3 **17** *1* **Dont Bother Me (IRE)**[37] 3332 6-8-13 **98** (t) SeamieHeffernan 8 77
(Niall Moran, Ire) *taken down early: mde most on far side to 2f out: wknd* **20/1**

0200 **18** *nk* **Emell**[14] 4152 6-9-2 **101** (b) PatDobbs 19 79
(Richard Hannon) *led centre gp to over 2f out: sn lost pl u.p* **50/1**

0000 **19** *1/2* **Balty Boys (IRE)**[14] 4165 7-9-3 **102** (b) JimCrowley 18 79
(Brian Ellison) *chsd ldrs in centre: u.p sn after 1/2-way: wknd over 1f out* **20/1**

41-0 **20** *3/4* **Mullionheir**[71] 2206 4-8-9 **94** KierenFox 3 69
(John Best) *taken down early: t.k.h: w ldrs far side tl wknd qckly 2f out* **25/1**

0000 **21** *4 1/2* **Majestic Moon (IRE)**[14] 4152 6-8-13 **98** JoeyHaynes 20 61
(John Gallagher) *pressed ldrs in centre: u.p wl over 2f out: sn wknd* **50/1**

2000 **22** *3 3/4* **Intransigent**[112] 1204 7-9-6 **105** DavidProbert 23 58
(Andrew Balding) *chsd ldrs in centre to 1/2-way: wknd over 2f out* **50/1**

3050 **23** *1/2* **King's Pavilion (IRE)**[14] 4163 3-8-1 **93** JoeFanning 5 41
(Mark Johnston) *chsd far side ldrs tl wknd qckly 2f out* **25/1**

0060 **24** *99* **Bossy Guest (IRE)**[14] 4152 4-9-5 **104** SilvestreDeSousa 10
(Mick Channon) *swvd lft s: virtually ref to r and effectively tk no part* **14/1**

1m 25.79s (-1.81) **Going Correction** 0.0s/f (Good)
WFA 3 from 4yo+ 7lb **24** Ran SP% **138.9**
Speed ratings (Par 109): **110,108,107,107,106 105,104,103,103,102 101,99,99,98,97 97,96,95,95,94 89,84,84,**
CSF £162.72 CT £4000.38 TOTE £5.20: £1.90, £8.90, £8.80, £3.90; EX 242.20 Trifecta £4840.80.
Owner Tony Bloom **Bred** Newsells Park Stud **Trained** Radlett, Herts

FOCUS
This valuable handicap looked competitive on paper, but it was won in dominant style by the well backed favourite. The field separated into similar-sized groups on the far side and down the centre, with just a pair racing on the stands' side. The first two both came from the rear of the ten-strong group in the centre. The runner-up has been rated better than ever, while the fourth helps set the standard on the far side.

4626 KING GEORGE VI AND QUEEN ELIZABETH STKS (SPONSORED BY QIPCO) (BRITISH CHAMPIONS SERIES) (GROUP 1) 1m 4f
4:30 (4:34) (Class 1) 3-Y-O+
£689,026 (£261,225; £130,734; £65,124; £32,683; £16,402) **Stalls** Low

Form RPR

-402 **1** **Highland Reel (IRE)**[35] 3384 4-9-7 119 RyanMoore 3 121+
(A P O'Brien, Ire) *swtg: mde all: clr 8f out to 5f out: sent for home 2f out: hrd rdn and styd on wl fnl f* **13/8**[1]

3114 **2** *1 1/4* **Wings of Desire**[49] 2896 3-8-9 113 FrankieDettori 2 119
(John Gosden) *trckd wnr after 3f: shkn up 2f out: styd on and clr of rest but no imp ins fnl f* **4/1**[3]

-111 **3** *2 3/4* **Dartmouth**[35] 3384 4-9-7 119 OlivierPeslier 5 115+
(Sir Michael Stoute) *hld up and sn in 5th: angled to outer and rdn 2f out: styd on fnl f to take 3rd last 75yds: no threat* **9/2**

-311 **4** *1/2* **Sir Isaac Newton**[27] 3692 4-9-7 109 SeamieHeffernan 1 114
(A P O'Brien, Ire) *t.k.h: sn trckd ldng trio: rdn 2f out: one pce and no imp after* **14/1**

6-02 **5** *nk* **Erupt (IRE)**[20] 3936 4-9-7 116 StephanePasquier 4 113
(F-H Graffard, France) *q str: lw: trckd wnr 3f: styd wl in tch: rdn 2f out: nt qckn over 1f out: lost 2 pls ins fnl f* **3/1**[2]

2236 **6** *1 1/4* **Western Hymn**[21] 3912 5-9-7 115 RobertHavlin 7 111
(John Gosden) *stdd s: hld up in last: shkn up and nt qckn over 2f out: no ch after* **25/1**

-355 **7** *nk* **Second Step (IRE)**[16] 4061 5-9-7 110 JamieSpencer 6 110
(Luca Cumani) *stdd s: hld up in 6th: rdn and no prog over 2f out: wl btn after* **33/1**

2m 28.97s (-3.53) **Going Correction** +0.075s/f (Good)
WFA 3 from 4yo+ 12lb **7** Ran SP% **114.7**
Speed ratings (Par 117): **114,113,111,111,110 109,109**
CSF £8.59 TOTE £2.40: £1.40, £2.10; EX 9.00 Trifecta £25.90.
Owner Derrick Smith & Mrs John Magnier & Michael Tabor **Bred** Hveger Syndicate **Trained** Cashel, Co Tipperary

FOCUS
This didn't look a vintage renewal of the showpiece middle-distance contest of the summer, as the seven runners didn't have much Group 1-winning form between them, and last year's winner Postponed, the 1-2 ante-post favourite, was taken out during the preceding week due to a respiratory infection. That said, it did go to a previous winner at the highest level. It was a shame that neither Minding or Harzand, the Oaks and Derby winners, didn't take their chance, especially the latter as a literal line of form through the runner-up would surely have meant the Aga Khan-owned colt would have taken the valuable prize. Incidentally, this was the first of 18 Breeders' Cup automatic qualifying races in Europe this season. The early gallop set by the winner didn't seem overly slow and the favourite gained a handy advantage, one he never relinquished. The winner has been rated to his Hong Kong win, with the runner-up building on his Dante win.

4627 LONGINES H'CAP STKS (LADIES' RACE) (FOR LADY AMATEUR RIDERS) 7f
5:00 (5:07) (Class 3) (0-90,90) 3-Y-O+ **£8,110** (£2,515; £1,257; £629) **Stalls** Centre

Form				RPR
0000	**1**		**Hawkeyethenoo (IRE)**[9] 4299 10-10-0 **80** MrsCBartley 12 (Jim Goldie) *hld up in rr: stdy prog over 2f out: rdn to chse ldr fnl f: led last 100yds: r.o wl and won gng away* **12/1**	91
1300	**2**	1 3/4	**Normandy Barriere (IRE)**[15] 4079 4-10-4 **84** MissJoannaMason 13 (Nigel Tinkler) *trckd ldrs: shkn up to ld wl over 1f out: styd on but hdd and outpcd last 100yds* **10/1**[3]	90
50-5	**3**	1 1/2	**Sakhee's Return**[22] 3848 4-10-1 **86** MissEEasterby(5) 11 (Tim Easterby) *lw: w ldrs: chal and upsides 2f out: chsd wnr to 1f out: one pce* **10/1**[3]	88
1100	**4**	1 1/4	**Classic Seniority**[12] 4193 4-10-0 **83** MissBeckySmith(3) 5 (Marjorie Fife) *cl up on far side of gp: rdn 2f out: outpcd and hung lft fr over 1f out: one pce* **25/1**	82
6003	**5**	1/2	**Chiswick Bey (IRE)**[15] 4081 8-9-0 **71** oh2 MissEmilyBullock(5) 9 (Richard Fahey) *taken down early: hld up in last pair: prog 2f out: rdn and styd on fnl f: nrst fin* **12/1**	68+
100	**6**	1	**Fieldsman (USA)**[15] 4109 4-10-10 **90** MsNCarberry 10 (George Scott) *towards rr: prog into midfield 2f out: rdn over 1f out: unable to make any imp after: kpt on same pce* **7/1**[2]	85
1125	**7**	1/2	**Flying Fantasy**[23] 3803 4-9-5 **76** MissPBridgwater(5) 16 (Stuart Williams) *towards rr: rdn over 2f out: prog over 1f out: one pce fnl f* **16/1**	69
0111	**8**	shd	**Robero**[8] 4362 4-9-11 **77** MissSBrotherton 8 (Brian Ellison) *w ldr: led over 2f out to wl over 1f out: hung lft and wknd* **5/2**[1]	70
5006	**9**	2 3/4	**Redvers (IRE)**[14] 4132 8-9-4 **75** (b) MissHMooney(5) 2 (Noel Wilson) *slowly away and stmbld s: mostly in last pair: effrt on far side over 2f out: no prog over 1f out* **25/1**	60
0606	**10**	1/2	**Majestic Myles (IRE)**[23] 3803 8-9-11 **80** MissHayleyMoore(3) 14 (Lee Carter) *mde most to over 2f out: wknd over 1f out* **25/1**	64
0-00	**11**	6	**Harwoods Volante (IRE)**[42] 3133 5-10-2 **82** MissCWalton 1 (David O'Meara) *nvr beyond midfield: rdn and no prog over 2f out: no ch after* **16/1**	50
0014	**12**	1/2	**Secret Glance**[30] 3571 4-10-3 **83** MsKWalsh 7 (Richard Rowe) *swtg: chsd ldrs over 4f: wknd wl over 1f out* **14/1**	50
5465	**13**	1 1/4	**Jammy Guest (IRE)**[4] 4474 6-9-5 **76** MissKMargarson(5) 4 (George Margarson) *nvr beyond midfield: struggling 2f out: wknd qckly over 1f out* **20/1**	39
0330	**14**	2	**Smokethatthunders (IRE)**[29] 3605 6-9-5 **71** oh1 MissMMullineaux 15 (James Unett) *chsd ldrs: rdn 3f out: wknd over 2f out* **33/1**	29
-150	**15**	2 3/4	**Dutch Golden Age (IRE)**[17] 4014 4-9-7 **76** MissPFuller(5) 6 (Gary Moore) *w ldrs over 4f: wknd qckly over 1f out* **50/1**	26
0405	**16**	2 3/4	**Childesplay**[35] 3405 5-9-10 **79** (p) MissAWaugh(3) 19 (Heather Main) *racd on nr side of gp: in tch over 4f: sn wknd* **14/1**	22
5603	**17**	1/2	**Burning Blaze**[35] 3421 6-9-11 **77** MissJMMangan 18 (Brian Ellison) *chsd ldrs 4f: sn wknd and bhd* **14/1**	19
0001	**18**	2	**Echo Of Lightning**[15] 4089 6-9-6 **75** (p) MissLWilson(3) 17 (Brian Ellison) *chsd ldrs over 4f: sn wknd qckly and bhd* **14/1**	11

1m 27.45s (-0.15) **Going Correction** 0.0s/f (Good) **18** Ran SP% **134.3**
Speed ratings (Par 107): **100,98,96,94,94 93,92,92,89,88 81,81,79,77,74 71,70,68**
CSF £127.83 CT £1288.47 TOTE £14.30: £2.70, £3.90, £2.90, £6.60; EX 193.10 Trifecta £3095.00.
Owner F J Connor & J S Goldie **Bred** S Leigh & R Leigh & Islandmore Stud **Trained** Uplawmoor, E Renfrews
■ Stewards' Enquiry : Miss Becky Smith four-day ban: used whip above permitted level (6-7 & 11-12 Aug)

FOCUS
Not a great deal of depth to this ladies' handicap, despite the large field. The field didn't split this time, and they raced centre-to-far side. The leaders appeared to go off quite quick and the time was 1.66sec slower than that of the earlier International Handicap. The runner-up has been rated back to form.

4628 CANISBAY BLOODSTOCK H'CAP 1m 4f
5:35 (5:35) (Class 4) (0-85,84) 3-Y-O **£7,762** (£2,310; £1,154; £577) **Stalls** Low

Form				RPR
3313	**1**		**Real Dominion (USA)**[15] 4092 3-9-5 **82** DavidProbert 4 (Andrew Balding) *hld up in 4th: prog to take 2nd jst over 2f out: hanging rt but rdn to ld over 1f out: sn clr* **4/1**[2]	94
5615	**2**	6	**Kesselring**[21] 3914 3-9-3 **80** PatDobbs 6 (Richard Hannon) *chsd clr ldr to 3f out: sn drvn: kpt on to take 2nd again jst over 1f out: no ch w wnr* **5/1**[3]	82
-110	**3**	5	**Opposition**[36] 3341 3-9-7 **84** FrankieDettori 2 (Ed Dunlop) *lw: trckd ldng pair: rdn to go 2nd 3f out to jst over 2f out: wknd jst over 1f out* **11/10**[1]	78
6300	**4**	1 1/2	**Second Serve (IRE)**[14] 4131 3-9-4 **81** (b[1]) JoeFanning 3 (Mark Johnston) *racd v freely: led and clr: 12 l ahd 1/2-way: stl clr 3f out: hdd & wknd over 1f out* **11/2**	73
-043	**5**	17	**Imari Kid (IRE)**[21] 3914 3-8-3 **71** HectorCrouch(5) 5 (Gary Moore) *stdd s: t.k.h and hld up in last: rdn and wknd over 2f out: eased over 1f out: t.o* **11/2**	35

2m 32.01s (-0.49) **Going Correction** +0.075s/f (Good) **5** Ran SP% **115.1**
Speed ratings (Par 102): **104,100,96,95,84**
CSF £23.84 TOTE £5.20: £2.40, £2.60; EX 24.90 Trifecta £38.40.
Owner Mick and Janice Mariscotti **Bred** Kendall E Hansen, M D Racing Llc **Trained** Kingsclere, Hants

FOCUS
The early leader went off at a strong gallop, which set things up for those who sat off the pace. Three closed in nicely but only one mattered late on. The runner-up has been rated to his latest form.
T/Jkpt: Not won. T/Plt: £341.30 to a £1 stake. Pool: £211,245.33 - 451.73 winning units. T/Qpdt: £105.20 to a £1 stake. Pool: £16,403.79 - 115.38 winning units. **Jonathan Neesom**

4133 CHESTER (L-H)
Saturday, July 23

OFFICIAL GOING: Good (good to soft in places; 6.6)
Wind: light 1/2 against Weather: fine, humid

4629 STELLA ARTOIS NURSERY H'CAP 5f 16y
2:15 (2:15) (Class 4) 2-Y-O **£6,225** (£1,864; £932; £466; £233) **Stalls** Low

Form				RPR
3225	**1**		**Northern Thunder (IRE)**[16] 4053 2-8-8 **74** TomMarquand 6 (Richard Hannon) *in rr: hdwy to chse ldrs over 2f out: styd on to take 2nd last 100yds: led nr fin* **6/1**	77
3140	**2**	nk	**Boundsy (IRE)**[7] 4394 2-8-8 **74** BarryMcHugh 3 (Richard Fahey) *led: shkn up over 1f out: edgd rt: hdd and no ex nr fin* **5/1**[3]	76
5421	**3**	hd	**The Nazca Lines (IRE)**[7] 4405 2-8-6 **79** (v) KillianLeonard(7) 1 (John Quinn) *chsd ldrs: n.m.r on inner over 1f out: kpt on fnl f: no ex clsng stages* **11/8**[1]	80
2121	**4**	4	**Poet's Society**[28] 3654 2-9-8 **88** JFEgan 5 (Mark Johnston) *w ldr: drvn over 1f out: wknd last 100yds: eased nr fin* **9/4**[2]	75
6202	**5**	2	**Gerrard's Fur Coat**[12] 4195 2-7-13 **72** CameronNoble(7) 2 (Tom Dascombe) *in rr: drvn over 2f out: wknd appr fnl f* **12/1**	52

1m 2.77s (1.77) **Going Correction** +0.425s/f (Yiel) **5** Ran SP% **111.5**
Speed ratings (Par 96): **102,101,101,94,91**
CSF £33.92 TOTE £6.50: £3.20, £3.20; EX 32.30 Trifecta £83.50.
Owner Ahmad Abdulla Al Shaikh **Bred** Peter & Hugh McCutcheon **Trained** East Everleigh, Wilts

FOCUS
Following 7mm of rain overnight the going was good, good to soft in places (GoingStick: 6.6). The entire length of the running rail was out by 3yds. Race distance increased by 10yds. The front two rather took each other on, setting things up for something to come over the top. The runner-up has been rated to his 6f form.

4630 TM CONTRACTORS FILLIES' H'CAP 7f 122y
2:50 (2:51) (Class 4) (0-85,85) 3-Y-O+ **£7,470** (£2,236; £1,118; £559; £279; £140) **Stalls** Low

Form				RPR
514	**1**		**Ionization (IRE)**[30] 3551 3-9-1 **80** TadhgO'Shea 3 (John Patrick Shanahan, Ire) *led: jnd over 1f out: fnd ex nr fin* **8/1**	89
3541	**2**	hd	**Breakable**[21] 3884 5-10-0 **85** JasonHart 6 (Tim Easterby) *trckd wnr: drvn upsides over 1f out: no ex cl home* **6/1**	95
-610	**3**	1 1/4	**Al Shahaniya (IRE)**[15] 4105 3-8-11 **83** KillianLeonard(7) 4 (John Quinn) *dwlt: hmpd bnd over 6f out: hdwy to trck ldrs over 4f out: n.m.r over 1f out: styd on fnl 150yds* **5/1**[3]	88
3104	**4**	1	**Golden Glimmer (IRE)**[14] 4130 3-9-4 **83** MartinHarley 2 (Tom Dascombe) *trckd ldrs: cl 3rd over 1f out: kpt on same pce last 150yds* **11/4**[1]	85
-331	**5**	1 1/2	**Sunnua (IRE)**[14] 4139 3-9-1 **80** PatrickMathers 5 (Richard Fahey) *in rr: drvn over 2f out: styd on appr fnl f* **7/2**[2]	79
6064	**6**	nse	**Queen Aggie (IRE)**[15] 4094 6-8-9 **69** GeorgeDowning(3) 7 (Tony Carroll) *dwlt: swtchd lft after s: checked bnd over 6f out: hld up in rr: hdwy over 1f out: keeping on at fin* **20/1**	70
-220	**7**	6	**Winter Rose (IRE)**[35] 3410 3-9-4 **83** TomMarquand 8 (Richard Hannon) *racd wd: rr-div: hdwy to chse ldrs over 2f out: lost pl over 1f out* **8/1**	67
3446	**8**	5	**Be Royale**[108] 1252 6-8-13 **70** JFEgan 1 (Michael Appleby) *trckd ldrs: t.k.h: wkng whn n.m.r on inner over 1f out* **9/1**	43

1m 36.05s (2.25) **Going Correction** +0.425s/f (Yiel)
WFA 3 from 5yo+ 8lb **8** Ran SP% **116.8**
Speed ratings (Par 102): **105,104,103,102,101 101,95,90**
CSF £56.14 CT £267.42 TOTE £10.40: £3.20, £2.00, £1.60; EX 56.10 Trifecta £555.80.
Owner Thistle Bloodstock Limited **Bred** Thistle Bloodstock Limited **Trained** Kells, Co Kilkenny

FOCUS
Race distance increased by 13yds. The pace was steady and suited those up front.

4631 STELLA ARTOIS CIDRE APPRENTICE H'CAP 7f 122y
3:25 (3:25) (Class 3) (0-90,88) 3-Y-O **£12,450** (£3,728; £1,864; £932; £466; £234) **Stalls** Low

Form				RPR
6414	**1**		**Viscount Barfield**[22] 3840 3-9-1 **82** RobHornby 4 (Andrew Balding) *hld up towards rr: hdwy on outside over 2f out: sn trcking ldrs: edgd lft and led last 75yds: rdr dropped rt rein nr line* **3/1**[2]	91
2-11	**2**	1 3/4	**War Glory (IRE)**[12] 4199 3-9-7 **88** TomMarquand 2 (Richard Hannon) *trckd ldr: drvn to ld over 1f out: hdd last 75yds: kpt on same pce* **15/8**[1]	92
0552	**3**	1 1/4	**Worlds His Oyster**[14] 4139 3-8-7 **79** KillianLeonard(5) 5 (John Quinn) *trckd ldrs: drvn over 3f out: kpt on same pce over 1f out: tk 3rd nr fin* **9/2**[3]	80
0354	**4**	nk	**Ninetta (IRE)**[16] 4042 3-8-10 **82** RowanScott(5) 3 (Ann Duffield) *led: shkn up over 1f out: kpt on same pce last 150yds* **12/1**	82
6020	**5**	1 3/4	**Bell Heather (IRE)**[14] 4139 3-8-5 **77** NatalieHambling(5) 1 (Richard Fahey) *mid-div: effrt over 2f out: hdwy on inner over 1f out: one pce* **20/1**	73
-004	**6**	7	**Dutch Gallery**[45] 3029 3-8-1 **73** CameronNoble(5) 7 (Tom Dascombe) *wnt rt s: sn trcking ldrs: drvn over 2f out: lost pl over 1f out* **14/1**	51
-000	**7**	8	**Still On Top**[42] 3165 3-9-6 **87** KevinStott 8 (Tim Easterby) *carried rt s: in rr: drvn over 3f out: sn bhd* **14/1**	45
432-	**8**	27	**Rock Warbler (IRE)**[304] 6644 3-8-1 **75** ManuelFernandes(7) 6 (Oliver Greenall) *s.s: hld up in rr: effrt over 3f out: lost pl over 2f out: sn wl bhd: t.o* **25/1**

1m 36.07s (2.27) **Going Correction** +0.425s/f (Yiel) **8** Ran SP% **113.9**
Speed ratings (Par 104): **105,103,102,101,99 92,84,57**
CSF £8.96 CT £23.47 TOTE £3.40: £1.70, £1.10, £1.10; EX 8.60 Trifecta £32.80.
Owner David Brownlow **Bred** Rockwell Bloodstock **Trained** Kingsclere, Hants

FOCUS
Race distance increased by 13yds. They went a solid gallop and the form looks pretty reliable. The runner-up has been rated similar to his AW latest, and the third and fourth close to their recent efforts.

4632 SEBASTIAN ARTOIS H'CAP 5f 16y
4:00 (4:01) (Class 3) (0-95,95) 3-Y-O+
£12,450 (£3,728; £1,864; £932; £466; £234) **Stalls** Low

Form RPR
5052 **1** **Blithe Spirit**[28] 3637 5-9-7 **90**.................. JasonHart 2 100
(Eric Alston) *mde all: drvn over 1f out: styd on gamely* **5/2**[1]
3031 **2** 2 1/4 **Powerallied (IRE)**[28] 3637 3-9-3 **90**.................. PatrickMathers 1 91
(Richard Fahey) *chsd ldrs: 2nd over 2f out: styd on same pce fnl 150yds* **5/2**[1]
5341 **3** 1 1/2 **Secret Asset (IRE)**[3] 4536 11-8-11 **83** 6ex..................(v) RobHornby(3) 3 80
(Lisa Williamson) *chsd ldrs: checked 3f out: kpt on same pce appr fnl f* **13/2**[2]
0200 **4** 1/2 **Seve**[8] 4373 4-9-6 **89**..................(t[1]) MartinHarley 11 84+
(Tom Dascombe) *s.i.s: in rr: hdwy on ins over 1f out: styd on to take 4th clsng stages* **16/1**
-000 **5** 1 3/4 **Ashpan Sam**[14] 4136 7-9-8 **94**..................(p) AlistairRawlinson(3) 9 82
(David W Drinkwater) *edgd lft s: chsd ldrs: one pce over 1f out* **33/1**
6621 **6** nk **Classy Anne**[15] 4100 6-8-10 **79**..................(p) KevinStott 4 66
(Jim Goldie) *s.i.s: in rr: hdwy and nt clr run over 1f out: sn swtchd rt: styd on* **9/1**
0022 **7** nk **Ballesteros**[28] 3638 7-9-1 **84**.................. BarryMcHugh 6 70
(Richard Fahey) *mid-div: drvn over 2f out: kpt on fnl f* **15/2**[3]
0313 **8** 1/2 **Lexi's Hero (IRE)**[28] 3637 8-8-8 **84**..................(v) NatalieHambling(7) 12 68
(Richard Fahey) *swtchd lft after s: in rr and pushed along: sme hdwy over 1f out: nvr a factor* **12/1**
00-5 **9** nk **Smart Daisy K**[28] 3637 6-8-11 **80**.................. PaulQuinn 5 63
(Sarah Hollinshead) *checked s: mid-div: effrt and n.m.r over 1f out: one pce: eased nr fin* **25/1**
0000 **10** 6 **Masamah (IRE)**[28] 3637 10-8-11 **80**..................(p) TomMarquand 10 42
(Patrick Morris) *chsd ldrs: lost pl over 1f out: bhd whn eased clsng stages* **50/1**
-000 **11** 1/2 **Red Stripes (USA)**[12] 4198 4-9-0 **83**.................. TadhgO'Shea 8 43
(Lisa Williamson) *checked s: mid-div: drvn over 2f out: lost pl over 1f out: bhd whn eased clsng stages* **28/1**

1m 1.95s (0.95) **Going Correction** +0.425s/f (Yiel)
WFA 3 from 4yo+ 4lb **11** Ran SP% **118.0**
Speed ratings (Par 107): **109,105,103,102,99 98,98,97,97,87 86**
CSF £7.60 CT £35.91 TOTE £3.80: £2.00, £1.80, £2.10; EX 8.00 Trifecta £63.60.
Owner Liam & Tony Ferguson **Bred** Liam & Tony Ferguson **Trained** Longton, Lancs

FOCUS
Race distance increased by 10yds. The winner dominated from the off and the others didn't really get a sniff. The bottom three stalls finished 2-1-3. It's been rated around the first two.

4633 CHALICE MAIDEN FILLIES' STKS 1m 4f 66y
4:35 (4:38) (Class 4) 3-Y-O+ **£6,283** (£1,922; £990; £524) **Stalls** Low

Form RPR
0-0 **1** **Great And Small**[31] 3535 3-8-11 0.................. RobHornby(3) 7 75+
(Andrew Balding) *in last: pushed along after 4f: modest 3rd over 2f out: styd on over 1f out: led fnl strides* **10/1**
6203 **2** nk **Pleasure Dome**[30] 3578 3-9-0 80.................. AdrianMcCarthy 9 74
(Peter Chapple-Hyam) *led: drvn over 1f out: hdd and no ex fnl strides* **5/2**[1]
0-2 **3** 2 **Pernickety**[107] 1289 3-8-7 0.................. KillianLeonard(7) 3 71
(Lucy Wadham) *trckd ldr: effrt 2f out: sn rdn: kpt on same pce fnl 150yds* **11/4**[2]
0-0 **4** 34 **Peppard**[72] 2182 3-9-0 0.................. TomMarquand 6 17
(Charles Hills) *stdd and swtchd lft s: t.k.h: sn trcking ldrs: drvn 3f out: sn lost pl and bhd: eased over 1f out: t.o* **4/1**[3]
2 **P** **Autumn Surprise (IRE)**[21] 3886 3-9-0 0.................. JasonHart 1
(Tim Easterby) *dwlt: sn trcking ldrs: lost pl and reminders over 5f out: sn wl bhd: t.o whn eased and p.u 3f out* **5/2**[1]

2m 43.5s (5.00) **Going Correction** +0.425s/f (Yiel)
WFA 3 from 7yo 12lb **5** Ran SP% **112.9**
Speed ratings (Par 102): **100,99,98,75,**
CSF £35.54 TOTE £13.00: £5.10, £1.10; EX 44.10 Trifecta £165.10.
Owner Nicholas Jones **Bred** Coln Valley Stud **Trained** Kingsclere, Hants

FOCUS
Race distance increased by 22yds. There was a bit of a shock result to this fillies' maiden. The runner-up has again been rated below her Goodwood figure and to her latest form.

4634 STELLA ARTOIS 4% H'CAP 1m 5f 89y
5:05 (5:11) (Class 4) (0-80,80) 4-Y-O+
£6,225 (£1,864; £932; £466; £233; £117) **Stalls** Low

Form RPR
6146 **1** **Marengo**[15] 4095 5-9-4 **77**..................(p) MartinHarley 4 84
(Bernard Llewellyn) *trckd ldr: led after 4f: drvn clr over 1f out: styd on* **10/1**
2556 **2** 2 1/4 **Medina Sidonia (IRE)**[11] 4237 4-8-11 **70**..................(p) JasonHart 8 73
(Tim Easterby) *chsd ldrs: drvn along 6f out: chsd wnr over 2f out: kpt on same pce over 1f out* **20/1**
3-24 **3** nk **Carbon Dating (IRE)**[9] 4312 4-9-2 **75**.................. TadhgO'Shea 11 78+
(John Patrick Shanahan, Ire) *hld up in mid-div: t.k.h: hdwy and 3rd over 1f out: kpt on same pce* **14/1**
0043 **4** 1 3/4 **Chebsey Beau**[19] 3942 6-8-7 **73**.................. KillianLeonard(7) 2 73
(John Quinn) *led 4f: chsd ldrs: kpt on one pce over 1f out* **6/1**[3]
5050 **5** nk **Nabhan**[28] 3639 4-9-2 **80**..................(t) RobJFitzpatrick(5) 7 80
(Bernard Llewellyn) *chsd ldrs: nt clr run and swtchd lft over 1f out: kpt on same pce fnl f* **12/1**
3610 **6** 3/4 **Itlaaq**[7] 4381 10-8-11 **77**..................(t) DanielleMooney(7) 3 76+
(Michael Easterby) *hld up in mid-div: nt clr run on inner over 2f out: bdly hmpd and wnt rt over 1f out: kpt on fnl f: nt rch ldrs* **10/1**
5406 **7** 1 1/4 **Celtic Power**[6] 4430 4-8-6 **65**.................. TomMarquand 12 62
(Jim Goldie) *mid-div: drvn on outer over 4f out: edgd lft and one pce fnl 2f* **25/1**
51-5 **8** 1/2 **Instant Karma (IRE)**[13] 1717 5-9-4 **80**.................. RobHornby(3) 9 76+
(Michael Bell) *hld up in last: effrt on ins 2f out: swtchd rt over 1f out: kpt on: nvr on terms* **9/2**[2]
5522 **9** 1 1/4 **Cottesloe (IRE)**[14] 4138 7-9-3 **76**..................(b) JFEgan 10 70+
(John Berry) *hld up towards rr: t.k.h: hdwy over 3f out: effrt on outside whn sltly hmpd over 1f out: nvr a factor* **7/2**[1]
620- **10** hd **Late Shipment**[38] 7876 5-9-0 **76**.................. GeorgeDowning(3) 1 70
(Nikki Evans) *chsd ldrs: effrt over 2f out: lost pl and hmpd over 1f out* **25/1**
4000 **11** hd **Gabrial The Duke (IRE)**[28] 3639 6-9-4 **77**.................. PatrickMathers 5 71+
(Richard Fahey) *s.i.s: drvn along early: a in rr: eased clsng stages* **8/1**
500- **12** 1 **Comedy King (IRE)**[343] 5391 5-9-5 **78**.................. BarryMcHugh 6 70
(Richard Fahey) *mid-div: hdwy on outer over 5f out: chsng ldrs over 2f out: edgd lft and wknd over 1f out: eased clsng stages* **8/1**

3m 1.39s (8.69) **Going Correction** +0.425s/f (Yiel) **12** Ran SP% **121.9**
Speed ratings (Par 105): **90,88,88,87,87 86,85,85,84,84 84,84**
CSF £200.29 CT £2422.14 TOTE £12.50: £3.80, £6.90, £4.50; EX 277.80 Trifecta £1190.40 Part won..
Owner Mrs Beth Williams **Bred** Lilly Hall Farm **Trained** Fochriw, Caerphilly

FOCUS
Race distance increased by 25yds. With the pace holding up, few got into this. It's been rated cautiously.
T/Plt: £297.70 to a £1 stake. Pool: £55,670.43 - 136.47 winning units. T/Qpdt: £37.70 to a £1 stake. Pool: £4,031.86 - 79.10 winning units. **Walter Glynn**

4523 LINGFIELD (L-H)
Saturday, July 23

OFFICIAL GOING: Good to firm (8.1)
Wind: light, behind Weather: sunny and warm

4635 GALWAY FESTIVAL BETTING AT 188BET H'CAP 1m 2f
5:40 (5:40) (Class 6) (0-65,73) 3-Y-O+ **£2,587** (£770; £384; £192) **Stalls** Low

Form RPR
0-55 **1** **Fast And Hot (IRE)**[9] 4288 3-8-11 **58**..................(p) KieranO'Neill 4 66
(Richard Hannon) *hld up in tch in midfield: effrt over 2f out: rdn to chal 2f out: led jst over 1f out: sn hdd: ev ch whn edgd rt ins fnl f: styd on to ld again towards fin* **8/1**
1040 **2** 1/2 **Rockliffe**[16] 4033 3-8-11 **58**.................. CharlesBishop 10 65
(Mick Channon) *hld up in tch in midfield: clsd to join ldrs 2f out: rdn to ld 1f out: edgd lft ins fnl f: hdd and unable qck towards fin* **7/1**[3]
0635 **3** 2 3/4 **Bognor (USA)**[9] 4305 5-9-6 **60**.................. EdwardGreatrex(3) 5 62
(Michael Attwater) *chsd ldrs: rdn to chse ldr over 2f out: ev ch 2f out tl unable qck 1f out: 3rd and wknd fnl 100yds* **33/1**
3461 **4** 1/2 **Cold Fusion (IRE)**[8] 4356 3-9-9 **73**.................. JosephineGordon(3) 1 74
(Ed Vaughan) *trckd ldrs: rdn wl over 2f out: drvn and unable qck over 1f out: styd on same pce after* **6/4**[1]
4235 **5** nk **Perfect Quest**[40] 3236 3-8-10 **64**..................(p) WilliamCox(7) 7 64
(Clive Cox) *s.i.s: niggled and detached in last tl clsd on to bk of field and travelling bttr 7f out: hdwy and swtchd rt over 1f out: styd on ins fnl f: nt rch ldrs* **9/2**[2]
4054 **6** 3/4 **Jackpot**[22] 3917 6-8-9 **46** oh1..................(p) DannyBrock 2 44
(Brendan Powell) *hld up in tch in last trio: clsd on inner and nt clr run 2f out: squeezed through and hdwy over 1f out: nt clr run again and swtchd rt ins fnl f: kpt on but no threat to ldrs* **33/1**
4133 **7** 1 1/4 **Betsalottie**[23] 3816 3-8-12 **59**.................. WilliamCarson 9 55
(John Bridger) *racd keenly: chsd ldr tl led wl over 2f out: rdn 2f out: hdd jst over 1f out: sn btn: wknd ins fnl f* **9/2**[2]
1300 **8** 1 1/2 **Togetherwecan (IRE)**[10] 4260 4-8-13 **55**..................(v[1]) RossCoakley(5) 6 48
(Mark Johnston) *s.i.s and bustled along early: hld up in tch in last pair: effrt over 2f out: no imp: wl hld and plugged on same pce ins fnl f* **14/1**
-005 **9** 15 **Who'sthedaddy**[9] 4293 4-9-9 **60**.................. SteveDrowne 8 23
(Daniel Kubler) *led: rdn and hdd wl over 2f out: lost pl and bhd over 1f out: wknd and eased wl ins fnl f* **12/1**

2m 10.58s (0.08) **Going Correction** +0.075s/f (Good)
WFA 3 from 4yo+ 10lb **9** Ran SP% **120.2**
Speed ratings (Par 101): **102,101,99,99,98 98,97,95,83**
CSF £65.32 CT £1755.81 TOTE £10.20: £2.70, £2.20, £6.20; EX 77.30 Trifecta £1006.90.
Owner Derek And Jean Clee **Bred** D D & Mrs J P Clee **Trained** East Everleigh, Wilts

FOCUS
A fair handicap. They went a respectable gallop on good to firm ground. The race developed into a battle between two 3yos in receipt of a hefty 10lb weight-for-age allowance. The winner has been rated to his best since his debut, with the runner-up back to the level of his Bath win.

4636 GLORIOUS GOODWOOD BETTING AT 188BET H'CAP 1m 6f
6:10 (6:10) (Class 5) (0-70,70) 3-Y-O **£3,234** (£962; £481; £240) **Stalls** Centre

Form RPR
2232 **1** **Scarpeta (FR)**[14] 4137 3-9-2 **70**.................. RossCoakley(5) 5 78
(Mark Johnston) *broke wl: led for 2f: chsd ldr after tl led again over 3f out: rdn 2f out: drvn over 1f out: kpt on u.p: grad being clsd down fnl 100yds: jst hld on* **5/4**[1]
345 **2** shd **Torquay**[10] 4265 3-9-5 **68**.................. SamHitchcott 6 75
(Harry Dunlop) *hld up in tch in last pair: clsd on outer 5f out: wnt 2nd 3f out: effrt over 1f out: rdn to press wnr 1f out: kpt on u.p and grad clsd fnl 100yds: jst hld* **7/1**
-202 **3** 4 1/2 **Argyle (IRE)**[24] 3778 3-9-3 **69**.................. JosephineGordon(3) 1 70
(William Muir) *trckd ldrs: effrt wl over 1f out: unable qck over 1f out: battling for 3rd and styd on same pce ins fnl f* **9/4**[2]
3343 **4** 3/4 **Dream Factory (IRE)**[10] 4277 3-9-4 **70**..................(b) DanielMuscutt(3) 2 70
(Marco Botti) *in tch in midfield: effrt and swtchd lft over 2f out: drvn and unable qck over 1f out: kpt on same pce after* **5/1**[3]
3030 **5** 7 **Sixties Idol**[12] 4210 3-8-3 **52**.................. KieranO'Neill 4 42
(Mick Channon) *a bhd and nvr travelling wl: in tch tl rdn and outpcd on downhill run over 4f out: drvn and no imp over 2f out* **20/1**
5164 **6** 29 **Trident Tested**[10] 4273 3-8-8 **57**.................. KierenFox 3 7
(John Best) *taken down early: chsd ldr tl led after 2f: hdd over 3f out: lost pl and btn 5th 2f out: wknd and wl bhd whn eased ins fnl f: t.o* **14/1**

3m 10.94s (0.94) **Going Correction** +0.075s/f (Good) **6** Ran SP% **115.8**
Speed ratings (Par 100): **100,99,97,96,92 76**
CSF £11.40 TOTE £2.20: £1.20, £3.40; EX 13.00 Trifecta £36.00.
Owner Brian Yeardley **Bred** Mme Michele Bliard **Trained** Middleham Moor, N Yorks

FOCUS
A modest 3yo handicap. The winning time was ordinary on quick ground. Muddling form. The winner has been rated as putting up a small pb, with the third rated close to form.

4637 188BET H'CAP 2m
6:40 (6:40) (Class 5) (0-70,70) 4-Y-O+ **£3,234** (£962; £481; £240) **Stalls** Centre

Form RPR
144- **1** **Leoncavallo (IRE)**[127] 1743 4-9-3 **66**.................. JamesDoyle 5 74+
(Charlie Appleby) *chsd ldr: pushed along to cl 2f out: rdn to ld over 1f out: forged ahd ins fnl f: styd on* **2/5**[1]

	2	3/4	**For Goodness Sake (IRE)**[27] 7380 4-8-13 **65**....... EdwardGreatrex(3) 4 *(Warren Greatrex) led: clr 8f out: rdn 2f out: drvn and hdd over 1f out: kpt on u.p but a hld ins fnl f* **5/1**[2]	72
1226	3	3 1/2	**Hurricane Volta (IRE)**[17] 4012 5-9-3 **66**....................(v[1]) CharlesBishop 7 *(Peter Hedger) pushed along leaving stalls: hld up in rr: effrt jst over 2f out: wnt 3rd and hung lft over 1f out: stl wanting to hang and r.o same pce fnl f* **6/1**[3]	69
0/5-	4	10	**Shalianzi (IRE)**[46] 4709 6-9-0 **63**...................................(b) SamHitchcott 6 *(Gary Moore) hld up in tch: wnt 3rd 5f out: rdn and little rspnse 2f out: 4th and btn over 1f out: wknd fnl f* **33/1**	54
4434	5	13	**Madame Lafite**[31] 3528 4-8-11 **63**.......................... JosephineGordon(3) 3 *(Jonathan Portman) chsd ldng pair tl 5f out: styd in tch: rdn jst over 2f out: sn btn: bhd and eased ins fnl f* **8/1**	38

3m 39.47s (4.67) **Going Correction** +0.075s/f (Good) **5** Ran SP% **116.4**
Speed ratings (Par 103): **91,90,88,83,77**
CSF £3.32 TOTE £1.30: £1.10, £1.70; EX 3.30 Trifecta £7.70.
Owner Godolphin **Bred** Darley **Trained** Newmarket, Suffolk

FOCUS
A modest staying handicap. Once again the winning time was a slow one on good to firm ground. The runner-up is the key to the form. The third has been rated close to form for now.

4638 188BET.CO.UK MAIDEN AUCTION STKS 5f
7:10 (7:10) (Class 5) 2-Y-O **£3,234** (£962; £481; £240) **Stalls** Centre

Form				RPR
535	1		**Marquee Club**[17] 4022 2-9-0 0.. WilliamCarson 5 *(Jamie Osborne) mde all and grad crossed to stands' rail: rdn over 1f out: drvn and asserted ins fnl f: styd on strly* **7/2**[3]	72
4330	2	1 3/4	**Zebspear (IRE)**[43] 3114 2-9-3 0.. JamesDoyle 8 *(Joseph Tuite) trckd ldng pair: wnt 2nd over 1f out: drvn to press wnr 1f out: no imp and btn 100yds out: clr 2nd and eased towards fin* **5/2**[1]	69
06	3	2 3/4	**Champagne Queen**[17] 4022 2-8-13 0...........................(t) RobertHavlin 9 *(Rae Guest) hld up in tch in midfield: nt clrest run wl over 1f out: hdwy 1f out: styd on to go 3rd wl ins fnl f: no threat to ldrs* **8/1**	55
36	4	3/4	**Luv U Always**[75] 2097 2-8-8 0.. JoeyHaynes 2 *(Jo Hughes) chsd ldrs: rdn jst over 2f out: drvn over 1f out: wnt 3rd but no imp jst ins fnl f: styd on same pce and lost 3rd wl ins fnl f* **7/1**	47
00	5	2 1/4	**Tigerfish (IRE)**[7] 4397 2-8-8 0... KieranO'Neill 4 *(William Stone) stdd after s: sn outpcd in last pair: clsd 1/2-way: rdn wl over 1f out: no imp: wl hld and plugged on same pce fnl f* **25/1**	39
2345	6	1/2	**Peachey Carnehan**[32] 3485 2-9-1 0........................ EdwardGreatrex(3) 7 *(Michael Attwater) taken down early: in tch in midfield: rdn 1/2-way: outpcd and btn over 1f out: wknd ins fnl f* **3/1**[2]	47
	7	3/4	**Blastofmagic** 2-9-3 0.. SteveDrowne 3 *(David Dennis) s.i.s: detached in last: clsd and in tch 1/2-way: rdn and no hdwy over 1f out: wl hld and kpt on same pce fnl f* **8/1**	46
052	8	1	**Chotto (IRE)**[23] 3820 2-8-3 0.. GeorgeWood(7) 1 *(George Scott) pressed wnr: rdn 2f out: lost 2nd and struggling over 1f out: wknd fnl f* **12/1**	33

57.95s (-0.25) **Going Correction** -0.05s/f (Good) **8** Ran SP% **122.1**
Speed ratings (Par 94): **100,97,92,91,88 87,86,84**
CSF £13.73 TOTE £4.80: £2.00, £1.10, £2.40; EX 14.10 Trifecta £73.50.
Owner The London Partnership **Bred** Norman Court Stud, P Taplin & McB Ltd **Trained** Upper Lambourn, Berks

FOCUS
An ordinary juvenile maiden. They went a decent gallop but the best winning time of the evening so far also suggests the straight track is riding quicker than on the round course.

4639 FREE SPINS AT 188BET CASINO MEDIAN AUCTION MAIDEN STKS 7f
7:40 (7:40) (Class 6) 3-5-Y-O **£2,587** (£770; £384; £192) **Stalls** Centre

Form				RPR
4366	1		**Clever Bob (IRE)**[14] 4158 3-9-5 69...............................(t) SamHitchcott 4 *(Joseph Tuite) chsd ldr tl led after 1f: rdn over 1f out: hld on wl ins fnl f: rdn out* **5/1**	75
6-	2	1/2	**Roman Holiday (IRE)**[276] 7392 3-8-11 0............ JosephineGordon(3) 11 *(Ed Vaughan) t.k.h: wnt rt s: hld up in tch: swtchd lft and hdwy over 1f out: chsd wnr 1f out: drifting lft ins fnl f: kpt on* **2/1**[1]	69
-24	3	2 1/2	**Spinners Ball (IRE)**[12] 4213 3-9-2 0....................... EdwardGreatrex(3) 3 *(Sylvester Kirk) chsd ldrs: effrt ent fnl 2f: wnt 3rd ins fnl f: styd on same pce and no imp after* **4/1**[3]	67
0	4	2 1/2	**Onesie (IRE)**[17] 4017 3-9-2 0....................................... DanielMuscutt(3) 9 *(Marco Botti) taken down early: sn prom: w wnr after 1f: rdn and unable qck over 1f out: wknd ins fnl f* **16/1**	60
0520	5	2 3/4	**Cadeaux Boxer**[14] 4149 3-9-5 80.. PatCosgrave 6 *(Martin Smith) t.k.h: hld up in tch in midfield: effrt jst over 2f out: 5th and no imp over 1f out: wknd ins fnl f* **5/2**[2]	53
	6	4 1/2	**Joanne Park** 3-9-0 0.. JohnFahy 7 *(Clive Cox) hld up in tch: rdn over 2f out: sn outpcd: rn green and hung rt 2f out: sn wknd* **7/1**	36
0	7	6	**Flying Sakhee**[19] 3958 3-9-0 0.. WilliamCarson 1 *(John Bridger) s.i.s: t.k.h: hld up in rr: hdwy into midfield 5f out: rdn and outpcd over 2f out: wkng whn hmpd and swtchd lft 2f out: bhd fnl f* **40/1**	19
	P		**Royal Phoenix** 3-8-9 0.. HectorCrouch(5) 10 *(Gary Moore) led for 1f: steadily lost pl and bhd 3f out: rdn over 2f out: sn lost tch and eased: p.u and dismntd ins fnl f* **25/1**	

1m 22.92s (-0.38) **Going Correction** -0.05s/f (Good)
WFA 3 from 4yo 7lb **8** Ran SP% **123.2**
Speed ratings (Par 101): **100,99,96,93,90 85,78,**
CSF £16.80 TOTE £6.60: £2.00, £1.20, £2.00; EX 20.70 Trifecta £85.50.
Owner Spear Family **Bred** Gerry Burke **Trained** Lambourn, Berks

FOCUS
An ordinary maiden. They went a respectable gallop. The third has been rated just shy of his pre-race level.

4640 BEST ODDS AT 188BET H'CAP 7f
8:10 (8:10) (Class 6) (0-65,65) 3-Y-O+ **£2,587** (£770; £384; £192) **Stalls** Centre

Form				RPR
0334	1		**Remember Me**[42] 3126 3-9-5 **63**.. HarryBentley 9 *(Hughie Morrison) chsd ldr tl led 3f out: rdn over 1f out: clr and r.o wl ins fnl f: readily* **5/1**[2]	70
0316	2	2 3/4	**Fairy Mist (IRE)**[7] 4389 9-9-5 **56**.................................(b) WilliamCarson 8 *(John Bridger) hld up in tch in midfield: hdwy u.p to chse wnr over 1f out: styd on but no imp ins fnl f* **11/1**	59
3555	3	nk	**Caledonia Laird**[31] 3514 5-10-0 **65**...................................... RobertHavlin 7 *(Jo Hughes) hld up in tch: shuffled bk and n.m.r 2f out: swtchd lft and effrt ent fnl f: nt clr run and hmpd ins fnl f: swtchd rt and r.o wl fnl 100yds: no threat to wnr* **7/1**[3]	70
0060	4	hd	**Sarmadee (IRE)**[14] 4155 4-9-13 **64**................................... CharlesBishop 2 *(Mick Channon) stdd and dropped in bhd after s: hld up in tch in rr: clsd and nt clr run over 1f out: hdwy u.p to chse ldrs 1f out: styd on same pce ins fnl f* **7/1**[3]	66
0-00	5	hd	**Windmills Girl**[18] 3987 3-8-8 **52**..............................(b[1]) AdamBeschizza 10 *(Jeremy Gask) chsd ldrs: rdn 2f out: drvn jst over 1f out: styd on same pce ins fnl f* **25/1**	50
4230	6	1 1/2	**Mrs Warren**[25] 3743 6-9-7 **58**.. PatCosgrave 4 *(George Baker) stdd s: t.k.h: hld up in tch: clsd and nt clrest of runs over 1f out: rdn and kpt on ins fnl f: nvr trbld ldrs* **5/1**[2]	55
46-3	7	3/4	**In Ken's Memory**[51] 2823 3-9-4 **65**........................ JosephineGordon(3) 6 *(John Butler) taken down early: chsd ldr over 2f out tl no ex u.p over 1f out: wknd ins fnl f* **8/1**	57
2566	8	1	**Viva Verglas (IRE)**[23] 3807 5-9-13 **64**.......................... RobertWinston 1 *(Daniel Mark Loughnane) t.k.h: wl in tch in midfield: rdn 2f out: little rspnse over 1f out: wknd ins fnl f: eased towards fin* **7/1**[3]	56
3312	9	1/2	**Gulland Rock**[9] 4289 5-9-6 **64**.. GeorgeWood(7) 5 *(Anthony Carson) hld up in tch: effrt 2f out: sme hdwy u.p over 1f out: no imp 1f out: wknd ins fnl f: eased towards fin* **4/1**[1]	55+
0065	10	nk	**Smoothtalkinrascal (IRE)**[19] 3953 6-9-7 **63**...........(t) HectorCrouch(5) 3 *(Peter Crate) hld up in tch: effrt and no hdwy over 1f out: wl hld whn nt clrest of runs and swtchd rt wl ins fnl f* **16/1**	56
-000	11	2 3/4	**Suzi Icon**[29] 3624 4-8-9 **49**.. DanielMuscutt(3) 11 *(John Butler) led tl 3f out: rdn over 2f out: lost pl and btn over 1f out: wknd fnl f* **25/1**	31

1m 23.39s (0.09) **Going Correction** -0.05s/f (Good)
WFA 3 from 4yo+ 7lb **11** Ran SP% **123.9**
Speed ratings (Par 101): **97,93,93,93,93 91,90,89,88,88 85**
CSF £62.48 CT £392.04 TOTE £7.10: £2.90, £3.30, £3.10; EX 79.40 Trifecta £651.70.
Owner Thurloe Thoroughbreds XXXVI **Bred** Aiden Murphy **Trained** East Ilsley, Berks

FOCUS
A modest handicap. They went a respectable gallop but four of the first five home were drawn in the four highest stalls. The runner-up helps set the level.

4641 £25 FREE BET AT 188BET H'CAP 7f
8:40 (8:40) (Class 5) (0-70,65) 3-Y-O **£3,234** (£962; £481; £240) **Stalls** Centre

Form				RPR
0026	1		**Arctic Flower (IRE)**[7] 4388 3-8-7 **51**.................................. DannyBrock 1 *(John Bridger) mde all: grad crossed to stands' rail: rdn and fnd ex over 1f out: in command and styd on ins fnl f: rdn out* **12/1**	58
020	2	1 1/4	**Marcle (IRE)**[10] 4269 3-9-7 **65**.. JohnFahy 8 *(Ed de Giles) chsd wnr thrght: swtchd lft and effrt over 1f out: clr 2nd but kpt on same pce ins fnl f* **3/1**[2]	69
-010	3	3 3/4	**R Bar Open (FR)**[25] 3740 3-9-7 **65**.................................. RobertWinston 4 *(Dean Ivory) stdd after s: t.k.h: hld up in rr: effrt jst over 2f out: styd on to pass btn horses 1f out: wnt 3rd ins fnl f: nvr trbld ldrs* **7/1**	59+
0006	4	3 1/2	**Lillyput (IRE)**[17] 3993 3-8-4 **53**... PaddyPilley(5) 6 *(Mick Channon) chsd ldrs: effrt 2f out: wnt 3rd and wnt lft 1f out: sn no imp: lost 3rd and wknd ins fnl f* **14/1**	37
-004	5	1 3/4	**Desirable**[31] 3513 3-8-12 **56**.. HarryBentley 7 *(Hughie Morrison) hld up in tch in midfield: rdn wl over 2f out: unable qck and no hdwy over 1f out: wknd ins fnl f* **8/1**	36+
-300	6	3/4	**Indigo**[12] 4206 3-9-1 **62**.. JosephineGordon(3) 3 *(Mark Usher) chsd ldrs: rdn 2f out: unable qck and btn over 1f out: wknd ins fnl f* **6/1**[3]	40
056	7	1	**Caledonia Duchess**[18] 3989 3-9-4 **62**.........................(v[1]) RobertHavlin 2 *(Jo Hughes) stdd s: t.k.h: hld up in tch: rdn jst over 2f out: no hdwy over 1f out: wknd ins fnl f* **9/1**	37+
-105	8	2	**Ebbisham (IRE)**[10] 4269 3-9-6 **64**.. PatCosgrave 5 *(Jim Boyle) in tch in last pair: effrt over 2f out: no imp and btn whn n.m.r over 1f out: wknd ins fnl f* **9/4**[1]	38+

1m 22.89s (-0.41) **Going Correction** -0.05s/f (Good) **8** Ran SP% **118.0**
Speed ratings (Par 100): **100,98,94,90,88 87,86,84**
CSF £49.67 CT £283.61 TOTE £11.60: £2.80, £2.10, £2.40; EX 70.60 Trifecta £553.10.
Owner Mr & Mrs K Finch **Bred** B Kennedy **Trained** Liphook, Hants

FOCUS
A modest 3yo handicap. They went a respectable gallop and the winner crossed over to make all from the lowest draw. The winner has been rated close to her maiden form here two starts back.
T/Plt: £174.80 to a £1 stake. Pool: £63,451.57 - 264.86 winning units. T/Qpdt: £7.30 to a £1 stake. Pool: £9,181.94 - 921.14 winning units. **Steve Payne**

3654 NEWCASTLE (A.W) (L-H)
Saturday, July 23

OFFICIAL GOING: Tapeta: standard
Wind: Almost nil Weather: Overcast, humid

4642 COLLINGWOOD INSURANCE COMPANY MAIDEN AUCTION STKS (PLUS 10 RACE) 7f 14y (Tp)
1:50 (1:54) (Class 4) 2-Y-O **£4,528** (£1,347; £673; £336) **Stalls** Centre

Form				RPR
6	1		**George Reme (IRE)**[16] 4040 2-9-5 0.................................. JackGarritty 9 *(John Quinn) hld up: pushed along and hdwy over 2f out: kpt on wl u.p fnl f to ld cl home* **12/1**	77
03	2	nse	**Drochaid**[14] 4128 2-9-5 0... PhillipMakin 10 *(Andrew Balding) pressed ldr: effrt and rdn over 2f out: led over 1f out: kpt on fnl f: hdd cl home* **2/1**[2]	77+
5	3	2 1/2	**Third Order (IRE)**[16] 4040 2-9-5 0................................. KeaganLatham 1 *(K R Burke) prom on outside: drvn and outpcd over 2f out: rallied fnl f: nt rch first two* **7/1**[3]	70
	4	3/4	**Moonlight Blue (IRE)** 2-9-5 0..................................... ConnorBeasley 4 *(Michael Dods) dwlt: bhd and green: drvn and hdwy over 1f out: kpt on fnl f: no imp* **25/1**	68+
3	5	nse	**Jive Talking (IRE)**[7] 4397 2-8-11 0.............................. LouisSteward(3) 3 *(Michael Bell) trckd ldrs: rdn over 2f out: outpcd ins fnl f* **7/4**[1]	63
30	6	3/4	**See The City (IRE)**[29] 3598 2-9-5 0.................................. PJMcDonald 7 *(Mark Johnston) led: rdn and hdd over 1f out: outpcd fnl f* **8/1**	66
45	7	1 1/4	**Steel Helmet (IRE)**[12] 4188 2-9-5 0...................................... DaleSwift 8 *(Brian Ellison) prom: sn drvn along: rallied fr 1/2-way: no ex over 1f out* **25/1**	63

6 **8** 1 3/4 **Dandy Place (IRE)**[9] 4297 2-9-5 0 JamesSullivan 2 58
(Tim Easterby) *hld up: rdn over 2f out: outpcd fr over 1f out* **66/1**
04 **9** 3 1/2 **Parkwarden (IRE)**[30] 3561 2-9-5 0 JoeDoyle 11 48
(Chris Grant) *hld up in tch: rdn over 2f out: wknd over 1f out* **66/1**
10 9 **Kelpie Spirit (IRE)** 2-9-5 0 LukeMorris 6 24
(John Weymes) *missed break: bhd: drvn 3f out: sn btn* **40/1**
1m 28.08s (1.88) **Going Correction** +0.175s/f (Slow) **10** Ran SP% **114.1**
Speed ratings (Par 96): **96,95,93,92,92 91,89,87,83,73**
CSF £33.02 TOTE £17.90: £3.20, £1.20, £2.40; EX 43.90 Trifecta £271.60.
Owner Robert Houlton **Bred** Shefford Valley Stud **Trained** Settrington, N Yorks
■ Harry George was withdrawn. Price at time of withdrawal 14-1. Rule 4 applies to all bets - deduction 5p in the pound.
■ Stewards' Enquiry : Jack Garritty two-day ban: used whip above permitted level (6-7 Aug)

FOCUS
There will be no speed figures at this track until there is sufficient data to calculate median times. Warm, overcast conditions, and clerk of the course James Armstrong expected the Tapeta to ride on the slow side once again, if perhaps not so markedly as it had on the first day of the Northumberland Plate fixture. Just a routine juvenile maiden to start with, but several shaped with conspicuous promise behind the winner. It's been rated as ordinary form.

4643 COLLINGWOOD FLEET INSURANCE H'CAP 6f (Tp)
2:20 (2:24) (Class 4) (0-85,85) 3-Y-O **£5,822** (£1,732; £865; £432) **Stalls** Centre

Form RPR
146 **1** **Mustallib (IRE)**[15] 4079 3-9-4 **82** MichaelJMMurphy 4 93
(Charles Hills) *trckd ldrs: effrt and ev ch over 1f out: led ins fnl f: hld on wl* **9/4**[2]
-13 **2** *hd* **Cocoa Beach (IRE)**[182] 315 3-8-12 **76** LukeMorris 1 86
(Sir Mark Prescott Bt) *t.k.h: cl up on outside: edgd rt and rdn to ld over 1f out: hdd ins fnl f: kpt on wl u.p: jst hld* **7/4**[1]
6003 **3** 2 1/4 **Be Kool (IRE)**[30] 3567 3-8-4 **68** AndrewElliott 11 71
(Brian Ellison) *hld up on nr side of gp: rdn over 2f out: kpt on wl fnl f: nt rch first two* **20/1**
4622 **4** *nk* **Wowcha (IRE)**[16] 4043 3-8-12 **76** (p) JackGarritty 10 78
(John Quinn) *s.i.s: hld up: rdn and hdwy 2f out: kpt on fnl f: nt gng pce to chal* **8/1**[3]
2326 **5** 3/4 **Bossipop**[8] 4344 3-9-5 **83** (p) JamesSullivan 5 83
(Tim Easterby) *hld up: hdwy on far side over 2f out: rdn over 1f out: one pce fnl f* **14/1**
6105 **6** 1/2 **Dodgy Bob**[21] 3893 3-9-3 **81** (p) KeaganLatham 2 79
(Kevin Ryan) *led to over 1f out: rdn and outpcd fnl f* **20/1**
4113 **7** 1 1/2 **In My Place**[20] 3924 3-8-3 **72** (p) CallumShepherd(5) 12 65
(Richard Fahey) *hld up on nr side of gp: drvn along over 2f out: kpt on fnl f: no imp* **16/1**
164- **8** 1/2 **Richter Scale (IRE)**[358] 4837 3-8-13 **77** ConnorBeasley 3 69
(Michael Dods) *in tch towards far side of gp: rdn over 2f out: edgd lft and outpcd over 1f out* **33/1**
6441 **9** 1 3/4 **Dark Defender**[19] 3944 3-9-7 **85** PhillipMakin 8 71
(Keith Dalgleish) *cl up: rdn over 2f out: wknd fnl f* **8/1**[3]
1160 **10** 1/2 **Ticking Away**[52] 2788 3-9-7 **85** ShaneGray 6 70
(David Brown) *hld up in tch: effrt over 2f out: wknd fnl f* **33/1**
2313 **11** 1 3/4 **General Alexander (IRE)**[57] 2650 3-8-7 **78** (p) BenRobinson(7) 13 57
(Brian Ellison) *hld up: rdn and edgd lft over 2f out: nvr on terms* **18/1**
300 **12** 2 1/4 **Insurplus (IRE)**[57] 2657 3-8-6 **70** JoeDoyle 9 42
(Jim Goldie) *bhd: struggling 1/2-way: nvr on terms* **50/1**
2464 **13** *nk* **Socialites Red**[10] 4256 3-8-5 **69** PJMcDonald 7 40
(Scott Dixon) *prom: rdn along over 2f out: wknd over 1f out* **50/1**
1m 12.34s (-0.16) **Going Correction** +0.175s/f (Slow) **13** Ran SP% **126.5**
Speed ratings (Par 102): **108,107,104,104,103 102,100,100,97,97 94,91,91**
CSF £6.46 CT £66.95 TOTE £3.60: £1.60, £1.40, £4.60; EX 8.30 Trifecta £107.60.
Owner Hamdan Al Maktoum **Bred** Wardstown Stud Ltd **Trained** Lambourn, Berks

FOCUS
A fair 3yo sprint handicap, but not many figured behind the pair who dominated the market. A pb from the winner, and a step up from the unexposed runner-up.

4644 COLLINGWOOD LEARNER DRIVER INSURANCE "BEESWING" H'CAP 7f 14y (Tp)
2:55 (2:58) (Class 3) (0-95,95) 3-Y-O+ **£16,172** (£4,812; £2,405; £1,202) **Stalls** Centre

Form RPR
5406 **1** **Barracuda Boy (IRE)**[39] 3250 6-10-0 **95** LukeMorris 1 103
(Tom Dascombe) *hld up: rdn and hdwy to chse ldrs over 1f out: drvn to ld wl ins fnl f* **20/1**
-003 **2** *shd* **Northgate Lad (IRE)**[30] 3566 4-9-1 **89** BenRobinson(7) 5 96
(Brian Ellison) *trckd ldrs: led and rdn over 2f out: hung rt appr fnl f: hdd wl ins fnl f: rallied: jst hld* **3/1**[1]
2055 **3** 1 3/4 **Candelisa (IRE)**[30] 3566 3-9-7 **95** (p) JackGarritty 7 94
(Jedd O'Keeffe) *chsd ldrs: rdn along over 2f out: kpt on ins fnl f: nt rch first two* **7/1**[2]
30-0 **4** 1 1/2 **Holiday Magic (IRE)**[8] 4374 5-9-4 **90** NathanEvans(5) 8 88
(Michael Easterby) *led to over 2f out: rdn and one pce fnl f* **12/1**
35 **5** *hd* **Margaret's Mission (IRE)**[14] 4130 5-9-4 **85** JoeDoyle 11 82
(Jim Goldie) *reluctant to enter stalls: sn wl bhd: hdwy over 1f out: kpt on wl fnl f: nrst fin* **7/1**[2]
6125 **6** 1 **Boots And Spurs**[14] 4163 7-9-1 **82** (v) DaleSwift 6 77
(Scott Dixon) *cl up: ev ch over 2f out: rdn whn carried rt appr fnl f: sn one pce* **7/1**[2]
0602 **7** 1 **Regal Dan (IRE)**[9] 4299 6-9-6 **87** SamJames 14 79
(David O'Meara) *in tch: drvn and outpcd over 2f out: no imp fr over 1f out* **7/1**[2]
601 **8** 3/4 **Lavetta**[49] 2890 4-9-2 **83** NeilFarley 10 73
(Alan Swinbank) *prom: drvn along over 2f out: no ex fr over 1f out* **12/1**
1020 **9** 4 **Justice First**[35] 3414 4-8-7 **81** HarryBurns(7) 4 60
(Ed Dunlop) *prom: rdn over 2f out: wknd wl over 1f out* **20/1**
3455 **10** *nk* **Father Bertie**[9] 4299 4-9-6 **87** (tp) JamesSullivan 3 65
(Tim Easterby) *hld up on far side of gp: rdn over 2f out: sn no imp* **8/1**[3]
-000 **11** 6 **Ocean Tempest**[28] 3672 7-9-6 **90** LouisSteward(3) 12 52
(John Ryan) *hld up: drvn and outpcd wl over 2f out: sn n.d* **11/1**
050- **12** 1 1/2 **Magic City (IRE)**[285] 7163 7-9-6 **92** AnnaHesketh(5) 13 50
(Michael Easterby) *s.v.s: nvr on terms* **25/1**
3000 **13** 3/4 **Fleckerl (IRE)**[59] 2581 6-9-7 **88** (p) KeaganLatham 2 44
(Conor Dore) *slowly away and wl bhd: no ch fr 1/2-way* **33/1**
1m 26.18s (-0.02) **Going Correction** +0.175s/f (Slow)
WFA 3 from 4yo+ 7lb **13** Ran SP% **126.1**
Speed ratings (Par 107): **107,106,104,103,102 101,100,99,95,94 88,86,85**
CSF £80.44 CT £508.48 TOTE £17.00: £4.00, £2.00, £2.60; EX 127.10 Trifecta £1787.40.
Owner Laurence Bellman **Bred** Mount Coote Partnership **Trained** Malpas, Cheshire
■ Stewards' Enquiry : Ben Robinson caution: careless riding

FOCUS
The first running on Tapeta of a long-established Newcastle event, and a third thrilling finish from as many races this afternoon. The runner-up and third are closely matched based on their C&D latest.

4645 COLLINGWOOD YOUNG DRIVER INSURANCE H'CAP 2m 56y (Tp)
3:30 (3:30) (Class 6) (0-60,60) 4-Y-O+ **£2,911** (£866; £432; £216) **Stalls** Low

Form RPR
46-4 **1** **Salford Dream**[49] 2916 7-8-10 **49** (p) JamesSullivan 6 56
(Pauline Robson) *t.k.h: trckd ldrs: effrt and rdn over 2f out: led over 1f out: edgd lft ins fnl f: drvn out* **15/2**
3-33 **2** 1 1/4 **Maple Stirrup (IRE)**[22] 3842 4-8-9 **55** PaulaMuir(7) 5 61
(Patrick Holmes) *trckd ldrs: rdn over 2f out: rallied to chse wnr ins fnl f: kpt on* **7/2**[1]
3435 **3** 1 **Hero's Story**[12] 4194 6-9-0 **53** JoeDoyle 12 57+
(Jim Goldie) *hld up: smooth hdwy 3f out: rdn over 1f out: kpt on ins fnl f* **10/1**
5500 **4** 1 **Another Lincolnday**[19] 3942 5-9-7 **60** (p) PhillipMakin 3 63
(Michael Herrington) *hld up in midfield on ins: rdn over 2f out: kpt on fnl f: nt gng pce to chal* **17/2**
0405 **5** *nk* **Noble Reach**[35] 3417 5-8-4 **46** oh1 (p) NoelGarbutt(3) 9 49
(Lawrence Mullaney) *s.i.s: hdwy and cl up after 2f: led after 6f: rdn and hdd over 1f out: no ex ins fnl f* **20/1**
-000 **6** 1/2 **Waltz Darling (IRE)**[23] 3191 8-8-4 **48** (b[1]) PhilDennis(5) 7 50
(Keith Reveley) *t.k.h: hld up: rdn over 2f out: kpt on fnl f: no imp* **9/1**
0100 **7** 1 1/2 **Desktop**[16] 4045 4-9-6 **59** LukeMorris 8 59
(Antony Brittain) *hld up: stdy hdwy over 3f out: rdn over 2f out: wknd fnl f* **5/1**[3]
-050 **8** 1/2 **Danzella**[6] 4430 4-8-7 **46** oh1 DuranFentiman 13 46
(Chris Fairhurst) *hld up in midfield: drvn and outpcd 3f out: rallied fnl f: no imp* **25/1**
5060 **9** *nk* **Yorkshireman (IRE)**[35] 3417 6-8-7 **46** oh1 (b) AndrewElliott 10 45
(Lynn Siddall) *hld up: rdn on outside 3f out: no imp fr 2f out* **10/1**
4010 **10** 3 **Byronegetonefree**[26] 3704 5-8-12 **51** PJMcDonald 4 47
(Stuart Coltherd) *led at ordinary gallop for 6f: pressed ldr: rdn and ev ch over 2f out: wknd fnl f* **4/1**[2]
4-00 **11** 1 3/4 **Zingiber**[65] 2409 4-8-7 **46** oh1 ShaneGray 11 40
(Wilf Storey) *in tch: rdn along over 2f out: wknd over 1f out* **50/1**
1054 **12** 1 3/4 **Solid Justice (IRE)**[30] 3547 5-8-13 **52** ConnorBeasley 2 44
(Kenny Johnson) *prom: drvn and outpcd over 2f out: sn btn* **18/1**
3m 39.37s (4.17) **Going Correction** +0.275s/f (Slow) **12** Ran SP% **125.2**
Speed ratings (Par 101): **100,99,98,98,98 97,97,96,96,95 94,93**
CSF £35.22 CT £277.41 TOTE £8.30: £2.80, £1.80, £3.60; EX 41.00 Trifecta £159.20.
Owner Hale Racing Limited **Bred** Jonathan Shack **Trained** Kirkharle, Northumberland

FOCUS
A low-grade affair run over the Northumberland Plate C&D, and the early pace appeared modest.

4646 COLLINGWOOD TAXI INSURANCE/EBFSTALLIONS.COM FILLIES' H'CAP 1m 4f 98y (Tp)
4:05 (4:05) (Class 4) (0-85,85) 4-Y-O+ **£6,469** (£1,925; £962; £481) **Stalls** High

Form RPR
21-0 **1** **Pecking Order (IRE)**[24] 3785 4-9-7 **85** ConnorBeasley 8 94
(James Fanshawe) *hld up: smooth hdwy on outside to ld appr 2f out: sn rdn: kpt on strly fnl f* **7/2**[2]
3000 **2** 3 **Intense Tango**[15] 4078 5-8-10 **81** (t) CliffordLee(7) 1 85
(K R Burke) *led: rdn and hdd appr 2f out: sn drvn and outpcd: rallied to chse (clr) wnr ins fnl f: kpt on* **4/1**[3]
2626 **3** 3/4 **Graceland (FR)**[38] 3278 4-9-1 **82** LouisSteward(3) 5 85
(Michael Bell) *hld up: rdn and hdwy over 2f out: kpt on same pce ins fnl f* **3/1**[1]
6016 **4** *shd* **Yorkindred Spirit**[5] 4455 4-8-9 **73** (v) PJMcDonald 6 76
(Mark Johnston) *hld up in tch: smooth hdwy to chal 2f out: sn rdn: edgd lft and lost 2 pls ins fnl f* **7/1**
6113 **5** 2 1/2 **Southern Storm (IRE)**[88] 1743 4-9-7 **85** (v) PhillipMakin 3 84
(Ralph Beckett) *hld up in tch: stdy hdwy over 2f out: sn rdn: no ex over 1f out* **3/1**[1]
4600 **6** 10 **Bayan Kasirga (IRE)**[16] 4049 6-8-8 **72** JamesSullivan 2 55
(Richard Fahey) *chsd ldr: drvn and ev ch briefly over 2f out: wknd over 1f out* **14/1**
6060 **7** 9 **Wor Lass**[15] 4101 8-8-5 **74** AnnaHesketh(5) 7 42
(Susan Corbett) *chsd ldrs tl rdn and wknd over 2f out* **10/1**
2m 41.05s (-0.05) **Going Correction** +0.275s/f (Slow) **7** Ran SP% **120.5**
Speed ratings (Par 102): **111,109,108,108,106 100,94**
CSF £19.23 CT £47.67 TOTE £4.20: £2.40, £3.20; EX 19.80 Trifecta £89.80.
Owner Merry Fox Stud Limited **Bred** Merry Fox Stud Ltd **Trained** Newmarket, Suffolk

FOCUS
A fairly competitive-looking fillies' handicap beforehand, but the winner made pretty short work of the rest. A step up from the winner on last year's maiden win, with the third rated close to her recent figures for now.

4647 COLLINGWOOD SHORT TERM LEARNER DRIVER INSURANCE H'CAP 5f (Tp)
4:40 (4:42) (Class 6) (0-60,66) 3-Y-O+ **£3,234** (£962; £481; £240) **Stalls** Centre

Form RPR
-032 **1** **Indastar**[30] 3549 6-9-6 **56** PJMcDonald 13 63
(Michael Herrington) *cl up towards nr side of gp: led 1/2-way: drvn out fnl f* **10/1**
5343 **2** 3/4 **Slim Chance (IRE)**[9] 4309 7-9-5 **58** (p) LouisSteward(3) 14 62
(Simon West) *hld up on nr side of gp: hdwy to chse wnr ent fnl f: kpt on fin* **14/1**
0000 **3** *shd* **Harpers Ruby**[24] 3776 6-9-0 **50** AndrewElliott 12 51
(Lynn Siddall) *led to over 2f out: rallied: kpt on same pce ins fnl f* **33/1**
1362 **4** 1/2 **Dream Ally (IRE)**[18] 3984 6-9-7 **57** (be) LukeMorris 11 56
(John Weymes) *hld up in tch towards nr side of gp: drvn along over 2f out: edgd lft: one pce* **8/1**[3]
0460 **5** *shd* **Little Belter (IRE)**[7] 4410 4-9-3 **53** (v) PhillipMakin 2 52
(Keith Dalgleish) *t.k.h: hld up: rdn over 2f out: hdwy over 1f out: kpt on same pce fnl f* **11/1**
4002 **6** 2 1/4 **Someone Exciting**[24] 3773 3-8-7 **52** NathanEvans(5) 9 42
(David Thompson) *s.i.s: bhd tl hdwy over 1f out: no imp fnl f* **12/1**
0214 **7** *shd* **Classic Flyer**[3] 4512 4-9-11 **66** (b) JoshDoyle(5) 10 57
(David O'Meara) *s.i.s: hld up: rdn 1/2-way: no imp over 1f out* **6/1**[2]
0000 **8** 3/4 **Majestic Manannan (IRE)**[4] 4492 7-8-13 **54** CallumShepherd(5) 7 42
(David Nicholls) *in tch: drvn along 1/2-way: no ex over 1f out* **16/1**
-060 **9** 1 **Sea Of Green**[7] 4410 4-9-0 **50** JoeDoyle 6 34
(Jim Goldie) *hld up: stdy hdwy 1/2-way: rdn over 1f out: sn outpcd* **25/1**

-011 **10** *nk* **Culloden**[4] 4472 4-9-2 **57** CharlieBennett(5) 5 40
(Shaun Harris) *cl up: rdn over 2f out: wknd ins fnl f* **15/8**[1]
6364 **11** *2 ¾* **Canford Belle**[24] 3786 3-8-12 **57** PhilDennis(5) 4 29
(Grant Tuer) *in tch on far side of gp: rdn over 2f out: wknd over 1f out* **14/1**
0005 **12** *nk* **Steel City Boy (IRE)**[11] 4229 13-8-7 **46** oh1 JacobButterfield(3) 3 18
(Shaun Harris) *prom on far side of gp to 1/2-way: wknd over 1f out* **50/1**
-002 **13** *10* **Lady Elizabeth (IRE)**[14] 4141 3-9-2 **56** (p) DaleSwift 8
(Scott Dixon) *chsd ldrs: drvn along 1/2-way: sn lost pl* **20/1**
6-03 **D** *¾* **Euxton**[11] 4229 4-9-1 **56** JordanNason(5) 1 58
(Lawrence Mullaney) *hld up on far side of gp: rdn over 2f out: kpt on fnl f: nrst fin* **9/1**

1m 0.74s (1.24) **Going Correction** +0.175s/f (Slow)
WFA 3 from 4yo+ 4lb **14** Ran SP% **128.0**
Speed ratings (Par 101): **97,95,94,93,93 89,89,88,86,86 82,81,65,94**
CSF £145.95 CT £1362.99 TOTE £12.30: £2.90, £4.30, £4.20; EX 178.30 Trifecta £1870.40.
Owner Tony Culhane Racing Club **Bred** Bearstone Stud Ltd **Trained** Cold Kirby, N Yorks

FOCUS
A pretty moderate affair, albeit with a good smattering of competitors in fair recent form at this sort of level.

4648 COLLINGWOOD CONVICTED DRIVER INSURANCE APPRENTICE H'CAP 1m 2f 42y (Tp)

5:10 (5:12) (Class 6) (0-60,60) 3-Y-O+ **£2,911** (£866; £432; £216) **Stalls** High

Form RPR
3/06 **1** **Gold Show**[26] 3706 7-9-10 **56** CliffordLee 2 64
(Grant Tuer) *hld up in midfield: smooth hdwy to ld 2f out: pushed out fnl f* **8/1**[3]
4402 **2** *2 ¾* **Kicking The Can (IRE)**[30] 3564 5-9-10 **60** LewisEdmunds(4) 8 63
(David Thompson) *trckd ldrs: smooth hdwy and ev ch over 2f out to over 1f out: sn rdn: kpt on same pce ins fnl f* **7/2**[2]
0044 **3** *1* **Kerry Icon**[15] 4098 3-8-0 **46** JamieGormley(4) 12 47
(Iain Jardine) *trckd ldrs: effrt and rdn 2f out: kpt on same pce ins fnl f* **9/1**
5-60 **4** *¾* **The Name's Bond**[47] 2958 4-8-10 **46** oh1 HayleyIrvine(4) 4 46
(Richard Fahey) *hld up: rdn over 2f out: kpt on fnl f: nvr able to chal* **8/1**[3]
0022 **5** *½* **Grandest**[6] 4425 5-9-6 **56** BenRobinson(4) 1 55
(Brian Ellison) *hld up: smooth hdwy and in tch over 2f out: rdn over 1f out: sn no imp* **11/10**[1]
5400 **6** *nk* **Silva Samourai**[15] 4099 7-9-0 **46** HarryBurns 10 44
(Susan Corbett) *cl up: led briefly over 2f out: rdn and outpcd fnl f* **25/1**
2160 **7** *¾* **Mount Cheiron (USA)**[12] 4214 5-9-5 **51** (p) CallumRodriguez 7 48
(Richard Ford) *hld up: stdy hdwy 2f out: sn rdn: no imp fnl f* **18/1**
6-00 **8** *7* **Papagayo (IRE)**[12] 4194 4-9-3 **53** (t) GerO'Neill(4) 3 36
(Barry Murtagh) *hld up: rdn over 2f out: wknd over 1f out* **20/1**
00-0 **9** *1* **Come On Lulu**[10] 4260 5-8-10 **46** oh1 (p) AledBeech(4) 11 28
(David Thompson) *midfield on outside: struggling over 2f out: sn btn* **33/1**
10 *2* **Devon River (FR)**[24] 6-8-10 **46** oh1 TomDonoghue(4) 5 24
(Simon Waugh) *in tch: rdn over 2f out: wknd over 1f out* **20/1**
00-0 **11** *12* **Tinseltown**[136] 674 10-9-4 **50** KieranSchofield 6 5
(Harriet Bethell) *hld up in tch: pushed along 1/2-way: wknd over 2f out* **25/1**
00-0 **12** *5* **Almost Spanish (IRE)**[58] 2608 3-8-0 **46** oh1 DavidEgan(4) 9
(Scott Dixon) *led to over 2f out: sn rdn and btn* **50/1**

2m 12.79s (2.39) **Going Correction** +0.275s/f (Slow)
WFA 3 from 4yo+ 10lb **12** Ran SP% **129.4**
Speed ratings (Par 101): **101,98,98,97,97 96,96,90,89,88 78,74**
CSF £36.56 CT £274.57 TOTE £12.30: £3.00, £1.90, £3.10; EX 45.60 Trifecta £713.00.
Owner E Tuer **Bred** Mr & Mrs A E Pakenham **Trained** Birkby, N Yorks

FOCUS
A weak finale. The fourth has been rated as running a pb on his debut for Richard Fahey.
T/Plt: £256.00 to a £1 stake. Pool: £72,857.72 - 207.69 winning tickets T/Qpdt: £48.60 to a £1 stake. Pool: £5,746.42 - 87.40 winning tickets **Richard Young**

4593 NEWMARKET (R-H)

Saturday, July 23

OFFICIAL GOING: Good to firm (7.7)
Wind: Light across Weather: Sunny spells

4649 ADNAMS SOUTHWOLD BITTER EBF STALLIONS MAIDEN STKS (PLUS 10 RACE) 7f

2:00 (2:00) (Class 4) 2-Y-O **£4,528** (£1,347; £673; £336) **Stalls** Low

Form RPR
2 **1** **D'bai (IRE)**[15] 4103 2-9-5 0 JamesMcDonald 3 84
(Charlie Appleby) *led early: racd keenly and remained w ldr: led over 1f out: rdn and hung lft fnl f: r.o* **1/5**[1]
2 *shd* **Hydroxide** 2-9-5 0 JackMitchell 2 84+
(Hugo Palmer) *s.s: hld up: swtchd lft over 2f out: hdwy over 1f out: rdn and ev ch wl ins fnl f: r.o* **17/2**[2]
4 **3** *1* **Hartswell**[28] 3661 2-9-5 0 NickyMackay 8 81
(John Gosden) *chsd ldrs: rdn and edgd lft over 1f out: r.o* **14/1**[3]
64 **4** *1 ¼* **Outre Mer (IRE)**[31] 3524 2-9-2 0 KieranShoemark(3) 1 78
(John Gosden) *chsd ldrs: rdn over 1f out: styd on same pce ins fnl f* **16/1**
5 *1* **Contrapposto (IRE)** 2-9-5 0 MartinDwyer 4 75
(David Menuisier) *s.i.s: hld up: nt clr run over 1f out: hung lft and styd on ins fnl f: nt trble ldrs* **50/1**
6 *1 ¼* **First Quest (USA)** 2-9-5 0 GeorgeBaker 5 72
(Ed Dunlop) *hld up: shkn up over 1f out: nt trble ldrs* **33/1**
7 *5* **Dahl (IRE)** 2-9-5 0 AdamKirby 7 58
(Mark Johnston) *sn led: rdn: hdd & wknd over 1f out* **14/1**[3]

1m 28.68s (2.98) **Going Correction** +0.20s/f (Good) **7** Ran SP% **118.0**
Speed ratings (Par 96): **90,89,88,87,86 84,79**
CSF £3.21 TOTE £1.10: £1.10, £3.10; EX 3.00 Trifecta £11.50.
Owner Godolphin **Bred** Lodge Park Stud **Trained** Newmarket, Suffolk

FOCUS
Stands' side used. Stalls on stands' side except 1m2f and 1m5f, centre. An interesting maiden. It was run at a sound pace with the field racing towards the stands' rail before edging to the centre inside the final furlong. The third and fourth have been rated as having progressed.

4650 ADNAMS BROADSIDE H'CAP 1m 2f

2:35 (2:36) (Class 3) (0-95,90) 3-Y-O+ **£9,703** (£2,887; £1,443; £721) **Stalls** Centre

Form RPR
1-01 **1** **Baydar**[36] 3355 3-9-2 **90** JackMitchell 6 102+
(Hugo Palmer) *hld up: hdwy over 1f out: rdn to ld and hung lft ins fnl f: r.o* **6/5**[1]
6241 **2** *nk* **Innocent Touch (IRE)**[20] 3920 5-9-9 **87** TedDurcan 3 98
(Richard Fahey) *chsd ldrs: rdn to ld jst over 1f out: hung rt and hdd ins fnl f: r.o* **11/2**[3]
0503 **3** *3 ¼* **Emerald (ITY)**[17] 4026 4-9-6 **87** (b) DanielMuscutt(3) 1 92
(Marco Botti) *hld up: hdwy and nt clr run over 1f out: cl up and rdn whn hmpd ins fnl f: styd on same pce* **10/1**
1564 **4** *1 ¾* **Haalan**[17] 4026 4-9-9 **87** JamesMcDonald 5 88
(James Tate) *sn led: hdd over 7f out: remained w ldr tl led wl over 1f out: rdn and hdd jst over 1f out: no ex ins fnl f* **9/2**[2]
200- **5** *5* **Mica Mika (IRE)**[250] 7470 8-9-11 **89** RoystonFfrench 4 80
(Richard Fahey) *hld up in tch: shkn up and edgd lft over 1f out: wknd fnl f* **33/1**
-236 **6** *1 ½* **Ansaab**[154] 656 8-9-9 **87** AndrewMullen 2 75
(Michael Appleby) *w ldr tl wnt on over 7f out: rdn and hung lft over 2f out: hdd wl over 1f out: wknd fnl f* **14/1**
0-14 **7** *7* **Arrowzone**[34] 3435 5-9-10 **88** AdamKirby 7 62
(Ivan Furtado) *chsd ldrs: rdn over 3f out: wknd over 1f out* **6/1**

2m 3.86s (-1.64) **Going Correction** +0.20s/f (Good)
WFA 3 from 4yo+ 10lb **7** Ran SP% **112.0**
Speed ratings (Par 107): **114,113,111,109,105 104,98**
CSF £7.83 TOTE £1.90: £1.40, £2.30; EX 8.00 Trifecta £30.40.
Owner V I Araci **Bred** Fittocks Stud **Trained** Newmarket, Suffolk

FOCUS
A tight handicap with only 3lb covering the field. It was run at a decent pace. Another step forward from the winner, with the second rated as running a length+ pb.

4651 ADNAMS GHOST SHIP FILLIES' H'CAP 7f

3:10 (3:11) (Class 2) (0-100,99) 3-Y-O+ **£12,938** (£3,850; £1,924; £962) **Stalls** Low

Form RPR
-105 **1** **Spangled**[15] 4114 4-10-0 **99** HarryBentley 3 106
(Roger Varian) *hld up: hdwy over 1f out: rdn and r.o to ld post* **5/2**[1]
5-02 **2** *shd* **Bahaarah (IRE)**[7] 4391 3-9-5 **97** SeanLevey 1 101
(Richard Hannon) *hld up: swtchd lft and hdwy over 1f out: rdn to ld and edgd rt wl ins fnl f: hdd post* **4/1**[2]
0261 **3** *½* **Dawaa**[15] 4116 3-9-0 **92** AdamKirby 5 95
(Mark Johnston) *led to 1/2-way: rdn to ld again over 1f out: sn hung lft: hdd wl ins fnl f* **4/1**[2]
0-33 **4** *1 ¼* **Sharaakah (IRE)**[21] 3911 3-9-5 **97** JamesMcDonald 6 96
(Ed Dunlop) *racd keenly: w ldr tl led 1/2-way: rdn and hdd over 1f out: no ex wl ins fnl f* **5/2**[1]
5004 **5** *1 ¾* **Rebel Surge (IRE)**[15] 4105 3-8-11 **89** PatCosgrave 7 84
(Richard Spencer) *a.p: rdn over 2f out: styd on same pce ins fnl f* **8/1**[3]
1 **6** *14* **Sabrewing (IRE)**[56] 2681 3-8-3 **81** AndrewMullen 4 38
(Robert Cowell) *plld hrd and prom: rdn 1/2-way: wknd over 1f out* **20/1**

1m 25.73s (0.03) **Going Correction** +0.20s/f (Good)
WFA 3 from 4yo 7lb **6** Ran SP% **113.0**
Speed ratings (Par 96): **107,106,106,104,102 86**
CSF £13.00 TOTE £3.40: £1.90, £1.80; EX 10.20 Trifecta £43.40.
Owner Cheveley Park Stud **Bred** Cheveley Park Stud Ltd **Trained** Newmarket, Suffolk

FOCUS
This was a decent fillies´ handicap. It was run at a sound pace and suited the closers. The winner has been rated close to her best, while the level is set by the second and third.

4652 ADNAMS EASE UP IPA H'CAP 6f

3:45 (3:46) (Class 2) (0-105,102) 3-Y-O
£31,125 (£9,320; £4,660; £2,330; £1,165; £585) **Stalls** Low

Form RPR
6025 **1** **Mont Kiara (FR)**[16] 4062 3-8-9 **90** HarryBentley 8 99
(Kevin Ryan) *racd centre: hld up: hdwy 2f out: rdn to chse ldr over 1f out: edgd lft ins fnl f: r.o u.p to ld post: 1st of 9 in gp* **11/2**[2]
-052 **2** *hd* **Priceless**[16] 4062 3-9-3 **98** AdamKirby 3 106
(Clive Cox) *overall ldr in centre: rdn and hung rt over 1f out: edgd lft u.p ins fnl f: hdd post: 2nd of 9 in gp* **7/2**[1]
-610 **3** *1 ¾* **Flying Pursuit**[16] 4062 3-8-8 **89** DarryllHolland 13 92
(Tim Easterby) *s.i.s: hld up: racd centre: hdwy over 1f out: rdn and hung rt ins fnl f: styd on: 3rd of 9 in gp* **14/1**
3340 **4** *2 ½* **Paddy Power (IRE)**[15] 4112 3-8-5 **86** RoystonFfrench 11 81
(Richard Fahey) *racd centre: hld up: pushed along and nt clr run over 1f out: swtchd lft and hdwy sn after: styd on same pce wl ins fnl f: 4th of 9 in gp* **25/1**
0-10 **5** *shd* **Show Stealer**[16] 4062 3-8-11 **92** MartinDwyer 4 86
(Rae Guest) *racd centre: hld up: hdwy over 3f out: rdn over 1f out: styd on same pce ins fnl f: 5th of 9 in gp* **6/1**[3]
2-34 **6** *nk* **Thetis (IRE)**[61] 2539 3-9-2 **97** TedDurcan 9 90
(Sir Michael Stoute) *hld up: rdn over 1f out: kpt on ins fnl f: nt trble ldrs: 6th of 9 in gp* **9/1**
0450 **7** *1* **Lady Clair (IRE)**[26] 3714 3-8-4 **85** NickyMackay 1 75
(K R Burke) *racd stands' side: chsd ldr: rdn and edgd lft over 2f out: wknd ins fnl f: 1st of 2 that side* **66/1**
013 **8** *shd* **The Commendatore**[39] 3266 3-8-0 **81** oh2 (b) AndrewMullen 2 71
(David Barron) *led stands' side pair and up w the pce in main gp: rdn over 2f out: wknd ins fnl f: last of 2 that side* **22/1**
-521 **9** *8* **Dutch Destiny**[8] 4344 3-8-9 **90** PatCosgrave 6 54
(William Haggas) *racd centre: chsd ldr: rdn over 2f out: edgd lft over 1f out: wknd fnl f: 7th of 9 in gp* **7/2**[1]
4-10 **10** *4* **Rah Rah**[77] 2034 3-9-7 **102** JamesMcDonald 10 54
(Mark Johnston) *racd centre: chsd ldrs: rdn whn hmpd over 1f out: sn wknd: 8th of 9 in gp* **14/1**
1112 **11** *¾* **Papa Luigi (IRE)**[11] 4223 3-8-8 **89** SeanLevey 12 38
(Richard Hannon) *prom: rdn over 2f out: hmpd and wknd over 1f out: lat of 9 in gp* **9/1**

1m 11.54s (-0.96) **Going Correction** +0.20s/f (Good) **11** Ran SP% **117.1**
Speed ratings (Par 106): **114,113,111,108,107 107,106,106,95,90 89**
CSF £24.48 CT £263.94 TOTE £6.20: £2.30, £1.60, £4.60; EX 24.20 Trifecta £295.70.
Owner JCG Chua & CK Ong 1 **Bred** Guy Pariente Holding Sprl **Trained** Hambleton, N Yorks

FOCUS
A cracking handicap run at a sound pace. The second and third help set the standard.

4653 ADNAMS MOSAIC EBF STALLIONS CONDITIONS STKS (PLUS 10 RACE) 6f

4:20 (4:20) (Class 3) 2-Y-O **£8,409** (£2,502; £1,250; £625) **Stalls** Low

Form RPR
13 **1** **Broken Stones (IRE)**[16] 4060 2-9-2 0 AdamKirby 4 97
(Kevin Ryan) *mde all: set stdy pce tl qcknd over 2f out: hung rt and rdn over 1f out: r.o* **1/1**[1]

1 **2** 1 3/4 **Unabated (IRE)**[30] 3569 2-9-4 0.. DarryllHolland 2 93
(Marco Botti) *hld up: hdwy over 1f out: rdn to chse wnr and edgd rt ins fnl f: styd on* **20/1**
5 **3** 3/4 **Van Der Decken**[39] 3243 2-9-4 0.................................. JamesMcDonald 3 91
(Charlie Appleby) *chsd ldrs: rdn and edgd rt over 1f out: styd on same pce ins fnl f* **5/4**[2]
6 **4** 2 1/2 **Dourado (IRE)**[44] 3058 2-9-0 0.. SeanLevey 1 79
(Richard Hannon) *chsd wnr: rdn over 1f out: no ex ins fnl f* **9/1**[3]
1m 13.15s (0.65) **Going Correction** +0.20s/f (Good) **4** Ran SP% **109.2**
Speed ratings (Par 98): **103,100,99,96**
CSF £15.43 TOTE £1.60; EX 13.20 Trifecta £20.00.
Owner Matt & Lauren Morgan **Bred** Highpark Bloodstock Ltd **Trained** Hambleton, N Yorks

FOCUS
A disappointing turnout but this truly run contest was won by a promising 2yo. The third has been rated close to form.

4654 ADNAMS EAST COAST VODKA H'CAP 1m
4:50 (4:51) (Class 3) (0-90,89) 3-Y-O+ **£9,703** (£2,887; £1,443; £721) **Stalls** Low

Form RPR
3410 **1** **Palmerston**[18] 3983 3-8-3 **72**.. AndrewMullen 1 79+
(Michael Appleby) *hld up: swtchd rt and hdwy over 1f out: rdn to ld and edgd lft wl ins fnl f* **20/1**
1541 **2** 1 1/4 **Dubai's Secret**[16] 4055 3-9-3 **86**.. SeanLevey 6 90
(Richard Hannon) *hld up: hdwy over 2f out: rdn over 1f out: styd on* **7/1**
5-45 **3** nk **Dubai Fashion (IRE)**[142] 807 3-9-3 **86**.................................. AdamKirby 5 89
(Saeed bin Suroor) *racd keenly: led at stdy pce tl qcknd over 2f out: rdn over 1f out: edgd lft and hdd wl ins fnl f* **5/1**[3]
3-05 **4** 1 1/4 **Mediciman**[15] 4104 3-8-9 **78**.. HarryBentley 3 78
(Henry Candy) *trckd ldrs: wnt 2nd 2f out: rdn over 1f out: edgd lft and styd on same pce ins fnl f* **3/1**[1]
5111 **5** 1 **Bastille Day**[16] 4048 4-10-0 **89**.. GeorgeBaker 7 89
(David Elsworth) *hld up: rdn and hung lft over 1f out: styd on: nt trble ldrs* **3/1**[1]
5214 **6** 1 1/2 **Marbooh (IRE)**[16] 4055 3-8-11 **80**................................... DarryllHolland 8 74
(Charles Hills) *hld up: hdwy u.p over 1f out: no ex ins fnl f* **8/1**
1001 **7** 5 **Huntlaw**[7] 4408 3-8-11 **80**.. NickyMackay 2 62
(Mark Johnston) *prom: jnd wnr 7f out tl rdn over 2f out: wknd fnl f* **4/1**[2]
0130 **8** 25 **Lunar Deity**[120] 1068 7-9-1 **76**.. PatCosgrave 4
(Stuart Williams) *plld hrd and prom: rdn and wknd over 1f out* **20/1**
1m 40.83s (0.83) **Going Correction** +0.20s/f (Good)
WFA 3 from 4yo+ 8lb **8** Ran SP% **119.8**
Speed ratings (Par 107): **103,101,101,100,99 97,92,67**
CSF £157.93 CT £822.36 TOTE £32.90: £6.60, £2.80, £1.70; EX 214.80 Trifecta £877.60.
Owner Infinity Racing **Bred** Carwell Equities Ltd **Trained** Oakham, Rutland

FOCUS
The pace was steady for this open handicap. The field raced up the centre. Muddling form. The third has been rated as running a pb having set the modest pace, while the fourth has been rated to form.

4655 SUE WESTON MEMORIAL H'CAP 1m 5f
5:25 (5:26) (Class 4) (0-80,84) 3-Y-O **£6,469** (£1,925; £962) **Stalls** Centre

Form RPR
4024 **1** **Clear Evidence**[16] 4033 3-8-3 **62**.. MartinDwyer 4 68
(Michael Bell) *hld up: hdwy to ld over 3f out: shkn up over 1f out: styd on wl* **7/2**[3]
21 **2** 2 1/2 **Rasmiya (IRE)**[31] 3508 3-9-7 **80**.. PatCosgrave 1 82
(William Haggas) *led 2f: chsd ldr: rdn over 3f out: edgd lft over 2f out: styd on same pce fnl f* **1/1**[1]
1 **3** 4 **Bachelorhood**[45] 3019 3-9-6 **79**...................................... JamesMcDonald 2 76
(Charlie Appleby) *led after 2f: hdd over 3f out: sn rdn and edgd lft: no ex appr fnl f* **7/4**[2]
2m 49.32s (5.32) **Going Correction** +0.20s/f (Good) **3** Ran SP% **108.6**
Speed ratings (Par 102): **91,89,87**
CSF £7.36 TOTE £4.20; EX 7.10 Trifecta £6.50.
Owner The Queen **Bred** The Queen **Trained** Newmarket, Suffolk
■ Stewards' Enquiry : Martin Dwyer caution: careless riding

FOCUS
A disappointing turnout for this handicap which was run at a steady tempo. The level is a bit fluid.
T/Plt: £33.70 to a £1 stake. Pool: £51,654.88 - 1116.23 winning units. T/Qpdt: £26.30 to a £1 stake. Pool: £3,757.49 - 105.47winning units. **Colin Roberts**

4154 SALISBURY (R-H)
Saturday, July 23

OFFICIAL GOING: Good to firm (good in places on straight course; 8.7)
Wind: light breeze against Weather: sunny periods

4656 PARTY CONTINUES AT THE CHAPEL NIGHTCLUB "CARNARVON" H'CAP (FOR GENTLEMAN AMATEUR RIDERS) 1m
5:15 (5:17) (Class 5) (0-70,70) 3-Y-O+ **£3,119** (£967; £483; £242) **Stalls** Low

Form RPR
056 **1** **Imperial State**[35] 3412 3-11-0 **70**..(t) MrSWalker 3 79
(George Scott) *untidy leaving stalls: hld up bhd ldrs: smooth hdwy 2f out: shkn up to ld over 1f out: edgd lft: kpt on wl to draw clr fnl 120yds* **5/2**[2]
6246 **2** 4 1/2 **George Baker (IRE)**[17] 4008 9-11-3 **65**................................. MrRBirkett 1 66
(George Baker) *chsd ldr tl lost pl after 3f: sn chsd along: hdwy 2f out: drifting rt but ch ent fnl f: no ex fnl 120yds* **8/1**[3]
3413 **3** 1/2 **Wordismybond**[1] 4589 7-11-0 **69**.................................... MrJEPerrett(7) 2 69
(Richard Hughes) *trckd ldr: ev ch briefly 2f out: sn rdn: kpt on same pce fnl f* **7/4**[1]
000- **4** 2 1/2 **Locommotion**[279] 7312 4-10-4 **57**.................................[1] MrWillPettis(5) 6 51
(Matthew Salaman) *sn led: rdn 2f out: hdd over 1f out: edgd rt and no ex fnl f* **20/1**
6036 **5** 14 **Jazri**[9] 4293 5-10-0 **55**..(v) MrJCJones(7) 4 17
(Milton Bradley) *awkward leaving stalls: chsd ldrs tl wknd over 1f out* **20/1**
04-4 **6** 19 **Bobby Benton (IRE)**[42] 3125 5-11-0 **69** ow3..........(v) MrDGBurchell(7) 5
(Jim Best) *hld up bhd ldrs: effrt over 2f out: wknd over 1f out* **10/1**
1m 44.84s (1.34) **Going Correction** +0.20s/f (Good)
WFA 3 from 4yo+ 8lb **6** Ran SP% **94.7**
Speed ratings (Par 103): **101,96,96,93,79 60**
CSF £14.75 TOTE £3.10: £1.90, £2.80; EX 13.80 Trifecta £23.70.
Owner The Harnage Partnership **Bred** Biddestone Stud Ltd **Trained** Newmarket, Suffolk
■ Rajadamri was withdrawn. Price at time of withdrawal 9-2. Rule 4 applies to all bets - deduction 15p in the pound.

FOCUS
Warm conditions and there had been 8mm of water applied to the track the previous day. There was a rail out up to 24ft off the permanent far-side rail between 6f and 2f. Rajadamri went down in his stall and was withdrawn. The winner was the only unexposed runner. Weak handicap form.

4657 GSI CONTRACT SERVICES LTD MAIDEN STKS 1m 1f 198y
5:50 (5:51) (Class 5) 3-Y-O+ **£3,557** (£1,058; £529; £264) **Stalls** Low

Form RPR
54 **1** **Desert Way (IRE)**[48] 2929 3-8-13 0........................... RichardKingscote 2 80
(Ralph Beckett) *trckd ldrs: rdn 2f out: led fnl 120yds: kpt on strly* **5/2**[2]
34 **2** 3/4 **Mubajal**[17] 3996 3-9-4 0.. SilvestreDeSousa 9 83
(Owen Burrows) *sn led: rdn whn strly pressed fr over 2f out: hld on gamely to narrow advantage tl hdd fnl 120yds: no ex* **6/1**
0-3 **3** 2 1/4 **Mujaamil**[58] 2614 3-9-4 0.. DaneO'Neill 3 79
(William Haggas) *trckd ldrs: chal over 2f out: sn rdn: ev ch ent fnl f: no ex fnl 120yds* **11/8**[1]
6 **4** 3 **Pc Dixon**[12] 4213 3-8-11 0... KillianHennessy(7) 5 73
(Mick Channon) *mid-div: rdn 2f out: kpt on ins fnl f: wnt 4th towards fin: nvr threatened ldrs* **28/1**
3 **5** 3/4 **Attest**[31] 3535 3-9-4 0.. JimCrowley 1 71
(Amanda Perrett) *trckd ldrs: chal over 2f out: sn rdn: hld jst over 1f out: fdd fnl 120yds* **10/3**[3]
00 **6** 15 **Three Loves (IRE)**[24] 3781 3-8-13 0.................................... OisinMurphy 7 36
(Andrew Balding) *a towards rr* **33/1**
7 5 **Briac (FR)**[18] 5-10-0 0.. TimmyMurphy 4 31
(Jim Best) *dwlt bdly: a towards rr* **66/1**
05- **8** nk **Silver Ghost (IRE)**[308] 6529 3-9-4 0................................ FrederikTylicki 8 30
(Geoffrey Deacon) *mid-div: hdwy over 4f out: wknd wl over 1f out* **20/1**
00 **9** 1 3/4 **Dance With Kate**[17] 3996 5-9-6 0.. TimClark(3) 6 22
(Polly Gundry) *mid-div tl wknd 2f out* **150/1**
2m 9.14s (-0.76) **Going Correction** -0.05s/f (Good)
WFA 3 from 5yo 10lb **9** Ran SP% **121.3**
Speed ratings (Par 103): **101,100,98,96,95 83,79,79,77**
CSF £17.88 TOTE £3.40: £1.10, £1.80, £1.10; EX 17.00 Trifecta £32.70.
Owner J H Richmond-Watson **Bred** J H Richmond-Watson **Trained** Kimpton, Hants

FOCUS
Just a fair maiden run at ordinary-looking gallop. Slight personal bests from the second and third, in line with the better view of their previous maiden form.

4658 JAN FULLER BIRTHDAY CELEBRATION H'CAP 5f
6:20 (6:22) (Class 6) (0-65,70) 3-Y-O+ **£2,911** (£866; £432; £216) **Stalls** Low

Form RPR
2321 **1** **Justice Lady (IRE)**[10] 4280 3-9-13 **70**................................. ShaneKelly 8 80+
(David Elsworth) *hld up last: in tch: hdwy in centre fr over 1f out: drifted rt ent fnl f: sn led: r.o srongly: readily* **5/4**[1]
6244 **2** 2 1/4 **Only Ten Per Cent (IRE)**[24] 3780 8-9-9 **62**...............(v) FrederikTylicki 4 65
(J R Jenkins) *hld up in tch: nt clr run briefly over 2f out: hdwy over 1f out: r.o fnl f: wnt 2nd towards fin: no ch w wnr* **17/2**
-053 **3** 1/2 **The Wee Chief (IRE)**[10] 4264 10-9-1 **54**............................. DaneO'Neill 2 55
(Jimmy Fox) *slowly away: sn in tch: hdwy 2f out: rdn over 1f out: ch ent fnl f: kpt on same pce* **7/1**
0600 **4** 1 1/4 **Hurricane Alert**[10] 4264 4-8-10 **52**....................................... EoinWalsh(3) 1 49
(Natalie Lloyd-Beavis) *prom: rdn over 2f out: led over 1f out: hdd jst ins fnl f: sn no ex* **66/1**
6/00 **5** 1 **Molly Jones**[17] 3994 7-8-11 **53**.. TimClark(3) 6 46
(Matthew Salaman) *trckd ldrs: rdn over 2f out: keeping on at same pce whn carried rt and hmpd jst ins fnl f* **20/1**
554 **6** 3 **Fabulous Flyer**[17] 3994 3-8-6 **49**.................................. SilvestreDeSousa 3 30
(Jeremy Gask) *led: rdn 2f out: hdd over 1f out: no ex fnl f* **9/2**[3]
0000 **7** 1 **Rubheira**[10] 4264 4-8-0 **46** oh1.....................................(b) MitchGodwin(7) 5 25
(Paul Burgoyne) *trckd ldrs: rdn over 2f out: nvr threatened: wknd ent fnl f* **100/1**
2106 **8** 2 1/4 **Lucky Clover**[17] 3994 5-9-8 **61**... OisinMurphy 7 32
(Malcolm Saunders) *hld up in tch: rdn to chse ldrs over 2f out: nt quite pce to chal: eased whn btn ins fnl f* **7/2**[2]
1m 1.4s (0.40) **Going Correction** +0.20s/f (Good)
WFA 3 from 4yo+ 4lb **8** Ran SP% **115.1**
Speed ratings (Par 101): **104,100,99,97,96 91,89,86**
CSF £13.25 CT £55.17 TOTE £2.10: £1.10, £2.40, £2.20; EX 12.00 Trifecta £52.60.
Owner Robert Ng **Bred** Miss Audrey F Thompson **Trained** Newmarket, Suffolk

FOCUS
The winner is better than this level and hammered some exposed sorts. The runner-up has been rated close to his AW figures.

4659 BATHWICK TYRES BRITISH STALLION STUDS EBF MAIDEN STKS (PLUS 10 RACE) 6f
6:50 (6:51) (Class 4) 2-Y-O **£4,528** (£1,347; £673; £336) **Stalls** Low

Form RPR
1 **Shozita** 2-9-0 0.. RichardKingscote 10 72+
(Ralph Beckett) *travelled wl: hld up: hdwy over 2f out: shkn up to ld jst ins fnl f: r.o wl: pushed out* **5/1**[3]
324 **2** 1 **Texas Katie**[8] 4350 2-9-0 0.. SilvestreDeSousa 5 70
(Mick Channon) *trckd ldrs: rdn to ld narrowly over 1f out: kpt on but nt pce of wnr whn hdd jst ins fnl f* **2/1**[1]
04 **3** 1 **Glory Of Paris (IRE)**[16] 4053 2-9-5 0................................ FrederikTylicki 2 71
(Rod Millman) *sn led: rdn and hdd over 1f out: hld ins fnl f but kpt on nicely fnl 120yds* **15/2**
4 **4** 3/4 **Neptunes Secret**[16] 4047 2-9-5 0.. FergusSweeney 6 68
(Sylvester Kirk) *trckd ldrs: chal over 2f out: rdn over 1f out: ev ch ent fnl f: kpt on same pce* **12/1**
00 **5** 3/4 **Lightoller (IRE)**[7] 4405 2-8-12 0................................... KillianHennessy(7) 3 66
(Mick Channon) *prom: rdn 2f out: ev ch ent fnl f: kpt on same pce* **50/1**
6 2 1/4 **Tawaafoq** 2-9-5 0... DaneO'Neill 8 59+
(Richard Hannon) *racd keenly in midfield: hdwy over 2f out: ev ch whn rdn wl over 1f out: wknd fnl f* **9/4**[2]
0 **7** 1 3/4 **Hollow Crown**[14] 4154 2-9-0 0.. ShaneKelly 1 48
(Denis Coakley) *racd keenly: trckd ldrs: effrt 2f out: wknd fnl f* **100/1**
6 **8** shd **Pass The Cristal (IRE)**[14] 4125 2-9-5 0............................. TimmyMurphy 9 53
(William Muir) *racd keenly in mid-div: nt pce to get on terms fnl 2f* **14/1**
50 **9** 3 3/4 **Eolian**[18] 3971 2-9-5 0.. JimCrowley 4 41
(William Knight) *s.i.s: sn pushed along: a in last pair* **14/1**
10 18 **Pastfact** 2-9-5 0.. OisinMurphy 7
(Malcolm Saunders) *sn outpcd in rr* **100/1**
1m 16.11s (1.31) **Going Correction** +0.20s/f (Good) **10** Ran SP% **117.5**
Speed ratings (Par 96): **99,97,96,95,94 91,89,88,83,59**
CSF £15.53 TOTE £6.50: £1.70, £1.40, £2.60; EX 16.00 Trifecta £79.00.
Owner Thurloe Thoroughbreds XXXVIII **Bred** Elusive Bloodstock **Trained** Kimpton, Hants

FOCUS
The 2nd and 3rd set a fair level and the winner is potentially above average. The race has been rated around the race average, and few down the field suggest caution.

4660 T & M GLASS MAIDEN STKS 6f
7:20 (7:20) (Class 5) 3-Y-O+ **£3,557** (£1,058; £529; £264) **Stalls** Low

Form RPR

33-3 **1** **Tanasoq (IRE)**[16] 4041 3-9-5 79 DaneO'Neill 5 83
(Owen Burrows) *mde all: battled on v gamely whn strly pressed fr 2f out: hld on wl: drvn rt out* **2/1**[2]

62-2 **2** *nk* **Catchment**[42] 3147 3-9-0 75 JimCrowley 9 77
(Amanda Perrett) *trckd ldrs: rdn 2f out: str chal ent fnl f: kpt on wl: hld nring fin* **9/2**[3]

-033 **3** *nk* **Menai (IRE)**[14] 4156 3-9-5 77 SilvestreDeSousa 7 81
(Charles Hills) *trckd wnr: rdn for str chal fr 2f out: ev ch fnl f: hld nring fin* **10/11**[1]

4 *7* **Wensara Dream** 3-9-0 0 OisinMurphy 4 54+
(Andrew Balding) *s.i.s: sn mid-div: rdn over 2f out: kpt on to go wl hld 4th ins fnl f: nt pce of front 3* **16/1**

0-4 **5** *¾* **Hereward The Wake**[14] 4156 3-8-12 0 MitchGodwin(7) 3 56
(Sylvester Kirk) *trckd ldrs: rdn over 2f out: outpcd over 1f out: no ex whn lost 4th ins fnl f* **11/1**

00 **6** *5* **Brooke's Point**[14] 4156 3-9-0 0 MeganNicholls(5) 2 40
(Neil Mulholland) *a towards rr* **150/1**

7 *8* **Hellarious** 3-9-5 0 TimmyMurphy 6 15
(Geoffrey Deacon) *mid-div tl wknd 2f out* **33/1**

8 *hd* **Back To Love (CAN)** 3-8-11 0 TimClark(3) 8 9
(Mark Gillard) *last pair: sme hdwy over 2f out: sn rdn: wknd over 1f out* **66/1**

1m 15.75s (0.95) **Going Correction** +0.20s/f (Good) **8 Ran SP% 123.2**
Speed ratings (Par 103): **101,100,100,90,89 83,72,72**
CSF £12.69 TOTE £2.90: £1.10, £1.60, £1.10; EX 11.00 Trifecta £16.90.
Owner Hamdan Al Maktoum **Bred** Mountarmstrong Stud **Trained** Lambourn, Berks

FOCUS
The first three had each had a few chances already and shown fair form. It's been rated around the second and third.

4661 DEREK BURRIDGE GOLF & RACING TROPHIES H'CAP 1m 6f 21y
7:50 (7:50) (Class 5) (0-75,75) 3-Y-O+ **£3,234** (£962; £481; £240) **Stalls** Far side

Form RPR

5-54 **1** **Flambeuse**[14] 4158 5-9-11 **72** DavidProbert 2 80
(Harry Dunlop) *mde all: rdn and drifted lft fr 2f out: styd on wl fnl 120yds: rdn out* **4/1**[3]

2320 **2** *2* **Ayr Of Elegance**[48] 2932 4-9-11 **72** RichardKingscote 7 77
(Philip Hide) *hld up: hdwy over 2f out: sn rdn: chsng wnr but hld whn sltly hmpd ins fnl f: styd on* **16/1**

000 **3** *2* **Lily Trotter**[24] 3781 3-8-6 **67** (p) SilvestreDeSousa 4 69
(Ralph Beckett) *trckd wnr most of way: rdn over 2f out: nt quite pce to get on terms: no ex fnl 120yds* **12/1**

-030 **4** *1 ¾* **King Calypso**[24] 3784 5-9-13 **74** JimCrowley 1 74
(Denis Coakley) *in tch: hdwy over 2f out: sn rdn to chse ldrs: styd on same pce* **15/2**

-601 **5** *2* **Sunny Future (IRE)**[14] 4158 10-10-0 **75** TimmyMurphy 5 72
(Malcolm Saunders) *racd keenly: trckd ldr tl lost pl after 6f: hdwy 3f out: rdn and ev ch briefly 2f out: one pce fnl f* **8/1**

3-65 **6** *1 ¼* **Denham Sound**[54] 2735 3-8-12 **73** FergusSweeney 6 68
(Henry Candy) *hld up in tch: hdwy 2f out: sn rdn: nt pce to get involved* **6/1**

0/0- **7** *½* **Alzammaar (USA)**[35] 7140 5-9-10 **71** (bt) OisinMurphy 8 66
(Warren Greatrex) *rousted along at times: in tch: trckd wnr after 6f tl drvn 4f out: sn hld* **10/3**[1]

424 **8** *25* **Zanjabeel**[26] 3727 3-9-0 **75** (t) DaneO'Neill 3 59
(Simon Crisford) *cl up: hdwy 4f out: veered lft whn rdn over 2f out: sn btn: eased fnl 2f* **7/2**[2]

3m 5.03s (-2.37) **Going Correction** -0.05s/f (Good)
WFA 3 from 4yo+ 14lb **8 Ran SP% 116.0**
Speed ratings (Par 103): **104,102,101,100,99 98,98,84**
CSF £64.44 CT £708.47 TOTE £5.00: £1.40, £4.50, £3.20; EX 62.20 Trifecta £2199.60.
Owner Glanvilles Stud Partners **Bred** Wertheimer Et Frere **Trained** Lambourn, Berks

FOCUS
Not a bad race - there was a case to be made for all of these beforehand. A length pb from the winner, with the runner-up confirming her penultimate Lingfield form.

4662 BATHWICK TYRES H'CAP 6f 212y
8:20 (8:21) (Class 4) (0-85,82) 3-Y-O **£7,762** (£2,310; £1,154; £577) **Stalls** Centre

Form RPR

1205 **1** **Ower Fly**[27] 3689 3-9-2 **82** MeganNicholls(5) 2 87
(Richard Hannon) *mde all: drifted lft whn rdn over 1f out: kpt on wl* **16/1**

3215 **2** *¾* **Musdam (USA)**[52] 2788 3-9-7 **82** StevieDonohoe 6 85+
(Sir Michael Stoute) *trckd ldrs: rdn and ev ch ent fnl f: kpt on but no ex nring fin* **9/4**[2]

6233 **3** *1 ½* **Kyllukey**[12] 4211 3-9-4 **79** SilvestreDeSousa 1 78+
(Charles Hills) *trckd ldrs: rdn 2f out: ch ent fnl f: kpt on same pce fnl 120yds* **7/2**[3]

10-0 **4** *1 ¾* **Inn The Bull (GER)**[16] 4055 3-9-2 **77** FergusSweeney 3 71
(Alan King) *s.i.s: last but in tch: rdn 2f out: kpt on into 4th ent fnl f but nt pce to get on terms* **16/1**

1-2 **5** *½* **King Cole (USA)**[88] 1763 3-9-7 **82** ShaneKelly 4 75+
(Robert Cowell) *racd keenly w little cover: hld up: hdwy 3f out: effrt 2f out: sn one pce* **6/4**[1]

-000 **6** *1* **Racquet**[15] 4079 3-9-3 **78** DaneO'Neill 5 68
(Richard Hannon) *prom: rdn over 2f out: sn hld: fdd fnl f* **10/1**

1m 29.67s (1.07) **Going Correction** +0.20s/f (Good) **6 Ran SP% 113.8**
Speed ratings (Par 102): **101,100,98,96,95 94**
CSF £53.20 TOTE £11.40: £4.50, £1.30; EX 39.00 Trifecta £174.30.
Owner Green Pastures Farm **Bred** Green Pastures Farm **Trained** East Everleigh, Wilts

FOCUS
A fair 3yo handicap. It's been rated cautiously given that the winner had been held off similar marks since his reappearance win.
T/Plt: £24.50 to a £1 stake. Pool: £49,235.53 - 1463.89 winning units. T/Qpdt: £8.10 to a £1 stake. Pool: £7,585.48 - 690.63 winning units. **Tim Mitchell**

4607 YORK (L-H)
Saturday, July 23

OFFICIAL GOING: Good to firm (7.4)
Wind: Virtually nil Weather: Fine & dry

4663 SKY BET MAKING BETTING BETTER MEDIAN AUCTION MAIDEN STKS (PLUS 10 RACE) 6f
1:55 (1:55) (Class 4) 2-Y-O **£6,469** (£1,925; £962; £481) **Stalls** High

Form RPR

63 **1** **Nautical Haven**[14] 4133 2-9-5 0 TomEaves 6 84
(Kevin Ryan) *mde all: rdn and qcknd wl over 1f out: drvn ins fnl f: kpt on wl towards fin* **5/1**[2]

0 **2** *¾* **Storm Cry**[17] 4011 2-9-0 0 FrannyNorton 11 76
(Mark Johnston) *a chsng wnr: rdn wl over 1f out: drvn and edgd rt ins fnl f: kpt on wl towards fin* **16/1**

6 **3** *1* **Battered**[14] 4161 2-9-5 0 BenCurtis 12 78
(William Haggas) *sn trcking ldrs on outer: effrt over 2f out: rdn along to chse ldng pair over 1f out: drvn and kpt on fnl f* **7/4**[1]

0 **4** *3* **Faulkwood**[8] 4371 2-9-0 0 JordanVaughan(5) 5 68+
(K R Burke) *towards rr: hdwy over 2f out: chsd ldrs over 1f out: rdn and kpt on same pce fnl f* **14/1**

60 **5** *3 ½* **Equity**[40] 3208 2-9-5 0 DanielTudhope 1 57
(David Brown) *chsd ldrs: rdn along wl over 1f out: drvn and wknd appr fnl f* **18/1**

6 *1 ¾* **Hersigh** 2-9-0 0 MartinLane 10 47+
(Saeed bin Suroor) *towards rr: hdwy over 2f out: rdn along wl over 1f out: sn no imp* **11/2**[3]

0 **7** *1 ¼* **Come On Percy**[14] 4161 2-9-5 0 GeorgeChaloner 2 48
(Richard Fahey) *in tch: rdn along wl over 2f out: sn wknd* **12/1**

46 **8** *2 ¼* **Rubiesnpearls**[15] 4110 2-9-0 0 PaulHanagan 9 35
(Richard Fahey) *chsd ldng pair: rdn along over 2f out: sn wknd* **12/1**

00 **9** *11* **Yorkshire Bounty**[15] 4110 2-9-5 0 DavidNolan 4 5
(Richard Fahey) *a towards rr* **25/1**

06 **10** *2* **Just Heather (IRE)**[28] 3640 2-9-0 0 PaddyAspell 7
(John Wainwright) *dwlt: a towards rr* **100/1**

3 **11** *99* **Eltanin (IRE)**[43] 3112 2-9-5 0 CamHardie 8
(John Quinn) *dwlt: in rr and sn pushed along: rdn along and outpcd bef 1/2-way: bhd whn eased over 2f out* **7/1**

1m 11.09s (-0.81) **Going Correction** -0.125s/f (Firm) **11 Ran SP% 118.9**
Speed ratings (Par 96): **100,99,97,93,89 86,85,82,67,64**
CSF £83.01 TOTE £6.20: £2.20, £4.40, £1.30; EX 93.10 Trifecta £302.70.
Owner J Hanson & Sir Alex Ferguson **Bred** Bearstone Stud Ltd **Trained** Hambleton, N Yorks

FOCUS
The rail around the home bend from 9f to the entrance to the home straight was realigned to produce fresh ground, reducing Races 2,4 & 6 by 25yds. The track had received 3mm of irrigation since the previous day's meeting and the going was good to firm. A fair maiden, in which it paid to race prominently. The third has been rated just off his C&D debut.

4664 SKY BET BEST ODDS GUARANTEED STKS (H'CAP) 2m 88y
2:25 (2:25) (Class 3) (0-90,90) 4-Y-O+ **£8,409** (£2,502; £1,250; £625) **Stalls** Low

Form RPR

0054 **1** **Full Day**[11] 4230 5-8-6 **75** BenCurtis 9 84
(Brian Ellison) *mde all: rdn wl over 2f out: drvn over 1f out: kpt on strly* **8/1**

-610 **2** *2 ¼* **Bulas Belle**[34] 3437 6-8-10 **79** GrahamLee 2 85
(Grant Tuer) *trckd ldrs on inner: hdwy over 2f out: rdn wl over 1f out: drvn and kpt on fnl f* **10/1**

-400 **3** *1 ¼* **Saved By The Bell (IRE)**[39] 3246 6-9-7 **90** (p) DanielTudhope 1 95
(David O'Meara) *trckd wnr: hdwy 3f out: pushed along over 2f out: rdn wl over 1f out: drvn appr fnl f: kpt on same pce* **7/2**[1]

5000 **4** *1 ¼* **Gabrial's King (IRE)**[14] 4162 7-9-4 **87** PaulHanagan 8 91+
(Richard Fahey) *hld up in rr: hdwy on inner over 2f out: swtchd rt and rdn wl over 1f out: drvn and kpt on fnl f* **5/1**[3]

1131 **5** *3 ¾* **Dew Pond**[17] 4004 4-8-4 **76** RachelRichardson(3) 5 75
(Tim Easterby) *trckd ldng pair: hdwy 3f out: cl up 2f out: sn rdn: drvn and wknd appr fnl f* **9/2**[2]

6560 **6** *1 ½* **Swaheen**[28] 3657 4-9-1 **84** GeorgeChaloner 4 81
(Julie Camacho) *hld up towards rr: hdwy 3f out: rdn along 2f out: sn drvn and n.d* **10/1**

1215 **7** *5* **Argent Knight**[28] 3639 6-8-12 **81** (p) TomEaves 3 72
(Christopher Kellett) *hld up in tch: effrt and sme hdwy over 3f out: rdn along wl over 2f out: sn wknd* **14/1**

60-6 **8** *1 ¾* **Perfect Summer (IRE)**[33] 1760 6-8-8 **77** (v) FrannyNorton 7 66
(Ian Williams) *hld up: a towards rr* **10/1**

2-30 **9** *4 ½* **Corona Borealis**[14] 4162 5-9-1 **84** PaulMulrennan 6 68
(Martin Todhunter) *trckd ldrs: hdwy and prom on outer over 3f out: rdn along over 2f out: sn wknd* **11/2**

3m 33.15s (-1.35) **Going Correction** -0.125s/f (Firm) **9 Ran SP% 117.5**
Speed ratings (Par 107): **98,96,96,95,93 93,90,89,87**
CSF £85.83 CT £333.61 TOTE £8.10: £2.50, £3.20, £1.70; EX 96.00 Trifecta £1081.20 Part won..
Owner Dan Gilbert **Bred** W And R Barnett Ltd **Trained** Norton, N Yorks

FOCUS
Distance reduced by 25yds. An open-looking, competitive staying handicap, but the pace was steady and it developed into a 3f sprint. The winner has been rated back to her best, with the runner-up and third close to form.

4665 READ RICHARD FAHEY'S COLUMN AT SPORTINGLIFE.COM STKS (H'CAP) 7f
3:00 (3:00) (Class 2) (0-105,102) 3-Y-O+
£15,562 (£4,660; £2,330; £1,165; £582; £292) **Stalls** Low

Form RPR

1326 **1** **Get Knotted (IRE)**[35] 3390 4-9-4 **92** (p) PaulMulrennan 4 100
(Michael Dods) *trckd ldrs: effrt 2f out: rdn over 1f out: chal ins fnl f: sn drvn and kpt on wl to ld nr fin* **11/2**[2]

0-05 **2** *nk* **Above The Rest (IRE)**[36] 3346 5-9-0 **88** [1] GrahamLee 8 98+
(David Barron) *t.k.h: hld up in rr: hdwy wl over 1f out: chsd ldrs whn n.m.r ins fnl f: sn swtchd rt and rdn: fin strly* **10/1**

1004 **3** *shd* **Calder Prince (IRE)**[14] 4136 3-9-4 **99** LiamJones 9 103
(Tom Dascombe) *trckd ldr: cl up 1/2-way: rdn to take slt advantage over 1f out: drvn ins fnl f: hdd and no ex towards fin* **14/1**

2265 **4** 1 1/4 **Atlantic Sun**[16] 4065 3-9-2 **102** GaryMahon(5) 2 103
(Richard Hannon) *hld up in tch: hdwy on inner over 2f out: chsd ldrs over 1f out: sn rdn and ev ch ins fnl f: drvn and kpt on same pce towards fin* **6/1**[3]

5030 **5** nk **Alfred Hutchinson**[30] 3565 8-9-12 **100** (p) DanielTudhope 5 103
(David O'Meara) *hld up: hdwy on outer over 2f out: chsd ldrs over 1f out and sn rdn: drvn ins fnl f and kpt on same pce* **8/1**

1161 **6** 1 **Swift Approval (IRE)**[15] 4109 4-9-8 **96** (p) TomEaves 7 96
(Kevin Ryan) *led: jnd over 3f out: rdn along over 2f out: drvn and hdd over 1f out: wknd ins fnl f* **11/2**[2]

1-30 **7** 3/4 **Predilection (USA)**[37] 3299 3-9-3 **98** PatSmullen 3 93
(John Gosden) *hld up: hdwy to chse ldrs over 2f out: sn rdn and wknd* **9/2**[1]

-006 **8** 1/2 **Farlow (IRE)**[14] 4152 8-9-12 **100** PaulHanagan 6 97
(Richard Fahey) *towards rr: effrt and sme hdwy on outer 3f out: rdn over 2f out and sn btn* **7/1**

0002 **9** 1 1/2 **Free Code (IRE)**[7] 4402 5-9-0 **88** GrahamGibbons 1 81
(David Barron) *chsd ldrs: rdn along over 2f out: sn drvn and wknd* **10/1**

0-00 **10** 2 3/4 **That Is The Spirit**[42] 3163 5-9-10 **98** DavidNolan 10 83
(David O'Meara) *hld up: a towards rr* **16/1**

1m 22.96s (-2.34) **Going Correction** -0.125s/f (Firm)
WFA 3 from 4yo+ 7lb **10** Ran SP% **117.6**
Speed ratings (Par 109): **108,107,107,106,105 104,103,103,101,98**
CSF £59.84 CT £752.18 TOTE £6.70: £1.90, £3.50, £5.00; EX 61.50 Trifecta £1318.80.
Owner D Neale **Bred** Rossenarra Bloodstock Limited **Trained** Denton, Co Durham

FOCUS
A well-contested handicap and solid form, despite there being very little between the three principals. A small pb from the winner, with the runner-up rated back to form and the third and fourth close to their marks.

4666 SKY BET YORK STKS (GROUP 2) 1m 2f 88y
3:35 (3:35) (Class 1) 3-Y-O+ **£56,710** (£21,500; £10,760; £5,360; £2,690) **Stalls** Low

Form RPR
0-13 **1** **Time Test**[21] 3912 4-9-3 121 PatSmullen 5 120
(Roger Charlton) *trckd ldrs: smooth hdwy 3f out: cl up over 2f out: sn slt ld: rdn over 1f out: drvn ins fnl f: kpt on wl last 100yds* **1/2**[1]

0-00 **2** 3/4 **Mondialiste (IRE)**[39] 3242 6-9-3 115 DanielTudhope 1 118
(David O'Meara) *hld up in rr: hdwy on inner over 2f out: chal wl over 1f out: sn rdn: drvn and ev ch ins fnl f: no ex last 100yds* **10/1**

0-24 **3** 3 1/4 **Countermeasure**[21] 3912 4-9-3 110 WilliamTwiston-Davies 4 112
(Roger Charlton) *led: pushed along 3f out: rdn and hdd 2f out: drvn over 1f out: kpt on same pce* **20/1**

-201 **4** 1 **Air Pilot**[31] 3544 7-9-3 113 GrahamLee 3 110
(Ralph Beckett) *trckd ldng pair: hdwy 3f out: cl up over 2f out: rdn wl over 1f out: sn drvn and kpt on same pce* **6/1**[3]

5-10 **5** 22 **Mahsoob**[70] 2243 5-9-3 116 PaulHanagan 2 66
(John Gosden) *sn trcking ldr: effrt 3f out and sn pushed along: rdn and lost pl qckly over 2f out: bhd and eased wl over 1f out* **9/2**[2]

2m 6.93s (-5.57) **Going Correction** -0.125s/f (Firm) **5** Ran SP% **113.0**
Speed ratings (Par 115): **117,116,113,113,95**
CSF £6.86 TOTE £1.40: £1.10, £4.20; EX 6.70 Trifecta £40.40.
Owner K Abdullah **Bred** Juddmonte Farms Ltd **Trained** Beckhampton, Wilts

FOCUS
Distance reduced by 25yds. A small-field renewal of this Group 2, but it served up a thrilling finish, with the short-priced favourite doing just enough. The runner-up is the key to the form - he's been rated to his best, although his US/Canadian form last year could be worth a bit more.

4667 SKY BET DASH STKS (H'CAP) 6f
4:10 (4:11) (Class 2) (0-105,101) 3-Y-O+
£31,125 (£9,320; £4,660; £2,330; £1,165; £585) **Stalls** Centre

Form RPR
2422 **1** **Kimberella**[14] 4136 6-9-8 **99** FrannyNorton 5 111
(David Nicholls) *t.k.h early: sn trcking ldr: smooth hdwy to ld ent fnl f: sn rdn and kpt on wl* **9/2**[1]

121 **2** 1 3/4 **Intisaab**[36] 3346 5-8-13 **93** (p) ShelleyBirkett(3) 14 99
(David O'Meara) *swtchd lft sn after s: midfield: hdwy 2f out: rdn over 1f out: drvn and kpt on wl fnl f* **7/1**[3]

0000 **3** hd **Related**[15] 4112 6-8-12 **89** (b) MartinLane 4 94
(Paul Midgley) *led: rdn along wl over 1f out: hdd ent fnl f: sn drvn and kpt on* **10/1**

2006 **4** 1 **Fast Track**[29] 3606 5-8-13 **90** GrahamGibbons 1 92
(David Barron) *trckd ldrs on inner: effrt 2f out: rdn over 1f out: drvn and kpt on wl fnl f* **20/1**

-133 **5** 1/2 **Lexington Abbey**[14] 4126 5-9-5 **96** PatSmullen 15 97
(Kevin Ryan) *hld up: hdwy wl over 1f out: sn rdn and styd on fnl f* **8/1**

00-0 **6** 1 **Tanzeel (IRE)**[14] 4152 5-9-7 **98** (t) PaulHanagan 6 95
(Charles Hills) *chsd ldrs on outer: rdn along 2f out: drvn over 1f out: no imp* **11/2**[2]

-403 **7** shd **Ninjago**[21] 3891 6-9-10 **101** PaulMulrennan 3 98
(Paul Midgley) *chsd ldrs: rdn along 2f out: drvn and wknd over 1f out* **7/1**[3]

0265 **8** nk **Cornwallville (IRE)**[8] 4338 4-9-5 **96** (v) BenCurtis 2 92
(David Loughnane) *sn rdn along and towards rr: hdwy wl over 1f out: kpt on fnl f* **12/1**

00-0 **9** 1 1/2 **Louis The Pious**[56] 2691 8-9-9 **100** (v) DanielTudhope 16 91
(David O'Meara) *stdd and swtchd lft s: hld up and bhd tl styd on fnl f* **20/1**

0-03 **10** 1/2 **Pipers Note**[39] 3250 6-9-6 **97** GeorgeChaloner 10 87
(Richard Whitaker) *chsd ldrs: rdn along wl over 1f out: sn wknd* **20/1**

0040 **11** nse **Tatlisu (IRE)**[8] 4338 6-9-5 **96** DavidNolan 8 86
(Richard Fahey) *chsd ldrs: rdn along 2f out: sn wknd* **12/1**

010 **12** 3/4 **Judicial (IRE)**[42] 3151 4-9-6 **97** (e) TomQueally 13 84
(Julie Camacho) *racd alone nr stands' rail: prom: rdn along over 2f out: sn outpcd* **16/1**

2000 **13** 3/4 **Patrick (IRE)**[14] 4126 4-8-12 **89** CamHardie 11 74
(Richard Fahey) *a towards rr* **33/1**

0644 **14** shd **Another Wise Kid (IRE)**[21] 3891 8-9-6 **97** GrahamLee 12 81
(Paul Midgley) *in tch on outer: chsd ldrs 1/2-way: rdn along over 2f out: sn wknd* **25/1**

0006 **15** 4 **Arctic Feeling (IRE)**[15] 4112 8-9-1 **92** TomEaves 9 64
(Richard Fahey) *a towards rr* **20/1**

1065 **16** 11 **See The Sun**[14] 4136 5-9-0 **91** DavidAllan 7 27
(Tim Easterby) *chsd ldng pair: rdn 2f out: drvn and wknd over 1f out: sn bhd and eased* **7/1**[3]

1m 9.66s (-2.24) **Going Correction** -0.125s/f (Firm) **16** Ran SP% **138.4**
Speed ratings (Par 109): **109,106,106,105,104 103,102,102,100,99 99,98,97,97,92 77**
CSF £36.50 CT £337.88 TOTE £5.20: £1.40, £2.00, £3.80, £6.10; EX 32.20 Trifecta £1988.70.
Owner C Titcomb **Bred** P And Mrs A G Venner **Trained** Sessay, N Yorks

FOCUS
A typically open handicap for the track, albeit not the strongest for the level with the top-weight rated 4lb below the ceiling, but solid sprint form. The winner is better than ever and this was another step forward off a career-high mark.

4668 SKY BET SUPPORTING NEW BEGINNINGS EBF FILLIES' STKS (H'CAP) 1m 2f 88y
4:45 (4:45) (Class 3) (0-90,88) 3-Y-O+ **£16,172** (£4,812; £2,405; £1,202) **Stalls** Low

Form RPR
1 **1** **Playful Sound**[41] 3194 3-8-12 **82** GrahamGibbons 2 91+
(Sir Michael Stoute) *t.k.h early: trckd ldrs: effrt and nt clr run wl over 1f out: rdn to ld jst ins fnl f: kpt on strly* **11/4**[2]

54-5 **2** 1 3/4 **Siren's Cove**[15] 4113 4-9-1 **75** PaulHanagan 3 79
(Richard Fahey) *hld up in rr: hdwy over 2f out: effrt and nt clr run wl over 1f out: swtchd rt to outer and rdn ent fnl f: sn drvn and no imp towards fin* **8/1**[3]

42-1 **3** 1/2 **Colonial Classic (FR)**[18] 3990 3-9-1 **85** GrahamLee 5 88
(John Gosden) *trckd ldng pair: hdwy on outer and cl up 2f out: rdn over 1f out and ev ch: drvn and kpt on fnl f* **11/4**[2]

3511 **4** 3 1/2 **My Lucille (IRE)**[14] 4145 3-8-8 **78** DavidAllan 1 74
(Tim Easterby) *set stdy pce: pushed along and qcknd 3f out: rdn over 2f out: drvn and hdd jst ins fnl f: wknd* **8/1**[3]

-121 **5** 5 **Sightline**[29] 3593 3-9-4 **88** PatSmullen 6 74
(Ralph Beckett) *trckd ldr: cl up 1/2-way: chal over 2f out: rdn wl over 1f out: sn drvn and wknd* **7/4**[1]

2m 12.29s (-0.21) **Going Correction** -0.125s/f (Firm)
WFA 3 from 4yo 10lb **5** Ran SP% **111.9**
Speed ratings (Par 104): **95,93,93,90,86**
CSF £22.81 TOTE £3.60: £1.70, £3.10; EX 28.30 Trifecta £86.20.
Owner Newsells Park Stud **Bred** Newsells Park Stud **Trained** Newmarket, Suffolk

FOCUS
Distance reduced by 25yds. A useful fillies' handicap, taken by the least exposed in the field. The winner was building on her maiden win, while the runner-up is the key to the form as her 3yo best could back this form being a bit better than currently rated.

4669 SKY BET SUPPORTING YORKSHIRE AIR AMBULANCE STKS (NURSERY H'CAP) 5f
5:20 (5:21) (Class 3) 2-Y-O **£7,762** (£2,310; £1,154; £577) **Stalls** High

Form RPR
102 **1** **Tahoo (IRE)**[15] 4111 2-8-10 **81** JordanVaughan(5) 4 88
(K R Burke) *in tch: hdwy over 1f out: sn rdn: chsd ldng pair ins fnl f: sn drvn and styd on strly to ld nr fin* **3/1**[2]

51 **2** hd **Equimou**[12] 4195 2-9-4 **84** PaoloSirigu 5 90
(Robert Eddery) *sn chsng clr ldr: hdwy and clsd over 1f out: sn rdn and led wl ins fnl f: hdd and no ex towards fin* **5/1**

3123 **3** 3 **Merry Banter**[15] 4111 2-8-5 **71** LiamJones 7 66
(Paul Midgley) *qckly away and sn clr at str pce: rdn along wl over 1f out: drvn and hdd wl ins fnl f: kpt on same pce* **7/1**

4104 **4** 1 1/2 **Vona (IRE)**[15] 4111 2-9-5 **85** PaulHanagan 3 75
(Richard Fahey) *chsd ldrs: pushed along 2f out: rdn wl over 1f out: kpt on one pce* **11/2**

113 **5** nse **Orewa (IRE)**[57] 2664 2-9-5 **85** BenCurtis 1 75
(Brian Ellison) *chsd ldng pair: rdn wl over 1f out: sn drvn and wknd* **4/1**[3]

2310 **6** 4 1/2 **Masham Star (IRE)**[35] 3382 2-9-7 **87** FrannyNorton 6 60
(Mark Johnston) *stdd and swtchd lft s: hld up in rr: hdwy and in tch over 2f out: sn rdn and wknd* **5/2**[1]

58.13s (-1.17) **Going Correction** -0.125s/f (Firm) **6** Ran SP% **118.1**
Speed ratings (Par 98): **104,103,98,96,96 89**
CSF £19.25 TOTE £3.80: £2.00, £3.30; EX 21.10 Trifecta £55.40.
Owner John Dance **Bred** Tally-Ho Stud **Trained** Middleham Moor, N Yorks

FOCUS
A useful nursery run at a strong pace.
T/Plt: £265.70 to a £1 stake. Pool: £123,780.78 - 340.02 winning units. T/Qpdt: £82.70 to a £1 stake. Pool: £9,160.24 - 81.87 winning units. **Joe Rowntree**

4670 - 4677a (Foreign Racing) - See Raceform Interactive

4032 CARLISLE (R-H)
Sunday, July 24

OFFICIAL GOING: Good (good to soft in places) changing to good to soft after race 1 (2.10)
Wind: Almost nil Weather: Overcast, raining races 1-3

4678 BOOKIES.COM NOVICE AUCTION STKS 5f 193y
2:10 (2:12) (Class 5) 2-Y-O **£2,911** (£866; £432; £216) **Stalls** Low

Form RPR
2 **1** **Phijee**[17] 4053 2-9-5 0 SamHitchcott 5 87+
(William Muir) *dwlt: hld up: hdwy over 2f out: rdn to ld over 1f out: sn clr: kpt on wl fnl f* **4/6**[1]

2 3 **Now Children (IRE)** 2-9-5 0 DougieCostello 1 76+
(Iain Jardine) *dwlt: hld up: stdy hdwy over 2f out: effrt and rdn over 1f out: chsd (clr) wnr ins fnl f: kpt on: improve* **50/1**

64 **3** 1 1/4 **Flash Of White**[12] 4227 2-9-5 0 PaulMulrennan 2 72
(Bryan Smart) *cl up: led over 2f out: rdn and hdd over 1f out: sn one pce* **14/1**

64 **4** 3 3/4 **Vintage Dream (IRE)**[41] 3222 2-9-5 0 PatrickMathers 10 61
(Noel Wilson) *hld up on outside: effrt and rdn over 2f out: edgd rt over 1f out: no imp* **14/1**

424 **5** 1/2 **Local Artist (IRE)**[20] 3947 2-9-0 0 JasonHart 11 55
(John Quinn) *prom: effrt over 2f out: rdn and ev ch over 1f out: wknd ins fnl f* **8/1**[3]

U2 **6** shd **Baie D'Amour (FR)**[15] 4140 2-9-0 0 JoeyHaynes 8 57
(K R Burke) *t.k.h: hld up in tch: rdn over 2f out: wknd over 1f out* **7/2**[2]

34 **7** 3 3/4 **Monte Cinq (IRE)**[104] 1377 2-9-5 0 BenCurtis 4 48
(Jason Ward) *t.k.h: trckd ldrs: rdn over 2f out: wknd over 1f out* **25/1**

66 **8** 4 1/2 **Red Savina**[43] 3148 2-9-0 0 ShaneGray 6 29
(Kevin Ryan) *cl up tl rdn and wknd fr 2f out* **66/1**

6 **9** 10 **Kirkby's Phantom**[15] 4140 2-8-9 0 PhilDennis(5) 7
(John David Riches) *dwlt: bhd and pushed along: struggling fr 1/2-way* **200/1**

5 **10** 1/2 **Bruny Island (IRE)**[15] 4140 2-9-5 0 JoeFanning 3
(Mark Johnston) *too t.k.h: led tl hung lft and hdd over 2f out: sn lost pl and struggling* **20/1**

1m 14.25s (0.55) **Going Correction** +0.10s/f (Good) **10** Ran SP% **119.2**
Speed ratings (Par 94): **100,96,94,89,88 88,83,77,64,63**
CSF £66.22 TOTE £1.60: £1.02, £6.20, £3.50; EX 39.70 Trifecta £494.20.

Owner Martin P Graham **Bred** Meon Valley Stud **Trained** Lambourn, Berks

FOCUS

The rail was at its innermost configuration, and all race distances were as advertised. Just a modest contest but the winner was comfortably the best and is well regarded.

4679 GET CARLISLE TIPS @BOOKIES.COM NURSERY H'CAP 5f
2:40 (2:41) (Class 5) 2-Y-O £2,911 (£866; £432; £216) **Stalls** Low

Form RPR

1054 **1** **Coolfitch (IRE)**[43] 3143 2-9-0 **70**.. SamJames 3 78+
(David O'Meara) *dwlt: hld up: hdwy whn nt clr run over 1f out tl swtchd lft ins fnl f: qckncd to ld towards fin* **6/1**

045 **2** *1/2* **Foxy Boy**[20] 3939 2-8-3 **59**.. JoeyHaynes 6 60
(Michael Dods) *sn cl up: rdn over 2f out: rallied over 1f out: led ins fnl f: hdd and no ex towards fin* **12/1**

664 **3** *nk* **Trick Of The Lyte (IRE)**[22] 3874 2-8-6 **62**......................... CamHardie 4 62
(John Quinn) *chsd ldrs: drvn along over 2f out: ev ch ins fnl f: kpt on: hld nr fin* **16/1**

522 **4** *shd* **Three C'S (IRE)**[17] 4047 2-9-7 **77**.................................. BenCurtis 2 77
(David Dennis) *trckd ldrs: effrt and rdn over 2f out: kpt on same pce ins fnl f* **11/4**[1]

4243 **5** *nk* **Katebird (IRE)**[19] 3977 2-8-4 **60**.................................. JoeFanning 8 59
(Mark Johnston) *led: rdn and edgd rt over 1f out: hdd ins fnl f: kpt on same pce* **5/1**[3]

443 **6** *1 1/2* **Harbour Lightning**[12] 4227 2-8-6 **67**........................... RowanScott(5) 9 61
(Ann Duffield) *hld up on outside: effrt over 2f out: edgd rt over 1f out: kpt on same pce fnl f* **17/2**

660 **7** *3/4* **Sheila's Return**[24] 3805 2-8-1 **57**.................................. DuranFentiman 1 48
(Bryan Smart) *in tch on ins: rdn along 2f out: one pce fnl f* **25/1**

2351 **8** *1 3/4* **Kodi Da Capo (IRE)**[39] 3282 2-9-4 **74**............................. JasonHart 7 59
(Keith Dalgleish) *checked and lost grnd s: bhd: rdn over 2f out: no imp fr over 1f out* **4/1**[2]

6665 **9** *10* **Zebedee Cat (IRE)**[22] 3881 2-8-11 **67** ow1...............(p) DougieCostello 5 16
(Iain Jardine) *t.k.h: prom tl rdn and wknd over 1f out* **11/1**

1m 2.39s (1.59) **Going Correction** +0.10s/f (Good) **9** Ran SP% **113.9**

Speed ratings (Par 94): **91,90,89,89,89 86,85,82,66**

CSF £73.56 CT £1086.80 TOTE £6.50: £1.80, £4.20, £4.40; EX 78.50 Trifecta £711.10.

Owner W Hoffman Racing **Bred** P Kelly **Trained** Upper Helmsley, N Yorks

FOCUS

Probably just a modest handicap, in which the first five weren't separated by a great deal.

4680 COMPARE BEST ODDS @BOOKIES.COM H'CAP 1m 3f 39y
3:15 (3:15) (Class 4) (0-85,85) 3-Y-O+ £5,175 (£1,540; £769; £384) **Stalls** High

Form RPR

0442 **1** **Top Of The Glas (IRE)**[29] 3659 5-9-2 **80**..................... BenRobinson(7) 8 87
(Brian Ellison) *in tch on outside: effrt and pushed along over 2f out: hdwy and hung rt over 1f out: kpt on wl fnl f to ld cl home* **10/3**[2]

4042 **2** *shd* **Mukhayyam**[4] 4520 4-9-9 **80**..(p) DavidAllan 2 87
(Tim Easterby) *led: rdn and qcknd over 2f out: edgd lft ins fnl f: kpt on: hdd cl home* **9/4**[1]

104 **3** *hd* **Tamayuz Magic (IRE)**[17] 4044 5-9-2 **78**...................(b) NathanEvans(5) 5 84
(Michael Easterby) *hld up: stdy hdwy on ins 2f out: rdn and ev ch ins fnl f: kpt on: hld cl home* **11/1**

4035 **4** *3 1/2* **Sennockian Star**[10] 4300 6-10-0 **85**.................................(v) JoeFanning 4 87
(Mark Johnston) *in tch: effrt and rdn over 2f out: keeping on same pce whn nt clr run appr fnl f: sn no ex* **10/3**[2]

-031 **5** *4 1/2* **Royal Regent**[13] 4190 4-9-6 **77**...................................... DougieCostello 1 69
(Lucy Normile) *s.i.s: hld up in tch: hdwy over 3f out: rdn over 2f out: one pce whn hmpd over 1f out* **7/1**[3]

4104 **6** *1/2* **Skiddaw Valleys**[20] 3942 4-9-2 **73**................................... DarryllHolland 6 64
(Alan Swinbank) *cl up: chal after 4f to over 3f out: rdn over 2f out: one pce whn hmpd over 1f out* **10/1**

45-0 **7** *56* **Only Orsenfoolsies**[99] 1493 7-10-0 **85**............................... JackGarritty 3
(Micky Hammond) *w ldr 4f: cl up: drvn and outpcd 3f out: lost tch fnl 2f* **22/1**

2m 24.74s (1.64) **Going Correction** +0.10s/f (Good) **7** Ran SP% **111.2**

Speed ratings (Par 105): **98,97,97,95,91 91,50**

CSF £10.61 CT £67.58 TOTE £3.80: £2.10, £1.70; EX 11.40 Trifecta £93.60.

Owner Market Avenue Racing Club Ltd **Bred** Seamus McConnon **Trained** Norton, N Yorks

■ Stewards' Enquiry : Ben Robinson caution: careless riding

FOCUS

The early pace for this middle-distance handicap was reasonably good and three passed the post almost in a line.

4681 BOOKIES.COM BETTING TIPS H'CAP 1m 1f
3:50 (3:51) (Class 5) (0-70,71) 3-Y-O £2,911 (£866; £432; £216) **Stalls** Low

Form RPR

2641 **1** **Blacklister**[8] 4382 3-9-8 **71**... PaulMulrennan 7 79
(Mick Channon) *mde all: rdn 2f out: kpt on strly fnl f* **4/1**[2]

5622 **2** *2 1/4* **Bit Of A Quirke**[19] 3982 3-8-10 **59**................................... JasonHart 4 61
(Mark Walford) *trckd ldrs: effrt and rdn over 2f out: chsd wnr over 1f out: no imp fnl f* **5/1**[3]

002 **3** *1/2* **Muroor**[17] 4036 3-9-1 **69**... JoshDoyle(5) 6 70
(David O'Meara) *missed break: hld up: rdn along 3f out: hdwy and swtchd rt over 1f out: kpt on fnl f: nvr able to chal* **8/1**

6503 **4** *1* **Calypso Delegator (IRE)**[10] 4301 3-8-2 **51** oh1.......... DuranFentiman 2 50
(Micky Hammond) *rn wout one of hind shoes: hld up: drvn along over 4f out: rallied over 2f out: kpt on fnl f: no imp* **33/1**

-042 **5** *1 1/2* **Page Of Wands**[16] 4098 3-9-2 **65**...................................... DavidNolan 1 60
(Karen McLintock) *in tch: rdn and edgd lft whn flashed tail repeatedly fr over 1f out: no imp fnl f* **5/1**[3]

2114 **6** *4 1/2* **Toffee Apple (IRE)**[6] 4449 3-8-6 **55**................................ JoeFanning 8 41
(Keith Dalgleish) *pressed wnr: rdn over 2f out: wknd over 1f out* **2/1**[1]

0-01 **7** *1* **Wootton Vale (IRE)**[9] 4370 3-8-6 **55**............................ PatrickMathers 3 38
(Richard Fahey) *in tch: drvn and outpcd over 2f out: n.d after* **10/1**

0-56 **8** *27* **Gilt Edged (IRE)**[40] 3249 3-8-7 **56**................................... CamHardie 5
(Julie Camacho) *t.k.h: hld up in tch on outside: drvn and struggling 3f out: btn and eased over 1f out* **33/1**

1m 58.15s (0.55) **Going Correction** +0.10s/f (Good) **8** Ran SP% **112.8**

Speed ratings (Par 100): **101,99,98,97,96 92,91,67**

CSF £23.55 CT £149.11 TOTE £4.70: £1.80, £1.40, £2.10; EX 25.80 Trifecta £111.40.

Owner Box 41 Racing **Bred** Aston House Stud **Trained** West Ilsley, Berks

FOCUS

A modest handicap won from the front by a horse in form.

4682 OPERA BINGO MAIDEN STKS 1m 1f
4:25 (4:25) (Class 5) 3-Y-O+ £2,911 (£866; £432; £216) **Stalls** Low

Form RPR

3 **1** **His Kyllachy (IRE)**[27] 3723 3-9-5 0.................................... BenCurtis 1 85
(William Haggas) *trckd ldrs: rdn and outpcd wl over 2f out: rallied and edgd lft over 1f out: hdwy to ld last 50yds: kpt on* **4/1**[3]

32 **2** *nk* **Apres Midi (IRE)**[37] 3343 3-9-0 0.................................. DougieCostello 4 79
(K R Burke) *led to over 2f out: sn rdn: regained ld over 1f out: edgd lft and hdd last 50yds: kpt on* **2/1**[1]

32 **3** *1 1/4* **Organza**[17] 4035 3-9-0 72.. PaulMulrennan 9 76
(Mick Channon) *pressed ldr: led and rdn over 2f out: hdd over 1f out: rallied: kpt on same pce last 100yds* **9/2**

3 **4** *3 3/4* **La Contessa (IRE)**[12] 4235 3-9-0 0.................................... DavidNolan 12 68
(Richard Fahey) *midfield: drvn and outpcd over 3f out: rallied over 1f out: kpt on: nt pce to chal* **14/1**

22 **5** *3/4* **Lastmanlastround (IRE)**[27] 3723 3-9-5 0......................... JoeFanning 7 71
(Rae Guest) *trckd ldrs: effrt and rdn whn edgd lft over 1f out: wknd ins fnl f* **3/1**[2]

0-5 **6** *11* **Toola Boola**[23] 3845 6-9-9 0... JackGarritty 11 43
(Jedd O'Keeffe) *hld up on ins: drvn and outpcd 4f out: rallied 2f out: nvr rchd ldrs* **25/1**

44 **7** *3/4* **Aislabie (FR)**[10] 4313 3-9-5 0... JasonHart 13 46
(Mark Walford) *v s.i.s: hld up: drvn over 4f out: struggling fnl 3f* **50/1**

2 **8** *4* **Miss Galidora (IRE)**[37] 3362 3-9-0 0................................. SamJames 10 32
(David O'Meara) *t.k.h: trckd ldrs tl rdn and wknd over 2f out* **14/1**

0 **9** *2 3/4* **Go George Go (IRE)**[23] 3856 3-9-5 0............................. DarryllHolland 2 31
(Alan Swinbank) *hld up: rdn and outpcd 4f out: btn fnl 2f* **50/1**

10 *3* **My Jamaican Guy (IRE)** 3-9-5 0.. TomEaves 5 24
(James Given) *s.i.s: bhd: struggling over 4f out: nvr on terms* **80/1**

11 *3/4* **Bilko's Back (IRE)**[14] 4-9-7 0.................................. JamesCorbett(7) 8 23
(Susan Corbett) *s.i.s: bhd: struggling fr over 4f out: sn btn* **200/1**

30 **12** *7* **Chiron (IRE)**[22] 3886 7-10-0 0.. JoeyHaynes 6 8
(Keith Dalgleish) *midfield: drvn and outpcd over 3f out: sn wknd* **125/1**

1m 57.22s (-0.38) **Going Correction** +0.10s/f (Good)

WFA 3 from 4yo+ 9lb **12** Ran SP% **120.1**

Speed ratings (Par 103): **105,104,103,100,99 89,89,85,83,80 79,73**

CSF £12.40 TOTE £5.20: £1.80, £1.50, £1.80; EX 14.00 Trifecta £58.90.

Owner Sheikh Juma Dalmook Al Maktoum **Bred** Mrs D Camacho **Trained** Newmarket, Suffolk

FOCUS

The market only wanted to know about four of these, and three of them dominated in the final furlong.

4683 BOOKIES.COM H'CAP 7f 173y
5:00 (5:01) (Class 5) (0-70,69) 4-Y-O+ £2,911 (£866; £432; £216) **Stalls** Low

Form RPR

12 **1** **Mister Royal (IRE)**[9] 4369 5-8-8 **56**..................................(p) BenCurtis 2 72
(Brian Ellison) *trckd ldrs: rdn to ld over 1f out: kpt on strly to draw clr ins fnl f* **8/11**[1]

0006 **2** *3* **Gun Case**[13] 4189 4-9-1 **63**..(p) DougieCostello 5 72
(Alistair Whillans) *pressed ldr: led briefly 2f out: sn rdn and hung lft: kpt on same pce fnl f* **33/1**

0050 **3** *1 1/4* **Character Onesie (IRE)**[16] 4089 4-9-7 **69**....................... DavidNolan 3 75
(Richard Fahey) *trckd ldrs: rdn along 3f out: rallied over 1f out: kpt on fnl f: nt pce to chal* **7/2**[2]

-660 **4** *3 1/2* **Yair Hill (IRE)**[46] 3016 8-8-2 **50** oh1..............................(p) JoeFanning 1 48
(Thomas Cuthbert) *hld up: smooth hdwy over 2f out: rdn and edgd lft over 1f out: sn outpcd* **33/1**

0024 **5** *1 3/4* **Circuitous**[5] 4490 8-8-12 **60**..(v) TomEaves 8 53
(Keith Dalgleish) *led tl rdn and hdd 2f out: outpcd fnl f* **12/1**

5000 **6** *1 1/4* **Osteopathic Remedy (IRE)**[38] 3327 12-9-3 **65**............... PhillipMakin 4 55
(John Davies) *hld up in tch: drvn and outpcd over 2f out: sn btn* **12/1**

6-06 **7** *nk* **Breton Blues**[15] 4146 6-8-3 **51**......................................(v[1]) CamHardie 9 41
(Fred Watson) *s.i.s: hld up: rdn along and outpcd over 3f out: sn btn* **80/1**

2444 **8** *12* **Knight Of The Air**[8] 4388 4-8-13 **61**............................. PaulMulrennan 6 22
(Mick Channon) *too t.k.h: hld up in tch: rdn along over 3f out: wknd over 2f out* **5/1**[3]

1m 40.03s (0.03) **Going Correction** +0.10s/f (Good) **8** Ran SP% **119.3**

Speed ratings (Par 103): **103,100,98,95,93 92,91,79**

CSF £37.16 CT £66.64 TOTE £1.60: £1.30, £3.50, £1.50; EX 27.90 Trifecta £114.30.

Owner Mrs J O'Sullivan **Bred** Michael Feeney **Trained** Norton, N Yorks

FOCUS

Almost certainly moderate form.

4684 FREE HORSE RACING BETS @BOOKIES.COM H'CAP 6f 195y
5:30 (5:30) (Class 5) (0-75,75) 3-Y-O+ £2,911 (£866; £432; £216) **Stalls** Low

Form RPR

4233 **1** **Yulong Xiongba (IRE)**[9] 4335 4-8-13 **65**..................(be[1]) JoshDoyle(5) 2 72
(Julie Camacho) *trckd ldrs: effrt and rdn 2f out: led ins fnl f: kpt on wl* **7/2**[1]

1235 **2** *1/2* **Bajan Rebel**[17] 4043 5-8-11 **63**..................................... NathanEvans(5) 1 69
(Michael Easterby) *led: rdn over 1f out: edgd lft and hdd ins fnl f: kpt on: hld nr fin* **13/2**[3]

5063 **3** *nk* **Cliff (IRE)**[22] 3880 6-8-10 **64**.................................. KieranSchofield(7) 10 69
(Nigel Tinkler) *hld up: hdwy on outside whn edgd rt 2f out: effrt and ev ch ins fnl f: kpt on: hld cl home* **8/1**

4505 **4** *6* **War Department (IRE)**[45] 3079 3-9-6 **74**......................... JoeFanning 9 60
(Keith Dalgleish) *dwlt: t.k.h in rr: effrt whn nt clr run briefly over 2f out: rdn wl over 1f out: kpt on fnl f: no ch w first three* **7/2**[1]

6233 **5** *1 1/2* **Strummer (IRE)**[17] 4036 3-8-11 **65**.................................... TomEaves 7 47
(Kevin Ryan) *hld up: hdwy 2f out: sn rdn: wknd fnl f* **11/2**[2]

120- **6** *4 1/2* **Destination Aim**[282] 7256 9-9-9 **70**...................................... JasonHart 4 43
(Fred Watson) *cl up: effrt and rdn over 2f out: wknd fnl f* **33/1**

206 **7** *2 1/4* **Star Of Spring (IRE)**[21] 3920 4-9-7 **68**....................... RoystonFfrench 6 35
(Iain Jardine) *in tch: effrt and rdn whn hmpd 2f out: sn btn* **10/1**

0-60 **8** *6* **In Focus (IRE)**[68] 2345 5-10-0 **75**................................ DarryllHolland 3 26
(Alan Swinbank) *pressed ldr: drvn along and one pce whn edgd lft and bmpd 2f out: sn wknd* **18/1**

0400 **9** *13* **Buccaneers Vault (IRE)**[32] 3517 4-10-0 **75**..............(b) PaulMulrennan 8
(Michael Dods) *stdd s: hld up in tch: rdn whn checked 2f out: sn btn* **13/2**[3]

1m 27.15s (0.05) **Going Correction** +0.10s/f (Good)

WFA 3 from 4yo+ 7lb **9** Ran SP% **114.9**

Speed ratings (Par 103): **103,102,102,95,93 88,85,78,64**

CSF £26.41 CT £169.84 TOTE £3.70: £1.60, £1.90, £2.20; EX 28.70 Trifecta £168.60.

Owner Owners Group 006 **Bred** Rockfield Farm **Trained** Norton, N Yorks

FOCUS
Most of these had some sort of chance 2f from home but they steadily thinned out from that point.
T/Jkpt: £3,418.40. Pool: £15,383 - 4.50 winning units. T/Plt: £53.50 to a £1 stake. Pool: £86,898.69 - 1186.07 winning units. T/Qpdt: £6.60 to a £1 stake. Pool: £7,541.98 - 842.37 winning units. **Richard Young**

4371 PONTEFRACT (L-H)
Sunday, July 24

OFFICIAL GOING: Good to firm (9.1)
Wind: light 1/2 against Weather: overcast, humid, showers

4685 FLY HIGH FAYE NICKELS MAIDEN STKS (PLUS 10 RACE) 5f
2:20 (2:20) (Class 4) 2-Y-O **£6,469** (£1,925; £962; £481) **Stalls** Low

Form RPR
5 **1** **Hemingway (IRE)**[15] 4161 2-9-5 0 KevinStott 1 79
(Kevin Ryan) *trckd ldrs: swtchd lft over 1f out: upsides last 75yds: led post* **7/4**[2]
20 **2** *nse* **Peach Pavlova (IRE)**[25] 3772 2-9-0 0 PJMcDonald 4 74
(Ann Duffield) *led tl over 2f out: led narrowly last 75yds: hdd post* **16/1**
32 **3** *1 1/2* **Savannah's Dream**[40] 3247 2-9-0 0 DanielTudhope 2 69
(David O'Meara) *w ldr: led over 2f out: edgd rt over 1f out: hdd and no ex last 75yds* **10/11**[1]
0 **4** *hd* **Party Tiger**[36] 3416 2-9-5 0 GeorgeChaloner 3 73
(Richard Fahey) *hld up in rr: hdwy on ins over 1f out: kpt on same pce* **25/1**
5 *1/2* **Kruger Park (IRE)** 2-9-5 0 TonyHamilton 5 71
(Richard Fahey) *dwlt: sn chsng ldrs: drvn over 2f out: kpt on same pce fnl f: will improve* **13/2**[3]
00 **6** *4 1/2* **Scotch Myst**[36] 3388 2-9-0 0 AdamMcNamara(5) 7 55
(Richard Fahey) *t.k.h on outer: trckd ldrs: lost pl over 2f out* **66/1**
1m 3.73s (0.43) **Going Correction** -0.175s/f (Firm) **6** Ran SP% **113.3**
Speed ratings (Par 96): **89,88,86,86,85 78**
CSF £27.68 TOTE £2.70: £1.20, £4.10; EX 26.20 Trifecta £38.80.
Owner Mrs Angie Bailey **Bred** Knocktoran Stud & Deerpark Stud **Trained** Hambleton, N Yorks

FOCUS
The ground had been watered and there was a shower before racing, but Kevin Stott agreed with the going description following this opener. The false rail that had been in place since the end of May was removed to provide fresh ground over the last 6f and the finishing order of this first race by draw was as follows: 1-4-2-3-5-7 (6 n/r). The third can't have run to her Royal Ascot level, but the winner and second had already shown plenty of ability and this was a fair enough juvenile maiden. The runner-up has been rated back to her debut form.

4686 PONTEFRACT AND DISTRICT GOLF CLUB H'CAP 1m 4f 8y
2:50 (2:50) (Class 5) (0-70,70) 3-Y-O+ **£4,528** (£1,347; £673; £336) **Stalls** Low

Form RPR
13-0 **1** **Chant (IRE)**[44] 3118 6-10-0 **70** PJMcDonald 4 78
(Ann Duffield) *mde all: clr after 3f: drvn over 1f out: styd on: unchal* **7/1**
0452 **2** *1 1/2* **Love Marmalade (IRE)**[20] 3942 6-9-12 **68** DanielTudhope 1 74
(David O'Meara) *sn trcking ldrs: effrt 2f out: chsd wnr fnl f: no imp* **15/8**[1]
4211 **3** *1 1/4* **Saint Thomas (IRE)**[10] 4320 9-9-3 **59** FrannyNorton 3 63
(John Mackie) *trckd ldrs: effrt over 2f out: kpt on same pce appr fnl f* **9/2**[3]
0343 **4** *3/4* **Stoneboat Bill**[10] 4320 4-9-0 **63** GerO'Neill(7) 6 65
(Declan Carroll) *hld up: t.k.h in rr: hdwy 8f out: chsng ldrs over 3f out: nt clr run wl over 1f out: kpt on same pce to take 4th 1f out* **10/1**
045 **5** *5* **Fastnet Blast (IRE)**[19] 3981 3-9-2 **70** ThomasBrown 2 64
(Ed Walker) *stdd s: hld up detached in last: hdwy over 5f out: chsng ldrs over 3f out: effrt on outer 2f out: wknd fnl 150yds: eased nr fin* **3/1**[2]
2644 **6** *2 1/2* **Bogardus (IRE)**[16] 4099 5-9-5 **61** GrahamLee 5 51
(Patrick Holmes) *trckd ldrs: t.k.h: drvn 4f out: wknd fnl f* **10/1**
2m 37.77s (-3.03) **Going Correction** -0.175s/f (Firm)
WFA 3 from 4yo+ 12lb **6** Ran SP% **108.6**
Speed ratings (Par 103): **103,102,101,100,97 95**
CSF £19.28 TOTE £6.70: £2.60, £1.50; EX 19.10 Trifecta £55.00.
Owner Mrs Ann Starkie & Mrs I Starkie **Bred** Roger K Lee **Trained** Constable Burton, N Yorks

FOCUS
A modest handicap and the winner was allowed too big a lead.

4687 SANDAL BMW H'CAP 1m 2f 6y
3:25 (3:25) (Class 4) (0-80,80) 3-Y-O+ **£7,115** (£2,117; £1,058; £529) **Stalls** Low

Form RPR
4310 **1** **Save The Bees**[15] 4138 8-9-0 **73** (b) GerO'Neill(7) 5 82
(Declan Carroll) *mde all: t.k.h: rdn 2f out: kpt on: unchal* **20/1**
0550 **2** *1 1/2* **Intiwin (IRE)**[16] 4113 4-9-6 **77** AdamMcNamara(5) 1 83
(Richard Fahey) *mid-div: effrt 3f out: chsng ldrs over 1f out: kpt on to take 2nd last 100yds* **5/1**
041 **3** *2 1/4* **Le Deluge (FR)**[7] 4424 6-9-0 **66** 6ex (t) PJMcDonald 2 68
(Micky Hammond) *mid-div: hdwy over 5f out: chsng ldrs over 1f out: kpt on same pce* **9/2**[3]
5000 **4** *1/2* **Green Howard**[8] 4408 8-9-11 **77** DanielTudhope 7 78
(Rebecca Bastiman) *hld up in rr: hdwy over 2f out: swtchd rt over 1f out: styd on to take 4th clsng stages* **25/1**
0400 **5** *1/2* **Sellingallthetime (IRE)**[16] 4115 5-10-0 **80** (p) AndrewMullen 4 80
(Michael Appleby) *chsd ldrs: drvn over 2f out: kpt on one pce over 1f out* **16/1**
0052 **6** *2 3/4* **Eutropius (IRE)**[6] 4455 7-9-7 **73** SilvestreDeSousa 3 67
(Alan Swinbank) *chsd wnr: drvn over 2f out: wknd last 75yds: b.b.v* **15/8**[1]
1452 **7** *11* **Street Duel (USA)**[5] 4476 3-9-0 **76** (b) FrannyNorton 8 48
(Mark Johnston) *in rr: sn pushed along: bhd over 2f out: eased clsng stages* **4/1**[2]
0122 **8** *6* **Miss Ranger (IRE)**[10] 4293 4-8-13 **70** CallumShepherd(5) 6 46
(Brian Ellison) *hld up in rr: hdwy over 5f out: drvn over 3f out: lost pl wl over 1f out: bhd whn heavily easaed clsng stages* **9/1**
2m 11.93s (-1.77) **Going Correction** -0.175s/f (Firm)
WFA 3 from 4yo+ 10lb **8** Ran SP% **114.1**
Speed ratings (Par 105): **100,98,97,96,96 94,85,80**
CSF £115.81 CT £538.31 TOTE £21.20: £3.90, £1.60, £1.50; EX 161.60 Trifecta £1895.40.
Owner Steve Ryan **Bred** S P Ryan **Trained** Malton, N Yorks

FOCUS
Like in the preceding race, the winner was completely unchallenged in front.

4688 SKY BET GO-RACING-IN-YORKSHIRE SUMMER FESTIVAL POMFRET STKS (LISTED RACE) 1m 4y
4:00 (4:01) (Class 1) 3-Y-O+
£25,519 (£9,675; £4,842; £2,412; £1,210; £607) **Stalls** Low

Form RPR
2200 **1** **Convey**[15] 4127 4-9-5 111 (p) RyanMoore 3 117
(Sir Michael Stoute) *trckd ldrs: t.k.h: 2nd over 2f out: led appr fnl f: drvn out* **5/6**[1]
10-0 **2** *3 1/4* **Algaith (USA)**[39] 3273 4-9-5 106 PaulHanagan 1 109
(Owen Burrows) *led: hdd appr fnl f: styd on same pce* **7/1**
3466 **3** *3/4* **Master Carpenter (IRE)**[8] 4392 5-9-5 108 SilvestreDeSousa 7 107
(Rod Millman) *hld up in rr: hdwy and nt clr run over 2f out: 3rd over 1f out: kpt on wl* **6/1**[2]
6105 **4** *7* **Gratzie**[8] 4391 5-9-0 94 GrahamGibbons 2 91
(Mick Channon) *s.s: racd in last: hdwy 4f out: modest 3rd over 1f out: one pce: eased clsng stages* **20/1**
5504 **5** *4 1/2* **Kentuckyconnection (USA)**[17] 4065 3-8-11 108 (p) ConnorBeasley 6 78
(Bryan Smart) *chsd ldrs: drvn over 2f out: lost pl over 1f out* **13/2**[3]
0414 **6** *nse* **Sound Advice**[36] 3390 7-9-5 102 RobertWinston 8 80
(Keith Dalgleish) *hld up in rr: hdwy to trck ldrs 4f out: drvn over 2f out: lost pl over 1f out* **12/1**
610 **7** *9* **Capo Rosso (IRE)**[36] 3390 6-9-5 99 (v) RichardKingscote 5 58
(Tom Dascombe) *chsd ldr: drvn over 2f out: lost pl wl over 1f out: eased whn bhd clsng stages* **16/1**
1m 41.94s (-3.96) **Going Correction** -0.175s/f (Firm)
WFA 3 from 4yo+ 8lb **7** Ran SP% **113.0**
Speed ratings (Par 111): **112,108,108,101,96 96,87**
CSF £7.11 TOTE £1.60: £1.60, £1.40; EX 7.30 Trifecta £25.40.
Owner K Abdullah **Bred** Juddmonte Farms Ltd **Trained** Newmarket, Suffolk

FOCUS
The winner was on a different level, despite compromising his chance.

4689 TIESPLANET.COM - TIES FOR EVERY OCCASION H'CAP 6f
4:35 (4:35) (Class 3) (0-90,84) 3-Y-O+
£9,337 (£2,796; £1,398; £699; £349; £175) **Stalls** Low

Form RPR
3464 **1** **Mishaal (IRE)**[11] 4259 6-9-8 **80** DanielTudhope 5 89
(Michael Herrington) *mde all: t.k.h: drvn over 1f out: hld on clsng stages* **4/1**[2]
0013 **2** *3/4* **Maureb (IRE)**[6] 4452 4-9-1 **73** (p) BarryMcHugh 2 79
(Tony Coyle) *mid-div: hdwy to chse wnr 2f out: edgd lft over 1f out: no ex clsng stages* **6/1**
0430 **3** *3/4* **Reputation (IRE)**[8] 4402 3-9-6 **83** (v) SilvestreDeSousa 3 91+
(John Quinn) *hld up in rr: hdwy on ins 2f out: trcking ldng pair whn hmpd and stmbld over 1f out: keeping on strly whn nt clr run last 50yds: nt rcvr* **3/1**[1]
6600 **4** *hd* **Yeeoow (IRE)**[9] 4366 7-9-0 **79** CliffordLee(7) 6 82
(K R Burke) *chsd ldrs: effrt over 2f out: kpt on fnl f* **9/1**
5103 **5** *3* **Eastern Racer (IRE)**[13] 4193 4-9-7 **84** (p) CallumShepherd(5) 9 77
(Brian Ellison) *dwlt: drvn along in rr: hdwy on outside over 1f out: tk modest 5th clsng stages* **12/1**
1602 **6** *1 1/4* **Explain**[7] 4428 4-9-11 **83** JamesSullivan 4 72
(Ruth Carr) *in rr: effrt and n.m.r over 2f out: hdwy over 1f out: wknd fnl 150yds* **9/2**[3]
2500 **7** *1* **Flicka's Boy**[6] 4452 4-8-13 **71** (t) PJMcDonald 1 57
(Tony Coyle) *w wnr: drvn over 2f out: wknd last 150yds* **14/1**
6010 **8** *hd* **Gran Canaria Queen**[8] 4398 7-9-8 **83** RachelRichardson(3) 8 69
(Tim Easterby) *chsd ldrs: drvn over 2f out: hung lft and lost pl over 1f out* **10/1**
-140 **9** *1/2* **Evangelical**[23] 3847 3-8-13 **76** TonyHamilton 7 59
(Richard Fahey) *chsd ldrs: lost pl over 1f out* **25/1**
1m 15.33s (-1.57) **Going Correction** -0.175s/f (Firm)
WFA 3 from 4yo+ 5lb **9** Ran SP% **114.8**
Speed ratings (Par 107): **103,102,101,100,96 95,93,93,92**
CSF £28.05 CT £81.05 TOTE £5.10: £2.00, £1.90, £1.60; EX 34.30 Trifecta £169.10.
Owner Kelvyn Gracie & Lawrence McCaughey **Bred** Darley **Trained** Cold Kirby, N Yorks

FOCUS
A fair sprint handicap in which the third probably should have won.

4690 GORDON DUKER MEMORIAL MAIDEN STKS 1m 4y
5:10 (5:10) (Class 5) 3-4-Y-O **£3,881** (£1,155; £577; £288) **Stalls** Low

Form RPR
2 **1** **Khairaat (IRE)**[15] 4156 3-9-5 0 PaulHanagan 3 92+
(Sir Michael Stoute) *hld up: t.k.h: hdwy to trck ldrs over 5f out: effrt and chsd ldr 2f out: led appr fnl f: pushed clr* **8/13**[1]
6-2 **2** *3 1/2* **Confident Kid**[23] 3856 3-9-5 0 MartinLane 2 81+
(Saeed bin Suroor) *trckd ldr: upsides over 2f out: led on bit wl over 1f out: sn hdd: kpt on same pce* **9/4**[2]
3 *1 3/4* **Russian Finale** 3-9-0 0 GrahamGibbons 5 72+
(William Haggas) *dwlt: racd in last: hdwy over 4f out: effrt over 2f out: modest 3rd over 1f out: kpt on same pce: will improve* **11/2**[3]
000- **4** *12* **Dream Serenade**[298] 6857 3-9-0 40 [1] AndrewMullen 1 43
(Michael Appleby) *wore ear plugs: dwlt: sn chsng ldrs: pushed along over 4f out: lost pl over 1f out: poor 4th clsng stages* **50/1**
0 **5** *2 3/4* **Bettercallphoenix**[30] 3609 3-9-5 0 PJMcDonald 4 41
(David C Griffiths) *led: hdd wl over 1f out: lost pl 1f out: sn bhd* **100/1**
1m 44.28s (-1.62) **Going Correction** -0.175s/f (Firm) **5** Ran SP% **111.0**
Speed ratings (Par 103): **101,97,95,83,81**
CSF £2.30 TOTE £1.40: £1.10, £1.40; EX 2.70 Trifecta £2.90.
Owner Hamdan Al Maktoum **Bred** Shadwell Estate Company Limited **Trained** Newmarket, Suffolk

FOCUS
A messy race, with the winner and second racing keenly off a steady pace, and the third in need of the experience and therefore in the wrong position given how things unfolded.

4691 NEW BEGINNINGS HORSES H'CAP 5f
5:40 (5:40) (Class 5) (0-70,69) 3-Y-O+ **£3,881** (£1,155; £577; £288) **Stalls** Low

Form RPR
0000 **1** **Jack Luey**[22] 3875 9-9-12 **69** (b) PaulHanagan 4 82
(Lawrence Mullaney) *mde all: drvn over 1f out: kpt on wl: unchal* **7/1**
0063 **2** *3 1/4* **Native Falls (IRE)**[22] 3882 5-9-9 **66** SilvestreDeSousa 2 67
(Alan Swinbank) *sn chsng wnr: drvn over 2f out: kpt on same pce fnl f* **7/2**[2]

0345 **3** 3/4 **Groundworker (IRE)**[6] 4452 5-9-9 **66**............................ GrahamLee 1 65
(Paul Midgley) *trckd ldrs: effrt on inner over 1f out: kpt on same pce* **2/1**[1]

3650 **4** *nk* **See Vermont**[10] 4295 8-9-4 **61**..........................(p) DanielTudhope 5 59+
(Rebecca Bastiman) *stmbld sltly s: in rr: hdwy and swtchd rt over 1f out: styd on wl* **11/1**

2422 **5** *nse* **Henley**[16] 4100 4-9-12 **69**.. DaleSwift 7 66
(Tracy Waggott) *chsd ldrs: drvn over 2f out: one pce over 1f out* **4/1**[3]

00-0 **6** *2* **Dark Castle**[51] 2856 7-9-2 **59**.. PJMcDonald 3 49
(Micky Hammond) *hld up in rr: hdwy on inner over 2f out: chsng ldrs over 1f out: fdd clsng stages* **22/1**

2306 **7** *5* **Taffetta**[8] 4378 4-9-6 **63**..(p) BarryMcHugh 9 35
(Tony Coyle) *in rr: drvn over 2f out: wknd fnl f* **16/1**

6-60 **8** *6* **Knockamany Bends (IRE)**[19] 3984 6-8-7 **50** oh2.....(p) AndrewMullen 8
(John Wainwright) *chsd ldrs: outpcd 2f out: wknd fnl f* **25/1**

5415 **9** *7* **David's Beauty (IRE)**[22] 3900 3-8-9 **56**...................... TonyHamilton 6
(Brian Baugh) *chsd ldrs: outpcd over 2f out: sn bhd* **20/1**

1m 2.09s (-1.21) **Going Correction** -0.175s/f (Firm)
WFA 3 from 4yo+ 4lb **9** Ran SP% **115.2**
Speed ratings (Par 103): **102,96,95,95,95 91,83,74,63**
CSF £30.76 CT £67.26 TOTE £6.70: £1.90, £2.20, £1.30; EX 29.10 Trifecta £123.10.
Owner The Jack Partnership & S Rimmer **Bred** Miss D A Johnson **Trained** Great Habton, N Yorks

FOCUS
Another front-running winner.
T/Plt: £74.60 to a £1 stake. Pool: £78,101.72 - 763.42 winning units. T/Qpdt: £8.10 to a £1 stake. Pool: £7,472.46 - 681.54 winning units. **Walter Glynn**

4692 - 4693a (Foreign Racing) - See Raceform Interactive

4439 MAISONS-LAFFITTE (R-H)
Sunday, July 24

OFFICIAL GOING: Turf: good

4694a PRIX ROBERT PAPIN (GROUP 2) (2YO COLTS & FILLIES) (TURF) 5f 110y
2:45 (12:00) 2-Y-O **£54,485** (£21,029; £10,036; £6,691; £3,345)

RPR

1 **Tis Marvellous**[13] 4203 2-9-2 0.. AdamKirby 2 110
(Clive Cox) *a in front rnk on inner: led 1/2-way: shkn up and qcknd clr 1 1/2f out: wandered rt ins fnl f: drvn out* **3/1**[3]

2 2 1/2 **Al Johrah**[39] 3270 2-8-13 0.. GregoryBenoist 4 98
(H-F Devin, France) *chsd ldng trio on outer: clsd over 2f out: styd on to chse eventual wnr fnl f: nvr able to chal* **11/4**[2]

3 *4* **Hargeisa (USA)**[28] 3701 2-8-13 0............................... AndreasSuborics 1 84
(Mario Hofer, Germany) *chsd ldrs on inner: rdn to chse ldr 2f out: styd on same pce fnl f* **11/1**

4 1 1/4 **Morigane Forlonge (FR)**[14] 2-8-13 0......................... CristianDemuro 3 80
(A Giorgi, Italy) *chsd front rnk between horses: outpcd over 2f out: kpt on again ins fnl f: nvr trbld ldrs* **40/1**

5 3/4 **Prince Of Lir (IRE)**[38] 3295 2-9-2 0................................ LukeMorris 6 81
(Robert Cowell) *virtually upsides ldr under restraint on outer: led narrowly after 1 1/2f: hdd 1/2-way: grad dropped away* **5/4**[1]

6 *hd* **Cosachope (FR)**[22] 3937 2-8-13 0.............................. MaximeGuyon 5 77
(P Sogorb, France) *led between horses: hdd after 1 1/2f and remained cl up: lost pl appr 2f out: sn wknd* **7/1**

1m 3.16s (-4.14) **6** Ran SP% **119.4**
WIN (incl. 1 euro stake): 4.50. PLACES: 2.90, 2.30. SF: 27.40.
Owner Miss J Deadman & S Barrow **Bred** Crossfields Bloodstock Ltd **Trained** Lambourn, Berks

FOCUS
The runner-up has been rated to her Queen Mary form.

4696a PRIX DE LA PEPINIERE (LISTED RACE) (4YO+ FILLIES & MARES) (STRAIGHT) (TURF) 1m 2f (S)
3:45 (12:00) 4-Y-O+ **£17,647** (£7,058; £5,294; £3,529; £1,764)

RPR

1 **Pacific Angel (IRE)**[38] 4-8-13 0..........................(b) AurelienLemaitre 1 105+
(M Delzangles, France) **245/10**

2 2 1/2 **Johara (IRE)**[18] 4030 5-8-13 0.. AlexisBadel 7 100
(H-F Devin, France) **9/1**

3 1 1/4 **Loaves And Fishes**[19] 3979 4-8-13 0............................ TonyPiccone 2 98
(David O'Meara) *cl up on inner: led overall after 2f and hdd stands' side gp of 3: jnd by main gp over 2f out: rdn and hdd by eventual wnr 1 1/2f out: styd on gamely u.p* **50/1**

4 *nse* **Contribution**[56] 2727 4-8-13 0................................ VincentCheminaud 8 97
(A Fabre, France) **8/5**[1]

5 1/2 **Weetles**[53] 2797 4-8-13 0.. GeraldMosse 3 96
(Clive Cox) *in last of 3 in stands' side gp: rdn to chse ldrs 2f out: styd on same pce fnl f* **11/1**

6 *hd* **Amona (IRE)**[59] 4-8-13 0.. FabriceVeron 10 96
(Andreas Lowe, Germany) **16/1**

6 *dht* **Game Theory (IRE)**[35] 3454 4-9-3 0.......................... StephanePasquier 9 100
(N Clement, France) **66/10**[2]

8 *hd* **Beautiful Heroine (IRE)**[56] 2727 5-9-3 0......... Pierre-CharlesBoudot 12 100
(F-H Graffard, France) **10/1**

9 *nk* **Spring Leaf (FR)**[32] 3544 4-8-13 0................................ TheoBachelot 6 95
(S Wattel, France) **89/10**[3]

10 1 1/4 **Salve Estelle (GER)**[35] 4-8-13 0................................ CristianDemuro 11 93
(Waldemar Hickst, Germany) **25/1**

11 1/2 **Madernia (IRE)**[18] 4030 4-8-13 0................................ OlivierPeslier 5 92
(C Laffon-Parias, France) **13/1**

12 *5* **Deauville Shower (IRE)**[35] 3454 5-8-13 0........................ MaximeGuyon 4 82
(E Libaud, France) **9/1**

2m 0.53s (-1.87) **12** Ran SP% **121.9**
WIN (incl. 1 euro stake): 25.50. PLACES: 7.00, 4.00, 13.40. DF: 128.70. SF: 347.90.
Owner Ballymore Thoroughbred Ltd **Bred** Dayton Investments Ltd **Trained** France

4695 - 4697a (Foreign Racing) - See Raceform Interactive

3917 LES LANDES
Sunday, July 24

OFFICIAL GOING: Firm (good to firm in places)

4698a LA VALLETTE 2016 JERSEY DERBY (TURF) 1m 4f
3:40 (3:41) 3-Y-O+ **£2,380** (£860; £510)

RPR

1 **Aussie Lyrics (FR)**[23] 3918 6-10-2 0......................(b) MattieBatchelor 5 67
(Mrs C Gilbert, Jersey) *a gng wl: trckd ldrs: chal on bit fr 3f out: qcknd clr ins fnl f: easily* **4/7**[1]

2 *10* **Bowl Imperior**[23] 3918 4-10-2 0................................ JemmaMarshall 4 51
(Mrs A Malzard, Jersey) *led: jnd and rdn fr 3f out: hdd ins fnl f: no ch w wnr* **13/2**

3 *10* **Blue Sea Of Ibrox (IRE)**[136] 884 8-9-13 0..................(p) NoraLooby 1 32
(Mrs A Corson, Jersey) *trckd ldrs tl outpcd and btn over 2f iout* **6/1**[3]

4 *25* **Benoordenhout (IRE)**[37] 3380 5-10-2 0.............................. TimClark 2
(T Le Brocq, Jersey) *w.r.s and uns rdr: rmntd: continued t.o* **6/4**[2]

Owner White Spot Racing **Bred** Hugh Hogg **Trained** Jersey

4442 AYR (L-H)
Monday, July 25

OFFICIAL GOING: Soft (heavy in places; 6.6)
Wind: Fresh, half against Weather: Overcast

4699 WILLIAM HILL RADIO/IRISH STALLION FARMS EBF NOVICE STKS 7f 50y
2:00 (2:00) (Class 5) 2-Y-O **£3,557** (£1,058; £529; £264) **Stalls** High

Form RPR

4 **1** **Temerity (IRE)**[31] 3597 2-8-11 0.................................. TonyHamilton 3 82+
(Richard Fahey) *trckd ldrs: hdwy on outside to ld wl over 1f out: edgd lft: rdn clr fnl f* **9/1**

1 **2** 3 1/2 **Permian (IRE)**[33] 3524 2-9-9 0.. JoeFanning 5 82
(Mark Johnston) *pressed ldr: led over 2f out to wl over 1f out: edgd lft and kpt on fnl f: no ch w wnr* **3/1**[2]

33 **3** 1 1/4 **Alfie's Angel (IRE)**[27] 3749 2-9-2 0............................ ConnorBeasley 6 72
(Bryan Smart) *sn pushed along bhd ldng gp: drvn and outpcd over 3f out: rallied over 1f out: kpt on wl fnl f: nt pce to chal* **6/1**

1 **4** 1 3/4 **Proud Archi (IRE)**[34] 3477 2-9-6 0................................ PaulMulrennan 1 72
(Michael Dods) *trckd ldrs: rdn over 2f out: rallied and ev ch briefly wl over 1f out: outpcd fnl f* **6/4**[1]

521 **5** 3 3/4 **Heir Of Excitement (IRE)**[14] 4188 2-9-9 0...................... ShaneGray 4 65
(Kevin Ryan) *led to over 2f out: rdn and wknd over 1f out* **9/2**[3]

6 *6* **Midge Hall (IRE)** 2-8-11 0.. PJMcDonald 2 38
(Ann Duffield) *jinked lft sn after s and s.i.s: rn green in rr: struggling over 3f out: sn btn* **40/1**

1m 39.93s (6.53) **Going Correction** +0.975s/f (Soft) **6** Ran SP% **109.9**
Speed ratings (Par 94): **101,97,95,93,89 82**
CSF £34.37 TOTE £12.30: £3.90, £1.50; EX 28.30 Trifecta £326.90.
Owner Cheveley Park Stud **Bred** Gamra Partnership **Trained** Musley Bank, N Yorks

FOCUS
Following 12mm of rain since the previous day the ground had eased to soft, heavy in places. The rail was in 2yds, increasing the distances of races 1, 2, 3, 4, 6 & 7 by 6yds and race 5 by 12yds. This opening contest wasn't a bad novice event at all, with a couple of these already having looked promising, and a nice step forward from the winner. The slow winning time shows just how testing conditions were.

4700 WILLIAM HILL IN THE APP STORE H'CAP 7f 50y
2:30 (2:30) (Class 4) (0-85,85) 3-Y-O+ **£5,498** (£1,636; £817; £408) **Stalls** High

Form RPR

5223 **1** **Vallarta (IRE)**[10] 4376 6-9-1 **72**.................................. JamesSullivan 5 80
(Ruth Carr) *in tch: rdn over 2f out: hdwy to ld last 50yds: hld on wl* **17/2**

-005 **2** *shd* **Invoke (IRE)**[7] 4443 5-10-0 **85**.................................... PhillipMakin 7 92
(Keith Dalgleish) *hld up: drvn and outpcd 3f out: rallied over 1f out: swtchd rt and kpt on wl fnl f: jst hld* **8/1**

0400 **3** 1/2 **Fullon Clarets**[14] 4193 4-9-1 **77**........................ AdamMcNamara(5) 4 82
(Richard Fahey) *t.k.h: cl up: rdn along over 2f: led ins fnl f: edgd lft: hdd and no ex last 50yds* **6/1**[3]

1101 **4** *2* **Cymraeg Bounty**[21] 3945 4-10-0 **85**................................ DavidNolan 3 85
(Iain Jardine) *t.k.h: led: rdn 2f out: hdd ins fnl f: sn no ex* **11/10**[1]

0060 **5** *hd* **Be Bold**[12] 4259 4-9-1 **72**.. BarryMcHugh 6 72
(Rebecca Bastiman) *pressed ldr: drvn over 2f out: one pce fr over 1f out* **25/1**

024 **6** *hd* **Sophie P**[14] 4193 3-8-6 **70**.. PJMcDonald 2 66
(R Mike Smith) *prom: rdn along over 2f out: outpcd fr over 1f out* **11/2**[2]

1430 **7** *21* **Alexandrakollontai (IRE)**[11] 4318 6-9-13 **84**...........(b) ConnorBeasley 1 29
(Alistair Whillans) *s.i.s: rdn in rr 1/2-way: struggling over 2f out: t.o* **10/1**

1m 39.38s (5.98) **Going Correction** +0.975s/f (Soft)
WFA 3 from 4yo+ 7lb **7** Ran SP% **111.9**
Speed ratings (Par 105): **104,103,103,101,100 100,76**
CSF £68.90 TOTE £8.30: £3.40, £3.70; EX 52.00 Trifecta £226.50.
Owner Douglas Renton **Bred** Frank O'Meara **Trained** Huby, N Yorks
■ Stewards' Enquiry : Phillip Makin two-day ban: used whip above permitted level (Aug 8-9)

FOCUS
Race distance increased by 6yds. A fair handicap and a race of changing fortunes, with almost four different leaders inside the last furlong. As in the opener, the winner made his effort up the centre of the track.

4701 WILLIAM HILL DAILY RACING PODCAST H'CAP 7f 50y
3:05 (3:06) (Class 6) (0-65,66) 3-Y-O+ **£2,587** (£770; £384; £192) **Stalls** High

Form RPR

201 **1** **Dark Crystal**[7] 4444 5-10-1 **66** 6ex.................................. DavidNolan 8 72
(Linda Perratt) *broke wl: chsd ldr: smooth hdwy to ld 2f out: sn rdn: hld on wl fnl f* **9/1**

0051 **2** 1 1/4 **Charava (IRE)**[7] 4445 4-10-0 **65** 6ex..........................(v) DanielTudhope 3 68
(Patrick Holmes) *hld up in tch: stdy hdwy whn n.m.r over 2f out: effrt and chsd wnr over 1f out: hung lft: kpt on ins fnl f: nt rch wnr* **7/2**[2]

4022 **3** *shd* **Dark Command**^{7} 4444 3-9-4 **62**..............................(p) ConnorBeasley 4 62
(Michael Dods) *hld up: hdwy whn nt clr run over 2f out to over 1f out: rdn and kpt on wl fnl f: nrst fin* **13/8**^{1}

4420 **4** *5* **Tanawar (IRE)**^{13} 4231 6-10-0 **65**..............................(b) JamesSullivan 10 55
(Ruth Carr) *t.k.h: trckd ldrs: rdn and hung lft over 1f out: wknd ins fnl f* **8/1**^{3}

0022 **5** *1 1/2* **Goninodaethat**^{14} 4191 8-9-6 **57**.............................. JoeDoyle 9 43
(Jim Goldie) *plld hrd: led to 2f out: rdn over 1f out: wknd fnl f* **9/1**

0363 **6** *2 3/4* **Mister Mischief**^{27} 3754 3-9-6 **64**.............................. JackGarritty 7 41
(Paul Midgley) *hld up: rdn along and outpcd over 2f out: n.d after* **12/1**

4-60 **7** *1 1/4* **She's Golden**^{10} 4370 3-8-13 **57**.............................. PJMcDonald 1 30
(Ann Duffield) *prom: rdn along over 2f out: wknd over 1f out* **25/1**

6506 **8** *6* **Justice Pleasing**^{12} 4256 3-9-5 **63**.............................. PaulMulrennan 6 21
(David Loughnane) *t.k.h: in tch: rdn over 2f out: wknd over 1f out* **28/1**

0-06 **9** *5* **Fire Diamond**^{34} 3478 3-8-13 **57**..............................(t) JoeFanning 5 3
(Tom Dascombe) *hld up: drvn and struggling 3f out: sn btn* **10/1**

1m 40.97s (7.57) **Going Correction** +0.975s/f (Soft)
WFA 3 from 4yo+ 7lb **9** Ran SP% **115.5**
Speed ratings (Par 101): **95,93,93,87,86 82,81,74,68**
CSF £40.60 CT £78.09 TOTE £9.20: £2.20, £1.60, £1.10; EX 37.70 Trifecta £108.60.
Owner Nil Sine Labore Partnership **Bred** R Biggs **Trained** East Kilbride, S Lanarks

FOCUS
Race distance increased by 6yds. A moderate handicap and a lopsided betting market. The early pace was generous, but the winning time ended up the slowest of the three 7f races on the card. The first two home had won different divisions of the same race here the previous week.

4702 WILLIAM HILL LIVE BETTING TV H'CAP 1m 2f
3:40 (3:40) (Class 5) (0-70,70) 3-Y-O+ **£3,557** (£1,058; £529; £264) **Stalls** Low

Form RPR

1U45 **1** **Sattelac**^{18} 4033 3-8-12 64.............................. PhillipMakin 5 70
(Keith Dalgleish) *hld up in tch: stdy hdwy over 2f out: led over 1f out: sn hrd pressed: hld on gamely u.p ins fnl f* **4/1**^{3}

2320 **2** *nse* **Sakhalin Star (IRE)**^{13} 4234 5-9-9 65..............................(e) ConnorBeasley 4 71
(Richard Guest) *hld up in last pl: stdy hdwy over 3f out: chal over 1f out: sn rdn: kpt on fnl f: jst hld* **9/2**

5054 **3** *1 3/4* **Age Of Elegance (IRE)**^{6} 4476 4-10-0 70.............................. DanielTudhope 7 73
(David Loughnane) *led: rdn over 2f out: hdd over 1f out: kpt on same pce ins fnl f* **3/1**^{2}

0050 **4** *13* **Haymarket**^{7} 4446 7-9-4 65.............................. GarryWhillans$^{(5)}$ 6 42
(R Mike Smith) *t.k.h: trckd ldrs: outpcd and hung lft over 2f out: btn over 1f out* **12/1**

00-4 **5** *14* **Assisted**^{191} 219 3-9-1 67.............................. JoeFanning 2 16
(Keith Dalgleish) *t.k.h: prom: hdwy to chse ldr after 4f: rdn over 2f out: hung rt and wknd over 1f out* **5/2**^{1}

3136 **6** *13* **Testa Rossa (IRE)**^{14} 4190 6-9-8 64..............................(b) JoeDoyle 3
(Jim Goldie) *hld up in tch: struggling 3f out: sn btn: t.o* **9/1**

5000 **7** *21* **Ralphy Lad (IRE)**^{16} 4143 5-10-0 70.............................. NeilFarley 1
(Alan Swinbank) *chsd ldr 4f: drvn and struggling over 3f out: sn btn: t.o* **16/1**

2m 20.83s (8.83) **Going Correction** +0.975s/f (Soft)
WFA 3 from 4yo+ 10lb **7** Ran SP% **115.3**
Speed ratings (Par 103): **103,102,101,91,79 69,52**
CSF £22.61 TOTE £5.20: £3.00, £1.90; EX 26.20 Trifecta £75.40.
Owner Tom Young **Bred** Jenny Hall Bloodstock & Sideways Bloodstock **Trained** Carluke, S Lanarks

FOCUS
Race distance increased by 6yds. An ordinary handicap, but a thrilling finish. The first three pulled well clear and a persinal best by the winner.

4703 WILLIAM HILL BET ON YOUR MOBILE H'CAP 1m 5f 13y
4:10 (4:11) (Class 4) (0-85,85) 3-Y-O+ **£5,498** (£1,636; £817; £408) **Stalls** Low

Form RPR

0002 **1** **Buonarroti (IRE)**^{22} 3920 5-9-10 **81**.............................. DanielTudhope 6 92+
(Declan Carroll) *hld up: smooth hdwy to ld over 2f out: qcknd clr on bridle fnl f: v easily* **5/2**^{1}

5003 **2** *2 3/4* **Multellie**^{18} 4044 4-9-10 **81**.............................. DavidAllan 4 86
(Tim Easterby) *pressed ldr: rdn over 2f out: chsd wnr over 1f out: no imp fnl f* **10/3**^{3}

/601 **3** *2* **Lexi's Boy (IRE)**^{9} 4381 8-10-0 **85**..............................(tp) DavidNolan 2 87
(Donald McCain) *led: rdn over 3f out: hdd over 2f out: one pce fr over 1f out* **3/1**^{2}

30/0 **4** *1/2* **Great Fighter**^{16} 4162 6-9-9 **80**.............................. JoeDoyle 7 81
(Jim Goldie) *hld up stdy hdwy over 2f out: sn pushed along: rdn and no imp over 1f out* **12/1**

5403 **5** *6* **Gabrial's Star**^{13} 4230 7-9-7 **83**..............................(b) AdamMcNamara$^{(5)}$ 3 75
(Richard Fahey) *prom: drvn and outpcd over 2f out: btn over 1f out* **9/2**

0430 **6** *14* **Stanarley Pic**^{36} 3437 5-8-9 **66**.............................. DarryllHolland 5 37
(Alan Swinbank) *chsd ldrs: lost pl over 2f out: sn pushed along and struggling: t.o* **10/1**

3m 9.17s (15.17) **Going Correction** +0.975s/f (Soft) **6** Ran SP% **111.6**
Speed ratings (Par 105): **92,90,89,88,85 76**
CSF £10.97 TOTE £3.10: £1.80, £1.40; EX 10.30 Trifecta £30.70.
Owner Denis Hardy **Bred** Beauty Is Truth Syndicate **Trained** Malton, N Yorks

FOCUS
Race distance increased by 12yds. A fair staying handicap in which the favourite hosed up. The runners came up the centre in the home straight and the winner ended up against the stands' rail.

4704 WILLIAM HILL DOWNLOAD THE APP H'CAP 1m
4:40 (4:40) (Class 4) (0-80,80) 3-Y-O+ **£5,498** (£1,636; £817; £408) **Stalls** Low

Form RPR

6416 **1** **Victoire De Lyphar (IRE)**^{24} 3840 9-9-9 **75**..............................(e) JamesSullivan 8 85
(Ruth Carr) *hld up: weaved through over 1f out: led and edgd lft ins fnl f: rdn and kpt on wl* **18/1**

0322 **2** *3/4* **Moonlightnavigator (USA)**^{7} 4443 4-10-0 **80**.............................. DougieCostello 7 88
(John Quinn) *trckd ldrs: rdn to ld over 1f out: edgd lft and hdd ins fnl f: kpt on: hld nr fin* **9/2**^{1}

603 **3** *4 1/2* **Terhaal (IRE)**^{11} 4312 4-9-11 **77**.............................. DanielTudhope 2 75
(David O'Meara) *hld up: stdy hdwy on outside over 2f out: rdn over 1f out: kpt on same pce fnl f* **9/2**^{1}

2434 **4** *1 1/2* **Gworn**^{7} 4448 6-10-0 **80**..............................(p) PJMcDonald 4 74
(R Mike Smith) *hld up in midfield: hdwy and cl up over 1f out: no ex ins fnl f* **5/1**^{2}

0060 **5** *1/2* **Tadaany (IRE)**^{40} 3286 4-9-10 **76**.............................. PhillipMakin 12 69
(David O'Meara) *hld up: pushed along and hdwy over 1f out: no imp ins fnl f* **11/1**

0652 **6** *2 1/2* **Ellaal**^{6} 4490 7-9-0 **66**.............................. JoeFanning 10 53
(Ruth Carr) *chsd ldr: led over 3f out: rdn and hdd over 1f out: sn btn* **10/1**

013- **7** *1 1/2* **Hibou**^{342} 5492 3-9-5 **79**.............................. DavidNolan 3 61
(Iain Jardine) *hld up: drvn along over 2f out: no imp over 1f out* **16/1**

6454 **8** *1 1/4* **Energia Flavio (BRZ)**^{10} 4348 6-9-0 **71**.............................. AdamMcNamara$^{(5)}$ 9 52
(Richard Fahey) *prom: drvn along over 2f out: wknd over 1f out* **12/1**

2313 **9** *3* **Eastern Dragon (IRE)**^{7} 4446 6-9-6 **77**.............................. GarryWhillans$^{(5)}$ 11 51
(Iain Jardine) *midfield: rdn along over 2f out: wknd wl over 1f out* **7/1**^{3}

050 **10** *20* **Lothair (IRE)**^{32} 3553 7-8-10 **62**.............................. DarryllHolland 13
(Alan Swinbank) *led to over 3f out: sn rdn and wknd* **25/1**

-044 **11** *18* **Optima Petamus**^{17} 4113 4-9-11 **77**..............................(p) JackGarritty 6
(Patrick Holmes) *prom: drvn along over 2f out: edgd lft and wknd wl over 1f out* **10/1**

1m 50.1s (6.30) **Going Correction** +0.975s/f (Soft)
WFA 3 from 4yo+ 8lb **11** Ran SP% **114.7**
Speed ratings (Par 105): **107,106,101,100,99 97,95,94,91,71 53**
CSF £94.97 CT £443.35 TOTE £18.00: £5.10, £1.90, £2.10; EX 114.70 Trifecta £886.70.
Owner P Newell & Mrs R Carr **Bred** Mrs Monica Hackett **Trained** Huby, N Yorks

FOCUS
Race distance increased by 6yds. A fair and competitive handicap, though the first two eventually pulled clear. The whole field came over to the stands' rail on turning in this time. The winner recorded his best rating since late 2014.

4705 WILLIAM HILL BEST ODDS GUARANTEED APPRENTICE H'CAP 1m
5:10 (5:10) (Class 6) (0-60,60) 3-Y-O+ **£2,587** (£770; £384; £192) **Stalls** Low

Form RPR

0606 **1** **Gone With The Wind (GER)**^{27} 3750 5-9-7 **59**....(t) LewisEdmunds$^{(6)}$ 1 64
(Rebecca Bastiman) *hld up: smooth hdwy over 2f out: led over 1f out: rdn out ins fnl f* **5/2**^{2}

0631 **2** *3/4* **Galilee Chapel (IRE)**^{11} 4314 7-9-4 **50**..............................(b) RowanScott 4 53
(Alistair Whillans) *t.k.h: led to over 1f out: rdn and kpt on fnl f* **7/4**^{1}

5004 **3** *3 1/2* **Magical Lasso (IRE)**^{10} 4337 3-9-4 **60**.............................. CliffordLee$^{(2)}$ 8 54
(Keith Dalgleish) *chsd ldr: chal briefly 1/2-way: effrt over 2f out: outpcd over 1f out* **6/1**

-000 **4** *28* **Canford Kilbey (IRE)**^{8} 4425 3-8-10 **52**.............................. PatrickVaughan$^{(2)}$ 3
(Michael Easterby) *s.i.s: hld up in tch: rdn and edgd lft over 2f out: sn wknd: t.o* **12/1**

0-00 **5** *36* **Bannock Town**^{11} 4309 5-8-8 **46** oh1..............................(p) JamieGormley$^{(6)}$ 2
(Linda Perratt) *chsd ldrs tl wknd over 3f out: sn lost tch: t.o* **100/1**

2006 **U** **Drinks For Losers (IRE)**^{7} 4444 5-9-0 **46** oh1.............................. AnnaHesketh 5
(R Mike Smith) *fly-jmpd and uns rdr leaving stalls* **7/2**^{3}

1m 54.11s (10.31) **Going Correction** +0.975s/f (Soft)
WFA 3 from 5yo+ 8lb **6** Ran SP% **110.1**
Speed ratings (Par 101): **87,86,82,54,18**
CSF £6.99 CT £19.46 TOTE £3.40: £1.80, £1.50; EX 7.10 Trifecta £18.20.
Owner Mrs P Bastiman **Bred** Graf And Grafin Von Stauffenberg **Trained** Cowthorpe, N Yorks

FOCUS
Race distance increased by 6yds. A moderate apprentice handicap and a rather messy start, including Drinks For Losers getting rid of his rider exiting the gate. The winner did it well, though, with his jockey gaining his first success.
T/Plt: £157.10 to a £1 stake. Pool: £64,298.43 - 298.65 winning tickets T/Qpdt: £11.60 to a £1 stake. Pool: £7,572.04 - 480.97 winning tickets **Richard Young**

4457 WINDSOR (R-H)
Monday, July 25

OFFICIAL GOING: Good to firm (good in places; 8.5)
Wind: Moderate to fresh, behind Weather: Fine becoming cloudy

4706 ROCHFORD CONSTRUSTION LTD MAIDEN STKS 5f 10y
5:55 (5:59) (Class 5) 2-Y-O **£2,911** (£866; £432; £216) **Stalls** Low

Form RPR

4 **1** **Grey Galleon (USA)**^{14} 4205 2-9-5 0.............................. JohnFahy 7 75
(Clive Cox) *trckd ldr: rdn to ld over 1f out: hrd pressed ins fnl f: hld on wl* **2/1**^{1}

2 *hd* **Tschierschen (IRE)** 2-9-0 0..............................^{1} JimCrowley 2 69
(William Haggas) *trckd ldrs: pushed along to take 2nd fnl f and sn chalng: shkn up and kpt on wl: jst hld* **2/1**^{1}

42 **3** *4* **Sheila's Palace**^{17} 4083 2-8-11 0.............................. JosephineGordon$^{(3)}$ 4 55
(J S Moore) *led to over 1f out: sn outpcd* **7/1**^{3}

00 **4** *2 1/4* **Surfina**^{21} 3954 2-9-0 0..............................^{1} KieranO'Neill 8 47
(Dean Ivory) *chsd ldrs: rdn 2f out: fdd over 1f out* **40/1**

5 *3/4* **Everkyllachy (IRE)** 2-9-0 0.............................. DannyBrock 1 44
(J S Moore) *s.i.s: mostly in last pair: shkn up and no prog 2f out* **50/1**

6 *1* **Money In My Pocket (IRE)** 2-9-0 0.............................. PatDobbs 3 40
(Richard Hannon) *in tch whn stmbld sltly over 3f out: pushed along 2f out: wknd over 1f out* **4/1**^{2}

7 *8* **Thomas Girtin (IRE)** 2-9-5 0.............................. GeorgeBaker 5 17
(Gary Moore) *s.i.s: a bhd in last pl* **12/1**

59.56s (-0.74) **Going Correction** -0.125s/f (Firm) **7** Ran SP% **111.3**
Speed ratings (Par 94): **100,99,93,89,88 86,74**
CSF £5.62 TOTE £2.40: £1.40, £1.60; EX 7.90 Trifecta £26.60.
Owner BA Racing & R G Levin **Bred** Jsm Equine Llc Et Al **Trained** Lambourn, Berks

FOCUS
The front pair came clear in a modest maiden lacking depth.

4707 SKY BET MAIDEN STKS (PLUS 10 RACE) 6f
6:25 (6:30) (Class 4) 2-Y-O **£3,946** (£1,174; £586; £293) **Stalls** Low

Form RPR

236 **1** **Evergate**^{17} 4103 2-9-5 0.............................. JimCrowley 3 86+
(Hugo Palmer) *trckd ldr: led 2f out: rdn over 1f out: styd on wl and drew clr fnl f* **2/1**^{2}

2 **2** *4* **Mr Pocket (IRE)**^{14} 4205 2-9-5 0.............................. LukeMorris 2 73
(Paul Cole) *trckd ldng pair: rdn 2f out: chsd wnr over 1f out: kpt on but readily lft bhd fnl f* **11/8**^{1}

0 **3** *2 1/2* **Inlawed**^{16} 4161 2-9-5 0.............................. GeorgeBaker 10 65
(Ed Walker) *led to 2f out: sn rdn and outpcd: kpt on* **33/1**

6 **4** *1 1/4* **Moi Moi Moi (IRE)**^{18} 4053 2-9-5 0.............................. JimmyFortune 9 61
(Brian Meehan) *settled in last pair: pushed along 2f out: styd on wl on outer fr over 1f out to take 4th last strides: shaped w promise* **8/1**

06 **5** *hd* **Saxagogo**^{14} 4203 2-9-0 0.............................. TomMarquand 4 56
(George Scott) *trckd ldrs: shkn up and in tch 2f out: disp 3rd jst over 1f out: wknd* **66/1**

0 **6** *shd* **Gala Celebration (IRE)**[21] 3954 2-9-5 0 JoeyHaynes 8 60
(John Gallagher) *trckd ldrs on outer: shkn up 2f out: disp 3rd jst over 1f out: wknd* **50/1**

3 **7** *1* **Company**[25] 3812 2-9-0 0 PatDobbs 1 52
(Richard Hannon) *trckd ldrs in 6th: rdn over 2f out: outpcd over 1f out* **6/1**[3]

0 **8** *1/2* **Rakematiz**[24] 3859 2-9-5 0 WilliamTwiston-Davies 7 55
(Brett Johnson) *a in rr: shkn up on outer 2f out and no prog: kpt on ins fnl f* **100/1**

9 *3/4* **King's Coinage (IRE)** 2-9-5 0 AndreaAtzeni 11 53
(Ed Walker) *s.i.s: a in rr: nvr a factor but pushed along and kpt on ins fnl f* **25/1**

10 *3 1/2* **Casaclare (IRE)** 2-9-5 0 FergusSweeney 6 42
(Jonjo O'Neill) *s.i.s: a wl in rr: shkn up and no prog 2f out* **50/1**

55 **11** *1/2* **Party Nights**[21] 3947 2-9-0 0 MartinLane 5 35
(Luca Cumani) *a towards rr: nudged along and wknd over 1f out* **20/1**

1m 12.04s (-0.96) **Going Correction** -0.125s/f (Firm) **11** Ran SP% **118.8**
Speed ratings (Par 96): **101,95,92,90,90 90,88,88,87,82 81**
CSF £4.86 TOTE £2.90: £1.10, £1.10, £8.60; EX 5.30 Trifecta £72.70.
Owner V I Araci **Bred** V I Araci **Trained** Newmarket, Suffolk

FOCUS
Average maiden form, but a nice step forward from the winner with more to come.

4708 SKY BET WINDSOR SERIES FILLIES' H'CAP (A QUALIFIER FOR THE WINDSOR SPRINT SERIES FINAL) 6f
7:00 (7:00) (Class 4) (0-80,80) 3-Y-O+ **£6,469** (£1,925; £962; £481) **Stalls** Low

Form RPR
1435 **1** **Pretty Bubbles**[60] 2621 7-9-10 78 (v) GeorgeBaker 8 90
(J R Jenkins) *hld up in last pair: smooth prog on outer over 2f out to ld over 1f out: in n.d whn shkn up fnl f: comf* **9/1**

3111 **2** *2 1/4* **Inclination (IRE)**[16] 4155 3-9-4 77 RyanTate 6 81
(Clive Cox) *trckd ldr: rdn to chal and upsides over 1f out: chsd wnr after: styd on but no ch* **15/8**[1]

0-43 **3** *2 1/4* **Symposium**[16] 4134 3-9-3 76 AndreaAtzeni 3 73
(William Haggas) *trckd ldrs: waiting for a gap over 2f out: eased out over 1f out: pushed along to chse ldng pair fnl f: no imp and jst hld on for 3rd* **2/1**[2]

513 **4** *nse* **Shypen**[31] 3625 3-8-7 73 JaneElliott(7) 1 70+
(George Margarson) *t.k.h: hld up bhd ldrs: nt clr run over 2f out and dropped to last over 1f out: shkn up and r.o fnl f: nrly snatched 3rd* **6/1**[3]

2300 **5** *1/2* **Lucky Di**[19] 4014 6-9-1 69 CharlesBishop 4 65
(Peter Hedger) *hld up in last pair: nt clr run over 2f out tl swtchd outside over 1f out: shuffled along and kpt on: nvr involved* **25/1**

410- **6** *1* **Bint Aldar**[319] 6244 3-9-7 80 LukeMorris 5 72
(Robert Cowell) *led to over 1f out: wknd fnl f* **12/1**

40-0 **7** *3 1/2* **Spiraea**[9] 4398 6-9-9 77 TomMarquand 7 59
(Andrew Reid) *chsd ldrs: drvn 2f out: lost pl over 1f out: wknd* **14/1**

-000 **8** *nk* **Veena (FR)**[9] 4398 3-9-4 77 FergusSweeney 2 57
(David Simcock) *in tch in midfield: rdn 2f out: wknd over 1f out* **16/1**

1m 11.37s (-1.63) **Going Correction** -0.125s/f (Firm)
WFA 3 from 6yo+ 5lb **8** Ran SP% **116.5**
Speed ratings (Par 102): **105,102,99,98,98 96,92,91**
CSF £26.87 CT £48.69 TOTE £10.10: £2.30, £1.30, £1.10; EX 29.10 Trifecta £93.00.
Owner Mark Goldstein **Bred** Southill Stud **Trained** Royston, Herts

FOCUS
A fair sprint with the winner rated close to her best.

4709 SKY BET TOP PRICE EVERY FAVOURITE H'CAP 1m 67y
7:30 (7:30) (Class 4) (0-80,80) 3-Y-O **£4,690** (£1,395; £697; £348) **Stalls** Low

Form RPR
-252 **1** **September Stars (IRE)**[20] 3990 3-9-5 80 JimCrowley 2 91+
(Ralph Beckett) *trckd ldr: pushed into ld wl over 1f out: shkn up sn after: drew clr fnl f: readily* **9/4**[1]

1241 **2** *3 1/2* **Feed The Goater (FR)**[11] 4288 3-9-3 78 TomMarquand 5 81
(Richard Hannon) *in tch: pushed along 3f out: rdn to chse wnr over 1f out: one pce and readily lft bhd* **11/4**[2]

4034 **3** *1 1/2* **Handytalk (IRE)**[16] 4157 3-8-10 78 GeorgeWood(7) 1 78
(Rod Millman) *racd in last: pushed along over 3f out: tried to cl 2f out: nvr gng pce to threaten but tk 3rd nr fin* **5/1**[3]

3-00 **4** *nse* **Ocean Eleven**[40] 3269 3-8-13 77 JosephineGordon(3) 4 76
(John Ryan) *chsd ldng pair: urged along over 3f out: lost pl but tried to cl 2f out: nvr gng pce to threaten* **20/1**

-436 **5** *hd* **Chester Street**[44] 3156 3-9-5 80 (b) GeorgeBaker 3 79
(Roger Charlton) *led and racd freely: shkn up and hdd wl over 1f out: sn btn: lost 2 pls nr fin* **9/4**[1]

1m 42.08s (-2.62) **Going Correction** -0.125s/f (Firm) **5** Ran SP% **109.6**
Speed ratings (Par 102): **108,104,103,102,102**
CSF £8.65 TOTE £3.00: £1.70, £1.60; EX 9.10 Trifecta £23.50.
Owner Andrew Rosen & Edward W Easton **Bred** John Connaughton **Trained** Kimpton, Hants

FOCUS
Race distance increased by 36yds. An ordinary handicap and the winner improved back down in trip.

4710 SKY BET H'CAP 1m 2f 7y
8:00 (8:01) (Class 4) (0-85,85) 3-Y-O+ **£4,690** (£1,395; £697; £348) **Stalls** Centre

Form RPR
1-34 **1** **Rock Steady (IRE)**[19] 4010 3-8-12 79 WilliamTwiston-Davies 5 86
(Roger Charlton) *awkward to post: hld up in midfield: prog on outer 2f out: rdn to chse ldr ins fnl f: styd on wl to ld nr fin* **7/2**[2]

0202 **2** *1/2* **Cape Banjo (USA)**[19] 3996 3-8-10 77 AndreaAtzeni 6 83
(Ralph Beckett) *sweating: hld up in midfield: pushed along and prog on outer to trck ldng pair 2f out: rdn to ld 1f out: kpt on but hdd nr fin* **9/1**

0201 **3** *1* **Prendergast Hill (IRE)**[14] 4208 4-9-13 84 (p) JimCrowley 4 88
(Ed de Giles) *led: rdn and hdd 2f out: kpt on and stl upsides 1f out: one pce fnl f* **3/1**[1]

4322 **4** *nk* **Rotherwick (IRE)**[14] 4208 4-10-0 85 (bt) LukeMorris 9 88
(Paul Cole) *t.k.h: pressed ldr: rdn to ld narrowly 2f out but sn u.str.p: hdd and nt qckn 1f out* **9/2**

-501 **5** *1 1/4* **Thames Knight**[18] 4050 4-9-7 78 RoystonFfrench 8 79
(Marcus Tregoning) *trckd ldng pair: drvn over 2f out: lost pl sn after: one pce and n.d fnl f* **16/1**

2102 **6** *1/2* **Banish (USA)**[21] 3957 3-9-4 85 (tp) GeorgeBaker 2 85
(Hugo Palmer) *s.s: hld up in detached last: taken wd and tried to cl on ldrs over 2f out: no imp over 1f out: fdd* **4/1**[3]

15 **7** *1/2* **Youre Always Right (IRE)**[32] 3574 3-9-1 82 JohnFahy 3 81
(Clive Cox) *trckd ldng pair: rdn over 2f out: sn lost pl on inner: no hdwy fnl f* **8/1**

0305 **8** *1* **Smaih (GER)**[14] 4199 4-9-10 81 TimmyMurphy 1 78
(Jamie Osborne) *hld up off the pce in 7th: dropped to last 3f out: pushed along over 2f out: no prog but kpt on whn rdn jst over 1f out* **33/1**

2m 7.49s (-1.21) **Going Correction** -0.125s/f (Firm)
WFA 3 from 4yo 10lb **8** Ran SP% **115.3**
Speed ratings (Par 105): **99,98,97,97,96 96,95,94**
CSF £34.94 CT £104.69 TOTE £4.50: £1.30, £3.10, £1.50; EX 39.00 Trifecta £182.80.
Owner Owners Group 011 **Bred** Martin Walsh **Trained** Beckhampton, Wilts

FOCUS
Race distance increased by 36yds. A useful handicap and no surprise to see one of the 3yos come out on top. The pace was pretty steady, though.

4711 PORSCHE WEST LONDON H'CAP 1m 3f 135y
8:30 (8:30) (Class 5) (0-70,70) 4-Y-O+ **£2,911** (£866; £432; £216) **Stalls** Centre

Form RPR
045 **1** **Ravenous**[25] 3817 5-9-6 69 KieranO'Neill 1 77
(Luke Dace) *trckd ldng pair: clsd to ld over 2f out: rdn clr over 1f out: pushed out last 100yds: readily* **4/1**[3]

56 **2** *2 3/4* **Officer Drivel (IRE)**[25] 3817 5-9-5 68 JimCrowley 2 71
(Jim Best) *trckd ldr: rdn to chal over 2f out: nt qckn w wnr sn after: kpt on same pce to win battle for 2nd* **11/2**

5433 **3** *nk* **Glens Wobbly**[25] 3817 8-9-5 68 FergusSweeney 3 71
(Jonathan Geake) *led and stretched field: rdn and hdd over 2f out: one pce after* **11/4**[2]

60- **4** *1 3/4* **Guantoshol (IRE)**[35] 7593 5-9-7 70 LukeMorris 8 70
(Ian Williams) *trckd ldng trio: clsd enough over 2f out but u.p: one pce and no imp after* **25/1**

5-23 **5** *1 1/2* **Chantecler**[26] 3766 5-9-7 70 GeorgeBaker 5 67
(Neil Mulholland) *restrained s: t.k.h and hld up in detached last: lot to do whn cajoled along over 2f out: plugged on but nvr a threat* **5/2**[1]

0-05 **6** *6* **Druot**[13] 4226 4-9-0 63 RyanTate 7 50
(Richard Hughes) *nvr bttr than 5th: shkn up over 2f out: sn wknd* **8/1**

00/- **7** *8* **King Muro**[9] 7304 6-9-6 69 (t) WilliamTwiston-Davies 4 43
(Fergal O'Brien) *hld up in 6th: shkn up wl over 2f out: wknd* **9/1**

2m 29.11s (-0.39) **Going Correction** -0.125s/f (Firm) **7** Ran SP% **115.6**
Speed ratings (Par 103): **96,94,93,92,91 87,82**
CSF £26.55 CT £69.92 TOTE £4.70: £2.40, £2.80; EX 27.00 Trifecta £145.70.
Owner Copped Hall Farm & Stud **Bred** Prince Of Wales And Duchess Of Cornwall **Trained** Pulborough, W Sussex

FOCUS
Race distance increased by 36yds. A modest handicap, the field were soon strung out but little got into it. The winner has been rated to this year's form.
T/Plt: £27.70 to a £1 stake. Pool: £75,863.00 - 1,992.11 winning tickets T/Qpdt: £14.20 to a £1 stake. Pool: £7,100.20 - 368.39 winning tickets **Jonathan Neesom**

4209 WOLVERHAMPTON (A.W) (L-H)
Monday, July 25

OFFICIAL GOING: Tapeta: standard
Wind: Fresh behind Weather: Showers

4712 FCL GLOBAL FORWARDING MAKING LOGISTICS PERSONAL NURSERY H'CAP 5f 20y (Tp)
5:40 (5:40) (Class 6) 2-Y-O **£2,425** (£721; £360; £180) **Stalls** Low

Form RPR
2536 **1** **Four Dragons**[11] 4296 2-8-12 62 RichardKingscote 7 66+
(Tom Dascombe) *chsd ldr: shkn up to ld over 1f out: rdn and edgd lft ins fnl f: r.o: comf* **7/2**[2]

303 **2** *1 1/4* **Makman (IRE)**[14] 4196 2-9-7 71 PaulHanagan 6 71
(Ed Dunlop) *hld up in tch: plld hrd: rdn to chse wnr ins fnl f: edgd lft: styd on* **11/4**[1]

0201 **3** *shd* **Mightaswellsmile**[23] 3902 2-9-5 69 TomEaves 2 68
(James Given) *prom: racd keenly: rdn over 1f out: edgd lft ins fnl f: r.o* **4/1**[3]

300 **4** *1 1/4* **Kings Heart (IRE)**[18] 4053 2-9-5 69 SteveDrowne 1 64
(Mark Usher) *hld up: hdwy over 1f out: swtchd rt ins fnl f: r.o* **20/1**

2053 **5** *3* **Affordability**[13] 4221 2-9-4 68 (p) RobertWinston 4 52
(Daniel Mark Loughnane) *trckd ldrs: rdn over 1f out: no ex ins fnl f* **9/2**

3324 **6** *1/2* **Princess Holly**[52] 2874 2-9-0 64 MartinHarley 8 46
(Robert Cowell) *sn led: rdn and hdd over 1f out: wknd ins fnl f* **8/1**

000 **7** *2 1/4* **Red Shanghai (IRE)**[49] 2970 2-7-7 52 oh5 HollieDoyle(7) 3 24
(Tom Dascombe) *hld up: rdn over 2f out: hung lft and wknd over 1f out* **80/1**

0505 **8** *1 1/2* **Wentwell Yesterday (IRE)**[9] 4386 2-8-9 59 WilliamCarson 5 28
(Jamie Osborne) *hld up: rdn over 2f out: wknd wl over 1f out* **7/1**

1m 2.27s (0.37) **Going Correction** -0.025s/f (Stan) **8** Ran SP% **116.7**
Speed ratings (Par 92): **96,94,93,91,87 86,82,80**
CSF £13.91 CT £39.97 TOTE £4.30: £1.40, £2.50, £1.30; EX 18.10 Trifecta £59.50.
Owner O'Halloran Owen Satchell Willcock **Bred** Grovewood Stud **Trained** Malpas, Cheshire

FOCUS
An ordinary nursery run at a moderate gallop in which the first four were clear. A clear personal best from the winner.

4713 FCL GLOBAL FORWARDING MAKING LOGISTICS PERSONAL MAIDEN STKS 5f 20y (Tp)
6:10 (6:10) (Class 5) 2-Y-O **£3,072** (£914; £456; £228) **Stalls** Low

Form RPR
0 **1** **Dandy Flame (IRE)**[14] 4205 2-9-5 0 RenatoSouza 8 75
(Jose Santos) *led 1f: chsd ldr who sn wnt clr: shkn up to ld over 1f out: r.o wl* **200/1**

50 **2** *2 3/4* **Elegantly Bound (IRE)**[10] 4363 2-9-5 0 TomEaves 1 65
(James Given) *hld up: hdwy 1/2-way: rdn over 1f out: r.o to go 2nd wl ins fnl f: no ch w wnr* **10/1**

04 **3** *1/2* **Goodwood Crusader (IRE)**[30] 3647 2-9-5 0 ShaneKelly 4 63
(Richard Hughes) *hld up in tch: carried rt 1/2-way: hmpd 2f out: rdn and r.o ins fnl f: nt rch ldrs* **3/1**[3]

50 **4** *1 1/4* **Khelly's Edge**[73] 2219 2-9-0 0 (b[1]) AdamBeschizza 5 54
(Scott Dixon) *hmpd s: sn pushed along and prom: led 4f out: sn wnt clr: rdn and hdd over 1f out: no ex wl ins fnl f* **10/1**

5 *1 1/2* **Ballyanna** 2-9-0 0 StevieDonohoe 10 48
(John Butler) *s.s: hdwy 2f out: rdn over 1f out: no ex ins fnl f* **33/1**

436 **6** 1 **Gerrard's Return**[45] 3093 2-9-5 0 .... RichardKingscote 7 50
(Tom Dascombe) *s.i.s: hld up: racd wd fr 3f out tl swtchd lft 2f out: nvr trbld ldrs* **6/4**[1]

7 6 **Wadood (IRE)** 2-9-5 0 .... MartinHarley 2 28+
(Robert Cowell) *chsd ldrs: hung rt 1/2-way: eased and wnt lft over 1f out* **5/2**[2]

0 **8** 9 **Tess Graham**[16] 4133 2-9-0 0 .... PatrickMathers 6
(Sarah Hollinshead) *hld up: wknd 2f out* **33/1**

06 **9** 3 3/4 **Rise Of Phoenix**[23] 3897 2-9-0 0 .... WilliamCarson 9
(John Spearing) *sn drvn along and prom: wknd 1/2-way* **50/1**

1m 2.29s (0.39) **Going Correction** -0.025s/f (Stan) **9** Ran SP% **120.1**
Speed ratings (Par 94): **95,90,89,87,85 83,74,59,53**
CSF £1603.83 TOTE £50.70: £19.90, £3.00, £1.80; EX 346.90 Trifecta £5614.80.
Owner Jose Santos **Bred** Limestone & Tara Studs **Trained** Upper Lambourn, Berks

FOCUS
A surprise winner to this juvenile maiden and it is hard to know what the form is worth. It has been rated around the placed horses.

4714 FCL GLOBAL FORWARDING MAKING LOGISTICS PERSONAL H'CAP 5f 216y (Tp)
6:40 (6:41) (Class 5) (0-75,75) 3-Y-O+ **£3,072** (£914; £456; £228) **Stalls** Low

Form RPR

0141 **1** **Eljaddaaf (IRE)**[26] 3780 5-9-10 **73** .... RobertWinston 6 82+
(Dean Ivory) *hmpd sn after s: hld up: hdwy over 2f out: swtchd rt 1f out: shkn up and r.o to ld nr fin* **11/8**[1]

0120 **2** 1/2 **Lucky Lodge**[44] 3153 6-9-4 **67** .... (p) SilvestreDeSousa 3 74
(Antony Brittain) *a.p: racd keenly: rdn over 1f out: led wl ins fnl f: hdd nr fin* **15/2**[3]

4403 **3** nk **Indian Affair**[6] 4485 6-9-1 **67** .... (bt) EdwardGreatrex(3) 9 73
(Milton Bradley) *chsd ldr 1f: remained handy: wnt 2nd again over 2f out: rdn over 1f out: ev ch ins fnl f: r.o* **12/1**

1366 **4** 1/2 **Desert Strike**[19] 4014 10-9-11 **74** .... (p) MartinHarley 7 78
(Conor Dore) *led: rdn over 1f out: hdd wl ins fnl f* **14/1**

0606 **5** 3 **Doctor Parkes**[14] 4211 10-9-4 **72** .... AaronJones(5) 1 67
(Stuart Williams) *hld up: hdwy over 1f out: r.o ins fnl f: nvr nrr* **7/1**[2]

3606 **6** 1 **Dark Forest**[5] 4517 3-8-9 **70** .... (p) SophieKilloran(7) 13 61
(Simon West) *prom: chsd ldr 5f out tl rdn over 2f out: no ex fnl f* **33/1**

1-00 **7** 1/2 **Murdanova (IRE)**[47] 3036 3-8-12 **71** .... PaddyBradley(5) 10 60
(Kevin Frost) *sn pushed along and prom: hmpd over 3f out: nt clr run over 1f out: sn rdn and swtchd lft: no ex fnl f* **33/1**

0050 **8** 2 **Piazon**[23] 3892 5-9-8 **71** .... WilliamCarson 5 55
(John Butler) *prom: rdn over 1f out: wknd ins fnl f* **20/1**

-113 **9** 3/4 **Pandar**[10] 4355 7-9-7 **73** .... DanielMuscutt(3) 12 54
(Patrick Chamings) *hld up: rdn over 2f out: nvr trbld ldrs* **11/1**

-006 **10** 1 3/4 **Billyoakes (IRE)**[162] 581 4-9-12 **75** .... AdamBeschizza 11 51
(Charlie Wallis) *prom: rdn over 2f out: wknd fnl f* **25/1**

1-06 **11** nk **Misu Mac**[24] 3847 6-9-1 **67** .... JacobButterfield(3) 2 42
(Neville Bycroft) *hld up: rdn over 1f out: nvr on terms* **66/1**

2-10 **12** 1/2 **Birkdale (IRE)**[27] 3753 3-9-7 **75** .... GrahamLee 4 47
(David O'Meara) *s.i.s: a in rr* **14/1**

0012 **13** 3/4 **City Of Angkor Wat (IRE)**[20] 3985 6-9-7 **70** .... (p) TomQueally 8 41
(Conor Dore) *hmpd sn after s: hld up: rdn over 2f out: a in rr* **16/1**

1m 14.05s (-0.45) **Going Correction** -0.025s/f (Stan)
WFA 3 from 4yo+ 5lb **13** Ran SP% **117.6**
Speed ratings (Par 103): **102,101,100,100,96 94,94,91,90,88 87,87,86**
CSF £10.33 CT £94.95 TOTE £2.00: £1.10, £2.30, £3.70; EX 12.70 Trifecta £118.90.
Owner Wentdale Ltd & Mrs L A Ivory **Bred** Shadwell Estate Company Limited **Trained** Radlett, Herts

■ Stewards' Enquiry : Aaron Jones two-day ban: careless riding (Aug 8-9)

FOCUS
Quite a competitive handicap with several coming into the race in decent form. The winner is an improving sort.

4715 LOGISTICS WITH FCL GLOBAL FORWARDING H'CAP 7f 32y (Tp)
7:10 (7:13) (Class 6) (0-65,65) 4-Y-O+ **£2,425** (£721; £360; £180) **Stalls** High

Form RPR

0000 **1** **Multitask**[19] 4014 6-9-2 **65** .... HectorCrouch(5) 6 75+
(Gary Moore) *hld up: nt clr run over 2f out: hdwy over 1f out: rdn to ld wl ins fnl f: r.o* **7/1**[3]

5002 **2** 2 1/2 **Red Unico (IRE)**[20] 3988 4-8-9 **60** .... JoshuaBryan(7) 2 64
(Brian Barr) *a.p: chsd ldr over 3f out: rdn and ev ch fr over 1f out tl styd on same pce wl ins fnl f* **7/1**[3]

2012 **3** 1 1/4 **Illusive Force (IRE)**[20] 3987 4-9-0 **61** .... (v) NoelGarbutt(3) 3 62
(Derek Shaw) *sn pushed along and prom: rdn over 1f out: styd on to go 3rd post* **9/1**

2500 **4** shd **Sooqaan**[38] 3344 5-9-6 **64** .... SilvestreDeSousa 4 65
(Antony Brittain) *led 6f out: rdn over 1f out: hdd and no ex wl ins fnl f* **7/1**[3]

0231 **5** 2 1/4 **Filament Of Gold (USA)**[28] 3732 5-8-12 **61** .... (p) GaryMahon(5) 1 56
(Roy Brotherton) *led 1f: chsd ldrs: rdn over 1f out: no ex fnl f* **5/1**[2]

2000 **6** 3 1/4 **Pyroclastic (IRE)**[19] 4005 4-9-0 **58** .... (p) RobertTart 5 45
(Nick Kent) *hld up in tch: rdn over 1f out: wknd fnl f* **33/1**

1560 **7** 3 1/2 **Hawk Moth (IRE)**[9] 4388 8-9-3 **61** .... (p) GrahamLee 8 40
(John Spearing) *rrd in stalls: hld up: nt clr run over 2f out: rdn over 1f out: nvr on terms* **25/1**

3205 **8** 2 3/4 **Veeraya**[59] 2643 6-9-4 **65** .... (bt) ShelleyBirkett(3) 12 37
(Julia Feilden) *s.i.s: hld up: nvr on terms* **8/1**

-505 **9** 3 1/4 **Steel Stockholder**[20] 3987 10-8-5 **56** .... MathewStill(7) 10 20
(Antony Brittain) *hld up: hdwy over 4f out: rdn and wknd over 2f out* **33/1**

0000 **10** hd **Nasri**[19] 4008 10-9-2 **60** .... TomQueally 7 23
(Emma Owen) *prom: chsd ldr over 5f out tl rdn over 3f out: wknd over 2f out* **40/1**

00-2 **11** 1 1/2 **What Usain**[35] 3476 4-9-1 **64** .... (v) JoshDoyle(5) 9 24
(David O'Meara) *unruly prior to the s: s.i.s: hld up: rdn over 2f out: sn wknd* **15/8**[1]

1m 28.44s (-0.36) **Going Correction** -0.025s/f (Stan) **11** Ran SP% **122.2**
Speed ratings (Par 101): **101,98,96,96,94 90,86,83,79,79 77**
CSF £55.62 CT £456.12 TOTE £11.40: £2.90, £2.40, £2.40; EX 79.60 Trifecta £1341.80.
Owner Power Geneva Ltd **Bred** Mrs L N Harmes **Trained** Lower Beeding, W Sussex

FOCUS
A decent gallop to this handicap which went to a well-supported winner who was rated in the low 80s last year.

4716 FCL GLOBAL FORWARDING H'CAP 1m 4f 50y (Tp)
7:40 (7:40) (Class 6) (0-65,65) 4-Y-O+ **£2,425** (£721; £360; £180) **Stalls** Low

Form RPR

00/0 **1** **Mr Lando**[8] 877 7-8-10 **54** .... (b[1]) StevieDonohoe 1 60
(Johnny Farrelly) *mde all: rdn over 2f out: styd on u.p* **8/1**

3534 **2** nk **Cool Music (IRE)**[24] 3842 6-8-12 **56** .... SilvestreDeSousa 9 62
(Antony Brittain) *a.p: rdn over 2f out: chsd wnr ins fnl f: styd on u.p* **10/3**[2]

00-0 **3** 1/2 **Gracesome (IRE)**[73] 2205 5-8-6 **50** .... HarryBentley 3 55
(Michael Blanshard) *hld up in tch: racd keenly: rdn over 3f out: nt clr run over 1f out: r.o* **50/1**

3311 **4** nk **Yasir (USA)**[14] 4212 8-8-10 **61** .... SophieKilloran(7) 6 65
(Conor Dore) *hld up: racd keenly: hdwy over 2f out: styd on* **3/1**[1]

56-2 **5** 1 1/4 **Cry Fury**[30] 3651 8-9-7 **65** .... SaleemGolam 7 67
(Sophie Leech) *chsd wnr: rdn over 2f out: no ex ins fnl f* **14/1**

-60U **6** nse **Kissy Suzuki**[35] 3470 4-8-13 **62** .... CharlieBennett(5) 5 66
(Hughie Morrison) *chsd ldrs: rdn over 3f out: nt clr run ins fnl f: styd on same pce* **7/2**[3]

/605 **7** 4 1/2 **Seven Summits (IRE)**[65] 2462 9-7-9 **46** oh1 .... (t) HollieDoyle(7) 2 41
(Sophie Leech) *hld up: rdn over 2f out: n.d* **8/1**

0061 **8** 3 1/4 **Diletta Tommasa (IRE)**[13] 4225 6-8-13 **62** .... (p) PaddyBradley(5) 8 52
(Daniel Mark Loughnane) *s.s: hld up: rdn over 2f out: wknd over 1f out* **9/1**

500/ **9** 78 **Alberto**[693] 5978 6-8-2 **46** oh1 .... PatrickMathers 4
(Sarah Hollinshead) *hld up: plld hrd: wknd over 3f out* **66/1**

2m 40.98s (0.18) **Going Correction** -0.025s/f (Stan) **9** Ran SP% **112.6**
Speed ratings (Par 101): **98,97,97,97,96 96,93,91,39**
CSF £33.85 CT £1242.73 TOTE £11.70: £4.20, £1.60, £3.30; EX 43.80 Trifecta £1390.80.
Owner Mrs Alison Batchelor **Bred** Capitana Partnership **Trained** Enmore, Somerset

FOCUS
A slow gallop and a result to treat with caution as it was run to suit to prominent racers.

4717 FCLGF.COM H'CAP 1m 141y (Tp)
8:10 (8:10) (Class 4) (0-85,85) 3-Y-O+ **£4,851** (£1,443; £721; £360) **Stalls** Low

Form RPR

4200 **1** **Ilzam (IRE)**[25] 3824 3-8-11 **77** .... (t) HarryBentley 5 84
(Marco Botti) *trckd ldrs: racd keenly: chsd ldr over 1f out: r.o to ld wl ins fnl f* **11/2**[3]

0014 **2** 3/4 **Ravenhoe (IRE)**[10] 4358 3-8-6 **72** .... SilvestreDeSousa 6 77
(Mark Johnston) *led at stdy pce tl qcknd over 3f out: rdn over 1f out: hdd wl ins fnl f* **4/1**[1]

5111 **3** shd **Vastly (USA)**[14] 4201 7-8-13 **70** .... (t) SaleemGolam 3 76+
(Sophie Leech) *hld up: rdn and r.o ins fnl f: nt quite rch ldrs* **12/1**

6000 **4** hd **Charlie Bear**[14] 4208 4-9-9 **80** .... WilliamCarson 9 85
(Jamie Osborne) *mid-div: shkn up over 2f out: rdn over 1f out: r.o ins fnl f: nt rch ldrs* **12/1**

0060 **5** 1 1/4 **Pivotman**[17] 4113 8-9-3 **74** .... (bt) MartinHarley 1 76+
(Michael Easterby) *hld up in tch: nt clr run fr over 2f out tl shkn up 1f out: styd on same pce ins fnl f* **9/1**

410 **6** 1/2 **Berlusca (IRE)**[17] 4113 7-9-9 **85** .... JoshDoyle(5) 2 86+
(David O'Meara) *hld up: nt clr run over 2f out: hdwy and nt clr run over 1f out: swtchd lft and styd on ins fnl f: nt rch ldrs* **14/1**

-544 **7** 1 1/2 **Dark Ocean (IRE)**[23] 3884 6-9-11 **82** .... GrahamLee 7 80
(Jedd O'Keeffe) *chsd ldr tl rdn over 1f out: no ex ins fnl f* **11/2**[3]

4060 **8** 3/4 **Burano (IRE)**[9] 4407 7-9-10 **84** .... ShelleyBirkett(3) 8 80
(David O'Meara) *hld up: pushed along 3f out: nvr nrr* **17/2**

-533 **9** 3 1/4 **Avalanche Express**[20] 3989 4-9-0 **71** .... MartinDwyer 4 60
(William Muir) *plld hrd and prom: rdn over 1f out: wknd ins fnl f* **5/1**[2]

0005 **10** 4 **St Patrick's Day (IRE)**[6] 4497 4-9-8 **79** .... (v) TomEaves 10 58
(J R Jenkins) *chsd ldrs: rdn over 1f out: wknd fnl f* **50/1**

1m 48.68s (-1.42) **Going Correction** -0.025s/f (Stan)
WFA 3 from 4yo+ 9lb **10** Ran SP% **112.0**
Speed ratings (Par 105): **105,104,104,104,102 102,101,100,97,94**
CSF £26.56 CT £248.90 TOTE £5.90: £2.10, £1.60, £2.30; EX 25.50 Trifecta £64.50.
Owner Khalid Bin Ali Al Khalifa **Bred** Denis McDonnell **Trained** Newmarket, Suffolk

FOCUS
Quite a competitive handicap, but run at just an ordinary gallop.

4718 FCL GLOBAL MAKING LOGISTICS PERSONAL MAIDEN H'CAP 1m 141y (Tp)
8:40 (8:41) (Class 6) (0-65,65) 3-Y-O+ **£2,425** (£721; £360; £180) **Stalls** Low

Form RPR

-333 **1** **Bonhomie**[32] 3558 3-9-5 **65** .... MartinHarley 3 72
(Michael Bell) *mde all: rdn over 1f out: edgd lft ins fnl f: styd on* **7/4**[1]

004 **2** nk **Encore Moi**[29] 3684 3-8-11 **60** .... DanielMuscutt(3) 2 66
(Marco Botti) *chsd ldrs: wnt 2nd over 1f out: sn edgd rt: rdn and ev ch whn bmpd ins fnl f: styd on* **5/1**[3]

-006 **3** 1 1/4 **Broughtons Vision**[31] 3614 3-9-4 **64** ....[1] StevieDonohoe 5 67
(Willie Musson) *a.p: rdn over 2f out: styd on* **9/1**

6005 **4** 1/2 **King Oswald (USA)**[14] 4214 3-8-12 **58** .... HarryBentley 9 60
(James Unett) *hdwy over 6f out: rdn over 1f out: styd on* **7/1**

404 **5** 1 1/2 **Brick Lane**[44] 3145 3-9-5 **65** .... AdrianMcCarthy 6 64
(Robyn Brisland) *trckd ldrs: racd keenly: rdn over 1f out: kpt on* **18/1**

5500 **6** 1 **Dwynant**[52] 2864 3-9-0 **60** .... RyanPowell 11 57
(Kevin Frost) *chsd wnr tl rdn over 1f out: no ex ins fnl f* **80/1**

6-64 **7** 1 **Lee Bay**[32] 3578 3-9-3 **63** .... (b) RobertHavlin 1 58+
(John Gosden) *hld up in tch: rdn over 1f out: styd on same pce* **9/2**[2]

4400 **8** 1 3/4 **Sabato (IRE)**[11] 4321 3-8-4 **55** .... MeganNicholls(5) 4 46+
(Fergal O'Brien) *hld up: effrt over 2f out: wknd fnl f* **25/1**

23-0 **9** 3/4 **Baker**[185] 295 4-9-7 **65** .... (bt[1]) SamuelClarke(7) 13 56+
(Robyn Brisland) *s.s: hld up: nvr nrr* **22/1**

040- **10** nk **Quina Brook (IRE)**[350] 5219 3-9-0 **65** .... CharlieBennett(5) 12 54+
(Daniel Mark Loughnane) *hld up: rdn over 1f out: nvr on terms* **50/1**

4500 **11** 2 **Hidden Gem**[10] 4375 3-9-2 **62** .... SilvestreDeSousa 10 47+
(Ed Walker) *hld up: rdn over 1f out: n.d* **14/1**

000 **12** 1/2 **Archipentura**[28] 3720 4-9-8 **59** .... TomQueally 8 44+
(J R Jenkins) *hld up: rdn over 3f out: a in rr* **66/1**

405 **13** 4 **Thatsthewaytodoit (IRE)**[140] 858 3-8-8 **57** .... JacobButterfield(3) 7 32+
(Kevin Frost) *hld up: effrt over 2f out: hung lft and wknd over 1f out* **50/1**

1m 52.46s (2.36) **Going Correction** -0.025s/f (Stan)
WFA 3 from 4yo 9lb **13** Ran SP% **121.5**
Speed ratings (Par 101): **88,87,86,86,84 83,83,81,80,80 78,78,74**
CSF £9.76 CT £65.12 TOTE £2.50: £1.10, £2.40, £3.20; EX 14.00 Trifecta £80.60.
Owner The Queen **Bred** The Queen **Trained** Newmarket, Suffolk

FOCUS
A maiden handicap run at a moderate gallop and so a muddling result with those ridden close to the pace greatly favoured.
T/Plt: £188.90 to a £1 stake. Pool: £73,792.63 - 285.07 winning tickets T/Qpdt: £41.10 to a £1 stake. Pool: £7,724.75 - 138.75 winning tickets **Colin Roberts**

4719 - 4720a (Foreign Racing) - See Raceform Interactive

GALWAY (R-H)
Monday, July 25

OFFICIAL GOING: Hurdle course - good (good to yielding in places); flat course - yielding (good in places)

4721a CONNACHT HOTEL (Q.R.) H'CAP 2m 179y
7:20 (7:21) (70-100,97) 4-Y-O+
£34,705 (£11,176; £5,294; £2,352; £1,176; £588)

RPR
1 **Swamp Fox (IRE)**[7] 4470 4-10-1 **77** ow1 (b) MrBBrowne(7) 18 84
(Joseph G Murphy, Ire) *hld up: tk clsr order 4f out: chsd ldr in 2nd over 2f out and sn led: rdn clr appr fnl f: kpt on wl* **16/1**
2 2 1/4 **Ted Veale (IRE)**[87] 7152 9-11-4 **90** ow1 MrSClements(3) 14 95+
(A J Martin, Ire) *hld up: prog over 2f out to chse ldrs in 5th: wnt 4th ent fnl f: styd on wl into 2nd fnl 100yds: nt rch wnr* **14/1**
3 3/4 **Benkei (IRE)**[3] 4615 6-11-12 **95** (p) MrJJCodd 15 100
(H Rogers, Ire) *chsd ldrs: clsr in 3rd 5f out: on terms under 4f out and sn led: hdd 2f out and nt qckn w wnr: no ex ins fnl f and dropped to 3rd fnl 100yds* **13/2**[2]
4 3/4 **Renneti (FR)**[31] 3630 7-11-7 **90** MrPWMullins 17 94+
(W P Mullins, Ire) *racd in mid-div: clsr to chse ldrs 4f out: rdn in 4th under 3f out: no imp over 1f out: kpt on same pce into 4th cl home* **9/1**
5 1/2 **Asbury Boss (IRE)**[8] 4436 5-11-8 **91** (p) MsKWalsh 16 95
(M Halford, Ire) *chsd ldr in 2nd tl led 6f out: hdd over 3f out: no imp in 3rd ent fnl f: kpt on same pce and dropped to 5th cl home* **16/1**
6 3 1/4 **Cardinal Palace (IRE)**[12] 831 6-10-6 **78** ow1 (b) MrDLQueally(3) 8 77
(J A Nash, Ire) *hld up: prog on outer under 2f out: kpt on wl fr over 1f out under hands and heels: nvr nrr* **33/1**
7 3/4 **Lagostovegas (IRE)**[39] 3333 4-10-4 **76** MrRPQuinlan(3) 2 75
(David Harry Kelly, Ire) *chsd ldrs: dropped to mid-div at 1/2-way: rdn to cl in 6th under 2f out: no imp ent fnl f: kpt on one pce* **16/1**
8 2 3/4 **Time To Inspire (IRE)**[31] 3630 4-11-6 **94** (v[1]) MrFMaguire(5) 5 90
(D K Weld, Ire) *racd in mid-div: rdn and nt qckn 3f out: sn no imp: kpt on one pce fr over 1f out* **9/2**[1]
9 shd **Always Resolute**[6] 4491 5-10-4 **80** JJSlevin(7) 9 76
(Brian Ellison) *chsd ldrs on inner in 3rd tl wknd into mid-div 3f out: sn no ex: kpt on again clsng stages* **12/1**
10 1/2 **Chadic**[17] 6330 4-10-12 **81** (vt) MrSCrawford 4 77
(R P McNamara, Ire) *chsd early ldrs on inner: dropped to rr of mid-div 6f out: kpt on again fr 1f out: nvr on terms* **16/1**
11 2 **Synopsis**[30] 3680 4-10-12 **81** [1] MsNCarberry 3 75
(G M Lyons, Ire) *racd in mid-div: towards rr 6f out: swtchd to outer 3f out: kpt on one pce in st: nvr on terms* **22/1**
12 1 **Roconga (IRE)**[15] 4181 6-10-11 **83** MrDGLavery(3) 10 75
(E J O'Grady, Ire) *racd in mid-div: chsd ldrs in 6th 4f out: nt qckn under 3f out: sn no ex* **10/1**
13 1 3/4 **Zafayan (IRE)**[274] 7493 5-11-7 **97** (b) MrDSinnott(7) 20 87
(D K Weld, Ire) *chsd ldrs: pushed along in 3rd over 3f out: sn wknd* **25/1**
14 4 1/2 **Weather Watch (IRE)**[30] 3680 6-10-9 **83** (p) MissKHarrington(5) 1 69
(Mrs John Harrington, Ire) *racd towards rr: rdn and no threat fr 3f out: nvr a factor* **7/1**[3]
15 3 1/4 **Sretaw (IRE)**[7] 4469 7-10-0 **76** (bt) MsLO'Neill(7) 7 58
(Gavin Cromwell, Ire) *racd in mid-div: rdn and wknd over 2f out* **28/1**
16 7 **Jocular**[13] 4252 5-10-1 **77** (b) MrNBashford(7) 11 51
(Edward U Hales, Ire) *led tl hdd 6f out: wknd fr 3f out* **50/1**
17 17 **Kalann (IRE)**[8] 4436 9-11-4 **92** (bt[1]) MrJFO'Meara(5) 12 48
(Denis Gerard Hogan, Ire) *chsd ldrs: dropped to mid-div 1/2-way: nt qckn 3f out: sn no ex* **16/1**
18 9 1/2 **Gusty Rocky (IRE)**[17] 2514 7-10-7 **79** MrROHarding(3) 19 24
(Patrick J Flynn, Ire) *a towards rr: nvr a factor: eased fr under 2f out* **11/1**
19 6 **Poitin**[74] 2194 6-10-10 **84** MrKHClarke(5) 6 23
(Keith Henry Clarke, Ire) *a towards rr: nvr a factor: easedfr under 2f out* **50/1**
20 14 **Enzani (IRE)**[15] 550 5-10-5 **77** (t) MrNMcParlan(3) 13
(John C McConnell, Ire) *a towards rr: adrift 4f out: nvr a factor: t.o* **33/1**

3m 45.44s (225.44) **20** Ran SP% **136.7**
CSF £230.67 CT £1643.75 TOTE £20.10: £3.90, £3.70, £2.10, £2.70; DF 433.30 Trifecta £4559.90.
Owner T Egan **Bred** John McEnery & M L Hanrahan **Trained** Fethard, Co Tipperary
■ Stewards' Enquiry : Mr S Clements two-day ban: weighed in 1lb heavy (tbn)

FOCUS
As competitive as ever and run at a decent gallop, the opening-night feature resulted in a worthy win for a lightly-weighted horse who has shown admirable consistency. A valuable 7lb claim was an important factor.

4722 - 4723a (Foreign Racing) - See Raceform Interactive

[4450]BEVERLEY (R-H)
Tuesday, July 26

OFFICIAL GOING: Good to firm (8.0)
Wind: Moderate across Weather: Cloudy

4724 PAT AND DAVID STILL GOING STRONG (S) H'CAP (BEVERLEY MIDDLE DISTANCE SERIES) 1m 4f 16y
2:10 (2:10) (Class 6) (0-65,61) 3-Y-O+ **£2,587** (£770; £384; £192) **Stalls** Low

Form RPR
6026 1 **Chauvelin**[7] 4489 5-9-4 **51** (b) ConnorBeasley 8 57
(Richard Guest) *hld up in rr: hdwy on inner 2f out: effrt and nt clr run ent fnl f: sn swtchd lft: squeezed through and rdn to ld last 100yds* **7/2**[1]
-420 2 1 **Impeccability**[7] 4499 6-9-0 **47** RoystonFfrench 7 51
(John Mackie) *trckd ldrs on inner: hdwy 2f out: sn swtchd lft and rdn over 1f out: drvn to chal ins fnl f: kpt on* **8/1**[3]
0065 3 1/2 **Monopoli**[8] 4456 7-9-3 **50** (p) DavidNolan 10 54
(Ivan Furtado) *chsd ldrs: hdwy over 2f out: rdn over 1f out: drvn and ev ch ins fnl f: kpt on* **7/2**[1]
-046 4 nk **Aneedh**[35] 3480 6-10-0 **61** (b) JamesSullivan 4 64
(Clive Mulhall) *trckd ldng pair: pushed along over 3f out: rdn wl over 2f out and sn chsng clr ldr: clsr order and drvn over 1f out: ev ch ent fnl f: hld whn sltly hmpd and one pce last 50yds* **5/1**[2]
-406 5 1 3/4 **Pencaitland**[29] 3704 4-8-12 **45** (p) PaulMulrennan 9 45
(Noel Wilson) *cl up: led after 2f: clr over 5f out: rdn along wl over 1f out: drvn and jnd ent fnl f: hdd & wknd last 100yds* **12/1**
0-06 6 2 **Christmas Light**[13] 4260 9-8-13 **46** CamHardie 11 43
(Alan Lockwood) *hld up towards rr: pushed along and hdwy 2f out: sn rdn and kpt on fnl f* **20/1**
5005 7 1 **Eeny Mac (IRE)**[35] 3480 9-8-12 **45** PaddyAspell 6 41
(John Wainwright) *chsd ldrs: rdn along over 2f out: drvn wl over 1f out: grad wknd* **20/1**
0520 8 1 3/4 **Troy Boy**[32] 3620 6-8-5 **45** (v) RPWalsh(7) 2 38
(Rebecca Bastiman) *led 2f: chsd ldr: rdn along wl over 2f out: drvn wl over 1f out: sn wknd* **20/1**
000 9 8 **Percy's Endeavour**[14] 4235 3-8-2 **47** ow2 DuranFentiman 12 27
(Mark Walford) *midfield: pushed along over 3f out: rdn over 2f out: sn outpcd* **33/1**
0045 10 2 3/4 **Samsonite (IRE)**[9] 4424 4-9-13 **60** BarryMcHugh 1 36
(Tony Coyle) *hld up towards rr: effrt and sme hdwy on outer over 2f out: sn rdn and wknd* **5/1**[2]
6000 11 4 **Playboy Bay**[9] 4424 4-9-3 **50** TomEaves 5 19
(Ron Barr) *a towards rr* **28/1**

2m 38.07s (-1.73) **Going Correction** -0.125s/f (Firm)
WFA 3 from 4yo+ 12lb **11** Ran SP% **117.3**
Speed ratings (Par 101): **100,99,99,98,97 96,95,94,89,87 84**
CSF £29.26 CT £105.69 TOTE £4.00: £1.70, £2.50, £1.80; EX 27.20 Trifecta £100.80.The winner was bought by N Tinkler for £6,500.
Owner Mrs Alison Guest **Bred** Mr & Mrs A E Pakenham **Trained** Ingmanthorpe, W Yorks
■ Stewards' Enquiry : Connor Beasley four-day ban: careless riding (Aug 9-12)

FOCUS
The going was good to firm (watered). Rail around bottom bend moved to its narrowest position, increasing distances of races on the round course, including the opener, by 23yds. A moderate selling handicap to start and not many came into it in much form.

4725 HOLDERNESS PONY CLUB MAIDEN AUCTION STKS 5f
2:45 (2:46) (Class 5) 2-Y-O **£3,780** (£1,131; £565; £283; £141) **Stalls** Low

Form RPR
432 1 **La Casa Tarifa (IRE)**[22] 3947 2-8-10 0 PaulMulrennan 4 80+
(Mark Johnston) *trckd ldrs: hdwy 2f out: sn swtchd lft and rdn to ld ent fnl f: sn clr: kpt on strly* **3/1**[3]
32 2 5 **Jeany (IRE)**[13] 4254 2-9-0 0 ConnorBeasley 6 66
(Bryan Smart) *cl up: chal 2f out: sn rdn: led over 1f out: drvn and hdd ent fnl f: kpt on same pce* **5/2**[1]
2 3 2 1/2 **Quiet Moment (IRE)**[24] 3902 2-8-10 0 JoeyHaynes 8 53
(Ben Haslam) *in tch on wd outside: pushed along 1/2-way: rdn and sltly outpcd wl over 1f out: kpt on u.p fnl f* **11/4**[2]
0 4 hd **Rebounded**[24] 3873 2-9-1 0 JamesSullivan 5 57
(Declan Carroll) *slt ld: rdn along over 2f out: drvn and hdd over 1f out: kpt on same pce* **20/1**
00 5 1 **Flying Hope (IRE)**[8] 4451 2-8-10 0 TomEaves 3 49+
(Nigel Tinkler) *towards rr: hdwy 2f out: rdn to chse ldrs over 1f out: one pce fnl f* **50/1**
6 3/4 **Justanotherbottle (IRE)** 2-9-5 0 BarryMcHugh 10 55
(Declan Carroll) *in rr: hdwy 2f out: swtchd rt to inner and rdn over 1f out: kpt on fnl f: nrst fin* **25/1**
34 7 1/2 **Nifty Niece (IRE)**[13] 4254 2-9-0 0 PJMcDonald 1 48
(Ann Duffield) *chsd ldrs: rdn along and outpcd 1/2-way: hdwy to chse ldrs wl over 1f out: grad wknd* **16/1**
4 8 2 **Western Presence**[17] 4140 2-8-12 0 TonyHamilton 7 39
(Richard Fahey) *chsd ldrs: rdn along over 2f out: sn drvn and wknd* **8/1**
4326 9 3 **Jollydee (IRE)**[43] 3223 2-8-10 0 GrahamLee 9 26
(Paul Midgley) *a towards rr* **9/1**

1m 2.9s (-0.60) **Going Correction** 0.0s/f (Good) **9** Ran SP% **117.8**
Speed ratings (Par 94): **104,96,92,91,90 88,88,84,80**
CSF £10.96 TOTE £4.00: £1.50, £1.20, £1.50; EX 12.50 Trifecta £35.10.
Owner Kingsley Park 5 **Bred** Tony Kilduff **Trained** Middleham Moor, N Yorks

FOCUS
Race distance as advertised. An ordinary maiden auction event, though several of these had already been placed. The winner continues to progress.

4726 ROBERTA MARSHALL MEMORIAL H'CAP 5f
3:20 (3:21) (Class 5) (0-75,74) 3-Y-O+ **£3,780** (£1,131; £565; £283; £141) **Stalls** Low

Form RPR
0122 1 **Bond Bombshell**[9] 4426 3-8-9 **67** JoshDoyle(5) 3 74
(David O'Meara) *led 1f: chsd clr ldr: hdwy wl over 1f out: sn rdn: drvn ins fnl f: kpt on wl to ld nr fin* **9/2**[3]
5000 2 1/2 **Flicka's Boy**[2] 4689 4-9-8 **71** (t) BarryMcHugh 1 77
(Tony Coyle) *chsd clr ldr: rdn along and hdwy wl over 1f out: drvn to ld last 100yds: hdd and no ex nr fin* **7/1**
2140 3 1 1/4 **Burtonwood**[8] 4452 4-8-12 **68** KieranSchofield(7) 6 70
(Julie Camacho) *towards rr: rdn along over 2f out: hdwy whn rdr lost irons over 1f out: kpt on ins fnl f* **14/1**
0550 4 3/4 **Captain Bob (IRE)**[18] 4079 5-9-10 **73** PaulMulrennan 5 72
(Robert Cowell) *wnt lft s and sn bhd: rdn along over 2f out: swtchd lft to wd outside and drvn over 1f out: fin wl* **11/4**[2]
5035 5 nse **Noodles Blue Boy**[12] 4295 10-9-2 **68** (p) JacobButterfield(3) 2 67
(Ollie Pears) *dwlt: rapid hdwy to ld after 1f and sn clr: rdn over 1f out: drvn ins fnl f: hdd & wknd last 100yds* **10/1**
-606 6 3/4 **Innocently (IRE)**[8] 4452 5-8-11 **67** (p) PatrickVaughan(7) 4 63
(David O'Meara) *t.k.h: cl up 1f: chsd clr ldr: rdn wl over 1f out: sn drvn and wknd* **10/1**
2212 7 2 **Oriental Splendour (IRE)**[8] 4452 4-9-8 **71** JamesSullivan 8 60
(Ruth Carr) *in tch: rdn along over 2f out: drvn wl over 1f out: sn btn* **9/4**[1]

1m 2.9s (-0.60) **Going Correction** 0.0s/f (Good)
WFA 3 from 4yo+ 4lb **7** Ran SP% **113.0**
Speed ratings (Par 103): **104,103,101,100,99 98,95**
CSF £34.28 CT £402.75 TOTE £4.60: £1.70, £4.10; EX 38.80 Trifecta £235.30.
Owner Trendy Ladies **Bred** Mrs P M A Avison **Trained** Upper Helmsley, N Yorks

FOCUS
Race distance as advertised. An ordinary sprint handicap, but quite a dramatic race and a small personal best from the winner.

4727 WILFORD WATTS MEMORIAL H'CAP — 1m 100y
3:55 (3:55) (Class 4) (0-85,88) 3-Y-O+ £6,301 (£1,886; £943; £472; £235) Stalls Low

Form RPR
0233 1 **Dawn Mirage**[12] 4307 4-9-5 76 ... TonyHamilton 4 85
(Richard Fahey) *cl up: led 7f out: stdd pce 5f out: jnd over 2f out: rdn and qcknd wl over 1f out: drvn and kpt on strly fnl f* **3/1**[3]
4511 2 2 **Final**[14] 4232 4-9-10 81 ... PaulMulrennan 2 85
(Mark Johnston) *trckd ldrs: pushed along 3f out: hdwy 2f out: rdn to chse ldng pair wl over 1f out: drvn and kpt on fnl f* **9/4**[2]
5021 3 hd **Jacbequick**[8] 4453 5-9-12 88 6ex ... (v) JoshDoyle(5) 1 92
(David O'Meara) *t.k.h: trckd ldng pair: hdwy to trck wnr over 4f out: chal jst over 2f out: sn rdn: drvn appr fnl f: kpt on same pce* **2/1**[1]
1062 4 3 **Dubai Dynamo**[10] 4408 11-10-0 85 ... PJMcDonald 6 82
(Ruth Carr) *hld up in rr: hdwy 2f out: rdn to chse ldrs over 1f out: sn drvn and no imp* **8/1**
1-05 5 2 **Bronte Flyer**[19] 4036 3-8-3 73 ... (p) RowanScott(5) 5 63
(Ann Duffield) *hld up in rr: hdwy on outer 3f out: rdn along 2f out: sn drvn and wknd* **20/1**
0003 6 19 **Homeland (IRE)**[14] 4232 4-9-2 73 ... (t) JamesSullivan 3 21
(Brian Rothwell) *led: hdd 7f out: trckd ldng pair on inner: rdn along wl over 2f out: sn wknd* **14/1**

1m 45.13s (-2.47) **Going Correction** -0.125s/f (Firm)
WFA 3 from 4yo+ 8lb 6 Ran SP% **111.6**
Speed ratings (Par 105): **107,105,104,101,99 80**
CSF £10.07 TOTE £3.50: £1.80, £1.50; EX 10.40 Trifecta £26.60.
Owner Merchants and Missionaries **Bred** Kilcarn Stud **Trained** Musley Bank, N Yorks

FOCUS
Race distance increased by 23yds. A fair handicap, but they didn't seem to go that quick and the winner was always best placed.

4728 IRISH STALLION FARMS EBF MAIDEN STKS — 7f 100y
4:30 (4:30) (Class 5) 2-Y-O £3,780 (£1,131; £565; £283) Stalls Low

Form RPR
0003 1 **Melesina (IRE)**[19] 4037 2-9-0 0 ... TonyHamilton 4 73+
(Richard Fahey) *cl up: led 3f out: rdn clr over 1f out: drvn ins fnl f: kpt on wl* **5/4**[2]
55 2 nk **Miss Bates**[29] 3705 2-9-0 0 ... PJMcDonald 2 72
(Ann Duffield) *towards rr: hdwy to chse ldng pair over 4f out: effrt over 2f out: rdn wl over 1f out: drvn to chse wnr ins fnl f: kpt on wl towards fin* **8/1**[3]
62 3 2 **Laureate**[19] 4037 2-9-0 0 ... PaulMulrennan 1 68+
(Mark Johnston) *sn slt ld: pushed along and hdd 3f out: rdn over 2f out: drvn over 1f out: kpt on same pce* **5/6**[1]
0246 4 57 **Smiley Riley (IRE)**[11] 4364 2-9-5 0 ... BarryMcHugh 3
(Tony Coyle) *sn outpcd and a wl bhd* **20/1**

1m 33.15s (-0.65) **Going Correction** -0.125s/f (Firm) 4 Ran SP% **114.9**
Speed ratings (Par 94): **98,97,95,30**
CSF £10.73 TOTE £2.00; EX 12.70 Trifecta £15.10.
Owner Nick Bradley Racing (Lastroseofsummer) **Bred** Duggan Bloodstock **Trained** Musley Bank, N Yorks

FOCUS
Race distance increased by 23yds. This maiden looked a match between two fillies who had met each other last time out, but the pair took each other on from the start and nearly conspired to hand the race to one of the outsiders.

4729 IN LOVING MEMORY OF AIDAN MCARDLE "MAC" H'CAP — 7f 100y
5:05 (5:06) (Class 5) (0-70,70) 3-Y-O+ £3,780 (£1,131; £565; £283; £141) Stalls Low

Form RPR
6030 1 **Arcane Dancer (IRE)**[8] 4454 3-8-12 61 ... (p) CamHardie 2 66+
(Lawrence Mullaney) *trckd ldrs on inner: hdwy wl over 1f out: n.m.r and swtchd lft jst ins fnl f: rdn and styd on wl to ld nr fin* **13/2**[3]
3020 2 1 **Talent Scout (IRE)**[14] 4231 10-9-4 65 ... (p) GemmaTutty(5) 7 70
(Karen Tutty) *trckd ldr on inner: effrt wl over 1f out and sn rdn: ev ch ins fnl f: no ex towards fin* **12/1**
0510 3 hd **Mercury**[12] 4314 4-9-4 60 ... (b) KevinStott 5 65
(Kevin Ryan) *trckd ldrs: hdwy 2f out: rdn to ld ins fnl f: sn drvn: hdd and no ex towards fin* **9/1**
0002 4 3/4 **Faintly (USA)**[8] 4454 5-9-9 65 ... JamesSullivan 3 68
(Ruth Carr) *hld up towards rr: hdwy on outer over 2f out: rdn to chse ldrs over 1f out: drvn and kpt on fnl f* **3/1**[1]
2233 5 3/4 **Relight My Fire**[8] 4453 6-9-9 68 ... (p) RachelRichardson(3) 13 69
(Tim Easterby) *trckd ldrs: hdwy over 2f out: rdn over 1f out: drvn and kpt on same pce fnl f* **3/1**[1]
0004 6 nk **Mr Cool Cash**[18] 4102 4-9-11 67 ... (t) ConnorBeasley 9 67
(Richard Guest) *trckd ldng pair: hdwy and cl up 3f out: rdn to chal over 1f out: drvn and led briefly ent fnl f: sn hdd & wknd* **6/1**[2]
-000 7 4 1/2 **Gambino (IRE)**[50] 2960 6-9-9 70 ... JordanVaughan(5) 11 59
(John David Riches) *rrd and lost several l s: bhd: tk cl order 4f out: rdn along wl over 2f out: plugged on* **12/1**
0 8 8 **Sekuras Girl (IRE)**[80] 2053 4-8-9 51 ... (p) BarryMcHugh 6 20
(Clive Mulhall) *led: rdn along 2f out: drvn over 1f out: hdd & wknd ins fnl f* **25/1**
4220 9 7 **Dasheen**[18] 4102 3-9-6 69 ... PaulMulrennan 8 17
(Mark Johnston) *a towards rr* **9/1**
2000 10 24 **Afkar (IRE)**[29] 3729 8-9-4 65 ... (p) LanceBetts(5) 4
(Ivan Furtado) *towards rr: stmbld bdly 5f out: bhd after* **25/1**

1m 32.17s (-1.63) **Going Correction** -0.125s/f (Firm)
WFA 3 from 4yo+ 7lb 10 Ran SP% **120.7**
Speed ratings (Par 103): **104,102,102,101,100 100,95,86,78,50**
CSF £84.38 CT £718.30 TOTE £7.80: £2.40, £2.70, £2.90; EX 100.70 Trifecta £1257.50.
Owner S Rimmer **Bred** Eimear Mulhern & Abbeville Stud **Trained** Great Habton, N Yorks

FOCUS
Race distance increased by 23yds. An ordinary handicap and the first six finished in a bit of a heap. The race has been rated around the placed horses.

4730 LADY JANE BETHELL MEMORIAL H'CAP (FOR LADY AMATEUR RIDERS) — 1m 1f 207y
5:35 (5:35) (Class 6) (0-65,65) 3-Y-O+ £2,495 (£774; £386; £193) Stalls Low

Form RPR
6030 1 **I'm Super Too (IRE)**[8] 4456 9-9-10 54 ... MissETodd(3) 3 62
(Karen Tutty) *hld up towards rr: hdwy wl over 2f out: chsd ldrs over 1f out: rdn to chal ins fnl f: kpt on to ld last 50yds* **10/1**
4566 2 3/4 **Rubis**[14] 4233 3-8-10 52 ... MissEmilyBullock(5) 8 59
(Richard Fahey) *chsd ldng pair: hdwy 2f out: rdn over 1f out: chsd ldr ent fnl f: sn drvn and kpt on* **8/1**
0U10 3 3/4 **Lean On Pete (IRE)**[25] 3842 7-10-4 59 ... MissCWalton 9 64
(Ollie Pears) *led: rdn clr wl over 1f out: drvn ent fnl f: hdd and no ex last 50yds* **9/1**
4551 4 1 1/2 **San Cassiano (IRE)**[14] 4234 9-10-9 64 ... (b) MissSBrotherton 6 66
(Ruth Carr) *trckd ldr: cl up 1/2-way: rdn along over 2f out: drvn wl over 1f out: kpt on same pce* **5/2**[1]
6644 5 2 **Jersey Jewel (FR)**[14] 4234 4-10-5 65 ... MissCAGreenway(5) 4 64
(Tom Dascombe) *trckd ldrs: pushed along over 2f out: rdn over 1f out: sn drvn and no imp fnl f* **8/1**
30 6 6 **Bollihope**[101] 1500 4-10-2 60 ... MissBeckySmith(3) 2 47
(Richard Guest) *chsd ldrs: wd st: rdn over 2f out: sn one pce* **7/1**[3]
60-0 7 3 1/4 **Yawail**[8] 4456 5-9-4 52 ow3 ... (p) MissFMcSharry(7) 11 33
(Brian Rothwell) *a towards rr* **50/1**
06/5 8 1/2 **Pevensey (IRE)**[14] 4234 14-10-4 59 ... MissJoannaMason 10 39
(Jacqueline Coward) *dwlt: a in rr* **16/1**
4643 9 2 1/2 **Weld Al Khawaneej (IRE)**[8] 4454 3-9-5 63 ... MissHTLees(7) 1 38
(Kevin Ryan) *hld up: a towards rr* **3/1**[2]
60-P 10 24 **Shavaughn**[6] 4516 4-9-11 55 ... (b) MissPFuller(3) 5
(Alexandra Dunn) *in tch: rdn along 4f out: sn wknd* **66/1**

2m 3.85s (-3.15) **Going Correction** -0.125s/f (Firm)
WFA 3 from 4yo+ 10lb 10 Ran SP% **116.7**
Speed ratings (Par 101): **107,106,105,104,103 98,95,95,93,74**
CSF £87.49 CT £752.43 TOTE £12.40: £2.30, £2.50, £2.20; EX 105.20 Trifecta £869.20.
Owner Grange Park Racing (Tutty Trio) **Bred** Norelands Bloodstock, J Hanly & H Lascelles **Trained** Osmotherley, N Yorks

FOCUS
Race distance increased by 23yds. A moderate lady amateurs' handicap with the winner, fourth and fifth having met each other here a fortnight earlier. The pace was sound and the race has been rated around the balance of the principals.
T/Plt: £98.50 to a £1 stake. Pool of £49338.88 - 365.65 winning tickets. T/Qpdt: £59.20 to a £1 stake. Pool of £2954.08 - 36.9 winning tickets. **Joe Rowntree**

3348 GOODWOOD (R-H)
Tuesday, July 26

OFFICIAL GOING: Straight course - good; round course - good to firm (good in places)
Wind: light, across Weather: overcast, bright spells after race 1

4731 MATCHBOOK BETTING EXCHANGE STKS (H'CAP) — 1m 1f 192y
2:00 (2:00) (Class 2) 4-Y-O+
£31,125 (£9,320; £4,660; £2,330; £1,165; £585) Stalls Low

Form RPR
0606 1 **Fire Fighting (IRE)**[17] 4165 5-9-5 102 ... (b) AdamKirby 16 113
(Mark Johnston) *lw: hld up in tch in midfield: rdn and hdwy to chal 2f out: drvn to ld jst over 1f out: styd on u.p to forge ahd ins fnl f: pressed towards fin but a holding on* **8/1**[1]
6120 2 nk **Oasis Fantasy (IRE)**[17] 4165 5-9-1 98 ... (b) SilvestreDeSousa 7 108
(Ed Dunlop) *hld up in tch in midfield: travelling wl and nt clr run over 2f out: rdn and hdwy to chse ldrs over 1f out: wnt 2nd and drifted rt 150yds out: styd on and clsng on wnr towards fin but nvr quite getting to wnr* **12/1**
/001 3 1 1/2 **Stars Over The Sea (USA)**[10] 4396 5-8-10 93 ... FrannyNorton 6 100
(Mark Johnston) *t.k.h: chsd ldr tl led 3f out: sn rdn and jnd 2f out: hdd jst over 1f out: no ex ins fnl f and one pce fnl 100yds* **8/1**[1]
41-2 4 1/2 **Second Wave (IRE)**[38] 3383 4-9-9 106 ... JamesDoyle 8 112
(Charlie Appleby) *lw: hld up in midfield: effrt 3f out: rdn and hdwy to chse ldrs over 1f out: styd on ins fnl f: nvr quite enough pce to get on terms* **8/1**[1]
-060 5 2 **Best Of Times**[24] 3910 4-9-8 105 ... (p) HarryBentley 12 107
(Saeed bin Suroor) *hld up in tch in midfield: gd hdwy over 2f out: ev ch 2f out: rdn over 1f out: no ex and btn ins fnl f: wknd fnl 75yds* **11/1**[3]
4142 6 2 1/2 **Snoano**[10] 4407 4-8-12 95 ... DavidAllan 17 92+
(Tim Easterby) *hld up in tch in last quartet: effrt and swtchd lft 2f out: sme hdwy u.p over 1f out: styd on same pce ins fnl f: nvr trbld ldrs* **14/1**
3010 7 nse **Mutamakkin (USA)**[24] 3910 4-8-13 96 ... PaulHanagan 1 93
(Sir Michael Stoute) *lw: hld up in midfield: effrt over 2f out: no imp u.p and outpcd over 1f out: kpt on same pce fnl f* **10/1**[2]
05-1 8 nse **Balmoral Castle**[90] 1775 7-8-12 95 ... RyanTate 18 92+
(Jonathan Portman) *broke wl and styd wd early: sn stdd bk and hld up towards rr: rdn and hdwy jst over 2f out: 6th and no imp 1f out: kpt on same pce after: nvr threatened ldrs* **16/1**
2324 9 2 1/4 **Erik The Red (FR)**[19] 4070 4-9-0 97 ... RyanMoore 14 89
(Kevin Ryan) *hld up in tch in last quartet: swtchd lft and effrt wl over 1f out: sme prog over 1f out but nvr on terms w ldrs: styd on same pce fnl f* **8/1**[1]
1200 10 1 1/2 **Silver Quay (IRE)**[86] 1885 4-8-9 92 ... SeanLevey 15 81
(Richard Hannon) *hld up in tch in last quartet: swtchd lft and effrt on outer wl over 1f out: kpt on to pass btn horses ins fnl f: nvr trbld ldrs* **50/1**
0020 11 hd **Watersmeet**[24] 3889 5-9-1 98 ... JoeFanning 11 87
(Mark Johnston) *chsd ldrs: rdn ent fnl 2f: outpcd u.p and btn over 1f out: wknd ins fnl f* **20/1**
0104 12 6 **Imshivalla (IRE)**[17] 4163 5-8-10 93 ... TomQueally 5 70
(Richard Fahey) *nvr really travelling wl: in midfield tl lost pl and towards rr 1/2-way: rdn over 3f out: wknd over 1f out* **33/1**
1300 13 2 3/4 **Noble Gift**[24] 3913 6-8-12 100 ... CallumShepherd(5) 2 71
(William Knight) *led tl 3f out: sn rdn and unable qck: lost pl and btn over 1f out: sn wknd* **25/1**
-451 14 1 3/4 **Shakopee**[12] 4300 4-8-9 92 ... JamieSpencer 3 60
(Luca Cumani) *hld up in midfield: effrt jst over 2f out: no imp and btn over 1f out: wknd fnl f* **8/1**[1]
1130 15 1 1/4 **Revolutionist (IRE)**[17] 4165 4-9-10 107 ... JamesMcDonald 13 72
(Mark Johnston) *chsd ldrs tl lost pl 3f out: bhd over 1f out* **11/1**[3]
006 16 6 **Storm Rock**[30] 3688 4-8-10 93 ... DavidProbert 9 46
(Harry Dunlop) *hld up in tch in last quartet: rdn 3f out: no hdwy: wl bhd over 1f out: eased ins fnl f* **33/1**

1100 **17** *12* **Our Channel (USA)**[17] 4165 5-9-1 **98**..........................(p) AndreaAtzeni 4 27
(William Haggas) *swtg: t.k.h: chsd ldrs tl lost pl qckly over 3f out: bhd 2f out: eased over 1f out: t.o* **20/1**

2m 3.6s (-4.50) **Going Correction** -0.05s/f (Good) **17** Ran SP% **122.8**
Speed ratings (Par 109): **116,115,114,114,112 110,110,110,108,107 107,102,100,98,97 93,83**
CSF £93.08 CT £807.97 TOTE £8.00: £1.90, £2.50, £2.70, £2.30; EX 114.70 Trifecta £2604.60.

Owner A D Spence **Bred** P Bellaiche **Trained** Middleham Moor, N Yorks

FOCUS
The watered ground (10mm a day) was given as good on the straight track and good to firm, good in places on the round course (GoingStick: 8.1). The rail from the 6f marker on the lower bend to the winning post was dolled out 6yds, increasing distances by 12yds. The top bend was dolled out 3yds, increasing race distances by 8yds. They went 8-1 the field in this fiercely competitive handicap, and the form looks very solid.

4732 QATAR VINTAGE STKS (GROUP 2) 7f
2:35 (2:35) (Class 1) 2-Y-O

£113,420 (£43,000; £21,520; £10,720; £5,380; £2,700) **Stalls** Low

Form RPR

2 **1** **War Decree (USA)**[17] 4150 2-9-1 0.................................... RyanMoore 1 113
(A P O'Brien, Ire) *trckd ldrs: swtchd lft and effrt to chse ldng pair and hdwy to ld 1f out: styd on wl and forged ahd ins fnl f: rdn out* **6/4**[1]

16 **2** *1 3/4* **Thunder Snow (IRE)**[42] 3243 2-9-1 0........................ JamesMcDonald 2 108
(Saeed bin Suroor) *lw: pressed ldng pair tl wnt 2nd 4f out: upsides ldr and rdn 2f out: drvn to ld jst over 1f out: sn hdd: no ex and styd on same pce fnl 100yds* **13/2**[3]

11 **3** *1* **Boynton (USA)**[17] 4150 2-9-4 0.. JamesDoyle 8 109
(Charlie Appleby) *lw: in tch in midfield: nt clr run and swtchd lft over 2f out: drvn over 1f out: styd on u.p ins fnl f: wnt 3rd fnl 50yds: nvr enough pce to threaten ldrs* **2/1**[2]

4131 **4** *1/2* **Pleaseletmewin (IRE)**[17] 4148 2-9-1 0............................ JimCrowley 7 104
(Ralph Beckett) *sn in tch in midfield: sltly hmpd 5f out: effrt on inner over 2f out: switching lft ent fnl f: styd on u.p ins fnl f: wnt 4th cl home: nvr enough pce to threaten ldrs* **33/1**

21 **5** *nk* **Repton (IRE)**[59] 2696 2-9-1 0... PatDobbs 3 103
(Richard Hannon) *led: rdn and jnd 2f out: hdd and drvn jst over 1f out: 3rd and btn ins fnl f: wknd fnl 100yds and lost 2 pls towards fin* **25/1**

221 **6** *2 1/4* **Isomer (USA)**[17] 4154 2-9-1 0....................................... JamieSpencer 6 98
(Andrew Balding) *bustled along sn after leaving stalls: in last pair and hmpd 5f out: clsd and in tch 3f out: no imp u.p over 1f out* **10/1**

1 **7** *nk* **Jackhammer (IRE)**[34] 3529 2-9-1 0................................ AndreaAtzeni 9 97
(William Knight) *tall: lw: bhd: hmpd 5f out: clsd and in tch 3f out: sn rdn and no imp: wl hld and styd on same pce fnl f* **33/1**

14 **8** *1 1/4* **Medieval (IRE)**[42] 3243 2-9-1 0... LukeMorris 10 93
(Paul Cole) *dropped into last trio after s: hmpd 5f out: clsd and in tch 3f out: sn rdn and no imp: wl hld and plugged on same pce fnl f* **16/1**

215 **9** *9* **Hakeem (FR)**[58] 2717 2-9-1 0... HarryBentley 5 69
(Richard Hannon) *chsd ldr tl 4f out: rdn jst over 2f out: sn lost pl: bhd over 1f out: wknd fnl f* **33/1**

1m 25.75s (-1.25) **Going Correction** -0.05s/f (Good) **9** Ran SP% **114.3**
Speed ratings (Par 106): **105,103,101,101,100 98,98,96,86**
CSF £11.30 TOTE £2.20: £1.10, £2.10, £1.30; EX 10.90 Trifecta £26.50.

Owner Andrew Rosen & Mrs John Magnier & Michael Tabor & **Bred** Ar Enterprises Llc **Trained** Cashel, Co Tipperary

FOCUS
Race distance increased by 12yds. Sound form for the level, although it was a bit of a rough race early and little featured from off the pace, with them not going particularly fast early. The winner may not have needed to improve on his Newmarket form.

4733 QATAR LENNOX STKS (GROUP 2) 7f
3:10 (3:12) (Class 1) 3-Y-O+

£170,130 (£64,500; £32,280; £16,080; £8,070; £4,050) **Stalls** Low

Form RPR

-202 **1** **Dutch Connection**[17] 4127 4-9-3 115......................... JamesMcDonald 4 119
(Charles Hills) *lw: hld up in midfield: hdwy to chse ldng pair and gng strly wl over 1f out: clsd and shkn up to chal 1f out: rdn to ld 100yds out: r.o wl: readily* **9/4**[1]

0-11 **2** *1 3/4* **Home Of The Brave (IRE)**[59] 2691 4-9-3 115...............(t) JamesDoyle 3 114
(Hugo Palmer) *racd keenly: chsd ldr: clsd and upsides ldr 2f out: rdn to ld ent fnl f: hdd 100yds: outpcd by wnr but kpt on for clr 2nd* **5/2**[2]

1130 **3** *1 3/4* **Gifted Master (IRE)**[41] 3269 3-8-10 114........................... JimCrowley 6 107
(Hugo Palmer) *led and sn clr: jnd and rdn 2f out: drvn and hdd ent fnl f: 3rd and btn ins fnl f: wknd but hld on for 3rd cl home* **13/2**[3]

-350 **4** *1/2* **Buckstay (IRE)**[17] 4152 6-9-3 109................................(p) JamieSpencer 1 108
(Peter Chapple-Hyam) *s.i.s: hld up in last trio: effrt in 5th 2f out: drvn ent fnl f: styd on but no threat to ldrs* **14/1**

-531 **5** *1/2* **Markaz (IRE)**[31] 3655 4-9-3 114... PaulHanagan 2 107
(Owen Burrows) *t.k.h: chsd ldng pair: rdn ent fnl 2f: unable qck and hld in 4th 1f out: kpt on same pce after* **7/1**

6600 **6** *3* **Tupi (IRE)**[17] 4135 4-9-3 105... FrankieDettori 7 99
(Richard Hannon) *swtg: stdd after s: hld up in rr: effrt 2f out: 6th and no imp over 1f out: wl hld and plugged on same pce after* **25/1**

-001 **7** *3 1/2* **Birchwood (IRE)**[17] 4135 3-8-10 113..................................(v) RyanMoore 8 86
(Richard Fahey) *swtg: stdd and wnt lft sn after s: t.k.h early: hld up in last trio: nvr on terms: pushed along and hung rt over 1f out: no prog and wl btn fnl f* **8/1**

1200 **8** *9* **Dream Dubai**[39] 3338 3-8-10 105.............................. SilvestreDeSousa 5 62
(Sylvester Kirk) *lw: in tch in midfield: rdn 3f out: struggling and lost pl 2f out: bhd and eased ins fnl f* **20/1**

1m 24.48s (-2.52) **Going Correction** -0.05s/f (Good)
WFA 3 from 4yo+ 7lb **8** Ran SP% **111.6**
Speed ratings (Par 115): **112,110,108,107,106 103,99,89**
CSF £7.61 TOTE £3.20: £1.20, £1.30, £2.30; EX 8.10 Trifecta £37.00.

Owner Godolphin **Bred** Mrs S M Roy **Trained** Lambourn, Berks

FOCUS
Race distance increased by 12yds. Quite a competitive Group 2, with the first five in the betting all officially rated within 2lb of each other. The question beforehand was how the race would unfold, given that both of Hugo Palmer's entries normally like to make the running. A small personal best from the winner.

4734 BETTER ODDS WITH MATCHBOOK SUMMER STKS (H'CAP) 1m 6f
3:45 (3:46) (Class 2) 3-Y-O+

£62,250 (£18,640; £9,320; £4,660; £2,330; £1,170) **Stalls** Low

Form RPR

-300 **1** **Elidor**[37] 3436 6-9-10 **105**... SilvestreDeSousa 8 114
(Mick Channon) *hld up in midfield: slipped bnd 12f out: effrt and pushed lft over 2f out: hdwy to chal and drifting rt over 1f out: led ent fnl f: styd on u.p and holding chalr cl home* **16/1**

50/2 **2** *nk* **Qewy (IRE)**[42] 3246 6-9-9 **104**.. JamesMcDonald 4 112
(Charlie Appleby) *lw: hld up in tch in midfield: swtchd lft and effrt over 2f out: hdwy u.p to chse ldng pair 1f out: wnt 2nd and ev ch ins fnl f: styd on but hld cl home* **8/1**[3]

3000 **3** *3/4* **Notarised**[24] 3889 5-9-3 **98**.. JoeFanning 5 105
(Mark Johnston) *chsd ldr: clsd and upsides ldr 4f out: rdn to ld wl over 2f out: drvn and hdd over 1f out: sn led again: hdd ent fnl f: stl ev ch tl no ex and jst outpcd fnl 75yds* **7/1**[2]

4300 **4** *3* **First Mohican**[38] 3387 8-8-10 **98**.................................. HollieDoyle(7) 1 100
(Alan King) *in tch in midfield: slipped bnd 12f out: effrt on inner and swtchd lft over 2f out: hdwy u.p to chse ldrs over 1f out: 4th and styd on same pce ins fnl f* **33/1**

2242 **5** *1/2* **Gold Prince (IRE)**[24] 3889 4-9-1 **96**..........................(b[1]) FrankieDettori 9 98
(Sylvester Kirk) *lw: t.k.h: chsd ldr for 2f: stdd bk but stl wl in tch in midfield: rdn and sltly short of room over 2f out: styd on same pce and no imp fr over 1f out* **9/1**

/0-4 **6** *2* **Francis Of Assisi (IRE)**[17] 4164 6-9-8 **103**........................ AdamKirby 3 102
(Charlie Appleby) *chsd ldrs after 2f: effrt to chse ldrs 3f out: sn drvn to chal: led over 1f out: sn hdd: no ex and btn jst ins fnl f: wknd qckly ins fnl f* **10/1**

-210 **7** *3/4* **My Reward**[31] 3658 4-9-1 **96**.. DavidAllan 10 94+
(Tim Easterby) *midfield: wd bnd after 2f and dropped towards rr: effrt 2f out: sme hdwy and swtchd rt 1f out: styd on ins fnl f: nvr trbld ldrs* **20/1**

1100 **8** *1 1/4* **Gang Warfare**[31] 3658 5-9-8 **103**..................................(p) RobertHavlin 12 99
(Simon Crisford) *hld up in midfield: effrt over 2f out: no imp tl sme modest hdwy ent fnl f: kpt on same pce after: nvr trbld ldrs* **25/1**

0-00 **9** *1/2* **Fun Mac (GER)**[24] 3913 5-9-8 **103**.............................(t) JimmyFortune 11 98+
(Hughie Morrison) *stdd s: hld up off pce in rr: effrt over 2f out: drvn over 1f out: plugged on to pass btn horses ins fnl f: nvr trbld ldrs* **14/1**

0-11 **10** *2 1/4* **King Bolete (IRE)**[48] 3027 4-9-9 **104**.............................. AndreaAtzeni 14 96
(Roger Varian) *chsd ldng pair tl 3f out: lost pl u.p 2f out: wknd over 1f out* **7/1**[2]

/0-6 **11** *3 1/2* **A Soldier's Life (IRE)**[39] 3340 5-9-4 **99**........................... JamesDoyle 2 86
(Charlie Appleby) *racd keenly: led but nvr totally settled in front: rdn and hdd wl over 2f out: sn btn and wknd over 1f out* **13/2**[1]

5210 **12** *2 1/4* **Tawdeea**[17] 4165 4-9-9 **104**... DanielTudhope 13 88
(David O'Meara) *lw: stdd s: hld up off the pce in rr: effrt over 2f out: no imp and swtchd rt jst over 1f out: n.d* **10/1**

3-40 **13** *1 1/4* **Havana Beat (IRE)**[24] 3889 6-9-3 **98**........................(t) RobertWinston 7 80
(Rod Millman) *stdd after s: hld up off the pce in last trio: effrt over 2f out: no hdwy: n.d* **7/1**[2]

/110 **14** *44* **Arch Villain (IRE)**[31] 3658 7-9-5 **100**..............................(v[1]) JimCrowley 6 21
(Amanda Perrett) *hld up in midfield: stmbld bdly bnd 12f out and dropped to last quartet: shkn up 3f out: sn eased: t.o* **25/1**

2m 59.33s (-4.27) **Going Correction** -0.05s/f (Good) **14** Ran SP% **118.1**
Speed ratings (Par 109): **110,109,109,107,107 106,105,105,104,103 101,100,99,74**
CSF £129.83 CT £991.26 TOTE £17.50: £4.80, £2.50, £2.80; EX 168.50 Trifecta £1375.60.

Owner Jon and Julia Aisbitt **Bred** Ashley House Stud **Trained** West Ilsley, Berks

■ Stewards' Enquiry : James McDonald 11-day ban: used whip above permitted levl without giving gelding time to respond (Aug 9-19); Fine: £250.

FOCUS
Race distance increased by 8yds. Rock-solid handicap form and it was a help to race in the first half of the field. A small personal best from the winner.

4735 WEATHERBYS PRIVATE BANK STKS (H'CAP) 5f
4:20 (4:28) (Class 2) (0-105,105) 4-Y-O+**£19,407** (£5,775; £2,886; £1,443) **Stalls** High

Form RPR

4000 **1** **Boom The Groom (IRE)**[17] 4126 5-9-0 **98**.......................... AdamKirby 6 107
(Tony Carroll) *taken down early: in tch in midfield: rdn and hdwy to chal over 1f out: drvn to ld ins fnl f: styd on* **13/2**[3]

0323 **2** *1/2* **Thesme**[18] 4112 4-8-12 **96**... FrankieDettori 17 103
(Nigel Tinkler) *taken down early: led: rdn and hdd over 1f out: stl ev ch ins fnl f: styd on but hld towards fin* **7/2**[1]

1226 **3** *1/2* **Bowson Fred**[17] 4126 4-8-11 **100**.............................. NathanEvans(5) 14 105
(Michael Easterby) *taken down early: chsd ldrs: rdn to ld over 1f out: hdd ins fnl f: styd on same pce wl ins fnl f* **14/1**

0000 **4** *1/2* **Humidor (IRE)**[24] 3909 9-9-0 **98**.................................. FergusSweeney 2 102
(George Baker) *taken down early and led to post: towards rr: hdwy 1/2-way: rdn to chse ldrs 1f out: styd on same pce ins fnl f* **25/1**

6100 **5** *3/4* **Harry Hurricane**[17] 4126 4-8-13 **97**................................... JamesDoyle 10 98
(George Baker) *awkward leaving stalls and slowly away: sn rcvrd and in midfield: hdwy to chse ldrs 1f out: styd on same pce ins fnl f* **15/2**

0415 **6** *hd* **Confessional**[11] 4373 9-8-6 **90**......................................(e) HarryBentley 11 90+
(Tim Easterby) *hld up in midfield: effrt over 1f out: nt clr run and swtchd lft ins fnl f: styd on towards fin: nt rch ldrs* **16/1**

-200 **7** *1/2* **Maljaa**[17] 4126 4-9-7 **105**..(b) PaulHanagan 7 103
(Roger Varian) *lw: wl in tch in midfield: effrt over 1f out: styd on same pce ins fnl f* **6/1**[2]

0000 **8** *nk* **Red Stripes (USA)**[3] 4632 4-8-2 **86** oh3.....................(b) FrannyNorton 8 83
(Lisa Williamson) *chsd ldrs: rdn over 1f out: unable qck jst ins fnl f: wknd towards fin* **100/1**

-030 **9** *1 1/4* **Abstraction (IRE)**[30] 3696 6-9-4 **102**................................ AndreaAtzeni 9 95
(Miss Natalia Lupini, Ire) *lw: chsd ldrs: rdn over 1f out: no ex 1f out: wknd wl ins fnl f* **20/1**

0002 **10** *nk* **Hay Chewed (IRE)**[11] 4359 5-8-11 **95**................................ JoeFanning 4 87
(Conrad Allen) *lw: chsd ldrs: rdn and n.m.r jst over 1f out: wknd wl ins fnl f* **14/1**

00 **11** *1* **Dutch Masterpiece**[30] 3696 6-9-2 **100**......................... JamesMcDonald 5 88+
(Gary Moore) *s.i.s: in rr: hdwy and nt clr run over 1f out: nvr able to cl: eased ins fnl f* **16/1**

The Form Book, Raceform Ltd, Newbury, RG14 5SJ

1260 **12** 1 ¼ **Brother Tiger**18 4112 7-8-6 **90** LukeMorris 18 74
(David C Griffiths) *taken down early: chsd ldrs: rdn ent fnl 2f: lost pl and btn over 1f out: wknd ins fnl f* **25/1**

63-4 **13** 3 **Shore Step (IRE)**81 1990 6-8-9 **93** SilvestreDeSousa 16 66+
(Mick Channon) *lw: s.i.s: bhd: nt clr run over 1f out: n.d* **7/1**

150- **14** 2 ¼ **Extrasolar**300 6870 6-8-2 **86** oh3 (t) JimmyQuinn 13 51
(Amanda Perrett) *in tch in midfield: rdn 2f out: sn lost pl: wknd 1f out* **50/1**

2000 **15** 1 ½ **Red Baron (IRE)**4 4584 7-9-1 **99** NeilFarley 12 58
(Eric Alston) *pressed ldrs tl jst over 2f out: lost pl over 1f out: wknd fnl f* **40/1**

0521 **16** ¾ **Blithe Spirit**3 4632 5-8-12 **96** 6ex JasonHart 19 53
(Eric Alston) *a towards rr: bhd and eased ins fnl f* **10/1**

57.11s (-3.09) **Going Correction** -0.325s/f (Firm) **16** Ran SP% **126.1**
Speed ratings (Par 109): **111,110,109,108,107 107,106,105,103,103 101,99,94,91,88 87**
CSF £28.48 CT £336.46 TOTE £7.30: £1.80, £1.50, £3.40, £6.70; EX 38.20 Trifecta £881.10.
Owner Gary Attwood **Bred** John Foley **Trained** Cropthorne, Worcs
■ Union Rose was withdrawn. Price at time of withdrawal 12/1. Rule 4 applies to bets struck prior to to withdrawal but not to SP bets - deduct 5p in the pound. New market formed.

FOCUS
There was good pace across the track and no apparent bias towards either the stands' side or the centre. The winner has been rated back to his best.

4736 IRISH THOROUGHBRED MARKETING EBF STALLIONS MAIDEN STKS (PLUS 10 RACE) 6f
4:55 (4:58) (Class 2) 2-Y-O **£12,938** (£3,850; £1,924; £962) **Stalls** High

Form RPR

3 **1** **Best Solution (IRE)**22 3954 2-9-0 0 JamesDoyle 7 86+
(Saeed bin Suroor) *athletic: lw: chsd ldr: rdn jst over 2f out: sltly outpcd by ldr over 1f out: rallied u.p ins fnl f: styd on to ld 50yds: sn in command* **11/2**2

2 1 **Rich And Famous (USA)** 2-9-0 0 JamesMcDonald 10 83+
(Mark Johnston) *str: broke fast: led: rdn and fnd ex over 1f out: drvn and pressed ins fnl f: hdd 50yds out: wknd cl home* **12/1**

0 **3** 3 **Sea Shack**18 4075 2-9-0 0 JimCrowley 3 74
(William Knight) *str: chsd ldrs: rdn 2f out: outpcd by ldng pair over 1f out: no ch w ldng pair but battled on u.p to hold 3rd ins fnl f* **66/1**

230 **4** ½ **Salouen (IRE)**11 4349 2-9-0 0 PatDobbs 6 73
(Sylvester Kirk) *in tch in midfield: effrt over 2f out: outpcd by ldng pair u.p: no ch w ldng pair but battling for 3rd ins fnl f: kpt on* **25/1**

20 **5** nk **Parys Mountain (IRE)**42 3243 2-9-0 0 SilvestreDeSousa 5 72
(Charles Hills) *stdd s: t.k.h: hld up in tch in last trio: hdwy over 2f out: no imp over 1f out: wl hld and styd on same pce ins fnl f* **8/1**3

6 1 **Mazyoun** 2-9-0 0 FrankieDettori 1 69+
(Hugo Palmer) *lengthy: lw: s.i.s and swtchd lft after s: hld up in last pair: pushed along 2f out: sme hdwy but nvr on terms over 1f out: kpt on same pce ins fnl f* **5/1**1

7 2 ½ **Tesko Fella (IRE)** 2-9-0 0 SeanLevey 8 61
(Richard Hannon) *lw: hld up in midfield: rdn over 2f out: struggling and lost pl over 1f out: wknd fnl f* **66/1**

8 ½ **Swag (IRE)** 2-9-0 0 (t) TomMarquand 9 60
(Richard Hannon) *cmpt: s.i.s: a in rr* **40/1**

9 1 ½ **Five Star Frank** 2-9-0 0 CharlesBishop 11 55
(Eve Johnson Houghton) *cmpt: t.k.h: hld up in tch in midfield: effrt 2f out: sme hdwy but no threat to ldrs over 1f out: wknd ins fnl f* **66/1**

10 shd **Poetic Principle (IRE)** 2-9-0 0 LukeMorris 12 55
(J S Moore) *leggy: chsd ldrs: rdn over 2f out: unable qck and btn over 1f out: wknd ins fnl f* **100/1**

1m 11.76s (-0.44) **Going Correction** -0.325s/f (Firm) **10** Ran SP% **62.6**
Speed ratings (Par 100): **89,87,83,83,82 81,77,77,75,75**
CSF £16.23 TOTE £3.10: £1.10, £2.30, £7.00; EX 22.20 Trifecta £342.60.
Owner Godolphin **Bred** Cecil And Martin McCracken **Trained** Newmarket, Suffolk
■ Harry Angel was withdrawn. Price at time of withdrawal 5/6F. Rule 4 applies to all bets - deduct 50p in the pound.

FOCUS
A maiden that didn't take as much winning as had looked likely after the short-priced favourite Harry Angel got down in the stalls and then had to be withdrawn. Still, two useful types fought out the finish.

4737 SMARTER BETS WITH MATCHBOOK BETTING EXCHANGE FILLIES' STKS (H'CAP) 1m
5:30 (5:32) (Class 3) (0-95,94) 3-Y-O+ **£12,938** (£3,850; £1,924; £962) **Stalls** Low

Form RPR

3113 **1** **Desert Haze**17 4130 3-8-9 **83** OisinMurphy 3 91
(Ralph Beckett) *awkward leaving stalls: sn rcvrd and in midfield: effrt to chse ldrs and swtchd lft ent fnl f: hdwy u.p to ld ins fnl f: sn edgd lft but kpt on: rdn out* **13/2**2

313- **2** 1 **Haggle**269 7631 3-9-5 **93** AndreaAtzeni 12 99
(Luca Cumani) *lw: stdd and dropped in after s: hld up in tch: effrt 2f out: rdn and hdwy to chse ldrs 1f out: styd on u.p to go 2nd cl home* **13/2**2

6431 **3** ½ **Home Cummins (IRE)**17 4163 4-9-11 **91** (p) PaulHanagan 2 98
(Richard Fahey) *chsd ldrs: clsd and rdn to chal wl over 1f out: led ent fnl f: edgd rt: hdd and one pce ins fnl f: lost 2nd cl home* **13/2**2

122 **4** hd **Pure Art**19 4042 3-8-8 **82** RichardKingscote 5 87
(Ralph Beckett) *athletic: hld up in tch in midfield: effrt 2f out: hdwy u.p to chse ldrs 1f out: nt clr run and swtchd rt ins fnl f: kpt on* **10/3**1

2311 **5** shd **Quebee**22 3957 3-8-12 **86** JohnFahy 11 90
(Clive Cox) *lw: hld up in tch towards rr: swtchd lft and effrt on outer over 1f out: kpt on u.p ins fnl f* **8/1**3

1501 **6** 2 ½ **Lyfka**18 4086 4-9-6 **86** (tp) LukeMorris 9 87
(Paul Cole) *swtg: s.i.s: bhd: rdn ent fnl 2f: styd on to pass btn horses ins fnl f: nvr trbld ldrs* **33/1**

1463 **7** ½ **Haley Bop (IRE)**6 4534 3-9-0 **88** JoeFanning 1 85
(Mark Johnston) *swtg: chsd ldrs: effrt and upsides ldrs 2f out: sn drvn: no ex and sltly hmpd ins fnl f: wknd fnl 100yds* **8/1**3

0512 **8** ½ **Pacolita (IRE)**15 4206 4-8-2 **75** oh1 MitchGodwin(7) 6 73
(Sylvester Kirk) *chsd ldr tl led over 2f out: sn rdn: hdd ent fnl f and rdr dropped reins 1f out: stl fumbling w reins and wknd fnl 100yds* **20/1**

-132 **9** ¾ **Inke (IRE)**12 4307 4-9-1 **81** (p) TomMarquand 8 78
(Jim Boyle) *stdd bk to last pair sn after s: hld up in tch: effrt 2f out: no hdwy u.p over 1f out: wl hld and one pce fnl f* **20/1**

-033 **10** nk **Shwaimsa (IRE)**10 4391 3-9-0 **88** FrankieDettori 13 82
(Richard Hannon) *broke wl enough and chsd ldrs early: grad stdd bk and in last quartet 5f out: rdn 2f out: drvn and no hdwy over 1f out* **8/1**3

5063 **11** 3 ¾ **Doubly Motivated (IRE)**12 4318 3-8-8 **82**1 SilvestreDeSousa 4 71
(Charles Hills) *led: rdn and hdd over 2f out: lost pl and btn over 1f out: wknd fnl f* **16/1**

1m 38.95s (-0.95) **Going Correction** -0.05s/f (Good)
WFA 3 from 4yo+ 8lb **11** Ran SP% **114.8**
Speed ratings (Par 104): **102,101,100,100,100 97,97,96,95,95 91**
CSF £45.78 CT £291.07 TOTE £7.50: £2.40, £2.30, £2.20; EX 62.50 Trifecta £344.60.
Owner H H Sheikh Mohammed Bin Khalifa Al Thani **Bred** Whatton Manor Stud & Robert Cornelius **Trained** Kimpton, Hants

FOCUS
Race distance increased by 12yds. The early pace was steady, several fought for their heads, and the race developed into a bit of a dash in the straight. The winner continues to progress.
T/Jkpt: Not won. T/Plt: £78.80 to a £1 stake. Pool of £287112.12 - 2659.65 winning tickets.
T/Qpdt: £40.50 to a £1 stake. Pool of £15145.26 - 276.59 winning tickets. **Steve Payne**

4564 YARMOUTH (L-H)
Tuesday, July 26

OFFICIAL GOING: Good to firm
Wind: Fresh across Weather: Cloudy

4738 GREAT YARMOUTH RACECOURSE AUGUST LIVE NIGHTS MAIDEN AUCTION STKS 7f 3y
1:50 (1:53) (Class 6) 2-Y-O **£2,975** (£885; £442; £221) **Stalls** Centre

Form RPR

4 **1** **Marilyn**26 3819 2-8-6 0 TedDurcan 5 72
(Chris Wall) *led main gp after 1f: overall ldr over 2f out: rdn and edgd rt over 1f out: styd on* **8/15**1

2 2 ¼ **Masonic (IRE)** 2-8-11 0 AdrianMcCarthy 3 71
(Robyn Brisland) *prom: lost pl after 1f: hdwy over 2f out: rdn to chse wnr over 1f out: styd on* **12/1**

0 **3** 3 **Drop Kick Murphi (IRE)**12 4287 2-8-11 0 SteveDrowne 4 63
(George Baker) *chsd ldrs: rdn over 2f out: styd on same pce fnl f* **6/1**3

043 **4** 2 ¼ **Elements Legacy**24 3897 2-9-0 0 (v) DougieCostello 8 60
(K R Burke) *racd alone on stands' side: overall ldr tl rdn: hdd and hung lft over 2f out: no ex fr over 1f out* **18/1**

5500 **5** nk **Apple Scruffs (IRE)**12 4315 2-9-0 0 AdamBeschizza 6 59
(Michael Attwater) *hld up: rdn over 2f out: styd on fr over 1f out: nvr trbld ldrs* **28/1**

6 5 **Bartholomew J (IRE)** 2-8-8 0 SimonPearce(3) 1 42
(Lydia Pearce) *led main gp 1f: chsd ldrs: rdn over 2f out: wknd over 1f out* **50/1**

4 **7** 6 **Pitch High (IRE)**13 4270 2-8-11 0 ShelleyBirkett(3) 7 29
(Julia Feilden) *sn prom: rdn over 2f out: wknd wl over 1f out* **3/1**2

8 2 ¾ **Chiconomic (IRE)** 2-8-7 0 ow1 MartinLane 9 15
(Rae Guest) *prom: pushed along 1/2-way: wknd over 2f out* **25/1**

1m 27.44s (0.84) **Going Correction** -0.125s/f (Firm) **8** Ran SP% **126.7**
Speed ratings (Par 92): **90,87,84,81,81 75,68,65**
CSF £10.86 TOTE £1.40: £1.02, £3.50, £1.80; EX 11.00 Trifecta £41.00.
Owner Lady Juliet Tadgell, D Swinburn & C Wall **Bred** Lady Juliet Tadgell **Trained** Newmarket, Suffolk

FOCUS
The ground was good to firm and there were no changes to race distances for the opener, a moderate juvenile maiden.

4739 WILLIAM (BILL) TAVERNER H'CAP 2m
2:20 (2:20) (Class 6) (0-65,63) 4-Y-O+ **£2,264** (£673; £336; £168) **Stalls** Centre

Form RPR

5035 **1** **La Fritillaire**7 4478 4-8-8 **50** AndrewMullen 5 59
(James Given) *chsd ldr tl led over 3f out: rdn over 1f out: styd on u.p* **7/2**3

-655 **2** hd **Lady Of Yue**45 3161 6-9-2 **63** AaronJones(5) 6 72
(Eugene Stanford) *a.p: chsd ldr over 2f out: rdn and ev ch fr over 1f out: sn hung lft: nt run on* **13/8**1

2234 **3** 12 **What A Party (IRE)**26 3825 4-8-13 **55** (p) DougieCostello 3 49
(Gay Kelleway) *s.i.s: hld up: rdn over 3f out: sn btn* **8/1**

4522 **4** 4 ½ **Theydon Bois**12 4320 4-8-11 **56** (p) RosieJessop(3) 4 45+
(Peter Charalambous) *led: hung rt thrght: hdd over 3f out: wknd over 2f out* **15/8**2

0006 **5** 1 ¾ **Sakhra**12 4320 5-8-0 **45** NoelGarbutt(3) 2 32
(Mark Brisbourne) *hld up: rdn over 4f out: wknd over 2f out* **25/1**

3m 30.46s (-1.94) **Going Correction** -0.05s/f (Good) **5** Ran SP% **110.1**
Speed ratings (Par 101): **102,101,95,93,92**
CSF £9.64 TOTE £4.70: £2.80, £1.20; EX 11.60 Trifecta £43.20.
Owner Ingram Racing **Bred** Mrs P M Ignarski **Trained** Willoughton, Lincs

FOCUS
A weak staying handicap in which they went a slow gallop.

4740 READE CATERING HOG ROASTS AT YARMOUTH H'CAP 1m 2f 23y
2:55 (2:55) (Class 6) (0-65,62) 3-Y-O+ **£2,264** (£673; £336; £168) **Stalls** Low

Form RPR

0061 **1** **We'll Shake Hands (FR)**7 4493 5-9-7 **62** CliffordLee(7) 6 68
(K R Burke) *disp ld tl wnt on over 6f out: rdn and hdd 1f out: edgd rt: rallied to ld post* **6/4**1

0660 **2** nse **Monna Valley**13 4278 4-9-8 **56** MartinHarley 5 62
(Stuart Williams) *hld up: hdwy and nt clr run 2f out: rdn to ld 1f out: r.o: edgd lft and hdd post* **7/1**

650- **3** nk **Buteo Bai (IRE)**266 7684 3-8-10 **54** ThomasBrown 4 59
(Lucy Wadham) *s.s: hld up: hdwy over 1f out: r.o* **9/1**

5-66 **4** 1 ¼ **Kilim**60 2666 3-9-3 **61** MartinLane 3 64
(Luca Cumani) *trckd ldrs: rdn over 2f out: styng on same pce whn nt clr run towards fin* **11/4**2

6-00 **5** 2 **Bethnal Green**45 3145 4-9-8 **56** AdrianMcCarthy 1 55
(Robyn Brisland) *chsd ldrs: rdn over 3f out: styd on same pce ins fnl f* **33/1**

003 **6** ½ **Captain Gerald**20 4021 3-8-7 **54** (p) JosephineGordon(3) 7 52
(John Ryan) *disp ld over 3f: remained handy: rdn and ev ch over 2f out: no ex ins fnl f* **13/2**3

00-0 **7** 1 ¾ **Work (IRE)**60 2653 3-8-6 **50** AndrewMullen 2 45
(David Simcock) *s.s: hld up: hdwy over 2f out: rdn over 1f out: edgd lft and no ex fnl f* **14/1**

2m 9.93s (-0.57) **Going Correction** -0.05s/f (Good)
WFA 3 from 4yo+ 10lb **7** Ran SP% **112.1**
Speed ratings (Par 101): **100,99,99,98,97 96,95**
CSF £12.24 TOTE £2.30: £1.20, £3.30; EX 13.20 Trifecta £60.00.
Owner Market Avenue Racing Club & Mrs E Burke **Bred** Eric Puerari **Trained** Middleham Moor, N Yorks

FOCUS
Modest form at best, but the winner was on a fair mark. He set a slow pace and they came down the centre of the home straight.

4741 MARTIN FOULGER MEMORIAL H'CAP 6f 3y
3:30 (3:31) (Class 3) (0-95,95) 3-Y-O+ **£7,762** (£2,310; £1,154; £577) **Stalls** Centre

Form RPR
1-50 **1** **Doctor Sardonicus**66 2488 5-9-8 **91** MartinHarley 3 99
(David Simcock) *chsd ldr tl led over 1f out: sn rdn: styd on u.p* **5/1**3
-540 **2** shd **Elronaq**45 3165 3-9-2 **90** DaneO'Neill 6 97
(Charles Hills) *hld up: racd keenly: hmpd by loose horse over 4f out: hdwy over 1f out: rdn and edgd rt ins fnl f: r.o* **6/1**
2212 **3** ½ **David's Duchess (IRE)**10 4398 3-8-3 **77** PatrickMathers 8 83+
(Richard Fahey) *trckd ldrs: racd keenly: nt clr run and swtchd lft 1f out: sn rdn: r.o* **11/4**1
4006 **4** 2 **Basil Berry**33 3573 5-9-12 **95** (p) SaleemGolam 7 95
(Chris Dwyer) *hld up in tch: rdn over 1f out: styd on* **16/1**
6004 **5** 2 **Yeeoow (IRE)**2 4689 7-8-4 **80** ow1 CliffordLee(7) 10 73
(K R Burke) *led: rdn and hdd over 1f out: no ex ins fnl f* **9/2**2
0453 **6** 3 **Showtime Star**10 4389 6-8-0 **76** oh12 DavidEgan(7) 4 60
(Gay Kelleway) *chsd ldrs: rdn 1/2-way: wknd over 1f out* **50/1**
R114 **7** 2½ **Gentlemen**14 4246 5-9-6 **92** JosephineGordon(3) 1 68
(Phil McEntee) *s.s: sn drvn along and a in rr* **8/1**
5350 **8** ½ **Honcho (IRE)**18 4100 4-8-7 **76** oh10 (p) RyanPowell 9 50
(John Ryan) *hood removed late and s.s: a bhd* **80/1**
1-04 **U** **Captain Colby (USA)**18 4112 4-9-12 **95** (b) DougieCostello 5
(Ed Walker) *hmpd and uns rdr over 5f out* **9/2**2

1m 12.31s (-2.09) **Going Correction** -0.125s/f (Firm)
WFA 3 from 4yo+ 5lb **9** Ran SP% **114.2**
Speed ratings (Par 107): **108,107,107,104,101 97,94,93,**
CSF £34.58 CT £98.60 TOTE £6.20: £2.00, £1.90, £1.70; EX 42.90 Trifecta £153.70.
Owner Charles Wentworth **Bred** D M James **Trained** Newmarket, Suffolk

FOCUS
A good sprint handicap in which they went a fair gallop, and there was drama at the start. A small personal best from the winner.

4742 SHIRLEY GILL MEMORIAL 10TH ANNIVERSARY H'CAP 7f 3y
4:05 (4:05) (Class 4) (0-80,79) 3-Y-O+ **£4,690** (£1,395; £697; £348) **Stalls** Centre

Form RPR
1 **1** **Takatul (USA)**42 3267 3-9-6 **78** DaneO'Neill 3 86+
(Charles Hills) *s.i.s: hld up: hdwy to ld and hung rt over 1f out: sn rdn: r.o* **11/8**1
5-13 **2** ¾ **Twin Point**191 231 5-9-9 **74** (t) StevieDonohoe 4 82
(Charlie Fellowes) *trckd ldrs: rdn to chse wnr fnl f r.o* **8/1**
4134 **3** ½ **Four Poets**18 4088 3-9-0 **72** ShaneKelly 1 76
(David Simcock) *hld up: hdwy and n.m.r over 1f out: sn rdn: r.o* **4/1**2
2631 **4** 6 **Coronation Day**13 4258 3-9-2 **74** MartinHarley 2 61
(James Tate) *led: hdd over 5f out: chsd ldr tl led again wl over 1f out: sn hdd: no ex ins fnl f* **7/1**
2136 **5** ½ **Johnny B Goode (IRE)**11 4360 4-8-10 **64** JosephineGordon(3) 7 53
(Chris Dwyer) *racd keenly: w ldr tl led over 5f out: rdn and hdd wl over 1f out: no ex fnl f* **14/1**
122 **6** shd **North Creek**20 4010 3-9-7 **79** TedDurcan 5 65
(Chris Wall) *hld up: rdn over 2f out: no ex fr over 1f out* **9/2**3

1m 25.55s (-1.05) **Going Correction** -0.125s/f (Firm)
WFA 3 from 4yo+ 7lb **6** Ran SP% **110.6**
Speed ratings (Par 105): **101,100,99,92,92 92**
CSF £12.69 TOTE £1.90: £1.10, £3.80; EX 12.20 Trifecta £51.70.
Owner Hamdan Al Maktoum **Bred** Shadwell Farm LLC **Trained** Lambourn, Berks

FOCUS
A competitive little handicap and an impressive winner who came from off a decent pace. There is more to come from him.

4743 RIVERSIDE RENTALS H'CAP 1m 3y
4:40 (4:40) (Class 5) (0-75,75) 3-Y-O+ **£2,911** (£866; £432; £216) **Stalls** Centre

Form RPR
6566 **1** **Blue Geranium (IRE)**12 4318 3-9-2 **71** 1 NickyMackay 6 77
(John Gosden) *hld up: racd keenly: shkn up over 2f out: hdwy to ld 1f out: rdn out* **12/1**
4-22 **2** ¾ **Hollywood Road (IRE)**12 4288 3-8-13 **75** (b1) GeorgeWood(7) 4 79
(Don Cantillon) *trckd ldrs: plld hrd: rdn and ev ch 1f out: styd on same pce wl ins fnl f* **7/4**1
-203 **3** 3 **Corked (IRE)**20 3996 3-9-3 **75** MarcMonaghan(3) 1 72
(Hugo Palmer) *chsd ldr: rdn and ev ch 1f out: styd on same pce ins fnl f* **9/2**3
-213 **4** ½ **Jawaayiz**19 4042 3-9-6 **75** DaneO'Neill 5 71
(Simon Crisford) *led: rdn and hdd 1f out: no ex ins fnl f* **5/2**2
1540 **5** 4½ **Trodero**89 1804 3-8-10 **68** JosephineGordon(3) 2 54
(Dr Jon Scargill) *prom: plld hrd: rdn over 2f out: wknd fnl f* **33/1**
3614 **6** 6 **Honey Badger**32 3612 5-8-6 **58** (v) AaronJones(5) 3 32
(Eugene Stanford) *s.i.s: hld up: rdn over 2f out: sn wknd* **11/2**

1m 39.85s (-0.75) **Going Correction** -0.125s/f (Firm)
WFA 3 from 5yo 8lb **6** Ran SP% **109.1**
Speed ratings (Par 103): **98,97,94,93,89 83**
CSF £31.74 TOTE £13.40: £5.60, £1.30; EX 43.60 Trifecta £134.20.
Owner Mrs Lucinda Freedman **Bred** Cliveden Stud Ltd **Trained** Newmarket, Suffolk

FOCUS
An ordinary handicap and the first two home were fitted with first-time headgear. They went a fair gallop and the winner has been rated back to her maiden best.

4744 FAT LARRY'S BURGERS AT YARMOUTH H'CAP 5f 42y
5:10 (5:10) (Class 5) (0-70,70) 3-Y-O+ **£2,911** (£866; £432; £216) **Stalls** Centre

Form RPR
0052 **1** **Outrage**7 4485 4-9-10 **68** DaneO'Neill 3 84
(Daniel Kubler) *hld up: hdwy over 1f out: led ins fnl f: r.o wl* **3/1**1
2616 **2** 3¼ **Racing Angel (IRE)**33 3559 4-9-10 **68** WilliamCarson 7 72
(Mick Quinn) *chsd ldrs: rdn over 1f out: sn swtchd lft: r.o to go 2nd wl ins fnl f* **11/2**
-043 **3** ¾ **Archimedes (IRE)**13 4280 3-9-6 **68** (b1) MartinHarley 5 68
(Robert Cowell) *edgd lft s: sn led on stands' side rail: rdn over 1f out: hdd ins fnl f: styd on same pce* **10/3**2
4062 **4** ½ **You're Cool**12 4295 4-9-5 **70** LewisEdmunds(7) 6 70
(John Balding) *trckd ldrs: rdn and edgd lft over 1f out: styd on same pce ins fnl f* **9/2**3
036 **5** 1¼ **Angel Way (IRE)**26 3811 7-9-10 **68** ShaneKelly 1 63
(John Gallagher) *racd alone towards far side: up w the pce: rdn 1/2-way: no ex fnl f* **14/1**
1150 **6** 1½ **Bring On A Spinner**46 3105 3-9-3 **70** AaronJones(5) 4 59
(Stuart Williams) *s.i.s and hmpd s: nvr on terms* **9/2**3
5000 **7** hd **Renounce (IRE)**20 3994 4-9-0 **58** (vt1) AdamBeschizza 2 47
(Charlie Wallis) *chsd ldrs: rdn over 1f out: no ex fnl f* **12/1**

1m 1.77s (-0.93) **Going Correction** -0.125s/f (Firm)
WFA 3 from 4yo+ 4lb **7** Ran SP% **114.2**
Speed ratings (Par 103): **102,96,95,94,92 90,90**
CSF £19.73 TOTE £3.70: £2.10, £3.50; EX 19.60 Trifecta £77.30.
Owner D Blunt & G Middlebrook **Bred** Trickledown Stud Limited **Trained** Lambourn, Berks

FOCUS
A modest sprint handicap to finish and a decent pace helped set things up for the ready winner who was quite impressive.
T/Plt: £23.50 to a £1 stake. Pool of £50645.59 - 1570.42 winning tickets. T/Qpdt: £8.70 to a £1 stake. Pool of £3664.93 - 310.02 winning tickets. **Colin Roberts**

4745 - 4746a (Foreign Racing) - See Raceform Interactive

4719 GALWAY (R-H)
Tuesday, July 26

OFFICIAL GOING: Jumps courses - good to yielding; flat course - yielding to soft

4747a COLM QUINN BMW MILE H'CAP (PREMIER HANDICAP) 1m 123y
7:20 (7:21) 3-Y-O+
£52,058 (£16,764; £7,941; £3,529; £1,764; £882)

RPR
1 **Creggs Pipes (IRE)**15 4218 4-9-7 **98** DeclanMcDonogh 5 107+
(Andrew Slattery, Ire) *mde all: stl gng wl and 3 l clr appr st: rdn into st and kpt on wl ins fnl f* **11/2**1
2 1¾ **Top Notch Tonto (IRE)**17 4165 6-9-3 **101** OisinOrr(7) 10 108+
(Brian Ellison) *hld up towards rr: hdwy on outer fr over 2f out and styd on wl into nvr nrr 2nd cl home: nt trble wnr* **12/1**
3 1 **Karalara (IRE)**45 3172 3-8-7 **92** LeighRoche 3 95
(D K Weld, Ire) *chsd ldrs: 3rd 1/2-way: rdn in 2nd 2f out and no imp on wnr u.p ent fnl f: kpt on same pce and dropped to 3rd cl home* **10/1**
4 ¾ **Stipulate**115 1196 7-9-6 **100** DonnachaO'Brien(3) 7 101
(Brian Ellison) *in tch: 6th 1/2-way: tk clsr order after 1/2-way: rdn in 3rd over 2f out and no imp on wnr u.p over 1f out: kpt on same pce and dropped to 4th ins fnl f* **16/1**
5 ½ **Baraweez (IRE)**17 4163 6-9-5 **103** DanielRedmond(7) 16 103+
(Brian Ellison) *chsd ldrs: gng wl in 4th 3f out: rdn in 4th 2f out and no imp on wnr into st: kpt on same pce ins fnl f* **10/1**
6 nse **Ringside Humour (IRE)**13 4282 4-9-3 **94** (t) KevinManning 14 94
(J S Bolger, Ire) *hld up: clsr in 7th at 1/2-way: rdn over 2f out and no imp u.p in 6th appr st: kpt on same pce* **25/1**
7 1¼ **Hasanour (USA)**31 3676 6-9-10 **101** ShaneFoley 2 98
(M Halford, Ire) *hooded to load: chsd ldrs early: 8th bef 1/2-way: rdn over 2f out and no imp u.p in 6th fr 2f out: one pce after* **11/1**
8 ¾ **Brendan Brackan (IRE)**31 3677 7-9-10 **101** (b1) GaryCarroll 13 96
(G M Lyons, Ire) *mid-div: pushed along fr 2f out and no imp into st: kpt on one pce* **16/1**
9 hd **Cailin Mor (IRE)**31 3682 4-8-12 **89** (t) NGMcCullagh 15 84
(M Halford, Ire) *in tch: 5th 1/2-way: rdn in 4th over 2f out and no imp on wnr into st: wknd fnl f* **33/1**
10 ½ **Whiskey Sour (IRE)**23 3931 3-8-6 **91** (t) DannyGrant 18 84
(Edward Lynam, Ire) *chsd ldrs early: 10th bef 1/2-way: n.m.r bhd horses appr st: rdn and no imp over 1f out: kpt on one pce ins fnl f* **20/1**
11 ¾ **Hat Alnasar (IRE)**14 4250 4-9-2 **93** (t) ConorHoban 17 85
(M Halford, Ire) *towards rr: 17th bef 1/2-way: rdn on inner under 2f out and kpt on ins fnl f: nvr nrr* **50/1**
12 ¾ **Fit For The Job (IRE)**290 7130 4-8-12 **89** 1 WayneLordan 12 79
(David Wachman, Ire) *in rr early: tk clsr order in mid-div fr 1/2-way: rdn 2f out and no ex into st: wknd over 1f out* **10/1**
13 1½ **Sea Wolf (IRE)**30 3693 4-9-4 **95** ColinKeane 11 82
(G M Lyons, Ire) *mid-div best: rdn and no imp 2f out: burst blood vessels* **13/2**2
14 nk **Gussy Goose (IRE)**15 4218 4-9-1 **92** (p) BillyLee 4 78
(David Wachman, Ire) *towards rr: tk clsr order after 1/2-way: rdn in mid-div appr st and no ex u.p in 7th 1 1/2f out: no imp whn sltly hmpd and checked ins fnl f: eased* **8/1**3
15 1¾ **Ashraf (IRE)**19 4070 4-9-11 **102** (v1) PatSmullen 1 84
(D K Weld, Ire) *hld up: niggled along in 11th bef 1/2-way and no imp appr st: eased over 1f out* **8/1**3
16 10 **Mohaayed**31 3676 4-9-0 **91** (b1) ChrisHayes 6 50
(Kevin Prendergast, Ire) *towards rr thrght: 15th bef 1/2-way: no imp appr st* **16/1**
17 4¾ **Lily's Rainbow (IRE)**31 3677 4-9-8 **99** RonanWhelan 9 47
(Mrs Denise Foster, Ire) *chsd ldr: 2nd bef 1/2-way: rdn in 2nd 3f out and sn no ex: wknd fr over 2f out* **25/1**
18 3¼ **Princess Aloof (IRE)**30 3698 5-8-12 **89** (p) ColmO'Donoghue 8 29
(Mrs John Harrington, Ire) *hld up: short of room early and sddle slipped: trailing in rr fr bef 1/2-way: nvr a factor* **16/1**

1m 48.86s (108.86)
WFA 3 from 4yo+ 9lb **18** Ran SP% **135.1**
CSF £73.45 CT £698.25 TOTE £5.80: £1.80, £2.70, £2.80, £4.50; DF 102.30 Trifecta £1433.90.
Owner Delphi Six Syndicate **Bred** John Hayes **Trained** Thurles, Co Tipperary
■ Stewards' Enquiry : N G McCullagh one-day ban: careless riding (tbn)

FOCUS
A spectacular performance from the front by the winner, a filly that just won't stop improving.

4748a CAULFIELD INDUSTRIAL H'CAP 7f
7:50 (7:52) (50-80,80) 4-Y-O+ **£6,783** (£2,095; £992; £441; £165)

RPR
1 **Beau Satchel**18 4123 6-9-9 **75** (t) DeclanMcDonogh 4 84
(Adrian McGuinness, Ire) *disp early tl settled bhd ldrs after 1f: 4th 1/2-way: tk clsr order into st and rdn to ld ins fnl f: kpt on wl* **11/4**1
2 ¾ **Severus (GER)**32 3612 6-9-7 **73** BillyLee 5 80
(Des Donovan, Ire) *hld up: gng wl in 9th appr st: prog on inner to chse ldrs ins fnl f where n.m.r: wnt 2nd in clsng stages and kpt on wl: hld* **16/1**

3 *1 1/4* **Strait Of Zanzibar (USA)**[6] 4542 7-10-0 **80**........(tp) ColmO'Donoghue 3 84
(K J Condon, Ire) *prom and reminders early: cl 2nd bef 1/2-way: rdn over 2f out and led narrowly into st: sn jnd and hdd u.p ins fnl f: no imp on wnr clsng stages where dropped to 3rd* **20/1**

4 *1/2* **Bainne (IRE)**[22] 3962 6-9-4 **77**................................(p) DMSimmonson(7) 8 79+
(M D O'Callaghan, Ire) *mid-div: 8th 2f out: hdwy fr over 1f out to chse ldrs ins fnl f where short of room on inner bhd horses: kpt on same pce in 4th clsng stages: nvr trbld ldrs* **10/1**

5 *1* **Plough Boy (IRE)**[19] 4071 5-9-10 **79**...................... RobbieDowney(3) 13 79
(Garvan Donnelly, Ire) *chsd ldrs: rdn in 7th 2f out and no imp on wnr u.p in 5th wl ins fnl f: kpt on same pce* **25/1**

6 *1/2* **Chestnut Fire**[10] 4412 4-9-13 **79**... ShaneFoley 1 77
(M Halford, Ire) *wnt lft s: chsd ldrs: 5th 1/2-way: rdn into st and n.m.r bhd horses in 4th ent fnl f: one pce after* **6/1**[3]

7 *hd* **Chillie Billie**[34] 3541 7-8-13 **68**.................................... RossCoakley(3) 16 66
(J Larkin, Ire) *sn chsd ldrs and led narrowly after 1f: rdn and pressed clly 2f out: hdd narrowly into st where rdr dropped rein briefly: sn disp tl no ex ins fnl f where wknd* **25/1**

8 *3/4* **Mister Martini (IRE)**[16] 4179 4-8-11 **70**............................. OisinOrr(7) 12 66
(Edward Lynam, Ire) *sn chsd ldrs: 3rd 1/2-way: rdn 2f out and sn no ex: wknd fnl f* **20/1**

9 *3/4* **Mzuri (IRE)**[6] 4542 4-9-5 **71**... GaryCarroll 10 65+
(Ms Sheila Lavery, Ire) *settled in mid-div: rdn in 10th 2f out and no imp on ldrs into st: kpt on one pce* **11/1**

10 *nk* **Liberty Jack (IRE)**[30] 3693 6-9-12 **78**...........................(v1) LeighRoche 2 71+
(Adrian Paul Keatley, Ire) *sltly hmpd s: hld up: rdn in 13th into st and no imp: kpt on one pce ins fnl f* **14/1**

11 *shd* **Excelli (IRE)**[10] 4412 6-9-13 **79**................................(p) MichaelHussey 11 72+
(Aidan Anthony Howard, Ire) *hld up: short of room briefly after 2f: rdn in 11th appr st and no imp: one pce fnl f* **40/1**

12 *1 3/4* **Fastidious**[16] 4177 7-9-0 **69**.. ShaneBKelly(3) 15 57+
(M D O'Callaghan, Ire) *hooded to load: rrd and s.i.s: settled in rr: gng wl in 15th appr st: kpt on one pce ins fnl f: nvr involved: coughing* **33/1**

13 *1* **Could Should Would (IRE)**[15] 4217 4-9-11 **77**..............[1] ChrisHayes 7 62
(A Oliver, Ire) *chsd ldrs: 6th 1/2-way: clsr in 5th appr st: pushed along and c wd into st: sn no ex under hands and heels: wknd and eased fnl f* **7/1**

14 *1* **Malinka (IRE)**[110] 1306 4-9-10 **76**.. PatSmullen 6 58+
(D K Weld, Ire) *hld up: pushed along in 12th 2f out and no imp into st: eased fnl f: nvr involved* **4/1**[2]

15 *5* **Beat The Ballot (IRE)**[34] 3541 7-9-10 **76**.................(p) RonanWhelan 14 45+
(Tracey Collins, Ire) *hld up: pushed along and no imp towards rr appr st: eased fnl f* **12/1**

16 *1/2* **Tunnel Creek**[15] 4217 4-9-11 **77**....................................[1] WayneLordan 9 45+
(T J O'Mara, Ire) *hld up: pushed along towards rr fr 1/2-way and no imp: one pce fnl 2f* **50/1**

1m 30.07s (-1.53) **16** Ran SP% **135.7**
CSF £52.71 CT £625.85 TOTE £3.70: £1.20, £4.20, £5.40, £2.60; DF 93.90 Trifecta £1520.20.
Owner Total Recall Racing Club **Bred** Advantage Chemicals Holdings Ltd **Trained** Lusk, Co Dublin

FOCUS
A good performance from the winner to land this contest for the second straight year.

4749 - (Foreign Racing) - See Raceform Interactive

4723 VICHY

Tuesday, July 26

OFFICIAL GOING: Turf: good to soft

4750a PRIX DES REVES D'OR - JACQUES BOUCHARA (LISTED RACE) (2YO) (TURF) 5f

1:20 (1:20) 2-Y-O **£20,220** (£8,088; £6,066; £4,044; £2,022)

RPR

1 **Afandem (IRE)**[18] 4076 2-9-2 0...................................... MaximeGuyon 5 101
(Hugo Palmer) *trckd ldr: rdn to chal and led over 1f out: qcknd and r.o wl: readily* **43/10**[2]

2 *1 1/4* **Boos (FR)**[16] 2-8-13 0.. CristianDemuro 10 93
(P Sogorb, France) **14/5**[1]

3 *3* **Ivory Choice (FR)**[26] 2-8-13 0................................... IoritzMendizabal 7 82
(F Chappet, France) **20/1**

4 *hd* **Becquamis (FR)**[18] 2-9-2 0.. AntoineWerle 4 84
(T Lemer, France) **9/1**[3]

5 *1 1/4* **California Tee**[14] 2-8-13 0...(b1) AntoineHamelin 3 77
(Matthieu Palussiere, France) **10/1**

6 *3/4* **Aiming For Rio (FR)**[38] 3382 2-8-13 0..................... MickaelBarzalona 9 74
(A Fabre, France) *in tch: rdn and outpcd over 1f out: fdd* **14/5**[1]

7 *2* **Notre Sage (FR)**[89] 1821 2-8-13 0...................... Pierre-CharlesBoudot 1 67
(P Decouz, France) **17/1**

8 *5 1/2* **Karyfanny (FR)**[39] 3378 2-8-13 0...................................(p) AlexisBadel 6 47
(S Labate, France) **15/1**

9 *2* **Sirma Traou Land (FR)**[11] 2-8-13 0.............................. JimmyMartin 8 40
(B De Montzey, France) **11/1**

10 *8* **Nazik**[28] 3742 2-9-2 0..(p) UmbertoRispoli 2 14
(J Reynier, France) **24/1**

59.5s (59.50) **10** Ran SP% **119.5**
PARI-MUTUEL (all including 1 euro stake): WIN 5.30; PLACE 1.90, 1.60, 3.70; DF 9.50; SF 19.90.
Owner Hamad Rashed Bin Ghedayer **Bred** Rabbah Bloodstock Limited **Trained** Newmarket, Suffolk

4751 - 5215a (Foreign Racing) - See Raceform Interactive

4731 GOODWOOD (R-H)

Wednesday, July 27

OFFICIAL GOING: Straight course - good (good to firm in places); round course - good to firm (8.1)
Wind: light, against Weather: overcast

4752 MATCHBOOK BETTING EXCHANGE GOODWOOD STKS (H'CAP) 2m 5f

2:00 (2:02) (Class 2) (0-100,96) 3-Y-O+
£31,125 (£9,320; £4,660; £2,330; £1,165; £585) **Stalls** Far side

Form RPR

1-33 **1** **Star Rider**[40] 3351 4-8-13 **85**.......................(p) JimmyFortune 12 94+
(Hughie Morrison) *hld up in midfield: pushed along and hdwy to chse ldrs over 2f out: rdn to ld and edgd rt over 1f out: clr and styd on wl ins fnl f: eased towards fin* **11/1**

0425 **2** *2* **Percy Veer**[12] 4353 4-8-10 **85**.................................. EdwardGreatrex(3) 1 91
(Sylvester Kirk) *swtg: chsd ldrs: rdn over 2f out: drvn and sltly outpcd over 1f out: swtchd lft and rallied ins fnl f: styd on u.p to go 2nd cl home* **14/1**

-401 **3** *hd* **Oceane (FR)**[19] 4077 4-9-0 **86**................................(p) FergusSweeney 13 94+
(Alan King) *lw: hld up towards rr: trying to cl but stuck bhd a wall of horses 2f out: swtchd lft and effrt over 1f out: r.o v strly ins fnl f: snatched 3rd last strides* **11/1**

2/23 **4** *hd* **Poyle Thomas**[32] 3657 7-9-6 **92**.............................. RichardKingscote 17 98
(Ralph Beckett) *hld up in midfield: hdwy to press ldrs 3f out: rdn and ev ch 2f out: unable qck whn sltly impeded and swtchd lft ent fnl f: chsd wnr 1f out: kpt on same pce: lost 2 pls cl home* **10/1**[3]

1560 **5** *1* **Planetoid (IRE)**[19] 4077 8-8-8 **80**..................................(b) JoeFanning 10 85
(Jim Best) *swtg: hld up in last quartet: clsd whn nt clr run over 2f out: squeezed through 2f out: hdwy u.p over 1f out: pressing for pls ins fnl f: styd on same pce fnl 100yds* **66/1**

3310 **6** *1/2* **Be My Sea (IRE)**[26] 3862 5-8-7 **79**.............................(p) JimmyQuinn 16 83
(Tony Carroll) *chsd ldng pair tl wnt 2nd 5f out tl led over 3f out: rdn and hrd pressed over 2f out: hdd over 1f out: no ex and styd on same pce ins fnl f* **33/1**

-001 **7** *1 1/2* **Wind Place And Sho**[38] 3437 4-9-4 **90**.............................. RyanTate 20 93
(James Eustace) *wl in tch in midfield: clsd to chse ldng trio: rdn and hung rt over 1f out: wknd ins fnl f* **11/1**

-244 **8** *2* **Moscato**[32] 3658 5-9-9 **95**..(p) LukeMorris 2 96
(Sir Mark Prescott Bt) *chsd ldrs: rdn over 3f out: drvn and unable qck over 1f out: wknd ins fnl f* **13/2**[2]

12-0 **9** *2* **Revision (FR)**[25] 3889 4-8-13 **85**... KierenFox 9 84
(John Best) *hld up towards rr: swtchd lft and effrt 3f out: no hdwy u.p 2f out: wl hld and plugged on same pce fnl f: fin lame* **25/1**

300- **10** *nk* **Teak (IRE)**[55] 7892 9-9-2 **88**..(p) AdamKirby 7 87
(Ian Williams) *t.k.h: hld up in midfield: rdn 3f out: no hdwy u.p over 1f out: wl hld and plugged on same pce ins fnl f* **20/1**

000 **11** *2 1/2* **Wordiness**[19] 4077 8-8-6 **83**...................................... HectorCrouch(5) 19 80
(David Evans) *hld up towards rr: swtchd lft 3f out: effrt and edging rt 2f out: no imp over 1f out: plugged on same pce fnl f* **25/1**

0-60 **12** *hd* **Perfect Summer (IRE)**[4] 4664 6-8-5 **77**....................(p) FrannyNorton 18 74
(Ian Williams) *t.k.h: hld up in midfield: effrt ent fnl 2f: no imp over 1f out: wl hld whn squeezed for room ins fnl f: wknd* **40/1**

3300 **13** *6* **Eton Rambler (USA)**[32] 3657 6-9-0 **86**........................ SteveDrowne 11 77
(George Baker) *hld up in last quartet: effrt ent fnl 2f: rdn and sme modest hdwy over 1f out: no ch and nt pushed ins fnl f* **50/1**

6-20 **14** *3 1/4* **The Cashel Man (IRE)**[32] 3657 4-9-3 **89**.................(p) JamieSpencer 15 77
(David Simcock) *lw: hld up in last quartet: swtchd lft and stl plenty to do over 2f out: no hdwy u.p over 1f out: wl btn and eased ins fnl f* **11/2**[1]

4663 **15** *3* **Communicator**[32] 3639 8-8-7 **79**..................................(v) DavidProbert 5 65
(Andrew Balding) *lw: hld up in tch in midfield: effrt over 2f out: no hdwy: btn whn sltly short of room over 1f out: sn wknd* **16/1**

5410 **16** *1 1/2* **Albahar (FR)**[32] 3657 5-9-4 **90**.................................(p) DaneO'Neill 14 74
(Chris Gordon) *hld up towards rr: effrt on inner but stl plenty to do whn nt clr run 2f out: swtchd lft but no ch over 1f out: eased fnl f* **20/1**

4-14 **17** *11* **Iftiraaq (IRE)**[11] 2897 5-8-9 **81**.......................................(p) AndreaAtzeni 6 55
(Seamus Durack) *swtg: t.k.h: chsd ldr tl 5f out: lost pl 3f out: wl bhd and eased over 1f out: t.o* **16/1**

24-2 **18** *16* **Diamond Joel**[32] 3639 4-8-8 **80**.............................. SilvestreDeSousa 3 40
(Mick Channon) *led tl over 3f out: lost pl qckly jst over 2f out: eased over 1f out: t.o* **12/1**

2600 **P** **Seaside Sizzler**[5] 4581 9-9-2 **88**.......................................(v) JimCrowley 4
(William Knight) *midfield tl pushed along and lost pl 6f out: bhd 2f out: sn lost tch: eased over 1f out: p.u and dismntd ins fnl f: lame* **28/1**

/100 **P** **No Heretic**[32] 3658 8-9-10 **96**.....................................(t1) JamesMcDonald 8
(Nicky Henderson) *hld up in last quartet: effrt over 2f out: no hdwy and lost action 2f out: sn eased and p.u (fatally injured)* **16/1**

4m 32.87s (1.87) **Going Correction** +0.025s/f (Good) **20** Ran SP% **124.3**
Speed ratings (Par 109): **97,96,96,96,95 95,94,94,93,93 92,92,89,88,87 87,82,76, ,**
CSF £137.92 CT £1756.33 TOTE £13.10: £3.50, £3.40, £3.00, £3.10; EX 228.00 Trifecta £3310.80.
Owner Ben & Sir Martyn Arbib **Bred** Arbib Bloodstock Partnership **Trained** East Ilsley, Berks

FOCUS
The running rail from the 6f marker on the lower bend to the winning post was dolled out 6yds, increasing distances by 12yds. The top bend had been dolled out 3yds, increasing race distances by 8yds. Dry overnight and, despite some rain in the morning, the going had apparently tightened up from the previous day. Traditionally an ultra-competitive marathon handicap, this year's edition was no different and the field were soon well strung out. The winner was an improver for the proper test and the runner-up ran close to form.

4753 BERINGICE GORDON STKS (GROUP 3) 1m 4f

2:35 (2:35) (Class 1) 3-Y-O
£56,710 (£21,500; £10,760; £5,360; £2,690; £1,350) **Stalls** High

Form RPR

-210 **1** **Ulysses (IRE)**[53] 2896 3-9-1 98.. AndreaAtzeni 5 111+
(Sir Michael Stoute) *t.k.h: hld up in tch in last trio: rdn and hdwy to ld jst over 1f out: hld on wl ins fnl f: rdn out* **9/2**[2]

14 **2** *1/2* **The Major General (IRE)**[33] 3631 3-9-1 102........... SeamieHeffernan 7 110
(A P O'Brien, Ire) *swtg: t.k.h: chsd ldrs tl led after 3f: rdn and hrd pressed 2f out: hdd over 1f out: battled on wl u.p and stl ev ch ins fnl f: hld towards fin* **11/1**

2500 **3** 1 ½ **Shogun (IRE)**[32] 3679 3-9-1 107 RyanMoore 1 109+
(A P O'Brien, Ire) *hld up in tch in midfield: effrt n.m.r wl over 1f: drvn and stl cl enough in 5th whn nt clrest of runs ent fnl f: kpt on u.p fnl 150yds: wnt 3rd wl ins fnl f* **13/2**

1 **4** shd **Qatari Hunter (IRE)**[20] 4070 3-9-1 102 KevinManning 4 107
(J S Bolger, Ire) *athletic: stdd s: hld up in rr: clsd over 2f out: hdwy u.p over 1f out: chsd ldrs 1f out: kpt on ins fnl f* **5/1**[3]

2220 **5** nk **Prize Money**[20] 4059 3-9-1 107 JamesDoyle 8 107
(Saeed bin Suroor) *broke wl and led early: sn stdd bk and chsd ldrs: rdn to chal 2f out: drvn to ld over 1f out: sn hdd: no ex and btn ins fnl f: wknd fnl 100yds: lost 2 pls cl home* **15/2**

5214 **6** 1 ¾ **Steel Of Madrid (IRE)**[41] 3296 3-9-1 104 PatDobbs 2 104
(Richard Hannon) *hld up in tch in midfield: effrt 2f out: 6th and no imp 1f out: styd on same pce ins fnl f* **10/1**

-016 **7** ½ **Goldmember**[20] 4059 3-9-1 99 OisinMurphy 3 103
(David Simcock) *swtg: t.k.h: hld up in tch in last trio: effrt and swtchd lft over 1f out: no imp and styd on same pce ins fnl f* **25/1**

-422 **8** 5 **Platitude**[20] 4059 3-9-1 103 FrankieDettori 6 95
(Sir Michael Stoute) *swtg: t.k.h: sn led: hdd after 2f: chsd ldrs after: rdn 2f out: lost pl and btn over 1f out: wknd fnl f* **4/1**[1]

3033 **9** 14 **Harrison**[20] 4059 3-9-1 103 SilvestreDeSousa 9 73
(Mick Channon) *t.k.h: led after 2f tl after 3f: chsd ldr tl lost pl and jostled over 2f out: bhd and eased 1f out* **15/2**

2m 38.37s (-0.03) **Going Correction** +0.025s/f (Good) **9** Ran SP% **113.0**
Speed ratings (Par 110): **101,100,99,99,99 98,97,94,85**
CSF £51.42 TOTE £4.00: £1.70, £2.80, £2.20; EX 45.10 Trifecta £376.10.
Owner Flaxman Stables Ireland Ltd **Bred** Flaxman Stables Ireland Ltd **Trained** Newmarket, Suffolk

FOCUS
Race distance increased by 8yds. A fourth win in this race in eight years for Sir Michael Stoute and, while the form doesn't look particularly strong on paper (they went steady early and plenty were keen), the winner is well regarded and can go on to rate higher.

4754 QATAR SUSSEX STKS (BRITISH CHAMPIONS SERIES) (GROUP 1) 1m
3:10 (3:13) (Class 1) 3-Y-0+
£560,200 (£213,300; £106,800; £53,300; £26,700; £13,400) **Stalls** Low

Form RPR

122 **1** **The Gurkha (IRE)**[25] 3912 3-9-0 121 (t) RyanMoore 3 124+
(A P O'Brien, Ire) *swtg: trckd ldr tl 1/2-way: styd handy in 3rd: hemmed in 2f out: gap opened and swtchd lft to press ldr ent fnl f: sn rdn to chal: led wl ins fnl f: r.o: rdn out* **11/8**[1]

-121 **2** nk **Galileo Gold**[43] 3245 3-9-0 123 FrankieDettori 6 123
(Hugo Palmer) *swtg: led: rdn wl over 1f out: hrd pressed and drvn jst ins fnl f: hdd wl ins fnl f: kpt on u.p but a hld after* **9/4**[2]

-231 **3** shd **Ribchester (IRE)**[42] 3269 3-9-0 117 JamesDoyle 2 123+
(Richard Fahey) *in tch in midfield: swtchd lft 2f out: in the clr and rdn over 1f out: hdwy to chse clr ldng pair jst ins fnl f: r.o strly fnl 100yds: nt quite rch ldrs* **8/1**

1540 **4** 3 **Toormore (IRE)**[18] 4127 5-9-8 115 JamesMcDonald 4 118
(Richard Hannon) *hld up in last trio: effrt 2f out: rdn and sltly impeded over 1f out: styd on u.p ins fnl f: no threat to ldrs* **16/1**

6513 **5** nk **Gabrial (IRE)**[18] 4127 7-9-8 113 JimmyFortune 1 117
(Richard Fahey) *hld up in midfield: effrt on inner: hdwy u.p 1f out: styd on ins fnl f: no threat to ldrs* **50/1**

30-3 **6** ¾ **Lightning Spear**[43] 3242 5-9-8 117 OisinMurphy 8 115
(David Simcock) *hld up in last pair: swtchd lft and effrt over 1f out: styd on ins fnl f: nvr trbld ldrs* **14/1**

-134 **7** nk **So Beloved**[32] 3664 6-9-8 113 DanielTudhope 9 114
(David O'Meara) *chsd ldng trio: rdn ent fnl 2f: edging rt u.p and unable qck ent fnl f: wknd ins fnl f* **40/1**

113 **8** hd **Awtaad (IRE)**[43] 3245 3-9-0 119 ChrisHayes 10 112
(Kevin Prendergast, Ire) *broke wl to press ldrs: wnt 2nd and pressing ldr 1/2-way: rdn ent fnl 2f: unable qck u.p ent fnl f: wknd ins fnl f* **13/2**[3]

-006 **9** ½ **Kodi Bear (IRE)**[18] 4127 4-9-8 111 [1] DaneO'Neill 5 113
(Clive Cox) *swtg: hld up in midfield: effrt and n.m.r 2f out: sn rdn and no imp whn drifted rt over 1f out: wl hld and styd on same pce ins fnl f* **25/1**

10-5 **10** 4 ½ **Richard Pankhurst**[18] 4127 4-9-8 113 AndreaAtzeni 7 102
(John Gosden) *swtg: hld up in last pair: effrt 2f out: rdn and btn over 1f out: wknd fnl f* **33/1**

1m 37.35s (-2.55) **Going Correction** +0.025s/f (Good)
WFA 3 from 4yo+ 8lb **10** Ran SP% **121.1**
Speed ratings (Par 117): **113,112,112,109,109 108,108,108,107,103**
CSF £4.57 CT £18.03 TOTE £2.10: £1.02, £1.70, £3.00; EX 5.10 Trifecta £22.40.
Owner Derrick Smith & Mrs John Magnier & Michael Tabor **Bred** Chintz Syndicate **Trained** Cashel, Co Tipperary

FOCUS
Race distance increased by 12yds. The highlight of the week, with the three Guineas winners facing off for a second time, and the winner managed to reverse form with his St James's Palace conqueror. The early pace was a steady one, with the runner-up dictating, and little got into it. The first two have been rated close to their marks, but we might have expected a bit more.

4755 VICTORIA RACING CLUB MOLECOMB STKS (GROUP 3) 5f
3:45 (3:47) (Class 1) 2-Y-0
£42,532 (£16,125; £8,070; £4,020; £2,017; £1,012) **Stalls** High

Form RPR

1100 **1** **Yalta (IRE)**[20] 4060 2-9-1 0 JamesDoyle 3 111
(Mark Johnston) *lw: mde all: shkn up ent fnl f: rdn and styd on strly to draw clr fnl 100yds: impressive* **8/1**

2221 **2** 3 **The Last Lion (IRE)**[26] 3858 2-9-1 0 FrannyNorton 2 100
(Mark Johnston) *swtg: chsd ldrs: wnt 2nd ent fnl 2f: rdn over 1f out: unable qck jst ins fnl f: outpcd by wnr but hld on for 2nd fnl 100yds* **3/1**[2]

1215 **3** ¾ **Global Applause**[41] 3295 2-9-1 0 FrankieDettori 1 98
(Ed Dunlop) *lw: hld up in tch in midfield: clsd to trck ldng pair over 1f out: rdn ent fnl f: styd on same pce ins fnl f* **2/1**[1]

4 ½ **Sportsmanship (USA)**[13] 4322 2-9-1 0 RyanMoore 7 96+
(A P O'Brien, Ire) *lengthy: str: lw: hld up in tch in last trio: clsd ent fnl 2f: rdn and effrt to chse ldng trio jst over 1f out: styd on ins fnl f: no ch w wnr* **11/2**[3]

101 **5** 3 ¾ **Big Time Baby (IRE)**[19] 4091 2-9-1 0 (t) RichardKingscote 8 82
(Tom Dascombe) *racd keenly: chsd wnr tl jst over 2f out: lost pl and btn 5th 1f out: drifted rt and wknd ins fnl f* **9/1**

41 **6** 1 **Kyllang Rock (IRE)**[16] 4205 2-9-1 0 AndreaAtzeni 9 79
(James Tate) *unf: taken down early: stdd s: t.k.h: hld up in last trio: effrt wl over 1f out: sn rdn and no imp: wl btn fnl f* **16/1**

303 **7** nk **Just An Idea (IRE)**[26] 3858 2-9-1 0 MartinHarley 4 78
(Harry Dunlop) *bmpd s: in tch in last trio: rdn ent fnl 2f: outpcd and btn over 1f out* **50/1**

1 **8** 4 ½ **Nayyar**[19] 4083 2-9-1 0 JamesMcDonald 5 61
(Charles Hills) *leggy: swtg: wnt rt s: in tch in midfield: rdn 1/2-way: sn struggling: wknd over 1f out: wl btn and eased ins fnl f* **10/1**

2115 **9** 4 ½ **Rapacity Alexander (IRE)**[25] 3937 2-8-12 0 JFEgan 10 42
(David Evans) *leggy: swtg: in tch in midfield: rdn over 2f out: sn struggling: wl bhd ins fnl f* **25/1**

57.14s (-3.06) **Going Correction** -0.375s/f (Firm) 2y crse rec **9** Ran SP% **115.6**
Speed ratings (Par 104): **109,104,103,102,96 94,94,86,79**
CSF £32.30 TOTE £9.80: £2.60, £1.30, £1.40; EX 29.20 Trifecta £93.80.
Owner Sheikh Hamdan bin Mohammed Al Maktoum **Bred** Darley **Trained** Middleham Moor, N Yorks

FOCUS
There was less early speed than predicted here, with the winner not really taken on in front. Setting middle fractions of 10.30, 10.64 and 10.70, he controlled the pace before pulling away inside the last and lowering the juvenile course record by 0.16sec.

4756 MARKEL INSURANCE MAIDEN FILLIES' STKS (PLUS 10 RACE) 6f
4:20 (4:22) (Class 2) 2-Y-0
£12,938 (£3,850; £1,924; £962) **Stalls** High

Form RPR

2 **1** **Perfect Angel (IRE)**[34] 3555 2-9-0 0 DavidProbert 3 90+
(Andrew Balding) *leggy: athletic: racd in centre: in tch in midfield: effrt to chal u.p over 1f out: led ins fnl f: hung lft but hld on wl fnl 100yds: rdn out* **8/1**[3]

2 nk **Promising (IRE)** 2-9-0 0 SeanLevey 11 89+
(Richard Hannon) *cmpt: hld up in tch in midfield: gd hdwy over 2f out: rdn to ld over 1f out: clr w wnr 1f out: hdd and carried lft ins fnl f: kpt on but hld towards fin* **33/1**

0 **3** 3 ½ **Bouquet De Flores (USA)**[20] 4064 2-9-0 0 JamesDoyle 10 79
(Charlie Appleby) *chsd ldrs: rdn to chse ldng pair jst over 1f out: clr 3rd but no imp fnl f: one pce* **5/4**[1]

36 **4** 2 ½ **Suffragette City (IRE)**[20] 4064 2-9-0 0 PatDobbs 18 71
(Richard Hannon) *stdd after s: hld up towards rr: hdwy 1/2-way: rdn over 1f out: kpt on to go 4th wl ins fnl f: nvr trbld ldrs* **12/1**

3242 **5** ½ **Texas Katie**[4] 4659 2-9-0 0 SilvestreDeSousa 20 70
(Mick Channon) *hld up towards rr: hdwy and hung rt over 1f out: kpt on ins fnl f: nvr trbld ldrs* **20/1**

3 **6** ¾ **Bithynia (IRE)**[69] 2410 2-9-0 0 JimCrowley 9 68
(Hugo Palmer) *athletic: racd freely: sn chsng ldr tl led 2f out: rdn and hdd over 1f out: sn struggling: hung rt and wknd ins fnl f* **5/1**[2]

7 nse **Fire Palace** 2-9-0 0 AndreaAtzeni 1 68+
(Robert Eddery) *athletic: stdd and swtchd lft after s: hld up towards rr: swtchd rt and hdwy 2f out: rdn over 1f out: styd on same pce ins fnl f: nvr trbld ldrs* **66/1**

8 ½ **Nepeta (USA)** 2-9-0 0 FrannyNorton 13 66+
(Mark Johnston) *tall: swtg: broke wl and chsd ldrs early: steadily lost pl: bhd 2f out: rallied and styd on to pass btn horses ins fnl f: no threat to ldrs* **33/1**

5 **9** nse **The Lacemaker**[20] 4063 2-9-0 0 FrankieDettori 5 66
(Ed Dunlop) *racd in centre: hld up in tch: rdn and unable qck: sn outpcd and wknd ins fnl f* **14/1**

0 **10** ½ **High Excitement (USA)**[53] 2885 2-9-0 0 [1] JamesMcDonald 4 64
(Charles Hills) *unf: swtg: racd in centre: t.k.h: hld up in tch in midfield: rdn and no hdwy over 1f out: wknd ins fnl f* **25/1**

0 **11** ¾ **Compton Poppy**[35] 3511 2-9-0 0 GeorgeDowning 8 62
(Tony Carroll) *cmpt: chsd ldrs tl rdn 2f out: sn struggling and lost pl over 1f out: wknd ins fnl f* **100/1**

4 **12** hd **Sky Ballerina**[27] 3812 2-9-0 0 RobertHavlin 12 62
(Simon Crisford) *chsd ldrs: rdn and unable qck whn edgd rt over 1f out: sn wknd* **14/1**

13 1 ¼ **Curry (IRE)** 2-9-0 0 DaneO'Neill 7 58
(Richard Hannon) *cmpt: hld up towards rr: nvr trbld ldrs* **28/1**

14 hd **Acertwo** 2-9-0 0 JFEgan 2 57
(Joseph Tuite) *w'like: racd in centre: hld up in tch in midfield: rdn and btn wl over 1f out: sn wknd* **100/1**

03 **15** hd **Grand Myla (IRE)**[20] 4064 2-9-0 0 RyanMoore 6 60
(Gary Moore) *racd in centre: led tl rdn and hdd wl over 1f out: sn btn: wknd and eased ins fnl f* **14/1**

30 **16** ¾ **Limelite (IRE)**[50] 2990 2-9-0 0 TomMarquand 17 54
(Richard Hannon) *hld up in tch in midfield: rdn and btn whn hung lft over 1f out: sn wknd* **50/1**

17 4 ½ **Paradwys (IRE)** 2-9-0 0 [1] TomQueally 19 41+
(Charles Hills) *tall: v.s.a: a bhd* **50/1**

0 **18** 1 ¼ **Nuptials (USA)**[61] 2637 2-9-0 0 JohnFahy 16 37
(Eve Johnson Houghton) *w'like: midfield tl lost pl 3f out: bhd over 1f out* **100/1**

1m 11.4s (-0.80) **Going Correction** -0.375s/f (Firm) **18** Ran SP% **126.2**
Speed ratings (Par 97): **90,89,84,81,80 79,79,79,79,78 77,77,75,75,75 74,68,66**
CSF £262.04 TOTE £8.70: £2.50, £10.30, £1.20; EX 225.40 Trifecta £2126.10.
Owner Mildmay Racing & D H Caslon **Bred** Yeomanstown Stud & Doc Bloodstock **Trained** Kingsclere, Hants

FOCUS
A fair fillies' maiden, the front pair drawing clear. The winner was up around a stone on her debut rating.

4757 EBF BREEDERS' SERIES VEUVE CLICQUOT FILLIES' H'CAP 1m 1f 192y
4:55 (4:55) (Class 2) (0-105,98) 3-Y-0+
£18,675 (£5,592; £2,796; £1,398; £699; £351) **Stalls** Low

Form RPR

5155 **1** **Sagaciously (IRE)**[32] 3662 4-9-11 **95** JamesDoyle 5 107
(Ed Dunlop) *hld up in tch in midfield: rdn and hdwy to chse ldr 2f out: led over 1f out: styd on wl fnl f: rdn out* **14/1**

1120 **2** 2 ¾ **Sagely (IRE)**[33] 3608 3-8-10 **90** SilvestreDeSousa 7 96
(Ed Dunlop) *hld up in tch in last pair: hdwy and drifting rt over 1f out: chsd clr wnr 1f out: styd on same pce ins fnl f* **7/1**[3]

1-00 **3** nk **Intimation**[33] 3608 4-9-6 **90** RyanMoore 4 95
(Sir Michael Stoute) *lw: in tch in midfield: effrt and drifted rt over 1f out: chsd ldrs 1f out: kpt on same pce u.p ins fnl f* **7/2**[2]

1231 **4** 2 ¼ **Shaan (IRE)**[11] 4403 3-8-12 **92** FrankieDettori 1 93+
(Richard Hannon) *t.k.h: chsd ldr tl 7f out: chsd ldrs after tl shuffled bk into midfield and nt clr run 2f out: rallied and swtchd rt jst over 1f out: kpt on same pce ins fnl f* **2/1**[1]

4215 **5** 1¾ **Motdaw**[19] 4078 3-8-8 **88** .... JFEgan 9 85
(Mick Channon) *hld up in last trio: rdn and hdwy 2f out: no imp and outpcd over 1f out: wknd ins fnl f* **25/1**

0045 **6** 1 **Dessertoflife (IRE)**[18] 4131 3-9-4 **98** .... JoeFanning 6 93
(Mark Johnston) *in tch in midfield: clsd chse ldrs 4f out: rdn to ld wl over 2f out: hdd over 1f out and sn outpcd: wknd ins fnl f* **8/1**

410- **7** 5 **Kiltara (IRE)**[292] 7076 4-9-5 **89** .... FrannyNorton 2 74
(Mark Johnston) *chsd ldrs tl wnt 2nd 7f out tl 3f out: losing pl and btn whn bdly hmpd over 1f out: sn wknd* **12/1**

142- **8** 1¼ **Rioca (IRE)**[270] 7631 3-8-13 **93** .... (p) LukeMorris 10 76
(Sir Mark Prescott Bt) *led tl hdd and rdn wl over 1f out: lost pl and towards rr whn bdly hmpd over 1f out: sn wknd* **15/2**

1430 **9** hd **Miss Van Gogh**[18] 4163 4-9-5 **89** .... PaulHanagan 8 72
(Richard Fahey) *lw: stdd s: hld up in last pair: effrt on outer 2f out: no prog over 1f out: sn wknd* **25/1**

-164 **10** 17 **Wholesome (USA)**[33] 3593 3-8-2 **82** .... JoeyHaynes 3 31
(K R Burke) *in tch in midfield: lost pl jst over 2f out: bhd and n.m.r 2f out: sn wknd: eased ins fnl f* **20/1**

2m 5.14s (-2.96) **Going Correction** +0.025s/f (Good)
WFA 3 from 4yo 10lb **10** Ran SP% **117.7**
Speed ratings (Par 96): **112,109,109,107,106 105,101,100,100,86**
CSF £106.48 CT £422.19 TOTE £19.40: £4.10, £2.10, £1.50; EX 90.10 Trifecta £503.80.
Owner The Sagacious Lot **Bred** Keatly Overseas Ltd **Trained** Newmarket, Suffolk

FOCUS
Race distance increased by 8yds. A decent fillies' handicap and a good training performance from Ed Dunlop, who saddled half-sisters to finish 1-2. Another improvement from the winner.

4758 NATWEST STKS (H'CAP) 7f
5:25 (5:26) (Class 3) (0-95,95) 3-Y-O+ **£12,938** (£3,850; £1,924; £962) **Stalls** Low

Form RPR

12-5 **1** **Shady McCoy (USA)**[25] 3890 6-9-6 **87** .... JamesDoyle 10 94
(Ian Williams) *hld up in midfield: effrt over 1f out: hdwy u.p and hung rt ins fnl f: str burst fnl 100yds to ld towards fin* **14/1**

5002 **2** ½ **Twin Sails**[19] 4116 3-9-7 **95** .... (b) DaneO'Neill 3 98
(Dean Ivory) *lw: in tch in midfield: effrt towards inner over 1f out: wnt 2nd ent fnl f: drvn and styd on to chal wl ins fnl f: kpt on* **7/1**[2]

1-03 **3** nse **Rex Imperator**[13] 4299 7-9-9 **90** .... (p) DanielTudhope 12 96
(David O'Meara) *stdd and bmpd s: t.k.h: hld up in midfield: clsd over 1f out: swtchd rt and chsd ldrs jst ins fnl f: kpt on wl fnl 100yds* **12/1**

4144 **4** hd **Magnus Maximus**[32] 3656 5-9-12 **93** .... MartinHarley 11 98
(Robyn Brisland) *led: clr and rdn over 1f out: hung lft ins fnl f: hdd towards fin: lost 2 pls cl home* **33/1**

0044 **5** ¾ **The Warrior (IRE)**[7] 4532 4-9-4 **85** .... JamesMcDonald 17 88
(Amanda Perrett) *hld up in last trio: rdn and hdwy on inner 2f out: styd on wl ins fnl f: nt quite rch ldrs* **16/1**

21-2 **6** hd **Afjaan (IRE)**[14] 4263 4-9-8 **89** .... FrankieDettori 1 92+
(William Haggas) *lw: t.k.h: chsd ldrs: hung rt fr 3f out: rdn and stl cl enough over 1f out: stl hanging and kpt on same pce ins fnl f* **11/8**[1]

2403 **7** nk **Plucky Dip**[5] 4599 5-9-4 **85** .... DannyBrock 15 87
(John Ryan) *chsd ldrs: rdn over 2f out: clsd and squeezed for room jst ins fnl f: kpt on same pce fnl 100yds* **50/1**

0012 **8** shd **Pastoral Player**[26] 3848 9-9-3 **89** .... CharlieBennett[(5)] 6 90
(Hughie Morrison) *hld up towards rr: clsd and swtchd rt ent fnl f: r.o wl fnl 100yds: nt rch ldrs* **10/1**

2100 **9** 2¼ **Al Khan (IRE)**[11] 4399 7-9-10 **91** .... JamieSpencer 2 86
(Kevin Ryan) *in tch in midfield: effrt 2f out: struggling to qckn whn nt clrest of runs ent fnl f: wknd ins fnl f* **25/1**

-600 **10** ½ **Fiftyshadesofgrey (IRE)**[54] 2862 5-9-11 **92** .... (p) SteveDrowne 18 86
(George Baker) *hld up towards rr: sme hdwy u.p over 1f out: no imp and styd on same pce ins fnl f* **25/1**

1002 **11** nk **Arnold Lane (IRE)**[13] 4305 7-9-9 **90** .... SilvestreDeSousa 8 83
(Mick Channon) *chsd ldr: rdn 2f out: unable qck and lost 2nd ent fnl f: wknd ins fnl f* **14/1**

1051 **12** nk **Mr Bossy Boots (IRE)**[34] 3566 5-9-5 **89** .... (t) KieranShoemark[(3)] 20 81
(Amanda Perrett) *hld up towards rr: c wd 3f out and sn rdn: no imp tl kpt on ins fnl f: nvr trbld ldrs* **33/1**

4603 **13** 2¼ **Fort Bastion (IRE)**[9] 4448 7-9-8 **94** .... (b) JoshDoyle[(5)] 13 80
(David O'Meara) *bmpd s: hld up towards rr: effrt towards inner 2f out: no imp u.p over 1f out: nvr trbld ldrs* **16/1**

00-4 **14** nk **Take A Note**[13] 4305 7-8-12 **86** .... (v) MitchGodwin[(7)] 9 71
(Patrick Chamings) *hld up in midfield: effrt on outer over 2f out: no hdwy and wl hld over 1f out: wknd fnl f* **66/1**

050 **15** ½ **Czech It Out (IRE)**[35] 3534 6-9-5 **86** .... PatDobbs 5 70
(Amanda Perrett) *midfield: rdn and no hdwy wl over 1f out: sn lost pl: wknd fnl f* **8/1**[3]

2035 **16** 20 **Jack's Revenge (IRE)**[19] 4109 8-9-5 **86** .... (bt) FergusSweeney 14 16
(George Baker) *hld up in rr: lost tch over 1f out: eased ins fnl f* **25/1**

1m 25.62s (-1.38) **Going Correction** +0.025s/f (Good)
WFA 3 from 4yo+ 7lb **16** Ran SP% **128.5**
Speed ratings (Par 107): **108,107,107,107,106 106,105,105,103,102 102,101,99,98,98 75**
CSF £108.13 CT £1293.44 TOTE £15.90: £3.20, £2.10, £2.70, £7.00; EX 129.80 Trifecta £7743.00 Part won..
Owner Allwins Stables **Bred** Bluegrass Hall Llc **Trained** Portway, Worcs

FOCUS
Race distance increased by 12yds. A useful handicap, although the short-priced favourite disappointed. The winner resumed last-year's progress.
T/Jkpt: Not won. T/Plt: £47.00 to a £1 stake. Pool: £297,854.16 - 4625.96 winning tickets.
T/Qpdt: £5.40 to a £1 stake. Pool: £21,608.7 - 2949.79 winning tickets. **Steve Payne**

4516 LEICESTER (R-H)
Wednesday, July 27

OFFICIAL GOING: Good to firm (good in places; 7.0)
Wind: Light across Weather: Fine

4759 EBF STALLIONS MEDIAN AUCTION MAIDEN FILLIES' STKS (PLUS 10 RACE) 6f
6:15 (6:17) (Class 5) 2-Y-O **£3,881** (£1,155; £577; £288) **Stalls** High

Form RPR

402 **1** **Bobby Vee**[14] 4261 2-9-0 0 .... RobertWinston 15 68
(Dean Ivory) *disp ld tl led 4f out: rdn over 1f out: styd on* **15/2**[3]

2 ½ **Prufrock (IRE)** 2-9-0 0 .... SaleemGolam 6 66
(David Simcock) *a.p: rdn to chse wnr over 1f out: r.o* **33/1**

0 **3** shd **Twiggy**[27] 3818 2-9-0 0 .... MartinDwyer 12 65
(Jane Chapple-Hyam) *unruly to post: s.i.s: hld up: hdwy over 1f out: shkn up and edgd lft ins fnl f: r.o* **7/2**[2]

4 ¾ **Tonahutu (IRE)** 2-9-0 0 .... HarryBentley 4 63
(Ed Vaughan) *hld up: hdwy over 2f out: rdn over 1f out: styd on* **12/1**

5 1¼ **Life On Mars** 2-9-0 0 .... WilliamTwiston-Davies 1 59+
(William Haggas) *hld up: pushed along 1/2-way: r.o ins fnl f: nvr nrr* **10/1**

6 nk **Gokena (FR)** 2-9-0 0 .... GrahamLee 16 58+
(Kevin Ryan) *prom: rdn and edgd lft over 1f out: styd on* **7/2**[2]

0 **7** ¾ **Seyasah (IRE)**[27] 3818 2-9-0 0 .... TedDurcan 9 56
(Chris Wall) *w ldrs: rdn and ev ch over 1f out: no ex ins fnl f* **2/1**[1]

6 **8** 2¾ **Topmeup**[9] 4457 2-9-0 0 .... CamHardie 7 47
(Stuart Edmunds) *prom: lost pl over 3f out: n.d after* **40/1**

9 3¾ **Loving Clarets (IRE)** 2-9-0 0 .... TonyHamilton 3 35
(Richard Fahey) *mid-div: racd on outer: racd keenly and hung rt almost thrght: sme hdwy 2f out: wknd over 1f out* **16/1**

10 6 **Elmley Queen** 2-8-9 0 .... GaryMahon[(5)] 13 16
(Roy Brotherton) *disp ld 2f out: sn pushed along: wknd 2f out* **200/1**

0 **11** 10 **Penuche**[16] 4195 2-8-11 0 .... NoelGarbutt[(3)] 2
(Derek Shaw) *chsd ldrs: rdn over 3f out: wknd over 2f out* **200/1**

1m 14.15s (1.15) **Going Correction** +0.05s/f (Good) **11** Ran SP% **118.6**
Speed ratings (Par 91): **94,93,93,92,90 90,89,85,80,72 59**
CSF £223.36 TOTE £7.90: £1.70, £5.00, £1.80; EX 83.60 Trifecta £1097.00.
Owner Roger S Beadle & Radlett Racing **Bred** Richard Kent **Trained** Radlett, Herts

FOCUS
No rail adjustments advised before this meeting. Not as deep a median auction as it might have been given the absence of a couple of possible market leaders, and a victory for the most experienced in the line-up.

4760 ILLSTON-ON-THE HILL (S) STKS 7f
6:50 (6:51) (Class 6) 3-Y-O **£2,587** (£770; £384; £192) **Stalls** High

Form RPR

6012 **1** **Boutan**[7] 4518 3-8-13 70 .... (p) LiamKeniry 7 69
(George Baker) *mde all: rdn over 1f out: styd on* **7/4**[1]

4024 **2** ¾ **Mecca's Missus (IRE)**[5] 4600 3-8-5 60 .... (p) AndrewMullen 1 59
(Michael Dods) *plld hrd and sn prom: chsd wnr over 2f out: rdn and stuck hd in the air over 1f out: nt run on* **2/1**[2]

-646 **3** 5 **Just Fab (IRE)**[19] 4087 3-8-5 62 .... (b[1]) CamHardie 4 46
(Ali Stronge) *stmbld sn after the s: hld up: hdwy over 2f out: rdn over 1f out: no ex fnl f* **8/1**

4064 **4** ½ **Zabdi**[7] 4518 3-8-10 66 .... KieranO'Neill 6 49
(Richard Hannon) *hld up: plld hrd: rdn over 2f out: wnt 4th ins fnl f: nvr trbld ldrs* **7/2**[3]

0-U0 **5** 2½ **Big Larry (IRE)**[7] 4518 3-8-10 49 .... GeorgeChaloner 3 42
(Nigel Tinkler) *chsd wnr tl rdn over 2f out: wknd over 1f out* **50/1**

0000 **6** 9 **Roman Urn**[14] 4267 3-8-10 52 .... WilliamCarson 5 18
(Brett Johnson) *s.i.s: sn chsng ldrs: rdn 1/2-way: wknd over 2f out* **33/1**

1m 26.4s (0.20) **Going Correction** +0.05s/f (Good) **6** Ran SP% **107.9**
Speed ratings (Par 98): **100,99,93,92,90 79**
CSF £5.05 TOTE £2.00: £1.20, £1.70; EX 5.00 Trifecta £13.70.
Owner Seaton Partnership **Bred** Seaton Partnership **Trained** Manton, Wilts

FOCUS
An ordinary seller and probably not a race to dwell on, with the first two closely matched on their meeting a fortnight earlier.

4761 BOSWORTH FIELD FILLIES' H'CAP 1m 1f 218y
7:20 (7:20) (Class 4) (0-80,80) 3-Y-O+ **£4,851** (£1,443; £721; £360) **Stalls** Low

Form RPR

052 **1** **Brief Visit**[22] 3981 3-9-2 **78** .... LiamKeniry 3 90
(Andrew Balding) *mde all: set stdy pce tl qcknd over 3f out: rdn over 1f out: styd on wl* **4/1**[2]

1233 **2** 2 **Bocking End (IRE)**[32] 3667 3-9-1 **77** .... WilliamCarson 4 85
(Michael Bell) *a.p: racd keenly: wnt 2nd over 2f out: rdn over 1f out: edgd rt ins fnl f: styd on: nt rch wnr* **6/1**

054 **3** ½ **Ghinia (IRE)**[32] 3667 5-9-9 **80** .... CallumShepherd[(5)] 1 87
(Pam Sly) *chsd ldrs: rdn over 2f out: styd on* **8/1**

1463 **4** 2½ **Intermittent**[16] 4206 3-9-2 **78** .... GeorgeBaker 2 80
(Roger Charlton) *trckd wnr tl rdn over 2f out: no ex ins fnl f* **6/4**[1]

-434 **5** ½ **Sepal (USA)**[16] 4207 3-8-13 **75** .... MichaelJMMurphy 6 76
(Charles Hills) *s.i.s: hld up: rdn over 2f out: r.o towards fin: nt trble ldrs* **9/2**[3]

4-05 **6** 5 **Colour Play (USA)**[15] 4235 3-8-8 **70** .... AndrewMullen 5 61
(Mark Johnston) *hld up: rdn over 2f out: sn btn* **20/1**

2m 10.57s (2.67) **Going Correction** +0.40s/f (Good)
WFA 3 from 5yo 10lb **6** Ran SP% **108.3**
Speed ratings (Par 102): **105,103,103,101,100 96**
CSF £25.24 TOTE £5.10: £2.40, £2.90; EX 29.60 Trifecta £120.40.
Owner Cliveden Stud **Bred** Cliveden Stud Ltd **Trained** Kingsclere, Hants

FOCUS
A fair fillies' handicap for the grade, dominated by a pretty taking winner who continues to progress.

4762 BRITISH STALLION STUDS EBF MAIDEN STKS (PLUS 10 RACE) 6f
7:50 (7:50) (Class 4) 2-Y-O **£4,528** (£1,347; £673; £336) **Stalls** High

Form RPR

1 **Senator** 2-9-5 0 .... TonyHamilton 8 77+
(Richard Fahey) *chsd ldrs: hung rt and outpcd over 2f out: rallied over 1f out: hung rt and r.o to ld to ld fnl 50yds: comfortable* **13/8**[1]

6042 **2** ½ **Father McKenzie**[8] 4473 2-9-5 0 .... GeorgeBaker 1 75
(Mick Channon) *w ldr tl led 2f out: rdn and hdd over 1f out: rallied to ld ins fnl f: hdd fnl 50yds* **8/1**

2 **3** ½ **Midaawi (IRE)**[23] 3939 2-9-5 0 ....[1] ShaneGray 4 73
(Kevin Ryan) *sn led: hdd 2f out: sn rdn: rallied and ev ch whn n.m.r wl ins fnl f: styd on* **3/1**[2]

4 ½ **Winning Return (IRE)** 2-9-0 0 .... WilliamCarson 2 66+
(Saeed bin Suroor) *trckd ldr: led over 1f out: rdn and hdd ins fnl f: no ex towards fin* **10/1**

5 1¼ **Braztime** 2-9-0 0 .... KieranO'Neill 7 62+
(Richard Hannon) *hld up: pushed along 1/2-way: hdwy over 1f out: r.o* **25/1**

5 **6** 3 **Imperial City (USA)**[21] 4011 2-9-0 0 .... MichaelJMMurphy 9 53
(Charles Hills) *hld up: pushed along over 2f out: nt trble ldrs* **7/2**[3]

06 **7** ½ **Booshbash (IRE)**[14] 4261 2-8-7 0 .... HarryBurns[(7)] 6 51
(Ed Dunlop) *hld up: shkn up over 1f out: n.d* **33/1**

8 7 **Deleyll** 2-9-5 0 .... WilliamTwiston-Davies 3 34
(William Haggas) *mid-div: pushed along 1/2-way: wknd over 1f out* **25/1**

56 **9** 1 ¾ **Time Down Under**[20] 4047 2-9-5 0 .... DarryllHolland 5 28
(Mark H Tompkins) *s.i.s: hld up: hdwy over 2f out: rdn and wknd over 1f out* **66/1**

1m 13.92s (0.92) **Going Correction** +0.05s/f (Good) **9** Ran SP% **117.6**
Speed ratings (Par 96): **95,94,93,93,91 87,86,77,75**
CSF £15.62 TOTE £2.10: £1.10, £3.00, £1.40; EX 14.10 Trifecta £46.20.
Owner Cheveley Park Stud **Bred** Cheveley Park Stud Ltd **Trained** Musley Bank, N Yorks

FOCUS
A fairly interesting juvenile maiden, and a winner's effort is worth marking up considerably. The first four finished clear and the race has been rated around the runner-up.

4763 ROTHLEY H'CAP 6f
8:20 (8:21) (Class 5) (0-70,68) 3-Y-O+ **£3,234** (£962; £481; £240) **Stalls** High

Form RPR
6211 **1** **Soaring Spirits (IRE)**[36] 3491 6-9-9 **65** ....(b) RobertWinston 6 79
(Dean Ivory) *w ldrs: led 1/2-way: rdn and hdd 2f out: hung rt over 1f out: rallied to ld wl ins fnl f: r.o* **5/2**[1]

0-43 **2** 1 ¼ **May Rose (IRE)**[62] 2606 3-9-5 **66** ....(t) GeorgeBaker 5 75+
(Charles Hills) *hld up: racd keenly: hdwy over 2f out: led over 1f out: hdd and unable qck wl ins fnl f* **9/2**[2]

0041 **3** 1 ¾ **Etienne Gerard**[23] 3953 4-9-5 **68** ....(p) DavidEgan[(7)] 2 72
(Nigel Tinkler) *trckd ldrs: led 2f out: rdn and hdd over 1f out: hung rt and no ex wl ins fnl f* **5/2**[1]

2653 **4** 4 ½ **Beau Mistral (IRE)**[25] 3898 7-8-8 **55** ....[1] PaddyPilley[(5)] 4 45
(Tony Carroll) *led to 1/2-way: sn rdn: styd on same pce fr over 1f out* **10/1**

2522 **5** ½ **New Rich**[35] 3530 6-9-10 **66** ....(v) CharlesBishop 7 54
(Eve Johnson Houghton) *hld up: rdn over 2f out: hung rt over 1f out: nt trble ldrs* **7/1**[3]

0100 **6** 5 **Goadby**[21] 4005 5-9-4 **60** .... RoystonFfrench 3 32
(John Holt) *w ldr tl over 3f out: rdn and wknd over 1f out* **16/1**

160 **7** 30 **Henryhudsonbridge (USA)**[19] 4088 4-9-3 **62** ....(b) EoinWalsh[(3)] 1
(Edward Bevan) *s.i.s: sn pushed along in rr: wknd and eased over 2f out* **12/1**

1m 12.83s (-0.17) **Going Correction** +0.05s/f (Good)
WFA 3 from 4yo+ 5lb **7** Ran SP% **110.5**
Speed ratings (Par 103): **103,101,99,93,92 85,45**
CSF £12.97 TOTE £2.50: £1.30, £2.60; EX 11.50 Trifecta £39.90.
Owner Mrs Doreen Carter **Bred** Kevin & Meta Cullen **Trained** Radlett, Herts

FOCUS
An okay race for the grade, and a definite sense that the placed horses could have run the winner closer. The winner continues his revival.

4764 SHANGTON H'CAP 1m 60y
8:50 (8:51) (Class 6) (0-65,63) 3-Y-O **£2,587** (£770; £384; £192) **Stalls** Low

Form RPR
0032 **1** **Pacific Salt (IRE)**[30] 3732 3-8-13 **60** .... CallumShepherd[(5)] 14 67+
(Pam Sly) *hld up: hdwy over 2f out: nt clr run fr over 1f out tl swtchd lft ins fnl f: r.o to ld post* **8/1**[3]

-630 **2** nk **Ripoll (IRE)**[61] 2652 3-9-0 **63** ....(t) MitchGodwin[(7)] 10 68
(Sylvester Kirk) *hld up: hdwy over 3f out: led over 2f out: rdn over 1f out: hdd post* **5/1**[2]

6006 **3** nk **Pivotal Dream (IRE)**[25] 3906 3-8-6 **48** .... KieranO'Neill 13 52
(Mark Brisbourne) *hld up: rdn over 2f out: hung rt and r.o wl ins fnl f: nt quite rch ldrs* **50/1**

6003 **4** ¾ **Harlequin Rock**[14] 4279 3-9-4 **60** .... MartinDwyer 5 63
(Mick Quinn) *hld up: hdwy over 2f out: nt clr run and hmpd over 1f out: r.o* **10/1**

00-0 **5** hd **St Dunstan (IRE)**[54] 2864 3-8-11 **53** ....(v[1]) CamHardie 11 55
(John Quinn) *prom: rdn over 2f out: hung rt and r.o ins fnl f* **22/1**

5234 **6** 1 ½ **Masterson (IRE)**[7] 4500 3-9-4 **60** ....(v) GeorgeBaker 7 59
(Mick Channon) *led over 6f out: rdn and hdd over 2f out: no ex ins fnl f* **7/2**[1]

4031 **7** 1 **Patanjali (IRE)**[14] 4275 3-9-1 **57** .... CharlesBishop 12 57+
(Eve Johnson Houghton) *hld up: hmpd over 3f out: nt clr run over 1f out: r.o ins fnl f: nvr nrr* **5/1**[2]

530 **8** ½ **Ramblow**[11] 4401 3-8-8 **57** .... GeorgiaCox[(7)] 3 52
(William Haggas) *chsd ldrs: rdn over 2f out: no ex ins fnl f* **10/1**

-400 **9** 2 ½ **Chelabella**[25] 3878 3-9-0 **63** ....[1] LuluStanford[(7)] 4 52
(Michael Bell) *prom: plld hrd: shkn up over 2f out: styd on same pce fr over 1f out* **20/1**

0430 **10** hd **Russian Ranger (IRE)**[14] 4269 3-9-4 **60** ....(p) MartinLane 1 49
(Jonathan Portman) *led: hdd over 6f out: chsd ldr: rdn and ev ch over 2f out: wknd fnl f* **33/1**

6555 **11** hd **Olympic Duel (IRE)**[12] 4370 3-9-2 **58** .... WilliamCarson 9 47
(Peter Hiatt) *prom: rdn over 2f out: wknd ins fnl f* **12/1**

12 ¾ **Vale Of Rock (IRE)**[280] 7403 3-8-10 **52** .... AndrewMullen 6 39
(Michael Appleby) *prom: rdn over 3f out: wknd fnl f* **10/1**

0055 **13** 1 **Long Island**[7] 4505 3-8-3 **48** .... NoelGarbutt[(3)] 8 33
(Mark Brisbourne) *s.s: hld up: hdwy over 2f out: wknd fnl f* **50/1**

0560 **14** 4 ½ **Ksenia (IRE)**[49] 3014 3-7-10 **45** .... DavidEgan[(7)] 2 19
(Nigel Tinkler) *s.i.s: hld up: plld hrd: hdwy over 3f out: wknd over 1f out* **66/1**

1m 48.11s (3.01) **Going Correction** +0.40s/f (Good) **14** Ran SP% **119.1**
Speed ratings (Par 98): **100,99,99,98,98 96,95,95,92,92 92,91,90,86**
CSF £44.20 CT £1335.42 TOTE £10.90: £2.80, £2.30, £11.00; EX 52.60 Trifecta £4312.30.
Owner D L Bayliss & G A Libson **Bred** Tally-Ho Stud **Trained** Thorney, Cambs

FOCUS
A moderate finale, though the winner at least looks mildly progressive. The race has been rated around the runner-up.
T/Plt: £128.30 to a £1 stake. Pool: £60,796.34 - 345.73 winning tickets T/Qpdt: £27.00 to a £1 stake. Pool: £7,956.21 - 218.05 winning tickets **Colin Roberts**

[4423]REDCAR (L-H)
Wednesday, July 27

OFFICIAL GOING: Good to firm (9.0)
Wind: light 1/2 against Weather: fine

4765 RACING UK CLUB DAY EBF MAIDEN STKS 6f
1:50 (1:59) (Class 5) 2-Y-O **£3,234** (£962; £481; £240) **Stalls** Centre

Form RPR
6 **1** **Lanjano**[12] 4363 2-9-5 0 .... KevinStott 3 79
(Kevin Ryan) *w ldrs: led over 1f out: edgd rt: drvn out* **7/1**

55 **2** 1 ¾ **Looting**[48] 3054 2-9-5 0 .... ShaneGray 1 73
(David Brown) *trckd ldrs: 2nd appr fnl f: edgd rt: styd on same pce last 75yds* **5/1**[3]

3 hd **Dawoodi** 2-9-2 0 .... MarcMonaghan[(3)] 10 73
(Hugo Palmer) *wnt rt s: mid-div: drvn over 2f out: chsng ldrs over 1f out: kpt on same pce last 100yds* **11/4**[2]

3 **4** hd **Double Touch**[20] 4040 2-9-5 0 .... DavidNolan 9 72
(Richard Fahey) *stdd s: hld up in rr: hdwy over 2f out: edgd lft over 1f out: styd on last 100yds* **2/1**[1]

6 **5** 1 ¾ **Halawain (USA)**[19] 4097 2-9-5 0 .... PhillipMakin 4 66
(John Quinn) *trckd ldrs: hmpd 1f out: kpt on wl* **16/1**

6 **6** ¾ **Wilderswood (IRE)**[11] 4405 2-9-5 0 .... PJMcDonald 7 64
(Ann Duffield) *led: hdd over 1f out: kpt on same pce* **33/1**

7 1 **Greenview Paradise (IRE)** 2-9-0 0 .... JackGarritty 2 56
(Richard Fahey) *dwlt: sn trcking ldrs: effrt and edgd rt over 1f out: kpt on one pce* **20/1**

8 1 ¼ **Anythingknappen (IRE)** 2-9-0 0 .... DavidAllan 6 52
(Tim Easterby) *dwlt in rr: reminders over 3f out: kpt on appr fnl f* **20/1**

00 **9** ½ **Magic Journey (IRE)**[12] 4371 2-9-5 0 .... CamHardie 8 55
(John Quinn) *mid-div: effrt over 2f out: one pce* **66/1**

0 **10** 4 ½ **Urban Spirit (IRE)**[53] 2913 2-9-5 0 .... PaulMulrennan 11 41
(David O'Meara) *chsd ldrs: lost pl over 1f out* **20/1**

11 ½ **Ronnie The Rooster** 2-9-5 0 .... JasonHart 12 39
(David Barron) *in rr: sn drvn along: reminders 3f out: nvr a factor* **20/1**

0 **12** nk **Hotfill**[68] 2417 2-9-5 0 .... TomEaves 14 38
(David Barron) *chsd ldrs: lost pl over 1f out* **40/1**

0 **13** 4 ½ **Northern Eclipse**[18] 4161 2-9-5 0 .... SamJames 13 24
(David O'Meara) *in rr-div: bhd fnl 2f* **25/1**

14 19 **Acombboy** 2-9-5 0 .... JamesSullivan 5
(Marjorie Fife) *in rr: bhd fnl 2f: eased clsng stages* **50/1**

1m 12.2s (0.40) **Going Correction** -0.05s/f (Good) **14** Ran SP% **126.8**
Speed ratings (Par 94): **95,92,92,92,89 88,87,85,85,79 78,78,72,46**
CSF £38.81 TOTE £8.30: £2.90, £2.20, £1.70; EX 55.50 Trifecta £223.60.
Owner Collier Holmes Racing **Bred** J A And Mrs Duffy **Trained** Hambleton, N Yorks

FOCUS
The watered ground had been hit with 4mm of overnight rain but the GoingStick still gave a reading of 9.0. A modest maiden.

4766 GALWAY FESTIVAL BETTING AT 188BET MAIDEN STKS 7f
2:20 (2:24) (Class 5) 3-Y-O+ **£2,911** (£866; £432; £216) **Stalls** Centre

Form RPR
44-3 **1** **Wrapped**[23] 3951 3-9-0 77 .... GrahamGibbons 6 74
(William Haggas) *mde all: rdn over 1f out: fnd ex clsng stages* **4/5**[1]

036- **2** ¾ **Manton Grange**[313] 6501 3-9-5 78 .... PJMcDonald 2 77
(George Baker) *wnt rt s: hld up: hdwy over 2f out: 2nd over 1f out: kpt on same pce last 50yds* **5/4**[2]

05 **3** 2 ½ **Lovin' Spoonful**[25] 3879 3-9-0 0 .... ConnorBeasley 7 65
(Bryan Smart) *chsd wnr: kpt on one pce over 1f out* **16/1**

60 **4** 11 **Snappydresser**[22] 3981 3-9-0 0 .... JasonHart 5 36
(Tracy Waggott) *trckd ldrs: drvn over 2f out: wknd over 1f out* **12/1**[3]

60-0 **5** 13 **Orobas (IRE)**[40] 3367 4-9-7 46 .... PhilDennis[(5)] 4 8
(Ron Barr) *hmpd s: mid-div: lost pl over 2f out* **50/1**

63-6 **6** 1 **Milu Mac**[15] 4236 5-9-4 39 ....(b[1]) JacobButterfield[(3)] 1 1
(Neville Bycroft) *chsd ldrs: reminders over 3f out: lost pl over 2f out* **33/1**

5 **7** ¾ **The Cheese Gang**[20] 4035 4-9-7 0 .... GarryWhillans[(5)] 3 4
(Susan Corbett) *hmpd s: t.k.h in mid-div: lost pl over 2f out* **66/1**

00-4 **8** 30 **Time Again**[64] 2560 3-9-0 50 ....(v[1]) ShaneGray 8
(David Brown) *wnt rt s: racd along towards stands' side: chsd ldrs: lost pl over 3f out: sn bhd: t.o whn heavily eased over 1f out: virtually p.u* **16/1**

1m 24.23s (-0.27) **Going Correction** -0.05s/f (Good)
WFA 3 from 4yo+ 7lb **8** Ran SP% **125.9**
Speed ratings (Par 103): **99,98,95,82,67 66,65,31**
CSF £2.34 TOTE £1.60: £1.10, £1.10, £4.00; EX 2.00 Trifecta £10.10.
Owner Cheveley Park Stud **Bred** Whatton Manor Stud **Trained** Newmarket, Suffolk

FOCUS
Essentially a match race, but there was a well-fought, close finish.

4767 GLORIOUS GOODWOOD BETTING AT 188BET (S) STKS 1m 2f
2:55 (2:55) (Class 6) 3-Y-O+ **£2,385** (£704; £352) **Stalls** Low

Form RPR
0523 **1** **Our Boy Jack (IRE)**[10] 4427 7-9-1 75 .... AdamMcNamara[(5)] 1 64+
(Richard Fahey) *mid-div: effrt and nt clr run over 3f out: drvn upsides over 1f out: kpt on to ld towards fin* **13/8**[2]

6021 **2** nk **Captain Felix**[10] 4427 4-9-11 72 .... GrahamGibbons 3 68+
(George Scott) *t.k.h: trckd ldrs: led over 3f out: drvn and edgd rt over 1f out: hdd and no ex clsng stages* **6/5**[1]

0000 **3** 4 **Thello**[10] 4424 4-9-8 50 .... JacobButterfield[(3)] 2 60
(Nigel Tinkler) *trckd ldrs: kpt on one pce appr fnl f* **20/1**

0505 **4** 2 ½ **Chorus of Lies**[10] 4427 4-9-6 57 ....(t) DaleSwift 4 50
(Tracy Waggott) *trckd ldrs: upsides over 3f out: one pce over 1f out* **10/1**[3]

4606 **5** 1 ½ **Elle Dorado**[9] 4456 4-9-1 46 ....(v) PJMcDonald 5 42
(David Loughnane) *s.i.s: in rr: drvn over 4f out: nvr a factor* **14/1**

0000 **6** 2 **Al Furat (USA)**[14] 4260 8-9-6 40 .... DavidAllan 6 43
(Ron Barr) *led: hdd over 3f out: fdd over 1f out* **50/1**

-000 **7** 2 **Kantara Castle (IRE)**[9] 4456 5-9-6 46 ....(tp) TomEaves 8 39
(John Mackie) *mid-div: effrt over 3f out: edgd lft and wknd over 1f out* **33/1**

0561 **8** 3 ½ **Gabrial's Hope (FR)**[9] 4456 7-9-11 52 .... JasonHart 7 37
(Tracy Waggott) *s.i.s: hld up in rr: hdwy over 3f out: wknd over 1f out: eased nr fin* **14/1**

2m 5.37s (-1.73) **Going Correction** -0.05s/f (Good) **8** Ran SP% **115.6**
Speed ratings (Par 101): **104,103,100,98,97 95,94,91**
CSF £3.87 TOTE £2.40: £1.10, £1.60, £3.80; EX 3.70 Trifecta £27.80.Captain Felix was the subject of a friendly claim for £6,000
Owner Middleham Park Racing XXXVI **Bred** Mrs Ian Fox **Trained** Musley Bank, N Yorks

FOCUS
A seller where only two could be considered such was their superiority on ratings.

4768 USPGA GOLF BETTING AT 188BET H'CAP 1m 2f
3:30 (3:30) (Class 5) (0-75,74) 3-Y-O+ **£2,911** (£866; £432; £216) **Stalls** Low

Form RPR
1260 **1** **Mysterial**[9] 4455 6-9-7 **74** .... GerO'Neill[(7)] 9 81
(Declan Carroll) *led: t.k.h: rdr dropped whip over 1f out: hdd briefly appr fnl f: kpt on wl last 150yds* **14/1**

3441 **2** 1 1/4 **Livella Fella (IRE)**[19] 4098 3-9-2 **72**.......... PhillipMakin 4 76
(Keith Dalgleish) *hld up towards rr: hdwy 3f out: led briefly appr fnl f: kpt on same pce* **3/1**[2]

2502 **3** 3/4 **Kiwi Bay**[10] 4427 11-10-0 **74**.......... PaulMulrennan 2 77
(Michael Dods) *mid-div: effrt 4f out: sn chsng ldrs: kpt on same pce appr fnl f* **11/4**[1]

-063 **4** 3/4 **Jan De Heem**[9] 4455 6-8-13 **59**..........(p) JamesSullivan 6 60
(Tina Jackson) *trckd ldrs: effrt over 2f out: one pce over 1f out* **17/2**

4040 **5** 2 3/4 **Nelson's Bay**[34] 3564 7-8-2 **55**.......... HollieDoyle(7) 7 51
(Wilf Storey) *mid-div: hdwy over 2f out: one pce over 1f out* **14/1**

3050 **6** 1/2 **Nonchalant**[9] 4455 5-9-12 **72**..........(e[1]) DavidNolan 5 67
(David O'Meara) *hld up in rr: hdwy on inner 4f out: drvn over 2f out: one pce* **8/1**

5466 **7** 3/4 **The Magic Pencil (IRE)**[23] 3952 3-8-11 **67**..........[1] TomEaves 3 60
(Kevin Ryan) *chsd ldrs: swtchd rt over 1f out: one pce* **4/1**[3]

0-00 **8** 1 **Exclusive Waters (IRE)**[34] 3564 6-8-9 **60**.......... PhilDennis(5) 1 51
(George Charlton) *sn chsng ldrs: drvn over 3f out: wknd over 1f out* **20/1**

0440 **9** 3/4 **Red Paladin (IRE)**[25] 3884 6-9-9 **69**..........(p) DougieCostello 8 59
(Kristin Stubbs) *swtchd lft after s: hld up in rr: sme hdwy over 2f out: nt clr run over 1f out: nvr a factor* **14/1**

2m 5.17s (-1.93) **Going Correction** -0.05s/f (Good)
WFA 3 from 5yo+ 10lb **9** Ran SP% **118.1**
Speed ratings (Par 103): **105,104,103,102,100 100,99,98,98**
CSF £57.24 CT £155.28 TOTE £16.70: £3.60, £1.50, £1.20; EX 67.80 Trifecta £181.10.
Owner Mrs Sarah Bryan **Bred** Ladyswood, Canning Down & D Farrington **Trained** Malton, N Yorks

FOCUS
They went a good pace, but just modest form.

4769 PINNACLE RACING SHARES AVAILABLE NOW H'CAP (QUAL FOR PINNACLE CUP STRAIGHT MILE SERIES FINAL) 1m
4:05 (4:09) (Class 4) (0-85,84) 3-Y-O **£6,469** (£1,925; £962; £481) **Stalls** Centre

Form RPR

-413 **1** **Weekend Offender (FR)**[53] 2907 3-9-7 **84**.......... TomEaves 7 89
(Kevin Ryan) *hld up: hdwy over 2f out: upsides over 1f out: styd on to ld fnl strides* **3/1**[2]

1212 **2** hd **Planetaria (IRE)**[15] 4232 3-9-2 **79**.......... DavidAllan 5 83
(Garry Moss) *led tl over 3f out: led over 1f out: sn drvn: edgd rt: hdd fnl strides* **9/4**[1]

1254 **3** 1 1/4 **Popsies Joy (IRE)**[25] 3877 3-8-6 **69**.......... DuranFentiman 6 71
(Tim Easterby) *stdd s: sn trcking ldrs: upsides over 1f out: hld whn short of room and eased fnl strides* **7/1**[3]

3005 **4** 3 **Picture Painter (IRE)**[24] 3920 3-8-5 **68**.......... JoeDoyle 2 62
(Jim Goldie) *swtchd rt s: trckd ldrs: effrt over 1f out: one pce* **8/1**

0016 **5** 1/2 **Furiant**[6] 4562 3-8-9 **72**.......... PaulMulrennan 3 65
(Mark Johnston) *racd wd: w ldrs: led over 3f out: drvn over 2f out: hdd over 1f out: grad wknd* **8/1**

1m 38.4s (1.80) **Going Correction** -0.05s/f (Good) **5** Ran SP% **90.5**
Speed ratings (Par 102): **89,88,87,84,84**
CSF £6.74 TOTE £3.50: £2.20, £1.10; EX 6.40 Trifecta £20.30.
Owner Matt & Lauren Morgan **Bred** Mathieu Daguzan-Garros Et Al **Trained** Hambleton, N Yorks
■ Midnight Macchiato was withdrawn. Price at time of withdrawal 4-1. Rule 4 applies to all bets - deduction 20p in the pound.

FOCUS
Nominally the best race on the card, but it was just a modest handicap for 3yos.

4770 £25 FREE BET AT 188BET H'CAP (DIV I) 6f
4:40 (4:41) (Class 6) (0-65,65) 3-Y-O+ **£2,264** (£673; £336; £168) **Stalls** Centre

Form RPR

54-0 **1** **Sugar Town**[15] 4240 6-8-3 **47**.......... NathanEvans(5) 3 57
(Peter Niven) *mde all: edgd rt 1f out: kpt on wl* **8/1**[3]

5320 **2** 2 **Tribesman**[5] 4612 3-9-2 **60**..........(b) JamesSullivan 7 63
(Marjorie Fife) *w wnr: checked sltly 1f out: kpt on same pce* **16/1**

046 **3** hd **Longroom**[21] 4006 4-8-12 **51**.......... BarryMcHugh 4 54
(Noel Wilson) *hld up towards rr: hdwy over 2f out: styd on fnl f: tk 3rd nr fin* **11/1**

3446 **4** hd **Mrs Biggs**[15] 4240 4-9-2 **62**..........(v[1]) GerO'Neill(7) 5 65+
(Declan Carroll) *hld up towards rr: hdwy whn nt clr run and swtchd lft 2f out: kpt on fnl f* **12/1**

0605 **5** 1 **Tom Sawyer**[25] 3882 8-9-7 **65**..........(b[1]) AdamMcNamara(5) 1 65
(Julie Camacho) *trckd ldrs: effrt over 1f out: kpt on one pce* **25/1**

2R55 **6** 2 **Teetotal (IRE)**[12] 4376 6-9-3 **56**..........(b[1]) GrahamGibbons 2 50
(Nigel Tinkler) *reluctant and v.s.a: hdwy over 2f out: one pce over 1f out* **11/1**

0600 **7** 1 **Sea Of Green**[4] 4647 4-8-11 **50**.......... JoeDoyle 9 41
(Jim Goldie) *hld up towards rr: hdwy over 2f out: n.m.r 1f out: kpt on one pce* **25/1**

5324 **8** hd **Enjoy Life (IRE)**[11] 4378 3-9-4 **62**.......... TomEaves 8 51
(Kevin Ryan) *trckd ldrs: effrt 2f out: one pce* **14/1**

0003 **9** nk **Tavener**[5] 4606 4-9-12 **65**.......... DavidNolan 10 54
(David O'Meara) *hld up towards rr: hdwy over 2f out: one pce over 1f out* **4/1**[2]

0311 **10** shd **Spirit Of Zebedee (IRE)**[7] 4513 3-9-5 **63** 6ex..........(p) PJMcDonald 12 51
(John Quinn) *chsd ldrs: one pce over 1f out* **15/8**[1]

0220 **11** 5 **Poolstock**[40] 3368 4-9-1 **54**..........(p) ConnorBeasley 11 28
(Michael Dods) *chsd ldrs: drvn over 2f out: lost pl over 1f out* **20/1**

036 **12** 2 1/4 **Dalalah**[12] 4365 3-8-4 **48**..........(v) PatrickMathers 6 14
(Richard Guest) *dwlt: hdwy to chse ldrs over 4f out: drvn over 3f out: outpcd over 2f out: swtchd lft over 1f out: sn bhd* **28/1**

2-00 **13** 1 1/2 **Wotnot (IRE)**[75] 2201 4-9-6 **59**.......... PaulMulrennan 13 22
(Bryan Smart) *hld up in tch: t.k.h: hung rt appr fnl f: sn eased* **28/1**

1m 11.61s (-0.19) **Going Correction** -0.05s/f (Good)
WFA 3 from 4yo+ 5lb **13** Ran SP% **122.2**
Speed ratings (Par 101): **99,96,96,95,94 91,90,90,89,89 83,80,78**
CSF £121.14 CT £1416.48 TOTE £10.10: £3.50, £5.30, £4.50; EX 177.60 Trifecta £4142.40 Part won..
Owner Mrs Heather Burley **Bred** Mrs S M Roy **Trained** Barton-le-Street, N Yorks

FOCUS
This looked slightly stronger than the second division, but was still moderate form.

4771 £25 FREE BET AT 188BET H'CAP (DIV II) 6f
5:15 (5:15) (Class 6) (0-65,65) 3-Y-O+ **£2,264** (£673; £336; £168) **Stalls** Centre

Form RPR

-524 **1** **El Principe**[9] 4445 3-9-2 **60**..........(t[1]) JasonHart 9 68
(Les Eyre) *w ldrs: led over 1f out: drvn out* **5/1**[2]

0003 **2** 1 1/2 **Caeser The Gaeser (IRE)**[7] 4516 4-8-6 **52**..........(p) LewisEdmunds(7) 12 56
(Nigel Tinkler) *chsd ldrs: upsides over 1f out: kpt on same pce last 75yds* **15/2**[3]

R04 **3** 1 **A J Cook (IRE)**[24] 3925 6-8-11 **50**.......... DavidAllan 3 51
(Ron Barr) *half-rrd s: in rr: hdwy over 1f out: styd on to take 3rd nr fin* **16/1**

4064 **4** nk **The Armed Man**[26] 3843 3-9-1 **59**.......... AndrewElliott 6 58
(Chris Fairhurst) *trckd ldrs: swtchd rt 100yds out: styng on at fin* **9/1**

2003 **5** 1/2 **Run Rio Run (IRE)**[13] 4310 3-9-4 **62**..........[1] ConnorBeasley 1 60
(Michael Dods) *led: hdd over 1f out: kpt on one pce* **20/1**

6360 **6** 1/2 **Cool Strutter (IRE)**[9] 4454 4-9-7 **65**..........(b) GemmaTutty(5) 4 62
(Karen Tutty) *racd towards far side: w ldrs: t.k.h: kpt on same pce fnl f* **14/1**

-006 **7** 3 3/4 **Amis Reunis**[7] 4513 7-8-9 **48**.......... TomEaves 2 34
(Colin Teague) *trckd ldrs: wknd last 100yds* **40/1**

6330 **8** 1 **Jebel Tara**[21] 4005 11-9-10 **63**..........(bt) DaleSwift 5 46
(Alan Brown) *racd towards far side: chsd ldrs: drvn 3f out: wknd appr fnl f* **14/1**

4555 **9** 1 1/2 **Saltarello (IRE)**[18] 4144 4-9-3 **56**..........(p) SamJames 8 34
(Marjorie Fife) *in rr: sme hdwy over 1f out: nvr on terms* **9/1**

6002 **10** 1 3/4 **Qortaaj**[7] 4517 3-8-13 **64**.......... CameronNoble(7) 7 36
(David Loughnane) *restless in stalls: in rr and sn drvn along: sme hdwy over 2f out: lost pl over 1f out* **15/8**[1]

-004 **11** nse **Aussie Ruler (IRE)**[23] 3953 4-9-8 **61**..........(b) GrahamGibbons 10 34
(Daniel Mark Loughnane) *mid-div: drvn over 2f out: lost pl over 1f out* **10/1**

-000 **12** 20 **Jessie Allan (IRE)**[8] 4486 5-8-7 **46** oh1..........[1] JoeDoyle 11
(Jim Goldie) *chsd ldrs: drvn 3f out: sn lost pl and bhd: eased fnl f: t.o* **66/1**

1m 11.19s (-0.61) **Going Correction** -0.05s/f (Good)
WFA 3 from 4yo+ 5lb **12** Ran SP% **120.2**
Speed ratings (Par 101): **102,100,98,98,97 96,91,90,88,86 86,59**
CSF £42.39 CT £578.45 TOTE £6.10: £2.00, £2.70, £5.90; EX 35.90 Trifecta £698.90.
Owner M Rozenbroek **Bred** Mrs Irene Clifford **Trained** Catwick, N Yorks

FOCUS
Moderate form, with all of these looking for their first win of season.

4772 BETFAIR NOVICE FLAT AMATEUR RIDERS' H'CAP 1m
5:50 (5:51) (Class 6) (0-65,64) 4-Y-O+ **£2,183** (£677; £338; £169) **Stalls** Centre

Form RPR

0-00 **1** **Broctune Papa Gio**[40] 3366 9-11-2 **59**.......... MissEEasterby 7 70
(Keith Reveley) *mid-div: hdwy over 2f out: led over 1f out: pushed out* **7/1**

4003 **2** 2 1/4 **Celtic Artisan (IRE)**[10] 4425 5-10-6 **52**..........(bt) MissFMcSharry(3) 3 58
(Rebecca Menzies) *led: hdd over 1f out: edgd lft: kpt on same pce* **11/2**[2]

6312 **3** 2 1/2 **Galilee Chapel (IRE)**[2] 4705 7-10-4 **50**..........(b) MrGaryBeaumont(3) 13 50
(Alistair Whillans) *chsd ldrs: kpt on same pce over 1f out* **5/1**[1]

6240 **4** 2 1/4 **Intensified (IRE)**[9] 4456 5-10-3 **46**..........(b) MissEmilyBullock 15 41
(Ruth Carr) *mid-div: swtchd lft after 1f: hdwy and swtchd lft over 2f out: kpt on over 1f out* **15/2**

0604 **5** 1 **Opt Out**[23] 3943 6-10-12 **58**..........(p) MissCarlyScott(3) 14 51
(David O'Meara) *dwlt: hld up in rr: hdwy and edgd lft over 1f out: kpt on* **6/1**[3]

005/ **6** nse **Tom's Anna (IRE)**[1102] 4561 6-10-12 **55**.......... MrJoeWright 4 47
(Sean Regan) *w ldrs: wknd appr fnl f* **33/1**

625 **7** 1 3/4 **Almanack**[12] 4369 6-10-13 **59**..........(t) MrSHawkins(3) 6 47
(Daniel Mark Loughnane) *mid-div: hdwy over 2f out: edgd rt and wknd over 1f out* **9/1**

0335 **8** 3 **Alans Pride (IRE)**[8] 4486 4-10-9 **55**..........(tp) MissSEDods(3) 11 37
(Michael Dods) *ldrs: edgd rt and wknd over 1f out* **11/2**[2]

3003 **9** 3 1/4 **Graceful Act**[14] 4260 8-10-3 **46**.......... MissKatyLyons 8 20
(Ron Barr) *rrd s: sn chsng ldrs: wknd over 1f out* **10/1**

50-0 **10** 2 1/4 **War Girl (USA)**[10] 4425 4-10-7 **50**.......... MrTGreenwood 10 19
(David Barron) *swtchd rt after s and racd stands' side: sn bhd: nvr on terms* **16/1**

-030 **11** 2 1/4 **Rosie Hall (IRE)**[15] 4240 6-10-2 **45**..........(p) MrMEnnis 16 9
(John Wainwright) *swtchd lft after s: in rr and sn drvn along: nvr on terms* **50/1**

0 **12** 6 **Qatea (IRE)**[98] 1560 4-11-7 **64**..........(t) MissAMcCain 12 14
(Donald McCain) *mid-div: reminders over 3f out: sn bhd* **25/1**

4000 **13** 9 **Fairy Pools**[55] 2810 5-9-13 **45**..........(b) MrMWBrown(3) 9
(Les Eyre) *chsd ldrs: lost pl over 3f out: sn bhd* **40/1**

-0 **14** nk **Shadow Of The Day**[15] 4228 9-9-13 **45**.....(bt) MrBenjaminStephens(3) 5
(Lee James) *lost pl over 3f out: sn bhd* **66/1**

1m 40.29s (3.69) **Going Correction** -0.05s/f (Good) **14** Ran SP% **123.6**
Speed ratings (Par 101): **79,76,74,72,71 70,69,66,62,60 58,52,43,43**
CSF £44.98 CT £222.29 TOTE £10.00: £3.40, £2.00, £2.10; EX 63.80 Trifecta £385.00.
Owner Thwaites Young Alessi & Reveley Farms **Bred** Lesley Winn And Reveley Farms **Trained** Lingdale, Redcar & Cleveland

FOCUS
Typically weak fare and half of these amateur jockeys were looking for their first winner.
T/Plt: £27.30 to a £1 stake. Pool: £50,364.49 - 1343.51 winning units. T/Qpdt: £14.30 to a £1 stake. Pool: £4,080.10 - 210.50 winning units. **Walter Glynn**

4558 SANDOWN (R-H)
Wednesday, July 27

OFFICIAL GOING: Good to firm (7.7)
Wind: Moderate, against Weather: Fine, warm

4773 WELLINGTON APPRENTICE H'CAP 1m 14y
5:55 (5:56) (Class 5) (0-70,70) 4-Y-O+ **£3,234** (£962; £481; £240) **Stalls** Low

Form RPR

006 **1** **Rightway (IRE)**[39] 3395 5-9-2 **65**.......... GeorgiaCox(5) 1 72
(Tony Carroll) *hld up in 5th: urged along 3f out: prog 2f out to chse ldr over 1f out: rdn to take narrow ld ins fnl f: hld on* **11/2**[3]

5112 **2** hd **Choral Clan (IRE)**[16] 4201 5-9-12 **70**.......... AlistairRawlinson 4 76
(Philip Mitchell) *hld up in 4th: prog on outer over 2f out: rdn to ld over 1f out: narrowly hdd ins fnl f: kpt on but jst hld* **9/2**[2]

6132 **3** 1 1/2 **Castle Talbot (IRE)**[11] 4388 4-9-7 **65**..........(p) JosephineGordon 7 67
(Richard Hughes) *hld up in last: rdn over 2f out: nt clrest of runs after: hdwy to take 3rd 1f out: kpt on but unable to chal* **6/4**[1]

2334 **4** 6 **Top Pocket**[49] 3031 4-8-7 **51**.......... DanielMuscutt 3 39
(Michael Madgwick) *rousted along s: led at gd pce: hdd over 2f out: wknd over 1f out* **9/1**

4462 **5** 1 **Tabla**[41] 3314 4-9-5 **68**.......... PaddyBradley(5) 2 54
(Lee Carter) *rousted along s but unable to ld: trckd ldr and t.k.h: rdn to ld over 2f out and edgd lft: hdd & wknd over 1f out* **9/2**[2]

4-02 **6** 9 **Ost Wind**[39] 3402 4-9-9 **67** RobHornby 6 31
(Michael Attwater) *chsd ldng pair to 2f out: wknd and sn bhd* **8/1**
1m 44.46s (1.16) **Going Correction** +0.05s/f (Good) **6** Ran SP% **112.9**
Speed ratings (Par 103): **96,95,94,88,87 78**
CSF £30.03 TOTE £7.40: £4.30, £2.30; EX 34.60 Trifecta £155.40.
Owner B J Millen **Bred** M Valade **Trained** Cropthorne, Worcs

FOCUS
Race distance increased by 12yds. The ground was officially described as good to firm on a warm and sunny evening. Only one of these had previously won a race on turf. The first three pulled clear in a strongly run affair, although the overall time was slow. The winner was on a good mark.

4774 CARDINAL WOLSEY H'CAP 1m 2f 7y
6:25 (6:26) (Class 5) (0-75,74) 4-Y-O+ **£3,234** (£962; £481; £240) **Stalls** Low

Form RPR
3215 **1** **Van Huysen (IRE)**[19] 4081 4-9-0 **70** JosephineGordon(3) 1 76
(Dominic Ffrench Davis) *trckd ldr 4f and again 3f out: led 2f out and gng best: rdn over 1f out: kpt on same pce and a holding on* **15/8**[1]
6036 **2** 1 ½ **Nosey Barker (IRE)**[7] 4531 4-9-3 **70** (p) JimmyFortune 4 73
(Richard Hannon) *led: drvn and hdd 2f out: kpt on but a hld by wnr* **6/1**
5120 **3** ½ **Pike Corner Cross (IRE)**[11] 4377 4-9-0 **67** JimCrowley 6 69
(Ed de Giles) *hld up in last: pushed along and prog 2f out: tk 3rd fnl f: rdn and kpt on but nvr able to chal* **9/4**[2]
0164 **4** ¾ **Fearless Lad (IRE)**[20] 4050 6-8-7 **60** KierenFox 3 60
(John Best) *chsd ldr after 4f to 3f out: sn u.p: styd cl up but nt qckn fr over 1f out* **7/1**
1204 **5** 3 ¼ **Mr Red Clubs (IRE)**[8] 4497 7-9-2 **74** (p) PaddyBradley(5) 2 68
(Michael Appleby) *hld up in 4th: shkn up 3f out: no prog 2f out: fdd over 1f out* **11/2**[3]
2m 10.43s (-0.07) **Going Correction** +0.05s/f (Good) **5** Ran SP% **107.7**
Speed ratings (Par 103): **102,100,100,99,97**
CSF £12.42 TOTE £2.60: £2.10, £2.70; EX 12.40 Trifecta £19.50.
Owner Prof C D Green **Bred** Prof C Green **Trained** Lambourn, Berks

FOCUS
Race distance increased by 12yds. A disappointing turnout and, with very little in the way of turf form to go on, it's unlikely it took much winning. A small turf best from the winner.

4775 BRITISH STALLION STUDS EBF MAIDEN STKS 7f 16y
7:00 (7:05) (Class 5) 2-Y-O **£3,881** (£1,155; £577; £288) **Stalls** Low

Form RPR
1 **Gemina (IRE)** 2-9-0 0 OisinMurphy 8 76+
(Ralph Beckett) *mde all: set stdy pce tl wound it up over 2f out: pushed along and in command over 1f out: styd on* **2/1**[1]
2 2 ¼ **Max Zorin (IRE)** 2-9-5 0 DavidProbert 6 75+
(Andrew Balding) *hld up: prog and squeezed through rivals to chse wnr over 1f out: styd on and clr of rest but no imp ins fnl f* **16/1**
3 3 ¼ **Spring Jig (USA)** 2-9-5 0 JimCrowley 5 66+
(Hugo Palmer) *trckd ldng trio: shkn up 2f out: kpt on to take 3rd fnl f: no ch w ldng pair* **5/2**[2]
4 1 ¼ **Envisaging (IRE)** 2-9-5 0 TomQueally 3 63+
(James Fanshawe) *dwlt: hld up in last: prog 2f out: shkn up 1f out: kpt on to take 4th nr fin: n.d* **13/2**[3]
5 ¾ **Emenem** 2-9-5 0 NickyMackay 11 61
(Simon Dow) *prom: chsd wnr after 3f to over 1f out: fdd* **25/1**
05 **6** ½ **Hi There Silver (IRE)**[44] 3231 2-9-2 0 DanielMuscutt(3) 2 59
(Michael Madgwick) *chsd wnr 3f: styd cl up tl easily outpcd fr 2f out* **66/1**
7 nk **Crystal Dome** 2-9-5 0 AndreaAtzeni 7 59+
(Ed Dunlop) *green preliminaries: a towards rr: pushed along and no prog 2f out* **16/1**
0 **8** ¾ **I'Vegotthepower (IRE)**[12] 4349 2-9-5 0 (b[1]) JimmyFortune 1 57
(Brian Meehan) *t.k.h: hld up in midfield: shkn up over 2f out and no prog: fdd over 1f out* **10/1**
9 hd **Matthioli (FR)** 2-9-5 0 KierenFox 9 56
(Michael Attwater) *in tch: shkn up and no prog over 2f out: fdd over 1f out* **50/1**
1m 34.94s (5.44) **Going Correction** +0.05s/f (Good) **9** Ran SP% **103.4**
Speed ratings (Par 94): **70,67,63,62,61 60,60,59,59**
CSF £26.62 TOTE £1.40: £3.30, £1.20; EX 23.50 Trifecta £57.40.
Owner Gillian, Lady Howard De Walden **Bred** Gillian, Lady Howard De Walden **Trained** Kimpton, Hants
■ Elucidation was withdrawn. Price at time of withdrawal 9/2. Rule 4 applies to all bets - deduction 15p in the pound.

FOCUS
Race distance increased by 12yds. This featured some interesting newcomers from big yards and looked a decent renewal. It was won in 2014 by subsequent Group 1 runner-up Latharnach. Derby entry Elucidation, who had two handlers in the parade ring, was withdrawn on veterinary advice. The winner fits the race averages but the form may not prove that solid.

4776 TRAFALGAR H'CAP 1m 14y
7:35 (7:35) (Class 3) (0-90,90) 3-Y-O+ **£7,439** (£2,213; £1,106; £553) **Stalls** Low

Form RPR
4-02 **1** **Laidback Romeo (IRE)**[20] 4055 4-9-10 **86** OisinMurphy 4 95+
(Clive Cox) *hld up in 8th: prog and waiting for room 2f out: hdwy over 1f out: drvn and clsd on ldrs ins fnl f: led last strides* **5/1**[3]
5103 **2** hd **Wimpole Hall**[21] 4010 3-8-10 **80** SilvestreDeSousa 8 86
(William Jarvis) *led 2f: styd cl up: rdn 2f out: tk 2nd fnl f: drvn ahd last 75yds: hdd nr fin* **10/1**
1-50 **3** 1 **Column**[19] 4104 3-9-2 **86** [1] TomQueally 2 90
(James Fanshawe) *prom: led 1/2-way: drvn 2f out: hanging over 1f out: kpt on but hdd and nt qckn last 75yds* **8/1**
0014 **4** nk **Pensax Boy**[19] 4104 4-9-4 **80** JimCrowley 10 85
(Ian Williams) *racd v wd first 2f then led whn crossed over: hdd 1/2-way: rdn 2f out: lost 2nd 1f out but stl chalng: no ex last 75yds* **14/1**
0-00 **5** 1 ½ **Faithful Creek (IRE)**[18] 4129 4-9-6 **89** [1] JordanUys(7) 6 91
(Brian Meehan) *trckd ldrs on inner: tried to cl fr 2f out: kpt on u.p fnl f but nvr quite able to chal: eased nr fin* **33/1**
1115 **6** 1 **Bastille Day**[4] 4654 4-9-13 **89** ShaneKelly 1 89
(David Elsworth) *cl up: rdn 2f out: nt qckn over 1f out: one pce last 150yds* **10/1**
-003 **7** ¾ **Directorship**[14] 4271 10-9-9 **90** HectorCrouch(5) 11 88
(Patrick Chamings) *stmbld s: hld up in last: modest prog and shkn up 2f out: rdn and styd on fnl f: nrst fin but no ch* **25/1**
-534 **8** 2 ¾ **Sky Ship**[32] 3635 3-8-11 **81** PatDobbs 3 71
(Sir Michael Stoute) *wl in tch: shkn up over 2f out: no imp over 1f out: wknd* **13/2**

1632 **9** 3 ¼ **War Story (IRE)**[19] 4080 3-9-5 **89** AndreaAtzeni 9 71
(Luca Cumani) *a in rr and rdn by 1/2-way: brief effrt on outer 2f out: sn no prog* **3/1**[1]
231- **10** 10 **Taqwaa (IRE)**[331] 5926 3-9-3 **87** PaulHanagan 5 46
(Richard Hannon) *wl in tch: shkn up over 2f out: wknd rapidly wl over 1f out: t.o* **9/2**[2]
3544 **11** 3 **Hot Mustard**[13] 4317 6-8-10 **72** SamHitchcott 7 26
(William Muir) *a in rr and struggling by 1/2-way: wknd 2f out: t.o* **33/1**
1m 42.23s (-1.07) **Going Correction** +0.05s/f (Good)
WFA 3 from 4yo+ 8lb **11** Ran SP% **118.9**
Speed ratings (Par 107): **107,106,105,105,104 103,102,99,96,86 83**
CSF £53.73 CT £400.95 TOTE £5.30: £1.70, £2.50, £2.90; EX 63.70 Trifecta £490.00.
Owner Robin Craddock **Bred** Mrs B Gardiner **Trained** Lambourn, Berks

FOCUS
Race distance increased by 12yds. A hotly contested feature but the market leaders disappointed. The pace was ordinary.

4777 WATERLOO FILLIES' H'CAP 1m 1f
8:10 (8:15) (Class 5) (0-75,74) 3-Y-O+ **£3,234** (£962; £481; £240) **Stalls** Low

Form RPR
36 **1** **Lulani (IRE)**[32] 3673 4-10-0 **74** SilvestreDeSousa 3 83
(Harry Dunlop) *mde all: shkn up 2f out: pressed over 1f out: styd on wl and drew away last 150yds* **11/2**[3]
-122 **2** 2 ½ **Kath's Legacy**[25] 3894 3-9-4 **73** OisinMurphy 4 76
(Ben De Haan) *mostly chsd wnr: rdn 2f out: no imp fnl f: kpt on* **9/4**[1]
005 **3** 1 ½ **Sante (IRE)**[23] 3951 3-8-13 **68** DavidProbert 1 67+
(Charles Hills) *hld up in tch: prog to dispute 2nd wl over 1f out and looked a threat: rdn sn after: flattened out fnl f* **7/1**
0003 **4** ¾ **Rock Palm (IRE)**[13] 4317 3-8-8 **63** JimmyQuinn 2 61
(Brendan Powell) *t.k.h: trckd ldng pair: awkward bnd 5f out: rdn over 2f out: one pce after* **12/1**
-046 **5** 3 ¾ **Princess Raihana**[16] 4206 3-9-1 **73** DanielMuscutt(3) 7 62
(Marco Botti) *hld up in 7th: shkn up 3f out: hanging and fnd nil 2f out: no prog* **8/1**
0-00 **6** 1 **Tea Gown (IRE)**[189] 256 5-9-10 **70** [1] JimCrowley 8 58
(Ed de Giles) *settled in detached last: pushed along over 2f out: minimal prog and nvr in it* **16/1**
5650 **7** ¾ **Gloryette**[20] 4057 3-9-1 **70** AndreaAtzeni 5 55
(Ed Dunlop) *wl in tch: rdn over 2f out: sn wknd* **4/1**[2]
-650 **8** 15 **Welsh Gem**[20] 4055 4-9-8 **68** [1] JohnFahy 6 21
(Clive Cox) *reluctant to enter stall: chsd ldrs rdn and wknd 3f out: t.o* **8/1**
1m 55.43s (-0.27) **Going Correction** +0.05s/f (Good)
WFA 3 from 4yo+ 9lb **8** Ran SP% **114.5**
Speed ratings (Par 100): **103,100,99,98,95 94,93,80**
CSF £18.33 CT £87.27 TOTE £6.60: £2.30, £1.30, £2.30; EX 17.80 Trifecta £126.30.
Owner Mr & Mrs James Blyth Currie **Bred** Oak Lodge Bloodstock **Trained** Lambourn, Berks

FOCUS
Race distance increased by 12yds. An ordinary fillies' handicap. The winner proved much to the best, posting a length+ pb..

4778 GRANBY H'CAP 1m 6f
8:40 (8:41) (Class 4) (0-80,78) 3-Y-O **£4,690** (£1,395; £697; £348) **Stalls** Low

Form RPR
5343 **1** **Yangtze**[27] 3814 3-9-5 **76** [1] AndreaAtzeni 2 85
(Sir Michael Stoute) *hld up in 4th: poised to chal over 2f out whn gng easily but wanting to hang: led over 1f out and sn pressed: hung lft jst ins fnl f: cajoled along tl drvn out last strides* **10/11**[1]
3103 **2** shd **Blakeney Point**[28] 3768 3-8-12 **72** [1] KieranShoemark(3) 3 80
(Roger Charlton) *hld up in last: prog on outer to chal over 1f out and edgd lft briefly: looked jst hld ins fnl f tl kpt on nr fin: jst failed* **6/1**[3]
-444 **3** 3 ¼ **Folly Bergere (IRE)**[37] 3468 3-9-2 **73** RyanTate 5 76
(James Eustace) *led 2f: rdn to ld again over 2f out: hdd over 1f out: one pce* **10/1**
0210 **4** 5 **Chelsea's Boy (IRE)**[18] 4131 3-9-7 **78** JohnFahy 6 74
(Clive Cox) *led after 2f to over 2f out: wknd over 1f out* **10/1**
0031 **5** 1 **Mystikana**[7] 4530 3-8-10 **67** 6ex (b) DannyBrock 1 62
(Marcus Tregoning) *cl up: nt clr run 3f out and swtchd lft and rt: rdn and no prog 2f out: wknd* **11/4**[2]
3m 11.86s (7.36) **Going Correction** +0.05s/f (Good) **5** Ran SP% **111.5**
Speed ratings (Par 102): **80,79,78,75,74**
CSF £7.07 TOTE £1.60: £1.10, £3.30; EX 5.30 Trifecta £39.50.
Owner Philip Newton **Bred** Philip Newton **Trained** Newmarket, Suffolk
■ Stewards' Enquiry : Kieran Shoemark two-day ban: used whip above permitted level (Aug 10-11)

FOCUS
Race distance increased by 12yds. An uncompetitive staying handicap run at a steady pace. The finish was fought out by two horses wearing first-time cheekpieces and the form is rated around the third.
T/Plt: £42.70 to a £1 stake. Pool: £47,782.83 - 815.87 winning units. T/Qpdt: £6.80 to a £1 stake. Pool: £6,779.89 - 733.61 winning units. **Jonathan Neesom**

4779 - 4782a (Foreign Racing) - See Raceform Interactive

[4750] VICHY
Wednesday, July 27

OFFICIAL GOING: Turf: good

4783a GRAND PRIX DE VICHY (GROUP 3) (3YO+) (TURF) 1m 2f
8:40 (12:00) 3-Y-O+ **£29,411** (£11,764; £8,823; £5,882; £2,941)

RPR
1 **Night Wish (GER)**[35] 3544 6-9-2 0 (p) TonyPiccone 8 105
(Frau S Steinberg, Germany) *trckd ldr: rdn to chal 2f out: led jst over 1f out: strly pressed fnl f: styd on wl and on top towards fin* **112/10**
2 ¾ **Black Sea (FR)**[45] 3-8-6 0 MaximeGuyon 6 104
(A De Royer-Dupre, France) *hld up in midfield: angled out and rdn 2f out: styd on and chal fnl f: hld in 2nd toward fin* **19/5**[3]
3 ½ **Prestige Vendome (FR)**[32] 3683 5-9-2 0 StephanePasquier 5 103
(N Clement, France) *hld up in midfield on inner: pushed along and looking for run 2f out: rdn over 1f out: styd on but nt quite pce to chal and hld in 3rd towards fin* **2/1**[1]
4 ½ **Garlingari (FR)**[24] 3936 5-9-8 0 (p) ThierryThulliez 2 108+
(Mme C Barande-Barbe, France) *midfield on inner: angled out 2f out: rdn and effrt over 1f out: styd on but hld fnl f: jst prevailed for 4th* **23/10**[2]

5 *shd* **Thank You Bye Bye (FR)**59 2727 4-8-13 0...... Pierre-CharlesBoudot 4 98+
(J-P Gauvin, France) *hld up: rdn and swtchd to outer over 1f out: styd on fnl f but nvr able to chal: jst missed 4th* **11/1**
6 *nk* **Royal Dolois (FR)**32 3683 4-9-2 0.............................. IoritzMendizabal 1 101
(J-M Lefebvre, France) *led: rdn and strly pressed 2f out: hdd jst over 1f out: no ex fnl f: fdd* **23/1**
7 *2* **Landym (FR)**38 5-9-2 0.. VincentCheminaud 3 97
(H-A Pantall, France) *dwlt and wnt lft s: hld up in rr: rdn 2f out: plugged on but no imp: n.d* **68/10**
8 *½* **Lili Moon (GER)**14 4286 7-8-13 0................................ UmbertoRispoli 7 93
(Werner Glanz, Germany) *midfield on outer: rdn and brief effrt 2f out: sn outpcd and fdd: dropped to last cl home* **62/1**

2m 5.17s (-3.43)
WFA 3 from 4yo+ 10lb **8** Ran SP% **119.6**
PARI-MUTUEL (all including 1 euro stake): WIN 12.20; PLACE 2.10, 1.60, 1.30; DF 22.70; SF 47.10.
Owner Stall Salzburg **Bred** Gestut Etzean **Trained** Germany

4302 EPSOM (L-H)

Thursday, July 28

OFFICIAL GOING: Good (good to firm in places)
Wind: Moderate, across Weather: Overcast becoming fine

4784 STEVE DONOGHUE APPRENTICE H'CAP 1m 2f 18y

5:50 (5:50) (Class 5) (0-70,71) 4-Y-O+ **£2,098** (£2,098; £481; £240) **Stalls** Low

Form RPR
3353 1 **Choral Festival**31 3721 10-9-9 **67**.. DannyBrock 1 74
(John Bridger) *trckd ldng pair: rdn over 2f out: clsd to chse ldr jst over 1f out: chal ins fnl f: n.m.r but led 50yds out: jnd post* **5/2**1
4235 1 *dht* **Ingleby Spring (IRE)**19 4145 4-8-9 **60**.................. NatalieHambling(7) 8 67
(Richard Fahey) *trckd ldr: led wl over 2f out: rdn over 1f out: edgd lft ins fnl f and hdd last 50yds: rallied to join ldr post* **9/2**2
1335 3 *4* **Tommys Geal**8 4531 4-9-6 **64**.. DanielMuscutt 4 63
(Michael Madgwick) *chsd ldng trio: rdn to chse ldr 2f out to jst over 1f out: fdd ins fnl f* **5/1**3
3006 4 *½* **Gaelic Silver (FR)**78 2150 10-9-9 **70**.......................(p) HectorCrouch(3) 6 68
(Gary Moore) *in tch: 5th st: drvn and nt qckn on outer over 2f out: no imp on ldrs over 1f out* **8/1**
2305 5 *¾* **Highlife Dancer**14 4294 8-8-8 **55**................................(v) PaddyPilley(3) 3 52
(Mick Channon) *led to wl over 2f out: grad fdd fr over 1f out* **11/2**
5062 6 *9* **Goodwood Moonlight**24 2872 4-8-7 **54**.............(p) CallumShepherd(3) 9 33
(Ian Williams) *s.s: a in rr: 6th st: sn rdn and no prog: wl btn after* **8/1**
464P 7 *5* **Spiritual Star (IRE)**40 3405 7-9-4 **69**............................ HarryBurns(7) 2 38
(Lee Carter) *stdd s: hld up: last st: shkn up and no real prog over 2f out* **14/1**
3-00 8 *31* **Ledbury (IRE)**17 4197 4-8-13 **62**................................ PaddyBradley(5) 7
(Lee Carter) *chsd ldrs: 7th and wkng st: t.o* **12/1**

2m 12.12s (2.42) **Going Correction** +0.225s/f (Good) **8** Ran SP% **115.4**
Speed ratings (Par 103): **99,99,95,95,94 87,83,58**
WIN: IS 2.80, CF 1.80; PL: IS 1.40, CF 1.30. TG 1.90; EX: CF-IS 7.60, IS-CF 9.10; CSF: CF-IS 6.94, IS-CF 8.18; TC: CF-IS-TG 25.84, IS-CF-TG 28.93; TF: CF-IS-TG 28.70, IS-CF-TG 42.10;.
Owner Mrs Liz Gardner **Bred** Cheveley Park Stud Ltd **Trained** Liphook, Hants
Owner Percy Green Racing 3 **Bred** Stephanie Von Schilcher & Gavan Kinch **Trained** Musley Bank, N Yorks

FOCUS
The rail was moved out from 1m to the winning post, adding 20yds to all races of 1m+ and 12yds to 7f races. This was an open-looking apprentice riders' handicap but the pace was very steady and it paid not to be too far back. The front two came clear in the final half-furlong and the judge couldn't split them on the line. The form is rated around them.

4785 MOLSON COORS H'CAP 1m 4f 10y

6:25 (6:26) (Class 5) (0-75,75) 4-Y-O+ **£4,528** (£1,347; £673; £336) **Stalls** Centre

Form RPR
-443 1 **Atwix**70 2415 4-9-3 **73**..(b) AaronJones(5) 4 83
(Lucy Wadham) *hld up in 5th: prog on outer early in st: led over 2f out: decisive move and sn clr: pushed out: readily* **15/2**
1433 2 *3* **Speculator**19 4158 4-9-3 **68**...(p) ShaneKelly 2 72
(David Menuisier) *trckd ldng pair: lost pl early in st but stl in tch and gng wl: effrt 2f out: rdn to take 2nd 1f out but wnr clr: no imp* **11/4**1
-633 3 *2¾* **Sunday Royal (FR)**21 4049 4-9-7 **72**............................... SamHitchcott 5 72
(Harry Dunlop) *chsd ldng trio: pushed along 1/2-way: rdn and prog to chal over 2f out: chsd wnr to 1f out but no ch: fdd* **7/2**2
540- 4 *1¾* **Jupiter Custos (FR)**12 8157 4-9-5 **75**.................. CallumShepherd(5) 1 72
(Michael Scudamore) *settled in 6th: rdn and no prog 3f out: plugged on to take 4th ins fnl f* **16/1**
4-15 5 *1* **Shalimah (IRE)**19 4158 4-9-7 **72**..(v) DaneO'Neill 3 67
(Clive Cox) *chsd ldr: chal over 3f out to over 2f out: wknd over 1f out* **4/1**3
3116 6 *1* **Roy Rocket (FR)**23 3972 6-9-9 **74**... JFEgan 6 68
(John Berry) *hld up in last: rdn and no prog 3f out* **5/1**
363 7 *¾* **Comanche Chieftain (CAN)**16 4237 4-9-2 **67**.........(p) AndrewMullen 7 59
(Michael Appleby) *led: rdn and hdd over 2f out: sn wknd* **8/1**

2m 43.34s (4.44) **Going Correction** +0.225s/f (Good) **7** Ran SP% **114.3**
Speed ratings (Par 103): **94,92,90,89,88 87,87**
CSF £28.40 TOTE £9.70: £4.20, £1.90; EX 35.00 Trifecta £124.90.
Owner The Calculated Speculators **Bred** Southcourt Stud **Trained** Newmarket, Suffolk

FOCUS
Add 20yds to race distance. A steadily run handicap won with a decisive move around home bend. The winner was not an obvious improver on profile.

4786 BRITISH STALLION STUDS EBF MAIDEN STKS 7f

7:00 (7:01) (Class 5) 2-Y-O **£3,881** (£1,155; £577; £288) **Stalls** Low

Form RPR
3 1 **Serengeti Sky (USA)**12 4390 2-9-5 0..............................(t) JamesDoyle 2 74+
(Charlie Appleby) *trckd ldr: led over 2f out: edgd rt sn after: shkn up over 1f out: styd on wl: comf* **2/13**1
003 2 *3* **Asfaar (IRE)**14 4297 2-9-5 0.. DaneO'Neill 5 66+
(Brian Meehan) *hld up in 5th: prog over 2f out: rdn to chse wnr over 1f out: kpt on but no imp* **8/1**3
4604 3 *2* **Crystal Secret**14 4304 2-9-0 0... DannyBrock 1 56
(John Bridger) *chsd ldrs: 4th st: rdn to dispute 2nd briefly over 1f out: outpcd after* **50/1**
0 4 *1* **Rashford's Double (IRE)**62 2648 2-9-5 0.......................... DavidNolan 4 58
(Richard Fahey) *trckd ldng pair: cl up whn sltly impeded jst over 2f out: sn rdn: outpcd over 1f out* **6/1**2
0 5 *3½* **Lemon Drop**10 4457 2-9-0 0.. SamHitchcott 7 44
(Jim Boyle) *sn in last: rdn and bhd over 2f out: plugged on to take modest 5th nr fin* **25/1**
00 6 *1¾* **Don't You Think**8 4533 2-9-5 0.......................................(b1) ShaneKelly 3 45
(Richard Hughes) *rousted to ld: hdd over 2f out: wknd qckly over 1f out* **40/1**
0 7 *13* **Rockaria**42 3315 2-9-5 0.. JFEgan 6 11
(Philip Hide) *a in last pair: wknd 3f out: t.o* **66/1**

1m 24.65s (1.35) **Going Correction** +0.225s/f (Good) **7** Ran SP% **121.8**
Speed ratings (Par 94): **101,97,95,94,90 88,73**
CSF £2.79 TOTE £1.10: £1.10, £3.00; EX 3.60 Trifecta £20.60.
Owner Godolphin **Bred** Mike G Rutherford **Trained** Newmarket, Suffolk

FOCUS
No depth at all to this maiden and it proved easy pickings for the very short-priced favourite, although he was not as impressive as might have been hoped. Improvement from the second and third.

4787 EBF STALLIONS BREEDING WINNERS FIFINELLA FILLIES' H'CAP 7f

7:30 (7:31) (Class 4) (0-80,72) 3-Y-O+ **£6,469** (£1,925; £962; £481) **Stalls** Low

Form RPR
0460 1 **Alyaa (IRE)**36 3519 3-9-5 **72**..1 MartinDwyer 7 76
(Conrad Allen) *trckd ldr gng wl: pushed into ld over 1f out: rdn and edgd lft fnl f: kpt on and nvr in any real danger* **4/1**3
2124 2 *1¼* **First Experience**28 3802 5-9-11 **71**..................................(p) KierenFox 1 75
(Lee Carter) *chsd ldrs: 3rd st: rdn 2f out: chsd wnr fnl f: one pce and nvr able to chal* **11/4**2
0521 3 *nse* **One Big Surprise**12 4389 4-9-9 **69**.................................(p) ShaneKelly 2 72
(Richard Hughes) *hld up: last tl wnt 5th st: effrt on inner and shkn up 2f out: kpt on to press for 2nd ins fnl f: nvr nr enough to chal* **2/1**1
3210 4 *3½* **Broughtons Fancy**15 4269 3-8-9 **69**............................ GeorgeWood(7) 5 60
(Andrew Reid) *in rr: last st: in tch over 2f out but sn rdn and no prog: one pce after* **5/1**
0304 5 *1¾* **Penny Dreadful**7 4548 4-9-12 **72**.. DavidNolan 6 61
(Scott Dixon) *racd freely: led: rdn over 2f out: hdd over 1f out: wknd* **10/1**
0030 6 *3* **Hipz (IRE)**13 4355 5-8-11 **62**....................................... MeganNicholls(5) 3 43
(Laura Mongan) *chsd ldrs: 4th st: rdn over 2f out: wknd over 1f out* **12/1**

1m 24.57s (1.27) **Going Correction** +0.225s/f (Good)
WFA 3 from 4yo+ 7lb **6** Ran SP% **113.4**
Speed ratings (Par 102): **101,99,99,95,93 90**
CSF £15.66 TOTE £4.50: £2.30, £2.00; EX 17.10 Trifecta £46.10.
Owner A Al Kathiri **Bred** N Hartery **Trained** Newmarket, Suffolk

FOCUS
Not a very competitive 0-80 with the top weight rated 8lb below the ceiling for the grade and not many of these brought solid recent form to the table. The winner is rated to form.

4788 NONSUCH PARK H'CAP 1m 114y

8:05 (8:05) (Class 4) (0-80,78) 3-Y-O+ **£5,175** (£1,540; £769; £384) **Stalls** Low

Form RPR
0-01 1 **Lorelina**30 3745 3-8-4 **66**.. EdwardGreatrex(3) 4 80
(Andrew Balding) *trckd ldr: chal over 2f out: drvn to ld 1f out: styd on wl* **9/2**3
-531 2 *¾* **Crowning Glory (FR)**17 4206 3-8-13 **72**.................. RichardKingscote 1 84
(Ralph Beckett) *led: pressed over 2f out: drvn and hdd 1f out: styd on and clr of rest but jst hld* **10/3**2
2000 3 *7* **Live Dangerously**21 4058 6-9-3 **67**.................................. WilliamCarson 7 64
(John Bridger) *t.k.h: trckd ldrs: 3rd st: rdn and easily lft bhd fr over 2f out: hld on for 3rd* **33/1**
5613 4 *nk* **Wind In My Sails**19 4157 4-9-11 **75**........................ MichaelJMMurphy 2 71
(Ed de Giles) *hld up in rr: prog and 5th st: pressed for 3rd pl fr 2f out but no ch w clr ldng pair* **7/1**
5232 5 *2½* **The Salmon Man**21 4048 4-9-10 **74**.................................... JimCrowley 8 65
(Brendan Powell) *dwlt: sn in tch: lost pl and 7th st: brief effrt over 2f out: no prog over 1f out* **3/1**1
6462 6 *3¼* **The Invisible Dog (IRE)**9 4480 3-9-5 **78**..................... TomMarquand 6 60
(Richard Hannon) *hld up: 6th st: rdn and floundering over 2f out: sn wl btn* **5/1**
0315 7 *10* **World's Greatest (USA)**50 3039 3-8-11 **70**...................(t) OisinMurphy 3 29
(Stuart Williams) *chsd ldng pair to 1/2-way: 4th st: sn wknd: t.o* **6/1**
0066 8 *5* **Forceful Appeal (USA)**21 4048 8-9-11 **75**...................... HarryBentley 5 24
(Simon Dow) *a last: struggling over 3f out: t.o* **25/1**

1m 46.85s (0.75) **Going Correction** +0.225s/f (Good)
WFA 3 from 4yo+ 9lb **8** Ran SP% **116.5**
Speed ratings (Par 105): **105,104,98,97,95 92,83,79**
CSF £20.34 CT £443.39 TOTE £5.50: £1.80, £1.60, £6.00; EX 20.80 Trifecta £355.20.
Owner Tim Wixted & Tony Anderson **Bred** Tony Anderson & Tim Wixted **Trained** Kingsclere, Hants

FOCUS
Add 12yds to race distance. A fairly competitive heat for the grade, on paper at least, but the front two filled those placed throughout and came clear up the straight. On the plus side, both are improving 3yo fillies who won last time, which gives the form a bit more solidity.

4789 LANGLANDS H'CAP 7f

8:40 (8:41) (Class 5) (0-75,81) 3-Y-O **£3,234** (£962; £481; £240) **Stalls** Low

Form RPR
3114 1 **Frank Bridge**15 4279 3-8-9 **63**.. ShaneKelly 3 74
(Eve Johnson Houghton) *hld up in tch: 6th st: prog on outer over 2f out: shkn up to ld over 1f out and sn clr: comf* **7/1**
5322 2 *4½* **Sonnet (IRE)**28 3810 3-8-13 **67**................................ MichaelJMMurphy 2 66
(Charles Hills) *trckd ldrs: 4th st: prog to ld over 2f out: drvn and hdd over 1f out: no ch w wnr: clung on for 2nd* **11/2**3
005 3 *½* **Tasteofexcellence (IRE)**24 3958 3-8-2 **63**................ RhiainIngram(7) 6 61
(Roger Ingram) *hld up: 7th st: rdn over 2f out: no prog tl styd on fr jst over 1f out: tk 3rd last stride* **25/1**
6056 4 *hd* **Willsy**13 4354 3-9-4 **72**.. JFEgan 1 69
(Mick Channon) *restless stalls and dwlt: in tch in rr: 5th st: cl up whn nt clr run and sltly hmpd wl over 2f out: tried to rally over 1f out: pressed for a pl nr fin but no ch* **12/1**
-001 5 *shd* **Able Jack**7 4563 3-9-13 **81** 6ex.......................................(v) OisinMurphy 5 78
(Andrew Balding) *s.i.s: in rr: last st: rdn over 2f out: no ch but kpt on fnl f to press for a pl nr fin* **9/4**2
2421 6 *shd* **Wakame (IRE)**13 4369 3-8-13 **67**.. JimCrowley 8 64
(Ed de Giles) *trckd ldng pair: rdn over 2f out: hanging and nt qckn wl over 1f out: one pce after* **2/1**1

-320 **7** 1 ¼ **Sandacres**[77] 2185 3-8-13 **67** DaneO'Neill 4 60
(Laura Mongan) *led to 4f out: led again 3f out to over 2f out: wknd and lost pls ins fnl f* **20/1**
0-05 **8** 1 ½ **Firedanser**[35] 3567 3-9-4 **72** DavidNolan 7 62
(Richard Fahey) *pressed ldr: led 4f out to 3f out: sn lost pl and btn* **12/1**
1m 24.18s (0.88) **Going Correction** +0.225s/f (Good) **8** Ran SP% **116.0**
Speed ratings (Par 100): **103,97,97,97,96 96,95,93**
CSF £45.67 CT £920.50 TOTE £8.40: £2.30, £1.90, £4.80; EX 56.00 Trifecta £604.60.
Owner John Dyer **Bred** Catherine Dyer **Trained** Blewbury, Oxon
FOCUS
A couple of last-time out winners in here so reasonably competitive for the grade, but they were all blown away by the winner who resumed his progress and bolted up in truth. The second and third are rated close to their marks.
T/Plt: £92.00 to a £1 stake. Pool: £56,313.12. 446.63 winning tickets. T/Qpdt: £17.90 to a £1 stake. Pool: £6,146.59. 253.24 winning tickets. **Jonathan Neesom**

4479 FFOS LAS (L-H)

Thursday, July 28

OFFICIAL GOING: Good to soft (8.0) changing to good to soft (soft in places) after 5.40 (race 1)

Wind: Fresh, half behind Weather: overcast, rain race 3

4790 BRITISH STALLION STUDS EBF MAIDEN STKS 6f

5:40 (5:40) (Class 5) 2-Y-O £3,234 (£962; £481; £240) **Stalls** Centre

Form RPR
44 **1** **Thammin**[20] 4075 2-9-5 0 WilliamTwiston-Davies 1 81
(Owen Burrows) *cl up: led over 4f out: shkn up appr fnl f: rdn out to hold on nr fin* **1/1**[1]
0 **2** *nk* **Intimate Art (IRE)**[12] 4390 2-9-5 0 DavidProbert 6 80
(Andrew Balding) *chsd ldrs: rdn and hdwy 2f out: wnt 2nd over 1f out: looked hld by wnr whn rdr dropped whip wl ins fnl f: clsng nr fin* **11/4**[2]
3 **3** 3 ¼ **Dixie's Double**[20] 4083 2-9-0 0 TimmyMurphy 2 65
(Daniel Kubler) *led 100yds: chsd ldrs: rdn and sltly outpcd over 1f out: styd on same pce fnl f* **7/1**[3]
45 **4** 2 ¼ **Black Bubba (IRE)**[28] 3808 2-9-5 0 RobertWinston 7 62
(David Evans) *led after 100yds: hdd over 4f out: styd prom: rdn over 2f out: wknd fnl f* **12/1**
50 **5** *hd* **Rita's Man (IRE)**[17] 4203 2-9-0 0 GaryMahon(5) 5 62
(Richard Hannon) *s.i.s: sn in tch: rdn over 2f out: one pce and nvr able to threaten ldrs* **14/1**
0 **6** 2 **Amberine**[15] 4261 2-9-0 0 JimmyQuinn 8 50
(Malcolm Saunders) *wnt rt leaving stalls: outpcd and a in rr: minor late hdwy* **66/1**
7 6 **John T Chance (IRE)** 2-9-5 0 JimmyFortune 3 36
(Brian Meehan) *s.s: a in rr* **10/1**
1m 13.77s (3.77) **Going Correction** +0.525s/f (Yiel) **7** Ran SP% **114.1**
Speed ratings (Par 94): **95,94,90,87,87 84,76**
CSF £3.85 TOTE £1.80: £1.50, £1.60; EX 5.10 Trifecta £14.60.
Owner Hamdan Al Maktoum **Bred** Stratford Place Stud & Willow Bloodstock **Trained** Lambourn, Berks
FOCUS
After 7mm of rain on Thursday, on top of 8mm on Tuesday night, the going was changed to good to soft, leading to several non-runners on the card. A modest maiden to open the meeting but won in good style by the favourite. He's rated a bit up on his Ascot form.

4791 HEINEKEN NURSERY H'CAP 5f

6:10 (6:10) (Class 5) 2-Y-O £3,234 (£962; £481) **Stalls** Centre

Form RPR
3302 **1** **Zebspear (IRE)**[5] 4638 2-8-12 **68** JosephineGordon(3) 1 72
(Joseph Tuite) *trckd ldr: rdn to ld wl over 1f out: kpt up to work fnl f and comf holding rival* **10/11**[1]
0321 **2** ¾ **Little Nosegay (IRE)**[16] 4221 2-8-6 **64** GaryMahon(5) 7 64
(David Evans) *led tl rdn and hdd wl over 1f out: kpt on u.p after but a being hld* **7/4**[2]
060 **3** 9 **Zebby Sizz (IRE)**[14] 4287 2-7-7 **53** oh5 TinaSmith(7) 3 21
(Richard Hannon) *nt as wl away as rivals: a last of 3: in tch tl rdn, hung lft and wknd qckly 2f out* **4/1**[3]
1m 1.23s (2.93) **Going Correction** +0.525s/f (Yiel) **3** Ran SP% **108.7**
Speed ratings (Par 94): **97,95,81**
CSF £2.82 TOTE £1.80; EX 2.30 Trifecta £2.30.
Owner Spear Family **Bred** Hyde Park Stud **Trained** Lambourn, Berks
FOCUS
Four non-runners took away some of the interest in this nursery but the two principals came here in form and it shouldn't be dismissed as a form guide on account of the small field. The 1-2 are rated close to their marks.

4792 HEINEKEN MAIDEN STKS 1m 4f (R)

6:45 (6:45) (Class 5) 3-Y-O+ £3,234 (£962; £481; £240) **Stalls** Low

Form RPR
5- **1** **To Be Wild (IRE)**[308] 6674 3-8-13 0 JosephineGordon(3) 11 87+
(Hugo Palmer) *w ldr: led 3f out: rdn over 1f out: edgd rt ins fnl f: comf* **4/6**[1]
53 **2** 1 ¾ **Sir Valentine (GER)**[14] 4319 3-9-2 0 WilliamTwiston-Davies 10 82
(Alan King) *trckd ldrs: rdn to chse wnr 2f out: swtchd lft ins fnl f: styd on: a hld by comfortable wnr* **5/1**[3]
5022 **3** 4 **Beauty Sleep (IRE)**[12] 4384 3-8-11 77 (p) RobertWinston 9 71
(William Haggas) *broke wl and led 100yds: sn in mid-div: hdwy to chse ldrs 4f out: one pce and no ch w ldng pair fnl f* **9/2**[2]
4 3 ¼ **Hannah Just Hannah**[68] 7-9-4 0 (t) LucyKBarry(5) 5 66
(Matthew Salaman) *hld up in rr: shkn up over 2f out: styd on down outer: tk 4th nr fin* **50/1**
30 **5** 1 **Tobougaloo**[27] 3845 5-9-9 0 TimmyMurphy 3 64+
(Stuart Kittow) *hld up towards rr: hdwy on ins 3f out: nudged along and styd on steadily fnl 2f* **28/1**
0 **6** *hd* **Maqam (IRE)**[13] 4367 3-8-11 0 JimmyQuinn 1 64
(Richard Hannon) *mid-div: hdwy 3f out: rdn 2f out: one pce* **28/1**
0 **7** 5 **Major Ben**[31] 3723 3-9-2 0 FrederikTylicki 4 61
(William Muir) *t.k.h in mid-div: pushed along 3f out: sn no ch but kpt on steadily* **50/1**
65 **8** 2 ½ **Last Summer**[94] 1722 5-9-9 0 CiaranMckee(5) 7 57
(Grace Harris) *a towards rr* **100/1**
05 **9** *shd* **Intercepted**[30] 3736 3-9-2 0 GeorgeBaker 6 57
(David Lanigan) *led after 100yds: rdn and hdd 3f out: wknd over 1f out* **8/1**
5 **10** 3 **Isaak (FR)**[91] 1806 3-9-2 0 DavidProbert 8 52
(Andrew Balding) *trckd ldrs tl lost pl and dropped towards rr after 2f: rdn 3f out: wknd 2f out* **33/1**
11 1 ¾ **Caracci Apache (IRE)**[264] 6-10-0 0 JimmyFortune 2 49
(Eve Johnson Houghton) *sn trcking ldrs: rdn 3f out: wknd 2f out* **16/1**
2m 40.71s (3.31) **Going Correction** +0.425s/f (Yiel)
WFA 3 from 5yo+ 12lb **11** Ran SP% **126.6**
Speed ratings (Par 103): **105,103,101,99,98 98,94,93,93,91 89**
CSF £4.73 TOTE £1.60: £1.10, £2.00, £1.70; EX 6.00 Trifecta £16.80.
Owner Carmichael Jennings **Bred** Miss Mary Davison **Trained** Newmarket, Suffolk
FOCUS
A steady pace for the 1m4f maiden but a taking performance from the well-regarded winner. There's a lot more to come from him.

4793 GEWS LTD H'CAP 1m 4f (R)

7:15 (7:16) (Class 4) (0-85,84) 3-Y-O+ **£5,175** (£1,540; £769; £384) **Stalls** Low

Form RPR
232 **1** **Swashbuckle**[22] 4001 3-8-5 **73** DavidProbert 1 84
(Andrew Balding) *mde all: set stdy gallop tl increased pce 3f out: rdn 2f out: sn jnd: r.o u.p: asserted nr fin* **5/2**[2]
3-15 **2** ½ **Pure Fantasy**[19] 4160 3-8-10 **78** WilliamTwiston-Davies 3 88
(Roger Charlton) *dwlt: hld up in last but wl in tch: hdwy gng wl 3f out: trckd wnr 2f out: chal over 1f out: r.o u.p: hld nr fin* **10/1**
0210 **3** 8 **Icebuster**[17] 4208 8-10-0 **84** FrederikTylicki 2 81
(Rod Millman) *t.k.h: sn trckd ldrs in 3rd: rdn and sltly hmpd over 2f out: one pce and no ch w 1st 2 appr fnl f* **8/1**
0506 **4** 4 **Vercingetorix (IRE)**[19] 4129 5-9-5 **80** GaryMahon(5) 6 71
(David Evans) *hld up and mainly in 4th: rdn 3f out: wknd over 1f out* **4/1**[3]
6-01 **5** 3 **Ravens Quest**[26] 3906 3-8-12 **80** RobertWinston 5 70
(Hughie Morrison) *plld hrd: trckd wnr: rdn over 2f out and sn lost 2nd: hung lft after: eased over 1f out* **5/4**[1]
2m 41.38s (3.98) **Going Correction** +0.425s/f (Yiel)
WFA 3 from 5yo+ 12lb **5** Ran SP% **113.2**
Speed ratings (Par 105): **103,102,97,94,92**
CSF £24.76 TOTE £3.40: £1.70, £3.60; EX 17.10 Trifecta £63.60.
Owner Kingsclere Racing Club **Bred** Kingsclere Stud **Trained** Kingsclere, Hants
FOCUS
One of the more interesting races on the card but run at a sedate pace and it didn't see them all to best effect. The first two both improved.

4794 FOSTERS H'CAP 1m 2f (R)

7:45 (7:48) (Class 6) (0-65,65) 3-Y-O £3,234 (£962; £481; £240) **Stalls** Low

Form RPR
-655 **1** **Pina**[15] 4279 3-9-3 **61** WilliamTwiston-Davies 9 73
(Roger Charlton) *hld up towards rr: stdy hdwy 4f out: shkn up to ld narrowly 2f out: drvn and styd on wl: plld away fnl 100yds* **4/1**[2]
-023 **2** 2 ¼ **Nanny Makfi**[37] 3493 3-8-3 **50** JosephineGordon(3) 12 57
(Stuart Kittow) *mid-div: hdwy 5f out: rdn and ev ch 2f out tl no ex fnl 100yds* **7/2**[1]
000 **3** 8 **Keyman (IRE)**[35] 3577 3-7-13 **49** ow2 MitchGodwin(7) 11 42
(Jeremy Gask) *towards rr: rdn and hdwy 3f out: hung lft 2f out: styd on same pce and no ch w 1st 2* **25/1**
1-03 **4** 1 **Hermarna (IRE)**[37] 3496 3-9-7 **65** DavidProbert 3 55
(Harry Dunlop) *t.k.h in mid-div: rdn and clsd 3f out: one pce fnl 2f* **7/2**[1]
0355 **5** 1 ½ **Rosie's Vision**[19] 4159 3-8-2 **46** (v[1]) JimmyQuinn 13 33
(Mark Usher) *s.i.s: hdwy to trck ldr after 2f and racd keenly: rdn and nt qckn over 2f out: one pce after and lost 4th ins fnl f* **12/1**
0652 **6** 1 ¾ **Wallangarra**[14] 4301 3-9-7 **65** AdamBeschizza 8 49
(Jeremy Gask) *s.i.s: towards rr: rdn 5f out: hdwy whn hmpd on rail over 2f out: swtchd rt over 1f out: no further imp* **7/1**[3]
-650 **7** 4 **Provoking (USA)**[22] 3998 3-9-1 **59** RobertWinston 5 35
(David Evans) *led: rdn over 2f out: sn hdd: wknd over 1f out* **25/1**
-000 **8** 15 **Mr Marchwood**[35] 3558 3-9-7 **65** LiamKeniry 7 13
(Sylvester Kirk) *mid-div: sme hdwy 4f out: rdn 3f out: sn wknd: t.o* **20/1**
0300 **9** 3 **Ocean Gale**[19] 4159 3-8-0 **47** NoelGarbutt(3) 2
(Richard Price) *chsd ldrs tl wknd 4f out: t.o* **40/1**
0300 **10** ¾ **The Detainee**[31] 3715 3-9-5 **63** (p) FrederikTylicki 1 4
(Jeremy Gask) *mid-div tl dropped to rr 6f out: lost tch over 3f out: t.o* **8/1**
656 **11** 3 **Walking In Rhythm (IRE)**[13] 4361 3-9-2 **65** GaryMahon(5) 10
(Richard Hannon) *trckd ldr 2f: styd prom: rdn 3f out: hung lft and wknd qckly: t.o* **8/1**
2m 12.04s (2.64) **Going Correction** +0.425s/f (Yiel) **11** Ran SP% **121.8**
Speed ratings (Par 98): **106,104,97,97,95 94,91,79,76,76 73**
CSF £18.27 CT £318.97 TOTE £4.20: £1.50, £1.90, £8.10; EX 18.00 Trifecta £391.60.
Owner David & Paul Hearson **Bred** Granham Farm Partnership **Trained** Beckhampton, Wilts
■ Stewards' Enquiry : Gary Mahon caution: careless riding
Mitch Godwin three-day ban: weighed in 2lb heavy (Aug 11-13)
FOCUS
Low-grade fare but a good finish with two pulling well clear. The form is rated slightly positively.

4795 KRONENBOURG H'CAP 2m (R)

8:20 (8:21) (Class 4) (0-80,80) 4-Y-O+ **£5,175** (£1,540; £769; £384) **Stalls** Low

Form RPR
4225 **1** **Champagne Champ**[27] 3862 4-9-4 **77** FrederikTylicki 7 87
(Rod Millman) *chsd ldrs: led over 3f out: rdn over 2f out: carried hd high but styd on wl* **2/1**[1]
60-6 **2** 2 ¼ **Kleitomachos (IRE)**[30] 3746 8-8-5 **67** (t) JosephineGordon(3) 4 73
(Stuart Kittow) *a.p and mainly in 2nd: rdn over 3f out: outpcd by wnr over 1f out: styd on wl fnl f* **7/1**
-646 **3** 7 **Spice Fair**[27] 3862 9-9-7 **80** LiamKeniry 8 78
(Mark Usher) *s.i.s: hld up in last pair: rdn over 3f out: hdwy 2f out: styd on to go modest 3rd ins fnl f* **5/1**[3]
0002 **4** *nk* **Bazooka (IRE)**[32] 3690 5-9-4 **77** GeorgeBaker 2 74
(David Flood) *wore hood in paddock: hld up in last pair: hdwy 3f out: shkn up 2f out: one pce* **8/1**
611 **5** *shd* **Medburn Cutler**[30] 3746 6-9-4 **77** (p) JimmyFortune 3 74
(Paul Henderson) *hld up in 5th: rdn 4f out: clsd to dispute 2nd 3f out to 2f out: wknd and lost modest 3rd fnl f* **7/2**[2]
0131 **6** 11 **Royal Reef (IRE)**[29] 3784 4-9-1 **74** JimmyQuinn 5 58
(William Knight) *chsd ldrs: rdn 4f out: wknd 2f out* **5/1**[3]
6250 **7** 7 **Moojaned (IRE)**[12] 4417 5-9-0 **80** AledBeech(7) 1 56
(David Evans) *led tl hdd over 3f out: sn wknd: bhd fnl 2f* **16/1**
3m 35.7s (5.70) **Going Correction** +0.425s/f (Yiel) **7** Ran SP% **118.4**
Speed ratings (Par 105): **102,100,97,97,97 91,88**
CSF £17.77 CT £63.39 TOTE £2.80: £2.20, £4.30; EX 17.80 Trifecta £68.50.
Owner Five Horses Ltd **Bred** Five Horses Ltd **Trained** Kentisbeare, Devon

FOCUS
A fair staying handicap featuring some in-form sorts, the winner further enhancing a good record at the track. The first two finished clear.

4796 STRONGBOW H'CAP 6f
8:55 (8:55) (Class 6) (0-60,60) 3-Y-O **£2,587** (£770; £384; £192) **Stalls** Centre

Form RPR
6060 **1** **Baz's Boy**[14] 4292 3-8-4 **46** oh1 NoelGarbutt(3) 3 50
(John Flint) *a.p: rdn over 2f out: r.o to ld wl ins fnl f* **14/1**
500 **2** *nk* **Arcanista (IRE)**[12] 4388 3-9-7 **60** (b[1]) JimmyFortune 2 63
(Richard Hughes) *s.i.s: sn cl up and racd alone towards far side: led narrowly over 2f out: rdn over 1f out: hdd wl ins fnl f* **4/1[3]**
5062 **3** *1* **Secretfact**[8] 4506 3-8-7 **46** oh1 JimmyQuinn 8 46
(Malcolm Saunders) *hld up: hdwy over 2f out: ev ch whn rdn over 1f out: unable qck and hld nr fin* **5/2[2]**
3064 **4** *1* **Concur (IRE)**[14] 4290 3-8-7 **46** DavidProbert 4 43
(Rod Millman) *led narrowly: rdn over 2f out: sn hdd: kpt on same pce fnl f* **6/4[1]**
0500 **5** *3/4* **Mostashreqah**[23] 3987 3-8-9 **51** (tp) JosephineGordon(3) 7 45
(Milton Bradley) *chsd ldrs: rdn over 2f out: one pce fnl f* **25/1**
6606 **6** *3 1/2* **Equal Point**[30] 3744 3-9-7 **60** FrederikTylicki 6 43
(William Knight) *chsd ldrs: ev ch 2f out: sn rdn: wknd fnl f* **8/1**
5060 **7** *23* **Tim The Taxi**[20] 4085 3-8-6 **50** (v[1]) GaryMahon(5) 11
(David Evans) *prom 2f: sn towards rr and rdn along: lost tch 2f out: t.o* **16/1**

1m 13.43s (3.43) **Going Correction** +0.525s/f (Yiel) **7** Ran SP% **116.1**
Speed ratings (Par 98): **98,97,96,94,93 89,58**
CSF £70.53 CT £190.47 TOTE £19.30: £7.80, £2.70; EX 94.70 Trifecta £249.00.
Owner B Jones & Son **Bred** B R Marsden **Trained** Kenfig Hill, Bridgend
■ Stewards' Enquiry : Noel Garbutt two-day ban: used whip above permitted level (Aug 11-12)

FOCUS
A very modest finale but run at a good pace. Unconvincing form.
T/Plt: £40.40 to a £1 stake. Pool: £53,269.62. 962.34 winning tickets. T/Qpdt: £10.90 to a £1 stake. Pool: £6,362.39. 430.44 winning tickets. **Richard Lowther**

4752 GOODWOOD (R-H)
Thursday, July 28

OFFICIAL GOING: Good to firm (overall 8.4, stands' side 8.3, far side 8.5)
Wind: light to medium, half against Weather: light rain, murky and poor visibility from races 3 to 6

4797 MATCHBOOK BETTING EXCHANGE STKS (H'CAP) 1m 1f 192y
2:00 (2:00) (Class 2) 3-Y-O **£31,125** (£9,320; £4,660; £2,330; £1,165; £585) **Stalls** Low

Form RPR
23-1 **1** **You're Hired**[19] 4156 3-8-2 **80** MartinDwyer 14 89
(Amanda Perrett) *chsd ldrs: hung lft and wd bnd 5f out: wnt 2nd over 2f out: wandered u.p wl over 1f out: chal 1f out: sustained effrt to ld towards fin: all out* **9/1**
5061 **2** *hd* **Ode To Evening**[20] 4108 3-9-7 **99** JamesMcDonald 9 107
(Mark Johnston) *led: rdn ent fnl 2f: hrd pressed 1f out: battled on wl u.p tl hdd and no ex towards fin* **10/1**
32-1 **3** *hd* **Stargazer (IRE)**[97] 1610 3-9-4 **96** RyanMoore 16 104+
(Sir Michael Stoute) *lw: hld up in tch in midfield but stuck wd: effrt 2f out: sltly hmpd wl over 1f out: hdwy to chse ldng trio ent fnl f: styd on wl u.p fnl 150yds: wnt 3rd towards fin: nt quite rch ldng pair* **11/2[1]**
4611 **4** *1/2* **Scarlet Dragon**[7] 4554 3-8-12 **90** 6ex TomMarquand 11 97
(Eve Johnson Houghton) *t.k.h: hld up in tch in midfield: nt clr run 3f out: rdn and hdwy to chse ldrs wl over 1f out: drvn to chal 1f out: kpt on but unable qck wl ins fnl f* **10/1**
1563 **5** *1 1/2* **Dwight D**[20] 4108 3-8-7 **85** (p) JamieSpencer 4 89+
(William Haggas) *stmbld leaving stalls: in tch in rr: clsd and nt clr run 3f out: hdwy over 1f out: chsng ldrs and drvn 1f out: kpt on but nvr able to get on terms: stuck bhd ldng quartet wl ins fnl f: eased nr fin* **8/1[3]**
1-4 **6** *1* **Red Rannagh (IRE)**[198] 154 3-8-9 **87** ow1 (t) JimCrowley 3 89+
(David Simcock) *s.i.s: hld up in rr: pushed along and nt clr run 3f out: hdwy u.p ent fnl f: styd on wl ins fnl f: nvr gng to rch ldrs* **14/1**
1604 **7** *1 3/4* **Carrington (FR)**[13] 4339 3-8-12 **90** JamesDoyle 2 89
(Charlie Appleby) *t.k.h: hld up in tch in midfield: swtchd rt and effrt 3f out: no imp u.p over 1f out: styd on same pce fnl f* **25/1**
3060 **8** *3/4* **Zhui Feng (IRE)**[42] 3299 3-9-6 **98** PatDobbs 13 95
(Amanda Perrett) *hld up in tch in midfield: rdn ent fnl 2f: unable qck and no imp over 1f out: kpt on but no threat to ldrs ins fnl f* **14/1**
-314 **9** *nk* **High Shields (IRE)**[19] 4131 3-8-12 **90** FrankieDettori 8 86
(Roger Charlton) *lw: trckd ldrs: swtchd lft and effrt wl over 2f out: struggling to qckn whn pushed lft and sltly impeded wl over 1f out: wknd fnl f* **7/1[2]**
-021 **10** *hd* **Goodwood Zodiac (IRE)**[32] 3687 3-9-1 **93** SilvestreDeSousa 6 89
(William Knight) *t.k.h: hld up in tch in midfield: stdd bk towards rr after 3f: nt clr run jst over 2f out: no real imp u.p over 1f out: kpt on same pce fnl f* **16/1**
2513 **11** *4 1/2* **Montsarrat (IRE)**[13] 4339 3-9-3 **95** FrannyNorton 17 82
(Mark Johnston) *hld up in tch towards rr but stuck wd: effrt over 2f out: no real imp and btn over 1f out: wknd fnl f* **14/1**
2215 **12** *3/4* **Banksea**[20] 4108 3-9-2 **94** AndreaAtzeni 7 80
(Luca Cumani) *t.k.h: hld up in tch in last quartet: swtchd lft and effrt over 2f out: no imp u.p and wl hld over 1f out: wknd fnl f* **8/1[3]**
0012 **13** *3/4* **Abareeq**[10] 4453 3-8-0 **78** oh1 JoeFanning 1 62
(Mark Johnston) *chsd ldrs: rdn 3f out: sn struggling and lost pl ent fnl 2f: bhd over 1f out: wknd* **16/1**
-403 **14** *1 1/4* **Champagne City**[26] 3887 3-8-13 **91** RichardKingscote 10 73
(Mark Johnston) *lw: chsd ldr tl over 2f out: sn lost pl and bhd over 1f out* **20/1**
1-00 **15** *8* **Top Beak (IRE)**[77] 2190 3-8-12 **90** (t) RobertHavlin 12 56
(Hughie Morrison) *hld up in tch in midfield: jostled 4f out: sn rdn and lost pl: bhd 2f out: eased ins fnl f* **40/1**

2m 5.49s (-2.61) **Going Correction** +0.025s/f (Good) **15** Ran SP% **121.1**
Speed ratings (Par 106): **111,110,110,110,109 108,106,106,106,105 102,101,101,100,93**
CSF £93.86 CT £551.23 TOTE £10.80: £3.30, £4.00, £2.00; EX 121.80 Trifecta £678.10.
Owner George Materna **Bred** Cheveley Park Stud Ltd **Trained** Pulborough, W Sussex

FOCUS
Watering took place overnight, but the going was still good to firm (GoingStick: 8.4). The running rail from the 6f marker on the lower bend to the 3f marker in the straight was dolled out 6yds, increasing distances by 8yds. The top bend was dolled out 3yds, increasing race distances by 8yds. A competitive handicap with plenty on the upgrade, and a tight finish. THe runner-up is perhaps the key.

4798 QATAR RICHMOND STKS (GROUP 2) (C&G) 6f
2:35 (2:35) (Class 1) 2-Y-O **£113,420** (£43,000; £21,520; £10,720) **Stalls** High

Form RPR
1221 **1** **Mehmas (IRE)**[21] 4060 2-9-3 0 FrankieDettori 3 114
(Richard Hannon) *lw: stdd s: trckd ldng pair: clsd and upsides ldrs 2f out: rdn and qcknd w ldr jst over 1f out: sustained chal u.p to ld wl ins fnl f: r.o wl* **7/2[3]**
11 **2** *nk* **Blue Point (IRE)**[14] 4297 2-9-0 0 JamesDoyle 2 110
(Charlie Appleby) *str: lengthy: lw: wnt rt s: sn led: jnd 2f out: rdn and qcknd jst over 1f out: sn drvn and hung rt 1f out: rdr changed hands and wnt further rt 100yds out: sn hdd: r.o but a hld after* **5/6[1]**
2 **3** *3* **Intelligence Cross (USA)**[21] 4060 2-9-0 0 (t) RyanMoore 4 101
(A P O'Brien, Ire) *sn trcking ldr: upsides ldr 2f out: rdn over 1f out: 3rd and unable qck 1f out: kpt on same pce and wl hld ins fnl f* **5/2[2]**
621 **4** *2 1/4* **Waqaas**[21] 4040 2-9-0 0 DaneO'Neill 5 94
(Charles Hills) *str: stdd s: hld up wl in tch in 4th: rdn 2f out: outpcd and btn over 1f out* **33/1**

1m 11.0s (-1.20) **Going Correction** -0.375s/f (Firm) **4** Ran SP% **108.3**
Speed ratings (Par 106): **93,92,88,85**
CSF £6.96 TOTE £4.00; EX 7.40 Trifecta £8.70.
Owner Al Shaqab Racing **Bred** Epona Bloodstock Ltd **Trained** East Everleigh, Wilts

FOCUS
Race distance as advertised. Despite the small field, a fascinating Richmond featuring the first two from the July Stakes up against an exciting and previously unbeaten Godolphin colt. The pace was good and the form looks solid. Mehmas improved again to defy a penalty, confirming July Stakes from with Intelligence Cross. Blue Point confirmed the merit of his Doncaster win.

4799 QATAR GOODWOOD CUP (BRITISH CHAMPIONS SERIES) (GROUP 2) 2m
3:10 (3:10) (Class 1) 3-Y-O+
£176,991 (£67,101; £33,581; £16,728; £8,395; £4,213) **Stalls** Low

Form RPR
-231 **1** **Big Orange**[21] 4061 5-9-8 117 (p) JamieSpencer 9 117
(Michael Bell) *lw: led: rdn and pressed 3f out: drvn and hdd over 1f out: sn regained ld and forged ahd 1f out: drifted rt: styd on v gamely u.p ins fnl f* **11/4[1]**
-104 **2** *1 1/4* **Pallasator**[26] 3913 7-9-8 112 OisinMurphy 15 116
(Sir Mark Prescott Bt) *mounted on crse and taken down early: chsd ldrs: clsd to press wnr and rdn 2f out: ev ch over 1f out: nt quite matching pce of wnr 1f out: wnt 2nd and kpt on same pce fnl 100yds* **9/1**
-103 **3** *hd* **Sheikhzayedroad**[42] 3298 7-9-8 113 MartinHarley 14 115
(David Simcock) *chsd ldrs: clsd to chse ldrs over 2f out: unable qck over 1f out: swtchd rt and rallied u.p jst ins fnl f: styd on* **11/1**
3-26 **4** *2* **Wicklow Brave**[40] 3384 7-9-8 111 AndreaAtzeni 12 113
(W P Mullins, Ire) *lw: hld up in tch in midfield: clsd to chse ldrs and rdn over 2f out: unable qck over 1f out: kpt on same pce ins fnl f* **16/1**
11 **5** *hd* **Sword Fighter (IRE)**[32] 3697 3-8-6 105 ow1 ColmO'Donoghue 1 114
(A P O'Brien, Ire) *chsd wnr: clsd and pressing wnr 2f out: drvn to ld over 1f out: sn hdd and no ex 1f out: 3rd and btn 100yds out: wknd towards fin* **9/2[2]**
0-23 **6** *hd* **Quest For More (IRE)**[19] 4164 6-9-8 109 (b) GeorgeBaker 2 113
(Roger Charlton) *swtg: hld up in midfield: clsd over 3f out: rdn and unable qck over 1f out: kpt on same pce ins fnl f* **7/1[3]**
-011 **7** *6* **Kinema (IRE)**[41] 3340 5-9-8 107 (b) RichardKingscote 11 105
(Ralph Beckett) *hld up in midfield: hdwy to chse ldrs 6f out: rdn over 2f out: no ex and btn over 1f out: wknd ins fnl f* **12/1**
4200 **8** *nk* **Suegioo (FR)**[19] 4164 7-9-8 108 (p) JamesDoyle 10 105
(Richard Fahey) *stdd s: hld up in rr of main gp: effrt over 2f out: sme hdwy over 1f out: nvr trbld ldrs* **66/1**
0-05 **9** *3 1/4* **Glaring**[76] 2221 5-9-8 105 JimCrowley 8 101
(Amanda Perrett) *hld up towards rr of main gp: rdn 3f out: sn struggling: wknd over 1f out* **100/1**
01-2 **10** *nk* **Curbyourenthusiasm (IRE)**[76] 2221 5-9-8 111 FergusSweeney 3 101
(David Simcock) *hld up in rr of main gp: rdn 4f out: no imp 3f out: wknd over 1f out* **8/1**
2651 **11** *4 1/2* **Sandro Botticelli (IRE)**[26] 3913 4-9-8 107 (p) FrankieDettori 13 95
(John Ryan) *hld up in midfield: rdn over 3f out: sn lost pl: wknd over 1f out* **25/1**
5-00 **12** *5* **The Twisler**[42] 3298 4-9-8 104 MartinDwyer 7 89
(Jane Chapple-Hyam) *hld up towards rr of main gp: rdn 3f out: no hdwy and sn btn: wknd over 1f out* **100/1**
-446 **13** *47* **Oriental Fox (GER)**[26] 3913 8-9-8 104 JoeFanning 4 33
(Mark Johnston) *midfield: bdly hmpd on inner and snatched up after 2f: lost pls but stl midfield: dropped to rr 3f out: sn eased: t.o* **25/1**
11/1 **P** **Commissioned (IRE)**[40] 3387 6-9-8 104 (p) AdamKirby 5
(Gordon Elliott, Ire) *s.i.s: sn rdn along in detached last and nvr gng wl: p.u and dismntd 11f out: lame* **11/1**

3m 24.93s (-4.07) **Going Correction** +0.025s/f (Good)
WFA 3 from 4yo+ 17lb **14** Ran SP% **119.9**
Speed ratings (Par 115): **111,110,110,109,109 109,106,105,104,104 101,99,75,**
CSF £27.06 TOTE £3.30: £1.50, £3.10, £3.30; EX 27.30 Trifecta £230.40.
Owner W J and T C O Gredley **Bred** Stetchworth & Middle Park Studs **Trained** Newmarket, Suffolk

FOCUS
Race distance increased by 8yds. The rain had started to fall prior to this race, but it's doubtful it had changed the ground much. An up-to-standard Goodwood Cup, but very little got into it from off the pace.

4800 MARKEL INSURANCE FILLIES' STKS (REGISTERED AS THE LILLIE LANGTRY STAKES) (GROUP 3) 1m 6f
3:45 (3:45) (Class 1) 3-Y-O+
£56,710 (£21,500; £10,760; £5,360; £2,690; £1,350) **Stalls** Low

Form RPR
061 **1** **California (IRE)**[20] 4078 4-9-6 98 RobertHavlin 2 103
(John Gosden) *chsd ldr: rdn and ev ch over 2f out: drvn to ld 1f out: styd on wl: rdn out* **9/2**
015 **2** *1* **Tioga Pass**[12] 4400 5-9-6 97 (tp) MartinHarley 6 102
(Paul Cole) *stdd s: hld up in tch in rr: slipped bnd 11f out: hdwy u.p over 1f out: chsd wnr ins fnl f: kpt on same pce fnl 100yds* **25/1**

3442 **3** 1 1/4 **Twitch (IRE)**[12] 4400 4-9-6 99....(p) JamesMcDonald 5 100
(Hugo Palmer) *t.k.h: hld up in tch: effrt on inner 2f out: styd on u.p ins fnl f: wnt 3rd towards fin* **4/1**[3]

1-03 **4** 1/2 **Mill Springs**[44] 3246 4-9-6 99.... FrankieDettori 1 100
(John Gosden) *lw: bustled along leaving stalls: sn led and set stdy gallop: rdn over 2f out: hdd 1f out: no ex: wknd ins fnl f* **5/1**

-001 **5** 2 1/4 **Pamona (IRE)**[19] 4164 4-9-6 104....(v) JimCrowley 3 96
(Ralph Beckett) *t.k.h: trckd ldng pair: effrt on inner 2f out: sn drvn and ev ch tl no ex 1f out: wknd ins fnl f* **5/2**[1]

0-01 **6** shd **Elysian Fields (GR)**[29] 3785 5-9-6 92.... PatDobbs 7 96
(Amanda Perrett) *hld up in tch: clsd to press ldrs and travelling wl 3f out: rdn and fnd little over 1f out: wknd ins fnl f* **25/1**

0-02 **7** 3/4 **Yarrow (IRE)**[39] 3436 4-9-6 100.... RyanMoore 4 95
(Sir Michael Stoute) *in tch in midfield: dropped to rr and rdn over 2f out: keeping on same pce and hld whn nt clr run ins fnl f: nt pushed after* **7/2**[2]

3m 3.71s (0.11) **Going Correction** +0.025s/f (Good) **7** Ran SP% **113.3**
Speed ratings (Par 110): **100,99,98,98,97 97,96**
CSF £93.67 TOTE £5.50: £2.50, £7.90; EX 76.40 Trifecta £311.40.
Owner Denford Stud **Bred** Epona Bloodstock Ltd And P A Byrne **Trained** Newmarket, Suffolk

FOCUS

Race distance increased by 8yds. The drizzle continued to fall and the visibility wasn't great. This Group 3 was won by Simple Verse last year before going on to dual Group 1 success, but no 3yos took part this time and it didn't look the strongest of races for the level, with the pace also looking an ordinary one. Five of these met in a Listed event over 1m4f here in May. California continued her progress.

4801 DOVE 100 COLOURS EBF BRITISH STALLION STUDS MAIDEN FILLIES' STKS (PLUS 10 RACE) 7f

4:20 (4:21) (Class 2) 2-Y-O **£16,172** (£4,812; £2,405; £1,202) **Stalls** Low

Form RPR

1 **Rhododendron (IRE)**[34] 3626 2-9-0 0.... RyanMoore 5 90+
(A P O'Brien, Ire) *str: lengthy: hld up in tch in midfield: effrt and wandered rt u.p over 1f out: str run 1f out: led 100yds out: sn in command and r.o strly: rdn out* **10/11**[1]

2 **2** 1 3/4 **Amabilis**[19] 4147 2-9-0 0.... FrankieDettori 6 85+
(Ralph Beckett) *lw: t.k.h: hld up in tch in midfield: smooth hdwy on inner over 2f out: led wl over 1f out: rdn ent fnl f: drvn and hdd 100yds out: kpt on same pce after* **7/4**[2]

3 1 **Argenterie** 2-9-0 0.... MartinDwyer 7 82+
(Marcus Tregoning) *cmpt: stdd s and dropped in bhd: hdwy on inner over 2f out: rdn to chse ldrs ent fnl f: r.o same pce ins fnl f* **66/1**

4 3/4 **Berengaria (IRE)** 2-9-0 0.... JoeFanning 4 80
(Mark Johnston) *str: led: hdd and rdn wl over 1f out: unable qck u.p: styd on same pce ins fnl f* **20/1**

0 **5** 1 **Sun Angel (IRE)**[21] 4063 2-9-0 0.... OisinMurphy 3 77
(Henry Candy) *hld up in tch in midfield: swtchd lft and effrt over 1f out: styd on same pce ins fnl f* **40/1**

2 **6** 4 1/2 **The Stalking Moon (IRE)**[8] 4508 2-9-0 0.... TomEaves 1 66+
(John Quinn) *neat: chsd ldrs tl wnt 2nd over 2f out: rdn and ev ch over 1f out tl no ex 1f out: wknd qckly ins fnl f* **33/1**

3 **7** nk **Helmsdale**[19] 4154 2-9-0 0.... PatDobbs 10 65
(Richard Hannon) *str: chsd ldr tl over 2f out: sn struggling u.p and lost pl over 1f out: wknd fnl f* **25/1**

8 3 1/4 **Lady Valdean** 2-9-0 0.... SilvestreDeSousa 9 56
(Jose Santos) *tall: stdd bk towards rr after 1f: effrt over 2f out: no ch but sme prog to pass btn horses 1f out: nvr trbld ldrs* **40/1**

9 3 1/2 **Silver Link (IRE)** 2-9-0 0.... HarryBentley 8 47
(Marcus Tregoning) *cmpt: in tch in midfield: rdn over 2f out and sn lost pl: wl btn over 1f out* **66/1**

0 **10** 2 1/4 **Cheeky Fox**[28] 3812 2-9-0 0.... HayleyTurner 12 41
(Marcus Tregoning) *lengthy: stdd bk to last pair after s: rdn over 2f out: no hdwy and wl bhd over 1f out* **33/1**

11 hd **Vrika Bay** 2-9-0 0.... AndreaAtzeni 13 41
(Robert Eddery) *w'like: hld up in rr: rdn over 2f out: sn btn and wl bhd over 1f out* **100/1**

2 **12** 2 3/4 **Manama (IRE)**[21] 4063 2-9-0 0.... JamesDoyle 11 34
(Charlie Appleby) *chsd ldrs: effrt over 2f out: sn hung lft and lost pl: wknd qckly over 1f out: bhd and eased ins fnl f* **7/1**[3]

1m 27.72s (0.72) **Going Correction** +0.025s/f (Good) **12** Ran SP% **124.6**
Speed ratings (Par 97): **96,94,92,92,90 85,85,81,77,75 74,71**
CSF £2.54 TOTE £1.90: £1.10, £1.50, £14.50; EX 3.30 Trifecta £100.20.
Owner Mrs John Magnier & Michael Tabor & Derrick Smith **Bred** Orpendale, Chelston & Wynatt **Trained** Cashel, Co Tipperary

FOCUS

Race distance increased by 8yds. The visibility had improved slightly since the previous contest, but it still wasn't wonderful. The last ten winners of this maiden all had previous experience and the betting for this year's renewal was dominated by a couple of fillies who had finished runner-up on their debuts. They duly filled the first two places, but there were also some eye-catchers in behind, so this is form to view positively. IT's rated up to race standard, although the time was 17lb slow compared with the following nursery.

4802 TELEGRAPH NURSERY STKS (H'CAP) 7f

4:55 (4:56) (Class 2) 2-Y-O **£12,938** (£3,850; £1,924; £962) **Stalls** Low

Form RPR

221 **1** **Bear Valley (IRE)**[14] 4304 2-9-6 82.... JamesMcDonald 6 97
(Mark Johnston) *chsd ldr tl led 2f out: sn rdn: clr 1f out: styd on strly ins fnl f: readily* **8/1**[3]

4111 **2** 4 **Montataire (IRE)**[6] 4595 2-9-13 89 6ex.... JamesDoyle 9 93
(Mark Johnston) *lw: chsd ldr: rdn to chse wnr 2f out: unable qck ent fnl f: no ch w wnr but kpt on to hold 2nd ins fnl f* **5/2**[1]

4131 **3** nk **Teofonic (IRE)**[8] 4510 2-9-11 87 6ex.... FrannyNorton 4 91
(Mark Johnston) *hld up in midfield: rdn and hdwy on inner 2f out: chsd ldrs and unable qck u.p over 1f out: no ch w wnr and battling for 2nd ins fnl f: kpt on* **10/1**

10 **4** 1 3/4 **Lady In Question (IRE)**[12] 4394 2-9-2 78.... JackGarritty 2 77
(Richard Fahey) *lw: chsd ldrs: unable qck u.p and edgd lft over 1f out: no ch w wnr and kpt on same pce fnl f* **11/1**

2231 **5** 3/4 **Tap Tap Boom**[28] 3799 2-8-12 74.... SteveDrowne 5 71
(George Baker) *lw: hld up in midfield: effrt 2f out: sme hdwy over 1f out: kpt on ins fnl f: no ch w wnr* **8/1**[3]

003 **6** 1 1/2 **Georgio (GER)**[12] 4387 2-8-1 67.... RyanPowell 7 56
(Andrew Balding) *hld up in midfield: n.m.r wl over 1f out: hdwy u.p over 1f out: kpt on ins fnl f: nvr trbld ldrs* **40/1**

004 **7** 1/2 **Brise De Mer (FR)**[23] 3971 2-8-4 66.... MartinDwyer 11 58
(George Baker) *hld up in last pair: swtchd rt and hdwy over 1f out: kpt on ins fnl f: nvr trbld ldrs* **66/1**

01 **8** 1/2 **Geneva Convention (IRE)**[19] 4125 2-9-4 80.... KieranO'Neill 13 71
(Richard Hannon) *hld up in last trio: effrt on outer and hung rt 2f out: hdwy over 1f out: kpt on ins fnl f: nvr trbld ldrs* **7/1**[2]

0401 **9** 1 **Global Revival (IRE)**[14] 4315 2-9-1 77.... SilvestreDeSousa 16 65
(Ed Dunlop) *hld up in midfield: effrt u.p over 1f out: no imp and btn 1f out: wknd ins fnl f* **25/1**

3524 **10** 1/2 **Logi (IRE)**[33] 3668 2-9-5 81....(b[1]) PatDobbs 1 68
(Richard Hannon) *chsd ldrs: effrt 2f out: unable qck and btn over 1f out: wknd fnl f* **16/1**

532 **11** 3 **Arc Royal**[49] 3054 2-9-2 78.... RichardKingscote 10 57
(Tom Dascombe) *hld up towards rr: effrt whn bmpd 2f out: struggling to qckn and n.m.r wl over 1f out: wknd fnl f* **11/1**

330 **12** 1 3/4 **Ivor's Magic (IRE)**[14] 4298 2-7-10 69.... DavidEgan(7) 14 39
(David Elsworth) *hld up in last pair: effrt on inner 2f out: no imp u.p whn swtchd lft jst over 1f out: wknd fnl f* **33/1**

600 **13** nk **Devilish Guest (IRE)**[28] 3813 2-8-8 70.... JoeFanning 8 44
(Mick Channon) *hld up towards rr: rdn over 2f out: no hdwy and btn whn nt clr run and hmpd over 1f out: bhd fnl f* **8/1**[3]

0436 **14** 5 **At The Beach**[12] 4386 2-8-6 68....(b[1]) TomMarquand 15 29
(Richard Hannon) *hld up towards rr: effrt over 2f out: no prog and wl btn over 1f out: bhd fnl f* **50/1**

5431 **15** 11 **Latest Quest (IRE)**[8] 4524 2-8-12 77 6ex.... EdwardGreatrex(3) 3 9
(Sylvester Kirk) *led tl over 2f out: lost pl: wl bhd and eased ins fnl f* **16/1**

1m 27.03s (0.03) **Going Correction** +0.025s/f (Good) **15** Ran SP% **124.6**
Speed ratings (Par 100): **100,95,95,93,92 90,89,89,88,87 84,82,81,76,63**
CSF £27.96 CT £214.92 TOTE £8.30: £2.70, £1.50, £3.50; EX 17.80 Trifecta £53.90.
Owner Sheikh Hamdan bin Mohammed Al Maktoum **Bred** Darley **Trained** Middleham Moor, N Yorks

FOCUS

Race distance increased by 8yds. This looked a pretty competitive nursery on paper, but the Mark Johnston trio (also top three in the weights) finished 1-2-3 and the winner looked a class above. The time compared well with the previous maiden.

4803 TATLER STKS (H'CAP) 5f

5:30 (5:33) (Class 3) (0-95,95) 3-Y-O

£12,450 (£3,728; £1,864; £932; £466; £234) **Stalls** High

Form RPR

3122 **1** **Laughton**[20] 4093 3-8-5 79.... ShaneGray 8 87
(Kevin Ryan) *racd in centre: hld up in midfield: clsd and gng strly over 1f out: rdn to chal 1f out: led ins fnl f: r.o: rdn out* **13/2**[2]

-611 **2** 1/2 **Kassia (IRE)**[16] 4223 3-9-5 93.... CharlesBishop 6 99+
(Mick Channon) *racd in centre: stdd after s: hld up in rr: clsd and nt clrest of runs over 1f out: rdn 1f out: wnt between horses and drvn to press wnr wl ins fnl f: r.o* **10/1**

00-4 **3** shd **Muhadathat**[30] 3752 3-9-7 95.... FrannyNorton 9 101+
(Mark Johnston) *racd in centre: wnt lft s: hld up in rr: trying to cl but nt clrest of runs over 1f out: hdwy ins fnl f: r.o strly fnl 100yds: nt quite rch ldrs* **25/1**

3210 **4** hd **Celebration**[20] 4112 3-8-13 87.... JackGarritty 11 92
(Richard Fahey) *racd in centre: chsd ldr: rdn and ev ch wl over 1f out: kpt on wl: unable qck and hld wl ins fnl f: lost 2 pls nr fin* **25/1**

0055 **5** nk **Lathom**[20] 4112 3-9-4 92.... DanielTudhope 3 96
(David O'Meara) *racd in centre: hld up in tch in midfield: clsd 2f out: rdn to chal 1f out: drvn and styd on same pce ins fnl f* **5/1**[1]

146 **6** 1/2 **Discreet Hero (IRE)**[6] 4612 3-8-10 84....(t) JimCrowley 13 86
(Simon Crisford) *racd in centre: hld up in tch in midfield: kpt on wl u.p ins fnl f: nvr quite getting to ldrs* **20/1**

1010 **7** hd **Sign Of The Kodiac (IRE)**[21] 4062 3-9-7 95.... TomEaves 2 96
(James Given) *racd in centre: chsd ldrs: rdn 2f out: unable qck u.p 1f out: styd on same pce ins fnl f* **33/1**

2111 **8** nse **Just Glamorous (IRE)**[6] 4612 3-9-6 94 6ex.... OisinMurphy 10 95
(Ronald Harris) *racd in centre: led: rdn over 1f out: hdd 100yds out: sn edgd lft and no ex towards fin* **7/1**[3]

5521 **9** 1 1/4 **September Issue**[34] 3611 3-8-4 78.... HarryBentley 16 75
(Gay Kelleway) *racd nr side tl gps merged 1/2-way: hld up in rr: swtchd rt 3f out: nt clr run 2f out tl over 1f out: kpt on u.p ins fnl f: nvr trbld ldrs* **28/1**

2640 **10** 1/2 **El Astronaute (IRE)**[20] 4112 3-8-12 86.... SilvestreDeSousa 17 84
(John Quinn) *racd nr side tl gps merged 1/2-way: led gp and chsd ldrs overall: rdn 2f out: hung rt fnl f: btn whn hmpd wl ins fnl f: wknd towards fin* **25/1**

3404 **11** nse **Paddy Power (IRE)**[5] 4652 3-8-12 86.... JamieSpencer 18 81
(Richard Fahey) *racd nr side tl gps merged 1/2-way: stdd s: hld up in rr: nt clr run 2f out: swtchd rt over 1f out: swtchd lft and carried lft ins fnl f: rdn and r.o wl fnl 100yds: nvr trbld ldrs* **16/1**

1332 **12** 1 **Gorokai (IRE)**[134] 954 3-8-4 78....(p) TomMarquand 15 69
(David Simcock) *racd nr side tl gps merged 1/2-way: in tch in midfield: unable qck and edgd lft over 1f out: styd on same pce ins fnl f* **33/1**

5340 **13** 3/4 **Sixties Sue**[47] 3165 3-8-6 87.... KillianHennessy(7) 5 75
(Mick Channon) *racd in centre: hld up in tch in midfield: effrt over 1f out: no imp jst ins fnl f: wknd fnl 100yds* **33/1**

-323 **14** nk **This Is For You**[20] 4093 3-8-0 77....[1] EdwardGreatrex(3) 14 64
(Andrew Balding) *swtchd lft after 1f and racd nr side tl gps merged 1/2-way: rdn 2f out: drvn and no imp: keeping on same pce and wl hld whn bdly hmpd and snatched up ins fnl f* **20/1**

516 **15** 4 **Olympic Runner**[6] 4585 3-8-8 82.... AndreaAtzeni 19 55
(William Haggas) *racd nr side tl gps merged 1/2-way: rdn: carried lft and no imp over 1f out: swtchd rt 1f out: no prog* **16/1**

3110 **16** 3/4 **A Momentofmadness**[21] 4062 3-9-2 90.... JamesMcDonald 12 60
(Charles Hills) *taken down early and led to post: racd in centre: chsd ldrs: rdn 2f out: lost pl u.p over 1f out: wknd ins fnl f* **12/1**

-045 **17** 1/2 **Exceed The Limit**[13] 4359 3-9-7 95....(p) AdamKirby 1 63
(Robert Cowell) *racd in centre: hld up in midfield: effrt to chse ldrs and drvn over 1f out: no ex and btn 1f out: sn wknd* **12/1**

4425 **18** 1 3/4 **Predetermined (IRE)**[13] 4344 3-8-2 76 oh1.... KieranO'Neill 7 38
(Andrew Balding) *racd in centre: in tch in midfield: rdn 1/2-way: sn struggling and lost pl over 1f out: bhd fnl f* **20/1**

5221 **19** 1 **Highly Sprung (IRE)**[31] 3716 3-8-3 77.... JoeFanning 4 35
(Mark Johnston) *racd in centre: chsd ldrs: rdn over 1f out: no ex u.p 1f out: btn and eased ins fnl f* **7/1**[3]

57.66s (-2.54) **Going Correction** -0.375s/f (Firm) **19** Ran SP% **129.3**
Speed ratings (Par 104): **105,104,104,103,103 102,102,102,100,99 99,97,96,95,89 88,87,84,83**
CSF £62.63 CT £1553.97 TOTE £7.90: £2.10, £2.60, £5.00, £5.90; EX 79.40 Trifecta £1889.40.
Owner Mrs Angie Bailey **Bred** Skymarc Farm Inc **Trained** Hambleton, N Yorks

The Form Book, Raceform Ltd, Newbury, RG14 5SJ

FOCUS
Race distance as advertised. A competitive 3yo sprint handicap and thankfully the visibility had improved immensely. Those that raced up the centre of the track were very much at an advantage and unsurprisingly there wasn't that much separating the principals at the end.
T/Jkpt: Not won. T/Plt: £476.90 to a £1 stake. Pool: £276,510.84. 423.20 winning tickets. T/Qpdt: £43.30 to a £1 stake. Pool: £21,948.23. 374.32 winning tickets. **Steve Payne**

[4493] NOTTINGHAM (L-H)

Thursday, July 28

OFFICIAL GOING: Good to firm (firm in places; 8.0) changing to good to firm after 2.20 (race 1)
Wind: Virtually nil Weather: Heavy grey cloud & light showers

4804 BRITISH STALLION STUDS EBF MAIDEN FILLIES' STKS (PLUS 10 RACE) 5f 13y

2:20 (2:22) (Class 5) 2-Y-O **£3,234** (£962; £481; £240) **Stalls** High

Form RPR
43 **1** **Fabric**[17] 4205 2-9-0 0 SeanLevey 3 74
(Richard Hannon) *trckd ldrs on outer: cl up 2f out: rdn and slt ld ins fnl f: edgd lft and kpt on towards fin* **9/4**[2]
3 **2** *nse* **Golden Easter (USA)**[20] 4110 2-9-0 0 GrahamLee 2 74
(Kevin Ryan) *trckd ldr: hdwy and cl up 2f out: rdn over 1f out: drvn and ev ch ins fnl f: edgd lft and kpt on wl towards fin* **9/2**[3]
2 **3** *hd* **Spinnaker Bay (IRE)**[13] 4350 2-9-0 0 PaulMulrennan 8 73
(William Jarvis) *led: pushed along over 1f out: rdn and hdd ins fnl f: rallied and kpt on wl towards fin* **2/1**[1]
53 **4** *1 3/4* **Whigwham**[12] 4405 2-9-0 0 TonyHamilton 5 67
(Richard Fahey) *chsd ldrs: effrt over 1f out: sn rdn and kpt on same pce* **7/1**
3 **5** *2 1/2* **Sky Gypsy**[14] 4308 2-9-0 0 PhillipMakin 4 58
(David Brown) *in tch: pushed along over 2f out: sn rdn and no imp* **25/1**
6 *1 3/4* **Kendamara (FR)** 2-9-0 0 MichaelJMMurphy 7 52
(Charles Hills) *wnt lft s: a in rr* **12/1**
B00 **7** *3/4* **Gabridan (IRE)**[16] 4227 2-8-10 0 ow1 AdamMcNamara(5) 1 50
(Richard Fahey) *in tch: rdn along 2f out: sn one pce* **50/1**
8 *19* **Lights** 2-9-0 0 DavidAllan 6
(Declan Carroll) *hmpd s: a in rr: outpcd and bhd fnl 2f* **25/1**

1m 0.87s (-0.63) **Going Correction** -0.175s/f (Firm) **8** Ran SP% **112.1**
Speed ratings (Par 91): **98,97,97,94,90 88,86,56**
CSF £12.19 TOTE £3.10: £1.10, £1.90, £1.10; EX 13.80 Trifecta £31.20.
Owner HighclereThoroughbredRacing-Oscar Wilde **Bred** Highclere Stud **Trained** East Everleigh, Wilts

FOCUS
Outer track used. A murky start to a meeting staged on fast ground. The rail was set out 4yds on the whole track. A fair maiden in which the gallop was sound throughout and the first three finished in a line. The form makes a lot of sense.

4805 BREEDERS BACKING RACING EBF MAIDEN STKS 6f 15y

2:55 (2:56) (Class 5) 2-Y-O **£3,234** (£962; £481; £240) **Stalls** High

Form RPR
1 **Eaton Square** 2-9-5 0 NickyMackay 6 78+
(John Gosden) *towards rr: hdwy to trck ldrs 2f out: effrt and green over 1f out: sn cl up: pushed into ld last 50yds: readily* **8/11**[1]
0 **2** *nk* **Rag Tatter**[13] 4371 2-9-5 0 KevinStott 1 75
(Kevin Ryan) *qckly away and led: pushed along wl over 1f out: rdn and edgd lft jst ins fnl f: drvn: hdd and nt qckn last 50yds* **25/1**
3 *1/2* **Vaulted** 2-9-0 0 TonyHamilton 7 68+
(Richard Fahey) *trckd ldrs: hdwy 2f out: cl up over 1f out: rdn and ev ch ins fnl f: kpt on same pce towards fin* **5/2**[2]
4 *4* **Enfolding (IRE)** 2-9-5 0 TomQueally 4 61
(James Fanshawe) *towards rr: hdwy on outer 1/2-way: effrt to chse ldrs over 1f out: rdn: green and no imp fnl f* **12/1**[3]
5 *3 1/4* **Outfox** 2-9-0 0 ConnorBeasley 2 45
(Bryan Smart) *chsd ldr: rdn along over 2f out: wknd wl over 1f out* **25/1**
6 *1/2* **Proud Show** 2-9-5 0 LukeMorris 3 49
(David Dennis) *a towards rr* **16/1**
0 **7** *nk* **Pursuing Steed**[55] 2847 2-9-5 0 MichaelJMMurphy 5 48
(John Gallagher) *dwlt: sn chsng ldrs: rdn along over 2f out: sn wknd* **33/1**

1m 14.97s (0.27) **Going Correction** -0.175s/f (Firm) **7** Ran SP% **110.7**
Speed ratings (Par 94): **91,90,89,84,80 79,79**
CSF £24.30 TOTE £1.50: £1.10, £10.00; EX 15.50 Trifecta £54.00.
Owner Derrick Smith & Michael Tabor & Mrs John Magnier **Bred** Highbank Stud Llp **Trained** Newmarket, Suffolk

FOCUS
The ground eased slightly to good to firm before this race. Not much in the way of strength in depth but fair form from the first three, who pulled clear in the closing stages. The runner-up is the key. The gallop was an ordinary one.

4806 RACINGUK.COM MEDIAN AUCTION MAIDEN STKS 1m 75y

3:25 (3:28) (Class 6) 3-4-Y-O **£2,264** (£673; £336; £168) **Stalls** Centre

Form RPR
2243 **1** **Torch**[21] 4055 3-9-5 81 (p) SeanLevey 8 84
(Richard Hannon) *trckd ldr: hdwy to ld wl over 3f out: rdn over 1f out: kpt on wl fnl f* **4/7**[1]
2 *3* **Loveable Helen (IRE)** 3-9-0 0 TonyHamilton 1 72
(Richard Fahey) *dwlt: sn trcking ldrs: hdwy over 3f out: rdn over 2f out: chal wl over 1f out: drvn appr fnl f and kpt on same pce* **8/1**[3]
02 **3** *3* **Best Laid Plans**[22] 4027 3-9-0 0 LukeMorris 9 65
(James Tate) *trckd ldrs: hdwy over 3f out and sn chsng wnr: rdn over 2f out: drvn wl over 1f out: sn one pce* **11/4**[2]
4 *1 3/4* **Lady Natasha (IRE)** 3-9-0 0 DougieCostello 2 61
(K R Burke) *dwlt and towards rr: hdwy over 2f out: rdn wl over 1f out: kpt on fnl f: nrst fin* **20/1**
5 *5* **Casablanca (IRE)** 3-8-11 0 RobHornby(3) 7 50
(Andrew Balding) *chsd ldng pair: rdn along wl over 2f out: sn drvn and wknd* **14/1**
0-6 **6** *2* **Noneedtotellme (IRE)**[22] 4017 3-8-11 0 TimClark(3) 10 45
(James Unett) *sn rdn along and outpcd in rr: sme hdwy over 2f out: n.d* **50/1**
00- **7** *42* **Face Of Glory (IRE)**[286] 7246 3-9-5 0 (t) ThomasBrown 3
(Ismail Mohammed) *led: pushed along and hdd wl over 3f out: sn wknd and bhd fnl 2f* **25/1**
0 **8** *8* **Late Starter (IRE)**[22] 4017 3-9-2 0 MarcMonaghan(3) 6
(Hugo Palmer) *sn rdn along and outpcd in rr: bhd fnl 3f* **20/1**

1m 45.81s (-3.19) **Going Correction** -0.175s/f (Firm)
WFA 3 from 4yo 8lb **8** Ran SP% **123.4**
Speed ratings (Par 101): **108,105,102,100,95 93,51,43**
CSF £6.75 TOTE £1.30: £1.02, £2.70, £1.10; EX 8.60 Trifecta £14.80.
Owner Highclere Thoroughbred Racing(Salisbury) **Bred** Whatton Manor Stud **Trained** East Everleigh, Wilts

FOCUS
Rail movements added 12yds onto the distance of this race. A fair gallop but a race that lacked anything in the way of strength. The winner is a reliable yardstick and the form is rated around his latest Newbury run.

4807 RACING UK PROFITS RETURNED TO RACING H'CAP 1m 75y

4:00 (4:00) (Class 5) (0-75,78) 3-Y-O+ **£2,911** (£866; £432; £216) **Stalls** Centre

Form RPR
3222 **1** **Shamaheart (IRE)**[9] 4497 6-10-0 75 (p) DavidAllan 4 83
(Geoffrey Harker) *t.k.h: trckd ldrs: swtchd rt to outer and smooth hdwy wl over 2f out: led 1 1/2f out: pushed out* **5/2**[1]
11-0 **2** *1 3/4* **Venutius**[72] 2347 9-9-12 73 DaleSwift 6 76
(Ed McMahon) *trckd ldng pair: hdwy over 3f out: chal over 2f out: rdn and ev ch wl over 1f out: drvn and kpt on same pce fnl f* **12/1**
2400 **3** *nk* **Molten Lava (IRE)**[14] 4288 4-9-13 74 LukeMorris 7 76
(Paul Cole) *dwlt and bhd: pushed along 1/2-way: rdn over 3f out: hdwy wl over 1f out: styd on u.p fnl f* **9/1**
5201 **4** *hd* **Thecornishbarron (IRE)**[7] 4568 4-10-3 78 6ex JackMitchell 1 80
(John Ryan) *t.k.h: trckd ldr: led after 2f: pushed along and jnd wl over 2f out: sn rdn: drvn and hdd 1 1/2f out: kpt on same pce* **7/1**
-525 **5** *1* **Celtic Sixpence (IRE)**[28] 3807 8-9-5 66 RobertTart 8 66
(Nick Kent) *led 2f: cl up: rdn along wl over 2f out: drvn over 1f out: kpt on one pce* **9/2**[3]
-260 **6** *2 1/4* **Rocket Ronnie (IRE)**[16] 4232 6-9-11 72 GrahamLee 5 66
(Ed McMahon) *hld up: a towards rr* **8/1**
0525 **7** *1 1/4* **Loading (IRE)**[15] 4272 3-9-6 75 SeanLevey 2 65
(Richard Hannon) *dwlt: sn chsng ldrs on inner: rdn along over 3f out: drvn and wknd over 2f out* **7/2**[2]

1m 46.71s (-2.29) **Going Correction** -0.175s/f (Firm)
WFA 3 from 4yo+ 8lb **7** Ran SP% **110.3**
Speed ratings (Par 103): **104,102,101,101,100 98,97**
CSF £30.38 CT £215.84 TOTE £2.90: £1.80, £5.30; EX 20.80 Trifecta £270.90.
Owner A S Ward **Bred** Gus Roche **Trained** Thirkleby, N Yorks

FOCUS
Rail movements meant that this race was 12yds longer than advertised. Exposed performers in a fair handicap. The gallop was an ordinary one. The winner has looked better than ever in recent starts.

4808 WATCH RACING UK TODAY JUST £10 H'CAP 1m 2f 50y

4:35 (4:35) (Class 4) (0-85,83) 3-Y-O+ **£4,690** (£1,395; £697; £348) **Stalls** Low

Form RPR
-454 **1** **Zest (IRE)**[40] 3410 3-9-2 82 TomQueally 3 92+
(James Fanshawe) *hld up: hdwy to trck ldrs 3f out: swtchd rt to outer and effrt 2f out: rdn to chse ldr ins fnl f: sn drvn and styd on wl to ld nr line* **4/1**[3]
1523 **2** *shd* **Both Sides**[27] 3861 3-8-13 82 RobHornby(3) 5 91
(Andrew Balding) *led: rdn along wl over 1f out: drvn ins fnl f: hdd nr line* **9/4**[2]
-003 **3** *2 1/4* **Ladurelli (IRE)**[12] 4396 4-9-11 81 LukeMorris 2 85
(Paul Cole) *t.k.h: trckd ldrs on inner: hdwy 3f out: rdn along wl over 1f out: drvn and kpt on same pce fnl f* **7/1**
0-31 **4** *nk* **Fidaawy**[21] 4035 3-9-2 82 TedDurcan 6 86+
(Sir Michael Stoute) *dwlt and hld up in rr: hdwy over 2f out: rdn over 1f out: kpt on fnl f: nrst fin* **2/1**[1]
2210 **5** *nk* **Belle Travers**[19] 4138 4-9-6 81 AdamMcNamara(5) 7 84
(Richard Fahey) *trckd ldrs: hdwy 3f out: chal 2f out and sn rdn: drvn and wknd ent fnl f* **25/1**
3521 **6** *1 1/2* **Eurystheus (IRE)**[19] 4138 7-9-6 81 (tp) GeorgeBuckell(5) 4 81
(Michael Appleby) *trckd ldr: cl up over 3f out: rdn along over 2f out: drvn over 1f out and grad wknd* **12/1**
134 **7** *4* **Auspicion**[31] 3717 4-9-8 78 JamesSullivan 8 70
(Tom Tate) *hld up in tch: pushed along wl over 2f out: sn rdn and btn wl over 1f out* **20/1**

2m 11.8s (-2.50) **Going Correction** -0.175s/f (Firm)
WFA 3 from 4yo+ 10lb **7** Ran SP% **112.9**
Speed ratings (Par 105): **103,102,101,100,100 99,96**
CSF £13.09 CT £58.86 TOTE £4.90: £2.40, £1.50; EX 12.90 Trifecta £58.10.
Owner Elite Racing Club **Bred** Elite Racing Club **Trained** Newmarket, Suffolk

FOCUS
Rail movements added 12yds onto the distance of this race. A useful handicap in which the gallop was on the steady side to the 2f pole and this bare form may be unreliable. The third helps with the standard.

4809 RACING UK IN GLORIOUS HD H'CAP 5f 13y

5:10 (5:11) (Class 5) (0-75,75) 3-Y-O+ **£2,911** (£866; £432; £216) **Stalls** High

Form RPR
3450 **1** **Musharrif**[17] 4211 4-9-8 73 DavidAllan 8 81
(Declan Carroll) *trckd ldrs: hdwy on inner 2f out: rdn to ld jst ins fnl f: styd on* **3/1**[2]
502 **2** *1/2* **Indian Tinker**[34] 3618 7-9-2 67 (v) DerekLeung 6 73
(Robert Cowell) *cl up: rdn to ld briefly jst over 1f out: hdd and drvn jst ins fnl f: ev ch tl no ex towards fin* **5/1**[3]
2220 **3** *1 3/4* **Bahamian Sunrise**[14] 4295 4-9-0 70 (p) GeorgeBuckell(5) 1 70
(John Gallagher) *wnt rt s: chsd ldrs on outer: hdwy wl over 1f out: sn rdn and kpt on fnl f* **8/1**
601 **4** *1/2* **Oriental Relation (IRE)**[9] 4495 5-9-3 73 6ex (b) AdamMcNamara(5) 5 71
(James Given) *cl up: led over 2f out and sn rdn: drvn and hdd jst over 1f out: wknd* **5/2**[1]
6064 **5** *nk* **Ruby's Day**[9] 4495 7-9-3 68 (p) PaulMulrennan 2 65
(David Brown) *bmpd s: a towards rr* **11/2**
0150 **6** *7* **Powerful Wind (IRE)**[22] 3995 7-9-10 75 (t) BenCurtis 3 47
(Charlie Wallis) *sn led: rdn along and hdd over 2f out: sn wknd* **8/1**
6015 **7** *24* **Sleepy Blue Ocean**[9] 4495 10-9-4 69 (p) PhillipMakin 7
(John Balding) *sn rdn along in rr: outpcd and bhd fr 1/2-way* **14/1**

1m 0.02s (-1.48) **Going Correction** -0.175s/f (Firm) **7** Ran SP% **114.5**
Speed ratings (Par 103): **104,103,100,99,99 87,49**
CSF £18.38 CT £107.37 TOTE £4.60: £2.20, £2.10; EX 20.70 Trifecta £157.20.
Owner Ray Flegg & John Bousfield **Bred** Mr & Mrs J Davis & P Mitchell B'Stock **Trained** Malton, N Yorks

FOCUS
A fair handicap in which the strong gallop suited those racing just behind the leaders. The winner is rated to form.

4810 RACING UK DAY PASS JUST £10 H'CAP 2m 9y
5:45 (5:45) (Class 6) (0-65,63) 3-Y-O **£2,264** (£673; £336; £168) **Stalls** Low

Form RPR

4013 **1** **Tyrell (IRE)**[15] 4273 3-9-4 **60**...(b) DougieCostello 4 70
(Alan King) *led: rdn along 3f out: jnd wl over 2f out and sn rdn: hdd wl over 1f out: swtchd rt and drvn: rallied gamely ent fnl f: styd on wl to ld nr fin* **11/4**[2]

5521 **2** *hd* **Mystique Heights**[15] 4273 3-9-6 **62**... LukeMorris 2 72+
(Sir Mark Prescott Bt) *trckd ldng pair: niggled along over 5f out: hdwy over 3f out and sn cl up: rdn to ld wl over 1f out: sn edgd lft: drvn ent fnl f: hdd and no ex nr fin* **4/7**[1]

-415 **3** *9* **Dusky Raider (IRE)**[29] 3778 3-9-7 **63**...(p) PaulMulrennan 5 62
(Michael Dods) *trckd ldr: effrt and cl up over 3f out: sn pushed along: rdn over 2f out and grad wknd* **7/1**[3]

5335 **4** *10* **Regal Galaxy**[17] 4210 3-8-6 **48**... JoeyHaynes 3 35
(Mark H Tompkins) *hld up in rr: sme hdwy to take clsr order over 4f out: rdn along over 3f out: sn outpcd* **25/1**

3m 34.87s (0.37) **Going Correction** -0.175s/f (Firm) **4** Ran SP% **106.7**
Speed ratings (Par 98): **92,91,87,82**
CSF £4.70 TOTE £3.10; EX 4.50 Trifecta £6.50.
Owner Apple Tree Stud **Bred** Gigginstown House Stud **Trained** Barbury Castle, Wilts

FOCUS
Rail movements meant that 24yds were added to the distance of this race. A modest and uncompetitive handicap in which the gallop was an ordinary one to the 3f marker. The first two pulled a long way clear. and the form is a bit fluid.
T/Plt: £16.80 to a £1 stake. Pool: £41,632.04. 1,799.93 winning tickets. T/Qpdt: £9.30 to a £1 stake. Pool: £2,890.44. 228.54 winning tickets. **Joe Rowntree**

4779 GALWAY (R-H)
Thursday, July 28

OFFICIAL GOING: Jumps courses - good to yielding; flat course - yielding to soft

4811a HOP HOUSE 13 H'CAP 1m 98y
3:00 (3:07) 4-Y-O+ **£9,044** (£2,794; £1,323; £588; £220)

RPR

1 **Total Demolition (IRE)**[1] 4780 4-8-7 **69**... ConorHoban 5 77+
(J Larkin, Ire) *hld up towards rr: 14th 1/2-way: pushed along and hdwy fr over 2f out to chse ldrs 1 1/2f out where n.m.r and brought wd: rdn in 6th over 1f out and r.o wl nr side to ld fnl strides* **10/1**

2 *3/4* **Marshall Jennings (IRE)**[7] 4577 4-9-11 **87**... ShaneFoley 9 93
(Mrs John Harrington, Ire) *cl up tl disp and led narrowly after 1f: over 1 l clr at 1/2-way: rdn into st and stl over 1 l clr ent fnl f: reduced advantage wl ins fnl f and hdd fnl strides* **14/1**

3 *1/2* **Dream Walker (FR)**[10] 4448 7-9-8 **91**...(t) OisinOrr[(7)] 15 96+
(Brian Ellison) *t.k.h to post: hld up: 11th 1/2-way: hdwy out wd over 2f out to chse ldrs: rdn into 3rd briefly ins fnl f: no imp on ldr in 4th clsng stages: kpt on same pce into 3rd fnl strides* **8/1**

4 *1/2* **Boherbuoy (IRE)**[289] 7205 4-9-11 **87**... WayneLordan 13 91
(David Wachman, Ire) *chsd ldrs: 3rd 1/2-way: rdn in 2nd into st and sn no imp on ldr: kpt on same pce ins fnl f and dropped to 4th cl home* **11/2**[3]

5 *1* **Maknificent (IRE)**[17] 4217 4-9-1 **80**...(v) ShaneBKelly[(3)] 8 81
(M D O'Callaghan, Ire) *reluctant on way to s: in rr of mid-div: 10th 1/2-way: pushed along 3f out and hdwy to chse ldrs u.p fr 2f out: wnt 4th briefly ent fnl f: no ex in 5th wl ins fnl f* **16/1**

6 *2* **Knockmaole Boy (IRE)**[10] 4467 4-8-13 **78**... RobbieDowney[(3)] 6 75
(J H Culloty, Ire) *in tch: 7th 1/2-way: hdwy bhd ldrs on inner into 3rd over 2f out: sn rdn and no ex 1 1/2f out: one pce in 6th wl ins fnl f* **8/1**

7 *2 3/4* **Hidden Oasis (IRE)**[17] 4217 5-9-4 **80**...(p) BillyLee 10 70
(David Wachman, Ire) *mid-div: 8th 1/2-way: rdn in 10th 2f out and no imp into st: kpt on ins fnl f into mod 7th: nvr nrr* **5/1**[2]

8 *2* **Ruler Of France**[10] 4467 5-9-1 **84**...(b) KillianLeonard[(7)] 14 70
(P Twomey, Ire) *chsd ldrs: racd keenly: 6th 1/2-way: rdn in 4th over 2f out and sn no imp on ldrs: dropped to 7th over 1f out and one pce after* **12/1**

9 *4 1/2* **Daredevil Day (IRE)**[10] 4467 5-9-0 **76**...(p) PatSmullen 3 52
(Joseph G Murphy, Ire) *chsd ldrs: 5th 1/2-way: rdn under 3f out and no ex u.p in 6th 2f out: sn wknd* **4/1**[1]

10 *3 1/4* **Sophie's World (IRE)**[46] 5772 5-9-2 **83**... DonaghO'Connor[(5)] 1 51
(Alan Fleming, Ire) *in rr of mid-div early: 13th 1/2-way: rdn and no imp 2f out* **14/1**

11 *1* **Voyageofdiscovery (USA)**[12] 4412 5-9-6 **82**...[1] MichaelHussey 4 48
(T J O'Mara, Ire) *towards rr: 12th 1/2-way: n.m.r briefly under 2f out: kpt on one pce ins fnl f* **25/1**

12 *4 1/2* **Dragon Fei (IRE)**[30] 3760 6-9-8 **84**... ColinKeane 11 39
(Dermot Anthony McLoughlin, Ire) *led narrowly tl jnd and hdd after 1f: 2nd 1/2-way: rdn and wknd fr over 2f out* **25/1**

13 *1/2* **Youceeyouceecee (IRE)**[25] 3932 4-9-0 **76**... SeamieHeffernan 7 30
(Miss Susan A Finn, Ire) *in rr of mid-div: 9th 1/2-way: rdn towards rr over 3f out and no imp bef st where n.m.r on inner and eased briefly: kpt on one pce ins fnl f* **16/1**

14 *3* **Maudlin Magdalen (IRE)**[21] 4070 6-9-3 **86**...[1] RobbieDolan[(7)] 12 33
(Donal Kinsella, Ire) *chsd ldrs: 4th 1/2-way: rdn and wknd fr over 2f out* **20/1**

15 *62* **Elusive In Paris (IRE)**[32] 3698 7-8-11 **76**... GaryHalpin[(3)] 16
(John James Feane, Ire) *on toes befhand: lost grnd s and t.o in rr thrght: nvr a factor* **14/1**

1m 43.5s (-6.70) **15** Ran SP% **135.3**
CSF £155.76 CT £1230.66 TOTE £11.60: £3.50, £5.10, £3.10; DF 225.50 Trifecta £3793.70.
Owner Breen White **Bred** Des Vere Hunt & Jack Ronan **Trained** Dunleer, Co. Louth
■ Poetic Choice was withdrawn. Price at time of withdrawal 16-1. Rule 4 does not apply.

FOCUS
A race with plenty of drama, a stalls malfunction led to a false start and in the subsequent flag start, Elusive In Paris was completely left when facing the wrong way as they broke away.

4812a ARTHUR GUINNESS EUROPEAN BREEDERS FUND CORRIB FILLIES STKS (LISTED RACE) 7f
3:30 (3:33) 3-Y-O+
£26,029 (£8,382; £3,970; £1,764; £882; £441)

RPR

1 **Planchart (USA)**[36] 3539 3-9-0 94... DeclanMcDonogh 5 98+
(Andrew Slattery, Ire) *chsd ldrs: 3rd bef 1/2-way: tk clsr order and disp 2nd fr 1/2-way: rdn in 2nd over 2f out and clsd u.p ins fnl f to ld ins fnl 100yds: kpt on wl* **10/3**[2]

2 *1/2* **Rayisa (IRE)**[11] 4434 3-9-0 95... ShaneFoley 1 97
(M Halford, Ire) *attempted to make all: over 1 l clr appr st: rdn into st and sn strly pressed: hdd ins fnl 100yds and kpt on wl wout matching wnr clsng stages* **5/2**[1]

3 *2 3/4* **Ibergman (IRE)**[24] 3962 4-9-7 85... RonanWhelan 7 93
(Ms Sheila Lavery, Ire) *hld up: 5th 1/2-way: rdn over 2f out and no imp on ldrs in 4th ent fnl f: kpt on u.p into 3rd fnl strides: nvr trbld ldrs* **9/1**

4 *nk* **Just Joan (IRE)**[17] 4218 3-9-0 83... BillyLee 3 89
(T Stack, Ire) *chsd ldrs: 4th 1/2-way: rdn into st and no imp on ldrs u.p in 3rd over 1f out: kpt on same pce and denied 3rd fnl strides* **14/1**

5 *1 3/4* **Gussy Goose (IRE)**[2] 4747 4-9-7 92...(p) WayneLordan 4 87
(David Wachman, Ire) *dwlt and pushed along in rr early: last at 1/2-way: sme hdwy into st where n.m.r: swtchd lft in 5th ins fnl f and kpt on same pce clsng stages: nvr trbld ldrs* **9/2**[3]

6 *16* **Emergent**[17] 4218 3-9-0 88... PatSmullen 6 41
(D K Weld, Ire) *cl up bhd ldr: jnd for 2nd fr 1/2-way: rdn in 3rd over 2f out and sn no imp on ldrs: wknd over 1f out: eased fnl f* **13/2**

7 *2 1/2* **Mothers Finest (IRE)**[23] 3979 4-9-7 102...(t) GaryCarroll 8 37
(Adrian Paul Keatley, Ire) *hld up: 6th 1/2-way: rdn over 2f out and no imp on ldrs into st: wknd* **6/1**

1m 28.76s (-2.84)
WFA 3 from 4yo+ 7lb **7** Ran SP% **114.1**
CSF £12.07 TOTE £3.90: £2.00, £1.80; DF 10.80 Trifecta £100.80.
Owner Pat Garvey **Bred** Taylor & Carr Estates Ltd **Trained** Thurles, Co Tipperary

FOCUS
This certainly was not a strong race for the grade, but it offered a good opportunity for something and the winner was very tough in victory.

4813a GUINNESS FOALS H'CAP 1m 4f
5:25 (5:26) (50-70,68) 3-Y-O+ **£6,783** (£2,095; £992; £441; £165)

RPR

1 **Tara Dylan (IRE)**[7] 4576 4-9-5 **61** 5ex... GaryCarroll 14 70+
(Thomas Mullins, Ire) *hld up: 12th 1/2-way: gd hdwy on outer fr 3f out to ld under 2f out: drvn clr over 1f out and kpt on wl ins fnl f where pressed* **7/1**[2]

2 *1 1/2* **Ondamoura (IRE)**[7] 4576 4-8-12 **54**...(bt) SeamieHeffernan 1 61
(T Hogan, Ire) *in tch: 6th 1/2-way: 5th 4f out: rdn into 2nd over 1f out and sn pressed wnr: kpt on wl wout matching wnr ins fnl f* **16/1**

3 *5* **Camlann (IRE)**[3] 3791 5-9-11 **67**... PatSmullen 3 66+
(John Joseph Hanlon, Ire) *chsd ldrs: 3rd 1/2-way: pushed along in 4th over 2f out and n.m.r into st: dropped to 6th briefly ins fnl f: kpt on again between horses into mod 3rd: nvr trbld ldrs* **7/4**[1]

4 *1* **Improver (IRE)**[73] 2060 5-9-6 **62**...[1] WayneLordan 12 59
(A J Martin, Ire) *in rr of mid-div: rdn over 3f out and hdwy u.p to chse ldrs in 5th over 1f out: wnt mod 3rd briefly ins fnl f: one pce in 4th wl ins fnl f* **7/1**[2]

5 *2 1/4* **Northern Sky (IRE)**[10] 4468 3-8-8 **62**...(b) LeighRoche 8 57
(Adrian Paul Keatley, Ire) *chsd ldrs tl sn wnt 2nd briefly: 4th 1/2-way: rdn almost on terms over 2f out: no imp on wnr into st and one pce in 3rd ent fnl f: sn wknd* **7/1**[2]

6 *2* **Letter Focus (IRE)**[64] 2594 4-9-10 **66**... RonanWhelan 9 57
(Brendan W Duke, Ire) *chsd ldrs: 5th 1/2-way: pushed along in 6th 4f out and no imp on ldrs u.p 2f out: kpt on one pce ins fnl f* **40/1**

7 *nse* **Greanta (IRE)**[17] 4219 5-9-0 **56**... RoryCleary 13 47
(Thomas Cleary, Ire) *mid-div: 9th 1/2-way: rdn 3f out and no imp appr st: kpt on one pce fnl 2f* **12/1**

8 *2* **Mischief Maisy (IRE)**[22] 4018 3-8-6 **60**... MichaelHussey 6 47
(Gordon Elliott, Ire) *mid-div: rdn 3f out and sme hdwy bhd ldrs 2f out where n.m.r on inner and checked briefly: no imp after and one pce fnl f* **22/1**

9 *shd* **Athenry Boy (IRE)**[17] 4219 4-9-6 **62**...(p) KevinManning 7 49
(J T Gorman, Ire) *chsd ldr: 2nd 1/2-way rdn to ld briefly 2f out tl sn hdd: sn no ex and wknd over 1f out* **10/1**[3]

10 *1 3/4* **Along The Shore (IRE)**[20] 4121 4-9-8 **67**...(t) DonnachaO'Brien[(3)] 10 51
(Joseph Patrick O'Brien, Ire) *hld up towards rr: rdn under 3f out and no imp into st: kpt on one pce ins fnl f* **14/1**

11 *1 1/2* **Rockview Emperor (IRE)**[5] 4674 6-9-0 **56**...(p) ColinKeane 2 38
(N Dooly, Ire) *in rr of mid-div early: rdn towards rr under 3f out and no imp appr st: one pce fnl 2f* **20/1**

12 *2 1/2* **Kennady (IRE)**[18] 4181 6-9-12 **68**...(t) DeclanMcDonogh 18 46
(Paul Nolan, Ire) *s.i.s and towards rr: last bef 1/2-way: no imp in rr appr st: kpt on one pce fnl 2f* **25/1**

13 *1* **Blue Skimmer (IRE)**[53] 2940 4-9-8 **67**...[1] JackKennedy[(3)] 4 43
(P J Prendergast, Ire) *in tch: 8th 1/2-way: rdn and no ex under 3f out: one pce after* **33/1**

14 *5 1/2* **Zero Euro (IRE)**[10] 4464 8-8-11 **56**...(b) GaryHalpin[(3)] 16 24
(H Rogers, Ire) *s.i.s and in rr early: rdn and no imp towards rr over 2f out where short of room briefly* **40/1**

15 *1* **Byron Beauty (IRE)**[10] 4468 8-8-11 **53**... ChrisHayes 5 19
(H Rogers, Ire) *led: rdn and hdd 2f out: no ex and wknd into st: eased fnl f* **16/1**

16 *1 1/4* **Dalaki (IRE)**[54] 2887 5-9-9 **65**...(p) BillyLee 17 29
(Des Donovan, Ire) *towards rr: rdn over 3f out and no ex: eased st* **25/1**

17 *9* **Miss Montana (IRE)**[15] 4281 3-8-7 **66**...[1] TomMadden[(5)] 15 16
(Mrs John Harrington, Ire) *chsd ldrs: 7th 1/2-way: rdn over 3f out and sn wknd* **33/1**

18 *2 3/4* **East Coker (IRE)**[34] 3632 3-8-10 **64**... ShaneFoley 11 9
(Mrs John Harrington, Ire) *mid-div: 11th 1/2-way: rdn and no ex over 2f out: eased st* **33/1**

2m 37.94s (-5.16)
WFA 3 from 4yo+ 12lb **18** Ran SP% **139.6**
CSF £115.58 CT £293.99 TOTE £8.30: £2.00, £3.20, £1.10, £2.40; DF 153.00 Trifecta £962.90.
Owner Melvyn J Kennedy **Bred** Mrs R McKeon **Trained** Goresbridge, Co Kilkenny

FOCUS
A run-of-the-mill festival handicap won by an improving filly

4814 - (Foreign Racing) - See Raceform Interactive

[4500]BATH (L-H)
Friday, July 29

OFFICIAL GOING: Good to firm (firm in places; 9.4)
Wind: light breeze half across Weather: sunny Rails: 10 yards need to be added for races that travel around the bottom bend into the home straight.

4815 BLACKMORE BUILDERS MAIDEN AUCTION STKS — 5f 161y
6:00 (6:00) (Class 5) 2-Y-O **£4,528** (£1,347; £673; £336) **Stalls** Centre

Form RPR
03 **1** **Drop Kick Murphi (IRE)**[3] 4738 2-8-11 0 SteveDrowne 6 70
(George Baker) *mde all: kpt on wl to assert fnl f: rdn out* **2/1**[1]
030 **2** 2 ¼ **Swan Serenade**[23] 4011 2-8-5 0 EdwardGreatrex(3) 5 59
(Jonathan Portman) *trckd wnr: swtchd rt wl over 1f out: sn rdn: kpt on but nt pce of wnr ins fnl f* **7/1**
346 **3** 3 **Zaatar (IRE)**[15] 4304 2-8-10 0 WilliamTwiston-Davies 1 51+
(Mick Channon) *s.i.s: in last pair: hdwy over 2f out: rdn to dispute 3rd ent fnl f: kpt on same pce* **5/1**[3]
06 **4** 1 **Tullinahoo (IRE)**[23] 4016 2-9-1 0 RobertWinston 2 53
(Denis Coakley) *racd keenly: in tch: hdwy over 2f out: sn rdn: disp 3rd over 1f out: kpt on same pce* **9/4**[2]
03 **5** 1 ¾ **Swallow Street (IRE)**[9] 4526 2-8-10 0 LucyKBarry(5) 7 47
(Jamie Osborne) *trckd ldrs: rdn over 2f out: sn one pce* **14/1**
55 **6** ¾ **Son Castello (IRE)**[71] 2390 2-8-8 0 JordanUys(7) 4 45
(Brian Meehan) *hld up in last pair: rdn 2f out: nvr threatened* **20/1**
5 **7** ½ **Newport Place (IRE)**[13] 4387 2-9-1 0 WilliamCarson 9 43
(Jamie Osborne) *trckd ldr: rdn 2f out: wknd jst over 1f out* **14/1**
8 10 **Black Tie Bob (IRE)** 2-8-8 0 RobHornby(3) 8 6
(J S Moore) *in tch: rdn over 2f out: wknd wl over 1f out* **14/1**

1m 13.24s (2.04) **Going Correction** +0.075s/f (Good) **8** Ran SP% **118.0**
Speed ratings (Par 94): **89,86,82,80,78 77,76,63**
CSF £17.46 TOTE £2.60: £1.10, £2.50, £1.90; EX 17.10 Trifecta £58.30.
Owner ININ Construction **Bred** Selman Tasbek **Trained** Manton, Wilts
■ Stewards' Enquiry : Edward Greatrex caution: careless riding

FOCUS
A modest maiden run at a steady pace. The first two were always prominent.

4816 SYMONDS FOUNDERS RESERVE H'CAP (BATH SUMMER STAYERS' SERIES QUALIFIER) — 2m 1f 34y
6:35 (6:35) (Class 5) (0-70,72) 4-Y-O+ **£3,881** (£1,155; £577; £288) **Stalls** Centre

Form RPR
0010 **1** shd **Delagoa Bay (IRE)**[23] 4012 8-7-13 55 MitchGodwin(7) 3 60
(Sylvester Kirk) *hld up in last pair: hdwy over 2f out: edgd lft: rdn to ld over 1f out: hdd ent fnl f: carried rt: kpt on: jst hld: fin 2nd: plcd 1st* **14/1**
51-3 **2** **Rainbow Pride (IRE)**[16] 4266 4-9-5 68 RobertWinston 2 75+
(Sir Mark Prescott Bt) *stdd s: t.k.h in last pair: hdwy but nt best of runs fr over 2f out: led ent fnl f: sn rdn and hung rt: hld on: fin 1st: plcd 2nd* **1/1**[1]
3402 **3** 2 ½ **Oratorio's Joy (IRE)**[9] 4507 6-9-2 65 WilliamCarson 6 67
(Jamie Osborne) *trckd ldrs: rdn over 2f out: nt pce to chal but styd on into 3rd ins fnl f* **4/1**[2]
202 **4** 1 **Tempuran**[16] 4266 7-9-4 70 GeorgeDowning(3) 4 71
(David Bridgwater) *led: rdn over 2f out: hdd over 1f out: no ex ins fnl f* **7/1**[3]
3311 **5** 1 ¾ **Urban Space**[7] 4592 10-9-4 72 12ex (t) HectorCrouch(5) 1 71
(John Flint) *trckd ldrs: rdn and ev ch over 2f out tl over 1f out: fdd fnl 120yds* **4/1**[2]
4446 **6** 21 **Agreement (IRE)**[7] 4591 6-8-6 58 (b) EdwardGreatrex(3) 5 34
(Nikki Evans) *chsd ldr: rdn 3f out: sn hld: wknd over 1f out* **16/1**

3m 52.92s (1.02) **Going Correction** +0.075s/f (Good) **6** Ran SP% **115.0**
Speed ratings (Par 103): **99,100,98,98,97 87**
CSF £29.87 TOTE £18.00: £6.70, £1.10; EX 34.20 Trifecta £164.20.
Owner Homebred Racing **Bred** J Ryan **Trained** Upper Lambourn, Berks

FOCUS
An interesting race for the grade. It was run at an honest pace and those held up dominated. There was drama after the finish as the stewards reversed the placings of the front two due to interference inside the final furlong.

4817 OLD MOUT H'CAP — 5f 11y
7:10 (7:10) (Class 4) (0-80,83) 4-Y-O+ **£6,469** (£1,925; £962; £481) **Stalls** Centre

Form RPR
-556 **1** **Newton's Law (IRE)**[9] 4536 5-8-12 76 (tp) JordanUys(7) 1 82
(Brian Meehan) *trckd ldrs: rdn over 1f out: led jst ins fnl f: r.o wl* **8/1**
5041 **2** 1 **Singeur (IRE)**[9] 4514 9-9-12 83 6ex LukeMorris 2 85
(Rebecca Bastiman) *nvr travelling and sn pushed along chsng ldrs: drvn over 2f out: kpt on to go 2nd cl home* **11/8**[1]
5055 **3** nk **Pensax Lad (IRE)**[14] 4345 5-9-1 75 GeorgeDowning(3) 5 76
(Ronald Harris) *prom: rdn to dispute ld fr 2f out tl jst ins fnl f: kpt on but no ex whn lost 2nd cl home* **11/4**[2]
-606 **4** nk **Noble Asset**[11] 4461 5-9-4 78 EdwardGreatrex(3) 4 78
(Milton Bradley) *led: drvn whn jnd 2f out: hdd jst ins fnl f: no ex nring fin* **7/1**
02-2 **5** 1 ¼ **Go Nani Go**[17] 4224 10-9-2 76 RobHornby(3) 7 72
(Ed de Giles) *hld up bhd ldrs: nt clr run and snatched up ent fnl f: nt clr run again sn after: nvr able to mount chal* **4/1**[3]

1m 2.02s (-0.48) **Going Correction** +0.075s/f (Good) **5** Ran SP% **112.4**
Speed ratings (Par 105): **106,104,103,103,101**
CSF £20.09 TOTE £10.40: £3.70, £1.30; EX 19.70 Trifecta £45.10.
Owner Bayardo **Bred** Ballylinch Stud **Trained** Manton, Wilts

FOCUS
They went a sound pace for this fair handicap.

4818 BULMERS LIVE COLOURFUL H'CAP — 1m 2f 46y
7:45 (7:45) (Class 4) (0-80,79) 3-Y-O **£7,762** (£2,310; £1,154; £577) **Stalls** Low

Form RPR
5211 **1** **Cote D'Azur**[7] 4607 3-9-7 79 6ex LukeMorris 3 89+
(Sir Mark Prescott Bt) *trckd ldrs: led 2f out: pushed clr ent fnl f: comf* **1/2**[1]
1615 **2** 2 ½ **Frozen Force (IRE)**[10] 4476 3-9-4 79 KieranShoemark(3) 4 82
(Amanda Perrett) *w ldr: rdn and ev ch 2f out: kpt on but comf hld by wnr fnl f* **12/1**[3]
2133 **3** 1 ½ **Melendez (USA)**[10] 4476 3-9-5 77 WilliamCarson 6 77
(Jamie Osborne) *trckd ldrs: rdn over 2f out: styd on but nt pce to chal: wnt 3rd cl home* **16/1**
5225 **4** hd **Red Hot Chilly (IRE)**[22] 4046 3-8-11 72 EdwardGreatrex(3) 1 72
(Joseph Tuite) *led: rdn and hdd 2f out: kpt on tl no ex fnl 75yds* **12/1**[3]
0031 **5** ½ **Lady Blanco (USA)**[9] 4500 3-8-6 64 6ex DavidProbert 2 63
(Andrew Balding) *racd in cl 5th: rdn 2f out: styd on but nt pce to chal* **7/2**[2]
4-40 **6** 8 **Bukle (IRE)**[73] 2341 3-8-10 68 RobertWinston 5 51
(Rod Millman) *stdd s: last but in tch: rdn over 2f out: nvr threatened* **25/1**

2m 9.61s (-1.39) **Going Correction** +0.075s/f (Good) **6** Ran SP% **114.0**
Speed ratings (Par 102): **108,106,104,104,104 97**
CSF £8.40 TOTE £1.30: £1.10, £2.50; EX 5.60 Trifecta £24.80.
Owner Neil Greig **Bred** W N Greig **Trained** Newmarket, Suffolk

FOCUS
Race distance 10yds further than advertised. A steadily run handicap.

4819 HUNTER SELECTION FILLIES' H'CAP — 1m 5y
8:15 (8:15) (Class 4) (0-80,78) 3-Y-O+ **£7,762** (£2,310; £1,154; £577) **Stalls** Low

Form RPR
-321 **1** **Red Tea**[7] 4593 3-9-8 78 6ex AdamBeschizza 6 85
(Peter Hiatt) *trckd ldr: led over 1f out: kpt on wl: rdn out* **13/8**[1]
0310 **2** 1 **Patanjali (IRE)**[2] 4764 3-8-1 57 NickyMackay 5 61
(Eve Johnson Houghton) *trckd ldrs: rdn to chse wnr over 1f out: kpt on but a being hld fnl 120yds* **7/2**[2]
334 **3** shd **Stosur (IRE)**[18] 4206 5-9-10 72 (v) LukeMorris 4 78
(Gay Kelleway) *sn led: rdn and hdd over 1f out: kpt chsng wnr but a being hld ins fnl f* **7/2**[2]
1313 **4** 3 ¾ **Bay Of St Malo (IRE)**[8] 4556 3-9-6 76 KieranO'Neill 2 71
(Richard Hannon) *hld up bhd ldrs: rdn over 2f out: nt quite pce to get on terms: fdd fnl 120yds* **9/2**[3]
0033 **5** nk **Golden Isles (IRE)**[11] 4463 3-8-0 59 EdwardGreatrex(3) 1 53
(J S Moore) *trckd ldrs: rdn over 2f out: no ex ins fnl f* **17/2**

1m 42.11s (1.31) **Going Correction** +0.075s/f (Good)
WFA 3 from 5yo 8lb **5** Ran SP% **111.2**
Speed ratings (Par 102): **96,95,94,91,90**
CSF £7.66 TOTE £2.00: £1.10, £4.00; EX 6.70 Trifecta £20.90.
Owner Ken Read Shelley Tucker Jimmy Cooper **Bred** Sheikh Hamdan Bin Maktoum Al Maktoum **Trained** Hook Norton, Oxon

FOCUS
Race distance 10yds further than advertised. Not a strong contest for the grade.

4820 TERRY NEILL 75TH BIRTHDAY H'CAP (BATH SUMMER SPRINT SERIES QUALIFIER) — 5f 11y
8:45 (8:47) (Class 5) (0-70,69) 3-Y-O **£5,175** (£1,540; £769; £384) **Stalls** Centre

Form RPR
0-30 **1** **Cherry Kool**[70] 2435 3-8-13 66 AaronJones(5) 2 73
(Stuart Williams) *trckd ldr: led jst over 1f out: kpt on wl* **6/1**
5- **2** 2 **Nora Batt (IRE)**[29] 3827 3-9-0 69 JoshuaBryan(7) 3 69
(John W Nicholson, Ire) *led: rdn and jst hdd over 1f out: kpt on same pce fnl f* **6/4**[1]
00-0 **3** ½ **Topsoil**[69] 2459 3-8-2 50 oh5 RaulDaSilva 5 48
(Ronald Harris) *last but in tch: hdwy over 2f out: sn rdn: kpt on same pce fnl f* **20/1**
0005 **4** 1 **Arlecchino's Rock**[16] 4262 3-9-1 63 (p) LiamKeniry 6 58
(Mark Usher) *trckd ldrs: rdn 2f out: kpt on same pce fnl f* **11/2**[3]
0033 **5** 3 **Swanton Blue (IRE)**[9] 4502 3-9-3 68 RobHornby(3) 1 52
(Ed de Giles) *trckd ldrs: rdn over 2f out: sn one pce* **9/4**[2]
41U0 **6** 2 ½ **Rampers (IRE)**[95] 1721 3-9-0 62 WilliamCarson 4 37
(Jamie Osborne) *s.i.s: cl up: rdn 2f out: fdd fnl f* **14/1**

1m 2.43s (-0.07) **Going Correction** +0.075s/f (Good) **6** Ran SP% **111.9**
Speed ratings (Par 100): **103,99,99,97,92 88**
CSF £15.42 TOTE £6.20: £3.50, £1.30; EX 16.70 Trifecta £198.90.
Owner B Piper & D Shekells **Bred** Old Mill Stud **Trained** Newmarket, Suffolk

FOCUS
The pace was sound for this modest handicap.
T/Plt: £8.80 to a £1 stake. Pool: £38,981.00 - 4,382.73 winning tickets T/Qpdt: £4.70 to a £1 stake. Pool: £3,384.00 - 707.80 winning tickets **Tim Mitchell**

[4797]GOODWOOD (R-H)
Friday, July 29

OFFICIAL GOING: Good to firm (stands' side 8.1, far side 8.2)
Wind: medium, across Weather: bright spells

4821 BETFRED GLORIOUS STKS (GROUP 3) — 1m 4f
2:00 (2:01) (Class 1) 4-Y-O+
£56,710 (£21,500; £10,760; £5,360; £2,690; £1,350) **Stalls** High

Form RPR
0/53 **1** **Kings Fete**[42] 3340 5-9-1 109 RyanMoore 4 114+
(Sir Michael Stoute) *chsd ldr: swtchd lft over 2f out and sn chsng ldr: rdn to chal and clr w ldr over 1f out: drvn to ld 1f out: styd on and forged ahd ins fnl f: rdn out* **5/2**[1]
3261 **2** ¾ **Ayrad (IRE)**[28] 3860 5-9-1 109 (p) FrankieDettori 5 113
(Roger Charlton) *led: rdn and clr w wnr over 1f out: hdd 1f out: kpt on same pce u.p ins fnl f* **6/1**
0001 **3** 5 **Majeed**[16] 4276 6-9-1 102 JamieSpencer 1 105
(David Simcock) *hld up in rr: swtchd rt and effrt on inner 2f out: chsd clr ldng trio 1f out: styd on same pce and no imp after* **16/1**
0-13 **4** ¾ **Loving Things**[27] 3888 4-8-12 108 MartinLane 7 101
(Luca Cumani) *in tch in midfield: rdn to chse ldng pair but outpcd by them wl over 1f out: wl hld 4th and plugged on same pce ins fnl f* **7/1**
/002 **5** 1 **Berkshire (IRE)**[13] 4392 5-9-1 110 (b) LukeMorris 2 102
(Paul Cole) *dwlt: hld up in last pair: swtchd lft over 2f out: sn rdn: drvn and no imp over 1f out: wl hld and plugged on same pce fnl f* **10/1**
2-14 **6** ½ **Mount Logan (IRE)**[41] 3384 5-9-1 110 AndreaAtzeni 8 101
(Roger Varian) *swtg: taken down early: chsd ldr tl over 2f out: sn drvn and lost pl 2f out: wl btn over 1f out: plugged on* **7/2**[2]
-126 **7** 18 **Elite Army**[22] 4061 5-9-1 109 JamesDoyle 6 73
(Saeed bin Suroor) *in tch in midfield: rdn and lost pl over 2f out: bhd over 1f out: virtually p.u wl ins fnl f* **4/1**[3]

2m 36.45s (-1.95) **Going Correction** -0.025s/f (Good) **7** Ran SP% **112.6**
Speed ratings (Par 113): **105,104,101,100,100 99,87**
CSF £17.30 TOTE £3.10: £1.80, £2.90; EX 18.00 Trifecta £106.50.
Owner K Abdullah **Bred** Juddmonte Farms Ltd **Trained** Newmarket, Suffolk

FOCUS
The top bend was dolled out three yards, so this was run over eight yards further than advertised. The rain the previous day amounted to only 1mm and there just a bit of drizzle in the morning, and the outer loop had been watered overnight. There was fresh ground on the inner around the lower bend from the 6f pole to the entrance to the straight. This was an ordinary Group 3. Kings Fete produced a similar level to Ascot latest.

4822 BONHAMS THOROUGHBRED STKS (GROUP 3) 1m
2:35 (2:36) (Class 1) 3-Y-O

£56,710 (£21,500; £10,760; £5,360; £2,690; £1,350) **Stalls** Low

Form RPR

-112 **1** **Thikriyaat (IRE)**[44] 3269 3-9-1 107 PaulHanagan 4 109+
(Sir Michael Stoute) *swtg: hld up in tch in midfield: n.m.r fr 2f out tl swtchd lft 1f out: hdwy u.p to ld wl ins fnl f: r.o: rdn out* **9/4**[1]

-133 **2** ½ **Forge**[44] 3269 3-9-1 106 RyanMoore 9 108+
(Sir Michael Stoute) *taken down early: t.k.h: hld up in midfield: effrt on outer over 1f out: hdwy u.p 1f out: str chal 100yds out: r.o but hld towards fin* **9/2**[3]

3601 **3** ¾ **Light Up Our World (IRE)**[27] 3911 3-8-12 103 PatDobbs 5 103
(Richard Hannon) *trckd ldr tl rdn to ld 2f out: drvn ent fnl f: hdd wl ins fnl f: no ex and outpcd towards fin* **25/1**

5-20 **4** hd **Dragon Mall (USA)**[13] 4395 3-9-1 102 JamieSpencer 6 107+
(David Simcock) *s.i.s and bustled along early: in tch in rr: clsd over 1f out: rdn and hdwy whn squeezed out and swtchd lft jst ins fnl f: r.o wl fnl 100yds: nt rch ldrs* **16/1**

6-44 **5** nk **Tony Curtis**[106] 1440 3-9-1 106 SeanLevey 2 105+
(Richard Hannon) *t.k.h: hld up in tch in last pair: swtchd rt 2f out: nt clr run and swtchd lft ent fnl f: gap opened and r.o wl fnl 100yds: nt rch ldrs* **20/1**

2235 **6** ½ **Promising Run (USA)**[42] 3339 3-8-12 107 (v[1]) AndreaAtzeni 3 101
(Saeed bin Suroor) *t.k.h: effrt and carried rt over 1f out: styd on same pce u.p ins fnl f* **6/1**

10-5 **7** 2½ **Emotionless (IRE)**[45] 3245 3-9-1 117 (p) JamesDoyle 1 98
(Charlie Appleby) *lw: led and set stdy gallop: rdn and hdd 2f out: styd upsides ldr tl no ex and btn jst ins fnl f: wknd qckly fnl 100yds* **10/3**[2]

0400 **8** shd **Buratino (IRE)**[13] 4393 3-9-1 110 JoeFanning 7 97
(Mark Johnston) *hld up in midfield on outer: clsd to chse ldrs 2f out: rdn and unable qck over 1f out: btn whn short of room jst ins fnl f: sn wknd* **14/1**

0542 **9** 7 **Cymric (USA)**[22] 4065 3-9-1 109 JamesMcDonald 10 81
(John Gosden) *chsd ldrs: rdn and unable qck over 1f out: struggling whn squeezed for room and lost pl 1f out: sn wknd* **14/1**

1m 38.16s (-1.74) **Going Correction** -0.025s/f (Good) **9** Ran SP% **114.1**
Speed ratings (Par 110): **107,106,105,105,105 104,102,102,95**
CSF £12.30 TOTE £3.00: £1.30, £1.70, £5.00; EX 10.30 Trifecta £241.30.
Owner Hamdan Al Maktoum **Bred** Kildaragh Stud **Trained** Newmarket, Suffolk

FOCUS
Race distance 8yds further due to rail movement. A very tight-looking Group 3 for 3yos. There was a muddling pace on and it got messy in the straight. That said, the best horse still won and, a 1-2 for Sir Michael Stoute, it saw another boost for the Jersey Stakes form. The third looks the key.

4823 BETFRED MILE (HERITAGE H'CAP) (FORMERLY KNOWN AS THE GOLDEN MILE) 1m
3:10 (3:13) (Class 2) 3-Y-O+

£93,375 (£27,960; £13,980; £6,990; £3,495; £1,755) **Stalls** Low

Form RPR

5321 **1** **Franklin D (USA)**[13] 4399 4-9-1 **99** 3ex (v) RyanMoore 1 110
(Michael Bell) *pushed along leaving stalls: chsd ldrs: effrt to chal ent fnl f: led ins fnl f: sn drvn: jst lasted home: all out* **7/4**[1]

5-50 **2** hd **Master The World (IRE)**[78] 2191 5-9-6 **104** (p) PatDobbs 5 114
(David Elsworth) *hld up towards rr: gd hdwy on inner 2f out: chsd ldrs 1f out: wnt 2nd and swtchd lft ins fnl f: r.o strly towards fin: nt quite get to wnr* **20/1**

2502 **3** 2 **Donncha (IRE)**[27] 3910 5-9-2 **100** AdamKirby 10 105
(Robert Eddery) *hld up in midfield: effrt 2f out: ev ch and edging rt over 1f out: stl edging rt and unable qck ins fnl f: 3rd and outpcd fnl 75yds* **10/1**[3]

050 **4** 1 **Belgian Bill**[20] 4165 8-9-4 **102** (b) PatCosgrave 9 106+
(George Baker) *t.k.h: chsd ldrs: rdn over 1f out: nt clr run 1f out tl swtchd lft and forced way out ins fnl f: r.o wl u.p fnl 100yds* **10/1**[3]

0501 **5** nk **Boomshackerlacker (IRE)**[13] 4395 6-9-2 **100** 3ex FergusSweeney 8 102
(George Baker) *hld up in midfield: swtchd lft wl over 1f out: rdn and hdwy ent fnl f: styd on wl u.p: nt rch ldrs* **20/1**

-100 **6** ½ **Carry On Deryck**[20] 4165 4-9-8 **106** JamesDoyle 21 107+
(Saeed bin Suroor) *led and grad crossed to inner: hdd 5f out: styd chsng ldr tl rdn to ld again over 1f out: drvn and hdd ins fnl f: wknd fnl 75yds* **25/1**

-633 **7** shd **One Word More (IRE)**[20] 4163 6-9-1 **99** DavidAllan 6 100+
(Tim Easterby) *hld up in midfield: nt clr run fr over 1f out tl gap fnlly opened ins fnl f: r.o fnl 100yds: nvr trbld ldrs* **14/1**

4600 **8** ½ **Solar Deity (IRE)**[13] 4399 7-8-11 **95** (p) MartinDwyer 15 95
(Jane Chapple-Hyam) *hld up in rr: effrt on outer 2f out: no imp tl hdwy jst ins fnl f: styd on wl fnl 100yds: nvr trbld ldrs* **80/1**

2140 **9** nk **Azraff (IRE)**[20] 4165 4-9-2 **100** AndreaAtzeni 4 99
(Marco Botti) *lw: hld up in midfield: n.m.r over 1f out tl effrt u.p 1f out: styd on same pce ins fnl f* **8/1**[2]

-452 **10** shd **Celestial Path (IRE)**[20] 4163 4-9-4 **102** (p) LukeMorris 17 101+
(Sir Mark Prescott Bt) *hld up in midfield: rdn over 2f out: drvn and hdwy 1f out: styd on u.p ins fnl f: nvr trbld ldrs* **10/1**[3]

1200 **11** hd **You're Fired (IRE)**[27] 3910 5-9-2 **105** JordanVaughan(5) 7 105
(K R Burke) *lw: in tch in midfield: effrt over 1f out: keeping on same pce whn squeezed for room and sltly impeded ins fnl f* **16/1**

1-10 **12** 1¾ **Can't Change It (IRE)**[36] 3566 5-8-12 **96** (p) JamieSpencer 19 90+
(David Simcock) *hld up in rr: clsd and nt clr run over 1f out: swtchd rt and briefly mde hdwy ins fnl f: nt clr run again and eased towards fin* **28/1**

1/12 **13** ½ **Jailawi (IRE)**[64] 2628 5-9-1 **99** SilvestreDeSousa 22 94
(Ismail Mohammed) *lw: in tch in midfield: drvn and unable qck over 1f out: squeezed for room and hmpd ins fnl f: one pce and hld whn hmpd again and snatched up 100yds out* **20/1**

5002 **14** 1¾ **Hors De Combat**[13] 4399 5-9-4 **102** OisinMurphy 18 93
(James Fanshawe) *hld up in tch in midfield: effrt over 1f out: unable qck u.p and btn whn squeezed for room and snatched up ins fnl f* **25/1**

312/ **15** ½ **Outlaw Country (IRE)**[664] 6925 4-9-4 **102** JamesMcDonald 13 90
(Charlie Appleby) *swtg: hld up and bhd: trying to cl on inner 2f out: nt clr run over 1f out: swtchd lft 1f out: kpt on ins fnl f: nvr trbld ldrs* **25/1**

0400 **16** 2 **Room Key**[6] 4625 4-8-9 **93** (p) JoeFanning 2 77
(Eve Johnson Houghton) *hld up towards rr: n.m.r wl over 1f out: rdn: hung rt and no hdwy over 1f out* **33/1**

0-0 **17** 1¾ **Red Avenger (USA)**[71] 2391 6-8-11 **95** (b) LiamKeniry 3 75
(Gary Moore) *hld up in midfield: swtchd rt and nt clr run over 1f out: hmpd 1f out: bhd after* **33/1**

2210 **18** ½ **Gabrial's Kaka (IRE)**[20] 4163 6-8-12 **96** TomEaves 14 74
(Richard Fahey) *broke wl: sn stdd bk and hld up in tch in midfield: pushed lft and lost pl 2f out: no hdwy u.p over 1f out* **50/1**

11-0 **19** ½ **Third Time Lucky (IRE)**[78] 2191 4-9-4 **102** PaulHanagan 12 79
(Richard Fahey) *chsd ldr tl led 5f out: rdn and hdd over 1f out: losing pl whn pushed rt and hmpd over 1f out: wknd fnl f* **14/1**

1m 37.19s (-2.71) **Going Correction** -0.025s/f (Good) **19** Ran SP% **132.3**
Speed ratings (Par 109): **112,111,109,108,108 108,107,107,107,107 106,105,104,102,102 100,98,98,97**
CSF £46.63 CT £323.71 TOTE £2.60: £1.30, £4.60, £2.70, £2.80; EX 41.80 Trifecta £520.50.
Owner W J and T C O Gredley **Bred** Grapestock LLC **Trained** Newmarket, Suffolk
■ Stewards' Enquiry : Pat Cosgrave four-day ban: careless riding (12-15 Aug)
James McDonald £140 fine: failed to report that the colt made a noise during the race

FOCUS
Race distance 8yds further due to rail movement.This fiercely competitive handicap was run at a strong pace and once again being drawn in double figures was a real disadvantage. The form looks solid. Franklin D was a bit off his Newmarket figure.

4824 QATAR KING GEORGE STKS (GROUP 2) 5f
3:45 (3:49) (Class 1) 3-Y-O+

£176,991 (£67,101; £33,581; £16,728; £8,395; £4,213) **Stalls** High

Form RPR

2510 **1** **Take Cover**[45] 3244 9-9-2 111 DavidAllan 11 117
(David C Griffiths) *swtg: mde all: rdn and drifting rt over 1f out: drvn ins fnl f: hld on gamely towards fin: all out* **8/1**[3]

1235 **2** nk **Washington DC (IRE)**[20] 4151 3-8-12 111 (t) RyanMoore 6 115
(A P O'Brien, Ire) *hld up towards rr: clsd over 1f out: swtchd lft 1f out: rdn and hdwy to chse wnr ins fnl f: str chal wl ins fnl f: r.o but hld cl home* **8/1**[3]

1-00 **3** hd **Goldream**[125] 1104 7-9-2 115 (p) MartinHarley 13 115
(Robert Cowell) *wl in tch in midfield: effrt over 1f out: hdwy u.p to chse ldrs ins fnl f: str chal towards fin: jst hld cl home* **12/1**

-112 **4** shd **Easton Angel (IRE)**[20] 4166 3-8-9 110 PaulMulrennan 4 111+
(Michael Dods) *lw: hld up towards rr: nt clr run 2f out tl gap opened 1f out: str run u.p ins fnl f: nt quite rch ldrs* **13/2**[2]

2511 **5** hd **Marsha (IRE)**[20] 4166 3-8-9 111 LukeMorris 8 110
(Sir Mark Prescott Bt) *t.k.h early: hld up in midfield: rdn 2f out: hdwy u.p ins fnl f: styd on strly fnl 100yds: nt quite rch ldrs* **5/1**[1]

3503 **6** 1¾ **Muthmir (IRE)**[20] 4166 6-9-2 114 (p) PaulHanagan 10 108
(William Haggas) *lw: t.k.h: hld up wl in tch in midfield: effrt over 1f out: drvn and no ex ins fnl f: wknd fnl 75yds* **5/1**[1]

4-40 **7** nse **Pearl Secret**[45] 3244 7-9-2 109 OisinMurphy 1 111+
(David Barron) *swtg: hld up towards rr: clsd over 1f out: nt clr run and swtchd lft 1f out: nt clr run and again and swtchd lft ins fnl f: r.o wl ins fnl f: no threat to ldrs* **25/1**

0220 **8** 1 **Cotai Glory**[20] 4151 4-9-2 114 GeorgeBaker 9 104+
(Charles Hills) *chsd wnr: rdn and ev ch over 1f out: carried rt and squeezed out 1f out: lost any ch: wknd ins fnl f* **9/1**

2134 **9** ½ **Finsbury Square (IRE)**[30] 3796 4-9-2 107 (b) OlivierPeslier 14 102
(F Chappet, France) *lw: hld up in midfield: effrt over 1f out: styd on same pce ins fnl f: nvr trbld ldrs* **50/1**

1626 **10** nk **Kachy**[20] 4166 3-8-12 112 RichardKingscote 3 100+
(Tom Dascombe) *lw: chsd ldrs: rdn and ev ch over 1f out: carried rt and squeezed for room 1f out: lost any ch: wknd ins fnl f* **14/1**

0030 **11** hd **Goken (FR)**[20] 4151 4-9-2 111 JamieSpencer 12 100
(Kevin Ryan) *midfield early: lost pl and towards rr whn rdn 2f out: kpt on ins fnl f: nvr trbld ldrs* **14/1**

0002 **12** shd **Move In Time**[31] 3752 8-9-2 107 (v) DanielTudhope 7 100
(David O'Meara) *wl in tch in midfield: effrt but unable qck u.p over 1f out: wl hld and kpt on same pce ins fnl f* **50/1**

4015 **13** 1½ **Spirit Quartz (IRE)**[27] 3909 8-9-2 108 (p) AdamKirby 2 95
(Robert Cowell) *chsd ldrs: rdn and ev ch over 1f out: carried rt and squeezed for room 1f out: lost any ch and wknd ins fnl f* **50/1**

4240 **14** nk **Jungle Cat (IRE)**[20] 4151 4-9-2 110 JamesDoyle 16 94
(Charlie Appleby) *midfield: rdn 1/2-way and sn struggling: wl hld and plugged on same pce fr over 1f out* **16/1**

4130 **15** nse **Line Of Reason (IRE)**[14] 4359 6-9-2 105 MartinLane 5 93
(Paul Midgley) *lw: hld up in midfield: clsd to chse ldrs and swtchd rt over 1f out: squeezed out on rail and bdly hmpd 1f out: nt rcvr* **66/1**

14-6 **16** 1 **Ajaya**[62] 2692 3-8-12 114 (p) AndreaAtzeni 17 89
(William Haggas) *racd along towards nr side: nvr bttr than midfield: rdn and btn over 1f out: bhd ins fnl f* **33/1**

6142 **17** 6 **Divine (IRE)**[13] 4393 5-8-13 110 SilvestreDeSousa 15 65
(Mick Channon) *restless in stalls: a bhd: eased wl ins fnl f* **20/1**

56.86s (-3.34) **Going Correction** -0.275s/f (Firm)
WFA 3 from 4yo+ 4lb **17** Ran SP% **124.7**
Speed ratings (Par 115): **115,114,114,114,113 110,110,109,108,107 107,107,105,104,104 102,93**
CSF £67.86 TOTE £11.00: £3.80, £2.30, £4.30; EX 95.10 Trifecta £1442.90.
Owner Norcroft Park Stud **Bred** Norcroft Park Stud **Trained** Bawtry, S Yorks

FOCUS
A typically competitive edition. All bar one of the field went towards the far side and, after a scorching pace, it threw up a cracking finish. The 3yos set the level and Take Cover is rated better than ever.

4825 BETFRED SUPPORTS JACK BERRY HOUSE NURSERY (H'CAP) 6f
4:20 (4:22) (Class 2) 2-Y-O **£12,938** (£3,850; £1,924; £962) **Stalls** High

Form RPR

421 **1** **Final Reckoning (IRE)**[35] 3619 2-9-1 **83** JamesMcDonald 1 89
(Charlie Appleby) *str: lw: racd towards far side: stdd s: hld up in rr: hdwy over 2f out: rdn to chal over 1f out: led 1f out: hld on wl: rdn out* **9/2**[1]

2101 **2** nk **Rusumaat (IRE)**[30] 3772 2-9-6 **88** PaulHanagan 3 93
(Mark Johnston) *racd far side: chsd ldr tl led 2f out: sn rdn and hdd over 1f out but stl ev ch over 1f out: kpt on u.p: jst hld wl ins fnl f* **11/2**[3]

310 **3** ¾ **Top Score**[45] 3247 2-9-5 **87** JamesDoyle 12 90
(Saeed bin Suroor) *racd centre to nr side: led gp and chsd ldrs overall: edgd rt u.p over 1f out: styd on same pce ins fnl f* **5/1**[2]

3315 **4** ¾ **El Torito (IRE)**[28] 3858 2-8-9 **77** SamHitchcott 5 77
(Jim Boyle) *racd far side: overall ldr tl rdn and hdd 2f out: sn wandered lft: kpt on same pce ins fnl f* **40/1**

441 **5** *hd* **Mailshot (USA)**[37] 3526 2-9-7 **89**.................................... FrannyNorton 18 89
(Mark Johnston) *racd centre to nr side: in tch in midfield: effrt and wanting to edge rt over 1f out: stl edging rt but styd on wl ins fnl f: nt rch ldrs* **10/1**

403 **6** *3/4* **Dusker (USA)**[36] 3562 2-8-3 **71**.................................... JoeFanning 2 68
(Mark Johnston) *str: racd far side: chsd ldrs: effrt to press ldrs 2f out: rdn to ld over 1f out: hdd 1f out: no ex ins fnl f: wknd wl ins fnl f* **10/1**

1106 **7** *1/2* **Monks Stand (USA)**[20] 4150 2-9-5 **87**......................(v) FrankieDettori 10 83
(Jeremy Noseda) *racd centre to nr side: in midfield in midfield: effrt and carried rt jst over 1f out: kpt on same pce ins fnl f* **8/1**

022 **8** *hd* **Notalot (IRE)**[30] 3772 2-7-7 **68**....................................(v) DavidEgan(7) 16 63
(Michael Bell) *w'like: lw: racd centre to nr side: w gp ldrs and prom overall: rdn and hung rt over 1f out: kpt on same pce ins fnl f* **33/1**

221 **9** *hd* **Naafer**[21] 4110 2-9-2 **84**.................................... MartinHarley 17 81+
(William Haggas) *w'like: racd centre to nr side: hld up in rr: nt clr run 2f out: swtchd rt and stl n.m.r over 1f out: gap opened and drvn 1f out: kpt on same pce after* **8/1**

13 **10** *1 1/4* **Scofflaw**[32] 3712 2-8-13 **81**.................................... JamieSpencer 4 71
(Richard Fahey) *unf: racd far side: in tch: effrt but unable qck over 1f out: kpt on same pce ins fnl f* **10/1**

4244 **11** *1 3/4* **Diable D'Or (IRE)**[13] 4394 2-9-2 **84**.................................... JohnFahy 15 73+
(Eve Johnson Houghton) *tall: racd centre to nr side: hld up towards rr: nt clr run 2f out: effrt whn jostled and hmpd over 1f out: no real imp u.p 1f out* **33/1**

3163 **12** *hd* **High Acclaim (USA)**[8] 4553 2-8-11 **79**...................... FergusSweeney 11 64+
(Roger Teal) *racd centre to nr side: hld up in tch in midfield: effrt 2f out: carried rt and hmpd over 1f out: wknd ins fnl f* **20/1**

13 **13** *3/4* **Naples Bay**[14] 4343 2-8-13 **81**.................................... CamHardie 6 63
(John Quinn) *neat: racd far side: in tch and effrt 2f out: sn hung lft and no hdwy: wknd ins fnl f* **25/1**

424 **14** *3/4* **Aventinus (IRE)**[18] 4188 2-8-12 **80**.......................... RichardKingscote 13 59
(Hugo Palmer) *racd centre to nr side: chsd gp ldrs: rdn over 2f out: losing pl whn squeezed and hmpd wl over 1f out: n.d after* **25/1**

6340 **15** *1 1/2* **Sayesse**[8] 4553 2-8-12 **80**.................................... CharlesBishop 14 56
(Mick Channon) *lw: racd centre to nr side: stdd s: hld up in rr: effrt whn squeezed for room and hmpd 2f out: n.d after* **66/1**

000 **16** *hd* **Buskin River (IRE)**[21] 4075 2-8-0 **68** oh2......................... KieranO'Neill 9 45
(Richard Hannon) *racd centre to nr side: pressed gp ldrs: rdn over 2f out: losing pl whn squeezed for room and hmpd 2f out: n.d after* **50/1**

102 **17** *6* **Prince Of Cool**[18] 4196 2-9-0 **82**.................................... TomEaves 7 37
(James Given) *racd centre to nr side: in tch in midfield: rdn and hung rt 2f out: wknd over 1f out* **20/1**

1m 11.5s (-0.70) **Going Correction** -0.275s/f (Firm) **17** Ran SP% **128.7**
Speed ratings (Par 100): **93,92,91,90,90 89,88,88,88,86 84,83,82,81,79 79,71**
CSF £26.75 CT £140.40 TOTE £4.60: £1.50, £1.80, £2.10, £8.60; EX 30.30 Trifecta £137.80.

Owner Godolphin **Bred** Azienda Agricola Loreto Luciani **Trained** Newmarket, Suffolk

FOCUS
A useful, competitive nursery - the first three finishers were among five runners who came into this with an entry in the Gimcrack - although the field split into two groups and the first two home raced in the smaller bunch towards the far side. The fourth looks the key to the form.

4826 L'ORMARINS QUEENS PLATE STKS (REGISTERED AS THE OAK TREE STAKES) (GROUP 3) (F&M) 7f

4:55 (4:55) (Class 1) 3-Y-O+

£45,368 (£17,200; £8,608; £4,288; £2,152; £1,080) **Stalls** Low

Form RPR

5- **1** **Al Jazi (IRE)**[25] 3967 3-8-10 100.................................... GregoryBenoist 1 110
(F Rohaut, France) *str: in tch: hdwy to chse ldrs after 2f: effrt and carried rt over 1f out: rdn to ld 1f out: in command and r.o wl ins fnl f* **12/1**

1301 **2** *1 3/4* **Mise En Rose (USA)**[21] 4105 3-8-10 101................. JamesMcDonald 7 105
(Charlie Appleby) *hld up in tch: effrt 2f out: swtchd rt and chsd ldrs over 1f out: wnt between rivals to chse wnr ins fnl f: kpt on but no imp* **5/1**[2]

3511 **3** *3/4* **Namhroodah (IRE)**[7] 4582 4-9-3 99.................................... LukeMorris 5 106
(James Tate) *chsd ldrs: effrt to chse ldr and drifted rt over 1f out: styd on same pce ins fnl f* **7/1**

-133 **4** *1 3/4* **Always Smile (IRE)**[21] 4107 4-9-3 110.......................(p) JamesDoyle 10 101
(Saeed bin Suroor) *lw: in tch in midfield: rdn over 3f out: hrd drvn and no imp over 1f out: styd on ins fnl f: no threat to wnr* **11/8**[1]

3402 **5** *1/2* **Besharah (IRE)**[21] 4114 3-8-10 110.................................... PatCosgrave 9 97
(William Haggas) *in tch in midfield: effrt 2f out: unable qck u.p over 1f out: no threat to wnr but kpt on ins fnl f* **11/2**[3]

-006 **6** *1/2* **Queen Catrine (IRE)**[19] 4178 5-9-6 105..........................(b) GaryCarroll 4 102
(G M Lyons, Ire) *sn led: rdn 2f out: hdd and no ex 1f out: wknd ins fnl f* **16/1**

-201 **7** *1 1/4* **Opal Tiara (IRE)**[37] 3519 3-8-10 95.................................... OisinMurphy 12 92
(Mick Channon) *hld up in tch towards rr: effrt 2f out: no imp u.p over 1f out: wl hld and plugged on same pce fnl f* **20/1**

663- **8** *1 3/4* **Growing Glory (FR)**[33] 4-9-3 99.......................... StephanePasquier 11 90
(F Rohaut, France) *w'like: swtg: hld up in tch in rr: effrt and hung rt over 1f out: no imp and wl hld fnl f* **33/1**

-110 **9** *nk* **Marenko**[42] 3339 3-8-13 105.................................... SeanLevey 6 90
(Richard Hannon) *chsd ldr tl unable qck and lost pl over 1f out: wknd ins fnl f* **20/1**

5-30 **10** *2* **Alfajer**[24] 3979 4-9-3 95.................................... AndreaAtzeni 3 84
(Marco Botti) *hld up in tch in rr: effrt 2f out: carried rt and hmpd over 1f out: no hdwy and wl hld after* **40/1**

0-06 **11** *nk* **Alamode**[27] 3911 3-8-10 95....................................(p) MartinDwyer 8 80
(Marcus Tregoning) *in tch towards rr: rdn jst over 2f out: sn dropped to rr and wl hld over 1f out* **50/1**

1m 24.92s (-2.08) **Going Correction** -0.025s/f (Good)
WFA 3 from 4yo+ 7lb **11** Ran SP% **117.1**
Speed ratings (Par 113): **110,108,107,105,104 104,102,100,100,97 97**
CSF £66.52 TOTE £13.90: £3.00, £1.80, £2.30; EX 64.90 Trifecta £386.00.

Owner Al Shaqab Racing **Bred** Skymarc Farm **Trained** Sauvagnon, France

FOCUS
This was run over eight yards further than advertised. The favourite was well below her best and it's hard to consider the form anything other than ordinary for a Group 3. Big improvement from Al Jazi, but it was no fluke.

4827 BETFRED MOBILE STKS (H'CAP) 1m 3f

5:30 (5:30) (Class 3) (0-90,88) 3-Y-O

£12,450 (£3,728; £1,864; £932; £466; £234) **Stalls** High

Form RPR

-314 **1** **Poet's Word (IRE)**[55] 2892 3-9-7 **88**.................................... RyanMoore 3 105+
(Sir Michael Stoute) *lw: chsd ldrs: nt clr run and shuffled bk over 2f out: swtchd rt 2f out: swtchd bk lft: rdn and hdwy over 1f out: chsd wnr 1f out: led ins fnl f: styd on strly* **7/4**[1]

0131 **2** *1 1/4* **Sixties Groove (IRE)**[22] 4046 3-9-2 **83**..........................(p) AdamKirby 11 95
(Jeremy Noseda) *lw: stdd s: hld up in tch: hdwy to chse ldrs 5f out: rdn to ld 2f out: hung lft and drvn over 1f out: stl hanging and hdd ins fnl f: no ex* **7/1**[3]

1202 **3** *3* **Carry Me Home**[23] 4013 3-9-1 **82**.............................. JamesMcDonald 15 89
(Charles Hills) *stdd after s: hld up in rr: hdwy on outer 2f out: kpt on to go 3rd wl ins fnl f* **20/1**

-532 **4** *hd* **Cosmeapolitan**[18] 4207 3-8-13 **80**................................ FergusSweeney 2 87
(Alan King) *dwlt: sn in tch in midfield: hmpd and dropped to rr after 1f: effrt and swtchd lft over 1f out: kpt on ins fnl f* **25/1**

156 **5** *hd* **Combative**[37] 3532 3-9-5 **86**.................................... PatDobbs 4 92
(Amanda Perrett) *w'like: hld up in midfield: effrt and n.m.r jst over 2f out: swtchd rt and hdwy over 1f out: kpt on ins fnl f* **20/1**

412 **6** *hd* **Indulged**[39] 3467 3-9-1 **82**.................................... TomQueally 9 88
(James Fanshawe) *in tch in midfield: rdn and hdwy to chal and edgd rt 2f out: wandered and dropped to 3rd 1f out: wknd ins fnl f* **7/1**[3]

-104 **7** *4 1/2* **Royal Reserve**[55] 2889 3-9-3 **84**.................................... MartinDwyer 1 82
(William Muir) *in tch in midfield: effrt on inner over 2f out: no hdwy u.p over 1f out: wknd ins fnl f* **40/1**

0513 **8** *1 1/4* **Theos Lolly (IRE)**[13] 4409 3-8-9 **76**.............................. PaulHanagan 13 72
(Richard Fahey) *lw: stdd after s: hld up in rr: effrt whn swtchd rt 2f out: no real imp: kpt on to pass btn horses fnl f: n.d* **40/1**

1542 **9** *2 1/2* **Sark (IRE)**[20] 4158 3-8-9 **76**.................................... SilvestreDeSousa 7 68
(David Evans) *stdd after s: hld up in rr: effrt 2f out: sn no imp: wl btn 1f out* **33/1**

1522 **10** *1 1/4* **Isharah (USA)**[20] 4143 3-8-11 **78**.................................... JoeFanning 6 68
(Mark Johnston) *lw: pressed ldr: rdn jst over 2f out: sn lost pl: wknd over 1f out* **12/1**

230 **11** *6* **Zzoro (IRE)**[69] 2479 3-9-4 **85**.................................... GeorgeBaker 5 74
(Amanda Perrett) *led tl hdd 2f out: sn rdn and btn: wknd jst over 1f out* **33/1**

-113 **12** *1 1/2* **Goldenfield (IRE)**[33] 3687 3-9-3 **84**..............................(p) LiamKeniry 12 61
(Gary Moore) *swtg: t.k.h: midfield tl hdwy to join ldrs after 2f: losing pl and wnt rt jst over 2f out: sn wknd* **33/1**

-060 **13** *23* **Welford**[13] 4407 3-9-6 **87**.................................... JamesDoyle 14 25
(Mark Johnston) *lw: in tch in midfield: rdn and struggling whn bmpd and lost pl jst over 2f out: no ch after and eased ins fnl f: t.o* **12/1**

311 **14** *11* **Al Neksh**[21] 4092 3-9-6 **87**.................................... FrankieDettori 8 6
(William Haggas) *str: swtg: t.k.h: chsd ldrs: rdn and losing pl whn bmpd and hmpd over 2f out: no ch and bhd after: eased ins fnl f: t.o* **7/2**[2]

2m 25.02s (-1.48) **Going Correction** -0.025s/f (Good) **14** Ran SP% **126.0**
Speed ratings (Par 104): **104,103,100,100,100 100,97,96,94,93 89,88,71,63**
CSF £13.54 CT £197.04 TOTE £2.40: £1.40, £2.40, £4.00; EX 17.10 Trifecta £177.80.
Owner Saeed Suhail **Bred** Woodcote Stud Ltd **Trained** Newmarket, Suffolk

FOCUS
A decent 3yo handicap run at a good pace. The winner rates better than the bare form.
T/Jkpt: Not won. T/Plt: £150.90 to a £1 stake. Pool: £328,172.70 - 1,587.36 winning tickets
T/Qpdt: £36.90 to a £1 stake. Pool: £23,636.50 - 473.36 winning tickets **Steve Payne**

4486 MUSSELBURGH (R-H)

Friday, July 29

OFFICIAL GOING: Good (good to firm in places; 7.3)
Wind: Almost nil Weather: Overcast

4828 WILKINSON AND ASSOCIATES AMATEUR RIDERS' H'CAP 1m 5f

5:40 (5:40) (Class 5) (0-70,69) 4-Y-O+ **£3,119** (£967; £483; £242) **Stalls** Low

Form RPR

-032 **1** **Amirli (IRE)**[21] 4099 5-10-7 **65**....................................(p) MrJamesKing(3) 1 73
(Alistair Whillans) *t.k.h: cl up: led over 2f out: rdn out fnl f* **5/2**[2]

2561 **2** *3/4* **Duke Of Yorkshire**[16] 4260 6-10-4 **64**....................(p) MissEEasterby(5) 3 70
(Tim Easterby) *led at modest gallop: rdn and hdd over 2f out: rallied to press wnr over 1f out: kpt on ins fnl f* **11/2**[3]

4522 **3** *3/4* **Love Marmalade (IRE)**[5] 4686 6-10-13 **68**.......................... MrRBirkett 4 73
(David O'Meara) *hld up in tch: hdwy to press wnr over 2f out to over 1f out: edgd rt: kpt on ins fnl f* **5/4**[1]

401 **4** *1* **Midnight Warrior**[12] 4430 6-9-8 **54**.............................. MrsVDavies(5) 2 57
(Ron Barr) *t.k.h: trckd ldrs: pushed along 2f out: kpt on ins fnl f* **10/1**

0502 **5** *3 3/4* **Merchant Of Dubai**[10] 4489 11-10-4 **59**.......................... MrsCBartley 5 57
(Jim Goldie) *cl up: lost pl over 2f out: rdn and outpcd over 1f out* **8/1**

2m 51.3s (-0.70) **Going Correction** -0.175s/f (Firm) **5** Ran SP% **108.6**
Speed ratings (Par 103): **95,94,94,93,91**
CSF £15.27 TOTE £2.90: £1.40, £2.20; EX 14.30 Trifecta £31.00.
Owner Paul & Clare Rooney **Bred** Haras De Son Altesse L'Aga Khan Scea **Trained** Newmill-On-Slitrig, Borders

FOCUS
Add 7yds to race distance. Just an ordinary pace to this handicap for amateur riders, and the first two were always close to the pace.

4829 IRISH STALLION FARMS EBF MAIDEN STKS (PLUS 10 RACE) 7f 30y

6:10 (6:10) (Class 4) 2-Y-O **£4,204** (£1,251; £625; £312) **Stalls** Low

Form RPR

52 **1** **Geophony (IRE)**[9] 4523 2-9-5 0.................................... RoystonFfrench 2 78+
(Mark Johnston) *trckd ldr: led over 2f out: rdn and edgd lft appr fnl f: kpt on strly* **5/2**[2]

32 **2** *2 1/4* **Lucky Esteem**[21] 4097 2-9-0 0.................................... GrahamLee 1 67
(Mark Johnston) *chsd ldrs: effrt and pushed along 2f out: chsd wnr wl ins fnl f: styd on* **4/5**[1]

06 **3** *1* **Permanent**[29] 3808 2-9-5 0.................................... ShaneGray 4 69
(Daniel Kubler) *led tl rdn and hdd over 2f out: chsd wnr to wl ins fnl f: one pce* **9/1**[3]

4 1 1/4 **Davy's Dilemma** 2-9-5 0 ConnorBeasley 3 66
(Michael Dods) *t.k.h: in tch: effrt and pushed along 2f out: outpcd fnl f* **9/1**[3]

06 5 6 **Hollywood Harry (IRE)**[53] 2956 2-9-0 0 ShirleyTeasdale[(5)] 5 50
(Keith Dalgleish) *hld up in tch: pushed along and outpcd over 2f out: wknd wl over 1f out* **40/1**

1m 30.56s (1.56) **Going Correction** -0.175s/f (Firm) **5** Ran SP% **106.6**
Speed ratings (Par 96): **84,81,80,78,72**
CSF £4.55 TOTE £3.10: £1.60, £1.10; EX 3.90 Trifecta £9.70.
Owner Thurloe XXXII & The Acorn Partnership **Bred** Carrigbeg Stud **Trained** Middleham Moor, N Yorks

FOCUS
Add 7yds to race distance. A moderate gallop to this juvenile maiden in which two Mark Johnston-trained horses dominated the market and finished first and second. However, the form is likely to prove modest.

4830 WILKINSON AND ASSOCIATES SCOTLAND H'CAP 7f 30y
6:45 (6:45) (Class 5) (0-75,75) 3-Y-O+ **£3,234** (£962; £481; £240) **Stalls** Low

Form RPR

4000 1 **Buccaneers Vault (IRE)**[5] 4684 4-10-0 **75** (p) ConnorBeasley 8 81
(Michael Dods) *hld up: stdy hdwy over 2f out: sn pushed along: kpt on wl fnl f to ld cl home* **17/2**

0050 2 nk **Ralphy Boy (IRE)**[21] 4094 7-9-6 **72** GarryWhillans[(5)] 7 77
(Alistair Whillans) *in tch: hdwy to ld over 2f out: rdn over 1f out: hrd pressed fnl f: kpt on: hdd cl home* **6/1**[3]

4222 3 nse **Chaplin Bay (IRE)**[21] 4094 4-9-13 **74** JackGarritty 5 79
(Ruth Carr) *trckd ldrs: hdwy and ev ch over 2f out: sn rdn: disp ld fnl f: kpt on: hld cl home* **7/4**[1]

001 4 1 3/4 **Rasaman (IRE)**[21] 4102 12-9-6 **67** JoeDoyle 3 72+
(Jim Goldie) *hld up in tch: stdy hdwy whn no room fr over 2f out: unlucky* **11/1**

3063 5 1 1/4 **Surewecan**[13] 4402 4-9-11 **72** GrahamLee 2 69+
(Mark Johnston) *missed break: hld up: rdn over 2f out: kpt on fnl f: nvr able to chal* **11/4**[2]

0245 6 1 1/4 **Circuitous**[5] 4683 8-8-8 **60** (v) ShirleyTeasdale[(5)] 4 54
(Keith Dalgleish) *dwlt: sn rcvrd and led after 2f: hdd over 2f out: rallied: wknd fnl f* **16/1**

0-00 7 2 1/2 **Thornaby Nash**[35] 3605 5-9-12 **73** RoystonFfrench 6 60
(Colin Teague) *hld up towards rr: drvn along over 2f out: no imp fr over 1f out* **40/1**

-061 8 4 **Bay Mirage (IRE)**[15] 4310 3-9-4 **72** (p) ShaneGray 1 45
(Kevin Ryan) *led 2f: pressed ldr: ev ch over 2f out: rdn and wknd over 1f out* **12/1**

1m 28.69s (-0.31) **Going Correction** -0.175s/f (Firm)
WFA 3 from 4yo+ 7lb **8** Ran SP% **112.2**
Speed ratings (Par 103): **94,93,93,91,90 88,85,81**
CSF £56.02 CT £129.02 TOTE £8.70: £2.40, £2.00, £1.10; EX 70.00 Trifecta £113.50.
Owner D Neale **Bred** Kilfrush Stud **Trained** Denton, Co Durham

FOCUS
Add 7yds to race distance. A stop-start gallop to this 7f handicap in which the first three finished line abreast, but it was a rather messy affair with some hard-luck stories, so the form is unlikely to prove reliable.

4831 RACING UK HD H'CAP 5f
7:20 (7:21) (Class 3) (0-90,90) 3-Y-O+ **£8,409** (£2,502; £1,250; £625) **Stalls** High

Form RPR

4030 1 **Kibaar**[13] 4415 4-9-5 **83** (p) KevinStott 8 92
(Kevin Ryan) *mde all: rdn over 1f out: kpt on wl fnl f* **13/2**[3]

2144 2 nk **Fumbo Jumbo (IRE)**[7] 4612 3-8-8 **81** RobJFitzpatrick[(5)] 12 88+
(Garry Moss) *awkward s: sn cl up: rdn and sltly outpcd over 1f out: rallied and chsd wnr ins fnl f: kpt on fin* **7/2**[1]

0146 3 1/2 **My Name Is Rio (IRE)**[14] 4338 6-9-12 **90** (p) ConnorBeasley 5 96
(Michael Dods) *hld up: rdn over 2f out: kpt on wl fnl f: nrst fin* **12/1**

2213 4 nk **Seamster**[8] 4544 9-8-0 **71** (t) CameronNoble[(7)] 6 76
(David Loughnane) *fly-jmpd s: hld up: hdwy on outside and cl up over 1f out: one pce wl ins fnl f* **14/1**

2104 5 1 **Lexington Place**[14] 4373 6-9-9 **87** JamesSullivan 9 88
(Ruth Carr) *dwlt: hld up: rdn and hdwy over 1f out: kpt on wl fnl f* **10/1**

114 6 3/4 **Rosealee (IRE)**[7] 4585 3-8-8 **76** RoystonFfrench 11 74
(Jeremy Gask) *cl up: effrt and chsd wnr over 2f out to over 1f out: no ex ins fnl f* **7/1**

6216 7 1 1/4 **Classy Anne**[6] 4632 6-9-1 **79** (p) JoeDoyle 4 73
(Jim Goldie) *in tch: nt clr run over 2f out to over 1f out: wknd fnl f* **20/1**

0226 8 1 1/2 **Olivia Fallow (IRE)**[41] 3392 4-9-10 **88** GrahamLee 2 77
(Paul Midgley) *in tch on outside: rdn over 2f out: wknd over 1f out* **17/2**

6302 9 nk **Desert Ace (IRE)**[9] 4514 5-9-3 **81** (p) DavidNolan 7 69
(Iain Jardine) *t.k.h: cl up tl rdn and wknd over 1f out* **6/1**[2]

0-61 10 1 1/4 **Economic Crisis (IRE)**[10] 4488 7-8-6 **75** 6ex NathanEvans[(5)] 3 58
(John David Riches) *chsd ldrs: rdn 1/2-way: wknd over 1f out* **9/1**

5433 11 3 3/4 **Pearl Acclaim (IRE)**[9] 4514 6-9-0 **78** (v) PaulQuinn 1 48
(David Nicholls) *s.v.s: hung rt thrght: a wl bhd* **12/1**

58.62s (-1.78) **Going Correction** -0.175s/f (Firm)
WFA 3 from 4yo+ 4lb **11** Ran SP% **118.8**
Speed ratings (Par 107): **107,106,105,105,103 102,100,98,97,95 89**
CSF £29.78 CT £277.03 TOTE £7.70: £3.20, £1.80, £4.90; EX 41.00 Trifecta £413.30.
Owner Course & Distance Racing 1 **Bred** Laundry Cottage Stud Farm **Trained** Hambleton, N Yorks

FOCUS
Quite a competitive sprint run at a sound gallop, though most were exposed sorts.

4832 TOR COATINGS PARTNER EVENT NURSERY H'CAP 5f
7:55 (7:55) (Class 5) 2-Y-O **£3,234** (£962; £481; £240) **Stalls** High

Form RPR

3510 1 **Kodi Da Capo (IRE)**[5] 4679 2-9-2 **74** JasonHart 4 79
(Keith Dalgleish) *prom: drvn to ld ins fnl f: kpt on strly* **3/1**[3]

403 2 1 1/4 **Yorkshiredebut (IRE)**[16] 4254 2-8-7 **65** JamesSullivan 3 65
(Paul Midgley) *dwlt: hld up in tch: smooth hdwy 1/2-way: led appr fnl f tl ins fnl f: kpt on same pce* **7/1**

6465 3 nse **Love Oasis**[17] 4221 2-8-10 **68** GrahamLee 1 68
(Mark Johnston) *prom on outside: pushed along and edgd rt 1/2-way: kpt on ins fnl f: no imp* **7/1**

1145 4 1 **Lawless Louis**[21] 4111 2-9-5 **82** JoshDoyle[(5)] 5 78
(David O'Meara) *cl up: rdn over 2f out: edgd rt and one pce fnl f* **9/4**[1]

41 5 hd **Reckless Serenade (IRE)**[20] 4140 2-8-11 **69** ConnorBeasley 2 65
(Keith Dalgleish) *led: rdn and hdd appr fnl f: sn no ex* **5/2**[2]

1m 0.06s (-0.34) **Going Correction** -0.175s/f (Firm) **5** Ran SP% **109.3**
Speed ratings (Par 94): **95,93,92,91,91**
CSF £21.78 TOTE £3.30: £2.30, £4.10; EX 16.30 Trifecta £60.10.
Owner Equus I **Bred** Tally-Ho Stud **Trained** Carluke, S Lanarks

FOCUS
This looked an ordinary nursery with only two and half lengths covering the five. The pace was sound.

4833 BERNARDHUNTER CELEBRATING 70 YEARS H'CAP 1m 1f
8:25 (8:25) (Class 5) (0-70,70) 3-Y-O+ **£3,234** (£962; £481; £240) **Stalls** Low

Form RPR

6526 1 **Ellaal**[4] 4704 7-9-10 **66** JamesSullivan 6 79
(Ruth Carr) *pressed ldr: led 3f out: rdn and clr over 1f out: kpt on wl fnl f* **2/1**[2]

0413 2 4 1/2 **Le Deluge (FR)**[5] 4687 6-9-5 **66** 6ex (t) AdamMcNamara[(5)] 2 70
(Micky Hammond) *s.i.s: hld up in tch: drvn and outpcd over 3f out: rallied to chse wnr over 2f out: kpt on fnl f: nt pce to chal* **6/4**[1]

3465 3 9 **Templier (IRE)**[15] 4312 3-9-3 **68** (b) GrahamLee 3 52
(Mark Johnston) *led tl rdn and hdd 3f out: wknd fr 2f out* **3/1**[3]

-600 4 5 **Spirit Of The Sea (IRE)**[11] 4446 4-9-0 **56** GeorgeChaloner 5 30
(Richard Whitaker) *trckd ldrs: drvn along over 3f out: wknd over 2f out* **20/1**

060 5 10 **Hightime Girl**[17] 4235 3-8-6 **64** (tp) CameronNoble[(7)] 8 16
(David Loughnane) *dwlt: hld up in tch: struggling over 3f out: sn btn* **14/1**

1m 51.84s (-2.06) **Going Correction** -0.175s/f (Firm)
WFA 3 from 4yo+ 9lb **5** Ran SP% **109.8**
Speed ratings (Par 103): **102,98,90,85,76**
CSF £5.37 TOTE £3.30: £2.00, £1.10; EX 4.70 Trifecta £13.40.
Owner The Bottom Liners & Paul Saxton **Bred** W And R Barnett Ltd **Trained** Huby, N Yorks

FOCUS
Add 7yds to race distance. A competitive handicap run at a moderate gallop and, although they finished well strung out, the form is ordinary.

4834 GREG AND JOHN MUSSELBURGH MEMPHIS H'CAP 5f
8:55 (8:55) (Class 6) (0-65,65) 3-Y-O+ **£2,587** (£770; £384; £192) **Stalls** High

Form RPR

0624 1 **Thornaby Princess**[10] 4492 5-8-8 **47** (p) RoystonFfrench 5 53
(Colin Teague) *towards rr: rdn and hdwy over 1f out: led ins fnl f: drvn out* **8/1**

560- 2 1/2 **Busy Bimbo (IRE)**[276] 7530 7-9-8 **61** DavidNolan 6 65
(John David Riches) *chsd ldrs: effrt and ev ch over 1f out to ins fnl f: kpt on: hld nr fin* **7/1**[3]

-11 3 1/2 **Rio Deva (IRE)**[20] 4141 3-9-7 **64** ConnorBeasley 1 65
(Keith Dalgleish) *cl up: led over 1f out to ins fnl f: kpt on: hld nr fin* **7/2**[2]

0550 4 1 **Bunce (IRE)**[10] 4488 8-9-10 **63** GrahamLee 3 62
(Linda Perratt) *in tch: effrt and rdn over 1f out: ev ch briefly ent fnl f: sn one pce* **15/2**

6355 5 3/4 **Miningold**[35] 3611 3-9-6 **63** JamesSullivan 9 61+
(Tim Easterby) *in tch: hdwy whn nt clr run over 1f out to ent fnl f: rdn and sn no imp* **3/1**[1]

556 6 3 **Summer Isles**[83] 2050 6-9-12 **65** JackGarritty 8 50
(Paul Midgley) *t.k.h: led to over 1f out: rdn and wknd fnl f* **3/1**[1]

0000 7 1 1/4 **Lowrie**[41] 3423 3-8-1 **49** 3ex oh1 NathanEvans[(5)] 2 29
(John David Riches) *dwlt: bhd on outside: rdn and drifted rt fr 2f out: sn btn* **40/1**

-605 8 5 **Ya Boy Sir (IRE)**[21] 4096 9-8-7 **46** oh1 (p) GeorgeChaloner 4 9
(Iain Jardine) *dwlt: hld up: drvn along over 2f out: wknd over 1f out* **20/1**

59.75s (-0.65) **Going Correction** -0.175s/f (Firm)
WFA 3 from 4yo+ 4lb **8** Ran SP% **114.8**
Speed ratings (Par 101): **98,97,96,94,93 88,86,78**
CSF £62.43 CT £233.44 TOTE £6.00: £1.50, £2.80, £1.70; EX 69.80 Trifecta £186.10.
Owner Dave Scott **Bred** Dave Scott **Trained** Station Town, Co Durham

FOCUS
A low-grade sprint handicap featuring mainly exposed sorts but the pace was sound.
T/Plt: £57.30 to a £1 stake. Pool: £26,230.00 - 457.38 winning tickets T/Qpdt: £30.80 to a £1 stake. Pool: £3,266.00 - 105.80 winning tickets **Richard Young**

4649 NEWMARKET (R-H)
Friday, July 29

OFFICIAL GOING: Good to firm
Wind: Light behind Weather: Cloudy with sunny spells

4835 DISCOVERNEWMARKET.CO.UK H'CAP 6f
5:20 (5:21) (Class 5) (0-75,75) 3-Y-O **£3,234** (£962; £481; £240) **Stalls** High

Form RPR

3331 1 **Lajatico**[9] 4525 3-9-9 **75** 6ex HarryBentley 2 91
(Ed Vaughan) *hld up: racd keenly: hdwy to ld 2f out: shkn up ins fnl f: r.o wl* **13/8**[1]

-303 2 3 3/4 **Mazzini**[51] 3036 3-9-7 **73** FrederikTylicki 9 77
(James Fanshawe) *trckd ldrs: rdn to chse wnr and edgd rt over 1f out: no ex wl ins fnl f* **9/4**[2]

1222 3 1 3/4 **Caitie (IRE)**[14] 4365 3-9-1 **72** (t) CallumShepherd[(5)] 1 70
(Paul Cole) *hld up: hdwy over 2f out: shkn up over 1f out: styd on same pce fnl f* **7/1**

1 4 1 3/4 **African Blessing**[121] 1151 3-9-5 **71** GrahamGibbons 8 64
(David Barron) *s.i.s: plld hrd and sn prom: led over 4f out: rdn and hdd 1f out: wknd ins fnl f* **5/1**[3]

0004 5 3 1/2 **Perfectly Fair**[9] 4517 3-7-9 **54** oh1 HollieDoyle[(7)] 7 36
(Simon West) *prom tl rdn and wknd over 1f out* **40/1**

0-36 6 1 1/2 **Poplar**[29] 3822 3-8-6 **58** TomMarquand 11 35
(Robyn Brisland) *disp ld tl over 4f out: remained handy: rdn over 2f out: sn ev ch: wknd over 1f out* **33/1**

6066 7 1/2 **Dark Forest**[4] 4714 3-8-11 **70** SophieKilloran[(7)] 6 45
(Simon West) *disp ld tl over 4f out: chsd ldrs tl rdn and wknd over 1f out* **20/1**

0000 8 1/2 **Show Legend**[35] 3604 3-8-6 **65** (p) LuluStanford[(7)] 3 39
(Michael Bell) *chsd ldrs: ev ch over 2f out: rdn and wknd over 1f out* **20/1**

00 9 13 **Lady Lloyd**[100] 1574 3-8-3 **58** (v) JosephineGordon[(3)] 4
(Phil McEntee) *in rr and sn pushed along: rdn and wknd over 2f out* **40/1**

1m 12.36s (-0.14) **Going Correction** +0.05s/f (Good) **9** Ran SP% **115.4**
Speed ratings (Par 100): **102,97,94,92,87 85,85,84,67**
CSF £5.00 CT £17.68 TOTE £2.40: £1.10, £1.40, £1.90; EX 5.90 Trifecta £14.60.
Owner D A Thorpe **Bred** Meon Valley Stud **Trained** Newmarket, Suffolk

The Form Book, Raceform Ltd, Newbury, RG14 5SJ

FOCUS
Far side used. Stalls on far side except 1m2f and 1m4f, centre. There was just 1.5mm of rain on Wednesday and a further 2.5mm on Thursday, and the going was given as good to firm (GoingStick: 7.8). The re-positioning of the bend into the home straight increased the distance of the 1m2f and 1m4f races by 13yds. A fair handicap won by an improving filly who is ahead of her mark. The runner-up is rated to form.

4836 PRICE BAILEY CHARTERED ACCOUNTANTS H'CAP 1m 4f
5:50 (5:50) (Class 5) (0-70,67) 3-Y-O **£3,234** (£962; £481; £240) **Stalls** Centre

Form RPR
2653 **1** **Duck A L'Orange (IRE)**[14] 4372 3-9-7 **67**..................(p) FrederikTylicki 2 75
(Michael Bell) *mde all: shkn up over 1f out: styd on wl: comf* **7/2**[1]
0-54 **2** 2 1/4 **Mamoo**[22] 4046 3-8-12 **58**.................................... HarryBentley 5 62
(Mike Murphy) *s.i.s: hld up: swtchd lft over 4f out: hdwy u.p and edgd rt over 1f out: chsd wnr ins fnl f: styd on same pce* **4/1**[2]
4-05 **3** 1/2 **Iona Island**[14] 4367 3-9-6 **66**.................................... DaneO'Neill 6 69
(Charles Hills) *hld up: hdwy over 3f out: chsd wnr over 2f out: sn rdn: styd on same pce ins fnl f* **6/1**
006 **4** 1 1/4 **Always Summer**[16] 4265 3-8-11 **64**............................ GeorgeWood(7) 4 65
(James Fanshawe) *hld up: racd keenly: rdn over 2f out: no imp fnl f* **4/1**[2]
6030 **5** 2 1/4 **Pennerley**[43] 3318 3-9-6 **66**.................................... RyanTate 1 63
(James Eustace) *chsd ldrs: rdn over 2f out: nt clr run over 1f out: wknd ins fnl f* **7/2**[1]
-633 **6** 9 **Free Bounty**[35] 3615 3-9-0 **60**.................................... RichardMullen 3 43
(Philip McBride) *chsd wnr: wnt upsides over 5f tl rdn over 3f out: wknd over 1f out* **11/2**[3]

2m 33.31s (0.41) **Going Correction** +0.05s/f (Good) **6** Ran SP% **114.1**
Speed ratings (Par 100): **100,98,98,97,95 89**
CSF £18.06 TOTE £4.10: £2.10, £2.40; EX 16.90 Trifecta £125.60.
Owner J Barnett & M Caine **Bred** Hascombe And Valiant Studs **Trained** Newmarket, Suffolk
FOCUS
Race distance increased by 13yds. This modest handicap lacked improvers and was dominated from the front by the winner.

4837 NGK SPARK PLUGS EBF STALLIONS MAIDEN STKS (PLUS 10 RACE) 6f
6:25 (6:25) (Class 4) 2-Y-O **£4,528** (£1,347; £673; £336) **Stalls** High

Form RPR
40 **1** **Monoshka (IRE)**[21] 4075 2-9-5 0.................................... TomMarquand 2 76+
(Richard Hannon) *w ldr: rdn over 2f out: led wl ins fnl f: r.o* **5/4**[1]
0 **2** 1/2 **Curve Ball (IRE)**[29] 3813 2-9-5 0.................................... ShaneKelly 5 74
(Richard Hughes) *led: rdn and edgd rt over 1f out: hdd wl ins fnl f: styd on u.p* **11/1**
3 2 **Dark Destroyer (IRE)** 2-9-5 0.................................... JFEgan 1 68
(Joseph Tuite) *wnt rt s: hld up: hdwy over 2f out: rdn to chal over 1f out: edgd rt and no ex wl ins fnl f* **10/1**
4 shd **Bizet (IRE)** 2-9-5 0.................................... DannyBrock 3 68
(John Ryan) *prom: rdn over 1f out: styd on same pce fnl f* **25/1**
2 **5** hd **Sakurajima (IRE)**[53] 2976 2-9-5 0.................................... DaneO'Neill 4 67
(Charles Hills) *s.i.s: hld up: hdwy over 1f out: sn rdn: styd on same pce fnl f* **5/2**[2]
6 3 3/4 **Tea El Tee (IRE)** 2-9-5 0.................................... DarrylHolland 7 55
(Gay Kelleway) *hld up: shkn up over 2f out: nt trble ldrs* **25/1**
05 **7** 5 **Ripper Street (IRE)**[10] 4473 2-9-5 0.................................... FrederikTylicki 6 39
(Ed Dunlop) *plld hrd and sn prom: edgd lft and wknd over 1f out* **6/1**[3]

1m 14.58s (2.08) **Going Correction** +0.05s/f (Good) **7** Ran SP% **112.4**
Speed ratings (Par 96): **88,87,84,84,84 79,72**
CSF £15.97 TOTE £2.20: £1.40, £4.80; EX 12.80 Trifecta £77.10.
Owner Michael Geoghegan **Bred** Lynn Lodge Stud **Trained** East Everleigh, Wilts
FOCUS
An ordinary maiden. The field finished compressed in a slow time.

4838 EVEREST HARRY LAUD CLASSIC H'CAP 1m 2f
7:00 (7:00) (Class 3) (0-90,89) 3-Y-O+ **£7,762** (£2,310; £1,154; £577) **Stalls** Centre

Form RPR
0423 **1** **Brorocco**[18] 4213 3-8-3 **74**.................................... JimmyQuinn 2 84+
(Andrew Balding) *hld up: hdwy to ld over 1f out: rdn and r.o wl* **13/2**[3]
1534 **2** 2 **Wild Hacked (USA)**[21] 4108 3-8-13 **84**.................................... HarryBentley 4 90
(Marco Botti) *chsd ldrs: rdn and ev ch over 1f out: styd on same pce ins fnl f* **11/10**[1]
4212 **3** 1/2 **The Gay Cavalier**[8] 4555 5-8-10 **74**..................(t) JosephineGordon(3) 1 79
(John Ryan) *a.p: rdn over 2f out: styd on same pce ins fnl f* **8/1**
1 **4** 2 **Erhaaf (USA)**[134] 968 4-9-9 **84**.................................... DaneO'Neill 3 85
(Owen Burrows) *chsd ldr: rdn over 2f out: ev ch over 1f out: no ex ins fnl f* **4/1**[2]
0511 **5** 3/4 **Nigel**[24] 3972 4-9-11 **86**.................................... ShaneKelly 6 86
(Richard Hughes) *led: rdn and hdd over 1f out: wknd wl ins fnl f* **7/1**
003 **6** 1 1/2 **Shell Bay (USA)**[30] 3785 4-10-0 **89**..........................(b[1]) TomMarquand 5 86
(Richard Hannon) *hld up in tch: effrt on outer over 2f out: wknd fnl f* **11/1**

2m 5.12s (-0.38) **Going Correction** +0.05s/f (Good)
WFA 3 from 4yo+ 10lb **6** Ran SP% **112.9**
Speed ratings (Par 107): **103,101,101,99,98 97**
CSF £14.40 TOTE £7.40: £2.80, £1.30; EX 16.20 Trifecta £62.30.
Owner Kingsclere Racing Club **Bred** Kingsclere Stud **Trained** Kingsclere, Hants
FOCUS
Race distance increased by 13yds. Not a bad handicap, and the 3yos finished 1-2.

4839 EBM-PAPST H'CAP 7f
7:35 (7:35) (Class 4) (0-85,83) 4-Y-O+ **£5,175** (£1,540; £769; £384) **Stalls** High

Form RPR
6-31 **1** **Alnashama**[20] 4157 4-9-1 **77**.................................... DaneO'Neill 3 89
(Charles Hills) *hld up: hdwy 1/2-way: rdn to ld over 1f out: hung lft ins fnl f: r.o* **4/1**[2]
-000 **2** hd **Carnival King (IRE)**[54] 2934 4-9-6 **82**..........................(b) TomQueally 6 93
(Brian Meehan) *sn led: rdn and hdd over 1f out: hung lft ins fnl f: r.o* **20/1**
4052 **3** 3 1/2 **Baltic Brave (IRE)**[7] 4599 5-9-2 **83**..........................(t) CharlieBennett(5) 4 85
(Hughie Morrison) *hld up: hdwy u.p over 1f out: styd on same pce ins fnl f: wnt 3rd nr fin* **9/2**[3]
5303 **4** 1/2 **Steal The Scene (IRE)**[10] 4474 4-9-2 **78**.................................... TomMarquand 7 79
(Richard Hannon) *led early: chsd ldrs: wnt 2nd over 2f out tl rdn over 1f out: no ex ins fnl f* **15/2**
0000 **5** 2 1/4 **Varsovian**[51] 3035 6-9-1 **77**..........................(v[1]) RenatoSouza 9 72
(Dean Ivory) *sn chsng ldr: rdn and lost 2nd over 2f out: edgd lft over 1f out: wknd ins fnl f* **20/1**
1253 **6** 2 1/4 **He's My Boy (IRE)**[14] 4362 5-8-1 **70**.................................... GeorgeWood(7) 5 59
(James Fanshawe) *hld up: hdwy 2f out: wknd ins fnl f* **11/2**
0305 **7** 4 1/2 **Athletic**[13] 4402 7-8-6 **71**..........................(v) JosephineGordon(3) 1 49
(Andrew Reid) *s.i.s: hld up: rdn over 2f out: wknd over 1f out* **11/2**
01 **8** 2 1/4 **Bunbury**[11] 4463 4-9-3 **79** 6ex.................................... ShaneKelly 8 51
(Richard Hughes) *chsd ldrs: rdn over 2f out: wknd over 1f out* **11/4**[1]

1m 24.1s (-1.60) **Going Correction** +0.05s/f (Good) **8** Ran SP% **116.9**
Speed ratings (Par 105): **111,110,106,106,103 101,95,93**
CSF £77.97 CT £369.26 TOTE £4.70: £1.60, £4.50, £1.40; EX 85.50 Trifecta £783.00.
Owner Hamdan Al Maktoum **Bred** Shadwell Estate Company Limited **Trained** Lambourn, Berks
FOCUS
The first two finished nicely clear and the form looks sound for the grade.

4840 RACING UK HD MAIDEN STKS 1m
8:05 (8:06) (Class 5) 3-Y-O+ **£3,881** (£1,155; £577; £288) **Stalls** High

Form RPR
4-2 **1** **In The City**[13] 4401 3-9-5 0.................................... PatCosgrave 3 78+
(William Haggas) *a.p: rdn over 1f out: r.o to ld wl ins fnl f* **8/11**[1]
-004 **2** 1 **Ocean Eleven**[4] 4709 3-9-2 77.................................... JosephineGordon(3) 8 76
(John Ryan) *chsd ldr: pushed along over 2f out: rdn to ld ins fnl f: sn hdd: styd on* **8/1**
3 1/2 **Chiefofchiefs** 3-9-5 0.................................... StevieDonohoe 2 75
(Charlie Fellowes) *s.i.s: hld up: hdwy over 2f out: rdn and ev ch whn edgd rt ins fnl f: kpt on* **9/1**
06 **4** shd **Iberica Road (USA)**[20] 4156 3-8-12 0..........................(t) WilliamCox(7) 9 75
(Andrew Balding) *led: clr 6f out tl over 2f out: rdn and edgd rt over 1f out: hdd ins fnl f: styd on same pce* **25/1**
5 4 **Howilat (USA)** 3-9-0 0.................................... MartinLane 6 60+
(Charlie Appleby) *hld up: rdn over 1f out: no imp fnl f* **5/2**[2]
0 **6** 6 **Enmeshing**[22] 4056 3-9-5 0.................................... TomQueally 7 51
(James Fanshawe) *s.i.s: hld up: rdn over 1f out: wknd fnl f* **6/1**[3]
0 **7** 7 **Briac (FR)**[6] 4657 5-9-13 0.................................... JFEgan 5 36
(Jim Best) *s.i.s: hld up: wknd over 2f out* **33/1**
8 2 **Q Cee** 3-9-5 0.................................... RichardMullen 4 29
(Eugene Stanford) *chsd ldrs: rdn over 3f out: wknd over 1f out* **33/1**

1m 40.19s (0.19) **Going Correction** +0.05s/f (Good)
WFA 3 from 5yo 8lb **8** Ran SP% **131.6**
Speed ratings (Par 103): **101,100,99,99,95 89,82,80**
CSF £9.94 TOTE £1.70: £1.10, £2.20, £3.20; EX 8.10 Trifecta £41.90.
Owner Simon Munir & Isaac Souede **Bred** Miss K Rausing **Trained** Newmarket, Suffolk
FOCUS
Just a fair maiden.

4841 QAV 15TH ANNIVERSARY CELEBRATION H'CAP 1m
8:35 (8:36) (Class 4) (0-80,80) 3-Y-O+ **£5,175** (£1,540; £769; £384) **Stalls** High

Form RPR
-136 **1** **Easter Mate (IRE)**[20] 4139 3-9-6 **80**..................(p) MartinLane 5 87+
(Ralph Beckett) *chsd ldr: rdn over 2f out: led ins fnl f: r.o* **7/2**[1]
0463 **2** 3/4 **Holy Grail (IRE)**[14] 4358 3-8-12 **79**.................................... HollieDoyle(7) 7 84
(Simon West) *led: clr 5f out tl rdn over 1f out: hdd ins fnl f: styd on* **7/1**
0132 **3** 1 1/4 **Exceeding Power**[22] 4058 5-8-13 **72**.................................... GeorgeWood(7) 11 76
(Martin Bosley) *hld up: racd keenly: hdwy over 2f out: rdn over 1f out: r.o* **9/2**[2]
5-00 **4** nk **Mister Music**[60] 2734 7-9-12 **78**.................................... TomMarquand 2 81+
(Tony Carroll) *hmpd s: hld up: rdn over 1f out: r.o ins fnl f: nt rch ldrs* **14/1**
15 **5** nk **Lawyer (IRE)**[13] 4408 5-9-7 **73**.................................... GrahamGibbons 9 76
(David Barron) *hld up: rdn over 2f out: r.o ins fnl f: nt rch ldrs* **8/1**
4255 **6** 3 1/4 **Rebel Lightning (IRE)**[23] 4010 3-8-13 **76**............(p) LouisSteward(3) 12 69
(Richard Spencer) *hld up: rdn over 2f out: hdwy over 1f out: styd on same pce ins fnl f* **5/1**[3]
3120 **7** 3 **Gulland Rock**[6] 4640 5-8-12 **64**.................................... JimmyQuinn 4 52
(Anthony Carson) *prom: rdn over 2f out: wknd fnl f* **25/1**
-230 **8** 3/4 **Stoked (IRE)**[14] 4362 4-9-4 **73**.................................... JosephineGordon(3) 10 60
(Chris Dwyer) *plld hrd and prom: rdn over 2f out: wknd fnl f* **20/1**
-341 **9** 2 1/2 **Hitman**[14] 4354 3-9-4 **78**.................................... SamHitchcott 3 57
(William Muir) *edgd rt s: hld up: rdn over 2f out: wknd fnl f* **9/2**[2]
020 **10** 1/2 **Western Way (IRE)**[17] 4235 7-9-8 **74**..........................(p) JFEgan 1 54
(Don Cantillon) *hld up: lost tch 2f out: eased fnl f* **20/1**

1m 39.81s (-0.19) **Going Correction** +0.05s/f (Good)
WFA 3 from 4yo+ 8lb **10** Ran SP% **118.9**
Speed ratings (Par 105): **102,101,100,99,99 96,93,92,89,89**
CSF £28.14 CT £113.94 TOTE £4.10: £1.30, £2.40, £1.80; EX 34.20 Trifecta £161.50.
Owner Robert Ng **Bred** J Hanly **Trained** Kimpton, Hants
FOCUS
The early gallop wasn't strong and it proved hard to challenge from off the pace.
T/Plt: £31.80 to a £1 stake. Pool: £52,129.28 - 1,193.11 winning tickets T/Qpdt: £6.70 to a £1 stake. Pool: £5,463.75 - 596.42 winning tickets **Colin Roberts**

4600 THIRSK (L-H)
Friday, July 29

OFFICIAL GOING: Good to soft (good in places; 7.4)
Wind: almost nil Weather: becoming fine and sunny

4842 £25 FREE BET AT 188BET (S) STKS 6f
1:50 (1:50) (Class 6) 2-Y-O **£2,587** (£770; £384; £192) **Stalls** High

Form RPR
00 **1** **Bismarck The Flyer (IRE)**[10] 4473 2-9-0 0.................................... TedDurcan 1 65
(Richard Hannon) *carried lft s: hld up: hdwy and trckd ldr over 2f out: led appr fnl f: pushed out* **9/2**[3]
2032 **2** 1 3/4 **London Grammar (IRE)**[9] 4509 2-8-9 0..........................(v[1]) JasonHart 3 54
(John Quinn) *t.k.h: trckd ldrs: led 2f out: hdd appr fnl f: fnd v little* **5/4**[1]
05 **3** 4 1/2 **Amy Gardner**[13] 4404 2-8-4 0.................................... NathanEvans(5) 5 40
(James Given) *chsd ldrs: pushed along over 2f out: swtchd lft over 1f out: tk modest 3rd last 150yds* **11/1**
5054 **4** 6 **Shadow Wing (IRE)**[23] 4002 2-8-9 0.................................... PJMcDonald 4 20
(Tom Dascombe) *trckd ldrs: wknd fnl f* **5/2**[2]
0320 **5** 3 1/2 **Irish Melody (IRE)**[17] 4221 2-9-0 0..........................(b[1]) DuranFentiman 2 14
(Bill Turner) *wnt lft s: led: hdd 2f out: lost pl fnl f* **9/1**
0 **6** 10 **Anshika (IRE)**[13] 4404 2-8-7 0 ow1..........................(p) JacobButterfield(3) 6
(Ollie Pears) *chsd ldrs: drvn over 4f out: lost pl wl over 1f out: sn wl bhd* **50/1**

1m 13.71s (1.01) **Going Correction** +0.10s/f (Good) **6** Ran SP% **111.5**
Speed ratings (Par 92): **97,94,88,80,76 62**
CSF £10.46 TOTE £5.30: £2.40, £1.30; EX 12.00 Trifecta £45.80.The winner was sold to Ollie Pears for £6,500.
Owner Leech, Morecombe, Anderson, Durkan **Bred** Edgeridge Ltd **Trained** East Everleigh, Wilts

FOCUS
The home bend was dolled out by approximately 6yds, adding around 20yds to the distances for all races of 7f and upwards. This was a weak seller won by a horse who had shown very little in two maidens.

4843 BRITISH STALLION STUDS 188BET.CO.UK EBF FILLIES' NURSERY H'CAP 5f
2:20 (2:21) (Class 4) 2-Y-O **£6,469** (£1,925; £962; £481) **Stalls** High

Form RPR
063 **1** **Savannah Slew**[40] 3433 2-8-9 **68** AndrewMullen 1 75+
(James Given) *dwlt: hdwy and swtchd rt jst over 2f out: chsd ldrs over 1f out: styd on wl to ld last 75yds* **7/1**[3]
0153 **2** *2* **Miss Rosina (IRE)**[33] 3686 2-8-3 **69** JaneElliott(7) 4 69
(George Margarson) *t.k.h: w ldr: led over 3f out: hdd and no ex last 75yds* **10/1**
053 **3** *3 3/4* **Samran Says (IRE)**[32] 3707 2-8-0 **59** PatrickMathers 5 46
(Richard Fahey) *hmpd s: sn chsng ldrs: one pce over 1f out* **11/1**
4062 **4** *1* **Coco La Belle (IRE)**[13] 4404 2-8-1 **60** DuranFentiman 8 43
(Tim Easterby) *wnt lft s: led over 1f: one pce over 1f out* **10/1**
4312 **5** *1* **Lexington Sky (IRE)**[37] 3511 2-9-7 **80** TedDurcan 2 59
(Richard Hannon) *chsd ldrs: one pce fnl 2f* **11/4**[2]
61 **6** *2 1/2* **Nile Empress**[23] 4022 2-9-5 **78** JackMitchell 7 48+
(Hugo Palmer) *hmpd s: chsd ldrs: hmpd and lost pl jst over 2f out* **6/5**[1]
59.85s (0.25) **Going Correction** +0.10s/f (Good) **6** Ran SP% **111.1**
Speed ratings (Par 93): **102,98,92,91,89 85**
CSF £66.65 CT £735.59 TOTE £8.30: £3.00, £3.80; EX 62.60 Trifecta £232.20.
Owner Dachel Stud **Bred** Dachel Stud **Trained** Willoughton, Lincs
■ Stewards' Enquiry : Andrew Mullen two-day ban: careless riding (12-13 Aug)

FOCUS
With both market leaders disappointing this might not be the strongest nursery form for the grade. The front two pulled clear though and both have some upside.

4844 TOMRODS STEEL H'CAP 1m
2:55 (2:55) (Class 5) (0-70,76) 3-Y-O **£3,234** (£962; £481; £240) **Stalls** Low

Form RPR
0561 **1** **Imperial State**[6] 4656 3-9-13 **76** 6ex (t) TedDurcan 3 85+
(George Scott) *sn trcking ldrs: smooth hdwy to ld over 2f out: wnt clr appr fnl f: heavily eased clsng stages* **11/10**[1]
0000 **2** *2 1/4* **Quoteline Direct**[17] 4241 3-9-4 **67** PJMcDonald 5 66
(Micky Hammond) *mid-div: drvn to chse ldrs over 2f out: kpt on same pce appr fnl f: tk modest 2nd post* **11/1**
0640 **3** *hd* **Mr Lucas (IRE)**[28] 3838 3-8-0 **54** oh6 ow3 (v) NathanEvans(5) 8 53
(Peter Niven) *led 1f: chsd ldrs: kpt on same pce appr fnl f* **33/1**
0030 **4** *nk* **Ginger Charlie**[8] 4567 3-8-2 **51** oh6 JamesSullivan 7 49
(Ruth Carr) *in rr: hdwy on outer over 2f out: kpt on same pce fnl f: tk modest 4th clsng stages* **50/1**
6430 **5** *3/4* **Weld Al Khawaneej (IRE)**[3] 4730 3-8-7 **63** (p) LewisEdmunds(7) 1 59+
(Kevin Ryan) *t.k.h: trckd ldrs: n.m.r and dropped bk 2f out: styd on fnl 100yds* **8/1**[3]
0542 **6** *nk* **Lozah**[7] 4600 3-7-13 **55** (tp) CameronNoble(7) 2 50
(David Loughnane) *stdd s: hld up in rr: hdwy on wd outside over 2f out: kpt on same pce fnl f* **6/1**[2]
-001 **7** *3 3/4* **Tan Arabiq**[17] 4241 3-9-3 **66** AndrewMullen 9 53
(Michael Appleby) *chsd ldrs on outer: drvn over 3f out: wknd fnl f* **8/1**[3]
-000 **8** *1 1/2* **Baltic Raider (IRE)**[31] 3753 3-9-7 **70** BarryMcHugh 12 53
(Michael Dods) *rn wout declared tongue strap: hld up in rr on outer: hdwy over 2f out: sn chsng ldrs: wknd fnl f* **40/1**
3630 **9** *1* **Saxon Gold (IRE)**[38] 3479 3-8-5 **54** (b[1]) SamJames 6 35
(John Davies) *w ldr: led after 1f: hdd over 2f out: sn wknd* **9/1**
435 **10** *1/2* **Hilltop Ranger (IRE)**[23] 3996 3-9-6 **69** TimmyMurphy 4 49
(Daniel Kubler) *hld up in rr: hdwy on ins over 2f out: wknd over 1f out* **12/1**
1m 43.81s (3.71) **Going Correction** +0.325s/f (Good) **10** Ran SP% **117.5**
Speed ratings (Par 100): **94,91,91,91,90 90,86,84,83,83**
CSF £14.75 CT £273.03 TOTE £2.00: £1.10, £3.40, £8.00; EX 15.40 Trifecta £331.40.
Owner The Harnage Partnership **Bred** Biddestone Stud Ltd **Trained** Newmarket, Suffolk

FOCUS
Add 20yds to race distance. This otherwise open but very modest handicap was turned into a procession by the one horse in the field who had looked ahead of his mark, and was value for 4l.

4845 PROJECT MANAGEMENT SCOTLAND MAIDEN STKS 5f
3:30 (3:30) (Class 5) 3-4-Y-O **£2,911** (£866; £432; £216) **Stalls** High

Form RPR
3-22 **1** **Magical Effect (IRE)**[10] 4496 4-9-9 74 JamesSullivan 6 74+
(Ruth Carr) *trckd ldrs: nt clr run on ins over 1f out: swtchd lft: styd on to ld last 100yds* **8/13**[1]
542- **2** *1 1/2* **Wernotfamusanymore (IRE)**[277] 7515 3-9-5 73 KeaganLatham 3 68
(Kevin Ryan) *led: hdd and no ex last 100yds* **7/2**[2]
5 **3** *hd* **By The Law**[9] 4521 3-9-2 0 RachelRichardson(3) 5 67
(Tim Easterby) *sn outpcd and drvn along detached in last: hdwy over 2f out: chsng ldrs over 1f out: kpt on same pce* **16/1**[3]
33- **4** *2* **Head East (IRE)**[405] 3390 3-9-5 0 AndrewMullen 1 60
(Ivan Furtado) *w ldr: drvn and rdr dropped whip over 1f out: hung lft and wknd fnl 150yds* **7/2**[2]
0-60 **5** *1/2* **Compton Mews**[10] 4492 3-9-0 15 BarryMcHugh 4 53?
(Les Eyre) *t.k.h: trckd ldrs: hung lft over 1f out: wknd fnl 150yds* **100/1**
1m 0.53s (0.93) **Going Correction** +0.10s/f (Good)
WFA 3 from 4yo 4lb **5** Ran SP% **113.2**
Speed ratings (Par 103): **96,93,93,90,89**
CSF £3.34 TOTE £1.50: £1.10, £2.00; EX 3.60 Trifecta £13.40.
Owner Miss Vanessa Church **Bred** W Maxwell Ervine **Trained** Huby, N Yorks

FOCUS
Nothing special in this maiden and it was won by a horse who had run well in defeat in handicaps the last twice, off marks in the low-to-mid 70s. THe winner didn't need to match his recent handicap efforts.

4846 BREEDERS BACKING RACING 188BET EBF CONDITIONS STKS 7f
4:05 (4:05) (Class 3) 3-Y-O+ **£9,056** (£2,695; £1,346; £673) **Stalls** Low

Form RPR
2402 **1** **Coulsty (IRE)**[27] 3891 5-9-4 104 (b) TedDurcan 5 111
(Richard Hannon) *wnt rt s: trckd ldrs: 2nd over 4f out: led over 2f out: drvn over 1f out: styd on wl* **1/1**[1]
4146 **2** *2* **Sound Advice**[5] 4688 7-9-4 102 PhillipMakin 4 106
(Keith Dalgleish) *trckd ldrs: drvn 3f out: 2nd over 1f out: kpt on same pce* **11/4**[2]
0640 **3** *5* **Birdman (IRE)**[20] 4165 6-9-4 100 SamJames 3 93
(David O'Meara) *chsd ldrs: drvn and outpcd over 4f out: modest 3rd 1f out: one pce* **7/2**[3]
0400 **4** *8* **B Fifty Two (IRE)**[20] 4152 7-9-6 97 MichaelJMMurphy 1 74
(Charles Hills) *led: hdd over 2f out: wknd over 1f out: eased clsng stages* **10/1**
1m 27.59s (0.39) **Going Correction** +0.325s/f (Good) **4** Ran SP% **108.0**
Speed ratings (Par 107): **110,107,102,92**
CSF £3.98 TOTE £1.80; EX 3.90 Trifecta £4.60.
Owner Lord Vestey **Bred** Peter & Sarah Fortune **Trained** East Everleigh, Wilts

FOCUS
Add 20yds to race distance. A reasonable conditions race but most of these had a bit to prove on recent efforts. The winner is rated to this year's form.

4847 MARKET CROSS JEWELLERS H'CAP 1m 4f
4:40 (4:40) (Class 6) (0-65,61) 3-Y-O **£2,587** (£770; £384; £192) **Stalls** High

Form RPR
4136 **1** **High On Light**[9] 4522 3-8-11 **54** RachelRichardson(3) 3 68+
(Tim Easterby) *hld up: hdwy to trck ldrs over 4f out: shkn up to ld over 1f out: sn clr: eased nr fin* **9/4**[1]
4442 **2** *5* **Becky The Thatcher**[16] 4255 3-9-7 **61** PJMcDonald 4 64
(Micky Hammond) *mid-div: hdwy and handy 3rd over 3f out: 2nd over 1f out: no ch w wnr* **5/2**[2]
6105 **3** *nk* **Rainbow Lad (IRE)**[16] 4255 3-9-1 **55** BenCurtis 7 58
(Michael Appleby) *trckd ldrs: led over 3f out: hdd over 1f out: one pce* **7/2**[3]
-000 **4** *11* **Top Of The Rocks (FR)**[16] 4255 3-9-1 **55** (vt) LiamJones 5 40
(Tom Dascombe) *led: hdd over 3f out: wknd over 2f out* **10/1**
3006 **5** *28* **Lady Canford (IRE)**[25] 3949 3-9-3 **57** TedDurcan 2
(James Bethell) *s.s: in rr: mod 5th over 3f out: sn bhd: eased over 1f out* **8/1**
0405 **6** *40* **Jon H The Lawman (IRE)**[17] 4233 3-8-5 **45** AndrewElliott 6
(Ronald Thompson) *chsd ldr: drvn over 6f out: lost pl over 4f out: sn bhd: t.o and eased fnl 2f* **16/1**
0-00 **7** *20* **Cockney Boy**[31] 3736 3-9-7 **61** MichaelJMMurphy 1
(John Gallagher) *mid-div: reminders and lost pl over 5f out: t.o 3f out: virtually p.u* **22/1**
2m 41.64s (5.44) **Going Correction** +0.325s/f (Good) **7** Ran SP% **112.0**
Speed ratings (Par 98): **94,90,90,83,64 37,24**
CSF £7.77 TOTE £3.30: £1.80, £1.20; EX 8.10 Trifecta £16.10.
Owner Habton Farms **Bred** Highclere Stud **Trained** Great Habton, N Yorks

FOCUS
Add 20yds to race distance. A very weak handicap in which few made any meaningful impact and the winner looks the only one of these who can hold her own at a higher level. The form is rated around the second and third.

4848 188BET GO RACING IN YORKSHIRE FUTURE STARS APPRENTICE H'CAP 6f
5:15 (5:18) (Class 5) (0-70,70) 3-Y-O+ **£2,911** (£866; £432; £216) **Stalls** High

Form RPR
6-50 **1** **Safe Voyage (IRE)**[22] 4041 3-9-4 **67** LewisEdmunds(2) 10 77
(John Quinn) *towards rr: hmpd after 2f: hdwy 2f out: styd on to ld last 75yds: drvn out* **4/1**[2]
-000 **2** *2 1/2* **Cuppatee (IRE)**[25] 3948 3-9-3 **64** RowanScott 7 65
(Ann Duffield) *in rr: outpcd over 3f out: hdwy and swtchd rt over 1f out: sn chsng ldrs: kpt on to take 2nd post* **20/1**
-010 **3** *shd* **Space War**[56] 2872 9-9-9 **65** (t) AnnaHesketh 3 67
(Michael Easterby) *mid-div: hdwy over 2f out: led briefly last 150yds: kpt on same pce* **20/1**
4000 **4** *1* **Carlovian**[24] 3988 3-8-0 **51** oh1 LiamLewis-Salter(4) 11 48
(Christopher Kellett) *mid-div: hdwy and swtchd rt over 2f out: chsng ldrs over 1f out: kpt on same pce* **40/1**
0043 **5** *1/2* **Fyrecracker (IRE)**[7] 4608 5-9-12 **70** CliffordLee(2) 5 67
(Grant Tuer) *w ldrs: led over 1f out: hdd last 150yds: kpt on same pce* **2/1**[1]
R556 **6** *1/2* **Teetotal (IRE)**[2] 4770 6-8-12 **56** (b) DanielleMooney(2) 8 51
(Nigel Tinkler) *t.k.h: mid-div: hdwy to chse ldrs over 1f out: n.m.r 150yds out: kpt on one pce* **8/1**
0030 **7** *1 3/4* **Tavener**[2] 4770 4-9-7 **65** PatrickVaughan(2) 9 54
(David O'Meara) *rr-div: edgd rt after 2f: drvn over 2f out: kpt on: nvr a factor* **11/2**[3]
0001 **8** *1 1/4* **Bold Spirit**[30] 3777 5-9-2 **60** (bt) BenRobinson(2) 4 44
(Declan Carroll) *led: hdd over 1f out: grad wknd* **16/1**
5050 **9** *1* **Jacob's Pillow**[15] 4291 5-9-8 **66** HarryBurns(2) 2 46
(Rebecca Bastiman) *racd wd: chsd ldrs: edgd rt appr fnl f: sn wknd* **10/1**
0020 **10** *11* **Llewellyn**[27] 3880 8-9-7 **65** (b) GerO'Neill(2) 1 6
(Declan Carroll) *racd wd: chsd ldrs: wknd over 1f out: sn eased* **12/1**
0040 **11** *28* **Clon Rocket (IRE)**[15] 4321 3-8-11 **62** (b) MeganEllingworth(4) 6
(John Holt) *uns rdr and rn loose to s: mid-div: lost pl over 2f out: bhd whn heavily eased over 1f out: t.o* **25/1**
1m 12.83s (0.13) **Going Correction** +0.10s/f (Good)
WFA 3 from 4yo+ 5lb **11** Ran SP% **118.3**
Speed ratings (Par 103): **103,99,99,98,97 96,94,92,91,76 39**
CSF £86.12 CT £1467.40 TOTE £5.40: £1.70, £5.90, £5.90; EX 82.00 Trifecta £874.00.
Owner Ross Harmon **Bred** Schneider Adolf **Trained** Settrington, N Yorks
■ Stewards' Enquiry : Lewis Edmunds caution: careless riding

FOCUS
A weak handicap which looked wide open entering the final furlong but the unexposed winner burst through towards the stands rail and forged clear. There are some doubts over the form.
T/Plt: £59.80 to a £1 stake. Pool: £41,544.09 - 507.05 winning tickets T/Qpdt: £3.60 to a £1 stake. Pool: £3,142.80 - 642.70 winning tickets **Walter Glynn**

4849a (Foreign Racing) - See Raceform Interactive

4811 GALWAY (R-H)

Friday, July 29

OFFICIAL GOING: Flat course - yielding (yielding to soft in places); jumps courses - good (good to yielding in places)

4850a GUINNESS H'CAP (PREMIER HANDICAP) 1m 4f

6:50 (6:51) 3-Y-O+

£43,382 (£13,970; £6,617; £2,941; £1,470; £735)

RPR

1 **Golden Spear**[278] 7493 5-8-4 **82** oh1 LeighRoche 3 86
(A J Martin, Ire) *hld up in tch: disp 5th at 1/2-way: lost pl after 1/2-way: gng wl towards rr over 2f out: hdwy on outer under 2f out to chal: rdn to ld ins fnl f and kpt on wl* **10/3**[1]

2 ½ **Abraham (IRE)**[34] 3680 4-8-4 **82** oh3 DannyGrant 5 85+
(J R Barry, Ire) *hld up: pushed along in 9th after 1/2-way: tk clsr order over 4f out: u.p in 8th appr st: swtchd lft over 1f out and r.o wl ins fnl f into 2nd cl home: hld by wnr* **20/1**

3 hd **Ringside Humour (IRE)**[3] 4747 4-9-2 **94** (t) KevinManning 2 97+
(J S Bolger, Ire) *chsd ldrs: 3rd 1/2-way: pushed along bhd ldrs over 2f out where n.m.r into st and dropped to 6th: r.o in 5th ins fnl f: nrst fin* **10/1**

4 ½ **Repeater**[55] 2897 7-8-6 **84** (b) ChrisHayes 12 86
(Miss Amanda Mooney, Ire) *hld up: 12th 1/2-way: hdwy on outer over 4f out: impr travelling wl in 4th fr 2f out: rdn to ld 1f out tl sn hdd and no ex cl home where dropped to 4th* **9/1**

5 nk **Le Vagabond (FR)**[22] 4070 4-8-2 **87** KillianLeonard(7) 6 88+
(E J O'Grady, Ire) *dwlt sltly: settled in rr of mid-div: 10th 1/2-way: rdn in 9th bef st and kpt on u.p on inner fr over 1f out: nrst fin* **8/1**

6 1 **Moonmeister (IRE)**[13] 4417 5-8-4 **82** (t) ConorHoban 8 82+
(A J Martin, Ire) *hooded to load: towards rr: 13th 1/2-way: rdn in 10th into st: sn swtchd lft and r.o ins fnl f: nvr trbld ldrs* **33/1**

7 nse **Torcedor (IRE)**[83] 2025 4-9-8 **100** (b) WayneLordan 13 100
(David Wachman, Ire) *chsd ldrs: 4th 1/2-way: lost pl and niggled along in 7th over 4f out: rdn into st and no imp on ldrs: kpt on one pce ins fnl f* **12/1**

8 nse **Queen Alphabet (IRE)**[6] 4675 7-8-4 **82** 5ex oh1 (t) NGMcCullagh 1 82
(Peter Fahey, Ire) *led early tl sn jnd and settled bhd ldr in 2nd after 1f: regained advantage under 3f out: rdn over 2f out and hdd u.p 1f out: no ex and one pce clsng stages* **5/1**[3]

9 3½ **Travertine (IRE)**[33] 3698 6-9-12 **104** NiallPMadden 4 98
(Niall Madden, Ire) *chsd ldrs: disp 5th at 1/2-way: sme hdwy on inner over 2f out where sn short of room and checked: no imp after: kpt on one pce ins fnl f* **16/1**

10 3¼ **Alveena (IRE)**[33] 3697 4-9-7 **99** (b[1]) PatSmullen 11 88
(D K Weld, Ire) *chsd ldrs: disp 5th at 1/2-way: impr bhd ldrs under 3f out: rdn in 2nd 2f out and no ex over 1f out where sltly hmpd: sn wknd and eased* **7/2**[2]

11 1½ **Ballybacka Queen (IRE)**[25] 3964 5-9-2 **97** DonnachaO'Brien(3) 10 83
(P A Fahy, Ire) *mid-div: 8th 1/2-way: tk clsr order bhd ldrs on outer 3f out: rdn in 3rd 2f out and sn no imp on ldrs: wknd 1f out* **20/1**

12 12 **Inis Meain (USA)**[40] 3447 9-9-2 **94** (v[1]) BillyLee 9 61
(Denis Gerard Hogan, Ire) *sn disp and led after 1f: over 1 l clr at 1/2-way: hdd under 3f out and sn no ex: wknd fnl 2f* **25/1**

13 ¾ **Coillte Cailin (IRE)**[141] 888 6-8-8 **86** ShaneFoley 7 52
(Daniel Mark Loughnane) *in rr: niggled along early: last 1/2-way: rdn and no imp over 2f out* **20/1**

14 37 **Lady Giselle (IRE)**[99] 1594 6-8-4 **82** oh3 (p) RoryCleary 14
(John J Walsh, Ire) *hld up: 11th 1/2-way: rdn on outer 3f out and no imp into st: wknd and eased: t.o* **33/1**

2m 36.33s (-6.77) **14** Ran SP% **129.8**

CSF £81.04 CT £637.26 TOTE £4.50: £1.70, £5.70, £2.90; DF 99.20 Trifecta £776.30.

Owner Newtown Anner Stud Farm Ltd **Bred** D P And Mrs J A Martin **Trained** Summerhill, Co. Meath

FOCUS

A gamble landed by the winner after his narrow defeat in this last year, and a fine training performance after an absence of nine months.

4851 - 4854a (Foreign Racing) - See Raceform Interactive

4544 DONCASTER (L-H)

Saturday, July 30

OFFICIAL GOING: Good (7.8)

Wind: Moderate against Weather: Cloudy with sunny periods

4855 THOMPSONS SOLICITORS ACTING FOR UNISON MEMBERS H'CAP 5f

1:45 (1:46) (Class 5) (0-70,72) 3-Y-O **£3,881** (£1,155; £577; £288) **Stalls** Centre

Form RPR

0400 1 **Showbizzy**[18] 4229 3-8-7 **56** (v[1]) GeorgeChaloner 6 71
(Richard Fahey) *t.k.h: trckd ldrs: hdwy 2f out: rdn to ld ent fnl f: kpt on strly* **20/1**

6341 2 2¼ **Noah Amor (IRE)**[18] 4229 3-9-2 **65** FrederikTylicki 1 72
(David Nicholls) *qckly away and led: rdn over 1f out: hdd and drvn ent fnl f: kpt on same pce* **7/4**[1]

1340 3 1¼ **Twentysvnthlancers**[17] 4256 3-9-3 **66** JackGarritty 2 68
(Paul Midgley) *chsd ldr: hdwy 2f out: sn rdn: drvn ent fnl f: kpt on same pce* **10/1**

300 4 2¼ **Chip Or Pellet**[13] 4426 3-7-13 **51** oh4 ShelleyBirkett(3) 4 45
(Nigel Tinkler) *awkward and dwlt s: sn in tch: hdwy 2f out: rdn to chse ldrs over 1f out: n.m.r ent fnl f: sn one pce* **16/1**

0531 5 ¾ **Dyllan (IRE)**[13] 4426 3-9-9 **72** JamesSullivan 9 64
(Ruth Carr) *towards rr: hdwy 2f out: rdn and hung lft over 1f out: sn no imp* **10/3**[3]

4231 6 10 **Lady Joanna Vassa (IRE)**[28] 3900 3-8-12 **61** AndreaAtzeni 7 17
(Richard Guest) *chsd ldng pair: pushed along over 2f out: rdn wl over 1f out: sn wknd* **11/4**[2]

-020 7 2¼ **Chandresh**[10] 4517 3-8-9 **58** OisinMurphy 8
(Robert Cowell) *a towards rr* **16/1**

500- 8 9 **Divasesque (IRE)**[261] 7808 3-7-13 **51** oh6 [1] NoelGarbutt(3) 5
(Derek Shaw) *towards rr: pushed along after 2f: sn outpcd and bhd fr 1/2-way* **100/1**

1m 0.14s (-0.36) **Going Correction** +0.125s/f (Good) **8** Ran SP% **112.7**

Speed ratings (Par 100): **107,103,101,97,96 80,77,62**

CSF £54.00 CT £387.04 TOTE £16.40: £4.10, £1.10, £2.40; EX 78.40 Trifecta £1116.90.

Owner Racegoers Club Owners Group **Bred** Whitsbury Manor Stud **Trained** Musley Bank, N Yorks

FOCUS

The round course was railed out from 1m2f to where the round joins the straight. A modest sprint and there was a bit of a turn up.

4856 UNISON SUPPORTING YOUR COMMUNITY MAIDEN AUCTION STKS (PLUS 10 RACE) 7f

2:20 (2:21) (Class 4) 2-Y-O **£4,528** (£1,347; £673; £336) **Stalls** Centre

Form RPR

5 1 **Western Duke (IRE)**[29] 3859 2-9-1 0 OisinMurphy 3 83+
(Ralph Beckett) *led 2f: cl up: led again 3f out: hdd wl over 1f out and sn rdn: styd on to chal ins fnl f: led last 100yds* **13/8**[1]

0 2 ¾ **Trooper's Gold**[9] 4545 2-8-13 0 NickyMackay 1 79+
(Kevin Ryan) *trckd ldrs: hdwy on outer over 2f out: led wl over 1f out: sn rdn and hung rt over 1f out: drvn ins fnl f: hdd and no ex last 100yds* **33/1**

0 3 1½ **Carducci**[14] 4397 2-8-10 0 TomQueally 2 72
(Richard Hannon) *trckd ldrs: hdwy over 2f out: rdn along wl over 1f out: drvn and kpt on fnl f* **16/1**

4 4 1 **Glorious Rocket**[37] 3569 2-9-1 0 AndreaAtzeni 8 74+
(Luca Cumani) *t.k.h: trckd ldrs: pushed along and sltly outpcd 2f out: sn rdn and kpt on fnl f* **5/1**[3]

33 5 1¾ **Pantera Negra (IRE)**[21] 4125 2-8-3 0 CallumShepherd(5) 4 63
(Ed Dunlop) *trckd ldrs: pushed along 2f out: rdn wl over 1f out: kpt on same pce* **8/1**

6 ½ **Armagnac (IRE)** 2-9-1 0 JackMitchell 6 68
(Michael Bell) *towards rr: hdwy on outer wl over 2f out: in tch and rdn over 1f out: sn wknd* **16/1**

7 hd **Charlie Rascal (FR)** 2-8-11 0 FrederikTylicki 10 64
(Peter Chapple-Hyam) *prom: rdn along 2f out: grad wknd* **20/1**

0 8 1½ **Chalieb**[23] 4040 2-8-13 0 WilliamTwiston-Davies 9 62
(Nigel Tinkler) *dwlt: a in rr* **66/1**

9 1½ **Trading Punches (IRE)** 2-9-1 0 ShaneGray 13 60
(David Brown) *in rr: green and rdn along bef 1/2-way: n.d* **14/1**

02 10 ¾ **Right Action**[15] 4371 2-8-13 0 JackGarritty 7 55+
(Richard Fahey) *plld hrd: cl up: led after 2f: hdd over 3f out: sn rdn and wknd fnl 2f* **10/3**[2]

5 11 ½ **Masterofdiscovery**[21] 4125 2-9-1 0 JohnFahy 11 56
(Clive Cox) *midfield: rdn along over 3f out: wknd over 2f out* **20/1**

12 2¼ **Prince Of Clappers** 2-8-11 0 AndrewElliott 12 46
(Tim Easterby) *dwlt: a in rr* **50/1**

1m 27.94s (1.64) **Going Correction** +0.125s/f (Good) **12** Ran SP% **123.3**

Speed ratings (Par 96): **95,94,92,91,89 88,88,86,85,84 83,81**

CSF £79.71 TOTE £2.40: £1.10, £11.00, £4.20; EX 76.90 Trifecta £1801.60.

Owner London City Bloodstock **Bred** Epona Bloodstock Ltd **Trained** Kimpton, Hants

FOCUS

Probably just a fair maiden.

4857 UNISON AND LV= LIVERPOOL VICTORIA CAR INSURANCE MAIDEN STKS 1m 2f 60y

2:55 (2:56) (Class 5) 3-Y-O **£3,881** (£1,155; £577; £288) **Stalls** Low

Form RPR

\- 1 **El Vip (IRE)** 3-9-5 0 AndreaAtzeni 8 92+
(Luca Cumani) *green and wnt rt s: sn in tch: hdwy to chse ldng pair 1/2-way: effrt over 2f out: rdn to chse clr ldr over 1f out: styd strly fnl f to ld last 50yds* **3/1**[2]

223- 2 ½ **Twobeelucky**[246] 8023 3-9-5 0 AndrewElliott 3 86
(Mark Johnston) *led: pushed along and qcknd over 3f out: rdn and qcknd wl clr over 2f out: rdn over 1f out: drvn ins fnl f: hdd and no ex last 50yds* **7/1**[3]

-222 3 5 **Stratum**[16] 4319 3-9-5 84 NickyMackay 7 76
(John Gosden) *sn trcking ldr: pushed along 3f out: rdn 2f out: sn drvn and kpt on one pce* **4/7**[1]

0 4 6 **Notion Of Beauty (USA)**[36] 3601 3-9-0 0 FrederikTylicki 5 59
(K R Burke) *hld up: hdwy over 3f out: rdn along over 2f out: kpt on one pce* **33/1**

0 5 6 **Foible**[16] 4319 3-9-5 0 (b[1]) RobertTart 2 52
(John Gosden) *in rr: pushed along and sme hdwy over 3f out: rdn along over 2f out: n.d* **40/1**

6 ¾ **Togetherness (IRE)** 3-9-5 0 OisinMurphy 1 51
(Harry Dunlop) *s.i.s: green: a in rr* **14/1**

7 3½ **Acrux** 3-9-5 0 GeorgeBaker 6 44
(David Lanigan) *prom: pushed along over 4f out: rdn over 3f out: sn wknd* **16/1**

2m 10.48s (1.08) **Going Correction** +0.125s/f (Good) **7** Ran SP% **119.1**

Speed ratings (Par 100): **100,99,95,90,86 85,82**

CSF £25.44 TOTE £4.10: £2.00, £3.20; EX 25.60 Trifecta £36.70.

Owner Al Shaqab Racing **Bred** Gestut Wittekindshof **Trained** Newmarket, Suffolk

FOCUS

Race distance increased by 9yds. The front pair came clear of the below-par favourite and it was probably a decent little maiden, with them getting racing a long way out.

4858 UNISON ESSENTIAL COVER WHEREVER YOU WORK H'CAP 1m 2f 60y

3:30 (3:30) (Class 2) (0-100,100) 3-Y-O+

£12,450 (£3,728; £1,864; £932; £466; £234) **Stalls** Low

Form RPR

1-40 1 **Oceanographer**[42] 3383 4-10-0 **100** [1] JackMitchell 6 109
(Charlie Appleby) *hld up in rr: hdwy 3f out: chsd ldrs over 1f out: rdn to chal and n.m.r ins fnl f: drvn and styd on to ld last 50yds* **6/1**

-062 2 nk **Scrutinise**[29] 3861 4-9-10 **96** GeorgeBaker 1 104
(Ed Dunlop) *led over 2f: trckd ldr: led again wl over 2f out: rdn over 1f out: drvn ins fnl f: hdd and no ex last 50yds* **5/1**[3]

-004 3 1¼ **Laurence**[24] 4026 4-8-13 **85** AndreaAtzeni 3 91
(Luca Cumani) *hld up: stdy hdwy 4f out: effrt 2f out: sn chsng ldr: rdn over 1f out: drvn and ch ins fnl f: kpt on same pce* **9/2**[2]

21/2 4 4 **Flight Officer**[35] 3666 5-9-2 **93** GaryMahon(5) 2 91
(Saeed bin Suroor) *trckd ldrs: hdwy 3f out: rdn 2f out: drvn over 1f out: kpt on one pce* **3/1**[1]

6000 **5** *3* **Hit The Jackpot (IRE)**[22] 4115 7-9-7 **96**.................... ShelleyBirkett(3) 5 88
(David O'Meara) *hld up in rr: effrt on outer over 3f out: sn rdn along and n.d* **12/1**

3306 **6** *5* **Swift Emperor (IRE)**[21] 4163 4-9-3 **89**.......................... FrederikTylicki 7 71
(David Barron) *t.k.h early: trckd ldrs: hdwy over 3f out: chsd ldr over 2f out: rdn wl over 1f out: grad wknd* **13/2**

1-05 **7** *hd* **Karraar**[35] 3670 5-9-0 **86**..............................(v[1]) OisinMurphy 4 67
(William Haggas) *t.k.h: trckd ldrs: led over 7f out: rdn along over 3f out: hdd wl over 2f out: sn wknd* **9/2**[2]

2m 9.85s (0.45) **Going Correction** +0.125s/f (Good) **7** Ran SP% **113.3**
Speed ratings (Par 109): **103,102,101,98,96 92,92**
CSF £34.93 TOTE £7.90: £5.10, £2.60; EX 29.40 Trifecta £300.10.

Owner Godolphin **Bred** Earle I Mack **Trained** Newmarket, Suffolk

FOCUS
Race distance increased by 9yds. A good handicap run at a fair enough gallop.

4859 UNISON CAMPAIGNING FOR PUBLIC SERVICES H'CAP 1m 4f
4:05 (4:06) (Class 4) (0-85,83) 3-Y-O **£5,175** (£1,540; £769; £384) **Stalls** Low

Form RPR

6231 **1** **Cape Cova (IRE)**[17] 4265 3-9-7 **83**.................................... TomQueally 5 93+
(John Gosden) *trckd ldr: hdwy and cl up 4f out: rdn to take slt ld over 2f out: drvn ent fnl f: kpt on wl towards fin* **4/1**[3]

3106 **2** *3/4* **Daphne**[15] 4351 3-9-6 **82**................................(p) WilliamTwiston-Davies 4 88
(William Haggas) *led: jnd wl over 2f out: sn rdn and hdd: cl up and drvn over 1f out: rallied gamely and ev ch ins fnl f tl no ex last 75yds* **10/1**

1662 **3** *1 1/2* **Michael's Mount**[26] 3949 3-8-10 **72**..............................(p) OisinMurphy 1 76
(Ed Dunlop) *hld up in rr: hdwy over 2f out: rdn wl over 1f out: styd on fnl f: nrst fin* **10/1**

31 **4** *3/4* **Pumblechook**[41] 3434 3-9-4 **80**.. GeorgeBaker 3 83
(Lucy Wadham) *trckd ldr: pushed along over 3f out: rdn 2f out: drvn over 1f out: kpt on same pce* **5/2**[2]

0012 **5** *13* **Diamond Geyser (IRE)**[23] 4057 3-9-1 **77**....................... AndreaAtzeni 6 59
(Luca Cumani) *hld up: niggled along wl over 3f out: pushed along wl over 2f out: sn rdn and btn* **11/10**[1]

2m 34.06s (-0.84) **Going Correction** +0.125s/f (Good) **5** Ran SP% **114.4**
Speed ratings (Par 102): **107,106,105,105,96**
CSF £38.06 TOTE £4.10: £1.60, £2.90; EX 21.50 Trifecta £177.20.

Owner Mohamed Obaida **Bred** Basil Brindley **Trained** Newmarket, Suffolk

FOCUS
Race distance increased by 9yds. A fair 3yo handicap won by a progressive type.

4860 UNISON DEFENDING YOUR NHS CONDITIONS STKS 6f
4:40 (4:40) (Class 3) 3-Y-O+ **£9,337** (£2,796; £1,398; £699; £349) **Stalls** Centre

Form RPR

0306 **1** **Naadirr (IRE)**[35] 3655 5-8-10 108................................ DanielMuscutt(3) 1 109
(Marco Botti) *trckd ldr: hdwy and cl up over 2f out: rdn to chal over 1f out: led ins fnl f: styd on* **11/4**[3]

-000 **2** *1* **Out Do**[21] 4166 7-8-13 105...(v) AndreaAtzeni 2 106
(David O'Meara) *hld up in rr: hdwy over 1f out: rdn to chal ins fnl f: sn edgd lft and kpt on same pce* **7/1**

0-46 **3** *3/4* **Strath Burn**[48] 3195 4-9-4 113... OisinMurphy 3 109
(Robert Cowell) *led: pushed along and jnd 2f out: rdn over 1f out: drvn and hdd ins fnl f: one pce* **7/4**[1]

-030 **4** *1 3/4* **Pipers Note**[7] 4667 6-8-13 95.. JackGarritty 6 98
(Richard Whitaker) *broke wl and stdd s: trckd ldr: effrt 2f out: sn rdn and no imp fnl f* **12/1**

0-06 **5** *1 1/2* **Burnt Sugar (IRE)**[42] 3386 4-8-8 105..........................(b) GaryMahon(5) 5 93
(Richard Hannon) *dwlt: sn chsng ldng pair: hdwy and cl up over 2f out: sn rdn and wknd ent fnl f* **5/2**[2]

1m 12.57s (-1.03) **Going Correction** +0.125s/f (Good) **5** Ran SP% **111.8**
Speed ratings (Par 107): **111,109,108,106,104**
CSF £20.73 TOTE £4.50: £2.10, £2.50; EX 15.90 Trifecta £58.40.

Owner Middleham Park Racing XXX **Bred** Castlemartin Sky & Skymarc Farm **Trained** Newmarket, Suffolk

FOCUS
A good-quality conditions race featuring four 105-plus rated sprinters.

4861 UNISON AND UIA MUTUAL HOME INSURANCE FILLIES' H'CAP 6f
5:15 (5:16) (Class 5) (0-70,79) 3-Y-O+ **£3,881** (£1,155; £577; £288) **Stalls** Centre

Form RPR

3112 **1** **Laila Honiwillow**[15] 4376 3-9-6 **69**..................................... JackGarritty 4 79+
(Jedd O'Keeffe) *cl up: rdn to ld over 1f out: drvn out* **2/1**[2]

000 **2** *1 1/2* **Isntshesomething**[11] 4498 4-8-4 **51** oh4.................(p) ShelleyBirkett(3) 8 56
(Richard Guest) *trckd ldrs: hdwy 2f out: sn rdn: drvn and kpt on fnl f* **16/1**

3211 **3** *1 1/4* **Justice Lady (IRE)**[7] 4658 3-10-2 **79**............................... GeorgeBaker 6 79+
(David Elsworth) *t.k.h: hld up in rr: hdwy over 2f out: chsd ldrs over 1f out: drvn and kpt on same pce fnl f* **13/8**[1]

0526 **4** *3/4* **Manipura**[11] 4472 3-8-3 **55**...(p) NoelGarbutt(3) 3 53
(Derek Shaw) *sn trcking ldrs on outer: hdwy 1/2-way: cl up 2f out: sn rdn: drvn and one pce ent fnl f* **25/1**

0-06 **5** *1/2* **Alpine Dream (IRE)**[23] 4043 3-8-13 **62**.........................[1] AndrewElliott 5 58
(Tim Easterby) *in tch: pushed along over 2f out: rdn wl over 1f out: no imp* **16/1**

206 **6** *hd* **Bad Girl Caoimhe (IRE)**[26] 3948 3-9-0 **68**............ CallumShepherd(5) 7 64
(Brian Ellison) *hld up: a towards rr* **6/1**[3]

6440 **7** *nk* **Fly True**[28] 3898 3-8-9 **63**.. DavidParkes(5) 1 58
(Jeremy Gask) *sn led: rdn along 2f out: hdd and drvn over 1f out: sn wknd* **16/1**

3553 **8** *7* **Full Of Promise**[12] 4445 3-8-12 **61**.................................... TomQueally 2 33
(Richard Fahey) *chsd ldrs: rdn along over 2f out: sn wknd* **7/1**

1m 13.8s (0.20) **Going Correction** +0.125s/f (Good)
WFA 3 from 4yo 5lb **8** Ran SP% **119.7**
Speed ratings (Par 100): **103,101,99,98,97 97,97,87**
CSF £35.48 CT £65.49 TOTE £2.70: £1.10, £3.40, £1.50; EX 40.90 Trifecta £122.70.

Owner Caron & Paul Chapman **Bred** J P Coggan **Trained** Middleham Moor, N Yorks

FOCUS
A modest handicap, but progressive types filled first and third.

T/Plt: £811.00 to a £1 stake. Pool of £78109.05 - 70.30 winning tickets. T/Qpdt: £72.50 to a £1 stake. Pool of £4792.92 - 48.90 winning tickets. **Joe Rowntree**

4821 GOODWOOD (R-H)
Saturday, July 30

OFFICIAL GOING: Good to firm (8.1)
Wind: virtually nil Weather: sunny spells after morning rain

4862 QATAR STEWARDS' SPRINT STKS (H'CAP) (CONSOLATION RACE FOR THE QATAR STEWARDS' CUP) 6f
2:00 (2:04) (Class 2) 3-Y-O+
£46,687 (£13,980; £6,990; £3,495; £1,312; £1,312) **Stalls** High

Form RPR

0012 **1** **Hoof It**[15] 4338 9-9-4 **95**.. NathanEvans(5) 11 105
(Michael Easterby) *racd centre to far side tl merged w far side 2f out: a.p: ev ch 2f out: rdn over 1f out: led ins fnl f: styd on* **8/1**[3]

0003 **2** *nk* **Related**[7] 4667 6-9-6 **92**...(b) LukeMorris 7 101
(Paul Midgley) *racd far side: led gp and chsd ldrs tl led overall over 2f out: drvn wl over 1f out: hdd ins fnl f: kpt on but hld towards fin* **16/1**

5615 **3** *3/4* **Nuno Tristan (USA)**[7] 4625 4-9-2 **93**.................... AdamMcNamara(5) 3 100+
(Richard Fahey) *racd far side: bmpd and squeezed out leaving stalls: hld up in rr: hdwy 2f out: rdn to chse ldrs and swtchd lft jst over 1f out: drifted lft 1f out: styd on wl u.p fnl 100yds* **13/2**[2]

2304 **4** *3/4* **Stellarta**[14] 4398 5-8-11 **83**... DavidProbert 20 88
(Michael Blanshard) *racd in centre: hld up in midfield: hdwy u.p over 1f out: styd on wl ins fnl f: no threat to ldng pair* **50/1**

41-4 **5** *3/4* **Projection**[23] 4062 3-9-8 **99**.. RyanMoore 22 103+
(Roger Charlton) *racd in centre: hld up in midfield: carried rt and nt clr run whn swtchd lft over 1f out: kpt on wl u.p ins fnl f: no threat to ldrs* **11/2**[1]

0060 **5** *dht* **Charles Molson**[15] 4366 5-9-2 **93**..........................(p) HectorCrouch(5) 2 95
(Patrick Chamings) *racd far side: pushed lft s: hld up towards rr: hdwy 2f out: rdn over 1f out: swtchd lft 1f out: drvn and kpt on ins fnl f: no threat to ldrs* **25/1**

2641 **7** *1* **Soie D'Leau**[23] 4066 4-9-8 **94** 6ex... JoeFanning 1 93
(Kristin Stubbs) *racd far side: wnt lft s: chsd ldrs: effrt to chal and rdn over 1f out: no ex ins fnl f: wknd towards fin* **33/1**

-216 **8** *1* **Seeking Magic**[56] 2895 8-9-10 **96**.......................................(t) RyanTate 8 92
(Clive Cox) *racd far side: chsd ldrs: effrt 2f out: rdn over 1f out: n.m.r and sltly impeded 1f out: styd on same pce ins fnl f* **14/1**

1004 **9** *hd* **Classic Seniority**[7] 4627 4-8-11 **83**................................. MartinHarley 4 78+
(Marjorie Fife) *racd far side: hld up in midfield: effrt 2f out: trying to cl whn nt clr run over 1f out: hdwy 1f out: styd on wl ins fnl f: no threat to ldrs* **33/1**

6500 **10** *shd* **Handsome Dude**[22] 4079 4-8-13 **88**............................(b) RobHornby(3) 5 83
(David Barron) *racd far side: in tch in midfield: effrt u.p over 1f out: unable qck and styd on same pce ins fnl f* **50/1**

0002 **11** *nk* **Grandad's World (IRE)**[15] 4366 4-9-0 **86**...................... BarryMcHugh 6 80
(Richard Fahey) *racd far side: w gp ldr and prom overall tl over 2f out: sn rdn and chsng ldrs over 1f out: no ex: wknd ins fnl f* **16/1**

1213 **12** *1/2* **Lightning Charlie**[12] 4460 4-8-13 **85** 6ex........................ JimCrowley 14 77
(Amanda Perrett) *racd in centre: chsd gp ldrs and handy overall: rdn and hung rt 2f out: unable qck over 1f out: wl hld and plugged on same pce ins fnl f* **25/1**

0064 **13** *hd* **Fast Track**[7] 4667 5-9-4 **90**.. DavidAllan 19 82
(David Barron) *racd in centre: hld up in rr: effrt 2f out: drvn and hdwy over 1f out: kpt on ins fnl f: no threat to ldrs* **25/1**

5514 **14** *1/2* **Shamshon (IRE)**[8] 4584 5-9-10 **96** 6ex............................. JamieSpencer 25 86
(Jamie Osborne) *racd in nr side sextet: hld up in rr: effrt and swtchd rt over 1f out: pushed along and no real imp ins fnl f: nvr a threat* **20/1**

0-0 **15** *hd* **Fairway To Heaven (IRE)**[14] 4415 7-8-8 **80**.................... KieranO'Neill 9 69+
(Michael Wigham) *racd far side: hld up in rr: clsd whn squeezed out and hmpd 2f out: rallied and sme hdwy whn nt clr run and swtchd rt ins fnl f: pushed along and kpt on same pce after* **25/1**

-056 **16** *shd* **El Viento (FR)**[15] 4373 8-9-3 **89**.......................................(v) JasonHart 18 78
(Richard Fahey) *racd in centre: rdn 2f out: no imp u.p over 1f out: wl hld and plugged on same pce ins fnl f* **40/1**

0422 **17** *1* **Gamesome (FR)**[15] 4373 5-9-7 **93**.............................. PaulMulrennan 26 79
(Paul Midgley) *racd in nr side sextet: chsd gp ldrs and midfield overall: effrt and rdn to ld gp but nt on terms w ldrs over 1f out: kpt on same pce fnl f* **16/1**

5000 **18** *1 3/4* **Barnet Fair**[22] 4079 8-8-12 **84**.. FrannyNorton 12 64+
(David Nicholls) *taken down early: racd centre to far side: awkward s and s.i.s: hld up in rr: clsd and nt clr run 2f out: bdly hmpd over 1f out: swtchd lft 1f out: pushed along and nvr any ch of getting involved fnl f* **16/1**

1330 **19** *1/2* **Dougan**[21] 4126 4-9-7 **93**... AdamKirby 21 72
(David Evans) *racd in centre: hld up in midfield: effrt 2f out: sme hdwy u.p over 1f out: no imp 1f out: wknd ins fnl f* **11/1**

0652 **20** *nk* **Ballymore Castle (IRE)**[9] 4569 4-9-0 **86**..................(p) PaulHanagan 17 64
(Richard Fahey) *racd in centre: midfield tl shuffled bk to rr and nt clr run 2f out: rallied and sme hdwy 1f out: nvr trbld ldrs* **25/1**

2502 **21** *1 3/4* **Iseemist (IRE)**[30] 3800 5-9-9 **95**............................ MichaelJMMurphy 27 67
(John Gallagher) *racd in nr side sextet: chsd gp ldr tl led gp 1/2-way: rdn 2f out: lost gp ld and wl hld over 1f out: wknd ins fnl f* **33/1**

0-00 **22** *4* **Elysian Flyer (IRE)**[12] 4461 4-9-4 **90**................................(p) PatDobbs 13 49
(Richard Hughes) *racd centre to far side tl merged w far side 2f out: midfield: losing pl whn pushed rt and bdly hmpd 2f out: n.d after* **66/1**

130 **23** *nse* **Muir Lodge**[22] 4109 5-9-7 **93**.......................................(t) PatCosgrave 10 52+
(George Baker) *racd centre to far side tl merged w far side 2f out: hld up towards rr: effrt whn squeezed out and bdly hmpd 2f out: no ch after: eased ins fnl f* **25/1**

-254 **24** *1 1/2* **Mukaynis (IRE)**[56] 2895 5-9-4 **90**..................................(b) TomEaves 15 44
(Kevin Ryan) *taken down early: racd in centre: overall ldr: hdd over 2f out: sn struggling: hung rt and wknd over 1f out* **20/1**

4314 **25** *1/2* **Misterioso (IRE)**[11] 4475 4-9-4 **90** 6ex............................ JamesDoyle 16 43
(Jamie Osborne) *racd in centre: hld up in midfield: effrt and hung rt 2f out: drvn and no hdwy over 1f out: wl hld and eased ins fnl f* **12/1**

-000 **26** *shd* **Secret Missile**[56] 2898 6-8-12 **84**..............................(b) SamHitchcott 28 36
(Gary Moore) *racd in nr side sextet: led gp tl 1/2-way: lost pl 2f out: wl bhd fnl f* **100/1**

0010 **27** *1 1/2* **Cool Bahamian (IRE)**[42] 3414 5-8-12 **84**..................(b) HarryBentley 24 32
(Eve Johnson Houghton) *racd in nr side sextet: nvr bttr than midfield: rdn 2f out: hung rt and no hdwy over 1f out: bhd and eased wl ins fnl f* **100/1**

50-0 **28** 5 **Extrasolar**[4] 4735 6-8-8 **83**....(t) KieranShoemark(3) 23 15
(Amanda Perrett) *racd in nr side sextet: nvr bttr than midfield: no hdwy u.p 2f out: bhd over 1f out: eased wl ins fnl f* **66/1**

1m 10.37s (-1.83) **Going Correction** -0.075s/f (Good)
WFA 3 from 4yo+ 5lb **28** Ran SP% **138.8**
Speed ratings (Par 109): **109,108,107,106,105 105,104,102,102,102 102,101,101,100,100 100,98,96,95,95 93,87,87,85,85 84**
CSF £112.62 CT £926.72 TOTE £13.40: £2.60, £5.50, £3.70, £14.40; EX 215.10 Trifecta £1744.20.
Owner A Chandler & L Westwood **Bred** Bond Thoroughbred Corporation **Trained** Sheriff Hutton, N Yorks
■ Stewards' Enquiry : James Doyle five-day ban; careless riding (13th-17th Aug)

FOCUS
All race distances were as advertsised. Rain on watered ground; 4mm of rain in the morning after 5mm of watering overnight. Conditions were still given as good to firm and the time of this opener was only 0.07sec slower than the previous year's edition of this race, which was run on the same going, although James Doyle said the ground was "very loose". The runners raced in four groups for much of the way, before the field merged in the closing stages, with those middle to far side dominating, and the stands' side bunch were beaten out of sight. This wasn't far off Hoof It's best run in the last three years.

4863 QATAR H'CAP 1m 4f
2:35 (2:38) (Class 2) (0-105,100) 3-Y-O
£46,687 (£13,980; £6,990; £3,495; £1,747; £877) **Stalls** High

Form RPR

-013 **1** **Dal Harraild**[21] 4131 3-9-5 **98**.... PatCosgrave 2 108+
(William Haggas) *trckd ldrs: rdn 2f out: styd on wl ins fnl f: led towards fin* **5/1**[2]

6310 **2** *shd* **Shraaoh (IRE)**[44] 3300 3-8-12 **91**.... FrankieDettori 7 98+
(Sir Michael Stoute) *hld up towards rr: pushed along over 6f out: rdn wl over 2f out: edgd sltly rt: hdwy over 1f out: styd on strly fnl f: ev ch fnl 120yds: jst hld* **7/1**

13-1 **3** *hd* **Move Up**[21] 4129 3-9-7 **100**.... JamesDoyle 11 106
(Saeed bin Suroor) *trckd ldrs: led wl over 2f out: sn rdn: styd on but no ex whn drifting lft and hdd towards fin* **6/1**[3]

-312 **4** *1/2* **Jaameh (IRE)**[14] 4409 3-8-3 **82**.... PaulHanagan 1 87
(Mark Johnston) *hld up towards rr: rdn over 2f out: hdwy over 1f out: styd on wl fnl f: wnt 4th towards fin* **18/1**

3231 **5** *3/4* **Emperor Napoleon**[31] 3768 3-8-9 **88**.... DavidProbert 9 92
(Andrew Balding) *mid-div: hdwy 3f out: rdn to chse ldr 2f out: ev ch ins fnl f: looking hld in cl 4th whn short of room fnl 75yds* **16/1**

1133 **6** *3/4* **Master Blueyes (IRE)**[21] 4137 3-8-4 **83**.... LukeMorris 6 87+
(Alan King) *hld up towards rr: hdwy over 2f out: swtchd lft jst ins fnl f: styng on in cl 5th/6th whn bdly squeezed out fnl 100yds: no ch after* **14/1**

6500 **7** *1* **Beaverbrook**[43] 3341 3-9-0 **93**.... JamesMcDonald 5 94
(Mark Johnston) *hld up towards rr: hdwy to trck ldrs 7f out: rdn to chse ldr 2f out: ch ent fnl f: no ex fnl 120yds* **16/1**

-521 **8** *1* **Gold Faith (IRE)**[21] 4153 3-8-6 **85**.... HarryBentley 3 85
(Ralph Beckett) *mid-div: rdn over 2f out: styd on but nt pce to get involved* **8/1**

2111 **9** *1 1/4* **Knights Table**[14] 4409 3-9-2 **95**.... DavidAllan 4 96
(James Tate) *mid-div: hdwy over 2f out: sn rdn: disputing 5th whn short of room and snatched up jst ins fnl f: no ch after* **8/1**

-001 **10** *1 3/4* **Wall Of Fire (IRE)**[28] 3887 3-9-1 **94**....(b) JimCrowley 13 92
(Hugo Palmer) *s.i.s: in last pair: rdn 3f out: hdwy over 1f out: styng on whn hmpd ent fnl f: no ch after* **20/1**

1112 **11** *17* **Shabbah (IRE)**[21] 4131 3-8-12 **91**.... RyanMoore 10 59
(Sir Michael Stoute) *trckd ldr: led briefly 3f out: sn rdn: wknd 2f out* **9/2**[1]

0001 **12** *20* **Soldier In Action (FR)**[14] 4407 3-9-1 **94**.... AdamKirby 14 30
(Mark Johnston) *wnt rt s: sn led: rdn and hdd 3f out: sn wknd* **10/1**

2m 37.68s (-0.72) **Going Correction** +0.05s/f (Good) **12** Ran SP% **121.4**
Speed ratings (Par 106): **104,103,103,103,102 102,101,101,100,99 87,74**
CSF £41.09 CT £220.04 TOTE £6.50: £2.40, £2.90, £2.70; EX 51.30 Trifecta £316.80.
Owner St Albans Bloodstock Limited **Bred** St Albans Bloodstock Llp **Trained** Newmarket, Suffolk
■ Stewards' Enquiry : Luke Morris five-day ban; careless riding (13th-17th Aug)

FOCUS
A cracking handicap, full of improving and unexposed 3yos, but it was a messy affair and there were some hard-luck stories. A slightly positive view has still been taken of the form.

4864 QATAR NASSAU STKS (BRITISH CHAMPIONS SERIES) (GROUP 1) (F&M) 1m 1f 192y
3:10 (3:15) (Class 1) 3-Y-**£340,260** (£129,000; £64,560; £32,160; £16,140) **Stalls** Low

Form RPR

1211 **1** **Minding (IRE)**[34] 3695 3-8-11 **120**.... RyanMoore 1 116+
(A P O'Brien, Ire) *trckd ldng pair tl shuffled bk to rr but stl wl in tch 4f out: effrt and rdn to ld wl over 1f out: forged ahd 1f out: drifted rt ins fnl f: styd on* **1/5**[1]

5-44 **2** *1 1/4* **Queen's Trust**[44] 3297 3-8-11 **105**.... JamesMcDonald 5 113
(Sir Michael Stoute) *sn chsng ldr: rdn and ev ch 1f out: unable to match pce of wnr 1f out: hld and keeping on same pce whn swtchd lft ins fnl f* **16/1**

2-10 **3** *1 1/4* **Jemayel (IRE)**[41] 3452 3-8-11 **110**....(p) GregoryBenoist 2 110
(J-C Rouget, France) *stdd bk after s: hld up in rr: effrt and swtchd lft wl over 1f out: drvn over 1f out: wnt 3rd ins fnl f: kpt on* **16/1**

-110 **4** *6* **Swiss Range**[41] 3452 3-8-11 **108**.... FrankieDettori 3 100
(John Gosden) *led: rdn and hdd wl over 1f out: unable qck and btn 3rd 1f out: wknd ins fnl f: eased towards fin* **7/1**[2]

3-15 **5** *11* **Beautiful Romance**[42] 3384 4-9-7 **112**....(v1) JamesDoyle 4 76
(Saeed bin Suroor) *dwlt: hld up in tch: hdwy on outer to chse ldrs: 4f out: rdn and lost pl jst over 2f out: wknd over 1f out: eased ins fnl f* **12/1**[3]

2m 5.05s (-3.05) **Going Correction** +0.05s/f (Good)
WFA 3 from 4yo 10lb **5** Ran SP% **115.3**
Speed ratings (Par 117): **114,113,112,107,98**
CSF £5.88 TOTE £1.10: £1.02, £4.60; EX 4.60 Trifecta £20.00.
Owner Derrick Smith & Mrs John Magnier & Michael Tabor **Bred** Orpendale, Chelston & Wynatt **Trained** Cashel, Co Tipperary

FOCUS
An uncompetitive Group 1, Minding being rated 8lb plus clear of the rest on both official ratings and RPRs. Already a five-time winner at this level, she took on only one rival who had previously won a Group 1, and was predictably sent off a short price. She didn't have to be at her best, with the second the key to the form.

4865 QATAR STEWARDS' CUP (HERITAGE H'CAP) 6f
3:45 (3:49) (Class 2) 3-Y-O+
£155,625 (£46,600; £23,300; £11,650; £5,825; £2,925) **Stalls** High

Form RPR

1121 **1** **Dancing Star**[23] 4062 3-8-12 **102** 6ex.... DavidProbert 4 113
(Andrew Balding) *racd far side: trckd ldrs: shkn up to ld jst ins fnl f: r.o wl: rdn out* **9/2**[1]

1111 **2** *1 1/4* **Orion's Bow**[15] 4338 5-9-4 **103** 6ex.... BarryMcHugh 12 111
(David Nicholls) *racd far side: trckd ldrs: chal over 1f out: rdn and ev ch ins fnl f: kpt on but nt quite pce of wnr* **6/1**[2]

5303 **3** *nse* **Raucous**[14] 4393 3-8-12 **102**....(tp) JimCrowley 20 109
(William Haggas) *racd centre: mid-div: hdwy 2f out: sn rdn: kpt on wl fnl f: wnt 3rd towards fin* **16/1**

4114 **4** *hd* **Growl**[21] 4152 4-9-0 **99**.... RyanMoore 26 106+
(Richard Fahey) *racd centre: hld up bhd: hdwy over 1f out: nt clr run briefly jst ins fnl f: qcknd up smartly whn clr fnl 120yds: snatched 4th cl home* **14/1**

3300 **5** *1/2* **Duke Of Firenze**[21] 4126 7-9-0 **99**.... DavidAllan 14 105
(David C Griffiths) *s.i.s: towards rr on far side: hdwy over 2f out: rdn over 1f out: kpt on wl fnl f* **66/1**

6000 **6** *nse* **Rivellino**[35] 3655 6-9-1 **100**.... HarryBentley 7 105
(K R Burke) *racd far side: mid-div: hdwy 2f out: sn rdn: r.o wl fnl f* **20/1**

1241 **7** *nk* **Ridge Ranger (IRE)**[22] 4114 5-9-10 **109** 6ex.... JasonHart 2 113
(Eric Alston) *racd far side: overall ldr: rdn 2f out: hdd jst ins fnl f: hung lft and sn no ex* **15/2**[3]

0322 **8** *1/2* **Red Pike (IRE)**[46] 3250 5-8-13 **98**.... PaulMulrennan 5 101
(Bryan Smart) *racd far side: trckd ldr: rdn and ev ch over 1f out: sltly hmpd ins fnl f: no ex fnl 120yds* **20/1**

3333 **9** *1 1/4* **Jamesie (IRE)**[21] 4135 8-9-3 **102**....(t) PatDobbs 3 101
(David Marnane, Ire) *racd far side: mid-div: rdn 2f out: kpt on ins fnl furlo ng but nt pce to get on terms* **25/1**

0100 **10** *hd* **Alben Star (IRE)**[98] 1644 8-9-3 **102**.... PaulHanagan 1 100
(Richard Fahey) *racd far side: mid-div: rdn 2f out: nt pce to get on terms* **12/1**

-020 **11** *shd* **Suzi's Connoisseur**[7] 4625 5-8-7 **97**....(vt) AaronJones(5) 11 95
(Stuart Williams) *racd far side: hld up towards rr: rdn 2f out: kpt on fnl f: nvr threatened ldrs* **33/1**

2430 **11** *dht* **Withernsea (IRE)**[7] 4625 5-8-12 **97**.... JamieSpencer 6 95
(Richard Fahey) *racd far side: a mid-div* **14/1**

4221 **13** *hd* **Kimberella**[7] 4667 6-9-4 **103** 6ex.... FrannyNorton 21 100
(David Nicholls) *racd centre: trckd ldrs: effrt 2f out: nt clrest of runs ent fnl f: kpt on but no ch fnl 120yds* **14/1**

6110 **14** *1/2* **Hoofalong**[21] 4126 6-8-10 **100**....(b) NathanEvans(5) 10 96
(Michael Easterby) *racd far side: in tch: rdn to chse ldrs 2f out: fdd ins fnl f* **25/1**

1620 **15** *nk* **Baccarat (IRE)**[68] 2546 7-9-10 **109**.... JamesDoyle 22 104
(Charlie Appleby) *racd centre: trckd ldr: rdn over 2f out: sn edging rt: fdd ins fnl f* **50/1**

1026 **16** *3/4* **Hold Tight**[22] 4109 4-8-12 **97**.... JamesMcDonald 17 89
(Saeed bin Suroor) *racd centre: trckd ldr: sddle slipped whn rdn over 1f out: nt rcvr* **33/1**

0-23 **17** *1/2* **Sir Robert Cheval**[35] 3656 5-8-10 **98**.... LouisSteward(3) 24 89
(Robert Cowell) *racd centre: a mid-div* **33/1**

0-20 **18** *3/4* **Go Far**[21] 4136 6-8-12 **97**....(v) MartinHarley 15 85
(Alan Bailey) *racd far side: nvr bttr than mid-div* **40/1**

1100 **19** *nk* **Spring Loaded (IRE)**[14] 4415 4-9-0 **99**.... FrankieDettori 27 86
(Paul D'Arcy) *racd centre: hld up bhd: pushed along over 2f out: making hdwy whn nt clr run ent fnl f: kpt on but no ch after* **33/1**

4030 **20** *nse* **Ninjago**[7] 4667 6-9-2 **101**....(b) LukeMorris 25 88
(Paul Midgley) *racd centre: mid-div: rdn 2f out: nvr threatened: fdd ins fnl f* **40/1**

0020 **21** *1/2* **Moonraker**[21] 4126 4-9-2 **101**.... CharlesBishop 18 87
(Mick Channon) *racd far side: a towards rr* **66/1**

4500 **22** *3/4* **Dinkum Diamond (IRE)**[21] 4152 8-8-11 **101**.... HectorCrouch(5) 13 84
(Henry Candy) *racd far side: mid-div: rdn over 2f out: wknd ent fnl f* **33/1**

4-00 **23** *nk* **Toofi (FR)**[42] 3386 5-9-3 **102**.... AdamKirby 23 84
(Robert Cowell) *racd centre: mid-div: rdn over 2f out: nvr any imp: wknd and eased fnl f* **12/1**

5603 **24** *1/2* **Poyle Vinnie**[21] 4136 6-9-3 **102**.... AndrewMullen 28 83
(Michael Appleby) *racd centre: stdd s and sn swtchd rt: mid-div after 1f: hdwy over 2f out: sn rdn: wknd ent fnl f* **66/1**

1616 **25** *1 3/4* **Swift Approval (IRE)**[7] 4665 4-8-13 **98** 6ex....(p) TomEaves 19 73
(Kevin Ryan) *led centre gp but chsd ldrs overall: rdn over 2f out: wknd over 1f out* **66/1**

0100 **26** *2 3/4* **Blaine**[15] 4338 6-8-13 **98**....(b) RoystonFfrench 16 64
(David Nicholls) *racd far side: a towards rr* **50/1**

0-56 **27** *3/4* **G Force (IRE)**[14] 4413 5-9-9 **108**....(tp) ChrisHayes 9 72
(Adrian Paul Keatley, Ire) *racd far side: a towards rr* **20/1**

1m 9.81s (-2.39) **Going Correction** -0.075s/f (Good)
WFA 3 from 4yo+ 5lb **27** Ran SP% **137.0**
Speed ratings (Par 109): **112,110,110,110,109 109,108,108,106,106 106,106,105,105,104 103,103,102,101,101 101,100,99,98,**
CSF £24.53 CT £428.26 TOTE £6.20: £2.00, £1.70, £6.20, £3.80; EX 23.60 Trifecta £774.80.
Owner J C Smith **Bred** Littleton Stud **Trained** Kingsclere, Hants
■ Stewards' Enquiry : Jason Hart caution; careless riding

FOCUS
There were two groups, with the main pace and majority of the runners towards the far side, but they all merged in the closing stages and those from the middle bunch had their chance as well. The time was 0.56sec quicker than the earlier consolation event and this race was won by a 3yo for the second straight year. Dancing Star improved a bit on her Newmarket win.

4866 QATAR EBF STALLIONS MAIDEN STKS (PLUS 10 RACE) (C&G) 7f
4:20 (4:23) (Class 2) 2-Y-O **£16,172** (£4,812; £2,405; £1,202) **Stalls** Low

Form RPR

2 **1** **Lockheed**[22] 4075 2-9-0 0.... RyanMoore 4 85+
(William Haggas) *hld up in tch in midfield: nt clr run and swtchd lft over 1f out: hdwy u.p to ld ins fnl f: r.o: rdn out* **1/1**[1]

2 **2** *1/2* **Ray's The Money (IRE)**[21] 4125 2-9-0 0.... JamieSpencer 3 83
(Michael Bell) *trckd ldrs: effrt to press ldrs over 1f out: drvn and ev ch 1f out: kpt on same pce fnl 75yds* **5/1**[2]

0 **3** *shd* **Black Trilby (IRE)**[60] 2757 2-9-0 0 AdamKirby 6 83+
(Clive Cox) *hld up in tch in midfield: edgd lft and effrt over 1f out: hdwy u.p to chse ldrs 1f out: styd on wl towards fin* **10/1**[3]

4 *½* **Star Stream** 2-9-0 0 RoystonFfrench 13 81
(Marcus Tregoning) *pressed ldr tl rdn to ld jst over 1f out: hdd ins fnl f: no ex and one pce wl ins fnl f* **50/1**

32 **5** *2 ½* **Abiento (IRE)**[15] 4343 2-9-0 0 PaulHanagan 12 75+
(Richard Fahey) *tool t.k.h: hld up in tch in last quartet: hmpd bnd 5f out: stuck bhd a wall of horses 2f out: swtchd rt and hdwy 1f out: kpt on wl ins fnl f: no threat to ldrs* **33/1**

52 **6** *½* **Manolito De Madrid (GER)**[30] 3799 2-9-0 0 DavidProbert 5 73
(Andrew Balding) *hld up in tch in midfield: unable qck u.p over 1f out: styd on same pce ins fnl f* **14/1**

0 **7** *2* **Syncopation (IRE)**[21] 4128 2-9-0 0 PatDobbs 10 68+
(Sylvester Kirk) *t.k.h: chsd ldrs: rdn over 1f out: no ex u.p and btn 1f out: wknd ins fnl f* **25/1**

8 *½* **Colibri (IRE)** 2-9-0 0 JimCrowley 8 67+
(Hugo Palmer) *dwlt: hld up in last trio: nt clr run 2f out: pushed along and rn green over 1f out: no threat to ldrs but kpt on steadily ins fnl f* **14/1**

54 **9** *1 ½* **Herm (IRE)**[21] 4154 2-9-0 0 KieranShoemark 9 62
(David Evans) *led: rdn 2f out: drvn and hdd over 1f out: sn struggling: wknd ins fnl f* **50/1**

10 *shd* **Imphal** 2-9-0 0 MartinDwyer 7 62
(Marcus Tregoning) *stdd after s: hld up in last trio: swtchd rt and effrt 2f out: rdn and outpcd over 1f out: wl hld and plugged on same pce fnl f* **50/1**

11 *2 ¼* **On To Victory** 2-9-0 0 PatCosgrave 14 56
(Eve Johnson Houghton) *stdd and dropped in bhd after s: t.k.h in last trio: swtchd lft and pushed along wl over 1f out: no hdwy: bhd fnl f* **66/1**

12 *nk* **Ghayyar (IRE)** 2-9-0 0 FrankieDettori 11 55+
(Richard Hannon) *hld up in tch in midfield: effrt whn intimidated: rn green and lost pl wl over 1f out: pushed along and no hdwy over 1f out: bhd fnl f* **5/1**[2]

13 *nk* **The Secrets Out** 2-9-0 0 KieranO'Neill 2 57+
(Luke Dace) *t.k.h: hld up in tch in midfield: hmpd bnd 5f out: rdn and rn green 2f out: sn struggling: bhd ins fnl f* **66/1**

1m 27.27s (0.27) **Going Correction** +0.05s/f (Good) **13** Ran SP% **121.4**
Speed ratings (Par 100): **100,99,99,98,95 95,93,92,90,90 88,87,87**
CSF £5.81 TOTE £2.20: £1.02, £2.30, £8.20; EX 12.80 Trifecta £59.50.
Owner China Horse Club **Bred** Cheveley Park Stud Ltd **Trained** Newmarket, Suffolk

FOCUS
Usually a decent maiden - three of the last eight winners have gone on to win in Group company - and a step up to Pattern company is now the plan for this year's winner. The form fits the race averages.

4867 QATAR STKS (H'CAP) 7f
4:55 (4:56) (Class 2) (0-105,101) 3-Y-O
£18,675 (£5,592; £2,796; £1,398; £699; £351) **Stalls** Low

Form RPR

6521 **1** **Hawatif (IRE)**[9] 4548 3-8-2 **82** JoeFanning 3 89
(Mark Johnston) *trckd ldr: led over 2f out: kpt on gamely fnl f: rdn out* **12/1**

3-01 **2** *½* **Bobby Wheeler (IRE)**[22] 4080 3-8-12 **92** FrankieDettori 16 98+
(Clive Cox) *led: hdd over 2f out: sn rdn: kpt on gamely fnl f: hld nring fin* **12/1**

4-34 **3** *hd* **Tigerwolf (IRE)**[96] 1701 3-8-5 **85** MartinDwyer 8 90+
(Mick Channon) *hld up towards rr: pushed along and hdwy whn nt clr run briefly over 1f out: fin strly fnl 170yds: snatched 3rd fnl strides* **20/1**

3-13 **4** *nse* **Hornsby**[21] 4149 3-8-13 **93** JamesDoyle 15 98
(Charlie Appleby) *s.i.s and pushed along in last early: hdwy in centre fr over 2f out: rdn and drifted rt over 1f out: r.o wl fnl f* **7/1**[2]

4303 **5** *hd* **Reputation (IRE)**[6] 4689 3-8-3 **83** (v) JimmyQuinn 6 87
(John Quinn) *mid-div: rdn 2f out: kpt on wl ins fnl f: chalng for 3rd cl home* **10/1**

21-0 **6** *1 ¾* **Estidraak (IRE)**[23] 4065 3-8-13 **93** PaulHanagan 2 93
(Sir Michael Stoute) *racd keenly: trckd ldrs: rdn 2f out: kpt on but nt pce to chal* **10/1**

3040 **7** *2 ¼* **Venturous (IRE)**[23] 4062 3-9-1 **95** JamesMcDonald 4 89
(Charlie Appleby) *hld up towards rr of midfield: sme minor prog u.p 2f out: no further imp* **9/2**[1]

1312 **8** *shd* **George William**[15] 4358 3-8-9 **89** JimCrowley 14 82
(Richard Hannon) *mid-div: hdwy over 2f out: sn rdn to chse ldrs: wknd fnl f* **9/1**

1552 **9** *1* **Stamp Hill (IRE)**[57] 2871 3-8-10 **90** BarryMcHugh 9 81
(Richard Fahey) *mid-div: rdn whn short of room briefly jst over 1f out: nt pce to get involved* **10/1**

1065 **10** *1* **Red Artist**[10] 4534 3-8-4 **84** (v) HarryBentley 10 72
(Simon Crisford) *trckd ldrs: rdn 2f out: wknd ent fnl f* **40/1**

0043 **11** *nse* **Calder Prince (IRE)**[7] 4665 3-9-7 **101** LiamJones 11 89
(Tom Dascombe) *mid-div on outer: effrt over 2f out: wknd over 1f out* **25/1**

2306 **12** *1 ½* **Monteverdi (FR)**[28] 3908 3-8-8 **88** (p) JamieSpencer 12 72
(Jamie Osborne) *a towards rr* **16/1**

2000 **13** *1* **Whitman**[7] 4625 3-8-11 **91** FrannyNorton 1 72
(Mark Johnston) *s.i.s: a towards rr* **10/1**

2-01 **14** *¾* **Mamillius**[53] 2999 3-8-8 **88** SteveDrowne 7 67
(George Baker) *mid-div: rdn over 2f out: wknd over 1f out* **8/1**[3]

1m 25.59s (-1.41) **Going Correction** +0.05s/f (Good) **14** Ran SP% **120.5**
Speed ratings (Par 106): **110,109,109,109,108 106,104,104,103,101 101,100,99,98**
CSF £145.51 CT £2924.61 TOTE £14.40: £3.90, £2.50, £6.70; EX 187.10 Trifecta £3512.50 Part won..
Owner Abdulla Al Mansoori **Bred** T Whitehead **Trained** Middleham Moor, N Yorks

FOCUS
A good 3yo handicap but the first two controlled things to suit, and a bit further back there were one or two for the notebook.

4868 QATAR APPRENTICE STKS (H'CAP) 1m 1f
6:00 (6:02) (Class 3) (0-90,90) 3-Y-O+ **£12,938** (£3,850; £1,924; £962) **Stalls** Low

Form RPR

5606 **1** **Illusive (IRE)**[16] 4300 5-9-7 **83** MarcMonaghan 16 91
(George Scott) *chsd ldng trio: effrt 2f out: clsd u.p and chal 1f out: led ins fnl f: kpt on: rdn out* **28/1**

6215 **2** *¾* **Freight Train (IRE)**[14] 4406 4-9-0 **76** (p) LouisSteward 2 82
(Mark Johnston) *sn led: rdn and edgd lft 2f out: stl drifting lft over 1f out: hdd ins fnl f: kpt on same pce fnl 100yds* **8/1**

064 **3** *¾* **Craftsmanship (FR)**[19] 4199 5-8-12 **81** DavidEgan[(7)] 4 86
(Robert Eddery) *hld up in midfield: swtchd rt and pushed along over 1f out: clsng whn nt clr run and swtchd lft ent fnl f: styd on to go 3rd wl ins fnl f* **25/1**

5155 **4** *½* **Pactolus (IRE)**[14] 4399 5-9-9 **88** (t) AaronJones[(3)] 3 92
(Stuart Williams) *hld up in tch in midfield: effrt ent fnl 2f: clsd u.p to press ldrs 1f out: styd on same pce ins fnl f* **14/1**

0053 **5** *1 ¼* **Aqua Ardens (GER)**[16] 4305 8-8-9 **78** (tp) WilliamCox[(7)] 6 79
(George Baker) *hld up in tch in midfield: effrt 2f out: hdwy u.p over 1f out: kpt on ins fnl f: nvr enough pce to threaten ldrs* **50/1**

0032 **6** *1* **Bold Prediction (IRE)**[24] 4026 6-9-11 **90** AdamMcNamara[(3)] 18 89
(Ed Walker) *broke wl: chsd ldr: swtchd rt and rdn 2f out: ev ch over 1f out tl no ex ins fnl f: wknd fnl 100yds* **25/1**

0-04 **7** *shd* **Holiday Magic (IRE)**[7] 4644 5-9-9 **88** NathanEvans[(3)] 12 87
(Michael Easterby) *chsd ldng pair: rdn 2f out: drvn and unable qck ent fnl f: no ex and wknd fnl 100yds* **16/1**

1024 **8** *½* **Bridge Of Sighs**[45] 3276 4-8-6 **73** NatalieHambling[(5)] 7 71
(Martin Smith) *hld up wl in tch in midfield: effrt 2f out: unable qck u.p over 1f out: styd on same pce and no imp ins fnl f* **20/1**

5024 **9** *3* **Fiftyshadesfreed (IRE)**[29] 3861 5-9-9 **85** (p) RobHornby 8 77
(George Baker) *hld up in tch in midfield: effrt 2f out: sn drvn and no imp: wl hld and plugged on same pce fnl f* **12/1**

4-01 **10** *hd* **Heisman (IRE)**[24] 4026 5-9-11 **87** (p) MichaelJMMurphy 9 78
(George Baker) *stmbld leaving stalls: hld up in last trio: effrt jst over 2f out: sme hdwy u.p over 1f out: plugged on fnl f: nvr trbld ldrs* **10/3**[1]

2151 **11** *5* **Van Huysen (IRE)**[3] 4774 4-8-9 **76** 6ex LuluStanford[(5)] 10 57
(Dominic Ffrench Davis) *hld up in tch but stuck wd: effrt over 2f out: drvn and no hdwy over 1f out: wknd fnl f* **11/1**

1000 **12** *nk* **Bathos (IRE)**[14] 4399 3-9-2 **87** RossCoakley 14 66
(Mark Johnston) *v awkward leaving stalls and slowly away: in rr: hdwy on outer into midfield after 3f: swtchd lft and rdn 3f out: no hdwy: wl btn and wknd over 1f out* **4/1**[2]

1540 **13** *2 ¼* **Berkeley Vale**[22] 4081 5-8-9 **76** KevinLundie[(5)] 17 51
(Roger Teal) *midfield early: grad stdd bk and in last quartet after 3f: rdn over 3f out: no hdwy: wl btn over 1f out: wknd* **50/1**

435- **14** *nk* **Open The Red**[313] 6590 4-8-13 **78** HectorCrouch[(3)] 15 53
(Amanda Perrett) *stdd bk after s: hld up in last quartet: effrt 3f out: no hdwy and nvr on terms: wknd over 1f out* **7/1**[3]

214/ **15** *2 ¾* **Artful Rogue (IRE)**[654] 7203 5-9-5 **81** KieranShoemark 13 50
(Amanda Perrett) *in tch in midfield: rdn and lost pl over 2f out: sn bhd: wl bhd and eased ins fnl f* **20/1**

1-02 **16** *shd* **Mr Quicksilver**[22] 4081 4-9-3 **79** (t) EdwardGreatrex 11 48
(Ed Walker) *stdd s: t.k.h: hld up in rr: effrt wl over 1f out: no hdwy and sn wl btn: wl bhd and eased ins fnl f* **11/1**

1m 55.06s (-1.24) **Going Correction** +0.05s/f (Good)
WFA 3 from 4yo+ 9lb **16** Ran SP% **128.2**
Speed ratings (Par 107): **107,106,105,105,104 103,103,102,100,99 95,95,93,92,90 90**
CSF £235.63 CT £5894.15 TOTE £38.20: £5.30, £2.60, £4.90, £3.40; EX 412.00 Trifecta £3149.30 Part won..
Owner The Done At One-O-Ones **Bred** Looking Back Syndicate **Trained** Newmarket, Suffolk
■ Stewards' Enquiry : William Cox two-day ban; used whip above the permitted level (13th-14th Aug)

FOCUS
An open handicap. The winner is rated back to form.
T/Jkpt: £12,655.90 to a £1 stake. Pool: £53,475.97 - 3 winning units T/Plt: £93.70 to a £1 stake. Pool: £296,338.72 - 2306.28 winning units T/Qpdt: £11.40 to a £1 stake. Pool: £20,669.08 - 1340.36 winning units **Steve Payne & Tim Mitchell**

4335 HAMILTON (R-H)
Saturday, July 30

OFFICIAL GOING: Good (good to soft in places; 6.2)
Wind: Breezy, half against Weather: Cloudy, bright

4869 HIGHLAND SPRING WATER NURSERY H'CAP (A £20,000 HIGHLAND SPRING WATER HAMILTON SERIES QUALIFIER) 6f 6y
5:40 (5:42) (Class 6) 2-Y-O **£2,911** (£866; £432; £216) **Stalls** High

Form RPR

3305 **1** **Percy Toplis**[8] 4602 2-8-12 **67** ow1 KeaganLatham 5 72
(Kevin Ryan) *t.k.h: trckd ldrs: led over 1f out: edgd rt and drew clr ins fnl f* **5/1**[3]

230 **2** *2 ¼* **Good Time Ahead (IRE)**[14] 4394 2-9-7 **76** DavidNolan 1 74
(Richard Fahey) *cl up: rdn and ev ch over 1f out: kpt on fnl f to take 2nd cl home: nt rch wnr* **9/5**[1]

535 **3** *nse* **Kroy**[47] 3208 2-8-6 **61** NeilFarley 6 59
(Ollie Pears) *prom: effrt and ev ch over 1f out: chsd wnr ins fnl f: no ex and lost 2nd cl home* **6/1**

000 **4** *1* **Flawed Diamond (FR)**[16] 4298 2-7-9 **57** ow1 PaulaMuir[(7)] 3 52
(K R Burke) *hld up: hdwy on outside over 2f out: rdn over 1f out: kpt on fnl f: no imp* **14/1**

0541 **5** *1 ¼* **Coolfitch (IRE)**[6] 4679 2-9-8 **77** 6ex SamJames 2 68
(David O'Meara) *t.k.h: trckd ldrs: smooth hdwy and ev ch over 1f out: rdn and wknd ins fnl f* **7/2**[2]

5003 **6** *2 ½* **Breaking Free**[15] 4364 2-8-3 **58** (v[1]) CamHardie 7 41
(John Quinn) *hld up in tch: rdn over 2f out: wknd over 1f out* **14/1**

100 **7** *2* **Katrine (IRE)**[22] 4111 2-9-5 **74** PhillipMakin 4 50
(Mark Johnston) *t.k.h: led to over 1f out: sn rdn and wknd* **8/1**

1m 14.95s (2.75) **Going Correction** +0.40s/f (Good) **7** Ran SP% **113.3**
Speed ratings (Par 92): **97,94,93,92,90 87,84**
CSF £14.19 TOTE £6.50: £3.10, £1.70; EX 16.30 Trifecta £134.30.
Owner K&J Bloodstock Ltd **Bred** Whatton Manor Stud **Trained** Hambleton, N Yorks

FOCUS
Race distances as advertised. The loop rail was on the innermost position and the going was good, good to soft in places. The went a fair pace in this nursery and the winner forged clear against the stands' rail.

4870 SCULLION LAW "AWARD WINNING CLIENT CARE" MAIDEN STKS 6f 6y
6:15 (6:15) (Class 5) 3-Y-O+ **£3,881** (£1,155; £577; £288) **Stalls** High

Form RPR

-244 **1** **Foresight (FR)**[28] 3892 3-9-5 78 SamJames 5 81
(David Simcock) *t.k.h: trckd ldrs: hdwy to ld appr fnl f: drvn clr* **5/4**[1]

2025 **2** *3* **Dance Alone**[14] 4410 3-9-5 70 (b[1]) KeaganLatham 2 71
(Kevin Ryan) *mde most tl hdd appr fnl f: kpt on: no pce of wnr* **6/1**[3]

-3 **3** 1 1/4 **Fivehundredmiles (IRE)**[37] 3550 3-9-5 0...................... TadhgO'Shea 7 67
(John Patrick Shanahan, Ire) *chsd ldng gp: rdn over 2f out: hdwy to chse ldrs over 1f out: kpt on same pce ins fnl f* **6/1**[3]

42 **4** 1/2 **Glengarry**[54] 2957 3-9-5 0...................................... PhillipMakin 4 65
(Keith Dalgleish) *dwlt: hld up: stdy hdwy over 2f out: rdn and hung rt over 1f out: one pce fnl f* **2/1**[2]

-000 **5** 1 3/4 **Fool's Dream**[29] 3850 3-8-9 44.. PhilDennis(5) 1 55?
(Bryan Smart) *in tch on outside: rdn over 2f out: edgd rt and outpcd over 1f out* **80/1**

650 **6** 10 **Diamond Avalanche (IRE)**[57] 2864 3-9-5 65................(p) DavidNolan 6 28
(Patrick Holmes) *chsd ldrs: rdn over 2f out: sn wknd* **25/1**

04 **7** 7 **Hellracer**[23] 4035 3-9-5 0.. CamHardie 3 5
(Bryan Smart) *chsd ldr: rdn along 1/2-way: edgd rt and wknd wl over 1f out* **50/1**

1m 14.87s (2.67) **Going Correction** +0.40s/f (Good) **7** Ran SP% **113.4**
Speed ratings (Par 103): **98,94,92,91,89 76,66**
CSF £9.31 TOTE £2.00: £1.10, £2.90; EX 7.80 Trifecta £25.70.
Owner HighclereThoroughbredRacing-Dream Ahead **Bred** Haras D'Ombreville Et Al **Trained** Newmarket, Suffolk

FOCUS
The favourite delivered in good style in this maiden.

4871 CAESAR'S ENTERTAINMENT H'CAP 1m 67y
6:45 (6:46) (Class 5) (0-75,78) 3-Y-O+ **£4,528** (£1,347; £673; £336) **Stalls** Low

Form RPR

4150 **1** **Normandie Lady**[38] 3521 3-9-4 73.................................... DavidNolan 2 80+
(Richard Fahey) *dwlt: sn in tch: rdn over 2f out: hdwy to ld ins fnl f: hung lft: drvn out* **5/1**[3]

2443 **2** 1 1/2 **Fidelma Moon (IRE)**[21] 4145 4-9-6 72..................... JordanVaughan(5) 6 78
(K R Burke) *t.k.h: led and sn clr: rdn over 2f out: hung lft over 1f out: hdd ins fnl f: r.o* **7/1**

033 **3** nk **Toboggan's Fire**[28] 3895 3-9-0 74................................. RowanScott(5) 9 77
(Ann Duffield) *hld up in tch: effrt and drvn along over 2f out: sn outpcd: kpt on fnl f: nrst fin* **5/2**[1]

3324 **4** nk **Tectonic (IRE)**[15] 4341 7-9-0 61.......................................(v) PhillipMakin 7 65
(Keith Dalgleish) *hld up: shkn up and hdwy over 1f out: kpt on same pce last 100yds* **20/1**

0203 **5** 1 1/4 **The Wee Barra (IRE)**[11] 4486 4-9-1 62..............................(p) JoeDoyle 1 63
(Kevin Ryan) *t.k.h: cl up: rdn over 2f out: outpcd fr over 1f out* **13/2**

-656 **6** 1/2 **Auxiliary**[18] 4241 3-8-13 75.......................................(p) PaulaMuir(7) 5 73
(Patrick Holmes) *s.i.s: hld up: rdn along and outpcd over 4f out: kpt on fnl f: no imp* **25/1**

2241 **7** 2 **Archie's Advice**[12] 4446 5-9-10 78................................ CliffordLee(7) 10 74
(Keith Dalgleish) *hld up: hdwy on outside over 2f out: edgd rt: wknd over 1f out* **4/1**[2]

023 **8** 1 1/2 **Muroor**[6] 4681 3-9-0 69... SamJames 4 59
(David O'Meara) *hld up: drvn along and effrt 3f out: wknd fr 2f out* **9/1**

6051 **9** 18 **The Lynch Man**[12] 4449 3-9-1 70.......................................(v) CamHardie 3 19
(John Quinn) *cl up: rdn and hung rt over 2f out: sn wknd: eased whn btn fnl f* **14/1**

1m 50.64s (2.24) **Going Correction** +0.40s/f (Good)
WFA 3 from 4yo+ 8lb **9** Ran SP% **116.3**
Speed ratings (Par 103): **104,103,103,102,101 101,99,97,79**
CSF £40.11 CT £108.26 TOTE £6.60: £2.10, £2.80, £1.80; EX 46.10 Trifecta £232.30.
Owner A B Phipps **Bred** A B Phipps **Trained** Musley Bank, N Yorks

FOCUS
The pace was decent but not many got involved in this handicap.

4872 GAS CALL SERVICES H'CAP 1m 1f 34y
7:15 (7:17) (Class 6) (0-60,60) 3-Y-O+ **£2,911** (£866; £432; £216) **Stalls** Low

Form RPR

3140 **1** **Jocks Wa Hae (IRE)**[16] 4314 3-8-13 56......................... TadhgO'Shea 1 65
(John Patrick Shanahan, Ire) *dwlt: hld up: rdn along 1/2-way: hdwy over 2f out: swtchd rt and led ins fnl f: kpt on strly* **10/3**[2]

2452 **2** 1 3/4 **Indian Giver**[12] 4456 8-9-3 56...............................(p) JordanVaughan(5) 2 62
(John David Riches) *hld up in tch: hdwy and cl up over 3f out: led appr fnl f: edgd lft and hdd ins fnl f: kpt on same pce* **5/2**[1]

5064 **3** 3 **Canny Style**[18] 4233 3-8-12 55.. JoeDoyle 8 54
(Kevin Ryan) *hld up: hdwy whn nt clr run over 2f out: sn rdn: rallied over 1f out: edgd lft and kpt on fnl f: nrst fin* **17/2**

443 **4** 3/4 **Kerry Icon**[7] 4648 3-7-12 46..................................... ShirleyTeasdale(5) 5 43
(Iain Jardine) *t.k.h: mde most tl rdn and hdd appr fnl f: wknd ins fnl f* **12/1**

6505 **5** 1 **Judith Gardenier**[16] 4314 4-8-5 46 oh1...................... JamieGormley(7) 9 42
(Iain Jardine) *hld up on outside: rdn over 3f out: rallied over 1f out: kpt on fnl f: nt pce to chal* **33/1**

0543 **6** 2 3/4 **Munjally**[16] 4314 5-9-1 56...(v) PaulaMuir(7) 10 46
(Patrick Holmes) *in tch: drvn along over 2f out: sn no ex* **14/1**

4326 **7** 2 1/4 **Incurs Four Faults**[11] 4486 5-8-10 51.......................(p) CliffordLee(7) 11 37
(Keith Dalgleish) *in tch: hdwy to chal after 3f to over 3f out: wknd fr 2f out* **12/1**

3303 **8** hd **L'Apogee**[13] 4424 3-9-1 58...(p) DavidNolan 7 42
(Richard Fahey) *prom: drvn along over 3f out: wknd wl over 1f out* **6/1**[3]

6-00 **9** 4 1/2 **Triassic (IRE)**[17] 4258 3-9-3 60.................................... PJMcDonald 3 35
(Mark Johnston) *chsd ldrs: pushed along 1/2-way: wknd fr 2f out* **12/1**

0043 **10** 6 **Magical Lasso (IRE)**[5] 4705 3-9-3 60............................(p) PhillipMakin 6 22
(Keith Dalgleish) *hld up towards rr: struggling over 3f out: sn btn* **16/1**

000 **11** 2 1/2 **Champagne Rules**[39] 3498 5-9-12 60............................. PaddyAspell 4 18
(Sharon Watt) *s.i.s: hld up: hdwy over 3f out: wknd fr 2f out* **33/1**

2m 2.76s (3.06) **Going Correction** +0.40s/f (Good)
WFA 3 from 4yo+ 9lb **11** Ran SP% **118.0**
Speed ratings (Par 101): **102,100,97,97,96 93,91,91,87,82 80**
CSF £12.10 CT £63.45 TOTE £4.50: £2.00, £1.60, £2.90; EX 12.80 Trifecta £86.00.
Owner Thistle Bloodstock Limited **Bred** Thistle Bloodstock Ltd **Trained** Kells, Co Kilkenny
■ Stewards' Enquiry : Jordan Vaughan four-day ban; used whip above the permitted level (13th-16th Aug)
Shirley Teasdale two-day ban; used whip above the permitted level (13th-14th Aug)
Tadhg O'Shea two-day ban; used whip above the permitted level (13th-14th Aug)

FOCUS
The first two pulled clear in this minor handicap.

4873 ALEA CASINO H'CAP 6f 6y
7:45 (7:46) (Class 4) (0-80,79) 3-Y-O+ **£6,469** (£1,925; £962; £481) **Stalls** High

Form RPR

-001 **1** **Naggers (IRE)**[19] 4191 5-9-7 74...................................... CamHardie 10 88+
(Paul Midgley) *in tch: effrt whn nt clr run over 2f out: plld out and hdwy over 1f out: led wl ins fnl f: drvn out* **4/1**[2]

0060 **2** 1 1/4 **Signore Piccolo**[8] 4608 5-9-8 75...................................... DavidNolan 11 85
(David O'Meara) *cl up: led over 2f out: rdn over 1f out: hdd wl ins fnl f: no ex nr fin* **10/1**

4015 **3** 1 1/2 **Specialv (IRE)**[14] 4382 3-8-5 70..............................(p) BenRobinson(7) 13 74
(Brian Ellison) *dwlt: hld up: hdwy to chse ldrs over 1f out: edgd lft and kpt on ins fnl f* **16/1**

3055 **4** 2 1/4 **Barkston Ash**[28] 3892 8-9-11 78...............................(p) DuranFentiman 14 76
(Eric Alston) *hld up: rdn and hdwy over 1f out: kpt on fnl f: nvr able to chal* **12/1**

5400 **5** 2 1/2 **Meshardal (GER)**[17] 4259 6-9-8 75............................... JamesSullivan 6 65+
(Ruth Carr) *stdd in rr: hdwy and far side of gp and ev ch briefly over 1f out: sn rdn: edgd lft and wknd ins fnl f* **13/2**

0660 **6** shd **Go Go Green (IRE)**[11] 4488 10-8-12 65.............................. JoeDoyle 12 55
(Jim Goldie) *dwlt: hld up: rdn and hdwy over 1f out: kpt on fnl f: nvr able to chal* **20/1**

4304 **7** 1/2 **The Name's Paver**[23] 4036 3-8-7 65.................................(b[1]) NeilFarley 4 52
(Noel Wilson) *chsd ldrs: rdn over 2f out: wknd over 1f out* **28/1**

0101 **8** 3 **Royal Connoisseur (IRE)**[15] 4337 5-9-0 74............... HayleyIrvine(7) 8 52
(Richard Fahey) *cl up: ev ch and rdn over 2f out: wknd over 1f out* **14/1**

6252 **9** 1 **Sir Domino (FR)**[23] 4032 4-9-9 76..............................(p) KeaganLatham 7 51
(Kevin Ryan) *t.k.h: led to over 2f out: rdn and wknd over 1f out* **10/1**

2313 **10** 1 1/2 **Brockholes**[17] 4259 3-9-4 76...................................... PJMcDonald 9 45
(Ann Duffield) *prom: drvn along over 2f out: wknd over 1f out* **7/2**[1]

2005 **11** 1 1/4 **Rita's Boy (IRE)**[26] 3944 4-9-7 79......................... JordanVaughan(5) 3 45
(K R Burke) *hld up in tch: effrt on outside over 2f out: wknd over 1f out* **16/1**

1512 **12** 6 **Born Innocent (IRE)**[32] 3753 3-8-13 71......................... TadhgO'Shea 1 17
(John Patrick Shanahan, Ire) *cl up: rdn over 2f out: wknd wl over 1f out* **11/2**[3]

1m 13.83s (1.63) **Going Correction** +0.40s/f (Good)
WFA 3 from 4yo+ 5lb **12** Ran SP% **123.5**
Speed ratings (Par 105): **105,103,101,98,95 94,94,90,88,86 85,77**
CSF £46.09 CT £597.32 TOTE £4.60: £1.10, £3.30, £5.40; EX 54.00 Trifecta £797.90.
Owner Taylor's Bloodstock Ltd **Bred** Azienda Agricola Rosati Colarieti **Trained** Westow, N Yorks

FOCUS
A decent handicap. The first four were all drawn in stall ten or higher and raced near the stands' rail in the closing stages.

4874 EXSEL GROUP - IT & COMMUNICATIONS H'CAP 5f 7y
8:15 (8:16) (Class 5) (0-70,69) 3-Y-O+ **£4,528** (£1,347; £673; £336) **Stalls** Centre

Form RPR

5-43 **1** **Showdaisy**[19] 4202 3-8-12 59 ow1.................................... PhillipMakin 8 69
(Keith Dalgleish) *taken early to post: mde virtually all: racd nr side of gp: rdn clr fr over 1f out: readily* **4/1**[1]

2003 **2** 2 1/4 **Kinloch Pride**[14] 4410 4-8-7 50...(p) NeilFarley 2 53
(Noel Wilson) *dwlt: hld up bhd ldng gp: effrt and hdwy over 2f out: chsd (clr) wnr ins fnl f: kpt on: no imp* **9/1**

3401 **3** 1 3/4 **Star Cracker (IRE)**[19] 4192 4-9-12 69..............................(p) JoeDoyle 4 66
(Jim Goldie) *hld up: rdn over 2f out: swtchd lft and hdwy over 1f out: kpt on fnl f: nvr able to chal* **4/1**[1]

100- **4** 1/2 **Raise A Billion**[270] 7680 5-8-7 50.. CamHardie 5 45
(John David Riches) *in tch: effrt and rdn over 2f out: no ex ins fnl f* **11/2**[2]

5100 **5** 2 1/2 **Bronze Beau**[12] 4452 9-9-9 66.......................................(tp) SamJames 3 52
(Kristin Stubbs) *w ldrs to over 2f out: wknd ins fnl f* **12/1**

6010 **6** 1 1/4 **Coiste Bodhar (IRE)**[23] 4039 5-9-8 65.......................... PJMcDonald 6 46
(Scott Dixon) *w ldrs: rdn over 2f out: wknd over 1f out* **10/1**

-500 **7** 1 **Amy Blair**[12] 4444 3-8-3 50 oh4......................................[1] JamesSullivan 7 27
(Keith Dalgleish) *bhd and sn drvn along: hung rt wl over 1f out: sme late hdwy: n.d* **33/1**

0503 **8** shd **Danzeb (IRE)**[17] 4256 3-8-13 65.................................(p) RowanScott(5) 9 41
(Ann Duffield) *prom: effrt and rdn over 2f out: wknd over 1f out* **8/1**[3]

0241 **9** 2 3/4 **Sarabi**[29] 3847 3-9-8 69...(p) DaleSwift 1 36
(Scott Dixon) *trckd ldrs: drvn along 1/2-way: wknd over 1f out* **4/1**[1]

1m 1.78s (1.78) **Going Correction** +0.40s/f (Good)
WFA 3 from 4yo+ 4lb **9** Ran SP% **116.2**
Speed ratings (Par 103): **101,97,94,93,89 87,86,86,81**
CSF £41.18 CT £154.48 TOTE £3.40: £1.10, £3.40, £2.20; EX 44.40 Trifecta £283.80.
Owner Ronnie Docherty **Bred** Patricia Ann Scott-Dunn **Trained** Carluke, S Lanarks

FOCUS
The winner forged clear from a high draw in this sprint handicap.

4875 PROCAST BUILDING CONTRACTORS LTD H'CAP 1m 3f 14y
8:45 (8:45) (Class 5) (0-75,76) 3-Y-O+ **£4,528** (£1,347; £673; £336) **Stalls** Low

Form RPR

-243 **1** **Carbon Dating (IRE)**[7] 4634 4-10-1 76........................... PhillipMakin 3 87
(John Patrick Shanahan, Ire) *chsd clr ldrs: smooth hdwy over 2f out: shkn up to ld over 1f out: kpt on strly fnl f* **4/1**[3]

226- **2** 3 1/4 **Al Destoor**[469] 1508 6-10-0 75... DavidNolan 2 80
(Jennie Candlish) *stdd s: hld up: stdy hdwy over 2f out: rdn and chsd (clr) wnr ins fnl f: kpt on: no imp* **11/4**[1]

2103 **3** 6 **Lara Carbonara (IRE)**[16] 4311 4-9-9 70......................... TadhgO'Shea 7 65
(John Patrick Shanahan, Ire) *hld up: rdn over 3f out: rallied over 2f out: kpt on fnl f: nvr able to chal* **9/2**

3015 **4** nse **Miningrocks (FR)**[27] 3921 4-8-6 58.............................. PhilDennis(5) 5 53
(Declan Carroll) *t.k.h: led and clr w one other to 4f out: rdn and hdd over 1f out: wknd ins fnl f* **16/1**

0235 **5** 5 **First Sargeant**[11] 4493 6-8-13 60......................................(p) CamHardie 4 46
(Lawrence Mullaney) *hld up: rdn along over 3f out: wknd fr 2f out* **12/1**

2412 **6** 11 **Falcon's Fire (IRE)**[12] 4447 3-8-5 63 ow1...................... PJMcDonald 8 31
(Keith Dalgleish) *hld up in tch: effrt over 3f out: rdn and wknd over 2f out* **3/1**[2]

6430 **7** 1 3/4 **King Of Paradise (IRE)**[28] 3903 7-9-2 63.......................(p) NeilFarley 1 28
(Eric Alston) *t.k.h: pressed ldr and clr of rest to 4f out: rdn and wknd fr 2f out* **8/1**

6030 **8** 12 **Arantes**[11] 4491 5-9-4 65...(p) JamesSullivan 6 9
(R Mike Smith) *prom chsng gp: drvn and outpcd over 3f out: sn btn* **20/1**

6650 **9** 33 **New Colours**[11] 4489 5-8-5 59 oh11 ow3......................(p) CliffordLee(7) 9
(Linda Perratt) *dwlt: bhd: drvn and struggling over 4f out: sn lost tch: t.o* **40/1**

2m 26.34s (0.74) **Going Correction** +0.40s/f (Good)
WFA 3 from 4yo+ 11lb **9** Ran SP% **121.7**
Speed ratings (Par 103): **113,110,106,106,102 94,93,84,60**
CSF £16.41 CT £53.14 TOTE £4.60: £1.80, £1.60, £1.90; EX 13.50 Trifecta £54.10.
Owner Thistle Bloodstock Limited **Bred** Thistle Bloodstock Ltd **Trained** Kells, Co Kilkenny

FOCUS
They went a good pace in this handicap and finished quite well strung out.

T/Plt: £78.90 to a £1 stake. Pool: £59,441.68 - 549.34 winning units T/Qpdt: £23.50 to a £1 stake. Pool: £5,819.35 - 182.80 winning units **Richard Young**

4635 LINGFIELD (L-H)

Saturday, July 30

OFFICIAL GOING: Turf course - good to firm (good in places; 7.7); all-weather: polytrack - standard

Wind: Almost nil Weather: Fine but cloudy

4876 MOBILE BETTING AT 188BET APPRENTICE H'CAP — 7f 140y

5:25 (5:25) (Class 6) (0-65,63) 4-Y-0+ **£2,587** (£770; £384; £192) **Stalls** Centre

Form — RPR

0001 **1** **Prince Of Cardamom (IRE)**^{16} **4290** 4-8-11 **51**....(p) CharlieBennett$^{(3)}$ 7 — 61
(Jonathan Geake) *racd against rail: led or disp: shkn up wl over 2f out: def advantage wl over 1f out and sn clr: kpt on wl* **4/1**^{2}

5552 **2** 3½ **Limerick Lord (IRE)**^{14} **4389** 4-8-12 **59**....................(p) LiamDoran$^{(10)}$ 1 — 60
(Julia Feilden) *taken down early: racd wdst: on terms w ldng pair: pushed along over 2f out: nt qckn wl over 1f out: one pce after* **9/4**^{1}

0206 **3** 3¼ **Believe It (IRE)**^{15} **4355** 4-8-13 **60**..........................(b^{1}) NicolaCurrie$^{(10)}$ 4 — 53
(Richard Hughes) *w wnr: gng strly 3f out: pushed along 2f out and nt qckn: fdd* **9/4**^{1}

3505 **4** ¾ **Whaleweigh Station**^{14} **4388** 5-8-12 **52**................(p) MeganNicholls$^{(3)}$ 5 — 43
(J R Jenkins) *restrained into last and nt gng wl after: rdn 3f out: effrt against rail to dispute 3rd ins fnl f: fdd nr fin* **7/1**^{3}

0401 **5** 5 **Nifty Kier**^{10} **4505** 7-8-9 **49**.. GeorgeWood$^{(3)}$ 3 — 28
(Phil McEntee) *trckd ldrs: rdn over 2f out: wknd over 1f out* **12/1**

5-00 **6** 2½ **Prim And Proper**^{16} **4288** 5-9-6 **60**........................(b^{1}) PaddyBradley$^{(3)}$ 6 — 32
(John Flint) *trckd ldrs: rdn wl over 2f out: wknd over 1f out* **7/1**^{3}

1m 31.67s (-0.63) **Going Correction** -0.05s/f (Good) **6** Ran SP% **114.2**
Speed ratings (Par 101): **101,97,94,93,88 86**
CSF £13.80 TOTE £5.10: £2.50, £1.60; EX 13.30 Trifecta £45.20.
Owner Mrs P D Gulliver **Bred** Kildaragh Stud **Trained** East Kennett, Wilts

FOCUS
A moderate handicap for apprentice riders. They went a muddling gallop on ground officially described as good to firm, good in places. Unsurprisingly, the winner stuck to the near stands' rail from a high draw, readily outstaying this weak opposition.

4877 OLYMPIC BETTING AT 188BET MEDIAN AUCTION MAIDEN STKS — 7f 140y

5:55 (5:56) (Class 6) 2-Y-0 **£2,587** (£770; £384; £192) **Stalls** Centre

Form — RPR

542 **1** **Harbour Master**^{8} **4594** 2-8-9 76.................................... LucyKBarry$^{(5)}$ 4 — 85+
(Jamie Osborne) *racd against rail: trckd ldr: gap appeared 3f out and led 2f out: shkn up and clr over 1f out: styd on strly* **11/4**^{2}

324 **2** 3¾ **Magical Forest (IRE)**^{56} **2885** 2-8-9 75.............................. LukeMorris 2 — 71+
(Marco Botti) *racd in 6th and pushed along over 4f out: prog on outer fr 3f out: styd on to take 2nd ins fnl f: no ch w wnr* **4/1**^{3}

2 **3** 3¼ **Harmonise**^{21} **4154** 2-8-9 0.. CharlesBishop 8 — 63+
(Mick Channon) *led against rail: hung lft fr 3f out and ended towards centre: hdd 2f out: fdd and lost 2nd ins fnl f* **7/4**^{1}

4 2 **Maldonado (FR)** 2-9-0 0.. MartinHarley 5 — 63+
(Charlie Appleby) *rn green in last pair: prog 3f out to chse ldrs 2f out: shkn up and no imp after* **5/1**

05 **5** ½ **Sufrah (USA)**^{33} **3730** 2-9-0 0... SamHitchcott 3 — 61
(Brian Meehan) *pushed along in midfield over 4f out: effrt u.p 3f out: chsd ldrs 2f out: no imp after* **8/1**

6 9 **Tis Wonderful (IRE)** 2-9-0 0...................................... TimmyMurphy 6 — 39
(Clive Cox) *restrained s: hld up in last pair: def last over 2f out: passed two rivals late on: nt knocked abt* **20/1**

7 2¼ **Miss Sayif** 2-8-9 0... JFEgan 7 — 28
(George Margarson) *wl in tch chsng ldrs tl wknd qckly over 2f out* **50/1**

8 5 **Aventus (IRE)** 2-9-0 0.. ShaneKelly 1 — 21
(Richard Hughes) *disp 2nd pl to 3f out: wknd rapidly over 2f out* **33/1**

1m 30.61s (-1.69) **Going Correction** -0.05s/f (Good) **8** Ran SP% **120.5**
Speed ratings (Par 92): **106,102,99,97,96 87,85,80**
CSF £14.87 TOTE £3.80: £1.20, £1.50, £1.20; EX 13.60 Trifecta £36.40.
Owner Michael Buckley & Charles E Noell **Bred** Mrs R F Johnson Houghton **Trained** Upper Lambourn, Berks

FOCUS
An ordinary juvenile maiden. They went a respectable gallop up the favoured stands' rail and an improver stretched nicely clear in the final furlong.

4878 188BET H'CAP — 6f

6:30 (6:30) (Class 6) (0-65,65) 3-Y-0+ **£2,587** (£770; £384; £192) **Stalls** Centre

Form — RPR

0021 **1** **Chetan**^{9} **4570** 4-9-8 **61**...(tp) AdamBeschizza 6 — 70
(Charlie Wallis) *taken down early: mde all and grabbed nr side rail: shkn up 2f out: styd on and a in command* **6/1**

0-40 **2** ¾ **Unnoticed**^{37} **3554** 4-9-12 **65**... LukeMorris 4 — 72+
(Luca Cumani) *hld up in last: prog on outer over 1f out: drvn and styd on to take 2nd ins fnl f: unable to chal* **4/1**^{2}

4503 **3** ¾ **Multi Quest**^{17} **4278** 4-8-12 **51**.......................................(b) SamHitchcott 7 — 55
(John E Long) *chsd wnr against rail: shkn up 2f out: one pce over 1f out: kpt on* **14/1**

4-01 **4** ¾ **Vincenzo Coccotti (USA)**^{17} **4278** 4-9-9 **62**..................(p) ShaneKelly 5 — 64
(Ken Cunningham-Brown) *chsd wnr: shkn up 2f out: kpt on same pce after* **4/1**^{2}

0453 **5** ½ **Angie's Girl**^{17} **4262** 3-9-4 **62**.. TimmyMurphy 8 — 61
(Clive Cox) *taken down early: t.k.h: hld up in last pair: swtchd lft and effrt 2f out: shkn up and no qckn over 1f out: one pce after* **11/2**^{3}

3421 **6** 10 **Shahaama**^{43} **3353** 3-9-7 **65**... MartinHarley 1 — 32
(Mick Channon) *chsd ldrs: pushed along 2f out: wknd qckly over 1f out* **7/4**^{1}

1m 11.63s (0.43) **Going Correction** -0.05s/f (Good)
WFA 3 from 4yo+ 5lb **6** Ran SP% **112.7**
Speed ratings (Par 101): **95,94,93,92,91 78**
CSF £29.88 CT £318.62 TOTE £7.10: £2.40, £1.90; EX 27.50 Trifecta £259.00.
Owner Roger & Val Miles, Tony Stamp **Bred** Andrew W Robson **Trained** Ardleigh, Essex

FOCUS
A modest handicap. They went an even gallop and the winner dominated up the favoured stands' rail.

4879 188BET.CO.UK BRITISH STALLION STUDS EBF MAIDEN STKS — 5f

7:00 (7:00) (Class 5) 2-Y-0 **£3,363** (£1,001; £500; £250) **Stalls** Centre

Form — RPR

2462 **1** **Stop The Wages (IRE)**^{11} **4494** 2-9-0 73........................ MartinDwyer 6 — 77+
(Brian Meehan) *mde all against rail: pushed along and drew clr fnl f* **8/13**^{1}

4303 **2** 4 **Speed Freak**^{14} **4386** 2-9-0 74......................................(v^{1}) MartinHarley 4 — 63
(Ralph Beckett) *racd against rail: trckd ldng pair: squeezed between them to take 2nd over 1f out: sn shkn up and outpcd by wnr* **13/8**^{2}

6 **3** 3½ **Debonaire David**^{80} **2147** 2-9-5 0.................................. ShaneKelly 5 — 55
(Richard Hughes) *chsd wnr to over 1f out: wknd ins fnl f* **10/1**^{3}

540 **4** 4½ **Daffodil Mulligan**^{39} **3507** 2-8-11 0.................. JosephineGordon$^{(3)}$ 2 — 34
(J S Moore) *a in last: pushed along after 2f: sn struggling* **20/1**

58.7s (0.50) **Going Correction** -0.05s/f (Good) **4** Ran SP% **113.9**
Speed ratings (Par 94): **94,87,82,74**
CSF £2.06 TOTE £1.50; EX 1.90 Trifecta £2.80.
Owner The Lets Do Lunch Partnership **Bred** David Cox & Dermot Farrington **Trained** Manton, Wilts

FOCUS
A fair little juvenile maiden. They went a respectable gallop and the winner built nicely on his recent promise under similar conditions.

4880 ASIAN H'CAP BETTING AT 188BET HANDICAP — 1m 4f (P)

7:30 (7:30) (Class 5) (0-70,73) 3-Y-0+ **£3,234** (£962; £481; £240) **Stalls** Low

Form — RPR

0002 **1** **Cliff Face (IRE)**^{24} **4018** 3-8-7 **61**.. LukeMorris 7 — 73+
(Sir Mark Prescott Bt) *trckd ldrs: wnt 3rd over 2f out: clsd to ld over 1f out: shkn up and sn clr: comf* **8/11**^{1}

2001 **2** 3½ **Brave Archibald (IRE)**^{10} **4522** 3-9-5 **73**........................ MartinHarley 6 — 79
(Paul Cole) *t.k.h: hld up tl quick move to join ldr after 4f: led 3f out: drvn and hdd over 1f out: kpt on and clr of rest but no ch w wnr* **3/1**^{2}

-066 **3** 3¼ **Perfect Rhythm**^{42} **3403** 5-9-7 **68**............................... CharlieBennett$^{(5)}$ 3 — 69
(Patrick Chamings) *hld up: last tl prog over 2f out: drvn over 1f out: styd on to take 3rd ins fnl f: no ch w ldng pair* **12/1**

5165 **4** 1¾ **Lady Lunchalot (USA)**^{19} **4201** 6-9-11 **67**......................(p) LiamKeniry 2 — 65
(Laura Mongan) *hld up in last trio: shkn up over 2f out: sme prog and briefly disp wl btn 3rd over 1f out: one pce after* **16/1**

6353 **5** 1¾ **Bognor (USA)**^{7} **4635** 5-9-9 **70**.................................. PaddyBradley$^{(5)}$ 5 — 65
(Michael Attwater) *led or disp to 3f out: sn u.p: fdd wl over 1f out* **25/1**

5040 **6** 4 **Chilworth Bells**^{10} **4531** 4-9-11 **70**....................(p) JosephineGordon$^{(3)}$ 4 — 59
(Conor Dore) *sn pushed along: in tch in last trio but nvr gng wl: drvn over 3f out: sn btn* **20/1**

0-10 **7** hd **Song And Dance Man**^{19} **4201** 6-9-12 **68**.....................(v) DannyBrock 8 — 56
(Jane Chapple-Hyam) *t.k.h: racd in ldng trio: chal 3f out: lost 2nd and wknd qckly wl over 1f out* **10/1**^{3}

-014 **8** hd **Merry Dancer (IRE)**^{33} **3722** 4-8-12 **61**....................... MitchGodwin$^{(7)}$ 9 — 49
(Patrick Chamings) *t.k.h: racd on outer: chsd ldrs: rdn and wknd over 2f out* **14/1**

22/5 **9** ¾ **Little Buxted (USA)**^{14} **4383** 6-10-0 **70**.....................(p) TimmyMurphy 1 — 57
(Jim Best) *in tch in midfield: rdn over 3f out: wknd 2f out* **20/1**

2m 32.73s (-0.27) **Going Correction** +0.075s/f (Slow)
WFA 3 from 4yo+ 12lb **9** Ran SP% **125.6**
Speed ratings (Par 103): **103,100,98,97,96 93,93,93,92**
CSF £3.32 CT £16.46 TOTE £1.50: £1.02, £1.40, £4.00; EX 3.60 Trifecta £22.90.
Owner Bluehills Racing Limited **Bred** Glashare House Stud **Trained** Newmarket, Suffolk

FOCUS
A modest middle-distance handicap. They went a respectable gallop, at best, on standard Polytrack. The improving 3yo winner proved particularly well treated in receipt a hefty 12lb weight-for-age allowance.

4881 BEST ODDS GUARANTEED AT 188BET H'CAP — 7f 1y(P)

8:00 (8:02) (Class 5) (0-75,75) 3-Y-0+ **£3,234** (£962; £481; £240) **Stalls** Low

Form — RPR

0613 **1** **Helfire**^{10} **4525** 3-8-3 **62**.. CharlieBennett$^{(5)}$ 3 — 69+
(Hughie Morrison) *taken down early: hld up bhd ldng trio: clsd over 2f out: drvn to ld over 1f out: kpt on wl fnl f* **9/2**^{2}

0051 **2** 1¼ **Danecase**^{9} **4557** 3-9-7 **75**.. FergusSweeney 7 — 79
(David Dennis) *hld up in midfield: prog on inner 2f out: rdn to chal and w wnr jst over 1f out: nt qckn ins fnl f* **5/1**^{3}

1000 **3** ¾ **Rosenborg Rider (IRE)**^{24} **4010** 3-9-5 **73**........................(t) ShaneKelly 1 — 75+
(Ralph Beckett) *hld up in midfield: effrt over 2f out: wd bnd wl over 1f out: rdn and styd on fnl f to take 3rd nr fin* **11/4**^{1}

65-2 **4** ½ **Gung Ho Jack**^{24} **4014** 7-9-12 **73**.. KierenFox 9 — 77
(John Best) *hld up in rr: gng strly on inner over 2f out: prog to chse ldrs 1f out and cl up: hrd rdn and one pce fnl f* **8/1**

0012 **5** shd **Dunnscotia**^{10} **4528** 4-9-2 **70**....................................(t) GeorgiaCox$^{(7)}$ 2 — 73+
(Paul Webber) *s.s: hld up in last pair: prog 2f out: chsd ldrs and in tch jst over 1f out: kpt on same pce after* **5/1**^{3}

6502 **6** 3¾ **With Approval (IRE)**^{24} **4008** 4-9-0 **66**..................(p) MeganNicholls$^{(5)}$ 5 — 59
(Laura Mongan) *disp ld at str pce to wl over 1f out: wknd* **16/1**

4104 **7** 2½ **Cliffhanger**^{35} **3649** 3-9-2 **70**.. LukeMorris 6 — 53
(Paul Cole) *settled towards rr: pushed along 3f out: no prog u.p over 1f out: fdd* **10/1**

6060 **8** 2¼ **Majestic Myles (IRE)**^{7} **4627** 8-9-9 **75**...................... PaddyBradley$^{(5)}$ 4 — 55
(Lee Carter) *disp ld at str pce tl hdd & wknd rapidly over 1f out* **8/1**

6500 **9** 6 **Cleverconversation (IRE)**^{19} **4215** 3-9-3 **71**................(e) DannyBrock 8 — 32
(Jane Chapple-Hyam) *pressed ldng pair on outer and clr of rest: rdn wl over 2f out: wknd wl over 1f out: eased* **20/1**

2136 **10** 32 **Layla's Hero (IRE)**^{16} **4291** 9-9-9 **73**...................(v) EdwardGreatrex$^{(3)}$ 11
(Roger Teal) *dwlt: a in last pair and nvr gng wl: t.o whn eased over 1f out* **25/1**

1m 24.36s (-0.44) **Going Correction** +0.075s/f (Slow)
WFA 3 from 4yo+ 7lb **10** Ran SP% **124.0**
Speed ratings (Par 103): **105,103,102,102,102 97,94,92,85,48**
CSF £29.30 CT £77.22 TOTE £5.30: £2.00, £1.60, £1.40; EX 28.80 Trifecta £130.90.
Owner Deborah Collett & M J Watson **Bred** M J Watson **Trained** East Ilsley, Berks

FOCUS
A fair handicap. They went a decent gallop and the first three home were 3yos in receipt of 7lb in weight-for-age allowances. The form should stand up to scrutiny in this sort of grade.

4882 FREE SPINS AT 188BET CASINO H'CAP 1m 2f (P)
8:30 (8:30) (Class 6) (0-60,59) 3-Y-O+ **£2,587** (£770; £384; £192) **Stalls** Low

Form RPR
004 1 **Embankment**[24] 4009 7-9-11 **56** KierenFox 3 63
(Michael Attwater) *prom: chsd ldr 4f: rdn to ld over 1f out: drvn and jst hld on* **10/1**
0550 2 *shd* **Power Up**[17] 4267 5-9-12 **57** DannyBrock 2 64
(Jane Chapple-Hyam) *chsd ldr to 4f out: rdn wl over 2f out: styd on fr over 1f out to take 2nd ins fnl f: clsd on wnr nr fin: jst failed* **8/1**[3]
0355 3 *1 1/4* **Sunshineandbubbles**[17] 4267 3-9-0 **58** (p) GeorgeDowning[(3)] 1 62
(Daniel Mark Loughnane) *chsd ldrs: lost pl and rdn on inner wl over 2f out: rallied over 1f out: styd on to take 3rd nr fin* **16/1**
5162 4 *1* **Megalala (IRE)**[17] 4267 15-9-2 **54** MitchGodwin[(7)] 4 56
(John Bridger) *led: rdn over 2f out: hdd over 1f out: fdd ins fnl f* **8/1**[3]
505- 5 *1/2* **Cartwright**[247] 8006 3-9-2 **57** LukeMorris 9 60+
(Sir Mark Prescott Bt) *s.i.s: racd in last pair: urged along fr 1/2-way: u.p on outer and no prog over 2f out: kpt on fr over 1f out: n.d* **11/10**[1]
5060 6 *3 1/4* **Protest (IRE)**[17] 4269 3-9-1 **56** (b[1]) LiamKeniry 7 51
(Sylvester Kirk) *t.k.h: hld up in last pair: shkn up over 2f out and no prog: wl btn after* **8/1**[3]
2541 7 *5* **Spinning Rose**[10] 4527 4-10-0 **59** (b) RobertWinston 6 44
(Dean Ivory) *in tch: prog to chse ldrs over 2f out: wknd rapidly over 1f out* **4/1**[2]
00-0 8 *2* **Passing Dream**[74] 2321 3-8-9 **55** CharlieBennett[(5)] 5 36
(Hughie Morrison) *dwlt: t.k.h: hld up in midfield: dropped to last and lost tch 3f out: bhd after* **14/1**

2m 7.61s (1.01) **Going Correction** +0.075s/f (Slow)
WFA 3 from 4yo+ 10lb **8** Ran SP% **122.6**
Speed ratings (Par 101): **98,97,96,96,95 93,89,87**
CSF £92.06 CT £1293.30 TOTE £12.60: £3.30, £2.50, £3.80; EX 85.30 Trifecta £1338.80.
Owner Canisbay Bloodstock **Bred** Juddmonte Farms Ltd **Trained** Epsom, Surrey

FOCUS
A moderate handicap. They went a modest gallop and the form is worth treating with a degree of caution.
T/Plt: £35.50 to a £1 stake. Pool: £57,346.50 - 1179.2 winning units T/Qpdt: £11.50 to a £1 stake. Pool: £6,416.82 - 409.6 winning units **Jonathan Neesom**

4835 NEWMARKET (R-H)
Saturday, July 30

OFFICIAL GOING: Good (good to firm in places; 7.5)
Wind: Fresh across Weather: Cloudy with sunny spells

4883 BRITISH STALLION STUDS EBF CHALICE STKS (LISTED RACE) (F&M) 1m 4f
2:15 (2:16) (Class 1) 3-Y-O+
£22,684 (£8,600; £4,304; £2,144; £1,076; £540) **Stalls** Centre

Form RPR
2052 1 **Fireglow**[8] 4610 3-8-8 105 SilvestreDeSousa 1 106
(Mark Johnston) *a.p: pushed along to chse ldr 3f out: led 2f out: rdn and hung lft over 1f out: r.o wl* **11/4**[2]
4-11 2 *2* **Abingdon (USA)**[51] 3060 3-8-11 100 TedDurcan 8 106
(Sir Michael Stoute) *hld up: rdn over 1f out: r.o to go 2nd nr fin: no ch w wnr* **2/1**[1]
1-55 3 *shd* **Tiptree (IRE)**[51] 3060 3-8-8 90 MartinLane 7 103
(Luca Cumani) *hld up: rdn over 2f out: hdwy over 1f out: styd on* **22/1**
-224 4 *1/2* **Sweeping Up**[41] 3436 5-9-6 104 (t) JimmyFortune 3 102
(Hughie Morrison) *led: rdn and hdd 2f out: styd on same pce ins fnl f* **8/1**[3]
5/15 5 *1 1/2* **Lady Of Camelot (IRE)**[28] 3888 4-9-6 107 RobertHavlin 6 100
(John Gosden) *prom: rdn and ev ch over 2f out: hung lft over 1f out: no ex ins fnl f* **2/1**[1]
1135 6 *7* **Southern Storm (IRE)**[7] 4646 4-9-6 84 (v) RichardKingscote 2 88
(Ralph Beckett) *hld up: rdn over 2f out: wknd over 1f out* **50/1**
0541 7 *3 1/4* **Full Day**[7] 4664 5-9-6 79 SeanLevey 4 83
(Brian Ellison) *chsd ldr 9f: sn rdn: wknd over 1f out* **66/1**

2m 33.09s (0.19) **Going Correction** +0.025s/f (Good)
WFA 3 from 4yo+ 12lb **7** Ran SP% **112.2**
Speed ratings (Par 111): **100,98,98,98,97 92,90**
CSF £8.32 TOTE £3.50: £1.70, £1.60; EX 9.50 Trifecta £96.60.
Owner Sheikh Hamdan bin Mohammed Al Maktoum **Bred** Darley **Trained** Middleham Moor, N Yorks

FOCUS
Far-side track used. Stalls stands' side except 1m4, centre. The ground had eased slightly and was now good, good to firm in places. Re-positioning of the bend into the home straight increased the distance of the 1m4f races (including the opener) by 13yds. An interesting fillies and mares' Listed event to start, but the pace looked ordinary and the winning time was 6.29sec outside standard. The runners made for the centre of the track on turning in. The winner has still to match the form of her Guineas fourth.

4884 BRITISH EBF FILLIES' NURSERY H'CAP 6f
2:50 (2:51) (Class 2) 2-Y-O
£24,900 (£7,456; £3,728; £1,864; £932; £468) **Stalls** Low

Form RPR
2611 1 **Rajar**[9] 4553 2-9-1 **82** SeanLevey 1 94+
(Richard Hannon) *chsd ldrs: led 5f out: shkn up over 1f out: r.o wl: comf* **8/1**
221 2 *2 1/2* **Paco's Angel**[33] 3718 2-8-9 **76** ShaneKelly 2 80
(Richard Hughes) *plld hrd and prom: rdn over 1f out: r.o to go 2nd wl ins fnl f* **7/1**[3]
122 3 *3/4* **Miss Sugars**[16] 4296 2-8-7 **74** MartinLane 15 76
(David Simcock) *a.p: rdn to chse wnr over 1f out: styd on same pce wl ins fnl f* **20/1**
311 4 *1* **Clef**[16] 4296 2-8-6 **73** PatrickMathers 10 72
(Richard Fahey) *hld up in tch: drvn and outpcd over 2f out: rallied over 1f out: r.o* **17/2**
1042 5 *nk* **Camargue**[10] 4503 2-9-4 **85** RobertHavlin 3 83+
(Mark Johnston) *hld up: hdwy whn nt clr run over 1f out: sn swtchd rt and rdn: r.o wl ins fnl f: nt rch ldrs* **20/1**
13 6 *3/4* **Appointed**[16] 4296 2-9-1 **82** RobertWinston 9 77
(Tim Easterby) *hld up: outpcd 1/2-way: rdn and hung lft over 1f out: styd on ins fnl f: nt trble ldrs* **9/1**
1130 7 *1/2* **Sea Of Snow (USA)**[43] 3336 2-9-4 **85** SilvestreDeSousa 12 79
(Mark Johnston) *free to post: led 1f: chsd wnr tl rdn over 2f out: no ex fnl f* **7/1**[3]
1 8 *nk* **Parsnip (IRE)**[16] 4287 2-8-13 **80** WilliamCarson 11 73
(Michael Bell) *chsd ldrs: rdn over 1f out: styd on same pce* **9/2**[1]
4041 9 *1/2* **Whiteley (IRE)**[14] 4386 2-8-3 **70** ow2 JFEgan 14 61
(Mick Channon) *hld up: hdwy over 2f out: sn rdn: no ex fnl f* **40/1**
14 10 *shd* **Funky Footsteps (IRE)**[16] 4296 2-8-7 **74** TedDurcan 13 65
(Eve Johnson Houghton) *s.i.s: hld up: rdn over 2f out: nvr on terms* **20/1**
011 11 *hd* **Franca Florio (IRE)**[21] 4167 2-7-13 **73** GeorgeWood[(7)] 4 63
(Kevin Ryan) *chsd ldrs: rdn over 1f out: wknd ins fnl f* **14/1**
531 12 *nse* **Pranceleya (IRE)**[9] 4564 2-8-5 **72** PaoloSirigu 7 62
(Marco Botti) *s.i.s: hld up: rdn over 2f out: nvr on terms* **16/1**
41 13 *shd* **Jumping Around (IRE)**[17] 4261 2-8-12 **79** DaneO'Neill 6 69
(William Haggas) *hld up: rdn over 2f out: n.d* **6/1**[2]

1m 12.2s (-0.30) **Going Correction** +0.025s/f (Good) **13** Ran SP% **118.4**
Speed ratings (Par 97): **103,99,98,97,96 95,95,94,94,94 93,93,93**
CSF £59.00 CT £1126.08 TOTE £8.50: £2.10, £2.50, £4.40; EX 60.90 Trifecta £846.60.
Owner Robin Blunt & Partners **Bred** Robin Blunt **Trained** East Everleigh, Wilts

FOCUS
A competitive fillies' nursery as it should be for the money, with eight of the 13 runners last-time-out winners, three of whom were bidding for a hat-trick. Again they came up the centre, but not many ever got into it and the winner bolted up. The form is rated around the race averages.

4885 NEWMARKET EQUINE HOSPITAL EBF STALLIONS MAIDEN FILLIES' STKS (PLUS 10 RACE) 7f
3:25 (3:25) (Class 4) 2-Y-O **£4,528** (£1,347; £673; £336) **Stalls** Low

Form RPR
3 1 **Blending**[15] 4357 2-9-0 0 RobertHavlin 8 81+
(John Gosden) *chsd ldr tl led 2f out: rdn and edgd rt ins fnl f: styd on* **7/4**[1]
2 *2* **Peak Princess (IRE)** 2-9-0 0 SeanLevey 4 76
(Richard Hannon) *led 5f: rdn over 1f out: styd on same pce ins fnl f* **7/1**
3 *3/4* **Blushing Rose** 2-9-0 0 TedDurcan 3 74+
(Sir Michael Stoute) *a.p: racd keenly: shkn up over 1f out: styd on same pce wl ins fnl f* **11/4**[2]
4 *3* **Raven's Lady** 2-9-0 0 DarryllHolland 5 66
(Marco Botti) *mid-div: hdwy over 2f out: rdn and hung lft over 1f out: styd on same pce* **25/1**
5 5 *1 3/4* **Carol (IRE)**[21] 4147 2-9-0 0 SilvestreDeSousa 9 61
(Ed Dunlop) *chsd ldrs: rdn over 2f out: wknd fnl f* **4/1**[3]
6 *4 1/2* **Mystical Nelly** 2-9-0 0 RichardKingscote 2 49
(Jonathan Portman) *hld up: shkn up over 2f out: nvr on terms* **28/1**
7 *2 1/4* **Rickrack (IRE)** 2-9-0 0 MartinLane 1 43
(Luca Cumani) *s.i.s: sn pushed along in rr: bhd 4f out: sme late hdwy* **12/1**
8 *7* **Satpura** 2-9-0 0 JFEgan 6 24
(Mick Channon) *sn given reminders in rr: bhd fnl 3f* **33/1**
9 *4 1/2* **Robin's Purse** 2-9-0 0 DaneO'Neill 7 12
(Charles Hills) *s.i.s: wnt lft sn after s: hld up: rdn over 2f out: wknd over 1f out* **25/1**

1m 26.44s (0.74) **Going Correction** +0.025s/f (Good) **9** Ran SP% **117.3**
Speed ratings (Par 93): **96,93,92,89,87 82,79,71,66**
CSF £14.42 TOTE £2.20: £1.10, £2.10, £1.30; EX 16.00 Trifecta £29.90.
Owner K Abdullah **Bred** Juddmonte Farms Ltd **Trained** Newmarket, Suffolk

FOCUS
An interesting fillies' maiden, with only two having raced before, and another race where few got into it. The winner built on her debut promise with the race rated around the race average.

4886 RACING UK HD H'CAP 7f
4:00 (4:01) (Class 3) (0-90,89) 3-Y-O **£7,762** (£2,310; £1,154; £577) **Stalls** Low

Form RPR
-220 1 **Fighting Temeraire (IRE)**[44] 3299 3-9-7 **89** RobertWinston 3 97
(Dean Ivory) *hld up: hdwy to ld over 1f out: sn rdn and hung lft: jst hld on* **2/1**[1]
2130 2 *shd* **Dream Mover (IRE)**[49] 3155 3-9-4 **86** (t) DarryllHolland 6 93
(Marco Botti) *w ldrs: rdn and ev ch over 1f out: edgd rt wl ins fnl f: r.o* **20/1**
5000 3 *2 1/4* **Take The Helm**[28] 3890 3-9-5 **87** JimmyFortune 5 89
(Brian Meehan) *w ldrs: rdn and ev ch over 1f out: styng on same pce whn n.m.r and eased wl ins fnl f* **25/1**
11 4 *1* **Miss Carbonia (IRE)**[16] 4317 3-9-1 **83** ThomasBrown 4 81
(Ismail Mohammed) *s.i.s: hld up: rdn over 1f out: styd on: nt trble ldrs* **8/1**
-242 5 *nk* **Silk Cravat**[28] 3908 3-9-2 **84** RobertHavlin 1 81
(Simon Crisford) *led: rdn and hdd over 2f out: no ex ins fnl f* **9/2**[3]
41 6 *4 1/2* **Justice Smart (IRE)**[24] 3996 3-9-2 **84** TedDurcan 7 69
(Sir Michael Stoute) *hld up: rdn over 2f out: wknd over 1f out* **5/1**
21 7 *nk* **Trenches (USA)**[14] 4401 3-9-1 **83** MartinLane 2 68
(Charlie Appleby) *w ldr tl led over 2f out: rdn and hdd over 1f out: wknd ins fnl f* **5/2**[2]

1m 24.78s (-0.92) **Going Correction** +0.025s/f (Good) **7** Ran SP% **116.5**
Speed ratings (Par 104): **106,105,103,102,101 96,96**
CSF £42.98 TOTE £4.90: £2.20, £3.60; EX 61.10 Trifecta £437.90.
Owner Michael & Heather Yarrow **Bred** Hot Ticket Partnership **Trained** Radlett, Herts

FOCUS
A good handicap which included some unexposed 3yos, but the finish was fought out by a couple of the more experienced horses. The pace was decent, with four of the seven runners disputing the advantage for much of the way. The winer built on earlier efforts.

4887 NEWMARKET NIGHTS H'CAP 7f
4:35 (4:35) (Class 2) (0-110,106) 3-Y-O+ **£16,172** (£4,812; £2,405; £1,202) **Stalls** Low

Form RPR
1100 1 **Oh This Is Us (IRE)**[7] 4624 3-8-9 **96** SeanLevey 3 100
(Richard Hannon) *hld up: hdwy over 1f out: r.o u.p to ld nr fin* **10/3**[3]
0553 2 *hd* **Highland Colori (IRE)**[28] 3910 8-9-2 **96** (v) LiamKeniry 1 102
(Andrew Balding) *racd alone on stands' side: up w the pce: overall ldr over 2f out: rdn and hung lft fr over 1f out: hdd nr fin* **7/1**
0-03 3 *2 1/4* **Windfast (IRE)**[14] 4395 5-9-5 **106** JordanUys[(7)] 5 106
(Brian Meehan) *chsd ldr: rdn over 1f out: styd on same pce ins fnl f* **13/2**
4-02 4 *3 1/4* **Squats (IRE)**[7] 4625 4-9-0 **101** GeorgiaCox[(7)] 4 92
(William Haggas) *prom: rdn over 1f out: styd on same pce* **5/2**[2]

6230 **5** 2 1/4 **Above N Beyond**[44] 3299 3-8-13 **100**......................(t) RichardKingscote 6 82
(Tom Dascombe) *overall ldr: rdn and hdd over 2f out: wknd fnl f* **9/4**[1]

1m 24.1s (-1.60) **Going Correction** +0.025s/f (Good)
WFA 3 from 4yo+ 7lb **5** Ran SP% **108.3**
Speed ratings (Par 109): **110,109,107,103,100**
CSF £23.52 TOTE £3.90: £2.80, £4.10; EX 27.20 Trifecta £67.40.
Owner Team Wallop **Bred** Herbertstown House Stud **Trained** East Everleigh, Wilts

FOCUS

A decent prize on offer, but the race conditions meant that two of the five runners were wrong at the weights and some of these have become hard to win with. Four of the five runners raced up the centre, while the runner-up raced up the stands' rail for most of the way. They went a good pace. Hard to read, with both the first two 4lb wrong and the market 1-2 disappointing.

4888 PRICE BAILEY CHARTERED ACCOUNTANTS H'CAP 1m 4f

5:10 (5:11) (Class 4) (0-85,85) 4-Y-O+ **£5,175** (£1,540; £769; £384) **Stalls** Centre

Form RPR

3543 **1** **Dolphin Village (IRE)**[24] 4013 6-9-0 **78**......................... DarryllHolland 6 87
(Jane Chapple-Hyam) *chsd ldr 8f: remained handy: led over 2f out: rdn and edgd lft over 1f out: styd on wl: eased nr fin* **8/1**[2]

2-10 **2** 2 1/2 **Slunovrat (FR)**[90] 1885 5-9-1 **79**...................................... JimmyFortune 3 84
(David Menuisier) *chsd ldrs: wnt 2nd 4f out tl led wl over 2f out: sn rdn and hdd: styd on same pce ins fnl f* **8/1**[2]

0-03 **3** 4 **Rydan (IRE)**[54] 2966 5-9-4 **82**....................................(v) LiamKeniry 4 81
(Gary Moore) *chsd ldrs: rdn over 2f out: styd on same pce fr over 1f out* **10/1**[3]

4323 **4** 3/4 **Brandon Castle**[14] 4381 4-8-11 **75**.................................. TomMarquand 7 72
(Simon West) *sn led: rdn and hdd wl over 2f out: no ex fnl f* **8/1**[2]

5210 **5** 5 **Knight Music**[22] 4077 4-9-7 **85**....................................... RobertHavlin 1 74
(Michael Attwater) *hld up: rdn over 2f out: wknd over 1f out* **10/1**[3]

04-3 **6** 1 1/2 **Al**[21] 4153 4-9-4 **82**.. MartinLane 2 69
(Luca Cumani) *hld up: hdwy u.p over 3f out: wknd 2f out* **4/6**[1]

2m 30.83s (-2.07) **Going Correction** +0.025s/f (Good) **6** Ran SP% **111.5**
Speed ratings (Par 105): **107,105,102,102,98 97**
CSF £64.57 CT £632.44 TOTE £6.80: £2.00, £3.10; EX 43.00 Trifecta £236.80.
Owner Martin Sellars **Bred** Gerrardstown House Stud **Trained** Dalham, Suffolk

FOCUS

Race distance increased by 13yds. A fair handicap and only one horse mattered according to the market, but despite punters seemingly prepared to take any price about the hot favourite, there was the distinct smell of sizzling fingers afterwards. Unconvincing form.

4889 FEDERATION OF BLOODSTOCK AGENTS H'CAP 6f

5:45 (5:45) (Class 3) (0-90,90) 3-Y-O+ **£7,762** (£2,310; £1,154; £577) **Stalls** Low

Form RPR

0400 **1** **Cartmell Cleave**[22] 4079 4-9-7 **85**.. TedDurcan 6 95
(Stuart Kittow) *hld up: gd hdwy and edgd lft ins fnl f: r.o to ld nr fin* **10/1**

0-10 **2** 1 **Aleef (IRE)**[54] 2972 3-9-1 **84**...[1] DaneO'Neill 1 90
(Charles Hills) *led: rdn over 1f out: edgd lft ins fnl f: hdd nr fin* **16/1**

1- **3** hd **Quick Look**[403] 3481 3-8-10 **79**.................................. SilvestreDeSousa 7 84
(William Jarvis) *dwlt: hld up: swtchd lft and hdwy over 1f out: sn rdn: r.o* **11/1**

0-46 **4** 1 **Ejbaar**[24] 3995 4-8-12 **76**.. RichardKingscote 2 79
(Robert Cowell) *chsd ldrs: rdn over 1f out: edgd lft: styd on* **12/1**

0632 **5** 3/4 **Amood (IRE)**[15] 4360 5-8-11 **75**................................(p) TomMarquand 11 76
(Simon West) *hld up: hdwy over 2f out: rdn and edgd lft over 1f out: nt clr run ins fnl f: r.o* **7/1**

1135 **6** 1/2 **Realize**[127] 1066 6-9-10 **88**..(t) SeanLevey 3 87
(Stuart Williams) *a.p: rdn over 1f out: edgd lft and nt clr run ins fnl f: styd on same pce towards fin* **6/1**[3]

103- **7** 1 **Valbchek (IRE)**[442] 2237 7-9-11 **89**................................ DarryllHolland 4 85
(Jane Chapple-Hyam) *hld up: shkn up over 1f out: nt trble ldrs* **20/1**

2643 **8** nse **Flowers On Venus (IRE)**[22] 4079 4-9-10 **88**...........(v[1]) RobertWinston 5 84
(David Evans) *hld up: rdn over 2f out: styd on towards fin: nvr trbld ldrs* **5/2**[1]

3431 **9** hd **Edward Lewis**[23] 4041 3-8-13 **82**..................................... RobertHavlin 8 76
(John Gosden) *chsd ldr: rdn and hung lft fr over 1f out: no ex ins fnl f* **5/1**[2]

0150 **10** 4 **Crew Cut (IRE)**[15] 4360 8-8-8 **79**................................ MillyNaseb[(7)] 9 61
(Stuart Williams) *prom: pushed along and lost pl 1/2-way: wknd over 1f out* **16/1**

0-00 **11** 9 **Strong Challenge (IRE)**[23] 4062 3-9-7 **90**.....................(t) MartinLane 10 42
(Saeed bin Suroor) *chsd ldrs: rdn over 2f out: wknd over 1f out* **10/1**

1m 11.79s (-0.71) **Going Correction** +0.025s/f (Good)
WFA 3 from 4yo+ 5lb **11** Ran SP% **122.8**
Speed ratings (Par 107): **105,103,103,102,101 100,99,99,98,93 81**
CSF £165.28 CT £1842.88 TOTE £13.90: £3.90, £4.20, £2.60; EX 294.60 Trifecta £1718.10 Part won..
Owner John Urquhart **Bred** D R Tucker **Trained** Blackborough, Devon

FOCUS

A decent sprint handicap with a dramatic conclusion. The first pair came from the rear.
T/Plt: £521.90 to a £1 stake. Pool: £82,446.39 - 115.3 winning units T/Qpdt: £58.50 to a £1 stake. Pool: £5,869.65 - 74.2 winning units **Colin Roberts**

4842 THIRSK (L-H)

Saturday, July 30

OFFICIAL GOING: Good to soft (good in places) changing to good (good to soft in places) after race 4 (3.35)

Wind: light 1/2 behind Weather: fine and sunny

4890 BRITISH STALLION STUDS EBF MAIDEN STKS (PLUS 10 RACE) 5f

1:50 (1:52) (Class 4) 2-Y-O **£4,851** (£1,443; £721; £360) **Stalls** High

Form RPR

30 **1** **Our Greta (IRE)**[63] 2670 2-9-0 0.. BenCurtis 7 72
(Michael Appleby) *chsd ldrs: outpcd over 2f out: hdwy and swtchd rt over 1f out: styd on to ld last 50yds* **9/1**[3]

2342 **2** nk **Full Intention**[21] 4133 2-9-5 93.. PJMcDonald 9 77
(Tom Dascombe) *sn chsng ldrs: edgd lft and squeezed through 1f out: rdr dropped rt hand rein and kpt on in clsng stages* **4/11**[1]

22 **3** nse **Perfect Symphony (IRE)**[18] 4227 2-9-5 0.......................... KevinStott 2 76
(Kevin Ryan) *chsd ldrs: edgd rt and led narrowly 1f out: hdd and no ex last 50yds* **7/2**[2]

5 **4** 7 **Vocalisation (IRE)**[8] 4601 2-9-0 0................................. DanielTudhope 6 46
(John Weymes) *w ldr: wandered over 2f out: n.m.r 1f out: sn wknd* **33/1**

5 1 3/4 **Can't Do Spells** 2-9-5 0.. DuranFentiman 1 45
(Tim Easterby) *dwlt: in rr: sme hdwy over 2f out: wknd over 1f out* **28/1**

30 **6** nse **My Cherry Blossom**[35] 3654 2-9-0 0.......................... GrahamGibbons 10 39
(Tim Easterby) *led: hdd 1f out: sn wknd* **12/1**

00 **7** 3 **Shake And Bakes**[26] 3939 2-9-5 0...................................... SamJames 5 34
(Marjorie Fife) *dwlt: hung lft and racd wd: sn bhd* **100/1**

50 **8** nse **Snookered (IRE)**[18] 4227 2-9-5 0.................................... TonyHamilton 3 33
(Richard Fahey) *dwlt: sn outpcd and in rr: carried lft over 3f out* **40/1**

6 **9** 1 3/4 **Zebedee Star**[31] 3772 2-9-0 0... PhillipMakin 8 22
(Keith Dalgleish) *s.i.s: sme hdwy over 2f out: lost pl over 1f out: sn eased* **10/1**

59.29s (-0.31) **Going Correction** -0.125s/f (Firm) **9** Ran SP% **132.1**
Speed ratings (Par 96): **97,96,96,85,82 82,77,77,74**
CSF £14.57 TOTE £16.00: £2.70, £1.02, £1.30; EX 29.00 Trifecta £71.80.
Owner Alan Gray **Bred** Rathbarry Stud **Trained** Oakham, Rutland

FOCUS

Home bend was dolled-out by approximately 6yds, adding approximately 20yds to standard distances for all races of 7f and upwards. The principals came clear in this modest 2yo maiden.

4891 TYERMAN FAMILY CELEBRATION NURSERY H'CAP 5f

2:25 (2:26) (Class 3) 2-Y-O **£8,086** (£2,406; £1,202; £601) **Stalls** High

Form RPR

430 **1** **Major Jumbo**[31] 3772 2-8-0 **67** oh2...................................... JoeyHaynes 2 69
(Kevin Ryan) *led: rdn and hung lft over 1f out: hld on nr fin* **16/1**

1 **2** nk **Wick Powell**[114] 1293 2-9-0 **80**..................................... GrahamGibbons 7 82+
(David Barron) *dwlt: swtchd lft after s: in rr: reminders 2f out: hdwy over 1f out: styd on wl last 100yds: nt quite get up* **6/5**[1]

21 **3** 1/2 **Dandy Highwayman (IRE)**[18] 4227 2-8-8 **77**........ JacobButterfield[(3)] 3 77
(Ollie Pears) *dwlt: drvn to join ldrs over 2f out: hung lft fr over 1f out: rdr dropped whip 100yds out: no ex in clsng stages* **7/1**[3]

1214 **4** nk **Poet's Society**[7] 4629 2-9-7 **87**.. GrahamLee 1 86
(Mark Johnston) *wnt lft s: drvn to join ldrs over 2f out: bmpd twice fnl f: no ex in clsng stages* **7/1**[3]

4213 **5** 1 3/4 **The Nazca Lines (IRE)**[7] 4629 2-9-1 **81**........................(v) BenCurtis 5 74
(John Quinn) *w wnr: drvn over 2f out: edgd lft over 1f out: wknd last 100yds* **11/4**[2]

2240 **6** 2 3/4 **Carson City**[14] 4394 2-8-8 **74**... TonyHamilton 4 57
(Richard Fahey) *chsd ldrs: drvn over 2f out: lost pl over 1f out* **9/1**

58.69s (-0.91) **Going Correction** -0.125s/f (Firm) **6** Ran SP% **113.0**
Speed ratings (Par 98): **102,101,100,100,97 93**
CSF £36.64 TOTE £18.20: £5.70, £1.30; EX 65.10 Trifecta £1872.70.
Owner T A Rahman **Bred** D R Botterill **Trained** Hambleton, N Yorks
■ Stewards' Enquiry : Jacob Butterfield caution; careless riding

FOCUS

There was a very tight finish in this fair little sprint nursery.

4892 TOTESCOOP6 THE MILLIONAIRE MAKER H'CAP 1m 4f

3:00 (3:00) (Class 4) (0-80,80) 3-Y-O+ **£4,851** (£1,443; £721; £360) **Stalls** High

Form RPR

6106 **1** **Itlaaq**[7] 4634 10-9-4 **77**..(t) DanielleMooney[(7)] 7 87
(Michael Easterby) *mid-div: hdwy 5f out: effrt over 2f out: led over 1f out: pushed out* **9/1**

2314 **2** 1 3/4 **Wotabreeze (IRE)**[15] 4340 3-8-8 **77**.......................... JordanVaughan[(5)] 3 84
(John Quinn) *trckd ldng pair: effrt 3f out: upsides over 1f out: styd on same pce* **5/1**[3]

0166 **3** 3 1/2 **Odeon**[14] 4407 5-10-0 **80**.. JoeDoyle 1 82
(James Given) *led: hdd over 3f out: lost pl over 2f out: rallied over 1f out: kpt on to take modest 3rd in clsng stages* **7/2**[1]

1266 **4** 1/2 **San Quentin (IRE)**[25] 3983 5-9-6 **72**..................................(b[1]) BenCurtis 4 73
(David Loughnane) *s.i.s: hld up in last: hdwy over 2f out: 3rd 1f out: one pce* **12/1**

6241 **5** 1/2 **Monsieur Glory**[12] 4455 3-8-2 **71**...........................(v) AnnaHesketh[(5)] 6 71
(Tom Dascombe) *awkward s: t.k.h: sn trcking ldr: led over 3f out: hdd over 1f out: edgd lft: one pce* **4/1**[2]

0-06 **6** 3 1/4 **Hot Spice**[16] 4311 8-9-10 **76**....................................... GrahamGibbons 8 71
(Michael Easterby) *hld up in rr: hdwy over 2f out: wknd over 1f out* **16/1**

0002 **7** hd **Correggio**[18] 4237 6-9-4 **70**.. PJMcDonald 2 64
(Micky Hammond) *mid-div: hdwy 5f out: drvn over 2f out: wknd over 1f out* **11/2**

3434 **8** 1 1/4 **Stoneboat Bill**[6] 4686 4-8-11 **63**....................................... TonyHamilton 5 55
(Declan Carroll) *hld up in rr: t.k.h: hdwy over 7f out: effrt on inner over 2f out: lost pl over 1f out* **4/1**[2]

2m 40.84s (4.64) **Going Correction** +0.275s/f (Good)
WFA 3 from 4yo+ 12lb **8** Ran SP% **117.8**
Speed ratings (Par 105): **95,93,91,91,90 88,88,87**
CSF £54.97 CT £191.05 TOTE £10.60: £2.90, £1.80, £1.80; EX 49.90 Trifecta £171.20.
Owner W H & Mrs J A Tinning 1 **Bred** Shadwell Estate Company Limited **Trained** Sheriff Hutton, N Yorks

FOCUS

Add 20yds to race distance. This modest handicap was run at a brisk pace but the closers still struggled to get seriously involved.

4893 PETER BELL MEMORIAL H'CAP 7f

3:35 (3:35) (Class 3) (0-90,90) 3-Y-O+ **£8,086** (£2,406; £1,202; £601) **Stalls** Low

Form RPR

3042 **1** **Muntadab (IRE)**[8] 4611 4-9-11 **87**..................................... PJMcDonald 6 97
(David Loughnane) *w ldr: led over 3f out: hdd narrowly over 1f out: rallied to regain ld nr fin* **9/2**[1]

3221 **2** hd **George Cinq**[29] 3848 6-10-0 **90**................................... GrahamGibbons 12 99
(George Scott) *anticipated s: trckd ldrs on outside: 2nd 3f out: led narrowly over 1f out: hdd and no ex nr fin* **5/1**[2]

5020 **3** 3 3/4 **Ocean Sheridan (IRE)**[25] 3980 4-9-7 **83**......................... ConnorBeasley 8 83
(Michael Dods) *chsd ldrs: kpt on one pce to take modest 3rd over 1f out* **10/1**

4400 **4** nk **Bertiewhittle**[16] 4299 8-9-11 **87**... BenCurtis 14 86
(David Barron) *in rr: hdwy 2f out: edgd lft over 1f out: kpt on to take modest 4th last 75yds* **9/1**

0206 **5** 1 1/2 **Steel Train (FR)**[44] 3324 5-9-11 **87**............................... DanielTudhope 11 82
(David O'Meara) *rr-div on outer: hdwy over 2f out: kpt on same pce appr fnl f* **12/1**

0-53 **6** nk **Sakhee's Return**[7] 4627 4-9-9 **85**............................... DuranFentiman 4 79
(Tim Easterby) *chsd ldrs: kpt on one pce fnl 2f* **10/1**

0010 **7** 1 3/4 **Slemy (IRE)**[16] 4299 5-9-4 **80**.. JamesSullivan 1 70
(Ruth Carr) *mid-div: drvn over 3f out: one pce fnl 2f* **16/1**

0-06 **8** 5 **He's No Saint**[51] 3055 5-9-6 **87**..................................(v) JoshDoyle[(5)] 13 64
(David O'Meara) *mid-div: swtchd lft after 2f: pushed along over 3f out: one pce fnl 2f* **11/1**

5010 **9** *4* **Kalk Bay (IRE)**[38] 3518 9-9-6 **85**........................(t) RachelRichardson(3) 7 51
(Michael Easterby) *sn bhd: hdwy over 1f out: nvr on terms* **10/1**

0203 **10** *4* **Pumaflor (IRE)**[8] 4611 4-9-1 **77**................................... GeorgeChaloner 2 33
(Richard Whitaker) *chsd ldrs: drvn over 3f out: wkng whn edgd lft over 1f out: bhd whn eased in clsng stages* **16/1**

2-54 **11** *4 1/2* **Shootingsta (IRE)**[71] 2421 4-9-3 **79**.............................(p) GrahamLee 10 23
(Bryan Smart) *trckd ldrs on outer: t.k.h: hung lft and lost pl over 1f out: eased whn bhd clsng stages* **8/1**[3]

0000 **12** *13* **Comino (IRE)**[33] 3708 5-9-1 **77**..(p) KevinStott 3
(Kevin Ryan) *led: hdd over 3f out: lost pl 2f out: hmpd on inner over 1f out: sn eased* **8/1**[3]

1m 27.03s (-0.17) **Going Correction** +0.275s/f (Good) **12** Ran SP% **122.1**
Speed ratings (Par 107): **111,110,106,106,104 104,102,96,91,87 82,67**
CSF £27.26 CT £223.77 TOTE £3.50: £1.90, £2.10, £4.10; EX 20.90 Trifecta £688.90.
Owner Fell & High Hopes Partnership **Bred** Mrs James Wigan **Trained** Market Drayton, Shropshire

FOCUS
Add 20yds to race distance. This looked highly competitive but the two at the top of the market dominated from 2f out.

4894 TOTESCOOP6 THIRSK SUMMER CUP H'CAP 1m
4:10 (4:11) (Class 3) (0-90,89) 3-Y-O+ **£19,407** (£5,775; £2,886; £1,443) **Stalls** Low

Form RPR

-015 **1** **Ginger Jack**[38] 3518 9-8-13 **83**................................ RobJFitzpatrick(5) 17 92
(Garry Moss) *w ldrs: t.k.h: led 2f out: hung lft over 1f out: drvn out* **9/2**[1]

2304 **2** *1* **Hard To Handel**[14] 4408 4-9-1 **85**.................................(p) JoshDoyle(5) 8 92
(David O'Meara) *trckd ldrs: drvn over 2f out: kpt on to take 2nd towards fin* **14/1**

-136 **3** *nk* **Rousayan (IRE)**[43] 3364 5-9-8 **87**............................... DanielTudhope 13 93
(David O'Meara) *mid-div: hdwy over 2f out: swtchd lft over 1f out: kpt on same pce last 100yds* **8/1**[3]

0014 **4** *3/4* **Silvery Moon (IRE)**[15] 4374 9-9-7 **89**................ RachelRichardson(3) 11 94
(Tim Easterby) *chsd ldrs: kpt on same pce fnl f* **14/1**

3436 **5** *nk* **Beardwood**[35] 3645 4-9-3 **82**... PJMcDonald 14 86+
(Mark Johnston) *mid-div: hdwy to chse ldrs over 2f out: kpt on in clsng stages* **9/2**[1]

2614 **6** *2 1/4* **Abushamah (IRE)**[15] 4368 5-9-6 **85**............................. JamesSullivan 2 84+
(Ruth Carr) *s.i.s: t.k.h in rr: hdwy over 2f out: kpt on same pce fnl f* **14/1**

1256 **7** *nse* **Boots And Spurs**[7] 4644 7-9-2 **81**.....................................(v) BenCurtis 1 80
(Scott Dixon) *led: hdd 2f out: fdd appr fnl f* **8/1**[3]

0506 **8** *nk* **Ingleby Angel (IRE)**[8] 4611 7-9-5 **84**.......................... DuranFentiman 7 82
(Colin Teague) *hld up in rr on outer: hdwy to chse ldrs over 2f out: fdd fnl f* **22/1**

1400 **9** *1/2* **Bahama Moon (IRE)**[28] 3895 4-9-4 **83**...................... GrahamGibbons 4 80
(David Barron) *mid-div: hdwy and swtchd ins over 2f out: one pce* **25/1**

0-05 **10** *shd* **Altharoos (IRE)**[15] 4374 6-9-7 **86**............................... TonyHamilton 12 83
(Sally Hall) *hld up in rr: hdwy whn nt clr run on outer 2f out: fdd fnl f* **18/1**

6614 **11** *1 1/4* **Hidden Rebel**[14] 4391 4-9-2 **81**................................... StevieDonohoe 15 75
(Alistair Whillans) *in tch on outer: hdwy 3f out: one pce over 1f out* **16/1**

1-0 **12** *2 1/2* **Strong Man**[28] 3884 8-9-3 **82**... KevinStott 18 70
(Michael Easterby) *chsd ldrs on outer: wknd over 1f out* **33/1**

3540 **13** *4* **Wilde Inspiration (IRE)**[37] 3566 5-9-10 **89**.................. ConnorBeasley 6 68
(Julie Camacho) *trckd ldrs: t.k.h: drvn 3f out: lost pl over 1f out: bhd whn eased in clsng stages* **7/1**[2]

/0-1 **14** *5* **Bluegrass Blues (IRE)**[22] 4081 6-9-6 **85**......................... GrahamLee 5 52
(Heather Main) *hld up towards rr: hdwy over 2f out: lost pl over 1f out: bhd whn eased in clsng stages* **10/1**

1m 42.22s (2.12) **Going Correction** +0.275s/f (Good) **14** Ran SP% **122.5**
Speed ratings (Par 107): **100,99,98,97,97 95,95,95,94,94 93,90,86,81**
CSF £70.02 CT £514.12 TOTE £4.10: £1.80, £3.40, £2.90; EX 68.80 TRIFECTA Not won..
Owner C H McGhie **Bred** Darley **Trained** Wynyard, Stockton-On-Tees

FOCUS
Add 20yds to race distance. They went a modest pace in this feature handicap and it paid to be handy.

4895 BREEDERS BACKING RACING EBF MAIDEN STKS 1m
4:45 (4:48) (Class 4) 3-Y-O+ **£5,175** (£1,540; £769; £384) **Stalls** Low

Form RPR

1 **Kharbetation (IRE)** 3-9-5 0.. DanielTudhope 4 95+
(David O'Meara) *gave problems loading: s.i.s: smooth hdwy on outer over 4f out: handy 2nd over 3f out: led 2f out: shkn up and qcknd wl clr: impressive* **11/2**[2]

-320 **2** *5* **Ehtiraas**[46] 3245 3-9-5 87.. GrahamLee 7 80
(Owen Burrows) *w ldr: t.k.h: led over 3f out: drvn over 2f out: hdd 2f out: no ch w wnr* **4/11**[1]

6 **3** *10* **Percy Verence**[18] 4235 3-9-5 0... JoeyHaynes 9 60
(K R Burke) *chsd ldrs: handy 3rd over 3f out: one pce* **8/1**[3]

0 **4** *2 3/4* **Old China**[9] 4546 3-9-5 0.. ConnorBeasley 8 51
(John Davies) *mid-div: drvn 3f out: tk poor 4th nr fin* **33/1**

5 *nk* **Westward Ho (IRE)** 3-9-5 0.. KevinStott 10 50
(James Bethell) *s.i.s: in rr: drvn 3f out: kpt on over 1f out: nvr on terms* **20/1**

6 *1* **Come Back King (IRE)** 3-9-5 0.. BenCurtis 6 48
(Michael Appleby) *mid-div: effrt 3f out: edgd lft and lost pl 2f out* **14/1**

05 **7** *1/2* **Southern Strife**[9] 4546 5-9-10 0.............................. RachelRichardson(3) 5 49+
(Tim Easterby) *hood removed v late: v.s.a: bhd: sme hdwy over 2f out: nvr on terms* **14/1**

02-0 **8** *12* **Frankster (FR)**[18] 4235 3-9-5 77.................................... TonyHamilton 1 19
(Micky Hammond) *chsd ldrs: outpcd over 3f out: lost pl over 2f out: bhd whn eased in clsng stages* **8/1**[3]

4-0 **9** *4* **Royal Acclaim (IRE)**[46] 3264 4-9-13 0........................ GeorgeChaloner 3 12
(Rebecca Bastiman) *mid-div: lost pl 3f out: bhd whn eased in clsng stages* **50/1**

00 **10** *16* **Fearless Poppy**[42] 3411 3-8-7 0...(p) RPWalsh(7) 2
(Christine Dunnett) *led: hdd over 3f out: lost pl over 2f out: sn bhd: eased fnl f* **100/1**

1m 43.17s (3.07) **Going Correction** +0.275s/f (Good)
WFA 3 from 4yo+ 8lb **10** Ran SP% **134.9**
Speed ratings (Par 105): **95,90,80,77,76 75,75,63,59,43**
CSF £9.03 TOTE £8.10: £2.20, £1.10, £2.20; EX 13.30 Trifecta £69.00.
Owner Salem Rashid **Bred** George Kent **Trained** Upper Helmsley, N Yorks

FOCUS
Add 20yds to race distance. This looked an ordinary maiden, but the winner rates a smart prospect.

4896 TOTEPOOL LIVE INFO DOWNLOAD THE APP H'CAP 6f
5:20 (5:20) (Class 4) (0-85,84) 3-Y-O+ **£4,851** (£1,443; £721; £360) **Stalls** High

Form RPR

2234 **1** **Cosmic Chatter**[9] 4569 6-9-3 **75**...(p) KevinStott 5 85+
(Ruth Carr) *dwlt: swtchd rt after s: in rr: hdwy 2f out: styd on wl to ld towards fin* **12/1**

212 **2** *3/4* **Pea Shooter**[11] 4488 7-9-7 **79**.. BenCurtis 2 87+
(Brian Ellison) *trckd 2 ldrs centre: effrt over 1f out: hung rt and led last 100yds: hdd and no ex towards fin* **6/1**[1]

0605 **3** *nk* **Highland Acclaim (IRE)**[13] 4428 5-9-11 **83**.............. DanielTudhope 13 90
(David O'Meara) *overall ldr stands' side: edgd lft and hdd last 100yds: no ex* **7/1**[2]

6500 **4** *1 3/4* **Whozthecat (IRE)**[8] 4608 9-8-8 **66**..................................(v) JoeyHaynes 6 67
(Declan Carroll) *led 3 others racing wd: w ldr: edgd lft over 1f out: kpt on same pce last 100yds* **9/1**

-050 **5** *hd* **Gin In The Inn (IRE)**[15] 4344 3-8-11 **74**.................... TonyHamilton 7 74
(Richard Fahey) *chsd ldrs: upsides over 1f out: kpt on same pce last 150yds* **16/1**

0001 **6** *nk* **Adam's Ale**[15] 4345 7-9-6 **81**................................ RachelRichardson(3) 10 81
(Mark Walford) *mid-div: drvn to chse ldrs over 2f out: kpt on same pce fnl f* **7/1**[2]

-000 **7** *shd* **Harwoods Volante (IRE)**[7] 4627 5-9-3 **80**..................... JoshDoyle(5) 8 80
(David O'Meara) *chsd ldrs: upsides over 1f out: kpt on same pce fnl f* **20/1**

6063 **8** *1 1/2* **Tiger Jim**[12] 4443 6-9-3 **82**... LewisEdmunds(7) 12 77
(Jim Goldie) *hood removed v late: in rr: hdwy over 1f out: nvr a threat* **8/1**[3]

2040 **9** *1 1/2* **Compton Park**[8] 4608 9-9-5 **77**.................................... StevieDonohoe 9 67
(Les Eyre) *dwlt: in rr: sme hdwy over 1f out: nvr a factor* **18/1**

-303 **10** *nk* **Bapak Asmara (IRE)**[26] 3956 4-9-9 **81**..........................(p) GrahamLee 4 70
(Kevin Ryan) *trckd ldr centre: wknd fnl f* **14/1**

3134 **11** *2 3/4* **Duke Cosimo**[15] 4366 6-9-11 **83**.. ShaneGray 3 63
(Michael Herrington) *hld up last of 4 towards centre: effrt over 2f out: nvr a factor* **7/1**[2]

1010 **12** *4* **Pomme De Terre (IRE)**[35] 3646 4-9-12 **84**............(b) ConnorBeasley 14 51
(Michael Dods) *chsd ldrs: drvn over 3f out: reminders 2f out: sn hung lft and lost pl* **6/1**[1]

0020 **13** *4 1/2* **Mappin Time (IRE)**[13] 4428 8-9-3 **75**....................(b) GrahamGibbons 11 28
(Tim Easterby) *dwlt: in rr: sn drvn along: nvr on terms: eased in clsng stages* **16/1**

1m 11.0s (-1.70) **Going Correction** -0.125s/f (Firm)
WFA 3 from 4yo+ 5lb **13** Ran SP% **123.3**
Speed ratings (Par 105): **106,105,104,102,102 101,101,99,97,97 93,88,82**
CSF £85.05 CT £574.78 TOTE £13.00: £4.20, £2.20, £3.20; EX 97.40 Trifecta £969.70 Part won..
Owner Grange Park Racing VII **Bred** Harrowgate Bloodstock Ltd **Trained** Huby, N Yorks
■ Stewards' Enquiry : Ben Curtis two-day ban; used whip above the permitted level (13th-14 Aug)

FOCUS
Competitive stuff. Those drawn high were at a real advantage.
T/Plt: £19.10 to a £1 stake. Pool of £62994.20 - 2402.07 winning tickets. T/Qpdt: £8.40 to a £1 stake. Pool of £3641.64 - 317.05 winning tickets. **Walter Glynn**

4897 - 4898a (Foreign Racing) - See Raceform Interactive

4849 GALWAY (R-H)
Saturday, July 30

OFFICIAL GOING: Hurdle course - good; flat course - yielding

4899a LADBROKES RED DAY H'CAP 7f
5:00 (5:00) (50-75,80) 3-Y-O+ **£6,783** (£2,095; £992; £441; £165)

RPR

1 **Tithonus (IRE)**[10] 4541 5-8-13 **63**.................................(tp) GaryHalpin(3) 11 73
(Denis Gerard Hogan, Ire) *sn led: rdn 2f out: pushed clr over 1f out: styd on wl ins fnl f* **12/1**

2 *3/4* **Cairdiuil (IRE)**[3] 4780 10-9-4 **65**...........................(v[1]) SeamieHeffernan 10 74+
(I Madden, Ire) *hld up: tk clsr order to chse ldrs 2f out: swtchd lft off home turn in 3rd: styd on strly into 2nd ins fnl f: nt rch wnr* **4/1**[2]

3 *3 3/4* **Beau Satchel**[4] 4748 6-9-12 **80** 5ex....................................(t) OisinOrr(7) 6 78
(Adrian McGuinness, Ire) *racd in mid-div: rdn over 2f out: wnt 8th 1f out: styd on strly clsng stages into 3rd on line: nrst fin* **7/4**[1]

4 *shd* **Ducky Mallon (IRE)**[56] 2922 5-9-5 **66**........................(t) EmmetMcNamara 13 64+
(Donal Kinsella, Ire) *bit slowly away: racd towards rr: gd prog under 2f out: c wd home turn: styd on strly into 4th cl home: nrst fin* **14/1**

5 *hd* **Afzal (FR)**[56] 2925 3-9-6 **74**..[1] BillyLee 2 68
(T J O'Mara, Ire) *chsd ldrs on inner: rdn in 3rd over 2f out: nt qckn over 1f out in 4th: kpt on same pce* **50/1**

6 *nk* **Little Miss Kodi (IRE)**[19] 4215 3-9-5 **73**.................. DeclanMcDonogh 3 66
(Daniel Mark Loughnane) *t.k.h to trck ldr in 2nd whn sltly hmpd after 1f: rdn in 2nd over 2f out: no imp appr fnl f and dropped to 3rd: wknd clsng stages* **20/1**

7 *nk* **Sister Slew (IRE)**[47] 3238 6-9-3 **67**......................(be) RobbieDowney(3) 5 62
(Shane Nolan, Ire) *racd in mid-div: rdn in 6th under 2f out: nt qckn over 1f out: kpt on one pce* **8/1**[3]

8 *2 1/4* **Miracle Ninetynine (IRE)**[63] 2703 4-9-12 **73**............[1] NGMcCullagh 15 62
(John James Feane, Ire) *racd in rr: prog over 1f out: kpt on wl ins fnl f: nvr nrr* **33/1**

9 *1/2* **Chillie Billie**[4] 4748 7-9-7 **68**.. ConorHoban 7 56
(J Larkin, Ire) *chsd ldrs: cl in 3rd after 2f: rdn and wknd under 2f out: no ex* **8/1**[3]

10 *1 1/2* **Seaforth (IRE)**[21] 4172 4-9-6 **67**......................................(bt) ColinKeane 1 51
(John Joseph Murphy, Ire) *racd in mid-div towards inner: rdn under 2f out: wknd appr fnl f* **12/1**

11 *2 1/2* **Hatton Cross (IRE)**[19] 4217 7-9-6 **67**..........................(tp) WayneLordan 9 44
(T J O'Mara, Ire) *racd in mid-div: rdn and nt qckn under 2f out: wknd fr 1f out* **25/1**

12 *nk* **True Companion (IRE)**[18] 4245 3-8-4 **65**..............(p) KillianLeonard(7) 4 38
(Adrian Brendan Joyce, Ire) *chsd ldrs: bmpd over 2f out and sn wknd* **25/1**

13 *nk* **Jembatt (IRE)**[21] 4170 9-9-4 **65**...(t) GaryCarroll 12 41
(Michael Mulvany, Ire) *hld up: towards rr fr 1/2-way: no threat under 2f out* **25/1**

14 12 **Siege Of Boston (IRE)**[5] 4720 3-9-1 **69**.................. MichaelHussey 16 9
(Gordon Elliott, Ire) *chsd ldrs on outer: wknd qckly under 2f out* **33/1**

15 13 **Chapter One (IRE)**[71] 2450 4-9-3 **64**.......................(v[1]) PatSmullen 14
(D K Weld, Ire) *racd in mid-div: rdn and dropped to rr over 2f out: eased in st* **8/1**[3]

1m 28.11s (-3.49)
WFA 3 from 4yo+ 7lb **15** Ran SP% **135.9**
CSF £62.48 CT £134.20 TOTE £15.30: £3.30, £1.70, £1.30; DF 89.90 Trifecta £224.70.
Owner T & M Racing Partnership **Bred** K N Dhunjibhoy & B M Desai **Trained** Cloughjordan, Co Tipperary
■ Stewards' Enquiry : Gary Halpin two-day ban: used whip with excessive frequency (tbn)

FOCUS
Competitive fare for the grade with some very familiar faces in action. A few of these were in action earlier in the week and the runner-up was once again agonisingly denied, for the second time in a few days.

4900 - (Foreign Racing) - See Raceform Interactive

4578 DEAUVILLE (R-H)
Saturday, July 30
OFFICIAL GOING: Turf: good; polytrack: standard

4901a PRIX ROYAL BARRIERE (CLAIMER) (4YO) (LADY AMATEUR RIDERS) (POLYTRACK) 1m 1f 110y
11:50 (12:00) 4-Y-O **£6,617** (£2,647; £1,985; £1,323; £661)

RPR

1 **Anantapur (FR)**[22] 4-9-12 0.................................. MissDeboraFioretti 6 73
(S Cerulis, France) **29/10**[1]

2 1 1/4 **Terra Fina**[66] 4-9-1 0..(b) MlleMarieArtu 1 59
(J-F Doucet, France) **79/10**

3 1/2 **Masterblaster (FR)**[43] 4-9-4 0................ MlleDelphineGarcia-Dubois 10 61
(C Lotoux, France) **53/10**[3]

4 3/4 **Yankee Mail (FR)**[15] 4356 4-9-12 0.......................... MlleLaraLeGeay 3 67
(Gay Kelleway) *wnt a little lft s: racd in fnl pair abt 15 l off the pce: clsd gap bef 1/2-way but stl towards rr: styd on to chse ldng gp over 2f out: kpt on at same pce fnl f: nvr looked likely to trble ldrs* **83/10**

5 nk **Rivolochop (FR)**[20] 4-9-8 0........................(p) MlleBlancheDeGranvilliers 7 63
(C Boutin, France) **15/1**

6 1/2 **Maply (FR)**[59] 4-9-7 0...(b) MissCelinaWeber 2 61
(Y Barberot, France) **11/1**

7 1/2 **Misty Love (FR)**[20] 4-10-1 0....................................... MissSiljaStoren 8 68
(F Vermeulen, France) **33/10**[2]

8 4 **Lotus (FR)**[43] 4-9-7 0.. MmeHanaJurankova 5 52
(Waldemar Hickst, Germany) **76/10**

9 4 **Charly Green (FR)**[17] 4-9-4 0.........................(p) MissJosephineChini 4 40
(P Leblanc, France) **21/1**

10 6 **Leonida (FR)**[130] 4-9-4 0.......................................(b) FrauLarissaBiess 9 28
(C Boutin, France) **33/1**

WIN (incl. 1 euro stake): 3.90. PLACES: 1.80, 2.70, 2.00. DF: 18.50. SF: 32.00.
Owner Mme Rosine Bouckhuyt **Bred** Mme A Gravereaux, E Puerari & Oceanic Bloodstock I **Trained** France

4902a PRIX SIX PERFECTIONS (LISTED RACE) (2YO FILLIES) (ROUND) (TURF) 7f
12:50 (12:00) 2-Y-O **£20,220** (£8,088; £6,066; £4,044; £2,022)

RPR

1 **Asidious Alexander (IRE)**[22] 4106 2-9-0 0................. MaximeGuyon 3 96
(Simon Crisford) *settled in midfield: cl 3rd 3f out: rdn along 2f out but unable to cl on ldrs: gd late run fnl f: led fnl 75yds* **29/10**[2]

2 snk **Calare (IRE)**[9] 4560 2-9-0 0..................................... MickaelBarzalona 4 96
(Charlie Appleby) *wl away: settled in midfield: 4th 3f out: effrt 2f out: c to chal and led jst ins fnl f: hdd 75yds out* **6/5**[1]

3 3/4 **Obedient**[38] 2-9-0 0.. VincentCheminaud 2 94
(P Bary, France) **41/10**[3]

4 hd **What's In A Kiss (IRE)**[27] 2-9-0 0.................(p) ChristopheSoumillon 6 93
(J-C Rouget, France) **26/5**

5 shd **Erica Bing**[32] 3763 2-9-0 0.. UmbertoRispoli 1 93
(Jo Hughes) *led: rdn along 2f out: hdd 1f out: kpt on* **9/1**

6 2 **Quandary Peak**[21] 4148 2-9-0 0.................................. IoritzMendizabal 5 88
(J S Moore) *niggled along in last early: 5th 4f out: rdn along 2f out but nvr involved* **23/1**

1m 27.94s (-0.36) **6** Ran SP% **121.0**
WIN (incl. 1 euro stake): 3.90. PLACES: 1.60, 1.40. SF: 7.80.
Owner Noel O'Callaghan **Bred** Martyn J McEnery **Trained** Newmarket, Suffolk

4903a 61ST PRIX GEORGES COURTOIS - EQUIDIA LIVE (CONDITIONS) (4YO+) (GENTLEMEN RIDERS) (POLYTRACK) 1m 1f 110y
1:20 (12:00) 4-Y-O+ **£8,823** (£3,529; £2,647; £1,764; £882)

RPR

1 **Gentora (FR)**[24] 4030 4-10-2 0.........................(p) MrVinzenzSchiergen 6 77
(P Sogorb, France) **71/10**

2 1 3/4 **No Mood**[295] 7103 5-10-6 0... MrAlexisLemer 3 77
(C Laffon-Parias, France) **14/1**

3 snk **Noray (FR)**[315] 6555 4-10-6 0...................................... MrKevinBraye 10 77
(Enrique Leon Penate, France) **48/10**[3]

4 1/2 **Stranger In Paris (FR)**[222] 9-10-6 0.......................... MrGuilainBertrand 7 76
(N Caullery, France) **17/1**

5 3 **Simba (FR)**[43] 3377 8-10-6 0.. MrFlorentGuy 5 70
(C Lerner, France) **23/10**[1]

6 3/4 **Saane (FR)**[647] 7394 5-10-12 0.......................... MrAntonioFerramosca 8 74
(J-C Rouget, France) **31/10**[2]

7 1/2 **Uphold**[329] 6091 9-10-6 0... MrMaxDenuault 9 67
(Gay Kelleway) *settled in tch on outer: rdn along 2f out but nt the pce to go w ldrs: sn btn* **64/1**

8 snk **It's A Privilege**[41] 7-10-8 0........................ MrIgnacioMelgarejoLoring 4 69
(Mme J Hendriks, Holland) **31/1**

9 nk **Sweet Thomas (GER)**[55] 4-10-12 0................. MrThomasGuineheux 1 72
(Christian Sprengel, Germany) **13/2**

10 1 1/2 **Becquarius (FR)**[354] 6-10-6 0.................. MrJean-PhilippeBoisgontier 2 63
(Eric Saint-Martin, France) **20/1**

Owner Guy Pariente **Bred** Guy Pariente Holding **Trained** France [illegible] 3.60, 2.20. DF: 37.70. SF: 95.80

4904a PRIX PSYCHE MOROCCO CUP BY SOREC (GROUP 3) (3YO FILLIES) (TURF) 1m 2f
1:50 (12:00) 3-Y-O **£29,411** (£11,764; £8,823; £5,882; £2,941)

RPR

1 **Left Hand**[41] 3452 3-8-11 0.. MaximeGuyon 4 107+
(C Laffon-Parias, France) *settled in tch in 3rd: moved up to chal 2f out: led 1 1/2f out: sn wnt 2 l clr: hld off late chal fnl f* **8/13**[1]

2 nk **Lakalas (FR)**[60] 3-8-11 0................................. ChristopheSoumillon 6 106+
(J-C Rouget, France) *settled in 6th: moved up to trck ldng pair 2f out: chsd ldr fnl 1 1/2f: fin wl u.str ride but jst hld* **11/2**[2]

3 2 **Apple Betty (IRE)**[62] 2726 3-8-11 0............................ HugoJourniac 2 102
(J-C Rouget, France) *sn led: jnd briefly 3f out but wnt clr again: chal 2f out: hdd 1 1/2f out: kpt on* **14/1**

4 4 1/2 **Zghorta Dance (FR)**[41] 3452 3-9-2 0.......................... IoritzMendizabal 5 98
(J-C Rouget, France) *settled in 5th: rdn along fr 2f out: no ch w ldrs* **13/2**[3]

5 2 1/2 **Gambissara (FR)**[27] 3935 3-8-11 0............................ AndraschStarke 3 88
(Lennart Hammer-Hansen, Germany) *broke wl and led briefly: sn hdd and settled in 4th: rdn along fr 2f out: no ch w ldrs* **18/1**

6 2 1/2 **Maquette (USA)**[20] 4184 3-8-11 0............................ VincentCheminaud 1 83
(A Fabre, France) *t.k.h in rr early: asked for an effrt over 2f out but unable qck: nvr on terms* **11/2**[2]

7 12 **Redcold (FR)**[61] 3-8-11 0...............................(p) AnthonyCrastus 7 59
(C Laffon-Parias, France) *settled in cl 2nd: jnd ldr 3f out: asked for an effrt over 2f out: qckly wknd: eased fnl f* **22/1**

2m 7.87s (-2.33) **7** Ran SP% **122.3**
WIN (incl. 1 euro stake): 1.80 (Left Hand coupled with Redcold); PLACES: 1.30, 2.00. SF: 6.20.
Owner Wertheimer & Frere **Bred** Wertheimer Et Frere **Trained** Chantilly, France

4905a PRIX DU CERCLE (LISTED RACE) (3YO+) (TURF) 5f
2:30 (12:00) 3-Y-O+ **£19,117** (£7,647; £5,735; £3,823; £1,911)

RPR

1 **Silver Rainbow (IRE)**[14] 4398 4-8-13 0............ ChristopheSoumillon 6 110+
(Charles Hills) *trckd ldr early: asked for an effrt over 1 1/2f out: c w a gd run to ld ins fnl f: wnt 2 l clr: comf* **39/10**[1]

2 1 1/2 **Monsieur Joe (IRE)**[15] 4359 9-9-6 0................ Pierre-CharlesBoudot 8 111
(Paul Midgley) *broke wl: led tl chal ins fnl f: no ch w wnr: kpt on wl for 2nd* **53/10**[2]

3 1/2 **Yakaba (FR)**[26] 3967 3-8-8 0.. MaximeGuyon 11 100
(F Head, France) **10/1**

4 hd **Largent Du Bonheur (FR)**[30] 3-8-11 0.............. VincentCheminaud 12 102
(M Delzangles, France) **89/10**

5 nk **Mirza**[55] 2943 9-9-2 0..(p) IoritzMendizabal 2 103
(Rae Guest) *midfield towards stands' side early: swtchd to rail 2f out: mde gd prog up rail fnl f: nrst fin* **78/10**

6 hd **Spiritfix**[24] 4029 3-8-8 0.. MickaelBarzalona 10 97
(A Fabre, France) **13/1**

7 1 1/2 **Porthilly (FR)**[26] 6-8-13 0.. GeraldMosse 1 94
(J E Hammond, France) **73/10**[3]

8 2 **Bolting (USA)**[45] 3269 3-9-2 0.................................. StephanePasquier 7 93
(F-H Graffard, France) **10/1**

9 shd **Lil's Joy (IRE)**[49] 3158 3-8-8 0...................................... CristianDemuro 3 85
(Giles Bravery) *wl away and hdd nr side gp: rdn along 2 1/2f out but unable to go w ldrs: eased fnl 110yds* **19/1**

10 nse **Fine Blend (IRE)**[42] 3392 3-8-13 0................................ UmbertoRispoli 4 89
(William Muir) *bmpd s: midfield towards stands' side early: effrt 2f out: chsd ldrs but unable to get on terms: btn and eased fnl 110yds* **11/1**

11 3/4 **Pupa Di Saronno (FR)**[31] 3796 5-8-13 0........................ FabriceVeron 5 84
(H-A Pantall, France) **9/1**

12 snk **Gamgoom**[62] 2722 5-9-2 0.. AndraschStarke 9 86
(Mario Hofer, Germany) **39/1**

57.71s (0.21)
WFA 3 from 4yo+ 4lb **12** Ran SP% **121.0**
WIN (incl. 1 euro stake): 4.90. PLACES: 2.20, 2.00, 2.80. DF: 11.80. SF: 27.00.
Owner R J Tufft **Bred** Austin Curran **Trained** Lambourn, Berks

4906a (Foreign Racing) - See Raceform Interactive

4586 CHEPSTOW (L-H)
Sunday, July 31
OFFICIAL GOING: Good (good to firm in places) changing to good to firm after race 3 (3.05)
Wind: slight across Weather: sunny spells

4907 POTTER GROUP EQUESTRIAN CARPET FIBRE SURFACES MAIDEN AUCTION STKS (PLUS 10 RACE) 7f 16y
2:00 (2:01) (Class 4) 2-Y-O **£5,175** (£1,540; £769; £384) **Stalls** Centre

Form RPR

6 1 **Accidental Agent**[18] 4270 2-9-5 0.................................. CharlesBishop 12 77
(Eve Johnson Houghton) *s.i.s: sn trcking ldrs: shkn up to ld over 1f out: hung sltly lft ins fnl f: pushed out: comf* **9/2**[2]

03 2 1 1/4 **Highland Lotus**[9] 4586 2-9-0 0..................(p) WilliamTwiston-Davies 13 67
(William Haggas) *cl up: led 3f out: rdn and hdd over 1f out: kpt on same pce* **6/1**[3]

3 2 **Gravity Wave (IRE)** 2-9-2 0.................................. EdwardGreatrex(3) 9 67
(Sylvester Kirk) *t.k.h towards rr: hdwy 3f out: pushed along to chse ldng pair 2f out: sn hung lft and no further imp* **28/1**

4 4 1/2 **Washington Blue** 2-9-0 0.. AdamKirby 5 50+
(Clive Cox) *in rr: rdn after 3f: hdwy over 2f out: one pce fnl f* **6/1**[3]

3 5 2 1/4 **Count Calabash (IRE)**[18] 4270 2-9-5 0.............................. LukeMorris 11 49
(Paul Cole) *chsd ldrs: rdn 3f out: bmpd over 2f out: unable qck and no ch after* **11/10**[1]

06 6 3/4 **Poetic Force (IRE)**[22] 4128 2-9-5 0................................ TimmyMurphy 10 47
(Jonathan Portman) *chsd ldrs: rdn whn bmpd over 2f out: one pce after: kpt on towards fin* **16/1**

400 7 1 1/4 **A Sure Welcome**[25] 4016 2-9-5 59.............................. TomMarquand 6 44
(John Spearing) *mid-div: rdn 3f out: one pce fnl 2f* **50/1**

0 8 1 **Sir Plato (IRE)**[39] 3529 2-8-12 0................................. GeorgeWood(7) 1 41
(Rod Millman) *dwlt: sn in mid-div: rdn 3f out: edgd lft over 1f out: wknd fnl f* **80/1**

00 9 7 **Stag Party (IRE)**[18] 4270 2-9-5 0.................................. DavidProbert 7 23
(Andrew Balding) *rdn over 2f out: a towards rr* **12/1**

10 ½ **Hoover Fever** 2-8-11 0 KieranShoemark(3) 8 17
(David Evans) *rdn along 1/2-way: a in rr* **50/1**

0 11 4½ **Viola Park**[33] 3742 2-9-5 0 RaulDaSilva 2 10
(Ronald Harris) *wnt sltly lft leaving stalls: sn swtchd rt: led tl hdd 3f out: wknd 2f out* **66/1**

12 3½ **Kissinger** 2-9-5 0 WilliamCarson 3
(Michael Bell) *s.s: towards rr and racd alone down centre: wknd over 2f out* **20/1**

1m 22.92s (-0.28) **Going Correction** -0.15s/f (Firm) **12** Ran SP% **122.8**
Speed ratings (Par 96): **95,93,90,85,83 82,80,79,71,71 65,61**
CSF £31.28 TOTE £5.00: £1.70, £2.80, £8.20; EX 31.00 Trifecta £1333.20.
Owner Mrs R F Johnson Houghton **Bred** Mrs R F Johnson Houghton **Trained** Blewbury, Oxon

FOCUS
Ground on the quick side of good and probably no more than an average maiden to kick-off the seven-race card. The front three pulled clear but, with the well-punted market leader bombing out completely and the front two having shown just reasonable form previously, it's hard to get too excited about the form.

4908 GALLERY LOFTS GALLOP H'CAP 7f 16y
2:30 (2:30) (Class 4) (0-80,80) 3-Y-O+ **£5,175** (£1,540; £769; £384) **Stalls** Centre

Form RPR
6636 1 **Corporal Maddox**[9] 4608 9-9-9 **75** (p) LukeMorris 8 83
(Ronald Harris) *racd stands' side: chsd ldrs: rdn over 3f out: stl 4th ent fnl f: r.o wl u.p to ld nr fin* **17/2**

3210 2 ½ **He's My Cracker**[35] 3689 3-9-7 **80** AdamKirby 6 84
(Clive Cox) *led gp on stands' side and in 2nd overall: rdn 2f out: ev ch u.p fnl f tl hld nr fin* **3/1**[1]

0003 3 shd **Sarangoo**[10] 4563 8-9-3 **72** JosephineGordon(3) 5 78+
(Malcolm Saunders) *led gp in centre and overall ldr: rdn over 2f out: edgd lft wl ins fnl f: hdd nr fin* **5/1**[3]

2425 4 ¾ **Gold Hunter (IRE)**[16] 4362 6-9-8 **74** TimmyMurphy 4 78
(Steve Flook) *s.i.s: racd in centre tl swtchd rt to stands' side gp over 4f out: sn prom and gng wl: rdn 2f out: unable qck fnl f* **4/1**[2]

0450 5 3 **Mister Musicmaster**[22] 4157 7-9-11 **77** SteveDrowne 7 74
(Ron Hodges) *racd stands' side: in rr: outpcd and rdn along 1/2-way: no hdwy tl r.o ins fnl f* **20/1**

0 6 1¼ **Show Me Again**[57] 2891 3-9-7 **80** FergusSweeney 9 70
(David Dennis) *racd stands' side: towards rr: rdn and hdwy over 2f out: one pce fnl f* **8/1**

6052 7 1¼ **Air Of York (IRE)**[12] 4481 4-9-6 **79** AledBeech(7) 2 69
(David Evans) *chsd overall ldr in centre: rdn wl over 1f out: sn outpcd and no ch* **8/1**

603 8 1 **Ambitious Boy**[11] 4506 7-8-6 **61** oh1 EdwardGreatrex(3) 3 49
(John O'Shea) *s.s: towards rr in centre: hdwy 3f out: wknd fnl f* **16/1**

5504 9 2¾ **See You When (IRE)**[11] 4519 3-9-2 **75** TomMarquand 1 52
(Richard Hannon) *s.i.s: sn in tch in centre: rdn over 2f out: wknd over 1f out* **6/1**

1m 22.51s (-0.69) **Going Correction** -0.15s/f (Firm)
WFA 3 from 4yo+ 7lb **9** Ran SP% **119.3**
Speed ratings (Par 105): **97,96,96,95,92 90,89,88,84**
CSF £35.46 CT £145.93 TOTE £8.80: £2.70, £1.50, £2.00; EX 34.70 Trifecta £100.60.
Owner S & A Mares & Ridge House Stables Ltd **Bred** Theobalds Stud **Trained** Earlswood, Monmouths

FOCUS
A difference of opinion here as Adam Kirby made an immediate beeline towards the stands rail, while Josephine Gordon led a group of four who stayed centre. The pace was strong and that set it up for a closer.

4909 WESSEX GARAGES NISSAN H'CAP 1m 14y
3:05 (3:05) (Class 4) (0-80,78) 3-Y-O+ **£5,175** (£1,540; £769; £384) **Stalls** Centre

Form RPR
5522 1 **Izmir (IRE)**[23] 4087 3-9-4 **78** (p) SeanLevey 2 82
(William Haggas) *trckd ldng pair: wnt 2nd gng wl over 3f out: rdn to ld appr fnl f: jst hld on* **9/4**[1]

5344 2 hd **Peak Storm**[23] 4086 7-9-10 **76** (p) LukeMorris 4 81
(John O'Shea) *chsd ldrs in 4th: rdn over 2f out: swtchd lft over 1f out: r.o ins fnl f: jst failed* **8/1**

5402 3 ¾ **Lilbourne Prince (IRE)**[9] 4589 3-8-8 **73** GaryMahon(5) 3 75
(David Evans) *wnt to post early: led and qckly brought field over to stands' side: rdn 2f out: hdd appr fnl f: unable qck* **3/1**[2]

5433 4 ¾ **Midnight Rider (IRE)**[12] 4481 8-9-3 **74** (b) AliceMills(5) 5 76
(Rod Millman) *dwlt: hld up in last: hdwy 2f out: rdn over 1f out: unable qck ins fnl f* **6/1**[3]

0310 5 7 **Bluff Crag**[19] 4241 3-8-12 **72** DavidProbert 6 56
(Andrew Balding) *trckd ldrs tl lost pl over 3f out: sn rdn: bhd fnl 2f* **9/4**[1]

1m 33.73s (-2.47) **Going Correction** -0.15s/f (Firm)
WFA 3 from 7yo+ 8lb **5** Ran SP% **111.9**
Speed ratings (Par 105): **106,105,105,104,97**
CSF £19.69 TOTE £2.20: £1.10, £2.80; EX 9.60 Trifecta £33.10.
Owner Mohamed Saeed Al Shahi **Bred** Michael Downey & Roalso Ltd **Trained** Newmarket, Suffolk

FOCUS
Not the strongest of 0-80 handicaps. The pace looked sound as they congregated up the stands rail and the front three were separated by just a length at the line.

4910 PANASONIC TOUGHBOOK TROPHY H'CAP 6f 16y
3:40 (3:40) (Class 4) (0-85,85) 3-Y-O+ **£5,175** (£1,540; £769; £384) **Stalls** Centre

Form RPR
-030 1 **Little Palaver**[23] 4079 4-9-12 **85** AdamKirby 2 94
(Clive Cox) *led pair on far rail and overall ldr: mde all: rdn over 2f out: hld on gamely u.p fnl f* **7/1**[3]

2232 2 nk **Pixeleen**[13] 4460 4-9-6 **82** JosephineGordon(3) 1 90
(Malcolm Saunders) *wnt to post early: trckd wnr on far side and a in 2nd overall: rdn over 2f out: ev ch fnl f: hld nr fin* **2/1**[1]

5441 3 1 **Ice Age (IRE)**[13] 4460 3-8-13 **77** RobertWinston 4 81+
(Eve Johnson Houghton) *racd centre tl swtchd to stands' side after 2f: chsd ldrs: led on side over 3f out: rdn over 2f out: r.o fnl f but hld by pair on far side* **7/2**[2]

2631 4 6 **Upstaging**[24] 4051 4-9-7 **80** (b) LukeMorris 7 66
(Paul Cole) *s.i.s: racd towards rr in centre: hdwy 3f out: sn rdn: one pce fnl f* **7/2**[2]

0600 5 shd **Francisco**[12] 4475 4-9-4 **82** GaryMahon(5) 5 67
(Richard Hannon) *racd in centre: prom: rdn 3f out and sn outpcd by ldrs: kpt on same pce fnl f* **14/1**

2004 6 2¼ **Light From Mars**[26] 3989 11-9-1 **74** (p) DavidProbert 6 52
(Ronald Harris) *racd centre tl swtchd to stands' side after 2f: towards rr overall: rdn wl over 2f out: kpt on same pce fnl f* **22/1**

4614 7 1 **Wiley Post**[55] 2982 3-9-1 **79** (b) TomMarquand 10 53
(Richard Hannon) *racd on stands' side and alone for 2f: led side tl over 3f out: sn rdn: grad wknd* **9/1**

6030 8 11 **Englishwoman**[9] 4585 3-8-8 **75** KieranShoemark(3) 3 14
(David Evans) *chsd ldrs in centre: rdn over 2f out: wknd over 1f out* **33/1**

0-00 9 ½ **Maymyo (IRE)**[103] 1545 5-8-4 **66** (t) EdwardGreatrex(3) 8 4
(Sylvester Kirk) *racd centre: sn outpcd in rr: swtchd to stands' side after 2f: bhd fnl 3f* **25/1**

1m 9.59s (-2.41) **Going Correction** -0.15s/f (Firm)
WFA 3 from 4yo+ 5lb **9** Ran SP% **118.1**
Speed ratings (Par 105): **110,109,108,100,100 97,95,81,80**
CSF £21.49 CT £59.08 TOTE £6.00: £1.90, £1.30, £1.70; EX 27.80 Trifecta £108.20.
Owner Trevor Fox **Bred** Mrs Sandra Fox **Trained** Lambourn, Berks

FOCUS
They were spread right across the track in this ordinary handicap but the front three finished some way clear.

4911 CAPITAL NETWORK SOLUTIONS H'CAP 5f 16y
4:15 (4:15) (Class 3) (0-90,89) 3-Y-O+ **£9,703** (£2,887; £1,443; £721) **Stalls** Centre

Form RPR
2353 1 **Majestic Hero (IRE)**[13] 4461 4-9-5 **84** AdamKirby 9 93
(Ronald Harris) *chsd ldrs: rdn to go 2nd over 2f out: chal 1f out: sn led: r.o* **13/2**

4504 2 1 **Rosie's Premiere (IRE)**[13] 4461 4-9-8 **87** (t) RobertWinston 6 92
(Dean Ivory) *in tch in rr: rdn over 2f out: only 7th ent fnl f: r.o down outer: wnt 2nd post* **5/1**

2050 3 nse **King Crimson**[11] 4514 4-9-2 **81** JFEgan 5 86
(Mick Channon) *led and tk field over to far side: rdn 2f out: hdd jst ins fnl f: no ex: ct for 2nd post* **16/1**

2214 4 nk **Dark Shot**[19] 4223 3-8-11 **80** (t) DavidProbert 7 83
(Andrew Balding) *in tch towards rr: rdn over 2f out: hdwy over 1f out: r.o* **9/4**[1]

6-10 5 1¾ **Edged Out**[58] 2846 6-8-5 **75** HectorCrouch(5) 1 73
(Christopher Mason) *chsd ldrs: rdn over 2f out: no ex and lost 2 pls wl ins fnl f* **20/1**

-410 6 ½ **Silverrica (IRE)**[25] 3995 6-8-9 **77** JosephineGordon(3) 4 73
(Malcolm Saunders) *trckd ldr tl rdn and lost pl over 2f out: kpt on same pce fnl f* **16/1**

1120 7 1¾ **Papa Luigi (IRE)**[8] 4652 3-9-1 **89** GaryMahon(5) 3 81
(Richard Hannon) *chsd ldrs: rdn over 2f out: outpcd over 1f out: no ch after* **4/1**[3]

5051 8 9 **Sydney Ruffdiamond**[17] 4291 4-9-6 **85** ShaneKelly 2 42
(Richard Hughes) *s.i.s: a towards rr: rdn 3f out: wknd over 1f out* **7/2**[2]

57.66s (-1.64) **Going Correction** -0.15s/f (Firm)
WFA 3 from 4yo+ 4lb **8** Ran SP% **119.5**
Speed ratings (Par 107): **107,105,105,104,102 101,98,84**
CSF £40.69 CT £507.98 TOTE £6.10: £2.30, £1.80, £4.00; EX 41.90 Trifecta £342.00.
Owner Mrs Jackie Jarrett & Ridge House Stables **Bred** Mrs Diane Williams **Trained** Earlswood, Monmouths

FOCUS
A competitive £15k handicap run at a strong pace and the form looks solid for the grade.

4912 INTERCITY TECHNOLOGY H'CAP 2m 49y
4:45 (4:46) (Class 4) (0-85,83) 4-Y-O+ **£6,469** (£1,925; £962; £481) **Stalls** Low

Form RPR
002 1 **Arty Campbell (IRE)**[25] 4012 6-9-0 **76** DavidProbert 1 83+
(Bernard Llewellyn) *towards rr: clsd 1/2-way: gng wl whn nt clr run over 2f out: sn swtchd rt: r.o to ld ins fnl f: all out* **10/3**[2]

0000 2 nk **Norab (GER)**[36] 3639 5-8-9 **74** (p) DanielMuscutt(3) 10 80
(Bernard Llewellyn) *mid-div: hdwy to trck ldr 7f out: rdn over 2f out: sn chal: led narrowly over 1f out tl hdd ins fnl f: rallied nr fin* **12/1**

0535 3 1¼ **Lungarno Palace (USA)**[10] 4550 5-9-1 **77** MichaelJMMurphy 2 82
(John Gallagher) *hld up in last pair: rdn and hdwy over 2f out: r.o to go 3rd ins fnl f* **6/1**

0245 4 ¾ **Cotton Club (IRE)**[11] 4535 5-8-6 **75** GeorgeWood(7) 3 79
(Rod Millman) *chsd ldrs: lost a couple of pls 1/2-way but stl wl in tch: rdn 3f out: styd on fnl f* **3/1**[1]

124/ 5 hd **Walter White (IRE)**[14] 428 6-8-2 **64** oh1 (t) LukeMorris 7 67
(Philip Hobbs) *led: rdn and jnd 2f out: hdd narrowly over 1f out: kpt on u.p tl no ex and lost 2 pls fnl 100yds* **7/1**

0004 6 4 **Kashgar**[12] 4483 7-7-12 **67** MitchGodwin(7) 8 66
(Bernard Llewellyn) *hld up in last pair: rdn and hdwy on outer over 3f out: nvr able to chal: wknd ins fnl f* **5/1**[3]

2150 7 1 **Argent Knight**[8] 4664 6-9-4 **80** (p) TimmyMurphy 6 77
(Christopher Kellett) *trckd ldr tl relegated to 3rd 7f out: rdn over 2f out: wknd over 1f out* **25/1**

0424 8 2½ **Fitzwilly**[18] 4266 6-8-13 **75** JFEgan 9 69
(Mick Channon) *chsd ldrs: rdn over 3f out: wknd over 2f out* **6/1**

3m 36.42s (-2.48) **Going Correction** -0.15s/f (Firm) **8** Ran SP% **117.4**
Speed ratings (Par 105): **100,99,99,98,98 96,96,95**
CSF £43.31 CT £233.53 TOTE £4.40: £1.30, £3.10, £2.20; EX 47.00 Trifecta £334.50.
Owner Alex James **Bred** Airlie Stud **Trained** Fochriw, Caerphilly

FOCUS
A steadily run staying event in in which the winner would have been an unlucky loser having had to wait for a run for most of the straight.

4913 BABYBELL'S SWIMMING LESSONS H'CAP 1m 4f 23y
5:15 (5:15) (Class 5) (0-70,68) 3-Y-O+ **£3,234** (£962; £481; £240) **Stalls** Low

Form RPR
4333 1 **Glens Wobbly**[6] 4711 8-9-9 **68** HectorCrouch(5) 5 79
(Jonathan Geake) *led and qckly clr: 15 l up 1/2-way: reduced ld 3f out: sn rdn to extend advantage again: unchal: eased nr fin* **3/1**[2]

0601 2 15 **Rum Swizzle**[11] 4507 4-9-12 **66** AdamKirby 6 53
(Harry Dunlop) *hld up: rdn 4f out: wnt 2nd wl over 1f out: styd on but nvr any imp on wnr who was wl clr* **5/1**[3]

0113 3 5 **Bernisdale**[11] 4507 8-9-8 **65** DanielMuscutt(3) 4 44
(John Flint) *chsd wnr who was sn clr: 15 l down in 2nd 1/2-way: effrt and clsd briefly 3f out: lost 2nd wl over 1f out: plugged on* **7/1**

0112 4 1¾ **Petrify**[9] 4592 6-8-9 **56** (tp) MitchGodwin(7) 1 32
(Bernard Llewellyn) *s.s: sn rcvrd and hld up in 4th: rdn to dispute mod 2nd 3f out but nvr any ch w wnr: one pce fnl 2f* **11/4**[1]

2241 5 5 **Ring Eye (IRE)**[9] 4591 8-9-3 **60** EdwardGreatrex(3) 2 28
(John O'Shea) *racd in 3rd but wl off wnr who was sn clr: rdn over 3f out: wknd over 2f out* **3/1**[2]

2004 **6** 2 1/4 **Distant High**[17] 4294 5-9-1 **62**....................................(p) GeorgeWood(7) 3 27
(Richard Price) *hld up in rr and wl off wnr who was sn clr: rdn over 3f out: wknd over 2f out* **14/1**

2m 34.62s (-4.38) **Going Correction** -0.15s/f (Firm) **6** Ran SP% **112.5**
Speed ratings (Par 103): **108,98,94,93,90 88**
CSF £18.11 TOTE £3.90: £1.80, £2.50; EX 24.70 Trifecta £58.10.
Owner Glen Symes **Bred** H J Manners **Trained** East Kennett, Wilts

FOCUS
This looked quite an open little heat but it turned into a procession as the I front-runner was gifted an unassailable lead and he came home in isolation. This is very unreliable form.
T/Jkpt: Not won. T/Plt: £160.90 to a £1 stake. Pool: £95,510.24 - 433.13 winning units. T/Qpdt: £20.70 to a £1 stake. Pool: £8,136.70 - 290.28 winning units. **Richard Lowther**

4629 CHESTER (L-H)
Sunday, July 31

OFFICIAL GOING: Good (good to firm in places; 7.2)
Wind: Light, against Weather: Cloudy

4914 CALDWELL CONSTRUCTION/EBF MAIDEN STKS (PLUS 10 RACE) 7f 2y
2:10 (2:11) (Class 4) 2-Y-O **£6,225** (£1,864; £932; £466; £233) **Stalls** Low

Form RPR
54 **1** **Thomas Cranmer (USA)**[12] 4473 2-9-5 0........................ FrannyNorton 3 82
(Mark Johnston) *mainly disp ld: hdd narrowly 2f out: rdn over 1f out: rallied to ld towards fin: gamely* **8/1**[3]

322 **2** *hd* **Devil's Bridge (IRE)**[16] 4349 2-9-5 89.................................... PatDobbs 2 81
(Richard Hannon) *mainly disp ld: led narrowly 2f out: rdn over 1f out: hdd towards fin and jst hld* **4/11**[1]

55 **3** 1 1/2 **Roaring Character (IRE)**[26] 3986 2-9-5 0............... RichardKingscote 1 77+
(Tom Dascombe) *dwlt: hld up: pushed along and outpcd over 1f out: styd on and tk 3rd towards fin: nt pce of front pair* **16/1**

33 **4** 3/4 **Navarone (IRE)**[17] 4304 2-9-5 0...................................... TonyHamilton 5 75
(Richard Fahey) *sltly rrd s: chsd ldrs: pushed along 2f out: unable to go pce of front pair over 1f out: no ex fnl 75yds* **4/1**[2]

04 **5** 7 **Albizu Campos**[22] 4133 2-9-5 0.. JasonHart 4 57
(Lawrence Mullaney) *in rr: pushed along and outpcd over 2f out: lft bhd fnl f* **66/1**

1m 28.37s (1.87) **Going Correction** +0.15s/f (Good) **5** Ran SP% **111.8**
Speed ratings (Par 96): **95,94,93,92,84**
CSF £11.90 TOTE £7.80: £2.90, £1.02; EX 12.70 Trifecta £56.10.
Owner Sheikh Hamdan bin Mohammed Al Maktoum **Bred** Darley **Trained** Middleham Moor, N Yorks

FOCUS
The going was given as good, good to firm in places (GoingStick: 7.6). Tony Hamilton said it's "nice ground - good, good to firm in places", while Richard Kingscote called it "good to firm." The rail between the 6f and 1 1/2f points was out 3yds since the last meeting, and the rail between the 1 1/2f and 6f point was in by 3yds since the last meeting, adding 24yds to races 1-5, 26yds to race 6 and 38yds to race 7. The favourite set a good standard in this maiden.

4915 CHITTY CHITTY BANG BANG AT THE LOWRY NURSERY H'CAP 6f 18y
2:40 (2:42) (Class 4) 2-Y-O
£6,225 (£1,864; £932; £466; £233; £117) **Stalls** Low

Form RPR
3341 **1** **Turanga Leela**[11] 4526 2-8-13 **74**................................ SilvestreDeSousa 4 78
(Ian Williams) *mde all: rdn and qcknd nrly 3 l clr over 1f out: kpt on gamely ins fnl f* **6/1**[3]

216 **2** 1 **Rosebride**[23] 4111 2-8-12 **73**.. TonyHamilton 3 74
(Richard Fahey) *hld up in midfield: swtchd rt and hdwy over 1f out: tk 2nd ins fnl f: styd on: nt quite able to get to wnr* **8/1**

163 **3** 1 1/4 **Tailor's Row (USA)**[22] 4167 2-9-7 **82**........................... FrannyNorton 1 79
(Mark Johnston) *racd keenly: chsd ldrs: 2nd whn rdn and nt qckn over 1f out: lost 2nd ins fnl f: styd on same pce fnl 100yds* **10/11**[1]

6643 **4** 1 1/2 **Trick Of The Lyte (IRE)**[7] 4679 2-8-2 **63**.............................. CamHardie 8 55+
(John Quinn) *hld up in rr: hdwy on inner wl over 1f out: sn chsd ldrs: kpt on ins fnl f and edgd rt: nvr able to mount serious chal* **25/1**

5220 **5** 2 1/4 **In First Place**[15] 4394 2-8-13 **79**.............................. AdamMcNamara(5) 6 64+
(Richard Fahey) *in rr: pushed along 3f out: sme hdwy ins fnl f: nvr able to trble ldrs* **9/2**[2]

4366 **6** 4 **Gerrard's Return**[6] 4713 2-9-0 **75**............................... RichardKingscote 5 47
(Tom Dascombe) *chsd wnr: pushed along 2f out: sn lost 2nd: wknd 1f out* **14/1**

2144 **7** 4 1/2 **Melaniemillie**[16] 4364 2-8-9 **73**................................ JacobButterfield(3) 2 31
(Ollie Pears) *chsd ldrs: pushed along over 2f out: wknd over 1f out* **12/1**

251U **8** 3 **Eva Gore**[11] 4526 2-8-4 **65**.. SamJames 7 13
(David O'Meara) *hld up: hung rt and lost pl wl over 2f out: sn bhd* **28/1**

1m 15.53s (1.73) **Going Correction** +0.15s/f (Good) **8** Ran SP% **117.6**
Speed ratings (Par 96): **94,92,91,89,86 80,74,70**
CSF £54.09 CT £82.83 TOTE £8.20: £2.00, £2.40, £1.10; EX 37.10 Trifecta £121.70.
Owner Eventmasters Racing **Bred** Chasemore Farm **Trained** Portway, Worcs
■ Stewards' Enquiry : Silvestre De Sousa Caution: Careless riding

FOCUS
Race distance increased by 24yds. A fair nursery. The first three raced on the rail into the straight.

4916 MANOR HOUSE STABLES QUEENSFERRY STKS (LISTED RACE) 6f 18y
3:15 (3:15) (Class 1) 3-Y-O+
£20,982 (£7,955; £3,981; £1,983; £995; £499) **Stalls** Low

Form RPR
4011 **1** **Hillbilly Boy (IRE)**[37] 3594 6-9-1 98........................ RichardKingscote 4 107
(Tom Dascombe) *mde all: rdn over 1f out: kpt finding for press ins fnl f: hld on wl* **8/1**[3]

-320 **2** 1/2 **Danzeno**[22] 4151 5-9-1 112.. AndrewMullen 10 105+
(Michael Appleby) *in tch: effrt over 1f out: wnt 2nd ins fnl f: sn edgd lft: r.o u.p: hld nr fin* **7/2**[2]

0-46 **3** 3/4 **Eastern Impact (IRE)**[22] 4151 5-9-1 110........................... JackGarritty 2 103
(Richard Fahey) *chsd wnr: pushed along 2f out: rdn and nt qckn over 1f out: lost 2nd ins fnl f: kpt on but a hld* **8/11**[1]

3500 **4** 3/4 **Scrutineer (IRE)**[24] 4062 3-8-10 98........................... SilvestreDeSousa 7 100
(Mick Channon) *in rr: effrt and hdwy over 1f out: styd on u.p on inner ins fnl f: eased whn hld towards fin* **20/1**

0-20 **5** 1/2 **Pretend (IRE)**[22] 4166 5-9-1 106.. PhillipMakin 9 99+
(Charlie Appleby) *hld up: rdn over 1f out and looked ill at ease on trck: kpt on ins fnl f: nvr able to trble ldrs* **11/1**

0000 **6** 1/2 **Intransigent**[8] 4625 7-9-1 100.. OisinMurphy 8 97
(Andrew Balding) *in tch: effrt over 1f out to chse ldrs: no ex fnl 75yds* **33/1**

0424 **7** 5 **Marsh Hawk**[71] 2474 4-8-10 99.. PatDobbs 5 76
(Richard Hannon) *chsd ldrs tl rdn and wknd over 1f out* **20/1**

1m 13.68s (-0.12) **Going Correction** +0.15s/f (Good)
WFA 3 from 4yo+ 5lb **7** Ran SP% **112.0**
Speed ratings (Par 111): **106,105,104,103,102 102,95**
CSF £34.12 TOTE £10.10: £4.00, £2.40; EX 37.10 Trifecta £70.30.
Owner Macguire's Bloodstock Ltd **Bred** Tipper House Stud **Trained** Malpas, Cheshire

FOCUS
Race distance increased by 24yds. Something of a shock based on the ratings, but there was market support for the winner. The pace held up once again.

4917 MBNA LITTLE LEGS MILE (H'CAP) 7f 122y
3:50 (3:50) (Class 3) (0-95,94) 3-Y-O+
£8,092 (£2,423; £1,211; £605; £302; £152) **Stalls** Low

Form RPR
1113 **1** **Ice Slice (IRE)**[30] 3855 5-9-11 **91**.. RyanTate 2 98
(James Eustace) *trckd ldrs: effrt to go 2nd ins fnl f: led fnl 110yds: kpt on and a doing enough nr fin* **11/4**[1]

0002 **2** 1/2 **Two For Two (IRE)**[28] 3923 8-9-12 **92**................(p) SilvestreDeSousa 9 98+
(David Loughnane) *hld up: rdn 2f out: hdwy ent fnl f: r.o: edgd lft and gng on towards fin* **8/1**

2214 **3** *nse* **Heir To A Throne (FR)**[29] 3885 3-8-9 **83**............................ ShaneGray 8 87
(Kevin Ryan) *in tch: pushed along 2f out: cl up ins fnl f: wanted to edge lft and bmpd rival: styd on u.p* **14/1**

5334 **4** *hd* **Fast Dancer (IRE)**[11] 4534 4-8-12 **83**.............................. JoshDoyle(5) 1 88
(Joseph Tuite) *midfield: rdn and waited for a run bef hdwy over 1f out: cl up whn wanted to edge rt and bmpd rival ins fnl f: styd on u.p: hld fnl strides* **6/1**

025 **5** 3/4 **Alejandro (IRE)**[9] 4611 7-9-6 **86**...................................... DanielTudhope 4 89
(David O'Meara) *led: rdn over 1f out: hdd fnl 110yds: no ex nr fin* **7/2**[2]

0111 **6** 1 1/2 **Gabrial The Tiger (IRE)**[23] 4094 4-9-3 **88**............... AdamMcNamara(5) 7 88
(Richard Fahey) *chsd ldr: rdn over 1f out: lost 2nd ins fnl f: no ex fnl 75yds* **5/1**[3]

-150 **7** *shd* **Zaeem**[17] 4299 7-9-5 **85**...(p) OisinMurphy 11 84
(Ivan Furtado) *hld up: rdn over 1f out: kpt on ins fnl f: nvr able to trble ldrs* **50/1**

0061 **8** 3/4 **Yourartisonfire**[30] 3849 6-8-13 **84**......................(p) JordanVaughan(5) 3 81
(Patrick Morris) *midfield: pushed along over 2f out: rdn and outpcd over 1f out: no imp after* **20/1**

2014 **9** 3/4 **Chosen Character (IRE)**[30] 3855 8-8-13 **79**.......(vt) RichardKingscote 5 75
(Tom Dascombe) *chsd ldrs: rdn 2f out: fdd ins fnl f* **14/1**

50-0 **10** 1 **Magic City (IRE)**[8] 4644 7-9-5 **90**................................ NathanEvans(5) 10 83
(Michael Easterby) *missed break: in rr: rdn over 1f out: kpt on ins fnl f: nvr able to get to ldrs* **33/1**

140- **11** 3/4 **Marcret (ITY)**[279] 7509 9-10-0 **94**.................................... StevieDonohoe 6 85
(James Unett) *missed break: hld up: rdn over 1f out: nvr threatened* **25/1**

1m 33.64s (-0.16) **Going Correction** +0.15s/f (Good)
WFA 3 from 4yo+ 8lb **11** Ran SP% **117.8**
Speed ratings (Par 107): **106,105,105,105,104 103,102,102,101,100 99**
CSF £24.38 CT £270.13 TOTE £3.00: £1.20, £2.70, £3.60; EX 25.90 Trifecta £270.70.
Owner The MacDougall Two **Bred** Kilfrush Stud **Trained** Newmarket, Suffolk

FOCUS
Race distance increased by 24yds. Not a bad handicap. There was an early dash for the lead (being on the pace was important in the previous races on the card) but this time they did a bit too much early. The winner was still fairly handy though, and on the rail.

4918 SOUTHPORT FLOWER SHOW/EBF STALLIONS CONDITIONS STKS (PLUS 10 RACE) (C&G) 6f 18y
4:25 (4:26) (Class 2) 2-Y-O **£12,450** (£3,728; £1,864) **Stalls** Low

Form RPR
4021 **1** **Leontes**[16] 4336 2-9-1 81.. OisinMurphy 3 94
(Andrew Balding) *in rr: effrt on inner over 1f out: sn wnt 2nd: led ins fnl f: r.o wl to draw clr ins fnl 100yds* **5/1**[2]

21 **2** 4 1/2 **Lonely The Brave (IRE)**[20] 4196 2-9-1 0......................... FrannyNorton 1 80
(Mark Johnston) *led: rdn over 1f out: hdd ins fnl f: outpcd by wnr and no ch ins fnl 100yds* **13/8**[1]

4216 **3** 2 **Super Julius**[15] 4394 2-9-1 88.. JohnFahy 2 75
(Eve Johnson Houghton) *chsd ldr: moved upsides wl over 2f out: sn pushed along: rdn whn lost 2nd over 1f out: one pce and btn ins fnl f* **13/8**[1]

1m 14.61s (0.81) **Going Correction** +0.15s/f (Good) **3** Ran SP% **92.9**
Speed ratings (Par 100): **100,94,91**
CSF £9.50 TOTE £5.30; EX 8.20 Trifecta £6.60.
Owner David Brownlow **Bred** D J Weston **Trained** Kingsclere, Hants
■ Kreb's Cycle was withdrawn. Price at time of withdrawal 6-1. Rule 4 applies to all bets - deduction 10p in the pound.

FOCUS
Race distance increased by 24yds. With the joint-favourites unproven at this trip and getting racing plenty soon enough, this was rather set up for the winner, who travelled well in behind them.

4919 BRITVIC H'CAP 1m 2f 75y
4:55 (4:56) (Class 4) (0-80,80) 3-Y-O+
£6,225 (£1,864; £932; £466; £233; £117) **Stalls** High

Form RPR
56 **1** **Toga Tiger (IRE)**[10] 4568 9-9-5 **71**............................ RichardKingscote 3 81
(Kevin Frost) *hld up: hdwy 2f out: led ins fnl f: r.o wl: comf* **20/1**

1523 **2** 1 3/4 **Mighty Lady**[37] 3593 3-9-0 **76**.. PatDobbs 8 83
(Robyn Brisland) *hld up: hdwy over 2f out: led over 1f out: hdd ins fnl f: unable to go w wnr fnl 75yds* **3/1**[1]

4361 **3** 3 3/4 **Lord Franklin**[29] 3905 7-9-13 **79**.. NeilFarley 2 78
(Eric Alston) *led: hdd after 2f: remained prom: rdn over 1f out: kpt on u.p ins fnl f: no ch w front two fnl 100yds* **9/2**[2]

5021 **4** *hd* **Lopito De Vega (IRE)**[15] 4377 4-9-0 **66**.................... GrahamGibbons 6 65
(David C Griffiths) *chsd ldrs: n.m.r over 1f out: sn rdn: kpt on u.p ins fnl f: nt pce of ldrs* **8/1**

0164 **5** 3/4 **Yorkindred Spirit**[8] 4646 4-9-6 **72**..................................(v) FrannyNorton 1 69
(Mark Johnston) *midfield: pushed along over 3f out: effrt on inner over 1f out: struggled to get gng: kpt on towards fin* **11/2**

3101 **6** 1/2 **Save The Bees**[7] 4687 8-9-6 **79** 6ex.................................(b) GerO'Neill(7) 9 75
(Declan Carroll) *racd keenly: chsd ldr: led after 2f: rdn over 2f out: hdd over 1f out: no ex ins fnl f: eased whn btn fnl 50yds: lost one pl nr fin* **9/1**

0110 **7** *hd* **Indian Chief (IRE)**[24] 4038 6-10-0 **80**................................ BarryMcHugh 10 76
(Rebecca Bastiman) *in rr: rdn over 1f out: sme hdwy ins fnl f: kpt on: nvr able to chal* **25/1**

3056 **8** 2 1/2 **Viewpoint (IRE)**[39] 3525 7-9-10 **76**................................ AndrewMullen 4 67
(Michael Appleby) *in tch: rdn 3f out: lost pl and outpcd over 1f out: eased whn btn fnl 50yds* **5/1**[3]

00-0 **9** 15 **Comedy King (IRE)**[8] 4634 5-9-9 **75**........................ SilvestreDeSousa 7 36
(Richard Fahey) *chsd ldrs: rdn over 2f out: wknd over 1f out: eased whn btn sn after* **7/1**

2m 10.95s (-0.25) **Going Correction** +0.15s/f (Good)
WFA 3 from 4yo+ 10lb **9** Ran SP% **117.5**
Speed ratings (Par 105): **107,105,102,102,101 101,101,99,87**
CSF £80.94 CT £330.57 TOTE £23.70: £4.90, £1.80, £1.80; EX 125.70 Trifecta £961.10.
Owner Jan Mead Kelly Gould **Bred** Daniel Spaight **Trained** Market Drayton, Shropshire

FOCUS
Race distance increased by 26yds. There was a good gallop on here and it was run to suit the hold-up horses.

4920 HAPPY RETIREMENT PHIL CUMMINS H'CAP 1m 4f 66y
5:25 (5:25) (Class 4) (0-85,85) 3-Y-O+

£6,225 (£1,864; £932; £466; £233; £117) **Stalls** Low

Form RPR

113- **1** **Who Dares Wins (IRE)**[135] 7090 4-10-0 **85**......................... PatDobbs 8 98
(Alan King) *hld up: gd hdwy over 2f out: led wl over 1f out: drew clr ins fnl f: styd on wl* **6/1**[3]

1441 **2** 5 **Against The Odds**[20] 4207 3-9-2 **85**.................................. JimCrowley 4 90
(Paul Cole) *bustled along to get position s: midfield: hdwy over 2f out: wnt 2nd whn rdn and ev ch wl over 1f out: unable to go w wnr fnl f* **11/4**[1]

-000 **3** 3 1/2 **Asian Wing (IRE)**[14] 4436 7-9-0 **71**.........................(p) DanielTudhope 11 70
(John James Feane, Ire) *hld up in rr: hdwy on wd outer over 2f out: chsd ldrs over 1f out: one pce and no imp fnl f* **20/1**

2601 **4** 10 **Mysterial**[4] 4768 6-9-1 **79** 6ex.. GerO'Neill[(7)] 7 62
(Declan Carroll) *led: rdn and hdd wl over 1f out: sn btn* **14/1**

40-4 **5** 2 **Energia Fox (BRZ)**[23] 4095 6-9-11 **82**.......................... FrannyNorton 10 62
(Richard Fahey) *prom: chsd ldr after 3f tl 7f out: rdn and wknd over 2f out* **11/2**[2]

5304 **6** 1 1/4 **Agent Gibbs**[17] 4311 4-9-8 **79**..(p) OisinMurphy 3 57
(John O'Shea) *prom: dropped to midfield 6f out: rdn and lost pl over 2f out: wknd over 1f out* **9/1**

4412 **7** 8 **Justice Grace (IRE)**[23] 4092 3-9-1 **84**.................(v[1]) RichardKingscote 2 49
(Ralph Beckett) *racd keenly: trckd ldrs: wnt 2nd 7f out: rdn over 2f out: sn wknd* **11/4**[1]

0505 **8** 2 **Nabhan**[8] 4634 4-9-9 **80**..(t) StevieDonohoe 1 42
(Bernard Llewellyn) *trckd ldrs: rdn 2f out: wknd over 1f out* **12/1**

0 **P** **Manny Owens (IRE)**[20] 4208 4-9-9 **80**.............................. JackGarritty 5
(Jonjo O'Neill) *hld up: pushed along over 5f out: t.o whn p.u 3f out: b.b.v* **20/1**

2m 38.28s (-0.22) **Going Correction** +0.15s/f (Good)
WFA 3 from 4yo+ 12lb **9** Ran SP% **116.9**
Speed ratings (Par 105): **106,102,100,93,92 91,86,84,**
CSF £23.18 CT £305.02 TOTE £7.20: £1.90, £1.30, £7.80; EX 27.50 Trifecta £607.80.
Owner W H Ponsonby **Bred** Mount Coote Stud **Trained** Barbury Castle, Wilts

FOCUS
Race distance increased by 38yds. Another race run at an overly strong gallop which suited those held up.
T/Plt: £139.10 to a £1 stake. Pool: £65,777.59 - 345.00 winning units. T/Qpdt: £72.70 to a £1 stake. Pool: £4,274.88 - 43.50 winning units. **Darren Owen**

4897 GALWAY (R-H)
Sunday, July 31

OFFICIAL GOING: Flat course - good to yielding; jumps courses - good

4921a IRISH STALLION FARMS EUROPEAN BREEDERS FUND "AHONOORA" H'CAP (PREMIER HANDICAP) 7f
3:20 (3:23) 3-Y-O+

£43,382 (£13,970; £6,617; £2,941; £1,470; £735)

RPR

1 **Dream Walker (FR)**[3] 4811 7-8-12 **91**...........................(t) ChrisHayes 12 99+
(Brian Ellison) *hld up: last appr st: gd hdwy 1 1/2f out and impr between horses through narrow gap ent fnl f: r.o wl to ld fnl strides* **7/1**

2 nk **Reckless Endeavour (IRE)**[55] 2984 3-8-11 **97**............... ColinKeane 13 101
(G M Lyons, Ire) *in tch: impr bhd ldrs on outer 2f out to chal in 2nd: led narrowly wl ins fnl f tl hdd fnl strides* **16/1**

3 1/2 **Tribal Path (IRE)**[30] 3865 6-8-7 **86**......................................(t) RoryCleary 92
(Damian Joseph English, Ire) *pushed along to ld after 1f: narrow advantage at 1/2-way: rdn into st and sn strly pressed: hdd wl ins fnl f and no ex in 3rd cl home* **14/1**

4 nk **Cailin Mor (IRE)**[5] 4747 4-8-10 **89**...............................(t) NGMcCullagh 8 94
(M Halford, Ire) *chsd ldrs: 5th 1/2-way: sn pushed along and rdn into st: kpt on u.p and swtchd rt ins fnl f: kpt on wl far side clsng stages: nvr on terms* **25/1**

5 1/2 **Baraweez (IRE)**[5] 4747 6-9-3 **103**.......................... DanielRedmond[(7)] 14 107
(Brian Ellison) *in tch: 7th bef 1/2-way: rdn into st and impr bhd ldrs on outer jst ins fnl f where sltly hmpd: kpt on same pce in 5th clsng stages* **6/1**[3]

6 1/2 **Canary Row (IRE)**[38] 3587 6-8-3 **89**........................(v) KillianLeonard[(7)] 6 91
(P J Prendergast, Ire) *hld up: 10th bef 1/2-way: kpt on u.p on outer ins fnl f where sltly hmpd: nrst fin* **8/1**

7 1 **Have A Nice Day**[15] 4412 6-8-7 **93**.......................... DMSimmonson[(7)] 9 93
(Sabrina J Harty, Ire) *chsd ldrs: disp 3rd at 1/2-way: rdn into st and no imp on ldrs whn sltly hmpd between horses jst ins fnl f: one pce clsng stages* **16/1**

8 hd **Eastern Rules (IRE)**[36] 3676 8-9-4 **97**................................ ShaneFoley 1 96
(M Halford, Ire) *chsd ldrs early: pushed along in 8th 2f out and no imp on ldrs into st: kpt on one pce fnl f* **16/1**

9 nk **Stipulate**[5] 4747 7-9-4 **100**.. DonnachaO'Brien[(3)] 3 98
(Brian Ellison) *hld up in mid-div: n.m.r on inner 2f out: rdn towards rr under 2f out and nt clr run over 1f out: kpt on same pce clsng stages* **7/2**[1]

10 1 3/4 **Kelinni (IRE)**[22] 4135 8-10-0 **107**......................................(p) PatSmullen 5 101
(Kevin Ryan) *broke wl to ld briefly tl sn settled bhd ldr: 2nd 1/2-way: rdn in 2nd into st and u.p in 3rd over 1f out: no ex and wknd ins fnl f* **9/2**[2]

11 nk **The Happy Prince (IRE)**[15] 4415 4-9-6 **99**...........(t) SeamieHeffernan 2 92
(A P O'Brien, Ire) *hld up: rdn towards rr on outer into st and no imp ent fnl f: kpt on one pce clsng stages: nvr nrr* **9/1**

12 1 1/4 **Downforce (IRE)**[15] 4415 4-9-0 **93**.. BillyLee 16 83
(W McCreery, Ire) *towards rr: rdn 2f out and no imp on outer into st: one pce after* **16/1**

13 nk **Pintura**[13] 4448 9-9-0 **93**..(b) TomQueally 10 82
(Alistair Whillans) *hld up: pushed along and sme hdwy into 9th fr 2f out: sn rdn and no ex ent fnl f: no imp whn sltly hmpd ins fnl f* **20/1**

14 1 3/4 **Fit For The Job (IRE)**[5] 4747 4-8-10 **89**..................(p) WayneLordan 11 73
(David Wachman, Ire) *dwlt and towards rr early: tk clsr order after 1/2-way: pushed along in 8th 2f out and sn no ex whn n.m.r between horses: dropped towards rr 1f out* **16/1**

15 3 1/2 **Seanie (IRE)**[11] 4543 7-9-6 **99**...................................(t) ColmO'Donoghue 4 74
(David Marnane, Ire) *sn led tl hdd after 1f: disp 3rd at 1/2-way: rdn over 2f out and sn no ex: wknd into st* **25/1**

1m 26.43s (-5.17)
WFA 3 from 4yo+ 7lb **15** Ran SP% **136.8**
CSF £126.51 CT £1608.57 TOTE £7.30: £2.50, £4.60, £4.00; DF 124.50 Trifecta £3860.10.
Owner Keith Brown **Bred** John Berry **Trained** Norton, N Yorks
■ Gussy Goose was withdrawn. Price at time of withdrawal 12-1. Rule 4 applies to bets place prior to withdrawal but not to SP bets - deduction 5p in the pound. New market formed.
■ Stewards' Enquiry : Chris Hayes one-day ban: careless riding (tbn)

FOCUS
The first, second and third came from stalls 12, 13 and 15 which is very rare in 7f handicaps around here. The third set a blistering pace. There were plenty of hard-luck stories. The winner got a superb ride and led in the final stride.

4922 - 4923a (Foreign Racing) - See Raceform Interactive

4901 DEAUVILLE (R-H)
Sunday, July 31

OFFICIAL GOING: Turf: good; polytrack: standard

4924a PRIX D'EXMES (MAIDEN) (2YO) (TURF) 6f
1:05 (1:05) 2-Y-O **£9,191** (£3,676; £2,757; £1,838; £919)

RPR

1 **Cavale Doree (FR)**[37] 2-8-13 0.. JulienAuge 8 98
(C Ferland, France) **27/10**[1]

2 7 **Facilitate**[23] 2-8-13 0... VincentCheminaud 3 77
(D Smaga, France) **14/5**[2]

3 3 **Alliance Secrete (FR)** 2-9-2 0...................................... MaximeGuyon 2 71
(T Castanheira, France) **11/1**

4 nk **Chantilly Fraise (FR)** 2-8-13 0................................ GregoryBenoist 7 67
(P Sogorb, France) **30/1**

5 2 1/2 **Broklyn Baby (FR)**[9] 2-9-2 0..................................... AntoineHamelin 10 63
(Matthieu Palussiere, France) **10/1**

6 3 1/2 **Samba Pa Ti (IRE)**[44] 2-8-13 0........................... ChristopheSoumillon 1 49
(J-C Rouget, France) **27/10**[1]

7 1 **Dolokhov**[15] 4394 2-9-2 0..(p) IoritzMendizabal 5 49
(J S Moore) *led: rdn 2f out: hdd appr 1 1/2f out: sn wknd* **13/2**[3]

8 4 **Rio Amare (FR)** 2-9-2 0.. EddyHardouin 4 37
(Matthieu Palussiere, France) **49/1**

9 2 1/2 **So Hoity Toity**[23] 4124 2-8-13 0.................................... CristianDemuro 6 27
(E J O'Neill, France) **21/1**

1m 11.6s (0.60) **9** Ran SP% **120.9**
WIN (incl. 1 euro stake): 3.70. PLACES: 1.40, 1.40, 2.30. DF: 6.30. SF: 11.60.
Owner Ecurie Mill Reef Sas **Bred** Mlle C Becq **Trained** France

4925a PRIX DE CABOURG (GROUP 3) (2YO) (TURF) 6f
2:45 (2:45) 2-Y-O **£29,411** (£11,764; £8,823; £5,882; £2,941)

RPR

1 **Alrahma**[60] 2-8-8 0.. AurelienLemaitre 6 103
(F Head, France) *a.p on outer: smooth prog to chal 1 1/2f out: sn rdn: led wl over 1f out: drvn out fnl f: readily* **5/1**[3]

2 1/2 **Fixette (IRE)**[29] 3937 2-8-8 0... MaximeGuyon 2 101
(F-H Graffard, France) *t.k.h: hld up in rr: swtchd to outer appr 1/2-way: shkn up 2f out: styd on u.p fr 1f out: run flattened out late on: a hld by wnr* **11/2**

3 nk **North Thunder (FR)**[32] 2-8-11 0................................ GregoryBenoist 3 103+
(A Fabre, France) *w.w in tch: n.m.r 2f out: angled ins and rdn 1 1/2f out: styd on fnl f: nt pce to ever look like winning* **1/1**[1]

4 hd **Biz Power (IRE)**[35] 3701 2-8-11 0.................................. SilvanoMulas 5 102
(Stefano Botti, Italy) *w.w in midfield: trckd ldr fr 1/2-way: rdn to ld 2f out: outpcd by eventual wnr and hdd over 1f out: styd on again cl home* **18/1**

5 7 **Hyper Hyper**[21] 2-8-11 0..................................... ChristopheSoumillon 4 80
(Mario Hofer, Germany) *led towards centre: hdd after 1 1/2f and remained cl up: rdn and nt qckn 1 1/2f out: grad wknd fnl f* **16/1**

6 1 1/4 **Nuit De Mai (FR)**[28] 2-8-8 0................................ Francois-XavierBertras 1 73
(B De Montzey, France) *dwlt: sn settled in fnl pair: rdn and no imp over 1 1/2f out: bhd fnl f* **25/1**

7 8 **Aardwolf (USA)**[23] 4090 2-8-11 0...................................... JamesDoyle 7 50
(Mark Johnston) *cl up on outer: led after 1 1/2f: rdn and hdd 2f out: sn btn: nt given a hrd time fnl f* **3/1**[2]

1m 10.91s (-0.09) **Going Correction** +0.10s/f (Good) **7** Ran SP% **122.0**
Speed ratings: **104,103,102,102,93 91,81**
WIN (incl. 1 euro stake): 5.10. PLACES: 3.50, 3.50. SF: 25.10.
Owner Hamdan Al Maktoum **Bred** Shadwell Estate Company Limited **Trained** France

4926a PRIX ROTHSCHILD (GROUP 1) (3YO+ FILLIES & MARES) (STRAIGHT) (TURF) 1m (R)
3:15 (3:15) 3-Y-O+ **£126,044** (£50,426; £25,213; £12,595; £6,308)

RPR

1 **Qemah (IRE)**[44] 3339 3-8-9 0...................................... GregoryBenoist 9 117+
(J-C Rouget, France) *settled in midfield on outer: clsd into 3rd and travelling wl appr 2f out: shkn up and qcknd to ld under 1 1/2f out: r.o fnl f: a too gd for runner-up* **11/4**[2]

2 1 1/4 **Volta (FR)**[42] 3452 3-8-9 0................................... ChristopheSoumillon 10 113
(F-H Graffard, France) *w.w in fnl trio: hdwy fr wl over 2 1/2f out: shkn up to chse eventual wnr ins fnl 1 1/2f: r.o but a hld by wnr* **5/1**

3 2 1/2 **Steip Amach (IRE)**[29] 3938 4-9-3 0................................ UmbertoRispoli 8 109
(D Smaga, France) *w.w in fnl pair: hdwy on inner 2f out: rdn appr fnl f: styd on under to go 3rd 75yds out: no further imp and nvr on terms w front two* **66/1**

4 *hd* **Esoterique (IRE)**[47] 4 3242 6-9-3 0........................ Pierre-CharlesBoudot 4 109
(A Fabre, France) *stmbld bdly leaving stalls: sn rcvrd and w.w towards rr: angled ins between horses and hdwy fr 1 1/2f out: styd on at same pce fnl f: nvr in contention* **9/1**

5 *snk* **Siyoushake (IRE)**[67] 2603 4-9-3 0.......................... StephanePasquier 11 108
(F Head, France) *w.w in rr: hdwy on outer wl over 2f out: 6th and rdn 1 1/2f out: styd on at same pce fnl f: nvr trbld ldrs* **40/1**

6 *hd* **Amazing Maria (IRE)**[23] 4107 5-9-3 0............................. JamesDoyle 7 108
(David O'Meara) *led: hdd wl after 1f and trckd new ldr: shkn up to ld appr 2f out: sn drvn and hdd under 1 1/2f out: qckly lft bhd by front two: plugged on at one pce fnl f* **20/1**

7 *6* **Impassable (IRE)**[42] 3451 4-9-3 0................................. MaximeGuyon 2 94
(C Laffon-Parias, France) *w.w in midfield on inner: cl 5th and rdn more than 1 1/2f out: sn btn: bhd fnl f* **18/1**

8 *3/4* **Alice Springs (IRE)**[23] 4107 3-8-9 0................................ RyanMoore 5 90
(A P O'Brien, Ire) *w.w in tch: 3rd and shkn up between horses under 2f out: sn rdn and btn wl over 1f out: eased ins fnl f* **15/8**[1]

9 *15* **Lumiere**[24] 4065 3-8-9 0... JoeFanning 3 56
(Mark Johnston) *racd a little freely: cl up towards inner: eased into ld 3f out: nudged along whn hdd appr 2f out: wknd qckly and eased* **9/2**[3]

10 *20* **Positive Vibration (IRE)**[21] 4185 3-8-9 0.................. IoritzMendizabal 6 10
(J-C Rouget, France) *pcemaker but missed the break: reminders and drvn to ld after wl over 1f: rousted along bef 1/2-way: hdd 3f out: wknd qckly and eased* **200/1**

1m 38.09s (-2.71) **Going Correction** +0.10s/f (Good)
WFA 3 from 4yo+ 8lb **10** Ran SP% **120.8**
Speed ratings: **117,115,113,113,112 112,106,105,90,70**
WIN (incl. 1 euro stake): 3.70 (Qemah coupled with Positive Vibration). PLACES: 1.50, 1.50, 10.20. DF: 4.50. SF: 9.50.
Owner Al Shaqab Racing **Bred** Ecurie Cadran Bissons Sas lei **Trained** Pau, France

FOCUS

A particularly classy renewal of the Prix Rothschild with half the field previously successful at Group 1 level, including the last two winners of this race. However, despite a strong overseas challenge the home-trained contingent dominated the finish. The pace was an even one, though it took the pacemaker \bPositive Vibration\p more than a furlong to get herself to the front.

4927a PRIX D'AUEVILLA - GRATIANNE BASCANS MAROQUINIER PARIS (CLAIMER) (5YO+) (AMATEUR RIDERS) (POLYTRACK) 1m 1f 110y

4:25 (4:25) 5-Y-O+ **£6,617** (£2,647; £1,985; £1,323; £661)

RPR

1 **High Star (FR)**[23] 9-10-3 0.................................. MrRomainBoisnard 10 66
(Y Barberot, France) **9/1**

2 *3/4* **Habeshia**[396] 6-9-11 0... MlleElisabethAllaire(6) 1 64
(C Lerner, France) **10/1**

3 *1* **Theo Danon (GER)**[42] 8-10-7 0.......................... MrVinzenzSchiergen 9 66
(Mario Hofer, Germany) **39/10**[2]

4 *1 1/4* **Menardais (FR)**[24] 4074 7-11-1 0............................ MrGuilainBertrand 8 71
(T Castanheira, France) **74/10**

5 *snk* **L'Ardent (FR)**[41] 5-10-10 0.. MrFlorentGuy 14 66
(J-C Rouget, France) **16/5**[1]

6 *nse* **Sindaco (GER)**[42] 8-10-8 0...................... MrJean-PhilippeBoisgontier 13 64
(H Blume, Germany) **12/1**

7 *2* **Time Dream (IRE)**[9] 5-10-1 0...............................(p) MrHugoBoutin(7) 11 60
(M Boutin, France) **12/1**

8 *1/2* **Harri Bizia (FR)**[233] 5-10-0 0............................(b) SebastienBouyssou 6 51
(F Sanchez, France) **76/1**

9 *snk* **Snap Call**[209] 6-10-3 0.. MrMaxDenuault 12 54
(C Lotoux, France) **57/1**

10 *shd* **Latin Charm (IRE)**[155] 747 5-10-7 0................. MrGonzagueCottreau 4 57
(Gay Kelleway) *w.w in midfield on inner: hdwy on rail 2f out: 5th and pushed along 1 1/2f out: no further imp: grad lft bhd fnl f* **49/1**

11 *3/4* **Arluno (FR)**[97] 7-10-3 0...(b) MlleMarieArtu 7 52
(J-Y Artu, France) **55/1**

12 *1* **Bonnoption**[23] 5-10-3 0.. MrHerveNaggar 3 50
(R Le Gal, France) **11/1**

13 *1 1/4* **Derwent (USA)**[78] 6-9-11 0............(p) MmeGratianneForcade-Dupuis(6) 5 47
(J-P Gallorini, France) **83/1**

14 *2* **Freud (FR)**[24] 4074 6-10-3 0............................... MrThomasGuineheux 2 43
(Ian Williams) *tk v t.k.h: restrained in tch on inner: disp 4th whn scrubbed along wl over 2 1/2f out: rdn and nt qckn wl over 1f out: wknd fnl f* **68/10**[3]

\n\x\x WIN (incl. 1 euro stake): 10.00. PLACES: 3.20, 3.80, 2.10. DF: 62.10. SF:
Owner Passion Racing Club **Bred** Scea De L'Aubay & S Bouvier **Trained** France

1908 MUNICH (L-H)

Sunday, July 31

OFFICIAL GOING: Turf: good

4928a GROSSER DALLMAYR-PREIS - BAYERISCHES ZUCHTRENNEN (GROUP 1) (3YO+) (TURF) 1m 2f

3:40 (12:00) 3-Y-O+ **£73,529** (£22,058; £11,029; £5,147; £2,205)

RPR

1 **Elliptique (IRE)**[39] 3544 5-9-6 0.................................. FrankieDettori 10 114+
(A Fabre, France) *t.k.h: hld up in fnl trio: rdn along 2 1/2f out: hdwy fr over 2f out: styd on wl u.p fnl f: led 50yds out* **27/10**[1]

2 *1/2* **Royal Solitaire (IRE)**[66] 2633 4-9-3 0......................... AndraschStarke 6 110
(P Schiergen, Germany) *racd in fnl trio: hdwy u.p fr 2f out: styd on along outer fnl f: nvr quite on terms w wnr* **9/1**

3 *1/2* **Potemkin (GER)**[35] 3699 5-9-6 0.............................. EduardoPedroza 12 112
(A Wohler, Germany) *settled in midfield: rdn and nt qckn wl over 1 1/2f out: styd on ins fnl f: tk 3rd cl home* **16/5**[3]

4 *shd* **Iquitos (GER)**[28] 3934 4-9-6 0.. IanFerguson 9 112
(H-J Groschel, Germany) *w.w in rr: outpcd and scrubbed along wl over 2f out: gd hdwy over 1 1/2f out: styd on u.p and led ins fnl f: hdd and no ex 50yds out: lost 3rd cl home* **6/1**

5 *1 1/2* **Articus (FR)**[19] 4253 4-9-6 0.. MarcLerner 5 109
(Waldemar Hickst, Germany) *a cl up on inner: rdn 2f out: drifter rt but styd on to ld 1f out: sn hdd and btn* **97/10**

6 *hd* **Nymeria (GER)**[29] 3916 4-9-3 0.................................. AndreasSuborics 3 105
(Waldemar Hickst, Germany) *w.w in midfield: rdn and no imp wl over 1 1/2f out: styd on at same pce fnl f* **21/1**

7 *1/2* **Brisanto**[36] 3683 4-9-6 0.. MartinSeidl 7 107
(M G Mintchev, Germany) *chsd ldng trio on inner: outpcd and scrubbed along fr 2f out: one pce fnl f* **51/1**

8 *3 1/2* **Ito (GER)**[63] 2723 5-9-6 0... FilipMinarik 2 100
(Jean-Pierre Carvalho, Germany) *led: kicked for home 2 1/2f out: hdd 1f out: sn btn* **14/5**[2]

9 *4* **Nacar (GER)**[35] 3699 3-8-10 0.. KoenClijmans 4 92
(Mario Hofer, Germany) *cl up on outer: rdn and nt qckn wl over 1 1/2f out: sn wknd* **48/1**

10 *9* **Diplomat (GER)**[14] 4438 5-9-6 0.. AdriedeVries 1 74
(Mario Hofer, Germany) *settled in midfield on inner: rdn and no imp fr 2f out: wknd wl over 1f out* **34/1**

11 *1/2* **Incantator (GER)**[19] 4253 4-9-6 0....................................... JozefBojko 11 73
(A Wohler, Germany) *chsd ldng trio on outer: rdn whn outpcd over 2f out: sn wknd: eased fnl f* **24/1**

12 *5 1/2* **Parthenius (GER)**[21] 4186 3-8-10 0.......................... AlexanderPietsch 8 62
(Mario Hofer, Germany) *hld up towards rr: no imp whn rdn over 2f out: sn bhd and eased fnl f* **35/1**

2m 7.83s (-1.14)
WFA 3 from 4yo+ 10lb **12** Ran SP% **128.9**
WIN (incl. 10 euro stake): 37. PLACES: 12, 15, 12, 13. SF: 507.
Owner Rothschild Family **Bred** Societe Civile Famille Rothschild **Trained** Chantilly, France

4678 CARLISLE (R-H)

Monday, August 1

OFFICIAL GOING: Good (good to soft in places down the hill; 7.0)

Wind: Almost nil Weather: Overcast

4929 SANDRA EICHENHOFER LADY RIDERS' INVITATIONAL H'CAP (FOR LADY AMATEUR RIDERS) 1m 1f

5:45 (5:45) (Class 6) (0-60,59) 4-Y-O+ **£3,119** (£967; £483; £242) **Stalls** Low

Form RPR

0050 **1** **Eeny Mac (IRE)**[6] 4724 9-9-7 **45**........................(p) MlleSaraVermeersch 2 52
(John Wainwright) *chsd clr ldr: effrt over 2f out: rdn to ld appr fnl f: hrd pressed ins fnl f: hld on wl* **14/1**

0000 **2** *hd* **Ted's Brother (IRE)**[15] 4424 8-9-7 **45**.................(e) MissJoannaMason 1 51
(Richard Guest) *s.i.s: hld up: hdwy over 2f out: effrt and ev ch ins fnl f: kpt on: jst hld* **7/2**[2]

1600 **3** *5* **Mount Cheiron (USA)**[9] 4648 5-9-12 **50**.................... MissMSlamanig 5 46
(Richard Ford) *dwlt: hld up: stdy hdwy 1/2-way: effrt and chsd ldrs over 1f out: outpcd ins fnl f* **12/1**

6061 **4** *2 1/4* **Gone With The Wind (GER)**[7] 4705 5-10-7 **59**.....(t) MissKHarrington 7 50
(Rebecca Bastiman) *t.k.h: hld up: stdy hdwy 1/2-way: effrt and rdn over 2f out: cl up over 1f out: wknd ins fnl f* **5/4**[1]

0640 **5** *1 3/4* **Outlaw Torn (IRE)**[15] 4425 7-9-10 **48**......(e) MissBethanyBaumgardner 6 35
(Richard Guest) *t.k.h: led: clr after 2f: rdn and hdd appr fnl f: sn wknd* **7/1**

-604 **6** *1/2* **The Name's Bond**[9] 4648 4-9-7 **45**...................... MissLilli-MarieEngels 3 31
(Richard Fahey) *chsd clr ldrs: lost pl 1/2-way: outpcd 4f out: plugged on fnl f: no imp* **9/2**[3]

1m 59.45s (1.85) **Going Correction** +0.15s/f (Good) **6** Ran SP% **111.7**
Speed ratings (Par 101): **97,96,92,90,88 88**
CSF £60.94 TOTE £18.30: £8.30, £3.90; EX 68.70 Trifecta £326.70.
Owner Gareth Davies **Bred** Kenneth Heelan **Trained** Kennythorpe, N Yorks

FOCUS

Race distance increased by 14yds. A low-grade handicap for invited lady amateurs opened the card on this annual meeting confined to female riders. There was a surprise winner, who has been rated close to recent form, and this is not form to rely on.

4930 CARLISLE YOUTHZONE (PRO-AM LADY RIDERS' RACE) LADIES RIDERS' H'CAP 1m 1f

6:15 (6:15) (Class 5) (0-75,75) 4-Y-O+ **£3,234** (£962; £481; £240) **Stalls** Low

Form RPR

00-5 **1** **Swiss Lait**[19] 4258 5-9-2 **56** oh7.. MissAWaugh 4 61
(Patrick Holmes) *dwlt: hld up: hdwy whn swtchd rt over 1f out: led ins fnl f: kpt on wl* **33/1**

506 **2** *1 1/2* **Warfare**[24] 4113 7-10-2 **75**.. MissHDukes(5) 1 77
(Tim Fitzgerald) *s.i.s: sn prom: hdwy to ld over 1f out: sn drvn: edgd lft and hdd ins fnl f: kpt on same pce* **3/1**[2]

4300 **3** *1 1/2* **Hernando Torres**[24] 4113 8-10-1 **69**........................ MissJoannaMason 8 67
(Michael Easterby) *hld up: hdwy to chse ldrs over 1f out: kpt on same pce ins fnl f* **15/2**

2335 **4** *nk* **Relight My Fire**[6] 4729 6-10-0 **68**..........................(p) RachelRichardson 2 66
(Tim Easterby) *t.k.h: cl up: rdn over 2f out: edgd rt and outpcd over 1f out: kpt on ins fnl f* **11/4**[1]

2641 **5** *1 1/4* **Framley Garth (IRE)**[17] 4335 4-10-1 **74**............................ PaulaMuir(5) 7 69
(Patrick Holmes) *t.k.h: cl up: effrt and rdn over 2f out: no ex over 1f out* **9/1**

0020 **6** *hd* **Royal Holiday (IRE)**[29] 3922 9-10-1 **69**..................(p) MissBeckySmith 3 64
(Marjorie Fife) *led at ordinary gallop: rdn and hdd over 1f out: sn btn* **11/1**

4564 **7** *4* **Mr Sundowner (USA)**[13] 4486 4-9-2 **56** oh2................(t) ShelleyBirkett 6 42
(Wilf Storey) *t.k.h: sn in tch: rdn and outpcd over 2f out: btn over 1f out* **9/1**

2452 **8** *4 1/2* **Rockwood**[21] 4190 5-10-4 **72**....................................(v) MissEmmaSayer 9 48
(Karen McLintock) *hld up in tch: drvn and struggling over 2f out: sn btn* **5/1**[3]

1m 58.47s (0.87) **Going Correction** +0.15s/f (Good) **8** Ran SP% **111.4**
Speed ratings (Par 103): **102,100,99,99,97 97,94,90**
CSF £123.73 CT £830.39 TOTE £42.90: £8.30, £1.50, £2.30; EX 218.60 TRIFECTA Not won..
Owner FPR Yorkshire Syndicate **Bred** A C M Spalding **Trained** Middleham, N Yorks
■ Stewards' Enquiry : Miss Joanna Mason Caution: careless riding

FOCUS

Race distance increased by 14yds. This fair handicap was run nearly a second faster than the opening contest, but the winner was hard to find and the form has been rated cautiously.

4931 COMPARE HORSE RACING AT BOOKIES.COM (PRO-AM LADY RIDERS' RACE) LADIES RIDERS' H'CAP 5f

6:45 (6:48) (Class 6) (0-65,65) 4-Y-O+ **£3,234** (£962; £481; £240) **Stalls** Low

Form RPR

R043 **1** **A J Cook (IRE)**[5] 4771 6-9-6 **50**.............................. RachelRichardson 14 58
(Ron Barr) *midfield on outside: hdwy 2f out: led ins fnl f: pushed out* **10/1**

0200 **2** *nk* **Hit The Lights (IRE)**[10] 4608 6-10-7 **65**..................... DanielleMooney 10 72
(David Nicholls) *cl up: led over 1f out: sn rdn: hdd ins fnl f: kpt on: hld nr fin* **13/2**[3]

5000 **3** ½ **Spring Bird**[39] 3549 7-9-11 **55** MeganNicholls 8 60
(Alan Swinbank) *trckd ldrs: effrt and rdn 2f out: kpt on ins fnl f: no ex towards fin* **28/1**

4314 **4** ½ **Perfect Words (IRE)**[19] 4257 6-10-7 **65** (p) MissBeckySmith 5 68
(Marjorie Fife) *chsd ldrs: rdn over 2f out: kpt on same pce ins fnl f* **12/1**

3432 **5** *nk* **Slim Chance (IRE)**[9] 4647 7-10-1 **59** (p) HollieDoyle 13 61
(Simon West) *towards rr: pushed along over 2f out: hdwy over 1f out: kpt on fnl f: no imp* **17/2**

5031 **6** *1* **Penny Royale**[10] 4606 4-10-1 **64** (p) MissEEasterby(5) 2 63
(Tim Easterby) *towards rr on ins: shkn up and hdwy over 1f out: kpt on fnl f: nvr able to chal* **9/2**[1]

6222 **7** ½ **Tinsill**[10] 4606 5-9-6 **50** (p) ShelleyBirkett 1 47
(Nigel Tinkler) *in tch: rdn along 2f out: no ex ins fnl f* **6/1**[2]

546 **8** ½ **Secret Millionaire (IRE)**[29] 3925 9-10-3 **61** (p) JosephineGordon 9 56
(Shaun Harris) *in tch: hmpd and lost grnd over 3f out: rdn 2f out: no imp fnl f* **16/1**

0344 **9** *nk* **Gaelic Wizard (IRE)**[10] 4606 8-10-0 **58** (v) GemmaTutty 7 52
(Karen Tutty) *dwlt: bhd and outpcd: hdwy over 1f out: nvr rchd ldrs* **12/1**

0100 **10** ½ **Captain Scooby**[56] 2974 10-10-7 **65** (b) MissSBrotherton 17 57
(Richard Guest) *s.i.s: outpcd in rr: sme late hdwy: nvr on terms* **12/1**

0302 **11** ½ **Spoken Words**[13] 4492 7-9-3 **47** (p) RosieJessop 11 37
(John David Riches) *in tch: n.m.r and lost grnd over 3f out: effrt and swtchd lft 2f out: sn no imp* **25/1**

6623 **12** *1 ¼* **Reflation**[21] 4192 4-9-5 **54** (p) MissCADods(5) 12 40
(Michael Dods) *sn pushed along in rr: sme late hdwy: nvr on terms* **12/1**

-600 **13** *3 ½* **Knockamany Bends (IRE)**[8] 4691 6-9-4 **48** (p) HayleyTurner 16 21
(John Wainwright) *led at decent gallop: edgd rt over 3f out: hdd over 1f out: sn wknd* **20/1**

0-05 **14** ¾ **Red Forever**[29] 3925 5-9-2 **46** MissHelenCuthbert 6 17
(Thomas Cuthbert) *rrd s: hdwy and prom over 3f out: rdn: edgd lft and wknd over 1f out* **16/1**

0040 **15** *1 ¼* **Simply Black (IRE)**[41] 3486 5-9-3 **47** (p) AnnStokell 15 13
(Ann Stokell) *chsd ldrs: rdn over 2f out: wknd wl over 1f out* **50/1**

1m 1.75s (0.95) **Going Correction** +0.025s/f (Good) **15** Ran SP% **122.0**
Speed ratings (Par 101): **93,92,91,90,90 88,88,87,86,85 85,83,77,76,74**
CSF £71.09 CT £1826.51 TOTE £13.50: £4.40, £2.40, £10.40; EX 99.80 Trifecta £2632.80 Part won..
Owner Mrs Victoria Davies **Bred** Francis Stynes **Trained** Seamer, N Yorks
■ Red Invader was withdrawn. Price at time of withdrawal 16/1 - Rule 4 does not apply

FOCUS
A big field for this modest sprint handicap and yet another double-figure priced winner, but straightforward form, with the fourth and fifth helping to set the level.

4932 GET THE BEST FREE BETS AT BOOKIES.COM (PRO-AM LADY RIDERS' RACE) LADIES RIDERS' H'CAP 5f 193y

7:15 (7:18) (Class 5) (0-75,74) 4-Y-O+ **£3,234 (**£962; £481; £240) **Stalls** Low

Form RPR

4322 **1** **Courier**[10] 4604 4-10-1 **68** (p) MissBeckySmith 10 77
(Marjorie Fife) *mde all: pushed along 2f out: hld on wl fnl f* **4/1**[2]

2343 **2** *1 ¾* **Honeysuckle Lil (IRE)**[18] 4318 4-10-7 **74** (p) RachelRichardson 5 78
(Tim Easterby) *prom: stdy hdwy to chse wnr over 2f out: effrt and rdn over 1f out: kpt on same pce last 100yds* **10/3**[1]

5300 **3** *hd* **Kenny The Captain (IRE)**[21] 4191 5-10-0 **72** MissEEasterby(5) 4 75
(Tim Easterby) *prom: effrt and pushed along 2f out: kpt on ins fnl f: nt pce to chal* **6/1**

0605 **4** *4 ½* **Percy's Gal**[10] 4604 5-9-10 **63** (p) GemmaTutty 6 52
(Karen Tutty) *hld up: rdn along over 2f out: hdwy over 1f out: sn no imp* **9/1**

5550 **5** *hd* **Saltarello (IRE)**[5] 4771 4-9-3 **56** HollieDoyle 2 44
(Marjorie Fife) *hld up in midfield: rdn over 2f out: no imp fr over 1f out* **12/1**

3120 **6** *nk* **Consistant**[18] 4321 8-9-10 **63** MissSBrotherton 8 50
(Brian Baugh) *sn bhd: hung lft over 3f out: hdwy over 2f out: no imp over 1f out* **17/2**

0550 **7** *1 ¾* **Musaaid (IRE)**[32] 3807 4-10-6 **73** MissJoannaMason 9 54
(Michael Easterby) *hld up on outside: outpcd over 2f out: hung rt and sn n.d* **9/2**[3]

0-00 **8** *9* **Centre Haafhd**[14] 4444 5-9-2 **55** oh2 (b) MrsCBartley 3 8
(Jim Goldie) *chsd wnr to over 2f out: rdn and wknd over 1f out* **33/1**

0500 **9** *6* **Speightowns Kid (USA)**[13] 4484 8-9-2 **55** oh1 (be) AnnStokell 11
(Ann Stokell) *chsd ldrs on outside: rdn over 2f out: sn lost pl and struggling* **50/1**

0-00 **10** *10* **Rock Canyon (IRE)**[13] 4488 7-9-9 **62** ShelleyBirkett 7
(Linda Perratt) *in tch: hmpd by loose horse and lost grnd over 4f out: wknd fr 1/2-way* **33/1**

1020 **U** **Mitchum**[24] 4089 7-9-12 **70** (p) MrsVDavies(5) 1
(Ron Barr) *rrd and uns rdr leaving stalls* **20/1**

1m 13.35s (-0.35) **Going Correction** +0.025s/f (Good) **11** Ran SP% **116.4**
Speed ratings (Par 103): **103,100,100,94,94 93,91,79,71,58**
CSF £16.85 CT £80.55 TOTE £5.30: £1.90, £1.60, £2.50; EX 22.30 Trifecta £82.30.
Owner Daniel Gath Homes Ltd **Bred** Stratford Place Stud And Watership Down **Trained** Stillington, N Yorks

FOCUS
A fair sprint handicap but few got into the race in the straight. The winner posted a length pb.

4933 PPM LTD (PRO-AM LADY RIDERS' RACE) LADIES RIDERS' H'CAP 7f 173y

7:45 (7:45) (Class 4) (0-85,85) 4-Y-O+ **£6,469 (**£1,925; £962; £481) **Stalls** Low

Form RPR

3222 **1** **Moonlightnavigator (USA)**[7] 4704 4-10-1 **79** JosephineGordon 2 87
(John Quinn) *pressed ldr: drvn and outpcd 2f out: rallied and led ins fnl f: rdn out* **5/4**[1]

0624 **2** ½ **Dubai Dynamo**[6] 4727 11-10-7 **85** HayleyTurner 4 92
(Ruth Carr) *hld up in last pl: pushed along 3f out: effrt and swtchd lft over 1f out: kpt on wl to take 2nd pl nr fin* **7/1**[2]

5140 **3** *nk* **Mustaqbal (IRE)**[29] 3922 4-9-4 **73** (p) MissSEDods(5) 6 79
(Michael Dods) *missed break: hld up: hdwy on outside over 2f out: chsd ldrs over 1f out: kpt on ins fnl f* **12/1**

5050 **4** *hd* **Mystic Miraaj**[10] 4611 4-9-13 **77** (b) RachelRichardson 3 83
(Tim Easterby) *t.k.h: trckd ldrs: led gng wl over 2f out: rdn over 1f out: hdd ins fnl f: sn no ex* **7/1**[2]

331 **5** *2 ¼* **Throckley**[31] 3856 5-10-2 **80** MeganNicholls 8 80
(John Davies) *plld hrd: in tch: rdn over 2f out: one pce fr over 1f out* **7/1**[2]

3035 **6** *1 ½* **Anton Chigurh**[17] 4348 7-9-7 **71** AnnaHesketh 5 68
(Tom Dascombe) *t.k.h: hld up on ins: nt clr run briefly over 2f out: sn pushed along: kpt on fnl f: no imp* **25/1**

0605 **7** *1 ½* **Pivotman**[7] 4717 8-9-2 **66** oh1 (bt) MissJoannaMason 10 59
(Michael Easterby) *hld up on outside: hdwy over 2f out: hung rt and wknd over 1f out* **9/1**[3]

011 **8** *1* **Dark Crystal**[7] 4701 5-9-7 **71** 6ex ShelleyBirkett 9 62
(Linda Perratt) *in tch: rdn over 2f out: hung rt and wknd over 1f out* **11/1**

-600 **9** *5* **In Focus (IRE)**[8] 4684 5-9-6 **75** MissRSharpe(5) 1 54
(Alan Swinbank) *led: rdn and hdd over 2f out: wknd wl over 1f out* **33/1**

1m 40.33s (0.33) **Going Correction** +0.15s/f (Good) **9** Ran SP% **114.8**
Speed ratings (Par 105): **104,103,103,103,100 99,97,96,91**
CSF £10.30 CT £72.50 TOTE £2.10: £1.10, £2.30, £4.10; EX 9.40 Trifecta £106.70.
Owner Malcolm Walker **Bred** Highfield Farm **Trained** Settrington, N Yorks

FOCUS
Race distance increased by 14yds. The feature race and a good mile handicap that produced a close finish. The winner was well in and the third and fourth help set the level.

4934 COMPARE BOOKIES AT BOOKIES.COM (PRO-AM LADY RIDERS' RACE) LADIES RIDERS' H'CAP 1m 3f 39y

8:15 (8:15) (Class 5) (0-70,70) 4-Y-O+ **£3,234 (**£962; £481; £240) **Stalls** High

Form RPR

222 **1** **Obboorr**[35] 3711 7-10-2 **70** MissHDukes(5) 7 79+
(Tim Fitzgerald) *hld up: smooth hdwy and ev ch wl over 1f out: edgd lft and led ins fnl f: hld on wl* **4/1**[1]

5612 **2** *hd* **Duke Of Yorkshire**[3] 4828 6-9-10 **64** (p) MissEEasterby(5) 2 72
(Tim Easterby) *hld up: gd hdwy on outside to ld wl over 1f out: sn hrd pressed: rdn and hdd ins fnl f: rallied: jst hld* **4/1**[1]

5341 **3** *3 ½* **Fillydelphia (IRE)**[33] 3774 5-9-8 **57** RachelRichardson 4 59
(Patrick Holmes) *hld up on outside: hdwy to chse ldrs wl over 1f out: sn rdn: edgd rt and one pce fnl f* **8/1**[2]

5-05 **4** *3 ½* **Latin Rebel (IRE)**[14] 4447 9-9-2 **51** oh1 (p) MrsCBartley 6 47
(Jim Goldie) *hld up: pushed along over 2f out: hdwy over 1f out: no imp fnl f* **16/1**

4456 **5** *2 ¼* **Northside Prince (IRE)**[39] 3547 10-10-2 **65** MeganNicholls 8 57
(Alan Swinbank) *in tch: rdn and outpcd over 2f out: kpt on fnl f: nvr able to chal* **10/1**[3]

4334 **6** *hd* **Triple Eight (IRE)**[14] 2962 8-10-1 **64** (p) JosephineGordon 3 56
(Philip Kirby) *t.k.h: prom: rdn over 2f out: wknd over 1f out* **8/1**[2]

3025 **7** *hd* **Sherman McCoy**[26] 4004 10-10-4 **67** MissBeckySmith 11 59
(Marjorie Fife) *led to over 3f out: rdn and wknd over 1f out* **14/1**

650- **8** *2 ¼* **Baileys Concerto (IRE)**[33] 6827 10-9-11 **60** (tp) MissEmmaSayer 10 48
(Dianne Sayer) *cl up: ev ch over 2f out: rdn and wknd over 1f out* **10/1**[3]

6/50 **9** *1 ¼* **Pevensey (IRE)**[6] 4730 14-9-10 **59** (b) MissJoannaMason 1 45
(Jacqueline Coward) *missed break: hld up: rdn over 3f out: wknd wl over 1f out* **14/1**

0054 **10** *shd* **Captain Swift (IRE)**[31] 3844 5-10-3 **66** ShelleyBirkett 5 51
(John Mackie) *hld up: rdn along 3f out: wknd wl over 1f out* **8/1**[2]

-100 **11** *1* **Van Mildert (IRE)**[35] 3704 7-8-11 **51** oh2 (p) MissAMSlack(5) 12 35
(Kenneth Slack) *pressed ldr: led over 3f out to wl over 1f out: sn wknd* **22/1**

0000 **12** *10* **That Be Grand**[37] 3641 5-9-2 **51** oh6 GemmaTutty 9 18
(Shaun Harris) *t.k.h: trckd ldrs tl rdn and wknd over 2f out* **50/1**

2m 26.93s (3.83) **Going Correction** +0.15s/f (Good) **12** Ran SP% **117.0**
Speed ratings (Par 103): **92,91,89,86,85 84,84,83,82,82 81,74**
CSF £17.53 CT £122.74 TOTE £4.50: £1.80, £1.70, £2.80; EX 13.30 Trifecta £71.30.
Owner Dukes Racing 1 **Bred** Darley **Trained** Norton, N Yorks

FOCUS
Race distance increased by 14yds. This modest middle-distance handicap appeared to be run at sound pace, as the first four were all held up. The market leaders fought out the finish and there was another small pb from the winner.

4935 LLOYDS GROUP (PRO-AM LADY RIDERS' RACE) LADIES RIDERS' H'CAP 2m 1f 47y

8:45 (8:47) (Class 5) (0-70,70) 4-Y-O+ **£3,234 (**£962; £481; £240) **Stalls** Low

Form RPR

60-5 **1** **Gold Chain (IRE)**[16] 3154 6-9-7 **56** (tp) MissEmmaSayer 2 65
(Dianne Sayer) *stdd in rr: smooth hdwy 3f out: led over 1f out: sn pushed along and edgd rt: kpt on wl fnl f* **13/2**[3]

5562 **2** *3 ¼* **Medina Sidonia (IRE)**[9] 4634 4-10-7 **70** (p) RachelRichardson 7 75
(Tim Easterby) *in tch: pushed along over 3f out: rallied to chse wnr over 1f out: kpt on same pce ins fnl f* **9/2**[2]

0454 **3** *1 ¾* **Jan Smuts (IRE)**[13] 4491 8-10-6 **69** (tp) HollieDoyle 9 72
(Wilf Storey) *hld up: pushed along 3f out: hdwy over 1f out: kpt on: nt pce to chal* **10/1**

-553 **4** *nk* **Bowdler's Magic**[25] 4045 9-10-2 **65** JosephineGordon 6 68
(David Thompson) *midfield: outpcd over 5f out: rallied on outside over 2f out: kpt on fnl f: nvr rchd ldrs* **8/1**

3224 **5** ¾ **Aldreth**[24] 4101 5-10-7 **70** (p) MissJoannaMason 11 72
(Michael Easterby) *prom: wnt 2nd over 3f out to over 1f out: outpcd ins fnl f* **7/2**[1]

0000 **6** *2 ¾* **La Bacouetteuse (FR)**[24] 4101 11-10-2 **65** (b) ShirleyTeasdale 8 64
(Iain Jardine) *hld up in midfield: effrt and pushed along whn edgd rt and bmpd rival over 2f out: wknd over 1f out* **25/1**

155 **7** *3 ¾* **An Fear Ciuin (IRE)**[28] 3942 5-10-7 **70** (p) MissBeckySmith 5 65
(Richard Ford) *pressed ldr: led after 3f: rdn and hdd over 1f out: sn wknd* **16/1**

0/0- **8** *14* **My Escapade (IRE)**[32] 1207 5-9-2 **51** oh6 MissAWaugh 12 30
(Simon Waugh) *chsd ldrs: drvn and outpcd over 3f out: btn fnl 2f* **20/1**

00-6 **9** *5* **Ronaldinho (IRE)**[14] 4099 6-9-1 **55** (tp) MissAMSlack(5) 3 29
(Dianne Sayer) *hld up in midfield: hdwy to trck ldrs 1/2-way: rdn and outpcd whn bmpd over 2f out: sn btn* **25/1**

0-00 **10** *9* **Goldan Jess (IRE)**[29] 3704 12-9-6 **55** ShelleyBirkett 4 19
(Philip Kirby) *led 3f: cl up tl rdn and wknd 3f out* **8/1**

0P-4 **11** *94* **Piper Bill**[29] 3919 5-9-2 **51** oh6 HayleyTurner 1
(Jim Goldie) *s.i.s: bhd: struggling 1/2-way: sn lost tch: virtually p.u fnl 2f* **33/1**

3m 53.81s (0.81) **Going Correction** +0.15s/f (Good) **11** Ran SP% **106.3**
Speed ratings (Par 103): **104,102,101,101,101 99,98,91,89,84 40**
CSF £27.73 CT £212.98 TOTE £8.40: £2.50, £1.60, £2.90; EX 42.30 Trifecta £301.10.
Owner Mrs Margaret Coppola **Bred** Sheikh Sultan Bin Khalifa Al Nahyan **Trained** Hackthorpe, Cumbria
■ Question Of Faith was withdrawn. Price at time of withdrawal 9/1. Rule 4 applies to all bets - deduction 10p in the pound.

FOCUS
Race distance increased by 23yds. A staying handicap to close the card. They went a decent gallop and the winner came from almost last turning in. The winner is rated close to her old Flat best.

T/Plt: £229.70 to a £1 stake. Pool: £70,714.67 - 224.71 winning units T/Qpdt: £13.60 to a £1 stake Pool: £9,285.44 - 502.74 winning units **Richard Young**

4008 KEMPTON (A.W) (R-H)

Monday, August 1

OFFICIAL GOING: Polytrack: standard to slow

Wind: virtually nil Weather: overcast, rain from race 3

4936 APOLLOBET BET THROUGH YOUR MOBILE H'CAP 1m (P)

2:00 (2:00) (Class 6) (0-60,60) 3-Y-O **£2,264** (£673; £336; £168) **Stalls** Low

Form RPR

3233 **1** **Music Major**62 2770 3-9-4 **57**........................ AdamBeschizza 6 65+
(Michael Attwater) *dwlt: hld up in last pair: effrt over 2f out: str run to chal 1f out: sn led: styd on wl: rdn out* **13/2**3

4040 **2** 3/4 **Bazzat (IRE)**11 4567 3-8-7 **46**...................(p) DannyBrock 1 52
(John Ryan) *led: rdn wl over 1f out: hdd briefly 2f out: sn drvn to ld again: hdd jst ins fnl f: styd on same pce fnl 100yds* **25/1**

00-4 **3** 2 **Zlatan (IRE)**13 4498 3-9-7 **60**.................... FrederikTylicki 2 61
(Ed de Giles) *chsd ldrs: effrt 2f out: ev ch u.p over 1f out: no ex and outpcd fnl 100yds* **7/2**1

400 **4** 1/2 **Broughtons Mystery**10 4596 3-8-13 **52**............ StevieDonohoe 3 52
(Willie Musson) *hld up in tch in midfield: effrt 2f out: hdwy to chal ent fnl f: no ex and outpcd fnl 100yds* **50/1**

2024 **5** 1 **Gladys Cooper (IRE)**21 4214 3-9-6 **59**............ LukeMorris 9 57
(Ed Walker) *broke wl: stdd bk to trck ldrs: rdn and unable qck over 1f out: no threat to ldrs but kpt on again ins fnl f* **7/1**

0510 **6** nk **Ventura Falcon (IRE)**35 3731 3-9-4 **57**............ PatDobbs 5 54
(Richard Hannon) *hld up in last pair: rdn over 1f out: hdwy ent fnl f: swtchd lft and styd on steadily ins fnl f: nvr trbld ldrs* **16/1**

1260 **7** 1/2 **New Abbey Angel (IRE)**19 4267 3-9-5 **58**............ DavidProbert 7 54
(Gay Kelleway) *hmpd sn after s and dropped to rr: effrt on inner 2f out: hdwy over 1f out: kpt on ins fnl f: nvr trbld ldrs* **14/1**

06- **8** 1 **Sweet Dream Lady (IRE)**279 7532 3-9-5 **58**............ GeorgeBaker 10 52
(Gary Moore) *t.k.h: hld up wl in tch: effrt 2f out: unable qck and btn over 1f out: wknd ins fnl f* **10/1**

-022 **9** 1 1/2 **Sparring Queen (USA)**21 4214 3-9-7 **60**...............(p) OisinMurphy 13 50
(Ralph Beckett) *pressed ldr: upsides and travelling bttr than ldr over 2f out: pushed into ld briefly 2f out: sn hdd and fnd little whn rdn: wknd ins fnl f* **4/1**2

0502 **10** 1 1/4 **African Showgirl**27 3973 3-9-4 **57**............ SteveDrowne 4 47
(George Baker) *hld up in tch: effrt on inner 2f out: chsd ldrs but unable qck over 1f out: wknd ins fnl f* **12/1**

1330 **11** 6 **Betsalottie**9 4635 3-9-7 **60**............ WilliamCarson 14 34
(John Bridger) *midfield early: hdwy to chse ldrs after 2f: lost pl u.p over 2f out: bhd fnl f* **7/1**

004 **12** 3/4 **Poetic Guest**13 4477 3-9-5 **58**............ TomQueally 12 30
(George Margarson) *chsd ldrs early: grad stdd bk into last quartet after 2f: rdn and no hdwy over 2f out: bhd fnl f* **50/1**

1m 40.81s (1.01) **Going Correction** +0.225s/f (Slow) **12 Ran SP% 117.7**
Speed ratings (Par 98): **103,102,100,99,98 98,97,96,95,94 88,87**
CSF £158.87 CT £668.36 TOTE £5.70: £2.30, £6.90, £1.50; EX 134.50 Trifecta £892.00.
Owner The Attwater Partnership & J Daniels **Bred** Kevin Daniel Crabb **Trained** Epsom, Surrey
■ Stewards' Enquiry : Steve Drowne Fine: £290 changed boots after weighing out

FOCUS
With the surface having been rewaxed, the official going was standard to slow, and there were no changes to race distances. The opener was a low-grade middle-distance handicap in which they went a slow gallop. Those drawn high struggled to get involved.

4937 APOLLOBET OLYMPIC GAMES CASHBACK NURSERY H'CAP 7f (P)

2:30 (2:32) (Class 6) (0-65,65) 2-Y-O **£2,264** (£673; £336; £168) **Stalls** Low

Form RPR

035 **1** **Jumping Jack (IRE)**40 3531 2-8-12 **56**............ ShaneKelly 4 62+
(Richard Hughes) *t.k.h: hld up in tch in midfield: effrt and rn green over 1f out: pushed along to chal 1f out: led wl ins fnl f: rdn out hands and heels* **16/1**

600 **2** 1/2 **Golden Guest**56 2976 2-9-7 **65**...............(v1) TomQueally 9 67
(George Margarson) *hld up in tch: effrt 2f out: str run u.p to ld ent fnl f: clr w wnr ins fnl f: hdd and unable qck wl ins fnl f* **8/1**

0323 **3** 2 **Coverham (IRE)**12 4510 2-9-2 **60**...............(p) TedDurcan 2 57
(James Bethell) *trckd ldrs: effrt on inner jst over 2f out: rdn and ev ch over 1f out tl no ex ins fnl f: outpcd fnl 100yds* **6/4**1

025 **4** 2 1/4 **Born To Please**19 4270 2-8-13 **62**............ RachealKneller(5) 5 53
(Mark Usher) *hld up in tch: effrt on inner wl over 1f out: hdwy to chse clr ldng trio jst ins fnl f: no imp after* **13/2**3

050 **5** 1 **Fanfair**25 4054 2-9-2 **60**............ PatDobbs 6 48
(Richard Hannon) *hld up in rr: effrt 2f out: no imp tl styd on to pass btn horses ins fnl f: nvr trbld ldrs* **5/1**2

6006 **6** nk **Hot N Sassy (IRE)**12 4524 2-8-1 **45**............ DannyBrock 8 32
(J S Moore) *trckd ldrs: effrt 2f out: drvn and unable qck over 1f out: wknd ins fnl f* **50/1**

066 **7** 2 1/2 **Crucial Moment**19 4274 2-9-7 **65**............ LukeMorris 10 46
(Bill Turner) *sn chsng ldr: rdn over 2f out: unable qck and lost pl over 1f out: wl hld whn nt clr run ins fnl f* **8/1**

601 **8** 4 1/2 **Mesmeric Moment**49 3232 2-8-13 **62**............ CharlieBennett(5) 3 31
(Shaun Harris) *led: rdn over 2f out: hdd ent fnl f: sn btn and fdd ins fnl f* **8/1**

1m 28.9s (2.90) **Going Correction** +0.225s/f (Slow) **8 Ran SP% 111.2**
Speed ratings (Par 92): **92,91,89,86,85 85,82,77**
CSF £128.29 CT £302.43 TOTE £10.60: £2.60, £2.90, £1.40; EX 105.90 Trifecta £497.40.
Owner Danny Waters **Bred** R & R Bloodstock **Trained** Upper Lambourn, Berkshire

FOCUS
A moderate nursery featuring a number of debutantes in this sphere. The two early pacesetters were the last pair to finish. The third has been rated close to form.

4938 APOLLOBET ONLINE CASINO & GAMES MAIDEN AUCTION STKS 6f (P)

3:00 (3:01) (Class 5) 2-Y-O **£3,234** (£962; £481; £240) **Stalls** Low

Form RPR

5 **1** **Just Maybe**42 3463 2-8-11 0............ RobertWinston 7 68
(Mike Murphy) *bmpd s: t.k.h: trckd ldr: rdn to ld over 1f out: r.o wl fnl f: readily* **4/1**3

0 **2** 1 1/4 **Happy Queen**26 4022 2-8-13 0............ TomQueally 11 66
(George Margarson) *hld up in tch in midfield: effrt to chse ldrs over 1f out: wnt 2nd ins fnl f: styd on but no imp on wnr* **10/1**

3 1/2 **Bubble Bath** 2-8-6 0............ LukeMorris 5 57+
(Daniel Kubler) *hld up in tch in midfield: rdn and unable qck over 1f out: rallied and styd on wl fnl 100yds: no threat to wnr* **8/1**

4 nk **Scorching Heat** 2-9-0 0............ OisinMurphy 4 65+
(Andrew Balding) *led: rdn 2f out: hdd and unable qck over 1f out: styd on same pce and lost 2 pls ins fnl f* **11/4**1

54 **5** shd **What A Boy**26 4016 2-9-0 0............ PatDobbs 12 64
(Ralph Beckett) *hld up in tch in midfield: rdn 2f out: no imp tl styd on ins fnl f: no threat to wnr* **3/1**2

03 **6** 3 1/2 **Epsom Secret**12 4524 2-8-6 0............ JFEgan 6 45
(Pat Phelan) *bmpd s: sn rdn along in rr: drvn over 2f out: no hdwy tl styd on to pass btn horses ins fnl f: n.d* **16/1**

02 **7** nk **Kath's Boy (IRE)**39 3576 2-8-11 0............ GeorgeDowning(3) 2 52
(Tony Carroll) *t.k.h: chsd ldrs: rdn and unable qck over 1f out: hung rt and wknd ins fnl f* **11/1**

8 1 **Captain Sue (IRE)** 2-8-9 0............ ShaneKelly 10 47
(Richard Hughes) *hld up in tch in last trio: effrt and sme hdwy 2f out: no imp over 1f out: wknd ins fnl f* **16/1**

9 1 1/4 **Secret Icon** 2-8-6 0............ WilliamCarson 8 37
(Jamie Osborne) *hld up in last pair: rdn jst over 2f out: no hdwy and wl hld over 1f out* **33/1**

66 **10** 1/2 **Aberdonian**21 4209 2-9-0 0............ NickyMackay 9 43
(Jeremy Gask) *hld up in tch in midfield: rdn and effrt towards inner jst over 2f out: no imp over 1f out: wknd fnl f* **50/1**

1m 15.51s (2.41) **Going Correction** +0.225s/f (Slow) **10 Ran SP% 116.9**
Speed ratings (Par 94): **92,90,89,89,89 84,84,82,81,80**
CSF £43.85 TOTE £6.00: £2.10, £3.10, £2.30; EX 42.70 Trifecta £346.30.
Owner The Maysonettes **Bred** James Patton & Greg Parsons **Trained** Westoning, Beds

FOCUS
Not the strongest of 2yo maidens and they went a steady pace. The level is fluid.

4939 APOLLOBET PREMIER LEAGUE CASHBACK MAIDEN STKS 7f (P)

3:30 (3:30) (Class 5) 3-Y-O+ **£3,234** (£962; £481; £240) **Stalls** Low

Form RPR

0 **1** **Enduring Power (IRE)**13 4480 3-9-5 0............ WilliamCarson 5 73
(Brendan Powell) *chsd ldrs: effrt 2f out: drvn to chal 1f out: led ins fnl f: r.o wl: rdn out* **33/1**

2 1/2 **James The Elder (IRE)** 3-9-5 0............ TimmyMurphy 2 72
(Seamus Durack) *hld up in tch in midfield: hdwy to chse ldng trio 2f out: wnt between horses to press wnr ins fnl f: r.o but hld towards fin* **50/1**

3234 **3** 1 1/4 **Sehayli (IRE)**20 4235 3-9-5 80...............(p) PatCosgrave 12 68
(William Haggas) *sn chsng ldr: rdn to ld over 2f out: drvn and hdd over 1f out: stl ev ch tl no ex and outpcd fnl 100yds* **9/4**2

4 **4** shd **Pearly Queen**11 4565 3-8-11 0............ JackDuern(3) 9 63
(Dean Ivory) *hld up in midfield: swtchd lft and effrt wl over 1f out: chsd clr ldng quartet over 1f out: styd on strly ins fnl f: nt rch ldrs* **16/1**3

6 **5** 2 **Sir Compton**92 1892 3-9-5 0............ TedDurcan 1 63
(Stuart Kittow) *hld up in midfield: effrt ent fnl 2f: hdwy 1f out: swtchd lft and kpt on ins fnl f: no threat to ldrs* **25/1**

6 nse **Saleh (IRE)** 3-9-5 0............ KierenFox 6 62
(Lee Carter) *dwlt: rn green in rr of main gp: hdwy over 1f out: kpt on ins fnl f: nvr trbld ldrs* **33/1**

3 **7** 3/4 **Poyle Emily**28 3958 3-9-0 0............ OisinMurphy 10 55
(Ralph Beckett) *sn led: hdd over 2f out: rdn to ld again over 1f out: hdd ins fnl f: sn btn and fdd wl ins fnl f* **4/5**1

30 **8** 3 1/4 **Gift From God**25 4041 3-9-5 0............ KieranO'Neill 7 52
(Hugo Froud) *hld up in tch in midfield: rdn over 2f out: sn struggling: wknd over 1f out* **50/1**

40 **9** 1 3/4 **Sund City (FR)**77 2312 3-9-0 0............ LukeMorris 14 42
(Harry Dunlop) *chsd ldrs tl over 2f out: sn rdn and lost pl: wknd over 1f out* **16/1**3

0-0 **10** 1 3/4 **Fast Play (IRE)**14 4458 4-9-6 0............ ShaneKelly 4 39
(Richard Hughes) *hld up in rr of main gp: rdn and rn green over 2f out: sn btn: wknd wl over 1f out* **33/1**

11 1/2 **Arquus (IRE)** 3-9-5 0............ LiamKeniry 8 41
(Ed de Giles) *s.i.s: in rr of main gp: rdn and btn over 2f out: bhd over 1f out* **50/1**

00 **12** 4 **Paca Punch**21 4213 3-9-0 0............ DavidProbert 11 25
(Michael Blanshard) *wl in tch in midfield: rdn over 2f out: sn lost pl and btn: wknd qckly over 1f out* **100/1**

13 5 **Unforeseen** 3-9-0 0............ SteveDrowne 3 12
(Daniel Kubler) *s.i.s: rn green and sn detached in last: nvr on terms* **33/1**

14 13 **Sams R Man** 4-9-11 0............ RobertHavlin 13
(Linda Jewell) *s.i.s: in rr of main gp: veered lft 5f out: bhd fr 1/2-way* **100/1**

1m 27.31s (1.31) **Going Correction** +0.225s/f (Slow)
WFA 3 from 4yo 6lb **14 Ran SP% 121.6**
Speed ratings (Par 103): **101,100,99,98,96 96,95,91,89,87 87,82,77,62**
CSF £1104.29 TOTE £44.80: £9.60, £10.00, £1.10; EX 485.40 TRIFECTA Not won..
Owner Saxon Gate Bloodstock **Bred** Fortbarrington Stud **Trained** Upper Lambourn, Berks

FOCUS
A weak maiden that centered around the well backed favourite, who set a steady pace, before giving way to a couple of outsiders. The level is fluid, with little to go on and form pair no guide.

4940 APOLLOBET RACING REFUNDS H'CAP (LONDON MIDDLE DISTANCE SERIES QUALIFIER) 1m 3f (P)

4:00 (4:01) (Class 4) (0-80,80) 4-Y-O+ **£4,690** (£1,395; £697; £348) **Stalls** Low

Form RPR

1- **1** **Anzhelika (IRE)**325 6282 4-9-4 **77**............ GeorgeBaker 6 91+
(David Lanigan) *trckd ldr after 1f: led on bit ent fnl 2f: shkn up and in command 1f out: nudged along fnl f: comf* **9/5**1

0/02 **2** 1 1/4 **Soul Intent (IRE)**11 4550 6-9-2 **75**............ BenCurtis 8 82
(Brian Ellison) *sn led and set stdy gallop: rdn and hdd ent fnl 2f: kpt on u.p but comf hld by wnr* **6/1**3

5444 **3** 2 3/4 **Dakota City**11 4566 5-9-4 **77**...............(v) AdamBeschizza 3 79
(Julia Feilden) *s.i.s: hld up in rr: hdwy u.p over 1f out: chsd clr ldng pair 1f out: no imp after* **10/1**

-060 **4** 1 **Plymouth Sound**25 4055 4-9-7 **80**...............(b1) JohnFahy 1 80
(Eve Johnson Houghton) *hld up in tch: effrt u.p and edgd rt over 1f out: kpt on ins fnl f: no threat to wnr* **12/1**

1215 **5** 3/4 **Lord Reason**18 4307 4-9-3 **76**............ JFEgan 2 75
(John Butler) *taken down early: led: sn hdd and settled in cl 3rd: rdn jst over 2f out: 3rd and outpcd over 1f out: kpt on same pce after* **16/1**

2221 **6** nk **I Am Not Here (IRE)**45 3345 5-9-2 **75**............ LiamKeniry 7 73
(Brian Ellison) *hld up in tch in midfield: rdn jst over 2f out: unable qck over 1f out: kpt on same pce and no imp after* **3/1**2

3036 **7** 3/4 **Clovelly Bay (IRE)**13 4476 5-8-8 **74**............ TylerSaunders(7) 5 71
(Marcus Tregoning) *hld up in tch in midfield: effrt on inner jst over 2f out: no imp over 1f out: wl hld and kpt on same pce fnl f* **8/1**

0250 **8** *18* **Warofindependence (USA)**[13] 4476 4-9-1 **74**...........(p) DavidProbert 4 39
(Alan Bailey) *hld up in tch in last trio: hung lft 5f out: v wd bnd 4f out: lost tch over 1f out: eased ins fnl f: fin lame* **25/1**

2m 23.76s (1.86) **Going Correction** +0.225s/f (Slow) **8** Ran SP% **112.6**
Speed ratings (Par 105): **102,101,99,98,97 97,97,83**
CSF £12.64 CT £81.85 TOTE £2.20: £1.40, £1.50, £2.60; EX 13.90 Trifecta £79.90.
Owner B E Nielsen **Bred** Bjorn Nielsen **Trained** Newmarket, Suffolk

FOCUS
An average handicap and an easy winner, who was up with a slow gallop throughout. The runner-up is rated close to form.

4941 APOLLOBET FREE SIGN-UP BONUS H'CAP 2m (P)

4:30 (4:30) (Class 4) (0-85,77) 4-Y-O+ **£4,690** (£1,395; £697; £348) **Stalls** Low

Form RPR

-041 **1** **Mister Bob (GER)**[26] 4012 7-9-0 **70**.................................(p) TedDurcan 1 78+
(James Bethell) *hld up in tch in last pair: swtchd rt and effrt in 3rd jst over 2f out: chsd clr ldr over 1f out: grad to ld wl ins fnl f: sn in command and eased cl home* **5/2**[2]

0010 **2** *1 1/4* **Saborido (USA)**[33] 3784 10-9-4 **77**.......................(b) KieranShoemark[(3)] 3 83
(Amanda Perrett) *led and dictated stdy gallop: grad qcknd gallop fr 4f out: rdn and 3 l clr over 1f out: hdd and no ex wl ins fnl f* **9/1**

3001 **3** *3 3/4* **Le Rock (IRE)**[19] 4266 4-9-3 **73**... DannyBrock 2 75
(J S Moore) *trckd ldr tl 12f out: styd handy in 3rd: wnt 2nd again and rdn 3f out: 3rd and styd on same pce fr over 1f out* **6/1**

-014 **4** *1 3/4* **Voice Control (IRE)**[26] 4012 4-9-2 **72**................................. LiamKeniry 5 71
(Laura Mongan) *bmpd s: hld up in tch in last pair: effrt over 2f out: no imp tl kpt on steadily ins fnl f: no threat to ldrs* **11/2**[3]

03- **5** *12* **Argante (FR)**[170] 6549 7-9-7 **77**.....................................(t) JamieSpencer 4 65
(Nicky Henderson) *wnt lft s: trckd ldng pair tl wnt 2nd 12f out: rdn and lost 2nd 3f out: dropped to rr and btn over 1f out: eased ins fnl f* **6/4**[1]

3m 32.57s (2.47) **Going Correction** +0.225s/f (Slow) **5** Ran SP% **108.2**
Speed ratings (Par 105): **102,101,99,98,92**
CSF £21.58 TOTE £3.20: £2.00, £3.50; EX 19.50 Trifecta £85.10.
Owner Robert Gibbons **Bred** Newsells Park Stud Ltd **Trained** Middleham Moor, N Yorks

FOCUS
A tight little staying handicap - even if below par for the grade - and the old-timer, who nearly stole it from the front, sets the standard.

4942 APOLLOBET BET THROUGH YOUR MOBILE H'CAP 1m 4f (P)

5:00 (5:02) (Class 6) (0-65,65) 3-Y-O **£2,264** (£673; £336; £168) **Stalls** Centre

Form RPR

401 **1** **Coarse Cut (IRE)**[8] 4024 3-9-0 **58**...................................(b[1]) JohnFahy 13 69
(Eve Johnson Houghton) *rdn along leaving stalls: hdwy to ld over 10f out: mde rest: clr and rdn over 2f out: styd on and nvr seriously chal after: rdn out* **20/1**

-024 **2** *2 1/2* **Denmead**[21] 4210 3-9-1 **59**... StevieDonohoe 4 66
(John Butler) *led tl over 10f out: chsd wnr after: rdn 3f out: drvn and styd on same pce fr over 1f out* **9/1**

6440 **3** *1 3/4* **Pinstripe**[27] 3991 3-9-6 **64**.. JamieSpencer 2 68+
(Luca Cumani) *hld up in last trio: swtchd lft and effrt but plenty to do over 2f out: hdwy u.p over 1f out: styd on to snatch 3rd last strides: nvr trbld ldrs* **7/2**[1]

0-14 **4** *hd* **Whitstable Pearl (IRE)**[26] 4021 3-8-8 **52**.............................. KierenFox 7 56+
(John Best) *hld up in midfield: rdn and hdwy between horses 2f out: styd on u.p to go 3rd towards fin: nvr a threat to ldrs: lost 3rd last strides* **9/1**

000 **5** *1/2* **Dream Free**[33] 3769 3-9-7 **65**.....................................(b[1]) GeorgeBaker 12 68
(David Lanigan) *chsd ldrs: 3rd and rdn over 2f out: no imp on wnr and plugged on same pce fnl 2f: lost 2 pls towards fin* **7/1**[3]

6260 **6** *3 1/4* **Le Tissier**[26] 3998 3-9-1 **62**.. RobHornby[(3)] 11 60+
(Michael Attwater) *s.i.s: hld up in last trio: effrt but stl plenty to do over 2f out: hdwy to pass btn horses over 1f out: nvr trbld ldrs* **25/1**

6046 **7** *1/2* **Persaverance**[54] 3033 3-9-7 **65**.................................... FergusSweeney 8 62+
(Gary Moore) *hld up in midfield: rdn over 2f out: no imp u.p and wl btn over 1f out: wknd ins fnl f* **7/1**[3]

1523 **8** *3* **Schoolboy Error (IRE)**[15] 3652 3-9-5 **63**...................... WilliamCarson 3 55+
(Jamie Osborne) *hld up in midfield: rdn 3f out: no imp u.p and btn 2f out: wknd over 1f out* **9/2**[2]

0055 **9** *2 3/4* **Shrubland**[17] 4342 3-8-13 **57**.. LukeMorris 10 45+
(Ed Walker) *hld up in midfield: rdn over 2f out: sn struggling and wl btn over 1f out* **10/1**

4226 **10** *2* **Dalavand (IRE)**[12] 4527 3-8-13 **57**....................................(t) LiamKeniry 9 42
(Laura Mongan) *hld up in midfield: rdn and no hdwy over 2f out: lost pl and bhd over 1f out* **25/1**

0362 **11** *2 3/4* **Strictly Art (IRE)**[38] 3596 3-9-4 **62**.................................(p) DavidProbert 1 42
(Alan Bailey) *t.k.h: w ldr for 1f: settled to chse ldrs after: rdn over 2f out: sn struggling: wknd over 1f out* **12/1**

600- **12** *16* **Careless Rapture**[263] 7811 3-7-13 **46** oh1.................... NoelGarbutt[(3)] 5
(Mark H Tompkins) *s.i.s: t.k.h in last trio: lost tch over 2f out: t.o* **66/1**

2m 35.1s (0.60) **Going Correction** +0.225s/f (Slow) **12** Ran SP% **116.1**
Speed ratings (Par 98): **107,105,104,104,103 101,101,99,97,96 94,83**
CSF £180.09 CT £788.59 TOTE £21.20: £6.20, £2.80, £1.70; EX 199.70 Trifecta £4200.20 Part won..
Owner Equi ex Incertis Partners **Bred** M E Wates **Trained** Blewbury, Oxon

■ Stewards' Enquiry : Stevie Donohoe three-day ban: careless riding (August 15,16,20)
George Baker two-day ban: used whip above permitted level (Aug 15-16)

FOCUS
A modest handicap featuring a number of unexposed types over this trip, though the winner set a slow pace from which he never came back to the pack. The runner-up sets the level.
T/Jkpt: Not won. T/Plt: £249.30 to a £1 stake. Pool: £59,232.10 - 173.41 winning units. T/Qpdt: £74.30 to a £1 stake. Pool: £5,287.36 - 52.61 winning units. **Steve Payne**

4404 RIPON (R-H)

Monday, August 1

OFFICIAL GOING: Good (8.2)
Wind: light 1/2 behind Weather: fine, becoming overcast with light rain races 3 & 4

4943 BRITISH STALLION STUDS EBF MAIDEN FILLIES' STKS (PLUS 10 RACE) 6f

2:15 (2:16) (Class 5) 2-Y-O **£3,881** (£1,155; £577; £288) **Stalls** High

Form RPR

02 **1** **Storm Cry**[9] 4663 2-9-0 0.. JoeFanning 11 83+
(Mark Johnston) *mde all: shkn up over 1f out: wnt clr: eased towards fin* **8/15**[1]

5 **2** *6* **Street Jazz**[14] 4451 2-9-0 0.. TomEaves 9 63
(James Given) *trckd ldrs: 2nd 2f out: kpt on same pce: no ch w wnr* **6/1**[3]

5 **3** *3/4* **Edged In Blue**[38] 3597 2-9-0 0.................................... DougieCostello 10 61
(K R Burke) *trckd wnr: edgd lft over 1f out: kpt on same pce* **17/2**

6 **4** *1/2* **Bloomin Lovely (IRE)**[14] 4451 2-9-0 0................................. JasonHart 5 59
(John Quinn) *dwlt: swtchd lft after s: sn chsng ldrs: swtchd rt 1f out: kpt on same pce* **5/1**[2]

03 **5** *nk* **Lucy's Law (IRE)**[28] 3947 2-9-0 0.................................... AndrewElliott 4 58
(Tom Tate) *dwlt: wl outpcd and pushed along: edgd rt 2f out: styd on fnl f* **25/1**

5 **6** *3/4* **Royal Cosmic**[17] 4336 2-9-0 0... TonyHamilton 8 56
(Richard Fahey) *swtchd rt after s: mid-div: hdwy over 1f out: kpt on* **14/1**

7 *3 1/2* **Princess Nearco (IRE)** 2-9-0 0.................................... DanielTudhope 6 44
(Patrick Holmes) *s.s: in rr on outside: hdwy over 2f out: wknd fnl f* **80/1**

04 **8** *1 1/4* **Our Lois (IRE)**[14] 4442 2-9-0 0... PhillipMakin 2 40
(Keith Dalgleish) *sn outpcd and in rr* **33/1**

60 **9** *2 3/4* **Sadieroseclifford (IRE)**[11] 4564 2-8-11 0......................... TimClark[(3)] 3 32
(Denis Quinn) *sn chsng ldrs: drvn over 2f out: lost pl over 1f out* **100/1**

6 **10** *7* **No Luck Penny**[28] 3939 2-9-0 0.. BarryMcHugh 1 9
(Noel Wilson) *wnt bdly rt s: swtchd lft after 1f: a bhd* **100/1**

1m 11.8s (-1.20) **Going Correction** -0.25s/f (Firm) **10** Ran SP% **123.4**
Speed ratings (Par 91): **98,90,89,88,87 86,82,80,76,67**
CSF £4.72 TOTE £1.40: £1.02, £2.20, £3.20; EX 5.00 Trifecta £22.70.
Owner A D Spence & Mr And Mrs P Hargreaves **Bred** Mr & Mrs P Hargreaves & A D Spence **Trained** Middleham Moor, N Yorks

FOCUS
Joe Fanning described the ground as "good, fast". Little depth to this maiden and an easy win for the hot favourite, who has been rated as improving a length.

4944 SIS ON-DEMAND RACING GAMES (S) H'CAP 5f

2:45 (2:45) (Class 6) (0-65,62) 3-Y-O **£2,587** (£770; £384; £192) **Stalls** High

Form RPR

2555 **1** **La Asomada**[12] 4512 3-9-1 **56**....................................... GrahamGibbons 1 62
(David Barron) *chsd ldrs: swtchd rt over 1f out: led last 150yds: drvn rt out* **7/2**[2]

5650 **2** *3/4* **Hashtag Frenzy**[12] 4512 3-8-4 **45**...............................(p) JamesSullivan 7 48
(Rebecca Menzies) *w ldrs: upsides 1f out: no ex nr fin* **13/2**

4130 **3** *3* **Birrafun (IRE)**[12] 4512 3-9-0 **55**....................................... PJMcDonald 8 48
(Ann Duffield) *led: shkn up over 1f out: hdd last 150yds: fdd* **5/1**[3]

5000 **4** *3/4* **Jazz Legend (USA)**[17] 4365 3-9-7 **62**................................. TomEaves 3 52
(James Given) *w ldrs: wknd last 100yds* **11/2**

0005 **5** *1 1/2* **Cautionary Note**[15] 4426 3-8-9 **50**........................(p) SilvestreDeSousa 2 34
(Nigel Tinkler) *n.m.r and lost pl sn after s: swtchd wd over 3f out: hdwy over 2f out: chsng ldrs over 1f out: wknd towards fin* **9/4**[1]

1065 **6** *4 1/2* **I T Guru**[20] 4236 3-9-2 **57**..(t) BarryMcHugh 5 25
(Noel Wilson) *wnt lft s: sn w ldrs: wknd over 1f out* **8/1**

000 **7** *4* **Lord Bopper (IRE)**[20] 4238 3-8-7 **53** ow1............(v[1]) RobJFitzpatrick[(5)] 4 7+
(Ben Haslam) *bdly hmpd s: a last and sn drvn along: rdn and wknd over 1f out* **40/1**

59.16s (-0.84) **Going Correction** -0.25s/f (Firm) **7** Ran SP% **111.9**
Speed ratings (Par 98): **96,94,90,88,86 79,72**
CSF £24.92 CT £110.48 TOTE £4.60: £1.80, £3.90; EX 24.90 Trifecta £119.10.
Owner J G Brown **Bred** A C M Spalding **Trained** Maunby, N Yorks

FOCUS
Weak sprint form.

4945 AMANDA REID FREE FRIDAY WINNER H'CAP 1m 1f 170y

3:15 (3:15) (Class 4) (0-85,85) 3-Y-O+ **£4,851** (£1,443; £721; £360) **Stalls** Low

Form RPR

031 **1** **Absolute Zero (IRE)**[14] 4459 3-9-0 **80**............................. HarryBentley 5 93+
(Roger Varian) *mde all: t.k.h: qcknd pce 3f out: pushed clr over 1f out: eased nr fin: readily* **1/1**[1]

1436 **2** *3* **Gulf Of Poets**[16] 4406 4-8-13 **75**................................(p) NathanEvans[(5)] 3 81
(Michael Easterby) *trckd ldng pair: effrt and swtchd lft 2f out: sn chsng wnr: no imp* **9/1**

2023 **3** *3/4* **Salmon Sushi**[18] 4300 5-9-11 **82**... DavidAllan 2 86
(Tim Easterby) *stdd s: hld up in last: t.k.h: hdwy to trck ldrs over 5f out: kpt on same pce fnl 2f* **9/4**[2]

0600 **4** *2 1/4* **Burano (IRE)**[7] 4717 7-9-13 **84**.. DanielTudhope 4 84
(David O'Meara) *sn trcking wnr: drvn over 2f out: sn checked sltly: wknd and eased last 75yds* **9/2**[3]

2m 4.63s (-0.77) **Going Correction** +0.05s/f (Good)
WFA 3 from 4yo+ 9lb **4** Ran SP% **109.0**
Speed ratings (Par 105): **105,102,102,100**
CSF £9.60 TOTE £1.80; EX 6.20 Trifecta £8.70.
Owner J Collins, C Fahy & S Piper **Bred** Mighty Universe Ltd **Trained** Newmarket, Suffolk

FOCUS
Race distance increased by 10yds. A small field, even more so after two came out, and it didn't take much winning, the favourite making all. But the form is taken at face value, with the winner progressing and the second and third close to form.

4946 ARMSTRONG MEMORIAL H'CAP 6f

3:45 (3:45) (Class 3) (0-95,91) 3-Y-O **£7,246** (£2,168; £1,084; £542; £270) **Stalls** High

Form RPR

4164 **1** **Snap Shots (IRE)**[25] 4066 4-9-11 **90**...................(tp) RichardKingscote 5 98
(Tom Dascombe) *w ldrs: led over 1f out: hdd narrowly last 100yds: led again post* **7/2**[2]

4225 **2** *nse* **Foxtrot Knight**[14] 4461 4-9-0 **79** JamesSullivan 10 87
(Ruth Carr) *chsd ldrs: edgd rt over 4f out: nt clr run over 1f out: led narrowly last 100yds: hdd post* **7/1**

-100 **3** *1 1/4* **Munfallet (IRE)**[17] 4338 5-9-2 **86** AdamMcNamara(5) 8 90
(David Brown) *w ldr: led after 1f: hdd over 1f out: kpt on same pce last 100yds* **9/1**

4600 **4** *1 1/4* **Love Island**[15] 4428 7-9-2 **81** GeorgeChaloner 4 81
(Richard Whitaker) *w ldrs on outer: drvn over 2f out: kpt on same pce fnl 150yds* **11/1**

00-0 **5** *1/2* **Willbeme**[17] 4366 8-9-3 **85** JacobButterfield(3) 9 83
(Neville Bycroft) *led 1f: chsd ldrs: kpt on same pce fnl f* **25/1**

-003 **6** *3 1/4* **Eccleston**[50] 3188 5-9-12 **91** (v) DanielTudhope 6 84
(David O'Meara) *mid-div: hdwy on outer over 2f out: chsng ldrs over 1f out: wl hld whn eased clsng stages* **9/4**[1]

6210 **7** *11* **Johnny Cavagin**[18] 4299 7-9-9 **88** (t[1]) JimmyQuinn 3 41
(Ronald Thompson) *rrd and v slow away: a detached: eased clsng stages* **6/1**[3]

5-10 **8** *3* **Yorkee Mo Sabee (IRE)**[13] 4481 3-8-12 **81** JoeFanning 7 23
(Mark Johnston) *chsd ldrs: bmpd over 4f out: outpcd 3f out: sn lost pl and bhd: eased last 100yds* **10/1**

1m 10.42s (-2.58) **Going Correction** -0.25s/f (Firm)
WFA 3 from 4yo+ 4lb **8** Ran SP% **111.0**
Speed ratings (Par 107): **107,106,105,103,102 98,83,79**
CSF £26.34 CT £194.81 TOTE £5.20: £1.80, £1.40, £3.00; EX 23.80 Trifecta £128.00.
Owner Gap Personnel **Bred** Tally-Ho Stud **Trained** Malpas, Cheshire

FOCUS
A decent sprint, little getting into it from off the pace, and the winner has been rated to the same sort of form as when runner-up in this last year.

4947 VISIT ATTHERACES.COM H'CAP 5f
4:15 (4:18) (Class 4) (0-85,85) 3-Y-O **£4,851** (£1,443; £721; £360) **Stalls** High

Form RPR

040 **1** **Excessable**[24] 4112 3-9-0 **78** (t) JasonHart 7 84
(Tim Easterby) *led 1f: trckd ldrs: styd on fnl f: led nr fin* **9/2**[3]

4130 **2** *1/2* **Rose Marmara**[10] 4612 3-9-1 **79** (t) JamesSullivan 4 83
(Brian Rothwell) *chsd ldrs: led over 1f out: hdd and no ex nr fin* **11/1**

0500 **3** *3/4* **Rosina**[47] 3292 3-9-4 **82** PJMcDonald 5 83
(Ann Duffield) *in rr: hdwy over 2f out: chsng ldrs over 1f out: kpt on same pce last 75yds* **5/1**

5455 **4** *1 1/4* **Sir Dudley (IRE)**[11] 4547 3-8-10 **74** (b) TomEaves 6 71
(James Given) *mid-div: effrt over 2f out: nt clr run over 1f out: swtchd rt and kpt on last 100yds* **5/1**

4500 **5** *2 1/4* **Lady Clair (IRE)**[9] 4652 3-8-13 **82** JordanVaughan(5) 3 71
(K R Burke) *wnt rt s: chsd ldrs: wknd fnl 150yds* **4/1**[2]

-41 **6** *nk* **L C Saloon**[20] 4238 3-9-7 **85** DavidAllan 1 73
(David C Griffiths) *swtchd lft after s: led after 1f: hdd over 1f out: wknd fnl 150yds* **11/4**[1]

0051 **7** *3/4* **New Road Side**[19] 4256 3-8-13 **77** (v) BarryMcHugh 2 62
(Tony Coyle) *sltly hmpd s: in rr: swtchd outside over 2f out: chsng ldrs over 1f out: wknd fnl f* **14/1**

58.69s (-1.31) **Going Correction** -0.25s/f (Firm) **7** Ran SP% **113.2**
Speed ratings (Par 102): **97,96,95,93,89 88,87**
CSF £49.45 TOTE £5.00: £2.60, £4.60; EX 44.90 Trifecta £159.60.
Owner B Guerin & Habton Farms **Bred** Whitsbury Manor Stud **Trained** Great Habton, N Yorks

FOCUS
A fair sprint but another on the straight course where it paid to race handy. The winner is rated back to the form of his C&D maiden win.

4948 SIS STREAM MAIDEN STKS 1m 4f 10y
4:45 (4:49) (Class 5) 3-Y-O+ **£2,911** (£866; £432; £216) **Stalls** High

Form RPR

65 **1** **Novalina (IRE)**[25] 4056 3-8-10 0 GrahamGibbons 2 80
(William Haggas) *mde all: qcknd pce 4f out: drvn over 2f out: hld on wl clsng stages* **6/1**

4220 **2** *1* **Withhold**[31] 3845 3-9-1 80 SilvestreDeSousa 3 83
(Charles Hills) *chsd wnr: shkn up 8f out: drvn over 5f out: upsides over 3f out: kpt on same pce fnl 100yds* **13/8**[1]

3 **3** *2 1/4* **Ardamir (FR)**[19] 4265 4-9-12 0 WilliamTwiston-Davies 1 79
(Alan King) *hood removed v late: s.s: hdwy to trck ldrs after 2f: drvn 4f out: rdn and hung bdly lft 2f out: tk modest 3rd clsng stages* **2/1**[2]

3342 **4** *1 1/2* **Just Hiss**[17] 4342 3-9-1 77 DavidAllan 4 77
(Tim Easterby) *trckd ldng pair: upsides over 2f out: sn drvn: edgd rt and fdd fnl f* **3/1**[3]

2m 36.49s (-0.21) **Going Correction** +0.05s/f (Good)
WFA 3 from 4yo 11lb **4** Ran SP% **110.7**
Speed ratings (Par 103): **102,101,99,98**
CSF £16.30 TOTE £6.50; EX 13.90 Trifecta £43.00.
Owner Messrs B Kantor & MJ Jooste **Bred** Barronstown Stud **Trained** Newmarket, Suffolk

FOCUS
Race distance increased by 10yds. Just the four runners but a fair maiden and the improved winner ensured it was a true test.

4949 FOSSGATE H'CAP 1m 4f 10y
5:15 (5:17) (Class 5) (0-75,75) 3-Y-O+ **£3,234** (£962; £481; £240) **Stalls** High

Form RPR

-401 **1** **Icefall (IRE)**[17] 4372 3-9-3 **75** DavidAllan 4 85+
(Tim Easterby) *trckd ldng pair: swtchd lft 3f out: 2nd 2f out: upsides appr fnl f: led last 100yds: styd on wl* **11/8**[1]

5-14 **2** *2 1/2* **Space Mountain**[38] 3621 3-9-0 **72** JoeFanning 7 78
(Mark Johnston) *led: qcknd pce 4f out: hdd and no ex last 100yds* **4/1**[2]

4-15 **3** *3* **Snow Prince**[25] 4044 5-9-9 **75** (p) AdamMcNamara(5) 3 76
(Steve Gollings) *in rr-div: hdwy over 5f out: drvn 3f out: kpt on one pce to take modest 3rd 1f out* **5/1**[3]

0222 **4** *nk* **Wishing Well**[20] 4239 4-9-6 **67** (p) PJMcDonald 2 68
(Micky Hammond) *hld up in rr: drvn over 3f out: kpt on one pce: tk modest 4th nr fin* **5/1**[3]

0340 **5** *1/2* **Kip**[14] 4455 4-9-10 **71** DanielTudhope 5 71
(David O'Meara) *trckd ldr: upsides over 4f out: drvn 3f out: fdd appr fnl f* **6/1**

140/ **U** **Hoist The Colours (IRE)**[53] 7020 5-10-0 **75** TonyHamilton 6
(Chris Grant) *hld up in last: wnt bdly wrong and uns rdr over 10f out: fatally injured* **33/1**

2m 36.35s (-0.35) **Going Correction** +0.05s/f (Good)
WFA 3 from 4yo+ 11lb **6** Ran SP% **112.7**
Speed ratings (Par 103): **103,101,99,99,98**
CSF £7.23 TOTE £2.40: £1.60, £2.70; EX 8.10 Trifecta £33.00.
Owner Ryedale Partners No 10 **Bred** Victor Stud Bloodstock Ltd **Trained** Great Habton, N Yorks

FOCUS
Race distance increased by 10yds. The 3yos predictably dominated this modest handicap, with the winner improving again.
T/Plt: £300.20 to a £1 stake. Pool: £62,462.32 - 151.85 winning units. T/Qpdt: £74.90 to a £1 stake. Pool: £5,105.62 - 50.40 winning units. **Walter Glynn**

4706 WINDSOR (R-H)
Monday, August 1

OFFICIAL GOING: Good (good to firm in places) changing to good after race 5 (7.30)
Wind: Light, behind Weather: Overcast with rain

4950 SKY BET AMATEUR RIDERS' H'CAP 1m 3f 135y
5:30 (5:33) (Class 6) (0-65,65) 3-Y-O+ **£2,183** (£677; £338; £169) **Stalls** Centre

Form RPR

6445 **1** **Jersey Jewel (FR)**[6] 4730 4-10-9 **65** MissCAGreenway(5) 6 74
(Tom Dascombe) *trckd ldng pair 5f: styd handy: clsd on outer to ld over 1f out: shkn up and kpt on wl* **4/1**[1]

325/ **2** *1 3/4* **Miss Tiger Lily**[27] 2419 6-10-6 **62** MissKatyLyons(5) 2 68
(Harry Dunlop) *trckd ldr: led over 3f out: rdn and hdd over 1f out: styd on but a hld* **10/1**

5/63 **3** *5* **Nafaath (IRE)**[11] 4551 10-10-9 **65** (v[1]) MissAMcCain(5) 9 63
(Donald McCain) *led to over 3f out: outpcd and struggling wl over 1f out: kpt on to take 3rd again ins fnl f* **5/1**[2]

065P **4** *1 3/4* **The Quarterjack**[46] 3302 7-10-4 **62** MissMorganKerr(7) 8 57
(Ron Hodges) *in tch: rdn to cl on ldrs 2f out: disp 3rd over 1f out: fdd ins fnl f* **10/1**

0243 **5** *1* **Dellbuoy**[18] 4303 7-9-13 **55** MissLDempster(5) 4 48
(Pat Phelan) *trckd ldng pair after 5f: chal over 3f out tl wl over 1f out: wknd ins fnl f* **7/1**

2060 **6** *3 1/4* **Primrose Brown**[10] 4596 5-10-8 **62** [1] MissLAllan(3) 10 50
(Conrad Allen) *wl in tch: rdn and cl up bhd ldrs over 2f out: wknd over 1f out* **33/1**

/014 **7** *1/2* **Eugenic**[39] 3560 5-10-2 **53** MrPMillman 5 40
(Rod Millman) *nvr quite on terms w ldrs: urged along and no prog 3f out: slipped up after fin* **5/1**[2]

8 *7* **Madness Light (FR)**[469] 7-9-6 **50** MissMESpencer(7) 1 26
(Daniel Steele) *s.v.s: a off the pce in last trio and nvr able to make significant grnd* **12/1**

-404 **9** *9* **Westerly**[25] 4052 5-10-1 **57** MrJDoe(5) 7 18
(Luke Dace) *lost tch w main gp after 2f: nvr on terms after* **11/2**[3]

0064 **10** *37* **Royal Etiquette (IRE)**[11] 4551 9-9-8 **50** (tp) MsVLPendleton(5) 3
(Lawney Hill) *rel to r: a wl t.o* **16/1**

2m 30.84s (1.34) **Going Correction** +0.125s/f (Good) **10** Ran SP% **115.9**
Speed ratings (Par 101): **100,98,95,94,93 91,91,86,80,55**
CSF £44.45 CT £204.39 TOTE £5.50: £1.80, £4.00, £2.20; EX 53.40 Trifecta £251.40.
Owner R Greenway **Bred** M Daguzan-Garros & F Bragato **Trained** Malpas, Cheshire

FOCUS
Inner of straight dolled out 6yds at 6f, and 3yds at the winning line. Top bend dolled out 10yds from normal inner configuration, adding 36yds to race distances of 1m-plus. The rain arrived prior to racing. They went a fair pace in this handicap for amateur riders and the first pair came clear. Not much solid form and it's been rated cautiously.

4951 SKY BET BRITISH STALLION STUDS EBF MAIDEN FILLIES' STKS (PLUS 10 RACE) 6f
6:00 (6:19) (Class 5) 2-Y-O **£3,234** (£962; £481; £240) **Stalls** Low

Form RPR

1 **Bahamadam** 2-9-0 0 RobertWinston 2 82+
(Eve Johnson Houghton) *dwlt: wl in tch against rail: prog over 2f out: led over 1f out: rdn and styd on wl* **33/1**

4 **2** *1 3/4* **Bee Case**[60] 2817 2-9-0 0 JimCrowley 12 73
(Hugo Palmer) *trckd ldrs: shkn up 2f out: clsd over 1f out: styd on to take 2nd ins fnl f: no real danger to wnr* **2/1**[2]

0 **3** *nk* **Miss Anticipation (IRE)**[25] 4054 2-8-11 0 [1] KieranShoemark(3) 10 72
(Roger Charlton) *taken down early: stdd s: hld up towards rr: prog 1/2-way: rdn and swtchd lft over 1f out: styd on to take 3rd nr fin* **25/1**

4 *nk* **Hathfa (FR)** 2-9-0 0 ShaneKelly 11 71+
(Richard Hughes) *s.i.s: sn in midfield: pushed along 2f out: styd on over 1f out to take 4th nr fin* **4/1**[3]

32 **5** *1* **Bellevarde (IRE)**[17] 4363 2-9-0 0 TomQueally 8 68
(James Fanshawe) *trckd ldrs: shkn up 2f out: weaved through to chal over 1f out: nt qckn and fdd ins fnl f* **6/4**[1]

6 *2* **Moonstone Rock** 2-9-0 0 PatCosgrave 15 61
(Jim Boyle) *racd on wd outside in midfield: pushed along and sme prog 2f out: no hdwy fnl f: nt disgracd* **66/1**

7 *2 3/4* **Mezyan (IRE)** 2-9-0 0 JFEgan 6 53
(David Evans) *pushed along in rr bef 1/2-way: nvr a factor but kpt on fr over 1f out* **66/1**

4 **8** *nk* **Ginger Truffle**[55] 2990 2-9-0 0 KieranO'Neill 13 52
(Brett Johnson) *racd freely: led to over 1f out: wknd* **66/1**

9 *nk* **Cuban Isabela** 2-9-0 0 OisinMurphy 5 51
(Stuart Williams) *dwlt: wl bhd in last pair: picked up quite wl fnl f: nrst fin* **66/1**

3 **10** *shd* **Queensbrydge**[26] 4011 2-9-0 0 MartinHarley 16 50
(Robyn Brisland) *pressed ldrs on outer: rt there 2f out: n.m.r over 1f out: wknd* **9/1**

54 **11** *1/2* **Highland Dream (IRE)**[19] 4261 2-9-0 0 AndrewMullen 9 49
(Clive Cox) *prom: rdn to chal wl over 1f out: wknd qckly fnl f* **25/1**

36 **12** *1 3/4* **Fair Selene**[74] 2410 2-9-0 0 JackMitchell 1 43
(Heather Main) *cl up bhd ldrs tl wknd fr 2f out* **50/1**

13 *1* **Venetian Proposal (IRE)** 2-8-11 0 DanielMuscutt(3) 7 40
(Zoe Davison) *a in rr: urged along and no prog 1/2-way* **100/1**

14 *1/2* **Harlequin Rose (IRE)** 2-9-0 0 CharlesBishop 4 38
(Mick Channon) *sn pushed along: a struggling in rr* **25/1**

0 **15** *5* **Gaia Princess (IRE)**[45] 3356 2-8-9 0 HectorCrouch(5) 14 22
(Gary Moore) *t.k.h: pressed ldr to over 2f out: losing pl whn squeezed out over 1f out: wknd rapidly* **25/1**

16 *3 3/4* **Melo Magic** 2-9-0 0 FrederikTylicki 3 10
(J R Jenkins) *dwlt: a wl bhd* **100/1**

1m 12.67s (-0.33) **Going Correction** -0.10s/f (Good) **16** Ran SP% **131.6**
Speed ratings (Par 91): **98,95,95,94,93 90,87,86,86,86 85,83,81,81,74 69**
CSF £101.87 TOTE £41.90: £6.80, £1.60, £5.40; EX 173.00 Trifecta £4542.30.
Owner J P Repard **Bred** J P Repard **Trained** Blewbury, Oxon

FOCUS
There was a 20-minute delay to this uncompetitive fillies' maiden due to officials inspecting the loose ground on the bend just after the winning line. The time suggested it was still quick underfoot. The winner is rated to the top end of the race averages.

4952 SKY BET H'CAP 5f 10y
6:30 (6:44) (Class 5) (0-70,70) 3-Y-O+ **£2,911** (£866; £432; £216) **Stalls** Low

Form RPR
040 **1** **Pink Martini (IRE)**[12] 4502 3-9-5 **68** OisinMurphy 8 77
(Joseph Tuite) *hld up in last trio: pushed along and prog on outer 2f out: rdn to chse ldr ins fnl f: styd on wl to ld last strides* **16/1**
0311 **2** *shd* **John Joiner**[19] 4264 4-8-12 **58** AndreaAtzeni 9 67
(Peter Hedger) *trckd ldrs gng wl: prog 2f out: led jst ins fnl f: rdn and kpt on wl but hdd last strides* **11/4**[1]
4414 **3** *3 1/4* **Stormflower**[19] 4268 3-9-4 **67** DannyBrock 1 64
(John Bridger) *racd freely: mde most to jst ins fnl f: outpcd but hld on for 3rd* **8/1**
0333 **4** *hd* **Toni's A Star**[31] 3851 4-8-12 **61** GeorgeDowning(3) 6 58
(Tony Carroll) *sn detached in last: pushed along 2f out: prog on outer fnl f: nrly snatched 3rd* **10/1**
2-30 **5** *shd* **Costa Filey**[33] 3780 5-9-6 **66** FrederikTylicki 7 63
(Ed Vaughan) *prom: rdn to dispute 2nd briefly over 1f out: fdd ins fnl f* **7/2**[2]
6500 **6** *1 1/2* **Whitecrest**[13] 4495 8-9-7 **67** RobertWinston 4 58
(John Spearing) *stmbld s: chsd ldrs: lost pl 2f out: n.d after* **12/1**
0650 **7** *nk* **Smoothtalkinrascal (IRE)**[9] 4640 6-9-0 **60** (bt[1]) ShaneKelly 3 50
(Peter Crate) *t.k.h: hld up in last trio: no ch whn shkn up jst over 1f out: nvr involved* **14/1**
30-0 **8** *1 1/4* **Balliol**[11] 4544 4-9-8 **68** RaulDaSilva 2 54
(Ronald Harris) *dwlt: rcvrd into midfield: cl up over 1f out: sn wknd* **7/1**
5461 **9** *10* **Fine 'n Dandy (IRE)**[10] 4590 5-9-10 **70** (t) TomQueally 5 20
(J R Jenkins) *w ldr to 2f out: wknd v rapidly* **5/1**[3]
59.32s (-0.98) **Going Correction** -0.10s/f (Good)
WFA 3 from 4yo+ 3lb **9** Ran SP% **118.5**
Speed ratings (Par 103): **103,102,97,97,97 94,94,92,76**
CSF £61.59 CT £396.78 TOTE £16.20: £4.00, £1.30, £2.50; EX 62.90 Trifecta £517.30.
Owner Pulse.Aero Partnership **Bred** E Ryan **Trained** Lambourn, Berks

FOCUS
A modest sprint handicap. The first pair pulled clear in a tight finish down the centre.

4953 MPM FLOORING LTD H'CAP 1m 67y
7:00 (7:07) (Class 4) (0-85,86) 3-Y-O+ **£4,690** (£1,395; £697; £348) **Stalls** Low

Form RPR
2521 **1** **September Stars (IRE)**[7] 4709 3-9-8 **86** 6ex JimCrowley 3 100
(Ralph Beckett) *mde all: drifted lft fr over 2f out: shkn up over 1f out and sn drew rt away* **8/13**[1]
5125 **2** *6* **Harlequin Striker (IRE)**[28] 3957 4-10-0 **85** RobertWinston 4 86
(Dean Ivory) *chsd wnr: rdn to try to chal whn carried sltly lft 2f out: wl outpcd over 1f out* **6/1**[3]
620 **3** *1* **Major Assault**[23] 4157 3-8-10 **74** JohnFahy 2 72
(Clive Cox) *chsd ldng trio: rdn to take 3rd over 2f out: outpcd fr over 1f out* **16/1**
4103 **4** *1/2* **Philadelphia (IRE)**[28] 3957 3-9-2 **80** AndreaAtzeni 5 77
(Roger Varian) *s.i.s: racd in 5th: rdn 3f out: tried to chal for a pl over 1f out: nvr a threat* **9/2**[2]
30-6 **5** *3* **Rahmah (IRE)**[21] 4208 4-9-4 **75** TimmyMurphy 8 66
(Geoffrey Deacon) *stdd s: sn detached in last: appeared to be hanging 3f out: tk remote 5th nr fin* **28/1**
512- **6** *2* **Bag Of Diamonds**[230] 8234 3-8-13 **77** KieranO'Neill 1 62
(Richard Hannon) *chsd ldng pair: rdn 3f out: sn lost 3rd and wknd* **12/1**
1m 44.6s (-0.10) **Going Correction** +0.125s/f (Good)
WFA 3 from 4yo+ 7lb **6** Ran SP% **111.4**
Speed ratings (Par 105): **105,99,98,97,94 92**
CSF £4.77 CT £26.55 TOTE £1.50: £1.10, £2.50; EX 4.80 Trifecta £19.60.
Owner Andrew Rosen & Edward W Easton **Bred** John Connaughton **Trained** Kimpton, Hants

FOCUS
Race distance increased by 36yds. This was all about the improved winner. The runner-up is a fair guide.

4954 SKY BET WINDSOR SPRINT SERIES H'CAP (QUALIFIER FOR THE WINDSOR SPRINT SERIES FINAL) 6f
7:30 (7:35) (Class 3) (0-95,90) 3-Y-O+ **£7,439** (£2,213; £1,106; £553) **Stalls** Low

Form RPR
2000 **1** **Goring (GER)**[24] 4081 4-9-3 **81** JohnFahy 4 88
(Eve Johnson Houghton) *settled in rr: rdn and prog 2f out: chsd ldng pair ins fnl f: drvn and styd on stoutly to ld last 50yds* **18/1**
0116 **2** *1/2* **Free Zone**[15] 4428 7-9-6 **84** (v) WilliamCarson 2 89
(Jamie Osborne) *led 1f: stayd prom: rdn 2f out: clsd to ld ins fnl f: hdd and nt qckn last 50yds* **12/1**
0160 **3** *1* **Stake Acclaim (IRE)**[31] 3857 4-9-9 **87** (p) RobertWinston 5 89
(Dean Ivory) *w ldr after 1f: rdn to ld over 1f out: hdd and one pce ins fnl f* **11/2**[3]
-000 **4** *2* **Musical Comedy**[10] 4584 5-9-12 **90** JimCrowley 6 85
(Mike Murphy) *trckd ldrs: trying to chal whn nt clr run over 1f out: one pce fnl f* **16/1**
-000 **5** *3/4* **Firmdecisions (IRE)**[12] 4534 6-9-9 **87** (v) PatCosgrave 7 80
(Dean Ivory) *pressed ldrs towards outer: rdn 2f out: nt qckn over 1f out: fdd* **14/1**
3314 **6** *3/4* **Escalating**[32] 3800 4-9-8 **86** (tp) AndrewMullen 10 77
(Michael Appleby) *mostly in midfield: drvn and tried to make prog wl over 1f out: sn no hdwy* **4/1**[1]
-011 **7** *nk* **Fang**[11] 4569 3-9-0 **82** (t) SeanLevey 3 71
(William Jarvis) *led after 1f to over 1f out: wknd* **9/2**[2]
-002 **8** *1/2* **Morache Music**[25] 4051 8-9-4 **85** DanielMuscutt(3) 9 73
(Patrick Chamings) *rdn in rr bef 1/2-way: a struggling* **15/2**
303 **9** *2 1/4* **Sir Billy Wright (IRE)**[17] 4366 5-9-8 **86** JFEgan 1 67
(David Evans) *slowly away: prog fr rr to chse ldrs 1/2-way: rdn and wknd over 1f out* **7/1**
3051 **10** *1 1/4* **Links Drive Lady**[49] 3233 8-9-6 **87** JackDuern(3) 11 64
(Dean Ivory) *slowly away: a in rr: racd towards far side fr 1/2-way and no ch over 1f out* **15/2**
4660 **11** *1/2* **Taajub (IRE)**[10] 4584 9-9-3 **81** ShaneKelly 8 56
(Peter Crate) *nvr beyond midfield: racd towards far side fr 1/2-way: no ch over 1f out* **33/1**
1m 12.07s (-0.93) **Going Correction** -0.10s/f (Good)
WFA 3 from 4yo+ 4lb **11** Ran SP% **118.0**
Speed ratings (Par 107): **102,101,100,97,96 95,94,94,91,89 88**
CSF £218.26 CT £1357.25 TOTE £19.10: £4.60, £4.40, £2.00; EX 294.50 Trifecta £3531.60.
Owner G C Stevens **Bred** Westminster Race Horses Gmbh **Trained** Blewbury, Oxon

FOCUS
A fair and competitive sprint handicap. The runners fanned across the track from 2f out. A small pb from the winner.

4955 SKY BET MAIDEN STKS 1m 2f 7y
8:00 (8:00) (Class 5) 3-4-Y-O **£3,067** (£905; £453) **Stalls** Centre

Form RPR
0-22 **1** **Julia Dream**[62] 2767 3-9-0 82 PatCosgrave 1 78
(William Haggas) *trckd ldr 3f: styd cl up: rdn wl over 1f out: tk 2nd again fnl f: drvn ahd last 100yds* **5/4**[1]
0-33 **2** *1/2* **Heartstone (IRE)**[17] 4356 3-9-0 72 MichaelJMMurphy 4 77
(Charles Hills) *mde most: rdn over 2f out: fought off one chalr over 1f out: hdd last 100yds: styd on* **8/1**
0-2 **3** *2 1/2* **Blaze Of Hearts (IRE)**[14] 4458 3-9-5 0 RobertWinston 5 77
(Dean Ivory) *trckd ldr after 3f: chal over 2f out: drvn and nt qckn over 1f out: lost 2nd and one pce fnl f* **11/4**[2]
64 **4** *2 3/4* **Pc Dixon**[9] 4657 3-8-12 0 KillianHennessy(7) 6 72
(Mick Channon) *mostly chsd ldng trio: rdn and on terms jst over 2f out: fdd over 1f out* **20/1**
0-0 **5** *3 1/2* **McCools Gold**[19] 4265 3-9-5 0 JohnFahy 7 65
(Eve Johnson Houghton) *dwlt: sn detached in last: nvr a factor but passed two wkng rivals fnl f* **14/1**
0 **6** *2 1/4* **Brahma**[14] 4458 3-9-5 0 RobertHavlin 2 60
(Hughie Morrison) *t.k.h: hld up in 6th and in tch: hanging bdly and wknd fr over 2f out* **40/1**
6 **7** *1* **Divine Quickstep (IRE)**[49] 3235 3-9-0 0 TedDurcan 3 53
(Sir Michael Stoute) *dwlt: pushed along early: in tch in 5th: pushed along and outpcd 3f out: wknd over 1f out* **7/2**[3]
2m 10.27s (1.57) **Going Correction** +0.125s/f (Good) **7** Ran SP% **118.3**
Speed ratings (Par 103): **98,97,95,93,90 88,88**
CSF £13.41 TOTE £2.10: £1.20, £2.80; EX 12.40 Trifecta £20.80.
Owner Mr & Mrs R Scott **Bred** Mr & Mrs R & P Scott **Trained** Newmarket, Suffolk

FOCUS
Race distance increased by 36yds. The going was changed to good all over after the preceding sprint handicap. A modest maiden and the winner probably didn't have to match her best. The level is fluid.

4956 SKY BET TOP PRICE EVERY FAVOURITE H'CAP 1m 2f 7y
8:30 (8:30) (Class 5) (0-70,70) 3-Y-O+ **£2,911** (£866; £432; £216) **Stalls** Centre

Form RPR
-013 **1** **Senza Una Donna**[18] 4293 3-9-0 **70** (t) CharlieBennett(5) 5 80
(Hughie Morrison) *hld up in last: smooth prog towards nr side over 2f out: led over 1f out: drvn and hrd pressed ins fnl f: hld on* **7/2**[2]
063 **2** *nk* **So Celebre (GER)**[17] 4341 3-9-3 **68** RobertHavlin 7 77
(Ian Williams) *trckd ldrs: rdn over 2f out and taken out wd: clsd to take 2nd 1f out and sn chalng: styd on but jst hld* **4/1**[3]
-304 **3** *4* **Apache Song**[74] 2415 3-9-4 **69** FrederikTylicki 8 70
(Rod Millman) *hld up in 6th: taken out wd and rdn over 2f out: clsd on ldrs jst over 1f out: readily outpcd fnl f* **6/1**
21-5 **4** *3 1/4* **Pendo**[179] 437 5-9-12 **68** KierenFox 6 63
(John Best) *fast away: led: rdn over 2f out: hdd & wknd over 1f out* **12/1**
053 **5** *4 1/2* **Princesse Eva (FR)**[26] 4025 3-8-13 **67** DanielMuscutt(3) 4 53
(James Fanshawe) *trckd ldr: chal over 2f out: wknd qckly over 1f out* **10/3**[1]
3103 **6** *1 3/4* **Tatawu (IRE)**[12] 4531 4-9-10 **66** WilliamCarson 2 48
(Peter Hiatt) *trckd ldng pair: rdn to chal over 2f out: wknd qckly wl over 1f out* **5/1**
3-06 **7** *9* **Dubawi Light**[18] 4302 5-9-9 **65** (b[1]) ShaneKelly 1 29
(Gary Moore) *in tch tl wknd u.p jst over 2f out: sn bhd* **9/1**
2m 8.82s (0.12) **Going Correction** +0.125s/f (Good)
WFA 3 from 4yo+ 9lb **7** Ran SP% **113.9**
Speed ratings (Par 103): **104,103,100,97,94 92,85**
CSF £17.72 CT £79.78 TOTE £4.80: £2.50, £2.00; EX 19.30 Trifecta £93.90.
Owner Castle Down Racing **Bred** Meon Valley Stud **Trained** East Ilsley, Berks
■ Stewards' Enquiry : Robert Havlin four-day ban: used whip above permitted level (August 15,16,20,21)

FOCUS
Race distance increased by 36yds. A modest handicap. There was a fair pace on and they got sorted out nearing the final furlong. The winner continued his progress, with the second to form.
T/Plt: £226.80 to a £1 stake. Pool: £84,710.71 - 272.65 winning units T/Qpdt: £28.50 to a £1 stake. Pool: £9,746.38 - 252.3 winning units **Jonathan Neesom**

4957 - 4964a (Foreign Racing) - See Raceform Interactive

4074 CLAIREFONTAINE (R-H)
Monday, August 1

OFFICIAL GOING: Turf: soft

4965a PRIX CLAUDE MONET (PRIX DES EGLANTINES) (CLAIMER) (2YO) (TURF) 7f
2:55 (12:00) 2-Y-O **£8,455** (£3,382; £2,536; £1,691; £845)

RPR
1 **Oncle Fernand (FR)**[80] 2-8-11 0 ChristopheSoumillon 7 74
(J-C Rouget, France) **1/2**[1]
2 *5* **Chababa Rosetgri (FR)**[22] 2-8-8 0 RonanThomas 9 58
(H De Nicolay, France) **139/10**
3 *3/4* **Etta (FR)**[8] 2-8-5 0 HugoJourniac(3) 8 56
(M Boutin, France) **11/2**[2]
4 *snk* **Sunday Winner (FR)**[14] 4471 2-8-11 0 (b) StephanePasquier 1 59
(Y Gourraud, France) **177/10**
5 *1/2* **Cholpon Ata (FR)**[14] 4471 2-8-11 0 AurelienLemaitre 6 57
(Mme P Butel, France) **219/10**
6 *1 1/2* **Countess Allegro (FR)**[22] 2-8-8 0 GregoryBenoist 3 50
(M Boutin, France) **93/10**
7 *5* **La Testerine (FR)**[14] 2-9-1 0 IoritzMendizabal 4 44
(F Chappet, France) **26/1**

8 *15* **Shaqoos (FR)** 2-8-8 0 MaximeGuyon 2
(Jo Hughes) *awkward leaving stalls: sn in rr under a tight hold: rdn and moved into midfield bef 1/2-way: in tch whn virtually p.u 1f out and cantered home* **8/1**[3]

1m 27.0s (87.00) **8** Ran SP% **123.0**
WIN (incl. 1 euro stake): 1.50. PLACES: 1.10, 1.70, 1.30. DF: 9.50. SF: 10.20.
Owner Daniel-Yves Treves **Bred** Mat Daguzan-Garros & Mme N La Fonta **Trained** Pau, France

4508 CATTERICK (L-H)

Tuesday, August 2

OFFICIAL GOING: Good to firm (8.9)
Wind: Moderate half behind Weather: Cloudy

4966 BRITISH STALLION STUDS EBF NOVICE STKS 7f

2:15 (2:17) (Class 5) 2-Y-O **£3,234** (£962; £481; £240) **Stalls** Low

Form RPR

51 **1** **Glitter Girl**[11] **4603** 2-9-4 81 BenCurtis 6 85+
(William Haggas) *cl up: led wl over 2f out: shkn up and pushed clr over 1f out: readily* **1/4**[1]

40 **2** *5* **Miss Danby (IRE)**[11] **4603** 2-8-11 0 FrannyNorton 2 62
(Mark Johnston) *sn slt ld on inner: pushed along and hdd wl over 2f out: sn rdn and kpt on: no ch w wnr* **28/1**[3]

3 *3 1/2* **Golconda Prince (IRE)** 2-9-2 0 TonyHamilton 5 57+
(Richard Fahey) *green and sn pushed along to chse ldrs: rdn along 3f out: styd on same pce fnl 2f* **7/1**[2]

0 **4** *1 1/4* **Sheriff Garrett (IRE)**[18] **4371** 2-9-2 0 DavidAllan 3 54
(Tim Easterby) *chsd ldrs on inner: rdn along wl over 2f out: sn one pce* **80/1**

0 **5** *2* **Dyna Might**[29] **3947** 2-8-8 0 JacobButterfield(3) 4 43
(Ollie Pears) *in rr: rdn along on inner over 2f out: kpt on one pce* **100/1**

00 **6** *2 1/4* **Mr Strutter (IRE)**[16] **4423** 2-9-2 0 CamHardie 7 42
(John Quinn) *chsd ldrs on outer: rdn along 1/2-way: wknd over 2f out* **66/1**

1m 26.23s (-0.77) **Going Correction** -0.20s/f (Firm) **6** Ran SP% **99.7**
Speed ratings (Par 94): **96,90,86,84,82 80**
CSF £7.59 TOTE £1.10: £1.02, £5.00; EX 5.40 Trifecta £8.90.
Owner Cheveley Park Stud **Bred** Cheveley Park Stud Ltd **Trained** Newmarket, Suffolk
■ Mere Brow was withdrawn. Price at time of withdrawal 15/2. Rule 4 applies to all bets - deduct 10p in the pound.

FOCUS
Rail on bend turning into home straight dolled out 2yds, increasing race distances by 6yds. Predictably one-way traffic for this novice, the red-hot favourite winning as she liked, and she's rated similar to her maiden win.

4967 SUPPORT ABF THE SOLDIERS' CHARITY CLASSIFIED CLAIMING STKS (A QUALIFIER FOR CATTERICK 12F SERIES) 1m 3f 214y

2:45 (2:45) (Class 5) 3-Y-O+ **£3,234** (£962; £481; £240) **Stalls** Low

Form RPR

-000 **1** **Brigadoon**[16] **4095** 9-9-4 75 AndrewMullen 1 73
(Michael Appleby) *mde all: pushed along 3f out: rdn 2f out: drvn over 1f out: styd on gamely fnl f* **9/1**[3]

1544 **2** *1/2* **The Kid**[12] **4550** 5-9-6 72 CamHardie 5 75+
(John Quinn) *hld up in rr: hdwy on inner 3f out: trckd ldng pair 2f out: effrt and nt clr run ent fnl f: sn swtchd rt and rdn: styd on wl towards fin* **5/2**[2]

3-01 **3** *1* **Chant (IRE)**[9] **4686** 6-9-11 70 PJMcDonald 4 77
(Ann Duffield) *trckd ldng pair: hdwy over 3f out: sn chal: rdn wl over 1f out and sn hung rt: drvn and edgd lft ent fnl f: ev ch tl no ex last 75yds* **6/4**[1]

30-0 **4** *5* **Gold Merlion (IRE)**[34] **3766** 3-8-5 75 FrannyNorton 2 60
(Mark Johnston) *t.k.h: trckd ldr: cl up over 4f out: rdn along over 3f out: sn drvn and wknd over 2f out* **5/2**[2]

2m 36.64s (-2.26) **Going Correction** -0.20s/f (Firm)
WFA 3 from 5yo+ 11lb **4** Ran SP% **107.1**
Speed ratings (Par 103): **99,98,98,94**
CSF £29.51 TOTE £8.00; EX 21.50 Trifecta £47.50.The Kid was subject to a friendly claim.
Owner Castle Racing **Bred** Biddestone Stud **Trained** Oakham, Rutland

FOCUS
Race distance increased by 6yds. An ordinary claimer that went to the outsider of the four - who hadn't been in any form this year and has been rated cautiously.

4968 DINE AND VIEW AT CATTERICK RACES H'CAP 5f

3:15 (3:16) (Class 6) (0-60,60) 3-Y-O+ **£2,264** (£673; £336; £168) **Stalls** Low

Form RPR

5021 **1** **Compton River**[21] **4228** 4-9-0 53 PaulMulrennan 7 61
(Bryan Smart) *cl up: led over 2f out: rdn 2 l clr over 1f out: drvn out* **5/1**[2]

-040 **2** *1* **Zebelini (IRE)**[21] **4229** 4-8-3 49 (b) RobertDodsworth(7) 8 53
(Ollie Pears) *led: hdd over 2f out and sn rdn: kpt on u.p fnl f* **18/1**

0-00 **3** *nk* **Horsforth**[21] **4228** 4-9-4 57 (b[1]) ConnorBeasley 5 60
(Richard Guest) *in tch: hdwy wl over 1f out: sn rdn: kpt on fnl f* **10/1**

-304 **4** *nk* **Pavers Star**[36] **3709** 7-9-1 54 (p) BarryMcHugh 9 56
(Noel Wilson) *chsd ldrs: rdn wl over 1f out: drvn and kpt on fnl f* **25/1**

5034 **5** *1* **Men United (FR)**[18] **4365** 3-8-9 54 (t) AlistairRawlinson(3) 13 51+
(Roy Bowring) *towards rr: hdwy on outer wl over 1f out: sn rdn and kpt on: nrst fin* **8/1**[3]

-403 **6** *1/2* **Loumarin (IRE)**[14] **4495** 4-9-4 57 AndrewMullen 4 53
(Michael Appleby) *chsd ldrs: rdn along wl over 1f out: drvn and kpt on same pce fnl f* **4/1**[1]

5433 **7** *1* **Tarnend Lass**[24] **4141** 3-8-7 49 (tp) JamesSullivan 2 41
(Tim Easterby) *prom: rdn 2f out: drvn over 1f out: sn wknd* **10/1**

6035 **8** *nk* **Lizzy's Dream**[14] **4492** 8-8-12 51 LukeMorris 11 43
(Rebecca Bastiman) *towards rr: rdn and hdwy wl over 1f out: sn drvn and no imp* **9/1**

5060 **9** *1 1/4* **Windforpower (IRE)**[15] **4452** 6-9-7 60 (p) DaleSwift 1 47
(Tracy Waggott) *towards rr on inner and sn pushed along: rdn and sme hdwy 2f out: sn drvn and btn* **10/1**

2003 **10** *1* **Minty Jones**[21] **4228** 7-8-10 49 (b) FrannyNorton 6 33
(Michael Mullineaux) *chsd ldrs: rdn along over 2f out: sn wknd* **8/1**[3]

0401 **11** *2 1/2* **Under Approval**[14] **4492** 5-8-8 52 (b) GemmaTutty(5) 3 27
(Karen Tutty) *wnt lft s: a towards rr* **12/1**

64 **12** *1 1/4* **Bahango (IRE)**[32] **3851** 4-9-2 55 (p) GrahamLee 10 25
(Patrick Morris) *stmbld bdly s: a in rr* **20/1**

58.81s (-0.99) **Going Correction** -0.15s/f (Firm)
WFA 3 from 4yo+ 3lb **12** Ran SP% **117.7**
Speed ratings (Par 101): **101,99,98,98,96 96,94,93,91,90 86,84**
CSF £90.85 CT £872.63 TOTE £6.10: £2.00, £6.10, £4.00; EX 107.10 Trifecta £1177.50.
Owner The Smart Inagh River Partnership **Bred** Glebe Farm Stud **Trained** Hambleton, N Yorks

FOCUS
Race distance increased by 6yds. Moderate sprinting form but it could be rated a length higher.

4969 CNG H'CAP (FOR THE ABF SOLDIER'S CHARITY PERPETUAL TROPHY) 1m 5f 175y

3:45 (3:45) (Class 4) (0-85,85) 3-Y-O+
£6,225 (£1,864; £932; £466; £233; £117) **Stalls** Low

Form RPR

4024 **1** **Project Bluebook (FR)**[24] **4137** 3-8-5 75 JasonHart 4 85
(John Quinn) *trckd ldrs on inner: hdwy 3f out: effrt wl over 1f and sn chal: rdn to ld ins fnl f: drvn and hld on wl towards fin* **6/4**[1]

5106 **2** *3/4* **Tartan Bute**[55] **3025** 3-8-2 72 FrannyNorton 1 81
(Mark Johnston) *in rr and niggled along after 4f: pushed along over 5f out: hdwy 3f out: swtchd rt and rdn over 1f out: styd on to chal ins fnl f: ev ch tl no ex towards fin* **7/2**[2]

-013 **3** *4 1/2* **Dominada (IRE)**[27] **4004** 4-9-12 83 BenCurtis 6 86
(Brian Ellison) *trckd ldng pair: hdwy on outer wl over 2f out: sn led: jnd and rdn over 1f out: drvn and hdd ins fnl f: kpt on same pce* **5/1**[3]

1306 **4** *12* **Russian Royale**[17] **4409** 6-9-3 74 PJMcDonald 5 60
(Micky Hammond) *dwlt and in rr: niggled along after 4f: in tch over 4f out: rdn over 3f out and sn wknd* **25/1**

0310 **5** *4* **Be Perfect (USA)**[19] **4311** 7-9-11 82 (p) JamesSullivan 7 63
(Ruth Carr) *led: hdd 7f out: cl up tl led again 4f out: rdn and hdd over 2f out: sn wknd* **13/2**

3112 **6** *5* **Ingleby Hollow**[16] **4430** 4-9-4 80 (p) JoshDoyle(5) 2 54
(David O'Meara) *trckd ldr: led 7f out: pushed along and hdd 4f out: rdn over 3f out: drvn over 2f out and sn wknd* **6/1**

2m 56.6s (-7.00) **Going Correction** -0.20s/f (Firm)
WFA 3 from 4yo+ 13lb **6** Ran SP% **110.4**
Speed ratings (Par 105): **112,111,109,102,99 97**
CSF £6.65 CT £17.95 TOTE £2.30: £1.60, £2.00; EX 7.20 Trifecta £24.50.
Owner Ross Harmon **Bred** S C E A Haras De La Perelle **Trained** Settrington, N Yorks

FOCUS
Race distance increased by 6yds. The 3yos predictably dominated this fair handicap, and the third has been rated to form.

4970 RACING UK PROFITS RETURNED TO RACING H'CAP 5f 212y

4:15 (4:15) (Class 5) (0-75,74) 3-Y-O+ **£2,911** (£866; £432; £216) **Stalls** Low

Form RPR

3110 **1** **Danish Duke (IRE)**[12] **4544** 5-9-6 68 (p) JamesSullivan 4 76
(Ruth Carr) *hld up in tch: hdwy over 2f out: chsd ldrs and n.m.r over 1f out: swtchd rt and rdn ent fnl f: styd on strly to ld nr line* **4/1**[2]

0341 **2** *hd* **Tricky Dicky**[13] **4512** 3-8-9 61 DuranFentiman 1 67
(Olly Williams) *chsd clr ldr: hdwy wl over 1f out: rdn to ld jst ins fnl f: sn drvn: hdd and no ex nr line* **5/2**[1]

0600 **3** *1 1/2* **Mercers Row**[18] **4376** 9-9-5 67 (p) DavidNolan 2 70
(Michael Herrington) *trckd ldrs on inner: effrt and squeezed through to chal ent fnl f: sn rdn and ev ch: kpt on same pce* **16/1**

0010 **4** *nk* **Bold Spirit**[4] **4848** 5-8-12 60 (vt) TomEaves 3 62
(Declan Carroll) *led and sn clr: rdn over 1f out: jnd ent fnl f: sn hdd and drvn: grad wknd* **14/1**

0/22 **5** *1/2* **More Beau (USA)**[18] **4337** 5-9-7 69 BarryMcHugh 8 69
(David Nicholls) *hld up in tch: hdwy on outer 2f out: rdn and ev ch ent fnl f: kpt on same pce* **5/2**[1]

1000 **6** *3 1/4* **Toledo**[47] **3326** 3-8-12 64 [1] SamJames 7 53
(Marjorie Fife) *chsd ldrs: hdwy 2f out and sn rdn: wknd ent fnl f* **50/1**

0000 **7** *2 1/4* **Clergyman**[11] **4608** 4-9-5 67 PaulMulrennan 9 49
(Rebecca Bastiman) *dwlt: hdwy on outer and in tch after 1/2f: rdn along over 2f out: sn wknd* **11/1**

6050 **8** *2 3/4* **Royal Normandy**[25] **4089** 4-9-4 66 BenCurtis 6 40
(David Loughnane) *sn outpcd and a bhd* **7/1**[3]

1m 12.04s (-1.56) **Going Correction** -0.20s/f (Firm)
WFA 3 from 4yo+ 4lb **8** Ran SP% **112.5**
Speed ratings (Par 103): **102,101,99,99,98 94,91,87**
CSF £13.93 CT £138.93 TOTE £4.80: £1.60, £1.20, £5.40; EX 15.30 Trifecta £147.80.
Owner Michael Hill **Bred** Dean Harron & Ciaran Conroy **Trained** Huby, N Yorks

FOCUS
Race distance increased by 6yds. Modest sprinting form, with the winner posting his best form since his early days in Ireland.

4971 RACING UK ANYWHERE H'CAP 1m 7f 177y

4:45 (4:47) (Class 6) (0-65,65) 3-Y-O+ **£2,587** (£770; £384; £192) **Stalls** Low

Form RPR

0000 **1** **Lightning Steps**[15] **4456** 4-8-9 46 oh1 DavidAllan 7 53
(Declan Carroll) *hld up: stdy hdwy over 4f out: chsd ldrs over 2f out: rdn over 1f out: led ent fnl f: drvn clr* **66/1**

5534 **2** *3 1/2* **Bowdler's Magic**[1] **4935** 9-10-0 65 PhillipMakin 1 68
(David Thompson) *hld up in rr: hdwy over 4f out: chsd ldrs on outer 2f out: rdn wl over 1f out: drvn to chse wnr ins fnl f: no imp* **7/1**[3]

440/ **3** *1 1/2* **Dynamic Drive (IRE)**[17] **6758** 9-8-12 49 (t) PaulMulrennan 12 50+
(Maurice Barnes) *hld up towards rr: stdy hdwy 6f out: trckd ldrs over 3f out: led jst over 2f out and sn rdn: drvn and hdd ent fnl f: kpt on same pce* **11/4**[2]

-264 **4** *1 1/2* **Exclusive Contract (IRE)**[21] **4239** 5-9-7 61 JacobButterfield(3) 11 60
(Ollie Pears) *trckd ldrs: hdwy over 4f out: chsd ldr over 3f out: rdn and cl up 2f out: drvn over 1f out: kpt on same pce* **12/1**

0600 **5** *1 3/4* **Yorkshireman (IRE)**[10] **4645** 6-8-10 47 oh1 ow1 (b) PaddyAspell 10 44
(Lynn Siddall) *trckd ldrs: hdwy to trck ldr after 7f: led over 4f out: rdn along over 3f out: hdd over 2f out: sn drvn and grad wknd* **33/1**

-0P0 **6** *1/2* **Kisumu**[21] **4237** 4-9-9 60 PJMcDonald 14 58
(Micky Hammond) *in tch: effrt 4f out: rdn along wl over 2f out: sn no imp* **18/1**

0-00 **7** *2 3/4* **Crakehall Lad (IRE)**[15] **4194** 5-8-12 49 NeilFarley 3 42
(Andrew Crook) *trckd ldrs on inner: effrt 4f out: rdn along over 2f out: sn drvn and wknd over 1f out* **12/1**

5-05 **8** *7* **Keep Up (GER)**[13] **4515** 4-8-9 46 oh1 (p) AndrewMullen 5 31
(Philip Kirby) *s.i.s: a in rr* **40/1**

4-06 **9** *3 1/4* **Arriella**[34] 3774 4-8-9 **46** oh1......(p) ConnorBeasley 9 27
(John Davies) *a in rr* **50/1**

05-0 **10** *5* **Rocky Two (IRE)**[23] 2745 6-8-4 **46** oh1......(p) PhilDennis(5) 13 21
(Philip Kirby) *prom: rdn along over 4f out: sn wknd* **33/1**

0056 **11** *18* **Invincible Bond**[18] 4340 3-8-1 **53** oh4 ow1...... PatrickMathers 6 7
(Simon Waugh) *prom: rdn along over 4f out: sn wknd* **40/1**

-052 **12** *66* **Monjeni**[15] 4450 3-8-10 **62**......(v) LukeMorris 2
(Sir Mark Prescott Bt) *plld hrd: led: stmbld bdly after 2f: rdn along 5f out: sn hdd & wknd rapidly* **11/10**[1]

3m 29.22s (-2.78) **Going Correction** -0.20s/f (Firm)
WFA 3 from 4yo+ 15lb **12** Ran SP% **121.6**
Speed ratings (Par 101): **98,96,95,94,93 93,92,88,87,84 75,42**
CSF £479.25 CT £1744.56 TOTE £64.30: £13.30, £2.30, £1.60; EX 608.90 Trifecta £4227.40.
Owner The Commissioning Team **Bred** Mrs S Hamilton & Kirtlington Stud Ltd **Trained** Malton, N Yorks

FOCUS
Race distance increased by 6yds. A race that set up for the closers, with the favourite going off too fast, and it has been rated around the second.

4972 12TH AUGUST IS LADIES' EVENING H'CAP (DIV I) 7f
5:15 (5:18) (Class 6) (0-65,65) 3-Y-O **£2,587** (£770; £384; £192) **Stalls** Low

Form RPR

040U **1** **Beadlam (IRE)**[31] 3877 3-8-6 **50**...... PJMcDonald 1 57
(David Loughnane) *chsd clr ldr: hdwy over 2f out: rdn to ld over 1f out: kpt on strly* **20/1**

05 **2** *2 3/4* **Indian Pursuit (IRE)**[13] 4517 3-9-7 **65**...... JasonHart 5 65+
(John Quinn) *hld up towards rr: hdwy over 2f out: rdn to chse ldrs over 1f out: drvn and kpt on fnl f* **13/2**

3501 **3** *hd* **Mango Chutney**[11] 4600 3-9-2 **60**......(p) PhillipMakin 4 59+
(John Davies) *midfield: hdwy to trck ldrs on inner whn slipped over 3f out: effrt and chsng ldrs 2f out: sn rdn: styd on same pce fnl f* **5/2**[1]

00-6 **4** *1 1/4* **Lilozza (IRE)**[16] 4429 3-8-5 **52**...... RachelRichardson(3) 7 48
(Tim Easterby) *in rr: hdwy over 2f out: sn rdn: styd on fnl f* **16/1**

2335 **5** *1 3/4* **Strummer (IRE)**[9] 4684 3-9-7 **65**......(b1) TomEaves 2 56
(Kevin Ryan) *led and sn clr: rdn: edgd rt and hdd over 1f out: sn drvn: hung bdly rt and wknd fnl f* **10/3**[2]

2602 **6** *3/4* **Ada Misobel (IRE)**[14] 4498 3-8-4 **55**......(p) KevinLundie(7) 8 44+
(Roy Bowring) *in tch: hdwy on outer over 3f out: wd st: rdn to chse ldrs 2f out: drvn over 1f out: sn one pce* **5/1**[3]

360 **7** *5* **Dalalah**[6] 4770 3-8-5 **49** ow1......(p) ConnorBeasley 9 25
(Richard Guest) *dwlt: a in rr* **25/1**

504 **8** *3 3/4* **Coquine**[20] 4258 3-8-10 **59**...... JoshDoyle(5) 11 25
(David O'Meara) *dwlt: a in rr* **16/1**

0-66 **9** *1* **Bigbadboy (IRE)**[42] 3483 3-8-8 **52**...... BarryMcHugh 6 15
(Clive Mulhall) *chsd ldrs: rdn along 3f out: sn drvn and wknd* **25/1**

0-03 **10** *11* **Bahrikate**[36] 3710 3-8-2 **46** oh1......(p) JamesSullivan 3
(Michael Herrington) *chsd ldrs: rdn along over 3f out: sn wknd* **14/1**

1m 26.41s (-0.59) **Going Correction** -0.20s/f (Firm) **10** Ran SP% **112.5**
Speed ratings (Par 98): **95,91,91,90,88 87,81,77,76,63**
CSF £136.68 CT £441.90 TOTE £13.50: £4.40, £2.20, £1.60; EX 72.10 Trifecta £742.20.
Owner R G Fell **Bred** Pipe View Stud **Trained** Market Drayton, Shropshire

FOCUS
A weak handicap. Race distance increased by 6yds.

4973 12TH AUGUST IS LADIES' EVENING H'CAP (DIV II) 7f
5:45 (5:51) (Class 6) (0-65,65) 3-Y-O **£2,587** (£770; £384; £192) **Stalls** Low

Form RPR

0003 **1** **Baby Ballerina**[27] 4003 3-9-7 **65**......(b) BenCurtis 1 72
(Brian Ellison) *trckd ldrs: hdwy over 2f out: rdn to ld 1 1/2f out: styd on strly fnl f* **5/2**[1]

S413 **2** *1 1/2* **Deben**[14] 4490 3-9-0 **58**...... JoeDoyle 4 61+
(Kevin Ryan) *hld up towards rr: hdwy over 2f out: rdn over 1f out: drvn to chse wnr ins fnl f: no imp towards fin* **5/2**[1]

0002 **3** *1/2* **Cuppatee (IRE)**[4] 4848 3-9-6 **64**...... PJMcDonald 6 66
(Ann Duffield) *trckd ldrs: hdwy on outer 2f out: rdn to chse wnr appr fnl f: sn drvn and kpt on same pce* **9/2**[2]

0004 **4** *1 1/2* **Kingfisher Girl**[34] 3777 3-8-4 **48**...... LukeMorris 10 46
(Michael Appleby) *sn chsng ldr: hdwy and cl up over 2f out: rdn wl over 1f out: sn drvn and kpt on same pce* **16/1**

4000 **5** *hd* **Bazula (IRE)**[11] 4600 3-8-7 **54**......(b) RachelRichardson(3) 3 51
(Tim Easterby) *led: rdn along over 2f out: hdd 1 1/2f out: sn drvn and grad wknd* **20/1**

0603 **6** *1 1/4* **A Boy Named Sue**[11] 4600 3-8-5 **49**...... JamesSullivan 9 43
(Peter Niven) *in tch: hdwy on outer to chse ldrs over 2f out: rdn along wl over 1f out: sn no imp* **15/2**[3]

0-00 **7** *1 1/2* **Canford Thompson**[78] 2306 3-8-13 **62**...... RobJFitzpatrick(5) 5 52
(Micky Hammond) *a in rr* **33/1**

0-00 **8** *1* **Fast Operator (IRE)**[19] 4316 3-8-8 **52**...... TomEaves 2 39
(Nigel Tinkler) *trckd ldrs: effrt 2f out: sn rdn and wknd* **33/1**

6300 **9** *1 3/4* **Dark Confidant (IRE)**[17] 4410 3-8-12 **56**...... ConnorBeasley 7 38
(Richard Guest) *a in rr* **12/1**

0-00 **10** *1 1/4* **Mission Mars**[70] 2553 3-8-6 **50**...... DuranFentiman 8 29
(Patrick Holmes) *a in rr* **40/1**

1m 26.17s (-0.83) **Going Correction** -0.20s/f (Firm) **10** Ran SP% **113.7**
Speed ratings (Par 98): **96,94,93,92,91 90,88,87,85,84**
CSF £7.73 CT £25.68 TOTE £3.60: £1.40, £1.40, £1.90; EX 9.70 Trifecta £29.20.
Owner Julie & Keith Hanson **Bred** Howard Barton Stud **Trained** Norton, N Yorks

FOCUS
The second division of the weak 7f handicap. It paid to be handy and the winner is rated back to form. Race distance increased by 6yds.
T/Plt: £600.90 to a £1 stake. Pool of £63358.88 - 76.97 winning tickets. T/Qpdt: £39.30 to a £1 stake. Pool of £7656.79 - 143.88 winning tickets. **Joe Rowntree**

4472 CHELMSFORD (A.W) (L-H)
Tuesday, August 2

OFFICIAL GOING: Polytrack: standard
Wind: light, behind Weather: cloudy, light rain at times

4974 TOTEPLACEPOT SIX PLACES IN SIX RACES NURSERY H'CAP 6f (P)
6:20 (6:20) (Class 4) (0-85,78) 2-Y-O **£6,469** (£1,925; £962; £481) **Stalls** Centre

Form RPR

15 **1** **Spiritual Lady**[17] 4394 2-9-7 **78**...... DanielTudhope 5 94+
(Philip McBride) *hld up in tch: clsd to trck ldrs and nt clr run 2f out: hdwy to ld on bit ent fnl f: nudged along and sn qcknd clr: v easily* **10/11**[1]

4321 **2** *3 3/4* **La Casa Tarifa (IRE)**[7] 4725 2-9-3 **74** 6ex...... JoeFanning 4 76
(Mark Johnston) *chsd ldng pair: clsd to press ldrs 2f out: drvn and ev ch over 1f out: wnt 2nd but nt matching pce of wnr 1f out: wl hld and kpt on same pce after* **9/2**[3]

522 **3** *3/4* **Wahash (IRE)**[13] 4533 2-9-4 **75**...... FrankieDettori 2 75
(Richard Hannon) *w ldr: rdn to ld wl over 1f out: hdd and unable qck w wnr ent fnl f: wl hld 3rd and styd on same pce fnl f* **9/4**[2]

3614 **4** *3 1/2* **Hi Milady (IRE)**[25] 4090 2-9-0 **71**......(b1) JimCrowley 1 60
(Dominic Ffrench Davis) *sn bustled up to ld: rdn and hdd wl over 1f out: sn outpcd: wknd fnl f* **20/1**

3004 **5** *12* **Kings Heart (IRE)**[8] 4712 2-8-13 **70**...... JamieSpencer 3 20
(Mark Usher) *s.i.s: a in rr: rdn 2f out: sn wl btn: wl bhd and eased wl ins fnl f* **12/1**

1m 11.96s (-1.74) **Going Correction** -0.10s/f (Stan) **5** Ran SP% **113.8**
Speed ratings (Par 96): **107,102,101,96,80**
CSF £5.82 TOTE £1.80: £1.10, £2.30; EX 5.50 Trifecta £9.30.
Owner PMRacing **Bred** J W Mitchell **Trained** Newmarket, Suffolk

FOCUS
An ordinary nursery that had an above-average winner and which was run at a sound pace despite the small field.

4975 TOTEPOOL LIVE INFO DOWNLOAD THE APP EBF MAIDEN STKS (PLUS 10 RACE) 1m (P)
6:50 (6:51) (Class 4) 2-Y-O **£6,469** (£1,925; £962; £481) **Stalls** Low

Form RPR

0 **1** **Walter Raleigh (IRE)**[93] 1889 2-9-5 0...... AdamKirby 3 83
(John Ryan) *pressed ldr: rdn and wnt clr w ldr wl over 1f out: rdn to ld ins fnl f: sn in command and r.o wl: readily* **8/1**[3]

4 **2** *2* **Al Hamdany (IRE)**[68] 2604 2-9-2 0...... DanielMuscutt(3) 2 78
(Marco Botti) *led and set stdy gallop: rdn and wnt clr w wnr wl over 1f out: edgd rt 1f out: edgd bk lft u.p and hdd ins fnl f: styd on same pce after* **11/4**[2]

F **3** *5* **Paddy A (IRE)**[29] 3954 2-9-5 0...... DanielTudhope 1 67
(Philip McBride) *hld up wl in tch in midfield: 3rd and rdn ent fnl 2f: outpcd over 1f out: wl hld but kpt on to hold 3rd fnl f* **25/1**

4 *1 1/2* **Mashadie Boy** 2-9-5 0...... JamieSpencer 5 63+
(David Simcock) *s.i.s: hld up in tch in rr: nt clr run over 2f out: effrt on inner wl over 1f out: wnt 4th ent fnl f: styd on same pce: no ch w ldrs* **2/1**[1]

5 *3 1/4* **Baileys Apprentice** 2-9-0 0...... JoeFanning 7 51
(Mark Johnston) *restless in stalls: in tch in last pair: effrt on outer over 2f out: outpcd and btn over 1f out: wknd fnl f* **8/1**[3]

00 **6** *4* **Pentito Rap (USA)**[18] 4363 2-9-5 0...... RyanPowell 4 46
(Sir Mark Prescott Bt) *t.k.h: hld up wl in tch in midfield: rdn 3f out: outpcd wl over 1f out: sn wknd* **66/1**

26 **7** *2 1/2* **See The Sea (IRE)**[19] 4298 2-9-0 0...... JimCrowley 6 36
(Richard Hannon) *pushed along leaving stalls: sn chsng ldng pair: rdn and lost pl over 2f out: bhd over 1f out* **11/4**[2]

1m 39.83s (-0.07) **Going Correction** -0.10s/f (Stan) **7** Ran SP% **114.2**
Speed ratings (Par 96): **96,94,89,87,84 80,77**
CSF £30.21 TOTE £10.20: £3.90, £2.50; EX 34.90 Trifecta £313.60.
Owner A Dee & G Smith Bernal **Bred** Deerfield Farm **Trained** Newmarket, Suffolk

FOCUS
An ordinary maiden dominated by the front-runners, and won in good style. The level is fluid.

4976 TOTEQUADPOT INSURE YOUR PLACEPOT LAST FOUR H'CAP 1m (P)
7:20 (7:24) (Class 3) (0-95,95) 3-Y-O+ **£9,703** (£2,887; £1,443; £721) **Stalls** Low

Form RPR

-124 **1** **Firmament**[17] 4399 4-9-10 **91**...... DanielTudhope 7 104+
(David O'Meara) *hld up in tch in midfield: effrt over 1f out: rdn and hdwy 1f out: chsd ldr ins fnl f: r.o wl to ld wl ins fnl f: sn in command* **9/2**[3]

-654 **2** *1 1/2* **Mustaaqeem (USA)**[24] 4129 4-9-5 **86**......(v1) PaulHanagan 5 95
(Sir Michael Stoute) *led: 3 l clr and rdn wl over 1f out: kpt on u.p tl hdd and no ex wl ins fnl f* **3/1**[1]

3661 **3** *2 1/2* **Fuwairt (IRE)**[14] 4474 4-8-8 **82**...... CameronNoble(7) 4 85
(David Loughnane) *chsd ldng pair: effrt to chse ldr over 1f out: no imp and lost 2nd ins fnl f: edgd lft and kpt on same pce after* **8/1**

2260 **4** *3/4* **Lazzam**[10] 4624 3-9-2 **93**......[1] DanielMuscutt(3) 9 94
(Marco Botti) *stdd s: hld up in tch in last pair: effrt on inner over 1f out: no imp on ldng pair ins fnl f: kpt on to go 4th last strides* **9/2**[3]

1215 **5** *hd* **Welliesinthewater (IRE)**[31] 3895 6-8-12 **82**......(v) NoelGarbutt(3) 1 83
(Derek Shaw) *chsd ldr: rdn 2f out: unable qck and lost 2nd over 1f out: wl hld and kpt on same pce ins fnl f* **20/1**

4351 **6** *3/4* **Strong Steps**[47] 3303 4-9-8 **92**......(p) MarcMonaghan(3) 2 91
(Hugo Palmer) *hld up in tch in midfield: effrt over 1f out: drvn and no hdwy 1f out: wl hld and kpt on same pce fnl f* **7/2**[2]

2041 **7** *46* **Ice Royal (IRE)**[13] 4532 3-8-13 **87**...... JamieSpencer 6
(Jamie Osborne) *dwlt: hld up in tch in last pair: rdn wl over 2f out: sn struggling and bhd over 1f out: heavily eased ins fnl f: t.o* **7/1**

1-26 **8** *4* **Ian's Memory (USA)**[139] 960 5-10-0 **95**......(b) MartinHarley 8
(Jeremy Noseda) *hld up in tch in last pair: hung rt bnd 3f out: btn 2f out: heavily eased ins fnl f: t.o* **20/1**

1m 36.92s (-2.98) **Going Correction** -0.10s/f (Stan)
WFA 3 from 4yo+ 7lb **8** Ran SP% **116.7**
Speed ratings (Par 107): **110,108,106,105,105 104,58,54**
CSF £18.86 CT £101.88 TOTE £5.50: £1.80, £1.70, £2.10; EX 19.20 Trifecta £110.70.
Owner Gallop Racing **Bred** Cheveley Park Stud Ltd **Trained** Upper Helmsley, N Yorks

FOCUS
A decent looking handicap for the course, with some improving sorts battling it out. The second has been rated to form.

4977 TOTETRIFECTA PICK THE 1,2,3 FILLIES' H'CAP 1m 2f (P)
7:50 (7:50) (Class 3) (0-90,84) 3-Y-O+ **£9,703** (£2,887; £1,443; £721) **Stalls** Low

Form RPR

615 **1** **Haddajah (IRE)**[38] 3665 3-9-5 **84**...... FrankieDettori 3 92
(Sir Michael Stoute) *pressed ldr: drvn ent fnl 2f out: stl ev ch and hrd drvn 1f out: styd on to ld last stride* **5/2**[2]

0543 **2** *shd* **Age Of Elegance (IRE)**[8] 4702 4-9-0 **70**......(p) DanielTudhope 1 77
(David Loughnane) *t.k.h: hld up in cl 3rd: rdn to ld over 1f out: stl hrd pressed and drvn 1f out: styd on u.p: hdd last stride* **4/1**[3]

41 **3** *3* **The Begum**[30] 3919 3-9-0 **79**...... JimCrowley 5 80
(Ralph Beckett) *hld up in cl 4th: effrt 2f out: drvn to go 3rd over 1f out: unable qck ent fnl f: outpcd fnl 150yds* **1/1**[1]

631 **4** 4 ½ **Della Valle (GER)**[43] 3467 3-9-1 **80**.................................... HarryBentley 4 72
(Mike Murphy) *led and set stdy gallop: grad qcknd gallop 3f out: rdn and hdd over 1f out: sn lost pl: wknd fnl f* **10/1**

2m 9.73s (1.13) **Going Correction** -0.10s/f (Stan)
WFA 3 from 4yo 9lb **4** Ran SP% **107.7**
Speed ratings (Par 104): **91,90,88,84**
CSF £11.67 TOTE £3.00; EX 8.10 Trifecta £12.10.
Owner Al Shaqab Racing **Bred** Sunderland Holding Inc & R P Blds Ltd **Trained** Newmarket, Suffolk

FOCUS
Muddling form, with the second setting the standard.

4978 TOTEPOOL FOLLOW US ON TWITTER MAIDEN FILLIES' STKS 1m 2f (P)
8:20 (8:22) (Class 4) 3-Y-O+ **£6,469** (£1,925; £962; £481) **Stalls** Low

Form RPR
-335 **1** **Ecureuil (IRE)**[28] 3990 3-9-0 76.................................... JimCrowley 1 83
(Hugo Palmer) *mde virtually all: pushed 3 l clr 2f out: drvn jst ins fnl f: pressed towards fin but a doing enough: rdn out* **6/1**

43 **2** ½ **Entsar (IRE)**[39] 3601 3-9-0 0.................................... FrankieDettori 6 82+
(William Haggas) *hld up in tch in midfield: effrt on outer to chse ldr over 2f out: drvn to chse clr wnr 1f out: styd on u.p and pressing wnr towards fin: a hld* **2/1**[1]

54- **3** 2 ¼ **Canonbury (IRE)**[311] 6737 3-9-0 0.................................... TedDurcan 5 78
(Sir Michael Stoute) *dwlt: steadily rcvrd and chsd ldrs after 2f: wnt 2nd over 3f out: rdn and unable qck 2f out: 3rd and styd on same pce ins fnl f* **9/2**[3]

3-5 **4** 7 **Nawkhatha (USA)**[18] 4361 3-9-0 0.................................... PaulHanagan 3 64
(Brian Meehan) *in tch in midfield: effrt in 4th over 2f out: sn outpcd and wl hld over 1f out: plugged on and hld modest 4th ins fnl f* **7/1**

5 ¾ **Blazing Mighty** 3-9-0 0.................................... AdrianMcCarthy 8 62
(Robyn Brisland) *s.i.s and rn green early: clsd and in tch in rr after 2f: rdn and outpcd over 2f out: edgd lft but passed btn rivals over 1f out: wl hld and plugged on ins fnl f* **66/1**

06 **6** ½ **Pure Innocence (IRE)**[19] 4319 3-9-0 0.................................... HarryBentley 9 61
(Ralph Beckett) *in tch in last trio: effrt over 2f out: sn no imp and wl hld 6th over 1f out: plugged on fnl f* **20/1**

3 **7** 3 ¼ **Blue Jean Baby**[18] 4367 3-9-0 0.................................... MartinHarley 10 55
(George Scott) *hld up in tch in last trio: effrt u.p in 5th over 2f out: hung lft: no hdwy and btn over 1f out: wknd ins fnl f* **11/4**[2]

0/2 **8** 5 **Medicean Queen (IRE)**[178] 487 5-9-2 0.................................... JaneElliott(7) 2 45
(Phil McEntee) *chsd ldrs: ducked rt and rdn along briefly 8f out: rdn and lost pl over 3f out: wl bhd over 1f out* **50/1**

-46 **9** 33 **Harikiri (IRE)**[78] 2312 3-9-0 0.................................... JamieSpencer 4
(Charles Hills) *w ldr tl lost pl over 3f out: bhd 2f out: virtually p.u fnl f: t.o* **25/1**

2m 5.96s (-2.64) **Going Correction** -0.10s/f (Stan)
WFA 3 from 5yo 9lb **9** Ran SP% **117.0**
Speed ratings (Par 102): **106,105,103,98,97 97,94,90,64**
CSF £18.18 TOTE £7.30: £1.80, £1.30, £1.90; EX 20.90 Trifecta £85.70.
Owner Al Asayl Bloodstock Ltd **Bred** J F Tuthill **Trained** Newmarket, Suffolk

FOCUS
Another front-running success in an okay fillies' maiden, with the winner rated to a better view of her previous form.

4979 TOTEPOOL LIKE US ON FACEBOOK H'CAP 2m (P)
8:50 (8:52) (Class 6) (0-65,65) 4-Y-O+ **£3,234** (£962; £481; £240) **Stalls** Low

Form RPR
3114 **1** **Yasir (USA)**[8] 4716 8-8-10 **61**.................................... SophieKilloran(7) 5 70
(Conor Dore) *stdd s: hld up off the pce in rr: clsd and wl in tch 3f out: rdn and hdwy over 1f out: led 1f out: r.o wl: rdn out* **9/1**

3/00 **2** 2 **Amantius**[28] 3991 7-9-1 **59**.................................... (b) MartinLane 4 65
(Johnny Farrelly) *hld up in rr of main gp: clsd and wl in tch over 3f out: effrt to chal on inner over 1f out: chsd wnr and styd on same pce ins fnl f* **12/1**

11/0 **3** 2 **Atalanta Bay (IRE)**[17] 4381 6-9-7 **65**.................................... RoystonFfrench 2 68
(Marcus Tregoning) *chsd clr ldr: steadily clsd fr 1/2-way: rdn to ld 2f out: drvn over 1f out: hdd 1f out: styd on same pce after* **5/1**

3232 **4** ¾ **Thomas Blossom (IRE)**[14] 4478 6-9-7 **65**.................................... (vt) AdamKirby 6 67
(Ali Stronge) *hld up in midfield: clsd and wl in tch over 3f out: drvn to chal over 1f out tl unable qck 1f out: styd on same pce fnl f* **3/1**[2]

1003 **5** 18 **King Olav (UAE)**[14] 4478 11-9-1 **62**.................................... GeorgeDowning(3) 7 43
(Tony Carroll) *rn in snatches: in midfield: clsd and wl in tch over 3f out: drvn and little rspnse over 2f out: wknd over 1f out* **8/1**

6044 **6** 3 ¾ **County Wexford (IRE)**[19] 4320 5-8-10 **57**.................................... (t) DanielMuscutt(3) 3 33
(Miss Joey Ellis) *led and sn clr: rdn and hdd 2f out: sn wknd* **9/2**[3]

05 **7** 55 **Endive**[56] 2994 4-9-3 **61**.................................... MartinHarley 1
(Robert Stephens) *prom in main gp: rdn and lost pl over 3f out: bhd 2f out: sn eased: t.o* **11/4**[1]

3m 27.62s (-2.38) **Going Correction** -0.10s/f (Stan) **7** Ran SP% **115.3**
Speed ratings (Par 101): **101,100,99,98,89 87,60**
CSF £106.07 TOTE £8.80: £3.90, £6.90; EX 117.00 Trifecta £685.80.
Owner Mrs Jennifer Marsh **Bred** Shadwell Farm LLC **Trained** Hubbert's Bridge, Lincs

FOCUS
A very modest staying handicap, with the winner weak in the market, and the level is fluid.

4980 JOOLS HOLLAND HERE ON 20TH AUGUST H'CAP 5f (P)
9:20 (9:21) (Class 6) (0-65,63) 3-Y-O+ **£3,234** (£962; £481; £240) **Stalls** Low

Form RPR
0066 **1** **The Burnham Mare (IRE)**[13] 4525 3-9-2 **63**.................................... (p) HollieDoyle(7) 7 69
(J S Moore) *led: rdn and hdd 1/2-way: rallied u.p to ld again jst ins fnl f: hld on gamely: rdn out* **7/1**

-366 **2** nk **Poplar**[4] 4835 3-9-4 **58**.................................... MartinHarley 1 63
(Robyn Brisland) *pressed ldr on inner tl led 1/2-way: rdn over 1f out: hdd jst ins fnl f: r.o u.p but a jst hld* **15/8**[1]

-250 **3** 2 ¼ **K'Gari Spirit**[21] 4238 3-9-8 **62**.................................... NickyMackay 5 59
(Jeremy Gask) *in rr: hdwy on inner to chse ldrs 2f out: rdn over 1f out: kpt on same pce ins fnl f* **11/1**

0110 **4** ¾ **Culloden**[10] 4647 4-9-6 **62**.................................... CharlieBennett(5) 6 57
(Shaun Harris) *sn pressing ldr on outer tl edgd rt and outpcd 2f out: sn rdn and unable qck: kpt on same pce fr over 1f out* **4/1**[2]

35-4 **5** 1 **Ryan Style (IRE)**[14] 4472 10-8-10 **52**.................................... (p) PaddyPilley(5) 3 44
(Lisa Williamson) *jostling w rival leaving stalls: midfield: rdn and edgd rt over 2f out: styd on same pce fr over 1f out* **8/1**

2200 **6** 3 ¼ **Excellent Aim**[35] 3741 9-9-5 **63**.................................... JaneElliott(7) 4 43
(George Margarson) *sn in last pair and wd: pushed along 3f out: no imp* **9/1**

4050 **7** 9 **Give Us A Belle (IRE)**[20] 4264 7-9-5 **56**.................................... (bt) AdamKirby 2 4
(Christine Dunnett) *rousted along leaving stalls and jostling w rival: chsd ldrs tl lost pl over 2f out: bhd 1f out* **9/2**[3]

(-0.20) **Going Correction** -0.10s/f (Stan)
WFA 3 from 4yo+ 3lb **7** Ran SP% **114.9**
Speed ratings (Par 101): **97,96,92,91,90 84,70**
CSF £20.82 TOTE £9.30: £4.00, £1.60; EX 24.80 Trifecta £143.00.
Owner The Swan Partnership **Bred** Patrick Cassidy **Trained** Upper Lambourn, Berks

FOCUS
A modest sprint handicap with the winner rated to her nursery form.
T/Plt: £348.90 to a £1 stake. Pool of £69178.56 - 144.73 winning tickets. T/Qpdt: £63.90 to a £1 stake. Pool of £6973.0 - 80.70 winning tickets. **Steve Payne**

4804 NOTTINGHAM (L-H)
Tuesday, August 2

OFFICIAL GOING: Good (good to firm in places) changing to good after race 2 (6.05)
Wind: almost nil Weather: overcast, humid, light drizzle at times

4981 32RED ONLINE CASINO MEDIAN AUCTION MAIDEN STKS 6f 15y
5:35 (5:36) (Class 5) 2-Y-O **£2,911** (£866; £432; £216) **Stalls** High

Form RPR
0 **1** **Gilgamesh**[25] 4103 2-9-5 0.................................... (t) WilliamBuick 5 79
(George Scott) *trckd ldr: led appr fnl f: drvn out* **5/2**[2]

5 **2** ¾ **One Too Many (IRE)**[14] 4494 2-9-0 0.................................... PatCosgrave 9 71
(David Brown) *led: hdd appr fnl f: kpt on same pce* **33/1**

42 **3** 2 **Singing Sands (IRE)**[27] 4011 2-9-0 0.................................... OisinMurphy 10 65
(Ralph Beckett) *trckd ldng pair: effrt over 2f out: kpt on same pce* **1/1**[1]

4 1 ¾ **Sheikspear** 2-9-5 0.................................... JFEgan 1 64
(Joseph Tuite) *swtchd rt after s: trckd ldrs: effrt over 2f out: edgd rt and kpt on same pce fnl f over 1f out* **10/1**[3]

5 1 **Angel Palanas** 2-9-5 0.................................... JoeyHaynes 7 61
(K R Burke) *chsd ldrs: drvn over 2f out: carried rt 1f out: kpt on same pce* **16/1**

00 **6** nk **Baker Street**[32] 3854 2-9-5 0.................................... RichardKingscote 6 60
(Tom Dascombe) *wnt rt s: t.k.h in rr: hdwy over 2f out: kpt on same pce over 1f out* **10/1**[3]

66 **7** 1 ½ **Opening Time**[24] 4154 2-9-0 0.................................... GaryMahon(5) 2 55
(Richard Hannon) *sn chsng ldrs on outside: drvn over 2f out: one pce* **10/1**[3]

8 ¾ **French Pass** 2-9-0 0.................................... AdamBeschizza 3 50+
(Stuart Williams) *in rr: hdwy over 2f out: one pce whn hmpd and nt clr run 1f out* **66/1**

9 5 **Like Minds** 2-9-0 0.................................... ShaneGray 8 32
(David Brown) *dwlt: drvn along in rr: bhd fnl 2f* **50/1**

10 13 **Lady Gwhinnyvere (IRE)** 2-9-0 0.................................... LiamJones 4
(John Spearing) *mid-div: lost pl over 2f out: sn bhd* **100/1**

1m 14.48s (-0.22) **Going Correction** -0.225s/f (Firm) **10** Ran SP% **119.1**
Speed ratings (Par 94): **92,91,88,86,84 84,82,81,74,57**
CSF £86.34 TOTE £3.20: £1.50, £8.40, £1.10; EX 94.40 Trifecta £301.90.
Owner Niarchos Family **Bred** Niarchos Family **Trained** Newmarket, Suffolk

FOCUS
Outer track. Rail was set out 6yds on the home bend adding approximately 18 yards to races 2, 3, 6 and 7. The winner improved on his debut form, although the level is fluid.

4982 32RED.COM NURSERY H'CAP 1m 75y
6:05 (6:05) (Class 5) (0-70,68) 2-Y-O **£2,911** (£866; £432; £216) **Stalls** Centre

Form RPR
306 **1** **See The City (IRE)**[10] 4642 2-9-6 **67**.................................... WilliamBuick 4 76+
(Mark Johnston) *sn chsng ldr: effrt 4f out: led 2f out: forged clr: eased in clsng stages* **2/1**[1]

5314 **2** 2 **Areyoutheway (IRE)**[13] 4509 2-9-4 **65**.................................... (v) RichardKingscote 1 66
(Tom Dascombe) *led: drvn 4f out: hdd 2f out: kpt on same pce* **16/1**

0642 **3** ¾ **Dewan (IRE)**[13] 4510 2-9-7 **68**.................................... CharlesBishop 2 67
(Mick Channon) *trckd ldrs: effrt over 3f out: kpt on same pce fnl 2f* **4/1**[2]

000 **4** 1 ¼ **Blast Of Faith (IRE)**[14] 4479 2-8-3 **57**.................................... DavidEgan(7) 7 53+
(Richard Hughes) *s.i.s: t.k.h: hdwy after 2f: chsng ldrs over 3f out: one pce fnl 2f* **16/1**

605 **5** 1 ¾ **Moneyoryourlife**[38] 3668 2-8-13 **65**.................................... GaryMahon(5) 3 57
(Richard Hannon) *dwlt: sn chsng ldrs: drvn 3f out: one pce* **8/1**

000 **6** 2 ¾ **Hawridge Glory (IRE)**[41] 3529 2-9-4 **65**.................................... FrederikTylicki 8 51
(Rod Millman) *in rr: drvn 4f out: sme hdwy 2f out: nvr a factor* **6/1**[3]

054 **7** 6 **Zamadance**[33] 3799 2-9-1 **62**.................................... OisinMurphy 6 38+
(Sylvester Kirk) *trckd ldrs: t.k.h: drvn 3f out: hung rt and wknd 2f out: bhd whn eased fnl f* **4/1**[2]

1m 48.94s (-0.06) **Going Correction** -0.075s/f (Good) **7** Ran SP% **110.5**
Speed ratings (Par 94): **97,95,94,93,91 88,82**
CSF £33.17 CT £110.27 TOTE £3.10: £1.60, £6.70; EX 22.30 Trifecta £70.30.
Owner Abdulla Al Mansoori **Bred** Epona Bloodstock Ltd And P A Byrne **Trained** Middleham Moor, N Yorks

FOCUS
Race distance increased by about 18yds. A stern test for 2yos. However, the decent early pace eased after a couple of furlongs and the first pair were always up there. An improving winner, with the second rated to a better view of his selling win.

4983 £10 FREE AT 32RED.COM MAIDEN STKS 1m 2f 50y
6:35 (6:35) (Class 5) 3-Y-O+ **£2,911** (£866; £432; £216) **Stalls** Low

Form RPR
04 **1** **Straw Hat (IRE)**[18] 4367 3-9-0 0.................................... PatCosgrave 1 65+
(William Haggas) *trckd ldr: led 3f out: pushed abt 6 l clr appr fnl f: heavily eased last 75yds* **30/100**[1]

6 **2** 1 ½ **Jonofark (IRE)**[18] 4347 3-9-5 0.................................... JFEgan 7 59
(Brian Rothwell) *hld up in rr: t.k.h: hdwy over 3f out: chsd wnr over 1f out: kpt on one pce* **100/1**

0 **3** ½ **Idyllic (IRE)**[92] 1931 3-9-0 0.................................... StevieDonohoe 3 53
(Sir Michael Stoute) *s.i.s: sn trcking ldrs: drvn over 3f out: hung lft and one pce fnl 2f* **4/1**[2]

0 **4** 2 ¼ **Zamindo**[19] 4313 3-9-5 0.................................... FrannyNorton 5 54
(Mark Johnston) *led: hdd 3f out: wknd fnl f: eased nr fin* **20/1**

5 2 **Macksville (IRE)** 3-9-5 0.................................... AdamBeschizza 6 50
(Jeremy Gask) *s.i.s: pushed along over 5f out: chsng ldrs over 3f out: wknd over 1f out* **25/1**

The Form Book, Raceform Ltd, Newbury, RG14 5SJ

5 **6** *13* **Eastern Shore (IRE)**[32] 3856 3-9-5 0................................ JoeyHaynes 2 25
(K R Burke) *in rr: drvn over 4f out: lost pl over 2f out* **12/1**[3]

2m 17.34s (3.04) **Going Correction** -0.075s/f (Good) **6** Ran SP% **114.2**
Speed ratings (Par 103): **84,82,82,80,79 68**
CSF £62.94 TOTE £1.20: £1.10, £13.70; EX 33.30 Trifecta £131.80.
Owner Old Harrovian Racing Club **Bred** Barronstown Stud **Trained** Newmarket, Suffolk

FOCUS
Race distance increased by about 18yds. The ground was downgraded to good all over prior to this uncompetitive maiden. There was an uneven pace on and this has been rated cautiously.

4984 32RED FILLIES' H'CAP — 6f 15y
7:05 (7:05) (Class 4) (0-85,85) 3-Y-O+ **£5,175** (£1,540; £769; £384) **Stalls** High

Form RPR

10-3 **1** **Southern Belle (IRE)**[21] 4223 3-9-6 **83**...................... GrahamGibbons 7 94
(Robert Cowell) *pushed along early to sn chse ldrs: 2nd over 3f out: led over 2f out: edgd rt and foraged clr last 75yds* **5/1**

2123 **2** *1 ¾* **Rococoa (IRE)**[18] 4360 3-8-13 **76**.................................... WilliamBuick 4 81
(Ed Walker) *hld up: effrt and nt clr run over 2f out: edgd lft and chsd wnr over 1f out: upsides 150yds out: kpt on same pce* **2/1**[1]

0121 **3** *5* **Emerald Loch**[26] 4034 3-9-2 **79**......................................(p) OisinMurphy 1 68
(Ralph Beckett) *trckd ldrs on outer: drvn over 2f out: wknd fnl f* **7/2**[3]

-211 **4** *nk* **Darma (IRE)**[14] 4496 4-9-1 **81**....................................... JoshuaBryan(7) 5 70
(Martyn Meade) *led 1f: trckd ldrs: drvn over 2f out: wknd over 1f out* **5/2**[2]

35 **5** *12* **Diamond Lady**[26] 4066 5-9-10 **83**................................... FrederikTylicki 3 34
(William Stone) *w ldr: led after 1f: hdd over 2f out: wkng whn hmpd over 1f out: sn eased and bhd* **10/1**

1m 12.75s (-1.95) **Going Correction** -0.225s/f (Firm)
WFA 3 from 4yo+ 4lb **5** Ran SP% **109.9**
Speed ratings (Par 102): **104,101,95,94,78**
CSF £15.33 TOTE £4.90: £2.70, £1.20; EX 15.30 Trifecta £32.80.
Owner Ahmed Jaber **Bred** Rabbah Bloodstock Limited **Trained** Six Mile Bottom, Cambs

FOCUS
Only one of these fillies had not previously won over C&D and the form looks strong with two coming well clear. A pb from the winner, with the second setting the standard.

4985 32RED.COM H'CAP — 6f 15y
7:35 (7:36) (Class 5) (0-75,75) 3-Y-O **£3,234** (£962; £481; £240) **Stalls** High

Form RPR

2501 **1** **King Of Spin**[14] 4485 3-9-1 **72**.......................................(t) RobHornby(3) 3 80
(William Muir) *trckd ldrs: effrt over 1f out: led last 75yds: drvn out* **5/1**[3]

1536 **2** *¾* **Semana Santa**[28] 3978 3-9-4 **72**.................................. GrahamGibbons 7 77
(David Barron) *sn trcking ldrs stands' side: effrt over 1f out: kpt on to take 2nd clsng stages* **8/1**

2015 **3** *¾* **Sir Theodore (IRE)**[33] 3806 3-9-2 **75**...................... CallumShepherd(5) 5 78
(Richard Spencer) *swtchd rt s: led: edgd lft over 1f out: hdd and no ex last 75yds* **10/1**

1-3 **4** *2* **Balance**[22] 4191 3-9-0 **73**... AdamMcNamara(5) 2 69
(Richard Fahey) *w ldrs: edgd rt and wknd last 50yds* **15/8**[1]

4-01 **5** *1 ½* **First Wheat**[27] 4007 3-8-13 **72**..................................... NathanEvans(5) 4 63
(Michael Easterby) *trckd ldrs: t.k.h: edgd lft to outside and reminders over 3f out: sn outpcd: kpt on fnl f* **4/1**[2]

041 **6** *1 ½* **Peter Park**[13] 4517 3-8-12 **73**.. WilliamCox(7) 6 60
(Clive Cox) *sn chsng ldrs: one pce over 1f out* **7/1**

5440 **7** *1 ¾* **Spice Mill (IRE)**[31] 3907 3-8-8 **62**...............................(tp) AndrewMullen 1 43
(Michael Appleby) *w ldrs: drvn over 2f out: lost pl over 1f out* **12/1**

1m 14.36s (-0.34) **Going Correction** -0.225s/f (Firm) **7** Ran SP% **111.8**
Speed ratings (Par 100): **93,92,91,88,86 84,82**
CSF £41.33 TOTE £5.00: £2.70, £4.10; EX 36.20 Trifecta £327.70.
Owner Muir Racing Partnership - Nottingham **Bred** Cheveley Park Stud Ltd **Trained** Lambourn, Berks

FOCUS
Not bad 3yo sprint handicap and it was run at a generous pace. It might prove better than rated.

4986 32REDSPORT.COM H'CAP — 1m 75y
8:05 (8:06) (Class 5) (0-75,73) 3-Y-O+ **£3,234** (£962; £481; £240) **Stalls** Centre

Form RPR

55 **1** **Lawyer (IRE)**[4] 4841 5-10-0 **73**.. PhillipMakin 1 82
(David Barron) *trckd ldrs: effrt and swtchd rt 2f out: styd on to ld 1f out: drvn out* **11/4**[1]

400 **2** *2* **Sunscape (IRE)**[12] 4549 3-9-4 **70**...................................[1] OisinMurphy 8 74
(Hughie Morrison) *sn trcking ldrs: t.k.h: led over 2f out: hdd 1f out: kpt on same pce* **12/1**

-023 **3** *1 ¼* **Arithmetic (IRE)**[51] 3189 3-9-4 **70**............................ MichaelJMMurphy 2 71
(Charles Hills) *sn w ldr: led after 2f: hdd over 2f out: kpt on same pce fnl f* **4/1**[3]

2514 **4** *½* **Cabal**[16] 4429 9-10-0 **73**...(v) DavidAllan 7 74
(Geoffrey Harker) *hld up in rr: effrt over 3f out: kpt on same pce fnl 2f* **10/1**

2352 **5** *½* **La Celebs Ville (IRE)**[17] 4382 3-9-6 **72**.................(p) RichardKingscote 6 71
(Tom Dascombe) *led 2f: chsd ldr: upsides over 2f out: one pce over 1f out* **7/2**[2]

2-15 **6** *3 ¼* **Billy Bond**[21] 4232 4-9-9 **73**...................................(v) AdamMcNamara(5) 3 65
(Richard Fahey) *hld up towards rr: hdwy on ins to chse ldrs over 3f out: wknd over 1f out: b.b.v* **8/1**

3463 **7** *6* **Overlord**[12] 4567 4-8-11 **56**.. GrahamLee 5 34
(Mark Rimell) *chsd ldrs: pushed along over 5f out: lost pl over 1f out: sn bhd* **8/1**

1m 48.04s (-0.96) **Going Correction** -0.075s/f (Good)
WFA 3 from 4yo+ 7lb **7** Ran SP% **107.9**
Speed ratings (Par 103): **101,99,97,97,96 93,87**
CSF £31.43 CT £111.78 TOTE £3.40: £2.00, £4.20; EX 26.20 Trifecta £140.00.
Owner John Knotts **Bred** Drumlin Bloodstock **Trained** Maunby, N Yorks

FOCUS
Race distance increased by about 18yds. A modest handicap, run at a routine pace. The winner is rated a length up on his Ripon victory.

4987 32RED ON THE APP STORE H'CAP — 1m 2f 50y
8:35 (8:36) (Class 6) (0-60,60) 3-Y-O **£2,264** (£673; £336; £168) **Stalls** Low

Form RPR

-000 **1** **File Of Facts (IRE)**[21] 4233 3-9-2 **55**.....................(vt) RichardKingscote 5 63
(Tom Dascombe) *led after 1f: reminders over 3f out: fnd ex and forged away last 75yds* **20/1**

3563 **2** *2 ¼* **Dor's Law**[61] 2829 3-9-6 **59**.. RobertWinston 11 63
(Dean Ivory) *mid-div: hdwy over 4f out: sn trcking ldrs: kpt on same pce last 150yds: tk 2nd nr fin* **11/4**[1]

-630 **3** *hd* **Primobella**[27] 3998 3-9-7 **60**.. DaleSwift 7 63
(Ed McMahon) *trckd ldrs: t.k.h: effrt over 3f out: upsides over 2f out: kpt on same pce last 100yds* **9/2**[3]

0661 **4** *hd* **Midnight Mood**[24] 4159 3-9-7 **60**....................................... LiamKeniry 3 63
(Dominic Ffrench Davis) *mid-div: hdwy over 2f out: kpt on fnl f: tk 4th in clsng stages* **4/1**[2]

6505 **5** *1 ¾* **Oyster Card**[14] 4498 3-8-13 **52**...................................... AndrewMullen 1 51
(Michael Appleby) *ldrs: drvn over 3f out: one pce appr fnl f* **5/1**

0-04 **6** *3 ¼* **Rosecomb (IRE)**[20] 4275 3-8-4 **50**............................... LuluStanford(7) 10 43
(Michael Bell) *s.i.s: swtchd lft after s: t.k.h: effrt on outside over 3f out: nvr a factor* **14/1**

0-05 **7** *hd* **Inwithachance (IRE)**[21] 4225 3-8-8 **47** oh1 ow1......(p) StevieDonohoe 6 39
(Daniel Mark Loughnane) *mid-div: drvn over 3f out: one pce* **20/1**

5-60 **8** *nk* **Nutzma**[68] 2608 3-8-7 **46**...[1] JohnFahy 2 38
(Mike Murphy) *hld up in rr: effrt on outer over 3f out: nvr a factor* **20/1**

5-00 **9** *3 ¼* **Karens Star**[13] 4522 3-9-2 **55**.................................... AdamBeschizza 12 40
(Steph Hollinshead) *led 1f: w wnr: wknd over 1f out* **12/1**

0-00 **10** *1 ¼* **Ingleby Erin**[36] 3710 3-8-2 **46** oh1............................... NathanEvans(5) 9 29
(Michael Easterby) *hld up towards rr: hdwy on ins 4f out: sn drvn: lost pl over 2f out* **33/1**

4500 **11** *9* **Gamesters Boy**[22] 4210 3-8-11 **50**...................................... LiamJones 8 15
(Mark Brisbourne) *chsd ldrs: drvn along 5f out: lost pl over 2f out: eased whn bhd in clsng stages* **33/1**

2m 15.63s (1.33) **Going Correction** -0.075s/f (Good) **11** Ran SP% **116.0**
Speed ratings (Par 98): **91,89,89,88,87 84,84,84,81,80 73**
CSF £69.66 TOTE £17.30: £5.10, £1.10, £2.00; EX 87.00.
Owner Chasemore Farm LLP & Owen Promotions Ltd **Bred** Bristen Ltd **Trained** Malpas, Cheshire

FOCUS
Race distance increased by about 18yds. There was no hanging about in this weak 3yo handicap. A length pb from the winner, with the second close to form and third helping to set the level.
T/Plt: £63.80 to £1 stake. Pool of £50725.20 - 579.61 winning tickets. T/Qpdt: £19.90 to a £1 stake. Pool of £4130.84 - 153.44 winning tickets. **Walter Glynn**

4656 SALISBURY (R-H)
Tuesday, August 2

OFFICIAL GOING: Soft (good to soft in places; 7.1)
Wind: almost nil Weather: drizzle

4988 M J CHURCH EBF STALLIONS MAIDEN STKS (PLUS 10 RACE) (DIV I) — 6f 212y
2:00 (2:00) (Class 4) 2-Y-O **£4,528** (£1,347; £673; £336) **Stalls** Centre

Form RPR

05 **1** **Arborist (IRE)**[13] 4533 2-9-5 0.. DaneO'Neill 4 77
(Sylvester Kirk) *trckd ldrs: rdn wl over 1f out: r.o to ld fnl 120yds: rdn out* **9/2**[3]

2 *nk* **Dance Teacher (IRE)** 2-9-0 0... PatDobbs 7 71+
(Ralph Beckett) *in tch: hdwy over 4f out: chal between horses jst over 1f out: led briefly jst ins fnl f: kpt on but a being jst hld fnl 100yds* **3/1**[1]

64 **3** *3 ¼* **Star Maker**[41] 3529 2-9-2 0.................................... EdwardGreatrex(3) 6 68
(Sylvester Kirk) *trckd ldrs tl lost pl and dropped to last pair over 4f out: hdwy over 2f out: styd on into 2nd fnl 120yds but no threat to ldrs* **4/1**[2]

0 **4** *1 ¾* **Never Surrender (IRE)**[18] 4349 2-9-5 0........................ SteveDrowne 2 63
(Charles Hills) *trckd ldr: rdn to chal over 2f out: ev ch tl jst ins fnl f: no ex* **3/1**[1]

06 **5** *2* **In The Spotlight (IRE)**[17] 4387 2-9-0 0............................ ShaneKelly 5 53
(Richard Hughes) *led: rdn and hdd jst ins fnl f: fdd fnl 120yds* **25/1**

0 **6** *½* **Kozier (GER)**[20] 4270 2-9-5 0............................. WilliamTwiston-Davies 8 57
(Alan King) *s.i.s: sn pushed along towards rr: nvr gng pce to get on terms* **12/1**

0 **7** *7* **Henry Did It (IRE)**[17] 4390 2-9-2 0.......................... GeorgeDowning(3) 3 39
(Tony Carroll) *s.i.s: towards rr: hdwy over 4f out: wknd jst over 1f out* **66/1**

8 *2* **Auric Goldfinger (IRE)** 2-9-5 0.. KieranO'Neill 9 34
(Richard Hannon) *in tch: rdn over 2f out: wknd jst over 1f out* **15/2**

9 *6* **License To Thrill (USA)** 2-9-5 0...................................... NickyMackay 1 18
(Simon Dow) *s.i.s: towards rr: effrt 3f out: wknd over 1f out* **33/1**

1m 29.98s (1.38) **Going Correction** +0.275s/f (Good) **9** Ran SP% **115.9**
Speed ratings (Par 96): **103,102,98,96,94 94,86,83,76**
CSF £18.24 TOTE £6.60: £1.80, £1.50, £1.40; EX 22.00 Trifecta £74.40.
Owner Malih L Al Basti **Bred** Yeomanstown Stud **Trained** Upper Lambourn, Berks

FOCUS
With 19mm of rain overnight the ground had eased considerably, from good to firm the day before. The time of the opener was almost 4sec outside the standard, suggesting that the ground wasn't all that testing. This looked an ordinary maiden, and the field came over to the stands' side. It's been rated around the third.

4989 M J CHURCH EBF STALLIONS MAIDEN STKS (PLUS 10 RACE) (DIV II) — 6f 212y
2:30 (2:31) (Class 4) 2-Y-O **£4,528** (£1,347; £673; £336) **Stalls** Centre

Form RPR

5 **1** **Galactic Prince**[11] 4580 2-9-5 0...................................... DavidProbert 8 73
(Andrew Balding) *trckd ldrs: shkn up over 1f out: led fnl 150yds: r.o wl: readily* **7/2**[2]

00 **2** *2* **Syncopation (IRE)**[3] 4866 2-9-5 0....................................... PatDobbs 9 68
(Sylvester Kirk) *trckd ldrs: pushed along but nowhere to go over 1f out: swtchd rt ent fnl f: kpt on wl to go 2nd cl home but no threat to wnr* **7/1**

3 *nk* **Coastal Cyclone** 2-9-5 0.. MartinHarley 5 67
(Harry Dunlop) *led: rdn over 1f out: hdd fnl 150yds: kpt on but lost 2nd cl home* **25/1**

0 **4** *¾* **City Dreamer (IRE)**[32] 3859 2-9-5 0............................ FergusSweeney 1 65+
(Alan King) *s.i.s: in last but in tch: rdn over 2f out: hdwy over 1f out: kpt on fnl f* **5/1**[3]

00 **5** *½* **Quothquan (FR)**[28] 3971 2-8-12 0.............................. GeorgeWood(7) 3 64
(Michael Madgwick) *trckd ldrs: rdn over 2f out: kpt on same pce fnl f* **100/1**

6 *hd* **Abatement** 2-9-2 0.. KieranShoemark(3) 4 63+
(Roger Charlton) *hld up in tch: rdn 2f out: hdwy whn swtchd rt over 1f out: kpt on same pce fnl f* **10/1**

7 *shd* **Percy Thrower (IRE)** 2-9-5 0................................. MichaelJMMurphy 7 63
(Charles Hills) *little slowly away: sn nudged along in tch: outpcd over 2f out: kpt on ins fnl f* **14/1**

3 **8** *1 ½* **Plant Pot Power (IRE)**[32] 3859 2-9-5 0............................ TomMarquand 2 59
(Richard Hannon) *hld up in tch: hdwy over 2f out: rdn and ev ch over 1f out: fdd ins fnl f* **6/4**[1]

6 **9** 1 ½ **Inner Circle (IRE)**[97] 1770 2-9-5 0 SeanLevey 6 55
(Richard Hannon) *trckd ldrs: rdn and ch 2f out: wknd ins fnl f* **20/1**

1m 30.58s (1.98) **Going Correction** +0.275s/f (Good) **9** Ran SP% **116.7**
Speed ratings (Par 96): **99,96,96,95,94 94,94,92,91**
CSF £27.90 TOTE £5.10: £1.80, £2.10, £7.80; EX 26.50 Trifecta £589.80.
Owner J C Smith **Bred** Littleton Stud **Trained** Kingsclere, Hants

FOCUS
This looked the stronger division on paper, but the time was slower by 0.6sec. Again they came over to the stands' side and the rail proved the place to be. This has been rated cautiously.

4990 PETER SYMONDS CATERING H'CAP 6f
3:00 (3:00) (Class 5) (0-75,75) 3-Y-O+ **£3,234** (£962; £481; £240) **Stalls** Low

Form RPR
402 **1** **Poole Belle (IRE)**[36] 3720 3-9-5 **73** DaneO'Neill 9 83
(Henry Candy) *trckd ldrs: led 2f out: r.o wl: rdn out* **4/1**[1]
0520 **2** 1 **Vincentti (IRE)**[19] 4291 6-9-7 **71** RaulDaSilva 13 79
(Ronald Harris) *hld up in last: hdwy over 1f out: swtchd rt ent fnl f: chsd wnr fnl 130yds: r.o but a being hld* **11/2**[3]
0063 **3** 1 **Quick March**[21] 4222 3-9-2 **73** KieranShoemark[(3)] 10 77
(Roger Charlton) *trckd ldrs: rdn 2f out: kpt on ins fnl f but nt ace to mount chal* **13/2**
0400 **4** ¾ **Tagula Night (IRE)**[45] 3414 10-9-8 **72** (tp) RobertWinston 6 74
(Dean Ivory) *cl up: drvn along fr 3f out: ev ch over 1f out: no ex fnl f* **9/2**[2]
436 **5** 1 ¼ **Fantasy Justifier (IRE)**[31] 3892 5-9-6 **70** DavidProbert 5 68
(Ronald Harris) *hld up: plld hrd and hdwy to trck ldrs 4f out: rdn 2f out: no ex fnl f* **6/1**
3165 **6** 1 ¾ **Showmethewayavrilo**[13] 4502 3-9-0 **71** NoelGarbutt[(3)] 14 63
(Malcolm Saunders) *prom: rdn 2f out: fdd ins fnl f* **10/1**
134- **7** *hd* **In Haste (IRE)**[405] 3520 3-9-7 **75** ShaneKelly 7 66
(Eve Johnson Houghton) *in tch: rdn whn sltly outpcd 3f out: no threat after* **9/1**
-004 **8** 2 ¼ **Dear Bruin (IRE)**[14] 4485 4-9-2 **66** (p) WilliamTwiston-Davies 4 51
(David W Drinkwater) *led: rdn and hdd 2f out: wknd over 1f out* **25/1**
2502 **9** 3 ¼ **Picket Line**[34] 3780 4-9-6 **75** PaddyPilley[(5)] 11 50
(Geoffrey Deacon) *hld up: rdn in tch over 2f out: wknd over 1f out* **8/1**

1m 15.14s (0.34) **Going Correction** +0.275s/f (Good)
WFA 3 from 4yo+ 4lb **9** Ran SP% **115.2**
Speed ratings (Par 103): **108,106,105,104,102 100,100,97,92**
CSF £25.97 CT £139.52 TOTE £4.60: £2.30, £2.00, £2.20; EX 25.50 Trifecta £203.40.
Owner Sir Edmund Loder **Bred** S P Tindall **Trained** Kingston Warren, Oxon

FOCUS
A modest sprint handicap but an improved winner. They came stands' side.

4991 CPA SCAFFOLDING MAIDEN FILLIES' STKS 1m
3:30 (3:30) (Class 5) 3-Y-O+ **£3,557** (£1,058; £529; £264) **Stalls** Low

Form RPR
42 **1** **Labyrinth (IRE)**[18] 4361 3-9-0 0 TedDurcan 2 76+
(Sir Michael Stoute) *trckd ldr: led jst over 1f out: pushed clr: easily* **8/11**[1]
323 **2** 2 ¼ **Organza**[9] 4682 3-9-0 72 MartinDwyer 6 67+
(Mick Channon) *led: rdn whn chal wl over 1f out: hdd jst outside fnl f: nt pce of wnr* **11/8**[2]
0 **3** 2 **Chandon Elysees**[54] 3059 3-9-0 0 FergusSweeney 3 62
(Gary Moore) *trckd ldrs: rdn over 2f out: kpt on but nt pce to get on terms* **66/1**
00 **4** 4 **Occasional Dream (IRE)**[14] 4480 3-8-7 0 SeanMooney[(7)] 7 53
(Joseph Tuite) *trckd ldr tl dropped to 5th u.p over 2f out: regained hld 4th ins fnl f* **33/1**[3]
0- **5** 1 ¾ **Mette**[439] 2438 3-9-0 0 SteveDrowne 1 49
(Rod Millman) *hld up 5th: tk clsr order over 2f out: effrt disputing 3rd over 1f out: fdd fnl f* **50/1**

1m 48.8s (5.30) **Going Correction** +0.275s/f (Good) **5** Ran SP% **106.4**
Speed ratings (Par 100): **84,81,79,75,74**
CSF £1.79 TOTE £1.50: £1.10, £1.10; EX 1.90 Trifecta £6.70.
Owner The Queen **Bred** Ballylinch Stud **Trained** Newmarket, Suffolk

FOCUS
This fillies' maiden lacked depth. Following the theme of the afternoon, they crossed over to the stands' side. The pace was steady, and this isn't form to take literally.

4992 VENTURE SECURITY H'CAP (DIV I) 1m
4:00 (4:01) (Class 6) (0-55,55) 3-Y-O+ **£2,911** (£866; £432; £216) **Stalls** Low

Form RPR
-000 **1** **Boychick (IRE)**[20] 4275 3-8-7 **48** AntonioFresu 9 54+
(Ed Walker) *trckd ldrs: chal 3f out: sn rdn: led over 1f out: looked in command whn idled towards fin: a holding on* **11/1**
0435 **2** *nk* **Ettie Hart (IRE)**[11] 4600 3-8-6 **54** KillianHennessy[(7)] 4 58
(Mick Channon) *trckd ldr: led over 2f out tl rdn over 1f out: rallied clsng stages whn wnr idled: kpt on* **9/2**[1]
403 **3** 1 ¼ **Altaira**[42] 3490 5-9-5 **53** WilliamCarson 2 55
(Tony Carroll) *mid-div: hdwy over 2f out: sn rdn: chal for 2nd ent fnl f: kpt on same pce* **5/1**[2]
0400 **4** 1 ¾ **Dandys Perier (IRE)**[19] 4289 5-9-4 **52** (p) RaulDaSilva 12 50
(Ronald Harris) *led tl rdn over 2f out: sn one pce* **8/1**
2060 **5** 1 **Blackdown Warrior**[22] 4202 3-7-12 **46** oh1 GeorgeWood[(7)] 8 41+
(Rod Millman) *hld up: hdwy 3f out: sn rdn: chal for 2nd ent fnl f: fdd fnl 120yds* **11/2**[3]
6-20 **6** 2 ¼ **Clevedon Court**[181] 436 3-9-0 **55** FergusSweeney 5 45
(Gary Moore) *mid-div: rdn over 2f out: nvr threatened: fdd fnl f* **8/1**
3344 **7** *nk* **Top Pocket**[6] 4773 4-9-3 **51** WilliamTwiston-Davies 3 41
(Michael Madgwick) *gate opened fractionally slower than the rest: sn mid-div: rdn over 2f out: nvr any imp* **5/1**[2]
5000 **8** 3 ½ **Miss Buckaroo (IRE)**[39] 3620 4-8-12 **46** oh1 (p) TomMarquand 6 28
(Peter Hedger) *trckd ldrs: rdn over 2f out: wknd over 1f out* **11/1**
00-0 **9** 14 **Admirals Choice**[208] 77 3-8-5 **46** oh1 MartinDwyer 1
(Robert Eddery) *a towards rr* **25/1**
005- **10** 12 **Oyster Pearl (IRE)**[246] 8057 3-8-12 **53** (t) ShaneKelly 11
(Carroll Gray) *a towards rr* **16/1**

1m 46.23s (2.73) **Going Correction** +0.275s/f (Good)
WFA 3 from 4yo+ 7lb **10** Ran SP% **115.5**
Speed ratings (Par 101): **97,96,95,93,92 90,90,86,72,60**
CSF £59.42 CT £288.91 TOTE £13.40: £4.20, £2.00, £1.90; EX 63.70 Trifecta £556.80.
Owner Laurence Bellman **Bred** Lynch Bages Ltd **Trained** Upper Lambourn, Berks
■ Stewards' Enquiry : Killian Hennessy two-day ban: use of whip (16 & 20 Aug)

FOCUS
They came stands' side again. Low-grade handicap form. A pb from the winner, with the second helping to set the level.

4993 VENTURE SECURITY H'CAP (DIV II) 1m
4:30 (4:30) (Class 6) (0-55,54) 3-Y-O+ **£2,911** (£866; £432; £216) **Stalls** Low

Form RPR
3565 **1** **Edge (IRE)**[13] 4504 5-9-1 **48** (b) DavidProbert 12 55
(Bernard Llewellyn) *hld up bhd: hdwy 4f out: rdn to chse ldrs over 1f out: edgd rt whn ldng ent fnl f: r.o wl* **9/1**
33U5 **2** 1 **Wild Flower (IRE)**[19] 4289 4-9-2 **49** KieranO'Neill 2 53
(Jimmy Fox) *hld up: hdwy 2f out: rdn over 1f out: mounting chal whn edgd rt ent fnl f: kpt on but nt pce of wnr* **7/1**[3]
00-0 **3** *nk* **Aspasius (GER)**[41] 3522 4-9-0 **52** HectorCrouch[(5)] 9 55
(Gary Moore) *trckd ldrs: rdn whn swtchd rt over 1f out: mounting chal whn bmpd sltly ent fnl f: kpt on same pce* **20/1**
0011 **4** 1 **Prince Of Cardamom (IRE)**[3] 4876 4-8-13 **51** (p) CharlieBennett[(5)] 3 52
(Jonathan Geake) *led: rdn over 2f out: edgd rt and hdd ent fnl f: no ex* **6/4**[1]
-050 **5** ¾ **Just Fred (IRE)**[19] 4290 3-8-1 **48** (p) GeorgeWood[(7)] 4 46
(Denis Coakley) *hld up: hdwy 2f out u.p: one pce fnl f* **9/1**
0-00 **6** ¾ **Dark Phantom (IRE)**[22] 4202 5-8-7 **45** PaddyPilley[(5)] 11 43
(Geoffrey Deacon) *w ldr: rdn over 2f out: ev ch over 1f out: fdd ins fnl f* **33/1**
6050 **7** ½ **Zeteah**[27] 3997 6-8-13 **46** TomMarquand 10 42
(Tony Carroll) *trckd ldrs: rdn over 2f out: sn one pce* **10/1**
0003 **8** *shd* **Infiniti (IRE)**[17] 4388 3-9-0 **54** SaleemGolam 7 49
(Rae Guest) *mid-div: swtchd rt over 2f out: effrt over 1f out: wknd ins fnl f* **9/2**[2]
0040 **9** 10 **Pursuit Of Time**[27] 3993 3-8-9 **49** (p) JackMitchell 6 21
(Neil Mulholland) *trckd ldrs: chal over 2f out: sn rdn: wknd over 1f out* **20/1**

1m 46.22s (2.72) **Going Correction** +0.275s/f (Good)
WFA 3 from 4yo+ 7lb **9** Ran SP% **112.2**
Speed ratings (Par 101): **97,96,95,94,93 93,92,92,82**
CSF £65.98 CT £1223.47 TOTE £7.20: £2.00, £1.90, £5.80; EX 40.20 Trifecta £809.60.
Owner B J Llewellyn **Bred** Swordlestown Stud **Trained** Fochriw, Caerphilly

FOCUS
They went off at a fair clip but the overall time was almost identical to that of the first division. Once more they came to the stands' side. This could be rated a bit higher.

4994 BATHWICK TYRES FILLIES' H'CAP 1m 4f
5:00 (5:00) (Class 4) (0-85,85) 3-Y-O+ **£7,762** (£2,310; £1,154; £577) **Stalls** Low

Form RPR
3331 **1** **Eager Beaver**[13] 4520 4-9-6 **77** MartinDwyer 6 85
(William Muir) *disp ld tl clr ldr after 2f out: racd far side of centre w one other 3f out: styd on strly to assert fnl f: readily* **6/1**[2]
6263 **2** 2 **Graceland (FR)**[10] 4646 4-9-7 **81** LouisSteward[(3)] 5 86
(Michael Bell) *slowly away: trckd ldrs: chsd wnr on far side of centre 3f out: styd on for clr 2nd but readily hld by wnr fnl f* **13/2**[3]
1531 **3** 5 **Hereawi**[24] 4137 3-9-2 **84** PatDobbs 2 81
(Ralph Beckett) *disp for 2f: trckd wnr tl swtchd to centre nrest stands' side 3f out: sn hld by far side gp: wknd fnl f* **4/9**[1]
3410 **4** 3 ½ **Genuine Approval (IRE)**[18] 4351 3-9-3 **85** DannyBrock 7 76
(Jonathan Portman) *trckd ldrs: swtchd w one other to centre nrest stands' side: sn hld by far side gp: wknd fnl f* **10/1**

2m 41.69s (3.69) **Going Correction** +0.35s/f (Good)
WFA 3 from 4yo 11lb **4** Ran SP% **106.0**
Speed ratings (Par 102): **101,99,96,94**
CSF £33.88 TOTE £5.40; EX 19.10 Trifecta £34.60.
Owner M J Caddy **Bred** Horizon Bloodstock Limited **Trained** Lambourn, Berks

FOCUS
A reasonable fillies' handicap, which became tactical. It was the first race of the day to use the loop and the small field came down the centre once into the home straight, only to split with over two furlongs to run. The first two home went nearer the far rail, with the other two coming down the stands' side. It has been rated around the front two, with the winner posting a small pb.

4995 BATHWICK TYRES SALISBURY H'CAP 1m 6f 21y
5:30 (5:30) (Class 6) (0-60,60) 4-Y-O+ **£2,911** (£866; £432; £216) **Stalls** Far side

Form RPR
0-00 **1** **Master Dancer**[35] 3737 5-8-7 **53** (p) MitchGodwin[(7)] 10 61
(Tim Vaughan) *plld hrd: trckd ldrs: led 3f out: sn drvn: styd on wl* **9/2**[3]
/002 **2** 2 ¼ **Double Dealites**[17] 4385 6-8-7 **46** KierenFox 14 51
(Jamie Poulton) *hld up: hdwy on rails and nt clrest of runs fr over 3f out: swtchd lft 2f out: sn rdn: styd on fnl f: wnt 2nd towards fin* **4/1**[2]
00-6 **3** 1 **Moon Trip**[27] 3999 7-8-4 **48** PaddyPilley[(5)] 1 52
(Geoffrey Deacon) *trckd ldr: led after 2f: rdn and hdd 3f out: kpt chsng wnr: hld ent fnl f: no ex whn lost 2nd towards fin* **6/1**
5625 **4** 3 **Captain George (IRE)**[27] 3999 5-9-5 **58** (p) SteveDrowne 5 58
(Michael Blake) *trckd ldrs: rdn wl over 2f out: styd on but nt pce to get on terms* **6/1**
3356 **5** 1 ¾ **Deepsand (IRE)**[34] 3767 7-9-7 **60** (tp) TomMarquand 13 58
(Ali Stronge) *hld up towards rr: rdn wl over 2f out: no imp tl styd on fnl f* **10/3**[1]
26-4 **6** ¾ **Captain Oats (IRE)**[21] 4225 13-8-8 **52** RachealKneller[(5)] 8 49
(Pam Ford) *hld up: hdwy over 3f out: effrt 2f out: fdd fnl f* **10/1**
6050 **7** 8 **Comedy House**[34] 3767 8-8-4 **50** (p) GeorgeWood[(7)] 11 36
(Michael Madgwick) *trckd ldrs: rdn whn hmpd over 2f out: wknd over 1f out* **25/1**
/00- **8** 14 **Asker (IRE)**[197] 8085 8-8-13 **55** (t) KieranShoemark[(3)] 9 23
(Nick Lampard) *led for 2f: prom: rdn 3f out: wknd 2f out* **18/1**
6000 **9** 3 **Abertillery**[13] 4531 4-8-4 **48** (b[1]) GeorgeBuckell[(5)] 6 12
(Michael Blanshard) *sn trcking ldrs: rdn over 3f out: wknd over 2f out: eased* **14/1**

3m 14.81s (7.41) **Going Correction** +0.35s/f (Good) **9** Ran SP% **114.7**
Speed ratings (Par 101): **92,90,90,88,87 87,82,74,72**
CSF £22.70 CT £108.02 TOTE £5.20: £1.70, £2.20, £2.40; EX 27.60 Trifecta £153.60.
Owner select-racing-club.co.uk & C Davies **Bred** D J Bloodstock, G Roddick & Wrottesley Ltd **Trained** Aberthin, Vale of Glamorgan

FOCUS
Few came into this lowly staying handicap in much sort of form. The pace was pretty steady and the field stayed towards the far side in the straight. It's muddling form, but rated around the second and third.
T/Jkpt: Not won. T/Plt: £48.60 to a £1 stake. Pool of £74503.73 - 1117.13 winning tickets.
T/Qpdt: £10.90 to a £1 stake. Pool of £6839.33 - 461.02 winning tickets. **Tim Mitchell**

4996 - 5001a (Foreign Racing) - See Raceform Interactive

3199 CORK (R-H)

Tuesday, August 2

OFFICIAL GOING: Yielding changing to good to yielding after race 3 (6.25)

5002a IRISH STALLION FARMS EUROPEAN BREEDERS FUND GIVE THANKS STKS (GROUP 3) (F&M) 1m 4f

8:25 (8:29) 3-Y-O+

£32,536 (£10,477; £4,963; £2,205; £1,102; £551)

RPR

1 **Best In The World (IRE)**[16] 4435 3-8-12 97 ColmO'Donoghue 3 105+
(A P O'Brien, Ire) *hld up: 7th 1/2-way: hdwy on outer to chal fr 2f out: rdn into 2nd 1f out and kpt on wl nr side wl ins fnl f where edgd rt to ld fnl strides* **12/1**

2 *nk* **Somehow (IRE)**[17] 4416 3-8-12 100 (v[1]) SeamieHeffernan 4 105+
(A P O'Brien, Ire) *dwlt and towards rr: clsr in 6th at 1/2-way: hdwy under 3f out and impr between horses to chal 2f out: led 1 1/2f out: strly pressed u.p wl ins fnl f and hdd fnl strides* **7/2**[2]

3 *½* **Harlequeen**[17] 4416 3-8-12 107 RonanWhelan 2 104
(Mick Channon) *chsd ldrs: 5th 1/2-way: pushed along in 5th appr st and impr bhd ldr u.p 2f out: rdn in 3rd over 1f out and kpt on wl ins fnl f where sltly impeded: hld by ldng pair* **11/10**[1]

4 *4 ½* **Shamreen (IRE)**[51] 3202 3-8-12 99 PatSmullen 7 98
(D K Weld, Ire) *trckd ldr tl dropped to 3rd at 1/2-way: impr into st and pushed along to ld narrowly over 2f out: hdd u.p 1 1/2f out and sn wknd in 4th* **5/1**[3]

5 *2 ¼* **Kallisha**[38] 3662 5-9-9 97 ChrisHayes 8 93
(Brendan Powell) *dismntd bef s: w.w towards rr: last at 1/2-way: niggled along in rr 5f out: rdn into mod 5th 1f out and kpt on one pce: nvr trbld ldrs* **25/1**

6 *6* **More Mischief**[39] 3608 4-9-9 99 DeclanMcDonogh 5 84
(Jedd O'Keeffe) *led: over 1 l clr at 1/2-way: rdn and hdd over 2f out: sn wknd qckly* **7/1**

7 *¾* **Arya Tara (IRE)**[19] 4327 3-8-12 96 (t) AnaO'Brien 9 82
(Joseph Patrick O'Brien, Ire) *chsd ldrs: tk clsr order in 2nd at 1/2-way: cl 2nd into st and disp briefly: hdd over 2f out and wknd qckly* **16/1**

8 *4 ¼* **Fact Or Folklore (IRE)**[11] 4615 4-9-9 94 BillyLee 1 76
(W McCreery, Ire) *hooded to load: chsd ldrs: 4th 1/2-way: pushed along in 4th 4f out and no ex over 2f out where wknd to rr* **33/1**

2m 35.14s (-12.76)
WFA 3 from 4yo+ 11lb **8** Ran SP% **119.4**
CSF £56.20 TOTE £14.30: £4.10, £2.20, £1.02; DF 73.80 Trifecta £206.10.
Owner Michael Tabor & Derrick Smith & Mrs John Magnier **Bred** Roncon, Wynatt & Chelston **Trained** Cashel, Co Tipperary

FOCUS
Aidan O'Brien has the best filly around in Minding and won the Irish Oaks with Seventh Heaven. Neither of those showed up here but he still sent out the first and second, confirming the suspicion that his squad of 3yo fillies are top-notch. There was nothing wrong with the early pace and the front three, all 3yos, pulled clear of the pack inside the final furlong. It's been rated around the second and third roughly to their Irish Oaks form.

5003 - (Foreign Racing) - See Raceform Interactive

4924 DEAUVILLE (R-H)

Tuesday, August 2

OFFICIAL GOING: Turf: good to soft; polytrack: standard

5004a PRIX CHEZ HERVE (PRIX DE TOURGEVILLE) (LISTED RACE) (3YO COLTS & GELDINGS) (ROUND) (TURF) 1m (R)

1:50 (12:00) 3-Y-O **£20,220** (£8,088; £6,066; £4,044; £2,022)

RPR

1 **Noor Al Hawa (FR)**[37] 3699 3-9-3 0 EduardoPedroza 3 105
(A Wohler, Germany) **9/2**[3]

2 *1* **Ghaaly**[30] 3-9-3 0 (b) ChristopheSoumillon 9 103
(J-C Rouget, France) **5/2**[1]

3 *hd* **London Protocol (FR)**[25] 4116 3-8-13 0 DougieCostello 7 99
(K R Burke) *midfield in tch: rdn and effrt over 1f out: ev ch fnl f: r.o but hld towards fin: jst missed 2nd* **72/1**

4 *¾* **Floodlight (USA)**[17] 4422 3-9-3 0 MickaelBarzalona 4 101
(A Fabre, France) *hld up: rdn 2f out: kpt on for 4th but nt quite pce to chal* **16/5**[2]

5 *1 ¼* **Moon Trouble (IRE)**[31] 3938 3-9-3 0 MaximeGuyon 6 98
(F Head, France) **47/10**

6 *1* **Barwod**[30] 3-8-13 0 Pierre-CharlesBoudot 1 92
(A Fabre, France) **79/10**

7 *snk* **Fourioso (FR)**[64] 2755 3-8-13 0 CristianDemuro 8 91
(P Sogorb, France) **13/1**

8 *3 ½* **No Education**[17] 4380 3-8-13 0 UmbertoRispoli 5 83
(Jo Hughes) *led: rdn and hdd over 1f out: wknd* **20/1**

9 *7* **Soho Starlight** 3-8-13 0 FabriceVeron 2 67
(H-A Pantall, France) **11/1**

1m 45.92s (5.12) **9** Ran SP% **121.0**
WIN (incl. 1 euro stake): 5.50. PLACES: 2.20, 1.70, 10.30. DF: 12.10. SF: 23.60.
Owner Jaber Abdullah **Bred** Rabbah Bloodstock Limited **Trained** Germany

5005a PRIX LE DRAKKAR (PRIX DU MEZERAY) (CONDITIONS) (2YO FILLIES) (TURF) 7f 110y

2:20 (12:00) 2-Y-O **£12,500** (£5,000; £3,750; £2,500; £1,250)

RPR

1 **Celanova (FR)**[39] 2-9-0 0 ChristopheSoumillon 6 93
(J-C Rouget, France) **4/5**[1]

2 *1* **Thais (FR)** 2-8-7 0 StephanePasquier 3 84
(P Bary, France) **23/5**[2]

3 *3* **Riviere Argentee (FR)**[26] 4037 2-9-0 0 DougieCostello 5 84
(K R Burke) *sn led: rdn into st: hdd over 1f out: readily outpcd by front pair fnl f but kpt on for wl hld 3rd* **36/5**[3]

4 *½* **Evalya Senora (FR)**[56] 2-8-9 0 TheoBachelot 9 77
(Y Barberot, France) **10/1**

5 *3* **Paisible Et Sage (FR)** 2-8-9 0 TonyPiccone 7 70
(F Chappet, France) **10/1**

6 *9* **Cazalys (FR)**[16] 2-8-9 0 CristianDemuro 8 49
(E J O'Neill, France) **19/1**

7 *4 ½* **Princess Of Snow (IRE)** 2-8-9 0 IoritzMendizabal 1 39
(H De Nicolay, France) **18/1**

8 *snk* **Vixenta (FR)**[27] 2-8-6 0 HugoJourniac(3) 4 38
(Eric Saint-Martin, France) **11/1**

1m 38.55s (10.15) **8** Ran SP% **122.4**
WIN (incl. 1 euro stake): 1.80. PLACES: 1.20, 1.70, 1.90. DF: 4.50. SF: 6.90.
Owner H H Aga Khan **Bred** His Highness The Aga Khan's Studs S C **Trained** Pau, France

5006a PRIX LA FLAMBEE (PRIX DE L'ABBAYE DE SAINT-LEONARD) (CONDITIONS) (3YO FILLIES) (POLYTRACK) 1m 1f 110y

2:55 (12:00) 3-Y-O **£12,500** (£5,000; £3,750; £2,500; £1,250)

RPR

1 **That Which Is Not (USA)**[24] 3-9-0 0 StephanePasquier 8 93
(F-H Graffard, France) **19/10**[1]

2 *hd* **Fresh Strike (IRE)**[22] 3-9-0 0 MaximeGuyon 4 93
(F Head, France) **12/1**

3 *½* **Secret Existence (IRE)**[50] 3241 3-8-9 0 IoritzMendizabal 7 87
(F Chappet, France) **47/10**[3]

4 *nk* **Coif (IRE)**[35] 3-9-0 0 MickaelBarzalona 9 91
(A Fabre, France) *hld up: rdn 2f out: styd on but nt quite pce to chal* **78/10**

5 *hd* **Identity Run Fast (IRE)**[19] 4334 3-9-0 0 Pierre-CharlesBoudot 5 91
(A Marcialis, Italy) **31/1**

6 *snk* **Happy Approach (FR)**[44] 3452 3-9-0 0 AntoineHamelin 11 90
(M Nigge, France) **9/1**

7 *3* **Daisy Bere (FR)**[39] 3596 3-9-0 0 DougieCostello 2 84
(K R Burke) *hld up: pushed along bef st: rdn and outpcd fnl 2f* **42/1**

8 *hd* **Myth**[80] 3-9-0 0 CristianDemuro 6 84
(Waldemar Hickst, Germany) **53/1**

9 *shd* **Roche Rose (IRE)**[34] 3797 3-9-0 0 TonyPiccone 3 84
(E Lellouche, France) **17/1**

10 *hd* **Jasmiralda (FR)**[33] 3-9-0 0 TheoBachelot 10 83
(S Wattel, France) **11/1**

11 *7* **Elennga (FR)**[38] 3-9-0 0 ChristopheSoumillon 1 69
(J-C Rouget, France) **9/2**[2]

1m 56.01s (116.01) **11** Ran SP% **120.5**
WIN (incl. 1 euro stake): 2.90. PLACES: 1.50, 2.50, 1.80. DF: 21.30. SF: 32.60.
Owner Flaxman Stables Ireland Ltd **Bred** Flaxman Holdings Limited **Trained** France

4815 BATH (L-H)

Wednesday, August 3

OFFICIAL GOING: Good to soft (good in places)
Wind: mild across Weather: sunny periods

5007 LORD'S TAVERNERS CHARITIES H'CAP (BATH SUMMER SPRINT SERIES QUALIFIER) 5f 11y

2:00 (2:02) (Class 6) (0-60,60) 3-Y-O+ **£2,264** (£673; £336; £168) **Stalls** Centre

Form RPR

0-03 1 **Topsoil**[5] 4820 3-8-4 **46** oh1 RaulDaSilva 7 53
(Ronald Harris) *hld up bhd: snatched up ins 1st f: hdwy over 2f out: squeezed through on rails to ld ent fnl f: kpt on wl: hld on* **8/1**

0322 2 *shd* **Essaka (IRE)**[23] 4202 4-8-12 **56** PaddyPilley(5) 11 64
(Tony Carroll) *s.i.s: towards rr: hdwy in centre fr over 2f out: drifting lft but ev ch ent fnl f: kpt on wl: jst hld* **7/2**[2]

-045 3 *1 ½* **Virile (IRE)**[20] 4292 5-9-0 **53** (b) RobertWinston 6 60+
(Sylvester Kirk) *trckd ldrs: nt clr run over 1f out: hmpd ent fnl f: r.o whn clr fnl 150yds* **11/4**[1]

6/00 4 *½* **Captain Devious**[20] 4289 5-8-7 **49** oh1 ow3 (t[1]) TimClark(3) 8 50
(Grace Harris) *in tch: rdn to chse ldrs 2f out: short of room briefly ent fnl f: kpt on same pce* **50/1**

5000 5 *shd* **Catalinas Diamond (IRE)**[22] 4224 8-9-1 **54** (t) SteveDrowne 2 54
(Pat Murphy) *towards rr: sn pushed along: nt clr run ent fnl f: rdn and r.o fnl 120yds* **12/1**

6134 6 *shd* **Captain Ryan**[14] 4506 5-9-4 **60** JosephineGordon(3) 12 60
(Geoffrey Deacon) *stdd s: in tch: effrt 2f out: short of room over 1f out: one pce fnl f* **4/1**[3]

0066 7 *¾* **Tally's Song**[20] 4292 3-7-11 **46** oh1 RPWalsh(7) 13 42
(Grace Harris) *prom: rdn and ev ch 2f out tl jst ins fnl f: no ex* **50/1**

2055 8 *¾* **Jaganory (IRE)**[15] 4484 4-9-0 **58** GaryMahon(5) 1 53+
(Christopher Mason) *led tl rdn over 2f out: remained cl up tl fdd ins fnl f* **12/1**

5546 9 *1* **Fabulous Flyer**[11] 4658 3-8-6 **48** LukeMorris 4 38
(Jeremy Gask) *racd keenly: in tch: effrt 2f out: nt clrest of runs over 1f out: fdd ins fnl f* **14/1**

3430 10 *nse* **Cerulean Silk**[28] 3993 6-8-1 **47** (p) GeorgeWood(7) 9 38
(Tony Carroll) *dwlt: sn in tch: rdn to chse ldrs 2f out: wknd ins fnl f* **25/1**

/005 11 *1 ½* **Molly Jones**[11] 4658 7-8-11 **50** DavidProbert 14 36+
(Matthew Salaman) *prom: led over 2f out: sn rdn: hdd ent fnl f: wknd* **16/1**

1m 4.05s (1.55) **Going Correction** +0.275s/f (Good)
WFA 3 from 4yo+ 3lb **11** Ran SP% **115.7**
Speed ratings (Par 101): **98,97,95,94,94 94,93,91,90,90 87**
CSF £35.08 CT £96.85 TOTE £8.60: £2.30, £1.60, £1.70; EX 36.10 Trifecta £119.70.
Owner Robert & Nina Bailey **Bred** Christopher & Annabelle Mason **Trained** Earlswood, Monmouths

FOCUS
Some starts have been moved at this track following remeasuring, so some races will not have speed figures until there is sufficient data to calculate updated median times. A further 4mm of rain overnight meant the going was good to soft, good in places. Races utilising bottom bend increased by 10yds. The opener was a weak sprint handicap and they didn't go hard early on, though that didn't prevent the winner from coming off the pace. The runner-up sets the standard.

5008 TAVERNERS DISABILITY SPORTS MEDIAN AUCTION MAIDEN STKS 5f 11y

2:30 (2:30) (Class 5) 2-Y-O **£2,911** (£866; £432; £216) **Stalls** Centre

Form RPR

40 1 **Secret Potion**[20] 4287 2-9-5 0 OisinMurphy 5 72
(Ronald Harris) *mde all: kpt on gamely fnl f: all out* **16/1**

2243 2 *hd* **Blue Suede (IRE)**[13] 4558 2-9-0 78 PatDobbs 4 66
(Richard Hannon) *t.k.h early: trckd wnr: rdn wl over 1f out: drifted rt briefly ent fnl f: kpt on fnl 120yds but nvr quite getting there* **4/11**[1]

0025 **3** 1¾ **Big Lachie**[13] 4553 2-9-2 72 JosephineGordon(3) 2 65
(Jamie Osborne) *little slowly away: trckd ldrs: disp 2nd over 2f out: rdn over 1f out: kpt on same pce fnl f* **3/1**[2]
0 **4** ¾ **Poetic Principle (IRE)**[8] 4736 2-9-5 0 KieranO'Neill 1 62
(J S Moore) *trckd ldrs: rdn 2f out: kpt on same pce fnl f* **12/1**[3]
060 **5** 25 **Rise Of Phoenix**[9] 4713 2-9-0 0 SamHitchcott 6
(John Spearing) *chsd ldrs: outpcd over 2f out: wknd over 1f out: eased* **66/1**

1m 4.72s (2.22) **Going Correction** +0.275s/f (Good) **5** Ran SP% **113.4**
Speed ratings (Par 94): **93,92,89,88,48**
CSF £23.95 TOTE £11.70: £5.60, £1.10; EX 27.90 Trifecta £49.80.
Owner RHS Ltd, R Fox, P Charter **Bred** Llety Farms **Trained** Earlswood, Monmouths
FOCUS
A weak maiden in which the market predicted a two-horse race, but there was an upset, with the winner a big improver.

5009 OVEN WIZARDS FILLIES' H'CAP 5f 161y
3:00 (3:00) (Class 5) (0-70,67) 3-Y-O+ **£2,911** (£866; £432; £216) **Stalls** Centre

Form RPR
0150 **1** **Dusty Blue**[28] 3994 4-9-2 **61** (t) EoinWalsh(3) 4 71
(Tony Carroll) *hld up in last pair: pushed along and hdwy over 2f out: rdn to ld ent fnl f: edgd lft: r.o wl* **3/1**[2]
6521 **2** 2 **Babyfact**[14] 4506 5-9-4 **63** JosephineGordon(3) 3 70+
(Malcolm Saunders) *trckd ldrs: nt clr run twice over 1f out: snatched up ent fnl f: swtchd rt: r.o wl to go 2nd cl home: unlucky* **9/4**[1]
-045 **3** ½ **Regal Miss**[22] 4222 4-9-3 **62** DanielMuscutt(3) 5 63
(Patrick Chamings) *prom: led 2f out: sn rdn: hdd ent fnl f: no ex whn lost 2nd cl home* **9/1**
043 **4** ¾ **Atalante**[13] 4565 3-9-7 **67** DavidProbert 6 65
(Andrew Balding) *trckd ldrs: rdn to chal wl over 1f out tl ent fnl f: kpt on same pce* **3/1**[2]
-121 **5** 6 **Go Amber Go**[15] 4484 4-9-1 **57** FrederikTylicki 2 36
(Rod Millman) *led: rdn and hdd 2f out: wknd ins fnl f* **7/2**[3]
00/0 **6** 25 **Saxony**[20] 4290 5-8-7 **49** oh4 (t) LukeMorris 1
(Matthew Salaman) *last pair: pushed along over 3f out: wknd over 2f out* **66/1**

1m 11.84s (0.64) **Going Correction** +0.275s/f (Good)
WFA 3 from 4yo+ 4lb **6** Ran SP% **114.5**
Speed ratings (Par 100): **106,103,102,101,93 60**
CSF £10.51 TOTE £5.10: £2.60, £1.60; EX 14.20 Trifecta £69.90.
Owner M Chung **Bred** Denford Stud Ltd **Trained** Cropthorne, Worcs
FOCUS
A fair sprint handicap in which the strong pace set it up for the closers. The winner is rated close to last year's form.

5010 DANIL'S SPORTING CHANCE FILLIES' H'CAP 1m 2f 46y
3:30 (3:31) (Class 5) (0-70,66) 3-Y-O+ **£3,234** (£962; £481; £240) **Stalls** Low

Form RPR
105 **1** **Pivotal Flame (IRE)**[39] 3652 3-9-5 **66** (p) LukeMorris 6 74
(James Tate) *trckd ldr: chal over 2f out: rdn into narrow advantage 2f out: styd on gamely and beginning to assert cl home: drvn out* **3/1**[2]
-633 **2** nk **Forecaster**[26] 4098 3-9-5 **66** (p) DavidProbert 4 73
(Michael Bell) *led: rdn whn narrowly hdd 2f out: kpt on w ev ch tl no ex cl home* **5/4**[1]
3006 **3** 2¼ **Indigo**[11] 4641 3-8-11 **58** SteveDrowne 2 60
(Mark Usher) *trckd ldng pair: rdn over 2f out: styd on but nt pce to mount chal* **14/1**
3000 **4** ½ **Togetherwecan (IRE)**[11] 4635 4-9-1 **53** (b) DerekLeung 8 54
(Mark Johnston) *hld up in tch: rdn over 2f out: styd on into 4th fnl f but nvr gng pce to threaten* **12/1**
3064 **5** 1½ **Azure Amour (IRE)**[14] 4507 4-8-6 **51** GeorgeWood(7) 7 49
(Rod Millman) *trckd ldrs: rdn to chal for cl 3rd over 2f out: no ex fnl f* **8/1**
0-04 **6** 1 **Amazing Charm**[13] 4568 4-9-10 **65** EoinWalsh(3) 3 61
(James Tate) *s.i.s: last but in tch: rdn over 3f out: nvr any imp* **7/1**[3]
0-50 **7** 26 **Sheer Honesty**[114] 1387 4-10-0 **66** OisinMurphy 5 13
(Anabel K Murphy) *in tch: rdn 3f out: wknd over 1f out: eased* **25/1**

2m 15.65s (4.65) **Going Correction** +0.275s/f (Good)
WFA 3 from 4yo 9lb **7** Ran SP% **111.3**
Speed ratings (Par 100): **92,91,89,89,87 87,66**
CSF £6.71 CT £38.56 TOTE £3.70: £2.20, £1.20; EX 7.10 Trifecta £53.20.
Owner Saeed Manana **Bred** Rabbah Bloodstock Limited **Trained** Newmarket, Suffolk
FOCUS
Race distance increased by 10yds. A moderate middle-distance handicap featuring several interesting types stepping up in trip. The slow gallop suited those ridden prominently. The runner-up's penultimate Hamilton form worked out well and this has been rated around that race.

5011 LORD'S TAVERNERS SENSORY ROOMS H'CAP 1m 2f 46y
4:00 (4:00) (Class 6) (0-65,65) 3-Y-O+ **£2,385** (£704; £352) **Stalls** Low

Form RPR
00-2 **1** **Hope Is High**[13] 4567 3-7-12 **47** JosephineGordon(3) 7 55+
(John Berry) *trckd ldrs: shkn up to ld jst ins fnl f: r.o wl: readily* **11/2**[3]
-551 **2** 1 **Fast And Hot (IRE)**[11] 4635 3-9-3 **63** (p) KieranO'Neill 1 68
(Richard Hannon) *trckd ldr: led over 6f out: rdn whn strly pressed over 2f out: edging rt whn hmpd jst ins fnl f: sn hdd: kpt on but nt pce of wnr* **4/1**[2]
0004 **3** ¾ **Opera Buffa (IRE)**[14] 4504 3-8-0 **46** (tp) LukeMorris 5 49
(Steve Flook) *led for over 3f: trckd ldr: rdn to chal 2f out: ev ch ent fnl f: kpt on same pce* **22/1**
/0 **4** ½ **Moss Street**[5] 2849 6-8-13 **53** DanielMuscutt(3) 4 55
(John Flint) *s.i.s: in last pair: tk clsr order after 2f: sltly outpcd over 2f out: hdwy over 1f out: styd on fnl f* **7/1**
5023 **5** ¾ **Patent**[14] 4522 3-9-5 **65** PatDobbs 6 66
(Richard Hannon) *trckd ldrs: rdn 2f out: styd on but nt pce to chal* **2/1**[1]
0-05 **6** 1¼ **Aurora Gray**[15] 4480 3-9-4 **64** FrederikTylicki 3 62
(Hughie Morrison) *trckd ldrs: rdn to chal 2f out: stl ev ch whn squeezed out ent fnl f: hld after* **6/1**
-000 **7** ¾ **Sunlit Waters**[28] 4018 3-8-12 **58** (v[1]) RobertWinston 8 55
(Eve Johnson Houghton) *stdd to last after 2f: hdwy over 2f out: sn rdn: wknd fnl f* **9/1**
0040 **8** 7 **Ferryview Place**[28] 3997 7-8-5 **49** (p) LukeCatton(7) 2 33
(Ian Williams) *s.i.s: in last pair: racd keenly and tk clsr order after 2f: effrt over 2f out: wknd jst over 1f out* **33/1**

2m 13.53s (2.53) **Going Correction** +0.275s/f (Good)
WFA 3 from 6yo+ 9lb **8** Ran SP% **112.8**
Speed ratings (Par 101): **100,99,98,98,97 96,96,90**
CSF £26.95 CT £442.31 TOTE £5.50: £1.60, £1.50, £3.90; EX 27.60 Trifecta £323.80.
Owner Mrs Emma Berry **Bred** Miss K Rausing **Trained** Newmarket, Suffolk
FOCUS
Race distance increased by 10yds. A moderate handicap, but an improving winner who recorded a 2.12sec faster time than the previous race over this trip. The pace was slow.

5012 IO ASSOCIATES H'CAP (BATH SUMMER STAYERS' SERIES QUALIFIER) 1m 6f
4:30 (4:30) (Class 6) (0-65,62) 3-Y-O **£2,264** (£673; £336; £168) **Stalls** Centre

Form RPR
5212 **1** **Mystique Heights**[6] 4810 3-9-7 **62** (v[1]) LukeMorris 1 69
(Sir Mark Prescott Bt) *dwlt: trckd ldrs: disp 2nd 1/2-way: led 6f out: rdn whn jnd over 2f out: drifted rt u.p: bmpd ent fnl f: edgd ahd towards fin: drvn out* **2/9**[1]
4016 **2** ½ **Kelvin Hall**[16] 4447 3-9-5 **60** DerekLeung 3 66
(Mark Johnston) *led tl 6f out: trckd wnr: rdn to dispute ld over 2f out: bmpd ent fnl f: no ex whn hdd towards fin* **16/1**[3]
1600 **3** 3¼ **Elocution**[28] 3998 3-9-1 **56** RobertWinston 4 57
(Denis Coakley) *trckd ldrs: rdn over 2f out: styd on same pce* **6/1**[2]
006 **4** 8 **Three Loves (IRE)**[11] 4657 3-9-3 **58** (v[1]) DavidProbert 2 48
(Andrew Balding) *trckd ldr most of way: rdn over 2f out: sn hld* **16/1**[3]

3m 12.23s (8.43) **4** Ran SP% **107.9**
CSF £4.88 TOTE £1.20; EX 5.00 Trifecta £7.20.
Owner G C Woodall **Bred** Brightwalton Stud **Trained** Newmarket, Suffolk
FOCUS
Race distance increased by 10yds. A low-grade staying handicap which revolved around the odds-on favourite. The pace was sedate and the first two came down the centre in the home straight.

5013 BUTFIELD CHARTERED SURVEYORS H'CAP 1m 5y
5:00 (5:00) (Class 6) (0-65,65) 3-Y-O **£2,264** (£673; £336; £168) **Stalls** Low

Form RPR
6214 **1** **You're A Goat**[21] 4269 3-8-12 **63** GeorgeWood(7) 10 73+
(Gary Moore) *little slowly away: in last pair: midfield after 2f: hdwy over 2f out: nt clr run over 1f out tl ent fnl f: r.o to ld cl home* **2/1**[1]
6302 **2** nk **Ripoll (IRE)**[7] 4764 3-9-0 **63** (t) GaryMahon(5) 1 72
(Sylvester Kirk) *trckd ldrs: rdn to ld over 1f out: kpt on: hdd cl home* **4/1**[2]
6-30 **3** 2½ **In Ken's Memory**[11] 4640 3-9-2 **63** JosephineGordon(3) 2 66
(John Butler) *led: rdn over 2f out: hdd over 1f out: kpt on but no ex fnl f* **16/1**
0-41 **4** 3 **Fantasy Queen**[12] 4587 3-9-2 **60** SteveDrowne 5 56
(Eve Johnson Houghton) *trckd ldrs: rdn 2f out: styd on same pce fnl f* **9/1**
0103 **5** 2¾ **R Bar Open (FR)**[11] 4641 3-9-7 **65** RobertWinston 11 55
(Dean Ivory) *in tch on outer: drvn over 2f out: drifted lft ent fnl f: fdd fnl 120yds* **13/2**
663 **6** 2¾ **Shongololo (IRE)**[28] 4017 3-9-4 **62** DavidProbert 9 46
(Andrew Balding) *rdn over 2f out: nvr bttr than mid-div* **7/1**
060 **7** 1¼ **Alaskan Breeze (IRE)**[19] 4367 3-9-7 **65** (b[1]) PatDobbs 7 46
(Brian Meehan) *s.i.s: in last pair: hdwy over 2f out: sn rdn: nvr threatened: fdd fnl f* **16/1**
0045 **8** ½ **Desirable**[11] 4641 3-8-8 **52** KieranO'Neill 8 32
(Hughie Morrison) *mid-div: struggling 5f out: drvn over 3f out: nvr gng pce to get involved* **20/1**
0646 **9** 1¾ **Sheila's Treat (IRE)**[16] 4463 3-9-5 **63** OisinMurphy 3 39
(Denis Coakley) *prom: rdn over 2f out: wknd over 1f out* **6/1**[3]
0600 **10** 2¼ **Secret Sonnet**[20] 4321 3-8-2 **46** oh1 (p[1]) NickyMackay 6 16
(Stuart Williams) *chsd ldrs: rdn over 2f out: wknd over 1f out* **50/1**

1m 42.55s (1.75) **Going Correction** +0.275s/f (Good) **10** Ran SP% **121.9**
Speed ratings (Par 98): **102,101,99,96,93 90,89,88,87,84**
CSF £10.33 CT £105.83 TOTE £3.50: £1.20, £1.60, £4.40; EX 13.40 Trifecta £125.70.
Owner Power Geneva Ltd **Bred** Mrs James Wigan **Trained** Lower Beeding, W Sussex
■ Stewards' Enquiry : George Wood two-day ban: used whip above permitted level (Aug 20-21)
FOCUS
Race distance increased by 10yds. A modest handicap but it featured a number of unexposed types over this trip. They went a good gallop and not many got into it.
T/Plt: £17.20 to a £1 stake. Pool: £57,011.60 - 2411.19 winning units. T/Qpdt: £10.20 to a £1 stake. Pool: £3,034.12 - 220.00 winning units. **Tim Mitchell**

3970 BRIGHTON (L-H)
Wednesday, August 3

OFFICIAL GOING: Good to soft (soft in places; 6.5)
Wind: medium, against Weather: cloudy, bright spells later

5014 THAMES VALLEY NURSERY H'CAP 5f 59y
1:50 (1:50) (Class 5) (0-75,74) 2-Y-O **£2,911** (£866; £432) **Stalls** Low

Form RPR
104 **1** **Quench Dolly**[14] 4503 2-9-7 **74** MichaelJMMurphy 2 77
(John Gallagher) *sn led and mde rest: rdn over 1f out: in command and styd on ins fnl f: pushed out towards fin* **2/1**[2]
005 **2** 1½ **Lightoller (IRE)**[11] 4659 2-9-1 **68** SilvestreDeSousa 6 66
(Mick Channon) *sn detached in 3rd: clsd and switched rt 2f out: sn rdn: chsd wnr and lugging lft 1f out: styd on same pce ins fnl f* **9/4**[3]
5351 **3** 4 **Marquee Club**[11] 4638 2-9-4 **71** WilliamCarson 3 58
(Jamie Osborne) *chsd wnr: rdn 2f out: sn hung lft: dropped to 3rd and btn 1f out: wl hld and eased towards fin* **5/4**[1]

1m 4.0s (1.70) **Going Correction** +0.375s/f (Good) **3** Ran SP% **108.5**
Speed ratings (Par 94): **101,98,92**
CSF £6.21 TOTE £2.70; EX 6.70 Trifecta £7.60.
Owner Quench Racing Partnership **Bred** Mrs R J Gallagher **Trained** Chastleton, Oxon
FOCUS
There had been 36mm of rain in the previous two days and 2mm overnight, turning good to firm at declaration time into good to soft, soft in places. The jockeys reported after the opener the ground was no worse than the easy side of good.

5015 SOUTH COAST/BRITISH STALLION STUDS EBF MAIDEN STKS 6f 209y
2:20 (2:20) (Class 5) 2-Y-O **£3,234** (£962; £481; £240) **Stalls** Low

Form RPR
24 **1** **Haulani (USA)**[48] 3315 2-9-5 0 WilliamTwiston-Davies 3 75
(Philip Hide) *broke wl and led early: sn stdd bk into 3rd: swtchd rt and clsd over 2f out: upsides gng best 2f out: led over 1f out: clr 1f out: r.o: rdn out: readily* **4/7**[1]
6 **2** 5 **Star Of The East (IRE)**[12] 4580 2-9-5 0 FrannyNorton 1 62
(Mark Johnston) *sn led: rdn 2f out: hdd over 1f out: outpcd by wnr and wl hld 1f out: lost 2nd ins fnl f: no ch w wnr but kpt on to regain 2nd last strides* **9/2**[2]

00 **3** hd **Varun's Bride (IRE)**[25] 4147 2-9-0 0 TomMarquand 4 56
(Richard Hannon) *sn detached in rr: rdn over 4f out: clsd and wl in tch 3f out: drvn over 1f out: outpcd by wnr 1f out: edgd lft and wnt modest 2nd ins fnl f: kpt on same pce after: lost 2nd last strides* **12/1**[3]

4250 **4** 4 1/2 **Vinnievanbaileys**[20] 4315 2-9-5 69 (b) SilvestreDeSousa 2 50
(Chris Dwyer) *sn w ldr: rdn ent fnl 2f: outpcd by wnr and btn 1f out: dropped to 4th and squeezed for room ins fnl f: wl btn and eased towards fin* **9/2**[2]

1m 25.37s (2.27) **Going Correction** +0.375s/f (Good) 4 Ran SP% **107.7**
Speed ratings (Par 94): **102,96,96,90**
CSF £3.44 TOTE £1.50; EX 3.10 Trifecta £10.20.
Owner S P C Woods **Bred** Bill Adair, Phyllis Adair & Connie Brown **Trained** Findon, W Sussex

FOCUS
It's hard to believe this will end up being anything other than modest form, but it gave the market leader a perfect chance to shed his maiden status. The pace didn't seem bad considering the lack of runners. This has been rated at the bottom end of the race averages.

5016 ESSEX & HERTFORDSHIRE (S) H'CAP 1m 3f 196y
2:50 (2:52) (Class 6) (0-55,52) 3-Y-O+ **£2,264** (£673; £336; £168) **Stalls** High

Form RPR
0-62 **1** **Goal (IRE)**[3] 3470 8-9-9 51 (vt) WilliamTwiston-Davies 3 61
(Sally Randell) *hld up in tch: trckd ldrs and gng wl 3f out: shkn up to ld 1f out: sn clr: r.o wl: pushed out: easily* **5/1**[3]

5320 **2** 7 **Elle Rebelle**[16] 4456 6-9-10 52 ShaneKelly 7 51
(Mark Brisbourne) *hld up in tch towards rr: clsd to chse ldrs 5f out: upsides ldr and travelling wl over 3f out: rdn and led over 1f out: sn hdd and outpcd by wnr: plugged on* **11/2**

-553 **3** 1 3/4 **Little Orchid**[23] 4212 3-8-10 52 AaronJones(3) 6 48
(Julia Feilden) *chsd ldrs tl led over 4f out: rdn over 2f out: hdd over 1f out and sn outpcd: wl hld and plugged on same pce fnl f* **11/4**[1]

0360 **4** 1 3/4 **Britannia Boy**[14] 4527 3-8-6 45 (p) DannyBrock 2 38
(Mark Usher) *hld up tch in rr: hdwy 5f out: cl enough in 4th and rdn over 2f out: drvn and no rspnse over 1f out: wl hld and plugged on same pce fnl f* **14/1**

0545 **5** 20 **Lucky Diva**[14] 4507 9-9-0 47 (p) HectorCrouch(5) 1 8
(Bill Turner) *hld up in tch in midfield: rdn over 3f out: wknd 2f out: wl bhd and eased ins fnl f* **7/2**[2]

-600 **6** 8 **Miss Mittens**[36] 3747 4-9-3 45 JohnFahy 5
(Geoffrey Deacon) *s.i.s: rdn along and flashing tail early: hdwy into midfield 9f out: dropped to rr again 7f out: rdn 5f out: wl bhd over 2f out: t.o and eased ins fnl f* **33/1**

0305 **7** 8 **Spring Overture**[23] 4204 4-9-3 45 JimCrowley 9
(Brendan Powell) *chsd ldr tl over 3f out: sn u.p and lost pl: t.o and eased ins fnl f* **10/1**

0005 **8** 31 **Pao De Acuca (IRE)**[23] 4212 4-9-10 52 (bt) SilvestreDeSousa 4
(Jose Santos) *led tl over 4f out: sn dropped out: t.o 2f out: eased fnl f* **7/1**

2m 39.22s (6.52) **Going Correction** +0.375s/f (Good)
WFA 3 from 4yo+ 11lb 8 Ran SP% **112.1**
Speed ratings (Par 101): **93,88,87,86,72 67,62,41**
CSF £31.16 CT £88.90 TOTE £5.20: £1.40, £1.80, £1.60; EX 22.50 Trifecta £82.70.
Owner Exors Of The Late Mark Hampson **Bred** A M F Persse **Trained** Broad Hinton, Wilts

FOCUS
Poor form whatever way you look at it, and only four counted from the 2f marker. The winning time was pretty slow compared to the standard. The winner is rated to last year's form.

5017 JOHN SMITH'S BRIGHTON MILE CHALLENGE TROPHY (H'CAP) 7f 214y
3:20 (3:21) (Class 4) (0-80,80) 3-Y-O+
£12,450 (£3,728; £1,864; £932; £466; £234) **Stalls** Low

Form RPR
4600 **1** **Cricklewood Green (USA)**[26] 4081 5-8-13 72 MitchGodwin(7) 4 79
(Sylvester Kirk) *hld up in last quartet: hdwy over 1f out: squeezed between horses 1f out: chsd ldrs ins fnl f: r.o wl to ld cl home* **12/1**

0423 **2** 1/2 **Pick A Little**[28] 4008 8-9-2 68 TimmyMurphy 8 74
(Michael Blake) *taken down early: chsd ldr tl 1/2-way: styd handy: rdn and ev ch over 1f out: led 1f out: sn hdd: battled bk and sn led again: hdd and no ex cl home* **22/1**

5120 **3** 1/2 **Pacolita (IRE)**[8] 4737 4-9-5 74 EdwardGreatrex(3) 15 79
(Sylvester Kirk) *t.k.h: hld up in tch in midfield but stuck wd: effrt over 1f out: hdwy u.p 1f out: styd on wl ins fnl f: wnt 3rd last stride* **13/2**[3]

5110 **4** shd **Pour La Victoire (IRE)**[53] 3159 6-9-3 76 (b) GeorgiaCox(7) 1 81
(Tony Carroll) *dwlt: sn rcvrd and in tch in midfield: hdwy 2f out: rdn and ev ch 1f out: led ins fnl f: sn hdd: no ex and wknd towards fin* **12/1**

3414 **5** nk **Duke Of North (IRE)**[20] 4302 4-8-8 67 RhiainIngram(7) 13 71
(Jim Boyle) *hld up in last quartet: clsd and nt clrest of runs over 1f out: hdwy 1f out: styd on wl ins fnl f: nt rch ldrs* **11/1**

0500 **6** 3 1/4 **Glenalmond (IRE)**[30] 3945 4-9-13 79 FergusSweeney 16 75
(Daniel Steele) *hld up in last quartet: rdn 2f out: no hdwy tl styd on to pass btn horses ins fnl f: nvr trbld ldrs* **25/1**

1202 **7** nk **Good Luck Charm**[19] 4354 7-9-6 77 (b) HectorCrouch(5) 2 73
(Gary Moore) *stdd after s: hld up in last quartet: hdwy over 2f out: rdn and no hdwy over 1f out: wknd ins fnl f* **16/1**

2360 **8** 1/2 **Mezzotint (IRE)**[26] 4081 7-9-9 75 KierenFox 7 70
(Lee Carter) *led: clr 1/2-way: rdn over 1f out: hdd 1f out: no ex and wknd ins fnl f* **16/1**

2152 **9** 2 1/2 **Freight Train (IRE)**[4] 4868 4-9-10 76 (p) NeilCallan 11 65
(Mark Johnston) *chsd ldrs tl wnt 2nd 1/2-way: rdn and unable qck over 1f out: wknd ins fnl f* **9/4**[1]

0142 **10** 1 3/4 **Ravenhoe (IRE)**[9] 4717 3-8-13 72 FrannyNorton 12 56
(Mark Johnston) *in tch in midfield: lost pl and rdn 2f out: sn struggling: wknd fnl f* **5/1**[2]

3126 **11** 3/4 **Qaffaal (USA)**[22] 4231 5-9-3 74 NathanEvans(5) 3 57
(Michael Easterby) *hld up in tch in midfield: effrt on inner over 1f out: n.m.r ent fnl f: wknd* **8/1**

-402 **12** 3 **Big Chill (IRE)**[25] 4157 4-9-10 76 JimCrowley 9 55
(Patrick Chamings) *in tch in midfield: 3f out: lost pl and btn over 1f out: bhd and eased ins fnl f* **14/1**

1m 37.17s (1.17) **Going Correction** +0.375s/f (Good)
WFA 3 from 4yo+ 7lb 12 Ran SP% **122.2**
Speed ratings (Par 105): **109,108,108,107,107 104,104,103,101,99 98,95**
CSF £256.04 CT £1904.06 TOTE £15.40: £4.50, £7.70, £2.20; EX 387.10 Trifecta £3609.70.
Owner Chris Wright & Andy MacDonald **Bred** Stratford Place Stud **Trained** Upper Lambourn, Berks

FOCUS
A tight finish to an ordinary race for the grade/money.

5018 KENT & SUSSEX/EBF STALLIONS BREEDING WINNERS FILLIES' H'CAP 6f 209y
3:50 (3:50) (Class 4) (0-85,78) 3-Y-O+ **£6,301** (£1,886; £943) **Stalls** Low

Form RPR
2445 **1** **Elusive Ellen (IRE)**[34] 3815 6-9-11 77 (t) ShaneKelly 3 85
(Brendan Powell) *chsd ldr tl moved rt off rail and rdn to ld over 2f out: drifting lft bk to rail over 1f out: r.o wl: rdn out* **7/2**[3]

-236 **2** 1 1/2 **Volition (IRE)**[27] 4042 3-9-6 78 TedDurcan 6 80
(Sir Michael Stoute) *stdd s: hld up in 3rd: followed wnr and c off rail over 2f out: effrt 2f out: chsd wnr 1f out: kpt on but no imp after* **2/1**[2]

2352 **3** nk **Bajan Rebel**[10] 4684 5-8-6 63 NathanEvans(5) 1 66
(Michael Easterby) *led tl over 2f out: rdn over 1f out: 3rd and styd on same pce ins fnl f* **10/11**[1]

1m 26.99s (3.89) **Going Correction** +0.375s/f (Good)
WFA 3 from 4yo+ 6lb 3 Ran SP% **107.9**
Speed ratings (Par 102): **92,90,89**
CSF £9.58 TOTE £4.00; EX 7.60 Trifecta £6.20.
Owner Con Harrington **Bred** Mrs Chris Harrington **Trained** Upper Lambourn, Berks

FOCUS
Not form to take overly seriously given the field size but it didn't appear to be run at really slow fractions. A decisive move by the winning jockey in the home straight was enough to see the other two off. A small pb from the winner, with the runner-up to her maiden form.

5019 LONDON H'CAP 1m 1f 209y
4:20 (4:20) (Class 6) (0-55,55) 3-Y-O+ **£2,587** (£770; £384; £192) **Stalls** High

Form RPR
-064 **1** **Iballisticvin**[35] 3765 3-8-0 46 oh1 NoelGarbutt(3) 4 53
(Gary Moore) *t.k.h: chsd ldrs: rdn to ld 2f out: forged ahd ins fnl f: styd on: rdn out* **11/2**

0-06 **2** 1 3/4 **Ahraam (IRE)**[15] 4498 3-8-5 55 JordanUys(7) 3 58
(Harry Whittington) *t.k.h early: led for 2f: chsd ldr after: ev ch and rdn 2f out: no ex and btn ins fnl f: wknd towards fin* **7/2**[2]

0-60 **3** shd **Fenner Hill Neasa (IRE)**[29] 3973 3-8-0 46 AaronJones(3) 10 49
(Pat Phelan) *stdd and dropped in after s: hld up in tch in rr: effrt over 2f out: hdwy to chse ldng pair and hung lft over 1f out: kpt on ins fnl f* **8/1**

0063 **4** 2 3/4 **Pivotal Dream (IRE)**[7] 4764 3-8-5 48 FrannyNorton 6 46
(Mark Brisbourne) *t.k.h: hld up in tch: effrt 2f out: wnt 4th 1f out: kpt on steadily but nvr threatened ldrs* **3/1**[1]

6-54 **5** 4 1/2 **Mystical Maze**[15] 4493 5-8-12 46 oh1 JimCrowley 2 35
(Mark Brisbourne) *hld up in tch in midfield: effrt 2f out: sn pushed along and hdwy: wl hld and plugged on same pce fnl f* **12/1**

-330 **6** 1 1/2 **Its A Sheila Thing**[21] 4267 3-8-10 53 RobertHavlin 12 39
(Linda Jewell) *hld up in tch in midfield: effrt 2f out: little rspnse and wl btn whn hmpd 1f out* **5/1**[3]

0-60 **7** 1 1/4 **Suni Dancer**[15] 4493 5-8-11 48 GeorgeDowning(3) 1 31
(Tony Carroll) *stdd after s: hld up in tch in rr: effrt jst over 2f out: no imp: wknd fnl f* **16/1**

0-03 **8** 1/2 **Santadelacruze**[14] 4527 7-9-6 54 (b) ShaneKelly 11 36
(Mark Hoad) *chsd ldrs tl led 8f out: c centre and field followed 3f out: rdn and hdd 2f out: sn btn: bhd 1f out* **10/1**

2m 7.25s (3.65) **Going Correction** +0.375s/f (Good)
WFA 3 from 4yo+ 9lb 8 Ran SP% **113.1**
Speed ratings (Par 101): **100,98,98,96,92 91,90,90**
CSF £24.47 CT £151.70 TOTE £6.40: £2.00, £2.00, £2.50; EX 31.60 Trifecta £229.10.
Owner Scuderia Vita Bella **Bred** Houghton-Barrons Partnership **Trained** Lower Beeding, W Sussex

FOCUS
A moderate contest.

5020 REGIONAL BREWERS H'CAP 5f 213y
4:50 (4:50) (Class 6) (0-55,54) 3-Y-O **£2,587** (£770; £384; £192) **Stalls** Low

Form RPR
0600 **1** **Oasis Moon**[21] 4275 3-9-3 50 (p) JimCrowley 2 60+
(William Haggas) *stdd s: t.k.h: trckd ldrs: angled rt and chal between horses over 1f out: rdn to ld ins fnl f: r.o wl: pushed out wl ins fnl f* **15/8**[1]

061 **2** 2 **Tahiti One**[37] 3725 3-9-7 54 WilliamCarson 4 58
(Tony Carroll) *led: rdn 2f out: drvn over 1f out: hdd ins fnl f: kpt on same pce after* **5/2**[3]

1204 **3** 3/4 **Guapo Bay**[20] 4289 3-8-11 51 (b) TinaSmith(7) 6 53
(Richard Hannon) *sltly hmpd and wnt rt s: in tch in last pair: hdwy to join ldrs over 2f out: rdn and ev ch over 1f out: 3rd and no ex 1f out: styd on same pce after* **9/4**[2]

0000 **4** 3 **Cecile Royale**[13] 4570 3-8-9 45 AaronJones(3) 5 37
(Stuart Williams) *chsd ldr tl over 2f out: sn rdn: outpcd and btn over 1f out: wknd ins fnl f* **9/1**

006- **5** 5 **Don't Tell Jo Jo**[228] 8306 3-8-7 45 HectorCrouch(5) 3 21
(Bill Turner) *stdd s: t.k.h: hld up in tch: effrt 2f out: no hdwy and hung lft over 1f out: wknd fnl f* **16/1**

1m 13.12s (2.92) **Going Correction** +0.375s/f (Good) 5 Ran SP% **110.0**
Speed ratings (Par 98): **95,92,91,87,80**
CSF £6.88 TOTE £2.80: £1.40, £1.70; EX 7.00 Trifecta £11.70.
Owner Sheikh Juma Dalmook Al Maktoum **Bred** Niarchos Family **Trained** Newmarket, Suffolk

FOCUS
The well-backed favourite/winner had shown virtually nothing previously, which helps to illustrates the weakness of this race.
T/Plt: £1025.80 to a £1 stake. Pool: £60,704.88 - 43.20 winning units. T/Qpdt: £115.90 to a £1 stake. Pool: £5,357.56 - 34.20 winning units. **Steve Payne**

4936 KEMPTON (A.W) (R-H)
Wednesday, August 3

OFFICIAL GOING: Polytrack: standard to slow
Wind: fresh across Weather: Warm

5021 RACING UK IN HD H'CAP 1m 4f (P)
6:10 (6:11) (Class 6) (0-60,60) 3-Y-O+ **£2,264** (£673; £336; £168) **Stalls** Centre

Form RPR
0200 **1** **Salient**[76] 2397 12-9-3 52 EdwardGreatrex(3) 9 62
(Michael Attwater) *racd in 2nd: rdn and led over 3f out: 5 l clr over 1f out: pressed ins fnl f: fnd more whn chal: rdn out* **25/1**

0-00 **2** 1/2 **Purple Lane (IRE)**[21] 4267 5-9-10 56 (t) TedDurcan 10 65
(Luke Dace) *racd in 6th: tk clsr order over 2f out: rdn to chse wnr over 1f out: ev ch ins fnl f: no ex tl styd on again nr fin* **14/1**

3002 **3** *4* **Awesome Rock (IRE)**[23] 4197 7-9-0 **46** oh1 DaneO'Neill 4 49
(Roger Ingram) *racd in 7th: shkn up 2f out: kpt on one pce fr over 1f out: no imp ins fnl f* **10/1**
2640 **4** *1 1/4* **Deluxe**[14] 4531 4-9-9 **60** PaddyBradley(5) 14 61
(Pat Phelan) *dropped out and wl in rr early: clsr at 1/2-way: rdn on outer over 2f out: kpt on wl tl one pce ins fnl f* **10/1**
0053 **5** *1 3/4* **Gunner Moyne**[21] 4267 4-10-0 **60** GeorgeBaker 6 58
(Gary Moore) *hld up in rr: tk clsr order over 2f out: shkn up 2f out: prog under hands heels fr over 1f out: nvr involved* **7/2**[2]
0-06 **6** *1 3/4* **Rizal Park (IRE)**[21] 336 5-10-0 **60** TimmyMurphy 13 55
(James Evans) *hld up in rr: rdn wl over 2f out: no imp fr over 1f out* **33/1**
0320 **7** *nse* **Bob's Boy**[21] 4275 3-8-12 **55** (p) RenatoSouza 5 50
(Jose Santos) *settled in 4th: niggled along over 4f out: rdn 4f out: kpt on tl wknd fr 1f out* **15/2**[3]
0001 **8** *6* **Munsarim (IRE)**[56] 3031 9-9-13 **59** (v) KierenFox 11 45
(Lee Carter) *s.s: in rr: rdn over 2f out: no ex* **9/1**
2112 **9** *4 1/2* **Zarliman (IRE)**[12] 3918 6-9-10 **56** (bt) LiamKeniry 1 34
(Neil Mulholland) *led tl hdd after 1f: restrained under t.k.h in 5th: rdn over 2f out: sn no ex and wknd* **3/1**[1]
5010 **10** *3/4* **Lily Edge**[14] 4527 7-9-6 **52** (v) DannyBrock 3 29
(John Bridger) *led after 1f tl hdd 2f: settled in 3rd: rdn over 2f out: sn no ex and wknd* **10/1**
06F5 **11** *8* **Machiavelian Storm (IRE)**[28] 4019 4-8-7 **46** oh1 LuluStanford(7) 7 10
(Richard Mitchell) *pushed up to ld after 2f: pressed and rdn over 3f out: sn hdd: no ex fr over 2f out and wknd* **25/1**

2m 36.34s (1.84) **Going Correction** +0.15s/f (Slow)
WFA 3 from 4yo+ 11lb **11** Ran SP% **113.6**
Speed ratings (Par 101): **99,98,96,95,94 92,92,88,85,85 79**
CSF £321.41 CT £3695.71 TOTE £27.20: £7.10, £4.50, £3.30; EX 353.60 Trifecta £3476.10.
Owner Canisbay Bloodstock **Bred** Hesmonds Stud Ltd **Trained** Epsom, Surrey

FOCUS
A moderate middle-distance handicap. They went an even gallop on standard to slow Polytrack and a veteran with previous form on this relatively rare type of going description came to the fore.

5022 BRITISH STALLION STUDS EBF MAIDEN FILLIES' STKS (PLUS 10 RACE) 7f (P)
6:40 (6:40) (Class 5) 2-Y-O **£3,234** (£962; £481; £240) **Stalls** Low

Form RPR
0 **1** **Fire Palace**[7] 4756 2-9-0 0 AndreaAtzeni 7 76
(Robert Eddery) *racd in 2nd: rdn and led over 1f out: racd nk and nk w runner-up and carried rt fr 1f out: hung sltly lft under drive fnl 55yds: jst got up* **4/1**[2]
03 **2** *shd* **Snow Squaw**[12] 4579 2-9-0 0 JimCrowley 3 75
(David Elsworth) *racd in 4th: gng wl over 2f out whn swtchd to outer: rdn over 1f out: hung rt gng nk and nk w wnr fr 1f out to wl ins fnl f: carried sltly lft fnl 55yds: jst hld* **10/11**[1]
0 **3** *6* **Vista Steppe**[20] 4298 2-9-0 0 FergusSweeney 2 59
(David Simcock) *racd in 3rd: rdn over 1f out: sn lft bhd by ldng pair: kpt on one pce fnl f: hld on for 3rd nr fin* **11/1**
4 *nk* **Flood Defence (IRE)** 2-9-0 0 TedDurcan 9 58
(Chris Wall) *in rr: pushed along 3f out: rdn over 1f out: kpt on one pce fnl f to press fr 3rd nr fin* **33/1**
5 *1/2* **Every Nice Girl (USA)** 2-9-0 0 HarryBentley 5 57
(Marco Botti) *settled in 5th: rdn along over 1f out: sn no imp on ldrs: one pce fnl f* **7/1**
0 **6** *3* **Onomatopoeia**[33] 3859 2-9-0 0 RobertHavlin 4 49
(Roger Ingram) *led: rdn and hdd over 1f out: ectra and wknd ins fnl f* **13/2**[3]
7 *7* **Demi's Quest** 2-9-0 0 JackMitchell 6 30
(Robert Eddery) *racd in 6th on outer: rn green ent st: rdn 2f out: hands and heels fr over 1f out* **33/1**

1m 27.61s (1.61) **Going Correction** +0.15s/f (Slow) **7** Ran SP% **112.4**
Speed ratings (Par 91): **96,95,89,88,88 84,76**
CSF £7.73 TOTE £4.00: £1.60, £1.40; EX 10.30 Trifecta £39.50.
Owner Edwin S Phillips **Bred** B & B Equine Limited **Trained** Newmarket, Suffolk

FOCUS
A fair juvenile fillies' maiden won by the smart Local Time in 2014 and the very smart Nemoralia in 2015 but this wasn't a vintage renewal despite the front two pulling clear. It's been rated around the bottom averages for the race.

5023 32RED ON THE APP STORE MAIDEN STKS 1m (P)
7:10 (7:11) (Class 5) 3-Y-O+ **£2,911** (£866; £432; £216) **Stalls** Low

Form RPR
2-52 **1** **Ballet Concerto**[22] 4235 3-9-5 86 AndreaAtzeni 10 91+
(Sir Michael Stoute) *broke wl and mde all: shkn up over 1f out: rdn and hung lft ins fnl f: kpt on wl and gng away nr fin* **7/4**[1]
2 *3* **Just For You** 3-8-11 0 [1] DanielMuscutt(3) 8 79+
(James Fanshawe) *settled in mid-div: prog on inner wl over 1f out to press wnr: kpt on wl tl wknd wl ins fnl f* **14/1**
23 **3** *1 3/4* **Toulson**[19] 4347 3-9-5 0 CharlesBishop 1 80
(Eve Johnson Houghton) *chsd ldr in 3rd on rail: ev ch whn rdn over 1f out: kpt on one pce ins fnl f* **10/3**[3]
4- **4** *1/2* **Curriculum**[278] 7592 3-9-5 0 GeorgeBaker 9 79+
(William Haggas) *settled in mid-div: shkn up on outer over 1f out: kpt on under hands and heels ins fnl f: nvr nrr* **5/2**[2]
0 **5** *1 1/2* **Donnerhall (IRE)**[46] 3411 3-9-5 0 RobertHavlin 7 75
(Simon Crisford) *settled in 4th: rdn over 1f out: sn no imp: no ex ins fnl f* **20/1**
5 **6** *9* **Nellie Deen (IRE)**[41] 3572 3-9-0 0 JimCrowley 12 49
(David Elsworth) *racd in 2nd: rdn over 2f out: no ex fr over 1f out: wknd qckly ins fnl f* **12/1**
00 **7** *7* **Moayadd (USA)**[16] 4458 4-9-12 0 FergusSweeney 11 38
(Neil Mulholland) *a in rr: rdn over 2f out: nvr gng pce* **100/1**
00 **8** *3* **Nightswift**[102] 1639 4-9-12 0 TimmyMurphy 2 31
(James Evans) *settled in mid-div: shkn up over 2f out: sn no ex and wknd fr over 1f out* **100/1**
9 *1 1/2* **Golden Muscade (USA)** 3-9-0 0 ThomasBrown 3 21
(Brian Barr) *in rr: shkn up over 2f out: sn no ex and wknd fr over 1f out* **100/1**
10 *5* **Pinkie Brown (FR)**[70] 4-9-12 0 LiamKeniry 5 15
(Neil Mulholland) *in rr: rdn 3f out: one pce over 2f out: no ex after* **25/1**
11 *57* **Joe Palooka (IRE)** 6-9-12 0 RyanPowell 4
(Alan Coogan) *racd in rr and rn green: no imp ent st and eased: t.o* **66/1**

1m 41.49s (1.69) **Going Correction** +0.15s/f (Slow)
WFA 3 from 4yo+ 7lb **11** Ran SP% **115.4**
Speed ratings (Par 103): **97,94,92,91,90 81,74,71,69,64 7**
CSF £26.52 TOTE £2.50: £1.10, £4.00, £1.50; EX 26.10 Trifecta £79.70.
Owner Saeed Suhail **Bred** Meon Valley Stud **Trained** Newmarket, Suffolk

FOCUS
A decent maiden won by the useful Don't Stare in 2013. The race was dictated from the front by the horse with clearly the best form beforehand and a reproduction proved more than enough. The third helps set the level.

5024 32RED.COM H'CAP (LONDON MILE SERIES QUALIFIER) 1m (P)
7:40 (7:40) (Class 4) (0-85,82) 3-Y-O+ **£4,690** (£1,395; £697; £348) **Stalls** Low

Form RPR
-063 **1** **Tournament**[19] 4368 5-9-9 **77** (t) GeorgeBaker 3 86
(Seamus Durack) *hld up in rr: smooth prog on outer over 2f out: stl on bridle over 1f out: rdn 1f out and qcknd wl to ld 100yds out: pushed out after: comf: p.u and dismntd sn after line* **4/1**[3]
2513 **2** *1 1/4* **Thaqaffa (IRE)**[19] 4374 3-9-6 **81** [1] DaneO'Neill 6 86
(Marcus Tregoning) *racd in 2nd: shkn up and rdn 2f out: sn led: kpt on on inner tl hdd 100yds out: one pce after* **2/1**[2]
111- **3** *1/2* **Fly**[287] 7388 4-9-12 **80** FrederikTylicki 4 85
(James Fanshawe) *racd in 4th: t.k.h: rdn 2f out: kpt on one pce* **13/8**[1]
031 **4** *3* **St Mary'S**[22] 4235 3-9-7 **82** OisinMurphy 1 79
(Andrew Balding) *racd in 5th: rdn over 2f out: no ex ins fnl f* **8/1**
3000 **5** *3 1/2* **Freddy With A Y (IRE)**[35] 3783 6-8-10 **69** DavidParkes(5) 2 58
(Paul Burgoyne) *settled in 3rd: rdn over 2f out: one pce and wknd fnl f* **50/1**
4215 **6** *1* **Shifting Star (IRE)**[16] 4463 11-9-5 **73** (vt) WilliamCarson 5 60
(John Bridger) *sn led: t.k.h: rdn and hdd 2f out: fnl f* **20/1**

1m 40.63s (0.83) **Going Correction** +0.15s/f (Slow)
WFA 3 from 4yo+ 7lb **6** Ran SP% **109.3**
Speed ratings (Par 105): **101,99,99,96,92 91**
CSF £11.75 TOTE £4.70: £1.80, £1.50; EX 12.00 Trifecta £28.20.
Owner Stephen Tucker **Bred** Juddmonte Farms Ltd **Trained** Upper Lambourn, Berkshire

FOCUS
A fairly decent handicap. They went a respectable gallop and the winner was able to pounce from off the pace. This has been rated around the second.

5025 £10 FREE BET AT 32REDSPORT.COM MAIDEN FILLIES' STKS 1m 4f (P)
8:10 (8:11) (Class 5) 3-Y-O+ **£2,911** (£866; £432; £216) **Stalls** Centre

Form RPR
3-24 **1** **Moorside**[65] 2735 3-9-0 96 MichaelJMMurphy 6 82
(Charles Hills) *settled in 2nd: shkn up over 2f out: rdn and led over 1f out: hung sltly rt ins fnl f: kpt on wl* **6/4**[1]
30-2 **2** *1 1/2* **Tuolumne Meadows**[35] 3781 3-9-0 78 LukeMorris 1 79
(Paul Cole) *settled in 3rd: rdn over 2f out: kpt on wl and ev ch on inner ent fnl f: carried sltly rt ins fnl f: dropped out of contention fr 110yds out: one pce* **10/1**[3]
64-3 **3** *3 1/2* **Lovely Story (IRE)**[26] 4078 5-9-11 92 GeorgeBaker 3 73
(Seamus Durack) *sn led: rdn 2f out: wknd between horses and hdd over 1f out: sn one pce* **6/4**[1]
04 **4** *12* **Adalene**[52] 3194 3-9-0 0 OisinMurphy 5 54
(David Simcock) *settled in 5th: rdn over 2f out: no imp and eased over 1f out* **11/2**[2]
50 **5** *1/2* **Notice (IRE)**[35] 3781 3-9-0 0 FergusSweeney 4 53
(David Simcock) *racd in 6th and rn green early: rdn along over 2f out: sn no imp: eased fr over 1f out* **40/1**
6 *43* **Alidara (IRE)** 4-9-11 0 TimmyMurphy 2
(Emma Owen) *racd in 4th: niggled along after 4f: rdn 4f out: no ex ent st and eased fr over 1f out: t.o* **100/1**

2m 35.81s (1.31) **Going Correction** +0.15s/f (Slow)
WFA 3 from 4yo+ 11lb **6** Ran SP% **107.9**
Speed ratings (Par 100): **101,100,97,89,89 60**
CSF £16.81 TOTE £2.40: £1.30, £2.10; EX 12.60 Trifecta £18.60.
Owner K Abdullah **Bred** Juddmonte Farms Ltd **Trained** Lambourn, Berks

FOCUS
A tricky maiden to read and the winner has been rated close to her previous maiden figures, rather than her standout Cheshire Oaks figure.

5026 32RED H'CAP (LONDON MIDDLE DISTANCE SERIES QUALIFIER) 1m 3f (P)
8:40 (8:40) (Class 4) (0-85,85) 3-Y-O+ **£4,690** (£1,395; £697; £348) **Stalls** Low

Form RPR
1314 **1** **West Coast Flyer**[19] 4346 3-8-11 **78** AndreaAtzeni 8 85+
(David Simcock) *racd in 6th: shkn up over 2f out: swtchd to outer over 1f out: str run to ld 110yds out: kpt on wl* **9/2**[2]
4020 **2** *1 1/4* **Sarsted**[42] 3525 4-9-12 **83** (b) JimCrowley 4 87
(Hughie Morrison) *settled in 4th: rdn over 2f out: hung sltly rt and bmpd rival 2f out: kpt on wl u.p: ev ch jst over 1f out: tk 2nd 100yds out: nt gng pce of wnr* **5/1**[3]
4-04 **3** *1/2* **Rehearse (IRE)**[42] 3535 3-8-7 **74** OisinMurphy 1 77
(Andrew Balding) *racd in 5th: nt clr run over 2f out whn sltly bmpd: gap opened and rdn 2f out: ev ch jst over 1f out: kpt on and tk 3rd nr fin* **14/1**
0033 **4** *hd* **Ladurelli (IRE)**[6] 4808 4-9-10 **81** TomMarquand 2 83
(Paul Cole) *t.k.h in 4th: rdn on inner over 2f out: led over 1f out: wknd and hdd 110yds out: lost two pls nr fin* **5/1**[3]
4225 **5** *1 1/4* **Sbraase**[25] 4153 5-10-0 **85** LukeMorris 3 85
(James Tate) *hld up in rr: shkn up over 2f out: swtchd to outer and kpt on one pce ins fnl f* **4/1**[1]
31 **6** *1/2* **Angrywhitepyjamas (IRE)**[23] 4213 3-8-10 **77** MartinDwyer 6 76
(William Muir) *pressed ldr: rdn 2f out where led briefly: one pce fr 1f out* **4/1**[1]
P-06 **7** *11* **London Citizen (USA)**[35] 3785 6-9-13 **84** GeorgeBaker 7 64
(Chris Wall) *sn led: rdn and hdd 2f out: wknd qckly fr over 1f out* **9/1**

2m 20.55s (-1.35) **Going Correction** +0.15s/f (Slow)
WFA 3 from 4yo+ 10lb **7** Ran SP% **108.2**
Speed ratings (Par 105): **110,109,108,108,107 107,99**
CSF £23.98 CT £251.35 TOTE £4.60: £2.20, £2.80; EX 27.80 Trifecta £205.30.
Owner Ali Saeed **Bred** Miss K Rausing **Trained** Newmarket, Suffolk

FOCUS
A decent middle-distance handicap. They went a respectable gallop and the form should prove reliable. The second helps set the level.

5027 32RED.COM CASINO H'CAP 7f (P)
9:10 (9:10) (Class 5) (0-75,75) 3-Y-O **£2,911** (£866; £432; £216) **Stalls** Low

Form RPR
-604 **1** **Consulting**[14] 4502 3-9-2 **70** HarryBentley 5 77
(Martyn Meade) *hld up in rr: tk clsr order and swtchd to outer 2f out: rdn over 1f out: styd on best to ld fnl 75yds* **4/1**[2]

6024 **2** *nk* **Finelcity (GER)**[18] 4382 3-9-5 **73**....(b) JimCrowley 10 79
(Harry Dunlop) *t.k.h and racd up fr outside draw to press ldr: rdn wl over 1f out where lost pl: kpt on again ins fnl f: tk 2nd fnl strides: jst hld* **11/4**[1]
0-42 **3** *½* **Palenville (IRE)**[34] 3821 3-9-7 **75**.... RobertHavlin 3 79
(Simon Crisford) *restrained in 4th: rdn over 1f out: tk 2nd 1f out: kpt on ins fnl f: one pce whn lost 2nd fnl strides* **11/4**[1]
P330 **4** *1 ¼* **Nassuvian Pearl**[27] 4043 3-9-3 **71**.... OisinMurphy 6 72
(Ralph Beckett) *wnt rt ss and in rr: plld way to front after 1f out: rdn over 2f out: kpt on wl tl wknd and hdd 75yds out: lost two pls nr fin* **4/1**[2]
-040 **5** *2 ½* **Port Gaverne (IRE)**[175] 519 3-8-8 **62**.... DannyBrock 1 56
(Marcus Tregoning) *led for 1f: racd on rail in 3rd: rdn over 2f out: ev ch over 1f out: wknd ins fnl f* **25/1**
4-40 **6** *hd* **Magic Strike (IRE)**[21] 4269 3-8-11 **65**.... LukeMorris 2 59
(Clive Cox) *settled in 7th: rdn on inner 2f out: sn one pce: sme prog under hands and heels ins fnl f* **14/1**[3]
-440 **7** *4* **Yensir**[20] 4307 3-9-2 **75**....(v) PaddyBradley(5) 9 58
(Pat Phelan) *s.s: sn settled in 5th: pushed along over 3f out: rdn over 2f out: sn hld and wknd: lost shoe* **20/1**
-030 **8** *17* **Song Of Paradise**[14] 4517 3-9-1 **69**.... TedDurcan 7 6
(Chris Wall) *racd in 6th on outer: rdn over 2f out: no ex and wknd qckly over 1f out: eased* **20/1**

1m 26.38s (0.38) **Going Correction** +0.15s/f (Slow) **8** Ran SP% **113.4**
Speed ratings (Par 100): **103,102,102,100,97 97,93,73**
CSF £14.80 CT £34.41 TOTE £4.40: £1.30, £1.30, £1.60; EX 15.50 Trifecta £48.70.
Owner J Anderson & J Spence 1 **Bred** Ladyswood Stud **Trained** Newmarket, Suffolk

FOCUS
The winner is rated back to the form of his 6f maiden win here, with the second posting a small pb. The third and fourth help set the level.
T/Plt: £217.70 to a £1 stake. Pool: £60,539.66 - 203.00 winning units. T/Qpdt: £16.50 to a £1 stake. Pool: £8,657.44 - 387.48 winning units. **Cathal Gahan**

4685 PONTEFRACT (L-H)
Wednesday, August 3

OFFICIAL GOING: Good to firm (8.9)
Wind: Moderate behind increasing to strong after 3.10 race Weather: Cloudy with sunny periods

5028 MOTORPOINT CASTLEFORD H'CAP (FOR GENTLEMAN AMATEUR RIDERS) 1m 2f 6y
2:10 (2:10) (Class 5) (0-75,75) 3-Y-O+ **£3,119** (£967; £483; £242) **Stalls** Low

Form RPR
0531 **1** **Silver Alliance**[27] 4052 8-11-0 **68**....(b) MrRBirkett 2 78+
(Julia Feilden) *trckd ldrs on inner: hdwy 3f out: effrt and nt clr run over 1f out: sn swtchd rt and rdn to ld ent fnl f: styd on wl* **11/4**[1]
6653 **2** *1 ¼* **Qibtee (FR)**[19] 4340 6-9-9 **56**.... MrMWBrown(7) 6 61
(Les Eyre) *hld up in rr: hdwy on outer 2f out: rdn over 1f out: styd on ins fnl f* **12/1**
4653 **3** *2* **Merchant Of Medici**[14] 4515 9-10-7 **61**.... MrSWalker 1 62
(Micky Hammond) *cl up on inner: slt ld wl over 2f out: rdn wl over 1f out: hdd and drvn ent fnl f: kpt on same pce* **4/1**[2]
5605 **4** *2* **Farham (USA)**[16] 4455 4-10-10 **69**....(p) MrMEnnis(5) 5 66
(Richard Fahey) *trckd ldrs: pushed along wl over 2f out: sn rdn and sltly outpcd: kpt on u.p fnl f* **11/2**[3]
U103 **5** *½* **Lean On Pete (IRE)**[8] 4730 7-10-2 **59**.... MrJamesKing(3) 4 55
(Ollie Pears) *cl up on outer: disp ld 1/2-way: rdn along over 2f out: drvn over 1f out: kpt on same pce* **6/1**
4444 **6** *6* **Proven Point (IRE)**[19] 4372 3-10-1 **69**....(p) MrHHunt(5) 3 53
(Tony Coyle) *t.k.h: slt ld: rdn along 3f out: sn hdd: drvn wl over 1f out: sn wknd* **6/1**
6624 **7** *¾* **Muqarred (USA)**[50] 3252 4-11-2 **75**....(t) MrJoeWright(5) 7 58
(David Loughnane) *hld up in tch: effrt 3f out: rdn along 2f out: sn drvn and btn* **7/1**

2m 15.09s (1.39) **Going Correction** -0.05s/f (Good)
WFA 3 from 4yo+ 9lb **7** Ran SP% **110.8**
Speed ratings (Par 103): **92,91,89,87,87 82,82**
CSF £33.65 TOTE £2.80: £1.50, £6.20; EX 28.80 Trifecta £123.40.
Owner In It To Win Partnership **Bred** Peter Harris **Trained** Exning, Suffolk

FOCUS
It was dry overnight and the watered ground was given as good to firm (GoingStick: 8.9). All distances as advertised. They didn't go much of a pace in this amateur riders' event. The winner is getting back towards last year's level, with the runner-up to this season's form.

5029 FRIENDS OF FRANCIS HAMILTON MEMORIAL EBF STALLIONS MAIDEN STKS (PLUS 10 RACE) 6f
2:40 (2:43) (Class 4) 2-Y-O **£5,175** (£1,540; £769; £384) **Stalls** Low

Form RPR
2300 **1** **Perfect Madge (IRE)**[18] 4394 2-9-0 81.... KevinStott 2 71
(Kevin Ryan) *trckd ldrs: hdwy over 2f out: swtchd rt and rdn over 1f out: drvn to ld ins fnl f: jst hld on* **13/8**[1]
2 *hd* **Mont Royal (FR)** 2-9-5 0.... DanielTudhope 7 75+
(Ollie Pears) *hld up in rr: hdwy on inner 2f out: swtchd rt to outer over 1f out: rdn and styng on strly whn green and edgd lft ins fnl f: fin wl: jst failed* **28/1**
3 *1 ¼* **Pudding Chare (IRE)** 2-9-5 0.... DavidNolan 1 71+
(Richard Fahey) *dwlt: hdwy to trck ldrs on inner after 2f: pushed along and hdwy wl over 1f out: rdn and ch ins fnl f: kpt on same pce* **13/2**
64 **4** *hd* **Glorious Artist (IRE)**[18] 4390 2-9-5 0.... GrahamLee 10 70
(Charles Hills) *trckd ldrs: hdwy on outer and cl up over 2f out: rdn and edgd lft and rt appr fnl f: sn drvn and kpt on* **2/1**[2]
0422 **5** *nk* **Father McKenzie**[7] 4762 2-9-5 71.... CharlesBishop 9 69
(Mick Channon) *prom: cl up over 2f out: rdn to ld wl over 1f out: drvn ent fnl f: sn hdd and kpt on same pce* **6/1**[3]
50 **6** *1* **Silk Mill Blue**[19] 4371 2-9-5 0.... GeorgeChaloner 11 66
(Richard Whitaker) *sn pushed along and towards rr: rdn over 2f out: kpt on u.p fnl f* **66/1**
50 **7** *2 ½* **Bruny Island (IRE)**[10] 4678 2-9-5 0.... JoeFanning 6 58
(Mark Johnston) *led: rdn along over 2f out: hdd wl over 1f out: grad wknd* **33/1**
8 *2 ¾* **Ideal Bounty (IRE)** 2-9-5 0.... NeilFarley 5 49
(Andrew Crook) *a towards rr* **66/1**
05 **9** *13* **Heaven's Rock (IRE)**[13] 4545 2-9-0 0....(t) AnnaHesketh(5) 8 7
(Tom Dascombe) *a in rr* **25/1**

0 **10** *27* **Maggi May (IRE)**[54] 3112 2-9-0 0.... PaulMulrennan 4
(David Brown) *chsd ldrs: rdn along wl over 2f out: sn wknd* **33/1**

1m 17.06s (0.16) **Going Correction** -0.05s/f (Good) **10** Ran SP% **115.2**
Speed ratings (Par 96): **96,95,94,93,93 92,88,85,67,31**
CSF £55.38 TOTE £2.60: £1.10, £5.70, £1.90; EX 46.10 Trifecta £297.50.
Owner T A Rahman **Bred** George Kent **Trained** Hambleton, N Yorks

FOCUS
There was a decent gallop on but they finished in a bit of a heap so it's hard to rate the form that highly.

5030 JAYNE AND STEVE ROBINSON - YOUR LOCAL BOOKMAKER H'CAP 1m 4y
3:10 (3:10) (Class 5) (0-70,70) 3-Y-O+ **£5,175** (£1,540; £769; £384) **Stalls** Low

Form RPR
2310 **1** **British Embassy (IRE)**[30] 3952 4-10-0 **70**.... PJMcDonald 1 81
(David Loughnane) *qckly away: mde all: clr 1/2-way: rdn wl over 1f out: drvn ins fnl f: hld on gamely towards fin* **10/3**[2]
6000 **2** *½* **Mime Dance**[39] 3646 5-9-12 **68**....(p) DanielTudhope 2 78
(David O'Meara) *trckd wnr: hdwy to take clsr order wl over 1f out: effrt ent fnl f: sn rdn and ev ch: drvn and kpt on same pce last 100yds* **7/4**[1]
5230 **3** *8* **John Caesar (IRE)**[15] 4486 5-9-8 **64**....(t) JamesSullivan 7 56
(Rebecca Bastiman) *dwlt and in rr: hdwy wl over 2f out: rdn wl over 1f out: kpt on fnl f* **16/1**
0000 **4** *2 ¼* **Border Bandit (USA)**[37] 3717 8-9-2 **58**....(p) ConnorBeasley 11 44
(Tracy Waggott) *dwlt and in rr: hdwy on outer wl over 2f out: rdn wl over 1f out: kpt on fnl f* **28/1**
3630 **5** *shd* **The King's Steed**[12] 4607 3-8-12 **68**.... LaurenSteade(7) 5 53
(Micky Hammond) *chsd ldng pair: rdn along 3f out: wknd 2f out* **25/1**
1460 **6** *2* **Palpitation (IRE)**[60] 2900 3-9-3 **66**.... PaulMulrennan 10 47
(David Brown) *chsd ldng pair: rdn along wl over 2f out: drvn and outpcd fr wl over 1f out* **9/1**
-044 **7** *3 ½* **Shadowtime**[16] 4454 11-9-4 **60**.... DaleSwift 3 34
(Tracy Waggott) *dwlt: sn in tch: rdn along 3f out: sn drvn and wknd* **9/1**
3261 **8** *6* **City Of Night (IRE)**[16] 4454 4-9-4 **65**....(e) JoshDoyle(5) 6 25
(Julie Camacho) *in tch: pushed along 3f out: rdn over 2f out: drvn and wknd wl over 1f out* **4/1**[3]

1m 45.16s (-0.74) **Going Correction** -0.05s/f (Good)
WFA 3 from 4yo+ 7lb **8** Ran SP% **112.6**
Speed ratings (Par 103): **101,100,92,90,90 88,84,78**
CSF £9.25 CT £76.71 TOTE £4.60: £1.80, £1.20, £3.70; EX 9.50 Trifecta £83.70.
Owner R G Fell **Bred** Corduff Stud Ltd & T J Rooney **Trained** Market Drayton, Shropshire

FOCUS
Few got into this.

5031 TIESPLANET.COM - LADIES LOVE GUYS IN TIES H'CAP 1m 4f 8y
3:40 (3:41) (Class 3) (0-95,93) 3-Y-O+
£9,337 (£2,796; £1,398; £699; £349; £175) **Stalls** Low

Form RPR
0013 **1** **Stars Over The Sea (USA)**[8] 4731 5-10-0 **93**.... JoeFanning 4 107+
(Mark Johnston) *mde all: rdn clr over 1f out: styd on strly* **10/11**[1]
0422 **2** *5* **Mukhayyam**[10] 4680 4-9-1 **80**....(p) DavidAllan 5 84
(Tim Easterby) *trckd ldrs: hdwy to chse wnr over 2f out: rdn wl over 1f out: drvn and no imp fnl f* **5/1**[2]
3000 **3** *4* **Hardstone (USA)**[26] 4077 5-9-8 **87**.... TomEaves 3 85
(Michael Dods) *trckd ldng pair on inner: pushed along wl over 2f out: sn rdn and kpt on same pce* **25/1**
3004 **4** *2 ¼* **Blue Hussar (IRE)**[18] 4407 5-9-7 **86**....(p) PJMcDonald 2 80
(Micky Hammond) *hld up in rr: hdwy 3f out: rdn along 2f out: sn no imp* **8/1**
-000 **5** *4* **Hernandoshideaway**[26] 4095 4-9-9 **88**.... PaulMulrennan 1 76
(Michael Dods) *hld up in rr: effrt and hdwy over 3f out: rdn along to chse ldrs over 2f out: sn drvn and one pce* **15/2**[3]
145 **6** *36* **Jam Session (IRE)**[40] 3602 4-9-1 **80**....(p) BenCurtis 6 10
(Ian Williams) *chsd wnr: rdn along over 3f out: drvn and wknd over 2f out: bhd and eased over 1f out* **15/2**[3]

2m 35.0s (-5.80) **Going Correction** -0.05s/f (Good) **6** Ran SP% **107.5**
Speed ratings (Par 107): **117,113,111,109,106 82**
CSF £5.13 TOTE £1.80: £1.40, £1.70; EX 5.40 Trifecta £58.10.
Owner R S Brookhouse **Bred** W S Farish & Watership Down Stud **Trained** Middleham Moor, N Yorks

FOCUS
This proved straightforward for the favourite, who was always in control out in front.

5032 CHAPLINS CLUB H'CAP 5f
4:10 (4:11) (Class 5) (0-75,75) 3-Y-O+ **£3,234** (£962; £481; £240) **Stalls** Low

Form RPR
4523 **1** **Sandra's Secret (IRE)**[12] 4612 3-9-2 **70**.... DavidAllan 9 79
(Les Eyre) *cl up: led wl over 1f out and sn rdn: drvn ins fnl f: kpt on strly* **15/2**[3]
3435 **2** *1 ½* **Royal Brave (IRE)**[15] 4488 5-9-7 **72**.... DanielTudhope 13 77+
(Rebecca Bastiman) *in rr: hdwy on wd outside over 1f out: sn rdn: styd on strly fnl f* **9/1**
1403 **3** *shd* **Burtonwood**[8] 4726 4-8-10 **66**.... JoshDoyle(5) 8 70
(Julie Camacho) *midfield: hdwy wl over 1f out: rdn to chse ldrs ent fnl f: sn drvn and kpt on* **11/1**
4000 **4** *¾* **Burning Thread (IRE)**[16] 4461 9-9-2 **74**....(b) AdamMcLean(7) 1 76
(David Elsworth) *stmbld s: sn chsng ldrs on inner: hdwy 2f out: swtchd rt and rdn to chse wnr over 1f out: drvn and kpt on same pce fnl f* **12/1**
5321 **5** *1* **Mr Orange (IRE)**[19] 4376 3-8-12 **66**....(p) CamHardie 7 63
(Paul Midgley) *chsd ldrs: rdn along over 2f out: drvn over 1f out: kpt on same pce* **6/1**[2]
0002 **6** *½* **Flicka's Boy**[8] 4726 4-9-3 **68**....(t) BarryMcHugh 3 64
(Tony Coyle) *in tch: hdwy over 2f out: rdn along wl over 1f out: sn drvn and no imp* **8/1**
0-00 **7** *shd* **Astrophysics**[12] 4608 4-9-7 **72**.... PaddyAspell 11 68
(Lynn Siddall) *towards rr: hdwy 2f out: rdn over 1f out: kpt on u.p fnl f* **40/1**
2405 **8** *½* **Flowing Clarets**[27] 4034 3-9-2 **75**.... AdamMcNamara(5) 5 70
(Richard Fahey) *hld up: hdwy 2f out: rdn wl over 1f out: sn drvn and no imp* **17/2**
3214 **9** *shd* **Flash City (ITY)**[14] 4514 8-9-9 **74**.... JamesSullivan 10 68
(Ruth Carr) *hld up: effrt and sme hdwy wl over 1f out: sn rdn and n.d* **10/1**
00/0 **10** *¾* **Storm Trooper (IRE)**[26] 4100 5-8-12 **63**.... RoystonFfrench 6 54
(David Nicholls) *led: rdn along 2f out: hdd and drvn over 1f out: sn wknd* **16/1**

0014 **11** 1½ **Eternitys Gate**[16] 4452 5-9-9 **74** .... DavidNolan 2 60
(Ivan Furtado) *chsd ldrs: rdn along wl over 1f out: sn drvn and wknd* **7/2**[1]

4464 **12** *hd* **Long Awaited (IRE)**[14] 4536 8-9-10 **75** .... (p) PaulMulrennan 12 60
(Conor Dore) *hld up: a in rr* **25/1**

1m 2.45s (-0.85) **Going Correction** -0.05s/f (Good)
WFA 3 from 4yo+ 3lb **12** Ran SP% **117.2**
Speed ratings (Par 103): **104,101,101,100,98 97,97,96,96,95 93,92**
CSF £72.55 CT £755.15 TOTE £7.60: £2.40, £3.20, £3.40; EX 80.90 Trifecta £820.10.
Owner Sunpak Potatoes **Bred** Tally-Ho Stud **Trained** Catwick, N Yorks

FOCUS
A competitive sprint but once again racing on the pace paid off. The winner is rated back to her 2yo level, with the third helping to set the standard.

5033 RIU HOTELS LADIES DAY VETERANS H'CAP 1m 4y
4:40 (4:40) (Class 4) (0-80,80) 6-Y-O+ **£5,175** (£1,540; £769; £384) **Stalls** Low

Form RPR

0502 **1** **Ralphy Boy (IRE)**[5] 4830 7-8-13 **72** .... PJMcDonald 2 78
(Alistair Whillans) *mde all: rdn wl over 1f out: drvn ins fnl f: hld on gamely towards fin* **11/4**[1]

0035 **2** *nk* **Chiswick Bey (IRE)**[11] 4627 8-8-10 **69** .... GeorgeChaloner 1 74
(Richard Fahey) *dwlt: sn in tch: trckd ldng pair over 3f out: rdn along on inner over 1f out: n.m.r and squeezed through ins fnl f: drvn and kpt on wl towards fin* **9/2**[3]

0010 **3** ½ **Echo Of Lightning**[11] 4627 6-8-11 **75** .... (p) CallumShepherd(5) 4 79
(Brian Ellison) *sn trcking wnr: effrt and cl up 2f out: sn rdn: drvn and ev ch ins fnl f: kpt on* **16/1**

5023 **4** ½ **Kiwi Bay**[7] 4768 11-9-1 **74** .... PaulMulrennan 7 76
(Michael Dods) *t.k.h: hld up in rr: hdwy on outer wl over 1f out: sn rdn: kpt on u.p fnl f* **9/1**

6060 **5** *nse* **Tommy's Secret**[34] 3823 6-8-2 **65** ow1 .... CharlieBennett(5) 6 68
(Jane Chapple-Hyam) *chsd ldrs: rdn and hdwy on outer 2f out: drvn jst over 1f out: kpt on u.p fnl f* **16/1**

1234 **6** 1¾ **Curzon Line**[26] 4089 7-8-9 **68** .... GrahamGibbons 8 66
(Michael Easterby) *trckd ldng pair: hdwy over 2f out: rdn to chal wl over 1f out: everty ch tl drvn and one pce fnl f* **11/2**

0616 **7** ½ **Janaab (IRE)**[22] 4232 6-8-7 **69** .... (t) RachelRichardson(3) 3 66
(Tim Easterby) *t.k.h: trckd ldrs: effrt 2f out: sn rdn and n.m.r appr fnl f: swtchd rt and kpt on* **10/1**

/P-3 **8** 12 **Like A Diamond (IRE)**[39] 3660 6-9-7 **80** .... DaleSwift 5 48
(Brian Ellison) *a in rr* **10/3**[2]

1m 44.64s (-1.26) **Going Correction** -0.05s/f (Good) **8** Ran SP% **114.2**
Speed ratings: **104,103,103,102,102 100,100,88**
CSF £15.31 CT £163.08 TOTE £3.60: £1.30, £1.60, £4.10; EX 17.10 Trifecta £179.80.
Owner Frank Lowe **Bred** Frank Lowe **Trained** Newmill-On-Slitrig, Borders

FOCUS
Another race on the card in which the winner was never headed.

5034 KEITH HAMMILL MEMORIAL H'CAP 6f
5:10 (5:10) (Class 4) (0-80,79) 3-Y-O+ **£5,175** (£1,540; £769; £384) **Stalls** Low

Form RPR

6553 **1** **Ace Master**[15] 4496 8-8-10 **71** .... (b) KevinLundie(7) 3 78
(Roy Bowring) *cl up on inner: led after 2f: rdn wl over 1f out: drvn ins fnl f: kpt on wl towards fin* **11/2**[3]

0045 **2** ¾ **Yeeoow (IRE)**[8] 4741 7-9-4 **79** .... CliffordLee(7) 8 83
(K R Burke) *qckly away and led 2f: cl up: rdn to chal over 1f out: drvn and ev ch ins fnl f: kpt on same pce towards fin* **6/1**

0103 **3** *shd* **Space War**[5] 4848 9-8-6 **65** .... AnnaHesketh(5) 4 69
(Michael Easterby) *hld up in rr: hdwy wl over 1f out: sn swtchd rt and rdn: styd on wl fnl f* **9/1**

0601 **4** 1½ **Sunraider (IRE)**[13] 4544 9-9-5 **73** .... GrahamLee 1 72
(Paul Midgley) *hld up in rr: hdwy on inner wl over 1f out: swtchd rt and rdn ent fnl f: kpt on* **4/1**[2]

2-40 **5** *shd* **Never In Doubt**[63] 2802 3-9-0 **72** .... GeorgeChaloner 5 70
(Richard Whitaker) *chsd ldrs: rdn wl over 1f out: drvn and kpt on same pce fnl f* **16/1**

0132 **6** 3¼ **Maureb (IRE)**[10] 4689 4-9-6 **74** .... (p) BenCurtis 6 62
(Tony Coyle) *chsd ldrs: rdn along 2f out: drvn over 1f out: grad wknd* **4/1**[2]

2333 **7** 5 **Kyllukey**[11] 4662 3-9-7 **79** .... GrahamGibbons 2 50
(Charles Hills) *hld up in tch: effrt 2f out: sn rdn and btn over 1f out* **7/2**[1]

0000 **8** 3½ **Clubland (IRE)**[15] 4496 7-9-2 **73** .... AlistairRawlinson(3) 7 34
(Roy Bowring) *chsd ldrs on outer: rdn along 2f out: sn drvn and wknd* **20/1**

1m 15.83s (-1.07) **Going Correction** -0.05s/f (Good)
WFA 3 from 4yo+ 4lb **8** Ran SP% **112.5**
Speed ratings (Par 105): **105,104,103,101,101 97,90,86**
CSF £36.93 CT £290.38 TOTE £6.80: £1.70, £2.00, £2.60; EX 40.80 Trifecta £230.50.
Owner S R Bowring **Bred** S R Bowring **Trained** Edwinstowe, Notts

FOCUS
An open handicap on paper, but once again the pace held up and the first two shared those positions throughout.
T/Jkpt: £6666.60 to a £1 stake. Pool: £10,000.00 - 1.50 winning units. T/Plt: £77.90 to a £1 stake. Pool: £70,244.48 - 657.83 winning units. T/Qpdt: £9.90 to a £1 stake. Pool: £5,795.05 - 432.81 winning units. **Joe Rowntree**

4738 YARMOUTH (L-H)
Wednesday, August 3

OFFICIAL GOING: Good to firm (7.8)
Wind: Fresh across Weather: Fine

5035 GOLD AND SILVER EXCHANGE OF GREAT YARMOUTH H'CAP 1m 6f 17y
5:20 (5:20) (Class 5) (0-75,75) 3-Y-O+ **£2,911** (£866; £432; £216) **Stalls** High

Form RPR

4453 **1** **Music Man (IRE)**[28] 4012 6-10-0 **75** .... PatCosgrave 4 80
(Laura Mongan) *chsd ldr: rdn to ld over 2f out: edgd lft over 1f out: styd on u.p* **9/4**[2]

4121 **2** 1¼ **Sandy Cove**[28] 4023 5-9-10 **71** .... RyanTate 3 74
(James Eustace) *hld up: hdwy over 2f out: rdn to chse wnr over 1f out: styd on* **13/8**[1]

0P-6 **3** *shd* **Meetings Man (IRE)**[27] 4057 9-9-11 **72** .... (p) DougieCostello 5 75
(Ali Stronge) *s.i.s: rcvrd to ld after 1f: clr 11f out tl over 5f out: rdn and hdd over 2f out: nt clr run wl over 1f out: styd on u.p* **15/2**

0252 **4** 6 **The Ducking Stool**[13] 4551 9-9-5 **69** .... ShelleyBirkett(3) 6 63
(Julia Feilden) *led 1f: chsd ldrs: rdn over 3f out: styd on same pce fnl 2f* **3/1**[3]

3m 4.97s (-2.63) **Going Correction** -0.10s/f (Good)
WFA 3 from 5yo+ 13lb **4** Ran SP% **105.6**
Speed ratings (Par 103): **103,102,102,98**
CSF £6.00 TOTE £2.80; EX 5.00 Trifecta £15.20.
Owner Mrs Jackie Cornwell **Bred** Swordlestown Stud **Trained** Epsom, Surrey

FOCUS
No rail adjustments advised. Racing took place in warm but windy conditions which prompted a going change (from good to firm, good in places) about an hour before racing. A modest stayers' event to begin with and the winner is rated to this year's AW level.

5036 BRITISH STALLION STUDS EBF "STALLION-RESTRICTED" MAIDEN STKS (PLUS 10 RACE) 7f 3y
5:50 (5:52) (Class 4) 2-Y-O **£6,301** (£1,886; £943; £472; £235) **Stalls** Centre

Form RPR

1 **Winston C (IRE)** 2-9-5 0 .... JamieSpencer 1 76+
(Michael Bell) *hld up: hdwy over 1f out: r.o u.p to ld post* **15/2**

62 **2** *nk* **Fortune Of War**[29] 3971 2-9-5 0 .... PatCosgrave 7 75
(Jane Chapple-Hyam) *led early: chsd ldr tl led again over 1f out: sn rdn: r.o: hdd post* **9/2**[3]

43 **3** *shd* **Hartswell**[11] 4649 2-9-5 0 .... WilliamBuick 8 75
(John Gosden) *sn led: hdd over 1f out: rdn and ev ch ins fnl f: r.o* **11/8**[1]

0 **4** 1 **Mungo Madness**[26] 4103 2-9-2 0 .... ShelleyBirkett(3) 5 72
(Julia Feilden) *a.p: shkn up over 1f out: styd on* **40/1**

02 **5** *nk* **Iconic Belle**[12] 4603 2-9-0 0 .... SilvestreDeSousa 6 67+
(Mick Channon) *chsd ldrs: pushed along 1/2-way: rdn and hung lft fr over 1f out: nt clr run ins fnl f: styd on* **5/2**[2]

6 1 **Seyadah** 2-9-0 0 .... LiamJones 3 64
(Marco Botti) *hld up: rdn over 1f out: styd on: nt trble ldrs* **20/1**

05 **7** 13 **Masterfilly (IRE)**[19] 4357 2-9-0 0 .... DougieCostello 2 28
(Ed Walker) *hld up: pushed along over 3f out: wknd wl over 1f out* **50/1**

1m 26.47s (-0.13) **Going Correction** -0.30s/f (Firm) **7** Ran SP% **109.8**
Speed ratings (Par 96): **88,87,87,86,86 84,70**
CSF £36.92 TOTE £8.30: £3.00, £2.50; EX 30.80 Trifecta £75.20.
Owner W J and T C O Gredley **Bred** Patrick F Kelly **Trained** Newmarket, Suffolk

FOCUS
There was a bunched finish off a modest pace.

5037 BANHAM POULTRY H'CAP 1m 3y
6:20 (6:21) (Class 4) (0-80,78) 4-Y-O+ **£4,690** (£1,395; £697; £348) **Stalls** Centre

Form RPR

-341 **1** **Carolinae**[48] 3314 4-8-10 **67** .... StevieDonohoe 3 79+
(Charlie Fellowes) *hld up in main gp: hdwy over 2f out: led overall over 1f out: rdn and edgd rt ins fnl f: styd on* **2/1**[1]

0515 **2** 1¼ **Kestrel Dot Com**[12] 4599 4-9-5 **76** ....[1] SilvestreDeSousa 7 84
(Chris Dwyer) *led one other away fr main gp: pushed along over 3f out: hdd that pair over 2f out: rallied to ld that duo over 1f out: edgd lft ins fnl f: styd on* **14/1**

204 **3** 3 **Snappy Guest**[16] 4463 4-9-0 **71** .... JamieSpencer 1 72
(George Margarson) *racd in main gp: hld up: hdwy over 1f out: sn rdn: no ex wl ins fnl f* **9/1**

2014 **4** 1¾ **Thecornishbarron (IRE)**[6] 4807 4-9-2 **76** .... LouisSteward(3) 2 73
(John Ryan) *racd in main gp: chsd clr ldr: rdn to take clsr order over 2f out: no ex ins fnl f* **15/2**

5521 **5** ½ **Trulee Scrumptious**[12] 4596 7-8-6 **63** .... (v) JimmyQuinn 4 58
(Peter Charalambous) *overall ldr in main gp and sn clr: c bk to the field over 2f out: rdn and hdd over 1f out: no ex fnl f* **13/2**[3]

6030 **6** 1¾ **Burning Blaze**[11] 4627 6-9-6 **77** .... (t) AdamBeschizza 8 68
(Brian Ellison) *s.i.s: chsd ldr away fr the main gp: led that pair over 2f out: rdn and hdd over 1f out: wknd ins fnl f* **18/1**

3-03 **7** *hd* **Courtsider**[19] 4361 4-8-11 **68** .... WilliamBuick 6 59
(Lucy Wadham) *hld up in main gp: rdn over 2f out: n.d* **7/1**

1-0 **8** 17 **Queen's Novel**[102] 1633 4-9-7 **78** .... MartinHarley 5 28
(James Tate) *racd in main gp: chsd ldrs: rdn over 2f out: sn wknd* **4/1**[2]

1m 37.05s (-3.55) **Going Correction** -0.30s/f (Firm) **8** Ran SP% **112.9**
Speed ratings (Par 105): **105,103,100,99,98 96,96,79**
CSF £31.37 CT £206.36 TOTE £2.80: £1.30, £3.10, £2.50; EX 23.60 Trifecta £203.80.
Owner The Dalmunzie Devils Partnership **Bred** Meon Valley Stud **Trained** Newmarket, Suffolk

FOCUS
A reasonable mile handicap with a few of these still looking to be on the up beforehand, but the favourite rather took it apart.

5038 3 SUN GROUP FILLIES' H'CAP 7f 3y
6:50 (6:50) (Class 5) (0-70,70) 3-Y-O+ **£2,911** (£866; £432; £216) **Stalls** Centre

Form RPR

223 **1** **Aflame**[46] 3406 3-9-6 **70** .... WilliamBuick 2 79+
(Sir Michael Stoute) *racd keenly: a.p: wnt 2nd 1/2-way: led over 2f out: rdn and edgd lft ins fnl f: styd on* **7/4**[1]

0-23 **2** *nk* **Dheyaa (IRE)**[28] 4009 3-9-2 **66** .... (p) PaulHanagan 1 74
(Owen Burrows) *hld up: hdwy over 2f out: rdn to chse wnr over 1f out: edgd lft ins fnl f: r.o* **9/4**[2]

-062 **3** 5 **Party Thyme**[21] 4279 3-8-13 **63** .... SilvestreDeSousa 7 58
(Chris Wall) *hld up in tch: shkn up over 2f out: styd on same pce fnl f* **7/2**[3]

3004 **4** 6 **Refuse Colette (IRE)**[32] 3898 7-9-9 **67** .... PatCosgrave 4 48
(Mick Quinn) *led over 4f: rdn and wknd over 1f out* **11/1**

000- **5** 1½ **Baileys Pursuit**[240] 8131 4-9-7 **65** .... (p) AdamBeschizza 6 43
(Christine Dunnett) *chsd ldr to 1/2-way: rdn over 2f out: wknd over 1f out* **33/1**

-246 **U** **Darrell Rivers**[68] 2655 4-9-5 **63** .... PatrickMathers 3
(Giles Bravery) *stmbld and uns rdr sn after s* **8/1**

1m 24.65s (-1.95) **Going Correction** -0.30s/f (Firm)
WFA 3 from 4yo+ 6lb **6** Ran SP% **111.7**
Speed ratings (Par 100): **99,98,92,86,84**
CSF £5.89 TOTE £2.50: £1.20, £2.10; EX 7.50 Trifecta £15.50.
Owner Lady Rothschild **Bred** Kincorth Investments Inc **Trained** Newmarket, Suffolk

FOCUS
A moderate fillies' handicap but drama from the outset, with Darrell Rivers losing Patrick Mathers as the stalls opened.

5039 PLEASUREWOOD HILLS H'CAP 6f 3y
7:20 (7:20) (Class 5) (0-75,75) 3-Y-O+ **£2,911** (£866; £432; £216) **Stalls** Centre

Form RPR

1160 **1** **Upavon**[19] 4362 6-9-8 **72**....(t) PatCosgrave 6 79
(Stuart Williams) *s.s: hld up: hdwy over 1f out: rdn to ld and edgd lft ins fnl f: r.o* **11/4**[2]

323 **2** 1 **Regal Parade**[32] 3907 12-9-6 **70**....(t) AdamBeschizza 4 73
(Charlie Wallis) *hld up: nt clr run over 1f out: rdn and r.o ins fnl f: wnt 2nd post: nt rch wnr* **8/1**

3056 **3** shd **Vimy Ridge**[27] 4066 4-9-4 **75**....(p) WilliamCox(7) 1 78
(Alan Bailey) *a.p: led over 1f out: rdn and hdd ins fnl f: styd on same pce* **10/1**

5504 **4** ½ **Captain Bob (IRE)**[8] 4726 5-9-9 **73**.... SilvestreDeSousa 2 74
(Robert Cowell) *racd keenly: wnt 2nd after 1f: led over 2f out: rdn and hdd over 1f out: styd on same pce ins fnl f* **9/4**[1]

556U **5** 1 **Fever Few**[19] 4355 7-9-10 **74**.... MartinHarley 7 72
(Chris Wall) *racd keenly: w ldrs tl stdd and lost pl after 1f: nt clr run over 1f out: r.o ins fnl f* **16/1**

5134 **6** 1¼ **Shypen**[9] 4708 3-8-12 **73**.... JaneElliott(7) 5 66
(George Margarson) *chsd ldrs: rdn and ev ch over 1f out: no ex ins fnl f* **4/1**[3]

3500 **7** ½ **Honcho (IRE)**[8] 4741 4-9-2 **66**.... StevieDonohoe 3 59
(John Ryan) *led: rdn and hdd over 2f out: no ex fnl f* **12/1**

1m 12.09s (-2.31) **Going Correction** -0.30s/f (Firm)
WFA 3 from 4yo+ 4lb **7** Ran SP% **111.2**
Speed ratings (Par 103): **103,101,101,100,99 97,97**
CSF £23.14 TOTE £3.70: £1.80, £3.10; EX 20.60 Trifecta £141.10.
Owner Morley, Reynolds & Watkins **Bred** Major-Gen Guy Watkins **Trained** Newmarket, Suffolk

FOCUS
Ordinary form but a small turf pb from the winner.

5040 MOULTON NURSERIES OF ACLE FILLIES' H'CAP 5f 42y
7:50 (7:50) (Class 4) (0-80,80) 3-Y-O+ **£4,690** (£1,395; £697; £348) **Stalls** Centre

Form RPR

6-63 **1** **Little Voice (USA)**[14] 4536 3-9-5 **78**.... WilliamBuick 9 84+
(Charles Hills) *hld up: shkn up over 1f out: qcknd to ld wl ins fnl f: sn clr: comf* **7/1**

0455 **2** 1¼ **Princess Tansy**[12] 4585 4-9-2 **72**.... DarryllHolland 7 75
(Gay Kelleway) *hld up: racd keenly: hdwy over 1f out: rdn to ld briefly wl ins fnl f: sn edgd lft and hdd: styd on same pce* **16/1**

0-12 **3** ½ **Cosmopolitan Girl (IRE)**[12] 4585 3-9-7 **80**.... MartinHarley 10 80
(Robert Cowell) *chsd ldr tl led over 1f out: rdn and hdd wl ins fnl f: styd on same pce* **2/1**[1]

2236 **4** ¾ **Silken Skies (IRE)**[22] 4223 3-9-0 **80**.... WilliamCox(7) 4 78+
(Clive Cox) *hmpd s: racd keenly and sn w ldrs: rdn and ev ch over 1f out: styng on same pce whn carried lft wl ins fnl f* **11/1**

325 **5** nk **Swirral Edge**[49] 3284 3-9-0 **73**.... JamieSpencer 6 73+
(David Brown) *hmpd s: hld up: nt clr run over 1f out: shkn up and running on whn hmpd and eased wl ins fnl f* **17/2**

1164 **6** hd **Saved My Bacon (IRE)**[33] 3847 5-9-7 **77**.... SilvestreDeSousa 8 74
(Chris Dwyer) *hld up: hdwy on outer over 1f out: sn rdn: styd on same pce wl ins fnl f* **9/1**

403 **7** 2¼ **Lydia's Place**[15] 4488 3-9-4 **80**.... RobHornby(3) 2 68
(Richard Guest) *edgd rt s: sn led: rdn and hdd over 1f out: wknd ins fnl f* **6/1**[3]

6162 **8** ¾ **Racing Angel (IRE)**[8] 4744 4-8-12 **68**.... PatCosgrave 3 54
(Mick Quinn) *hmpd s: sn chsng ldrs: rdn over 1f out: wknd fnl f* **9/2**[2]

1m 0.77s (-1.93) **Going Correction** -0.30s/f (Firm)
WFA 3 from 4yo+ 3lb **8** Ran SP% **113.0**
Speed ratings (Par 102): **103,101,100,99,98 98,94,93**
CSF £105.05 CT £303.59 TOTE £7.80: £2.00, £4.50, £1.30; EX 85.80 Trifecta £312.40.
Owner Mr & Mrs T O'Donohoe **Bred** Summerhill Stud **Trained** Lambourn, Berks

FOCUS
This looks ordinary form, set around the second.

5041 GREENE KING FESTIVAL AT YARMOUTH RACECOURSE H'CAP 5f 42y
8:20 (8:21) (Class 6) (0-60,60) 3-Y-O **£2,264** (£673; £336; £168) **Stalls** Centre

Form RPR

2-00 **1** **Annie Salts**[57] 3000 3-9-7 **60**.... SilvestreDeSousa 1 69
(Chris Dwyer) *mde all: sn clr: shkn up over 1f out: r.o: unchal* **14/1**

004 **2** 1½ **Chip Or Pellet**[4] 4855 3-8-8 **47**.... AndrewMullen 3 50
(Nigel Tinkler) *hld up: hdwy 1/2-way: rdn to go 2nd over 1f out: nt rch wnr* **7/2**[2]

0-00 **3** nk **Fleeting Dream (IRE)**[27] 4041 3-9-3 **56**....(b[1]) PatCosgrave 10 58
(William Haggas) *wnt rt s: hld up: hdwy over 1f out: r.o: nt rch ldrs* **5/2**[1]

6055 **4** 1½ **Justice Rock**[13] 4570 3-8-13 **52**.... LiamJones 5 48
(Phil McEntee) *chsd wnr: rdn over 2f out: lost 2nd over 1f out: styd on same pce* **14/1**

6400 **5** nk **Edith Weston**[29] 3970 3-8-7 **46** oh1....(p) JimmyQuinn 2 41
(Robert Cowell) *hld up: hdwy 1/2-way: rdn over 1f out: styd on same pce ins fnl f* **28/1**

4540 **6** ½ **Westbourne Grove (USA)**[21] 4278 3-9-0 **53**.... AdamBeschizza 9 47
(John Butler) *hld up: pushed along 1/2-way: nvr nrr* **11/2**

2034 **7** 1 **Sacred Harp**[14] 4521 3-8-13 **59**....(t) MillyNaseb(7) 6 49
(Stuart Williams) *chsd ldrs: rdn over 1f out: no ex* **4/1**[3]

6505 **8** 2 **Another Desperado (IRE)**[49] 3293 3-8-0 **46** oh1.... RPWalsh(7) 4 29
(Rebecca Bastiman) *prom: rdn over 1f out: wknd fnl f* **20/1**

1000 **9** 7 **Let There Be Light**[21] 4262 3-8-12 **58**....(v) DavidEgan(7) 8 17
(Gay Kelleway) *sn pushed along in rr: swtchd rt 3f out: wknd 1/2-way* **14/1**

1m 0.99s (-1.71) **Going Correction** -0.30s/f (Firm) **9** Ran SP% **114.4**
Speed ratings (Par 98): **101,98,98,95,95 94,92,89,78**
CSF £62.07 CT £167.05 TOTE £8.20: £2.20, £1.50, £1.60; EX 53.80 Trifecta £184.40.
Owner Mrs Shelley Dwyer **Bred** D R Botterill **Trained** Newmarket, Suffolk

FOCUS
Nothing got into this behind the tearaway winner, who is rated a length up on her nursery form. The second helps set the level.
T/Plt: £194.40 to a £1 stake. Pool: £52,543.54 - 197.23 winning units. T/Qpdt: £8.70 to a £1 stake. Pool: £6,891.72 - 580.58 winning units. **Colin Roberts**

5042 - 5049a (Foreign Racing) - See Raceform Interactive

5014 BRIGHTON (L-H)
Thursday, August 4

OFFICIAL GOING: Good (7.9)
Wind: medium, against Weather: fine, light cloud

5050 CELEBRATING 233YRS OF RACING AT BRIGHTON H'CAP 5f 59y
2:00 (2:00) (Class 5) (0-75,79) 4-Y-O+ **£3,234** (£962; £481; £240) **Stalls** Centre

Form RPR

0606 **1** **Storm Lightning**[13] 4606 7-8-8 **60**.... FrannyNorton 3 69
(Mark Brisbourne) *chsd ldng pair tl over 2f out: clsd and n.m.r 1f out: swtchd rt and hdwy ins fnl f: r.o wl to ld towards fin* **16/1**

5006 **2** ½ **Whitecrest**[3] 4952 8-9-1 **67**.... WilliamTwiston-Davies 5 74
(John Spearing) *midfield: chsd clr ldng pair and pushed along over 2f out: rdn and clsd over 1f out: drvn to ld ins fnl f: kpt on tl hdd and no ex towards fin* **10/1**

5561 **3** 1¾ **Newton's Law (IRE)**[6] 4817 5-9-6 **79** 6ex....(tp) JordanUys(7) 4 80
(Brian Meehan) *awkward leaving stalls: hld up in rr: clsd 2f out: drvn over 1f out: chsd ldrs ins fnl f: r.o same pce fnl 100yds* **2/1**[1]

532 **4** 1 **Time Medicean**[30] 3970 10-8-7 **62**....(t) GeorgeDowning(3) 2 59
(Tony Carroll) *hld up in last pair: clsd over 1f out: nt clrest of runs jst ins fnl f: swtchd rt and kpt on fnl 100yds: no threat to ldrs* **7/1**

6436 **5** ¾ **Monumental Man**[16] 4475 7-9-6 **72**....(p) SilvestreDeSousa 7 67
(Michael Attwater) *bustled along leaving stalls: sn w ldr and wnt clr after 1f: drvn to ld over 1f out: hdd ins fnl f: sn btn and wknd fnl 100yds* **5/2**[2]

416 **6** 6 **Rainbow Orse**[28] 4039 4-9-7 **73**....(p) JimCrowley 1 47
(Robert Cowell) *led: wnt clr w rival after 1f: rdn and hdd over 1f out: btn whn short of room 1f out: sn wknd and eased towards fin* **7/2**[3]

1m 3.05s (0.75) **Going Correction** +0.30s/f (Good) **6** Ran SP% **111.6**
Speed ratings (Par 103): **106,105,102,100,99 90**
CSF £147.90 TOTE £16.70: £5.70, £3.70; EX 82.90 Trifecta £1186.80.
Owner Law Abiding Citizens **Bred** New England Stud And Partners **Trained** Great Ness, Shropshire

FOCUS
The rail was dolled out between the 6f marker and 3.5f out, adding 5 yards to each race distance. The jockeys reported the ground had dried out from the previous day's meeting and that good was the right description. An ordinary race in which the leaders probably went too quickly early on.

5051 GENTING CASINO BRIGHTON AMERICAN ROULETTE (S) H'CAP 6f 209y
2:30 (2:32) (Class 6) (0-60,60) 3-Y-O+ **£2,264** (£673; £336; £168) **Stalls** Centre

Form RPR

000 **1** **Monsieur Valentine**[37] 3745 4-8-13 **56**.... GeorgiaCox(7) 1 66
(Tony Carroll) *hld up off the pce in last trio: pushed along 1/2-way: hdwy over 1f out: nt clr run and swtchd rt 1f out: chsd clr wnr jst ins fnl f: r.o strly to ld last strides* **8/1**

-001 **2** shd **Indus Valley (IRE)**[30] 3970 9-9-5 **55**....(v) SilvestreDeSousa 3 64
(Lee Carter) *stdd s: hld up off the pce in last trio: pushed along and stdy hdwy 3f out: rdn to ld ent fnl f: drvn and edging lft ins fnl f: kpt on hdd last stride* **7/2**[3]

6650 **3** 6 **Ocean Bentley (IRE)**[21] 4290 4-8-5 **46** oh1....(b[1]) MeganNicholls(5) 6 39
(Tony Carroll) *midfield: clsd 2f out: hung lft u.p over 1f out: no ch w ldrs but kpt on to go 3rd wl ins fnl f* **20/1**

0230 **4** 1¾ **Malaysian Boleh**[30] 3985 6-9-3 **53**....(b) FrannyNorton 5 42
(Shaun Lycett) *midfield: clsd on inner over 1f out: rdn to press ldrs whn squeezed of room on rail 1f out: no threat to ldrs after: plugged on* **3/1**[2]

0200 **5** 1 **Harry Bosch**[57] 3043 6-8-12 **48**....(b) AdamBeschizza 7 34+
(Julia Feilden) *chsd ldr: drvn and clsd to chal over 1f out: pushed lft 1f out: sn btn: wknd ins fnl f* **9/1**

2001 **6** 1¼ **The Lillster**[22] 4257 3-9-1 **60**.... GeorgeDowning(3) 8 41+
(Tony Carroll) *taken down early: led and sn clr: rdn over 1f out: hdd and ducked lft ent fnl f: sn btn and wknd ins fnl f* **12/1**

0550 **7** 2¼ **Long Island**[8] 4764 3-8-4 **46**.... KieranO'Neill 9 21
(Mark Brisbourne) *mounted on crse and taken down early: dwlt: sn rcvrd to chse ldng pair: rdn 2f out: no imp and btn over 1f out: wknd fnl f* **20/1**

0464 **8** 8 **Miss Inga Sock (IRE)**[19] 4389 4-9-10 **60**....(p) JimCrowley 2 16
(Eve Johnson Houghton) *midfield: effrt u.p jst over 2f out: no imp over 1f out: wl btn and heavily eased ins fnl f* **9/4**[1]

-000 **9** 35 **Overstone Lass (IRE)**[21] 4290 4-8-7 **46** oh1....(b) EdwardGreatrex(3) 4
(John Spearing) *a in rr and nvr on terms: rdn over 3f out: lost tch over 1f out: virtually p.u fnl f: t.o* **40/1**

1m 24.08s (0.98) **Going Correction** +0.30s/f (Good)
WFA 3 from 4yo+ 6lb **9** Ran SP% **118.8**
Speed ratings (Par 101): **106,105,99,97,95 94,91,82,42**
CSF £36.36 CT £556.11 TOTE £10.20: £2.30, £1.90, £5.60; EX 49.30 Trifecta £940.70.There was no bid for the winner.
Owner Mayden Stud **Bred** Mayden Stud, J A And D S Dewhurst **Trained** Cropthorne, Worcs

FOCUS
The rail was dolled out between the 6f marker and 3.5f out, adding 5 yards to each race distance. This moderate contest was run at an overly strong gallop thanks to The Lillster, who was trying the trip for the first time, which meant those off the pace were always going to be favoured.

5052 JURYS BRIGHTON WATERFRONT MAIDEN AUCTION STKS 7f 214y
3:00 (3:00) (Class 5) 2-Y-O **£2,911** (£866; £432; £216) **Stalls** Centre

Form RPR

35 **1** **Count Calabash (IRE)**[4] 4907 2-9-2 0.... JimCrowley 7 74
(Paul Cole) *t.k.h: hld up in tch in midfield: effrt to chal over 1f out: ev ch and bmpd ins fnl f: styd on wl u.p to ld on post* **7/4**[1]

4 **2** nse **Showtime Lady (IRE)**[16] 4487 2-8-11 0.... FrannyNorton 1 69
(Mark Johnston) *led: hung rt fr 3f out: rdn and hrd pressed over 1f out: wnt lft u.p and bmpd chalr ins fnl f: styd on: hdd on post* **7/4**[1]

0 **3** 6 **Let's Be Happy (IRE)**[15] 4523 2-8-10 0.... ShaneKelly 5 54
(Richard Hughes) *hld up in tch in midfield: effrt 2f out: pushed along and unable qck jst over 1f out: chsd clr ldng pair ins fnl f: no imp* **14/1**

00 **4** 1 **Girlofinkandstars (IRE)**[25] 4187 2-8-12 0.... AdamBeschizza 2 54
(Rae Guest) *hld up in last pair: effrt u.p to chse ldrs over 1f out: no imp 1f out: lost 3rd and kpt on same pce ins fnl f* **25/1**

5 3 **Falcon Rising** 2-9-3 0.... SilvestreDeSousa 4 52
(Sylvester Kirk) *dwlt: hld up in rr: effrt 2f out: swtchd lft over 1f out: no imp: wl hld 5th whn nt clr run and eased wl ins fnl f* **5/1**[2]

5005 **6** 3 **Apple Scruffs (IRE)**[9] 4738 2-8-10 64.... EdwardGreatrex(3) 6 41
(Michael Attwater) *t.k.h: chsd ldrs: unable qck u.p and lost pl over 1f out: wknd fnl f* **10/1**[3]

0 **7** *4* **Chamasay**[66] 2748 2-8-11 0 .... KieranO'Neill 3 30
(J S Moore) *t.k.h: chsd ldr tl lost pl over 1f out: hung lft and wl btn 1f out: sn wknd* **40/1**

1m 37.77s (1.77) **Going Correction** +0.30s/f (Good) **7** Ran SP% **111.4**
Speed ratings (Par 94): **103,102,96,95,92 89,85**
CSF £4.44 TOTE £2.40: £1.50, £1.70; EX 5.00 Trifecta £34.50.
Owner Trish Hall & Colin Fletcher **Bred** Miss S Von Schilcher **Trained** Whatcombe, Oxon
■ Stewards' Enquiry : Franny Norton caution: careless riding

FOCUS
The rail was dolled out between the 6f marker and 3.5f out, adding 5 yards to each race distance. The two market leaders pulled clear in this modest contest, with the whole field fanning out and the first and second ending up coming home closest to the stands' rail.

5053 FROSTS4CARS.CO.UK BRIGHTON CHALLENGE CUP H'CAP 1m 3f 196y
3:30 (3:31) (Class 4) (0-80,80) 3-Y-O+
£12,450 (£3,728; £1,864; £932; £466; £234) **Stalls** High

Form RPR

5213 **1** **William Hunter**[15] 4535 4-9-11 **77** .... WilliamTwiston-Davies 9 84+
(Alan King) *hld up in tch in midfield: effrt on inner 2f out: drvn to ld 1f out: styd on wl: rdn out* **9/2**[2]

5015 **2** *1 1/4* **Thames Knight**[10] 4710 4-9-12 **78** .... JimCrowley 2 83
(Marcus Tregoning) *chsd ldrs: wnt 2nd over 2f tl rdn to ld over 1f out: hdd 1f out: styd on same pce ins fnl f* **6/1**[3]

3004 **3** *3/4* **Second Serve (IRE)**[12] 4628 3-9-3 **80** .... FrannyNorton 6 84
(Mark Johnston) *led and set stdy gallop: rdn over 2f out: drvn and hdd over 1f out: styd on same pce ins fnl f* **4/1**[1]

451 **4** *1 1/2* **Ravenous**[10] 4711 5-9-9 **75** 6ex .... KieranO'Neill 3 77
(Luke Dace) *v.s.a: sn rcvrd and hld up in tch in rr: rdn and effrt over 1f out: 4th and styd on same pce fnl f* **8/1**

202 **5** *1/2* **Rose Above**[30] 3972 4-9-9 **78** .... EdwardGreatrex(3) 8 79
(Andrew Balding) *hld up in tch in last pair: effrt ent fnl 2f: no imp u.p over 1f out: styd on same pce fnl f* **9/1**

2200 **6** *3/4* **Whinging Willie (IRE)**[34] 3861 7-9-9 **80** ....(v) HectorCrouch(5) 4 80
(Gary Moore) *t.k.h: hld up wl in tch in last trio: clsd whn nt clr run and swtchd rt over 1f out: sn rdn and no hdwy 1f out: wl hld fnl f* **6/1**[3]

-000 **7** *4 1/2* **Cockney Boy**[6] 4847 3-7-8 **64** oh2 ow1 .... RhiainIngram(7) 5 56
(John Gallagher) *chsd ldr tl drifted rt and rdn over 2f out: btn and hung lft jst over 1f out: wknd fnl f* **40/1**

5213 **8** *16* **Smoky Hill (IRE)**[28] 4052 7-8-5 **64** .... GeorgiaCox(7) 7 31
(Tony Carroll) *hld up in tch in midfield: rdn 2f out: sn lost pl: wl btn and eased ins fnl f* **16/1**

4431 **9** *18* **Atwix**[7] 4785 4-9-10 **79** 6ex ....(b) AaronJones(3) 1 17+
(Lucy Wadham) *hld up wl in tch in midfield: effrt whn wnt lft and hit rail 2f out: unbalanced and nt rcvr: eased: t.o* **4/1**[1]

2m 36.89s (4.19) **Going Correction** +0.30s/f (Good)
WFA 3 from 4yo+ 11lb **9** Ran SP% **116.2**
Speed ratings (Par 105): **98,97,96,95,95 94,91,81,69**
CSF £31.86 CT £116.96 TOTE £4.00: £1.20, £2.00, £2.30; EX 24.90 Trifecta £194.10.
Owner Incipe Partnership **Bred** Barbury Castle Stud **Trained** Barbury Castle, Wilts

FOCUS
The rail was dolled out between the 6f marker and 3.5f out, adding 5 yards to each race distance. Quite a competitive contest but the early gallop wasn't that quick, and the time was 8.59 seconds slower than standard. Improvement from the winner and second, with the third close to form.

5054 JAMES ROSS JEWELLERS FILLIES' H'CAP 1m 1f 209y
4:00 (4:00) (Class 4) (0-85,83) 3-Y-O+ **£5,175** (£1,540; £769; £384) **Stalls** High

Form RPR

231 **1** **Trainnah**[30] 3981 3-9-3 **81** ....(p) JimCrowley 4 91
(William Haggas) *sn led and mde rest: rdn and drifted rt 2f out: drvn ins fnl f: rn green u.p but a doing enough: rdn out* **1/1**[1]

3110 **2** *1/2* **Singyoursong (IRE)**[19] 4391 3-9-3 **81** .... ShaneKelly 2 90
(David Simcock) *hld up in tch: effrt over 1f out: sn chalng: drvn and ev ch ins fnl f: kpt on but a hld* **3/1**[2]

2065 **3** *6* **Lady Marl**[15] 4501 5-9-9 **83** .... HectorCrouch(5) 3 80
(Gary Moore) *stdd after s: hld up in tch in rr: effrt to chse ldrs over 1f out: 3rd and no ex 1f out: wknd ins fnl f* **16/1**

502 **4** *3 1/2* **Visage Blanc**[26] 4160 3-8-11 **75** .... SilvestreDeSousa 1 65
(Mick Channon) *sn chsng ldr tl rdn over 2f out: lost pl and btn over 1f out: wknd ins fnl f* **7/2**[3]

1234 **5** *2* **Solveig's Song**[15] 4531 4-8-9 **67** ....(p) EdwardGreatrex(3) 5 53
(Steve Woodman) *broke wl: sn stdd and trckd ldng pair: rdn to chse ldr over 2f out tl lost pl over 1f out: wknd fnl f* **12/1**

2m 5.97s (2.37) **Going Correction** +0.30s/f (Good)
WFA 3 from 4yo+ 9lb **5** Ran SP% **110.8**
Speed ratings (Par 102): **102,101,96,94,92**
CSF £4.31 TOTE £1.90: £1.10, £1.60; EX 3.80 Trifecta £22.90.
Owner Al Shaqab Racing **Bred** Stetchworth & Middle Park Studs Ltd **Trained** Newmarket, Suffolk

FOCUS
The rail was dolled out between the 6f marker and 3.5f out, adding 5 yards to each race distance. A decent handicap for fillies.

5055 HUNDREDS OF USED CARS AT FROSTS4CARS.CO.UK H'CAP 7f 214y
4:30 (4:30) (Class 6) (0-60,59) 3-Y-O+ **£2,911** (£866; £432; £216) **Stalls** Centre

Form RPR

5020 **1** **African Showgirl**[3] 4936 3-9-3 **57** .... SteveDrowne 7 64
(George Baker) *hld up in tch in rr: hdwy to chse ldrs and swtchd lft ent fnl f: ev ch ins fnl f: r.o wl to ld fnl 50yds* **7/2**[2]

6-05 **2** *nk* **Nona Blu**[29] 3997 4-9-12 **59** .... FrannyNorton 2 66
(Michael Wigham) *stdd s: hld up in tch in midfield: clsd and swtchd rt jst over 1f out: rdn and hdwy to ld ins fnl f: hdd and unable qck fnl 50yds* **7/2**[2]

033 **3** *1 1/4* **Altaira**[2] 4992 5-9-1 **53** .... MeganNicholls(5) 4 57
(Tony Carroll) *broke wl: stdd and hld up in tch in midfield: effrt and rdn to chse ldrs over 1f out: led jst over 1f out: hdd 100yds out: no ex and outpcd fnl 100yds* **5/2**[1]

0202 **4** *1 3/4* **Lutine Charlie (IRE)**[15] 4505 9-9-4 **51** ....(p) ShaneKelly 8 51
(Emma Owen) *hld up in tch in last trio: effrt over 1f out: swtchd rt jst ins fnl f: styd on u.p: no threat to ldrs* **7/1**[3]

-600 **5** *1 1/2* **Suni Dancer**[1] 5019 5-8-12 **48** .... GeorgeDowning(3) 10 45
(Tony Carroll) *t.k.h: sn chsng ldr: rdn and ev ch 2f out: led over 1f out: sn hdd and no ex: wknd ins fnl f* **16/1**

0000 **6** *hd* **Miss Buckaroo (IRE)**[2] 4992 4-8-12 **45** ....(p) MichaelJMMurphy 1 42
(Peter Hedger) *hld up in tch in last trio: hdwy 2f out: rdn to chse ldrs over 1f out: unable qck and btn 1f out: wknd ins fnl f* **12/1**

55-5 **7** *1 3/4* **Bunker Hill Lass**[196] 277 4-9-7 **57** ....(p) TimClark(3) 6 49
(Michael Appleby) *t.k.h: sn led: rdn 2f out: hdd over 1f out: sn outpcd: wknd ins fnl f* **10/1**

1064 **8** *41* **Palace Moon**[51] 3255 11-9-6 **56** ....(t) EdwardGreatrex(3) 3
(Michael Attwater) *chsd ldrs: rdn over 1f out: unable qck: btn whn eased 1f out: virtually p.u fnl f: t.o* **12/1**

1m 38.2s (2.20) **Going Correction** +0.30s/f (Good)
WFA 3 from 4yo+ 7lb **8** Ran SP% **115.9**
Speed ratings (Par 101): **101,100,99,97,96 96,94,53**
CSF £16.46 CT £35.63 TOTE £5.40: £1.60, £1.80, £1.30; EX 19.90 Trifecta £74.20.
Owner PJL Racing 1 **Bred** Ballabeg Stables **Trained** Manton, Wilts

FOCUS
The rail was dolled out between the 6f marker and 3.5f out, adding 5 yards to each race distance. Nothing more than a modest handicap.

5056 PARTY AT THE RACES 1ST OCT LADY AMATEUR RIDERS' H'CAP 1m 1f 209y
5:00 (5:01) (Class 5) (0-70,70) 3-Y-O+ **£2,807** (£870; £435; £217) **Stalls** High

Form RPR

-122 **1** **City Ground (USA)**[34] 3917 9-10-8 **68** .... MissSBrotherton 3 74
(Michael Appleby) *led: rdn and hdd wl over 1f out: stl ev ch tl led again and edgd lft ins fnl f: styd on: rdn out* **2/5**[1]

0064 **2** *1 1/2* **Gaelic Silver (FR)**[7] 4784 10-10-3 **70** ....(p) MissBeckyButler(7) 1 73
(Gary Moore) *trckd ldng pair tl clsd to join wnr 3f out: reminder to ld wl over 1f out: pushed along over 1f out: hdd and styd on same pce ins fnl f* **3/1**[2]

3156 **3** *1 1/2* **My Lord**[19] 4383 8-10-5 **70** .... MissMBryant(5) 2 70
(Paddy Butler) *hld up in tch in 4th: clsd to chse ldng pair 3f out: swtchd lft and rdn over 1f out: styd on same pce ins fnl f* **8/1**[3]

/00- **4** *72* **Queen Of Norway (IRE)**[523] 730 5-8-12 **51** oh1 .... MissJMOlliver(7) 5
(Paddy Butler) *pressed wnr tl 3f out: sn dropped to last and lost tch: t.o and eased ins fnl f* **20/1**

2m 9.09s (5.49) **Going Correction** +0.30s/f (Good) **4** Ran SP% **112.3**
Speed ratings (Par 103): **90,88,87,30**
CSF £2.07 TOTE £1.20; EX 2.10 Trifecta £2.50.
Owner Mrs D R Brotherton **Bred** Mrs E Scott Jr & Mrs L Macelree **Trained** Oakham, Rutland

FOCUS
The rail was dolled out between the 6f marker and 3.5f out, adding 5 yards to each race distance. Two leading players for this came out during the afternoon, which weakened an already modest event, and the winner probably didn't need to improve on his recent form.
T/Plt: £210.80 to a £1 stake. Pool of £65805.61 - 227.84 winning tickets. T/Qpdt: £3.60 to a £1 stake. Pool of £7256.71 - 1459.70 winning tickets. **Steve Payne**

4377 HAYDOCK (L-H)
Thursday, August 4

OFFICIAL GOING: Good to firm (8.9)
Wind: Moderate against Weather: Cloudy with sunny periods

5057 APOLLOBET HOME OF CASHBACK OFFERS H'CAP (GRASSROOTS FLAT MIDDLE DISTANCE SERIES QUALIFIER) 1m 2f 95y
1:50 (1:50) (Class 5) (0-70,69) 3-Y-O+ **£2,911** (£866; £432; £216) **Stalls** Centre

Form RPR

3315 **1** **Raven Banner (IRE)**[27] 4098 3-9-3 **67** .... DaleSwift 3 73
(Daniel Mark Loughnane) *trckd ldng pair: hdwy 4f out: cl up over 2f out: rdn to chal over 1f out: led ent fnl f: kpt on wl* **7/2**[3]

6003 **2** *1 1/4* **Tiga Tuan (FR)**[18] 4429 3-8-13 **63** .... GrahamLee 7 66
(Kevin Ryan) *led and sn clr: pushed along wl over 2f out: jnd and rdn over 1f out: hdd ent fnl f: sn drvn: kpt on same pce last 100yds* **3/1**[2]

1203 **3** *nk* **Pike Corner Cross (IRE)**[8] 4774 4-9-9 **67** .... JosephineGordon(3) 4 69
(Ed de Giles) *hld up in tch: hdwy on outer over 3f out: cl up over 2f out: rdn to chal over 1f out and ev ch: drvn ent fnl f: sn edgd lft and kpt on same pce* **9/4**[1]

30-0 **4** *1 1/4* **Best Boy**[17] 4455 4-9-9 **64** ....(t) DavidAllan 2 64
(David C Griffiths) *chsd ldr: rdn along 3f out: drvn wl over 1f out: sn one pce* **5/1**

0464 **5** *3 1/4* **Aneedh**[9] 4724 6-9-6 **61** ....(b) JoeDoyle 5 54
(Clive Mulhall) *hld up in tch: hdwy on inner to chse ldrs over 2f out: sn rdn along and no imp* **13/2**

2m 13.69s (-1.81) **Going Correction** -0.175s/f (Firm)
WFA 3 from 4yo+ 9lb **5** Ran SP% **108.0**
Speed ratings (Par 103): **100,99,98,97,95**
CSF £13.58 TOTE £3.20: £2.00, £1.90; EX 13.30 Trifecta £28.80.
Owner David Slater **Bred** F Dunne **Trained** Baldwin's Gate, Staffs
■ Stewards' Enquiry : Dale Swift two-day ban: used whip above permitted level (Aug 20-21)

FOCUS
Going was Good to firm all round following 3mm of rain overnight and showers in the morning. All races took place on the inner track, with rail movements adding 3yds to the race distance. A modest handicap with the field reduced by almost half owing to withdrawals. The finish was dominated by the 3yo fillies. Muddling form. The front-running runner-up has been rated to her maiden form.

5058 APOLLOBET DAILY RACING REFUNDS EBF NOVICE STKS (PLUS 10 RACE) 6f
2:20 (2:22) (Class 4) 2-Y-O **£4,269** (£1,270; £634; £317) **Stalls** Centre

Form RPR

1 **1** **Mubtasim (IRE)**[35] 3819 2-9-8 0 .... PatCosgrave 7 102+
(William Haggas) *trckd ldrs: smooth hdwy over 2f out: sn cl up: shkn up and qcknd to ld ent fnl f: clr whn green and drifted lft last 100yds: readily* **4/6**[1]

21 **2** *4 1/2* **Town Charter (USA)**[31] 3939 2-9-8 0 .... JoeFanning 1 87
(Mark Johnston) *led: jnd 2f out and sn rdn along: hdd and drvn ent fnl f: kpt on: no ch w wnr* **15/8**[2]

01 **3** *3 1/2* **Private Matter**[52] 3216 2-9-5 0 .... TonyHamilton 2 73
(Richard Fahey) *trckd ldr: effrt over 2f out: rdn wl over 1f out: drvn appr fnl f and sn one pce* **10/1**[3]

0 **4** *3 1/2* **Infatuated**[69] 2648 2-9-2 0 .... DavidAllan 3 59
(Tim Easterby) *chsd ldrs on outer: rdn along 2f out: sn drvn and wknd* **66/1**

5 *1* **Ashurst Beacon** 2-9-2 0 .... BenCurtis 4 55
(Richard Fahey) *chsd ldrs: rdn along over 2f out: sn wknd* **33/1**

60 **6** *10* **Bahkit (IRE)**[34] 3854 2-9-2 0 .... ShaneGray 6 23
(Alan Swinbank) *in rr: rdn along 1/2-way: sn outpcd and bhd* **100/1**

1m 14.01s (0.21) **Going Correction** +0.025s/f (Good) **6** Ran SP% **109.3**
Speed ratings (Par 96): **99,93,88,83,82 69**
CSF £1.97 TOTE £1.50: £1.10, £1.40; EX 2.20 Trifecta £3.50.

Owner Sheikh Rashid Dalmook Al Maktoum **Bred** Mrs Natasha Drennan **Trained** Newmarket, Suffolk

FOCUS

An interesting juvenile novice stakes that featured three previous winners. They dominated the market and the race. The time was 0.07secs slower than the following 3yo contest.

5059 APOLLOBET CASHBACK IF 2ND H'CAP (THE JOCKEY CLUB GRASSROOTS FLAT SPRINT SERIES QUALIFIER) 6f

2:50 (2:52) (Class 5) (0-70,67) 3-Y-O **£2,911** (£866; £432; £216) **Stalls** Centre

Form RPR

26-1 **1** **Tanaasub (IRE)**[50] 3293 3-9-7 **67**.. JoeFanning 5 75+
(Robert Cowell) *wnt rt s: trckd ldr: hdwy to ld 2f out: rdn clr ent fnl f: kpt on wl* **7/4**[1]

6006 **2** ¾ **Big Amigo (IRE)**[24] 4215 3-9-5 **65**........................(e[1]) RichardKingscote 1 70
(Tom Dascombe) *hld up towards rr: hdwy 2f out: rdn and edgd lft 1f out: drvn to chse wnr whn hung lft wl ins fnl f: no imp after* **9/1**

1603 **3** 1 ¾ **Ponty Royale (IRE)**[13] 4604 3-9-3 **63**........................... DavidAllan 6 62
(Tim Easterby) *hmpd s: sn swtchd lft and trckd ldrs: swtchd lft to outer 1/2-way and sn prom: rdn 2f out: drvn over 1f out: kpt on same pce* **7/2**[2]

0514 **4** hd **Hamish McGonagain**[22] 4262 3-8-11 **62**..................(p) DavidParkes[(5)] 2 60
(Jeremy Gask) *trckd ldrs: rdn along and outpcd 2f out: drvn over 1f out: kpt on fnl f* **11/1**

4016 **5** 2 ½ **Round The Island**[20] 4376 3-8-12 **63**........................(p) NathanEvans[(5)] 7 53
(Richard Whitaker) *trckd ldrs: effrt 2f out: rdn over 1f out: sn drvn and wknd* **8/1**[3]

0651 **6** ¾ **Le Manege Enchante (IRE)**[20] 4365 3-8-10 **61**(p) CallumShepherd[(5)] 3 49
(Derek Shaw) *hld up towards rr: swtchd rt to outer and hdwy wl over 2f out: rdn to chse ldrs wl over 1f out: sn drvn and wknd* **12/1**

6050 **7** 4 **Born To Finish (IRE)**[29] 4009 3-9-3 **63**..........................(b) MartinLane 8 38
(Jeremy Gask) *chsd ldrs: rdn along 2f out: sn drvn and btn* **10/1**

0060 **8** nk **Gowanless**[30] 3978 3-9-7 **67**..(p) PaulMulrennan 4 41
(Michael Dods) *led: rdn along and hdd 2f out: sn drvn and wknd* **12/1**

1m 13.94s (0.14) **Going Correction** +0.025s/f (Good) **8** Ran SP% **112.5**

Speed ratings (Par 100): **100,99,96,96,93 92,86,86**

CSF £17.83 CT £49.78 TOTE £2.20: £1.10, £2.30, £1.10; EX 16.60 Trifecta £54.30.

Owner Abdulla Al Mansoori **Bred** J F Tuthill **Trained** Six Mile Bottom, Cambs

FOCUS

This modest 3yo sprint handicap was run 0.07secs faster than the preceding juvenile contest and fractionally faster than the following older horse contest. It could be rated a length or so higher, but not the strongest of form.

5060 APOLLOBET WEEKLY GOLF RETURNS H'CAP 6f

3:20 (3:21) (Class 5) (0-70,70) 4-Y-O+ **£2,911** (£866; £432; £216) **Stalls** Centre

Form RPR

-240 **1** **Classic Pursuit**[41] 3610 5-9-3 **66**....................................(p) RaulDaSilva 2 75
(Ivan Furtado) *towards rr: hdwy on inner 2f out: rdn over 1f out: led ins fnl f: drvn out* **14/1**

3660 **2** nk **Salvatore Fury (IRE)**[27] 4100 6-8-13 **62**.......................(p) JoeFanning 11 70
(Keith Dalgleish) *sltly hmpd s and in rr: hdwy 2f out: rdn ent fnl f: chal and ev ch whn hung lft last 75yds: no ex nr fin* **14/1**

3156 **3** 1 ¾ **Spirit Of Wedza (IRE)**[16] 4496 4-9-2 **65**...........................(p) JoeDoyle 5 67
(Julie Camacho) *cl up: led over 2f out: rdn over 1f out: hdd and drvn ins fnl f: kpt on same pce* **11/1**

1032 **4** ¾ **Razin' Hell**[14] 4544 5-9-7 **70**..(v) BenCurtis 7 70
(John Balding) *trckd ldrs: hdwy over 2f out: rdn and ev ch ent fnl f: sn drvn and kpt on same pce* **8/1**

0634 **5** nk **Champagne Bob**[20] 4354 4-8-6 **60**................................ JoshDoyle[(5)] 14 59
(Richard Price) *midfield: hdwy 2f out: rdn to chse ldrs over 1f out: kpt on same pce* **16/1**

5-45 **6** 1 **Ryan Style (IRE)**[2] 4980 10-8-0 **52**...................(p) JosephineGordon[(3)] 10 48
(Lisa Williamson) *in rr: hdwy wl over 1f out: sn rdn and kpt on fnl f* **33/1**

0413 **7** ½ **Etienne Gerard**[8] 4763 4-9-2 **68**......................(p) RachelRichardson[(3)] 13 62
(Nigel Tinkler) *in tch on outer: hdwy to chse ldrs 2f out: sn rdn and one pce appr fnl f* **15/2**[3]

0210 **8** shd **Mad Endeavour**[26] 4155 5-9-1 **64**....................................... MartinLane 3 58
(Stuart Kittow) *prom: cl up 2f out: rdn and ev ch over 1f out: wknd ins fnl f* **8/1**

0052 **9** ½ **Bop It**[13] 4608 7-9-7 **70**...(be) DanielTudhope 9 62
(David O'Meara) *trckd ldrs: effrt 2f out: sn rdn and wknd* **11/4**[1]

5004 **10** nk **Whozthecat (IRE)**[5] 4896 9-9-3 **66**.....................................(v) JasonHart 6 57
(Declan Carroll) *led: rdn along and hdd 2f out: sn drvn and wknd over 1f out* **7/1**[2]

0504 **11** 5 **Ypres**[14] 4544 7-8-9 **63** ow2....................................(p) CallumShepherd[(5)] 1 38
(Jason Ward) *chsd ldrs: rdn along 2f out: sn wknd* **20/1**

0632 **12** 4 ½ **Native Falls (IRE)**[11] 4691 5-9-3 **66**................................... DavidAllan 12 27
(Alan Swinbank) *chsd ldrs: rdn along 2f out: sn drvn and wknd* **11/1**

1m 13.98s (0.18) **Going Correction** +0.025s/f (Good) **12** Ran SP% **116.7**

Speed ratings (Par 103): **99,98,96,95,94 93,92,92,92,91 85,79**

CSF £193.04 CT £2267.26 TOTE £18.30: £5.80, £4.90, £4.50; EX 274.70 Trifecta £1792.20.

Owner From The Front Racing **Bred** B & B Equine Limited **Trained** Wiseton, Nottinghamshire

■ Stewards' Enquiry : Callum Shepherd one-day ban: weighed in 2lb heavy (Aug 20)

FOCUS

An ordinary sprint handicap that was run 0.04secs slower than the preceding 3yo contest. The runner-up has been rated to this year's form.

5061 APOLLOBET ONLINE CASINO AND GAMES H'CAP 1m 6f

3:50 (3:50) (Class 4) (0-80,80) 4-Y-O+ **£5,175** (£1,540; £769; £384) **Stalls** Low

Form RPR

1-44 **1** **Trevisani (IRE)**[29] 4013 4-9-5 **78**....................................(v[1]) GeorgeBaker 4 86+
(David Lanigan) *mde most: rdn wl over 1f out: drvn ins fnl f: kpt on strly* **7/4**[1]

-205 **2** 1 ¾ **Snowy Dawn**[36] 3767 6-8-9 **68**.. RoystonFfrench 3 73
(Steph Hollinshead) *trckd ldrs: pushed along wl over 2f out: hdwy and rdn wl over 1f out: drvn appr fnl f: kpt on: no imp towards fin* **9/2**[2]

0434 **3** 2 ¼ **Chebsey Beau**[12] 4634 6-8-9 **73**..........................(p) CallumShepherd[(5)] 1 75
(John Quinn) *hld up: hdwy on outer over 3f out: chsd wnr 2f out and sn rdn: drvn over 1f out: kpt on same pce fnl f* **9/2**[2]

0000 **4** ¾ **Gabrial The Duke (IRE)**[12] 4634 6-8-13 **75**.....(v) RachelRichardson[(3)] 6 76
(Richard Fahey) *s.i.s and bhd: too clsr order 1/2-way: chsd ldrs and rdn over 2f out: drvn wl over 1f out: kpt on one pce* **7/1**

0024 **5** 7 **Moshe (IRE)**[19] 4381 5-9-3 **76**... JoeFanning 8 67
(Philip Kirby) *prom: pushed along wl over 3f out: rdn over 2f out: sn drvn and wknd* **11/2**[3]

052 **6** ½ **Maoi Chinn Tire (IRE)**[27] 4101 9-9-3 **76**.........................(p) DavidNolan 5 66
(Jennie Candlish) *trckd kldng pair: hdwy to trck wnr 6f out: rdn along 3f out: drvn over 2f out and sn wknd* **15/2**

2m 59.03s (-2.97) **Going Correction** -0.175s/f (Firm) **6** Ran SP% **112.4**

Speed ratings (Par 105): **101,100,98,98,94 94**

CSF £9.88 CT £28.96 TOTE £2.20: £1.10, £3.30; EX 8.10 Trifecta £32.40.

Owner Cheveley Park Stud **Bred** Bjorn Nielsen **Trained** Newmarket, Suffolk

FOCUS

Rail movements added 3yds to the race distance. One of the feature races and not a bad staying handicap in which they went a sound enough pace. The third has been rated close to his earlier fast ground form this year.

5062 APOLLOBET BET ON LOTTERIES FILLIES' H'CAP 1m

4:20 (4:20) (Class 5) (0-75,75) 3-Y-O+ **£2,911** (£866; £432; £216) **Stalls** Low

Form RPR

2106 **1** **Lincoln Rocks**[26] 4145 3-9-5 **73**...................................... DanielTudhope 6 82
(David O'Meara) *trckd ldrs: hdwy over 2f out: rdn to ld over 1f out: edgd lft fnl f: styd on wl* **7/1**

0205 **2** 1 ¾ **Bell Heather (IRE)**[12] 4631 3-9-7 **75**.................................. JoeFanning 4 79
(Richard Fahey) *hld up in rr: hdwy over 2f out: rdn over 1f out: chsd wnr ins fnl f: sn drvn and no imp* **9/2**[2]

-055 **3** 3 **Simply Me**[24] 4206 3-8-6 **60**.. LiamJones 3 57
(Tom Dascombe) *led over 2f: cl up: rdn to ld again over 2f out: drvn and hdd over 1f out: sn one pce* **9/2**[2]

0312 **4** ½ **Zaria**[21] 4302 5-8-10 **64**...(p) HollieDoyle[(7)] 2 61
(Richard Price) *trckd ldrs: hdwy and cl up 1/2-way: rdn along over 2f out: n.m.r and sltly outpcd over 1f out: kpt on fnl f* **5/1**[3]

-040 **5** 2 **Sister Dude**[52] 3213 3-8-7 **68**...(t) CliffordLee[(7)] 1 59
(K R Burke) *prom: led over 5f out: rdn along and hdd over 2f out: drvn over 1f out: grad wknd* **7/1**

541 **6** 1 ¾ **La Havrese (FR)**[16] 4486 5-9-0 **66**.................................. JoshDoyle[(5)] 5 54
(Lynn Siddall) *hld up: hdwy wl over 2f out: chsd ldrs wl over 1f out sn rdn and ev ch: drvn and wknd ent fnl f* **13/2**

1532 **7** 4 **Bush Beauty (IRE)**[20] 4348 5-9-2 **70**.............................. GerO'Neill[(7)] 7 49
(Eric Alston) *t.k.h: hld up in rr: effrt over 3f out: sn rdn along and nvr a factor* **4/1**[1]

1m 40.67s (-3.03) **Going Correction** -0.175s/f (Firm)

WFA 3 from 5yo 7lb **7** Ran SP% **111.4**

Speed ratings (Par 100): **108,106,103,102,100 99,95**

CSF £36.10 TOTE £10.10: £3.90, £1.90; EX 37.80 Trifecta £328.30.

Owner Peter Smith P C Coaches Limited **Bred** James Ortega Bloodstock **Trained** Upper Helmsley, N Yorks

FOCUS

Rail movements added 3yds to the race distance. This fillies' handicap looked a tightly knit affair, but did not work out as the market expected. The runner-up has been rated close to his C&D reappearance run.

5063 APOLLOBET BET THROUGH YOUR MOBILE H'CAP 1m

4:50 (4:51) (Class 4) (0-85,83) 3-Y-O **£5,175** (£1,540; £769; £384) **Stalls** Low

Form RPR

5523 **1** **Worlds His Oyster**[12] 4631 3-8-12 **79**.................(p) CallumShepherd[(5)] 4 85
(John Quinn) *trckd ldng pair: hdwy over 2f out: rdn to ld over 1f out: drvn and kpt on wl fnl f* **2/1**[1]

2232 **2** 1 **Haraz (IRE)**[21] 4313 3-9-3 **79**..[1] DanielTudhope 5 83
(David O'Meara) *hld up: hdwy over 2f out: effrt and nt clr run over 1f out and again ins fnl f: sn rdn and kpt on* **3/1**[2]

2362 **3** nk **Deansgate (IRE)**[23] 4241 3-8-11 **73**...................................(e) JoeDoyle 2 76
(Julie Camacho) *t.k.h: trckd ldr: pushed along 2f out: rdn and ev ch over 1f out: drvn ins fnl f: kpt on same pce* **4/1**[3]

3601 **4** 3 **Lido Lady (IRE)**[18] 4429 3-8-10 **72**...................................... JoeFanning 7 68
(Mark Johnston) *led: pushed along wl over 2f out: rdn wl over 1f out: sn hdd & wknd fnl f* **3/1**[2]

2350 **5** 13 **Steccando (IRE)**[61] 2907 3-8-13 **75**...................................... NeilFarley 8 42
(Alan Swinbank) *hld up: hdwy on outer over 3f out: rdn along 2f out: sn drvn and btn* **9/1**

1m 41.74s (-1.96) **Going Correction** -0.175s/f (Firm) **5** Ran SP% **113.3**

Speed ratings (Par 102): **102,101,100,97,84**

CSF £8.57 TOTE £2.80: £1.40, £1.30; EX 9.20 Trifecta £15.80.

Owner Ross Harmon **Bred** Cheveley Park Stud Ltd **Trained** Settrington, N Yorks

FOCUS

Rail movements added 3yds to the race distance. This mile handicap was weakened by the absence of the top weight. It developed into something of a sprint in the straight and the time was 1.07secs slower than the preceding fillies' contest. The first three have been rated close to their recent marks.

T/Jkpt: £6666.60 to a £1 stake. Pool of £10,000.00 - 1.50 winning units. T/Plt: £89.20 to a £1 stake. Pool of £57319.65 - 469.03 winning tickets. T/Qpdt: £76.30 to a £1 stake. Pool of £4510.25 - 43.70 winning tickets. **Joe Rowntree**

4642 NEWCASTLE (A.W) (L-H)

Thursday, August 4

OFFICIAL GOING: Tapeta: standard

Wind: Breezy, half against Weather: Overcast, showers after race 1 (5.50)

5064 OLYMPICS BETTING AT 188BET APPRENTICE H'CAP 1m 2f 42y (Tp)

5:50 (5:51) (Class 6) (0-60,60) 3-Y-O+ **£2,587** (£770; £384; £192) **Stalls** High

Form RPR

6003 **1** **Mount Cheiron (USA)**[3] 4929 5-8-13 **50**............(b) CallumRodriguez[(3)] 6 57
(Richard Ford) *s.i.s: sn prom: smooth hdwy to ld over 2f out: rdn fnl f: hld on wl nr fin* **20/1**

4-31 **2** ¾ **Reckless Wave (IRE)**[22] 4267 3-9-3 **60**.............................. GeorgeWood 5 65
(Ed Walker) *hld up towards rr: niggled along after 2f: rdn over 2f out: hdwy over 1f out: kpt on to take 2nd towards fin: nt rch wnr* **1/1**[1]

1460 **3** hd **Diamond Runner (IRE)**[76] 2448 4-8-13 **52**...............(p) AledBeech[(5)] 14 57
(John Norton) *hld up in tch: stdy hdwy over 2f out: effrt and chsd wnr over 1f out: kpt on fnl f: no ex and lost 2nd nr fin* **50/1**

5242 **4** 2 ¾ **Exclusive Diamond**[18] 4424 4-9-5 **56**........................ PatrickVaughan[(3)] 13 56
(David O'Meara) *pressed ldr: rdn and ev ch over 2f out: outpcd and lost 2nd over 1f out: no imp after* **8/1**[2]

4006 **5** 1 ¼ **Table Manners**[18] 4425 4-9-4 **52**..................................... NatalieHambling 7 49
(Wilf Storey) *t.k.h: in tch: lost pl bef 1/2-way: rdn over 2f out: rallied over 1f out: nt pce to chal* **25/1**

4434 **6** 2 ½ **Kerry Icon**[5] 4872 3-7-11 **47** 1ex.. JamieGormley[(7)] 3 39
(Iain Jardine) *t.k.h: trckd ldrs: rdn over 2f out: wknd over 1f out* **9/1**[3]

0056 **7** *1* **Free One (IRE)**[16] 4493 4-9-9 **60**...........................(p) CameronNoble[(3)] 10 50
(Ivan Furtado) *hld up on outside: pushed along over 3f out: hdwy on outside over 1f out: kpt on: nvr able to chal* **14/1**

0663 **8** *shd* **Allfredandnobell (IRE)**[20] 4375 3-8-11 **54**...................... RowanScott 1 44
(Micky Hammond) *midfield on ins: rdn and effrt over 2f out: wknd over 1f out* **9/1**[3]

6405 **9** *1/2* **Outlaw Torn (IRE)**[3] 4929 7-8-9 **48**...........................(e) BenRobinson[(5)] 2 37
(Richard Guest) *towards rr: shortlived effrt on ins over 2f out: wknd over 1f out* **25/1**

4022 **10** *1/2* **Kicking The Can (IRE)**[12] 4648 5-9-12 **60**.................... KevinLundie 11 48
(David Thompson) *led at modest gallop: rdn and hdd over 2f out: wknd over 1f out* **8/1**[2]

060 **11** *5* **Adrakhan (FR)**[23] 4235 5-9-0 **48**................................ AnnaHesketh 9 26
(Wilf Storey) *t.k.h: hld up: rdn and outpcd over 3f out: nvr on terms* **66/1**

044- **12** *2 1/4* **Stamp Duty (IRE)**[382] 4424 8-8-13 **47**............................ LuluStanford 4 20
(Suzzanne France) *t.k.h in rr: struggling wl over 2f out: sn btn* **25/1**

2m 14.9s (4.50) **Going Correction** +0.325s/f (Slow)
WFA 3 from 4yo+ 9lb **12** Ran SP% **118.6**
Speed ratings (Par 101): **95,94,94,92,91 89,88,88,87,87 83,81**
CSF £38.51 CT £1103.24 TOTE £18.30: £4.20, £1.30, £6.80; EX 70.30 TRIFECTA Not won..
Owner The Style Council **Bred** Swettenham Stud **Trained** Garstang, Lancs

FOCUS
A low-grade handicap for apprentices in which the pace was ordinary.

5065 PARKLANDS MINI GOLF TEAM BUILDING EVENTS H'CAP 1m 4f 98y (Tp)
6:20 (6:21) (Class 5) (0-70,69) 3-Y-O+ **£3,881** (£866; £866; £288) **Stalls** High

Form RPR

-103 **1** **Major Rowan**[44] 3480 5-9-5 **60**.. PhillipMakin 4 76+
(John Davies) *hld up in last pl: stdy hdwy over 2f out: qcknd to ld over 1f out: shkn up and sn clr: v easily* **7/2**[2]

23-1 **2** *9* **Intrigue**[20] 4375 4-9-10 **65**..(b) DougieCostello 5 67
(Daniel Kubler) *trckd ldr: led over 2f out: rdn and hdd over 1f out: plugged on but no ch w easy wnr fnl f: jnd for 2nd on line* **11/4**[1]

6451 **2** *dht* **Whitchurch**[15] 4515 4-8-12 **53**.. PJMcDonald 8 55
(Philip Kirby) *t.k.h: hld up in tch: rdn over 2f out: rallied over 1f out: kpt on fnl f to dead-heat for 2nd on line: no ch w easy wnr* **7/1**

6126 **4** *2 1/4* **Nonagon**[47] 3418 5-9-5 **63**..(t) ShelleyBirkett[(3)] 7 61
(Wilf Storey) *dwlt: sn prom: rdn over 2f out: kpt on same pce fnl f* **6/1**

0004 **5** *nk* **Kopassus (IRE)**[18] 4424 4-8-10 **51**..............................(be) CamHardie 6 49
(Lawrence Mullaney) *led at ordinary gallop: rdn along and hdd over 2f out: outpcd over 1f out* **8/1**

-200 **6** *1 1/2* **Applejack Lad**[22] 4260 5-9-2 **57**...............................(tp) PaulMulrennan 3 53
(Michael Smith) *trckd ldrs: rdn and outpcd over 2f out: no imp fr over 1f out* **12/1**

-54R **R** **Clear Spell (IRE)**[37] 3751 5-10-0 **69**................................ GrahamLee 1
(Alistair Whillans) *ref to r* **5/1**[3]

2m 42.44s (1.34) **Going Correction** +0.325s/f (Slow) **7** Ran SP% **111.1**
Speed ratings (Par 103): **108,102,102,100,100 99,**
WIN: £3.30 Major Rowan; PL: Whitchurch £1.30, Major Rowan £1.40, Whitchurch £1.00; EX: MR/I £7.50, MR/W £10.70; CSF: MR/I £6.38, MJ/W £13.03; TRICAST: £29.56, £36.28; TRIFECTA: MR/I/W £24.10, MR/W/I £31.50;.
Owner J J Davies **Bred** David H Cox **Trained** Piercebridge, Durham

FOCUS
Not the strongest of handicaps and the pace wasn't great either, but the winner scored in fine style. The level is fluid.

5066 NEWLY REFURBISHED BORDER MINSTREL FILLIES' NURSERY H'CAP 7f 14y (Tp)
6:55 (6:55) (Class 4) (0-85,80) 2-Y-O **£5,175** (£1,540; £769; £384) **Stalls** Centre

Form RPR

0451 **1** **Bongrace (IRE)**[16] 4487 2-8-8 **67**.. KevinStott 5 73
(Kevin Ryan) *trckd ldrs: smooth hdwy to ld over 1f out: rdn and edgd lft ins fnl f: kpt on strly* **9/2**[3]

61 **2** *2 1/2* **Micolys (FR)**[17] 4442 2-8-9 **68**.. BenCurtis 1 67
(K R Burke) *pressed ldr: rdn and led over 2f out: hdd over 1f out: kpt on same pce ins fnl f* **9/4**[2]

51 **3** *1 1/4* **Island Vision (IRE)**[50] 3275 2-9-7 **80**................................ TomEaves 4 76
(David Simcock) *stdd in tch: stdy hdwy over 2f out: rdn and ev ch briefly over 1f out: drvn and no ex ins fnl f* **1/1**[1]

165 **4** *8* **Fancy Day (IRE)**[20] 4364 2-8-13 **72**............................ PaulMulrennan 3 47
(Mark Johnston) *led: rdn and hdd over 2f out: wknd over 1f out* **8/1**

1m 27.57s (1.37) **Going Correction** 0.0s/f (Stan) **4** Ran SP% **110.1**
Speed ratings (Par 93): **92,89,87,78**
CSF £14.67 TOTE £5.60; EX 12.90 Trifecta £17.40.
Owner Bongrace Partners **Bred** Mrs Celine Collins **Trained** Hambleton, N Yorks

FOCUS
Just four runners for this fillies' nursery but they were all previous winners. It's tricky to pin down the level but this could be rated a bit higher.

5067 FOOTBALL BETTING AT 188BET MEDIAN AUCTION MAIDEN STKS 6f (Tp)
7:30 (7:32) (Class 5) 2-Y-O **£2,911** (£866; £432; £216) **Stalls** Centre

Form RPR

1 **Parnassian (IRE)** 2-9-5 0.. DougieCostello 8 85+
(K R Burke) *hld up in tch: smooth hdwy over 2f out: shkn up to ld over 1f out: qcknd clr w ears pricked fnl f: readily* **10/1**

20 **2** *4 1/2* **Lucky Mistake (IRE)**[19] 4394 2-9-5 0.............................. DavidNolan 9 71
(Richard Fahey) *trckd ldrs: rdn and ev ch briefly over 1f out: sn chsng wnr: kpt on fnl f: nt pce to chal* **1/2**[1]

0 **3** *3/4* **Hot Hannah**[13] 4601 2-9-0 0.. ConnorBeasley 11 63
(Michael Dods) *led: rdn and hdd over 1f out: kpt on same pce* **33/1**

0 **4** *3 3/4* **Dream Team**[63] 2830 2-9-5 0.. PaulMulrennan 3 56
(Michael Dods) *trckd ldrs: rdn over 2f out: outpcd fr over 1f out* **9/1**[3]

06 **5** *3/4* **Lil's Affair (IRE)**[28] 4037 2-9-0 0.................................... DavidAllan 7 49
(Bryan Smart) *cl up on outside of gp: drvn along over 2f out: wknd over 1f out* **20/1**

4 **6** *nk* **Peny Arcade**[27] 4097 2-9-0 0... CamHardie 13 48
(Alistair Whillans) *hld up bhd ldng gp: effrt and rdn 2f out: edgd lft and sn no imp* **14/1**

0 **7** *2 1/4* **Shakabula (IRE)**[40] 3654 2-9-5 0.................................... BenCurtis 14 46
(Brian Ellison) *hld up: drvn and outpcd over 3f out: plugged on fnl f: nvr able to chal* **16/1**

8 *1/2* **Wily Rumpus (IRE)** 2-9-5 0.. AntonioFresu 1 44
(Ed Walker) *prom on outside of gp: outpcd and hung lft over 2f out: btn over 1f out* **11/2**[2]

9 *2 1/4* **Metisian** 2-9-5 0.. GrahamLee 12 37
(Jedd O'Keeffe) *s.i.s: bhd: drvn along 1/2-way: nvr on terms* **28/1**

10 *40* **Thornton Frank** 2-9-5 0.. BarryMcHugh 5
(Brian Rothwell) *s.v.s: a t.o* **66/1**

1m 13.14s (0.64) **Going Correction** 0.0s/f (Stan) **10** Ran SP% **126.3**
Speed ratings (Par 94): **95,89,88,83,82 81,78,77,74,21**
CSF £16.36 TOTE £13.20: £2.90, £1.02, £7.20; EX 28.50 Trifecta £625.10.
Owner Ontoawinner 14 & Mrs E Burke **Bred** Ballyhane Stud Ltd **Trained** Middleham Moor, N Yorks

FOCUS
A juvenile maiden run at a sound pace, and an interesting winner.

5068 ROA/RACING POST OWNERS' JACKPOT H'CAP 7f 14y (Tp)
8:05 (8:06) (Class 6) (0-65,65) 3-Y-O+ **£3,234** (£962; £481; £240) **Stalls** Centre

Form RPR

0062 **1** **Gun Case**[11] 4683 4-9-10 **63**..(p) DougieCostello 9 73
(Alistair Whillans) *hld up: hdwy to ld over 1f out: rdn and sn hung lft: kpt on ins fnl f* **10/1**[3]

0000 **2** *1 1/4* **Inshaa**[31] 3946 4-9-10 **63**..(p) GrahamLee 4 70
(Michael Herrington) *prom: hdwy to ld over 2f out: hdd over 1f out: kpt on fnl f: nt pce of wnr* **25/1**

341 **3** *2* **Hardy Black (IRE)**[30] 3987 5-9-4 **64**.....................(p) CameronNoble[(7)] 11 66
(Kevin Frost) *hld up: rdn over 2f out: hdwy over 1f out: kpt on fnl f: nt pce to chal* **12/1**

1105 **4** *1/2* **Barwah (USA)**[18] 4429 5-9-0 **58**.................................. NathanEvans[(5)] 13 58
(Peter Niven) *hld up: gd hdwy over 1f out: sn rdn and edgd lft: kpt on same pce fnl f* **17/2**[2]

0405 **5** *1/2* **Nelson's Bay**[8] 4768 7-9-2 **55**...................................... CamHardie 8 54
(Wilf Storey) *dwlt: bhd: rdn and hdwy over 2f out: kpt on same pce ins fnl f* **25/1**

040 **6** *nk* **Truly**[57] 3012 5-9-12 **65**.. TomEaves 1 63
(Colin Teague) *hld up in tch on far side of gp: rdn over 2f out: wknd over 1f out* **33/1**

0055 **7** *2 1/2* **Just Paul (IRE)**[51] 3262 6-9-2 **55**..................................[1] PJMcDonald 10 47
(Micky Hammond) *midfield: outpcd and hung lft 2f out: sn btn* **14/1**

0032 **8** *1 1/4* **Caeser The Gaeser (IRE)**[8] 4771 4-8-7 **53**............(p) GeorgeWood[(7)] 7 41
(Nigel Tinkler) *trckd ldrs: rdn over 2f out: wknd over 1f out* **16/1**

5360 **9** *6* **For Shia And Lula (IRE)**[30] 3989 7-9-1 **61**..................... TobyEley[(7)] 12 34
(Daniel Mark Loughnane) *prom: rdn and outpcd over 2f out: edgd lft and sn wknd* **33/1**

3350 **10** *1/2* **Alans Pride (IRE)**[8] 4772 4-9-1 **54**...........................(tp) ConnorBeasley 2 26
(Michael Dods) *disp ld to over 2f out: rdn and wknd over 1f out* **12/1**

5060 **11** *2 1/2* **Justice Pleasing**[10] 4701 3-9-4 **63**.............................. PaulMulrennan 6 26
(David Loughnane) *slt ld to over 2f out: rdn and wknd over 1f out* **50/1**

0044 **12** *3 3/4* **Cascading Stars (IRE)**[29] 4006 4-9-8 **61**................... DanielTudhope 14 16
(Daniel Mark Loughnane) *hld up: drvn along on nr side of gp over 2f out: sn wknd* **12/1**

5640 **13** *9* **Mr Sundowner (USA)**[3] 4930 4-8-12 **54**..................(t) ShelleyBirkett[(3)] 5
(Wilf Storey) *chsd ldrs tl rdn and wknd fr over 2f out* **16/1**

121 **P** **Mister Royal (IRE)**[11] 4683 5-9-9 **62** 6ex...........................(p) BenCurtis 3
(Brian Ellison) *in tch on far side of gp: pushed along whn lost action and p.u over 2f out: lame* **11/10**[1]

1m 26.29s (0.09) **Going Correction** 0.0s/f (Stan)
WFA 3 from 4yo+ 6lb **14** Ran SP% **124.3**
Speed ratings (Par 101): **99,97,95,94,94 93,90,89,82,82 79,74,64,**
CSF £251.19 CT £3104.14 TOTE £10.90: £3.50, £6.10, £2.40; EX 326.80 TRIFECTA Not won..
Owner A C Whillans **Bred** Mildmay Bloodstock Ltd **Trained** Newmill-On-Slitrig, Borders

FOCUS
A run-of-the-mile handicap which was run at a good gallop. The hot favourite went wrong and was pulled up.

5069 @NEWCASTLERACES FOLLOW US ON INSTAGRAM H'CAP 6f (Tp)
8:40 (8:41) (Class 6) (0-65,65) 3-Y-O+ **£2,911** (£866; £432; £216) **Stalls** Centre

Form RPR

4-01 **1** **Sugar Town**[8] 4770 6-8-9 **53** 6ex.............................. NathanEvans[(5)] 5 62
(Peter Niven) *mde all: rdn along wl over 1f out: kpt on strly fnl f: unchal* **4/1**[1]

5660 **2** *1* **Viva Verglas (IRE)**[12] 4640 5-9-9 **62**.........................(e[1]) DanielTudhope 3 67
(Daniel Mark Loughnane) *chsd wnr thrght: rdn along over 1f out: kpt on ins fnl f: nt pce of wnr* **11/2**[2]

2330 **3** *1/2* **Gypsy Major**[17] 4454 4-8-8 **47**..(v) DavidAllan 9 50+
(Garry Moss) *hld up: hdwy to chse ldrs over 2f out: sn rdn: disp 2nd pl appr fnl f: edgd lft: no ex towards fin* **11/2**[2]

0644 **4** *1/2* **The Armed Man**[8] 4771 3-9-2 **59**..............................(p) AndrewElliott 2 59
(Chris Fairhurst) *prom: rdn over 2f out: edgd lft: kpt on ins fnl f* **8/1**[3]

1000 **5** *nk* **Captain Scooby**[3] 4931 10-9-0 **53**...........................(b) ConnorBeasley 6 53+
(Richard Guest) *hld up: rdn along over 2f out: hdwy over 1f out: kpt on same pce wl ins fnl f* **14/1**

033 **6** *5* **Euxton**[12] 4647 4-9-3 **56**.. CamHardie 14 40
(Lawrence Mullaney) *hld up: rdn along over 2f out: kpt on fnl f: nvr able to chal* **10/1**

040 **7** *1* **Questo**[18] 4428 4-9-12 **65**.. DaleSwift 11 46
(Tracy Waggott) *hld up in midfield: hdwy and prom over 2f out: wknd over 1f out* **12/1**

-006 **8** *1* **Wilsons Ruby (IRE)**[42] 3568 3-9-7 **64**................................ BenCurtis 10 41
(Brian Ellison) *hld up: drvn along over 2f out: sn no imp* **9/1**

3340 **9** *1 1/4* **Whispering Wolf**[15] 4513 3-8-6 **49**.................................... JoeDoyle 8 22
(Suzzanne France) *t.k.h: trckd ldrs: rdn along over 2f out: wknd over 1f out* **25/1**

0000 **10** *1* **Majestic Manannan (IRE)**[12] 4647 7-8-12 **51**............ BarryMcHugh 12 22
(David Nicholls) *prom tl rdn and wknd wl over 1f out* **22/1**

-046 **11** *1/2* **Cape Crusader (IRE)**[17] 4445 3-8-2 **50**.......................(p) PhilDennis[(5)] 1 18
(Michael Dods) *prom: rdn over 2f out: edgd lft and sn wknd* **20/1**

4450 **12** *1/2* **Keene's Pointe**[14] 4544 6-9-8 **61**.................................. PJMcDonald 4 29
(Kristin Stubbs) *hld up: drvn and hung lft over 2f out: sn btn* **9/1**

1510 **13** *7* **Hab Reeh**[14] 4570 8-9-2 **55**..(p) TomEaves 13
(Ruth Carr) *hld up: rdn over 2f out: sn wknd* **25/1**

0-00 **14** *shd* **Sunnyhills Belford**[23] 4238 3-8-3 **46** oh1...................... PatrickMathers 7
(Noel Wilson) *s.i.s: bhd and sn pushed along: struggling fr 1/2-way* **66/1**

1m 12.18s (-0.32) **Going Correction** 0.0s/f (Stan)
WFA 3 from 4yo+ 4lb **14** Ran SP% **123.6**
Speed ratings (Par 101): **102,100,100,99,98 92,90,89,87,86 85,85,75,75**
CSF £23.90 CT £129.25 TOTE £4.80: £1.70, £2.00, £2.70; EX 27.70 Trifecta £157.40.
Owner Mrs Heather Burley **Bred** Mrs S M Roy **Trained** Barton-le-Street, N Yorks

FOCUS
An ordinary sprint handicap, but the pace was sound and the first five were clear of the remainder.

5070 ANNUAL MEMBERS H'CAP 5f (Tp)
9:10 (9:10) (Class 5) (0-75,75) 3-Y-O **£3,881** (£1,155; £577; £288) **Stalls** Centre

Form RPR
1435 **1** **Futoon (IRE)**[19] 4398 3-9-7 **75** JoeDoyle 5 86
(Kevin Ryan) *trckd ldrs: effrt and rdn over 1f out: led wl ins fnl f: kpt on wl* **15/8**[1]
2050 **2** ½ **First Bombardment**[13] 4612 3-9-7 **75** DanielTudhope 7 84
(David O'Meara) *pressed ldr: rdn over 1f out: led briefly ins fnl f: kpt on: hld towards fin* **11/2**[3]
3231 **3** 1 **Hilary J**[13] 4604 3-9-6 **74** PJMcDonald 1 79
(Ann Duffield) *led: rdn over 1f out: hdd ins fnl f: kpt on same pce* **9/4**[2]
6344 **4** 2 **Emerald Asset (IRE)**[24] 4192 3-8-2 **56** CamHardie 6 54
(Paul Midgley) *dwlt: bhd and sn pushed along: drvn and outpcd 1/2-way: hdwy fnl f: nrst fin* **16/1**
2526 **5** 2½ **Roaring Rory**[18] 4426 3-8-10 **67** (p) JacobButterfield(3) 2 56
(Ollie Pears) *trckd ldrs: rdn over 2f out: wknd appr fnl f* **12/1**
265- **6** nk **Ingleby Valley**[344] 5738 3-8-13 **67** GeorgeChaloner 4 55
(Richard Fahey) *prom: sn pushed along: drvn along over 2f out: edgd lft and wknd over 1f out* **9/1**
0050 **7** 2½ **Farkle Minkus**[16] 4488 3-9-6 **74** (p) DougieCostello 3 53
(Keith Dalgleish) *rrd in stalls: missed break: sn in tch: rdn along over 2f out: edgd lft and wknd wl over 1f out* **8/1**

58.83s (-0.67) **Going Correction** 0.0s/f (Stan) **7** Ran SP% **115.6**
Speed ratings (Par 100): **105,104,102,99,95 94,90**
CSF £13.10 TOTE £2.90: £1.60, £3.90; EX 13.10 Trifecta £41.40.
Owner Course & Distance Racing **Bred** Melchior Bloodstock & Partners **Trained** Hambleton, N Yorks

FOCUS
This looked the most competitive of the handicaps on the card. The winner built on her recent form, and a small pb from the second.
T/Plt: £144.80 to a £1 stake. Pool of £52016.73 - 262.12 winning tickets. T/Qpdt: £80.10 to a £1 stake. Pool of £4550.24 - 42.0 winning tickets. **Richard Young**

4773 SANDOWN (R-H)
Thursday, August 4

OFFICIAL GOING: Good (good to firm in places on round course)
Wind: Moderate, against Weather: Fine but cloudy, warm

5071 SLUG AND LETTUCE 2-4-1 COCKTAILS GENTLEMAN AMATEUR RIDERS' H'CAP 1m 2f 7y
5:35 (5:36) (Class 4) (0-80,80) 3-Y-O+ **£4,991** (£1,548; £773; £387) **Stalls** Low

Form RPR
2212 **1** **Palisade**[22] 4277 3-10-5 **73** (v) MrSWalker 4 85+
(Sir Mark Prescott Bt) *hld up: nt clr run briefly 3f out: prog 2f out to ld jst over 1f out: sn rdn clr* **1/1**[1]
5514 **2** 3¼ **Compton Mill**[14] 4561 4-10-13 **77** (t) MrRPooles(5) 6 82
(Hughie Morrison) *pressed ldr: led 1/2-way: sent for home over 3f out: hdd and no ex jst over 1f out* **4/1**[2]
4060 **3** ¾ **Biotic**[29] 4013 5-11-4 **77** (t) MrPMillman 3 81
(Rod Millman) *hld up in last: prog over 3f out to chse ldr jst over 2f out: rdn to cl over 1f out but sn lost 2nd and nt qckn* **10/1**
-656 **4** 6 **Zoffanys Pride (IRE)**[68] 2694 3-10-2 **75** MrHHunt(5) 7 67
(Andrew Balding) *in tch: chsd ldr briefly over 2f out: wknd over 1f out* **8/1**[3]
3-05 **5** 6 **River Dart (IRE)**[24] 4208 4-11-0 **80** (v[1]) MrGTregoning(7) 2 60
(Marcus Tregoning) *chsd ldng pair to wl over 2f out: wknd* **4/1**[2]
/05- **6** 5 **Classic Colori (IRE)**[18] 190 9-10-3 **65** (bt) MrJamesKing(3) 1 35
(Martin Keighley) *rn wout declared tongue-strap: mde most to 1/2-way: lost 2nd over 2f out and wknd* **66/1**

2m 11.39s (0.89) **Going Correction** +0.10s/f (Good)
WFA 3 from 4yo+ 9lb **6** Ran SP% **111.7**
Speed ratings (Par 105): **100,97,96,92,87 83**
CSF £5.27 TOTE £1.80: £1.40, £2.20; EX 5.30 Trifecta £17.30.
Owner Cheveley Park Stud **Bred** Cheveley Park Stud Ltd **Trained** Newmarket, Suffolk

FOCUS
The going was given as good, good to firm in places on the Round course, and good on the Sprint course (GoingStick: Round 7.5; Sprint 7.2). The far side rail on the Sprint course was in 4yds, while the Round course was railed out from 7f and wide up the home straight, adding 17yds to all Round course distances. A fair handicap for amateur riders. The pace picked up a fair way out. It's been rated around the second and third.

5072 SLUG AND LETTUCE CHRISTMAS/EBF STALLIONS MAIDEN STKS (PLUS 10 RACE) 5f 6y
6:10 (6:10) (Class 4) 2-Y-O **£4,528** (£1,347; £673; £336) **Stalls** Low

Form RPR
3 **1** **Tadkhirah**[22] 4261 2-9-0 **0** FrankieDettori 2 72
(William Haggas) *rousted along to ld after 100yds: mde most after against rail: rdn for home wl over 1f out: at least 2 l clr fnl f: drvn out and jst lasted* **13/8**[1]
64 **2** nk **Moi Moi Moi (IRE)**[10] 4707 2-9-5 **0** JimCrowley 1 76
(Brian Meehan) *s.i.s: hld up in last pair against rail: waiting for room 2f out: prog over 1f out: chsd wnr 100yds: clsd fin but jst too much to do* **9/2**[3]
3 1 **Connacht Girl (IRE)** 2-9-0 **0** JoeyHaynes 4 67+
(K R Burke) *s.i.s: w.w in last pair: rdn and prog on outer over 1f out: chsd wnr jst ins fnl f: tried to cl but lost 2nd 100yds out: kpt on* **8/1**
3 **4** 8 **Coronation Cottage**[21] 4287 2-9-0 **0** RyanTate 8 39
(Malcolm Saunders) *pressed ldrs on outer: w wnr 1/2-way: outpcd over 1f out: lost 2nd and wknd qckly jst ins fnl f* **5/1**
00 **5** 3¼ **Whatalove**[17] 4457 2-9-0 **0** SamHitchcott 3 27
(Martin Keighley) *w wnr after 100yds to 1/2-way: sn wknd qckly* **100/1**
2200 **6** ½ **Cappananty Con**[19] 4394 2-9-5 **73** RobertWinston 6 30
(Dean Ivory) *broke best: led 100yds: cl up: chal 1/2-way: rdn and wknd over 1f out: heavily eased fnl f* **3/1**[2]

1m 3.48s (1.88) **Going Correction** +0.30s/f (Good) **6** Ran SP% **110.0**
Speed ratings (Par 96): **96,95,93,81,75 75**
CSF £8.94 TOTE £2.20: £1.40, £2.50; EX 7.90 Trifecta £43.40.
Owner Hamdan Al Maktoum **Bred** Horizon Bloodstock Limited **Trained** Newmarket, Suffolk

FOCUS
No more than a fair maiden, and the early pace wasn't breakneck.

5073 SLUG AND LETTUCE FAST & FRESH/EBF STALLIONS MAIDEN STKS (PLUS 10 RACE) 1m 14y
6:45 (6:45) (Class 4) 2-Y-O **£4,528** (£1,347; £673; £336) **Stalls** Low

Form RPR
6 **1** **First Quest (USA)**[12] 4649 2-9-5 **0** WilliamBuick 5 77
(Ed Dunlop) *trckd ldrs: rdn over 2f out: narrow ld over 1f out but hotly pressed after: drvn out and jst hld on* **9/2**[3]
5 **2** shd **Whip Nae Nae (IRE)**[13] 4594 2-9-5 **0** SeanLevey 2 76
(Richard Hannon) *trckd ldrs: shkn up 2f out: swtchd lft and clsd on ldng pair fnl f: tk 2nd last 75yds and chal: jst hld* **5/1**
0 **3** ¾ **Glendun (USA)**[34] 3859 2-9-5 **0** JimCrowley 3 74
(Brian Meehan) *mostly pressed ldr tl narrow ld jst over 2f out: hdd over 1f out but styd w wnr: gd battle tl no ex and lost 2nd last 75yds* **3/1**[2]
4 nk **Zenon (IRE)** 2-9-5 **0** FrankieDettori 6 73+
(John Gosden) *rn green: hld up in last: pushed along wl over 2f out: effrt over 1f out: styd on ins fnl f: nrst fin* **9/4**[1]
5 1¾ **Mount Moriah** 2-9-5 **0** OisinMurphy 7 69
(Ralph Beckett) *led at mod pce: narrowly hdd jst over 2f out: styd cl up fdd fnl f* **5/1**
4 **6** 8 **Peace And Plenty**[16] 4479 2-9-5 **0** SamHitchcott 1 51
(William Muir) *dwlt: in tch: shkn up wl over 2f out: wknd over 1f out* **11/1**

1m 45.98s (2.68) **Going Correction** +0.10s/f (Good) **6** Ran SP% **115.6**
Speed ratings (Par 96): **90,89,89,88,87 79**
CSF £27.53 TOTE £5.20: £3.00, £2.90; EX 29.60 Trifecta £76.40.
Owner The First Quest Partnership **Bred** Paul Tackett **Trained** Newmarket, Suffolk

FOCUS
Race distance increased by 17yds. An ordinary maiden.

5074 FIZZ-FRIDAYS AT SLUG AND LETTUCE H'CAP 1m 2f 7y
7:20 (7:22) (Class 3) (0-90,90) 3-Y-O **£9,337** (£2,796; £1,398; £699; £349) **Stalls** Low

Form RPR
0531 **1** **Proctor**[22] 4272 3-8-12 **81** OisinMurphy 5 87
(Stuart Kittow) *mde virtually all: rdn and jnd 2f out: kpt finding after: edgd lft ins fnl f but jst asserted last 75yds* **5/1**[2]
3-43 **2** nk **Four On Eight**[41] 3617 3-8-10 **79** AndreaAtzeni 4 84
(Luca Cumani) *trckd ldng pair: rdn over 2f out: clsd to chal over 1f out: w wnr fnl f tl nt qckn last 75yds* **9/1**
2210 **3** shd **Wave Reviews**[26] 4131 3-9-1 **84** (p) JimCrowley 2 89
(William Haggas) *trckd wnr: chal 2f out: lost 2nd 1f out but stl rt on terms: kpt on but jst hld* **11/2**[3]
31 **4** 1½ **Frontiersman**[28] 4056 3-9-7 **90** WilliamBuick 1 92
(Charlie Appleby) *a in 4th: shkn up over 2f out and little rspnse: swtchd wd over 1f out and drvn: kpt on but nt qckn and nvr chal* **10/11**[1]
4041 **5** 15 **Shahbar**[35] 3824 3-9-4 **87** (b) FrankieDettori 3 73
(Marco Botti) *hld up in last: pushed along 3f out: no prog and btn 2f out: eased and t.o* **5/1**[2]

2m 9.39s (-1.11) **Going Correction** +0.10s/f (Good) **5** Ran SP% **111.1**
Speed ratings (Par 104): **108,107,107,106,94**
CSF £42.48 TOTE £6.10: £2.60, £4.00; EX 39.20 Trifecta £96.80.
Owner Qatar Racing Limited **Bred** Qatar Bloodstock Ltd **Trained** Blackborough, Devon

FOCUS
Race distance increased by 17yds. With the favourite disappointing and one of the second-favourites finishing tailed off, this probably didn't take as much winning as had been expected, but nevertheless there was plenty to like about the way the winner refused to be beaten. A small pb from the runner-up, with the third rated to the better view of his maiden form.

5075 PARTY BOOKING AT SLUG AND LETTUCE H'CAP 7f 16y
7:55 (7:55) (Class 4) (0-85,85) 3-Y-O+ **£6,469** (£1,925; £962; £481) **Stalls** Low

Form RPR
2223 **1** **Chaplin Bay (IRE)**[6] 4830 4-9-1 **74** JamesSullivan 11 82+
(Ruth Carr) *hld up in last: gd prog on outer 2f out to chse ldr 1f out and sn on terms: edgd rt but cajoled into ld last 75yds: kpt on* **11/2**[1]
0033 **2** nk **Sarangoo**[4] 4908 8-8-13 **72** JimCrowley 5 79
(Malcolm Saunders) *led: drew 3 l clr 3f out: rdn 2f out: kpt on but hdd last 75yds: jst hld whn n.m.r nr fin* **10/1**
-220 **3** 1¼ **Doctor Bong**[35] 3803 4-8-7 **73** (b[1]) JoshuaBryan(7) 3 77
(Andrew Balding) *chsd ldr: rdn over 2f out: lost 2nd 1f out and one pce after* **8/1**
1102 **4** nse **Marcano (IRE)**[20] 4368 4-9-3 **76** (t) FrederikTylicki 4 80+
(Rod Millman) *hld up in rr: trapped bhd rivals fr 2f out to fnl f: r.o last 150yds: nrly snatched 3rd* **7/1**[3]
1242 **5** ¾ **First Experience**[7] 4787 5-8-12 **71** KierenFox 1 73
(Lee Carter) *trckd ldrs: rdn 2f out: wl hld whn n.m.r jst ins fnl f: kpt on* **14/1**
-204 **6** ½ **Commodore (IRE)**[21] 4299 4-9-12 **85** SteveDrowne 9 85+
(George Baker) *hld up: pushed along and nt making much prog whn squeezed out over 1f out: kpt on ins fnl f* **7/1**[3]
1352 **7** ¾ **Koptoon**[15] 4534 4-9-7 **80** RobertWinston 6 78
(Jo Hughes) *chsd ldrs: rdn and nt qckn 2f out: no imp after* **7/1**[3]
0306 **8** 1 **Outback Ruler (IRE)**[21] 4306 4-9-9 **82** (p) OisinMurphy 2 78
(Clive Cox) *dwlt: a towards rr: rdn and no prog 2f out* **8/1**
0512 **9** 1¾ **Danecase**[5] 4881 3-8-10 **75** FergusSweeney 8 64
(David Dennis) *trckd ldrs: moved up and looked a threat jst over 2f out: fnd little and wknd over 1f out* **6/1**[2]
4-22 **10** 8 **Great Fun**[38] 3729 5-9-6 **79** SilvestreDeSousa 7 49
(Michael Blake) *t.k.h: trckd ldrs: rdn 3f out: wknd 2f out: eased* **7/1**[3]

1m 29.05s (-0.45) **Going Correction** +0.10s/f (Good)
WFA 3 from 4yo+ 6lb **10** Ran SP% **117.7**
Speed ratings (Par 105): **106,105,104,104,103 102,101,100,98,89**
CSF £60.64 CT £451.73 TOTE £6.90: £2.40, £3.50, £2.70; EX 63.50 Trifecta £593.90.
Owner Miss B Houlston,Mrs M Chapman,Mrs R Carr **Bred** Stonethorn Stud Farms Ltd **Trained** Huby, N Yorks

FOCUS
Race distance increased by 17yds. A competitive handicap. The form is a bit messy.

5076 DEVINE HOMES H'CAP 1m 14y
8:25 (8:27) (Class 5) (0-75,75) 3-Y-O+ **£5,175** (£1,540; £769; £384) **Stalls** Low

Form RPR
06-5 **1** **Unison (IRE)**[28] 4052 6-9-6 **67** SilvestreDeSousa 2 73
(Jeremy Scott) *kpt on the move bhd stalls: led: steered lft after 2f and sn hdd: rdn to chal over 2f out: drvn to ld 1f out: jst hld on* **7/2**[3]

1401 **2** *hd* **Boycie**[13] 4588 3-9-7 **75**....................(b) KieranO'Neill 6 79
(Richard Hannon) *hld up in last pair: rdn over 3f out: fnlly mde prog 2f out: tk 3rd fnl f: styd on to take 2nd last 75yds: clsd on wnr but jst failed* **5/1**

4432 **3** *1 1/4* **Fidelma Moon (IRE)**[5] 4871 4-9-6 **72**.................... JordanVaughan(5) 3 74
(K R Burke) *pressed ldr: carried lft after 2f but sn led and stretched on: pressed over 2f out but gng bttr than rivals: rdn and hdd 1f out: nt qckn and lost 2nd last 75yds* **3/1**[2]

1122 **4** *4* **Choral Clan (IRE)**[8] 4773 5-9-9 **70**.................... AndreaAtzeni 4 63
(Philip Mitchell) *hld up in last pair: rdn over 2f out: tried to make prog over 1f out: sn no hdwy* **11/4**[1]

3002 **5** *1 3/4* **Saint Pois (FR)**[24] 4200 5-9-4 **68**.................... GeorgeDowning(3) 5 57
(Tony Carroll) *t.k.h: hld up bhd ldrs: rdn over 2f out: no imp over 1f out: wknd* **9/1**

3413 **6** *6* **Cooperess**[14] 4562 3-8-3 **57**....................(bt) JoeyHaynes 1 31
(Ali Stronge) *trckd ldrs: rdn to chal over 2f out: wknd qckly over 1f out* **6/1**

1m 43.1s (-0.20) **Going Correction** +0.10s/f (Good)
WFA 3 from 4yo+ 7lb **6** Ran SP% **114.8**
Speed ratings (Par 103): **105,104,103,99,97 91**
CSF £21.54 TOTE £4.20: £1.90, £2.60; EX 21.40 Trifecta £99.40.
Owner J P Carrington **Bred** Alan Dargan **Trained** Brompton Regis, Somerset

FOCUS
Race distance increased by 17yds. A regular handicap.
T/Plt: £390.40 to a £1 stake. Pool of £50918.24 - 95.20 winning tickets. T/Qpdt: £135.40 to a £1 stake. Pool of £4214.81 - 23.02 winning tickets. **Jonathan Neesom**

4712 WOLVERHAMPTON (A.W) (L-H)
Thursday, August 4

OFFICIAL GOING: Tapeta: standard
Wind: light across Weather: Cloudy

5077 G.M. TREBLE LTD MAIDEN STKS 5f 216y (Tp)
5:55 (6:01) (Class 5) 2-Y-O **£2,911** (£866; £432; £216) **Stalls** Low

Form RPR

3 **1** **The Amber Fort (USA)**[38] 3730 2-9-5 0.................... RobertHavlin 2 81
(John Gosden) *dwlt: sn trckd ldng pair: rdn over 1f out: led ins fnl f: kpt on* **2/1**[2]

6 **2** *1/2* **Colonel Frank**[35] 3818 2-9-5 0.................... LukeMorris 7 79
(Ed Walker) *trckd ldng pair: rdn 2f out: drvn and ev ch 1f out: kpt on* **9/2**[3]

4224 **3** *1 1/4* **Tafaakhor (IRE)**[20] 4363 2-9-5 84.................... DaneO'Neill 1 75
(Richard Hannon) *w ldr: pushed along to ld wl over 1f out: sn rdn: hdd ins fnl f: no ex* **11/8**[1]

0 **4** *3* **Broughtons Story**[58] 2997 2-9-5 0.................... JFEgan 9 65
(Willie Musson) *hld up: pushed along and hdwy on outside 2f out: one pce* **50/1**

5 *5* **Fluorescent Rock (IRE)**[35] 3826 2-9-0 0.................... PatCosgrave 4 44
(Damian Joseph English, Ire) *midfield: rdn 2f out: wknd over 1f out* **16/1**

6 **6** *3/4* **Sir Harry Collins (IRE)**[16] 4494 2-9-5 0.................... HarryBentley 8 47
(Richard Spencer) *hld up in midfield: rdn 2f out: nvr threatened* **33/1**

5 **7** *nk* **Dashing Poet**[14] 4558 2-9-0 0.................... MartinLane 5 41+
(Jeremy Gask) *led narrowly: rdn whn hdd wl over 1f out: wknd* **16/1**

8 *shd* **Oh So Dandy (IRE)** 2-9-5 0.................... JasonHart 3 46
(Derek Shaw) *slowly away: a towards rr* **100/1**

9 *shd* **Abundant Courage (IRE)** 2-9-5 0.................... RichardKingscote 6 45
(Brian Meehan) *s.i.s: sn midfield: pushed along 2f out: sn wknd* **22/1**

1m 14.96s (0.46) **Going Correction** +0.025s/f (Slow) **9** Ran SP% **115.6**
Speed ratings (Par 94): **97,96,94,90,84 83,82,82,82**
CSF £11.20 TOTE £3.80: £1.80, £1.80, £1.02; EX 13.20 Trifecta £23.10.
Owner Rachel Hood & Elaine Lawlor **Bred** Mr & Mrs Oliver S Tait **Trained** Newmarket, Suffolk

FOCUS
A fair maiden and the three market principals fought out the finish.

5078 G.M. TREBLE - GRUNDFOS FILLIES' H'CAP 5f 216y (Tp)
6:30 (6:31) (Class 5) (0-75,73) 3-Y-O+ **£2,911** (£866; £432; £216) **Stalls** Low

Form RPR

21-4 **1** **Jameerah**[42] 3568 3-9-7 **73**.................... LukeMorris 3 81
(James Tate) *dwlt: sn in tch racing keenly: trckd ldrs gng wl 2f out: pushed along and qcknd to ld jst ins fnl f: kpt on pushed out* **5/2**[1]

0422 **2** *1* **Tigserin (IRE)**[15] 4525 3-9-2 **68**.................... SamJames 1 73
(Giles Bravery) *trckd ldng pair: rdn to ld appr fnl f: hdd jst ins fnl f: kpt on but a hld* **7/2**[2]

24-0 **3** *hd* **Welsh Rose**[19] 4398 3-9-6 **72**.................... MartinDwyer 8 76
(William Muir) *hld up: rdn 2f out: hdwy over 1f out: kpt on* **8/1**

-432 **4** *4 1/2* **Andalusite**[16] 4472 3-8-8 **60**.................... RoystonFfrench 7 50
(Ed McMahon) *chsd ldng pair: rdn to chal on outer 2f out: wknd ins fnl f* **8/1**

0035 **5** *1 3/4* **Abberley Dancer (IRE)**[27] 4085 3-8-10 **65**.......... JosephineGordon(3) 6 49
(J S Moore) *hld up in rr: pushed along over 3f out: sme late hdwy: nvr threatened* **11/2**[3]

6526 **6** *2 1/2* **Chookie's Lass**[16] 4488 5-9-0 **62**.................... JasonHart 5 39
(Keith Dalgleish) *pressed ldr: rdn 2f out: wknd fnl f* **10/1**

000- **7** *2* **Camino**[266] 7807 3-8-8 **60**....................[1] NickyMackay 2 30
(Willie Musson) *dwlt: hld up: rdn over 1f out: nvr threatened* **33/1**

0034 **8** *1 3/4* **Lady Nayef**[22] 4280 3-9-2 **68**.................... JFEgan 4 32
(John Butler) *led narrowly: rdn over 2f out: hdd appr fnl f: wknd* **8/1**

1m 13.55s (-0.95) **Going Correction** +0.025s/f (Slow)
WFA 3 from 5yo 4lb **8** Ran SP% **111.5**
Speed ratings (Par 100): **107,105,105,99,97 93,91,88**
CSF £10.61 CT £57.07 TOTE £3.30: £1.30, £1.60, £2.30; EX 12.10 Trifecta £43.70.
Owner Saeed Manana **Bred** Rabbah Bloodstock Limited **Trained** Newmarket, Suffolk

FOCUS
A fair fillies' handicap and it could be rated a length higher.

5079 G.M. TREBLE - WILO H'CAP 1m 5f 194y (Tp)
7:05 (7:06) (Class 6) (0-60,60) 3-Y-O **£2,264** (£673; £336; £168) **Stalls** Low

Form RPR

0002 **1** **Miss Marina Bay**[13] 4591 3-8-13 **52**....................(p) LukeMorris 4 61+
(Sir Mark Prescott Bt) *midfield: rdn along to chse clr ldr 5f out: clsr 2f out: drvn to ld 1f out: edgd rt: styd on* **11/1**

0003 **2** *1* **Ryan The Giant**[24] 4210 3-8-7 **46**....................(p) JoeFanning 7 54
(Keith Dalgleish) *chsd ldr: rdn 4f out: outpcd over 2f out: styd on fr over 1f out* **7/1**

0242 **3** *4 1/2* **Denmead**[3] 4942 3-9-6 **59**.................... GrahamGibbons 2 61
(John Butler) *led: clr 7f out: stl 6 l up whn rdn 3f out: reduced advantage 2 out: hdd 1f out: wknd* **15/8**[1]

0344 **4** *3* **Harry's Endeavour**[23] 4226 3-9-7 **60**.................... TimmyMurphy 3 58
(Daniel Kubler) *midfield: rdn over 4f out: no imp* **8/1**

-300 **5** *10* **Kazoey**[22] 4255 3-8-7 **46** oh1.................... DuranFentiman 8 30
(Chris Fairhurst) *hld up: nvr threatened* **50/1**

0323 **6** *3 3/4* **Chestnut Storm (IRE)**[17] 4450 3-9-3 **56**....................(p) PatCosgrave 5 34
(Ed Dunlop) *sn in tch: rdn over 4f out: sn struggling* **5/1**[3]

0-04 **7** *99* **Rob's Legacy**[17] 4450 3-8-3 **47** oh1 ow1.................... CharlieBennett(5) 6
(Shaun Harris) *hld up: already struggling whn hung bdly rt on bnd over 5f out: t.o* **100/1**

000 **P** **Placedela Concorde**[73] 2548 3-9-3 **56**.................... RichardKingscote 1
(Anthony Carson) *hld up: hung rt on bnd 7f out and sn p.u* **3/1**[2]

3m 4.66s (-0.14) **Going Correction** +0.025s/f (Slow) **8** Ran SP% **111.3**
Speed ratings (Par 98): **101,100,97,96,90 88,31,**
CSF £80.30 CT £203.83 TOTE £9.40: £2.50, £2.00, £1.30; EX 58.80 Trifecta £190.90.
Owner J L C Pearce **Bred** J L C Pearce **Trained** Newmarket, Suffolk

FOCUS
Only a modest staying handicap.

5080 G.M. TREBLE 50TH ANNIVERSARY H'CAP 7f 32y (Tp)
7:40 (7:41) (Class 6) (0-55,55) 3-Y-O+ **£2,264** (£673; £336; £168) **Stalls** High

Form RPR

40-0 **1** **Quiet Warrior (IRE)**[43] 3510 5-9-4 **52**....................[1] JFEgan 1 61
(Tony Carroll) *racd keenly hld up: rdn and hdwy on outer fr 2f out: r.o fnl f: led towards fin* **7/4**[1]

0504 **2** *1* **Major Muscari (IRE)**[30] 3988 8-9-2 **55**....................(p) CharlieBennett(5) 6 61
(Shaun Harris) *chsd ldr: rdn over 2f out: led 110yds out: hdd towards fin* **14/1**

0000 **3** *1* **Lobster Cocktail (IRE)**[18] 4424 3-9-0 **54**.................... LukeMorris 7 56
(Ed Walker) *chsd ldr: rdn over 2f out: drvn over 1f out: one pce fnl f* **9/2**[2]

-050 **4** *hd* **Deftera Lad (IRE)**[31] 3953 4-9-1 **52**.................... EoinWalsh(3) 4 55
(Natalie Lloyd-Beavis) *hld up in rr: rdn along 3f out: bhd tl kpt on fr appr fnl f: nrst fin* **20/1**

0030 **5** *nse* **Gavarnie Encore**[29] 4009 4-9-6 **54**.................... HarryBentley 5 57
(Michael Blanshard) *hld up in midfield: stl to be asked for effrt whn briefly short of room over 1f out: rdn and kpt on* **5/1**[3]

4-05 **6** *shd* **Decisive (IRE)**[30] 3973 4-9-4 **52**....................(t) RichardKingscote 10 55
(Anthony Carson) *led: rdn 2f out: hdd 110yds out: no ex* **9/2**[2]

4-00 **7** *7* **Magician Coutinho**[38] 3731 4-9-5 **53**.................... GrahamGibbons 8 37
(David O'Meara) *midfield: rdn over 2f out: wknd over 1f out* **16/1**

5636 **8** *shd* **Fossa**[21] 4290 6-9-3 **51**....................(p) RyanClark 11 34
(Mark Brisbourne) *s.i.s: sn midfield on outer racing keenly: rdn over 2f out: wknd over 1f out* **22/1**

650/ **9** *12* **Decibelle**[667] 7014 4-9-0 **48**.................... RyanPowell 3
(Barry Brennan) *midfield: rdn over 2f out: sn wknd* **66/1**

1m 29.02s (0.22) **Going Correction** +0.025s/f (Slow)
WFA 3 from 4yo+ 6lb **9** Ran SP% **112.5**
Speed ratings (Par 101): **99,97,96,96,96 96,88,88,74**
CSF £27.90 CT £95.46 TOTE £2.40: £1.10, £3.70, £2.60; EX 26.30 Trifecta £127.20.
Owner Miss G Spence **Bred** John R Jeffers **Trained** Cropthorne, Worcs

FOCUS
A low-grade handicap, in which the well-backed favourite pounced late in the day.

5081 G.M. TREBLE - XYLEM MEDIAN AUCTION MAIDEN STKS 7f 32y (Tp)
8:15 (8:16) (Class 6) 2-Y-O **£2,264** (£673; £336; £168) **Stalls** High

Form RPR

2425 **1** **Texas Katie**[8] 4756 2-9-0 74.................... CharlesBishop 8 70
(Mick Channon) *wnt lft s: trckd ldr: pressed ldr over 2f out: pushed along to ld appr fnl f: rdn ins fnl f: kpt on* **9/4**[2]

0 **2** *1* **Zymyran**[21] 4287 2-9-5 0.................... HarryBentley 6 72
(David Simcock) *sltly hmpd s: sn in midfield: pushed along to chse ldng pair 2f out: rdn over 1f out: kpt on fnl f: wnt 2nd post* **7/1**

5522 **3** *shd* **Major Cornwallis (IRE)**[33] 3872 2-9-5 72.................... JackGarritty 3 72
(Richard Fahey) *led: pressed over 2f out: rdn whn hdd appr fnl f: one pce: lost 2nd post* **2/1**[1]

4 *1/2* **Hernandes (FR)** 2-9-5 0.................... GeorgeBaker 2 71
(Ed Walker) *trckd ldr: pushed along over 1f out: kpt on fnl f* **4/1**[3]

5 *nk* **Vanderbilt (IRE)** 2-9-2 0.................... JosephineGordon(3) 4 70
(Martyn Meade) *hmpd s: hld up: pushed along and hdwy on inner over 1f out: kpt on fnl f: nrst fin* **9/1**

6 *5* **Amadeus Rox (FR)** 2-9-5 0.................... WilliamTwiston-Davies 7 57
(Alan King) *slowly away: hld up: pushed along 2f out: nvr threatened* **20/1**

00 **7** *1* **Oxford Blu**[21] 4287 2-9-5 0.................... LukeMorris 1 54
(Sir Mark Prescott Bt) *midfield: pushed along over 2f out: wknd over 1f out* **50/1**

1m 31.82s (3.02) **Going Correction** +0.025s/f (Slow) **7** Ran SP% **113.3**
Speed ratings (Par 92): **83,81,81,81,80 75,73**
CSF £17.94 TOTE £3.50: £1.60, £3.80; EX 18.60 Trifecta £51.50.
Owner Norman Court Stud **Bred** Norman Court Stud **Trained** West Ilsley, Berks

FOCUS
A fair maiden and they finished in a heap, so the form is probably ordinary, although a few shaped with a bit of promise in behind.

5082 G.M. TREBLE PUMP SPECIALIST H'CAP 1m 141y (Tp)
8:50 (8:50) (Class 4) (0-85,85) 3-Y-O+ **£4,690** (£1,395; £523; £523) **Stalls** Low

Form RPR

00-0 **1** **Gold Sands (IRE)**[59] 2978 4-9-12 **83**.................... LukeMorris 3 93
(James Tate) *prom: rdn 2f out: led appr fnl f: edgd rt: kpt on* **10/1**[3]

4230 **2** *2 1/4* **Gold Flash**[24] 4193 4-9-2 **73**....................(b) JoeFanning 4 78
(Keith Dalgleish) *midfield: rdn over 1f out: chsd ldr ins fnl f: kpt on* **14/1**

0-24 **3** *1* **Divisionist**[73] 2541 3-9-0 **79**.................... GrahamGibbons 2 82
(Sir Michael Stoute) *led: pushed along over 2f out: rdn wl over 1f out: hdd appr fnl f: one pce* **1/1**[1]

2100 **3** *dht* **Pushaq (IRE)**[53] 3187 3-8-13 **78**....................(b[1]) HarryBentley 1 81
(Marco Botti) *in tch: gng wl whn briefly short of room over 1f out: swtchd lft: sn rdn: one pce* **10/1**[3]

0046 **5** *nk* **Mustaqqil (IRE)**[24] 4199 4-9-0 **76**....................(v[1]) JoshDoyle(5) 7 78
(David O'Meara) *racd keenly: hld up: rdn 2f out: kpt on fnl f: nvr threatened* **12/1**

3144 **6** *nse* **Mountain Rescue (IRE)**[21] 4300 4-9-11 **82**.................... GeorgeBaker 5 84
(Chris Wall) *midfield towards outer: rdn 2f out: one pce* **7/2**[2]

1506 **7** *10* **Idol Deputy (FR)**[126] 1166 10-9-1 **77**....................(p) RachealKneller(5) 8 56
(James Bennett) *hld up: rdn over 2f out: wknd over 1f out* **28/1**

006 **8** *9* **Spes Nostra**[21] 4312 8-10-0 **85**........................(bt) MartinDwyer 6 43
(Iain Jardine) *slowly away: sn rdn and looked reluctant: a wl bhd* **12/1**

1m 47.74s (-2.36) **Going Correction** +0.025s/f (Slow)
WFA 3 from 4yo+ 8lb **8** Ran SP% **115.9**
Speed ratings (Par 105): **111,109,108,108,107 107,98,90**
WIN: £9.30 Gold Sands; PL: £2.70 Gold Sands, £5.20 Gold Flash, £.60 Divisionist; EX: £59.60; CSF: £137.07; TRICAST: GS/GF/P £717.90, GS/GF/D £131.30; TRIFECTA: GS/GF/D £234.20, GS/GF/P £268.00..
Owner Saeed Manana **Bred** Razza Pallorsi **Trained** Newmarket, Suffolk

FOCUS
A useful handicap but the pace was only ordinary. An improved performance from the winner, with the runner-up a fair guide.

5083 G.M. TREBLE, PUMP SERVICE SPECIALIST H'CAP 1m 4f 50y (Tp)
9:20 (9:20) (Class 5) (0-70,70) 3-Y-O+ **£2,911** (£866; £432) **Stalls** Low

Form RPR
224 **1** **Introductory (IRE)**[92] 1961 3-9-0 **67**........................ JFEgan 1 79+
(Keith Dalgleish) *in tch in 3rd: pushed along and qcknd to ld appr fnl f: rdn and kpt on* **9/2**[3]

6532 **2** *3 1/2* **Machine Learner**[21] 4303 3-9-3 **70**........................(v) LukeMorris 6 76
(Michael Bell) *trckd ldr in 2nd: rdn to ld narrowly 2f out: hdd appr fnl f: sn drvn and hung lft: one pce* **8/13**[1]

5342 **3** *6* **Cool Music (IRE)**[10] 4716 6-9-0 **56**........................(p) PatCosgrave 4 55
(Antony Brittain) *led at stdy pce: rdn over 2f out: wknd fnl f* **11/4**[2]

2m 44.11s (3.31) **Going Correction** +0.025s/f (Slow)
WFA 3 from 4yo+ 11lb **3** Ran SP% **106.8**
Speed ratings (Par 103): **89,86,82**
CSF £7.85 TOTE £3.90; EX 9.90 Trifecta £7.30.
Owner Michael Beaumont **Bred** Ballyhane Stud **Trained** Carluke, S Lanarks

FOCUS
A modest handicap, in which the pace was steady, and the least exposed runner proved far too good. The winner improved, with the second to his recent level.
T/Plt: £10.10 to a £1 stake. Pool of £57310.46 - 4129.41 winning tickets. T/Qpdt: £8.50 to a £1 stake. Pool of £5271.86 - 456.20 winning tickets. **Andrew Sheret**

5035 YARMOUTH (L-H)
Thursday, August 4

OFFICIAL GOING: Good to firm
Wind: Fresh across Weather: Overcast

5084 BRITISH STALLION STUDS EBF MAIDEN STKS (PLUS 10 RACE) 6f 3y
2:10 (2:11) (Class 4) 2-Y-O **£4,657** (£1,386; £692; £346) **Stalls** Centre

Form RPR
1 **Ernststavroblofeld (USA)** 2-9-5 0........................ TomMarquand 4 83+
(Martyn Meade) *trckd ldrs: shkn up over 2f out: rdn to ld wl ins fnl f: r.o* **6/4**[1]

23 **2** *1 1/4* **Stanhope**[13] 4594 2-9-5 0........................ TomQueally 5 77
(Mick Quinn) *w ldr tl led over 1f out: rdn: edgd lft and hdd wl ins fnl f* **4/1**[3]

3 *1* **Millie's Kiss** 2-8-10 0 ow1........................ AdamMcNamara(5) 1 70
(Philip McBride) *s.i.s: hld up: hdwy over 1f out: styd on* **25/1**

63 **4** *1* **Elementary**[27] 4097 2-9-5 0........................ MartinHarley 3 71
(Michael Bell) *led: rdn and hdd over 1f out: styd on same pce ins fnl f* **7/1**

0 **5** *11* **Deleyll**[8] 4762 2-9-5 0........................ JamieSpencer 2 35
(William Haggas) *chsd ldrs tl wknd over 1f out* **14/1**

6 *2 1/2* **Fareeq** 2-9-5 0........................ PaulHanagan 6 27+
(William Haggas) *s.s: hld up: rdn over 2f out: sn hung lft and eased* **11/4**[2]

1m 13.8s (-0.60) **Going Correction** -0.15s/f (Firm) **6** Ran SP% **109.7**
Speed ratings (Par 96): **98,96,95,93,79 75**
CSF £7.43 TOTE £1.90: £1.20, £2.10; EX 7.10 Trifecta £139.60.
Owner Chelsea Thoroughbreds - Diamonds **Bred** Airlie Stud & Mrs S M Rogers **Trained** Newmarket, Suffolk

FOCUS
Around 4mm of water was put on the home straight and the bends during the morning. This looked a reasonable little maiden.

5085 FAMILY FUNDAY AT YARMOUTH RACECOURSE H'CAP 1m 1f 21y
2:40 (2:40) (Class 6) (0-65,65) 3-Y-O+ **£2,264** (£673; £336; £168) **Stalls** Low

Form RPR
2163 **1** **Rustique**[24] 4200 4-9-11 **62**........................ ThomasBrown 10 68
(Ed Walker) *a.p: rdn over 2f out: led ins fnl f: sn hung lft: styd on wl* **7/2**[2]

-034 **2** *1 1/4* **My Mistress (IRE)**[14] 4567 4-8-12 **49**........................ JamieSpencer 6 52
(Phil McEntee) *hld up: swtchd lft and hdwy over 1f out: rdn and ev ch ins fnl f: no ex towards fin* **14/1**

4203 **3** *hd* **The Dukkerer (IRE)**[16] 4493 5-9-6 **62**........................ AdamMcNamara(5) 11 65
(James Given) *s.i.s: sn prom: rdn over 2f out: ev ch fr over 1f out tl ins fnl f: styng on same pce whn hmpd towards fin* **6/1**[3]

0005 **4** *3/4* **Heat Storm (IRE)**[38] 3732 5-8-6 **46** oh1........................(v[1]) RobHornby(3) 5 47
(James Unett) *mid-div: hdwy whn hmpd over 1f out: r.o towards fin: nt rch ldrs* **33/1**

0201 **5** *3/4* **Port Paradise**[15] 4518 3-8-13 **65**........................ SamuelClarke(7) 2 65
(William Jarvis) *chsd ldrs: rdn over 1f out: styd on same pce ins fnl f* **7/2**[2]

3-64 **6** *hd* **Fast Sprite (IRE)**[20] 4362 4-9-10 **61**........................ KierenFox 8 60
(John Best) *chsd ldr tl rdn to ld and hung rt over 1f out: hdd ins fnl f: styng on same pce whn hmpd towards fin* **10/3**[1]

0400 **7** *3 3/4* **World Record (IRE)**[35] 3823 6-9-9 **60**........................ TomQueally 12 52
(Mick Quinn) *sn led: rdn over 2f out: hdd over 1f out: wknd ins fnl f* **12/1**

3314 **8** *1* **Miss Lillie**[13] 4589 5-9-11 **62**........................(p) TomMarquand 3 51
(Roger Teal) *hld up: rdn over 2f out: styd on same pce fr over 1f out* **14/1**

0 **9** *2 3/4* **Vale Of Rock (IRE)**[8] 4764 3-8-7 **52**........................ AndrewMullen 7 36
(Michael Appleby) *s.i.s: hld up: rdn 1/2-way: nvr on terms* **25/1**

0-00 **10** *8* **Mr Turner**[56] 3080 3-8-8 **53**........................ StevieDonohoe 9 20
(Mark H Tompkins) *hld up: rdn over 2f out: wknd over 1f out* **20/1**

1m 54.32s (-1.48) **Going Correction** -0.15s/f (Firm)
WFA 3 from 4yo+ 8lb **10** Ran SP% **114.4**
Speed ratings (Par 101): **100,98,98,98,97 97,93,92,90,83**
CSF £48.65 CT £284.26 TOTE £4.70: £1.80, £2.60, £2.00; EX 55.20 Trifecta £314.30.
Owner Dubai Thoroughbred Racing **Bred** D Lancaster-Smith & Moreton Manor Stud **Trained** Upper Lambourn, Berks

FOCUS
Modest handicap form, and a bit of a messy race in the latter stages.

5086 MOULTON NURSERIES OF ACLE H'CAP 1m 2f 23y
3:10 (3:10) (Class 5) (0-70,69) 3-Y-O **£2,911** (£866; £432; £216) **Stalls** Low

Form RPR
-051 **1** **Pacharana**[14] 4567 3-9-0 **62**........................ JamieSpencer 3 79+
(Luca Cumani) *chsd ldrs: rdn to go 2nd over 2f out: led over 1f out: styd on u.p* **11/8**[1]

5-66 **2** *1 1/4* **Master Gunner (USA)**[56] 3066 3-9-7 **69**........................(b[1]) TedDurcan 2 83
(Sir Michael Stoute) *led: clr over 6f out tl over 3f out: rdn and hdd over 1f out: styd on same pce wl ins fnl f* **9/4**[2]

0402 **3** *10* **Rockliffe**[12] 4635 3-9-0 **62**........................ PaulHanagan 6 56
(Mick Channon) *chsd ldr tl rdn over 2f out: edgd lft and wknd over 1f out* **9/2**[3]

4410 **4** *1* **Ubla (IRE)**[74] 2506 3-9-4 **66**........................ TomMarquand 1 58
(Gay Kelleway) *hld up: rdn over 2f out: wknd over 1f out* **33/1**

50-3 **5** *nk* **Buteo Bai (IRE)**[9] 4740 3-8-7 **55** ow1........................ ThomasBrown 4 46
(Lucy Wadham) *hld up: shkn up over 3f out: rdn and wknd over 1f out* **11/2**

2m 8.75s (-1.75) **Going Correction** -0.15s/f (Firm) **5** Ran SP% **109.4**
Speed ratings (Par 100): **101,100,92,91,90**
CSF £4.65 TOTE £2.30: £1.40, £1.10; EX 5.30 Trifecta £15.00.
Owner S Stuckey **Bred** Stuart Stuckey **Trained** Newmarket, Suffolk

FOCUS
The first two, unexposed 3yos from top yards, finished well clear but it's hard to pin down the level.

5087 GREENE KING FESTIVAL AT YARMOUTH RACECOURSE (S) H'CAP 7f 3y
3:40 (3:40) (Class 6) (0-65,65) 3-Y-O **£2,264** (£673; £336; £168) **Stalls** Centre

Form RPR
363 **1** **Masqueraded (USA)**[15] 4518 3-8-11 **55**........................(v) JamieSpencer 8 61
(Gay Kelleway) *w ldr: c stands' side over 5f out and led that trio: led overall over 2f out: sn rdn and hung lft: styd on u.p* **10/3**[1]

0000 **2** *nk* **Art Echo**[20] 4365 3-9-7 **65**........................(t) MartinHarley 6 70
(Jonathan Portman) *hld up: racd centre: edgd towards stands' side 3f out: hdwy over 2f out: rdn to chse wnr over 1f out: hung lft u.p ins fnl f: styd on* **11/2**[3]

-600 **3** *6* **Forest Lakes (IRE)**[13] 4587 3-9-4 **62**........................ TomMarquand 3 51
(George Scott) *racd centre: chsd ldrs: edgd towards stands' side 3f out: nt clr run over 2f out: styd on same pce fr over 1f out* **6/1**

0064 **4** *1* **Lillyput (IRE)**[12] 4641 3-8-7 **51**........................ AndrewMullen 5 37
(Mick Channon) *overall ldr in centre: edgd towards stands' side 3f out: rdn and hdd over 2f out: wknd fnl f* **9/2**[2]

-600 **5** *4 1/2* **She's Golden**[10] 4701 3-8-13 **57**........................ PaulHanagan 1 31
(Ann Duffield) *chsd ldrs in centre: lft 2nd in that gp over 5f out: edgd towards stands' side 3f out: rdn over 2f out: wknd over 1f out* **8/1**

6634 **6** *6* **Sunbaked (IRE)**[13] 4588 3-8-13 **57**........................(p) JohnFahy 10 15
(Eve Johnson Houghton) *prom: c stands' side and chsd wnr over 5f out: lost 2nd 4f out: chsd wnr again over 2f out: rdn and wknd over 1f out* **6/1**

2260 **7** *7* **Ashford Island**[21] 4316 3-8-7 **51**........................(p[1]) TedDurcan 7
(Mike Murphy) *hld up: plld hrd: c stands over 5f out: chsd wnr 4f out tl rdn over 2f out: sn wknd* **11/2**[3]

1m 27.02s (0.42) **Going Correction** -0.15s/f (Firm) **7** Ran SP% **111.7**
Speed ratings (Par 98): **91,90,83,82,77 70,62**
CSF £20.69 CT £101.75 TOTE £3.00: £1.60, £2.90; EX 20.50 Trifecta £147.80.The winner was bought in for 7,000gns.
Owner Bubbly Racing **Bred** Hargus & S Sexton & Silver Fern Farm **Trained** Exning, Suffolk

FOCUS
A difference of opinion in this seller, with the field splitting after two furlongs and three runners coming stands' side with the rest down the centre. The groups merged again after a couple of furlongs and the first two home, who finished clear, drifted to the far side late on.

5088 NORFOLK CHAMBER OF COMMERCE MAIDEN H'CAP 6f 3y
4:10 (4:12) (Class 6) (0-65,65) 3-Y-O+ **£2,975** (£885; £442; £221) **Stalls** Centre

Form RPR
4-40 **1** **Himalayan Queen**[71] 2586 3-8-12 **62**........................ SophieKilloran(7) 1 69
(William Jarvis) *hld up in tch: led and hung lft over 1f out: styd on: eased nr fin* **16/1**

0-06 **2** *3/4* **Guanabara Bay (IRE)**[19] 4410 3-9-7 **64**........................ JamieSpencer 11 67
(Martyn Meade) *hld up: hdwy over 1f out: rdn to chse wnr and hung lft ins fnl f: styd on* **6/1**[3]

050 **3** *2* **Vivre La Reve**[30] 3973 4-8-8 **50**........................(v) RobHornby(3) 5 48
(James Unett) *chsd ldrs: rdn over 2f out: styd on same pce wl ins fnl f* **50/1**

50 **4** *hd* **The Special One (IRE)**[29] 3994 3-9-3 **60**........................ JohnFahy 6 56
(Clive Cox) *chsd ldrs: lost pl after 1f: swtchd lft and hdwy over 1f out: styd on same pce wl ins fnl f* **7/1**

6240 **5** *3/4* **Lucky Louie**[56] 3062 3-9-8 **65**........................ TomMarquand 10 59
(Roger Teal) *hld up: rdn over 1f out: styd on ins fnl f: nt trble ldrs* **9/2**[2]

0420 **6** *nk* **Dream Dana (IRE)**[38] 3725 3-9-3 **65**........................ LucyKBarry(5) 4 58
(Jamie Osborne) *chsd ldrs: rdn over 1f out: styd on same pce ins fnl f* **14/1**

006 **7** *3/4* **Luang Prabang (IRE)**[19] 4401 3-9-7 **64**........................ TedDurcan 9 55
(Chris Wall) *sn prom: rdn over 1f out: no ex ins fnl f* **4/1**[1]

0323 **8** *1* **Malvia**[20] 4337 4-9-6 **59**........................(b) StevieDonohoe 8 47+
(Ian Williams) *s.s: hld up: nvr nrr* **4/1**[1]

4060 **9** *hd* **Aegean Boy**[85] 2143 3-9-1 **58**........................ AndrewMullen 7 45
(Michael Appleby) *s.i.s: hdwy to join ldrs after 1f: rdn to ld wl over 1f out: sn hdd: wknd wl ins fnl f* **16/1**

050 **10** *2 1/2* **Gomez**[19] 4401 3-9-8 **65**........................(b[1]) SaleemGolam 2 44
(Rae Guest) *plld hrd and sn w ldr: rdn and ev ch over 2f out: wknd fnl f* **10/1**

-450 **11** *9* **Majestic Girl (IRE)**[22] 4256 3-8-12 **55**........................(p) MartinHarley 3 5
(Robert Cowell) *sn led: rdn and hdd wl over 1f out: sn wknd* **33/1**

1m 12.86s (-1.54) **Going Correction** -0.15s/f (Firm)
WFA 3 from 4yo 4lb **11** Ran SP% **117.4**
Speed ratings (Par 101): **104,103,100,100,99 98,97,96,96,92 80**
CSF £108.95 CT £4736.47 TOTE £20.40: £5.00, £2.10, £10.30; EX 132.80 Trifecta £7081.90.
Owner Miss Samantha Dare **Bred** Usk Valley Stud **Trained** Newmarket, Suffolk

FOCUS
A typically moderate race of its type.

5089 RACING WELFARE FILLIES' H'CAP — 1m 3y
4:40 (4:42) (Class 4) (0-85,83) 3-Y-O **£4,690** (£1,395; £697; £348) **Stalls** Centre

Form | | | | RPR
1051 **1** **Kylla Instinct**[24] 4215 3-8-11 **78**.............................. AdamMcNamara(5) 1 84+
(Philip McBride) *hld up in tch: led on bit 1f out: sn hdd: rallied to ld wl ins fnl f: r.o* **5/1**[2]

4210 **2** *hd* **Dot Green (IRE)**[33] 3914 3-9-4 **80**.................................. DarryllHolland 6 85
(Mark H Tompkins) *hld up: hdwy over 1f out: rdn to ld and edgd lft ins fnl f: sn hdd: r.o* **10/1**

2-10 **3** *2 ¼* **De Veer Cliffs (IRE)**[27] 4113 3-9-6 **82**.......................... JamieSpencer 7 81
(Martyn Meade) *led at stdy pce tl qcknd over 2f out: rdn and hdd 1f out: edgd lft and styd on same pce ins fnl f* **13/2**

5-10 **4** *1 ½* **Malmostosa**[64] 2789 3-9-6 **82**... MartinHarley 5 78
(Marco Botti) *hld up: hdwy over 1f out: sn rdn and ev ch: styd on same pce ins fnl f* **11/2**[3]

31- **5** *nk* **Mirror City**[344] 5747 3-9-7 **83**.. JackMitchell 4 78+
(Charlie Appleby) *plld hrd: racd in 2nd pl: rdn and ev ch over 1f out: no ex ins fnl f* **11/8**[1]

0-23 **6** *¾* **Pernickety**[12] 4633 3-8-10 **72**.. ThomasBrown 2 66
(Lucy Wadham) *s.i.s: sn chsng ldrs: rdn over 1f out: no ex ins fnl f* **12/1**

-505 **7** *nk* **Salvo**[29] 4028 3-9-3 **79**... StevieDonohoe 3 72
(Charlie Fellowes) *chsd ldrs: rdn over 2f out: styd on same pce fr over 1f out* **12/1**

1m 39.85s (-0.75) **Going Correction** -0.15s/f (Firm) **7** Ran SP% **112.0**
Speed ratings (Par 99): **97,96,94,93,92 92,91**
CSF £49.54 TOTE £5.80: £2.70, £4.30; EX 46.20 Trifecta £213.40.
Owner PMRacing **Bred** Whatton Manor Stud **Trained** Newmarket, Suffolk

FOCUS
They didn't go much of a gallop in this fair fillies' handicap, and the first two did well to pull clear. A hard race to read but a pb from the winner.

5090 CONFERENCES AT GREAT YARMOUTH RACECOURSE APPRENTICE H'CAP — 7f 3y
5:10 (5:10) (Class 5) (0-70,68) 4-Y-O+ **£2,911** (£866; £432; £216) **Stalls** Centre

Form | | | | RPR
5040 **1** **Anastazia**[20] 4362 4-9-5 **66**.. DavidEgan(5) 3 74
(Paul D'Arcy) *s.i.s: hld up: hdwy to ld over 2f out: rdn out* **3/1**[2]

0000 **2** *2* **Zeshov (IRE)**[17] 4454 5-9-4 **65**.. LewisEdmunds(5) 1 68
(Rebecca Bastiman) *hld up: hdwy over 2f out: chsd wnr over 1f out: styd on same pce ins fnl f* **7/2**[3]

5522 **3** *4 ½* **Limerick Lord (IRE)**[5] 4876 4-8-12 **59**.........................(p) LiamDoran(5) 4 49
(Julia Feilden) *racd keenly: sn w ldrs: rdn and ev ch over 2f out: no ex fnl f* **85/40**[1]

00-0 **4** *4* **Perfect Orange**[37] 3739 4-8-9 **56**.................................... WilliamCox(5) 6 36
(Lucy Wadham) *hld up: hdwy over 2f out: rdn and hung lft over 1f out: wknd fnl f* **18/1**

3550 **5** *10* **Jonnie Skull (IRE)**[15] 4504 10-8-7 **49** oh4.......................(vt) JaneElliott 7 2
(Phil McEntee) *led: hdd over 4f out: sn pushed along: wknd wl over 1f out* **20/1**

5452 **6** *3* **Ocean Legend (IRE)**[38] 3719 11-9-7 **63**............................ HarryBurns 2 8
(Tony Carroll) *w ldrs: rdn over 2f out: wknd wl over 1f out* **7/1**

4460 **7** *¾* **Be Royale**[12] 4630 6-9-7 **68**... BenSanderson(5) 5 11
(Michael Appleby) *racd keenly: sn w ldr: led over 4f out: hdd over 2f out: wknd wl over 1f out* **10/1**

1m 24.0s (-2.60) **Going Correction** -0.15s/f (Firm) **7** Ran SP% **110.8**
Speed ratings (Par 103): **108,105,100,96,84 81,80**
CSF £13.01 TOTE £3.30: £1.10, £3.70; EX 25.70 Trifecta £76.00.
Owner K Snell **Bred** K Snell **Trained** Newmarket, Suffolk

FOCUS
A moderate event for apprentices who'd ridden no more than ten winners. The first two have better than back form than they have been rated this time, but this didn't look much of a race.
T/Plt: £475.00 to a £1 stake. Pool of £55904.71 - 85.91 winning tickets. T/Qpdt: £82.20 to a £1 stake. Pool of £4370.74 - 39.30 winning tickets. **Colin Roberts**

5091 - 5094a (Foreign Racing) - See Raceform Interactive

4571 LEOPARDSTOWN (L-H)
Thursday, August 4

OFFICIAL GOING: Good

5095a BALLYROAN STKS (GROUP 3) — 1m 4f
7:25 (7:28) 3-Y-O+
£27,352 (£8,823; £4,191; £1,875; £948; £485)

| | | | RPR
1 **Stellar Mass (IRE)**[13] 4615 3-8-12 112........................... KevinManning 6 114+
(J S Bolger, Ire) *chsd ldrs: disp 3rd at 1/2-way: pushed along bhd ldrs in 4th into st: sn rdn on outer and clsd u.p to ld ins fnl 100yds: kpt on wl to assert cl home* **7/2**[2]

2 *½* **Almela (IRE)**[291] 7321 4-9-6 100... PatSmullen 1 110
(D K Weld, Ire) *cl up bhd ldr tl dropped to 3rd after 1f where sltly hmpd: disp 3rd at 1/2-way: prog on inner into st to ld under 2f out: strly pressed ins fnl f and hdd ins fnl 100yds: no ex cl home* **7/1**

3 *1 ½* **Bondi Beach (IRE)**[81] 2275 4-9-12 118.................... SeamieHeffernan 2 114+
(A P O'Brien, Ire) *w.w towards rr: 5th 1/2-way: sme hdwy bhd ldrs over 1f out: n.m.r briefly and wnt 3rd ins fnl f: kpt on same pce clsng stages: nvr trbld ldrs* **5/4**[1]

4 *1* **Shogun (IRE)**[8] 4753 3-8-12 107..............................[1] DonnachaO'Brien 3 109
(A P O'Brien, Ire) *chsd ldrs tl wnt 2nd after 1f where edgd sltly lft: cl 2nd appr st: rdn in 2nd 1 1/2f out and no ex in 3rd ins fnl f whn swtchd rt: kpt on same pce in 4th cl home* **9/2**[3]

5 *8 ½* **Lustrous Light (IRE)**[25] 4182 3-8-12 100.......................... ColinKeane 4 96
(G M Lyons, Ire) *led: racd keenly early: over 1 l clr at 1/2-way: narrow advantage appr st: rdn and hdd under 2f out and no ex in 5th over 1f out: wknd* **7/1**

6 *1 ½* **Agnes Stewart (IRE)**[39] 3692 4-9-6 102.............................(v[1]) BillyLee 5 90
(Edward Lynam, Ire) *w.w: last at 1/2-way: rdn and lost tch 2f out: wknd* **28/1**

2m 36.9s (1.60)
WFA 3 from 4yo 11lb **6** Ran SP% **113.3**
CSF £27.40 TOTE £4.00: £1.80, £2.50; DF 28.60 Trifecta £76.30.
Owner Mrs June Judd **Bred** Tinnakill House & Alan Byrne **Trained** Coolcullen, Co Carlow

FOCUS
Dermot Weld and Aidan O'Brien had shared this prize between them since 2009. This looked a decent renewal with the entire field rated 100 or higher. The pace was strong from the outset. The winner, third and fourth have been rated in line with this year's best.

5096a STRYPES APPRENTICE H'CAP — 1m 1f
8:00 (8:01) (45-70,70) 3-Y-O+ **£4,522** (£1,397; £661; £294; £110)

| | | | RPR
1 **Mcguigan (IRE)**[14] 4575 4-9-12 **70**.........................(t) DanielRedmond(2) 2 84
(J S Bolger, Ire) *chsd ldrs tl led after 2f: drvn into st over 2 l clr: extended advantage 1 1/2f out and in command ins fnl f: kpt on wl: comf* **13/2**[1]

2 *2 ¾* **Kubali (IRE)**[13] 4616 3-9-2 **70**...(t) ETDaly(4) 18 78+
(G M Lyons, Ire) *in tch: 6th 1/2-way: tk clsr order bhd ldrs over 2f out: rdn in 3rd 1 1/2f out and no imp on easy wnr u.p in 2nd ins fnl f: kpt on same pce* **8/1**[2]

3 *¾* **Danse Rouge (IRE)**[401] 3766 4-8-2 **46** oh1................ DamienMelia(2) 17 52+
(Patrick J Flynn, Ire) *cl up early: 3rd 1/2-way: rdn disputing 4th into st and wnt 3rd u.p ins fnl f where no imp on easy wnr: kpt on same pce* **16/1**

4 *½* **Settle For Red (IRE)**[21] 4328 6-9-12 **68**.................... DonaghO'Connor 6 73+
(David Marnane, Ire) *in tch: 8th 1/2-way: pushed along in 7th bef st: rdn over 2f out and clsd u.p to chse ldrs ent fnl f: kpt on same pce in 4th clsng stages* **10/1**[3]

5 *1 ½* **Royal Blessing**[35] 3836 4-9-0 **58**..............................(b[1]) RobbieDolan(2) 7 60+
(Peter Fahey, Ire) *chsd ldrs: 7th 3f out: rdn over 1f out and kpt on u.p on outer wl ins fnl f into nvr threatening 5th clsng stages* **11/1**

6 *½* **Dark Amber**[13] 4593 6-9-4 **60**..(p) TomMadden 8 61+
(Brendan Powell) *mid-div: sme hdwy u.p fr under 2f out to chse ldrs ins fnl f: kpt on clsng stages: nvr trbld ldrs* **10/1**[3]

7 *½* **Liberality**[25] 4181 4-8-12 **61**.................................[1] ColmanComerford(7) 1 61
(Miss Evanna McCutcheon, Ire) *sn chsd ldrs: rdn in 4th under 4f out and no imp on ldrs into st: one pce fnl 2f* **33/1**

8 *½* **Path Of Silver (IRE)**[22] 4283 3-8-7 **59**............................... OisinOrr(2) 19 58
(Richard Brabazon, Ire) *mid-div: rdn into st and no imp on ldrs: kpt on one pce fnl 2f* **12/1**

9 *hd* **Shukhov (IRE)**[23] 4242 7-9-3 **61**................................... KeithMoriarty(2) 3 60
(Gerard O'Leary, Ire) *in rr of mid-div: rdn in 12th under 2f out and kpt on one pce ins fnl f* **33/1**

10 *nk* **Lightening Sticks (IRE)**[15] 4541 9-8-5 **51**.................(t) PJO'Hanlon(4) 5 49
(Liam Roche, Ire) *chsd ldrs: 4th 1/2-way: rdn in 2nd into st and no imp on easy wnr: wknd fnl f* **10/1**[3]

11 *shd* **Oromo (IRE)**[36] 3792 3-8-9 **66**.. CJMadden(7) 14 64
(T Stack, Ire) *hld up: no imp in 17th into st: kpt on one pce fnl 2f* **10/1**[3]

12 *nk* **William Ashford (IRE)**[35] 3833 4-8-3 **49**......................... KeithQuinn(4) 4 46
(J C Hayden, Ire) *mid-div: rdn and no ex over 2f out: one pce after* **10/1**[3]

13 *1 ½* **Rathbride Raven**[23] 4245 3-9-3 **69**................................ DylanHogan(2) 9 63
(Kevin Prendergast, Ire) *mid-div: pushed along in 12th appr st and no imp: one pce fnl 2f* **8/1**[2]

14 *nse* **Keukenhof (IRE)**[23] 4244 3-9-2 **68**...........................(t) DenisLinehan(2) 12 62
(J P Murtagh, Ire) *sn led narrowly tl hdd after 2f: 2nd 1/2-way: rdn into st and sn no imp on wnr in 3rd: wknd 1 1/2f out* **8/1**[2]

15 *nk* **Primal Snow (USA)**[28] 4071 4-9-9 **65**..........................(tp) AnaO'Brien 16 58
(James M Ryan, Ire) *towards rr thrght: rdn and no imp over 2f out* **12/1**

16 *½* **Any Time**[79] 2351 3-8-0 **54**.. KarenReidy(4) 13 46
(John Joseph Murphy, Ire) *hld up towards rr: pushed along bef 1/2-way and tk clsr order in rr of mid-div 2f out: no ex and wknd ins fnl f* **33/1**

17 *1 ¾* **Queen Alpha (IRE)**[44] 3502 3-8-2 **54** oh7.............(b) KillianLeonard(2) 10 43
(Denis Gerard Hogan, Ire) *in rr of mid-div: rdn over 3f out and no imp: wknd fnl 2f* **25/1**

18 *4 ¾* **Papal Parade (IRE)**[292] 7304 5-8-0 **46**.................... AndrewBreslin(4) 11 25
(Eamonn O'Connell, Ire) *dwlt and a bhd: pushed along trailing fr 1/2-way: kpt on one pce fnl 3f* **40/1**

19 *5 ½* **Roter Baron (IRE)**[134] 1056 7-8-1 **50**.................. ConorMcNamara(7) 15 17
(Eamonn O'Connell, Ire) *dwlt and sltly awkward s: a bhd: pushed along and trailing fr 1/2-way* **33/1**

1m 57.2s (3.10)
WFA 3 from 4yo+ 8lb **19** Ran SP% **139.8**
CSF £59.94 CT £870.37 TOTE £7.10: £2.50, £1.80, £8.40, £2.20; DF 51.90 Trifecta £1277.90.
Owner Mrs J S Bolger **Bred** J S Bolger **Trained** Coolcullen, Co Carlow

FOCUS
A competitive apprentice handicap won in emphatic fashion by the favourite. Very few got into this. The winner has been rated to the best view of his maiden form.

5097 - (Foreign Racing) - See Raceform Interactive

4329 OVREVOLL (R-H)
Thursday, August 4

OFFICIAL GOING: Turf: heavy

5098a POLAR CUP (GROUP 3) (3YO+) (TURF) — 6f 187y
7:35 (7:35) 3-Y-O+ **£23,006** (£7,668; £3,834; £2,300; £1,533)

| | | | RPR
1 **Brownie (FR)**[21] 4-9-4 0.. JacobJohansen 8 104
(Bent Olsen, Denmark) **31/10**[2]

2 *1 ½* **Easy Road**[30] 3992 6-9-8 0... NelsonDeSouza 3 104
(Cathrine Erichsen, Norway) **42/10**

3 *2 ½* **Giftorm (USA)**[19] 4421 6-9-8 0.. CarlosLopez 4 96
(Fredrik Reuterskiold, Sweden) **11/5**[1]

4 *nk* **Over The Ocean (USA)**[19] 4421 6-9-4 0.............. Per-AndersGraberg 7 92
(Niels Petersen, Norway) **9/1**

5 *5* **Ragazzo (NOR)**[63] 7-9-4 0.. OliverWilson 2 77
(Annike Bye Hansen, Norway) **7/2**[3]

6 *5 ¼* **Boomerang Bob (IRE)**[40] 3656 7-9-4 0........................ WilliamCarson 5 62
(Jamie Osborne) *hld up: a in rr: rdn into st: no imp fnl 2f: wl btn* **111/10**

7 *11 ¼* **Secret Hint**[26] 4136 5-9-1 0.. DavidProbert 6 26
(Andrew Balding) *hld up: a in rr: rdn into st: no imp fnl 2f: wl btn and t.o* **44/5**

Owner Lone Kaj-Nielsen **Bred** Mme Sylviane Jeffroy **Trained** Denmark

5050 BRIGHTON (L-H)

Friday, August 5

OFFICIAL GOING: Good (good to firm in places; 8.2)

Wind: light, across Weather: mainly sunny

5099 CHECKATRAINER/BRITISH STALLION STUDS EBF MAIDEN STKS 5f 213y

2:10 (2:10) (Class 5) 2-Y-O **£3,557** (£1,058; £529; £264) **Stalls** Centre

Form RPR

0 **1** **Hidden Stash**[15] 4552 2-9-5 0 .... LiamKeniry 1 75
(Andrew Balding) *hld up wl in tch: swtchd lft and effrt towards inner 2f out: hdwy u.p to ld ent fnl f: r.o wl: readily* **7/2**[2]

06 **2** 4 ½ **Rebel Heart**[27] 4133 2-8-11 0 .... EdwardGreatrex(3) 4 56
(Bill Turner) *led: hung rt fr over 2f out: drvn 2f out: hdd ent fnl f: outpcd and wandered ins fnl f: wknd fnl 100yds* **25/1**

5224 **3** 4 **Three C'S (IRE)**[12] 4679 2-9-5 78 .... LukeMorris 5 49
(David Dennis) *w ldr: rdn over 1f out: sn drvn and no rspnse: wknd fnl f* **4/11**[1]

40 **4** 1 **Ginger Truffle**[4] 4951 2-9-0 0 .... JimCrowley 3 41
(Brett Johnson) *t.k.h: trckd ldrs: effrt 2f out: drvn and unable qck over 1f out: wknd fnl f* **8/1**[3]

0 **5** 3 ¾ **Take This Waltz**[30] 4011 2-8-9 0 .... HectorCrouch(5) 2 30
(Bill Turner) *awkward leaving stalls and s.i.s: a detached in last: nvr on terms: eased wl ins fnl f* **66/1**

1m 11.92s (1.72) **Going Correction** +0.20s/f (Good) 5 Ran SP% **112.0**
Speed ratings (Par 94): **96,90,84,83,78**
CSF £57.72 TOTE £5.60: £2.20, £7.00; EX 53.10 Trifecta £77.20.
Owner Kingsclere Racing Club **Bred** Kingsclere Stud **Trained** Kingsclere, Hants

FOCUS
The going was upgraded to Good, good to firm in places prior to racing on this third and final day of the festival here. This was a weak 2yo maiden. The level is fluid.

5100 JOBMAN H'CAP 1m 3f 196y

2:40 (2:40) (Class 6) (0-65,67) 3-Y-O+ **£2,911** (£866; £432; £216) **Stalls** High

Form RPR

0021 **1** **Cliff Face (IRE)**[6] 4880 3-9-6 67 6ex .... LukeMorris 7 80+
(Sir Mark Prescott Bt) *hld up in tch: clsd to ld on bit over 2f out: cruised wl clr over 1f out: v easily* **1/7**[1]

05-6 **2** 3 ¾ **Zarawi (IRE)**[29] 4050 5-9-11 61 ....(p) MichaelJMMurphy 5 62
(John Gallagher) *chsd ldr: rdn and ev ch briefly over 2f out: clr 2nd but no ch w wnr 1f out: plugged on* **12/1**

20-0 **3** 9 **Hermosa Vaquera (IRE)**[24] 4225 6-9-0 55 ....(p) HectorCrouch(5) 4 42
(Gary Moore) *led: rdn and hdd over 2f out: 3rd and wl btn over 1f out: wknd fnl f* **7/1**[2]

0065 **4** 1 ¾ **Sakhra**[10] 4739 5-8-9 45 .... KieranO'Neill 3 29
(Mark Brisbourne) *chsd ldng pair tl rdn and lost pl over 3f out: bhd fnl 2f* **33/1**

3306 **5** 11 **Its A Sheila Thing**[2] 5019 3-8-3 53 .... EdwardGreatrex(3) 2 19
(Linda Jewell) *hld up in rr: short-lived effrt over 3f out: wl btn 2f out: bhd and eased wl ins fnl f* **10/1**[3]

2m 36.67s (3.97) **Going Correction** +0.20s/f (Good)
WFA 3 from 5yo+ 11lb 5 Ran SP% **119.7**
Speed ratings (Par 101): **94,91,85,84,77**
CSF £4.29 TOTE £1.10: £1.02, £5.50; EX 5.20 Trifecta £12.80.
Owner Bluehills Racing Limited **Bred** Glashare House Stud **Trained** Newmarket, Suffolk

FOCUS
After the two defections this was all about the penalised winner. The balance of the second and third back this solid level.

5101 VANTAINER H'CAP 1m 1f 209y

3:10 (3:12) (Class 6) (0-60,59) 3-Y-O **£2,911** (£866; £432; £216) **Stalls** High

Form RPR

45 **1** **Becca Campbell (IRE)**[30] 4021 3-9-1 53 ....(p) JimCrowley 11 58
(Eve Johnson Houghton) *a.p: effrt over 2f out: rdn and ev ch over 1f out: led jst ins fnl f: hld on wl fnl 100yds: drvn out* **9/2**[3]

2322 **2** hd **Go On Gal (IRE)**[23] 4275 3-8-13 51 .... AdamBeschizza 9 56
(Julia Feilden) *hld up in tch in midfield: effrt over 2f out: hdwy u.p over 1f out: str chal ins fnl f: r.o u.p but a jst hld* **3/1**[1]

00-5 **3** 1 ¼ **Lilly Bonbon (IRE)**[37] 3765 3-9-6 58 .... DavidProbert 8 60
(Gary Moore) *t.k.h: hld up in tch towards rr: rdn and hdwy jst over 2f out: ev ch and wnt lft over 1f out: led 1f out: sn hdd and styd on same pce ins fnl f* **8/1**

-000 **4** 1 ½ **Onehelluvatouch**[55] 3141 3-8-12 53 .... EdwardGreatrex(3) 6 52
(Philip Hide) *squeezed out and dropped to rr sn after s: pushed along for 1f: hdwy to chse ldr 7f out tl led 3f out: rdn and hdd over 1f out: wknd ins fnl f* **10/1**

2346 **5** 2 ¾ **Masterson (IRE)**[9] 4764 3-9-0 59 .... KillianHennessy(7) 2 53
(Mick Channon) *t.k.h: chsd ldr early: sn stdd bk and hld up in tch in midfield: effrt and rdn to chse ldrs over 1f out: unable qck: wknd ins fnl f* **9/2**[3]

0634 **6** ¾ **Pivotal Dream (IRE)**[2] 5019 3-8-10 48 .... LukeMorris 3 41
(Mark Brisbourne) *t.k.h: hld up in tch in midfield: effrt 3f out: drvn to chsd ldrs over 1f out: unable qck and btn 1f out: wknd ins fnl f* **4/1**[2]

000 **7** 1 ½ **Dancing Rainbow (GR)**[32] 3958 3-8-6 49 .... HectorCrouch(5) 1 39
(Amanda Perrett) *hld up in tch in midfield: dropped to rr but stl wl in tch 7f out: effrt over 2f out: no hdwy u.p over 1f out: wknd fnl f* **20/1**

0-60 **8** 3 ¼ **Mooizo (IRE)**[21] 4367 3-8-10 48 .... AdrianMcCarthy 10 32
(Peter Chapple-Hyam) *hld up in tch towards rr: effrt 2f out: sn struggling u.p: wknd fnl f* **14/1**

000- **9** 31 **Suuki**[290] 7353 3-8-0 45 ....(t) SeanMooney(7) 7
(Adam West) *t.k.h: mde most tl 3f out: sn rdn and lost pl: bhd over 1f out: fdd fnl f: eased wl ins fnl f: t.o* **50/1**

2m 6.28s (2.68) **Going Correction** +0.20s/f (Good) 9 Ran SP% **115.0**
Speed ratings (Par 98): **97,96,95,94,92 91,90,88,63**
CSF £18.31 CT £104.04 TOTE £4.20: £1.80, £1.70, £2.20; EX 19.80 Trifecta £123.90.
Owner Miss E Johnson Houghton **Bred** Lynn Lodge Stud **Trained** Blewbury, Oxon

FOCUS
They went an ordinary pace in this weak handicap. Straightforward low-grade handicap form, rated around the principals.

5102 CHECKATRADE FOUNDATION CHARITY H'CAP 1m 1f 209y

3:40 (3:40) (Class 4) (0-80,80) 3-Y-O+ **£6,301** (£1,886; £943; £472) **Stalls** High

Form RPR

6152 **1** **Frozen Force (IRE)**[7] 4818 3-9-4 79 ....(p) JimCrowley 3 87
(Amanda Perrett) *chsd clr ldr: grad clsd fr 1/2-way and upsides 3f out: led over 2f out: rdn over 1f out: styd on and in command ins fnl f: rdn out* **13/8**[2]

-343 **2** 2 **Melabi (IRE)**[23] 4272 3-9-2 77 .... BenCurtis 1 81
(William Haggas) *awkward leaving stalls: hld up off the pce in last: plld out and t.k.h 4f out: clsd to trck ldrs over 2f out: effrt to chse wnr over 1f out: styd on same pce u.p fnl f* **1/1**[1]

1264 **3** 3 ¼ **Best Tamayuz**[20] 4377 5-8-12 64 .... LukeMorris 6 62
(Scott Dixon) *led and sn clr: jnd 3f out: sn hdd: unable qck u.p: 3rd and btn 1f out: wknd ins fnl f* **9/1**[3]

1225 **4** 2 **Innoko (FR)**[12] 3748 6-8-7 62 .... GeorgeDowning(3) 2 56
(Tony Carroll) *hld up off the pce in 3rd: clsd and trcking ldrs 3f out: effrt u.p on inner over 1f out: sn outpcd and btn 1f out* **10/1**

2m 4.68s (1.08) **Going Correction** +0.20s/f (Good)
WFA 3 from 4yo+ 9lb 4 Ran SP% **107.2**
Speed ratings (Par 105): **103,101,98,97**
CSF £3.58 TOTE £2.80; EX 3.30 Trifecta £7.20.
Owner A D Spence **Bred** J Kenny **Trained** Pulborough, W Sussex

FOCUS
Not a bad little handicap, run at a fair pace. It's been rated in line with the better view of the winner's form.

5103 HARRY BLOOM MEMORIAL "BRIGHTON BULLET" H'CAP 5f 213y

4:10 (4:10) (Class 4) (0-80,80) 3-Y-O- **£7,561** (£2,263; £1,131; £566; £282) **Stalls** Centre

Form RPR

5202 **1** **Vincentti (IRE)**[3] 4990 6-9-3 71 .... RaulDaSilva 8 79
(Ronald Harris) *stdd s: hld up in tch in rr: rdn and hdwy over 1f out: r.o wl to ld fnl 50yds: rdn out* **5/1**[3]

545 **2** ½ **Summer Chorus**[17] 4496 3-9-5 77 .... DavidProbert 1 82
(Andrew Balding) *taken down early: t.k.h: trckd ldrs: effrt to chal over 1f out: led ent fnl f: hdd and no ex fnl 50yds* **5/1**[3]

0401 **3** nk **Pink Martini (IRE)**[4] 4952 3-8-13 74 6ex .... EdwardGreatrex(3) 6 78
(Joseph Tuite) *stdd bk after s: hld up in tch in last pair: effrt over 1f out: swtchd rt ent fnl f: r.o strly u.p fnl 100yds: nt quite rch ldrs* **10/1**

641 **4** ½ **Under Siege (IRE)**[17] 4475 4-9-9 80 ....(t) AaronJones(3) 10 84
(Stuart Williams) *pressed ldr: rdn and ev ch over 1f out: styd on same pce ins fnl f* **7/1**

1104 **5** nk **Pour La Victoire (IRE)**[2] 5017 6-9-1 76 ....(b) GeorgiaCox(7) 3 79
(Tony Carroll) *dwlt and pushed along early: in tch in midfield: swtchd lft and effrt towards inner jst over 2f out: hdwy and rdn to ld over 1f out: sn hdd: no ex and wknd wl ins fnl f* **5/2**[1]

0630 **6** 1 ½ **Heartsong (IRE)**[21] 4355 7-9-2 70 .... MichaelJMMurphy 5 68
(John Gallagher) *chsd ldrs: drvn and ev ch over 1f out: unable qck 1f out: wknd ins fnl f* **16/1**

1234 **7** shd **Capolavoro (FR)**[30] 4008 5-8-12 66 .... JimCrowley 9 64
(Robert Cowell) *trckd ldrs: clsd to press ldrs 1/2-way: rdn and ev ch over 1f out: unable qck 1f out: wknd ins fnl f* **7/2**[2]

0010 **8** 6 **Noverre To Go (IRE)**[17] 4485 10-8-8 62 ....(p) LukeMorris 4 41
(Ronald Harris) *led: rdn and hdd over 1f out: lost pl and btn 1f out: wknd ins fnl f* **16/1**

1m 10.23s (0.03) **Going Correction** +0.20s/f (Good)
WFA 3 from 4yo+ 4lb 8 Ran SP% **117.5**
Speed ratings (Par 105): **107,106,105,105,104 102,102,94**
CSF £31.02 CT £244.10 TOTE £6.10: £1.70, £1.60, £2.50; EX 34.10 Trifecta £274.70.
Owner Robert & Nina Bailey **Bred** Stephanie Hanly **Trained** Earlswood, Monmouths

FOCUS
A competitive sprint handicap. Sound form. The runner-up has been rated as running as well as ever.

5104 CHECKAPROFESSIONAL.COM H'CAP 6f 209y

4:40 (4:40) (Class 5) (0-75,71) 3-Y-O+ **£2,911** (£866; £432; £216) **Stalls** Centre

Form RPR

0604 **1** **Sarmadee (IRE)**[13] 4640 4-8-12 64 .... KillianHennessy(7) 1 71
(Mick Channon) *stdd s: hld up in detached last: effrt on inner 2f out: hdwy to chse ldr 1f out: str chal ins fnl f: r.o wl to ld last strides* **7/1**[3]

02 **2** hd **Baltic Prince (IRE)**[28] 4089 6-9-5 67 .... GeorgeDowning(3) 7 73
(Tony Carroll) *led: rdn over 1f out: drvn ins fnl f: kpt on u.p: hdd and no ex last strides* **10/1**

030 **3** 1 ¼ **German Whip**[20] 4401 3-8-6 62 .... HectorCrouch(5) 8 63
(Gary Moore) *in tch in midfield: rdn over 2f out: lugging lft and no imp over 1f out: styd on again ins fnl f* **14/1**

0565 **4** 1 ½ **Dr Red Eye**[30] 4005 8-9-4 63 .... LukeMorris 6 62
(Scott Dixon) *chsd ldr: rdn over 2f out: unable qck u.p over 1f out: styd on same pce ins fnl f* **10/1**

0202 **5** 1 **Marcle (IRE)**[13] 4641 3-9-1 66 .... JimCrowley 4 60
(Ed de Giles) *chsd ldrs: rdn over 2f out: chsd wnr over 1f out tl 1f out: wknd ins fnl f* **4/1**[2]

4443 **6** 1 **Port Lairge**[21] 4354 6-9-4 63 ....(v) MichaelJMMurphy 3 56
(John Gallagher) *in tch in rr of main gp: rdn over 2f out: no imp and wl hld whn hung lft ins fnl f* **8/1**

1141 **7** 10 **Frank Bridge**[8] 4789 3-9-4 69 6ex .... ShaneKelly 2 33
(Eve Johnson Houghton) *hld up in tch in rr of main gp: effrt 3f out: hdwy u.p to chse ldrs over 1f out: sn struggling and btn 1f out: wl btn and heavily eased ins fnl f* **5/4**[1]

1m 23.97s (0.87) **Going Correction** +0.20s/f (Good)
WFA 3 from 4yo+ 6lb 7 Ran SP% **112.9**
Speed ratings (Par 103): **103,102,101,99,98 97,85**
CSF £69.45 CT £945.58 TOTE £5.20: £2.50, £4.30; EX 72.80 Trifecta £1136.80.
Owner M Channon **Bred** Airlie Stud **Trained** West Ilsley, Berks

FOCUS
A modest handicap. It's been rated around the front-running runner-up.

5105 NORMAN SHARP FLOWER OF SCOTLAND MEMORIAL H'CAP 5f 59y

5:10 (5:11) (Class 6) (0-60,66) 3-Y-O+ **£2,911** (£866; £432; £216) **Stalls** Centre

Form RPR

6534 **1** **Beau Mistral (IRE)**[9] 4763 7-8-13 55 ....(b[1]) GeorgeDowning(3) 6 62
(Tony Carroll) *v.s.a: t.k.h: hld up in rr: effrt over 1f out: stl in last pair and hrd drvn ent fnl f: str burst ins fnl f: led last strides* **11/2**[3]

5310 **2** *nk* **Assertive Agent**[30] 3993 6-9-4 **57** DavidProbert 1 63
(Tony Carroll) *hld up in tch towards rr: clsd and swtchd lft jst over 1f out: rdn to ld jst ins fnl f: edgd rt but kpt on u.p: hdd last strides* **9/2**[1]

0600 **3** *1 ½* **Ask The Guru**[16] 4536 6-9-6 **59** (p) KierenFox 5 60
(Michael Attwater) *chsd ldr: rdn and effrt over 1f out: drvn and ev ch 1f out: unable qck and styd on same pce ins fnl f* **5/1**[2]

3515 **4** *hd* **Our Lord**[16] 4529 4-9-7 **60** LukeMorris 3 60
(Bill Turner) *chsd ldrs: clsd u.p over 1f out: drvn and pressing ldrs 1f out: unable qck and one pce after* **7/1**

5613 **5** *1 ¼* **Quantum Dot (IRE)**[14] 4590 5-9-5 **58** (b) JimCrowley 4 53
(Ed de Giles) *sn led and wnt clr 4f out: rdn jst over 1f out: hdd ins fnl f: sn btn and wknd fnl 100yds* **5/1**[2]

0322 **6** *nk* **Picansort**[50] 3317 9-9-5 **58** ShaneKelly 8 52
(Peter Crate) *hld up in tch in midfield: clsd and effrt over 1f out: drvn to press ldrs 1f out: sn no ex and wknd fnl 100yds* **11/2**[3]

6061 **7** *nse* **Storm Lightning**[1] 5050 7-9-13 **66** 6ex KieranO'Neill 2 60
(Mark Brisbourne) *in tch in midfield: lost pl and rdn 3f out: bhd 2f out: kpt on ins fnl f but nvr threatening ldrs* **7/1**

505 **8** *¾* **Go Charlie**[17] 4472 5-8-7 **46** AdamBeschizza 7 37
(Lisa Williamson) *taken down early: stdd s: t.k.h: hld up in tch in midfield: hdwy u.p over 1f out: chalng ent fnl f: sn no ex: wknd ins fnl f* **12/1**

1m 3.02s (0.72) **Going Correction** +0.20s/f (Good) **8** Ran SP% **115.0**
Speed ratings (Par 101): **102,101,99,98,96 96,96,95**
CSF £30.58 CT £132.58 TOTE £7.10: £2.00, £1.20, £3.30; EX 35.60 Trifecta £190.60.
Owner A Mills **Bred** John McEnery **Trained** Cropthorne, Worcs

FOCUS
There was no hanging around in this wide-open looking handicap. It saw a 1-2 for Tony Carroll. It's been rated as very ordinary form.
T/Plt: £486.80 to a £1 stake. Pool: £65,263.42 - 97.86 winning tickets T/Qpdt: £81.10 to a £1 stake. Pool: £8,154.28 - 74.40 winning tickets **Steve Payne**

5057 HAYDOCK (L-H)
Friday, August 5

OFFICIAL GOING: Good to firm (8.5)
Wind: Moderate, against Weather: fairly cloudy

5106 BETFRED GOALS GALORE HAYDOCK PARK APPRENTICE TRAINING SERIES H'CAP (RACING EXCELLENCE INITIATIVE) 1m 3f 200y
5:45 (5:45) (Class 5) (0-75,75) 4-Y-O+ **£2,911** (£866; £432; £216) **Stalls** Centre

Form RPR

10/4 **1** **Zamoyski**[29] 4049 6-9-12 **75** (p) AdamMcNamara 3 81
(Steve Gollings) *prom: wnt 2nd 7f out: rdn 3f out: led jst over 1f out: edgd lft ins fnl f: kpt on wl* **11/8**[1]

4300 **2** *¾* **King Of Paradise (IRE)**[6] 4875 7-8-9 **63** GerO'Neill(5) 4 67
(Eric Alston) *racd keenly: led: rdn over 2f out: hdd jst over 1f out: hld nr fin* **11/4**[2]

3022 **3** *2 ¼* **Cape Spirit (IRE)**[17] 4499 4-8-2 **56** oh1 (v) WilliamCox(5) 2 56
(Andrew Balding) *prom: dropped to rr 6f out: hdwy 3f out: effrt to chal over 1f out: no ex fnl 110yds* **10/3**[3]

6533 **4** *1 ½* **Merchant Of Medici**[2] 5028 9-8-7 **61** CameronNoble(5) 1 59
(Micky Hammond) *racd keenly: chsd ldr tl 7f out: rdn over 2f out: sn outpcd: kpt on but n.d ins fnl f* **5/1**

2m 28.41s (-5.39) **Going Correction** -0.35s/f (Firm) **4** Ran SP% **108.5**
Speed ratings (Par 103): **103,102,101,100**
CSF £5.38 TOTE £2.00; EX 5.20 Trifecta £12.30.
Owner Irvin S Naylor **Bred** N C Appleton & Cheveley Park Stud **Trained** Scamblesby, Lincs

FOCUS
All races on inner home straight. Races on Round course increased by 3yds. A stop-start gallop to this apprentice handicap and the form is unlikely to be anything special. The runner-up has been rated to his recent form.

5107 BETFRED "LOOKING FORWARD TO LISA STANSFIELD" MAIDEN STKS (PLUS 10 RACE) 1m
6:15 (6:16) (Class 4) 2-Y-O **£3,946** (£1,174; £586; £293) **Stalls** Low

Form RPR

032 **1** **Drochaid**[13] 4642 2-9-5 76 OisinMurphy 5 77
(Andrew Balding) *led early: chsd ldr: led over 2f out: rdn over 1f out: kpt finding for press and r.o gamely ins fnl f* **5/2**[3]

4 **2** *¾* **Sofia's Rock (FR)**[19] 4423 2-9-5 0 FrannyNorton 3 75
(Mark Johnston) *racd keenly: sn led: hdd over 2f out: stl ev ch ins fnl f: hld nr fin* **9/4**[2]

4 **3** *shd* **Procurator (IRE)**[16] 4533 2-9-5 0 TomMarquand 6 75
(Richard Hannon) *hld up in rr: hdwy over 2f out: rdn to chal over 1f out: ev ch ins fnl f: no ex nr fin* **2/1**[1]

43 **4** *3* **Actualisation**[25] 4188 2-9-5 0 JasonHart 2 68
(John Quinn) *trckd ldrs: rdn over 2f out: lost pl over 1f out: one pce ins fnl f* **8/1**

0 **5** *15* **Ravenoak (IRE)**[27] 4125 2-9-5 0 RichardKingscote 1 32
(Tom Dascombe) *trckd ldrs: rdn and lost pl over 2f out: dropped away over 1f out: eased whn wl btn ins fnl f* **16/1**

1m 40.67s (-3.03) **Going Correction** -0.35s/f (Firm) **5** Ran SP% **109.7**
Speed ratings (Par 96): **101,100,100,97,82**
CSF £8.44 TOTE £3.40: £1.80, £1.50; EX 7.60 Trifecta £14.50.
Owner Mick and Janice Mariscotti **Bred** Meon Valley Stud **Trained** Kingsclere, Hants

FOCUS
Race distance increased by 3yds. Something of a tactical affair with no real pace early and it became rather a sprint up the straight. The first three had a good tussle but it is unlikely to be as strong a race as last year when it was won by Foundation. It's been rated around the winner for now.

5108 BETFRED TV EBF NOVICE STKS (PLUS 10 RACE) 7f
6:50 (6:51) (Class 4) 2-Y-O **£4,269** (£1,270; £634; £317) **Stalls** Low

Form RPR

4 **1** **Contrast (IRE)**[20] 4387 2-9-2 0 TomMarquand 4 88+
(Richard Hannon) *racd keenly: hld up: hdwy 2f out: led over 1f out: r.o ins fnl f: pushed out and in command fnl 100yds* **12/1**

0 **2** *3 ½* **War Of Succession**[84] 2203 2-9-2 0 OisinMurphy 5 79
(Andrew Balding) *upset in stalls: hld up: swtchd rt fr inner over 1f out: styd on to take 2nd fnl 120yds: no imp on wnr* **11/4**[2]

15 **3** *2 ¼* **White Tower (IRE)**[27] 4150 2-9-8 0 FrannyNorton 1 78
(Mark Johnston) *led: rdn and hdd over 1f out: no ex fnl 150yds* **8/11**[1]

0 **4** *2 ½* **Justice Frederick (IRE)**[48] 3382 2-9-3 0 AdamMcNamara(5) 3 72
(Paul D'Arcy) *chsd ldr: rdn and ev ch wl over 1f out: sn lost 2nd: one pce fnl f* **5/1**[3]

1m 27.57s (-3.13) **Going Correction** -0.35s/f (Firm) 2y crse rec **4** Ran SP% **108.9**
Speed ratings (Par 96): **103,99,96,93**
CSF £41.69 TOTE £9.90; EX 30.60 Trifecta £40.90.
Owner Highclere T'Bred Racing - Thomas Hardy **Bred** Lynn Lodge Stud **Trained** East Everleigh, Wilts

FOCUS
Race distance increased by 3yds. Just the four runners, a moderate gallop and a surprise result. The opening level is fluid.

5109 COUNTRYWIDE FREIGHT NURSERY H'CAP 7f
7:20 (7:21) (Class 4) (0-85,83) 2-Y-O **£4,528** (£1,347; £673; £336) **Stalls** Low

Form RPR

413 **1** **Londinium**[20] 4379 2-9-3 **79** FrannyNorton 3 82
(Mark Johnston) *hld up: rdn over 1f out: hdwy ins fnl f: r.o to ld towards fin* **2/1**[2]

21 **2** *nk* **Tommy Taylor (USA)**[14] 4609 2-9-7 **83** TomEaves 4 85
(Kevin Ryan) *hld up in rr: hdwy 3f out: led over 1f out: hrd pressed ins fnl f: hdd towards fin* **10/11**[1]

100 **3** *hd* **Fayez (IRE)**[27] 4167 2-9-6 **82** PhillipMakin 5 84
(David O'Meara) *midfield: hdwy over 2f out: sn chalng: styd on u.p and upsides ins fnl f: hld nr fin* **10/1**[3]

1464 **4** *1 ¼* **Springwood (IRE)**[31] 3977 2-8-10 **72** (v[1]) BarryMcHugh 6 70
(Richard Fahey) *led: rdn and hdd over 1f out: kpt on u.p ins fnl f: no ex fnl 75yds* **25/1**

053 **5** *hd* **Our Boy John (IRE)**[27] 4140 2-8-2 **64** PatrickMathers 2 62
(Richard Fahey) *chsd ldrs: rdn and outpcd over 2f out: styng on bhd ldrs and cl up whn denied a run fnl 75yds: eased nr fin* **11/1**

053 **6** *10* **Quantum Field (USA)**[19] 4423 2-8-4 **66** ShaneGray 7 37
(David Brown) *racd keenly: chsd ldr tl rdn and lost 2nd over 2f out: wknd over 1f out* **14/1**

1m 29.22s (-1.48) **Going Correction** -0.35s/f (Firm) **6** Ran SP% **113.7**
Speed ratings (Par 96): **94,93,93,92,91 80**
CSF £4.25 TOTE £3.10: £1.60, £1.20; EX 4.60 Trifecta £18.10.
Owner Sheikh Hamdan bin Mohammed Al Maktoum **Bred** Darley **Trained** Middleham Moor, N Yorks

FOCUS
Race distance increased by 3yds. Plenty pulled hard in this nursery which was run at a moderate gallop, and only two lengths covered five of the six runners. It may prove muddling form. The winner has been rated to his pre-race form.

5110 BETFRED "BE PART OF THE ACTION" FILLIES' H'CAP 5f
7:55 (7:55) (Class 5) (0-70,69) 3-Y-O+ **£2,911** (£866; £432; £216) **Stalls** Centre

Form RPR

1223 **1** **Rose Eclair**[20] 4378 3-9-7 **69** (b) JasonHart 5 73+
(Tim Easterby) *in tch: rdn and hdwy over 1f out: r.o u.p ins fnl f: led nr fin* **6/1**

-431 **2** *nk* **Showdaisy**[6] 4874 3-9-2 **64** 6ex DougieCostello 8 67+
(Keith Dalgleish) *racd keenly: prom: rdn and nt qckn over 1f out: r.o u.p towards fin* **2/1**[1]

0000 **3** *½* **Lowrie**[7] 4834 3-8-0 **53** oh5 ow3 (p[1]) NathanEvans(5) 6 54
(John David Riches) *led: rdn over 1f out: hrd pressed ins fnl f: hdd nr fin* **50/1**

60-2 **4** *nk* **Busy Bimbo (IRE)**[7] 4834 7-9-2 **61** (b) TomEaves 4 62
(John David Riches) *hld up: rdn and hdwy over 1f out: ev ch and r.o fnl 100yds: hld nr fin* **7/1**

0645 **5** *3 ¼* **Ruby's Day**[8] 4809 7-9-3 **67** (p) AdamMcNamara(5) 2 56
(David Brown) *hld up: hdwy 2f out: rdn over 1f out: chsd ldrs ins fnl f: no imp fnl 150yds* **11/2**[3]

0412 **6** *1 ¾* **Lydiate Lady**[20] 4378 4-8-13 **58** FrannyNorton 7 41
(Paul Green) *racd keenly: chsd ldrs: rdn over 1f out: wknd fnl 150yds* **5/1**[2]

032 **7** *1 ¼* **Shesthedream (IRE)**[16] 4521 3-9-5 **67** PhillipMakin 3 45
(David O'Meara) *hld up: pushed along and outpcd over 1f out: n.d after* **5/1**[2]

6400 **8** *5* **Seraphima**[127] 1164 6-7-12 **50** oh5 (p) RPWalsh(7) 1 11
(Lisa Williamson) *in tch: pushed along over 2f out: wknd over 1f out* **50/1**

1m 0.15s (-0.65) **Going Correction** -0.35s/f (Firm)
WFA 3 from 4yo+ 3lb **8** Ran SP% **112.8**
Speed ratings (Par 100): **91,90,89,89,84 81,79,71**
CSF £17.90 CT £536.22 TOTE £6.90: £2.10, £1.10, £7.50; EX 20.80 Trifecta £852.70.
Owner James Bowers **Bred** J Bowers **Trained** Great Habton, N Yorks
■ Stewards' Enquiry : Dougie Costello two-day ban; used whip above permitted level.

FOCUS
A modest fillies' event which, surprisingly for a 5f handicap, wasn't run at a flat-out gallop and resulted in several spoiling their chances by racing keenly. Muddling form. The first two have been rated close to form for now.

5111 BETFRED GREAT VALUE EVERY DAY H'CAP 1m 3f 200y
8:30 (8:30) (Class 4) (0-80,77) 3-Y-O **£5,175** (£1,540; £769; £384) **Stalls** Centre

Form RPR

2333 **1** **Kajaki (IRE)**[21] 4346 3-8-13 **69** (p) TomEaves 5 74
(Kevin Ryan) *led: rdn over 2f out: hdd narrowly over 1f out: rallied gamely wl ins fnl f: led on the nod* **11/2**

6535 **2** *nse* **Monaco Rose**[27] 4137 3-8-9 **65** PatrickMathers 3 70
(Richard Fahey) *chsd ldr: rdn and chalng fr 3f out: led narrowly over 1f out: hdd and lost out on the nod* **4/1**[3]

324 **3** *¾* **Rasasee (IRE)**[58] 3025 3-9-4 **77** DanielMuscutt(3) 1 81
(Marco Botti) *a.p: rdn over 3f out: ev ch wl ins fnl f: styd on u.p: hld nr fin* **9/2**

1062 **4** *¾* **Tartan Bute**[3] 4969 3-9-2 **72** (p) FrannyNorton 4 75
(Mark Johnston) *hld up: niggled along 6f out: pushed along to chse ldrs 4f out: outpcd 2f out: styd on towards fin: nt pce to chal* **2/1**[1]

-522 **5** *1 ¾* **Nucky Thompson**[39] 3728 3-9-2 **75** LouisSteward(3) 2 75
(Richard Spencer) *racd keenly: hld up: rdn and hdwy to chse ldrs over 2f out: no ex fnl 100yds: eased whn btn towards fin* **3/1**[2]

2m 31.31s (-2.49) **Going Correction** -0.35s/f (Firm) **5** Ran SP% **111.9**
Speed ratings (Par 102): **94,93,93,92,91**
CSF £26.89 TOTE £5.00: £2.60, £2.00; EX 18.70 Trifecta £59.60.
Owner F Gillespie **Bred** Epona Bloodstock Ltd **Trained** Hambleton, N Yorks

FOCUS
Race distance increased by 3yds. Quite a competitive 1m4f handicap for three-year-olds but only two of the five had won a race. The pace was ordinary, the first three were the first three throughout, and a length and a half separated the first four home. Muddling form, but the winner has been rated to form.

T/Plt: £399.10 to a £1 stake. Pool: £58,446.59 - 106.90 winning tickets T/Qpdt: £62.10 to a £1 stake. Pool: £5214.12 - 62.10 winning tickets **Darren Owen**

4828 MUSSELBURGH (R-H)

Friday, August 5

OFFICIAL GOING: Good (good to firm in places; watered) changing to good after race 1 (2.00)

Wind: Almost nil Weather: Sunny

5112 QUILTER CHEVIOT NURSERY H'CAP 7f 30y

2:00 (2:00) (Class 6) (0-65,64) 2-Y-O **£2,587** (£770; £384; £192) **Stalls** Low

Form RPR

000 **1** **Ray Donovan (IRE)**[24] 4227 2-9-5 **62**.......................... DanielTudhope 7 66
(David O'Meara) *pressed ldr: led over 2f out: sn rdn: edgd rt ent fnl f: rdn out* **7/1**

5030 **2** 3/4 **Mulwith (IRE)**[14] 4602 2-9-4 **61**..............................(b[1]) GrahamGibbons 1 63
(David Barron) *t.k.h: led: rdn and hdd over 2f out: rallied: kpt on fnl f: hld nr fin* **13/2**[3]

2332 **3** 1/2 **Bridal March**[17] 4487 2-9-7 **64**.......................... JoeFanning 2 65
(Mark Johnston) *fly-jmpd and lost grnd s: sn prom on outside: effrt and pushed along over 2f out: kpt on ins fnl f* **13/8**[1]

0022 **4** 1 1/2 **Kilbaha Lady (IRE)**[14] 4602 2-9-5 **62**.......................... AndrewMullen 4 59
(Nigel Tinkler) *trckd ldrs on ins: rdn over 2f out: kpt on same pce appr fnl f* **3/1**[2]

050 **5** 1 **Belle's Angel (IRE)**[53] 3222 2-8-5 **53**.......................... RowanScott(5) 5 47
(Ann Duffield) *stdd in last pl: pushed along over 4f out: effrt over 2f out: no ex fr over 1f out* **10/1**

6065 **6** 4 1/2 **Geego**[22] 4315 2-9-0 **57**.......................... GeorgeChaloner 6 39
(Richard Fahey) *t.k.h: prom: rdn over 2f out: wknd over 1f out* **15/2**

1m 32.4s (3.40) **Going Correction** +0.20s/f (Good) **6** Ran SP% **109.8**

Speed ratings (Par 92): **88,87,86,84,83 78**

CSF £47.16 TOTE £6.10: £2.80, £3.70; EX 37.30 Trifecta £73.10.

Owner Sterling Racing **Bred** Rbr Bloodstock Ltd **Trained** Upper Helmsley, N Yorks

FOCUS

Rail movements added 7yds to the race distance. A modest nursery in which the pace was modest and first two held those positions throughout. The winning jockey felt the ground was good. Ordinary form.

5113 BRITISH STALLION STUDS EBF STALLIONS CONDITIONS STKS (PLUS 10 RACE) 5f

2:30 (2:31) (Class 3) 2-Y-O **£8,086** (£2,406; £1,202; £601) **Stalls** High

Form RPR

5101 **1** **Kodi Da Capo (IRE)**[7] 4832 2-8-8 74.......................... ConnorBeasley 5 79
(Keith Dalgleish) *prom: rdn over 2f out: hdwy over 1f out: kpt on wl fnl f to ld cl home* **10/1**

12 **2** nse **Wick Powell**[6] 4891 2-8-13 80.......................... GrahamGibbons 4 84
(David Barron) *dwlt: t.k.h: trckd ldrs: wnt 2nd over 3f out: rdn over 1f out: led ins fnl f: kpt on: hdd cl home* **13/8**[1]

2144 **3** hd **Poet's Society**[6] 4891 2-9-2 87.......................... JoeFanning 2 86
(Mark Johnston) *led: rdn over 1f out: hdd ins fnl f: kpt on wl cl home: jst hld* **3/1**[3]

21 **4** 1 **Whirl Me Round**[22] 4308 2-8-13 0.......................... JoeDoyle 3 82
(Kevin Ryan) *pressed ldr to over 3f out: cl up: effrt and pushed along whn n.m.r briefly over 1f out and n.m.r thrght fnl 150yds: nt rcvr* **11/4**[2]

2135 **5** 8 **The Nazca Lines (IRE)**[6] 4891 2-8-8 81............(v) CallumShepherd(5) 1 51
(John Quinn) *wnt bdly rt s: hld up in tch on outside: effrt over 2f out: blkd and outpcd over 1f out: wknd and eased fnl f* **10/1**

1m 0.99s (0.59) **Going Correction** +0.20s/f (Good) **5** Ran SP% **107.9**

Speed ratings (Par 98): **103,102,102,101,88**

CSF £25.79 TOTE £12.20: £4.90, £1.20; EX 32.30 Trifecta £91.50.

Owner Equus I **Bred** Tally-Ho Stud **Trained** Carluke, S Lanarks

FOCUS

The going was changed to Good before this race. Plenty of interest in this good juvenile conditions race, despite the small field, and it produced a really close finish. Straightforward form.

5114 GANG OF FOUR H'CAP 1m

3:00 (3:00) (Class 6) (0-65,60) 3-Y-O+ **£2,587** (£770; £384; £192) **Stalls** Low

Form RPR

5406 **1** **Almuhalab**[18] 4446 5-9-4 **56**..........................(p) JamesSullivan 4 63
(Ruth Carr) *t.k.h: prom: effrt and rdn over 1f out: led ins fnl f: kpt on wl* **9/2**[3]

052- **2** 1 1/4 **Playtothewhistle**[276] 7683 5-9-8 **60**..........................(v) ConnorBeasley 2 64
(Bryan Smart) *t.k.h: cl up: effrt and ev ch over 1f out: kpt on fnl f to take 2nd pl cl home* **11/1**

0 **3** hd **Let Right Be Done**[32] 3943 4-9-3 **55**.......................... GeorgeChaloner 5 59
(Linda Perratt) *t.k.h: cl up: led and rdn over 2f out: hdd ins fnl f: kpt on: no ex and lost 2nd cl home* **22/1**

0032 **4** 2 3/4 **Celtic Artisan (IRE)**[9] 4772 5-9-2 **54**..........................(bt) JoeFanning 7 51
(Rebecca Menzies) *t.k.h: hld up in tch: effrt and pushed along over 2f out: kpt on ins fnl f: nt pce to chal* **4/1**[2]

6045 **5** 2 1/2 **Opt Out**[9] 4772 6-9-6 **58**..........................(p) DanielTudhope 6 49
(David O'Meara) *s.i.s: hld up: rdn over 2f out: no imp fr over 1f out* **11/4**[1]

2456 **6** nk **Circuitous**[7] 4830 8-9-2 **59**..........................(v) ShirleyTeasdale(5) 3 49
(Keith Dalgleish) *led at ordinary gallop: rdn and hdd over 2f out: rallied: wknd over 1f out* **16/1**

1334 **7** 4 **Charles De Mille**[19] 4425 8-9-8 **60**.......................... GrahamLee 1 41
(Jedd O'Keeffe) *in tch: drvn over 2f out: wknd wl over 1f out* **4/1**[2]

032 **8** hd **Top Offer**[31] 3989 7-9-6 **58**.......................... DavidNolan 8 38
(Patrick Morris) *dwlt: hld up: drvn along over 2f out: sn btn* **8/1**

1m 41.39s (0.19) **Going Correction** +0.20s/f (Good) **8** Ran SP% **114.5**

Speed ratings (Par 101): **107,105,105,102,100 100,96,95**

CSF £52.00 CT £977.33 TOTE £6.30: £2.70, £2.90, £4.50; EX 48.20 Trifecta £456.60.

Owner Michael Hill **Bred** Shadwell Estate Company Limited **Trained** Huby, N Yorks

FOCUS

Rail movements added 7yds to the race distance. A low-grade mile handicap and the pace looked ordinary.

5115 EBF SCOTTISH PREMIER SERIES FILLIES' H'CAP 7f 30y

3:30 (3:30) (Class 4) (0-80,78) 3-Y-O+ **£8,086** (£2,406; £1,202; £601) **Stalls** Low

Form RPR

5522 **1** **Lucky Violet (IRE)**[17] 4486 4-9-1 **67**.......................... DanielTudhope 5 77
(Iain Jardine) *trckd ldrs: led wl over 1f out: sn rdn and edgd rt: kpt on strly fnl f* **7/1**

-350 **2** 2 1/4 **Mustique (IRE)**[20] 4398 3-9-5 **77**.......................... JackGarritty 7 79
(Richard Fahey) *hld up in tch: effrt and swtchd rt wl over 1f out: squeezed through to chse (clr) wnr ins fnl f: kpt on: no imp* **10/3**[1]

-251 **3** nk **Dark Intention (IRE)**[41] 3634 3-9-1 **73**.......................... CamHardie 2 74
(Lawrence Mullaney) *s.i.s: sn outpcd: hdwy on outside and prom over 1f out: kpt on ins fnl f* **4/1**[3]

-433 **4** 3 1/2 **Symposium**[11] 4708 3-9-4 **76**..........................(p) GrahamGibbons 3 68
(William Haggas) *led: rdn and hdd wl over 1f out: chsd wnr to ins fnl f: sn wknd* **7/2**[2]

2543 **5** 5 **Popsies Joy (IRE)**[9] 4769 3-8-11 **69**.......................... DuranFentiman 4 48
(Tim Easterby) *t.k.h: w ldr: ev ch to over 1f out: outpcd whn checked ins fnl f: sn btn* **7/1**

221 **6** 5 **Forever A Lady (IRE)**[18] 4443 3-9-6 **78**.......................... JoeFanning 1 44
(Keith Dalgleish) *hld up in tch: rdn over 2f out: edgd rt and wknd over 1f out* **9/2**

0110 **7** 2 1/2 **Dark Crystal**[4] 4933 5-9-5 **71** 6ex.......................... DavidNolan 6 33
(Linda Perratt) *prom on outside: swtchd to ins over 4f out: rdn over 2f out: wknd wl over 1f out* **14/1**

1m 29.39s (0.39) **Going Correction** +0.20s/f (Good)

WFA 3 from 4yo+ 6lb **7** Ran SP% **115.1**

Speed ratings (Par 102): **105,102,102,98,92 86,83**

CSF £30.91 TOTE £8.90: £3.70, £1.80; EX 35.40 Trifecta £155.50.

Owner Richard Allan **Bred** O F Ryan **Trained** Carrutherstown, D'fries & G'way

FOCUS

Rail movements added 7yds to the race distance. A fair and competitive fillies' handicap that was run just over 3secs faster than the opening nursery. The runner-up has been rated close to her reappearance effort.

5116 ARCHERFIELD CUP (H'CAP) 1m 6f

4:00 (4:00) (Class 2) (0-100,97) 3-Y-O+ **£16,172** (£4,812; £2,405; £1,202) **Stalls** Low

Form RPR

0002 **1** **Intense Tango**[13] 4646 5-8-7 **83** ow2..........................(t) CliffordLee(7) 1 91
(K R Burke) *trckd ldr: led over 4f out: hrd pressed and drvn along fnl 2f: hld on gamely towards fin* **15/2**

1-46 **2** hd **Gabrial The Hero (USA)**[41] 3658 7-9-11 **94**.......................... DavidNolan 7 101
(Richard Fahey) *hld up in tch: stdy hdwy to trck ldrs 5f out: effrt and ev ch fr 2f out: kpt on u.p fnl f: jst hld* **7/2**[1]

6330 **3** 3 1/4 **Vive Ma Fille (GER)**[21] 4353 4-9-12 **95**.......................... JoeFanning 5 97
(Mark Johnston) *t.k.h: hld up: smooth hdwy on outside to chse ldrs over 2f out: sn rdn: kpt on ins fnl f: nt rch first two* **5/1**[3]

66/0 **4** 1 3/4 **Mijhaar**[27] 4165 8-10-0 **97**.......................... DanielTudhope 3 97
(David O'Meara) *in tch: pushed along 5f out: drvn and hdwy to chse ldrs 3f out: kpt on same pce fr over 1f out* **15/2**

1002 **5** 10 **Steve Rogers (IRE)**[28] 4077 5-9-12 **95**.......................... AndrewMullen 2 81
(Roger Varian) *trckd ldrs: drvn and outpcd over 2f out: sn wknd* **7/2**[1]

0-00 **6** nk **Dawn Missile**[28] 4077 4-9-6 **89**..........................(p) GrahamGibbons 8 74
(William Haggas) *awkward s: t.k.h: hld up: rdn along and effrt over 2f out: wknd over 1f out: eased whn btn ins fnl f* **9/2**[2]

4205 **7** 8 **Zand (IRE)**[14] 4583 6-9-0 **83**.......................... GrahamLee 6 57
(Mark Johnston) *led at ordinary gallop: hdd over 4f out: rdn and wknd over 2f out* **14/1**

3m 2.51s (-2.79) **Going Correction** +0.20s/f (Good)

WFA 3 from 4yo+ 13lb **7** Ran SP% **109.5**

Speed ratings (Par 109): **115,114,113,112,106 106,101**

CSF £30.89 CT £131.91 TOTE £9.10: £3.40, £2.00; EX 32.50 Trifecta £127.30.

Owner Cosy Seal Racing Limited **Bred** Newsells Park Stud **Trained** Middleham Moor, N Yorks

FOCUS

Rail movements added 7yds to the race distance. The feature race and good prizemoney attracted some useful performers from major yards. The race was run at a sound gallop and produced another close finish. The winner has been rated to her turf best, and the third close to form.

5117 FISHER GROUP H'CAP 1m 4f 100y

4:30 (4:30) (Class 6) (0-65,63) 3-Y-O+ **£3,234** (£962; £481; £240) **Stalls** Low

Form RPR

1361 **1** **High On Light**[7] 4847 3-8-10 **59** 6ex.......................... RachelRichardson(3) 4 68+
(Tim Easterby) *t.k.h: cl up: led gng wl over 2f out: rdn over 1f out: kpt on wl fnl f* **6/5**[1]

0033 **2** 3/4 **Neuf Des Coeurs**[17] 4489 5-9-9 **58**..........................(p) JoeFanning 2 64
(Iain Jardine) *hld up: stdy hdwy over 2f out: effrt and rdn over 1f out: kpt on fnl f to take 2nd nr fin* **4/1**[2]

2355 **3** hd **First Sargeant**[6] 4875 6-9-11 **60**..........................(p) CamHardie 6 65
(Lawrence Mullaney) *wnt lft s: sn cl up: rdn and ev ch over 2f out to over 1f out: kpt on fnl f: lost 2nd nr fin* **10/1**

0261 **4** 2 3/4 **Chauvelin**[10] 4724 5-9-8 **57** 6ex..........................(b) AndrewMullen 5 58
(Nigel Tinkler) *in tch: effrt and pushed along over 2f out: outpcd fnl f* **12/1**

0056 **5** 3/4 **Gabrial The Terror (IRE)**[25] 4194 6-10-0 **63**..........................(p) DavidNolan 3 63
(Richard Fahey) *hld up in tch: stdy hdwy over 2f out: sn rdn: no ex fr over 1f out* **6/1**[3]

0540 **6** nk **Annigoni (IRE)**[17] 4489 4-9-0 **49**..........................(p) JamesSullivan 1 48
(Ruth Carr) *t.k.h: led: rdn and hdd over 2f out: wknd ins fnl f* **13/2**

2m 46.19s (4.19) **Going Correction** +0.20s/f (Good)

WFA 3 from 4yo+ 11lb **6** Ran SP% **109.9**

Speed ratings (Par 101): **94,93,93,91,91 90**

CSF £5.86 TOTE £2.20: £1.70, £1.40; EX 6.10 Trifecta £26.00.

Owner Habton Farms **Bred** Highclere Stud **Trained** Great Habton, N Yorks

FOCUS

Rail movements added 7yds to the race distance. The feature race and good prizemoney attracted some useful performers from major yards. The race was run at a sound gallop and produced another close finish. Straightforward form.

5118 EDGEN MURRAY AMATEUR RIDERS' H'CAP 2m

5:00 (5:00) (Class 6) (0-65,71) 4-Y-O+ **£3,119** (£967; £483; £242) **Stalls** High

Form RPR

0611 **1** **Stoneham**[39] 3704 5-10-5 **63**.......................... MrBLynn(7) 1 70
(Iain Jardine) *hld up in tch: smooth hdwy on outside to ld over 2f out: pushed clr fr over 1f out: rdn and edgd lft ins fnl f: comf* **3/1**[3]

/00- **2** 2 **Strobe**[36] 5140 12-9-9 **46** oh1..........................(p) MissJoannaMason 5 49
(Lucy Normile) *pressed ldr: led over 4f out to over 2f out: sn drvn: rallied to chse (clr) wnr ins fnl f: r.o* **25/1**

0321 **3** nk **Amirli (IRE)**[7] 4828 5-11-3 **71** 6ex..........................(p) MrJamesKing(3) 2 73
(Alistair Whillans) *t.k.h: cl up: rdn over 2f out: chsd wnr wl over 1f out to ins fnl f: kpt on same pce* **2/1**[2]

4541 **4** 4 1/2 **Rosette**[29] 4045 4-10-10 **61**.......................... MrSWalker 4 58
(Alan Swinbank) *prom: effrt and rdn over 2f out: edgd rt and wknd over 1f out* **13/8**[1]

4353 **5** *5* **Hero's Story**[13] 4645 6-10-3 **54**.. MrsCBartley 3 45
(Jim Goldie) *led at ordinary gallop: hdd over 4f out: rdn and wknd fr over 2f out* **8/1**
3m 40.71s (7.21) **Going Correction** +0.20s/f (Good) **5** Ran SP% **111.4**
Speed ratings (Par 101): **89,88,87,85,83**
CSF £50.51 TOTE £3.10: £1.60, £8.30; EX 33.00 Trifecta £129.90.
Owner The Dregs Of Humanity & Partner **Bred** Norman Court Stud **Trained** Carrutherstown, D'fries & G'way

FOCUS
Rail movements added 7yds to the race distance. A small field for this amateur riders' staying handicap and the pace was leisurely before picking up late. The form could possibly be rated a shade higher, but given the lack of depth it makes sense to start cautiously.
T/Plt: £616.00 to a £1 stake. Pool: £56,209.28 - 66.61 winning tickets T/Qpdt: £92.00 to a £1 stake. Pool: £4,665.06 - 37.52 winning tickets **Richard Young**

4883 NEWMARKET (R-H)
Friday, August 5

OFFICIAL GOING: Good to firm (good in places)
Wind: Light across Weather: Cloudy

5119 TRICONNEX MAIDEN FILLIES' STKS (PLUS 10 RACE) 6f
5:35 (5:35) (Class 4) 2-Y-O **£4,528** (£1,347; £673; £336) **Stalls** High

Form RPR
1 **Elliptical** 2-9-0 0.. AndreaAtzeni 2 79
(Robert Cowell) *s.i.s and wnt rt s: hld up: hdwy over 2f out: shkn up to ld over 1f out: edgd lft ins fnl f: r.o* **16/1**
2 *1 ½* **Bequia (IRE)** 2-9-0 0.. PaulMulrennan 7 74
(Martyn Meade) *hld up: hdwy over 1f out: r.o to go 2nd nr fin* **10/1**
4 **3** *¾* **Island In The Sky (IRE)**[29] 4064 2-9-0 0.................... PatCosgrave 5 72
(David Simcock) *chsd ldr tl shkn up to ld over 2f out: hdd over 1f out: rdn and edgd lft ins fnl f: styd on same pce* **5/2**[1]
6 **4** *hd* **Heavenly Angel**[21] 4350 2-9-0 0.................... SeanLevey 8 71
(Richard Hannon) *led over 3f: rdn over 1f out: nt clr run and swtchd rt ins fnl f: styd on* **15/2**
55 **5** *1* **Bassmah**[22] 4298 2-9-0 0.................................(p) ThomasBrown 6 68
(Ismail Mohammed) *prom: rdn over 2f out: edgd rt over 1f out: styd on same pce fnl f* **12/1**
3 **6** *2 ¼* **Elas Ruby**[37] 3782 2-9-0 0.. FrankieDettori 3 61
(John Gosden) *prom: shkn up over 1f out: styd on same pce* **3/1**[2]
7 *hd* **Claire's Secret** 2-9-0 0.. NickyMackay 1 60+
(Philip McBride) *dwlt and wnt rt s: hld up: rdn over 2f out: nvr trbld ldrs* **25/1**
5 **8** *3 ¾* **Sparkle**[21] 4350 2-9-0 0.. SilvestreDeSousa 4 48
(Ed Dunlop) *hld up: rdn over 2f out: no ch whn eased ins fnl f* **7/2**[3]
0 **9** *½* **Ashazuri**[36] 3812 2-9-0 0.. FrederikTylicki 9 47
(Jonathan Portman) *prom tl wknd over 1f out* **50/1**
1m 12.5s **Going Correction** +0.075s/f (Good) **9** Ran SP% **116.0**
Speed ratings (Par 93): **103,101,100,99,98 95,95,90,89**
CSF £165.11 TOTE £19.40: £4.70, £3.70, £1.10; EX 215.20 Trifecta £1782.90.
Owner Cheveley Park Stud **Bred** Cheveley Park Stud Ltd **Trained** Six Mile Bottom, Cambs

FOCUS
Stands' side course used. Stalls far side except 1m2f: centre. The watered ground (5mm Thursday evening) was given as good to firm, good in places (GoingStick: 7.5). A fair fillies' maiden and a nice performance from the winner. The third and fifth offer an early guide to the level.

5120 TAMDOWN (S) STKS 7f
6:05 (6:05) (Class 5) 2-Y-O **£3,881** (£1,155; £577; £288) **Stalls** High

Form RPR
3300 **1** **Ivor's Magic (IRE)**[8] 4802 2-8-1 65.................... AdamMcLean(7) 2 64
(David Elsworth) *hld up: hdwy over 2f out: chsd ldr and hung lft over 1f out: sn carried rt: rdn to ld and hung lft wl ins fnl f: styd on* **6/4**[1]
0540 **2** *¾* **If I Say So**[23] 4270 2-8-13 63.................... SilvestreDeSousa 6 67
(J S Moore) *sn led: qcknd over 2f out: rdn and hung rt fr over 1f out: hdd wl ins fnl f: bmpd sn after: unable qck towards fin* **7/1**[3]
05 **3** *6* **Cautious Choice (IRE)**[16] 4526 2-8-1 0.................... HollieDoyle(7) 5 46
(J S Moore) *chsd ldr: rdn over 2f out: hung lft and lost 2nd over 1f out: no ex ins fnl f* **16/1**
035 **4** *½* **Swallow Street (IRE)**[7] 4815 2-8-13 0.................... WilliamCarson 1 49
(Jamie Osborne) *hld up: rdn over 2f out: no imp fnl f* **15/2**
00 **5** *1 ¾* **Single Estate**[23] 4274 2-8-10 0.................... (b[1]) RosieJessop(3) 7 45
(Sir Mark Prescott Bt) *chsd ldrs: rdn over 2f out: wknd fnl f* **9/1**
50 **6** *14* **Dusty Berry**[22] 4287 2-8-8 0.. JohnFahy 3 2
(Eve Johnson Houghton) *s.s: sn drvn along in rr: wknd over 2f out* **5/2**[2]
1m 26.04s (0.34) **Going Correction** +0.075s/f (Good) **6** Ran SP% **108.7**
Speed ratings (Par 94): **101,100,93,92,90 74**
CSF £11.66 TOTE £2.40: £1.30, £2.30; EX 12.00 Trifecta £72.50.
Owner Ivor Perry & David Elsworth **Bred** Tally-Ho Stud **Trained** Newmarket, Suffolk

FOCUS
The first two pulled well clear in this seller. It's been rated around the first two.

5121 WESTON GROUP MAIDEN STKS (PLUS 10 RACE) 7f
6:40 (6:40) (Class 4) 2-Y-O **£4,528** (£1,347; £673; £336) **Stalls** High

Form RPR
1 **Seniority** 2-9-5 0.. PatCosgrave 6 86+
(William Haggas) *s.i.s: sn prom: shkn up to ld 1f out: r.o wl* **7/1**[3]
2 *½* **Zefferino** 2-9-5 0.. AndreaAtzeni 1 85+
(Roger Charlton) *trckd ldrs: racd keenly: shkn up and ev ch thrght fnl f: r.o wl* **8/15**[1]
3 *6* **Endless Gold** 2-9-5 0.. WilliamBuick 7 69
(Charlie Appleby) *pushed along to ld after 1f: shkn up over 2f out: hdd 1f out: sn outpcd* **11/4**[2]
4 *4* **American Patrol (IRE)** 2-9-5 0.................... WilliamCarson 2 58
(Michael Bell) *sn led: hdd 6f out: remained w ldr: rdn and ev ch over 1f out: wknd fnl f* **14/1**
1m 27.76s (2.06) **Going Correction** +0.075s/f (Good) **4** Ran SP% **111.1**
Speed ratings (Par 96): **91,90,83,79**
CSF £11.94 TOTE £5.60; EX 12.30 Trifecta £18.20.
Owner The Queen **Bred** Darley **Trained** Newmarket, Suffolk

FOCUS
Often a good maiden (won by Emotionless last year), this was steadily run and it developed into a bit of a dash to the line. The first two look useful types. The level is fluid.

5122 TAMDOWN H'CAP 1m 2f
7:10 (7:11) (Class 5) (0-75,75) 3-Y-O+ **£3,234** (£962; £481; £240) **Stalls** Centre

Form RPR
-222 **1** **Hollywood Road (IRE)**[10] 4743 3-9-5 **75**.................... (b) FrankieDettori 13 86
(Don Cantillon) *hld up: hdwy over 2f out: rdn to ld over 1f out: sn hung lft: styd on* **11/4**[1]
-042 **2** *1 ¼* **Kismet Hardy**[49] 3348 3-9-1 **71**.. SeanLevey 1 79
(Richard Hannon) *led over 7f: sn rdn: styd on* **10/1**
2123 **3** *hd* **The Gay Cavalier**[7] 4838 5-9-10 **74**.................... (t) JosephineGordon(3) 12 82
(John Ryan) *hld up: racd keenly: hdwy over 7f out: rdn over 1f out: styd on* **6/1**[3]
5215 **4** *½* **Trulee Scrumptious**[2] 5037 7-8-9 **63**.................... (v) GeorgeWood(7) 9 70
(Peter Charalambous) *hld up: hdwy over 1f out: sn rdn: styd on* **6/1**[3]
4010 **5** *2 ¼* **Edge Of Reason**[20] 4400 3-9-5 **75**.................... AntonioFresu 4 78
(Ed Walker) *s.i.s: hld up: hdwy over 3f out: rdn and hung rt over 1f out: styd on same pce* **14/1**
1502 **6** *3* **Wings Of Esteem (IRE)**[30] 4025 3-8-13 **69**.................... JamesDoyle 2 66
(Martin Smith) *chsd ldrs: rdn to ld over 2f out: hdd over 1f out: wknd ins fnl f* **5/1**[2]
6100 **7** *7* **Cat Royale (IRE)**[42] 3617 3-9-0 **75**.................... (p) CharlieBennett(5) 5 58
(Jane Chapple-Hyam) *chsd ldrs: rdn over 2f out: hung rt and wknd over 1f out* **25/1**
54-0 **8** *3 ¼* **Pure Vanity**[107] 1577 3-8-11 **67**.................... [1] SilvestreDeSousa 6 43
(Roger Charlton) *hld up in tch: plld hrd: stdd and lost pl over 7f out: rdn and wknd over 2f out* **12/1**
036 **9** *7* **Captain Gerald**[10] 4740 3-8-0 **56** oh2.................... (p) RyanPowell 7 18
(John Ryan) *chsd ldr over 7f: sn rdn and wknd* **33/1**
10 *8* **Yasood (IRE)**[60] 2987 3-8-7 **70**.................... GeorgiaDobie(7) 3 16
(Phil McEntee) *chsd ldrs: rdn over 3f out: wknd over 2f out* **66/1**
0004 **11** *1 ½* **Marshal Dan Troop (IRE)**[23] 4272 3-9-1 **71**.................... (p) AndreaAtzeni 11 14
(Peter Chapple-Hyam) *prom: rdn over 3f out: wknd over 2f out* **8/1**
1005 **12** *9* **Artful Prince**[15] 4568 6-9-10 **71**.................... (b) PaulMulrennan 8
(James Given) *hld up: rdn and wknd over 2f out* **16/1**
2m 6.63s (1.13) **Going Correction** +0.075s/f (Good)
WFA 3 from 4yo+ 9lb **12** Ran SP% **120.6**
Speed ratings (Par 103): **98,97,96,96,94 92,86,84,78,72 70,63**
CSF £31.83 CT £158.16 TOTE £3.70: £1.70, £3.00, £2.00; EX 36.80 Trifecta £139.00.
Owner Mrs Catherine Reed **Bred** Tally-Ho Stud **Trained** Newmarket, Suffolk

FOCUS
Just an ordinary handicap run at a fairly steady early gallop. The third and fourth help set the standard.

5123 TAMDOWN EBF STALLIONS FILLIES' H'CAP 1m
7:45 (7:46) (Class 3) (0-95,88) 3-Y-O+ **£9,056** (£2,695; £1,346; £673) **Stalls** High

Form RPR
30-5 **1** **Up In Lights (IRE)**[64] 2819 4-10-0 **88**.................... TomQueally 4 95+
(James Fanshawe) *hld up: hdwy and nt clr run over 1f out: rdn to ld wl ins fnl f: r.o* **5/1**[2]
200 **2** *1* **Yeah Baby Yeah (IRE)**[23] 4263 3-9-2 **86**.................... (p) JosephineGordon(3) 8 90
(Gay Kelleway) *a.p: racd keenly: rdn and ev ch fr over 1f out tl styd on same pce towards fin* **16/1**
0123 **3** *shd* **Invermere**[18] 4453 3-8-9 **76**.. AndreaAtzeni 7 80
(Richard Fahey) *edgd rt s: plld hrd and prom: led over 1f out: sn rdn: hdd wl ins fnl f* **7/1**[3]
6-65 **4** *½* **Aqua Libre**[15] 4548 3-9-1 **82**.................... SilvestreDeSousa 5 85
(Philip McBride) *plld hrd and sn prom: rdn and ev ch whn hung lft over 1f out: styd on same pce wl ins fnl f* **8/1**
2410 **5** *2* **Ejayteekay**[34] 3911 3-8-3 **77**.................... GeorgeWood(7) 6 75
(Hughie Morrison) *bmpd s: sn chsng ldr: led 5f out: rdn and hdd over 1f out: no ex ins fnl f* **10/1**
24-0 **6** *1 ¼* **Ceaseless (IRE)**[65] 2797 4-9-13 **87**.................... MartinHarley 2 83
(James Tate) *hld up: rdn and edgd lft over 1f out: nt trble ldrs* **12/1**
01- **7** *shd* **City Chic (USA)**[347] 5697 3-9-4 **85**.................... WilliamBuick 3 80
(Charlie Appleby) *hld up: shkn up over 1f out: nvr trbld ldrs* **15/8**[1]
2312 **8** *1 ¾* **Shafafya**[35] 3846 3-9-4 **85**.. PaulHanagan 9 75
(Ed Dunlop) *led 3f: chsd ldr: rdn over 1f out: wknd ins fnl f* **5/1**[2]
1m 40.23s (0.23) **Going Correction** +0.075s/f (Good)
WFA 3 from 4yo 7lb **8** Ran SP% **114.4**
Speed ratings (Par 104): **101,100,99,99,97 96,96,94**
CSF £78.25 CT £561.56 TOTE £5.20: £1.70, £3.00, £2.00; EX 71.90 Trifecta £346.10.
Owner Mohamed Obaida **Bred** Bluehills Racing Limited **Trained** Newmarket, Suffolk

FOCUS
Quite a competitive fillies' handicap. The runner-up has been rated close to form.

5124 TRICONNEX H'CAP 6f
8:20 (8:20) (Class 3) (0-95,94) 3-Y-O+ **£7,762** (£2,310; £1,154; £577) **Stalls** High

Form RPR
-134 **1** **Mehronissa**[42] 3616 4-9-11 **93**.................... FrederikTylicki 2 106
(Ed Vaughan) *hld up: swtchd rt over 2f out: hdwy over 1f out: rdn to ld wl ins fnl f: r.o* **5/1**[3]
5401 **2** *nk* **Solar Flair**[21] 4366 4-9-12 **94**.. JamesDoyle 8 106
(William Knight) *hld up: nt clr run over 2f: swtchd rt over 1f out: led sn after: rdn and hdd wl ins fnl f: r.o* **7/2**[1]
1040 **3** *2 ½* **Exchequer (IRE)**[41] 3656 5-9-7 **89**.................... PatCosgrave 9 93
(David Brown) *hld up: hdwy over 1f out: sn rdn and edgd rt: styd on same pce ins fnl f* **9/1**
5012 **4** *½* **Merhoob (IRE)**[28] 4079 4-9-1 **86**.................... JosephineGordon(3) 3 88
(John Ryan) *sn pushed along in rr: rdn over 2f out: styd on ins fnl f: nt trble ldrs* **9/2**[2]
6113 **5** *1 ¾* **Guishan**[20] 4398 6-9-6 **91**.. TimClark(3) 7 88
(Michael Appleby) *led: rdn over 2f out: hdd over 1f out: no ex ins fnl f* **7/1**
4133 **6** *1 ¾* **Intense Style (IRE)**[21] 4338 4-9-9 **91**.................... DavidAllan 4 82
(Les Eyre) *chsd ldrs: rdn over 2f out: hmpd over 1f out: wknd ins fnl f* **5/1**[3]
3-61 **7** *nk* **Excellent George**[21] 4360 4-9-0 **82**.................... (t) AndreaAtzeni 5 72
(Stuart Williams) *chsd ldr: rdn over 2f out: lost 2nd and hmpd over 1f out: wknd ins fnl f* **5/1**[3]
1m 11.44s (-1.06) **Going Correction** +0.075s/f (Good) **7** Ran SP% **112.9**
Speed ratings (Par 107): **110,109,106,105,103 100,100**
CSF £22.17 CT £150.80 TOTE £5.90: £3.20, £1.80; EX 24.60 Trifecta £138.90.
Owner Salem Rashid **Bred** Carmel Stud **Trained** Newmarket, Suffolk

FOCUS
A tight handicap on paper, but the first two separated themselves from the rest and both look ahead of the game.

T/Jkpt: Not won. T/Plt: £341.60 to a £1 stake. Pool: £77,192.41 - 164.92 winning tickets T/Qpdt: £78.60 to a £1 stake. Pool: £6,345.46 - 59.68 winning tickets **Colin Roberts**

5077 WOLVERHAMPTON (A.W) (L-H)

Friday, August 5

OFFICIAL GOING: Tapeta: standard

Wind: Light behind Weather: Sunny

5125 FCL GLOBAL FORWARDING MAKING LOGISTICS PERSONAL NOVICE STKS 5f 20y (Tp)

1:50 (1:50) (Class 5) 2-Y-O **£3,234** (£962; £481; £240) **Stalls** Low

Form RPR

1550 **1** **Simmie (IRE)**[20] 4394 2-8-6 89 MitchGodwin(7) 4 81+
(Sylvester Kirk) *hld up in tch: pushed along and hdwy 2f out: rdn to ld jst ins fnl f: kpt on wl* **5/4**[1]

1233 **2** *4* **Merry Banter**[13] 4669 2-8-11 69 AdamMcNamara(5) 6 70
(Paul Midgley) *led: rdn 2f out: hdd jst ins fnl f: sn no ch w wnr* **4/1**[3]

0 **3** *2* **Wearethepeople**[36] 3813 2-9-0 0 RichardKingscote 3 61
(William Muir) *s.i.s: hld up: pushed along and outpcd 1/2-way: kpt on fnl f: nvr able to chal* **2/1**[2]

364 **4** *1 1/4* **Luv U Always**[13] 4638 2-8-9 56 FrannyNorton 7 51
(Jo Hughes) *chsd ldr: rdn 2f out: wknd fnl f* **25/1**

3021 **5** *2* **Zebspear (IRE)**[8] 4791 2-9-4 69 JosephineGordon(3) 2 56
(Joseph Tuite) *in tch: rdn 2f out: wknd over 1f out* **17/2**

00 **6** *14* **Penuche**[9] 4759 2-8-6 0 NoelGarbutt(3) 5
(Derek Shaw) *dwlt: a towards rr* **200/1**

1m 1.26s (-0.64) **Going Correction** 0.0s/f (Stan) **6** Ran SP% **112.6**
Speed ratings (Par 94): **105,98,95,93,90 67**
CSF £6.85 TOTE £2.20: £1.10, £2.70; EX 7.20 Trifecta £13.30.
Owner Neil Simpson **Bred** D Ryan, D S Ryan & R A Williams **Trained** Upper Lambourn, Berks

FOCUS
The winner stood out at the figures in this novice event. The runner-up has been rated close to her best pre-race form.

5126 PORSCHE CENTRE WOLVERHAMPTON LAUNCH H'CAP (DIV I) 5f 216y (Tp)

2:20 (2:21) (Class 6) (0-60,60) 3-Y-O+ **£2,587** (£770; £384; £192) **Stalls** Low

Form RPR

0005 **1** **Compton Prince**[20] 4389 7-9-9 59 (b) FrannyNorton 4 65
(Milton Bradley) *sn trckd ldrs: pushed along to chal strly ent fnl f: edgd ahd 110yds out: rdn and hld on wl* **5/1**[2]

305 **2** *hd* **Intense Starlet (IRE)**[16] 4513 5-8-13 52 (p) JacobButterfield(3) 7 57
(Marjorie Fife) *chsd ldrs on outside: rdn over 2f out: led wl over 1f out: edgd lft and jnd ent fnl f: hdd narrowly 110yds out: kpt on* **4/1**[1]

6610 **3** *shd* **Curious Fox**[23] 4262 3-9-5 59 RichardKingscote 6 63
(Anthony Carson) *chsd ldrs: rdn and briefly outpcd 2f out: kpt on wl fnl f* **4/1**[1]

0000 **4** *2 3/4* **Ershaad (IRE)**[57] 3069 4-9-5 60 (b[1]) CharlieBennett(5) 3 56
(Shaun Harris) *hld up in tch: rdn over 2f out: kpt on fnl f: nvr threatened ldrs* **6/1**

5050 **5** *1/2* **Cuban Queen (USA)**[25] 4202 3-8-11 51 MartinLane 1 46
(Jeremy Gask) *trckd ldrs on inner: rdn 2f out: lost pl over 1f out: one pce fnl f* **11/2**[3]

0000 **6** *nk* **Burauq**[22] 4292 4-8-7 46 (b) JosephineGordon(3) 8 42
(Milton Bradley) *pressed ldr on outer: led narrowly over 1f out: rdn whn hdd wl over 1f out: wknd ins fnl f* **10/1**

0400 **7** *9* **Emerald Bay**[58] 3009 3-9-4 58 MartinHarley 5 53
(Ivan Furtado) *led narrowly: hdd over 3f out: remained cl up tl wknd appr fnl f* **10/1**

-000 **8** *3 1/4* **Sun In His Eyes**[15] 4546 4-8-10 46 oh1 (p) ShaneGray 9 42
(Ed de Giles) *hld up: rdn over 2f out: sn btn* **40/1**

6040 **9** *3 1/2* **Guilded Rock**[28] 4085 3-9-0 54 (t) TedDurcan 2 49
(Stuart Kittow) *s.i.s: sn pushed along in rr: a bhd* **14/1**

1m 15.14s (0.64) **Going Correction** 0.0s/f (Stan)
WFA 3 from 4yo+ 4lb **9** Ran SP% **113.6**
Speed ratings (Par 101): **95,94,94,90,90 89,77,73,68**
CSF £24.87 CT £86.67 TOTE £4.70: £1.80, £1.70, £2.00; EX 28.40 Trifecta £123.10.
Owner E A Hayward **Bred** Whitsbury Manor Stud **Trained** Sedbury, Gloucs

FOCUS
A tight finish to this distinctly moderate handicap, which was the slower division by 0.25sec. Straightforward low-grade form.

5127 PORSCHE CENTRE WOLVERHAMPTON LAUNCH H'CAP (DIV II) 5f 216y (Tp)

2:50 (2:53) (Class 6) (0-60,59) 3-Y-O+ **£2,587** (£770; £384; £192) **Stalls** Low

Form RPR

0453 **1** **Virile (IRE)**[2] 5007 5-8-11 53 (bt) MitchGodwin(7) 9 64
(Sylvester Kirk) *sn trckd ldr racing keenly: led on bit over 1f out: sn pushed clr: comf* **10/11**[1]

0054 **2** *2 1/4* **Whipphound**[16] 4513 8-9-1 50 (p) TomEaves 3 54
(Ruth Carr) *midfield: hdwy 2f out: rdn to chse ldr 1f out: kpt on but no ch w wnr* **7/1**[3]

3625 **3** *3 1/4* **Dream Ally (IRE)**[13] 4647 6-9-7 56 (be) DarryllHolland 5 49
(John Weymes) *led: rdn whn hdd over 1f out: wknd ins fnl f* **5/1**[2]

2000 **4** *1 3/4* **Orlando Rogue (IRE)**[16] 4528 4-9-7 59 (b[1]) JosephineGordon(3) 4 47
(Conor Dore) *midfield towards outer: rdn over 2f out: no imp* **9/1**

0-04 **5** *nk* **Bilash**[127] 1164 9-8-12 47 PaulQuinn 7 34
(Sarah Hollinshead) *hld up: rdn over 2f out: nvr threatened* **33/1**

0063 **6** *1* **Tulip Dress**[15] 4570 3-9-5 58 RichardKingscote 1 41
(Anthony Carson) *s.i.s: hld up in midfield: rdn 2f out: nvr threatened* **7/1**[3]

-004 **7** *1 1/2* **Indian Tim**[17] 4484 4-8-10 45 FrannyNorton 2 24
(Milton Bradley) *chsd ldr: rdn over 2f out: wknd over 1f out* **12/1**

1400 **8** *8* **My Time**[16] 4516 7-8-10 48 (be) RobHornby(3) 6
(Michael Mullineaux) *slowly away: a in rr* **50/1**

1m 14.89s (0.39) **Going Correction** 0.0s/f (Stan)
WFA 3 from 4yo+ 4lb **8** Ran SP% **116.6**
Speed ratings (Par 101): **97,94,89,87,86 85,83,72**
CSF £8.28 CT £22.55 TOTE £2.20: £1.30, £2.00, £1.20; EX 8.60 Trifecta £25.70.
Owner Gerry Dolan **Bred** B Holland, S Hillen & J Cullinan **Trained** Upper Lambourn, Berks

FOCUS
The quicker division by 0.25sec.

5128 FCL GLOBAL FORWARDING MAKING LOGISTICS PERSONAL FILLIES' (S) STKS 5f 216y (Tp)

3:20 (3:23) (Class 6) 2-Y-O **£2,587** (£770; £384; £192) **Stalls** Low

Form RPR

0605 **1** **Tennessee Rose (IRE)**[18] 4457 2-8-12 58 RichardKingscote 2 59
(Tom Dascombe) *trckd ldr on inner: pushed along to ld ins fnl f: rdn out fnl 110yds: shade cosily* **5/4**[1]

51U0 **2** *3/4* **Eva Gore**[5] 4915 2-8-11 65 JoshDoyle(5) 6 61
(David O'Meara) *led: rdn 2f out: hdd ins fnl f: kpt on but a hld* **5/2**[2]

2005 **3** *2 1/4* **Black Redstart**[42] 3592 2-8-5 60[1] MitchGodwin(7) 1 49+
(Alan Bailey) *awkward s and lost 5 l: sn rcvrd and hld up in tch: rdn and hdwy on outer 2f out: one pce fnl f* **5/1**[3]

555 **4** *7* **Secret Coin (IRE)**[61] 2933 2-8-12 58 TimmyMurphy 9 27
(Jamie Osborne) *trckd ldr: rdn 2f out: lost pl over 1f out and sn btn* **6/1**

0 **5** *1/2* **Elmley Queen**[9] 4759 2-8-5 0 JoshuaBryan(7) 5 25
(Roy Brotherton) *racd keenly in tch on outer: rdn to briefly chse ldr over 1f out: wknd fnl f* **28/1**

1m 16.22s (1.72) **Going Correction** 0.0s/f (Stan) **5** Ran SP% **107.4**
Speed ratings (Par 89): **88,87,84,74,74**
CSF £4.33 TOTE £1.90: £1.10, £2.90; EX 4.60 Trifecta £12.50.There was no bid winner
Owner The Roaring Twenties **Bred** Peter McCutcheon **Trained** Malpas, Cheshire

FOCUS
Four came out of this very modest event.

5129 FCL GLOBAL FORWARDING MAKING LOGISTICS PERSONAL MAIDEN STKS 1m 4f 50y (Tp)

3:50 (3:51) (Class 5) 3-Y-O+ **£3,234** (£962; £481; £240) **Stalls** Low

Form RPR

22 **1** **To Eternity**[21] 4367 3-8-10 0 RobertHavlin 8 77+
(John Gosden) *mde all: pushed clr over 1f out: rdn out ins fnl f: comf* **2/11**[1]

0 **2** *3* **Fashion Design (IRE)**[53] 3235 3-8-10 0 TedDurcan 7 72+
(Sir Michael Stoute) *trckd ldr: rdn over 3f out: one pce and a hld* **9/2**[2]

5 **3** *nk* **Rasmee**[43] 3578 3-8-12 0 DanielMuscutt(3) 3 77
(Marco Botti) *midfield: sme hdwy over 3f out: rdn to go 3rd over 2f out: one pce* **10/1**[3]

4 *5* **Versant** 4-9-12 0 (t) MartinHarley 5 69
(Seamus Durack) *slowly away: hld up: pushed along and hdwy over 3f out: rdn over 2f out: no further imp* **16/1**

50 **5** *1 3/4* **Coeur De Lion**[29] 4056 3-9-1 0 FergusSweeney 4 66
(Alan King) *trckd ldr: rdn and outpcd over 2f out: wknd fnl f* **10/1**[3]

0P **6** *39* **Super Seer**[140] 980 3-9-1 0 WilliamTwiston-Davies 6 4
(Philip Hide) *in tch: pushed along over 6f out: lost pl 4f out: wknd over 2f out: eased* **50/1**

7 *3/4* **Rayanne** 3-8-10 0[1] PatrickMathers 9
(Sarah Hollinshead) *s.i.s: a towards rr* **50/1**

0/00 **8** *3* **Not Another Bill**[35] 3845 5-9-12 0 GeorgeBaker 1
(Chris Wall) *midfield: rdn over 3f out: sn wknd and eased* **50/1**

9 *9* **Kindled** 3-8-7 0 RobHornby(3) 2
(Ed McMahon) *a bhd* **50/1**

2m 37.63s (-3.17) **Going Correction** 0.0s/f (Stan)
WFA 3 from 4yo+ 11lb **9** Ran SP% **134.7**
Speed ratings (Par 103): **110,108,107,104,103 77,76,74,68**
CSF £2.38 TOTE £1.10: £1.02, £1.50, £2.30; EX 2.80 Trifecta £8.80.
Owner Lady Bamford **Bred** Lady Bamford **Trained** Newmarket, Suffolk
■ Stewards' Enquiry : Robert Havlin two-day ban; used his whip down the shoulder (22nd-23rd Aug)

FOCUS
This lacked depth and proved straightforward for the short-priced favourite. The level is a bit fluid.

5130 FCLGF.COM H'CAP 1m 1f 103y (Tp)

4:20 (4:20) (Class 6) (0-65,65) 3-Y-O+ **£2,587** (£770; £384; £192) **Stalls** Low

Form RPR

10/3 **1** **Amthal (IRE)**[41] 3642 7-9-13 64 TedDurcan 10 71
(Lucy Wadham) *midfield: hdwy over 2f out: rdn to ld wl over 1f out: drvn fnl f: kpt on: all out* **5/2**[2]

0035 **2** *nk* **Hussar Ballad (USA)**[49] 3342 7-9-13 64 PJMcDonald 1 70
(Antony Brittain) *hld up in midfield: stl bit to do 2f out: rdn and hdwy over 1f out: kpt on wl fnl f: jst hld* **13/2**[3]

000 **3** *1* **Tenerezza (IRE)**[21] 4361 3-9-6 65 GeorgeBaker 3 69
(David Lanigan) *in tch on inner: angled towards outer 2f out: rn wd on bnd wl over 1f out: sn rdn to chse ldr: hung lft appr fnl f: one pce fnl 110yds* **2/1**[1]

2315 **4** *8* **Filament Of Gold (USA)**[11] 4715 5-9-3 61 (p) MitchGodwin(7) 7 50
(Roy Brotherton) *trckd ldr: rdn over 2f out: wknd over 1f out* **13/2**[3]

2400 **5** *3* **Shining Romeo**[36] 3823 4-9-11 65 TimClark(3) 11 48
(Denis Quinn) *trckd ldr on outer: led 3f out: rdn whn hdd wl over 1f out: sn wknd* **12/1**

0506 **6** *2 3/4* **Andaz**[14] 4600 3-9-1 63 (e) JacobButterfield(3) 2 41
(Marjorie Fife) *hld up: rdn over 3f out: sn btn* **28/1**

40-0 **7** *1 1/2* **Quina Brook (IRE)**[11] 4718 3-9-6 65 DaleSwift 12 40
(Daniel Mark Loughnane) *swtchd lft s: hld up: a towards rr* **33/1**

2600 **8** *hd* **Cahar Fad (IRE)**[18] 4456 4-9-4 55 (bt) RobertHavlin 6 30
(Steph Hollinshead) *led: hdd 3f out: wknd* **17/2**

2m 0.64s (-0.16) **Going Correction** 0.0s/f (Stan)
WFA 3 from 4yo+ 8lb **8** Ran SP% **113.2**
Speed ratings (Par 101): **100,99,98,91,89 86,85,85**
CSF £18.76 CT £37.07 TOTE £2.90: £1.40, £1.30, £1.40; EX 17.50 Trifecta £54.80.
Owner C E Brittain **Bred** Shadwell Estate Company Limited **Trained** Newmarket, Suffolk

FOCUS
Three finished clear in this low-grade handicap.

5131 INCO CONTRACTS H'CAP 2m 119y (Tp)

4:50 (4:51) (Class 5) (0-75,73) 4-Y-O+ **£3,234** (£962; £481; £240) **Stalls** Low

Form RPR

1011 **1** **Lady Makfi (IRE)**[17] 4478 4-9-7 73 StevieDonohoe 1 84+
(Johnny Farrelly) *hld up: hdwy and trckd ldr gng wl 4f out: led on bit 2f out: pushed 5 l clr tl eased fnl 110yds* **11/8**[2]

-464 **2** *1* **Dovils Date**[24] 1550 7-8-11 70 MitchGodwin(7) 2 74
(Tim Vaughan) *hld up in rr: rdn over 6f out: sme hdwy over 2f out: wnt 2nd over 1f out: styd on but flattered by proximity to eased wnr* **11/1**[3]

6-25 **3** *10* **Cry Fury**[11] 4716 8-8-13 **65**........ SaleemGolam 3 60
(Sophie Leech) *chsd ldr: rdn over 3f out: led over 2f out: hdd 2f out: already wkng whn briefly short of room on inner wl over 1f out* **20/1**

1-31 **4** *47* **Rainbow Pride (IRE)**[7] 4816 4-9-2 **68**........(p) MartinHarley 4 4
(Sir Mark Prescott Bt) *led: racd keenly and sn clr: reduced advantage 10f out: rdn over 3f out: hdd over 2f out: wknd qckly: eased* **10/11**[1]

3m 40.79s (-2.91) **Going Correction** 0.0s/f (Stan) **4** Ran SP% **107.6**
Speed ratings (Par 103): **106,105,100,78**
CSF £13.09 TOTE £2.00; EX 15.70 Trifecta £45.40.
Owner The Lansdowners **Bred** Coleman Bloodstock Limited **Trained** Enmore, Somerset

FOCUS
The first part of this was run at a strong gallop, before the pace slowed with a circuit left. The winner continues to progress, but there's a bit of a doubt about what else ran its race.

5132 FCL GLOBAL FORWARDING MAKING LOGISTICS PERSONAL H'CAP 1m 141y (Tp)
5:20 (5:20) (Class 6) (0-60,60) 3-Y-O+ **£2,587** (£770; £384; £192) **Stalls** Low

Form RPR
0054 **1** **King Oswald (USA)**[11] 4718 3-8-11 **58**........ RobHornby(3) 4 66
(James Unett) *hld up: stl plenty to do 2f out: rdn and gd hdwy on outer over 1f out: led ins fnl f: kpt on wl* **3/1**[1]

060 **2** *3/4* **Gold Return (IRE)**[25] 4213 3-8-12 **56**........ StevieDonohoe 11 62
(David Lanigan) *trckd ldrs: rdn over 2f out: kpt on wl fnl f* **14/1**

620 **3** *2* **Schottische**[39] 3731 6-8-10 **53**........(p) MitchGodwin(7) 8 55
(Alan Bailey) *trckd ldr: rdn to chal 2f out: led narrowly appr fnl f: hdd ins fnl f: no ex* **14/1**

5465 **4** *nk* **Check 'Em Tuesday (IRE)**[14] 4587 3-9-2 **60**........ DaleSwift 7 62
(Daniel Mark Loughnane) *trckd ldr: rdn over 2f out: no ex fnl 110yds* **10/1**

0203 **5** *1/2* **Grey Destiny**[31] 3988 6-9-9 **59**........ PJMcDonald 10 60
(Antony Brittain) *s.i.s: hld up in midfield: rdn and hdwy over 1f out: swtchd lft ent fnl f: one pce* **11/2**

6 *1/2* **Chatterton (IRE)**[24] 4242 6-9-4 **54**........(t) WilliamTwiston-Davies 3 53
(Paul W Flynn, Ire) *midfield: rdn and outpcd 2f out: sltly hmpd ent fnl f: kpt on* **7/2**[2]

-006 **7** *2 1/4* **Haames (IRE)**[41] 3648 9-8-7 **46** oh1........ EoinWalsh(3) 5 41
(Kevin Morgan) *midfield: rdn over 2f out: wknd fnl 110yds* **25/1**

4440 **8** *1* **Ixelles Diamond (IRE)**[70] 2646 5-9-3 **60**........ NatalieHambling(7) 1 53
(Andrew Reid) *dwlt: hld up: rdn over 2f out: nvr threatened* **12/1**

0-05 **9** *1* **Zamastar**[25] 4200 5-9-4 **54**........(p) JackMitchell 6 45
(Brendan Powell) *led: rdn over 2f out: hdd appr fnl f: wknd* **9/2**[3]

660 **10** *7* **On The Clock**[21] 4361 3-7-13 **46** oh1........ NoelGarbutt(3) 2 22
(Denis Quinn) *in tch on inner: rdn over 2f out: wknd over 1f out* **50/1**

0 **11** *24* **Duke Of Dance (IRE)**[31] 3973 6-8-7 **46** oh1........(p) TimClark(3) 12
(Denis Quinn) *hld up in rr: rdn 4f out: sn wknd and t.o* **66/1**

1m 50.42s (0.32) **Going Correction** 0.0s/f (Stan)
WFA 3 from 5yo+ 8lb **11** Ran SP% **118.2**
Speed ratings (Par 101): **98,97,95,95,94 94,92,91,90,84 63**
CSF £46.51 CT £527.23 TOTE £4.50: £1.70, £5.50, £3.80; EX 75.50 Trifecta £536.30.
Owner M Watkinson & P Steadman **Bred** Darley **Trained** Wolverhampton, West Midlands

FOCUS
This modest handicap was run at a steady gallop and not many got into it.
T/Plt: £3.90 to a £1 stake. Pool: £55,038.33 - 10,174.02 winning tickets T/Qpdt: £1.50 to a £1 stake. Pool: £5,112.73 - 2,436.91 winning tickets **Andrew Sheret**

5133 - 5135a (Foreign Racing) - See Raceform Interactive

4168 TIPPERARY (L-H)
Friday, August 5

OFFICIAL GOING: Yielding to soft

5136a COOLMORE CANFORD CLIFFS STKS (LISTED RACE) 7f 100y
5:55 (5:56) 2-Y-O
£23,860 (£7,683; £3,639; £1,617; £808; £404)

RPR
1 **Capri (IRE)**[6] 4897 2-9-3........(t) SeamieHeffernan 5 103
(A P O'Brien, Ire) *led after 1f: rdn to extend advantage under 2f out: styd on wl ins fnl f* **8/11**[1]

2 *2* **Boyfriend Brian (IRE)**[25] 4216 2-9-3........ ColinKeane 7 98+
(G M Lyons, Ire) *hld up in 5th: travelled wl to take clsr order under 2f out: rdn to chse ldr in 2nd over 1f out: kpt on wl in clr 2nd: nt rch wnr* **10/1**

3 *3 3/4* **Intern (IRE)**[22] 4323 2-9-3........ WayneLordan 1 89
(David Wachman, Ire) *chsd ldrs in 4th on inner: pushed along under 3f out: wnt 3rd under 2f out: no imp ent fnl f: kpt on same pce* **11/1**

4 *3/4* **Elusive Beauty (IRE)**[40] 3694 2-8-12........ ShaneFoley 6 83
(K J Condon, Ire) *hld up in 6th: pushed along under 3f out in rr: kpt on into 5th ent fnl f: wnt 4th fnl 50yds: nvr nrr* **16/1**

5 *1* **Branch Line (IRE)**[53] 3237 2-9-3........ BillyLee 3 85
(Andrew Slattery, Ire) *sn chsd ldrs in 3rd: rdn and nt qckn in 5th over 1f out: kpt on same pce fnl f* **6/1**[3]

6 *nk* **Right Honourable (IRE)**[11] 4719 2-9-3........ PatSmullen 2 85
(D K Weld, Ire) *led for 1f: chsd ldr in 2nd: nt qckn w ldr under 2f out: no imp in 4th 1f out: wknd* **5/1**[2]

7 *16* **Elizabeth Browning (IRE)**[13] 4670 2-8-12........ ColmO'Donoghue 4 42
(A P O'Brien, Ire) *a towards rr: rdn and no imp under 2f out: wknd ins fnl f and eased fnl 100yds* **25/1**

1m 36.43s (96.43) **7** Ran SP% **116.0**
CSF £9.74 TOTE £1.50: £1.10, £3.10; DF 9.50 Trifecta £45.10.
Owner Derrick Smith & Mrs John Magnier & Michael Tabor **Bred** Lynch Bages Ltd & Camas Park Stud **Trained** Cashel, Co Tipperary

FOCUS
This was a high-quality renewal. The winner made all and looks a top-class prospect. The front two pulled nicely clear.

5137 - 5140a (Foreign Racing) - See Raceform Interactive

5004 DEAUVILLE (R-H)
Friday, August 5

OFFICIAL GOING: Turf: soft; polytrack: standard

5141a PRIX DE BAVENT (CLAIMER) (2YO COLTS & GELDINGS) (TURF) 6f
1:45 (12:00) 2-Y-O **£9,926** (£3,970; £2,977; £1,985; £992)

RPR
1 **Forty Foot (IRE)** 2-8-11........(b) EddyHardouin 8 68
(Matthieu Palussiere, France) **26/1**

2 *3/4* **Fankairos Ranger (USA)** 2-9-4........ ChristopheSoumillon 1 73
(Cedric Rossi, France) **14/5**[2]

3 *nse* **Dolokhov**[5] 4924 2-8-11........(p) HugoJourniac(4) 3 70
(J S Moore) *nudged along in fnl trio: last and nt clr run wl over 2f out: sn in clr and rdn: styd on u.p fr over 1f out: jst missed 2nd* **19/5**[3]

4 *3/4* **Alfa Manifesto (FR)**[8] 2-9-4........(p) AntoineHamelin 7 71
(Matthieu Palussiere, France) **9/5**[1]

5 *3* **Ultimate Fight (FR)**[22] 2-9-1........ StephanePasquier 5 59
(F Monnier, France) **54/10**

6 *6* **Rinky Dink Dawn (IRE)**[18] 4471 2-8-11........ IoritzMendizabal 6 37
(J S Moore) *hld up in fnl trio: rdn and shortlived effrt 2f out: sn no imp: bhd fnl f* **14/1**

7 *2* **Battle Of Wits (IRE)**[20] 4386 2-8-11........ LouisBeuzelin 4 31
(J S Moore) *chsd ldng pair: rdn but nt qckn appr 2f out: sn btn* **19/1**

8 *2 1/2* **Backontheroadagain (IRE)**[6] 2-9-1........(b) TonyPiccone 2 27
(Matthieu Palussiere, France) **15/1**

1m 14.8s (3.80) **8** Ran SP% **120.1**
WIN (incl. 1 euro stake): 2.20 (Forty Foot coupled with Alfa Manifesto & Backontheroadagain). PLACES: 3.20, 1.80, 1.70. DF: 37.30. SF: 95.90.
Owner Mrs Theresa Marnane **Bred** A Cunningham, A Grace & O Hegarty **Trained** France

5142a PRIX D'HEROUVILLE (CLAIMER) (2YO FILLIES) (TURF) 6f
3:20 (12:00) 2-Y-O **£9,926** (£3,970; £2,977; £1,985; £992)

RPR
1 **Holy Makfi**[22] 4330 2-8-11........ StephanePasquier 9 75
(Y Gourraud, France) **69/10**[3]

2 *hd* **Rajeline (FR)**[33] 2-8-11........ HugoJourniac(4) 4 78
(M Nigge, France) **17/5**[1]

3 *1 1/2* **Tawaret (FR)**[36] 2-8-10........(p) ClementLecoeuvre(6) 12 75
(Mme M-C Naim, France) **11/1**

4 *shd* **Fongani (FR)**[73] 2-9-1........ Pierre-CharlesBoudot 11 73
(P Sogorb, France) **58/10**[2]

5 *3 1/2* **Sabawa (FR)** 2-9-1........ UmbertoRispoli 3 63
(R Rohne, Germany) **17/2**

6 *snk* **Secret Lady**[108] 2-8-11........ AlexisBadel 14 58
(Mme M Bollack-Badel, France) **8/1**

7 *1 1/2* **Miss Charlotte (IRE)**[18] 2-8-9........ MathieuPelletan(6) 15 58
(M Delcher Sanchez, France) **15/1**

8 *1* **Nadeschda (FR)**[26] 4187 2-9-1........ TonyPiccone 10 55
(Mario Hofer, Germany) **32/1**

9 *1 3/4* **Lady Sidney (FR)** 2-9-1........ ChristopheSoumillon 8 50
(R Le Dren Doleuze, France) **26/1**

10 *3/4* **Joyful Dream (IRE)**[14] 4586 2-8-11........ LouisBeuzelin 6 43
(J S Moore) *w ldrs: lost pl and rdn sn after 1/2-way: bhd fr wl over 1f out* **58/1**

11 *3/4* **Malagueta (FR)**[12] 2-9-1........ ThierryJarnet 2 45
(A De Watrigant, France) **10/1**

12 *6* **Fast Kar (IRE)**[59] 3006 2-8-11........ EddyHardouin 1 23
(Matthieu Palussiere, France) **42/1**

13 *1 1/4* **Kitgame (FR)**[42] 2-9-1........(p) MickaelBarzalona 5 23
(D Prod'Homme, France) **10/1**

P **Kalinka (FR)**[28] 2-9-1........ JulienAuge 7
(C Ferland, France) **19/1**

1m 14.28s (3.28) **14** Ran SP% **120.2**
WIN (incl. 1 euro stake): 7.90. PLACES: 2.30, 1.70, 3.10. DF: 12.10. SF: 35.40.
Owner Remy Dupuy-Naulot **Bred** S Lock **Trained** France

4622 ASCOT (R-H)
Saturday, August 6

OFFICIAL GOING: Good to firm (good in places on the round course; straight 8.8, round 8.0)
Wind: Light, across Weather: Fine, warm

5143 DUBAI DUTY FREE SHERGAR CUP DASH (H'CAP) 5f
1:15 (1:17) (Class 2) (0-105,105) 3-Y-O+
£22,131 (£7,749; £3,541; £2,763; £2,434; £1,773) **Stalls** High

Form RPR
32-4 **1** **In Salutem**[21] 4415 6-9-7 **98**........(t) ThierryJarnet 7 107
(K J Condon, Ire) *trckd ldng quartet: smooth prog to ld over 1f out: in command fnl f: rdn out* **9/2**[1]

1300 **2** *2* **Line Of Reason (IRE)**[8] 4824 6-10-0 **105**........ Kenichilkezoe 5 107
(Paul Midgley) *awkward s: wl in rr: pushed along and prog fr 2f out on outer: rdn and styd on to take 2nd last 100yds: no threat to wnr* **12/1**

0002 **3** *nk* **Out Do**[7] 4860 7-10-0 **105**........(v) Pierre-CharlesBoudot 12 106
(David O'Meara) *cl up: tried to chal on inner over 1f out: styd on same pce fnl f* **7/1**[3]

3203 **4** *nk* **Willytheconqueror (IRE)**[22] 4359 3-9-8 **102**........ JoeFanning 6 101
(William Muir) *trckd ldrs: wnt 2nd 2f out to over 1f out: kpt on same pce after* **8/1**

0666 **5** *nk* **Medicean Man**[15] 4584 10-9-13 **104**........(tp) FrankieDettori 1 103
(Jeremy Gask) *wl in rr: cajoled along and prog on outer over 1f out: chsd ldrs fnl f: one pce last 100yds* **5/1**[2]

0000 **6** *nk* **Stepper Point**[15] 4584 7-9-3 **97**........(p) JosephineGordon(3) 9 94
(William Muir) *led to over 1f out: fdd* **14/1**

6030 **7** *1/2* **Poyle Vinnie**[7] 4865 6-9-10 **101**........ HayleyTurner 10 97
(Michael Appleby) *taken down early: dwlt: towards rr: urged along 2f out: hanging and nt qckn over 1f out: plugged on* **12/1**

 The Form Book, Raceform Ltd, Newbury, RG14 5SJ

0-25 **8** 1 3/4 **Union Rose**[28] 4126 4-9-6 **97**........................ SilvestreDeSousa 8 86
(Ronald Harris) *chsd ldr to 2f out: wknd* **5/1**[2]

0300 **9** 2 **Ninjago**[7] 4865 6-9-6 **97**........................(b) Emma-JayneWilson 11 79
(Paul Midgley) *a towards rr: rdn and no prog over 1f out* **12/1**

-065 **10** 1 3/4 **Burnt Sugar (IRE)**[7] 4860 4-9-13 **104**........................(b) MartinHarley 4 80
(Richard Hannon) *s.s: a wl in rr: nvr a factor* **8/1**

59.47s (-1.03) **Going Correction** -0.025s/f (Good)
WFA 3 from 4yo+ 3lb **10** Ran SP% **116.0**
Speed ratings (Par 109): **107,103,103,102,102 101,101,98,95,92**
CSF £58.28 CT £384.14 TOTE £5.40: £1.80, £3.80, £2.60; EX 55.80 Trifecta £482.70.
Owner Declan R Ryan & Mrs Pauline Condon **Bred** Mrs R Wilson **Trained** Rathbride, Co Kildare

FOCUS
A glorious day for the unique annual event and the ground was upgraded to Good to firm on the straight course, while it was Good to firm, good in places on the round. The rail on the round course was positioned approx 3yds out from its innermost position from the 1m4f start increasing to 9yds out at the bend entering the home straight. This good-quality sprint handicap was run at a decent pace and the main action was near the stands' rail. Solid form. The third has been rated close to his latest.

5144 DUBAI DUTY FREE SHERGAR CUP STAYERS (H'CAP) 2m

1:45 (1:45) (Class 2) (0-100,100) 4-Y-O+

£22,192 (£7,810; £3,603; £2,824; £2,496; £1,834) **Stalls** Low

Form RPR

1100 **1** **Arch Villain (IRE)**[11] 4734 7-10-0 **100**........................(b) GLerena 12 107
(Amanda Perrett) *prog to ld after 2f: hdd 5f out and sn in 3rd: effrt to chal and w ldr 2f out: narrow ld fnl f: kpt on wl* **25/1**

-021 **2** nk **Sea Of Heaven (IRE)**[15] 4581 4-9-4 **90**........................ Kenichilkezoe 1 96+
(Sir Mark Prescott Bt) *t.k.h: hld up in 5th: plld out and prog to ld 5f out and sent for home: jnd 2f out: narrowly hdd fnl f: kpt on wl but jst hld* **3/1**[1]

-015 **3** 1 1/4 **Saigon City**[42] 3658 6-9-3 **92**........................ JosephineGordon(3) 3 98+
(Declan Carroll) *hld up in 7th: rdn and prog over 2f out: styd on to take 3rd last 100yds: unable to chal* **6/1**[2]

2425 **4** 1/2 **Gold Prince (IRE)**[11] 4734 4-9-10 **96**........................(b) HayleyTurner 2 100
(Sylvester Kirk) *hld up in 6th: prog over 2f out: drvn to chse ldng pair over 1f out: kpt on but unable to chal: lost 3rd last 100yds* **12/1**

0-66 **5** 1 1/4 **Noble Silk**[15] 4581 7-9-4 **90**........................(v) ThierryJarnet 10 93
(Lucy Wadham) *hld up in last: effrt on wd outside 3f out: rdn and prog 2f out: tried to cl on ldrs jst over 1f out: one pce after* **7/1**

1452 **6** hd **Haines**[42] 3657 5-9-5 **91**........................ Emma-JayneWilson 7 93
(Andrew Balding) *hld up in 8th: dropped to last and pushed along 3f out: kpt on same pce fnl 2f: n.d* **16/1**

-012 **7** 1 **Serena Grae**[52] 3278 5-9-5 **91**........................ OisinMurphy 11 92
(Marcus Tregoning) *trckd ldr after 2f: chal jst over 5f out but sn chsd new ldr: lost 2nd and fdd fr 2f out* **12/1**

3452 **8** 6 **Two Jabs**[28] 4162 6-9-1 **87**........................ FrankieDettori 6 81
(Michael Appleby) *taken down early: led 2f: chsd ldng pair: rdn and lost pl 3f out: wknd over 1f out* **13/2**[3]

-210 **9** 3 3/4 **Green Light**[35] 3889 5-9-8 **94**........................(v) SilvestreDeSousa 5 84
(Ralph Beckett) *s.s: mostly in last trio: rdn 3f out: wknd 2f out* **10/1**

0003 **P** **Notarised**[11] 4734 5-10-0 **100**........................ JoeFanning 8
(Mark Johnston) *trckd ldng trio: hmpd over 5f out: pushed along and disputing 4th whn broke down jst over 2f out: p.u: fatally injured* **6/1**[2]

3m 27.35s (-1.65) **Going Correction** +0.05s/f (Good) **10** Ran SP% **113.6**
Speed ratings (Par 109): **106,105,105,104,104 104,103,100,98,**
CSF £96.74 CT £523.80 TOTE £27.50: £7.60, £1.50, £2.00; EX 136.30 Trifecta £1974.40.
Owner Mr & Mrs F Cotton, Mr & Mrs P Conway **Bred** Summerhill Bloodstock **Trained** Pulborough, W Sussex

■ Stewards' Enquiry : Emma-Jayne Wilson four-day ban: used whip above permitted level (Aug 20-23)

FOCUS
Race distance increased 16yds. There was a messy pace on in this decent staying handicap. The form looks pretty limited. The fourth has been rated to his recent form at shorter.

5145 DUBAI DUTY FREE SHERGAR CUP CHALLENGE (H'CAP) 1m 4f

2:20 (2:21) (Class 3) (0-95,95) 4-Y-O+

£22,131 (£7,749; £3,541; £2,763; £2,434; £1,773) **Stalls** Low

Form RPR

0001 **1** **Mistiroc**[29] 4095 5-9-9 **91**........................(v) MartinHarley 6 100
(John Quinn) *mde all: gng strly over 2f out: drew clr over 1f out: drvn out and nvr in any real danger* **12/1**

-250 **2** 1 1/4 **Duretto**[35] 3889 4-9-12 **94**........................ Emma-JayneWilson 10 101+
(Andrew Balding) *hld up disputing 5th: prog 2f out: rdn to chse ldng pair over 1f out: tk 2nd last 100yds: clsd on wnr but nvr able to threaten* **11/2**[3]

0023 **3** 1 1/4 **Darshini**[24] 4276 4-9-8 **90**........................ JoeFanning 9 95
(Sir Michael Stoute) *chsd wnr: rdn and no imp over 2f out: lost 2nd last 100yds: kpt on* **7/1**

40-1 **4** 1 3/4 **Great Glen**[21] 4384 4-9-13 **95**........................ OisinMurphy 8 97
(Ralph Beckett) *t.k.h: trckd ldng pair 3f: styd cl up: rdn and outpcd over 2f out: kpt on one pce after* **5/1**[2]

2000 **5** 2 1/4 **Silver Quay (IRE)**[11] 4731 4-9-8 **90**........................ SilvestreDeSousa 12 89+
(Richard Hannon) *hld up in last pair: plenty to do 3f out: rdn and no prog over 2f out: sn pushed along: nrst fin but n.d* **14/1**

334 **6** 1 **Plutocracy (IRE)**[15] 4583 6-9-5 **90**........................(b[1]) JosephineGordon(3) 11 87+
(Gary Moore) *hld up in last pair: plenty to do 3f out: sn rdn and no prog: kpt on fnl f* **17/2**

2211 **7** hd **Ruwasi**[15] 4598 5-9-10 **92**........................ FrankieDettori 4 89
(James Tate) *t.k.h: hld up disputing 5th: rdn wl over 2f out and no prog: n.d after* **3/1**[1]

0-46 **8** shd **Leah Freya (IRE)**[22] 4353 5-9-8 **90**........................ Pierre-CharlesBoudot 7 87
(Pat Phelan) *hld up towards rr: rdn and slt prog over 2f out: sn no imp on ldrs* **20/1**

5506 **9** hd **Blue Surf**[42] 3670 7-9-11 **93**........................ Kenichilkezoe 2 89
(Amanda Perrett) *trckd ldng pair after 3f to over 2f out: wknd* **20/1**

114 **10** 3 1/2 **Baadi**[42] 3670 4-9-6 **88**........................(v[1]) GLerena 5 79
(Charlie Fellowes) *hld up towards rr: rdn and no real prog over 2f out: no ch after* **8/1**

2m 31.74s (-0.76) **Going Correction** +0.05s/f (Good) **10** Ran SP% **115.1**
Speed ratings (Par 107): **104,103,102,101,99 99,98,98,98,96**
CSF £75.65 CT £498.90 TOTE £12.60: £3.50, £2.30, £2.20; EX 101.80 Trifecta £806.60.
Owner Drew & Ailsa Russell **Bred** Jethro Bloodstock **Trained** Settrington, N Yorks

FOCUS
Race distance increased 13yds. This quality handicap was another race where it proved tricky to get involved from off the pace and the winner dictated. The third helps set the standard.

5146 DUBAI DUTY FREE SHERGAR CUP MILE (H'CAP) 1m (R)

2:55 (2:55) (Class 2) (0-100,99) 4-Y-O+

£22,131 (£7,749; £3,541; £2,763; £2,434; £1,773) **Stalls** Low

Form RPR

-100 **1** **Early Morning (IRE)**[28] 4163 5-9-10 **98**........................ HayleyTurner 12 104
(Harry Dunlop) *wl away fr wd draw: trckd ldr: led 2f out gng wl: rdn and edgd rt over 1f out: hrd pressed fnl f: hld on wl* **6/1**[2]

2000 **2** 1/2 **Emell**[14] 4625 6-9-10 **98**........................(b) JoeFanning 3 103
(Richard Hannon) *hld up off the pce in 9th: prog over 2f out: swtchd ins over 1f out: drvn and styd on to take 2nd nr fin* **12/1**

5532 **3** nk **Highland Colori (IRE)**[7] 4887 8-9-10 **98**........................(v) Pierre-CharlesBoudot 5 102
(Andrew Balding) *chsd ldng trio: rdn over 2f out: clsd over 1f out to dispute 2nd fnl f: kpt on but a hld* **6/1**[2]

-000 **4** nk **Bancnuanaheireann (IRE)**[177] 540 9-9-8 **96**........................ ThierryJarnet 2 99
(Michael Appleby) *chsd ldrs disputing 5th: rdn to cl fr 2f out: disp 2nd 1f out: one pce ins fnl f* **8/1**

4620 **5** 1/2 **Beach Bar (IRE)**[126] 1196 5-9-8 **99**........................ JosephineGordon(3) 9 101
(Brendan Powell) *taken down early: led at gd pce: hdd 2f out: lost 2nd and one pce fnl f* **10/1**

5400 **6** 1 1/4 **Glory Awaits (IRE)**[28] 4152 6-9-9 **97**........................(b) GLerena 7 96
(David Simcock) *hld up disputing 7th: rdn and no rspnse over 2f out: plugged on fnl f: nrst fin but no ch* **7/1**[3]

100 **7** 3/4 **Capo Rosso (IRE)**[13] 4688 6-9-11 **99**........................ SilvestreDeSousa 1 97
(Tom Dascombe) *chsd ldng pair: rdn wl over 2f out: lost 3rd and wknd over 1f out* **12/1**

0000 **8** 3/4 **Balty Boys (IRE)**[14] 4625 7-9-10 **98**........................(b) OisinMurphy 4 94
(Brian Ellison) *hld up in detached last: drvn and no prog wl over 2f out: kpt on fnl f: nrst fin* **8/1**

2212 **9** 2 1/2 **George Cinq**[7] 4893 6-9-7 **95**........................ MartinHarley 10 85
(George Scott) *chsd ldrs on outer: rdn to cl over 2f out: n.m.r briefly over 1f out and sn wknd* **4/1**[1]

0000 **10** 4 1/2 **Majestic Moon (IRE)**[14] 4625 6-9-9 **97**........................ FrankieDettori 6 77
(John Gallagher) *hld up disputing 7th: rdn and no prog over 2f out: sn btn* **12/1**

1m 39.97s (-0.73) **Going Correction** +0.05s/f (Good) **10** Ran SP% **115.5**
Speed ratings (Par 109): **105,104,104,103,103 102,101,100,98,93**
CSF £74.63 CT £461.26 TOTE £6.00: £2.00, £3.30, £2.30; EX 74.90 Trifecta £620.20.
Owner Early Risers **Bred** Lakin Bloodstock/Wardley Bloodstock **Trained** Lambourn, Berks

■ Stewards' Enquiry : Hayley Turner four-day ban: used whip above permitted level (Aug 20-23)

FOCUS
Race distance increased 10yds. This competitive 1m handicap was run at a sound pace and the third gives it a good look. The third has been rated to his Newmarket latest.

5147 DUBAI DUTY FREE SHERGAR CUP CLASSIC (H'CAP) 1m 4f

3:30 (3:30) (Class 3) (0-95,91) 3-Y-O

£22,131 (£7,749; £3,541; £2,763; £2,434; £1,773) **Stalls** Low

Form RPR

4354 **1** **Danehill Kodiac (IRE)**[21] 4396 3-9-7 **84**........................ GLerena 6 96
(Richard Hannon) *hld up bhd two clr ldrs: lost 3rd 3f out but styd wl in tch: rdn and clsd to ld 2f out: styd on wl and in command fnl f* **10/1**

1565 **2** 2 **Combative**[8] 4827 3-9-9 **86**........................ SilvestreDeSousa 2 95
(Amanda Perrett) *trckd ldrs in 5th: lost pl over 3f out: drvn and prog over 2f out: chsd wnr over 1f out: styd on but no imp fnl f* **5/1**[2]

3131 **3** 3 **Real Dominion (USA)**[14] 4628 3-10-0 **91**........................ Emma-JayneWilson 4 95+
(Andrew Balding) *hld up in 9th: rapid prog on outer over 4f out to press ldng pair 3f out: chal and w wnr 2f out to over 1f out: no ex* **6/1**

4412 **4** 2 **Against The Odds**[6] 4920 3-9-8 **85**........................ OisinMurphy 9 86
(Paul Cole) *hld up in rr: rdn over 3f out: prog on outer over 2f out: one pce in 4th and no imp fnl f* **9/2**[1]

5 2 1/2 **Full Court Press (IRE)**[15] 4616 3-9-9 **86**........................ MartinHarley 1 83
(J P Murtagh, Ire) *hld up towards rr: rdn and prog to cl on ldrs whn nt clr run 2f out and lost momentum: no hdwy after: fdd ins fnl f* **15/2**

6152 **6** 1 **Kesselring**[14] 4628 3-9-3 **80**........................ Pierre-CharlesBoudot 12 75
(Richard Hannon) *in tch in chsng gp: rdn 3f out: lost pl 2f out: no ch after* **10/1**

2512 **7** 1 **Lord Yeats**[23] 4311 3-9-10 **87**........................ Kenichilkezoe 3 81
(Jedd O'Keeffe) *led at v str pce: hdd & wknd 2f out* **10/1**

312 **8** 9 **White Shaheen**[35] 3914 3-9-8 **88**........................ JosephineGordon(3) 8 67
(William Muir) *prom in chsng gp: wknd qckly jst over 2f out* **11/2**[3]

2-16 **9** 3 1/2 **King Of Dreams**[89] 2099 3-9-2 **79**........................(b[1]) ThierryJarnet 5 53
(David Simcock) *rushed up to press ldr and clr of rest: lost 2nd and wknd qckly jst over 2f out* **16/1**

0420 **10** 31 **Juste Pour Nous**[16] 4561 3-9-6 **83**........................ HayleyTurner 10 7
(Mark Johnston) *sn detached in last and tk no interest: t.o* **14/1**

2m 30.27s (-2.23) **Going Correction** +0.05s/f (Good) **10** Ran SP% **116.1**
Speed ratings (Par 104): **109,107,105,104,102 102,101,95,93,72**
CSF £59.15 CT £330.94 TOTE £14.00: £3.90, £2.00, £2.20; EX 77.40 Trifecta £523.70.
Owner Davies Smith Govier & Brown **Bred** Rathbarry Stud **Trained** East Everleigh, Wilts

FOCUS
Race distance increased 13yds. There was no hanging about in this fair 3yo handicap as the leaders went too hard. The runner-up has been rated as building on his Goodwood latest.

5148 DUBAI DUTY FREE SHERGAR CUP SPRINT (H'CAP) 6f

4:05 (4:05) (Class 2) (0-100,98) 3-Y-O

£22,131 (£7,749; £3,541; £2,763; £2,434; £1,773) **Stalls** High

Form RPR

2350 **1** **Kadrizzi (FR)**[30] 4062 3-9-13 **97**........................ ThierryJarnet 5 107
(Dean Ivory) *hld up in last: prog on wd outside 2f out: led 1f out: rdn out and styd on wl* **6/1**[3]

6103 **2** 2 **Flying Pursuit**[14] 4652 3-9-6 **90**........................ Pierre-CharlesBoudot 12 94
(Tim Easterby) *sltly awkward s: racd nr side and prom in chsng gp: clsd to ld wl over 1f out: hdd and one pce 1f out* **11/4**[1]

0-43 **3** 1 3/4 **Muhadathat**[9] 4803 3-9-12 **96**........................ Emma-JayneWilson 1 94
(Mark Johnston) *hld up on outer: prog over 2f out: disp 2nd briefly over 1f out: sn outpcd in 3rd* **4/1**[2]

1026 **4** 3 1/2 **Suqoor**[47] 3466 3-9-3 **87**........................ Kenichilkezoe 10 74
(Chris Dwyer) *prom in chsng gp: drvn to dispute 2nd briefly over 1f out: sn wl btn in 4th: fdd ins fnl f* **16/1**

16-0 **5** 1 **Sunflower**[84] 2242 3-9-11 **95**........................ MartinHarley 6 79
(Andrew Balding) *prom in chsng gp: rdn over 2f out: no prog and btn over 1f out: fdd* **10/1**

1200 **6** ½ **Papa Luigi (IRE)**[6] 4911 3-9-5 **89** .... OisinMurphy 8 71
(Richard Hannon) *in tch in chsng gp: rdn and dropped to last 2f out and no ch: plugged on fnl f* **8/1**

1311 **7** 2 **Black Bess**[23] 4306 3-9-2 **86** .... HayleyTurner 7 62
(Jim Boyle) *racd on outer: prom in chsng gp: lost pl u.p 2f out: wl btn after* **7/1**

0450 **8** ¾ **Exceed The Limit**[9] 4803 3-9-8 **92** .... GLerena 11 65
(Robert Cowell) *racd towards nr side: prom in chsng gp: wknd 2f out* **14/1**

2506 **9** 4 ½ **Field Of Vision (IRE)**[68] 2751 3-9-13 **97** .... JoeFanning 9 56
(Joseph Tuite) *prom in chsng gp: rdn and wknd 2f out* **20/1**

5-40 **10** 3 ¾ **Soapy Aitken**[35] 3909 3-10-0 **98** ....(b) FrankieDettori 4 45
(Clive Cox) *blasted off in ld: clr tl hdd & wknd rapidly wl over 1f out: eased* **8/1**

1m 13.15s (-1.35) **Going Correction** -0.025s/f (Good) **10** Ran SP% **122.1**
Speed ratings (Par 106): **108,105,103,98,97 96,93,92,86,81**
CSF £24.02 CT £78.59 TOTE £8.60: £2.40, £1.70, £1.90; EX 27.50 Trifecta £143.20.
Owner A Chapman & Wentdale Limited **Bred** Simon Urizzi & Yann Loizeau **Trained** Radlett, Herts

FOCUS
This decent 3yo sprint handicap saw a difference of opinion as to the best ground. The main action was down the middle. The winner has been rated back to the level of his AW form.
T/Plt: £81.20 to a £1 stake. Pool: £196,574.84 - 1,765.63 winning tickets T/Qpdt: £17.80 to a £1 stake. Pool: £10,723.86 - 443.69 winning tickets **Jonathan Neesom**

4699 AYR (L-H)

Saturday, August 6

OFFICIAL GOING: Good to soft (7.8)
Wind: fresh 1/2 against Weather: fine becoming overcast, breezy

5149 QTS INVESTORS IN YOUNG PEOPLE LADY RIDERS' H'CAP (FOR PROFESSIONAL AND AMATEUR LADY RIDERS) 1m

5:40 (5:41) (Class 6) (0-65,63) 4-Y-O+ **£2,587** (£770; £384; £192) **Stalls** Low

Form RPR

0002 **1** **Ted's Brother (IRE)**[5] 4929 8-9-3 **45** ....(e) MissAWaugh 3 51
(Richard Guest) *s.i.s: in rr: drvn and hdwy over 2f out: kpt on fnl f: led nr fin* **5/1**[3]

006U **2** nk **Drinks For Losers (IRE)**[12] 4705 5-9-3 **45** .... AnnaHesketh 1 50
(R Mike Smith) *trckd ldrs: 2nd over 3f out: led appr fnl f: hdd nr fin* **16/1**

022 **3** ¾ **Dolphin Rock**[22] 4335 9-10-7 **63** ....(b) MissSBrotherton 5 67
(Richard Ford) *led: hdd appr fnl f: kpt on same pce last 100yds* **5/2**[1]

00-0 **4** 1 ½ **Lipstickandpowder (IRE)**[40] 3706 4-8-12 **45** ....(bt[1]) PaulaMuir[(5)] 8 45
(Dianne Sayer) *trckd ldrs: edgd rt fnl 2f: kpt on one pce fnl f* **20/1**

3260 **5** 1 ¼ **Incurs Four Faults**[7] 4872 5-9-2 **49** ....(p) MissKWeir[(5)] 9 47
(Keith Dalgleish) *s.s: t.k.h: hdwy to trck ldrs 6f out: hung lft over 2f out: one pce* **11/2**

6604 **6** 1 ¾ **Yair Hill (IRE)**[13] 4683 8-9-5 **47** ....(p) MissHelenCuthbert 4 41
(Thomas Cuthbert) *hld up in rr: hdwy 2f out: styng on at fin* **22/1**

1113 **7** 1 ¾ **Vastly (USA)**[12] 4717 7-10-4 **60** ....(t) MrsClaireHardwick 2 50
(Sophie Leech) *mid-div: drvn and swtchd rt over 2f out: one pce* **3/1**[2]

0040 **8** hd **Haidees Reflection**[19] 4449 6-10-5 **61** .... MrsCBartley 6 51
(Jim Goldie) *hld up towards rr: pushed along over 3f out: kpt on one pce: nvr a factor* **16/1**

-042 **9** 5 **Poor Duke (IRE)**[23] 4290 6-9-5 **47** .... MissMMullineaux 7 26
(Michael Mullineaux) *mid-div: t.k.h: drvn and checked over 2f out: lost pl over 1f out* **9/1**

1m 44.72s (0.92) **Going Correction** +0.075s/f (Good) **9** Ran SP% **116.5**
Speed ratings (Par 101): **98,97,96,95,94 92,90,90,85**
CSF £80.83 CT £247.92 TOTE £5.90: £1.90, £3.80, £1.70; EX 75.90 Trifecta £483.70.
Owner Mrs Alison Guest **Bred** T Counihan **Trained** Ingmanthorpe, W Yorks
■ Stewards' Enquiry : Miss K Weir caution: careless riding
Anna Hesketh two-day ban: used whip above permitted level (Aug 20-21)

FOCUS
Race distance increased by 15yds. A low-grade pro-am handicap for women riders run at a good gallop with mostly exposed performers.

5150 QTS MISS SCOTLAND/BRITISH STALLION STUDS EBF MAIDEN STKS 7f 50y

6:10 (6:11) (Class 5) 2-Y-O **£3,234** (£962; £481; £240) **Stalls** High

Form RPR

2 **1** **Kings Gift (IRE)**[20] 4423 2-9-5 0 .... PaulMulrennan 4 77+
(Michael Dods) *trckd ldrs: t.k.h: effrt and edgd rt over 1f out: styd on to ld last 50yds* **2/1**[1]

5 **2** 1 ¼ **Thorndyke**[23] 4297 2-9-5 0 .... JoeDoyle 7 74
(Kevin Ryan) *led: shkn up 2f out: hdd narrowly 1f out: no ex last 50yds* **22/1**

4 **3** nse **Election Day**[23] 4297 2-9-5 0 .... GrahamLee 8 74
(Mark Johnston) *trckd ldrs: upsides over 3f out: led narrowly 1f out: kpt on same pce last 50yds* **15/2**

4 ½ **Souter** 2-9-5 0 .... JasonHart 5 73+
(Keith Dalgleish) *mid-div: pushed along over 4f out: chsng ldrs over 2f out: kpt on fnl 100yds* **20/1**

0 **5** 1 ½ **Yarmouk (FR)**[16] 4545 2-9-5 0 .... GeorgeChaloner 6 69
(Richard Fahey) *trckd ldrs: effrt over 2f out: fdd clsng stages* **7/2**[3]

6 8 **Quiet Weekend** 2-9-5 0 .... JoeyHaynes 2 49
(James Bethell) *s.i.s: hdwy after 2f: chsng ldrs over 4f out: hung lft: lost pl over 1f out* **20/1**

7 2 ½ **American Craftsman (IRE)** 2-9-5 0 .... DuranFentiman 3 43
(Jedd O'Keeffe) *dwlt: in rr: bhd fnl 3f* **33/1**

0322 **8** 15 **Wigan Warrior**[21] 4379 2-9-5 75 .... ShaneGray 1 5
(David Brown) *s.i.s: reminders after s: sn drvn along and detached in last: reminders over 3f out: eased clsng stages: lame* **9/4**[2]

1m 34.12s (0.72) **Going Correction** +0.075s/f (Good) **8** Ran SP% **114.9**
Speed ratings (Par 94): **98,96,96,95,94 85,82,65**
CSF £49.27 TOTE £2.50: £1.10, £4.30, £2.50; EX 48.00 Trifecta £267.10.
Owner Geoff & Sandra Turnbull **Bred** Old Carhue & Graeng Bloodstock **Trained** Denton, Co Durham
■ Stewards' Enquiry : Shane Gray vet said colt finished lame right-hind

FOCUS
Race distance increased by 15yds. Quite an interesting 7f juvenile maiden in which most were unexposed and the first five were clear.

5151 QTS TRAINING H'CAP 7f 50y

6:40 (6:41) (Class 5) (0-70,70) 3-Y-O+ **£3,234** (£962; £481; £240) **Stalls** High

Form RPR

0-54 **1** **Bahamian Bird**[15] 4604 3-8-8 **58** .... GeorgeChaloner 10 66
(Richard Fahey) *trckd ldrs: pushed along over 3f out: 2nd over 1f out: styd on wl to ld post* **16/1**

502 **2** shd **Jay Kay**[26] 4189 7-9-12 **70** .... JoeyHaynes 3 80
(K R Burke) *led: shkn up over 2f out: abt 3 l clr over 1f out: kpt on wl: hdd post* **9/2**[3]

0432 **3** 3 **Niqnaaqpaadiwaaq**[19] 4445 4-9-8 **66** .... NeilFarley 9 68
(Eric Alston) *trckd ldrs: t.k.h: effrt over 2f out: hung rt and kpt on same pce over 1f out* **8/1**

014 **4** shd **Rasaman (IRE)**[8] 4830 12-9-9 **67** .... JoeDoyle 7 69+
(Jim Goldie) *in rr: hdwy on outside over 2f out: kpt on fnl f* **14/1**

5 ½ **Crazy Tornado (IRE)**[45] 3541 3-9-6 **70** .... JasonHart 5 69
(Keith Dalgleish) *mid-div: effrt 3f out: swtchd outside over 1f out: styng on at fin* **28/1**

0246 **6** nk **Sophie P**[12] 4700 3-9-0 **69** .... GarryWhillans[(5)] 1 67
(R Mike Smith) *dwlt: in rr: hdwy over 4f out: chsng ldrs whn swtchd rt over 1f out: kpt on* **12/1**

0223 **7** ½ **Dark Command**[12] 4701 3-9-2 **66** ....(p) PaulMulrennan 2 63
(Michael Dods) *trckd ldrs: effrt over 2f out: one pce over 1f out: wl hld whn n.m.r and eased nr fin* **4/1**[2]

0046 **8** 1 **Mr Cool Cash**[11] 4729 4-9-1 **66** ....(t) BenRobinson[(7)] 4 62
(Richard Guest) *in rr: drvn 3f out: hdwy over 1f out: kpt on: nvr a threat* **15/2**

0002 **9** 3 ½ **Mime Dance**[3] 5030 5-9-5 **68** ....(p) JoshDoyle[(5)] 6 55
(David O'Meara) *hld up in mid-div: trcking ldrs over 4f out: rdn over 2f out: nvr a factor: wknd over 1f out: eased clsng stages* **11/4**[1]

3403 **10** 7 **Depth Charge (IRE)**[18] 4497 4-9-11 **69** ....(vt) ShaneGray 8 38
(Kristin Stubbs) *hld up in rr: sme hdwy over 2f out: lost pl over 1f out: eased clsng stages* **14/1**

1m 32.82s (-0.58) **Going Correction** +0.075s/f (Good)
WFA 3 from 4yo+ 6lb **10** Ran SP% **118.1**
Speed ratings (Par 103): **106,105,102,102,101 101,100,99,95,87**
CSF £87.77 CT £650.39 TOTE £22.20: £4.50, £2.00, £2.90; EX 145.10 Trifecta £2412.10.
Owner Lady Juliet Tadgell **Bred** Lady Juliet Tadgell **Trained** Musley Bank, N Yorks
■ Stewards' Enquiry : Joey Haynes two-day ban: used whip above permitted level (Aug 20-21)

FOCUS
Race distance increased by 15yds. A fair 7f handicap run at no more than a fair gallop with the first three in the first three virtually throughout. The runner-up has been rated similar to when winning this race last year off 1lb lower.

5152 GAS SURE & JAMES FREW H'CAP 6f

7:10 (7:12) (Class 6) (0-65,65) 3-Y-O+ **£2,587** (£770; £384; £192) **Stalls** High

Form RPR

3412 **1** **Tricky Dicky**[4] 4970 3-9-4 **61** .... DuranFentiman 6 68
(Olly Williams) *w ldrs: led after 1f: drvn rt out* **5/4**[1]

-000 **2** ¾ **Rock Canyon (IRE)**[5] 4932 7-9-4 **62** .... JoshDoyle[(5)] 9 67
(Linda Perratt) *mid-div: hdwy to chse ldrs over 1f out: kpt on to take 2nd last 75yds* **25/1**

206 **3** 2 **Lady Wootton**[35] 3882 3-8-11 **59** ....(v) ShirleyTeasdale[(5)] 2 57
(Keith Dalgleish) *trckd ldrs on outside: effrt over 1f out: kpt on same pce* **18/1**

3500 **4** 1 ½ **Blue Sonic**[18] 4488 6-9-12 **65** .... PaulMulrennan 3 60
(Linda Perratt) *half-rrd s: in rr: hdwy over 1f out: kpt on to take 4th last 50yds* **7/1**[3]

00-4 **5** ½ **Raise A Billion**[7] 4874 5-8-10 **49** .... GeorgeChaloner 7 42
(John David Riches) *led 1f: chsd ldrs: drvn over 2f out: one pce over 1f out* **5/1**[2]

0225 **6** ¾ **Goninodaethat**[12] 4701 8-9-4 **57** .... GrahamLee 5 48
(Jim Goldie) *chsd ldrs: hung lft: effrt over 2f out: one pce over 1f out* **7/1**[3]

10 **7** 4 ½ **Lady Cordie**[19] 4445 4-8-10 **49** .... JoeDoyle 1 26
(Jim Goldie) *mid-div: drvn over 2f out: lost pl over 1f out* **16/1**

5000 **8** nk **Amy Blair**[7] 4874 3-8-3 **46** .... JoeyHaynes 8 21
(Keith Dalgleish) *mid-div: lost pl over 2f out* **33/1**

113 **9** ¾ **Rio Deva (IRE)**[8] 4834 3-9-7 **64** .... JasonHart 10 37
(Keith Dalgleish) *chsd ldrs: drvn over 2f out: lost pl over 1f out* **8/1**

1m 12.76s (0.36) **Going Correction** +0.075s/f (Good)
WFA 3 from 4yo+ 4lb **9** Ran SP% **115.2**
Speed ratings (Par 101): **100,99,96,94,93 92,86,86,85**
CSF £39.26 CT £400.02 TOTE £2.10: £1.10, £6.80, £5.30; EX 37.20 Trifecta £811.00.
Owner Eight Gents and a Lady **Bred** Onslow, Stratton & Parry **Trained** Market Rasen, Lincs

FOCUS
A run-of-the-mill sprint with the winner a well-supported favourite.

5153 QTS LADIES' NIGHT GRAND SPECTACULAR H'CAP 5f

7:40 (7:43) (Class 4) (0-85,85) 3-Y-O+ **£5,498** (£1,636; £817; £408) **Stalls** High

Form RPR

1-00 **1** **Invincible Ridge (IRE)**[22] 4366 8-9-6 **81** .... NeilFarley 1 89
(Eric Alston) *racd wd: w ldrs: led last 100yds: all out* **17/2**

2160 **2** hd **Classy Anne**[8] 4831 6-9-3 **78** ....(p) JoeDoyle 8 85
(Jim Goldie) *trckd ldrs: effrt over 1f out: kpt on to take cl 2nd clsng stages: jst hld* **15/2**

4410 **3** ½ **Dark Defender**[14] 4643 3-9-7 **85** ....(v) JasonHart 5 89
(Keith Dalgleish) *led: drvn over 1f out: hdd and no ex last 100yds* **4/1**[1]

1631 **4** ½ **Ladweb**[36] 3857 6-9-8 **83** .... MichaelJMMurphy 6 86
(John Gallagher) *chsd ldrs: drvn 2f out: kpt on same pce last 150yds* **9/2**[2]

1300 **5** ¾ **Fredricka**[15] 4585 5-9-3 **83** .... JoshDoyle[(5)] 2 84
(David Barron) *mid-div: effrt over 2f out: chsng ldrs over 1f out: kpt on one pce* **7/1**[3]

0220 **6** 1 ½ **Ballesteros**[14] 4632 7-9-8 **83** .... GeorgeChaloner 9 78
(Richard Fahey) *mid-div: effrt over 2f out: kpt on same pce fnl f* **17/2**

3020 **7** ½ **Desert Ace (IRE)**[8] 4831 5-9-1 **81** ....(p) ShirleyTeasdale[(5)] 7 75
(Iain Jardine) *mid-div: effrt over 2f out: chsng ldrs over 1f out: kpt on one pce* **9/1**

-610 **8** 4 ½ **Economic Crisis (IRE)**[8] 4831 7-9-1 **76** .... PaulMulrennan 10 53
(John David Riches) *rrd s: sn chsng ldrs: lost pl over 1f out* **12/1**

1603 **9** 2 ¾ **Soul Brother (IRE)**[33] 3944 5-9-7 **82** ....(b) GrahamLee 3 49
(Tim Easterby) *in rr: lost pl over 3f out* **9/1**

6430 **10** *nk* **Something Lucky (IRE)**[15] 4608 4-9-4 **79**......................(p) ShaneGray 4 45
(Kristin Stubbs) *mid-div: hdwy over 2f out: lost pl over 1f out* **20/1**

59.02s (-0.38) **Going Correction** +0.075s/f (Good)
WFA 3 from 4yo+ 3lb **10** Ran SP% **116.0**
Speed ratings (Par 105): **106,105,104,104,102 100,99,92,88,87**
CSF £70.31 CT £304.42 TOTE £10.90: £3.50, £2.50, £1.40; EX 81.70 Trifecta £1291.90.
Owner Paul Buist & John Thompson **Bred** Con Harrington **Trained** Longton, Lancs

FOCUS

Quite a competitive sprint run at a decent gallop. The winner has been rated back to his best form over the past year or so.

5154 QTS GROUP H'CAP 1m 2f

8:10 (8:10) (Class 5) (0-75,75) 3-Y-O+ **£3,234** (£962; £481; £240) **Stalls** Low

Form RPR

3244 **1** **Tectonic (IRE)**[7] 4871 7-8-13 **60**..(v) JasonHart 7 67
(Keith Dalgleish) *stdd s: t.k.h: hdwy to trck ldrs after 3f: effrt 1f out: led last 100yds: hld on nr fin* **12/1**

201 **2** *shd* **Henpecked**[22] 4341 6-9-3 **69**......................................(p) GarryWhillans(5) 6 75
(Alistair Whillans) *hld up wl in tch: hdwy over 2f out: led narrowly 1f out: hdd last 100yds: kpt on: jst hld* **5/1**

0463 **3** *1 ¼* **Onda District (IRE)**[21] 4377 4-9-1 **69**...................... CallumRodriguez(7) 4 72+
(Richard Ford) *sn hld up in rr: hdwy over 2f out: nt clr run and swtchd rt over 1f out: styd on to take 3rd last 50yds* **9/1**

1453 **4** *2 ½* **Carnageo (FR)**[21] 4406 3-9-5 **75**.................................. GeorgeChaloner 5 73
(Richard Fahey) *led early: trckd ldrs: effrt over 2f out: fdd last 150yds* **11/4**[1]

4 **5** *2 ¼* **Khabaray (IRE)**[15] 4607 3-8-10 **71**.................................... JoshDoyle(5) 3 65
(David O'Meara) *trckd ldrs: led over 3f out: hdd 1f out: wknd last 100yds* **7/2**[3]

0504 **6** *7* **Haymarket**[12] 4702 7-9-1 **62**.. GrahamLee 2 42
(R Mike Smith) *trckd ldrs: effrt over 2f out: lost pl over 1f out* **18/1**

0300 **7** *3* **Arantes**[7] 4875 5-9-1 **62**.. PaulMulrennan 1 36
(R Mike Smith) *sn led: hdd over 3f out: lost pl over 1f out* **18/1**

8 *7* **Forcefull (IRE)**[12] 4722 3-8-4 **67**...................................... RobbieDolan(7) 8 27
(Adrian Paul Keatley, Ire) *s.i.s: jnd ldrs after 2f: drvn 3f out: lost pl wl over 1f out* **3/1**[2]

2m 11.97s (-0.03) **Going Correction** +0.075s/f (Good)
WFA 3 from 4yo+ 9lb **8** Ran SP% **118.8**
Speed ratings (Par 103): **103,102,101,99,98 92,90,84**
CSF £73.31 CT £578.46 TOTE £11.00: £2.70, £1.50, £3.40; EX 61.20 Trifecta £485.10.
Owner Mrs L A Ogilvie **Bred** W Maxwell Ervine **Trained** Carluke, S Lanarks

FOCUS

Race distance increased by 15yds. A handicap for three-year-olds in which the first three finished clear. The early pace was moderate but it picked up in the straight and the first and third were the last two turning for home. The third has been rated to his latest form.

5155 DAWN HOMES H'CAP 1m 7f

8:40 (8:40) (Class 6) (0-65,69) 4-Y-O+ **£2,587** (£770; £384; £192) **Stalls** Low

Form RPR

420- **1** **Bell Weir**[68] 7124 8-9-7 **65**..(bt[1]) PaulMulrennan 5 72
(Dianne Sayer) *hld up in mid-div: hdwy and swtchd rt over 3f out: led over 2f out: pushed abt 3 l clr 150yds out: idled: drvn out nr line* **12/1**

4-20 **2** *½* **Feeltherhythm (IRE)**[191] 368 5-8-4 **48**...........................(p) ShaneGray 8 52
(Chris Grant) *trckd ldrs: chsd wnr 2f out: kpt on fnl 75yds* **6/1**[2]

3535 **3** *1 ½* **Hero's Story**[1] 5118 6-8-10 **54**...(p) JoeDoyle 2 56
(Jim Goldie) *hld up in rr: t.k.h: hdwy over 2f out: kpt on to take 3rd last 50yds* **4/1**[1]

0006 **4** *½* **La Bacouetteuse (FR)**[5] 4935 11-9-2 **65**................(b) GarryWhillans(5) 6 67
(Iain Jardine) *hld up towards rr: hdwy over 3f out: kpt on over 1f out* **6/1**[2]

0563 **5** *2 ¼* **No Not Yet**[40] 3704 4-8-2 **46** oh1.. JoeyHaynes 7 45
(Michael Dods) *led: hdd over 2f out: wknd appr fnl f* **4/1**[1]

-032 **6** *8* **Gunner Lindley (IRE)**[27] 3706 9-9-1 **59**................................ JasonHart 1 48
(Stuart Coltherd) *dwlt: drvn along to sn chse ldrs: lost pl over 1f out* **7/1**[3]

-332 **7** *nk* **Maple Stirrup (IRE)**[14] 4645 4-8-6 **57**............................ PaulaMuir(7) 9 46
(Patrick Holmes) *mid-div: hdwy to trck ldrs after 5f: drvn along 4f out: lost pl over 2f out* **4/1**[1]

0 **8** *4* **Macalla (IRE)**[11] 2525 4-8-2 **46** oh1..........................(p) DuranFentiman 10 30
(R Mike Smith) *chsd ldrs: upside over 4f out: lost pl 2f out: sn bhd* **20/1**

5200 **9** *17* **Troy Boy**[11] 4724 6-7-9 **46** oh1..(v) RPWalsh(7) 3 10
(Rebecca Bastiman) *s.i.s: in rr: bhd and pushed along 6f out* **22/1**

3m 28.68s (8.28) **Going Correction** +0.075s/f (Good) **9** Ran SP% **117.9**
Speed ratings (Par 101): **80,79,78,78,77 73,73,70,61**
CSF £83.69 CT £345.55 TOTE £10.80: £3.50, £3.00, £1.80; EX 103.40 Trifecta £385.90.
Owner Sjd Racing & Dianne Sayer **Bred** Mrs I Russell **Trained** Hackthorpe, Cumbria

FOCUS

Race distance increased by 30yds. Just an ordinary staying handicap run at just an ordinary gallop. The winner pulled himself up inside the last furlong and is value for more than the winning margin.

T/Plt: £361.40 to a £1 stake. Pool: £75,403.89 - 152.30 winning units. T/Qpdt: £106.90 to a £1 stake. Pool: £6,112.59 - 42.30 winning units. **Walter Glynn**

5106 HAYDOCK (L-H)

Saturday, August 6

OFFICIAL GOING: Good to firm (8.5)
Wind: Moderate, across Weather: Fine

5156 BETFRED DUKE OF LANCASTER'S OWN YEOMANRY H'CAP (LONDON MILE SERIES QUALIFIER) 1m

2:00 (2:00) (Class 3) (0-95,95) 3-Y-O+ **£8,086** (£2,406; £1,202; £601) **Stalls** Low

Form RPR

1415 **1** **Treasury Notes (IRE)**[49] 3390 4-9-11 **92**...................... DanielTudhope 4 103+
(David O'Meara) *hld up in midfield: nt clr run over 2f out: hdwy over 1f out: r.o ins fnl f: led towards fin* **15/2**

3200 **2** *¾* **Lat Hawill (IRE)**[19] 4448 5-10-0 **95**...............................(v[1]) PhillipMakin 2 104
(Keith Dalgleish) *midfield: hdwy whn n.m.r over 2f out: sn swtchd lft: rdn to ld over 1f out: kpt on for press ins fnl f: hdd and nt pce of wnr towards fin* **25/1**

1642 **3** *hd* **Spring Offensive (IRE)**[22] 4374 4-9-5 **91**........... AdamMcNamara(5) 6 99
(Richard Fahey) *chsd ldrs: nt clr run over 2f out: rdn to ld wl over 1f out: sn hdd: continued to chal ins fnl f: hld towards fin* **8/1**

-005 **4** *3 ½* **Faithful Creek (IRE)**[10] 4776 4-9-0 **88**..................(tp) JordanUys(7) 10 88
(Brian Meehan) *hld up: pushed along whn nt clr run over 2f out: hdwy over 1f out: styd on ins fnl f: unable to trble ldrs* **14/1**

020 **5** *nk* **Free Code (IRE)**[14] 4665 5-9-7 **88**.................................. HarryBentley 3 87
(David Barron) *midfield: niggled along over 4f out: rdn and hdwy 2f out: kpt on for press ins fnl f: nvr able to chal* **20/1**

4623 **6** *½* **Archie (IRE)**[29] 4104 4-9-8 **89**... LukeMorris 7 87
(Clive Cox) *in tch: effrt over 2f out: led briefly under 2f out: stl chsng ldrs u.p 1f out: no ex fnl 100yds* **5/1**[2]

6520 **7** *3* **Grand Inquisitor**[21] 4399 4-10-0 **95**.................................. AndreaAtzeni 1 86+
(Sir Michael Stoute) *s.i.s: bustled along early: sn in midfield: n.m.r on inner whn hmpd over 2f out: one pce and no imp fnl f* **4/1**[1]

0022 **8** *nk* **Two For Two (IRE)**[6] 4917 8-9-11 **92**..........................(p) ShaneFoley 8 83+
(David Loughnane) *sltly worse than midfield: pushed along 4f out: rdn over 3f out: nt clr run over 2f out and over 1f out: no imp fnl f* **6/1**[3]

0200 **9** *1* **Off Art**[28] 4163 6-9-11 **92**...(p) JackGarritty 13 80+
(Tim Easterby) *late removal of blindfold and missed break: in rr: rdn 4f out: switch to outer over 2f out: plugged on fnl f: n.d* **16/1**

5600 **10** *4* **Mont Ras (IRE)**[15] 4611 9-9-7 **88**.. BenCurtis 14 67
(David Loughnane) *prom: upsides 3f out: led over 2f out: hdd under 2f out: wknd over 1f out* **16/1**

0144 **11** *4* **Silvery Moon (IRE)**[7] 4894 9-9-5 **89**................. RachelRichardson(3) 12 59
(Tim Easterby) *missed break: in rr: rdn 4f out: nvr a threat* **20/1**

0140 **12** *nk* **Chosen Character (IRE)**[6] 4917 8-8-12 **79**.......(vt) RichardKingscote 11 48
(Tom Dascombe) *prom: rdn and ev ch 2f out: wknd over 1f out* **16/1**

/140 **13** *3 ½* **Cape Icon**[14] 4625 5-9-3 **84**.. PaulMulrennan 9 45
(Clive Cox) *led: rdn and hdd over 2f out: wknd over 1f out: eased whn btn ins fnl f* **10/1**

1m 39.7s (-4.00) **Going Correction** -0.35s/f (Firm) **13** Ran SP% **120.6**
Speed ratings (Par 107): **106,105,105,101,101 100,97,97,96,92 88,88,84**
CSF £187.48 CT £1055.68 TOTE £8.60: £2.90, £7.10, £2.40; EX 202.00 Trifecta £1289.20.
Owner T Proctor **Bred** Ammerland Verwaltung Gmbh & Co Kg **Trained** Upper Helmsley, N Yorks

FOCUS

All races were run on the stands' side home straight. Allowing for rail positioning on the bends, this was run over approximately 1m 43yds. It was a warm, dry day and the ground was fast. The leaders went too quick, three horses who forced the pace finishing among the last four runners. The runner-up has been rated as running as well as ever.

5157 BETFRED HAYDOCK PARK LADIES' TROPHY H'CAP (PRO-AM LADY RIDERS' RACE) 1m 3f 200y

2:35 (2:35) (Class 3) (0-90,88) 3-Y-O+ **£12,938** (£3,850; £1,924; £962) **Stalls** Centre

Form RPR

2216 **1** **I Am Not Here (IRE)**[5] 4940 5-9-8 **75**........................ MissEmmaSayer 4 82
(Brian Ellison) *hld up: hdwy 2f out: rdn to go chalng 2nd over 1f out: r.o to ld fnl 75yds* **7/2**[2]

0004 **2** *1* **Gabrial's King (IRE)**[14] 4664 7-10-1 **87**......................... HayleyIrvine(5) 7 92
(Richard Fahey) *sn led: hdd 5f out: regained ld 3f out: rdn over 2f out: hdd fnl 75yds: hld nr fin* **9/1**

0635 **3** *2 ½* **English Summer**[29] 4095 9-10-7 **88**...........................(t) NatalieHambling 5 89
(Richard Fahey) *in tch: pushed along over 3f out: rdn to chal over 1f out: edgd lft fnl 100yds: styd on same pce* **7/1**

0032 **4** *1 ½* **Multellie**[12] 4703 4-9-9 **81**..................................... MissEEasterby(5) 6 80
(Tim Easterby) *chsd ldrs: wnt 2nd 9f out: led 5f out: hdd 3f out: kpt on same pce ins fnl f* **3/1**[1]

0313 **5** *2 ¾* **Tapis Libre**[21] 4407 8-10-2 **83**..................................(p) MissJoannaMason 2 77
(Jacqueline Coward) *chsd ldr to 9f out: rdn over 2f out: one pce fnl f* **4/1**[3]

0365 **6** *2* **Dance King**[21] 4407 6-10-7 **88**..................................(tp) RachelRichardson 3 79
(Tim Easterby) *hld up: effrt 2f out: no imp over 1f out* **7/2**[2]

2m 30.15s (-3.65) **Going Correction** -0.35s/f (Firm) **6** Ran SP% **111.9**
Speed ratings (Par 107): **89,88,86,85,83 82**
CSF £32.48 TOTE £3.80: £2.00, £4.00; EX 30.00 Trifecta £226.10.
Owner Koo's Racing Club **Bred** John Reilly **Trained** Norton, N Yorks

FOCUS

This was run over approximately 1m4f 23yds. There was a 20,000GBP development award for any rider successful on the all-girls card at Carlisle on August 1 and in this race, and two of these jockeys were eligible, including the winner. The runner-up has been rated close to form.

5158 BETFRED TV/EBF STALLIONS DICK HERN FILLIES' STKS (LISTED RACE) 1m

3:10 (3:11) (Class 1) 3-Y-O+

£26,653 (£10,105; £5,057; £2,519; £1,264; £634) **Stalls** Low

Form RPR

1-40 **1** **Aljazzi**[97] 1888 3-8-9 98..[1] AndreaAtzeni 5 103
(Marco Botti) *missed break: trckd ldrs: pushed along over 3f out: rdn and hung lft 2f out: plld off rail ins fnl f: r.o to ld towards fin* **12/1**

-405 **2** *nk* **Mix And Mingle (IRE)**[15] 4582 3-8-9 104.................. FergusSweeney 2 102
(Chris Wall) *trckd ldrs: wnt 2nd 2f out: rdn and chalng over 1f out: led narrowly ins fnl f: hdd towards fin* **15/2**

-112 **3** *hd* **Pirouette**[14] 4624 3-8-9 84.. TomQueally 1 101
(Hughie Morrison) *led: rdn and pressed over 1f out: hdd narrowly ins fnl f: hld nr fin* **14/1**

40-0 **4** *1* **Muffri'Ha (IRE)**[15] 4582 4-9-2 98.. BenCurtis 6 100
(William Haggas) *racd keenly: in tch: rdn over 2f out: styd on ins fnl f: no imp nr fin* **20/1**

1625 **5** *½* **Lucy The Painter (IRE)**[32] 3979 4-9-2 88...................... HarryBentley 11 99
(Ed de Giles) *hld up: rdn over 2f out: hdwy over 1f out: styd on u.p ins fnl f: nt pce to get to ldrs* **33/1**

1212 **6** *½* **Red Box**[15] 4582 3-9-0 101... LukeMorris 14 102+
(Sir Mark Prescott Bt) *hld up: pushed along over 3f out: hdwy whn nt clr run over 2f out: rdn over 1f out: struggled to get gng: kpt on ins fnl f: nvr able to trble ldrs* **4/1**[2]

3114 **7** *hd* **Light And Shade**[15] 4582 4-9-2 96...................................... NeilCallan 9 97
(James Tate) *midfield: pushed along over 2f out: rdn over 1f out: chsd ldrs ins fnl f: kpt on u.p* **14/1**

2111 **8** *1 ¼* **Golden Stunner (IRE)**[21] 4391 3-8-9 93.............. RichardKingscote 12 97+
(Ralph Beckett) *hld up: nt clr run on inner over 1f out: sn swtchd rt: kpt on ins fnl f: nvr trbld ldrs* **5/1**[3]

-334 **9** *¾* **Sharaakah (IRE)**[14] 4651 3-8-9 97.. ShaneFoley 7 94
(Ed Dunlop) *missed break: midfield: effrt over 2f out: sn n.m.r on inner and hmpd: one pce and no imp fnl f* **20/1**

054 **10** *3 ¾* **Gratzie**[13] 4688 5-9-2 94... GeorgeBaker 3 84
(Mick Channon) *missed break: in rr: rdn 2f out: plugged on fnl f: nvr a threat* **33/1**

212 **11** *1 ¾* **Wilamina (IRE)**[35] 3911 3-8-9 100.......................... ColmO'Donoghue 4 79
(Martyn Meade) *chsd ldr: rdn and ev ch 2f out: wkng whn n.m.r 1f out: eased* **7/2**[1]

-661 **12** *6* **Peru**[16] 4556 3-8-9 87.. JackMitchell 8 65
(Hugo Palmer) *chsd ldrs: rdn over 2f out: sn wknd* **25/1**

513 **13** *15* **Manaboo (USA)**[30] 4065 3-8-9 101 WilliamBuick 10 31
(Charlie Appleby) *midfield: lost pl u.p over 2f out: eased whn wl btn ins fnl f* **8/1**

1m 40.12s (-3.58) **Going Correction** -0.35s/f (Firm)
WFA 3 from 4yo+ 7lb **13** Ran SP% **122.0**
Speed ratings (Par 108): **103,102,102,101,101 100,100,99,98,94 92,86,71**
CSF £94.32 TOTE £15.20: £4.60, £3.20, £3.70; EX 142.10 Trifecta £1888.70.
Owner Saleh Al Homaizi & Imad Al Sagar **Bred** Saleh Al Homaizi & Imad Al Sagar **Trained** Newmarket, Suffolk

FOCUS
This was run over approximately 1m 43yds. A muddling fillies' Listed race in which few got involved. The fourth helps set the standard.

5159 BETFRED ROSE OF LANCASTER STKS (GROUP 3) 1m 2f 95y
3:45 (3:46) (Class 1) 3-Y-O+
£35,727 (£13,545; £6,778; £3,376; £1,694; £850) **Stalls** Centre

Form RPR
1-45 **1** **Royal Artillery (USA)**[51] 3296 3-8-8 99 (t) ColmO'Donoghue 6 117
(John Gosden) *chsd ldr: pushed along over 3f out: rdn whn chalng over 2f out: led 1f out: leant on rival wl ins fnl f: kpt on* **10/1**
1-31 **2** *1 ¼* **Scottish (IRE)**[21] 4392 4-9-3 115 WilliamBuick 2 115
(Charlie Appleby) *led: rdn whn hdd 1f out: bmpd wl ins fnl f: eased whn hld nr fin: jst hld on for 2nd* **7/4**[1]
/12- **3** *nse* **Arab Spring (IRE)**[436] 2645 6-9-3 112 AndreaAtzeni 1 114
(Sir Michael Stoute) *coltish on way to post: racd keenly: trckd ldrs: rdn and nt gng pce of front two whn swtchd rt off ins rail over 1f out: styd on towards fin: jst failed to get up for 2nd* **9/4**[2]
5135 **4** *1* **Gabrial (IRE)**[10] 4754 7-9-3 113 PhillipMakin 7 112
(Richard Fahey) *dwlt: hld up: rdn over 1f out: kpt on ins fnl f: nvr able to chal* **11/1**
-230 **5** *nk* **Foundation (IRE)**[62] 2946 3-8-8 110 (b[1]) RobertHavlin 5 111
(John Gosden) *missed break: hld up: hdwy over 2f out: rdn whn chsng ldrs over 1f out: styd on same pce ins fnl f* **4/1**[3]
6061 **6** *2 ¾* **Fire Fighting (IRE)**[11] 4731 5-9-3 108 (b) NeilCallan 4 106
(Mark Johnston) *trckd ldrs: rdn over 2f out: one pce fnl f* **12/1**

2m 7.71s (-7.79) **Going Correction** -0.35s/f (Firm) course record
WFA 3 from 4yo+ 9lb **6** Ran SP% **112.2**
Speed ratings (Par 113): **108,107,106,106,105 103**
CSF £28.06 TOTE £11.30: £4.20, £1.20; EX 29.50 Trifecta £94.80.
Owner Mrs John Magnier & Michael Tabor & Derrick Smith **Bred** Jpr Stable Llc **Trained** Newmarket, Suffolk

FOCUS
This was run over approximately 1m2f 138yds. A decent, interesting Group 3, but they didn't go that fast, with the 1-2 racing 2-1 for much of the way. It's been rated around the front-running runner-up.

5160 BETFRED MOBILE H'CAP 1m 2f 95y
4:15 (4:15) (Class 2) (0-105,102) 3-Y-O+**£16,172** (£4,812; £2,405; £1,202) **Stalls** Centre

Form RPR
1-20 **1** **Abdon**[51] 3296 3-9-5 **102** AndreaAtzeni 2 113
(Sir Michael Stoute) *hld up: hdwy over 2f out: led whn rdn and hung rt over 1f out: continually pressed ins fnl f: kpt on towards fin* **7/2**[3]
-612 **2** *½* **Gershwin**[28] 4129 3-9-1 **98** GeorgeBaker 7 108
(David Lanigan) *hld up: hdwy on bit over 2f out: 2nd and chalng fr over 1f out: hld nr fin* **1/1**[1]
0612 **3** *7* **Ode To Evening**[9] 4797 3-9-5 **102** WilliamBuick 5 99
(Mark Johnston) *chsd ldrs: pushed along 3f out: edgd lft whn outpcd over 1f out: coasted home but stl tk 3rd nr fin: no ch w front two* **3/1**[2]
0151 **4** *nk* **Gurkha Friend**[22] 4374 4-8-12 **86** TomQueally 1 82
(Karen McLintock) *led: rdn and hung rt over 2f out: hdd over 1f out: one pce and unable to go w front two ins fnl f* **14/1**
2135 **5** *nk* **Demonstration (IRE)**[24] 4276 4-8-9 **83** oh1 (p) RichardKingscote 3 79
(William Jarvis) *w ldr: pushed along over 2f out: rdn and nt qckn over 1f out: one pce and unable to go w front two ins fnl f* **12/1**

2m 8.31s (-7.19) **Going Correction** -0.35s/f (Firm)
WFA 3 from 4yo+ 9lb **5** Ran SP% **111.6**
Speed ratings (Par 109): **105,104,99,98,98**
CSF £7.61 TOTE £3.90: £1.70, £1.30; EX 8.00 Trifecta £15.00.
Owner Al Shaqab Racing **Bred** Newsells Park Stud **Trained** Newmarket, Suffolk

FOCUS
This was run over approximately 1m2f 138yds. Two well regarded, promising colts pulled a long way clear.

5161 BETFRED SUPPORTS JACK BERRY HOUSE H'CAP 6f
4:45 (4:47) (Class 4) (0-85,85) 3-Y-O+ **£6,469** (£1,925; £962; £481) **Stalls** Centre

Form RPR
3002 **1** **Normandy Barriere (IRE)**[14] 4627 4-9-10 **84** WilliamBuick 3 98
(Nigel Tinkler) *hld up: hdwy 2f out: r.o to ld ins fnl f: wl in command towards fin* **3/1**[1]
6-10 **2** *2* **Mickey (IRE)**[22] 4338 3-9-7 **85** (t) RichardKingscote 7 92
(Tom Dascombe) *led: rdn over 1f out: hdd ins fnl f: outpcd by wnr fnl 100yds* **11/2**
6026 **3** *2 ¼* **Explain**[13] 4689 4-9-9 **83** JackGarritty 5 84
(Ruth Carr) *stdd s: hld up: rdn and hdwy over 1f out: chsd ldrs ins fnl f: kpt on but no imp fnl 100yds* **9/1**
1056 **4** *1 ¼* **Dodgy Bob**[14] 4643 3-9-2 **80** (p) NeilCallan 2 76
(Kevin Ryan) *a.p: rdn 2f out: styd on same pce ins fnl f* **14/1**
3312 **5** *hd* **Spirit Of Zeb (IRE)**[24] 4259 4-9-3 **82** AdamMcNamara[(5)] 8 78
(Richard Fahey) *prom: rdn over 2f out: lost pl and outpcd over 1f out: kpt on same pce and no imp ins fnl f* **5/1**[3]
0000 **6** *1* **Canyari (IRE)**[56] 3168 5-9-4 **78** (p) AndreaAtzeni 1 71
(Richard Fahey) *in tch: rdn over 2f out: one pce u.p ins fnl f* **9/1**
10-5 **7** *¾* **Ustinov**[24] 4259 4-9-11 **85** DanielTudhope 6 76
(David O'Meara) *racd keenly: hld up in midfield: rdn and outpcd over 1f out: no imp: wl hld ins fnl f* **7/2**[2]
0554 **8** *4 ½* **Barkston Ash**[7] 4873 8-9-2 **76** (p) PhillipMakin 9 52
(Eric Alston) *in tch: rdn and lost pl 2f out: eased whn wl btn fnl 100yds* **8/1**

1m 11.14s (-2.66) **Going Correction** -0.35s/f (Firm)
WFA 3 from 4yo+ 4lb **8** Ran SP% **117.1**
Speed ratings (Par 105): **103,100,97,95,95 94,93,87**
CSF £20.39 CT £133.86 TOTE £3.60: £1.30, £2.70, £3.10; EX 20.10 Trifecta £144.30.
Owner Eddie Carswell **Bred** Tinnakill Bloodstock & L Cantillon **Trained** Langton, N Yorks

FOCUS
A fair sprint handicap and a likeable winner. The runner-up has been rated as running a small pb in defeat.

5162 BETFRED "LIKE US ON FACEBOOK" H'CAP 5f
5:15 (5:15) (Class 5) (0-70,77) 3-Y-O+ **£4,528** (£1,347; £673; £336) **Stalls** Centre

Form RPR
0521 **1** **Outrage**[11] 4744 4-10-3 **77** GeorgeBaker 9 87+
(Daniel Kubler) *hld up: swtchd rt over 1f out: hdwy on nrside rail ins fnl f: str run to ld post* **2/1**[1]
6066 **2** *nse* **Innocently (IRE)**[11] 4726 5-9-5 **65** (v) DanielTudhope 4 74
(David O'Meara) *led: rdn over 1f out: nrly 2 l clr ent fnl f: hdd post* **6/1**
33 **3** *1 ½* **Flying Bear (IRE)**[23] 4295 5-9-10 **70** RichardKingscote 3 74
(Jeremy Gask) *hld up: hdwy over 1f out: styd on to chse ldrs fnl 100yds: nt pce of front two* **9/4**[2]
4126 **4** *2* **Lydiate Lady**[1] 5110 4-8-12 **58** TomQueally 5 54
(Paul Green) *in tch: rdn over 1f out: kpt on u.p ins fnl f: nvr able to chal* **11/2**[3]
0400 **5** *hd* **Pushkin Museum (IRE)**[19] 4452 5-8-12 **63** AdamMcNamara[(5)] 7 59
(Richard Fahey) *chsd ldrs: pushed along 2f out: rdn and nt qckn over 1f out: styd on same pce ins fnl f* **11/1**
640- **6** *hd* **Cruise Tothelimit (IRE)**[283] 7565 8-9-7 **67** JackGarritty 1 62
(Patrick Morris) *w ldr: pushed along 2f out: rdn and lost 2nd over 1f out: kpt on same pce ins fnl f* **16/1**
666 **7** *2 ½* **Ten Rocks**[32] 3985 3-9-1 **64** (b) BenCurtis 2 49
(Lisa Williamson) *racd keenly: chsd ldrs: rdn and lost pl over 1f out: outpcd ins fnl f* **28/1**
261 **8** *5* **Frank The Barber (IRE)**[17] 4529 4-8-13 **59** (t) RoystonFfrench 6 27
(Steph Hollinshead) *sed awkwardly: hld up: rdn over 1f out: nvr a threat* **14/1**

58.91s (-1.89) **Going Correction** -0.35s/f (Firm)
WFA 3 from 4yo+ 3lb **8** Ran SP% **118.1**
Speed ratings (Par 103): **101,100,98,95,95 94,90,82**
CSF £15.30 CT £29.43 TOTE £2.90: £1.10, £2.00, £1.40; EX 15.30 Trifecta £50.70.
Owner D Blunt & G Middlebrook **Bred** Trickledown Stud Limited **Trained** Lambourn, Berks

FOCUS
A reasonable sprint handicap. The runner-up has been rated as running close to his winter AW level. The third has been rated to his latest form.
T/Jkpt: Not won. T/Plt: £383.90 to a £1 stake. Pool: £127,473.82 - 242.39 winning units. T/Qpdt: £29.10 to a £1 stake. Pool: £8,006.42 - 203.23 winning units. **Darren Owen**

4876 LINGFIELD (L-H)
Saturday, August 6

OFFICIAL GOING: Good (good to firm in places) changing to good to firm (good in places) after race 1 (5.20)
Wind: light, half behind Weather: sunny and warm

5163 OLYMPICS BETTING AT 188BET MEDIAN AUCTION MAIDEN STKS 1m 2f
5:20 (5:20) (Class 6) 3-4-Y-O **£2,587** (£770; £384; £192) **Stalls** Low

Form RPR
3362 **1** **California Lad**[26] 4213 3-9-5 76 (v) PatCosgrave 2 76
(Harry Dunlop) *chsd ldr: effrt ent fnl 2f: drvn to ld 1f out: styd on and forged ahd fnl 100yds: rdn out* **11/4**[2]
23-2 **2** *2 ½* **Twobeelucky**[7] 4857 3-9-5 89 NickyMackay 1 71
(Mark Johnston) *led: rdn ent fnl 2f: drvn and hdd 1f out: high hd carriage and one pce ins fnl f* **1/3**[1]
0 **3** *½* **Iconic Sky**[22] 4367 3-9-0 0 DougieCostello 3 65
(Lucy Wadham) *trckd ldng pair: rdn over 2f out: stl cl enough 1f out: styd on same pce ins fnl f* **16/1**[3]
4 *63* **Marcmywords (IRE)** 3-9-5 0 AdamBeschizza 4
(Christine Dunnett) *s.i.s: a last: rdn 5f out: lost tch over 3f out: t.o* **50/1**

2m 10.54s (0.04) **Going Correction** 0.0s/f (Good) **4** Ran SP% **109.5**
Speed ratings (Par 101): **99,97,96,46**
CSF £4.19 TOTE £3.30; EX 4.40 Trifecta £5.40.
Owner Daniel Macauliffe & Anoj Don **Bred** Miss K Rausing **Trained** Lambourn, Berks

FOCUS
Ground on the fast side of good for this seven-race card.\n\x\x This looked a straightforward task for the market leader on paper but he proved disappointing and was readily seen off by a rival rated 13lb inferior on official figures.

5164 FOOTBALL BETTING AT 188BET H'CAP 1m 3f 106y
5:50 (5:50) (Class 5) (0-75,73) 3-Y-O **£3,234** (£962; £481) **Stalls** High

Form RPR
1035 **1** **Pack It In (IRE)**[16] 4554 3-9-2 **70** (b) MartinDwyer 2 74
(Brian Meehan) *chsd ldr tl led over 3f out: drifting rt and racing in centre fnl 3f: hrd drvn over 1f out: styd on* **2/1**[2]
3452 **2** *¾* **Torquay**[14] 4636 3-9-4 **72** SamHitchcott 4 75
(Harry Dunlop) *hld up in cl 3rd: wnt 2nd 3f out and racing on inner rail: rdn 2f out: styd on steadily ins fnl f: nvr quite getting on terms w wnr* **10/11**[1]
0-04 **3** *54* **Sautter**[32] 3981 3-9-3 **71** ShaneKelly 6
(Peter Chapple-Hyam) *led tl over 3f out: sn rdn and dropped to last: lost tch over 2f out: heavily eased over 1f out: t.o* **7/2**[3]

2m 33.15s (1.65) **Going Correction** 0.0s/f (Good) **3** Ran SP% **107.9**
Speed ratings (Par 100): **94,93,54**
CSF £4.25 TOTE £2.80; EX 3.60 Trifecta £3.30.
Owner The C3 Partnership **Bred** Lisa Kelly & Skymarc Farm **Trained** Manton, Wilts

FOCUS
A depleted field and this developed into a match up the straight, with the pair wide apart. Modest form. The runner-up has been rated to his 1m6f latest here.

5165 PRB ESTATES LTD NURSERY H'CAP 6f
6:20 (6:21) (Class 6) (0-60,60) 2-Y-O **£2,587** (£770; £384; £192) **Stalls** Centre

Form RPR
560 **1** **Glenys The Menace (FR)**[71] 2649 2-9-4 **57** KierenFox 1 61
(John Best) *chsd ldr: effrt and edgd lft over 1f out: rdn to chal 1f out: styd on to ld wl ins fnl f: rdn out* **5/1**[2]
050 **2** *½* **Waves (IRE)**[31] 4022 2-9-7 **60** ShaneKelly 3 63
(Eve Johnson Houghton) *led and crossed to r against stands' rail: rdn over 1f out: hrd pressed and drvn 1f out: hdd and one pce wl ins fnl f* **4/1**[1]

005 **3** nk **Tigerfish (IRE)**[14] 4638 2-8-8 **47** .... KieranO'Neill 5 49
(William Stone) *stdd after s: hld up in rr: effrt and swtchd lft 2f out: hdwy and racing in centre 1f out: wnt 3rd 100yds out: styd on wl: nt quite rch ldrs* **9/1**

0004 **4** 1 ½ **Flawed Diamond (FR)**[7] 4869 2-9-1 **54** .... DougieCostello 2 51
(K R Burke) *wl in tch in midfield: effrt to chse ldrs over 1f out: styd on same pce u.p fnl f* **4/1**[1]

564 **5** 4 **Brexit**[17] 4524 2-9-1 **59** .... PaddyBradley(5) 6 44
(Pat Phelan) *t.k.h: hld up in tch in midfield: effrt and swtchd rt over 1f out: sn outpcd: wl hld and plugged on same pce fnl f* **4/1**[1]

4606 **6** 2 ¾ **Patrouille De Nuit (IRE)**[25] 4221 2-8-8 **54** ....(b) HollieDoyle(7) 7 31
(J S Moore) *hld up in last pair: swtchd lft and effrt u.p over 1f out: no imp and btn 1f out: wknd ins fnl f* **8/1**[3]

000 **7** nse **Myredbush (IRE)**[37] 3799 2-8-9 **48** ....(b[1]) NickyMackay 8 25
(Simon Dow) *trckd ldrs: effrt over 1f out: sn outpcd and btn: wknd ins fnl f* **14/1**

050 **8** 1 ½ **Seminole Dream (IRE)**[52] 3290 2-8-6 **45** .... JimmyQuinn 4 17
(Philip Kirby) *hld up in tch in midfield: rdn and lost pl jst over 2f out: drvn and wl btn over 1f out: wknd fnl f* **5/1**[2]

1m 12.01s (0.81) **Going Correction** -0.05s/f (Good) **8** Ran SP% **121.1**
Speed ratings (Par 92): **92,91,90,88,83 79,79,77**
CSF £26.97 CT £181.26 TOTE £6.80: £2.40, £1.40, £2.70; EX 30.30 Trifecta £274.80.
Owner Curtis, Malt & Jenkins **Bred** Haras D'Etreham & Georges Lugon **Trained** Oad Street, Kent

FOCUS
A very modest event on paper but a few of these have some potential to improve now handicapping.

5166 ACCA INSURANCE AT 188BET EBF MAIDEN STKS 7f 140y
6:50 (6:51) (Class 5) 2-Y-O **£3,363** (£1,001; £500; £250) **Stalls** Centre

Form RPR

64 **1** **Dourado (IRE)**[14] 4653 2-9-5 0 .... TomMarquand 7 76
(Richard Hannon) *trckd ldng pair: swtchd lft and clsd to join ldr over 2f out: led wl over 1f out: sn rdn clr: r.o wl and rdn out hands and heels fnl f* **4/5**[1]

0 **2** 2 ½ **Too Many Shots**[37] 3799 2-9-5 0 .... KierenFox 2 68
(John Best) *hld up in tch in midfield: effrt over 2f out: drvn and battling for placings over 1f out: wnt 2nd 100yds out: kpt on but no ch w wnr* **16/1**

60 **3** 1 **Rock On Dandy (FR)**[57] 3093 2-9-5 0 ....(b[1]) ShaneKelly 6 65
(Harry Dunlop) *led: rdn and hdd wl over 1f out: sn outpcd by wnr: kpt on same pce u.p after: lost 2nd 100yds out* **14/1**

4 hd **Ettihadi (IRE)** 2-9-5 0 .... PatCosgrave 4 65
(Hugo Palmer) *dwlt: rn green: hld up in tch: swtchd lft and effrt 2f out: rdn and battling for placings 1f out: no threat to wnr and styd on same pce ins fnl f* **13/8**[2]

5 1 **Sassoferrato (IRE)** 2-9-5 0 .... SaleemGolam 1 62
(Alan Bailey) *s.i.s: hld up in tch in last pair: swtchd lft and effrt 2f out: nvr threatening wnr and styd on same pce fnl f: swtchd lft cl home* **12/1**[3]

0 **6** 11 **Gog Elles (IRE)**[40] 3730 2-9-0 0 .... DannyBrock 3 32
(J S Moore) *chsd ldr: rdn 1/2-way: lost 2nd over 2f out and losing pl whn squeezed for room 2f out: bhd fnl f* **40/1**

0 **7** 1 ¼ **Maysonri**[31] 4016 2-9-5 0 ....(p) AdamBeschizza 5 32
(Mark Hoad) *s.i.s: a bhd: rdn 5f out: wknd 2f out* **100/1**

1m 32.4s (0.10) **Going Correction** -0.05s/f (Good) **7** Ran SP% **117.3**
Speed ratings (Par 94): **97,94,93,93,92 81,80**
CSF £17.54 TOTE £1.60: £1.10, £7.30; EX 16.90 Trifecta £80.00.
Owner Saleh Al Homaizi & Imad Al Sagar **Bred** Canice M Farrell Jnr **Trained** East Everleigh, Wilts

FOCUS
Little depth to this maiden and the clear form choice got the job done, although he had to be kept up to his work in the closing stages to maintain his advantage.

5167 CORE GROUP H'CAP 7f 140y
7:20 (7:22) (Class 6) (0-60,62) 3-Y-O **£2,587** (£770; £384; £192) **Stalls** Centre

Form RPR

-662 **1** **Rock Icon**[17] 4504 3-8-10 **49** .... JimmyQuinn 10 69
(Patrick Chamings) *hld up in tch towards rr: nt clr run 3f out: swtchd lft and hdwy 2f out: chsng ldrs and swtchd rt over 1f out: squeezed through on stands' rail to ld over 1f out: stormed clr fnl f: easily* **7/2**[2]

0005 **2** 8 **Pacohontas**[39] 3734 3-8-12 **51** .... SamHitchcott 4 51
(John E Long) *sn outpcd in detached: rdn 1/2-way: styng on to pass btn rivals and switching lft over 1f out: kpt on ins fnl f to go 2nd last strides: no ch w wnr* **14/1**

5002 **3** hd **Arcanista (IRE)**[9] 4796 3-9-9 **62** ....(b) ShaneKelly 9 62
(Richard Hughes) *chsd ldr for 1f: chsd ldrs: swtchd lft 5f out: wnt 2nd again 4f out: rdn to ld and edgd rt ent fnl 2f: hdd over 1f out: no ch w wnr ins fnl f: plugged on same pce* **7/1**[3]

5005 **4** hd **Mostashreqah**[9] 4796 3-8-6 **48** ....(tp) EdwardGreatrex(3) 1 47
(Milton Bradley) *hld up in tch in midfield: clsd 3f out: rdn and ev ch briefly over 1f out: outpcd by wnr and wl hld 2nd 1f out: wandering and tiring ins fnl f: lost 2 pls cl home* **25/1**

0606 **5** ½ **Protest (IRE)**[7] 4882 3-8-13 **52** ....(b) LiamKeniry 8 50
(Sylvester Kirk) *led for 1f: chsd ldr tl 4f out: rdn and unable qck whn hung lft 2f out: sn outpcd and wl btn over 1f out: plugged on* **7/2**[2]

0261 **6** 6 **Arctic Flower (IRE)**[14] 4641 3-9-3 **56** .... DannyBrock 7 39
(John Bridger) *in tch in midfield: rdn and hdwy to chse ldrs over 3f out: wnt 2nd 2f out: sn struggling and lost 2nd: wknd fnl f* **5/2**[1]

-000 **7** 1 ½ **Lee's Hall (IRE)**[24] 4279 3-9-7 **60** ....(b[1]) DougieCostello 2 39
(Murty McGrath) *dwlt: rcvrd to ld after 1f: rdn and hdd ent fnl 2f: sn struggling: wknd qckly over 1f out* **12/1**

000- **8** 10 **Robbie Roo Roo**[301] 7107 3-9-4 **57** ....(t) SaleemGolam 6 12
(Mrs Ilka Gansera-Leveque) *hld up in tch: pushed lft 5f out: rdn over 2f out: sn struggling: wl btn and hung rt wl over 1f out: eased wl ins fnl f* **18/1**

2430 **9** 14 **Kristoff (IRE)**[17] 4528 3-8-13 **52** .... PatCosgrave 3
(Jim Boyle) *in tch in midfield: rdn over 2f out: sn btn: wl bhd and eased fnl f: t.o* **8/1**

1m 31.68s (-0.62) **Going Correction** -0.05s/f (Good) **9** Ran SP% **120.1**
Speed ratings (Par 98): **101,93,92,92,92 86,84,74,60**
CSF £53.36 CT £335.61 TOTE £4.80: £1.50, £3.80, £2.00; EX 57.70 Trifecta £970.90.
Owner M J Black **Bred** Maurice Black **Trained** Baughurst, Hants

FOCUS
A weak handicap run at what looked a reasonable gallop and the winner shot clear up the stands rail in the final furlong to win by a wide margin.

5168 188BET MAIDEN STKS 6f
7:50 (7:50) (Class 5) 3-Y-O+ **£3,234** (£962; £481; £240) **Stalls** Centre

Form RPR

0333 **1** **Menai (IRE)**[14] 4660 3-8-10 77 .... SteveDrowne 5 82
(Charles Hills) *mde all: rdn and fnd ex over 1f out: clr whn idled and hung lft 100yds out: pressed towards fin but a doing enough* **7/4**[1]

2-22 **2** ½ **Catchment**[14] 4660 3-8-5 73 ....(p) JimmyQuinn 7 75
(Amanda Perrett) *t.k.h: hld up in tch in midfield: effrt to chse ldrs over 1f out: sn drvn: wnt 2nd 100yds out and sn pressing wnr: kpt on but hld towards fin* **9/4**[3]

0 **3** 2 ¼ **Manshood (IRE)**[21] 4401 3-8-10 0 ....(b) PatCosgrave 6 73
(William Haggas) *chsd ldrs: wnt 2nd over 3f out: rdn and unable qck over 1f out: lost 2nd 100yds out and eased cl home* **2/1**[2]

0P-0 **4** 1 ¾ **Bigmouth Strikes (IRE)**[17] 4521 3-8-10 0 .... MartinDwyer 3 67
(David Menuisier) *taken down early and led to post: chsd ldrs: 3rd and unable qck u.p over 1f out: wknd ins fnl f* **25/1**

04 **5** 2 ¾ **Corella (IRE)**[36] 3850 3-8-5 0 .... RyanTate 4 53
(Clive Cox) *dwlt: hld up in tch in midfield: rdn 2f out: unable qck u.p: wknd fnl f* **22/1**

5-00 **6** 1 ¾ **Canford Lilli (IRE)**[40] 3720 3-8-5 72 ....(p) JohnFahy 10 48
(Eve Johnson Houghton) *chsd ldr tl over 3f out: styd chsng ldrs: nt clrest of run 2f out: sn pushed along and btn: wknd fnl f* **14/1**

00 **7** 1 **Flying Sakhee**[14] 4639 3-8-5 0 .... DannyBrock 8 45
(John Bridger) *hld up in tch in last trio: rdn 2f out: sn outpcd: wknd over 1f out* **100/1**

0 **8** 4 **Gorgeous (FR)**[61] 2980 3-8-5 0 .... TomMarquand 1 32
(Tony Carroll) *dwlt: hld up in tch in last trio: swtchd lft and rdn over 2f out: rn green and no hdwy: wknd over 1f out* **50/1**

9 nk **Sharp Boy (IRE)** 3-8-7 0 .... AaronJones(3) 2 36
(Stuart Williams) *s.i.s: hld up in tch in rr: swtchd lft 3f out: sn rdn and no imp: wknd over 1f out* **16/1**

1m 10.9s (-0.30) **Going Correction** -0.05s/f (Good) **9** Ran SP% **124.2**
Speed ratings (Par 103): **100,99,96,94,90 88,86,81,80**
CSF £6.44 TOTE £2.80: £1.10, £1.40, £1.20; EX 7.10 Trifecta £14.70.
Owner Julie Martin & David R Martin & Partner **Bred** Yeomanstown Stud **Trained** Lambourn, Berks

FOCUS
Probably not form to go overboard about given the front two are fairly exposed now. It's been rated around the first two.

5169 188BET.CO.UK H'CAP 6f
8:20 (8:20) (Class 5) (0-75,75) 3-Y-O+ **£3,234** (£962; £481; £240) **Stalls** Centre

Form RPR

2-20 **1** **Ballylare**[28] 4134 3-9-7 **75** .... KierenFox 4 83
(John Best) *mde all: rdn wl over 1f out: styd on wl ins fnl f: drifted lft u.p fnl 75yds: rdn out* **10/1**

0060 **2** 1 **Billyoakes (IRE)**[12] 4714 4-9-8 **72** .... AdamBeschizza 2 78
(Charlie Wallis) *chsd ldr: rdn 2f out: stl pressing ldr but unable qck 1f out: styd on same pce ins fnl f* **20/1**

5213 **3** shd **One Big Surprise**[9] 4787 4-9-5 **69** ....(p) ShaneKelly 5 78+
(Richard Hughes) *hld up in tch: nt clr run 2f out: clsd to trck ldrs but hemmed in on stands' rail 1f out: swtchd lft and bmpd rival 1f out: gap fnlly opened on rail 75yds out: r.o: nvr threatening wnr* **11/4**[1]

6065 **4** ¾ **Doctor Parkes**[12] 4714 10-9-3 **70** .... AaronJones(3) 3 73
(Stuart Williams) *chsd ldrs: rdn ent fnl 2f: unable qck u.p over 1f out: styd on same pce ins fnl f* **9/1**[3]

0446 **5** 1 **Great Expectations**[23] 4321 8-8-13 **63** ....(vt) DougieCostello 7 63
(J R Jenkins) *hld up in tch: rdn and hdwy over 1f out: chsng ldrs but no ex ins fnl f: styd on same pce fnl 100yds* **10/1**

30-4 **6** 2 ¾ **Surety (IRE)**[105] 1648 5-9-8 **72** .... PatCosgrave 8 74+
(James Tate) *chsd ldrs: rdn ent fnl 2f: drvn and unable qck jst over 1f out: styng on same pce and hld whn pushed lft and hmpd 100yds out* **11/4**[1]

0-06 **7** 1 **Evening Attire**[56] 3144 5-9-0 **71** .... GeorgeWood(7) 1 59
(William Stone) *stdd s: t.k.h: hld up in midfield: rdn over 2f out: no imp u.p over 1f out: wknd ins fnl f* **12/1**

0000 **8** shd **Divine Call**[23] 4291 9-8-5 **58** ....(v) EdwardGreatrex(3) 9 46
(Milton Bradley) *t.k.h: hld up in rr: effrt 2f out: sme hdwy 1f out: swtchd rt ins fnl f: nvr trbld ldrs* **14/1**

602- **9** 7 **The Perfect Show**[316] 6702 3-9-3 **71** ....[1] AntonioFresu 6 35
(Ed Walker) *dwlt: hld up in tch in midfield: rdn jst over 2f out: sn struggling and lost pl over 1f out: wknd fnl f* **4/1**[2]

1m 11.59s (0.39) **Going Correction** -0.05s/f (Good)
WFA 3 from 4yo+ 4lb **9** Ran SP% **120.6**
Speed ratings (Par 103): **95,93,93,92,91 87,86,86,76**
CSF £192.97 CT £706.99 TOTE £13.90: £2.90, £5.30, £1.40; EX 299.00 Trifecta £1182.70.
Owner Curtis, Malt & Williams **Bred** J H Mayne **Trained** Oad Street, Kent

FOCUS
A modest handicap but there was trouble for one or two behind the leader entering the final furlong and the result might have been different had the third-placed horse got a run. The unlucky third has been rated as finishing upsides the winner.
T/Plt: £106.80 to a £1 stake. Pool: £49,065.38 - 335.11 winning units. T/Qpdt: £9.00 to a £1 stake. Pool: £6,499.62 - 528.70 winning units. **Steve Payne**

5119 NEWMARKET (R-H)
Saturday, August 6

OFFICIAL GOING: Good to firm (7.4)
Wind: Light across Weather: Cloudy with sunny spells

5170 SEA THE MOON MAIDEN FILLIES' STKS (PLUS 10 RACE) 7f
2:05 (2:05) (Class 4) 2-Y-O **£4,528** (£1,347; £673; £336) **Stalls** Low

Form RPR

1 **Wuheida** 2-9-0 0 .... JamesDoyle 1 83+
(Charlie Appleby) *chsd ldrs: shkn up to ld over 1f out: sn rdn and edgd lft: r.o* **15/8**[1]

2 1 ¼ **Spatial** 2-9-0 0 .... TedDurcan 2 79+
(Sir Michael Stoute) *hld up: hdwy over 2f out: rdn and ev ch over 1f out: styd on same pce wl ins fnl f* **2/1**[2]

3 nk **Nathania** 2-9-0 0 .... ShaneKelly 5 78+
(Richard Hughes) *led: rdn: hdd and hung lft over 1f out: styd on same pce wl ins fnl f* **11/1**

4 6 **Poet's Vanity** 2-9-0 0 DavidProbert 6 62
(Andrew Balding) *sn chsng ldr: rdn and wknd over 1f out* **9/1**

5 3/4 **Forest Angel (IRE)** 2-9-0 0 SeanLevey 3 60
(Richard Hannon) *prom: rdn over 2f out: wknd over 1f out* **9/2**3

6 9 **Kitsey (IRE)** 2-9-0 0 PatDobbs 4 35
(Richard Hannon) *sn pushed along in rr: rdn and wknd over 2f out* **11/1**

1m 26.55s (0.85) **Going Correction** +0.10s/f (Good) **6** Ran SP% **113.0**
Speed ratings (Par 93): **99,97,97,90,89 79**
CSF £6.04 TOTE £2.60: £1.60, £1.40; EX 6.20 Trifecta £39.80.
Owner Godolphin **Bred** Darley **Trained** Newmarket, Suffolk

FOCUS
Stands' side course used. Stalls stands' side except 1m2f & 2m: centre. A juvenile contest for fillies that have never run, won by Passage Of Time and Winsili in 2006 and 2012, who both became Group 1 winners over 1m2f. They went a respectable gallop on good to firm ground and the winner beat a promising bunch of fillies in taking style.

5171 ROYAL BRITISH LEGION NURSERY H'CAP 7f

2:40 (2:40) (Class 4) (0-85,83) 2-Y-O **£5,175** (£1,540; £769; £384) **Stalls** Low

Form RPR

61 **1** **Majoris (IRE)**32 3971 2-9-0 **76** (t) JimCrowley 3 91+
(Hugo Palmer) *mde all: set stdy pce tl qcknd 1/2-way: shkn up and c readily clr fnl f: impressive* **8/11**1

365 **2** 7 **Book Of Poetry (IRE)**30 4047 2-8-6 **68** FrannyNorton 1 64
(Mark Johnston) *disp cl 2nd: rdn over 1f out: sn outpcd* **10/1**

3223 **3** nk **Prerogative (IRE)**18 4479 2-9-7 **83** PatDobbs 5 78
(Richard Hannon) *disp cl 2nd: shkn up and hung lft over 2f out: rdn over 1f out: sn outpcd* **4/1**2

443 **4** 3/4 **Law Power**18 4473 2-8-10 **72** RyanPowell 6 65
(Sir Mark Prescott Bt) *sn pushed along in rr: sme hdwy u.p over 1f out: sn outpcd* **7/1**3

443 **5** 1 1/4 **Heatongrad (IRE)**40 3705 2-8-10 **72** TonyHamilton 4 62
(Richard Fahey) *hld up in tch: rdn over 2f out: btn over 1f out* **8/1**

1m 25.48s (-0.22) **Going Correction** +0.10s/f (Good) **5** Ran SP% **110.6**
Speed ratings (Par 96): **105,97,96,95,94**
CSF £8.88 TOTE £1.50: £1.20, £3.40; EX 9.10 Trifecta £23.70.
Owner Al Asayl Bloodstock Ltd **Bred** Al Asayl Bloodstock Ltd **Trained** Newmarket, Suffolk

FOCUS
A decent nursery handicap won by the smart Tobosa and Battle Of Hastings in 2006 and 2008. Another promising colt by Frankel turned this race into a procession from over 1f out.

5172 GERMAN-THOROUGHBRED.COM SWEET SOLERA STKS (GROUP 3) (FILLIES) 7f

3:15 (3:15) (Class 1) 2-Y-O

£22,684 (£8,600; £4,304; £2,144; £1,076; £540) **Stalls** Low

Form RPR

2213 **1** **Nations Alexander (IRE)**29 4106 2-9-0 101 PatDobbs 1 103
(Richard Hannon) *mde all: shkn up over 1f out: rdn ins fnl f: r.o* **4/1**2

1 **2** 1 1/2 **Grecian Light (IRE)**22 4357 2-9-0 0 JamesDoyle 8 99
(Charlie Appleby) *hld up: hdwy 1/2-way: rdn and hung lft over 2f out: chsd wnr ins fnl f: styd on* **9/2**3

3111 **3** nk **On Her Toes (IRE)**16 4560 2-9-0 95 PatCosgrave 9 98
(William Haggas) *chsd wnr: rdn over 1f out: styd on* **5/1**

114 **4** nse **Urban Fox**16 4560 2-9-0 91 JimCrowley 6 98
(James Tate) *hld up: plld hrd: hdwy over 1f out: sn rdn: styd on* **16/1**

51 **5** 1 **Tiburtina (IRE)**22 4350 2-9-0 76 TedDurcan 2 95
(Sylvester Kirk) *chsd ldrs: rdn over 1f out: hung lft ins fnl f: styd on same pce* **50/1**

1103 **6** 2 1/2 **Grizzel (IRE)**16 4560 2-9-0 93 SeanLevey 7 89
(Richard Hannon) *hld up: rdn over 2f out: hdwy over 1f out: no ex ins fnl f* **10/1**

1 **7** 1/2 **Belle Meade (IRE)**22 4371 2-9-0 0 TonyHamilton 4 87
(Richard Fahey) *awkward leaving stalls: hld up: rdn over 1f out: nt trble ldrs* **10/1**

1 **8** hd **Easy Victory**30 4064 2-9-0 0 DavidProbert 5 87
(Saeed bin Suroor) *plld hrd and prom: rdn over 1f out: wknd ins fnl f* **15/8**1

1 **9** 3/4 **San Sebastiana**23 4298 2-9-0 78 DougieCostello 3 85
(K R Burke) *hld up: rdn over 1f out: nvr on terms* **25/1**

1m 26.03s (0.33) **Going Correction** +0.10s/f (Good) **9** Ran SP% **119.5**
Speed ratings (Par 101): **102,100,99,99,98 95,95,95,94**
CSF £23.30 TOTE £4.10: £1.20, £1.60, £2.00; EX 26.00 Trifecta £87.70.
Owner Noel O'Callaghan **Bred** Oakhill Stud **Trained** East Everleigh, Wilts

FOCUS
A competitive renewal of this Group 3 juvenile fillies' contest won by the high-class Rainbow View in 2008. The winner dominated from start to finish at a decent tempo.

5173 BUY, BREED AND TRAIN IN GERMANY H'CAP 1m 2f

3:50 (3:51) (Class 2) (0-100,100) 3-Y-O+ **£12,938** (£3,850; £1,924; £962) **Stalls** Centre

Form RPR

0140 **1** **First Sitting**35 3889 5-10-0 **100** JamesDoyle 2 109
(Chris Wall) *hld up: hdwy over 2f out: chsd ldr over 1f out: rdn to ld and edgd rt ins fnl f: r.o: eased nr fin* **9/2**3

5332 **2** 1 3/4 **Passover**42 3670 5-9-6 **92** DavidProbert 4 97
(Andrew Balding) *sn led: rdn over 1f out: hdd and edgd lft ins fnl f: styd on same pce* **7/1**

0354 **3** 1 1/4 **Sennockian Star**13 4680 6-8-11 **83** (v) FrannyNorton 6 86
(Mark Johnston) *sn chsng ldr: lost 2nd over 3f out: sn rdn: styd on same pce ins fnl f* **5/1**

1440 **4** hd **Speed Company (IRE)**51 3299 3-9-0 **95** 1 FrederikTylicki 5 97
(John Quinn) *plld hrd and sn prom: rdn over 2f out: styd on same pce ins fnl f* **12/1**

2412 **5** 1 **Innocent Touch (IRE)**14 4650 5-9-4 **90** TonyHamilton 3 90
(Richard Fahey) *chsd ldrs: wnt 2nd over 3f out tl rdn over 1f out: no ex ins fnl f* **7/2**2

1-16 **6** nk **Barye**156 793 5-9-12 **98** ShaneKelly 1 98
(Richard Hughes) *hld up: hdwy over 2f out: sn rdn: no ex ins fnl f* **25/1**

0-00 **7** 8 **Spanish Squeeze (IRE)**24 4276 4-9-7 **96** NoelGarbutt(3) 9 80
(Hugo Palmer) *hld up: wnt centre and chsd ldr of that pair over 7f out: rdn over 2f out: hung rt and wknd over 1f out* **16/1**

5000 **8** 11 **Beaverbrook**7 4863 3-8-10 **91** JimCrowley 8 53
(Mark Johnston) *prom: wnt centre and led that pair over 7f out: up w the pce tl rdn 3f out: wknd 2f out* **11/4**1

2m 3.39s (-2.11) **Going Correction** +0.10s/f (Good)
WFA 3 from 4yo+ 9lb **8** Ran SP% **113.7**
Speed ratings (Par 109): **112,110,109,109,108 108,102,93**
CSF £35.23 CT £161.82 TOTE £4.90: £1.70, £1.90, £1.70; EX 33.00 Trifecta £168.20.
Owner Bringloe & Clarke **Bred** Juddmonte Farms Ltd **Trained** Newmarket, Suffolk

FOCUS
A good quality handicap won by the smart Sir John Hawkwood in 2012. They went a decent gallop and it should prove reliable form. The runner-up has been rated to his latest.

5174 BBAG-SALES-DE-THE GERMAN BLOODSTOCK SALES SILVER SALVER STKS (H'CAP) 7f

4:25 (4:25) (Class 2) (0-105,99) 3-Y-O+ **£12,938** (£3,850; £1,924; £962) **Stalls** Low

Form RPR

5221 **1** **Dutch Law**21 4402 4-8-9 **87** CharlieBennett(5) 8 96
(Hughie Morrison) *sn pushed along in rr: hdwy u.p over 1f out: led and hung rt ins fnl f: drvn out* **3/1**1

1000 **2** 2 **Accession (IRE)**28 4152 7-9-11 **98** MartinLane 10 102
(Charlie Fellowes) *chsd ldrs: rdn over 2f out: styd on* **10/1**

0423 **3** hd **Ifwecan**21 4399 5-9-5 **92** JimCrowley 9 95
(Martin Smith) *led: rdn over 1f out: hdd ins fnl f: styd on same pce* **11/2**2

-006 **4** nk **Miracle Of Medinah**21 4399 5-9-5 **92** LiamKeniry 3 94
(Mark Usher) *hld up: hdwy over 2f out: sn edgd rt: rdn and ev ch over 1f out: styd on same pce ins fnl f* **11/1**

2020 **5** nk **Ghalib (IRE)**28 4163 4-9-9 **96** JamesDoyle 1 97
(Ed Walker) *a.p: rdn over 2f out: ev ch over 1f out: styd on same pce ins fnl f* **6/1**3

3033 **6** hd **Scottish Glen**14 4625 10-9-3 **95** HectorCrouch(5) 6 96
(Patrick Chamings) *hld up: rdn over 2f out: hdwy u.p over 1f out: styd on same pce ins fnl f* **11/2**2

0060 **7** 2 **Farlow (IRE)**14 4665 8-9-12 **99** TonyHamilton 2 94
(Richard Fahey) *hld up in tch: rdn over 2f out: styng on same pce whn edgd rt fnl f* **12/1**

0-06 **8** 3/4 **Tanzeel (IRE)**14 4667 5-9-9 **96** (t) PaulHanagan 4 89
(Charles Hills) *chsd ldr: rdn over 2f out: ev ch over 1f out: wknd wl ins fnl f* **11/2**2

5001 **9** 1 1/2 **Outer Space**17 4534 5-9-3 **90** WilliamCarson 7 79
(Jamie Osborne) *s.i.s: hld up: rdn over 2f out: n.d* **22/1**

4030 **10** 20 **Plucky Dip**10 4758 5-8-10 **83** DannyBrock 5 18
(John Ryan) *chsd ldrs: rdn 1/2-way: wknd and eased over 1f out* **16/1**

1m 24.67s (-1.03) **Going Correction** +0.10s/f (Good) **10** Ran SP% **120.8**
Speed ratings (Par 109): **109,106,106,106,105 105,103,102,100,77**
CSF £36.09 CT £147.29 TOTE £4.10: £1.70, £3.20, £2.10; EX 34.60 Trifecta £345.10.
Owner Raymond Tooth **Bred** Raymond Clive Tooth **Trained** East Ilsley, Berks

FOCUS
Another good quality handicap won by the smart subsequent Ayr Gold Cup winners Captain Ramius and Highland Colori in 2011 and 2012. They went a decent gallop and, once again, the form should stand up to close scrutiny. The third helps with the standard.

5175 ROYAL BRITISH LEGION H'CAP 1m

5:00 (5:00) (Class 2) (0-100,99) 3-Y-O **£12,938** (£3,850; £1,924; £962) **Stalls** Low

Form RPR

-200 **1** **Another Touch**19 4448 3-9-0 **92** TonyHamilton 2 99
(Richard Fahey) *a.p: rdn and swtchd lft 1f out: led wl ins fnl f: r.o u.p* **16/1**

111 **2** nk **Sir Roderic (IRE)**24 4271 3-9-3 **95** FrederikTylicki 5 101
(Rod Millman) *hld up: hdwy over 2f out: rdn and ev ch wl ins fnl f: r.o* **6/1**

0022 **3** 3/4 **Twin Sails**10 4758 3-9-4 **96** (b) RobertWinston 8 100
(Dean Ivory) *trckd ldrs: plld hrd: wnt 2nd 1/2-way: rdn to ld over 1f out: hdd and unable qck wl ins fnl f* **11/2**3

41- **4** 2 1/4 **Daily Bulletin (USA)**267 7836 3-8-11 **89** JamesDoyle 6 88
(John Gosden) *led at stdy pce: qcknd over 2f out: rdn and hdd over 1f out: no ex ins fnl f* **15/8**1

1035 **5** 1 1/2 **Taurean Star (IRE)**14 4624 3-8-11 **89** WilliamCarson 1 84
(Michael Bell) *hld up: hdwy u.p over 1f out: no ex ins fnl f* **5/1**2

-022 **6** 1 3/4 **Bahaarah (IRE)**14 4651 3-9-7 **99** SeanLevey 7 90
(Richard Hannon) *s.s: hld up: racd keenly: hdwy and hung lft over 1f out: wknd fnl f* **17/2**

-101 **7** 14 **Galvanize (USA)**59 3026 3-8-9 **87** TedDurcan 4 44
(Sir Michael Stoute) *chsd ldr to 1/2-way: rdn over 2f out: wknd over 1f out* **11/2**3

1m 41.22s (1.22) **Going Correction** +0.10s/f (Good) **7** Ran SP% **112.9**
Speed ratings (Par 106): **97,96,95,93,92 90,76**
CSF £103.55 CT £600.84 TOTE £16.70: £6.90, £2.60; EX 92.80 Trifecta £310.70.
Owner Nicholas Wrigley & Kevin Hart **Bred** Shadwell Estate Company Limited **Trained** Musley Bank, N Yorks

FOCUS
A good quality 3yo handicap. They went a muddling gallop, though, and the form is worth treating with a degree of caution. A clear pb from the winner, and another step forward from the runner-up, with the third helping to set the standard.

5176 PRICE BAILEY CHARTERED ACCOUNTANTS H'CAP 2m 24y

5:30 (5:30) (Class 3) (0-90,86) 3-Y-O+ **£9,703** (£2,887; £1,443; £721) **Stalls** Centre

Form RPR

1212 **1** **St Michel**16 4559 3-8-13 **86** LukeMorris 2 98+
(Sir Mark Prescott Bt) *a.p: led over 1f out: shkn up and styd on wl: comf* **4/5**1

5605 **2** 3 1/4 **Planetoid (IRE)**10 4752 8-9-8 **80** (b) TimmyMurphy 8 85
(Jim Best) *hld up: hdwy over and swtchd rt over 1f out: sn rdn: chsd wnr and edgd lft ins fnl f: no imp* **20/1**

6213 **3** 1 **Stetchworth Park**16 4559 3-8-5 **78** (p) CamHardie 5 82
(Michael Bell) *chsd ldr: rdn and ev ch over 1f out: styd on same pce fnl f* **7/2**2

2321 **4** hd **Scarpeta (FR)**14 4636 3-8-2 **75** FrannyNorton 7 79
(Mark Johnston) *led: rdn and hdd over 1f out: styd on same pce* **9/2**3

1422 **5** 4 1/2 **Safira Menina**19 4462 4-9-0 **72** JimCrowley 4 70
(Martin Smith) *s.i.s: hld up: hdwy over 2f out: rdn over 1f out: wknd fnl f* **25/1**

0004 **6** 2 1/2 **See And Be Seen**15 4581 6-8-10 **75** (p) MitchGodwin(7) 6 70
(Sylvester Kirk) *chsd ldrs: rdn over 2f out: wknd over 1f out* **12/1**

-000 **7** 35 **Amber Flush**15 3913 7-9-2 **77** TimClark(3) 3 30
(Martin Smith) *hld up: bhd fnl 4f* **33/1**

3m 27.7s (0.70) **Going Correction** +0.10s/f (Good)
WFA 3 from 4yo+ 15lb **7** Ran SP% **115.2**
Speed ratings (Par 107): **102,100,99,99,97 96,78**
CSF £22.31 CT £41.95 TOTE £1.70: £1.10, £6.30; EX 20.70 Trifecta £62.90.
Owner J L C Pearce **Bred** J L C Pearce **Trained** Newmarket, Suffolk

FOCUS
A decent staying handicap. They went an, at best, respectable gallop which wasn't going to unduly effect the versatile and progressive winner. The form is set by the second, third and fourth.
T/Plt: £129.20 to a £1 stake. Pool: £81,868.65 - 462.30 winning units. T/Qpdt: £49.40 to a £1 stake. Pool: £5,014.85 - 75.10 winning units. **Colin Roberts**

The Form Book, Raceform Ltd, Newbury, RG14 5SJ

4765 REDCAR (L-H)
Saturday, August 6

OFFICIAL GOING: Good to firm (9.5)
Wind: Light against Weather: Sunny

5177 RACING UK FREE DAY PASS AUGUST 6 (S) STKS 6f
2:15 (2:16) (Class 6) 2-Y-O **£2,385** (£704; £352) **Stalls** Centre

Form				RPR
1U02	**1**		**Eva Gore**[1] 5128 2-8-12 64 GrahamGibbons 2 (David O'Meara) *mde all: rdn clr over 1f out: nudged out fnl 110yds: comf* **5/2**[2]	65
001	**2**	1 ¾	**Bismarck The Flyer (IRE)**[8] 4842 2-9-0 69 JacobButterfield(3) 4 (Ollie Pears) *hld up in tch: pushed along over 2f out: rdn over 2f out: kpt on fnl f: wnt 2nd post* **11/10**[1]	63
030	**3**	hd	**Forster Square (IRE)**[31] 4000 2-8-11 64 BarryMcHugh 5 (Richard Fahey) *trckd ldr: rdn 2f out: wandered u.p over 1f out: one pce fnl f: lost 2nd post* **11/2**[3]	56
60	**4**	8	**Whitby Bay**[15] 4601 2-8-1 0 NathanEvans(5) 3 (Michael Easterby) *hld up in tch: rdn over 2f out: wknd over 1f out* **7/1**	27
004	**5**	1 ½	**Ey Up**[31] 4000 2-8-6 43 PJMcDonald 1 (Paul Midgley) *racd keenly: trckd ldr: rdn over 2f out: wknd over 1f out* **20/1**	23

1m 12.54s (0.74) **Going Correction** -0.05s/f (Good) **5** Ran SP% **108.8**
Speed ratings (Par 92): **93,90,90,79,77**
CSF £5.52 TOTE £3.20: £1.60, £1.20; EX 5.70 Trifecta £13.00.
Owner Nick Bradley Racing (Inagh River) **Bred** Glebe Farm Stud **Trained** Upper Helmsley, N Yorks

FOCUS
Quick ground which had been watered, with 6mm applied to the whole track on Thursday and another 4mm on Friday. Very moderate fare, but a tight event pre-race on both BHA ratings and RPRs. The runners made their way towards the stands' side.

5178 RACINGUK.COM/FREEDAYPASS MEDIAN AUCTION MAIDEN STKS 7f
2:50 (2:52) (Class 5) 3-4-Y-O **£2,911** (£866; £432; £216) **Stalls** Centre

Form				RPR
	1		**Pointillism**[218] 4-9-11 0 PJMcDonald 2 (Iain Jardine) *wnt rt s: sn in midfield: rdn over 3f out: hdwy 2f out: led appr fnl f: kpt on* **13/2**[3]	66+
6	**2**	1 ¾	**Alice Thornton**[44] 3550 4-9-6 0 DavidNolan 3 (Martin Todhunter) *s.i.s: hld up: rdn over 3f out: hdwy over 1f out: styd on fnl f* **50/1**	56
6	**3**	nk	**The Big Day (IRE)**[16] 4546 3-9-0 0 AndrewMullen 12 (Nigel Tinkler) *hld up: rdn over 3f out: hdwy over 1f out: styd on fnl f* **10/1**	53
-000	**4**	2	**Euro Mac**[36] 3850 4-9-3 42 JacobButterfield(3) 8 (Neville Bycroft) *dwlt: sn in midfield: rdn and hdwy to chse ldr over 1f out: no ex fnl 110yds* **25/1**	50?
63	**5**	3	**Percy Verence**[7] 4895 3-9-0 0 JordanVaughan(5) 1 (K R Burke) *chsd ldr: rdn 3f out: wknd ins fnl f* **6/4**[1]	45
0	**6**	½	**Lukoutoldmakezebak**[24] 4258 3-9-0 0 NathanEvans(5) 10 (James Bethell) *midfield: rdn and edgd rt over 2f out: no imp* **33/1**	44
04	**7**	1 ½	**Onesie (IRE)**[14] 4639 3-9-2 0 DanielMuscutt(3) 4 (Marco Botti) *dwlt: hld up: rdn over 3f out: sn no imp* **9/4**[2]	40
00-0	**8**	nk	**Mr Conundrum**[21] 4382 3-9-5 50 PaddyAspell 5 (Lynn Siddall) *hld up: rdn over 3f out: sme hdwy over 1f out: wknd fnl f* **50/1**	39
50	**9**	3 ¾	**The Cheese Gang**[10] 4766 4-9-11 0 ConnorBeasley 6 (Susan Corbett) *led: rdn 3f out: hdd appr fnl f: wknd* **100/1**	31
	10	3 ¾	**Secret Dreamer** 4-9-8 0 EoinWalsh(3) 9 (Kevin Morgan) *hld up: rdn and edgd rt over 2f out: sn wknd* **11/1**	20
000/	**11**	17	**Sir Veillance**[598] 8192 4-9-11 0 RaulDaSilva 7 (Ivan Furtado) *trckd ldr: rdn over 3f out: wknd 2f out: eased* **33/1**	

1m 24.36s (-0.14) **Going Correction** -0.05s/f (Good)
WFA 3 from 4yo 6lb **11** Ran SP% **116.2**
Speed ratings (Par 103): **98,96,95,93,89 89,87,87,83,78 59**
CSF £291.55 TOTE £6.00: £2.20, £11.00, £2.70; EX 267.10 Trifecta £2708.70.
Owner Jim Beaumont & Douglas Pryde **Bred** Darley **Trained** Carrutherstown, D'fries & G'way

FOCUS
A seriously weak maiden. This time the runners remained in the centre of the track.

5179 MARKET CROSS JEWELLERS H'CAP 7f
3:25 (3:26) (Class 4) (0-80,84) 3-Y-O+ **£6,469** (£1,925; £962; £481) **Stalls** Centre

Form				RPR
2221	**1**		**Shamaheart (IRE)**[9] 4807 6-10-0 80 (p) DavidAllan 2 (Geoffrey Harker) *hld up: pushed along and gd hdwy over 1f out: rdn to ld narrowly ins fnl f: kpt on* **11/2**[3]	89
130	**2**	shd	**The Commendatore**[14] 4652 3-9-6 78 (b) GrahamGibbons 1 (David Barron) *led: rdn 2f out: hdd ins fnl f: briefly dropped to 3rd: rallied fnl 110yds: jst failed* **9/2**[2]	84
-452	**3**	1	**Company Asset (IRE)**[16] 4548 3-9-7 79 TomEaves 3 (Kevin Ryan) *hld up in midfield: pushed along 2f out: rdn and kpt on fnl f: wnt 3rd post* **7/1**	83
0000	**4**	hd	**Harwoods Volante (IRE)**[7] 4896 5-9-11 77 SamJames 7 (David O'Meara) *in tch: rdn over 1f out: hdwy and ev ch 1f out: no ex fnl 50yds* **9/1**	82
1050	**5**	1 ½	**Nonno Giulio (IRE)**[21] 4408 5-9-10 76 DavidNolan 6 (David Loughnane) *trckd ldr: rdn 2f out: ev ch appr fnl f: no ex fnl 110yds* **18/1**	77
3440	**6**	1 ½	**Favourite Treat (USA)**[19] 4453 6-9-11 77 (e) JamesSullivan 9 (Ruth Carr) *hld up: rdn over 1f out: nvr threatened* **16/1**	74
0001	**7**	nk	**Buccaneers Vault (IRE)**[8] 4830 4-9-11 77 (p) ConnorBeasley 4 (Michael Dods) *hld up: rdn 2f out: nvr threatened* **12/1**	73
0024	**8**	nk	**Faintly (USA)**[11] 4729 5-9-3 69 (b) KevinStott 5 (Ruth Carr) *in tch: rdn over 1f out: wknd ins fnl f* **16/1**	64
2004	**9**	1 ¼	**Athollblair Boy (IRE)**[15] 4605 3-8-13 71 AndrewMullen 10 (Nigel Tinkler) *midfield: rdn 2f out: wknd fnl f* **50/1**	61
5611	**10**	7	**Imperial State**[8] 4844 3-9-9 84 (t) MarcMonaghan(3) 8 (George Scott) *hld up: racd wd of main field: rdn over 2f out: sn btn* **5/2**[1]	55
6200	**11**	½	**Balducci**[15] 4611 9-9-10 76 PJMcDonald 11 (David Loughnane) *chsd ldr: racd wd of main field: rdn 3f out: wknd over 1f out* **20/1**	48

1m 23.51s (-0.99) **Going Correction** -0.05s/f (Good)
WFA 3 from 4yo+ 6lb **11** Ran SP% **116.1**
Speed ratings (Par 105): **103,102,101,101,99 98,97,97,95,87 87**
CSF £30.03 CT £153.65 TOTE £6.90: £1.70, £2.10, £1.60; EX 33.90 Trifecta £150.30.
Owner A S Ward **Bred** Gus Roche **Trained** Thirkleby, N Yorks

FOCUS
A decent race for the grade. They came down the centre, bar the last two home who raced nearer to the stands' side, and the first three home came from the three lowest stalls. The winner has been rated better than ever, and the fifth has been rated similar to his penultimate C&D form.

5180 PINNACLE RACING SYNDICATE SHARES NOW AVAILABLE H'CAP (PINNACLE CUP STRAIGHT MILE QUALIFIER) 1m
4:00 (4:00) (Class 4) (0-85,85) 3-Y-O+ **£6,469** (£1,925; £962; £481) **Stalls** Centre

Form				RPR
1000	**1**		**Normandy Knight**[15] 4593 4-9-1 72 PatrickMathers 11 (Richard Fahey) *racd keenly: trckd ldr: rdn 2f out: led jst ins fnl f: kpt on* **20/1**	78
5433	**2**	nk	**Quick N Quirky (IRE)**[16] 4548 3-9-3 81 (tp) AndrewMullen 10 (Tim Easterby) *hld up: pushed along 3f out: rdn and hdwy over 1f out: kpt on* **18/1**	85
4550	**3**	½	**Father Bertie**[14] 4644 4-10-0 85 (tp) GrahamGibbons 5 (Tim Easterby) *led: rdn 2f out: hdd jst ins fnl f: one pce* **7/1**[3]	89
0/00	**4**	nk	**Storm King**[65] 2819 7-9-9 80 PJMcDonald 4 (David C Griffiths) *trckd ldr: rdn over 2f out: kpt on fnl f* **25/1**	83
531	**5**	½	**Briyouni (FR)**[15] 4605 3-9-4 82 KevinStott 9 (Kevin Ryan) *midfield: rdn 2f out: kpt on fnl f* **3/1**[1]	83
5144	**6**	nk	**Cabal**[4] 4986 9-9-2 73 (v) DavidAllan 8 (Geoffrey Harker) *midfield: rdn 2f out: one pce* **16/1**	75
3042	**7**	1 ¼	**Hard To Handel**[7] 4894 4-9-11 85 (p) ShelleyBirkett(3) 7 (David O'Meara) *slowly away: hld up: pushed along 2f out: rdn ins fnl f: nvr threatened* **11/2**[2]	84
5060	**8**	shd	**Ingleby Angel (IRE)**[7] 4894 7-9-11 82 TomEaves 2 (Colin Teague) *hld up: rdn over 2f out: nvr threatened* **10/1**	81
3544	**9**	nk	**Ninetta (IRE)**[14] 4631 3-8-12 81 RowanScott(5) 1 (Ann Duffield) *in tch: rdn over 2f out: wknd ins fnl f* **16/1**	78
0000	**10**	¾	**El Beau (IRE)**[23] 4300 5-9-4 75 BarryMcHugh 3 (John Quinn) *midfield: rdn over 2f out: lost pl over 1f out* **22/1**	71
6146	**11**	1	**Abushamah (IRE)**[7] 4894 5-9-13 84 JamesSullivan 13 (Ruth Carr) *slowly away: hld up: nvr threatened* **17/2**	78
10	**12**	2	**Muhaafiz (IRE)**[57] 3113 4-9-11 85 (p) MarcMonaghan(3) 12 (David Brown) *dwlt: midfield: rdn 3f out: wknd over 1f out* **16/1**	74

1m 36.36s (-0.24) **Going Correction** -0.05s/f (Good)
WFA 3 from 4yo+ 7lb **12** Ran SP% **108.4**
Speed ratings (Par 105): **99,98,98,97,97 97,95,95,95,94 93,91**
CSF £274.55 CT £2083.45 TOTE £24.40: £7.10, £3.00, £2.80; EX 263.80 Trifecta £2269.10.
Owner Mrs H Steel **Bred** Al-Baha Bloodstock **Trained** Musley Bank, N Yorks

FOCUS
A competitive handicap. This time they stayed in the centre, with the first two positioned towards the stands' side of the pack. The first six home were separated by under two lengths. The third helps with the standard.

5181 HIGH DEFINITION RACING UK CLAIMING STKS 1m
4:35 (4:35) (Class 6) 3-Y-O **£2,385** (£704; £352) **Stalls** Centre

Form				RPR
60-0	**1**		**Scruffy McGuffy**[23] 4314 3-8-5 57 PJMcDonald 3 (Ann Duffield) *in tch: pushed along 2f out: rdn to ld narrowly appr fnl f: kpt on wl* **7/1**	64
1000	**2**	¾	**Back To Bond**[15] 4607 3-8-5 68 PatrickMathers 1 (Richard Fahey) *trckd ldr: rdn to chal 2f out: no ex towards fin* **11/8**[1]	62
1650	**3**	nse	**Intalza (IRE)**[52] 3287 3-8-0 52 (p) JamesSullivan 4 (Michael Herrington) *hld up: rdn 2f out: hdwy over 1f out: kpt on* **3/1**[2]	57
-000	**4**	4 ½	**Colombe Bleu**[43] 3604 3-8-0 58 AndrewMullen 6 (Tony Coyle) *trckd ldr: led over 5f out: rdn over 2f out: hdd appr fnl f: sn wknd* **10/1**	46
6403	**5**	2 ¼	**Mr Lucas (IRE)**[8] 4844 3-8-0 53 (v) NathanEvans(5) 5 (Peter Niven) *trcked ldr: rdn over 2f out: wknd fnl f* **4/1**[3]	46
00	**6**	22	**Olympus Mons (FR)**[31] 4001 3-8-11 0 SamJames 2 (David O'Meara) *tk str hold: led: hdd 5f out: sn dropped to rr: t.o fnl 2f* **25/1**	

1m 37.09s (0.49) **Going Correction** -0.05s/f (Good) **6** Ran SP% **112.5**
Speed ratings (Par 98): **95,94,94,89,87 65**
CSF £17.30 TOTE £8.40: £3.50, £1.10; EX 21.10 Trifecta £60.80.
Owner John Sagar & Partner **Bred** Mrs Doreen Addison & Mrs Ann Duffield **Trained** Constable Burton, N Yorks

FOCUS
A weak claimer in which they came down the centre of the track.

5182 RACING UK FREE DAY PASS TODAY H'CAP 6f
5:05 (5:06) (Class 4) (0-85,85) 3-Y-O+ **£6,469** (£1,925; £962; £481) **Stalls** Centre

Form				RPR
1014	**1**		**Cymraeg Bounty**[12] 4700 4-9-12 85 PJMcDonald 11 (Iain Jardine) *chsd ldr: rdn over 2f out: r.o fnl f: led post* **7/1**	94
6053	**2**	nse	**Highland Acclaim (IRE)**[7] 4896 5-9-12 85 DavidNolan 1 (David O'Meara) *led: clr 4f out: reduced ins fnl f: sn drvn: hdd post* **9/2**[3]	94
2341	**3**	nk	**Cosmic Chatter**[7] 4896 6-9-7 80 (p) KevinStott 4 (Ruth Carr) *midfield: pushed along and hdwy over 1f out: rdn to chse ldr ins fnl f: kpt on* **7/2**[1]	88
3130	**4**	2 ¼	**Lexi's Hero (IRE)**[14] 4632 8-9-10 83 (v) PatrickMathers 6 (Richard Fahey) *chsd ldr: rdn over 2f out: no ex ins fnl f* **14/1**	84
5200	**5**	¾	**Tikthebox (IRE)**[16] 4547 3-8-11 77 MarcMonaghan(3) 7 (David Brown) *chsd ldr: rdn over 2f out: wknd ins fnl f* **33/1**	74
000	**6**	shd	**Funding Deficit (IRE)**[20] 4428 6-9-0 78 NathanEvans(5) 8 (Jim Goldie) *midfield: rdn over 2f out: one pce and nvr threatened ldrs* **25/1**	76
4005	**7**	¾	**Meshardal (GER)**[7] 4873 6-9-1 74 JamesSullivan 5 (Ruth Carr) *hld up: rdn over 1f out: nvr threatened* **4/1**[2]	70
00	**8**	hd	**Steelriver (IRE)**[24] 4259 6-9-9 82 GrahamGibbons 9 (David Barron) *s.i.s: hld up: rdn over 1f out: nvr threatened* **12/1**	77
0410	**9**	1 ¾	**Art Obsession (IRE)**[15] 4608 5-9-3 76 BarryMcHugh 3 (Paul Midgley) *midfield: rdn along over 3f out: wknd fnl f* **8/1**	65
3004	**10**	2 ¼	**Mass Rally (IRE)**[15] 4608 9-9-7 80 (b) ConnorBeasley 2 (Michael Dods) *a towards rr* **13/2**	62

1m 9.63s (-2.17) **Going Correction** -0.05s/f (Good)
WFA 3 from 4yo+ 4lb **10** Ran SP% **118.5**
Speed ratings (Par 105): **112,111,111,108,107 107,106,106,103,100**
CSF £39.23 CT £134.22 TOTE £6.30: £2.70, £2.10, £1.30; EX 42.70 Trifecta £115.50.
Owner M Andrews **Bred** Richard Evans **Trained** Carrutherstown, D'fries & G'way

FOCUS
A fair sprint handicap in which the first three finished a little way clear. The field raced down the middle and the time was just 0.33sec outside standard. The third has been rated back to the best of his form from last year.

5183 LADIES' & GENTS' EVENING 27TH AUGUST H'CAP 1m 6f 19y
5:35 (5:37) (Class 6) (0-65,65) 3-Y-O+ **£2,264** (£673; £336; £168) **Stalls** Low

Form				RPR
4153	1		**Dusky Raider (IRE)**[9] 4810 3-8-13 **63**.......................(p) ConnorBeasley 1 (Michael Dods) *trckd ldr: rdn over 3f out: styd on fnl f: led nr fin* **3/1**[1]	68
6605	2	shd	**Next Edition (IRE)**[20] 4430 8-9-11 **62**............................(p) PJMcDonald 4 (Philip Kirby) *midfield: smooth hdwy 3f out: rdn to chal over 1f out: edgd ahd 50yds out: hdd nr fin* **10/1**	67
014	3	nk	**Midnight Warrior**[8] 4828 6-9-1 **57**.................................. RowanScott(5) 2 (Ron Barr) *in tch: rdn and hdwy to chal 3f out: led narrowly 2f out: hdd 50yds out: one pce* **5/1**[3]	62
-604	4	2 1/4	**Bridey's Lettuce (IRE)**[55] 3191 4-9-11 **62**......................... RaulDaSilva 9 (Ivan Furtado) *trckd ldr: pressed ldr over 5f out: led 4f out: sn rdn: hdd 2f out: remained cl up tl no ex fnl 110yds* **9/2**[2]	64
4060	5	3/4	**Celtic Power**[14] 4634 4-9-7 **63**.................................. NathanEvans(5) 8 (Jim Goldie) *midfield: rdn over 3f out: one pce and nvr threatened* **12/1**	64
P440	6	1/2	**Perennial**[16] 4045 7-8-10 **52**...(p) PhilDennis(5) 11 (Philip Kirby) *s.i.s: hld up: rdn and sme hdwy on outer over 2f out: one pce fr over 1f out* **25/1**	52
3446	7	5	**Frosty The Snowman (IRE)**[18] 4499 5-9-2 **53**............ JamesSullivan 5 (Ruth Carr) *hld up: nvr threatened* **8/1**	47
3-50	8	3/4	**Slipper Satin (IRE)**[21] 4381 6-9-13 **64**............................(t) AndrewElliott 6 (Simon West) *led: jnd over 5f out: hdd 4f out: sn rdn: wknd over 2f out* **10/1**	57
3-03	9	11	**Cavalieri (IRE)**[20] 4430 6-9-8 **59**..................................(p) AndrewMullen 12 (Philip Kirby) *hld up: rdn over 3f out: sn wknd* **16/1**	37
0-06	10	3/4	**Sigurd (GER)**[36] 3842 4-9-2 **53**..(p) TomEaves 3 (Kevin Ryan) *midfield: rdn along over 5f out: wknd over 2f out* **18/1**	30
2206	11	3/4	**Hallstatt (IRE)**[16] 4550 10-10-0 **65**..........................(t) GrahamGibbons 10 (John Mackie) *in tch: rdn over 3f out: wknd 2f out* **11/1**	41

3m 0.07s (-4.63) **Going Correction** -0.05s/f (Good)
WFA 3 from 4yo+ 13lb **11** Ran SP% **120.2**
Speed ratings (Par 101): **111,110,110,109,109 108,105,105,99,98 98**
CSF £35.03 CT £149.68 TOTE £3.10: £1.20, £3.10, £2.50; EX 39.20 Trifecta £317.90.
Owner A Wynn Williams & D Graham **Bred** Spratstown Bloodstock Ltd **Trained** Denton, Co Durham

FOCUS
A good finish to this moderate staying handicap.
T/Plt: £577.60 to a £1 stake.. Pool: £57,451.39 - 72.60 winning units. T/Qpdt: £26.80 to a £1 stake. Pool: £4,343.02 - 119.80 winning units. **Andrew Sheret**

5184 - (Foreign Racing) - See Raceform Interactive

4906 SARATOGA (R-H)
Saturday, August 6

OFFICIAL GOING: Dirt: fast; turf: firm

5185a FASIG-TIPTON DE LA ROSE STKS (LISTED RACE) (4YO+ FILLIES & MARES) (TURF) 1m
11:54 (12:00) 4-Y-O+
£40,816 (£13,605; £6,802; £3,401; £2,040; £340)

			RPR
1		**Lady Lara (IRE)**[56] 3178 5-8-11 0.................................... JoseLezcano 3 (William Mott, U.S.A) **16/5**[2]	107
2	1	**Stormy Victoria (FR)**[34] 4-8-7 0.. IradOrtizJr 2 (Christophe Clement, U.S.A) **63/10**	101
3	1	**Zindaya (USA)**[400] 5-8-9 0.. JavierCastellano 7 (Chad C Brown, U.S.A) **79/20**[3]	100
4	nk	**Roca Rojo (IRE)**[437] 2620 4-8-5 0................................ JohnRVelazquez 1 (Chad C Brown, U.S.A) **21/10**[1]	96
5	nse	**My Sweet Girl (USA)**[35] 4-8-9 0................................(b) ManuelFranco 8 (Barclay Tagg, U.S.A) **118/10**	100
6	1	**Robillard (USA)**[44] 4-8-5 0.................................... KendrickCarmouche 6 (Kiaran McLaughlin, U.S.A) **106/10**	93
7	nk	**Excilly**[35] 3916 4-8-9 0.. JulienRLeparoux 5 (Tom Dascombe) **146/10**	97
8	1 1/2	**Bitty Kitty (USA)**[28] 6-8-3 0.. JoseLOrtiz 9 (Brendan P Walsh, U.S.A) **248/10**	87
9	3/4	**Mayla (USA)**[42] 4-8-9 0.. LuisSaez 4 (W Bret Calhoun, U.S.A) **30/1**	91

1m 35.88s (95.88) **9** Ran SP% **119.9**

Owner B V Sangster **Bred** Shanty Syndicate **Trained** USA

4854 VICHY
Saturday, August 6

OFFICIAL GOING: Turf: soft

5186a PRIX DES JOUVENCEAUX ET DES JOUVENCELLES (LISTED RACE) (2YO) (TURF) 7f
6:05 (12:00) 2-Y-O **£20,220** (£8,088; £6,066; £4,044; £2,022)

			RPR
1		**Miss Infinity (IRE)**[22] 4352 2-8-13 0................................ IoritzMendizabal 6 (Mark Johnston) *led or disp ld early: hdd bef 1/2-way but styd handy: cl 3rd and rdn over 1 1/2f out: styd on u.p to ld fnl 100yds* **23/5**[3]	94
2	nk	**Body Sculpt (FR)**[42] 2-8-13 0.. AlexisBadel 1 (S Kobayashi, France) **25/1**	93
3	1 1/4	**Belle De Belle (FR)**[9] 2-8-13 0.................................. MickaelBarzalona 2 (P Sogorb, France) **89/10**	90
4	shd	**My Bo Chop (FR)** 2-9-2 0... MickaelForest 9 (A Chopard, France) **41/10**[2]	93
5	snk	**Tornibush (IRE)**[36] 3871 2-9-2 0................................... FranckBlondel 5 (P Decouz, France) **16/1**	92
6	1 1/2	**Icalo (FR)**[23] 4330 2-9-2 0.. FabriceVeron 4 (H-A Pantall, France) **6/4**[1]	88
7	9	**Neelanjali (FR)**[50] 3378 2-8-13 0.................................. AnthonyCrastus 3 (N Caullery, France) **26/5**	62
8	4 1/2	**Affoburg (FR)**[32] 2-9-2 0.. CristianDemuro 8 (Simone Brogi, France) **17/1**	53
9	3/4	**Silver Poker (FR)** 2-9-2 0... ThibaultSpeicher 7 (D Chenu, France) **99/1**	51

1m 27.39s (87.39) **9** Ran SP% **120.0**
WIN (incl. 1 euro stake): 5.60. PLACES: 2.70, 4.90, 3.00. DF: 73.00. SF: 166.10.
Owner Mrs Jane Newett **Bred** Desert Star Phoenix Jvc **Trained** Middleham Moor, N Yorks

KLAMPENBORG
Saturday, August 6

OFFICIAL GOING: Turf: good

5187a CHESS RACING SCANDINAVIAN OPEN CHAMPIONSHIP (GROUP 3) (3YO+) (TURF) 1m 4f
3:30 (12:00) 3-Y-O+ **£24,703** (£9,881; £4,940; £2,964; £1,976)

			RPR
1		**Quarterback (GER)**[23] 4329 4-9-4 0.........................(p) Jan-ErikNeuroth 3 (Rune Haugen) **17/2**	99
2	nse	**Inaya**[308] 6949 5-9-1 0.. NelsonDeSouza 6 (Jessica Long, Sweden) **207/10**	96
3	1/2	**Bank Of Burden (USA)**[23] 4329 9-9-6 0............ Per-AndersGraberg 12 (Niels Petersen, Norway) **596/100**[3]	99
4	nk	**Giuseppe Piazzi (IRE)** 4-9-4 0................................ JorgeHorcajada 11 (Flemming Velin, Denmark) **67/10**	97
5	hd	**Hurricane Red (IRE)**[23] 4329 6-9-6 0......................... JacobJohansen 10 (Lennart Reuterskiold Jr, Sweden) **51/20**[2]	98
6	1/2	**Matauri (IRE)**[23] 4329 5-9-4 0....................................(p) ElioneChaves 8 (Niels Petersen, Norway) **29/1**	95
7	nk	**Fields Of Athenry (IRE)**[329] 6314 4-9-6 0........................ OliverWilson 5 (Flemming Velin, Denmark) **5/2**[1]	97
8	1/2	**Jubilance (IRE)**[23] 4329 7-9-4 0.............................. MrFredrikJanetzky 7 (Bent Olsen, Denmark) **40/1**	94
9	4	**Berling (IRE)**[23] 9-9-6 0... ValmirDeAzeredo 4 (Jessica Long, Sweden) **106/10**	88
10	1/2	**Captain Morgan (DEN)**[303] 5-9-4 0.................................. NikolajStott 1 (Marc Stott, Denmark) **233/10**	85
11	5	**Falconet (DEN)**[62] 6-9-4 0... ManuelSantos 2 (Bent Olsen, Denmark) **18/1**	77
12	3	**Stinger (DEN)**[636] 4-9-4 0.. CarlosLopez 9 (Hanne Bechmann, Denmark) **42/1**	72

2m 28.0s (148.00) **12** Ran SP% **125.3**

Owner Team MK **Bred** Stiftung Gestut Fahrhof **Trained** Newmarket, Suffolk

4974 CHELMSFORD (A.W) (L-H)
Sunday, August 7

OFFICIAL GOING: Polytrack: standard
Wind: medium, half behind Weather: sunny, breezy

5188 JOOLS HOLLAND HERE ON 20TH AUGUST MAIDEN STKS (PLUS 10 RACE) 5f (P)
2:20 (2:21) (Class 4) 2-Y-O **£6,469** (£1,925; £962; £481) **Stalls** Low

Form				RPR
2004	1		**Megan Lily (IRE)**[16] 4586 2-9-0 77............................[1] GeorgeChaloner 6 (Richard Fahey) *led for 1f: styd pressing ldr: rdn to chal over 1f out: led ent fnl f: r.o wl: rdn out* **4/1**[2]	73
22	2	1 1/4	**Mr Pocket (IRE)**[13] 4707 2-9-5 0.. LukeMorris 1 (Paul Cole) *wnt sharply rt leaving stalls: hung rt thrght: led after 1f: shkn up over 1f out: rdn and hdd ent fnl f: one pce fnl f* **1/4**[1]	74
66	3	1 3/4	**Precious Plum**[19] 4473 2-8-11 0............................ JosephineGordon(3) 4 (Chris Dwyer) *dwlt: outpcd in 5th: pushed and clsd 2f out: hdwy to chse clr ldng pair ins fnl f: styd on steadily wout threatening ldrs* **20/1**[3]	62
0	4	1 3/4	**Prancelina (IRE)**[32] 4022 2-9-0 0............................ SilvestreDeSousa 7 (Phil McEntee) *racd keenly early: pressed ldrs tl dropped in to 3rd after 1f: rdn and hung lft over 1f out: lost 3rd and wknd ins fnl f* **20/1**[3]	56
0	5	1/2	**Erissimus Maximus (FR)**[19] 4473 2-9-5 0................. LemosdeSouza 3 (Chris Dwyer) *s.i.s: outpcd in rr: c wd 2f out: rdn over 1f out: kpt on steadily ins fnl f: nvr trbld ldrs* **50/1**	59
4	6	7	**The Lady Hysteria (IRE)**[27] 4196 2-8-7 0........................ JaneElliott(7) 2 (Phil McEntee) *taken down early: in tch in 4th: rdn over 1f out: sn struggling and lost pl: wknd fnl f* **66/1**	29

1m 0.49s (0.29) **Going Correction** +0.025s/f (Slow) **6** Ran SP% **113.0**
Speed ratings (Par 96): **98,96,93,90,89 78**
CSF £5.51 TOTE £4.10: £1.70, £1.10; EX 7.10 Trifecta £15.40.
Owner Nick Bradley Racing 1 **Bred** Irish National Stud **Trained** Musley Bank, N Yorks

FOCUS
Weak form as only two made any obvious appeal, and the odds-on favourite proved to be really disappointing.

5189 WE ARE MACMILLAN CANCER SUPPORT H'CAP 5f (P)
2:50 (2:52) (Class 4) (0-80,80) 3-Y-O+ **£8,086** (£2,406; £1,202; £601) **Stalls** Low

Form				RPR
4546	1		**Dynamo Walt (IRE)**[27] 4198 5-9-2 **75**.........................(v) NoelGarbutt(3) 7 (Derek Shaw) *chsd ldng pair: effrt on inner to chal over 1f out: drvn to ld ins fnl f: r.o wl: rdn out* **4/1**[1]	85
2100	2	3/4	**Elusivity (IRE)**[23] 4345 8-9-2 **79**..............................(p) SophieKilloran(7) 3 (Conor Dore) *w ldr tl led wl over 1f out: edgd lft u.p jst over 1f out: hdd ins fnl f: styd on same pce after* **16/1**	86
4640	3	2 3/4	**Long Awaited (IRE)**[4] 5032 8-9-2 **75**.................(b) JosephineGordon(3) 8 (Conor Dore) *hld up in midfield: rdn and effrt over 1f out: styd on ins fnl f: wnt 3rd fnl 75yds out: nvr threatened ldrs* **10/1**	72
0434	4	nk	**Top Boy**[23] 4345 6-9-9 **79**..(v) MartinLane 10 (Derek Shaw) *hld up in last trio: hung rt and wd bnd 2f out: sn rdn: hdwy 1f out: r.o wl ins fnl f: wnt 4th last stride: nvr trbld ldrs* **5/1**[2]	75+

5301 **5** *shd* **Jaarih (IRE)**[26] 4236 4-9-2 **72**.......................................(p) PaulMulrennan 6 68
(Conor Dore) *swtchd lft sn after s: hld up in midfield: hdwy on inner over 1f out: battling for 3rd 100yds out: kpt on: nvr trbld ldrs* **12/1**

5545 **6** *½* **Diamond Charlie (IRE)**[25] 4264 8-9-3 **73**..................(p) NickyMackay 11 67
(Simon Dow) *s.i.s and swtchd lft after s: hld up in last trio: rdn and hdwy over 1f out: styd on ins fnl f: nvr trbld ldrs* **25/1**

6064 **7** *½* **Noble Asset**[9] 4817 5-9-5 **75**.. FrannyNorton 2 67
(Milton Bradley) *led tl wl over 1f out: 3rd and outpcd u.p whn swtchd rt over 1f out: lost 2 pls and wknd wl ins fnl f* **7/1**

6253 **8** *½* **Welease Bwian (IRE)**[19] 4475 7-9-1 **78**....................(v) MillyNaseb(7) 12 68
(Stuart Williams) *s.i.s: racd in last trio: effrt over 1f out: hdwy 1f out: clsng but stl plenty to do whn nt clr run ins fnl f: swtchd rt and styd on towards fin: nvr trbld ldrs* **6/1**3

3664 **9** *nk* **Desert Strike**[13] 4714 10-9-4 **74**....................................(p) MartinHarley 5 63
(Conor Dore) *taken down early: chsd ldng trio: hung rt 2f out: rdn and unable qck over 1f out: wknd ins fnl f* **7/1**

1506 **10** *25* **Powerful Wind (IRE)**[10] 4809 7-9-3 **73**........................ AdamBeschizza 9
(Charlie Wallis) *midfield: lost pl and bhd 2f out: lost tch over 1f out: t.o* **20/1**

59.51s (-0.69) **Going Correction** +0.025s/f (Slow)
WFA 3 from 4yo+ 3lb **10** Ran SP% **107.2**
Speed ratings (Par 105): **106,104,100,99,99 98,98,97,96,56**
CSF £57.60 CT £437.71 TOTE £4.70: £1.60, £6.20, £4.00; EX 70.50 Trifecta £551.10.
Owner Brian Johnson (Northamptonshire) **Bred** Dan Major **Trained** Sproxton, Leics
■ Rocking Rudolph was withdrawn. Price at time of withdrawal 6-1. Rule 4 applies to all bets - deduction 10p in the pound.

FOCUS
They went a good pace in this fair handicap, and not many got into it.

5190 MACMILLAN NOT ALONE CAMPAIGN FILLIES' H'CAP 7f (P)
3:20 (3:21) (Class 3) (0-95,93) 4-Y-O+ **£9,703** (£2,887; £1,443; £721) **Stalls** Low

Form RPR
343 **1** **Stosur (IRE)**[9] 4819 5-7-9 **74** oh2..................................(b) DavidEgan(7) 3 82
(Gay Kelleway) *t.k.h: sn w ldr tl led 5f out: rdn over 1f out: hrd pressed ins fnl f: kpt on and hld on cl home* **5/1**2

4404 **2** *hd* **Bint Dandy (IRE)**[37] 3848 5-9-7 **93**.......................(b) SilvestreDeSousa 6 100
(Chris Dwyer) *chsd ldrs: rdn jst over 2f out: drvn to chse wnr over 1f out: pressing wnr ins fnl f: styd on u.p: nt quite get to wnr* **7/4**1

2245 **3** *1 ½* **Gleaming Girl**[30] 4087 4-7-9 **74**.................................. SophieKilloran(7) 1 77
(David Simcock) *hld up in last pair: effrt and hdwy whn swtchd rt over 1f out: rdn and nt clrest of runs 1f out: styd on wl ins fnl f: nt rch ldrs* **5/1**2

200 **4** *½* **Perfect Alchemy (IRE)**[38] 3815 5-8-4 **76**........................ FrannyNorton 4 78
(Patrick Chamings) *t.k.h: chsd ldrs: effrt and hung lft over 1f out: stl pressing ldrs ins fnl f: no ex and lost 3rd 100yds out: wknd towards fin* **8/1**3

1326 **5** *4* **Maureb (IRE)**[4] 5034 4-7-10 **75**.......................................(p) RPWalsh(7) 5 66
(Tony Coyle) *t.k.h: hld up in tch in midfield: hdwy on outer to chse ldrs 2f out: unable qck u.p over 1f out: wknd ins fnl f* **8/1**3

4-54 **6** *2* **Maggie Pink**[193] 351 7-8-12 **87**............................ AlistairRawlinson(3) 2 73
(Michael Appleby) *taken down early: t.k.h: led for 2f: styd upsides ldr tl unable qck and outpcd over 1f out: wknd ins fnl f* **8/1**3

0646 **7** *¾* **Queen Aggie (IRE)**[15] 4630 6-8-2 **77**................... JosephineGordon(3) 7 61
(Tony Carroll) *hld up in tch in rr: rdn over 2f out: no imp u.p over 1f out: wknd fnl f* **8/1**3

1m 26.39s (-0.81) **Going Correction** +0.025s/f (Slow) **7** Ran SP% **114.1**
Speed ratings (Par 104): **105,104,103,102,97 95,94**
CSF £14.16 TOTE £6.70: £4.00, £1.90; EX 16.40 Trifecta £100.10.
Owner Brian C Oakley **Bred** Mervyn Stewkesbury **Trained** Exning, Suffolk

FOCUS
Ordinary form for the level. The runner-up produced a fine effort giving both the winner and the third 26lb.

5191 MACMILLAN.ORG.UK H'CAP 1m (P)
3:50 (3:53) (Class 4) (0-85,84) 3-Y-O+ **£8,086** (£2,406; £1,202; £601) **Stalls** Low

Form RPR
1032 **1** **Nouvelli Dancer (IRE)**[21] 4429 3-9-0 **77**.................. SilvestreDeSousa 3 86
(Ivan Furtado) *chsd ldng pair tl wnt 2nd 3f out: effrt and hanging rt over 1f out: drvn and str chal ins fnl f: styd on to ld last strides* **9/2**3

-150 **2** *hd* **Symbolic**[30] 4080 3-9-7 **84**.......................................[1] RobertHavlin 4 92
(John Gosden) *sn led: hung rt and rdn over 1f out: drvn and hrd pressed ins fnl f: hdd last strides* **2/1**2

12 **3** *¾* **Misty Lord (IRE)**[16] 4593 3-8-11 **77**.........................(t) DanielMuscutt(3) 1 83
(Marco Botti) *dwlt: hld up in tch: stmbld after 1f: effrt to chse ldng pair and swtchd rt 2f out: carried rt and swtchd lft over 1f out: styd on u.p ins fnl f* **13/8**1

004 **4** *5* **Starboard**[44] 3623 7-9-9 **84**.......................................(p) GeorgeBuckell(5) 2 80
(David Simcock) *broke wl: sn stdd to rr and sn niggled along: effrt on outer bnd 2f out: 4th and swtchd lft over 1f out: no imp 1f out: wknd ins fnl f* **8/1**

1101 **5** *18* **Just Be Lucky (IRE)**[18] 4511 4-9-10 **80**....................(p) PaulMulrennan 5 34
(Conor Dore) *sn chsng ldr: lost 2nd 3f out and sn u.p: lost pl 2f out and sn bhd* **12/1**

1m 39.92s (0.02) **Going Correction** +0.025s/f (Slow)
WFA 3 from 4yo+ 7lb **5** Ran SP% **108.4**
Speed ratings (Par 105): **100,99,99,94,76**
CSF £13.46 TOTE £5.10: £2.20, £1.60; EX 14.30 Trifecta £25.90.
Owner S Laffan **Bred** Colin Kennedy **Trained** Wiseton, Nottinghamshire
■ Stewards' Enquiry : Silvestre De Sousa caution: careless riding

FOCUS
The three that headed the market pulled nicely clear, and the form is probably okay for the level. The first and third were sired by Lilbourne Lad.

5192 BE.MACMILLAN MEDIAN AUCTION MAIDEN FILLIES' STKS 1m (P)
4:20 (4:23) (Class 5) 3-4-Y-O **£5,175** (£1,540; £769; £384) **Stalls** Low

Form RPR
05 **1** **Rebel Sky**[17] 4565 3-9-0 0...................................... KierenFox 5 64
(J R Jenkins) *broke wl: sn stdd bk to last and t.k.h: rdn over 2f out: hdwy u.p 1f out: styd on wl to ld towards fin* **33/1**

6-2 **2** *nk* **Roman Holiday (IRE)**[15] 4639 3-9-0 0............................. TedDurcan 4 63
(Ed Vaughan) *stdd s: hld up in tch: effrt to press ldr 2f out: rdn to chal over 1f out: led ins fnl f: sn hrd pressed: hdd last strides* **1/2**1

033 **3** *3 ½* **Ms Gillard**[120] 1346 3-9-0 65...................................... SilvestreDeSousa 1 55
(David Simcock) *restless in stalls: trckd ldrs: effrt over 2f out: nt clr run and swtchd rt over 1f out: drvn and unable qck 1f out: outpcd by ldng pair ins fnl f: wnt 3rd but wknd fnl 100yds* **9/4**2

0 **4** *¾* **Summertime Lucy (IRE)**[142] 984 3-9-0 0........................ JackMitchell 3 53
(Giles Bravery) *pressed ldr tl rdn to ld 3f out: drvn over 1f out: hdd jst ins fnl f: wknd fnl 100yds* **25/1**

000 **5** *9* **Lady Lloyd**[9] 4835 3-8-11 54...............................(p) JosephineGordon(3) 2 33
(Phil McEntee) *led tl 3f out: sn rdn: outpcd and btn over 1f out: wknd fnl f* **16/1**3

1m 43.03s (3.13) **Going Correction** +0.025s/f (Slow) **5** Ran SP% **110.1**
Speed ratings (Par 100): **85,84,81,80,71**
CSF £52.23 TOTE £25.40: £13.50, £1.10; EX 70.00 Trifecta £145.90.
Owner Barry Polkey **Bred** Philippa Casey & David Bryans **Trained** Royston, Herts

FOCUS
They didn't go any great pace early in this fillies maiden, and it produced a surprise result.

5193 NO ONE SHOULD FACE CANCER ALONE H'CAP 1m 2f (P)
4:50 (4:53) (Class 5) (0-75,74) 3-Y-O **£5,175** (£1,540; £769; £384) **Stalls** Low

Form RPR
5-45 **1** **Possible Future**[18] 4522 3-9-2 **69**............................ SilvestreDeSousa 2 79
(Ismail Mohammed) *mde all: pushed clr over 2f out: 4 l clr 1f out: drvn ins fnl f: a jst gng to hold on* **9/4**2

5-05 **2** *hd* **Rubensian**[36] 3904 3-8-7 **65**.. GeorgeBuckell(5) 3 74
(David Simcock) *stdd s: hld up in rr: swtchd rt and effrt 2f out: chsd clr wnr and hung lft over 1f out: styd on wl ins fnl f and clsng qckly towards fin: nvr quite getting to wnr* **6/1**

-443 **3** *13* **Hardington**[24] 4288 3-9-3 **70**.. FergusSweeney 1 53
(Alan King) *in tch: wnt 3rd 7f out: rdn over 3f out: struggling and outpcd over 2f out: wknd over 1f out* **7/4**1

2242 **4** *4 ½* **The Major**[43] 3653 3-9-4 **74**.. LouisSteward(3) 5 48
(Michael Bell) *chsd ldng pair tl 7f out: styd handy in 4th: rdn 3f out: sn struggling: wknd over 1f out* **9/2**3

050 **5** *15* **Stamford Raffles**[20] 4458 3-8-12 **65**............................ MartinHarley 4 9
(Stuart Williams) *chsd ldr: rdn over 2f out: getting outpcd whn hung lft and eased wl over 1f out: wl bhd fnl f: t.o* **6/1**

2m 6.65s (-1.95) **Going Correction** +0.025s/f (Slow) **5** Ran SP% **113.9**
Speed ratings (Par 100): **108,107,97,93,81**
CSF £15.81 TOTE £3.30: £1.50, £3.60; EX 17.50 Trifecta £38.20.
Owner Saeed H Al Tayer **Bred** Jeremy Green And Sons **Trained** Newmarket, Suffolk

FOCUS
None of these had won previously, so it's hard to know quite what the value of the form is. The gallop appeared fairly sound but the winner kicked off the front.

5194 CHELMSFORD CITY RACECOURSE SUPPORTING MACMILLAN H'CAP 6f (P)
5:20 (5:20) (Class 6) (0-60,65) 4-Y-O+ **£3,234** (£962; £481; £240) **Stalls** Centre

Form RPR
3213 **1** **Not Your Call (IRE)**[48] 3474 5-9-7 **60**............................ KierenFox 2 70
(Lee Carter) *taken down early: mde all: rdn 2f out: styd on wl and in command ins fnl f: rdn out* **6/4**1

3500 **2** *1 ¼* **Encapsulated**[97] 1928 6-9-0 **60**..................................... RhiainIngram(7) 8 67
(Roger Ingram) *taken down early: chsd ldrs on outer: effrt to press ldrs 2f out: drvn to chse wnr 1f out: styd on same pce ins fnl f* **8/1**3

200 **3** *1 ½* **Wattaboutsteve**[19] 4472 5-8-9 **48**.............................. SilvestreDeSousa 6 50
(Ralph J Smith) *chsd wnr: rdn over 2f out: lost 2nd and unable qck 1f out: styd on same pce after* **8/1**3

0045 **4** *2 ½* **Rocket Rob (IRE)**[37] 3843 10-9-3 **56**............................ StevieDonohoe 5 51
(Willie Musson) *hld up in tch in midfield: effrt over 1f out: styd on same pce and no imp ins fnl f* **10/1**

3214 **5** *shd* **Wedgewood Estates**[33] 3984 5-9-3 **56**............................ LukeMorris 7 50
(Tony Carroll) *hld up in tch in last pair: effrt over 1f out: no imp u.p: kpt on same pce fnl f* **4/1**2

0051 **6** *½* **Compton Prince**[2] 5126 7-9-12 **65** 6ex.........................(b) FrannyNorton 4 58
(Milton Bradley) *hld up in tch in midfield: rdn and unable qck over 1f out: wl hld and plugged on same pce fnl f* **4/1**2

0-00 **7** *6* **Interchoice Star**[40] 3735 11-8-13 **52**...............................(p) MartinLane 3 27
(Ray Peacock) *in tch in midfield: rdn over 2f out: lost pl u.p over 1f out: bhd fnl f* **25/1**

1m 13.27s (-0.43) **Going Correction** +0.025s/f (Slow) **7** Ran SP% **115.2**
Speed ratings (Par 101): **103,101,99,96,95 95,87**
CSF £14.88 CT £73.49 TOTE £2.20: £2.90, £3.20; EX 15.10 Trifecta £101.70.
Owner Clear Racing **Bred** Castleton Lyons & Kilboy Estate **Trained** Epsom, Surrey

FOCUS
Being in a prominent position was beneficial as the first three home were in the first three places entering the home straight.
T/Jkpt: Not won. T/Plt: £26.20 to a £1 stake. Pool: £57,659.02 - 1603.91 winning units. T/Qpdt: £17.20 to a £1 stake. Pool: £3,624.05 - 155.75 winning units. **Steve Payne**

4759 LEICESTER (R-H)
Sunday, August 7

OFFICIAL GOING: Good to firm (7.7)
Wind: Light across Weather: Fine

5195 ROBERT COX 60TH BIRTHDAY CELEBRATION H'CAP 6f
2:00 (2:00) (Class 5) (0-70,70) 3-Y-O **£3,234** (£962; £481; £240) **Stalls** High

Form RPR
3006 **1** **Case Key**[50] 3407 3-9-7 **70**.. AndrewMullen 4 77
(Michael Appleby) *prom: pushed along and outpcd over 3f out: hdwy to chse ldr over 1f out: sn rdn: styd on u.p to ld nr fin* **9/2**3

0252 **2** *nk* **Dance Alone**[8] 4870 3-9-0 **70**.................................(b) LewisEdmunds(7) 3 76
(Kevin Ryan) *led: pushed clr wl over 1f out: sn rdn and hung rt: hdd nr fin* **11/4**1

3154 **3** *4 ½* **Belle Mare Plage**[18] 4525 3-8-9 **61**.........................(t) AaronJones(3) 6 53
(Stuart Williams) *hld up: hdwy over 3f out: rdn over 2f out: hung rt fr over 1f out: styd on same pce ins fnl f* **8/1**

5433 **4** *nk* **Iceaxe**[23] 4365 3-9-1 **64**.. RoystonFfrench 5 55
(John Holt) *chsd ldr tl rdn over 2f out: sn outpcd: styd on towards fin* **4/1**2

6200 **5** *¾* **Take Charge**[18] 4517 3-9-4 **67**.. SeanLevey 7 55
(David Brown) *dwlt: bhd: styd on towards fin: nvr nrr* **14/1**

1542 **6** *3* **Bahamian Sunshine**[65] 2864 3-9-0 **68**...............(p) AdamMcNamara(5) 1 47
(Richard Fahey) *chsd ldrs: wnt 2nd over 2f out tl rdn over 1f out: sn wknd* **11/4**1

1m 11.58s (-1.42) **Going Correction** -0.20s/f (Firm) **6** Ran SP% **109.3**
Speed ratings (Par 100): **101,100,94,94,93 89**
CSF £16.27 TOTE £6.20: £2.80, £1.10; EX 21.70 Trifecta £95.30.
Owner Terry Pryke **Bred** Lady Cobham **Trained** Oakham, Rutland

FOCUS
An ordinary 3yo sprint handicap.

5196 BRITISH STALLION STUDS EBF MAIDEN STKS (PLUS 10 RACE) 7f
2:30 (2:30) (Class 4) 2-Y-O **£6,469** (£1,925; £962; £481) **Stalls** High

Form RPR

4 **1** **Berengaria (IRE)**[10] 4801 2-9-0 0 JoeFanning 2 80+
(Mark Johnston) *mde all: racd keenly early: shkn up over 1f out: r.o: comf* **10/11**[1]

56 **2** *1 ½* **Mr Tyrrell (IRE)**[23] 4349 2-9-5 0 PatDobbs 4 78
(Richard Hannon) *chsd wnr: rdn over 2f out: styd on same pce wl ins fnl f* **5/2**[2]

3 *2 ¼* **Zainhom (USA)** 2-9-5 0 PaulHanagan 5 72
(Sir Michael Stoute) *s.i.s: hld up: shkn up over 2f out: hdwy over 1f out: rdn and edgd rt ins fnl f: styd on same pce* **3/1**[3]

0 **4** *2 ½* **Trading Punches (IRE)**[8] 4856 2-9-5 0 ShaneGray 1 65
(David Brown) *s.i.s: hld up: pushed along 1/2-way: rdn and outpcd over 2f out: nvr on terms* **33/1**

0 **5** *shd* **Cambridge Favorite**[59] 3074 2-9-0 0 SaleemGolam 3 60
(Mrs Ilka Gansera-Leveque) *chsd ldrs: rdn over 2f out: wknd fnl f* **50/1**

1m 25.38s (-0.82) **Going Correction** -0.20s/f (Firm) **5** Ran SP% **110.9**
Speed ratings (Par 96): **96,94,91,88,88**
CSF £3.53 TOTE £1.80: £1.10, £1.80; EX 3.90 Trifecta £5.40.
Owner Sheikh Hamdan bin Mohammed Al Maktoum **Bred** Darley **Trained** Middleham Moor, N Yorks

FOCUS
Probably not a bad little 2yo maiden.

5197 THURMASTON (S) STKS 7f
3:00 (3:00) (Class 6) 3-4-Y-O **£2,587** (£770; £384; £192) **Stalls** High

Form RPR

0242 **1** **Mecca's Missus (IRE)**[11] 4760 3-8-4 59 (be) ConnorBeasley 4 64
(Michael Dods) *racd keenly: sn w ldrs: led wl over 1f out: sn rdn and edgd lft: styd on u.p* **5/2**[2]

1622 **2** *1 ½* **Smart Mover (IRE)**[18] 4511 3-8-8 70 CallumShepherd(5) 9 69
(John Quinn) *w ldr tl rdn over 2f out: styd on same pce ins fnl f* **11/4**[3]

0121 **3** *3 ¼* **Boutan**[11] 4760 3-8-13 69 (p) LiamKeniry 7 60
(George Baker) *edgd rt s: sn led: rdn and hdd wl over 1f out: edgd rt: no ex ins fnl f* **2/1**[1]

4060 **4** *1 ¼* **Stormy Art (IRE)**[16] 4600 3-8-9 50 AndrewMullen 6 53
(Michael Dods) *hmpd s: sn prom: rdn over 2f out: no ex fnl f* **12/1**

0500 **5** *6* **Popeswood (IRE)**[17] 4557 4-9-6 72 SeanLevey 8 44
(Ron Hodges) *hld up: drvn along 1/2-way: nt trble ldrs* **6/1**

0400 **6** *6* **Hodgkins Trust (IRE)**[33] 3975 3-8-10 40 ow1 (b[1]) RobertTart 5 21
(Jeremy Gask) *hmpd s: a in rr* **66/1**

0-00 **7** *1 ¾* **Miss Mozaico**[32] 4001 3-8-4 27 (b) PaulQuinn 1 11
(Richard Whitaker) *s.i.s: racd keenly and sn prom: rdn and wknd over 2f out* **100/1**

00-0 **8** *8* **Teepee Time**[158] 785 3-8-4 48 RoystonFfrench 3
(Brian Baugh) *hld up: plld hrd: rdn and wknd 1/2-way* **50/1**

1m 24.71s (-1.49) **Going Correction** -0.20s/f (Firm)
WFA 3 from 4yo 6lb **8** Ran SP% **115.0**
Speed ratings (Par 101): **100,98,94,93,86 79,77,68**
CSF £9.91 TOTE £3.10: £1.10, £1.30, £1.10; EX 11.30 Trifecta £20.00.Meccas Missus was bought by James Lay for 4200gns; Boutan was claimed by Bernard Llewellyn for £7000; Smart Mover was claimed by Nikki Evans for £7000
Owner David T J Metcalfe **Bred** Kabansk Ltd & Rathbarry Stud **Trained** Denton, Co Durham

FOCUS
Straightforward plating-class form.

5198 MICHAEL JOHN FLOORING H'CAP 1m 1f 218y
3:30 (3:30) (Class 4) (0-85,85) 3-Y-O+ **£6,301** (£1,886; £943; £472; £235) **Stalls** Low

Form RPR

4122 **1** **Paling**[17] 4561 3-8-12 81 KieranShoemark(3) 5 94
(Roger Charlton) *hld up: plld hrd: hdwy over 2f out: shkn up to ld and edgd rt over 1f out: rdn clr ins fnl f: eased nr fin* **6/4**[1]

31 **2** *5* **His Kyllachy (IRE)**[14] 4682 3-9-1 81 GrahamGibbons 3 84
(William Haggas) *plld hrd early: trckd ldrs: rdn over 2f out: styd on same pce fnl f* **3/1**[2]

2366 **3** *¾* **Ansaab**[15] 4650 8-10-0 85 AndrewMullen 1 87
(Michael Appleby) *led: hdd over 8f out: chsd ldr tl rdn to ld over 2f out: hdd over 1f out: styd on same pce fnl f* **12/1**

2022 **4** *1 ¼* **Cape Banjo (USA)**[13] 4710 3-8-13 79 PatDobbs 6 78
(Ralph Beckett) *s.i.s: hld up: rdn over 2f out: nt trble ldrs* **11/2**[3]

5156 **5** *nse* **Daisy Boy (IRE)**[17] 4561 5-9-7 81 (t) AaronJones(3) 4 80
(Stuart Williams) *pushed along early and prom: led over 8f out: rdn and hdd over 2f out: no ex fr over 1f out* **10/1**

1040 **6** *3 ¾* **Royal Reserve**[9] 4827 3-9-2 82 MartinDwyer 2 73
(William Muir) *hld up: rdn over 2f out: wknd over 1f out* **7/1**

2m 5.5s (-2.40) **Going Correction** -0.20s/f (Firm)
WFA 3 from 5yo+ 9lb **6** Ran SP% **109.7**
Speed ratings (Par 105): **101,97,96,95,95 92**
CSF £5.80 TOTE £2.00: £2.20, £1.40; EX 6.70 Trifecta £40.30.
Owner K Abdullah **Bred** Juddmonte Farms Ltd **Trained** Beckhampton, Wilts

FOCUS
This fair handicap was run at a sound pace.

5199 COPLOW H'CAP 6f
4:00 (4:01) (Class 3) (0-90,89) 3-Y-O **£9,451** (£2,829; £1,414; £708; £352) **Stalls** High

Form RPR

1461 **1** **Mustallib (IRE)**[15] 4643 3-9-6 88 PaulHanagan 5 101
(Charles Hills) *w ldr: shkn up to ld over 2f out: rdn over 1f out: styd on u.p* **5/2**[1]

2210 **2** *½* **Highly Sprung (IRE)**[10] 4803 3-8-9 77 JoeFanning 8 88
(Mark Johnston) *led: hdd over 3f out: remained handy: rdn and ev ch fr over 1f out: styd on* **14/1**

-304 **3** *1 ½* **Vibrant Chords**[30] 4079 3-9-6 88 GrahamLee 2 94
(Henry Candy) *trckd ldrs: plld hrd: rdn over 1f out: styd on same pce ins fnl f* **5/2**[1]

4016 **4** *nk* **Florenza**[22] 4398 3-8-11 79 AndrewElliott 6 84
(Chris Fairhurst) *chsd ldrs: rdn and hung rt over 1f out: styd on* **16/1**

11 **5** *2* **Toriano**[82] 2322 3-8-13 81 RyanTate 1 80
(James Eustace) *s.i.s: hld up: plld hrd: hdwy on outer over 2f out: rdn over 1f out: no ex ins fnl f* **11/4**[2]

10-0 **6** *1 ½* **Appleton**[57] 3131 3-9-4 86 (v[1]) GrahamGibbons 4 80
(David O'Meara) *s.i.s: sn given reminders: hdwy over 4f out: led over 3f out tl rdn over 2f out: no ex fnl f* **20/1**

4200 **7** *½* **Madrinho (IRE)**[31] 4062 3-9-7 89 PatDobbs 3 81
(Richard Hannon) *dwlt: hld up: shkn up over 2f out: nvr on terms* **8/1**[3]

1m 10.45s (-2.55) **Going Correction** -0.20s/f (Firm) **7** Ran SP% **112.2**
Speed ratings (Par 104): **109,108,106,105,103 101,100**
CSF £35.39 CT £93.94 TOTE £3.30: £2.30, £3.80; EX 28.60 Trifecta £108.60.
Owner Hamdan Al Maktoum **Bred** Wardstown Stud Ltd **Trained** Lambourn, Berks

FOCUS
The feature 3yo sprint handicap. Decent form.

5200 ROTHERBY H'CAP 5f
4:30 (4:30) (Class 6) (0-65,65) 3-Y-O+ **£3,234** (£962; £481; £240) **Stalls** High

Form RPR

443 **1** **Noble Act**[18] 4521 3-9-7 65 PaulHanagan 6 70
(Rae Guest) *hld up in tch: racd keenly: pushed along 1/2-way: rdn over 1f out: r.o u.p to ld post* **9/4**[2]

-000 **2** *shd* **Wotnot (IRE)**[11] 4770 4-9-0 55 (p) ConnorBeasley 4 61
(Bryan Smart) *w ldr: pushed along 1/2-way: rdn to ld over 1f out: hdd post* **9/1**

4150 **3** *hd* **David's Beauty (IRE)**[14] 4691 3-8-11 55 (p) GrahamLee 5 59
(Brian Baugh) *led: rdn and hdd over 1f out: rallied and ev ch ins fnl f: r.o* **14/1**

0-44 **4** *3* **Golden Rosanna**[16] 4590 3-8-2 46 oh1 RoystonFfrench 1 39
(Steph Hollinshead) *s.i.s and hmpd s: pushed along in rr: rdn over 1f out: styd on to go 4th wl ins fnl f: nt trble ldrs* **18/1**

0134 **5** *4 ½* **Very First Blade**[24] 4292 7-8-8 49 (p) RobertTart 3 27
(Michael Mullineaux) *chsd ldrs: rdn 1/2-way: wknd fnl f* **5/1**[3]

1222 **6** *nk* **Jack The Laird (IRE)**[25] 4280 3-9-6 64 (b) RobertWinston 2 40+
(Dean Ivory) *edgd rt s: sn prom: rdn over 1f out: btn whn appeared to take a false step ins fnl f: eased* **11/8**[1]

59.06s (-0.94) **Going Correction** -0.20s/f (Firm)
WFA 3 from 4yo+ 3lb **6** Ran SP% **111.5**
Speed ratings (Par 101): **99,98,98,93,86 86**
CSF £21.41 TOTE £3.50: £1.80, £3.90; EX 22.40 Trifecta £107.70.
Owner C J Murfitt **Bred** Pantile Stud **Trained** Newmarket, Suffolk

FOCUS
There was a desperate three-way finish in this moderate sprint handicap.

5201 BOOK YOUR CHRISTMAS PARTY AT LEICESTER H'CAP 1m 60y
5:00 (5:03) (Class 5) (0-75,77) 3-Y-O **£3,234** (£962; £481; £240) **Stalls** Low

Form RPR

6411 **1** **Blacklister**[14] 4681 3-9-9 77 PaulHanagan 8 83
(Mick Channon) *chsd ldr who sn wnt clr: tk clsr order over 3f out: led over 2f out: sn rdn: styd on u.p* **7/2**[2]

13 **2** *1 ¼* **Tomahawk Kid**[22] 4382 3-9-0 71 GeorgeDowning(3) 5 74
(Ian Williams) *s.i.s: hld up: hdwy over 2f out: sn rdn: styd on to go 2nd wl ins fnl f: nt rch wnr* **5/2**[1]

5-06 **3** *½* **Indrapura (IRE)**[102] 1777 3-9-2 70 (t) GrahamLee 7 72
(Paul Cole) *chsd ldrs: jnd wnr over 2f out: sn rdn: styd on same pce ins fnl f* **20/1**

52 **4** *3 ¼* **Cosmic Storm**[17] 4549 3-9-2 70 PatDobbs 1 64
(Ralph Beckett) *hld up: racd keenly: hdwy over 2f out: rdn over 1f out: no ex ins fnl f* **5/2**[1]

0165 **5** *9* **Furiant**[11] 4769 3-9-4 72 (b) JoeFanning 4 46
(Mark Johnston) *led: plld hrd: wnt clr over 6f out: c bk to the field over 3f out: hdd over 2f out: wknd wl over 1f out* **6/1**[3]

54-0 **6** *1 ¼* **Executive Bay**[23] 4347 3-8-4 63 AnnaHesketh(5) 3 34
(Tom Dascombe) *chsd ldrs: rdn over 3f out: wknd over 2f out* **20/1**

210 **7** *hd* **Simply Clever**[53] 3285 3-8-1 58 AaronJones(3) 2 28
(David Brown) *hld up: rdn and wknd over 2f out* **12/1**

1m 43.71s (-1.39) **Going Correction** -0.20s/f (Firm) **7** Ran SP% **110.9**
Speed ratings (Par 100): **98,96,96,93,84 82,82**
CSF £11.87 CT £138.94 TOTE £4.40: £1.90, £1.70; EX 12.80 Trifecta £79.60.
Owner Box 41 Racing **Bred** Aston House Stud **Trained** West Ilsley, Berks

FOCUS
A modest 3yo handicap. Sound form for the class.
T/Plt: £32.70 to a £1 stake. Pool: £70,004.44 - 1559.40 winning units. T/Qpdt: £8.90 to a £1 stake. Pool: £4,292.77 - 355.70 winning units. **Colin Roberts**

4950 WINDSOR (R-H)
Sunday, August 7

OFFICIAL GOING: Good to firm (8.5)
Wind: Fresh, behind Weather: Fine, warm

5202 DR JOHN BUSH 60TH BIRTHDAY MAIDEN AUCTION STKS 6f
2:10 (2:12) (Class 5) 2-Y-O **£3,234** (£962; £481; £240) **Stalls** Low

Form RPR

65 **1** **Angel Down**[38] 3813 2-9-3 0 OisinMurphy 12 80
(Henry Candy) *mde virtually all and sn crossed to nr side: rdn and pressed over 1f out: edgd lft but kpt on wl* **5/4**[1]

02 **2** *2* **Happy Queen**[6] 4938 2-8-10 0 TomQueally 2 67
(George Margarson) *cl up: chsd wnr 2f out: shkn up to chal over 1f out: nt qckn and hld fnl f* **13/2**

3 *1 ¼* **Gracious Tom (IRE)** 2-8-11 0 ShaneKelly 10 64
(David Evans) *chsd wnr to 2f out: one pce u.p but clr of rest in 3rd* **28/1**

00 **4** *3* **Intisha (IRE)**[23] 4350 2-8-10 0 DannyBrock 6 54
(Jonathan Portman) *in tch on outer: rdn 2f out: kpt on to win battle for 4th but nvr a threat* **9/1**

00 **5** *½* **Rakematiz**[13] 4707 2-8-13 0 RobHornby(3) 8 59
(Brett Johnson) *chsd ldrs: rdn 2f out: sn outpcd: one pce after* **66/1**

0 **6** *1 ¾* **Secret Icon**[6] 4938 2-8-7 0 WilliamCarson 9 45
(Jamie Osborne) *t.k.h bhd ldrs: outpcd 2f out: fdd fnl f* **50/1**

6 **7** *¾* **Feel The Vibes**[17] 4552 2-9-3 0 TomMarquand 7 52+
(Richard Hannon) *wl in rr: rdn over 2f out: modest late prog: no ch* **5/1**[2]

60 **8** *nk* **Felstead Queen**[71] 2696 2-8-10 0 SteveDrowne 5 44+
(Joseph Tuite) *awkward s: mostly wl in rr: kpt on fnl f* **28/1**

0 **9** *nk* **Chiconomic (IRE)**[12] 4738 2-8-7 0 LiamJones 11 40
(Rae Guest) *in tch in midfield: outpcd 2f out: n.d after* **66/1**

10 *12* **Bay Of Angels (IRE)** 2-8-7 0 JoeyHaynes 1
(Stuart Williams) *slowly away: a bhd: t.o* **20/1**

0 11 ¾ **Equal Rights**31 4053 2-9-2 0 .... JimCrowley 3 11
(Eve Johnson Houghton) *sn lost gd early pl: wknd over 2f out: t.o* **6/1**3

1m 10.95s (-2.05) **Going Correction** -0.45s/f (Firm) **11** Ran SP% **115.3**
Speed ratings (Par 94): **95,92,90,86,86 83,82,82,81,65 64**
CSF £8.73 TOTE £2.30: £1.50, £2.00, £5.20; EX 10.80 Trifecta £108.60.
Owner Thurloe Thoroughbreds XX **Bred** Kirtlington Stud & C Budgett **Trained** Kingston Warren, Oxon

FOCUS
The going was good to firm. There was a strong tailwind helping the runners up the straight. Not a great maiden but it was run at a sound pace and the winner did it well.

5203 ACADEMY INSURANCE MAIDEN STKS 1m 67y
2:40 (2:41) (Class 5) 2-Y-O **£3,234** (£962; £481; £240) **Stalls** Low

Form RPR
304 1 **Salouen (IRE)**12 4736 2-9-5 78 .... GeorgeBaker 7 91
(Sylvester Kirk) *hld up in last pair: prog 1/2-way: trckd ldr over 2f out: led over 1f out: sn clr: easily* **4/1**2

2 2 3 ¼ **Star Archer**16 4609 2-9-5 0 .... JimCrowley 5 84+
(Hugo Palmer) *rousted s: wd bnd after 2f but pressed ldr: pushed into ld 3f out: drvn 2f out: sn hdd: no ch w wnr after* **4/11**1

3 6 **Genetics (FR)** 2-9-5 0 .... OisinMurphy 4 70
(Andrew Balding) *hld up in last pair: prog 1/2-way: cl up in 3rd 3f out: sn rdn: fdd fr 2f out* **25/1**

0 4 3 ¾ **Go On Mayson**23 4349 2-9-5 0 .... ShaneKelly 2 61
(David Evans) *chsd ldng pair after 3f to over 3f out: drvn and btn wl over 2f out* **10/1**3

0 5 3 ¼ **Midnight Man (FR)**59 3054 2-9-5 0 .... DougieCostello 1 54+
(K R Burke) *led to 3f out: sn wknd* **18/1**

36 6 13 **Padleyourowncanoe**60 3032 2-9-5 0 .... (p) AdamKirby 3 24+
(Daniel Mark Loughnane) *chsd ldr 2f: sn lost pl qckly: t.o* **50/1**

1m 41.73s (-2.97) **Going Correction** -0.225s/f (Firm) 2y crse rec **6** Ran SP% **113.5**
Speed ratings (Par 94): **105,101,95,92,88 75**
CSF £5.95 TOTE £4.00: £1.90, £1.10; EX 7.20 Trifecta £37.40.
Owner H Balasuriya **Bred** Silvercon Edgerodge Ltd **Trained** Upper Lambourn, Berks

FOCUS
Add 16yds to race distance. An uncompetitive maiden run at an honest pace.

5204 DENNING LEGAL H'CAP 1m 3f 135y
3:10 (3:11) (Class 6) (0-60,60) 3-Y-O **£2,264** (£673; £336; £168) **Stalls** Centre

Form RPR
1 **Tasty Ginger (IRE)**59 3087 3-9-4 57 .... (v1) AdamKirby 4 62
(J R Jenkins) *racd in 4th: rdn wl over 3f out: clsd u.p 2f out: led 1f out: kpt on* **3/1**2

6060 2 2 **Mister Showman**22 4385 3-9-7 60 .... GeorgeBaker 5 62
(Jonathan Portman) *led 1f: styd cl up: rdn over 2f out: nt qckn wl over 1f out: kpt on to win battle for 2nd last strides* **8/1**

3003 3 hd **Ochos Rios**18 4500 3-9-1 54 .... ShaneKelly 8 55
(David Evans) *s.s: rapid prog to ld after 1f: rdn 3f out: hdd 2f out: nt qckn over 1f out: kpt on nr fin* **9/2**3

6003 4 hd **Elocution**4 5012 3-9-3 56 .... OisinMurphy 6 57
(Denis Coakley) *trckd ldr after 3f: rdn to chal over 3f out: led 2f out: hdd and one pce 1f out: lost 2 pls last strides* **5/2**1

2145 5 ¾ **Frivolous Prince (IRE)**18 4527 3-8-12 51 .... (vt) SteveDrowne 1 52
(David Evans) *hld up: effrt and shkn up on outer over 2f out: wl in tch over 1f out: one pce* **8/1**

-603 6 4 **Fenner Hill Neasa (IRE)**4 5019 3-8-7 46 .... WilliamCarson 3 40
(Pat Phelan) *hld up: prog to trck ldrs 3f out gng strly: trapped bhd them and weaving abt looking for room over 2f out to over 1f out: wknd and eased* **9/2**3

2m 31.88s (2.38) **Going Correction** -0.225s/f (Firm) **6** Ran SP% **112.2**
Speed ratings (Par 98): **83,81,81,81,80 78**
CSF £25.80 CT £104.29 TOTE £3.80: £2.40, £4.50; EX 27.00 Trifecta £85.60.
Owner B Dowling **Bred** Hadi Al Tajir **Trained** Royston, Herts

FOCUS
Add 16yds to race distance. They went a steady pace for this modest handicap.

5205 OSSIE & HUTCH MEMORIAL FILLIES' H'CAP 6f
3:40 (3:42) (Class 4) (0-85,85) 3-Y-O+ **£6,469** (£1,925; £962; £481) **Stalls** Low

Form RPR
2-11 1 **Gravity Flow (IRE)**17 4547 3-9-7 84 .... PatCosgrave 3 97+
(William Haggas) *fast away: mde all: gng best whn hung lft fr wl over 1f out: rdn out* **2/1**1

1411 2 1 ½ **Battlement**16 4599 3-9-8 85 .... (p) GeorgeBaker 5 91
(Roger Charlton) *hld up: pushed along on outer 2f out: rdn and effrt over 1f out: kpt on to take 2nd nr fin: unable to chal* **2/1**1

-123 3 nk **Cersei**43 3644 3-9-0 77 .... (t) JimCrowley 2 82
(David Simcock) *chsd wnr: rdn over 2f out: no imp over 1f out: lost 2nd nr fin* **6/1**3

0-00 4 5 **Immediate**16 4585 4-9-10 83 .... AdamKirby 1 73
(Robert Cowell) *chsd ldrs: rdn over 2f out: wknd over 1f out* **16/1**

410- 5 1 ½ **Love On The Rocks (IRE)**331 6269 3-9-6 83 .... MichaelJMMurphy 4 67
(Charles Hills) *t.k.h: hld up in last: shkn up and effrt over 2f out: wknd over 1f out* **16/1**

2114 6 20 **Very Honest (IRE)**38 3815 3-9-7 84 .... OisinMurphy 6 4
(Brett Johnson) *disp 2nd pl to 1/2-way: wknd over 2f out: eased and t.o* **9/2**2

1m 9.7s (-3.30) **Going Correction** -0.45s/f (Firm)
WFA 3 from 4yo 4lb **6** Ran SP% **110.9**
Speed ratings (Par 102): **104,102,101,94,92 66**
CSF £5.84 TOTE £2.70: £1.70, £1.80; EX 4.80 Trifecta £9.60.
Owner Sheikh Juma Dalmook Al Maktoum **Bred** Eimear Mulhern & Abbeville Stud **Trained** Newmarket, Suffolk

FOCUS
A fair handicap run at a sound pace. The front three finished clear.

5206 DEBBIE PARRISH BIRTHDAY CELEBRATION H'CAP 1m 67y
4:10 (4:10) (Class 3) (0-90,89) 3-Y-O+ **£7,439** (£2,213; £1,106; £553) **Stalls** Low

Form RPR
-021 1 **Laidback Romeo (IRE)**11 4776 4-10-0 89 .... AdamKirby 3 97
(Clive Cox) *chsd ldng pair: pushed along 3f out: dropped to last and looked btn over 1f out: gap appeared against rail and rallied u.p: led last 100yds: drvn out* **6/4**1

5151 2 ¾ **Raising Sand**19 4481 4-9-13 88 .... GeorgeBaker 5 94
(Jamie Osborne) *hld up in last: clsd on outer and shkn up 2f out: rdn to ld jst ins fnl f: hdd and jst outpcd last 100yds* **2/1**2

0530 3 1 ½ **Essenaitch (IRE)**30 4080 3-8-8 76 .... JimCrowley 4 78
(David Evans) *led: pushed along over 2f out: drvn and hdd jst ins fnl f: one pce* **6/1**

1043 4 1 ¾ **Short Work**43 3635 3-8-13 81 .... (p) OisinMurphy 2 79
(Ralph Beckett) *pressed ldr: urged along over 3f out: stl chalng over 1f out: sn lost 2nd and fdd* **3/1**3

1m 41.4s (-3.30) **Going Correction** -0.225s/f (Firm)
WFA 3 from 4yo 7lb **4** Ran SP% **112.6**
Speed ratings (Par 107): **107,106,104,103**
CSF £5.05 TOTE £2.30; EX 4.50 Trifecta £14.40.
Owner Robin Craddock **Bred** Mrs B Gardiner **Trained** Lambourn, Berks

FOCUS
Add 16yds to race distance. They went a decent pace for this fair handicap.

5207 EQUESTRIAN SURFACES H'CAP 1m 2f 7y
4:40 (4:41) (Class 5) (0-70,70) 3-Y-O+ **£2,911** (£866; £432; £216) **Stalls** Centre

Form RPR
1503 1 **Pink Ribbon (IRE)**22 4383 4-9-7 63 .... (p) GeorgeBaker 3 72
(Sylvester Kirk) *hld up in last pair: stdy prog to trck ldrs 3f out: shkn up to chal over 1f out: rdn to ld last 75yds: won narrowly but quite decisively* **4/1**3

-605 2 ½ **Free Passage**17 4562 3-8-11 62 .... OisinMurphy 6 70
(Henry Candy) *cl up: pushed along to take 2nd and chal over 3f out: rdn to ld 2f out: styd on but hdd and jst outpcd last 75yds* **7/2**2

3212 3 3 ¾ **Zephyros (GER)**22 4383 5-9-8 64 .... AdamKirby 8 65
(David Bridgwater) *restrained into last after s: prog on outer 3f out: chal 2f out: nt qckn over 1f out: fdd fnl f* **11/4**1

-053 4 1 ½ **Iona Island**9 4836 3-9-0 65 .... MichaelJMMurphy 1 63
(Charles Hills) *led: rdn 3f out: hdd 2f out: steadily fdd* **5/1**

3531 5 3 ¾ **Choral Festival**10 4784 10-10-0 70 .... DannyBrock 2 60
(John Bridger) *trckd ldrs: tried to chal against rail over 2f out but no room and lost momentum: wknd over 1f out* **6/1**

1-00 6 14 **Seven Clans (IRE)**20 4463 4-9-7 63 .... (t) DougieCostello 4 25
(Neil Mulholland) *cl up tl wknd tamely 3f out: sn bhd* **33/1**

066 7 16 **Magnificent Madiba**72 2640 3-8-12 63 .... SteveDrowne 7
(George Baker) *pressed ldr to over 3f out: wknd rapidly: t.o* **10/1**

2m 6.47s (-2.23) **Going Correction** -0.225s/f (Firm)
WFA 3 from 4yo+ 9lb **7** Ran SP% **111.9**
Speed ratings (Par 103): **99,98,95,94,91 80,67**
CSF £17.52 CT £42.99 TOTE £4.60: £2.60, £2.50; EX 21.10 Trifecta £58.50.
Owner Mrs Michelle Cousins **Bred** Ann & Joe Hallinan **Trained** Upper Lambourn, Berks

FOCUS
Add 16yds to race distance. The pace was honest for this open handicap.

5208 BETFAIR NOVICE FLAT AMATEUR RIDERS' H'CAP (FOR NOVICE AMATEUR RIDERS) 1m 3f 135y
5:10 (5:11) (Class 5) (0-70,70) 4-Y-O+ **£2,807** (£870; £435; £217) **Stalls** Centre

Form RPR
640 1 **Shirataki (IRE)**48 3470 8-9-9 51 oh4 .... MissMollyKing 2 59
(Peter Hiatt) *dwlt: sn wl in tch: trckd ldrs 5f out: led 2f out: sn in command: jst pushed out fnl f* **20/1**

25/2 2 1 ½ **Miss Tiger Lily**6 4950 6-10-6 62 .... MissKatyLyons 4 67
(Harry Dunlop) *dwlt: sn pressed ldr: led 3f out: rdn and hdd 2f out: one pce* **2/1**1

-235 3 1 ¼ **Chantecler**13 4711 5-11-0 70 .... (t) MrJamesKing 8 73
(Neil Mulholland) *t.k.h early: trckd ldrs: gng wl 3f out: rdn 2f out: fnd little and wl hld in 3rd fnl f* **9/2**3

2024 4 3 ¼ **Tempuran**9 4816 7-11-0 70 .... MissPBridgwater 6 68
(David Bridgwater) *prom: led after 4f: rdn and hdd 3f out: one pce after: wknd last 150yds* **7/1**

365/ 5 7 **Another Squeeze**1068 6097 8-9-9 51 oh6 .... KatherineGlenister 1 37
(Peter Hiatt) *led 4f: styd prom tl wknd over 2f out: wandered u.p after* **33/1**

0-52 6 7 **Sawwala**167 673 6-9-6 51 oh6 .... MrSSayers(3) 9 26
(J R Jenkins) *hmpd 10f out: in tch to over 4f out: sn no ch* **28/1**

0100 7 ¾ **Lily Edge**4 5021 7-9-7 52 .... (v) MissTannyaBagoban(3) 5 25
(John Bridger) *sn struggling in last: nvr a factor* **16/1**

4/0- 8 16 **Minority Interest**17 8164 7-9-12 54 .... (b) MrJPearce 3
(Daniel O'Brien) *lost tch 1/2-way: bhd fr 4f out: t.o* **33/1**

4451 U **Jersey Jewel (FR)**6 4950 4-11-0 70 6ex .... MissCAGreenway 7
(Tom Dascombe) *cl up whn squeezed for room and uns rdr bnd 10f out* **9/4**2

2m 30.87s (1.37) **Going Correction** -0.225s/f (Firm) **9** Ran SP% **114.8**
Speed ratings (Par 103): **86,85,84,82,77 72,72,61,**
CSF £58.20 CT £218.79 TOTE £21.20: £5.20, £1.30, £2.00; EX 89.10 Trifecta £293.50.
Owner Simon King **Bred** Deerfield Farm **Trained** Hook Norton, Oxon

FOCUS
Add 16yds to race distance. A modest handicap for the grade. There was drama as the favourite was hampered early and unseated her rider.
T/Plt: £41.80 to a £1 stake. Pool: £79,672.56 - 1389.59 winning units. T/Qpdt: £39.20 to a £1 stake. Pool: £3,651.48 - 68.85 winning units. **Jonathan Neesom**

5209 - 5211a (Foreign Racing) - See Raceform Interactive

4431 CURRAGH (R-H)
Sunday, August 7

OFFICIAL GOING: Good to firm (good in places)

5212a KEENELAND PHOENIX STKS (GROUP 1) 6f
3:35 (3:35) 2-Y-O **£104,779** (£34,926; £16,544; £7,352; £3,676)

RPR
1 **Caravaggio (USA)**54 3243 2-9-3 116 .... SeamieHeffernan 3 118
(A P O'Brien, Ire) *w.w bhd ldrs in 4th: smooth hdwy on outer after 1/2-way where edgd sltly lft to chal and led travelling wl 1 1/2f out: sn pushed clr and in command: easily* **1/8**1

2 4 **Courage Under Fire (USA)**13 4719 2-9-3 0 .... (t) MichaelHussey 2 105
(A P O'Brien, Ire) *sltly awkward s: sn led: 2 l clr at 1/2-way: rdn over 2f out and sn strly pressed: hdd 1 1/2f out and no ch w easy wnr ent fnl f: kpt on same pce* **33/1**

3 2 ¾ **Medicine Jack**43 3678 2-9-3 108 .... ColinKeane 4 96
(G M Lyons, Ire) *chsd ldrs: 3rd 1/2-way: tk clsr order bhd ldr after 1/2-way: short of room briefly and sn rdn in 3rd: no imp on easy wnr ent fnl f: kpt on same pce* **4/1**2

4 2 1/4 **Grand Coalition (IRE)**[16] 4613 2-9-3 92 PatSmullen 1 89
(J P Murtagh, Ire) *chsd ldr: racd keenly early: 2nd 1/2-way: lost pl after 1/2-way and no ex u.p in 4th fr 2f out: one pce after* **25/1**[3]

5 2 **Ambiguity (IRE)**[22] 4414 2-9-3 91 (t) DonnachaO'Brien 5 82
(Joseph Patrick O'Brien, Ire) *prom tl sn settled in rr: last at 1/2-way: pushed along after 1/2-way: rdn and no imp fr 2f out: one pce after* **50/1**

1m 11.79s (-3.71) **Going Correction** -0.875s/f (Hard) **5** Ran SP% **117.6**
Speed ratings: **89,83,80,77,74**
CSF £12.06 TOTE £1.10: £1.02, £2.60; DF 6.20 Trifecta £11.10.
Owner Mrs John Magnier & Michael Tabor & Derrick Smith **Bred** Windmill Manor Farms Inc Et Al **Trained** Cashel, Co Tipperary

FOCUS

An absolute stroll for the winner, a horse of immense speed and class, and a horse that potentially could be a champion sprinter for a few years to come.

5213a QATAR RACING & EQUESTRIAN CLUB PHOENIX SPRINT STKS (GROUP 3) 6f

4:05 (4:06) 3-Y-O+

£26,029 (£8,382; £3,970; £1,764; £882; £441)

RPR

1 **Toscanini (IRE)**[21] 4433 4-9-7 110 JamesDoyle 2 114
(M Halford, Ire) *sn trckd ldr tl tacked over to dispute ld bef 1/2-way: led narrowly 1 1/2f out where edgd sltly lft and bmpd rival: rdn ent fnl f and pressed clly: kpt on wl to assert clsng stages* **5/1**[3]

2 1 1/4 **Eastern Impact (IRE)**[7] 4916 5-9-7 110 PatSmullen 7 110
(Richard Fahey) *chsd ldrs: 3rd 1/2-way: rdn into 2nd ins fnl f and pressed wnr briefly: no imp on wnr ins fnl 100yds: kpt on same pce* **9/2**[2]

3 2 **Lord Of The Land (IRE)**[22] 4393 5-9-7 102 (v) RonanWhelan 6 104
(David O'Meara) *sn led tl jnd bef 1/2-way: hdd 1 1/2f out where bmpd on inner: no imp on wnr ins fnl f where dropped to 3rd: kpt on same pce* **20/1**

4 1 **Fort Del Oro (IRE)**[18] 4540 4-9-4 105 BillyLee 3 98+
(Edward Lynam, Ire) *w.w: last at 1/2-way: sme hdwy gng wl on outer fr 2f out: rdn in 4th ent fnl f and no imp on ldrs ins fnl 150yds: kpt on same pce* **6/1**

5 1 1/4 **Flight Risk (IRE)**[5] 5000 5-9-7 108 KevinManning 1 97
(J S Bolger, Ire) *chsd ldrs: disp 4th at 1/2-way: rdn over 2f out and no imp on ldrs in 5th ent fnl f: one pce after* **8/1**

6 1 1/2 **Jamesie (IRE)**[8] 4865 8-9-7 105 [1] WayneLordan 5 92
(David Marnane, Ire) *prom tl sn settled bhd ldrs: pushed along fr 1/2-way and no imp on ldrs u.p in 6th under 2f out: one pce after* **40/1**

7 11 **Air Force Blue (USA)**[29] 4151 3-9-3 118 (t) SeamieHeffernan 4 56
(A P O'Brien, Ire) *dwlt sltly: w.w: tk clsr order and disp 4th briefly at 1/2-way: sn pushed along and wknd u.p to rr fr 2f out: eased fnl f* **1/1**[1]

1m 10.17s (-5.33) **Going Correction** -0.875s/f (Hard)
WFA 3 from 4yo+ 4lb **7** Ran SP% **117.4**
Speed ratings: **100,98,95,94,92 90,76**
CSF £28.70 TOTE £4.90: £1.20, £2.40; DF 27.40 Trifecta £253.30.
Owner Godolphin **Bred** Darley **Trained** Doneany, Co Kildare

FOCUS

A really solid performance from the winner, demonstrating how far he has come in quite a short space of time. The second and third have been rated in line with this year's turf best.

5214 - 5215a (Foreign Racing) - See Raceform Interactive

5141 DEAUVILLE (R-H)

Sunday, August 7

OFFICIAL GOING: Turf: good; polytrack: standard

5216a PRIX DU HARAS DON ALFREDO (URUGUAY) (CLAIMER) (4YO+) (TURF) 1m 7f

1:10 (12:00) 4-Y-O+ **£6,985** (£2,794; £2,095; £1,397; £698)

RPR

1 **Django James (IRE)**[141] 5-9-4 0 (p) ThomasHuet 9 61
(Mlle A Rosa, France) **40/1**

2 nk **Mohadjer (FR)**[304] 4-9-1 0 CristianDemuro 11 58
(Waldemar Hickst, Germany) **31/10**[2]

3 1 3/4 **Trigger Flash (FR)**[17] 5-9-2 0 GeraldMosse 3 57
(F Cheyer, France) **19/1**

4 snk **Wolverine (FR)**[30] 9-9-1 0 (p) AurelienLemaitre 2 56
(H Billot, France) **17/1**

5 hd **Ataman Ermak (IRE)**[100] 1846 5-8-11 0 (b) JeremyCrocquevieille 14 52
(S Gouyette, France) **33/1**

6 2 **Belga Bere (FR)**[25] 5-8-11 0 (p) Pierre-CharlesBoudot 7 49
(E Leenders, France) **9/1**

7 1/2 **Vero (GER)**[25] 4-9-5 0 MaximeGuyon 5 57
(Jean-Pierre Carvalho, Germany) **27/10**[1]

8 snk **Vardaris (IRE)**[98] 6-8-11 0 TonyPiccone 4 48
(J Bertin, France) **69/1**

9 1 1/4 **Hier Encore (FR)**[32] 4019 4-8-11 0 OlivierPeslier 13 47
(David Menuisier) *w.w in midfield on outer: 6th and pushed along to hold pl over 4f out: hrd rdn and nt qckn 1 1/2f out: plugged on at one pce fnl f* **58/10**[3]

10 1 1/2 **Toxaris (IRE)**[83] 2292 4-8-8 0 FabriceVeron 15 42
(Mlle M Henry, France) **71/1**

11 20 **Maldon (IRE)**[64] 4-8-11 0 JeromeClaudic 10 21
(Patrice Quinton, France) **29/1**

12 3/4 **Corybas (FR)**[412] 4-9-4 0 FabienLefebvre 8 27
(Mlle A Voraz, France) **32/1**

13 4 **Monsieur Opera (FR)**[89] 7-9-1 0 ChristopheSoumillon 1 19
(Barbara Valenti, Spain) **7/1**

14 8 **Notaire (IRE)**[850] 6-9-4 0 AlexandreRoussel 12 13
(J Bourgeais, France) **18/1**

15 15 **Bahia Del Duque (FR)**[436] 8-8-11 0 IoritzMendizabal 6
(J-P Domalain, France) **80/1**

3m 14.89s (-4.21) **15** Ran SP% **120.2**
WIN (incl. 1 euro stake): 41.10. PLACES: 9.80, 2.10, 5.70. DF: 92.60. SF: 292.20.
Owner Mlle Alexandra Rosa **Bred** H Honore, Scuderia De Moubray & Entry Point **Trained** France

5217a LARC PRIX MAURICE DE GHEEST (GROUP 1) (3YO+) (TURF) 6f 110y(S)

2:15 (12:00) 3-Y-O+ **£159,655** (£63,873; £31,936; £15,954; £7,991)

RPR

1 **Signs Of Blessing (IRE)**[50] 3385 5-9-2 0 StephanePasquier 10 119
(F Rohaut, France) *mde all: broke wl and led towards centre of trck: drvn clr ins fnl 2f: rdn wl over 1f out: edgd lft and styd on wl fnl f: nvr really chal* **12/1**

2 1 1/4 **Donjuan Triumphant (IRE)**[51] 3338 3-8-11 0 AlexisBadel 8 115
(Richard Fahey) *w.w towards rr: tk clsr order 1/2-way: hrd rdn 1 1/2f out: styd on u.p fnl f: wnt 2nd 80yds out: nvr on terms w wnr* **10/1**

3 nk **Jimmy Two Times (FR)**[36] 3938 3-8-11 0 VincentCheminaud 16 114
(A Fabre, France) *hld up towards rr: hdwy 2f out: hrd rdn to chse ldrs over 1f out: styd on fnl f: nt pce to chal* **11/1**

4 nk **Suedois (FR)**[29] 4151 5-9-2 0 DanielTudhope 15 114
(David O'Meara) *a cl up on far side: 2nd and rdn 2f out: styd on u.p: labouring fnl 1/2f: lost 2nd 80yds out* **7/1**[3]

5 shd **Dutch Connection**[12] 4733 4-9-2 0 WilliamBuick 1 114
(Charles Hills) *settled last of three in stands' side gp: towards rr overall whn hdwy 2f out: styd on u.p and edgd rt ins fnl f: nt pce to get on terms* **7/2**[2]

6 1/2 **Attendu (FR)**[64] 2927 3-8-11 0 MaximeGuyon 12 111
(C Laffon-Parias, France) *w.w in tch: chsd front rnk whn rdn 2f out: kpt on at same pce* **12/1**

7 1 3/4 **Damila (FR)**[39] 3796 3-8-8 0 CristianDemuro 5 103
(H-A Pantall, France) *w.w towards rr: hdwy over 2f out: styd on fr over 1f out: run flattened out last 75yds* **33/1**

8 2 1/2 **Gordon Lord Byron (IRE)**[21] 4433 8-9-2 0 RichardKingscote 11 100
(T Hogan, Ire) *chsd ldr: 3rd and rdn 2f out: dropped away wl over 1f out* **11/1**

9 1/2 **Black Max (FR)**[35] 3-8-11 0 FabriceVeron 13 98
(H-A Pantall, France) *w.w in midfield: sltly outpcd towards rr bef 1/2-way: hrd rdn 1 1/2f out: nvr in contention* **66/1**

10 4 **Schang (GER)**[33] 3992 3-8-11 0 IoritzMendizabal 7 86
(P Vovcenko, Germany) *settled in midfield: rdn and nt qckn 2f out: sn btn* **25/1**

11 1/2 **The Right Man**[59] 3090 4-9-2 0 Francois-XavierBertras 3 86
(D Guillemin, France) *chsd ldr in stands' side gp of three: rdn and wknd wl over 2f out* **22/1**

12 1 1/2 **Gifted Master (IRE)**[12] 4733 3-8-11 0 MickaelBarzalona 2 80
(Hugo Palmer) *led stands' side gp of three: rdn and struggling fr 1/2-way: bhd whn hmpd by faller 75yds out* **14/1**

13 3 **Love Spirit**[39] 3796 6-9-2 0 Pierre-CharlesBoudot 14 73
(Louis Baudron, France) *w.w in tch: rdn 2 1/2f out: lost pl 2f out: bhd whn heavily eased fnl f* **33/1**

14 10 **Ross Castle (IRE)**[39] 3796 3-8-11 0 TonyPiccone 9 43
(Matthieu Palussiere, France) *a among bkmarkers: wl bhd fnl f* **66/1**

F **Gold-Fun (IRE)**[50] 3385 7-9-2 0 (b) ChristopheSoumillon 6
(Richard Gibson, Hong Kong) *chsd ldr travelling strly: disp 3rd and rdn ins fnl 2f: hung lft u.p 1 1/2f out: 7th and looked hld whn fell fatally 75yds out* **11/4**[1]

1m 16.74s (-0.46)
WFA 3 from 4yo+ 4lb **15** Ran SP% **126.3**
WIN (incl. 1 euro stake): 10.20. PLACES: 3.40, 5.40, 3.40. DF: 96.40. SF: 218.00.
Owner Mme Isabelle Corbani **Bred** S Boucheron **Trained** Sauvagnon, France

FOCUS

Already behind schedule, there was a further delay when Jimmy Two Times, having seemed to force his stall open, broke out along with Suedois and Love Spirit. The whole field were in the gates at the time and were unloaded, with the race was eventually almost 13 minutes late off. From a form standpoint these are an unexceptional group of horses and it was an event marred by Gold-Fun suffering a fatal injury in the closing stages. The first seven have been rated close to their marks.

5218a HARAS DE LA POMME (ARGENTINE) PRIX DE REUX (GROUP 3) (3YO+) (TURF) 1m 4f 110y

2:50 (12:00) 3-Y-O+ **£29,411** (£11,764; £8,823; £5,882; £2,941)

RPR

1 **Ventura Storm (IRE)**[23] 4339 3-8-7 0 GregoryBenoist 6 111+
(Richard Hannon) *a cl up: pressed ldr fr after 1/2-way: led 3f out: drvn clr more than 1f out: readily* **4/1**[3]

2 3 1/2 **Moonshiner (GER)**[42] 3-8-7 0 MaximeGuyon 4 105
(Jean-Pierre Carvalho, Germany) *hld up in fnl pair: rdn and clsd 2f out: styd on u.p fnl f: tk 2nd cl home: no ch w wnr* **10/1**

3 hd **Big Blue**[25] 4286 4-9-5 0 MickaelBarzalona 3 105
(A Fabre, France) *w.w in tch: rdn to chse ldr 2f out: no match for eventual wnr wl over 1f out: styd on at same pce fnl f: lost 2nd cl home* **15/8**[1]

4 nse **Pacific Angel (IRE)**[14] 4696 4-9-2 0 (b) AurelienLemaitre 7 102
(M Delzangles, France) *w.w in rr: rdn and no immediate imp over 2f out: styd on u.p fnl f: nvr plcd to chal* **7/1**

5 2 1/2 **Techno Queen (IRE)**[35] 3934 5-9-2 0 StephanePasquier 1 98
(T Potters, Germany) *settled in midfield: rdn and short-lived effrt over 2f out: plugged on at one pce fnl f: nvr in contention* **8/1**

6 2 1/2 **Cohesion**[39] 3795 3-8-7 0 VincentCheminaud 2 97
(D Smaga, France) *led: hdd 3f out: grad dropped away fnl 2f* **9/4**[2]

2m 44.37s (-2.03)
WFA 3 from 4yo+ 11lb **6** Ran SP% **118.3**
WIN (incl. 1 euro stake): 3.80. PLACES: 2.40, 3.40. SF: 27.30.
Owner Middleham Park Racing LXXII **Bred** Laurence Kennedy **Trained** East Everleigh, Wilts

4438 DUSSELDORF (R-H)

Sunday, August 7

OFFICIAL GOING: Turf: good

5219a FRITZ HENKEL STIFTUNGS-RENNEN (LISTED RACE) (3YO+) (TURF) 1m 3f

2:00 (12:00) 3-Y-O+ **£10,294** (£4,779; £2,205; £1,102)

RPR

1 **Fair Mountain (GER)**[35] 3934 4-9-4 0 EduardoPedroza 6 104
(A Wohler, Germany) **53/10**[3]

2 1 **Mighty Mouse (GER)**[273] 7769 8-9-2 0 DanielePorcu 8 100
(Annika Fust, Germany) **109/10**

3 3/4 **Rose Rized (GER)**[49] 4-8-13 0.................................. AndraschStarke 4 96
(P Schiergen, Germany) **98/10**

4 3/4 **Novano (GER)**[17] 4578 4-9-4 0.................................. AndreasSuborics 5 99
(Waldemar Hickst, Germany) **143/10**

5 1 3/4 **Capitano (GER)**[35] 3-8-7 0 ow1.................................. AlexanderPietsch 2 95
(J Hirschberger, Germany) **12/5**[2]

6 3/4 **Yorkidding**[16] 4583 4-8-13 0.. FrankieDettori 1 90
(Mark Johnston) *chsd ldrs early: sn settled in midfield on inner: 5th and nudged along 3f out: rdn and nt qckn 2f out: n.m.r whn angled out appr fnl f: sn btn* **6/5**[1]

7 shd **Nordwienerin (IRE)**[26] 3-8-3 0.. FilipMinarik 3 90
(P Schiergen, Germany) **84/10**

8 2 1/4 **Vif Monsieur (GER)**[26] 4253 6-9-2 0..........................(p) KoenClijmans 7 89
(Mario Hofer, Germany) **144/10**

WIN (incl. 10 euro stake): 63. PLACES: 20, 29, 28. SF: 1,265
Owner Stall Margarethe **Bred** Frau Margrit Wetzel **Trained** Germany

5220a 158 HENKEL-PREIS DER DIANA - GERMAN OAKS (GROUP 1) (3YO FILLIES) (TURF) 1m 3f

3:45 (12:00) 3-Y-O

£220,588 (£73,529; £36,764; £19,852; £9,558; £7,352)

RPR

1 **Serienholde (GER)**[43] 3-9-2 0.................................. EduardoPedroza 7 106
(A Wohler, Germany) *settled in tch of ldng gp: rdn to take clsr order fr 2 1/2f out: styd on wl u.p to chal 1f out: r.o and led 100yds out* **61/10**[2]

2 1/2 **Sarandia (GER)**[21] 3-9-2 0.................................. AndraschStarke 14 105
(P Schiergen, Germany) *led under a t.k.h: wnt wd into first bnd and hdd: hld up bhd new ldr: rdn and led over 2f out: styd on gamely u.p: hdd 100yds out: no ex* **8/1**

3 1 3/4 **Architecture (IRE)**[22] 4416 3-9-2 0.................................. FrankieDettori 10 102
(Hugo Palmer) *cl up: disp 4th between horses whn rdn 2f out: styd on u.p: wnt 3rd ins fnl f: kpt on at same pce* **1/1**[1]

4 nk **Kasalla (GER)**[29] 4175 3-9-2 0.. AdriedeVries 4 101
(Markus Klug, Germany) *hld up in midfield: rdn and styd on fr 1 1/2f out: tk 4th cl home: nvr on terms* **115/10**

5 1/2 **Parvaneh (IRE)**[63] 2949 3-9-2 0.................................. AndreaAtzeni 16 100
(Waldemar Hickst, Germany) *w.w in rr: hdwy on outer appr 2f out: styd on wl fnl f: nrest at fin* **184/10**

6 nk **She's Gina (GER)**[29] 4175 3-9-2 0.................................. MaximPecheur 9 100
(Markus Klug, Germany) *cl up: led gng into first bnd: sn clr: hdd over 2f out: kpt on at one pce* **51/1**

7 1/2 **Pagella (GER)**[56] 3207 3-9-2 0.................................. AlexanderPietsch 1 99
(J Hirschberger, Germany) *settled towards rr on inner: prog 2f out: n.m.r 1 1/2f out: styd on again ins fnl f: nvr in contention* **68/10**[3]

8 hd **La Dynamite (IRE)**[26] 3-9-2 0.. FilipMinarik 5 98
(Markus Klug, Germany) *racd in midfield: rdn and no prog 3f out: kpt on at one pce* **38/1**

9 1 1/4 **Milenia (GER)**[43] 3-9-2 0.. AndreasSuborics 2 96
(Markus Klug, Germany) *settled in midfield: kpt on at same pce u.p fr 2f out: nvr a factor* **59/1**

10 hd **Meergorl (GER)**[56] 3207 3-9-2 0.................................. FrederikTylicki 15 96
(R Dzubasz, Germany) *w.w in midfield on outer: rdn and no imp 2 1/2f out: styd on at same pce fnl 1 1/2f out: nvr threatened* **112/10**

11 hd **Night Music (GER)**[29] 4175 3-9-2 0.................................. JozefBojko 12 95
(A Wohler, Germany) *nvr beyond midfield: rdn and btn 2f out* **25/1**

12 1 1/4 **Near England (IRE)**[29] 4175 3-9-2 0.......................... AndreasHelfenbein 8 93
(Markus Klug, Germany) *w.w towards rr: last and rdn 1 1/2f out: styd on late past btn horses: nvr involved* **269/10**

13 1/2 **Dhaba (GER)**[29] 4175 3-9-2 0.. MartinSeidl 6 92
(Markus Klug, Germany) *settled in midfield: rdn and no imp over 2f out: sn btn* **45/1**

14 2 1/4 **Flemish Duchesse (FR)**[43] 3-9-2 0.................................. StephenHellyn 11 88
(Andreas Lowe, Germany) *cl up: outpcd whn scrubbed along wl over 2f out: sn wknd* **246/10**

15 1/2 **Lopera (GER)**[26] 3-9-2 0.. DanielePorcu 13 87
(P Schiergen, Germany) *hld up in midfield: lost pl 3f out: sn btn* **40/1**

16 1 1/4 **Fosun (GER)**[43] 3-9-2 0.. IanFerguson 3 85
(Markus Klug, Germany) *w.w in fnl trio: short-lived effrt whn rdn 3f out: sn wknd* **67/1**

2m 14.49s (134.49) **16** Ran SP% **132.9**
WIN (incl. 10 euro stake): 71. PLACES: 16, 17, 13, 19. SF: 385.
Owner Gestut Wittekindshof **Bred** Gestut Wittekindshof **Trained** Germany

5149 AYR (L-H)
Monday, August 8

OFFICIAL GOING: Good to soft (7.8)
Wind: breezy 1/2 against Weather: fine but breezy

5221 BRITISH STALLION STUDS EBF MAIDEN FILLIES' STKS (PLUS 10 RACE) 7f 50y

2:00 (2:03) (Class 4) 2-Y-O **£4,528** (£1,347; £673; £336) **Stalls** High

Form RPR

1 **Whatsthemessage (IRE)** 2-9-0 0.................................. PhillipMakin 2 75
(Keith Dalgleish) *dwlt: sn trcking ldng pair: nt clr run over 1f out: led last 100yds: drvn out* **20/1**

4 2 1 **Honourable**[17] 4609 2-9-0 0.................................. TonyHamilton 1 72
(Richard Fahey) *led: shkn up over 2f out: hdd and no ex last 100yds* **10/11**[1]

6 3 2 1/2 **Mistress Viz (IRE)**[17] 4603 2-9-0 0.................................. PJMcDonald 4 66
(John Mackie) *chsd ldrs: shkn up over 3f out: 3rd 1f out: hung lft: kpt on one pce* **14/1**

0 4 1 3/4 **Nepeta (USA)**[12] 4756 2-9-0 0.................................. JoeFanning 3 62
(Mark Johnston) *w ldr: shkn up over 2f out: fdd last 100yds* **13/8**[2]

0 5 6 **Savannah Moon (IRE)**[25] 4298 2-9-0 0.................................. TomEaves 5 46
(Kevin Ryan) *hld up in last: effrt 3f out: wknd over 1f out* **11/1**[3]

1m 37.54s (4.14) **Going Correction** +0.325s/f (Good) **5** Ran SP% **110.2**
Speed ratings (Par 93): **89,87,85,83,76**
CSF £39.79 TOTE £12.90: £5.50, £1.10; EX 36.10 Trifecta £115.90.
Owner Equus I **Bred** Lynn Lodge Stud **Trained** Carluke, S Lanarks

FOCUS
Inside rail in 7yds; Races 7f to 1m2f increased 21yds. There was 5mm of rain during the past day and the going was on the easy side. They went a fair pace in this modest 2yo fillies' maiden, and the runner-up had shaped well at York on debut.

5222 RACING UK H'CAP 7f 50y

2:30 (2:32) (Class 6) (0-60,58) 3-Y-O+ **£2,587** (£770; £384; £192) **Stalls** High

Form RPR

00-0 1 **Norville (IRE)**[17] 4619 9-9-4 52..........................(b) PaulMulrennan 3 60
(Lee Smyth, Ire) *sn trcking ldrs: 3rd over 2f out: styd on to ld last 50yds* **15/2**

2600 2 3/4 **New Abbey Angel (IRE)**[7] 4936 3-9-4 58..........................(p) PhillipMakin 6 62
(Keith Dalgleish) *trckd ldrs: t.k.h: 2nd 3f out: led over 1f out: hdd and no ex last 50yds* **2/1**[1]

002- 3 1/2 **Cheers Buddy (IRE)**[17] 4619 8-9-4 52.................................. JackGarritty 12 57
(Lee Smyth, Ire) *hld up towards rr: hdwy over 2f out: chsng ldrs over 1f out: kpt on same pce last 75yds* **20/1**

-010 4 2 3/4 **Madam Mai Tai**[24] 4369 4-9-3 51.................................. DanielTudhope 10 50
(Rebecca Bastiman) *hld up in rr: hdwy over 2f out: kpt on one pce to take modest 4th nr fin* **11/2**[2]

0 5 1 **Buzz Boy (ITY)**[25] 4290 3-7-13 46..........................(b) RobbieDolan(7) 1 39
(Adrian Paul Keatley, Ire) *sn chsng ldr: led 4f out: hung rt over 2f out: hdd over 1f out: wknd last 100yds* **6/1**[3]

4554 6 3 **Fine Example**[35] 3946 3-9-3 57..........................(p) TomEaves 11 43
(Kevin Ryan) *mid-div: hdwy to chse ldrs over 2f out: wknd appr fnl f* **6/1**[3]

00 7 3 **Lady Cordie**[2] 5152 4-9-1 49.................................. JoeDoyle 8 29
(Jim Goldie) *s.i.s: in rr: kpt on fnl 2f: nvr a factor* **16/1**

0030 8 6 **Indego Blues**[35] 3940 7-9-5 53..........................(p) PaulQuinn 2 18
(David Nicholls) *hld up in mid-div: effrt over 2f out: wknd over 1f out: eased in clsng stages* **11/1**

5000 9 3 1/2 **Ready Steady (USA)**[61] 3015 3-8-6 46..........................(b[1]) AndrewMullen 7 1
(Kenneth Slack) *in rr: bhd fnl 2f* **20/1**

-005 10 36 **Bannock Town**[14] 4705 5-8-11 45..........................(p) PJMcDonald 4
(Linda Perratt) *led: hdd 4f out: lost pl 3f out: sn bhd: heavily eased fnl 100yds: virtually p.u: t.o* **200/1**

1m 35.81s (2.41) **Going Correction** +0.325s/f (Good)
WFA 3 from 4yo+ 6lb **10** Ran SP% **113.3**
Speed ratings (Par 101): **99,98,97,94,93 89,86,79,75,34**
CSF £21.74 CT £296.86 TOTE £9.80: £2.80, £1.10, £4.80; EX 28.10 Trifecta £280.80.
Owner Richard Auld **Bred** R N Auld **Trained** Magheralin, Co Down
■ Stewards' Enquiry : Robbie Dolan two-day ban: use of whip (22-23 Aug)

FOCUS
A modest handicap. The pace picked up generously after a furlong and the principals came clear, with the winner capable of rating a bit higher in the short term.

5223 RACING UK HD ON SKY432 H'CAP 1m

3:00 (3:01) (Class 5) (0-75,79) 3-Y-O+ **£3,557** (£1,058; £529; £264) **Stalls** Low

Form RPR

0605 1 **Tadaany (IRE)**[14] 4704 4-10-0 74.................................. DanielTudhope 2 83
(David O'Meara) *led 1f: trckd ldrs: led over 2f out: drvn rt out* **4/1**[1]

0503 2 3/4 **Character Onesie (IRE)**[15] 4683 4-9-8 68.................................. DavidNolan 9 75
(Richard Fahey) *prom: effrt over 2f out: 2nd 1f out: kpt on towards fin* **9/1**

1403 3 1 **Mustaqbal (IRE)**[7] 4933 4-9-8 73..........................(p) PhilDennis(5) 3 78
(Michael Dods) *s.i.s: hdwy over 2f out: nt clr run over 1f out: 3rd 1f out: kpt on same pce* **7/1**[3]

551 4 2 **Lawyer (IRE)**[6] 4986 5-10-0 79 6ex.................................. AdamMcNamara(5) 6 79
(David Barron) *mid-div: effrt over 1f out: nt clr run over 1f out: kpt on to take 4th nr fin* **9/2**[2]

5054 5 nk **War Department (IRE)**[15] 4684 3-9-5 72.................................. JoeFanning 5 71
(Keith Dalgleish) *hld up in mid-div: hdwy over 2f out: chsng ldrs over 1f out: kpt on one pce* **9/2**[2]

4204 6 1/2 **Tanawar (IRE)**[14] 4701 6-9-4 64..........................(v) JamesSullivan 8 63
(Ruth Carr) *in rr: hdwy over 2f out: hung lft: kpt on one pce over 1f out* **16/1**

5 7 nk **Black Agnes (IRE)**[25] 4313 3-8-9 62.................................. JackGarritty 10 59
(Lee Smyth, Ire) *led after 1f: hdd over 2f out: fdd fnl f* **33/1**

0442 8 1/2 **Fray**[21] 4446 5-9-12 72.. JoeDoyle 4 69
(Jim Goldie) *in rr: drvn over 3f out: sme hdwy over 2f out: nvr a factor* **9/2**[2]

060 9 1 1/2 **Star Of Spring (IRE)**[15] 4684 4-9-6 66.................................. AndrewMullen 7 59
(Iain Jardine) *trckd ldrs: t.k.h: hung rt and fdd over 1f out* **20/1**

0406 10 7 **Truly**[4] 5068 5-9-5 65.. TomEaves 1 42
(Colin Teague) *trckd ldrs: lost pl over 1f out: sn bhd* **33/1**

1m 45.44s (1.64) **Going Correction** +0.325s/f (Good)
WFA 3 from 4yo+ 7lb **10** Ran SP% **113.6**
Speed ratings (Par 103): **104,103,102,100,99 99,99,98,97,90**
CSF £38.27 CT £247.08 TOTE £3.60: £2.10, £3.50, £2.40; EX 43.80 Trifecta £227.80.
Owner Ebor Racing Club V **Bred** Gerard Phelan **Trained** Upper Helmsley, N Yorks

FOCUS
This was competitive and they went a fair pace. The winner got a good trip tracking the pace and is rated back to his best.

5224 RACING UK PROFITS RETURNED TO RACING H'CAP 6f

3:30 (3:30) (Class 5) (0-75,74) 3-Y-O+ **£3,557** (£1,058; £529; £264) **Stalls** High

Form RPR

0153 1 **Specialv (IRE)**[9] 4873 3-9-4 70..........................(p) BenCurtis 6 80+
(Brian Ellison) *hld up in rr: hdwy and swtchd lft over 1f out: nt clr run and swtchd rt 1f out: styd on wl to ld nr fin* **5/1**[3]

0000 2 1/2 **Aprovado (IRE)**[18] 4544 4-9-4 66..........................(p) PaulMulrennan 3 75
(Michael Dods) *trckd ldr: led over 1f out: hdd and no ex nr fin* **20/1**

14 3 2 **African Blessing**[10] 4835 3-9-5 71.................................. GrahamGibbons 5 73
(David Barron) *hld up in mid-div: t.k.h: effrt over 2f out: edgd lft 1f out: kpt on same pce* **7/2**[1]

1524 4 3 **Mo Henry**[25] 4291 4-9-1 63..........................(v) TonyHamilton 4 56
(Adrian Paul Keatley, Ire) *mid-div: effrt over 2f out: edgd lft and wknd 1f out* **13/2**

2231 5 3 **Vallarta (IRE)**[14] 4700 6-9-12 74.................................. JamesSullivan 8 58
(Ruth Carr) *hld up in rr: hdwy over 2f out: kpt on last 100yds: tk 5th nr fin* **9/2**[2]

0002 6 3/4 **Rock Canyon (IRE)**[2] 5152 7-9-0 62.................................. TomEaves 1 43
(Linda Perratt) *mid-div: drvn over 2f out: sn chsng ldrs: wknd appr fnl f* **11/1**

-300 7 1 1/4 **Townsville**[77] 2531 4-9-10 72.................................. JoeFanning 2 49
(Keith Dalgleish) *led: hdd over 1f out: sn wknd* **16/1**

0605 8 1 **Be Bold**[14] 4700 4-9-8 70.................................. DanielTudhope 10 44
(Rebecca Bastiman) *chsd ldrs: drvn over 2f out: lost pl over 1f out* **17/2**

-200 **9** *2 1/4* **Master Mirasol (IRE)**[36] 3924 3-9-7 **73**....................(p) KeaganLatham 7 39
(Kevin Ryan) *chsd ldrs: lost pl wl over 1f out* **33/1**

1130 **10** *1/2* **In My Place**[16] 4643 3-9-0 **71**........................(p) AdamMcNamara[(5)] 9 35
(Richard Fahey) *dwlt: in rr: drvn and n.m.r on inner 2f out: swtchd lft: nvr a factor* **8/1**

1m 15.21s (2.81) **Going Correction** +0.55s/f (Yiel)
WFA 3 from 4yo+ 4lb **10** Ran SP% **114.0**
Speed ratings (Par 103): **103,102,99,95,91 90,89,87,84,84**
CSF £96.22 CT £392.51 TOTE £5.50: £1.80, £5.30, £1.80; EX 99.70 Trifecta £906.20.
Owner D Gilbert, M Lawrence, A Bruce **Bred** Peter & Hugh McCutcheon **Trained** Norton, N Yorks

FOCUS

This modest sprint handicap was run at just an average pace on the stands' side. The potentially well handicapped runner-up was split by a couple of 3yos.

5225 RACING UK IN GLORIOUS HD H'CAP 5f

4:00 (4:00) (Class 6) (0-65,65) 3-Y-O+ **£2,587** (£770; £384; £192) **Stalls** High

Form RPR

5504 **1** **Bunce (IRE)**[10] 4834 8-9-6 **61**... PJMcDonald 8 69
(Linda Perratt) *in rr: hdwy 2f out: chsd ldr 1f out: styd on to ld post* **9/1**

40-0 **2** *nse* **Catwilldo (IRE)**[17] 4614 6-8-13 **59**.....................(b) AdamMcNamara[(5)] 10 67
(Garvan Donnelly, Ire) *w ldrs: led 2f out: hdd post* **4/1**[1]

5004 **3** *2 1/4* **Blue Sonic**[2] 5152 6-9-10 **65**.. DanielTudhope 4 65+
(Linda Perratt) *half rrd s: hld up in rr: hdwy over 2f out: nt clr run over 1f: styd on wl to go 3rd in clsng stages* **4/1**[1]

3044 **4** *nk* **Pavers Star**[6] 4968 7-8-13 **54**....................................(p) PatrickMathers 9 53
(Noel Wilson) *hood removed v late: sn chsng ldrs: kpt on same pce appr fnl f* **11/1**

2256 **5** *1 3/4* **Goninodaethat**[2] 5152 8-9-2 **57**... JoeDoyle 5 49
(Jim Goldie) *chsd ldrs: one pce over 1f out* **17/2**[3]

164/ **6** *2* **Strategic Heights (IRE)**[7] 4960 7-9-9 **64**.......................(p) DavidNolan 3 49
(John James Feane, Ire) *chsd ldrs: fdd over 1f out* **9/2**[2]

7 *nk* **Jingle Jangle**[133] 1129 3-9-7 **65**..............................(v[1]) GrahamGibbons 1 48
(Adrian Paul Keatley, Ire) *mid-div: drvn over 2f out: wknd fnl f* **20/1**

0000 **8** *nk* **Amber Crystal**[67] 2812 4-8-11 **52**.................................. JamesSullivan 2 35
(Linda Perratt) *chsd ldrs: outpcd over 2f out: lost pl over 1f out* **22/1**

2063 **9** *1* **Lady Wootton**[2] 5152 3-8-10 **59**.............................(v) ShirleyTeasdale[(5)] 7 37
(Keith Dalgleish) *awkward s: stmbld sn after s: in rr: hdwy over 2f out: edgd lft and lost pl over 1f out* **10/1**

130 **10** *4* **Rio Deva (IRE)**[2] 5152 3-9-6 **64**.................................... ConnorBeasley 6 28
(Keith Dalgleish) *led tl 2f out: sn lost pl* **10/1**

1m 1.97s (2.57) **Going Correction** +0.55s/f (Yiel)
WFA 3 from 4yo+ 3lb **10** Ran SP% **114.3**
Speed ratings (Par 101): **101,100,97,96,94 90,90,89,88,81**
CSF £44.03 CT £171.89 TOTE £9.50: £3.40, £1.80, £1.90; EX 45.70 Trifecta £260.70.
Owner Peter Tsim & The Late Mrs Helen Perratt **Bred** John Doyle **Trained** East Kilbride, S Lanarks

FOCUS

This moderate sprint handicap looked wide open. The near rail was shunned this time, but the first two raced nearest. Bunce got on top passing the post to get past the enterprisingly ridden runner-up.

5226 FOLLOW @RACING_UK ON TWITTER H'CAP 1m 2f

4:30 (4:32) (Class 3) (0-90,88) 3-Y-O+ **£7,762** (£2,310; £1,154; £577) **Stalls** Low

Form RPR

3421 **1** **Robinnielly (IRE)**[25] 4312 3-9-4 **87**................................ PhillipMakin 10 95+
(Keith Dalgleish) *hld up in mid-div: smooth hdwy to trck ldrs over 3f out: led appr fnl f: drvn out* **4/1**[2]

104 **2** *1/2* **Navajo War Dance**[37] 3887 3-8-7 **83**.............................. CliffordLee[(7)] 2 90
(K R Burke) *trckd ldr after 1f: led over 2f out: hdd appr fnl f: styd on: no ex last 50yds* **11/2**[3]

00-5 **3** *1* **Mica Mika (IRE)**[16] 4650 8-9-7 **86**.......................... AdamMcNamara[(5)] 3 91
(Richard Fahey) *chsd ldrs: upsides over 2f out: kpt on same pce last 150yds* **12/1**

540 **4** *hd* **Nietzsche**[53] 3300 3-8-7 **76**... BenCurtis 7 81
(Brian Ellison) *hld up in rr: t.k.h: hdwy 4f out: effrt 3f out: chsng ldrs over 1f out: edgd lft and kpt on same pce last 150yds* **3/1**[1]

1230 **5** *1 1/2* **Nicholas T**[21] 4448 4-9-5 **79**... JoeDoyle 4 81
(Jim Goldie) *hld up in mid-div: t.k.h: hdwy over 3f out: chsng ldrs 2f out: kpt on one pce* **15/2**

0000 **6** *3/4* **Finn Class (IRE)**[21] 4448 5-10-0 **88**............................ PaulMulrennan 11 88
(Michael Dods) *hld up in rr: effrt over 3f out: chsng ldrs over 1f out: one pce whn n.m.r last 100yds* **18/1**

13-0 **7** *1 1/4* **Hibou**[14] 4704 3-8-10 **79**... PJMcDonald 9 77
(Iain Jardine) *s.i.s: racd in last: drvn over 4f out: hung lft over 1f out: kpt on fnl 150yds* **20/1**

4344 **8** *hd* **Gworn**[14] 4704 6-9-0 **79**.. GarryWhillans[(5)] 1 76
(R Mike Smith) *led 1f: trckd ldrs: t.k.h: one pce fnl 2f* **8/1**

0315 **9** *1 3/4* **Royal Regent**[15] 4680 4-9-3 **77**.. JoeFanning 5 71
(Lucy Normile) *led after 1f: hdd over 2f out: wknd over 1f out* **15/2**

2m 12.94s (0.94) **Going Correction** +0.325s/f (Good)
WFA 3 from 4yo+ 9lb **9** Ran SP% **112.7**
Speed ratings (Par 107): **109,108,107,107,106 105,104,104,103**
CSF £25.54 CT £238.27 TOTE £5.40: £1.80, £1.60, £3.90; EX 29.10 Trifecta £282.20.
Owner Prestige Thoroughbred Racing **Bred** Kellsgrange Stud **Trained** Carluke, S Lanarks

FOCUS

The feature handicap was a competitive affair and there was a fair enough pace on. Robinnielly backed up his improved Hamilton run.

5227 RACING UK DAY PASS JUST £10 H'CAP (DIV I) 1m 2f

5:00 (5:03) (Class 6) (0-65,65) 3-Y-O+ **£2,587** (£770; £384; £192) **Stalls** Low

Form RPR

5556 **1** **Highway Robber**[22] 4424 3-8-3 **49**....................................... CamHardie 6 53
(Wilf Storey) *mid-div: hdwy to chse ldrs over 2f out: swtchd lft and led over 1f out: hld on towards fin* **12/1**

3-24 **2** *nk* **Penelope Pitstop**[25] 4314 4-8-10 **47**................................ JackGarritty 3 50
(Lee Smyth, Ire) *chsd ldrs: tk 2nd last 150yds: kpt on* **5/1**[2]

4006 **3** *1 1/4* **Silva Samourai**[16] 4648 7-8-9 **46** oh1................................ JoeyHaynes 12 47
(Susan Corbett) *chsd ldrs: led 3f out: hdd over 1f out: kpt on same pce* **25/1**

4063 **4** *1 1/2* **Remember Rocky**[21] 4449 7-9-7 **63**...................(b) AdamMcNamara[(5)] 8 62
(Lucy Normile) *chsd ldrs: drvn over 4f out: nt clr run 3f out: kpt on one pce* **7/1**

5046 **5** *2 1/2* **Haymarket**[2] 5154 7-9-6 **62**.. GarryWhillans[(5)] 9 56
(R Mike Smith) *led early: chsd ldrs: fdd appr fnl f* **15/2**

5055 **6** *2 1/2* **Judith Gardenier**[9] 4872 4-8-2 **46** oh1....................(p) JamieGormley[(7)] 1 36
(Iain Jardine) *in rr-div: sn pushed along: kpt on fnl 2f: nvr a threat* **12/1**

0054 **7** *3/4* **Picture Painter (IRE)**[12] 4769 3-9-5 **65**.................................[1] JoeDoyle 10 53
(Jim Goldie) *mid-div: hdwy over 4f out: one pce fnl 3f* **3/1**[1]

4400 **8** *1 1/4* **Frightened Rabbit (USA)**[11] 4314 4-9-6 **57**................. ConnorBeasley 11 43
(Susan Corbett) *in rr: sn drvn along: kpt on fnl 2f: nvr a factor* **25/1**

0-10 **9** *1/2* **Tonto's Spirit**[42] 3706 4-8-12 **49**...................................... AndrewMullen 4 34
(Kenneth Slack) *sn led: hdd 3f out: wknd over 1f out* **6/1**[3]

000/ **10** *hd* **Hundred Acre Wood**[1054] 6558 6-8-4 **46** oh1.................. PhilDennis[(5)] 5 31
(Sandy Thomson) *mid-div: drvn over 3f out: nvr a factor* **50/1**

2404 **11** *16* **Intensified (IRE)**[12] 4772 5-8-9 **46** oh1.......................(b) JamesSullivan 2 2
(Ruth Carr) *hld up: sn detached in last: sme hdwy 3f out: lost pl over 1f out: bhd whn eased* **10/1**

2m 14.32s (2.32) **Going Correction** +0.55s/f (Yiel)
WFA 3 from 4yo+ 9lb **11** Ran SP% **114.3**
Speed ratings (Par 101): **103,102,101,100,98 96,95,94,94,94 81**
CSF £67.80 CT £1479.13 TOTE £15.70: £4.00, £1.70, £5.60; EX 72.20 Trifecta £2547.20.
Owner Gremlin Racing **Bred** Raymond Clive Tooth **Trained** Muggleswick, Co Durham

FOCUS

Division one of a lowly handicap, one of the 3yos came to the fore. This looks weak form.

5228 RACING UK DAY PASS JUST £10 H'CAP (DIV II) 1m 2f

5:35 (5:35) (Class 6) (0-65,66) 3-Y-O+ **£2,587** (£770; £384; £192) **Stalls** Low

Form RPR

0154 **1** **Miningrocks (FR)**[9] 4875 4-9-2 **57**...................................... GerO'Neill[(7)] 6 64
(Declan Carroll) *mde all: pushed abt 6 l clr 3f out: edgd rt over 1f out: drvn rt out: unchal* **5/1**[3]

/061 **2** *1 3/4* **Gold Show**[16] 4648 7-9-7 **62**.. CliffordLee[(7)] 4 66
(Grant Tuer) *sn mid-div: hdwy over 2f out: wnt 2nd 1f out: kpt on same pce* **9/2**[2]

3 *3* **Dea Dia (IRE)**[21] 4464 4-8-11 **45**..............................(vt[1]) GrahamGibbons 5 43
(Adrian Paul Keatley, Ire) *chsd ldrs: 3rd over 3f out: kpt on same pce: tk modest 3rd nr fin* **5/2**[1]

-010 **4** *nk* **Wootton Vale (IRE)**[15] 4681 3-8-11 **54**........................... TonyHamilton 7 52
(Richard Fahey) *chsd ldrs: 2nd over 3f out: one pce* **14/1**

1366 **5** *1 3/4* **Testa Rossa (IRE)**[14] 4702 6-10-0 **62**..................................(b) JoeDoyle 8 57
(Jim Goldie) *mid-div: drvn over 2f out: one pce* **16/1**

5-26 **6** *nk* **Highfield Lass**[25] 4314 5-9-0 **48**.................................. ConnorBeasley 12 42
(Michael Dods) *hld up towards rr: hdwy 3f out: one pce fnl 2f* **9/2**[2]

7 *8* **Maritime Law (IRE)**[16] 4676 4-8-6 **45**...................(p) ShirleyTeasdale[(5)] 10 25
(Garvan Donnelly, Ire) *in rr-div: hdwy 5f out: wknd fnl 2f* **33/1**

-000 **8** *26* **Wisteria**[20] 4489 4-8-11 **45**..(tp) RaulDaSilva 2
(Susan Corbett) *chsd ldrs: wknd over 2f out: heavily eased fnl f: t.o* **100/1**

000- **9** *2 3/4* **Bassett Bleu**[300] 7183 3-8-2 **45**...(p) JoeyHaynes 9
(Iain Jardine) *chsd ldrs: drvn and lost pl after 3f: sn bhd: t.o over 2f out: eased fnl f* **33/1**

0004 **10** *7* **Togetherwecan (IRE)**[5] 5010 4-9-5 **53**.............................(b) JoeFanning 3
(Mark Johnston) *s.i.s: in rr: pushed along 5f out: sn bhd: t.o whn eased over 1f out* **6/1**

2m 15.82s (3.82) **Going Correction** +0.55s/f (Yiel)
WFA 3 from 4yo+ 9lb **10** Ran SP% **115.3**
Speed ratings (Par 101): **97,95,93,92,91 91,84,64,61,56**
CSF £27.17 CT £68.93 TOTE £8.50: £2.10, £1.80, £1.80; EX 31.10 Trifecta £106.70.
Owner Mrs Sarah Bryan **Bred** M Daguzan-Garros & Rolling Hills Farm **Trained** Malton, N Yorks

FOCUS

Little got into this, the slower of the two divisions, with the winner making all. The level is set near the runner-up's recent Tapeta win.

T/Jkpt: Not won. T/Plt: £119.20 to a £1 stake. Pool of £84850.65 - 519.31 winning tickets. T/Qpdt: £28.90 to a £1 stake. Pool of £7188.28 - 183.70 winning tickets. **Walter Glynn**

4790 FFOS LAS (L-H)

Monday, August 8

OFFICIAL GOING: Good

Wind: medium half against Weather: sunny spells

5229 FOOTBALL BETTING AT 188BET MEDIAN AUCTION MAIDEN STKS 6f

5:30 (5:31) (Class 5) 2-Y-O **£3,234** (£962; £481; £240) **Stalls** Centre

Form RPR

6 **1** **Chaplin (FR)**[17] 4594 2-9-5 0.. ShaneKelly 4 73
(Richard Hughes) *hld up wl in tch: clsd over 2f out: led 1f out: sn edgd lft: rdn out* **5/1**[2]

4 **2** *3/4* **Arzaak (IRE)**[69] 2756 2-9-5 0.. DavidProbert 3 71
(Owen Burrows) *trckd ldrs: shkn up 2f out: sn ev ch: rdn fnl f: jst hld by wnr* **4/6**[1]

3 *1 1/4* **Twilight Spirit** 2-9-0 0... FrannyNorton 5 62+
(Tony Carroll) *s.i.s: hld up: stl last whn shkn up over 1f out: r.o wl fnl f: tk 3rd last strides* **20/1**

043 **4** *nk* **Glory Of Paris (IRE)**[16] 4659 2-9-5 73................................... RyanTate 6 66
(Rod Millman) *trckd ldr: rdn to ld over 2f out: hdd 1f out: 3rd whn sltly hmpd sn after: one pce after and lost 3rd last strides* **8/1**[3]

5 *1 1/4* **Oh Geno** 2-9-5 0.. JimCrowley 2 63
(Richard Spencer) *hld up wl in tch: rdn 2f out: sn outpcd by ldrs: kpt on fnl f* **10/1**

4222 **6** *1 1/2* **Bazwind (IRE)**[23] 4386 2-9-5 71.. SteveDrowne 1 58
(David Evans) *led tl rdn and hdd over 2f out: wknd fnl f* **9/1**

1m 13.75s (3.75) **Going Correction** +0.15s/f (Good) **6** Ran SP% **111.6**
Speed ratings (Par 94): **81,80,78,77,76 74**
CSF £8.70 TOTE £5.20: £1.90, £1.30; EX 10.60 Trifecta £133.00.
Owner Macdonald,Wright,Creed,Jiggins & Miller **Bred** Monsieur William Huntingdon **Trained** Upper Lambourn, Berkshire

FOCUS

An ordinary juvenile maiden, which is rated in line with the runner up's debut effort.

5230 £25 FREE BET AT 188BET H'CAP 5f

6:00 (6:01) (Class 5) (0-75,75) 3-Y-O+ **£2,911** (£866; £432; £216) **Stalls** Centre

Form RPR

0600 **1** **Bonjour Steve**[56] 3217 5-8-7 **58**....................................(p) DavidProbert 4 65
(Richard Price) *chsd ldng trio: rdn over 2f out: wnt 2nd 1f out: led narrowly ins fnl f: all out* **9/2**[3]

0661 **2** *nk* **The Burnham Mare (IRE)**[6] 4980 3-8-2 **63** 6ex..........(p) HollieDoyle[(7)] 2 68
(J S Moore) *led 1f: styd cl up: rdn 1/2-way: led again over 1f out: hdd narrowly ins fnl f: kpt on* **5/1**

2342 **3** *3/4* **Head Space (IRE)**[17] 4590 8-8-8 **66**............................(v) JoshuaBryan[(7)] 5 69
(Brian Barr) *s.i.s: hld up in last: effrt 2f out: r.o wl fnl f: tk 3rd fnl 75yds: clsng on first two nr fin* **11/4**[2]

0016 **4** 3/4 **Addicted To Luck**[37] 3898 3-8-11 **65**.................... ShaneKelly 3 64
(Jo Hughes) *cl up: led after 1f tl rdn and hdd over 1f out: no ex fnl f: lost 3rd fnl 75yds* **10/1**

0153 **5** 6 **Sir Theodore (IRE)**[6] 4985 3-9-7 **75**.................... JimCrowley 1 53
(Richard Spencer) *cl up: rdn 2f out: wknd 1f out* **11/8**[1]

59.62s (1.32) **Going Correction** +0.15s/f (Good)
WFA 3 from 5yo+ 3lb **5** Ran SP% **112.7**
Speed ratings (Par 103): **95,94,93,92,82**
CSF £26.08 TOTE £5.40: £2.20, £2.50; EX 32.20 Trifecta £89.50.
Owner Barry Veasey **Bred** The Pocock Family **Trained** Ullingswick, H'fords

FOCUS
Modest sprinting form, with the favourite disappointing. The winner was on a good mark and found a little on this year's form.

5231 3A'S LEISURE H'CAP 1m 4f (R)
6:30 (6:30) (Class 4) (0-85,78) 3-Y-O+ **£4,690** (£1,395; £697; £348) **Stalls** Low

Form RPR
2321 **1** **Swashbuckle**[11] 4793 3-9-2 **78**.................... DavidProbert 6 87+
(Andrew Balding) *trckd ldr in share of 2nd: rdn over 2f out: led over 1f out: styd on strly* **7/4**[1]

-230 **2** 2 **Desdichado**[38] 3862 4-9-13 **78**.................... JimCrowley 3 84
(Ralph Beckett) *hld up in last pair: rdn and hdwy on outer over 2f out: chsd wnr ent fnl f: one pce and no imp* **8/1**

5220 **3** nk **Isharah (USA)**[10] 4827 3-9-2 **78**.................... FrannyNorton 4 83
(Mark Johnston) *hld up and mainly in 4th: rdn 3f out: sn sltly outpcd by ldrs: edgd rt ins fnl f: styd on wl towards fin* **10/3**[3]

22-3 **4** 1 3/4 **Nonios (IRE)**[21] 4458 4-9-10 **75**.................... ShaneKelly 1 78
(David Simcock) *trckd ldr in share of 2nd: rdn over 3f out: led over 2f out tl over 1f out: lost 2nd ent fnl f: no ex* **5/2**[2]

2500 **5** 3/4 **Moojaned (IRE)**[11] 4795 5-9-6 **78**.................... MitchGodwin(7) 5 79
(David Evans) *led tl hdd over 2f out: kpt on u.p tl no ex appr fnl f: hld whn swtchd rt 110yds out* **16/1**

013 **6** 1/2 **Swift Cedar (IRE)**[124] 1250 6-9-6 **78**.................... AledBeech(7) 2 79
(David Evans) *s.i.s: racd keenly in last pair: clsd 4f out: rdn over 2f out: one pce and no further imp* **16/1**

2m 35.63s (-1.77) **Going Correction** +0.15s/f (Good)
WFA 3 from 4yo+ 11lb **6** Ran SP% **110.9**
Speed ratings (Par 105): **111,109,109,108,107 107**
CSF £15.84 TOTE £2.50: £1.50, £2.80; EX 13.30 Trifecta £38.50.
Owner Kingsclere Racing Club **Bred** Kingsclere Stud **Trained** Kingsclere, Hants

FOCUS
A fair handicap that went to a progressive 3yo, who found plenty for pressure. The runner-up is rated to have run to form.

5232 188BET H'CAP 1m 4f (R)
7:00 (7:00) (Class 6) (0-65,65) 3-Y-O+ **£2,264** (£673; £336; £168) **Stalls** Low

Form RPR
642 **1** **Captain Peacock**[26] 4273 3-9-2 **64**....................(v) JimCrowley 3 74
(William Knight) *squeezed out s: in rr tl hdwy on outer to go 2nd after 3f: led gng wl 3f out: jnd whn rdn and veered lft over 1f out: r.o u.p: edgd lft wl ins fnl f: won on nod* **6/4**[1]

003 **2** hd **Fandango (GER)**[33] 3998 3-8-10 **63**.................... DavidParkes(5) 2 73
(Jeremy Gask) *hld up towards rr: rdn and hdwy over 2f out: chal and carried lft over 1f out: ev ch fnl f: lost on nod* **7/2**[2]

1133 **3** 9 **Bernisdale**[8] 4913 8-9-7 **65**.................... MitchGodwin(7) 1 60
(John Flint) *chsd ldrs: rdn over 2f out: hung lft over 1f out: one pce and no ch w first two fnl f* **7/1**

0561 **4** 1 3/4 **Street Outlaw (IRE)**[28] 4210 3-9-2 **64**....................(p) FrannyNorton 7 56
(Daniel Mark Loughnane) *hld up: rdn 3f out: sn outpcd by ldrs: styd on to take mod 4th ins fnl f* **9/2**[3]

-525 **5** 1 1/2 **Grams And Ounces**[17] 4592 9-9-5 **61**....................(t) CiaranMckee(5) 8 51
(Grace Harris) *chsd ldrs: rdn over 2f out: wknd over 1f out* **14/1**

5042 **6** 2 3/4 **Doctor Kehoe**[27] 4225 4-9-6 **57**....................(vt) ShaneKelly 6 43
(David Evans) *s.i.s: sn rcvrd to ld at stdy pce: brought field into centre home st: rdn and hdd 3f out: wknd wl over 1f out* **8/1**

6000 **7** 2 **Antonio Joli (IRE)**[110] 1561 4-9-11 **62**.................... AdamBeschizza 5 44
(Jo Hughes) *led early: trckd ldrs after tl rdn and lost pl over 3f out: wknd wl over 1f out* **25/1**

2m 39.22s (1.82) **Going Correction** +0.15s/f (Good)
WFA 3 from 4yo+ 11lb **7** Ran SP% **114.5**
Speed ratings (Par 101): **99,98,92,91,90 88,87**
CSF £6.91 CT £26.75 TOTE £2.30: £1.80, £1.70; EX 6.00 Trifecta £23.40.
Owner Chasemore Farm **Bred** Chasemore Farm **Trained** Patching, W Sussex
■ Stewards' Enquiry : Jim Crowley caution: careless riding

FOCUS
The 3yos predictably dominated this modest handicap that had little depth.

5233 188BET.CO.UK MEDIAN AUCTION MAIDEN STKS 1m (R)
7:30 (7:31) (Class 6) 3-4-Y-O **£2,587** (£770; £384; £192) **Stalls** Low

Form RPR
2-43 **1** **High Hopes**[81] 2395 3-9-0 79.................... JimCrowley 4 69+
(David Simcock) *hld up in 3rd: wnt 2nd gng wl over 2f out: led early ins fnl f: pushed clr: easily* **1/8**[1]

04 **2** 4 1/2 **Zamindo**[6] 4983 3-9-5 0.................... FrannyNorton 3 56
(Mark Johnston) *chsd ldr who wnt clr after 2f: lost 2nd over 2f out: sn rdn: one pce and no ch w wnr: wnt 2nd 100yds out: edgd rt sn after* **8/1**[2]

00-4 **3** 1 1/4 **Locommotion**[16] 4656 4-9-7 55.................... LucyKBarry(5) 1 54
(Matthew Salaman) *led and racd freely: clr after 2f: stl 10 l up 4f out: rdn over 1f out: reduced ld whn rdn over 1f out: hdd and no ex early ins fnl f: lost 2nd 100yds out* **16/1**[3]

0 **4** 40 **Scarlet Not Blue**[30] 4156 4-9-5 0.................... MitchGodwin(7) 2
(Matthew Salaman) *t.k.h in last: rdn 4f out: lost tch 3f out: t.o* **66/1**

1m 41.48s (0.48) **Going Correction** +0.15s/f (Good)
WFA 3 from 4yo 7lb **4** Ran SP% **107.4**
Speed ratings (Par 101): **103,98,97,57**
CSF £1.66 TOTE £1.10; EX 1.70 Trifecta £1.80.
Owner Major M G Wyatt **Bred** Charlie Wyatt **Trained** Newmarket, Suffolk
■ Stewards' Enquiry : Franny Norton caution: careless riding

FOCUS
No depth to this maiden and it was little more than an exercise canter for the favourite. The third is the form marker, as he is rated cose to his previous start.

5234 OLYMPICS BETTING AT 188BET H'CAP 1m (R)
8:00 (8:02) (Class 4) (0-85,83) 3-Y-O+ **£4,690** (£1,395; £697; £348) **Stalls** Low

Form RPR
-061 **1** **Kummiya**[20] 4497 3-8-12 **77**.................... KieranShoemark(3) 1 92+
(Roger Charlton) *hld up: swtchd lft and hdwy over 2f out: rdn to ld wl over 1f out: sn c clr: eased nr fin* **15/8**[1]

0566 **2** 2 **Force (IRE)**[19] 4534 3-9-2 **78**.................... DavidProbert 3 82
(Charles Hills) *hld up: hdwy on outer 3f out: sn rdn: wnt 2nd over 1f out: kpt on but a hld by wnr* **7/1**

446 **3** 1 **Alcatraz (IRE)**[31] 4081 4-9-12 **81**....................(p) SteveDrowne 7 84
(George Baker) *s.i.s: sn chsng ldrs: rdn 2f out: kpt on same pce* **9/2**

060 **4** 1 1/4 **Fire Ship**[37] 3910 7-10-0 **83**....................(v) JimCrowley 5 83
(William Knight) *led: rdn over 2f out: hdd wl over 1f out: one pce* **3/1**[2]

4023 **5** 2 1/2 **Lilbourne Prince (IRE)**[8] 4909 3-8-4 **73**.................... MitchGodwin(7) 6 66
(David Evans) *trckd ldr: rdn over 2f out and sn lost 2nd: wknd appr fnl f* **4/1**[3]

-000 **6** 1 **Yamllik**[30] 4158 4-8-10 **72**.................... JoshuaBryan(7) 4 63
(Brian Barr) *t.k.h: trckd ldrs: rdn over 2f out: wknd over 1f out* **25/1**

1m 40.7s (-0.30) **Going Correction** +0.15s/f (Good)
WFA 3 from 4yo+ 7lb **6** Ran SP% **114.3**
Speed ratings (Par 105): **107,105,104,102,100 99**
CSF £16.04 TOTE £2.60: £1.70, £3.30; EX 15.40 Trifecta £52.40.
Owner A E Oppenheimer **Bred** Hascombe And Valiant Studs **Trained** Beckhampton, Wilts
■ Stewards' Enquiry : Jim Crowley jockey said that the gelding lost a front shoe

FOCUS
A fair handicap that saw quite a taking win from the favourite. The pace was ordinary but the runner-up is rated to have run to his best form.

5235 EDWARDS COACHES H'CAP 7f 80y(R)
8:30 (8:31) (Class 6) (0-60,58) 3-Y-O+ **£2,264** (£673; £336; £168) **Stalls** Low

Form RPR
1330 **1** **Satchville Flyer**[23] 4389 5-9-7 **58**.................... KieranShoemark(3) 4 67
(David Evans) *t.k.h in 5th: hdwy 4f out: rdn to ld and hung lft over 1f out: continued to hang but r.o wl: comf* **9/2**

5010 **2** 2 3/4 **Carcharias (IRE)**[19] 4506 3-9-0 **54**.................... JimCrowley 5 54
(Ed de Giles) *trckd ldr: rdn over 2f out and briefly in 3rd: one pce and hld by comfortable wnr fnl f* **4/1**[3]

-005 **3** 1 1/4 **Windmills Girl**[16] 4640 3-8-11 **51**....................(b) AdamBeschizza 3 48
(Jeremy Gask) *set stdy pce: rdn 2f out: sn hdd: one pce fnl f: jst hld 3rd* **8/1**

2243 **4** hd **Funny Oyster (IRE)**[42] 3724 3-9-4 **58**....................(p) SteveDrowne 7 54
(George Baker) *hld up: rdn 3f out: hdwy on outer 2f out: r.o fnl f: jst missed 3rd* **9/4**[1]

-003 **5** 1 **Just Isla**[19] 4504 6-9-0 **55**....................(b) MitchGodwin(7) 6 50
(John Flint) *mounted in chute: s.s: hld up: rdn 2f out: one pce and nvr able to chal* **7/2**[2]

0500 **6** 1 **Outlaw Kate (IRE)**[25] 4289 4-8-11 **45**....................(b[1]) RobertTart 2 38
(Michael Mullineaux) *chsd ldrs: rdn over 2f out: one pce and hld after* **14/1**

3600 **7** 2 1/4 **Malvesi**[143] 986 7-8-11 **45**....................(b[1]) FrannyNorton 1 32
(Daniel Mark Loughnane) *plld hrd: trckd ldrs: rdn 2f out: wknd appr fnl f* **16/1**

1m 32.98s (-0.02) **Going Correction** +0.15s/f (Good)
WFA 3 from 4yo+ 6lb **7** Ran SP% **114.8**
Speed ratings (Par 101): **106,102,101,101,100 98,96**
CSF £22.93 TOTE £6.00: £2.50, £3.00; EX 31.30 Trifecta £197.40.
Owner Mr A Cooke & Lynn Cullimore 1 **Bred** Newsells Park Stud **Trained** Pandy, Monmouths

FOCUS
A pretty weak handicap, run at a steady pace, and is rated around the first three. The winner was the pick of the weights on this year's 6f form.
T/Plt: £41.00 to a £1 stake. Pool of £44458.05 - 790.13 winning tickets. T/Qpdt: £5.10 to a £1 stake. Pool of £4255.05 - 612.80 winning tickets. **Richard Lowther**

5202 WINDSOR (R-H)
Monday, August 8

OFFICIAL GOING: Good to firm (8.7)
Wind: Fresh, behind Weather: Overcast

5236 SKYBET APPRENTICE H'CAP 6f
5:50 (5:52) (Class 5) (0-70,69) 3-Y-O+ **£2,911** (£866; £432; £216) **Stalls** Low

Form RPR
0556 **1** **Perfect Pastime**[35] 3953 8-9-3 **63**.................... PaddyBradley(5) 1 70
(Jim Boyle) *c out of stalls bef rest but stdd and hdd after 100yds: sn in rr: prog 2f out: swtchd to rail fnl f: drvn and r.o to ld nr fin* **14/1**

2204 **2** 1/2 **Straits Of Malacca**[32] 4051 5-10-0 **69**....................(p) JosephineGordon 2 74+
(Simon Dow) *trckd ldrs: wnt 2nd over 2f out: rdn to ld over 1f out: kpt on but hdd nr fin* **3/1**[2]

4320 **3** 3/4 **Wahaab (IRE)**[41] 3743 5-9-0 **60**....................(p) NicolaCurrie(5) 3 63
(Richard Hughes) *taken down early: hld up in last and off the pce: prog and shkn up 2f out: rdn and styd on to take 3rd nr fin: too much to do* **11/4**[1]

5612 **4** 3/4 **Generalyse**[18] 4570 7-9-5 **60**....................(b) RobHornby 5 60
(Anabel K Murphy) *hld up off the pce: prog 2f out: shkn up and styd on to press for a pl fnl f: one pce nr fin* **13/2**

-500 **5** 4 **State Of The Union (IRE)**[154] 856 4-9-1 **61**....................(t) JordanUys(5) 4 48
(Willie Musson) *chsd ldr after 2f to over 2f out: wknd over 1f out* **9/1**

3626 **6** nse **Swendab (IRE)**[17] 4590 8-10-0 **69**....................(b) EdwardGreatrex 7 56
(John O'Shea) *led after 100yds and set str pce: rdn over 2f out: hdd over 1f out: wknd fnl f* **14/1**

0000 **7** 2 1/2 **Pop Culture**[26] 4262 3-8-13 **58**.................... DannyBrock 6 36
(Jonathan Portman) *chsd ldr after 100yds tl after 2f: sn pushed along: lost pl wl over 1f out: wknd* **9/1**

0306 **8** 1/2 **Hipz (IRE)**[11] 4787 5-9-0 **60**....................(p) MeganNicholls(5) 8 38
(Laura Mongan) *a in rr: rdn and brief effrt 2f out: sn wknd* **6/1**[3]

1m 12.08s (-0.92) **Going Correction** -0.075s/f (Good)
WFA 3 from 4yo+ 4lb **8** Ran SP% **112.6**
Speed ratings (Par 103): **103,102,101,100,95 94,91,90**
CSF £54.26 CT £149.92 TOTE £10.00: £2.70, £1.50, £1.30; EX 57.70 Trifecta £225.30.
Owner The Paddock Space Partnership 2 **Bred** R G & T E Levin **Trained** Epsom, Surrey

FOCUS
Races of 1m and further increased by 16yds. A modest sprint handicap for apprentice riders. They went a strong gallop on heavily watered, officially good to firm, ground and the winner benefited from a delayed challenge despite gaining a length when forcing his head through the gate at the start. The runner-up can be marked up a but for racing on the speed.

5237 MTS RECRUITMENT MAIDEN STKS 6f
6:20 (6:21) (Class 5) 2-Y-O **£2,911** (£866; £432; £216) **Stalls** Low

Form RPR
45 **1** **Himself**[30] 4154 2-9-5 0 TomMarquand 5 74
(Richard Hannon) *led 1f: pressed ldr: shkn up over 2f out: chalng whn carried lft fr over 1f out: led ins fnl f: rdn out* **4/1**[3]
2 3/4 **Lovely Acclamation (IRE)** 2-9-0 0 SilvestreDeSousa 1 67
(Ismail Mohammed) *led after 1f: rdn and hung lft fr over 1f out: hdd and no ex ins fnl f* **15/2**
44 **3** 1 1/4 **Act Of Freedom (IRE)**[32] 4040 2-9-5 0 WilliamBuick 4 68
(Charlie Appleby) *sn in 5th: pushed along and no prog jst over 2f out: hdwy and rdn 1f out: r.o to take 3rd last 100yds: nt rch ldng pair* **9/4**[2]
4 1 3/4 **Ourmullion** 2-9-5 0 KierenFox 8 62
(John Best) *sn pushed along in 6th: effrt on wd outside 2f out: shkn up and kpt on same pce fnl f* **33/1**
02 **5** 1 **Curve Ball (IRE)**[10] 4837 2-9-5 0 PatDobbs 7 59
(Richard Hughes) *trckd ldrs: shkn up 2f out: nt qckn over 1f out: fdd ins fnl f* **11/8**[1]
6 2 3/4 **Red Alert** 2-9-5 0 OisinMurphy 2 50
(Joseph Tuite) *dwlt: sn trckd ldng pair: pushed along over 1f out: steadily wknd* **33/1**
7 18 **Av A Word** 2-9-5 0 DougieCostello 3
(Daniel Kubler) *slowly away: rn green and a detached in last* **33/1**

1m 12.82s (-0.18) **Going Correction** -0.075s/f (Good) **7** Ran SP% **113.5**
Speed ratings (Par 94): **98,97,95,93,91 88,64**
CSF £31.68 TOTE £5.10: £2.30, £2.70; EX 39.00 Trifecta £122.50.
Owner Mrs E Roberts **Bred** Mrs E C Roberts **Trained** East Everleigh, Wilts

FOCUS
A fair juvenile maiden, won by a colt down to 6f again. They went a decent gallop but the two horses coming in with the best form disappointed to certain degrees.

5238 MPM FLOORING LTD MAIDEN STKS 5f 10y
6:50 (6:50) (Class 4) 3-4-Y-O **£4,690** (£1,395; £697; £348) **Stalls** Low

Form RPR
-432 **1** **May Rose (IRE)**[12] 4763 3-9-0 68 (t) AndreaAtzeni 5 83+
(Charles Hills) *trckd ldng pair: clsd fr 2f out: pushed into 2nd over 1f out: shkn up to ld last 150yds: readily* **1/1**[1]
-22 **2** 1 **Sirajiah (IRE)**[27] 4238 3-9-0 74 (p) PatCosgrave 4 78
(William Haggas) *led: rdn over 1f out: hdd last 150yds: styd on but readily hld by wnr* **7/4**[2]
04 **3** 3 3/4 **Website**[27] 4238 4-9-8 73 SilvestreDeSousa 3 70
(Robert Cowell) *chsd ldr: urged along 1/2-way: lost 2nd over 1f out: fdd ins fnl f* **7/1**[3]
4 **4** 5 **Wensara Dream**[16] 4660 3-9-0 0 OisinMurphy 2 46
(Andrew Balding) *pushed along and outpcd by ldng trio: stl pushed along and no imp fnl 2f: nvr really involved* **9/1**
0 **5** 9 **Sams R Man**[7] 4939 4-9-5 0 (p) GeorgeDowning[(3)] 1 20
(Linda Jewell) *outpcd and pushed along after 2f: sn bhd* **100/1**
0 **6** 2 1/2 **Back To Love (CAN)**[16] 4660 3-9-0 0 TomQueally 6 5
(Mark Gillard) *v awkward s and swvd lft: detached in last: a bhd* **100/1**

59.27s (-1.03) **Going Correction** -0.075s/f (Good)
WFA 3 from 4yo 3lb **6** Ran SP% **110.8**
Speed ratings (Par 105): **105,103,97,89,75 71**
CSF £2.87 TOTE £1.80: £1.10, £1.50; EX 2.70 Trifecta £5.90.
Owner Saleh Al Homaizi & Imad Al Sagar **Bred** Irish National Stud **Trained** Lambourn, Berks

FOCUS
A fair maiden sprint, in which the winner built on the recent promise of his stable debut. They went a decent gallop and the improving winner benefited from a patient ride. The runner-up, who'd had a few chances, seemingly ran his race from the front.

5239 ODDFELLOWS NURSERY H'CAP 1m 67y
7:20 (7:20) (Class 4) (0-85,83) 2-Y-O **£4,690** (£1,395; £697; £348) **Stalls** Low

Form RPR
12 **1** **Permian (IRE)**[14] 4699 2-9-7 **83** WilliamBuick 2 93+
(Mark Johnston) *mde all: sltly awkward bnd 5f out: shkn up over 2f out: drew clr over 1f out: styd on wl* **11/10**[1]
553 **2** 4 **Challow (IRE)**[31] 4076 2-8-9 **71** LiamKeniry 6 70
(Sylvester Kirk) *hld up: shkn up 1/2-way: prog u.p to go 2nd over 1f out: styd on but no ch w wnr* **3/1**[2]
6055 **3** 4 **Moneyoryourlife**[6] 4982 2-8-3 **65** KieranO'Neill 4 54
(Richard Hannon) *trckd ldng pair tl chsd wnr over 3f out: drvn over 2f out: lost 2nd over 1f out: edgd rt jst ins fnl f: fdd* **11/1**
6002 **4** 3/4 **Golden Guest**[7] 4937 2-8-3 **65** (v) RyanPowell 3 54
(George Margarson) *sltly awkward s: hld up in last: pushed along over 2f out: clsng to chal for 3rd whn stuck bhd rivals over 1f out and then squeezed out jst ins fnl f: nt rcvr* **9/1**
4106 **5** 2 **Nibras Bounty (IRE)**[31] 4076 2-9-4 **80** PatDobbs 5 62
(Richard Hannon) *chsd wnr to over 3f out: drvn and wknd 2f out* **4/1**[3]

1m 44.28s (-0.42) **Going Correction** -0.075s/f (Good) **5** Ran SP% **111.0**
Speed ratings (Par 96): **99,95,91,90,88**
CSF £4.69 TOTE £1.90: £1.30, £1.50; EX 4.70 Trifecta £22.90.
Owner Sheikh Hamdan bin Mohammed Al Maktoum **Bred** Darley **Trained** Middleham Moor, N Yorks

FOCUS
A decent, if not particularly competitive, nursery handicap. The winner set the tempo until kicking on from past halfway in a thoroughly dominant victory. The runner-up is rated to have run near to form.

5240 SKYBET H'CAP 1m 2f 7y
7:50 (7:50) (Class 3) (0-90,88) 3-Y-O+ **£7,439** (£2,213; £1,106; £553) **Stalls** Centre

Form RPR
260- **1** **Landwade Lad**[273] 7779 4-10-0 **88** OisinMurphy 3 97
(James Fanshawe) *hld up in last pair: swtchd to nr side and clsd over 1f out: drvn to ld jst ins fnl f: hung bdly lft after: jst hld on* **9/1**
-341 **2** shd **Rock Steady (IRE)**[14] 4710 3-8-13 **82** WilliamTwiston-Davies 6 90
(Roger Charlton) *hld up in last pair: clsd steadily on outer fr 2f out: rdn to chal ins fnl f: sltly impeded nr fin: jst failed* **9/4**[2]
2013 **3** 1 3/4 **Prendergast Hill (IRE)**[14] 4710 4-9-7 **84** (p) JosephineGordon[(3)] 5 90+
(Ed de Giles) *t.k.h: trckd ldng pair: clsd to ld 2f out: hdd jst ins fnl f: cl 3rd but hld whn squeezed out nr fin* **5/1**[3]
6-56 **4** 4 **Jelly Monger (IRE)**[23] 4391 4-9-12 **86** SilvestreDeSousa 2 82
(Dominic Ffrench Davis) *t.k.h: led after 3f: drvn and hdd 2f out: nt qckn over 1f out: hld in 4th whn squeezed out ins fnl f: wknd* **14/1**
311 **5** 2 3/4 **Absolute Zero (IRE)**[7] 4945 3-9-3 **86** 6ex AndreaAtzeni 1 77
(Roger Varian) *t.k.h: led: stdd after 3f and hdd: chal again 3f out: wknd over 1f out* **11/10**[1]

2m 7.14s (-1.56) **Going Correction** -0.075s/f (Good)
WFA 3 from 4yo 9lb **5** Ran SP% **111.7**
Speed ratings (Par 107): **103,102,101,98,96**
CSF £29.74 TOTE £8.90: £3.50, £1.30; EX 30.60 Trifecta £94.50.
Owner Pearl Bloodstock Ltd **Bred** Shutford Stud **Trained** Newmarket, Suffolk
■ Stewards' Enquiry : Oisin Murphy two-day ban: careless riding (22-23 Aug)

FOCUS
The feature contest was a decent handicap. The jockeys were wary of doing too much too soon, though, which resulted in a muddling gallop and the fourth and fifth running keen. The winner has a progressive profile, and the runner-up is on the upgrade as well.

5241 DENNING LEGAL H'CAP 1m 67y
8:20 (8:20) (Class 5) (0-70,73) 3-Y-O+ **£2,911** (£866; £432) **Stalls** Low

Form RPR
6416 **1** **Reaver (IRE)**[26] 4269 3-9-7 **70** CharlesBishop 7 76+
(Eve Johnson Houghton) *hld up in 3rd: clsd steadily over 2f out: shkn up to ld over 1f out: in command after: comf* **4/5**[1]
1054 **2** 1 1/4 **Blushes (FR)**[24] 4370 3-8-12 **61** (b[1]) SilvestreDeSousa 4 62
(Ed Dunlop) *chsd ldr: rdn and dropped to 3rd 2f out: kpt on to take 2nd again fnl f: no real threat to wnr* **2/1**[2]
0003 **3** 1 1/4 **Live Dangerously**[11] 4788 6-9-11 **67** WilliamCarson 1 66
(John Bridger) *racd freely: led and hanging lft: drvn 2f out: hdd over 1f out: one pce* **4/1**[3]

1m 44.76s (0.06) **Going Correction** -0.075s/f (Good)
WFA 3 from 4yo+ 7lb **3** Ran SP% **108.9**
Speed ratings (Par 103): **96,94,93**
CSF £2.72 TOTE £1.80; EX 2.20 Trifecta £3.00.
Owner Anthony Pye-Jeary **Bred** Kildaragh Stud **Trained** Blewbury, Oxon

FOCUS
An ordinary handicap decimated by four morning non-runners. The right horse came to the fore off an, at best, respectable gallop and may have more to offer.
T/Plt: £50.10 to a £1 stake. Pool of £81025.90 - 1180.25 winning tickets. T/Qpdt: £5.60 to a £1 stake. Pool of £6746.78 - 879.41 winning tickets. **Jonathan Neesom**

5125 WOLVERHAMPTON (A.W) (L-H)
Monday, August 8

OFFICIAL GOING: Tapeta: standard
Wind: medium, behind Weather: light cloud, sunny spells

5242 FCL GLOBAL FORWARDING EBF STALLIONS MAIDEN FILLIES' STKS (PLUS 10) 5f 216y (Tp)
2:15 (2:18) (Class 5) 2-Y-O **£3,234** (£962; £481; £240) **Stalls** Low

Form RPR
1 **Many A Tale** 2-9-0 0 ThomasBrown 12 76+
(Ismail Mohammed) *chsd ldrs: rdn and effrt to chal 2f out: led 1f out: styd on wl: rdn out* **28/1**
32 **2** 3/4 **Golden Easter (USA)**[11] 4804 2-9-0 0 RichardKingscote 11 74
(Kevin Ryan) *taken down early: led: rdn and hung lft over 1f out: hdd 1f out: styd on same pce ins fnl f* **13/8**[1]
5 **3** 1/2 **Braztime**[12] 4762 2-9-0 0 SeanLevey 1 72
(Richard Hannon) *hld up in tch in midfield: effrt and hdwy 2f out: chsd clr ldng pair 150yds out: styd on wl: nt rch ldrs* **7/2**[2]
3 **4** 2 1/4 **Moonlit Show**[21] 4457 2-9-0 0 StevieDonohoe 7 66
(Charlie Fellowes) *chsd ldr tl ent fnl 2f: 3rd and unable qck u.p over 1f out: kpt on same pce fnl f* **4/1**[3]
0 **5** 1 **Impassioned**[37] 3881 2-9-0 0 LukeMorris 3 63
(Sir Mark Prescott Bt) *in tch in midfield: effrt and hdwy over 2f out: drvn: styd on same pce and no imp over 1f out* **16/1**
0 **6** 3 **Faith In Me (IRE)**[24] 4350 2-9-0 0 RobertHavlin 10 54
(Simon Crisford) *hld up in tch in midfield but stuck wd: outpcd and rdn 2f out: no hdwy and btn over 1f out: wknd fnl f* **20/1**
7 3/4 **Fast Lily (IRE)**[19] 4537 2-9-0 0 (v) TedDurcan 2 51
(P J Prendergast, Ire) *chsd ldrs: rdn and no rspnse 2f out: lost pl and btn over 1f out: wknd and eased wl ins fnl f* **15/2**
45 **8** 3 1/2 **Cape Falcone**[18] 4564 2-8-11 0 EoinWalsh[(3)] 8 41
(James Tate) *in tch in midfield: rdn 3f out: sn struggling: wknd wl over 1f out* **14/1**
60 **9** 1 1/2 **Topmeup**[12] 4759 2-9-0 0 JFEgan 6 36
(Stuart Edmunds) *s.i.s: a in last quartet: rdn 4f out: wknd 2f out* **66/1**
10 shd **Glyder** 2-9-0 0 RoystonFfrench 5 36
(John Holt) *s.i.s: a in last quartet: swtchd rt 3f out: sn rdn and struggling: wknd 2f out* **100/1**
11 3/4 **I Dare To Dream** 2-8-9 0 CharlieBennett[(5)] 4 34
(Lisa Williamson) *a in last quartet: rdn over 4f out: drvn and wknd 2f out* **100/1**
0 **12** 7 **Henrietta's Dream**[21] 4451 2-9-0 0 PaddyAspell 9 13
(John Wainwright) *sn stdd bk to last quartet: rdn and no rspnse 2f out: sn wknd* **200/1**

1m 13.97s (-0.53) **Going Correction** -0.10s/f (Stan) **12** Ran SP% **116.8**
Speed ratings (Par 91): **99,98,97,94,93 89,88,83,81,81 80,70**
CSF £72.03 TOTE £34.00: £7.20, £1.20, £1.50; EX 85.70 Trifecta £525.10.
Owner Saeed Manana **Bred** Whatton Manor Stud & Robert Cornelius **Trained** Newmarket, Suffolk

FOCUS
Fairly useful form from the principals in this fillies' maiden, the winner deserving credit for seeing off a more experienced rival on debut. The two widest stalls dominated the finish.

5243 FCL GLOBAL FORWARDING MAKING LOGISTICS PERSONAL CLAIMING STKS 5f 20y (Tp)
2:45 (2:47) (Class 6) 2-Y-O **£2,264** (£673; £336; £168) **Stalls** Low

Form RPR
3212 **1** **Little Nosegay (IRE)**[11] 4791 2-8-9 64 JFEgan 5 65
(David Evans) *sn pushed into ld: mde rest: wnt clr 2f out: in command and r.o wl fnl f: rdn out* **1/1**[1]
6105 **2** 4 1/2 **King Of Castilla**[49] 3472 2-9-4 67 LukeMorris 4 58
(Gay Kelleway) *chsd wnr: rdn over 2f out: sn outpcd and no imp whn hung lft over 1f out: wl hld and plugged on same pce fnl f* **2/1**[2]

3 1 1/4 **Gold Locket (IRE)**[22] 4432 2-9-3 0 (v[1]) TedDurcan 1 52
(P J Prendergast, Ire) *chsd ldng pair: rdn over 2f out: sn outpcd by wnr: wl hld 3rd and plugged on same pce fr over 1f out* **13/2**[3]

50 4 2 3/4 **Newport Place (IRE)**[10] 4815 2-9-4 0 WilliamCarson 6 43
(Jamie Osborne) *hld up in tch in 4th tl outpcd and rdn after 1f: nvr on terms after: kpt on ins fnl f* **12/1**

5 5 **Meadow View Madam** 2-8-4 0 (b[1]) GeorgeWood[(7)] 2 18
(David Flood) *s.i.s: sn rdn and a outpcd in last: nvr on terms* **33/1**

1m 2.4s (0.50) **Going Correction** -0.10s/f (Stan) **5** Ran SP% **107.3**
Speed ratings (Par 92): **92,84,82,78,70**
CSF £3.00 TOTE £1.70: £1.10, £1.50; EX 3.20 Trifecta £5.30.Little Nosegay was subject to a friendly claim.
Owner David Berry **Bred** Mrs Amanda McCreery **Trained** Pandy, Monmouths

FOCUS
A claimer which was dominated throughout by the short-priced favourite who kept on gamely. The second and third are rated to have run to recent form.

5244 FCL GLOBAL FORWARDING MAKING LOGISTICS PERSONAL MEDIAN AUCTION MAIDEN STKS 5f 20y (Tp)
3:15 (3:15) (Class 6) 2-Y-O **£2,264** (£673; £336; £168) **Stalls** Low

Form RPR

1 **Storm Over (IRE)** 2-9-5 0 LukeMorris 2 72+
(Robert Cowell) *trckd ldng pair: rdn 2f out: nt clr run and swtchd lft ent fnl f: str run ins fnl f to ld fnl 50yds: sn in command* **9/4**[2]

0 2 1 **Cheerful Character (IRE)**[17] 4601 2-9-0 0 BarryMcHugh 6 62
(Richard Fahey) *pressed ldr: rdn wl over 1f out: ev ch and hung lft ins fnl f: led wl ins fnl f: sn hdd: stl hanging and outpcd towards fin* **9/1**

340 3 3/4 **Monte Cinq (IRE)**[15] 4678 2-9-5 66 JFEgan 3 64
(Jason Ward) *led: rdn wl over 1f out: drvn ent fnl f: hdd and no ex wl ins fnl f: hld whn squeezed for room and hmpd towards fin* **9/2**[3]

6 4 3 1/2 **Oakley Pride (IRE)**[18] 4564 2-9-5 0 RyanPowell 7 51
(Gay Kelleway) *dwlt and rdn along leaving stalls: racd in midfield: effrt ent fnl 2f: no imp and hung lft over 1f out: wl hld and one pce fnl f* **12/1**

0 5 4 1/2 **Miss Salt**[32] 4054 2-9-0 0 TimmyMurphy 5 30
(Dominic Ffrench Davis) *a towards rr: rdn 3f out: sn outpcd and wl btn fnl 2f* **33/1**

6 2 1/2 **Wagoner** 2-9-2 0 GeorgeDowning[(3)] 4 26
(Tony Carroll) *sn dropped to rr: rdn 3f out: sn struggling and wl btn fnl 2f* **16/1**

0 7 4 1/2 **Still Waiting**[17] 4594 2-9-5 0 CharlesBishop 1 10
(William Jarvis) *short of room on inner after s: hdwy into midfield 4f out: rdn and no rspnse 2f out: wknd over 1f out* **2/1**[1]

1m 1.9s **Going Correction** -0.10s/f (Stan) **7** Ran SP% **108.8**
Speed ratings (Par 92): **96,94,93,87,80 76,69**
CSF £20.10 TOTE £2.90: £1.70, £4.20; EX 17.80 Trifecta £58.90.
Owner Abdulla Al Mansoori **Bred** J Dorrian **Trained** Six Mile Bottom, Cambs

FOCUS
Not a strong maiden overall but the winner could be quite useful. It's best rated around the third.

5245 FCL GLOBAL FORWARDING MAKING LOGISTICS PERSONAL FILLIES' H'CAP 1m 4f 50y (Tp)
3:45 (3:45) (Class 5) (0-75,75) 3-Y-O+ **£2,911** (£866; £432; £216) **Stalls** Low

Form RPR

-353 1 **Great Thoughts (IRE)**[21] 4462 3-9-0 72 FrederikTylicki 3 83
(David Simcock) *hld up in tch: effrt to chse ldrs 2f out: hdwy to ld 1f out: styd on strly and drew clr fnl f: readily* **15/8**[1]

04 2 6 **Saga Sprint (IRE)**[37] 3904 3-9-1 73 PaulHanagan 5 74
(J R Jenkins) *stdd s: hld up in tch in rr: effrt over 3f out: 4th and hung lft ent fnl f: kpt on same pce ins fnl f: wnt 2nd last strides: no ch w wnr* **11/2**

21- 3 nk **Falcon's Song (USA)**[468] 1770 4-10-0 75 ThomasBrown 4 76
(Ismail Mohammed) *chsd ldr: rdn and ev ch ent fnl 2f: drvn to ld over 1f out: hdd 1f out and immediately outpcd: wknd fnl 100yds: lost 2nd last strides* **9/2**[3]

003 4 3 3/4 **Disquotational**[33] 4001 3-8-10 68 HarryBentley 1 63
(David Simcock) *led: rdn and hrd pressed wl over 1f out: hdd over 1f out: no ex and wknd ins fnl f* **11/4**[2]

625 5 2 1/4 **Martha McCandles**[24] 4347 5-9-9 75 DannyBurton[(5)] 2 66
(Alan King) *chsd ldrs: rdn 3f out: sn lost pl: bhd over 1f out* **7/1**

2m 39.32s (-1.48) **Going Correction** -0.10s/f (Stan)
WFA 3 from 4yo+ 11lb **5** Ran SP% **107.5**
Speed ratings (Par 100): **100,96,95,93,91**
CSF £11.60 TOTE £3.10: £1.60, £3.50; EX 10.70 Trifecta £40.90.
Owner Sultan Ali **Bred** Ennistown Stud **Trained** Newmarket, Suffolk

FOCUS
Not a strong handicap, a few performing below expectations, but that's not to knock the winner who has clearly found some improvement. The gallop looked more than modest for a long way, and the runner-up is rated to have run close to form.

5246 FCLGF.COM H'CAP 1m 141y (Tp)
4:15 (4:15) (Class 4) (0-85,84) 3-Y-O+ **£5,175** (£1,540; £769; £384) **Stalls** Low

Form RPR

154- 1 **Shawaahid (IRE)**[324] 6513 3-9-6 84 PaulHanagan 6 92
(Richard Hannon) *sn led and mde rest: rdn and hung rt over 1f out: flashed tail u.p: bmpd but lft in command wl ins fnl f: rdn out* **3/1**[2]

2302 2 1 1/4 **Gold Flash**[4] 5082 4-9-3 73 (b) LukeMorris 7 79
(Keith Dalgleish) *t.k.h: chsd ldrs tl wnt 2nd 7f out: upsides wnr and shkn up over 1f out: rdn: wnt lft and bmpd wnr wl ins fnl f: unbalanced: lost impetus and could nt rcvr* **4/1**[3]

106 3 1/2 **Berlusca (IRE)**[14] 4717 7-9-9 84 JoshDoyle[(5)] 2 88
(David O'Meara) *taken down early: squeezed for room leaving stalls: hld up in last pair: hdwy over 2f out: swtchd rt and drvn over 1f out: sn chsng ldng pair: kpt on ins fnl f* **13/2**

3006 4 3 1/2 **Torrid**[47] 3517 5-9-1 76 NathanEvans[(5)] 1 72
(Michael Easterby) *hld up in last pair: nt clr run over 2f out: swtchd rt and rdn 2f out: no threat to ldrs but kpt on ins fnl f* **5/1**

5060 5 3 3/4 **Idol Deputy (FR)**[4] 5082 10-9-2 77 (p) RachealKneller[(5)] 5 64
(James Bennett) *hld up in tch in midfield but stuck wd: rdn 2f out: drvn and unable qck over 1f out: hung lft and wknd ins fnl f* **33/1**

2001 6 1 3/4 **Ilzam (IRE)**[14] 4717 3-9-1 79 (t) HarryBentley 4 62
(Marco Botti) *taken down early: hld up in tch in midfield: effrt to chse ldrs 2f out: drvn and unable qck over 1f out: wknd fnl f* **9/4**[1]

32-0 7 30 **Rock Warbler (IRE)**[16] 4631 3-8-6 70 (t) BarryMcHugh 3
(Oliver Greenall) *t.k.h: chsd ldr tl 7f out: styd chsng ldrs tl rdn and lost pl 3f out: wl bhd fnl f: t.o* **33/1**

1m 48.02s (-2.08) **Going Correction** -0.10s/f (Stan)
WFA 3 from 4yo+ 8lb **7** Ran SP% **111.7**
Speed ratings (Par 105): **105,103,103,100,97 95,68**
CSF £14.63 TOTE £3.40: £2.20, £2.30; EX 15.40 Trifecta £47.10.
Owner Hamdan Al Maktoum **Bred** Cecil And Martin McCracken **Trained** East Everleigh, Wilts
■ Stewards' Enquiry : Paul Hanagan caution: careless riding

FOCUS
A fairly useful handicap; the gallop didn't look strong, the leading pair, who got involved in a bit of a barging match late on, holding those positions almost throughout.

5247 FCL GLOBAL FORWARDING MAKING LOGISTICS PERSONAL FILLIES' H'CAP 7f 32y (Tp)
4:45 (4:45) (Class 5) (0-75,71) 3-Y-O+ **£2,911** (£866; £432; £216) **Stalls** High

Form RPR

0024 1 **Mallymkun**[37] 3880 4-9-4 68 JordanVaughan[(5)] 2 76
(K R Burke) *hld up in tch in midfield: swtchd lft and effrt towards inner over 1f out: rdn to ld jst ins fnl f: hung rt ins fnl f: hld on wl towards fin: rdn out* **8/1**

6314 2 nk **Coronation Day**[13] 4742 3-9-6 71 LukeMorris 3 76
(James Tate) *t.k.h: hld up in tch in last pair: c wd and effrt wl over 1f out: hdwy 1f out: drvn and str chal wl ins fnl f: hld towards fin* **5/2**[1]

1513 3 1 **Figurante (IRE)**[64] 2935 3-9-6 71 WilliamCarson 1 73+
(Jamie Osborne) *dwlt: hld up in tch in last pair: nt clr run 2f out: swtchd lft and effrt on inner over 1f out: hdwy u.p to chse ldrs ins fnl f: kpt on* **4/1**[2]

0514 4 1/2 **Magical Daze**[20] 4496 4-9-6 70 NathanEvans[(5)] 7 73
(John Mackie) *t.k.h: chsd ldr tl 6f out: styd chsng ldrs: rdn over 1f out: swtchd lft jst ins fnl f: styd on same pce u.p fnl 100yds* **8/1**

3105 5 1/2 **Colourfilly**[27] 4240 4-9-9 68 (p) RichardKingscote 4 70
(Tom Dascombe) *led: rdn wl over 1f out: hdd jst ins fnl f: no ex: wknd wl ins fnl f* **11/2**[3]

335 6 1/2 **Totally Magic (IRE)**[21] 4449 4-8-11 61 (p) JoshDoyle[(5)] 6 61
(Richard Whitaker) *dwlt: in tch in midfield but stuck wd: effrt over 2f out: chsd ldrs but unable qck 1f out: wknd ins fnl f* **11/1**

3222 7 6 **Sonnet (IRE)**[11] 4789 3-9-2 67 MichaelJMMurphy 5 49
(Charles Hills) *chsd ldr 6f out: rdn and pressing ldr 3f out tl unable qck and lost pl over 1f out: wknd fnl f* **13/2**

1m 28.89s (0.09) **Going Correction** -0.10s/f (Stan)
WFA 3 from 4yo 6lb **7** Ran SP% **107.8**
Speed ratings (Par 100): **95,94,93,92,92 91,84**
CSF £25.13 TOTE £8.60: £3.40, £1.90; EX 28.00 Trifecta £153.60.
Owner Ray Bailey **Bred** Ray Bailey **Trained** Middleham Moor, N Yorks

FOCUS
Fair form in this fillies' handicap. The pace looked sound and the winner has a good record at the track, while the second and third sat in rear early.

5248 PERSONAL LOGISTICS FROM FCL GLOBAL FORWARDING APPRENTICE H'CAP 7f 32y (Tp)
5:15 (5:15) (Class 6) (0-65,65) 3-Y-O **£2,264** (£673; £336; £168) **Stalls** High

Form RPR

0-05 1 **Always A Dream**[42] 3731 3-9-0 58 SamuelClarke[(5)] 2 67
(Chris Wall) *chsd ldrs tl wnt 2nd 2f out: effrt over 1f out: kpt on to ld wl ins fnl f: rdn out* **13/2**

4423 2 1 **Harmony Bay (IRE)**[26] 4269 3-9-8 61 MichaelJMMurphy 8 68
(Sylvester Kirk) *chsd ldr tl led 3f out: rdn over 1f out: sn hung rt: continued to hang bdly and hdd wl ins fnl f: one pce and racing against stands' rail at fin* **9/2**[2]

00-3 3 2 **Rebel State (IRE)**[98] 1917 3-9-10 63 LouisSteward 9 65
(Richard Spencer) *dwlt: hld up in tch in last pair: nt clr run over 2f out tl rdn and hdwy to chse clr ldng pair over 1f out: swtchd lft 1f out: styd on wl: nt rch ldrs* **9/2**[2]

2500 4 7 **Bahamian Boy**[20] 4498 3-9-5 61 CharlieBennett[(3)] 7 46
(Hughie Morrison) *s.i.s: hld up in rr: rdn over 3f out: sme hdwy but stl plenty to do whn nt clr run jst over 1f out: kpt on u.p ins fnl f: wnt modest 4th nr fin* **6/1**[3]

064 5 1/2 **Last Star Falling (IRE)**[25] 4316 3-9-5 65 DavidEgan[(7)] 3 49
(Henry Spiller) *hld up in tch in midfield: effrt over 2f out: chsd clr ldng pair wl over 1f out: no imp and wl hld 4th 1f out: wknd ins fnl f* **10/1**

2043 6 1 1/4 **Guapo Bay**[5] 5020 3-8-5 51 (b) TinaSmith[(7)] 5 32
(Richard Hannon) *dwlt and sltly impeded leaving stalls: hld up in tch: effrt over 2f out: no imp and wl hld whn hung bdly rt ins fnl f* **10/1**

665 7 1/2 **Tell The Stars**[48] 3483 3-9-1 54 JacobButterfield 10 33
(Ollie Pears) *in tch in midfield but stuck wd: shkn up 4f out: rallied and sme hdwy over 2f out: carried v wd and lost any ch bnd 2f out: no ch whn cannoned into ins fnl f* **25/1**

2050 8 1/2 **Atrayu (IRE)**[37] 3906 3-9-6 62 [1] NathanEvans[(3)] 1 40
(Paul D'Arcy) *led tl 3f out: sn struggling u.p: lost 2nd 2f out and sn wknd* **4/1**[1]

5006 9 9 **Dwynant**[14] 4718 3-9-5 58 KevinStott 4 14
(Kevin Frost) *hld up wl in tch in midfield: rdn over 2f out: hung bdly rt and v wd bnd 2f out: bhd and eased fnl f* **11/1**

1m 28.92s (0.12) **Going Correction** -0.10s/f (Stan) **9** Ran SP% **114.3**
Speed ratings (Par 98): **95,93,91,83,83 81,81,80,70**
CSF £35.45 CT £145.85 TOTE £7.30: £2.00, £1.80, £1.80; EX 35.70 Trifecta £180.50.
Owner Ms Aida Fustoq **Bred** Deerfield Farm **Trained** Newmarket, Suffolk

FOCUS
A low-grade finale, but there are reasons to be positive about the first three who came well clear. The winner is improving and the third ran to his mark.
T/Plt: £79.70 to a £1 stake. Pool of £48915.39 - 447.77 winning tickets. T/Qpdt: £31.40 to a £1 stake. Pool of £4036.33 - 94.85 winning tickets. **Steve Payne**

SAN SEBASTIAN (R-H)

Monday, August 8

OFFICIAL GOING: Turf: good

5249a GRAN PREMIO HOTEL MARIA CRISTINA (CONDITIONS) (3YO+ FILLIES & MARES) (TURF) 1m 3f

5:55 (12:00) 3-Y-0+ £13,235 (£5,294; £2,647; £1,323)

RPR

1 **Rock Eyes**374 4-9-4 0 (b) JoseLuisMartinez 9 91
(G Arizkorreta Elosegui, Spain) **73/10**

2 5 1/4 **Sureness (IRE)**32 4049 6-9-4 0 (vt) Roberto-CarlosMontenegro 8 82
(Charlie Mann) *sn led: pushed along to maintain narrow ld 3f out: hdd and qckly passed 2 1/2f out: no ch w wnr fnl 2f: kpt on wl for clr 2nd* **2/1**[1]

3 3 **Musique Sacree (FR)**43 4-9-4 0 JoseLuisBorrego 5 77
(J C Rosell, Spain) **43/10**

4 1/2 **Andalucia (SPA)**412 5-9-4 0 VaclavJanacek 3 76
(G Arizkorreta Elosegui, Spain) **104/10**

5 2 1/4 **Avenue Dargent (FR)**78 3-8-8 0 BorjaFayosMartin 7 72
(J-M Osorio, Spain) **17/5**[3]

6 1 1/4 **Cascabel (SPA)**361 5324 7-9-4 0 RicardoSousaFerreira 1 69
(Barbara Valenti, Spain) **135/10**

7 1 1/4 **Lady Dari (IRE)** 3-8-8 0 NicolasDeJulian 2 67
(Alfonso Nunez, Spain) **125/10**

8 3/4 **Poti (SPA)**117 5-9-4 0 ClementCadel 4 66
(R Avial Lopez, Spain) **3/1**[2]

9 1 1/4 **Lady Madiba (FR)** 3-8-8 0 EJArguinzones 6 64
(Alfonso Nunez, Spain) **125/10**

Owner Cuadra Medreal **Bred** D Curran **Trained** Spain

4907 CHEPSTOW (L-H)

Tuesday, August 9

OFFICIAL GOING: Good to firm (9.1)

Wind: Light half-behind Weather: Cloudy with sunny spells

5250 PTL MAIDEN STKS 7f 16y

2:15 (2:15) (Class 5) 2-Y-O £3,234 (£962; £481; £240) **Stalls** Centre

Form RPR

4 1 **Shipping Forecast**31 4128 2-9-5 0 JimmyFortune 6 73+
(Brian Meehan) *trckd ldrs: led wl over 1f out: r.o: comf* **4/7**[1]

0 2 1 1/4 **Dahl (IRE)**17 4649 2-9-5 0 FrannyNorton 4 66
(Mark Johnston) *led: rdn and hdd wl over 1f out: sn outpcd: styd on again to go 2nd towards fin* **10/3**[2]

56 3 nk **Express (IRE)**29 4205 2-9-0 0 PatDobbs 3 60
(Richard Hannon) *w ldr: rdn and ev ch wl over 1f out: styd on same pce ins fnl f: lost 2nd towards fin* **12/1**

4 3 **Tawfik (IRE)** 2-9-5 0 AdamKirby 2 57
(Harry Dunlop) *s.i.s: sn chsng ldrs: rdn over 2f out: edgd lft over 1f out: no ex ins fnl f* **15/2**[3]

5 5 **Holyroman Princess** 2-9-0 0 FrederikTylicki 1 39
(Rod Millman) *s.s: sn pushed along in rr: rdn over 2f out: sn wknd* **22/1**

6 8 **Meadow View Girl** 2-8-7 0 KillianHennessy(7) 5 17
(David Flood) *s.s: a in rr: rdn and wknd over 2f out* **66/1**

1m 23.62s (0.42) **Going Correction** -0.325s/f (Firm) 6 Ran SP% **112.0**

Speed ratings (Par 94): **84,82,82,78,73 63**

CSF £2.74 TOTE £1.50: £1.10, £1.90; EX 2.60 Trifecta £8.00.

Owner M Wilmshurst, Mrs L Mann, N Attenborough **Bred** Mr & Mrs G E M Wates **Trained** Manton, Wilts

FOCUS

Franny Norton described the ground as "firm". They raced centre-field in what was just an ordinary maiden. The winner did at least confirm the ability he showed on debut.

5251 ROA/RACING POST OWNERS' JACKPOT NURSERY H'CAP 7f 16y

2:45 (2:45) (Class 5) (0-70,70) 2-Y-O £3,234 (£962; £481; £240) **Stalls** Centre

Form RPR

0220 1 **Notalot (IRE)**11 4825 2-9-1 **67** (v) LouisSteward(3) 6 79+
(Michael Bell) *hld up in tch: led 2f out: rdn clr fnl f: eased nr fin* **2/1**[1]

2222 2 3 3/4 **Bayston Hill**35 3986 2-9-7 **70** LiamKeniry 5 71
(Mark Usher) *w ldr: led wl over 2f out: hdd 2f out: sn rdn: styd on same pce ins fnl f* **5/1**

300 3 1 1/2 **Madam Prancealot (IRE)**78 2536 2-8-3 **52** FrannyNorton 7 49
(David Evans) *w ldrs over 4f: sn rdn: styd on same pce fnl f* **10/1**

012 4 3/4 **Luduamf (IRE)**18 4595 2-9-0 **63** TomMarquand 4 58
(Richard Hannon) *led: rdn: edgd lft and hdd wl over 2f out: no ex fnl f* **7/2**[2]

440 5 nk **Cj Parker**27 4270 2-9-6 **69** SamHitchcott 2 63
(Jim Boyle) *hld up: hdwy 3f out: rdn over 1f out: no ex fnl f* **14/1**

005 6 3 **Dravid**21 4479 2-8-13 **62** FrederikTylicki 3 48
(Rod Millman) *plld hrd and prom: lost pl 3f out: rdn and wknd over 1f out* **11/1**

6000 7 1/2 **Devilish Guest (IRE)**12 4802 2-8-13 **69** KillianHennessy(7) 1 54
(Mick Channon) *trckd ldrs: plld hrd: rdn and wknd over 1f out* **9/2**[3]

1m 22.42s (-0.78) **Going Correction** -0.325s/f (Firm) 7 Ran SP% **114.5**

Speed ratings (Par 94): **91,86,85,84,83 80,79**

CSF £12.43 TOTE £2.70: £1.40, £2.40; EX 10.00 Trifecta £71.90.

Owner The Fitzrovians **Bred** Tally-Ho Stud **Trained** Newmarket, Suffolk

FOCUS

A modest nursery in which they raced stands' side. The winner was down in class and in command during the final furlong, while the runner-up ran close to his best.

5252 DIAMOND RACING H'CAP 1m 14y

3:15 (3:16) (Class 6) (0-65,65) 3-Y-O+ £2,587 (£770; £384; £192) **Stalls** Centre

Form RPR

-006 1 **Prim And Proper**10 4876 5-9-4 **58** (b) DanielMuscutt(3) 6 65
(John Flint) *chsd ldrs: n.m.r and wnt 2nd over 2f out: led over 1f out: rdn out* **8/1**

2065 2 3/4 **Stanlow**20 4516 6-8-10 **47** RobertTart 5 52
(Michael Mullineaux) *sn pushed along in rr: hdwy over 2f out: rdn to chse wnr ins fnl f: r.o* **5/1**[3]

0611 3 3/4 **Diamonds A Dancing**18 4589 6-9-6 **62** (be) CiaranMckee(5) 9 65
(John O'Shea) *racd keenly: sn trcking ldr: lost 2nd and pushed along over 4f out: rdn and hung lft over 2f out: styd on ins fnl f* **7/4**[1]

5000 4 1 1/4 **Hidden Gem**15 4718 3-9-1 **59** AdamKirby 4 58
(Ed Walker) *sn led: rdn and hdd over 1f out: no ex ins fnl f* **12/1**

1323 5 4 **Castle Talbot (IRE)**13 4773 4-10-0 **65** (p) ShaneKelly 1 56
(Richard Hughes) *hld up: pushed along over 6f out: hdwy to go prom over 5f out: chsd ldr over 4f out: rdn: hung lft and lost 2nd over 2f out: wknd fnl f* **2/1**[2]

-500 6 3 3/4 **Avon Scent**26 4290 6-8-2 **46** oh1 (p) RPWalsh(7) 8 28
(Christopher Mason) *hld up: plld hrd: rdn and wknd over 2f out* **33/1**

3000 7 12 **Ocean Gale**12 4794 3-7-13 **46** oh1 NoelGarbutt(3) 3
(Richard Price) *prom: lost pl wl over 4f out: wknd 3f out* **33/1**

1m 33.52s (-2.68) **Going Correction** -0.325s/f (Firm)

WFA 3 from 4yo+ 7lb 7 Ran SP% **111.0**

Speed ratings (Par 101): **100,99,98,97,93 89,77**

CSF £44.32 CT £97.66 TOTE £9.20: £3.70, £2.50; EX 49.40 Trifecta £135.20.

Owner Mr & Mrs A J Mutch **Bred** Mrs J L Egan **Trained** Kenfig Hill, Bridgend

FOCUS

Low-grade stuff, they again came stands' side. The winner, previously successful over C&D, bounced back to form from nowhere.

5253 DRIBUILD DASH H'CAP 6f 16y

3:45 (3:45) (Class 4) (0-85,84) 3-Y-O+ £5,175 (£1,540; £769; £384) **Stalls** Centre

Form RPR

4254 1 **Gold Hunter (IRE)**9 4908 6-9-2 **74** (p) TomMarquand 1 82
(Steve Flook) *sn chsng ldr: rdn to ld over 1f out: r.o: edgd lft towards fin* **3/1**[1]

0416 2 1 **Alizoom (IRE)**44 3689 3-9-6 **82** HarryBentley 4 86
(Roger Varian) *a.p: rdn over 2f out: chsd wnr ins fnl f: r.o* **7/2**[2]

0102 3 1 1/2 **Monarch Maid**26 4291 5-9-3 **75** WilliamCarson 7 75
(Peter Hiatt) *led: shkn up over 2f out: rdn and hdd over 1f out: styd on same pce ins fnl f* **4/1**[3]

4334 4 1 3/4 **Midnight Rider (IRE)**9 4909 8-9-1 **73** (b) FrederikTylicki 2 67
(Rod Millman) *hld up: pushed along over 2f out: sme hdwy on outer over 1f out: no imp fnl f* **7/2**[2]

1413 5 2 **Gilmer (IRE)**26 4291 5-8-10 **71** NoelGarbutt(3) 9 59
(Laura Young) *chsd ldrs: rdn over 2f out: styd on same pce fr over 1f out* **9/2**

3150 6 1 3/4 **Operative**21 4496 3-9-3 **79** (b[1]) LiamKeniry 8 60
(Ed de Giles) *hld up: rdn over 1f out: nvr on terms* **12/1**

1m 9.05s (-2.95) **Going Correction** -0.325s/f (Firm)

WFA 3 from 5yo+ 4lb 6 Ran SP% **115.3**

Speed ratings (Par 105): **106,104,102,100,97 95**

CSF £14.28 CT £41.62 TOTE £4.60: £3.40, £2.20; EX 17.60 Trifecta £71.90.

Owner Glyn Byard **Bred** Airlie Stud And Sir Thomas Pilkington **Trained** Leominster, Herefordshire

FOCUS

A fair handicap in which they headed stands' side. The winner had been threatening to come good again off this sort of mark, and was down to 6f for the first time since his 3yo campaign.

5254 STABLESOFT-EUROPE EQUESTRIAN SURFACES FILLIES' H'CAP 1m 2f 36y

4:15 (4:15) (Class 5) (0-70,68) 3-Y-O+ £3,234 (£962; £481; £240) **Stalls** Low

Form RPR

2355 1 **Perfect Quest**17 4635 3-9-1 **64** (b[1]) AdamKirby 3 71
(Clive Cox) *trckd ldrs: shkn up over 2f out: rdn to ld over 1f out: r.o* **11/8**[1]

0431 2 2 1/2 **Pastoral Star**21 4482 3-8-9 **63** CharlieBennett(5) 6 65
(Hughie Morrison) *led: rdn over 2f out: hdd over 1f out: styd on same pce ins fnl f* **15/8**[2]

4305 3 7 **Evidence (FR)**34 4018 3-9-5 **68** SamHitchcott 4 56
(Harry Dunlop) *hld up: hdwy to go 3rd 7f out: rdn over 2f out: wknd over 1f out* **6/1**

5106 4 4 1/2 **Ventura Falcon (IRE)**8 4936 3-8-8 **57** TomMarquand 1 36
(Richard Hannon) *chsd ldrs: lost pl 7f out: pushed along over 5f out: sn outpcd: rallied u.p over 2f out: wknd over 1f out* **5/1**[3]

2m 13.38s (2.78) **Going Correction** -0.15s/f (Firm)

WFA 3 from 5yo 9lb 4 Ran SP% **107.8**

Speed ratings (Par 100): **82,80,74,70**

CSF £4.21 TOTE £2.00; EX 3.70 Trifecta £6.50.

Owner Hants and Herts **Bred** Mrs S J Walker **Trained** Lambourn, Berks

FOCUS

A modest handicap that was dominated by the two at the head of the market. The winner was wearing first-time blinkers, while the runner-up enjoyed an easy lead.

5255 AGEAS INSURANCE LTD MAIDEN STKS 1m 4f 23y

4:45 (4:46) (Class 5) 3-Y-O+ £3,234 (£962; £481; £240) **Stalls** Low

Form RPR

03 1 **Dance The Dream**33 4056 3-8-12 0 MartinDwyer 13 82+
(Marcus Tregoning) *plld hrd early: sn w ldr: led 10f: c readily clr fr over 4f out: easily* **1/2**[1]

6 2 5 **Togetherness (IRE)**10 4857 3-9-3 0 RichardKingscote 3 74
(Harry Dunlop) *led 2f: chsd wnr tl 8f out: remained handy: rdn over 2f out: styd on same pce fr over 1f out: wnt 2nd post* **6/1**[3]

43 3 nse **Alberta (IRE)**24 4384 7-10-0 0 TimmyMurphy 4 74
(Jim Best) *chsd ldrs: chsd wnr over 3f out: rdn over 1f out: styd on same pce* **3/1**[2]

4 7 **L Stig**324 6-9-9 0 CiaranMckee(5) 2 63
(John O'Shea) *s.s: hld up: styd on appr fnl f: nvr nrr* **50/1**

0 5 8 **Alfredo (IRE)**82 2414 4-10-0 0 (tp) AdamKirby 10 50
(Seamus Durack) *hld up in tch: rdn over 3f out: wknd 2f out* **16/1**

40 6 1 **Rue Balzac (IRE)**48 3508 3-9-3 0 TomMarquand 6 48
(Neil King) *s.s: sn pushed along in rr: rdn over 5f out: nvr on terms* **16/1**

40 7 2 1/2 **Buachaillnaheirean (IRE)**48 3508 3-9-3 0 LiamJones 12 44
(Neil King) *hld up in tch: rdn over 5f out: wknd over 3f out* **66/1**

8 2 3/4 **Certain Time**18 4-10-0 0 WilliamCarson 5 40
(Peter Hiatt) *prom: chsd wnr 8f out tl rdn over 3f out: wknd over 2f out* **28/1**

9 29 **Atlantic Splash**73 6-9-11 0 NoelGarbutt(3) 7
(Nikki Evans) *s.s: hld up: drvn along over 5f out: sn wknd* **100/1**

2m 39.02s (0.02) **Going Correction** -0.15s/f (Firm)

WFA 3 from 4yo+ 11lb 9 Ran SP% **125.6**

Speed ratings (Par 103): **93,89,89,84,79 78,77,75,56**

CSF £5.05 TOTE £1.50: £1.02, £2.80, £1.50; EX 6.40 Trifecta £12.60.

Owner Mrs Hugh Dalgety **Bred** Minster Stud And Mrs H Dalgety **Trained** Whitsbury, Hants

The Form Book, Raceform Ltd, Newbury, RG14 5SJ

FOCUS
A pretty weak maiden in terms of depth, but a useful winner with a future. Dance The Dream did not need to match his encouraging Newbury effort to take this.

5256 GEORGE SMITH HORSEBOXES H'CAP — 1m 4f 23y
5:20 (5:20) (Class 5) (0-70,70) 3-Y-O+ — **£3,234** (£962; £481; £240) **Stalls** Low

Form — RPR

0256 **1** **Rosie Royale (IRE)**[34] 4019 4-9-3 **59**........................ TomMarquand 7 — 67
(Roger Teal) *prom: chsd ldr over 10f out: rdn to ld over 2f out: edgd lft ins fnl f: styd on gamely* **8/1**

0001 **2** 2½ **File Of Facts (IRE)**[7] 4987 3-8-8 **61** 6ex..............(vt) RichardKingscote 4 — 65
(Tom Dascombe) *led: rdn and hdd over 2f out: nt clr run ins fnl f: styd on same pce* **7/2**[3]

2102 **3** 3 **Bigger And Better**[38] 3905 3-9-1 **68**........................ PatDobbs 6 — 67
(Richard Hannon) *hld up in tch: jnd wnr over 2f out: rdn and ev ch over 1f out: wknd ins fnl f* **1/1**[1]

6333 **4** 4 **Sunday Royal (FR)**[12] 4785 4-10-0 **70**........................ AdamKirby 1 — 63
(Harry Dunlop) *chsd ldrs: rdn over 4f out: wknd over 1f out* **11/4**[2]

000 **5** 11 **Dance With Kate**[17] 4657 5-8-6 **51** oh6........................ TimClark(3) 8 — 26
(Polly Gundry) *s.s: hld up: rdn over 3f out: sn wknd* **50/1**

2m 35.46s (-3.54) **Going Correction** -0.15s/f (Firm)
WFA 3 from 4yo+ 11lb — 5 Ran SP% **112.0**
Speed ratings (Par 103): **105,103,101,98,91**
CSF £35.28 TOTE £8.50: £3.50, £2.00; EX 33.10 Trifecta £98.80.
Owner The Idle B's **Bred** Fergus Cousins **Trained** Great Shefford, Berks

FOCUS
Not a bad little race for the level, although the early pace was steady. The market leader shaped like a non-stayer, but the winner recorded a personal best.
T/Plt: £63.30 to a 31 stake. Pool: £68,543.81 - 789.73 winning units. T/Qpdt: £33.00 to a £1 stake. Pool: £5,238.32 - 117.40 winning units. **Colin Roberts**

5163 LINGFIELD (L-H)
Tuesday, August 9

OFFICIAL GOING: Turf course - good to firm (good in places; 8.0); all-weather - polytrack: standard
Wind: light, across Weather: light cloud, shower race 6

5257 PREMIER LEAGUE BETTING AT 188BET NURSERY H'CAP — 5f
5:10 (5:12) (Class 6) (0-65,65) 2-Y-O — **£2,587** (£770; £384; £192) **Stalls** Centre

Form — RPR

060 **1** **Rose Berry**[46] 3597 2-8-13 **60**........................[1] JosephineGordon(3) 2 — 66+
(Chris Dwyer) *dwlt: sn rcvrd and in tch in midfield: hdwy 2f out: rdn to chal over 1f out: led 1f out: pushed along and readily drew clr fnl f: comf* **8/1**

66 **2** 2½ **Seprani**[29] 4195 2-9-3 **61**........................ SaleemGolam 5 — 61
(Mrs Ilka Gansera-Leveque) *chsd ldr: rdn and ev ch whn squeezed for room and hmpd over 1f out: rallied ins fnl f to snatch 2nd last stride: no ch w wnr* **20/1**

005 **3** shd **Roundabout Magic (IRE)**[29] 4205 2-9-7 **65**........................ NickyMackay 6 — 62
(Simon Dow) *led: rdn and hung lft over 1f out: hdd 1f out: sn outpcd by wnr: wknd towards fin and lost 2nd last stride* **8/1**

506 **4** 1¼ **Spin Top**[19] 4553 2-9-2 **63**........................(v) EdwardGreatrex(3) 9 — 56
(Joseph Tuite) *hld up in tch towards rr: swtchd lft and effrt 2f out: hung lft u.p 1f out: kpt on ins fnl f: no ch w wnr* **9/2**[2]

004 **5** 2¼ **Surfina**[15] 4706 2-8-12 **56**........................ KieranO'Neill 1 — 40
(Dean Ivory) *t.k.h: chsd ldrs: flashed tail after 1f: rdn 2f out: unable qck over 1f out: wknd ins fnl f* **12/1**

063 **6** 2¼ **Champagne Queen**[17] 4638 2-9-0 **58**........................(t) MartinHarley 7 — 34
(Rae Guest) *in tch in midfield: effrt 2f out: struggling to qckn and no imp whn short of room over 1f out: wknd ins fnl f* **4/1**[1]

0530 **7** ½ **Royal Melody**[25] 4350 2-8-9 **58**........................ HectorCrouch(5) 10 — 33
(Heather Main) *hld up in rr: effrt 2f out: no real imp: nvr trbld ldrs* **14/1**

630 **8** ½ **Mary Brady**[28] 4227 2-9-7 **65**........................ JamesDoyle 3 — 38+
(David O'Meara) *dwlt: in tch towards rr: effrt and rdn 2f out: no imp and btn 1f out: wl btn and eased ins fnl f* **6/1**[3]

0535 **9** 1 **Affordability**[15] 4712 2-9-7 **65**........................ LukeMorris 8 — 34
(Daniel Mark Loughnane) *in tch in midfield: rdn 1/2-way: drvn and no hdwy over 1f out: wknd fnl f* **9/2**[2]

59.38s (1.18) **Going Correction** +0.125s/f (Good) — 9 Ran SP% **112.0**
Speed ratings (Par 92): **95,91,90,88,85 81,80,80,78**
CSF £144.81 CT £1307.50 TOTE £8.10: £2.00, £4.50, £3.30; EX 177.40 Trifecta £3964.30.
Owner Strawberry Fields Stud **Bred** Aljw Bloodstock **Trained** Newmarket, Suffolk

FOCUS
The watered ground was given as good to firm, good in places (GoingStick: 8.0). The stands' rail, which had been an advantage in recent meetings, looked much less so here. A low-grade nursery with an ordinary feel about it. The runner-up would have been closer with a bit of luck.

5258 £25 FREE BET AT 188BET MEDIAN AUCTION MAIDEN FILLIES' STKS (PLUS 10 RACE) — 5f
5:45 (5:45) (Class 5) 2-Y-O — **£3,234** (£962; £481; £240) **Stalls** Centre

Form — RPR

33 **1** **Dixie's Double**[12] 4790 2-9-0 0........................ LukeMorris 7 — 69
(Daniel Kubler) *swtchd lft after s and racd in centre: chsd ldrs: rdn to ld and hung lft over 1f out: clr and wnt bk rt u.p ins fnl f: styd on: rdn out* **8/11**[1]

0 **2** 2¾ **Acertwo**[13] 4756 2-9-0 0........................ JFEgan 8 — 59
(Joseph Tuite) *racd nr stands' rail: chsd ldr: effrt ent fnl 2f: 3rd and drvn 1f out: chsd clr wnr 100yds out: kpt on* **9/2**[2]

3 2¼ **Luxford** 2-9-0 0........................ KierenFox 2 — 51
(John Best) *racd nr stands' rail: s.i.s: outpcd in last trio: rdn and hdwy over 1f out: styd on ins fnl f to go 3rd nr fin: nvr trbld ldrs* **20/1**

4 ¾ **Zipedee** 2-8-11 0........................ JosephineGordon(3) 3 — 48
(John Ryan) *racd nr stands' rail: chsd ldrs: effrt 2f out: rdn to ld gp and chse clr wnr 1f out: no imp: lost 2nd and wknd fnl 100yds* **8/1**

5 ¾ **Mercers** 2-9-0 0........................ TomQueally 1 — 46+
(Peter Crate) *racd in centre: rn green and ducked sharply lft leaving stalls: lost many l and wl off the pce in rr: rdn and hdwy over 1f out: kpt on ins fnl f: nvr trbld ldrs* **33/1**

3246 **6** 3 **Princess Holly**[15] 4712 2-9-0 63........................(v[1]) DannyBrock 4 — 35
(Robert Cowell) *racd nr stands' rail: led: rdn and hdd over 1f out: lost 2nd and btn 1f out: fdd ins fnl f* **5/1**[3]

7 ½ **Silver Penny** 2-9-0 0........................ PatCosgrave 6 — 33
(Jim Boyle) *racd nr stands' rail: s.i.s: a outpcd in rr* **16/1**

59.92s (1.72) **Going Correction** +0.125s/f (Good) — 7 Ran SP% **117.4**
Speed ratings (Par 91): **91,86,83,81,80 75,75**
CSF £4.69 TOTE £1.60: £1.20, £2.50; EX 4.20 Trifecta £38.50.
Owner Peter Onslow & Kevin Nash **Bred** Peter Onslow **Trained** Lambourn, Berks
■ Stewards' Enquiry : Danny Brock caution: careless riding

FOCUS
Ordinary maiden form. Once again the normally favourable stands' rail didn't look the place to be. The well-backed winner can be given a slight personal best.

5259 188BET H'CAP — 6f
6:15 (6:15) (Class 5) (0-70,70) 3-Y-O+ — **£3,234** (£962; £481; £240) **Stalls** Centre

Form — RPR

0040 **1** **Dear Bruin (IRE)**[7] 4990 4-9-6 **66**........................(p) WilliamTwiston-Davies 4 — 73
(David W Drinkwater) *led: rdn and hdd over 1f out: drvn and rallied ins fnl f: styd on to ld post* **16/1**

0654 **2** nse **Doctor Parkes**[3] 5169 10-9-10 **70**........................ PatCosgrave 7 — 77
(Stuart Williams) *t.k.h: wl in tch in midfield: rdn to ld over 1f out: drvn ins fnl f: hdd on post* **4/1**[3]

0645 **3** ¾ **Summersault (IRE)**[21] 4485 5-9-4 **64**........................(b[1]) GeorgeBaker 6 — 68
(Jamie Osborne) *stdd after s: hld up in rr: clsd over 1f out: rdn and hdwy to chse ldrs whn swtchd lft ins fnl f: kpt on: nt rch ldrs* **3/1**[1]

0563 **4** nk **Storm Melody**[20] 4517 3-9-6 **70**........................(p) LukeMorris 8 — 72
(Jonjo O'Neill) *stdd s: t.k.h: hld up in tch in rr: hdwy 2f out: rdn to chse ldrs and edgd lft over 1f out: styd on same pce u.p wl ins fnl f* **7/2**[2]

-555 **5** 3 **Tilsworth Micky**[186] 460 4-9-2 **62**........................ TomQueally 9 — 56
(J R Jenkins) *hld up wl in tch in midfield: pushed along and hung lft over 1f out: stl hanging and kpt on same pce ins fnl f* **33/1**

-450 **6** 1¼ **Sexton Blake (IRE)**[27] 4269 3-8-11 **66**........................ HectorCrouch(5) 1 — 55
(Gary Moore) *hld up in tch towards rr: rdn over 2f out: hdwy u.p over 1f out: no imp 1f out: wknd ins fnl f* **9/1**

4465 **7** 1 **Great Expectations**[3] 5169 8-9-3 **63**........................(vt) DarryllHolland 5 — 50
(J R Jenkins) *t.k.h: chsd ldrs: effrt and rdn over 1f out: unable qck and wknd ins fnl f* **5/1**

0124 **8** ½ **Bush Warrior (IRE)**[130] 1178 5-9-10 **70**........................(v) MartinHarley 3 — 55
(Anabel K Murphy) *pressed ldr tl no ex u.p and lost pl over 1f out: wknd ins fnl f* **8/1**

-060 **9** hd **Captain Marmalade (IRE)**[33] 4058 4-9-6 **66**........................(b[1]) KieranO'Neill 2 — 50
(Jimmy Fox) *t.k.h: hld up in tch in midfield: squeezed for room and lost pl over 1f out: sn swtchd lft and no hdwy u.p: bhd ins fnl f* **16/1**

1m 11.0s (-0.20) **Going Correction** +0.125s/f (Good)
WFA 3 from 4yo+ 4lb — 9 Ran SP% **119.7**
Speed ratings (Par 103): **106,105,104,104,100 98,97,96,96**
CSF £81.92 CT £253.17 TOTE £17.70: £4.50, £1.90, £1.40; EX 82.70 Trifecta £351.30.
Owner Advantage Chemicals Holdings Ltd **Bred** Advantage Chemicals Holdings Ltd **Trained** Hanley Castle, Worcs

FOCUS
A modest sprint. This time they mostly shunned the stands' rail. The winner had gone well here in the past, while the second appeared to run to his recent best.

5260 188BET.CO.UK MAIDEN STKS — 7f
6:45 (6:46) (Class 5) 3-Y-O — **£3,234** (£962; £481; £240) **Stalls** Centre

Form — RPR

02 **1** **Zwayyan**[19] 4546 3-9-5 0........................ PatCosgrave 1 — 83+
(William Haggas) *trckd ldr tl nudged into ld over 1f out: cruised clr on bit ins fnl f: v easily* **4/6**[1]

5 **2** 3 **Thundering Blue (USA)**[118] 1421 3-9-5 0........................ LukeMorris 3 — 69
(David Menuisier) *t.k.h: trckd ldrs: effrt over 2f out: upsides ldrs but wnr gng much bttr over 1f out: wl hld 2nd and kpt on same pce fnl f* **11/8**[2]

0 **3** 3¼ **African Trader (USA)**[33] 4041 3-9-5 0........................(t) GeorgeBaker 4 — 60
(Daniel Mark Loughnane) *stdd after s: t.k.h: hld up in rr: pushed along and swtchd rt over 1f out: wnt 3rd ins fnl f: nvr trbld ldrs* **16/1**[3]

-06 **4** 2¾ **Cytringan**[19] 4565 3-8-11 0........................ SimonPearce(3) 5 — 48
(Lydia Pearce) *led: rdn and hdd over 1f out: sn btn: wknd ins fnl f* **33/1**

B0 **5** 5 **Squire Hockey**[24] 4401 3-9-0 0........................ HectorCrouch(5) 2 — 39
(Gary Moore) *t.k.h: trckd ldrs: j. path 5f out: rdn 2f out: sn lost pl: bhd ins fnl f* **66/1**

1m 25.33s (2.03) **Going Correction** +0.125s/f (Good) — 5 Ran SP% **112.4**
Speed ratings (Par 100): **93,89,85,82,77**
CSF £1.89 TOTE £1.70: £1.10, £1.10; EX 2.00 Trifecta £2.80.
Owner Al Shaqab Racing **Bred** Newsells Park Stud & Cheveley Park Stud **Trained** Newmarket, Suffolk

FOCUS
They went fairly steady early on, and the favourite only had to be shaken up to win. The runner-up was below form.

5261 INCHCAPE AUDI H'CAP — 1m 4f (P)
7:15 (7:15) (Class 6) (0-60,60) 4-Y-O+ — **£2,587** (£770; £384; £192) **Stalls** Low

Form — RPR

0500 **1** **Fleetwood Poppy**[24] 4385 4-8-4 **46**........................ EdwardGreatrex(3) 7 — 51
(Michael Attwater) *chsd ldr tl over 4f out: styd chsng ldrs: rdn 2f out: styd on u.p to ld 100yds out: jst hld on: all out* **9/1**

4244 **2** shd **Fair Comment**[113] 781 6-9-7 **60**........................ MartinHarley 8 — 65
(Michael Blanshard) *t.k.h: chsd ldrs: wnt 2nd over 4f out: rdn and ev ch 2f out: kpt on u.p towards fin: jst hld* **7/2**[1]

4054 **3** nk **Peeps**[63] 2995 4-9-1 **54**........................(b) DarryllHolland 5 — 58
(Mark H Tompkins) *stdd s: hld up in rr: hdwy on outer to press ldrs 2f out: rdn and ev ch 1f out: styd on same pce wl ins fnl f* **5/1**

0050 **4** ¾ **Pao De Acuca (IRE)**[6] 5016 4-8-6 **52**........................ SeanMooney(7) 1 — 55
(Jose Santos) *led: rdn 2f out: hdd 100yds out: no ex and wknd towards fin* **10/1**

0023 **5** 1¼ **Awesome Rock (IRE)**[6] 5021 7-8-0 **46** oh1........................ RhiainIngram(7) 3 — 47
(Roger Ingram) *hld up in tch in midfield: nt clr run and shuffled bk over 2f out: rdn and hdwy over 1f out: switching rt and styd on same pce ins fnl f* **6/1**

446- **6** 1 **Top Set (IRE)**[35] 1765 6-8-9 **48**........................ LukeMorris 4 — 48
(Richard Phillips) *hld up in tch in midfield: rdn 3f out: unable qck over 1f out: drvn and styd on same pce ins fnl f* **16/1**

013- **7** 1 **Illustration (IRE)**[262] 7947 8-8-10 **52**........................ NathanAlison(3) 2 — 50
(George Margarson) *s.i.s: hld up in tch in midfield: rdn and dropped to rr over 3f out: styd on same pce u.p fnl 2f* **4/1**[2]

6035 **8** 1 1/4 **Galuppi**[62] 3041 5-9-5 **58**....(p) GeorgeBaker 6 54
(J R Jenkins) *hld up in tch in last pair: clsd and swtchd rt over 2f out: wd bnd 2f out: rdn over 1f out: no imp ins fnl f* **9/2**[3]

2m 36.47s (3.47) **Going Correction** +0.10s/f (Slow) **8** Ran SP% **116.3**
Speed ratings (Par 101): **92,91,91,91,90 89,89,88**
CSF £41.30 CT £178.32 TOTE £7.60: £2.70, £1.50, £2.10; EX 47.10 Trifecta £351.00.
Owner Canisbay Bloodstock **Bred** Canisbay Bloodstock Ltd **Trained** Epsom, Surrey

FOCUS
A weak handicap. Three of the first four raced in the first three positions virtually throughout.

5262 FOLLOW US ON TWITTER AT 188BET H'CAP 1m 7f 169y(P)
7:45 (7:45) (Class 5) (0-75,75) 4-Y-O+ **£3,234** (£962; £481; £240) **Stalls** Low

Form RPR
24/5 **1** **Charlie Wells (IRE)**[167] 693 5-9-7 **75**.... JohnFahy 1 83+
(Eve Johnson Houghton) *hld up off the pce in rr: clsd and in tch 4f out: nt clr run 2f out: gap opened on inner and hdwy to chse clr ldng pair ent fnl f: str run fnl f to ld last strides* **5/1**[3]

-446 **2** hd **Kristjano (GER)**[34] 4023 4-8-13 **67**....(p) MartinHarley 6 74
(Chris Wall) *chsd ldr: upsides and rdn over 2f out: sustained duel w rival after: drvn over 1f out: led wl ins fnl f: styd on: hdd last strides* **7/2**[2]

2 **3** 3/4 **For Goodness Sake (IRE)**[17] 4637 4-8-10 **67**.... EdwardGreatrex(3) 4 73
(Warren Greatrex) *led: rdn 3f out: sustained duel w rival after: rdr dropped whip jst over 2f out: hdd wl ins fnl f: no ex* **11/4**[1]

1500 **4** 8 **Bohemian Rhapsody (IRE)**[24] 4381 7-9-1 **69**....(p) PatCosgrave 5 66
(Brendan Powell) *chsd ldng pair: rdn over 2f out: outpcd and btn 2f out: wknd over 1f out* **10/1**

-340 **5** 4 **Carpe Vita (IRE)**[19] 4550 4-9-3 **71**.... JamesDoyle 2 63
(David O'Meara) *hld up off the pce in 4th: clsd and in tch 6f out: rdn over 2f out: outpcd and btn 2f out: wknd over 1f out* **8/1**

3202 **P** **Ayr Of Elegance**[17] 4661 4-9-5 **73**.... GeorgeBaker 3
(Philip Hide) *nose ct in stall gate and v.s.a: immediately p.u* **11/4**[1]

3m 26.08s (0.38) **Going Correction** +0.10s/f (Slow) **6** Ran SP% **112.4**
Speed ratings (Par 103): **103,102,102,98,96**
CSF £22.64 TOTE £6.30: £2.90, £1.90; EX 19.30 Trifecta £73.00.
Owner Eden Racing **Bred** Carlingford Breeding Syndicate **Trained** Blewbury, Oxon

FOCUS
This was run at a good gallop and the leaders got racing plenty soon enough. The winner finished strongly and looks to have more to offer at 2m. The placed horses ran to form.

5263 MOBILE BETTING AT 188BET H'CAP 1m 2f (P)
8:15 (8:15) (Class 6) (0-60,58) 3-Y-O **£2,587** (£770; £384; £192) **Stalls** Low

Form RPR
05-5 **1** **Cartwright**[10] 4882 3-9-6 **57**.... LukeMorris 2 65+
(Sir Mark Prescott Bt) *rdn along early: racd in tch in midfield: effrt and c wd wl over 1f out: chsd ldng pair 1f out: str run ins fnl f to ld cl home* **10/11**[1]

5300 **2** nk **Ramblow**[13] 4764 3-8-11 **55**.... GeorgiaCox(7) 8 62
(William Haggas) *chsd ldrs tl wnt 2nd 8f out: rdn to ld over 2f out: kpt on u.p: hdd and no ex cl home* **10/1**

3553 **3** 1 1/2 **Sunshineandbubbles**[10] 4882 3-9-4 **58**....(p) GeorgeDowning(3) 7 62
(Daniel Mark Loughnane) *in tch in midfield: rdn and hdwy to press ldr 2f out: unable qck over 1f out: styd on same pce ins fnl f: lost 2nd wl ins fnl f* **8/1**[3]

0402 **4** 4 1/2 **Bazzat (IRE)**[8] 4936 3-8-9 **46**....(p) DannyBrock 1 42
(John Ryan) *chsd ldr for 2f: styd chsng ldrs: rdn and cl 3rd 2f out: no ex 1f out: wknd ins fnl f* **3/1**[2]

6463 **5** 2 3/4 **Just Fab (IRE)**[13] 4760 3-9-7 **58**....(b) PatCosgrave 6 48
(Ali Stronge) *led: hdd and rdn over 2f out: sn struggling: wknd over 1f out* **16/1**

000 **6** 3 **Icons Image**[95] 2008 3-8-13 **50**.... DarrylIHolland 9 35
(Brian McMath) *stdd s: t.k.h: hld up in rr: effrt 3f out: 6th and no imp 2f out: sn wknd* **25/1**

05-0 **7** 11 **Oyster Pearl (IRE)**[7] 4992 3-8-9 **53**....(t) WilliamCox(7) 5 17
(Carroll Gray) *in tch in midfield: rdn and lost pl 3f out: bhd over 1f out* **66/1**

0004 **8** 1 **Wassail**[20] 4505 3-8-6 **46**.... JosephineGordon(3) 3 8
(Ed de Giles) *rn in snatches: in tch in last pair: rdn over 3f out: sn struggling: bhd over 1f out* **12/1**

2m 7.3s (0.70) **Going Correction** +0.10s/f (Slow) **8** Ran SP% **116.5**
Speed ratings (Par 98): **101,100,99,95,93 91,82,81**
CSF £12.05 CT £49.13 TOTE £1.70: £1.10, £3.00, £2.00; EX 14.50 Trifecta £68.60.
Owner J L C Pearce **Bred** Meon Valley Stud **Trained** Newmarket, Suffolk

FOCUS
A moderate handicap but the winner looks the type to go in again. The third is rated as running to his mark.
T/Plt: £178.30 to a £1 stake. Pool: £67,978.18 - 278.18 winning units. T/Qpdt: £19.70 to a £1 stake. Pool: £6,243.16 - 234.33 winning units. **Steve Payne**

4981 NOTTINGHAM (L-H)
Tuesday, August 9

OFFICIAL GOING: Good to firm (good in places; 8.2)
Wind: fresh across Weather: fine but breezy

5264 RACINGUK.COM APPRENTICE H'CAP 1m 2f 50y
5:30 (5:30) (Class 6) (0-60,60) 4-Y-O+ **£2,264** (£673; £336; £168) **Stalls** Low

Form RPR
6446 **1** **Bogardus (IRE)**[16] 4686 5-9-3 **58**.... PaulaMuir(5) 6 67
(Patrick Holmes) *in rr: hdwy over 2f out: styd on on inner to ld last 75yds* **4/1**[1]

5526 **2** 1/2 **First Summer**[24] 3564 4-9-5 **55**.... GeorgeWood 1 63
(Shaun Harris) *trckd ldr: led over 2f out: hdd and no ex last 75yds* **16/1**

0003 **3** 1 1/4 **Thello**[13] 4767 4-9-0 **55**.... LewisEdmunds(5) 2 61
(Nigel Tinkler) *mid-div: hdwy 3f out: n.m.r 1f out: kpt on* **9/2**[2]

125 **4** 3 3/4 **Ifan (IRE)**[42] 3738 8-9-10 **60**....(p) MitchGodwin 8 59
(Tim Vaughan) *led: hdd over 2f out: one pce fnl f* **7/1**[3]

016 **5** 3 **Frantical**[35] 3973 4-9-2 **57**....(v[1]) JoshuaBryan(5) 7 50
(Tony Carroll) *sn trcking ldr: upsides over 2f out: wknd fnl f* **4/1**[1]

353 **6** 1 1/2 **Little Choosey**[22] 4456 6-9-3 **56**....(tp) HarryBurns(3) 4 46
(Roy Bowring) *mid-div: hdwy to join ldrs over 2f out: wknd fnl 150yds* **4/1**[1]

-545 **7** 7 **Mystical Maze**[6] 5019 5-8-5 **46** oh1.... DavidEgan(5) 10 23
(Mark Brisbourne) *s.i.s: mid-div: wd bnd and drvn over 4f out: lost pl over 2f out* **25/1**

050 **8** 6 **Scot Daddy (USA)**[18] 951 4-9-4 **54**....(t) PaddyBradley 9 19
(David Dennis) *trckd ldr: lost pl over 2f out* **25/1**

-060 **9** 2 1/4 **Secret Lightning (FR)**[45] 3642 4-9-10 **60**....(p) MeganNicholls 3 21
(Michael Appleby) *s.i.s: t.k.h in rr: wd bnd over 4f out: bhd fnl 2f* **12/1**

2m 10.55s (-3.75) **Going Correction** -0.35s/f (Firm) **9** Ran SP% **111.9**
Speed ratings (Par 101): **101,100,99,96,94 93,87,82,80**
CSF £65.05 CT £294.50 TOTE £5.40: £2.00, £3.90, £1.80; EX 74.80 Trifecta £403.00.
Owner Peter Acheson & Foulrice Park Racing **Bred** Grangecon Stud **Trained** Middleham, N Yorks

FOCUS
Outer track used and all distances as advertised. A total of 14mm of water had been added to the track over the previous couple of days and the going was good to firm, good in places. A modest handicap run at a good pace, which collapsed late on. The class-dropping winner picked up the pieces.

5265 WATCH RACING UK TODAY JUST £10 NURSERY H'CAP 6f 15y
6:00 (6:01) (Class 5) (0-75,75) 2-Y-O **£2,911** (£866; £432; £216) **Stalls** Centre

Form RPR
6016 **1** **Allux Boy (IRE)**[31] 4167 2-8-13 **67**.... AndrewMullen 5 72
(Nigel Tinkler) *wnt lft s: led: hdd over 3f out: wandered appr fnl f: led last 100yds: drvn out* **25/1**

552 **2** 1 1/4 **Looting**[13] 4765 2-9-0 **71**.... KieranShoemark(3) 7 72+
(David Brown) *hood removed v late: dwlt: hdwy stands' side over 3f out: led over 2f out: hung rt appr fnl f: hdd and no ex last 100yds* **5/1**[2]

0454 **3** 1 1/2 **Champion Harbour (IRE)**[18] 4595 2-8-11 **65**.... PaulHanagan 3 62
(Richard Fahey) *hmpd s: t.k.h: sn trcking ldrs: hmpd and swtchd rt 150yds out: kpt on to take 3rd clsng stages* **5/1**[2]

605 **4** nk **Equity**[17] 4663 2-8-11 **65**.... SilvestreDeSousa 1 62
(David Brown) *carried lft and hmpd s: sn chsng ldrs: edgd lft over 1f out: kpt on same pce last 150yds* **8/1**[3]

031 **5** 1 1/4 **Drop Kick Murphi (IRE)**[11] 4815 2-9-3 **71**.... SteveDrowne 4 63
(George Baker) *carried lft s: sn chsng ldrs: drvn over 2f out: one pce fnl f* **12/1**

352 **6** nk **Kodiac Khan (IRE)**[18] 4601 2-9-7 **75**....(b[1]) JimCrowley 2 66
(Hugo Palmer) *carried lft s: sn chsng ldrs: drvn over 2f out: one pce fnl f* **9/4**[1]

3323 **7** nk **Pulsating (IRE)**[20] 4508 2-9-1 **69**.... JoeyHaynes 6 59
(Rebecca Menzies) *chsd ldrs: drvn over 2f out: sn outpcd: kpt on one pce fnl f* **16/1**

220 **8** 3 3/4 **Princeofthequeen (USA)**[29] 4209 2-9-5 **73**.... DanielTudhope 8 52
(David O'Meara) *w ldrs: led over 3f out: hdd over 2f out: wknd over 1f out: eased clsng stages* **8/1**[3]

4046 **9** 6 **Restore (IRE)**[26] 4315 2-8-10 **64**.... SeanLevey 9 25
(Richard Hannon) *chsd ldrs: drvn over 2f out: sn lost pl and bhd* **10/1**

1m 14.82s (0.12) **Going Correction** -0.35s/f (Firm) **9** Ran SP% **112.8**
Speed ratings (Par 94): **85,83,81,80,79 78,78,73,65**
CSF £142.02 CT £740.13 TOTE £27.40: £5.00, £1.70, £2.20; EX 156.00 Trifecta £1064.90.
Owner M Webb **Bred** Victor Stud Bloodstock Ltd **Trained** Langton, N Yorks

FOCUS
Just a fair nursery, where the winner was always prominent. The runner-up's hood was removed late.

5266 BRITISH STALLION STUDS EBF FILLIES' MAIDEN STKS (PLUS 10 RACE) 1m 75y
6:30 (6:31) (Class 5) 2-Y-O **£3,234** (£962; £481; £240) **Stalls** Centre

Form RPR
3 **1** **Vanity Queen**[26] 4298 2-9-0 0.... JamieSpencer 5 73+
(Luca Cumani) *t.k.h in rr: effrt over 2f out: sn swtchd wd: hdwy over 1f out: edgd lft 100yds out: styd on to ld fnl strides* **5/6**[1]

623 **2** 1/2 **Laureate**[14] 4728 2-9-0 73.... JoeFanning 8 72
(Mark Johnston) *chsd ldrs: edgd rt 100yds out: no ex nr fin* **8/1**[3]

0 **3** nk **Tomorrowcomes (IRE)**[18] 4603 2-9-0 0.... PaulHanagan 3 71
(Richard Fahey) *led tl over 6f out: chsd ldrs: led narrowly last 50yds: no ex and hdd fnl strides* **25/1**

4 1 1/4 **For The Roses** 2-9-0 0.... OisinMurphy 2 68
(Ralph Beckett) *trckd ldrs: led over 6f out: drvn 3f out: hdd and fdd last 50yds* **10/1**

025 **5** shd **Iconic Belle**[6] 5036 2-9-0 0.... SilvestreDeSousa 7 68+
(Mick Channon) *chsd ldrs: one pce whn hmpd 100yds out: eased* **9/2**[2]

365 **6** 1 1/2 **Ocean Temptress**[24] 4397 2-9-0 66.... JimCrowley 6 65
(John Ryan) *s.v.s: detached in last: hdwy over 6f out: drvn on inner to chse ldrs over 2f out: wknd last 50yds* **14/1**

0 **7** nk **Mary Anne Evans**[31] 4147 2-9-0 0.... RobertHavlin 4 64
(John Gosden) *s.i.s: sn chsng ldrs: drvn over 2f out: one pce* **8/1**[3]

00 **8** 5 **Hazy Manor (IRE)**[26] 4298 2-8-9 0.... AnnaHesketh(5) 1 53
(Tom Dascombe) *chsd ldrs: drvn 4f out: lost pl appr fnl f* **100/1**

1m 46.73s (-2.27) **Going Correction** -0.35s/f (Firm) **8** Ran SP% **115.6**
Speed ratings (Par 91): **97,96,96,94,94 93,93,88**
CSF £8.61 TOTE £2.00: £1.10, £2.70, £6.10; EX 8.10 Trifecta £90.30.
Owner S Stuckey **Bred** Stuart Stuckey **Trained** Newmarket, Suffolk

FOCUS
A fair maiden and they finished in a bunch. The winner did not need to improve on her debut run to take this.

5267 RACING UK PROFITS RETURNED TO RACING H'CAP 1m 6f 15y
7:00 (7:00) (Class 5) (0-75,75) 3-Y-O+
£2,801 (£838; £419; £209; £104; £52) **Stalls** Low

Form RPR
1203 **1** **Bertie Moon**[19] 4550 6-9-7 **75**....(p) CliffordLee(7) 4 84+
(Lydia Pearce) *led after 1f: qcknd pce over 3f out: over 2 l clr whn stmbld: wnt lft and hit rail 1f out: jst hld on* **8/1**

3433 **2** shd **Ivanhoe**[21] 4483 6-9-3 **64**....(v[1]) DavidProbert 3 71
(Michael Blanshard) *hld up in rr: hdwy 4f out: chsd wnr over 2f out: styd on fnl 150yds: jst hld* **5/1**[3]

0-04 **3** 5 **Fix Up Look Sharp**[33] 4057 5-9-1 **62**.... RobertHavlin 6 62
(Jamie Poulton) *hld up in rr: hdwy 4f out: hung lft and 3rd 1f out: one pce* **7/2**[2]

-656 **4** 3/4 **Denham Sound**[17] 4661 3-8-12 **72**.... FergusSweeney 5 71
(Henry Candy) *chsd wnr after 1f: rdn over 3f out: one pce fnl 2f* **7/2**[2]

-166 **5** 7 **Atalan**[20] 4535 4-9-9 **70**....(b[1]) JimCrowley 7 59
(Hughie Morrison) *chsd ldrs: rdn over 3f out: wknd over 1f out* **3/1**[1]

0503 **6** 23 **Lineman**[21] 4499 6-8-10 **57**....(b) SilvestreDeSousa 1 14
(Sarah Hollinshead) *led 1f: chsd ldrs: wknd 2f out: sn eased and bhd: t.o* **16/1**

2210 **7** *25* **Longside**[35] 3972 4-9-9 **70** .... RyanTate 2
(James Eustace) *ldrs: pushed along over 5f out: lost pl over 3f out: wl bhd whn eased over 1f out: t.o* **10/1**
3m 0.9s (-6.10) **Going Correction** -0.35s/f (Firm)
WFA 3 from 4yo+ 13lb **7** Ran SP% **112.2**
Speed ratings (Par 103): **103,102,100,99,95 82,68**
CSF £45.24 TOTE £10.30: £4.50, £2.50; EX 51.40 Trifecta £154.90.
Owner SC Oliver Racing Limited **Bred** M E Wates **Trained** Newmarket, Suffolk

FOCUS
Not the strongest staying handicap for the grade and the winner made all even after hitting the rail late.

5268 EBFSTALLIONS.COM CONDITIONS STKS 5f 13y
7:30 (7:31) (Class 3) 3-Y-O+
£9,960 (£2,982; £1,491; £745; £372; £187) **Stalls** Centre

Form RPR
0500 **1** **Kingsgate Native (IRE)**[25] 4359 11-8-11 100 ....(p) JimCrowley 7 111
(Robert Cowell) *trckd ldrs: drvn upsides appr fnl f: led last 100yds: kpt on wl* **20/1**
3232 **2** *1/2* **Thesme**[14] 4735 4-8-6 99 .... TomEaves 4 104
(Nigel Tinkler) *led: shkn up appr fnl f: hdd last 100yds: no ex* **11/4**[2]
-463 **3** *1 1/4* **Strath Burn**[10] 4860 4-8-11 111 ....(p) OisinMurphy 5 105
(Robert Cowell) *in rr: outpcd over 2f out: hdwy and swtchd lft over 1f out: kpt on to take 3rd post* **5/2**[1]
2000 **4** *shd* **Maljaa**[14] 4735 4-8-11 104 ....(b) PaulHanagan 1 104
(Roger Varian) *wnt lft s: sn chsng ldrs: outpcd over 2f out: hdwy over 1f out: kpt on same pce last 150yds* **9/2**[3]
-236 **5** *shd* **Ornate**[25] 4359 3-8-8 105 ....[1] AndreaAtzeni 2 103
(William Haggas) *chsd ldrs: drvn 2f out: kpt on clsng stages* **13/2**
0020 **6** *2 1/2* **Hay Chewed (IRE)**[14] 4735 5-8-6 92 .... SilvestreDeSousa 8 90
(Conrad Allen) *trckd ldrs: t.k.h: drvn over 2f out: wknd fnl f* **8/1**
5300 **7** *2 1/2* **Desert Law (IRE)**[18] 4584 8-9-0 97 .... MartinLane 3 89
(Paul Midgley) *chsd ldr: wknd over 1f out* **12/1**
5560 **8** *shd* **King Of Rooks**[33] 4062 3-8-8 98 ....[1] SeanLevey 6 84
(Richard Hannon) *in rr and sn drvn along: nvr a factor* **20/1**
58.47s (-3.03) **Going Correction** -0.35s/f (Firm)
WFA 3 from 4yo+ 3lb **8** Ran SP% **115.1**
Speed ratings (Par 107): **110,109,107,107,106 102,98,98**
CSF £75.31 TOTE £16.80: £5.40, £1.20, £1.50; EX 68.90 Trifecta £537.60.
Owner Cheveley Park Stud **Bred** Peter McCutcheon **Trained** Six Mile Bottom, Cambs

FOCUS
A good-quality conditions event and there was a shock winner, with a charismatic 11yo rolling back the years. The runner-up helps set the start considering he recent progressive handicap form.

5269 RACING UK IN GLORIOUS HD H'CAP 5f 13y
8:00 (8:00) (Class 5) (0-70,72) 3-Y-O+ **£2,911** (£866; £432; £216) **Stalls** Centre

Form RPR
4212 **1** **Orient Class**[25] 4345 5-9-5 **70** .... AdamMcNamara(5) 3 81
(Paul Midgley) *chsd ldrs: led over 1f out: hung lft fnl 150yds: drvn out* **7/2**[2]
0624 **2** *1 1/4* **You're Cool**[14] 4744 4-9-2 **69** .... LewisEdmunds(7) 5 75
(John Balding) *trckd ldrs: outpcd over 2f out: hdwy over 1f out: styd on wl to take 2nd last 50yds* **13/2**
2401 **3** *1 1/4* **Classic Pursuit**[5] 5060 5-9-12 **72** 6ex ....(p) RaulDaSilva 2 74+
(Ivan Furtado) *awkward s: detached in last: hdwy over 1f out: styd on wl to take n3rd nr fin* **3/1**[1]
0300 **4** *3/4* **Tavener**[11] 4848 4-9-3 **63** .... DanielTudhope 7 62
(David O'Meara) *chsd ldrs stands' side: 2nd over 1f out: hung bdly lft last 150yds: demoted 2 pls last 50yds* **7/2**[2]
610 **5** *2 1/4* **Frank The Barber (IRE)**[3] 5162 4-8-13 **59** ....(t) AdamBeschizza 6 50
(Steph Hollinshead) *chsd ldrs: led over 2f out: hdd over 1f out: wknd last 50yds* **16/1**
2660 **6** *6* **Royal Bajan (USA)**[65] 2931 8-9-7 **67** ....(p) JimCrowley 4 36
(Robert Cowell) *led tl over 2f out: lost pl appr fnl f* **8/1**
-154 **7** *6* **Dominance**[85] 2288 3-9-2 **65** .... DavidProbert 1 12
(Rae Guest) *trckd ldrs far side: t.k.h: edgd lft and lost pl over 1f out: eased clsng stages* **6/1**[3]
59.77s (-1.73) **Going Correction** -0.35s/f (Firm)
WFA 3 from 4yo+ 3lb **7** Ran SP% **114.1**
Speed ratings (Par 103): **99,97,95,93,90 80,71**
CSF £25.95 TOTE £4.20: £2.20, £2.50; EX 20.30 Trifecta £28.20.
Owner F Brady,A Williams,P Lindley,S Wibberley **Bred** Frank Brady **Trained** Westow, N Yorks
■ Stewards' Enquiry : Raul Da Silva ten-day ban: serious misjudgement (Aug 23-Sep 1)

FOCUS
A fair and competitive sprint, run at an even pace. The winner recorded a small personal best on old form with help from a good claiming rider.

5270 COLWICK CUP FAMILY DAY 12TH AUGUST H'CAP 6f 15y
8:30 (8:31) (Class 6) (0-60,59) 3-Y-O+ **£2,264** (£673; £336; £168) **Stalls** Centre

Form RPR
000 **1** **Kaaber (USA)**[42] 3748 5-8-3 **45** ....(b) MitchGodwin(7) 3 54
(Roy Brotherton) *chsd ldrs: led over 1f out: drvn out* **25/1**
3302 **2** *2* **First Excel**[26] 4321 4-8-13 **55** ....(b) KevinLundie(7) 5 58
(Roy Bowring) *s.s: detached in last: hdwy over 2f out: chsd wnr last 100yds* **11/4**[1]
0004 **3** *3* **Carlovian**[11] 4848 3-8-10 **49** .... JimCrowley 2 41
(Christopher Kellett) *sn chsng ldrs: kpt on same pce appr fnl f* **8/1**
0345 **4** *nk* **Men United (FR)**[7] 4968 3-8-12 **54** ....(t) AlistairRawlinson(3) 9 45
(Roy Bowring) *trckd ldrs: led over 2f out: hdd over 1f out: kpt on one pce* **9/2**[2]
4036 **5** *1 1/2* **Loumarin (IRE)**[7] 4968 4-9-8 **57** .... AndrewMullen 10 45
(Michael Appleby) *mid-div: edgd lft and kpt on fnl f* **6/1**[3]
0060 **6** *1/2* **Kodimoor (IRE)**[28] 4228 3-9-4 **57** ....(b[1]) JoeyHaynes 4 42
(Christopher Kellett) *w ldr: led after 1f: hdd over 2f out: fdd fnl f* **25/1**
2445 **7** *1* **Camdora (IRE)**[42] 3743 4-9-10 **59** .... TimmyMurphy 6 42
(Jamie Osborne) *chsd ldrs: one pce fnl 2f* **9/2**[2]
0-03 **8** *7* **Jacksonfire**[42] 3743 4-8-10 **45** ....(p) RobertTart 11 5
(Michael Mullineaux) *outpcd: bhd fnl 2f* **10/1**
3110 **9** *1/2* **Triple Dream**[26] 4292 11-9-1 **50** .... OisinMurphy 1 15
(Milton Bradley) *led 1f: chsd ldrs: wknd over 1f out: sn eased* **11/1**
0000 **10** *3/4* **Kylla**[36] 3941 3-7-13 **45** .... RPWalsh(7) 8
(Shaun Harris) *w ldrs: lost pl over 1f out: sn bhd* **66/1**
1m 13.51s (-1.19) **Going Correction** -0.35s/f (Firm)
WFA 3 from 4yo+ 4lb **10** Ran SP% **115.0**
Speed ratings (Par 101): **93,90,86,85,83 83,81,72,71,70**
CSF £90.87 CT £621.77 TOTE £20.90: £6.20, £1.50, £2.60; EX 168.80 Trifecta £2254.10.
Owner Jeremy Holt **Bred** Shadwell Farm LLC **Trained** Elmley Castle, Worcs

FOCUS
Moderate form.
T/Plt: £120.60 to a £1 stake. Pool: £70,696.03 - 427.83 winning units. T/Qpdt: £8.10 to a £1 stake. Pool: £4,941.61 - 448.32 winning units. **Walter Glynn**

4890 THIRSK (L-H)
Tuesday, August 9

OFFICIAL GOING: Good to firm (good in places; 8.7)
Wind: Fresh across - gusting Weather: Cloudy& blustery

5271 RACINGUK.COM/HD MAIDEN AUCTION STKS 7f
2:00 (2:01) (Class 6) 2-Y-O **£2,587** (£770; £384; £192) **Stalls** Low

Form RPR
1 **Society Red** 2-8-12 0 .... TonyHamilton 7 74+
(Richard Fahey) *midfield: hdwy to trck ldrs 1/2-way: effrt over 2f out: rdn to ld wl over 1f out: edgd lft and kpt on wl fnl f* **5/1**[2]
6 **2** *2 3/4* **Stevie Brown**[19] 4545 2-8-11 0 .... ShaneGray 6 65
(David Brown) *trckd ldrs: hdwy 3f out: rdn to ld briefly 2f out: sn hdd and drvn: kpt on fnl f* **6/1**[3]
2302 **3** *nk* **Good Time Ahead (IRE)**[10] 4869 2-9-2 75 .... AndrewMullen 9 69
(Philip Kirby) *slt ld: pushed along and rn wd home turn: rdn and hdd 2f out: sn drvn: kpt on fnl f* **5/2**[1]
4 *nk* **Doctor Cross (IRE)** 2-9-0 0 ow1 .... DavidNolan 4 66
(Richard Fahey) *midfield: hdwy over 2f out: rdn along to chse ldrs over 1f out: kpt on fnl f: nrst fin* **15/2**
60 **5** *3/4* **Dandy Place (IRE)**[17] 4642 2-9-2 0 .... DavidAllan 3 66
(Tim Easterby) *midfield: hdwy wl over 2f out: pushed along to chse ldrs wl over 1f out: sn rdn and kpt on fnl f* **14/1**
5 **6** *nk* **Inglorious**[68] 2807 2-8-13 0 .... JasonHart 11 64+
(Keith Dalgleish) *cl up: edgd rt bnd over 4f out: disp ld whn carried rt home turn: rdn along over 2f out: drvn over 1f out: grad wknd* **6/1**[3]
644 **7** *2 1/4* **Traveltalk (IRE)**[48] 3515 2-8-13 67 .... BenCurtis 2 56
(Brian Ellison) *chsd ldrs: rdn along over 2f out: drvn over 1f out: sn wknd* **8/1**
65 **8** *2 1/4* **Gold Patch (IRE)**[20] 4508 2-8-7 0 .... NathanEvans(5) 5 49
(Michael Easterby) *chsd ldng pair: rdn along over 2f out: sn wknd* **66/1**
9 *1/2* **Archi's Affaire** 2-8-13 0 .... PaulMulrennan 1 49
(Michael Dods) *dwlt: a bhd* **20/1**
50 **10** *1* **Spanish Beauty**[36] 3947 2-7-13 0 .... RobertDodsworth(7) 8 39
(Ollie Pears) *towards rr: sme hdwy on outer and in tch 2f out: sn rdn and wknd over 1f out* **50/1**
11 *17* **Where's Stewart** 2-8-12 0 .... TomEaves 10
(Nigel Tinkler) *sn outpcd and a bhd* **28/1**
1m 28.6s (1.40) **Going Correction** +0.15s/f (Good) **11** Ran SP% **115.0**
Speed ratings (Par 92): **98,94,94,94,93 92,90,87,87,86 66**
CSF £33.02 TOTE £5.50: £1.90, £1.80, £1.40; EX 35.80 Trifecta £81.00.
Owner M J Macleod **Bred** Select Bloodstock **Trained** Musley Bank, N Yorks

FOCUS
The home bend was out 8yds, adding approximately 25yds for all races of 7f and upwards. Additionally, half of the away bend was out from the winning line onwards adding an additional 5yds to the standard distance for the 1m4f Start, therefore making it 30 yds longer than standard. This modest 2yo maiden was run at a brisk pace, and the winner was quite impressive.

5272 RACING UK PROFITS RETURNED TO RACING MAIDEN FILLIES' STKS (PLUS 10 RACE) 6f
2:30 (2:35) (Class 5) 2-Y-O **£2,911** (£866; £432; £216) **Stalls** High

Form RPR
1 **Delectation** 2-9-0 0 .... PaulMulrennan 5 80+
(Bryan Smart) *trckd ldrs: smooth hdwy over 2f out: led over 1f out: sn rdn and edgd lft: kpt on wl towards fin* **28/1**
2 **2** *2* **Tschierschen (IRE)**[15] 4706 2-9-0 0 .... BenCurtis 6 74
(William Haggas) *trckd ldrs: hdwy wl over 1f out: rdn to chse wnr ent fnl f: sn drvn and edgd rt: kpt on same pce* **10/11**[1]
3 **3** *1/2* **Vaulted**[12] 4805 2-9-0 0 .... TonyHamilton 4 72
(Richard Fahey) *cl up: led 2f out: rdn and hdd over 1f out: kpt on same pce* **9/2**[2]
60 **4** *3 3/4* **Zebedee Star**[10] 4890 2-9-0 0 .... JasonHart 11 60
(Keith Dalgleish) *led: hdd and rdn 2f out: grad wknd appr fnl f* **50/1**
00 **5** *2* **Chalieb**[10] 4856 2-8-11 0 .... RachelRichardson(3) 2 54
(Nigel Tinkler) *midfield: hdwy 2f out: sn rdn and kpt on fnl f* **50/1**
0 **6** *1/2* **Poppy May (IRE)**[18] 4603 2-9-0 0 .... TomEaves 12 52
(James Given) *chsd ldrs on inner: rdn along 2f out: wknd over 1f out* **25/1**
7 *nk* **Doria Road (USA)** 2-9-0 0 .... KevinStott 1 51+
(Kevin Ryan) *wnt lft s: in rr: rdn along and sme hdwy on wd outside over 2f out: n.d* **22/1**
3 **8** *1 1/2* **Coping Stone**[70] 2771 2-9-0 0 .... ShaneGray 10 47
(David Brown) *wnt rt s: trckd ldrs on inner: swtchd lft 2f out: sn rdn and wknd* **7/1**
9 *1 1/2* **Navajo Thunder (IRE)** 2-9-0 0 .... AndrewMullen 7 42
(Michael Appleby) *a towards rr* **66/1**
00 **10** *3/4* **Can Can Dream**[33] 4040 2-9-0 0 .... CamHardie 8 39
(Olly Williams) *dwlt: a towards rr* **100/1**
6 **11** *hd* **Volta Do Mar (IRE)**[99] 1921 2-9-0 0 .... DavidNolan 3 39
(Richard Fahey) *dwlt: a towards rr* **33/1**
12 *2 1/2* **Kulgri** 2-9-0 0 .... JoeDoyle 9 31
(Kevin Ryan) *a towards rr* **40/1**
13 *nk* **Rutherford (IRE)** 2-9-0 0 .... GrahamLee 13 30+
(Kevin Ryan) *dwlt: a towards rr* **6/1**[3]
1m 11.32s (-1.38) **Going Correction** -0.125s/f (Firm) **13** Ran SP% **120.8**
Speed ratings (Par 91): **104,101,100,95,93 92,91,89,87,86 86,83,82**
CSF £52.68 TOTE £33.90: £8.60, £1.02, £1.90; EX 79.40 Trifecta £302.70.
Owner Crossfields Racing **Bred** Crossfields Bloodstock Ltd **Trained** Hambleton, N Yorks

FOCUS
An average 2yo fillies' maiden. The winner was always travelling nicely and was well on top passing the post, while Vaulted is rated a small improver.

5273 TOBEY STEWART 1ST BIRTHDAY H'CAP 1m
3:00 (3:01) (Class 5) (0-70,70) 3-Y-O+ **£3,234** (£962; £481; £240) **Stalls** Low

Form RPR
-350 **1** **Hijran (IRE)**[62] 3033 3-8-13 **62** ....(p) AndrewMullen 7 69
(Michael Appleby) *midfield: hdwy over 2f out: rdn wl over 1f out: narrow ld appr fnl f: sn drvn and kpt on wl towards fin* **16/1**

0310 **2** *nk* **Whitkirk**[35] 3982 3-9-0 **63** JoeyHaynes 5 69+
(Jedd O'Keeffe) *hld up towards rr: stdy hdwy on outer wl over 2f out: chsd ldrs wl over 1f out: sn chal and rdn: drvn and ev ch ins fnl f: no ex towards fin* **5/1**[2]

-052 **3** *1 ½* **Midlight**[36] 3952 4-9-0 **56** (t) GeorgeChaloner 12 60
(Richard Whitaker) *trckd ldrs: hdwy 3f out and sn cl up: rdn to ld wl over 1f out: hdd and drvn appr fnl f: kpt on same pce* **6/1**[3]

4326 **4** *shd* **Ferdy (IRE)**[38] 3883 7-9-1 **57** PJMcDonald 4 60+
(Paul Green) *in rr: hdwy over 2f out: rdn along wl over 1f out: styd on strly fnl f: nrst fin* **12/1**

6331 **5** *½* **Ronya (IRE)**[23] 4425 5-9-4 **60** RoystonFfrench 11 62
(Tracy Waggott) *cl up: led 3f out: rdn along and hdd wl over 1f out: sn drvn and grad wknd appr fnl f* **9/1**

54-2 **6** *2 ½* **Dark Wonder (IRE)**[56] 3262 4-9-10 **66** RobertWinston 1 62
(Ivan Furtado) *trckd ldrs on inner: effrt over 2f out: sn rdn: drvn and no imp fr over 1f out* **3/1**[1]

-200 **7** *2 ¼* **She's Electric (IRE)**[66] 2906 3-9-6 **69** (p) JoeFanning 9 59
(Keith Dalgleish) *chsd ldrs: rdn along over 2f out: drvn and wknd over 1f out* **16/1**

5103 **8** *7* **Mercury**[14] 4729 4-9-4 **60** (b) KevinStott 3 34
(Kevin Ryan) *t.k.h: in tch: hdwy over 2f out: rdn along wl over 1f out: sn btn* **9/1**

2606 **9** *¾* **Rocket Ronnie (IRE)**[12] 4807 6-10-0 **70** (b) GrahamLee 2 42
(Ed McMahon) *hld up: a in rr* **8/1**

0000 **10** *8* **Afkar (IRE)**[14] 4729 8-9-6 **62** RaulDaSilva 10 15
(Ivan Furtado) *led: pushed along over 3f out: sn hdd and rdn: wknd 2f out* **33/1**

6360 **11** *34* **Young Christian**[28] 4241 3-9-7 **70** JamesSullivan 6
(Tom Tate) *chsd ldrs on inner: rdn along wl over 2f out: sn wknd and bhd whn eased over 1f out* **20/1**

1m 41.22s (1.12) **Going Correction** +0.15s/f (Good)
WFA 3 from 4yo+ 7lb **11** Ran SP% **114.2**
Speed ratings (Par 103): **100,99,98,98,97 95,92,85,85,77 43**
CSF £91.52 CT £551.59 TOTE £19.60: £6.60, £2.10, £2.10; EX 128.20 Trifecta £914.90.
Owner L A Hill & C L Bacon **Bred** C Farrell **Trained** Oakham, Rutland

FOCUS
A moderate handicap, run at a sound pace. The winner was making is debut for Michael Appleby and ran to his 2yo level. The third was always well placed and helps set the level.

5274 FOLLOW @RACING_UK ON TWITTER H'CAP 5f
3:30 (3:30) (Class 4) (0-80,80) 3-Y-0+ **£4,851** (£1,443; £721; £360) **Stalls** High

Form RPR
2134 **1** **Seamster**[11] 4831 9-8-8 **71** (t) CameronNoble(7) 16 81
(David Loughnane) *trckd ldrs: smooth hdwy wl over 1f out: rdn to ld appr fnl f: kpt on wl towards fin* **9/2**[2]

0/01 **2** *½* **Ziggy Lee**[22] 4452 10-9-8 **78** DougieCostello 13 86
(Lawrence Mullaney) *hld up in tch: hdwy on inner over 2f out: swtchd lft and rdn over 1f out: drvn to chse wnr ins fnl f: kpt on* **18/1**

4501 **3** *1 ¼* **Musharrif**[12] 4809 4-9-6 **76** DavidAllan 9 80
(Declan Carroll) *hld up: hdwy 2f out: swtchd lft and rdn over 1f out: kpt on fnl f* **4/1**[1]

0400 **4** *1 ¼* **Captain Dunne (IRE)**[20] 4514 11-9-0 **73** RachelRichardson(3) 8 72
(Tim Easterby) *led: rdn along 2f out: hdd and drvn appr fnl f: kpt on same pce* **12/1**

0016 **5** *½* **Adam's Ale**[10] 4896 7-9-10 **80** JackGarritty 10 77
(Mark Walford) *chsd ldrs: rdn over 1f out: drvn and kpt on same pce fnl f* **6/1**[3]

030 **6** *½* **Lydia's Place**[6] 5040 3-9-4 **80** RobHornby(3) 5 75
(Richard Guest) *stmbld s: chsd ldrs: rdn along wl over 1f out: sn drvn and kpt on same pce* **11/1**

1300 **7** *nk* **Money Team (IRE)**[20] 4514 5-9-7 **77** GrahamGibbons 14 72
(David Barron) *hld up and bhd: hdwy jst over 1f out: tenderly rdn and styd on wl fnl f: nrst fin* **8/1**

014 **8** *¾* **Oriental Relation (IRE)**[12] 4809 5-9-1 **71** (b) TomEaves 3 63
(James Given) *cl up: rdn along 2f out: drvn and wkng whn n.m.r ent fnl f* **14/1**

2005 **9** *nse* **Tikthebox (IRE)**[3] 5182 3-9-4 **77** (p) JamieSpencer 2 68
(David Brown) *chsd ldrs on outer: rdn along 2f out: sn wknd* **10/1**

64-0 **10** *1 ½* **Richter Scale (IRE)**[17] 4643 3-9-2 **75** PaulMulrennan 11 60
(Michael Dods) *wnt lft s: a in rr* **14/1**

6646 **11** *2* **Rusty Rocket (IRE)**[20] 4514 7-9-9 **79** PJMcDonald 7 58
(Paul Green) *chsd ldrs: rdn along over 2f out: sn wknd* **12/1**

4-00 **12** *½* **Space Artist (IRE)**[101] 1874 6-9-2 **72** (vt) GrahamLee 1 49
(Nigel Tinkler) *a towards rr* **50/1**

1600 **13** *4 ½* **Ticking Away**[17] 4643 3-9-6 **79** (v[1]) ShaneGray 4 39
(David Brown) *a in rr* **33/1**

57.23s (-2.37) **Going Correction** -0.125s/f (Firm)
WFA 3 from 4yo+ 3lb **13** Ran SP% **119.9**
Speed ratings (Par 105): **113,112,110,108,107 106,106,104,104,102 99,98,91**
CSF £83.53 CT £356.09 TOTE £4.90: £2.00, £6.80, £1.60; EX 88.00 Trifecta £384.40.
Owner Bamford and Fell **Bred** D G Hardisty Bloodstock **Trained** Market Drayton, Shropshire

FOCUS
A competitive sprint handicap. Predictably those drawn high held the aces.

5275 JW 4X4 NORTHALLERTON H'CAP 1m 4f
4:00 (4:00) (Class 4) (0-85,85) 4-Y-0+ **£4,851** (£1,443; £721; £360) **Stalls** High

Form RPR
-113 **1** **Walpole (IRE)**[80] 2487 4-9-4 **82** JamieSpencer 6 90+
(Hugo Palmer) *trckd clr ldr: tk clsr order 3f out: smooth hdwy and cl up 2f out: tk narrow advantage over 1f out and sn rdn: edgd lft ins fnl f: drvn out* **4/5**[1]

1663 **2** *¾* **Odeon**[10] 4892 5-9-1 **79** TomEaves 4 85
(James Given) *led and sn clr: pushed along over 2f out: sn jnd and rdn: hdd narrowly and drvn over 1f out: rallied gamely ins fnl f: no ex last 75yds* **6/1**[3]

043 **3** *1* **Tamayuz Magic (IRE)**[16] 4680 5-8-9 **78** (b) NathanEvans(5) 3 82
(Michael Easterby) *hld up: hdwy to chse ldng pair over 3f out: effrt over 2f out: rdn and ch over 1f out: drvn: edgd lft and kpt on same pce fnl f* **5/1**[2]

-051 **4** *shd* **Carthage (IRE)**[28] 4237 5-8-10 **74** BenCurtis 5 78
(Brian Ellison) *hld up: hdwy to chse ldng pair 1/2-way: rdn along 3f out and sn sltly outpcd: drvn and styd on wl fnl f* **7/1**

0000 **5** *8* **Min Alemarat (IRE)**[45] 3657 5-9-4 **85** RachelRichardson(3) 1 76
(Tim Easterby) *hld up: a towards rr* **12/1**

5-00 **6** *34* **Only Orsenfoolsies**[16] 4680 7-9-4 **82** PJMcDonald 2 19
(Micky Hammond) *chsd ldng pair to 1/2-way: sn lost pl and bhd fnl 3f* **33/1**

2m 36.92s (0.72) **Going Correction** +0.15s/f (Good) **6** Ran SP% **109.6**
Speed ratings (Par 105): **103,102,101,101,96 73**
CSF £5.74 TOTE £1.50: £1.10, £3.70; EX 5.50 Trifecta £13.30.
Owner Roldvale Limited **Bred** Roundhill Stud **Trained** Newmarket, Suffolk

FOCUS
This fair little handicap was a proper test of the distance. The winner is progressive but didn't win as far as seemed likely 2f out, but that won't harm his mark too much.

5276 RACING UK HD ON SKY 432 FILLIES' H'CAP 7f
4:30 (4:31) (Class 5) (0-70,75) 3-Y-0+ **£2,911** (£866; £432; £216) **Stalls** Low

Form RPR
3221 **1** **Courier**[8] 4932 4-9-12 **75** 7ex (p) HollieDoyle(7) 6 85
(Marjorie Fife) *mde all: pushed along over 2f out: rdn clr wl over 1f out: kpt on strly* **7/4**[1]

5426 **2** *2 ¼* **Lozah**[11] 4844 3-8-8 **56** (tp) PJMcDonald 2 58
(David Loughnane) *dwlt: hld up in rr: hdwy over 2f out: rdn wl over 1f out: chsd wnr ins fnl f: sn drvn and no imp* **7/1**

2664 **3** *hd* **Desire**[31] 4142 4-9-5 **61** (v[1]) GeorgeChaloner 5 64
(Richard Fahey) *trckd ldng pair on inner: pushed along over 2f out: rdn wl over 1f out: sn drvn and kpt on same pce* **5/1**[3]

0335 **4** *2 ¼* **Make On Madam (IRE)**[22] 4454 4-9-7 **63** DavidAllan 9 60
(Les Eyre) *trckd ldrs: effrt over 2f out and sn rdn: drvn over 1f out and sn one pce* **4/1**[2]

002 **5** *1* **Isntshesomething**[10] 4861 4-8-10 **52** (p) PaulMulrennan 7 47
(Richard Guest) *chsd wnr: rdn along over 2f out: drvn wl over 1f out: sn wknd* **10/1**

00U1 **6** *¾* **White Flag**[20] 4516 5-8-12 **57** RachelRichardson(3) 3 50
(Tim Easterby) *in tch: pushed along 1/2-way: rdn wl over 2f out and sn btn* **7/1**

6-50 **7** *11* **Tweetheart**[85] 2302 3-8-4 **57** PhilDennis(5) 4 18
(Ron Barr) *dwlt: a towards rr: outpcd and bhd fnl 2f* **40/1**

1m 27.5s (0.30) **Going Correction** +0.15s/f (Good)
WFA 3 from 4yo+ 6lb **7** Ran SP% **109.6**
Speed ratings (Par 100): **104,101,101,98,97 96,84**
CSF £13.31 CT £45.73 TOTE £2.80: £1.70, £2.70; EX 12.30 Trifecta £54.30.
Owner Daniel Gath Homes Ltd **Bred** Stratford Place Stud And Watership Down **Trained** Stillington, N Yorks

FOCUS
An ordinary fillies' handicap in which the winner dictated, recording a new personal best.

5277 RACINGUK.COM/DAYPASS H'CAP (DIV I) 6f
5:00 (5:01) (Class 6) (0-60,60) 3-Y-0+ **£2,587** (£770; £384; £192) **Stalls** High

Form RPR
0020 **1** **Someone Exciting**[17] 4647 3-8-11 **51** PatrickMathers 12 58
(David Thompson) *trckd ldrs on inner: swtchd lft and hdwy over 1f out: rdn ins fnl f: styd on wl to ld last 75yds* **12/1**

6241 **2** *1 ¼* **Thornaby Princess**[11] 4834 5-9-0 **50** (p) RoystonFfrench 7 54
(Colin Teague) *prom: hdwy 2f out: rdn to ld over 1f out: drvn ins fnl f: hdd and no ex last 75yds* **16/1**

0362 **3** *shd* **Bogsnog (IRE)**[20] 4513 6-9-4 **54** TonyHamilton 2 58
(Kristin Stubbs) *chsd ldrs: hdwy 2f out: rdn over 1f out: drvn and kpt on wl fnl f* **6/1**[3]

6000 **4** *½* **Sea Of Green**[13] 4770 4-8-11 **47** JoeDoyle 8 49
(Jim Goldie) *in rr: hdwy 2f out: rdn over 1f out: styd on strly: nrst fin* **14/1**

-500 **5** *hd* **Cosmic Dust**[24] 4410 3-8-1 **46** oh1 NathanEvans(5) 1 47
(Richard Whitaker) *qckly away and sn cl up nr stands' rail: rdn to take slt ld wl over 1f out: hdd and drvn ent fnl f: kpt on same pce* **16/1**

3202 **6** *½* **Tribesman**[13] 4770 3-9-6 **60** (b) RobertWinston 3 59
(Marjorie Fife) *chsd ldrs: rdn along and outpcd 1/2-way: hdwy over 1f out: kpt on u.p fnl f* **7/2**[1]

3440 **7** *hd* **Gaelic Wizard (IRE)**[8] 4931 8-9-3 **58** (v) GemmaTutty(5) 10 64
(Karen Tutty) *hld up in rr whn n.m.r and stmbld after 1f: rdr lost iron: rcvrd 1/2-way: hdwy and nt clr run over 1f out: kpt on ins fnl f: nrst fin* **10/1**

0402 **8** *½* **Sir Geoffrey (IRE)**[20] 4512 10-9-4 **54** (b) BenCurtis 5 52
(Scott Dixon) *slt ld nr stands' rail: rdn along over 2f out: hdd wl over 1f out: sn drvn and grad wknd ent fnl f* **10/1**

40U1 **9** *nk* **Beadlam (IRE)**[7] 4972 3-9-2 **56** 6ex PJMcDonald 6 52
(David Loughnane) *in tch whn n.m.r after 1f and sn towards rr: hdwy 2f: sn rdn and no imp fnl f* **9/2**[2]

0004 **10** *2* **George Bailey (IRE)**[28] 4229 4-8-13 **49** BarryMcHugh 9 40
(Suzzanne France) *chsd ldrs whn n.m.r after 1f: rdn along over 2f out: n.d* **33/1**

0410 **11** *3 ¼* **King's Currency**[25] 4365 3-9-5 **59** (p) JackGarritty 4 39
(Jedd O'Keeffe) *chsd ldrs: rdn along over 2f out: sn drvn and wknd over 1f out* **10/1**

0-06 **12** *7* **Miss Popov**[83] 2359 3-8-6 **46** oh1 (p) JamesSullivan 13 5
(Noel Wilson) *chsd ldrs on inner: rdn along 1/2-way: sn lost pl and bhd* **40/1**

0506 **13** *13* **Sunrise Dance**[18] 4604 7-8-10 **46** oh1 (p) ShaneGray 11
(Kenny Johnson) *chsd ldrs: rdn along 1/2-way: sn lost pl and bhd* **25/1**

1m 13.05s (0.35) **Going Correction** -0.125s/f (Firm)
WFA 3 from 4yo+ 4lb **13** Ran SP% **117.3**
Speed ratings (Par 101): **92,90,90,89,89 88,88,87,87,84 80,70,53**
CSF £183.48 CT £1313.39 TOTE £13.20: £3.60, £4.60, £2.30; EX 232.90 Trifecta £3420.10.
Owner Wayne Fleming **Bred** Trebles Holford Farm Thoroughbreds **Trained** Bolam, Co Durham

FOCUS
The heavens opened prior to this run-of-the-mill sprint handicap. Once again there was a dash for the stands' side.

5278 RACINGUK.COM/DAYPASS H'CAP (DIV II) 6f
5:35 (5:35) (Class 6) (0-60,56) 3-Y-0+ **£2,587** (£770; £384; £192) **Stalls** High

Form RPR
2200 **1** **Poolstock**[13] 4770 4-9-6 **52** (b[1]) PaulMulrennan 6 60
(Michael Dods) *hld up towards rr: hdwy over 2f out: chsd ldrs over 1f out: rdn to chal jst ins fnl f: led last 100yds: kpt on* **7/1**

3020 **2** *1 ½* **Spoken Words**[8] 4931 7-9-1 **47** (p) PatrickMathers 4 51
(John David Riches) *trckd ldrs on inner: swtchd lft and hdwy over 2f out: sn cl up: rdn to chal over 1f out: ev ch ins fnl f: drvn and no ex last 100yds* **14/1**

5566 **3** *nk* **Teetotal (IRE)**[11] 4848 6-9-8 **54** (b) GrahamGibbons 9 58
(Nigel Tinkler) *swtchd rt to stands' rail s: in rr: hdwy 2f out: sn swtchd lft and effrt wl over 1f out: rdn and n.m.r jst ins fnl f: styd on wl towards fin* **11/4**[1]

0431 **4** *1 1/4* **A J Cook (IRE)**[8] **4931** 6-9-7 **56** 6ex........................ RachelRichardson[(3)] 3 55
(Ron Barr) *in tch on outer: hdwy 1/2-way: chsd ldrs 2f out: rdn over 1f out: drvn and kpt on same pce fnl f* **11/2**[3]

0005 **5** *1* **Bazula (IRE)**[7] **4973** 3-9-4 **54**..(b) JasonHart 2 49
(Tim Easterby) *cl up: led after 2f: jnd and rdn wl over 1f out: drvn ent fnl f: sn hdd & wknd* **16/1**

0060 **6** *hd* **Amis Reunis**[13] **4771** 7-8-8 **45**........................... NathanEvans[(5)] 12 40
(Colin Teague) *chsd ldrs: rdn along wl over 1f out: drvn appr fnl f: kpt on same pce* **9/1**

306- **7** *2 3/4* **Molivias Gem**[288] **7517** 3-9-3 **53**.. GrahamLee 11 41
(David Thompson) *in tch: rdn along over 2f out: sn no hdwy* **25/1**

0343 **8** *shd* **Secret City (IRE)**[20] **4513** 10-9-4 **55**.............................(b) RowanScott[(5)] 8 44
(Rebecca Bastiman) *a towards rr* **5/1**[2]

0-06 **9** *3/4* **Dark Castle**[16] **4691** 7-9-10 **56**.. PJMcDonald 10 40
(Micky Hammond) *a towards rr* **8/1**

-000 **10** *2 1/4* **Anushka Noo Noo**[22] **4454** 3-9-3 **56**...................(b) JacobButterfield[(3)] 5 33
(Ollie Pears) *qckly away and led 2f: cl up and rdn wl over 2f out: sn drvn and wknd* **20/1**

0465 **11** *9* **Bomber Etches**[77] **2560** 3-8-9 **45**.. BenCurtis 7
(Scott Dixon) *chsd ldrs on outer: rdn along 1/2-way: sn lost pl and bhd* **25/1**

46-0 **12** *1* **Good Move (IRE)**[34] **4006** 4-8-13 **45**...........................(p) JamesSullivan 1
(Brian Rothwell) *prom: rdn along over 2f out: sn wknd* **50/1**

1m 13.2s (0.50) **Going Correction** -0.125s/f (Firm)
WFA 3 from 4yo+ 4lb **12** Ran SP% **119.3**
Speed ratings (Par 101): **91,89,88,86,85 85,81,81,80,77 65,64**
CSF £96.19 CT £342.15 TOTE £6.80: £2.30, £4.00, £2.10; EX 103.10 Trifecta £655.90.
Owner Dunham Trading Ltd **Bred** R F And S D Knipe **Trained** Denton, Co Durham

FOCUS
This second division of the 46-60 sprint handicap looked wide open. Poolstock was entitled to win on this year's peak form, and the runner-up is rated to his best of this campaign.
T/Jkpt: Not won. T/Plt: £31.90 to a £1 stake. Pool: £55,294.07 - 1263.16 winning units. T/Qpdt: £27.30 to a £1 stake. Pool: £4,418.32 - 119.48 winning units. **Joe Rowntree**

5216 DEAUVILLE (R-H)
Tuesday, August 9

OFFICIAL GOING: Polytrack: standard; turf: good

5279a ~~PRIX DU MONT CANISY (CLAIMER) (2YO) (POLYTRACK)~~ ~~7f 110y~~
1:50 (12:00) 2-Y-O **£8,455** (£3,382; £2,536; £1,691; £845)

RPR

1 **Larno (FR)** 2-9-4 0.. Pierre-CharlesBoudot 6 76
(B De Montzey, France) **92/10**

2 *snk* **If I Say So**[4] **5120** 2-8-11 0... IoritzMendizabal 1 69
(J S Moore) *rowed along leaving stalls to ld: 2 l clr and rdn under 2f out: edgd lft u.p under 1 1/2f out: kpt on gamely fnl f: hdd 25yds out: no ex* **7/1**[3]

3 *1 1/2* **Elfy James (FR)** 2-8-8 0... HugoJourniac[(3)] 5 65
(D Windrif, France) **16/1**

4 *1 3/4* **Incantu (IRE)**[41] 2-9-1 0...(b) TonyPiccone 2 65
(F Chappet, France) **10/1**

5 *nse* **Power Of The Cross**[107] 2-9-1 0.................................... ThierryJarnet 4 65
(D Guillemin, France) **12/5**[2]

6 *2 1/2* **Dibaba Traou Land (FR)** 2-8-11 0................................ OlivierPeslier 3 55
(C Gourdain, France) **17/1**

7 *1 3/4* **Chababa Rosetgri (FR)**[8] **4965** 2-8-11 0........................ RonanThomas 9 51
(H De Nicolay, France) **15/2**

8 *3 1/2* **Jantine (FR)**[42] **3763** 2-8-11 0.. AlexisBadel 8 43
(Mme M Bollack-Badel, France) **20/1**

9 *6* **Jenychope (FR)**[22] **4471** 2-9-5 0........................... ChristopheSoumillon 7 37
(D Windrif, France) **23/10**[1]

10 *1 1/2* **Supercopa (SPA)** 2-8-9 0.................................... JeremieCatineau[(6)] 10 29
(C Laffon-Parias, France) **54/1**

WIN (incl. 1 euro stake): 10.20. PLACES: 3.50, 3.10, 4.60. DF: 33.60.

Owner Bruno De Montzey **Bred** Scea Plessis **Trained** France

5280a PRIX DE TORTISAMBERT (CLAIMER) (3YO) (APPRENTICES & YOUNG JOCKEYS) (POLYTRACK) 7f 110y
2:25 (12:00) 3-Y-O **£8,455** (£3,382; £2,536; £1,691; £845)

RPR

1 **Michele Strogoff**[34] **4029** 3-8-13 0............................ HugoJourniac[(3)] 10 75
(Simone Brogi, France) **3/1**[1]

2 *2* **Kizomba (FR)**[36] 3-8-2 0...(b) KyllanBarbaud[(6)] 13 62
(N Caullery, France) **9/1**

3 *nk* **Rip Van Suzy (IRE)**[29] **4220** 3-8-6 0....................... JeromeMoutard[(10)] 4 69
(Jo Hughes) *sn led narrowly: hdd after 1 1/2f: chsd ldr between horses: 3rd and rdn 2f out: styd on at same pce u.p fnl f* **83/10**

4 *1/2* **Octavia (FR)**[22] 3-8-6 0.. FlorentGavilan[(5)] 1 63
(H-A Pantall, France) **16/1**

5 *nk* **Des Annees Folles (FR)**[7] 3-8-7 0..................(p) NicolasBarzalona[(6)] 8 64
(P Adda, France) **14/1**

6 *shd* **Filzeto (FR)**[10] 3-8-6 0......................................(b) ClementLecoeuvre[(12)] 9 69
(E Lellouche, France) **26/1**

7 *snk* **Trento (FR)**[242] **8188** 3-8-11 0.. GabrielBon[(4)] 12 66
(L A Urbano-Grajales, France) **14/1**

8 *shd* **Passeport (IRE)**[18] 3-8-7 0.................................. NathanKasztelan[(8)] 14 65
(S Jesus, France) **22/1**

9 *3/4* **Sopran Secreter (ITY)**[275] **7765** 3-8-10 0............ JeremieMonteiro[(10)] 7 69
(Carina Fey, France) **22/5**[2]

10 *1/2* **Great Dora (FR)**[18] 3-8-6 0..............................(p) EmmanuelEtienne[(5)] 6 58
(S Wattel, France) **53/10**[3]

11 *1 1/2* **Minminwin (IRE)**[42] **3735** 3-8-3 0.................................. RichardOliver[(5)] 2 52
(Gay Kelleway) *chsd ldrs: scrubbed along 2 1/2f out: lost pl wl over 1 1/2f out: one pce fnl f* **41/1**

12 *nk* **Santorina (FR)**[48] **3546** 3-8-5 0..........................(p) NicolasLarenaudie[(3)] 5 51
(Mlle M-L Mortier, France) **47/1**

13 *1* **Ihaveadream (POL)**[29] **4220** 3-8-5 0......................... JeffersonSmith[(3)] 11 48
(W Mongil, Germany) **16/1**

14 *4 1/2* **Fica Comigo**[57] 3-8-4 0... JeremyMoisan[(7)] 16 40
(M Delzangles, France) **84/1**

15 *7* **Zarzis Beauty (FR)**[18] 3-8-5 0............................ LudovicBoisseau[(3)] 3 20
(D Prod'Homme, France) **46/1**

WIN (incl. 1 euro stake): 4.00. PLACES: 1.80, 3.00, 2.70. DF: 19.60. SF: 27.90
Trained France **Bred** Razza Del Sole Societa Agricola Srl

5281a PRIX DE LA BAIE (H'CAP) (5YO+) (POLYTRACK) 1m 4f 110y
2:55 (12:00) 5-Y-O+ **£5,882** (£2,352; £1,764; £1,176; £588)

RPR

1 **Spiritueux (IRE)**[9] 5-8-9 **0**.. GeraldMosse 6 54
(C Laffon-Parias, France) **18/5**[1]

2 *nk* **Volzapone (FR)**[670] 6-9-1 **0**............................ ChristopheSoumillon 14 60
(Y Fertillet, France) **74/10**

3 *1 1/4* **Ismane (FR)**[32] 7-9-3 **0**.. JulienGuillochon 10 60
(L Cendra, France) **16/1**

4 *shd* **Coeur Dolois (IRE)**[9] 5-9-0 **0**..................................(b) GregoryBenoist 1 57
(A Bonin, France) **67/10**[3]

5 *nse* **Veneziano (FR)**[19] 7-8-11 **0**.. EddyHardouin 7 54
(Robert Collet, France) **35/1**

6 *nk* **Conte Colorate (FR)**[9] 7-9-1 **0**.............................. AdrienMoreau[(3)] 12 60
(Mlle M Henry, France) **26/5**[2]

7 *hd* **Laguna Sun (FR)**[213] 7-8-7 **0**.................................(p) LudovicBoisseau 3 49
(L Cendra, France) **35/1**

8 *snk* **Coressos (FR)**[513] 5-9-6 **0**..(b) CristianDemuro 11 62
(Roberto Di Paolo, Italy) **18/1**

9 *1/2* **Testarossa (POL)**[22] 5-9-6 **0**................................ MickaelBarzalona 5 61
(P Sobry, France) **15/1**

10 *1* **Enfin Seuls (FR)**[19] 5-9-6 **0**.. MaximeGuyon 8 59
(Yves de Nicolay, France) **77/10**

11 *3/4* **Uphold**[10] **4903** 9-9-3 **0**............................(b) Pierre-CharlesBoudot 4 55
(Gay Kelleway) *broke wl and led: hdd after 1 1/2f but remained cl up: 5th and scrubbed along wl over 2f out: n.m.r 1 1/2f out but then no imp: one pce fnl f* **10/1**

12 *1/2* **Apollon (FR)**[32] 8-8-2 **0**.. AntoineCoutier 15 39
(A Bonin, France) **76/1**

13 *2* **Private Lesson's (FR)**[42] 8-9-3 **0**................................ TheoBachelot 2 51
(P Bigot, France) **11/1**

14 *2* **Zhayrem (FR)**[19] 5-8-5 **0**.. AlexisBadel 13 36
(P Van De Poele, France) **49/1**

15 *2 1/2* **Medaillon (FR)**[373] 5-9-6 **0**....................................(p) IoritzMendizabal 9 47
(Mario Hofer, Germany) **36/1**

Owner Mme Carlos Laffon-Parias **Bred** Wertheimer Et Frere **Trained** Chantilly, France

5007 BATH (L-H)
Wednesday, August 10

OFFICIAL GOING: Firm
Wind: almost nil Weather: cloudy with light rain at times

5282 HAPPY 50TH BIRTHDAY KIM DASH H'CAP (BATH SUMMER SPRINT SERIES QUALIFIER) 5f 11y
5:20 (5:21) (Class 6) (0-60,60) 4-Y-O+ **£2,264** (£673; £336; £168) **Stalls** Centre

Form RPR

0050 **1** **Molly Jones**[7] **5007** 7-8-11 **50**................................. SilvestreDeSousa 5 55
(Matthew Salaman) *disp ld: rdn over 2f out: tk narrow advantage ins fnl f: jst hld on* **9/1**

0005 **2** *nse* **Catalinas Diamond (IRE)**[7] **5007** 8-9-1 **54**...................(t) SteveDrowne 1 59
(Pat Murphy) *last but in tch: sn pushed along: hdwy 2f out: sn rdn: ev ch fnl 120yds: kpt on: jst hld* **10/1**

1215 **3** *hd* **Go Amber Go**[7] **5009** 4-9-4 **57**.. RyanTate 4 61
(Rod Millman) *disp ld: rdn over 1f out: narrowly hdd ins fnl f: kpt on* **3/1**[2]

4531 **4** *1 1/4* **Virile (IRE)**[5] **5127** 5-8-13 **59** 6ex.............................(bt) MitchGodwin[(7)] 3 59
(Sylvester Kirk) *trckd ldrs: rdn over 1f out: kpt on but no ex towards fin* **6/5**[1]

6504 **5** *1 1/2* **See Vermont**[17] **4691** 8-9-7 **60**..(p) LukeMorris 2 54
(Rebecca Bastiman) *stdd bk bhd ldrs after breaking wl: rdn 2f out: kpt chsng ldrs tl no ex fnl 75yds* **9/2**[3]

45/0 **6** *8* **Ignight**[22] **4484** 5-8-4 **46** oh1................................... NoelGarbutt[(3)] 6 11
(Matthew Salaman) *awkward leaving stalls: trckd ldrs: rdn 2f out: sn wknd* **25/1**

1m 3.29s (0.79) **Going Correction** -0.125s/f (Firm) **6** Ran SP% **111.6**
Speed ratings (Par 101): **88,87,87,85,83 70**
CSF £85.32 TOTE £10.20: £3.00, £4.20; EX 101.10 Trifecta £332.80.
Owner Mrs D J Hughes **Bred** Mrs M L Parry & P M Steele-Mortimer **Trained** Tonyrefail, Rhondda Cynon Taff

FOCUS
The rail had been moved out on the bottom bend, adding 10yds to races run on the round course. The ground was firm all over. This opening sprint was reasonably competitive given the small field size and the low grade but the early pace looked fairly steady for a 5f contest. It produced a thrilling finish with three horses virtually in line as they hit the wire. The third is rated as running to her mark.

5283 CHARTWELL FUNDING MORTGAGE CLASSIC MAIDEN STKS 5f 11y
5:50 (5:50) (Class 5) 2-Y-O **£2,911** (£866; £432; £216) **Stalls** Centre

Form RPR

2432 **1** **Blue Suede (IRE)**[7] **5008** 2-9-0 78.................................... TomMarquand 5 78
(Richard Hannon) *mde all: rdn clr ent fnl f: comf* **8/13**[1]

2 *3 1/2* **Kiribati** 2-9-5 0.. AdamKirby 1 70+
(Mark Johnston) *s.i.s: sn trcking ldrs: rdn to chse wnr jst over 2f out: sn edgd rt: kpt on same pce fnl f* **2/1**[2]

00 **3** *8* **Fethiye Boy**[100] **1915** 2-9-5 0.............................. SilvestreDeSousa 4 42
(Ronald Harris) *hld up in last: racing keenly whn short of room and snatched up after 1f: nt clr run briefly 2f out: wnt 3rd over 1f out: kpt on but nt pce of front pair* **10/1**[3]

00 **4** *1 1/2* **Viola Park**[10] **4907** 2-9-5 0... RaulDaSilva 3 36
(Ronald Harris) *chsd ldrs: rdn over 2f out: sn one pce* **40/1**

5 *2 1/2* **Stopdworldnletmeof** 2-9-5 0.. MartinDwyer 2 27
(David Flood) *trckd wnr tl rdn over 2f out: wknd fnl f* **16/1**

1m 1.76s (-0.74) **Going Correction** -0.125s/f (Firm) **5** Ran SP% **112.7**
Speed ratings (Par 94): **100,94,81,79,75**
CSF £2.16 TOTE £1.40: £1.02, £1.80; EX 2.50 Trifecta £4.20.
Owner Mrs J Wood **Bred** Andrew Brazil **Trained** East Everleigh, Wilts

FOCUS
A very weak maiden which represented a golden opportunity for the 78-rated market leader and she had this wrapped up from some way out. The winner made all.

5284 SIMONSTONE BRISTOL H'CAP 5f 161y
6:20 (6:20) (Class 5) (0-75,75) 3-Y-O+ **£2,911** (£866; £432; £216) **Stalls** Centre

Form RPR

1064 **1** **Belledesert**[20] 4547 3-9-7 **74** .... RoystonFfrench 1 88
(Steph Hollinshead) *disp ld: overall ldr over 2f out: rdn clr over 1f out: readily* **6/1**[2]

5315 **2** 3 ¼ **Dyllan (IRE)**[11] 4855 3-9-5 **72** .... TomMarquand 4 75
(Ruth Carr) *trckd ldrs: rdn to chse wnr over 1f out: hung sltly rt: kpt on but nt pce to get on terms* **9/1**

0006 **3** 1 ¾ **Racquet**[18] 4662 3-9-8 **75** .... SeanLevey 3 73
(Richard Hannon) *disp ld tl rdn jst over 2f out: kpt on same pce fnl f* **8/1**

4033 **4** nk **Indian Affair**[16] 4714 6-9-2 **65** ....(bt) FrannyNorton 8 63
(Milton Bradley) *chsd ldrs: rdn over 2f out: kpt on but nt pce mount chal* **6/1**[2]

4352 **5** 3 **Royal Brave (IRE)**[7] 5032 5-9-9 **72** .... LukeMorris 9 60
(Rebecca Bastiman) *hld up in tch: drvn in centre 2f out: nvr threatened to get on terms* **7/2**[1]

1332 **6** hd **Nag's Wag (IRE)**[29] 4222 3-9-4 **71** .... SteveDrowne 6 57
(George Baker) *s.i.s: pushed along in tch: rdn over 2f out: sn one pce* **9/1**

1406 **7** 1 **Rhythm And Blues**[66] 2935 3-9-5 **72** ....(b[1]) AdamKirby 10 55
(Clive Cox) *rousted along on outer: in tch: drvn over 2f out: nvr threatened to get on terms fr over 1f out* **6/1**[2]

2-25 **8** 2 ¼ **Go Nani Go**[12] 4817 10-9-12 **75** .... SilvestreDeSousa 7 51
(Ed de Giles) *hld up in tch: rdn over 2f out: nvr any imp* **10/1**

005 **9** 1 ¼ **Where Next**[25] 4401 3-9-4 **71** .... HarryBentley 5 42
(Henry Candy) *trckd ldrs: rdn over 2f out: wknd over 1f out* **13/2**[3]

1m 9.61s (-1.59) **Going Correction** -0.125s/f (Firm)
WFA 3 from 5yo+ 4lb **9** Ran SP% **118.6**
Speed ratings (Par 103): **105,100,98,97,93 93,92,89,87**
CSF £60.20 CT £344.63 TOTE £7.80: £2.20, £3.20, £2.00; EX 65.30 Trifecta £481.40.
Owner K Meredith, D Hodson, The Ocean Four **Bred** M Pyle & Mrs T Pyle **Trained** Upper Longdon, Staffs

FOCUS
An open event with several holding sound claims on paper but very little got into it and the winner blew them away in the closing stages. The winner was taking her record to 3/3 over C&D on decent ground.

5285 BRAKES H'CAP 5f 11y
6:50 (6:51) (Class 3) (0-90,89) 3-Y-O+ **£7,439** (£2,213; £1,106; £553) **Stalls** Centre

Form RPR

3511 **1** **Go On Go On Go On**[23] 4461 3-9-7 **89** .... AdamKirby 1 101+
(Clive Cox) *prom: led over 2f out: r.o wl to assert fnl f: rdn out* **13/8**[1]

0-00 **2** 2 ½ **Extrasolar**[11] 4862 6-9-2 **81** ....(t) JimmyQuinn 5 85
(Amanda Perrett) *hld up: hdwy 2f out: nt clr run briefly ent fnl f: kpt on to go 2nd cl home* **12/1**

105 **3** nk **Edged Out**[10] 4911 6-8-10 **75** .... TomMarquand 4 78
(Christopher Mason) *trckd ldrs: rdn over 2f out: kpt on fnl f: snatched 3rd fnl stride* **20/1**

301 **4** nse **Cherry Kool**[12] 4820 3-8-1 **72** .... AaronJones(3) 2 74
(Stuart Williams) *chsd ldrs: rdn to chse wnr over 2f out: kpt on but no ex whn lost 2 pls cl home* **11/1**

1046 **5** ¾ **Equally Fast**[37] 3956 4-9-4 **83** .... MartinDwyer 8 83
(William Muir) *slowly away: bhd: hdwy 2f out: sn rdn and hung lft: kpt on same pce fnl f* **8/1**[3]

-000 **6** 3 **Nocturn**[23] 4461 7-8-12 **77** ....(p) RaulDaSilva 6 66
(Ronald Harris) *hld up: nt clr run and swtchd rt 2f out: sn rdn and hung lft: fdd fnl 120yds* **20/1**

0640 **7** 4 ½ **Noble Asset**[3] 5189 5-8-10 **75** ....[1] FrannyNorton 10 48
(Milton Bradley) *sn prom: rdn over 2f out: wknd over 1f out* **16/1**

-132 **8** 4 ½ **Cocoa Beach (IRE)**[18] 4643 3-8-13 **81** .... LukeMorris 9 37
(Sir Mark Prescott Bt) *led tl rdn over 2f out: wknd over 1f out* **15/8**[2]

1m 0.89s (-1.61) **Going Correction** -0.125s/f (Firm)
WFA 3 from 4yo+ 3lb **8** Ran SP% **115.4**
Speed ratings (Par 107): **107,103,102,102,101 96,89,82**
CSF £22.72 CT £279.32 TOTE £2.00: £1.10, £4.10, £6.30; EX 21.40 Trifecta £167.30.
Owner Paul & Clare Rooney **Bred** Richard Kent & Robert Percival **Trained** Lambourn, Berks

FOCUS
Not a particularly competitive heat for the grade with only a few of these bringing solid recent form to the table. The inside rail was once again the place to be. The winner did much the best of the three that raced prominently, and those placed ran close to their marks.

5286 BYP H'CAP (BATH SUMMER STAYERS' SERIES QUALIFIER) 1m 6f
7:20 (7:21) (Class 5) (0-70,67) 3-Y-O **£2,911** (£866; £432; £216) **Stalls** Centre

Form RPR

4011 **1** **Coarse Cut (IRE)**[9] 4942 3-9-4 **64** 6ex........(b) JohnFahy 3 69
(Eve Johnson Houghton) *trckd ldr: rdn to ld over 2f out: sn in command: styd on wl: pushed out* **7/4**[2]

0003 **2** 2 ¾ **Lily Trotter**[18] 4661 3-9-7 **67** ....(p) SilvestreDeSousa 4 68
(Ralph Beckett) *slipped leaving stalls: hld up bhd ldng trio: pushed along over 4f out: rdn and stdy prog over 2f out: styd on to go 2nd ins fnl f: nvr any threat to wnr* **6/5**[1]

-306 **3** nk **Shine**[39] 3878 3-9-0 **60** .... LukeMorris 2 61
(Jonathan Portman) *uns rdr and galloped loose bef s: trckd ldng pair: rdn over 4f out: chsd wnr 2f out but nvr threatened: no ex fnl 120yds* **10/1**

0-00 **4** 16 **Hamilton Terrace**[74] 2700 3-8-7 **53** ....(b[1]) HarryBentley 1 31
(Henry Candy) *led: rdn and hdd over 2f out: sn wknd* **5/1**[3]

3m 4.06s (0.26) **Going Correction** -0.10s/f (Good) **4** Ran SP% **107.6**
CSF £4.20 TOTE £2.60; EX 3.80 Trifecta £9.70.
Owner Equi ex Incertis Partners **Bred** M E Wates **Trained** Blewbury, Oxon

FOCUS
This turned out to be pretty uncompetitive with the favourite never really looking any sort of threat, but the winner is on a roll for his in-form yard. The runner-up is rated as running close to her recent best.

5287 DRIBUILD GROUP LTD H'CAP 1m 2f 46y
7:50 (7:50) (Class 5) (0-75,77) 3-Y-O+ **£2,911** (£866; £432; £216) **Stalls** Low

Form RPR

4-24 **1** **Exoteric**[76] 2619 3-9-4 **74** .... SilvestreDeSousa 3 83
(Charles Hills) *trckd ldr: rdn 3f out: led 2f out: strly pressed sn after: styd on wl to assert nring fin* **11/10**[1]

0406 **2** ¾ **Not Touch**[20] 4554 3-8-12 **68** .... SeanLevey 2 75
(Richard Hannon) *trckd ldrs: rdn over 2f out: str chal fr wl over 1f out: ev ch fnl f: hld nring fin* **7/2**[2]

3066 **3** 4 **Magnum (IRE)**[28] 4272 3-9-5 **75** ....(p) JimmyFortune 1 74
(Brian Meehan) *led: rdn and hdd 2f out: kpt pressing wnr tl ent fnl f: no ex fnl 120yds* **8/1**

561 **4** ½ **Toga Tiger (IRE)**[10] 4919 9-9-11 **77** 6ex........ PaddyBradley(5) 4 75
(Kevin Frost) *hld up: rdn over 2f out: kpt on fnl f but nt pce to get on terms* **6/1**

1200 **5** 2 **Beauty Night**[27] 4288 3-9-2 **72** .... AdamKirby 5 66
(Clive Cox) *trckd ldrs: rdn over 2f out: nt quite pce to chal: wknd fnl 120yds* **5/1**[3]

2m 9.14s (-1.86) **Going Correction** -0.10s/f (Good)
WFA 3 from 9yo 9lb **5** Ran SP% **111.9**
Speed ratings (Par 103): **103,102,99,98,97**
CSF £5.34 TOTE £2.00: £1.50, £2.00; EX 6.70 Trifecta £22.20.
Owner K Abdullah **Bred** Juddmonte Farms Ltd **Trained** Lambourn, Berks

FOCUS
A modest little handicap run at what looked a steady pace and the favourite needed lifting home by an inspired Silvestre De Sousa, so it's hard to get exciting about this form.

5288 PREMIER CONSERVATORY ROOFS H'CAP 1m 2f 46y
8:20 (8:21) (Class 5) (0-70,67) 3-Y-O **£2,911** (£866; £432; £216) **Stalls** Low

Form RPR

00-0 **1** **Totally Committed**[41] 3816 3-9-7 **67** .... AdamKirby 3 76
(Clive Cox) *trckd ldrs: chal 2f out: rdn to ld sn after: kpt on wl fnl 100yds: rdn out* **5/1**

0-44 **2** 1 ½ **Rajadamri**[27] 4288 3-8-13 **59** .... RyanTate 1 65
(Rod Millman) *led for 1f: trckd ldrs: rdn wl over 1f out: disputing cl 2nd ent fnl f: kpt on same pce fnl 120yds* **4/1**[3]

6332 **3** 1 ½ **Forecaster**[7] 5010 3-9-6 **66** ....(v[1]) LukeMorris 6 69
(Michael Bell) *trckd ldrs: wnt 2nd over 6f out: led 2f out: sn rdn and hdd: hld ent fnl f: kpt on same pce* **13/8**[1]

4023 **4** 3 **Rockliffe**[6] 5086 3-9-2 **62** .... SilvestreDeSousa 4 60
(Mick Channon) *led after 1f: rdn and hdd 2f out: kpt on tl no ex ins fnl f* **11/4**[2]

0-45 **5** 15 **Hereward The Wake**[18] 4660 3-9-0 **67** .... MitchGodwin(7) 5 40
(Sylvester Kirk) *chsd ldrs: struggling over 4f out: wknd 2f out* **9/1**

2m 10.38s (-0.62) **Going Correction** -0.10s/f (Good) **5** Ran SP% **111.4**
Speed ratings (Par 100): **98,96,95,93,81**
CSF £24.45 TOTE £6.40: £3.10, £2.80; EX 8.50 Trifecta £84.10.
Owner Con Harrington **Bred** Usk Valley Stud And C Harrington **Trained** Lambourn, Berks

FOCUS
This ordinary handicap was run at what appeared quite a strong gallop and the two market leaders, who raced on the front end, both disappointed. The winner was an improver up in trip.
T/Plt: £357.10 to a £1 stake. Pool of £41414.91 - 84.66 winning tickets. T/Qpdt: £32.40 to a £1 stake. Pool of £6145.32 - 140.30 winning tickets. **Tim Mitchell**

4724 BEVERLEY (R-H)
Wednesday, August 10

OFFICIAL GOING: Good to firm (8.0)
Wind: Light half against Weather: Cloudy with sunny periods

5289 ST STEPHEN'S MAIDEN AUCTION STKS 5f
2:00 (2:00) (Class 5) 2-Y-O **£3,780** (£1,131; £565; £283; £141) **Stalls** Low

Form RPR

043 **1** **Sir Viktor (IRE)**[20] 4564 2-9-5 70........(v) DougieCostello 7 74
(K R Burke) *trckd ldrs on outer: hdwy and cl up over 1f out: rdn and edgd rt ent fnl f: sn led: styd on wl* **4/1**[3]

4436 **2** 1 ¾ **Harbour Lightning**[17] 4679 2-9-0 65........ PJMcDonald 4 63
(Ann Duffield) *trckd ldrs: hdwy over 1f out: rdn and ev ch whn n.m.r jst ins fnl f: sn drvn and kpt on* **8/1**

02 **3** nk **Rag Tatter**[13] 4805 2-9-5 0........ KevinStott 3 67
(Kevin Ryan) *led: rdn wl over 1f out: drvn ent fnl f: sn hdd: kpt on towards fin* **2/1**[1]

4 ¾ **Celestation** 2-9-0 0........ JoeFanning 1 59+
(Mark Johnston) *trckd ldrs: hdwy and cl up over 1f out: sn rdn and ev ch: drvn and kpt on fnl f* **8/1**

40 **5** ½ **Western Presence**[15] 4725 2-9-5 0........ TonyHamilton 2 62
(Richard Fahey) *chsd ldrs: rdn along wl over 1f out: sn drvn and kpt on same pce* **25/1**

23 **6** nse **Mama Africa (IRE)**[19] 4601 2-9-0 0........ GrahamGibbons 8 57
(David Barron) *wnt lft s: sn swtchd rt to inner rail: in rr: hdwy on inner wl over 1f out: rdn appr fnl f: no imp ins fnl f* **7/2**[2]

04 **7** 1 **Lou's Diamond**[19] 4601 2-8-9 0........ NathanEvans(5) 6 53
(Michael Easterby) *cl up: rdn along wl over 1f out: wkng whn n.m.r jst ins fnl f* **9/1**

020 **8** ½ **Little Miss Lola**[39] 3881 2-9-0 65........ NeilFarley 5 52
(Alan Swinbank) *in tch: rdn along wl over 1f out: sn one pce* **12/1**

1m 3.89s (0.39) **Going Correction** -0.15s/f (Firm) **8** Ran SP% **119.3**
Speed ratings (Par 94): **90,87,86,85,84 84,83,82**
CSF £37.34 TOTE £5.60: £1.80, £2.20, £1.40; EX 36.10 Trifecta £191.80.
Owner Kristian Strangeway **Bred** Max Morris **Trained** Middleham Moor, N Yorks

FOCUS
The watered ground was officially given as good to firm and after the first the jockeys praised the surface as "beautiful racing ground". Races around the bottom bend were extended by 23yds and a modest maiden opened the card. The winner stepped forward in form again for the drop in trip.

5290 HULL DAILY MAIL/BRITISH STALLION STUDS EBF MAIDEN STKS 7f 100y
2:30 (2:31) (Class 5) 2-Y-O **£3,780** (£1,131; £565; £283; £141) **Stalls** Low

Form RPR

2 **1** **Total Star**[20] 4545 2-9-5 0........ DanielTudhope 2 80
(Luca Cumani) *trckd ldng pair: hdwy to trck ldr over 2f out: chal over 1f out: rdn to ld ins fnl f: sn clr: kpt on strly* **4/9**[1]

2 5 **Sue's Angel (IRE)** 2-9-0 0........ GeorgeChaloner 6 61
(Richard Fahey) *dwlt: green and in rr: hdwy over 2f out: rdn along to chse ldng pair over 1f out: styd on ins fnl f* **7/1**[2]

5 **3** ¾ **Baileys Apprentice**[8] 4975 2-9-0 0........ JoeFanning 1 59
(Mark Johnston) *led: pushed along 2f out: rdn over 1f out: drvn and hdd ins fnl f: kpt on same pce* **8/1**[3]

4 2 ¼ **Dominating (GER)** 2-9-5 0........ PaulMulrennan 7 59+
(Mark Johnston) *chsd ldrs: rn green thrght: rdn and hung bdly lft 2f out: edgd rt over 1f out: kpt on same pce* **10/1**

556 **5** *1* **Mister Moosah (IRE)**[24] 4423 2-9-5 75 PJMcDonald 8 57
(Micky Hammond) *towards rr: rdn along 3f out: sme late hdwy* **14/1**

0 **6** *nk* **Hellomoto**[24] 4423 2-9-5 0 ShaneGray 3 56
(Kevin Ryan) *chsd ldr: pushed along 3f out: sn rdn and wknd* **14/1**

0 **7** *5* **The Batham Boy (IRE)**[48] 3576 2-9-5 0 GrahamGibbons 5 44
(Daniel Mark Loughnane) *green: sn pushed along in rr: rdn 3f out: sn outpcd* **40/1**

1m 33.35s (-0.45) **Going Correction** -0.275s/f (Firm) **7** Ran SP% **117.7**
Speed ratings (Par 94): **91,85,84,81,80 80,74**
CSF £4.66 TOTE £1.30: £1.10, £2.90; EX 5.20 Trifecta £14.40.
Owner Fittocks Stud **Bred** Fittocks Stud **Trained** Newmarket, Suffolk

FOCUS
A lop-sided look to the betting, with the favourite in command some way out. The race took place over 23yds further than advertised.

5291 JOURNAL CLASSIFIED CLAIMING STKS 7f 100y
3:00 (3:00) (Class 6) 3-Y-O+ **£2,587** (£770; £384; £192) **Stalls** Low

Form RPR

0202 **1** **Talent Scout (IRE)**[15] 4729 10-8-7 65 (p) GemmaTutty(5) 4 71
(Karen Tutty) *mde all: rdn over 1f out: drvn and kpt on wl towards fin* **7/2**[2]

5231 **2** *1/2* **Our Boy Jack (IRE)**[14] 4767 7-9-3 75 AdamMcNamara(5) 5 80
(Richard Fahey) *trckd wnr: pushed along wl over 1f out: sn rdn: drvn ins fnl f: kpt on towards fin* **9/2**[3]

0234 **3** *1 1/4* **Kiwi Bay**[7] 5033 11-9-6 74 PaulMulrennan 1 75
(Michael Dods) *t.k.h: trckd ldng pair: effrt 2f out and sn pushed along: rdn over 1f out: drvn and kpt on same pce fnl f* **3/1**[1]

0156 **4** *3/4* **Beautiful Stranger (IRE)**[26] 4335 5-9-10 72 (p) PhillipMakin 3 77
(Keith Dalgleish) *trckd ldrs on inner: hdwy over 2f out: rdn over 1f out: sn drvn and no imp* **11/2**

6014 **5** *1 1/2* **Sunraider (IRE)**[7] 5034 9-8-12 73 GrahamLee 6 62+
(Paul Midgley) *trckd ldrs: pushed along over 4f out: rdn 3f out: n.d* **9/2**[3]

6050 **6** *2 3/4* **Order Of Service**[33] 4089 6-9-3 74 JacobButterfield(3) 2 63
(Shaun Harris) *dwlt: a in rr* **11/2**

1m 32.43s (-1.37) **Going Correction** -0.275s/f (Firm) **6** Ran SP% **114.4**
Speed ratings (Par 101): **96,95,94,93,91 88**
CSF £19.81 TOTE £4.10: £2.20, £2.50; EX 22.60 Trifecta £65.20.
Owner Thoroughbred Homes Ltd **Bred** Johnston King **Trained** Osmotherley, N Yorks

FOCUS
A fair claimer, which was extended by 23yds due to rail movement. The first three were in the first three throughout.

5292 RACING UK H'CAP 1m 1f 207y
3:30 (3:30) (Class 4) (0-85,79) 3-Y-O+ **£6,301** (£1,886; £943; £472; £235) **Stalls** Low

Form RPR

5432 **1** **Age Of Elegance (IRE)**[8] 4977 4-9-3 70 (p) PJMcDonald 1 77
(David Loughnane) *trckd ldrs on inner: hdwy over 2f out: swtchd lft and effrt to chal over 1f out: sn rdn: drvn ins fnl f: styd on wl to ld nr fin* **5/1**[3]

1016 **2** *hd* **Save The Bees**[10] 4919 8-9-3 77 (b) GerO'Neill(7) 5 83
(Declan Carroll) *led: pushed along wl over 2f out: rdn wl over 1f out: hdd and no ex nr fin* **8/1**

0304 **3** *1 1/4* **Purple Rock (IRE)**[19] 4611 4-9-2 74 (t) NathanEvans(5) 3 77
(Michael Easterby) *hld up in rr: hdwy on inner 2f out: rdn over 1f out: drvn and kpt on fnl f* **13/2**

6323 **4** *1 3/4* **Peterhouse (USA)**[50] 3481 4-9-8 75 BenCurtis 7 75
(Jason Ward) *s.i.s and sn pushed along in rr: hdwy on wd outside 3f out: rdn 2f out: drvn: wandered and flashed tail 1f out: kpt on same pce* **7/2**[2]

5502 **5** *1* **Intiwin (IRE)**[17] 4687 4-9-6 78 AdamMcNamara(5) 2 76
(Richard Fahey) *in tch: pushed along over 4f out: rdn over 3f out: drvn 2f out: sn one pce* **5/1**[3]

0120 **6** *nse* **Abareeq**[13] 4797 3-9-2 78 JoeFanning 6 75
(Mark Johnston) *chsd ldng pair: rdn along over 2f out: drvn over 1f out: wknd fnl f* **10/3**[1]

02-0 **7** *2 1/4* **Taraz**[72] 2743 4-9-12 79 DanielTudhope 4 72
(David O'Meara) *trckd ldr: hdwy over 2f out: rdn wl over 1f out: drvn and wknd fnl f* **7/1**

2m 4.58s (-2.42) **Going Correction** -0.275s/f (Firm)
WFA 3 from 4yo+ 9lb **7** Ran SP% **115.6**
Speed ratings (Par 105): **98,97,96,95,94 94,92**
CSF £44.20 TOTE £5.60: £3.00, £4.60; EX 40.70 Trifecta £231.30.
Owner R G Fell **Bred** Ladyswood Stud **Trained** Market Drayton, Shropshire

FOCUS
A fair small-field handicap which looked wide open. The official distance was extended by 23yds. The runner-up got an easy lead but rated to best.

5293 BRITISH LAND H'CAP 1m 1f 207y
4:00 (4:01) (Class 5) (0-70,70) 3-Y-O+ **£3,780** (£1,131; £565; £283; £141) **Stalls** Low

Form RPR

2664 **1** **San Quentin (IRE)**[11] 4892 5-10-0 70 (b) BenCurtis 9 77
(David Loughnane) *wnt lft s and in rr: hdwy on outer wl over 2f out: sn chsng ldrs: chal over 1f out: rdn to ld ent fnl f and sn edgd lft: drvn last 100yds: jst hld on* **11/2**[3]

0454 **2** *shd* **Judicious**[23] 4456 9-8-12 54 (p) DavidAllan 2 61+
(Geoffrey Harker) *hld up in rr: hdwy on outer 2f out: chsd ldrs over 1f out: swtchd rt and rdn jst ins fnl f: sn rdn and swtchd rt: drvn and kpt on wl: jst failed* **7/2**[1]

0020 **3** *2 1/2* **Correggio**[11] 4892 6-10-0 70 PJMcDonald 6 72+
(Micky Hammond) *hld up: hdwy on inner over 2f out: rdn to chse ldrs over 1f out: styng on whn n.m.r and hmpd wl ins fnl f: styd on to take 3rd on line* **8/1**

4653 **4** *nse* **Templier (IRE)**[12] 4833 3-8-13 64 (b) JoeFanning 5 65
(Mark Johnston) *led: pushed along 2f out: rdn over 1f out: hdd ent fnl f: sn drvn and kpt on same pce* **6/1**

5514 **5** *3* **San Cassiano (IRE)**[15] 4730 9-9-8 64 (b) JamesSullivan 1 59
(Ruth Carr) *trckd ldr: effrt and cl up over 2f out: rdn wl over 1f out: drvn and wknd appr fnl f* **11/2**[3]

6164 **6** *1 1/2* **King Of The Celts (IRE)**[23] 4455 8-9-10 69 RachelRichardson(3) 8 61
(Tim Easterby) *trckd ldrs: hdwy over 2f out: rdn over 1f out: sn drvn and no imp* **5/1**[2]

1515 **7** *1 1/2* **Hydrant**[39] 3901 10-9-2 65 BenRobinson(7) 7 54
(Richard Guest) *trckd ldng pair: pushed along wl over 2f out: rdn wl over 1f out: sn wknd* **11/1**

6000 **8** *3 1/4* **Mariners Moon (IRE)**[22] 4498 5-8-10 52 (v[1]) JackGarritty 3 34
(Patrick Holmes) *chsd ldrs: rdn along over 2f out: sn wknd* **14/1**

2m 3.44s (-3.56) **Going Correction** -0.275s/f (Firm)
WFA 3 from 5yo+ 9lb **8** Ran SP% **110.1**
Speed ratings (Par 103): **103,102,100,100,98 97,96,93**
CSF £23.10 CT £131.20 TOTE £4.80: £2.00, £2.10, £1.50; EX 27.80 Trifecta £168.90.
Owner Stephen Louch **Bred** London Thoroughbred Services Ltd **Trained** Market Drayton, Shropshire
■ Morocco was withdrawn. Price at time of withdrawal 10/1. Rule 4 applies to all bets - deduct 5p in the pound.

FOCUS
Not many could be confidently ruled out of this modest handicap which took place over 23yds further than the official distance. The first three sat in the last three three positions early, and the winner is rated to have run to his best.

5294 BEVERLEY ADVERTISER H'CAP 1m 4f 16y
4:30 (4:30) (Class 5) (0-75,72) 3-Y-O+ **£3,780** (£1,131; £565; £283; £141) **Stalls** Low

Form RPR

-142 **1** **Space Mountain**[9] 4949 3-9-3 72 JoeFanning 2 79
(Mark Johnston) *trckd ldr: led 7f out: rdn and qcknd 2f out: drvn ins fnl f: kpt on strly* **5/6**[1]

-320 **2** *1* **Dry Your Eyes (IRE)**[74] 2678 5-9-10 68 DanielTudhope 5 73
(David O'Meara) *hld up in rr: hdwy 5f out: trckd ldrs 3f out: chsd wnr over 1f out: sn rdn and ch ins fnl f: drvn and kpt on same pce towards fin* **13/2**[2]

0634 **3** *1/2* **Jan De Heem**[14] 4768 6-9-0 58 (p) JamesSullivan 3 62
(Tina Jackson) *trckd ldng pair on inner: shuffled bk towards rr over 4f out: hdwy 2f out: swtchd rt to inner over 1f out: sn drvn and kpt on wl towards fin* **8/1**

1334 **4** *1 1/4* **Ghostly Arc (IRE)**[34] 4038 4-9-4 62 BarryMcHugh 6 64
(Noel Wilson) *set stdy pce: hdd 7f out: trckd ldng pair: effrt on inner and n.m.r wl over 1f out: swtchd lft and rdn to chse wnr ent fnl f: sn drvn and kpt on same pce* **13/2**[2]

2113 **5** *2 1/4* **Saint Thomas (IRE)**[17] 4686 9-9-1 59 GrahamGibbons 4 58
(John Mackie) *trckd ldng pair: hdwy to trck ldr 1/2-way: cl up 2f out: sn rdn and wknd over 1f out* **7/1**[3]

6230 **6** *1/2* **Taurian**[33] 4082 5-9-4 65 GeorgeDowning(3) 1 63
(Ian Williams) *hld up in rr: effrt and hdwy over 2f out: rdn wl over 1f out: sn drvn and n.d* **8/1**

2m 44.36s (4.56) **Going Correction** -0.275s/f (Firm)
WFA 3 from 4yo+ 11lb **6** Ran SP% **115.9**
Speed ratings (Par 103): **73,72,72,71,69 69**
CSF £7.32 TOTE £1.60: £1.10, £3.00; EX 9.60 Trifecta £32.30.
Owner J M Brown **Bred** Qatar Bloodstock Ltd **Trained** Middleham Moor, N Yorks

FOCUS
The official distance was extended by 23yds. Mark Johnston had won three of the last four renewals of this race, two with 3yos, and the sole candidate from that trainer/age group was backed as if defeat was out of the question. He found plenty for pressure to beat a couple of rivals that appeared to run to form.

5295 LADIES DAY H'CAP (DIV I) 5f
5:00 (5:00) (Class 5) (0-75,75) 3-Y-O+ **£5,040** (£1,508; £754; £377; £188) **Stalls** Low

Form RPR

0000 **1** **Bosham**[21] 4514 6-9-3 73 (bt) NathanEvans(5) 4 81
(Michael Easterby) *qckly away and mde all: rdn over 1f out: kpt on strly* **12/1**

4345 **2** *nk* **Geno (IRE)**[19] 4612 3-9-6 74 (p) KevinStott 6 80
(Kevin Ryan) *chsd wnr on inner: rdn along wl over 1f out: drvn and kpt on wl fnl f* **4/1**[2]

0502 **3** *hd* **First Bombardment**[6] 5070 3-9-7 75 DanielTudhope 8 80
(David O'Meara) *prom: hdwy to chse wnr 2f out: rdn over 1f out: drvn and kpt on fnl f* **11/2**

6602 **4** *3/4* **Salvatore Fury (IRE)**[6] 5060 6-8-11 62 (p) JoeFanning 3 66+
(Keith Dalgleish) *hld up towards rr: hdwy 2f out: swtchd lft and rdn to chse ldrs over 1f out: drvn ins fnl f: no imp towards fin* **7/2**[1]

0435 **5** *1* **Fyrecracker (IRE)**[12] 4848 5-9-6 71 TomEaves 1 71
(Grant Tuer) *chsd ldrs on inner: rdn along wl over 1f out: kpt on same pce fnl f* **9/2**[3]

0355 **6** *3 1/2* **Noodles Blue Boy**[15] 4726 10-9-1 66 (p) PJMcDonald 2 53
(Ollie Pears) *chsd ldrs: rdn along wl over 1f out: drvn appr fnl f: sn wknd* **8/1**

60 **7** *nk* **Savannah Beau**[24] 4428 4-9-9 74 DavidNolan 10 60
(Marjorie Fife) *dwlt and wnt lft s: in rr and sn swtchd rt to inner rail: sme hdwy 2f out: sn rdn and n.d* **8/1**

460 **8** *1/2* **Secret Millionaire (IRE)**[9] 4931 9-8-5 61 (p) CharlieBennett(5) 5 45
(Shaun Harris) *dwlt: a in rr* **25/1**

2120 **9** *1/2* **Oriental Splendour (IRE)**[15] 4726 4-9-8 73 JamesSullivan 9 56
(Ruth Carr) *a in rr* **12/1**

026- **10** *8* **Lilvanita (IRE)**[384] 4558 3-9-0 68 BenCurtis 7 21
(Brian Ellison) *chsd ldrs on outer: rdn along over 2f out: sn wknd* **33/1**

1m 2.37s (-1.13) **Going Correction** -0.15s/f (Firm)
WFA 3 from 4yo+ 3lb **10** Ran SP% **120.2**
Speed ratings (Par 103): **103,102,102,101,99 93,93,92,91,78**
CSF £61.49 CT £303.98 TOTE £12.50: £3.90, £1.70, £2.00; EX 72.30 Trifecta £442.60.
Owner Peter Easterby **Bred** Rabbah Bloodstock Limited **Trained** Sheriff Hutton, N Yorks

FOCUS
A modest sprint handicap, which looked wide open on paper. However, not much got into it, with the first three occupying those positions throughout. It was run faster than the second division thanks to the winner, who recorded a turf personal best.

5296 LADIES DAY H'CAP (DIV II) 5f
5:35 (5:36) (Class 5) (0-75,75) 3-Y-O+ **£5,040** (£1,508; £754; £377; £188) **Stalls** Low

Form RPR

0200 **1** **Mappin Time (IRE)**[11] 4896 8-9-8 73 (b) DavidAllan 2 81
(Tim Easterby) *in rr: gd hdwy 1 1/2f out: rdn ent fnl f: styd on strly to ld last 100yds* **9/2**[3]

05-0 **2** *3/4* **I'll Be Good**[33] 4100 7-9-9 74 BenCurtis 6 79
(Brian Ellison) *wnt lft s: sn slt ld: hung lft to stands' rail 1/2-way: rdn over 1f out: drvn ins fnl f: hdd and kpt on same pce last 100yds* **7/1**

2020 **3** *1 1/2* **Fujin**[116] 1489 5-8-11 67 CharlieBennett(5) 5 67
(Shaun Harris) *chsd ldrs: rdn and ev ch over 1f out: sn drvn and hung rt: kpt on same pce fnl f* **14/1**

0026 **4** *1 1/2* **Flicka's Boy**[7] 5032 4-9-7 72 (t) BarryMcHugh 4 67
(Tony Coyle) *towards rr: hdwy wl over 1f out: rdn to chse ldrs over 1f out: cl up whn n.m.r and hmpd ent fnl f: sn swtchd rt: drvn and styd on wl towards fin* **10/1**

4300 **5** *3/4* **One Boy (IRE)**[24] 4428 5-9-1 71 (b[1]) AdamMcNamara(5) 8 66
(Richard Fahey) *sltly hmpd s and towards rr: hdwy wl over 1f out: sn rdn and ev ch ent fnl f: sn drvn and kpt on* **6/1**

1221 **6** *1 3/4* **Bond Bombshell**[15] 4726 3-8-12 71 JoshDoyle(5) 1 56
(David O'Meara) *cl up on inner: rdn over 1f out and ev ch tl drvn and wknd ins fnl f* **3/1**[1]

504 **7** *2* **Krystallite**[30] 4198 3-9-7 **75** DaleSwift 3 52
(Scott Dixon) *prom: rdn along over 1f out: grad wknd* **10/1**

0040 **8** *4* **Whozthecat (IRE)**[6] 5060 9-8-13 **64** (v) DanielTudhope 9 28
(Declan Carroll) *sltly hmpd s: chsd ldrs on outer: rdn wl over 1f out: sn wknd* **4/1**[2]

566 **9** *43* **Summer Isles**[12] 4834 6-8-11 **62** PaulMulrennan 7
(Paul Midgley) *sddle slipped and bolted 6f bef s: chsd ldrs to 1/2-way: sn lost pl and bhd* **16/1**

1m 2.85s (-0.65) **Going Correction** -0.15s/f (Firm)
WFA 3 from 4yo+ 3lb **9** Ran SP% **120.7**
Speed ratings (Par 103): **99,97,95,93,91 89,85,79,10**
CSF £37.77 CT £418.91 TOTE £4.10: £1.10, £2.80, £5.90; EX 38.20 Trifecta £697.80.
Owner P Baillie **Bred** J Jamgotchian **Trained** Great Habton, N Yorks
■ Stewards' Enquiry : Charlie Bennett caution: careless riding

FOCUS
The second division was half a second slower than the first division, but it looked pretty competitive for the grade. The winner came from off the pace, while the runner-up made a solid debut for Brian Ellison.
T/Plt: £47.70 to a £1 stake. Pool of £64640.84 - 988.16 winning tickets. T/Qpdt: £25.20 to a £1 stake. Pool of £4100.41 - 120.40 winning tickets. **Joe Rowntree**

5021 KEMPTON (A.W) (R-H)
Wednesday, August 10

OFFICIAL GOING: Polytrack: standard to slow
Wind: Almost nil Weather: Fine

5297 BOOK NOW FOR LADIES DAY 03.09.16 NURSERY H'CAP 7f (P)
6:10 (6:10) (Class 6) (0-60,62) 2-Y-O **£2,264** (£673; £336; £168) **Stalls** Low

Form RPR

5404 **1** **Daffodil Mulligan**[11] 4879 2-8-8 **50** [1] JosephineGordon[(3)] 4 57
(J S Moore) *mde all: kpt on u.p fnl 2f: jst hld on* **25/1**

0351 **2** *nk* **Jumping Jack (IRE)**[9] 4937 2-9-9 **62** 6ex ShaneKelly 6 68+
(Richard Hughes) *stdd s: hld up in 5th: hdwy 2f out: clsd on wnr fnl f: jst failed* **2/1**[1]

040 **3** *5* **Wakened (IRE)**[35] 4011 2-9-6 **59** RichardKingscote 3 52
(Tom Dascombe) *in tch: rdn over 2f out: one pce* **10/3**[3]

060 **4** *shd* **Booshbash (IRE)**[14] 4762 2-8-13 **59** HarryBurns[(7)] 1 52
(Ed Dunlop) *hld up in rr: effrt 2f out: nvr able to chal* **9/4**[2]

0434 **5** *nk* **Elements Legacy**[15] 4738 2-9-2 **60** (v) JordanVaughan[(5)] 2 51
(K R Burke) *chsd ldrs tl no ex over 1f out* **7/1**

056 **6** *2 1/4* **Hi There Silver (IRE)**[14] 4775 2-9-7 **60** LiamKeniry 5 45
(Michael Madgwick) *pressed wnr: rdn over 2f out: wknd over 1f out* **12/1**

1m 27.97s (1.97) **Going Correction** +0.05s/f (Slow) **6** Ran SP% **111.2**
Speed ratings (Par 92): **90,89,83,83,83 80**
CSF £73.81 TOTE £20.30: £7.10, £1.40; EX 62.10 Trifecta £182.20.
Owner Kieron Badger & J S Moore **Bred** Kassala Limited **Trained** Upper Lambourn, Berks
■ Stewards' Enquiry : Harry Burns seven-day ban: failed to take all reasonable and permissable measures to obtain best possible placing (Aug 24-30)

FOCUS
The going was standard to slow. They went a steady pace in this ordinary nursery and there was a surprise result as the outsider made all, kicking at the right time. The runner-up made a nice step forward as well.

5298 BRITISH STALLION STUDS EBF MAIDEN FILLIES' STKS (PLUS 10 RACE) 7f (P)
6:40 (6:41) (Class 5) 2-Y-O **£3,234** (£962; £481; £240) **Stalls** Low

Form RPR

2 **1** **Soldier's Girl (IRE)**[19] 4579 2-9-0 0 PatDobbs 2 82+
(Richard Hannon) *mde all: rdn 2f out: styd on wl* **4/5**[1]

53 **2** *1 1/4* **Dubara**[32] 4147 2-9-0 0 AndreaAtzeni 5 78
(Luca Cumani) *prom: chsd wnr fnl 2f: kpt on: a hld* **11/4**[2]

3 *5* **Brogan** 2-9-0 0 RichardKingscote 1 64+
(Tom Dascombe) *t.k.h: sn stdd in 5th: rdn and one pce fnl 2f* **20/1**

4 **4** *nk* **Midnight Vixen**[26] 4357 2-9-0 0 JimCrowley 7 63
(Sir Michael Stoute) *prom: chsd wnr after 2f tl 2f out: sn outpcd* **7/1**[3]

0 **5** *3/4* **Lady Kaviar (IRE)**[62] 3074 2-9-0 0 TomQueally 8 61
(George Margarson) *bhd tl r.o fnl f: nrest at fin* **40/1**

6 *1/2* **Subatomic** 2-9-0 0 OisinMurphy 3 60+
(Ralph Beckett) *dwlt: hld up towards rr: shkn up over 2f out: nvr rchd ldrs* **9/1**

7 *3 1/4* **Let's Sway** 2-8-11 0 JosephineGordon[(3)] 9 51
(Martyn Meade) *dwlt: a in rr* **33/1**

8 *shd* **Prairie Light** 2-9-0 0 DavidProbert 4 51
(Sylvester Kirk) *plld hrd: in tch tl wknd 2f out* **20/1**

0 **9** *1/2* **Pemberley House (IRE)**[47] 3613 2-9-0 0 ShaneKelly 6 50
(Paul D'Arcy) *prom tl wknd 2f out* **50/1**

1m 26.32s (0.32) **Going Correction** +0.05s/f (Slow) **9** Ran SP% **121.6**
Speed ratings (Par 91): **100,98,92,92,91 91,87,87,86**
CSF £3.12 TOTE £1.80: £1.10, £1.10, £4.70; EX 4.70 Trifecta £39.00.
Owner Saeed Manana **Bred** Soc Finanza Locale Consulting Srl **Trained** East Everleigh, Wilts

FOCUS
The two leading form contenders pulled clear in this maiden. The winner had the run of things in front to build on the promise of her debut, while the runner-up also improved.

5299 32RED CASINO NURSERY H'CAP 6f (P)
7:10 (7:10) (Class 4) (0-85,85) 2-Y-O **£3,946** (£1,174; £586; £293) **Stalls** Low

Form RPR

2251 **1** **Northern Thunder (IRE)**[18] 4629 2-8-13 **77** PatDobbs 1 80
(Richard Hannon) *mde all: rdn 2f out: edgd lft fnl f: hld on wl* **3/1**[3]

1060 **2** *nk* **Monks Stand (USA)**[12] 4825 2-9-7 **85** (v) JimCrowley 3 87
(Jeremy Noseda) *hld up: hdwy over 1f out: drvn to chal ins fnl f: carried lft: r.o* **6/5**[1]

51 **3** *3* **Morning Suit (USA)**[63] 3032 2-9-0 **78** JamesDoyle 4 73
(Mark Johnston) *pressed ldrs: n.m.r ent fnl f: one pce* **2/1**[2]

055 **4** *2 3/4* **Xenon**[30] 4195 2-8-0 **64** oh1 RyanPowell 2 49
(Sir Mark Prescott Bt) *chsd wnr tl outpcd 2f out* **10/1**

1m 14.3s (1.20) **Going Correction** +0.05s/f (Slow) **4** Ran SP% **112.9**
Speed ratings (Par 96): **94,93,89,85**
CSF £7.40 TOTE £4.20; EX 6.80 Trifecta £9.50.
Owner Ahmad Abdulla Al Shaikh **Bred** Peter & Hugh McCutcheon **Trained** East Everleigh, Wilts
■ Stewards' Enquiry : Pat Dobbs caution: careless riding

FOCUS
They went a very steady pace in this small-field nursery and there was an all-the-way winner, who held on from a well-backed runner-up.

5300 32RED/BREEDERS BACKING RACING EBF MAIDEN FILLIES' STKS 7f (P)
7:40 (7:41) (Class 5) 3-Y-O+ **£4,204** (£1,251; £625; £312) **Stalls** Low

Form RPR

-320 **1** **Aristocratic**[33] 4105 3-9-0 79 AndreaAtzeni 1 79+
(Sir Michael Stoute) *led tl 4f out: led 2f out tl narrowly hdd ins fnl f: rallied to ld fnl 50yds: gamely* **11/10**[1]

0-6 **2** *nk* **Sunset Dream (IRE)**[77] 2578 3-9-0 0 PatDobbs 4 78
(Richard Hannon) *pressed ldr: led 4f out tl 2f out: slt ld ins fnl f: hdd fnl 50yds: kpt on wl* **12/1**[3]

3 *3* **Right Rebel** 4-9-3 0 EoinWalsh[(3)] 5 72
(Alan Bailey) *prom on inner: rdn over 2f out: one pce appr fnl f* **33/1**

2 **4** *2 3/4* **Showreel**[81] 2470 3-9-0 0 JimCrowley 6 63
(Amanda Perrett) *prom tl no ex over 1f out* **7/4**[2]

5 *1* **Ducissa** 3-9-0 0 TomQueally 3 60+
(Daniel Kubler) *mid-div: rdn over 2f out: styd on same pce* **25/1**

44 **6** *3 1/4* **Pearly Queen**[9] 4939 3-9-0 0 RobertWinston 7 51
(Dean Ivory) *prom tl wknd 2f out* **12/1**[3]

7 *1* **Serangoon** 3-9-0 0 OisinMurphy 2 48
(Michael Appleby) *dwlt: nvr nr ldrs* **40/1**

40- **8** *2* **Rouge Noir**[252] 8073 3-9-0 0 MartinHarley 10 43
(Jeremy Noseda) *a in rr* **25/1**

0- **9** *1/2* **Lady Perignon**[377] 4790 3-9-0 0 DavidProbert 9 42
(Andrew Balding) *sn in midfield: wknd 3f out* **14/1**

10 *16* **Autumn Chorus** 3-9-0 0 DannyBrock 8
(John Bridger) *dwlt: sn in midfield: wknd over 2f out* **100/1**

1m 25.9s (-0.10) **Going Correction** +0.05s/f (Slow)
WFA 3 from 4yo 6lb **10** Ran SP% **120.1**
Speed ratings (Par 100): **102,101,98,95,93 90,89,86,86,67**
CSF £16.11 TOTE £1.90: £1.02, £4.00, £13.20; EX 20.70 Trifecta £513.30.
Owner Cheveley Park Stud **Bred** Cheveley Park Stud Ltd **Trained** Newmarket, Suffolk

FOCUS
The well-backed favourite battled well under a positive ride in this maiden and pulled clear with the runner-up. The time was modest.

5301 32RED.COM H'CAP 7f (P)
8:10 (8:10) (Class 4) (0-85,83) 3-Y-O+ **£4,690** (£1,395; £697; £348) **Stalls** Low

Form RPR

0242 **1** **Finelcity (GER)**[7] 5027 3-8-10 **73** (v[1]) JimCrowley 9 79
(Harry Dunlop) *chsd ldr: led 1f out: drvn out* **5/2**[1]

3-56 **2** *1 1/4* **Song Of Norway**[21] 4519 5-9-6 **77** TedDurcan 5 82+
(Chris Wall) *bmpd and stdd s: patiently rdn towards rr: hdwy over 1f out: fin wl* **8/1**

2-55 **3** *3/4* **Poet's Song (IRE)**[20] 4557 3-8-10 **73** DannyBrock 1 74
(Marcus Tregoning) *hmpd s: sn in midfield: nt clr run 2f out: hdwy and hrd rdn over 1f out: styd on* **10/1**

1200 **4** *1/2* **Frenchman (FR)**[32] 4132 3-8-13 **76** MichaelJMMurphy 4 76
(Charles Hills) *plld hrd: wnt lft s: sn led: hdd 1f out: one pce* **4/1**[3]

0630 **5** *nk* **Personal Touch**[36] 3980 7-9-8 **82** (p) TimClark[(3)] 3 83
(Michael Appleby) *plld hrd: prom: kpt on u.p fnl 2f* **12/1**

-000 **6** *1/2* **Bold**[48] 3571 4-9-3 **74** (t) OisinMurphy 7 73
(Stuart Williams) *in tch: effrt over 2f out: one pce appr fnl f* **16/1**

4015 **7** *1* **Mezmaar**[47] 3622 7-9-9 **80** PatCosgrave 6 77
(Kevin Morgan) *t.k.h towards rr: shkn up 2f out: styng on but hld whn nt clr run fnl 50yds* **7/2**[2]

2000 **8** *3 3/4* **Quintus Cerialis (IRE)**[68] 2846 4-9-3 **74** DarryllHolland 2 61
(Karen George) *wnt rt s: a in rr* **28/1**

0-40 **9** *2 1/4* **Take A Note**[14] 4758 7-9-7 **83** (v) HectorCrouch[(5)] 10 64
(Patrick Chamings) *in tch on outer: drvn along over 2f out: sn wknd* **12/1**

1m 25.92s (-0.08) **Going Correction** +0.05s/f (Slow)
WFA 3 from 4yo+ 6lb **9** Ran SP% **115.7**
Speed ratings (Par 105): **102,100,99,99,98 98,97,92,90**
CSF £23.41 CT £172.69 TOTE £3.60: £1.60, £2.60, £4.00; EX 27.70 Trifecta £164.70.
Owner The Blue Bar Partnership **Bred** Gestut Hofgut Heymann **Trained** Lambourn, Berks

FOCUS
The pace was not very strong but the favourite delivered, in a first-time visor, with authority in this fair handicap. The runner-up made late gains and has a bit more to offer.

5302 32RED ON THE APP STORE H'CAP (LONDON MILE SERIES QUALIFIER) 1m (P)
8:40 (8:43) (Class 5) (0-70,70) 3-Y-O **£2,911** (£866; £432; £216) **Stalls** Low

Form RPR

4104 **1** **Ubla (IRE)**[6] 5086 3-8-10 **66** [1] DavidEgan[(7)] 12 73
(Gay Kelleway) *hld up in rr: plld to centre and effrt over 1f out: str run to ld fnl 75yds: in control whn edgd rt nr fin* **22/1**

2005 **2** *1 1/2* **Cryptic (IRE)**[19] 4607 3-9-7 **70** AndreaAtzeni 10 73
(Luca Cumani) *hld up towards rr: hdwy and nt clr run over 1f out: swtchd lft: r.o to take 2nd nr fin* **9/2**[2]

1600 **3** *1/2* **Papou Tony**[35] 4010 3-9-7 **70** LiamKeniry 7 72
(George Baker) *towards rr: gd hdwy over 1f out: r.o* **14/1**

-553 **4** *hd* **Aberlady (USA)**[47] 3599 3-9-4 **67** (b) RichardKingscote 3 69
(Sir Michael Stoute) *in tch: rdn to ld 1f out: hdd and one pce fnl 75yds* **4/1**[1]

-040 **5** *2 1/4* **Mercifilly (FR)**[33] 4087 3-9-2 **65** [1] ThomasBrown 2 61
(Ed Walker) *s.i.s and rdn along in rr: hdwy on inner over 1f out: styd on* **14/1**

4002 **6** *1* **Sunscape (IRE)**[8] 4986 3-9-7 **70** OisinMurphy 11 64+
(Hughie Morrison) *prom on outer: led briefly over 1f out: no ex* **10/1**

6546 **7** *1* **Miss Phillyjinks (IRE)**[35] 4009 3-9-0 **63** [1] ShaneKelly 1 55
(Paul D'Arcy) *chsd ldrs tl wknd over 1f out* **14/1**

5555 **8** *1 1/2* **Ruby Wednesday**[48] 3558 3-9-7 **70** KierenFox 6 58
(John Best) *mid-div: effrt whn nt clr run wl over 1f out: sn btn* **7/1**

3331 **9** *1 1/4* **Bonhomie**[16] 4718 3-9-5 **68** MartinHarley 8 53
(Michael Bell) *trckd ldr: led 2f out tl wknd over 1f out* **6/1**[3]

0050 **10** *8* **Premier Currency (IRE)**[28] 4269 3-9-2 **65** (b[1]) RobertWinston 4 32
(Mike Murphy) *t.k.h: led tl wknd 2f out* **6/1**[3]

3-05 **11** *5* **Cause And Effect (IRE)**[43] 3744 3-9-7 **70** JimCrowley 9 26
(Ralph Beckett) *t.k.h: in tch: rdn 3f out: sn wknd* **10/1**

1m 38.94s (-0.86) **Going Correction** +0.05s/f (Slow) **11** Ran SP% **121.8**
Speed ratings (Par 100): **106,104,104,103,101 100,99,98,96,88 83**
CSF £122.69 CT £1505.65 TOTE £23.00: £4.70, £2.40, £3.70; EX 108.90 Trifecta £3817.10.
Owner Peter Petrovic **Bred** Tenuta Genzianella **Trained** Exning, Suffolk
■ Pepper was withdrawn. Price at time of withdrawal 50/1. Rule 4 does not apply

FOCUS
The pace was decent and this handicap and it was a race of changing fortunes. The leading few were in rear early, and the third is rated to have run to a small personal best.

5303 £10 FREE BET AT 32REDSPORT.COM H'CAP 1m 4f (P)
9:10 (9:12) (Class 6) (0-60,60) 3-Y-O+ **£2,264** (£673; £336; £168) **Stalls** Centre

Form RPR

0250 **1** **Gabster (IRE)**[28] 4267 3-9-2 **59** PatDobbs 3 66
(Amanda Perrett) *led for 1f: a.p: rdn to ld fnl 100yds* **7/1**

20-2 **2** *1 1/4* **Tingo In The Tale (IRE)**[37] 949 7-9-11 **57** JimCrowley 6 62
(David Arbuthnot) *mid-div: hdwy 2f out: styd on wl to take 2nd on line* **5/1**[2]

0/01 **3** *shd* **Mr Lando**[16] 4716 7-9-11 **57** (b) StevieDonohoe 12 62
(Johnny Farrelly) *led after 1f tl fnl 100yds: kpt on u.p: lost 2nd on line* **9/2**[1]

0-03 **4** *1/2* **Gracesome (IRE)**[16] 4716 5-9-4 **50** DavidProbert 13 54
(Michael Blanshard) *chsd ldrs: lost pl 1/2-way: drvn along over 2f out: gd late hdwy* **11/1**

0625 **5** *1 1/2* **Monday Club**[21] 4500 3-8-11 **57** (b[1]) JosephineGordon[(3)] 4 59
(Dominic Ffrench Davis) *chsd ldrs: one pce fnl 2f* **6/1**[3]

0020 **6** *1/2* **Ali Bin Nayef**[10] 1500 4-9-6 **52** RobertHavlin 8 53
(Michael Wigham) *towards rr tl styd on fnl 2f* **14/1**

6404 **7** *1/2* **Deluxe**[7] 5021 4-10-0 **60** JFEgan 9 60
(Pat Phelan) *towards rr: hdwy 2f out: no imp fnl f* **9/1**

4/55 **8** *3/4* **Barnacle**[30] 4197 7-9-0 **46** oh1 (v) TomQueally 1 45
(Emma Owen) *towards rr: hrd rdn 2f out: nvr rchd ldrs* **25/1**

0-05 **9** *1* **Enchanted Moment**[39] 3903 4-10-0 **60** (p) TedDurcan 2 57
(Chris Wall) *in tch: n.m.r after 2f: rdn to chse ldrs 2f out: no ex appr fnl f* **8/1**

-056 **10** *2 1/2* **Druot**[16] 4711 4-9-13 **59** [1] ShaneKelly 7 52
(Richard Hughes) *s.i.s: bhd: mod hdwy over 1f out: sn wknd* **8/1**

3000 **11** *4 1/2* **The Detainee**[13] 4794 3-9-2 **59** (b[1]) AdamBeschizza 10 45
(Jeremy Gask) *a in rr* **16/1**

-040 **12** *15* **Street Art (IRE)**[71] 2781 4-9-5 **51** RobertWinston 5 13
(Mike Murphy) *prom tl wknd 2f out* **16/1**

650 **13** *14* **Last Summer**[13] 4792 5-9-9 **60** CiaranMckee[(5)] 11
(Grace Harris) *s.s: sn rdn into midfield: wknd 3f out: eased whn no ch over 2f out* **22/1**

2m 36.04s (1.54) **Going Correction** +0.05s/f (Slow)
WFA 3 from 4yo+ 11lb **13** Ran SP% **128.8**
Speed ratings (Par 101): **96,95,95,94,93 93,93,92,91,90 87,77,67**
CSF £45.37 CT £184.27 TOTE £7.70: £2.20, £2.40, £2.30; EX 45.30 Trifecta £327.20.
Owner Cordage Racing Ltd **Bred** T Whitehead **Trained** Pulborough, W Sussex

FOCUS
They went a steady gallop and not many got involved from off the pace in this minor handicap, with the winner always being well placed. The time was 7.04 seconds slower than standard.
T/Plt: £233.60 to a £1 stake. Pool of £66333.25 - 207.23 winning tickets. T/Qpdt: £62.30 to a £1 stake. Pool of £5695.03 - 67.61 winning tickets. **Lee McKenzie**

4988 SALISBURY (R-H)
Wednesday, August 10

OFFICIAL GOING: Good to firm (good in places; 8.6)
Wind: light, across Weather: bright spells and light cloud

5304 BRITISH STALLION STUDS EBF MOLSON COORS MAIDEN STKS (PLUS 10 RACE) 6f
2:20 (2:20) (Class 4) 2-Y-O **£4,528** (£1,347; £673; £336) **Stalls** Low

Form RPR

1 **Akhlaaq** 2-9-5 0 PaulHanagan 5 87+
(Owen Burrows) *t.k.h: hld up wl in tch: effrt to chse clr ldng pair over 1f out: rn green u.p and wandered jst ins fnl f: qcknd smartly under hands and heels riding 100yds out: r.o wl to ld cl home* **11/4**[2]

05 **2** *nk* **Sfumato**[20] 4552 2-9-5 0 [1] GeorgeBaker 2 81
(Roger Charlton) *led: pushed along over 1f out: rdn ins fnl f and kpt on: hdd cl home* **7/2**[3]

3 **3** *1/2* **Beck And Call**[26] 4350 2-9-0 0 FergusSweeney 6 74
(Henry Candy) *chsd ldr: rdn and ev ch over 1f out: drvn and kpt on same pce ins fnl f* **2/1**[1]

4 *3 3/4* **Dimitre** 2-9-5 0 MartinHarley 8 67+
(Henry Candy) *hld up in tch: effrt and rn green over 1f out: hdwy 1f out and styd on wl ins fnl f: gng on wl fin and wnt 4th last strides* **20/1**

60 **5** *hd* **Inner Circle (IRE)**[8] 4989 2-9-5 0 SeanLevey 1 66
(Richard Hannon) *chsd ldrs: rdn 2f out: 4th and outpcd by ldrs over 1f out: kpt on same pce fnl f: lost 4th last strides* **16/1**

6 *1 1/4* **Belle Diva (IRE)** 2-9-0 0 OisinMurphy 10 57
(Ralph Beckett) *hld up in tch towards rr: pushed along and hdwy over 1f out: kpt on steadily but no threat to ldrs fnl f* **6/1**

0 **7** *nk* **Pastfact**[18] 4659 2-9-5 0 RyanTate 12 61
(Malcolm Saunders) *chsd ldrs: rdn 1/2-way: swtchd lft and drvn over 2f out: 6th and outpcd over 1f out: wl hld and plugged on same pce fnl f* **150/1**

50 **8** *1 1/2* **Altiko Tommy (IRE)**[43] 3742 2-9-5 0 LiamKeniry 4 57
(George Baker) *stdd s: t.k.h: hld up in tch in rr: swtchd rt over 2f out: nudged along and sme hdwy 2f out: no imp over 1f out: nvr trbld ldrs* **66/1**

0 **9** *3/4* **Aventus (IRE)**[11] 4877 2-9-5 0 ShaneKelly 13 54
(Richard Hughes) *stdd and swtchd lft after s: hld up in tch in rr: pushed along 2f out: no imp over 1f out: nvr trbld ldrs* **66/1**

0 **10** *1 1/4* **Raj Balaraaj (GER)**[51] 3463 2-9-5 0 [1] SteveDrowne 9 50
(George Baker) *hld up in tch in rr: rdn 2f out: sn outpcd: wknd over 1f out* **66/1**

0 **11** *shd* **John T Chance (IRE)**[13] 4790 2-9-5 0 JimmyFortune 11 50
(Brian Meehan) *stdd s: t.k.h: hld up in tch in midfield: rdn and lost pl 2f out: wknd over 1f out* **33/1**

0 **12** *nk* **Sweet Pursuit**[23] 4457 2-9-0 0 FrederikTylicki 3 44
(Rod Millman) *in tch in midfield: rdn 2f out: lost pl u.p over 1f out: wknd fnl f* **25/1**

00 **13** *3 3/4* **Hollow Crown**[18] 4659 2-9-0 0 DavidProbert 7 32
(Denis Coakley) *stdd s: hld up in midfield: rdn 2f out: sn struggling and lost pl over 1f out: bhd fnl f* **50/1**

1m 15.12s (0.32) **Going Correction** -0.075s/f (Good) **13** Ran SP% **121.0**
Speed ratings (Par 96): **94,93,92,87,87 86,85,83,82,80 80,80,75**
CSF £12.28 TOTE £3.20: £1.20, £1.70, £1.30; EX 13.20 Trifecta £33.90.
Owner Hamdan Al Maktoum **Bred** Rabbah Bloodstock Limited **Trained** Lambourn, Berks

FOCUS
Race distances as advertised. A fair maiden, run at a steady pace, and it saw quite a taking performance from the winner, who is likely to do considerably better. The third probably posted some small improvement in form.

5305 S H JONES WINES H'CAP 5f
2:50 (2:50) (Class 4) (0-80,79) 3-Y-O+ **£5,175** (£1,540; £769; £384) **Stalls** Low

Form RPR

5031 **1** **Pine Ridge**[21] 4502 3-9-4 **76** AdamKirby 6 82
(Clive Cox) *mde all: rdn over 1f out: hrd pressed and drvn ins fnl f: hld on gamely cl home* **3/1**[1]

1330 **2** *nk* **Ginzan**[27] 4291 8-9-9 **78** JimCrowley 5 84
(Malcolm Saunders) *hld up in tch in midfield: hdwy u.p to chse ldrs over 1f out: pressing ldrs ins fnl f: kpt on wl to go 2nd towards fin: nvr quite getting to wnr* **10/1**

3546 **3** *1/2* **Verne Castle**[21] 4502 3-8-9 **67** DavidProbert 8 70
(Andrew Balding) *t.k.h: chsd ldrs tl wnt 2nd over 3f out: rdn over 1f out: ev ch ins fnl f: styd on same pce and lost 2nd towards fin* **8/1**[2]

-252 **4** *nk* **Jack Nevison**[32] 4155 3-9-3 **75** FergusSweeney 9 77
(Henry Candy) *hld up in midfield: hdwy u.p over 1f out: chsd ldrs ins fnl f: kpt on wl u.p towards fin* **3/1**[1]

5403 **5** *2* **Point Of Woods**[28] 4268 3-9-4 **76** PatDobbs 7 71
(Ralph Beckett) *hld up in tch in midfield: swtchd rt and effrt on inner 2f out: hdwy over 1f out: no imp 1f out: wknd ins fnl f* **9/1**

0004 **6** *2 1/4* **Burning Thread (IRE)**[7] 5032 9-8-12 **74** (b) AdamMcLean[(7)] 4 62
(David Elsworth) *t.k.h: chsd ldr: bmpd rival and lost 2nd over 3f out: styd chsng ldrs tl unable qck u.p over 1f out: wknd ins fnl f* **17/2**[3]

2140 **7** *4* **Shackled N Drawn (USA)**[30] 4198 4-9-10 **79** CharlesBishop 1 52
(Peter Hedger) *taken down early: t.k.h: chsd ldrs: bmpd over 3f out: rdn and no rspnse over 1f out: wknd fnl f* **12/1**

4106 **8** *1/2* **Silverrica (IRE)**[10] 4911 6-9-0 **76** GeorgiaCox[(7)] 10 48
(Malcolm Saunders) *stmbld bdly leaving stalls: a in rr: no hdwy u.p and hung rt over 1f out: bhd ins fnl f* **9/1**

130- **9** *5* **Kashtan**[243] 8180 3-9-2 **74** LukeMorris 2 27
(Harry Dunlop) *a outpcd in rr: rdn 1/2-way: drvn and no hdwy 2f out: lost tch over 1f out* **12/1**

1m 0.49s (-0.51) **Going Correction** -0.075s/f (Good)
WFA 3 from 4yo+ 3lb **9** Ran SP% **116.1**
Speed ratings (Par 105): **101,100,99,99,96 92,86,85,77**
CSF £35.25 CT £219.33 TOTE £3.90: £1.70, £2.30, £2.70; EX 31.30 Trifecta £205.90.
Owner Wood Hall Stud Limited **Bred** Wood Hall Stud **Trained** Lambourn, Berks

FOCUS
A reasonable little sprint, the winner making all in game fashion.

5306 SAM FM PEMBROKE CUP (H'CAP) 1m
3:20 (3:21) (Class 4) (0-85,85) 3-Y-O **£6,469** (£1,925; £962; £481) **Stalls** Low

Form RPR

11 **1** **Takatul (USA)**[15] 4742 3-9-3 **81** PaulHanagan 1 90+
(Charles Hills) *t.k.h: trckd ldng pair: clsd to join ldrs 2f out: rdn to ld over 1f out: hung lft 1f out: stl hanging but in command ins fnl f: r.o wl: comf* **8/11**[1]

015 **2** *1 1/2* **Staunch**[25] 4403 3-9-7 **85** [1] AdamKirby 4 90
(Clive Cox) *chsd ldr: rdn over 2f out: ev ch over 1f out: chsd wnr and kpt on same pce ins fnl f: hld whn sltly impeded and swtchd rt wl ins fnl f* **9/2**[3]

2431 **3** *1 1/2* **Torch**[13] 4806 3-9-3 **81** (p) SeanLevey 2 83
(Richard Hannon) *led: rdn ent fnl 2f out: hdd and unable qck over 1f out: in 3rd and kpt on same pce fnl f* **11/4**[2]

0-04 **4** *9* **Inn The Bull (GER)**[18] 4662 3-8-9 **73** FergusSweeney 3 54
(Alan King) *stdd s: hld up in tch in rr: swtchd lft and effrt over 2f out: no hdwy u.p over 1f out: wknd fnl f* **16/1**

1m 42.5s (-1.00) **Going Correction** -0.075s/f (Good) **4** Ran SP% **108.6**
Speed ratings (Par 102): **102,100,99,90**
CSF £4.38 TOTE £1.60; EX 4.30 Trifecta £4.40.
Owner Hamdan Al Maktoum **Bred** Shadwell Farm LLC **Trained** Lambourn, Berks

FOCUS
Just the four runners but a decent handicap and the winner maintained his unbeaten record. He looks to have more to come. The second is rated to have run to his maiden success.

5307 EBF STALLIONS UPAVON FILLIES' STKS (LISTED RACE) 1m 1f 198y
3:50 (3:51) (Class 1) 3-Y-O+
£23,818 (£9,030; £4,519; £2,251; £1,129; £567) **Stalls** Low

Form RPR

1-05 **1** **Chain Of Daisies**[47] 3608 4-9-2 101 FergusSweeney 6 107
(Henry Candy) *mde all: rdn 2f out: styd on wl u.p and a doing enough fnl f: rdn out* **11/2**[3]

1551 **2** *1* **Sagaciously (IRE)**[14] 4757 4-9-2 102 JamesDoyle 1 105
(Ed Dunlop) *hld up in tch in last trio: rdn and hdwy over 2f out: chsd ldng pair over 1f out: wnt 2nd 100yds out: styd on but nvr getting to wnr* **7/2**[2]

20-3 **3** *1* **Maybelater**[137] 1088 4-9-2 90 RichardKingscote 3 103
(Jonathan Portman) *chsd wnr for 2f: chsd ldrs tl wnt 2nd again over 2f out: sn rdn: styd on same pce u.p fnl 2f: lost 2nd 100yds out* **20/1**

02-1 **4** *2 3/4* **Very Dashing**[26] 4367 3-8-7 86 FrederikTylicki 2 98
(Luca Cumani) *in tch in midfield: lost pl and rdn over 2f out: rallied u.p over 1f out: 4th and no imp fnl f* **7/1**

-021 **5** *4* **Sharja Queen**[32] 4160 3-8-7 102 AndreaAtzeni 4 90
(Roger Varian) *in tch in midfield: effrt over 2f out: chsd ldrs but no imp u.p 2f out: 5th and wl hld 1f out: wknd fnl f* **6/4**[1]

0204 **6** *hd* **Beauly**[19] 4610 3-8-7 98 DavidProbert 8 89
(Charles Hills) *hld up in tch in last trio: rdn over 2f out: no hdwy and sn struggling: wl btn over 1f out* **10/1**

-120 **7** *20* **Tears Of The Sun**[47] 3608 5-9-2 97 AdamKirby 5 49
(Clive Cox) *dwlt: hld up in tch in last trio: rdn over 2f out: sn btn: wl bhd fnl f* **16/1**

5030 **8** *3 1/2* **Australian Queen**[39] 3911 3-8-7 90 OisinMurphy 7 42
(David Elsworth) *chsd ldrs: wnt 2nd 8f out tl lost pl u.p over 2f out: sn wl btn: bhd fnl f: t.o* **16/1**

2m 4.0s (-5.90) **Going Correction** -0.30s/f (Firm) course record
WFA 3 from 4yo+ 9lb **8** Ran SP% **115.7**
Speed ratings (Par 108): **111,110,109,107,104 103,87,85**
CSF £25.42 TOTE £7.00: £1.70, £1.30, £5.20; EX 30.90 Trifecta £281.20.
Owner Girsonfield Ltd **Bred** Girsonfield Ltd **Trained** Kingston Warren, Oxon

FOCUS
Sound form for the level, the winner making all in course record time, returning to her best. The third was a surprise improver.

5308 CHAMPAGNE JOSEPH PERRIER H'CAP — 1m 1f 198y
4:20 (4:20) (Class 5) (0-70,69) 3-Y-O+ **£3,234** (£962; £481; £240) **Stalls** Low

Form RPR

0632 **1** **So Celebre (GER)**[9] 4956 3-9-4 **68** JamesDoyle 1 83
(Ian Williams) *in tch in midfield: effrt to press ldr and wnt clr of field 2f out: led ins fnl f: styd on: rdn out* **2/1**[2]

-662 **2** *1* **Master Gunner (USA)**[6] 5086 3-9-5 **69** (b) TedDurcan 6 82
(Sir Michael Stoute) *racd keenly: led: rdn and clr w wnr over 1f out: hdd and one pce ins fnl f* **5/4**[1]

6526 **3** *7* **Wallangarra**[13] 4794 3-9-1 **65** AdamBeschizza 2 64
(Jeremy Gask) *chsd ldrs: wnt 2nd and rdn over 2f out: 3rd and outpcd 2f out: wl hld but plugged on to hold 3rd after* **14/1**

0235 **4** *1 ¼* **Patent**[7] 5011 3-9-1 **65** SeanLevey 3 61
(Richard Hannon) *hld up in tch in last pair: rdn over 2f out: no ch w ldrs but kpt on to pass btn horses fnl f* **11/2**[3]

0-04 **5** *hd* **Peppard**[18] 4633 3-9-1 **65** JimCrowley 5 60
(Charles Hills) *t.k.h: hld up wl in tch in midfield: effrt and hung rt 2f out: hung rt and wknd over 1f out* **20/1**

604- **6** *2* **Cranwell**[259] 7976 4-9-3 **58** FergusSweeney 4 49
(George Baker) *stdd after s: hld up in rr: effrt over 2f out: no imp and wl btn over 1f out* **33/1**

000- **7** *29* **Avocadeau (IRE)**[239] 8228 5-9-7 **62** (p) OisinMurphy 7
(Stuart Kittow) *chsd wnr tl over 2f out: sn u.p and dropped out: t.o and eased ins fnl f* **20/1**

2m 7.18s (-2.72) **Going Correction** -0.30s/f (Firm)
WFA 3 from 4yo+ 9lb **7** Ran SP% **112.3**
Speed ratings (Par 103): **98,97,91,90,90 88,65**
CSF £4.62 TOTE £2.50: £1.60, £1.10; EX 5.10 Trifecta £23.80.
Owner Miss Jekaterina Melnika **Bred** Gestut Wittekindshof **Trained** Portway, Worcs

FOCUS
The front pair, both well in at the weights, came clear in what was a modest handicap. The pace was a pretty steady one and the winner is rated as stepping forward in form..

5309 LITTLETON STUD RACING EXCELLENCE APPRENTICE H'CAP (WHIPS SHALL BE CARRIED BUT NOT USED) — 6f 212y
4:50 (4:50) (Class 5) (0-70,69) 3-Y-O+ **£3,234** (£962; £481; £240) **Stalls** Centre

Form RPR

2355 **1** **Exoplanet Blue**[48] 3575 4-9-13 **69** GeorgeWood 6 78
(Henry Candy) *mde all: rdn over 1f out: styd on wl fnl f* **4/1**

00-2 **2** *2* **Polymnia**[19] 4587 3-9-5 **67** HollieDoyle 4 69
(Richard Hannon) *wnt rt and bmpd rival s: hmpd and stmbld after 1f: hld up in rr: hdwy 1/2-way: rdn to chse wnr 1f out: one pce fnl f* **7/2**[3]

3341 **3** *1* **Remember Me**[18] 4640 3-9-7 **69** CameronNoble 1 68
(Hughie Morrison) *t.k.h: chsd ldr for 2f: chsd wnr again over 2f out: rdn and unable qck over 1f out: 3rd and one pce fnl f* **10/3**[2]

3203 **4** *½* **Wahaab (IRE)**[2] 5236 5-9-1 **60** (p) NicolaCurrie(3) 2 60
(Richard Hughes) *trckd ldrs: effrt on inner 2f out: styd on same pce fnl f* **9/4**[1]

5550 **5** *4* **Olympic Duel (IRE)**[14] 4764 3-8-8 **56** LuluStanford 5 43
(Peter Hiatt) *hld up in tch: rdn over 2f out: wknd over 1f out* **17/2**

0-00 **6** *5* **Meroula (FR)**[34] 4058 3-8-8 **59** (v[1]) WilliamCox(3) 3 32
(Harry Dunlop) *bmpd s and slowly away: swtchd lft sn after s: steadily rcvrd to chse wnr 5f out tl over 2f out: sn wknd* **20/1**

1m 29.27s (0.67) **Going Correction** -0.075s/f (Good)
WFA 3 from 4yo+ 6lb **6** Ran SP% **111.4**
Speed ratings (Par 103): **93,90,89,89,84 78**
CSF £17.90 TOTE £4.50: £2.30, £2.60; EX 15.50 Trifecta £27.90.
Owner One Too Many Partners **Bred** H J Strecker **Trained** Kingston Warren, Oxon
■ Stewards' Enquiry : William Cox two-day ban

FOCUS
Modest handicap form and yet another all-the-way winner on the card. He is rated as running close to his 3yo peak.
T/Jkpt: £5245.20 to a £1 stake. Pool of £26226.36 - 5.00 winning units. T/Plt: £32.70 to a £1 stake. Pool of £65125.59 - 1452.54 winning tickets. T/Qpdt: £14.60 to a £1 stake. Pool of £3082.44 - 155.48 winning tickets. **Steve Payne**

5310 - 5312a (Foreign Racing) - See Raceform Interactive

4670 GOWRAN PARK (R-H)
Wednesday, August 10
OFFICIAL GOING: Good (good to firm in places)

5313a IRISH STALLION FARMS EUROPEAN BREEDERS FUND HURRY HARRIET STKS (LISTED RACE) (F&M) — 1m 1f 100y
7:00 (7:01) 3-Y-O+
£23,860 (£7,683; £3,639; £1,617; £808; £404)

RPR

1 **Adool (IRE)**[27] 4326 3-9-0 0 PatSmullen 13 94+
(D K Weld, Ire) *sn chsd ldrs in 3rd: pushed along 2f out on outer: pressed ldr in 2nd appr fnl f: led fnl 100yds: kpt on strly in clsng stages* **7/4**[1]

2 *½* **Santa Monica**[24] 4435 3-9-0 97 DeclanMcDonogh 1 93
(Charles O'Brien, Ire) *pressed ldr in 2nd: rdn to ld 2f out: pressed appr fnl f: kpt on wl: hdd fnl 100yds* **9/2**[3]

3 *½* **Assume (IRE)**[30] 4218 4-9-8 99 WayneLordan 6 92
(David Wachman, Ire) *chsd ldrs in 4th: rdn in 5th under 2f out: kpt on wl to press ldr over 1f out in 2nd: dropped to 3rd ins fnl f: kpt on wl* **7/2**[2]

4 *2 ¾* **Molly Dolly (IRE)**[31] 4178 4-9-8 96 ChrisHayes 8 86+
(W T Farrell, Ire) *racd towards rr: rdn and prog over 1f out: 6th ent fnl f: kpt on wl into 4th cl home: nvr nrr* **16/1**

5 *hd* **Glenmayne (IRE)**[27] 4327 3-9-0 86 [1] ColmO'Donoghue 4 86
(Mrs John Harrington, Ire) *racd in mid-div: early reminders: chsd ldrs on inner 4f out: rdn in 5th appr fnl f: nt qckn ins fnl f: kpt on same pce* **20/1**

6 *¾* **Flirt (IRE)**[30] 4218 3-9-0 80 (p) GaryCarroll 5 84
(David Wachman, Ire) *chsd early ldrs: mid-div 1/2-way: kpt on wl fr over 1f out: nvr nrr* **50/1**

7 *hd* **Uninhibited (IRE)**[18] 4672 3-9-0 88 ColinKeane 9 84
(Charles O'Brien, Ire) *racd in rr: prog over 1f out on outer: kpt on strly clsng stages: nrst fin* **20/1**

8 *3* **Burma Star**[23] 4465 3-9-0 76 (b) LeighRoche 11 78
(D K Weld, Ire) *racd in mid-div: pushed along under 3f out: no imp towards rr 2f out: kpt on again clsng stages: nvr on terms* **33/1**

9 *nk* **Midnight Crossing (IRE)**[8] 5000 3-9-0 91 BillyLee 7 77
(Edward Lynam, Ire) *hld up: towards rr 4f out: kpt on fr over 1f out: nvr on terms* **14/1**

10 *shd* **Siamsaiocht (IRE)**[20] 4577 3-9-0 91 (tp) KevinManning 14 77
(J S Bolger, Ire) *chsd ldrs: rdn and nt qckn on outer under 2f out: wknd fnl f* **12/1**

11 *2 ½* **Etched (IRE)**[9] 4964 3-9-0 84 SeamieHeffernan 2 72
(A P O'Brien, Ire) *led tl hdd 2f out: wknd appr fnl f* **12/1**

12 *2* **Orcia (IRE)**[30] 4218 4-9-8 94 ConorHoban 10 68
(M Halford, Ire) *racd in mid-div: pushed along and nt qckn under 2f out: sn one pce: nt hrd rdn ins fnl f* **16/1**

13 *nk* **Mothers Finest (IRE)**[13] 4812 4-9-8 99 (t) MichaelHussey 3 67
(Adrian Paul Keatley, Ire) *bit slowly away: sn mid-div: rdn towards inner under 3f out: no imp under 2f out* **25/1**

14 *7* **Diamond Rio (IRE)**[24] 4434 4-9-8 77 (t) RoryCleary 12 53
(Anthony Mullins, Ire) *hld up: mid-div at 1/2-way: rdn 3f out: wknd to rr over 1f out: eased fnl 100yds* **50/1**

2m 0.38s (-6.62)
WFA 3 from 4yo 8lb **14** Ran SP% **130.8**
CSF £9.55 TOTE £3.10: £1.40, £2.40, £2.00; DF 16.10 Trifecta £72.10.
Owner Hamdan Al Maktoum **Bred** Shadwell Estate Comany Limited **Trained** Curragh, Co Kildare

FOCUS
This feature Listed event was run at a routine sort of pace. The market leaders fought it out.

5314 - 5316a (Foreign Racing) - See Raceform Interactive

5289 BEVERLEY (R-H)
Thursday, August 11
OFFICIAL GOING: Good to firm (good in places; 7.9)
Wind: Strong against Weather: Cloudy & blustery

5317 RACING UK HD EBF MAIDEN FILLIES' STKS (PLUS 10 RACE) — 5f
1:50 (1:50) (Class 5) 2-Y-O **£3,780** (£1,131; £565; £283; £141) **Stalls** Low

Form RPR

1 **Bay Station** 2-9-0 0 PaulQuinn 1 74
(David Nicholls) *dwlt and in rr: hdwy 2f out: rdn over 1f out: swtchd rt to inner ins fnl f: styd on strly to ld last 50yds* **33/1**

2 *½* **Queen In Waiting (IRE)** 2-9-0 0 JoeFanning 9 72+
(Mark Johnston) *wnt lft s: sn cl up: led 1 1/2f out: rdn and edgd rt ent fnl f: sn jnd and drvn: hdd and no ex last 50yds* **6/1**

52 **3** *1 ¼* **Street Jazz**[10] 4943 2-9-0 0 TomEaves 5 67
(James Given) *wnt rt s: chsd ldrs: hdwy over 1f out and sn rdn: drvn and kpt on fnl f* **5/1**[3]

52 **4** *½* **One Too Many (IRE)**[9] 4981 2-9-0 0 ShaneGray 2 66
(David Brown) *trckd ldrs: pushed along and hdwy wl over 1f out: rdn and kpt on fnl f* **9/2**[2]

5 *2 ¾* **Tivra (IRE)** 2-9-0 0 SamJames 7 56+
(Bryan Smart) *green and towards rr: hdwy on outer 2f out: rdn and edgd rt ent fnl f: kpt on: nrst fin* **7/1**

36 **6** *½* **Bithynia (IRE)**[15] 4756 2-8-11 0 JosephineGordon(3) 8 54
(Hugo Palmer) *t.k.h: cl up: led over 3f out: rdn and hdd 1 1/2f out: sn drvn and wknd ins fnl f* **6/4**[1]

036 **7** *1 ½* **La Haule Lady**[54] 3388 2-9-0 68 GrahamLee 4 48
(Paul Midgley) *hmpd s: a towards rr* **25/1**

0 **8** *7* **Loving Clarets (IRE)**[15] 4759 2-9-0 0 TonyHamilton 3 23
(Richard Fahey) *hmpd s: a towards rr* **12/1**

060 **9** *2* **Newgate Sioux**[61] 3128 2-9-0 34 BarryMcHugh 6 16
(Tony Coyle) *slt ld: hdd over 3f out: rdn along over 2f out: wknd wl over 1f out* **200/1**

1m 4.36s (0.86) **Going Correction** +0.05s/f (Good) **9** Ran SP% **116.6**
Speed ratings (Par 91): **95,94,92,91,87 86,83,72,69**
CSF £219.68 TOTE £35.50: £8.30, £2.30, £1.60; EX 177.20 Trifecta £2497.60.
Owner Sporting Lives Racing **Bred** Richard & Fraser Kent **Trained** Sessay, N Yorks

FOCUS
The inside rail on the bottom bed had been realigned, adding 23yds to Races 2,3,5,6 & 7. Following 3mm of overnight rain the going description was changed to good to firm, good in places. After riding in the opener Joe Fanning said: "There is a bit of juice but it is good ground" and Sam James said: "It is on the slow side of good." An ordinary maiden, in which a couple of debutantes fought out the finish. The third and fourth set the level.

5318 ERIC'S MAGIC NURSERY H'CAP — 7f 100y
2:20 (2:20) (Class 5) (0-75,75) 2-Y-O **£3,780** (£1,131; £565; £283; £141) **Stalls** Low

Form RPR

031 **1** **Muirsheen Durkin**[40] 3872 2-9-7 **75** (p) RichardKingscote 7 80+
(Tom Dascombe) *trckd ldng pair: hdwy on inner wl over 1f out: rdn to chal ent fnl f: sn led and kpt on strly* **3/1**[3]

400 **2** *1 ¼* **Vatican Hill (IRE)**[27] 4371 2-8-0 **54** oh2 (v[1]) PatrickMathers 1 56
(Richard Fahey) *hld up: hdwy and swtchd to inner over 1f out: sn rdn: styd on wl towards fin* **14/1**

0224 **3** *nk* **Kilbaha Lady (IRE)**[6] 5112 2-8-7 **61** (t) AndrewMullen 2 62
(Nigel Tinkler) *hld up: hdwy 2f out: rdn over 1f out: drvn and styd on wl fnl f* **14/1**

3061 **4** *hd* **See The City (IRE)**[9] 4982 2-9-5 **73** 6ex JoeFanning 8 74
(Mark Johnston) *sn led: pushed along 2f out: rdn over 1f out: drvn and hdd ins fnl f: kpt on same pce* **2/1**[1]

333 **5** *3 ½* **Alfie's Angel (IRE)**[17] 4699 2-9-5 **73** PaulMulrennan 3 66
(Bryan Smart) *trckd ldrs: hdwy to chse ldr 5f out: cl up 3f out: rdn along 2f out: drvn over 1f out: grad wknd* **5/2**[2]

552 **6** *¾* **Miss Bates**[16] 4728 2-9-5 **73** PJMcDonald 4 64
(Ann Duffield) *trckd ldrs: effrt on outer wl over 2f out: rdn along wl over 1f out: sn wknd* **10/1**

006 **7** *6* **Pontecarlo Boy**[20] 4609 2-8-0 **54** JamesSullivan 6 31
(Richard Whitaker) *dwlt: a bhd* **33/1**

1m 33.95s (0.15) **Going Correction** 0.0s/f (Good) **7** Ran SP% **112.3**
Speed ratings (Par 94): **99,97,97,97,93 92,85**
CSF £40.42 CT £501.33 TOTE £3.80: £1.70, £4.70; EX 39.60 Trifecta £399.20.
Owner The Roaring Twenties **Bred** Lady Bamford **Trained** Malpas, Cheshire

FOCUS
Race distance increased by 23yds. A fair nursery and an improving winner. The runner-up returned to his best.

5319 BULLET DAY NEXT ON 27TH AUGUST (BEVERLEY MIDDLE DISTANCE SERIES) (S) H'CAP 1m 4f 16y

2:50 (2:50) (Class 6) (0-60,60) 3-Y-O+ **£2,587** (£770; £384; £192) **Stalls** Low

Form RPR

0004 **1** **Top Of The Rocks (FR)**[13] 4847 3-8-5 **50**........................(tp) BenCurtis 1 59
(Tom Dascombe) *prom: effrt on inner wl over 1f out: rdn to chal ent fnl f: kpt on to ld last 100yds: drvn out* **7/2**[2]

0032 **2** ¾ **Ryan The Giant**[7] 5079 3-8-1 **46**..(p) RaulDaSilva 4 54
(Keith Dalgleish) *led: pushed along over 3f out: rdn wl over 2f out: drvn over 1f out: hdd and no ex last 100yds* **9/4**[1]

1655 **3** 7 **Master Of Song**[42] 3825 9-9-6 **57**........................(p) AlistairRawlinson(3) 8 54
(Roy Bowring) *midfield: hdwy on outer to trck ldrs 5f out: effrt over 2f out: rdn wl over 1f out: kpt on same pce* **16/1**

4202 **4** 3 **Impeccability**[16] 4724 6-8-13 **47**.................................(p) RoystonFfrench 12 39
(John Mackie) *hld up: hdwy over 3f out: chsd ldrs 2f out and sn rdn: drvn over 1f out: no imp* **9/1**

2000 **5** *hd* **Golly Miss Molly**[36] 4012 5-9-5 **58**.................................(b) DavidParkes(5) 7 49
(Jeremy Gask) *hld up: hdwy on wd outside 3f out: rdn to chse ldrs wl over 1f out: drvn and kpt on one pce fnl f* **10/1**

0540 **6** 5 **Solid Justice (IRE)**[19] 4645 5-9-2 **50**.................................... JoeFanning 5 33
(Kenny Johnson) *chsd ldrs: rdn along over 2f out: drvn wl over 1f out: sn wknd* **7/1**[3]

4065 **7** 1 **Pencaitland**[16] 4724 4-8-12 **46** oh1...............................(p) BarryMcHugh 9 28
(Noel Wilson) *trckd ldr: cl up 4f out: rdn along over 2f out: drvn wl over 1f out: grad wknd* **14/1**

0000 **8** ½ **Belle Peinture (FR)**[30] 4234 5-8-12 **46** oh1.....................(p) CamHardie 6 27
(Alan Lockwood) *nvr bttr than midfield* **50/1**

4056 **9** ½ **Jon H The Lawman (IRE)**[13] 4847 3-8-1 **46** oh1............ JimmyQuinn 3 26
(Ronald Thompson) *a towards rr* **20/1**

3-66 **10** 1¾ **Milu Mac**[15] 4766 5-8-9 **46** oh1................................... JacobButterfield(3) 10 23
(Neville Bycroft) *midfield: rdn along wl over 3f out: drvn 2f out: sn wknd* **40/1**

4203 **11** 14 **Golden Thread**[73] 2397 6-9-12 **60**...................................... LiamJones 11 15
(Neil King) *awkward s: sn in tch: trckd ldrs after 3f: rdn along over 3f out: wknd over 2f out* **8/1**

4000 **12** 4 **Judicial Enquiry**[22] 4527 3-8-10 **55**.................................(p) TomEaves 2 4
(Mike Sowersby) *a in rr: bhd fnl 4f* **25/1**

2m 40.29s (0.49) **Going Correction** 0.0s/f (Good)
WFA 3 from 4yo+ 11lb 12 Ran SP% **121.3**
Speed ratings (Par 101): **98,97,92,90,90 87,86,86,86,84 75,72**
CSF £11.58 CT £114.27 TOTE £4.40: £1.70, £1.60, £5.80; EX 13.00 Trifecta £187.60.
Owner The Mad March Hares **Bred** Dermot Cantillon & Mrs Meta Cantillon **Trained** Malpas, Cheshire

FOCUS
Race distance increased by 23yds. The first two pulled clear of the rest, with the winner given a decent chance by the handicapper.

5320 COLIN TINKLER SNR PROFESSIONAL LADY JOCKEYS H'CAP 5f

3:20 (3:21) (Class 5) (0-70,68) 3-Y-O+ **£3,881** (£1,155; £577; £288) **Stalls** Low

Form RPR

3555 **1** **Mininggold**[13] 4834 3-8-13 **63**............................ RachelRichardson(3) 12 74
(Tim Easterby) *qckly away and trckd ldrs: hdwy over 1f out: sn rdn: led ins fnl f: kpt on strly* **16/1**

4130 **2** 1¼ **Etienne Gerard**[7] 5060 4-9-5 **68**.................................(p) AnnaHesketh(5) 9 75
(Nigel Tinkler) *in tch: swtchd rt and n.m.r over 1f out: sn rdn: chsd wnr ins fnl f: no imp towards fin* **8/1**

4001 **3** ¾ **Showbizzy**[12] 4855 3-8-9 **63**...................................(v) NatalieHambling(7) 7 66+
(Richard Fahey) *in tch: swtchd lft and hdwy over 1f out: rdn to chal whn carried lft towards stands' rail ins fnl f: styd on wl towards fin* **11/1**

3216 **4** ½ **Poppy In The Wind**[21] 4544 4-8-13 **64**........................(v) HollieDoyle(7) 4 67
(Alan Brown) *dwlt: sn rdn along and outpcd in rr: swtchd lft to outer and hdwy wl over 1f out: rdn to chse ldrs whn carried lft to stands' rail ins fnl f: kpt on* **7/2**[2]

2220 **5** 1¼ **Tinsill**[10] 4931 5-7-13 **50**..(p) DanielleMooney(7) 6 48
(Nigel Tinkler) *towards rr: hdwy wl over 1f out: sn rdn and kpt on fnl f: nrst fin* **12/1**

4312 **6** *nk* **Showdaisy**[6] 5110 3-9-1 **67**.. ShirleyTeasdale(5) 11 63
(Keith Dalgleish) *sn trcking ldr: hdwy 2f out: rdn over 1f out: chal whn hung bdly lft ent fnl f: sn wknd* **6/1**[3]

4033 **7** ¾ **Burtonwood**[8] 5032 4-9-5 **66**.................................... JosephineGordon(3) 3 60+
(Julie Camacho) *in tch on inner whn n.m.r wl over 2f out: sn rdn along and plugged on: one pce appr fnl f* **5/2**[1]

4640 **8** 1¼ **Socialites Red**[19] 4643 3-9-0 **68**................................... SophieKilloran(7) 1 57
(Scott Dixon) *chsd ldrs: rdn along on inner 2f out: sn drvn and grad wknd* **8/1**

1005 **9** 1¼ **Bronze Beau**[12] 4874 9-9-0 **65**...(tp) JaneElliott(7) 5 50
(Kristin Stubbs) *led: rdn along over 1f out: drvn and hdd ins fnl f: sn wknd* **25/1**

33P0 **10** *nk* **Penny Pot Lane**[48] 3603 3-9-1 **67**................................ MeganNicholls(5) 8 50
(Richard Whitaker) *dwlt: a towards rr* **22/1**

22-4 **11** 2¾ **Redalani (IRE)**[219] 46 6-7-12 **49**................................ RhiainIngram(7) 10 23
(Alan Brown) *chsd ldrs: rdn along 2f out: sn wknd* **33/1**

1m 3.26s (-0.24) **Going Correction** +0.05s/f (Good)
WFA 3 from 4yo+ 3lb 11 Ran SP% **120.3**
Speed ratings (Par 103): **103,101,99,99,97 96,95,93,91,90 86**
CSF £138.29 CT £1510.02 TOTE £14.50: £4.40, £3.20, £3.50; EX 209.10 Trifecta £2056.40.
Owner Middleham Park Racing XII & Partner **Bred** Mrs G S Rees **Trained** Great Habton, N Yorks

FOCUS
A modest sprint handicap run at a sound pace. The winner was drawn high but ended up on the far rail, while the runner-up is rated as running to form.

5321 RB H'CAP 2m 35y

3:50 (3:51) (Class 4) (0-85,80) 3-Y-O+
£6,225 (£1,864; £932; £466; £233; £117) **Stalls** Low

Form RPR

4035 **1** **Gabrial's Star**[17] 4703 7-9-12 **80**......................................(b) TonyHamilton 2 92
(Richard Fahey) *hld up in tch: hdwy to trck ldng pair over 4f out: tk cl order 2f out: swtchd rt and effrt over 1f out: rdn to ld ent fnl f: kpt on wl* **11/2**

5410 **2** 7 **Full Day**[12] 4883 5-9-11 **79**..(p) BenCurtis 3 83
(Brian Ellison) *trckd ldng pair: hdwy to trck ldr over 4f out: cl up 3f out: rdn to ld over 2f out: jnd and drvn over 1f out: hdd ent fnl f: kpt on same pce* **7/2**[2]

5622 **3** 1¾ **Medina Sidonia (IRE)**[10] 4935 4-8-13 **70**........(p) RachelRichardson(3) 6 72
(Tim Easterby) *hld up in rr: hdwy over 3f out: chsd ldrs on inner over 2f out: rdn wl over 1f out: kpt on same pce u.p fnl f* **5/1**[3]

020 **4** 10 **Sisyphus**[20] 4581 4-9-12 **80**.. AndrewMullen 5 70
(Ollie Pears) *sn led: pushed along over 3f out: rdn and hdd over 2f out: sn drvn and wknd wl over 1f out* **10/1**

-034 **5** 14 **Air Squadron**[27] 4353 6-9-11 **79**................................ RichardKingscote 4 52
(Ralph Beckett) *hld up in rr: pushed along wl over 3f out: rdn wl over 2f out: sn btn* **2/1**[1]

6102 **6** 3½ **Bulas Belle**[19] 4664 6-9-12 **80**.. GrahamLee 1 49
(Grant Tuer) *trckd ldr: pushed along and lost pl over 5f out: sn bhd* **5/1**[3]

3m 37.67s (-2.13) **Going Correction** 0.0s/f (Good) 6 Ran SP% **113.4**
Speed ratings (Par 105): **105,101,100,95,88 86**
CSF £25.18 TOTE £5.40: £1.50, £2.20; EX 30.30 Trifecta £103.20.
Owner Dr Marwan Koukash **Bred** Miss K Rausing **Trained** Musley Bank, N Yorks

FOCUS
Race distance increased by 23yds. A competitive staying handicap, albeit not the strongest for the grade. The winner had been given a chance by the handicapper and duly took it.

5322 MARGARET AND BRIAN MARCHANT DIAMOND WEDDING ANNIVERSARY H'CAP 1m 100y

4:20 (4:20) (Class 5) (0-70,69) 3-Y-O **£3,780** (£1,131; £565; £283; £141) **Stalls** Low

Form RPR

0430 **1** **Big Time Dancer (IRE)**[59] 3210 3-8-5 **53**............................ BenCurtis 9 72
(Brian Ellison) *mde all: rdn and qcknd clr over 1f out: kpt on strly* **4/1**[3]

0301 **2** 7 **Arcane Dancer (IRE)**[16] 4729 3-9-1 **63**...........................(p) CamHardie 7 66
(Lawrence Mullaney) *trckd ldrs: hdwy over 2f out: chsd wnr over 1f out: sn rdn and no ch w wnr* **5/1**

065 **3** 2 **Lady Canford (IRE)**[13] 4847 3-8-1 **52**.................. JosephineGordon(3) 8 50
(James Bethell) *hld up towards rr: hdwy on outer over 2f out: sn rdn and kpt on fnl f* **10/1**

200 **4** 1 **Beverley Bullet**[75] 2674 3-9-1 **63**...................................... DavidAllan 2 59
(Les Eyre) *trckd ldrs: effrt over 2f out: rdn wl over 1f out: sn drvn and one pce* **3/1**[1]

4446 **5** ¾ **Proven Point (IRE)**[8] 5028 3-9-7 **69**.............................. BarryMcHugh 1 63
(Tony Coyle) *t.k.h: trckd ldrs on inner: effrt over 2f out: sn rdn along: drvn wl over 1f out: one pce* **12/1**

2200 **6** *hd* **Dasheen**[16] 4729 3-9-5 **67**.. JoeFanning 6 61
(Mark Johnston) *trckd wnr: cl up and rdn along over 2f out: drvn wl over 1f out: wknd appr fnl f* **12/1**

0304 **7** 4 **Ginger Charlie**[13] 4844 3-8-2 **50** oh1................................. JamesSullivan 4 35
(Ruth Carr) *in tch: effrt over 3f out: rdn along wl over 2f out: sn outpcd* **16/1**

0321 **8** *nse* **Pacific Salt (IRE)**[15] 4764 3-8-12 **65**........................ CallumShepherd(5) 5 50
(Pam Sly) *hld up: a in rr* **7/2**[2]

000- **9** 22 **Great Colaci**[300] 7251 3-8-2 **50** oh2.............................. AndrewMullen 3
(Keith Reveley) *a towards rr: outpcd and bhd fnl 3f* **25/1**

1m 45.92s (-1.68) **Going Correction** 0.0s/f (Good) 9 Ran SP% **118.1**
Speed ratings (Par 100): **108,101,99,98,97 97,93,93,71**
CSF £25.00 CT £165.20 TOTE £4.20: £1.20, £2.10, £3.30; EX 28.10 Trifecta £256.90.
Owner Andy Bell Anna Noble Arnie Flower **Bred** Gerard Callanan **Trained** Norton, N Yorks

FOCUS
Race distance increased by 23yds. A modest handicap and the unexposed winner, on debut for Brian Ellison, proved far too good. The runner-up can be rated close to his best form.

5323 WHITE ROSE SADDLERY AMATEUR RIDERS' H'CAP 1m 100y

4:50 (4:51) (Class 6) (0-65,64) 4-Y-O+ **£2,495** (£774; £386; £193) **Stalls** Low

Form RPR

4050 **1** **Outlaw Torn (IRE)**[7] 5064 7-9-12 **48**....................(e) MissJoannaMason 6 56
(Richard Guest) *trckd ldrs: hdwy 2f out: rdn to chal over 1f out: drvn and styd on wl to ld last 100yds* **14/1**

0301 **2** 1½ **I'm Super Too (IRE)**[16] 4730 9-10-7 **57**............................. MrPMillman 7 62
(Karen Tutty) *hld up towards rr: hdwy 2f out: swtchd lft and rdn on outer over 1f out: styd on strly fnl f* **5/1**[3]

2303 **3** ½ **John Caesar (IRE)**[8] 5030 5-11-0 **64**.................................(t) MrSWalker 2 68
(Rebecca Bastiman) *in tch on inner: hdwy over 2f out: rdn over 1f out: drvn and ev ch ins fnl f: kpt on same pce towards fin* **7/2**[2]

4040 **4** *nse* **Intensified (IRE)**[3] 5227 5-9-4 **45**......................(b) MissEmilyBullock(5) 4 48
(Ruth Carr) *n.m.r and hmpd shortly after s: hld up in rr: effrt and n.m.r over 2f out: swtchd lft to outer and rdn over 1f out: styd on strly fnl f* **13/2**

60-0 **5** *shd* **Mayfield Boy**[154] 893 5-10-10 **60**................................... MissSBrotherton 8 63
(Antony Brittain) *awkward s and t.k.h: sn led and clr: stdd 1/2-way: rdn along wl over 1f out: drvn ent fnl f: hdd and no ex last 100yds* **8/1**

0633 **6** 2¾ **Cliff (IRE)**[18] 4684 6-11-0 **64**.. MrRBirkett 10 63
(Nigel Tinkler) *hld up in tch: hdwy over 2f out: chsd ldrs over 1f out: sn rdn and one pce fnl f* **11/4**[1]

6046 **7** *nk* **Yair Hill (IRE)**[5] 5149 8-9-8 **47**...........................(p) MissHelenCuthbert(3) 5 44
(Thomas Cuthbert) *hld up in rr: smooth hdwy over 2f out: rdn and ev ch over 1f out: wknd ent fnl f* **20/1**

0656 **8** 1 **L'Es Fremantle (FR)**[30] 4234 5-9-4 **45**................................ MrJPearce(5) 9 39
(Michael Chapman) *prom: chsd ldr after 2f: rdn along over 2f out: drvn and wknd wl over 1f out* **20/1**

0501 **9** *nse* **Eeny Mac (IRE)**[10] 4929 9-10-1 **51** 6ex.........................(p) MissCWalton 1 45
(John Wainwright) *chsd ldrs on inner: rdn along over 2f out: drvn wl over 1f out: grad wknd* **15/2**

0300 **10** 18 **Rosie Hall (IRE)**[15] 4772 6-9-4 **45**......................................(v) MrMEnnis(5) 3
(John Wainwright) *towards rr: rdn along 1/2-way: sn outpcd and bhd* **50/1**

1m 48.55s (0.95) **Going Correction** 0.0s/f (Good) 10 Ran SP% **119.9**
Speed ratings (Par 101): **95,93,93,92,92 90,89,88,88,70**
CSF £83.06 CT £313.06 TOTE £17.60: £3.70, £2.10, £1.50; EX 123.80 Trifecta £546.50.
Owner James S Kennerley **Bred** Derek Veitch & Rory O'Brien **Trained** Ingmanthorpe, W Yorks

FOCUS
Race distance increased by 23yds. A modest handicap for amateur riders and they went a good pace. The winner ran to the best of this summer's form.
T/Jkpt: Not won. T/Plt: £2984.20 to a £1 stake. Pool: £66,020.46 - 16.15 winning units. T/Qpdt: £77.80 to a £1 stake. Pool: £5,841.39 - 55.52 winning units. **Joe Rowntree**

5304 SALISBURY (R-H)

Thursday, August 11

OFFICIAL GOING: Good to firm (8.9)

Wind: almost nil Weather: sunny

5324 TOTEPLACEPOT SIX PLACES IN SIX RACES MAIDEN AUCTION STKS (DIV I) 6f 212y

1:40 (1:40) (Class 5) 2-Y-O **£3,881** (£1,155; £577; £288) **Stalls** Centre

Form RPR

3 **1** **Gravity Wave (IRE)**[11] 4907 2-8-13 0 PatDobbs 8 77
(Sylvester Kirk) *unf: swtg: wnt lft s: rcvrd to trck ldr after 2f: rdn over 2f out: kpt on wl: led fnl strides* **2/1**[2]

03 **2** *shd* **Carducci**[12] 4856 2-8-8 0 SeanLevey 7 72
(Richard Hannon) *tall: lw: led: rdn 2f out: kpt on: hdd fnl strides* **5/4**[1]

550 **3** *1 ½* **Party Nights**[17] 4707 2-8-6 0 AntonioFresu 2 66
(Luca Cumani) *str: trckd ldrs: rdn 3f out: kpt on but nt pce to mount chal* **16/1**

4 *1 ½* **Vibes (IRE)** 2-9-2 0 WilliamCarson 5 72
(Jamie Osborne) *str: bit bkwd: s.i.s: last: hdwy over 2f out: pushed along over 1f out: kpt on fnl f but nt pce to get involved* **10/1**[3]

5 **5** *½* **Makkadangdang**[22] 4524 2-8-13 0 OisinMurphy 4 68
(Andrew Balding) *medium-sized: w'like: hld up in tch: rdn over 2f out: nt pce to get on terms* **10/1**[3]

0 **6** *2 ½* **Silver Chimes**[26] 4397 2-8-4 0 MartinDwyer 1 52
(William Knight) *cls cpld: trckd ldrs: squeezed up on rails ins 1st f and lost pl: in tch: rdn 3f out: no imp: wknd fnl 100yds* **10/1**[3]

00 **7** *1* **Sir Plato (IRE)**[11] 4907 2-8-9 0 RyanTate 6 54
(Rod Millman) *trckd ldrs: pushed along over 4f out: rdn over 3f out: nt pce to threaten: wknd ins fnl f* **66/1**

1m 30.62s (2.02) **Going Correction** +0.075s/f (Good) **7** Ran SP% **112.4**
Speed ratings (Par 94): **91,90,89,87,86 84,82**
CSF £4.66 TOTE £3.10: £1.60, £1.20; EX 5.00 Trifecta £22.20.
Owner Deauville Daze Partnership **Bred** Paget Bloodstock & Eadling Farm **Trained** Upper Lambourn, Berks

FOCUS

The ground had dried out to Good to firm and the jockeys said it was "quick but safe". The first division of this maiden auction was dominated by the market leaders. The early pace was very steady and the winner did well to overcome a poorish start.

5325 TOTEPLACEPOT SIX PLACES IN SIX RACES MAIDEN AUCTION STKS (DIV II) 6f 212y

2:10 (2:11) (Class 5) 2-Y-O **£3,881** (£1,155; £577; £288) **Stalls** Centre

Form RPR

0 **1** **Seafarer (IRE)**[28] 4287 2-8-11 0 PatDobbs 1 76+
(Marcus Tregoning) *broke wl: stdd bk to trck ldrs: swtchd lft 2f out: gd hdwy over 1f out: r.o wl to ld fnl 100yds: drifted lft: readily* **6/4**[1]

05 **2** *¾* **Famous Dynasty (IRE)**[22] 4523 2-8-9 0 TomMarquand 2 70
(Michael Blanshard) *last pair: nt clr run briefly over 2f out and bmpd: sn swtchd lft: rdn and hdwy over 1f out: r.o wl w wnr ins fnl f but a being hld* **20/1**

4 **3** *1* **Scorching Heat**[10] 4938 2-8-11 0 OisinMurphy 6 69
(Andrew Balding) *str: sn led: rdn 2f out: no ex whn hdd fnl 100yds* **9/2**[3]

60 **4** *¾* **Feel The Vibes**[4] 5202 2-8-13 0 KieranO'Neill 4 69
(Richard Hannon) *medium-sized: w'like: trckd ldr: rdn wl over 2f out: kpt on same pce fnl f* **9/1**

5 *2* **Manners Please** 2-8-11 0 JohnFahy 5 62
(Ralph Beckett) *cmpt: bit bkwd: s.i.s: racd green in rr: kpt on ins fnl f: nvr any threat to ldrs* **14/1**

5220 **6** *½* **King Of Spades (FR)**[19] 4622 2-9-2 80 (v[1]) SilvestreDeSousa 9 66
(Mick Channon) *trckd ldrs: effrt over 2f out: nt quite pce to chal: fdd ins fnl f* **11/4**[2]

6043 **7** *9* **Crystal Secret**[14] 4786 2-8-5 58 ow1 WilliamCarson 3 30
(John Bridger) *in tch: rdn over 3f out: wkng whn bmpd 2f out* **16/1**

0 **8** *1 ½* **Lord Cooper**[35] 4053 2-8-13 0 MartinDwyer 7 34
(Jose Santos) *w'like: s.i.s: sn trcking ldrs: rdn 3f out: wknd over 1f out: eased* **25/1**

1m 29.1s (0.50) **Going Correction** +0.075s/f (Good) **8** Ran SP% **116.0**
Speed ratings (Par 94): **100,99,98,97,94 94,84,82**
CSF £35.93 TOTE £2.50: £1.40, £6.90, £1.80; EX 32.90 Trifecta £157.20.
Owner Green, Hoare, Raw & Tregoning **Bred** Airlie Stud **Trained** Whitsbury, Hants

FOCUS

The second leg of this maiden was run at a better gallop early and the time was 1.52secs faster than the first division. The winner built on his eye-catching debut and may have a good bit more to come.

5326 TOTEQUADPOT AVAILABLE AT ALL UK MEETINGS H'CAP 1m

2:40 (2:42) (Class 6) (0-65,65) 3-Y-O+ **£2,911** (£866; £432; £216) **Stalls** Low

Form RPR

0-11 **1** **Mia Tesoro (IRE)**[28] 4301 3-9-7 **65** JimCrowley 3 75
(Charlie Fellowes) *in tch: hdwy 3f out: led 2f out: sn rdn: edgd lft fnl f: jst hld on* **7/2**[1]

-052 **2** *hd* **Nona Blu**[7] 5055 4-9-8 **59** AdamKirby 5 70
(Michael Wigham) *lw: mid-div: hdwy over 2f out: rdn to chse wnr ent fnl f: kpt on wl clsng stages: jst failed* **5/1**[2]

-652 **3** *6* **Aye Aye Skipper (IRE)**[45] 3724 6-9-4 **55** (p) PatDobbs 9 52
(Ken Cunningham-Brown) *hld up: hdwy 2f out: rdn into 3rd jst over 1f out: kpt on but outpcd by front pair fnl f* **8/1**[3]

5100 **4** *2 ½* **Elegant Annie**[20] 4596 3-8-6 **57** LuluStanford[(7)] 7 47
(Jonathan Portman) *in tch: rdn to chse ldrs over 2f out: kpt on same pce fnl f* **9/1**

0305 **5** *1 ¼* **Gavarnie Encore**[7] 5080 4-9-3 **54** KieranO'Neill 13 42
(Michael Blanshard) *hld up towards rr: swtchd to centre 2f out: sn rdn and hdwy: styd on same pce fnl 120yds* **25/1**

0-40 **6** *hd* **The Greedy Boy**[22] 4505 3-8-9 **53** CharlesBishop 12 39
(Mick Channon) *mid-div: rdn and hdwy over 1f out: styd on fnl f* **25/1**

0006 **7** *1 ½* **Miss Buckaroo (IRE)**[7] 5055 4-8-9 **46** oh1 TomMarquand 14 30
(Peter Hedger) *s.i.s: towards rr: styd on past btn horses fnl f: nvr any threat* **50/1**

054 **8** *7* **Senor George (IRE)**[61] 3121 9-9-9 **60** RyanClark 1 27
(Simon Hodgson) *led for 1f: trckd ldrs: rdn over 3f out: wknd over 1f out* **33/1**

4435 **9** *¾* **Corpus Chorister (FR)**[40] 3906 3-9-7 **65** MartinDwyer 2 29
(David Menuisier) *trckd ldrs: rdn over 2f out: wknd over 1f out* **5/1**[2]

0600 **10** *1 ½* **Attitude Rocks**[29] 4269 3-8-13 **57** (b) JohnFahy 4 17
(Clive Cox) *s.i.s: drvn over 3f out: a towards rr* **16/1**

0036 **11** *½* **Oat Couture**[21] 4557 4-9-12 **63** FergusSweeney 8 23
(Henry Candy) *trckd ldr: rdn to ld briefly over 2f out: wknd ent fnl f* **12/1**

4440 **12** *1 ¾* **Knight Of The Air**[18] 4683 4-9-9 **60** SilvestreDeSousa 6 16
(Mick Channon) *mid-div: nt clr run twice over 2f out and again briefly over 1f out: hld whn eased ins fnl f* **9/1**

0-43 **13** *7* **Zlatan (IRE)**[10] 4936 3-9-2 **60** (b[1]) LiamKeniry 10
(Ed de Giles) *led after 1f: rdn and hdd over 2f out: wknd over 1f out* **10/1**

1m 43.54s (0.04) **Going Correction** +0.075s/f (Good)
WFA 3 from 4yo+ 7lb **13** Ran SP% **121.9**
Speed ratings (Par 101): **102,101,95,93,92 91,90,83,82,81 80,78,71**
CSF £19.86 CT £139.47 TOTE £5.40: £2.00, £1.90, £2.70; EX 18.50 Trifecta £50.30.
Owner Deron Pearson **Bred** D Pearson **Trained** Newmarket, Suffolk

FOCUS

A good sized field for this modest 1m handicap but the market leaders came well clear. Both were in form heading into this.

5327 TOTEPOOL LIVE INFO DOWNLOAD THE APP MAIDEN STKS 6f 212y

3:10 (3:10) (Class 5) 3-4-Y-O **£3,881** (£1,155; £577; £288) **Stalls** Centre

Form RPR

-343 **1** **Tigerwolf (IRE)**[12] 4867 3-9-5 86 CharlesBishop 3 79
(Mick Channon) *trckd ldrs: barged through on rails over 2f out: led over 1f out: sn rdn and hung bdly lft: hld on* **2/9**[1]

2 *hd* **Port Isaac (IRE)** 3-9-5 0 MartinDwyer 6 78
(Marcus Tregoning) *tall: lengthy: travelled wl in 4th: chal over 2f out: ev ch whn rdn wl over 1f out but sn drifted lft: r.o strly fnl 120yds: jst hld* **9/1**[3]

35 **3** *5* **Land Of Dubai (IRE)**[33] 4156 3-9-0 0 AdamKirby 2 60
(Clive Cox) *trckd ldr: led over 2f out: rdn and hdd over 1f out: no ex fnl f* **7/1**[2]

65 **4** *3 ¼* **Sir Compton**[10] 4939 3-9-5 0 TedDurcan 7 56
(Stuart Kittow) *tall: hld up 5th: pushed along over 4f out: rdn over 2f out: wnt hld 4th ent fnl f: styd on same pce* **25/1**

60- **5** *1 ¾* **Kylea (IRE)**[327] 6538 3-9-0 0 PatDobbs 4 46
(Richard Hannon) *sn led: hdd and hmpd over 2f out: sn hld: wknd fnl f* **16/1**

1m 30.42s (1.82) **Going Correction** +0.075s/f (Good) **5** Ran SP% **114.1**
Speed ratings (Par 103): **92,91,86,82,80**
CSF £3.47 TOTE £1.10: £1.02, £3.10; EX 3.00 Trifecta £7.30.
Owner George Materna & Roger Badley **Bred** Ballyreddin Stud **Trained** West Ilsley, Berks
■ Stewards' Enquiry : Charles Bishop two-day ban: careless riding (Aug 25-26)

FOCUS

Tigerwolf set a decent standard in what otherwise looked a moderate older horse maiden but had to work hard to land the odds. The time was 1.32 secs slower than the second leg of the earlier juvenile maiden.

5328 EBF BREEDERS' SERIES FILLIES' H'CAP 1m 4f

3:40 (3:40) (Class 2) (0-100,95) 3-Y-O+

£18,675 (£5,592; £2,796; £1,398; £699; £351) **Stalls** Low

Form RPR

611 **1** **Dubka**[41] 3846 3-8-9 **87** TedDurcan 6 96+
(Sir Michael Stoute) *w'like: str: trckd ldrs: nudged along over 4f out: rdn to ld wl over 1f out: styd on: all out* **11/8**[1]

-436 **2** *shd* **Perestroika**[34] 4078 4-9-6 **87** FergusSweeney 1 95
(Henry Candy) *nvr really travelling: pushed along in last trio early: dropped to last 6f out: rdn over 3f out: hdwy over 2f out: styd on strly fnl f: jst failed* **17/2**

2632 **3** *1* **Graceland (FR)**[9] 4994 4-8-11 **81** LouisSteward[(3)] 5 87
(Michael Bell) *dwlt: detached in last early: hdwy over 3f out: rdn to chse wnr over 1f out tl jst ins fnl f: styd on* **10/1**

31-0 **4** *1 ¾* **Bess Of Hardwick**[34] 4078 4-9-6 **87** AdamKirby 2 90
(Luca Cumani) *str: lw: s.i.s: in last trio: rdn 3f out: no imp tl styd on to go 4th ins fnl f* **9/2**[2]

-016 **5** *shd* **Elysian Fields (GR)**[14] 4800 5-9-11 **92** PatDobbs 3 95
(Amanda Perrett) *led for 4f: trckd ldrs: rdn 3f out: kpt chsng ldrs tl no ex ins fnl f* **12/1**

3303 **6** *1* **Vive Ma Fille (GER)**[6] 5116 4-10-0 **95** FrannyNorton 4 96
(Mark Johnston) *trckd ldrs: pressed ldr after 5f: led over 2f out: sn rdn: hdd wl over 1f out: fdd ins fnl f* **7/1**[3]

3311 **7** *33* **Eager Beaver**[9] 4994 4-9-2 **83** 6ex MartinDwyer 7 32
(William Muir) *pressed ldr: led after 4f: rdn and hdd over 2f out: wknd and eased over 1f out* **7/1**[3]

2m 34.0s (-4.00) **Going Correction** -0.125s/f (Firm)
WFA 3 from 4yo+ 11lb **7** Ran SP% **112.6**
Speed ratings (Par 96): **108,107,107,106,106 105,83**
CSF £13.51 TOTE £2.40: £1.50, £4.40; EX 13.30 Trifecta £72.70.
Owner Sir Evelyn De Rothschild **Bred** Southcourt Stud **Trained** Newmarket, Suffolk
■ Stewards' Enquiry : Ted Durcan two-day ban: used whip above permitted level (Aug 25-26)

FOCUS

This good fillies' handicap was run at a good pace early as several battled for the lead. Apart from the winner, the principals were held up. The runner-up recorded a small personal best.

5329 TOTEPOOL SOVEREIGN STKS (GROUP 3) (C&G) 1m

4:10 (4:10) (Class 1) 3-Y-O+

£42,532 (£16,125; £8,070; £4,020; £2,017; £1,012) **Stalls** Low

Form RPR

-610 **1** **Zonderland**[32] 4185 3-8-7 107 OisinMurphy 5 114+
(Clive Cox) *prom for 1f: trckd ldrs: led over 2f out: sn rdn: edgd lft ins fnl f: kpt on strly: rdn out* **4/1**[2]

502 **2** *1 ¾* **Master The World (IRE)**[13] 4823 5-9-0 108 (p) JimCrowley 2 111
(David Elsworth) *hld up in last pair: hdwy 3f out: rdn to chse wnr over 1f out: kpt on but a being hld fnl f* **11/2**[3]

6006 **3** *1 ½* **Tupi (IRE)**[16] 4733 4-9-0 105 PatDobbs 1 108
(Richard Hannon) *hld up: rdn and hdwy 2f out: kpt on fnl f: snatched 3rd cl home* **33/1**

-445 **4** *hd* **Tony Curtis**[13] 4822 3-8-7 106 SeanLevey 8 106
(Richard Hannon) *trckd ldrs: rdn to chse wnr briefly 2f out: kpt on same pce fnl f: lost 3rd cl home* **8/1**

4663 **5** *4 ½* **Master Carpenter (IRE)**[18] 4688 5-9-0 107 FrederikTylicki 3 97
(Rod Millman) *lw: trckd ldrs: flattered briefly 2f out: one pce after* **20/1**

504 **6** *11* **Belgian Bill**[13] 4823 8-9-0 102 (b) SteveDrowne 9 71
(George Baker) *lw: chsd ldr: rdn 3f out: sn btn* **25/1**

2-20 **7** *21* **Massaat (IRE)**[68] 2896 3-8-7 116.. PaulHanagan 6 22
(Owen Burrows) *led: rdn and hdd over 2f out: wknd qckly and sn eased*
4/5[1]

1m 40.35s (-3.15) **Going Correction** +0.075s/f (Good)
WFA 3 from 4yo+ 7lb **7** Ran SP% **113.6**
Speed ratings (Par 113): **118,116,114,114,110 99,78**
CSF £25.03 TOTE £5.40: £2.20, £2.10; EX 23.80 Trifecta £194.20.
Owner Cheveley Park Stud **Bred** Cheveley Park Stud Ltd **Trained** Lambourn, Berks

FOCUS
The feature race and a solid looking Group 3, despite the withdrawal of previous winner Tullius with the 2,000 Guineas second and sixth bidding to bounce back from lesser efforts. The time was 3.19 secs faster than the earlier handicap and unsurprisingly the best time of the day. It produced a step forward in form from the highly regarded winner, but the favourite was really disappointing.

5330 BILL GARNETT MEMORIAL FILLIES' H'CAP 6f
4:40 (4:40) (Class 5) (0-70,68) 3-Y-O+ **£3,234** (£962; £481; £240) **Stalls** Low

Form RPR
1245 **1** **Dynamic Girl (IRE)**[27] 4354 3-9-6 **66**.............................(p[1]) OisinMurphy 2 75+
(Brendan Powell) *trckd ldrs: pushed along over 3f out: nt clr run over 1f out: swtchd rt ent fnl f: led fnl 100yds: qcknd clr* **4/1**[2]

5212 **2** *1 ¼* **Babyfact**[8] 5009 5-9-6 **62**.. JimCrowley 8 68
(Malcolm Saunders) *lw: travelled wl most of way: trckd ldrs: led wl over 1f out: sn rdn: hdd and outpcd by wnr fnl 100yds* **9/4**[1]

3205 **3** *1* **Naziba (IRE)**[44] 3740 3-9-3 **63**.. JimmyFortune 7 65+
(David Menuisier) *hld up: swtchd lft 2f out: hdwy over 1f out: rdn and r.o wl fnl f: snatched 3rd fnl stride* **14/1**

340- **4** *hd* **Rosie Royce**[304] 7167 3-9-7 **67**....................................... FergusSweeney 11 68
(Henry Candy) *racd keenly: trckd ldrs: rdn to chse wnr over briefly jst over 1f out: kpt on: lost 3rd fnl stride* **14/1**

6560 **5** *½* **Walking In Rhythm (IRE)**[14] 4794 3-9-1 **61**.......................... PatDobbs 1 60
(Richard Hannon) *mid-div: hdwy whn nt clr run over 1f out: kpt on whn clr fnl f but no ch* **25/1**

3405 **6** *½* **Quite A Story**[24] 4460 4-9-5 **66**.................................... HectorCrouch(5) 10 65
(Patrick Chamings) *s.i.s: towards rr: rdn and hdwy ent fnl f: r.o* **14/1**

3005 **7** *½* **Lucky Di**[17] 4708 6-9-12 **68**.. CharlesBishop 4 65
(Peter Hedger) *hld up: rdn 2f out: kpt on ins fnl f* **10/1**

-350 **8** *2 ¾* **Romancingthestone**[199] 327 3-8-3 **49**.. RyanTate 3 36
(Karen George) *mid-div: drvn over 2f out: nvr any imp* **50/1**

560 **9** *1 ¼* **Caledonia Duchess**[19] 4641 3-8-12 **58**............................. PaulHanagan 9 41
(Jo Hughes) *trckd ldrs: rdn 2f out: wknd fnl f* **18/1**

4535 **10** *½* **Angie's Girl**[12] 4878 3-9-0 **60**.. AdamKirby 6 45
(Clive Cox) *led: rdn and hdd wl over 1f out: cl up but hld whn hmpd jst ins fnl f: wknd* **13/2**[3]

4216 **11** *2 ¾* **Shahaama**[12] 4878 3-9-5 **65**.................................... SilvestreDeSousa 5 38
(Mick Channon) *s.i.s: sn mid-div: rdn over 2f out: wknd over 1f out* **13/2**[3]

1m 15.47s (0.67) **Going Correction** +0.075s/f (Good)
WFA 3 from 4yo+ 4lb **11** Ran SP% **117.6**
Speed ratings (Par 100): **98,96,95,94,94 93,92,89,87,86 83**
CSF £13.35 CT £116.94 TOTE £4.70: £2.00, £1.10, £4.30; EX 15.90 Trifecta £145.90.
Owner Wajid Ali Abdul Qayyum **Bred** Swordlestown Stud **Trained** Upper Lambourn, Berks
■ Stewards' Enquiry : Oisin Murphy caution: careless riding

FOCUS
A modest but competitive sprint handicap for fillies, although most had questions to answer. The winner took it after being off the bridle before halfway.

5331 KEVIN HALL & PAT BOAKES MEMORIAL H'CAP 1m 6f 21y
5:15 (5:16) (Class 4) (0-85,85) 3-Y-O **£5,175** (£1,540; £769; £384) **Stalls** Far side

Form RPR
-311 **1** **Alyssa**[28] 4303 3-9-7 **85**.. SilvestreDeSousa 4 97+
(Ralph Beckett) *mde all: styd on strly: rdn out* **5/6**[1]

3242 **2** *2 ½* **Rainbow Dreamer**[27] 4346 3-9-6 **84**.......................... WilliamTwiston-Davies 6 92
(Alan King) *trckd ldrs: wnt 2nd 3f out: sn rdn: styd on but nt pce to mount chal* **9/2**[3]

0241 **3** *3 ½* **Clear Evidence**[19] 4655 3-8-2 **66**.. MartinDwyer 3 69
(Michael Bell) *lw: hld up 5th: hdwy into 3rd 3f out: sn rdn: styd on same pce fnl 2f* **4/1**[2]

2104 **4** *8* **Chelsea's Boy (IRE)**[15] 4778 3-8-13 **77**................................ JohnFahy 1 69
(Clive Cox) *trckd wnr tl rdn over 3f out: sn one pce* **14/1**

3411 **5** *shd* **Fashion Parade**[24] 4462 3-9-7 **85**.. JimCrowley 2 77
(Charles Hills) *hld up 4th: rdn 3f out: hung rt: sn one pce* **6/1**

3m 2.9s (-4.50) **Going Correction** -0.125s/f (Firm) **5** Ran SP% **113.7**
Speed ratings (Par 102): **107,105,103,99,98**
CSF £5.28 TOTE £1.70: £1.10, £2.70; EX 5.40 Trifecta £11.40.
Owner Miss K Rausing **Bred** Miss K Rausing **Trained** Kimpton, Hants

FOCUS
Despite the small field this looked a decent staying handicap and the gallop was sound, with the winner making all. The runner-up is handed a personal best in beating the remainder.
T/Plt: £33.50 to a £1 stake. Pool: £57,701.44 - 1255.41 winning units. T/Qpdt: £36.10 to a £1 stake. Pool: £4,441.54 - 90.92 winning units. **Tim Mitchell**

[5084] YARMOUTH (L-H)
Thursday, August 11

OFFICIAL GOING: Good to firm changing to good after race 1 (5.05)
Wind: light, across Weather: overcast, brightening up after race 2

5332 TOTEPLACEPOT SIX PLACES IN SIX RACES EBF MAIDEN STKS (PLUS 10 RACE) 7f 3y
5:05 (5:08) (Class 4) 2-Y-O **£4,657** (£1,386; £692; £346) **Stalls** Centre

Form RPR
1 **Salsabeel (IRE)** 2-9-5 0.. WilliamBuick 10 83+
(Charlie Appleby) *t.k.h: trckd ldrs: rdn 2f out: rn green over 1f out: hdwy to press ldrs 1f out: wnt between rivals to chal ins fnl f: pushed into ld 75yds out: r.o wl* **5/1**[3]

3 **2** *½* **Novoman (IRE)**[42] 3799 2-9-5 0.. PatCosgrave 11 80+
(William Haggas) *led: rdn over 1f out: hrd pressed ins fnl f: hdd and one pce fnl 75yds* **3/1**[2]

3 *½* **Law And Order (IRE)** 2-9-5 0.. MartinHarley 3 79+
(James Tate) *trckd ldrs: effrt to chse ldr wl over 1f out: drvn and ev ch jst ins fnl f: one pce fnl 100yds* **5/2**[1]

4 *6* **Intrepidly (USA)** 2-9-5 0.. JamieSpencer 1 62
(Jeremy Noseda) *s.i.s: hld up in rr: pushed along and hdwy ent fnl f: drifting rt but kpt on ins fnl f: wnt 4th towards fin: nvr trbld ldrs* **13/2**

4 **5** *¾* **Bizet (IRE)**[13] 4837 2-9-5 0.. DannyBrock 4 60
(John Ryan) *chsd ldr: rdn 2f out: drvn and outpcd over 1f out: 4th and btn 1f out: wknd ins fnl f* **12/1**

6 *¾* **Presence Process** 2-9-5 0.. AndreaAtzeni 9 58
(Luca Cumani) *hld up in tch in midfield: nt clr run 2f out and shuffled bk towards rr: pushed along and rallied 1f out: kpt on ins fnl f: nvr trbld ldrs* **10/1**

0 **7** *nk* **Crystal Dome**[15] 4775 2-9-5 0.. LukeMorris 2 58
(Ed Dunlop) *dwlt: sn rcvrd and in tch in midfield: rdn 2f out: outpcd over 1f out: wl hld and plugged on same pce fnl f* **50/1**

8 *1 ¼* **Merlin** 2-9-5 0.. DavidProbert 7 54
(Michael Bell) *t.k.h: hld up in tch in midfield: rdn over 1f out: unable qck and sn outpcd: wknd fnl f* **9/1**

6 **9** *hd* **Shadow Warrior**[50] 3524 2-9-0 0.............................. AdamMcNamara(5) 5 54
(Paul D'Arcy) *taken down early: t.k.h: hld up in tch: effrt 2f out: sn rdn and unable qck: wknd fnl f* **40/1**

5 **10** *1 ¼* **Sassoferrato (IRE)**[5] 5166 2-9-5 0.................................... SaleemGolam 8 50
(Alan Bailey) *hld up in tch in last trio: pushed along 2f out: no hdwy: bhd fnl f* **40/1**

6 **11** *9* **Bartholomew J (IRE)**[16] 4738 2-9-2 0............................ SimonPearce(3) 6 26
(Lydia Pearce) *stdd s: t.k.h: hld up in rr: swtchd lft over 2f out: rdn and btn 2f out: sn wknd* **100/1**

1m 25.84s (-0.76) **Going Correction** -0.10s/f (Good) **11** Ran SP% **118.2**
Speed ratings (Par 96): **100,99,98,92,91 90,89,88,88,86 76**
CSF £20.24 TOTE £5.50: £1.30, £1.80, £1.60; EX 20.50 Trifecta £77.60.
Owner Godolphin **Bred** Darley **Trained** Newmarket, Suffolk

FOCUS
No alterations to race distances advised. Probably the most intriguing race on the entire card to begin, with many top yards represented among the line-up of this juvenile maiden. The first three finished well clear.

5333 TOTEPOOL LIVE INFO DOWNLOAD THE APP H'CAP 1m 1f 21y
5:35 (5:35) (Class 4) (0-80,79) 3-Y-O+ **£4,690** (£1,395; £697; £348) **Stalls** Low

Form RPR
4231 **1** **Brorocco**[13] 4838 3-9-6 **79**.. DavidProbert 3 89+
(Andrew Balding) *t.k.h: hld up in tch in last pair: clsd to press ldrs and travelling strly 2f out: rdn to ld over 1f out: pushed along and a doing enough ins fnl f* **5/4**[1]

1004 **2** *½* **Mirsaalah**[41] 3846 3-9-6 **79**.. LukeMorris 1 88
(James Tate) *led for 1f: styd chsng ldr tl led again on bit wl over 2f out: drvn and hdd over 1f out: kpt on gamely u.p but a hld* **7/1**

-020 **3** *3 ½* **Mr Quicksilver**[12] 4868 4-10-0 **79**..................................(t) ThomasBrown 7 81
(Ed Walker) *stdd s: hld up in rr: clsd and wl in tch over 2f out: effrt to chse ldng pair over 1f out: no imp ins fnl f* **14/1**

3426 **4** *¾* **Sands Chorus**[45] 3717 4-9-7 **77**................................ AdamMcNamara(5) 5 77
(James Given) *led after 1f: rdn over 3f out: hdd wl over 2f out: outpcd u.p over 1f out: wl hld and styd on same pce fnl f* **5/1**[2]

620 **5** *hd* **Buckland Beau**[33] 4129 5-9-12 **77**.................................... StevieDonohoe 2 77
(Charlie Fellowes) *t.k.h: hld up in tch: wnt 3rd 5f out: nt clr run and swtchd rt 2f out: unable qck u.p over 1f out: wl hld and plugged on same pce ins fnl f* **6/1**[3]

1004 **6** *5* **Ban Shoof**[21] 4549 3-9-1 **74**.......................................(p) WilliamBuick 6 68
(Ismail Mohammed) *t.k.h: chsd ldng pair tl 5f out: rdn to press ldrs 3f out: bmpd over 1f out: sn lost pl and btn: wknd 1f out: eased towards fin* **5/1**[2]

1m 54.36s (-1.44) **Going Correction** -0.025s/f (Good)
WFA 3 from 4yo+ 8lb **6** Ran SP% **111.2**
Speed ratings (Par 105): **105,104,101,100,100 96**
CSF £10.40 TOTE £2.50: £1.30, £3.70; EX 6.90 Trifecta £54.30.
Owner Kingsclere Racing Club **Bred** Kingsclere Stud **Trained** Kingsclere, Hants

FOCUS
A pretty competitive event for the grade run at an ordinary pace, with all bar one racing off 3lb or fewer below the ratings ceiling.

5334 TOTEQUADPOT INSURE YOUR PLACEPOT LAST FOUR H'CAP 2m
6:05 (6:05) (Class 5) (0-75,81) 4-Y-O+ **£2,911** (£866; £432; £216) **Stalls** Centre

Form RPR
2031 **1** **Bertie Moon**[2] 5267 6-9-4 **81** 6ex....................................(p) CliffordLee(7) 1 86
(Lydia Pearce) *mde all: rdn 2f out: drvn ins fnl f: hld on wl towards fin* **2/1**[1]

0411 **2** *shd* **Duke Of Diamonds**[41] 3844 4-8-13 **72**........................ ShelleyBirkett(3) 4 77
(Julia Feilden) *chsd ldr for 4f: dropped to last 6f out: effrt and hung rt over 2f out: rdn and ev ch over 1f out: styd on u.p: hld towards fin* **2/1**[1]

0013 **3** *2 ½* **Le Rock (IRE)**[10] 4941 4-9-3 **73**.. DannyBrock 2 75
(J S Moore) *chsd ldrs: wnt 2nd 12f out tl 3rd and unable qck 2f out: styd on same pce u.p fr over 1f out* **9/2**[3]

2004 **4** *6* **Knight's Parade (IRE)**[13] 4023 6-9-2 **72**.......................(tp) LukeMorris 3 67
(Sarah Humphrey) *hld up in tch: effrt on inner over 3f out: unable qck u.p over 2f out: wknd fnl f* **3/1**[2]

3m 31.55s (-0.85) **Going Correction** -0.025s/f (Good) **4** Ran SP% **109.8**
Speed ratings (Par 103): **101,100,99,96**
CSF £6.34 TOTE £3.70; EX 6.30 Trifecta £14.30.
Owner SC Oliver Racing Limited **Bred** M E Wates **Trained** Newmarket, Suffolk

FOCUS
A fair little stayers' event despite the small field, and a sensible gallop throughout set by the winner. The third is rated as running to his latest form.

5335 TOTEPOOL RACECOURSE CASH BACK AVAILABLE H'CAP 5f 42y
6:35 (6:35) (Class 6) (0-55,55) 3-Y-O+ **£2,264** (£673; £336; £168) **Stalls** Centre

Form RPR
0016 **1** **Willow Spring**[29] 4264 4-9-0 **48**.. SaleemGolam 5 55
(Conrad Allen) *hld up in tch in midfield: hdwy to chse ldr over 1f out: rdn to ld 1f out: r.o wl: rdn out* **6/1**[2]

0500 **2** *1 ¼* **Give Us A Belle (IRE)**[9] 4980 7-8-10 **51**..........................(p) RPWalsh(7) 6 54
(Christine Dunnett) *led: rdn wl over 1f out: hdd 1f out: styd on same pce u.p ins fnl f* **16/1**

60-0 **3** *shd* **Plantation (IRE)**[29] 4278 3-9-1 **52**.. DannyBrock 9 53
(Robert Cowell) *in tch in midfield: effrt over 1f out: chsd ldng pair 1f out: kpt on same pce u.p fnl 150yds* **12/1**

6004 **4** *3 ¼* **Hurricane Alert**[19] 4658 4-8-13 **50**.................................... EoinWalsh(3) 7 40
(Natalie Lloyd-Beavis) *taken down early: jostled leaving stalls: sn rcvrd to chse ldr after 1f: rdn and unable qck over 1f out: high hd carriage and wknd ins fnl f* **11/1**

0350 **5** *1* **Lizzy's Dream**[9] 4968 8-9-3 **51**.. LukeMorris 4 38
(Rebecca Bastiman) *in tch towards rr: effrt 2f out: sme hdwy 1f out: plugged on same pce and no threat to ldrs fnl f* **8/1**

0025 **6** *1 ¼* **Frangarry (IRE)**[20] 4606 4-9-7 **55**................................(v) DarryllHolland 10 37
(Alan Bailey) *chsd ldr for 1f: styd chsng ldrs tl unable qck over 1f out: wknd fnl f* **3/1**[1]

503 **7** *4* **Vivre La Reve**[7] 5088 4-8-13 **50**....................................(v) RobHornby(3) 2 18
(James Unett) *racd towards centre: midfield: lost pl u.p and towards rr whn drvn 2f out: no rspnse: wknd over 1f out* **13/2**[3]

0644 **8** *nse* **Lillyput (IRE)**[7] 5087 3-9-0 **51**...................................... JFEgan 1 18
(Mick Channon) *racd towards centre: in tch in midfield: rdn 1/2-way: struggling u.p 2f out: sn btn: wknd fnl f* **7/1**

-500 **9** *2* **Burnt Cream**[69] 2845 9-9-2 **50**...(t) MartinHarley 3 11
(Martin Bosley) *restless in stalls: stdd and dropped in bhd after s: hld up in rr: rdn over 1f out: no rspnse: bhd ins fnl f* **13/2**[3]

1m 2.1s (-0.60) **Going Correction** -0.10s/f (Good)
WFA 3 from 4yo+ 3lb **9** Ran SP% **111.5**
Speed ratings (Par 101): **100,98,97,92,91 89,82,82,79**
CSF £90.60 CT £1084.20 TOTE £7.00: £2.00, £3.90, £4.30; EX 108.70 Trifecta £952.00.
Owner John C Davies **Bred** Kirtlington Stud Ltd **Trained** Newmarket, Suffolk

FOCUS
Very ordinary fare, though the winner could yet prove better than this grade in the right circumstances.

5336 TOTEEXACTA PICK THE 1ST AND 2ND H'CAP 7f 3y
7:05 (7:07) (Class 5) (0-75,75) 3-Y-O **£2,911** (£866; £432; £216) **Stalls** Centre

Form RPR

1040 **1** **Mywayistheonlyway (IRE)**[48] 3614 3-9-7 **75**............(bt¹) HarryBentley 3 82
(Martyn Meade) *sn trcking ldr: rdn to ld over 1f out: in command and r.o wl ins fnl f: comf* **11/8**[1]

2-01 **2** *1 ½* **Desert River (IRE)**[57] 3280 3-8-7 **61**............................ StevieDonohoe 4 64
(Mark H Tompkins) *trckd ldng pair: effrt over 1f out: chsd wnr ent fnl f: styd on but no imp on wnr* **8/1**

0564 **3** *2 ½* **Willsy**[14] 4789 3-9-4 **72**.. JFEgan 1 69
(Mick Channon) *t.k.h early: hld up in tch: rdn over 2f out: styd on same pce fnl f and no threat to wnr: wnt 3rd 100yds out* **9/2**[3]

064 **4** *hd* **Iberica Road (USA)**[13] 4840 3-9-6 **74**............................(t) DavidProbert 2 70
(Andrew Balding) *racd keenly: led and set stdy gallop: rdn 2f out: hdd over 1f out: wl hld and plugged on same pce ins fnl f: lost 3rd 100yds out* **7/2**[2]

4010 **5** *3 ¾* **Joules**[27] 4365 3-9-6 **74**...(t) TimmyMurphy 5 60
(Natalie Lloyd-Beavis) *t.k.h: hld up in tch in last: pushed along and hung lft over 1f out: sn wl btn* **5/1**

1m 26.19s (-0.41) **Going Correction** -0.10s/f (Good) **5** Ran SP% **110.3**
Speed ratings (Par 100): **98,96,93,93,88**
CSF £12.71 TOTE £2.50: £1.30, £3.10; EX 12.70 Trifecta £36.90.
Owner Richard Morecombe **Bred** M Duffy **Trained** Newmarket, Suffolk

FOCUS
An okay race for the grade. The well-backed winner was wearing first-time blinkers and is rated above his reappearance win.

5337 TOTETRIFECTA PICK THE 1,2,3 H'CAP 7f 3y
7:35 (7:35) (Class 5) (0-75,74) 4-Y-O+ **£2,911** (£866; £432; £216) **Stalls** Centre

Form RPR

-132 **1** **Twin Point**[16] 4742 5-9-7 **74**...(t) StevieDonohoe 1 81+
(Charlie Fellowes) *taken down early: mde all: set stdy gallop: rdn over 1f out: asserted 1f out: r.o wl and in command ins fnl f: pushed out* **6/4**[2]

2050 **2** *1 ½* **Veeraya**[17] 4715 6-8-10 **63**...(t) AdamBeschizza 4 66
(Julia Feilden) *trckd ldng pair: wnt 2nd 2f out and sn drvn to press wnr: unable qck 1f out: styd on same pce ins fnl f* **16/1**

2536 **3** *½* **He's My Boy (IRE)**[13] 4839 5-8-9 **69**........................... GeorgeWood(7) 2 71
(James Fanshawe) *stdd after s: t.k.h: hld up in tch in rr: effrt to chse ldrs over 1f out: styd on same pce u.p fnl f* **6/1**[3]

0401 **4** *nse* **Anastazia**[7] 5090 4-8-6 **66**.. DavidEgan(7) 5 67
(Paul D'Arcy) *s.i.s: hld up in tch in last pair: effrt over 1f out: styd on same pce u.p ins fnl f* **5/4**[1]

2300 **5** *3* **Stoked (IRE)**[13] 4841 4-9-4 **71**...................................... LemosdeSouza 3 64
(Chris Dwyer) *t.k.h: chsd wnr tl 2f out: sn lost pl and drvn: bhd and styd on same pce fnl f* **20/1**

1m 29.75s (3.15) **Going Correction** -0.10s/f (Good) **5** Ran SP% **109.4**
Speed ratings (Par 103): **78,76,75,75,72**
CSF £21.21 TOTE £2.30: £1.10, £3.80; EX 18.90 Trifecta £64.80.
Owner F J Perry **Bred** V I Araci **Trained** Newmarket, Suffolk

FOCUS
Just a steady gallop to this third race of the evening over the 7f trip, and the winner was allowed to dictate. The second and third didn't come into the race in the best of form.

5338 COLLECT TOTEPOOL WINNINGS AT BETFRED SHOPS H'CAP 7f 3y
8:05 (8:05) (Class 6) (0-55,54) 3-Y-O **£2,264** (£673; £336; £168) **Stalls** Centre

Form RPR

2404 **1** **Intimately**[31] 4202 3-8-10 **50**.. GeorgeWood(7) 6 57
(Jonathan Portman) *hld up in last trio: rdn and hdwy ent fnl 2f: led over 1f out: sustained duel w runner-up after: hld on wl u.p ins fnl f: all out* **6/1**[2]

0030 **2** *nk* **Infiniti (IRE)**[9] 4993 3-9-7 **54**... SaleemGolam 2 60
(Rae Guest) *hld up in tch in midfield: effrt ent fnl 2f: rdn and hdwy to chal over 1f out: sustained duel w wnr after: unable qck towards fin* **9/2**[1]

0-06 **3** *1 ½* **Color Force (IRE)**[68] 2904 3-9-5 **52**...............................(t) LukeMorris 4 54
(Gay Kelleway) *in tch in midfield: rdn over 2f out: hdwy u.p over 1f out: chsd ldng pair 1f out: styd on same pce ins fnl f* **8/1**[3]

-060 **4** *1 ½* **Any Guest (IRE)**[44] 3734 3-9-4 **51**..................................... TomQueally 5 49
(George Margarson) *t.k.h: hld up in tch in midfield: swtchd rt and hdwy over 1f out: rdn to chse ldng trio 1f out: styd on same pce ins fnl f* **6/1**[2]

406 **5** *9* **Cadland Lad (IRE)**[22] 4518 3-9-2 **49**................................ DannyBrock 10 23
(John Ryan) *chsd ldrs tl rdn to ld 2f out: sn hdd: 5th and btn 1f out: wknd qckly ins fnl f* **12/1**

0041 **6** *1 ¼* **Castlerea Tess**[73] 2741 3-9-3 **50**................................ PatrickMathers 14 20
(Sarah Hollinshead) *s.i.s: hld up in rr: effrt over 2f out: switching lft and hdwy u.p over 1f out: no imp and wl hld fnl f* **14/1**

4352 **7** *½* **Ettie Hart (IRE)**[9] 4992 3-9-0 **54**........................... KillianHennessy(7) 12 23
(Mick Channon) *chsd ldr: rdn and ev ch 2f out: unable qck and sn btn: wknd jst over 1f out* **9/2**[1]

5406 **8** *1* **Westbourne Grove (USA)**[8] 5041 3-9-6 **53**........................ JFEgan 8 19
(John Butler) *taken down early: t.k.h: hld up in tch in midfield: rdn and lost pl over 2f out: wknd over 1f out* **12/1**

0-06 **9** *¾* **Royal Mighty**[21] 4567 3-8-6 **46**................................... MillyNaseb(7) 13 10
(Jane Chapple-Hyam) *led tl 2f out: sn btn and hung lft over 1f out: wknd* **20/1**

0-66 **10** *1 ¾* **Noneedtotellme (IRE)**[14] 4806 3-8-9 **45**...................(v¹) RobHornby(3) 1 5
(James Unett) *in tch in midfield: effrt to chse ldrs 2f out: sn u.p and btn: wknd qckly jst over 1f out* **14/1**

0000 **11** *1 ¼* **Serendib's Glory (IRE)**[22] 4525 3-9-3 **50**................(p) AdamBeschizza 7 6
(Julia Feilden) *a towards rr: rdn over 2f out: sn struggling: bhd fnl f* **20/1**

000 **12** *5* **Fearless Poppy**[12] 4895 3-8-5 **45**..................................(b¹) RPWalsh(7) 3
(Christine Dunnett) *midfield tl 1/2-way: sn rdn and struggling: bhd over 1f out* **40/1**

1m 24.98s (-1.62) **Going Correction** -0.10s/f (Good) **12** Ran SP% **116.7**
Speed ratings (Par 98): **105,104,102,101,90 89,88,87,86,84 83,77**
CSF £31.71 CT £219.33 TOTE £10.00: £2.70, £2.00, £3.10; EX 45.70 Trifecta £227.40.
Owner Whitcoombe Park Racing **Bred** S Emmet And Miss R Emmet **Trained** Upper Lambourn, Berks

FOCUS
A low-grade finale for 3yos, but also the fastest of the evening's four 7f contests and they finished fairly well strung out.
T/Plt: £175.90 to a £1 stake. Pool: £56,593.47 - 234.84 winning units. T/Qpdt: £76.20 to a £1 stake. Pool: £3,967.23 - 38.51 winning units. **Steve Payne**

5339 - 5342a (Foreign Racing) - See Raceform Interactive

5091 LEOPARDSTOWN (L-H)
Thursday, August 11

OFFICIAL GOING: Good to firm

5343a INVESCO PENSION CONSULTANTS DESMOND STKS (GROUP 3) 1m
7:30 (7:30) 3-Y-O+
£27,113 (£8,731; £4,136; £1,838; £919; £459)

RPR

1 **Tribal Beat (IRE)**[292] 7478 3-9-2 101...........................(p) KevinManning 8 114+
(J S Bolger, Ire) *hld up bhd ldrs in 5th early: 6th 1/2-way: rdn in 5th 1 1/2f out and impr into 3rd ins fnl f: r.o wl u.p to ld ins fnl 100yds: asserted cl home* **9/1**

2 *1 ¾* **Cougar Mountain (IRE)**[47] 3677 5-9-9 110..........(tp) DonnachaO'Brien 2 111+
(A P O'Brien, Ire) *chsd ldrs early and pushed along: sn settled towards rr in 7th: rdn and gd hdwy fr over 1f out to chal on outer in cl 4th: kpt on wl into 2nd clsng stages: nt trble wnr* **7/2**[3]

3 *nk* **Hit It A Bomb (USA)**[286] 7624 3-9-2 116.................. SeamieHeffernan 6 109
(A P O'Brien, Ire) *on toes befhand: chsd ldrs: 4th 1/2-way: gng wl in 3rd fr 2f out and impr on outer to dispute over 1f out: rdn and hdd ins fnl f and no imp on wnr in 3rd cl home* **13/8**[1]

4 *hd* **Custom Cut (IRE)**[33] 4127 7-9-9 114............................ DanielTudhope 7 110
(David O'Meara) *settled bhd ldrs tl wnt 2nd bef 1/2-way: impr to ld on outer over 2f out: sn rdn and jnd u.p over 1f out: hdd ins fnl 100yds and no ex: dropped to 4th cl home* **2/1**[2]

5 *5* **Captain Joy (IRE)**[28] 4326 7-9-9 103................................. PatSmullen 3 98
(Tracey Collins, Ire) *led narrowly tl sn hdd and settled bhd ldr: dropped to 3rd bef 1/2-way: pushed along in 4th fr 2f out and no imp on ldrs u.p ent fnl f: one pce in mod 5th wl ins fnl f* **25/1**

6 *1 ¾* **Elleval (IRE)**[28] 4326 6-9-9 103....................................(p) WayneLordan 1 94
(David Marnane, Ire) *w.w in rr: last at 1/2-way: pushed along into st and no imp u.p in rr ent fnl f: kpt on one pce into mod 6th cl home: nvr nrr* **33/1**

7 *½* **General Macarthur (USA)**[22] 4543 3-9-2 103.......(t) ColmO'Donoghue 5 92
(A P O'Brien, Ire) *hld up in 6th early: 5th 1/2-way: n.m.r briefly 1 1/2f out and lost pl: no imp in 7th over 1f out: one pce after* **14/1**

8 *nse* **Dont Bother Me (IRE)**[19] 4625 6-9-9 97..........................(t) GaryHalpin 4 93
(Niall Moran, Ire) *sn led: 1 l clr at 1/2-way: rdn and hdd over 2f out: sn no ex u.p in 3rd and wknd fr over 1f out* **50/1**

1m 41.9s (0.70) **Going Correction** +0.45s/f (Yiel)
WFA 3 from 5yo+ 7lb **8** Ran SP% **119.1**
Speed ratings: **114,112,111,111,106 105,104,104**
CSF £41.64 TOTE £10.10: £2.50, £1.80, £1.02; DF 85.50 Trifecta £144.40.
Owner Godolphin **Bred** Darley **Trained** Coolcullen, Co Carlow

FOCUS
A belated reappearance winner for the 3yo ranks, but not the one the market expected.

5344 - 5347a (Foreign Racing) - See Raceform Interactive

5279 DEAUVILLE (R-H)
Thursday, August 11

OFFICIAL GOING: Turf: good; polytrack: standard

5348a PRIX DE TOUR-EN-BESSIN (MAIDEN) (2YO COLTS & GELDINGS) (ROUND) (TURF) 7f
11:55 (12:00) 2-Y-O **£9,191** (£3,676; £2,757; £1,838; £919)

RPR

1 **Kontrastat (FR)**[28] 2-9-2 0.. TheoBachelot 6 78
(S Wattel, France) **58/10**

2 *1 ¾* **Brise De Mer (FR)**[14] 4802 2-9-2 0............................ UmbertoRispoli 4 73
(George Baker) *led: rdn 2f out: strly pressed over 1f out and hdd ent fnl f: kpt on wout matching wnr after* **24/1**

3 *nk* **Mysterious Boy (FR)**[71] 2-9-2 0.............................. StephanePasquier 5 72
(Y Gourraud, France) **23/5**[3]

4 *1 ¼* **Goji Berry (FR)** 2-8-13 0... SebastienMaillot 10 66
(M Boutin, France) **39/1**

5 *nse* **Aufsteiger (FR)** 2-9-2 0.. AndraschStarke 7 68
(P Schiergen, Germany) **14/5**[2]

6 *nk* **Tresor (IRE)**[12] 2-9-2 0.. MaximeGuyon 9 68
(F Head, France) **76/10**

7 *shd* **Ascot Angel (FR)**[50] 2-9-2 0.............................. ChristopheSoumillon 3 67
(J-C Rouget, France) **27/10**[1]

8 *hd* **Beslon (FR)** 2-9-2 0.. CristianDemuro 1 67
(C Ferland, France) **9/1**

9 *2* **Nil Dream (FR)**[39] 2-9-2 0.. EddyHardouin 8 61
(J-P Gallorini, France) **26/1**

10 *7* **Out Of Ideas (FR)** 2-8-13 0... TonyPiccone 2 40
(Andrew Hollinshead, France) **56/1**

1m 29.21s (0.91) **10** Ran SP% **119.5**
WIN (incl. 1 euro stake): 6.80. PLACES: 2.90, 6.30, 2.10. DF: 61.20. SF: 110.30.
Owner B Plainfosse & Ecurie Palos De Moguer **Bred** B Plainfosse **Trained** France

5349a PRIX DE VILLERVILLE (CLAIMER) (3YO) (POLYTRACK) 1m 1f 110y
1:05 (12:00) 3-Y-O **£9,926** (£3,970; £2,977; £1,985; £992)

RPR

1 **Illustrissime (USA)**[71] 3-9-1 0................................ StephanePasquier 9 72
(N Clement, France) **1/1**[1]

2 3/4 **Little Ghetto Boy**[50] 3546 3-8-10 0............................ HugoJourniac(6) 7 71
(J-C Rouget, France) **13/1**

3 hd **Van Dyke**[31] 4213 3-8-11 0.. UmbertoRispoli 13 66
(Hughie Morrison) *prom on outer: rdn and effrt into st: styd on wl u.p but nt quite pce of wnr: jst missed 2nd* **18/1**

4 nk **Ipanemo (FR)**[48] 3-9-4 0.. CristianDemuro 2 72
(P Sogorb, France) **48/10**[2]

5 1 1/4 **Rougeoyant (FR)**[261] 7970 3-8-10 0.................... MlleAdelineMerou(8) 8 70
(B De Montzey, France) **13/1**

6 hd **Corroyer (IRE)**[9] 3-9-2 0...................................... EmmanuelEtienne(3) 4 70
(F Alloncle, France) **107/1**

7 nse **Roderic Queen (IRE)**[18] 3-8-13 0...................... ChristopheSoumillon 6 64
(Simone Brogi, France) **32/5**[3]

8 3 **Blonville (FR)**[38] 3-8-11 0................................ Pierre-CharlesBoudot 10 56
(Robert Collet, France) **9/1**

9 nk **Diamond Fragance (FR)**[46] 3-8-8 0........................... EddyHardouin 11 53
(C Lotoux, France) **50/1**

10 1 1/2 **Rosamaria (FR)**[25] 3-8-13 0.................................... MickaelBarzalona 3 54
(H-A Pantall, France) **31/1**

11 nk **Top Sensation (FR)**[25] 3-8-8 0...................................... GeraldMosse 12 49
(T Castanheira, France) **15/1**

WIN (incl. 1 euro stake): 2.00. PLACES: 1.30, 2.50, 3.10. DF: 11.90. SF: 18.50
Owner Frederic Sauque **Bred** Goldmark Farm Llc **Trained** Chantilly, France

4966 CATTERICK (L-H)
Friday, August 12

OFFICIAL GOING: Good (good to firm in places 8.4)
Wind: moderate 1/2 behind Weather: fine

5350 HAUGHTY HATS AMATEUR RIDERS' H'CAP 1m 3f 214y
5:40 (5:40) (Class 5) (0-75,77) 3-Y-O+ **£3,119** (£967; £483; £242) **Stalls** Centre

Form RPR

0332 **1** **Neuf Des Coeurs**[7] 5117 5-9-6 **58**................................(p) MrBLynn(5) 6 67
(Iain Jardine) *in rr: pushed along over 6f out: hdwy over 3f out: nt clr run and swtchd rt 2f out: 2nd appr fnl f: kpt on to ld last 100yds* **16/1**

0211 **2** 1 1/4 **Cliff Face (IRE)**[7] 5100 3-10-5 **77** 6ex....................... MissSBrotherton 2 84
(Sir Mark Prescott Bt) *hld up in mid-div: nt clr run and swtchd rt over 2f out: led appr fnl f: hdd and no ex last 100yds* **11/10**[1]

401 **3** 3 **Shirataki (IRE)**[5] 5208 8-9-4 **53** 6ex.......................... MissMollyKing(5) 4 58
(Peter Hiatt) *dwlt: in rr: hdwy to trck ldrs after 3f: nt clr run over 1f out: swtchd rt: kpt on to take 3rd nr fin* **22/1**

2221 **4** nk **Obboorr**[11] 4934 7-10-10 **76** 6ex.................................... MissHDukes(5) 3 78
(Tim Fitzgerald) *hld up towards rr: hdwy to trck ldrs 7f out: drvn over 3f out: one pce over 1f out* **8/1**[3]

5442 **5** nk **The Kid**[10] 4967 5-10-6 **72**... MrHHunt(5) 7 74
(John Quinn) *mid-div: chsng ldrs over 3f out: hung lft and one pce over 1f out* **10/1**

2245 **6** 2 **Aldreth**[11] 4935 5-10-9 **70**....................................(b) MissJoannaMason 9 68
(Michael Easterby) *led: hdd 7f out: led over 3f out: hdd appr fnl f: wknd* **16/1**

0030 **7** 8 **Graceful Act**[16] 4772 8-9-6 **56** oh10............................ MissAWaugh(3) 8 42
(Ron Barr) *hld up in rr: jnd ldr after 3f: led 7f out tl over 3f out: wknd over 1f out: bhd whn eased in clsng stages* **66/1**

0/41 **8** 1 1/2 **Zamoyski**[7] 5106 6-11-0 **75**...(p) MrSWalker 1 58
(Steve Gollings) *chsd ldrs: drvn over 4f out: lost pl over 1f out: eased in clsng stages* **10/3**[2]

3064 **9** 8 **Russian Royale**[10] 4969 6-10-8 **74**................................. MrJoeWright(5) 5 44
(Micky Hammond) *chsd ldrs: lost pl 2f out: bhd whn eased in clsng stages* **22/1**

2m 39.97s (1.07) **Going Correction** +0.05s/f (Good)
WFA 3 from 5yo+ 11lb **9** Ran SP% **112.9**
Speed ratings (Par 103): **98,97,95,94,94 93,88,87,81**
CSF £32.90 CT £408.86 TOTE £15.80: £3.70, £1.10, £4.50; EX 50.30 Trifecta £1057.80.
Owner Iain Livingstone **Bred** Conor J Colgan **Trained** Carrutherstown, D'fries & G'way

FOCUS
Rail movement added 9yds to race distance. A 56-75 handicap for amateur riders run at a moderate gallop, though the winner came from last to first and has been rated as stepping up on recent efforts.

5351 OOPS A DAISY FLORISTS (S) STKS 7f
6:10 (6:10) (Class 6) 2-Y-O **£2,587** (£770; £384; £192) **Stalls** Low

Form RPR

0012 **1** **Bismarck The Flyer (IRE)**[6] 5177 2-8-8 69........... JacobButterfield(3) 2 60
(Ollie Pears) *trckd ldng pair: effrt over 3f out: led 1f out: hld on in clsng stages* **8/11**[1]

053 **2** nk **Amy Gardner**[14] 4842 2-8-1 47...................................... NathanEvans(5) 4 54
(James Given) *led 1f: trckd ldr: pushed along over 3f out: rallied over 1f out: kpt on to take 2nd last 50yds* **9/2**[3]

0303 **3** 1 1/2 **Forster Square (IRE)**[6] 5177 2-8-11 64......................... TonyHamilton 3 55
(Richard Fahey) *trckd ldng pair: t.k.h: 2nd over 3f out: led narrowly 2f out: hdd 1f out: kpt on one pce* **10/3**[2]

2464 **4** 5 **Smiley Riley (IRE)**[17] 4728 2-8-11 64...........................(p) BarryMcHugh 6 41
(Tony Coyle) *led after 1f: pushed along over 3f out: hdd 2f out: wknd fnl f* **11/1**

1m 28.57s (1.57) **Going Correction** +0.05s/f (Good) **4** Ran SP% **107.5**
Speed ratings (Par 92): **93,92,90,85**
CSF £4.26 TOTE £2.10; EX 4.40 Trifecta £7.30.There was no bid for the winner.
Owner Ontoawinner & Ollie Pears **Bred** Edgeridge Ltd **Trained** Norton, N Yorks

FOCUS
Rail movement added 9yds to race distance. Probably just an ordinary juvenile seller, but the winner is better than the bare form.

5352 KEITH PARTRIDGE MEMORIAL NURSERY H'CAP 5f 212y
6:45 (6:45) (Class 4) (0-85,78) 2-Y-O **£5,175** (£1,540; £769; £384) **Stalls** Low

Form RPR

6434 **1** **Trick Of The Lyte (IRE)**[12] 4915 2-8-6 **63**........................... CamHardie 3 66
(John Quinn) *trckd ldrs: nt clr run on ins fr 2f out tl squeezed through to ld last 50yds* **9/2**

310 **2** 3/4 **Harome (IRE)**[51] 3515 2-9-2 **73**.. SamJames 1 74
(David Loughnane) *w ldr: led 4f out: hdd and no ex last 50yds* **9/1**

213 **3** nse **Dandy Highwayman (IRE)**[13] 4891 2-9-7 **78**................. PJMcDonald 5 78
(Ollie Pears) *trckd ldrs: effrt 3f out: upsides over 1f out: kpt on same pce in clsng stages* **2/1**[1]

234 **4** 3 **Climax**[27] 4405 2-8-10 **67**.. FrannyNorton 2 58
(Mark Johnston) *led 2f: w ldrs: wknd fnl f* **7/2**[3]

4301 **5** 2 1/2 **Major Jumbo**[13] 4891 2-8-12 **69**.. ShaneGray 6 52+
(Kevin Ryan) *chsd ldrs: drvn over 3f out: sn outpcd and last* **3/1**[2]

1m 13.94s (0.34) **Going Correction** +0.05s/f (Good) **5** Ran SP% **108.7**
Speed ratings (Par 96): **99,98,97,93,90**
CSF £37.31 TOTE £4.60: £3.00, £3.70; EX 33.00 Trifecta £152.00.
Owner The Lyteproducts Partnership **Bred** Mrs M Fox **Trained** Settrington, N Yorks

FOCUS
Rail movement added 9yds to race distance. A decent gallop to this nursery though the form is unlikely to prove anything special. The winner has improved marginally.

5353 ALAN CLOUGH MAIDEN STKS 1m 3f 214y
7:20 (7:20) (Class 5) 3-Y-O+ **£3,234** (£962; £481; £240) **Stalls** Centre

Form RPR

5 **1** **Gala**[49] 3601 3-8-12 0.. GrahamLee 1 78+
(John Gosden) *hld up in last: hdwy 7f out: sn trcking ldrs: led over 2f out: drvn over 1f out: styd on* **5/6**[1]

2032 **2** 1 1/4 **Pleasure Dome**[20] 4633 3-8-12 77.............................. AdrianMcCarthy 2 76
(Peter Chapple-Hyam) *led early: trckd ldrs: 2nd 2f out: sn drvn: kpt on same pce fnl f* **6/4**[2]

04 **3** 7 **Notion Of Beauty (USA)**[13] 4857 3-8-7 0.............. JordanVaughan(5) 3 65
(K R Burke) *trckd ldrs: 2nd after 2f: led 4f out: hdd over 2f out: wknd fnl f* **8/1**[3]

4 41 **Feisty Girl**[378] 6-9-9 0.. RobertTart 4
(Michael Mullineaux) *s.s: sn chsng ldrs: pushed along over 7f out: lost pl over 3f out: sn wl bhd: t.o* **100/1**

5 1/2 **Python**[43] 4-10-0 0.. NeilFarley 5
(Andrew Crook) *t.k.h: sn led: hdd 4f out: lost pl over 3f out: sn wl bhd: t.o* **100/1**

2m 39.75s (0.85) **Going Correction** +0.05s/f (Good)
WFA 3 from 4yo+ 11lb **5** Ran SP% **107.6**
Speed ratings (Par 103): **99,98,93,66,65**
CSF £2.18 TOTE £1.60: £1.10, £1.10; EX 2.20 Trifecta £2.60.
Owner Denford Stud **Bred** Denford Stud Ltd **Trained** Newmarket, Suffolk

FOCUS
Rail movement added 9yds to race distance. An uncompetitive maiden run at just an ordinary gallop, but the winner improved on her debut effort and should do even better.

5354 BLACK BULL INN MOULTON H'CAP 5f
7:50 (7:52) (Class 6) (0-65,65) 3-Y-O+ **£2,587** (£770; £384; £192) **Stalls** Low

Form RPR

6024 **1** **Salvatore Fury (IRE)**[2] 5295 6-9-7 **62**..................(p) GrahamGibbons 5 71+
(Keith Dalgleish) *mid-div: effrt over 2f out: nt clr run over 1f out: swtchd rt: hung lft and kpt on to ld last 75yds* **7/2**[1]

0211 **2** 1 **Compton River**[10] 4968 4-9-4 **59** 6ex............................ PaulMulrennan 9 64
(Bryan Smart) *chsd ldrs: led over 1f out: hdd and no ex last 75yds* **5/1**[3]

5040 **3** 3/4 **Ypres**[8] 5060 7-9-6 **61**.. FrannyNorton 13 64
(Jason Ward) *s.i.s: swtchd lft after s: in rr: hdwy over 1f out: styd on wl to take 3rd nr fin* **18/1**

0662 **4** 1/2 **Innocently (IRE)**[6] 5162 5-9-5 **65**...............................(b[1]) JoshDoyle(5) 6 66
(David O'Meara) *mid-div: drvn over 2f out: kpt on wl fnl f: tk 4th cl home* **4/1**[2]

3144 **5** shd **Perfect Words (IRE)**[11] 4931 6-9-7 **65**................(p) JacobButterfield(3) 7 66
(Marjorie Fife) *mid-div: hdwy 2f out: kpt on fnl f* **25/1**

0500 **6** nk **Jacob's Pillow**[14] 4848 5-9-4 **64**............................ AdamMcNamara(5) 14 63
(Rebecca Bastiman) *in rr: hdwy over 1f out: keeping on at fin* **16/1**

0444 **7** shd **Pavers Star**[4] 5225 7-8-13 **54**...(p) BarryMcHugh 2 53
(Noel Wilson) *led: hdd over 1f out: fdd in clsng stages* **17/2**

0600 **8** 1/2 **Windforpower (IRE)**[10] 4968 6-9-5 **60**.............................(p) JasonHart 3 57
(Tracy Waggott) *chsd ldrs: one pce appr fnl f* **28/1**

0430 **9** 1/2 **Boxing Shadows**[59] 3268 6-9-9 **64**....................................... DavidAllan 8 60
(Les Eyre) *chsd ldrs: one pce over 1f out* **12/1**

3453 **10** 3/4 **Groundworker (IRE)**[19] 4691 5-9-10 **65**.........................(p) GrahamLee 1 58
(Paul Midgley) *chsd ldrs: one pce fnl 2f* **15/2**

0060 **11** 4 1/2 **Wilsons Ruby (IRE)**[8] 5069 3-8-11 **62**....................(b[1]) BenRobinson(7) 4 38
(Brian Ellison) *s.i.s: nvr on terms* **20/1**

0104 **12** 1 1/4 **Bold Spirit**[10] 4970 5-9-5 **60**..(vt) TomEaves 11 32
(Declan Carroll) *chsd ldrs: lost pl over 1f out* **20/1**

5050 **13** 11 **Another Desperado (IRE)**[9] 5041 3-7-9 **46** oh1..........(p) RPWalsh(7) 12
(Rebecca Bastiman) *racd wd: chsd ldrs: lost pl 2f out: sn bhd: eased in clsng stages* **100/1**

59.8s **Going Correction** +0.05s/f (Good)
WFA 3 from 4yo+ 3lb **13** Ran SP% **117.8**
Speed ratings (Par 101): **102,100,99,98,98 97,97,96,96,94 87,85,68**
CSF £18.89 CT £287.89 TOTE £4.30: £1.90, £1.80, £5.10; EX 25.40 Trifecta £293.60.
Owner Prestige Thoroughbred Racing **Bred** Ken Harris & Dr Brid Corkery **Trained** Carluke, S Lanarks

FOCUS
Exposed performers in this 46-65 sprint handicap in which 11 of the 15 runners had some sort of headgear, but the winner won in the style of one with more to offer in the short term.

5355 24TH AUGUST IS FAMILY DAY H'CAP 7f
8:25 (8:27) (Class 6) (0-60,58) 3-Y-O+ **£2,587** (£770; £384; £192) **Stalls** Low

Form RPR

5203 **1** **Emblaze**[25] 4444 4-9-9 **57**.. PaulMulrennan 10 68
(Bryan Smart) *swtchd lft after s: mde all: kpt on wl fnl f* **10/1**

4132 **2** 2 1/4 **Deben**[10] 4973 3-9-4 **58**.. JoeDoyle 2 61
(Kevin Ryan) *chsd ldrs: 2nd 1f out: kpt on same pce: no imp* **3/1**[1]

0000 **3** 1¼ **Coolcalmcollected (IRE)**[45] 3750 4-9-4 **52**............... GrahamGibbons 4 56+
(David Loughnane) *s.i.s: hdwy into mid-div over 3f out: effrt over 2f out: kpt on fnl f: tk 3rd post* **4/1**[2]
0U10 **4** shd **Beadlam (IRE)**[3] 5277 3-9-2 **56** 6ex.................................. PJMcDonald 14 55
(David Loughnane) *mid-div: hdwy over 2f out: kpt on fnl f* **8/1**[3]
3640 **5** ¾ **Canford Belle**[20] 4647 3-8-11 **56**............................... PhilDennis(5) 12 53
(Grant Tuer) *in rr: hdwy 2f out: kpt on wl last 150yds* **33/1**
0-35 **6** hd **Lord Rob**[26] 4425 5-8-11 **45**.. PatrickMathers 11 44
(David Thompson) *mid-div: hdwy over 2f out: kpt on fnl f* **9/1**
4055 **7** hd **Nelson's Bay**[8] 5068 7-9-5 **53**.. CamHardie 1 51
(Wilf Storey) *mid-div: effrt over 2f out: kpt on fnl f* **14/1**
2200 **8** hd **Mr Potter**[21] 4600 3-9-2 **56**.. FrannyNorton 8 52
(Richard Guest) *chsd ldrs: kpt on one pce appr fnl f* **25/1**
05/6 **9** 1 **Tom's Anna (IRE)**[16] 4772 6-8-9 **50**.................................. PaulaMuir(7) 7 45
(Sean Regan) *chsd ldrs: one pce whn n.m.r and swtchd lft 1f out* **25/1**
0550 **10** shd **Just Paul (IRE)**[8] 5068 6-9-7 **55**.....................................(p) JackGarritty 6 51
(Micky Hammond) *chsd ldrs: nt clr run on inner over 1f out: one pce* **10/1**
0206 **11** ½ **Adiator**[25] 4454 8-9-1 **56**...(p) CliffordLee(7) 5 49
(Neville Bycroft) *chsd ldrs: drvn over 2f out: fdd appr fnl f* **12/1**
5505 **12** 3¼ **Saltarello (IRE)**[11] 4932 4-9-6 **54**.. SamJames 9 39
(Marjorie Fife) *hld up in mid-div: effrt over 2f out: lost pl over 1f out* **12/1**
0430 **13** 2¼ **Magical Lasso (IRE)**[13] 4872 3-8-11 **56**............(p) ShirleyTeasdale(5) 15 33
(Keith Dalgleish) *a towards rr* **33/1**
0004 **14** 5 **Canford Kilbey (IRE)**[18] 4705 3-8-8 **48**...................(b1) BarryMcHugh 13 11
(Michael Easterby) *in rr: bhd fnl 2f* **66/1**
00-0 **15** 7 **Suuki**[7] 5101 3-8-5 **45**...(t) RoystonFfrench 3
(Adam West) *in rr: bhd fnl 2f* **80/1**

1m 27.9s (0.90) **Going Correction** +0.05s/f (Good)
WFA 3 from 4yo+ 6lb **15** Ran SP% **122.6**
Speed ratings (Par 101): **96,93,92,91,91 90,90,90,89,89 88,84,82,76,68**
CSF £38.36 CT £149.84 TOTE £11.40: £3.30, £1.60, £2.40; EX 41.70 Trifecta £208.00.
Owner Crossfields Racing **Bred** Crossfields Bloodstock Ltd **Trained** Hambleton, N Yorks

FOCUS
Rail movement added 9yds to race distance. A low-grade 7f handicap featuring plenty of exposed and hard-to-win with sorts. The pace was moderate and the winner made all having enjoyed a good trip..
T/Plt: £65.80 to a £1 stake. Pool of £53160.77 - 589.73 winning tickets. T/Qpdt: £20.20 to a £1 stake. Pool of £4160.35 - 152.20 winning tickets. **Walter Glynn**

4551 NEWBURY (L-H)

Friday, August 12

OFFICIAL GOING: Good to firm (good in places)
Wind: Moderate, against Weather: Sunny and warm

5356 DON DEADMAN MEMORIAL EBF STALLIONS MAIDEN STKS (PLUS 10 RACE) 7f (S)

2:20 (2:21) (Class 4) 2-Y-O **£4,528** (£1,347; £673; £336) **Stalls** Centre

Form RPR
3 **1** **Ultimate Avenue (IRE)**[30] 4274 2-9-5 0.......................... GeorgeBaker 4 85+
(Ed Walker) *t.k.h: mde virtually all: rdn clr 1f out: readily* **7/4**[1]
2 1¾ **Syndicate** 2-9-0 0.. JamesDoyle 12 74+
(Ralph Beckett) *mid-div: hdwy over 2f out: drvn to chse wnr fnl f: r.o* **7/1**
3 hd **Muhajjal** 2-9-5 0... PaulHanagan 9 79+
(Owen Burrows) *mid-div: hdwy over 1f out: r.o fnl f* **14/1**
0 **4** ½ **Colibri (IRE)**[13] 4866 2-9-5 0.. JimCrowley 2 77
(Hugo Palmer) *a.p: kpt on u.p fnl 2f* **10/1**
43 **5** hd **Procurator (IRE)**[7] 5107 2-9-5 0... SeanLevey 5 77
(Richard Hannon) *stdd s: plld hrd in midfield: hdwy over 1f out: styd on* **6/1**[3]
6 1¼ **Hushood (IRE)** 2-9-5 0.. DavidProbert 11 73
(Richard Hannon) *dwlt: towards rr tl styd on fnl 2f* **33/1**
30 **7** ¾ **Plant Pot Power (IRE)**[10] 4989 2-9-5 0................... RichardKingscote 7 72
(Richard Hannon) *w wnr tl no ex over 1f out* **14/1**
8 1¾ **Flying North** 2-9-0 0.. PatDobbs 6 62+
(Richard Hannon) *stdd s: hld up in rr: hung lft 2f out: effrt and n.m.r jst over 1f out: nvr nrr* **33/1**
9 1½ **Meyrick** 2-9-5 0... AndreaAtzeni 3 63
(William Haggas) *t.k.h: in tch tl outpcd fnl 2f* **9/2**[2]
6 **10** ¾ **Tis Wonderful (IRE)**[13] 4877 2-9-5 0.................................. AdamKirby 1 61
(Clive Cox) *prom: rdn over 2f out: edgd rt and wknd over 1f out* **50/1**
11 nk **Padrinho (IRE)** 2-9-5 0... KierenFox 10 60
(John Best) *chsd ldrs tl wknd 2f out* **100/1**
12 1½ **Sixties Sheila** 2-9-0 0... CharlesBishop 8 53+
(Mick Channon) *towards rr: effrt over 2f out: n.d whn hmpd jst over 1f out* **66/1**
13 2½ **Young Officer (IRE)** 2-9-5 0.. JimmyFortune 14 49
(Brian Meehan) *a bhd* **50/1**

1m 28.22s (2.52) **Going Correction** +0.125s/f (Good) **13** Ran SP% **116.0**
Speed ratings (Par 96): **90,88,87,87,86 85,84,82,80,80 79,78,75**
CSF £13.16 TOTE £2.70: £1.10, £2.90, £3.10; EX 17.30 Trifecta £100.30.
Owner P K Siu **Bred** Brian O'Neill **Trained** Upper Lambourn, Berks

FOCUS
Watered ground but a warm, sunny day. The rail had been moved in on the round course from the 8f to the 5f to give fresh ground. Probably a good maiden - the first, third, fourth and ninth came into this entered in Group company this year. The winner won well and nice starts from the placed horses.

5357 CHRISTOPHER SMITH ASSOCIATES H'CAP 1m (S)

2:50 (2:53) (Class 4) (0-80,81) 3-Y-O+ **£4,690** (£1,395; £697; £348) **Stalls** Centre

Form RPR
6134 **1** **Wind In My Sails**[15] 4788 4-9-5 **75**.....................................[1] LiamKeniry 9 88
(Ed de Giles) *patiently rdn in rr: shkn up 2f out: smooth hdwy over 1f out: drvn to ld ins fnl f* **10/1**[3]
1323 **2** 1¾ **Exceeding Power**[14] 4841 5-8-9 **72**.............................. GeorgeWood(7) 6 81
(Martin Bosley) *chsd ldrs: led over 1f out tl ins fnl f: unable qck* **4/1**[2]
3034 **3** 4 **Steal The Scene (IRE)**[14] 4839 4-9-6 **76**............................. SeanLevey 1 76
(Richard Hannon) *prom: led over 2f out: edgd lft and hdd over 1f out: one pce* **4/1**[2]
6361 **4** 3 **Corporal Maddox**[12] 4908 9-9-11 **81** 6ex.........................(p) AdamKirby 3 74
(Ronald Harris) *towards rr: hdwy to chse ldrs 2f out: no ex fnl f* **16/1**
1024 **5** 1¼ **Marcano (IRE)**[8] 5075 4-9-6 **76**.................................(t) FrederikTylicki 4 66
(Rod Millman) *chsd ldrs tl wknd over 1f out* **7/2**[1]
0-00 **6** 1½ **Monsieur Chevalier (IRE)**[87] 2328 9-9-7 **77**...............(v) DavidProbert 8 64
(Nikki Evans) *in tch tl edgd rt and btn 2f out* **66/1**

4505 **7** 5 **Mister Musicmaster**[12] 4908 7-9-7 **77**............................ SteveDrowne 5 52
(Ron Hodges) *mid-div: effrt over 2f out: hrd rdn and wknd over 1f out* **14/1**
361 **8** 3½ **Lulani (IRE)**[16] 4777 4-9-10 **80**... JimCrowley 2 47
(Harry Dunlop) *prom: hung lft 2f out: sn wknd* **4/1**[2]
5045 **9** 1 **Cordite (IRE)**[23] 4532 5-9-7 **77**.......................................(p) SamHitchcott 7 42
(Jim Boyle) *racd alone towards stands' rail: led tl over 2f out: sn wknd* **14/1**

1m 39.52s (-0.18) **Going Correction** +0.125s/f (Good) **9** Ran SP% **112.0**
Speed ratings (Par 105): **105,103,99,96,95 93,88,85,84**
CSF £47.86 CT £188.39 TOTE £11.40: £3.20, £1.70, £1.60; EX 55.20 Trifecta £256.10.
Owner John Manser **Bred** Meon Valley Stud **Trained** Ledbury, H'fords

FOCUS
The pace was fast. Plenty went right for the winner and the race has been rated around the runner-up.

5358 BERRY BROS. & RUDD CELLAR PLAN H'CAP 1m 5f 61y

3:20 (3:22) (Class 3) (0-90,90) 3-Y-O+ **£7,762** (£2,310; £1,154; £577) **Stalls** Centre

Form RPR
1416 **1** **The Graduate (IRE)**[34] 4137 3-8-6 **80**.............................. DavidProbert 7 88+
(Andrew Balding) *prom: outpcd 3f out: rallied 2f out: edgd lft: slt ld fnl 100yds: all out* **3/1**[1]
-000 **2** shd **Continuum**[21] 4581 7-9-12 **88**..................................(v) RichardKingscote 3 95
(Peter Hedger) *s.s: hld up in rr: rdn and hdwy over 1f out: drvn nrly level fnl 100yds: r.o* **8/1**
1000 **3** 1¾ **Sunblazer (IRE)**[48] 3658 6-9-7 **90**.............................(t) JoshuaBryan(7) 10 94
(Kim Bailey) *hld up in 5th: hdwy 4f out: led 3f out tl fnl 100yds: one pce* **20/1**
1134 **4** ½ **Touch The Sky**[23] 4535 5-9-9 **85**...................................... JamesDoyle 4 89
(David Elsworth) *chsd ldr: hrd rdn 3f out: lost 2nd 2f out: kpt on u.p* **9/2**[3]
-245 **5** 2 **Faithful Mount**[29] 4311 7-9-7 **83**... AdamKirby 5 84
(Ian Williams) *chsd ldrs: effrt and nt clr run over 1f out tl ins fnl f: no ex* **13/2**
5031 **6** ¾ **Niceonecenturion**[36] 4057 3-8-5 **79**............................... MartinDwyer 1 79
(William Knight) *dwlt: t.k.h off the pce in 6th: drvn along over 2f out: styd on same pce* **7/2**[2]
26/3 **7** 7 **Cool Macavity (IRE)**[35] 4077 8-9-10 **86**...................... DougieCostello 9 75
(Nicky Henderson) *dwlt: bhd: effrt and hrd rdn 2f out: sn wknd* **11/1**
12 **8** 10 **Zambeasy**[81] 2549 5-9-8 **84**.. GeorgeBaker 6 58
(Philip Hide) *racd freely: led at gd pce tl 3f out: wknd over 2f out* **9/1**

2m 48.87s (-3.13) **Going Correction** -0.05s/f (Good)
WFA 3 from 4yo+ 12lb **8** Ran SP% **112.9**
Speed ratings (Par 107): **107,106,105,105,104 103,99,93**
CSF £26.70 CT £399.87 TOTE £3.40: £1.70, £2.90, £4.20; EX 29.90 Trifecta £564.70.
Owner Mick and Janice Mariscotti **Bred** Daniel Chassagneux **Trained** Kingsclere, Hants

FOCUS
This was run over 7yds further than advertised. Just an ordinary-looking race for the grade, but a sound pace and the winner seems likely to rate a bit better yet.

5359 BATHWICK TYRES ST HUGH'S FILLIES' STKS (LISTED RACE) 5f 34y

3:55 (3:57) (Class 1) 2-Y-O

£14,461 (£5,482; £2,743; £1,366; £685; £344) **Stalls** Centre

Form RPR
111 **1** **Mrs Danvers**[27] 4394 2-9-0 89.................................... RichardKingscote 1 104+
(Jonathan Portman) *prom: drvn to ld 1f out: pushed out* **5/2**[1]
512 **2** 2 **Equimou**[20] 4669 2-9-0 90... AndreaAtzeni 6 97
(Robert Eddery) *chsd ldr: led briefly over 1f out: unable qck fnl f* **9/1**
0002 **3** 1¼ **Stormy Clouds (IRE)**[27] 4394 2-9-0 88.............................(b) PatDobbs 3 93
(Richard Hannon) *outpcd and bhd: hdwy and edgd lft over 1f out: nrest at fin* **12/1**
2161 **4** ¾ **Barroche (IRE)**[23] 4503 2-9-0 89.. AdamKirby 7 90
(Clive Cox) *led tl over 1f out: one pce* **8/1**
6111 **5** nk **Rajar**[13] 4884 2-9-0 91.. SeanLevey 2 89
(Richard Hannon) *towards rr: hung lft and sme hdwy 2f out: no imp fnl f* **7/2**[2]
4621 **6** 3 **Stop The Wages (IRE)**[13] 4879 2-9-0 77......................... MartinDwyer 5 78
(Brian Meehan) *stdd s: t.k.h towards rr: effrt and in tch 2f out: wknd over 1f out* **25/1**
323 **7** 2 **Savannah's Dream**[19] 4685 2-9-0 88............................... DanielTudhope 8 71
(David O'Meara) *prom tl hrd rdn and wknd wl over 1f out* **25/1**
030 **8** 2½ **Grand Myla (IRE)**[16] 4756 2-9-0 77................................ DougieCostello 4 62
(Gary Moore) *outpcd: a wl bhd* **50/1**
1021 **9** 2½ **Tahoo (IRE)**[20] 4669 2-9-0 88... JoeyHaynes 10 53
(K R Burke) *in tch: rdn 2f out: sn wknd* **25/1**
103 **10** 6 **Dainty Dandy (IRE)**[20] 4623 2-9-0 98............................ PaulHanagan 11 31
(Paul Cole) *prom tl wknd 2f out* **11/2**[3]
314 **11** 2 **Tallulah Rose**[20] 4623 2-9-0 94.. SteveDrowne 9 24
(George Baker) *mid-div: rdn over 2f out: sn wknd* **14/1**

1m 1.3s (-0.10) **Going Correction** +0.125s/f (Good) **11** Ran SP% **115.1**
Speed ratings (Par 99): **105,101,99,98,98 93,90,86,82,72 69**
CSF £24.06 TOTE £2.90: £1.10, £3.10, £4.60; EX 25.30 Trifecta £261.50.
Owner Turf Club 2014 **Bred** M A Burton & Connie Hopper **Trained** Upper Lambourn, Berks

FOCUS
Just an ordinary juvenile fillies' Listed event, but there's no knocking the winner who just keeps on getting better.

5360 INSPIRATION INC. H'CAP 5f 34y

4:30 (4:30) (Class 4) (0-85,90) 3-Y-O+ **£5,175** (£1,540; £769; £384) **Stalls** Centre

Form RPR
300 **1** **Sandfrankskipsgo**[36] 4066 7-9-6 **83**................................ GeorgeBaker 6 91
(Peter Crate) *hld up: hdwy to ld jst over 1f out: rdn out* **8/1**
-631 **2** ¾ **Little Voice (USA)**[9] 5040 3-9-4 **84** 6ex.......................... JamesDoyle 1 88
(Charles Hills) *hld up: hdwy and carried lft over 1f out: drvn to chal ins fnl f: kpt on* **5/2**[1]
3531 **3** ¾ **Majestic Hero (IRE)**[12] 4911 4-9-13 **90** 6ex..................... AdamKirby 3 92
(Ronald Harris) *prom: hrd rdn and hung lft over 1f out: kpt on* **11/4**[2]
3413 **4** ¾ **Secret Asset (IRE)**[20] 4632 11-9-3 **83**.........................(v) RobHornby(3) 5 83
(Lisa Williamson) *chsd ldrs: kpt on u.p fnl 2f* **8/1**
0503 **5** 1¾ **King Crimson**[12] 4911 4-9-4 **81**... CharlesBishop 4 74
(Mick Channon) *led tl jst over 1f out: no ex ins fnl f* **13/2**[3]
5613 **6** nk **Newton's Law (IRE)**[8] 5050 5-8-9 **79**.........................(tp) JordanUys(7) 2 71
(Brian Meehan) *s.s: outpcd in rr: styng on at fin* **13/2**[3]
0000 **7** 6 **Red Stripes (USA)**[17] 4735 4-9-3 **80**......................(b) RichardKingscote 7 51
(Lisa Williamson) *racd alone towards stands' rail: w ldr for 3f* **12/1**

1m 1.42s (0.02) **Going Correction** +0.125s/f (Good)
WFA 3 from 4yo+ 3lb **7** Ran SP% **111.8**
Speed ratings (Par 105): **104,102,101,100,97 97,87**
CSF £27.08 TOTE £8.90: £3.90, £1.90; EX 34.40 Trifecta £159.50.

The Form Book, Raceform Ltd, Newbury, RG14 5SJ

Owner Peter Crate **Bred** Peter Crate **Trained** Newdigate, Surrey

FOCUS

A fair sprint handicap which was set up for the closers. The winner is back to form off a good mark.

5361 BREEDERS BACKING RACING AND TUTTS CLUMP CIDER EBF MAIDEN FILLIES' STKS 1m 2f 6y

5:00 (5:01) (Class 5) 3-Y-O+ **£5,175** (£1,540; £769; £384) **Stalls** Centre

Form RPR

2- **1** **Myopic**[339] 6186 3-9-0 0 ... AdamKirby 2 84+
(Luca Cumani) *chsd tearaway ldr: rdn over 3f out: kpt on dourly to ld 100yds out* **7/4**[1]

2 *1 1/4* **Scattered Stars** 3-9-0 0 ... JamesDoyle 1 81+
(Charlie Appleby) *dwlt: sn chsng ldng pair: rdn 4f out: plugged on to take 2nd nr fin* **9/4**[2]

-234 **3** *1 3/4* **Malmoosa (IRE)**[34] 4160 3-9-0 82 ...(p) PaulHanagan 4 77
(Brian Meehan) *led at fast pce: rdn and tiring 2f out: wknd and hdd 100yds out* **5/2**[3]

0 **4** *6* **Poppy Time**[102] 1931 3-9-0 0 ... RyanTate 6 65
(James Eustace) *outpcd: modest 4th thrght* **50/1**

5 *3* **Wink And Win (IRE)** 3-9-0 0 ... SteveDrowne 3 59
(Charles Hills) *outpcd: modest 5th thrght* **20/1**

4 **6** *4 1/2* **Lady Natasha (IRE)**[15] 4806 3-9-0 0 ... DougieCostello 7 50
(K R Burke) *outpcd: a last: n.d fnl 3f* **14/1**

2m 6.37s (-2.43) **Going Correction** -0.05s/f (Good) **6** Ran SP% **109.1**

Speed ratings (Par 100): **107,106,104,99,97 93**

CSF £5.59 TOTE £2.20: £1.10, £2.80; EX 6.00 Trifecta £9.80.

Owner The Dukes Of Devonshire & Roxburghe **Bred** Floors Farming & The Duke Of Devonshire **Trained** Newmarket, Suffolk

FOCUS

This was run over 7yds further than advertised. The front three have a fair amount of ability, with the winner and second the least exposed. The third went off hard with the first two visibly tiring late on.

5362 MOBILE PIMM'S BARS APPRENTICE H'CAP 1m 1f

5:35 (5:35) (Class 5) (0-75,75) 3-Y-O+ **£3,234** (£962; £481; £240) **Stalls** Centre

Form RPR

0422 **1** **Kismet Hardy**[7] 5122 3-8-13 **71** ...(p) MeganNicholls(3) 2 79
(Richard Hannon) *mde virtually all: drvn clr over 1f out: styd on wl* **6/4**[1]

0042 **2** *2 1/2* **Ocean Eleven**[14] 4840 3-8-13 **75** ... JonathanFisher(7) 6 78
(John Ryan) *w wnr: rdn 2f out: styd on same pce* **7/1**

0233 **3** *2* **Arithmetic (IRE)**[10] 4986 3-8-10 **70** ... JordanUys(5) 7 68
(Charles Hills) *hld up in 5th: effrt 2f out: one pce* **7/2**[3]

5634 **4** *1 1/4* **Silhouette (IRE)**[22] 4562 3-9-2 **71** ... PaddyPilley 5 66
(Daniel Kubler) *hld up in 4th: effrt 2f out: btn over 1f out* **3/1**[2]

060 **5** *3 3/4* **Royal Occassion**[25] 4458 4-9-5 **69** ... HollieDoyle(3) 3 56
(Jim Boyle) *prom tl hrd rdn and wknd 2f out* **12/1**

0050 **6** *11* **Dukes Meadow**[29] 4302 5-8-9 **59** ...(p[1]) RhiainIngram(3) 8 22
(Roger Ingram) *a in rr: n.d fnl 4f* **16/1**

1m 56.05s (0.55) **Going Correction** -0.05s/f (Good)

WFA 3 from 4yo+ 8lb **6** Ran SP% **113.3**

Speed ratings (Par 103): **95,92,91,89,86 76**

CSF £12.99 CT £31.24 TOTE £2.10: £1.10, £2.90; EX 10.80 Trifecta £35.40.

Owner Mason Brown Partnership 2 **Bred** Andrew Parrish **Trained** East Everleigh, Wilts

FOCUS

This was run over 7yds further than advertised. Only two of these had won before, including the winner. The pace wasn't quick and the front pair were never out of the first two. The winner built slightly on his Newmarket run.

T/Jkpt: Not won. T/Plt: £117.50 to a £1 stake. Pool of £98181.08 - 609.54 winning tickets. T/Qpdt: £23.50 to a £1 stake. Pool of £5613.54 - 176.17 winning tickets. **Lee McKenzie**

5064 NEWCASTLE (A.W) (L-H)

Friday, August 12

OFFICIAL GOING: Tapeta: standard

Wind: fresh half against Weather: cloudy

5363 BREEDERS SUPPORTING RACING EBF MAIDEN STKS (PLUS 10 RACE) (STALLION-RESTRICTED) 1m 5y (Tp)

1:30 (1:30) (Class 4) 2-Y-O **£6,469** (£1,925; £962) **Stalls** Centre

Form RPR

3222 **1** **Devil's Bridge (IRE)**[12] 4914 2-9-5 89 ... SilvestreDeSousa 3 85
(Richard Hannon) *led: hdd narrowly 6f out: led again 4f out: pushed clr over 1f out: kpt on* **1/3**[1]

4 **2** *3 1/2* **Davy's Dilemma**[14] 4829 2-9-5 0 ... PaulMulrennan 2 75
(Michael Dods) *trckd ldng pair: pushed along over 3f out: rdn 2f out: sn one pce and hld in 2nd* **16/1**[3]

45 **3** *10* **Lester Kris (IRE)**[27] 4379 2-9-5 0 ... TonyHamilton 4 51+
(Richard Hannon) *prom: led narrowly 6 out: hdd 4f out: rdn over 2f out: sn wknd* **11/4**[2]

1m 40.35s (1.75) **Going Correction** +0.225s/f (Slow) **3** Ran SP% **107.6**

Speed ratings (Par 96): **100,96,86**

CSF £5.34 TOTE £1.20; EX 4.60 Trifecta £4.60.

Owner Middleham Park Racing IX & D Shapiro **Bred** D G Iceton **Trained** East Everleigh, Wilts

FOCUS

This maiden was open to those which were sired by the winner of a race of a 1m 2f or over. It attracted only three runners and proved uncompetitive with the winner rated to his mark.

5364 VALUED NURSERY H'CAP 5f (Tp)

2:00 (2:00) (Class 6) (0-60,60) 2-Y-O **£2,911** (£866; £432; £216) **Stalls** Centre

Form RPR

065 **1** **Saxagogo**[18] 4707 2-9-4 **57** ... SilvestreDeSousa 13 65+
(George Scott) *hld up in midfield: gd hdwy 1/2-way: pushed along to ld over 1f out: kpt on wl* **3/1**[1]

6600 **2** *2* **Sheila's Return**[19] 4679 2-9-2 **55** ... PaulMulrennan 5 56
(Bryan Smart) *trckd ldrs: rdn 2f out: kpt on: wnt 2nd 110yds out* **12/1**

2435 **3** *3/4* **Katebird (IRE)**[19] 4679 2-9-7 **60** ... FrannyNorton 1 58
(Mark Johnston) *prom: rdn 2f out: kpt on same pce* **4/1**[2]

660 **4** *3/4* **Red Savina**[19] 4678 2-8-6 **45** ... ShaneGray 2 41
(Kevin Ryan) *led: rdn whn hdd 2f out: one pce fnl f* **20/1**

045 **5** *1/2* **Regal Decree**[31] 4227 2-9-4 **57** ... JackGarritty 12 51+
(Jedd O'Keeffe) *hld up: pushed along 1/2-way: sme hdwy over 1f out: kpt on fnl f* **9/2**[3]

6504 **6** *1 1/4* **Chickenfortea (IRE)**[29] 4308 2-9-7 **60** ... NeilFarley 4 49
(Eric Alston) *prom: rdn to ld 2f out: hdd over 1f out: wknd ins fnl f* **14/1**

5634 **7** *2* **George Ravenscar**[31] 4221 2-9-1 **54** ...(t) LukeMorris 11 36
(Ed Vaughan) *midfield: rdn 1/2-way: wknd fnl f* **13/2**

005 **8** *1/2* **Flying Hope (IRE)**[17] 4725 2-9-2 **55** ... TomEaves 8 38
(Nigel Tinkler) *racd keenly in midfield: rdn over 1f out: sn no imp* **10/1**

3260 **9** *nse* **Jollydee (IRE)**[17] 4725 2-9-2 **60** ... AdamMcNamara(5) 9 40
(Paul Midgley) *in tch: rdn 1/2-way: wknd over 1f out* **25/1**

0624 **10** *1 1/2* **Coco La Belle (IRE)**[14] 4843 2-9-6 **59** ... DuranFentiman 10 34
(Tim Easterby) *chsd ldrs: rdn 1/2-way: wknd over 1f out* **14/1**

000 **11** *4* **Miss Island Ruler**[39] 3947 2-7-13 **45** ... RPWalsh(7) 3 5
(Shaun Harris) *sn pushed along in rr: a bhd* **100/1**

600 **12** *3 1/2* **Queens Parade (IRE)**[54] 3433 2-8-1 **45** ... PhilDennis(5) 6
(Sharon Watt) *dwlt: a in rr* **100/1**

1m 0.31s (0.81) **Going Correction** +0.225s/f (Slow) **12** Ran SP% **117.2**

Speed ratings (Par 92): **102,98,97,96,95 93,90,89,89,87 80,75**

CSF £39.17 CT £148.19 TOTE £3.30: £1.40, £3.30, £2.40; EX 38.80 Trifecta £181.40.

Owner The Roughies and Rags Partnership **Bred** Mrs C R Philipson & Mrs H G Lascelles **Trained** Newmarket, Suffolk

FOCUS

This featured six nursery debutants and is difficult form to assess, though there is probably more to come from the winner. The market proved a key guide.

5365 TDX H'CAP 1m 2f 42y (Tp)

2:30 (2:32) (Class 5) (0-75,79) 3-Y-O **£3,557** (£1,058; £529; £264) **Stalls** Low

Form RPR

2121 **1** **Palisade**[8] 5071 3-9-11 **79** 6ex ...(v) LukeMorris 3 89+
(Sir Mark Prescott Bt) *hld up: angled rt to outer over 2f out: sn pushed along and hdwy: led 1f out: edgd lft: styd on* **5/4**[1]

-055 **2** *2 1/4* **Southern Gailes (IRE)**[47] 3687 3-9-2 **75** ...(t) JordanVaughan(5) 2 80
(K R Burke) *trckd ldr: pushed along to ld 2f out: rdn whn hdd 1f out: one pce fnl 110yds* **3/1**[2]

-401 **3** *3/4* **Airton**[22] 4549 3-9-0 **68** ... PJMcDonald 4 72
(James Bethell) *midfield: rdn over 2f out: chsd ldrs over 1f out: kpt on* **7/2**[3]

0455 **4** *6* **Ronnie Baird**[22] 4549 3-9-4 **72** ...(b) TonyHamilton 5 64
(Kristin Stubbs) *hld up in rr: rdn over 2f out: plugged on to go pooer 4th towards fin* **16/1**

2334 **5** *1/2* **Torremar (FR)**[28] 4342 3-9-4 **72** ...(p) TomEaves 8 63
(Kevin Ryan) *led: rdn over 2f out: hdd 2f out: wknd fnl f* **8/1**

0425 **6** *1 1/2* **Page Of Wands**[19] 4681 3-8-11 **65** ... GrahamLee 6 53
(Karen McLintock) *trckd ldr: rdn over 2f out: wknd over 1f out* **20/1**

-000 **7** *4 1/2* **Canford Thompson**[10] 4973 3-8-3 **62** ... RobJFitzpatrick(5) 1 41
(Micky Hammond) *dwlt: sn midfield: rdn 3f out: wknd over 1f out* **50/1**

0453 **8** *9* **Smirnova (IRE)**[29] 4316 3-8-1 **60** ...(p) PhilDennis(5) 7 21
(Kenny Johnson) *racd keenly in midfield: rdn over 2f out: sn wknd* **50/1**

2m 9.99s (-0.41) **Going Correction** +0.025s/f (Slow) **8** Ran SP% **117.3**

Speed ratings (Par 100): **102,100,99,94,94 93,89,82**

CSF £5.26 CT £9.91 TOTE £2.10: £1.02, £1.70, £1.60; EX 5.70 Trifecta £12.30.

Owner Cheveley Park Stud **Bred** Cheveley Park Stud Ltd **Trained** Newmarket, Suffolk

FOCUS

A fair handicap, which revolved heavily around the penalised favourite who continues to progress.

5366 CONSTRUCTING EXCELLENCE FOUNDATION MAIDEN STKS 1m 2f 42y (Tp)

3:00 (3:00) (Class 5) 3-Y-O+ **£3,557** (£1,058; £529; £264) **Stalls** Low

Form RPR

2 **1** **Loveable Helen (IRE)**[15] 4806 3-8-13 0 ... TonyHamilton 2 80
(Richard Fahey) *trckd ldr: upsides gng wl 3f out: led 2f out: pushed clr: easily* **5/2**[2]

-224 **2** *7* **Plenary (USA)**[56] 3359 3-9-4 86 ... SilvestreDeSousa 4 71
(Jeremy Noseda) *led: jnd 3f out: sn rdn: hdd 2f out: grad wknd* **1/3**[1]

-060 **3** *11* **Breton Blues**[19] 4683 6-9-13 45 ...(p) CamHardie 1 49?
(Fred Watson) *dwlt: sn in tch racing keenly: rdn over 2f out: sn wknd* **100/1**

4 *1 1/2* **Ajman Prince (IRE)** 3-8-13 0 ... RowanScott(5) 3 46
(Alistair Whillans) *hld up: rdn over 2f out: sn wknd* **14/1**[3]

0 **5** *37* **Bilko's Back (IRE)**[19] 4682 4-9-13 0 ... RaulDaSilva 5
(Susan Corbett) *in tch: rdn over 3f out: sn wknd: eased and t.o* **100/1**

2m 10.39s (-0.01) **Going Correction** +0.025s/f (Slow)

WFA 3 from 4yo+ 9lb **5** Ran SP% **112.2**

Speed ratings (Par 103): **101,95,86,85,55**

CSF £3.77 TOTE £3.70: £1.40, £1.02; EX 4.40 Trifecta £27.50.

Owner Mrs A M Riney **Bred** Mrs A M Riney **Trained** Musley Bank, N Yorks

FOCUS

They came home at long intervals in what was little more than a match.

5367 BARBOUR H'CAP 7f 14y (Tp)

3:35 (3:35) (Class 5) (0-75,75) 3-Y-O+ **£3,557** (£1,058; £529; £264) **Stalls** Centre

Form RPR

4030 **1** **Depth Charge (IRE)**[6] 5151 4-9-6 **69** ...(vt) TonyHamilton 5 81
(Kristin Stubbs) *hld up: smooth hdwy 2f out: pushed along to ld ent fnl f: kpt on wl* **18/1**

224 **2** *3* **Wowcha (IRE)**[20] 4643 3-9-6 **75** ...(p) JasonHart 6 77
(John Quinn) *midfield: pushed along over 3f out: rdn and hdwy to ld over 1f out: hdd ent fnl f: kpt on but sn no ch w wnr* **5/1**[2]

-616 **3** *2 1/4* **Awesome Quality (USA)**[43] 3821 3-9-6 **75** ...(p) LukeMorris 4 71
(James Tate) *midfield: hdwy over 2f out: rdn over 1f out: sn one pce* **5/4**[1]

0002 **4** *3/4* **Inshaa**[8] 5068 4-9-0 **63** ...(p) GrahamLee 3 59
(Michael Herrington) *midfield: rdn 3f out: plugged on fnl f* **7/1**[3]

5166 **5** *1* **Foie Gras**[24] 4474 6-9-2 **65** ...(p) SilvestreDeSousa 8 58
(Chris Dwyer) *hld up: rdn over 3f out: plugged on fnl f: nvr threatened* **20/1**

6444 **6** *1/2* **The Armed Man**[8] 5069 3-8-3 **58** ...(p) AndrewElliott 7 48
(Chris Fairhurst) *chsd ldrs: rdn over 2f out: wknd ins fnl f* **10/1**

-001 **7** *1 1/2* **Broctune Papa Gio**[16] 4772 9-9-2 **65** ... TomEaves 2 53
(Keith Reveley) *hld up: rdn over 3f out: nvr threatened* **25/1**

161- **8** *1* **Let's Twist**[325] 6616 4-9-4 **67** ...(b) ShaneGray 10 52
(Kristin Stubbs) *sn led: rdn whn hdd over 1f out: sn wknd* **25/1**

4350 **9** *2 1/2* **Know Your Name**[35] 4094 5-9-9 **72** ...(b) NeilFarley 9 50
(Eric Alston) *prom: rdn over 2f out: wknd over 1f out* **16/1**

0010 **10** *9* **Slingsby**[21] 4608 5-9-7 **70** ...(p) GrahamGibbons 1 24
(Michael Easterby) *prom: rdn over 3f out: wknd over 2f out: eased* **8/1**

1m 27.34s (1.14) **Going Correction** +0.225s/f (Slow)

WFA 3 from 4yo+ 6lb **10** Ran SP% **117.4**

Speed ratings (Par 103): **102,98,96,95,94 93,91,90,87,77**

CSF £103.72 CT £197.29 TOTE £20.80: £4.20, £1.80, £1.30; EX 97.90 Trifecta £534.10.

Owner Paramount Racing III **Bred** Budget Stable **Trained** Norton, N Yorks

FOCUS
This looked far more competitive than the market suggested. The winner's effort was hard to predict, while the runner-up has been rated to form.

5368 ASBESTOS SPECIALISTS H'CAP (DIV I) 6f (Tp)
4:10 (4:10) (Class 6) (0-65,65) 3-Y-O+ **£2,911** (£866; £432; £216) **Stalls** Centre

Form RPR

2140 **1** **Classic Flyer**[20] 4647 4-9-12 **65**..(v) PhillipMakin 7 72
(David O'Meara) *hld up: pushed along and gd hdwy over 1f out: rdn to ld 110yds out: kpt on* **12/1**

630 **2** *nk* **Letbygonesbeicons**[41] 3896 3-8-10 **58**......................... RowanScott(5) 8 63
(Ann Duffield) *in tch: pushed along and shuffled bk a bit over 1f out: rdn ins fnl f: r.o wl fnl 110yds: wnt 2nd post* **20/1**

2442 **3** *hd* **Only Ten Per Cent (IRE)**[20] 4658 8-9-6 **62**.......(v) AlistairRawlinson(3) 9 68
(J R Jenkins) *midfield: hdwy over 1f out: rdn to chal ins fnl f: kpt on* **9/1**

052 **4** *3/4* **Intense Starlet (IRE)**[7] 5126 5-8-10 **52**..............(p) JacobButterfield(3) 6 55
(Marjorie Fife) *midfield: rdn over 2f out: kpt on fnl f* **4/1**[2]

0321 **5** *nk* **Indastar**[20] 4647 6-9-6 **59**.. PJMcDonald 1 61
(Michael Herrington) *chsd ldrs: rdn over 2f out: led over 1f out: hdd 110yds out: no ex* **9/2**[3]

1563 **6** *1/2* **Spirit Of Wedza (IRE)**[8] 5060 4-9-7 **65**.......................(p) JoshDoyle(5) 3 66
(Julie Camacho) *led narrowly: rdn over 2f out: hdd over 1f out: no ex fnl f* **7/2**[1]

0400 **7** *1/2* **Clon Rocket (IRE)**[14] 4848 3-9-5 **62**......................... RoystonFfrench 10 60
(John Holt) *hld up: rdn over 3f out: kpt on fnl f: nvr threatened* **16/1**

6606 **8** *3/4* **Go Go Green (IRE)**[13] 4873 10-9-10 **63**............................[1] JoeDoyle 11 60
(Jim Goldie) *s.i.s: hld up in rr: rdn over 2f out: kpt on ins fnl f: nvr threatened* **10/1**

0542 **9** *2 1/4* **Whipphound**[7] 5127 8-8-11 **50**..(p) TomEaves 2 40
(Ruth Carr) *midfield: rdn 2f out: wknd ins fnl f* **10/1**

3606 **10** *1 3/4* **Cool Strutter (IRE)**[16] 4771 4-9-2 **60**.......................(b) GemmaTutty(5) 4 45
(Karen Tutty) *pressed ldr: rdn over 2f out: wknd appr fnl f* **10/1**

5060 **11** *2 3/4* **Sunrise Dance**[3] 5277 7-8-2 **46** oh1..........................(tp) PhilDennis(5) 12 23
(Kenny Johnson) *prom: rdn over 2f out: wknd appr fnl f* **50/1**

000 **12** *10* **Declined**[30] 4258 4-8-7 **46** oh1....................................... PatrickMathers 5
(David C Griffiths) *chsd ldrs: rdn and lost pl over 3f out: sn btn: bhd over 1f out* **66/1**

1m 14.18s (1.68) **Going Correction** +0.225s/f (Slow)
WFA 3 from 4yo+ 4lb **12** Ran SP% **119.5**
Speed ratings (Par 101): **97,96,96,95,94 94,93,92,89,87 83,70**
CSF £230.35 CT £2262.83 TOTE £13.50: £3.90, £8.00, £3.40; EX 173.60 Trifecta £1583.80.
Owner The Classic Strollers Partnership **Bred** Pippa Bloodstock **Trained** Upper Helmsley, N Yorks

FOCUS
This looked the stronger of the two divisions with the winner rated back close to the best of his 6f form.

5369 ASBESTOS SPECIALISTS H'CAP (DIV II) 6f (Tp)
4:40 (4:41) (Class 6) (0-65,65) 3-Y-O+ **£2,911** (£866; £432; £108; £108) **Stalls** Centre

Form RPR

3303 **1** **Gypsy Major**[8] 5069 4-8-4 **48** ow1..........................(v) RobJFitzpatrick(5) 5 58+
(Garry Moss) *hld up: pushed along and gd hdwy over 2f out: rdn to ld over 1f out: kpt on wl* **3/1**[1]

6055 **2** *3* **Tom Sawyer**[16] 4770 8-9-6 **64**..............................(b) AdamMcNamara(5) 1 65
(Julie Camacho) *chsd clr ldr: rdn over 2f out: ev ch over 1f out: one pce fnl f* **11/1**

5040 **3** *nk* **Coquine**[10] 4972 3-9-2 **59**... PaulMulrennan 11 58
(David O'Meara) *dwlt: hld up: pushed along and gd hdwy over 2f out: rdn and ev ch over 1f out: one pce fnl f* **33/1**

1365 **4** *1* **Johnny B Goode (IRE)**[17] 4742 4-9-10 **63**............[1] SilvestreDeSousa 2 60
(Chris Dwyer) *chsd clr ldr: rdn over 2f out: no ex ins fnl f* **7/2**[2]

3444 **4** *dht* **Emerald Asset (IRE)**[8] 5070 3-8-13 **56**............................ JackGarritty 8 52
(Paul Midgley) *racd keenly in midfield: rdn 2f out: one pce* **7/1**

0023 **6** *1/2* **Cuppatee (IRE)**[10] 4973 3-9-7 **64**.. PJMcDonald 10 59
(Ann Duffield) *hld up: rdn over 3f out: kpt on ins fnl f* **10/1**

-000 **7** *1/2* **Centre Haafhd**[11] 4932 5-9-0 **53**... JoeDoyle 7 47
(Jim Goldie) *hld up: rdn 3f out: nvr threatened* **20/1**

400 **8** *6* **A Fitting Finale**[30] 4258 3-8-6 **49**.. ShaneGray 4 24
(Kevin Ryan) *midfield: rdn 3f out: wknd over 1f out* **33/1**

3412 **9** *1* **Oscars Journey**[53] 3469 6-9-12 **65**..................................(v) TomEaves 9 38+
(J R Jenkins) *led: sn clr: reduced advantage 2f out: hdd over 1f out: wknd* **5/1**[3]

0466 **10** *3 1/4* **Studio Star**[25] 4449 4-8-4 **46** oh1.................................. NoelGarbutt(3) 12 9
(Wilf Storey) *midfield: rdn 3f out: wknd* **33/1**

0020 **11** *1 1/4* **Frozon**[24] 4498 3-9-5 **62**... LukeMorris 3 21
(Brian Ellison) *midfield: sn pushed along: wknd over 2f out* **7/1**

1m 14.04s (1.54) **Going Correction** +0.225s/f (Slow)
WFA 3 from 4yo+ 4lb **11** Ran SP% **119.9**
Speed ratings (Par 101): **98,94,93,92,92 91,90,82,81,77 75**
CSF £36.26 CT £915.66 TOTE £3.40: £1.20, £4.00, £10.30; EX 34.90 Trifecta £1666.80.
Owner Pinnacle Duo Partnership **Bred** Bearstone Stud Ltd **Trained** Wynyard, Stockton-On-Tees

FOCUS
This was run at a furious early pace and played into the hands of the patiently ridden favourite who has the scope to win again. The winning time was marginally quicker than the first division.

5370 SIR BOBBY ROBSON FOUNDATION H'CAP 5f (Tp)
5:10 (5:10) (Class 5) (0-70,68) 3-Y-O **£3,557** (£1,058; £529; £264) **Stalls** Centre

Form RPR

0035 **1** **Run Rio Run (IRE)**[16] 4771 3-8-13 **60**......................(p) PaulMulrennan 2 67
(Michael Dods) *mde all: rdn 2f out: strly pressed thrght fnl f: hld on wl* **6/1**[3]

4022 **2** *nk* **Fruit Salad**[42] 3847 3-9-2 **68**...................................... AdamMcNamara(5) 1 74
(James Bethell) *wnt lft s and s.i.s: sn in tch: rdn to chal strly 1f out: kpt on* **7/4**[1]

5016 **3** *3/4* **Searanger (USA)**[46] 3709 3-9-6 **67**.................................. PJMcDonald 5 70
(Rebecca Menzies) *trckd ldrs: rdn 2f out: one pce fnl f* **13/2**

-060 **4** *1 1/2* **Our Place In Loule**[31] 4238 3-8-8 **55**.......................... PatrickMathers 7 53
(Noel Wilson) *hld up: rdn 1/2-way: one pce and nvr threatened ldrs* **20/1**

0540 **5** *nk* **Nefetari**[31] 4229 3-8-2 **49** oh4..(b) LukeMorris 6 46
(Alan Brown) *prom: rdn 1/2-way: outpcd over 1f out: plugged on fnl f* **25/1**

001 **6** *8* **Annie Salts**[9] 5041 3-9-5 **66** 6ex.............................. SilvestreDeSousa 3 34
(Chris Dwyer) *dwlt: sn chsd ldrs: rdn 2f out: wknd over 1f out* **15/8**[2]

-000 **7** *1/2* **Emilie Bronte**[65] 3009 3-8-3 **50** ow1.............................(v[1]) AndrewElliott 4 16
(Chris Fairhurst) *hld up: rdn 1/2-way: wknd* **22/1**

1m 0.64s (1.14) **Going Correction** +0.225s/f (Slow) **7** Ran SP% **111.7**
Speed ratings (Par 100): **99,98,97,94,94 81,80**
CSF £16.15 TOTE £8.60: £3.20, £1.20; EX 18.40 Trifecta £67.30.
Owner Mrs Suzanne Kirkup Michael Dods **Bred** L Wright **Trained** Denton, Co Durham

FOCUS
This ordinary sprint handicap served up a good finish. The winner has been rated up slightly on this year's form.
T/Plt: £18.20 to a £1 stake. Pool of £59824.95 - 2389.57 winning tickets. T/Qpdt: £8.30 to a £1 stake. Pool of £4829.96 - 426.60 winning tickets. **Andrew Sheret**

[5170]NEWMARKET (R-H)
Friday, August 12

OFFICIAL GOING: Good to firm
Wind: Light half-behind Weather: Fine

5371 32RED.COM MEDIAN AUCTION MAIDEN STKS (PLUS 10 RACE) 7f
5:30 (5:30) (Class 4) 2-Y-O **£3,946** (£1,174; £586; £293) **Stalls** High

Form RPR

1 **Rich Legacy (IRE)** 2-9-0 0... OisinMurphy 8 84+
(Ralph Beckett) *hld up: hdwy over 2f out: rdn to ld ins fnl f: r.o* **6/1**[3]

4 **2** *1 1/2* **Maldonado (FR)**[13] 4877 2-9-5 0.................................... WilliamBuick 10 85
(Charlie Appleby) *led: rdn and hdd over 2f out: led again over 1f out: hdd ins fnl f: styd on same pce* **13/2**

3 *nk* **Firefright (IRE)** 2-9-5 0.. JimCrowley 11 84+
(Jeremy Noseda) *w ldr: rdn and ev ch fr over 1f out tl styd on same pce ins fnl f* **8/1**

023 **4** *6* **Used To Be**[21] 4609 2-9-5 **76**... BenCurtis 4 68
(K R Burke) *racd keenly: w ldrs: rdn to ld over 2f out: hdd over 1f out: wknd ins fnl f* **5/1**[1]

5 *1* **Phalaborwa** 2-9-0 0... FrederikTylicki 12 60+
(Ed Vaughan) *dwlt: hld up: shkn up over 1f out: r.o ins fnl f: nvr nrr* **11/2**[2]

5 **6** *nk* **Forgivethenforget**[34] 4128 2-9-5 0................................. ThomasBrown 1 64
(Ismail Mohammed) *w ldrs: rdn and ev ch over 2f out: wknd fnl f* **5/1**[1]

7 *1/2* **Cool Climate (IRE)** 2-9-5 0.. DavidNolan 5 63
(Richard Fahey) *prom: rdn 1/2-way: outpcd over 2f out: styd on ins fnl f* **12/1**

6 **8** *3* **Armagnac (IRE)**[13] 4856 2-9-5 0..................................... WilliamCarson 9 55
(Michael Bell) *hld up: hdwy 1/2-way: rdn and wknd over 1f out* **12/1**

9 *2* **Houndstooth (IRE)** 2-8-12 0................................... GabrieleMalune(7) 7 50
(Luca Cumani) *prom tl wknd over 1f out* **14/1**

10 *2 1/2* **Thetrioandme (IRE)** 2-9-5 0.. KierenFox 6 43
(John Best) *s.i.s: hld up: hung rt over 2f out: sn wknd* **25/1**

6 **11** *1* **Tea El Tee (IRE)**[14] 4837 2-9-5 0.................................... TomMarquand 3 40
(Gay Kelleway) *s.i.s: a in rr: wknd over 2f out* **50/1**

1m 25.92s (0.22) **Going Correction** +0.075s/f (Good) **11** Ran SP% **115.3**
Speed ratings (Par 96): **101,99,98,92,90 90,90,86,84,81 80**
CSF £43.86 TOTE £6.70: £2.20, £2.30, £3.70; EX 45.60 Trifecta £288.90.
Owner Qatar Racing Limited **Bred** Gestut Ammerland **Trained** Kimpton, Hants

FOCUS
The far-side track was used with the stalls on the far side except for the 10f race (centre). The going was good to firm on a watered track. They went a fair pace in this interesting maiden and the first three pulled clear.

5372 FIRESTONE BUILDING PRODUCTS H'CAP 6f
6:00 (6:01) (Class 4) (0-85,83) 3-Y-O+ **£5,175** (£1,540; £769; £384) **Stalls** High

Form RPR

2102 **1** **Highly Sprung (IRE)**[5] 5199 3-9-2 **77**............................ WilliamBuick 3 89
(Mark Johnston) *chsd ldrs: rdn over 2f out: led over 1f out: r.o u.p* **7/2**[2]

3413 **2** *2* **Cosmic Chatter**[6] 5182 6-9-9 **80**...............................(p) JamesSullivan 5 87
(Ruth Carr) *pushed along early then hld up and racd keenly: rdn over 1f out: r.o ins fnl f: wnt 2nd nr fin: nt rch wnr* **11/2**

1-3 **3** *1 1/4* **Quick Look**[13] 4889 3-9-6 **81**.. DavidProbert 7 83
(William Jarvis) *dwlt: hld up: racd keenly: hdwy 2f out: rdn over 1f out: styd on same pce wl ins fnl f* **4/1**[3]

2123 **4** *1 1/4* **David's Duchess (IRE)**[17] 4741 3-9-2 **77**.......................... DavidNolan 8 75
(Richard Fahey) *led 5f out: rdn and hdd over 1f out: no ex ins fnl f* **5/2**[1]

3051 **5** *4* **Kestrel Call (IRE)**[48] 3644 3-9-1 **76**.............................(t) TomMarquand 6 61
(Michael Appleby) *led 1f: chsd ldr: rdn over 2f out: wknd fnl f* **16/1**

0553 **6** *6* **Bahamian Heights**[22] 4569 5-9-6 **77**................................ OisinMurphy 4 44
(Robert Cowell) *s.i.s: hld up: hdwy 1/2-way: rdn over 1f out: wknd fnl f: eased* **8/1**

1240 **7** *17* **Until Midnight (IRE)**[28] 4360 6-9-1 **72**............................ JimCrowley 2
(Eugene Stanford) *prom over 4f* **14/1**

1m 12.65s (0.15) **Going Correction** +0.075s/f (Good)
WFA 3 from 5yo+ 4lb **7** Ran SP% **109.8**
Speed ratings (Par 105): **102,99,97,96,90 82,60**
CSF £20.95 CT £72.35 TOTE £4.30: £2.20, £2.90; EX 18.90 Trifecta £82.00.
Owner Douglas Livingston **Bred** Patrick J Moloney **Trained** Middleham Moor, N Yorks

FOCUS
This looked competitive but the winner justified support with plenty in hand. The runner-up helps set the standard.

5373 NGK SPARK PLUGS EBF STALLIONS MAIDEN STKS (PLUS 10 RACE) 1m
6:35 (6:35) (Class 4) 2-Y-O **£4,528** (£1,347; £673; £336) **Stalls** High

Form RPR

0 **1** **Ghayyar (IRE)**[13] 4866 2-9-5 0....................................... FrankieDettori 5 84
(Richard Hannon) *mde all: qcknd 3f out: rdn and edgd rt over 1f out: c clr and edgd lft ins fnl f: styd on* **10/3**[3]

2 *3/4* **Glencadam Glory** 2-9-5 0.. RobertHavlin 2 82+
(John Gosden) *free to post: s.i.s: hld up: hdwy 2f out: edgd rt and rdn to chse wnr sn after: outpcd 1f out: r.o towards fin* **2/1**[1]

3 *5* **Hamada** 2-9-5 0.. WilliamBuick 3 70
(Charlie Appleby) *hld up: rdn over 2f out: hdwy over 1f out: rdn: edgd lft and styd on same pce fnl f* **3/1**[2]

3 **4** *1* **Spring Jig (USA)**[16] 4775 2-9-5 0.. JimCrowley 4 68
(Hugo Palmer) *chsd wnr tl rdn over 2f out: styd on same pce fr over 1f out* **10/3**[3]

5 *10* **Alapinta** 2-9-0 0... OisinMurphy 8 39
(Ralph Beckett) *s.i.s: sn chsng ldrs: wnt 2nd over 2f out: sn ev ch: wknd over 1f out* **14/1**

1m 40.47s (0.47) **Going Correction** +0.075s/f (Good) **5** Ran SP% **111.2**
Speed ratings (Par 96): **100,99,94,93,83**
CSF £10.53 TOTE £3.50: £1.70, £1.80; EX 12.30 Trifecta £33.70.
Owner Al Shaqab Racing **Bred** Rjb Bloodstock **Trained** East Everleigh, Wilts

The Form Book, Raceform Ltd, Newbury, RG14 5SJ

FOCUS
This maiden was won by the mighty Frankel in 2010 and subsequent Derby hero Motivator in 2004. This didn't look the strongest renewal and there were a few withdrawals, but the winner beat the favourite with something in hand and they pulled 5l clear.

5374 FIRESTONE BUILDING PRODUCTS EUROPE H'CAP 1m
7:10 (7:11) (Class 5) (0-75,75) 3-Y-O+ **£3,234** (£962; £481; £240) **Stalls** High

Form RPR
5261 **1** **Ellaal**[14] 4833 7-9-11 **72**.................................... JamesSullivan 5 81
(Ruth Carr) *prom: lost pl 5f out: hdwy over 2f out: swtchd rt and chsd ldr over 1f out: rdn to ld ins fnl f: styd on* **5/1**[2]
100 **2** *2* **Tellovoi (IRE)**[62] 3166 8-9-11 **72**....................................(v) JimCrowley 8 76
(Richard Guest) *led: rdn over 1f out: edgd rt and hdd ins fnl f: no ex towards fin* **9/1**
2556 **3** *9* **Rebel Lightning (IRE)**[14] 4841 3-9-7 **75**.....(b[1]) WilliamTwiston-Davies 3 58
(Richard Spencer) *prom: chsd ldr over 4f out: rdn over 2f out: edgd rt and lost 2nd over 1f out: wknd fnl f* **6/1**[3]
1300 **4** *4 1/2* **Lunar Deity**[20] 4654 7-9-11 **72**....................................(t) OisinMurphy 7 45
(Stuart Williams) *hld up: hdwy 5f out: rdn over 2f out: wknd over 1f out* **15/2**
0264 **5** *3/4* **Gannicus**[27] 4383 5-9-8 **69**....................................(vt) ShaneKelly 1 41
(Brendan Powell) *hld up: rdn 1/2-way: hung lft fr over 2f out: sme hdwy sn after: wknd over 1f out* **5/1**[2]
5661 **6** *12* **Blue Geranium (IRE)**[17] 4743 3-9-7 **75**.................... FrankieDettori 4 18
(John Gosden) *hld up: rdn 1/2-way: wknd 2f out* **2/1**[1]
1200 **7** *5* **Gulland Rock**[14] 4841 5-9-1 **62**.................................... WilliamCarson 2
(Anthony Carson) *chsd ldr over 3f: remained handy: rdn over 2f out: wknd wl over 1f out* **20/1**
5000 **8** *1/2* **Cleverconversation (IRE)**[13] 4881 3-8-12 **71**.....(b[1]) CharlieBennett(5) 6
(Jane Chapple-Hyam) *s.s: looked reluctant and a bhd* **12/1**

1m 39.64s (-0.36) **Going Correction** +0.075s/f (Good)
WFA 3 from 5yo+ 7lb 8 Ran SP% **115.2**
Speed ratings (Par 103): **104,102,93,88,87 75,70,70**
CSF £48.96 CT £279.02 TOTE £5.80: £1.80, £2.80, £2.20; EX 57.70 Trifecta £311.40.
Owner The Bottom Liners & Paul Saxton **Bred** W And R Barnett Ltd **Trained** Huby, N Yorks

FOCUS
They went a decent pace in this minor handicap and the first two finished a long way clear. The winner has been rated to his best in the past two years.

5375 TILBROOKS LANDSCAPE & TUDDENHAM NURSERIES H'CAP 1m 2f
7:40 (7:41) (Class 5) (0-70,70) 3-Y-O+ **£3,234** (£962; £481; £240) **Stalls** Centre

Form RPR
000 **1** **Fire Jet (IRE)**[38] 3990 3-9-0 **65**.................................... TomQueally 11 74+
(John Mackie) *in rr and pushed along 8f out: hdwy to chse ldr over 2f out: rdn and edgd lft over 1f out: styd on u.p to ld nr fin* **16/1**
2154 **2** *nk* **Trulee Scrumptious**[7] 5122 7-9-7 **63**....................(v) JimmyQuinn 3 71
(Peter Charalambous) *led: clr over 5f out: hrd rdn fr over 1f out: sn edgd rt: styd on gamely u.p: hdd nr fin* **11/4**[1]
04-3 **3** *10* **Thahab Ifraj (IRE)**[76] 2701 3-9-2 **67**.............................. WilliamBuick 7 55
(Ismail Mohammed) *chsd ldrs: wnt 2nd over 4f out tl rdn over 2f out: wknd over 1f out* **10/3**[3]
000 **4** *3/4* **Glorious Legend (IRE)**[70] 2861 3-8-11 **62**................ ThomasBrown 12 49
(Ed Walker) *s.i.s: hld up: hdwy over 3f out: rdn over 2f out: wkng whn edgd rt over 1f out* **7/1**
5 *2 3/4* **Cutty Sark**[100] 3-9-3 **68**.................................... AndreaAtzeni 10 49
(Luca Cumani) *prom: rdn over 2f out: wknd over 1f out* **3/1**[2]
1500 **6** *6* **Aldair**[22] 4562 3-9-5 **70**.................................... TomMarquand 8 39
(Richard Hannon) *sn chsng ldr: rdn and lost 2nd over 4f out: wknd over 2f out* **15/2**
0342 **7** *9* **My Mistress (IRE)**[8] 5085 4-8-4 **51** oh2.................... CharlieBennett(5) 4 2
(Phil McEntee) *s.s: hld up: rdn and wknd over 2f out* **14/1**
60-5 **8** *6* **Kirtling**[22] 4566 5-9-6 **62**....................................(t) MartinLane 5 1
(Andi Brown) *s.i.s: hld up: rdn over 3f out: wknd over 2f out* **20/1**

2m 5.83s (0.33) **Going Correction** +0.075s/f (Good)
WFA 3 from 4yo+ 9lb 8 Ran SP% **116.3**
Speed ratings (Par 103): **101,100,92,92,89 85,77,73**
CSF £61.08 CT £188.78 TOTE £23.80: £4.60, £1.30, £1.30; EX 81.00 Trifecta £171.60.
Owner Ladas **Bred** Ladas **Trained** Church Broughton , Derbys

FOCUS
Race distance increased by 15 yards. The leader set a good pace and the first two finished a long way clear. The winner improved from her maidens, while the runner-up has a good record here and has been rated close to her best.

5376 JAMES HARDIE CLADDING @ U.PLASTICS H'CAP 1m
8:15 (8:15) (Class 3) (0-95,95) 3-Y-O+ **£9,056** (£2,695; £1,346; £673) **Stalls** High

Form RPR
-300 **1** **Predilection (USA)**[20] 4665 3-9-6 **94**.............................. FrankieDettori 4 102
(John Gosden) *mde all: set stdy pce tl qcknd over 2f out: shkn up over 1f out: rdn and hung lft ins fnl f: r.o* **7/2**[2]
4101 **2** *1/2* **Palmerston**[20] 4654 3-8-2 **76**.................................... TomMarquand 8 83
(Michael Appleby) *stdd s: hld up: shkn up over 2f out: rdn: hung lft and r.o to go 2nd nr fin: nt rch wnr* **11/2**
2211 **3** *3/4* **Dutch Law**[6] 5174 4-9-7 **93** 6ex.................................. CharlieBennett(5) 3 99
(Hughie Morrison) *hld up: hdwy over 3f out: rdn over 1f out: styd on* **9/4**[1]
0121 **4** *1 3/4* **Briardale (IRE)**[21] 4611 4-9-3 **84**....................................[1] TedDurcan 2 86
(James Bethell) *trckd ldrs: rdn over 1f out: styd on same pce ins fnl f* **5/1**[3]
6242 **5** *3/4* **Dubai Dynamo**[11] 4933 11-9-4 **85**.............................. JamesSullivan 5 85
(Ruth Carr) *hld up: racd keenly: rdn over 1f out: no imp ins fnl f* **12/1**
1361 **6** *1/2* **Easter Mate (IRE)**[14] 4841 3-8-10 **84**..............................(p) JimCrowley 7 82
(Ralph Beckett) *trckd wnr: rdn over 1f out: no ex ins fnl f* **7/2**[2]

1m 40.96s (0.96) **Going Correction** +0.075s/f (Good)
WFA 3 from 4yo+ 7lb 6 Ran SP% **115.0**
Speed ratings (Par 107): **98,97,96,95,94 93**
CSF £23.17 CT £51.59 TOTE £3.70: £2.00, £2.90; EX 8.50 Trifecta £89.40.
Owner K Abdullah **Bred** Juddmonte Farms Inc **Trained** Newmarket, Suffolk

FOCUS
Four last-time-out winners lined up in this good handicap. The winner made all under Frankie Dettori, who recorded his 3,000th win in Britain. He has been rated back to his AW form.
T/Plt: £147.00 to a £1 stake. Pool of £78047.05 - 387.41 winning tickets. T/Qpdt: £21.20 to a £1 stake. Pool of £7253.42 - 252.11 winning tickets. **Colin Roberts**

5264 NOTTINGHAM (L-H)
Friday, August 12

OFFICIAL GOING: Good to firm
Wind: Fresh against Weather: Fine & dry

5377 BRITISH STALLION STUDS EBF MAIDEN STKS 6f 15y
2:10 (2:12) (Class 5) 2-Y-O **£3,234** (£962; £481; £240) **Stalls** Centre

Form RPR
65 **1** **Halawain (USA)**[16] 4765 2-9-5 0.................................... MartinHarley 7 75
(John Quinn) *mde all: rdn over 1f out: edgd lft ins fnl f: kpt on wl towards fin* **13/2**
04 **2** *3/4* **Party Tiger**[19] 4685 2-9-5 0.................................... GeorgeChaloner 10 73
(Richard Fahey) *trckd ldrs: hdwy over 2f out: pushed along and sltly outpcd over 1f out: sn rdn: styd on wl fnl f* **9/2**[3]
0 **3** *shd* **Desert Sport (USA)**[24] 4473 2-9-5 0.............................. JoeFanning 1 73
(Robert Cowell) *racd wd: cl up: rdn and ev ch over 1f out: drvn and kpt on wl fnl f* **12/1**
03 **4** *3* **Inlawed**[18] 4707 2-9-5 0.................................... JamieSpencer 9 63
(Ed Walker) *trckd ldrs: hdwy and cl up over 2f out: sn pushed along: rdn over 1f out: kpt on same pce* **3/1**[2]
5 *4 1/2* **Lady Cleo (IRE)** 2-9-0 0.................................... OisinMurphy 8 44
(Stuart Williams) *in tch on outer: pushed along 2f out: sn rdn and no hdwy* **8/1**
6 *3/4* **King Of Paris** 2-9-5 0.................................... ShaneKelly 5 46
(Richard Hughes) *trckd ldrs: hdwy wl over 2f out: sn trcking ldrs: shkn up wl over 1f out: sn rdn and btn* **11/4**[1]
05 **7** *1 1/2* **Deleyll**[8] 5084 2-9-5 0.................................... WilliamTwiston-Davies 4 41
(William Haggas) *dwlt: a towards rr* **25/1**
8 *nse* **Different Views (USA)** 2-9-5 0.................................... JFEgan 2 41
(Mick Channon) *prom: pushed along bef 1/2-way: rdn wl over 2f out: sn wknd* **12/1**
000 **9** *3/4* **Can Can Dream**[3] 5272 2-9-0 0.................................... JamesSullivan 3 34
(Olly Williams) *towards rr: rdn along after 2f: nvr a factor* **100/1**

1m 15.8s (1.10) **Going Correction** +0.05s/f (Good) 9 Ran SP% **114.5**
Speed ratings (Par 94): **94,93,92,88,82 81,79,79,78**
CSF £35.51 TOTE £7.90: £2.50, £1.50, £3.80; EX 42.40 Trifecta £329.50.
Owner Sheikh Abdullah Almalek Alsabah **Bred** George Krikorian **Trained** Settrington, N Yorks

FOCUS
A warm, sunny day and the ground was riding on the quick side of good for this seven-race card. This opening maiden featured some well-bred newcomers but, despite the modest standard set by those who had already run, it was the horses with previous experience who came to the fore. The winning jockey reported afterwards there was quite a strong headwind in the straight. The winner has improved while the runner-up has been rated to his mark.

5378 RACING UK PROFITS RETURNED TO RACING H'CAP 5f 13y
2:40 (2:41) (Class 6) (0-60,58) 3-Y-O+ **£2,264** (£673; £336; £168) **Stalls** Centre

Form RPR
-045 **1** **Bilash**[7] 5127 9-8-7 **47**.................................... JackDuern(3) 1 54
(Sarah Hollinshead) *hld up towards rr: gd hdwy on outer 2f out: rdn to ld ent fnl f: sn drvn and kpt on* **10/1**
4005 **2** *hd* **Edith Weston**[9] 5041 3-8-5 **45**....................................(p) JimmyQuinn 2 50
(Robert Cowell) *bhd: gd hdwy wl over 1f out: sn rdn: str run ins fnl f: jst failed* **14/1**
6430 **3** *1 3/4* **Prigsnov Dancer (IRE)**[23] 4513 11-8-13 **57**............ LewisEdmunds(7) 4 57
(John Balding) *hld up: hdwy over 1f out: rdn and styd on fnl f* **5/1**[2]
0402 **4** *1 1/4* **Zebelini (IRE)**[10] 4968 4-8-5 **49**....................(b) RobertDodsworth(7) 10 44
(Ollie Pears) *racd towards stands' rail: cl up: led after 1f: rdn and hdd 1 1/2f out: drvn and kpt on same pce fnl f* **9/2**[1]
0660 **5** *1/2* **Tally's Song**[9] 5007 3-8-2 **45**.............................. EdwardGreatrex(3) 8 38
(Grace Harris) *cl up: rdn to ld 1 1/2f out: drvn and hdd ent fnl f: grad wknd* **10/1**
4000 **6** *nk* **Emerald Bay**[7] 5126 3-9-4 **58**.................................... MartinHarley 9 50
(Ivan Furtado) *slt ld towards stands' rail: hdd after 1f: cl up: rdn along wl over 1f out: grad wknd* **10/1**
6502 **7** *1/2* **Hashtag Frenzy**[11] 4944 3-8-5 **45**..............................(p) JamesSullivan 6 35
(Rebecca Menzies) *trckd ldrs: hdwy 2f out: rdn over 1f out: sn wknd* **6/1**[3]
2210 **8** *3/4* **Whispering Soul (IRE)**[23] 4513 3-9-2 **56**....................(b) JoeFanning 5 43
(Brian Baugh) *dwlt and a in rr* **5/1**[2]
/004 **9** *2 1/4* **Captain Devious**[9] 5007 5-8-5 **48**..............................(t) AaronJones(3) 7 25
(Grace Harris) *cl up: rdn along 2f out: sn drvn and wknd* **8/1**
5050 **10** *nk* **Go Charlie**[7] 5105 5-8-9 **46**.................................... LemosdeSouza 3 25
(Lisa Williamson) *cl up on outer ev ch 2f out: sn rdn and wknd* **12/1**

1m 1.6s (0.10) **Going Correction** +0.05s/f (Good)
WFA 3 from 4yo+ 3lb 10 Ran SP% **118.5**
Speed ratings (Par 101): **101,100,97,95,95 94,93,92,89,88**
CSF £142.52 CT £593.84 TOTE £13.00: £3.40, £5.10, £1.70; EX 165.30 Trifecta £917.50.
Owner Pyle & Hollinshead **Bred** M Pyle & Mrs T Pyle **Trained** Upper Longdon, Staffs
■ Stewards' Enquiry : Jack Duern four-day ban: use of whip (26-29 Aug)

FOCUS
A wide-open sprint handicap run at what looked a strong gallop and the headwind may have been a factor because the finish was dominated by horses who came from off the pace. The winner is not the force of old, but has always gone well here.

5379 KIND FILLIES' H'CAP (JOCKEY CLUB GRASSROOTS SPRINT SERIES QUALIFIER) 6f 15y
3:10 (3:10) (Class 4) (0-80,80) 3-Y-O+ **£4,690** (£1,395; £697; £348) **Stalls** Centre

Form RPR
0641 **1** **Belledesert**[2] 5284 3-9-11 **80** 6ex.............................. AdamBeschizza 1 90
(Steph Hollinshead) *trckd ldrs: smooth hdwy 2f out: led appr fnl f: sn rdn clr: styd on* **11/4**[1]
2132 **2** *2 1/4* **Invade (IRE)**[106] 1811 4-8-13 **67**..............................(t) AaronJones(3) 2 70
(Stuart Williams) *in tch on outer: hdwy 2f out and sn pushed along rdn over 1f out: styd on ins fnl f* **11/1**
0435 **3** *shd* **Meandmyshadow**[21] 4608 8-9-9 **74**....................(b) FergusSweeney 7 77
(Alan Brown) *led towards stands' rail: hdd over 3f out: rdn along: edgd ;lft and outpcd 2f out: drvn over 1f out: edgd lft and styd on fnl f* **8/1**
3432 **4** *4* **Honeysuckle Lil (IRE)**[11] 4932 4-9-9 **74**....................(v[1]) DavidAllan 4 64
(Tim Easterby) *cl up in centre: led over 3f out: rdn 2f out: drvn and hdd appr fnl f: sn wknd* **11/4**[1]
60-0 **5** *2* **Augusta Ada**[26] 4428 5-9-7 **72**.................................... JoeFanning 5 55
(Bryan Smart) *trckd ldrs: hdwy over 2f out: rdn to chse ldrs over 1f out: sn wknd* **4/1**[2]

4013 **6** 1 1/2 **Pink Martini (IRE)**[7] 5103 3-9-2 **74** 6ex.................. EdwardGreatrex(3) 6 52
(Joseph Tuite) *in tch: rdn along 2f out: sn outpcd and bhd* **5/1**[3]
1m 14.17s (-0.53) **Going Correction** +0.05s/f (Good)
WFA 3 from 4yo+ 4lb **6** Ran SP% **109.4**
Speed ratings (Par 102): **105,102,101,96,93 91**
CSF £30.46 CT £194.30 TOTE £2.80: £1.40, £3.20; EX 24.20 Trifecta £126.30.
Owner K Meredith, D Hodson, The Ocean Four **Bred** M Pyle & Mrs T Pyle **Trained** Upper Longdon, Staffs

FOCUS
An ordinary little sprint handicap and most of these looked to be floundering in the headwind in the closing stages, but the in-form winner powered clear to follow up her recent Bath success.

5380 NK MOTORS MAIDEN STKS 1m 75y
3:45 (3:46) (Class 5) 3-Y-O+ **£2,911** (£866; £432; £216) **Stalls** Centre

Form RPR
02 **1** **Jantina**[39] 3958 3-9-0 0.. TedDurcan 7 73+
(Sir Michael Stoute) *trckd ldr: pushed along 3f out: rdn to chal over 1f out: led ent fnl f: sn edgd lft: kpt on* **3/1**[2]
0-33 **2** 2 **Mujaamil**[20] 4657 3-9-5 80...........................(p) WilliamTwiston-Davies 6 72
(William Haggas) *led: pushed along over 2f out: rdn and jnd over 1f out: hdd ent fnl f: sn n.m.r: swtchd rt and drvn: kpt on same pce* **8/15**[1]
34 **3** 1 3/4 **Booborowie (IRE)**[28] 4347 3-9-0 0.......................... DavidParkes(5) 1 68
(Jeremy Gask) *trckd ldrs: hdwy 4f out: rdn along to chse ldng pair 2f out: drvn over 1f out: kpt on same pce* **16/1**
05 **4** 2 **Donnerhall (IRE)**[9] 5023 3-9-5 0.............................. HarryBentley 2 63
(Simon Crisford) *hld up in rr: hdwy over 2f out: rdn to chse ldrs over 1f out: sn drvn and no imp* **8/1**[3]
5 nk **Annoushka** 3-9-0 0..(t) SaleemGolam 3 57?
(Mrs Ilka Gansera-Leveque) *hld up in tch: effrt over 2f out and sn pushed along: rdn and kpt on fnl f* **40/1**
-300 **6** 3 3/4 **Ormering**[30] 4262 3-8-11 43...............................(p) EdwardGreatrex(3) 4 48?
(Roger Teal) *trckd ldng pair on inner: rdn along 3f out: wknd over 2f out* **100/1**
004 **7** 9 **Lmntrix**[169] 710 4-9-12 0... RyanPowell 5 32
(George Margarson) *chsd ldrs on outer: pushed along over 3f out: rdn wl over 2f out: sn wknd* **100/1**
1m 46.4s (-2.60) **Going Correction** -0.25s/f (Firm)
WFA 3 from 4yo 7lb **7** Ran SP% **111.6**
Speed ratings (Par 103): **103,101,99,97,96 93,84**
CSF £4.69 TOTE £3.50: £1.90, £1.10; EX 5.20 Trifecta £16.20.
Owner Cheveley Park Stud **Bred** Cheveley Park Stud Ltd **Trained** Newmarket, Suffolk

FOCUS
Add 6yds to the race distance. Probably no more than ordinary maiden form with the favourite disappointing, but one or two of these are of definite interest in the near future.

5381 RACING UK IN HD COLWICK CUP (H'CAP) 1m 6f 15y
4:20 (4:20) (Class 3) (0-95,94) 3-Y-O+ **£22,641** (£6,737; £3,367; £1,683) **Stalls** Low

Form RPR
4514 **1** **Ravenous**[8] 5053 5-8-6 **75**.................................. DanielMuscutt(3) 7 86
(Luke Dace) *trckd ldr: hdwy to ld over 3f out: rdn clr wl over 1f out: drvn out* **25/1**
0021 **2** 1 3/4 **Intense Tango**[7] 5116 5-9-0 **87** 6ex..........................(t) CliffordLee(7) 8 96
(K R Burke) *led: hdd over 3f out and sn pushed along: rdn over 2f out: drvn over 1f out: kpt on wl u.p fnl f* **10/1**
13-1 **3** 1 3/4 **Who Dares Wins (IRE)**[12] 4920 4-9-11 **91** 6ex.......... FergusSweeney 3 97
(Alan King) *trckd ldng trio: effrt over 3f out and sn pushed along: rdn wl over 2f out: drvn wl over 1f out: kpt on u.p fnl f* **2/1**[1]
-242 **4** 1/2 **Engage (IRE)**[28] 4351 3-8-9 **88**.................................. TedDurcan 2 93
(Sir Michael Stoute) *trckd ldrs: hdwy over 3f out: chsd ldng pair wl over 2f out: sn rdn: drvn wl over 1f out: sn one pce* **11/4**[2]
3-12 **5** 4 **Jack Bear**[27] 4381 5-8-13 **79**...................................... MartinHarley 10 79
(Harry Whittington) *in tch: hdwy over 3f out: rdn along to chse ldrs over 2f out: sn drvn and no imp* **8/1**
/55- **6** 1 1/4 **Roman Flight (IRE)**[17] 2040 8-8-13 **79**.........................(v) MartinLane 12 77
(David Dennis) *hld up in midfield: hdwy and in tch over 4f out: rdn along 3f out: drvn over 2f out and sn wknd* **50/1**
4005 **7** 1/2 **Sellingallthetime (IRE)**[19] 4687 5-8-7 **78**............(p) GeorgeBuckell(5) 11 75
(Michael Appleby) *hld up: a towards rr* **28/1**
5422 **8** 1/2 **Forgotten Hero (IRE)**[35] 4115 7-10-0 **94**............(t) MichaelJMMurphy 4 91
(Kim Bailey) *hld up in rr: sme hdwy on wd outside over 3f out: rdn along wl over 2f out: nvr a factor* **17/2**
206- **9** 31 **Deauville Dancer (IRE)**[15] 7493 5-9-6 **86**...............(tp) TimmyMurphy 1 39
(David Dennis) *trckd ldng pair: rdn along on inner over 4f out: wknd over 3f out* **33/1**
5/40 **10** 62 **Cardinal Walter (IRE)**[48] 3657 7-9-10 **90**.................... JamieSpencer 5
(Nicky Henderson) *stdd s: hld up and bhd tl awkward and lost tch wl over 3f out: sn t.o* **7/1**[3]
3m 0.6s (-6.40) **Going Correction** -0.25s/f (Firm)
WFA 3 from 4yo+ 13lb **10** Ran SP% **115.4**
Speed ratings (Par 107): **108,107,106,105,103 102,102,102,84,49**
CSF £244.10 CT £734.58 TOTE £21.40: £6.10, £3.00, £1.40; EX 319.40 Trifecta £4112.50.
Owner Copped Hall Farm & Stud **Bred** Prince Of Wales And Duchess Of Cornwall **Trained** Pulborough, W Sussex

FOCUS
Add 6yds to the race distance. A competitive handicap, as it should have been for the money, but it paid to race close to the speed and the race has been rated cautiously in view of that.

5382 EBF STALLIONS BREEDING WINNERS FILLIES' H'CAP 1m 2f 50y
4:50 (4:51) (Class 3) (0-95,89) 3-Y-O+ **£9,056** (£2,695; £1,346; £673) **Stalls** Low

Form RPR
5644 **1** **Haalan**[20] 4650 4-9-11 **86**.. MartinHarley 3 97
(James Tate) *set stdy pce: qcknd wl over 2f out: rdn along wl over 1f out: drvn ent fnl f: kpt on gamely* **5/1**[3]
2-13 **2** 1 3/4 **Colonial Classic (FR)**[20] 4668 3-9-1 **85**....................... NickyMackay 1 93
(John Gosden) *trckd wnr: effrt over 2f out: rdn wl over 1f out: drvn appr fnl f: no imp towards fin* **2/1**[1]
541 **3** 3/4 **Desert Way (IRE)**[20] 4657 3-8-11 **81**......................... HarryBentley 2 87
(Ralph Beckett) *trckd ldng pair on inner: effrt 3f out: rdn along over 2f out: drvn wl over 1f out: kpt on same pce* **4/1**[2]
1102 **4** 3 3/4 **Singyoursong (IRE)**[8] 5054 3-8-11 **81**......................... JamieSpencer 5 80
(David Simcock) *hld up in rr: sme hdwy 3f out: rdn along wl over 1f out: sn no imp* **2/1**[1]
10-0 **5** 5 **Kiltara (IRE)**[16] 4757 4-10-0 **89**.. JoeFanning 4 78
(Mark Johnston) *trckd ldrs on outer: pushed along wl over 2f out: sn rdn and wknd wl over 1f out* **10/1**
2m 10.19s (-4.11) **Going Correction** -0.25s/f (Firm)
WFA 3 from 4yo 9lb **5** Ran SP% **112.4**
Speed ratings (Par 104): **106,104,104,101,97**
CSF £15.74 TOTE £6.70: £2.60, £1.50; EX 19.90 Trifecta £61.60.
Owner Saeed Manana **Bred** Kirtlington Stud Ltd **Trained** Newmarket, Suffolk

FOCUS
Add 6yds to the race distance. A quality fillies' handicap on paper, but it was run at a steady pace and, when conditions are quick around here, it's always difficult to reel in the leader. The race has been rated around the winner, while the next three home all look unexposed/progressive.

5383 BETFAIR NOVICE RIDERS SERIES AMATEUR RIDERS' H'CAP 1m 2f 50y
5:20 (5:23) (Class 6) (0-60,60) 3-Y-O+ **£2,183** (£677; £338; £169) **Stalls** Low

Form RPR
3055 **1** **Highlife Dancer**[15] 4784 8-10-7 **53**.............................. MissKatyLyons 6 59
(Mick Channon) *set str pce: hdd wl over 2f out and sn rdn: drvn wl over 1f out: rallied ent fnl f: hrd drvn and sn led again: rdr unbalanced nr fin: hld on* **9/4**[2]
-000 **2** 3/4 **Mister Marcasite**[82] 2507 6-10-5 **51**.................................... MrMEnnis 5 56
(Antony Brittain) *chsd ldng pair: tk clsr order over 4f out: cl up over 3f out: rdn to ld wl over 2f out: drvn over 1f out: hdd ins fnl f: kpt on* **8/1**[3]
00-4 **3** 2 **Dream Serenade**[19] 4690 3-9-2 **46** oh1............... MrJamesKendrick(3) 7 47
(Michael Appleby) *t.k.h early: in tch: hdwy over 3f out: chsd ldng pair over 2f out: sn rdn: kpt on fnl f* **10/1**
6532 **4** 6 **Qibtee (FR)**[9] 5028 6-10-7 **56**.................................. MrMWBrown(3) 1 46
(Les Eyre) *hld up towards rr: hdwy on outer 3f out: rdn along 2f out: sn drvn and no imp* **2/1**[1]
-000 **5** 3 3/4 **Fledermaus (IRE)**[25] 4456 6-9-11 **46**........................(t) MissBJohnson(3) 8 28
(Tina Jackson) *dwlt and in rr: plugged on fnl 3f* **11/1**
0406 **6** 1/2 **Natalia**[23] 4516 7-9-11 **46** oh1..................................(p) DrMVoikhansky(3) 3 28
(Sarah Hollinshead) *chsd ldrs: rdn along 3f out: drvn 2f out: sn one pce* **12/1**
-006 **7** 3/4 **Savannah Star**[28] 4369 3-9-2 **46** oh1..................... [1] MrTPBroughton(3) 10 26
(Nick Kent) *hld up towards rr: hdwy 3f out: rdn along over 2f out: n.d* **14/1**
300 **8** 1/2 **Thrtypointstothree (IRE)**[156] 870 5-9-11 **46** oh1......... MrsDScott(3) 2 25
(Nikki Evans) *hld up: a towards rr* **16/1**
00 **9** 1 3/4 **Qatea (IRE)**[16] 4772 4-11-0 **60**....................................(tp) MissAMcCain 9 36
(Donald McCain) *cl up: disp ld after 2f tl rdn along over 4f out: sn wknd* **25/1**
2m 14.51s (0.21) **Going Correction** -0.25s/f (Firm)
WFA 3 from 4yo+ 9lb **9** Ran SP% **116.7**
Speed ratings (Par 101): **89,88,86,82,79 78,78,77,76**
CSF £21.15 CT £151.85 TOTE £4.70: £1.30, £2.80, £4.20; EX 27.70 Trifecta £219.80.
Owner The Highlife Racing Club **Bred** Imperial & Mike Channon Bloodstock Ltd **Trained** West Ilsley, Berks
■ Stewards' Enquiry : Miss Katy Lyons 17-day ban: use of whip (TBC)

FOCUS
Add 6yds to the race distance. They went hard in this modest amateur riders' handicap, but the winner was on the sharp end throughout and repeated his victory in this race from 12 months earlier. He has been rated near this year's peak.
T/Plt: £344.30 to a £1 stake. Pool of £60320.59 - 127.87 winning tickets. T/Qpdt: £19.80 to a £1 stake. Pool of £4452.94 - 166.40 winning tickets. **Joe Rowntree**

4965 CLAIREFONTAINE (R-H)
Friday, August 12

OFFICIAL GOING: Turf: good to soft

5384a PRIX LUTH ENCHANTEE (LISTED RACE) (4YO+ FILLIES & MARES) (TURF) 1m 1f
3:05 (12:00) 4-Y-O+ **£17,647** (£7,058; £5,294; £3,529; £1,764)

RPR
1 **Banzari**[54] 3454 4-9-0 0.. GregoryBenoist 11 102
(H-F Devin, France) **12/1**
2 1/2 **Thank You Bye Bye (FR)**[16] 4783 4-9-0 0........ Pierre-CharlesBoudot 3 101+
(J-P Gauvin, France) **48/10**[2]
3 3/4 **Incahoots**[54] 3451 4-9-0 0... MaximeGuyon 6 99
(F Head, France) **9/1**
4 1/2 **Johara (IRE)**[19] 4696 5-9-0 0.. AlexisBadel 10 98+
(H-F Devin, France) **33/10**[1]
5 shd **Persona Grata**[69] 2893 5-9-0 0............................... StephanePasquier 7 98
(Ed Walker) *w.w towards rr: hdwy under 2f out: sn short of room and nt clr run: gap appeared ins fnl f: styd on late: nvr on terms* **11/1**
6 1 1/4 **Sainte Amarante (FR)**[22] 4-9-0 0................................ TheoBachelot 2 96
(Yves de Nicolay, France) **73/10**
7 1/2 **Kayenne (FR)**[106] 4-9-0 0.. IoritzMendizabal 5 94
(P Khozian, France) **9/1**
8 1 1/2 **Loaves And Fishes**[19] 4696 4-9-0 0.............................. TonyPiccone 8 91
(David O'Meara) *led: sn clr: 3 l clr and rdn ent fnl 2f: hdd wl over 1f out: grad dropped away* **19/1**
9 nse **Taniya (FR)**[104] 1876 4-9-4 0............................ ChristopheSoumillon 9 95
(J-C Rouget, France) **49/10**[3]
10 3 **Gentora (FR)**[13] 4903 4-9-0 0.................................. MickaelBarzalona 4 85
(P Sogorb, France) **22/1**
11 8 **Lady Marl**[8] 5054 5-9-0 0.. VincentCheminaud 1 68
(Gary Moore) *awkward leaving stalls and nrly dislodged rdr: in rr early: sn rcvrd to be cl up in main gp bhd clr ldr: 3rd and hrd rdn 1 1/2f out but no imp: bhd whn eased ins fnl f* **16/1**
WIN (incl. 1 euro stake): 3.30 (Banzari coupled with Johara). PLACES: 3.70,2.30, 2.90. DF: 48.10. SF: 102.90
Owner Mrs R G Hillen **Bred** New England Stud & Barton Stud **Trained** France

5385a PRIX BELLYPHA (MAIDEN) (3YO) (TURF) 1m
3:35 (12:00) 3-Y-O **£9,191** (£3,676; £2,757; £1,838; £919)

RPR
1 **Grand Jete**[35] 3-8-13 0.. VincentVion 7 80
(D Smaga, France) **14/5**[2]
2 1 3/4 **Hout Bay (FR)**[49] 3-9-2 0...................................... NicolasLarenaudie 13 79
(Mario Hofer, Germany) **31/1**
3 1 1/2 **Lord Of The North (IRE)**[27] 4401 3-9-2 0................ YohannBourgois 1 76
(Gay Kelleway) *chsd ldrs on inner: 2nd and rdn wl over 1 1/2f out: chal between horses fnl f: no ex last 100yds* **17/2**[3]

The Form Book, Raceform Ltd, Newbury, RG14 5SJ

4 ½ **Step In Late (FR)**[35] 3-8-13 0.......................... RichardOliver 2 72
(Mme C Head-Maarek, France) **42/1**
5 shd **Witchcraft (FR)**[34] 3-9-2 0.......................... SylvainRuis 4 75
(J-M Beguigne, France) **1/1**[1]
6 snk **La Milva (FR)** 3-8-9 0.......................... ClementLecoeuvre 6 67
(Alex Fracas, France) **98/1**
7 7 **Shere Calm (FR)**[295] 3-9-2 0.......................... MikeDoleuze 8 58
(G Doleuze, France) **16/1**
8 ¾ **American Whipper (FR)**[35] 3-9-2 0.......................... MatthiasLauron 12 56
(J-C Rouget, France) **17/2**[3]
9 hd **Laquyood** 3-8-13 0..........................(b[1]) AntonioPolli 10 53
(Werner Glanz, Germany) **107/1**
10 1 ¾ **Dayli Love Royale (FR)**[21] 3-8-13 0..........................(b) MlleJohannaHeitz 14 49
(P Capelle, France) **154/1**
11 ½ **Ciacona (IRE)**[24] 3-8-13 0.......................... CyrilleStefan 9 48
(A De Royer-Dupre, France) **19/1**
12 1 **Almunther (IRE)** 3-8-13 0.......................... CesarPasserat 11 46
(J E Hammond, France) **29/1**
13 1 **Carosamel (IRE)**[34] 3-8-13 0.......................... PaulineProd'homme 5 43
(D Prod'Homme, France) **34/1**

1m 39.6s (99.60) **13** Ran SP% **122.5**
WIN (incl. 1 euro stake): 3.80. PLACES: 1.90, 7.50, 2.70. DF: 55.90. SF: 94.60.
Owner K Abdullah **Bred** Juddmonte Farms Ltd **Trained** Lamorlaye, France

4855 DONCASTER (L-H)

Saturday, August 13

OFFICIAL GOING: Good (good to firm in places) changing to good to firm after race 1 (2.05)
Wind: Fresh against Weather: Fine & dry

5386 BETFRED "LOOKING FORWARD TO SIMPLY RED" H'CAP 7f

2:05 (2:06) (Class 5) (0-70,70) 3-Y-O+ **£3,881** (£1,155; £577; £288) **Stalls** Centre

Form RPR
4400 1 **Red Paladin (IRE)**[17] 4768 6-9-11 **69**..........................(p) ShaneKelly 4 79
(Kristin Stubbs) *dwlt and in rr: hdwy 3f out: trckd ldrs wl over 1f out: sn swtchd lft and effrt: rdn to ld ins fnl f: kpt on wl* **6/1**[2]
3600 2 1 ¼ **Danot (IRE)**[58] 3327 4-9-7 **65**.......................... GrahamLee 7 71
(Jedd O'Keeffe) *trckd ldrs: hdwy and cl up over 2f out: rdn to ld jst over 1f out: hdd and drvn ins fnl f: kpt on* **10/1**
5553 3 1 **Caledonia Laird**[21] 4640 5-9-7 **65**.......................... JoeyHaynes 8 68
(Jo Hughes) *midfield: hdwy 3f out: chsd ldrs wl over 1f out: sn rdn and kpt on same pce fnl f* **7/1**[3]
0500 4 1 ¼ **Royal Normandy**[11] 4970 4-9-6 **64**.......................... TomEaves 6 64
(David Loughnane) *towards rr: hdwy over 2f out: sn rdn: styd on wl fnl f: nrst fin* **25/1**
6 5 nk **Frozen Lake (USA)**[92] 2213 4-9-12 **70**.......... WilliamTwiston-Davies 9 69
(Mary Hambro) *cl up: led over 3f out: rdn along 2f out: hdd and drvn appr fnl f: grad wknd* **11/2**[1]
3000 6 1 **Insurplus (IRE)**[21] 4643 3-9-1 **65**.......................... JoeDoyle 14 59
(Jim Goldie) *towards rr: hdwy wl over 1f out: rdn and kpt on fnl f: nrst fin* **20/1**
5255 7 ½ **Celtic Sixpence (IRE)**[16] 4807 8-8-13 **64**.......................... RPWalsh(7) 12 59
(Nick Kent) *cl up: rdn along over 2f out: drvn wl over 1f out and kpt on one pce* **8/1**
0004 8 2 ¼ **Firgrove Bridge (IRE)**[23] 4557 4-8-11 **55**..........................(p) RoystonFfrench 13 44
(Steph Hollinshead) *towards rr: hdwy 3f out: rdn along to chse ldrs wl over 1f out: wknd appr fnl f* **16/1**
0020 9 6 **Qortaaj**[17] 4771 3-9-4 **68**..........................(b[1]) PJMcDonald 11 38
(David Loughnane) *chsd ldrs: rdn along 2f out: drvn and wknd over 1f out* **8/1**
600 10 5 **Rupert Boy (IRE)**[57] 3357 3-8-5 **55**..........................(b) LiamJones 15 12
(Scott Dixon) *chsd ldrs: rdn along 4f out: sn lost pl and bhd* **33/1**
0006 11 2 ¾ **My Dad Syd (USA)**[29] 4362 4-9-9 **70**.......................... GeorgeDowning(3) 3 21
(Ian Williams) *in tch on wd outside: effrt over 2f out: sn rdn and btn over 1f out* **12/1**
0060 12 1 **Lackaday**[60] 3262 4-9-2 **65**..........................(p) CallumShepherd(5) 5 14
(Mark Walford) *chsd ldrs: rdn along over 2f out: sn drvn and wknd* **12/1**
-203 13 42 **The Knave (IRE)**[53] 3499 3-8-8 **58**..........................(p) BenCurtis 2
(Scott Dixon) *racd wd: sn led: pushed along and hdd over 3f out: rdn along wl over 2f: sn wknd and bhd whn eased fnl f* **9/1**

1m 26.44s (0.14) **Going Correction** -0.075s/f (Good)
WFA 3 from 4yo+ 6lb **13** Ran SP% **122.9**
Speed ratings (Par 103): **96,94,93,92,91 90,89,87,80,74 71,70,22**
CSF £65.28 CT £440.00 TOTE £6.80: £1.90, £4.40, £2.30; EX 71.50 Trifecta £676.80.
Owner K Stubbs, Dr Grieve, T Baker & Clark **Bred** Noel O'Callaghan **Trained** Norton, N Yorks

FOCUS
The rail on the round course was railed out from 1m2f to where it meets the straight, adding about 9yds to races 6 and 7. The ground was officially good, good to firm in places, with clerk of the course Roderick Duncan stating: "It is quickest in the last 2f and the first furlong of the mile. After riding in the opener Ben Curtis said: "The ground is good to firm", and Joe Doyle and PJ McDonald both said: "It is quick." The opener was an average handicap featuring mainly out-of-form sorts, but they went a good pace. The winner has a good record here and was back down to his last winning mark.

5387 BETFRED TV EBF STALLIONS MAIDEN FILLIES' STKS (PLUS 10 RACE) 1m (S)

2:35 (2:36) (Class 5) 2-Y-O **£3,881** (£1,155; £577; £288) **Stalls** Centre

Form RPR
1 **Aljezeera** 2-9-0 0.......................... ShaneKelly 3 83+
(Luca Cumani) *trckd ldrs: hdwy 3f out: led jst over 2f out: rdn clr appr fnl f: kpt on wl* **10/11**[1]
232 2 2 ½ **Conqueress (IRE)**[28] 4397 2-9-0 76.......................... LiamJones 2 77
(Tom Dascombe) *led: pushed along and hdd jst over 2f out: sn rdn: drvn and kpt on same pce fnl f* **10/3**[2]
3 1 ¼ **Show Me The Music** 2-9-0 0.......................... TomEaves 1 74
(Richard Fahey) *hld up in rr: hdwy wl over 2f out: swtchd lft to outer and effrt to chse ldrs over 1f out: kpt on fnl f* **9/2**[3]
0 4 1 **Satpura**[14] 4885 2-9-0 0.......................... CharlesBishop 4 72
(Mick Channon) *hld up towards rr: hdwy over 3f out: chsd ldrs 2f out: sn rdn and kpt on same pce* **33/1**
5 11 **Devoran** 2-9-0 0.......................... WilliamTwiston-Davies 10 47
(Alan King) *a in rr* **10/1**
05 6 1 **Junoesque**[22] 4579 2-9-0 0.......................... MichaelJMMurphy 5 44
(John Gallagher) *chsd ldr: rdn along wl over 2f out: sn wknd* **18/1**
0 7 nk **Melcano**[74] 2757 2-8-11 0.......................... JacobButterfield(3) 7 44
(Shaun Harris) *in tch: rdn along wl over 2f out: sn outpcd* **100/1**
8 2 ¼ **Astrolabe (IRE)** 2-9-0 0.......................... AndrewElliott 9 38
(Tom Dascombe) *chsd ldrs: rdn along 3f out: sn wknd* **25/1**
0 9 2 ¾ **Silver Gleam (IRE)**[30] 4298 2-9-0 0.......................... CamHardie 6 32
(Tim Easterby) *t.k.h: trckd ldr: rdn along befr 1/2-way: sn outpcd* **12/1**

1m 39.86s (0.56) **Going Correction** -0.075s/f (Good) **9** Ran SP% **123.5**
Speed ratings (Par 91): **94,91,90,89,78 77,76,74,71**
CSF £4.48 TOTE £2.00: £1.10, £1.10, £1.60; EX 4.60 Trifecta £13.60.
Owner Al Shaqab Racing **Bred** Newsells Park Stud **Trained** Newmarket, Suffolk

FOCUS
The ground was changed to good to firm before the second race, a fair maiden in which the form can be rated around the runner-up. They went an honest gallop and the form looks solid with the first four coming clear, from which an impressive winner emerged.

5388 BETFRED "1400 SHOPS NATIONWIDE" MAIDEN STKS 6f

3:10 (3:10) (Class 4) 3-Y-O+ **£5,175** (£1,540; £769; £384) **Stalls** Centre

Form RPR
04 1 **Time To Exceed (IRE)**[70] 2904 3-9-0 0.......................... BenCurtis 7 81
(Henry Candy) *trckd ldrs: hdwy over 2f out: cl up over 1f out: sn chal: rdn to ld ins fnl f: kpt on wl towards fin* **4/1**[3]
62 2 nk **Soundstrings**[23] 4565 3-9-0 0.......................... WilliamTwiston-Davies 9 80
(William Haggas) *hld up: hdwy over 2f out: rdn to chse ldrs over 1f out: drvn to chal and edgd persistently lft ins fnl f: no ex towards fin* **5/2**[2]
2 3 3 ¾ **Thankyou Stars**[113] 1597 3-9-0 0.......................... JoeyHaynes 8 68
(K R Burke) *trckd ldr: led 1/2-way: jnd wl over 1f out and sn rdn: drvn and hdd ins fnl f: grad wknd* **15/8**[1]
6 4 2 ¼ **Joanne Park**[21] 4639 3-9-0 0.......................... JohnFahy 2 61
(Clive Cox) *in tch: effrt and hdwy over 2f out: rdn along wl over 1f out: sn no imp* **16/1**
5 ½ **Eternalist** 3-9-0 0..........................[1] JoeDoyle 3 59
(Jim Goldie) *led: hdd 1/2-way: cl up tl rdn along 2f out and sn wknd* **40/1**
6 5 **Young Tiger** 3-9-5 0.......................... AndrewElliott 6 48
(Tom Tate) *prom: rdn along over 2f out: sn wknd* **33/1**
33-4 7 2 ½ **Head East (IRE)**[15] 4845 3-9-5 80.......................... MartinHarley 4 40
(Ivan Furtado) *hld up towards rr: sme hdwy wl over 2f out: sn rdn along and n.d* **7/1**
53 8 4 **By The Law**[15] 4845 3-9-5 0.......................... CamHardie 1 27
(Tim Easterby) *dwlt: a in rr* **16/1**
0 9 ½ **Mrs Frosty (IRE)**[37] 4041 3-9-0 0.......................... TomEaves 5 21
(Clive Mulhall) *a towards rr* **100/1**
10 3 ½ **Sense Of Snow (IRE)** 3-9-2 0..........................(t) RobHornby(3) 10 15
(William Muir) *dwlt: a towards rr* **16/1**
11 20 **Escapade** 3-9-0 0.......................... RoystonFfrench 11
(Les Eyre) *s.i.s: green and a bhd* **66/1**

1m 12.37s (-1.23) **Going Correction** -0.075s/f (Good) **11** Ran SP% **121.4**
Speed ratings (Par 105): **105,104,99,96,95 89,85,80,79,75 48**
CSF £14.76 TOTE £5.50: £1.60, £1.20, £1.30; EX 16.60 Trifecta £34.30.
Owner Hunscote Stud **Bred** Hunscote Stud **Trained** Kingston Warren, Oxon

FOCUS
A fair maiden in which those with experience came out on top. They went a good pace and the winner improved down at 6f.

5389 BETFRED "BE PART OF THE ACTION" H'CAP 7f

3:45 (3:45) (Class 2) (0-105,99) 3-Y-O+
£15,562 (£4,660; £2,330; £1,165; £582; £292) **Stalls** Centre

Form RPR
-226 1 **Certificate**[51] 3566 5-9-10 **97**.......................... JackMitchell 4 108+
(Roger Varian) *trckd ldrs: smooth hdwy to ld 1 1/2f out: rdn ins fnl f: kpt on strly* **7/1**[3]
4004 2 2 **Bertiewhittle**[14] 4893 8-8-8 **86**.......................... RowanScott(5) 2 92
(David Barron) *dwlt and in rr: hdwy into midfield 1/2-way: effrt to chse ldrs wl over 1f out: sn rdn: styd on to chse wnr ins fnl f: sn drvn and no imp towards fin* **12/1**
3261 3 shd **Get Knotted (IRE)**[21] 4665 4-9-8 **95**..........................(p) TomEaves 9 102+
(Michael Dods) *hld up towards rr: hdwy over 2f out: rdn over 1f out: drvn and kpt on wl fnl f* **8/1**
0100 4 2 **Kalk Bay (IRE)**[14] 4893 9-8-12 **85**..........................(t) CamHardie 1 85
(Michael Easterby) *midfield: hdwy on outer wl over 1f out: rdn and kpt on fnl f* **40/1**
-660 5 nk **Salateen**[56] 3386 4-9-12 **99**.......................... GrahamLee 6 99
(David O'Meara) *cl up: ev ch 2f out and sn rdn: drvn over 1f out and grad wknd* **17/2**
1000 6 ½ **Spring Loaded (IRE)**[14] 4865 4-9-11 **98**.......................... ShaneKelly 7 96
(Paul D'Arcy) *towards rr: hdwy 2f out: rdn over 1f out: styd on fnl f: nrst fin* **12/1**
4061 7 1 ¼ **Barracuda Boy (IRE)**[21] 4644 6-9-12 **99**.......................... ThomasBrown 10 94
(Tom Dascombe) *towards rr: hdwy on outer wl over 1f out: sn rdn: kpt on fnl f* **20/1**
5056 8 ¾ **Lincoln (IRE)**[21] 4625 5-9-1 **88**.......................... CharlesBishop 8 81
(Mick Channon) *bhd: hdwy 2f out: sn rdn and plugged on fnl f: n.d* **11/2**[1]
-536 9 1 **Sakhee's Return**[14] 4893 4-8-11 **84**.......................... JasonHart 12 74
(Tim Easterby) *led: rdn along over 2f out: hdd and drvn 1 1/2f out: sn wknd* **16/1**
6410 10 ½ **Brazos (IRE)**[21] 4625 5-9-6 **93**..........................(b) MartinHarley 14 82
(James Tate) *chsd ldrs: rdn along over 2f out: drvn wl over 1f out: sn wknd* **13/2**[2]
0600 11 nk **Farlow (IRE)**[7] 5174 8-9-3 **97**.......................... NatalieHambling(7) 15 85
(Richard Fahey) *a towards rr* **9/1**
61- 12 7 **Newstead Abbey**[463] 2034 6-9-12 **99**.......................... PJMcDonald 11 68
(David Barron) *trckd ldrs: rdn along wl over 2f out: sn wknd* **33/1**
205 13 3 ¼ **Free Code (IRE)**[7] 5156 5-9-0 **87**.......................... FrederikTylicki 16 47
(David Barron) *chsd ldrs: rdn along 1/2-way: sn lost pl and bhd* **14/1**
2121 14 9 **Shanghai Glory (IRE)**[44] 3800 3-9-1 **94**.......................... MichaelJMMurphy 3 28
(Charles Hills) *chsd ldng pair: rdn along wl over 2f out: sn drvn and wknd* **8/1**

1m 24.12s (-2.18) **Going Correction** -0.075s/f (Good)
WFA 3 from 4yo+ 6lb **14** Ran SP% **122.0**
Speed ratings (Par 109): **109,106,106,104,103 103,101,101,99,99 99,91,87,77**
CSF £87.95 CT £717.10 TOTE £7.20: £2.50, £4.10, £2.50; EX 103.90 Trifecta £1857.20 Part won..
Owner Cheveley Park Stud **Bred** Cheveley Park Stud Ltd **Trained** Newmarket, Suffolk

FOCUS
A quality handicap, although the top weights were rated 6lb below the ceiling for the grade. They went a good pace and the form looks solid with a progressive winner leading them home. The runner-up helps set the standard.

5390 BETFRED "FOLLOW US ON TWITTER" H'CAP 5f
4:20 (4:21) (Class 3) (0-95,95) 3-Y-O+ **£7,762** (£2,310; £1,154; £577) **Stalls** Centre

Form RPR
3514 **1** **Bashiba (IRE)**[25] 4488 5-8-4 **80**.................................(t) RowanScott(5) 17 94+
(Nigel Tinkler) *hld up towards rr: smooth hdwy on outer wl over 1f out: rdn and qcknd wl to ld ins fnl f: sn clr: readily* **12/1**
4156 **2** 1 ¾ **Confessional**[18] 4735 9-9-4 **89**.......................................(be) JasonHart 16 95
(Tim Easterby) *in tch on outer: hdwy wl over 1f out: rdn ent fnl f: kpt on wl towards fin* **20/1**
4220 **3** nk **Gamesome (FR)**[14] 4862 5-9-10 **95**.............................. MartinHarley 10 100
(Paul Midgley) *prom: rdn over 1f out: ev ch ent fnl f: sn drvn and kpt on* **9/2**[1]
0005 **4** nk **Ashpan Sam**[21] 4632 7-9-6 **91**........................(p) WilliamTwiston-Davies 2 95
(David W Drinkwater) *led: rdn over 1f out: drvn and hdd ins fnl f: kpt on* **18/1**
6410 **5** hd **Soie D'Leau**[14] 4862 4-9-8 **93**.. ShaneKelly 12 96
(Kristin Stubbs) *in tch: hdwy wl over 1f out: rdn to chse ldrs appr fnl f and ev ch: sn drvn and kpt on* **8/1**[3]
0555 **6** ½ **Lathom**[16] 4803 3-8-13 **92**.. JoshDoyle(5) 15 92
(David O'Meara) *midfield: hdwy wl over 1f out: rdn to chse ldrs ent fnl f: sn n.m.r: kpt on towards fin* **5/1**[2]
1045 **7** 1 ¼ **Lexington Place**[15] 4831 6-9-1 **86**................................... PJMcDonald 7 83
(Ruth Carr) *in tch: hdwy to chse ldrs wl over 1f out: rdn and ch ent fnl f: sn drvn and no imp* **10/1**
2260 **8** ½ **Olivia Fallow (IRE)**[15] 4831 4-9-2 **87**.............................. GrahamLee 11 86
(Paul Midgley) *s.i.s and bhd: hdwy 2f out: styng on whn nt clr run jst over 1f out: swtchd rt and rdn: kpt on: nrst fin* **16/1**
0000 **9** shd **Barnet Fair**[14] 4862 8-8-10 **81**.. CamHardie 8 76
(David Nicholls) *chsd ldrs: pushed along over 2f out: rdn wl over 1f out: grad wknd* **12/1**
0020 **10** 1 ¼ **Primrose Valley**[22] 4584 4-9-5 **90**...............................(b) FrederikTylicki 6 80
(Ed Vaughan) *prom: rdn along wl over 1f out: grad wknd* **14/1**
3-40 **11** ½ **Shore Step (IRE)**[18] 4735 6-9-8 **93**.............................. CharlesBishop 13 81
(Mick Channon) *prom: rdn over 2f out: sn drvn and wknd* **10/1**
0020 **12** 1 ¼ **New Bidder**[29] 4338 5-9-5 **93**.......................................(b) RobHornby(3) 1 77
(David Barron) *a towards rr* **9/1**
200- **13** 3 ½ **Thorntoun Lady (USA)**[322] 6747 6-8-5 **76** oh4.................. JoeDoyle 14 47
(Jim Goldie) *dwlt: a towards rr* **50/1**
6004 **14** 2 ¼ **Love Island**[12] 4946 7-8-3 **79**... PhilDennis(5) 4 42
(Richard Whitaker) *dwlt: sn in tch: rdn along 1/2-way: sn wknd* **10/1**
0100 **15** ½ **Sign Of The Kodiac (IRE)**[16] 4803 3-9-6 **94**..................... TomEaves 9 54
(James Given) *chsd ldrs: rdn along whn n.m.r and hmpd over 2f out: sn wknd* **18/1**

58.89s (-1.61) **Going Correction** -0.075s/f (Good) **15** Ran SP% **128.4**
WFA 3 from 4yo+ 3lb
Speed ratings (Par 107): **109,106,105,105,104 104,102,101,101,99 98,96,90,87,86**
CSF £245.48 CT £1293.14 TOTE £9.20: £3.30, £5.80, £2.10; EX 237.20 Trifecta £1574.40.
Owner M Webb **Bred** John T Heffernan & Grainne Dooley **Trained** Langton, N Yorks

FOCUS
A fair sprint handicap for the grade and yet another impressive winner on the card. He looks much improved, while the runner-up helps set the standard.

5391 BETFRED "RACINGS BIGGEST SUPPORTER" H'CAP 1m 2f 60y
4:50 (4:51) (Class 4) (0-85,84) 3-Y-O **£5,175** (£1,540; £769; £384) **Stalls** Low

Form RPR
-314 **1** **Fidaawy**[16] 4808 3-9-5 **82**.. GrahamLee 1 99
(Sir Michael Stoute) *mde all: pushed along over 2f out: rdn wl over 1f out: clr ins fnl f: kpt on wl* **5/4**[1]
-221 **2** 7 **Fastnet Tempest (IRE)**[29] 4347 3-9-7 **84**.....(p) WilliamTwiston-Davies 6 88
(William Haggas) *hld up: hdwy 3f out: chsd wnr over 2f out: rdn and ch over 1f out: sn drvn and kpt on same pce* **9/4**[2]
51- **3** 4 **Richie McCaw**[303] 7237 3-8-11 **77**........................... GeorgeDowning(3) 2 73
(Ian Williams) *trckd ldrs: pushed along wl over 2f out: sn rdn and plugged on one pce* **12/1**
0064 **4** 1 **Jim Dandy**[23] 4554 3-8-13 **76**.. MartinHarley 3 71
(Alan King) *chsd wnr: rdn along 3f out: drvn 2f out: sn one pce* **4/1**[3]
1110 **5** ¾ **Caponova (IRE)**[29] 4342 3-8-12 **75**..................................... LiamJones 5 68
(Tom Dascombe) *hld up in rr: hdwy 3f out: rdn 2f out: sn drvn and no imp* **10/1**

2m 9.54s (0.14) **Going Correction** +0.15s/f (Good) **5** Ran SP% **112.0**
Speed ratings (Par 102): **105,99,96,95,94**
CSF £4.43 TOTE £2.00: £1.40, £1.50; EX 4.20 Trifecta £21.50.
Owner Hamdan Al Maktoum **Bred** Shadwell Estate Company Limited **Trained** Newmarket, Suffolk

FOCUS
Rail movement added about 9yds to the race distance. Several improving types lined up for this tight little handicap, but in the end it was easy work for the front-running favourite who looked much more straightforward and is a big improver.

5392 BETFRED "LIKE US ON FACEBOOK" APPRENTICE H'CAP 1m 2f 60y
5:25 (5:25) (Class 5) (0-75,76) 4-Y-O+ **£3,881** (£1,155; £577; £288) **Stalls** Low

Form RPR
3043 **1** **Purple Rock (IRE)**[3] 5292 4-9-8 **74**.......................(t) DanielleMooney(3) 9 84
(Michael Easterby) *hld up towards rr: gd hdwy on outer wl over 2f out: led 2f out: sn rdn and kpt on strly fnl f* **4/1**[1]
5025 **2** 2 ¾ **Merchant Of Dubai**[15] 4828 11-8-6 **60**.................. LewisEdmunds(5) 10 65
(Jim Goldie) *hld up in tch: hdwy 3f out and sn chsng ldrs: rdn wl over 1f out: drvn and kpt on wl fnl f* **20/1**
2351 **3** 1 **Ingleby Spring (IRE)**[16] 4784 4-8-11 **63**................ NatalieHambling(3) 1 66
(Richard Fahey) *trckd ldrs on inner: hdwy to ld over 3f out: rdn along over 2f out: sn hdd and drvn: kpt on fnl f* **8/1**
6641 **4** hd **San Quentin (IRE)**[3] 5293 5-9-8 **76** 6ex..............(b) CameronNoble(5) 11 79
(David Loughnane) *hld up in rr: gd hdwy on inner wl over 2f out: rdn to chal over 1f out and ev ch: kpt on same pce fnl f* **5/1**[2]
3-54 **5** 1 ½ **Zabeel Star (IRE)**[28] 4406 4-9-7 **75**...................... PatrickVaughan(5) 5 75
(Graeme McPherson) *in tch: effrt 3f out: rdn along 2f out: sn drvn and no imp* **5/1**[2]
1220 **6** ½ **Miss Ranger (IRE)**[20] 4687 4-9-6 **69**........................... CallumShepherd 2 68
(Brian Ellison) *hld up towards rr: hdwy over 4f out: cl up 3f out: rdn and ev ch 2f out: drvn over 1f out: wknd ent fnl f* **7/1**[3]
016 **7** 6 **Almutamarred (USA)**[31] 4277 4-8-9 **58**.............................. PhilDennis 4 46
(Kevin Morgan) *in tch: effrt over 3f out: rdn along wl 2f out: sn outpcd* **20/1**
0600 **8** 1 **My Mo (FR)**[16] 2507 4-8-8 **57**.......................................(p) GeorgeBuckell 7 43
(David Dennis) *prom: rdn along over 3f out: drvn wl over 2f out and sn wknd* **8/1**
0611 **9** ¾ **We'll Shake Hands (FR)**[18] 4740 5-9-0 **66**..................... CliffordLee(3) 3 50
(K R Burke) *slt ld: pushed along and hdd wl over 3f out: sn drvn and wknd over 2f out* **5/1**[2]
1036 **10** ½ **Tatawu (IRE)**[12] 4956 4-8-13 **65**................................... LuluStanford(3) 12 48
(Peter Hiatt) *cl up: rdn along 4f out: drvn over 3f out: sn wknd* **10/1**

2m 9.85s (0.45) **Going Correction** +0.15s/f (Good) **10** Ran SP% **123.3**
Speed ratings (Par 103): **104,101,101,100,99 99,94,93,93,92**
CSF £91.84 CT £619.96 TOTE £5.00: £1.80, £5.90, £2.70; EX 82.90 Trifecta £814.30.
Owner S Hull, M Blades, S Hollings & D Swales **Bred** Barronstown Stud **Trained** Sheriff Hutton, N Yorks

FOCUS
Rail movement added about 9yds to the race distance. The finale was an apprentice handicap run at a good gallop and the trio who set the pace were well beaten. The winner improved slightly on this year's better form, while the runner-up helps set the level.
T/Plt: £24.70 to a £1 stake. Pool: £62,856.79 - 1852.4 winning units T/Qpdt: £8.50 to a £1 stake. Pool: £5,446.68 - 472.27 winning units **Joe Rowntree**

5257 LINGFIELD (L-H)
Saturday, August 13

OFFICIAL GOING: Turf course - good to firm (8.2); all-weather - polytrack: standard
Wind: light, across Weather: fine, sunny spells

5393 LADBROKES APPRENTICE TRAINING SERIES H'CAP (PART OF THE RACING EXCELLENCE INITIATIVE) 7f 140y
4:55 (4:55) (Class 5) (0-70,68) 4-Y-O+ **£3,234** (£962; £481; £240) **Stalls** Centre

Form RPR
4133 **1** **Wordismybond**[21] 4656 7-9-7 **68**........................(p) StephenCummins(5) 6 75
(Richard Hughes) *mde all: pushed along along over 1f out: edgd lft ins fnl f: kpt on wl* **5/2**[1]
6041 **2** ½ **Sarmadee (IRE)**[8] 5104 4-9-10 **66**............................... KillianHennessy 4 72
(Mick Channon) *hld up in rr of main gp: swtchd lft and hdwy in centre over 2f out: rdn to chse ldrs over 1f out: ev ch ins fnl f: kpt on* **7/2**[3]
5223 **3** 1 ¾ **Limerick Lord (IRE)**[9] 5090 4-8-11 **58**.........................(p) LiamDoran(5) 7 59
(Julia Feilden) *taken down early: chsd wnr: upsides 2f out: rdn over 1f out: unable qck 1f out: styd on same pce ins fnl f* **3/1**[2]
5046 **4** ½ **Two In The Pink (IRE)**[33] 4201 6-9-4 **60**....................... RhiainIngram 3 60
(Ralph J Smith) *hld up in tch: effrt 2f out: sme hdwy whn nt clr run and swtchd rt ins fnl f: styd on towards fin: no threat to wnr* **10/1**
0022 **5** ½ **Red Unico (IRE)**[19] 4715 4-9-0 **61**.................................. JoshuaBryan(5) 2 60
(Brian Barr) *chsd ldng trio: swtchd lft and drvn over 1f out: styd on same pce ins fnl f* **6/1**
0440 **6** 1 **Cascading Stars (IRE)**[9] 5068 4-8-13 **60**.......................... TobyEley(5) 1 56
(Daniel Mark Loughnane) *chsd ldrs: rdn and hung lft over 1f out: no imp 1f out: wknd ins fnl f* **11/1**
0010 **7** 24 **Munsarim (IRE)**[10] 5021 9-8-12 **59**...............................(b) JordanUys(5) 5
(Lee Carter) *v.s.a: nvr rcvrd and a detached in last* **16/1**

1m 31.32s (-0.98) **Going Correction** -0.15s/f (Firm) **7** Ran SP% **113.4**
Speed ratings (Par 103): **98,97,95,95,94 93,69**
CSF £11.31 TOTE £4.00: £2.20, £2.40; EX 12.00 Trifecta £35.00.
Owner T W Wellard & Partners **Bred** Henry And Mrs Rosemary Moszkowicz **Trained** Upper Lambourn, Berkshire

FOCUS
A modest apprentice handicap. They went at best a respectable gallop on ground officially described as good to firm, good in places. The winner stuck to the stands' rail and the runner-up challenged centrally.

5394 DOWNLOAD THE LADBROKES APP EBF NOVICE STKS 7f
5:30 (5:30) (Class 5) 2-Y-O **£3,881** (£1,155) **Stalls** Centre

Form RPR
1 **1** **Rodaini (USA)**[74] 2757 2-9-9 0.................................... SilvestreDeSousa 2 81+
(Simon Crisford) *dwlt: sn trcking ldr: led over 4f out: stl on bridle: in command and ears pricked fr over 1f out: nt extended* **4/6**[1]
0 **2** 4 ½ **Matthioli (FR)**[17] 4775 2-9-2 0....................................... AdamBeschizza 3 56
(Michael Attwater) *broke wl: led tl over 4f out: rdn over 2f out: wl hld and plugged on same pce fr over 1f out* **22/1**[2]

1m 25.29s (1.99) **Going Correction** -0.15s/f (Firm) **2** Ran SP% **64.3**
Speed ratings (Par 94): **82,76**
TOTE £1.10.Harbour Master was withdrawn. Price at time of withdrawal 11/8. Rule 4 applies to all bets - deduction 40p in the pound.
Owner Abdullah Saeed Al Naboodah **Bred** Greenwood Lodge Farm **Trained** Newmarket, Suffolk

FOCUS
A juvenile novice contest which lost most of its lustre when the second-favourite was withdrawn after losing a shoe on the way down to the start. Winner has the scope to do much better.

5395 CASHOUT AVAILABLE ON THE APP AT LADBROKES MAIDEN AUCTION STKS 6f
6:00 (6:00) (Class 6) 2-Y-O **£2,911** (£866; £432; £216) **Stalls** Centre

Form RPR
22 **1** **Grey Britain**[23] 4564 2-9-1 0...(b[1]) JimCrowley 6 83
(John Ryan) *travelled strly thrght: chsd ldrs tl wnt 2nd 1/2-way: rdn to ld 1f out: asserted u.p ins fnl f: r.o wl and gng away at fin* **2/1**[1]
3 **2** 2 **Miss Icon**[24] 4523 2-8-5 0... NickyMackay 10 67
(Patrick Chamings) *chsd ldrs: effrt u.p over 1f out: chsd wnr ins fnl f: styd on same pce fnl 100yds* **16/1**
5 **3** ½ **Wind In Her Sails (IRE)**[37] 4054 2-8-7 0............ JosephineGordon(3) 8 70
(Giles Bravery) *t.k.h: hld up in tch in midfield: effrt to chse ldrs over 1f out: styd on same pce ins fnl f* **3/1**[2]
05 **4** shd **Erissimus Maximus (FR)**[6] 5188 2-8-11 0................. LemosdeSouza 4 71
(Chris Dwyer) *led: rdn over 1f out: hdd 1f out: styd on same pce ins fnl f and lost 2 pls fnl 150yds* **33/1**
5 2 ½ **Swift Mover (IRE)** 2-8-8 0... TomMarquand 12 60
(Richard Hannon) *hld up in tch in midfield: swtchd lft and effrt u.p over 1f out: no imp and styd on same pce ins fnl f* **10/1**
4 **6** 3 ½ **Ejabah (IRE)**[23] 4564 2-8-10 0... TedDurcan 9 53
(Chris Wall) *hld up in midfield: pushed along over 1f out: sn outpcd and btn: wknd ins fnl f* **7/2**[3]

4 **7** *nk* **Ruby Woo**[65] 3073 2-8-8 0 AaronJones(3) 11 51
(Stuart Williams) *chsd ldr tl 1/2-way: rdn and unable qck over 1f out: sn lost pl and btn 1f out: wknd ins fnl f* **8/1**

8 *1 1/2* **Derek Duval (USA)** 2-9-1 0 (t) AdamBeschizza 7 50
(Stuart Williams) *s.i.s: a towards rr: sltly hmpd after 1f: rdn 2f out: no imp and edgd rt over 1f out: wknd fnl f* **25/1**

53 **9** *hd* **Spiritofedinburgh (IRE)**[82] 2535 2-9-2 0 StevieDonohoe 3 50
(Brendan Powell) *a last trio: swtchd rt after 1f: rdn and no hdwy 2f out: wknd over 1f out* **16/1**

06 **10** *3 1/2* **Secret Icon**[6] 5202 2-8-3 0 EdwardGreatrex(3) 1 29
(Jamie Osborne) *stdd and swtchd rt after s: a in rr: rdn 2f out: sn btn and wknd over 1f out* **33/1**

1m 10.36s (-0.84) **Going Correction** -0.15s/f (Firm) **10** Ran SP% **122.3**
Speed ratings (Par 92): **99,96,95,95,92 87,87,85,84,80**
CSF £39.03 TOTE £2.60: £1.10, £5.60, £1.40; EX 27.50 Trifecta £117.30.
Owner G Smith-Bernal **Bred** D R Tucker **Trained** Newmarket, Suffolk
■ Stewards' Enquiry : Adam Beschizza caution: careless riding

FOCUS
A fair juvenile maiden. They went a decent gallop and the form should prove reliable with winner rated has up to his mark.

5396 EUROPEAN BREEDERS FUND SERIES EBF FILLIES' H'CAP 7f 140y
6:35 (6:36) (Class 3) (0-95,93) 3-Y-O+ **£12,602** (£3,772; £1,886; £944; £470) **Stalls** Centre

Form RPR
-132 **1** **Eternally**[36] 4105 3-9-4 **90** RobertHavlin 5 107+
(John Gosden) *led tl 6f out: settled bk to trck ldng pair: shkn up and qcknd to ld over 1f out: r.o strly and drew clr fnl f: readily* **5/4**[1]

4630 **2** *4 1/2* **Haley Bop (IRE)**[18] 4737 3-9-2 **88** AdamKirby 1 94
(Mark Johnston) *chsd ldrs: wnt 2nd 6f out tl led 3f out: rdn ent fnl 2f: hdd and unable qck over 1f out: no ch w wnr but kpt on for clr 2nd ins fnl f* **8/1**

3521 **3** *2 3/4* **Subtle Knife**[30] 4318 7-9-4 **86** JosephineGordon(3) 3 86
(Giles Bravery) *hld up in tch in midfield: effrt 2f out: edging rt u.p 1f out: no ch w wnr but kpt on to go 3rd last strides* **12/1**

0045 **4** *hd* **Rebel Surge (IRE)**[21] 4651 3-8-12 **87** EdwardGreatrex(3) 4 86
(Richard Spencer) *hld up in tch: effrt ent fnl 2f: drvn to chse ldng pair over 1f out: no imp and plugged on same pce after: lost 3rd last strides* **6/1**[3]

5016 **5** *2 1/2* **Lyfka**[18] 4737 4-9-6 **85** (tp) JimCrowley 7 78
(Paul Cole) *hld up in tch in midfield: lost pl and rdn jst over 2f out: wknd over 1f out: no ch whn swtchd lft ins fnl f* **10/1**

0540 **6** *nse* **Gratzie**[7] 5158 5-9-7 **93** KillianHennessy(7) 2 86
(Mick Channon) *s.i.s: a in rr: nvr on terms* **16/1**

4042 **7** *4 1/2* **Bint Dandy (IRE)**[6] 5190 5-9-8 **87** (b) SilvestreDeSousa 6 69
(Chris Dwyer) *chsd ldr tl led 6f out: hdd and rdn 3f out: lost pl and btn over 1f out: bhd and eased wl ins fnl f* **7/2**[2]

1m 28.67s (-3.63) **Going Correction** -0.15s/f (Firm)
WFA 3 from 4yo+ 7lb **7** Ran SP% **114.7**
Speed ratings (Par 104): **112,107,104,104,102 102,97**
CSF £12.39 TOTE £1.90: £1.70, £4.40; EX 13.30 Trifecta £63.10.
Owner Cheveley Park Stud **Bred** Cheveley Park Stud Ltd **Trained** Newmarket, Suffolk

FOCUS
The feature contest was a good fillies' handicap. They went a decent gallop and a young improver stamped her quality on the race. The race has been rated around the runner-up.

5397 LADBROKES H'CAP 1m 4f (P)
7:05 (7:05) (Class 5) (0-70,70) 3-Y-O+ **£3,234** (£962; £481; £240) **Stalls** Low

Form RPR
-243 **1** **Spinners Ball (IRE)**[21] 4639 3-9-3 **70** TomMarquand 6 77+
(Sylvester Kirk) *hld up in tch in midfield: effrt to chse ldrs 2f out: rdn to ld 1f out: styd on wl: rdn out* **3/1**[2]

1644 **2** *3/4* **Fearless Lad (IRE)**[17] 4774 6-9-8 **64** KierenFox 5 69+
(John Best) *in tch in rr: rdn briefly 4f out: rdn and swtchd rt bnd 2f out: hdwy u.p ent fnl f: styd on strly ins fnl f: snatched 2nd last strides: nt rch wnr* **8/1**

5322 **3** *hd* **Machine Learner**[9] 5083 3-9-3 **70** (v) AdamKirby 3 74
(Michael Bell) *in tch in midfield: effrt 2f out: hdwy u.p over 1f out: styd on ins fnl f: wnt 2nd wl ins fnl f: kpt on but nvr getting to wnr and lost 2nd last strides* **2/1**[1]

62 **4** *1* **Officer Drivel (IRE)**[19] 4711 5-9-12 **68** JimCrowley 2 71
(Jim Best) *chsd ldr for 2f: styd chsng ldrs: rdn to ld wl over 1f out: hdd 1f out: no ex and styd on same pce ins fnl f: lost 2 pls wl ins fnl f* **9/2**[3]

0610 **5** *3 1/2* **Diletta Tommasa (IRE)**[19] 4716 6-9-6 **62** (p) SilvestreDeSousa 9 59
(Daniel Mark Loughnane) *v.s.a: sn rcvrd and t.k.h in last trio: effrt and switching rt bnd 2f out: styd on ins fnl f: no threat to ldrs* **22/1**

1654 **6** *1 3/4* **Lady Lunchalot (USA)**[14] 4880 6-9-9 **65** (p) LiamKeniry 1 59
(Laura Mongan) *dwlt and early reminders: in tch in midfield: effrt on inner 2f out: nt clrest of runs and swtchd lft ent fnl f: sn drvn and no imp: wknd ins fnl f* **14/1**

-260 **7** *3/4* **Putaringonit (IRE)**[28] 4383 4-9-8 **69** DavidParkes(5) 8 62
(Jeremy Gask) *t.k.h: sn led and set stdy gallop: rdn and hdd wl over 1f out: sn edgd rt u.p and no ex: wknd ins fnl f* **16/1**

5022 **8** *2* **Clive Clifton (IRE)**[33] 4204 3-8-11 **64** StevieDonohoe 7 54
(Phil York) *chsd ldrs tl wnt 2nd after 2f tl 2f out: sn lost pl u.p: wknd fnl f* **14/1**

2/50 **9** *2 3/4* **Little Buxted (USA)**[14] 4880 6-9-11 **67** (b) TimmyMurphy 4 53
(Jim Best) *in tch in last trio: rdn and dropped to last over 2f out: no rspnse and wknd over 1f out* **20/1**

2m 34.01s (1.01) **Going Correction** -0.025s/f (Stan)
WFA 3 from 4yo+ 11lb **9** Ran SP% **116.0**
Speed ratings (Par 103): **95,94,94,93,91 90,89,88,86**
CSF £27.46 CT £58.32 TOTE £4.30: £1.70, £2.00, £1.20; EX 28.00 Trifecta £98.00.
Owner E McCay **Bred** Lynch-Bages Ltd **Trained** Upper Lambourn, Berks

FOCUS
A modest middle-distance handicap. They went a sedate gallop on standard Polytrack and an unexposed 3yo came to the fore. The race has been rated around the fourth.

5398 BET NOW WITH THE LADBROKES APP H'CAP 1m 7f 169y(P)
7:35 (7:35) (Class 5) (0-70,72) 3-Y-O **£3,234** (£962; £481; £240) **Stalls** Low

Form RPR
421 **1** **Captain Peacock**[5] 5232 3-9-9 **72** 6ex (v) JimCrowley 6 78+
(William Knight) *hld up in tch: effrt bnd 2f out: wnt 3rd but stl 4 l down over 1f out: hdwy ins fnl f: styd on strly to ld towards fin: sn in command and eased last strides* **10/11**[1]

060 **2** *1* **Contingency**[29] 4367 3-9-2 **70** CharlieBennett(5) 4 75
(Jane Chapple-Hyam) *chsd ldr for 3f: styd handy in 3rd: rdn to chse ldr again over 2f out: sltly outpcd over 1f out: rallied u.p 1f out: styd on to ld wl ins fnl f: sn hdd and one pce towards fin* **16/1**

2023 **3** *1 1/2* **Argyle (IRE)**[21] 4636 3-9-5 **68** SilvestreDeSousa 1 71
(William Muir) *chsd ldrs tl led after 3f: rdn 2f out and sn kicked 3 l clr: drvn ins fnl f: hdd wl ins fnl f: sn btn and wknd towards fin* **11/4**[2]

0553 **4** *4* **Marshall Aid (IRE)**[39] 3991 3-9-7 **70** LiamKeniry 5 68
(Mark Usher) *hld up in tch: effrt on inner 2f out: hung lft and no imp over 1f out: wl hld and plugged on same pce fnl f* **10/1**

3354 **5** *18* **Regal Galaxy**[16] 4810 3-8-2 **51** oh5 NickyMackay 2 28
(Mark H Tompkins) *led for 3f: chsd ldr tl over 2f out: sn u.p and unable qck: wknd over 1f out* **33/1**

5614 **P** **Street Outlaw (IRE)**[5] 5232 3-9-1 **64** (p) AdamKirby 3
(Daniel Mark Loughnane) *nvr gng wl and a last: clsd and in tch 9f out: eased and p.u 7f out: dismntd: lame* **6/1**[3]

3m 24.76s (-0.94) **Going Correction** -0.025s/f (Stan) **6** Ran SP% **111.3**
Speed ratings (Par 100): **101,100,99,97,88**
CSF £17.16 TOTE £1.80: £1.10, £4.50; EX 13.70 Trifecta £47.30.
Owner Chasemore Farm **Bred** Chasemore Farm **Trained** Patching, W Sussex

FOCUS
An ordinary 3yo staying handicap. They went a modest gallop and the winner needed every yard to assert his superiority. The race has been rated around the third.

5399 TRACK YOUR FOOTBALL ACCA WITH LADBROKES H'CAP 1m 2f (P)
8:05 (8:05) (Class 6) (0-60,60) 3-Y-O+ **£2,587** (£770; £384; £192) **Stalls** Low

Form RPR
6602 **1** **Monna Valley**[18] 4740 4-9-4 **57** AaronJones(3) 5 63
(Stuart Williams) *midfield but nt on terms w ldng quartet: effrt in 4th and clsng over 2f out: chsd ldr 1f out: styd on to ld 100yds out: rdn out* **5/1**[2]

5502 **2** *3/4* **Power Up**[14] 4882 5-9-4 **59** CharlieBennett(5) 7 64
(Jane Chapple-Hyam) *chsd ldrs and clr in ldng quartet: effrt to chse ldr 2f out: kpt on u.p: chsd wnr wl ins fnl f: kpt on but no imp fnl 50yds* **8/1**[3]

1624 **3** *3/4* **Megalala (IRE)**[14] 4882 15-9-4 **54** DannyBrock 6 57
(John Bridger) *chsd ldr and clr in ldng quartet tl rdn to ld wl over 2f out: drvn 2 l clr 2f out: hdd 100yds out: no ex and kpt on same pce after* **14/1**

0046 **4** *1 1/4* **Chella Thriller (SPA)**[33] 4200 7-9-10 **60** (b) SilvestreDeSousa 11 61
(Ralph J Smith) *s.i.s: hld up in last trio: effrt on outer over 2f out: styd on u.p ins fnl f: nvr trbld ldrs* **8/1**[3]

5533 **5** *2 3/4* **Sunshineandbubbles**[4] 5263 3-8-13 **58** (p) JimCrowley 4 54
(Daniel Mark Loughnane) *hld up off the pce in midfield: effrt over 2f out: drvn and no imp over 1f out: wl hld and plugged on same pce fnl f* **3/1**[1]

041 **6** *hd* **Embankment**[14] 4882 7-9-6 **59** EdwardGreatrex(3) 1 54
(Michael Attwater) *hld up in tch in midfield: effrt on inner jst over 2f out: no imp u.p over 1f out: wl hld and plugged on same pce fnl f* **8/1**[3]

-144 **7** *8* **Whitstable Pearl (IRE)**[12] 4942 3-8-7 **52** KierenFox 8 32
(John Best) *led and clr in ldng quartet: hdd and rdn wl over 2f out: lost pl and btn over 1f out: eased fnl f* **3/1**[1]

-000 **8** *5* **Ledbury (IRE)**[16] 4784 4-9-7 **57** (b) AmirQuinn 10 27
(Lee Carter) *dwlt: hld up off the pce in rr: rdn over 3f out: no hdwy: wl btn fnl 2f* **25/1**

0360 **9** *1 3/4* **Captain Gerald**[8] 5122 3-8-5 **53** (p) JosephineGordon(3) 3 20
(John Ryan) *hld up off the pce in lat trio: drvn and no rspnse 3f out: wl btn fnl 2f* **8/1**[3]

6040 **10** *nse* **Zebedee's Son (IRE)**[52] 3509 3-8-2 **52** AliceMills(5) 2 19
(Phil York) *chsd ldrs and clr in ldng quartet: rdn and lost pl over 2f out: wknd 2f out: bhd ins fnl f* **20/1**

2m 6.06s (-0.54) **Going Correction** -0.025s/f (Stan)
WFA 3 from 4yo+ 9lb **10** Ran SP% **126.4**
Speed ratings (Par 101): **101,100,99,98,96 96,90,86,84,84**
CSF £48.85 CT £547.25 TOTE £7.90: £2.60, £3.10, £4.10; EX 48.00 Trifecta £320.10.
Owner Happy Valley Racing & Breeding Limited **Bred** Mrs Rebecca Philipps **Trained** Newmarket, Suffolk

FOCUS
A moderate handicap. They went a muddling stop-start gallop, but the form makes sense.
T/Plt: £6.60 to a £1 stake. Pool: £42,044.35 - 4624.02 winning units T/Qpdt: £4.10 to a £1 stake. Pool: £6,931.23 - 1248.66 winning units **Steve Payne**

5356 NEWBURY (L-H)
Saturday, August 13

OFFICIAL GOING: Good to firm (7.5)
Wind: light breeze against Weather: sunny periods

5400 BETFRED "SUPPORTS JACK BERRY HOUSE" EBF STALLIONS MAIDEN FILLIES' STKS (PLUS 10 RACE) 6f 8y
1:55 (1:58) (Class 4) 2-Y-O **£5,822** (£1,732; £865; £432) **Stalls** Centre

Form RPR
0 **1** **Partitia**[29] 4350 2-9-0 0 PatSmullen 7 84
(Sir Michael Stoute) *a.p: led jst over 2f out: rdn whn strly chal fr over 1f out: kpt on gamely: drvn out* **10/1**

2 *nk* **Considered Opinion** 2-9-0 0 AndreaAtzeni 5 83
(Ralph Beckett) *s.i.s: sn mid-div: hdwy over 2f out: rdn for str chal fr over 1f out: ev ch thrght fnl f: hld cl home* **33/1**

2 **3** *nk* **Promising (IRE)**[17] 4756 2-9-0 0 SeanLevey 13 82
(Richard Hannon) *racd keenly: mid-div: lost pl over 2f out: hdwy whn nt clr run briefly over 1f out: r.o wl fnl f: lft 3rd fnl 60yds* **11/8**[1]

4 *1 1/2* **Contentment** 2-9-0 0 RobertHavlin 2 78+
(William Haggas) *s.i.s: towards rr: hdwy into midfield over 1f out: r.o fnl f: lft 4th fnl 60yds* **14/1**

5 *1 3/4* **Amelia Dream** 2-9-0 0 TimmyMurphy 8 72+
(Mick Channon) *s.i.s: towards rr: hdwy over 1f out: kpt on nicely on fnl f but nvr any threat* **33/1**

4 **6** *1 1/4* **Hathfa (FR)**[12] 4951 2-9-0 0 FrankieDettori 9 71
(Richard Hughes) *trckd ldrs: nt clr run 2f out: sn rdn: kpt on same pce* **3/1**[2]

0 **7** *2 1/4* **Heart Of Gold**[23] 4558 2-9-0 0 PaulHanagan 4 62
(William Muir) *trckd ldrs: rdn over 1f out: fdd fnl 120yds* **50/1**

8 *1* **Think Fashion (IRE)** 2-9-0 0 JimmyFortune 15 59
(Brian Meehan) *s.i.s: towards rr: hdwy over 2f out: effrt over 1f out: fdd ins fnl f* **66/1**

9 *2 1/4* **Magicinthemaking (USA)** 2-9-0 0 JimCrowley 3 52
(Jeremy Noseda) *mid-div: rdn 2f out: wknd fnl f* **14/1**

0 **10** *1 1/2* **Foxcatcher**[29] 4350 2-9-0 0 AdamKirby 14 48
(Clive Cox) *mid-div: hdwy 3f out to trck ldrs: rdn over 1f out: wknd ent fnl f* **9/1**[3]

00 **11** *1 3/4* **Nuptials (USA)**[17] 4756 2-9-0 0 RobertWinston 10 42
(Eve Johnson Houghton) *led tl 2f out: sn wknd* **200/1**

0 **12** ¾ **Harlequin Rose (IRE)**[12] 4951 2-9-0 0 .... LiamKeniry 6 40
(Mick Channon) *trckd ldrs: rdn over 2f out: wknd over 1f out* **66/1**

13 *nk* **Guiding Star** 2-9-0 0 .... OisinMurphy 12 39
(Henry Candy) *mid-div: effrt 2f out: sn wknd* **14/1**

06 **14** 7 **Sukiwarrior (IRE)**[44] 3812 2-9-0 0 .... SteveDrowne 11 18
(Charles Hills) *trckd ldrs: rdn over 2f out: sn wknd* **100/1**

56 **U** **Chica De La Noche**[67] 2990 2-9-0 0 .... NickyMackay 1 78+
(Simon Dow) *hld up towards rr: hdwy 3f out: str chal over 1f out: sddle slipped ent fnl f: stl upsides w jockey unable to ride fin whn sddle slipped further and uns rdr fnl 60yds* **100/1**

1m 14.25s (1.25) **Going Correction** +0.125s/f (Good) **15** Ran SP% **119.5**
Speed ratings (Par 93): **96,95,95,93,90 89,86,84,81,79 77,76,76,66,**
CSF £307.78 TOTE £10.70: £2.70, £10.10, £1.10; EX 300.90 Trifecta £1023.80.
Owner K Abdullah **Bred** Juddmonte Farms Ltd **Trained** Newmarket, Suffolk

FOCUS
Another warm, sunny day and no rain or watering since the previous afternoon's fixture, so proper fast, summer ground. The rail was moved out overnight to give fresh ground from the 8f to the 5f on the round course. The third, fourth, sixth and ninth were entered in Group company coming into this, but there might have been a 100-1 shocker had Chic De La Noche's saddle not slipped. Improved effort by winner amd third rated a bit below promising debut efffort.

5401 DENFORD STUD WASHINGTON SINGER STKS (LISTED RACE) 7f (S)
2:30 (2:31) (Class 1) 2-Y-O **£14,461** (£5,482; £2,743; £1,366) **Stalls** Centre

Form RPR

1 **1** **Escobar (IRE)**[29] 4349 2-9-1 0 .... FrankieDettori 1 104+
(Hugo Palmer) *trckd ldng trio: hdwy to ld wl over 1f out: qcknd clr: kpt on wl: pushed out* **1/1**[1]

1343 **2** 1¼ **Mr Scaramanga**[35] 4150 2-9-1 99 .... SeanLevey 3 101
(Richard Hannon) *trckd ldr: drifting lft whn led briefly 2f out: outpcd whn wnr kicked over 1f out: hld after but kpt on fnl 100yds* **6/1**

22 **3** 5 **Amabilis**[16] 4801 2-8-10 0 .... PatSmullen 2 83
(Ralph Beckett) *trckd ldr: chal briefly 2f out: rdn in cl 3rd but sn hld: kpt on same pce fnl f* **4/1**[3]

153 **4** *shd* **Frankuus (IRE)**[21] 4622 2-9-1 95 .... AdamKirby 5 87
(Mark Johnston) *led: rdn and hdd 2f out where squeezed up: nt pce to get bk on terms but kpt on again ins fnl f* **3/1**[2]

1m 26.17s (0.47) **Going Correction** +0.125s/f (Good) **4** Ran SP% **109.3**
Speed ratings (Par 102): **102,100,94,94**
CSF £7.21 TOTE £1.70; EX 5.40 Trifecta £17.90.
Owner Carmichael Jennings **Bred** Peter Evans **Trained** Newmarket, Suffolk

FOCUS
Only four runners for the third straight year, but this is often a good race. Indeed, two of the last four winners, Just The Judge (2012) and Belardo (2014), were subsequently successful at the highest level. Winner and runner-up taken to have progressed.

5402 BETFRED GEOFFREY FREER STKS (GROUP 3) 1m 5f 61y
3:05 (3:05) (Class 1) 3-Y-O+ **£34,026** (£12,900; £6,456; £3,216; £1,614) **Stalls** Centre

Form RPR

/531 **1** **Kings Fete**[15] 4821 5-9-7 112 .... PatSmullen 3 109+
(Sir Michael Stoute) *mde all: qcknd pce over 2f out: rdn ent fnl f: styd on strly* **1/1**[1]

3302 **2** 1¼ **Ormito (GER)**[29] 4339 3-8-7 98 .... OisinMurphy 2 104
(Andrew Balding) *hld up bhd ldng trio: outpcd over 2f out: styd on wl fnl f: edging lft fnl 120yds: snatched 2nd fnl stride* **8/1**

-111 **3** *hd* **Red Cardinal (IRE)**[50] 3621 4-9-5 95 .... JamieSpencer 4 104
(David Simcock) *trckd ldrs: trckd wnr 6f out: rdn to chal 2f out: sn hld: styd on: lost 2nd fnl stride* **6/1**[3]

1560 **4** 1½ **Humphrey Bogart (IRE)**[35] 4173 3-8-7 105 .... SeanLevey 5 101
(Richard Hannon) *racd keenly: hld up bhd ldng trio: rdn 2f out: styd on but nt pce to mount chal* **9/2**[2]

-144 **5** ¾ **Battersea**[37] 4061 5-9-5 107 .... AndreaAtzeni 1 100
(Roger Varian) *trckd wnr tl 6f out: racd in cl 3rd: rdn over 2f out: nt pce to get on terms: no ex fnl 100yds* **6/1**[3]

2m 52.97s (0.97) **Going Correction** +0.175s/f (Good)
WFA 3 from 4yo+ 12lb **5** Ran SP% **107.9**
Speed ratings (Par 113): **104,103,103,102,101**
CSF £9.00 TOTE £1.90: £1.20, £2.70; EX 8.80 Trifecta £27.50.
Owner K Abdullah **Bred** Juddmonte Farms Ltd **Trained** Newmarket, Suffolk

FOCUS
This was run over 13yds further than advertised. Already an uncompetitive-looking race, the favourite was allowed a totally uncontested lead, while the second choice pulled too hard under a hold-up ride, so not much of a contest.

5403 BETFRED TV LADIES DAY H'CAP 7f (S)
3:40 (3:41) (Class 3) (0-95,94) 3-Y-O+
£12,450 (£3,728; £1,864; £932; £466; £234) **Stalls** Centre

Form RPR

2650 **1** **Cornwallville (IRE)**[21] 4667 4-9-12 94 ....(v) AdamKirby 5 103
(David Loughnane) *racd centre: trckd ldrs: rdn to ld over 1f out: 1 ¾ l clr ent fnl f: drifted rt: fin on stands' side: jst hld on* **10/1**

-410 **2** *shd* **Von Blucher (IRE)**[21] 4624 3-9-5 93 ....(t) FrankieDettori 14 99+
(John Gosden) *racd stands' side: hld up: hdwy over 2f out: rdn in 4th ent fnl f: r.o wl clsng stages: jst hld* **4/1**[1]

0605 **3** *nse* **Charles Molson**[14] 4862 5-9-4 91 ....(p) HectorCrouch(5) 9 99
(Patrick Chamings) *racd centre: hld up: hdwy over 2f out: swtchd rt over 1f out: sn rdn: wnt 3rd ent fnl f: r.o wl clsng stages: jst hld* **20/1**

0204 **4** 1¼ **Valley Of Fire**[28] 4402 4-9-4 86 .... JamieSpencer 12 90+
(William Haggas) *hld up stands' side: hdwy fr 2f out: kpt on ins fnl f but nt pce to get on terms* **12/1**

2110 **5** 2½ **Gunmetal (IRE)**[37] 4062 3-9-0 88 .... SteveDrowne 8 83
(Charles Hills) *racd centre: disp ld tl rdn into def advantage 2f out: hdd over 1f out: no ex ins fnl f* **15/2**[3]

0421 **6** 1 **Muntadab (IRE)**[14] 4893 4-9-11 93 .... PatSmullen 2 88
(David Loughnane) *racd centre: disp ld tl rdn 2f out: kpt on same pce* **8/1**

0120 **7** 1 **Pastoral Player**[17] 4758 9-9-2 89 .... CharlieBennett(5) 4 81
(Hughie Morrison) *hld up centre: hdwy into midfield over 2f out: sn rdn: no further imp fnl f* **16/1**

0522 **8** ¾ **Dollar Reward**[25] 4474 3-8-8 82 .... AndreaAtzeni 6 70
(Sir Michael Stoute) *racd centre: trckd ldrs: rdn over 2f out: sn one pce* **9/2**[2]

0040 **9** 2½ **Classic Seniority**[14] 4862 4-8-13 81 .... PaulHanagan 3 64
(Marjorie Fife) *racd centre: hld up towards rr: rdn and hdwy into mid-div over 1f out: fdd ins fnl f* **16/1**

0523 **10** 1¾ **Baltic Brave (IRE)**[15] 4839 5-9-3 85 ....(tp) JimCrowley 11 64
(Hughie Morrison) *racd stands' side: mid-div: rdn over 2f out: nvr on terms* **20/1**

0005 **11** 4½ **Firmdecisions (IRE)**[12] 4954 6-9-4 86 .... RobertWinston 16 52
(Dean Ivory) *racd stands' side: disp overall ld tl rdn over 2f out: sn wknd* **16/1**

0002 **12** 1¼ **Carnival King (IRE)**[15] 4839 4-9-4 86 ....(b) JimmyFortune 10 49
(Brian Meehan) *racd stands' side: chsd ldr in gp but overall mid-div: struggling wl over 2f out: wknd over 1f out* **16/1**

046 **13** 3¾ **Palawan**[35] 4149 3-9-5 93 ....[1] SeanLevey 13 44
(Richard Hannon) *racd stands' side: chsd ldr in gp but overall mid-div: wknd over 1f out* **20/1**

2051 **14** ½ **Ower Fly**[21] 4662 3-8-8 87 .... MeganNicholls(5) 7 37
(Richard Hannon) *racd centre: prom for 3f: sn struggling: wknd over 1f out* **25/1**

0520 **15** 2¼ **Air Of York (IRE)**[13] 4908 4-8-10 78 .... AdamBeschizza 1 23
(David Evans) *racd centre: mid-div: struggling 1/2-way: sn bhd* **50/1**

-104 **16** 13 **Noble Peace**[64] 3105 3-8-8 82 .... OisinMurphy 15
(Henry Candy) *chsd ldr in stands' side gp for 3f: sn bhd: eased fnl 2f* **16/1**

1m 25.12s (-0.58) **Going Correction** +0.125s/f (Good)
WFA 3 from 4yo+ 6lb **16** Ran SP% **127.3**
Speed ratings (Par 107): **108,107,107,106,103 102,101,100,97,95 90,88,84,84,81 66**
CSF £48.12 CT £854.29 TOTE £11.10: £2.60, £1.60, £4.10, £2.60; EX 60.30 Trifecta £1741.20.
Owner Stephen Louch **Bred** Corrin Stud & Blackwater Bloodstock Ltd **Trained** Market Drayton, Shropshire

FOCUS
A decent handicap. They split into two groups but merged in the closing stages and there was no obvious speed/track bias. The winner was back to the same mark as when chasing home a progressive sort in June.

5404 BETFRED HUNGERFORD STKS (GROUP 2) 7f (S)
4:10 (4:15) (Class 1) 3-Y-O+
£85,065 (£32,250; £16,140; £8,040; £4,035; £2,025) **Stalls** Centre

Form RPR

0-50 **1** **Richard Pankhurst**[17] 4754 4-9-6 111 .... RobertHavlin 6 117
(John Gosden) *hld up but wl in tch: travelled wl: smooth hdwy but nt clr run over 1f out tl ent fnl f: led fnl 150yds: r.o wl: readily* **11/1**

-112 **2** 1 **Home Of The Brave (IRE)**[18] 4733 4-9-6 115 ....(t) JimCrowley 3 114
(Hugo Palmer) *led: rdn and edgd rt ent fnl f: hdd fnl 150yds: kpt on but no ex* **7/4**[1]

4062 **3** ¾ **Dark Emerald (IRE)**[28] 4395 6-9-6 108 ....(v) AdamKirby 2 112
(Brendan Powell) *trckd ldrs: rdn over 2f out: wnt cl 3rd ent fnl f: kpt on same pce* **10/1**

5315 **4** ¾ **Markaz (IRE)**[18] 4733 4-9-6 112 .... PaulHanagan 4 110
(Owen Burrows) *hld up in last pair but wl in tch: hdwy 2f out: sn rdn to chse ldrs: kpt on same pce fnl f* **13/2**[3]

1421 **5** *nk* **Jallota**[28] 4380 5-9-6 110 .... JamieSpencer 1 109
(Charles Hills) *trckd ldr: rdn over 2f out: kpt on same pce fnl f* **7/1**

2001 **6** 1¾ **Convey**[20] 4688 4-9-6 113 ....(p) PatSmullen 5 104
(Sir Michael Stoute) *trckd ldrs: rdn and cl up whn hmpd ent fnl f: no ch after* **9/4**[2]

1m 24.43s (-1.27) **Going Correction** +0.125s/f (Good) **6** Ran SP% **110.4**
Speed ratings (Par 115): **112,110,110,109,108 106**
CSF £29.80 TOTE £12.70: £5.20, £1.60; EX 28.40 Trifecta £316.70.
Owner Godolphin **Bred** Rachel D S Hood **Trained** Newmarket, Suffolk

FOCUS
Not a bad Group 2 with the winner belatedly delivering on 2yo promise.

5405 BETFRED "CELEBRATING AIDEN KELLY'S 81ST BIRTHDAY" H'CAP 1m 2f 6y
4:45 (4:46) (Class 4) (0-85,85) 3-Y-O+ **£5,175** (£1,540; £769; £384) **Stalls** Centre

Form RPR

-114 **1** **Muzdawaj**[28] 4403 3-9-5 85 ....(p) PaulHanagan 6 94+
(William Haggas) *hld up in tch: hdwy over 2f out: rdn to chal ent fnl f: kpt on: led cl home* **9/4**[1]

2005 **2** *nk* **Croquembouche (IRE)**[23] 4561 7-9-6 84 .... GeorgiaCox(7) 7 92
(Ed de Giles) *led: rdn over 2f out: kpt on gamely whn strly chal ent fnl f: hdd cl home* **7/1**

021- **3** ½ **Wapping (USA)**[300] 7309 3-8-12 78 .... PatSmullen 8 85+
(David Lanigan) *stdd s: in last pair: hdwy 2f out: rdn and ev ch ent fnl f: kpt on tl no ex nring fin* **3/1**[2]

-553 **4** 3 **Vincent's Forever**[23] 4554 3-9-2 82 .... RobertHavlin 5 83
(John Gosden) *trckd ldrs: rdn to chse ldr over 1f out tl ent fnl f: kpt on same pce* **4/1**[3]

401- **5** 3¼ **Maestro Mac (IRE)**[329] 6548 3-9-1 81 .... OisinMurphy 3 76
(Hughie Morrison) *hld up in tch: pushed along and sme hdwy over 2f out: nvr threatened: fdd ins fnl f* **8/1**

4151 **6** 1 **Loving Your Work**[44] 3817 5-8-11 68 .... SeanLevey 2 61
(Ken Cunningham-Brown) *trckd ldrs: rdn to chse ldr 2f out tl over 1f out: fdd fnl f* **10/1**

024 **7** 2½ **Bazooka (IRE)**[16] 4795 5-9-6 77 ....(b) RobertWinston 1 65
(David Flood) *hld up in last pair: rdn over 2f out: nvr threatened: wknd fnl f* **25/1**

432 **8** *shd* **Mazalto (IRE)**[22] 4597 3-8-11 77 .... TimmyMurphy 4 64
(Pat Phelan) *trckd ldr tl rdn over 2f out: wknd ent fnl f* **25/1**

2m 8.83s (0.03) **Going Correction** +0.175s/f (Good)
WFA 3 from 5yo+ 9lb **8** Ran SP% **116.2**
Speed ratings (Par 105): **106,105,105,102,100 99,97,97**
CSF £19.14 CT £46.42 TOTE £3.20: £1.20, £2.20, £1.60; EX 21.80 Trifecta £81.80.
Owner Hamdan Al Maktoum **Bred** Shadwell Estate Company Limited **Trained** Newmarket, Suffolk
■ Stewards' Enquiry : Georgia Cox two-day ban: use of whip (27-28 Aug)

FOCUS
This was run over 13yds further than advertised. A fair handicap with the runner-up rated to this year's form.

5406 BETFRED LADIES DERBY H'CAP (FOR LADY AMATEUR RIDERS) 1m 4f 5y
5:20 (5:20) (Class 4) (0-80,80) 3-Y-O+ **£5,615** (£1,741; £870; £435) **Stalls** Centre

Form RPR

5324 **1** **Cosmeapolitan**[15] 4827 3-10-0 80 .... MissSBrotherton 3 97+
(Alan King) *in tch: smooth hdwy to ld 2f out: pushed clr: easily* **10/11**[1]

2P5- **2** 10 **Samtu (IRE)**[32] 4229 5-10-3 75 .... MissBeckySmith(3) 4 76
(Marjorie Fife) *trckd ldrs: rdn 3f out: sn hld by wnr: styd on same pce* **20/1**

2006 **3** 3¾ **Whinging Willie (IRE)**[9] 5053 7-10-7 79 ....(v) MissHayleyMoore(3) 1 74
(Gary Moore) *trckd ldrs: nt clr run and swtchd rt 2f out: sn rdn: styd on fnl f: snatched 3rd fnl strides* **6/1**[3]

/022 **4** *shd* **Soul Intent (IRE)**[12] 4940 6-10-6 **75**........................ MissJoannaMason 6 70
(Brian Ellison) *trckd ldrs: rdn 3f out: one pce fnl 2f: lost 3rd fnl strides* **9/2**[2]

2101 **5** *2 1/4* **Onorina (IRE)**[23] 4551 4-9-12 **70**.................................. MissAWaugh(3) 8 61
(Jim Boyle) *hld up: hdwy 4f out: rdn to chse ldrs over 3f out: nvr threatened: fdd ins fnl f* **15/2**

5503 **6** *3/4* **Miss Minuty**[24] 4501 4-10-5 **77**.............................. MissJodieHughes(3) 7 67
(Alexandra Dunn) *hld up last: hdwy over 4f out: rdn to chse ldrs 3f out: nvr threatened: fdd ins fnl f* **20/1**

5005 **7** *3 3/4* **Moojaned (IRE)**[5] 5231 5-10-4 **78**........................ KatherineGlenister(5) 2 62
(David Evans) *led: rdn and hdd over 3f out: wknd over 1f out* **12/1**

1563 **8** *6* **My Lord**[9] 5056 8-9-11 **71** ow2....................................... MissMBryant(5) 5 45
(Paddy Butler) *a in rr* **33/1**

2m 35.45s (-0.05) **Going Correction** +0.175s/f (Good)
WFA 3 from 4yo+ 11lb **8** Ran SP% **116.8**
Speed ratings (Par 105): **107,100,97,97,96 95,93,89**
CSF £25.87 CT £79.01 TOTE £1.80: £1.10, £4.10, £1.60; EX 18.80 Trifecta £81.40.
Owner Barbury Castle Stud **Bred** Barbury Castle Stud **Trained** Barbury Castle, Wilts

FOCUS
This was run over 13yds further than advertised. The sole 3yo hammered his more exposed rivals.
T/Plt: £12.80 to a £1 stake. Pool: £57,321.0 - 4469.1 winning units T/Qpdt: £7.70 to a £1 stake. Pool: £4,400.0 - 568.91 winning units **Tim Mitchell**

5371 NEWMARKET (R-H)

Saturday, August 13

OFFICIAL GOING: Good to firm (7.2)
Wind: Fresh half-behind Weather: Cloudy with sunny spells

5407 RIDGEONS FILLIES' NURSERY H'CAP 7f
2:15 (2:15) (Class 2) 2-Y-O **£12,938** (£3,850; £1,924; £962) **Stalls** Low

Form RPR
3114 **1** **Clef**[14] 4884 2-8-3 **73**.. JoeFanning 8 86
(Richard Fahey) *chsd ldr tl shkn up to ld over 1f out: rdn out* **5/1**[2]

5105 **2** *3* **High On Love (IRE)**[23] 4560 2-8-12 **82**...................... StevieDonohoe 1 87
(Charlie Fellowes) *led: rdn and hdd over 1f out: edgd rt and styd on same pce ins fnl f* **8/1**

1 **3** *2 3/4* **Shozita**[21] 4659 2-8-5 **75**.. SilvestreDeSousa 9 73
(Ralph Beckett) *dwlt: hld up: hdwy over 2f out: sn rdn: hung rt over 1f out: no ex ins fnl f* **2/1**[1]

104 **4** *hd* **Lady In Question (IRE)**[16] 4802 2-8-8 **78**.................... PatrickMathers 5 75
(Richard Fahey) *trckd ldrs: racd keenly: rdn over 2f out: outpcd over 1f out: kpt on ins fnl f* **6/1**[3]

100 **5** *1 3/4* **Somebody To Love (IRE)**[36] 4106 2-9-7 **91**...................... PatDobbs 4 83
(Richard Hannon) *s.i.s: hld up: rdn over 2f out: nvr nrr* **8/1**

4511 **6** *1* **Bongrace (IRE)**[9] 5066 2-8-5 **75**.. ShaneGray 3 65
(Kevin Ryan) *hld up: rdn over 2f out: nvr on terms* **9/1**

4251 **7** *1 3/4* **Texas Katie**[9] 5081 2-8-2 **72**.. AndrewMullen 6 57
(Mick Channon) *plld hrd and prom: rdn over 2f out: wkng whn nt clr run 1f out* **10/1**

3125 **8** *7* **Lexington Sky (IRE)**[15] 4843 2-8-11 **81**........................ TomMarquand 2 47
(Richard Hannon) *a in rr: pushed along 1/2-way: rdn over 2f out: sn wknd* **16/1**

1m 25.85s (0.15) **Going Correction** +0.05s/f (Good) **8** Ran SP% **111.5**
Speed ratings (Par 97): **101,97,94,94,92 91,89,81**
CSF £41.79 CT £102.74 TOTE £5.90: £1.90, £2.80, £1.10; EX 37.10 Trifecta £163.80.
Owner Cheveley Park Stud **Bred** Cheveley Park Stud Ltd **Trained** Musley Bank, N Yorks

FOCUS
A warm afternoon, with the going officially described as good to firm (watered) ahead of the first of seven races. Rail movements increased the distances of races 5 & 7 by 15 yards. An informative nursery and a taking performance from the winner, who relished the step up from 6f. Runner-up rated on par with prevuious effort.

5408 PANTILE STUD GREY HORSE H'CAP (FOR GREY HORSES ONLY) 6f
2:45 (2:46) (Class 4) (0-85,79) 3-Y-O+
£12,450 (£3,728; £1,864; £932; £466; £234) **Stalls** Low

Form RPR
0010 **1** **Syrian Pearl**[29] 4360 5-9-10 **79**.. TedDurcan 5 88
(Chris Wall) *broke wl: sn stdd and lost pl: hld up: hdwy and nt clr run over 1f out: rdn to ld ins fnl f: r.o* **6/1**[3]

6345 **2** *1/2* **Champagne Bob**[9] 5060 4-8-1 **59**........................... EdwardGreatrex(3) 7 66
(Richard Price) *hld up: hdwy over 2f out: sn rdn: ev ch over 1f out: styd on* **9/1**

0061 **3** *1/2* **Case Key**[6] 5195 3-9-3 **76** 6ex.. AndrewMullen 2 80
(Michael Appleby) *chsd ldrs: rdn over 2f out: ev ch over 1f out: edgd lft ins fnl f: styd on u.p* **9/2**[1]

5000 **4** *1/2* **Honcho (IRE)**[10] 5039 4-8-5 **63**.........................(v) JosephineGordon(3) 8 67
(John Ryan) *prom: racd keenly: rdn and ev ch over 1f out: styd on same pce wl ins fnl f* **12/1**

1500 **5** *nk* **Crew Cut (IRE)**[14] 4889 8-9-8 **77**.. PatDobbs 9 80
(Stuart Williams) *led: rdn over 1f out: hdd ins fnl f: no ex towards fin* **5/1**[2]

2253 **6** *nk* **Andar**[29] 4344 3-9-4 **77**..(b[1]) NeilCallan 11 78
(Clive Cox) *w ldr: rdn and ev ch over 1f out: no ex wl ins fnl f* **5/1**[2]

324 **7** *shd* **Time Medicean**[9] 5050 10-8-0 **62**.................................(t) DavidEgan(7) 10 64
(Tony Carroll) *hld up: rdn over 2f out: styd on ins fnl f: nt trble ldrs* **14/1**

0046 **8** *1* **Light From Mars**[13] 4910 11-9-4 **73**.............................(p) DavidProbert 6 71
(Ronald Harris) *chsd ldrs: rdn and ev ch over 1f out: no ex ins fnl f* **12/1**

553 **9** *2 1/4* **Pensax Lad (IRE)**[15] 4817 5-9-5 **74**............................ TomMarquand 3 65
(Ronald Harris) *hld up: rdn over 1f out: n.d* **8/1**

6516 **10** *6* **Le Manege Enchante (IRE)**[9] 5059 3-7-13 **61**.........(p) NoelGarbutt(3) 1 32
(Derek Shaw) *s.s: hld up: rdn over 2f out: wknd over 1f out* **20/1**

1m 12.05s (-0.45) **Going Correction** +0.05s/f (Good)
WFA 3 from 4yo+ 4lb **10** Ran SP% **113.7**
Speed ratings (Par 105): **105,104,103,103,102 102,102,100,97,89**
CSF £57.35 CT £264.50 TOTE £6.30: £1.80, £2.60, £1.30; EX 58.10 Trifecta £365.30.
Owner The Clodhoppers **Bred** Jeremy Green And Sons **Trained** Newmarket, Suffolk

FOCUS
Another exciting renewal of this grey horse handicap. It represents only fair handicap form, however, with the winner close to her best and the second rated to recent form.

5409 C J MURFITT LTD H'CAP 6f
3:20 (3:20) (Class 2) (0-105,100) 3-Y-O
£28,012 (£8,388; £4,194; £2,097; £1,048; £526) **Stalls** Low

Form RPR
452 **1** **Summer Chorus**[8] 5103 3-8-0 **79**.................................... JimmyQuinn 2 90+
(Andrew Balding) *hld up: shkn up over 2f out: rdn over 1f out: edgd lft and r.o ins fnl f to ld post* **14/1**

4351 **2** *shd* **Futoon (IRE)**[9] 5070 3-7-12 **80** ow1............... JosephineGordon(3) 10 90
(Kevin Ryan) *a.p: chsd ldr over 3f out: rdn over 1f out: led towards fin: hdd post* **28/1**

1-45 **3** *shd* **Projection**[14] 4862 3-9-7 **100**... GeorgeBaker 7 110
(Roger Charlton) *hld up in tch: rdn over 1f out: ev ch wl ins fnl f: r.o* **9/4**[1]

1142 **4** *1/2* **East Street Revue**[22] 4612 3-8-2 **81**..........................(b) DuranFentiman 9 89
(Tim Easterby) *led: rdn over 1f out: hdd and unable qck towards fin* **16/1**

1360 **5** *1 1/2* **Aclaim (IRE)**[28] 4393 3-9-4 **97**..(t) DavidProbert 5 100
(Martyn Meade) *hld up: rdn over 2f out: hdwy over 1f out: styd on* **8/1**

4040 **6** *2 1/4* **Paddy Power (IRE)**[16] 4803 3-8-5 **84**........................ PatrickMathers 11 80
(Richard Fahey) *hld up: plld hrd: hdwy over 2f out: rdn over 1f out: no ex ins fnl f* **16/1**

-433 **7** *shd* **Muhadathat**[7] 5148 3-9-3 **96**... JoeFanning 13 92
(Mark Johnston) *s.i.s: hdwy over 4f out: rdn over 1f out: styd on same pce* **14/1**

3400 **8** *1* **Sixties Sue**[16] 4803 3-8-5 **84**.. AndrewMullen 6 77
(Mick Channon) *chsd ldrs: rdn over 2f out: no ex ins fnl f* **33/1**

0251 **9** *2 1/4* **Mont Kiara (FR)**[21] 4652 3-9-2 **95**.. NeilCallan 8 80
(Kevin Ryan) *hld up: plld hrd: hdwy over 3f out: rdn over 1f out: wknd ins fnl f* **7/1**[3]

110 **10** *nk* **Udontdodou**[63] 3165 3-8-10 **89**... JFEgan 4 73
(Richard Guest) *hld up: rdn over 2f out: n.d* **8/1**

1402 **11** *1* **Fashaak (IRE)**[51] 3574 3-8-3 **82**................................... TomMarquand 14 63
(Richard Hannon) *w ldr 2f: remained handy: rdn over 2f out: wknd fnl f* **16/1**

5402 **12** *4* **Elronaq**[18] 4741 3-8-12 **91**... SilvestreDeSousa 3 59
(Charles Hills) *hld up in tch: shkn up over 2f out: wknd over 1f out* **13/2**[2]

0000 **13** *12* **Still On Top**[21] 4631 3-8-3 **82**... ShaneGray 12 12
(Tim Easterby) *prom: lost pl over 2f out: sn rdn: wknd over 1f out* **50/1**

1m 11.17s (-1.33) **Going Correction** +0.05s/f (Good) **13** Ran SP% **118.2**
Speed ratings (Par 106): **110,109,109,109,107 104,103,102,99,99 97,92,76**
CSF £357.25 CT £1260.80 TOTE £16.80: £4.70, £8.30, £1.40; EX 305.70 Trifecta £922.80.
Owner Sheikh Juma Dalmook Al Maktoum **Bred** Genesis Green Stud Ltd And Thurso Ltd **Trained** Kingsclere, Hants

FOCUS
A fiercely competitive renewal of this feature handicap, though the market suggested it was all about one horse. Two short-heads separated the first three home and the race has been rated positively.

5410 LONGINES IRISH CHAMPIONS WEEKEND EBF STALLIONS MAIDEN STKS (PLUS 10 RACE) 6f
3:50 (3:52) (Class 4) 2-Y-O **£4,528** (£1,347; £673; £336) **Stalls** Low

Form RPR
2 **1** **Rich And Famous (USA)**[18] 4736 2-9-5 0........................ JoeFanning 1 83+
(Mark Johnston) *sn led: shkn up over 1f out: edgd lft and c readily clr fnl f* **1/2**[1]

4225 **2** *3 1/4* **Father McKenzie**[10] 5029 2-9-5 75................................ GeorgeBaker 7 73
(Mick Channon) *chsd ldrs: rdn to chse wnr over 1f out: sn outpcd* **10/1**[3]

3 *1 1/2* **Anfaass (IRE)** 2-9-5 0.. NeilCallan 2 68
(George Margarson) *prom: chsd wnr 1/2-way tl rdn over 1f out: styd on same pce* **33/1**

6 **4** *nse* **Tawaafoq**[21] 4659 2-9-5 0.. PatDobbs 5 68+
(Richard Hannon) *s.i.s: hld up: racd keenly: styd on ins fnl f: nrst fin* **7/1**[2]

0 **5** *3/4* **Swag (IRE)**[18] 4736 2-9-5 0...(t) TedDurcan 4 66
(Richard Hannon) *sn chsng wnr: lost 2nd 1/2-way: rdn over 1f out: styd on same pce* **14/1**

03 **6** *1 1/4* **Twiggy**[17] 4759 2-9-0 0...[1] MartinDwyer 3 57
(Jane Chapple-Hyam) *hld up: plld hrd: rdn over 2f out: edgd lft and sme hdwy over 1f out: no ex fnl f* **12/1**

0 **7** *1/2* **Amherst Rock**[23] 4545 2-9-5 0.. DavidProbert 8 60
(Charlie Appleby) *hld up: racd keenly: rdn over 2f out: nt clr run over 1f out: nvr trbld ldrs* **7/1**[2]

8 *1* **Hajaj (IRE)** 2-9-5 0... StevieDonohoe 9 57
(Charlie Fellowes) *s.i.s: hld up: a in rr* **16/1**

66 **9** *13* **Sir Harry Collins (IRE)**[9] 5077 2-9-2 0........................ LouisSteward(3) 6 15
(Richard Spencer) *broke wl: sn stdd to trck ldrs and racd keenly: lost pl over 2f out: wknd over 1f out* **66/1**

1m 12.96s (0.46) **Going Correction** +0.05s/f (Good) **9** Ran SP% **125.4**
Speed ratings (Par 96): **98,93,91,91,90 88,88,86,69**
CSF £8.13 TOTE £1.30: £1.10, £2.70, £14.10; EX 6.50 Trifecta £199.70.
Owner Sheikh Hamdan bin Mohammed Al Maktoum **Bred** Darley **Trained** Middleham Moor, N Yorks
■ Stewards' Enquiry : Neil Callan £140 fine: passport irregularity

FOCUS
The odds-on favourite proved in a different league to his rivals and should be capable of mixing it at Pattern level.

5411 EAGLE HOME INTERIORS H'CAP 1m 4f
4:25 (4:25) (Class 2) (0-110,108) 3-Y-O+**£16,172** (£4,812; £2,405; £1,202) **Stalls** Centre

Form RPR
0616 **1** **Fire Fighting (IRE)**[7] 5159 5-10-0 **108**...............................(b) NeilCallan 5 116
(Mark Johnston) *a.p: racd keenly: shkn up to ld over 1f out: styd on strly* **11/2**

1110 **2** *4* **Knights Table**[14] 4863 3-8-5 **95**....................................... AndrewMullen 1 98
(James Tate) *chsd ldrs: led 3f out: rdn and hdd over 1f out: no ex ins fnl f* **3/1**[1]

3322 **3** *1 1/2* **Passover**[7] 5173 5-9-2 **93**... DavidProbert 6 95
(Andrew Balding) *chsd ldrs: wnt upsides over 5f out tl rdn over 2f out: edgd lft over 1f out: styd on same pce* **4/1**[2]

000- **4** *nse* **Great Hall**[48] 6082 6-9-3 **97**.. WilliamCarson 2 96
(Mick Quinn) *disp ld over 2f: chsd ldr tl over 5f out: rdn over 3f out: hung lft over 1f out: styd on same pce* **33/1**

-056 **5** *3* **Niceofyoutotellme**[31] 4276 7-9-3 **97**...................................... PatDobbs 8 91
(Ralph Beckett) *hld up: rdn over 2f out: nt trble ldrs* **9/1**

1-30 **6** 3/4 **Missed Call (IRE)**[57] 3340 6-8-11 **98** .... GeorgeWood(7) 4 91
(James Fanshawe) *hld up in tch: rdn over 2f out: wknd fnl f* **9/2**[3]

0200 **7** 1/2 **Watersmeet**[18] 4731 5-9-3 **97** .... JoeFanning 3 89
(Mark Johnston) *disp ld tl wnt on over 9f out: hdd 3f out: rdn over 1f out: wknd fnl f* **6/1**

-050 **8** 5 **Glaring**[16] 4799 5-9-9 **103** .... MartinDwyer 7 87
(Amanda Perrett) *hld up: rdn over 2f out: wknd wl over 1f out* **10/1**

2m 29.97s (-2.93) **Going Correction** +0.05s/f (Good)
WFA 3 from 5yo+ 11lb **8** Ran SP% **114.9**
Speed ratings (Par 109): **111,108,107,107,105 104,104,101**
CSF £22.51 CT £73.00 TOTE £6.70: £2.00, £1.50, £1.40; EX 23.40 Trifecta £74.30.
Owner A D Spence **Bred** P Bellaiche **Trained** Middleham Moor, N Yorks

FOCUS
A competitive handicap was turned into a procession by the admirable Fire Fighting with the second running to form. Rail movements added 15 yards to the race distance.

5412 N & C GLASS H'CAP 7f
5:00 (5:01) (Class 4) (0-80,80) 3-Y-O **£5,175** (£1,540; £577; £577) **Stalls** Low

Form RPR

0112 **1** **Roll On Rory**[23] 4547 3-9-7 **80** ....(v) JFEgan 7 89
(Jason Ward) *chsd ldr: rdn and hung rt fr over 1f out: led ins fnl f: r.o wl* **11/2**[2]

-206 **2** 2 **Captain Dion**[45] 3775 3-9-2 **75** .... NeilCallan 10 81+
(Kevin Ryan) *led: rdn and hung rt fr over 1f out: hdd ins fnl f: rdr dropped reins sn after: styd on same pce* **17/2**

1006 **3** 1/2 **Destroyer**[25] 4481 3-9-7 **80** ....(p) MartinDwyer 8 82
(William Muir) *prom: racd keenly: rdn over 1f out: styd on* **16/1**

4365 **3** dht **Chester Street**[19] 4709 3-9-5 **78** .... GeorgeBaker 9 80
(Roger Charlton) *stdd s: hld up: plld hrd: hdwy u.p over 1f out: styd on* **10/3**[1]

0-16 **5** 1 3/4 **Showing Off (IRE)**[77] 2695 3-9-6 **79** .... FergusSweeney 1 85+
(Henry Candy) *hld up: plld hrd: hdwy over 2f out: rdn and ev ch whn hmpd ins fnl f: nt rcvr* **10/3**[1]

4012 **6** 2 **Boycie**[9] 5076 3-9-5 **78** ....(b) PatDobbs 3 70
(Richard Hannon) *hld up: rdn over 1f out: nvr on terms* **6/1**[3]

-044 **7** hd **Harry Champion**[22] 4593 3-8-13 **75** .... MarcMonaghan(3) 11 67
(Hugo Palmer) *hld up: rdn over 2f out: nvr nrr* **10/1**

1630 **8** 1 1/2 **Irish Eclare (IRE)**[36] 4086 3-9-5 **78** .... DavidProbert 2 66
(Charles Hills) *chsd ldrs: rdn over 2f out: wknd fnl f* **12/1**

3150 **9** 5 **World's Greatest (USA)**[16] 4788 3-8-11 **70** ....(t) JoeFanning 4 44
(Stuart Williams) *hld up in tch: rdn over 2f out: wknd over 1f out* **20/1**

1m 25.49s (-0.21) **Going Correction** +0.05s/f (Good) **9** Ran SP% **113.8**
Speed ratings (Par 102): **103,100,100,100,98 95,95,93,88**
Place: D 2.70, CS 0.70; Tricast: ROR/CD/D 349.53, ROR/CD/CS 89.30; Trifecta: ROR/CD/D 705.30, ROR/CD/CS 155.20 CSF £50.48 TOTE £5.90: £1.70, £2.20; EX 52.30.
Owner P Adams, P Clarke, T Wickins, J Sutton **Bred** Stuart Matheson **Trained** Middleham, N Yorks

FOCUS
A moderate race for the level, but it produced another clear winner on the card. The joint thirds set the level.

5413 ANDREW FLEET H'CAP 1m 4f
5:35 (5:35) (Class 4) (0-85,85) 3-Y-O+ **£5,175** (£1,540; £769; £384) **Stalls** Centre

Form RPR

2023 **1** **Carry Me Home**[15] 4827 3-9-0 **82** .... DavidProbert 3 89+
(Charles Hills) *hld up: hdwy over 3f out: chsd ldr over 1f out: sn rdn: led wl ins fnl f: styd on* **9/4**[1]

6531 **2** 3/4 **Duck A L'Orange (IRE)**[15] 4836 3-8-5 **73** ....(p) WilliamCarson 7 78
(Michael Bell) *led over 10f out: rdn over 1f out: hdd wl ins fnl f: styd on* **8/1**

5431 **3** 1/2 **Dolphin Village (IRE)**[14] 4888 6-9-12 **83** .... DarryllHolland 2 87
(Jane Chapple-Hyam) *chsd ldrs: wnt 2nd over 9f out: ev ch over 2f out: sn rdn: unable qck wl ins fnl f* **10/3**[3]

14/0 **4** 2 1/4 **Artful Rogue (IRE)**[14] 4868 5-9-8 **79** .... MartinDwyer 6 79
(Amanda Perrett) *hld up: hdwy over 2f out: rdn over 1f out: styd on same pce ins fnl f* **6/1**

40-4 **5** 4 1/2 **Jupiter Custos (FR)**[16] 4785 4-9-1 **72** .... NeilCallan 4 65
(Michael Scudamore) *stmbld s: sn led: hdd over 10f out: chsd ldrs: rdn over 2f out: wknd ins fnl f* **16/1**

2151 **6** 7 **Snan (IRE)**[29] 4346 3-9-3 **85** ....(b) PatDobbs 1 67
(Richard Hannon) *chsd ldrs: rdn over 3f out: wknd 2f out* **3/1**[2]

2m 34.16s (1.26) **Going Correction** +0.05s/f (Good)
WFA 3 from 4yo+ 11lb **6** Ran SP% **110.1**
Speed ratings (Par 105): **97,96,96,94,91 87**
CSF £19.54 TOTE £2.50: £1.60, £2.30; EX 13.10 Trifecta £71.90.
Owner Gary And Linnet Woodward **Bred** Gary Woodward **Trained** Lambourn, Berks

FOCUS
Movements of the rail added 15 yards to the race distance. A tight handicap, featuring three last-time-out winners but it was very steadily run. The race has been rated around the third.
T/Plt: £28.30 to a £1 stake. Pool: £127,800.48 - 3296.1 winning units T/Qpdt: £7.80 to a £1 stake. Pool: £5,757.4 - 544.35 winning units **Colin Roberts**

4943 RIPON (R-H)
Saturday, August 13

OFFICIAL GOING: Good (8.0)
Wind: fresh across Weather: Sunny

5414 CHS VEHICLES MAIDEN AUCTION STKS 6f
1:50 (1:50) (Class 5) 2-Y-O **£4,528** (£1,347; £673; £336) **Stalls** High

Form RPR

4 **1** **Robben Rainbow**[29] 4336 2-9-3 0 .... GrahamGibbons 2 79
(David Barron) *trckd ldrs: pushed along to ld 110yds out: cosily* **3/1**[1]

26 **2** 1 **The Stalking Moon (IRE)**[16] 4801 2-8-10 0 .... JasonHart 6 69
(John Quinn) *pressed ldr: led narrowly over 3f out: rdn over 2f out: hdd 110yds out: kpt on* **3/1**[1]

6 **3** nse **Golden Apollo**[44] 3805 2-9-5 0 ....(be[1]) DavidAllan 5 78
(Tim Easterby) *prom: rdn over 2f out: kpt on* **6/1**[3]

020 **4** 2 3/4 **Right Action**[14] 4856 2-9-1 82 .... TonyHamilton 7 66
(Richard Fahey) *dwlt but sn led narrowly: hdd over 3f out: rdn and outpcd in 4th over 1f out: plugged on fnl f* **9/2**[2]

23 **5** 3 1/4 **Quiet Moment (IRE)**[18] 4725 2-8-8 0 .... DougieCostello 4 49
(Ben Haslam) *chsd ldrs towards outer: rdn over 2f out: wknd ins fnl f* **9/1**

0 **6** 1 **Princess Nearco (IRE)**[12] 4943 2-7-13 0 .... PaulaMuir(7) 8 44+
(Patrick Holmes) *slowly away: hld up in rr: pushed along 1/2-way: bhd tl kpt on fr over 1f out* **100/1**

7 1/2 **Hint Of A Smile (USA)** 2-9-0 0 .... DavidNolan 1 50
(Richard Fahey) *midfield towards outer: rdn over 2f out: wknd ins fnl f* **11/1**

6 **8** 3/4 **Breakwater Bay (IRE)**[60] 3248 2-9-0 0 .... RachelRichardson(3) 11 51
(Tim Easterby) *in tch: rdn over 2f out: wknd fnl f* **25/1**

555 **9** 13 **Nordic Combined (IRE)**[61] 3223 2-8-11 0 .... MartinLane 9 6
(Brian Ellison) *sn outpcd towards rr: a bhd* **28/1**

10 1 **Hamba Kashe (IRE)** 2-8-13 0 .... JamesSullivan 10 5
(Tim Easterby) *a outpcd in rr* **20/1**

11 1 3/4 **Equipe** 2-8-8 0 .... PaulQuinn 3
(Richard Whitaker) *dwlt: a towards rr* **50/1**

1m 12.43s (-0.57) **Going Correction** -0.175s/f (Firm) **11** Ran SP% **115.8**
Speed ratings (Par 94): **96,94,94,90,86 85,84,83,66,64 62**
CSF £10.77 TOTE £3.50: £1.10, £2.60, £1.40; EX 14.10 Trifecta £83.80.
Owner Mrs Christine Barron **Bred** Miss A J Rawding & D Macham **Trained** Maunby, N Yorks

FOCUS
The rail was at its innermost position and there were no additional yardage to any races during the afternoon. An open-looking maiden started off the meeting. Race rated around runner-up returning to debut mark.

5415 BRITISH STALLION STUDS EBF FILLIES' H'CAP 1m 1f 170y
2:20 (2:20) (Class 4) (0-80,79) 3-Y-O+ **£6,469** (£1,925; £962; £481) **Stalls** Low

Form RPR

2332 **1** **Bocking End (IRE)**[17] 4761 3-9-3 **77** .... PaulMulrennan 3 88
(Michael Bell) *midfield: smooth hdwy to ld wl over 2f out: rdn clr* **3/1**[2]

1061 **2** 9 **Lincoln Rocks**[9] 5062 3-9-5 **79** .... PhillipMakin 6 72
(David O'Meara) *trckd ldr: rdn 3f out: one pce* **9/2**[3]

0612 **3** 3/4 **Gold Show**[5] 5228 7-8-11 **62** .... KevinStott 2 53
(Grant Tuer) *trckd ldr: rdn over 3f out: one pce* **5/1**

4103 **4** 2 **Island Flame (IRE)**[23] 4549 3-9-0 **74** .... TonyHamilton 4 61
(Richard Fahey) *hld up: rdn over 3f out: no imp* **5/1**

0600 **5** 1/2 **Secret Lightning (FR)**[4] 5264 4-8-4 **60** ....(b[1]) NathanEvans(5) 5 46
(Michael Appleby) *led: rdn whn hdd wl over 2f out: grad wknd* **18/1**

1- **6** 2 **Stoney Broke**[318] 6858 3-9-1 **75** .... TomQueally 1 57
(James Fanshawe) *slowly away: hld up in rr: rdn wl over 2f out: sn no imp* **5/2**[1]

2m 2.06s (-3.34) **Going Correction** -0.175s/f (Firm)
WFA 3 from 4yo+ 9lb **6** Ran SP% **110.3**
Speed ratings (Par 102): **106,98,98,96,96 94**
CSF £16.04 TOTE £3.50: £1.30, £3.70; EX 18.80 Trifecta £66.40.
Owner W J and T C O Gredley **Bred** Howard Barton Stud **Trained** Newmarket, Suffolk

FOCUS
Despite the small field, this was run at a decent tempo and there was an impressive winner though it may not have been the deepest of races.

5416 WILLIAM HILL RIPON HORN BLOWER CONDITIONS STKS (PLUS 10 RACE) 6f
2:55 (2:55) (Class 3) 2-Y-O **£9,451** (£2,829; £1,414; £708; £352) **Stalls** High

Form RPR

21 **1** **Phijee**[20] 4678 2-9-2 84 .... SamHitchcott 1 95
(William Muir) *in tch on outer: rdn to chal over 1f out: kpt on wl: led 50yds out* **11/4**[1]

2010 **2** nk **Madam Dancealot (IRE)**[21] 4623 2-8-11 88 .... TomQueally 2 89
(Joseph Tuite) *prom: pushed along to ld 2f out: rdn over 1f out: strly pressed ent fnl f: edgd lft: kpt on: hdd 50yds out* **7/2**[2]

510 **3** 3 1/4 **Seduce Me**[21] 4623 2-8-11 85 .... DougieCostello 6 79
(K R Burke) *led narrowly: rdn whn hdd 2f out: outpcd over 1f out: plugged on fnl f* **9/2**

214 **4** nk **Kreb's Cycle (IRE)**[35] 4148 2-9-2 85 .... DavidAllan 5 83
(Richard Hannon) *prom: rdn 2f out: sn outpcd by ldng pair: one pce fnl f* **9/2**

1410 **5** 3/4 **Aardwolf (USA)**[13] 4925 2-9-2 92 .... FrannyNorton 3 81
(Mark Johnston) *dwlt sltly: sn chsd ldrs: rdn over 2f out: edgd rt over 1f out: one pce* **4/1**[3]

01 **6** 8 **My Dear Baby (IRE)**[33] 4209 2-8-11 81 .... GrahamGibbons 4 52
(Robert Cowell) *hld up in tch: rdn over 2f out: wknd over 1f out: eased* **14/1**

1m 11.58s (-1.42) **Going Correction** -0.175s/f (Firm) **6** Ran SP% **111.9**
Speed ratings (Par 98): **102,101,97,96,95 85**
CSF £12.50 TOTE £4.10: £2.50, £1.90; EX 13.00 Trifecta £40.10.
Owner Martin P Graham **Bred** Meon Valley Stud **Trained** Lambourn, Berks

FOCUS
This well-established race has had a mixed history in recent times, but has produced Group performers with the July Cup winner Mayson being easily the best of them in 2010. Highly-regarded winner who is expected to improve; fourth puts race into persepective.

5417 WILLIAM HILL SILVER TROPHY H'CAP (CONSOLATION RACE FOR WILLIAM HILL GREAT ST WILFRID STKS) 6f
3:25 (3:25) (Class 2) 3-Y-O+ **£12,602** (£3,772; £1,886; £944; £470) **Stalls** High

Form RPR

2000 **1** **Roudee**[35] 4136 4-9-10 **93** .... RichardKingscote 20 102
(Tom Dascombe) *chsd ldrs stands' side: rdn over 2f out: r.o fnl f: led towards fin* **16/1**

4641 **2** nk **Mishaal (IRE)**[20] 4689 6-9-1 **84** .... BarryMcHugh 18 92
(Michael Herrington) *led narrowly stands' side and overall ldr: rdn over 2f out: kpt on: hdd towards fin: 2nd of 10 in gp* **14/1**

-033 **3** shd **Rex Imperator**[17] 4758 7-9-8 **91** ....(p) DavidNolan 12 99
(David O'Meara) *hld up stands' side: pushed along and hdwy over 1f out: angled rt to outer ent fnl f: r.o strly: 3rd of 10 in gp* **11/2**[1]

122 **4** 1 1/4 **Pea Shooter**[14] 4896 7-8-7 **83** .... BenRobinson(7) 17 87
(Brian Ellison) *chsd ldrs stands' side: rdn and ev ch appr fnl f: no ex fnl 50yds: 4th of 10 in gp* **10/1**[3]

-060 **5** nk **Fendale**[30] 4299 4-9-4 **87** .... PaulMulrennan 1 90+
(Michael Dods) *midfield far side: pushed along over 1f out: rdn fnl f: kpt on wl: led gp 50yds out: 1st of 10 in gp* **14/1**

3205 **6** shd **Shipyard (USA)**[29] 4366 7-9-6 **89** .... TomQueally 13 92
(Michael Appleby) *trckd ldrs stands' side: rdn to chal 2f out: no ex fnl 50yds: 5th of 10 in gp* **8/1**[2]

0600 **7** 1 **George Bowen (IRE)**[28] 4415 4-9-10 **93** ....(b[1]) TonyHamilton 6 93
(Richard Fahey) *chsd ldr far side: rdn 2f out: led gp 1f out: no ex and hdd in gp 50yds out: 2nd of 10 in gp* **8/1**[2]

5000 **8** 3/4 **Handsome Dude**[14] 4862 4-9-2 **85** ....(b) GrahamGibbons 16 82
(David Barron) *midfield stands' side: rdn 2f out: carried rt to outside ent fnl f: one pce: 6th of 10 in gp* **16/1**

-040 **9** hd **Holiday Magic (IRE)**[14] 4868 5-9-4 **87** JamesSullivan 5 83
(Michael Easterby) *chsd ldrs far side: rdn over 2f out: kpt on: 3rd of 10 in gp* **28/1**

5010 **10** 2 **Best Trip (IRE)**[24] 4514 9-9-6 **89** SamJames 15 79
(Marjorie Fife) *w ldr stands' side: rdn over 2f out: wknd ins fnl f: 7th of 10 in gp* **33/1**

035- **11** nk **Twin Appeal (IRE)**[235] 8342 5-9-4 **87** (b) DougieCostello 19 76
(David Barron) *dwlt: hld up stands' side: nvr threatened: 8th of 10 in gp* **33/1**

0-00 **12** ½ **Magic City (IRE)**[13] 4917 7-8-11 **85** NathanEvans(5) 2 73
(Michael Easterby) *dwlt: sn midfield far side: rdn over 2f out: one pce: 4th of 10 in gp* **33/1**

0640 **13** hd **Fast Track**[14] 4862 5-9-5 **88** PhillipMakin 8 75
(David Barron) *nvr bttr than midfield far side: 5th of 10 in gp* **12/1**

023 **14** hd **Dragon King (IRE)**[29] 4373 4-9-5 **88** ConnorBeasley 10 74
(Michael Dods) *led far side: prom overall: rdn over 2f out: hdd 1f out: wknd: 6th of 10 in gp* **8/1**[2]

1003 **15** 2½ **Munfallet (IRE)**[12] 4946 5-8-12 **86** AdamMcNamara(5) 14 64
(David Brown) *a towards rr far side: 9th of 10 in gp* **16/1**

0000 **16** ¾ **Patrick (IRE)**[21] 4667 4-9-3 **86** (b[1]) GeorgeChaloner 3 62
(Richard Fahey) *hld up and nvr threatened far side: 7th of 10 in gp* **25/1**

4135 **17** shd **Avon Breeze**[90] 2267 7-9-8 **91** KeaganLatham 7 67
(Richard Whitaker) *dwlt: nvr bttr than midfield far side: 8th of 10 in gp* **25/1**

0020 **18** ½ **Grandad's World (IRE)**[14] 4862 4-9-4 **87** JackGarritty 9 61
(Richard Fahey) *prom far side: rdn over 2f out: wknd over 1f out: 9th of 10 in gp* **11/1**

1003 **19** 1¼ **Khelman (IRE)**[44] 3800 6-8-9 **85** HayleyIrvine(7) 4 55
(Richard Fahey) *a towards rr far side: edgd lft fr over 1f out: last of 10 in gp* **25/1**

0650 **20** 8 **See The Sun**[21] 4667 5-9-7 **90** DavidAllan 11 34
(Tim Easterby) *racd on outside of stands' side gp: chsd ldrs: rdn 1/2-way: wknd over 1f out: eased* **20/1**

1m 10.84s (-2.16) **Going Correction** -0.175s/f (Firm) **20** Ran SP% **133.4**
Speed ratings (Par 109): **107,106,106,104,104 104,102,101,101,99 98,97,97,97,94 93,92,92,90,79**
CSF £216.50 CT £1444.19 TOTE £21.80: £3.00, £3.50, £2.40, £3.40; EX 352.20 Trifecta £1827.50 Part won..

Owner Edwards Hughes Jenkins Roberts & Partner **Bred** Miss D Fleming **Trained** Malpas, Cheshire

■ Stewards' Enquiry : Barry McHugh two-day ban: use of whip (27-28 Aug)

FOCUS
As could have have been reasonably expected, they split in two groups leaving the stalls, with those who raced down the stands' side favoured. A small personal best from the winner and a turf personal best from the second.

5418 WILLIAM HILL GREAT ST WILFRID STKS (H'CAP) 6f

3:55 (4:00) (Class 2) 3-Y-O+
£43,575 (£13,048; £6,524; £3,262; £1,631; £819) **Stalls** High

Form RPR

0-30 **1** **Nameitwhatyoulike**[29] 4338 7-8-13 **98** ConnorBeasley 13 107
(Bryan Smart) *mde all: rdn 2f out: kpt on wl* **16/1**

1212 **2** nk **Intisaab**[21] 4667 5-8-6 **94** (p) ShelleyBirkett(3) 17 102+
(David O'Meara) *midfield: pushed along over 2f out: bit tight for room a couple of times over 1f out: nt fully clr tl ent fnl f: kpt on wl: 2nd of 13 in gp* **7/1**[2]

6200 **3** hd **Baccarat (IRE)**[14] 4865 7-9-8 **107** KevinStott 11 114
(Charlie Appleby) *slowly away: hld up stands' side: rdn and gd hdwy on outside over 1f out: r.o strly fnl f: 3rd of 13 in gp* **20/1**

0304 **4** 1 **Pipers Note**[14] 4860 6-8-10 **95** GeorgeChaloner 14 99
(Richard Whitaker) *chsd ldrs stands' side: rdn over 2f out: kpt on: 4th of 13 in gp* **16/1**

-200 **5** shd **George Dryden (IRE)**[49] 3655 4-9-3 **102** JamesSullivan 10 106+
(Ann Duffield) *midfield stands' side: rdn over 2f out: kpt on wl fnl f: 5th of 13 in gp* **33/1**

1641 **6** 1 **Snap Shots (IRE)**[12] 4946 4-8-9 **94** (tp) RichardKingscote 7 95
(Tom Dascombe) *chsd ldr far side: rdn over 2f out: kpt on 1st of 7 in gp* **16/1**

1U20 **7** shd **Mythmaker**[49] 3656 4-8-11 **96** PaulMulrennan 6 96
(Bryan Smart) *led far side gp: rdn 2f out: no ex fnl 50yds: 2nd of 7 in gp* **22/1**

1112 **8** 1¾ **Orion's Bow**[14] 4865 5-9-7 **106** BarryMcHugh 9 101
(David Nicholls) *swtchd lft s to r stands' side: chsd ldrs: rdn 2f out: wknd ins fnl f: 6th of 13 in gp* **5/1**[1]

6153 **9** ¾ **Nuno Tristan (USA)**[14] 4862 4-8-9 **94** TonyHamilton 12 86
(Richard Fahey) *hld up in midfield stands' side: rdn over 2f out: no imp: 7th of 13 in gp* **15/2**[3]

2210 **10** hd **Kimberella**[14] 4865 6-9-6 **105** FrannyNorton 16 97
(David Nicholls) *prom stands' side: rdn over 2f out: wknd ins fnl f: 8th of 13 in gp* **15/2**[3]

0303 **11** 1 **Mujassam**[50] 3622 4-8-9 **94** (v) PhillipMakin 4 83
(David O'Meara) *chsd ldr far side: rdn over 2f out: one pce: 3rd of 7 in gp* **28/1**

1000 **12** 1 **Alben Star (IRE)**[14] 4865 8-9-1 **100** DavidNolan 19 85
(Richard Fahey) *midfield stands' side: rdn over 2f out: wknd ins fnl f: 9th of 13 in gp* **16/1**

0200 **13** ¾ **Moonraker**[14] 4865 4-9-0 **99** SamHitchcott 2 82
(Mick Channon) *midfield far side: rdn over 2f out: wknd fnl f: 4th of 7 in gp* **50/1**

-000 **14** 1½ **Toofi (FR)**[14] 4865 5-8-10 **100** AdamMcNamara(5) 3 78
(Robert Cowell) *chsd ldrs far side: rdn over 2f out: wknd over 1f out: 5th of 7 in gp* **14/1**

0032 **15** ½ **Related**[14] 4862 6-8-10 **95** (b) MartinLane 18 72
(Paul Midgley) *dwlt: hld up stands' side: nvr threatened: 10th of 13 in gp* **9/1**

0-00 **16** nk **Louis The Pious**[21] 4667 8-8-13 **98** (v) GrahamGibbons 15 74
(David O'Meara) *dwlt: hld up and nvr threatened stands' side: 11th of 13 in gp* **25/1**

0400 **17** 1¾ **Tatlisu (IRE)**[21] 4667 6-8-9 **94** SamJames 5 64
(Richard Fahey) *hld up and nvr a threat far side: 6th of 7 in gp* **25/1**

0056 **18** 4 **Son Of Africa**[29] 4366 4-8-9 **94** JackGarritty 20 51
(Henry Candy) *prom stands' side: rdn 2f out: sn wknd: 12th of 13 in gp* **12/1**

-200 **19** ½ **Go Far**[14] 4865 6-8-11 **96** (b) DougieCostello 1 52
(Alan Bailey) *a bhd far side: last of 7 in gp* **66/1**

0031 **20** 6 **Perfect Pasture**[28] 4415 6-9-5 **109** (v) NathanEvans(5) 8 45
(Michael Easterby) *swtchd lft s to r stands' side: midfield: hung violently rt fr over 2f out and sn bhd* **20/1**

1m 10.14s (-2.86) **Going Correction** -0.175s/f (Firm) **20** Ran SP% **132.0**
Speed ratings (Par 109): **112,111,111,110,109 108,108,106,105,104 103,102,101,99,98 98,95,90,89,81**
CSF £116.17 CT £2319.05 TOTE £17.30: £4.40, £2.00, £5.00, £4.50; EX 184.80 Trifecta £5626.20.

Owner S Chappell **Bred** A E Smith And Co **Trained** Hambleton, N Yorks

FOCUS
Following the consolation race, it was no massive shock that plenty of the field headed towards the stands' rail. The first five did come down that part of the track, but those who raced on the inside weren't beaten that far. A small personal best from the winner.

5419 ATTHERACES.COM H'CAP 1m

4:30 (4:32) (Class 3) (0-90,90) 3-Y-O **£9,451** (£2,829; £1,414; £708; £352) **Stalls** Low

Form RPR

5412 **1** **Breakable**[21] 4630 5-9-7 **87** RachelRichardson(3) 4 95
(Tim Easterby) *trckd ldr on inner: rdn to ld 1f out: kpt on wl* **9/1**

1460 **2** ¾ **Abushamah (IRE)**[7] 5180 5-9-6 **83** JamesSullivan 10 89
(Ruth Carr) *midfield: rdn and hdwy over 1f out: kpt on* **18/1**

1363 **3** shd **Rousayan (IRE)**[14] 4894 5-9-7 **87** ShelleyBirkett(3) 11 93+
(David O'Meara) *hld up in midfield: rdn and hdwy on outer 2f out: chal ent fnl f: kpt on* **11/1**

0151 **4** ¾ **Ginger Jack**[14] 4894 9-9-10 **87** DavidAllan 7 91
(Garry Moss) *trckd ldrs: pushed along 2f out: nt a much room tl ins fnl f: kpt on* **9/2**[1]

0326 **5** ¾ **Bold Prediction (IRE)**[14] 4868 6-9-8 **90** AdamMcNamara(5) 14 92
(Ed Walker) *prom towards outer: rdn over 2 out: no ex ins fnl f* **11/1**

-00 **6** ½ **Strong Man**[14] 4894 8-8-12 **80** NathanEvans(5) 5 81
(Michael Easterby) *led narrowly: rdn over 2f out: hdd 1f out: wknd ins fnl f* **40/1**

0213 **7** nse **Jacbequick**[18] 4727 5-9-13 **90** (v) SamJames 6 91
(David O'Meara) *prom: rdn over 2f out: no ex ins fnl f* **14/1**

5514 **8** ½ **Lawyer (IRE)**[5] 5223 5-9-2 **79** PhillipMakin 1 79
(David Barron) *hld up in midfield: rdn over 2 out: one pce* **8/1**[3]

4300 **9** ¾ **Alexandrakollontai (IRE)**[19] 4700 6-9-6 **83** (b) ConnorBeasley 13 81
(Alistair Whillans) *hld up in rr: rdn over 3f out: kpt on fnl f: nvr threatened ldrs* **40/1**

01 **10** hd **Little Lady Katie (IRE)**[49] 3667 4-9-10 **87** RichardKingscote 2 85
(K R Burke) *midfield on inner: pushed along 2f out: nt a much room and nvr threatened* **5/1**[2]

0500 **11** ½ **Gerry The Glover (IRE)**[50] 3605 4-8-12 **82** BenRobinson(7) 8 79
(Brian Ellison) *midfield: rdn 2f out: no imp* **10/1**

3316 **12** nk **Spryt (IRE)**[26] 4453 4-9-5 **82** (v) DavidNolan 16 78
(David O'Meara) *swtchd rt s: hld up: pushed along and n.m.r over 1f out: nvr threatened* **14/1**

-50 **13** 2¾ **Lord Ben Stack (IRE)**[26] 4448 4-9-13 **90** DougieCostello 3 80
(K R Burke) *dwlt: sn in tch towards inner: n.m.r fr over 2f out and lost pl over 1f out* **10/1**

0020 **14** hd **Arnold Lane (IRE)**[17] 4758 7-9-11 **88** SamHitchcott 12 77
(Mick Channon) *trckd ldrs: rdn over 2f out: wknd appr fnl f* **25/1**

0052 **15** nk **Invoke (IRE)**[19] 4700 5-9-9 **86** TomQueally 9 74
(Keith Dalgleish) *midfield towards outer: rdn 3f out: wknd over 1f out* **14/1**

0610 **16** 11 **Yourartisonfire**[13] 4917 6-9-7 **84** FrannyNorton 15 47
(Patrick Morris) *a towards rr* **33/1**

1m 38.6s (-2.80) **Going Correction** -0.175s/f (Firm) **16** Ran SP% **127.7**
Speed ratings (Par 107): **107,106,106,105,104 104,104,103,102,102 102,101,99,98,98 87**
CSF £163.87 CT £1897.67 TOTE £7.70: £1.30, £4.70, £3.70, £2.10; EX 243.70 Trifecta £978.60.

Owner Ryedale Partners No 9 **Bred** Habton Farms **Trained** Great Habton, N Yorks

FOCUS
Plenty of these held a chance about a furlong from home and not a lot separated the first 12, so this may not be reliable form. A small personal best from the winner, though.

5420 WILLIAM HILL DOWNLOAD THE APP H'CAP 1m 4f 10y

5:05 (5:05) (Class 5) (0-75,80) 3-Y-O **£4,528** (£1,347; £673; £336) **Stalls** Centre

Form RPR

5130 **1** **Theos Lolly (IRE)**[15] 4827 3-9-2 **75** AdamMcNamara(5) 4 83
(Richard Fahey) *midfield: pushed along over 2f out: bit short of room in bhd ldng pair over 1f out: swtchd rt and in clr ent fnl f: rdn to ld 110yds out: kpt on wl* **9/2**[2]

4011 **2** 1½ **Icefall (IRE)**[12] 4949 3-9-12 **80** DavidAllan 3 86
(Tim Easterby) *in tch: pushed along over 2f out: rdn to chal strly over 1f out: one pce fnl 110yds* **6/5**[1]

4233 **3** nk **Kings Gold (IRE)**[29] 4342 3-9-4 **72** (p) PaulMulrennan 5 77
(Michael Dods) *trckd ldr: upsides over 3f out: rdn to ld over 2f out: strly pressed over 1f out: hdd 110yds out: one pce* **5/1**[3]

3465 **4** 2¾ **Masterson (IRE)**[8] 5101 3-8-3 **57** FrannyNorton 1 58
(Mick Channon) *hld up in tch: rdn over 2f out: nvr threatened* **9/1**

0216 **5** 1 **Sporty Yankee (USA)**[40] 3959 3-8-13 **67** DougieCostello 6 66
(K R Burke) *dwlt: hld up in rr: rdn over 3f out: nvr threatened* **10/1**

4422 **6** 1 **Becky The Thatcher**[15] 4847 3-8-8 **62** ow1 GrahamGibbons 2 60
(Micky Hammond) *led: jnd over 3f out: rdn whn hdd over 2f out: wknd over 1f out* **7/1**

2m 35.48s (-1.22) **Going Correction** -0.175s/f (Firm) **6** Ran SP% **111.9**
Speed ratings (Par 100): **97,96,95,93,93 92**
CSF £10.31 TOTE £5.90: £2.20, £1.10; EX 8.30 Trifecta £46.60.

Owner M J Macleod **Bred** Mrs Claire Doyle **Trained** Musley Bank, N Yorks

FOCUS
A fair handicap in which three pulled away. The winner and third recorded small personal bests.

T/Jkpt: Not Won. T/Plt: £163.50 to a £1 stake. Pool of £58,271.56 - 260.04 winning units T/Qpdt: £39.20 to a £1 stake. Pool of £6,867.91 - 129.40 winning units **Andrew Sheret**

5421 - 5427a (Foreign Racing) - See Raceform Interactive

ARLINGTON PARK (L-H)
Saturday, August 13

OFFICIAL GOING: Turf: firm

5428a AMERICAN ST. LEGER STKS (GRADE 3) (3YO+) (TURF) 1m 5f 110y
9:05 (12:00) 3-Y-O+

£118,775 (£39,591; £19,795; £9,897; £5,938; £3,959)

RPR

1 **Da Big Hoss (USA)**64 5-9-0 0 FlorentGeroux 5 113+
(Michael J Maker, U.S.A) **4/5**1

2 1 3/4 **Clondaw Warrior (IRE)**16 3387 9-8-11 0 SeamieHeffernan 7 107+
(W P Mullins, Ire) *hld up in rr: rdn bef st: styd on down outer and up for 2nd cl home: no threat to wnr* **61/10**3

3 nk **Wasir (GER)**58 3298 4-8-9 0 WilliamBuick 6 105
(A Wohler, Germany) **145/10**

4 3 1/2 **Montclair (IRE)**34 6-8-7 0 (b) MikeESmith 2 98
(Roger Brueggemann, U.S.A) **158/10**

5 1/2 **Billabong (MOR)**168 757 7-8-7 0 FlavienPrat 8 97
(P Bary, France) **59/10**2

6 3/4 **Tobias (USA)**17 7-8-7 0 CarlosHMarquezJr 4 96
(Rafael A Fernandez, U.S.A) **81/1**

7 2 1/2 **Generous Kitten (USA)**41 5-8-7 0 (b) RobbyAlbarado 1 92
(Michael J Maker, U.S.A) **97/10**

8 4 **Hart Hills Road (USA)**20 5-8-7 0 (b) SantoSanjur 3 86
(Michael B Campbell, U.S.A) **84/1**

9 3 1/2 **O'Prado Ole (USA)**35 6-8-7 0 CoreyJLanerie 9 81
(Dale Romans, U.S.A) **67/10**

2m 49.47s (169.47) **9** Ran SP% **121.3**

Owner Skychai Racing LLC **Bred** Gary & Mary West Stables Inc **Trained** USA

5429a SECRETARIAT STKS (GRADE 1) (3YO) (TURF) 1m 2f
9:43 (12:00) 3-Y-O

£178,163 (£59,387; £29,693; £14,846; £8,908; £5,938)

RPR

1 **Beach Patrol (USA)**35 4173 3-8-7 0 (b) FlorentGeroux 9 104
(Chad C Brown, U.S.A) **14/5**1

2 hd **Long Island Sound (USA)**35 4173 3-8-7 0 SeamieHeffernan 8 104
(A P O'Brien, Ire) **31/10**2

3 3/4 **American Patriot (USA)**28 3-8-11 0 (b) WilliamBuick 2 106
(Todd Pletcher, U.S.A) **31/10**2

4 1/2 **One Mean Man (USA)**35 3-8-9 0 RobbyAlbarado 4 103
(Bernard Flint, U.S.A) **117/10**

5 nse **Oscar Nominated (USA)**35 3-8-11 0 (b) CoreyJLanerie 6 105
(Michael J Maker, U.S.A) **109/10**

6 2 3/4 **Cordon (USA)**34 3-8-7 0 CarlosHMarquezJr 5 95
(Pavel Vashchenko, U.S.A) **55/1**

7 1 1/4 **Surgical Strike (USA)**35 4173 3-8-7 0 (b) FlavienPrat 7 93
(Ben Colebrook, U.S.A) **67/10**

8 5 **Cherry Wine (USA)**27 3-8-7 0 MikeESmith 1 83
(Dale Romans, U.S.A) **6/1**3

9 14 **Scissors And Tape (USA)**57 3-8-7 0 (b) ShaunBridgmohan 3 55
(Michael J Maker, U.S.A) **74/1**

2m 1.95s (0.31) **9** Ran SP% **121.8**
PARI-MUTUEL (all including 2 usd stake): WIN 7.60; PLACE (1-2) 3.80, 4.40; SHOW (1-2-3) 3.00, 3.00, 3.00; SF 25.80.
Owner James Covello, Sheep Pond Partners & Head Of Plain **Bred** Nancy C Shuford **Trained** USA

5430a BEVERLY D. STKS (GRADE 1) (3YO+ FILLIES & MARES) (TURF) 1m 1f 110y
10:21 (12:00) 3-Y-O+

£262,857 (£87,619; £43,809; £21,904; £13,142; £8,761)

RPR

1 **Sea Calisi (FR)**64 3119 4-8-11 0 FlorentGeroux 13 111+
(Chad C Brown, U.S.A) **11/10**1

2 1/2 **Al's Gal (USA)**35 5-8-11 0 CoreyJLanerie 2 110
(Michael J Maker, U.S.A) **202/10**

3 1 1/4 **Zipessa (USA)**40 4-8-11 0 JoeBravo 9 107
(Michael Stidham, U.S.A) **104/10**

4 1 **Tuttipaesi (IRE)**40 6-8-11 0 ChristopherPDeCarlo 5 105
(William Mott, U.S.A) **19/1**

5 3/4 **Faufiler (IRE)**35 5-8-11 0 JoseValdiviaJr 12 104
(H Graham Motion, U.S.A) **32/5**

6 3/4 **No Fault Of Mine (USA)**35 4-8-11 0 WilliamBuick 4 102
(Chris Block, U.S.A) **48/1**

7 2 3/4 **Pretty Girl (ARG)**18 4751 5-8-11 0 BriceBlanc 14 96
(M Delzangles, France) **38/1**

8 1/2 **Secret Someone (USA)**35 5-8-11 0 RobbyAlbarado 10 95
(Michael Stidham, U.S.A) **66/1**

9 2 1/4 **Personal Diary (USA)**35 5-8-11 0 (b) MikeESmith 8 91
(Victoria H Oliver, U.S.A) **86/1**

10 1/2 **Coolmore (IRE)**35 4174 3-8-5 0 (p) ColmO'Donoghue 6 92
(A P O'Brien, Ire) **56/10**2

11 1/2 **Marypop (FR)**35 4-8-11 0 (b1) FlavienPrat 3 88
(Michael Stidham, U.S.A) **226/10**

12 1 1/4 **Ballydoyle (IRE)**35 4174 3-8-5 0 SeamieHeffernan 1 89
(A P O'Brien, Ire) **59/10**3

13 11 1/4 **Lots O' Lex (USA)**294 5-8-11 0 EdgarPerez 7 62
(Gerald Russel Aschinger, U.S.A) **115/1**

14 32 **Elusive Million (IRE)**51 3590 3-8-5 0 JulioEFelix 11
(Chad C Brown, U.S.A) **98/1**

1m 54.93s (-0.54)
WFA 3 from 4yo+ 8lb **14** Ran SP% **122.6**
PARI-MUTUEL (all including 2 usd stake): WIN 4.20; PLACE (1-2) 3.40, 10.40; SHOW (1-2-3) 2.60, 6.40, 7.40; SF 68.60.
Owner Martin S Schwartz **Bred** Derek Bloodstock **Trained** USA

5431a ARLINGTON MILLION XXXIV STKS (GRADE 1) (3YO) (TURF) 1m 2f
11:09 (12:00) 3-Y-O

£387,755 (£129,251; £64,625; £32,312; £19,387; £12,925)

RPR

1 **Mondialiste (IRE)**21 4666 6-9-0 0 DanielTudhope 7 115
(David O'Meara) **22/5**3

2 nk **Kasaqui (ARG)**35 6-9-0 0 RobbyAlbarado 5 114
(Ignacio Correas IV, U.S.A) **122/10**

3 nk **Deauville (IRE)**35 4173 3-8-8 0 SeamieHeffernan 11 117
(A P O'Brien, Ire) **79/10**

4 3/4 **Greengrassofyoming (USA)**35 6-9-0 0 (b) ShaunBridgmohan 2 112
(Michael J Maker, U.S.A) **47/1**

5 nk **Danish Dynaformer (CAN)**41 4-9-0 0 (b) PatrickHusbands 1 112
(Roger L Attfield, Canada) **26/1**

6 hd **The Pizza Man (USA)**35 7-9-0 0 MikeESmith 4 111
(Roger Brueggemann, U.S.A) **6/1**

7 nk **World Approval (USA)**41 4-9-0 0 (b) FlorentGeroux 9 110
(Mark Casse, Canada) **37/10**1

8 1 **Tryster (IRE)**59 3272 5-9-0 0 WilliamBuick 10 108
(Charlie Appleby) **41/10**2

9 nse **Pumpkin Rumble (USA)**35 5-9-0 0 MitchellMurrill 3 108
(Gary Scherer, U.S.A) **73/1**

10 1 1/2 **Wake Forest (GER)**41 6-9-0 0 FlavienPrat 8 105
(Chad C Brown, U.S.A) **59/10**

11 nk **Take The Stand (ARG)**140 5-9-0 0 (b) EdgarSPrado 6 105
(William Mott, U.S.A) **133/10**

2m 1.87s (0.23)
WFA 3 from 4yo+ 9lb **11** Ran SP% **121.1**
PARI-MUTUEL (all including 2 usd stake): WIN 10.80; PLACE (1-2) 6.40, 13.20; SHOW (1-2-3) 4.80, 9.40, 7.00; SF 149.80.
Owner Geoff & Sandra Turnbull **Bred** Wertheimer Et Frere **Trained** Upper Helmsley, N Yorks

5028 PONTEFRACT (L-H)
Sunday, August 14

OFFICIAL GOING: Good (good to firm in places; 8.5)
Wind: Moderate across Weather: Cloudy with sunny periods

5433 BRITISH STALLION STUDS EBF TREVOR WOODS MEMORIAL MAIDEN STKS (PLUS 10 RACE) 5f
2:15 (2:17) (Class 4) 2-Y-O **£5,175** (£1,540; £769; £384) **Stalls** Low

Form RPR

35 1 **Sky Gypsy**17 4804 2-9-0 0 TomEaves 11 70+
(David Brown) *qckly away: mde all: rdn over 1f out: kpt on wl towards fin* **10/1**

025 2 3/4 **Sheepscar Lad (IRE)**29 4405 2-9-5 75 AndrewMullen 4 72
(Nigel Tinkler) *dwlt: sn trcking ldrs: hdwy 2f out: rdn over 1f out: chsd wnr ins fnl f: kpt on* **4/1**2

0052 3 1 1/4 **Lightoller (IRE)**11 5014 2-9-5 68 CharlesBishop 5 68
(Mick Channon) *t.k.h: trckd ldng pair on inner: effrt wl over 1f out: rdn and n.m.r ins fnl f: sn swtchd rt and kpt on* **11/2**

5 4 2 3/4 **Ashurst Beacon**10 5058 2-9-5 0 SilvestreDeSousa 7 58
(Brian Ellison) *dwlt and towards rr: pushed along 2f out: rdn over 1f out: styd on fnl f: nrst fin* **7/2**1

655 5 nk **Emerald Secret (IRE)**37 4110 2-9-0 65 PaulMulrennan 9 52
(Paul Midgley) *sn cl up: rdn along wl over 1f out: wknd fnl f* **5/1**3

6 6 1 1/2 **Justanotherbottle (IRE)**19 4725 2-9-5 0 BarryMcHugh 1 51
(Declan Carroll) *t.k.h: in tch on inner: pushed along 2f out: rdn over 1f out: sn no imp* **8/1**

0 7 1 3/4 **Dusty Bin**33 4227 2-9-5 0 ShaneGray 2 45
(Kevin Ryan) *a towards rr* **6/1**

8 11 **Yelow Bird** 2-9-5 0 DougieCostello 8 5
(Chris Grant) *dwlt and wnt rt s: green and a outpcd in rr* **33/1**

05 9 10 **Nyx**52 3576 2-9-0 0 ConnorBeasley 6
(Richard Guest) *chsd ldrs: rdn along wl over 1f out: sn wknd* **25/1**

1m 3.81s (0.51) **Going Correction** -0.20s/f (Firm) **9** Ran SP% **115.5**
Speed ratings (Par 96): **87,85,83,79,78 76,73,56,40**
CSF £49.84 TOTE £10.70: £2.70, £1.70, £1.70; EX 54.40 Trifecta £185.10.
Owner A Birkle, P Boden & S Brown **Bred** A C Birkle **Trained** Averham Park, Notts

FOCUS
The ground was officially good, good to firm in places and clerk of the course Norman Gundill said: "We put 4mm of water on yesterday and the forecast is for it to stay dry today." This was an ordinary 2yo maiden.

5434 TOTEPOOL LIVE INFO DOWNLOAD THE APP H'CAP 1m 4f 8y
2:45 (2:47) (Class 3) (0-90,88) 3-Y-O+

£7,470 (£2,236; £1,118; £559; £279; £140) **Stalls** Low

Form RPR

312 1 **Regal Monarch**23 4598 3-9-0 **85** FrannyNorton 6 96+
(Mark Johnston) *trckd ldng pair: hdwy wl over 1f out: rdn to ld jst ins fnl f: sn drvn and kpt on wl* **7/4**1

1453 2 1 **Mainstream**29 4403 3-9-3 **88** StevieDonohoe 2 97+
(Sir Michael Stoute) *hld up towards rr: hdwy on inner 2f out: effrt and nt clr run over 1f out: sn swtchd rt and rdn to chse wnr ins fnl f: kpt on* **2/1**2

010 3 2 1/4 **Plane Song (IRE)**53 3520 4-9-5 **79** SilvestreDeSousa 1 84
(Alan Swinbank) *trckd ldr: hdwy and cl up over 2f out: rdn to ld wl over 1f out: drvn and hdd jst ins fnl f: kpt on same pce* **10/1**

2230 4 3 3/4 **Modernism**29 4407 7-9-12 **86** PaulHanagan 3 85
(Richard Fahey) *hld up in tch: hdwy 4f out: rdn along 2f out: drvn over 1f out: sn one pce* **7/1**3

6014 5 1 **Mysterial**14 4920 6-8-10 **77** GerO'Neill(7) 4 75
(Declan Carroll) *led: pushed along 3f out: jnd and rdn over 2f out: drvn and hdd wl over 1f out: wknd* **14/1**

3105 6 1 1/2 **Be Perfect (USA)**12 4969 7-9-7 **81** (b1) JamesSullivan 5 76
(Ruth Carr) *hld up: a in rr* **16/1**

2204 7 14 **Busy Street**79 2663 4-9-5 **79** NeilFarley 7 52
(Alan Swinbank) *chsd ldrs: rdn along wl over 2f out: sn wknd* **11/1**

2m 36.15s (-4.65) **Going Correction** -0.20s/f (Firm)
WFA 3 from 4yo+ 11lb **7** Ran SP% **112.2**
Speed ratings (Par 107): **107,106,104,102,101 100,91**
CSF £5.24 TOTE £2.60: £1.60, £1.50; EX 5.60 Trifecta £37.00.

Owner Highclere T'Bred Racing East Layton Stud **Bred** A H Bennett **Trained** Middleham Moor, N Yorks

FOCUS

A fair handicap, run at something of an uneven pace.

5435 MOOR TOP FARM SHOP HEMSWORTH H'CAP 2m 1f 22y

3:15 (3:17) (Class 5) (0-70,70) 3-Y-O+ **£3,234** (£962; £481; £240) **Stalls** Low

Form RPR

5004 **1** **Another Lincolnday**[22] 4645 5-9-4 **60**....(p) TomEaves 1 68
(Michael Herrington) *mde: rdn wl over 2f out: drvn clr over 1f out: kpt on gamely* **9/2**[2]

4420 **2** 1/2 **Riptide**[47] 3746 10-9-9 **65**.... DougieCostello 2 72
(Michael Scudamore) *hld up towards rr: hdwy 3f out: rdn to chse ldng pair over 1f out: drvn and styd on wl to chse wnr ins fnl f: kpt on wl towards fin* **9/2**[2]

6-63 **3** 3 1/4 **RockthERunway (IRE)**[33] 4239 7-9-13 **69**....(p) ConnorBeasley 4 72
(Michael Dods) *trckd ldrs: hdwy 4f out: cl up 3f out: rdn to chal over 2f out: drvn wl over 1f out and kpt on same pce* **2/1**[1]

2505 **4** 3 3/4 **Tuscan Gold**[27] 2971 9-10-0 **70**....(p) PJMcDonald 8 69
(Micky Hammond) *hld up in rr: hdwy 3f out: rdn along over 2f out: plugged on one pce* **7/1**

6005 **5** 5 **Yorkshireman (IRE)**[12] 4971 6-8-10 **56** oh6 ow1....(b) PaddyAspell 3 46
(Lynn Siddall) *trckd ldrs: hdwy 4f out: rdn to chse ldng pair 3f out: drvn wl over 1f out and sn wknd* **20/1**

2005 **6** 18 **Madam Lilibet (IRE)**[56] 3437 7-9-7 **63**.... JoeyHaynes 7 37
(Sharon Watt) *trckd ldng pair: pushed along 5f out: rdn along 4f out: sn drvn and wknd* **8/1**

4-05 **7** 99 **Sthenic (FR)**[78] 2678 4-9-8 **64**....(p) SilvestreDeSousa 5
(Micky Hammond) *chsd wnr: rdn along 5f out: sn lost pl and bhd whn eased over 2f out* **11/2**[3]

3m 50.65s (6.05) **Going Correction** -0.20s/f (Firm) **7** Ran SP% **113.5**

Speed ratings (Par 103): **77,76,75,73,71 62,16**

CSF £24.45 CT £51.78 TOTE £5.20: £1.90, £2.80; EX 27.00 Trifecta £65.90.

Owner J D Spensley & Mrs M A Spensley **Bred** J D Spensley & Mrs M A Spensley **Trained** Cold Kirby, N Yorks

FOCUS

An ordinary staying handicap.

5436 EBF STALLIONS HIGHFIELD FARM FLYING FILLIES' STKS (LISTED RACE) 6f

3:45 (3:45) (Class 1) 3-Y-O+

£28,355 (£10,750; £5,380; £2,680; £1,345; £675) **Stalls** Low

Form RPR

1341 **1** **Mehronissa**[9] 5124 4-9-2 98.... FrederikTylicki 1 108
(Ed Vaughan) *trckd ldr on inner: hdwy over 1f out: swtchd rt and rdn ins fnl f: styd on wl to ld towards fin* **5/1**[3]

2410 **2** 3/4 **Ridge Ranger (IRE)**[15] 4865 5-9-9 110.... JasonHart 3 113
(Eric Alston) *led: rdn wl over 1f out: drvn ins fnl f: hdd and no ex towards fin* **10/3**[2]

-543 **3** 3 3/4 **La Rioja**[37] 4114 3-8-12 107.... MartinHarley 5 93
(Henry Candy) *trckd ldrs: swtchd rt and hdwy wl over 1f out: sn rdn: drvn ins fnl f and kpt on same pce* **11/4**[1]

0522 **4** nk **Priceless**[22] 4652 3-8-12 102.... SilvestreDeSousa 7 92
(Clive Cox) *chsd ldr: hdwy and cl up over 2f out: rdn wl over 1f out: drvn and edgd rt ins fnl f: wknd* **11/4**[1]

2-46 **5** 6 **Imtiyaaz (IRE)**[85] 2474 4-9-2 92.... HarryBentley 2 73
(Roger Varian) *hld up: effrt 2f out: sn rdn along and n.d* **14/1**

5-16 **6** nk **Mayfair Lady**[37] 4114 3-8-12 107.... JackGarritty 10 71
(Richard Fahey) *in tch: hdwy on outer and cl up over 2f out: rdn along wl over 1f out: sn wknd* **8/1**

-200 **7** 33 **Raaqy (IRE)**[23] 4582 3-8-12 92.... PaulHanagan 8
(Owen Burrows) *in tch: pushed along over 2f out: sn rdn: wknd wl over 1f out: sn eased* **22/1**

1m 14.04s (-2.86) **Going Correction** -0.20s/f (Firm)

WFA 3 from 4yo+ 4lb **7** Ran SP% **115.2**

Speed ratings (Par 108): **111,110,105,104,96 96,52**

CSF £22.32 TOTE £7.00: £3.30, £1.60; EX 23.30 Trifecta £80.20.

Owner Salem Rashid **Bred** Carmel Stud **Trained** Newmarket, Suffolk

FOCUS

The first pair dominated the finish of this feature Listed sprint and the runner-up is a decent guide.

5437 IN LOVING MEMORY OF ALISON CLARK H'CAP 1m 4y

4:20 (4:20) (Class 3) (0-95,94) 3-Y-O **£7,470** (£2,236; £1,118; £559; £279) **Stalls** Low

Form RPR

0010 **1** **Huntlaw**[22] 4654 3-8-7 **80**.... FrannyNorton 5 93
(Mark Johnston) *trckd ldng pair: hdwy to trck ldr over 3f out: cl up over 2f out: rdn to ld wl over 1f out: clr fnl f: kpt on strly* **6/4**[1]

5114 **2** 4 **My Lucille (IRE)**[22] 4668 3-8-5 **78**.... AndrewMullen 4 81
(Tim Easterby) *trckd ldr: cl up on inner 3f out: rdn to chse wnr over 1f out: sn drvn and no imp* **9/2**[3]

10-0 **3** 1 3/4 **Drifting Spirit (IRE)**[37] 4105 3-9-1 **88**.... TonyHamilton 6 87
(Richard Fahey) *hld up in tch: hdwy on outer over 2f out: rdn wl over 1f out: sn drvn and kpt on same pce* **9/2**[3]

1100 **4** 9 **Cape Speed (FR)**[122] 1438 3-9-7 **94**.... JoeFanning 8 72
(Mark Johnston) *hld up: effrt and sme hdwy over 2f out: sn rdn and n.d* **15/2**

1215 **5** nk **Billy Roberts (IRE)**[57] 3389 3-8-9 **82**.... ConnorBeasley 7 59
(Richard Guest) *led: jnd and rdn along over 2f out: hdd wl over 1f out: sn drvn and wknd* **7/2**[2]

1m 43.74s (-2.16) **Going Correction** -0.20s/f (Firm) **5** Ran SP% **110.4**

Speed ratings (Par 104): **102,98,96,87,86**

CSF £8.56 TOTE £2.10: £1.30, £2.00; EX 9.50 Trifecta £26.20.

Owner Duke Of Roxburghe **Bred** Floors Farming **Trained** Middleham Moor, N Yorks

FOCUS

This was always likely to be run at a decent pace and so it proved. The runner-up sets the level.

5438 TOTEPOOLLIVEINFO.COM MAIDEN STKS 1m 4y

4:50 (4:50) (Class 4) 3-Y-O+ **£5,175** (£1,540; £769; £384) **Stalls** Low

Form RPR

23 **1** **Hilldale**[24] 4546 3-9-0 0.... PaulMulrennan 8 74
(Michael Dods) *led: pushed along wl over 1f out: sn rdn: hdd narrowly ent fnl f: rallied gamely u.p to ld again last 75yds* **5/1**[3]

3424 **2** nk **Just Hiss**[13] 4948 3-9-5 77.... DavidAllan 7 78
(Tim Easterby) *trckd ldng pair: hdwy wl over 1f out: rdn to take narrow ld ent fnl f: sn drvn: hdd and no ex last 75yds* **6/1**

3232 **3** 3 1/2 **Organza**[12] 4991 3-9-0 73.... SilvestreDeSousa 4 65
(Mick Channon) *trckd ldrs: swtchd rt to outer and hdwy 2f out: rdn over 1f out: drvn and kpt on fnl f* **5/2**[2]

6 **4** 3/4 **Come Back King (IRE)**[15] 4895 3-9-5 0.... AndrewMullen 3 68
(Michael Appleby) *chsd ldrs on inner: pushed along over 3f out: rdn 2f out: drvn and kpt on fnl f* **22/1**

3 **5** nk **Russian Finale**[21] 4690 3-9-0 0.... GrahamGibbons 9 63
(William Haggas) *prom: trckd ldr 1/2-way: cl up over 2f out: rdn to chal wl over 1f out and ev ch tl drvn appr fnl f and grad wknd* **2/1**[1]

6 3/4 **Going Up (IRE)** 3-9-5 0.... PaulHanagan 1 66
(Rae Guest) *in rr: green: pushed along and hdwy 2f out: kpt on wl fnl f: nrst fin* **7/1**

7 1/2 **Spinart** 3-9-2 0.... RobHornby[(3)] 6 65
(Pam Sly) *towards rr: pushed along over 2f out: rdn wl over 1f out: kpt on fnl f: nrst fin* **50/1**

04 **8** 1 1/4 **Old China**[15] 4895 3-9-5 0.... ConnorBeasley 2 62
(John Davies) *chsd ldrs: rdn along over 2f out: sn drvn and wknd* **33/1**

9 42 **Dark Enemy (IRE)** 3-9-5 0.... DougieCostello 5
(Brendan Powell) *towards rr: rdn along 3f out: sn outpcd and bhd fnl 2f* **25/1**

1m 44.34s (-1.56) **Going Correction** -0.20s/f (Firm) **9** Ran SP% **118.5**

Speed ratings (Par 105): **99,98,95,94,94 93,92,91,49**

CSF £34.19 TOTE £5.40: £1.70, £1.60, £1.20; EX 29.20 Trifecta £93.70.

Owner David W Armstrong **Bred** Equine Breeding Limited **Trained** Denton, Co Durham

FOCUS

A modest maiden.

5439 NOVA DISPLAY H'CAP 6f

5:20 (5:20) (Class 5) (0-75,74) 3-Y-O+ **£3,234** (£962; £481; £240) **Stalls** Low

Form RPR

0505 **1** **Gin In The Inn (IRE)**[15] 4896 3-9-5 **72**.... PaulHanagan 10 83
(Richard Fahey) *hld up in rr: gd hdwy over 1f out: rdn appr fnl f: styd on strly to ld last 100yds: sn clr* **11/2**[2]

44 **2** 2 3/4 **Van Gerwen**[48] 3716 3-9-7 **74**.... DavidAllan 1 76
(Les Eyre) *cl up on inner: slt ld over 3f out: rdn along wl over 1f out: drvn ent fnl f: hdd last 100yds* **3/1**[1]

/225 **3** nk **More Beau (USA)**[12] 4970 5-9-5 **68**.... BarryMcHugh 3 70
(David Nicholls) *midfield: hdwy 2f out: effrt and n.m.r over 1f out: sn rdn and styd on fnl f* **7/1**[3]

0000 **4** 1 1/4 **Mon Beau Visage (IRE)**[52] 3568 3-9-2 **69**.... DavidNolan 8 66
(David O'Meara) *in tch: hdwy on wd outside over 1f out: rdn to chal and hung rt ins fnl f: sn drvn and kpt on same pce* **20/1**

0300 **5** 1 **Mon Brav**[23] 4608 9-9-9 **72**.... SilvestreDeSousa 6 67+
(Brian Ellison) *hld up: hdwy over 1f out: n.m.r ent fnl f: sn rdn and styd on towards fin* **8/1**

5-06 **6** nk **Spike (IRE)**[74] 2802 3-9-5 **72**.... GrahamGibbons 4 65
(David Barron) *trckd ldrs on inner: effrt wl over 1f out: sn rdn and n.m.r ent fnl f: kpt on same pce* **7/1**[3]

3003 **7** 3 1/2 **Dominium (USA)**[39] 4014 9-9-4 **72**....(b) DavidParkes[(5)] 7 55
(Jeremy Gask) *dwlt: a towards rr* **14/1**

0140 **8** 1 3/4 **Eternitys Gate**[11] 5032 5-9-11 **74**.... RobertWinston 2 51
(Ivan Furtado) *slt ld: hdd over 3f out: cl up: rdn wl over 1f out and ev ch: sn drvn and wknd fnl f* **8/1**

0036 **9** 1/2 **Market Choice (IRE)**[24] 4547 3-9-7 **74**.... PaulMulrennan 5 49
(Michael Dods) *trckd ldrs: rdn along wl over 1f out: sn drvn and wknd* **8/1**

2002 **10** 1 1/4 **Hit The Lights (IRE)**[13] 4931 6-8-11 **67**.... DanielleMooney[(7)] 12 39
(David Nicholls) *qckly away and cl up on outer: rdn along 2f out: sn wknd* **12/1**

1m 15.58s (-1.32) **Going Correction** -0.20s/f (Firm)

WFA 3 from 5yo+ 4lb **10** Ran SP% **117.8**

Speed ratings (Par 103): **100,96,95,94,92 92,87,85,84,83**

CSF £22.61 CT £121.40 TOTE £6.30: £1.70, £1.70, £1.80; EX 28.40 Trifecta £200.50.

Owner Dean Hardman and Stella Hardman **Bred** Colman O'Flynn **Trained** Musley Bank, N Yorks

FOCUS

A run-of-the-mill sprint handicap, run at a decent tempo.

T/Jkpt: Not Won. T/Plt: £61.10 to a £1 stake. Pool: £63,031.51 - 752.89 winning units T/Qpdt: £22.10 to a £1 stake. Pool: £5,779.56 - 193.13 winning units **Joe Rowntree**

5440 - (Foreign Racing) - See Raceform Interactive

4242 DUNDALK (A.W) (L-H)

Sunday, August 14

OFFICIAL GOING: Polytrack: standard

5441a CROWNE PLAZA RACE & STAY RATED RACE 5f (P)

2:40 (2:46) 3-Y-O+ **£7,687** (£2,375; £1,125; £500; £187)

RPR

1 **Primo Uomo (IRE)**[9] 5135 4-8-11 76....(t) KillianLeonard[(7)] 1 90
(Gerard O'Leary, Ire) *chsd ldrs in 3rd: clsr over 1f out and led ent fnl f: pushed clr fnl 100yds* **2/1**[1]

2 2 1/2 **Golden Pearl**[33] 4246 3-9-8 87.... ShaneFoley 8 87
(M Halford, Ire) *chsd ldrs in 4th: rdn under 2f out: kpt on wl into 3rd ins fnl f: wnt 2nd cl home: nt rch wnr* **5/1**[3]

3 nk **Tylery Wonder (IRE)**[9] 5135 6-9-4 79....(b) BillyLee 9 80
(W McCreery, Ire) *pressed ldr tl led after 1f: hdd ent fnl f: no imp on wnr fnl 100yds and dropped to 3rd cl home* **6/1**

4 1 1/4 **Split The Atom (IRE)**[9] 5135 4-9-10 86.... ConorHoban 5 81
(David Marnane, Ire) *hld up: rdn in 6th under 2f out: kpt on ins fnl f whn short of room fnl 100yds: kpt on cl home into 4th* **7/1**

5 hd **Anonymous Lady (IRE)**[25] 4540 4-9-3 86....(t) RobbieDolan[(7)] 3 81
(Adrian Paul Keatley, Ire) *hld up: rdn in 5th appr fnl f: kpt on one pce: no imp fnl 100yds* **9/1**

6 shd **Shanghai Beauty (IRE)**[9] 5135 4-8-10 82....(tp) AndrewBreslin[(10)] 2 76
(K J Condon, Ire) *led for 1f: trckd ldr in 2nd tl 1f out: wknd ins fnl f* **8/1**

7 8 **Seychelloise**[188] 503 4-10-0 90....(b) DeclanMcDonogh 7 56
(Sir Mark Prescott Bt) *hld up: hung rt off home turn and sn rdn: no imp in rr over 1f out: eased ins fnl f* **3/1**[2]

59.0s (59.00)

WFA 3 from 4yo+ 3lb **7** Ran SP% **122.9**

CSF £13.89 TOTE £3.30: £1.60, £2.30; DF 16.30 Trifecta £96.10.

Owner Lance Bloodstock Limited **Bred** D J Sweeney **Trained** Kildare, Co. Kildare

■ Lady Mega was withdrawn. Price at time of withdrawal 7/2. Rule 4 applies to bets struck prior to withdrawal but not to SP bets. Deduct 20 cent in the euro.

FOCUS
Competitive stuff for this sprint, though it was weakened somewhat by the withdrawal of second-favourite Lady Mega, who got loose from the stalls. They went a good pace and the winner came down the middle.

5442 - 5446a (Foreign Racing) - See Raceform Interactive

[5460]DEAUVILLE (R-H)
Sunday, August 14

OFFICIAL GOING: Turf: good; polytrack: standard

5447a PRIX DE L'AUGERON (CONDITIONS) (2YO) (POLYTRACK) 7f 110y
1:05 (12:00) 2-Y-O **£12,500** (£5,000; £3,750; £2,500; £1,250)

RPR

1 **Toulifaut (IRE)**[36] 2-8-10 0 ...... ChristopheSoumillon 2 85
(J-C Rouget, France) **1/2**[1]

2 2 **Dolokhov**[9] 5141 2-8-9 0 ...... (p) TonyPiccone 6 79
(J S Moore) *chsd ldr: rdn to chal fr 2f out: led appr 1 1/2f out: styd on and edgd lft u.p ins fnl f: hdd 75yds out: no ex* **19/1**

3 1½ **Barbarigo (IRE)**[35] 4183 2-8-4 0 ...... NicolasLarenaudie(5) 5 75
(F Chappet, France) **13/1**[3]

4 ¾ **Admiralty Arch**[31] 4330 2-9-0 0 ...... MickaelBarzalona 1 79
(Richard Hannon) *chsd ldrs on inner: rdn and nt qckn fr 1 1/2f out: one pce fnl f* **19/10**[2]

5 2½ **Elfy James (FR)**[5] 5279 2-8-4 0 ...... HugoJourniac(2) 3 65
(D Windrif, France) **20/1**

6 3½ **Quandary Peak**[15] 4902 2-8-10 0 ...... IoritzMendizabal 4 61
(J S Moore) *led: hdd appr 1 1/2f out: sn outpcd by ldrs: fdd ins fnl f* **21/1**

WIN (incl. 1 euro stake): 1.50. PLACES: 1.10, 2.90. SF: 14.10
Owner Andrew-James Smith **Bred** Barronstown Stud **Trained** Pau, France

5448a PRIX MICHEL HOUYVET (LISTED RACE) (3YO) (TURF) 1m 7f
1:35 (12:00) 3-Y-O **£20,220** (£8,088; £6,066; £4,044; £2,022)

RPR

1 **Cleonte (IRE)**[23] 3-8-11 0 ...... Pierre-CharlesBoudot 4 98+
(A Fabre, France) **23/10**[1]

2 2½ **Marmelo**[44] 3845 3-8-11 0 ...... UmbertoRispoli 1 95
(Hughie Morrison) *dwlt: shkn up and sn chsng ldr: rdn along to press ldr fr 3f out: hrd rdn 1 1/2f out: styd on fnl f: nt pce of wnr* **57/10**

3 snk **Peribsen (IRE)**[59] 3-8-11 0 ...... AurelienLemaitre 2 95
(F Head, France) **43/5**

4 hd **Mint Julep (FR)**[24] 3-8-8 0 ...... MaximeGuyon 6 92
(F-H Graffard, France) **22/1**

5 ½ **Magnentius (FR)**[22] 3-8-11 0 ...... CristianDemuro 7 94
(Rod Collet, France) **11/1**

6 5 **Shalakar (FR)**[32] 4285 3-8-11 0 ...... ChristopheSoumillon 5 88
(M Delzangles, France) **13/5**[2]

7 12 **Fixed Rate**[10] 3-8-11 0 ...... VincentCheminaud 3 74
(D Smaga, France) **16/5**[3]

3m 16.03s (-3.07) **Going Correction** 0.0s/f (Good) 7 Ran SP% **119.9**
Speed ratings: **108,106,106,106,106 103,97**
WIN (incl. 1 euro stake): 3.30. PLACES: 1.70, 2.20. SF: 13.70.
Owner Baron Edouard De Rothschild **Bred** Sc Ecurie De Meautry **Trained** Chantilly, France

5449a PRIX DU HARAS DE FRESNAY-LE-BUFFARD - JACQUES LE MAROIS (GROUP 1) (3YO+ NO GELDINGS) (STR) (TURF) 1m (R)
2:55 (12:00) 3-Y-O+ **£294,102** (£117,661; £58,830; £29,389; £14,720)

RPR

1 **Ribchester (IRE)**[18] 4754 3-8-13 0 ...... WilliamBuick 2 123
(Richard Fahey) *w.w in midfield: clsd to chse ldrs 1 1/2f out: rdn and sustained run to ld fnl 120yds: drvn out: readily* **11/4**[2]

2 ½ **Vadamos (FR)**[28] 4441 5-9-5 0 ...... VincentCheminaud 8 122
(A Fabre, France) *w.w towards rr: clsd into midfield bef 1/2-way: pressed ldrs 2f out: rdn and led under 1 1/2f out: styd on u.p: hdd fnl 120yds: no ex* **5/1**[3]

3 1¾ **Ervedya (FR)**[61] 3242 4-9-2 0 ...... ChristopheSoumillon 4 115
(J-C Rouget, France) *w.w in fnl trio: tk clsr order fr 3f out: 6th and clsng 1 1/2f out: styd on fnl f: nt pce to get on terms* **15/2**

4 nse **Spectre (FR)**[35] 4185 3-8-9 0 ...... CristianDemuro 7 114
(M Munch, Germany) *w.w in rr: clsd sn after 1/2-way: 5th and rdn 1 1/2f out: styd on fnl f: nvr able to chal* **40/1**

5 nk **Dicton**[70] 2946 3-8-13 0 ...... OlivierPeslier 3 117
(Gianluca Bietolini, Italy) *w.w in fnl trio: hdwy on outer 2f out: sn rdn: styd on wl fnl f: nrest at fin* **33/1**

6 nk **Esoterique (IRE)**[14] 4926 6-9-2 0 ...... Pierre-CharlesBoudot 5 113
(A Fabre, France) *settled in midfield: sltly outpcd and scrubbed along in fnl trio appr 2f out: styd on fr wl over 1f out: run flattened out last 75yds: nvr in contention* **14/1**

7 nse **Stormy Antarctic**[35] 4185 3-8-13 0 ...... AndreaAtzeni 11 116
(Ed Walker) *propped sltly leaving stalls: hld up bhd ldrs: 7th and rdn 2f out: kpt on at same pce fnl f* **25/1**

8 nk **Galileo Gold**[18] 4754 3-8-13 0 ...... FrankieDettori 10 116
(Hugo Palmer) *tk v t.k.h: led after 1f: hdd bef 1/2-way and chsd ldr: rdn and led again briefly 1 1/2f out: sn hdd: fdd ins fnl f* **11/8**[1]

9 snk **Lightning Spear**[18] 4754 5-9-5 0 ...... OisinMurphy 9 115
(David Simcock) *t.k.h: hld up in midfield: towards rr bef 1/2-way: rdn and no real imp over 1 1/2f out: kpt on at one pce* **18/1**

10 2 **Arod (IRE)**[36] 4151 5-9-5 0 ...... (p) JamieSpencer 1 111
(Peter Chapple-Hyam) *broke wl and led: hdd after 1f: cl up and led gain bef 1/2-way: hdd 1 1/2f out: sn dropped away and eased* **33/1**

11 5 **Grand Vintage (FR)**[81] 2603 7-9-5 0 ...... MickaelForest 6 99
(Carina Fey, France) *cl up: lost pl after 1/2-way: sn btn* **100/1**

1m 36.16s (-4.64) **Going Correction** -0.225s/f (Firm)
WFA 3 from 4yo+ 7lb 11 Ran SP% **122.3**
Speed ratings: **114,113,111,111,111 111,111,110,110,108 103**
WIN (incl. 1 euro stake): 4.70. PLACES: 1.90, 2.30, 2.00. DF: 16.60. SF: 35.30.
Owner Godolphin **Bred** A Thompson & M O'Brien **Trained** Musley Bank, N Yorks

FOCUS
A really good renewal of this top 1m contest. The pace looked fair if unspectacular, but those that raced close up from at least halfway seemed favoured. There looks to be even more to come from the winner.

5450a PRIX FRANCOIS BOUTIN (LISTED RACE) (2YO) (STRAIGHT) (TURF) 7f
3:30 (12:00) 2-Y-O **£20,220** (£8,088; £6,066; £4,044; £2,022)

RPR

1 **Xaarino (FR)**[35] 2-9-2 0 ...... MickaelBarzalona 6 103
(A Fabre, France) **9/5**[1]

2 ¾ **Medieval (IRE)**[19] 4732 2-9-2 0 ...... (b[1]) JamieSpencer 4 101
(Paul Cole) *chsd ldr: shkn up and qcknd to ld 1f out: sn hrd pressed: hdd fnl 100yds: no ex* **14/5**[2]

3 2½ **Red Onion**[23] 4620 2-9-2 0 ...... ThierryThulliez 2 94
(C Lerner, France) **38/1**

4 nse **Euginio (IRE)**[48] 3730 2-9-2 0 ...... StephanePasquier 5 94
(Richard Hannon) *settled in share of 3rd: rdn and no immediate imp fr 2 1/2f out: kpt on at same pce fnl f* **16/5**[3]

5 nk **Erica Bing**[15] 4902 2-8-13 0 ...... UmbertoRispoli 3 90
(Jo Hughes) *led: sn 2 l clr: rdn along 2f out: hdd 1f out: sn btn* **22/1**

6 1½ **Phoceen (FR)**[44] 3871 2-9-2 0 ...... Pierre-CharlesBoudot 1 89
(F Chappet, France) **19/1**

1m 26.32s (-1.98) **Going Correction** -0.225s/f (Firm) 6 Ran SP% **97.8**
Speed ratings: **102,101,98,98,97 96**
WIN (incl. 1 euro stake): 2.80. PLACES: 1.40, 2.10. SF: 8.10.
Owner HRH Prince Faisal Bin Khaled **Bred** Guy Pariente Holding **Trained** Chantilly, France

5451a PRIX MINERVE (GROUP 3) (3YO FILLIES) (TURF) 1m 4f 110y
4:10 (12:00) 3-Y-O **£29,411** (£11,764; £8,823; £5,882; £2,941)

RPR

1 **Golden Valentine (FR)**[31] 4331 3-8-9 0 ...... AurelienLemaitre 9 105
(F Head, France) *w.w in rr: stdy hdwy on outer 2f out: rdn to ld 1f out: styd on wl to assert fnl 100yds* **11/4**[2]

2 1½ **The Juliet Rose (FR)**[56] 3452 3-9-0 0 ...... StephanePasquier 1 108
(N Clement, France) *a cl up: chsd ldr: rdn and wandered briefly 1 1/2f out: styd on to chal 1f out: kpt on gamely but nt match pce of wnr* **4/1**[3]

3 snk **Sotteville (FR)**[58] 3379 3-8-9 0 ...... CristianDemuro 6 103
(J-C Rouget, France) *settled in midfield on outer: clsd to chse ldr bef 1/2-way: 3rd and rdn 2 1/2f out: edgd lft u.p under 1 1/2f out: styd on to chal 1f out: nt pce of wnr fnl f* **8/1**

4 ¾ **Do Re Mi Fa Sol (FR)**[42] 3935 3-8-9 0 ...... FranckBlondel 7 102
(P Decouz, France) *w.w in fnl trio: tk clsr order fr 2 1/2f out: rdn whn sltly impeded ins fnl 1 1/2f and dropped to last but wl in tch: styd on u.p fnl f* **9/1**

5 ½ **Pakora (FR)**[19] 3-8-9 0 ...... MaximeGuyon 4 101
(P Sogorb, France) *hld up in tch: drvn to chal between horses 1 1/2f out: one pce u.p fnl f: lost 4th cl home* **22/1**

6 nk **Deremah (USA)**[74] 3-8-9 0 ...... ChristopheSoumillon 2 100
(A De Royer-Dupre, France) *settled in fnl 3rd: rdn to chse ldng gp wl over 1 1/2f out: one pce fnl f* **2/1**[1]

7 ½ **Impressionist (IRE)**[42] 3935 3-8-9 0 ...... Pierre-CharlesBoudot 8 99
(A Fabre, France) *hld up in fnl pair: rdn and effrt 2f out: sn no further imp: plugged on late but nvr in contention* **15/2**

8 1 **Son Macia (GER)**[36] 4175 3-8-9 0 ...... IoritzMendizabal 3 98
(Andreas Lowe, Germany) *w.w in midfield on inner: tk clsr order bef 1/2-way: 4th and scrubbed along 3f out: grad lft bhd fnl f* **20/1**

9 hd **Khaleesy (IRE)**[20] 4723 3-8-9 0 ...... Francois-XavierBertras 5 98
(F Rohaut, France) *led: rdn whn hrd pressed fr all sides 1 1/2f out: hdd 1f out: sn btn* **20/1**

2m 44.7s (-1.70) **Going Correction** 0.0s/f (Good) 9 Ran SP% **126.7**
Speed ratings: **105,104,103,103,103 103,102,102,101**
WIN (incl. 1 euro stake): 3.80. PLACES: 1.80, 2.00, 2.30. DF: 9.60. SF: 16.80.
Owner LNJ Foxwoods **Bred** Foxwood Stables **Trained** France

5452a PRIX DE PRE-EN-PAIL (CLAIMER) (4YO+) (POLYTRACK) 1m 1f 110y
4:50 (12:00) 4-Y-O+ **£5,882** (£2,352; £1,764; £1,176; £588)

RPR

1 **L'Ardent (FR)**[14] 4927 5-9-4 0 ...... ChristopheSoumillon 1 65
(J-C Rouget, France) **12/5**[1]

2 nk **Babel Ouest (FR)**[126] 8-9-2 0 ...... AurelienLemaitre 7 63
(W Mongil, Germany) **79/10**

3 ¾ **Yankee Mail (FR)**[15] 4901 4-9-5 0 ...... (p) Pierre-CharlesBoudot 8 64
(Gay Kelleway) *dwlt sltly: hld up in rr of main gp: rdn and hdwy on inner 2f out: styd on u.p fnl f: jst hld on to 3rd* **10/1**

4 nse **Steel Blade (GER)**[96] 7-9-4 0 ...... StephanePasquier 12 63
(H Blume, Germany) **32/5**[2]

5 snk **Claudia Octavia**[365] 5-9-5 0 ...... (p) AntoineHamelin 10 64
(Werner Glanz, Germany) **12/1**

6 hd **Rethra (IRE)**[257] 4-8-7 0 ...... (p) MlleIsisMagnin(8) 3 59
(J-P Gauvin, France) **18/1**

7 shd **Volpe Fiona (GER)**[14] 5-8-3 0 ...... KyllanBarbaud(5) 2 52
(M Munch, Germany) **36/1**

8 nk **Arizona (GER)**[230] 4-8-9 0 ...... HugoJourniac(4) 11 56
(Waldemar Hickst, Germany) **69/10**[3]

9 1¼ **Hokulaya (FR)**[242] 5-8-8 0 ...... TonyPiccone 14 49
(A Kleinkorres, Germany) **39/1**

10 shd **Albert Hall (USA)**[401] 11-8-11 0 ...... TeddySoulat 4 52
(A Chaille-Chaille, France) **69/10**[3]

11 ¾ **Shakko (FR)**[32] 6-9-5 0 ...... (b) MlleJessicaMarcialis 9 58
(Charley Rossi, France) **56/1**

12 2½ **Imago Live (IRE)**[1785] 8-9-5 0 ...... (p) UmbertoRispoli 6 53
(N Minner, Belgium) **41/1**

13 3 **Lykastos (IRE)**[74] 2806 6-9-4 0 ...... DelphineSantiago 13 46
(Mlle K Hoste, Belgium) **16/1**

14 15 **Falco Junior (FR)**[466] 2012 6-9-4 0 ...... MickaelBarzalona 5 15
(Charley Rossi, France) **30/1**

WIN (incl. 1 euro stake): 3.70. PLACES: 1.50, 2.60, 2.70. DF: 12.10. SF: 15.10
Owner Bernard Magrez Horses **Bred** F Bayrou **Trained** Pau, France

5453 - (Foreign Racing) - See Raceform Interactive

3207 HOPPEGARTEN (R-H)

Sunday, August 14

OFFICIAL GOING: Turf: good

5454a 126 LONGINES GROSSER PREIS VON BERLIN (GROUP 1) (3YO+) (TURF) 1m 4f

3:40 (12:00) 3-Y-O+ **£80,882** (£29,411; £11,029; £7,352)

RPR

1 **Protectionist (GER)**[42] 3934 6-9-6 0 .... EduardoPedroza 2 116+
(A Wohler, Germany) *mde all: led under a tight hold: qcknd tempo over 2 1/2f out: rdn whn pressed 2f out: styd on strly fnl 1 1/2f: won easing down* **2/5**[1]

2 *2 1/2* **Nightflower (IRE)**[43] 3888 4-9-3 0 .... AndraschStarke 4 107
(P Schiergen, Germany) *w.w in rr: tk clsr order after 1/2-way: chsd ldr on outer 2 1/2f out: tried to chal 2f out: no match for wnr fnl 1 1/2f* **18/5**[2]

3 *1 1/4* **Guignol (GER)**[42] 3934 4-9-6 0 .... FilipMinarik 5 108
(Jean-Pierre Carvalho, Germany) *t.k.h: a cl up: chsd ldr on inner fr 2 1/2f out: styd on at same pce* **9/1**

4 *2 1/4* **Shivajia (GER)**[98] 2075 4-9-3 0 .... MichaelCadeddu 6 101
(U Stech, Germany) *hld up in fnl pair: styd on fnl 1 1/2f: nvr trbld ldrs* **18/1**

5 *1/2* **Caccini (FR)**[42] 3-8-9 0 .... TomLukasek 1 104
(Adam Wyrzyk, Poland) *t.k.h: cl up on inner: lost pl 2 1/2f out: grad lft bhd* **42/10**[3]

6 *3 1/2* **Amona (IRE)**[21] 4696 4-9-3 0 .... AlexanderPietsch 3 95
(Andreas Lowe, Germany) *chsd ldng trio: lost pl 3f out: nvr seen w a ch* **171/10**

2m 41.1s (11.80)
WFA 3 from 4yo+ 11lb **6** Ran SP% **133.2**
WIN (incl. 10 euro stake): 14. PLACES: 12, 16. SF: 30.
Owner Australian Bloodstock Stable **Bred** Dr Christoph Berglar **Trained** Germany

4698 LES LANDES

Sunday, August 14

OFFICIAL GOING: Turf: good (good to firm in places)

Wind: Light, across away from stands Weather: Fine and warm

5456a LADBROKES GRID PRICE SURGE H'CAP 7f

3:05 (3:06) 3-Y-O+ **£1,780** (£860; £380)

RPR

1 **Swiss Cross**[23] 4593 9-10-12 0 ....(t) TimClark 4 70
(Phil McEntee) *mde all: c to stands' rail ent st: clr over 1f out: comf* **13/8**[1]

2 *6* **First Cat**[21] 9-9-6 0 .... PhilipPrince 1 34
(K Kukk, Jersey) *trckd ldrs: hrd rdn over 1f out: hung lft: one pce* **9/4**[2]

3 *1/2* **Pas D'Action**[21] 8-10-8 0 ....(p) JemmaMarshall 2 49
(Mrs A Malzard, Jersey) *hld up in 4th: effrt on inner and chal 2f out: one pce* **3/1**[3]

4 *1 1/2* **Chapeau Bleu (IRE)**[21] 4-10-8 0 .... AliceMills 5 45
(Mrs C Gilbert, Jersey) *chsd wnr tl 2f out: no ex over 1f out* **3/1**[3]

5 *2 1/2* **Spanish Bounty**[21] 11-10-1 0 .... MattieBatchelor 3 31
(Mrs A Malzard, Jersey) *hld up in 5th: effrt over 2f out: wknd over 1f out* **9/1**

Owner Steve Jakes **Bred** Lordship Stud **Trained** Newmarket, Suffolk

5457a COUTTS H'CAP 1m 100y

3:40 (3:39) (0-55,0) 3-Y-O+ **£2,380** (£860; £415)

RPR

1 **Mendacious Harpy (IRE)**[25] 4516 5-10-12 0 ....(p) MattieBatchelor 3 57
(George Baker) *hld up in rr: gd hdwy to ld over 1f out: rdn clr* **6/4**[1]

2 *4* **Too Many Diamonds (IRE)**[23] 7273 5-10-3 0 ....(tp) PaddyPilley 1 39
(Clare Ellam) *in tch: effrt over 2f out: styd on to take 2nd nr fin* **4/1**[3]

3 *1/2* **Fast Freddie**[21] 12-9-0 0 ....(p) NoraLooby 4 21
(Mrs A Corson, Jersey) *led tl over 1f out: kpt on same pce* **10/1**

4 *1 1/2* **Brown Velvet**[21] 4-10-6 0 ....(p) PhilipPrince 7 38
(K Kukk, Jersey) *sn chsng ldr: hrd rdn and no ex over 1f out* **13/2**

5 *5* **Ocean Crystal**[21] 4-10-1 0 .... MrFTett 6 22
(Mrs A Malzard, Jersey) *hld up in 5th: outpcd over 3f out: sn btn* **7/1**

6 *nk* **Larch (IRE)**[21] 4-9-11 0 .... JemmaMarshall 5 17
(Mrs A Malzard, Jersey) *a abt same pl: nvr able to chal* **11/2**

7 *7* **Grey Panel (FR)**[21] 8-10-5 0 .... TimClark 2 10
(T Le Brocq, Jersey) *prom tl hrd rdn and wknd over 1f out* **3/1**[2]

Owner On The Game Partnership **Bred** Val & Angela Leeson **Trained** Manton, Wilts

5458a LADBROKES LADIES DAY H'CAP 1m 2f

4:15 (4:14) 3-Y-O+ **£1,780** (£640; £380)

RPR

1 **Flutterbee**[26] 4482 4-10-12 0 ....(p) MattieBatchelor 7 69
(George Baker) *trckd ldrs: led 4f out: sn qcknd clr: rdn out* **8/11**[1]

2 *4* **Captain James (FR)**[21] 6-8-9 0 .... AliceMills 3 30
(Mrs C Gilbert, Jersey) *hld up towards rr: styd on to chse wnr over 1f out: no imp* **4/1**[3]

3 *8* **Lady Petrus**[21] 11-8-8 0 oh10 ow3 ....(p) PhilipPrince 5 13
(K Kukk, Jersey) *outpcd and bhd tl styd on u.p fnl 2f* **14/1**

4 *1* **Spring Dixie (IRE)**[21] 4-9-9 0 .... MrFTett 1 26
(Mrs A Malzard, Jersey) *chsd ldr: led 5f out tl 4f out: lost 2nd and wknd over 1f out* **9/1**

5 *20* **Benoordenhout (IRE)**[21] 4698 5-10-8 0 .... TimClark 4
(T Le Brocq, Jersey) *prom tl lost pl 5f out* **2/1**[2]

6 *1 1/2* **Frankki M**[21] 3917 6-8-5 0 oh15 .... NoraLooby 2
(Mrs A Corson, Jersey) *in tch: outpcd 3f out: grad fdd* **22/1**

7 *8* **Engaging Smile**[21] 4-10-0 0 .... RichardHodson 8
(J Moon, Jersey) *led tl 5f out: sn lost pl* **9/1**

8 *1* **Rebel Woman**[21] 10-8-5 0 oh17 ....(p) MissMHooper 6
(Mrs A Corson, Jersey) *a bhd* **20/1**

Owner PJL Racing **Bred** Mill House Stud **Trained** Manton, Wilts

5459a LADBROKES BEST ODDS GUARANTEED H'CAP 1m 4f

4:50 (4:51) 3-Y-O+ **£1,780** (£640; £380)

RPR

1 **River Du Nord (FR)**[107] 1830 9-8-5 0 oh1 .... JemmaMarshall 2 40
(Sue Gardner) *hld up in rr: stdy hdwy fr 5f out: squeezed through and led wl over 1f out: drvn ahd fnl 50yds* **5/1**[3]

2 *1/2* **Aussie Lyrics (FR)**[21] 4698 6-10-12 0 ....(b) MarcGoldstein 5 74
(Mrs C Gilbert, Jersey) *trckd ldrs gng wl: pressed wnr over 1f out: shkn up and drew level: hrd rdn and unable qck fnl 50yds* **4/5**[1]

3 *8* **King Kenny**[21] 11-8-8 0 .... NoraLooby 4 29
(Mrs A Corson, Jersey) *in tch: effrt and brought wd into st: one pce* **5/1**[3]

4 *4* **Candelita**[21] 8003 9-8-8 0 ....(p) PaddyPilley 3 23
(Clare Ellam) *led tl 3f out: w ldrs tl wknd wl over 1f out* **9/1**

5 *nk* **Mr Opulence**[21] 7-9-11 0 .... TimClark 7 40
(T Le Brocq, Jersey) *hld up in 6th: rdn and wknd 3f out* **7/4**[2]

6 *5 1/2* **Bowl Imperior**[21] 4698 4-9-10 0 .... MattieBatchelor 1 30
(Mrs A Malzard, Jersey) *pressed ldr: slt ld 3f out tl wknd wl over 1f out* **8/1**

7 *30* **Blue Sea Of Ibrox (IRE)**[21] 4698 8-10-7 0 ....(p) MrFTett 6
(Mrs A Corson, Jersey) *chsd ldrs: wknd 6f out: wl bhd fnl 4f* **8/1**

Owner Miss Jane Edgar **Bred** Mrs Jane Edgar & John Mercier **Trained** Longdown, Devon

5347 DEAUVILLE (R-H)

Saturday, August 13

OFFICIAL GOING: Turf: good; polytrack: standard

5460a FEE - PRIX SHADWELL FARM (MAIDEN) (UNRACED 2YO FILLIES) (POLYTRACK) 6f 110y

1:35 (12:00) 2-Y-O **£9,191** (£3,676; £2,757; £1,838; £919)

RPR

1 **Kestila** 2-9-0 0 .... ChristopheSoumillon 2 80
(J-C Rouget, France) **17/10**[1]

2 *2* **Angel Baby (FR)** 2-8-8 0 .... HugoJourniac(6) 7 74
(J-C Rouget, France) **7/1**

3 *3* **Grande Bleue (IRE)** 2-9-0 0 .... MaximeGuyon 1 66
(C Laffon-Parias, France) **19/10**[2]

4 *1 1/4* **Key Success (IRE)** 2-9-0 0 .... GregoryBenoist 3 63
(Y Barberot, France) **30/1**

5 *3* **So You Go (IRE)** 2-9-0 0 .... Pierre-CharlesBoudot 6 54
(Mme C Head-Maarek, France) **15/2**

6 *nk* **Mary Arden (FR)** 2-9-0 0 .... CristianDemuro 8 53
(P Bary, France) **69/10**[3]

7 *8* **Wind In The Trees (FR)** 2-9-0 0 ....(p) UmbertoRispoli 5 31
(George Baker) *pushed along early: settled towards rr on outer: pushed along 3f out: outpcd and wl bhd 2f out: eased fnl f* **23/1**

Owner H H Aga Khan **Bred** H H The Aga Khan's Studs S C **Trained** Pau, France [overprinted] SF: 9.80

5461a SHADWELL PRIX DE POMONE (GROUP 2) (3YO+ FILLIES & MARES) (TURF) 1m 4f 110y

3:55 (12:00) 3-Y-O+ **£54,485** (£21,029; £10,036; £6,691; £3,345)

RPR

1 **Highlands Queen (FR)**[55] 3452 3-8-7 0 .... StephanePasquier 4 111+
(Y Gourraud, France) *settled towards rr: pushed along over 2f out: picked up wl to ld ent fnl f: sn wnt clr: impressive* **5/2**[2]

2 *2 1/2* **Mango Tango (FR)**[41] 3935 3-8-7 0 .... LouisBeuzelin 6 106
(P Bary, France) *midfield: cl 3rd 5f out: chal u.str ride fr 2f out: led briefly jst over 1f out: no ch w wnr fnl f* **10/1**

3 *2* **Contribution**[20] 4696 4-9-5 0 .... VincentCheminaud 7 103
(A Fabre, France) *settled in rr: stl last whn effrt fr 3f out: c to chal 1 1/2f out but no ch w ldrs fnl f: kpt on wl for cl 3rd* **15/2**

4 *1/2* **Mambomiss (FR)**[51] 5-9-5 0 .... FranckBlondel 1 102
(D De Watrigant, France) *settled towards rr: effrt fr 3f out: chal and led narrowly fr 2f out to jst over 1f out: no ch w ldrs fnl f* **20/1**

5 *3/4* **Gargotiere (FR)**[30] 4331 3-8-7 0 .... AlexisBadel 3 101
(H-F Devin, France) *led after 2f: hdd after 5f: disp ld 2f out: unable to go w ldrs* **14/1**

6 *1* **Forever Popular (USA)**[28] 4400 4-9-5 0 ....(p) ChristopheSoumillon 5 99
(William Haggas) *led after 100yds: hdd and settled in 2nd after 2f: regained ld after 5f: hdd 2f out: sn btn* **3/1**[3]

7 *8* **Al Wathna**[41] 3935 3-8-11 0 .... GregoryBenoist 2 90
(J-C Rouget, France) *broke wl to ld early: hdd after 100yds and settled bhd ldrs: rdn along over 2f out but unable qck: eased fnl f* **7/4**[1]

2m 45.57s (-0.83)
WFA 3 from 4yo+ 11lb **7** Ran SP% **122.2**
WIN (incl. 1 euro stake): 3.70. PLACES: 2.10, 2.50. SF: 16.30.
Owner Mme N Kerjean & S Kumin **Bred** S.C.E.A. Domaine De L'Argos **Trained** France

5221 AYR (L-H)

Monday, August 15

5462 Meeting Abandoned - Waterlogged

5188 CHELMSFORD (A.W) (L-H)

Monday, August 15

OFFICIAL GOING: Polytrack: standard

Wind: Light, across Weather: Sunny and warm

5469 JOOLS HOLLAND HERE ON SATURDAY MAIDEN FILLIES' STKS (PLUS 10 RACE) 6f (P)

2:00 (2:00) (Class 4) 2-Y-O **£6,469** (£1,925; £962; £481) **Stalls** Centre

Form RPR

42 1 **Bee Case**[14] 4951 2-9-0 0 .... JimCrowley 9 83
(Hugo Palmer) *chsd ldr: rdn to ld ent fnl f: edgd lft but gng clr jst ins fnl f: r.o wl: eased towards fin* **4/1**[3]

30 **2** 2 1/4 **Queensbrydge**[14] 4951 2-9-0 0 AdrianMcCarthy 2 76
(Robyn Brisland) *hld up in tch in midfield: effrt to chse clr ldng and swtchd rt over 1f out: styd on wl to chse wnr wl ins fnl f: no threat to wnr but keeping on wl at fin* **14/1**

3 1 1/2 **Muthmira** 2-9-0 0 SilvestreDeSousa 7 75+
(Simon Crisford) *v.s.a: detached in last tl clsd on to bk of field after 2f: swtchd lft and hdwy over 1f out: wnt 3rd wl ins fnl f: styd on wl but nvr a threat to wnr: eased cl home* **5/2**[1]

2 **4** 3 **Prufrock (IRE)**[19] 4759 2-9-0 0 JamieSpencer 1 62
(David Simcock) *hld up in tch towards rr of main gp: nt clr run 2f out tl over 1f out: pushed along and hdwy ent fnl f: n.d but styd on steadily ins fnl f* **3/1**[2]

0 **5** nk **Believable**[39] 4063 2-9-0 0 TedDurcan 6 61
(Sir Michael Stoute) *wl in tch in midfield: rdn and unable qck over 2f out: wl hld and plugged on same pce fr over 1f out* **3/1**[2]

35 **6** 1 **Apamurra (USA)**[66] 3106 2-9-0 0 RichardKingscote 11 57
(Mark Johnston) *led: rdn over 1f out: hdd ent fnl f: sn outpcd: wknd fnl 100yds* **12/1**

60 **7** 1 1/4 **Newz Watch**[25] 4558 2-9-0 0 WilliamCarson 4 53
(Mick Quinn) *chsd ldng pair: rdn and unable qck over 2f out: wl hld over 1f out: wknd ins fnl f* **100/1**

6 **8** 3/4 **Sandwood Bay**[67] 3073 2-9-0 0 DarryllHolland 3 51
(Mark H Tompkins) *t.k.h: hld up in tch in midfield: rdn over 2f out: sn outpcd: wknd over 1f out* **50/1**

9 3 **Oudwood** 2-8-11 0 MarcMonaghan(3) 8 41
(Hugo Palmer) *t.k.h: hld up in tch in midfield but stuck wd: rdn and lost pl over 1f out: sn btn: bhd ins fnl f* **33/1**

10 9 **Tilly Devine** 2-9-0 0 MartinLane 5 13
(Scott Dixon) *rn green: sn outpcd in rr and rdn along: lost tch 2f out* **66/1**

1m 13.92s (0.22) **Going Correction** +0.075s/f (Slow) **10** Ran SP% **120.3**
Speed ratings (Par 93): **101,98,96,92,91 90,88,87,83,71**
CSF £58.23 TOTE £4.60: £1.50, £4.00, £1.30; EX 42.50 Trifecta £275.50.
Owner K Abdullah **Bred** Millsec Limited **Trained** Newmarket, Suffolk

FOCUS
A modest 2yo fillies' maiden. The winner stepped up on her previous form.

5470 BOMBAY SAPPHIRE PREMIUM GIN H'CAP 5f (P)
2:30 (2:30) (Class 6) (0-65,64) 3-Y-O+ **£3,234** (£962; £481; £240) **Stalls** Low

Form RPR

000 **1** **Red Invader (IRE)**[55] 3494 6-9-7 **61** WilliamCarson 6 71
(Paul D'Arcy) *chsd ldrs: effrt wl over 1f out: hdwy u.p to ld and hung lft ent fnl f: styd on: rdn out* **9/1**

2226 **2** 1/2 **Jack The Laird (IRE)**[8] 5200 3-9-7 **64** (b) RobertWinston 1 71
(Dean Ivory) *sn led: rdn over 1f out: hdd ent fnl f: sltly hmpd and swtchd rt ins fnl f: rallied towards fin but a hld* **6/4**[1]

0555 **3** 4 **Strictly Carter**[41] 3970 3-8-13 **56** (p) JimCrowley 3 49
(Alan Bailey) *pressed ldr: rdn and unable qck over 1f out: 3rd and outpcd 1f out: wknd ins fnl f* **7/2**[2]

2503 **4** 1/2 **K'Gari Spirit**[13] 4980 3-9-2 **59** (t) NickyMackay 7 50
(Jeremy Gask) *s.i.s and swtchd lft after s: hld up in tch in last pair: effrt on inner over 1f out: 4th and no imp 1f out: wl hld and plugged on same pce after* **8/1**

0554 **5** nk **Justice Rock**[12] 5041 3-8-6 **52** JosephineGordon(3) 2 42
(Phil McEntee) *chsd ldrs: rdn over 2f out: drvn and outpcd whn swtchd rt jst over 1f out: wl hld and plugged on same pce ins fnl f* **6/1**[3]

5002 **6** 3 1/2 **Give Us A Belle (IRE)**[4] 5335 7-8-8 **55** (p) RPWalsh(7) 5 33
(Christine Dunnett) *hld up in tch: rdn 2f out: sn swtchd rt and outpcd u.p: wknd 1f out* **12/1**

333- **7** 3 1/2 **Wimboldsley**[263] 7995 5-8-10 **50** MartinLane 4 16
(Scott Dixon) *half-rrd as stalls opened and s.i.s: t.k.h: hld up in tch towards rr: effrt on outer 1/2-way: wknd 1f out* **9/1**

1m 0.36s (0.16) **Going Correction** +0.075s/f (Slow)
WFA 3 from 5yo+ 3lb **7** Ran SP% **115.3**
Speed ratings (Par 101): **101,100,93,93,92 86,81**
CSF £23.45 CT £58.19 TOTE £10.20: £3.70, £1.20; EX 24.90 Trifecta £116.80.
Owner C M Wilson **Bred** Tally-Ho Stud **Trained** Newmarket, Suffolk

FOCUS
A moderate sprint handicap. The winner is entitled to rate this high.

5471 COCA COLA ZERO H'CAP 1m 2f (P)
3:00 (3:01) (Class 5) (0-70,70) 3-Y-O+ **£4,528** (£1,347; £673; £336) **Stalls** Low

Form RPR

050 **1** **Intercepted**[18] 4792 3-9-5 **70** GeorgeBaker 6 82+
(David Lanigan) *s.i.s: niggled along early and off the pce in last trio: clsd and in tch 4f out: rdn and switching rt ent fnl 2f: hdwy to chse ldrs 1f out: styd on to ld wl ins fnl f: sn in command* **15/8**[1]

30-0 **2** 1 1/2 **Dream Ruler**[26] 4531 5-9-4 **65** (tp) DavidParkes(5) 3 71
(Jeremy Gask) *chsd ldrs: clsd to trck ldr and nt clr run over 2f out: rdn and ev ch over 1f out: chsd wnr and kpt on same pce ins fnl f* **20/1**

2223 **3** 1 **Santiburi Spring**[80] 2652 3-9-0 **65** KierenFox 5 69
(John Best) *chsd ldrs: jnd ldr and travelling strly over 2f out: rdn to ld over 1f out: hrd drvn ins fnl f: hdd wl ins fnl f: sn btn* **3/1**[2]

2034 **4** 5 **Sky Of Stars (IRE)**[26] 4530 3-9-5 **70** (v) SilvestreDeSousa 8 64
(William Knight) *sn dropped to rr and nt travelling wl in rr: reminders over 6f out: clsd and in tch 4f out: effrt wd 2f out: no imp over 1f out: hung lft and plugged on same pce fnl f* **5/1**[3]

040 **5** 3/4 **Tyrsal (IRE)**[40] 4013 5-9-4 **60** DarryllHolland 7 53
(Clifford Lines) *racd off the pce in last trio: clsd and in tch 4f out: drvn and outpcd wl over 1f out: no threat to ldrs and plugged on same pce fnl f* **10/1**

2000 **6** 1 3/4 **Estibdaad (IRE)**[40] 4013 6-9-8 **67** (t) JosephineGordon(3) 4 56
(Paddy Butler) *led: hdd and hung lft 4f out: sn led again: rdn and hrd pressed over 1f out: sn hdd and btn: wknd ins fnl f* **20/1**

3-00 **7** 2 **Baker**[21] 4718 4-9-7 **63** (t) MartinHarley 1 48
(Robyn Brisland) *hld up in midfield: effrt over 2f out: drvn and btn over 1f out: sn wknd* **7/1**

04 **8** 26 **Albert Boy (IRE)**[45] 3841 3-8-12 **63** MartinLane 2
(Scott Dixon) *pressed ldr tl led 4f out: sn rdn and hdd: dropped out qckly and bhd 2f out: eased fnl f: t.o* **10/1**

2m 8.56s (-0.04) **Going Correction** +0.075s/f (Slow)
WFA 3 from 4yo+ 9lb **8** Ran SP% **116.7**
Speed ratings (Par 103): **103,101,101,97,96 95,93,72**
CSF £43.30 CT £107.69 TOTE £2.60: £1.60, £5.00, £1.60; EX 41.00 Trifecta £163.80.
Owner B E Nielsen **Bred** Hascombe And Valiant Studs **Trained** Newmarket, Suffolk
■ Stewards' Enquiry : Josephine Gordon caution: careless riding

FOCUS
An ordinary handicap with an unexposed winner. The second is rated to last year's form.

5472 MALIBU COCONUT CUP CONDITIONS STKS 7f (P)
3:30 (3:31) (Class 3) 3-Y-O+ **£9,056** (£2,695; £1,346; £673) **Stalls** Low

Form RPR

3504 **1** **Buckstay (IRE)**[20] 4733 6-9-4 110 (p) JamieSpencer 4 110
(Peter Chapple-Hyam) *chsd ldr for 1f: styd trcking ldrs: effrt over 1f out: rdn to go between rivals and ld jst ins fnl f: r.o under hands and heels riding* **10/3**[2]

2-03 **2** hd **Mitchum Swagger**[61] 3273 4-9-4 110 GeorgeBaker 2 109+
(David Lanigan) *hld up in tch in last pair: effrt and hung lft over 1f out hdwy u.p ins fnl f: wnt 2nd wl ins fnl f: r.o wl towards fin: nvr quite getting to wnr* **13/8**[1]

2654 **3** 1 1/4 **Atlantic Sun**[23] 4665 3-8-12 101 SilvestreDeSousa 1 104
(Richard Hannon) *led: rdn and qcknd ent fnl 2f: drvn and hdd jst ins fnl f: no ex and lost 2nd wl ins fnl f: wknd towards fin* **7/2**[3]

-020 **4** 1/2 **Golden Amber (IRE)**[38] 4114 5-8-13 97 RobertWinston 5 99
(Dean Ivory) *s.i.s: sn rcvrd and chsd ldr after 1f: rdn and ev ch 2f out tl unable qck jst ins fnl f: wknd wl ins fnl f* **16/1**

3036 **5** hd **Here Comes When (IRE)**[37] 4135 6-9-4 107 JimCrowley 3 104
(Andrew Balding) *stdd after s: t.k.h: hld up in tch in last pair: effrt over 1f out: styd on same pce ins fnl f* **7/2**[3]

1m 26.53s (-0.67) **Going Correction** +0.075s/f (Slow)
WFA 3 from 4yo+ 6lb **5** Ran SP% **111.5**
Speed ratings (Par 107): **106,105,104,103,103**
CSF £9.35 TOTE £3.30: £1.60, £1.30; EX 8.10 Trifecta £18.80.
Owner Mrs Fitri Hay **Bred** M Phelan & Lawman Syndicate **Trained** Newmarket, Suffolk

FOCUS
A good-quality affair. Despite the small field there was a fair enough pace on. The first two are rated below their bests.

5473 HOP HOUSE 13 H'CAP 2m (P)
4:00 (4:01) (Class 6) (0-65,64) 3-Y-O+ **£3,234** (£962; £481; £240) **Stalls** Low

Form RPR

6662 **1** **Hiorne Tower (FR)**[133] 1236 5-9-5 **55** KierenFox 7 62
(John Best) *t.k.h: chsd ldr tl led after 1f: mde rest: wnt clr 4f out: rdn over 2f out: styd on and unchal after: eased wl ins fnl f* **5/1**[3]

0520 **2** 3 3/4 **Monjeni**[13] 4971 3-8-11 **62** (p) JimCrowley 2 65
(Sir Mark Prescott Bt) *t.k.h: hld up off the pce in last trio: effrt in 4th but stl plenty to do 3f out: styd on to chse clr wnr ins fnl f: nvr a threat* **2/1**[1]

0053 **3** 2 1/4 **Racing Knight (IRE)**[34] 4226 4-9-9 **59** SteveDrowne 1 59
(David Evans) *chsd ldrs: chsd clr ldr 4f out: sn rdn and no real imp on wnr: lost 2nd and plugged on same pce ins fnl f* **6/1**

1141 **4** 4 **Yasir (USA)**[13] 4979 8-9-7 **64** SophieKilloran(7) 4 59
(Conor Dore) *s.i.s: hld up off the pce in last: effrt in 5th but stl plenty to do 3f out: kpt on but nvr on terms w wnr* **5/2**[2]

0102 **5** 4 **Delagoa Bay (IRE)**[17] 4816 8-9-3 **60** MitchGodwin(7) 5 50
(Sylvester Kirk) *hld up in midfield: effrt in 3rd over 3f out: no imp and wl hld whn lost 3rd over 1f out: wknd fnl f* **7/1**

0/00 **6** 2 1/4 **Magnus Romeo**[40] 3999 5-9-4 **54** (t) TimmyMurphy 8 42
(Johnny Farrelly) *hld up in last trio: effrt in 6th 3f out: no imp and nvr on terms w ldrs: wknd over 1f out* **16/1**

00-0 **7** 45 **Careless Rapture**[14] 4942 3-7-11 **51** oh6 (b[1]) NoelGarbutt(3) 3
(Mark H Tompkins) *t.k.h: chsd ldrs tl wnt 2nd 1/2-way: clr w wnr 6f out tl 4f out: sn rdn and lost pl: t.o fnl 2f* **33/1**

506 **8** 54 **Tilsworth Phyllis**[82] 2589 4-8-9 **45** (e[1]) TomMarquand 6
(J R Jenkins) *led for 1f: chsd ldr tl 1/2-way: sn u.p and lost pl: bhd 4f out: t.o fnl 3f: lame* **33/1**

3m 31.81s (1.81) **Going Correction** +0.075s/f (Slow)
WFA 3 from 4yo+ 15lb **8** Ran SP% **117.1**
Speed ratings (Par 101): **98,96,95,93,91 89,67,40**
CSF £15.86 CT £60.48 TOTE £6.70: £2.00, £1.40, £1.60; EX 19.50 Trifecta £101.30.
Owner Mrs Jackie Jones **Bred** David Menuisier & Christiane Head Maarek **Trained** Oad Street, Kent

FOCUS
The winner was given too much rope in this weak staying handicap and the form should be treated with a little caution, although it makes sense around the second and third.

5474 HILLS PROSPECT DRINKS DISTRIBUTOR MEDIAN AUCTION MAIDEN STKS 5f (P)
4:30 (4:32) (Class 5) 3-4-Y-O **£4,528** (£1,347; £673; £336) **Stalls** Low

Form RPR

5463 **1** **Verne Castle**[5] 5305 3-9-5 67 DavidProbert 5 72
(Andrew Balding) *t.k.h: trckd ldrs: effrt to chal 1f out: rdn hands and heels to ld 75yds out: r.o* **5/4**[1]

0453 **2** 1/2 **Regal Miss**[12] 5009 4-9-0 62 DanielMuscutt(3) 4 66
(Patrick Chamings) *led: rdn over 1f out: drvn ins fnl f: hdd and unable qck fnl 75yds* **7/2**[2]

06 **3** hd **Vale Of Flight (IRE)**[34] 4238 3-9-0 0 JimCrowley 2 64
(Rae Guest) *t.k.h: pressed ldr: rdn and ev ch ent fnl f: unable qck and styd on same pce ins fnl f* **5/1**[3]

3662 **4** 2 1/4 **Poplar**[13] 4980 3-9-5 60 MartinHarley 3 61
(Robyn Brisland) *trckd ldrs: effrt over 1f out: sn drvn and unable qck: styd on same pce ins fnl f* **7/2**[2]

0 **5** 3/4 **Sharp Boy (IRE)**[9] 5168 3-9-2 0 AaronJones(3) 1 58
(Stuart Williams) *s.i.s: t.k.h: hld up in tch in last pair: effrt and wnt lft over 1f out: no imp and styd on same pce ins fnl f* **14/1**

04- **6** 6 **Bella's Boy (IRE)**[301] 7344 3-9-5 0 RyanPowell 7 37
(John Ryan) *t.k.h: hld up in tch in last pair: rdn 2f out: sn outpcd: bhd fnl f* **25/1**

1m 1.58s (1.38) **Going Correction** +0.075s/f (Slow)
WFA 3 from 4yo 3lb **6** Ran SP% **116.1**
Speed ratings (Par 103): **91,90,89,86,85 75**
CSF £6.28 TOTE £1.90: £1.20, £1.90; EX 6.00 Trifecta £14.30.
Owner J C Smith **Bred** Littleton Stud **Trained** Kingsclere, Hants

FOCUS
An ordinary sprint maiden and for that's rated slightly negatively.

5475 BOOK TICKETS ON CHELMSFORDCITYRACECOURSE.COM H'CAP 6f (P)
5:00 (5:00) (Class 6) (0-60,66) 3-Y-O+ **£3,234** (£962; £481; £240) **Stalls** Centre

Form RPR

2131 **1** **Not Your Call (IRE)**[8] 5194 5-9-13 **66** 6ex KierenFox 3 73
(Lee Carter) *sn led and mde rest: rdn over 1f out: styd on wl u.p fnl f* **11/4**[1]

5002 **2** ½ **Encapsulated**[8] 5194 6-9-0 **60**........................ RhiainIngram(7) 1 65
(Roger Ingram) *taken down early: t.k.h: hld up in tch in midfield: effrt to chse ldrs and swtchd rt wl over 1f out: kpt on u.p ins fnl f: wnt 2nd towards fin* **11/4**[1]

0340 **3** ¾ **Sacred Harp**[12] 5041 3-8-13 **59**........................(t) AaronJones(3) 2 61
(Stuart Williams) *broke wl and led early: sn stdd and pressed ldr: rdn and ev ch over 1f out: unable qck 1f out: styd on same pce ins fnl f* **11/1**

-056 **4** 1½ **Decisive (IRE)**[11] 5080 4-8-13 **52**........................(t) WilliamCarson 8 50
(Anthony Carson) *swtchd lft after 1f: hld up in tch in midfield: effrt over 1f out: kpt on u.p ins fnl f* **8/1**[3]

5042 **5** 1 **Major Muscari (IRE)**[11] 5080 8-8-13 **57**..............(p) CharlieBennett(5) 6 52
(Shaun Harris) *squeezed out sn after s: in tch in rr: hdwy over 1f out: styd on same pce ins fnl f* **10/1**

3301 **6** 8 **Satchville Flyer**[7] 5235 5-9-11 **64** 6ex........................ JimCrowley 4 33
(David Evans) *chsd ldrs: rdn over 2f out: lost pl qckly over 1f out: sn wknd* **7/2**[2]

0-00 **7** 1½ **Romantic Angel (USA)**[73] 2848 3-9-1 **58**.................... ThomasBrown 5 22
(Ismail Mohammed) *chsd ldrs: rdn and unable qck over 1f out: losing pl whn squeezed for room 1f out: wknd fnl f* **11/1**

5033 **8** 9 **Multi Quest**[16] 4878 4-8-12 **51**........................(b) RyanPowell 7
(John E Long) *stuck wd: chsd ldrs tl rdn and lost pl 2f out: sn bhd* **16/1**

1m 13.73s (0.03) **Going Correction** +0.075s/f (Slow)
WFA 3 from 4yo+ 4lb **8** Ran SP% **118.3**
Speed ratings (Par 101): **102,101,100,98,97 86,84,72**
CSF £10.80 CT £71.77 TOTE £3.30: £1.30, £1.20, £3.50; EX 10.00 Trifecta £74.40.
Owner Clear Racing **Bred** Castleton Lyons & Kilboy Estate **Trained** Epsom, Surrey

FOCUS
The principals came from the lowest three stalls in this moderate sprint handicap. The second and third set a atraightforward level.
T/Plt: £12.20 to a £1 stake. Pool: £74,681.32. 4,448.43 winning tickets. T/Qpdt: £3.80 to a £1 stake. Pool: £6,730.58. 1,306.87 winning tickets. **Steve Payne**

5271 THIRSK (L-H)
Monday, August 15

OFFICIAL GOING: Good (good to soft in places) changing to good after race 3 (3.15)
Wind: Light, half against Weather: Fine and sunny, very warm

5476 BRITISH STALLION STUDS EBF MAIDEN STKS (PLUS 10 RACE) (DIV I) 6f
2:15 (2:17) (Class 4) 2-Y-O **£4,269** (£1,270; £634; £317) **Stalls** High

Form RPR

1 **Koropick (IRE)** 2-9-5 0........................ JackMitchell 4 90+
(Hugo Palmer) *dwlt: sn trcking ldrs: smooth hdwy on outer 1/2-way: shkn up to ld wl over 1f out: clr whn edgd rt ent fnl f: kpt on strly* **3/1**[2]

3 **2** 4½ **Prazeres**[25] 4552 2-9-5 0........................ PaulHanagan 7 70
(William Haggas) *trckd ldrs on inner: effrt 2f out and sn pushed along: rdn over 1f out: kpt on fnl f* **8/11**[1]

3 nk **Dakota Gold** 2-9-5 0........................ ConnorBeasley 8 68
(Michael Dods) *dwlt and towards rr on inner: swtchd lft: pushed along and hdwy 2f out: chsd ldrs and nt clr run whn swtchd lft over 1f out: sn rdn: green and edgd lft: styd on wl towards fin* **25/1**

5 **4** 1¼ **Angel Palanas**[13] 4981 2-9-5 0........................ JoeyHaynes 10 64
(K R Burke) *cl up on inner: slt ld after 2f: rdn 2f out and sn hdd: drvn and kpt on same pce fnl f* **12/1**

00 **5** hd **Dreamorchid (IRE)**[28] 4451 2-9-0 0........................ DavidAllan 1 59
(Tim Easterby) *qckly away and led 2f: cl up: rdn along 2f out: drvn over 1f out: kpt on same pce* **100/1**

00 **6** ½ **Come On Percy**[23] 4663 2-9-5 0........................ TonyHamilton 5 62
(Richard Fahey) *chsd ldrs: swtchd lft and rdn along 2f out: sn drvn and one pce* **16/1**

3 **7** ¾ **Lualiwa**[31] 4336 2-9-5 0........................ ShaneGray 2 60
(Kevin Ryan) *dwlt: a towards rr* **7/1**[3]

0 **8** 1 **Nobility (IRE)**[114] 1641 2-9-5 0........................ CamHardie 3 57
(Tim Easterby) *chsd ldrs: cl up over 2f out: sn rdn and wknd over 1f out* **100/1**

9 3¾ **Haworth** 2-9-5 0........................ AndrewElliott 9 46
(James Bethell) *in rr: outpcd and bhd fr 1/2-way* **50/1**

10 7 **Aegean Secret** 2-9-5 0........................ KevinStott 6 25
(Kevin Ryan) *in rr: outpcd and bhd fr 1/2-way* **50/1**

1m 12.26s (-0.44) **Going Correction** -0.10s/f (Good) **10** Ran SP% **118.7**
Speed ratings (Par 96): **98,92,91,89,89 89,88,86,81,72**
CSF £5.52 TOTE £3.90: £1.40, £1.02, £8.80; EX 6.70 Trifecta £76.30.
Owner V I Araci **Bred** C M Farrell **Trained** Newmarket, Suffolk

FOCUS
The ground was given as just on the easy side of good but it was a warm, dry day. The home bend was dolled out circa 8yds and circa half of the away bend was out from the winning line onwards. The time was 0.60sec quicker than the second division. THE winner was impressive, but the bare form of the main bunch is probably not great.

5477 BRITISH STALLION STUDS EBF MAIDEN STKS (PLUS 10 RACE) (DIV II) 6f
2:45 (2:48) (Class 4) 2-Y-O **£4,269** (£1,270; £634; £317) **Stalls** High

Form RPR

2 **1** **Silent Assassin (IRE)**[35] 4203 2-9-5 0........................ GrahamLee 7 74
(Ed Walker) *trckd ldng pair: hdwy 2f out: cl up over 1f out: rdn ent fnl f: kpt on wl to ld nr fin* **10/11**[1]

2 hd **Humbert (IRE)** 2-9-5 0........................ GrahamGibbons 4 74
(Hugo Palmer) *trckd ldrs: swtchd lft and gd hdwy over 2f out: rdn to take slt ld jst over 1f out: green and edgd rt ins fnl f: hdd nr fin* **4/1**[2]

04 **3** 2¾ **Infatuated**[11] 5058 2-9-5 0........................ DavidAllan 5 65+
(Tim Easterby) *trckd ldrs on inner: pushed along wl over 2f out: rdn wl over 1f out: kpt on fnl f* **28/1**

202 **4** ½ **Peach Pavlova (IRE)**[22] 4685 2-9-0 75........................ PJMcDonald 2 58
(Ann Duffield) *slt ld: rdn along 2f out: hdd jst over 1f out: sn drvn and kpt on same pce* **4/1**[2]

6 **5** nk **Fareeq**[11] 5084 2-9-5 0........................ PaulHanagan 10 62
(William Haggas) *dwlt and in rr: pushed along bef 1/2-way: hdwy 2f out: sn rdn and styd on fnl f* **8/1**[3]

0 **6** 1½ **Four Wishes**[54] 3516 2-9-5 0........................ JamesSullivan 8 58
(Tim Easterby) *towards rr: hdwy 2f out: sn rdn: kpt on fnl f* **20/1**

7 1 **Pavers Pride** 2-9-5 0........................ TonyHamilton 9 54
(Noel Wilson) *towards rr: hdwy on outer 1/2-way: chsd ldrs over 2f out: sn rdn and wknd over 1f out* **100/1**

8 1 **Atrafan (IRE)** 2-9-5 0........................ ConnorBeasley 6 51
(Alan Brown) *in rr: pushed along after 2f: rdn 1/2-way: kpt on u.p appr fnl f* **100/1**

4 **9** ¾ **Jorvik Prince**[26] 4508 2-9-5 0........................ SamJames 3 49
(Karen Tutty) *t.k.h: chsd ldrs: rdn along 2f out: sn drvn and wknd over 1f out* **66/1**

0 **10** ¾ **Backinanger**[29] 4423 2-9-5 0........................ TomEaves 1 49
(Kevin Ryan) *wnt lft s: sn cl up: disp ld 1/2-way: rdn along over 2f out: sn wknd* **50/1**

1m 12.86s (0.16) **Going Correction** -0.10s/f (Good) **10** Ran SP% **117.1**
Speed ratings (Par 96): **94,93,90,89,89 87,85,84,83,82**
CSF £4.58 TOTE £2.00: £1.02, £1.80, £5.70; EX 6.20 Trifecta £65.00.
Owner Mrs M Gittins **Bred** Rabbah Bloodstock Limited **Trained** Upper Lambourn, Berks

FOCUS
None with Group-race entries, compared to three in the first leg, and the time was 0.60sec slower, so probably just fair form. A step up from the winner.

5478 PIRATES FAMILY DAY FRIDAY 26TH AUGUST H'CAP 7f
3:15 (3:16) (Class 5) (0-75,74) 3-Y-O **£3,234** (£962; £481; £240) **Stalls** Low

Form RPR

3142 **1** **Coronation Day**[7] 5247 3-9-4 **71**........................ DavidAllan 8 79
(James Tate) *sn trcking ldr: smooth hdwy to ld over 2f out: rdn clr over 1f out: kpt on strly* **9/4**[1]

5435 **2** 2 **Popsies Joy (IRE)**[10] 5115 3-8-12 **68**.............. RachelRichardson(3) 6 70
(Tim Easterby) *trckd ldrs: hdwy on outer 3f out: rdn wl over 1f out: sn chsng wnr: drvn and no imp fnl f* **4/1**[2]

5-44 **3** 1½ **Pickett's Charge**[63] 3224 3-9-3 **70**........................ BarryMcHugh 5 68
(Tony Coyle) *chsd ldrs: pushed along 3f out: rdn over 2f out: drvn over 1f out: kpt on same pce* **4/1**[2]

3040 **4** shd **The Name's Paver**[16] 4873 3-8-10 **63**........................(v[1]) TonyHamilton 7 61
(Noel Wilson) *led: rdn along and hdd over 2f out: drvn over 1f out: kpt on same pce* **16/1**

4305 **5** shd **Weld Al Khawaneej (IRE)**[17] 4844 3-8-8 **61**..................(p) TomEaves 2 58
(Kevin Ryan) *hld up in tch on inner: hdwy over 2f out: nt clr run and swtchd rt wl over 1f out: sn rdn: drvn ent fnl f and one pce* **12/1**

600 **6** ½ **Be Bop Tango (FR)**[43] 3924 3-8-13 **66**........................(v[1]) JoeyHaynes 4 62
(K R Burke) *hld up in tch: hdwy over 2f out: rdn wl over 1f out: drvn and no imp fnl f* **16/1**

5362 **7** 8 **Semana Santa**[13] 4985 3-9-7 **74**........................ GrahamGibbons 1 49
(David Barron) *t.k.h early: trckd ldng pair: pushed along 3f out: rdn over 2f out: sn btn* **13/2**[3]

000- **8** 1¼ **Baileys Galaxy (FR)**[277] 7809 3-8-9 **62**........................ FrannyNorton 3 33
(Mark Johnston) *a in rr: rdn along 3f out: sn outpcd and bhd* **12/1**

1m 28.34s (1.14) **Going Correction** +0.175s/f (Good) **8** Ran SP% **111.3**
Speed ratings (Par 100): **100,97,96,95,95 95,86,84**
CSF £10.51 CT £31.32 TOTE £3.10: £1.40, £1.50, £1.50; EX 11.10 Trifecta £38.90.
Owner James Tate Racing Limited **Bred** Whitsbury Manor Stud **Trained** Newmarket, Suffolk

FOCUS
This was run over approximately 25 yards further than advertised. A modest handicap and few were involved. The winner seems to be getting his act together.

5479 MARKET CROSS JEWELLERS H'CAP 5f
3:45 (3:46) (Class 4) (0-85,85) 4-Y-O+ **£4,851** (£1,443; £721; £360) **Stalls** High

Form RPR

2150 **1** **Stanghow**[31] 4373 4-9-3 **81**........................ PJMcDonald 7 90
(Antony Brittain) *qckly away: mde all: rdn over 1f out: kpt on strly* **10/1**

1050 **2** 1½ **Apricot Sky**[24] 4608 6-8-12 **76**........................ FrannyNorton 9 80
(David Nicholls) *t.k.h early: trckd ldrs: hdwy over 1f out: rdn ent fnl f: kpt on* **10/1**

1341 **3** nse **Seamster**[6] 5274 9-8-6 **77** 6ex........................(t) CameronNoble(7) 11 80
(David Loughnane) *trckd wnr on inner: effrt and n.m.r over 1f out: sn rdn and chsd wnr ins fnl f: kpt on* **7/2**[1]

0500 **4** ½ **Silvanus (IRE)**[31] 4373 11-9-7 **85**........................ PaulMulrennan 12 87+
(Paul Midgley) *t.k.h: trckd ldrs: effrt and nt clr run over 1f out: rdn ins fnl f: styd on strly towards fin* **15/2**[3]

4013 **5** nk **Star Cracker (IRE)**[16] 4874 4-8-0 **69**........................(p) NathanEvans(5) 1 70
(Jim Goldie) *racd wd: cl up: rdn along wl over 1f out: drvn and kpt on same pce fnl f* **20/1**

4100 **6** ½ **Bondi Beach Boy**[31] 4373 7-9-6 **84**........................ GeorgeChaloner 2 83
(James Turner) *cl up: rdn wl over 1f out: drvn and kpt on same pce fnl f* **12/1**

2140 **7** 1 **Flash City (ITY)**[12] 5032 8-8-9 **73**........................(b) JamesSullivan 8 68
(Ruth Carr) *hld up: sme hdwy whn n.m.r wl over 1f out: n.d* **11/1**

0412 **8** hd **Singeur (IRE)**[17] 4817 9-9-5 **83**........................ DanielTudhope 3 77
(Rebecca Bastiman) *in tch: hdwy on outer to chse ldrs over 2f out: rdn wl over 1f out: wknd fnl f* **7/1**[2]

3005 **9** ½ **Fredricka**[9] 5153 5-9-4 **82**........................ GrahamGibbons 5 75
(David Barron) *trckd ldrs: hdwy 2f out: rdn wl over 1f out: wknd fnl f* **8/1**

00 **10** hd **Savannah Beau**[5] 5295 4-8-10 **74**........................(p) SamJames 6 66
(Marjorie Fife) *dwlt: t.k.h: a towards rr* **12/1**

6030 **11** 7 **Soul Brother (IRE)**[9] 5153 5-9-2 **80**........................(b) DavidAllan 4 47
(Tim Easterby) *stdd s: hld up: a in rr* **14/1**

0-10 **12** hd **Kommander Kirkup**[81] 2613 5-8-13 **82**........................ PhilDennis(5) 10 48
(John Davies) *a towards rr* **20/1**

58.26s (-1.34) **Going Correction** -0.10s/f (Good) **12** Ran SP% **115.7**
Speed ratings (Par 105): **106,103,103,102,102 101,99,99,98,98 87,86**
CSF £103.61 CT £418.46 TOTE £11.90: £3.40, £3.50, £1.50; EX 124.20 Trifecta £851.90.
Owner Antony Brittain **Bred** Mel Brittain **Trained** Warthill, N Yorks

FOCUS
A fair sprint handicap. The winner is rated around his Pontefract May win.

5480 BREEDERS BACKING RACING EBF MAIDEN STKS 7f
4:15 (4:20) (Class 4) 3-Y-O+ **£5,498** (£1,636; £817; £408) **Stalls** Low

Form RPR

225 **1** **Lastmanlastround (IRE)**[22] 4682 3-9-5 78........................ DavidAllan 3 75+
(Rae Guest) *mde all: rdn wl over 1f out: drvn out* **5/4**[1]

03 **2** 1¼ **Manshood (IRE)**[9] 5168 3-9-5 0........................ PaulHanagan 6 71
(William Haggas) *trckd wnr: effrt over 2f out: rdn wl over 1f out: drvn ent fnl f: no imp* **11/4**[2]

3 ½ **New Signal** 3-9-5 0........................ DanielTudhope 2 70+
(David O'Meara) *t.k.h: trckd ldrs: effrt on outer over 2f out: rdn and green wl over 1f out: kpt on same pce* **3/1**[3]

4 1 1/2 **Interlink (USA)** 3-9-5 0 PJMcDonald 8 66
(Tony Coyle) *towards rr: rdn along 2f out: styd on wl fnl f: nrst fin* **10/1**

0044 5 5 **The Resdev Way**30 4410 3-9-5 46 GeorgeChaloner 4 52
(Richard Whitaker) *t.k.h: chsd ldng pair on inner: rdn along over 2f out: drvn wl over 1f out: sn wknd* **66/1**

050 6 1 1/4 **Southern Strife**16 4895 5-9-11 0 CamHardie 7 51
(Tim Easterby) *a in rr: rdn along wl over 2f out: sn outpcd* **20/1**

1m 29.22s (2.02) **Going Correction** +0.175s/f (Good)
WFA 3 from 5yo 6lb **6** Ran SP% **111.5**
Speed ratings (Par 105): **95,93,93,91,85 84**
CSF £4.87 TOTE £2.40: £1.20, £1.50; EX 5.00 Trifecta £9.00.
Owner The Boot Sarratt Racing Syndicate **Bred** Duggan Bloodstock **Trained** Newmarket, Suffolk

FOCUS
This was run over approximately 25 yards further than advertised. Very ordinary maiden form, the time a stone slower than the 3yo handicap. The winner didn't need to improve.

5481 RACING UK CLUB DAY HERE TODAY H'CAP 1m 4f
4:45 (4:45) (Class 6) (0-65,65) 3-Y-O+ **£2,587** (£770; £384; £192) **Stalls** High

Form RPR
-000 1 **Calliope**37 4159 3-8-7 55 JamesSullivan 6 65
(Kenneth Slack) *trckd ldrs: hdwy over 3f out: led 2f out: rdn over 1f out: kpt on strly towards fin* **12/1**

3611 2 2 1/4 **High On Light**10 5117 3-9-0 65 RachelRichardson(3) 5 71
(Tim Easterby) *hld up towards rr: gd hdwy on inner over 3f out: swtchd rt and effrt to chse ldrs 2f out: rdn over 1f out: drvn ins fnl f: kpt on same pce towards fin* **11/4**1

300 3 nk **Moon Over Rio (IRE)**55 3498 5-9-8 59 GrahamLee 12 65
(Ben Haslam) *hld up towards rr: hdwy on outer 3f out: chsd ldrs wl over 1f out: sn rdn: chsd wnr ent fnl f: sn drvn and kpt on same pce* **20/1**

3030 4 4 1/2 **L'Apogee**16 4872 3-8-9 57 (p) TonyHamilton 11 56
(Richard Fahey) *trckd ldrs: hdwy over 3f out and sn chsng ldr: rdn along and ev ch 2f out: sn drvn and one pce* **10/1**

0-04 5 1/2 **Best Boy**11 5057 4-9-11 62 (t) DavidAllan 9 60
(David C Griffiths) *hld up towards rr: hdwy over 3f out: rdn along over 2f out: swtchd rt to outer and drvn over 1f out: kpt on fnl f* **9/1**

0300 6 shd **Graceful Act**3 5350 8-8-9 46 KevinStott 7 44
(Ron Barr) *prom: rdn along over 3f out: outpcd wl over 2f out: drvn and plugged on fnl f* **50/1**

4512 7 nk **Whitchurch**11 5065 4-9-2 53 PJMcDonald 8 50
(Philip Kirby) *hld up in midfield: hdwy to trck ldrs over 4f out: rdn along over 2f out: drvn wl over 1f out: sn wknd* **14/1**

6044 8 3/4 **Bridey's Lettuce (IRE)**9 5183 4-9-10 61 RaulDaSilva 4 57+
(Ivan Furtado) *chsd clr ldr: tk clsr order 3f out: cl up over 2f out and sn rdn: drvn and wknd over 1f out* **5/1**2

-030 9 3 **Cavalieri (IRE)**9 5183 6-9-6 57 (p) AndrewMullen 10 48
(Philip Kirby) *a towards rr* **25/1**

2156 10 2 1/4 **Mcvicar**74 2836 7-9-11 62 (p) DanielTudhope 2 50
(John Davies) *hld up: a towards rr* **7/1**3

2003 11 5 **Tamujin (IRE)**34 4225 8-8-13 50 CamHardie 3 30
(Ken Cunningham-Brown) *a towards rr* **33/1**

1035 12 4 1/2 **Lean On Pete (IRE)**12 5028 7-9-1 59 RobertDodsworth(7) 13 32+
(Ollie Pears) *sn led and clr: pushed along 3f out: hdd 2f out and sn wknd* **20/1**

2643 13 6 **Adherence**15 4255 3-8-11 59 BarryMcHugh 1 22
(Tony Coyle) *chsd ldrs on inner: rdn along 4f out: wknd wl over 2f out* **11/1**

2m 37.37s (1.17) **Going Correction** +0.175s/f (Good)
WFA 3 from 4yo+ 11lb **13** Ran SP% **115.9**
Speed ratings (Par 101): **103,101,101,98,97 97,97,97,95,93 90,87,83**
CSF £40.73 CT £670.69 TOTE £15.70: £4.60, £1.60, £6.70; EX 58.00 Trifecta £1249.00.
Owner E G Tunstall **Bred** G B Partnership **Trained** Hilton, Cumbria

FOCUS
This was run over approximately 30 yards further than advertised. A moderate handicap run at a strong pace. The winner improved for her new yard.

5482 JAMES HERRIOT CENTENARY ANNIVERSARY H'CAP 1m
5:15 (5:18) (Class 4) (0-80,80) 3-Y-O+ **£4,851** (£1,443; £721; £360) **Stalls** Low

Form RPR
2301 1 **Sovereign Bounty**34 4231 4-9-9 75 GrahamLee 13 86+
(Jedd O'Keeffe) *trckd ldrs: hdwy over 2f out: rdn to ld wl over 1f out: drvn and kpt on wl fnl f* **10/1**

6130 2 1 1/2 **Hanseatic**38 4113 7-9-9 75 (bt1) CamHardie 10 82
(Michael Easterby) *in tch: hdwy on outer wl over 2f out: chsd ldrs wl over 1f out: sn rdn: drvn and kpt on fnl f* **10/1**

044 3 hd **Dutch Artist (IRE)**34 4232 4-9-12 78 DanielTudhope 9 85
(David O'Meara) *trckd ldng pair: hdwy 3f out: cl up 2f out: sn rdn and ev ch: drvn ent fnl f and kpt on same pce* **13/2**1

1430 4 1 1/2 **Woody Bay**24 4611 6-9-9 80 NathanEvans(5) 6 83
(Mark Walford) *in tch: hdwy to chse ldrs over 2f out: rdn wl over 1f out: kpt on fnl f* **12/1**

6500 5 shd **Darrington**66 3113 4-9-7 78 AdamMcNamara(5) 18 81
(Richard Fahey) *hld up: hdwy 3f out: rdn along 2f out: chsd ldrs and drvn over 1f out: kpt on* **7/1**2

3315 6 1/2 **Throckley**14 4933 5-10-0 80 SamJames 1 82
(John Davies) *chsd ldrs: rdn along over 2f out: drvn wl over 1f out: kpt on same pce fnl f* **22/1**

0-02 7 hd **Le Roi Du Temps (USA)**26 4519 3-9-4 77 (p) RaulDaSilva 12 77
(Ivan Furtado) *cl up: rdn along over 2f out: drvn and hdd wl over 1f out: grad wknd* **9/1**3

4026 8 1 **Trinity Star (IRE)**31 4374 5-9-11 77 (p) PaulMulrennan 17 76+
(Michael Dods) *hld up in rr: hdwy wl over 2f out: n.m.r wl over 1f out: sn swtchd lft and nt clr run ent fnl f: swtchd rt and rdn: kpt on towards fin* **10/1**

1560 9 hd **Shouranour (IRE)**24 4611 6-9-11 77 (b) ConnorBeasley 7 76
(Alan Brown) *slt ld: rdn along 3f out: drvn 2f out: hdd wl over 1f out: grad wknd* **16/1**

033 10 nse **Terhaal (IRE)**21 4704 4-9-5 76 JoshDoyle(5) 11 74
(David O'Meara) *midfield: hdwy on inner 3f out: rdn along 2f out: drvn over 1f out: no imp* **10/1**

4406 11 hd **Favourite Treat (USA)**9 5179 6-9-9 75 (e) JamesSullivan 8 73
(Ruth Carr) *hld up: a in rr* **25/1**

0505 12 1 1/2 **Nonno Giulio (IRE)**9 5179 5-9-9 75 DavidNolan 15 69
(David Loughnane) *midfield: effrt wl over 2f out: sn rdn along and n.d* **20/1**

0504 13 shd **Mystic Miraaj**14 4933 4-9-11 77 (b) DavidAllan 5 71
(Tim Easterby) *midfield: hdwy and in tch 3f out: rdn along wl over 2f out: drvn and wknd wl over 1f out* **7/1**2

2502 14 2 **King Of Swing**24 4605 3-9-5 78 (b) TomEaves 2 66
(James Given) *t.k.h on inner: chsd ldrs: rdn along over 2f out: sn wknd* **12/1**

5021 15 6 **Ralphy Boy (IRE)**12 5033 7-9-8 74 PJMcDonald 4 49
(Alistair Whillans) *a towards rr* **18/1**

-000 16 3 1/4 **Thornaby Nash**17 4830 5-9-5 71 RoystonFfrench 14 38
(Colin Teague) *a towards rr* **50/1**

0200 17 29 **Western Way (IRE)**17 4841 7-9-6 72 FrannyNorton 16
(Don Cantillon) *a towards rr: outpcd 1/2-way and sn wl bhd* **33/1**

1m 40.5s (0.40) **Going Correction** +0.175s/f (Good)
WFA 3 from 4yo+ 7lb **17** Ran SP% **129.1**
Speed ratings (Par 105): **105,103,103,101,101 101,101,100,99,99 99,98,97,95,89 86,57**
CSF £105.28 CT £722.21 TOTE £11.60: £2.80, £4.10, £2.60, £3.50; EX 187.20 Trifecta £1613.40.
Owner Caron & Paul Chapman **Bred** West Dereham Abbey Stud **Trained** Middleham Moor, N Yorks

FOCUS
This was run over approximately 25 yards further than advertised. A fair handicap but it wasn't strong run. It was rated around the second and third.

5483 LADIES' DAY SATURDAY 3RD SEPTEMBER BOOK NOW H'CAP (FOR LADY AMATEUR RIDERS) 6f
5:45 (5:47) (Class 6) (0-60,60) 3-Y-O+ **£2,495** (£774; £386; £193) **Stalls** High

Form RPR
5663 1 **Teetotal (IRE)**6 5278 6-9-10 54 (b) MissKMargarson(5) 4 64
(Nigel Tinkler) *hood removed v late: sn trcking ldrs centre: hdwy over 2f out: led over 1f out: edgd lft: drvn out* **8/1**

4400 2 1 1/4 **Gaelic Wizard (IRE)**6 5277 8-10-5 58 (v) MissEmmaSayer 13 64
(Karen Tutty) *chsd ldrs stands' side: effrt over 1f out: led that side 100yds out: kpt on* **8/1**

-011 3 1 1/2 **Sugar Town**11 5069 6-10-4 57 MissJoannaMason 15 58
(Peter Niven) *overall ldr stands' side: hdd that gp and no ex last 100yds* **7/2**1

2026 4 nk **Tribesman**6 5277 3-10-0 60 MissBeckySmith(3) 8 59
(Marjorie Fife) *chsd ldrs: kpt on same pce fnl f* **9/2**2

6124 5 1/2 **Generalyse**7 5236 7-10-7 60 (v) MrsCBartley 3 59
(Anabel K Murphy) *mid-div: drvn over 2f out: chsng ldrs whn edgd lft over 1f out: kpt on same pce* **12/1**

0606 6 3/4 **Amis Reunis**6 5278 7-9-0 46 oh1 MissRSharpe(7) 12 42
(Colin Teague) *half-rrd s: bhd: hdwy over 1f out: styng on at fin* **25/1**

5100 7 3/4 **Hab Reeh**11 5069 8-9-10 54 (p) MissEmilyBullock(5) 7 48
(Ruth Carr) *chsd ldrs: one pce over 1f out* **25/1**

6230 8 1/2 **Reflation**14 4931 4-9-7 53 (v1) MissCADods(7) 2 45
(Michael Dods) *chsd ldrs centre: hung lft and one pce over 1f out* **20/1**

1345 9 1/2 **Very First Blade**8 5200 7-9-10 49 (p) MissMMullineaux 1 40
(Michael Mullineaux) *chsd ldr centre: outpcd over 2f out: kpt on fnl f* **33/1**

4314 10 hd **A J Cook (IRE)**6 5278 6-9-11 53 MissAWaugh(3) 14 43
(Ron Barr) *w ldrs stands' side: fdd fnl f* **8/1**

-050 11 1 3/4 **Red Forever**14 4931 5-9-4 46 oh1 MissHelenCuthbert(3) 9 30
(Thomas Cuthbert) *trckd ldrs: effrt appr fnl f: sn fdd* **40/1**

0004 12 shd **Colombe Bleu**9 5181 3-9-7 55 MissHDukes(5) 10 38
(Tony Coyle) *mid-div: effrt over 2f out: wknd over 1f out* **33/1**

2001 13 2 1/4 **Poolstock**6 5278 4-9-12 58 6ex (b) MissSEDods(7) 11 35
(Michael Dods) *t.k.h: trckd ldrs stands' side: wknd over 1f out* **15/2**3

400- 14 7 **Shesnotforturning (IRE)**297 7437 6-9-6 50 (p) MissPBridgwater(5) 5 4
(Ben Haslam) *sn outpcd in rr: hung bdly rt 2f out: sn bhd* **25/1**

1m 12.39s (-0.31) **Going Correction** -0.10s/f (Good)
WFA 3 from 4yo+ 4lb **14** Ran SP% **117.8**
Speed ratings (Par 101): **98,96,94,93,93 92,91,90,89,89 87,87,84,74**
CSF £62.82 CT £274.13 TOTE £8.50: £2.70, £2.30, £1.50; EX 83.50 Trifecta £325.50.
Owner J Raybould **Bred** T Jones **Trained** Langton, N Yorks

FOCUS
A moderate handicap and the runners were all over the place in the closing stages. Straightforward form.
T/Jkpt: £15,349.20 to a £1 stake. Pool: £15,349.20 - 1.00 winning ticket. T/Plt: £8.00 to a £1 stake. Pool: £82,458.11. 7,484.53 winning tickets. T/Qpdt: £4.80 to a £1 stake. Pool: £6,356.96. 971.08 winning tickets. **Joe Rowntree**

5236 WINDSOR (R-H)
Monday, August 15

OFFICIAL GOING: Good to firm (8.4)
Wind: Light, against Weather: Sunny, warm

5484 SKY BET BRITISH STALLION STUDS EBF MAIDEN STKS 6f
5:30 (5:35) (Class 5) 2-Y-O **£3,234** (£962; £481; £240) **Stalls** Low

Form RPR
226 1 **Smokey Lane (IRE)**31 4352 2-9-5 96 ShaneKelly 2 84
(David Evans) *trckd ldrs: clsd 2f out: shkn up to ld jst over 1f out: edgd rt jst ins fnl f: rdn out and styd on wl* **6/4**1

05 2 1 1/2 **Sun Angel (IRE)**18 4801 2-9-0 0 OisinMurphy 7 74
(Henry Candy) *pressed ldr: rdn to ld wl over 1f out to jst over 1f out: hld whn sltly checked jst ins fnl f: styd on* **7/4**2

3 1 3/4 **Endeavour (IRE)** 2-9-5 0 SeanLevey 4 73
(Richard Hannon) *dwlt: sn chsd ldrs: swtchd lft wl over 1f out: drvn to chse ldng pair fnl f: one pce* **9/2**3

6 4 4 **Tranquil Daze (IRE)**24 4601 2-9-5 0 AdamKirby 9 61
(David Brown) *fast away: led and crossed to nr side: rdn and hdd wl over 1f out: fdd* **20/1**

04 5 1 1/2 **Trading Punches (IRE)**9 5196 2-9-5 0 TedDurcan 5 56
(David Brown) *stdd after s: hld up and sn wl bhd: nudged along and passed rivals fnl 2f: likely improver* **14/1**

00 6 4 **Makemerichjohn (IRE)**31 4349 2-9-5 0 JFEgan 1 43
(David Evans) *chsd ldng pair to jst over 2f out: wknd* **33/1**

0 7 1 1/2 **Thomas Girtin (IRE)**21 4706 2-9-5 0 FergusSweeney 6 38+
(Gary Moore) *chsd ldrs: in tch over 2f out: sn wknd* **40/1**

405 8 3 1/4 **Gentleman Giles (IRE)**26 4503 2-9-0 0 LucyKBarry(5) 3 28
(Jamie Osborne) *sn wl off the pce in 7th: light reminder 2f out: no prog* **50/1**

9 32 **Reach For Glory** 2-9-0 0 .... HectorCrouch(5) 8
(Bill Turner) *dwlt: bdly outpcd: t.o* **28/1**

1m 13.26s (0.26) **Going Correction** -0.125s/f (Firm) **9** Ran SP% **116.8**
Speed ratings (Par 94): **93,91,88,83,81 76,74,69,27**
CSF £4.14 TOTE £2.40: £1.10, £1.30, £2.00; EX 4.50 Trifecta £10.30.
Owner Walters Plant Hire P T Civil Engineering **Bred** Miss Philippa Proctor Quinn **Trained** Pandy, Monmouths

FOCUS
An interesting maiden run at a sound pace. The winner didn't need to replicate his best.

5485 SKY BET (S) STKS — 1m 3f 135y
6:00 (6:05) (Class 5) 3-Y-O+ **£2,911** (£866; £432; £216) **Stalls** Centre

Form / RPR

0642 **1** **Gaelic Silver (FR)**[11] 5056 10-9-6 69 .... (p) HectorCrouch(5) 3 — 65+
(Gary Moore) *hld up in 3rd: clsd smoothly to ld 2f out: shkn up and clr fnl f* **8/11**[1]

01-2 **2** 2 3/4 **Mount Shamsan**[70] 2977 6-9-11 72 .... GeorgeBaker 1 — 58
(Gary Moore) *led 1f: trckd ldr: upsides and shkn up whn wnr eased past 2f out: chsng after and no imp* **13/8**[2]

05-6 **3** 2 1/2 **Classic Colori (IRE)**[11] 5071 9-9-11 57 .... (v) TomQueally 5 — 54
(Martin Keighley) *dwlt: pushed up to ld after 1f: urged along bnd 5f out: rdn and hdd 2f out: one pce and sn btn* **8/1**[3]

0-00 **4** 38 **Praise N Glory**[41] 3970 5-9-3 32 .... [1] GeorgeDowning(3) 4
(Linda Jewell) *a last: rdn and lost tch 4f out: t.o* **100/1**

2m 29.91s (0.41) **Going Correction** -0.125s/f (Firm)
WFA 3 from 5yo+ 11lb **4** Ran SP% **108.1**
Speed ratings (Par 103): **93,91,89,64**
CSF £2.16 TOTE £1.60; EX 2.10 Trifecta £2.70.There was no bid for the winner.
Owner The Winning Hand **Bred** Earl Haras Du Camp Bernard Et Al **Trained** Lower Beeding, W Sussex

FOCUS
Add 20yds to advertised race distance. This weak seller looked a match between the two Gary Moore-trained runners, and they were in control from some way out.

5486 SKY BET MAIDEN STKS — 1m 2f 7y
6:30 (6:36) (Class 5) 3-4-Y-O **£2,911** (£866; £432; £216) **Stalls** Centre

Form / RPR

2223 **1** **Stratum**[16] 4857 3-9-5 84 .... NickyMackay 2 — 84+
(John Gosden) *mde all: drew clr 3f out: easily* **8/13**[1]

2 8 **Capton** 3-9-5 0 .... FergusSweeney 9 — 68
(Henry Candy) *in tch disputing 7th: shkn up over 3f out: prog on outer to chse wnr wl over 1f out: no ch but kpt on* **7/1**[3]

00 **3** 1/2 **Angelical (IRE)**[25] 4546 3-9-0 0 .... JFEgan 7 — 62
(Daniel Mark Loughnane) *in tch disputing 5th: reminder 4f out: prog and swtchd to outer fr 2f out: tk 3rd ins fnl f: kpt on* **100/1**

4 1 **Transmitting** 3-9-5 0 .... TedDurcan 3 — 65+
(Sir Michael Stoute) *trckd ldng pair: outpcd 4f out: shkn up 3f out: effrt to chal for 2nd 2f out: one pce after* **4/1**[2]

5 **5** 1 1/4 **Macksville (IRE)**[13] 4983 3-9-0 0 .... DavidParkes(5) 4 — 63
(Jeremy Gask) *in tch disputing 7th: pushed along 3f out: shkn up and kpt on fr over 1f out: nvr a threat* **50/1**

00 **6** 3 3/4 **Major Ben**[18] 4792 3-9-5 0 .... MartinDwyer 5 — 55
(William Muir) *s.i.s: pushed up to chse wnr: tried to chal over 3f out and clr of rest: sn btn off: lost 2nd and wknd wl over 1f out* **25/1**

06 **7** 1 1/2 **Brahma**[14] 4955 3-9-5 0 .... RobertWinston 6 — 52
(Hughie Morrison) *chsd ldng trio: ch of a pl over 2f out: racd awkwardly and wknd wl over 1f out* **20/1**

365 **8** 5 **Hellavashock**[51] 3653 3-9-5 74 .... AdamKirby 10 — 42
(Giles Bravery) *chsd ldrs disputing 5th: shkn up and no imp 3f out: wknd wl over 1f out* **8/1**

0 **9** 1/2 **Buckle Street**[47] 3769 3-9-5 0 .... TomQueally 1 — 41
(Martin Keighley) *dwlt: a in last trio: bhd 4f out* **50/1**

000 **10** 1 1/2 **Moayadd (USA)**[12] 5023 4-10-0 0 .... GeorgeBaker 8 — 38
(Neil Mulholland) *hld up in 9th: bhd 4f out: pushed along and nvr involved after* **100/1**

0 **11** 1 1/4 **Pinkie Brown (FR)**[12] 5023 4-10-0 0 .... LiamKeniry 11 — 36
(Neil Mulholland) *dwlt: a in last pair: bhd fnl 4f* **28/1**

2m 6.22s (-2.48) **Going Correction** -0.125s/f (Firm)
WFA 3 from 4yo 9lb **11** Ran SP% **123.5**
Speed ratings (Par 103): **104,97,97,96,95 92,91,87,86,85 84**
CSF £5.81 TOTE £1.60: £1.02, £3.00, £21.00; EX 7.60 Trifecta £1051.00.
Owner Al Asayl Bloodstock Ltd **Bred** Al Asayl Bloodstock Ltd **Trained** Newmarket, Suffolk

FOCUS
Add 20yds to advertised race distance. The pace was sound for this uncompetitive maiden and the time good compared with the later handicap. The winner is rated a bit below his best.

5487 SKY BET FILLIES' H'CAP — 1m 67y
7:00 (7:05) (Class 4) (0-85,84) 3-Y-O+ **£4,690** (£1,395; £697; £348) **Stalls** Low

Form / RPR

1- **1** **Materialistic**[311] 7077 3-9-7 84 .... AdamKirby 5 — 92+
(Luca Cumani) *hld up bhd ldng pair: rdn over 2f out: grad clsd u.p: drvn ahd ins fnl f: kpt on* **4/5**[1]

0543 **2** 1/2 **Ghinia (IRE)**[19] 4761 5-9-6 79 .... RobHornby(3) 4 — 87
(Pam Sly) *pressed ldr: rdn 2f out: narrow ld over 1f out: hdd and nt qckn ins fnl f: kpt on* **11/2**[3]

3211 **3** 2 1/2 **Red Tea**[17] 4819 3-9-3 80 .... AdamBeschizza 2 — 81
(Peter Hiatt) *led: rdn 2f out: narrowly hdd over 1f out: one pce fnl f* **9/4**[2]

5050 **4** 5 **Salvo**[11] 5089 3-8-13 76 .... ShaneKelly 1 — 66
(Charlie Fellowes) *hld up: rdn and no prog over 2f out: wknd over 1f out* **12/1**

1m 42.52s (-2.18) **Going Correction** -0.125s/f (Firm)
WFA 3 from 5yo 7lb **4** Ran SP% **109.4**
Speed ratings (Par 102): **105,104,102,97**
CSF £5.63 TOTE £1.40; EX 5.50 Trifecta £7.10.
Owner Fittocks Stud **Bred** Fittocks Stud **Trained** Newmarket, Suffolk

FOCUS
Add 20yds to advertised race distance. A fair contest despite the small field. The winner has the potential to do better.

5488 SKY BET WINDSOR SPRINT SERIES FINALE H'CAP — 6f
7:30 (7:37) (Class 2) 3-Y-O+ **£48,517** (£14,437; £7,215; £3,607) **Stalls** Low

Form / RPR

3044 **1** **Stellarta**[16] 4862 5-8-4 82 .... TomMarquand 5 — 96
(Michael Blanshard) *towards rr: rdn and prog 2f out: clsd to ld jst ins fnl f: stormed clr* **7/1**[3]

4351 **2** 3 3/4 **Pretty Bubbles**[21] 4708 7-8-7 85 .... (v) FrederikTylicki 2 — 87
(J R Jenkins) *trckd ldrs gng wl: rdn to chal over 1f out: upsides whn wnr stormed past jst ins fnl f: outpcd* **16/1**

4413 **3** 1/2 **Ice Age (IRE)**[15] 4910 3-7-7 82 oh4 .... SophieKilloran(7) 10 — 81+
(Eve Johnson Houghton) *pressed ldr: rdn 2f out: led briefly 1f out: sn outpcd* **9/1**

0100 **4** nse **Cool Bahamian (IRE)**[16] 4862 5-8-2 83 .... (v) EdwardGreatrex(3) 14 — 83
(Eve Johnson Houghton) *dwlt: wl in rr: prog on wd outside 2f out: kpt on u.p fnl f* **33/1**

0001 **5** nk **Goring (GER)**[14] 4954 4-8-7 85 .... JohnFahy 8 — 84
(Eve Johnson Houghton) *hld up towards rr: prog and tried to weave through fr 2f out: kpt on same pce u.p fnl f* **8/1**

2252 **6** 1/2 **Foxtrot Knight**[14] 4946 4-8-4 82 .... SilvestreDeSousa 9 — 80
(Ruth Carr) *fast away: led against nr side: rdn 2f out: hdd & wknd 1f out* **13/2**[2]

5042 **6** dht **Rosie's Premiere (IRE)**[15] 4911 4-8-9 87 .... (t) RobertWinston 4 — 85
(Dean Ivory) *s.i.s: wl in rr: rdn 2f out: styd on wl fnl f: gng on at fin* **13/2**[2]

3110 **8** nk **Black Bess**[9] 5148 3-7-11 86 .... RhiainIngram(7) 7 — 82
(Jim Boyle) *nvr bttr than midfield: rdn and one pce fr 2f out: no imp on ldrs* **22/1**

1255 **9** 1/2 **Rio Ronaldo (IRE)**[24] 4584 4-8-10 88 .... OisinMurphy 12 — 83
(Mike Murphy) *s.v.s: wl off the pce in last: rdn and sme prog fr 2f out: kpt on but no ch to threaten* **5/1**[1]

6430 **10** 2 1/2 **Flowers On Venus (IRE)**[16] 4889 4-8-10 88 .... JFEgan 6 — 83
(David Evans) *cl up: rdn over 2f out: nt qckn and lost pl over 1f out: eased last 100yds* **15/2**

3510 **11** 1 3/4 **Young John (IRE)**[38] 4079 3-8-3 85 .... PatrickMathers 1 — 66
(Richard Fahey) *chsd ldrs to over 2f out: sn btn* **20/1**

162 **12** 1 1/4 **Free Zone**[14] 4954 7-8-8 86 .... (v) WilliamCarson 11 — 64
(Jamie Osborne) *chsd ldrs 4f: wknd* **20/1**

54 **13** 12 **Clear Spring (IRE)**[51] 3671 8-9-10 102 .... AdamKirby 13 — 41
(John Spearing) *chsd ldrs on outer over 3f: wknd rapidly: t.o* **14/1**

0510 **14** 2 **Sydney Ruffdiamond**[15] 4911 4-8-7 85 .... (b[1]) ShaneKelly 3 — 18
(Richard Hughes) *pressed ldng pair to over 2f out: wknd rapidly over 1f out: t.o* **33/1**

1m 10.73s (-2.27) **Going Correction** -0.125s/f (Firm)
WFA 3 from 4yo+ 4lb **14** Ran SP% **121.0**
Speed ratings (Par 109): **110,105,104,104,103 103,103,102,102,98 96,94,78,76**
CSF £105.16 CT £1049.20 TOTE £8.20: £2.90, £4.10, £3.10; EX 143.90 Trifecta £1037.40.
Owner Vincent Ward **Bred** Whitsbury Manor Stud & Pigeon House Stud **Trained** Upper Lambourn, Berks

FOCUS
A competitive first running of this sprint finale, which included winners from four of the nine qualifiers. It was run at a sound pace with the winner pulling clear for an impressive success. She posted a clear pb, with the next two close to their recent form.

5489 SKY BET CASH OUT FILLIES' H'CAP — 1m 2f 7y
8:00 (8:05) (Class 4) (0-80,80) 4-Y-O+ **£4,690** (£1,395; £697; £348) **Stalls** Centre

Form / RPR

3121 **1** **Ickymasho**[30] 4383 4-9-7 80 .... GeorgeBaker 5 — 89
(Jonathan Portman) *mde all: in total command fr 2f out: jst pushed out: fin lame* **6/4**[1]

452 **2** 1 3/4 **Sahara (IRE)**[25] 4568 4-9-4 77 .... TedDurcan 2 — 82
(Chris Wall) *mostly chsd wnr: drvn and no imp over 2f out: n.d after but kpt on* **10/3**[2]

0-60 **3** 1 1/4 **Starlit Cantata**[201] 353 5-9-6 79 .... JohnFahy 6 — 81
(Eve Johnson Houghton) *hld up in last trio: rdn over 2f out: kpt on one pce and nvr a threat* **8/1**

1645 **4** 1 1/2 **Yorkindred Spirit**[15] 4919 4-8-12 71 .... (v) SilvestreDeSousa 4 — 70
(Mark Johnston) *hld up in last trio: rdn over 2f out: no real prog* **9/2**[3]

2345 **5** hd **Solveig's Song**[11] 5054 4-8-4 66 .... (p) EdwardGreatrex(3) 3 — 65
(Steve Woodman) *chsd ldng pair: u.p and struggling wl over 2f out: fdd over 1f out* **11/1**

1230 **6** shd **Coillte Cailin (IRE)**[17] 4850 6-9-7 80 .... AdamKirby 1 — 78
(Daniel Mark Loughnane) *hld up in last trio: rdn and no rspnse wl over 2f out: wl btn over 1f out* **7/1**

2m 7.96s (-0.74) **Going Correction** -0.125s/f (Firm) **6** Ran SP% **113.2**
Speed ratings (Par 102): **97,95,94,93,93 93**
CSF £6.81 TOTE £2.10: £1.30, £1.80; EX 6.70 Trifecta £42.80.
Owner C R Lambourne, M Forbes, D Losse **Bred** Allseasons Bloodstock **Trained** Upper Lambourn, Berks

FOCUS
Add 20yds to advertised race distance. A fair handicap run at a steady pace. The second and third set the standard.
T/Plt: £23.60 to a £1 stake. Pool: £92,213.93. 2,851.29 winning tickets. T/Qpdt: £9.80 to a £1 stake. Pool: £6,611.27. 494.95 winning tickets. **Jonathan Neesom**

5490 - 5496a (Foreign Racing) - See Raceform Interactive

5447 DEAUVILLE (R-H)
Monday, August 15

OFFICIAL GOING: Turf: good; polytrack: standard

5497a PRIX DE LA VALLEE D'AUGE (LISTED RACE) (2YO) (TURF) — 5f
1:50 (12:00) 2-Y-O **£20,220** (£8,088; £6,066; £4,044; £2,022)

RPR

1 **Sans Equivoque (GER)**[44] 3937 2-8-13 0 .... ThierryJarnet 3 — 99
(D Guillemin, France) **7/5**[1]

2 1 1/2 **Ivory Choice (FR)**[20] 4750 2-8-13 0 .... IoritzMendizabal 1 — 94
(F Chappet, France) **58/10**

3 1 1/4 **Aladdine**[28] 2-8-13 0 .... AurelienLemaitre 2 — 89
(F Head, France) **27/10**[2]

4 1 3/4 **Just An Idea (IRE)**[19] 4755 2-9-2 0 .... TonyPiccone 6 — 86
(Harry Dunlop) *awkward s: towards rr early: pushed along and hdwy appr 2f out: unable to go w ldrs fnl f* **53/10**[3]

5 3/4 **California Tee**[20] 4750 2-8-13 0 .... AntoineHamelin 7 — 80
(Matthieu Palussiere, France) **135/10**

6 1 3/4 **Becquamis (FR)**[20] 4750 2-9-2 0 .... AntoineWerle 4 — 77
(T Lemer, France) **32/5**

58.88s (1.38) **6** Ran SP% **119.7**
PARI-MUTUEL (all including 1 euro stake): WIN 2.40; PLACE 1.40, 2.10; SF 9.00.
Owner Haras D'Etreham **Bred** Pontchartrain Stud Et Al **Trained** France

5498a PRIX DE LIEUREY (GROUP 3) (3YO FILLIES) (TURF) (ROUND) 1m (R)

2:25 (12:00) 3-Y-O £29,411 (£11,764; £8,823; £5,882; £2,941)

RPR

1 **Trixia (FR)**117 1581 3-8-11 0 OlivierPeslier 7 109
(A De Royer-Dupre, France) *settled in fnl 3rd: impeded and snatched up 3f out: shkn up and hdwy over 1 1/2f out: r.o u.p fnl f: chal between horses 75yds out: led post* **11/2**2

2 nse **Chartreuse (IRE)**36 4184 3-8-11 0 ThierryJarnet 2 109
(F Head, France) *chsd ldr on inner early: sn hld up bhd ldng gp: shkn up to press ldr 2f out: qcknd to ld 1 1/2f out: r.o fnl f: hdd post* **4/1**1

3 1 **Aim To Please (FR)**71 2945 3-8-11 0 GeraldMosse 10 106
(F Doumen, France) *hld up in rr: hdwy into midfield bef 1/2-way: rdn to chse ldr fr 1 1/2f out: styd on fnl f* **239/10**

4 nk **Midweek**42 3967 3-8-11 0 ThierryThulliez 5 106
(Mme C Head-Maarek, France) *t.k.h: hld up in tch: rdn to chse ldrs over 1f out: styd on u.p fnl f: nt pce to chal* **13/2**3

5 1 **Switching (USA)**113 1687 3-8-11 0 Pierre-CharlesBoudot 8 103
(A Fabre, France) *chsd ldng gp: dropped into midfield bef 1/2-way: rdn and styd on fr over 1f out: nt pce to get on terms* **30/1**

6 nk **Come Alive**42 3967 3-8-11 0 MickaelBarzalona 13 103
(A Fabre, France) *hld up in fnl pair: hdwy sn after 1/2-way: rdn to chse ldng trio 1f out: run flattened out last 100yds* **71/10**

7 1 1/4 **Kenriya (FR)**92 2282 3-8-11 0 StephanePasquier 3 100
(C Ferland, France) *settled in midfield on inner: rushed up to ld after 3f: rdn whn pressed 2f out: hdd 1 1/2f out: wknd wl ins fnl f* **224/10**

8 1 **Mise En Rose (USA)**17 4826 3-8-11 0 WilliamBuick 14 97
(Charlie Appleby) *settled in midfield: dropped towards rr after 1/2-way: sme prog fr over 1f out: rn petered out last 100yds: nvr trbld ldrs* **122/10**

9 1/2 **Rosay (IRE)**71 2945 3-8-11 0 CristianDemuro 12 98+
(J-C Rouget, France) *w.w in fnl 3rd: dropped among bkmarkers 1/2-way: rdn and effrt whn nt clr run wl over 1f out: kpt on fnl f wout being given a hrd time* **157/10**

10 1 3/4 **Magnanime**37 4174 3-8-11 0 TonyPiccone 15 92
(F Chappet, France) *racd in midfield: lost pl appr 1/2-way: sme mod late prog: nvr in contention* **35/1**

11 3 1/2 **Antonoe (USA)**92 2282 3-8-11 0 VincentCheminaud 4 83
(P Bary, France) *settled in midfield: rdn and nt qckn 2f out: wknd fnl f* **121/10**

12 nk **Light Up Our World (IRE)**17 4822 3-8-11 0 ChristopheSoumillon 11 83
(Richard Hannon) *chsd ldrs: cl 4th and rdn 2 1/2f out: no imp: wknd appr fnl 1 1/2f* **149/10**

13 1 3/4 **Silver Step (FR)**22 4695 3-8-11 0 MaximeGuyon 9 79
(Mme Pia Brandt, France) *scrubbed along early: a among bkmarkers: last and rdn 2 1/2f out: nvr a factor* **109/10**

14 1 1/2 **Gherdaiya**22 4695 3-8-11 0 GregoryBenoist 6 75
(A Fabre, France) *hld up in midfield: outpcd and rdn 2f out: sn btn* **60/1**

15 1/2 **Surava**14 3-8-11 0 JulienAuge 1 74
(C Ferland, France) *led: hdd after 3f: remained prom: wknd 1 1/2f out* **143/10**

1m 43.33s (2.53) **15** Ran SP% **119.4**
PARI-MUTUEL (all including 1 euro stake): WIN 6.50; PLACE 2.40, 1.90, 5.50; DF 14.90; SF 40.70.
Owner Jean-Claude Seroul **Bred** Dr Georges Sandor & Mme Jacqueline Sandor **Trained** Chantilly, France

5499a PRIX GUILLAUME D'ORNANO - HARAS DU LOGIS SAINT-GERMAIN (GROUP 2) (3YO) (TURF) 1m 2f

3:00 (12:00) 3-Y-O £167,647 (£64,705; £30,882; £20,588; £10,294)

RPR

1 **Almanzor (FR)**71 2946 3-9-2 0 Jean-BernardEyquem 5 118+
(J-C Rouget, France) *settled towards rr: rdn along fr 2f out: gd hdwy and c to chal ins fnl f: led 75yds out* **3/1**3

2 1 **Zarak (FR)**71 2946 3-9-2 0 ChristopheSoumillon 3 116
(A De Royer-Dupre, France) *midfield: hdwy appr 2f out: rdn along to ld 1 1/2f out: hdd 75yds out* **29/10**2

3 1 1/4 **Royal Artillery (USA)**9 5159 3-9-2 0 FrankieDettori 6 114
(John Gosden) *slt stumble s: led: rdn along u.p 2f out: hdd 1 1/2f out: unable to go w ldrs but kpt on wl for 3rd* **8/1**

4 2 **Taareef (USA)**54 3543 3-9-2 0 IoritzMendizabal 7 110
(J-C Rouget, France) *towards rr early: hdwy between runners fr 2f out: unable to go w ldrs fnl f* **209/10**

5 snk **Steel Of Madrid (IRE)**19 4753 3-9-2 0 StephanePasquier 8 110
(Richard Hannon) *settled in midfield: rdn along 2 1/2f out: nt the pce to chal: kpt on* **80/1**

6 1/2 **Ultra (IRE)**29 4439 3-9-2 0 MickaelBarzalona 9 109
(A Fabre, France) *settled in rr: stl last whn asked for effrt 2f out: unable to get on terms w ldrs* **23/10**1

7 1 1/4 **Heshem (IRE)**29 4439 3-9-2 0 GregoryBenoist 1 106
(C Ferland, France) *prom early: effrt 2f out: unable qck and sn btn* **42/10**

8 3/4 **Sky Kingdom (IRE)**107 1866 3-9-2 0 GeraldMosse 2 105
(William Haggas) *midfield: pushed along 3f out: unable to get on terms w ldrs: eased fnl f* **43/1**

9 5 **Lamarck**29 4439 3-9-2 0 AndreasHelfenbein 4 95
(M G Mintchev, Germany) *prom early: hrd rdn 2f out: unable to pick up: wl btn and wknd fnl f* **146/1**

2m 9.63s (-0.57) **9** Ran SP% **120.0**
PARI-MUTUEL (all including 1 euro stake): WIN 4.00; PLACE 1.60, 1.70, 2.30; DF 7.10; SF 12.80.
Owner Ecurie Antonio Caro & Gerard Augustin-Normand **Bred** Haras D'Etreham **Trained** Pau, France

5500a PRIX GONTAUT-BIRON HONG KONG JOCKEY CLUB (GROUP 3) (4YO+) (TURF) 1m 2f

3:40 (12:00) 4-Y-O+ £29,411 (£11,764; £8,823; £5,882; £2,941)

RPR

1 **New Bay**83 2568 4-8-9 0 VincentCheminaud 4 113+
(A Fabre, France) *led briefly s: settled in 2nd: 3rd 5f out: hdwy fr 3f out: moved comf into ld jst over 2f out: kpt up to work fnl f: a holding chalrs* **30/100**1

2 1 1/2 **Arthenus**37 4165 4-8-9 0 (p) Pierre-CharlesBoudot 1 107
(James Fanshawe) *sn led: hdd over 2f out: kpt on wl but unable to get bk on terms w wnr* **106/10**3

3 1 1/4 **Garlingari (FR)**19 4783 5-9-4 0 (p) ThierryThulliez 3 114
(Mme C Barande-Barbe, France) *towards rr early: rdn along 2f out: nt the pce to chal but kpt on wl for 3rd* **18/5**2

4 1 3/4 **Brisanto**15 4928 4-8-9 0 AndreasHelfenbein 2 101
(M G Mintchev, Germany) *3rd early: moved up to 2nd 5f out: rdn along to chal over 2f out: sn btn: wknd fnl f* **167/10**

5 snk **Royal Dolois (FR)**19 4783 4-8-9 0 IoritzMendizabal 5 101
(J-M Lefebvre, France) *awkward s: a in rr: nvr on terms* **138/10**

2m 12.67s (2.47) **5** Ran SP% **119.7**
PARI-MUTUEL (all including 1 euro stake): WIN 1.30; PLACE 1.10, 1.10; SF 4.60.
Owner K Abdullah **Bred** Juddmonte Farms Ltd **Trained** Chantilly, France

5501a PRIX LADIES DAY (PRIX DE BOIS CARROUGES) (CLAIMER) (4YO+) (POLYTRACK) 1m 1f 110y

4:15 (12:00) 4-Y-O+ £6,985 (£2,794; £2,095; £1,397; £698)

RPR

1 **Saane (FR)**16 4903 5-9-1 0 CristianDemuro 7 74
(J-C Rouget, France) **8/5**1

2 3/4 **Anantapur (FR)**16 4901 4-9-4 0 KyllanBarbaud(6) 3 81
(S Cerulis, France) **32/5**

3 1/2 **Madiva (FR)**36 4-8-11 0 (p) AlexisBadel 2 67
(Mme M Bollack-Badel, France) **193/10**

4 shd **Polkarena (FR)**38 4-9-5 0 AntoineHamelin 4 75
(J-P Gauvin, France) **11/2**2

5 1 **Pistoletto (SPA)**28 5-9-4 0 AnthonyCrastus 5 72
(N Caullery, France) **96/10**

6 nk **Danileo (IRE)**434 5-9-5 0 HugoJourniac(3) 1 75
(F Rossi, France) **56/10**3

7 1/2 **Kingspone (FR)**42 5-9-5 0 (p) GregoryBenoist 6 71
(Mme P Butel, France) **109/10**

8 1 1/2 **Kassim (IRE)**96 4-9-4 0 MlleIsisMagnin(6) 8 73
(J-M Lefebvre, France) **40/1**

9 1 1/4 **Maply (FR)**16 4901 4-8-9 0 MlleAlisonMassin(6) 9 61
(Y Barberot, France) **51/1**

10 snk **Latin Charm (IRE)**15 4927 5-9-1 0 (p) Pierre-CharlesBoudot 11 61
(Gay Kelleway) *midfield on outer early: moved up to ld 6f out: hdd over 3f out: rdn along but unable qck: wl btn whn eased fnl f* **51/1**

11 nse **Misty Love (FR)**16 4901 4-9-2 0 ChristopheSoumillon 10 62
(F Vermeulen, France) **117/10**

\n\x\x PARI-MUTUEL (all including 1 euro stake): WIN 2.60; PLACE 1.50, 2.40, 3.30;
Owner Gerard Augustin-Normand **Bred** Franklin Finance S.A. **Trained** Pau, France

5249 SAN SEBASTIAN (R-H)

Monday, August 15

OFFICIAL GOING: Turf: good

5502a COPA DE ORO DE SAN SEBASTIAN (LISTED RACE) (3YO+) (TURF) 1m 4f

5:00 (12:00) 3-Y-O+ £29,411 (£11,764; £5,882; £2,941)

RPR

1 **Flanders Flame**50 3-8-7 0 RicardoSousa 15 102
(Helder Pereira, Spain) **23/5**3

2 1/2 **Madrileno**50 4-9-4 0 VaclavJanacek 7 101
(G Arizkorreta Elosegui, Spain) **2/1**1

3 nk **Rooke**79 2713 6-9-4 0 ThomasHenderson 8 101
(D Henderson, France) **6/1**

4 2 **Gwafa (IRE)**30 6127 5-9-4 0 OscarUrbina 10 97
(Paul Webber) *w.w towards rr: rdn along and no immediate imp 4f out: persevered w and styd on fr over 2f out: gng on wl fnl f: tk 4th post: nvr nrr* **41/5**

5 nse **Nemqueteba (FR)**78 3-8-7 0 BorjaFayosMartin 13 97
(J-M Osorio, Spain) **18/5**2

6 4 3/4 **Eric (GER)**43 3934 5-9-4 0 AlexanderPietsch 4 90
(C Von Der Recke, Germany) **198/10**

7 3/4 **Alaraz (SPA)**85 4-9-4 0 JulienGrosjean 5 88
(G Arizkorreta Elosegui, Spain) **23/1**

8 1 1/4 **Striving (GER)**50 5-9-4 0 FranckBlondel 9 86
(F Rohaut, France) **29/1**

9 2 1/4 **Santo Spirito**50 5-9-4 0 Francois-XavierBertras 11 83
(F Rohaut, France) **161/10**

10 1 1/4 **Lateran Accord (IRE)**50 7-9-4 0 (v) JaimeGelabert 16 81
(G Arizkorreta Elosegui, Spain) **2/1**1

11 1 1/2 **Sant'Alberto (ITY)**399 8-9-4 0 SoufianeSaadi 6 78
(D Teixeira, Spain) **51/1**

12 dist **Keshiro (IRE)**50 6-9-4 0 (b) MarinoGomes 3
(Michaella Augelli, Spain) **42/1**

13 5 3/4 **Intaglio (POR)**78 3-8-7 0 Jean-BaptisteHamel 1
(Ana Imaz Ceca, Spain) **35/1**

14 1 3/4 **Atacama (SPA)** 3-8-7 0 Roberto-CarlosMontenegro 14
(Ana Imaz Ceca, Spain) **36/1**

15 nk **Arkaitz (SPA)**295 7500 5-9-4 0 JoseLuisMartinez 2
(Ana Imaz Ceca, Spain) **114/10**

16 2 1/2 **Vizcaya (IRE)**363 4-9-1 0 IvanBorrego 12
(G Arizkorreta Elosegui, Spain) **2/1**1

2m 31.3s (151.30)
WFA 3 from 4yo+ 11lb **16** Ran SP% **200.7**
.
Owner Nossa Senhora Do Vale **Bred** Dukes Stud & Overbury Stallions Ltd **Trained** Spain

[5297]KEMPTON (A.W) (R-H)

Tuesday, August 16

OFFICIAL GOING: Polytrack: standard to slow

Wind: Moderate, half behind Weather: Fine, warm

5503 APOLLOBET ONLINE CASINO & GAMES H'CAP 1m (P)

2:15 (2:16) (Class 5) (0-70,70) 3-Y-O+ **£2,911** (£866; £432; £216) **Stalls** Low

Form RPR

2033 **1** **Pike Corner Cross (IRE)**[12] 5057 4-9-9 **67**.................... JimCrowley 12 80+
(Ed de Giles) *stdd s: hld up in last: stl great deal to do over 2f out: rapid prog on outer over 1f out: drvn and r.o wl to ld last strides* **11/2**[1]

1-54 **2** *nk* **Pendo**[15] 4956 5-9-9 **67**.................................... KierenFox 1 76
(John Best) *led after 1f: clr w one rival 2f out: drvn and kpt on wl fr over 1f out: looked sure to win but mown down last strides* **15/2**

0164 **3** *1 ½* **Star Of The Stage**[27] 4528 4-9-12 **70**....................(p) AdamBeschizza 3 75
(Julia Feilden) *led 1f: chsd ldr: rdn and clr of rest fr 2f out: kpt on but no imp and lost 2nd last 50yds* **8/1**

0525 **4** *3 ½* **Cornelious (IRE)**[27] 4528 4-9-8 **66**....................(v) DarryllHolland 13 63
(Clifford Lines) *racd on outer: chsd ldng trio: rdn and outpcd 2f out: one pce after* **13/2**[3]

250 **5** *2* **Almanack**[20] 4772 6-9-2 **63**....................(t) NathanAlison(3) 2 55
(Daniel Mark Loughnane) *dwlt: sn in midfield: rdn over 2f out: limited rspnse and sn outpcd: plugged on* **20/1**

0052 **6** *1* **Dana's Present**[29] 4463 7-9-9 **67**.................................... LiamKeniry 10 56
(Tom Dascombe) *hld up in last trio: gng wl enough 3f out: asked to make prog over 2f out but only plugged on past btn rivals* **6/1**[2]

0034 **7** *3* **Rock Palm (IRE)**[20] 4777 3-8-12 **62**....................(p) MartinDwyer 5 43
(Brendan Powell) *t.k.h: hld up in midfield: shkn up over 2f out: no great prog and nvr really figured* **8/1**

0005 **8** *shd* **Freddy With A Y (IRE)**[13] 5024 6-9-9 **67**....................(p) JimmyQuinn 11 49
(Paul Burgoyne) *chsd ldrs: rdn and outpcd over 2f out: wl btn after* **15/2**

0000 **9** *nse* **Welsh Inlet (IRE)**[33] 4302 8-8-9 **53**.................................... WilliamCarson 6 35
(John Bridger) *chsd ldng pair: outpcd 2f out: wknd over 1f out* **25/1**

0123 **10** *1 ¾* **Illusive Force (IRE)**[22] 4715 4-9-3 **61**....................(v) MartinLane 4 39
(Derek Shaw) *nvr bttr than midfield: wknd over 1f out* **10/1**

6460 **11** *3* **Sheila's Treat (IRE)**[13] 5013 3-9-6 **70**....................(p) OisinMurphy 8 39
(Denis Coakley) *hld up in rr: shkn up and no prog over 2f out: wl btn after* **12/1**

-500 **12** *14* **Sheer Honesty**[13] 5010 4-9-0 **65**.................................... JoshuaBryan(7) 7 2
(Anabel K Murphy) *a in rr: wknd wl over 2f out: t.o* **66/1**

1m 39.06s (-0.74) **Going Correction** +0.05s/f (Slow)
WFA 3 from 4yo+ 6lb **12** Ran SP% **115.6**
Speed ratings (Par 103): **105,104,103,99,97 96,93,93,93,91 88,74**
CSF £43.99 CT £333.25 TOTE £5.30: £1.90, £2.70, £2.40; EX 32.90 Trifecta £154.20.
Owner Tight Lines Partnership **Bred** Rockfield Farm **Trained** Ledbury, H'fords
■ Dunnscotia was withdrawn. Price at time of withdrawal 13/2. Rule 4 applies to bets struck prior to withdrawal but not to SP bets - deduction 10p in the pound. New market formed.

FOCUS
This wide-open looking handicap wasn't run to suit the closers. The winner is worth better than the bare form.

5504 APOLLOBET PREMIER LEAGUE CASHBACK MAIDEN FILLIES' STKS 1m (P)

2:45 (2:46) (Class 5) 3-Y-O+ **£2,911** (£866; £432; £216) **Stalls** Low

Form RPR

22-0 **1** **Honorina**[32] 4367 3-9-0 78.................................... OisinMurphy 9 76+
(Sir Michael Stoute) *pressed ldr: shkn up to ld 2f out: rdn and steadily drew clr over 1f out: styd on wl* **5/6**[1]

2 *2 ¼* **Trishuli Rock (IRE)** 3-8-11 0.................................... DanielMuscutt(3) 2 71+
(Marco Botti) *dwlt: sn in midfield: prog over 2f out: rdn to chse wnr jst ins fnl f: no imp but styd on steadily* **16/1**

45 **3** *2 ¾* **Entrench**[60] 3350 3-9-0 0.................................... PatDobbs 3 65
(Amanda Perrett) *mde most: shkn up and hdd 2f out: wl hld over 1f out: fdd and lost 2nd jst ins fnl f: sddle slipped* **3/1**[2]

4 *¾* **Flower Of Love** 3-9-0 0....................(t) AndreaAtzeni 5 62+
(Simon Crisford) *towards rr: pushed along over 2f out: no real prog tl styd on wl fnl f: nrst fin* **7/1**

5 *1* **Electrify (IRE)** 3-9-0 0.................................... JimCrowley 6 60
(Jeremy Noseda) *chsd ldng pair: no imp over 1f out: fdd fnl f* **6/1**[3]

0 **6** *¾* **Golden Muscade (USA)**[13] 5023 3-8-7 0.................................... JoshuaBryan(7) 1 58?
(Brian Barr) *chsd ldrs: shkn up over 2f out: outpcd and n.d sn after* **150/1**

60 **7** *shd* **Just For Show (IRE)**[43] 3958 3-9-0 0.................................... WilliamCarson 8 58?
(Shaun Lycett) *chsd ldrs: rdn and outpcd over 2f out: sn btn* **50/1**

0- **8** *3 ¼* **Royal Alstroemeria**[309] 7160 3-8-11 0.................................... ShelleyBirkett(3) 10 50
(Stuart Kittow) *hld up in rr: shkn up and struggling over 2f out: fdd* **33/1**

30 **9** *10* **Embroidery (IRE)**[55] 3508 3-9-0 0.................................... SamHitchcott 4 26
(Harry Dunlop) *racd on outer: towards rr: struggling 1/2-way: wknd wl over 2f out: bhd over 1f out* **50/1**

0 **10** *25* **Twilight Pursuits**[70] 2998 3-9-0 0.................................... JimmyQuinn 7
(Natalie Lloyd-Beavis) *a in last pair: t.o* **250/1**

1m 40.2s (0.40) **Going Correction** +0.05s/f (Slow) **10** Ran SP% **120.1**
Speed ratings (Par 100): **100,97,95,94,93 92,92,89,79,54**
CSF £18.74 TOTE £1.80: £1.10, £5.40, £1.60; EX 21.10 Trifecta £57.50.
Owner Qatar Racing Limited **Bred** Qatar Bloodstock Ltd **Trained** Newmarket, Suffolk

FOCUS
An uncompetitive fillies' maiden, run at a fair enough pace. The winner didn't need to improve.

5505 APOLLOBET RACING REFUNDS/BRITISH STALLION STUDS EBF MAIDEN STKS 1m (P)

3:15 (3:16) (Class 5) 2-Y-O **£3,234** (£962; £481; £240) **Stalls** Low

Form RPR

3 **1** **Red Ensign (IRE)**[32] 4349 2-9-5 0.................................... AndreaAtzeni 7 84+
(Simon Crisford) *led after 2f: mde rest: pushed clr wl over 1f out: comf* **2/5**[1]

42 **2** *3 ¼* **Al Hamdany (IRE)**[14] 4975 2-9-2 0.................................... DanielMuscutt(3) 3 76
(Marco Botti) *led 2f: sn in 3rd: rdn to chse wnr wl over 1f out: styd on but n.d* **15/2**[3]

3 *2 ½* **Draw Swords** 2-9-5 0.................................... WilliamBuick 9 70+
(John Gosden) *pressed wnr over 5f out: shkn up over 2f out: lost 2nd and outpcd wl over 1f out* **7/1**[2]

0 **4** *2 ¼* **Percy Thrower (IRE)**[14] 4989 2-9-5 0.................................... MichaelJMMurphy 1 65
(Charles Hills) *dwlt: in rr: prog on inner to take 4th 2f out: one pce and no imp after* **14/1**

5 *3 ¾* **Mr Maximum (USA)** 2-9-5 0.................................... JimCrowley 4 56
(Harry Dunlop) *prom: rdn over 2f out: sn lft bhd* **25/1**

0 **6** *2 ¼* **Auric Goldfinger (IRE)**[14] 4988 2-9-5 0.................................... PatDobbs 5 50+
(Richard Hannon) *dwlt: towards rr: pushed along and readily lft bhd over 2f out* **50/1**

7 *1 ¼* **City Limits** 2-9-5 0.................................... JamieSpencer 8 47
(Luca Cumani) *dwlt: prog on outer to chse ldrs 1/2-way: shkn up and rn green wl over 2f out: sn wknd* **8/1**

8 *6* **Designamento (IRE)** 2-9-5 0.................................... LiamKeniry 6 33
(Ed de Giles) *dwlt: struggling in last bef 1/2-way: bhd over 2f out* **66/1**

1m 40.85s (1.05) **Going Correction** +0.05s/f (Slow) **8** Ran SP% **120.8**
Speed ratings (Par 94): **96,92,90,88,84 82,80,74**
CSF £4.71 TOTE £1.40: £1.02, £1.60, £2.10; EX 4.80 Trifecta £18.10.
Owner Sheikh Mohammed Obaid Al Maktoum **Bred** New Line Stud Ltd **Trained** Newmarket, Suffolk

FOCUS
An interesting 2yo maiden, rated around the runner-up. The winner looks sure to improve.

5506 APOLLOBET OLYMPIC GAMES CASHBACK NURSERY H'CAP 7f (P)

3:45 (3:47) (Class 4) (0-85,79) 2-Y-O **£3,946** (£1,174; £586; £293) **Stalls** Low

Form RPR

1 **1** **Fly At Dawn (USA)**[25] 4594 2-9-6 **79**.................................... WilliamBuick 2 90+
(Charlie Appleby) *trckd ldr after 1f: led 2f out: pushed along quite firmly and drew clr fnl f: readily* **30/100**[1]

01 **2** *3* **Northdown**[27] 4523 2-9-4 **77**.................................... ShaneKelly 1 78
(David Lanigan) *chsd ldr 1f: urged along 3f out: kpt on u.p to win battle for 2nd nr fin: no ch w wnr* **6/1**[2]

602 **3** *nk* **Mums The Word**[29] 4457 2-9-2 **75**.................................... PatDobbs 3 75
(Richard Hannon) *led: shkn up and hdd 2f out: no ch w wnr fnl f: lost 2nd nr fin* **14/1**

1203 **4** *½* **Spirit Of Sarwan (IRE)**[25] 4595 2-9-2 **75**.................................... AdamBeschizza 4 74
(Julia Feilden) *in tch in last: rdn wl over 2f out: nvr any ch but kpt on fnl f* **10/1**[3]

1m 27.23s (1.23) **Going Correction** +0.05s/f (Slow) **4** Ran SP% **107.0**
Speed ratings (Par 96): **94,90,90,89**
CSF £2.44 TOTE £1.20; EX 2.70 Trifecta £5.10.
Owner Godolphin **Bred** Darley **Trained** Newmarket, Suffolk

FOCUS
Not a bad little nursery and a talented winner. The form is rated around the runner-up's maiden.

5507 APOLLOBET BET THROUGH YOUR MOBILE H'CAP 7f (P)

4:15 (4:15) (Class 3) (0-90,88) 3-Y-O+

£7,158 (£2,143; £1,071; £535; £267; £134) **Stalls** Low

Form RPR

2301 **1** **Loaded (IRE)**[28] 4480 3-9-0 **81**.................................... OisinMurphy 3 95
(Andrew Balding) *disp ld at decent pce: def advantage 3f out: rdn clr over 2f out: drvn out and kpt on wl* **3/1**[2]

1005 **2** *2 ¾* **Gambit**[28] 4475 3-9-6 **87**.................................... RichardKingscote 1 93
(Tom Dascombe) *chsd ldng pair: wnt 2nd over 2f out: drvn and styd on but nvr any imp on wnr* **5/1**[3]

2456 **3** *3 ½* **Arab Poet**[31] 4402 3-9-4 **85**.................................... AndreaAtzeni 2 81
(Sir Michael Stoute) *racd in 5th and off the pce: rdn and prog over 2f out: styd on to take 3rd jst ins fnl f: nvr able to threaten* **9/4**[1]

3155 **4** *1 ¾* **King Of Naples**[57] 3466 3-9-0 **88**.................................... GeorgeWood(7) 9 79
(James Fanshawe) *chsd ldng trio: rdn to go 3rd wl over 1f out to jst ins fnl f: nvr a threat and fdd nr fin* **12/1**

31-0 **5** *shd* **Taqwaa (IRE)**[20] 4776 3-9-6 **87**.................................... PatDobbs 5 78
(Richard Hannon) *dwlt: wl off the pce in rr: rdn over 2f out: kpt on fr over 1f out but nvr really a factor* **7/1**

0020 **6** *2* **Morache Music**[15] 4954 8-9-6 **85**.................................... DanielMuscutt(3) 8 73
(Patrick Chamings) *settled in last pair and wl off the pce: rdn over 2f out: plugged on same pce* **25/1**

0140 **7** *1 ¼* **Secret Glance**[24] 4627 4-8-13 **75**.................................... AdamBeschizza 6 59
(Richard Rowe) *off the pce in 6th: rdn and struggling 3f out: sn no ch* **16/1**

3420 **8** *3 ¾* **Captain Lars (SAF)**[108] 1869 7-9-1 **77**....................(p) MartinLane 4 51
(Derek Shaw) *hld up in last pair: pushed along and no prog over 2f out: wknd over 1f out* **33/1**

0332 **9** *1 ¼* **Sarangoo**[12] 5075 8-8-12 **74**.................................... JimCrowley 7 45
(Malcolm Saunders) *disp ld at decent pce to 3f out: wknd qckly over 2f out* **12/1**

1m 25.05s (-0.95) **Going Correction** +0.05s/f (Slow)
WFA 3 from 4yo+ 5lb **9** Ran SP% **113.0**
Speed ratings (Par 107): **107,103,99,97,97 95,94,89,88**
CSF £18.01 CT £38.34 TOTE £3.30: £1.10, £2.40, £1.40; EX 20.10 Trifecta £66.70.
Owner Mr & Mrs R M Gorell **Bred** Ms Alice Fitzgerald **Trained** Kingsclere, Hants

FOCUS
Despite setting a decent pace in this fair handicap the leaders weren't for catching. Another improved run from the winner.

5508 APOLLOBET FREE SIGN-UP BONUS FILLIES' H'CAP 1m 4f (P)

4:45 (4:47) (Class 5) (0-75,78) 3-Y-O+ **£2,911** (£866; £432; £216) **Stalls** Centre

Form RPR

3531 **1** **Great Thoughts (IRE)**[8] 5245 3-9-9 **78** 6ex.................... FrederikTylicki 4 86+
(David Simcock) *last after 4f but wl in tch: shkn up and clsng whn lft in ld and handed r 2f out: mde most of it and styd on strly fr over 1f out* **7/2**[3]

-602 **2** *3 ½* **Percy's Romance**[60] 3355 3-9-4 **73**.................................... AndreaAtzeni 1 76+
(Sir Michael Stoute) *trckd ldng pair: wnt 2nd and chalng whn bdly hmpd over 2f out: no ch w wnr after: kpt on to take 2nd again nr fin* **7/4**[1]

4-00 **3** *½* **Pure Vanity**[11] 5122 3-8-3 **65**.................................... MitchGodwin(7) 5 65
(Roger Charlton) *led: rdn and hung bdly lft over 2f out causing carnage: sn hdd: continued hanging lft and no ch w wnr: lost 2nd nr fin* **25/1**

0021 **4** *4 ½* **Zain Arion (IRE)**[34] 4277 3-8-13 **68**.................................... WilliamBuick 3 63+
(Charlie Fellowes) *chsd ldng trio after 4f: urged along over 3f out: looked to be struggling whn hmpd over 2f out: no ch after* **2/1**[2]

4614 **5** *18* **Cold Fusion (IRE)**[24] 4635 3-9-4 **73**.................................... OisinMurphy 2 65+
(Ed Vaughan) *trckd ldr: rdn and dropped to 3rd whn hmpd over 2f out: lost all ch and eased* **6/1**

2m 35.06s (0.56) **Going Correction** +0.05s/f (Slow) **5** Ran SP% **110.1**
Speed ratings (Par 100): **100,97,97,94,82**
CSF £10.07 TOTE £3.90: £1.90, £1.10; EX 10.00 Trifecta £81.90.
Owner Sultan Ali **Bred** Ennistown Stud **Trained** Newmarket, Suffolk

FOCUS
This fillies' handicap was always likely to prove tactical and there was drama in the home straight. Form to treat with caution.

5509 APOLLOBET DOWNLOAD THE FREE APP H'CAP 6f (P)
5:15 (5:16) (Class 6) (0-60,60) 3-Y-O+ £2,264 (£673; £336; £168) Stalls Low

Form RPR
0630 1 **For Ayman**[41] 4008 5-9-0 **60**....(t) SeanMooney(7) 11 71
(Joseph Tuite) *hld up in midfield fr wd draw: shkn up over 1f out: clsd qckly to ld 150yds out and sn clr* **8/1**[3]
3445 2 2 ¾ **Foxford**[27] 4525 5-8-8 **54**.... MitchGodwin(7) 10 57
(Patrick Chamings) *spd fr wd draw to ld after 1f: gng strly over 2f out: rdn and hanging rt over 1f out: hdd and qckly outpcd last 150yds* **5/1**[1]
2003 3 1 ½ **Wattaboutsteve**[9] 5194 5-8-9 **48**.... JimCrowley 8 46
(Ralph J Smith) *chsd ldrs: rdn 2f out: trying to cl whn wnr shot past fnl f: one pce after* **8/1**[3]
0006 4 1 **Burauq**[11] 5126 4-8-7 **46** oh1....(b) JimmyQuinn 6 41
(Milton Bradley) *trckd ldng pair: chsd ldr over 2f out: rdn and no imp over 1f out: lost 2nd jst ins fnl f: fdd* **16/1**
6500 5 nse **Smoothtalkinrascal (IRE)**[15] 4952 6-9-5 **58**....(t) TomQueally 7 53
(Peter Crate) *sn in last pair: shkn up and no prog over 2f out: no ch after but kpt on fnl f: nrst fin* **7/1**[2]
0405 6 hd **Port Gaverne (IRE)**[13] 5027 3-8-11 **60**....(p) TylerSaunders(7) 3 55
(Marcus Tregoning) *chsd ldrs: rdn and no imp 2f out: one pce after* **8/1**[3]
2440 7 1 **Little Indian**[41] 4008 6-9-5 **58**.... FrederikTylicki 2 50
(J R Jenkins) *chsd ldrs: rdn and no prog over 2f out: n.d after* **5/1**[1]
0600 8 1 ½ **Alketios (GR)**[55] 3522 5-9-4 **57**.... LiamKeniry 9 44
(Chris Gordon) *dwlt: in tch in rr: rdn and no prog over 2f out: wl btn after* **16/1**
5000 9 ½ **Bubbly Bailey**[109] 1833 6-9-1 **57**....(v) AlistairRawlinson(3) 4 43
(J R Jenkins) *led 1f: chsd ldr to over 2f out: sn wknd* **33/1**
10 3 ¾ **Another Day**[44] 3-8-9 **51**.... OisinMurphy 1 25
(Robert Cowell) *dwlt: mostly in last and a struggling* **5/1**[1]
043- 11 7 **On The Huh**[307] 7216 4-8-9 **51**....(p) NoelGarbutt(3) 5
(Derek Shaw) *chsd ldrs to over 2f out: wknd rapidly: t.o* **25/1**

1m 13.4s (0.30) **Going Correction** +0.05s/f (Slow)
WFA 3 from 4yo+ 3lb **11** Ran SP% **114.4**
Speed ratings (Par 101): **100,96,94,93,92 92,91,89,88,83 74**
CSF £46.38 CT £267.37 TOTE £9.60: £2.60, £1.90, £2.40; EX 58.40 Trifecta £313.20.
Owner I & K Prince **Bred** Anthony Byrne **Trained** Lambourn, Berks

FOCUS
A weak sprint handicap. The winner is rated back to last year's late-season form.
T/Jkpt: £133.30 to a £1 stake. Pool: £10,000.00 - 75 winning tickets. T/Plt: £5.70 to a £1 stake. Pool: £67,844.30 - 8,634.31 winning tickets. T/Qpdt: £2.30 to a £1 stake. Pool: £4,032.28 - 1,265.48 winning tickets. **Jonathan Neesom**

5195 LEICESTER (R-H)
Tuesday, August 16

OFFICIAL GOING: Good to firm (7.1) (watered)
Wind: Light across Weather: Fine and sunny

5510 KIRKBY MALLORY NURSERY H'CAP 5f
5:40 (5:41) (Class 4) (0-85,85) 2-Y-O £4,528 (£1,347; £673; £336) Stalls High

Form RPR
3400 1 **Sayesse**[18] 4825 2-9-1 **79**.... GrahamLee 8 83
(Mick Channon) *sn outpcd: swtchd rt and hdwy over 1f out: rdn and r.o to ld wl ins fnl f* **20/1**
1020 2 1 **Prince Of Cool**[18] 4825 2-9-1 **79**.... TomEaves 7 79
(James Given) *in rr: outpcd over 3f out: rdn 1/2-way: r.o wl ins fnl f: wnt 2nd post* **10/1**[3]
61 3 hd **Lanjano**[20] 4765 2-8-12 **76**.... KevinStott 6 76
(Kevin Ryan) *chsd ldrs: rdn to ld over 1f out: hdd wl ins fnl f* **7/2**[2]
142 4 1 ½ **Shamsaya (IRE)**[33] 4297 2-9-3 **84**.... JosephineGordon(3) 3 78
(Simon Crisford) *sn pushed along to chse ldrs: rdn over 1f out: styd on same pce ins fnl f* **7/2**[2]
1454 5 shd **Lawless Louis**[18] 4832 2-8-12 **81**.... JoshDoyle(5) 4 75
(David O'Meara) *led: rdn and hdd over 1f out: styd on same pce ins fnl f* **11/1**
41 6 2 ¾ **Grey Galleon (USA)**[22] 4706 2-9-4 **82**.... AdamKirby 2 66
(Clive Cox) *prom: rdn 2f out: wknd wl ins fnl f* **13/8**[1]
1356 7 ½ **Awesome Allan (IRE)**[90] 2371 2-9-2 **80**.... JFEgan 5 62
(David Evans) *w ldr tl rdn 1/2-way: wknd ins fnl f* **16/1**

59.01s (-0.99) **Going Correction** -0.125s/f (Firm) **7** Ran SP% **110.6**
Speed ratings (Par 96): **102,100,100,97,97 93,92**
CSF £182.90 CT £835.48 TOTE £15.40: £7.50, £5.20; EX 112.40 Trifecta £761.40.
Owner Lord Ilsley Racing (Steele Syndicate) **Bred** Llety Farms **Trained** West Ilsley, Berks

FOCUS
A decent nursery run at a strong tempo, in which the first two home couldn't go the early pace. Straightforward form.

5511 BEEBY MAIDEN AUCTION FILLIES' STKS (PLUS 10 RACE) 5f
6:10 (6:12) (Class 5) 2-Y-O £3,234 (£962; £481; £240) Stalls High

Form RPR
304 1 **Snuggy (IRE)**[32] 4371 2-8-8 67.... SilvestreDeSousa 7 67
(David Barron) *sn chsng ldrs: rdn 2f out: led ins fnl f: r.o* **13/2**[3]
4245 2 1 ¼ **Local Artist (IRE)**[23] 4678 2-8-10 63.... JasonHart 5 65
(John Quinn) *chsd ldr: rdn to ld over 1f out: edgd lft and hdd ins fnl f: styd on same pce* **7/1**
4 3 hd **Vote**[67] 3106 2-8-8 0.... RyanTate 4 62
(James Eustace) *hld up: hdwy over 1f out: styd on* **3/1**[2]
02 4 2 **Acertwo**[7] 5258 2-8-8 0.... JFEgan 6 55
(Joseph Tuite) *sn led: rdn 1/2-way: hdd over 1f out: no ex ins fnl f* **14/1**
5 1 ¼ **Free At Last (IRE)** 2-8-10 0.... TomEaves 3 52
(Richard Fahey) *hld up: hdwy and racd keenly 3f out: hung lft and nt clr run fr over 1f out tl swtchd rt ins fnl f: styd on same pce* **16/1**
242 6 3 ¼ **Broadhaven Honey (IRE)**[29] 4451 2-8-10 68.... GrahamLee 8 40
(Ed McMahon) *w ldr tl over 3f out: rdn 1/2-way: wknd over 1f out* **9/4**[1]
0 7 ½ **Seaview**[43] 3954 2-8-12 0.... RobertWinston 2 41
(Dean Ivory) *prom: rdn 1/2-way: wknd fnl f* **8/1**
0302 8 3 ½ **Swan Serenade**[18] 4815 2-8-5 61.... EdwardGreatrex(3) 1 24
(Jonathan Portman) *hld up: hdwy 2f out: sn rdn: wknd fnl f* **16/1**

1m 0.75s (0.75) **Going Correction** -0.125s/f (Firm) **8** Ran SP% **111.1**
Speed ratings (Par 91): **89,87,86,83,81 76,75,69**
CSF £47.96 TOTE £7.30: £2.20, £2.10, £1.30; EX 45.10 Trifecta £247.60.
Owner A G Greenwood **Bred** Ballyhane Stud **Trained** Maunby, N Yorks

FOCUS
The pace wasn't as strong as in the nursery, and the time was 1.74 seconds slower. Pretty weak form.

5512 GRAHAM'S PEARL YEAR AT MEASOM H'CAP 6f
6:40 (6:40) (Class 4) (0-85,85) 3-Y-O+ £4,690 (£1,395; £697; £348) Stalls High

Form RPR
3035 1 **Reputation (IRE)**[17] 4867 3-9-7 **85**....(v) SilvestreDeSousa 1 98
(John Quinn) *s.i.s: hld up: swtchd lft 5f out: shkn up: hdwy and nt clr run over 1f out: r.o to ld wl ins fnl f: sn clr: comf* **11/4**[1]
-150 2 1 ¾ **Straightothepoint**[66] 3133 4-9-5 **80**.... ConnorBeasley 6 87
(Bryan Smart) *sn led: hdd wl over 4f out: chsd ldr tl led again over 2f out: rdn over 1f out: hdd and unable qck wl ins fnl f* **11/2**[3]
0602 3 ¾ **Signore Piccolo**[17] 4873 5-9-4 **79**.... DavidNolan 7 84
(David O'Meara) *sn w ldr: led wl over 4f out: rdn and hdd over 2f out: styd on* **12/1**
3-31 4 ¾ **Tanasoq (IRE)**[24] 4660 3-9-1 **79**.... PaulHanagan 2 81
(Owen Burrows) *hld up: hdwy over 2f out: sn hung lft: rdn over 1f out: styd on same pce ins fnl f* **7/1**
6520 5 shd **Ballymore Castle (IRE)**[17] 4862 4-9-5 **85**.... AdamMcNamara(5) 9 88
(Richard Fahey) *prom: rdn over 1f out: styd on same pce ins fnl f* **5/1**[2]
4013 6 1 **Classic Pursuit**[7] 5269 5-8-5 **69**....(p) JosephineGordon(3) 4 68
(Ivan Furtado) *s.s: hdwy 5f out: racd keenly after: rdn over 2f out: nt clr run and no ex ins fnl f* **7/1**
0263 7 shd **Explain**[10] 5161 4-9-8 **83**.... JamesSullivan 3 81
(Ruth Carr) *hld up: rdn over 2f out: nt clr run fr over 1f out: nt trble ldrs* **10/1**
1-00 8 1 ¾ **Easy Code**[39] 4116 3-8-7 **78**.... GeorgiaCox(7) 8 71
(William Haggas) *trckd ldrs: plld hrd: rdn and nt clr run over 1f out: sn swtchd rt: wknd ins fnl f* **40/1**
0303 9 nk **Mississippi**[30] 4428 7-9-4 **79**.... GrahamLee 5 71
(Paul Midgley) *prom: racd keenly: rdn over 2f out: wknd ins fnl f* **12/1**

1m 11.3s (-1.70) **Going Correction** -0.125s/f (Firm)
WFA 3 from 4yo+ 3lb **9** Ran SP% **110.6**
Speed ratings (Par 105): **106,103,102,101,101 100,100,97,97**
CSF £16.44 CT £144.50 TOTE £3.30: £1.40, £2.20, £4.30; EX 18.80 Trifecta £160.60.
Owner Highclere Thoroughbred Racing (Applause) **Bred** Moyns Park Estate And Stud Ltd **Trained** Settrington, N Yorks

FOCUS
A competitive mid-range sprint handicap. The winner built on his unlucky penultimate start.

5513 QDOS CONSULTING H'CAP 1m 1f 218y
7:10 (7:10) (Class 6) (0-60,58) 3-Y-O+ £2,911 (£866; £432; £216) Stalls Low

Form RPR
2424 1 **Exclusive Diamond**[12] 5064 4-9-7 **55**.... DavidNolan 11 61
(David O'Meara) *led after 1f: sn hdd: chsd ldr tl over 4f out: remained handy: rdn to chse ldr again over 1f out: r.o to ld nr fin* **5/1**[1]
0001 2 ½ **Anneani (IRE)**[36] 4214 4-9-7 **55**.... JFEgan 7 60
(David Evans) *hld up: hdwy over 5f out: chsd ldr over 4f out tl led over 2f out: rdn over 1f out: hdd nr fin* **7/1**
51 3 1 ¼ **Becca Campbell (IRE)**[11] 5101 3-9-0 **56**....(p) JohnFahy 6 60
(Eve Johnson Houghton) *chsd ldrs: nt clr run and lost pl 3f out: hdwy over 1f out: styd on* **11/2**[2]
0653 4 3 **Monopoli**[21] 4724 7-9-2 **50**....(p) RaulDaSilva 3 47
(Ivan Furtado) *led 1f: chsd ldrs: lost pl over 3f out: hdwy: nt clr run and swtchd lft over 2f out: rdn over 1f out: edgd rt ins fnl f: styd on* **7/1**
0000 5 1 ¼ **Kantara Castle (IRE)**[20] 4767 5-8-11 **45**....(tp) RoystonFfrench 9 40
(John Mackie) *chsd ldrs: rdn over 3f out: sn outpcd: hdwy over 1f out: styd on* **16/1**
-540 6 ½ **Graceful Lady**[26] 4562 3-9-2 **58**.... PaoloSirigu 10 52
(Robert Eddery) *s.s: hld up: rdn over 4f out: r.o ins fnl f: nvr nrr* **25/1**
0643 7 ½ **Canny Style**[17] 4872 3-8-12 **54**.... TomEaves 13 47
(Kevin Ryan) *stdd s: hld up: rdn over 2f out: r.o ins fnl f: nvr on terms* **9/1**
0626 8 1 **Goodwood Moonlight**[19] 4784 4-9-5 **53**....(p) AdamKirby 1 44
(Ian Williams) *hld up: hdwy over 3f out: rdn and ev ch over 2f out: wknd ins fnl f* **17/2**
6036 9 ¾ **Invincible Wish (IRE)**[39] 4082 4-9-7 **58**.... EoinWalsh(3) 5 47
(Trevor Wall) *hld up: hdwy over 3f out: jnd ldrs over 2f out: sn rdn: wknd fnl f* **16/1**
5-50 10 4 **Bunker Hill Lass**[12] 5055 4-9-6 **57**....(p) TimClark(3) 8 39
(Michael Appleby) *s.i.s: hld up: plld hrd: sme hdwy whn nt clr run over 1f out: sn wknd* **20/1**
0560 11 2 **Free One (IRE)**[12] 5064 4-9-9 **57**....(p) SilvestreDeSousa 12 35
(Ivan Furtado) *racd keenly and wd: led over 8f out: sn swtchd ins: clr over 5f out tl over 3f out: hdd over 2f out: wknd over 1f out* **13/2**[3]
006/ 12 28 **Master Choice (IRE)**[666] 7328 4-9-2 **50**.... GrahamLee 2
(Paul Green) *hld up: rdn and wknd over 3f out* **25/1**

2m 7.25s (-0.65) **Going Correction** 0.0s/f (Good)
WFA 3 from 4yo+ 8lb **12** Ran SP% **115.1**
Speed ratings (Par 101): **102,101,100,98,97 96,96,95,95,91 90,67**
CSF £37.10 CT £196.28 TOTE £5.50: £1.80, £2.60, £2.20; EX 39.20 Trifecta £245.50.
Owner R C Bond & C S Bond **Bred** Whatton Manor Stud **Trained** Upper Helmsley, N Yorks

FOCUS
A moderate handicap run at a decent pace. The right horses came to the fore.

5514 BARKBY THORPE H'CAP 1m 60y
7:40 (7:40) (Class 4) (0-85,85) 3-Y-O+ £4,690 (£1,395; £697; £348) Stalls Low

Form RPR
-311 1 **Alnashama**[18] 4839 4-9-7 **82**.... PaulHanagan 6 92+
(Charles Hills) *chsd ldrs: rdn to ld over 1f out: hung lft ins fnl f: r.o* **2/1**[1]
-000 2 ¾ **Top Beak (IRE)**[19] 4797 3-9-4 **85**....(t) JimmyFortune 5 92+
(Hughie Morrison) *hld up: hdwy and hung rt over 1f out: rdn and ev ch whn carried lft ins fnl f: nt qckn towards fin* **25/1**
2065 3 1 ½ **Steel Train (FR)**[17] 4893 5-9-7 **85**.... ShelleyBirkett(3) 4 90
(David O'Meara) *hld up: racd keenly: hdwy and nt clr run over 1f out: r.o* **16/1**
4602 4 1 ¾ **Abushamah (IRE)**[3] 5419 5-9-8 **83**.... JamesSullivan 9 84
(Ruth Carr) *s.i.s: hld up: hdwy and nt clr run over 1f out: styd on same pce ins fnl f* **4/1**[2]
6-60 5 ½ **Postbag**[59] 3410 4-9-4 **79**.... FergusSweeney 2 79
(Henry Candy) *chsd ldrs: rdn and ev ch over 1f out: no ex ins fnl f* **8/1**
060 6 hd **He's No Saint**[17] 4893 5-9-10 **85**....(v) DavidNolan 8 84
(David O'Meara) *sn led: rdn and hdd over 1f out: no ex ins fnl f* **11/1**
4523 7 ¾ **Company Asset (IRE)**[10] 5179 3-8-13 **80**.... GrahamLee 7 77
(Kevin Ryan) *hld up in tch: rdn over 2f out: nt clr run over 1f out: no ex ins fnl f* **5/1**[3]

1005 **8** 1 1/2 **Hulcolt (IRE)**[29] 4453 5-9-4 **82**.......................... JosephineGordon[(3)] 1 76
(Ivan Furtado) *chsd ldr: rdn and ev ch wl over 1f out: wknd ins fnl f* **12/1**
065 **9** *hd* **Intrude**[32] 4368 4-9-4 **79**.......................... PatCosgrave 3 73
(Stuart Williams) *hld up: effrt over 2f out: styd on same pce fr over 1f out* **25/1**

1m 43.8s (-1.30) **Going Correction** 0.0s/f (Good)
WFA 3 from 4yo+ 6lb **9** Ran SP% **110.7**
Speed ratings (Par 105): **106,105,103,102,101 101,100,99,98**
CSF £54.29 CT £593.33 TOTE £2.40: £1.30, £3.80, £3.60; EX 56.40 Trifecta £739.10.
Owner Hamdan Al Maktoum **Bred** Shadwell Estate Company Limited **Trained** Lambourn, Berks

FOCUS
A decent handicap run at just a medium pace even though two of the runners soon went clear of the others. The winner took another step forward.

5515 SHEARSBY H'CAP 7f
8:10 (8:11) (Class 6) (0-65,65) 3-Y-O **£2,587** (£770; £384; £192) **Stalls** High

Form RPR
0636 **1** **Tulip Dress**[11] 5127 3-8-13 **57**.......................... PaulHanagan 16 65
(Anthony Carson) *sn outpcd: hdwy wl over 1f out: sn edgd rt: led 1f out: hung rt ins fnl f: r.o wl* **33/1**
2025 **2** 1 3/4 **Marcle (IRE)**[11] 5104 3-9-7 **65**.......................... PatCosgrave 3 68
(Ed de Giles) *led 2f: remained w ldrs: rdn over 2f out: styd on u.p* **7/1**[3]
33-5 **3** 1/2 **Artists Model (IRE)**[74] 2848 3-9-5 **63**.......................... FergusSweeney 2 65
(Henry Candy) *w ldrs: rdn over 2f out: styd on same pce ins fnl f* **14/1**
0005 **4** *hd* **Fool's Dream**[17] 4870 3-8-7 **51**..........................(p) ConnorBeasley 1 52
(Bryan Smart) *w ldrs: rdn to ld over 1f out: sn hdd: no ex wl ins fnl f* **25/1**
6-40 **5** 1 3/4 **Beatbybeatbybeat**[110] 1804 3-9-7 **65**.......................... SilvestreDeSousa 12 62
(Ismail Mohammed) *hld up: hdwy and hung rt over 2f out: rdn and ev ch over 1f out: no ex ins fnl f* **9/1**
060 **6** 2 **Touch Of Color**[45] 3906 3-9-2 **60**.......................... DannyBrock 11 51
(Jane Chapple-Hyam) *mid-div: rdn 1/2-way: hdwy over 1f out: nt trble ldrs* **25/1**
5120 **7** *shd* **Moi Aussie**[42] 3988 3-9-2 **60**.......................... RoystonFfrench 10 51
(Ed McMahon) *w ldrs: led 5f out: rdn and hdd over 1f out: wknd ins fnl f* **16/1**
-051 **8** 1 3/4 **Always A Dream**[8] 5248 3-8-7 **58**.......................... SamuelClarke[(7)] 4 44
(Chris Wall) *prom: pushed along over 2f out: no ex fnl f* **7/2**[1]
5320 **9** 1 1/4 **Mustn't Grumble (IRE)**[53] 3604 3-9-6 **64**.......................... DavidNolan 14 47+
(Ivan Furtado) *hld up: rdn and swtchd lft over 2f out: nvr on terms* **20/1**
0-33 **10** 1 1/2 **Rebel State (IRE)**[8] 5248 3-9-5 **63**.......................... WilliamTwiston-Davies 5 42
(Richard Spencer) *mid-div: effrt over 2f out: wknd fnl f* **6/1**[2]
-406 **11** 2 1/4 **Magic Strike (IRE)**[13] 5027 3-9-6 **64**..........................(b[1]) AdamKirby 9 37
(Clive Cox) *trckd ldrs: rdn over 1f out: wknd ins fnl f* **12/1**
2421 **12** 3 1/2 **Mecca's Missus (IRE)**[9] 5197 3-9-7 **65** 6ex..........................(be) GrahamLee 8 28
(Michael Wigham) *mid-div: rdn over 2f out: wknd over 1f out* **11/1**
1035 **13** 2 1/2 **R Bar Open (FR)**[13] 5013 3-9-5 **63**.......................... RobertWinston 6 20
(Dean Ivory) *chsd ldrs: lost pl 1/2-way: sn rdn: wknd over 1f out* **8/1**
0-02 **14** 5 **Gabbys Lad (IRE)**[33] 4310 3-8-7 **51** oh1.......................... NeilFarley 13
(Eric Alston) *chsd ldrs: rdn over 2f out: sn wknd* **33/1**

1m 25.49s (-0.71) **Going Correction** -0.125s/f (Firm) **14** Ran SP% **117.0**
Speed ratings (Par 98): **99,97,96,96,94 91,91,89,88,86 84,80,77,71**
CSF £232.74 CT £3470.78 TOTE £21.70: £6.90, £2.30, £5.00; EX 395.50 TRIFECTA Not won..
Owner Hugh & Mindi Byrne & Minster Stud **Bred** Minster Stud **Trained** Newmarket, Suffolk

FOCUS
A routine handicap run at a solid pace, enabling the winner to come from last to first.
T/Plt: £2,012.10 to a £1 stake. Pool: £82,279.16 - 29.85 winning tickets. T/Qpdt: £45.00 to a £1 stake. Pool: £9,270.24 - 152.20 winning tickets. **Colin Roberts**

5414 RIPON (R-H)
Tuesday, August 16

OFFICIAL GOING: Good (good to firm in places; 8.2) (watered)
Wind: almost nil Weather: fine and sunny, very warm

5516 AT THE RACES SKY 415 MAIDEN FILLIES' STKS (PLUS 10 RACE) 6f
2:00 (2:00) (Class 5) 2-Y-O **£2,911** (£866; £432; £216) **Stalls** High

Form RPR
0 **1** **Arwa (IRE)**[40] 4063 2-9-0 0.......................... DanielTudhope 6 82+
(Charles Hills) *dwlt: t.k.h: trckd ldrs: smooth hdwy over 2f out: shkn up to ld 1f out: pushed clr: readily* **9/2**[3]
2 2 1/4 **Sugar Beach (FR)** 2-9-0 0.......................... PJMcDonald 3 72+
(Ann Duffield) *mid-div: effrt over 2f out: sn chsng ldrs: kpt on to take 2nd post* **8/1**
2 **3** *shd* **Hamidans Girl (IRE)**[99] 2090 2-9-0 0.......................... PhillipMakin 2 71
(Keith Dalgleish) *swtchd lft after s: led: hdd 1f out: kpt on same pce* **15/8**[1]
03 **4** 3 1/4 **Miss Anticipation (IRE)**[15] 4951 2-9-0 0.......................... SeanLevey 1 61
(Roger Charlton) *wnt rt s: chsd ldrs: drvn 2f out: fdd appr fnl f* **9/4**[2]
0 **5** 1 1/2 **Anythingknappen (IRE)**[20] 4765 2-9-0 0.......................... DavidAllan 4 56
(Tim Easterby) *in rr: drvn over 2f out: nvr a factor* **16/1**
0 **6** *nk* **Greenview Paradise (IRE)**[20] 4765 2-9-0 0.......................... TonyHamilton 5 55
(Richard Fahey) *mid-div: drvn over 2f out: sn outpcd: nvr a factor* **11/1**

1m 12.03s (-0.97) **Going Correction** -0.30s/f (Firm) **6** Ran SP% **109.1**
Speed ratings (Par 91): **94,91,90,86,84 84**
CSF £35.67 TOTE £4.90: £2.50, £3.90; EX 40.80 Trifecta £137.90.
Owner Saleh Al Homaizi & Imad Al Sagar **Bred** Paget Bloodstock **Trained** Lambourn, Berks

FOCUS
The watered ground (2mm applied overnight Sunday into Monday) was given as good, good to firm in places (GoingStick: 8.2). The rail was at its innermost position, so distances were as advertised. A fair maiden with a nice step up from the winner..

5517 DOWNLOAD THE AWARD-WINNING AT THE RACES APP (S) STKS 1m 1f 170y
2:30 (2:32) (Class 6) 3-4-Y-O **£2,587** (£770; £384; £192) **Stalls** Low

Form RPR
0033 **1** **Thello**[7] 5264 4-9-5 55.......................... LewisEdmunds[(7)] 8 61
(Nigel Tinkler) *w ldrs: t.k.h: 2nd over 7f out: drvn over 2f out: led last 150yds: jst hld on* **11/4**[2]
2006 **2** *nse* **Indulgent**[32] 4375 3-8-12 51.......................... BarryMcHugh 7 55
(Tony Coyle) *in rr: drvn 4f out: hdwy 2f out: styd on fnl f: tk 2nd post: jst denied* **10/1**
5054 **3** *hd* **Chorus of Lies**[20] 4767 4-9-6 55.......................... DaleSwift 4 55
(Tracy Waggott) *stmbld s: t.k.h: sn trcking ldrs: led after 2f: hdd 2f out: kpt on to take 2nd last 100yds: no ex cl home* **7/1**
0-45 **4** 2 **Assisted**[22] 4702 3-8-12 66.......................... PhillipMakin 1 51
(Keith Dalgleish) *led 2f: trckd ldrs: led over 2f out: hdd last 150yds: wknd last 50yds* **10/3**[3]
3500 **5** *nk* **Alans Pride (IRE)**[12] 5068 4-9-12 52..........................(b) ConnorBeasley 5 56
(Michael Dods) *trckd ldrs: t.k.h: hung rt over 2f out: one pce over 1f out* **14/1**
0063 **6** 3 **Cautious Optimism**[28] 4482 3-8-12 67.......................... FrannyNorton 2 44
(William Muir) *prom: lost pl after 3f: effrt 3f out: one pce whn n.m.r over 1f out* **9/4**[1]
0000 **7** 1 **Playboy Bay**[21] 4724 4-9-6 45.......................... DavidAllan 9 43
(Ron Barr) *chsd ldrs: hung rt 2f out: one pce* **40/1**
0405 **8** 29 **Citadel**[29] 4450 3-8-12 43..........................(v) PaddyAspell 6
(John Wainwright) *t.k.h towards rr: lost pl over 3f out: sn bhd: t.o* **100/1**

2m 3.6s (-1.80) **Going Correction** -0.30s/f (Firm)
WFA 3 from 4yo 8lb **8** Ran SP% **112.2**
Speed ratings (Par 101): **95,94,94,93,92 90,89,66**
CSF £28.87 TOTE £3.60: £1.30, £2.60, £1.80; EX 26.90 Trifecta £149.10.There was no bid for the winner.
Owner Y T Szeto **Bred** Mickley Stud & Mr W T Whittle **Trained** Langton, N Yorks
■ Karch was withdrawn. Price at time of withdrawal 50/1. Rule 4 does not apply.

FOCUS
An ordinary seller and a tight finish. The form is rated around the first two.

5518 AT THE RACES VIRGIN 535 NURSERY H'CAP 1m
3:00 (3:00) (Class 4) (0-85,84) 2-Y-O **£4,204** (£1,251; £625) **Stalls** Low

Form RPR
21 **1** **Maths Prize**[28] 4479 2-9-7 **84**.......................... SeanLevey 2 85+
(Roger Charlton) *trckd ldng pair: t.k.h: 2nd over 3f out: upsides and drvn over 1f out: styd on to ld last 75yds* **4/6**[1]
14 **2** *nk* **Proud Archi (IRE)**[22] 4699 2-9-1 **78**.......................... PaulMulrennan 1 78
(Michael Dods) *led: clr after 1f: drvn over 3f out: edgd lft 2f out: hdd and no ex last 75yds* **5/2**[2]
6232 **3** 7 **Laureate**[7] 5266 2-8-10 **73**.......................... FrannyNorton 3 59
(Mark Johnston) *chsd wnr: pushed along over 3f out: outpcd over 2f out* **9/2**[3]

1m 39.92s (-1.48) **Going Correction** -0.30s/f (Firm) **3** Ran SP% **106.7**
Speed ratings (Par 96): **95,94,87**
CSF £2.55 TOTE £1.50; EX 1.90 Trifecta £1.70.
Owner The Queen **Bred** The Queen **Trained** Beckhampton, Wilts

FOCUS
Just the three runners, but a nice enough performance by the winner, who probably has more to offer.

5519 DOWNLOAD THE FREE AT THE RACES APP CONDITIONS STKS (PLUS 10 RACE) 1m
3:30 (3:30) (Class 3) 2-Y-O **£6,469** (£1,925; £962) **Stalls** Low

Form RPR
121 **1** **Permian (IRE)**[8] 5239 2-9-2 83.......................... FrannyNorton 2 89+
(Mark Johnston) *mde all: qcknd pce 3f out: edgd lft clsng stages: pushed out: cosily* **4/9**[1]
51 **2** 3/4 **Western Duke (IRE)**[17] 4856 2-9-2 84.......................... PhillipMakin 1 87+
(Ralph Beckett) *trckd wnr: effrt 2f out: edgd lft: kpt on same pce fnl f: a hld* **11/4**[2]
1003 **3** 3 1/2 **Fayez (IRE)**[11] 5109 2-9-2 83.......................... DanielTudhope 3 80
(David O'Meara) *t.k.h in last: effrt and swtchd lft over 2f out: wl hld whn edgd rt 1f out: eased clsng stages* **9/1**[3]

1m 40.23s (-1.17) **Going Correction** -0.30s/f (Firm) **3** Ran SP% **105.9**
Speed ratings (Par 98): **93,92,88**
CSF £1.89 TOTE £1.30; EX 1.30 Trifecta £1.10.
Owner Sheikh Hamdan bin Mohammed Al Maktoum **Bred** Darley **Trained** Middleham Moor, N Yorks

FOCUS
Another small field. The winner set an ordinary pace and is not quite rated to his latest win.

5520 ATTHERACES.COM CITY OF RIPON STKS (H'CAP) 1m 1f 170y
4:00 (4:00) (Class 3) (0-90,88) 3-Y-O-**£7,246** (£2,168; £1,084; £542; £270) **Stalls** Low

Form RPR
2111 **1** **Cote D'Azur**[18] 4818 3-9-5 **87**.......................... DavidAllan 5 95
(Les Eyre) *stdd s: t.k.h: trckd ldrs: 2nd over 2f out: shkn up to ld over 1f out: pushed out* **9/4**[1]
166 **2** 1 1/2 **Cape Of Glory (IRE)**[38] 4153 3-9-4 **86**.......................... PhillipMakin 1 91
(Keith Dalgleish) *led: shkn up over 2f out: hdd over 1f out: kpt on same pce* **6/1**
5112 **3** 1/2 **Final**[21] 4727 4-9-9 **83**.......................... FrannyNorton 6 87+
(Mark Johnston) *in rr: effrt 3f out: sn chsng ldrs: kpt on same pce over 1f out: tk 3rd nr fin* **5/1**[3]
-152 **4** 1/2 **Pure Fantasy**[19] 4793 3-9-0 **82**.......................... SeanLevey 4 85+
(Roger Charlton) *stdd s: hld up in rr: effrt 2f out: kpt on same pce: tk 4th cl home* **11/4**[2]
0004 **5** 1/2 **Green Howard**[23] 4687 8-9-2 **76**.......................... DanielTudhope 2 78
(Rebecca Bastiman) *hld up in mid-div: effrt over 2f out: n.m.r over 1f out: kpt on one pce* **8/1**
1440 **6** 1 1/4 **Silvery Moon (IRE)**[10] 5156 9-9-11 **88**.......................... RachelRichardson[(3)] 3 87
(Tim Easterby) *trckd ldr: n.m.r on ins over 1f out: fdd last 50yds* **9/1**

2m 2.56s (-2.84) **Going Correction** -0.30s/f (Firm)
WFA 3 from 4yo+ 8lb **6** Ran SP% **109.5**
Speed ratings (Par 107): **99,97,97,97,96 95**
CSF £15.10 TOTE £2.60: £1.80, £2.80; EX 14.30 Trifecta £41.40.
Owner Billy Parker & Steven Parker **Bred** W N Greig **Trained** Catwick, N Yorks

FOCUS
Not a bad handicap, but they went fairly steady early on. The winner continues to progress.

5521 RACE REPLAYS ON THE ATR APP H'CAP 1m
4:30 (4:30) (Class 5) (0-75,80) 3-Y-O+ **£3,234** (£962; £481; £240) **Stalls** Low

Form RPR
1-02 **1** **Venutius**[19] 4807 9-9-11 **73**.......................... DaleSwift 8 82
(Ed McMahon) *chsd ldrs: effrt 3f out: styd on to take 2nd last 100yds: led post* **9/1**
3354 **2** *shd* **Relight My Fire**[15] 4930 6-9-5 **67**..........................(b) DavidAllan 5 76
(Tim Easterby) *trckd ldr: led over 6f out: rdn 2f out: hdd and no ex fnl strides* **5/1**[3]
0523 **3** 2 **Midlight**[7] 5273 4-8-8 **56**..........................(t) GeorgeChaloner 2 60
(Richard Whitaker) *led over 1f: trckd ldr: drvn over 3f out: kpt on same pce fnl f* **7/2**[2]

0004 **4** 4 1/2 **Border Bandit (USA)**[13] 5030 8-8-8 **56**............................(p) JoeFanning 7 50
(Tracy Waggott) *rr-div: hdwy over 3f out: chsng ldrs over 2f out: wknd fnl f* **12/1**

6051 **5** 1 **Tadaany (IRE)**[8] 5223 4-10-4 **80** 6ex.............................. DanielTudhope 6 71
(David O'Meara) *chsd ldrs: effrt over 2f out: wknd appr fnl f: eased nr fin* **9/4**[1]

6160 **6** 2 3/4 **Janaab (IRE)**[13] 5033 6-9-3 **68**............................(t) RachelRichardson[(3)] 4 53
(Tim Easterby) *hld up in rr: drvn 3f out: kpt on fnl f: nvr a factor* **13/2**

1446 **7** 7 **Cabal**[10] 5180 9-9-10 **72**..(p) FrannyNorton 3 41
(Geoffrey Harker) *rr-div: effrt over 2f out: sn lost pl and bhd* **17/2**

6305 **8** 3 **The King's Steed**[13] 5030 3-8-6 **67**.............................. LaurenSteade[(7)] 1 28
(Micky Hammond) *in rr: sme hdwy over 3f out: sn lost pl: bhd fnl 2f* **40/1**

1m 37.83s (-3.57) **Going Correction** -0.30s/f (Firm)
WFA 3 from 4yo+ 6lb **8** Ran SP% **113.6**
Speed ratings (Par 103): **105,104,102,98,97 94,87,84**
CSF £52.62 CT £189.82 TOTE £9.80: £2.30, £1.60, £1.50; EX 33.20 Trifecta £164.50.
Owner Mrs Fiona Williams **Bred** Mrs F S Williams **Trained** Lichfield, Staffs

FOCUS
A fair handicap run at a sound pace. The winner's best form for four years.

5522 VISIT ATTHERACES.COM STAYERS H'CAP 2m

5:00 (5:01) (Class 6) (0-65,63) 3-Y-O+ **£2,587** (£770; £384; £192) **Stalls** High

Form RPR

0351 **1** **La Fritillaire**[21] 4739 4-9-4 **53**.. JackGarritty 10 60
(James Given) *w ldr: led after 1f: hdd after 2f: upsides 4f out: led 2f out: hld on towards fin: all out* **9/2**[2]

0P06 **2** hd **Kisumu**[14] 4971 4-9-11 **60**... FrannyNorton 7 67
(Micky Hammond) *hld up in mid-div: hdwy over 3f out: sn chsng ldrs: cl 2nd 1f out: kpt on: jst hld* **8/1**[3]

0064 **3** 2 3/4 **La Bacouetteuse (FR)**[10] 5155 11-9-9 **63**..............(p) GarryWhillans[(5)] 2 67
(Iain Jardine) *hld up in rr: hdwy on ins 3f out: kpt on same pce to take 3rd last 100yds* **9/2**[2]

6052 **4** 1 **Next Edition (IRE)**[10] 5183 8-10-0 **63**...........................(p) PJMcDonald 4 66
(Philip Kirby) *dwlt: sn mid-div: hdwy to chse ldrs 3f out: kpt on one pce over 1f out: tk 4th nr fin* **4/1**[1]

-500 **5** 1/2 **Slipper Satin (IRE)**[10] 5183 6-9-8 **60**......................(t) LouisSteward[(3)] 11 62
(Simon West) *racd v wd: chsd ldrs: swtchd rt and led after 2f: hdd 2f out: one pce* **8/1**[3]

0001 **6** 1 1/4 **Lightning Steps**[14] 4971 4-9-3 **52**.. DavidAllan 1 52
(Declan Carroll) *hld up in rr: drvn over 3f out: kpt on fnl f: nvr a threat* **4/1**[1]

0500 **7** nk **Danzella**[24] 4645 4-8-10 **45**...(v[1]) AndrewElliott 6 45
(Chris Fairhurst) *led 1f: chsd ldrs: drvn over 3f out: one pce* **25/1**

3346 **8** 1 1/4 **Triple Eight (IRE)**[3] 4934 8-9-13 **62**..............................(p) JoeyHaynes 9 61
(Philip Kirby) *s.i.s: hld up in rr: effrt over 3f out: kpt on one pce fnl 2f: nvr a factor* **8/1**[3]

00-0 **9** 23 **Kheskianto (IRE)**[61] 3325 10-8-5 **45**................................. AliceMills[(5)] 8 16
(Michael Chapman) *chsd ldrs: drvn over 4f out: lost pl over 2f out: wl bhd whn eased clsng stages: t.o* **150/1**

3m 30.15s (-1.65) **Going Correction** -0.30s/f (Firm)
WFA 3 from 4yo+ 14lb **9** Ran SP% **114.2**
Speed ratings (Par 101): **92,91,90,90,89 89,89,88,76**
CSF £39.70 CT £170.10 TOTE £5.00: £1.90, £2.40, £2.20; EX 34.40 Trifecta £210.90.
Owner Ingram Racing **Bred** Mrs P M Ignarski **Trained** Willoughton, Lincs

FOCUS
A moderate affair, but competitive. The winner only needed to repeat her Yarmouth form.
T/Plt: £131.40 to a £1 stake. Pool: £62,969.88 - 349.79 winning tickets. T/Qpdt: £10.80 to a £1 stake. Pool: £5,222.70 - 356.34 winning tickets. **Walter Glynn**

5242 WOLVERHAMPTON (A.W) (L-H)

Tuesday, August 16

OFFICIAL GOING: Tapeta: standard
Wind: light, across Weather: sunny and warm

5523 DOWNLOAD THE AT THE RACES APP FILLIES' H'CAP 5f 216y (Tp)

6:00 (6:00) (Class 5) (0-70,74) 3-Y-O+ **£2,911** (£866; £432; £216) **Stalls** Low

Form RPR

4321 **1** **May Rose (IRE)**[8] 5238 3-9-13 **74** 6ex.............................(t) DavidProbert 6 81+
(Charles Hills) *dwlt: hld up in rr: stdy hdwy on outer over 3f out: effrt over 1f out: str run to ld ins fnl f: r.o wl: pushed out* **11/8**[1]

5303 **2** 1 **Inner Knowing (IRE)**[25] 4587 3-8-9 **63**......................(b) CliffordLee[(7)] 5 66
(K R Burke) *hld up in tch in midfield: effrt 2f out: hdwy u.p 1f out: chsd wnr 100yds: kpt on but no serious threat to wnr* **6/1**[2]

1055 **3** 1 **Colourfilly**[8] 5247 4-9-5 **68**...(p) AnnaHesketh[(5)] 3 70+
(Tom Dascombe) *bustled along early: towards rr: dropped to last over 3f out: gd hdwy over 1f out: chsd ldrs and nt clr run jst ins fnl f: fnlly in the clr wl ins fnl f: kpt on wl towards fin: no ch w wnr* **13/2**[3]

612 **4** 3 **Tahiti One**[12] 5020 3-8-7 **54**.. HarryBentley 7 44
(Tony Carroll) *w ldr: rdn and ev ch over 2f out tl unable qck w wnr ins fnl f: wknd fnl 100yds* **11/1**

3523 **5** 3/4 **Bajan Rebel**[13] 5018 5-9-0 **63**.......................................(p) NathanEvans[(5)] 2 51
(Michael Easterby) *sn led: rdn wl over 1f out: hdd ins fnl f: no ex and wknd fnl 100yds* **7/1**

-211 **6** 2 1/2 **Jumeirah Star (USA)**[34] 4262 3-9-7 **68**..............................(v) MartinHarley 4 48
(Robert Cowell) *chsd ldng pair: rdn 2f out: struggling whn squeezed for room 1f out: sn wknd* **6/1**[2]

5551 **7** 7 **La Asomada**[15] 4944 3-9-1 **62**... GrahamGibbons 1 19
(David Barron) *in tch in midfield: struggling u.p and lost pl over 2f out: bhd and eased ins fnl f* **16/1**

1m 14.36s (-0.14) **Going Correction** +0.05s/f (Slow)
WFA 3 from 4yo+ 3lb **7** Ran SP% **110.7**
Speed ratings (Par 100): **102,100,99,95,94 91,81**
CSF £9.25 TOTE £2.50: £1.40, £4.30; EX 9.90 Trifecta £53.50.
Owner Saleh Al Homaizi & Imad Al Sagar **Bred** Irish National Stud **Trained** Lambourn, Berks

FOCUS
A fair fillies' handicap, in which the pace was strong, and those ridden with restraint were favoured. The winner was well in and has more to offer.

5524 UNIVERSITY OF WOLVERHAMPTON RACING MAIDEN FILLIES' STKS (PLUS 10 RACE) 7f 32y (Tp)

6:30 (6:32) (Class 5) 2-Y-O **£3,234** (£962; £481; £240) **Stalls** High

Form RPR

1 **Goya Girl (IRE)** 2-9-0 0.. MartinHarley 2 73+
(Ralph Beckett) *hld up in tch in midfield: clsd to chse ldrs and travelling wl over 2f out: effrt and rn green jst over 1f out: rdn and hdwy ins fnl f: styd on to ld 50yds out: gng away at fin* **10/1**

364 **2** 1 **Suffragette City (IRE)**[20] 4756 2-9-0 73........................ TomMarquand 4 71
(Richard Hannon) *chsd ldrs tl wnt 2nd 1/2-way: rdn and ev ch over 1f out tl unable to match pce of wnr fnl 50yds: kpt on same pce* **2/1**[1]

23 **3** 1/2 **Harmonise**[17] 4877 2-9-0 0... GrahamGibbons 8 70
(Mick Channon) *sn led: rdn and hrd pressed over 1f out: hdd 50yds out: no ex towards fin* **6/1**[3]

40 **4** 1/2 **Sky Ballerina**[20] 4756 2-9-0 0... HarryBentley 9 69
(Simon Crisford) *hld up in tch: effrt over 2f out: hdwy u.p over 1f out: styd on wl ins fnl f: nt rch ldrs* **4/1**[2]

4 **5** hd **Miss Laila (IRE)**[29] 4457 2-9-0 0...................................... DavidProbert 3 68
(Richard Hughes) *led early: sn hdd and chsd ldr tl 1/2-way: chsd ldrs after: rdn over 1f out: unable qck and styd on same pce ins fnl f* **11/1**

4 **6** 1 1/4 **Starlite Sienna (IRE)**[31] 4397 2-9-0 0............................ TonyHamilton 10 65
(Richard Fahey) *dwlt: sn rcvrd and chsd ldrs after 1f: rdn 2f out: unable qck u.p and btn 1f out: wknd ins fnl f* **4/1**[2]

7 8 **Dazacam** 2-9-0 0.. DougieCostello 6 45
(Michael Herrington) *stdd after s: t.k.h: hld up in tch in last pair: sme hdwy over 2f out: rdn and rn green over 1f out: sn btn and wknd fnl f* **100/1**

8 4 1/2 **French Silver (FR)** 2-8-11 0.................................. GeorgeDowning[(3)] 7 34
(Tony Carroll) *in tch in last trio: rdn 3f out: sn struggling and wl btn: lost tch over 1f out* **100/1**

9 23 **Counterweight (IRE)** 2-9-0 0... TedDurcan 1
(Sir Michael Stoute) *dwlt: in tch but nvr gng wl in rr: lost tch 3f out: t.o and eased fnl f* **10/1**

1m 29.74s (0.94) **Going Correction** +0.05s/f (Slow) **9** Ran SP% **116.1**
Speed ratings (Par 91): **96,94,94,93,93 92,82,77,51**
CSF £30.55 TOTE £10.70: £3.00, £1.10, £2.70; EX 48.90 Trifecta £372.10.
Owner Duke Of Roxburghe **Bred** Floors Farming And Newbyth Stud **Trained** Kimpton, Hants

FOCUS
Not a bad maiden for the track. They went a good gallop and a nicely-bred filly proved good enough to make a winning debut. The field finished compressed and can only be rated as ordinary.

5525 VISIT ATTHERACES.COM H'CAP 7f 32y (Tp)

7:00 (7:01) (Class 5) (0-70,69) 3-Y-O **£3,234** (£962; £481; £240) **Stalls** High

Form RPR

3022 **1** **Ripoll (IRE)**[13] 5013 3-9-5 **67**..(t) TomMarquand 8 74
(Sylvester Kirk) *chsd ldng trio: effrt to chal and carried rt over 1f out: stl being carried rt but sustained chal to ld towards fin: rdn out* **9/2**[2]

5402 **2** nk **Ballyer Rallyer (IRE)**[34] 4258 3-9-5 **67**...................... GrahamGibbons 5 73
(Daniel Mark Loughnane) *chsd ldrs: wnt 2nd 4f out: rdn to ld and hung rt over 1f out: stl hanging and sustained duel w wnr fnl f: hdd and no ex towards fin* **12/1**

-401 **3** 2 3/4 **Himalayan Queen**[12] 5088 3-8-11 **66**......................... SophieKilloran[(7)] 7 65+
(William Jarvis) *wnt lft and bmpd s: hld up in tch in last pair: rdn and hdwy ent fnl f: kpt on wl to go 3rd wl ins fnl f: no threat to ldng pair* **10/1**

6033 **4** nk **Ponty Royale (IRE)**[12] 5059 3-9-1 **63**............................. AndrewMullen 2 61
(Tim Easterby) *t.k.h: chsd ldrs: effrt u.p over 1f out: unable qck 1f out: styd on same pce after: lost 3rd wl ins fnl f* **16/1**

0-30 **5** 3/4 **Matilda's Law**[50] 3724 3-9-2 **64**... TedDurcan 1 60
(Chris Wall) *in tch in midfield: effrt ent fnl 2f: unable qck u.p over 1f out: styd on same pce ins fnl f* **16/1**

6632 **6** 2 1/4 **Bryght Boy**[34] 4269 3-9-3 **65**... ThomasBrown 3 55
(Ed Walker) *t.k.h: hld up in tch towards rr: effrt ent fnl 2f: no imp over 1f out: swtchd lft ins fnl f: nvr trbld ldrs* **11/8**[1]

-006 **7** shd **Canford Lilli (IRE)**[10] 5168 3-9-6 **68**.................................(p) ShaneKelly 9 57
(Eve Johnson Houghton) *led: rdn ent fnl 2f: hdd over 1f out: drifted rt and wknd ins fnl f* **50/1**

-003 **8** 3/4 **So Much Fun (IRE)**[36] 4215 3-9-0 **69**......................(p) CameronNoble[(7)] 4 56
(Ismail Mohammed) *hld up in tch: effrt 2f out: no hdwy u.p over 1f out: wl hld and plugged on same pce fnl f* **13/2**[3]

051- **9** 10 **Rock Of Monaco**[260] 8053 3-8-8 **56**................................. TonyHamilton 6 16
(Antony Brittain) *squeezed for room and hmpd leaving stalls: t.k.h: hld up in tch in rr: effrt 2f out: no imp over 1f out: wl btn and eased ins fnl f* **11/1**

1m 29.6s (0.80) **Going Correction** +0.05s/f (Slow) **9** Ran SP% **112.5**
Speed ratings (Par 100): **97,96,93,93,92 89,89,88,77**
CSF £54.86 CT £506.65 TOTE £5.60: £1.20, £3.30, £3.10; EX 58.60 Trifecta £334.20.
Owner D Harding, C Conroy & P Reglar **Bred** Mrs Bridget Delaney **Trained** Upper Lambourn, Berks

FOCUS
A modest handicap run at an ordinary pace, in which the short-priced favourite ran below expectations. The form is rated around the second.

5526 ROA/RACING POST OWNERS JACKPOT H'CAP 1m 4f 50y (Tp)

7:30 (7:30) (Class 4) (0-80,80) 3-Y-O+ **£5,175** (£1,540; £769; £384) **Stalls** Low

Form RPR

0233 **1** **Salmon Sushi**[15] 4945 5-10-0 **80**.................................... AndrewMullen 3 92
(Tim Easterby) *taken down early: stdd s: hld up in rr: clsd and nt clr run over 2f out: hdwy to chse ldrs on inner 2f out: rdn to ld 1f out: sn clr and r.o strly: readily* **8/1**

-335 **2** 5 **All My Love (IRE)**[29] 4462 4-9-6 **75**............................... RobHornby[(3)] 6 79
(Pam Sly) *hld up in tch towards rr: rdn: hdwy and swtchd rt 3f out: chsd ldrs over 1f out: swtchd rt 1f out: styd on to go 2nd fnl 100yds: kpt on but no ch w wnr* **12/1**

0004 **3** 3 **Charlie Bear**[22] 4717 4-10-0 **80**...................................... WilliamCarson 8 79
(Jamie Osborne) *dwlt: hdwy to ld over 10f out and racd keenly in front: rdn wl over 1f out: drifted rt and hdd 1f out: sn btn: lost 2nd and wknd fnl 100yds* **9/1**

-231 **4** 1 1/2 **Mayasa (IRE)**[42] 3991 3-9-4 **80**..(b) MartinHarley 5 77
(James Tate) *chsd ldrs: wnt 2nd 7f out: rdn over 3f out: stl cl enough but unable qck over 1f out: wknd ins fnl f* **15/8**[1]

6226 **5** 10 **Patriotic (IRE)**[76] 2791 8-9-8 **74**.................................(p) LemosdeSouza 4 55
(Chris Dwyer) *hld up in tch: effrt over 2f out: no imp and wl btn over 1f out: wknd and hung rt wl ins fnl f* **25/1**

1510 **6** 1 1/2 **Van Huysen (IRE)**[17] 4868 4-9-4 **77**........ GeorgeWood(7) 7 55
(Dominic Ffrench Davis) *hld up in tch: rdn and hdwy on outer 3f out: no imp 2f out: wkng whn hung bdly lft over 1f out* **18/1**

6312 **7** hd **Blenheim Warrior**[28] 4483 4-9-5 **71**........ ShaneKelly 1 49
(Richard Hughes) *bustled along leaving stalls: in tch in midfield: effrt to chse clr ldng pair 3f out: lost pl and btn 2f out: no ch whn hmpd over 1f out* **11/4**[2]

050 **8** 34 **Fisher Green (IRE)**[45] 3914 3-9-0 **76**........ PaulMulrennan 2
(Michael Dods) *led tl over 10f out: chsd ldr tl 7f out: chsd ldrs after tl lost pl u.p 3f out: t.o and eased fnl f* **15/2**[3]

2m 37.57s (-3.23) **Going Correction** +0.05s/f (Slow)
WFA 3 from 4yo+ 10lb **8** Ran SP% **111.1**
Speed ratings (Par 105): **112,108,106,105,99 98,97,75**
CSF £91.24 CT £851.52 TOTE £8.20: £1.40, £2.70, £2.80; EX 65.80 Trifecta £791.40.
Owner S A Heley **Bred** Arbib Bloodstock Partnership **Trained** Great Habton, N Yorks

FOCUS
A decent middle-distance handicap and a wide-margin winner. It looked a well run race.

5527 JOIN THE BLACK COUNTRY CHAMBER OF COMMERCE MAIDEN FILLIES' STKS 1m 141y (Tp)
8:00 (8:01) (Class 5) 3-Y-O+ **£3,234** (£962; £481; £240) **Stalls** Low

Form RPR

42 **1** **Side Hill (USA)**[68] 3059 3-9-0 0........(t) NickyMackay 5 88+
(John Gosden) *restless in stalls: s.i.s: hdwy on outer to ld over 6f out: mde rest: pushed clr over 1f out: in command whn hung bdly rt ins fnl f: eased towards fin* **8/15**[1]

255 **2** 5 **Dame Judi (IRE)**[51] 3684 3-9-0 78........ HarryBentley 7 75
(Simon Crisford) *chsd ldrs: wnt clr in ldng trio 3f out: rdn to chse wnr 2f out: outpcd and btn over 1f out: plugged on same pce ins fnl f: eased towards fin* **6/1**[3]

0346 **3** 2 1/2 **Shadow Spirit**[46] 3853 3-9-0 73........ TomMarquand 4 69
(Iain Jardine) *led tl over 6f out: chsd wnr tl 2f out: 3rd and outpcd over 1f out: wknd wl ins fnl f* **8/1**

4 nse **Gamrah (IRE)** 3-9-0 0........ MartinHarley 3 69+
(James Tate) *hld up in rr: swtchd rt and hdwy over 2f out: modest 4th over 1f out: kpt on steadily ins fnl f: no ch w wnr* **7/2**[2]

3-0 **5** hd **Tranquil Time**[32] 4361 3-9-0 0........ PaulMulrennan 8 68+
(James Tate) *hld up in rr: pushed along and wnt modest 6th wl over 1f out: carried rt over 1f out: swtchd lft and rdn ins fnl f: kpt on towards fin: nvr trbld ldrs* **14/1**

00 **6** 7 **Shift On Sheila**[33] 4319 3-8-11 0........ RobHornby(3) 1 52
(Pam Sly) *in tch in midfield: rdn and outpcd in 4th 3f out: wl hld whn drifted rt over 1f out: wknd fnl f* **40/1**

0 **7** 7 **Serangoon**[6] 5300 3-9-0 0........ AndrewMullen 2 36
(Michael Appleby) *t.k.h: dropped to rr 7f out: rdn and rn green over 3f out: sn struggling: bhd fnl 2f* **50/1**

0 **8** 4 **Tanera Mor (IRE)**[53] 3601 3-8-7 0........ HollieDoyle(7) 6 27
(Alan Bailey) *in tch in midfield: rdn over 3f out: sn struggling and lost pl over 2f out: bhd over 1f out* **100/1**

1m 50.37s (0.27) **Going Correction** +0.05s/f (Slow) **8** Ran SP% **124.9**
Speed ratings (Par 100): **100,95,93,93,93 86,80,77**
CSF £5.38 TOTE £1.50: £1.02, £1.80, £2.80; EX 5.50 Trifecta £15.10.
Owner K Abdullah **Bred** Juddmonte Farms Inc **Trained** Newmarket, Suffolk

FOCUS
Not a strong maiden and the market leader took advantage of a good opportunity. The winner increased her superiority over the second.

5528 TOAST OF NEW YORK NURSERY H'CAP 1m 141y (Tp)
8:30 (8:31) (Class 6) (0-65,64) 2-Y-O **£2,425** (£721; £360; £180) **Stalls** Low

Form RPR

3512 **1** **Jumping Jack (IRE)**[6] 5297 2-9-7 **64**........ ShaneKelly 8 70+
(Richard Hughes) *t.k.h: chsd ldrs tl wnt 2nd over 6f out: upsides ldr 2f out: rdn to ld 1f out: styd on wl under hands and heels riding ins fnl f: readily* **10/11**[1]

0124 **2** 2 **Luduamf (IRE)**[7] 5251 2-8-13 **63**........ HollieDoyle(7) 4 64
(Richard Hannon) *t.k.h: chsd ldr tl led after 1f and set stdy gallop: rdn and qcknd 2f out: hdd 1f out: kpt on same pce after* **10/3**[2]

600 **3** nk **Hazell Berry (IRE)**[57] 3472 2-8-6 **49**........ AdamBeschizza 2 49
(David Evans) *t.k.h: led for 1f: chsd ldng pair after: rdn 3f out: kpt on same pce u.p fr over 1f out* **16/1**

0500 **4** 1 3/4 **Seminole Dream (IRE)**[10] 5165 2-8-2 **45**........ AndrewMullen 1 41
(Philip Kirby) *t.k.h: chsd ldng trio: effrt over 2f out: unable qck over 1f out: kpt on same pce ins fnl f* **25/1**

000 **5** 3 1/4 **Reinstorm**[25] 4609 2-8-12 **55**........ TonyHamilton 7 45
(Richard Fahey) *hld up in tch in midfield: rdn over 2f out: drvn and outpcd 2f out: wl hld and styd on same pce fr over 1f out* **6/1**[3]

053 **6** 2 1/4 **Cautious Choice (IRE)**[11] 5120 2-8-2 **45**........ RyanPowell 9 30
(J S Moore) *hld up in tch in last pair: effrt 2f out: no imp and sn btn: wknd fnl f* **25/1**

0053 **7** nk **Black Redstart**[11] 5128 2-8-8 **58**........ MitchGodwin(7) 5 42
(Alan Bailey) *hld up in last pair: nt clr run and swtchd rt wl over 1f out: no hdwy u.p over 1f out: wknd fnl f* **20/1**

0505 **8** 6 **Fanfair**[15] 4937 2-9-0 **57**........ TomMarquand 3 29
(Richard Hannon) *in tch in midfield: rdn over 3f out: drvn and lost pl over 2f out: bhd fnl f* **10/1**

1m 54.55s (4.45) **Going Correction** +0.05s/f (Slow) **8** Ran SP% **117.2**
Speed ratings (Par 92): **82,80,79,78,75 73,73,67**
CSF £4.04 CT £25.49 TOTE £1.90: £1.02, £1.70, £4.20; EX 4.90 Trifecta £33.90.
Owner Danny Waters **Bred** R & R Bloodstock **Trained** Upper Lambourn, Berkshire

FOCUS
A modest nursery that went to an improver. The pace was ordinary and the first four were always prominent.

5529 FOLLOW AT THE RACES ON TWITTER H'CAP 1m 1f 103y (Tp)
9:00 (9:00) (Class 6) (0-65,65) 3-Y-O+ **£2,425** (£721; £360; £180) **Stalls** Low

Form RPR

-040 **1** **Cape Crystal (IRE)**[66] 3141 3-9-1 **59**........(p) RyanPowell 3 71+
(Sir Mark Prescott Bt) *trckd ldrs: travelling wl but nt clrest of runs 2f out: swtchd rt and hdwy between rivals jst over 1f out: rdn to ld jst ins fnl f: styd on strly: rdn out* **13/2**[3]

-344 **2** 3 1/4 **Cacica**[33] 4301 3-9-7 **65**........(b[1]) TomMarquand 5 69
(George Scott) *dwlt: hld up in tch in midfield: nt clr run over 2f out: swtchd rt and hdwy over 2f out: clsd and swtchd lft ins fnl f: styd in to go 2nd nr fin: no ch w wnr* **7/1**

0302 **3** 1/2 **Roman De Brut (IRE)**[27] 4527 4-9-11 **62**........ GrahamGibbons 8 65
(Daniel Mark Loughnane) *hld up in tch in midfield: rdn and hdwy ent fnl 2f: chsd ldrs and hung lft over 1f out: led 1f out: sn hdd and outpcd by wnr: lost 2nd towards fin* **7/1**

1302 **4** 1 1/4 **Spinning Pearl (IRE)**[27] 4522 3-9-5 **63**........ CharlesBishop 1 64
(Eve Johnson Houghton) *led tl over 6f out: chsd ldr tl clsd and upsides over 2f out: sn rdn: unable qck 1f out: wknd fnl 100yds* **8/1**

0-00 **5** 1 1/2 **Fast Play (IRE)**[15] 4939 4-9-11 **62**........ ShaneKelly 12 60
(Richard Hughes) *chsd ldng trio: effrt and hung lft whn hmpd over 1f out: wl hld and styd on same pce ins fnl f* **33/1**

0541 **6** 1/2 **King Oswald (USA)**[11] 5132 3-9-3 **64**........ RobHornby(3) 7 61
(James Unett) *hld up in last quartet: effrt on outer over 2f out: midfield and racing on centre over 1f out: no imp fnl f* **3/1**[1]

0060 **7** 1/2 **Tafahom (IRE)**[42] 3983 4-9-7 **63**........(b[1]) NathanEvans(5) 6 59
(Michael Easterby) *pressed ldr tl led over 6f out: rdn 2f out: hdd and no ex jst ins fnl f: wknd fnl 100yds* **11/2**[2]

4005 **8** 6 **Shining Romeo**[11] 5130 4-9-11 **62**........(v[1]) MartinHarley 2 47
(Denis Quinn) *hld up in tch in midfield: effrt over 2f out: hung lft and btn over 1f out: fdd ins fnl f* **11/1**

0/00 **9** 1 **Whitstable Native**[39] 4088 8-8-9 **46** oh1........(t) KierenFox 9 29
(Sophie Leech) *hld up in last quartet: effrt over 2f out: sn outpcd and no hdwy u.p over 1f out: wknd fnl f* **33/1**

0-00 **10** 9 **Sharp Jack**[26] 4546 3-8-3 **47**........(p) WilliamCarson 4 13
(Tom Dascombe) *in tch in midfield: drvn and no rspnse 3f out: lost pl and wl btn 2f out: wknd over 1f out* **22/1**

0-00 **11** 6 **Lisala (FR)**[43] 3958 3-9-4 **62**........ HarryBentley 11 16
(George Peckham) *hld up in last quartet: rdn over 2f out: sn btn: bhd fnl f* **28/1**

160 **12** 11 **Frivolous Lady (IRE)**[36] 4206 3-9-1 **59**........(v) AdamBeschizza 13
(David Evans) *a bhd and nvr gng wl: lost tch over 2f out: t.o* **40/1**

2m 0.16s (-0.64) **Going Correction** +0.05s/f (Slow)
WFA 3 from 4yo+ 7lb **12** Ran SP% **114.3**
Speed ratings (Par 101): **104,101,100,99,98 97,97,92,91,83 77,68**
CSF £46.38 CT £327.74 TOTE £6.80: £2.20, £2.80, £2.60; EX 67.80 Trifecta £448.20.
Owner Axom LVII **Bred** Rockfield Farm **Trained** Newmarket, Suffolk

FOCUS
Just a modest handicap but an impressive winner. The next three help set a straightforward level.
T/Plt: £92.40 to a £1 stake. Pool: £69,598.62 - 549.67 winning tickets. T/Qpdt: £30.50 to a £1 stake. Pool: £6,805.91 - 164.84 winning tickets. **Steve Payne**

5530 - 5534a (Foreign Racing) - See Raceform Interactive

[4929]CARLISLE (R-H)
Wednesday, August 17

OFFICIAL GOING: Good to firm (7.3)
Wind: fresh across Weather: Sunny

5535 BETFAIR AMATEUR RIDERS' H'CAP (FOR NOVICE AMATEUR RIDERS) 5f 193y
2:10 (2:13) (Class 6) (0-65,65) 4-Y-O+ **£2,495** (£774; £386; £193) **Stalls** Low

Form RPR

0320 **1** **Caeser The Gaeser (IRE)**[13] 5068 4-10-9 **53**........(p) MrBLynn 2 65
(Nigel Tinkler) *in tch: rdn and hdwy over 1f out: led ins fnl f: edgd lft: kpt on wl* **9/2**[1]

3305 **2** 2 1/2 **Picks Pinta**[27] 4544 5-11-6 **64**........(b) MrTGreenwood 9 68
(John David Riches) *chsd ldr: rdn over 2f out: led appr fnl f: hdd ins fnl f: one pce* **5/1**[2]

40-6 **3** 2 1/4 **Cruise Tothelimit (IRE)**[11] 5162 8-11-7 **65**........ MrMEnnis 5 62
(Patrick Morris) *midfield: rdn over 2f out: kpt on fr over 1f out: wnt 3rd towards fin* **12/1**

6320 **4** nk **Native Falls (IRE)**[13] 5060 5-11-4 **65**........ MissRSharpe(3) 1 61+
(Alan Swinbank) *led: rdn over 2f out: hdd appr fnl f: wknd ins fnl f* **14/1**

0316 **5** 1/2 **Penny Royale**[16] 4931 4-11-6 **64**........(p) MissEEasterby 4 58
(Tim Easterby) *midfield on inner: bit short of room over 1f out: angled lft appr fnl f: kpt on: nvr threatened ldrs* **9/2**[1]

0-45 **6** nk **Raise A Billion**[11] 5152 5-10-4 **48**........ MissAMcCain 12 41
(John David Riches) *hld up on outer: rdn over 2f out: kpt on fr over 1f out: nvr threatened ldrs* **10/1**

0010 **7** 1/2 **Poolstock**[2] 5483 4-10-11 **58** 6ex........(b) MissSEDods(3) 8 50
(Michael Dods) *hld up: nvr threatened* **9/1**[3]

-060 **8** 1 1/4 **Dark Castle**[8] 5278 7-10-12 **56**........ MrJoeWright 10 44
(Micky Hammond) *midfield: rdn over 2f out: no imp* **50/1**

2300 **9** nse **Reflation**[2] 5483 4-10-6 **53**........(v) MissCADods(3) 11 41
(Michael Dods) *dwlt: hld up: nvr threatened* **18/1**

4566 **10** 1 1/4 **Circuitous**[12] 5114 8-10-10 **57**........(v) MissKWeir(3) 6 41
(Keith Dalgleish) *chsd ldrs: rdn over 2f out: wknd fnl f* **11/1**

4500 **11** 1/2 **Keene's Pointe**[13] 5069 6-10-12 **59**........ MrBenjaminStephens(3) 7 41
(Kristin Stubbs) *hld up: rdn 3f out: nvr threatened* **10/1**

0030 **12** 3 1/4 **Minty Jones**[15] 4968 7-10-5 **49**........(v) MrLewisStones 3 21
(Michael Mullineaux) *rrd s and slowly away: a towards rr* **33/1**

1m 13.66s (-0.04) **Going Correction** -0.10s/f (Good) **12** Ran SP% **114.1**
Speed ratings (Par 101): **96,92,89,89,88 88,87,85,85,84 83,79**
CSF £25.26 CT £253.63 TOTE £4.70: £2.00, £2.00, £3.20; EX 27.60 Trifecta £284.40.
Owner Flying High Racing Club **Bred** Tom Foley **Trained** Langton, N Yorks

FOCUS
Race distance as advertised. Not many played a part in this moderate handicap for novice amateur riders. The winner repeated last August's C&D win.

5536 APOLLOBET IRISH STALLION FARMS EBF NOVICE STKS 5f 193y
2:45 (2:46) (Class 5) 2-Y-O **£3,234** (£962; £481; £240) **Stalls** Low

Form RPR

1 **1** **Senator**[21] 4762 2-9-9 0........ TonyHamilton 4 87+
(Richard Fahey) *trckd ldrs: pushed along to chal 2f out: led appr fnl f: edgd rt ins fnl f: kpt on pushed out* **4/6**[1]

2511 **2** 1 3/4 **Racemaker**[28] 4509 2-9-2 74........ NeilFarley 6 72
(Andrew Crook) *led: hdd over 3f out: chsd ldrs: rdn 2f out: angled lft to outer appr fnl f: kpt on: wnt 2nd fnl 75yds* **50/1**

214 **3** 1 1/4 **Whirl Me Round**[12] 5113 2-9-9 85........ JoeDoyle 7 75
(Kevin Ryan) *trckd ldr: led over 3f out: jnd 2f out: rdn appr fnl f: wknd and lost 2nd fnl 75yds* **11/4**[2]

5 **4** 3/4 **Can't Do Spells**[18] 4890 2-8-13 0........ RachelRichardson(3) 3 66
(Tim Easterby) *hld up in tch: pushed along over 2f out: hdwy over 1f out: kpt on fnl f* **25/1**

0 **5** 27 **Where's Stewart**[8] 5271 2-9-2 0........ GrahamLee 1
(Nigel Tinkler) *chsd ldrs: pushed along and lost pl over 3f out: sn wknd* **200/1**

153 **6** 2 **White Tower (IRE)**[12] 5108 2-9-9 93 JoeFanning 5
(Mark Johnston) *stmbld sltly leaving stalls: sn chsd ldrs: rdn over 2f out: wknd over 1f out: eased* **4/1**[3]

0 **7** 23 **Piccolino**[30] 4451 2-8-8 0 ow2 JoshDoyle(5) 2
(John David Riches) *a bhd* **300/1**

1m 13.58s (-0.12) **Going Correction** -0.10s/f (Good) **7** Ran SP% **113.3**
Speed ratings (Par 94): **96,93,92,91,55 52,21**
CSF £42.77 TOTE £1.50: £1.10, £6.40; EX 19.10 Trifecta £50.40.
Owner Cheveley Park Stud **Bred** Cheveley Park Stud Ltd **Trained** Musley Bank, N Yorks

FOCUS
Race distance as advertised. They went hard early on in this fair novice event. The fourth may be the key to the level of this bare form.

5537 APOLLOBET ONLINE CASINO H'CAP (JOCKEY CLUB GRASSROOTS FLAT SPRINT SERIES QUALIFIER) 5f 193y
3:20 (3:22) (Class 5) (0-70,69) 3-Y-O **£2,911** (£866; £432; £216) **Stalls** Low

Form RPR

6421 **1** **Portland Street (IRE)**[44] 3948 3-9-1 63 [1] PaulMulrennan 6 71+
(Bryan Smart) *dwlt: sn in midfield racing keenly: hdwy over 2f out: rdn to ld over 1f out: sn strly pressed: edgd rt ins fnl f: hld on wl* **5/2**[1]

-065 **2** nk **Alpine Dream (IRE)**[18] 4861 3-8-12 60 AndrewElliott 8 67
(Tim Easterby) *hld up: rdn and hdwy on outer over 2f out: chal strly appr fnl f: kpt on* **25/1**

0040 **3** ¾ **Athollblair Boy (IRE)**[11] 5179 3-8-13 68 LewisEdmunds(7) 11 73
(Nigel Tinkler) *hld up on outside: hdwy over 2f out: rdn and ev ch over 1f out: no ex fnl 50yds* **12/1**

0-25 **4** 1¾ **Reinforced**[35] 4278 3-8-9 57 [1] JoeFanning 10 56
(Michael Dods) *in tch towards outer: hdwy over 2f out: rdn to chal 2f out: no ex fnl f* **8/1**

5 **5** 1 **Crazy Tornado (IRE)**[11] 5151 3-9-6 68 PhillipMakin 1 64
(Keith Dalgleish) *midfield: rdn and outpcd over 2f out: kpt on ins fnl f: nvr threatened ldrs* **5/1**[2]

0031 **6** nk **Baby Ballerina**[15] 4973 3-9-7 69 (b) BenCurtis 5 64
(Brian Ellison) *hld up in midfield: rdn over 2f out: one pce and nvr threatened* **13/2**[3]

3355 **7** ¾ **Strummer (IRE)**[15] 4972 3-9-2 64 [1] KevinStott 7 56
(Kevin Ryan) *trckd ldr: led over 2f out: sn rdn: hdd over 1f out: wknd ins fnl f* **15/2**

052 **8** 7 **Indian Pursuit (IRE)**[15] 4972 3-9-3 65 JasonHart 3 35
(John Quinn) *chsd ldr: rdn over 3f out: lost pl whn hmpd over 1f out: wknd* **17/2**

0610 **9** 3 **Bay Mirage (IRE)**[19] 4830 3-9-7 69 (b[1]) GrahamLee 2 29
(Kevin Ryan) *led: rdn whn hdd over 2f out: sn wknd* **18/1**

-030 **10** 6 **Bahrikate**[15] 4972 3-8-2 50 oh5 (p) JamesSullivan 9
(Michael Herrington) *chsd ldrs: rdn over 3f out: wknd over 2f out* **100/1**

65-6 **P** **Ingleby Valley**[13] 5070 3-8-12 65 AdamMcNamara(5) 4
(Richard Fahey) *slowly away: sn wl bhd: p.u and dismntd over 3f out* **18/1**

1m 13.09s (-0.61) **Going Correction** -0.10s/f (Good) **11** Ran SP% **115.0**
Speed ratings (Par 100): **100,99,98,96,94 94,93,84,80,72**
CSF £73.27 CT £651.63 TOTE £3.40: £1.50, £6.50, £4.10; EX 67.90 Trifecta £750.40.
Owner Michael Moses & Terry Moses **Bred** Ballylinch Stud **Trained** Hambleton, N Yorks

FOCUS
Race distance as advertised. Not a bad sprint handicap for the class, run to suit the closers. The first four came from towards the outer and the winner has more to offer.

5538 APOLLOBET BET THROUGH YOUR MOBILE H'CAP (LONDON MILE SERIES QUALIFIER) 7f 173y
3:55 (3:55) (Class 4) (0-85,84) 3-Y-O+ **£5,175** (£1,540; £769; £384) **Stalls** Low

Form RPR

6140 **1** **Hidden Rebel**[18] 4894 4-9-8 80 PaulMulrennan 6 91
(Alistair Whillans) *hld up: rdn and hdwy on outer 2f out: led appr fnl f: kpt on pushed out* **9/2**[3]

2331 **2** 2¼ **Dawn Mirage**[22] 4727 4-9-10 82 TonyHamilton 5 88
(Richard Fahey) *sn led: rdn over 2f out: hdd appr fnl f: one pce* **9/4**[1]

0635 **3** 1½ **Surewecan**[19] 4830 4-9-0 72 JoeFanning 2 74
(Mark Johnston) *midfield: rdn to briefly chse ldr over 1f out: one pce* **13/2**

0100 **4** ¾ **Slemy (IRE)**[18] 4893 5-9-8 80 JamesSullivan 4 81
(Ruth Carr) *hld up: pushed along whn short of room over 1f out: swtchd lft: sn rdn and one pce* **6/1**

2221 **5** 1¼ **Moonlightnavigator (USA)**[16] 4933 4-9-12 84 [1] JasonHart 1 82
(John Quinn) *racd keenly: trckd ldr: rdn over 2f out: wknd fnl f* **5/2**[2]

6000 **6** 6 **In Focus (IRE)**[16] 4933 5-8-12 70 BenCurtis 3 54
(Alan Swinbank) *racd keenly: trckd ldr: rdn over 2f out: wknd over 1f out* **20/1**

1m 38.0s (-2.00) **Going Correction** -0.10s/f (Good) **6** Ran SP% **109.9**
Speed ratings (Par 105): **106,103,102,101,100 94**
CSF £14.39 TOTE £6.30: £2.60, £1.50; EX 15.20 Trifecta £61.40.
Owner J D Wright **Bred** D Curran **Trained** Newmill-On-Slitrig, Borders

FOCUS
Add 5yds to official race distance. They went a sound pace in this modest handicap, resulting in a good winning time. The form is rated around the second.

5539 APOLLOBET CASHBACK IF 2ND H'CAP 7f 173y
4:30 (4:30) (Class 5) (0-75,72) 3-Y-O **£2,911** (£866; £432; £216) **Stalls** Low

Form RPR

633- **1** **Rainbow Rebel (IRE)**[295] 7540 3-9-2 67 JoeFanning 1 76
(Mark Johnston) *led: hdd over 5f out: trckd ldr on inner: briefly had to wait for gap over 2f out: rdn to ld over 1f out: kpt on wl* **4/1**[2]

-000 **2** 3¼ **Jordan James (IRE)**[55] 3567 3-8-13 64 BenCurtis 5 66
(Brian Ellison) *in tch on outer: rdn over 2f out: chal 2f out: one pce and no ch w wnr fnl f* **8/1**

-050 **3** ½ **Firedanser**[20] 4789 3-9-4 69 TonyHamilton 6 70
(Richard Fahey) *hld up: swtchd lft over 2f out: sn rdn and hdwy: kpt on one pce fr over 1f out* **6/1**[3]

6002 **4** 2¾ **New Abbey Angel (IRE)**[9] 5222 3-8-6 57 (p) JoeyHaynes 2 52
(Keith Dalgleish) *in tch: rdn over 2f out: bit short of room and lost pl 2f out: one pce fr over 1f out* **9/4**[1]

2000 **5** 6 **She's Electric (IRE)**[8] 5273 3-9-4 69 (p) PhillipMakin 7 50
(Keith Dalgleish) *trckd ldr: led over 5f out: rdn over 2f out: hung lft over 1f out: sn hdd: wknd* **10/1**

0002 **6** 11 **Quoteline Direct**[19] 4844 3-9-1 66 PaulMulrennan 3 21
(Micky Hammond) *trckd ldr: rdn over 2f out: wknd over 1f out* **13/2**

-015 **7** 26 **First Wheat**[15] 4985 3-9-7 72 JamesSullivan 4
(Michael Easterby) *dwlt: hld up: rdn over 3f out: sn wknd: eased* **6/1**[3]

1m 39.59s (-0.41) **Going Correction** -0.10s/f (Good) **7** Ran SP% **112.9**
Speed ratings (Par 100): **98,94,94,91,85 74,48**
CSF £34.04 TOTE £4.90: £2.10, £4.20; EX 41.00 Trifecta £147.20.
Owner Owners Group 004 **Bred** Pier House Stud **Trained** Middleham Moor, N Yorks

FOCUS
Add 5yds to official race distance. An ordinary 3yo handicap, run at a sound pace. An improved display from the winner.

5540 APOLLOBET WEEKLY GOLF REFUNDS H'CAP (JOCKEY CLUB GRASSROOTS FLAT MIDDLE DISTANCE SERIES QUALIFIER 1m 1f
5:05 (5:07) (Class 5) (0-70,70) 3-Y-O+ **£2,911** (£866; £432; £216) **Stalls** Low

Form RPR

1 **1** **Pointillism**[11] 5178 4-9-11 67 DavidNolan 5 74
(Iain Jardine) *midfield: rdn over 2f out: chsd ldr over 1f out: styd on: led 50yds out* **4/1**[2]

2035 **2** shd **The Wee Barra (IRE)**[18] 4871 4-9-5 61 (p) KevinStott 2 68
(Kevin Ryan) *trckd ldr: rdn to ld 2f out: strly pressed ent fnl f: kpt on: hdd 50yds out* **9/2**[3]

0-50 **3** ½ **Taopix**[33] 4375 4-8-9 51 oh3 GrahamLee 1 57
(Karen McLintock) *trckd ldrs: rdn and lost pl over 2f out: kpt on fnl f* **28/1**

0050 **4** 1¼ **Artful Prince**[12] 5122 6-10-0 70 (b) JoeDoyle 9 73
(James Given) *hld up in rr: rdn and hdwy on outer fr over 2f out: ev ch ent fnl f: no ex fnl 75yds* **8/1**

3003 **5** nse **Hernando Torres**[16] 4930 8-9-13 69 CamHardie 7 72
(Michael Easterby) *hld up: rdn and hdwy over 2f out: ev ch ent fnl f: no ex fnl 75yds* **14/1**

0352 **6** 1¾ **Chiswick Bey (IRE)**[14] 5033 8-9-9 70 AdamMcNamara(5) 6 69
(Richard Fahey) *hld up: rdn over 2f out: one pce and nvr threatened* **10/3**[1]

6503 **7** 2¾ **Intalza (IRE)**[11] 5181 3-8-3 52 (p) JamesSullivan 3 46
(Michael Herrington) *led: rdn whn hdd 2f out: sn wknd* **14/1**

4-60 **8** ½ **Catastrophe**[26] 4607 3-9-6 69 JackGarritty 4 62
(John Quinn) *trckd ldrs: rdn over 2f out: wknd over 1f out* **11/1**

2441 **9** shd **Tectonic (IRE)**[11] 5154 7-9-7 63 (v) JasonHart 8 55
(Keith Dalgleish) *dwlt: sn midfield on inner: rdn over 2f out: wknd fnl f* **5/1**

1m 56.46s (-1.14) **Going Correction** -0.10s/f (Good)
WFA 3 from 4yo+ 7lb **9** Ran SP% **114.2**
Speed ratings (Par 103): **101,100,100,99,99 97,95,94,94**
CSF £22.09 CT £440.45 TOTE £5.00: £1.60, £1.50, £7.30; EX 24.10 Trifecta £679.30.
Owner Jim Beaumont & Douglas Pryde **Bred** Darley **Trained** Carrutherstown, D'fries & G'way
■ Stewards' Enquiry : David Nolan four-day ban: used whip above permitted level (Aug 31-Sep 2,4)

FOCUS
Add 5yds to official race distance. This was competitive for the class and there was a brisk pace on. The winner improved on the bare form of his Redcar win.

5541 APOLLOBET DAILY RACING REFUNDS H'CAP 1m 6f 32y
5:40 (5:40) (Class 4) (0-85,85) 3-Y-O+ **£5,175** (£1,540; £769; £384) **Stalls** Low

Form RPR

-304 **1** **Trendsetter (IRE)**[67] 3129 5-9-13 84 [1] JackGarritty 4 90+
(John Quinn) *hld up in tch: hdwy to trck ldr gng wl over 1f out: pushed along to ld ins fnl f: rdn out* **2/1**[2]

4543 **2** 1 **Jan Smuts (IRE)**[16] 4935 8-8-12 69 (tp) CamHardie 8 73
(Wilf Storey) *hld up: rdn and hdwy on outer 2f out: styd on fnl f* **12/1**

20-1 **3** nk **Bell Weir**[11] 5155 8-8-12 69 (bt) JamesSullivan 7 72
(Dianne Sayer) *hld up in tch: rdn over 2f out: bit outpcd over 1f out: styd on ins fnl f* **8/1**

0003 **4** ½ **Hardstone (USA)**[14] 5031 5-10-0 85 PaulMulrennan 6 87
(Michael Dods) *trckd ldr: rdn to ld 2f out: hdd ins fnl f: no ex* **15/8**[1]

0600 **5** 2¼ **Wor Lass**[25] 4646 8-8-9 71 GarryWhillans(5) 1 70
(Susan Corbett) *trckd ldr: rdn over 2f out: lost pl over 1f out* **22/1**

6013 **6** 6 **Lexi's Boy (IRE)**[23] 4703 8-10-0 85 (tp) DavidNolan 3 76
(Donald McCain) *led: rdn whn hdd 2f out: wknd fnl f* **4/1**[3]

3m 5.12s (-2.38) **Going Correction** -0.10s/f (Good)
WFA 3 from 5yo+ 12lb **6** Ran SP% **111.3**
Speed ratings (Par 105): **102,101,101,100,99 96**
CSF £24.00 CT £152.11 TOTE £2.80: £1.50, £5.50; EX 30.40 Trifecta £130.00.
Owner Maxilead Limited **Bred** Denis McDonnell **Trained** Settrington, N Yorks

FOCUS
Add 5yds to official race distance. Something of a mixed bag in this staying handicap. It was a decent test. The winner is rated to his best.
T/Plt: £168.70 to a £1 stake. Pool of £48759.77 - 210.94 winning tickets. T/Qpdt: £71.00 to a £1 stake. Pool of £3081.92 - 32.10 winning tickets. **Andrew Sheret**

5250 CHEPSTOW (L-H)
Wednesday, August 17

OFFICIAL GOING: Good to firm (good in places; 8.5)
Wind: slight half behind Weather: fine

5542 EQUESTRIAN SURFACES MAIDEN FILLIES' STKS (PLUS 10 RACE) 5f 16y
2:20 (2:20) (Class 5) 2-Y-O **£3,234** (£962; £481; £240) **Stalls** Centre

Form RPR

00 **1** **Compton Poppy**[21] 4756 2-8-11 0 GeorgeDowning(3) 1 83+
(Tony Carroll) *chsd ldrs: rdn and hdwy over 2f out: led over 1f out: r.o wl* **22/1**

22 **2** 2¾ **Tschierschen (IRE)**[8] 5272 2-9-0 0 PatCosgrave 3 71
(William Haggas) *wnt to post early: cl up: led wl over 2f out: sn rdn: hdd over 1f out: qckly outpcd by wnr but kpt on to hold 2nd* **7/4**[2]

23 **3** 1¼ **Coral Sea**[28] 4503 2-9-0 0 [1] SilvestreDeSousa 4 67
(Charles Hills) *led tl rdn and hdd wl over 2f out: styd prom: n.m.r over 1f out: one pce fnl f but tk 3rd towards fin* **7/2**[3]

43 **4** ½ **Island In The Sky (IRE)**[12] 5119 2-9-0 0 JimCrowley 9 65
(David Simcock) *cl up: shkn up 2f out: sn hung lft: continued to hang and unable qck: lost 3rd towards fin* **5/4**[1]

34 **5** 1 **Coronation Cottage**[13] 5072 2-9-0 0 RyanTate 7 61
(Malcolm Saunders) *chsd ldrs: rdn 3f out: hung lft over 1f out: unable qck and hld after* **16/1**

423 **6** nk **Sheila's Palace**[23] 4706 2-8-11 67 JosephineGordon(3) 5 60
(J S Moore) *racd keenly: chsd ldrs: rdn 2f out: one pce after but keeping on whn hmpd on rail 100yds out* **16/1**

7 2 **Polkadot Princess (IRE)** 2-8-11 0 EdwardGreatrex(3) 6 53
(Nikki Evans) *s.i.s: in rr: veered rt over 1f out: modest late prog* **200/1**

05 **8** 2 **Elmley Queen**[12] 5128 2-8-7 0 MitchGodwin(7) 2 46
(Roy Brotherton) *hld up: rdn 1/2-way: a towards rr* **200/1**

9 1 1/2 **Glam'Selle** 2-9-0 0 RaulDaSilva 8 40
(Ronald Harris) *s.i.s: t.k.h: a towards rr* **66/1**

58.96s (-0.34) **Going Correction** -0.15s/f (Firm) 9 Ran SP% **121.6**
Speed ratings (Par 91): **96,91,89,88,87 86,83,80,77**
CSF £64.22 TOTE £26.90: £7.00, £1.02, £1.50; EX 127.70 Trifecta £611.80.
Owner Paul Downing **Bred** Llety Farms **Trained** Cropthorne, Worcs

FOCUS
A fair juvenile fillies' maiden sprint. They went a decent gallop on ground officially described as good to firm, good in places. The race developed towards the far rail, with the first two horses home drawn that side, and the relatively unconsidered winner appreciated the quicker ground more than most. It appeared no fluke.

5543 EQUESTRIAN SURFACES NURSERY H'CAP 6f 16y
2:55 (2:55) (Class 5) (0-75,75) 2-Y-O **£3,234** (£962; £481; £240) **Stalls** Centre

Form RPR

2201 **1** **Notalot (IRE)**[8] 5251 2-9-2 **73** 6ex (v) LouisSteward(3) 8 81+
(Michael Bell) *hld up: racd towards stands' side tl swtchd lft over 4f out: sn chsng ldrs: rdn to ld wl over 1f out: sn edgd rt: drvn out* **6/4**[1]

3513 **2** 2 1/4 **Marquee Club**[14] 5014 2-9-3 **71** WilliamCarson 1 71
(Jamie Osborne) *led and racd keenly: rdn and hdd 2f out: hung rt fnl f but rallied to take 2nd fnl 75yds* **14/1**

064 **3** *nk* **Spin Top**[8] 5257 2-8-9 **63** (v) TomMarquand 3 62
(Joseph Tuite) *chsd ldr: rdn to ld 2f out: sn hdd: hung rt and unable qck fnl f: lost 2nd 75yds out* **25/1**

4404 **4** 3 1/4 **Primrose Place**[64] 3254 2-8-12 **66** PatDobbs 4 55
(Richard Hannon) *towards rr: hdwy 2f out: one pce fnl f* **14/1**

3666 **5** 2 1/4 **Gerrard's Return**[17] 4915 2-9-3 **71** RichardKingscote 6 52
(Tom Dascombe) *hld up: rdn 2f out: swtchd lft over 1f out: nvr able to chal* **16/1**

31 **6** 5 **Tadkhirah**[13] 5072 2-9-3 **71** DaneO'Neill 7 36
(William Haggas) *s.i.s: towards rr: racd towards stands' side tl swtchd lft over 4f out: hdwy 1/2-way: rdn and unable qck 2f out: wknd 1f out* **4/1**[3]

01 **7** 3 1/4 **Hidden Stash**[12] 5099 2-9-4 **75** EdwardGreatrex(3) 5 30
(Andrew Balding) *t.k.h: mid-div tl lost pl over 3f out: no ch fnl 2f* **3/1**[2]

2266 **8** 2 1/4 **Davarde (IRE)**[40] 4083 2-9-0 **68** JimCrowley 2 16
(David Evans) *chsd ldrs: rdn 1/2-way: wknd 2f out* **16/1**

1m 10.9s (-1.10) **Going Correction** -0.15s/f (Firm) 8 Ran SP% **113.9**
Speed ratings (Par 94): **101,98,97,93,90 83,79,76**
CSF £24.96 CT £376.65 TOTE £2.30: £1.20, £3.30, £6.20; EX 22.00 Trifecta £471.40.
Owner The Fitzrovians **Bred** Tally-Ho Stud **Trained** Newmarket, Suffolk

FOCUS
A fair nursery handicap. They went over to race far side at a decent tempo but drifted back towards the stands' rail under pressure in the final furlong. The winner was heavily backed and the next two were close to their pre-race marks.

5544 ALL-WEATHER RIDING SURFACES FROM EQUESTRIAN SURFACES MAIDEN STKS 7f 16y
3:30 (3:30) (Class 5) 3-Y-O+ **£3,234** (£962; £481; £240) **Stalls** Centre

Form RPR

0053 **1** **Sante (IRE)**[21] 4777 3-9-0 68 SilvestreDeSousa 8 86
(Charles Hills) *t.k.h: cl up: led over 2f out: rdn clr over 1f out: eased cl home* **9/4**[2]

4020 **2** 9 **Big Chill (IRE)**[14] 5017 4-9-3 75 MitchGodwin(7) 4 69
(Patrick Chamings) *led tl rdn and hdd over 2f out: outpcd by wnr over 1f out and no ch after: kpt on for modest 2nd* **7/2**[3]

4-4 **3** 4 **Curriculum**[14] 5023 3-9-5 0 [1] PatCosgrave 5 56
(William Haggas) *wnt to post early: chsd ldrs: rdn over 3f out: unable qck and sn outpcd by ldng pair* **5/4**[1]

4 7 **Outrath (IRE)**[261] 6-9-10 0 TimmyMurphy 9 39
(Jim Best) *s.i.s: in rr: rdn over 2f out: hdwy into modest 4th ins fnl f but nvr any ch* **20/1**

0- **5** 3 1/4 **Josh Perry**[310] 7159 3-9-5 0 RyanTate 2 29
(Rod Millman) *s.i.s: sn in mid-div: a tending to hang lft: rdn and no ch fr 1/2-way* **80/1**

6 *hd* **Magic Mirror** 3-9-0 0 TomMarquand 7 23
(Mark Rimell) *towards rr: rdn and sme hdwy over 3f out: nvr any ch and lost modest 4th ins fnl f* **28/1**

6 **7** 7 **Saleh (IRE)**[16] 4939 3-9-5 0 KierenFox 3 9
(Lee Carter) *mid-div: rdn 1/2-way and qckly no ch: nudged along and fdd fnl 2f* **9/1**

00-0 **8** 1 **Love In The Dark**[42] 3996 3-8-11 55 JosephineGordon(3) 6
(Nikki Evans) *chsd ldrs tl rdn and lost pl over 3f out: bhd fnl 2f* **150/1**

00 **9** 6 **Briac (FR)**[19] 4840 5-9-10 0 JFEgan 10
(Jim Best) *s.s: a bhd* **100/1**

1m 21.02s (-2.18) **Going Correction** -0.15s/f (Firm)
WFA 3 from 4yo+ 5lb 9 Ran SP% **118.5**
Speed ratings (Par 103): **106,95,91,83,79 79,71,70,63**
CSF £10.62 TOTE £3.30: £1.50, £1.80, £1.02; EX 9.80 Trifecta £16.20.
Owner Mr & Mrs R Kelvin-Hughes **Bred** Knocktoran Stud **Trained** Lambourn, Berks

FOCUS
A fair maiden. They went a decent gallop central to stands' side and the winner stretched clear in the manner of a horse much more at home on fast ground than most of her opponents. There are some doubts over the form.

5545 EQUESTRIAN SURFACES H'CAP 1m 14y
4:05 (4:05) (Class 4) (0-85,85) 3-Y-O+ **£6,469** (£1,925; £962; £481) **Stalls** Centre

Form RPR

5662 **1** **Force (IRE)**[9] 5234 3-8-12 **77** SilvestreDeSousa 3 84
(Charles Hills) *dwlt: t.k.h and sn trcking ldrs: rdn over 2f out: led over 1f out: pressed wl ins fnl f: hld on u.p* **2/1**[1]

0-10 **2** *hd* **Bluegrass Blues (IRE)**[18] 4894 6-9-7 **85** HectorCrouch(5) 2 92
(Heather Main) *hld up wl in tch: rdn over 2f out: swtchd rt over 1f out: r.o to chal wl ins fnl f: jst hld* **7/1**

5221 **3** 1 3/4 **Izmir (IRE)**[17] 4909 3-9-1 **80** (p) DaneO'Neill 5 82
(William Haggas) *led narrowly: rdn over 2f out: hdd over 1f out: unable qck fnl f* **2/1**[1]

2440 **4** 1/2 **Outback Blue**[39] 4139 3-8-13 **78** (t) JFEgan 4 79
(David Evans) *hld up wl in tch: effrt over 2f out: r.o fnl f but nvr cl enough to chal* **5/1**[2]

3442 **5** 2 1/2 **Peak Storm**[17] 4909 7-9-1 **77** (p) EdwardGreatrex(3) 1 73
(John O'Shea) *w ldr tl rdn over 2f out: wknd over 1f out* **11/2**[3]

1m 35.39s (-0.81) **Going Correction** -0.15s/f (Firm)
WFA 3 from 6yo+ 6lb 5 Ran SP% **111.2**
Speed ratings (Par 105): **98,97,96,95,93**
CSF £16.34 TOTE £3.20: £1.20, £2.60; EX 18.10 Trifecta £46.50.
Owner Highclere Thoroughbred Racing(Hardwicke) **Bred** Brian Walsh **Trained** Lambourn, Berks

FOCUS
The feature contest was a decent little handicap and they went an, at best, respectable gallop. An ability to work hard for a victory on quick ground proved paramount. The winner confirmed his latest form.

5546 DRIBUILD DASH (ROUND 6 OF THE CHEPSTOW SPRINT SERIES) H'CAP 5f 16y
4:40 (4:40) (Class 5) (0-70,69) 3-Y-O+ **£3,234** (£962; £481; £240) **Stalls** Centre

Form RPR

6135 **1** **Quantum Dot (IRE)**[12] 5105 5-8-13 **58** (b) LiamKeniry 2 68
(Ed de Giles) *mde all: shkn up 2f out: rdn out fnl f* **9/2**[3]

150- **2** 1 3/4 **Dreams Of Glory**[264] 8011 8-9-10 **69** AdamBeschizza 5 73
(Ron Hodges) *chsd wnr thrght: rdn over 1f out: r.o but hld fnl f* **10/1**

6001 **3** *shd* **Bonjour Steve**[9] 5230 5-9-5 **64** 6ex (p) TomMarquand 3 68
(Richard Price) *chsd ldrs: rdn over 2f out: kpt on to chal for 2nd ins fnl f but hld by wnr* **10/3**[1]

0100 **4** *nk* **Noverre To Go (IRE)**[12] 5103 10-9-2 **61** (p) SilvestreDeSousa 6 64
(Ronald Harris) *hld up: hdwy after 2f: rdn over 1f out: r.o fnl f* **5/1**

0550 **5** 2 **Jaganory (IRE)**[14] 5007 4-8-9 **57** (p) EdwardGreatrex(3) 7 52
(Christopher Mason) *chsd ldrs: rdn 1/2-way: one pce appr fnl f* **5/1**

06-0 **6** *hd* **Dishy Guru**[174] 714 7-9-9 **68** WilliamTwiston-Davies 1 63
(Michael Blanshard) *towards rr: hdwy 1/2-way: rdn over 1f out: wknd ins fnl f* **16/1**

0-00 **7** 1/2 **Balliol**[16] 4952 4-9-7 **66** (t) RaulDaSilva 4 59
(Ronald Harris) *v.s.a: a bhd: edgd lft u.p over 1f out* **7/2**[2]

58.6s (-0.70) **Going Correction** -0.15s/f (Firm) 7 Ran SP% **111.8**
Speed ratings (Par 103): **99,96,96,95,92 92,91**
CSF £44.67 TOTE £5.20: £2.40, £3.80; EX 51.10 Trifecta £204.80.
Owner Mrs Yvonne Fleet **Bred** R N Auld **Trained** Ledbury, H'fords

FOCUS
A modest sprint handicap. The winner dominated at a good tempo and in a decent time for the grade.

5547 ALL-WEATHER RIDING SURFACES FROM EQUESTRIAN SURFACES H'CAP 1m 2f 36y
5:15 (5:15) (Class 5) (0-75,75) 4-Y-O+ **£3,234** (£962; £481; £240) **Stalls** Low

Form RPR

5064 **1** **Vercingetorix (IRE)**[20] 4793 5-9-7 **75** SilvestreDeSousa 4 80
(David Evans) *trckd ldr after 1f: lost 2nd over 5f out: drvn over 2f out: chal over 1f out: led ins fnl f: edgd sltly lft 75yds out: all out* **4/6**[1]

0-65 **2** *hd* **Rahmah (IRE)**[16] 4953 4-9-4 **72** TimmyMurphy 5 76
(Geoffrey Deacon) *broke wl: sn hld up bhd ldng pair: wnt 2nd over 5f out: rdn to ld narrowly over 1f out: hdd ins fnl f: sn carried sltly lft: jst hld* **7/2**[2]

0305 **3** 1 3/4 **Classic Mission**[27] 4551 5-8-8 **69** (b) MitchGodwin(7) 1 70
(Jonathan Portman) *led: rdn 2f out: sn hdd: one pce* **4/1**[3]

0100 **4** 10 **Munsarim (IRE)**[4] 5393 9-8-5 **59** TomMarquand 3 40
(Lee Carter) *hld up and a last: rdn 4f out: wknd and edgd rt 2f out* **16/1**

2m 9.37s (-1.23) **Going Correction** -0.15s/f (Firm) 4 Ran SP% **108.1**
Speed ratings (Par 103): **98,97,96,88**
CSF £3.29 TOTE £1.60; EX 3.00 Trifecta £4.80.
Owner Simon Munir & Isaac Souede **Bred** M Henochsberg & Madame D Ades-Hazan **Trained** Pandy, Monmouths

FOCUS
A weakish handicap. They went an, at best, respectable gallop and the odds-on favourite was nursed home in fine style by the champion jockey Silvestre De Sousa.

5548 ALL-WEATHER RIDING SURFACES FROM EQUESTRIAN SURFACES APPRENTICE H'CAP 1m 4f 23y
5:45 (5:45) (Class 6) (0-65,65) 3-Y-O **£2,587** (£770; £384; £192) **Stalls** Low

Form RPR

0032 **1** **Fandango (GER)**[9] 5232 3-9-7 **63** HectorCrouch(3) 3 73+
(Jeremy Gask) *hld up: hdwy 3f out: sn rdn: led over 1f out: edgd lft ins fnl f: asserted nr fin* **2/1**[1]

0315 **2** 1 **Lady Blanco (USA)**[19] 4818 3-9-12 **65** EdwardGreatrex 4 73
(Andrew Balding) *chsd ldrs: rdn to ld over 2f out: hdd over 1f out: kpt on tl no ex nr fin* **4/1**[2]

3444 **3** 3 3/4 **Harry's Endeavour**[13] 5079 3-9-4 **57** (b[1]) JosephineGordon 10 59
(Daniel Kubler) *t.k.h: disp 2nd: rdn over 2f out: unable qck: hld in 3rd fnl f* **9/2**[3]

0-05 **4** 1 **McCools Gold**[16] 4955 3-9-12 **65** GeorgeDowning 8 66
(Eve Johnson Houghton) *hld up: rdn over 3f out: no hdwy tl styd on fnl f: tk 4th cl home* **14/1**

-664 **5** *hd* **Kilim**[22] 4740 3-9-0 **60** GabrieleMalune(7) 7 60
(Luca Cumani) *t.k.h: mid-div: rdn over 2f out: unable qck and hld by ldrs after: lost 4th cl home* **6/1**

0602 **6** *hd* **Mister Showman**[10] 5204 3-9-7 **60** TomMarquand 5 60
(Jonathan Portman) *disp 2nd tl rdn and lost pl 3f out: styd on again fnl f* **14/1**

0012 **7** 1 3/4 **File Of Facts (IRE)**[8] 5256 3-9-1 **59** (vt) AnnaHesketh(5) 6 56
(Tom Dascombe) *led at stdy gallop: rdn over 3f out: hdd over 2f out: wknd appr fnl f* **7/1**

-046 **8** 94 **Rosecomb (IRE)**[15] 4987 3-8-2 **48** (t[1]) SophieScardifield(7) 2
(Michael Bell) *virtually ref to r: emerged fr stalls over a f bhd and completed crse in own time* **25/1**

2m 37.44s (-1.56) **Going Correction** -0.15s/f (Firm) 8 Ran SP% **115.5**
Speed ratings (Par 98): **99,98,95,95,95 94,93,31**
CSF £10.15 CT £31.58 TOTE £2.60: £1.02, £2.20, £2.30; EX 10.10 Trifecta £36.70.
Owner Anglo Australian Racing **Bred** Gestut Etzean **Trained** Stockbridge, Hants

FOCUS
A modest 3yo middle-distance handicap for apprentice riders. They went quite steadily until the top of the straight but the right horse still came to fore. Straightforward form.

T/Plt: £66.70 to a £1 stake. Pool of £61351.01 - 670.79 winning tickets. T/Qpdt: £12.70 to a £1 stake. Pool of £3684.11 - 214.10 winning tickets. **Richard Lowther**

5503KEMPTON (A.W) (R-H)

Wednesday, August 17

OFFICIAL GOING: Polytrack: standard to slow

Wind: Light, half behind Weather: Sunny, very warm

5549 32RED CASINO MAIDEN AUCTION STKS (PLUS 10 RACE) 7f (P)
6:40 (6:42) (Class 4) 2-Y-O £3,946 (£1,174; £586; £293) Stalls Low

Form RPR

0 1 **Sir Dancealot (IRE)**44 3954 2-9-3 0 JimCrowley 6 92+
(David Elsworth) *dwlt: sn chsd ldrs but pushed along at various stages: shkn up and clsd to ld wl over 1f out: sn clr: rdn out and styd on strly* **4/1**2

4 2 6 **Tonahutu (IRE)**21 4759 2-8-10 0 HarryBentley 11 69
(Ed Vaughan) *in tch in midfield: prog 2f out to chse wnr over 1f out: kpt on but no threat at all* **8/1**

3242 3 1 **Magical Forest (IRE)**18 4877 2-8-8 75 (b1) DanielMuscutt(3) 4 70
(Marco Botti) *t.k.h: trckd ldrs: stmbld after 1f: trying to cl whn nt clr run 2f out: renewed effrt and kpt on to take 3rd fnl f* **3/1**1

036 4 1 1/2 **Three Duchesses**30 4442 2-8-4 74 LuluStanford(7) 8 63
(Michael Bell) *settled wl in rr: shkn up over 2f out: gd prog over 1f out to press for 3rd fnl f: one pce last 100yds* **16/1**

0 5 4 **Viking Hoard (IRE)**35 4270 2-9-3 0 TomQueally 12 58
(Harry Dunlop) *wl bhd in 11th: prog 2f out: nvr any ch but kpt on past wkng rivals fr jst over 1f out* **33/1**

0 6 4 1/2 **Captain Sue (IRE)**16 4938 2-8-8 0 ShaneKelly 1 37
(Richard Hughes) *led to wl over 1f out: wknd qckly* **40/1**

3 7 hd **Bubble Bath**16 4938 2-8-7 0 RoystonFfrench 7 36
(Daniel Kubler) *pressed ldr after 2f to 2f out: wknd qckly* **14/1**

032 8 1/2 **Highland Lotus**17 4907 2-8-7 67 (p) WilliamCarson 2 34
(William Haggas) *trckd ldr 2f: styd prom tl wknd over 2f out* **5/1**3

2 9 1 1/2 **Masonic (IRE)**22 4738 2-8-12 0 AdrianMcCarthy 9 35
(Robyn Brisland) *racd in 8th: rdn and no prog wl over 2f out: wl btn after* **6/1**

255 10 6 **Conistone**26 4603 2-8-11 70 TedDurcan 5 18
(James Bethell) *trckd ldrs: rdn and wknd qckly over 2f out* **14/1**

0 11 1 **Ultimat Power (IRE)**35 4270 2-8-12 0 SteveDrowne 13 16
(Mark Hoad) *detached in last: virtually t.o 3f out: plugged on fnl 150yds* **250/1**

0 12 1 3/4 **Black Tie Bob (IRE)**19 4815 2-8-12 0 JohnFahy 10
(J S Moore) *hld up: pushed along and brief effrt over 2f out: sn wknd qckly* **100/1**

1m 26.22s (0.22) **Going Correction** +0.05s/f (Slow) **12** Ran SP% **113.0**

Speed ratings (Par 96): **100,93,92,90,85 80,80,79,78,71 70,68**

CSF £33.78 TOTE £4.50: £2.10, £2.60, £1.70; EX 48.70 Trifecta £121.80.

Owner C Benham/ D Whitford/ L Quinn/ K Quinn **Bred** Vincent Duignan **Trained** Newmarket, Suffolk

■ Master Billie was withdrawn. Price at time of withdrawal 20/1. Rule 4 does not apply.

FOCUS

A modest maiden auction to open proceedings but it produced a very impressive winner. This rating could underplay him.

5550 £10 FREE BET AT 32REDSPORT.COM MEDIAN AUCTION MAIDEN FILLIES' STKS 1m 4f (P)
7:10 (7:13) (Class 4) 3-5-Y-O £4,690 (£1,395; £697; £348) Stalls Centre

Form RPR

3364 1 **Taffeta Lady**46 3894 3-9-0 77 (v1) JimCrowley 6 79
(Lucy Wadham) *t.k.h: hld up tl prog to trck ldr 1/2-way: chalng whn carried lft fr over 2f out: drvn over 1f out: led jst ins fnl f: styd on* **7/4**2

5 2 1 **Casablanca (IRE)**20 4806 3-9-0 0 LiamKeniry 3 77
(Andrew Balding) *trckd ldng pair: cl up whn lft in ld wl over 1f out: hdd jst ins fnl f: styd on but hld fnl 100yds* **16/1**

4522 3 6 **Torquay**11 5164 3-9-0 72 PatCosgrave 4 70
(Harry Dunlop) *led and dictated stdy pce: rdn and hung bdly lft over 2f out: hdd wl over 1f out: sn wl btn: eased last 100yds* **4/5**1

5 4 1/2 **Blazing Mighty**15 4978 3-9-0 0 AdrianMcCarthy 1 67
(Robyn Brisland) *trckd ldrs: urged along over 4f out: outpcd over 3f out and carried wd bnd sn after: looked likely to fin wl btn but fin to sme effect fnl f* **12/1**3

00 5 3 **Want The Fairytale**33 4367 3-9-0 0 JohnFahy 7 62
(Clive Cox) *trckd in last pair: lost tch w ldrs and pushed along over 3f out: tk modest 4th over 2f out tl fnl f: nvr involved* **20/1**

6 6 16 **Alidara (IRE)**14 5025 4-9-10 0 TomQueally 2 37
(Emma Owen) *mostly in last pair tl tk modest 4th over 3f out to over 2f out: wknd qckly* **200/1**

-00 7 39 **The Black Cygnet**33 4367 3-9-0 0 (t1) WilliamCarson 5
(David Menuisier) *trckd ldr to 1/2-way: sltly checked sn after and lost interest: wkng whn wd bnd 3f out: t.o* **100/1**

2m 37.62s (3.12) **Going Correction** +0.05s/f (Slow)

WFA 3 from 4yo 10lb **7** Ran SP% **111.7**

Speed ratings (Par 102): **91,90,86,86,84 73,47**

CSF £25.83 TOTE £2.90: £1.80, £3.30; EX 25.60 Trifecta £52.40.

Owner Mr And Mrs A E Pakenham **Bred** Mr & Mrs A E Pakenham **Trained** Newmarket, Suffolk

FOCUS

Little depth to this fillies' maiden but the winner, who set the standard, wasn't scoring out of turn - the early pace was very steady.

5551 32RED.COM FILLIES' H'CAP 7f (P)
7:40 (7:41) (Class 4) (0-85,84) 3-Y-O+ £5,175 (£1,540; £769; £384) Stalls Low

Form RPR

-222 1 **Catchment**11 5168 3-8-10 73 PatDobbs 7 82
(Amanda Perrett) *t.k.h: hld up bhd ldrs: prog to go 2nd over 1f out: pushed along to cl on ldr: rdn fnl 100yds and r.o to ld nr fin* **8/1**

14 2 nk **Owaseyf (USA)**75 2855 3-8-12 75 HarryBentley 6 83
(Roger Varian) *led after 1f: drvn for home 2f out: kpt on but hdd nr fin* **9/2**2

0221 3 1 3/4 **Excellent Sounds**28 4528 3-9-0 77 JimCrowley 1 80+
(Hughie Morrison) *sn shuffled bk to rr on inner: effrt 2f out: rdn and prog to take 3rd ins fnl f: nt pce to threaten* **15/8**1

241 4 2 3/4 **Sweet Dragon Fly**75 2848 3-9-7 84 JimmyFortune 5 80
(Paul Cole) *led 1f: trckd ldrs: shkn up and nt qckn 2f out: outpcd fr over 1f out* **5/1**3

4-03 5 2 1/4 **Welsh Rose**13 5078 3-8-11 74 MartinDwyer 9 64
(William Muir) *t.k.h: trckd ldr over 5f out to over 1f out: wknd* **12/1**

-104 6 nk **Malmostosa**13 5089 3-9-0 80 DanielMuscutt(3) 4 69
(Marco Botti) *hld up in last: shkn up over 2f out: modest late prog: nvr involved* **11/1**

1-10 7 2 1/2 **Certified (IRE)**29 4474 3-9-6 83 FrederikTylicki 10 65
(James Tate) *hld up in rr: rdn and struggling wl over 2f out: sn no ch* **10/1**

004 8 1 3/4 **Perfect Alchemy (IRE)**10 5190 5-9-4 76 PatCosgrave 8 56
(Patrick Chamings) *chsd ldrs to over 2f out: wknd* **25/1**

1m 25.92s (-0.08) **Going Correction** +0.05s/f (Slow)

WFA 3 from 4yo+ 5lb **8** Ran SP% **109.7**

Speed ratings (Par 102): **102,101,99,96,93 93,90,88**

CSF £40.18 CT £88.83 TOTE £9.20: £2.00, £2.20, £1.10; EX 48.80 Trifecta £64.00.

Owner K Abdullah **Bred** Juddmonte Farms Ltd **Trained** Pulborough, W Sussex

FOCUS

A couple of non-runners detracted slightly from this fillies' handicap and the pace, dictated by the runner-up, was steady but the first three all have something to recommend them in the short term.

5552 32RED ON THE APP STORE H'CAP (LONDON MILE SERIES QUALIFIER) 1m (P)
8:10 (8:11) (Class 3) (0-95,95) 3-Y-O+

£7,470 (£2,236; £1,118; £559; £279; £140) Stalls Low

Form RPR

1122 1 **Dommersen (IRE)**32 4396 3-9-2 91 NickyMackay 2 102+
(John Gosden) *dwlt: towards rr: pushed along and prog on inner over 2f out: drvn to chse ldr jst over 1f out: styd on wl u.p to ld nr fin* **4/1**2

1-26 2 hd **Afjaan (IRE)**21 4758 4-9-6 89 PatCosgrave 10 101+
(William Haggas) *hld up in 8th: smooth prog on outer over 2f out: pushed into ld over 1f out: hrd pressed and drvn fnl f: hdd nr fin* **3/1**1

0602 3 2 **Sirius Prospect (USA)**32 4380 8-9-12 95 (p) JFEgan 3 102
(Dean Ivory) *trckd ldrs: shake up jst over 2f out: prog to take 3rd fnl f: styd on wl but no match for ldng pair* **20/1**

6542 4 2 1/2 **Mustaaqeem (USA)**15 4976 4-9-5 88 DaneO'Neill 12 89
(Sir Michael Stoute) *chsd ldrs: urged along over 3f out: hdwy u.p 2f out to go 4th fnl f: nvr pce to threaten* **5/1**3

0341 5 1 **Secret Art (IRE)**46 3910 6-9-12 95 MartinDwyer 5 94
(William Knight) *in tch in midfield: rdn over 2f out: styd on same pce fr over 1f out: n.d* **12/1**

3500 6 nk **Georgian Bay (IRE)**55 3566 6-9-12 95 (v) HarryBentley 7 93
(K R Burke) *hld up in rr: rdn over 2f out: prog over 1f out: kpt on same pce fnl f and no ch* **8/1**

-101 7 1/2 **Replenish (FR)**74 2917 3-9-2 91 FrederikTylicki 13 87
(James Fanshawe) *hld up wl in rr: pushed along on wd outside over 2f out: reminder over 1f out: kpt on but nvr involved* **5/1**3

00 8 1 **Red Avenger (USA)**19 4823 6-9-7 90 (b) JimmyFortune 8 85
(Gary Moore) *trckd ldrs: rdn to go 2nd briefly 2f out: wknd fnl f* **40/1**

1056 9 1 **Jack Of Diamonds (IRE)**28 4532 7-9-8 91 OisinMurphy 9 84
(Roger Teal) *hld up wl in rr: shkn up over 2f out: modest prog over 1f out: nvr involved* **50/1**

0-15 10 3/4 **Primogeniture (IRE)**47 3861 5-9-7 90 RichardKingscote 6 81
(Mary Hambro) *led at gd pce to over 1f out: wknd qckly fnl f* **18/1**

6400 11 5 **Baddilini**66 3185 6-9-2 92 MitchGodwin(7) 11 71
(Alan Bailey) *t.k.h: trckd ldr after 2f to 2f out: wknd rapidly* **66/1**

3240 12 4 1/2 **Unforgiving Minute**83 2628 5-9-9 92 SaleemGolam 4 61
(John Butler) *chsd ldr 2f: styd prom tl wknd rapidly jst over 2f out* **20/1**

6000 13 6 **Ticking Away**8 5274 3-8-8 83 TedDurcan 14 37
(David Brown) *t.k.h: hld up in last: detached after 3f: t.o over 2f out* **125/1**

1m 38.33s (-1.47) **Going Correction** +0.05s/f (Slow)

WFA 3 from 4yo+ 6lb **13** Ran SP% **118.6**

Speed ratings (Par 107): **109,108,106,104,103 103,102,101,100,99 94,90,84**

CSF £15.26 CT £222.71 TOTE £5.50: £1.70, £1.50, £5.50; EX 20.70 Trifecta £303.80.

Owner Al Mirqab Racing **Bred** The Lavington Stud **Trained** Newmarket, Suffolk

■ Stewards' Enquiry : Nicky Mackay four-day ban: used whip above permitted level (Aug 31-Sep 2,4)

FOCUS

A good-quality handicap and with two of the more progressive runners in the field pulling nicely clear, it looks a solid piece of form.

5553 32RED.COM H'CAP 2m (P)
8:40 (8:40) (Class 4) (0-85,85) 4-Y-O+ £5,175 (£1,540; £769; £384) Stalls Low

Form RPR

021 1 **Arty Campbell (IRE)**17 4912 6-8-12 79 DanielMuscutt(3) 2 87
(Bernard Llewellyn) *t.k.h: hld up in 4th: prog to press ldr over 6f out: led 4f out gng strly: drvn and edgd lft over 2f out: hdd over 1f out: pressed ldr after: kpt on to ld fnl strides* **7/1**

0102 2 hd **Saborido (USA)**16 4941 10-8-13 77 (b) JimCrowley 6 84
(Amanda Perrett) *trckd ldrs: wnt 2nd wl over 2f out: drvn into narrow ld over 1f out: kpt on but hdd last strides* **12/1**

0304 3 2 **King Calypso**25 4661 5-9-2 80 OisinMurphy 8 84
(Denis Coakley) *trckd ldr to over 6f out: rdn 3f out: kpt on to take 3rd over 1f out: one pce after* **12/1**

12 4 1 1/2 **Jacob Cats**47 3862 7-9-7 85 (v) FrederikTylicki 3 88+
(William Knight) *hld up in last: lot to do once field stretched out 4f out: drvn 3f out: prog over 2f out: tk 4th fnl f but no imp on ldrs after* **11/2**3

2454 5 2 **Cotton Club (IRE)**17 4912 5-9-7 85 RyanTate 4 85
(Rod Millman) *hld up in 7th: rdn 3f out: sme prog u.p 2f out: one pce and no imp fnl f* **12/1**

0411 6 1 3/4 **Mister Bob (GER)**16 4941 7-8-9 73 (p) TedDurcan 7 71
(James Bethell) *stdd s: hld up in 7th: rdn 3f out: no great prog after* **13/2**

3106 7 9 **Be My Sea (IRE)**21 4752 5-9-1 79 (p) JimmyQuinn 5 66
(Tony Carroll) *led to 4f out: wknd qckly over 2f out* **4/1**2

111 8 26 **Hatsaway (IRE)**48 3798 5-8-8 72 JFEgan 1 28
(Pat Phelan) *trckd ldrs in 5th: rdn 5f out: sn btn: bhd and eased 2f out: t.o* **11/4**1

3m 30.37s (0.27) **Going Correction** +0.05s/f (Slow) **8** Ran SP% **111.0**

Speed ratings (Par 105): **101,100,99,99,98 97,92,79**

CSF £80.03 CT £950.53 TOTE £9.00: £2.50, £3.70, £2.90; EX 90.10 Trifecta £548.90.

Owner Alex James **Bred** Airlie Stud **Trained** Fochriw, Caerphilly

FOCUS

Some in-form stayers in opposition here and an exciting finish - little got into it from off the pace.

5554 RACING UK IN HD H'CAP 6f (P)
9:10 (9:12) (Class 6) (0-60,60) 3-Y-O £2,587 (£770; £384; £192) Stalls Low

Form RPR

6103 1 **Curious Fox**12 5126 3-9-7 60 WilliamCarson 10 67
(Anthony Carson) *trckd ldr: rdn over 1f out: led last 150yds: drvn out* **12/1**

5043 **2** 1 1/2 **Deer Song**28 4529 3-9-3 **56** DannyBrock 6 58
(John Bridger) *led: rdn over 2f out: hdd and no ex last 150yds: hld on for 2nd* **16/1**

-000 **3** nk **Keiba (IRE)**49 3786 3-9-7 **60** 1 ShaneKelly 12 61
(Gary Moore) *chsd ldrs: rdn 2f out: styd on fnl f to take 3rd nr fin* **8/1**

6350 **4** hd **Kenstone (FR)**43 3987 3-8-11 **50** (p) JFEgan 3 51+
(David Dennis) *towards rr and pushed along: rdn on outer over 2f out: styd on wl fnl f: nrly snatched 3rd* **10/1**

6001 **5** nk **Oasis Moon**14 5020 3-9-2 **55** (p) JimCrowley 1 55
(William Haggas) *trckd ldrs: shkn up 2f out: nt qckn over 1f out: styd on ins fnl f but nt pce to chal* **2/1**1

2253 **6** 1 **Lady McGuffy (IRE)**29 4484 3-9-6 **59** (t) AdamBeschizza 2 56
(David Evans) *chsd ldng pair: rdn 2f out: tried to chal 1f out: fdd last 100yds* **6/1**3

00-0 **7** hd **Robbie Roo Roo**11 5167 3-9-1 **54** (t) SaleemGolam 11 50
(Mrs Ilka Gansera-Leveque) *nvr beyond midfield: rdn 2f out: kpt on one pce: n.d* **50/1**

065 **8** 2 **Protest (IRE)**11 5167 3-8-5 **51** MitchGodwin(7) 5 41
(Sylvester Kirk) *sn pushed along and a struggling to go the pce: nvr on terms* **4/1**2

-230 **9** 2 **Secret Interlude (IRE)**43 3970 3-8-11 **55** LucyKBarry(5) 4 39
(Jamie Osborne) *hld up in last pair: a bhd: no ch whn rdn over 1f out: nvr involved* **12/1**

0-50 **10** 13 **Storming Ambition**126 1414 3-8-12 **51** JimmyQuinn 7
(Conrad Allen) *a struggling: t.o* **20/1**

1m 13.19s (0.09) **Going Correction** +0.05s/f (Slow) **10** Ran SP% **115.8**
Speed ratings (Par 98): **101,99,98,98,97 96,96,93,91,73**
CSF £185.44 CT £1627.08 TOTE £11.10: £3.40, £4.20, £2.40; EX 121.20.
Owner Carson, Francis, Ghauri & Percy **Bred** Minster Stud **Trained** Newmarket, Suffolk

FOCUS
A low-grade finale but a taking performance from the winner who looked better than the grade. Pace held up.
T/Plt: £185.30 to a £1 stake. Pool of £70585.08 - 278.06 winning units. T/Qpdt: £62.00 to a £1 stake. Pool of £5694.19 - 67.88 winning units. **Jonathan Neesom**

4663YORK (L-H)
Wednesday, August 17

OFFICIAL GOING: Good to firm (7.3)
Wind: Light half behind Weather: Cloudy, warm with sunny periods

5555 SYMPHONY GROUP STKS (H'CAP) 5f 89y
1:55 (1:57) (Class 2) (0-105,105) 3-Y-O+
£40,462 (£12,116; £6,058; £3,029; £1,514; £760) **Stalls** Centre

Form RPR
0001 **1** **Boom The Groom (IRE)**22 4735 5-9-7 **102** AndreaAtzeni 5 111
(Tony Carroll) *chsd ldrs: drvn 3f out: led over 1f out: fnd ex nr fin* **11/1**3

3005 **2** hd **Duke Of Firenze**18 4865 7-9-4 **99** DavidAllan 2 107
(David C Griffiths) *hld up in mid-div: hdwy over 2f out: upsides last 100yds: no ex nr fin* **8/1**1

-04U **3** 1 1/2 **Captain Colby (USA)**22 4741 4-9-0 **95** (b) WilliamBuick 19 98
(Ed Walker) *swtg: on toes: racd stands' side: chsd ldrs: kpt on wl fnl f* **14/1**

3002 **4** 1 1/4 **Line Of Reason (IRE)**11 5143 6-9-10 **105** MartinLane 4 103
(Paul Midgley) *chsd ldrs: upsides over 1f out: kpt on same pce* **11/1**3

1005 **5** 1 **Harry Hurricane**22 4735 4-9-1 **96** RobertWinston 12 91
(George Baker) *chsd ldrs: edgd rt over 1f out: kpt on same pce* **12/1**

6665 **6** nk **Medicean Man**11 5143 10-9-3 **103** (tp) DavidParkes(5) 6 96
(Jeremy Gask) *s.i.s: in rr: hdwy over 1f out: styng on at fin* **25/1**

0206 **7** 1/2 **Hay Chewed (IRE)**8 5268 5-8-8 **92** NoelGarbutt(3) 20 84
(Conrad Allen) *racd stands' side: mid-div: hdwy over 1f out: kpt on* **33/1**

1100 **8** hd **Hoofalong**18 4865 6-8-13 **99** (b) NathanEvans(5) 13 90
(Michael Easterby) *mid-div: drvn over 2f out: kpt on fnl f* **20/1**

0060 **9** 1/2 **Arctic Feeling (IRE)**25 4667 8-8-8 **89** PaulHanagan 1 78
(Richard Fahey) *racd far side: mid-div: effrt over 2f out: kpt on fnl f* **25/1**

1335 **10** nk **Lexington Abbey**25 4667 5-9-0 **95** JamieSpencer 17 83
(Kevin Ryan) *racd stands' side: towards rr: hdwy and swtchd rt over 1f out: kpt on: nvr a factor* **11/1**3

-620 **11** 3/4 **Robot Boy (IRE)**26 4584 6-9-1 **96** (b1) GrahamGibbons 7 81
(David Barron) *w ldr: led 4f out: hdd over 1f out: sn wknd* **10/1**2

0113 **12** hd **Royal Birth**26 4584 5-8-10 **94** (t) AaronJones(3) 16 82
(Stuart Williams) *mid-div: keeping on one pce whn hmpd over 1f out* **11/1**3

6055 **13** hd **Baraweez (IRE)**17 4921 6-9-7 **102** DaleSwift 3 86
(Brian Ellison) *in rr and sn drvn along: sme hdwy over 1f out: nvr a factor* **16/1**

2263 **14** 3/4 **Bowson Fred**22 4735 4-9-5 **100** FrankieDettori 11 81
(Michael Easterby) *chsd ldrs: edgd lft and wknd over 1f out* **10/1**2

3000 **15** shd **Ninjago**11 5143 6-9-0 **95** PatSmullen 18 76
(Paul Midgley) *lw: racd stands' side: towards rr: nvr a factor* **16/1**

-250 **16** 3/4 **Union Rose**11 5143 4-9-1 **96** (p) MartinHarley 14 74
(Ronald Harris) *sltly on toes: mid-div: effrt over 2f out: one pce whn n.m.r over 1f out* **25/1**

0020 **17** 1/2 **Move In Time**19 4824 8-9-10 **105** (v) DanielTudhope 10 81
(David O'Meara) *chsd ldrs: wkng whn hmpd over 1f out: eased in clsng stages* **14/1**

-400 **18** 2 1/2 **Zanetto**46 3890 6-8-12 **93** PJMcDonald 15 60
(John Quinn) *lw: a towards rr* **25/1**

-400 **19** 1 1/2 **Soapy Aitken**11 5148 3-9-1 **98** AdamKirby 8 60
(Clive Cox) *swtg: on toes: mid-div: wknd over 1f out* **25/1**

6010 **20** 2 **Meadway**54 3606 5-9-1 **96** (p) ConnorBeasley 9 51
(Bryan Smart) *led 2f: wkng whn hmpd over 1f out: sn eased* **25/1**

1m 1.77s (-2.33) **Going Correction** -0.20s/f (Firm)
WFA 3 from 4yo+ 2lb **20** Ran SP% **126.2**
Speed ratings (Par 109): **110,109,107,105,103 103,102,102,101,100 99,99,98,97,97 96,95,91,89,86**
CSF £85.54 CT £1295.84 TOTE £11.40: £2.90, £2.20, £4.70, £3.30; EX 97.30 Trifecta £2032.30.
Owner Gary Attwood **Bred** John Foley **Trained** Cropthorne, Worcs

FOCUS
The watered ground (2mm overnight) was given as good to firm (GoingStick: 7.3. Home straight - far side 7.3: centre 7.3: stands' side 7.2). After riding in the opener William Buick and Frankie Dettori called the ground good to firm, Robert Winston said: "It is quick ground" and PJ McDonald said: "It is quick enough but it is safe, proper summer ground." The rail was on its traditional racing line and there were no adjustments to race distances. A wide-open sprint handicap, but the race developed centre to far side and four of the first six were drawn in the lowest six stalls. The winner backed up his Goodwood win with another pb.

5556 TATTERSALLS ACOMB STKS (GROUP 3) 7f
2:30 (2:31) (Class 1) 2-Y-O
£48,203 (£18,275; £9,146; £4,556; £2,286; £1,147) **Stalls** Low

Form RPR
1 **1** **Syphax (USA)**40 4097 2-9-1 77 JamieSpencer 6 109
(Kevin Ryan) *w'like: bit on the leg: swtchd lft after s: in last and sn pushed along: hdwy on outer over 2f out: styd on wl fnl f: led fnl strides* **16/1**

1 **2** hd **Best Of Days**28 4533 2-9-1 0 WilliamBuick 1 108
(Hugo Palmer) *str: trckd ldrs: effrt over 2f out: led over 1f out: hdd and no ex fnl strides* **10/11**1

21 **3** 3/4 **Lockheed**18 4866 2-9-1 83 FrankieDettori 2 106
(William Haggas) *lengthy: hld up: hdwy over 2f out: chsng ldrs over 1f out: no ex last 50yds* **7/2**2

212 **4** 2 1/4 **Tommy Taylor (USA)**12 5109 2-9-1 84 TomEaves 3 100
(Kevin Ryan) *q str: warm: hld up in rr: hdwy over 3f out: swtchd rt 2f out: kpt on to take 4th nr fin* **33/1**

2 **5** 1/2 **Courage Under Fire (USA)**10 5212 2-9-1 0 (t) SeamieHeffernan 7 99
(A P O'Brien, Ire) *trckd ldrs: effrt over 2f out: upsides over 1f out: kpt on one pce* **7/1**

2211 **6** 3 3/4 **Bear Valley (IRE)**20 4802 2-9-1 95 FrannyNorton 8 88
(Mark Johnston) *sltly on toes; trckd ldr: effrt over 2f out: wknd fnl f* **11/2**3

51 **7** 3 1/4 **Galactic Prince**15 4989 2-9-1 76 DavidProbert 5 80
(Andrew Balding) *cmpt: led: hdd & wknd over 1f out* **25/1**

1m 23.46s (-1.84) **Going Correction** -0.15s/f (Firm) **7** Ran SP% **115.2**
Speed ratings (Par 104): **104,103,102,100,99 95,91**
CSF £31.83 TOTE £19.40: £5.80, £1.40; EX 47.00 Trifecta £160.90.
Owner K&J Bloodstock Ltd **Bred** Pin Oak Stud LLC **Trained** Hambleton, N Yorks

FOCUS
Race distance as advertised. Not a terribly strong race for the grade, and rated towards the lower end of the race average, although the winner did well to come from last place, overcoming greenness.

5557 BETWAY GREAT VOLTIGEUR STKS (GROUP 2) (C&G) 1m 4f
3:05 (3:05) (Class 1) 3-Y-O
£90,736 (£34,400; £17,216; £8,576; £4,304; £2,160) **Stalls** Centre

Form RPR
2332 **1** **Idaho (IRE)**53 3679 3-9-0 120 SeamieHeffernan 2 116+
(A P O'Brien, Ire) *swtg: on toes: hld up in last: hdwy over 2f out: shkn up and hung rt: rdn to chal 1f out: sn led: styd on wl to forge clr clsng stages* **5/6**1

3441 **2** 1 3/4 **Housesofparliament (IRE)**41 4059 3-9-0 105 (t) JamieSpencer 6 113
(A P O'Brien, Ire) *lw: led: qcknd pce over 3f out: hdd and no ex last 150yds* **6/1**3

1301 **3** 1 3/4 **Across The Stars (IRE)**61 3337 3-9-3 111 FrankieDettori 5 113
(Sir Michael Stoute) *trckd ldrs: t.k.h: effrt 3f out: hung lft and chsd ldr briefly over 1f out: kpt on same pce* **9/2**2

0330 **4** 4 1/2 **Harrison**21 4753 3-9-0 103 AndreaAtzeni 3 103
(Mick Channon) *chsd ldr: drvn over 3f out: one pce fnl 2f* **33/1**

-110 **5** 4 1/2 **Imperial Aviator**73 2946 3-9-0 99 OisinMurphy 1 96
(Roger Charlton) *hld up in rr: hdwy on inner over 3f out: wknd appr fnl f* **10/1**

142 **6** 4 **The Major General (IRE)**21 4753 3-9-0 109 ColmO'Donoghue 4 89
(A P O'Brien, Ire) *swtg: trckd ldrs: effrt over 2f out: lost pl over 1f out* **9/1**

2m 29.41s (-3.79) **Going Correction** -0.05s/f (Good) **6** Ran SP% **109.1**
Speed ratings (Par 112): **110,108,107,104,101 99**
CSF £5.87 TOTE £1.70: £1.20, £2.60; EX 5.50 Trifecta £17.60.
Owner Michael Tabor & Derrick Smith & Mrs John Magnier **Bred** Hveger Syndicate **Trained** Cashel, Co Tipperary

FOCUS
Race distance as advertised. This looked an up-to-standard Voltigeur on paper, and the winner, coming off placed efforts in the Epsom and Irish Derby, stamped himself a strong favourite for the St Leger. Idaho is rated a bit below his best, with the second reversing Ascot form with the third.

5558 JUDDMONTE INTERNATIONAL STKS (BRITISH CHAMPIONS SERIES) (GROUP 1) 1m 2f 88y
3:40 (3:41) (Class 1) 3-Y-O+
£546,542 (£207,206; £103,699; £51,657; £25,924; £13,010) **Stalls** Low

Form RPR
-111 **1** **Postponed (IRE)**74 2894 5-9-6 124 AndreaAtzeni 6 126
(Roger Varian) *lw: trckd ldrs: led 3f out: edgd rt fnl f: drvn out* **15/8**1

4021 **2** 1 1/4 **Highland Reel (IRE)**25 4626 4-9-6 121 SeamieHeffernan 3 123
(A P O'Brien, Ire) *swtg: led 1f: trckd ldrs: upsides 3f out: kpt on same pce last 150yds* **6/1**2

3-11 **3** 1 **Mutakayyef**39 4127 5-9-6 118 PaulHanagan 8 122
(William Haggas) *lw: hld up in mid-div: hdwy 3f out: chsng ldrs over 1f out: carried rt: keeping on same pce whn nt clr run last 50yds* **15/2**3

3114 **4** 2 **Sir Isaac Newton**25 4626 4-9-6 112 ColmO'Donoghue 4 117
(A P O'Brien, Ire) *swtg: hld up towards rr: t.k.h: hdwy 3f out: chsng ldrs over 1f out: kpt on same pce* **25/1**

-103 **5** hd **Exosphere**41 4061 4-9-6 117 PatSmullen 2 116
(Sir Michael Stoute) *hld up in mid-div: t.k.h: hdwy 3f out: chsng ldrs over 1f out: kpt on same pce* **28/1**

6-42 **6** 6 **The Grey Gatsby (IRE)**41 4061 5-9-6 115 (p) DanielTudhope 10 104
(Kevin Ryan) *in rr: hdwy 3f out: swtchd lft over 1f out: kpt on: nvr a threat* **10/1**

2-13 **7** 3/4 **Almodovar (IRE)**60 3384 4-9-6 113 GeorgeBaker 9 103
(David Lanigan) *lw: hld up in rr: sme hdwy over 2f out: nvr a factor* **20/1**

-111 **8** hd **Hawkbill (USA)**46 3912 3-8-12 122 WilliamBuick 13 102
(Charlie Appleby) *trckd ldrs: t.k.h: effrt 3f out: wknd over 1f out: eased clsng stages* **6/1**2

1142 **9** 4 1/2 **Wings of Desire**25 4626 3-8-12 115 FrankieDettori 12 93
(John Gosden) *hld up toward rr: drvn 4f out: nvr a factor: eased clsng stages* **8/1**

6125 **10** 5 **Dariyan (FR)**31 4441 4-9-6 120 ChristopheSoumillon 5 83
(A De Royer-Dupre, France) *rr-div: effrt over 2f out: lost pl over 1f out: eased clsng stages* **14/1**

12-3 **11** *7* **Arab Spring (IRE)**[11] 5159 6-9-6 112 JamieSpencer 1 69
(Sir Michael Stoute) *chsd ldrs: lost pl over 2f out: heavily eased last 100yds* **25/1**

-110 **12** *¾* **King Bolete (IRE)**[22] 4734 4-9-6 102 (b[1]) JackMitchell 11 68
(Roger Varian) *led after 1f: hung lft over 4f out: hdd 3f out: lost pl 2f out: heavily eased last 100yds* **150/1**

2m 6.58s (-5.92) **Going Correction** -0.05s/f (Good)
WFA 3 from 4yo+ 8lb **12** Ran SP% **118.6**
Speed ratings (Par 117): **121,120,119,117,117 112,112,111,108,104 98,98**
CSF £11.92 CT £70.83 TOTE £2.50: £1.50, £1.90, £2.50; EX 16.60 Trifecta £86.70.
Owner Sheikh Mohammed Obaid Al Maktoum **Bred** St Albans Bloodstock Llp **Trained** Newmarket, Suffolk

■ Exosphere ran under the name Exosphere in this and all his previous races.
■ Stewards' Enquiry : Andrea Atzeni two-day ban: careless riding (Aug 31-Sep 1)

FOCUS
Race distance as advertised. Run at a fair pace, not much got into this, with the first two home, incidentally the last two King George winners, sitting third and second respectively for the early stages of the race. The 3yos failed to live up to expectations, but this is rock-solid form nonetheless. Postponed confirmed his position as Europe's leading middle-distance horse, with Highland Reel building on his King George win.

5559 FINE EQUINITY STKS (H'CAP) 2m 88y
4:20 (4:20) (Class 2) (0-100,97) 4-Y-0+
£37,350 (£11,184; £5,592; £2,796; £1,398; £702) **Stalls** Low

Form RPR

4013 **1** **Oceane (FR)**[21] 4752 4-8-11 87 (p) FergusSweeney 17 96+
(Alan King) *mid-div: hdwy over 3f out: 2nd over 2f out: hung lft and led over 1f out: styd on clsng stages* **7/1[2]**

2042 **2** *1 ½* **Nakeeta**[26] 4581 5-9-0 97 CliffordLee(7) 14 105
(Iain Jardine) *lw: trckd ldrs: 2nd 7f out: led 4f out: hdd over 1f out: sn crowded on inner: kpt on same pce last 100yds* **8/1[3]**

-200 **3** *1 ¼* **The Cashel Man (IRE)**[21] 4752 4-8-7 88 (p) GeorgeBuckell(5) 8 94
(David Simcock) *hld up in rr: hdwy 3f out: wnt lft over 2f out: chsng ldrs whn wnt bdly lft over 1f out: kpt on same pce* **14/1**

4111 **4** *nk* **Sweet Selection**[33] 4353 4-8-11 87 PJMcDonald 3 93+
(Hughie Morrison) *towards rr: drvn 5f out: hdwy over 3f out: swtchd rt over 1f out: styd on wl* **8/1[3]**

0-45 **5** *nk* **Botany Bay (IRE)**[41] 4072 4-9-2 92 FrankieDettori 1 97
(Charles O'Brien, Ire) *lw: mid-div: effrt over 3f out: keeping on one pce whn hmpd over 1f out* **7/1[2]**

31-0 **6** *hd* **Eshtiaal (USA)**[32] 3246 6-9-1 91 (tp) GrahamGibbons 6 97+
(Gordon Elliott, Ire) *mid-div: drvn over 3f out: no imp whn n.m.r over 1f out* **16/1**

-400 **7** *1* **Havana Beat (IRE)**[22] 4734 6-9-5 95 (t) RobertWinston 9 99
(Rod Millman) *lw: chsd ldrs: one pce whn hmpd over 1f out* **12/1**

2221 **8** *½* **Life Less Ordinary (IRE)**[28] 4535 4-8-12 88 JamieSpencer 13 91
(Jamie Osborne) *lw: s.i.s: swtchd lft after s: in rr: hdwy 3f out: one pce whn hmpd over 1f out* **10/1**

2100 **9** *1* **My Reward**[22] 4734 4-9-6 96 DavidAllan 11 99
(Tim Easterby) *led 1f: chsd ldrs: one pce whn carried lft over 1f out* **20/1**

/234 **10** *1* **Poyle Thomas**[21] 4752 7-9-2 92 WilliamBuick 12 93
(Ralph Beckett) *lw: in rr: sme hdwy and swtchd rt over 2f out: nvr a factor* **10/1**

0323 **11** *1 ¾* **Modem**[20] 4417 6-9-0 90 (b) ColmO'Donoghue 16 90
(Mrs John Harrington, Ire) *trckd ldrs: effrt over 2f out: one pce whn hmpd over 1f out* **25/1**

00-0 **12** *3 ½* **Teak (IRE)**[21] 4752 9-8-10 86 (v) FrannyNorton 4 81
(Ian Williams) *chsd ldrs: drvn over 3f out: lost pl 2f out* **50/1**

4-04 **13** *8* **Renneti (FR)**[23] 4721 7-9-1 91 PatSmullen 15 76
(W P Mullins, Ire) *hld up in rr: hdwy into mid-div over 6f out: effrt on outer over 3f out: lost pl 2f out: sn eased* **13/2[1]**

/234 **14** *1 ¼* **Repeater**[19] 4850 7-8-1 84 (b) KillianLeonard(7) 5 67
(Miss Amanda Mooney, Ire) *hld up in rr: drvn 3f out: nvr on terms: eased over 1f out* **16/1**

4003 **15** *nk* **Saved By The Bell (IRE)**[25] 4664 6-9-0 90 (p) DanielTudhope 7 73
(David O'Meara) *led after 1f: hdd 4f out: lost pl over 2f out: bhd whn eased over 1f out* **25/1**

3m 30.03s (-4.47) **Going Correction** -0.05s/f (Good) **15** Ran SP% **119.3**
Speed ratings (Par 109): **109,108,107,107,107 107,106,106,105,105 104,102,98,98,98**
CSF £58.21 CT £772.77 TOTE £7.20: £2.30, £2.80, £5.40; EX 49.40 Trifecta £810.00.
Owner McNeill Family **Bred** S C E A Haras De Manneville **Trained** Barbury Castle, Wilts

FOCUS
Race distance as advertised. A competitive staying handicap, but very few actually got seriously involved. The winner has more to offer, and the second ran a pb.

5560 BETWAY STKS (NURSERY H'CAP) 6f
4:55 (4:58) (Class 2) 2-Y-O
£37,350 (£11,184; £5,592; £2,796; £1,398; £702) **Stalls** Low

Form RPR

1 **1** **The Wagon Wheel (IRE)**[30] 4451 2-8-3 73 PatrickMathers 6 84+
(Richard Fahey) *w'like: bit on the leg: mde all: edgd rt over 1f out: drvn and kpt on wl fnl f* **13/2[3]**

3212 **2** *1 ¾* **La Casa Tarifa (IRE)**[15] 4974 2-8-7 77 AndrewMullen 3 83
(Mark Johnston) *chsd ldrs: kpt on same pce fnl f* **20/1**

021 **3** *½* **Storm Cry**[16] 4943 2-8-9 79 FrannyNorton 20 83
(Mark Johnston) *mid-div: hdwy over 1f out: kpt on wl* **10/1**

3106 **4** *hd* **Masham Star (IRE)**[25] 4669 2-9-1 85 PJMcDonald 18 88
(Mark Johnston) *in rr: hdwy over 1f out: styd on* **50/1**

1620 **5** *¾* **Letmestopyouthere (IRE)**[32] 4394 2-8-13 83 SamJames 2 84
(David Evans) *chsd ldrs: kpt on same pce appr fnl f* **33/1**

214 **6** *hd* **Mutawatheb (IRE)**[25] 4622 2-9-7 91 SeanLevey 12 91
(Richard Hannon) *chsd ldrs: kpt on same pce over 1f out* **5/1[1]**

122 **7** *¾* **Wick Powell**[12] 5113 2-9-1 85 GrahamGibbons 5 83
(David Barron) *athletic: swtg: mid-div: drvn over 2f out: sn chsng ldrs: one pce over 1f out* **14/1**

610 **8** *½* **Farleigh Mac**[33] 4352 2-8-11 81 [1] DavidProbert 10 77
(Andrew Balding) *lw: mid-div: hdwy over 2f out: one pce over 1f out* **14/1**

3154 **9** *hd* **El Torito (IRE)**[19] 4825 2-8-9 79 SamHitchcott 19 75
(Jim Boyle) *in rr: hdwy over 1f out: kpt on last 150yds* **50/1**

2210 **10** *nk* **Naafer**[19] 4825 2-9-0 84 PaulHanagan 15 79
(William Haggas) *chsd ldrs: one pce over 1f out* **6/1[2]**

3411 **11** *hd* **Turanga Leela**[17] 4915 2-8-9 79 DavidAllan 17 73
(Ian Williams) *w ldrs: one pce fnl 2f* **33/1**

010 **12** *1* **Burrishoole Abbey (IRE)**[25] 4622 2-9-1 85 DougieCostello 9 76
(K R Burke) *in rr: rdn over 2f out: kpt on fnl f* **25/1**

205 **13** *¾* **Parys Mountain (IRE)**[22] 4736 2-8-11 81 [1] WilliamBuick 4 69
(Charles Hills) *mid-div: drvn over 2f out: edgd lft over 1f out: one pce* **10/1**

521 **14** *nk* **Kamra (USA)**[29] 4494 2-9-0 84 (v) FrankieDettori 8 72
(Jeremy Noseda) *q str: sltly on toes: trckd ldrs: fdd over 1f out* **14/1**

2163 **15** *2 ¾* **Super Julius**[17] 4918 2-9-2 86 RobertWinston 13 65
(Eve Johnson Houghton) *str: trckd ldrs: t.k.h: hung lft and lost pl over 1f out* **16/1**

130 **16** *4 ½* **Spin Doctor**[61] 3336 2-8-13 83 JamieSpencer 7 47
(Richard Fahey) *chsd ldrs: lost pl over 1f out: eased fnl 100yds* **20/1**

631 **17** *1 ¼* **Nautical Haven**[25] 4663 2-9-0 84 TomEaves 14 44
(Kevin Ryan) *cl-cpld: chsd ldrs: lost pl over 1f out: eased clsng stages* **10/1**

212 **18** *8* **Lonely The Brave (IRE)**[17] 4918 2-9-0 84 AndreaAtzeni 1 19
(Mark Johnston) *chsd ldrs: lost pl over 1f out: sn heavily eased* **16/1**

4310 **19** *7* **Latest Quest (IRE)**[20] 4802 2-7-13 72 NoelGarbutt(3) 16
(Sylvester Kirk) *chsd ldrs: lost pl 2f out: bhd whn eased last 100yds* **80/1**

1m 10.61s (-1.29) **Going Correction** -0.20s/f (Firm) **19** Ran SP% **127.7**
Speed ratings (Par 100): **100,97,97,96,95 95,94,93,93,93 92,91,90,90,86 80,78,68,58**
CSF £140.85 CT £1353.82 TOTE £7.10: £2.30, £4.80, £2.60, £9.20; EX 170.30 Trifecta £2777.20.
Owner T Proctor **Bred** Rathbarry Stud & Abbeylands Farm **Trained** Musley Bank, N Yorks

FOCUS
Pace across the track, the first two came from low stalls on the far side, but there seemed no significant advantage. A very deep and competitive nursery.
T/Jkpt: Not won. T/Plt: £51.70 to a £1 stake. Pool of £323310.5 - 4563.77 winning tickets.
T/Qpdt: £17.30 to a £1 stake. Pool of £15120.70 - 644.71 winning tickets. **Walter Glynn**

5561 - 5563a (Foreign Racing) - See Raceform Interactive

4281 KILLARNEY (L-H)
Wednesday, August 17

OFFICIAL GOING: Good to firm

5564a VINCENT O'BRIEN RUBY STKS (LISTED RACE) 1m 70y
6:50 (6:50) 3-Y-O+
£19,522 (£6,286; £2,977; £1,323; £661; £330)

RPR

1 **Erysimum (IRE)**[80] 2719 3-8-12 93 BillyLee 1 93
(W McCreery, Ire) *led: strly pressed over 1f out: jnd appr fnl f: rallied wl to reassert clsng stages: hld on gamely* **5/1[2]**

2 *shd* **Marshall Jennings (IRE)**[20] 4811 4-9-9 91 ColinKeane 7 99
(Mrs John Harrington, Ire) *racd in mid-div: disp 4th at 1/2-way: travelled wl to cl 2f out: on terms appr fnl f: kpt on wl clsng stages in 2nd: jst hld* **12/1**

3 *shd* **Cailin Mor (IRE)**[17] 4921 4-9-4 89 (t) NGMcCullagh 8 94+
(M Halford, Ire) *hld up towards rr: prog 2f out: rdn to chse ldrs in 5th over 1f out: swtchd rt ins fnl f and styd on strly clsng stages into 3rd: nrst fin* **12/1**

4 *shd* **Colour Blue (IRE)**[37] 4218 5-9-4 91 GaryCarroll 2 94
(W McCreery, Ire) *chsd ldr in 2nd: clsr to press ldr over 1f out and sn on terms: kpt on wl fnl 100yds: dropped to 4th on line* **12/1**

5 *hd* **Assume (IRE)**[7] 5313 4-9-4 99 WayneLordan 5 93
(David Wachman, Ire) *chsd ldrs in 3rd: travelled wl over 2f out: sn rdn to chal over 1f out: disp ins fnl f: no ex clsng strides in 5th* **7/4[1]**

6 *1 ¾* **Flirt (IRE)**[7] 5313 3-8-12 88 (p) ChrisHayes 10 88+
(David Wachman, Ire) *racd in rr: rdn and prog under 2f out: 8th 1f out: styd on wl into 6th clsng stages: nvr nrr* **20/1**

7 *2* **Military Angel (USA)**[109] 1858 4-9-4 102 KevinManning 3 84
(M D O'Callaghan, Ire) *chsd ldrs in 5th: disp 4th at 1/2-way: rdn and nt qckn over 1f out: no ex ins fnl f* **8/1[3]**

8 *1* **General Macarthur (USA)**[6] 5343 3-9-3 102 (t) DonnachaO'Brien 4 86
(A P O'Brien, Ire) *racd in mid-div on inner: rdn and nt qckn over 1f out: sn one pce* **8/1[3]**

9 *7* **Wychwood Warrior (IRE)**[28] 4543 4-9-9 98 ShaneFoley 11 71
(M Halford, Ire) *racd in mid-div: rdn over 2f out and dropped towards rr over 1f out: no ex and eased clsng stages* **11/1**

10 *2 ¼* **Just Joan (IRE)**[20] 4812 3-8-12 89 DeclanMcDonogh 6 60
(T Stack, Ire) *a towards rr: rdn and no imp 2f out: sn no ex and eased ins fnl f* **20/1**

1m 42.16s (-4.94)
WFA 3 from 4yo+ 6lb **10** Ran SP% **116.2**
CSF £63.10 TOTE £5.50: £2.20, £3.70, £4.20; DF 65.00 Trifecta £1370.30.
Owner Barouche Stud (Ireland) Ltd **Bred** Nesco II **Trained** Rathbride, Co Kildare

FOCUS
An absolutely gripping finish at the end of this mile, one could say that the handicapper got it right but it was certainly more like a handicap than a Listed race. The time does not support this race being rated any higher, and the winner, third and fourth have been rated in line with their latest efforts.

5565 - 5567a (Foreign Racing) - See Raceform Interactive

5384 CLAIREFONTAINE (R-H)
Wednesday, August 17

OFFICIAL GOING: Turf: good to firm

5568a PRIX TUNISIE TELECOM (PRIX NORTH JET) (CONDITIONS) (2YO) (TURF) 1m
5:30 (12:00) 2-Y-O **£10,661** (£4,264; £3,198; £2,132; £1,066)

RPR

1 **Pazeer (FR)**[47] 3871 2-9-0 0 AlexisBadel 6 86
(J-C Rouget, France) **30/100[1]**

2 *1 ¾* **If I Say So**[8] 5370 2-9-0 0 (b[1]) IoritzMendizabal 5 77
(J S Moore) *broke wl and led: sn 5 l clr: kicked for home and c stands' side over 2f out: hrd rdn wl over 1f out and rallied: styd on gamely: hdd last 100yds: no ex* **76/10[3]**

3 *snk* **Sunderia (FR)**[34] 4330 2-8-6 0 AnthonyCrastus 7 73
(Mme S Allouche, France) **26/5[2]**

4 *2 ½* **Iggy Chop (FR)** 2-8-9 0 TonyPiccone 4 70
(C Boutin, France) **41/1**

5 *1 ½* **Alfa Manifesto (FR)**[6] 2-9-0 0 (b) AntoineHamelin 2 72
(Matthieu Palussiere, France) **12/1**

6 7 **Jenychope (FR)**[8] 5279 2-8-6 0 UmbertoRispoli 1 47
(D Windrif, France) **22/1**
7 1 1/4 **Silver Top (FR)**[71] 3006 2-8-9 0 GeraldMosse 3 47
(N Caullery, France) **34/1**
1m 37.0s (97.00) **7** Ran SP% **122.0**
WIN (incl. 1 euro stake): 1.30. PLACES: 1.10, 1.80. SF: 5.70.
Owner H H Aga Khan **Bred** Haras De S.A. Aga Khan Scea **Trained** Pau, France

5542 CHEPSTOW (L-H)

Thursday, August 18

OFFICIAL GOING: Good to firm (9.2)
Wind: Almost nil Weather: Cloudy and warm

5569 BET365/EBF MAIDEN STKS 5f 16y
2:10 (2:10) (Class 5) 2-Y-O **£3,881** (£1,155; £577; £288) **Stalls** Centre

Form RPR
2440 1 **Diable D'Or (IRE)**[20] 4825 2-9-5 83 ShaneKelly 1 82
(Eve Johnson Houghton) *mde all: nudged along fnl f: easily* **2/11**[1]
00 2 3 1/2 **Pastfact**[8] 5304 2-9-5 0 RyanTate 4 63
(Malcolm Saunders) *last and sn rdn along to stay in tch: clsd 2f out: stl only 4th 1f out: styd on to go 2nd 100yds out: no ch w easy wnr* **25/1**
03 3 1 1/4 **Wearethepeople**[13] 5125 2-9-5 0 SamHitchcott 5 59
(William Muir) *racd alone in centre bef edging lft to join others over 3f out: sn chsng wnr: rdn 2f out and unable to chal: one pce and lost 2nd 100yds out* **5/1**[2]
4 2 **Jack Blane** 2-9-5 0 LukeMorris 3 51
(Daniel Kubler) *rousted along early: chsd ldrs: rdn and hung lft over 1f out: wknd fnl f* **22/1**
4236 5 4 **Sheila's Palace**[1] 5542 2-9-0 67 LiamKeniry 2 32
(J S Moore) *s.i.s: chsd ldrs: pushed along over 1f out: sn wknd* **10/1**[3]
58.62s (-0.68) **Going Correction** -0.30s/f (Firm) **5** Ran SP% **118.6**
Speed ratings (Par 94): **93,87,85,82,75**
CSF £9.62 TOTE £1.10: £1.02, £7.90; EX 8.50 Trifecta £25.30.
Owner Astor, Baring, Brown & Cochrane **Bred** Nicholas Hartery **Trained** Blewbury, Oxon

FOCUS
There was just a light shower overnight and the going had quickened up to good to firm all round (GoingStick: 9.2, compared with 8.5 the previous day). This maiden proved straightforward for the short-priced favourite.

5570 BET365.COM H'CAP 5f 16y
2:45 (2:46) (Class 6) (0-60,60) 3-Y-O **£3,234** (£962; £481; £240) **Stalls** Centre

Form RPR
0623 1 **Secretfact**[21] 4796 3-8-7 46 JimmyQuinn 5 56
(Malcolm Saunders) *t.k.h in mid-div: swtchd rt over 1f out: drvn and r.o wl to ld ins fnl f: readily* **9/2**
1503 2 1 1/2 **David's Beauty (IRE)**[11] 5200 3-9-2 55 (p) LukeMorris 2 60
(Brian Baugh) *led: rdn 2f out: sn hdd: kpt on u.p* **7/1**
4324 3 1/2 **Andalusite**[14] 5078 3-9-7 60 JimCrowley 4 63
(Ed McMahon) *cl up: rdn to ld over 1f out: hdd ins fnl f: unable qck* **11/4**[1]
0200 4 3 **Silver Springs (IRE)**[29] 4525 3-9-4 57 ShaneKelly 3 49
(David Evans) *chsd ldrs: rdn 2f out: edgd rt and one pce ins fnl f* **12/1**
5505 5 3/4 **Master Pekan**[27] 4590 3-8-0 46 MitchGodwin[(7)] 6 36
(Roy Brotherton) *chsd ldrs: rdn 1/2-way: wknd fnl f* **33/1**
-031 6 1 **Topsoil**[15] 5007 3-8-12 51 RaulDaSilva 7 37
(Ronald Harris) *bucked and kicked in paddock: t.k.h towards rr: rdn and unable qck 2f out: hld whn sltly hmpd appr fnl f* **4/1**[3]
0644 7 1 **Concur (IRE)**[21] 4796 3-8-7 46 DavidProbert 1 29
(Rod Millman) *hld up: rdn 2f out: no imp* **7/2**[2]
1U06 8 1/2 **Rampers (IRE)**[20] 4820 3-9-7 60 WilliamCarson 8 41
(Jamie Osborne) *racd alone stands' rail and up w ldrs on opposite side: rdn 2f out: wknd appr fnl f* **25/1**
58.17s (-1.13) **Going Correction** -0.30s/f (Firm) **8** Ran SP% **114.1**
Speed ratings (Par 98): **97,94,93,89,87 86,84,83**
CSF £35.48 CT £101.35 TOTE £5.40: £1.50, £2.30, £1.80; EX 35.00 Trifecta £109.80.
Owner Premier Conservatory Roofs **Bred** M S Saunders & D Collier **Trained** Green Ore, Somerset

FOCUS
A moderate sprint handicap.

5571 BET365 FILLIES' H'CAP 1m 14y
3:20 (3:23) (Class 5) (0-75,70) 3-Y-O+ **£3,234** (£962; £481; £240) **Stalls** Centre

Form RPR
-414 1 **Fantasy Queen**[15] 5013 3-8-10 60 JohnFahy 2 65
(Eve Johnson Houghton) *hld up: rdn and hdwy 2f out: led 1f out: drvn out* **9/4**[1]
0335 2 1/2 **Golden Isles (IRE)**[20] 4819 3-8-7 57 LukeMorris 4 61
(J S Moore) *led: rdn over 2f out: hdd 1f out: kpt on u.p* **5/1**
6222 3 2 1/4 **Smart Mover (IRE)**[11] 5197 3-9-1 70 CallumShepherd[(5)] 1 69
(Nikki Evans) *trckd ldrs: rdn 3f out: swtchd rt over 2f out: sn one pce: kpt on to take 3rd cl home* **20/1**
4134 4 nk **Lady Bayside**[41] 4087 8-9-11 69 JimCrowley 3 68
(Malcolm Saunders) *reluctant to enter stalls: hld up bhd ldrs: clsd 1/2-way: rdn over 2f out: no ex fnl f: lost 3rd cl home* **3/1**[3]
404 5 4 1/2 **Zebedee's Girl (IRE)**[27] 4587 3-8-10 60 ShaneKelly 6 48
(David Evans) *t.k.h in rr: rdn 2f out: sn outpcd by ldrs and nvr able to chal* **12/1**
3124 6 2 3/4 **Zaria**[14] 5062 5-8-12 63 (p) HollieDoyle[(7)] 5 45
(Richard Price) *cl up: rdn over 2f out: wknd over 1f out* **5/2**[2]
1m 34.04s (-2.16) **Going Correction** -0.30s/f (Firm)
WFA 3 from 5yo+ 6lb **6** Ran SP% **113.5**
Speed ratings (Par 100): **98,97,95,94,90 87**
CSF £14.13 TOTE £2.70: £1.50, £2.50; EX 14.10 Trifecta £152.60.
Owner Mrs Zara Campbell-Harris **Bred** Mrs Z C Campbell-Harris **Trained** Blewbury, Oxon

FOCUS
A modest fillies' handicap, rated around the second.

5572 CASH OUT AT BET365 H'CAP 1m 14y
3:55 (3:57) (Class 6) (0-55,55) 3-Y-O+ **£2,587** (£770; £384; £192) **Stalls** Centre

Form RPR
0102 1 **Carcharias (IRE)**[10] 5235 3-9-0 54 JimCrowley 8 61
(Ed de Giles) *chsd ldrs: rdn to ld wl over 1f out: drvn out to hold on fnl f* **5/2**[1]
006 2 nk **Brooke's Point**[26] 4660 3-8-6 46 oh1 SamHitchcott 10 52
(Neil Mulholland) *mid-div: rdn over 2f out: swtchd rt over 1f out: r.o wl to take 2nd last strides: jst hld by wnr* **25/1**
0420 3 shd **Poor Duke (IRE)**[12] 5149 6-8-13 47 (p) RobertTart 3 54
(Michael Mullineaux) *towards rr: rdn over 3f out: hdwy over 2f out: chal fnl f: kpt on u.p: jst hld and lost 2nd last strides* **7/1**
4-01 4 6 **No No Cardinal (IRE)**[29] 4504 7-9-2 50 TimmyMurphy 5 43
(Mark Gillard) *hld up towards rr: hdwy 1/2-way: rdn 2f out: styd on same pce fnl f and no ch w ldrs* **8/1**
6450 5 1 1/2 **Pensax Lady (IRE)**[52] 3732 3-8-12 55 GeorgeDowning[(3)] 11 44
(Daniel Mark Loughnane) *racd w one other stands' side tl gps merged after 2f: chsd ldrs: rdn 3f out: one pce whn n.m.r over 1f out* **25/1**
3-40 6 3/4 **The Reel Way (GR)**[35] 4289 5-8-7 48 MitchGodwin[(7)] 6 36
(Patrick Chamings) *racd keenly: prom: led 1/2-way: rdn over 2f out: hdd wl over 1f out: wknd fnl f* **6/1**[3]
0043 7 2 **Opera Buffa (IRE)**[15] 5011 3-8-7 47 (tp) LukeMorris 12 29
(Steve Flook) *led pair on stands' side: prom whn gps merged after 2f: rdn 3f out: wknd 1f out* **5/1**[2]
6-04 8 3/4 **Burning Love (IRE)**[187] 565 3-9-1 55 [1] HarryPoulton 1 36
(Adam West) *chsd ldrs: ev ch 3f out tl over 1f out: wknd fnl f* **25/1**
3555 9 4 1/2 **Rosie's Vision**[21] 4794 3-8-6 46 oh1 (p[1]) JimmyQuinn 4 16
(Mark Usher) *a in rr* **8/1**
5346 10 16 **Faster Company (IRE)**[176] 700 3-8-0 47 HollieDoyle[(7)] 9
(J S Moore) *s.i.s: sn pushed along: bhd fr 1/2-way: t.o* **10/1**
000/ 11 16 **Liddle Dwiggs**[1009] 7854 5-8-7 46 oh1 DavidParkes[(5)] 7
(Peter Hiatt) *led to 1/2-way: wknd qckly: bhd fnl 2f: t.o* **50/1**
1m 33.8s (-2.40) **Going Correction** -0.30s/f (Firm)
WFA 3 from 5yo+ 6lb **11** Ran SP% **116.8**
Speed ratings (Par 101): **100,99,99,93,92 91,89,88,84,68 52**
CSF £77.17 CT £404.91 TOTE £2.90: £2.30, £7.60, £2.30; EX 67.00 Trifecta £734.30.
Owner Boardman, Golder, Sercombe & Viall I **Bred** Mrs Helen Walsh **Trained** Ledbury, H'fords

FOCUS
A moderate affair, but the first three finished nicely clear.

5573 CASINO AT BET365 H'CAP 2m 2f
4:30 (4:30) (Class 6) (0-65,65) 3-Y-O+ **£2,587** (£770; £384; £192) **Stalls** Low

Form RPR
0500 1 **Danglydontask**[43] 4019 5-9-5 56 (b) JimCrowley 2 64
(David Arbuthnot) *hld up: hdwy 7f out: led over 3f out: styd on to draw clr appr fnl f: drvn out* **13/2**
0022 2 4 **Double Dealites**[16] 4995 6-8-11 48 KierenFox 5 51
(Jamie Poulton) *trckd ldrs: rdn 4f out: styd on same pce u.p: tk 2nd ins fnl f but no threat to wnr* **4/1**[3]
2415 3 3/4 **Ring Eye (IRE)**[18] 4913 8-9-6 60 EdwardGreatrex[(3)] 7 62
(John O'Shea) *hld up in last: hdwy on outer 3f out: sn rdn and chsd wnr: no imp and lost 2nd ins fnl f* **7/2**[2]
0-05 4 1 3/4 **The Lampo Genie**[7] 3528 4-9-11 62 (p) StevieDonohoe 6 62
(Johnny Farrelly) *rousted fr stalls to ld: hung rt at path on bnd after 3f: drvn and hdd over 4f out: sn outpcd in last: styd on fnl f* **15/2**
0021 5 1/2 **Miss Marina Bay**[14] 5079 3-8-5 58 (p) LukeMorris 9 59
(Sir Mark Prescott Bt) *flashed tail regularly: hld up in 4th: drvn 3f out: one pce and no imp fnl 2f* **2/1**[1]
636- 6 1 **Albert Herring**[72] 5805 4-8-13 50 RyanTate 8 48
(Jonathan Portman) *mainly trckd ldr tl led over 4f out: hdd over 3f out: kpt on u.p tl wknd fnl f* **9/1**
4m 1.14s (-2.46) **Going Correction** -0.30s/f (Firm)
WFA 3 from 4yo+ 16lb **6** Ran SP% **110.7**
Speed ratings (Par 101): **93,91,90,90,89 89**
CSF £31.11 CT £99.98 TOTE £6.90: £3.70, £1.80; EX 31.00 Trifecta £108.80.
Owner Philip Banfield **Bred** P Banfield **Trained** Beare Green, Surrey

FOCUS
An ordinary staying race, but a good winner.

5574 BET365 H'CAP 1m 4f 23y
5:05 (5:05) (Class 4) (0-85,84) 3-Y-O+ **£6,469** (£1,925; £962; £481) **Stalls** Low

Form RPR
0131 1 **Senza Una Donna**[17] 4956 3-8-4 75 (t) CharlieBennett[(5)] 5 86
(Hughie Morrison) *hld up in last: hdwy 3f out: chal gng wl over 2f out: rdn to ld 1f out: r.o wl* **4/1**[2]
2025 2 2 **Rose Above**[14] 5053 4-9-7 77 DavidProbert 7 85
(Andrew Balding) *hld up towards rr: hdwy 3f out: rdn to ld 2f out: hdd 1f out: one pce* **8/1**
2/24 3 5 **What A Scorcher**[32] 3094 5-8-12 71 EdwardGreatrex[(3)] 3 71
(Nikki Evans) *rousted along fr stalls: chsd ldrs: wnt 2nd after 3f: rdn to ld over 2f out: sn hdd: no ch w first two appr fnl f* **25/1**
3046 4 hd **Agent Gibbs**[18] 4920 4-9-3 78 (p) CiaranMckee[(5)] 2 80+
(John O'Shea) *chsd ldrs: rdn over 2f out: nt clr run over 1f out: styd on ins fnl f* **12/1**
0133 5 1 1/2 **Prendergast Hill (IRE)**[10] 5240 4-10-0 84 (p) JimCrowley 8 81
(Ed de Giles) *chsd ldrs: rdn and ev ch over 2f out: outpcd by ldrs over 1f out: fdd fnl f* **11/4**[1]
0152 6 2 **Thames Knight**[14] 5053 4-9-9 79 RoystonFfrench 6 73
(Marcus Tregoning) *trckd ldr 3f: styd prom tl rdn and lost pl over 3f out: styd on same pce fnl f and no threat* **11/2**[3]
5220 7 1 **Cottesloe (IRE)**[26] 4634 7-8-13 76 DavidEgan[(7)] 4 68
(John Berry) *t.k.h in rr: rdn 3f out: hung lft over 1f out and no imp* **11/2**[3]
3331 8 2 1/2 **Glens Wobbly**[18] 4913 8-9-0 75 HectorCrouch[(5)] 1 63
(Jonathan Geake) *led: rdn 3f out: sn hdd: wknd over 1f out* **13/2**
2m 31.87s (-7.13) **Going Correction** -0.30s/f (Firm)
WFA 3 from 4yo+ 10lb **8** Ran SP% **113.4**
Speed ratings (Par 105): **111,109,106,106,105 103,103,101**
CSF £34.98 CT £697.43 TOTE £5.00: £1.50, £2.10, £4.10; EX 44.20 Trifecta £338.90.
Owner Castle Down Racing **Bred** Meon Valley Stud **Trained** East Ilsley, Berks

FOCUS
This appeared to be run at a solid gallop and the first two drew clear. The winner continues to progress, as does the second.

5575 BET365 LADY RIDERS' H'CAP (FOR LADY AMATEUR RIDERS) 1m 2f 36y
5:35 (5:36) (Class 6) (0-65,59) 3-Y-O+ **£2,495** (£774; £386; £193) **Stalls** Low

Form RPR
0066 1 **Desert Tango**[50] 3765 3-9-6 47 MissMMullineaux 6 56
(Michael Mullineaux) *hld up in last: hdwy into 4 l 3rd 3f out: drvn 2f out: led 1f out: styd on wl to draw clr* **7/1**[2]
4013 2 5 **Shirataki (IRE)**[6] 5350 8-10-1 53 6ex MissMollyKing[(5)] 5 53+
(Peter Hiatt) *t.k.h: chsd ldrs: wnt 2nd after 3f: pressed ldr 5f out: led 2f out: sn rdn: hdd 1f out: no ex* **6/4**[1]

6-46 **3** ½ **Captain Oats (IRE)**[16] 4995 13-9-12 **52**.................... MissSLBowen(7) 4 51
(Pam Ford) *chsd ldrs: outpcd 4f out: pushed along on outer over 2f out: styd on fnl f* **15/2**[3]
0551 **4** 1 **Highlife Dancer**[6] 5383 8-10-7 **59** 6ex........................ MissKatyLyons(5) 8 56+
(Mick Channon) *led: jnd 5f out: drvn and hdd 2f out: wknd fnl f* **6/4**[1]
46 **5** 2½ **Surprise Us**[24] 4225 9-9-7 **45**..............................(p) MissAMcCain(5) 7 37
(Mark Gillard) *trckd ldr tl lost 2nd after 3f: 8 l off first two 4f out: drvn and lost 3rd 3f out: one pce after* **16/1**

2m 9.95s (-0.65) **Going Correction** -0.30s/f (Firm)
WFA 3 from 4yo+ 8lb **5** Ran SP% **110.1**
Speed ratings (Par 101): **90,86,85,84,82**
CSF £18.10 TOTE £6.60: £3.70, £1.30; EX 15.30 Trifecta £58.00.
Owner Ogwen Valley Racing **Bred** Mrs Hugh Maitland-Jones **Trained** Alpraham, Cheshire

FOCUS
The joint-favourites took each other on from a long way out and that set things up for the winner to come through and beat them both.
T/Plt: £78.90 to a £1 stake. Pool: £54,587.64. 504.84 winning tickets. T/Qpdt: £72.90 to a £1 stake. Pool: £3,464.15. 35.14 winning tickets. **Richard Lowther**

4869 HAMILTON (R-H)
Thursday, August 18

OFFICIAL GOING: Good to firm (good in places; 7.3)
Wind: Virtually Nil Weather: Fine

5576 JORDAN ELECTRICS "HANDS AND HEELS" APPRENTICE H'CAP 1m 67y
5:10 (5:12) (Class 6) (0-55,59) 3-Y-O+ **£2,911** (£866; £432; £216) **Stalls** Low

Form RPR
4301 **1** **Big Time Dancer (IRE)**[7] 5322 3-9-3 **59** 6ex.............. BenRobinson(6) 6 69
(Brian Ellison) *led narrowly: hdd over 4f out: led again 3f out: pushed along 2f out: 2 l up over 1f out: idled fnl f* **4/6**[1]
3123 **2** ½ **Galilee Chapel (IRE)**[22] 4772 7-9-7 **51**..................(b) AdamMcNamara 3 57
(Alistair Whillans) *midfield: pushed along over 2f out: hdwy to chse ldr ent fnl f: kpt on* **10/1**[2]
0030 **3** 3½ **Call Me Crockett (IRE)**[31] 4456 4-9-6 **50**................(p) PatrickVaughan 8 48
(Noel Wilson) *trckd ldrs: pushed along over 2f out: one pce* **25/1**
02-3 **4** shd **Cheers Buddy (IRE)**[10] 5222 8-9-8 **52**........................ DanielleMooney 5 49
(Lee Smyth, Ire) *midfield: pushed along and outpcd over 3f out: styd on fr over 1f out* **28/1**
0021 **5** 1¼ **Ted's Brother (IRE)**[12] 5149 8-9-0 **47**..........................(e) GerO'Neill(3) 12 41
(Richard Guest) *dwlt: hld up in rr: pushed along over 2f out: kpt on fnl f: nvr threatened ldrs* **25/1**
06U2 **6** 1 **Drinks For Losers (IRE)**[12] 5149 5-9-2 **46**.............. CallumRodriguez 1 38
(R Mike Smith) *s.i.s: hld up in rr: plugged on fnl f: nvr threatened* **16/1**
0-01 **7** shd **Norville (IRE)**[10] 5222 9-10-0 **58** 6ex........................(b) NatalieHambling 4 50
(Lee Smyth, Ire) *trckd ldrs: lost pl over 3f out: no threat after* **25/1**
-242 **8** ¾ **Penelope Pitstop**[10] 5227 4-9-0 **47**............................ HayleyIrvine(3) 11 37
(Lee Smyth, Ire) *midfield on outer racing keenly: plld way into narrow ld over 4f out: hdd 3f out: grad wknd fnl 2f* **14/1**
4346 **9** 2 **Kerry Icon**[14] 5064 3-8-1 **45**.. JamieGormley(8) 2 29
(Iain Jardine) *stdd s: hld up: racd keenly: nvr threatened* **12/1**[3]
0052 **10** nse **Wayside Magic**[31] 4449 3-9-4 **54**...................................(p) CliffordLee 7 38
(Michael Dods) *pressed ldr: pushed along over 2f out: wknd appr fnl f* **20/1**
5-02 **11** 2¾ **No Refund (IRE)**[29] 4516 5-9-8 **52**................................ CameronNoble 9 30
(David Loughnane) *in tch: pushed along 3f out: wknd appr fnl f* **10/1**[2]
0-64 **12** 1 **Lilozza (IRE)**[16] 4972 3-8-9 **51**................................ HannahWorrall(6) 10 26
(Tim Easterby) *hld up: nvr threatened* **33/1**

1m 49.44s (1.04) **Going Correction** -0.075s/f (Good)
WFA 3 from 4yo+ 6lb **12** Ran SP% **121.1**
Speed ratings (Par 101): **91,90,87,86,85 84,84,83,81,81 79,78**
CSF £6.88 CT £105.21 TOTE £1.40: £1.10, £2.90, £10.00; EX 8.80 Trifecta £159.20.
Owner Andy Bell Anna Noble Arnie Flower **Bred** Gerard Callanan **Trained** Norton, N Yorks

FOCUS
Race distance increased by 12yds. A low-grade handicap for apprentices run at a slow gallop with those who raced prominently favoured. Most were exposed sorts ad the winner was well ahead of the handicapper.

5577 BRITISH STALLIONS STUDS DEBUTANTS' EBF MAIDEN STKS (PLUS 10 RACE) 6f 6y
5:40 (5:40) (Class 4) 2-Y-O **£4,528** (£1,347; £673; £336) **Stalls** High

Form RPR
1 **Bamber Bridge (IRE)** 2-9-5 0.................................... PaulMulrennan 1 86+
(Michael Dods) *slowly away: hld up: pushed along and hdwy over 2f out: rdn to ld ent fnl f: kpt on fnl f: wl to go clr* **8/13**[1]
2 6 **Hee Haw (IRE)** 2-9-5 0.................................... ConnorBeasley 5 68
(Keith Dalgleish) *led: rdn 2f out: hdd ent fnl f: one pce and sn no ch w wnr* **5/1**[3]
3 1½ **X Rated (IRE)** 2-9-5 0.................................... FrannyNorton 2 64
(Mark Johnston) *pressed ldr: rdn over 2f out: one pce and hld in 3rd fr over 1f out* **10/3**[2]
4 1¼ **Cool Run Girl (IRE)** 2-9-0 0.................................... DougieCostello 3 55
(Iain Jardine) *in tch: pushed along and outpcd in 4th 1/2-way: no threat after* **14/1**

1m 12.9s (0.70) **Going Correction** -0.025s/f (Good) **4** Ran SP% **108.3**
Speed ratings (Par 96): **94,86,84,82**
CSF £4.07 TOTE £1.60; EX 4.30 Trifecta £7.50.
Owner David W Armstrong **Bred** Old Peartree Stud **Trained** Denton, Co Durham

FOCUS
A four-runner race for newcomers which produced a wide-margin, well-backed winner.

5578 WATCH RACING UK IN HD H'CAP 6f 6y
6:10 (6:10) (Class 6) (0-60,57) 3-Y-O **£2,911** (£866; £432; £216) **Stalls** High

Form RPR
26-0 **1** **Roman Times (IRE)**[203] 365 3-8-13 **54**...................(p) NathanEvans(5) 9 59
(John David Riches) *mde all: rdn over 1f out: pressed ent fnl f: kpt on wl* **14/1**
0043 **2** 1¼ **Carlovian**[9] 5270 3-8-6 **49**.. CliffordLee(7) 10 50
(Christopher Kellett) *chsd ldng pair: rdn over 2f out: chal ent fnl f: hung rt and one pce ins fnl f* **5/1**[3]
0-00 **3** 1¼ **Mr Conundrum**[12] 5178 3-8-12 **48**.................................... PaddyAspell 5 46
(Lynn Siddall) *sltly hmpd s: hld up: rdn over 2f out: hdwy over 1f out: kpt on fnl f* **33/1**
0-55 **4** nk **Duncan Of Scotland (IRE)**[35] 4309 3-9-3 **53**...........(b) PaulMulrennan 1 50
(Lee Smyth, Ire) *pressed ldr: rdn over 2f out: outpcd over 1f out: kpt on fnl f* **9/1**
63 **5** hd **The Big Day (IRE)**[12] 5178 3-9-7 **57**.............................. AndrewMullen 8 53
(Nigel Tinkler) *midfield: pushed along and outpcd over 3f out: edgd lft to stands' rail over 2f out: hdwy over 1f out: kpt on* **4/1**[1]
0-66 **6** 1 **Man Of La Mancha (IRE)**[83] 2667 3-9-1 **51**...................... GrahamLee 4 44
(Ben Haslam) *midfield: rdn and outpcd 1/2-way: kpt on ins fnl f: nvr threatened* **15/2**
0000 **7** ½ **Amy Blair**[12] 5152 3-8-4 **45**.. ShirleyTeasdale(5) 6 37
(Keith Dalgleish) *chsd ldng pair: rdn over 2f out: grad wknd over 1f out* **25/1**
6435 **8** 3½ **Ss Vega**[31] 4444 3-8-13 **49**...[1] JoeyHaynes 3 30
(James Bethell) *sn outpcd in rr: a bhd* **9/2**[2]
6460 **9** ¾ **Wishing Tree**[35] 4289 3-8-9 **52**...................................... BenRobinson(7) 2 31
(Brian Ellison) *midfield: rdn 1/2-way: wknd over 1f out* **9/1**
4330 **10** ½ **Tarnend Lass**[16] 4968 3-8-12 **48**.................................(tp) JamesSullivan 7 25
(Tim Easterby) *midfield: rdn over 2f out: wknd fnl f* **7/1**

1m 12.39s (0.19) **Going Correction** -0.025s/f (Good) **10** Ran SP% **112.6**
Speed ratings (Par 98): **97,95,93,93,93 91,91,86,85,84**
CSF £79.74 CT £2301.15 TOTE £15.10: £4.10, £2.00, £6.40; EX 79.00 Trifecta £3916.50.
Owner A B Parr **Bred** Times Of Wigan Ltd **Trained** Pilling, Lancashire

FOCUS
Not a great deal of strength in depth in this low-grade sprint for three-year-olds.

5579 JORDAN ELECTRICS SCOTTISH TROPHY H'CAP 1m 1f 34y
6:40 (6:40) (Class 4) (0-80,80) 3-Y-O+
£7,470 (£2,236; £1,118; £559; £279; £140) **Stalls** Low

Form RPR
3613 **1** **Lord Franklin**[18] 4919 7-9-9 **79**.. NeilFarley 5 88
(Eric Alston) *mde all: rdn over 2f out: kpt on wl* **10/1**
2322 **2** 2¼ **Haraz (IRE)**[14] 5063 3-9-0 **80**.. ShelleyBirkett(3) 6 84
(David O'Meara) *midfield: pushed along over 2f out: angled lft into clr over 1f out: rdn and kpt on: wnt 2nd 110yds out* **8/1**
2325 **3** 1½ **Warp Factor (IRE)**[34] 4339 3-9-3 **80**................................ TadhgO'Shea 3 81
(John Patrick Shanahan, Ire) *midfield: rdn and hdwy to chse ldr over 2f out: one pce fnl f: lost 2nd 110yds out* **3/1**[1]
3130 **4** ½ **Eastern Dragon (IRE)**[24] 4704 6-9-1 **76**..................... GarryWhillans(5) 1 76
(Iain Jardine) *in tch: rdn over 2f out: one pce* **16/1**
543- **5** 1¼ **Cadeau Magnifique**[381] 4938 4-9-2 **77**................. AdamMcNamara(5) 7 74
(Richard Fahey) *hld up in midfield: pushed along and hdwy on outer over 3f out: rdn over 2f out: no ex fnl f* **7/2**[2]
0526 **6** hd **Eutropius (IRE)**[25] 4687 7-9-5 **75**...................................... DaleSwift 4 71
(Alan Swinbank) *dwlt: hld up in rr: rdn over 2f out: kpt on fnl f: nvr threatened* **12/1**
0440 **7** 1 **Optima Petamus**[24] 4704 4-9-6 **76**.................................(p) GrahamLee 12 70
(Patrick Holmes) *hld up in midfield: rdn over 2f out: no imp* **25/1**
0162 **8** 2 **Save The Bees**[8] 5292 8-9-0 **77**....................................(b) GerO'Neill(7) 11 67
(Declan Carroll) *trckd ldr: rdn over 3f out: wknd 2f out* **9/1**
6240 **9** shd **Muqarred (USA)**[15] 5028 4-8-10 **73**........................[1] CameronNoble(7) 8 63
(David Loughnane) *hld up: pushed along and hdwy on outside over 3f out: rdn to briefly chse ldr over 2f out: wknd over 1f out* **14/1**
000- **10** 1 **Seagull Star**[391] 4592 5-9-10 **80**...................................... ConnorBeasley 9 67
(Keith Dalgleish) *trckd ldr: rdn 3f out: wknd over 1f out* **13/2**[3]

1m 57.84s (-1.86) **Going Correction** -0.075s/f (Good)
WFA 3 from 4yo+ 7lb **10** Ran SP% **114.8**
Speed ratings (Par 105): **105,103,101,101,100 99,99,97,97,96**
CSF £86.06 CT £300.19 TOTE £10.80: £2.80, £2.40, £1.30; EX 91.70 Trifecta £242.70.
Owner Whitehills Racing Syndicate **Bred** Tony Ferguson & Liam Ferguson **Trained** Longton, Lancs

FOCUS
Race distance increased by 12yds. The most competitive race on the card, but not a true test as the pace was slow and it suited the prominent racers. The winner had the run of the race which developed into a bit of sprint over the last 2f. A pb from the winner.

5580 RACING UK PROFITS RETURNED TO RACING H'CAP 1m 4f 14y
7:10 (7:11) (Class 5) (0-70,70) 3-Y-O+ **£3,881** (£1,155; £577; £288) **Stalls** High

Form RPR
3321 **1** **Neuf Des Coeurs**[6] 5350 5-9-1 **64** 6ex..........................(p) CliffordLee(7) 2 71
(Iain Jardine) *hld up: hdwy on inner 3f out: swtchd lft 2f out: in clr over 1f out: sn rdn: led 1f out: kpt on wl* **9/2**[2]
1033 **2** ¾ **Lara Carbonara (IRE)**[19] 4875 4-10-0 **70**.................... DougieCostello 3 76
(John Patrick Shanahan, Ire) *midfield: pushed along and hdwy on outer 3f out: rdn to ld 2f out: hdd 1f out: kpt on* **8/1**[3]
3344 **3** 2 **Ghostly Arc (IRE)**[8] 5294 4-9-6 **62**.............................. GrahamGibbons 9 65
(Noel Wilson) *led: rdn over 2f out: hdd 2f out: kpt on same pce* **9/1**
-054 **4** 1 **Latin Rebel (IRE)**[17] 4934 9-8-9 **51** oh2.............................(p) JoeDoyle 6 52
(Jim Goldie) *hld up: rdn over 2f out: sme hdwy over 1f out: kpt on fnl f* **28/1**
455 **5** 1 **Eez Eh (IRE)**[56] 3550 3-9-2 **68**.. ConnorBeasley 5 68
(Keith Dalgleish) *trckd ldrs: bit short of room and lost pl over 2f out: rdn 2f out: one pce fnl f* **12/1**
3553 **6** 2¾ **First Sargeant**[13] 5117 6-9-2 **58**......................................(v[1]) CamHardie 8 53
(Lawrence Mullaney) *in tch: rdn over 2f out: sn ev ch: wknd ins fnl f* **11/1**
5223 **7** ¾ **Love Marmalade (IRE)**[20] 4828 6-9-7 **68**..................(p) JoshDoyle(5) 12 62
(David O'Meara) *trckd ldr: rdn over 2f out: wknd appr fnl f* **9/2**[2]
1401 **8** 2¼ **Jocks Wa Hae (IRE)**[19] 4872 3-8-9 **61**........................... TadhgO'Shea 4 51
(John Patrick Shanahan, Ire) *hld up in midfield: rdn and sme hdwy on outer over 2f out: hung rt and wknd over 1f out* **3/1**[1]

2m 39.26s (0.66) **Going Correction** -0.075s/f (Good)
WFA 3 from 4yo+ 10lb **8** Ran SP% **101.9**
Speed ratings (Par 103): **94,93,92,91,90 89,88,87**
CSF £31.15 CT £216.32 TOTE £3.70: £2.10, £2.30, £2.40; EX 14.50 Trifecta £155.70.
Owner Iain Livingstone **Bred** Conor J Colgan **Trained** Carrutherstown, D'fries & G'way
■ Head High was withdrawn. Price at time of withdrawal 9-1. Rule 4 applies to all bets - deduction 10p in the pound.

FOCUS
Race distance increased by 12yds. The early pace was slow for this 1m4f handicap but they began racing a fair way out so a reasonable test. The winner is rated close to her old best.

5581 OVERTON FARM MAIDEN STKS 1m 1f 34y
7:40 (7:40) (Class 5) 3-Y-O+ **£3,881** (£1,155; £577; £288) **Stalls** Low

Form RPR
322 **1** **Apres Midi (IRE)**[25] 4682 3-9-0 75.................................... DougieCostello 5 82
(K R Burke) *mde all: sn 3 l clr: pushed along 2f out: kpt on: unchal* **5/6**[1]

3-22 **2** 3 **Twobeelucky**[12] 5163 3-9-5 85 FrannyNorton 3 80
(Mark Johnston) *trckd ldr: sn 3 l down in 2nd: pushed along over 2f out: drvn over 1f out: kpt on* **11/4**[2]

-33 **3** 7 **Fivehundredmiles (IRE)**[19] 4870 3-9-5 0 TadhgO'Shea 6 65
(John Patrick Shanahan, Ire) *hld up in tch: pushed along over 3f out: wnt poor 3rd over 2f out: wknd fnl f* **8/1**

4 11 **Traditional Dancer (IRE)**[22] 5952 4-9-12 0 PaulMulrennan 1 41
(Iain Jardine) *in tch in 3rd: rdn over 3f out: wknd over 2f out* **13/2**[3]

5 55 **Sinamas (IRE)** 3-9-0 0 JasonHart 2
(Eric Alston) *unruly in preliminaries: dwlt: hld up in rr: rdn over 4f out: sn t.o* **50/1**

1m 58.13s (-1.57) **Going Correction** -0.075s/f (Good)
WFA 3 from 4yo 7lb **5** Ran SP% **107.6**
Speed ratings (Par 103): **103,100,94,84,35**
CSF £3.14 TOTE £1.40: £1.10, £1.80; EX 3.30 Trifecta £6.90.
Owner Mrs Melba Bryce **Bred** B V Sangster **Trained** Middleham Moor, N Yorks

FOCUS
Race distance increased by 12yds. A fairly uncompetitive maiden though it was run at a reasonable gallop, the winner enjoying an easy lead..He has been accorded a bit of credit in the ratings.

5582 RACING UK HD ON SKY 432 H'CAP 5f 7y
8:10 (8:11) (Class 5) (0-70,70) 3-Y-O+ **£3,881** (£1,155; £577; £288) **Stalls** Centre

Form RPR

0241 **1** **Salvatore Fury (IRE)**[6] 5354 6-9-10 **70** 6ex (p) GrahamGibbons 6 77+
(Keith Dalgleish) *hld up stands' side: smooth hdwy over 1f out: pushed along to ld ins fnl f: sn drvn: all out* **11/4**[1]

0026 **2** nse **Rock Canyon (IRE)**[10] 5224 7-8-11 **62** JoshDoyle(5) 10 69
(Linda Perratt) *hld up stands' side: rdn 1/2-way: r.o strly fnl f: jst failed: 2nd of 6 in gp* **25/1**

0032 **3** 1 **Kinloch Pride**[19] 4874 4-8-5 **51** oh1 (p) NeilFarley 8 54
(Noel Wilson) *chsd ldrs stands' side: rdn 2f out: edgd rt ent fnl f: kpt on: 3rd of 6 in gp* **7/1**

-000 **4** ½ **Astrophysics**[15] 5032 4-9-10 **70** PaddyAspell 1 71+
(Lynn Siddall) *hld up centre: rdn 1/2-way: hdwy over 1f out: kpt on fnl f: 1st of 4 in gp* **13/2**[3]

0000 **5** ¾ **Amber Crystal**[10] 5225 4-8-6 **52** CamHardie 11 51
(Linda Perratt) *racd stands' side: pressed ldr: rdn 1/2-way: no ex ins fnl f: 4th of 6 in gp* **40/1**

0600 **6** nk **Gowanless**[14] 5059 3-9-1 **63** (b[1]) PaulMulrennan 9 61
(Michael Dods) *racd stands' side: led narrowly: rdn 1/2-way: hdd ins fnl f: no ex: 5th of 6 in gp* **14/1**

2205 **7** 1 **Tinsill**[7] 5320 5-8-5 **51** oh1 (p) AndrewMullen 7 45
(Nigel Tinkler) *dwlt: hld up stands' side: rdn 2f out: keeping on whn short of room 75yds out: last of 6 in gp* **9/1**

46 **8** 1¼ **Encantar**[60] 3439 3-9-8 **70** (b[1]) FrannyNorton 4 60
(Ann Duffield) *hld up centre: rdn 1/2-way: nvr threatened: 2nd of 4 in gp* **8/1**

0050 **9** 1 **Bronze Beau**[7] 5320 9-9-5 **65** (tp) JamesSullivan 3 51
(Kristin Stubbs) *racd isolated against far rail: prom: rdn 1/2-way: wknd over 1f out* **20/1**

0-24 **10** 2¼ **Busy Bimbo (IRE)**[13] 5110 7-8-11 **62** (b) NathanEvans(5) 2 40
(John David Riches) *chsd ldrs centre: rdn 1/2-way: wknd fnl f: 3rd of 4 in gp* **8/1**

42-2 **11** 2½ **Wernotfamusanymore (IRE)**[20] 4845 3-9-8 **70** GrahamLee 5 39
(Kevin Ryan) *prom centre: rdn 1/2-way: wknd over 1f out* **6/1**[2]

59.39s (-0.61) **Going Correction** -0.025s/f (Good)
WFA 3 from 4yo+ 2lb **11** Ran SP% **116.7**
Speed ratings (Par 103): **103,102,101,100,99 98,97,95,93,90 86**
CSF £84.24 CT £443.75 TOTE £3.30: £1.50, £7.80, £2.60; EX 98.30 Trifecta £495.00.
Owner Prestige Thoroughbred Racing **Bred** Ken Harris & Dr Brid Corkery **Trained** Carluke, S Lanarks

FOCUS
A low-grade sprint run at a decent gallop and the field were spread across the course with the stand side holding the call. The winner is rated back to his turf best.
T/Plt: £88.40 to a £1 stake. Pool: £48,694.73. 402.03 winning tickets. T/Qpdt: £16.70 to a £1 stake. Pool: £5,633.46. 249.06 winning tickets. **Andrew Sheret**

5555 YORK (L-H)
Thursday, August 18

OFFICIAL GOING: Good to firm (7.2)
Wind: Light, half behind Weather: Cloudy with sunny periods

5583 GOFFS PREMIER YEARLING STKS 6f
1:55 (1:55) (Class 2) 2-Y-O **£147,540** (£59,040; £29,520; £14,730; £7,380; £7,380) **Stalls** Low

Form RPR

0023 **1** **Stormy Clouds (IRE)**[6] 5359 2-8-9 88 (b) SeanLevey 4 98
(Richard Hannon) *prom: led wl over 2f out: rdn clr over 1f out: kpt on wl towards fin* **13/2**[2]

1012 **2** 1¾ **Rusumaat (IRE)**[20] 4825 2-8-11 94 PaulHanagan 14 94
(Mark Johnston) *lw: chsd ldrs: rdn along 2f out: drvn to chse wnr over 1f out: kpt on* **11/2**[1]

3230 **3** 1¾ **Savannah's Dream**[6] 5359 2-8-6 88 HarryBentley 19 83
(David O'Meara) *in tch towards outer: pushed along 1/2-way: rdn wl over 1f out: styd on wl fnl f: nrst fin* **25/1**

6216 **4** hd **Stop The Wages (IRE)**[6] 5359 2-8-6 77 MartinDwyer 13 83
(Brian Meehan) *chsd ldrs: rdn along wl over 1f out: drvn to chse ldng pair ins fnl f: kpt on same pce* **28/1**

1151 **5** 1¼ **Miss Infinity (IRE)**[12] 5186 2-8-11 94 JoeFanning 9 84
(Mark Johnston) *prom: pushed along over 2f out: rdn wl over 1f out: drvn appr fnl f and grad wknd* **8/1**

3001 **6** nk **Perfect Madge (IRE)**[15] 5029 2-8-6 81 JoeDoyle 16 78
(Kevin Ryan) *dwlt and towards rr: rdn along wl over 2f out: hdwy wl over 1f out: kpt on wl fnl f: nrst fin* **25/1**

1331 **7** ½ **Rainbow Mist (IRE)**[41] 4111 2-8-11 95 PJMcDonald 15 81
(Ann Duffield) *w'like: towards rr: rdn along 2f out: styd on wl fnl f: nrst fin* **7/1**[3]

3 **8** nk **Dark Destroyer (IRE)**[20] 4837 2-8-11 0 JFEgan 2 80+
(Joseph Tuite) *q str: hld up far side: in tch and swtchd lft 2f out: hdwy and sn rdn to chse ldrs: sn drvn and kpt on same pce* **25/1**

51 **9** hd **Hemingway (IRE)**[25] 4685 2-8-11 81 TomEaves 6 80
(Kevin Ryan) *str: led: pushed along and hdd wl over 2f out: rdn wl over 1f out: sn drvn and grad wknd* **12/1**

301 **10** nk **Our Greta (IRE)**[19] 4890 2-8-6 74 BenCurtis 1 75
(Michael Appleby) *t.k.h: chsd ldrs towards far side: rdn along 2f out: n.m.r and sltly hmpd over 1f out: no imp after* **25/1**

3221 **11** hd **Mr Hobbs**[42] 4053 2-8-11 81 FrankieDettori 8 78
(Sylvester Kirk) *towards rr: hdwy over 2f out: rdn wl over 1f out: kpt on fnl f: nrst fin* **12/1**

026 **12** 1½ **Computable**[69] 3112 2-8-11 79 JasonHart 11 73
(Tim Easterby) *t.k.h: chsd ldrs: hdwy 2f out: rdn and edgd lft over 1f out: sn drvn and kpt on same pce* **33/1**

223 **13** 1 **Perfect Symphony (IRE)**[19] 4890 2-8-11 78 KevinStott 12 70
(Kevin Ryan) *chsd ldrs: rdn along wl over 2f out: sn wknd* **20/1**

212 **14** 1½ **Danielsflyer (IRE)**[76] 2865 2-8-11 94 PhillipMakin 18 65
(David Barron) *a towards rr far side* **8/1**

5215 **15** 2 **Heir Of Excitement (IRE)**[24] 4699 2-8-11 77 ShaneGray 5 59
(Kevin Ryan) *lw: chsd ldrs towards far side: rdn along 2f out: n.m.r over 1f out: wknd* **66/1**

651 **16** ½ **Angel Down**[11] 5202 2-8-11 0 OisinMurphy 20 57
(Henry Candy) *racd towards stands' side: a towards rr* **14/1**

125 **17** 1¾ **Wedding Dress**[67] 3186 2-8-6 79 AndreaAtzeni 10 47
(David Brown) *w'like: chsd ldrs: rdn along bef 1/2-way: sn lost pl and bhd* **25/1**

40 **18** 6 **Man About Town (IRE)**[40] 4161 2-8-11 0[1] PatSmullen 3 32
(K R Burke) *cmpt: chsd ldrs towards far side: rdn along over 2f out: sn lost pl and bhd* **33/1**

1m 10.43s (-1.47) **Going Correction** -0.15s/f (Firm) **18** Ran SP% **120.3**
Speed ratings (Par 100): **103,100,98,98,96 96,95,94,94,94 94,92,90,88,86 85,83,75**
CSF £35.15 TOTE £7.00: £2.50, £2.30, £8.30; EX 46.80 Trifecta £1070.60.
Owner Chris Giles & Richard Webb **Bred** Tally-Ho Stud **Trained** East Everleigh, Wilts

FOCUS
All distances as advertised. This was hugely competitive, as it should have been for the money on offer. The field didn't split on exiting the stalls and ran in a group towards the centre of the track. It's hard to say the draw made a significant difference but the winner, drawn low, never looked like being caught from about the furlong marker. Interestingly, three of the first four ran six days previously and give a boost to that talents of Mrs Danvers. A straightforward renewal in which Stormy Clouds improved notably.

5584 SKY BET LOWTHER STKS (GROUP 2) (FILLIES) 6f
2:30 (2:30) (Class 1) 2-Y-O **£113,420** (£43,000; £21,520; £10,720; £5,380; £2,700) **Stalls** Low

Form RPR

131 **1** **Queen Kindly**[36] 4254 2-9-0 102 JamieSpencer 4 112
(Richard Fahey) *hld up: hdwy over 2f out: rdn over 1f out: qcknd to ld ins fnl f: kpt on wl towards fin* **9/2**[2]

4011 **2** ¾ **Roly Poly (USA)**[41] 4106 2-9-3 0 SeamieHeffernan 5 112
(A P O'Brien, Ire) *lw: slt ld: rdn along wl over 1f out: drvn ent fnl f: sn hdd: kpt on* **15/2**[3]

11 **3** ¾ **Fair Eva**[26] 4623 2-9-0 0 PatSmullen 7 107
(Roger Charlton) *warm: hld up: gd hdwy on outer 2f out: rdn to chal over 1f out: ev ch tl drvn ins fnl f and kpt on same pce* **4/11**[1]

2131 **4** 4½ **Nations Alexander (IRE)**[12] 5172 2-9-0 101 PatDobbs 8 92
(Richard Hannon) *chsd ldrs: hdwy over 2f out: rdn along wl over 1f out: drvn appr fnl f: wknd* **16/1**

21 **5** ½ **Fashion Queen**[27] 4601 2-9-0 81 DanielTudhope 6 91
(David O'Meara) *athletic: prom: cl up 1/2-way: rdn 2f out: drvn over 1f out: sn wknd* **25/1**

1233 **6** 2¾ **Clem Fandango (FR)**[33] 4394 2-9-0 93 PhillipMakin 1 82
(Keith Dalgleish) *prom: cl up 1/2-way: rdn along 2f out: sn drvn and wknd* **33/1**

1642 **7** 1¼ **Kilmah**[26] 4623 2-9-0 101 JoeFanning 3 78
(Mark Johnston) *dwlt: sn chsng ldrs: cl up 1/2-way: rdn along over 2f out: sn wknd* **16/1**

552 **8** 1¾ **Magical Fire (IRE)**[41] 4106 2-9-0 0 ColmO'Donoghue 2 72
(M D O'Callaghan, Ire) *cl up: rdn along over 2f out: sn drvn and wknd* **20/1**

1m 9.84s (-2.06) **Going Correction** -0.15s/f (Firm) **8** Ran SP% **126.6**
Speed ratings (Par 103): **107,106,105,99,98 94,93,90**
CSF £40.65 TOTE £6.30: £1.50, £2.20, £1.02; EX 54.70 Trifecta £61.40.
Owner Jaber Abdullah **Bred** Rabbah Bloodstock Limited **Trained** Musley Bank, N Yorks

FOCUS
Strong form with three very smart 2yo fillies coming clear. Queen Kindly took a nice step forward, Roly Poly remains progressive and Fair Eva was 2l below her Ascot form.

5585 CLIPPER LOGISTICS STKS (H'CAP) 1m
3:05 (3:09) (Class 2) 3-Y-O+ **£52,912** (£15,844; £7,922; £3,961; £1,980; £994) **Stalls** Low

Form RPR

1241 **1** **Firmament**[16] 4976 4-8-13 **96** DanielTudhope 1 105+
(David O'Meara) *lw: trckd ldrs: hdwy 3f out: chal over 1f out: sn rdn: led ins fnl f: kpt on* **8/1**[2]

2101 **2** ½ **Mustashry**[26] 4624 3-8-11 **100** PaulHanagan 17 107+
(Sir Michael Stoute) *towards rr: rdn along 1/2-way: hdwy on inner wl over 2f out: chsd ldrs over 1f out: sn drvn: kpt on wl fnl f* **5/1**[1]

01 **3** ¾ **Red Napoleon (USA)**[28] 4555 4-8-12 **95** JamesDoyle 2 101
(Ralph Beckett) *lw: trckd ldng pair: hdwy over 3f out: cl up over 2f out: rdn to ld over 1f out: drvn and hdd ins fnl f: kpt on* **8/1**[2]

5025 **4** ½ **Spark Plug (IRE)**[33] 4392 5-9-7 **104** (p) SeanLevey 10 109
(Brian Meehan) *towards rr: hdwy over 2f out: rdn wl over 1f out: kpt on wl fnl f* **14/1**

1-00 **5** nse **Third Time Lucky (IRE)**[20] 4823 4-9-3 **100** TonyHamilton 3 106+
(Richard Fahey) *lw: in tch: hdwy over 2f out: chsd ldrs over 1f out: sn rdn: n.m.r and swtchd rt ins fnl f: sn drvn and kpt on towards fin* **16/1**

0440 **6** 2 **Kelinni (IRE)**[18] 4921 8-9-8 **105** ShaneGray 13 105
(Kevin Ryan) *chsd clr ldr: tk clsr order over 3f out: rdn to ld 2f out: drvn and hdd over 1f out: kpt on same pce* **20/1**

1000 **7** ½ **Fanciful Angel (IRE)**[26] 4625 4-9-5 **105** DanielMuscutt(3) 9 104
(Marco Botti) *towards rr: hdwy over 2f out: rdn along wl over 1f out: kpt on fnl f* **25/1**

5000 **8** 1 **Dinkum Diamond (IRE)**[19] 4865 8-9-3 **100** OisinMurphy 4 97
(Henry Candy) *midfield: hdwy 3f out: rdn along 2f out: sn drvn and no imp* **40/1**

1400 **9** shd **Azraff (IRE)**[20] 4823 4-9-2 **99** (b) AndreaAtzeni 16 96
(Marco Botti) *towards rr: pushed along and hdwy over 2f out: sn rdn and kpt on fnl f* **14/1**

-000 **10** 2¼ **That Is The Spirit**[26] 4665 5-8-12 **95** GrahamGibbons 11 86
(David O'Meara) *led and sn clr: pushed along 3f out: rdn and hdd 2f out: grad wknd* **80/1**

2000 **11** *3/4* **You're Fired (IRE)**[20] 4823 5-9-2 **104** .... JordanVaughan(5) 14 94
(K R Burke) *in tch: hdwy 3f out: rdn along over 2f out: sn drvn and no imp* **20/1**

/120 **12** *hd* **Jailawi (IRE)**[20] 4823 5-9-2 **99** .... SilvestreDeSousa 20 88
(Ismail Mohammed) *bhd: hdwy on inner wl over 2f out and sn rdn: sn drvn: edgd lft and no imp* **10/1**[3]

6330 **13** *1 1/4* **One Word More (IRE)**[20] 4823 6-9-3 **100** .... DavidAllan 7 86
(Tim Easterby) *s.i.s: a towards rr* **8/1**[2]

0305 **14** *1 1/2* **Alfred Hutchinson**[26] 4665 8-9-2 **99** ....(p) PatSmullen 6 82
(David O'Meara) *in tch: hdwy to chse ldrs 3f out: rdn over 2f out: sn drvn and wknd* **16/1**

6403 **15** *2 3/4* **Birdman (IRE)**[20] 4846 6-9-3 **100** .... DavidNolan 12 77
(David O'Meara) *midfield: pushed along 4f out: rdn along 3f out: n.d* **25/1**

6-40 **16** *3/4* **Chil The Kite**[33] 4392 7-9-10 **107** .... GeorgeBaker 19 82
(Hughie Morrison) *a bhd* **14/1**

6000 **17** *1 3/4* **Solar Deity (IRE)**[20] 4823 7-8-10 **93** ....(p) MartinDwyer 8 64
(Jane Chapple-Hyam) *a towards rr* **28/1**

2002 **18** *3 3/4* **Lat Hawill (IRE)**[12] 5156 5-9-1 **98** ....(v) PhillipMakin 15 60
(Keith Dalgleish) *a towards rr* **14/1**

1160 **19** *1/2* **Mister Universe**[103] 2027 4-9-5 **102** .... JoeFanning 5 63
(Mark Johnston) *chsd ldrs: rdn along wl over 2f out: sn wknd* **25/1**

6030 **20** *8* **Fort Bastion (IRE)**[22] 4758 7-8-10 **93** ....(b) WilliamBuick 18 36
(David O'Meara) *s.i.s: a bhd* **28/1**

1m 36.7s (-2.30) **Going Correction** 0.0s/f (Good)
WFA 3 from 4yo+ 6lb **20** Ran SP% **129.2**
Speed ratings (Par 109): **111,110,109,109,109 107,106,105,105,103 102,102,101,99,96 96,94,90,90,82**
CSF £42.95 CT £354.21 TOTE £9.40: £2.50, £1.90, £2.70, £2.90; EX 54.10 Trifecta £464.10.
Owner Gallop Racing **Bred** Cheveley Park Stud Ltd **Trained** Upper Helmsley, N Yorks

FOCUS
A fiercely competitive mile handicap. The pace was quick, with the field being well spread out on the home bend, and hardly anything got into it. That said, it's best to treat this as strong form and quite a few winners may emerge from it before the close of the turf season. A pb from the winner whose previous best came on the AW.

5586 DARLEY YORKSHIRE OAKS (BRITISH CHAMPIONS SERIES) (GROUP 1) (F&M) 1m 4f

3:40 (3:41) (Class 1) 3-Y-O+

£207,416 (£78,636; £39,354; £19,604; £9,838; £4,937) **Stalls** Centre

Form RPR

-161 **1** **Seventh Heaven (IRE)**[33] 4416 3-8-11 114 .... ColmO'Donoghue 10 121
(A P O'Brien, Ire) *hld up towards rr: hdwy over 3f out: trckd ldrs over 2f out: rdn to chal over 1f out: sn led: kpt on strly* **10/3**[2]

1222 **2** *2 3/4* **Found (IRE)**[64] 3272 4-9-7 119 .... SeamieHeffernan 1 117
(A P O'Brien, Ire) *hld up towards rr: hdwy 3f out: chsd ldrs wl over 1f out: sn rdn: styd on fnl f* **2/1**[1]

-442 **3** *1 1/4* **Queen's Trust**[19] 4864 3-8-11 112 .... AndreaAtzeni 2 115
(Sir Michael Stoute) *lw: trckd ldrs: smooth hdwy and cl up 3f out: led over 2f out: jnd and rdn over 1f out: sn hdd and drvn: kpt on same pce fnl f* **6/1**[3]

2010 **4** *5* **Pretty Perfect (IRE)**[33] 4416 3-8-11 105 .... PaulHanagan 7 107
(A P O'Brien, Ire) *led: pushed along 3f out: rdn and hdd jst over 2f out: sn drvn and grad wknd* **25/1**

-604 **5** *1/2* **Turret Rocks (IRE)**[33] 4416 3-8-11 106 ....(t) KevinManning 12 106
(J S Bolger, Ire) *hld up in rr: hdwy on inner 3f out: rdn to chse ldrs 2f out: sn drvn and kpt on one pce* **20/1**

3522 **6** *11* **Furia Cruzada (CHI)**[47] 3888 5-9-7 110 .... FrankieDettori 4 88
(John Gosden) *lw: in tch: hdwy on outer to chse ldrs 4f out: rdn along 3f out: drvn over 2f out: sn wknd and eased* **16/1**

310 **7** *1* **Even Song (IRE)**[33] 4416 3-8-11 110 .... PatSmullen 3 87
(A P O'Brien, Ire) *trckd ldng pair: hdwy 4f out: rdn along 3f out: sn drvn and wknd: bhd whn eased wl over 1f out* **12/1**

-134 **8** *6* **Loving Things**[20] 4821 4-9-7 108 .... MartinLane 8 77
(Luca Cumani) *hld up: effrt over 4f out: rdn along over 3f out: nvr a factor* **50/1**

11-1 **9** *12* **Endless Time (IRE)**[47] 3888 4-9-7 110 .... WilliamBuick 5 58
(Charlie Appleby) *lw: trckd ldrs: hdwy on outer 4f out: rdn along 3f out: sn drvn and btn: bhd and eased fr wl over 1f out* **9/1**

1-24 **10** *2* **Koora**[53] 3695 4-9-7 109 .... JamieSpencer 6 55
(Luca Cumani) *hld up: a towards rr* **20/1**

4333 **11** *1 1/2* **Harlequeen**[16] 5002 3-8-11 110 .... SilvestreDeSousa 9 52
(Mick Channon) *cl up: rdn along wl over 3f out: sn lost pl and bhd* **20/1**

0521 **12** *16* **Fireglow**[19] 4883 3-8-11 105 .... JamesDoyle 11 27
(Mark Johnston) *chsd ldrs on outer: rdn along wl over 4f out: sn lost pl and bhd* **20/1**

2m 28.5s (-4.70) **Going Correction** 0.0s/f (Good)
WFA 3 from 4yo+ 10lb **12** Ran SP% **119.1**
Speed ratings (Par 117): **115,113,112,109,108 101,100,96,88,87 86,75**
CSF £9.17 CT £38.62 TOTE £4.60: £1.50, £1.40, £1.70; EX 12.80 Trifecta £51.30.
Owner Derrick Smith & Mrs John Magnier & Michael Tabor **Bred** La Traviata Syndicate **Trained** Cashel, Co Tipperary

FOCUS
Run at a sound pace, the right horses came to the fore and the form looks strong, with the Irish Oaks winner beating an extremely reliable yardstick at the top level. Only the principals showed their form, with Seventh Heaven rated an up-to-scratch winner.

5587 EBF & SIR HENRY CECIL GALTRES STKS (LISTED RACE) (F&M) 1m 4f

4:20 (4:20) (Class 1) 3-Y-O+

£34,026 (£12,900; £6,456; £3,216; £1,614; £810) **Stalls** Centre

Form RPR

-112 **1** **Abingdon (USA)**[19] 4883 3-9-1 102 .... AndreaAtzeni 6 111+
(Sir Michael Stoute) *lw: trckd ldrs: hdwy on inner 3f out: rdn to ld 1 1/2f out: kpt on wl fnl f* **13/8**[1]

221 **2** *1 1/4* **To Eternity**[13] 5129 3-8-11 85 .... FrankieDettori 5 104
(John Gosden) *athletic: led 2f: trckd ldr: led again over 3f out: rdn over 2f out: hdd 1 1/2f out and sn drvn: kpt on u.p fnl f* **11/2**[2]

-013 **3** *1/2* **Pandora (IRE)**[27] 4610 4-9-7 99 .... PhillipMakin 3 103+
(David O'Meara) *s.i.s and hld up in rr: hdwy 2f out: in tch whn hmpd and carried bdly lft over 1f out: sn rcvrd and nt clr run jst ins fnl f: swtchd rt: rdn and styd on strly towards fin* **10/1**

-425 **4** *2* **Glamorous Approach (IRE)**[32] 4436 3-8-11 102 .... KevinManning 2 100
(J S Bolger, Ire) *trckd ldrs on inner: hdwy and cl up 4f out: rdn along wl over 2f out: drvn over 1f out: kpt on same pce* **13/2**[3]

1202 **5** *hd* **Sagely (IRE)**[22] 4757 3-8-11 91 .... SilvestreDeSousa 4 100
(Ed Dunlop) *hld up in tch: hdwy over 4f out: chsd ldrs 3f out: rdn 2f out: drvn and kpt on same pce appr fnl f* **16/1**

1-1 **6** *1 3/4* **Anzhelika (IRE)**[17] 4940 4-9-7 86 .... GeorgeBaker 8 97
(David Lanigan) *hld up towards rr: hdwy on outer 3f out: chsd ldrs whn rdn and hung bdly lft over 1f out: one pce after* **9/1**

4423 **7** *hd* **Twitch (IRE)**[21] 4800 4-9-7 100 ....(p) JamesDoyle 1 97
(Hugo Palmer) *lw: prom: led after 2f: rdn along and hdd over 3f out: drvn over 2f out: grad wknd* **10/1**

-553 **8** *4 1/2* **Tiptree (IRE)**[19] 4883 3-8-11 98 .... JamieSpencer 7 89
(Luca Cumani) *trckd ldrs: hdwy over 4f out: cl up over 3f out: rdn over 2f out: sn ev ch: drvn appr fnl f: wknd* **8/1**

2m 33.84s (0.64) **Going Correction** 0.0s/f (Good)
WFA 3 from 4yo+ 10lb **8** Ran SP% **112.0**
Speed ratings (Par 111): **97,96,95,94,94 93,93,90**
CSF £10.09 TOTE £2.50: £1.20, £1.70, £2.30; EX 11.50 Trifecta £53.60.
Owner Ballymacoll Stud **Bred** Ballymacoll Stud **Trained** Newmarket, Suffolk

FOCUS
The last five renewals of this had gone to a 3yo, so it wasn't surprising to see horses of that age group heading the betting. None of the fillies were keen to set a searching gallop so this wasn't a true test (time over 5 seconds slower than the Yorkshire Oaks that preceded it), but the winner is an exciting prospect for a team renowned for significantly improving horses. The form is rated around the race averages.

5588 EVENTMASTERS.CO.UK EBF FILLIES' STKS (H'CAP) 7f

4:55 (4:55) (Class 2) (0-105,97) 3-Y-O+

£37,350 (£11,184; £5,592; £2,796; £1,398; £702) **Stalls** Low

Form RPR

2010 **1** **Opal Tiara (IRE)**[20] 4826 3-9-8 **95** .... OisinMurphy 13 106
(Mick Channon) *trckd ldrs: hdwy 3f out: rdn to ld 1 1/2f out: drvn out* **8/1**[3]

24-1 **2** *1 3/4* **Jadaayil**[126] 1436 3-8-11 **84** .... DaneO'Neill 9 89+
(Charles Hills) *lw: hld up towards rr: hdwy 2f out: rdn over 1f out: fin strly* **6/1**[1]

0164 **3** *nk* **Florenza**[11] 5199 3-8-6 **79** .... AndrewElliott 3 83
(Chris Fairhurst) *lw: wnt lft s: slt ld: rdn along and hdd narrowly over 2f out: cl up and sn drvn: kpt on gamely u.p fnl f* **25/1**

-105 **4** *3/4* **Show Stealer**[26] 4652 3-9-4 **91** .... MartinDwyer 12 93+
(Rae Guest) *rrd and dwlt s: bhd: hdwy on inner over 2f out: rdn to chse ldrs over 1f out: drvn and kpt on same pce fnl f* **15/2**[2]

353 **5** *3/4* **Lil Sophella (IRE)**[44] 3979 7-9-7 **89** .... JackGarritty 8 91+
(Patrick Holmes) *lw: hld up in rr: hdwy on outer 2f out: rdn over 1f out: kpt on fnl f* **16/1**

2613 **6** *nk* **Dawaa**[26] 4651 3-9-7 **94** .... PaulHanagan 7 94
(Mark Johnston) *cl up: rdn and slt ld over 2f out: hdd 1 1/2f out and sn drvn: kpt on same pce fnl f* **8/1**[3]

3502 **7** *1/2* **Mustique (IRE)**[13] 5115 3-8-4 **77** .... PatrickMathers 5 75
(Richard Fahey) *chsd ldrs: rdn along over 2f out: drvn wl over 1f out: kpt on same pce* **8/1**[3]

4332 **8** *3/4* **Quick N Quirky (IRE)**[12] 5180 3-8-9 **82** ....(tp) DavidAllan 4 78
(Tim Easterby) *hld up: hdwy 3f out: rdn along 2f out: n.m.r and drvn over 1f out: kpt on fnl f* **9/1**

3340 **9** *3/4* **Sharaakah (IRE)**[12] 5158 3-9-7 **97** .... JosephineGordon(3) 14 91
(Ed Dunlop) *a towards rr* **14/1**

4601 **10** *1/2* **Alyaa (IRE)**[21] 4787 3-7-13 **75** .... NoelGarbutt(3) 2 68
(Conrad Allen) *sltly hmpd s: chsd ldrs on inner: rdn along 2f out: sn wknd* **20/1**

-200 **11** *1/2* **Light Music**[42] 4062 3-9-9 **96** .... PatCosgrave 1 88
(William Haggas) *t.k.h: chsd ldrs: rdn along over 2f out: sn btn* **11/1**

5211 **12** *1/2* **Hawatif (IRE)**[19] 4867 3-8-13 **86** .... JoeFanning 6 76
(Mark Johnston) *hld up in tch: effrt and pushed along wl over 2f out: rdn wl over 1f out: sn wknd* **6/1**[1]

6302 **13** *1 1/4* **Haley Bop (IRE)**[5] 5396 3-9-1 **88** .... JamesDoyle 10 75
(Mark Johnston) *chsd ldrs: rdn along 3f out: drvn over 2f out: sn wknd* **14/1**

1m 22.99s (-2.31) **Going Correction** -0.10s/f (Good)
WFA 3 from 7yo 5lb **13** Ran SP% **119.8**
Speed ratings (Par 96): **109,107,106,105,104 104,104,103,102,101 101,100,99**
CSF £55.58 CT £1203.11 TOTE £11.00: £3.10, £2.50, £8.00; EX 64.60 Trifecta £1498.30.
Owner Qatar Racing & The Sweet Partnership **Bred** Mcb Ltd & Mrs G Hedley **Trained** West Ilsley, Berks

FOCUS
Race distance as advertised. They went a decent gallop and the form looks good, with the winner doing it nicely. She's accorded a pb.
T/Jkpt: Not won. T/Plt: £24.90 to a £1 stake. Pool: £337,048.61. 9,867.92 winning tickets. T/Qpdt: £9.80 to a £1 stake. Pool: £17,053.90. 1,282.46 winning tickets. **Joe Rowntree**

5589 - 5591a (Foreign Racing) - See Raceform Interactive

5324 SALISBURY (R-H)

Friday, August 19

OFFICIAL GOING: Good (good to firm in places; 8.1)
Wind: light breeze against Weather: sunny periods

5592 SHIPSEYS MARQUEES LADY RIDERS' H'CAP (FOR LADY AMATEUR RIDERS) 1m

5:30 (5:31) (Class 5) (0-70,70) 3-Y-O+ **£3,119** (£967; £483; £242) **Stalls** Low

Form RPR

524 **1** **Cosmic Storm**[12] 5201 3-10-4 **70** .... MissSBrotherton 5 78
(Ralph Beckett) *racd keenly: prom: led after 2f: hld on wl whn chal ins fnl f: pushed out* **9/4**[2]

0522 **2** *nk* **Nona Blu**[8] 5326 4-10-1 **61** .... MsLO'Neill 1 69
(Michael Wigham) *led for 1f: trckd ldrs: rdn 2f out: chal jst ins fnl f: kpt on: hld nring fin* **11/10**[1]

2315 **3** *4* **Stormbound (IRE)**[28] 4589 7-10-7 **67** .... MissJoannaMason 2 66
(Paul Cole) *hld up in 4th: pushed along 3f out: rdn and stdy prog fr 2f out: wnt 3rd jst ins fnl f but nt pce to get on terms* **9/2**[3]

004 **4** *7* **Living Leader**[36] 4293 7-9-9 **60** ....(tp) MissCRobinson(5) 4 43
(Grace Harris) *led after 1f tl 6f out: prom: rdn over 2f out: wknd ins fnl f* **16/1**

0050 **5** *6* **Victor's Bet (SPA)**[30] 4531 7-10-0 **65** .... MissEllaSmith(5) 3 34
(Ralph J Smith) *awkward leaving stalls: hld up 5th: rdn 3f out: sn wknd* **8/1**

1m 46.4s (2.90) **Going Correction** +0.125s/f (Good)
WFA 3 from 4yo+ 6lb **5** Ran SP% **113.6**
Speed ratings (Par 103): **90,89,85,78,72**
CSF £5.34 TOTE £2.70: £1.80, £1.20; EX 5.30 Trifecta £12.20.

Owner The Eclipse Partnership **Bred** Car Colston Hall Stud **Trained** Kimpton, Hants

FOCUS

There was 9mm of rain earlier in the day and the going was given as good, good to firm in places (GoingStick: 8.1). Something of a tactical affair, with no pace on early. The form has been rated at face value, with the runner-up to his latest C&D effort.

5593 BATHWICK TYRES MAIDEN AUCTION STKS 6f

6:05 (6:08) (Class 5) 2-Y-O **£3,557** (£1,058; £529; £264) **Stalls** Low

Form RPR

5 **1** **Swift Mover (IRE)**[6] 5395 2-7-13 0.......... HollieDoyle(7) 2 70
(Richard Hannon) *trckd ldrs: led over 1f out: drifted lft: r.o: rdn out* **4/1**[3]

2 3/4 **Shabeeh (IRE)** 2-9-2 0.......... FrannyNorton 7 78
(Mark Johnston) *prom: led 3f out: rdn and hdd over 1f out: kpt on towards fin but a being hld* **3/1**[1]

0 **3** 2 1/2 **Darkroom Angel**[29] 4558 2-8-11 0.......... SamHitchcott 9 65
(Clive Cox) *trckd ldrs: rdn 2f out: kpt on but nt pce to get on terms* **9/1**

3 **4** 3/4 **Gracious Tom (IRE)**[12] 5202 2-8-9 0.......... SteveDrowne 4 61
(David Evans) *led for 3f: sn rdn: kpt on tl no ex fnl 120yds* **4/1**[3]

0 **5** 4 **King's Coinage (IRE)**[25] 4707 2-9-2 0.......... LiamKeniry 5 56
(Ed Walker) *trckd ldrs: rdn over 2f out: sn hld: fdd fnl f* **7/2**[2]

6 1 1/2 **Esloobaha (IRE)** 2-8-11 0.......... MichaelJMMurphy 1 47+
(Charles Hills) *s.i.s: in last pair: sme prog 2f out: nvr threatened: wknd fnl f* **9/1**

63 **7** 6 **Debonaire David**[20] 4879 2-9-2 0.......... RyanTate 6 34
(Richard Hughes) *racd keenly: trckd ldrs: rdn over 2f out: wknd over 1f out* **20/1**

8 6 **Modhilah (IRE)** 2-8-3 0.......... EdwardGreatrex(3) 3 6
(Harry Dunlop) *slowly int stride: a in last pair: wknd 2f out* **11/1**

1m 16.17s (1.37) **Going Correction** +0.125s/f (Good) **8** Ran SP% **120.3**

Speed ratings (Par 94): **95,94,90,89,84 82,74,66**

CSF £17.45 TOTE £5.10: £1.80, £1.40, £3.10; EX 23.70 Trifecta £229.20.

Owner Sheikh Juma Dalmook Al Maktoum **Bred** Tally-Ho Stud **Trained** East Everleigh, Wilts

FOCUS

An ordinary maiden. The opening level is fluid.

5594 BATHWICK CAR & VAN HIRE NURSERY H'CAP 1m

6:35 (6:37) (Class 5) (0-75,74) 2-Y-O **£3,234** (£962; £481; £240) **Stalls** Low

Form RPR

241 **1** **Haulani (USA)**[16] 5015 2-9-6 **73**.......... WilliamTwiston-Davies 2 82+
(Philip Hide) *mid-div: hdwy 2f out: led jst ins fnl f: r.o strly to draw clr: readily* **3/1**[2]

005 **2** 4 **Quothquan (FR)**[17] 4989 2-8-8 **64**.......... EdwardGreatrex(3) 1 64
(Michael Madgwick) *outpcd in last pair: swtchd to centre 2f out: hdwy over 1f out: r.o strly fnl f: snatched 2nd cl home: nvr any ch w wnr* **28/1**

423 **3** nk **Singing Sands (IRE)**[17] 4981 2-9-7 **74**.......... FrederikTylicki 9 73
(Ralph Beckett) *led: rdn over 1f out: hdd jst ins fnl f: sn outpcd by wnr: no ex whn lost 2nd cl home* **5/1**[3]

055 **4** 1 **Sufrah (USA)**[20] 4877 2-9-4 **71**..........[1] DaneO'Neill 8 68+
(Brian Meehan) *s.i.s and wnt rt: rousted along and sn trcking ldr: rdn over 2f out: kpt on same pce fnl f* **13/2**

012 **5** 1 1/2 **Fastnet Spin (IRE)**[110] 1895 2-9-5 **72**.......... SteveDrowne 5 68
(David Evans) *trckd ldr: rdn wl over 2f out: kpt on but nt pce to chal* **25/1**

0006 **6** 2 1/2 **Hawridge Glory (IRE)**[17] 4982 2-8-9 **62**..........(b[1]) RyanTate 6 50
(Rod Millman) *slowly away and hmpd s: nvr bttr than mid-div* **20/1**

500 **7** 1 **Eolian**[27] 4659 2-8-12 **65**.......... MartinDwyer 4 51
(William Knight) *outpcd in rr: sme hdwy 2f out: no further imp fnl f* **10/1**

2222 **8** 14 **Bayston Hill**[10] 5251 2-9-3 **70**.......... LiamKeniry 7 23
(Mark Usher) *trckd ldr: rdn 3f out: wknd 2f out* **10/1**

643 **9** 3 1/2 **Star Maker**[17] 4988 2-9-3 **70**.......... SamHitchcott 3 15
(Sylvester Kirk) *mid-div: hdwy over 4f out: rdn 3f out: wknd 2f out: eased* **9/4**[1]

1m 44.27s (0.77) **Going Correction** +0.125s/f (Good) **9** Ran SP% **116.0**

Speed ratings (Par 94): **101,97,96,95,94 91,90,76,73**

CSF £86.16 CT £412.72 TOTE £3.20: £1.60, £7.80, £1.80; EX 91.20 Trifecta £742.90.

Owner S P C Woods **Bred** Bill Adair, Phyllis Adair & Connie Brown **Trained** Findon, W Sussex

FOCUS

A fair nursery and, although the favourite ran no sort of race, the convincing winner looks one to keep on side.

5595 EBF STALLIONS STONEHENGE STKS (LISTED RACE) 1m

7:05 (7:06) (Class 1) 2-Y-O

£17,013 (£6,450; £3,228; £1,608; £807; £405) **Stalls** Low

Form RPR

1112 **1** **Montataire (IRE)**[22] 4802 2-9-1 93.......... FrannyNorton 7 105
(Mark Johnston) *mde all: pushed clr over 1f out: r.o strly: rdn out* **7/1**[3]

1 **2** 5 **Gemina (IRE)**[23] 4775 2-8-10 0.......... SteveDrowne 3 89
(Ralph Beckett) *trckd ldrs: edging rt u.p fr 2f out: chsd wnr over 1f out: kpt on but nt pce to threaten* **16/1**

221 **3** 3/4 **Sea Fox (IRE)**[44] 4016 2-9-1 83.......... WilliamTwiston-Davies 4 92
(David Evans) *s.i.s: last: swtchd lft and rdn over 2f out: hanging rt but hdwy over 1f out: styd on fnl f* **20/1**

134 **4** 2 **Cunco (IRE)**[41] 4150 2-9-1 97..........[1] RobertHavlin 8 87
(John Gosden) *trckd wnr: rdn over 2f out: nt pce to chal: lost 2nd over 1f out: no ex ins fnl f where lost 3rd* **3/1**[1]

3432 **5** 10 **Mr Scaramanga**[6] 5401 2-9-1 99.......... SeanLevey 10 64
(Richard Hannon) *mid-div: hdwy 3f out: sn rdn to chse ldrs: wknd over 1f out* **4/1**[2]

341 **6** 1/2 **Rebel De Lope**[34] 4387 2-9-1 86.......... MichaelJMMurphy 5 63
(Charles Hills) *racd keenly in midfield: no imp u.p whn hmpd over 1f out: sn wknd* **11/1**

4126 **7** nk **Hellofahaste**[29] 4560 2-8-10 87.......... FrederikTylicki 2 57
(Rod Millman) *mid-div: rdn wl over 2f out: nvr any imp: wknd over 1f out* **40/1**

31 **8** 3/4 **Ronald R (IRE)**[37] 4274 2-9-1 85.......... JamieSpencer 9 61
(Michael Bell) *hld up towards rr: hdwy 3f out: rdn in midfield whn hmpd over 1f out: sn wknd* **3/1**[1]

051 **9** 1 1/2 **Arborist (IRE)**[17] 4988 2-9-1 77.......... DaneO'Neill 1 57
(Sylvester Kirk) *struggling 4f out: a in rr* **33/1**

10 **10** 1 3/4 **Jackhammer (IRE)**[24] 4732 2-9-1 0.......... MartinDwyer 6 53
(William Knight) *prom tl pushed along over 4f out: rdn over 3f out: wknd 2f out* **9/1**

1m 42.63s (-0.87) **Going Correction** +0.125s/f (Good) **10** Ran SP% **116.9**

Speed ratings (Par 102): **109,104,103,101,91 90,90,89,88,86**

CSF £108.47 TOTE £9.30: £2.50, £3.90, £4.50; EX 97.70 Trifecta £570.30.

Owner Sheikh Hamdan bin Mohammed Al Maktoum **Bred** Tinnakill, P Lawlor & C Beale **Trained** Middleham Moor, N Yorks

FOCUS

Questionable form to an extent, with several failing to run up to form, but the winner was impressive nevertheless. The second and third have been rated as improvers but there are no real anchors for the form.

5596 RICHARD MACLELLAN, SAGE OF BARTON H'CAP 1m 4f

7:35 (7:35) (Class 4) (0-85,87) 3-Y-O **£5,175** (£1,540; £769; £384) **Stalls** Low

Form RPR

2 **1** **Guns Of Leros (USA)**[46] 3959 3-8-11 **73**.......... FergusSweeney 6 80
(Gary Moore) *trckd ldr: led over 3f out: rdn whn strly pressed over 2f out: styd on gamely fnl f: drvn out* **13/2**

024 **2** 1/2 **Visage Blanc**[15] 5054 3-8-12 **74**.......... FrannyNorton 5 80
(Mick Channon) *hld up bhd ldrs: hdwy over 2f out: rdn over 1f out: chal ins fnl f: no ex cl home* **7/1**

025 **3** 2 3/4 **Knight Commander**[37] 4277 3-8-8 **70**.......... MartinDwyer 3 72
(William Knight) *slowly away: detached in last: hdwy over 2f out: rdn over 1f out: styd on into 3rd fnl 120yds: nt pce to get on terms w front pair* **7/1**

1-63 **4** 1 1/2 **Zaakhir (IRE)**[41] 4160 3-9-7 **83**.......... DaneO'Neill 1 82
(Charles Hills) *trckd ldr: chal wnr over 3f out: rdn and ev ch over 2f out tl jst over 1f out: kpt on same pce* **7/2**[3]

651 **5** 5 **Novalina (IRE)**[18] 4948 3-9-2 **78**.......... WilliamTwiston-Davies 4 69
(William Haggas) *trckd ldrs: rdn over 3f out: nt pce to chal: wknd fnl f* **11/4**[1]

5312 **6** 7 **Duck A L'Orange (IRE)**[6] 5413 3-8-11 **73**..........(p) JamieSpencer 2 53
(Michael Bell) *led: rdn and hdd over 3f out: wknd 2f out* **3/1**[2]

2m 37.73s (-0.27) **Going Correction** +0.125s/f (Good) **6** Ran SP% **112.2**

Speed ratings (Par 102): **105,104,102,101,98 93**

CSF £48.48 TOTE £7.70: £3.30, £3.20; EX 39.20 Trifecta £170.00.

Owner Paul Hunt **Bred** Woodcote Stud Ltd **Trained** Lower Beeding, W Sussex

FOCUS

A fair handicap. They came stands' side in the straight this time. The runner-up has been rated to form.

5597 SARAH JANE SMITH MEMORIAL H'CAP 1m 6f 21y

8:05 (8:06) (Class 5) (0-75,75) 3-Y-O+ **£3,234** (£962; £481; £240) **Stalls** Far side

Form RPR

4332 **1** **Ivanhoe**[10] 5267 6-9-3 **64**..........(v) DaneO'Neill 8 71
(Michael Blanshard) *mid-div: hdwy over 2f out: sn rdn: str chal ent fnl f: led cl home* **3/1**[1]

2263 **2** nk **Hurricane Volta (IRE)**[27] 4637 5-9-4 **65**..........(b) CharlesBishop 10 71
(Peter Hedger) *led: rdn and strly pressed fr wl over 2f out: hld on gamely tl hdd cl home* **9/1**

24/5 **3** 1 1/4 **Walter White (IRE)**[19] 4912 6-9-2 **63**..........(t) WilliamTwiston-Davies 6 67
(Philip Hobbs) *trckd ldrs: rdn 3f out: styd on but nt quite pce to chal* **10/1**

-314 **4** hd **Rainbow Pride (IRE)**[14] 5131 4-9-12 **73**.......... JamieSpencer 2 77
(Sir Mark Prescott Bt) *hld up bhd: hdwy over 2f out: sn rdn: chal for hld 3rd ins fnl f: styd on* **6/1**

0032 **5** hd **Lily Trotter**[9] 5286 3-8-5 **67**..........(b[1]) EdwardGreatrex(3) 9 71
(Ralph Beckett) *pressed ldr: rdn 3f out: hld over 1f out: styd on same pce* **4/1**[3]

-642 **6** 6 **Lady Hare (IRE)**[38] 4226 4-8-9 **56** oh1.......... SamHitchcott 7 51
(Ken Cunningham-Brown) *racd keenly: towards rr: rdn over 2f out: styd on past btn horses fnl f: nvr trbld ldrs* **14/1**

305 **7** 1 **Tobougaloo**[22] 4792 5-9-11 **72**.......... LiamKeniry 11 66
(Stuart Kittow) *hld up in last trio: hdwy over 4f out: effrt over 2f out: wknd over 1f out* **7/2**[2]

3063 **8** 3 1/4 **Shine**[9] 5286 3-8-1 **60**.......... NickyMackay 5 49
(Jonathan Portman) *trckd ldrs: rdn 3f out: wknd over 1f out* **20/1**

60-4 **9** 5 **Guantoshol (IRE)**[25] 4711 5-9-4 **68**.......... GeorgeDowning(3) 4 50
(Ian Williams) *mid-div: effrt 3f out: wknd over 1f out* **14/1**

3m 14.66s (7.26) **Going Correction** +0.125s/f (Good)

WFA 3 from 4yo+ 12lb **9** Ran SP% **118.7**

Speed ratings (Par 103): **84,83,83,83,82 79,78,77,74**

CSF £31.80 CT £244.68 TOTE £4.30: £1.40, £2.50, £3.00; EX 31.00 Trifecta £145.80.

Owner The Ivanhoe Partnership **Bred** Simon Balding **Trained** Upper Lambourn, Berks

FOCUS

A modest stayers event, and once again they headed over to the stands' rail in the straight. The runner-up has been rated to form.

T/Plt: £610.80 to a £1 stake. Pool: £51,743.78 - 61.84 winning units T/Qpdt: £148.30 to a £1 stake. Pool: £6,147.96 - 30.66 winning units **Tim Mitchell**

5071 SANDOWN (R-H)

Friday, August 19

OFFICIAL GOING: Good to firm (good in places; rnd 7.4, spr 7.5)

Wind: Almost nil Weather: Overcast, humid

5598 ABU DHABI SPORTS COUNCIL NURSERY H'CAP 5f 6y

2:20 (2:23) (Class 5) (0-75,74) 2-Y-O **£3,881** (£1,155; £577; £288) **Stalls** Low

Form RPR

5522 **1** **Looting**[10] 5265 2-9-4 **71**.......... SeanLevey 2 87
(David Brown) *mde all against rail: clr bef 1/2-way: shkn up 2f out: eased last 100yds* **5/2**[1]

0253 **2** 5 **Big Lachie**[16] 5008 2-9-4 **71**.......... WilliamCarson 6 69
(Jamie Osborne) *hld up in last gng wl: prog and nt clr run wl over 2f out: hdwy and squeezed through to take 2nd wl over 1f out: sn rdn: styd on but no imp on wnr: eased last 75yds* **10/1**[3]

006 **3** 2 **Zumran**[29] 4558 2-8-10 **66**.......... MarcMonaghan(3) 3 57
(Hugo Palmer) *chsd wnr 1f: rdn to go 2nd again briefly 2f out: sn outpcd and wl hld* **8/1**[2]

0045 **4** 3 1/4 **Kings Heart (IRE)**[17] 4974 2-8-13 **66**..........[1] SteveDrowne 4 45
(Mark Usher) *chsd ldrs: shkn up 2f out: outpcd and no imp after* **16/1**

5361 **5** 1 1/4 **Four Dragons**[25] 4712 2-9-1 **68**.......... LiamJones 8 43
(Tom Dascombe) *prom: chsd wnr 4f out to 2f out: hung lft and wknd* **12/1**

0410 **6** 2 3/4 **Whiteley (IRE)**[20] 4884 2-9-0 **67**.......... JFEgan 5 32
(Mick Channon) *prom: lost pl and drvn after 2f: sn struggling in rr* **8/1**[2]

454 **7** 2 1/4 **Snoozy Sioux (IRE)**[92] 2410 2-8-10 **66**.......... TimClark(3) 9 23+
(Martin Smith) *chsd ldrs on outer to 1/2-way: sn wknd* **8/1**[2]

020 **8** 32 **Kath's Boy (IRE)**[18] 4938 2-8-8 **61**.......... LukeMorris 7
(Tony Carroll) *lost tch 1/2-way: t.o* **33/1**

1m 2.35s (0.75) **Going Correction** +0.275s/f (Good) **8** Ran SP% **87.5**

Speed ratings (Par 94): **105,97,93,88,86 82,78,27**

CSF £15.41 CT £66.83 TOTE £2.20: £1.10, £2.70, £2.30; EX 17.90 Trifecta £76.50.

Owner J C Fretwell **Bred** Dunchurch Lodge Stud Company **Trained** Averham Park, Notts

■ Fabric with withdrawn. Price at time of withdrawal 11/4. Rule 4 applies to all bets - deduction 25p in the pound

FOCUS
Following 2mm of rain leading up to the meeting the the going was good to firm, good in places on both tracks and the jockeys in the first race were very complimentary about the ground. The rail was out from the 7f marker to the winning post, adding 12yds to race distances on the round course. A fair sprint nursery to start which took less winning after the second-favourite Fabric was withdrawn at the start on vet's advice, but they finished well spread out and the form looks solid enough for the grade.

5599 UAE NATIONAL ARCHIVE H'CAP 5f 6y
2:55 (2:58) (Class 5) (0-75,75) 3-Y-O+ **£3,234** (£962; £481; £240) **Stalls** Low

Form RPR
2122 **1** **Babyfact**[8] 5330 5-8-12 **63**.. JimCrowley 12 73
(Malcolm Saunders) *prom on outer: chsd ldr 2f out: drvn and str chal fnl f: r.o to ld last 50yds* **6/1**[2]
-464 **2** ½ **Ejbaar**[20] 4889 4-9-10 **75**.. SilvestreDeSousa 4 83
(Robert Cowell) *led but racd off far rail: rdn over 1f out: edgd lft fnl f: hdd and nt qckn last 50yds* **15/8**[1]
6003 **3** 1 **Ask The Guru**[14] 5105 6-8-8 **59**..(p) LukeMorris 2 63
(Michael Attwater) *prom: disp 2nd 1/2-way to 2f out: kpt on same pce u.p over 1f out* **12/1**
5561 **4** ½ **Perfect Pastime**[11] 5236 8-8-12 **63**................................. PatCosgrave 1 66
(Jim Boyle) *nt that wl away: towards rr: rdn wl over 1f out: kpt on fnl f to press for a pl nr fin* **7/1**[3]
-305 **5** nk **Costa Filey**[18] 4952 5-9-0 **65**.. FrederikTylicki 11 67
(Ed Vaughan) *prom: disp 2nd 1/2-way to 2f out: kpt on one pce after* **7/1**[3]
6542 **6** 3 **Doctor Parkes**[10] 5259 10-9-2 **70**.................................. AaronJones(3) 13 61
(Stuart Williams) *sn in rr: rdn over 2f out: kpt on fnl f: n.d* **12/1**
0004 **7** nk **Keep It Dark**[58] 3530 7-9-4 **69**... JamesDoyle 8 59+
(William Knight) *hld up: lost pl and in last pair 2f out: nt clr run twice over 1f out: nudged along after: nvr involved* **14/1**
2042 **8** 1¼ **Straits Of Malacca**[11] 5236 5-9-4 **69**................................(v[1]) JFEgan 10 54
(Simon Dow) *s.s: mostly in last: effrt on outer over 1f out: no great prog* **8/1**
3100 **9** 1 **Ada Lovelace**[28] 4585 6-9-10 **75**............................(p) FergusSweeney 9 57
(John Gallagher) *chsd ldrs tl wknd wl over 1f out* **50/1**
6403 **10** 4½ **Long Awaited (IRE)**[12] 5189 8-9-4 **72**..............(b) JosephineGordon(3) 6 37
(Conor Dore) *chsd ldr to 1/2-way: wknd qckly 2f out* **20/1**

1m 2.45s (0.85) **Going Correction** +0.275s/f (Good)
WFA 3 from 4yo+ 2lb **10** Ran SP% **114.0**
Speed ratings (Par 103): **104,103,101,100,100 95,95,93,91,84**
CSF £17.15 CT £132.65 TOTE £6.90: £2.50, £1.10, £3.20; EX 18.20 Trifecta £262.50.
Owner Mrs Ginny Nicholas **Bred** M S Saunders And Chris Scott **Trained** Green Ore, Somerset

FOCUS
It started to rain again before this race. An ordinary sprint handicap and not that many got into it. The third has been rated to his recent C&D form.

5600 TCA ABU DHABI/BRITISH STALLION STUDS EBF MAIDEN STKS 7f 16y
3:30 (3:31) (Class 5) 2-Y-O **£3,881** (£1,155; £577; £288) **Stalls** Low

Form RPR
32 **1** **Deningy**[29] 4552 2-9-5 0... JamesDoyle 11 84
(Charlie Appleby) *trckd ldr: chal 2f out gng wl: rdn to ld jst over 1f out: drvn out* **7/4**[1]
3 **2** 1 **Calibration (IRE)**[28] 4580 2-9-5 0....................................... JimCrowley 3 81
(Martyn Meade) *chsd ldng pair: clr of rest fr 3f out: pushed along over 2f out: no imp tl styd on to take 2nd last 100yds: clsng at fin* **2/1**[2]
52 **3** 1¼ **Whip Nae Nae (IRE)**[15] 5073 2-9-5 0................................. SeanLevey 4 78
(Richard Hannon) *led: rdn 2f out: hdd jst over 1f out: one pce and lost 2nd last 100yds* **8/1**
4 1½ **Eynhallow** 2-9-5 0.. DaneO'Neill 8 74+
(Roger Charlton) *in tch in chsng gp: pushed along 2f out: tk 4th over 1f out: nvr a threat but kpt on steadily: fair debut* **33/1**
5 1½ **City Of Joy** 2-9-5 0... PatDobbs 5 73+
(Sir Michael Stoute) *dwlt: mostly in last trio tl pushed along and prog jst over 2f out: tk 5th fnl f and styd on: shaped w real promise* **10/1**
6 2 **Reverend Jacobs** 2-9-5 0... PatCosgrave 16 67+
(William Haggas) *veered lft s: hld up in last pair: nt clr run 2f out and swtchd lft: styd on in encouraging fashion fr over 1f out* **25/1**
7 2½ **Meteor Light (IRE)** 2-9-5 0... FrederikTylicki 7 61+
(Ed Vaughan) *settled in midfield: no ch but gng wl enough whn twice into trble over 1f out: styd on fnl f: nt disgracd* **66/1**
8 2¼ **Leapt** 2-9-5 0.. JimmyFortune 1 51
(Roger Charlton) *prom in chsng gp: shkn up to go 4th 3f out to over 1f out: wknd* **20/1**
9 2½ **Sound Bar** 2-9-5 0... TedDurcan 2 45
(Ralph Beckett) *dwlt: rcvrd to chse ldrs: shkn up over 2f out: no prog and wknd over 1f out* **6/1**[3]
0 **10** nk **Silver Link (IRE)**[22] 4801 2-9-0 0.................................... SteveDrowne 12 43
(Marcus Tregoning) *settled in midfield: no ch but gng wl enough whn hmpd on inner over 1f out: eased* **100/1**
11 ½ **Exspectation (IRE)** 2-9-5 0... RobertHavlin 9 42
(Michael Blanshard) *chsd ldng trio to 3f out: wknd* **100/1**
0 **12** 1¼ **Imphal**[20] 4866 2-9-5 0... MartinDwyer 14 39
(Marcus Tregoning) *a towards rr: bhd fnl 2f* **50/1**
50 **13** 6 **Masterofdiscovery**[20] 4856 2-9-5 0................................... LukeMorris 10 23
(Clive Cox) *racd on outer in midfield: no prog over 2f out: pushed along and wknd* **100/1**
14 11 **Reynardo De Silver** 2-9-5 0.. FergusSweeney 15
(Gary Moore) *s.s: rn green in last and a bhd* **100/1**

1m 31.27s (1.77) **Going Correction** +0.225s/f (Good) **14** Ran SP% **123.1**
Speed ratings (Par 94): **98,96,95,93,92 89,86,84,81,81 80,79,72,59**
CSF £5.17 TOTE £2.50: £1.02, £1.80, £3.10; EX 6.10 Trifecta £20.80.
Owner Godolphin **Bred** Bolton Grange **Trained** Newmarket, Suffolk

FOCUS
Rail movement added 12yds to race distance. This maiden can go to a good one, with Time Test and Stormy Antarctic amongst the recent winners. This year's renewal was dominated by the form horses, but unsurprisingly there were a few eye-catching performances in behind.

5601 NATIONAL FEED & FLOUR PRODUCTION H'CAP 1m 14y
4:05 (4:09) (Class 3) (0-90,89) 3-Y-O **£7,439** (£2,213; £1,106; £553) **Stalls** Low

Form RPR
032 **1** **Wimpole Hall**[23] 4776 3-9-0 **82**..................................[1] SilvestreDeSousa 4 91
(William Jarvis) *mde all: rdn over 1f out: kpt on wl and nvr seriously threatened* **3/1**[2]
125- **2** 2 **Fleeting Visit**[336] 6501 3-9-1 **83**... JohnFahy 1 87+
(Eve Johnson Houghton) *hld up in last pair: prog on inner over 2f out: drvn over 1f out: styd on to take 2nd last strides* **14/1**
320 **3** shd **Midnight Macchiato (IRE)**[76] 2907 3-8-11 **79**................. PatCosgrave 2 83
(David Brown) *reluctant to enter stalls: trckd ldrs: rdn to chse wnr 2f out: kpt on but no imp: lost 2nd last strides* **10/1**
6320 **4** ¾ **War Story (IRE)**[23] 4776 3-9-7 **89**...................................... JimCrowley 3 92
(Luca Cumani) *hld up in midfield: trckd ldrs and waiting for room 2f out: swtchd lft over 1f out: drvn and kpt on but nvr able to chal* **13/2**[3]
3120 **5** 1¼ **George William**[20] 4867 3-9-7 **89**...................................... SeanLevey 10 88
(Richard Hannon) *hld up in last trio: rdn and gd prog on outer over 2f out: disp 2nd wl over 1f out to jst ins fnl f: fdd* **15/2**
2000 **6** 6 **Madrinho (IRE)**[12] 5199 3-9-7 **89**... PatDobbs 9 75
(Richard Hannon) *hld up in last pair: shkn up over 2f out: passed a few wkng rivals but nvr on terms* **33/1**
5132 **7** 12 **Thaqaffa (IRE)**[16] 5024 3-9-0 **82**....................................... DaneO'Neill 11 40
(Marcus Tregoning) *chsd ldrs: shoved along 3f out: wknd rapidly jst over 2f out: t.o* **7/1**
41-4 **8** 10 **Daily Bulletin (USA)**[13] 5175 3-9-7 **89**............................... JamesDoyle 5 24
(John Gosden) *t.k.h: trckd ldrs: rdn and n.m.r over 2f out: sn wknd rapidly: t.o and virtually p.u nr fin* **11/4**[1]
1105 **9** 4½ **Medburn Dream**[60] 3465 3-9-0 **82**................................... JimmyFortune 8 7
(Paul Henderson) *chsd wnr to 2f out: wknd rapidly: t.o and virtually p.u nr fin* **14/1**

1m 43.68s (0.38) **Going Correction** +0.225s/f (Good) **9** Ran SP% **114.6**
Speed ratings (Par 104): **107,105,104,104,102 96,84,74,70**
CSF £43.81 CT £372.98 TOTE £4.40: £1.70, £4.10, £3.30; EX 45.60 Trifecta £323.00.
Owner Ms E L Banks **Bred** R F And S D Knipe **Trained** Newmarket, Suffolk

FOCUS
Rail movement added 12yds to race distance. A decent handicap run at just a fair pace. The third has been rated to form.

5602 IPIC FILLIES' H'CAP 1m 14y
4:40 (4:42) (Class 5) (0-75,74) 3-Y-O+ **£3,234** (£962; £481; £240) **Stalls** Low

Form RPR
22-1 **1** **Carenot (IRE)**[120] 1589 3-9-4 **72**..................................(v[1]) PatCosgrave 5 83
(William Haggas) *trckd ldr: led 2f out gng easily: sn pressed and rdn: drew clr 1f out: readily* **1/1**[1]
0063 **2** 3 **Indigo**[16] 5010 3-8-1 **58**.. JosephineGordon(3) 4 62
(Mark Usher) *chsd ldng pair: pushed along and nt clr run 3f out: rallied u.p to take 2nd wl over 1f out and pressed wnr: one pce after* **8/1**
5133 **3** 1½ **Figurante (IRE)**[11] 5247 3-9-3 **71**.................................. WilliamCarson 7 72
(Jamie Osborne) *hld up in last: shkn up and nt qckn over 2f out: one pce and n.d after* **9/4**[2]
4-35 **4** 6 **Wall Of Light**[70] 3107 3-9-2 **70**.................................. SilvestreDeSousa 1 62
(Tom Dascombe) *led: rdn and hdd 2f out: sn lost 2nd: wknd and eased fnl f* **9/2**[3]

1m 46.53s (3.23) **Going Correction** +0.225s/f (Good)
WFA 3 from 4yo 6lb **4** Ran SP% **110.1**
Speed ratings (Par 100): **92,89,87,81**
CSF £8.95 TOTE £1.70; EX 8.20 Trifecta £14.50.
Owner P Makin **Bred** Swordlestown Stud **Trained** Newmarket, Suffolk

FOCUS
Rail movement added 12yds to race distance. A modest fillies' handicap contested by four 3yos following the withdrawals. The pace was steady and the unexposed winner proved far too good. The runner-up has been rated to her turf form.

5603 GLOBAL UNITED VETERINARY SERVICES H'CAP 1m 2f 7y
5:15 (5:18) (Class 4) (0-80,86) 3-Y-O **£4,690** (£1,395; £697; £348) **Stalls** Low

Form RPR
2221 **1** **Hollywood Road (IRE)**[14] 5122 3-8-13 **79**...............(b) GeorgeWood(7) 3 87
(Don Cantillon) *t.k.h: trckd ldng pair: rdn over 2f out: chal over 1f out: sustained effrt to ld last strides* **5/1**[3]
1 **2** hd **Blind Faith (IRE)**[64] 3305 3-9-3 **76**................................... JimCrowley 8 83
(Luca Cumani) *t.k.h: trckd ldr: rdn 2f out: sn chalng: drvn ahd briefly 50yds out: jst outpcd* **11/2**
3301 **3** nk **Jimenez (IRE)**[29] 4562 3-9-7 **80**....................................(p) JimmyFortune 5 86
(Brian Meehan) *led: stretched field 1/2-way: rdn 2f out: fought on wl but hdd 50yds out and sn jst hld in 3rd* **10/1**
1211 **4** 5 **Palisade**[7] 5365 3-9-13 **86** 6ex...(v) LukeMorris 2 82
(Sir Mark Prescott Bt) *hld up: shkn up to take 4th over 2f out and cl enough: no imp on ldng trio over 1f out: wknd fnl f* **5/2**[2]
306 **5** 6 **Irrevocable (IRE)**[31] 4480 3-8-11 **73**.................... JosephineGordon(3) 1 57
(Roger Charlton) *s.s: in tch in last tl shoved along over 3f out: sn no ch: tk remote 5th nr fin* **20/1**
0611 **6** nk **Kummiya**[11] 5234 3-9-10 **83** 6ex... JamesDoyle 4 71
(Roger Charlton) *hld up in last pair: prog on outer over 2f out: sn rdn: nt qckn and btn wl over 1f out: wknd and eased* **2/1**[1]
3261 **7** 2¾ **Glance My Way (IRE)**[35] 4342 3-9-3 **76**................................ PatDobbs 7 54
(Richard Hannon) *chsd ldng trio to over 2f out: wknd* **12/1**

2m 13.87s (3.37) **Going Correction** +0.225s/f (Good) **7** Ran SP% **115.5**
Speed ratings (Par 102): **95,94,94,90,85 85,83**
CSF £32.81 CT £264.97 TOTE £7.70: £3.20, £2.60; EX 35.30 Trifecta £175.80.
Owner Mrs Catherine Reed **Bred** Tally-Ho Stud **Trained** Newmarket, Suffolk

FOCUS
Rail movement added 12yds to race distance. An interesting 3yo handicap with six of the seven remaining runners last-time-out winners, two of them bidding for a hat-trick, but they went a modest early pace and this was a race where you just had to be handy. The jockeys decided to take the wide route racing down the back straight. The level is a bit fluid, with the third rated to the better view of his previous win here.
T/Plt: £32.70 to a £1 stake. Pool: £66,144.29 - 1476.07 winning units T/Qpdt: £11.80 to a £1 stake. Pool: £3,401.32 - 211.82 winning units **Jonathan Neesom**

5523 WOLVERHAMPTON (A.W) (L-H)
Friday, August 19

OFFICIAL GOING: Tapeta: standard
Wind: Light behind turning fresh from race 3 Weather: Cloudy with sunny spells and heavy rain for race 3

5604 GLAZERITE UK GROUP LTD APPRENTICE H'CAP 1m 141y (Tp)
6:20 (6:20) (Class 6) (0-55,55) 3-Y-O+ **£2,264** (£673; £336; £168) **Stalls** Low

Form RPR
0031 **1** **Mount Cheiron (USA)**[15] 5064 5-9-4 **54**............(v) CallumRodriguez(5) 8 60
(Richard Ford) *chsd ldrs: wnt 2nd over 1f out: rdn to ld and hung lft ins fnl f: styd on* **9/2**[1]

-050 **2** 1 ½ **Zamastar**[14] 5132 5-9-6 **51**....(p) DannyBrock 6 54
(Brendan Powell) *mid-div: hdwy u.p 2f out: rdn to chse wnr and hung lft ins fnl f: styd on* **11/2**[2]

0600 **3** ¾ **Mops Angel**[44] 4025 5-9-8 **53**.... AlistairRawlinson 2 54
(Michael Appleby) *s.s: hld up: hdwy 2f out: rdn over 1f out: styd on* **7/1**

0505 **4** ½ **Just Fred (IRE)**[17] 4993 3-8-6 **47**....(p) PaddyPilley(3) 9 48
(Denis Coakley) *hld up: rdn over 3f out: nt clr run over 1f out: styd on: nt rch ldrs* **7/1**

6346 **5** nk **Pivotal Dream (IRE)**[14] 5101 3-8-5 **48**.... KillianHennessy(5) 7 48
(Mark Brisbourne) *hld up: rdn and hung lft fr over 1f out: styd on: nt rch ldrs* **8/1**

6-50 **6** ½ **Rafaaf (IRE)**[60] 3474 8-9-5 **55**.... MeganNicholls(5) 4 54
(Richard Phillips) *prom: chsd ldr over 5f out: led over 2f out: hdd and no ex ins fnl f* **16/1**

023 **7** nk **Rosie Crowe (IRE)**[31] 4498 4-9-0 **48**....(v) CharlieBennett(3) 5 46+
(Shaun Harris) *led: hdd 8f out: chsd ldrs: rdn over 2f out: no ex ins fnl f* **13/2**

0500 **8** 3 ¼ **Zeteah**[17] 4993 6-9-1 **46** oh1.... RobHornby 1 37+
(Tony Carroll) *led 8f out: rdn and hdd over 2f out: wknd fnl f* **11/1**

4603 **9** shd **Diamond Runner (IRE)**[15] 5064 4-9-2 **54**....(p) AledBeech(7) 3 45
(John Norton) *hld up: rdn over 2f out: wknd fnl f* **6/1**[3]

600 **10** nk **Outback Guy (IRE)**[80] 2780 3-8-12 **55**.... RowanScott(5) 10 45
(Kevin Frost) *hld up: rdn 1/2-way: wknd over 1f out* **66/1**

1m 49.72s (-0.38) **Going Correction** -0.075s/f (Stan)
WFA 3 from 4yo+ 7lb **10** Ran SP% **113.0**
Speed ratings (Par 101): **98,96,96,95,95 94,94,91,91,91**
CSF £27.87 CT £172.91 TOTE £5.00: £1.50, £2.70, £2.40; EX 25.50 Trifecta £124.80.
Owner The Style Council **Bred** Swettenham Stud **Trained** Garstang, Lancs

FOCUS
Dry conditions and standard going for a low-key evening card. This was a weakish opener for apprentices, but the pace at least looked sound.

5605 QATAR AIRWAYS H'CAP 5f 216y (Tp)
6:50 (6:51) (Class 6) (0-65,71) 3-Y-O+ **£2,587** (£770; £384; £192) **Stalls** Low

Form RPR

0061 **1** **Langley Vale**[45] 3984 7-9-8 **63**....(v) JackMitchell 2 70
(Roger Teal) *chsd ldrs: wnt 2nd over 2f out: rdn to ld and edgd rt wl ins fnl f* **4/1**[3]

6602 **2** ½ **Viva Verglas (IRE)**[15] 5069 5-9-7 **62**....(e) GrahamGibbons 4 67
(Daniel Mark Loughnane) *sn led: rdn and hung rt fr over 1f out: hdd wl ins fnl f* **7/2**[2]

5314 **3** shd **Virile (IRE)**[9] 5282 5-9-6 **61**....(bt) RobertWinston 7 66+
(Sylvester Kirk) *hld up: racd keenly: hdwy over 1f out: r.o to go 2rd post* **9/4**[1]

0054 **4** ½ **Arlecchino's Rock**[21] 4820 3-9-3 **61**....(p) DannyBrock 6 64
(Mark Usher) *chsd ldrs: rdn over 2f out: ev ch fr over 1f out: styd on* **11/1**

3000 **5** ¾ **Sakhee's Rose**[45] 3984 6-8-12 **56**....(b) RobHornby(3) 1 57
(Ed McMahon) *hld up: hdwy over 2f out: rdn and ev ch fr over 1f out: no ex towards fin* **20/1**

3200 **6** 2 ¼ **Sandacres**[22] 4789 3-9-2 **65**.... DavidParkes(5) 11 59
(Laura Mongan) *hld up: rdn over 2f out: r.o ins fnl f: nrst fin* **20/1**

0610 **7** 1 **Storm Lightning**[14] 5105 7-9-9 **64**.... ShaneKelly 5 55
(Mark Brisbourne) *chsd ldrs: rdn over 2f out: styd on same pce fr over 1f out* **25/1**

5/06 **8** nk **Ignight**[9] 5282 5-8-0 **48** oh1 ow2....(t[1]) MitchGodwin(7) 10 38
(Matthew Salaman) *sn pushed along in rr: sme hdwy u.p over 1f out: no ex fnl f* **100/1**

1401 **9** 2 **Classic Flyer**[7] 5368 4-9-11 **71** 6ex....(v) JoshDoyle(5) 9 54
(David O'Meara) *hld up: on outer over 2f out: nvr trbld ldrs* **11/1**

0000 **10** 7 **Sun In His Eyes**[14] 5126 4-8-2 **46** oh1....(p) NoelGarbutt(3) 8 7
(Ed de Giles) *chsd ldr tl rdn over 2f out: wknd over 1f out* **100/1**

6635 **11** 1 **Misu Pete**[76] 2918 4-9-2 **62**.... RachealKneller(5) 12 20+
(Mark Usher) *s.s: outpcd* **7/1**

1m 14.16s (-0.34) **Going Correction** -0.075s/f (Stan)
WFA 3 from 4yo+ 3lb **11** Ran SP% **117.5**
Speed ratings (Par 101): **99,98,98,97,96 93,92,91,89,79 78**
CSF £17.38 CT £38.62 TOTE £5.40: £1.80, £1.80, £1.20; EX 23.10 Trifecta £53.10.
Owner Mrs Muriel Forward & Dr G C Forward **Bred** Miss Brooke Sanders **Trained** Great Shefford, Berks

FOCUS
A modest but reasonably competitive sprint, in which the first five finished fanned right across the track and clear of the remainder.

5606 GOLIATH HOMEWORLD LTD FILLIES' (S) STKS 5f 20y (Tp)
7:20 (7:20) (Class 6) 2-Y-O **£2,264** (£673; £336; £168) **Stalls** Low

Form RPR

5 **1** **Ballyanna**[25] 4713 2-8-12 0.... RobertWinston 3 60+
(John Butler) *hld up: hdwy over 1f out: shkn up to ld ins fnl f: r.o wl* **4/1**[3]

4464 **2** 2 ½ **Princess Way (IRE)**[36] 4315 2-8-12 58.... ShaneKelly 2 51
(David Evans) *chsd ldrs: rdn over 1f out: styd on to go 2nd nr fin* **11/4**[2]

3644 **3** nk **Luv U Always**[14] 5125 2-8-12 56.... AndrewMullen 5 50
(Jo Hughes) *led: rdn over 1f out: edgd rt and hdd ins fnl f: styd on same pce* **2/1**[1]

0000 **4** 1 ¼ **Miss Island Ruler**[7] 5364 2-8-9 20....(b[1]) JacobButterfield(3) 8 45
(Shaun Harris) *chsd ldrs: rdn and hung lft over 1f out: no ex ins fnl f* **100/1**

5554 **5** shd **Secret Coin (IRE)**[14] 5128 2-8-9 56.... RobHornby(3) 4 45
(Jamie Osborne) *hld up in tch: rdn over 1f out: styd on same pce* **12/1**

2466 **6** ¾ **Princess Holly**[10] 5258 2-8-12 63.... GrahamGibbons 7 42
(Robert Cowell) *chsd ldr: rdn whn hmpd over 1f out: edgd rt and no ex ins fnl f* **4/1**[3]

05 **7** nk **Miss Salt**[11] 5244 2-8-12 0.... TimmyMurphy 6 41
(Dominic Ffrench Davis) *sn pushed along in rr: rdn 1/2-way: n.d* **28/1**

0 **8** 11 **Tisnowornever (IRE)**[30] 4526 2-8-12 0.... DannyBrock 1 2
(J S Moore) *s.i.s: outpcd* **33/1**

1m 2.21s (0.31) **Going Correction** -0.075s/f (Stan) **8** Ran SP% **115.1**
Speed ratings (Par 89): **94,90,89,87,87 86,85,68**
CSF £15.40 TOTE £4.80: £1.50, £1.50, £1.10; EX 18.70 Trifecta £45.40.The winner was bought in by David Evans for 5000gns. Luv U Always was claimed by Mr I J Jardine for £6000
Owner John O'Donnell & Noel Kelly **Bred** J O'Donnell & N Kelly **Trained** Newmarket, Suffolk

FOCUS
A very ordinary seller for juvenile fillies, run in driving rain at an initially overly strong gallop. It's been rated around the par for the level.

5607 QATAR AIRWAYS - GOING PLACES TOGETHER H'CAP 1m 4f 50y (Tp)
7:50 (7:51) (Class 5) (0-70,70) 3-Y-O+ **£3,234** (£962; £481; £240) **Stalls** Low

Form RPR

-052 **1** **Rubensian**[12] 5193 3-8-8 **65**.... GeorgeBuckell(5) 4 80
(David Simcock) *trckd ldrs: plld hrd: rdn to ld over 1f out: c clr fnl f* **8/11**[1]

635 **2** 6 **Stonecoldsoba**[34] 4385 3-8-6 **58**.... DannyBrock 2 64
(David Evans) *led 5f: chsd ldrs: rdn over 3f out: hmpd over 2f out: styd on same pce fr over 1f out: wnt 2nd nr fin* **10/1**

3223 **3** nk **Machine Learner**[6] 5397 3-9-1 **70**....(v) LouisSteward(3) 1 75
(Michael Bell) *w ldr tl settled into 2nd after 1f: led 7f out: rdn over 2f out: hdd over 1f out: no ex ins fnl f* **7/2**[2]

0350 **4** 1 **Woofie (IRE)**[32] 4463 4-9-8 **69**.... CallumShepherd(5) 5 73
(Laura Mongan) *hld up: hdwy over 1f out: wnt 4th nr fin: nvr trbld ldrs* **20/1**

0455 **5** 1 ¾ **Fastnet Blast (IRE)**[26] 4686 3-9-2 **68**....(b) ThomasBrown 7 69
(Ed Walker) *s.i.s: hdwy 8f out: chsd ldr over 6f out: rdn and ev ch over 1f out: wknd ins fnl f* **13/2**[3]

0050 **6** 14 **U S Navy Seal (USA)**[29] 4568 4-9-11 **70**....(v) AlistairRawlinson(3) 3 49
(J R Jenkins) *hld up: rdn and wknd over 2f out* **12/1**

0-00 **7** 2 ¾ **Tinseltown**[27] 4648 10-8-2 **51** oh5....(p) SophieKilloran(7) 8 25
(Harriet Bethell) *hld up: rdn over 3f out: wknd over 2f out* **66/1**

0200 **8** 99 **Wildomar**[91] 2445 7-9-5 **61**.... GrahamGibbons 6
(Peter Hiatt) *chsd ldrs tl rdn and wknd over 2f out: eased* **25/1**

2m 38.38s (-2.42) **Going Correction** -0.075s/f (Stan)
WFA 3 from 4yo+ 10lb **8** Ran SP% **120.3**
Speed ratings (Par 103): **105,101,100,100,98 89,87,21**
CSF £10.16 CT £19.67 TOTE £1.60: £1.02, £2.50, £1.60; EX 11.00 Trifecta £27.90.
Owner Roger & Yvonne Allsop **Bred** Cheveley Park Stud Ltd **Trained** Newmarket, Suffolk
■ Stewards' Enquiry : Graham Gibbons jockey said gelding stopped quickly
Callum Shepherd jockey said gelding was denied a clear run app home turn
Louis Steward jockey cautioned as to his future conduct in races

FOCUS
The eight runners here were collectively 0-39 for the calendar year prior to racing, so not a strong contest by any means. The pace was reasonable, however, and one of those with most time on his side won well. The runner-up and third have been rated close to form.

5608 GLAZERITE WINDOWS & NETWORK VEKA PARTNERSHIP MEDIAN AUCTION MAIDEN STKS 1m 141y (Tp)
8:20 (8:20) (Class 5) 3-4-Y-O **£3,234** (£962; £481; £240) **Stalls** Low

Form RPR

2253 **1** **Van Dyke**[8] 5349 3-9-0 75.... CharlieBennett(5) 4 78
(Hughie Morrison) *mde all rdn over 1f out: styd on u.p* **1/2**[1]

023 **2** ¾ **Best Laid Plans**[22] 4806 3-9-0 73.... AndrewMullen 1 71
(James Tate) *chsd wnr: rdn over 2f out: styd on u.p* **2/1**[2]

3 16 **Hangman Jury** 3-9-5 0.... ShaneKelly 3 39
(Richard Hughes) *s.s: sn chsng ldrs: pushed along over 3f out: wknd over 2f out* **12/1**[3]

0- **4** 1 **Demand Respect**[361] 5701 3-9-2 0.... LouisSteward(3) 2 37
(Henry Spiller) *hld up: rdn and wknd over 2f out* **28/1**

1m 50.58s (0.48) **Going Correction** -0.075s/f (Stan) **4** Ran SP% **111.1**
Speed ratings (Par 103): **94,93,79,78**
CSF £1.85 TOTE £1.50; EX 2.30 Trifecta £4.60.
Owner The Fairy Story Partnership **Bred** Deepwood Farm Stud **Trained** East Ilsley, Berks

FOCUS
This concerned just the two market leaders virtually throughout. A small pb from the winner, with the runner-up to form.

5609 BIRMINGHAM TO DOHA AND BEYOND H'CAP 1m 141y (Tp)
8:50 (8:50) (Class 5) (0-75,75) 3-Y-O+ **£3,234** (£962; £481; £240) **Stalls** Low

Form RPR

333 **1** **Toboggan's Fire**[20] 4871 3-9-1 **74**.... RowanScott(5) 3 82
(Ann Duffield) *w ldrs 1f: remained handy: rdn to ld over 1f out: sn hung rt: bmpd ins fnl f: styd on wl* **13/2**[3]

4505 **2** 1 ¼ **The Third Man**[57] 3563 5-9-6 **70**....(p) LouisSteward(3) 2 75
(Henry Spiller) *hld up: hdwy over 2f out: rdn over 1f out: styd on same pce towards fin* **7/2**[1]

0465 **3** hd **Mustaqqil (IRE)**[15] 5082 4-10-0 **75**....(v) GrahamGibbons 1 80
(David O'Meara) *hld up in tch: rdn and ev ch whn hung lft over 1f out: bmpd ins fnl f: no ex towards fin* **7/2**[1]

4606 **4** 1 ½ **Palpitation (IRE)**[16] 5030 3-8-11 **68**.... AaronJones(3) 7 70
(David Brown) *disp ld tl wnt on over 7f out: hdd over 6f out: chsd ldr: rdn over 2f out: ev ch over 1f out: nt clr run sn after: edgd lft and no ex ins fnl f* **8/1**

2340 **5** nse **Jayjinski (IRE)**[41] 4155 3-9-5 **73**.... ShaneKelly 5 74
(Richard Hughes) *hld up: rdn over 3f out: styd on ins fnl f: nt trble ldrs* **12/1**

3101 **6** ¾ **British Embassy (IRE)**[16] 5030 4-9-9 **75**.... DavidParkes(5) 4 75
(Simon Hodgson) *led to post: w ldrs: led over 6f out: rdn and hdd over 1f out: styd on same pce* **12/1**

0046 **7** 1 ¾ **Dutch Gallery**[27] 4631 3-9-2 **70**.... RichardKingscote 8 66
(Tom Dascombe) *hld up: rdn over 1f out: no imp fnl f* **4/1**[2]

5400 **8** nk **Berkeley Vale**[20] 4868 5-10-0 **75**....(v) TomMarquand 6 70
(Roger Teal) *chsd ldrs: pushed along over 6f out: rdn over 2f out: styd on same pce fr over 1f out* **13/2**[3]

1m 48.11s (-1.99) **Going Correction** -0.075s/f (Stan)
WFA 3 from 4yo+ 7lb **8** Ran SP% **117.6**
Speed ratings (Par 103): **105,103,103,102,102 101,100,99**
CSF £30.42 CT £92.13 TOTE £8.60: £2.20, £1.80, £1.80; EX 31.50 Trifecta £311.20.
Owner Grange Park Racing X, T P & D McMahon **Bred** D McMahon **Trained** Constable Burton, N Yorks
■ Stewards' Enquiry : Rowan Scott two-day ban: careless riding (2-4 sep)

FOCUS
The best-quality handicap on the card, with all bar one of these rated within 5lb of the ratings ceiling, but not a race that took as much winning as expected. The fourth have been rated close to his Wolverhampton spring form.

5610 BIRMINGHAM TO THE WORLD H'CAP 1m 1f 103y (Tp)
9:20 (9:21) (Class 6) (0-60,65) 3-Y-O+ **£2,587** (£770; £384; £192) **Stalls** Low

Form RPR

0401 **1** **Cape Crystal (IRE)**[3] 5529 3-9-10 **65** 6ex....(p) LukeMorris 4 78+
(Sir Mark Prescott Bt) *trckd ldrs: shkn up to ld over 1f out: pushed out* **10/11**[1]

0012 **2** *2 1/4* **Anneani (IRE)**[3] 5513 4-9-7 **55**.................................... JFEgan 1 62
(David Evans) *hld up in tch: plld hrd: rdn to chse wnr over 1f out: styd on* **5/1**[3]

-062 **3** *2 1/2* **Ahraam (IRE)**[16] 5019 3-9-1 **56**.................................... JackMitchell 10 58
(Harry Whittington) *chsd ldrs: rdn and hung lft over 1f out: no ex fnl f* **18/1**

0245 **4** *1/2* **Gladys Cooper (IRE)**[18] 4936 3-9-3 **58**.......................... ThomasBrown 5 59
(Ed Walker) *led: hdd over 5f out: led again over 3f out: rdn and hdd over 1f out: wknd ins fnl f* **12/1**

6000 **5** *1 1/4* **Cahar Fad (IRE)**[14] 5130 4-9-4 **52**..........................(bt) AdamBeschizza 7 51
(Steph Hollinshead) *hld up: hdwy over 6f out: led over 5f out tl over 3f out: rdn and nt clr run over 1f out: wknd fnl f* **28/1**

3235 **6** *hd* **Castle Talbot (IRE)**[10] 5252 4-9-10 **58**..........................(p) ShaneKelly 6 57
(Richard Hughes) *s.i.s: hld up: rdn and hung lft over 1f out: nvr nrr* **16/1**

3154 **7** *1/2* **Filament Of Gold (USA)**[14] 5130 5-9-5 **60**...........(p) MitchGodwin(7) 11 58
(Roy Brotherton) *hld up: pushed along over 5f out: rdn over 2f out: nvr on terms* **22/1**

050- **8** *1 1/4* **King Of Cornwall (IRE)**[332] 6628 3-8-12 **53**.........[1] RichardKingscote 9 48
(David Lanigan) *prom: rdn over 2f out: wknd fnl f* **3/1**[2]

00 **9** *3 1/2* **Vale Of Rock (IRE)**[15] 5085 3-8-6 **47**.......................... AndrewMullen 3 36
(Michael Appleby) *mid-div: rdn 1/2-way: wknd 2f out* **66/1**

-450 **10** *4* **Miss Fortune**[178] 688 3-8-5 **46** oh1.................................... DannyBrock 2 27
(Mark Usher) *hld up: rdn over 2f out: wknd over 1f out* **66/1**

1m 59.81s (-0.99) **Going Correction** -0.075s/f (Stan)
WFA 3 from 4yo+ 7lb **10** Ran SP% **123.7**
Speed ratings (Par 101): **101,99,96,96,95 95,94,93,90,86**
CSF £6.30 CT £54.06 TOTE £1.90: £1.10, £1.60, £4.50; EX 6.90 Trifecta £55.30.
Owner Axom LVII **Bred** Rockfield Farm **Trained** Newmarket, Suffolk

FOCUS
A modest finale, taken apart by the penalised winner. The third has been rated close to his recent form.
T/Plt: £9.40 to a £1 stake. Pool: £73,650.71 - 5705.39 winning units T/Qpdt: £3.30 to a £1 stake. Pool: £5,518.77 - 1231.88 winning units **Colin Roberts**

5583 YORK (L-H)
Friday, August 19

OFFICIAL GOING: Good to firm changing to good after race 2 (2.30)
Wind: Light across Weather: Heavy cloud and showers

5611 SKY BET FIRST RACE SPECIAL STKS (H'CAP) 1m 4f
1:55 (1:55) (Class 2) (0-105,105) 3-Y-O+

£40,462 (£12,116; £6,058; £3,029; £1,514; £760) **Stalls** Centre

Form RPR

1132 **1** **Barsanti (IRE)**[41] 4164 4-9-10 **105**.................................... AndreaAtzeni 2 114
(Roger Varian) *lw: hld up towards rr: smooth hdwy 3f out: cl up 2f out: rdn to take narrow advantage over 1f out: drvn ins fnl f: kpt on wl towards fin* **5/1**[1]

4510 **2** *nk* **Shakopee**[24] 4731 4-8-11 **92**.................................... JamieSpencer 8 100
(Luca Cumani) *hld up in rr: hdwy 3f out: chsd ldrs wl over 1f out: rdn to chal ent fnl f: sn drvn and ev ch tl no ex towards fin* **8/1**[2]

0-06 **3** *hd* **Moonmeister (IRE)**[21] 4850 5-8-1 **82**..........................(t) FrannyNorton 4 90
(A J Martin, Ire) *lw: dwlt and towards rr: hdwy on inner 3f out: chsd ldrs 2f out: sn rdn and chal jst over 1f out: drvn and ev ch ins fnl f: sn edgd rt and no ex towards fin* **8/1**[2]

0131 **4** *2* **Stars Over The Sea (USA)**[16] 5031 5-9-5 **100**.................. JoeFanning 6 105
(Mark Johnston) *t.k.h: trckd ldng pair on inner: hdwy to ld 3f out: jnd and rdn 2f out: hdd over 1f out: cl up ent fnl f: drvn and hld whn n.m.r and hmpd last 100yds* **5/1**[1]

0116 **5** *nk* **Yorkidding**[12] 5219 4-8-12 **93**.................................... PJMcDonald 14 97
(Mark Johnston) *hld up in midfield: rdn along and hdwy on outer wl over 2f out: drvn and edgd lft over 1f out: kpt on fnl f: nrst fin* **11/1**

0042 **6** *nk* **Gabrial's King (IRE)**[13] 5157 7-8-9 **90**...................... GeorgeChaloner 12 94
(Richard Fahey) *lw: trckd ldrs: hdwy 3f out: rdn along 2f out: drvn over 1f out: kpt on same pce* **20/1**

-006 **7** *3/4* **Dawn Missile**[14] 5116 4-8-6 **87**.................................... PaulHanagan 15 89
(William Haggas) *lw: stdd and swtchd lft s: hld up and bhd: gd hdwy 3f out: rdn along whn n.m.r and swtchd lft over 1f out: styd on wl fnl f: nrst fin* **16/1**

-166 **8** *3 1/4* **Barye**[13] 5173 5-9-1 **96**.................................... ShaneKelly 1 93
(Richard Hughes) *in tch: hdwy over 3f out: chsd ldrs over 2f out: sn rdn: drvn wl over 1f out: grad wknd* **25/1**

0133 **9** *3 1/4* **Dominada (IRE)**[17] 4969 4-8-1 **82**.................................[1] JoeyHaynes 13 74
(Brian Ellison) *chsd ldrs on outer: pushed along over 4f out: rdn over 3f out: drvn wl over 1f out: grad wknd* **25/1**

100/ **10** *1/2* **Restraint Of Trade (IRE)**[398] 2142 6-8-7 **88**.............. ConnorBeasley 3 79
(Jennie Candlish) *a towards rr* **66/1**

6632 **11** *2 1/2* **Odeon**[10] 5275 5-8-0 **81** oh2.................................... AndrewMullen 11 68
(James Given) *swtg: cl up: disp ld over 3f out: rdn along over 2f out: sn wknd* **25/1**

4254 **12** *9* **Gold Prince (IRE)**[13] 5144 4-9-1 **96**..........................(b) FrankieDettori 10 69
(Sylvester Kirk) *trckd ldrs: effrt on outer over 3f out and sn rdn along: drvn 2f out and sn wknd* **10/1**[3]

0044 **13** *1* **Blue Hussar (IRE)**[16] 5031 5-8-3 **84**..........................(p) TomMarquand 5 55
(Micky Hammond) *a towards rr* **25/1**

110 **14** *10* **Sindarban (IRE)**[34] 4407 5-8-10 **91**.................................... PhillipMakin 9 46
(Keith Dalgleish) *chsd ldrs: rdn along 3f out: sn wknd* **8/1**[2]

6/04 **15** *21* **Mijhaar**[14] 5116 8-9-0 **95**..........................(v[1]) DanielTudhope 7 17
(David O'Meara) *lw: slt ld: rdn along 4f out: hdd 3f out and sn wknd* **14/1**

2m 30.38s (-2.82) **Going Correction** +0.025s/f (Good) **15** Ran SP% **118.3**
Speed ratings (Par 109): **110,109,109,108,108 107,107,105,103,102 101,95,94,87,73**
CSF £38.41 CT £319.06 TOTE £5.00: £1.80, £2.90, £3.10; EX 28.10 Trifecta £207.50.
Owner Sheikh Mohammed Obaid Al Maktoum **Bred** Glenvale Stud **Trained** Newmarket, Suffolk

FOCUS
Rail moved out 3 yards, adding 9 yards to race distance. The forecast rain began at around noon, only light at first, and after winning the opener Andrea Atzeni said of the ground: "It's sort of getting in, it's probably a bit loose on top but still firm underneath." This warm handicap was run at a solid gallop, the first three coming from the latter half of the field, with the time 2.38sec outside the standard. The runners came up the centre of the track in the straight. The fifth helps set the standard, while the sixth has been rated to his latest form.

5612 WEATHERBYS HAMILTON LONSDALE CUP (BRITISH CHAMPIONS SERIES) (GROUP 2) 2m 88y
2:30 (2:30) (Class 1) 3-Y-O+

£113,420 (£43,000; £21,520; £10,720; £5,380; £2,700) **Stalls** Low

Form RPR

-236 **1** **Quest For More (IRE)**[22] 4799 6-9-3 111......................(b) GeorgeBaker 7 116
(Roger Charlton) *swtg: mde all and sn clr: pushed along and qcknd over 3f out: rdn and qcknd 2f out: drvn ent fnl f: kpt on strly towards fin* **9/2**[3]

1042 **2** *3 1/2* **Pallasator**[22] 4799 7-9-3 113.................................... OisinMurphy 2 113
(Sir Mark Prescott Bt) *trckd clr ldr: tk clsr order over 4f out: rdn along over 2f out and sn sltly outpcd: drvn over 1f out: kpt on wl u.p fnl f* **7/2**[2]

-264 **3** *nk* **Wicklow Brave**[22] 4799 7-9-3 111.................................... PatSmullen 3 111
(W P Mullins, Ire) *hld up in rr: smooth hdwy over 3f out: trckd ldrs 2f out: chal over 1f out: sn rdn and ev ch: drvn ins fnl f: kpt on same pce last 100yds* **6/1**

40-3 **4** *3 1/4* **Trip To Paris (IRE)**[34] 4392 5-9-3 116.............................. GrahamLee 1 108
(Ed Dunlop) *trckd ldng pair: hdwy over 3f out and sn pushed along: rdn to chse ldrs 2f out: sn drvn and wknd over 1f out* **10/3**[1]

2210 **5** *1* **Clever Cookie**[64] 3298 8-9-3 113..........................(p) PJMcDonald 4 106
(Peter Niven) *lw: hld up: hdwy and in tch over 4f out: pushed along 3f out: rdn along 2f out: sn no imp* **7/2**[2]

2000 **6** *13* **Suegioo (FR)**[22] 4799 7-9-3 107..........................(b) PaulHanagan 5 91
(Richard Fahey) *in tch: pushed along 5f out: rdn along over 3f out: outpcd and eased fnl 2f* **28/1**

1-20 **7** *8* **Curbyourenthusiasm (IRE)**[22] 4799 5-9-3 109........... JamieSpencer 6 81
(David Simcock) *hld up in rr: effrt 4f out: rdn along 3f out: nvr a factor* **7/1**

3m 32.57s (-1.93) **Going Correction** +0.025s/f (Good) **7** Ran SP% **115.9**
Speed ratings (Par 115): **105,103,103,101,100 94,90**
CSF £21.17 TOTE £5.70: £2.80, £2.10; EX 20.70 Trifecta £109.30.
Owner H R H Sultan Ahmad Shah **Bred** Epona Bloodstock Ltd **Trained** Beckhampton, Wilts

FOCUS
Add 9 yards to race distance. A fair edition of this Group 2 staying prize. The runners kicked up turf along the way and it threw up a tight three-way finish. The winner has been rated as running a small pb for now, while the second and third help set the level.

5613 SKY BET CITY OF YORK STKS (GROUP 3) 7f
3:05 (3:05) (Class 1) 3-Y-O+

£85,065 (£32,250; £16,140; £8,040; £4,035; £1,012) **Stalls** Low

Form RPR

-124 **1** **Nemoralia (USA)**[40] 4185 3-8-7 112 ow1.......................... JamieSpencer 7 114
(Jeremy Noseda) *hld up in tch: gd hdwy over 2f out: rdn to ld appr fnl f and sn edgd rt: drvn out* **15/8**[1]

1340 **2** *1 1/4* **So Beloved**[23] 4754 6-9-0 113.................................... DanielTudhope 4 115
(David O'Meara) *lw: hld up in tch: hdwy over 2f out: effrt and chsd ldrs whn n.m.r and sltly hmpd ent fnl f: sn rdn and kpt on* **11/2**

4215 **3** *1/2* **Jallota**[6] 5404 5-9-0 110.................................... MartinHarley 5 114
(Charles Hills) *trckd ldrs: hdwy whn n.m.r and hmpd over 1f out: sn rdn and chsd wnr ins fnl f: sn drvn and kpt on same pce* **14/1**

-121 **4** *1 1/4* **Librisa Breeze**[27] 4625 4-9-0 107.................................... RobertWinston 11 110
(Dean Ivory) *hld up in rr: hdwy over 2f out: rdn over 1f out: kpt on wl u.p fnl f* **9/2**[2]

0010 **5** *1 3/4* **Birchwood (IRE)**[24] 4733 3-8-9 113.................................... PaulHanagan 8 104
(Richard Fahey) *lw: cl up: rdn to ld 2f out: drvn and hdd appr fnl f: one pce after* **14/1**

1332 **6** *1* **Forge**[21] 4822 3-8-9 108.................................... PatSmullen 2 101
(Sir Michael Stoute) *chsd ldng pair: rdn along over 2f out: drvn and edgd rt over 1f out: sn wknd* **5/1**[3]

2000 **6** *dht* **Dream Dubai**[24] 4733 3-8-9 105.................................... OisinMurphy 6 101
(Sylvester Kirk) *towards rr: hdwy 2f out: rdn over 1f out: drvn and kpt on fnl f* **50/1**

1054 **8** *1/2* **Flash Fire (IRE)**[27] 4625 4-9-0 109.................................... MartinLane 3 102
(Charlie Appleby) *swtg: chsd ldng pair: rdn over 2f out: drvn and edgd lft over 1f out: sn wknd* **16/1**

1/46 **9** *4* **Charming Thought**[34] 4393 4-9-0 111..........................(t) WilliamBuick 9 91
(Charlie Appleby) *a towards rr* **12/1**

5331 **10** *2 3/4* **Glen Moss (IRE)**[48] 3891 7-9-0 104.................................... PaulMulrennan 1 83
(Michael Dods) *set str pce: rdn along 3f out: hdd 2f out and sn wknd* **25/1**

1m 22.16s (-3.14) **Going Correction** -0.10s/f (Good)
WFA 3 from 4yo+ 5lb **10** Ran SP% **117.7**
Speed ratings (Par 113): **113,111,111,109,107 106,106,105,101,98**
CSF £12.36 TOTE £2.60: £1.20, £1.90, £3.60; EX 11.40 Trifecta £114.20.
Owner T Allan, J Lovat & C Pigram **Bred** Alberta Davies **Trained** Newmarket, Suffolk

FOCUS
The going was officially changed to good prior to this race, after the track had taken 3mm of rain during the day, but the time of this truly run event was almost bang on the standard, suggesting that this was still decent ground. This looked a quality Group 3. They raced more towards the inside rail this time. The runner-up has been rated close to form, and the third as running a small pb.

5614 COOLMORE NUNTHORPE STKS (BRITISH CHAMPIONS SERIES) (GROUP 1) 5f
3:40 (3:41) (Class 1) 2-Y-O+

£236,622 (£89,708; £44,896; £22,364; £11,224; £5,632) **Stalls** Centre

Form RPR

-201 **1** **Mecca's Angel (IRE)**[34] 4413 5-9-8 120.......................... PaulMulrennan 7 125
(Michael Dods) *warm: cl up: shkn up 2f out and sn led: rdn over 1f out: kpt on strly* **9/2**[2]

2-41 **2** *2* **Limato (IRE)**[41] 4151 4-9-11 121.................................... HarryBentley 4 121
(Henry Candy) *trckd ldrs: hdwy and swtchd lft over 1f out: rdn to chse wnr ins fnl f: sn drvn and no imp* **15/8**[1]

5101 **3** *2* **Take Cover**[21] 4824 9-9-11 113.................................... DavidAllan 12 114
(David C Griffiths) *wnt rt s: slt ld to 1/2-way: cl up: rdn wl over 1f out: drvn ent fnl f: kpt on* **25/1**

2200 **4** *nk* **Cotai Glory**[21] 4824 4-9-11 112.................................... GeorgeBaker 10 113
(Charles Hills) *in tch: hdwy 2f out and sn rdn: styd on fnl f: nrst fin* **33/1**

2322 **5** *hd* **Thesme**[10] 5268 4-9-8 99 .... AndreaAtzeni 9 109
(Nigel Tinkler) *lw: cl up: led 1/2-way: rdn and hdd wl over 1f out: sn drvn and kpt on same pce* **66/1**

1114 **6** *nse* **Profitable (IRE)**[41] 4151 4-9-11 117 .... AdamKirby 13 112+
(Clive Cox) *lw: bmpd s and midfield: hdwy wl over 1f out: sn swtchd rt and rdn: styd on fnl f: nrst fin* **7/1**[3]

003 **7** *1/2* **Goldream**[21] 4824 7-9-11 114 ....(p) MartinHarley 2 110
(Robert Cowell) *chsd ldrs: hdwy on inner over 1f out: sn rdn: kpt on same pce fnl f* **14/1**

004 **8** *1/2* **Sole Power**[34] 4413 9-9-11 111 .... PatSmullen 15 108
(Edward Lynam, Ire) *towards rr: rdn and hdwy over 1f out: kpt on fnl f: n.d* **28/1**

2212 **9** *1* **Brando**[34] 4413 4-9-11 110 .... TomEaves 5 105
(Kevin Ryan) *lw: chsd ldrs: rdn wl over 1f out: wknd appr fnl f* **20/1**

3202 **10** *hd* **Danzeno**[19] 4916 5-9-11 112 .... TomQueally 11 104
(Michael Appleby) *dwlt and towards rr: sme hdwy wl over 1f out: sn rdn and n.d* **16/1**

-400 **11** *hd* **Pearl Secret**[21] 4824 7-9-11 109 .... OisinMurphy 3 103
(David Barron) *towards rr: hdwy 2f out: sn rdn and n.d* **33/1**

0300 **12** *2 1/4* **Goken (FR)**[21] 4824 4-9-11 109 .... JamieSpencer 1 95
(Kevin Ryan) *lw: a towards rr* **25/1**

115 **13** *3/4* **Prince Of Lir (IRE)**[26] 4694 2-8-1 0 .... TomMarquand 14 85
(Robert Cowell) *chsd ldrs on outer: rdn along 2f out: sn wknd* **33/1**

3111 **14** *hd* **Silver Rainbow (IRE)**[20] 4905 4-9-8 106 .... WilliamBuick 16 89
(Charles Hills) *a towards rr* **33/1**

1124 **15** *nk* **Easton Angel (IRE)**[21] 4824 3-9-6 110 .... FrankieDettori 17 88+
(Michael Dods) *dwlt: racd wd: a towards rr* **12/1**

0046 **16** *3/4* **Iffranesia (FR)**[48] 3909 6-9-8 100 .... AdamBeschizza 6 85
(Robert Cowell) *chsd ldrs on inner: rdn wl over 1f out: sn drvn and wknd* **100/1**

2352 **17** *hd* **Washington DC (IRE)**[21] 4824 3-9-9 112 ....(t) SeamieHeffernan 18 87
(A P O'Brien, Ire) *midfield on outer: effrt and hdwy over 2f out: sn rdn and btn* **20/1**

0023 **18** *1 3/4* **Out Do**[13] 5143 7-9-11 105 ....(b[1]) DanielTudhope 20 81
(David O'Meara) *a in rr* **66/1**

1001 **19** *6* **Yalta (IRE)**[23] 4755 2-8-1 111 .... JoeFanning 19 51
(Mark Johnston) *chsd ldrs on outer: rdn along 2f out: sn wknd* **12/1**

56.24s (-3.06) **Going Correction** -0.175s/f (Firm) **19 Ran SP% 129.8**
Speed ratings: **117,113,110,110,109 109,108,108,106,106 105,102,101,100,100 99,98,95,86**
CSF £11.86 CT £213.77 TOTE £5.40: £2.10, £1.60, £6.50; EX 17.60 Trifecta £366.60.
Owner David T J Metcalfe **Bred** Yeomanstown Stud & Doc Bloodstock **Trained** Denton, Co Durham

FOCUS
This was a strong Nunthorpe no doubt and the form is rock-solid. However, those drawn high were at a real disadvantage and it paid to be up there. The third helps set the standard and, while the fifth is a slight doubt, she is progressive and this race played to her strengths. The winner has been rated as running the best Nunthorpe figure since Oasis Dream (129, 2003) and the same figure as Lochsong back in 1993.

5615 BRITISH STALLION STUDS EBF CONVIVIAL MAIDEN STKS (PLUS 10 RACE) 7f

4:20 (4:22) (Class 2) 2-Y-O

£37,350 (£11,184; £5,592; £2,796; £1,398; £702) **Stalls** Low

Form RPR

2 **1** **Rivet (IRE)**[28] 4580 2-9-5 0 .... FrankieDettori 4 93+
(William Haggas) *str: gd-bodied: scope: warm: wnt rt s: hld up: hdwy on outer over 2f out: rdn to ld and hung bdly lft jst over 1f out: kpt on strly* **15/8**[1]

5 **2** *3 1/4* **Contrapposto (IRE)**[27] 4649 2-9-5 0 .... PaulHanagan 5 82
(David Menuisier) *q str: hld up in rr: gd hdwy wl over 1f out: rdn and styd on strly fnl f* **50/1**

3 *nk* **Via Serendipity** 2-9-5 0 .... PatSmullen 2 81+
(Hugo Palmer) *tall: lengthy: lw: trckd ldrs on inner: smooth hdwy to chal wl over 1f out: rdn and ev ch ent fnl f: sn drvn and kpt on same pce* **3/1**[2]

4 **4** *nk* **Celestation**[9] 5289 2-9-0 0 .... JoeFanning 3 75
(Mark Johnston) *leggy: prom: led over 2f out: rdn over 1f out: hdd appr fnl f: kpt on same pce* **50/1**

5 *3/4* **First Up (IRE)** 2-9-5 0 .... JamieSpencer 8 78+
(Jeremy Noseda) *q str: towards rr: hdwy over 2f out: rdn over 1f out: kpt on fnl f* **28/1**

3 **6** *nk* **Portledge (IRE)**[29] 4545 2-9-5 0 .... PJMcDonald 1 77
(James Bethell) *leggy: hld up: hdwy over 2f out: rdn wl over 1f out: kpt on fnl f* **33/1**

03 **7** *1/2* **Black Trilby (IRE)**[20] 4866 2-9-5 0 .... AdamKirby 7 78
(Clive Cox) *str: lw: led 2f: cl up: rdn along 2f out: drvn whn hmpd jst over 1f out: sn one pce* **11/2**[3]

325 **8** *nse* **Abiento (IRE)**[20] 4866 2-9-5 78 .... TonyHamilton 6 76
(Richard Fahey) *unf: t.k.h: in tch: hdwy to chse ldrs over 2f out: rdn wl over 1f out: kpt on same pce* **25/1**

9 *nse* **Capezzano (USA)** 2-9-5 0 .... WilliamBuick 11 76+
(Charlie Appleby) *athletic: a towards rr* **14/1**

2 **10** *4* **Max Zorin (IRE)**[23] 4775 2-9-5 0 .... DavidProbert 14 69+
(Andrew Balding) *str: trckd ldng pair on outer: pushed along over 2f out: rdn wl over 1f out: hld whn hmpd jst over 1f out: wknd after* **14/1**

4 **11** *nk* **Star Stream**[20] 4866 2-9-5 0 .... RoystonFfrench 10 65
(Marcus Tregoning) *leggy: chsd ldrs: rdn along over 2f out: sn wknd* **12/1**

2 **12** *3 1/4* **Dance Teacher (IRE)**[17] 4988 2-9-0 0 .... OisinMurphy 12 54+
(Ralph Beckett) *angular: lw: cl up: led over 4f out: rdn along and hdd over 2f out: sn wknd* **11/1**

13 *1/2* **Upgrade** 2-9-5 0 .... BenCurtis 13 55+
(K R Burke) *leggy: a in rr* **40/1**

1m 24.33s (-0.97) **Going Correction** -0.10s/f (Good) **13 Ran SP% 121.1**
Speed ratings (Par 100): **101,97,96,96,95 95,94,94,94,90 89,86,85**
Midaawi was withdrawn. Price at time of withdrawal 33/1 - Rule 4 does not apply CSF £133.51 TOTE £2.70: £1.30, £14.50, £1.70; EX 121.30 Trifecta £719.20.
Owner The Starship Partnership **Bred** Des Scott **Trained** Newmarket, Suffolk

FOCUS
Britain's richest maiden worth, with the Plus 10 bonus Rivet qualified for, a scarcely believable 47,350GBP to the winner. It hasn't thrown up any true stars since becoming a 7f race in 2010 but this year's edition looks sure to prove a fertile source of winners. Low draws did best. Eleven of the next dozen to chase home Beautiful Morning last year have won since.

5616 NATIONWIDE ACCIDENT REPAIR SERVICES STKS (H'CAP) 1m

4:55 (5:00) (Class 2) (0-100,100) 3-Y-O

£37,350 (£11,184; £5,592; £2,796; £1,398; £702) **Stalls** Low

Form RPR

1041 **1** **Arcanada (IRE)**[55] 3635 3-9-6 99 .... RoystonFfrench 2 109
(Tom Dascombe) *lw: trckd ldrs: hdwy over 2f out: led 1 1/2f out and sn rdn clr: drvn out* **5/1**[1]

2150 **2** *3/4* **Banksea**[22] 4797 3-9-1 94 .... AndreaAtzeni 7 102+
(Luca Cumani) *hld up: hdwy and in tch 3f out: effrt and n.m.r wl over 1f out: sn rdn: styd on to chse wnr ins fnl f: sn drvn and kpt on* **5/1**[1]

0553 **3** *1 3/4* **Candelisa (IRE)**[27] 4644 3-9-1 94 ....(p) GrahamLee 1 98
(Jedd O'Keeffe) *warm: hld up in midfield: hdwy on inner over 2f out: rdn wl over 1f out: drvn and kpt on fnl f* **20/1**

4131 **4** *1 1/4* **Weekend Offender (FR)**[23] 4769 3-8-7 86 .... TomEaves 17 87
(Kevin Ryan) *in rr: hdwy wl over 2f out: rdn wl over 1f out: styd on wl fnl f: nrst fin* **25/1**

2001 **5** *1 1/4* **Another Touch**[13] 5175 3-9-2 95 .... TonyHamilton 19 93+
(Richard Fahey) *in rr: hdwy wl over 2f out: rdn wl over 1f out: styd on wl fnl f: nrst fin* **16/1**

4141 **6** *nk* **Viscount Barfield**[27] 4631 3-8-9 88 .... DavidProbert 8 86
(Andrew Balding) *towards rr: hdwy wl over 2f out: rdn wl over 1f out: kpt on strly fnl f: nrst fin* **6/1**[2]

2143 **7** *1 3/4* **Heir To A Throne (FR)**[19] 4917 3-8-5 84 .... ShaneGray 5 78
(Kevin Ryan) *prom: cl up 1/2-way: rdn along over 2f out: drvn wl over 1f out: grad wknd* **25/1**

1040 **8** *1 1/4* **Manson**[27] 4624 3-9-1 94 .... FrankieDettori 13 85
(Dominic Ffrench Davis) *in rr: hdwy wl over 2f out: rdn wl over 1f out: kpt on fnl f* **12/1**[3]

4- **9** *hd* **Markhan (USA)**[30] 4542 3-9-1 94 ....(t) MartinHarley 14 84
(David Marnane, Ire) *dwlt and in rr: hdwy 3f out: rdn along 2f out: kpt on fnl f* **20/1**

10 *1 1/2* **Spruce Meadows (IRE)**[25] 4720 3-8-9 88 ....(p) PaulMulrennan 9 75
(John James Feane, Ire) *in tch: hdwy on outer to chse ldrs 3f out: rdn along 2f out: sn drvn and wknd* **12/1**[3]

1302 **11** *3/4* **Dream Mover (IRE)**[20] 4886 3-8-11 90 ....(t) DarryllHolland 18 75
(Marco Botti) *lw: t.k.h: chsd ldrs: rdn along over 2f out: drvn and edgd lft over 1f out: wknd* **25/1**

0223 **12** *1 1/4* **Twin Sails**[13] 5175 3-9-3 96 ....(b) PJMcDonald 16 78
(Dean Ivory) *chsd ldrs: rdn along over 2f out: wknd wl over 1f out* **14/1**

4632 **13** *nk* **Holy Grail (IRE)**[21] 4841 3-8-2 81 .... JoeFanning 15 62
(Simon West) *chsd ldrs: rdn along 3f out: drvn over 2f out: sn wknd* **50/1**

-012 **14** *nk* **Bobby Wheeler (IRE)**[20] 4867 3-9-0 93 .... AdamKirby 11 74+
(Clive Cox) *led: rdn along over 2f out: drvn and hdd 1 1/2f out: sn wknd* **5/1**[1]

4111 **15** *1 1/2* **Blacklister**[12] 5201 3-8-4 83 6ex .... PaulHanagan 4 60
(Mick Channon) *lw: chsd ldrs: rdn along 3f out: sn wknd* **16/1**

010 **16** *6* **Zealous (IRE)**[49] 3855 3-8-4 83 ow1 .... BenCurtis 10 47
(Alan Swinbank) *in tch on outer: rdn along wl over 2f out: sn wknd* **25/1**

2102 **17** *nse* **Dot Green (IRE)**[15] 5089 3-8-4 83 .... JoeyHaynes 3 46
(Mark H Tompkins) *in tch: rdn along 3f out: sn wknd* **66/1**

1m 37.47s (-1.53) **Going Correction** +0.025s/f (Good) **17 Ran SP% 126.5**
Speed ratings (Par 106): **108,107,105,104,103 102,100,99,99,98 97,96,95,95,93 87,87**
CSF £26.27 CT £372.45 TOTE £6.20: £1.90, £1.80, £4.50, £4.90; EX 37.80 Trifecta £604.10.
Owner The Arcanada Partnership **Bred** C J Foy **Trained** Malpas, Cheshire

FOCUS
Add 8 yards to race distance. This top 3yo handicap was run at a strong pace. The runner-up is still on the upgrade, while the third and fourth help set the standard.
T/Jkpt: £16,654.70 to a £1 stake. Pool: £16,654.70 - 1 winning unit T/Plt: £56.50 to a £1 stake. Pool: £337,088.84 - 4348.74 winning units T/Qpdt: £9.60 to a £1 stake. Pool: £20,764.1 - 1599.45 winning units **Joe Rowntree**

5617 - 5619a (Foreign Racing) - See Raceform Interactive

5589 KILLARNEY (L-H)

Friday, August 19

OFFICIAL GOING: Flat course - good to yielding changing to yielding after race 2 (5.55) changing to yielding to soft after race 3 (6.25) hurdle course - yielding

5620a PLAZA HOTEL H'CAP 1m 6f

6:55 (6:56) 3-Y-O+ **£4,748** (£1,466; £694; £308; £115)

RPR

1 **Prickly (IRE)**[21] 4576 6-9-4 69 .... BillyLee 4 81+
(E J O'Grady, Ire) *chsd ldrs in 4th: travelled wl into 2nd 4f out: led gng easily under 3f out and sn clr: eased ins fnl f: nt extended* **4/1**[2]

2 *6* **Sword Of The Lord**[8] 2174 6-9-2 70 .... DonnachaO'Brien(3) 12 74
(Nigel Twiston-Davies) *racd in rr: sme prog into mid-div 4f out: sn rdn: styd on wl into 2nd ins fnl f: no trble easy wnr* **11/1**

3 *1/2* **Three Star General**[23] 4779 3-8-7 75 ....(b) AnaO'Brien(5) 9 78
(A P O'Brien, Ire) *sn cl up on outer: tacked across to ld after 2f: hdd under 3f out and sn no match for wnr: kpt on one pce and dropped to 3rd ins fnl f* **8/1**[3]

4 *1/2* **Zemario (IRE)**[37] 4284 10-8-1 57 ....(p) KillianLeonard(5) 5 60
(Joseph G Murphy, Ire) *led early: sn hdd: chsd ldng pair in 3rd: pushed along in 4th 4f out: rdn in 3rd over 2f out: sn no imp: kpt on one pce* **20/1**

5 *1 1/2* **Hazariban (IRE)**[6] 5426 7-9-1 66 ....(t) GaryCarroll 11 67
(Seamus Fahey, Ire) *hld up: dropped to rr at 1/2-way: prog 2f out: kpt on wl into 5th ins fnl f: nrst fin* **12/1**

6 *8 1/2* **Sea's Aria (IRE)**[6] 5427 5-8-7 58 ....(t) LeighRoche 1 48
(Denis Gerard Hogan, Ire) *hld up: 9th at 1/2-way: rdn and prog in modest 5th under 2f out: no ex fnl f and wknd* **4/1**[2]

7 *22* **Whats The Plot (IRE)**[19] 4922 4-9-2 67 .... ColinKeane 3 25
(A L T Moore, Ire) *racd in mid-div on inner: rdn and no imp in 6th under 2f out: no ex* **7/2**[1]

8 *6 1/2* **Fly Round The Bend (IRE)**[17] 5003 5-8-4 55 oh7 .... ChrisHayes 8 4
(John J Walsh, Ire) *hld up: rdn 5f out: dropped towards rr over 3f out and sn no ex* **11/1**

9 7 **Moone Dancer (IRE)**[15] 5097 4-9-7 **72**.................... ColmO'Donoghue 2 11
(Mrs John Harrington, Ire) *led on inner tl narrowly hdd after 2f: chsd ldrs tl rdn and wknd to rr 4f out and sn detached: no ex* **10/1**

10 22 **Runmhar (IRE)**[3] 5534 3-8-5 **68**..(t) RoryCleary 7
(J S Bolger, Ire) *bit slowly away: sn mid-div: keen and clsr to chse ldrs after 6f in 3rd: wknd qckly 4f out: eased fnl f: t.o* **8/1**[3]

11 18 **Shamar (FR)**[14] 5133 8-9-7 **72**..[1] KevinManning 6
(R K Watson, Ire) *chsd ldrs: rdn in mid-div 5f out: sn dropped towards rr: eased fr over 2f out: t.o* **25/1**

3m 12.93s (-3.57)
WFA 3 from 4yo+ 12lb **11** Ran SP% **126.5**
CSF £51.83 CT £352.26 TOTE £4.40: £1.60, £4.30, £2.60; DF 37.00 Trifecta £151.60.
Owner Simon J H Davis **Bred** Pat McCarthy **Trained** Ballynonty, Co Tipperary

FOCUS
In deteriorating conditions, this open-looking handicap was turned into a procession. The winner has been rated in line with the best view of his jumps form.

5621 - 5622 - VOID

5282 BATH (L-H)

Saturday, August 20

OFFICIAL GOING: Firm changing to good to firm (firm in places) after race 2 (5.40) changing to good after race 4 (6.35)
Wind: Fresh against Weather: Showers

5623 CUTLER & GROSS MAIDEN STKS 1m 5f 22y

5:10 (5:10) (Class 5) 3-Y-O+ **£3,067** (£905; £453) **Stalls** High

Form RPR

2202 **1** **Withhold**[19] 4948 3-9-3 79... SteveDrowne 2 81
(Charles Hills) *mde all: rdn over 2f out: styd on u.p* **1/1**[1]

2 1/2 **Arthur Mc Bride (IRE)**[25] 7-10-0 0...................................(t) ShaneKelly 3 80
(Nigel Twiston-Davies) *a.p: chsd wnr over 2f out: rdn over 1f out: ev ch ins fnl f: unable qck nr fin* **10/1**

4-04 **3** 3/4 **Satish**[29] 4597 3-9-3 80...(b) NickyMackay 7 79
(John Gosden) *hld up in tch: racd keenly: rdn and hung lft over 1f out: nt run on* **11/4**[2]

06 **4** 7 **Maqam (IRE)**[23] 4792 3-8-12 0... JimmyQuinn 5 64
(Richard Hannon) *chsd ldrs: rdn and ev ch over 2f out: wknd over 1f out* **12/1**

644 **5** 6 **Pc Dixon**[19] 4955 3-8-10 75....................................... KillianHennessy(7) 4 60
(Mick Channon) *plld hrd and prom: hdwy to join wnr over 10f out tl settled into 2nd 7f out: rdn and lost pl over 2f out: wknd wl over 1f out* **7/1**[3]

4 **6** 5 **L Stig**[11] 5255 6-9-9 0.. CiaranMckee(5) 8 52
(John O'Shea) *hld up: sme hdwy over 4f out: wknd over 2f out* **50/1**

4 **7** 14 **Hannah Just Hannah**[23] 4792 7-9-4 0.........................(t) LucyKBarry(5) 1 26
(Matthew Salaman) *s.i.s: a in rr: lost tch fnl 3f* **12/1**

2m 53.1s (1.10) **Going Correction** +0.20s/f (Good)
WFA 3 from 6yo+ 11lb **7** Ran SP% **115.6**
Speed ratings (Par 103): **104,103,103,98,95 92,83**
CSF £13.01 TOTE £1.90: £1.20, £3.30; EX 9.20 Trifecta £22.10.
Owner K Abdullah **Bred** Millsec Limited **Trained** Lambourn, Berks

FOCUS
Races incorporating bottom bend increased by 10yds. An ordinary staying maiden and the winner, who brought the best form into the race, showed a good attitude to get the job done. The winner, third and fourth have been rated close to their marks.

5624 EF MEDISPA BRISTOL H'CAP (BATH SUMMER STAYERS' SERIES QUALIFIER) 1m 5f 22y

5:40 (5:41) (Class 5) (0-70,68) 4-Y-O+ **£2,911** (£866; £432; £216) **Stalls** High

Form RPR

2561 **1** **Rosie Royale (IRE)**[11] 5256 4-8-9 **63**.......................... GeorgeWood(7) 5 71
(Roger Teal) *chsd ldr: wnt upsides over 6f out: rdn to ld over 1f out: edgd lft ins fnl f: drvn out* **3/1**[1]

6012 **2** nk **Rum Swizzle**[20] 4913 4-9-5 **66**.. JohnFahy 7 73
(Harry Dunlop) *hld up: hdwy over 2f out: chsd wnr over 1f out: sn rdn and ev ch: edgd lft: styd on* **7/2**[2]

/04 **3** 3 **Moss Street**[9] 5011 6-8-2 **52**... NoelGarbutt(3) 3 55
(John Flint) *hld up in tch: pushed along over 4f out: rdn over 2f out: no ex wl ins fnl f* **9/2**[3]

4023 **4** nk **Oratorio's Joy (IRE)**[22] 4816 6-9-7 **68**........................[1] WilliamCarson 4 70
(Jamie Osborne) *chsd ldrs: rdn over 2f out: styd on same pce fnl f* **11/2**

1U13 **5** 1 1/4 **Dynamo (IRE)**[34] 2850 5-9-0 **61**..(t) ShaneKelly 8 61
(Richard Hughes) *sn led: qcknd over 2f out: rdn and hdd over 1f out: wknd ins fnl f* **3/1**[1]

3565 **6** 5 **Deepsand (IRE)**[18] 4995 7-8-12 **59**..............................(bt) SteveDrowne 6 52
(Ali Stronge) *s.s: hld up: rdn over 1f out: styng on whn hmpd ent fnl f: no ch after* **9/1**

2m 56.52s (4.52) **Going Correction** +0.20s/f (Good) **6** Ran SP% **115.8**
Speed ratings (Par 103): **94,93,91,91,91 87**
CSF £14.35 CT £45.96 TOTE £3.00: £1.80, £1.90; EX 12.70 Trifecta £57.90.
Owner The Idle B's **Bred** Fergus Cousins **Trained** Great Shefford, Berks

FOCUS
Race distance increased by 10yds. A modest staying handicap run at 3.42sec slower than the opening maiden. The third has been rated to his latest.

5625 MJ CHURCH H'CAP 1m 2f 46y

6:05 (6:05) (Class 6) (0-55,55) 3-Y-O+ **£2,264** (£673; £336; £168) **Stalls** Low

Form RPR

3200 **1** **Bob's Boy**[17] 5021 3-8-11 **53**...(p) RenatoSouza 13 61
(Jose Santos) *chsd ldrs: led over 8f out: clr over 4f out tl rdn wl over 1f out: edgd lft and styd on u.p* **12/1**

0645 **2** 1 1/2 **Azure Amour (IRE)**[17] 5010 4-8-8 **49**.......................[1] GeorgeWood(7) 10 54
(Rod Millman) *hld up: hdwy over 2f out: rdn to chse wnr fnl f: styd on* **12/1**

0-21 **3** 1/2 **Hope Is High**[17] 5011 3-8-7 **52**.............................. JosephineGordon(3) 6 58
(John Berry) *hmpd s: wnt prom over 6f out: rdn over 1f out: styng on whn nt clr run wl ins fnl f* **6/4**[1]

0030 **4** 1/2 **Tamujin (IRE)**[5] 5481 8-9-2 **50**.. SamHitchcott 2 53
(Ken Cunningham-Brown) *hld up: hdwy u.p over 1f out: nt rch ldrs* **28/1**

0232 **5** 3/4 **Nanny Makfi**[23] 4794 3-8-11 **53**...................................... AdamBeschizza 9 55
(Stuart Kittow) *led: hdd over 8f out: remained handy: chsd wnr over 3f out tl rdn over 2f out: styd on same pce ins fnl f* **10/3**[2]

0333 **6** 2 1/4 **Altaira**[16] 5055 5-9-5 **53**.. WilliamCarson 3 51
(Tony Carroll) *prom: chsd wnr over 2f out: sn rdn: lost 2nd 1f out: wknd ins fnl f* **14/1**

0641 **7** 6 **Iballisticvin**[17] 5019 3-8-5 **50**...................................... NoelGarbutt(3) 5 36
(Gary Moore) *hmpd s: hld up: hdwy over 2f out: rdn: hung lft and wknd over 1f out* **5/1**[3]

0040 **8** 3 1/2 **Wassail**[11] 5263 3-8-4 **46** oh1...[1] RaulDaSilva 8 26
(Ed de Giles) *w ldr tl chse wnr over 8f out: rdn and lost 2nd over 3f out: wknd 2f out* **33/1**

4630 **9** 13 **Overlord**[18] 4986 4-9-7 **55**.. JohnFahy 1 10
(Mark Rimell) *hld up: rdn over 2f out: sn wknd* **20/1**

0430 **10** 28 **Opera Buffa (IRE)**[2] 5572 3-8-5 **47**...............................(tp) JimmyQuinn 4
(Steve Flook) *edgd rt s: chsd ldrs: rdn over 3f out: sn wknd* **16/1**

3460 **11** 18 **Faster Company (IRE)**[2] 5572 3-8-5 **47**.............................. RyanPowell 7
(J S Moore) *hmpd s: a bhd* **50/1**

2m 11.51s (0.51) **Going Correction** +0.20s/f (Good)
WFA 3 from 4yo+ 8lb **11** Ran SP% **120.8**
Speed ratings (Par 101): **105,103,103,103,102 100,95,93,82,60 45**
CSF £144.14 CT £344.82 TOTE £10.10: £2.50, £3.80, £1.30; EX 117.60 Trifecta £448.40.
Owner R Cooper Racing Ltd **Bred** Bob Cooper & Val Dean **Trained** Upper Lambourn, Berks

FOCUS
Race distance increased by 10yds. A weak handicap won from the front by a 53-rated 3yo.

5626 SOUTHGATE BATH H'CAP (BATH SUMMER SPRINT SERIES QUALIFIER) 5f 161y

6:35 (6:35) (Class 5) (0-70,70) 3-Y-O **£3,234** (£962; £481; £240) **Stalls** Centre

Form RPR

0013 **1** **Showbizzy**[9] 5320 3-9-0 **63**...(v) ShaneKelly 5 72
(Richard Fahey) *hld up: hdwy over 1f out: rdn to ld and edgd lft wl ins fnl f: styd on* **3/1**[2]

-003 **2** nk **Fleeting Dream (IRE)**[17] 5041 3-8-7 **56**...................(b) WilliamCarson 3 64
(William Haggas) *a.p: chsd ldr 2f out: rdn and hung lft over 1f out: rallied and ev ch wl ins fnl f: styd on* **7/1**

5634 **3** 2 1/2 **Storm Melody**[11] 5259 3-9-7 **70**.................................(b[1]) SteveDrowne 4 70
(Jonjo O'Neill) *s.i.s: hdwy over 3f out: rdn over 1f out: nt clr run ins fnl f: styd on same pce* **3/1**[2]

1656 **4** hd **Showmethewayavrilo**[18] 4990 3-9-4 **70**.................. EdwardGreatrex(3) 1 69
(Malcolm Saunders) *led: rdn over 2f out: hdd and no ex wl ins fnl f* **9/4**[1]

3520 **5** 3/4 **Waneen (IRE)**[81] 2776 3-9-1 **67**............................ JosephineGordon(3) 2 63
(Joseph Tuite) *trckd ldrs: plld hrd: lost pl over 3f out: rdn over 1f out: no imp ins fnl f* **5/1**[3]

0200 **6** 7 **Chandresh**[21] 4855 3-8-7 **56**..[1] JimmyQuinn 6 27
(Robert Cowell) *w ldr 2f: rdn and lost 2nd 2f out: nt clr run and wknd sn after* **25/1**

1m 12.13s (0.93) **Going Correction** +0.20s/f (Good) **6** Ran SP% **113.8**
Speed ratings (Par 100): **101,100,97,97,96 86**
CSF £23.84 TOTE £4.10: £1.90, £2.60; EX 15.80 Trifecta £53.90.
Owner Racegoers Club Owners Group **Bred** Whitsbury Manor Stud **Trained** Musley Bank, N Yorks

FOCUS
An ordinary sprint handicap but the winner has struck form this summer and is going the right way now. The fourth has been rated close to his recent form, and the third to his recent fast ground form.

5627 NOVIA H'CAP 1m 5y

7:05 (7:05) (Class 5) (0-70,70) 3-Y-O+ **£2,911** (£866; £432; £216) **Stalls** Low

Form RPR

4216 **1** **Wakame (IRE)**[23] 4789 3-9-0 **67**.............................. JosephineGordon(3) 1 75
(Ed de Giles) *chsd ldr tl led over 4f out: rdn and hung lft fr over 1f out: hdd whn rdr lost whip wl ins fnl f: rallied to ld post* **13/8**[1]

4400 **2** nse **Knight Of The Air**[9] 5326 4-9-0 **58**...................................... ShaneKelly 2 67
(Mick Channon) *hdwy over 6f out: rdn to ld wl ins fnl f: hdd post* **12/1**

5440 **3** 3 1/4 **Hot Mustard**[24] 4776 6-9-12 **70**.. SamHitchcott 4 72
(William Muir) *sn pushed along to chse ldrs: ev ch over 1f out: sn rdn: no ex wl ins fnl f* **9/2**[2]

-056 **4** 1/2 **Aurora Gray**[17] 5011 3-8-10 **63**.................................. EdwardGreatrex(3) 6 62+
(Hughie Morrison) *hld up: rdn over 2f out: hdwy over 1f out: nt rch ldrs* **6/1**

-063 **5** 3 1/4 **Indrapura (IRE)**[13] 5201 3-9-6 **70**..(t) JohnFahy 5 62
(Paul Cole) *prom: lost pl after 1f: hdwy over 2f out: rdn over 1f out: wknd ins fnl f* **7/1**

5210 **6** 3/4 **Saint Helena (IRE)**[37] 4288 8-9-5 **70**.........................(b) GeorgeWood(7) 3 61
(Mark Gillard) *s.s: hdwy over 5f out: rdn over 3f out: wknd fnl f* **5/1**[3]

4206 **7** 5 **Plauseabella**[29] 4589 5-9-2 **60**.....................................(p) WilliamCarson 7 40
(Stuart Kittow) *led: stdd pce 5f out: sn hdd: rdn over 2f out: wknd fnl f* **14/1**

1m 42.73s (1.93) **Going Correction** +0.20s/f (Good)
WFA 3 from 4yo+ 6lb **7** Ran SP% **114.1**
Speed ratings (Par 103): **98,97,94,94,90 90,85**
CSF £22.88 TOTE £2.40: £1.50, £4.00; EX 20.40 Trifecta £80.10.
Owner Simon Treacher **Bred** Tally-Ho Stud **Trained** Ledbury, H'fords
■ Stewards' Enquiry : Shane Kelly 4-day ban: improper use of the whip (4-7 sept)

FOCUS
Race distance increased by 10yds. Quite a competitive 0-70 with three of the seven runners carrying the ceiling rating for the grade. The runner-up has been rated to form.

5628 BE WISER H'CAP 5f 11y

7:35 (7:36) (Class 6) (0-55,56) 3-Y-O+ **£2,264** (£673; £336; £168) **Stalls** Centre

Form RPR

0004 **1** **Mambo Spirit (IRE)**[30] 4570 12-9-3 **54**........................ EoinWalsh(3) 10 66
(Tony Newcombe) *hld up: hdwy over 1f out: rdn to ld ins fnl f: edgd lft: r.o wl* **8/1**[3]

0052 **2** 3 **Catalinas Diamond (IRE)**[10] 5282 8-9-8 **56**...............(t) SteveDrowne 11 57
(Pat Murphy) *s.i.s: hld up: hdwy over 1f out: r.o* **9/1**

0161 **3** nk **Willow Spring**[9] 5335 4-9-1 **52**... NoelGarbutt(3) 8 52
(Conrad Allen) *a.p: led over 1f out: rdn and hdd ins fnl f: styd on same pce* **6/1**[2]

6605 **4** 2 **Tally's Song**[8] 5378 3-8-7 **46** oh1..............................[1] EdwardGreatrex(3) 6 39
(Grace Harris) *led: hdd over 3f out: led again 1/2-way: rdn and hdd over 1f out: no ex ins fnl f* **25/1**

0010 **5** hd **Captain Devious**[8] 5378 5-9-13 **47**.................................(t) TimmyMurphy 7 39
(Grace Harris) *w ldrs: rdn and ev ch over 1f out: styd on same pce* **25/1**

06-5 **6** 1 **Don't Tell Jo Jo**[17] 5020 3-8-10 **46** oh1............................ SamHitchcott 9 34
(Bill Turner) *prom: rdn over 1f out: no ex fnl f* **50/1**

2004 **7** 1 1/4 **Magic Garden (IRE)**[177] 711 3-8-12 **55**...................[1] GeorgeWood(7) 13 39
(Jonathan Portman) *s.i.s: in rr and sn pushed along: hdwy 2f out: rdn over 1f out: no ex fnl f* **10/1**

6231 **8** 1/2 **Secretfact**[2] 5570 3-9-2 **52** 6ex..[1] JimmyQuinn 1 34
(Malcolm Saunders) *trckd ldrs: plld hrd: hung lft 1/2-way: rdn over 1f out: wknd ins fnl f* **11/8**[1]

60/0 **9** *nse* **Portrush Storm**[40] 4202 11-8-12 **46** oh1 AdamBeschizza 3 28
(Ray Peacock) *prom: rdn 1/2-way: wknd fnl f* **66/1**
10 *3/4* **Les Darcy**[395] 4532 5-8-12 **46** oh1 ShaneKelly 12 25
(Ken Cunningham-Brown) *in rr whn swtchd lft 4f out: hdwy 1/2-way: rdn and wknd over 1f out* **20/1**
0501 **11** *8* **Molly Jones**[10] 5282 7-9-1 **52** JosephineGordon(3) 5 2
(Matthew Salaman) *s.i.s: hld up: rdn 1/2-way: hmpd and wknd over 1f out* **12/1**
4325 **12** *8* **Blistering Dancer (IRE)**[40] 4202 6-9-2 **50** (p) WilliamCarson 4
(Tony Carroll) *w ldr: led over 3f out: hdd 1/2-way: rdn and wknd over 1f out* **6/1**[2]

1m 3.07s (0.57) **Going Correction** +0.20s/f (Good)
WFA 3 from 4yo+ 2lb 12 Ran SP% **124.5**
Speed ratings (Par 101): **103,98,97,94,94 92,90,89,89,88 75,62**
CSF £77.33 CT £475.45 TOTE £9.60: £2.90, £2.50, £1.90; EX 81.10 Trifecta £645.70.
Owner Nigel Hardy **Bred** R Warren **Trained** Yarnscombe, Devon

FOCUS
A weak handicap won emphatically by a thoroughly exposed veteran.

5629 SIMPLY THE BEST DRIFTWOOD HORSES H'CAP 1m 2f 46y
8:05 (8:05) (Class 5) (0-70,70) 3-Y-O+ **£2,911** (£866; £432; £216) **Stalls** Low

Form RPR
-442 **1** **Rajadamri**[10] 5288 3-8-3 **60** GeorgeWood(7) 6 66
(Rod Millman) *chsd ldrs: wnt 2nd over 3f out: rdn to ld over 1f out: all out* **5/1**[3]
2353 **2** *hd* **Chantecler**[13] 5208 5-10-0 **70** (t) JackMitchell 1 75
(Neil Mulholland) *plld hrd: sn led at stdy pce: qcknd over 3f out: rdn and hdd whn rdr dropped whip over 1f out: rallied ins fnl f: styd on* **11/2**
6551 **3** *1 1/2* **Pina**[23] 4794 3-9-1 **68** JosephineGordon(3) 2 70
(Roger Charlton) *hld up: rdn over 3f out: sn outpcd: nt clr run ins fnl f: swtchd rt and r.o wl* **1/1**[1]
1051 **4** *1/2* **Pivotal Flame (IRE)**[17] 5010 3-9-6 **70** (p) ShaneKelly 3 71
(James Tate) *hld up in tch: rdn over 2f out: styd on same pce ins fnl f* **7/2**[2]
0360 **5** *shd* **Tatawu (IRE)**[7] 5392 4-9-7 **63** WilliamCarson 7 64
(Peter Hiatt) *chsd ldr over 6f: rdn over 2f out: styd on same pce ins fnl f* **10/1**

2m 12.86s (1.86) **Going Correction** +0.20s/f (Good)
WFA 3 from 4yo+ 8lb 5 Ran SP% **113.4**
Speed ratings (Par 103): **100,99,98,98,98**
CSF £30.94 TOTE £6.60: £2.20, £2.10; EX 28.00 Trifecta £87.90.
Owner Mustajed Partnership **Bred** Redmyre Bloodstock & Tweenhills Stud **Trained** Kentisbeare, Devon

FOCUS
Race distance increased by 10yds. A modest heat in which the only obviously progressive runner in the field proved disappointing, so not form to get excited about. It's been rated a bit cautiously.
T/Plt: £42.50 to a £1 stake. Pool: £30,183.73 - 518.13 winning tickets. T/Qpdt: £16.90 to a £1 stake. Pool: £4,793.63 - 209.64 winning tickets. **Colin Roberts**

5469 CHELMSFORD (A.W) (L-H)
Saturday, August 20

OFFICIAL GOING: Polytrack: standard
Wind: strong, half behind Weather: dry, blustery

5630 TOTEPLACEPOT SIX PLACES IN SIX RACES APPRENTICE H'CAP 1m 2f (P)
5:45 (5:46) (Class 6) (0-55,54) 3-Y-O+ **£3,234** (£962; £481; £240) **Stalls** Low

Form RPR
0633 **1** **Unsuspected Girl (IRE)**[30] 4566 3-9-1 **53** GeorgeBuckell 7 62
(David Simcock) *stdd after s: hld up in rr: hdwy and swtchd rt over 1f out: led jst ins fnl f: r.o wl* **4/1**[3]
0001 **2** *1 1/2* **Boychick (IRE)**[18] 4992 3-8-9 **52** CameronNoble(5) 6 58
(Ed Walker) *chsd ldrs: effrt 2f out: rdn and chal over 1f out: led 1f out: sn hdd and one pce fnl 100yds* **7/2**[2]
0004 **3** *nk* **Onehelluvatouch**[15] 5101 3-8-10 **51** MeganNicholls(3) 9 56
(Philip Hide) *hld up in tch: stdy hdwy 5f out: chsd ldrs and rdn over 2f out: ev ch 1f out: styd on same pce ins fnl f* **8/1**
-600 **4** *1 3/4* **Esspeegee**[117] 1698 3-8-7 **48** DavidParkes(3) 10 50
(Alan Bailey) *in tch in midfield: pushed along 4f out: rdn over 1f out: styd on wl ins fnl f: nt rch ldrs* **16/1**
4305 **5** *1/2* **Music Hall (FR)**[47] 3943 6-8-12 **45** SophieKilloran(3) 5 46
(Shaun Harris) *t.k.h: in tch in midfield: rdn and effrt over 1f out: styd on same pce ins fnl f* **14/1**
-005 **6** *1 1/2* **Bethnal Green**[25] 4740 4-9-4 **53** SamuelClarke(5) 8 51
(Robyn Brisland) *led: rdn 2f out: hdd 1f out: no ex and wknd fnl 100yds* **12/1**
3222 **7** *1 1/4* **Go On Gal (IRE)**[15] 5101 3-8-8 **53** LiamDoran(7) 11 49
(Julia Feilden) *w ldr: rdn ent fnl 2f: unable qck over 1f out: losing pl whn squeezed for room jst ins fnl f: sn wknd* **3/1**[1]
-060 **8** *3 1/4* **Royal Mighty**[9] 5338 3-8-2 **45** MillyNaseb(5) 3 35
(Jane Chapple-Hyam) *hld up towards rr: rdn over 1f out: no hdwy and nvr trbld ldrs* **25/1**
0546 **9** *4 1/2* **Jackpot**[28] 4635 6-8-12 **45** (p) RhiainIngram(3) 1 26
(Brendan Powell) *hld up towards rr: swtchd rt and effrt wl over 1f out: no hdwy and wknd fnl f* **16/1**
0U50 **10** *8* **Topalova**[88] 2563 3-8-9 **54** (b[1]) GeorgiaDobie(7) 2 20
(Mark H Tompkins) *t.k.h: midfield tl hdwy to chse ldrs 1/2-way: lost pl qckly over 2f out: bhd fnl f* **8/1**

2m 7.88s (-0.72) **Going Correction** -0.025s/f (Stan)
WFA 3 from 4yo+ 8lb 10 Ran SP% **119.4**
Speed ratings (Par 101): **101,99,99,98,97 96,95,92,89,82**
CSF £18.94 CT £108.94 TOTE £4.50: £1.50, £1.50, £2.30; EX 22.40 Trifecta £123.00.
Owner Tick Tock Partnership **Bred** Mrs E Henry **Trained** Newmarket, Suffolk

FOCUS
A modest apprentice handicap with very little recent winning form on display. A step forward from the winner, with the race rated around the second and third.

5631 VISIT TOTEPOOLLIVEINFO.COM FOR RACING RESULTS MAIDEN STKS (PLUS 10 RACE) 5f (P)
6:15 (6:15) (Class 4) 2-Y-O **£7,115** (£2,117; £1,058; £529) **Stalls** Low

Form RPR
2 **1** **Queen In Waiting (IRE)**[9] 5317 2-9-0 0 JamesDoyle 6 77+
(Mark Johnston) *in tch in midfield but wd bnd 3f out: rdn and hdwy over 2f out: chal u.p 1f out: led wl ins fnl f: styd on* **10/11**[1]
450 **2** *1/2* **Nuclear Power**[65] 3295 2-9-0 85 RowanScott(5) 4 80
(William Muir) *w ldr tl led 1/2-way: rdn over 1f out: hrd pressed 1f out: hdd wl ins fnl f: kpt on for clr 2nd but a hld after* **5/2**[2]
2252 **3** *2 1/2* **Father McKenzie**[7] 5410 2-9-5 75 CharlesBishop 9 71
(Mick Channon) *hld up in tch: swtchd rt and hdwy over 1f out: chsd ldrs and styd on same pce ins fnl f* **7/1**[3]
0 **4** *1/2* **Five Star Frank**[25] 4736 2-9-5 0 JimCrowley 7 69
(Eve Johnson Houghton) *in tch in midfield: n.m.r and effrt over 1f out: kpt on same pce and no threat to ldng pair fnl f* **12/1**
600 **5** *3/4* **Sadieroseclifford (IRE)**[19] 4943 2-8-7 52 CameronNoble(7) 3 62
(Denis Quinn) *trckd ldrs: effrt on inner over 1f out: unable qck 1f out: kpt on same pce fnl f* **66/1**
6 *2* **Supreme Power (IRE)** 2-9-2 0 LouisSteward(3) 8 59+
(Philip McBride) *s.i.s: rn green and detached in last: pushed along and hdwy 1f out: kpt on ins fnl f: nvr trbld ldrs* **20/1**
7 *1/4* **See You Mush** 2-9-5 0 LemosdeSouza 10 58
(Chris Dwyer) *hld up in tch: swtchd rt and effrt over 1f out: no imp and styd on same pce after* **66/1**
5 **8** *1 1/4* **Wild Approach (IRE)**[78] 2852 2-9-5 0 MartinHarley 2 54
(Robert Cowell) *t.k.h and hung rt thrght: led tl 1/2-way: dropped out over 1f out: eased fnl f: sddle slipped* **20/1**
9 *1 3/4* **Desert Gift (IRE)** 2-9-0 0 LukeMorris 11 43
(Robert Cowell) *hld up in tch in rr of main gp: nt clr run and swtchd rt over 1f out: sn btn: wknd fnl f* **25/1**
4 **10** *shd* **Zipedee**[11] 5258 2-9-0 0 DannyBrock 5 42
(John Ryan) *wl in tch in midfield: nt clr run over 1f out: sn swtchd rt and no hdwy: wknd ins fnl f* **33/1**
46 **11** *4* **The Lady Hysteria (IRE)**[13] 5188 2-9-0 0 KierenFox 12 28
(Phil McEntee) *racd wd: a towards rr: bhd over 1f out* **66/1**

59.72s (-0.48) **Going Correction** -0.025s/f (Stan) 11 Ran SP% **121.9**
Speed ratings (Par 96): **102,101,97,96,95 92,91,89,86,86 80**
CSF £3.07 TOTE £1.90: £1.10, £1.40, £2.00; EX 4.60 Trifecta £10.50.
Owner Sheikh Hamdan bin Mohammed Al Maktoum **Bred** Darley **Trained** Middleham Moor, N Yorks

FOCUS
A juvenile maiden featuring a couple of runners who had shown signs of ability on their previous outings. The form makes sense rated around the second and third.

5632 TOTEQUADPOT FOUR PLACES IN FOUR RACES FILLIES' CONDITIONS STKS (PLUS 10 RACE) 7f (P)
6:50 (6:50) (Class 2) 2-Y-O **£16,172** (£4,812; £2,405; £1,202) **Stalls** Low

Form RPR
302 **1** **Queensbrydge**[5] 5469 2-8-12 0 LukeMorris 4 83
(Robyn Brisland) *hld up wl in tch: effrt to chal over 1f out: drvn and ev ch ins fnl f: r.o wl to ld last stride* **8/1**
10 **2** *nse* **Soul Silver (IRE)**[43] 4106 2-9-2 81 MartinHarley 3 87
(David Simcock) *trckd ldr: upsides and gng wl ent fnl 2f: rdn to ld over 1f out: kpt on wl u.p ins fnl f: hdd last stride* **9/1**
21 **3** *1* **Soldier's Girl (IRE)**[10] 5298 2-9-2 83 TomMarquand 1 84
(Richard Hannon) *trckd ldng pair: effrt on inner over 1f out: rdn and ev ch ins fnl f: unable qck fnl 75yds* **7/2**[3]
41 **4** *1/2* **Berengaria (IRE)**[13] 5196 2-9-2 83 JamesDoyle 2 83
(Mark Johnston) *led: rdn ent fnl 2f: drvn and hdd over 1f out: styd on same pce u.p fnl f* **9/4**[2]
1 **5** *nk* **Bahamadam**[19] 4951 2-9-2 0 RobertWinston 5 82+
(Eve Johnson Houghton) *dropped in bhd after s: effrt over 1f out: no imp u.p 1f out: styd on towards fin: nvr threatened ldrs* **7/4**[1]

1m 28.46s (1.26) **Going Correction** -0.025s/f (Stan) 5 Ran SP% **110.5**
Speed ratings (Par 97): **91,90,89,89,88**
CSF £65.72 TOTE £10.50: £4.50, £4.50; EX 49.40 Trifecta £232.80.
Owner Franconson Partners **Bred** D Curran **Trained** Newmarket, Suffolk

FOCUS
A competitive race with three last-time-out winners among the five who went to post for this valuable prize. They went a steady gallop through the early stages and this ended up a mad dash up the straight.

5633 TOTEEXACTA PICK 1ST AND 2ND H'CAP 1m 5f 66y(P)
7:20 (7:20) (Class 4) (0-85,85) 3-Y-O+ **£8,086** (£2,406; £1,202; £601) **Stalls** Low

Form RPR
0115 **1** **Tenzing Norgay**[78] 2859 3-8-9 **77** (p) LukeMorris 1 81+
(Sir Mark Prescott Bt) *stdd s: t.k.h: trckd ldrs: effrt on inner over 1f out: drvn 1f out: str chal 100yds out: r.o to ld last stride* **5/2**[2]
1421 **2** *shd* **Space Mountain**[10] 5294 3-8-8 **76** JoeFanning 2 79
(Mark Johnston) *led and set stdy gallop: rdn and qcknd 2f out: drvn 1f out: kpt on u.p: hdd last stride* **6/1**
2255 **3** *3/4* **Sbraase**[17] 5026 5-9-13 **84** MartinHarley 3 86
(James Tate) *stdd s: hld up in tch in last pair: clsd over 1f out: chsng ldrs and nt clrest of runs ins fnl f: gap opened and r.o under hands and heels riding wl ins fnl f* **9/2**[3]
3431 **4** *1/2* **Yangtze**[24] 4778 3-8-13 **81** (p) JimCrowley 5 82+
(Sir Michael Stoute) *hld up in tch in last pair: effrt wl over 1f out: styd on u.p ins fnl f: nt quite enough pce to rch ldrs* **6/4**[1]
2300 **5** *nk* **Street Artist (IRE)**[39] 4230 6-9-7 **85** DanielleMooney(7) 6 86
(David Nicholls) *pressed ldr: rdn and ev ch wl over 1f out tl unable qck and lost 2nd 100yds out: outpcd towards fin* **20/1**
2105 **6** *2 1/2* **Knight Music**[21] 4888 4-9-13 **84** RobertHavlin 4 81
(Michael Attwater) *t.k.h: hld up in midfield: rdn 2f out: unable qck u.p ent fnl f: wknd ins fnl f* **20/1**

2m 59.28s (5.68) **Going Correction** -0.025s/f (Stan)
WFA 3 from 4yo+ 11lb 6 Ran SP% **110.6**
Speed ratings (Par 105): **81,80,80,80,79 78**
CSF £16.89 TOTE £3.20: £1.80, £2.70; EX 18.00 Trifecta £48.20.
Owner J L C Pearce **Bred** J L C Pearce **Trained** Newmarket, Suffolk

FOCUS
A trio of progressive 3yos took on their elders in this competitive heat where they again went steadily for much of the race. It's been rated around the runner-up.

5634 TOTETRIFECTA PICK THE 1, 2 AND 3 MAIDEN STKS 1m 2f (P)
7:50 (7:50) (Class 4) 3-Y-O+ **£8,086** (£2,406; £1,202) **Stalls** Low

Form RPR
342 **1** **Mubajal**[28] 4657 3-9-5 84 JimCrowley 2 91+
(Owen Burrows) *swtchd lft after s and niggled along early: chsd ldr tl 7f out: nudged into ld on inner over 1f out: sn clr: v easily* **8/11**[1]
-332 **2** *9* **Heartstone (IRE)**[19] 4955 3-9-0 77 JamesDoyle 1 71
(Charles Hills) *led tl rdn and hdd over 1f out: sn brushed aside by wnr and wl btn fnl f* **9/4**[2]

3 **3** *6* **Dubawi Hundred (IRE)**[64] 3362 3-9-5 0 LukeMorris 3 64
(James Tate) *chsd rivals tl wnt 2nd 7f out: rdn over 3f out: dropped to last 2f out: sn btn: hung lft and eased 1f out* **4/1**[3]

2m 7.15s (-1.45) **Going Correction** -0.025s/f (Stan) **3** Ran SP% **108.7**
Speed ratings (Par 105): **104,96,92**
CSF £2.67 TOTE £2.00; EX 2.40 Trifecta £3.10.

Owner Hamdan Al Maktoum **Bred** Shadwell Estate Company Limited **Trained** Lambourn, Berks

FOCUS
Just the three runners in this maiden but all of them had shown encouraging signs on their limited racecourse experience. The runner-up has been rated close to his form before last time out.

5635 TOTEPOOL LIVE INFO DOWNLOAD OUR APP H'CAP 1m (P)
8:20 (8:21) (Class 6) (0-65,65) 3-Y-O+ **£3,234** (£962; £481; £240) **Stalls** Low

Form RPR

-646 **1** **Fast Sprite (IRE)**[16] 5085 4-9-10 **61** KierenFox 3 72+
(John Best) *hld up in tch in midfield: effrt on inner over 1f out: led and hung rt 1f out: r.o wl and drew clr ins fnl f: eased towards fin* **11/8**[1]

-303 **2** *3 ½* **In Ken's Memory**[17] 5013 3-9-6 **63** TomQueally 7 63
(John Butler) *sn chsng ldr: rdn 2f out: drvn and unable qck over 1f out: styd on same pce ins fnl f* **6/1**[3]

6203 **3** *½* **Schottische**[15] 5132 6-8-9 **53** (p) LiamLewis-Salter(7) 2 52
(Alan Bailey) *in tch in midfield: effrt over 1f out: no threat to wnr and kpt on same pce ins fnl f* **16/1**

5410 **4** *shd* **Spinning Rose**[21] 4882 4-9-8 **59** (b) RobertWinston 1 59
(Dean Ivory) *chsd ldrs: effrt over 1f out: struggling to qckn u.p and hmpd 1f out: styd on same pce after* **5/1**[2]

3654 **5** *nse* **Johnny B Goode (IRE)**[8] 5369 4-9-12 **63** MartinHarley 8 62
(Chris Dwyer) *taken down early: led: drvn over 1f out: hdd 1f out: styd on same pce u.p ins fnl f* **9/1**

0 **6** *¾* **Yasood (IRE)**[15] 5122 3-9-1 **65** GeorgiaDobie(7) 6 61
(Phil McEntee) *hld up in tch in last pair: effrt over 1f out: kpt on same pce ins fnl f* **50/1**

6300 **7** *hd* **Roxie Lot**[29] 4596 4-9-13 **64** [1] LukeMorris 5 61
(Pam Sly) *hld up in tch in midfield: effrt and nt clr run over 1f out: styd on same pce ins fnl f* **5/1**[2]

0506 **8** *¾* **Dukes Meadow**[8] 5362 5-9-1 **59** RhiainIngram(7) 4 54
(Roger Ingram) *squeezed for room leaving stalls: hld up in tch in last pair: clsd and nt clr run over 1f out tl ins fnl f: styd on same pce after* **6/1**[3]

1m 39.13s (-0.77) **Going Correction** -0.025s/f (Stan)
WFA 3 from 4yo+ 6lb **8** Ran SP% **121.9**
Speed ratings (Par 101): **102,98,98,97,97 97,96,96**
CSF £11.23 CT £100.06 TOTE £2.40: £1.40, £1.70, £3.00; EX 10.40 Trifecta £92.80.

Owner N Dyshaev & The Boys Partnership **Bred** John Costello **Trained** Oad Street, Kent

FOCUS
A modest handicap contested by a largely out of form bunch. The winner has been rated as posting an effort in keeping with his previous efforts here, and those in behind help set a straightforward level.

5636 BOOK TICKETS ONLINE AT CHELMSFORDCITYRACECOURSE.COM H'CAP 6f (P)
8:50 (8:51) (Class 6) (0-55,54) 3-Y-O+ **£3,234** (£962; £481; £240) **Stalls** Centre

Form RPR

5264 **1** **Manipura**[21] 4861 3-9-0 **53** (p) MatthewCosham(3) 7 60
(Derek Shaw) *hld up in tch in midfield: rdn and hdwy to chse ldrs jst over 1f out: led ins fnl f: r.o wl* **10/1**

0564 **2** *1* **Decisive (IRE)**[5] 5475 4-9-2 **52** (t) LouisSteward(3) 5 56
(Anthony Carson) *hld up in tch in midfield: rdn and hdwy over 1f out: led 1f out: hdd and styd on same pce ins fnl f* **2/1**[1]

065 **3** *1 ¾* **Cadland Lad (IRE)**[9] 5338 3-8-12 **48** (t) DannyBrock 11 47
(John Ryan) *chsd ldrs effrt to press ldr ent fnl 2f: drvn to ld over 1f out: hdd 1f out: no ex ins fnl f: outpcd towards fin* **8/1**

0033 **4** *4 ½* **Wattaboutsteve**[4] 5509 5-9-1 **48** JimCrowley 4 33
(Ralph J Smith) *chsd ldrs: effrt towards inner over 1f out: 4th and no ex 1f out: wknd ins fnl f* **3/1**[2]

0050 **5** *¾* **Steel City Boy (IRE)**[28] 4647 13-8-5 **45** RPWalsh(7) 2 28
(Shaun Harris) *taken down early: led: rdn and hdd over 1f out: no ex and wknd ins fnl f* **40/1**

5545 **6** *2 ½* **Justice Rock**[5] 5470 3-9-2 **52** LukeMorris 12 28
(Phil McEntee) *chsd ldr tl ent fnl 2f: drvn and unable qck over 1f out: wknd fnl f* **16/1**

5044 **7** *¾* **Fiftytintsofsilver (IRE)**[61] 3473 3-8-9 **45** TomMarquand 6 18
(Jeremy Gask) *hld up in tch in midfield: swtchd rt and effrt wl over 1f out: no hdwy and sn btn: wknd ins fnl f* **10/1**

-000 **8** *1 ¼* **Mr Turner**[16] 5085 3-8-12 **48** (b[1]) DarryllHolland 1 18
(Mark H Tompkins) *a bhd: n.d* **9/1**

1303 **9** *1* **Birrafun (IRE)**[19] 4944 3-8-13 **54** RowanScott(5) 10 21
(Ann Duffield) *hld up in tch in midfield: effrt and no hdwy over 1f out: wknd ins fnl f* **5/1**[3]

0004 **10** *1 ¼* **Blackasyourhat (IRE)**[143] 1138 4-8-5 **45** (t) RhiainIngram(7) 9 8
(Michael Attwater) *hld up in last trio: struggling 3f out: rdn and no hdwy over 1f out: n.d* **25/1**

00-0 **11** *1 ½* **Divasesque (IRE)**[21] 4855 3-8-6 **45** AaronJones(3) 3 3
(Derek Shaw) *a towards rr: pushed along 4f out: rdn and struggling 3f out: n.d after* **66/1**

1m 12.34s (-1.36) **Going Correction** -0.025s/f (Stan)
WFA 3 from 4yo+ 3lb **11** Ran SP% **128.0**
Speed ratings (Par 101): **108,106,104,98,97 94,93,91,90,88 86**
CSF £32.78 CT £187.87 TOTE £12.90: £3.10, £1.40, £2.40; EX 43.90 Trifecta £361.90.

Owner Paddy Barrett **Bred** P E Barrett **Trained** Sproxton, Leics

FOCUS
A moderate handicap in which only two of the 11 had previously tasted victory.

T/Plt: £164.50 to a £1 stake. Pool: £38,781.79 - 172.06 winning tickets. T/Qpdt: £86.40 to a £1 stake. Pool: £4,747.66 - 40.63 winning tickets. **Steve Payne**

4914 CHESTER (L-H)
Saturday, August 20

OFFICIAL GOING: Good (good to firm in places) changing to good after race 1 (2.05)
Wind: fresh 1/2 behind Weather: overcast, very breezy, showers, becoming fine and sunny

5637 ANS MEANS BUSINESS/EBF STALLIONS MAIDEN STKS (PLUS 10 RACE) 7f 2y
2:05 (2:10) (Class 4) 2-Y-O
£6,225 (£1,864; £932; £466; £233; £117) **Stalls** Low

Form RPR

34 **1** **Double Touch**[24] 4765 2-9-5 0 DavidNolan 2 84+
(Richard Fahey) *wnt rt s: hld up towards rr: hdwy and 4th over 3f out: trcking ldrs whn nt clr run over 1f out: swtchd rt and r.o wl to ld last 75yds* **5/1**[3]

5320 **2** *2 ¼* **Arc Royal**[23] 4802 2-9-5 77 RichardKingscote 4 78
(Tom Dascombe) *led: drvn 3f out: hdd and no ex last 75yds* **7/2**[2]

64 **3** *nk* **Bloomin Lovely (IRE)**[19] 4943 2-9-0 0 JasonHart 3 72+
(John Quinn) *carried rt s: hld up towards rr: hdwy over 3f out: chsng ldrs over 1f out: styd on to take 3rd nr fin* **20/1**

5223 **4** *1 ½* **Wahash (IRE)**[18] 4974 2-9-5 76 SeanLevey 10 73
(Richard Hannon) *trckd ldr: upsides 2f out: keeping on same pce whn carried rt 75yds out* **9/1**

22 **5** *¾* **Ray's The Money (IRE)**[21] 4866 2-9-5 0 DavidProbert 8 71
(Michael Bell) *chsd ldrs: drvn and hung lft over 1f out: one pce* **13/8**[1]

433 **6** *11* **Hartswell**[17] 5036 2-9-5 77 [1] GrahamLee 5 41
(John Gosden) *half-rrd s: t.k.h in mid-div: effrt and outpcd over 2f out: tk modest 6th clsng stages* **5/1**[3]

0 **7** *1 ¾* **Bollin Ted**[29] 4609 2-9-5 0 DavidAllan 9 37
(Tim Easterby) *in rr: sn drvn along: nvr on terms* **40/1**

8 *2 ¼* **Blue Rocks** 2-8-12 0 JordanUys(7) 7 31
(Lisa Williamson) *s.i.s: sn drvn along in rr: nvr on terms* **50/1**

0 **9** *½* **Jenji (IRE)**[147] 1086 2-9-0 0 SamJames 6 24
(David Evans) *t.k.h in rr: hdwy into mid-div 5f out: lost pl over 2f out* **66/1**

00 **10** *9* **Shadow Of Hercules (IRE)**[30] 4545 2-9-5 0 TomEaves 1 5
(Michael Mullineaux) *chsd ldrs: drvn over 3f out: lost pl over 2f out: sn bhd* **150/1**

11 *4* **Zacchetto (USA)** 2-9-5 0 JFEgan 11
(Mark Johnston) *in rr: sn drvn along: reminders over 4f out: wl bhd fnl 2f: sn eased* **25/1**

1m 27.06s (0.56) **Going Correction** +0.125s/f (Good) **11** Ran SP% **118.8**
Speed ratings (Par 96): **101,98,98,96,95 82,80,78,77,67 62**
CSF £21.99 TOTE £6.90: £1.60, £1.50, £5.80; EX 23.40 Trifecta £227.00.

Owner Nicholas Wrigley & Kevin Hart **Bred** Honeypuddle Stud **Trained** Musley Bank, N Yorks

FOCUS
There was 6mm of rain on Friday and a further 2mm since 6am, leaving the going as good, good to firm in places (GoingStick: 7.4). The running rail was on the very inside and all race distances were as advertised. A fair maiden. The level is a bit fluid.

5638 &FEELINGFRUITY/EBFSTALLIONS.COM FILLIES' CONDITIONS STKS (PLUS 10 RACE) 6f 18y
2:40 (2:42) (Class 2) 2-Y-O
£12,450 (£3,728; £1,864; £932; £466; £234) **Stalls** Low

Form RPR

01 **1** **Partitia**[7] 5400 2-9-1 85 GrahamLee 1 93+
(Sir Michael Stoute) *trckd ldrs: swtchd rt 2f out: styd on to ld last 75yds* **13/8**[1]

213 **2** *1 ¾* **Rosabelle**[40] 4195 2-9-1 78 GrahamGibbons 2 88
(Alan Bailey) *led: hdd and no ex last 75yds* **7/1**

1036 **3** *4 ½* **Grizzel (IRE)**[14] 5172 2-9-5 93 SeanLevey 6 78+
(Richard Hannon) *hld up in rr: hdwy over 2f out: sn carried lft: kpt on same pce over 1f out* **4/1**[2]

541 **4** *1 ¼* **Night Law**[30] 4558 2-8-12 79 DavidProbert 7 67
(Andrew Balding) *in rr: hdwy to chse ldrs over 2f out: one pce over 1f out* **8/1**

100 **5** *4 ½* **Kachess**[28] 4623 2-8-12 81 RichardKingscote 8 54+
(Tom Dascombe) *rrd s and v.s.a: hdwy on inner whn hmpd over 2f out: kpt on fnl f* **11/1**

2121 **6** *4 ½* **Little Nosegay (IRE)**[12] 5243 2-8-12 63 SamJames 3 40
(David Evans) *w ldr: wknd over 1f out* **25/1**

0425 **7** *11* **Camargue**[21] 4884 2-9-1 85 JFEgan 5 10
(Mark Johnston) *mid-div: sn drvn along: reminders 3f out: lost pl over 2f out: eased fnl 100yds* **5/1**[3]

145 **8** *17* **Fiery Character (IRE)**[36] 4343 2-9-1 77 LiamJones 4
(Tom Dascombe) *chsd ldrs: lost pl and edgd lft over 2f out: sn bhd: eased fnl f* **16/1**

1m 14.04s (0.24) **Going Correction** +0.125s/f (Good) **8** Ran SP% **116.4**
Speed ratings (Par 97): **103,100,94,93,87 81,66,43**
CSF £14.11 TOTE £2.30: £1.10, £2.70, £1.50; EX 11.20 Trifecta £68.50.

Owner K Abdullah **Bred** Juddmonte Farms Ltd **Trained** Newmarket, Suffolk

FOCUS
The going was changed to good before this race, with Jason Hart saying it was loose on top and that it wouldn't take much for it to be on the easy side. This didn't look a particularly strong conditions race but the well-related winner is progressing. The level is a bit fluid.

5639 CRABBIE'S ALCOHOLIC GINGER BEER CHESTER STKS (H'CAP) (LISTED RACE) 1m 5f 89y
3:15 (3:16) (Class 1) (0-110,108) 3-Y-O+
£20,982 (£7,955; £3,981; £1,983; £995; £499) **Stalls** Low

Form RPR

3213 **1** **Muntahaa (IRE)**[64] 3337 3-9-0 **108** GrahamLee 5 116
(John Gosden) *wnt rt s: sn led: pushed along over 3f out: kpt on fnl f: jst hld on* **15/8**[1]

2502 **2** *shd* **Duretto**[14] 5145 4-8-13 **96** DavidProbert 6 104+
(Andrew Balding) *hmpd s: in rr: hdwy on ins over 3f out: 3rd over 2f out: chsd wnr 1f out: styd on: jst hld* **6/1**[3]

3-25 **3** *2 ¾* **Fabricate**[64] 3340 4-9-0 **97** (p) WilliamTwiston-Davies 2 101
(Michael Bell) *led early: chsd ldr: 2nd over 2f out: kpt on same pce fnl f* **4/1**[2]

3004 **4** *nk* **First Mohican**[25] 4734 8-9-1 **98**.. HollieDoyle 9 101
(Alan King) *s.i.s: hdwy over 3f out: 4th over 1f out: kpt on same pce* **25/1**

0212 **5** *1 3/4* **Sea Of Heaven (IRE)**[14] 5144 4-8-11 **94** oh1.................... DavidAllan 7 95+
(Sir Mark Prescott Bt) *hmpd s: in rr: hdwy on outside over 2f out: kpt on: nt rch ldrs* **4/1**[2]

0015 **6** *4 1/2* **Pamona (IRE)**[23] 4800 4-9-7 **104**..............................(v) GrahamGibbons 1 98
(Ralph Beckett) *trckd ldrs: t.k.h: effrt over 2f out: wknd appr fnl f* **20/1**

3036 **7** *1 1/2* **Vive Ma Fille (GER)**[9] 5328 4-8-11 **94**.................................. JFEgan 10 86
(Mark Johnston) *hld up in rr: hdwy on ins over 2f out: hung lft over 1f out: nvr a factor* **50/1**

-462 **8** *nk* **Gabrial The Hero (USA)**[15] 5116 7-9-0 **97**..................... DavidNolan 12 88
(Richard Fahey) *trckd ldrs: drvn over 2f out: lost pl over 1f out* **14/1**

0103 **9** *6* **John Reel (FR)**[56] 3662 7-9-3 **100**...................................... SamJames 3 82
(David Evans) *chsd ldrs: drvn over 3f out: lost pl over 2f out* **33/1**

1404 **10** *5* **Cymro (IRE)**[55] 3697 4-9-5 **102**................................ RichardKingscote 8 77
(Tom Dascombe) *hmpd s: hld up in rr: racd wd: hdwy after 4f: lost pl 2f out: eased fnl 150yds* **14/1**

0011 **11** *2 1/4* **Mistiroc**[14] 5145 5-8-13 **96**...(v) TomEaves 11 67
(John Quinn) *sn chsng ldrs: drvn 3f out: lost pl 2f out: sn bhd* **25/1**

2m 50.89s (-1.81) **Going Correction** +0.125s/f (Good)
WFA 3 from 4yo+ 11lb **11** Ran SP% **119.8**
Speed ratings (Par 111): **110,109,108,108,106 104,103,103,99,96 94**
CSF £12.86 CT £42.14 TOTE £2.40: £1.50, £2.20, £1.70; EX 12.80 Trifecta £41.80.
Owner Hamdan Al Maktoum **Bred** Shadwell Estate Company Limited **Trained** Newmarket, Suffolk

FOCUS
A decent race and a good performance from the winner to beat his elders, even allowing for him controlling things from the front. The third helps set the standard.

5640 BRITISH STALLIONS STUDS EBF H'CAP 7f 122y
3:50 (3:53) (Class 2) 3-Y-O+

£28,012 (£8,388; £4,194; £2,097; £1,048; £526) **Stalls** Low

Form RPR

4121 **1** **Breakable**[7] 5419 5-8-13 **90**.. DavidAllan 7 100
(Tim Easterby) *w ldr: led after 1f: drvn over 1f out: styd on gamely* **11/2**

0041 **2** *1* **Right Touch**[42] 4136 6-9-8 **99**.. TonyHamilton 3 106
(Richard Fahey) *sn trcking ldrs: 2nd 1f out: styd on same pce: no real imp* **4/1**[2]

-052 **3** *3/4* **Above The Rest (IRE)**[28] 4665 5-9-0 **91**................... GrahamGibbons 6 96+
(David Barron) *rrd s: hld up in rr: hdwy over 2f out: 4th over 1f out: kpt on to take 3rd post* **3/1**[1]

1131 **4** *hd* **Ice Slice (IRE)**[20] 4917 5-9-2 **93**...................................... RyanTate 10 98
(James Eustace) *led 1f: w wnr: kpt on same pce fnl f* **5/1**[3]

0006 **5** *5* **Intransigent**[20] 4916 7-9-8 **99**.. DavidProbert 5 91
(Andrew Balding) *hld up in mid-div: effrt and modest 5th over 1f out: kpt on one pce* **10/1**

2100 **6** *3/4* **Gabrial's Kaka (IRE)**[22] 4823 6-9-4 **95**.................... GeorgeChaloner 11 85
(Richard Fahey) *mid-div: sn drvn along: outpcd over 2f out: kpt on fnl f* **14/1**

1000 **7** *2* **Al Khan (IRE)**[24] 4758 7-8-12 **89**...................................... TomEaves 9 74
(Kevin Ryan) *hood removed v late: s.i.s: in rr: sme hdwy over 1f out: nvr a factor* **50/1**

40-0 **8** *1/2* **Marcret (ITY)**[20] 4917 9-9-1 **92**... GrahamLee 1 76
(James Unett) *hld up in rr: t.k.h: sme hdwy on inner over 2f out: nvr a factor* **16/1**

1462 **9** *1/2* **Sound Advice**[22] 4846 7-9-10 **101**.................................. PhillipMakin 8 84
(Keith Dalgleish) *chsd ldrs on outer: wd bnd 2f out: sn lost pl* **7/1**

4-00 **10** *4* **Winklemann (IRE)**[177] 723 4-9-6 **97**................................ LiamJones 4 70
(Marco Botti) *chsd ldrs: lost pl wl over 1f out* **25/1**

000 **11** *13* **Capo Rosso (IRE)**[14] 5146 6-9-6 **97**....................... RichardKingscote 12 37
(Tom Dascombe) *racd v wd: mid-div: lost pl over 2f out: bhd whn eased fnl f* **25/1**

1m 33.2s (-0.60) **Going Correction** +0.125s/f (Good) **11** Ran SP% **120.8**
Speed ratings (Par 109): **108,107,106,106,101 100,98,97,97,93 80**
CSF £28.12 CT £80.21 TOTE £5.90: £1.50, £1.90, £1.70; EX 30.70 Trifecta £90.10.
Owner Ryedale Partners No 9 **Bred** Habton Farms **Trained** Great Habton, N Yorks

FOCUS
A good handicap but, with the pace holding up, few got into it. Another pb from the winner, while the runner-up helps set the standard, along with the fourth.

5641 SPORTINGBET.COM H'CAP 5f 110y
4:25 (4:27) (Class 2) (0-100,99) 3-Y-O+

£11,827 (£3,541; £1,770; £885; £442; £222) **Stalls** Low

Form RPR

100 **1** **Judicial (IRE)**[28] 4667 4-9-6 **95**..(e) GrahamLee 1 105
(Julie Camacho) *trckd ldrs on ins: swtchd rt appr fnl f: styd on to ld last 75yds* **4/1**[1]

3410 **2** *1* **Lightscameraction (IRE)**[148] 1066 4-9-7 **96**........................(b) JFEgan 2 102
(Gay Kelleway) *trckd ldrs: led appr fnl f: hdd and no ex last 75yds* **9/1**

0300 **3** *nk* **Poyle Vinnie**[14] 5143 6-9-10 **99**................................... AndrewMullen 3 104
(Michael Appleby) *s.i.s: hld up: hdwy over 2f out: hmpd over 1f out: swtchd rt over 1f out: styd on* **5/1**[3]

6400 **4** *1/2* **Fast Track**[7] 5417 5-8-12 **87**..................................... GrahamGibbons 12 90+
(David Barron) *stmbld sltly s: in rr: swtchd lft after s: hdwy over 1f out: edgd lft 100yds out: styd on to take 4th fnl strides* **20/1**

1562 **5** *1/2* **Confessional**[7] 5390 9-9-1 **90**..(e) DavidAllan 5 92
(Tim Easterby) *chsd ldrs: drvn over 2f out: n.m.r over 1f out: swtchd rt and kpt on last 150yds* **9/2**[2]

5210 **6** *nk* **Blithe Spirit**[25] 4735 5-9-7 **96**... JasonHart 9 97+
(Eric Alston) *in rr: hdwy on ins over 2f out: nt clr run over 1f out: kpt on fnl 100yds* **11/1**

0100 **7** *3/4* **Best Trip (IRE)**[7] 5417 9-8-13 **88**....................................... SamJames 4 86
(Marjorie Fife) *led: hdd appr fnl f: fdd last 100yds* **20/1**

2004 **8** *1 1/2* **Seve**[28] 4632 4-8-12 **87**...(t) RichardKingscote 10 80
(Tom Dascombe) *dwlt: in rr: hdwy over 1f out: one pce whn short of room on inner 100yds out* **14/1**

0054 **9** *hd* **Ashpan Sam**[7] 5390 7-9-1 **90**.........................(p) WilliamTwiston-Davies 7 83
(David W Drinkwater) *chsd ldrs on outer: fdd appr fnl f* **16/1**

0301 **10** *1 1/2* **Kibaar**[22] 4831 4-8-11 **86**...(p) TomEaves 6 74
(Kevin Ryan) *w ldr: wknd fnl f* **17/2**

0312 **11** *3/4* **Powerallied (IRE)**[28] 4632 3-8-12 **90**............................... TonyHamilton 8 75
(Richard Fahey) *chsd ldrs: lost pl over 1f out* **8/1**

2540 **12** *2 1/2* **Mukaynis (IRE)**[21] 4862 5-9-0 **89**....................................(p) ShaneGray 11 66
(Kevin Ryan) *in rr and drvn along: nvr on terms* **16/1**

1m 5.81s (-0.39) **Going Correction** +0.125s/f (Good)
WFA 3 from 4yo+ 2lb **12** Ran SP% **122.8**
Speed ratings (Par 109): **107,105,105,104,103 103,102,100,100,98 97,93**
CSF £41.89 CT £162.42 TOTE £5.40: £2.50, £3.30, £1.40; EX 45.20 Trifecta £259.70.
Owner Elite Racing Club **Bred** Elite Racing Club **Trained** Norton, N Yorks

FOCUS
A good sprint handicap, and a treble on the card for Graham Lee. A turf pb from the runner-up.

5642 SPORTINGBET H'CAP 1m 7f 195y
5:00 (5:03) (Class 4) (0-85,87) 3-Y-O+

£6,225 (£1,864; £932; £466; £233; £117) **Stalls** Low

Form RPR

231/ **1** **Chocala (IRE)**[834] 2108 6-10-0 **85**.................. WilliamTwiston-Davies 8 92+
(Alan King) *hld up in rr: hdwy on outer over 3f out: effrt over 2f out: edgd lft and kpt on to ld towards fin* **5/1**[3]

-600 **2** *nk* **Perfect Summer (IRE)**[24] 4752 6-9-4 **75**........................(p) GrahamLee 6 81
(Ian Williams) *trckd ldrs: led after 5f: pushed along 4f out: kpt on: hdd and no ex nr fin* **22/1**

0351 **3** *hd* **Gabrial's Star**[9] 5321 7-10-2 **87**....................................(b) TonyHamilton 4 93+
(Richard Fahey) *hld up in mid-div: effrt over 3f out: sn chsng ldrs: keeping on same pce whn n.m.r clsng stages* **3/1**[1]

0000 **4** *1/2* **Wordiness**[24] 4752 8-9-10 **81**.. SamJames 10 86
(David Evans) *sn trcking ldrs: chal over 1f out: edgd rt 100yds out: kpt on same pce* **16/1**

6223 **5** *2 1/4* **Medina Sidonia (IRE)**[9] 5321 4-9-1 **72**..........................(p) DavidAllan 9 74
(Tim Easterby) *chsd ldrs: drvn 6f out: one pce over 1f out* **12/1**

6630 **6** *hd* **Communicator**[24] 4752 8-9-6 **77**...................................(v) DavidProbert 2 79
(Andrew Balding) *hld up in rr: hdwy over 1f out: kpt on one pce: nvr a threat* **9/2**[2]

2052 **7** *2 1/2* **Snowy Dawn**[16] 5061 6-8-12 **69**...................................... RoystonFfrench 3 68
(Steph Hollinshead) *mid-div: effrt over 2f out: one pce whn nt clr run over 1f out* **9/2**[2]

1-62 **8** *hd* **Cotillion**[105] 2041 10-8-12 **69**.......................................(p) RichardKingscote 1 68
(Ian Williams) *mid-div: nt clr run and swtchd rt over 1f out: kpt on: nvr a factor* **12/1**

201- **9** *1 1/2* **Gleese The Devil (IRE)**[315] 7124 5-9-11 **82**.............. GeorgeChaloner 5 79
(Richard Fahey) *chsd ldrs: drvn over 2f out: fdd appr fnl f* **16/1**

136 **10** *3 1/2* **Swift Cedar (IRE)**[12] 5231 6-8-11 **75**................................ AledBeech[(7)] 7 68
(David Evans) *stdd s: hld up in rr: drvn over 3f out: hung rt and bhd fnl 2f: lame* **33/1**

4-20 **11** *6* **Diamond Joel**[24] 4752 4-9-9 **80**.. JFEgan 12 66
(Mick Channon) *t.k.h: led: hdd after 5f: upsides over 5f out: wknd over 1f out: eased last 150yds* **9/1**

3m 31.19s (3.19) **Going Correction** +0.125s/f (Good) **11** Ran SP% **122.5**
Speed ratings (Par 105): **97,96,96,96,95 95,94,93,93,91 88**
CSF £113.09 CT £394.46 TOTE £5.00: £2.40, £6.90, £2.20; EX 159.10 Trifecta £1016.30.
Owner High 5 **Bred** Peter Harris **Trained** Barbury Castle, Wilts

FOCUS
A fair staying event and a good training performance to get the winner back from a long absence. Muddling form. The third has been rated to this year's form and the fourth to his turf best, but this is not necessarily solid form.

5643 CONTROLLED EVENT SOLUTIONS H'CAP 5f 110y
5:35 (5:37) (Class 4) (0-85,88) 3-Y-O

£6,225 (£1,864; £932; £466; £233; £117) **Stalls** Low

Form RPR

5005 **1** **Lady Clair (IRE)**[19] 4947 3-9-2 **80**...................................... JoeyHaynes 3 87
(K R Burke) *mid-div: hdwy over 2f out: chsng ldrs over 1f out: styd on to ld nr fin* **12/1**

3452 **2** *1/2* **Geno (IRE)**[10] 5295 3-8-13 **77**...(p) TomEaves 2 82
(Kevin Ryan) *trckd ldrs on ins: nt clr run over 1f out: swtchd lft 150yds out: kpt on to take 2nd post* **7/2**[2]

5231 **3** *shd* **Sandra's Secret (IRE)**[17] 5032 3-8-11 **75**.......................... DavidAllan 5 80
(Les Eyre) *led: edgd rt 150yds out: hdd and no ex nr fin* **10/3**[1]

4103 **4** *1 1/4* **Dark Defender**[14] 5153 3-9-7 **85**.................................(v) PhillipMakin 6 86
(Keith Dalgleish) *trckd ldrs on outer: kpt on same pce last 150yds* **5/1**[3]

143 **5** *1 1/2* **African Blessing**[12] 5224 3-8-7 **71**................................ DavidProbert 8 67+
(David Barron) *dwlt: in rr: hdwy appr fnl f: styd on wl to take 4th nr fin* **13/2**

21 **6** *1 1/4* **Acclaim The Nation (IRE)**[49] 3879 3-8-13 **77**.................. JasonHart 12 68+
(Eric Alston) *sn chsng ldrs: upsides over 1f out: fdd last 75yds* **10/1**

4000 **7** *1 1/4* **Sixties Sue**[7] 5409 3-9-3 **81**... GrahamLee 10 68
(Mick Channon) *mid-div: effrt on outer over 2f out: kpt on fnl f: nvr a threat* **14/1**

0062 **8** *shd* **Big Amigo (IRE)**[16] 5059 3-8-5 **69**..................................(e) ShaneGray 4 56
(Tom Dascombe) *in rr: effrt over 2f out: sme hdwy and edgd lft last 150yds: nvr a factor* **16/1**

3265 **9** *1 1/2* **Bossipop**[28] 4643 3-9-4 **82**...(p) GrahamGibbons 9 64
(Tim Easterby) *gave problems in stalls: s.i.s: in rr: sme hdwy on inner over 1f out: n.m.r 100yds out: nvr a factor* **10/1**

6- **10** *1/2* **Birdcage**[330] 6722 3-9-6 **84**... TonyHamilton 7 64
(Richard Fahey) *mid-div: effrt over 2f out: nvr on terms* **20/1**

1m 6.89s (0.69) **Going Correction** +0.125s/f (Good) **10** Ran SP% **118.5**
Speed ratings (Par 102): **100,99,99,97,95 93,92,92,90,89**
CSF £54.74 CT £165.92 TOTE £16.60: £3.90, £1.10, £2.00; EX 64.00 Trifecta £195.50.
Owner White Rose Racing **Bred** Kilcarn Stud **Trained** Middleham Moor, N Yorks

FOCUS
There was a contested lead here and that helped set things up for a closer.
T/Plt: £48.10 to a £1 stake. Pool: £70,436.91 - 1,068.55 winning tickets. T/Qpdt: £9.60 to a £1 stake. Pool: £3,938.77 - 302.71 winning tickets. **Walter Glynn**

5598 SANDOWN (R-H)

Saturday, August 20

OFFICIAL GOING: Round course - good to soft (good in places); sprint course - good (good to soft in places)

Wind: Fresh, half against Weather: Fine but cloudy

5644 OMEIR TRAVEL AGENCY NURSERY H'CAP — 7f 16y

1:55 (1:57) (Class 4) (0-85,82) 2-Y-O **£4,528** (£1,347; £673; £336) **Stalls** Low

Form RPR

5421 **1** **Harbour Master**[21] 4877 2-9-7 **82** GeorgeBaker 5 93+
(Jamie Osborne) *hld up in detached last: stdy prog to trck ldng trio 2f out: shkn up and clsd to ld 150yds out: sn clr: readily* **11/4**[2]

5312 **2** 2 ½ **Mister Blue Sky (IRE)**[43] 4076 2-8-13 **74** OisinMurphy 1 78
(Sylvester Kirk) *chsd ldng pair: pushed along over 2f out: chal u.p over 1f out: led briefly jst ins fnl f and edgd lft: kpt on but readily outpcd last 150yds* **9/2**[3]

31 **3** 2 ¼ **Serengeti Sky (USA)**[23] 4786 2-9-6 **81** (t) JamesDoyle 8 79
(Charlie Appleby) *trckd ldr: upsides over 2f out gng wl: rdn to take narrow ld over 1f out: hdd and outpcd jst ins fnl f* **15/8**[1]

641 **4** ¾ **Dourado (IRE)**[14] 5166 2-9-5 **80** PatDobbs 3 76
(Richard Hannon) *racd freely: led: tk field to centre in st: rdn and hdd over 1f out: cl up but hld whn squeezed for room jst ins fnl f: one pce* **15/2**

401 **5** 9 **Monoshka (IRE)**[22] 4837 2-9-4 **79** TomMarquand 7 52
(Richard Hannon) *shoved along in 5th pl bef 1/2-way: struggling after* **10/1**

521 **6** 1 ¼ **Geophony (IRE)**[22] 4829 2-9-2 **77** JoeFanning 2 47
(Mark Johnston) *t.k.h: chsd ldng trio to 2f out: wknd qckly* **8/1**

1m 31.14s (1.64) **Going Correction** +0.225s/f (Good) **6** Ran SP% **111.6**

Speed ratings (Par 96): **99,96,93,92,82 81**

CSF £15.14 CT £26.70 TOTE £2.80: £1.20, £2.00; EX 13.20 Trifecta £36.20.

Owner Michael Buckley & Charles E Noell **Bred** Mrs R F Johnson Houghton **Trained** Upper Lambourn, Berks

■ Stewards' Enquiry : Oisin Murphy caution: careless riding

FOCUS

After a heavy morning shower, the going was officially good to soft, good in places on the round course and good, good to soft in places on the 5f track. There was also a headwind in the straight, so conditions were quite testing, and the opening contest was over 4sec over standard. Add 3yds to race distance. No shortage of potentially well handicapped horses on show in this nursery and the pace looked fairly strong, with some of these colts looking particularly tired in the closing stages. The runner-up's previous effort could be rated this good, and the third fits, so this form should work out.

5645 REDROCK ENTERTAINMENT ATALANTA FILLIES' STKS (GROUP 3) — 1m 14y

2:30 (2:33) (Class 1) 3-Y-O+

£36,861 (£13,975; £6,994; £3,484; £1,748; £877) **Stalls** Low

Form RPR

-111 **1** **Persuasive (IRE)**[66] 3274 3-8-9 104 RobertHavlin 4 113+
(John Gosden) *hld up in midfield: pushed along and gd prog fr 2f out to ld jst over 1f out: sn clr: impressive* **6/4**[1]

-100 **2** 3 **Blond Me (IRE)**[42] 4127 4-9-1 107 OisinMurphy 12 107
(Andrew Balding) *racd wd in bk st: midfield: rdn and prog on outer 2f out: drvn to take 2nd ins fnl f: no ch w wnr* **9/1**[2]

6255 **3** ¾ **Lucy The Painter (IRE)**[14] 5158 4-9-1 96 HarryBentley 5 105
(Ed de Giles) *hld up in last pair: rdn on outer over 2f out: prog whn nt clr run over 1f out and again jst ins fnl f: styd on to take 3rd fnl 75yds* **20/1**

4052 **4** 1 ¼ **Mix And Mingle (IRE)**[14] 5158 3-8-9 100 TedDurcan 9 101
(Chris Wall) *hld up in last trio: rdn and prog on outer over 2f out: kpt on to take 4th nr fin: nvr pce to threaten* **10/1**[3]

1123 **5** nk **Pirouette**[14] 5158 3-8-10 100 ow1 TomQueally 8 102
(Hughie Morrison) *trckd ldr: rdn to ld 2f out: hdd & wknd jst over 1f out* **14/1**

-101 **6** 1 ¼ **Spirit Raiser (IRE)**[46] 3979 5-9-1 103 FrederikTylicki 6 99
(James Fanshawe) *trckd ldrs: rdn to chal 2f out: sn outpcd: n.d fnl f* **9/1**[2]

2126 **7** ½ **Red Box**[14] 5158 3-8-9 101 MartinHarley 1 97
(Sir Mark Prescott Bt) *hld up in midfield: prog towards inner 2f out: racd awkwardly and nt qckn over 1f out: one pce after* **9/1**[2]

0514 **8** 3 ¼ **Epsom Icon**[34] 4435 3-8-13 105 JamesDoyle 7 93
(Mick Channon) *a in midfield: rdn over 2f out: no imp on ldrs over 1f out: wknd fnl f* **16/1**

5211 **9** hd **September Stars (IRE)**[19] 4953 3-8-9 97 JimCrowley 11 89
(Ralph Beckett) *racd wd in bk st: trckd ldng pair: rdn and lost pl fr over 2f out: wknd* **10/1**[3]

0300 **10** nk **Australian Queen**[10] 5307 3-8-9 90 (b[1]) JoeFanning 10 88
(David Elsworth) *chsd ldrs to over 2f out: sn lost pl and in rr* **66/1**

3026 **11** nk **Black Cherry**[29] 4582 4-9-1 100 TomMarquand 2 88
(Richard Hannon) *led to 2f out: wknd* **20/1**

1230 **12** 8 **Clotilde**[46] 3979 4-9-1 100 MartinDwyer 3 70
(William Knight) *s.i.s and urged along early in last pl: nvr a factor: wknd over 2f out: t.o* **25/1**

1m 42.74s (-0.56) **Going Correction** +0.225s/f (Good)

WFA 3 from 4yo+ 6lb **12** Ran SP% **115.6**

Speed ratings (Par 110): **111,108,107,106,105 104,103,100,100,100 99,91**

CSF £13.71 TOTE £2.10: £1.40, £2.60, £5.20; EX 12.80 Trifecta £192.20.

Owner Cheveley Park Stud **Bred** J F Tuthill **Trained** Newmarket, Suffolk

■ Stewards' Enquiry : Harry Bentley jockey said filly was denied a clear run

FOCUS

Add 3yds to race distance. A big field for this Group 3 prize but, with more than half the field rated no higher than 100, it didn't look as deep as the numbers suggested. However, the winner is a filly going places, and going places quickly because she looks top class. The runner-up has a good record here and has been rated similar to her effort in this race last year.

5646 TCA ABU DHABI SOLARIO STKS (GROUP 3) — 7f 16y

3:05 (3:06) (Class 1) 2-Y-O

£25,519 (£9,675; £4,842; £2,412; £1,210; £607) **Stalls** Low

Form RPR

11 **1** **South Seas (IRE)**[36] 4343 2-9-1 0 OisinMurphy 3 107
(Andrew Balding) *awkward s and slowly away: sn in midfield: prog over 2f out: led over 1f out and sn clr: drvn out tl last 50yds: decisively* **9/4**[1]

041 **2** 2 ¼ **Salouen (IRE)**[13] 5203 2-9-1 86 TomMarquand 10 101+
(Sylvester Kirk) *hld up and sn in last: rdn over 2f out and no prog: stl last over 1f out: r.o wl fnl f to take 2nd last 50yds* **16/1**

1 **3** 1 **Eqtiraan (IRE)**[29] 4580 2-9-1 0 TimmyMurphy 1 99
(Richard Hannon) *t.k.h: trckd ldr: tried to cl fr 2f out but wnr sn shot past: chsd wnr and wandering 1f out: no imp and lost 2nd last 50yds* **8/1**[3]

011 **4** ½ **Apex King (IRE)**[28] 4622 2-9-1 92 GeorgeBaker 6 97
(Ed Dunlop) *hld up in rr: stl in last pair 2f out but gng bttr than many: shkn up and weaved through fr over 1f out: tk 4th nr fin but no ch to threaten* **8/1**[3]

611 **5** 1 **Majoris (IRE)**[14] 5171 2-9-1 95 (t) JimCrowley 4 95
(Hugo Palmer) *trckd ldrs: rdn over 2f out: outpcd over 1f out: no imp after* **13/2**[2]

112 **6** 1 ¼ **Monticello (IRE)**[28] 4622 2-9-1 92 JoeFanning 8 91
(Mark Johnston) *led: clr 1/2-way: drvn and hdd over 1f out: wknd fnl f* **8/1**[3]

53 **7** nse **Van Der Decken**[28] 4653 2-9-1 0 JamesDoyle 7 91
(Charlie Appleby) *chsd ldng pair: first one rdn wl over 2f out: lost pl and struggling sn after* **12/1**

215 **8** nk **Repton (IRE)**[25] 4732 2-9-1 103 PatDobbs 5 90
(Richard Hannon) *a in midfield: rdn over 2f out: tried to cl briefly wl over 1f out: sn no prog* **9/1**

21 **9** ½ **Total Star**[10] 5290 2-9-1 83 AdamKirby 2 89
(Luca Cumani) *chsd ldrs: rdn over 2f out: no prog over 1f out: fdd* **14/1**

1 **10** 2 ¾ **Seniority**[15] 5121 2-9-1 0 MartinHarley 12 82
(William Haggas) *awkward s: hld up in last trio: rdn and tried to make prog over 2f out: no hdwy over 1f out: wknd* **12/1**

1m 30.81s (1.31) **Going Correction** +0.225s/f (Good) **10** Ran SP% **115.4**

Speed ratings (Par 104): **101,98,97,96,95 94,94,93,93,90**

CSF £41.81 TOTE £2.90: £1.50, £5.70, £2.20; EX 46.30 Trifecta £487.50.

Owner Qatar Racing Limited **Bred** Stonepark Farms **Trained** Kingsclere, Hants

■ Stewards' Enquiry : Timmy Murphy jockey said colt ran green

Pat Dobbs jockey said colt ran too freely

FOCUS

Add 3yds to race distance. Plenty of progressive colts on show in what looked a competitive Solario Stakes, but the winner got the job done in pretty emphatic style ultimately, and looks capable of holding his own in better company. The opening level is a bit guessy.

5647 NATIONAL FEED & FLOUR PRODUCTION H'CAP — 1m 2f 7y

3:40 (3:42) (Class 2) 3-Y-O+

£31,125 (£9,320; £4,660; £2,330; £1,165; £585) **Stalls** Low

Form RPR

-011 **1** **Baydar**[28] 4650 3-7-12 **95** JosephineGordon[(3)] 1 103+
(Hugo Palmer) *hld up in 7th: squeezed through on inner fr 2f out: drvn to chal and edgd lft ins fnl f: led fnl 75yds: jst hld on* **9/4**[1]

0321 **2** shd **Goodwood Mirage (IRE)**[30] 4561 6-7-13 **88** EdwardGreatrex[(3)] 4 95+
(Michael Bell) *trckd ldng pair: wnt 2nd over 2f out: rdn to ld over 1f out: idled in front: hdd fnl 75yds: kpt on wl once hdd: jst failed* **12/1**

5060 **3** hd **Blue Surf**[14] 5145 7-8-4 **90** (p) MartinDwyer 5 97
(Amanda Perrett) *led: rdn and hdd over 1f out: kpt on wl and nrly upsides ldr 100yds out: jst outpcd* **25/1**

3-16 **4** 1 **Bermondsey**[29] 4583 4-8-6 **92** OisinMurphy 7 97+
(Luca Cumani) *hld up in 9th: waiting for a clr run over 2f out: stdy prog over 1f out: kpt on wl to take 4th nr fin: nvr able to chal* **6/1**[2]

1202 **5** ½ **Oasis Fantasy (IRE)**[25] 4731 5-9-5 **105** (b) GeorgeBaker 2 109
(Ed Dunlop) *trckd ldrs in 6th: clsd up fr 2f out: rdn to try to chal jst over 1f out but racd awkwardly and nt qckn: one pce after* **7/1**[3]

0622 **6** 1 **Scrutinise**[21] 4858 4-8-12 **98** RobertHavlin 8 100
(Ed Dunlop) *trckd ldng trio: rdn 2f out: kpt on but nvr fnd enough pce to chal* **12/1**

0-04 **7** ½ **Muffri'Ha (IRE)**[14] 5158 4-8-12 **98** JoeFanning 9 99
(William Haggas) *hld up in 8th: gng wl bhd ldrs 2f out and looked sure to chal: shkn up and fnd nil over 1f out* **25/1**

0036 **8** ½ **Shell Bay (USA)**[22] 4838 4-8-2 **88** ow1 (b) TomMarquand 3 88
(Richard Hannon) *trckd ldng quartet: rdn to chal 2f out but racd awkwardly and nt qckn: lost pl over 1f out: n.d after* **66/1**

022 **9** ¾ **Master The World (IRE)**[9] 5329 5-9-8 **108** (p) JimCrowley 12 107
(David Elsworth) *hld up in last: rdn over 2f out: racd awkwardly and no prog: nvr a factor* **8/1**

3000 **10** nk **What About Carlo (FR)**[42] 4165 5-8-11 **97** RobertWinston 11 95
(Eve Johnson Houghton) *hld up in last trio: shkn up and no prog over 2f out: no ch after* **10/1**

6161 **11** 1 ¼ **Fire Fighting (IRE)**[7] 5411 5-9-13 **113** (b) AdamKirby 10 108
(Mark Johnston) *v s.i.s: mostly in last trio: brief effrt over 2f out: sn no prog* **11/1**

1300 **12** 18 **Revolutionist (IRE)**[25] 4731 4-9-7 **107** JamesDoyle 6 66
(Mark Johnston) *chsd ldr to over 2f out: wknd rapidly and eased fnl f: t.o* **8/1**

2m 9.57s (-0.93) **Going Correction** +0.225s/f (Good)

WFA 3 from 4yo+ 8lb **12** Ran SP% **121.8**

Speed ratings (Par 109): **112,111,111,110,110 109,109,108,108,108 107,92**

CSF £32.13 CT £560.39 TOTE £3.10: £1.40, £4.30, £9.30; EX 35.90 Trifecta £569.40.

Owner V I Araci **Bred** Fittocks Stud **Trained** Newmarket, Suffolk

FOCUS

Race distance increased by 3yds. A red hot handicap run at what appeared an even gallop, and it was won, narrowly, by the only 3yo in the line-up. The fourth has been rated close to his penultimate C&D win.

5648 GLOBAL UNITED VETERINARY SERVICES H'CAP — 5f 6y

4:15 (4:18) (Class 3) (0-95,95) 3-Y-O+

£9,337 (£2,796; £1,398; £699; £349; £175) **Stalls** Low

Form RPR

0560 **1** **Son Of Africa**[7] 5418 4-9-8 **93** HarryBentley 14 103
(Henry Candy) *slowly away: hld up in last trio: gd prog on wd outside over 1f out: swept into ld last 75yds: sn clr* **10/1**

2056 **2** 1 ¼ **Shipyard (USA)**[7] 5417 7-9-4 **89** (p) TomQueally 13 95
(Michael Appleby) *dwlt: hld up in rr: prog on outer over 1f out: clsd to chal 100yds out: sn outpcd by wnr: kpt on* **11/1**

2160 **3** ¾ **Seeking Magic**[21] 4862 8-9-10 **95** (t) AdamKirby 8 98
(Clive Cox) *led against rail: drvn over 1f out: hdd and outpcd fnl 75yds* **7/1**[3]

5140 **4** shd **Shamshon (IRE)**[21] 4862 5-9-10 **95** GeorgeBaker 3 97+
(Jamie Osborne) *hld up towards rr against rail: gng easily whn waiting for a gap fr 2f out: swtchd lft and r.o strly ins fnl f: gaining at fin* **11/4**[1]

4105 **5** 1 **Soie D'Leau**[7] 5390 4-9-8 **93** JoeFanning 2 92+
(Kristin Stubbs) *trckd ldng pair: gng wl enough whn waiting for a gap fr wl over 1f out: rdn and outpcd ins fnl f* **6/1**[2]

012 **6** nk **Ziggy Lee**[11] 5274 10-8-9 **80** OisinMurphy 4 78+
(Lawrence Mullaney) *trckd ldrs against rail: gng wl enough whn waiting for a gap fr over 1f out: rdn and outpcd ins fnl f* **11/1**

4001 **7** 1 1/4 **Cartmell Cleave**[21] 4889 4-9-5 **90** TedDurcan 12 83+
(Stuart Kittow) *slowly away: hld up in last against rail: gng easily whn trying to cl and waiting for a gap over 1f out: nvr a clr run and allowed to coast home* **14/1**

2203 **8** hd **Gamesome (FR)**[7] 5390 5-9-10 **95** MartinHarley 9 88
(Paul Midgley) *chsd ldr: rdn over 1f out: lost 2nd and wknd jst ins fnl f* **6/1**[2]

0006 **9** 1 **Stepper Point**[14] 5143 7-9-10 **95** (p) MartinDwyer 5 84
(William Muir) *dwlt: a in rr: rdn whn nt clr run over 1f out: no real prog* **8/1**

4134 **10** hd **Secret Asset (IRE)**[8] 5360 11-8-10 **81** (v) TadhgO'Shea 7 69
(Lisa Williamson) *dwlt: chsd ldrs on outer: lost pl over 1f out: fdd* **25/1**

-000 **11** 1 **Elysian Flyer (IRE)**[21] 4862 4-8-13 **84** JimCrowley 10 69
(Richard Hughes) *sn chsd ldrs: drvn 2f out: sn lost pl and btn* **33/1**

0500 **12** 2 **Foxy Forever (IRE)**[29] 4584 6-9-6 **91** [1] RobertHavlin 6 68
(Michael Wigham) *chsd ldrs 3f: wknd* **33/1**

1m 2.28s (0.68) **Going Correction** +0.325s/f (Good) **12** Ran SP% **117.8**
Speed ratings (Par 107): **107,105,103,103,102 101,99,99,97,97 95,92**
CSF £176.65 CT £1365.85 TOTE £20.10: £5.70, £3.40, £2.40; EX 210.40 Trifecta £3667.10 Part Won..
Owner One Too Many Partners **Bred** Mrs P A Clark **Trained** Kingston Warren, Oxon

FOCUS
A wide open sprint but it looks unreliable form given the hard luck stories from runners who raced towards the inside rail. The winner ran a pb here last year and has been rated in line with that.

5649 YAS TV H'CAP 1m 14y
4:50 (4:52) (Class 4) (0-80,82) 3-Y-O+ **£4,690** (£1,395; £697; £348) **Stalls** Low

Form RPR

6-51 **1** **Unison (IRE)**[16] 5076 6-9-3 **71** GeorgeBaker 2 83
(Jeremy Scott) *trckd ldr: cajoled along to ld jst over 1f out: styd on wl: readily* **3/1**[1]

3060 **2** 3 3/4 **Outback Ruler (IRE)**[16] 5075 4-9-12 **80** (p) AdamKirby 8 83
(Clive Cox) *trckd ldr: shkn up to chal 2f out: upsides tl outpcd fnl f: hanging but hld on for 2nd* **4/1**[3]

1643 **3** hd **Bernie's Boy**[31] 4532 3-9-5 **79** OisinMurphy 12 81
(Andrew Balding) *led: racd freely but set mod pce and wd in bk st: rdn and pressed 2f out: hdd jst over 1f out: outpcd* **7/2**[2]

0655 **4** 3/4 **Justice Lass (IRE)**[42] 4157 3-9-0 **74** TedDurcan 11 74
(David Elsworth) *chsd ldng trio: stmbld bnd 5f out: shkn up over 2f out: kpt on same pce and nvr able to chal* **6/1**

0603 **5** 1/2 **Biotic**[16] 5071 5-9-8 **76** (t) FrederikTylicki 10 76
(Rod Millman) *stdd s: hld up in last in modly run event: shkn up over 2f out: no prog and nvr able to threaten: r.o fnl 00yds* **8/1**

12-6 **6** hd **Bag Of Diamonds**[19] 4953 3-9-0 **74** TimmyMurphy 7 73
(Richard Hannon) *chsd ldng trio: stmbld sltly bnd 5f out: shkn up over 2f out: one pce and nvr able to chal* **25/1**

320- **7** 3/4 **Hungerford**[409] 4015 4-9-8 **76** TomQueally 5 74
(Eve Johnson Houghton) *stdd s: hld up in 6th in modly run event: shkn up over 2f out: nvr able to threaten as ldrs weren't stopping* **16/1**

1034 **8** hd **Philadelphia (IRE)**[19] 4953 3-8-13 **80** DavidEgan[(7)] 6 76
(Roger Varian) *stdd s: hld up in 7th in modly run event: shkn up over 2f out: nvr able to get involved* **8/1**

1m 45.03s (1.73) **Going Correction** +0.225s/f (Good)
WFA 3 from 4yo+ 6lb **8** Ran SP% **113.5**
Speed ratings (Par 105): **100,96,96,95,94 94,93,93**
CSF £14.92 CT £42.61 TOTE £3.20: £1.40, £1.40, £1.40; EX 14.60 Trifecta £29.80.
Owner J P Carrington **Bred** Alan Dargan **Trained** Brompton Regis, Somerset

FOCUS
Race distance increased by 3yds. Ordinary handicap form and nothing could get in a blow from off the pace, with the front three filling those positions throughout. The winner has been rated back to his old best.

5650 ABU DHABI SPORTS COUNCIL H'CAP 1m 2f 7y
5:25 (5:25) (Class 4) (0-85,88) 3-Y-O+ **£4,690** (£1,395; £697; £348) **Stalls** Low

Form RPR

1224 **1** **Pure Art**[25] 4737 3-9-5 **84** HarryBentley 6 95+
(Ralph Beckett) *hld up disputing 5th: smooth prog on outer over 2f out: led fnl f: sn rdn and limited rspnse: fnd jst enough to hold on* **6/5**[1]

2110 **2** shd **Man Look**[43] 4095 4-9-13 **84** OisinMurphy 8 94
(Andrew Balding) *trckd ldr after 2f: rdn to chal 2f out: narrow ld over 1f out: hdd fnl f: battled on wl: jst hld* **6/1**[3]

-033 **3** 1 3/4 **Rydan (IRE)**[21] 4888 5-9-9 **80** (v) TomQueally 5 86
(Gary Moore) *hld up disputing 5th: waiting for a gap on inner over 2f out: swtchd lft and rdn over 1f out: styd on to take 3rd ins fnl f: unable to chal* **10/1**

5232 **4** 1 **Perceived**[54] 3721 4-8-13 **75** HectorCrouch[(5)] 2 79
(Henry Candy) *trckd ldng pair: pushed along whn waiting for a gap over 2f out: drvn and kpt on same pce fnl f* **4/1**[2]

5031 **5** 4 **Pink Ribbon (IRE)**[13] 5207 4-8-4 **68** (p) MitchGodwin[(7)] 9 64
(Sylvester Kirk) *t.k.h: trckd ldr 2f: drvn over 2f out: wknd over 1f out* **16/1**

1136 **6** 1/2 **Inniscastle Lad**[59] 3520 4-9-9 **80** (b) GeorgeBaker 11 75
(Stuart Williams) *led: rdn over 2f out: hdd & wknd over 1f out* **12/1**

4425 **7** 9 **Franco's Secret**[52] 3783 5-9-11 **82** (p) MartinDwyer 7 59
(Peter Hedger) *a in last pair: awkward bnd over 4f out to over 3f out: sn wl btn* **14/1**

2103 **8** 26 **Icebuster**[23] 4793 8-9-11 **82** FrederikTylicki 1 7
(Rod Millman) *stdd s: hld up in last pair: wknd 3f out: eased and t.o* **16/1**

2m 11.28s (0.78) **Going Correction** +0.225s/f (Good)
WFA 3 from 4yo+ 8lb **8** Ran SP% **115.0**
Speed ratings (Par 105): **105,104,103,102,99 99,91,71**
CSF £8.88 CT £49.19 TOTE £2.00: £1.10, £2.20, £2.80; EX 8.00 Trifecta £57.00.
Owner R Barnett **Bred** W And R Barnett Ltd **Trained** Kimpton, Hants

FOCUS
Race distance increased by 3yds. This looked quite an open handicap on paper but the market told a different story, with justification as things transpired. The third has been rated close to his recent form for now.
T/Plt: £172.10 to a £1 stake. Pool: £103,878.80 - 440.42 winning tickets T/Qpdt: £42.60 to a £1 stake. Pool: £5,819.19 - 101.06 winning tickets **Jonathan Neesom**

5611 YORK (L-H)
Saturday, August 20

OFFICIAL GOING: Good (home straight 6.9, centre 6.9, stands' 6.8)
Wind: Strong behind Weather: Cloudy and blustery with sunny periods and showers

5651 BETFRED SUPPORTS JACK BERRY HOUSE STKS (H'CAP) 1m 2f 88y
1:45 (1:46) (Class 2) (0-105,104) 3-Y-O+
£37,350 (£11,184; £5,592; £2,796; £1,398; £702) **Stalls** Low

Form RPR

6114 **1** **Scarlet Dragon**[23] 4797 3-8-4 **92** LukeMorris 2 106
(Eve Johnson Houghton) *trckd ldrs on inner: hdwy over 2f out: rdn to ld jst appr fnl f: styd on strly* **11/2**[1]

1114 **2** 2 3/4 **Dark Red (IRE)**[78] 2866 4-9-1 **95** FrankieDettori 12 103
(Ed Dunlop) *lw: trckd ldr: led over 2f out: rdn over 1f out: hung lft and hdd appr fnl f: sn drvn: kpt on same pce* **15/2**[2]

3240 **3** 1 3/4 **Erik The Red (FR)**[25] 4731 4-9-2 **96** DeclanMcDonogh 13 101+
(Kevin Ryan) *midfield: hdwy on outer over 2f out: rdn wl over 1f out: styd on fnl f: nrst fin* **8/1**[3]

3543 **4** nk **Sennockian Star**[14] 5173 6-8-3 **83** (v) AndrewMullen 6 87
(Mark Johnston) *cl up: rdn along and ev ch over 2f out: drvn over 1f out: n.m.r jst ins fnl f: grad wknd* **16/1**

4560 **5** 1 1/4 **Battalion (IRE)**[63] 3383 6-9-10 **104** (p) JimmyFortune 4 105+
(William Haggas) *hld up and bhd: gd hdwy on inner 2f out: rdn over 1f out: styd on wl fnl f: nrst fin* **16/1**

/040 **6** nk **Stipulate**[20] 4921 7-9-6 **100** BenCurtis 15 101
(Brian Ellison) *towards rr: hdwy on outer 2f out: rdn over 1f out: kpt on fnl f: nrst fin* **14/1**

0610 **7** 1 **Master Of Irony (IRE)**[71] 3109 4-8-11 **91** (v) PatCosgrave 10 90+
(Ralph Beckett) *dwlt and towards rr: hdwy into midfield 3f out: rdn along 2f out: kpt on fnl f* **14/1**

5130 **8** 3/4 **Montsarrat (IRE)**[23] 4797 3-8-7 **95** FrannyNorton 7 92
(Mark Johnston) *lw: slt ld: rdn along and hdd over 2f out: cl up and drvn over 1f out: hld whn n.m.r and squeezed out jst ins fnl f: wknd* **20/1**

1040 **9** 1 1/4 **Imshivalla (IRE)**[25] 4731 5-8-12 **92** PaulHanagan 11 87
(Richard Fahey) *chsd ldrs: rdn along over 2f out: drvn wl over 1f out: grad wknd* **16/1**

1426 **10** nk **Snoano**[25] 4731 4-9-1 **95** PaulMulrennan 16 89
(Tim Easterby) *in tch: hdwy 3f out: rdn along 2f out: sn no imp* **15/2**[2]

4050 **11** 1 1/4 **Chancery (USA)**[35] 4407 8-9-1 **95** (p) DanielTudhope 5 87
(David O'Meara) *midfield: effrt 3f out: rdn along over 2f out: n.d* **12/1**

3000 **12** 1/2 **Afonso De Sousa (USA)**[119] 1629 6-9-2 **99** AlistairRawlinson[(3)] 9 90
(Michael Appleby) *chsd ldrs: rdn along 3f out: wknd fnl 2f* **50/1**

-460 **13** 1 1/2 **Mohab**[28] 4624 3-8-8 **96** KevinStott 14 84
(Kevin Ryan) *in rr: effrt on outer 3f out: sn rdn along and nvr a factor* **28/1**

6123 **14** 1/2 **Ode To Evening**[14] 5160 3-9-0 **102** WilliamBuick 1 89
(Mark Johnston) *a towards rr* **9/1**

-614 **15** shd **Fallen For A Star**[38] 4276 4-8-11 **91** JamieSpencer 8 78
(Luca Cumani) *a towards rr* **10/1**

-043 **16** 1/2 **Awake My Soul (IRE)**[56] 3666 7-9-2 **96** JamesSullivan 18 82
(Tom Tate) *lw: towards rr: effrt and sme hdwy on outer over 3f out: sn rdn and n.d* **16/1**

2m 9.2s (-3.30) **Going Correction** -0.225s/f (Firm)
WFA 3 from 4yo+ 8lb **16** Ran SP% **123.8**
Speed ratings (Par 109): **104,101,100,100,99 98,98,97,96,96 95,94,93,93,93 92**
CSF £43.96 CT £339.52 TOTE £6.00: £1.70, £2.10, £2.10, £4.60; EX 36.20 Trifecta £80.30.
Owner W H Ponsonby **Bred** Usk Valley Stud **Trained** Blewbury, Oxon

FOCUS
Rail realigned on to inner track on home bend from 9f to entrance to home straight. There was a fierce tailwind in the final 3f. This decent opening handicap was run at a sound pace. The field kept to the centre after turning in but the main action developed on the far side late on. Race distance reduced by 32yds. The runner-up has been rated back to form off a break and the third as close to form.

5652 BETFRED MOBILE STRENSALL STKS (GROUP 3) 1m 208y
2:15 (2:16) (Class 1) 3-Y-O+
£48,203 (£18,275; £9,146; £4,556; £2,286; £1,147) **Stalls** Low

Form RPR

-312 **1** **Scottish (IRE)**[14] 5159 4-9-5 113 WilliamBuick 10 119
(Charlie Appleby) *lw: trckd ldr on outer: cl up 1/2-way: led over 2f out: rdn clr over 1f out: edgd lft ins fnl f: kpt on wl* **5/1**[2]

2 1 1/4 **Yorker (SAF)**[805] 7-9-5 118 PatCosgrave 7 116
(William Haggas) *swtg: dwlt and hld up in rr: hdwy 3f out: trckd ldrs on inner 2f out: rdn over 1f out: drvn ins fnl f and sn chsng wnr: kpt on* **14/1**

0344 **3** nk **Custom Cut (IRE)**[7] 5343 7-9-5 114 DanielTudhope 3 115
(David O'Meara) *led: pushed along 3f out: hdd over 2f out and sn rdn: drvn over 1f out: kpt on wl u.p fnl f* **6/1**[3]

1354 **4** 3 1/4 **Gabrial (IRE)**[14] 5159 7-9-5 113 PaulHanagan 9 108
(Richard Fahey) *towards rr: hdwy on outer to trck ldrs 1/2-way: pushed along wl over 2f out: rdn wl over 1f out: kpt on same pce* **16/1**

-251 **5** 3 1/2 **Educate**[42] 4165 7-9-5 112 ThomasBrown 8 100
(Ismail Mohammed) *hld up: hdwy wl over 2f out: rdn wl over 1f out: no imp fnl f* **11/1**

-243 **6** 1 **Countermeasure**[28] 4666 4-9-5 112 FrankieDettori 5 98
(Roger Charlton) *lw: trckd ldrs: hdwy 3f out: rdn along 2f out: sn drvn and wknd over 1f out* **9/1**

4520 **7** 2 **Celestial Path (IRE)**[22] 4823 4-9-5 104 (v[1]) LukeMorris 2 94
(Sir Mark Prescott Bt) *swtg: hld up: hdwy over 3f out: chsd ldrs 2f out: sn rdn and wknd over 1f out* **12/1**

-151 **8** 3 3/4 **Diploma**[29] 4610 3-8-9 110 AndreaAtzeni 4 82
(Sir Michael Stoute) *in tch: pushed along to chse ldrs 3f out: rdn over 2f out and sn wknd* **11/4**[1]

5351 **9** 1/2 **Tullius (IRE)**[78] 2867 8-9-9 110 (v) JimmyFortune 6 88
(Andrew Balding) *hld up towards rr: hdwy 3f out: rdn along over 2f out: sn btn* **12/1**

2014 **10** 5 **Air Pilot**[28] 4666 7-9-9 113 PaulMulrennan 1 77
(Ralph Beckett) *trckd ldrs on inner: hdwy over 3f out: rdn along over 2f out: sn drvn and wknd* **7/1**

1m 46.61s (-5.39) **Going Correction** -0.225s/f (Firm) course record
WFA 3 from 4yo+ 7lb **10** Ran SP% **116.4**
Speed ratings (Par 113): **114,112,112,109,106 105,103,100,100,95**
CSF £72.26 TOTE £4.90: £1.80, £4.20, £2.40; EX 63.40 Trifecta £435.80.
Owner Godolphin **Bred** Knocktoran Stud **Trained** Newmarket, Suffolk

FOCUS
A decent Group 3. Those racing handily held the advantage and again the main action was far side late on. The principals finished clear. Race distance reduced by 31yds. The third has been rated close to form.

5653 BETFRED MELROSE STKS (H'CAP) 1m 6f
2:50 (2:50) (Class 2) (0-105,95) 3-Y-O

£52,912 (£15,844; £7,922; £3,961; £1,980; £994) **Stalls** Low

Form RPR

0010 **1** **Wall Of Fire (IRE)**[21] 4863 3-9-6 **94**..............(b) WilliamBuick 4 107
(Hugo Palmer) *bhd: hdwy 3f out: swtchd lft 2f and sn rdn to chse ldrs: swtchd rt and drvn ent fnl f: styd on strly to ld last 100yds* **16/1**

121 **2** 2 ¾ **Regal Monarch**[6] 5434 3-9-3 **91** 6ex.............. FrannyNorton 7 100
(Mark Johnston) *lw: prom: cl up over 4f out: rdn over 2f out: led ent fnl f: sn drvn: hdd and no ex last 100yds* **8/1**

0- **3** 1 ¼ **Unicorn (IRE)**[328] 6793 3-9-7 **95**..............(p) JamieSpencer 5 103
(A P O'Brien, Ire) *hld up in rr: stdy hdwy over 3f out: chsd ldrs wl over 1f out: drvn and ev ch ent fnl f: kpt on same pce* **14/1**

1336 **4** 1 **Master Blueyes (IRE)**[21] 4863 3-8-9 **83**.............. FergusSweeney 9 89
(Alan King) *hld up in rr: hdwy on wd outside 3f out: rdn to chse ldrs over 1f out: sltly hmpd and drvn ent fnl f: drvn and kpt on towards fin* **7/1**[3]

3102 **5** hd **Shraaoh (IRE)**[21] 4863 3-9-5 **93**.............. FrankieDettori 12 99
(Sir Michael Stoute) *hld up in tch: hdwy to chse ldrs 3f out: pushed along over 2f out: sn rdn on inner and n.m.r wl over 1f out: drvn ent fnl f: kpt on same pce* **3/1**[1]

2315 **6** ½ **Emperor Napoleon**[21] 4863 3-9-0 **88**.............. LiamKeniry 1 93+
(Andrew Balding) *lw: t.k.h: trckd ldrs on inner: hdwy 4f out: led wl over 2f out: rdn wl over 1f out: drvn and hdd ent fnl f: grad wknd* **8/1**

0112 **7** 5 **Icefall (IRE)**[7] 5420 3-8-7 **81**.............. JamesSullivan 11 79
(Tim Easterby) *swtg: in tch: hdwy on outer to chse ldrs 3f out: rdn along 2f out: sn drvn and grad wknd* **33/1**

3124 **8** 3 ¼ **Jaameh (IRE)**[21] 4863 3-8-9 **83**.............. PaulHanagan 13 77
(Mark Johnston) *cl up: led after 2f: pushed along 4f out: rdn over 3f out: hdd wl over 2f out: cl up and drvn over 1f out: sn wknd* **11/1**

9 6 **Kellstorm (IRE)**[101] 2169 3-9-4 **92**..............[1] SeamieHeffernan 8 77
(A P O'Brien, Ire) *midfield: hdwy 4f out: rdn along wl over 2f out: sn drvn and wknd* **6/1**[2]

1301 **10** 1 **Theos Lolly (IRE)**[7] 5420 3-8-6 **80**.............. PatrickMathers 2 64
(Richard Fahey) *lw: in tch on inner: rdn along over 4f out: sn wknd* **25/1**

2321 **11** 1 ½ **Injam (IRE)**[51] 3809 3-8-10 **84**.............. PaulMulrennan 6 66
(Jedd O'Keeffe) *led 2f: prom: rdn along over 4f out: sn wknd* **11/1**

321 **12** 2 ½ **Forth Bridge**[73] 3028 3-9-1 **89**.............. AndreaAtzeni 3 67
(Michael Bell) *trckd ldrs: pushed along and hdwy 4f out: rdn wl over 2f out: sn drvn and wknd* **11/1**

2105 **13** 20 **Girling (IRE)**[36] 4351 3-8-13 **87**.............. DanielTudhope 10 37
(Ralph Beckett) *towards rr: rapid hdwy on outer to chse ldrs after 4f: rdn along 5f out: wknd 4f out: sn bhd and eased* **25/1**

2m 56.94s (-3.26) **Going Correction** -0.225s/f (Firm) **13** Ran SP% **122.2**
Speed ratings (Par 106): **100,98,97,97,97 96,93,92,88,88 87,85,74**
CSF £139.05 CT £1863.44 TOTE £20.70: £5.30, £2.70, £4.50; EX 177.20 Trifecta £4250.90 Part Won..

Owner Carmichael Jennings **Bred** B V Sangster **Trained** Newmarket, Suffolk

FOCUS
There was a brisk pace on in this long-established 3yo staying handicap. The runner-up is a solid benchmark. Race distance reduced by 32yds. The runner-up has been rated better than ever, while the fourth, fifth and sixth all came out of the same Goodwood race and have been rated similar.

5654 IRISH THOROUGHBRED MARKETING GIMCRACK STKS (GROUP 2) (C&G) 6f
3:25 (3:26) (Class 1) 2-Y-O

£124,762 (£47,300; £23,672; £11,792; £5,918; £2,970) **Stalls** Low

Form RPR

112 **1** **Blue Point (IRE)**[23] 4798 2-9-0 109.............. WilliamBuick 4 116+
(Charlie Appleby) *lw: trckd ldrs: cl up over 2f out: led 1 1/2f out: rdn and qcknd clr ins fnl f: kpt on strly* **11/8**[1]

101 **2** 3 **Mokarris (USA)**[36] 4352 2-9-0 105.............. PaulHanagan 10 106
(Simon Crisford) *trckd ldrs: hdwy and cl up over 2f out: sn ev ch: rdn over 1f out: drvn and kpt on fnl f* **11/2**[3]

2212 **3** 1 ¾ **The Last Lion (IRE)**[24] 4755 2-9-0 105.............. FrannyNorton 7 100
(Mark Johnston) *lw: trckd ldr: hdwy and cl up 1/2-way: disp ld 2f out and ev ch: rdn over 1f out: drvn ins fnl f: kpt on same pce* **14/1**

2153 **4** shd **Global Applause**[24] 4755 2-9-0 105.............. AndreaAtzeni 9 100
(Ed Dunlop) *hld up towards rr: hdwy wl over 1f out: sn rdn and styd on wl fnl f: nrst fin* **20/1**

221 **5** 1 **Grey Britain**[7] 5395 2-9-0 80.............. JimmyFortune 6 97
(John Ryan) *slt ld: jnd over 2f out: rdn and hdd wl over 1f out: sn drvn and grad wknd* **50/1**

215 **6** ¾ **Medici Banchiere**[44] 4060 2-9-0 99.............. DougieCostello 1 94
(K R Burke) *racd wd: cl up: rdn along over 2f out: drvn wl over 1f out: grad wknd* **33/1**

110 **7** 1 ½ **Ardad (IRE)**[44] 4060 2-9-0 101.............. FrankieDettori 5 90
(John Gosden) *t.k.h: chsd ldrs: rdn along over 2f out: sn wknd* **7/1**

11 **8** ¾ **Mubtasim (IRE)**[16] 5058 2-9-0 0.............. PatCosgrave 3 87
(William Haggas) *lw: dwlt and towards rr: hdwy 1/2-way: trckd ldrs 2f out and sn rdn: wknd over 1f out* **4/1**[2]

12 **9** 30 **Unabated (IRE)**[28] 4653 2-9-0 0.............. DarryllHolland 2
(Marco Botti) *t.k.h: in tch towards far rail: rdn along wl over 2f out: sn outpcd and bhd* **33/1**

213 **P** **Dream Of Dreams (IRE)**[56] 3678 2-9-0 102.............. JamieSpencer 8
(Kevin Ryan) *trckd ldrs: lost action and p.u qckly bef 1/2-way: dismntd* **10/1**

1m 9.0s (-2.90) **Going Correction** -0.225s/f (Firm) **10** Ran SP% **118.4**
Speed ratings (Par 106): **110,106,103,103,102 101,99,98,58,**
CSF £8.97 TOTE £2.30: £1.20, £2.00, £3.00; EX 10.90 Trifecta £91.00.

Owner Godolphin **Bred** Oak Lodge Bloodstock **Trained** Newmarket, Suffolk

FOCUS
This was a strong Gimcrack and the form is straightforward. The winner has been rated the best winner since Turtle Island (119) in 1993, while the runner-up travelled well and more than confirmed his latest effort. The third has been rated to his recent level and gives a solid guide to the form.

5655 BETFRED EBOR (HERITAGE H'CAP) 1m 6f
4:00 (4:00) (Class 2) 3-Y-O+

£174,300 (£52,192; £26,096; £13,048; £6,524; £3,276) **Stalls** Low

Form RPR

00-0 **1** **Heartbreak City (FR)**[22] 1967 6-9-1 **103**..............(t) AdamMcNamara(5) 15 115
(A J Martin, Ire) *hld up: smooth hdwy over 3f out: trckd ldrs over 2f out: chal wl over 1f out: rdn to ld appr fnl f: styd on strly* **15/2**[3]

515 **2** 4 **Shrewd**[42] 4164 6-8-10 **100**.............. CliffordLee(7) 10 106
(Iain Jardine) *hld up and bhd: hdwy on wd outside 3f out: rdn along 2f out: styd on strly appr fnl f* **12/1**

03-6 **3** hd **Quick Jack (IRE)**[23] 1967 7-8-13 **103**.............. OisinOrr(7) 8 109
(A J Martin, Ire) *hld up in rr: hdwy on outer over 3f out: rdn along 2f out: sn chsng ldrs: drvn and kpt on wl fnl f* **10/1**

1445 **4** 1 ½ **Battersea**[7] 5402 5-9-10 **107**..............[1] AndreaAtzeni 18 111
(Roger Varian) *hld up in rr: hdwy 3f out: in tch and rdn 2f out: drvn over 1f out: kpt on fnl f* **16/1**

-620 **5** nk **Seamour (IRE)**[42] 4164 5-9-6 **103**.............. BenCurtis 22 107
(Brian Ellison) *lw: trckd ldr: effrt to ld wl over 2f out: rdn and edgd lft wl over 1f out: hdd and drvn appr fnl f: kpt on same pce* **14/1**

4460 **6** 2 ½ **Oriental Fox (GER)**[23] 4799 8-9-7 **104**.............. FrannyNorton 13 104
(Mark Johnston) *prom: cl up 4f out: rdn over 2f out and ev ch: drvn over 1f out and grad wknd* **20/1**

-401 **7** ¾ **Oceanographer**[21] 4858 4-9-7 **104** 4ex.............. MartinLane 2 104
(Charlie Appleby) *lw: dwlt and in rr: hdwy wl over 2f out: swtchd lft to inner and rdn wl over 1f out: kpt on: nrst fin* **20/1**

0-41 **8** 2 **Antiquarium (IRE)**[56] 3658 4-9-8 **105**.............. WilliamBuick 7 101
(Charlie Appleby) *hld up in midfield: hdwy on outer 3f out: rdn to chse ldrs wl over 1f out: drvn appr fnl f: sn wknd* **13/2**[2]

-300 **9** ¾ **Seismos (IRE)**[56] 3658 8-9-3 **103**.............. MarcMonaghan(3) 16 98
(Marco Botti) *in tch: hdwy to chse ldrs 3f out: rdn over 2f out: sn drvn and grad wknd* **25/1**

-000 **10** shd **Fun Mac (GER)**[25] 4734 5-9-1 **103**..............(t) CharlieBennett(5) 6 98
(Hughie Morrison) *dwlt and towards rr: hdwy 3f out: rdn along over 2f out: kpt on* **25/1**

0110 **11** 2 **Kinema (IRE)**[23] 4799 5-9-10 **107**.............. PatCosgrave 20 99
(Ralph Beckett) *towards rr: hdwy over 3f out: rdn along over 2f out: n.d* **9/1**

1303 **12** 2 ¾ **Top Tug (IRE)**[43] 4115 5-9-2 **99**.............. FergusSweeney 4 87
(Alan King) *in tch: hdwy 3f out: chsd ldrs over 2f out: sn rdn and wknd over 1f out* **11/1**

2100 **13** 2 **Tawdeea**[25] 4734 4-9-7 **104**.............. DanielTudhope 3 90
(David O'Meara) *in tch on inner: hdwy 4f out: cl up over 2f out: sn rdn and ev ch: drvn over 1f out and grad wknd* **16/1**

-212 **14** 1 **She Is No Lady**[49] 3913 4-9-4 **101**.............. FrankieDettori 5 85
(Ralph Beckett) *trckd ldrs: hdwy 4f out: cl up 3f out: sn chal: rdn over 2f out and ev ch: drvn over 1f out: sn wknd and eased* **4/1**[1]

4000 **15** 3 ¼ **Havana Beat (IRE)**[3] 5559 6-9-1 **98**..............(vt) DougieCostello 14 77
(Rod Millman) *led: and sn clr: pushed along over 4f out: rdn over 3f out: hdd wl over 2f out and sn wknd* **33/1**

60-0 **16** 8 **Vent De Force**[49] 3913 5-9-9 **106**.............. PJMcDonald 11 74
(Hughie Morrison) *nvr bttr than midfield* **20/1**

-000 **17** 4 **The Twisler**[23] 4799 4-9-7 **104**.............. DarryllHolland 17 66
(Jane Chapple-Hyam) *a towards rr* **50/1**

6230 **18** 7 **Ballynanty (IRE)**[49] 3913 4-9-5 **102**..............(t) LiamKeniry 1 54
(Andrew Balding) *midfield: hdwy and in tch 6f out: rdn along 4f out: sn wknd* **50/1**

3001 **19** ¾ **Elidor**[25] 4734 6-9-12 **109** 4ex.............. PaulHanagan 9 60
(Mick Channon) *trckd ldrs: hdwy over 3f out: rdn along wl over 2f out: sn drvn and wknd* **20/1**

1346 **20** 5 **Sir Chauvelin**[42] 4164 4-9-2 **99**.............. PaulMulrennan 12 43
(Jim Goldie) *lw: a towards rr* **25/1**

2m 56.13s (-4.07) **Going Correction** -0.225s/f (Firm) **20** Ran SP% **136.1**
Speed ratings (Par 109): **102,99,99,98,98 97,96,95,95,95 93,92,91,90,88 83,81,77,77,74**
CSF £90.01 CT £943.32 TOTE £9.20: £2.80, £3.80, £3.20, £4.70; EX 115.30 Trifecta £1153.90.
Owner Here For The Craic Partnership **Bred** Mrs Isabelle Corbani **Trained** Summerhill, Co. Meath

FOCUS
Race distance reduced by 32yds. What had looked a typically competitive edition of the race produced a clear-cut winner and, although run at a pretty steady pace early, the closers came to the fore and the form looks solid in behind the winner. The field headed centre-to-far side in the straight. The fourth and fifth help set the standard.

5656 JULIA GRAVES ROSES STKS (LISTED RACE) 5f
4:35 (4:36) (Class 1) 2-Y-O

£34,026 (£12,900; £6,456; £3,216; £1,614; £810) **Stalls** Low

Form RPR

1015 **1** **Big Time Baby (IRE)**[24] 4755 2-9-0 93..............(t) FrankieDettori 5 105
(Tom Dascombe) *cl up: led over 2f out: rdn wl over 1f out: clr ins fnl f: sn drvn and jst hld on* **6/1**[3]

3151 **2** hd **Afandem (IRE)**[25] 4750 2-9-3 103.............. AndreaAtzeni 8 107
(Hugo Palmer) *lw: in tch: hdwy 2f out: rdn over 1f out: chsd wnr ins fnl f: kpt on strly towards fin: jst failed* **7/2**[2]

2261 **3** 4 **Smokey Lane (IRE)**[5] 5484 2-9-0 96.............. DeclanMcDonogh 1 90
(David Evans) *sltly hmpd s: sn pushed along and outpcd towards rr: hdwy on inner 2f out: swtchd rt and rdn ent fnl f: kpt on wl towards fin* **10/1**

11 **4** 1 ½ **Sutter County**[129] 1422 2-9-0 0.............. FrannyNorton 3 84
(Mark Johnston) *lw: wnt lft s: cl up: rdn along 2f out and ev ch tl drvn and wknd ent fnl f* **15/8**[1]

4211 **5** ½ **Final Reckoning (IRE)**[22] 4825 2-9-0 90.............. WilliamBuick 4 84+
(Charlie Appleby) *towards rr: hdwy 2f out: sn rdn and noo imp fnl f* **7/2**[2]

0041 **6** 1 ½ **Megan Lily (IRE)**[13] 5188 2-8-9 77.............. JackGarritty 6 72
(Richard Fahey) *t.k.h: chsd ldrs: rdn along 2f out: sn wknd* **20/1**

416 **7** 2 ¼ **Kyllang Rock (IRE)**[24] 4755 2-9-0 86.............. PaulMulrennan 2 69
(James Tate) *sltly hmpd s: sn slt ld: pushed along and hdd over 2f out: sn rdn and wknd over 1f out* **14/1**

401 **8** 2 ¼ **Secret Potion**[17] 5008 2-9-0 77.............. LiamKeniry 7 61
(Ronald Harris) *w'like: dwlt and a bhd* **50/1**

57.11s (-2.19) **Going Correction** -0.225s/f (Firm) 2y crse rec **8** Ran SP% **116.0**
Speed ratings (Par 102): **108,107,101,98,98 95,92,88**
CSF £27.73 TOTE £6.70: £1.80, £1.70, £2.80; EX 29.70 Trifecta £212.50.

Owner Jones & Owen Promotions Ltd **Bred** Paul & Billy McEnery **Trained** Malpas, Cheshire

FOCUS

No hanging around here, with the winner one of three runners to go tearing off, and the front pair came clear. Strong form for the grade.

5657 BETFRED APPRENTICE STKS (H'CAP) 5f

5:05 (5:10) (Class 2) (0-105,95) 3-Y-O

£37,350 (£11,184; £5,592; £2,796; £1,398; £702) **Stalls** Centre

Form RPR

1424 **1** **East Street Revue**[7] 5409 3-8-10 **84**..............................(b) RobHornby 11 94
(Tim Easterby) *dwlt and sltly hmpd s: sn swtchd lft and in tch: hdwy to trck ldrs 2f out: rdn over 1f out: drvn ins fnl f: kpt on to ld nr fin* **8/1**[3]

10-5 **2** ½ **Love On The Rocks (IRE)**[13] 5205 3-8-7 **81**......... MichaelJMMurphy 8 89
(Charles Hills) *led: rdn along wl over 1f out: drvn ins fnl f: hdd and no ex nr fin* **20/1**

1110 **3** ½ **Just Glamorous (IRE)**[23] 4803 3-9-4 **92**.................. GeorgeDowning 16 98
(Ronald Harris) *racd alone nr stands' rail: cl up: rdn along and disp ld over 1f out: drvn and ev ch ins fnl f: no ex towards fin* **14/1**

6400 **4** *shd* **El Astronaute (IRE)**[23] 4803 3-8-7 **84**.................. CallumShepherd[(3)] 14 90
(John Quinn) *hld up towards rr: hdwy 2f out: rdn over 1f out: drvn and edgd lft ins fnl f: styd on wl towards fin* **20/1**

1221 **5** ½ **Laughton**[23] 4803 3-8-9 **83**... KevinStott 5 87+
(Kevin Ryan) *hld up in rr: hdwy wl over 1f out: swtchd lft and rdn ins fnl f: kpt on: nrst fin* **11/4**[1]

2104 **6** *nk* **Celebration**[23] 4803 3-8-11 **88**..............................(p) AdamMcNamara[(3)] 9 91
(Richard Fahey) *chsd ldrs: hdwy 2f out: rdn over 1f out: drvn and hld whn n.m.r ins fnl f* **7/1**[2]

041 **7** *1* **Lady Macapa**[55] 3685 3-9-2 **95**.................................. PaddyBradley[(5)] 12 95
(William Knight) *dwlt and wnt lft s: towards rr: hdwy 2f out: rdn to chse ldrs over 1f out: drvn and n.m.r ins fnl f: kpt on same pce* **16/1**

401 **8** *nk* **Excessable**[19] 4947 3-8-5 **82**..(t) NathanEvans[(3)] 7 84+
(Tim Easterby) *cl up: rdn wl over 1f out: drvn and ev ch ent fnl f: hld whn n.m.r last 100yds* **16/1**

5060 **9** *hd* **Field Of Vision (IRE)**[14] 5148 3-8-13 **94**................... SeanMooney[(7)] 13 92
(Joseph Tuite) *chsd ldrs on outer: rdn along 2f out: drvn over 1f out: one pce fnl f* **33/1**

5556 **10** ½ **Lathom**[7] 5390 3-9-0 **91**...(v[1]) JoshDoyle[(3)] 10 87
(David O'Meara) *chsd ldrs: rdn along wl over 1f out: wknd appr fnl f* **7/1**[2]

1000 **11** *1* **Sign Of The Kodiac (IRE)**[7] 5390 3-8-12 **93**.........[1] LewisEdmunds[(7)] 3 85
(James Given) *in tch: rdn along and outpcd 1/2-way: towards rr after* **14/1**

0264 **12** *1* **Suqoor**[14] 5148 3-8-6 **85**.. CliffordLee[(5)] 6 74
(Chris Dwyer) *chsd ldrs: rdn along over 2f out: sn wknd* **20/1**

11-4 **13** 1½ **Quatrieme Ami**[148] 1070 3-9-6 **94**.............................. MarcMonaghan 15 77
(Philip McBride) *a towards rr* **16/1**

306 **14** ¾ **Lydia's Place**[11] 5274 3-7-11 **78**.. PaulaMuir[(7)] 4 59
(Richard Guest) *awkward s: a towards rr* **25/1**

0 **15** *2* **Top Of The Bank**[30] 4547 3-8-4 **78**......................................(p) JoeDoyle 2 51
(Kevin Ryan) *chsd ldrs on inner: rdn along 1/2-way and sn wknd* **20/1**

57.19s (-2.11) **Going Correction** -0.225s/f (Firm) **15** Ran SP% **119.6**

Speed ratings (Par 106): **107,106,105,105,104 103,102,101,101,100 99,97,95,93,90**

CSF £141.40 CT £1685.83 TOTE £9.20: £3.10, £3.20, £2.80; EX 190.20 Trifecta £2525.00 Part Won..

Owner S A Heley **Bred** Habton Farms & A Heley **Trained** Great Habton, N Yorks

■ Midnight Malibu was withdrawn. Price at time of withdrawal 7/1. Rule 4 applies to all bets - deduction 10p in the pound

■ Stewards' Enquiry : Michael J M Murphy caution: careless riding

FOCUS

A useful sprint handicap, with all bar third racing far side. The form is set around the fourth to his recent efforts.

T/Jkpt: Not Won. T/Plt: £423.30 to a £1 stake. Pool: £290,388.75 - 500.74 winning tickets. T/Qpdt: £79.00 to a £1 stake. Pool: £16,678.09 - 156.13 winning tickets. **Joe Rowntree**

5658 - 5659a (Foreign Racing) - See Raceform Interactive

5209 CURRAGH (R-H)

Saturday, August 20

OFFICIAL GOING: Good (good to yielding in places on straight course)

5660a PALMERSTOWN HOUSE ESTATE IRISH ST LEGER TRIAL STKS (GROUP 3) 1m 6f

2:45 (2:45) 3-Y-O+ **£27,352** (£8,823; £4,191; £1,875; £948)

RPR

1 **Order Of St George (IRE)**[65] 3298 4-10-0 124........ DonnachaO'Brien 4 117+
(A P O'Brien, Ire) *settled in 4th: travelled wl to cl on ldng pair over 1f out: led 1f out and sn in command under hands and heels: comf* **2/11**[1]

2 1½ **Twilight Payment (IRE)**[35] 4418 3-8-11 100..............(p) KevinManning 2 109
(J S Bolger, Ire) *led and hdd after 1f: chsd ldr in 2nd: pushed along to cl over 3f out: on terms appr fnl f: hdd 1f out and no match for wnr but kpt on wl in clr 2nd* **6/1**[2]

3 *9* **Arya Tara (IRE)**[18] 5002 3-8-8 96..(t) AnaO'Brien 1 94
(Joseph Patrick O'Brien, Ire) *led after 1f: strly pressed over 1f out and hdd 1f out: sn no ex* **25/1**

4 2¼ **Benkei (IRE)**[26] 4721 6-9-9 100.. ChrisHayes 3 93
(H Rogers, Ire) *chsd ldrs in 3rd: rdn over 3f out: no imp in 4th over 1f out: sn one pce* **20/1**

5 *15* **Charming Kitten (USA)**[29] 4615 6-9-9 108....................(b) PatSmullen 5 72
(D K Weld, Ire) *racd in rr thrght: rdn and detached 3f out: eased ins fnl f* **12/1**[3]

3m 9.2s (-0.20) **Going Correction** +0.325s/f (Good)

WFA 3 from 4yo+ 12lb **5** Ran SP% **115.2**

Speed ratings: **113,112,107,105,97**

CSF £2.16 TOTE £1.10: £1.10, £1.50; DF 2.70 Trifecta £9.80.

Owner L J Williams/Mrs J Magnier/M Tabor/D Smith **Bred** Paget Bloodstock **Trained** Cashel, Co Tipperary

FOCUS

A very convincing performance from the winner, and a considerable honourable mention for the runner-up. The third has been rated to her best.

5661a JIMMY O'NEILL IRISH RACING EXCELLENCE CURRAGH STKS (GROUP 3) 5f

3:20 (3:21) 2-Y-O

£26,029 (£8,382; £3,970; £1,764; £882; £441)

RPR

1 **Hit The Bid**[91] 2494 2-9-3 0.. LeighRoche 3 101
(D J Bunyan, Ire) *broke wl and chsd ldrs on far side in 4th: tacked across to stands' side over 1f out where led: hung lft and styd on wl clsng stages* **50/1**

2 ½ **Mur Hiba (IRE)**[13] 5209 2-9-0 87.................................... KevinManning 6 97
(M D O'Callaghan, Ire) *racd in mid-div: rdn and clsr 1f out in 4th: kpt on wl into 2nd fnl 100yds: nt rch wnr* **10/1**

3 ½ **Yulong Baobei (IRE)**[42] 4171 2-9-0 107............................ ShaneFoley 2 95
(M Halford, Ire) *led in centre of trck: tacked across to stands' rails at 1/2-way: hdd over 1f out: short of room against rails fnl 150yds: kpt on same pce in 3rd* **9/4**[2]

4 ¾ **Velveteen**[34] 4431 2-9-0 0... ColinKeane 4 92
(G M Lyons, Ire) *sn chsd ldrs in 3rd: almost on terms over 1f out: no imp in 4th fnl 100yds: kpt on same pce* **10/1**

5 *shd* **Sportsmanship (USA)**[24] 4755 2-9-3 0.................... DonnachaO'Brien 8 96
(A P O'Brien, Ire) *hld up towards rr: prog whn nt clr run over 1f out in 8th: kpt on wl clsng stages into 5th: nrst fin* **3/1**[3]

6 *hd* **Mayleaf Shine (IRE)**[15] 5134 2-9-0 90.............................. GaryCarroll 1 91
(Joseph G Murphy, Ire) *hld up: prog on outer appr fnl f in 6th: kpt on wl clsng stages: nvr on terms* **16/1**

7 *hd* **Miss Cogent (IRE)**[15] 5134 2-9-0 80......................................[1] BillyLee 9 90
(J P Murtagh, Ire) *racd in rr tl prog on outer ent fnl f: kpt on strly clsng stages: nrst fin* **50/1**

8 *hd* **Giselle's Charm (IRE)**[29] 4613 2-9-0 90......................... ShaneBKelly 10 91
(M D O'Callaghan, Ire) *chsd ldrs in 5th: rdn and nt qckn ent fnl f: kpt on same pce* **25/1**

9 *1* **Swish (IRE)**[6] 5440 2-9-0 96... NGMcCullagh 11 86
(John James Feane, Ire) *racd in mid-div on stands' rails: rdn and dropped towards rr after 1/2-way: kpt on one pce ins fnl f* **16/1**

10 2½ **Leo Minor (USA)**[19] 4957 2-9-3 0............................... ColmO'Donoghue 7 92+
(A P O'Brien, Ire) *chsd ldr in 2nd on stands' side: 4th at 1/2-way and sn lost position: kpt on again whn short of room ins fnl f: eased fnl 100yds* **2/1**[1]

1m 0.04s (-2.86) **Going Correction** -0.625s/f (Hard) **10** Ran SP% **126.8**

Speed ratings: **97,96,95,94,94 93,93,93,91,87**

CSF £519.11 TOTE £20.10: £3.80, £2.80, £1.02; DF 293.60 Trifecta £652.80.

Owner Straight To Victory Syndicate **Bred** W And R Barnett Ltd **Trained** The Curragh, Co Kildare

■ Stewards' Enquiry : Leigh Roche one-day ban: careless riding

FOCUS

After a lengthy enquiry the winner kept the race. A shock result no doubt, but not to connections. The form has been rated at face value for now.

5662 - 5665a (Foreign Racing) - See Raceform Interactive

5666 - 5667a VOID

5099 BRIGHTON (L-H)

Sunday, August 21

OFFICIAL GOING: Good to firm (good in places)

Wind: Fresh across Weather: Overcast

5668 DELIVEROO.CO.UK MAIDEN AUCTION STKS 5f 59y

2:00 (2:00) (Class 6) 2-Y-O **£2,587** (£770; £384; £192) **Stalls** Low

Form RPR

1 **Lord Clenaghcastle (IRE)** 2-8-6 0.......................... HectorCrouch[(5)] 3 61
(Gary Moore) *chsd ldrs: rdn over 1f out: r.o to ld post* **7/2**[2]

00 **2** *nse* **Chiconomic (IRE)**[14] 5202 2-8-6 0...................................... LiamJones 1 56
(Rae Guest) *chsd ldrs: rdn over 1f out: r.o to ld wl ins fnl f: hdd post* **10/1**

0 **3** 1¼ **Blastofmagic**[29] 4638 2-9-1 0... TimmyMurphy 4 60
(David Dennis) *chsd ldr tl led over 2f out: rdn and hdd wl ins fnl f* **9/2**[3]

0045 **4** *2* **Surfina**[12] 5257 2-8-8 54...[1] DavidParkes[(5)] 5 51
(Dean Ivory) *plld hrd and prom: rdn and outpcd 1/2-way: nt clr run over 1f out: styd on ins fnl f* **5/1**

064 **5** *3* **Tullinahoo (IRE)**[23] 4815 2-9-4 64.....................................[1] TomQueally 6 45
(Denis Coakley) *hld up: hdwy over 3f out: hung rt 1/2-way: sn rdn: wknd fnl f* **13/8**[1]

0 **6** *4* **Lady Gwhinnyvere (IRE)**[19] 4981 2-8-9 0 ow1....................... JFEgan 2 22
(John Spearing) *led: hdd over 2f out: sn rdn: wknd fnl f* **33/1**

7 *12* **General Gerrard** 2-8-11 0... LiamKeniry 7
(Michael Madgwick) *s.s: outpcd* **20/1**

1m 4.77s (2.47) **Going Correction** +0.35s/f (Good) **7** Ran SP% **112.0**

Speed ratings (Par 92): **94,93,91,88,83 77,58**

CSF £35.33 TOTE £4.30: £2.30, £4.40; EX 32.20 Trifecta £164.60.

Owner Michael Baldry **Bred** D McCarthy **Trained** Lower Beeding, W Sussex

FOCUS

A weak maiden and no great surprise to see it go to a newcomer. The level is fluid.

5669 HARRINGTONS LETTINGS H'CAP 5f 59y

2:30 (2:30) (Class 4) (0-85,85) 3-Y-O+ **£6,301** (£1,886; £943; £472; £235) **Stalls** Low

Form RPR

5035 **1** **King Crimson**[9] 5360 4-9-5 **80**.. CharlesBishop 4 88
(Mick Channon) *mde all: rdn over 1f out: styd on* **5/1**[3]

4340 **2** ½ **Waseem Faris (IRE)**[59] 3573 7-9-10 **85**.............................. JFEgan 2 91
(Joseph Tuite) *a.p: rdn to chse wnr over 1f out: r.o* **4/1**[2]

0465 **3** *nk* **Equally Fast**[11] 5285 4-9-3 **81**.. RobHornby[(3)] 7 86
(William Muir) *s.i.s: hld up: rdn: hdwy and hung lft fr over 1f out: r.o* **7/2**[1]

6136 **4** *2* **Newton's Law (IRE)**[9] 5360 5-8-10 **78**........................(tp) JordanUys[(7)] 9 76
(Brian Meehan) *hld up in tch: rdn over 1f out: styd on same pce ins fnl f* **10/1**

6600 **5** 1¼ **Taajub (IRE)**[20] 4954 9-9-4 **79**.. ShaneKelly 3 73
(Peter Crate) *hld up: hdwy and hung lft fr over 1f out: sn rdn: no ex ins fnl f* **10/1**

0062 **6** 2¾ **Whitecrest**[17] 5050 8-8-9 **70**... FrannyNorton 6 54
(John Spearing) *chsd ldrs: rdn 1/2-way: wknd over 1f out* **12/1**

2513 **7** 1½ **Pucon**[40] 4224 7-8-13 **74**...(p) LiamKeniry 1 53
(Roger Teal) *chsd wnr tl rdn over 1f out: wknd ins fnl f* **10/1**

1400 **8** *8* **Shackled N Drawn (USA)**[11] 5305 4-9-3 **78**................(t) HarryBentley 5 29
(Peter Hedger) *hld up: plld hrd: rdn and nt clr run over 1f out: wknd fnl f: eased* **12/1**

-002 **9** *3 ½* **Extrasolar**[11] 5285 6-9-6 **81**...[1] JimmyQuinn 8 20
(Amanda Perrett) *hld up: nt clr run and hung lft over 1f out: sn wknd and eased* **5/1**[3]

1m 2.94s (0.64) **Going Correction** +0.35s/f (Good) **9** Ran SP% **118.2**
Speed ratings (Par 105): **108,107,106,103,101 97,94,81,76**
CSF £26.00 CT £80.34 TOTE £5.70: £2.20, £1.50, £1.70; EX 25.60 Trifecta £116.10.
Owner Billy Parish **Bred** Mickley Stud **Trained** West Ilsley, Berks

FOCUS
A fair sprint, with the winner making all.

5670 GENTING CASINO BRIGHTON MAIDEN STKS (PLUS 10 RACE) 6f 209y
3:00 (3:00) (Class 4) 2-Y-O **£4,204** (£1,251; £625; £312) **Stalls** Low

Form RPR

32 **1** **Novoman (IRE)**[10] 5332 2-9-5 0.. PatCosgrave 6 80
(William Haggas) *hld up in tch: racd keenly: shkn up to ld over 1f out: edgd lft ins fnl f: r.o wl* **4/11**[1]

0 **2** *3* **Getgo**[43] 4128 2-9-5 0... ShaneKelly 2 72
(David Lanigan) *pushed along in rr early: rdn over 2f out: r.o ins fnl f: wnt 2nd nr fin: no ch w wnr* **50/1**

03 **3** *¾* **Glendun (USA)**[17] 5073 2-9-5 0..................................... JimmyFortune 3 70
(Brian Meehan) *chsd ldrs: wnt 2nd over 5f out: led wl over 4f out: rdn and hdd over 1f out: styd on same pce ins fnl f* **5/1**[2]

44 **4** *½* **Neptunes Secret**[29] 4659 2-9-2 0........................... EdwardGreatrex[(3)] 1 69
(Sylvester Kirk) *led: hung rt over 5f out: hdd wl over 4f out: chsd ldr tl rdn over 1f out: styd on same pce ins fnl f* **12/1**

02 **5** *4* **Dahl (IRE)**[12] 5250 2-9-5 0... FrannyNorton 7 58
(Mark Johnston) *chsd ldr tl over 5f out: remained handy: rdn over 1f out: wknd ins fnl f* **8/1**[3]

063 **6** *7* **Permanent**[23] 4829 2-9-5 69.. TomQueally 5 39
(Daniel Kubler) *hld up: sme hdwy over 2f out: rdn and wknd over 1f out* **33/1**

1m 24.97s (1.87) **Going Correction** +0.35s/f (Good) **6** Ran SP% **113.7**
Speed ratings (Par 96): **103,99,98,98,93 85**
CSF £25.57 TOTE £1.40: £1.10, £13.30; EX 25.40 Trifecta £70.50.
Owner Sheikh Ahmed Al Maktoum **Bred** Gerard Mullins **Trained** Newmarket, Suffolk

FOCUS
No depth to this maiden and the red-hot favourite won as expected.

5671 BRITISH STALLIONS STUDS EBF FILLIES' H'CAP 1m 1f 209y
3:30 (3:30) (Class 4) (0-85,83) 3-Y-O **£7,876** (£2,357; £1,178; £590; £293) **Stalls** High

Form RPR

2134 **1** **Jawaayiz**[26] 4743 3-8-12 **75**... PaulHanagan 5 82
(Simon Crisford) *chsd ldrs: led over 2f out: rdn over 1f out: jst hld on* **3/1**[2]

6103 **2** *shd* **Al Shahaniya (IRE)**[29] 4630 3-9-1 **83**.................... AdamMcNamara[(5)] 3 89
(John Quinn) *s.i.s: hld up: hdwy over 2f out: rdn to chse wnr over 1f out: sn edgd lft: r.o* **11/4**[1]

1222 **3** *4 ½* **Kath's Legacy**[25] 4777 3-8-12 **75**... RyanTate 1 72
(Ben De Haan) *chsd ldrs: lost pl over 5f out: hdwy over 2f out: sn rdn: styd on same pce fnl f* **4/1**[3]

6454 **4** *8* **Yorkindred Spirit**[6] 5489 4-9-2 **71**................................(v) FrannyNorton 2 59
(Mark Johnston) *s.i.s: hdwy over 5f out: cl up whn hmpd and lost pl over 2f out: n.d after* **8/1**

4104 **5** *1 ½* **Genuine Approval (IRE)**[19] 4994 3-8-13 **83**.............. MitchGodwin[(7)] 4 61
(Jonathan Portman) *led 1f: chsd ldr tl rdn over 2f out: wknd over 1f out* **7/1**

1542 **6** *2 ¼* **Trulee Scrumptious**[9] 5375 7-8-12 **67**..........................(v) JimmyQuinn 6 41
(Peter Charalambous) *led after 1f: sn clr tl rdn and c bk to the field over 3f out: hdd over 2f out: sn wknd* **5/1**

2m 5.17s (1.57) **Going Correction** +0.35s/f (Good)
WFA 3 from 4yo+ 8lb **6** Ran SP% **111.9**
Speed ratings (Par 102): **107,106,103,96,95 93**
CSF £11.59 TOTE £3.80: £1.60, £1.50; EX 11.60 Trifecta £39.70.
Owner Hamdan Al Maktoum **Bred** D R Botterill **Trained** Newmarket, Suffolk

FOCUS
The front pair, representing leading owners, came clear in what was a reasonable little handicap.

5672 LOVEFAIRS.COM ANTIQUES FAIR 28TH AUG H'CAP 1m 3f 196y
4:00 (4:02) (Class 6) (0-65,65) 3-Y-O+ **£2,587** (£770; £384; £192) **Stalls** High

Form RPR

6050 **1** **Maria's Choice (IRE)**[115] 1810 7-9-11 **62**.................(v) TimmyMurphy 7 67
(Jim Best) *hld up: hdwy over 2f out: rdn to chse ldr over 1f out: styd on to ld post* **16/1**

0534 **2** *shd* **Iona Island**[14] 5207 3-9-3 **64**...................................... MichaelJMMurphy 6 69
(Charles Hills) *w ldr tl led over 2f out: rdn and edgd lft over 1f out: hdd post* **5/6**[1]

2606 **3** *½* **Le Tissier**[20] 4942 3-8-12 **62**...[1] RobHornby[(3)] 5 66
(Michael Attwater) *chsd ldrs: rdn over 3f out: edgd lft over 1f out: styd on* **7/2**[2]

0-35 **4** *1 ¼* **Buteo Bai (IRE)**[17] 5086 3-8-9 **56**................................... ThomasBrown 3 58
(Lucy Wadham) *s.i.s: sn prom: rdn over 2f out: styd on same pce wl ins fnl f* **4/1**[3]

2001 **5** *29* **Salient**[18] 5021 12-9-3 **57**.. EdwardGreatrex[(3)] 1 37
(Michael Attwater) *led at stdy pce: qcknd over 3f out: rdn and hdd over 2f out: nt clr run over 1f out: wknd and eased fnl f* **8/1**

2m 37.93s (5.23) **Going Correction** +0.35s/f (Good)
WFA 3 from 4yo+ 10lb **5** Ran SP% **113.8**
Speed ratings (Par 101): **96,95,95,94,75**
CSF £31.68 TOTE £16.60: £6.30, £1.10; EX 26.90 Trifecta £71.80.
Owner Philip Arrow **Bred** A Christodoulou **Trained** Lewes, E Sussex
■ Intrigue was withdrawn. Price at time of withdrawal 5/2. Rule 4 applies to bets struck prices prior to withdrawal but not to SP bets. Deduct 25p in the pound. New market formed.

FOCUS
A modest handicap run at a steady gallop early.

5673 FRIGHT FESTIVAL BRIGHTON 29TH OCT H'CAP 5f 213y
4:30 (4:31) (Class 5) (0-75,75) 3-Y-O+ **£3,557** (£1,058; £529; £264) **Stalls** Low

Form RPR

1601 **1** **Upavon**[18] 5039 6-9-6 **75**..(t) PatCosgrave 4 83
(Stuart Williams) *trckd ldrs: plld hrd: wnt 2nd over 4f out: rdn and edgd lft fr over 1f out: r.o to ld wl ins fnl f* **5/4**[1]

2111 **2** *shd* **Soaring Spirits (IRE)**[25] 4763 6-9-2 **71**....................(b) RobertWinston 3 79
(Dean Ivory) *led at stdy pce: qcknd over 2f out: rdn over 1f out: n.m.r and hdd wl ins fnl f: r.o: bmpd nr fin* **7/4**[2]

2021 **3** *1 ½* **Vincentti (IRE)**[16] 5103 6-9-5 **74**.. RaulDaSilva 2 77
(Ronald Harris) *s.s: hld up: outpcd 2f out: r.o to go 3rd nr fin: nt rch ldrs* **4/1**[3]

0602 **4** *¾* **Billyoakes (IRE)**[15] 5169 4-9-4 **73**................................ AdamBeschizza 1 74
(Charlie Wallis) *chsd ldr tl over 4f out: remained handy: rdn over 1f out: no ex ins fnl f* **10/1**

1m 12.07s (1.87) **Going Correction** +0.35s/f (Good) **4** Ran SP% **109.9**
Speed ratings (Par 103): **101,100,98,97**
CSF £3.81 TOTE £1.80; EX 3.70 Trifecta £7.50.
Owner Morley, Reynolds & Watkins **Bred** Major-Gen Guy Watkins **Trained** Newmarket, Suffolk

FOCUS
They went pretty steady in this fair sprint.

5674 HARRINGTONS LETTINGS APPRENTICE H'CAP 7f 214y
5:00 (5:00) (Class 5) (0-75,75) 4-Y-O+ **£3,234** (£962; £481; £240) **Stalls** Low

Form RPR

6001 **1** **Cricklewood Green (USA)**[18] 5017 5-9-6 **75**............ MitchGodwin[(5)] 3 82
(Sylvester Kirk) *hld up: hdwy over 2f out: rdn over 1f out: edgd lft and r.o to ld wl ins fnl f* **6/4**[1]

113 **2** *1 ½* **Giovanni Di Bicci**[118] 1699 4-9-3 **72**......................(t) RhiainIngram[(5)] 2 76
(Jim Boyle) *plld hrd: trckd ldr tl led 2f out: rdn over 1f out: hdd wl ins fnl f* **7/1**

1331 **3** *nk* **Wordismybond**[8] 5393 7-9-1 **72**.........................(p) StephenCummins[(7)] 5 75
(Richard Hughes) *sn led at stdy pce: plld hrd: qcknd over 2f out: sn hdd: rdn and ev ch 1f out: no ex wl ins fnl f* **7/2**[3]

0-00 **4** *hd* **Tee It Up Tommo (IRE)**[124] 1546 7-9-2 **66**..............(t) EdwardGreatrex 1 69
(Daniel Steele) *s.i.s: hld up: pushed along over 2f out: r.o ins fnl f: nrst fin* **16/1**

4232 **5** *1 ¼* **Pick A Little**[18] 5017 8-9-5 **69**.................................... MichaelJMMurphy 4 69
(Michael Blake) *trckd ldrs: racd keenly: rdn over 2f out: styd on same pce fnl f* **9/4**[2]

1m 40.3s (4.30) **Going Correction** +0.35s/f (Good) **5** Ran SP% **111.4**
Speed ratings (Par 103): **92,90,90,90,88**
CSF £12.38 TOTE £2.50: £1.20, £2.20; EX 10.40 Trifecta £32.60.
Owner Chris Wright & Andy MacDonald **Bred** Stratford Place Stud **Trained** Upper Lambourn, Berks

FOCUS
No great gallop on here in what was a modest handicap.
T/Plt: £57.80 to a £1 stake. Pool of £75378.48 - 951.71 winning tickets. T/Qpdt: £7.40 to a £1 stake. Pool of £5377.85 - 532.98 winning tickets.. **Colin Roberts**

5630 CHELMSFORD (A.W) (L-H)
Sunday, August 21

OFFICIAL GOING: Polytrack: standard
Wind: light to medium, across Weather: bright spells

5675 TOTEPLACEPOT NURSERY H'CAP 6f (P)
2:10 (2:10) (Class 6) (0-60,65) 2-Y-O **£3,234** (£962; £481; £240) **Stalls** Centre

Form RPR

0635 **1** **Roys Dream**[38] 4296 2-9-7 **60**.. JimCrowley 1 69
(Kristin Stubbs) *hld up in tch in midfield: rdn and hdwy over 1f out: led jst ins fnl f: r.o wl u.p: gng away at fin* **6/1**[3]

5050 **2** *2 ¼* **Wentwell Yesterday (IRE)**[27] 4712 2-9-4 **57**.................. GeorgeBaker 3 59
(Jamie Osborne) *led for 1f: stdd bk to trck ldrs: effrt to chal over 1f out: drvn to ld ent fnl f: hdd jst ins fnl f: no ex and outpcd fnl 100yds* **14/1**

0651 **3** *1 ¼* **Saxagogo**[9] 5364 2-9-12 **65**... TomMarquand 7 63
(George Scott) *dwlt: hld up in rr: pushed along ent fnl 2f: hdwy u.p over 1f out: styd on ins fnl f to snatch 3rd last strides: nvr trbld ldrs* **4/5**[1]

3233 **4** *hd* **Coverham (IRE)**[20] 4937 2-9-6 **59**..................................(b[1]) TedDurcan 4 57
(James Bethell) *dwlt: sn rcvrd and racd keenly in midfield: effrt to chal and carried rt wl over 1f out: ev ch but finding little and edging lft jst over 1f out: wknd ins fnl f: lost 3rd last strides* **9/2**[2]

646 **5** *1 ½* **Iftitah (IRE)**[90] 2543 2-8-13 **52**.. LukeMorris 5 45
(George Peckham) *stdd s: t.k.h: hld up in last pair: effrt and swtchd rt over 1f out: drvn and kpt on same pce ins fnl f* **20/1**

504 **6** *3* **Newport Place (IRE)**[13] 5243 2-8-11 **50**........................ WilliamCarson 2 34
(Jamie Osborne) *in tch towards rr: rdn over 2f out: no imp over 1f out: wl hld and plugged on same pce ins fnl f* **50/1**

062 **7** *¾* **Rebel Heart**[16] 5099 2-9-4 **57**.. PaulMulrennan 9 39
(Bill Turner) *wl in tch in midfield but stuck wd: rdn 2f out: sn outpcd and btn: wknd fnl f* **25/1**

010 **8** *1* **Mesmeric Moment**[20] 4937 2-9-2 **60**........................ CharlieBennett[(5)] 11 39
(Shaun Harris) *taken down early: dwlt: rcvrd to ld after 1f and crossed to inner: rdn and edgd rt wl over 1f out: hdd ent fnl f: sn btn and fdd ins fnl f* **33/1**

500 **9** *11* **Bruny Island (IRE)**[18] 5029 2-9-6 **59**................................ JoeFanning 8 5
(Mark Johnston) *t.k.h: chsd ldr after 1f tl lost pl qckly wl over 1f out: wl bhd and eased ins fnl f* **12/1**

1m 12.96s (-0.74) **Going Correction** -0.15s/f (Stan) **9** Ran SP% **115.9**
Speed ratings (Par 92): **98,95,93,93,91 87,86,84,70**
CSF £77.94 CT £137.23 TOTE £9.90: £2.10, £3.50, £1.02; EX 97.60 Trifecta £194.30.
Owner Mrs A Pickering **Bred** Dr A Gillespie **Trained** Norton, N Yorks

FOCUS
A low grade nursery dominated by runners who had already taken their chance in this sphere.

5676 TOTEEXACTA MAIDEN STKS (PLUS 10 RACE) 7f (P)
2:40 (2:42) (Class 4) 2-Y-O **£7,115** (£2,117; £1,058; £529) **Stalls** Low

Form RPR

0 **1** **Hajaj (IRE)**[8] 5410 2-9-5 0.. StevieDonohoe 3 77
(Charlie Fellowes) *trckd ldrs: swtchd rt and chsd ldr 2f out: sn rdn to chal: led 1f out: kpt on: pressed towards fin but a doing enough* **16/1**

2 *nk* **Qatar Man (IRE)** 2-9-5 0.. DarryllHolland 2 76+
(Marco Botti) *dwlt: rn green: in tch in midfield: swtchd rt over 3f out: effrt and hung rt over 1f out: str run ins fnl f: wnt 2nd fnl 50yds: clsng qckly towards fin but nvr quite getting to wnr* **4/1**[3]

4 **3** *1 ¼* **Accento**[31] 4545 2-9-5 0... JimCrowley 1 73
(Hugo Palmer) *led: rdn wl over 1f out: hdd 1f out: no ex and one pce ins fnl f* **8/11**[1]

4 *½* **Tuscany (IRE)** 2-9-5 0... MartinHarley 8 71
(Paul Cole) *hld up in tch in last trio: pushed along and hdwy on inner over 1f out: chsd ldrs and kpt on same pce ins fnl f* **16/1**

5 2 3/4 **Ningaloo (GER)** 2-9-5 0 AndreaAtzeni 6 64+
(Simon Crisford) *dwlt and bustled along early: rcvrd and travelled wl in midfield after 1f: rn green and pushed along over 3f out: rdn and hdwy to chse ldrs over 2f out: carried rt and outpcd over 1f out: edgd lft and one pce fnl f* **11/4**[2]

00 6 1 3/4 **Crystal Dome**[10] 5332 2-9-5 0 GeorgeBaker 9 59
(Ed Dunlop) *s.i.s: t.k.h: hld up in last pair: effrt and swtchd lft over 1f out: no threat to ldrs: carried lft and plugged on same pce ins fnl f* **50/1**

0 7 nse **Av A Word**[13] 5237 2-9-0 0 PaddyPilley(5) 5 59
(Daniel Kubler) *chsd ldrs on outer: wnt 2nd 4f out tl 2f out: sn drifted rt and outpcd: wl hld: carried lft and kpt on same pce fnl f* **100/1**

8 2 1/4 **Flauto (IRE)** 2-9-5 0 PaoloSirigu 7 53
(Marco Botti) *dwlt: hld up in last pair: swtchd rt and effrt wl over 1f out: no hdwy and wl btn 1f out* **25/1**

0 9 25 **Reach For Glory**[6] 5484 2-9-5 0 PaulMulrennan 4
(Bill Turner) *chsd ldr tl 4f out: sn rdn: hung rt and lost pl: wl bhd over 1f out* **100/1**

1m 27.56s (0.36) **Going Correction** -0.15s/f (Stan) 9 Ran SP% **124.1**
Speed ratings (Par 96): **91,90,89,88,85 83,83,80,52**
CSF £83.62 TOTE £27.00: £4.10, £1.40, £1.10; EX 124.50 Trifecta £347.40.
Owner Khalifa Bin Hamad Al Attiyah **Bred** Lismacue Mare Syndicate **Trained** Newmarket, Suffolk

FOCUS
Little strength in depth in this maiden although there was good support at different times during the day for two runners who were subsequently beaten.

5677 TOTETRIFECTA H'CAP 1m (P)
3:10 (3:15) (Class 4) (0-80,80) 3-Y-O+ **£8,086** (£2,406; £1,202; £601) **Stalls** Low

Form RPR

123 1 **Misty Lord (IRE)**[14] 5191 3-9-3 **77** (t) AndreaAtzeni 10 85+
(Marco Botti) *dwlt: sn rcvrd and in tch in midfield: rdn and hdwy to chal over 1f out: led ent fnl f: styd on wl and in command ins fnl f: rdn out* **7/2**[3]

-350 2 3/4 **Sacred Trust**[71] 3156 3-9-3 **77** [1] JimCrowley 7 83+
(Hugo Palmer) *dwlt: hld up in tch in last quartet: rdn and hdwy on inner over 1f out: styd on u.p and wnt 2nd wl ins fnl f: nvr getting to wnr* **11/4**[2]

3600 3 1/2 **Mezzotint (IRE)**[18] 5017 7-9-12 **80** PaulMulrennan 1 86
(Lee Carter) *hld up in tch in midfield: swtchd rt and effrt over 1f out: rdn and hdwy ent fnl f: styd on u.p fnl 150yds: wnt 3rd towards fin: no threat to wnr* **12/1**

0-14 4 1 **Acclio (IRE)**[64] 3405 5-9-12 **80** MartinHarley 11 84
(James Tate) *trckd ldrs: clsd to press ldr 2f out: rdn to ld over 1f out: hdd ent fnl f: drvn and hdd ent fnl f: no ex ins fnl f: lost 2nd and wknd wl ins fnl f* **8/1**

2425 5 2 3/4 **First Experience**[17] 5075 5-8-12 **71** CallumShepherd(5) 2 68
(Lee Carter) *in tch in midfield: effrt u.p over 1f out: styd on same pce and no imp ins fnl f* **20/1**

411 6 1 1/4 **Carolinae**[18] 5037 4-9-7 **75** StevieDonohoe 3 70
(Charlie Fellowes) *t.k.h: hld up wl in tch in midfield: swtchd rt and effrt over 1f out: no rspnse u.p: wknd ins fnl f* **5/2**[1]

1420 7 1 1/2 **Ravenhoe (IRE)**[18] 5017 3-8-12 **72** JoeFanning 9 62
(Mark Johnston) *hld up in tch towards rr: rdn over 2f out: no imp u.p: wl hld and kpt on same pce fr over 1f out* **16/1**

0605 8 1 1/2 **Tommy's Secret**[18] 5033 6-8-12 **71** CharlieBennett(5) 4 59
(Jane Chapple-Hyam) *a towards rr: rdn in last pair 4f out: nvr trbld ldrs* **14/1**

04-0 9 8 **Myboydaniel**[233] 1 4-9-2 **73** NoelGarbutt(3) 8 42
(Derek Shaw) *racd keenly: led tl rdn and hdd over 1f out: sn btn: fdd fnl f* **50/1**

400/ 10 1 **Two No Bids (IRE)**[793] 3427 6-9-3 **74** JosephineGordon(3) 5 41
(Phil McEntee) *w ldr tl ent fnl 2f: lost pl u.p over 1f out: fdd fnl f* **66/1**

0000 11 16 **Cleverconversation (IRE)**[9] 5374 3-8-7 **67** ow1 (b) DannyBrock 6
(Jane Chapple-Hyam) *s.i.s: nvr gng wl in rr: lost tch and eased jst over 1f out* **50/1**

1m 39.01s (-0.89) **Going Correction** -0.15s/f (Stan)
WFA 3 from 4yo+ 6lb 11 Ran SP% **119.0**
Speed ratings (Par 105): **98,97,96,95,93 91,90,88,80,79 63**
CSF £13.39 CT £106.80 TOTE £4.50: £1.60, £1.50, £3.60; EX 15.80 Trifecta £130.10.
Owner Fabfive **Bred** Skymarc Farm **Trained** Newmarket, Suffolk

FOCUS
A competitive race ran at a frantic pace.

5678 TOTESWINGER H'CAP 6f (P)
3:40 (3:42) (Class 3) (0-95,95) 3-Y-O+ **£16,172** (£4,812; £2,405; £1,202) **Stalls** Centre

Form RPR

1444 1 **Magnus Maximus**[25] 4758 5-9-8 **93** MartinHarley 13 110
(Robyn Brisland) *mde all: rdn and qcknd clr over 1f out: in n.d and r.o wl fnl f: rdn out* **5/1**[2]

0320 2 5 **Related**[8] 5418 6-9-10 **95** (b) LukeMorris 14 96
(Paul Midgley) *dwlt and bustled along early: hdwy to chse wnr after 1f: rdn and unable qck w wnr over 1f out: wl hld but kpt on to hold 2nd ins fnl f* **8/1**

6020 3 nse **Regal Dan (IRE)**[29] 4644 6-9-2 **87** SamJames 6 88
(David O'Meara) *chsd ldng pair after 1f: rdn and unable qck w wnr over 1f out: wl hld but battling for 2nd fnl f: kpt on* **10/1**

1140 4 nk **Gentlemen**[26] 4741 5-9-7 **95** JosephineGordon(3) 3 95+
(Phil McEntee) *taken down early: s.i.s: hld up in rr: rdn and hdwy towards inner over 1f out: chalng for placings wl ins fnl f: kpt on: no ch w wnr* **4/1**[1]

03-0 5 1 1/2 **Valbchek (IRE)**[22] 4889 7-9-8 **93** (p) DannyBrock 8 88
(Jane Chapple-Hyam) *s.i.s and rdn along early: hld up towards rr: clsd over 1f out: nt clr run and swtchd lft 1f out: kpt on ins fnl f: no ch w wnr* **8/1**

0256 6 1 1/2 **Boomerang Bob (IRE)**[17] 5098 7-9-8 **93** WilliamCarson 5 83
(Jamie Osborne) *hld up in tch in midfield: effrt and no imp over 1f out: wl hld and plugged on same pce fnl f* **7/1**[3]

4004 7 nse **B Fifty Two (IRE)**[23] 4846 7-9-10 **95** (b) SteveDrowne 10 85
(Charles Hills) *hld up wl in tch in midfield: effrt 2f out: sme hdwy into 4th but no ch w wnr 1f out: wknd ins fnl f* **20/1**

100- 8 nk **Picture Dealer**[369] 5472 7-9-0 **88** SimonPearce(3) 7 77
(Lydia Pearce) *hld up in tch in midfield: rdn and unable qck over 1f out: sn btn: wknd ins fnl f* **20/1**

3140 9 1/2 **Misterioso (IRE)**[22] 4862 4-9-4 **89** GeorgeBaker 9 77
(Jamie Osborne) *hld up in last pair: c wd and effrt wl over 1f out: no imp: n.d* **4/1**[1]

0004 10 1 **Musical Comedy**[20] 4954 5-9-4 **89** JimCrowley 12 73
(Mike Murphy) *chsd wnr for 1f: stdd bk to chse ldng trio: rdn and unable qck over 1f out: wknd ins fnl f* **14/1**

4000 11 1 3/4 **Baddilini**[4] 5552 6-9-2 **92** CallumShepherd(5) 2 71
(Alan Bailey) *hld up in midfield: lost pl over 2f out: rdn and no hdwy over 1f out: bhd fnl f* **16/1**

6205 12 6 **Crosse Fire**[32] 4514 4-9-2 **87** DarryllHolland 4 47
(Scott Dixon) *t.k.h: hld up in midfield: rdn and lost pl over 2f out: bhd over 1f out* **50/1**

1m 11.01s (-2.69) **Going Correction** -0.15s/f (Stan) 12 Ran SP% **124.5**
Speed ratings (Par 107): **111,104,104,103,101 99,99,99,98,97 95,87**
CSF £46.21 CT £404.40 TOTE £6.10: £1.90, £3.10, £3.30; EX 45.40 Trifecta £457.10.
Owner Franconson Partners **Bred** St Albans Bloodstock Llp **Trained** Newmarket, Suffolk

FOCUS
A competitive looking sprint in which a whole host of runners had looked to be in with a chance although in the end few got into it.

5679 TOTEPOOL LIVE INFO DOWNLOAD OUR APP H'CAP 5f (P)
4:10 (4:12) (Class 4) (0-80,82) 3-Y-O+ **£8,086** (£2,406; £1,202; £601) **Stalls** Low

Form RPR

4344 1 **Top Boy**[14] 5189 6-9-7 **78** (v) MartinLane 6 89
(Derek Shaw) *hld up wl in tch in midfield: swtchd lft and hdwy to chse ldr over 1f out: drvn to ld ins fnl f: r.o wl* **7/1**[3]

5461 2 1 3/4 **Dynamo Walt (IRE)**[14] 5189 5-9-7 **81** (v) NoelGarbutt(3) 2 86
(Derek Shaw) *trckd ldng pair: rdn to ld over 1f out: drvn and hdd jst ins fnl f: styd on same pce after* **9/2**[1]

5536 3 3/4 **Bahamian Heights**[9] 5372 5-9-6 **77** (e[1]) JimCrowley 4 79
(Robert Cowell) *hld up in midfield: swtchd lft and hdwy over 1f out: wnt 3rd 100yds out: kpt on but nvr a threat to wnr* **6/1**[2]

2520 4 1/2 **Sir Domino (FR)**[22] 4873 4-9-4 **75** (b) GeorgeBaker 8 76
(Kevin Ryan) *hld up in tch in midfield: clsd 1f out: swtchd lft and shkn up ins fnl f: hung lft and styd on same pce fnl 100yds* **14/1**

1002 5 1/2 **Elusivity (IRE)**[14] 5189 8-9-11 **82** (p) PaulMulrennan 3 81
(Conor Dore) *led for 1f: styd w ldr tl unable qck u.p over 1f out: wknd ins fnl f* **9/1**

1400 6 nk **Eternitys Gate**[7] 5439 5-9-3 **74** (v[1]) JoeFanning 12 72
(Ivan Furtado) *wnt rt s: hld up towards rr and wd: effrt over 1f out: hdwy ins fnl f: styd on but no threat to wnr* **20/1**

51 7 1/2 **Rich Again (IRE)**[41] 4211 7-9-6 **77** (b) TedDurcan 5 73
(James Bethell) *s.i.s: hld up in rr: effrt over 1f out: sme hdwy but stl plenty to do whn nt clr run 1f out: swtchd rt ins fnl f: kpt on: nvr trbld ldrs* **6/1**[2]

5023 8 hd **First Bombardment**[11] 5295 3-9-5 **78** (v[1]) AndreaAtzeni 10 73
(David O'Meara) *t.k.h: chsd ldng trio: rdn and unable qck over 1f out: wknd ins fnl f* **12/1**

0563 9 hd **Vimy Ridge**[18] 5039 4-9-4 **75** (p) SamJames 9 69
(Alan Bailey) *hld up in tch towards rr: rdn and effrt over 1f out: kpt on same pce and no imp ins fnl f: nvr trbld ldrs* **10/1**

2530 10 3/4 **Welease Bwian (IRE)**[14] 5189 7-8-13 **77** (v) MillyNaseb(7) 7 69
(Stuart Williams) *s.i.s: effrt over 1f out: rdn and sme hdwy but stl plenty to do 1f out: nt clr run and no hdwy fnl 100yds: n.d* **14/1**

0030 11 1 3/4 **It Must Be Faith**[33] 4496 6-9-5 **76** (p) LukeMorris 1 61
(Michael Appleby) *chsd ldrs tl led after 1f: rdn and hdd over 1f out: wknd fnl f* **6/1**[2]

6640 12 3/4 **Desert Strike**[14] 5189 10-9-2 **73** (p) MartinHarley 11 56
(Conor Dore) *taken down early: stuck wd in midfield: wnt v wd and lost pl bnd 2f out: sn bhd and wknd fnl f* **33/1**

58.72s (-1.48) **Going Correction** -0.15s/f (Stan)
WFA 3 from 4yo+ 2lb 12 Ran SP% **121.4**
Speed ratings (Par 105): **105,102,101,100,99 98,98,97,97,96 93,92**
CSF £39.47 CT £206.27 TOTE £9.30: £2.70, £1.80, £2.90; EX 47.30 Trifecta £354.50.
Owner Brian Johnson (Northamptonshire) **Bred** Mrs C R Philipson & Mrs H G Lascelles **Trained** Sproxton, Leics

FOCUS
Another competitive sprint featuring a host of in-form runners and a number of course and distance winners.

5680 TOTEPOOL RACING'S BIGGEST SUPPORTER H'CAP 1m 6f (P)
4:40 (4:40) (Class 6) (0-65,65) 3-Y-O+ **£3,234** (£962; £481; £240) **Stalls** Low

Form RPR

3126 1 **Ballyfarsoon (IRE)**[40] 4226 5-9-3 **54** (v) LukeMorris 8 65
(Ian Williams) *chsd ldrs: rdn to chse ldr wl over 2f out: led over 1f out: sn asserted but hung lft: eased wl ins fnl f* **10/1**

0064 2 7 **Always Summer**[23] 4836 3-8-13 **62** JoeFanning 1 63
(James Fanshawe) *led for 2f: chsd ldr after tl led again over 3f out: rdn and hdd over 1f out: sn btn: plugged on same pce fnl f* **2/1**[1]

/013 3 10 **Mr Lando**[11] 5303 7-9-7 **58** (b) StevieDonohoe 7 46
(Johnny Farrelly) *chsd ldrs tl hdwy to ld 7f out: rdn and hdd over 3f out: 3rd and btn over 2f out: wknd over 1f out* **4/1**[3]

0543 4 2 1/2 **Peeps**[12] 5261 4-9-3 **54** (b) DarryllHolland 9 39+
(Mark H Tompkins) *v.s.a: wl detached in last but steadily rcvrd: in tch 6f out: 4th and rdn 3f out: sn btn: wknd over 1f out* **11/1**

-000 5 9 **Par Three (IRE)**[33] 4493 5-9-4 **58** GeorgeDowning(3) 4 31
(Tony Carroll) *hld up in tch in midfield: reminder 5f out: drvn and struggling over 3f out: 5th and no ch over 2f out* **11/1**

6253 6 17 **Mexican Mick**[38] 4294 7-9-3 **54** WilliamCarson 2 5
(Peter Hiatt) *hld up in tch in rr of main gp: shuffled bk and swtchd rt 6f out: rdn and struggling over 4f out: wl bhd 3f out: t.o* **6/1**

6004 7 133 **Madame Chow (IRE)**[36] 4385 3-8-13 **62** JimCrowley 3
(Ralph Beckett) *t.k.h: chsd ldr tl led after 2f: hdd 7f out and sn u.p: dropped to last over 5f out: lost tch 4f out and sn t.o* **11/4**[2]

3m 2.03s (-1.17) **Going Correction** -0.15s/f (Stan)
WFA 3 from 4yo+ 12lb 7 Ran SP% **120.0**
Speed ratings (Par 101): **97,93,87,85,80 71,**
CSF £32.46 CT £98.58 TOTE £10.90: £3.20, £2.10; EX 42.80 Trifecta £172.90.
Owner Patrick Kelly **Bred** A O'Sullivan **Trained** Portway, Worcs

FOCUS
Very little recent winning form in this moderate staying handicap which would not have taken a lot of winning.

5681 FOLLOW US @CHELMSFORDCRC ON TWITTER MAIDEN STKS 1m 2f (P)
5:10 (5:12) (Class 5) 3-Y-O+ **£5,175** (£1,540; £769; £384) **Stalls** Low

Form RPR

0223 1 **Beauty Sleep (IRE)**[24] 4792 3-9-0 75 (p) MartinHarley 4 77
(William Haggas) *in tch in midfield tl hdwy to ld 8f out: mde rest: rdn over 2f out: sn hrd pressed: battled on wl u.p: bmpd 100yds out: hld on: gamely: all out* **4/1**[3]

0-6 **2** ½ **Vermeulen**[34] 4458 3-9-5 0 RobertHavlin 7 81
(John Gosden) *mostly chsd ldr: pushed along to chal 2f out: sustained duel w wnr after: drvn and edging lft ins fnl f: bmpd wnr 100yds out: kpt on but hld towards fin* **9/4**[2]

53 **3** 3¼ **Rasmee**[16] 5129 3-9-5 0 LukeMorris 5 75
(Marco Botti) *dwlt and bustled along early: chsd ldrs: effrt ent fnl 2f out: no imp and u.p over 1f out: in 3rd and kpt on same pce fnl f* **5/1**

3-5 **4** 2½ **Cap Canaille (USA)**[34] 4458 3-9-5 0 JimCrowley 2 70
(Jeremy Noseda) *led for 2f: 3rd and pushed along 6f out: rdn and unable qck over 2f out: 4th and wl hld 1f out: plugged on* **7/4**[1]

24 **5** 6 **Aid To Africa (IRE)**[176] 746 3-9-5 0 WilliamCarson 1 58
(Michael Bell) *hld up in tch in midfield: rdn over 2f out: drifted rt and outpcd over 1f out: wknd fnl f* **16/1**

6 4 **Fastnet Monsoon (IRE)** 3-8-12 0 GabrieleMalune[(7)] 3 50
(Luca Cumani) *s.i.s and niggled along early: a in rr: rdn 4f out: no prog and wl btn after* **20/1**

7 12 **Clandon** 3-9-5 0 StevieDonohoe 6 26
(Brett Johnson) *stdd and swtchd lft after s: hld up in last pair: rdn over 3f out: sn btn and lost tch 2f out* **66/1**

2m 5.79s (-2.81) **Going Correction** -0.15s/f (Stan) **7** Ran SP% **115.9**
Speed ratings (Par 103): **105,104,102,100,95 92,82**
CSF £13.85 TOTE £4.30: £2.10, £2.10; EX 14.20 Trifecta £39.20.
Owner Liam Sheridan **Bred** Kabansk Ltd & Rathbarry Stud **Trained** Newmarket, Suffolk

FOCUS
Very little strength in depth as is often the case in these races.
T/Jkpt: Not won. T/Plt: £74.50 to a £1 stake. Pool of £100345.22 - 982.51 winning tickets. T/Qpdt: £40.50 to a £1 stake. Pool of £6482.84 - 118.38 winning tickets. **Steve Payne**

5682 & 5684a- (Foreign Racing) - See Raceform Interactive

5658 CURRAGH (R-H)
Sunday, August 21

OFFICIAL GOING: Round course - yielding; straight course - yielding to soft

5683a GALILEO EUROPEAN BREEDERS FUND FUTURITY STKS (GROUP 2) 7f
2:45 (2:45) 2-Y-O **£56,397** (£18,161; £8,602; £3,823)

RPR

1 **Churchill (IRE)**[31] 4574 2-9-3 109 SeamieHeffernan 2 111+
(A P O'Brien, Ire) *settled in 3rd: clsr in 2nd over 2f out: shkn up to ld ins fnl f: strly pressed: styd on strly to assert ins fnl 100yds: gng away at fin* **1/4**[1]

2 2 **Radio Silence (USA)**[36] 4414 2-9-3 0 KevinManning 3 105
(J S Bolger, Ire) *racd in rr: clsd in 3rd appr fnl f: pressed ldr in 2nd ins fnl f: kpt on wl: no imp ins fnl 100yds* **5/1**[2]

3 ¾ **Arcada (IRE)**[36] 4411 2-9-3 0 DonnachaO'Brien 5 103
(Joseph Patrick O'Brien, Ire) *sn led: rdn under 2f out: hdd ins fnl f and sn dropped to 3rd: kpt on same pce* **12/1**[3]

4 2¾ **Lancaster Bomber (USA)**[17] 5092 2-9-3 0 EmmetMcNamara 1 96
(A P O'Brien, Ire) *led early but sn hdd: chsd ldr in 2nd: dropped to 3rd over 2f out: rdn and dropped to rr appr fnl f: no ex* **14/1**

1m 27.36s (-3.44) **Going Correction** -0.225s/f (Firm) **4** Ran SP% **111.0**
Speed ratings: **110,107,106,103**
CSF £2.07 TOTE £1.20; DF 1.90 Trifecta £2.80.
Owner Michael Tabor & Derrick Smith & Mrs John Magnier **Bred** Liberty Bloodstock **Trained** Cashel, Co Tipperary

FOCUS
Like many of the season's better juvenile races this was short on numbers. Ballydoyle's contribution was reduced to two by the defection of Capri, the apparent second-string on paper. The long odds-on winner was completing a notable hat-trick. Another step forward from the winner, looking the type to do just what is needed. Time will tell the merit of this race, but it's hard to rate much higher than this for now.

5685a KILFRUSH STUD ROYAL WHIP STKS (GROUP 3) 1m 2f
3:45 (3:46) 3-Y-O+

£28,198 (£9,080; £4,301; £1,911; £955; £477)

RPR

1 **Success Days (IRE)**[91] 2512 4-9-9 114 ShaneFoley 2 116+
(K J Condon, Ire) *mde all: rdn and extended advantage under 2f out: styd on wl ins fnl f: advantage reduced cl home* **10/1**

2 ¾ **Fascinating Rock (IRE)**[91] 2512 5-10-0 123 PatSmullen 3 119+
(D K Weld, Ire) *chsd ldr in 2nd: rdn and no imp under 2f out: kpt on wl to reduce deficit clsng stages: nvr nrr* **2/1**[2]

3 2½ **Moonlight Magic**[57] 3679 3-9-4 109 KevinManning 5 112
(J S Bolger, Ire) *settled off ldrs in 3rd: rdn under 3f out: nt qckn in 4th over 1f out: kpt on fnl f into 3rd clsng stages: nvr nrr* **14/1**

4 ¾ **US Army Ranger (IRE)**[78] 2896 3-9-4 121 SeamieHeffernan 7 110
(A P O'Brien, Ire) *racd in rr: bit clsr over 3f out: sn rdn in 5th: no imp over 1f out: kpt on ins fnl f: nvr nrr* **1/1**[1]

5 nse **Endless Drama (IRE)**[32] 4543 4-9-9 116[1] ColinKeane 4 107
(G M Lyons, Ire) *settled off ldrs in 4th: clsr in 3rd over 1f out: kpt on same pce fnl f and dropped to 4th cl home* **7/1**[3]

6 6½ **Maneen**[91] 2513 3-9-1 99 LeighRoche 1 94
(D K Weld, Ire) *hld up in 6th: dropped to rr over 3f out: sn rdn and no threat fr 2f out: wnt 6th ins fnl f* **33/1**

7 3¼ **The Steward (USA)**[91] 2512 5-9-9 96 DeclanMcDonogh 6 87
(D K Weld, Ire) *hld up in 5th: bit clsr under 3f out: rdn and nt qckn 2f out: no ex and dropped to rr ent fnl f* **200/1**

2m 13.27s (3.97) **Going Correction** +0.475s/f (Yiel)
WFA 3 from 4yo+ 8lb **7** Ran SP% **115.0**
Speed ratings: **103,102,100,99,99 94,91**
CSF £30.84 TOTE £15.40: £4.50, £1.80; DF 38.60 Trifecta £233.50.
Owner Robert Ng **Bred** Robert Ng & Dermot Farrington **Trained** Rathbride, Co Kildare

FOCUS
Billed as a clash between a five-year-old dual Group 1 winner and this season's Derby second, this produced a minor upset, but a deserving winner for all that. The third has been rated as running a fair pb.

5686a BREAST CANCER RESEARCH DEBUTANTE STKS (GROUP 2) 7f
4:15 (4:16) 2-Y-O

£49,889 (£16,066; £7,610; £3,382; £1,691; £845)

RPR

1 **Rhododendron (IRE)**[24] 4801 2-9-0 SeamieHeffernan 6 108
(A P O'Brien, Ire) *racd in mid-div: gd hdwy on outer to chse ldrs in 4th 2f out: led ent fnl f: hung rt fnl 100yds: kpt on wl* **11/8**[1]

2 hd **Hydrangea (IRE)**[14] 5210 2-9-0 PBBeggy 5 107
(A P O'Brien, Ire) *sn led: strly pressed 1f out and sn hdd: rallied wl on inner clsng stages in 2nd: jst hld* **10/1**

3 1¼ **Intricately (IRE)**[31] 4573 2-9-0 DonnachaO'Brien 9 104
(Joseph Patrick O'Brien, Ire) *chsd ldrs in 4th: rdn in 3rd over 2f out: dropped to 4th 1f out: kpt on same pce into 3rd clsng stages* **14/1**

4 ¾ **Rehana (IRE)**[58] 3626 2-9-0 PatSmullen 4 102
(M Halford, Ire) *trckd ldrs in 3rd: clsr in 2nd under 3f out: pressed ldr appr fnl f: nt qckn in 3rd fnl 100yds: kpt on same pce and dropped to 4th clsng stages* **2/1**[2]

5 2½ **Drumfad Bay (IRE)**[31] 4573 2-9-0 BillyLee 3 96
(Mrs John Harrington, Ire) *racd in mid-div: pushed along in 5th under 2f out: nt qckn appr fnl f: kpt on same pce* **33/1**

6 2¼ **Brave Anna (USA)**[65] 3336 2-9-0 MichaelHussey 7 90
(A P O'Brien, Ire) *racd in rr: pushed along 3f out: prog into 6th over 1f out: no imp ins fnl f: sn one pce* **5/1**[3]

7 shd **Brooklyn's Rose (IRE)**[31] 4573 2-9-0 97 ColinKeane 8 90
(G M Lyons, Ire) *racd in rr: wnt 7th 1f out: kpt on wl fnl f: nvr on terms* **25/1**

8 6½ **Elusive Beauty (IRE)**[16] 5136 2-9-0 94 ShaneFoley 2 73
(K J Condon, Ire) *hld up: rdn under 3f out: no imp over 1f out in 8th: eased ins fnl f* **50/1**

9 6½ **Oh Grace (IRE)**[31] 4573 2-9-0 97 (p) KevinManning 1 56
(J S Bolger, Ire) *sn trckd ldr in 2nd: rdn under 3f out: wknd under 2f out to rr: eased ins fnl f* **50/1**

1m 27.06s (-3.74) **Going Correction** -0.225s/f (Firm) **9** Ran SP% **118.6**
Speed ratings: **112,111,110,109,106 104,103,96,89**
CSF £16.69 TOTE £2.20: £1.02, £2.60, £3.80; DF 16.20 Trifecta £162.60.
Owner Mrs John Magnier & Michael Tabor & Derrick Smith **Bred** Orpendale, Chelston & Wynatt **Trained** Cashel, Co Tipperary

FOCUS
A Ballydoyle one-two in this Group 2 event for the second year in succession. A race which should provide a good guide to the form of the leading Irish-trained fillies. The level is a bit fluid and this looks a sensible starting off point, but it could easily go up slightly.

5687 - 5689a (Foreign Racing) - See Raceform Interactive

5701 DEAUVILLE (R-H)
Sunday, August 21

OFFICIAL GOING: Turf: good; polytrack: standard

5690a DARLEY PRIX MORNY (GROUP 1) (2YO COLTS & FILLIES) (TURF) 6f
2:45 (12:00) 2-Y-O **£147,051** (£58,830; £29,415; £14,694; £7,360)

RPR

1 **Lady Aurelia (USA)**[67] 3270 2-8-10 0 (b) FrankieDettori 2 112
(Wesley A Ward, U.S.A) *mde all: broke wl and led under a tight hold: shkn up under 2f out and rallied: r.o fnl f: a in command* **2/7**[1]

2 ¾ **Alrahma**[21] 4925 2-8-10 0 AurelienLemaitre 3 110
(F Head, France) *t.k.h: hld up in fnl pair: clsd 1 1/2f out: rdn to chse ldr ins fnl f: r.o but nvr quite on terms* **14/1**

3 hd **Peace Envoy (FR)**[36] 4414 2-9-0 0 ColmO'Donoghue 1 113
(A P O'Brien, Ire) *t.k.h: hld up in rr: 6 l last under 1 1/2f out: stl last and rdn 1f out: styd on wl fnl f: jst missed 2nd: nrest at fin* **12/1**[3]

4 hd **Al Johrah**[28] 4694 2-8-10 0 GregoryBenoist 4 109
(H-F Devin, France) *a tch keen: hld up in 3rd: hrd rdn wl over 1f out: styd on ins fnl f: nvr able to chal* **22/1**

5 2½ **Tis Marvellous**[28] 4694 2-9-0 0 AdamKirby 5 105
(Clive Cox) *chsd ldr: 2 1/2 l 2nd and scrubbed along wl over 1f out: sn hrd rdn and no imp: grad dropped away* **11/2**[2]

1m 10.61s (-0.39) **5** Ran SP% **111.9**
WIN (incl. 1 euro stake): 1.30. PLACES: 1.10, 1.20. SF: 5.00.
Owner Stonestreet Stables LLC/G Bolton/P Leidel **Bred** Stonestreet Thoroughbred Holdings LLC **Trained** North America

FOCUS
The race has been rated in line with the race average. The runner-up has been rated as taking a nice step forward.

5691a DARLEY PRIX JEAN ROMANET (GROUP 1) (4YO+ FILLIES & MARES) (TURF) 1m 2f
3:20 (12:00) 4-Y-O+ **£105,036** (£42,022; £21,011; £10,496; £5,257)

RPR

1 **Speedy Boarding**[56] 3695 4-9-0 0 FrederikTylicki 7 111
(James Fanshawe) *w.w bhd ldrs: shkn up to chal 2f out: led appr 1 1/2f out: drvn clr ent fnl f: r.o* **6/1**

2 1¾ **Ame Bleue**[46] 4030 4-9-0 0 Pierre-CharlesBoudot 1 107
(A Fabre, France) *t.k.h: a wl in tch: rdn to chal fr 2f out: outpcd by wnr ent fnl f: styd on at same pce fnl f* **22/1**

3 hd **Steip Amach (IRE)**[21] 4926 4-9-0 0 UmbertoRispoli 2 107
(D Smaga, France) *w.w in midfield: rdn to chse ldrs but nt clr run 1 1/2f out: angled out and styd on u.p fnl f: nt pce to chal* **16/1**

4 ½ **Sea Front (FR)**[63] 3451 5-9-0 0 VincentCheminaud 10 106+
(E Libaud, France) *w.w in fnl pair: hdwy on outer wl over 1 1/2f out: sn rdn: styd on fnl f: nt pce to get on terms* **22/1**

5 snk **Bateel (IRE)**[57] 3662 4-9-0 0 WilliamBuick 5 106+
(David Simcock) *dwlt: w.w in rr: last and rdn under 1 1/2f out: styd on ins fnl f: nvr in contention* **7/1**

6 snk **Game Theory (IRE)**[28] 4696 4-9-0 0 StephanePasquier 6 105
(N Clement, France) *w.w towards rr: rdn and no real imp over 1 1/2f out: kpt on u.p fnl f: nvr nrr* **40/1**

7 nse **Royal Solitaire (IRE)**[21] 4928 4-9-0 0 AndraschStarke 4 105
(P Schiergen, Germany) *settled towards rr: rdn and kpt on appr 1f out: nvr trbld ldrs* **11/2**[3]

8 nk **Sayana (FR)**[78] 2893 4-9-0 0 ChristopheSoumillon 3 105
(A De Royer-Dupre, France) *led: hdd 1/2-way and followed ldr: rdn and ev ch 2f out: grad dropped away fnl 1 1/2f* **3/1**[2]

9 snk **Carnachy (IRE)**[50] 3888 4-9-0 0 JamieSpencer 8 104
(David Simcock) *sn settled in midfield on outer: rdn and nt qckn 2f out: plugged on at same pce fnl f* **16/1**

10 10 **Bocca Baciata (IRE)**[35] 4435 4-9-0 0 ColmO'Donoghue 9 84
(Mrs John Harrington, Ire) *cl up on outer: led 1/2-way: hdd appr 1 1/2f out: wknd over 1f out* **15/8**[1]

2m 7.1s (-3.10) **10** Ran SP% **124.9**
WIN (incl. 1 euro stake): 5.30. PLACES: 2.30, 4.90, 2.80. DF: 47.00. SF: 99.70.
Owner Helena Springfield Ltd **Bred** Meon Valley Stud **Trained** Newmarket, Suffolk

FOCUS
The runner-up, fourth, sixth and eighth offer perspective in what was a tight finish behind the winner.

5692a DARLEY PRIX KERGORLAY (GROUP 2) (3YO+) (TURF) 1m 7f
3:55 (12:00) 3-Y-O+ **£54,485** (£21,029; £10,036; £6,691; £3,345)

RPR

1 **Nearly Caught (IRE)**[31] 4578 6-9-4 0 UmbertoRispoli 2 115+
(Hughie Morrison) *mde all: broke wl and led: drvn clr wl over 1 1/2f out: styd on strly fnl f: won easing down* **7/1**

2 3 1/2 **Candarliya (FR)**[38] 4333 4-9-3 0 ChristopheSoumillon 1 109+
(A De Royer-Dupre, France) *slow to stride: w.w fnl pair: rdn over 2f out: hdwy and nt clr run 1 1/2f out: sn angled out and styd on fnl f: tk 2nd last 30yds: no ch w wnr* **4/5**[1]

3 snk **Trip To Rhodos (FR)**[92] 7-9-4 0 CristianDemuro 6 110
(Pavel Tuma, Czech Republic) *w.w in fnl f: rdn and hdwy on outer 1 1/2f out: styd on fnl f: nvr on terms* **20/1**

4 hd **Harlem**[49] 3936 4-9-4 0 VincentCheminaud 8 110
(A Fabre, France) *sn cl up on outer: 3rd and rdn 2 1/2f out: chsd clr ldr wl over 1f out: sn rdn and no imp: lost two pls fnl 30yds* **13/2**[3]

5 1 3/4 **Walzertakt (GER)**[38] 4333 7-9-4 0 AndraschStarke 3 107
(Jean-Pierre Carvalho, Germany) *w.w in tch on inner: cl 4th and n.m.r 2f out: rdn to chse plcd horse over 1f out: plugged on at one pce* **33/1**

6 3/4 **Launched (IRE)**[38] 4333 4-9-4 0 StephanePasquier 4 106
(P Bary, France) *sn settled in midfield: 4th and rdn 2 1/2f out: rdn and lost pl ins fnl 1 1/2f: kpt on at once pce ins fnl f* **7/1**

7 1 1/2 **Fly With Me (FR)**[84] 2725 6-9-4 0 (p) MaximeGuyon 7 104
(E Libaud, France) *w.w in midfield: in fnl trio fr 1/2-way: scrubbed along 3f out: no imp fnl 1 1/2f* **9/2**[2]

8 snk **Grey Lion (IRE)**[77] 2947 4-9-4 0 Pierre-CharlesBoudot 5 104
(A Fabre, France) *sn chsng ldr: 2nd and nudged along under 3f out: outpcd by ldr wl over 1f out: dropped away ins fnl f* **22/1**

3m 13.41s (-5.69) **8** Ran SP% **124.1**
WIN (incl. 1 euro stake): 6.50. PLACES: 1.90, 1.30, 2.40. DF: 6.10. SF: 14.60.
Owner A N Solomons **Bred** Irish National Stud **Trained** East Ilsley, Berks

FOCUS
The standard is set by the third, fourth and fifth.

5693 - 5694a (Foreign Racing) - See Raceform Interactive

5219 DUSSELDORF (R-H)
Sunday, August 21

OFFICIAL GOING: Turf: good to soft

5695a GROSSER SPARKASSENPREIS - PREIS DER STADTSPARKASSE DUSSELDORF (LISTED RACE) (3YO+ FILLIES & MARES) 7f
4:10 (12:00) 3-Y-O+
£12,867 (£5,147; £3,676; £2,205; £1,102; £735)

RPR

1 **Dynamic Lips (IRE)**[40] 3-8-13 0 AndreasHelfenbein 10 99
(Andreas Lowe, Germany) **43/10**[3]

2 1 3/4 **Subtle Knife**[8] 5396 7-9-2 0 JackMitchell 9 94
(Giles Bravery) *chsd ldrs: rdn to chal over 1f out: styd on u.p fnl f: nt pce of wnr* **128/10**

3 3/4 **Lips Planet (GER)**[28] 3-8-10 0 Eva-MariaZwingelstein 7 89
(Andreas Lowe, Germany) **222/10**

4 1 1/2 **Donna Doria (GER)**[108] 3-8-10 0 MrVinzenzSchiergen 8 85
(J Hirschberger, Germany) **105/10**

5 3/4 **Pabouche (IRE)**[20] 3-8-10 0 FabriceVeron 6 83
(H-A Pantall, France) *t.k.h: hld up in tch early: dropped into fnl trio bef 1/2-way: rdn and hdwy 2f out: styd on ins fnl f: nvr on terms* **58/10**

6 nk **Halli Galli (GER)**[98] 3-8-10 0 MiguelLopez 5 82
(U Stech, Germany) **42/10**[2]

7 3/4 **Schutzenpost (GER)**[50] 3916 4-9-4 0 AlexanderPietsch 2 85
(J Hirschberger, Germany) **19/10**[1]

8 5 1/2 **Antalya (GER)**[63] 5-9-2 0 MaximPecheur 3 68
(Markus Klug, Germany) **124/10**

9 3 **Manisa (FR)**[495] 7-9-2 0 (b) FranciscoDaSilva 12 60
(Steffen Schwarz, Germany) **35/1**

10 4 **Irish Valley (GER)**[40] 3-8-10 0 StephenHellyn 4 46
(K Demme, Germany) **26/1**

11 2 1/2 **Matara (FR)**[46] 3-8-10 0 AndreasSuborics 1 40
(H-A Pantall, France) **43/5**

1m 25.46s (85.46)
WFA 3 from 4yo+ 5lb **11** Ran SP% **131.9**
WIN (incl. 10 euro stake): 53, PLACES: 22, 34, 46. SF: 902.
Owner Stall Lintec **Bred** Stall Parthenaue **Trained** Germany

4253 HANOVER (L-H)
Sunday, August 21

OFFICIAL GOING: Turf: good

5696a GROSSER AUDI SPORT PREIS DES AUDI ZENTRUM HANNOVER (FURSTENBERG-RENNEN) (GROUP 3) (3YO) (TURF) 1m 2f
3:50 (12:00) 3-Y-O **£23,529** (£8,823; £4,411; £2,205; £1,470)

RPR

1 **Wai Key Star (GER)**[42] 4186 3-9-2 0 EduardoPedroza 5 109
(A Wohler, Germany) *settled one fr last: shkn up and hdwy 2f out: led 1 1/2f out: drvn clr fnl f: won easing down* **1/2**[1]

2 4 1/2 **Capitano (GER)**[14] 5219 3-9-0 0 FilipMinarik 1 98
(J Hirschberger, Germany) *wnt sltly lft s: sn led: hdd after 2f: led again 1/2-way: shkn up and kicked for home 2 1/2f out: hdd 1 1/2f out: rallied u.p flat: no ch w wnr* **94/10**

3 nk **El Loco (GER)**[42] 4186 3-9-0 0 AdriedeVries 4 97
(Markus Klug, Germany) *t.k.h: led after 2f to 1/2-way: chsd ldr tl outpcd and hrd rdn 2f out: rallied u.p fnl f* **13/5**[2]

4 nk **Noble House (GER)**[42] 4186 3-8-11 0 KoenClijmans 2 94
(Mario Hofer, Germany) *w.w in rr: rdn and effrt wl after 1/2-way: kpt on fnl f: nvr in contention* **9/1**

5 1 1/4 **Tickle Me Blue (GER)**[42] 4184 3-8-10 0 MartinSeidl 3 90
(Markus Klug, Germany) *chsd ldng pair: lost pl wl over 2f out: plugged on but wl hld fnl f* **39/10**[3]

2m 10.35s (130.35) **5** Ran SP% **134.5**
WIN (incl. 10 euro stake): 15. PLACES: 13, 22. SF: 108.
Owner Stall Salzburg **Bred** Gestut Park Wiedingen **Trained** Germany

5697 - (Foreign Racing) - See Raceform Interactive

5568 CLAIREFONTAINE (R-H)
Friday, August 19

OFFICIAL GOING: Turf: good

5698a PRIX DE TOLLEVILLE (CONDITIONS) (2YO FILLIES) (TURF) 7f
1:15 (12:00) 2-Y-O **£9,191** (£3,676; £2,757; £1,838; £919)

RPR

1 **Normandel (FR)** 2-8-13 0 CristianDemuro 14 76
(Mme Pia Brandt, France) **31/10**[1]

2 3/4 **Upendi (FR)**[8] 2-9-2 0 LouisBeuzelin 2 77
(Robert Collet, France) **88/1**

3 hd **Samba Pa Ti (IRE)**[19] 4924 2-9-2 0 ChristopheSoumillon 11 76
(J-C Rouget, France) **51/10**

4 3/4 **Baie D'Amour (FR)**[26] 4678 2-9-2 0 DougieCostello 10 74
(K R Burke) *a cl up: nudged along bhd front rnk 1/2-way: rdn to chal between horses 1 1/2f out: sltly outpcd appr 1f out: styd on again fnl 110yds* **27/1**

5 1/2 **Baileys Temptress (FR)** 2-9-2 0 GeraldMosse 3 73
(F Doumen, France) **65/1**

6 snk **La Cumparsita (FR)**[51] 2-9-2 0 ThierryThulliez 13 72
(C Lerner, France) **18/1**

7 nk **Karyfanny (FR)**[24] 4750 2-9-2 0 (p) FranckBlondel 5 71
(S Labate, France) **9/1**

8 nk **Vue Du Ciel (FR)**[20] 2-9-2 0 IoritzMendizabal 6 71
(J-C Rouget, France) **18/5**[3]

9 1 **La Berlioz (FR)**[33] 2-9-2 0 StephanePasquier 8 68
(P De Chevigny, France) **34/1**

10 snk **Nasive De Cerisy (FR)** 2-8-9 0 EmmanuelEtienne(4) 15 65
(G Elbaz, France) **119/1**

11 shd **Eblouissante (FR)**[20] 2-9-2 0 AlexisBadel 1 67
(R Chotard, France) **29/1**

12 2 1/2 **Bering Empress (IRE)**[32] 2-9-2 0 Pierre-CharlesBoudot 9 61
(Mme C Head-Maarek, France) **17/5**[2]

13 3 **Crystal Money (FR)**[10] 2-9-2 0 EddyHardouin 12 52
(J-Y Artu, France) **52/1**

14 3 **Volstora (FR)** 2-8-13 0 TheoBachelot 4 41
(T Castanheira, France) **54/1**

15 dist **Abba Forever (FR)** 2-8-13 0 UmbertoRispoli 7
(R Rohne, Germany) **39/1**

1m 27.5s (87.50) **15** Ran SP% **120.0**
WIN (incl. 1 euro stake): 4.10. PLACES: 2.00, 13.40, 2.40. DF: 180.80. SF: 213.20.
Owner Gerard Augustin-Normand **Bred** Franklin Finance S.A. **Trained** France

5699a PRIX PELLEAS (LISTED RACE) (3YO COLTS & GELDINGS) (TURF) 1m 1f
2:15 (12:00) 3-Y-O **£20,220** (£8,088; £6,066; £4,044; £2,022)

RPR

1 **Alignement**[40] 4185 3-9-0 0 MaximeGuyon 9 102+
(C Laffon-Parias, France) **14/5**[2]

2 1 **Caribbean Blue (ITY)**[17] 3-9-0 0 (b) CristianDemuro 10 100
(G Botti, France) **30/1**

3 nk **Zhui Feng (IRE)**[22] 4797 3-9-0 0 OlivierPeslier 3 99
(Amanda Perrett) *led: racd away fr ins rail: led field towards stands' side st: rdn and kicked for home wl over 1 1/2f out: styd on fnl f but edgd a little rt: hdd 125yds out: no ex* **45/1**

4 3/4 **Spectroscope (USA)**[33] 4439 3-9-0 0 MickaelBarzalona 2 97
(A Fabre, France) *sltly outpcd early: sn settled towards rr on inner: hdwy 2f out: disputing 4th and rdn over 1 1/2f out: styd on to chse ldr over 1f out: one pce u.p fnl f* **6/5**[1]

5 1 1/4 **Jorvick (USA)**[17] 3-9-0 0 VincentCheminaud 1 95
(D Smaga, France) **73/10**

6 shd **Vedevani (FR)**[88] 2551 3-9-4 0 ChristopheSoumillon 5 99
(A De Royer-Dupre, France) **59/10**[3]

7 2 1/2 **Guizot (IRE)**[26] 4693 3-9-0 0 Pierre-CharlesBoudot 8 89
(Jean-Pierre Carvalho, Germany) **22/1**

8 1 **Aubenas (FR)**[40] 3-9-0 0 TonyPiccone 4 87
(F Chappet, France) **9/1**

9 *5* **Percy Street**[35] 4339 3-9-0 0 DougieCostello 6 77
(K R Burke) *cl up: 3rd and scrubbed along 2f out: lost pl wl over 1 1/2f out: bhd fnl f* **38/1**
1m 51.3s (111.30) **9** Ran SP% **120.6**
WIN (incl. 1 euro stake): 3.80. PLACES: 1.90, 5.00, 7.90. DF: 47.70. SF: 61.80.
Owner Wertheimer & Frere **Bred** Wertheimer & Frere **Trained** Chantilly, France

5700a PRIX DES MARGUERITES (CLAIMER) (4YO+) (TURF) 1m 6f 110y
3:15 (12:00) 4-Y-0+ **£5,882** (£2,352; £1,764; £1,176; £588)

RPR
1 **Book Of Days (FR)**[701] 5-8-13 0 (p) MickaelBerto 10 61
(M Rulec, Germany) **6/1**
2 *3 1/2* **Stock Exchange (FR)**[52] 9-9-1 0 LudovicBoisseau(5) 11 63
(J-F Doucet, France) **11/2**[3]
3 *6* **Funky Mary (GER)**[56] 7-9-6 0 (b) RonanThomas 7 55
(C Plisson, France) **17/1**
4 *1 1/4* **Testarossa (POL)**[10] 5281 5-8-11 0 MickaelBarzalona 5 44
(P Sobry, France) **12/1**
5 *1 1/2* **Ataman Ermak (IRE)**[12] 5216 5-9-4 0 (b) JeremyCrocquevieille 6 49
(S Gouyette, France) **15/1**
6 *snk* **Apollon (FR)**[10] 5281 8-8-4 0 (p) ClementLecoeuvre(7) 13 42
(A Bonin, France) **51/1**
7 *snk* **Dynamis (FR)**[442] 8-9-8 0 StephaneLaurent 1 52
(G Elbaz, France) **48/10**[2]
8 *2 1/2* **Wave Power (FR)**[28] 4-8-11 0 (b) AlexisBadel 8 38
(D Windrif, France) **87/10**
9 *6* **Latin Charm (IRE)**[4] 5501 5-9-1 0 (b) Pierre-CharlesBoudot 4 34
(Gay Kelleway) *t.k.h: hld up towards rr: in fnl pair and scrubbed along 2 1/2f out: sn rdn and no imp fr wl over 1 1/2f out: wl hld whn eased fnl f* **11/1**
10 *5* **Modern Palace (FR)** 4-8-11 0 (b) AntoineHamelin 12 23
(M Nigge, France) **43/1**
11 *nk* **Zhayrem (FR)**[10] 5281 5-8-11 0 TheoBachelot 3 22
(P Van De Poele, France) **42/1**
12 *9* **L'Heritier (FR)**[509] 5-8-4 0 MmeAlexiaCeccarello(7) 9 10
(M Seror, France) **120/1**
13 *20* **Pelvoux (FR)**[77] 11-9-2 0 MaximeGuyon 2
(W Mongil, Germany) **27/10**[1]
WIN (incl. 1 euro stake): 7.00. PLACES: 2.90, 2.70, 4.50. DF: 26.00. SF: 50.10
Owner Diamonds Stable **Bred** Earl Elevage Des Loge **Trained** Germany

5497 DEAUVILLE (R-H)
Saturday, August 20
OFFICIAL GOING: Turf: good; polytrack: standard

5701a PRIX D'AUQUAINVILLE (MAIDEN) (2YO COLTS & GELDINGS) (TURF) 6f
1:05 (12:00) 2-Y-0 **£9,191** (£3,676; £2,757; £1,838; £919)

RPR
1 **Fas (IRE)** 2-8-13 0 MaximeGuyon 1 80
(Mme Pia Brandt, France) **9/5**[2]
2 *2* **Dolokhov**[6] 5447 2-9-2 0 (p) TonyPiccone 4 77
(J S Moore) *chsd ldr: rdn to ld narrowly 2f out: sn hdd: styd on wl but nt pce of wnr* **6/4**[1]
3 *2* **Ucel (IRE)**[33] 2-9-2 0 IoritzMendizabal 6 71
(F Chappet, France) **59/10**
4 *1 1/2* **Zangokari (FR)**[52] 2-9-2 0 OlivierPeslier 2 67
(T Lemer, France) **33/10**[3]
5 *1/2* **Mamadysh (FR)** 2-8-13 0 FabriceVeron 3 62
(A Savujev, Czech Republic) **15/1**
6 *dist* **Keltetu**[135] 2-9-2 0 AntonioPolli 7
(E Large, France) **45/1**
1m 12.36s (1.36) **6** Ran SP% **121.9**
WIN (incl. 1 euro stake): 2.80. PLACES: 1.40, 1.40. SF: 5.70.
Owner Zalim Bifov **Bred** Zalim Bifov **Trained** France

5703a PRIX DU CALVADOS - ASSOCIATION DES JOCKEYS (GROUP 3) (2YO FILLIES) (STRAIGHT) (TURF) 7f
3:15 (12:00) 2-Y-0 **£29,411** (£11,764; £8,823; £5,882; £2,941)

RPR
1 **Cavale Doree (FR)**[20] 4924 2-8-11 0 JulienAuge 9 103+
(C Ferland, France) *hld up in rr: hdwy fr 3f out: drvn 2f out: led ins fnl f: rdn out* **23/10**[1]
2 *1 1/4* **Asidious Alexander (IRE)**[21] 4902 2-8-11 0 MaximeGuyon 8 100
(Simon Crisford) *prom tl led 3f out: drvn 2f out: hdd and no ex ins fnl f* **51/10**[3]
3 *3/4* **Baileys Showgirl (FR)**[29] 4620 2-8-11 0 IoritzMendizabal 3 98
(Mark Johnston) *midfield: drvn over 2f out: styd on fnl f: nt pce of front pair* **5/1**[2]
4 *shd* **Obedient**[21] 4902 2-8-11 0 VincentCheminaud 2 99+
(P Bary, France) *t.k.h in midfield: nt clr run on inner 2f out: styd on fnl f: nt able to chal* **10/1**
5 *1 1/2* **Dame Du Roi (IRE)**[34] 2-8-11 0 AurelienLemaitre 7 93
(F Head, France) *midfield: hdwy to trck ldrs over 2f out: drvn and unable qck 1 1/2f out: kpt on same pce* **56/10**
6 *3/4* **Spanish Fly (IRE)**[34] 2-8-11 0 GeraldMosse 5 91
(M Delcher Sanchez, France) *stdd s: towards rr: drvn and gd hdwy on outer to press ldrs over 1f out: wknd 1/2f out* **21/1**
7 *2* **Calare (IRE)**[21] 4902 2-8-11 0 MickaelBarzalona 6 86
(Charlie Appleby) *trckd ldrs: hmpd 5f out and bmpd sn afterwards: rdn and unable qck over 2f out: wknd 1f out* **67/10**
8 *4* **Morigane Forlonge (FR)**[27] 4694 2-8-11 0 CristianDemuro 1 75
(A Giorgi, Italy) *trckd ldrs: hmpd 5f out and bmpd rival sn afterwards: lost pl 2f out: eased whn btn fnl f* **21/1**
9 *2 1/2* **Emmie (IRE)**[58] 3556 2-8-13 0 ow2 ChristopheSoumillon 4 70
(Harry Dunlop) *led: edgd lft and hmpd two rivals 5f out: hdd 3f out: wknd 2f out: eased fnl f* **17/2**
1m 25.31s (-2.99) **9** Ran SP% **120.2**
WIN (incl. 1 euro stake): 3.30. PLACES: 1.70, 1.80, 1.80. DF: 9.50. SF: 17.70.
Owner Ecurie Mill Reef Sas **Bred** Mlle C Becq **Trained** France

5704a PRIX PMU (PRIX DU PETIT COTIL) (CLAIMER) (3YO) (POLYTRACK) 1m 4f 110y
4:20 (12:00) 3-Y-0 **£8,455** (£3,382; £2,536; £1,691; £845)

RPR
1 **Brave Archibald (IRE)**[21] 4880 3-9-8 0 ChristopheSoumillon 7 79
(Paul Cole) *trckd ldrs: rdn over 2f out: led narrowly over 1f out: drvn out* **8/5**[1]
2 *nk* **Cork (FR)**[22] 3-9-2 0 OlivierPeslier 1 72
(F Monnier, France) **11/1**
3 *nk* **Brancaio (FR)**[165] 3-8-11 0 (b) Pierre-CharlesBoudot 10 67
(K Borgel, France) **68/10**
4 *1 1/4* **More Than This (FR)**[7] 3-9-5 0 MaximeGuyon 4 73
(Y Barberot, France) **42/10**[2]
5 *1/2* **Sparkle Jack (FR)**[53] 3-8-8 0 ThomasHuet 2 61
(Mlle A Rosa, France) **43/1**
6 *hd* **Dberto (IRE)**[70] 3-8-13 0 HugoJourniac(3) 8 69
(M Delcher Sanchez, France) **76/10**
7 *3/4* **Scandaleux (FR)**[27] 3-8-10 0 ClementLecoeuvre(8) 9 70
(E Lellouche, France) **11/2**[3]
8 *1 1/4* **Naousa (FR)**[34] 3-8-8 0 AntoineHamelin 5 58
(R Schoof, Belgium) **10/1**
9 *12* **Leo Le Lion**[45] 3-8-11 0 TheoBachelot 6 41
(S Cerulis, France) **28/1**
Owner PJL Racing/Wright Asprey Meyrick Wilcock **Bred** Peter J Magnier **Trained** Whatcombe, Oxon
WIN (incl. 1 euro stake): 2.60. PLACES: 1.50, 2.60, 1.80. DF: 18.80. SF: 27.50

5668 BRIGHTON (L-H)
Monday, August 22
OFFICIAL GOING: Good (good to firm in places; 8.0)
Wind: medium, half against Weather: bright spells

5705 ABF THE SOLDIERS' CHARITY MAIDEN FILLIES' STKS (PLUS 10 RACE) 5f 213y
2:00 (2:00) (Class 5) 2-Y-0 **£3,234** (£962; £481; £240) **Stalls** Centre

Form RPR
1 **Mystic Dawn (IRE)** 2-9-0 0 PatCosgrave 4 80+
(David Simcock) *dwlt: hld up in last: rdn and hdwy 2f out: led 1f out: sn in command and r.o wl: readily* **7/2**[2]
2 *2 3/4* **Spinnaka (IRE)** 2-9-0 0 AdamKirby 1 72+
(Luca Cumani) *s.i.s: hld up in rr: rdn and hdwy over 1f out: chsd clr wnr ins fnl f: kpt on wl but nvr a threat to wnr* **11/2**
6 3 *2 1/4* **Money In My Pocket (IRE)**[28] 4706 2-9-0 0 TomMarquand 2 65
(Richard Hannon) *chsd ldrs: effrt on inner over 1f out: n.m.r ent fnl f: 3rd and styd on same pce ins fnl f* **12/1**
5 4 *1* **Amelia Dream**[9] 5400 2-9-0 0 TimmyMurphy 8 64+
(Mick Channon) *dwlt and pushed along leaving stalls: sn rcvrd and in tch in midfield: rdn: rn green and outpcd whn sltly impeded wl over 1f out: rallied and nt clr run jst ins fnl f: kpt on fnl 100yds: no ch w ldrs* **9/4**[1]
5 *nk* **Favourite Royal (IRE)** 2-9-0 0 RobertWinston 7 61+
(Eve Johnson Houghton) *awkward leaving stalls and flashing taill early: sn rcvrd to chse ldr: led 2f out: immediately rn green and wandering: edgd lft and hdd 1f out: wknd ins fnl f* **25/1**
0300 6 *hd* **Grand Myla (IRE)**[10] 5359 2-9-0 76 ShaneKelly 3 61
(Gary Moore) *chsd ldrs: effrt 2f out: unable qck u.p over 1f out: wknd ins fnl f* **4/1**[3]
30 7 *1 1/2* **Company**[28] 4707 2-8-7 0 HollieDoyle(7) 6 60
(Richard Hannon) *hld up in tch in last trio: effrt whn nt clr run and hmpd wl over 1f out: n.d after* **6/1**
04 8 *3/4* **Prancelina (IRE)**[15] 5188 2-8-11 0 JosephineGordon(3) 5 54
(Phil McEntee) *led: rdn and hdd 2f out: no ex and edging lft over 1f out: wknd ins fnl f* **66/1**
1m 12.16s (1.96) **Going Correction** +0.30s/f (Good) **8** Ran SP% **115.7**
Speed ratings (Par 91): **98,94,91,90,89 89,87,86**
CSF £23.38 TOTE £5.30: £1.60, £1.90, £4.40; EX 22.10 Trifecta £208.00.
Owner Al Asayl Bloodstock Ltd **Bred** Al Asayl Bloodstock Ltd **Trained** Newmarket, Suffolk

FOCUS
Add 3 yards to advertised race distance. The ground was eased to good (good to firm in places) following 2mm of overnight rain and there was a breeze against the runners in the home straight. What looked only a moderate juvenile maiden beforehand was dominated by a couple of promising newcomers who came clear down the middle of the track. They went a good pace. The level is fluid.

5706 IAN CARNABY (S) H'CAP 5f 213y
2:30 (2:32) (Class 6) (0-60,60) 3-Y-0+ **£2,328** (£693; £346; £173) **Stalls** Centre

Form RPR
2034 1 **Wahaab (IRE)**[12] 5309 5-9-7 60 (p) ShaneKelly 4 67
(Richard Hughes) *hld up in tch in midfield: effrt and carried rt 2f out: hdwy and rdn to chal ent fnl f: drvn to ld wl ins fnl f: kpt on but wnt rt cl home* **11/4**[1]
3240 2 *1* **Time Medicean**[9] 5408 10-9-4 60 GeorgeDowning(3) 7 64
(Tony Carroll) *hld up in tch in last: hdwy u.p over 1f out: led ent fnl f: hdd wl ins fnl f: no ex towards fin* **4/1**[3]
0005 3 *2* **Sakhee's Rose**[3] 5605 6-9-3 56 (b) MartinLane 5 54
(Ed McMahon) *in tch in rr: clsd and nt clr run over 1f out: rdn ent fnl f: hdwy ins fnl f: kpt on u.p to snatch 3rd last strides: no threat to ldrs* **8/1**
0601 4 *hd* **Baz's Boy**[25] 4796 3-8-4 49 NoelGarbutt(3) 3 46
(John Flint) *chsd ldrs: rdn 2f out: unable qck over 1f out: rallied to chse ldng pair ins fnl f: no imp: lost 3rd last strides* **12/1**
6360 5 *5* **Fossa**[18] 5080 6-8-7 46 oh1 WilliamCarson 6 28
(Mark Brisbourne) *t.k.h: hld up in tch in last trio: effrt 2f out: drvn and btn over 1f out: wknd and drifted rt ins fnl f* **16/1**
0012 6 *shd* **Indus Valley (IRE)**[18] 5051 9-9-7 60 (v) KierenFox 2 42
(Lee Carter) *dwlt: sn rcvrd and in tch in midfield: effrt u.p on inner over 1f out: no imp 1f out: wknd ins fnl f: fin lame* **3/1**[2]
6404 7 *3/4* **Zipedeedodah (IRE)**[67] 3316 4-9-6 59 AdamKirby 1 39
(Joseph Tuite) *led: rdn wl over 1f out: hdd ent fnl f: sn btn: wknd qckly ins fnl f* **6/1**

0400 **8** 1 3/4 **Pursuit Of Time**[20] 4993 3-8-6 **48**..............................(bt[1]) TomMarquand 8 23
(Neil Mulholland) *sn w ldr: rdn: drifted rt and unable qck 2f out: lost pl over 1f out: wknd fnl f* **33/1**

1m 11.87s (1.67) **Going Correction** +0.30s/f (Good)
WFA 3 from 4yo+ 3lb **8** Ran SP% **113.6**
Speed ratings (Par 101): **100,98,96,95,89 88,87,85**
CSF £13.85 CT £76.06 TOTE £3.30: £1.30, £1.60, £2.90; EX 14.00 Trifecta £85.50.No bid for the winner
Owner Martin Clarke **Bred** Shadwell Estate Company Limited **Trained** Upper Lambourn, Berkshire

FOCUS
Add 3 yards to advertised race distance. A selling handicap in which they went a good pace, and the first two came from behind to battle it out down the middle. The second and thid offer perspective for the level.

5707 LCS ROOFING & CLADDING LTD NURSERY H'CAP 5f 213y
3:00 (3:01) (Class 5) (0-70,70) 2-Y-O **£3,234** (£962; £481; £240) **Stalls** Centre

Form RPR
0315 **1** **Drop Kick Murphi (IRE)**[13] 5265 2-9-5 **68**...................... SteveDrowne 4 73
(George Baker) *in tch in midfield: effrt and swtchd rt 2f out: hdwy to chse ldr over 1f out: styd on u.p ins fnl f: led towards fin* **9/2**[3]

1000 **2** 1/2 **Katrine (IRE)**[23] 4869 2-9-7 **70**..[1] PatCosgrave 2 73
(William Knight) *stdd s: t.k.h: hld up in tch in last pair: clsd on inner to ld 2f out: rdn over 1f out: drvn ins fnl f: hdd and no ex towards fin* **9/1**

4021 **3** 1 **Bobby Vee**[26] 4759 2-9-5 **68**.. RobertWinston 1 68
(Dean Ivory) *broke okay but stdd and sn detached in last: clsd and in tch after 2f out: hdwy u.p to chse ldng pair over 1f out: styd on ins fnl f* **5/2**[1]

043 **4** 2 1/4 **Goodwood Crusader (IRE)**[28] 4713 2-9-5 **68**................... ShaneKelly 5 61
(Richard Hughes) *hld up in tch in midfield: swtchd rt wl over 2f out: drvn and unable qck over 1f out: styd on same pce to go 4th 100yds out* **3/1**[2]

4360 **5** 2 **At The Beach**[25] 4802 2-9-3 **66**....................................(b) TomMarquand 6 53
(Richard Hannon) *sn led: hdd and rdn 2f out: unable qck over 1f out and btn whn wandered 1f out: wknd ins fnl f* **14/1**

331 **6** 8 **Dixie's Double**[13] 5258 2-9-7 **70**.. TomQueally 3 33
(Daniel Kubler) *chsd ldrs: rdn and drifted rt 2f out: lost pl u.p over 1f out: wknd 1f out: eased wl ins fnl f* **6/1**

0225 **7** 5 **Hope Against Hope (IRE)**[47] 4002 2-9-2 **65**.................... AdamKirby 7 13
(Mark Johnston) *chsd ldr: rdn and edgd rt wl over 2f out: squeezed out and dropped to rr 2f out: sn wl btn: bhd and eased wl ins fnl f* **8/1**

1m 12.36s (2.16) **Going Correction** +0.30s/f (Good) **7** Ran SP% **113.8**
Speed ratings (Par 94): **97,96,95,92,89 78,72**
CSF £42.58 TOTE £5.80: £2.80, £5.60; EX 47.30 Trifecta £173.50.
Owner ININ Construction **Bred** Selman Tasbek **Trained** Manton, Wilts

FOCUS
Add 3 yards to advertised race distance. A fair nursery featuring a couple of recent maiden winners. Once again, they went a good gallop and the trio who set the pace were the last three to finish. The runner-up has been rated back to the level of his debut effort.

5708 CALL STAR SPORTS ON 08000 521 321 AMATEUR RIDERS' H'CAP 1m 1f 209y
3:30 (3:31) (Class 6) (0-60,60) 3-Y-O+ **£2,183** (£677; £338; £169) **Stalls** High

Form RPR
0660 **1** **Magnificent Madiba**[15] 5207 3-10-13 **60**........................... MrSWalker 8 68
(George Baker) *stdd s: t.k.h: hld up in tch towards rr: hdwy over 2f out: rn green but rdn to chal 1f out: led ins fnl f: styd on wl and drew clr fnl 100yds: comf* **5/1**[3]

232 **2** 3 1/4 **Flag Of Glory**[51] 3901 9-10-8 **52**..................................(b) MissMEdden(5) 6 54
(Peter Hiatt) *wl in tch in midfield: hdwy to chse ldrs over 3f out: rdn to ld ent fnl 2f: hrd pressed 1f out: hdd ins fnl f: sn brushed aside and plugged on same pce fnl 100yds* **13/2**

0-53 **3** 1 1/4 **Lilly Bonbon (IRE)**[17] 5101 3-10-8 **58**................. MissHayleyMoore(3) 7 58
(Gary Moore) *stdd s: hld up in tch in rr: hdwy on inner 3f out: rdn to chse ldrs over 1f out: edgd lft and unable qck 1f out: styd on same pce ins fnl f* **9/4**[1]

3202 **4** 1 1/2 **Elle Rebelle**[19] 5016 6-10-9 **51**...................................... MrJamesKing(3) 2 48
(Mark Brisbourne) *stdd s: t.k.h: hld up in tch in midfield: effrt on inner jst over 2f out: chsd ldrs but unable qck whn n.m.r 1f out: wknd ins fnl f* **10/1**

004- **5** hd **Leyland (IRE)**[393] 4688 7-10-9 **53**................................... MrWillPettis(5) 1 49
(Natalie Lloyd-Beavis) *led tl 7f out: lost pl and rdn over 4f out: no threat to ldrs but rallied 1f out: kpt on steadily ins fnl f* **100/1**

5450 **6** 2 1/2 **Mystical Maze**[13] 5264 5-10-1 **45**.. MrHHunt(5) 3 37
(Mark Brisbourne) *chsd ldr tl 7f out: styd chsng ldrs: rdn ent fnl 2f: lost pl and btn over 1f out: wknd fnl f* **33/1**

6036 **7** 7 **Fenner Hill Neasa (IRE)**[15] 5204 3-9-13 **46**............. MissSBrotherton 9 24
(Pat Phelan) *hld up in tch in midfield: effrt ent fnl 2f: drifted lft and btn over 1f out: sn wknd* **4/1**[2]

4015 **8** 11 **Nifty Kier**[23] 4876 7-10-10 **49**... MrRBirkett 4 6
(Phil McEntee) *t.k.h: sn chsng ldrs: rdn 2f out: no rspnse and sn btn: wknd over 1f out* **16/1**

0464 **9** 60 **Chella Thriller (SPA)**[9] 5399 7-10-4 **48**..................(b) MissEllaSmith(5) 5
(Ralph J Smith) *stdd s: hld up in rr: gd hdwy to ld 7f out and sn clr: hdd ent fnl 2f: sn dropped out: t.o fnl f: burst blood vessel* **6/1**

2m 9.62s (6.02) **Going Correction** +0.30s/f (Good)
WFA 3 from 5yo+ 8lb **9** Ran SP% **114.0**
Speed ratings (Par 101): **87,84,83,82,82 80,74,65,17**
CSF £36.86 CT £91.97 TOTE £6.10: £2.20, £2.20, £1.30; EX 39.40 Trifecta £123.80.
Owner PJL Racing 1 **Bred** K Bosley **Trained** Manton, Wilts
■ Stewards' Enquiry : Mr James King nine-day ban: used whip above permitted level (Sep 9,20, Oct 3,4,5,17,24,26, Nov 1)

FOCUS
Add 3 yards to advertised race distance. A weak amateur riders handicap in which they went a fair pace and the winner was delivered wide and late in recording a double for trainer, George Baker. The second, third and fourth help pin the opening level.

5709 STARSPORTSBET.CO.UK MAIDEN STKS 1m 1f 209y
4:00 (4:00) (Class 5) 3-Y-O+ **£3,234** (£962; £481; £240) **Stalls** High

Form RPR
1 **Testimonio** 3-9-5 0... AdamKirby 3 79+
(Luca Cumani) *hld up in 3rd: clsd and in tch 4f out: rdn over 2f out: hdwy u.p to press ldr over 1f out: led ins fnl f: styd on wl* **2/1**[2]

3533 **2** 1 1/4 **Golden Reign (IRE)**[31] 4597 3-9-0 74..........................(p) PatCosgrave 1 71
(William Haggas) *chsd ldr: effrt ent fnl 2f: rdn to ld wl over 1f out: drvn ent fnl f: hdd ins fnl f: kpt on same pce after* **4/5**[1]

3 17 **Art Of Swing (IRE)**[254] 4-9-8 0.................................... HectorCrouch(5) 4 42
(Gary Moore) *led: rdn ent fnl 2f: hdd wl over 1f out: sn btn: wknd fnl f* **25/1**

4 3 1/4 **Boru's Brook (IRE)**[212] 8-9-13 0.................................... TimmyMurphy 2 36
(Jim Best) *s.i.s: hld up in rr and nvr on terms: pushed along 3f out: sn lost tch* **13/2**[3]

2m 7.97s (4.37) **Going Correction** +0.30s/f (Good)
WFA 3 from 4yo+ 8lb **4** Ran SP% **106.1**
Speed ratings (Par 103): **94,93,79,76**
CSF £3.86 TOTE £3.10; EX 3.60 Trifecta £12.70.
Owner O T I Racing **Bred** Stowell Hill Ltd **Trained** Newmarket, Suffolk

FOCUS
Add 3 yards to advertised race distance. Some of the bigger yards won this modest maiden in recent years and the trend continued. They went a fair gallop and raced in Indian file prior to the straight. The form can be rated around the runner-up, who came clear of the third. The runner-up has been rated close to his efforts since his debut.

5710 FOLLOW US ON TWITTER @STARSPORTS_BET H'CAP 7f 214y
4:30 (4:34) (Class 6) (0-55,55) 3-Y-O+ **£2,587** (£770; £384; £192) **Stalls** Centre

Form RPR
0001 **1** **Multitask**[28] 4715 6-9-5 **53**.. AdamKirby 2 70+
(Gary Moore) *stdd after s and t.k.h early: hld up in rr: clsd to trck ldrs and travelling strly 2f out: pushed into ld over 1f out: rdn clr and in command 1f out: eased towards fin: easily* **6/4**[1]

3U52 **2** 3 3/4 **Wild Flower (IRE)**[20] 4993 4-8-11 **50**.......................... MeganNicholls(5) 4 55
(Jimmy Fox) *t.k.h: hld up in tch in midfield: hdwy to chse ldr over 3f out: rdn to ld 2f out: hdd over 1f out: no ch w wnr but kpt on for clr 2nd ins fnl f* **4/1**[2]

3465 **3** 1 3/4 **Pivotal Dream (IRE)**[3] 5604 3-8-8 **48**........................... WilliamCarson 3 48
(Mark Brisbourne) *hld up in tch towards rr: hdwy over 2f out: nt clr run and swtchd rt over 1f out: kpt on u.p ins fnl f to go 3rd towards fin: no ch w wnr* **8/1**

-406 **4** 1 **The Greedy Boy**[11] 5326 3-8-11 **51**............................... CharlesBishop 5 49
(Mick Channon) *hld up in tch in last pair: hdwy over 2f out: rdn and ev ch 2f out: outpcd by wnr and btn over 1f out: wknd ins fnl f* **8/1**

0053 **5** 7 **Windmills Girl**[14] 5235 3-8-10 **50**..(b) MartinLane 6 32
(Jeremy Gask) *t.k.h: chsd ldrs: rdn ent fnl f: unable qck w wnr and btn over 1f out: sn wknd* **11/1**

350- **6** 3/4 **Tanzina**[315] 7162 4-9-2 **55**.. DavidParkes(5) 1 40
(Laura Mongan) *hld up in tch in midfield: nt clr run and hmpd on inner over 2f out: effrt u.p 2f out: no imp and sn wknd* **40/1**

2024 **7** 7 **Lutine Charlie (IRE)**[18] 5055 9-9-3 **51**..........................(p) TomQueally 10 16
(Emma Owen) *dwlt: sn rcvrd and in tch in midfield on outer: rdn over 2f out: sn btn: wknd over 1f out* **11/1**

0446 **8** 12 **County Wexford (IRE)**[20] 4979 5-9-7 **55**...................(t) StevieDonohoe 8
(Miss Joey Ellis) *led: rdn and hdd 2f out: sn dropped out: wl bhd fnl f: burst blood vessel* **7/1**[3]

400/ **9** 7 **Jenny Sparks**[662] 7546 5-8-12 **46** oh1.............................. HarryPoulton 9
(Sheena West) *chsd ldr tl 4f out: sn lost pl: t.o over 1f out* **80/1**

00-4 **10** 12 **Queen Of Norway (IRE)**[18] 5056 5-8-6 **47**................. VictoriaWood(7) 7
(Paddy Butler) *hld up in tch in midfield: lost pl and rdn over 2f out: sn bhd: t.o over 1f out* **100/1**

1m 37.36s (1.36) **Going Correction** +0.30s/f (Good)
WFA 3 from 4yo+ 6lb **10** Ran SP% **116.1**
Speed ratings (Par 101): **105,101,99,98,91 90,83,71,64,52**
CSF £7.22 CT £35.61 TOTE £2.50: £1.40, £1.30, £2.60; EX 9.10 Trifecta £45.80.
Owner Power Geneva Ltd **Bred** Mrs L N Harmes **Trained** Lower Beeding, W Sussex

FOCUS
Add 3 yards to advertised race distance. A weak handicap featuring mainly infrequent winners, and it was the only last time out winner who followed-up. They went a fair tempo and the winner came from last place. Those in behind the winner help set the opening level.

5711 STARSPREADS.COM H'CAP 6f 209y
5:00 (5:00) (Class 5) (0-70,70) 3-Y-O+ **£3,234** (£962; £481; £240) **Stalls** Centre

Form RPR
5026 **1** **With Approval (IRE)**[23] 4881 4-9-5 **65**...........................(p) PatCosgrave 5 71
(Laura Mongan) *led for 1f: chsd ldr after: rdn and ev ch over 2f out: stl ev ch but looked hld ins fnl f: styd on u.p last 50yds: led last strides* **14/1**

0002 **2** shd **Art Echo**[18] 5087 3-9-4 **69**..(t) MartinLane 6 73
(Jonathan Portman) *stdd s: hld up in tch in rr: hdwy u.p ent fnl f: chsd ldrs wl ins fnl f: styd on and ev ch towards fin: snatched 2nd last stride: jst failed* **10/1**

0-22 **3** shd **Polymnia**[12] 5309 3-8-13 **69**.. MeganNicholls(5) 2 72+
(Richard Hannon) *t.k.h: hld up wl in tch in midfield: hdwy on inner to ld wl over 1f out: sn rdn: looked like holding on ins fnl f: hdd and lost 2 pls last strides* **9/2**[2]

-300 **4** 1/2 **Bingo George (IRE)**[97] 2322 3-8-8 **62**............................ RobHornby(3) 8 66+
(Andrew Balding) *t.k.h: hld up wl in tch in midfield: chsng ldrs whn short of room and jostled ent fnl f: gap opened and kpt on wl fnl 75yds* **5/1**[3]

001 **5** 2 **Monsieur Valentine**[18] 5051 4-8-13 **62**.................. GeorgeDowning(3) 3 61
(Tony Carroll) *taken down early: stdd s: hld up in rr: effrt but hanging lft over 1f out swtchd rt 1f out: styd on ins fnl f: no threat to ldrs* **6/1**

003 **6** hd **Jan Steen (IRE)**[32] 4557 3-9-5 **70**.. TomQueally 7 66
(Denis Coakley) *t.k.h: hld up in tch in midfield: ev ch over 2f out: edging lft and short of room ent fnl f: wknd ins fnl f* **6/1**

0412 **7** 1/2 **Sarmadee (IRE)**[9] 5393 4-9-2 **69**............................ KillianHennessy(7) 1 66+
(Mick Channon) *t.k.h: hld up in tch in last trio: rdn and effrt on inner over 1f out: nt clr run ent fnl f: swtchd rt ins fnl f: kpt on but no ch of chalng* **7/2**[1]

4436 **8** hd **Port Lairge**[17] 5104 6-9-2 **62**..................................(v) MichaelJMMurphy 4 58
(John Gallagher) *led after 1f: rdn ent fnl 2f: hdd wl over 1f out: struggling to qckn whn jostled ent fnl f: wknd fnl 100yds* **13/2**

1m 24.65s (1.55) **Going Correction** +0.30s/f (Good)
WFA 3 from 4yo+ 5lb **8** Ran SP% **114.7**
Speed ratings (Par 103): **103,102,102,102,99 99,99,98**
CSF £142.90 CT £739.18 TOTE £17.30: £3.70, £2.90, £2.00; EX 169.90 Trifecta £782.10.
Owner Mrs P J Sheen **Bred** Yeomanstown Stud **Trained** Epsom, Surrey

FOCUS
Add 3 yards to advertised race distance. A competitive little handicap in which things got tight on the inside and there was a close three-way finish. A turf pb from the winner and close to his AW best.

T/Plt: £627.40 to a £1 stake. Pool: £58,776.99 - 68.38 winning units T/Qpdt: £45.00 to a £1 stake. Pool: £8,410.56 - 138.3 winning units **Steve Payne**

5535 CARLISLE (R-H)

Monday, August 22

OFFICIAL GOING: Good (good to soft in places; 6.5)

Wind: Fresh, half against Weather: Overcast

5712 APOLLOBET WEEKLY GOLF RETURNS NURSERY H'CAP 5f

2:15 (2:17) (Class 5) (0-75,74) 2-Y-O **£3,881** (£1,155; £577; £288) **Stalls** Low

Form RPR

0452 **1** **Foxy Boy**[29] 4679 2-8-7 **60** ConnorBeasley 7 62
(Michael Dods) *dwlt: hld up: hdwy on outside wl over 1f out: edgd rt and led ins fnl f: kpt on strly* **6/1**

000 **2** ¾ **Myllachy**[31] 4601 2-8-1 **54** oh4 ow1 DuranFentiman 10 53
(Tim Easterby) *hld up: rdn and hdwy on outside 2f out: kpt on fnl f to take 2nd nr fin* **40/1**

0560 **3** *hd* **Redrosezorro**[44] 4133 2-8-8 **61** PatrickMathers 4 60
(Eric Alston) *t.k.h: led: rdn and edgd rt over 1f out: edgd lft and hdd ins fnl f: no ex and lost 2nd nr fin* **40/1**

236 **4** ¾ **Mama Africa (IRE)**[12] 5289 2-8-13 **66** GrahamGibbons 8 63
(David Barron) *trckd ldrs: effrt and wnt 2nd over 1f out to ins fnl f: one pce whn hmpd ins fnl f* **9/2**[3]

006 **5** *shd* **Scotch Myst**[29] 4685 2-8-6 **59** JamesSullivan 6 55
(Richard Fahey) *in tch: rdn along over 2f out: kpt on ins fnl f* **33/1**

5023 **6** 1 **Lady Cristal (IRE)**[31] 4602 2-9-2 **74** JordanVaughan(5) 2 66
(K R Burke) *t.k.h: hld up: rdn along 2f out: kpt on ins fnl f: nt pce to chal* **4/1**[2]

415 **7** ½ **Reckless Serenade (IRE)**[24] 4832 2-9-0 **67** PhillipMakin 1 57
(Keith Dalgleish) *prom: rdn along 2f out: outpcd fnl f* **12/1**

0330 **8** *nk* **Clear As A Bell (IRE)**[35] 4451 2-8-13 **66** DavidAllan 3 55
(Tim Easterby) *s.i.s: hld up on ins: stdy hdwy over 3f out: rdn and no imp fr over 1f out* **10/1**

2013 **9** 1 **Mightaswellsmile**[28] 4712 2-9-3 **70** TomEaves 11 55
(James Given) *t.k.h: cl up: rdn over 2f out: wknd over 1f out* **15/2**

3051 **10** 1 **Percy Toplis**[23] 4869 2-8-12 **72** LewisEdmunds(7) 12 54
(Kevin Ryan) *t.k.h: cl up: rdn and edgd rt over 1f out: wknd fnl f* **7/2**[1]

340 **11** ¾ **Nifty Niece (IRE)**[27] 4725 2-8-7 **60** FrannyNorton 9 39
(Ann Duffield) *bhd: rdn over 2f out: edgd rt and wknd over 1f out* **25/1**

1m 3.28s (2.48) **Going Correction** +0.325s/f (Good) **11** Ran SP% **114.9**

Speed ratings (Par 94): **93,91,91,90,90 88,87,87,85,84 82**

CSF £226.91 CT £8605.91 TOTE £5.20: £1.50, £13.60, £10.00; EX 203.70 Trifecta £4281.30.

Owner Sekura Group **Bred** Giles W Pritchard-Gordon (farming) Ltd **Trained** Denton, Co Durham

FOCUS

Due to 2mm of overnight rain the going was downgraded to good, good to soft in places. This was a moderate nursery, run at a strong pace. Those who finished close up suggest that the form is no better than rated.

5713 APOLLOBET HOME OF CASHBACK OFFERS NOVICE MEDIAN AUCTION STKS 5f 193y

2:45 (2:46) (Class 5) 2-Y-O **£2,911** (£866; £432; £216) **Stalls** Low

Form RPR

1 **1** **Parnassian (IRE)**[18] 5067 2-9-2 0 CliffordLee(7) 1 88+
(K R Burke) *cl up: led over 2f out: rdn clr fnl f: readily* **7/4**[1]

6 **2** 2 ¼ **Grinty (IRE)**[38] 4371 2-9-2 0 PaulMulrennan 2 75
(Michael Dods) *s.i.s: hld up: shkn up and hdwy over 1f out: kpt on steadily to take 2nd under hands and heels riding nr fin: no ch w wnr* **22/1**

2 **3** ½ **Mont Royal (FR)**[19] 5029 2-9-2 0 DanielTudhope 9 75
(Ollie Pears) *wnt bdly lft s: hld up: smooth hdwy on outside to chse wnr over 1f out: edgd rt: kpt on fnl f: no ex and lost 2nd nr fin* **11/4**[2]

5 **4** 1 ¼ **Outfox**[25] 4805 2-8-11 0 ConnorBeasley 8 64
(Bryan Smart) *sn pushed along bhd ldng gp: rdn over 2f out: kpt on same pce fr over 1f out* **28/1**

0 **5** 2 ¼ **Metisian**[18] 5067 2-9-2 0 GrahamLee 4 63
(Jedd O'Keeffe) *prom: drvn along over 3f out: rallied 2f out: kpt on same pce fnl f* **66/1**

4 **6** ¾ **Mere Brow**[35] 4451 2-8-11 0 PJMcDonald 5 55
(Ann Duffield) *t.k.h: trckd ldrs: effrt and disp 2nd pl over 1f out: wknd ins fnl f* **15/2**

56 **7** 1 ½ **Inglorious**[13] 5271 2-9-2 0 PhillipMakin 3 56
(Keith Dalgleish) *sn pushed along bhd ldng gp: outpcd whn edgd rt over 1f out: nvr on terms* **33/1**

0 **8** ¾ **Ronnie The Rooster**[26] 4765 2-9-2 0 GrahamGibbons 7 54
(David Barron) *t.k.h: cl up: rdn over 2f out: wknd wl over 1f out* **33/1**

334 **9** 11 **Navarone (IRE)**[22] 4914 2-9-2 80 TonyHamilton 6 21
(Richard Fahey) *led: rdn along and hdd over 2f out: wknd over 1f out* **10/3**[3]

1m 15.9s (2.20) **Going Correction** +0.325s/f (Good) **9** Ran SP% **113.0**

Speed ratings (Par 94): **98,95,94,92,89 88,86,85,71**

CSF £45.03 TOTE £2.70: £1.30, £5.90, £1.50; EX 37.60 Trifecta £171.50.

Owner Ontoawinner 14 & Mrs E Burke **Bred** Ballyhane Stud Ltd **Trained** Middleham Moor, N Yorks

FOCUS

Not a bad novice event. The level is a bit fluid.

5714 APOLLOBET CASHBACK IF 2ND H'CAP 5f 193y

3:15 (3:18) (Class 5) (0-70,70) 3-Y-O+ **£3,234** (£962; £481; £240) **Stalls** Low

Form RPR

3240 **1** **Enjoy Life (IRE)**[26] 4770 3-8-11 **60** TomEaves 1 69+
(Kevin Ryan) *trckd ldrs: effrt and squeezed through over 1f out: led wl ins fnl f: kpt on* **7/1**[2]

5006 **2** ¾ **Jacob's Pillow**[10] 5354 5-9-2 **62** DanielTudhope 2 68
(Rebecca Bastiman) *led: rdn over 2f out: hdd wl ins fnl f: kpt on* **7/2**[1]

3P00 **3** *nk* **Penny Pot Lane**[11] 5320 3-9-1 **64** ConnorBeasley 14 69
(Richard Whitaker) *hld up: hdwy on outside over 1f out: ev ch ins fnl f: kpt on: hld nr fin* **14/1**

4005 **4** 1 ¼ **Pushkin Museum (IRE)**[16] 5162 5-9-1 **61** TonyHamilton 10 65+
(Richard Fahey) *s.i.s: t.k.h: hld up: stdy hdwy whn nt clr run over 2f out: effrt whn hmpd over 1f out: rdn and kpt on fnl f* **11/1**

0002 **5** 5 **Aprovado (IRE)**[14] 5224 4-9-9 **69** (p) PaulMulrennan 15 54
(Michael Dods) *cl up on outside: effrt and rdn over 2f out: wknd fnl f* **7/2**[1]

6003 **6** 2 **Mercers Row**[20] 4970 9-9-7 **67** (p) DavidNolan 9 46
(Michael Herrington) *t.k.h: cl up tl rdn and wknd over 1f out* **7/1**[2]

3300 **7** ¾ **Jebel Tara**[26] 4771 11-9-1 **61** (bt) PhillipMakin 12 37
(Alan Brown) *pressed ldr: ev ch over 2f out: rdn and wknd over 1f out* **10/1**

000 **8** 2 ¼ **Lady Cordie**[14] 5222 4-8-5 **51** oh4 JoeDoyle 7 20
(Jim Goldie) *bhd: drvn along and outpcd over 3f out: n.d after* **40/1**

1264 **9** *nk* **Lydiate Lady**[16] 5162 4-8-11 **57** GrahamLee 6 25
(Paul Green) *dwlt: bhd: drvn and effrt over 2f out: btn over 1f out* **10/1**

-000 **10** 6 **Murdanova (IRE)**[28] 4714 3-9-5 **68** GrahamGibbons 11 17
(Kevin Frost) *t.k.h: hld up bhd ldng gp: drvn along 1/2-way: wknd wl over 1f out* **17/2**[3]

1m 15.53s (1.83) **Going Correction** +0.325s/f (Good)

WFA 3 from 4yo+ 3lb **10** Ran SP% **115.6**

Speed ratings (Par 103): **100,99,98,96,90 87,86,83,83,75**

CSF £31.43 CT £343.93 TOTE £6.90: £2.10, £1.80, £4.10; EX 32.90 Trifecta £386.10.

Owner CN Farm Limited **Bred** E Puerari & Mme D Ades-Hazan **Trained** Hambleton, N Yorks

FOCUS

This moderate sprint handicap was hit by non-runners. The third has been rated to form.

5715 APOLLOBET H'CAP 1m 1f

3:45 (3:45) (Class 6) (0-65,63) 3-Y-O+ **£2,911** (£866; £432; £216) **Stalls** Low

Form RPR

5030 **1** **Intalza (IRE)**[5] 5540 3-8-10 **52** (p) JoeDoyle 2 60
(Michael Herrington) *mde all: j. path after 4f: rdn 2f out: kpt on wl fnl f: unchal* **10/1**

4340 **2** 2 **Stoneboat Bill**[23] 4892 4-9-5 **61** GerO'Neill(7) 11 65
(Declan Carroll) *hld up: hdwy on outside 3f out: rdn: hung rt and chsd wnr 1f out: kpt on: nt pce to chal* **10/3**[1]

0634 **3** 2 ¼ **Remember Rocky**[14] 5227 7-9-8 **62** (b) AdamMcNamara(5) 8 62
(Lucy Normile) *trckd ldrs: wnt 2nd over 3f out to 1f out: kpt on same pce u.p* **7/1**[3]

4410 **4** 2 ¾ **Tectonic (IRE)**[5] 5540 7-10-0 **63** (v) JasonHart 7 57
(Keith Dalgleish) *hld up in midfield on ins: rdn over 2f out: kpt on same pce fr over 1f out* **8/1**

6046 **5** ½ **The Name's Bond**[21] 4929 4-8-10 **45** TonyHamilton 14 38
(Richard Fahey) *prom: rdn over 2f out: hung rt and no ex over 1f out* **25/1**

3264 **6** 1 **Ferdy (IRE)**[13] 5273 7-9-7 **56** GrahamLee 10 47
(Paul Green) *hld up towards rr: rdn and effrt over 2f out: edgd rt and no imp over 1f out* **9/1**

-356 **7** ½ **Lord Rob**[10] 5355 5-8-10 **45** PatrickMathers 12 35
(David Thompson) *hld up in midfield: hdwy over 2f out: carried hd high and wknd over 1f out* **11/1**

3000 **8** 9 **Arantes**[16] 5154 5-9-5 **59** (b[1]) GarryWhillans(5) 5 31
(R Mike Smith) *s.i.s: sn midfield: rdn and struggling over 2f out: sn btn* **16/1**

3033 **9** 4 ½ **John Caesar (IRE)**[11] 5323 5-10-0 **63** (t) DanielTudhope 6 26
(Rebecca Bastiman) *hld up: rdn over 3f out: struggling fnl 2f* **8/1**

0-51 **10** 3 **Swiss Lait**[21] 4930 5-9-7 **59** RachelRichardson(3) 3 16
(Patrick Holmes) *s.i.s: hld up: drvn along over 3f out: struggling fnl 2f* **5/1**[2]

000- **11** 42 **Arousal**[384] 4964 4-8-10 **45** TomEaves 4
(Tina Jackson) *chsd wnr to over 3f out: sn rdn and lost pl: lost tch fr 2f out: t.o* **125/1**

1m 59.73s (2.13) **Going Correction** +0.325s/f (Good)

WFA 3 from 4yo+ 7lb **11** Ran SP% **112.4**

Speed ratings (Par 101): **103,101,99,96,96 95,95,87,83,80 43**

CSF £41.31 CT £254.76 TOTE £10.90: £3.20, £1.70, £2.10; EX 47.30 Trifecta £363.20.

Owner K Fitzsimons **Bred** Patrick Ryan **Trained** Cold Kirby, N Yorks

FOCUS

Add 5 yards to advertised race distance. This ordinary handicap saw the winner dictate at an uneven tempo. The third sets the level. It's been rated as modest form to begin with.

5716 APOLLOBET DAILY RACING REFUNDS MAIDEN STKS 1m 1f

4:15 (4:16) (Class 5) 3-4-Y-O **£3,234** (£962; £481; £240) **Stalls** Low

Form RPR

1 **Gaelic Tiger** 3-9-5 0 FrannyNorton 7 84+
(Mark Johnston) *rn green in tch: rdn and outpcd over 3f out: rallied 2f out: led last 50yds: pushed out* **5/2**[2]

6 **2** ¾ **Going Up (IRE)**[8] 5438 3-9-5 0 DavidAllan 8 82
(Rae Guest) *prom: hdwy to press ldr over 5f out: rdn and led 2f out: hdd last 50yds: kpt on* **6/5**[1]

4 **3** 11 **Interlink (USA)**[7] 5480 3-9-5 0 BenCurtis 6 58
(Tony Coyle) *t.k.h: led after 1f: rdn and hdd 2f out: wknd fnl f* **7/2**[3]

00 **4** 10 **Go George Go (IRE)**[29] 4682 3-9-5 0 NeilFarley 5 36
(Alan Swinbank) *led 1f: cl up: rdn over 3f out: wknd fr 2f out* **40/1**

50 **5** 4 **Isaak (FR)**[25] 4792 3-9-5 0 DavidNolan 3 27
(Donald McCain) *hld up in tch: drvn and outpcd over 3f out: btn fnl 2f* **22/1**

6 *hd* **Calarules** 3-9-5 0 JasonHart 2 27
(Tim Easterby) *s.i.s: rn green in rr: drvn along 4f out: nvr on terms* **14/1**

4 **7** 2 ½ **Ajman Prince (IRE)**[10] 5366 3-9-0 0 RowanScott(5) 4 21
(Alistair Whillans) *hld up: drvn and struggling over 3f out: sn btn* **22/1**

0/0- **8** 30 **Newspeak (IRE)**[385] 4947 4-9-12 0 GrahamLee 1
(Fred Watson) *pressed ldr after 1f to over 5f out: wknd over 3f out: t.o* **100/1**

1m 59.47s (1.87) **Going Correction** +0.325s/f (Good)

WFA 3 from 4yo 7lb **8** Ran SP% **115.0**

Speed ratings (Par 103): **104,103,93,84,81 80,78,52**

CSF £5.72 TOTE £3.40: £1.30, £1.10, £1.80; EX 7.30 Trifecta £12.50.

Owner Newsells Park Stud **Bred** Newsells Park Stud **Trained** Middleham Moor, N Yorks

FOCUS

Add 5 yards to advertised race distance. Two interesting prospects came clear in this average maiden.

5717 APOLLOBET BET ON LOTTERIES H'CAP 6f 195y

4:45 (4:46) (Class 5) (0-70,70) 3-Y-O+ **£3,234** (£962; £481; £240) **Stalls** Low

Form RPR

0223 **1** **Dolphin Rock**[16] 5149 9-8-12 **63** (b) CallumRodriguez(7) 3 70
(Richard Ford) *pressed ldr: pushed along 2f out: drvn ent fnl f: kpt on to ld last 25yds* **10/1**

2031 **2** ½ **Emblaze**[10] 5355 4-9-5 **63** ConnorBeasley 1 68+
(Bryan Smart) *t.k.h: led: rdn over 1f out: kpt on fnl f: hdd and no ex last 25yds* **5/1**[3]

55 **3** 2 **Crazy Tornado (IRE)**[5] 5537 3-9-5 **68** JasonHart 5 66
(Keith Dalgleish) *trckd ldrs: rdn along over 2f out: kpt on same pce fnl f* **4/1**[1]

0460 **4** 1 ¾ **Yair Hill (IRE)**[11] 5323 8-8-7 **51** oh6 (p) AndrewElliott 8 46
(Thomas Cuthbert) *hld up on outside: hdwy over 2f out: rdn over 1f out: kpt on same pce ins fnl f* **80/1**

2046 **5** 1 ½ **Tanawar (IRE)**[14] 5223 6-9-4 **62** (v) JamesSullivan 7 53
(Ruth Carr) *hld up: drvn along 3f out: kpt on same pce fr over 1f out* **13/2**

20-6 **6** 1 **Destination Aim**[29] 4684 9-9-10 **68** GrahamLee 10 57
(Fred Watson) *dwlt: sn cl up: rdn along over 2f out: edgd rt and wknd over 1f out* **20/1**

32-5 **7** 5 **Mockinbird (IRE)**[229] 59 3-9-7 **70** LukeMorris 12 43
(Sir Mark Prescott Bt) *hld up in tch: drvn along over 3f out: wknd 2f out* **9/2**[2]

0512 **8** 1 3/4 **Charava (IRE)**[28] 4701 4-9-9 **67** (p) DanielTudhope 9 37
(Patrick Holmes) *hld up towards rr: drvn along over 3f out: nvr able to chal* **6/1**

0005 **9** 6 **Captain Scooby**[18] 5069 10-9-6 **64** (b) FrannyNorton 11 18
(Richard Guest) *hld up: struggling over 3f out: nvr on terms* **22/1**

5004 **10** hd **Royal Normandy**[9] 5386 4-9-4 **62** BenCurtis 2 16
(David Loughnane) *dwlt: hld up: struggling over 3f out: btn fnl 2f* **7/1**

1m 29.24s (2.14) **Going Correction** +0.325s/f (Good)
WFA 3 from 4yo+ 5lb **10** Ran SP% **114.4**
Speed ratings (Par 103): **100,99,97,95,93 92,86,84,77,77**
CSF £57.04 CT £205.04 TOTE £11.40: £2.80, £2.00, £1.90; EX 58.10 Trifecta £508.30.
Owner Mia Racing **Bred** Mia Racing **Trained** Garstang, Lancs
■ Rosy Ryan was withdrawn. Price at time of withdrawal 50/1. Rule 4 does not apply

FOCUS
Add 5 yards to advertised race distance. This looked competitive. However, the closers struggled to get in a blow. A small step up from the winner, with the third rated a length off his penultimate run.

5718 APOLLOBET ONLINE GAMES & CASINO H'CAP 1m 3f 39y
5:15 (5:15) (Class 5) (0-70,68) 3-Y-0+ **£3,234** (£962; £481; £240) **Stalls** High

Form RPR

5-51 **1** **Cartwright**[13] 5263 3-9-0 **63** LukeMorris 4 78+
(Sir Mark Prescott Bt) *s.i.s: hld up in tch: drvn along over 3f out: rallied and led over 1f out: pricked ears ins fnl f: drvn clr* **5/6**[1]

4555 **2** 2 3/4 **Eez Eh (IRE)**[4] 5580 3-9-5 **68** ConnorBeasley 7 77
(Keith Dalgleish) *trckd ldrs: hdwy and ev ch whn edgd lft over 1f out: kpt on fnl f: nt pce of wnr* **10/1**

5352 **3** 2 3/4 **Monaco Rose**[17] 5111 3-9-3 **66** TonyHamilton 3 70
(Richard Fahey) *trckd ldrs: smooth hdwy to ld over 2f out: rdn and hdd over 1f out: outpcd ins fnl f* **3/1**[2]

6343 **4** 1 1/4 **Jan De Heem**[12] 5294 6-9-4 **58** (p) TomEaves 6 60
(Tina Jackson) *bhd: hdwy 3f out: rdn and kpt on fnl f: nvr able to chal* **18/1**

6000 **5** 3/4 **Heaven Scent**[22] 4233 3-8-4 **58** RowanScott(5) 9 59
(Ann Duffield) *hld up: drvn and outpcd 5f out: rallied 3f out: no ex over 1f out* **14/1**

3002 **6** 11 **King Of Paradise (IRE)**[17] 5106 7-9-8 **62** JasonHart 2 44
(Eric Alston) *led: rdn over 3f out: hdd over 2f out: wknd over 1f out* **9/1**[3]

-040 **7** 3 3/4 **Voice From Above (IRE)**[113] 1881 7-8-6 **53** PaulaMuir(7) 1 29
(Patrick Holmes) *bhd: drvn and struggling over 3f out: sn btn* **33/1**

0405 **8** 9 **Sister Dude**[18] 5062 3-8-10 **66** (t) CliffordLee(7) 8 26
(K R Burke) *t.k.h: pressed ldr to 3f out: struggling fr 2f out* **12/1**

2m 28.63s (5.53) **Going Correction** +0.325s/f (Good)
WFA 3 from 6yo+ 9lb **8** Ran SP% **121.2**
Speed ratings (Par 103): **92,90,88,87,86 78,75,69**
CSF £11.95 CT £21.07 TOTE £1.50: £1.10, £2.90, £1.40; EX 11.00 Trifecta £42.40.
Owner J L C Pearce **Bred** Meon Valley Stud **Trained** Newmarket, Suffolk

FOCUS
Add 5 yards to advertised race distance. This wasn't a bad handicap for the class and it was run at a sound tempo. It's been rated at face value, with the third and fourth close to their marks.
T/Jkpt: Not Won. T/Plt: £122.80 to a £1 stake. Pool: £88,126.9 - 523.58 winning units T/Qpdt: £11.70 to a £1 stake. Pool: £8,726.15 - 550.96 winning units **Richard Young**

5549 KEMPTON (A.W) (R-H)
Monday, August 22

OFFICIAL GOING: Polytrack: standard to slow
Wind: Moderate, across (away from stands) Weather: Fine, warm

5719 HAPPY 60TH BIRTHDAY TIM ROWBOTHAM NURSERY H'CAP 1m (P)
5:50 (5:51) (Class 6) (0-60,59) 2-Y-0 **£2,264** (£673; £336; £168) **Stalls** Low

Form RPR

0540 **1** **Zamadance**[20] 4982 2-9-7 **59** TomMarquand 2 61
(Sylvester Kirk) *t.k.h early: hld up in rr: prog on inner over 2f out: rdn over 1f out: led ins fnl f: styd on* **11/2**

0604 **2** 1/2 **Booshbash (IRE)**[12] 5297 2-9-5 **57** JamesDoyle 3 58
(Ed Dunlop) *trckd ldr: rdn to take narrow ld over 1f out: edgd rt u.p: hdd ins fnl f: kpt on* **5/2**[1]

6003 **3** 1 1/2 **Hazell Berry (IRE)**[6] 5528 2-8-11 **49** JimCrowley 7 46
(David Evans) *led: rdn over 2f out: narrowly hdd over 1f out: kpt on tl one pce ins fnl f* **5/1**[3]

0505 **4** 1 **Belle's Angel (IRE)**[17] 5112 2-8-12 **50** JimmyQuinn 1 45
(Ann Duffield) *trckd ldrs: rdn 2f out: cl enough 1f out: one pce* **20/1**

036 **5** shd **Epsom Secret**[21] 4938 2-9-0 **52** JFEgan 4 47
(Pat Phelan) *towards rr: rdn 2f out: tried to cl on ldrs over 1f out: kpt on same pce* **7/1**

0254 **6** 4 1/2 **Born To Please**[21] 4937 2-9-7 **59** LiamKeniry 5 43
(Mark Usher) *chsd ldr: rdn over 2f out: sn lost pl and btn* **10/1**

0004 **7** 5 **Blast Of Faith (IRE)**[20] 4982 2-9-2 **54** (b[1]) ShaneKelly 6 26
(Richard Hughes) *s.i.s and urged along to get in tch: effrt on wd outside bnd over 3f out: wknd over 2f out: sn bhd* **3/1**[2]

1m 41.77s (1.97) **Going Correction** 0.0s/f (Stan) **7** Ran SP% **112.0**
Speed ratings (Par 92): **90,89,88,87,86 82,77**
CSF £18.82 TOTE £6.40: £3.20, £1.60; EX 20.20 Trifecta £97.40.
Owner J C Smith **Bred** Littleton Stud **Trained** Upper Lambourn, Berks

FOCUS
Standard to slow ground for a seven-race card on a warm, dry evening. A line-up with a combined record of 0-31 entering the contest marked this out as a decidedly ordinary nursery, but the first two may yet transcend the grade.

5720 RACINGUK.COM/HD H'CAP 1m (P)
6:20 (6:20) (Class 6) (0-65,65) 3-Y-0 **£2,264** (£673; £336; £168) **Stalls** Low

Form RPR

0063 **1** **Broughtons Vision**[28] 4718 3-9-6 **64** JamesDoyle 6 72
(Willie Musson) *trckd ldrs: clsd to ld over 1f out: sn in command: rdn out* **9/2**[2]

2015 **2** 1 1/2 **Port Paradise**[18] 5085 3-9-0 **65** SamuelClarke(7) 4 69
(William Jarvis) *hld up in midfield: gng strly over 2f out: pushed along and prog over 1f out: styd on to take 2nd last 100yds: nt rch wnr* **8/1**

0042 **3** 1 1/4 **Encore Moi**[28] 4718 3-9-4 **62** HarryBentley 2 63
(Marco Botti) *trckd ldrs on inner: prog 2f out: tried to chal over 1f out jst as wnr tk it up: chsd after but outpcd: lost 2nd last 100yds* **9/2**[2]

2233 **4** 2 **Santiburi Spring**[7] 5471 3-9-7 **65** KierenFox 7 62
(John Best) *led after 1f: hdd over 1f out: steadily wknd* **4/1**[1]

0-65 **5** 2 **Ice Alert (IRE)**[116] 1816 3-9-4 **65** JosephineGordon(3) 11 57
(John Ryan) *trapped out wd: chsd ldrs: urged along over 4f out: nvr able to threaten but kpt on one pce u.p fr over 2f out* **25/1**

-430 **6** 3/4 **Zlatan (IRE)**[11] 5326 3-9-1 **59** JimCrowley 8 49
(Ed de Giles) *nvr bttr than midfield: urged along over 3f out: one pce over 2f out* **7/1**[3]

0300 **7** nk **Nidnod**[40] 4262 3-8-4 **48** DannyBrock 5 37
(John Bridger) *led 1f: styd cl up: rdn to chal on inner 2f out: sn lost pl and btn* **50/1**

6500 **8** 1/2 **Provoking (USA)**[25] 4794 3-8-11 **55** JFEgan 10 43
(David Evans) *chsd ldr after 2f to jst over 2f out: sn lost pl and btn* **20/1**

4266 **9** 1/2 **Buzz Lightyere**[40] 4267 3-8-12 **59** EdwardGreatrex(3) 12 46
(Michael Attwater) *trapped out wd in rr: rdn wl over 2f out: no great prog* **20/1**

0053 **10** 10 **Tasteofexcellence (IRE)**[25] 4789 3-8-12 **63** RhiainIngram(7) 1 26
(Roger Ingram) *sn dropped to last and pushed along: nvr a factor: wl bhd over 1f out* **16/1**

0623 **11** 11 **Party Thyme**[19] 5038 3-9-5 **63** [1] GeorgeBaker 9
(Chris Wall) *sn in last pair: brief effrt 3f out: no prog and btn over 2f out: heavily eased and t.o* **8/1**

524 **12** 4 1/2 **Fishergate**[39] 4303 3-9-6 **64** AdamBeschizza 3
(Richard Rowe) *a struggling in last trio: t.o* **20/1**

1m 39.89s (0.09) **Going Correction** 0.0s/f (Stan) **12** Ran SP% **117.1**
Speed ratings (Par 98): **99,97,96,94,92 91,91,90,90,80 69,64**
CSF £36.29 CT £172.32 TOTE £5.00: £1.60, £2.40, £1.70; EX 39.60 Trifecta £263.60.
Owner Broughton Thermal Insulation **Bred** Broughton Bloodstock **Trained** Newmarket, Suffolk

FOCUS
A modest but fairly tight-knit handicap, in which nothing barring the runner-up made much impact from the rear. The third suggests the form might be a bit better than this, but this is a sensible starting point.

5721 £10 FREE BET AT 32REDSPORT.COM H'CAP 7f (P)
6:50 (6:50) (Class 6) (0-60,60) 3-Y-0 **£2,264** (£673; £336; £168) **Stalls** Low

Form RPR

0303 **1** **German Whip**[17] 5104 3-9-2 **60** HectorCrouch(5) 11 66
(Gary Moore) *in tch in midfield: shkn up and prog 2f out: chsd ldr ins fnl f: styd on to ld last strides* **4/1**[2]

0553 **2** nk **Simply Me**[18] 5062 3-9-4 **57** [1] RichardKingscote 9 62
(Tom Dascombe) *prom: chsd ldr over 2f out: shkn up to ld over 1f out: more than a l in front fnl f and looked sure to win: idled bdly and hdd last strides* **9/4**[1]

3403 **3** 1 **Sacred Harp**[7] 5475 3-9-3 **59** (t) AaronJones(3) 1 61
(Stuart Williams) *led: rdn and hdd over 1f out: kpt on same pce and lost 2nd ins fnl f* **6/1**[3]

040 **4** 1 3/4 **Onesie (IRE)**[16] 5178 3-9-7 **60** AdamKirby 4 57
(Marco Botti) *prom: disp 2nd on inner over 2f out: sn rdn: steadily fdd jst over 1f out* **6/1**[3]

6346 **5** nk **Sunbaked (IRE)**[18] 5087 3-9-7 **60** (b[1]) CharlesBishop 6 56
(Eve Johnson Houghton) *settled towards rr: shkn up 2f out: sme prog over 1f out: no imp on ldrs and one pce fnl f* **16/1**

0054 **6** 3 1/4 **Mostashreqah**[16] 5167 3-8-6 **48** (tp) EdwardGreatrex(3) 2 36
(Milton Bradley) *chsd ldrs: drvn to try to cl jst over 2f out: wknd over 1f out* **16/1**

000 **7** nse **Home Again**[67] 3319 3-9-4 **57** KierenFox 12 45
(Lee Carter) *struggling in last pair by 1/2-way: plugged on fnl 2f* **33/1**

3500 **8** 3 1/4 **Romancingthestone**[11] 5330 3-8-8 **47** TomMarquand 10 26
(Karen George) *struggling bdly in last bef 1/2-way: nvr a factor* **40/1**

0006 **9** 5 **Roman Urn**[26] 4760 3-8-11 **50** (vt) WilliamCarson 7 15
(Brett Johnson) *s.i.s and pushed along: a in rr: no ch fr 2f out* **66/1**

2616 **10** 7 **Arctic Flower (IRE)**[16] 5167 3-9-2 **55** DannyBrock 5 1
(John Bridger) *chsd ldr to over 2f out: wknd rapidly* **8/1**

0 **11** 10 **Another Day**[6] 5509 3-8-12 **51** (v[1]) ShaneKelly 8
(Robert Cowell) *rdn in midfield after 3f: sn wknd: t.o* **20/1**

4300 **P** **Kristoff (IRE)**[16] 5167 3-8-4 **50** RhiainIngram(7) 3
(Jim Boyle) *towards rr whn lost action after 2f and p.u* **14/1**

1m 26.62s (0.62) **Going Correction** 0.0s/f (Stan) **12** Ran SP% **120.5**
Speed ratings (Par 98): **96,95,94,92,92 88,88,84,78,70 59,**
CSF £13.17 CT £55.48 TOTE £5.20: £1.70, £1.50, £1.70; EX 16.30 Trifecta £60.80.
Owner G L Moore **Bred** Brightwalton Stud **Trained** Lower Beeding, W Sussex

FOCUS
Competitive enough for the level, and a race of late changing fortunes.

5722 32RED.COM/BRITISH STALLION STUDS EBF MAIDEN FILLIES' STKS (PLUS 10 RACE) 7f (P)
7:20 (7:21) (Class 4) 2-Y-0 **£4,269** (£1,270; £634; £317) **Stalls** Low

Form RPR

3 **1** **Blushing Rose**[23] 4885 2-9-0 0 TedDurcan 10 82+
(Sir Michael Stoute) *trckd ldrs: clsd to ld 2f out: sn more than 2 l clr: drvn fnl f: styd on wl* **1/1**[1]

4 **2** 1 **Raven's Lady**[23] 4885 2-9-0 0 DarryllHolland 3 79+
(Marco Botti) *s.i.s: hld up in 10th: long way off the pce whn distracted by tail swisher in front of her over 3f out: rapid prog on outer 2f out: tk 2nd and looked a threat ins fnl f: no imp last 75yds* **14/1**

30 **3** 2 **Helmsdale**[25] 4801 2-9-0 0 SeanLevey 9 74
(Richard Hannon) *towards rr: rdn and prog over 2f out: chsd wnr over 1f out: no imp and lost 2nd ins fnl f: jst hld on for 3rd* **14/1**

45 **4** nse **Pacofilha**[54] 3782 2-9-0 0 MartinHarley 6 74
(Paul Cole) *towards rr: rdn over 2f out: prog over 1f out: styd on fnl f: nrly snatched 3rd* **50/1**

3 **5** 2 1/2 **Millie's Kiss**[18] 5084 2-8-11 0 LouisSteward(3) 5 67
(Philip McBride) *wl in tch: shkn up over 2f out: pressed for a pl over 1f out: fdd fnl f* **12/1**

6 4 **Lawfilly** 2-9-0 0 ShaneKelly 11 56
(Richard Hughes) *wl in rr and swishing tail: sme prog on inner 2f out: pushed along and no hdwy over 1f out* **66/1**

20 **7** 6 **Manama (IRE)**[25] 4801 2-9-0 0 WilliamBuick 4 40
(Charlie Appleby) *chsd ldr: lft in ld over 2f out: sn hdd & wknd rapidly* **6/1**[3]

032 **8** nk **Snow Squaw**[19] 5022 2-9-0 76 JimCrowley 7 39
(David Elsworth) *prom: lft in cl 2nd over 2f out: sn rdn and wknd rapidly* **3/1**[2]

9 4 ½ **Fleeting Francesca** 2-9-0 0 AdamBeschizza 2 27
(Chris Gordon) *sn detached in last: a bhd* **100/1**

10 2 **Iron Lady (IRE)** 2-8-11 0 RobHornby(3) 8 22
(William Muir) *nvr on terms w ldrs: bhd fnl 2f* **33/1**

0 11 3 ½ **I Dare To Dream**14 5242 2-8-9 0 CharlieBennett(5) 1 12
(Lisa Williamson) *led: more than 2 l up whn hung bdly lft bnd 3f out and ended against nr side rail: sn hdd & wknd* **100/1**

1m 25.35s (-0.65) **Going Correction** 0.0s/f (Stan) **11** Ran SP% **118.7**
Speed ratings (Par 93): **103,101,99,99,96 92,85,84,79,77 73**
CSF £18.49 TOTE £1.90: £1.10, £3.60, £4.10; EX 16.80 Trifecta £128.40.
Owner Sir Evelyn De Rothschild **Bred** Southcourt Stud **Trained** Newmarket, Suffolk

FOCUS
Plenty of top yards represented in an interesting juvenile fillies' maiden, and a winning time nearly 1.3 seconds quicker than that of the preceding 0-60 event for three-year-olds. The front pair have been rated as taking steps forward.

5723 32RED ON THE APP STORE MAIDEN STKS 1m 4f (P)
7:50 (7:52) (Class 4) 3-Y-O+ **£4,690** (£1,395; £697; £348) **Stalls** Centre

Form RPR
532 1 **Sir Valentine (GER)**25 4792 3-9-4 84 WilliamTwiston-Davies 1 88
(Alan King) *pushed along early: sn in 3rd: rdn over 2f out: sn chsd ldr but outpcd: styd on wl fnl f to ld last 50yds* **11/4**2

-02 2 ¾ **Eyeshine**73 3094 3-8-13 0 1 FrankieDettori 7 82
(John Gosden) *trckd ldr after 1f: led over 2f out and kicked for home: abt 3 l clr over 1f out: kpt on but hdd last 50yds* **4/5**1

3 6 **Snobbery (IRE)** 3-9-4 0 GeorgeBaker 5 77
(Roger Charlton) *slowly away: settled in detached last: pushed along and stdy prog fr 2f out: styd on to take 3rd nr fin* **12/1**

00 4 1 **Pray For Paris**52 3845 3-8-10 0 JosephineGordon(3) 2 71
(Martyn Meade) *led 1f: t.k.h after bhd ldrs: outpcd 2f out: pushed along and tk 3rd over 1f out to ins fnl f: kpt on* **66/1**

0-22 5 4 ½ **Tuolumne Meadows**19 5025 3-8-13 80 MartinHarley 3 64
(Paul Cole) *led after 1f to over 2f out: sn outpcd: fdd over 1f out* **4/1**3

35 6 2 ½ **Attest**30 4657 3-9-4 0 JimCrowley 8 65
(Amanda Perrett) *hld up towards rr: outpcd whn wnt 5th over 2f out: nvr on terms* **15/2**

0- 7 shd **Mere Anarchy (IRE)**32 7640 5-10-0 0 AdamBeschizza 4 64
(Robert Stephens) *in tch to over 2f out: sn btn* **66/1**

0 8 90 **Certain Time**13 5255 4-10-0 0 WilliamCarson 6
(Peter Hiatt) *a in last pair: t.o* **100/1**

2m 32.1s (-2.40) **Going Correction** 0.0s/f (Stan)
WFA 3 from 4yo+ 10lb **8** Ran SP% **125.7**
Speed ratings (Par 105): **108,107,103,102,99 98,98,38**
CSF £5.96 TOTE £3.70: £1.40, £1.10, £3.20; EX 8.20 Trifecta £51.70.
Owner Walters Plant Hire & James & Jean Potter **Bred** Stiftung Gestut Fahrhof **Trained** Barbury Castle, Wilts

FOCUS
Not too bad a middle-distance maiden, and another race whose outcome was determined only late on. It's been rated fairly positively for now, with the runner-up to the better view of his latest effort.

5724 32RED H'CAP 1m 4f (P)
8:20 (8:23) (Class 4) (0-80,80) 3-Y-O+ **£4,690** (£1,395; £697; £348) **Stalls** Centre

Form RPR
4211 1 **Athlon (IRE)**49 3959 3-9-4 80 GeorgeBaker 9 94+
(David Lanigan) *trckd ldrs: smooth prog over 2f out to ld wl over 1f out: sn rdn and edgd lft: styd on wl fnl f* **9/4**1

3031 2 1 ½ **Pointel (FR)**51 3904 3-9-2 78 FrederikTylicki 7 89+
(James Fanshawe) *settled in midfield: rdn and prog over 2f out: chsd wnr over 1f out and intimidated sn after: styd on but no imp fnl f* **9/4**1

0604 3 3 ¾ **Plymouth Sound**21 4940 4-9-12 78 (b) JohnFahy 6 84
(Eve Johnson Houghton) *hld up and sn in last pair: gng wl enough over 2f out in 9th: gd prog over 1f out but racing sltly awkwardly: r.o fnl f to take 3rd last 50yds* **20/1**

3506 4 ¾ **Charlies Mate**81 2827 5-9-11 77 KierenFox 12 82
(John Best) *trckd ldrs: rapid prog to ld over 7f out: tried to kick for home 3f out: hdd wl over 1f out: outpcd after: lost 3rd last 50yds* **25/1**

1130 5 3 **Vastly (USA)**16 5149 7-9-4 70 (t) SaleemGolam 4 70
(Sophie Leech) *in tch in midfield: rdn over 2f out: sme prog over 1f out but nt on terms: fdd fnl f* **50/1**

-043 6 ½ **Rehearse (IRE)**19 5026 3-8-12 74 WilliamBuick 8 73
(Andrew Balding) *t.k.h: hld up towards rr: effrt and rdn over 2f out: nt qckn wl over 1f out: no imp after* **7/2**2

10-6 7 hd **Syncopate**46 4049 7-9-8 77 RobHornby(3) 10 76
(Pam Sly) *wl in rr: last over 4f out: rdn and no prog over 2f out: styd on fnl f: gng on at fin* **50/1**

004 8 2 **Sabre Rock**58 3659 6-9-12 78 (t) RichardKingscote 1 74
(Julia Feilden) *prom: rdn over 2f out: sn wknd* **16/1**3

1212 9 1 ¼ **Sandy Cove**19 5035 5-9-5 71 RyanTate 5 65
(James Eustace) *slowly away: rapid prog to ld after 2f: stdd and hdd over 7f out: chsd ldr to 2f out: wknd* **16/1**3

5534 10 2 ¾ **Marshall Aid (IRE)**9 5398 3-8-4 69 JosephineGordon(3) 11 58
(Mark Usher) *dwlt: t.k.h: hld up in last pair early: nvr a factor: bhd fnl 2f* **33/1**

-060 11 7 **London Citizen (USA)**19 5026 6-10-0 80 TedDurcan 3 58
(Chris Wall) *wl in tch: urged along over 3f out: wknd rapidly 2f out* **25/1**

00/6 12 58 **Art History (IRE)**80 2876 8-9-1 67 MartinHarley 2
(Zoe Davison) *led 2f: wknd rapidly 4f out: sn t.o* **100/1**

2m 32.75s (-1.75) **Going Correction** 0.0s/f (Stan)
WFA 3 from 4yo+ 10lb **12** Ran SP% **115.8**
Speed ratings (Par 105): **105,104,101,101,99 99,98,97,96,94 90,51**
CSF £6.34 CT £76.34 TOTE £3.00: £1.30, £1.50, £4.40; EX 8.80 Trifecta £97.20.
Owner The Athlon Partnership **Bred** Thomas Maher **Trained** Newmarket, Suffolk

FOCUS
A fair middle-distance handicap dominated by the joint-favourites, but a winning time 0.65 seconds slower than the maiden which preceded it. The third has been rated in line with his latest effort, and the fourth close to form.

5725 32RED CASINO FILLIES' H'CAP 6f (P)
8:50 (8:50) (Class 5) (0-70,70) 3-Y-O+ **£2,911** (£866; £432; £216) **Stalls** Low

Form RPR
3326 1 **Nag's Wag (IRE)**12 5284 3-9-7 70 PatCosgrave 2 78
(George Baker) *chsd ldrs: rdn over 2f out: clsd on outer to take 2nd jst over 1f out: drvn ahd last 75yds: styd on wl* **7/2**2

5050 2 nk **Lolita**31 4587 4-9-7 67 FrederikTylicki 4 74
(J R Jenkins) *led: jnd after 1f: rdn 2f out and def advantage: hrd pressed fnl f: fought on wl but hdd and jst hld last 75yds* **12/1**

0015 3 2 **Oasis Moon**5 5554 3-8-6 55 (p) LiamJones 3 56
(William Haggas) *trckd ldng pair: rdn to chse ldr wl over 1f out and tried to chal: nt qckn and lost 2nd jst over 1f out: one pce* **5/1**3

2133 4 nk **One Big Surprise**16 5169 4-9-10 70 (p) ShaneKelly 1 70
(Richard Hughes) *n.m.r sn after s: towards rr: prog on inner over 2f out: disp 2nd and drvn over 1f out: one pce fnl f* **5/2**1

003- 5 2 ½ **Fashionable Spirit (IRE)**277 7896 3-9-2 65 JimCrowley 7 57
(Amanda Perrett) *towards rr: rdn and no prog 2f out: wl hld after* **13/2**

0536 6 ½ **Langham**40 4280 3-9-2 68 1 JosephineGordon(3) 5 58
(Martyn Meade) *jnd ldr after 1f to jst over 2f out: sn btn* **9/1**

00-0 7 1 ½ **Camino**18 5078 3-8-8 57 StevieDonohoe 8 42
(Willie Musson) *hld up in detached last: no ch whn rdn over 1f out: nvr involved* **50/1**

2104 8 2 ½ **Broughtons Fancy**25 4787 3-9-0 63 TomMarquand 6 40
(Andrew Reid) *racd wd: towards rr: rdn and btn 2f out* **11/2**

1m 12.95s (-0.15) **Going Correction** 0.0s/f (Stan)
WFA 3 from 4yo 3lb **8** Ran SP% **115.8**
Speed ratings (Par 100): **101,100,97,97,94 93,91,88**
CSF £44.67 CT £210.25 TOTE £4.40: £1.30, £3.50, £2.10; EX 41.60 Trifecta £254.50.
Owner Nag's Wag Partnership **Bred** Mrs Ann Foley & Mr William Neville **Trained** Manton, Wilts

FOCUS
A reasonably competitive fillies' sprint. A length pb from the winner, with the third to her latest C&D effort.
T/Plt: £15.40 to a £1 stake. Pool: £84,941.34 - 4006.87 winning units T/Qpdt: £2.80 to a £1 stake. Pool: £8,964.03 - 2324.82 winning units **Jonathan Neesom**

5476 THIRSK (L-H)
Monday, August 22

OFFICIAL GOING: Soft (good to soft in places; 6.4)
Wind: Light behind Weather: Cloudy

5726 BETFAIR NOVICE FLAT AMATEUR RIDERS' H'CAP 2m
5:05 (5:05) (Class 6) (0-65,64) 4-Y-O+ **£2,495** (£774; £386; £193) **Stalls** Centre

Form RPR
363 1 **Question Of Faith**42 4194 5-10-3 46 1 MrGaryBeaumont 4 55
(Martin Todhunter) *hld up towards rr: hdwy 6f out: trckd ldrs over 4f out: cl up 3f out: led 2f out: sn rdn clr* **4/1**1

5353 2 3 ¾ **Hero's Story**16 5155 6-10-10 53 (p) MrMEnnis 7 56
(Jim Goldie) *trckd ldrs: hdwy over 4f out: clsd up 3f out: ev ch 2f out: sn rdn and kpt on same pce* **8/1**3

0000 3 6 **Belle Peinture (FR)**11 5319 5-10-2 45 (p) MissEmilyBullock 1 41
(Alan Lockwood) *led: pushed along over 3f out: rdn and hdd 2f out: plugged on same pce* **50/1**

2614 4 8 **Chauvelin**17 5117 5-10-11 54 (b) MrBLynn 11 40
(Nigel Tinkler) *hld up and bhd: hdwy 4f out: effrt on outer 3f out: rdn along 2f out: sn drvn and no imp* **4/1**1

5455 5 3 ½ **Lucky Diva**19 5016 9-10-1 47 (p) MissPSkipper(3) 2 29
(Bill Turner) *midfield: hdwy over 4f out: in tch and rdn along 3f out: sn one pce* **14/1**

0-00 6 2 ½ **Come On Lulu**30 4648 5-10-2 45 MrBJames 5 24
(David Thompson) *midfield: hdwy 4f out: in tch and rdn along on outer 3f out: sn drvn and one pce* **100/1**

1040 7 nk **Dark Diamond (IRE)**9 4234 6-11-4 61 (b) MrCJMiller 3 40
(Michael Chapman) *trckd ldrs: pushed along over 4f out: rdn over 3f out: wknd over 2f out* **14/1**

/633 8 3 ¾ **Nafaath (IRE)**21 4950 10-11-7 64 (v) MissAMcCain 8 38
(Donald McCain) *chsd ldr: rdn along over 3f out: sn wknd* **9/2**2

000- 9 1 ¼ **Cool Baranca (GER)**124 7290 10-10-5 51 MissAMSlack(3) 10 24
(Dianne Sayer) *hld up: a bhd* **18/1**

30-0 10 29 **Rayadour (IRE)**41 4239 7-10-11 54 MrJoeWright 9
(Micky Hammond) *hld up towards rr: pushed along 1/2-way: rdn 6f out: outpcd and bhd fr over 3f out* **16/1**

6064 11 25 **Kirkman (IRE)**34 4478 5-10-5 48 MissMollyKing 6
(Peter Hiatt) *chsd ldng pair: pushed along over 4f out: rdn along over 3f out: sn wknd* **4/1**1

3m 40.24s (11.94) **Going Correction** +0.425s/f (Yiel) **11** Ran SP% **116.7**
Speed ratings (Par 101): **87,85,82,78,76 75,74,73,72,57 45**
CSF £36.20 CT £1386.78 TOTE £4.90: £1.80, £1.90, £14.00; EX 38.60 Trifecta £691.50.
Owner K Fitzsimons & G Fell **Bred** Sir Robert Ogden **Trained** Orton, Cumbria

FOCUS
Race distances as advertised. After 5mm of overnight rain and a further 7mm prior to racing, the official going was changed to soft, good to soft in places. A modest staying handicap and they finished well strung out. A minor pb from the winner, with the runner-up fitting.

5727 BRITISH STALLION STUDS EBF MAIDEN STKS (PLUS 10 RACE) 5f
5:35 (5:36) (Class 4) 2-Y-O **£4,269** (£1,270; £634; £317) **Stalls** High

Form RPR
66 1 **Norwegian Highness (FR)**100 2254 2-9-0 0 ShaneGray 6 77
(Kevin Ryan) *wnt rt s: cl up: rdn to ld wl over 1f out: drvn ins fnl f: kpt on wl towards fin* **14/1**

3 2 1 ¼ **Connacht Girl (IRE)**18 5072 2-9-0 0 JoeyHaynes 5 72
(K R Burke) *trckd ldrs: cl up 1/2-way: rdn to chal over 1f out: drvn and ev ch ins fnl f: no ex towards fin* **5/2**2

0 3 ¾ **Ocelot**68 3290 2-9-0 0 AndrewMullen 12 69
(Tim Easterby) *slt ld: pushed along over 2f out: rdn and hdd wl over 1f out: kpt on wl fnl f* **25/1**

0252 4 2 ¼ **Sheepscar Lad (IRE)**8 5433 2-9-5 75 PaulHanagan 8 66
(Nigel Tinkler) *wnt lft s: towards rr: hdwy 1/2-way: rdn to chse ldrs whn hung bdly lft over 1f out: no imp after* **7/2**3

04 5 ½ **Not Now Nadia (IRE)**51 3873 2-9-0 0 PaulMulrennan 9 59
(Michael Dods) *chsd ldrs: rdn along 2f out: sn drvn and kpt on same pce* **25/1**

04 6 1 **Rebounded**27 4725 2-9-5 0 JoeFanning 1 61
(Declan Carroll) *in tch: hdwy on outer and cl up after 2f: rdn along 2f out: grad wknd* **25/1**

7 ¾ **Mr Black** 2-9-5 0 JamieSpencer 2 58+
(George Scott) *dwlt and towards rr: hdwy over 2f out: in tch and rdn wl over 1f out: sn no imp* **9/4**1

8 3 **Miss Pepper (IRE)** 2-9-0 0 CamHardie 4 42
(Paul Midgley) *chsd ldrs: rdn along 2f out: sn edgd lft and wknd* **100/1**

66 9 ½ **Wilderswood (IRE)**26 4765 2-9-5 0 PJMcDonald 13 46
(Ann Duffield) *chsd ldrs on inner: pushed along and lost pl 1/2-way: sn bhd* **20/1**

10 3/4 **Gaval** 2-9-5 0 GrahamGibbons 10 32
(David Barron) *a in rr* **16/1**

0 11 3/4 **Lights**[25] 4804 2-9-0 0 BarryMcHugh 7 24
(Declan Carroll) *hmpd s: t.k.h: chsd ldrs: rdn along over 2f out: grad wknd* **100/1**

56 12 nk **Royal Cosmic**[21] 4943 2-9-0 0 JackGarritty 11 23
(Richard Fahey) *a in rr* **22/1**

1m 0.44s (0.84) **Going Correction** +0.10s/f (Good) **12** Ran SP% **116.7**
Speed ratings (Par 96): **97,95,93,90,89 87,86,81,81,75 73,73**
CSF £45.12 TOTE £22.10: £5.50, £1.60, £6.10; EX 71.90 Trifecta £1815.80.
Owner Guy Pariente **Bred** Guy Pariente Holding Sprl **Trained** Hambleton, N Yorks

FOCUS
Not many got into this fair maiden, with the stands' rail proving the place to be. The time reads well and the form is probably at least as good as rated.

5728 ANDERSON BARROWCLIFF CHARTERED ACCOUNTANTS MAIDEN AUCTION STKS 7f
6:05 (6:05) (Class 5) 2-Y-O **£3,234** (£962; £481; £240) **Stalls** Low

Form RPR

5 1 **Manners Please**[11] 5325 2-9-0 0 GrahamGibbons 5 73+
(Ralph Beckett) *sn led: racd centre in st: pushed clr 2f out: shkn up last 75yds: jst hld on* **10/11**[1]

2 hd **Free To Dance (IRE)** 2-8-12 0 JoeyHaynes 6 68+
(K R Burke) *trckd ldrs: racd wd and pushed along 3f out: rdn and green 2f out: styd on to chse wnr ins fnl f: sn swtchd lft and fin strly: jst failed* **11/1**

3 2 3/4 **Fortuities (IRE)** 2-8-9 0 PaulHanagan 9 58
(Jedd O'Keeffe) *in tch: pushed along and hdwy over 2f out: rdn over 1f out: kpt on wl fnl f* **22/1**

05 4 shd **Midnight Man (FR)**[15] 5203 2-9-0 0 DougieCostello 10 63
(K R Burke) *towards rr: racd wd st and hdwy 3f out: pushed along wl over 2f out: rdn wl over 1f out: styd on fnl f* **7/1**[3]

04 5 1 1/2 **Dream Team**[18] 5067 2-8-11 0 PaulMulrennan 2 56
(Michael Dods) *chsd wnr: racd wd st: rdn along over 2f out: drvn wl over 1f out: grad wknd* **12/1**

605 6 2 1/2 **Dandy Place (IRE)**[13] 5271 2-9-3 72 DuranFentiman 1 56
(Tim Easterby) *plld hrd: chsd ldrs on inner: rdn to chal 2f out: sn drvn and wknd 1f out* **14/1**

7 2 **Bodacious Name (IRE)** 2-9-3 0 JackGarritty 4 51
(John Quinn) *chsd ldrs: rdn along over 2f out: wknd wl over 1f out* **33/1**

05 8 4 **Dyna Might**[20] 4966 2-7-13 0 RobertDodsworth(7) 8 30
(Ollie Pears) *a towards rr* **100/1**

9 hd **Spin A Disc (GER)** 2-9-3 0 JoeFanning 7 40
(Mark Johnston) *s.i.s: green and a in rr* **9/2**[2]

10 1 **Cryogenics (IRE)** 2-9-0 0 PJMcDonald 11 35
(Rebecca Menzies) *a in rr* **66/1**

1m 32.47s (5.27) **Going Correction** +0.425s/f (Yiel) **10** Ran SP% **115.5**
Speed ratings (Par 94): **86,85,82,82,80 77,75,71,70,69**
CSF £11.92 TOTE £1.80: £1.10, £3.30, £4.90; EX 12.50 Trifecta £122.10.
Owner R Roberts **Bred** C A Cyzer **Trained** Kimpton, Hants

FOCUS
An ordinary maiden with little depth, in which the winner was given a scare late on. The level is a bit fluid.

5729 MARKET CROSS JEWELLERS (S) H'CAP 1m
6:35 (6:36) (Class 6) (0-65,65) 3-Y-O+ **£2,587** (£770; £384; £192) **Stalls** Low

Form RPR

0-01 1 **Scruffy McGuffy**[16] 5181 3-9-1 58 PJMcDonald 3 67
(Ann Duffield) *trckd ldrs: hdwy over 3f out: chsd ldr wl over 1f out: sn rdn: led jst ins fnl f: drvn out* **7/1**[3]

4460 2 1 1/2 **Bertha Burnett (IRE)**[49] 3952 5-8-11 48 BarryMcHugh 15 55
(Brian Rothwell) *hld up: hdwy 3f out: chsd ldrs wl over 1f out: sn rdn: drvn and styd on wl fnl f* **16/1**

5005 3 1 1/4 **Alans Pride (IRE)**[6] 5517 4-9-1 52 (b) PaulMulrennan 18 56
(Michael Dods) *sn led: rdn clr over 2f out: drvn over 1f out: hdd jst ins fnl f: kpt on same pce* **13/2**[2]

0044 4 4 1/2 **Border Bandit (USA)**[6] 5521 8-9-5 56 (p) JoeFanning 10 50
(Tracy Waggott) *in rr: hdwy on wd outside over 2f out: sn rdn: styd on fnl f: nrst fin* **7/1**[3]

6400 5 nse **Mr Sundowner (USA)**[18] 5068 4-9-2 53 (t) CamHardie 5 47
(Wilf Storey) *midfield: hdwy 3f out: rdn to chse ldrs wl over 1f out: drvn and no imp fnl f* **14/1**

6005 6 2 **Secret Lightning (FR)**[9] 5415 4-9-4 55 (b) AndrewMullen 16 45
(Michael Appleby) *trckd ldrs: hdwy to chse ldr 3f out: rdn 2f out: drvn over 1f out: wknd fnl f* **11/1**

6022 7 shd **Handheld**[34] 4493 9-9-9 63 (p) ShelleyBirkett(3) 14 53
(Julia Feilden) *trckd ldrs: hdwy 3f out: rdn along 2f out: sn drvn and no imp* **5/1**[1]

5050 8 nk **Saltarello (IRE)**[10] 5355 4-8-9 51 (b) NathanEvans(5) 11 40
(Marjorie Fife) *bhd: hdwy on inner wl over 2f out: sn rdn and plugged on* **7/1**[3]

0000 9 5 **Centre Haafhd**[10] 5369 5-8-7 51 LewisEdmunds(7) 9 29
(Jim Goldie) *a towards rr* **28/1**

0000 10 8 **Afkar (IRE)**[13] 5273 8-9-6 57 RaulDaSilva 7 17
(Ivan Furtado) *chsd ldr: rdn along over 3f out: sn drvn and outpcd fnl 2f* **50/1**

0055 11 7 **Striking Nigella**[67] 3322 6-8-9 46 oh1 JoeyHaynes 8
(Michael Chapman) *a towards rr* **150/1**

0-04 12 20 **Lipstickandpowder (IRE)**[16] 5149 4-8-9 46 oh1 (bt) KevinStott 4
(Dianne Sayer) *in tch: pushed along 1/2-way: sn rdn and wknd* **16/1**

0000 13 6 **Shearian**[65] 3421 6-9-1 52 (p) RoystonFfrench 1
(Tracy Waggott) *a towards rr* **12/1**

0002 14 2 **Back To Bond**[16] 5181 3-9-3 65 AdamMcNamara(5) 13
(Richard Fahey) *a in rr* **10/1**

5563 15 5 **Grenade**[33] 4511 4-8-9 46 oh1 DuranFentiman 2
(Patrick Holmes) *chsd ldrs on inner: rdn along over 3f out: sn wknd* **50/1**

1m 42.98s (2.88) **Going Correction** +0.425s/f (Yiel)
WFA 3 from 4yo+ 6lb **15** Ran SP% **119.1**
Speed ratings (Par 101): **102,100,99,94,94 92,92,92,87,79 72,52,46,44,39**
CSF £110.17 CT £784.39 TOTE £8.20: £3.00, £4.70, £2.40; EX 124.50 Trifecta £1682.60.No bid for the winner
Owner John Sagar & Partner **Bred** Mrs Doreen Addison & Mrs Ann Duffield **Trained** Constable Burton, N Yorks

FOCUS
A typically modest selling handicap. The second and third help confirm the solid but limited standard.

5730 CALVERTS CARPETS H'CAP 5f
7:05 (7:05) (Class 4) (0-85,85) 3-Y-O **£4,851** (£1,443; £721; £360) **Stalls** High

Form RPR

255 1 **Swirral Edge**[19] 5040 3-8-8 72 JoeFanning 6 83+
(David Brown) *hld up towards rr: swtchd rt to inner and gd hdwy over 1f out: qcknd to ld ent fnl f: sn rdn and kpt on* **13/2**[2]

0222 2 1 1/4 **Fruit Salad**[10] 5370 3-8-1 70 NathanEvans(5) 9 75
(James Bethell) *trckd ldrs: hdwy wl over 1f out: swtchd rt ins fnl f: sn rdn to chse wnr: no imp towards fin* **9/2**[1]

1302 3 1 3/4 **Rose Marmara**[21] 4947 3-9-3 81 (t) JamesSullivan 4 80
(Brian Rothwell) *trckd ldrs: pushed along over 2f out: rdn wl over 1f out: styd on fnl f* **10/1**

6055 4 1 1/2 **Crombay (IRE)**[40] 4256 3-8-2 69 RachelRichardson(3) 11 62
(Tim Easterby) *led: rdn along wl over 1f out: hdd ent fnl f: sn drvn and kpt on same pce* **9/1**[3]

416 5 1 1/4 **L C Saloon**[21] 4947 3-9-4 82 DavidAllan 8 71
(David C Griffiths) *chsd ldrs: rdn along wl over 1f out: drvn and one pce fnl f* **9/2**[1]

0510 6 1 **New Road Side**[21] 4947 3-8-13 77 (v) BarryMcHugh 5 62
(Tony Coyle) *cl up: rdn along 2f out: sn drvn and wknd* **25/1**

1333 7 1 **Gwendolyn (GER)**[65] 3413 3-9-0 85 GeorgeWood(7) 7 67
(Robert Cowell) *dwlt: sn swtchd lft to outer: rdn along and in tch 1/2-way: sn wknd* **9/2**[1]

8 1 **Jenniechild (IRE)**[71] 3200 3-8-10 74 JamieSpencer 3 52
(Peter Fahey, Ire) *prom: cl up 2f out: rdn over 1f out: sn drvn and wknd* **9/2**[1]

0515 9 8 **Kestrel Call (IRE)**[10] 5372 3-8-12 76 (t) AndrewMullen 2 25
(Michael Appleby) *chsd ldrs: rdn along 2f out: sn drvn and wknd over 1f out* **12/1**

1m 0.1s (0.50) **Going Correction** +0.10s/f (Good) **9** Ran SP% **116.7**
Speed ratings (Par 102): **100,98,95,92,90 89,87,86,73**
CSF £36.24 CT £294.57 TOTE £7.60: £2.50, £2.10, £2.90; EX 33.60 Trifecta £484.50.
Owner D H Brown **Bred** Bolton Grange **Trained** Averham Park, Notts

FOCUS
A decent 3yo sprint handicap and again it paid to race close to the stands' rail. The third has been rated close to her latest form.

5731 RACING UK PROFITS RETURNED TO RACING MAIDEN STKS 1m
7:35 (7:37) (Class 5) 3-4-Y-O **£3,234** (£962; £481; £240) **Stalls** Low

Form RPR

3202 1 **Ehtiraas**[23] 4895 3-9-5 83 PaulHanagan 4 81+
(Owen Burrows) *trckd ldng pair: hdwy 3f out: rdn to ld 2f out: sn drvn: kpt on u.p fnl f* **2/7**[1]

64 2 5 **Come Back King (IRE)**[8] 5438 3-9-5 0 AndrewMullen 2 69
(Michael Appleby) *led 1f: chsd ldr: cl up 3f out: rdn and ev ch 2f out: sn drvn and kpt on same pce* **13/2**[2]

3 3 1 3/4 **Captain Peaky**[40] 4258 3-9-5 0 JackGarritty 3 65
(Patrick Holmes) *trckd ldrs: hdwy 3f out: rdn along 2f out: drvn and no imp fnl f* **10/1**[3]

0- 4 3/4 **Merriment**[303] 7467 3-9-0 0 TomEaves 1 58
(Peter Niven) *dwlt and in rr: hdwy wl over 2f out: rdn along wl over 1f out: kpt on fnl f* **50/1**

6 5 8 **Bemusement**[227] 102 3-9-0 0 JoeFanning 7 47+
(Mark Johnston) *plld hrd: led after 1f: pushed along 3f out: hdd and rdn 2f out: sn wknd and eased fnl f* **10/1**[3]

2-00 6 2 3/4 **Frankster (FR)**[23] 4895 3-9-5 72 (t[1]) PJMcDonald 6 39
(Micky Hammond) *a in rr* **25/1**

00- 7 7 **No Pleasing You (IRE)**[382] 5063 3-8-9 0 NathanEvans(5) 5 17
(Bill Turner) *a in rr* **125/1**

1m 45.08s (4.98) **Going Correction** +0.425s/f (Yiel) **7** Ran SP% **115.9**
Speed ratings (Par 103): **92,87,85,84,76 73,66**
CSF £2.92 TOTE £1.10: £1.02, £2.90; EX 3.10 Trifecta £7.50.
Owner Hamdan Al Maktoum **Bred** Shadwell Estate Company Limited **Trained** Lambourn, Berks

FOCUS
An uncompetitive maiden and the short-priced favourite made no mistake. The second and third have bee rated close to their previous early maiden figures for now.

5732 RACING UK HD H'CAP 7f
8:05 (8:05) (Class 5) (0-70,69) 3-Y-O **£3,234** (£962; £481; £240) **Stalls** Low

Form RPR

4334 1 **Iceaxe**[15] 5195 3-9-1 63 RoystonFfrench 15 71
(John Holt) *led 1f: cl up: led again 2f out: sn rdn: drvn and kpt on wl fnl f* **12/1**

5013 2 2 **Mango Chutney**[20] 4972 3-8-12 60 (p) PhillipMakin 9 63
(John Davies) *trckd ldrs: hdwy over 2f out: rdn wl over 1f out: sn chal and ev ch: drvn and kpt on same pce fnl f* **11/2**[2]

3040 3 1 **Ginger Charlie**[11] 5322 3-8-2 50 oh1 JamesSullivan 13 50+
(Ruth Carr) *in rr: hdwy on outer 2f out: rdn wl over 1f out: swtchd lft and styd on strly fnl f: nrst fin* **25/1**

-300 4 1/2 **Kirkham**[60] 3567 3-9-5 67 JoeDoyle 11 66
(Julie Camacho) *prom: effrt 2f out: sn rdn and ev ch: drvn and n.m.r ins fnl f: kpt on* **9/1**

4352 5 1 1/4 **Popsies Joy (IRE)**[7] 5478 3-9-3 68 RachelRichardson(3) 7 64
(Tim Easterby) *in tch: hdwy to trck ldrs 3f out: cl up 2f out: sn rdn and ev ch: drvn ent fnl f and kpt on same pce* **7/2**[1]

5000 6 1/2 **Firesnake (IRE)**[54] 3775 3-9-0 69 LewisEdmunds(7) 14 64
(Lisa Williamson) *trckd ldrs: effrt over 2f out and sn rdn along: drvn over 1f out: hld whn n.m.r ins fnl f* **50/1**

004 7 2 **Beverley Bullet**[11] 5322 3-8-13 61 DavidAllan 1 50
(Les Eyre) *towards rr: hdwy over 2f out: rdn to chse ldrs over 1f out: sn drvn and no imp* **8/1**

5426 8 1 3/4 **Bahamian Sunshine**[15] 5195 3-9-1 68 (p) AdamMcNamara(5) 4 53
(Richard Fahey) *dwlt and towards rr: hdwy wl over 2f out: rdn along wl over 1f out: kpt on fnl f* **12/1**

0-0 9 2 3/4 **Epeius (IRE)**[80] 2864 3-9-6 68 GrahamLee 12 46
(Ben Haslam) *a towards rr* **15/2**[3]

6036 10 2 1/4 **A Boy Named Sue**[20] 4973 3-7-13 52 oh1 ow2[1] NathanEvans(5) 3 24
(Peter Niven) *a towards rr* **14/1**

3200 11 1/2 **Mustn't Grumble (IRE)**[6] 5515 3-9-2 64 PJMcDonald 2 35
(Ivan Furtado) *chsd ldrs: pushed along 3f out: rdn over 2f out and grad wknd* **16/1**

4305 **12** 3/4 **Miramonte Dancer (IRE)**[62] 3479 3-8-12 **60**..........(p) GrahamGibbons 5 29
(David C Griffiths) *cl up on inner: led after 1f: rdn along 3f out: hdd 2f out: sn drvn and wknd* **15/2**[3]
4035 **13** 6 **Mr Lucas (IRE)**[16] 5181 3-8-4 **52**..................................(v) JoeFanning 10 5
(Peter Niven) *chsd ldrs: rdn along 3f out: sn wknd* **25/1**
1m 29.52s (2.32) **Going Correction** +0.425s/f (Yiel) **13** Ran SP% **119.8**
Speed ratings (Par 100): **103,100,99,99,97 97,94,92,89,87 86,85,78**
CSF £75.62 CT £1706.22 TOTE £14.60: £3.90, £1.80, £8.10; EX 66.00 Trifecta £1975.00 Part Won..
Owner J R Holt **Bred** Llety Farms **Trained** Peckleton, Leics
FOCUS
A fair 3yo handicap, in which they came down the middle of the course in the home straight. The runner-up helps set the standard.
T/Plt: £114.80 to a £1 stake. Pool: £62,327.17 - 396.03 winning units T/Qpdt: £19.30 to a £1 stake. Pool: £6,111.97 - 234.17 winning units **Joe Rowntree**

5733 - (Foreign Racing) - See Raceform Interactive

5675 CHELMSFORD (A.W) (L-H)
Tuesday, August 23

OFFICIAL GOING: Polytrack: standard
Wind: light, half behind Weather: sunny and warm

5734 TOTEPLACEPOT H'CAP 7f (P)
6:10 (6:10) (Class 6) (0-60,60) 4-Y-O+ **£3,234** (£962; £481; £240) **Stalls** Low

Form RPR
0-60 **1** **O Dee**[127] 1533 4-9-4 **57**.. RenatoSouza 2 63
(Jose Santos) *racd keenly: w ldr tl led after 1f: mde rest: travelling best and wnt clr 2f out: rdn over 1f out: tiring wl ins fnl f but a doing enough* **12/1**
3600 **2** 1 1/4 **For Shia And Lula (IRE)**[19] 5068 7-9-3 **59**......... JosephineGordon(3) 5 62
(Daniel Mark Loughnane) *bustled along leaving stalls: led for 1f: chsd wnr after: rdn over 2f out: outpcd 2f out: kpt on u.p: clsng on tiring wnr towards fin but nvr enough pce to chal* **7/1**
0003 **3** 1/2 **Coolcalmcollected (IRE)**[11] 5355 4-8-13 **52**................. PJMcDonald 3 54
(David Loughnane) *w ldrs tl stdd bk to chse ldrs after 1f: effrt in 3rd wl over 1f out: sn drvn: plugged on u.p ins fnl f: nvr enough pce to chal* **5/4**[1]
0004 **4** 2 1/4 **Orlando Rogue (IRE)**[18] 5127 4-9-4 **57**...................(b) PaulMulrennan 4 53
(Conor Dore) *bhd: rdn over 2f out: drvn over 1f out: styd on ins fnl f: nvr trbld ldrs* **10/1**
1140 **5** 1 **Theydon Thunder**[39] 4362 4-9-0 **60**............................ GeorgeWood(7) 8 53
(Peter Charalambous) *dwlt and niggled along leaving stalls: a towards rr: drvn 2f out: plugged on ins fnl f: nvr trbld ldrs* **6/1**[3]
2233 **6** 1 **Limerick Lord (IRE)**[10] 5393 4-9-1 **57**.....................(p) ShelleyBirkett(3) 7 47
(Julia Feilden) *taken down early: in tch in midfield but stuck wd: clsd to chse ldrs 3f out: rdn and unable qck wl over 1f out: wknd ins fnl f* **9/2**[2]
0-50 **7** 3/4 **Royal Caper**[38] 4388 6-9-5 **58**.. RobertHavlin 6 46
(Miss Joey Ellis) *dwlt and bustled along along early: a towards rr: effrt on inner over 1f out: no imp ins fnl f* **12/1**
60-0 **8** 71 **Magic Ice**[76] 3043 6-8-7 **46** oh1.................................... AdamBeschizza 1
(John Berry) *wl in tch in midfield: lost pl qckly over 2f out: lost tch wl over 1f out: sn eased: t.o: burst blood vessel* **66/1**
1m 27.84s (0.64) **Going Correction** +0.025s/f (Slow) **8** Ran SP% **115.4**
Speed ratings (Par 101): **97,95,95,92,91 90,89,8**
CSF £92.96 CT £180.10 TOTE £14.40: £4.20, £2.30, £1.10; EX 131.40 Trifecta £416.30.
Owner Jose Santos **Bred** Lofts Hall Stud & B Sangster **Trained** Upper Lambourn, Berks
FOCUS
A weak handicap won by a 57-rated maiden who had them all in trouble from the home turn.

5735 TOTEEXACTA MAIDEN FILLIES' STKS 1m (P)
6:40 (6:41) (Class 5) 3-5-Y-O **£5,175** (£1,540; £769; £384) **Stalls** Low

Form RPR
0-62 **1** **Sunset Dream (IRE)**[13] 5300 3-9-0 78......................... TimmyMurphy 3 83
(Richard Hannon) *t.k.h: mde all: wnt clr on bridle 2f out: rdn ent fnl f: kpt on: unchal* **5/6**[1]
2 **2** 6 **Trishuli Rock (IRE)**[7] 5504 3-8-11 0....................... MarcMonaghan(3) 4 69
(Marco Botti) *trckd ldng pair: chsd wnr and rdn over 2f out: drvn and no hdwy over 1f out: wl hld and plugged on same pce fnl f* **7/4**[2]
3 8 **Tanzania Road (USA)** 3-9-0 0.. LukeMorris 5 51
(James Tate) *chsd wnr tl over 2f out: u.p and no rspnse after: 3rd and wl btn over 1f out* **6/1**[3]
4 3/4 **Whispered Kiss** 3-9-0 0..[1] RoystonFfrench 2 49
(Mike Murphy) *s.i.s: rn green and pushed in rr: wnt modest 4th over 3f out: no imp* **25/1**
5 22 **Rianna Star** 3-9-0 0.. LiamKeniry 1
(Gary Moore) *dwlt: rn green and sn pushed along in last pair: dropped to last over 3f out: t.o fnl 2f* **25/1**
1m 38.59s (-1.31) **Going Correction** +0.025s/f (Slow) **5** Ran SP% **112.9**
Speed ratings (Par 100): **107,101,93,92,70**
CSF £2.64 TOTE £1.70: £1.10, £1.50; EX 2.70 Trifecta £4.00.
Owner Ecurie Des Charmes **Bred** Gigginstown House Stud **Trained** East Everleigh, Wilts
FOCUS
Little depth to this fillies' maiden and they finished well strung out. The result never looked in any doubt. The runner-up has been rated close to her debut mark.

5736 TOTETRIFECTA H'CAP 6f (P)
7:10 (7:10) (Class 5) (0-70,70) 4-Y-O+ **£5,175** (£1,540; £769; £384) **Stalls** Centre

Form RPR
0211 **1** **Chetan**[24] 4878 4-9-4 **67**..(tp) AdamBeschizza 1 77
(Charlie Wallis) *taken down early: sn led and mde rest: rdn and kicked clr over 1f out: in command and styd on wl fnl f* **7/2**[2]
0203 **2** 2 1/2 **Fujin**[13] 5296 5-9-7 **70**.. TomEaves 8 72
(Shaun Harris) *sn chsng wnr: rdn and unable qck over 1f out: drifted rt 1f out: styd on same pce ins fnl f* **11/1**
3452 **3** nk **Champagne Bob**[10] 5408 4-8-4 **60**.............................. GeorgeWood(7) 5 61
(Richard Price) *t.k.h: chsd ldrs: effrt over 1f out: styd on same pce ins fnl f* **9/2**[3]
-402 **4** 1/2 **Unnoticed**[24] 4878 4-9-2 **65**.. LukeMorris 7 64+
(Luca Cumani) *hld up in tch in midfield: effrt and c centre wl over 1f out: sn drvn: styd on same pce ins fnl f* **9/4**[1]
0516 **5** 3/4 **Compton Prince**[16] 5194 7-8-12 **61**................................(b) JoeFanning 6 58
(Milton Bradley) *hld up in tch in midfield: swtchd lft and effrt over 1f out: no imp and styd on same pce fnl f* **20/1**
0500 **6** 2 1/2 **Run With Pride (IRE)**[68] 3303 6-9-4 **67**........................... MartinLane 9 56
(Derek Shaw) *v.s.a: off the pce in last trio: swtchd lft and sme hdwy u.p over 1f out: no imp ins fnl f* **5/1**

1100 **7** 1 3/4 **Triple Dream**[14] 5270 11-9-1 **67**................................ EdwardGreatrex(3) 2 50
(Milton Bradley) *pushed stall open early: stdd and chsd ldrs: effrt 2f out: unable qck u.p over 1f out: wknd ins fnl f* **20/1**
0120 **8** 2 **City Of Angkor Wat (IRE)**[29] 4714 6-9-5 **68**...........(p) PaulMulrennan 3 45
(Conor Dore) *chsd ldrs: rdn and unable qck over 1f out: lost pl and bhd 1f out: wknd fnl f* **8/1**
5000 **9** 3 3/4 **Speightowns Kid (USA)**[22] 4932 8-8-11 **65** ow3......(be) AnnStokell(5) 4 30
(Ann Stokell) *s.i.s: a bhd: sddle slipped* **66/1**
1m 12.79s (-0.91) **Going Correction** +0.025s/f (Slow) **9** Ran SP% **118.3**
Speed ratings (Par 103): **107,103,103,102,101 98,95,93,88**
CSF £41.11 CT £179.43 TOTE £4.70: £1.50, £2.50, £1.90; EX 36.00 Trifecta £184.10.
Owner Roger & Val Miles, Tony Stamp **Bred** Andrew W Robson **Trained** Ardleigh, Essex
FOCUS
A wide open sprint handicap on paper but it was dominated by those racing on the front end. Another pb from the winner, with the runner-up rated to his February C&D form.

5737 TOTEPOOL BETTING ON ALL UK RACING H'CAP 1m 5f 66y(P)
7:40 (7:40) (Class 5) (0-70,68) 4-Y-O+ **£5,175** (£1,540; £769; £384) **Stalls** Low

Form RPR
1414 **1** **Yasir (USA)**[8] 5473 8-9-6 **64**... PaulMulrennan 2 71
(Conor Dore) *stdd s: hld up in tch in last pair: clsd to ld 2f out: sn rdn: 1 l clr 1f out: drvn ins fnl f: hld on towards fin* **5/2**[2]
1/03 **2** hd **Atalanta Bay (IRE)**[21] 4979 6-9-6 **64**......................... RoystonFfrench 5 70
(Marcus Tregoning) *t.k.h: chsd ldr: led 10f out tl 8f out: styd chsng ldrs: rdn over 2f out: drvn to chse wnr ent fnl f: kpt on u.p and ev ch wl ins fnl f: nvr quite getting to wnr* **11/8**[1]
224 **3** 3 1/2 **Theydon Bois**[28] 4739 4-8-12 **56**...................................(p) JimmyQuinn 3 56
(Peter Charalambous) *t.k.h: hld up in tch: hdwy to join ldr 7f out: rdn and ev ch over 2f out: unable qck w wnr over 1f out: 3rd and btn 1f out: kpt on same pce after* **7/1**
00-0 **4** 4 **Sov (IRE)**[215] 273 5-8-13 **57**.. TomEaves 6 51
(James Given) *chsd ldrs: hdwy to join ldr 10f out tl led 8f out: rdn over 2f out: hdd 2f out: sn outpcd: wl hld 4th and one pce fr over 1f out* **7/2**[3]
0/20 **5** 9 **Medicean Queen (IRE)**[21] 4978 5-9-4 **65**........... JosephineGordon(3) 1 46
(Phil McEntee) *t.k.h: led tl 10f out: stdd bk to rr but stl wl in tch 6f out: rdn and unable qck over 2f out: wknd over 1f out* **14/1**
2m 54.67s (1.07) **Going Correction** +0.025s/f (Slow) **5** Ran SP% **112.1**
Speed ratings (Par 103): **97,96,94,92,86**
CSF £6.51 TOTE £2.60: £1.70, £1.40; EX 5.80 Trifecta £10.80.
Owner Mrs Jennifer Marsh **Bred** Shadwell Farm LLC **Trained** Hubbert's Bridge, Lincs
FOCUS
A weak 0-70 given the highest-rated horse in here was racing off 65, and the pace was muddling. However, the two form horses dominated the finish and drew clear of the rest. Muddling form.

5738 TOTESWINGER H'CAP 1m 2f (P)
8:10 (8:10) (Class 4) (0-85,85) 3-Y-O **£8,086** (£2,406; £1,202; £601) **Stalls** Low

Form RPR
5342 **1** **Wild Hacked (USA)**[25] 4838 3-9-6 **84**............................... LukeMorris 1 94
(Marco Botti) *chsd ldrs: shkn up over 2f out: rdn and hdwy on inner to chal over 1f out: led ins fnl f: r.o wl: rdn out* **4/5**[1]
1130 **2** 2 1/4 **Goldenfield (IRE)**[25] 4827 3-9-6 **84**..............................(p) LiamKeniry 2 89
(Gary Moore) *racd keenly: sn led: rdn over 1f out: drvn and hdd ins fnl f: styd on same pce after* **10/1**
0600 **3** 1 1/2 **Welford**[25] 4827 3-9-7 **85**... JoeFanning 4 87
(Mark Johnston) *hld up in tch in last pair: nt clr run 2f out: sn swtchd rt: effrt and pushed rt over 1f out: led on same pce u.p ins fnl f* **5/1**[3]
0552 **4** nse **Southern Gailes (IRE)**[11] 5365 3-8-8 **77**..............(t) JordanVaughan(5) 5 79
(K R Burke) *chsd ldr tl over 1f out: sn swtchd rt: kpt on same pce u.p ins fnl f* **7/2**[2]
0314 **5** shd **St Mary'S**[20] 5024 3-8-13 **80**..................................... EdwardGreatrex(3) 6 82
(Andrew Balding) *t.k.h early: hld up in tch in last pair: effrt 2f out: pushed rt over 1f out: styd on same pce u.p ins fnl f* **10/1**
2m 5.64s (-2.96) **Going Correction** +0.025s/f (Slow) **5** Ran SP% **112.6**
Speed ratings (Par 102): **112,110,109,108,108**
CSF £10.00 TOTE £1.80: £1.10, £4.90; EX 8.70 Trifecta £29.30.
Owner Khalid Bin Ali Al Khalifa **Bred** Moyglare Stud **Trained** Newmarket, Suffolk
FOCUS
A reasonably competitive Class 4 handicap despite the small field and the pace looked fairly even, resulting in a time around 6secs quicker than the concluding handicap, run over the same trip. The runner-up has been rated to the better view of his earlier form.

5739 TOTEPOOL LIVE INFO DOWNLOAD OUR APP H'CAP 1m 2f (P)
8:40 (8:40) (Class 6) (0-60,60) 4-Y-O+ **£3,234** (£962; £481; £240) **Stalls** Low

Form RPR
5262 **1** **First Summer**[14] 5264 4-8-11 **57**.................................. GeorgeWood(7) 2 63
(Shaun Harris) *trckd ldng pair: effrt and ev ch 2f out: sustained duel w runner-up fr over 1f out: drvn ins fnl f: styd on to ld towards fin* **5/2**[2]
5400 **2** shd **Thane Of Cawdor (IRE)**[132] 1413 7-9-2 **58**......... JosephineGordon(3) 7 64
(Joseph Tuite) *t.k.h: hld up wl in tch in 4th: effrt and ev ch ent fnl 2f: rdn to ld over 1f out: kpt on u.p: hdd towards fin* **7/1**
2441 **3** 2 1/4 **Sexy Secret**[33] 4566 5-9-1 **57**.......................................(p) SimonPearce(3) 5 59
(Lydia Pearce) *led: rdn ent fnl 2f: hdd and unable qck over 1f out: 3rd and kpt on same pce ins fnl f* **15/8**[1]
0054 **4** 2 3/4 **Heat Storm (IRE)**[19] 5085 5-8-7 **46**...............................(v) RyanPowell 3 42
(James Unett) *hld up in tch in rr: bdly hmpd over 2f out: sn rdn: no ch of rcvring but kpt on ins fnl f* **9/1**
3054 **P** **Capelena**[43] 4200 5-9-2 **55**... RobertHavlin 6
(Miss Joey Ellis) *pressed ldr: ev ch whn lost action and p.u over 2f out: dismntd* **3/1**[3]
2m 11.65s (3.05) **Going Correction** +0.025s/f (Slow) **5** Ran SP% **110.9**
Speed ratings (Par 101): **88,87,86,83,**
CSF £18.84 TOTE £3.60: £1.40, £1.90; EX 20.80 Trifecta £51.20.
Owner Vision Bloodstock **Bred** The C H F Partnership **Trained** Carburton, Notts
FOCUS
A weak handicap run at a steady pace and the winner was an exposed maiden coming into this. Straightforward form.
T/Plt: £13.60 to a £1 stake. Pool of £64142.91 - 3437.44 winning units. T/Qpdt: £6.00 to a £1 stake. Pool of £5934.71 - 723.29 winning units. **Steve Payne**

5400 NEWBURY (L-H)

Tuesday, August 23

OFFICIAL GOING: Good to firm (good in places)

Wind: Moderate, half behind Weather: Sunny, hot

5740 BATHWICK TYRES MAIDEN AUCTION STKS 1m (S)

4:40 (4:42) (Class 5) 2-Y-O **£3,946** (£1,174; £586; £293) **Stalls** High

Form				RPR
3	**1**		**Genetics (FR)**[16] 5203 2-8-13 0 RobHornby[(3)] 3	80
			(Andrew Balding) *trckd ldng pair: led wl over 2f out: clr wl over 1f out: in n.d after: rdn out* **7/2**[2]	
	2	1 ¼	**Raheen House (IRE)** 2-9-3 0 RichardKingscote 7	79+
			(Brian Meehan) *trckd ldrs: lost pl sltly over 2f out: nt clr run over 1f out: r.o wl to take 2nd ins fnl f: clsd on wnr but no ch to chal* **6/1**[3]	
	3	3	**Temple Church (IRE)** 2-8-11 0 CharlieBennett[(5)] 4	70
			(Hughie Morrison) *dwlt: sn chsd ldrs: rdn to chse wnr 2f: no imp: lost 2nd ins fnl f* **16/1**	
2	**4**	1	**Fields Of Fortune**[41] 4270 2-8-12 0 TomMarquand 8	63
			(Richard Hannon) *towards rr: pushed along 3f out: prog over 2f out: chal for a pl fr over 1f out but no ch w wnr: one pce* **7/4**[1]	
4	**5**	½	**Ettihadi (IRE)**[17] 5166 2-9-2 0 WilliamBuick 5	66
			(Hugo Palmer) *trckd ldr: chal over 3f out tl wnr wnt past wl over 2f out: rn green and hanging after: fdd ins fnl f* **8/1**	
	6	3 ¾	**Je Suis Charlie** 2-8-12 0 LouisSteward[(3)] 6	56
			(Michael Bell) *awkward s: sn in tch: effrt on wd outside over 2f out: wknd over 1f out* **20/1**	
052	**7**	½	**Famous Dynasty (IRE)**[12] 5325 2-8-12 70 KieranO'Neill 1	52
			(Michael Blanshard) *sn chsd ldrs: effrt on outer over 2f out: wknd over 1f out* **12/1**	
04	**8**	1 ¾	**City Dreamer (IRE)**[21] 4989 2-9-0 0 FergusSweeney 13	50
			(Alan King) *dwlt: settled in last pair: gng wl enough 3f out: steadily fdd fr 2f out* **10/1**	
0	**9**	2 ¾	**Bianca Minola (FR)**[38] 4397 2-8-7 0 MartinDwyer 10	36
			(David Menuisier) *swtchd to r against nr side rail: led to wl over 2f out: wknd* **100/1**	
06	**10**	2 ¼	**Kozier (GER)**[21] 4988 2-9-2 0 JimmyFortune 9	40
			(Alan King) *chsd ldrs to 1/2-way: sn lost pl and wknd* **50/1**	
6	**11**	1 ¾	**Amadeus Rox (FR)**[19] 5081 2-9-2 0 WilliamTwiston-Davies 11	36
			(Alan King) *a in last pair: wknd over 2f out* **100/1**	

1m 37.99s (-1.71) **Going Correction** -0.15s/f (Firm) **11** Ran SP% **115.4**

Speed ratings (Par 94): **102,100,97,96,96 92,92,90,87,85 83**

CSF £23.82 TOTE £4.70: £1.50, £2.60, £4.10; EX 28.50 Trifecta £302.30.

Owner DJT Racing Partnership **Bred** S C E A De Maulepaire & David Taylor **Trained** Kingsclere, Hants

FOCUS

A dry and hot day, and the going, officially given as good to firm (GoingStick: 7.1), was described by William Twiston-Davies as "Very fast", while Jimmy Fortune said: "It's quick, good to firm", and Martin Dwyer said "It's rattling." The rail was in the same position as the last meeting, with the 7f and 5f bends out 6yds from the measured distance. Just a fair maiden. The level is a bit fluid.

5741 BATHWICK TYRES NURSERY H'CAP 5f 34y

5:10 (5:11) (Class 4) (0-85,85) 2-Y-O **£4,690** (£1,395; £697; £348) **Stalls** High

Form				RPR
10	**1**		**Nayyar**[27] 4755 2-9-7 **81** WilliamBuick 5	86
			(Charles Hills) *trckd ldng pair: wnt 2nd over 1f out: rdn to ld last 150yds: styd on steadily* **13/8**[1]	
4321	**2**	1 ¼	**Blue Suede (IRE)**[13] 5283 2-9-4 **78** TomMarquand 1	78
			(Richard Hannon) *wl away: led: rdn 2f out: edgd rt over 1f out: hdd and one pce last 150yds* **3/1**[2]	
5415	**3**	1 ½	**Coolfitch (IRE)**[24] 4869 2-9-2 **76** SamJames 3	71
			(David O'Meara) *racd in 4th and off the pce early: pushed along to cl 2f out: shkn up to take 3rd ins fnl f: nvr nr to chal* **8/1**	
1041	**4**	3 ¼	**Quench Dolly**[20] 5014 2-9-5 **79** MichaelJMMurphy 6	62
			(John Gallagher) *pressed ldr: rdn over 2f out: lost 2nd over 1f out: wknd fnl f* **15/2**[3]	
4001	**5**	7	**Sayesse**[7] 5510 2-9-11 **85** 6ex GeorgeBaker 4	43
			(Mick Channon) *stdd s and sn way adrift in last: nvr mde any grnd and a bhd* **3/1**[2]	

1m 0.27s (-1.13) **Going Correction** -0.15s/f (Firm) **5** Ran SP% **111.0**

Speed ratings (Par 96): **103,101,98,93,82**

CSF £6.83 TOTE £2.50: £1.30, £1.20; EX 6.40 Trifecta £17.50.

Owner Abdulla Al Khalifa **Bred** Sheikh Abdulla Bin Isa Al Khalifa **Trained** Lambourn, Berks

FOCUS

They went a good pace in this nursery. The third has been rated as matching her previous fast-ground form.

5742 BATHWICK TYRES MAIDEN STKS 1m 4f 5y

5:45 (5:45) (Class 5) 3-Y-O+ **£3,234** (£962; £481; £240) **Stalls** Centre

Form				RPR
2	**1**		**Scattered Stars**[11] 5361 3-8-13 0 WilliamBuick 2	75+
			(Charlie Appleby) *trckd ldr: pushed into ld over 2f out: drvn over 1f out: narrow ld after and kpt on at same pce: a holding on* **11/10**[1]	
662	**2**	nk	**Henry Croft**[56] 3736 3-9-4 84 JamesDoyle 1	79
			(John Gosden) *led after nthing else wanted to: set mod pce to over 4f out: pushed along over 3f out: drvn and hdd over 2f out: kpt on to press wnr after but a jst hld* **13/8**[2]	
33	**3**	1	**Ardamir (FR)**[22] 4948 4-10-0 0 WilliamTwiston-Davies 4	77
			(Alan King) *hld up in 5th: prog to chse ldng pair over 2f out: sn drvn: kpt on same pce and nvr quite able to chal* **12/1**	
02	**4**	hd	**Fashion Design (IRE)**[18] 5129 3-8-13 0 [1] TedDurcan 5	72
			(Sir Michael Stoute) *hld up in 4th: pushed along to chse ldng pair over 3f out to over 2f out: sn rdn and nt qckn: kpt on same pce fr over 1f out* **7/1**[3]	
62	**5**	nk	**Togetherness (IRE)**[14] 5255 3-9-4 0 RichardKingscote 3	76
			(Harry Dunlop) *trckd ldng pair to over 3f out: styd wl in tch: rdn and kpt on same pce fnl 2f out and nvr pce to chal* **33/1**	
04	**6**	2	**Poppy Time**[11] 5361 3-8-13 0 RyanTate 7	68
			(James Eustace) *settled in last: prog on outer 3f out: sn rdn: fdd fr 2f out* **66/1**	

2m 35.38s (-0.12) **Going Correction** -0.15s/f (Firm)

WFA 3 from 4yo 10lb **6** Ran SP% **110.3**

Speed ratings (Par 103): **94,93,93,93,92 91**

CSF £2.97 TOTE £2.00: £1.10, £1.30; EX 3.90 Trifecta £11.00.

Owner Godolphin **Bred** Newsells Park Stud **Trained** Newmarket, Suffolk

FOCUS

Race distance increased by 13yds. Not a bad maiden on paper, but the pace held up, they all finished in a heap and it's hard to rate the race too highly. The first two have been rated below their pre-race marks, with the third and fourth setting the level.

5743 BATHWICK TYRES NEWBURY H'CAP 7f (S)

6:20 (6:20) (Class 4) (0-85,85) 3-Y-O **£4,690** (£1,395; £697; £348) **Stalls** High

Form				RPR
-345	**1**		**Calvados Spirit**[39] 4358 3-8-13 **77** MartinDwyer 7	85
			(William Muir) *trckd ldng pair: wnt 2nd over 2f out: rdn to ld over 1f out: drvn out and styd on wl* **9/2**[2]	
-201	**2**	1 ½	**Ballylare**[17] 5169 3-9-1 **79** KierenFox 4	83
			(John Best) *led: rdn over 2f out: hdd over 1f out: kpt on same pce* **7/1**[3]	
4162	**3**	½	**Alizoom (IRE)**[14] 5253 3-9-6 **84** JackMitchell 3	87
			(Roger Varian) *t.k.h: hld up in last pair: prog 2f out: rdn over 1f out: disp 2nd fnl f but nt qckn* **9/2**[2]	
0511	**4**	2 ¼	**Kylla Instinct**[19] 5089 3-8-12 **83** RhiainIngram[(7)] 6	80
			(Philip McBride) *trckd ldrs: gng strly 2f out: rdn and fnd nil over 1f out: wknd* **8/1**	
4-31	**5**	1 ¼	**Wrapped**[27] 4766 3-8-13 **77** [1] PatCosgrave 9	70
			(William Haggas) *racd against rail: chsd ldr to over 2f out: sn wknd u.p* **9/2**[2]	
4514	**6**	½	**Horrah**[41] 4271 3-9-7 **85** GeorgeBaker 8	77
			(Roger Charlton) *hld up in last pair: stl last 2f out: shuffled along and no prog: nvr involved* **4/1**[1]	
3410	**7**	20	**Hitman**[25] 4841 3-8-13 **77** SamHitchcott 2	15
			(William Muir) *pushed along early to get in tch: rdn on outer sn after 3f out: wknd: t.o* **15/2**	

1m 24.83s (-0.87) **Going Correction** -0.15s/f (Firm) **7** Ran SP% **109.9**

Speed ratings (Par 102): **98,96,95,93,91 91,68**

CSF £32.38 CT £137.58 TOTE £5.40: £3.20, £3.30; EX 31.60 Trifecta £158.00.

Owner Muir Racing Partnership - Deauville **Bred** Newsells Park Stud **Trained** Lambourn, Berks

FOCUS

A tight little handicap. It's been rated around the second and third.

5744 BATHWICK TYRES H'CAP 6f 8y

6:50 (6:52) (Class 4) (0-85,84) 3-Y-O+ **£6,469** (£1,925; £962; £481) **Stalls** High

Form				RPR
6	**1**		**Boy In The Bar**[61] 3580 5-9-1 **75** (b) JamesDoyle 12	86
			(Ian Williams) *settled towards rr: prog over 2f out: brought to nr side rail and rdn to ld over 1f out: styd on wl* **7/1**[3]	
6005	**2**	1 ¼	**Francisco**[23] 4910 4-9-6 **80** SeanLevey 9	87
			(Richard Hannon) *hld up in rr: rdn over 2f out: prog over 1f out and weaved through rivals: styd on wl to take 2nd last 75yds* **10/1**	
3354	**3**	1	**Major Crispies**[55] 3783 5-9-5 **84** (b) DavidParkes[(5)] 2	88
			(Jeremy Gask) *awkward s: hld up in rr: prog on wd outside and pushed along 2f out: tried to cl 1f out: racd awkwardly but kpt on to take 3rd* **14/1**	
0000	**4**	nk	**Souville**[38] 4398 5-9-8 **82** GeorgeBaker 3	85
			(Chris Wall) *led: edgd towards nr side over 2f out: rdn and hdd over 1f out: one pce and lost 2 pls last 100yds* **12/1**	
2130	**5**	1 ¾	**Lightning Charlie**[24] 4862 4-9-9 **83** JimmyFortune 5	80
			(Amanda Perrett) *dwlt: hld up in tch: looked to be gng wl whn nt clr run over 2f out: swtchd to nr side over 1f out but sn rdn and nt qckn: wl hld whn no room nr fin* **5/1**[2]	
-41	**6**	1	**Gale Song**[33] 4565 3-9-0 **77** WilliamBuick 6	71
			(Ed Walker) *prom: rdn and lost pl sltly over 1f out: steadily fdd* **5/1**[2]	
5044	**7**	½	**Captain Bob (IRE)**[20] 5039 5-8-12 **72** TomMarquand 10	64
			(Robert Cowell) *dwlt: hld up in rr: rdn over 2f out: tried to cl over 1f out but nvr pce to make much imp* **12/1**	
0010	**8**	2	**Field Game**[32] 4608 4-9-0 **79** (t) CharlieBennett[(5)] 13	65
			(Hughie Morrison) *hld up and sn detached in last of main gp: rdn 2f out: swtchd to wd outside jst over 1f out: kpt on but nvr a factor* **10/1**	
0620	**9**	1 ½	**Calypso Choir**[38] 4398 3-9-6 **83** OisinMurphy 4	68
			(Sylvester Kirk) *t.k.h: pressed ldr: rdn to chal over 1f out: wknd qckly fnl f* **16/1**	
20F-	**10**	1 ¾	**Panther Patrol (IRE)**[458] 2510 6-9-1 **75** (v) JohnFahy 15	51
			(Eve Johnson Houghton) *dwlt: racd along towards nr side: sn wl off the pce: a bhd* **25/1**	
4060	**11**	½	**Brazen Spirit**[40] 4291 4-8-9 **69** (v) RyanTate 1	43
			(Clive Cox) *pressed ldr to 2f out: wknd rapidly jst over 1f out* **33/1**	
4021	**P**		**Poole Belle (IRE)**[21] 4990 3-9-2 **79** FergusSweeney 7	
			(Henry Candy) *trckd ldrs in 5th: lost action 1/2-way and p.u* **4/1**[1]	

1m 11.06s (-1.94) **Going Correction** -0.15s/f (Firm)

WFA 3 from 4yo+ 3lb **12** Ran SP% **118.7**

Speed ratings (Par 105): **106,104,103,102,100 98,98,95,93,91 90,**

CSF £75.38 CT £978.82 TOTE £7.40: £2.30, £3.70, £4.60; EX 92.30 Trifecta £1025.30.

Owner Sovereign Racing **Bred** Brinkley Stud S R L **Trained** Portway, Worcs

FOCUS

A competitive sprint handicap in which the closers came to the fore. The second and third could back this form being rated a bit higher.

5745 BATHWICK TYRES ANDOVER H'CAP 2m

7:20 (7:21) (Class 5) (0-75,73) 3-Y-O+ **£3,234** (£962; £481; £240) **Stalls** Centre

Form				RPR
0-62	**1**		**Kleitomachos (IRE)**[26] 4795 8-9-8 **67** (t) OisinMurphy 3	76
			(Stuart Kittow) *led: stretched on over 4f out: pushed along over 3f out: hdd and rdn wl over 2f out: rallied to ld again over 1f out: drvn out and kpt on wl* **11/4**[2]	
4443	**2**	1 ¾	**Folly Bergere (IRE)**[27] 4778 3-9-0 **73** RyanTate 9	80
			(James Eustace) *trckd ldr: pushed into ld wl over 2f out: sn rdn: hdd over 1f out: kpt on and clr of rest but hld fnl f* **2/1**[1]	
/002	**3**	6	**Amantius**[21] 4979 7-9-1 **60** (b) StevieDonohoe 4	60
			(Johnny Farrelly) *t.k.h: hld up in 4th: chsd ldng pair over 4f out: rdn and limited rspnse 3f out: steadily lft bhd after* **8/1**	
45-4	**4**	¾	**Laser Blazer**[38] 78 8-9-11 **70** (p) FergusSweeney 2	69
			(Alan King) *dwlt: hld up in 5th: pushed along 4f out: rdn and no prog 3f out: one pce after* **6/1**	
0144	**5**	¾	**Voice Control (IRE)**[22] 4941 4-9-12 **71** GeorgeBaker 5	69
			(Laura Mongan) *hld up in detached last: plenty to do whn asked to improve 3f out: sn rdn and no real prog* **9/2**[3]	
1025	**6**	2 ¾	**Delagoa Bay (IRE)**[8] 5473 8-8-8 **60** MitchGodwin[(7)] 6	55
			(Sylvester Kirk) *chsd ldng pair to over 4f out: sn rdn and struggling: in last and wl btn 2f out* **16/1**	

3m 32.37s (0.37) **Going Correction** -0.15s/f (Firm)

WFA 3 from 4yo+ 14lb **6** Ran SP% **109.5**

Speed ratings (Par 103): **93,92,89,88,88 87**

CSF £8.21 CT £32.30 TOTE £3.40: £1.40, £1.80; EX 8.90 Trifecta £42.00.

Owner Eric Gadsden **Bred** Carrigbeg Stud Co Ltd **Trained** Blackborough, Devon

FOCUS

Race distance increased by 13yds. The front two dominated throughout in this staying contest. The level is a bit fluid.

5746 BATHWICK TYRES SWINDON H'CAP — 1m 4f 5y

7:50 (7:50) (Class 5) (0-70,70) 3-Y-O — **£3,234** (£962; £481; £240) **Stalls** Centre

Form — RPR

4350 **1** — **Corpus Chorister (FR)**[12] 5326 3-9-1 **64** .... MartinDwyer 2 — 74
(David Menuisier) *mde all: upped the pce over 4f out: rdn 2f out: styd on wl to draw clr fnl f* **13/2**

0111 **2** 3¾ **Coarse Cut (IRE)**[13] 5286 3-9-6 **69** .... (b) JohnFahy 3 — 74
(Eve Johnson Houghton) *trckd ldng pair: wnt 2nd over 3f out: rdn to chal 2f out: one pce and lft bhd fnl f* **7/2**[3]

2254 **3** 1¼ **Red Hot Chilly (IRE)**[25] 4818 3-9-7 **70** .... OisinMurphy 6 — 72
(Joseph Tuite) *t.k.h: hld up in last pair: shkn up over 2f out: tk 3rd over 1f out but nvr a threat and no prog after* **3/1**[2]

44-6 **4** ½ **Wynford (IRE)**[39] 4372 3-9-4 **70** .... RobHornby(3) 5 — 71
(Andrew Balding) *t.k.h: hld up in 4th: rdn on outer 3f out: hanging and nt qckn over 2f out: no imp after* **10/1**

0214 **5** 3¼ **Zain Arion (IRE)**[7] 5508 3-9-5 **68** .... StevieDonohoe 8 — 64
(Charlie Fellowes) *dwlt: hld up in last pair: brought out wdst of all and rdn 3f out: sn no prog: wknd over 1f out* **9/4**[1]

400 **6** 3¾ **Sund City (FR)**[22] 4939 3-8-8 **57** .... TomMarquand 4 — 47
(Harry Dunlop) *chsd wnr to over 3f out: wknd 2f out* **10/1**

2m 33.37s (-2.13) **Going Correction** -0.15s/f (Firm) — **6** Ran SP% **109.5**

Speed ratings (Par 100): **101,98,97,97,95 92**

CSF £27.66 CT £74.82 TOTE £7.40: £2.70, £1.80; EX 31.70 Trifecta £70.70.

Owner Clive Washbourn **Bred** Mme Elisabeth Erbeya **Trained** Pulborough, W Sussex

FOCUS

Race distance increased by 12yds. This was another race in which the pace held up. The first two have been rated as improving, with the third and fourth fitting.

T/Jkpt: £7394.60 to a £1 stake. Pool of £11092.02 - 1.50 winning units. T/Plt: £207.40 to a £1 stake. Pool of £61377.40 - 216.02 winning tickets. T/Qpdt: £65.00 to a £1 stake. Pool of £7346.10 - 83.53 winning tickets. **Jonathan Neesom**

5332 YARMOUTH (L-H)

Tuesday, August 23

OFFICIAL GOING: Good to firm (good in places)

Wind: Light across Weather: Fine

5747 TOTEPLACEPOT MAIDEN FILLIES' STKS (PLUS 10 RACE) — 1m 3y

2:00 (2:01) (Class 5) 2-Y-O — **£3,557** (£1,058; £529; £264) **Stalls** Centre

Form — RPR

1 — **Kind Of Beauty (IRE)** 2-9-0 0 .... JimCrowley 5 — 74+
(Hugo Palmer) *dwlt: hld up: hdwy over 1f out: rdn and r.o to ld nr fin* **9/2**[3]

03 **2** ½ **Tomorrowcomes (IRE)**[14] 5266 2-9-0 0 .... PaulHanagan 6 — 73
(Richard Fahey) *led: rdn and hung rt over 1f out: hdd nr fin* **2/1**[2]

0 **3** 1 **Rickrack (IRE)**[24] 4885 2-9-0 0 .... JamieSpencer 7 — 71
(Luca Cumani) *trckd ldrs: rdn over 1f out: unable qck wl ins fnl f* **7/4**[1]

60 **4** 1¾ **Sandwood Bay**[8] 5469 2-9-0 0 .... DarryllHolland 2 — 66
(Mark H Tompkins) *hld up: pushed along over 3f out: r.o ins fnl f: nt trble ldrs* **50/1**

3656 **5** 2½ **Ocean Temptress**[14] 5266 2-8-11 69 .... JosephineGordon(3) 8 — 60
(John Ryan) *chsd ldrs: wnt 2nd over 5f out tl rdn over 2f out: wknd ins fnl f* **8/1**

5 **6** 2 **Every Nice Girl (USA)**[20] 5022 2-9-0 0 .... HarryBentley 3 — 56
(Marco Botti) *hld up: nt clr run over 2f out: rdn over 1f out: wknd ins fnl f* **14/1**

40 **7** 1 **Speciale Di Giorno (IRE)**[38] 4397 2-9-0 0 .... LukeMorris 1 — 53
(Marco Botti) *prom: stdd and lost pl over 6f out: rdn over 2f out: wknd over 1f out* **25/1**

0 **8** 7 **Navajo Thunder (IRE)**[14] 5272 2-9-0 0 .... AndrewMullen 4 — 36
(Michael Appleby) *chsd ldr over 2f: remained handy: rdn over 3f out: wknd over 1f out* **50/1**

1m 39.79s (-0.81) **Going Correction** -0.175s/f (Firm) — **8** Ran SP% **113.4**

Speed ratings (Par 91): **97,96,95,93,91 89,88,81**

CSF £13.67 TOTE £5.60: £1.90, £1.20, £1.10; EX 14.50 Trifecta £31.70.

Owner Dr Ali Ridha **Bred** Rabbah Bloodstock Limited **Trained** Newmarket, Suffolk

FOCUS

Race distances as advertised. A warm day and the ground had quickened up from the overnight description of Good. They came down the centre of the track in this modest maiden, although the principals ended up nearer the stands' rail. It was won by the only newcomer in the field. The runner-up sets the opening level.

5748 TOTEPOOL LIVE INFO DOWNLOAD THE APP MEDIAN AUCTION MAIDEN STKS — 6f 3y

2:30 (2:30) (Class 6) 3-5-Y-O — **£2,975** (£885; £442; £221) **Stalls** Centre

Form — RPR

056- **1** — **Sakhee's Jem**[278] 7895 3-9-0 63 .... LukeMorris 6 — 70
(Gay Kelleway) *hld up: hdwy to chse ldr over 1f out: rdn to ld wl ins fnl f: styd on* **8/1**[3]

2243 **2** 1 **Hyland Heather (IRE)**[33] 4547 3-9-0 78 .... PaulHanagan 5 — 67
(Richard Fahey) *chsd ldrs: shkn up to ld over 1f out: rdn and hdd wl ins fnl f* **2/7**[1]

5- **3** 7 **Fanci That (IRE)**[310] 7310 3-9-0 0 .... JimCrowley 2 — 44
(Rae Guest) *prom: racd keenly: rdn over 1f out: wknd ins fnl f* **5/1**[2]

05 **4** 1½ **Sharp Boy (IRE)**[8] 5474 3-9-2 0 .... AaronJones(3) 3 — 45
(Stuart Williams) *chsd ldrs tl led over 4f out: rdn: hung lft and hdd over 1f out: wknd fnl f* **40/1**

44 **5** ¾ **Wensara Dream**[15] 5238 3-9-0 0 .... LiamKeniry 4 — 37
(Andrew Balding) *sn led: hdd over 4f out: rdn and wknd over 1f out* **16/1**

1m 13.4s (-1.00) **Going Correction** -0.175s/f (Firm) — **5** Ran SP% **113.9**

Speed ratings (Par 101): **99,97,88,86,85**

CSF £11.47 TOTE £12.00: £3.00, £1.10; EX 13.70 Trifecta £22.40.

Owner M M Foulger **Bred** Giles Wates **Trained** Exning, Suffolk

FOCUS

This seriously lacked depth and the first two came well clear. The winner has been rated to her previous best.

5749 TOTEQUADPOT MAIDEN H'CAP — 1m 3f 104y

3:00 (3:00) (Class 5) (0-70,70) 3-Y-O+ — **£3,557** (£1,058; £529; £264) **Stalls** Low

Form — RPR

505 **1** — **Notice (IRE)**[20] 5025 3-9-2 **67** .... JamieSpencer 1 — 74+
(David Simcock) *s.i.s: hld up: hdwy over 1f out: rdn and r.o to ld wl ins fnl f* **9/2**[2]

0535 **2** ¾ **Princesse Eva (FR)**[22] 4956 3-9-0 **65** .... TomQueally 4 — 70
(James Fanshawe) *hld up in tch: led over 1f out: rdn: edgd lft and hdd wl ins fnl f* **8/1**[3]

405- **3** 1½ **Alsacienne**[305] 7442 3-8-11 **62** .... LukeMorris 2 — 65+
(Sir Mark Prescott Bt) *hld up tch: shkn up and nt clr run over 2f out: rdn ins fnl f: styd on same pce* **4/5**[1]

0465 **4** ½ **Princess Raihana**[27] 4777 3-9-5 **70** .... HarryBentley 5 — 72
(Marco Botti) *chsd ldr: rdn and ev ch over 1f out: no ex wl ins fnl f* **8/1**[3]

-046 **5** 1 **Amazing Charm**[20] 5010 4-9-4 **63** .... EoinWalsh(3) 7 — 63
(James Tate) *hld up: rdn over 2f out: styd on: nt rch ldrs* **16/1**

4063 **6** 2½ **Heavensfield**[50] 3949 3-9-5 **70** .... DarryllHolland 6 — 66
(Mark H Tompkins) *led: rdn and hdd over 1f out: wknd wl ins fnl f* **20/1**

0206 **7** ½ **Ali Bin Nayef**[13] 5303 4-8-9 **51** .... RobertHavlin 3 — 46
(Michael Wigham) *chsd ldrs: pushed along over 3f out: wknd fnl f* **33/1**

2m 26.72s (-1.98) **Going Correction** -0.175s/f (Firm)

WFA 3 from 4yo 9lb — **7** Ran SP% **109.5**

Speed ratings (Par 103): **100,99,98,98,97 95,95**

CSF £35.79 TOTE £5.80: £2.20, £3.40; EX 38.70 Trifecta £60.60.

Owner Anthony Rogers & Mrs Sonia Rogers **Bred** Airlie Stud & Mrs S M Rogers **Trained** Newmarket, Suffolk

FOCUS

This was run at just an ordinary gallop. It's been rated around the fourth.

5750 TOTEEXACTA H'CAP — 1m 1f 21y

3:30 (3:30) (Class 5) (0-75,75) 4-Y-O+ — **£2,911** (£866; £432; £216) **Stalls** Low

Form — RPR

5032 **1** — **Character Onesie (IRE)**[15] 5223 4-9-2 **70** .... AdamMcNamara(5) 8 — 77
(Richard Fahey) *chsd ldrs: wnt 2nd over 6f out: led over 2f out: rdn over 1f out: edgd lft ins fnl f: styd on* **7/2**[2]

1233 **2** hd **The Gay Cavalier**[18] 5122 5-9-12 **75** .... (t) JimCrowley 5 — 81
(John Ryan) *a.p: rdn over 1f out: r.o* **9/4**[1]

1631 **3** 1¾ **Rustique**[19] 5085 4-9-2 **65** .... ThomasBrown 4 — 67
(Ed Walker) *led at stdy pce: hdd 8f out: remained handy: rdn and ev ch over 1f out: styd on same pce ins fnl f* **7/2**[2]

0212 **4** ¾ **Captain Felix**[27] 4767 4-9-9 **72** .... JamieSpencer 2 — 73
(George Scott) *led at stdy pce 8f out: qcknd over 3f out: hdd over 2f out: no ex wl ins fnl f* **9/2**[3]

5363 **5** 1½ **He's My Boy (IRE)**[12] 5337 5-8-11 **67** .... GeorgeWood(7) 3 — 64
(James Fanshawe) *hld up: rdn over 1f out: nt trble ldrs* **7/1**

4003 **6** nse **Molten Lava (IRE)**[26] 4807 4-9-11 **74** .... (b) LukeMorris 6 — 71
(Paul Cole) *hld up: plld hrd: rdn over 2f out: nt trble ldrs* **12/1**

0614 **7** 9 **Gone With The Wind (GER)**[22] 4929 5-8-13 **62** .... (t) TomQueally 1 — 39
(Rebecca Bastiman) *plld hrd and prom: stdd and lost pl over 7f out: hdwy over 3f out: wknd over 1f out* **40/1**

1m 56.44s (0.64) **Going Correction** -0.175s/f (Firm) — **7** Ran SP% **116.0**

Speed ratings (Par 103): **90,89,88,87,86 86,78**

CSF £12.20 CT £28.91 TOTE £5.80: £2.50, £2.00; EX 15.70 Trifecta £43.10.

Owner Aykroyd And Sons Ltd **Bred** Ms A R Nugent **Trained** Musley Bank, N Yorks

FOCUS

This was run at a pretty steady pace, and the time was slow. The runners came over towards the stands' side once into the home straight. The first three have been rated close to their recent form.

5751 TOTETRIFECTA H'CAP — 5f 42y

4:00 (4:02) (Class 5) (0-75,75) 3-Y-O+ — **£2,911** (£866; £432; £216) **Stalls** Centre

Form — RPR

10 **1** — **Lapilli**[113] 1935 3-9-1 **75** .... GeorgiaCox(7) 6 — 89+
(William Haggas) *hld up in tch: racd keenly: shkn up and qcknd to ld 1f out: edgd lft: r.o wl* **15/8**[1]

0046 **2** 3 **Burning Thread (IRE)**[13] 5305 9-9-7 **72** .... (b) JamieSpencer 5 — 75
(David Elsworth) *hld up: rdn over 1f out: wnt 2nd wl ins fnl f: no ch w wnr* **7/1**[3]

022 **3** nk **Indian Tinker**[26] 4809 7-8-12 **68** .... (v) AdamMcNamara(5) 4 — 70
(Robert Cowell) *chsd ldr: rdn over 1f out: styd on same pce fnl f* **11/4**[2]

4431 **4** nse **Noble Act**[16] 5200 3-9-1 **68** .... JimCrowley 1 — 70
(Rae Guest) *chsd ldrs: rdn and ev ch over 1f out: no ex ins fnl f* **11/4**[2]

4610 **5** 3¼ **Fine 'n Dandy (IRE)**[22] 4952 5-9-5 **70** .... (t) PaulHanagan 3 — 60
(J R Jenkins) *led: rdn and hdd 1f out: wknd ins fnl f* **14/1**

1m 0.98s (-1.72) **Going Correction** -0.175s/f (Firm)

WFA 3 from 4yo+ 2lb — **5** Ran SP% **107.3**

Speed ratings (Par 103): **106,101,100,100,95**

CSF £14.02 TOTE £2.40: £1.40, £2.90; EX 11.20 Trifecta £26.40.

Owner Sheikh Ahmed Al Maktoum **Bred** Whitsbury Manor Stud **Trained** Newmarket, Suffolk

FOCUS

They gradually came over to the stands' side in this modest sprint handicap, which proved a one-horse race. The winner has been rated as building on his impressive debut win.

5752 TOTEPOOL SUPPORTING THE HORSE COMES FIRST H'CAP — 7f 3y

4:30 (4:30) (Class 4) (0-80,79) 3-Y-O+ — **£4,690** (£1,395; £697; £348) **Stalls** Centre

Form — RPR

2231 **1** — **Aflame**[20] 5038 3-9-3 **75** .... JimCrowley 2 — 84+
(Sir Michael Stoute) *w ldrs: shkn up to ld over 1f out: rdn out* **13/8**[1]

650 **2** 1¼ **Intrude**[7] 5514 4-9-12 **79** .... HarryBentley 6 — 85
(Stuart Williams) *hld up: hdwy u.p over 1f out: styd on to go 2nd nr fin* **14/1**

1343 **3** nk **Four Poets**[28] 4742 3-9-0 **72** .... JamieSpencer 4 — 75
(David Simcock) *trckd ldrs: nt clr run over 1f out: sn rdn: styd on* **15/8**[2]

4003 **4** nk **Fullon Clarets**[29] 4700 4-9-5 **77** .... AdamMcNamara(5) 3 — 81
(Richard Fahey) *led at stdy pce tl qcknd over 2f out: rdn and hdd over 1f out: no ex wl ins fnl f* **6/1**[3]

2203 **5** 2¼ **Doctor Bong**[19] 5075 4-8-13 **73** .... (b) JoshuaBryan(7) 5 — 71
(Andrew Balding) *w ldr: rdn over 2f out: no ex ins fnl f* **13/2**

1m 25.09s (-1.51) **Going Correction** -0.175s/f (Firm)

WFA 3 from 4yo 5lb — **5** Ran SP% **107.2**

Speed ratings (Par 105): **101,99,99,98,96**

CSF £20.44 TOTE £2.00: £1.20, £5.20; EX 19.50 Trifecta £50.30.

Owner Lady Rothschild **Bred** Kincorth Investments Inc **Trained** Newmarket, Suffolk

FOCUS
Fair handicap form. The second has been rated to his past turf best.

5753 COLLECT TOTEPOOL WINNINGS AT BETFRED SHOPS APPRENTICE TRAINING SERIES H'CAP — 1m 3y

5:05 (5:05) (Class 6) (0-65,65) 4-Y-O+ **£2,264** (£673; £336; £168) **Stalls** Centre

Form	RPR
5640 **1** **Titan Goddess**[35] 4498 4-8-11 **52** .... KevinLundie 7	59
(Mike Murphy) *chsd ldrs: led over 2f out: rdn and edgd rt fr over 1f out: styd on* **9/1**
0400 **2** *nk* **Whozthecat (IRE)**[13] 5296 9-9-3 **63** .... (t) GerO'Neill(5) 3	70
(Declan Carroll) *led over 5f: rdn over 1f out: nt clr run ins fnl f: styd on* **9/1**
001 **3** *3/4* **McDelta**[71] 3214 6-9-6 **61** .... (p) MeganNicholls 4	67
(Ian Williams) *hld up: hdwy over 1f out: nt clr run ins fnl f: r.o to go 3rd nr fin* **9/4**[1]
0002 **4** *1/2* **Zeshov (IRE)**[19] 5090 5-9-5 **65** .... LewisEdmunds(5) 8	69
(Rebecca Bastiman) *prom: rdn over 1f out: styd on same pce wl ins fnl f* **11/4**[2]
6003 **5** *3 1/2* **Mops Angel**[4] 5604 5-8-7 **53** .... BenSanderson(5) 6	49
(Michael Appleby) *hld up: racd keenly: hdwy over 2f out: rdn over 1f out: no ex ins fnl f* **8/1**
3420 **6** *8* **My Mistress (IRE)**[11] 5375 4-8-5 **49** .... CameronNoble(3) 1	26
(Phil McEntee) *s.s: sn pushed along in rr: nvr nrr* **16/1**
0000 **7** *9* **Archipentura**[29] 4718 4-9-0 **55** .... GeorgiaCox 5	12
(J R Jenkins) *chsd ldrs tl rdn and wknd 2f out* **50/1**
-630 **8** *20* **Sublimation (IRE)**[52] 3901 6-9-8 **63** .... AdamMcNamara 2
(Steve Gollings) *w ldr over 2f: remained handy tl rdn 1/2-way: wknd over 2f out: eased* **6/1**[3]

1m 38.34s (-2.26) **Going Correction** -0.175s/f (Firm) **8** Ran SP% **110.7**
Speed ratings (Par 101): **104,103,102,102,98 90,81,61**
CSF £80.09 CT £235.67 TOTE £13.50: £3.00, £2.70, £1.10; EX 89.70 Trifecta £262.10.
Owner Phoebe's Friends **Bred** Mrs A D Bourne **Trained** Westoning, Beds
■ Stewards' Enquiry : Kevin Lundie caution: careless riding

FOCUS
A very modest handicap. The field ended up towards the stands' side. The third has been rated to his recent win.
T/Plt: £38.90 to a £1 stake. Pool of £79043.23 - 1480.87 winning tickets. T/Qpdt: £34.10 to a £1 stake. Pool of £4335.56 - 93.90 winning tickets. **Colin Roberts**

5690 DEAUVILLE (R-H)

Tuesday, August 23

OFFICIAL GOING: Polytrack: standard; turf: good

5754a PRIX DE LA NONETTE BEACHCOMBER HOTELS LE ROYAL PALM ILE MAURICE (GROUP 2) (3YO FILLIES) (TURF) — 1m 2f

1:20 (12:00) 3-Y-O **£54,485** (£21,029; £10,036; £6,691; £3,345)

| RPR
---|---
1 **La Cressonniere (FR)**[65] 3452 3-9-0 0 .... CristianDemuro 3 | 115+
(J-C Rouget, France) *stmbld and propped leaving stalls: qckly rcvrd and hld up in tch in 3rd: clsd 1 1/2f out: shkn up and qcknd to ld appr fnl f: drvn clr: comf* **2/9**[1] |
2 *2* **Jemayel (IRE)**[24] 4864 3-9-0 0 .... GregoryBenoist 5 | 110
(J-C Rouget, France) *t.k.h: sn chsng ldr under a tight hold: rdn to chal 1 1/2f out and sn upsides ldr: hdd 1f out: r.o but no ch w wnr* **7/1**[2] |
3 *5* **Lakalas (FR)**[24] 4904 3-9-0 0 .... ChristopheSoumillon 6 | 100+
(J-C Rouget, France) *w.w in rr: rdn and sme prog over 1f out: styd on to go 3rd but nvr in contention* **10/1**[3] |
4 *1 1/4* **Ouezy (IRE)**[16] 3-9-0 0 .... IoritzMendizabal 1 | 98
(J-C Rouget, France) *rousted along to take up pcemaking duties: kicked for home 2f out: jnd ins fnl 1 1/2f: hdd 1f out: sn dropped away: jst hld on for 4th* **100/1** |
5 *nse* **Nezwaah**[60] 3608 3-9-0 0 .... AndreaAtzeni 4 | 97+
(Roger Varian) *t.k.h: hld up in fnl pair: rdn and no imp over 1 1/2f out: plugged on at one pce: jst missed 4th* **10/1**[3] |

2m 11.77s (1.57) **5** Ran SP% **113.5**
WIN (incl. 1 euro stake): 1.20 (La Cressonniere coupled with Ouezy). PLACES: 1.10, 1.10. SF: 2.90.
Owner Ecurie Antonio Caro & Gerard Augustin-Normand **Bred** Franklin Finance **Trained** Pau, France

FOCUS
The always-handy runner-up helps set the standard, in line with her Goodwood latest. The unbeaten winner has been rated in line with the better view of her bunchy Classic form.

5755a PRIX MTPA - OFFICE DU TOURISME DE L'ILE MAURICE (CLAIMER) (2YO) (POLYTRACK) — 6f 110y

1:50 (12:00) 2-Y-O **£9,926** (£3,970; £2,977; £1,985; £992)

| RPR
---|---
1 **La Fibre (FR)** 2-9-1 0 .... FranckBlondel 5 | 78
(M Pimbonnet, France) **19/2** |
2 *1 1/2* **Tawaret (FR)**[18] 5142 2-8-7 0 .... (p) ClementLecoeuvre(6) 2 | 72
(Mme M-C Naim, France) **15/1** |
3 *hd* **Douceur D'Antan (FR)**[20] 5049 2-9-2 0 .... MaximeGuyon 7 | 74
(K Borgel, France) *fin 4th: plcd 3rd* **42/10**[1] |
4 *shd* **Imperial Tango (FR)**[12] 2-9-1 0 .... ChristopheSoumillon 15 | 73
(G Botti, France) *fin 5th: plcd 4th* **11/2**[3] |
5 *nk* **Martini Gin (IRE)** 2-8-8 0 .... EddyHardouin 12 | 65
(J-P Perruchot, France) *fin 3rd: disqualified and plcd 5th* **63/1** |
6 *hd* **Beslon (FR)**[12] 5348 2-9-1 0 .... (p) CristianDemuro 8 | 72
(C Ferland, France) **13/1** |
7 *3/4* **Ngendha (FR)**[24] 2-8-4 0 .... KyllanBarbaud(7) 13 | 65
(N Caullery, France) **35/1** |
8 *1/2* **Elusiva (FR)**[48] 2-8-8 0 .... UmbertoRispoli 3 | 61
(K Borgel, France) **34/1** |
9 *1/2* **Nuit De Mai (FR)**[23] 4925 2-8-5 0 .... HugoJourniac(3) 6 | 60
(B De Montzey, France) **47/10**[2] |
10 *1 1/4* **Alfa Manifesto (FR)**[6] 5568 2-9-4 0 .... (b) AntoineHamelin 1 | 66
(Matthieu Palussiere, France) **17/1** |
11 *3* **Efichope (FR)**[77] 3006 2-8-8 0 .... SylvainRuis 9 | 48
(S Culin, France) **26/1** |
12 *2* **Morgan Blond (IRE)**[24] 2-8-11 0 .... MickaelForest 11 | 45
(A Giorgi, Italy) **16/1** |
13 *1 3/4* **Daffodil Mulligan**[13] 5297 2-8-13 0 .... (p) TonyPiccone 4 | 42
(J S Moore) *chsd ldng gp on inner: 6th and n.m.r over 3f out: rdn and lost pl 2f out: wl hld whn eased 100yds out* **10/1** |
14 *1 3/4* **Sirma Traou Land (FR)**[28] 4750 2-8-11 0 .... ThierryJarnet 14 | 35
(B De Montzey, France) **79/10** |
15 *2 1/2* **Vixenta (FR)**[21] 5005 2-8-11 0 .... IoritzMendizabal 10 | 28
(Eric Saint-Martin, France) **31/1** |

WIN (incl. 1 euro stake): 10.50. PLACES: 3.30, 3.90, 2.60. DF: 63.60. SF: 155.00.
Owner Fabrice Petit **Bred** C Barel **Trained** France

5350 CATTERICK (L-H)

Wednesday, August 24

OFFICIAL GOING: Good to soft (soft in places; 7.7)
Wind: Virtually nil Weather: Fine & dry

5756 BETFRED TV NOVICE MEDIAN AUCTION STKS — 5f

1:50 (1:51) (Class 5) 2-Y-O **£2,911** (£866; £432; £216) **Stalls** Low

Form	RPR
160 **1** **Kyllang Rock (IRE)**[4] 5656 2-9-9 86 .... DanielTudhope 9	85+
(James Tate) *trckd ldrs: hdwy to ld 1 1/2f out: rdn clr ent fnl f: kpt on* **7/5**[1]
0140 **2** *1 3/4* **Ventura Secret (IRE)**[39] 4394 2-9-9 76 .... DavidAllan 4	78
(Tim Easterby) *trckd ldrs effrt 2f out: rdn over 1f out: chsd wnr ins fnl f: no imp towards fin* **9/1**
1 **3** *3/4* **Fields Of Song (IRE)**[53] 3873 2-9-4 71 .... GrahamLee 5	70
(Kevin Ryan) *trckd ldrs: pushed along over 2f out: rdn on outer and hdwy wl over 1f out: kpt on same pce fnl f* **3/1**[2]
63 **4** *1/2* **Amathyst**[61] 3613 2-8-11 0 .... AndrewMullen 7	62
(Michael Appleby) *trckd ldng pair: pushed along over 2f out: rdn wl over 1f out: drvn and kpt on same pce fnl f* **5/1**[3]
03 **5** *nk* **Hot Hannah**[20] 5067 2-8-11 0 .... ConnorBeasley 2	60
(Michael Dods) *cl up: led over 2f out: rdn and hdd 1 1/2f out: sn drvn and kpt on same pce* **16/1**
6 *3 1/2* **A Bit Of Ginger** 2-8-11 0 .... PJMcDonald 10	48
(Ann Duffield) *towards rr: rdn along over 2f out: n.d* **22/1**
60 **7** *1 1/4* **Volta Do Mar (IRE)**[15] 5272 2-8-11 0 .... PatrickMathers 6	43
(Richard Fahey) *sn rdn along and outpcd in rr: sme late hdwy* **40/1**
0600 **8** *2 3/4* **Newgate Sioux**[13] 5317 2-8-11 34 .... NeilFarley 1	33
(Tony Coyle) *slt ld on inner: rdn along 1/2-way: sn hdd & wknd* **250/1**
3 **9** *4 1/2* **Best Away (FR)**[82] 2852 2-9-2 0 .... JamesSullivan 3	22
(Ruth Carr) *in tch: rdn along 1/2-way: sn wknd* **12/1**

59.56s (-0.24) **Going Correction** 0.0s/f (Good) **9** Ran SP% **114.1**
Speed ratings (Par 94): **97,94,93,92,91 86,84,79,72**
CSF £15.01 TOTE £2.00: £1.10, £3.00, £1.70; EX 15.10 Trifecta £37.20.
Owner Sheikh Juma Dalmook Al Maktoum **Bred** Old Carhue & Graeng Bloodstock **Trained** Newmarket, Suffolk

FOCUS
The ground was good to soft, soft in places. An interesting contest run at a decent pace. After riding in the opener Connor Beasley and Danny Tudhope described the ground as 'just on the easy side of good'. The race has been rated around the runner-up to his best.

5757 BETFRED SUPPORTS JACK BERRY HOUSE MAIDEN FILLIES' STKS — 7f

2:20 (2:22) (Class 5) 3-Y-O+ **£2,911** (£866; £432; £216) **Stalls** Low

Form	RPR
622 **1** **Soundstrings**[11] 5388 3-9-0 75 .... GrahamGibbons 5	69
(William Haggas) *dwlt and sltly hmpd s: in rr: hdwy on outer 1/2-way: chsd ldr over 2f out: rdn to take slt ld wl over 1f out: sn drvn and kpt on towards fin* **4/9**[1]
253 **2** *3/4* **Al Hawraa**[41] 4313 3-9-0 68 .... KevinStott 6	67
(Kevin Ryan) *sn led: jnd and rdn over 2f out: hdd and cl up over 1f out: drvn and ev ch ent fnl f tl no ex towards fin* **5/1**[2]
0305 **3** *3/4* **American Hustle (IRE)**[36] 4490 4-9-5 62 .... (b[1]) BenCurtis 4	67
(Brian Ellison) *trckd ldrs: effrt on outer over 2f out and sn rdn: drvn to chse ldng pair over 1f out: ch ent fnl f: kpt on same pce* **5/1**[2]
62 **4** *1/2* **Alice Thornton**[18] 5178 4-9-5 0 .... GrahamLee 1	66
(Martin Todhunter) *cl up on inner: pushed along 3f out: rdn over 2f out: drvn wl over 1f out: kpt on same pce* **33/1**[3]
56 **5** *6* **Any Joy (IRE)**[110] 1998 3-9-0 0 .... JoeyHaynes 2	47
(Ben Haslam) *towards rr: pushed along 3f out: rdn over 2f out: sn one pce* **33/1**[3]
00 **6** *19* **Culturehull**[43] 4235 3-9-0 0 .... DavidAllan 7
(Les Eyre) *chsd ldng pair: rdn along wl 3f out: drvn: drvn over 2f out: sn outpcd and bhd* **150/1**

1m 27.41s (0.41) **Going Correction** +0.075s/f (Good)
WFA 3 from 4yo 5lb **6** Ran SP% **109.1**
Speed ratings (Par 100): **100,99,98,97,90 69**
CSF £2.82 TOTE £1.20: £1.10, £2.50; EX 3.30 Trifecta £5.00.
Owner Lael Stable **Bred** S Boucheron **Trained** Newmarket, Suffolk

FOCUS
Add 9yds to advertised race distance. An uncompetitive fillies' maiden run at a sound pace. It's been rated around the second and third.

5758 BETFRED DOUBLE DELIGHT H'CAP — 1m 7f 177y

2:50 (2:51) (Class 5) (0-70,69) 3-Y-O+ **£3,234** (£962; £481; £240) **Stalls** Low

Form	RPR
1550 **1** **An Fear Ciuin (IRE)**[23] 4935 5-9-7 **69** .... (p) CallumRodriguez(7) 3	78+
(Richard Ford) *mde all: clr 1/2-way: rdn along 2f out: drvn ent fnl f: kpt on strly* **6/1**
0431 **2** *1* **Arthurs Secret**[53] 3903 6-10-0 **69** .... (v) DougieCostello 7	75
(John Quinn) *trckd wnr thrght: hdwy to take clsr order 3f out: rdn 2f out: drvn and kpt on same pce fnl f* **5/1**[2]
3-02 **3** *1/2* **Silver Shuffle (IRE)**[59] 2558 9-9-6 **61** .... (t) JamesSullivan 8	66+
(Dianne Sayer) *hld up in rr: hdwy wl over 2f out: rdn wl over 1f out: styd on wl fnl f: nrst fin* **12/1**
143 **4** *nk* **Midnight Warrior**[18] 5183 6-8-11 **57** .... RowanScott(5) 4	62
(Ron Barr) *trckd ldng pair: pushed along wl over 2f out: rdn wl over 1f out: drvn and kpt on same pce fnl f* **9/1**
P062 **5** *1/2* **Kisumu**[8] 5522 4-9-5 **60** .... PJMcDonald 5	64
(Micky Hammond) *hld up: hdwy 4f out: rdn to chse ldrs over 2f out: drvn wl over 1f out: kpt on* **11/2**[3]
0300 **6** *14* **Cavalieri (IRE)**[9] 5481 6-9-2 **57** .... (p) AndrewMullen 6	45
(Philip Kirby) *chsd ldrs: rdn along over 5f out: sn outpcd and bhd* **33/1**

-562 **7** 7 **Rockabilly Riot (IRE)**[35] 4515 6-8-13 **59** .... AdamMcNamara(5) 9 38
(Martin Todhunter) *dwlt: a in rr* **10/1**
0-66 **8** 2 1/4 **Di's Gift**[73] 3191 7-9-9 **69** .... CharlieBennett(5) 2 46
(Shaun Harris) *hld up: a towards rr* **11/2**[3]
6111 **9** 8 **Stoneham**[19] 5118 5-9-13 **68** .... DanielTudhope 1 35
(Iain Jardine) *trckd ldrs: pushed along 4f out: rdn 3f out: sn wknd* **3/1**[1]
3m 33.33s (1.33) **Going Correction** +0.075s/f (Good) **9** Ran SP% **116.4**
Speed ratings (Par 103): **99,98,98,98,97 90,87,86,82**
CSF £36.37 CT £351.21 TOTE £6.80: £2.10, £2.30, £3.00; EX 43.80 Trifecta £426.90.
Owner D M Proos **Bred** Miss S A McManus **Trained** Garstang, Lancs
FOCUS
Add 18yds to advertised race distance. The pace was sound for this open handicap. It paid to race handy. The form has been rated at face value around the second down to the fifth.

5759 BETFRED HAT-TRICK HEAVEN H'CAP 7f
3:20 (3:24) (Class 4) (0-85,84) 3-Y-O **£5,822** (£1,732; £865; £432) **Stalls** Low

Form RPR
6231 **1** **Baron Bolt**[49] 4003 3-9-7 **84** .... (p) PJMcDonald 7 96
(Paul Cole) *hld up in rr: gd hdwy on inner over 2f out: rdn to ld over 1f out and sn hung rt: drvn clr ins fnl f* **2/1**[1]
6135 **2** 3 3/4 **Like No Other**[43] 4231 3-8-9 **72** ow1 .... GrahamGibbons 9 74
(Les Eyre) *hld up: hdwy on outer over 2f out: rdn to chse wnr over 1f out: drvn and kpt on same pce fnl f* **17/2**[3]
3501 **3** 1 **Hijran (IRE)**[15] 5273 3-8-3 **66** .... (p) AndrewMullen 5 65
(Michael Appleby) *cl up: disp ld over 2f and sn rdn: drvn over 1f out: kpt on same pce* **11/1**
-405 **4** nk **Never In Doubt**[21] 5034 3-8-7 **70** .... GeorgeChaloner 6 68
(Richard Whitaker) *chsd ldrs: rdn along over 2f out: drvn wl over 1f out: kpt on same pce* **18/1**
0316 **5** 2 **Baby Ballerina**[7] 5537 3-8-6 **69** .... (b) BenCurtis 3 62
(Brian Ellison) *chsd ldrs: rdn along 2f out: sn drvn and wknd over 1f out* **17/2**[3]
0165 **6** 1 1/4 **Brilliant Vanguard (IRE)**[53] 3908 3-9-5 **82** .... GrahamLee 2 71
(Kevin Ryan) *slt ld: rdn over 2f out: drvn and hdd over 1f out: sn wknd* **11/2**[2]
0401 **7** 6 **Mywayistheonlyway (IRE)**[13] 5336 3-9-5 **82** .... (vt[1]) KevinStott 1 55
(Grant Tuer) *chsd ldrs on inner: rdn along over 2f out: sn wknd* **9/1**
1m 27.01s (0.01) **Going Correction** +0.075s/f (Good) **7** Ran SP% **93.4**
Speed ratings (Par 102): **102,97,96,96,93 92,85**
CSF £12.30 CT £69.40 TOTE £2.30: £1.80, £3.10; EX 15.00 Trifecta £94.70.
Owner Asprey Wright Meyrick PJL Racing Wilcock **Bred** J A And M A Knox **Trained** Whatcombe, Oxon
■ Piccolo Grande was withdrawn. Price at time of withdrawal 7/2. Rule 4 applies to all bets - deduct 20p in the pound.
FOCUS
Add 9yds to advertised race distance. A fair handicap run at an honest pace. The runner-up has been rated in line with his turf form.

5760 BETFRED RACING'S BIGGEST SUPPORTER H'CAP 5f 212y
3:50 (3:50) (Class 6) (0-60,60) 3-Y-O+ **£2,264** (£673; £336; £168) **Stalls** Low

Form RPR
1040 **1** **Bold Spirit**[12] 5354 5-9-6 **59** .... (vt) DanielTudhope 6 67
(Declan Carroll) *qckly away and sn clr: rdn over 1f out: drvn and kpt on wl fnl f* **6/1**[3]
6000 **2** 1 3/4 **Windforpower (IRE)**[12] 5354 6-9-5 **58** .... (p) DaleSwift 12 61
(Tracy Waggott) *trckd ldrs: hdwy 2f out: rdn wl over 1f out: drvn to chse wnr ins fnl f: kpt on* **16/1**
302 **3** 1/2 **Letbygonesbeicons**[12] 5368 3-8-13 **60** .... RowanScott(5) 9 62
(Ann Duffield) *in tch: hdwy over 2f out: rdn to chse ldrs wl over 1f out: kpt on fnl f* **5/1**[2]
0300 **4** 1 **Indego Blues**[16] 5222 7-8-6 **52** .... (p) DanielleMooney(7) 5 51
(David Nicholls) *chsd ldrs: rdn along wl over 1f out: drvn and kpt on same pce fnl f* **8/1**
0006 **5** nk **Toledo**[22] 4970 3-9-3 **59** .... SamJames 8 57
(Marjorie Fife) *chsd wnr: rdn along 2f out: drvn over 1f out: one pce* **33/1**
0063 **6** 1/2 **Kyllach Me (IRE)**[35] 4512 4-9-5 **58** .... (p) ConnorBeasley 2 54
(Bryan Smart) *chsd ldrs: rdn along wl over 1f out: sn drvn and no imp* **4/1**[1]
-506 **7** 1/2 **Grandad Chunk (IRE)**[35] 4512 5-8-13 **52** .... PatrickMathers 7 47
(Colin Teague) *towards rr: hdwy 2f out: sn rdn: kpt on fnl f: nrst fin* **8/1**
5600 **8** 5 **National Service (USA)**[50] 3985 5-9-4 **57** .... (tp) PJMcDonald 1 37
(Rebecca Menzies) *s.i.s: a in rr* **11/1**
1006 **9** hd **Goadby**[28] 4763 5-9-5 **58** .... GrahamGibbons 3 37
(John Holt) *chsd ldng pair: rdn along over 2f out: sn drvn and wknd* **6/1**[3]
4400 **10** 1 **Spice Mill (IRE)**[22] 4985 3-9-4 **60** .... (tp) AndrewMullen 11 36
(Michael Appleby) *a in rr* **9/1**
1m 15.05s (1.45) **Going Correction** +0.075s/f (Good)
WFA 3 from 4yo+ 3lb **10** Ran SP% **114.6**
Speed ratings (Par 101): **93,90,90,88,88 87,86,80,80,78**
CSF £94.92 CT £526.28 TOTE £7.40: £2.90, £5.70, £1.70; EX 109.70 Trifecta £989.60.
Owner Mrs Sarah Bryan **Bred** The Queen **Trained** Malton, N Yorks
FOCUS
Add 9yds to advertised race distance. The pace was strong for this modest handicap. Straightforward form rated around those in behind the winner.

5761 BETFRED GOALS GALORE EXTRA H'CAP (A QUALIFIER FOR THE 2016 CATTERICK TWELVE FURLONG SERIES FINAL) 1m 3f 214y
4:20 (4:20) (Class 4) (0-85,85) 3-Y-O **£6,469** (£1,925; £962; £481) **Stalls** Centre

Form RPR
404 **1** **Nietzsche**[16] 5226 3-8-7 **76** .... CallumShepherd(5) 1 86
(Brian Ellison) *hld up in tch: hdwy to trck ldrs 1/2-way: effrt on inner and cl up 2f out: rdn to ld over 1f out: drvn out* **5/2**[2]
3142 **2** 3/4 **Wotabreeze (IRE)**[25] 4892 3-8-9 **78** .... AdamMcNamara(5) 6 86
(John Quinn) *hld up in tch: hdwy on outer 2f out: rdn over 1f out: chsd wnr ent fnl f: sn drvn and kpt on* **6/1**
4124 **3** 4 1/2 **Against The Odds**[18] 5147 3-9-7 **85** .... PJMcDonald 5 86
(Paul Cole) *in rr: pushed along 1/2-way: rdn wl over 2f out: hdwy wl over 1f out: drvn and kpt on fnl f* **2/1**[1]
1640 **4** 1 1/2 **Wholesome (USA)**[28] 4757 3-9-4 **82** .... DougieCostello 3 80
(K R Burke) *trckd ldr: hdwy over 2f out: sn rdn: drvn wl over 1f out: wknd* **25/1**
-316 **5** nk **Young Tom**[48] 4033 3-8-2 **66** oh2 .... AndrewMullen 7 64
(Michael Appleby) *led: pushed along over 3f out: rdn along over 2f out: drvn and hdd over 1f out: sn wknd* **11/1**

0043 **6** 5 **Second Serve (IRE)**[20] 5053 3-9-2 **80** .... FrannyNorton 2 70
(Mark Johnston) *dwlt and hld up towards rr: effrt and sme hdwy over 3f out: rdn along 2f out: sn btn* **4/1**[3]
2m 40.72s (1.82) **Going Correction** +0.075s/f (Good) **6** Ran SP% **108.4**
Speed ratings (Par 102): **96,95,92,91,91 87**
CSF £16.15 TOTE £2.90: £2.30, £1.90; EX 18.10 Trifecta £54.00.
Owner D Gilbert, M Lawrence, A Bruce, G Wills **Bred** West Stow Stud Ltd **Trained** Norton, N Yorks
FOCUS
Add 9yds to advertised race distance. A fair handicap run at a decent pace. A pb from the winner, with the runner-up rated to the better view of his latest effort.

5762 BETFRED MOBILE H'CAP 5f
4:55 (4:56) (Class 5) (0-75,75) 3-Y-O+ **£2,911** (£866; £432; £216) **Stalls** Low

Form RPR
3413 **1** **Seamster**[9] 5479 9-9-3 **75** .... (t) CameronNoble(7) 9 85
(David Loughnane) *hld up: hdwy 2f out: rdn to ld appr fnl f: kpt on strly* **5/2**[1]
6624 **2** 1 1/4 **Innocently (IRE)**[12] 5354 5-9-3 **68** .... (b) DanielTudhope 6 73
(David O'Meara) *trckd ldrs: hdwy wl over 1f out: rdn ent fnl f: kpt on* **9/2**[2]
0-63 **3** 1/2 **Cruise Tothelimit (IRE)**[7] 5535 8-8-9 **65** .... AdamMcNamara(5) 2 68
(Patrick Morris) *trckd ldrs: hdwy 2f out: rdn to ld briefly 1 1/2f out: sn hdd and drvn: kpt on same pce* **6/1**[3]
1445 **4** 3/4 **Perfect Words (IRE)**[12] 5354 6-8-10 **64** .... (p) JacobButterfield(3) 3 65
(Marjorie Fife) *sn outpcd and rdn along in rr: hdwy wl over 1f out: kpt on fnl f: nrst fin* **12/1**
1104 **5** nk **Culloden**[22] 4980 4-8-6 **62** .... CharlieBennett(5) 8 61
(Shaun Harris) *cl up on outer: rdn along 2f out: drvn over 1f out: kpt on same pce* **18/1**
4225 **6** 1 **Henley**[31] 4691 4-9-3 **68** .... DaleSwift 1 64
(Tracy Waggott) *chsd ldrs: cl up 1/2-way: rdn along wl over 1f out: grad wknd* **9/2**[2]
4004 **7** 4 1/2 **Captain Dunne (IRE)**[15] 5274 11-9-3 **71** .... RachelRichardson(3) 4 51
(Tim Easterby) *led: rdn along 2f sn hdd & wknd* **7/1**
6214 **8** 1 1/4 **Quickaswecan**[47] 4084 5-9-6 **71** .... (p) FrannyNorton 5 46
(Milton Bradley) *dwlt: sn cl up: rdn along 2f out: sn drvn and wknd* **12/1**
59.33s (-0.47) **Going Correction** 0.0s/f (Good)
WFA 3 from 4yo+ 2lb **8** Ran SP% **112.4**
Speed ratings (Par 103): **99,97,96,95,94 92,85,83**
CSF £13.17 CT £59.02 TOTE £3.30: £1.40, £1.70, £2.20; EX 14.80 Trifecta £83.70.
Owner Miss Sarah Hoyland **Bred** D G Hardisty Bloodstock **Trained** Market Drayton, Shropshire
FOCUS
A strongly run handicap. A pb from the winner, with the fourth close to his C&D latest.
T/Plt: £29.80 to a £1 stake. Pool of £53573.23 - 1310.30 winning tickets. T/Qpdt: £34.30 to a £1 stake. Pool of £3631.99 - 78.20 winning tickets. **Joe Rowntree**

5719 KEMPTON (A.W) (R-H)
Wednesday, August 24
OFFICIAL GOING: Polytrack: standard to slow
Wind: Virtually nil Weather: Warm, thundery after Race 4

5763 £10 FREE BET AT 32REDSPORT.COM FILLIES' H'CAP 1m 4f (P)
5:40 (5:41) (Class 5) (0-70,73) 3-Y-O+ **£2,911** (£866; £432; £216) **Stalls** Centre

Form RPR
0511 **1** **Pacharana**[20] 5086 3-9-4 **70** .... JamieSpencer 7 78+
(Luca Cumani) *s.s: sn cl up bhd ldr on outer: shkn up 2f out: rdn and led over 1f out: sn hung to far side rail under rt hand drive: hrd rdn nr fin: jst hld on* **1/1**[1]
331 **2** shd **Unsuspected Girl (IRE)**[4] 5630 3-7-8 **53** .... SophieKilloran(7) 4 61+
(David Simcock) *s.s and hld up wl in rr: cl up in rr by 1/2-way: shkn up in rr jst over 2f out: rdn and drifted to nrside rail wl over 1f out: styd on wl ins fnl f: jst failed* **2/1**[2]
-034 **3** 3 **Gracesome (IRE)**[14] 5303 5-8-9 **51** oh1 .... TomMarquand 1 54
(Michael Blanshard) *hld up in cl up 5th: rdn over 1f out: kpt on ins fnl f but no ch w ldng pair* **16/1**
600 **4** 3 **Astrosecret**[50] 3990 3-9-2 **68** .... DarryllHolland 3 66
(Mark H Tompkins) *racd in 4th: nudged along 3f out: rdn over 2f out: kpt on one pce* **25/1**
4-22 **5** 3/4 **O'Connor's Girl**[226] 139 3-9-1 **67** .... LukeMorris 2 64
(Sir Mark Prescott Bt) *sn led: shkn up 2f out: sn rdn: hdd over 1f out: wknd ins fnl f* **5/1**[3]
333 **6** 3 **Ms Gillard**[17] 5192 3-8-12 **64** .... MartinHarley 6 56
(David Simcock) *settled in 3rd: rdn wl over 2f out: lft bhd wl over 1f out: sn wknd* **20/1**
2m 36.49s (1.99) **Going Correction** +0.10s/f (Slow)
WFA 3 from 5yo 10lb **6** Ran SP% **114.5**
Speed ratings (Par 100): **97,96,94,92,92 90**
CSF £3.34 TOTE £1.70: £1.10, £2.00; EX 3.30 Trifecta £16.90.
Owner S Stuckey **Bred** Stuart Stuckey **Trained** Newmarket, Suffolk
FOCUS
A very warm, humid summer's evening and the Polytrack surface was still officially standard to slow. A modest middle-distance handicap for fillies only where they seemed to go a steady pace. It's been rated around the third to his C&D latest.

5764 BRITISH STALLION STUDS EBF MAIDEN STKS 1m (P)
6:10 (6:12) (Class 5) 2-Y-O **£3,234** (£962; £481; £240) **Stalls** Low

Form RPR
5 **1** **Mount Moriah**[20] 5073 2-9-5 0 .... FMBerry 3 73
(Ralph Beckett) *pushed up on inner to sn ld: mde all: shkn up wl over 2f out: rdn jst under 2f out: kpt on wl ins fnl f: comf* **9/2**[3]
5 **2** 3 **Emenem**[28] 4775 2-9-5 0 .... NickyMackay 5 66
(Simon Dow) *settled in 4th between horses: rdn over 2f out: tk 2nd jst over 1f out: kpt on to hold 2nd nr fin* **16/1**
3 hd **Kissoffire (IRE)** 2-9-5 0 .... AndreaAtzeni 10 65+
(Marco Botti) *missed break and in rr: stl plenty to do over 3f out: shkn up 3f out: gd prog fr over 1f out to press for 2nd nr fin: bttr for run* **10/1**
4 1 1/2 **Balashakh (USA)** 2-9-5 0 .... JamieSpencer 8 62+
(David Simcock) *settled in mid-div on outer: shkn up jst over 2f out: sn rdn: kpt on wl ins fnl f* **6/4**[1]
00 **5** 1 **Henry Did It (IRE)**[22] 4988 2-9-5 0 .... JimmyFortune 4 59
(Tony Carroll) *racd in 3rd on inner: rdn over 2f out: kpt on wl tl wknd and lost two pls nr fin* **100/1**
6 nk **Keepup Kevin** 2-9-2 0 .... RobHornby(3) 9 59
(Pam Sly) *hld up in rr: rdn along on inner 2f out: sn no imp* **66/1**

06 **7** *nk* **Auric Goldfinger (IRE)**[8] 5505 2-9-5 0 SeanLevey 7 58
(Richard Hannon) *t.k.h on inner in mid-div: rdn 2f out: nt qckn over 1f out: pushed out ins fnl f* **40/1**

3 **8** *2 1/2* **Endless Gold**[19] 5121 2-9-5 0 WilliamBuick 11 52
(Charlie Appleby) *racd in 2nd: pushed along to hold pl over 3f out: rdn 3f out: stl there 2f out: no ex fr over 1f out: eased* **2/1**[2]

60 **9** *4 1/2* **Ablaze**[37] 4457 2-9-0 0 LiamKeniry 6 36
(Laura Mongan) *settled in 6th: shkn up on bnd ent st: no imp fr 2f out* **100/1**

10 *31* **Casina Di Notte (IRE)** 2-9-5 0 LukeMorris 2
(Marco Botti) *missed break and green: sn given reminders: racd in rr in centre: rdn over 3f out: no imp and eased fr over 1f out* **25/1**

1m 42.37s (2.57) **Going Correction** +0.10s/f (Slow) **10** Ran SP% **116.2**
Speed ratings (Par 94): **91,88,87,86,85 85,84,82,77,46**
CSF £66.87 TOTE £6.10: £1.70, £4.70, £3.10; EX 92.40 Trifecta £622.10.
Owner Norman Brunskill **Bred** Lady Bland And Newsells Park Stud Ltd **Trained** Kimpton, Hants

FOCUS
Just a modest maiden.

5765 32RED.COM H'CAP (LONDON MILE SERIES QUALIFIER) 1m (P)
6:40 (6:41) (Class 4) (0-80,80) 3-Y-O **£4,690** (£1,395; £697; £348) **Stalls** Low

Form RPR

1324 **1** **Mukaabra**[34] 4556 3-9-7 80 [1] MartinHarley 9 89
(James Tate) *hld up in rr-div: tk clsr order over 3f out: rdn in centre and led over 1f out: kpt on wl ins fnl f gng hd to hd w runner-up: on top fnl strides* **10/1**

4161 **2** *hd* **Reaver (IRE)**[16] 5241 3-9-1 74 CharlesBishop 11 82
(Eve Johnson Houghton) *s.s: hld up in rr: prog in centre over 2f out: rdn and upsides ent fnl f: kpt on wl gng hd to hd w wnr ins fnl f: hld fnl strides* **9/1**[3]

226 **3** *3/4* **North Creek**[29] 4742 3-9-6 79 JamesDoyle 6 85
(Chris Wall) *t.k.h in mid-div: rdn 2f out: kpt on ins fnl f: nt rchd ldrs* **7/2**[1]

0063 **4** *1* **Destroyer**[11] 5412 3-9-7 80 (p) SamHitchcott 8 83
(William Muir) *racd in 2nd tl led after 5f: rdn wl over 2f out: hdd over 1f out: kpt on again ins fnl f* **20/1**

-553 **5** *1 1/4* **Poet's Song (IRE)**[14] 5301 3-8-13 72 WilliamBuick 3 72
(Marcus Tregoning) *settled in mid-div on inner: pushed along over 2f out: kpt on fr over 1f out* **6/1**[2]

0422 **6** *3/4* **Ocean Eleven**[12] 5362 3-9-2 75 AdamKirby 1 74
(John Ryan) *sn led: hdd after 5f: bhd ldrs after: rdn 2f out: no ex fr over 1f out* **12/1**

0-16 **7** *3/4* **House Of Commons (IRE)**[65] 3465 3-9-6 79 [1] JamieSpencer 13 76
(Paul Cole) *taken bk and hld up in rr: swtchd to rail over 2f out: rdn and no imp fr over 1f out: nvr involved* **16/1**

31-0 **8** *2 1/2* **Graceful James (IRE)**[83] 2818 3-9-7 80 KieranO'Neill 4 71
(Jimmy Fox) *hld up in rr: pushed along over 2f out: nt qckn and hld fr over 1f out* **20/1**

0-23 **9** *3/4* **Blaze Of Hearts (IRE)**[23] 4955 3-9-5 78 RobertWinston 12 70
(Dean Ivory) *racd in 4th on outer: rdn 2f out: no imp over 1f out and wknd ins fnl f* **12/1**

01 **10** *hd* **Enduring Power (IRE)**[23] 4939 3-9-3 76 WilliamCarson 5 65
(Brendan Powell) *settled bhd ldrs on rail: rdn over 2f out: sn no ex and wknd* **16/1**

11 *1/2* **Pinwood (IRE)**[59] 3693 3-9-4 77 (t) HarryPoulton 10 64
(Adam West) *cl up: rdn over 2f out: no ex ent fnl f and wknd* **66/1**

31- **12** *1* **Notary**[391] 4790 3-9-6 79 AndreaAtzeni 7 64
(Roger Varian) *tk fierce hold bhd ldrs: lost pl over 2f out: no ex over 1f out and wknd: lame* **7/2**[1]

1m 39.0s (-0.80) **Going Correction** +0.10s/f (Slow) **12** Ran SP% **116.0**
Speed ratings (Par 102): **108,107,107,106,104 104,103,100,100,99 99,98**
CSF £92.63 CT £387.11 TOTE £9.40: £2.70, £2.70, £1.30; EX 61.20 Trifecta £223.10.
Owner Sheikh Juma Dalmook Al Maktoum **Bred** Biddestone Stud Ltd **Trained** Newmarket, Suffolk

FOCUS
An above-average, competitive handicap for 3yos, which played host to a good finish between the front two. The third's penultimate C&D form has worked out quite well and backs this pb.

5766 32RED CASINO MAIDEN FILLIES' STKS 7f (P)
7:10 (7:13) (Class 5) 3-Y-O+ **£2,911** (£866; £432; £216) **Stalls** Low

Form RPR

3-4 **1** **Tegara**[51] 3951 3-9-0 0 TomQueally 9 76+
(James Fanshawe) *hld up under restraint bhd ldrs: gng wl jst over 2f out: shkn up in centre 2f out: pushed into ld under 1f out: hands and heels wl ins fnl f: comf* **8/13**[1]

36-2 **2** *1 3/4* **Cinders (IRE)**[110] 2004 3-9-0 74 JimmyFortune 7 68
(Hughie Morrison) *t.k.h in ld: shkn up over 1f out: sn rdn and hdd under 1f out: kpt on one pce* **7/2**[2]

5 **3** *1 1/2* **Ducissa**[14] 5300 3-9-0 0 LukeMorris 6 63
(Daniel Kubler) *settled bhd ldr in 3rd on rail: rdn along over 2f out: kpt on one pce ins fnl f* **6/1**[3]

56 **4** *shd* **Nellie Deen (IRE)**[21] 5023 3-9-0 0 JimCrowley 4 63
(David Elsworth) *t.k.h on rail in 4th: shkn up and swtchd to centre over 1f out: sn rdn: kpt on wl to press for 3rd nr fin* **7/1**

5 *8* **Harbour Star** 3-9-0 0 OisinMurphy 5 41
(Laura Mongan) *settled in 2nd bhd ldr: stl in 2nd whn rdn over 2f out: wknd fr over 1f out* **25/1**

00-0 **6** *1 1/2* **Purple Belle**[42] 4264 3-8-7 32 MitchGodwin(7) 3 37?
(Jimmy Fox) *hld up in rr: rdn over 2f out: sn no imp* **100/1**

06 **7** *2 1/4* **Back To Love (CAN)**[16] 5238 3-9-0 0 TimmyMurphy 8 31
(Mark Gillard) *half-rrd s and wnt lft: t.k.h in rr: shkn up over 2f out: wknd fr over 1f out* **100/1**

00 **8** *2* **Gorgeous (FR)**[18] 5168 3-8-11 0 GeorgeDowning(3) 2 26
(Tony Carroll) *a in rr: rdn over 2f out: nvr gng pce* **100/1**

9 *nk* **Miss Geronimo** 4-9-5 0 SamHitchcott 1 27
(Ken Cunningham-Brown) *green in rr: racd wd bnd: prog to chse ldrs on outer over 3f out: rdn over 2f out: sn wknd* **66/1**

1m 27.24s (1.24) **Going Correction** +0.10s/f (Slow)
WFA 3 from 4yo 5lb **9** Ran SP% **119.2**
Speed ratings (Par 100): **96,94,92,92,83 81,78,76,76**
CSF £3.22 TOTE £1.60: £1.10, £1.40, £1.80; EX 3.70 Trifecta £8.30.
Owner Mohamed Obaida **Bred** Rabbah Bloodstock Limited **Trained** Newmarket, Suffolk

FOCUS
Not many could be seriously considered in this modest fillies' maiden and the first four duly came clear. Muddling form rated around the first four.

5767 32RED H'CAP 2m (P)
7:40 (7:40) (Class 4) (0-85,82) 4-Y-O+ **£4,690** (£1,395; £697; £348) **Stalls** Low

Form RPR

-441 **1** **Trevisani (IRE)**[20] 5061 4-9-7 82 (v) GeorgeBaker 4 91+
(David Lanigan) *sn led and mde rest: increased pce over 4f out: shkn up and briefly wandered over 1f out: sn stened up under drive and pushed out ins fnl f* **11/10**[1]

1022 **2** *1 1/2* **Saborido (USA)**[7] 5553 10-9-2 77 (b) JimCrowley 1 84
(Amanda Perrett) *racd in 2nd: rdn over 2f out: kpt on one pce but nvr getting to wnr* **13/2**

1316 **3** *1 3/4* **Royal Reef (IRE)**[27] 4795 4-8-13 74 SilvestreDeSousa 2 79
(William Knight) *hld up in 3rd: rdn on inner over 2f out: no imp on ldr over 1f out* **3/1**[2]

4/51 **4** *2* **Charlie Wells (IRE)**[15] 5262 5-9-2 77 JohnFahy 5 80
(Eve Johnson Houghton) *hld up in rr: rdn over 2f out: hld fr over 1f and hung lft after: spread an off-fore shoe* **4/1**[3]

3m 30.2s (0.10) **Going Correction** +0.10s/f (Slow) **4** Ran SP% **106.0**
Speed ratings (Par 105): **103,102,101,100**
CSF £7.82 TOTE £1.80; EX 5.40 Trifecta £9.90.
Owner Cheveley Park Stud **Bred** Bjorn Nielsen **Trained** Newmarket, Suffolk

FOCUS
A depleted field, but it still looked like a fair staying handicap. The runner-up has been rated to his C&D latest.

5768 32RED ON THE APP STORE H'CAP (LONDON MIDDLE DISTANCE SERIES QUALIFIER) 1m 3f (P)
8:10 (8:11) (Class 4) (0-85,85) 3-Y-O **£4,690** (£1,395; £697; £348) **Stalls** Low

Form RPR

5534 **1** **Vincent's Forever**[11] 5405 3-9-2 80 RobertHavlin 3 87
(John Gosden) *settled bhd ldr: pressed ldr over 3f out: rdn and led wl over 1f out: kpt on wl ins fnl f* **8/1**

-432 **2** *3/4* **Four On Eight**[20] 5074 3-9-1 79 AndreaAtzeni 6 85
(Luca Cumani) *hld up in 3rd: rdn over 2f out: tk 2nd under 1f out: kpt on ins fnl f but a hld* **10/3**[2]

5-12 **3** *1 1/2* **Dune Dancer (IRE)**[68] 3365 3-9-3 81 GeorgeBaker 4 84
(David Lanigan) *settled in rr: swtchd to outer and rdn 2f out: nt qckn: kpt on one pce to take 3rd fnl strides* **5/6**[1]

212 **4** *hd* **Rasmiya (IRE)**[32] 4655 3-9-2 80 PatCosgrave 2 82
(William Haggas) *led: rdn over 2f out: hdd wl over 1f out: lost 2nd under 1f out: one pce after and lost 3rd fnl strides* **5/1**[3]

2m 20.56s (-1.34) **Going Correction** +0.10s/f (Slow) **4** Ran SP% **105.4**
Speed ratings (Par 102): **108,107,106,106**
CSF £30.09 TOTE £9.80; EX 25.50 Trifecta £48.20.
Owner R J H Geffen & P Bennett-Jones **Bred** Newsells Park Stud **Trained** Newmarket, Suffolk

FOCUS
A thundery shower preceded this small-field handicap. The second, third and fourth have been rated close to their marks.

5769 PAY AND WATCH RACING UK VIA MOBILE H'CAP 6f (P)
8:40 (8:44) (Class 6) (0-65,65) 3-Y-O **£2,264** (£673; £336; £168) **Stalls** Low

Form RPR

2-44 **1** **Don't Blame Me**[57] 3743 3-9-7 65 AdamKirby 7 73
(Clive Cox) *sn led and mde rest: rdn over 2f out: hrd rdn in centre over 1f out: kpt on wl to maintain advantage wl ins fnl f* **4/1**[2]

4206 **2** *3/4* **Dream Dana (IRE)**[20] 5088 3-9-6 64 TimmyMurphy 4 70
(Jamie Osborne) *racd in 6th: nt clr run and swtchd lft over 2f out: sn rdn: kpt on wl ins fnl f to take 2nd cl home: nvr nrr* **20/1**

653 **3** *3/4* **Cadland Lad (IRE)**[4] 5636 3-8-1 48 (t) JosephineGordon(3) 1 52
(John Ryan) *racd in 3rd: rdn bhd ldr over 2f out: tk 2nd 1f out: lost 2nd cl home: jst hld 3rd* **7/2**[1]

0060 **4** *nse* **Luang Prabang (IRE)**[20] 5088 3-9-6 64 TedDurcan 9 68
(Chris Wall) *hld up in rr under restraint: rdn and angled wd over 2f out: stl in last jst over 1f out: kpt on wl ins fnl f* **12/1**

2405 **5** *shd* **Lucky Louie**[20] 5088 3-9-6 64 (v[1]) OisinMurphy 10 67
(Roger Teal) *s.s and wnt lft s: in rr: c wd bnd: rdn over 2f out: nt much prog tl kpt on wl ins fnl f* **8/1**

2006 **6** *1 1/4* **Sandacres**[5] 5605 3-9-7 65 GeorgeBaker 2 65
(Laura Mongan) *racd in 4th on outer: shkn up over 2f out: rdn 2f out: styd on one pce ins fnl f: eased fnl strides* **5/1**[3]

0500 **7** *nk* **Born To Finish (IRE)**[20] 5059 3-9-4 62 (bt) MartinLane 11 61
(Jeremy Gask) *taken lft s and t.k.h in rr: rdn on inner 2f out: 4th ent fnl f: wknd nr fin and lost numerous pls* **25/1**

660 **8** *1 3/4* **Ten Rocks**[18] 5162 3-8-10 61 JordanUys(7) 3 54
(Lisa Williamson) *hld up on rail in 5th: rdn over 2f out: 3rd ent fnl f: wknd ins fnl f* **33/1**

0004 **9** *5* **Jazz Legend (USA)**[23] 4944 3-9-2 60 JimCrowley 8 38
(Robert Cowell) *pressed ldr: rdn over 2f out: nt qckn and wknd qckly fr over 1f out* **12/1**

1m 13.44s (0.34) **Going Correction** +0.10s/f (Slow) **9** Ran SP% **96.9**
Speed ratings (Par 98): **101,100,99,98,98 97,96,94,87**
CSF £51.22 CT £138.61 TOTE £3.50: £1.30, £6.00, £1.30; EX 67.30 Trifecta £206.80.
Owner Paul & Clare Rooney **Bred** Mickley Stud And Mick Quinn **Trained** Lambourn, Berks
■ Desert River was withdrawn. Price at time of withdrawal 3/1F. Rule 4 applies to all bets - deduct 25p in the pound.

FOCUS
A weak handicap to close the card, but it looked competitive enough for the level. Ordinary form.
T/Plt: £426.00 to a £1 stake. Pool of £62816.17- 107.63 winning tickets. T/Qpdt: £48.00 to a £1 stake. Pool of £6937.72 - 106.87 winning tickets. **Cathal Gahan**

5393 LINGFIELD (L-H)
Wednesday, August 24

OFFICIAL GOING: Good to firm (8.0)
Wind: virtually nil Weather: sunny and hot

5770 RYAN VEHICLES NURSERY H'CAP 7f
1:40 (1:42) (Class 6) (0-60,58) 2-Y-O **£2,911** (£866; £432; £216) **Stalls** Centre

Form RPR

3003 **1** **Madam Prancealot (IRE)**[15] 5251 2-8-13 50 JimCrowley 8 56
(David Evans) *chsd ldrs: rdn to chal wl over 1f out: drvn to ld jst over 1f out: hdd wl ins fnl f: battled on gamely to ld again on post* **6/1**[2]

500 **2** *nse* **Altiko Tommy (IRE)**[14] 5304 2-9-7 **58**.................................. LiamKeniry 3 64
(George Baker) *hld up in rr: hdwy and switching lft over 1f out: upsides ldrs and rdn ins fnl f: led wl ins fnl f: kpt on: hdd on post* **12/1**

0053 **3** *3* **Tigerfish (IRE)**[18] 5165 2-8-11 **48**.................................. KieranO'Neill 12 48
(William Stone) *chsd ldrs: effrt and switching lft over 1f out: drvn and chsng ldrs whn nt clr run and swtchd rt ins fnl f: styd on same pce after: wnt 3rd towards fin* **7/1**

000 **4** *3/4* **Nuptials (USA)**[11] 5400 2-9-5 **56**.................................. RobertWinston 4 52
(Eve Johnson Houghton) *chsd ldrs: rdn and ev ch wl over 1f out tl no ex ins fnl f: wknd fnl 100yds* **18/1**

4000 **5** *2 1/4* **A Sure Welcome**[24] 4907 2-9-5 **56**.................................. TomMarquand 5 46
(John Spearing) *hld up in tch in midfield: swtchd lft and effrt u.p: no imp tl kpt on steadily u.p ins fnl f: nvr trbld ldrs* **10/1**

0430 **6** *nse* **Crystal Secret**[13] 5325 2-9-5 **56**.................................. DannyBrock 1 46
(John Bridger) *in tch in midfield: rdn over 2f out: no imp tl kpt on ins fnl f: no threat to ldrs* **16/1**

000 **7** *1/2* **On Show (IRE)**[33] 4601 2-8-5 **45**.................................. AaronJones(3) 6 33
(David Brown) *dwlt: hld up towards rr: effrt 2f out: no imp u.p over 1f out: pushed along and kpt on steadily ins fnl f: nvr trbld ldrs* **8/1**

0403 **8** *nk* **Wakened (IRE)**[14] 5297 2-9-6 **57**..................................1 RichardKingscote 13 44
(Tom Dascombe) *led tl rdn and hdd 2f out: lost pl and btn ent fnl f: wknd ins fnl f* **13/2**[3]

4002 **9** *1* **Vatican Hill (IRE)**[13] 5318 2-9-4 **55**..................................(v) DavidNolan 11 40
(Richard Fahey) *hld up in tch in midfield: rdn and lost pl 2f out: n.d after: swtchd lft and plugged on same pce ins fnl f* **5/2**[1]

5300 **10** *3/4* **Royal Melody**[15] 5257 2-8-13 **55**.................................. HectorCrouch(5) 7 38
(Heather Main) *stdd s: t.k.h: hld up in tch in rr: effrt 2f out: no imp over 1f out: n.d* **33/1**

556 **11** *1 1/4* **Son Castello (IRE)**[26] 4815 2-8-11 **48**..................................(b[1]) SeanLevey 9 27
(Brian Meehan) *t.k.h: chsd ldr tl led 2f out: rdn and hdd jst over 1f out: sn btn: wknd ins fnl f* **14/1**

0566 **12** *5* **Hi There Silver (IRE)**[14] 5297 2-9-1 **57**.................................. GeorgeWood(5) 10 23
(Michael Madgwick) *in tch in midfield: rdn 1/2-way: struggling 2f out: bhd ins fnl f* **25/1**

004 **P** **Viola Park**[14] 5283 2-8-8 **45**.................................. SilvestreDeSousa 2
(Ronald Harris) *hld up in tch towards rr: stmbld after 1f: sn eased: p.u and dismntd 5f out* **33/1**

1m 24.19s (0.89) **Going Correction** -0.125s/f (Firm) **13** Ran SP% **124.1**
Speed ratings (Par 92): **89,88,85,84,82 82,81,81,79,79 77,71,**
CSF £77.85 CT £540.58 TOTE £5.80: £2.30, £3.80, £2.90; EX 85.90 Trifecta £534.20.
Owner Mrs E Evans **Bred** Martin Butler **Trained** Pandy, Monmouths

FOCUS
A weak nursery in which the first pair came clear. The third sets the standard.

5771 ROCKINGHORSE CHILDREN'S CHARITY EBF MEDIAN AUCTION MAIDEN FILLIES' STKS (PLUS 10 RACE) (DIV I) 7f

2:10 (2:12) (Class 5) 2-Y-O **£3,881** (£1,155; £577; £288) **Stalls** Centre

Form RPR

1 **Hidden Steps** 2-9-0 0.................................. OisinMurphy 4 74+
(Andrew Balding) *s.i.s: rn green in last pair: shkn up and hdwy over 1f out: chsd ldr and rdn 1f out: styd on wl to ld towards fin* **5/1**[3]

4 **2** *1/2* **Aimez La Vie (IRE)**[41] 4298 2-9-0 0.................................. DavidNolan 7 74+
(Richard Fahey) *chsd ldr tl led jst over 2f out: pushed along and edging lft over 1f out: rdn and hung lft ins fnl f: hdd and no ex towards fin* **1/1**[1]

3 *3 1/2* **Miss Fay (IRE)** 2-9-0 0.................................. AndreaAtzeni 9 64
(Michael Bell) *in tch in midfield: pushed and effrt to chse ldrs 1f out: wnt lft and no ex ins fnl f: wknd fnl 100yds* **4/1**[2]

05 **4** *2 1/4* **Lemon Drop**[27] 4786 2-9-0 0.................................. PatCosgrave 5 57
(Jim Boyle) *chsd ldrs: swtchd lft and chsd ldr 2f out tl no ex u.p 1f out: wknd ins fnl f* **16/1**

5 *3 1/2* **B B Queen (IRE)** 2-9-0 0.................................. AdamKirby 2 48
(Clive Cox) *hld up towards rr: swtchd lft and hdwy 1/2-way: chsd ldrs and rdn 2f out: no ex and btn ent fnl f: sn wknd* **10/1**

30 **6** *2* **Coping Stone**[15] 5272 2-9-0 0.................................. SeanLevey 1 43
(David Brown) *t.k.h: hld up in tch in midfield: effrt 2f out: sn rdn and btn: wknd fnl f* **6/1**

7 *7* **Sea My Diamond (IRE)** 2-9-0 0.................................. AdamBeschizza 6 24
(Mark Hoad) *led tl hdd ust over 2f out: sn hanging lft: lost pl and wnt bdly lft over 1f out: sn bhd and eased fnl f* **66/1**

0 **8** *8* **Sixties Symphony**[40] 4349 2-9-0 0.................................. WilliamTwiston-Davies 3
(Michael Blanshard) *s.i.s: rn green in rr: swtchd lft 4f out: rdn 2f out: sn btn: bhd 1f out* **66/1**

1m 24.13s (0.83) **Going Correction** -0.125s/f (Firm) **8** Ran SP% **118.9**
Speed ratings (Par 91): **90,89,85,82,78 76,68,59**
CSF £10.85 TOTE £6.20: £1.60, £1.10, £1.80; EX 12.20 Trifecta £35.50.
Owner Kingsclere Racing Club **Bred** Kingsclere Stud **Trained** Kingsclere, Hants

FOCUS
This didn't look a bad 2yo fillies' maiden. The opening level is fluid.

5772 ROCKINGHORSE CHILDREN'S CHARITY EBF MEDIAN AUCTION MAIDEN FILLIES' STKS (PLUS 10 RACE) (DIV II) 7f

2:40 (2:43) (Class 5) 2-Y-O **£3,881** (£1,155; £577; £288) **Stalls** Centre

Form RPR

2322 **1** **Conqueress (IRE)**[11] 5387 2-9-0 76.................................. RichardKingscote 5 73
(Tom Dascombe) *led: rdn wl over 1f out: hdd ent fnl f: rallied u.p ins fnl f: styd on to ld again last stride* **5/4**[1]

24 **2** *shd* **Prufrock (IRE)**[9] 5469 2-9-0 0.................................. JamieSpencer 4 73
(David Simcock) *hld up in tch in midfield: hdwy to chse ldr ent fnl f: sn chalng: rdn to ld ent fnl f: edgd rt ins fnl f: hdd last stride* **3/1**[2]

0 **3** *1 3/4* **Robin's Purse**[25] 4885 2-9-0 0.................................. MichaelJMMurphy 3 68
(Charles Hills) *hld up in tch towards rr: hdwy over 2f out: rdn and ev ch over 1f out tl drifted lft and no ex ins fnl f: outpcd towards fin* **25/1**

0 **4** *nk* **Cuban Isabela**[23] 4951 2-9-0 0.................................. HarryBentley 8 67
(Stuart Williams) *hld up in tch in midfield: pushed along to chse ldrs over 1f out: kpt on same pce ins fnl f* **16/1**

5 **5** *1 1/4* **Life On Mars**[28] 4759 2-9-0 0.................................. PatCosgrave 6 64
(William Haggas) *chsd ldrs: wnt 2nd 4f out tl over 2f out: 5th and unable qck u.p over 1f out: edgd rt 1f out: pushed along and wknd ins fnl f* **4/1**[3]

4 **6** *1* **Washington Blue**[24] 4907 2-9-0 0.................................. AdamKirby 9 61
(Clive Cox) *chsd ldr tl 4f out: lost pl over 2f out: 6th and edgd lft whn rdn over 1f out: styd on same pce ins fnl f* **11/2**

05 **7** *15* **Dragon Dream (IRE)**[41] 4304 2-8-7 0..................................1 RhiainIngram(7) 7 21
(Roger Ingram) *stdd s: t.k.h: hld up in tch in last pair: rdn wl over 2f out: sn btn and bhd* **66/1**

8 *2 3/4* **Giveitsomeginger** 2-9-0 0.................................. ShaneKelly 1 13
(Jo Hughes) *s.i.s: a in rr: hung lft 3f out: sn bhd* **33/1**

1m 24.55s (1.25) **Going Correction** -0.125s/f (Firm) **8** Ran SP% **119.0**
Speed ratings (Par 91): **87,86,84,84,83 81,64,61**
CSF £5.40 TOTE £2.20: £1.02, £1.70, £5.30; EX 5.80 Trifecta £54.30.
Owner Deva Racing Dandy Man Partnership **Bred** Powerstown Stud **Trained** Malpas, Cheshire

FOCUS
The second division of the 2yo fillies' maiden, run in a time 0.42secs slower than the first. The third has been rated as taking a step forward.

5773 LADBROKES (S) STKS 6f

3:10 (3:10) (Class 6) 3-Y-O+ **£2,587** (£770; £384; £192) **Stalls** Centre

Form RPR

1130 **1** **Pandar**[30] 4714 7-10-0 72.................................. DanielMuscutt 1 79+
(Patrick Chamings) *chsd ldr: upsides and travelling best 2f out: shkn up to ld over 1f out: sn rdn clr: eased towards fin: easily* **5/1**[3]

0034 **2** *4* **Anonymous John (IRE)**[37] 4460 4-9-9 80.................................. AdamKirby 8 59
(David Evans) *chsd ldng trio: effrt ent fnl 2f: sn rdn and litle rspnse: plugged on to go 2nd ins fnl f: no ch w wnr* **4/5**[1]

0600 **3** *1* **Majestic Myles (IRE)**[25] 4881 8-10-0 78.................................. KierenFox 5 61
(Lee Carter) *led: rdn ent fnl 2f: hdd over 1f out: sn brushed aside by wnr: lost 2nd and wknd ins fnl f* **9/2**[2]

3423 **4** *1 3/4* **Head Space (IRE)**[16] 5230 8-8-11 66.................................. JoshuaBryan(7) 3 45
(Brian Barr) *hld up in tch in midfield: effrt 2f out: sn outpcd and swtchd rt: wl hld and plugged on same pce ins fnl f* **10/1**

0302 **5** *nse* **Agerzam**[36] 4484 6-9-4 62..................................(p) OisinMurphy 6 45
(Ronald Harris) *in tch in midfield: effrt and hung lft ent fnl 2f: racing against far rail and no imp over 1f out: wknd ins fnl f* **12/1**

5005 **6** *5* **Popeswood (IRE)**[17] 5197 4-9-9 70..................................1 JimCrowley 2 34
(Ron Hodges) *taken down early: dwlt: a towards rr: pushed along wl over 1f out: sn btn* **20/1**

0500 **7** *3* **Gomez**[20] 5088 3-9-1 63..................................(b) SaleemGolam 9 20
(Rae Guest) *stdd s: hld up in tch in rr: rdn ent fnl 2f: sn btn and bhd over 1f out* **33/1**

1m 9.89s (-1.31) **Going Correction** -0.125s/f (Firm)
WFA 3 from 4yo+ 3lb **7** Ran SP% **114.9**
Speed ratings (Par 101): **103,97,96,94,93 87,83**
CSF £9.51 TOTE £8.80: £3.60, £1.10; EX 16.30 Trifecta £33.80.The winner was bought in 4,000gns. Anonymous John was claimed by D. J. Ffrench Davis for £5000, Head Space was claimed by P. D. Evans for £5000 and Popeswood was claimed by L. A. Carter for £5000.
Owner P R Chamings **Bred** Miss F Vittadini **Trained** Baughurst, Hants

FOCUS
This moderate seller rather fell apart from 2f out. The winner has been rated to this year's form.

5774 GARHIGH SOUTHERN LTD H'CAP 6f

3:40 (3:41) (Class 4) (0-80,80) 3-Y-O+ **£5,175** (£1,540; £769; £384) **Stalls** Centre

Form RPR

1301 **1** **Staintondale Lass (IRE)**[43] 4222 3-9-7 **80**.................................. HarryBentley 8 91+
(Ed Vaughan) *chsd ldrs: clsd to press ldrs and travelling strly over 1f out: pushed along and qcknd to ld ent fnl f: sn in command: pushed out: comf* **11/4**[2]

0213 **2** *2 1/4* **Vincentti (IRE)**[3] 5673 6-9-4 **74**.................................. OisinMurphy 7 78+
(Ronald Harris) *dwlt: hld up in tch in last pair: switching lft and hdwy over 1f out: r.o u.p to go 2nd 50yds out: no ch w wnr* **9/2**[3]

34-0 **3** *3/4* **In Haste (IRE)**[22] 4990 3-9-1 **74**.................................. ShaneKelly 5 76
(Eve Johnson Houghton) *in tch in midfield: effrt ent fnl 2f: sme hdwy jst over 1f out: kpt on ins fnl f: wnt 3rd last strides: no ch w wnr* **10/1**

5051 **4** *shd* **Gin In The Inn (IRE)**[10] 5439 3-9-5 **78** 6ex.................................. DavidNolan 1 79+
(Richard Fahey) *stdd and swtchd rt leaving stalls: t.k.h: hld up in midfield: effrt and swtchd rt over 1f out: nt clr run and swtchd rt again ent fnl f: kpt on u.p ins fnl f: no ch w wnr* **2/1**[1]

0000 **5** *hd* **Red Stripes (USA)**[12] 5360 4-9-2 **79**..................................(b) JordanUys(7) 11 80
(Lisa Williamson) *t.k.h: chsd ldr: swtchd lft after 1f: rdn and hung lft 2f out: led over 1f out: sn hdd and unable qck: kpt on same pce: lost 3 pls fnl 50yds* **25/1**

0006 **6** *4 1/2* **Nocturn**[14] 5285 7-9-4 **74**..................................(p) AdamKirby 6 60
(Ronald Harris) *hld up in tch in midfield: rdn 2f out: unable qck u.p over 1f out: wknd fnl f* **12/1**

1023 **7** *nk* **Monarch Maid**[15] 5253 5-9-5 **75**.................................. WilliamCarson 9 60
(Peter Hiatt) *racd keenly: led: rdn and hdd over 1f out: no ex and btn whn hmpd ent fnl f: sn wknd* **6/1**

1500 **8** *5* **Dutch Golden Age (IRE)**[32] 4627 4-9-4 **74**.................................. FergusSweeney 4 43
(Gary Moore) *s.i.s: a in rr: n.d* **16/1**

1m 9.91s (-1.29) **Going Correction** -0.125s/f (Firm)
WFA 3 from 4yo+ 3lb **8** Ran SP% **119.0**
Speed ratings (Par 105): **103,100,99,98,98 92,92,85**
CSF £16.41 CT £109.63 TOTE £3.80: £1.50, £1.60, £2.70; EX 16.70 Trifecta £122.80.
Owner A M Pickering **Bred** Ringfort Stud **Trained** Newmarket, Suffolk

FOCUS
This sprint handicap was weakened by non-runners, but it's still decent form for the class. It's been rated around the second and third.

5775 DOWNLOAD THE LADBROKES APP CLAIMING STKS 1m 1f

4:10 (4:10) (Class 6) 3-Y-O **£2,587** (£770; £384; £192) **Stalls** Low

Form RPR

1550 **1** **Adventure Zone (IRE)**[35] 4518 3-8-7 65..................................(b[1]) KieranO'Neill 1 55
(Richard Hannon) *mde all: rdn over 2f out: edgd rt 1f out: styd on wl: rdn out* **5/1**[3]

0034 **2** *2 1/4* **Harlequin Rock**[28] 4764 3-9-7 60.................................. WilliamCarson 5 65
(Mick Quinn) *stdd after s: hld up in tch in rr: effrt ent fnl 2f: drvn chse ldrs over 1f out: kpt on same pce ins fnl f: snatched 2nd last strides* **5/2**[2]

-040 **3** *nk* **Burning Love (IRE)**[6] 5572 3-8-4 55..................................(p) NickyMackay 3 47
(Adam West) *stdd s: t.k.h: chsd ldrs after 2f: rdn to chse ldr and swtchd rt over 2f out: drvn over 1f out: swtchd lft jst ins fnl f: kpt on same pce after: lost 2nd last strides* **8/1**

631 **4** *7* **Masqueraded (USA)**[20] 5087 3-8-13 60..................................(v) SilvestreDeSousa 2 45
(Gay Kelleway) *t.k.h: hld up in tch: effrt over 3f out: no ex u.p and edgd lft over 1f out: wknd fnl f* **1/1**[1]

006 **5** *9* **Links Bar Marbella (IRE)**[41] 4316 3-8-13 44..................................(b) JimCrowley 4 24
(Eric Wheeler) *chsd ldr tl rdn and hung lft over 2f out: dropped to last and btn wl over 1f out: eased ins fnl f* **33/1**

1m 56.3s (-0.30) **Going Correction** -0.05s/f (Good) **5** Ran SP% **109.3**
Speed ratings (Par 98): **99,97,96,90,82**
CSF £17.42 TOTE £4.70: £2.30, £2.00; EX 13.40 Trifecta £57.00.Adventure Zone was claimed by L. A. Carter for £5000.
Owner R Hannon **Bred** Lynn Lodge Stud **Trained** East Everleigh, Wilts

FOCUS
A 3yo moderate claimer. The runner-up is a good guide to the level.

5776 DANNY TRAYNOR MEMORIAL H'CAP 1m 2f
4:40 (4:40) (Class 6) (0-65,65) 4-Y-O+ **£2,911** (£866; £432; £216) **Stalls** Low

Form RPR
4043 **1** **Roly Tricks**[40] 4370 5-9-2 **63** AaronJones(3) 2 69
(Natalie Lloyd-Beavis) *hld up in tch in rr: effrt ent fnl f: hdwy to chal 1f out: styd on wl to ld towards fin: rdn out* **11/2**
3353 **2** ½ **Tommys Geal**[27] 4784 4-9-5 **63** DanielMuscutt 5 68
(Michael Madgwick) *hld up in tch in 4th: rdn and qcknd to ld over 2f out: drvn and hrd pressed 1f out: hdd and no ex towards fin* **7/2**[3]
6546 **3** 2¾ **Lady Lunchalot (USA)**[11] 5397 6-9-5 **63** (p) JimCrowley 8 63
(Laura Mongan) *chsd ldr: rdn 3f out: outpcd and drvn 2f out: 3rd and kpt on same pce ins fnl f* **11/4**[2]
5514 **4** 2½ **Highlife Dancer**[6] 5575 8-8-13 **57** SilvestreDeSousa 6 52
(Mick Channon) *led: rdn and qcknd over 3f out: hdd over 2f out: outpcd u.p over 1f out: wknd ins fnl f* **6/4**[1]
00-0 **5** 4½ **Avocadeau (IRE)**[14] 5308 5-9-1 **59** (b) OisinMurphy 3 46
(Stuart Kittow) *trckd ldng pair: effrt over 2f out: sn drvn and unable qck: wknd over 1f out* **10/1**

2m 12.81s (2.31) **Going Correction** -0.05s/f (Good) **5** Ran SP% **113.4**
Speed ratings (Par 101): **88,87,85,83,79**
CSF £24.90 TOTE £6.20: £2.40, £1.90; EX 21.00 Trifecta £50.60.
Owner R Eagle **Bred** Iain Wilson **Trained** East Garston, Berks

FOCUS
This moderate handicap suited the closers and two came well clear. The front two set a straightforward level.

5777 RACING WELFARE H'CAP 1m 3f 106y
5:10 (5:11) (Class 6) (0-55,55) 3-Y-O+ **£3,234** (£962; £481; £240) **Stalls** High

Form RPR
4654 **1** **Masterson (IRE)**[11] 5420 3-9-1 **55** SilvestreDeSousa 9 63
(Mick Channon) *hld up in last pair: hdwy ent fnl 2f: rdn to ld over 1f out: forged ahd ins fnl f: styd on wl* **11/4**[1]
1440 **2** ¾ **Whitstable Pearl (IRE)**[11] 5399 3-8-11 **51** KierenFox 8 58
(John Best) *v s.i.s: hld up in rr: hdwy on outer and bmpd over 2f out: drvn to chal over 1f out: no ex and one pce ins fnl f* **4/1**[2]
0-03 **3** 3 **Hermosa Vaquera (IRE)**[19] 5100 6-9-1 **51** (tp) HectorCrouch(5) 14 53
(Gary Moore) *hld up in tch in midfield: clsd to trck ldrs over 3f out: led gng wl over 2f out: rdn 2f out: hdd over 1f out: sn outpcd and one pce fnl f* **10/1**
46-6 **4** ¾ **Top Set (IRE)**[15] 5261 6-9-1 **46** (p) WilliamTwiston-Davies 4 47
(Richard Phillips) *hld up in tch in midfield: clsd to chse ldrs and nt clr run 2f out: swtchd rt over 1f out: kpt on u.p ins fnl f: no threat to ldrs* **20/1**
0560 **5** 1 **Druot**[14] 5303 4-9-10 **55** (b[1]) ShaneKelly 10 54
(Richard Hughes) *hld up in last quartet: hdwy on outer whn bmpd over 2f out: hdwy ent fnl f: kpt on: nvr trbld ldrs* **8/1**
1455 **6** hd **Frivolous Prince (IRE)**[17] 5204 3-8-11 **51** (vt) PatCosgrave 6 51
(David Evans) *hld up in last quartet: hdwy on inner over 2f out: rdn over 1f out: nt clr run and swtchd rt 1f out: kpt on same pce after* **6/1**
0223 **7** ¾ **Cape Spirit (IRE)**[19] 5106 4-9-3 **55** (v) JoshuaBryan(7) 1 53
(Andrew Balding) *chsd ldrs: effrt and swtchd rt over 2f out: drvn and unable qck over 1f out: wknd ins fnl f* **5/1**[3]
0-00 **8** ¾ **Rod Of Iron**[56] 3765 3-8-8 **48** DanielMuscutt 5 46
(Michael Madgwick) *hld up in midfield: effrt and pushed rt over 2f out: squeezed out and hmpd wl over 1f out: swtchd lft over 1f out: kpt on same pce ins fnl f* **20/1**
0235 **9** ½ **Awesome Rock (IRE)**[15] 5261 7-9-1 **46** oh1 MartinLane 2 42
(Roger Ingram) *chsd ldng trio: clsd to chse ldr 3f out: sn rdn and ev ch 2f: unable qck over 1f out: wknd ins fnl f* **14/1**
0000 **10** 3 **Dancing Rainbow (GR)**[19] 5101 3-8-6 **46** oh1 (b[1]) MartinDwyer 12 37
(Amanda Perrett) *chsd ldr tl led over 3f out: rdn and hdd over 2f out: lost pl and bhd 1f out: wknd ins fnl f* **14/1**
0000 **11** 50 **Ledbury (IRE)**[11] 5399 4-9-8 **53** (v[1]) AmirQuinn 3
(Lee Carter) *led: hdd over 3f out: lost pl and bhd 2f out: t.o ins fnl f* **33/1**

2m 31.18s (-0.32) **Going Correction** -0.05s/f (Good)
WFA 3 from 4yo+ 9lb **11** Ran SP% **123.6**
Speed ratings (Par 101): **99,98,96,95,95 94,94,93,93,91 54**
CSF £13.85 CT £100.66 TOTE £3.50: £1.50, £1.80, £3.60; EX 16.70 Trifecta £163.00.
Owner Box 41 Racing **Bred** Star Pointe Ltd **Trained** West Ilsley, Berks

FOCUS
This weak handicap suited those coming from off the pace. The runner-up had hinted she could rate this high, while the fourth has been rated to his latest effort.
T/Jkpt: Not won. T/Plt: £30.90 to a £1 stake. Pool of £67595.47 - 1592.38 winning tickets.
T/Qpdt: £9.40 to a £1 stake. Pool of £5156.03 - 405.87 winning tickets. **Steve Payne**

5112 MUSSELBURGH (R-H)
Wednesday, August 24

OFFICIAL GOING: Good to firm (good in places; 8.2)
Wind: Light, half against Weather: Sunny

5778 DAM GOOD BRITISH STALLION STUDS EBF MAIDEN STKS (PLUS 10 RACE) 7f 30y
2:00 (2:01) (Class 4) 2-Y-O **£4,204** (£1,251; £625; £312) **Stalls** Low

Form RPR
04 **1** **Nepeta (USA)**[16] 5221 2-9-0 0 JoeFanning 4 71+
(Mark Johnston) *mde all: rdn along 2f out: edgd lft and kpt on wl ins fnl f* **7/2**[3]
4 **2** 1 **Souter**[18] 5150 2-9-5 0 JasonHart 1 73+
(Keith Dalgleish) *trckd ldrs: rdn whn n.m.r briefly over 2f out: rallied: chsd wnr ins fnl f: kpt on* **7/4**[1]
4 **3** nk **Doctor Cross (IRE)**[15] 5271 2-9-5 0 JackGarritty 6 72
(Richard Fahey) *pressed ldr: rdn over 2f out: sn edgd lft: lost 2nd ins fnl f: styd on* **11/4**[2]
04 **4** 2½ **Rashford's Double (IRE)**[27] 4786 2-9-5 0 TonyHamilton 8 65
(Richard Fahey) *s.i.s: hld up: pushed along over 2f out: effrt whn checked ent fnl f: kpt on: no imp* **11/2**
04 **5** ½ **Sheriff Garrett (IRE)**[22] 4966 2-9-5 0 DuranFentiman 9 64
(Tim Easterby) *s.i.s: sn prom on outside: stdy hdwy over 2f out: rdn wl over 1f out: outpcd fnl f* **40/1**
6 6 **Performing (IRE)** 2-9-5 0 TomEaves 2 48
(John Quinn) *prom: rdn along over 2f out: wknd over 1f out* **11/1**
7 6 **Good Boy Jasper** 2-9-5 0 ShaneGray 3 32
(Linda Perratt) *s.i.s: racd awkwardly in rr and sn struggling: sme hdwy 1/2-way: rdn and wknd over 2f out* **100/1**

1m 29.48s (0.48) **Going Correction** -0.125s/f (Firm) **7** Ran SP% **112.4**
Speed ratings (Par 96): **92,90,90,87,87 80,73**
CSF £9.69 TOTE £5.30: £3.00, £1.10; EX 11.80 Trifecta £27.20.
Owner N Browne,M Bradford,S Frosell,S Richards **Bred** Kenneth L Ramsey & Sarah K Ramsey **Trained** Middleham Moor, N Yorks

FOCUS
Rails were moved out 4yds on the bottom bend, adding 14yds to this race. A step forward from the winner, with the runner-up rated to his debut form.

5779 WORLD HORSE WELFARE H'CAP (SUPPORTED BY PAUL AND CLAIRE ROONEY) 1m
2:30 (2:30) (Class 5) (0-75,75) 3-Y-O+ **£3,234** (£962; £481; £240) **Stalls** Low

Form RPR
33-1 **1** **Rainbow Rebel (IRE)**[7] 5539 3-9-3 **73** 6ex JoeFanning 6 80+
(Mark Johnston) *led over 3f out: pressed ldr: rdn 2f out: regained ld ins fnl f: kpt on strly* **8/11**[1]
0210 **2** 1¼ **Ralphy Boy (IRE)**[9] 5482 7-9-10 **74** PaulMulrennan 7 79
(Alistair Whillans) *pressed ldr: led over 3f out: rdn 2f out: hdd ins fnl f: kpt on same pce* **9/2**[2]
0144 **3** ¾ **Rasaman (IRE)**[18] 5151 12-8-9 **66** LewisEdmunds(7) 2 69
(Jim Goldie) *t.k.h: prom: plld out over 2f out: rdn and edgd rt over 1f out: kpt on ins fnl f* **9/1**
-156 **4** ¾ **Billy Bond**[22] 4986 4-9-6 **70** (v) TonyHamilton 4 71
(Richard Fahey) *s.i.s: hld up: rdn over 2f out: hdwy and hung rt over 1f out: kpt on fnl f: no imp* **14/1**
1564 **5** 2¼ **Beautiful Stranger (IRE)**[14] 5291 5-9-8 **72** (v) PhillipMakin 5 68
(Keith Dalgleish) *hld up in tch: rdn and outpcd over 2f out: n.d after* **13/2**[3]
1100 **6** 2¾ **Dark Crystal**[19] 5115 5-9-1 **70** PhilDennis(5) 3 59
(Linda Perratt) *prom: drvn along over 2f out: wknd over 1f out* **28/1**

1m 39.55s (-1.65) **Going Correction** -0.125s/f (Firm)
WFA 3 from 4yo+ 6lb **6** Ran SP% **109.5**
Speed ratings (Par 103): **103,101,101,100,98 95**
CSF £4.02 CT £12.79 TOTE £1.70: £1.20, £1.70; EX 4.50 Trifecta £12.70.
Owner Owners Group 004 **Bred** Pier House Stud **Trained** Middleham Moor, N Yorks

FOCUS
Race distance increased by 14yds. A modest handicap that went to the short-price favourite. Little got into it. It's been rated around the runner-up.

5780 MAX RECYCLE H'CAP 5f
3:00 (3:01) (Class 4) (0-85,85) 3-Y-O+ **£5,175** (£1,540; £769; £384) **Stalls** High

Form RPR
6100 **1** **Economic Crisis (IRE)**[18] 5153 7-8-9 **75** NathanEvans(5) 6 83
(John David Riches) *pressed ldr: rdn and led over 1f out: hld on wl ins fnl f* **11/1**
2600 **2** hd **Olivia Fallow (IRE)**[11] 5390 4-9-10 **85** PaulMulrennan 5 92
(Paul Midgley) *trckd ldrs: effrt and swtchd rt over 1f out: chsd wnr ins fnl f: kpt on fin* **5/2**[1]
3005 **3** nk **One Boy (IRE)**[14] 5296 5-8-8 **69** (v) TonyHamilton 8 75
(Richard Fahey) *trckd ldrs: effrt whn n.m.r briefly over 1f out: drvn and kpt on ins fnl f* **15/2**[3]
4330 **4** ½ **Pearl Acclaim (IRE)**[26] 4831 6-9-2 **77** (p) BarryMcHugh 1 81
(David Nicholls) *stmbld leaving stalls: t.k.h and sn cl up: effrt and ev ch over 1f out: no ex ins fnl f* **8/1**
5003 **5** ¾ **Rosina**[23] 4947 3-9-5 **82** PhillipMakin 9 83
(Ann Duffield) *hld up: rdn and hdwy over 1f out: kpt on ins fnl f* **5/1**[2]
0165 **6** nk **Adam's Ale**[15] 5274 7-9-4 **79** (b) JackGarritty 10 79
(Mark Walford) *dwlt: hld up on ins: drvn and outpcd over 1f out: rallied ins fnl f: nvr able to chal* **5/1**[2]
0600 **7** ½ **Fast Act (IRE)**[35] 4514 4-9-4 **79** TomEaves 7 77
(Kevin Ryan) *led to over 1f out: rdn and wknd ins fnl f* **14/1**
5041 **8** 1½ **Bunce (IRE)**[16] 5225 8-8-5 **66** oh1 JoeFanning 4 59
(Linda Perratt) *bhd: drvn along 1/2-way: no imp fr over 1f out* **33/1**
2001 **9** shd **Mappin Time (IRE)**[14] 5296 8-9-2 **77** (b) JasonHart 2 70
(Tim Easterby) *towards rr and sn niggled along: drvn 1/2-way: wknd over 1f out* **14/1**
00-0 **10** ½ **Thorntoun Lady (USA)**[11] 5390 6-8-10 **71** JoeDoyle 3 62
(Jim Goldie) *bhd and outpcd: no imp whn hung rt over 1f out: nvr on terms* **25/1**

58.91s (-1.49) **Going Correction** -0.15s/f (Firm)
WFA 3 from 4yo+ 2lb **10** Ran SP% **113.2**
Speed ratings (Par 105): **105,104,104,103,102 101,100,98,98,97**
CSF £37.54 CT £222.78 TOTE £12.60: £3.50, £1.30, £2.40; EX 55.40 Trifecta £379.80.
Owner William Burns & Alan Berry **Bred** Philip Hore Jnr **Trained** Pilling, Lancashire

FOCUS
Ordinary sprint form. A pb from the winner, with the runner-up close to form. The fourth has been rated close to this year's C&D form, with the fifth to this year's form.

5781 GLORIA ROCHE H'CAP 2m
3:30 (3:30) (Class 6) (0-65,63) 4-Y-O+ **£2,587** (£770; £384; £192) **Stalls** High

Form RPR
5560 **1** **Cosmic Tigress**[77] 3018 5-8-13 **55** JasonHart 4 61
(John Quinn) *dwlt: t.k.h and sn trckd ldrs: effrt and rdn over 1f out: led ins fnl f: kpt on strly* **7/2**[3]
0643 **2** 1¾ **La Bacouetteuse (FR)**[8] 5522 11-9-2 **63** (p) GarryWhillans(5) 2 67
(Iain Jardine) *pressed ldr: rdn to ld over 2f out: hdd ins fnl f: kpt on same pce* **5/2**[2]
3511 **3** 2¼ **La Fritillaire**[8] 5522 4-9-3 **59** 6ex JackGarritty 1 60
(James Given) *led at slow pce: rdn and hdd over 2f out: rallied: outpcd fnl f* **6/5**[1]
0650 **4** ¾ **Pencaitland**[13] 5319 4-8-3 **45** JoeFanning 5 45
(Noel Wilson) *t.k.h: hld up in tch: effrt and pushed along over 1f out: edgd rt and outpcd fnl f* **7/1**

3m 35.34s (1.84) **Going Correction** -0.125s/f (Firm) **4** Ran SP% **108.7**
Speed ratings (Par 101): **90,89,88,87**
CSF £12.14 TOTE £4.50; EX 13.30 Trifecta £21.10.
Owner The Cosmic Cases **Bred** The Cosmic Cases **Trained** Settrington, N Yorks

FOCUS
Race distance increased by 14yds. A moderate staying contest that was run at a steady pace. Limited form.

5782 RAE HAWTHORNE MEMORIAL H'CAP 7f 30y
4:00 (4:00) (Class 5) (0-80,77) 3-Y-O **£5,175** (£1,540; £769; £384) **Stalls** Low

Form RPR

424 **1** **Glengarry**[25] 4870 3-9-7 **77**.......... PhillipMakin 5 89+
(Keith Dalgleish) *t.k.h early: pressed ldr: led gng wl over 2f out: edgd rt and rdn clr fr over 1f out* **11/2**

2466 **2** 2 1/4 **Sophie P**[18] 5151 3-8-6 **67**.......... NathanEvans(5) 4 71
(R Mike Smith) *trckd ldrs: rdn over 2f out: chsd (clr) wnr 1f out: kpt on: no pce to chal* **4/1[2]**

1033 **3** 3/4 **Irish Optimism (IRE)**[51] 3945 3-9-5 **75**..........(v[1]) JasonHart 7 77
(John Quinn) *t.k.h: sn prom: rdn and outpcd over 2f out: rallied over 1f out: kpt on ins fnl f: no imp* **9/4[1]**

3012 **4** nk **Arcane Dancer (IRE)**[13] 5322 3-8-8 **64**..........(p) CamHardie 9 65
(Lawrence Mullaney) *hld up: hdwy on outside over 2f out: rdn and edgd rt over 1f out: kpt on same pce fnl f* **8/1**

0404 **5** 2 **The Name's Paver**[9] 5478 3-8-7 **63**.......... TomEaves 3 59
(Noel Wilson) *hld up: drvn and outpcd over 2f out: kpt on fnl f: no imp* **18/1**

1655 **6** hd **Furiant**[17] 5201 3-9-0 **70**.......... JoeFanning 6 65
(Mark Johnston) *led: rdn and hdd over 2f out: rallied: wknd ins fnl f* **10/1**

2-43 **7** 6 **Regal Response (IRE)**[33] 4605 3-9-5 **75**..........(p) PaulMulrennan 2 54
(Michael Dods) *t.k.h: hld up in tch: drvn and outpcd 3f out: struggling fr 2f out* **9/2[3]**

1m 28.16s (-0.84) **Going Correction** -0.125s/f (Firm) 7 Ran SP% **109.8**
Speed ratings (Par 100): **99,96,95,95,92 92,85**
CSF £25.34 CT £57.99 TOTE £9.50: £4.60, £4.50; EX 35.20 Trifecta £123.30.
Owner Mrs Janis Macpherson **Bred** Laundry Cottage Stud Farm **Trained** Carluke, S Lanarks

FOCUS
Race distance increased by 14yds. No great gallop on here and the winner was much too good. The second, third and fourth have been rated close to their marks.

5783 PARTNERSHIP CHALLENGE H'CAP 1m 6f
4:30 (4:32) (Class 6) (0-65,71) 3-Y-O+ **£2,587** (£770; £384; £192) **Stalls** Low

Form RPR

6534 **1** **Templier (IRE)**[14] 5293 3-9-0 **63**..........[1] JoeFanning 8 69
(Mark Johnston) *mde all: rdn and edgd lft over 1f out: hld on wl fnl f* **9/4[1]**

0322 **2** 1/2 **Ryan The Giant**[13] 5319 3-8-1 **50**..........(p) CamHardie 5 55
(Keith Dalgleish) *pressed wnr: drvn along and edgd lft fr over 2f out: kpt on ins fnl f* **9/2[2]**

5202 **3** nk **Stone Quercus (IRE)**[38] 2015 3-8-9 **58**..........(p) TomEaves 7 63
(Donald McCain) *trckd ldrs: effrt and rdn 2f out: styd on ins fnl f* **10/1**

3211 **4** 1 1/2 **Neuf Des Coeurs**[6] 5580 5-9-13 **71** 6ex..........(p) CliffordLee(7) 2 74
(Iain Jardine) *hld up: stdy hdwy over 5f out: rdn and effrt 2f out: kpt on same pce ins fnl f* **9/4[1]**

0556 **5** 1/2 **Judith Gardenier**[16] 5227 4-8-9 **46** oh1..........(p) JasonHart 1 48
(Iain Jardine) *in tch: stdy hdwy 5f out: rdn over 2f out: hung lft: one pce fr over 1f out* **10/1**

0252 **6** 8 **Merchant Of Dubai**[11] 5392 11-9-2 **60**.......... LewisEdmunds(7) 6 52
(Jim Goldie) *hld up: rdn and struggling over 2f out: sn btn* **7/1[3]**

00/0 **7** 1/2 **Hundred Acre Wood**[16] 5227 6-8-4 **46** oh1..........[1] PhilDennis(5) 3 37
(Sandy Thomson) *dwlt: t.k.h: hld up in tch: struggling over 2f out: sn wknd* **40/1**

3m 3.28s (-2.02) **Going Correction** -0.125s/f (Firm)
WFA 3 from 4yo+ 12lb 7 Ran SP% **112.8**
Speed ratings (Par 101): **100,99,99,98,98 93,93**
CSF £12.41 CT £80.95 TOTE £3.80: £2.70, £1.40; EX 13.10 Trifecta £68.10.
Owner Gerry Ryan **Bred** Monsieur J C Coude **Trained** Middleham Moor, N Yorks

FOCUS
Race distance increased by 14yds. A modest staying handicap, it paid to race prominent and the winner made all. The runner-up has been rated to his recent form.
T/Plt: £360.20 to a £1 stake. Pool of £52968.69 - 107.32 winning tickets. T/Qpdt: £117.50 to a £1 stake. Pool of £2821.52 - 17.76 winning tickets. **Richard Young**

5784 - 5789a (Foreign Racing) - See Raceform Interactive

3863 BELLEWSTOWN (L-H)
Wednesday, August 24

OFFICIAL GOING: Yielding (soft in places) changing to yielding after race 3 (5.00)

5790a DROGHEDA TRADERS PLATE H'CAP 1m 4f
7:00 (7:01) 3-Y-O+ **£9,044** (£2,794; £1,323; £588; £220)

RPR

1 **Xebec (USA)**[7] 5566 4-9-13 **86**..........(b) DeclanMcDonogh 3 90
(John M Oxx, Ire) *hooded to load: mde all: pushed along 1 l clr over 2f out: rdn and extended ld over 1f out: reduced advantage u.p wl ins fnl f: hld on wl* **3/1[2]**

2 3/4 **Hint Of Frost (IRE)**[8] 5534 3-8-2 **76**.......... TomMadden(5) 2 79+
(Mrs John Harrington, Ire) *hld up bhd ldrs in 5th: hdwy on outer fr under 2f out to chse ldrs u.p in 3rd over 1f out: wnt 2nd ins fnl f and pressed wnr clsng stages: a hld* **6/1[3]**

3 1 1/4 **Sretaw (IRE)**[6] 5591 7-9-2 **75**..........(bt) WayneLordan 4 76+
(Gavin Cromwell, Ire) *dwlt and sltly awkward s: settled towards rr: 6th 1/2-way: hdwy far side over 1f out to chse ldrs: rdn in 4th ins fnl f and no imp on wnr in 3rd clsng stages: kpt on same pce* **9/1**

4 1/2 **Tarazani (IRE)**[24] 4922 3-9-6 **89**..........(v) PatSmullen 5 89
(D K Weld, Ire) *trckd ldr: pushed along in 2nd over 2f out and no ex ent fnl f: one pce in 3rd ins fnl f and dropped to 4th clsng stages* **7/4[1]**

5 1 3/4 **Political Policy (IRE)**[10] 5444 5-9-2 **75**..........(tp) RonanWhelan 1 72
(Gavin Cromwell, Ire) *attempted to duck under stall briefly bef s: chsd ldrs: 4th 1/2-way: tk clsr order bhd ldrs under 2f out: rdn over 1f out and sn no imp on wnr in 5th: kpt on one pce fnl f* **16/1**

6 1 **Remarkable Lady (IRE)**[11] 5421 3-8-6 **75**..........(t) ChrisHayes 9 71
(H Rogers, Ire) *dismntd bef s: hld up towards rr: 7th 1/2-way: rdn 2f out and no imp on ldrs in 7th 1f out: kpt on wl ins fnl f into nvr nrr 6th fnl strides* **8/1**

7 hd **Mica Mika (IRE)**[16] 5226 8-9-10 **86**.......... RobbieDowney(3) 8 81
(Richard Fahey) *jinked and uns rdr on way to s: chsd ldrs: 3rd 1/2-way: rdn over 2f out and sn no imp on wnr: wknd into 6th 1f out: denied 6th fnl strides* **7/1**

8 2 3/4 **Gretzky**[306] 7450 9-8-11 **77**..........(t) OisinOrr(7) 6 68
(Matthew J Smith, Ire) *hmpd sltly and uns rdr on way to s: dwlt and w.w in rr: rdn under 2f out and no imp stl in rr ent fnl f: kpt on one pce* **40/1**

2m 40.3s (160.30)
WFA 3 from 4yo+ 10lb 8 Ran SP% **117.6**
CSF £22.11 CT £146.73 TOTE £4.20: £1.30, £1.70, £1.90; DF 19.70 Trifecta £148.70.
Owner Francois Vincent Fabre **Bred** Horse Breeding Company **Trained** Currabeg, Co Kildare

FOCUS
A good front-running display from the winner, who was registering a deserved success. The first three have been rated as running small personal bests.

5791 - (Foreign Racing) - See Raceform Interactive

5510 LEICESTER (R-H)
Thursday, August 25

OFFICIAL GOING: Good (good to firm in places on the round course) changing to good to soft after race 5 (4.10)
Wind: Light; across Weather: Showers

5792 GLEBE MAIDEN AUCTION STKS 7f
2:10 (2:10) (Class 5) 2-Y-O **£2,911** (£866; £432; £216) **Stalls** High

Form RPR

1 **Ocean Air (FR)** 2-9-3 0.......... MartinHarley 1 73+
(James Tate) *s.i.s: hld up: hdwy over 1f out: rdn and r.o to ld post* **12/1**

0 **2** hd **Claire's Secret**[20] 5119 2-8-7 0.......... NickyMackay 7 62
(Philip McBride) *s.i.s: hdwy over 4f out: rdn to ld wl ins fnl f: hdd post* **11/4[1]**

2444 **3** hd **Sidewinder (IRE)**[55] 3852 2-9-3 72.......... RichardKingscote 6 71
(Tom Dascombe) *w ldr tl over 4f out: racd in 2nd tl led over 1f out: rdn: edgd rt and hdd wl ins fnl f: styd on* **4/1[3]**

0 **4** 2 1/4 **Charlie Rascal (FR)**[26] 4856 2-8-12 0.......... JamesDoyle 5 60
(Peter Chapple-Hyam) *led: rdn and hdd over 1f out: styd on same pce ins fnl f* **3/1[2]**

0 **5** 1 1/2 **Prince Of Clappers**[26] 4856 2-8-12 0.......... DavidAllan 9 56
(Tim Easterby) *in rr and sn pushed along: styd on ins fnl f: nt rch ldrs* **33/1**

0 **6** 1 3/4 **Daring Guest (IRE)**[43] 4270 2-9-3 0.......... TomQueally 8 56
(George Margarson) *plld hrd: w ldrs 2f: rdn over 2f out: sn outpcd: rallied u.p over 1f out: no ex ins fnl f* **12/1**

7 6 **Master Billie (IRE)** 2-9-3 0.......... MartinDwyer 2 40
(William Muir) *in rr: pushed along over 4f out: outpcd fr over 2f out* **25/1**

0 **8** 3 3/4 **Young Officer (IRE)**[13] 5356 2-9-2 0.......... JimmyFortune 4 29
(Brian Meehan) *prom: rdn over 2f out: wknd over 1f out* **25/1**

9 14 **Aqshion Stations** 2-8-13 0.......... SilvestreDeSousa 3
(William Jarvis) *hld up: plld hrd early: rdn over 2f out: sn wknd and eased* **11/2**

1m 27.74s (1.54) **Going Correction** +0.075s/f (Good) 9 Ran SP% **113.1**
Speed ratings (Par 94): **94,93,93,90,89 87,80,76,60**
CSF £43.36 TOTE £11.10: £3.80, £1.40, £1.10; EX 37.50 Trifecta £115.10.
Owner Saeed Manana **Bred** D R Tucker **Trained** Newmarket, Suffolk

FOCUS
There was 5mm of rain overnight and the going was given as good, good to firm in places on the round course (GoingStick: 6.9). No more than a fair maiden. The third helps with the opening level.

5793 DALE HALL AND HICKMAN ASSOCIATES H'CAP 7f
2:40 (2:40) (Class 4) (0-80,78) 3-Y-O+ **£4,851** (£1,443; £721; £360) **Stalls** High

Form RPR

4001 **1** **Red Paladin (IRE)**[12] 5386 6-9-9 **75**..........(p) ShaneKelly 1 83
(Kristin Stubbs) *s.s: sn given reminders in rr: hung rt at various stages: hdwy u.p over 1f out: styd on to ld nr fin* **15/2**

0004 **2** shd **Harwoods Volante (IRE)**[19] 5179 5-9-11 **77**.......... JimCrowley 7 84
(David O'Meara) *trckd ldrs: plld hrd: led over 4f out: rdn over 1f out: hdd nr fin* **10/3[2]**

1321 **3** 2 1/2 **Twin Point**[14] 5337 5-9-12 **78**..........(t) StevieDonohoe 2 78
(Charlie Fellowes) *led: edgd lft over 5f out: hdd over 4f out: chsd ldr: rdn over 1f out: styd on same pce ins fnl f* **9/4[1]**

0535 **4** nk **Aqua Ardens (GER)**[26] 4868 8-9-11 **77**..........(p) PatCosgrave 6 76
(George Baker) *chsd ldrs: rdn over 2f out: styd on same pce ins fnl f* **9/2[3]**

06 **5** 3 3/4 **Show Me Again**[25] 4908 3-9-5 **76**..........[1] MartinLane 5 63
(David Dennis) *stdd s: hld up: rdn over 2f out: nt trble ldrs* **20/1**

3614 **6** 7 **Corporal Maddox**[13] 5357 9-9-12 **78**..........(p) AdamKirby 4 48
(Ronald Harris) *chsd ldrs: rdn and hung rt over 2f out: wknd and eased over 1f out* **11/1**

246U **7** 1/2 **Darrell Rivers**[22] 5038 4-8-11 **63**.......... PatrickMathers 8 32
(Giles Bravery) *plld hrd and prom: lost pl over 5f out: rdn over 2f out: wknd over 1f out* **9/1**

0-00 **8** 5 **Cosmic Ray**[87] 2734 4-9-6 **72**..........[1] JFEgan 3 27
(Daniel Mark Loughnane) *w ldr whn hmpd over 5f out: sn lost pl: rdn 1/2-way: sn wknd and eased* **33/1**

1m 25.35s (-0.85) **Going Correction** +0.075s/f (Good)
WFA 3 from 4yo+ 5lb 8 Ran SP% **109.8**
Speed ratings (Par 105): **107,106,104,103,99 91,90,85**
CSF £30.10 CT £69.15 TOTE £9.60: £2.40, £1.20, £1.20; EX 35.70 Trifecta £138.30.
Owner K Stubbs, Dr Grieve, T Baker & Clark **Bred** Noel O'Callaghan **Trained** Norton, N Yorks
■ Stewards' Enquiry : Stevie Donohoe three-day ban: careless riding (Sep 8,9,11)

FOCUS
They went fairly steady early on, but the pace picked up once Harwoods Volante went on, and the winner came from last place. Limited form for the grade.

5794 IRISH STALLION FARMS EBF FILLIES' NURSERY H'CAP 6f
3:10 (3:13) (Class 4) (0-80,80) 2-Y-O **£6,469** (£1,925; £962; £481) **Stalls** High

Form RPR

2162 **1** **Rosebride**[25] 4915 2-8-12 **76**..........[1] AdamMcNamara(5) 11 90+
(Richard Fahey) *hld up: racd keenly: hdwy to ld over 1f out: r.o wl* **10/1**

10 **2** 3 **Parsnip (IRE)**[26] 4884 2-9-5 **78**..........[1] JamesDoyle 10 83
(Michael Bell) *prom: rdn over 2f out: styd on to go 2nd wl ins fnl f* **7/1[3]**

0213 **3** 1 3/4 **Storm Cry**[8] 5560 2-9-6 **79**.......... FrannyNorton 6 79
(Mark Johnston) *hld up: pushed along and hdwy over 1f out: styd on to go 3rd nr fin* **15/8[1]**

1 **4** nk **Many A Tale**[17] 5242 2-9-5 **78**.......... ThomasBrown 1 77+
(Ismail Mohammed) *chsd ldrs: rdn and ev ch over 1f out: styd on same pce ins fnl f* **8/1**

2510 **5** 1/2 **Texas Katie**[12] 5407 2-8-12 **71**.......... SilvestreDeSousa 5 68
(Mick Channon) *led: racd keenly: rdn and hdd over 1f out: no ex ins fnl f* **12/1**

321 **6** 2 1/2 **Ariena (IRE)**[34] 4586 2-9-7 **80**.. AdamKirby 3 70
(Clive Cox) *trckd ldrs: racd keenly: rdn over 2f out: wknd fnl f* **3/1**[2]
631 **7** 2 3/4 **Savannah Slew**[27] 4843 2-9-2 **75**.. AndrewMullen 2 57
(James Given) *uns rdr and got loose on the way to post: chsd ldrs: rdn over 2f out: wknd over 1f out* **16/1**
5310 **8** 2 1/2 **Pranceleya (IRE)**[26] 4884 2-8-13 **72**.. LiamJones 8 46
(Marco Botti) *prom: rdn 1/2-way: wknd wl over 1f out* **20/1**
6023 **9** 20 **Mums The Word**[9] 5506 2-9-2 **75**.. SeanLevey 9
(Richard Hannon) *chsd ldrs: rdn over 2f out: wknd wl over 1f out* **25/1**
060 **10** dist **Sukiwarrior (IRE)**[12] 5400 2-8-7 **66**.. MartinLane 4
(Charles Hills) *sn pushed along in rr: bhd fr 1/2-way* **66/1**

1m 13.32s (0.32) **Going Correction** +0.075s/f (Good) **10** Ran SP% **116.2**
Speed ratings (Par 93): **100,96,93,93,92 89,85,82,55,**
CSF £76.17 CT £189.75 TOTE £10.70: £2.90, £2.20, £1.10; EX 63.00 Trifecta £328.80.
Owner Cheveley Park Stud **Bred** Cheveley Park Stud Ltd **Trained** Musley Bank, N Yorks

FOCUS
Not a bad fillies' nursery, and it should throw up a winner or two. The runner-up has been rated as posting an effort in keeping with her debut, while the third has been rated a bit below her latest form.

5795 NELSON H'CAP — 1m 3f 183y
3:40 (3:41) (Class 5) (0-70,66) 3-Y-O+ **£2,911** (£866; £432; £216) **Stalls** Low

Form RPR
5254 **1** **Cornelious (IRE)**[9] 5503 4-10-0 **66**..............................(v) DarryllHolland 3 71
(Clifford Lines) *hld up: hdwy over 2f out: rdn to ld wl ins fnl f: styd on* **4/1**[3]
-542 **2** hd **Mamoo**[27] 4836 3-8-10 **58**.. MartinDwyer 2 63
(Mike Murphy) *chsd ldr: shkn up and ev ch fr over 2f out: rdn and hmpd over 1f out: styd on* **5/4**[1]
5335 **3** nk **Percys Princess**[11] 4320 5-9-8 **60**.. AndrewMullen 6 64
(Michael Appleby) *led: rdn over 2f out: wnt lft over 1f out: hdd wl ins fnl f: kpt on* **15/2**
1135 **4** 3 3/4 **Saint Thomas (IRE)**[15] 5294 9-9-6 **58**.. FrannyNorton 4 56
(John Mackie) *chsd ldrs: rdn over 2f out: styd on same pce fr over 1f out* **3/1**[2]
0-50 **5** 1/2 **Kirtling**[13] 5375 5-9-8 **60**..............................(t) MartinLane 7 57
(Andi Brown) *s.i.s: hld up: rdn over 2f out: hdwy over 1f out: edgd rt and no ex ins fnl f* **16/1**
6600 **6** 21 **On The Clock**[20] 5132 3-7-11 **48** oh3.. NoelGarbutt(3) 1 11
(Denis Quinn) *plld hrd and prom: rdn over 3f out: wknd over 2f out* **100/1**

2m 38.13s (4.23) **Going Correction** +0.075s/f (Good)
WFA 3 from 4yo+ 10lb **6** Ran SP% **108.1**
Speed ratings (Par 103): **88,87,87,85,84 70**
CSF £8.72 TOTE £4.80: £2.30, £1.20; EX 10.00 Trifecta £33.50.
Owner Prima Racing Partnership **Bred** Gerard Kerin **Trained** Exning, Suffolk

FOCUS
They went fairly steady here and, while they finished in a heap up front, the winner did quite well to come from behind and get by the first two.

5796 GALLOWGATE NURSERY H'CAP — 7f
4:10 (4:11) (Class 5) (0-70,69) 2-Y-O **£2,911** (£866; £432; £216) **Stalls** High

Form RPR
605 **1** **Inner Circle (IRE)**[15] 5304 2-9-4 **66**.. SeanLevey 2 71
(Richard Hannon) *w ldr tl led over 2f out: rdn over 1f out: styd on* **6/1**[3]
500 **2** 1 **Snookered (IRE)**[26] 4890 2-8-1 **49**.. PatrickMathers 9 51
(Richard Fahey) *plld hrd and prom: rdn over 2f out: outpcd over 1f out: r.o wl towards fin* **12/1**
002 **3** 3/4 **Syncopation (IRE)**[23] 4989 2-9-6 **68**.. DaneO'Neill 6 68
(Sylvester Kirk) *w ldrs: plld hrd: rdn over 1f out: hung rt ins fnl f: styd on* **7/4**[1]
604 **4** hd **Feel The Vibes**[14] 5325 2-9-7 **69**.. KieranO'Neill 1 69
(Richard Hannon) *prom: racd keenly: rdn over 2f out: styd on same pce wl ins fnl f* **4/1**[2]
6440 **5** 1 **Traveltalk (IRE)**[16] 5271 2-8-13 **66**..............................[1] CallumShepherd(5) 7 63+
(Brian Ellison) *wnt lft s: hld up: rdn over 2f out: r.o ins fnl f: nvr nrr* **20/1**
040 **6** 1 3/4 **Jasmincita (IRE)**[63] 3556 2-9-5 **67**.. SteveDrowne 4 59
(George Baker) *prom: rdn over 2f out: no ex wl ins fnl f: eased nr fin* **8/1**
050 **7** 1/2 **Ripper Street (IRE)**[27] 4837 2-9-6 **68**.. SilvestreDeSousa 8 59
(Ed Dunlop) *hmpd s: hld up: rdn over 2f out: nt trble ldrs* **9/1**
6144 **8** 2 1/2 **Hi Milady (IRE)**[23] 4974 2-9-6 **68**.. FrederikTylicki 3 52
(Dominic Ffrench Davis) *led: rdn and hdd over 2f out: wknd ins fnl f* **12/1**
650 **9** 6 **Powerless (IRE)**[65] 3477 2-8-2 **50**.. AndrewMullen 5 18
(Tim Easterby) *chsd ldrs: rdn over 2f out: wknd over 1f out* **40/1**

1m 28.42s (2.22) **Going Correction** +0.075s/f (Good) **9** Ran SP% **114.3**
Speed ratings (Par 94): **90,88,88,87,86 84,84,81,74**
CSF £73.86 CT £178.14 TOTE £6.50: £2.00, £3.50, £1.10; EX 85.30 Trifecta £293.80.
Owner Mrs J Wood **Bred** Anthony Morris **Trained** East Everleigh, Wilts

FOCUS
A modest nursery run at a fairly pedestrian early gallop. Not form to trust implicitly.

5797 CHARLES STREET H'CAP — 6f
4:45 (4:45) (Class 5) (0-70,70) 3-Y-O+ **£2,911** (£866; £432; £216) **Stalls** High

Form RPR
302 **1** **Etienne Gerard**[14] 5320 4-9-2 **69**..............................(p) LewisEdmunds(7) 15 80
(Nigel Tinkler) *hld up: hdwy to ld 1f out: edgd rt and r.o wl* **6/1**[2]
1400 **2** 3 **Rigolleto (IRE)**[104] 2217 8-9-10 **70**.. KieranO'Neill 16 72
(Anabel K Murphy) *prom: rdn over 2f out: styd on same pce ins fnl f* **66/1**
2100 **3** 3/4 **Mad Endeavour**[21] 5060 5-9-3 **63**..............................[1] MartinLane 12 63
(Stuart Kittow) *chsd ldrs: rdn over 1f out: styd on same pce fnl f* **15/2**[3]
0430 **4** hd **Commanche**[43] 4278 7-8-7 **53**..............................(b) SilvestreDeSousa 10 52
(Chris Dwyer) *w ldrs: rdn over 2f out: led over 1f out: sn hdd: no ex ins fnl f* **15/2**[3]
0040 **5** 1 3/4 **Firgrove Bridge (IRE)**[12] 5386 4-8-4 **55**..............................(p) PaddyPilley(5) 11 49
(Steph Hollinshead) *s.i.s: hdwy over 4f out: rdn over 2f out: no ex fnl f* **25/1**
0401 **6** nk **Dear Bruin (IRE)**[16] 5259 4-9-10 **70**..............................(p) WilliamTwiston-Davies 14 63
(David W Drinkwater) *prom: rdn and lost pl over 3f out: styd on ins fnl f* **16/1**
232 **7** 2 1/4 **Regal Parade**[22] 5039 12-9-10 **70**..............................(t) AdamBeschizza 13 56
(Charlie Wallis) *hld up: pushed along over 2f out: styd on ins fnl f: nvr nrr* **8/1**
00 **8** 1/2 **Maymyo (IRE)**[25] 4910 5-9-4 **64**..............................(t) DaneO'Neill 7 49
(Sylvester Kirk) *hld up: rdn over 1f out: nt trble ldrs* **14/1**
-500 **9** nk **Bunker Hill Lass**[9] 5513 4-8-11 **57**..............................(p) AndrewMullen 1 41
(Michael Appleby) *s.i.s: sn pushed along and prom: rdn and lost pl over 3f out: rallied over 1f out: wknd ins fnl f* **33/1**

0000 **10** 1/2 **Clubland (IRE)**[22] 5034 7-9-7 **70**.. AlistairRawlinson(3) 2 52
(Roy Bowring) *led 2f: led again over 2f out: rdn and hdd over 1f out: wknd ins fnl f* **20/1**
1206 **11** 1 1/2 **Consistant**[24] 4932 8-8-13 **62**..............................[1] EoinWalsh(3) 9 40
(Brian Baugh) *mid-div: drvn along over 2f out: wknd over 1f out* **16/1**
1245 **12** nk **Generalyse**[10] 5483 7-8-7 **60**..............................(b) JoshuaBryan(7) 3 37
(Anabel K Murphy) *w ldrs 2f: sn lost pl: sme hdwy u.p over 1f out: sn wknd* **8/1**
0000 **13** 1 1/4 **Divine Call**[19] 5169 9-8-11 **57**..............................(v) FrannyNorton 5 30
(Milton Bradley) *hld up: effrt and nt clr run over 1f out: nvr on terms* **25/1**
-000 **14** 10 **Balliol**[8] 5546 4-9-6 **66**.. AdamKirby 8 9
(Ronald Harris) *s.i.s: sn prom: led 4f out tl rdn: edgd lft and hdd over 2f out: wknd over 1f out* **16/1**
660- **15** 4 **Thrilled (IRE)**[316] 7212 3-9-3 **66**..............................[1] GeorgeBaker 4
(David Lanigan) *s.i.s: hld up: wknd over 2f out* **9/2**[1]

1m 13.15s (0.15) **Going Correction** +0.075s/f (Good)
WFA 3 from 4yo+ 3lb **15** Ran SP% **119.4**
Speed ratings (Par 103): **102,98,97,96,94 94,91,90,89,89 87,86,85,71,66**
CSF £378.07 CT £2028.91 TOTE £6.90: £1.90, £11.30, £2.90; EX 209.80 Trifecta £4188.90.
Owner welovewhitby.com **Bred** R Biggs **Trained** Langton, N Yorks

FOCUS
The going was changed to good to soft before this race. The race developed centre to stands' side, with the seven horses drawn in double figure stalls filling the first seven places. The race could be rated higher but this is a sensible starting point.
T/Plt: £16.80 to a £1 stake. Pool: £76,671.81 - 3,316.10 winning units T/Qpdt: £8.30 to a £1 stake. Pool: £4,993.71 - 444.70 winning units **Colin Roberts**

[5778]MUSSELBURGH (R-H)
Thursday, August 25

OFFICIAL GOING: Good to firm (8.1)
Wind: Breezy; across Weather: Overcast

5798 RACINGUK.COM MAIDEN AUCTION STKS — 5f
2:00 (2:00) (Class 5) 2-Y-O **£2,911** (£866; £432; £216) **Stalls** High

Form RPR
4032 **1** **Yorkshiredebut (IRE)**[27] 4832 2-8-9 65.. PaulMulrennan 3 70
(Paul Midgley) *mde all: crossed to stands' rail after 2f: rdn over 1f out: kpt on wl fnl f* **13/2**[2]
202 **2** 1 1/4 **Lucky Mistake (IRE)**[21] 5067 2-8-13 81.. TonyHamilton 6 69
(Richard Fahey) *pressed wnr: effrt and drvn along wl over 1f out: kpt on same pce last 100yds* **4/9**[1]
3 2 1/2 **Lady Molly (IRE)** 2-8-9 0.. JoeFanning 2 56
(Keith Dalgleish) *in tch: hdwy and hung rt over 2f out: rdn and outpcd ins fnl f* **10/1**
4 1 1/2 **Hueston**[20] 5134 2-9-2 0.. GrahamGibbons 7 58
(Conor O'Dwyer, Ire) *awkward s: chsd ldrs: rdn along over 2f out: no ex fnl f* **15/2**[3]
46 **5** 1 **Peny Arcade**[21] 5067 2-8-6 0.. PJMcDonald 1 44
(Alistair Whillans) *bhd and sn struggling: sme late hdwy: nvr on terms* **20/1**

58.35s (-2.05) **Going Correction** -0.45s/f (Firm) **5** Ran SP% **108.2**
Speed ratings (Par 94): **98,96,92,89,88**
CSF £9.71 TOTE £6.80: £2.80, £1.10; EX 7.80 Trifecta £33.90.
Owner Taylor's Bloodstock Ltd **Bred** Yasmeena Partnership **Trained** Westow, N Yorks

FOCUS
Rails were moved out 4yds on the bottom bend, adding 14yds to all races bar 5f. There was a bit of a turn-up in this opening maiden. The level is fluid.

5799 DICKSON MINTO NURSERY H'CAP — 7f 30y
2:30 (2:30) (Class 6) (0-65,62) 2-Y-O **£2,587** (£770; £384; £192) **Stalls** Low

Form RPR
050 **1** **Our Charlie Brown**[54] 3872 2-9-7 **62**.. JamesSullivan 2 76+
(Tim Easterby) *t.k.h: trckd ldr: led gng wl over 2f out: rdn over 1f out: drew clr ins fnl f: eased nr fin* **11/4**[1]
2243 **2** 2 1/2 **Kilbaha Lady (IRE)**[14] 5318 2-9-6 **61**..............................(t) TomEaves 3 63
(Nigel Tinkler) *chsd ldrs: drvn along 3f out: rallied to chse wnr over 1f out: kpt on fnl f: nt pce to chal* **4/1**[3]
065 **3** 3 **Lil's Affair (IRE)**[21] 5067 2-8-12 **53**.. PaulMulrennan 8 47
(Bryan Smart) *stdd s: hld up: rdn along 1/2-way: hdwy over 1f out: kpt on fnl f: nt rch first two* **6/1**
040 **4** 2 1/4 **Our Lois (IRE)**[24] 4943 2-9-2 **57**.. JasonHart 5 45
(Keith Dalgleish) *in tch: drvn along and outpcd wl over 2f out: rallied over 1f out: sn no imp* **6/1**
045 **5** 1 1/4 **Albizu Campos**[25] 4914 2-9-7 **62**..............................(b[1]) CamHardie 1 46
(Lawrence Mullaney) *s.i.s: hld up: drvn and outpcd over 2f out: n.d after* **10/1**
665 **6** 1/2 **Lavender Skye (IRE)**[102] 2266 2-8-4 **45**.. JoeyHaynes 7 28
(K R Burke) *hld up in tch: drvn and struggling wl over 2f out: sn n.d* **18/1**
0302 **7** 1 **Mulwith (IRE)**[20] 5112 2-9-7 **62**..............................(b) GrahamGibbons 4 42
(David Barron) *t.k.h: led: qcknd 1/2-way: hdd over 2f out: rdn and lost 2nd over 1f out: sn wknd* **7/2**[2]

1m 29.23s (0.23) **Going Correction** -0.20s/f (Firm) **7** Ran SP% **111.8**
Speed ratings (Par 92): **90,87,83,81,79 79,78**
CSF £13.29 CT £57.94 TOTE £3.30: £2.30, £1.80; EX 12.10 Trifecta £51.30.
Owner Ontoawinner, SDH Project Services Ltd 2 **Bred** North Bradon Stud & D R Tucker **Trained** Great Habton, N Yorks

FOCUS
Race distance increased by 14yds. Little got into this moderate nursery. The winner has been rated value for further, while the runner-up fits.

5800 HBJ GATELY H'CAP — 1m 208y
3:00 (3:00) (Class 6) (0-60,61) 3-Y-O+ **£2,587** (£770; £384; £192) **Stalls** Low

Form RPR
4241 **1** **Exclusive Diamond**[9] 5513 4-9-11 **61** 6ex.. DanielTudhope 5 68
(David O'Meara) *trckd ldrs: smooth hdwy to ld 2f out: rdn and hrd pressed fnl f: hld on wl towards fin* **5/6**[1]
0550 **2** hd **Nelson's Bay**[13] 5355 7-9-1 **51**.. CamHardie 1 58
(Wilf Storey) *hld up: rdn and hdwy over 2f out: ev ch ins fnl f: kpt on: hld nr fin* **7/1**[3]
0404 **3** 3 1/2 **Intensified (IRE)**[14] 5323 5-8-10 **46** oh1..............................(b) JamesSullivan 4 46
(Ruth Carr) *in tch: rdn along 3f out: hdwy and edgd rt over 1f out: kpt on ins fnl f* **8/1**

-040 **4** 2 1/2 **Lipstickandpowder (IRE)**[3] 5729 4-8-10 **46** oh1....(bt) PaulMulrennan 2 40
(Dianne Sayer) *prom: pushed along whn n.m.r briefly over 2f out: drvn and outpcd fnl f* **16/1**

4300 **5** nk **Magical Lasso (IRE)**[13] 5355 3-8-5 **53**................(p) ShirleyTeasdale[(5)] 8 47
(Keith Dalgleish) *led 4f: cl up: ev ch and rdn over 2f out: edgd rt over 1f out: wknd fnl f* **20/1**

3315 **6** 4 **Ronya (IRE)**[16] 5273 5-9-10 **60**.................................... RoystonFfrench 3 45
(Tracy Waggott) *pressed ldr: led after 4f: rdn and hdd 2f out: sn wknd* **4/1**[2]

3000 **7** 6 **Rosie Hall (IRE)**[14] 5323 6-8-10 **46** oh1..........................(v) TomEaves 6 19
(John Wainwright) *hld up: drvn and outpcd 3f out: btn fnl 2f* **125/1**

1m 51.32s (-2.58) **Going Correction** -0.20s/f (Firm)
WFA 3 from 4yo+ 7lb **7** Ran SP% **109.6**
Speed ratings (Par 101): **103,102,99,97,97 93,88**
CSF £6.63 CT £24.12 TOTE £1.60: £1.10, £3.50; EX 6.90 Trifecta £21.10.
Owner R C Bond & C S Bond **Bred** Whatton Manor Stud **Trained** Upper Helmsley, N Yorks

FOCUS
A race originally advertised as being run over 1m2f, it only became apparent it was to be run over a furlong shorter earlier in the day. The front pair came clear in what was a lowly handicap, the early leaders getting tired late. A small step forward from the winner.

5801 RACING UK NOW IN HD! H'CAP 1m 4f 100y
3:30 (3:30) (Class 5) (0-75,73) 3-Y-O+ **£2,911** (£866; £432; £216) **Stalls** Low

Form RPR

2241 **1** **Introductory (IRE)**[21] 5083 3-9-4 **73**................................ PhillipMakin 5 79+
(Keith Dalgleish) *mde all: set stdy pce: shkn up and qcknd clr over 1f out: eased last 100yds: readily* **5/6**[1]

0-60 **2** 1 1/2 **Ronaldinho (IRE)**[24] 4935 6-8-9 **54** oh4...................(bt) JamesSullivan 1 54
(Dianne Sayer) *prom: rdn over 2f out: rallied to take 2nd pl over 1f out: kpt on fnl f: flattered by proximity to eased-down wnr* **18/1**

0565 **3** 2 **Gabrial The Terror (IRE)**[20] 5117 6-9-2 **61**...............(p) TonyHamilton 4 58
(Richard Fahey) *dwlt: hld up in tch: hdwy over 3f out: drvn and chsd (clr) wnr briefly over 1f out: kpt on same pce fnl f* **5/1**[3]

3202 **4** 9 **Dry Your Eyes (IRE)**[15] 5294 5-9-10 **69**...................... DanielTudhope 2 56
(David O'Meara) *t.k.h: trckd wnr: rdn over 2f out: wknd over 1f out: eased whn btn ins fnl f* **9/4**[2]

2m 42.8s (0.80) **Going Correction** -0.20s/f (Firm)
WFA 3 from 5yo+ 10lb **4** Ran SP% **107.3**
Speed ratings (Par 103): **89,88,86,80**
CSF £13.21 TOTE £1.90; EX 11.50 Trifecta £39.40.
Owner Michael Beaumont **Bred** Ballyhane Stud **Trained** Carluke, S Lanarks

FOCUS
Race distance increased by 14yds. They went no gallop and the winner dictated. The runner-up limits the form.

5802 SCOTT COPPOLA ELECTRICAL DISTRIBUTOR H'CAP 1m
4:00 (4:00) (Class 3) (0-90,90) 3-Y-O+ **£7,762** (£2,310; £1,154; £577) **Stalls** Low

Form RPR

1514 **1** **Ginger Jack**[12] 5419 9-9-11 **87**.. JasonHart 9 93
(Garry Moss) *hld up in tch: drvn along over 2f out: rallied over 1f out: kpt on wl fnl f to ld towards fin* **9/4**[1]

0-00 **2** nk **Argaki (IRE)**[64] 3518 6-8-13 **80**............................... ShirleyTeasdale[(5)] 7 85
(Keith Dalgleish) *led: rdn along 2f out: kpt on fnl f: hdd towards fin* **40/1**

3-00 **3** hd **Hibou**[17] 5226 3-8-1 **76**... JamieGormley[(7)] 1 80
(Iain Jardine) *hld up: shkn up and outpcd after 3f: hdwy and swtchd rt wl over 1f out: nt clr run briefly ent fnl f: kpt on steadily under hands and heels: improve* **15/2**

1233 **4** 3/4 **Invermere**[20] 5123 3-8-10 **78**... TonyHamilton 4 80
(Richard Fahey) *dwlt: hld up: rdn and plld out over 2f out: kpt on wl fnl f: nrst fin* **5/1**[3]

0000 **5** 2 **Whitman**[26] 4867 3-9-6 **88**... JoeFanning 10 85
(Mark Johnston) *trckd ldrs: rdn along and effrt over 2f out: kpt on same pce fnl f* **8/1**

2130 **6** 2 1/4 **Jacbequick**[12] 5419 5-10-0 **90**...................................(v) DanielTudhope 3 83
(David O'Meara) *dwlt: sn w ldr: rdn over 2f out: wknd ins fnl f* **7/2**[2]

3440 **7** 6 **Gworn**[17] 5226 6-8-10 **77**... GarryWhillans[(5)] 5 55
(R Mike Smith) *hld up: effrt and drvn over 2f out: wknd over 1f out* **9/1**

6000 **8** 10 **Mont Ras (IRE)**[19] 5156 9-9-10 **86**................................. PJMcDonald 6 40
(David Loughnane) *prom: rdn along over 2f out: edgd rt: wknd over 1f out* **17/2**

1m 38.06s (-3.14) **Going Correction** -0.20s/f (Firm)
WFA 3 from 5yo+ 6lb **8** Ran SP% **115.5**
Speed ratings (Par 107): **107,106,106,105,103 101,95,85**
CSF £91.82 CT £593.94 TOTE £3.00: £1.30, £6.80, £3.10; EX 82.70 Trifecta £1157.60.
Owner C H McGhie **Bred** Darley **Trained** Wynyard, Stockton-On-Tees

FOCUS
Race distance increased by 14yds. They pressed on a fair way out here and it was no surprise to see one of the closers triumph. Straightforward form, with the winner near his best of recent times, and the second, third and fourth to their respective levels.

5803 BOOGIE IN THE MORNING H'CAP 7f 30y
4:30 (4:31) (Class 6) (0-60,60) 3-Y-O **£2,587** (£770; £384; £192) **Stalls** Low

Form RPR

5546 **1** **Fine Example**[17] 5222 3-9-2 **55**.......................................(b[1]) KevinStott 2 67+
(Kevin Ryan) *t.k.h early: mde all: qcknd clr jst bef 1/2-way: rdn 1f out: kpt on strly: eased fnl 75yds: unchal* **6/1**

U104 **2** 2 1/2 **Beadlam (IRE)**[13] 5355 3-9-3 **56**...................................... PJMcDonald 10 57
(David Loughnane) *hld up in midfield: hdwy on outside over 2f out: kpt on wl to take 2nd nr fin: no ch w eased-down wnr* **5/1**[3]

-060 **3** hd **Fire Diamond**[31] 4701 3-9-1 **54**..(t) BenCurtis 8 54
(Tom Dascombe) *chsd ldrs: hdwy to chse (clr) wnr over 2f out: sn rdn and edgd rt: kpt on fnl f: lost 2nd nr fin* **8/1**

0024 **4** nk **New Abbey Angel (IRE)**[8] 5539 3-9-7 **60**.....................(p) PhillipMakin 5 60
(Keith Dalgleish) *hld up: rdn along and outpcd over 2f out: hdwy over 1f out: kpt on ins fnl f: nvr able to chal* **5/2**[1]

6405 **5** 2 1/2 **Canford Belle**[13] 5355 3-8-11 **55**...................................... PhilDennis[(5)] 6 48
(Grant Tuer) *s.i.s: hld up: effrt whn nt clr run briefly 3f out: hdwy over 1f out: edgd rt and kpt on same pce fnl f* **17/2**

6 2 1/2 **Trump Card (IRE)**[43] 4283 3-8-7 **46** oh1...................(t) JamesSullivan 11 32
(Conor O'Dwyer, Ire) *s.i.s: hld up: rdn along over 3f out: sme late hdwy: nvr rchd ldrs* **14/1**

0604 **7** 4 **Stormy Art (IRE)**[18] 5197 3-8-11 **50**............................[1] PaulMulrennan 1 25
(Michael Dods) *in tch: effrt whn nt clr run over 2f out to over 1f out: sn rdn and btn* **4/1**[2]

604 **8** nk **Snappydresser**[29] 4766 3-9-2 **55**................................ RoystonFfrench 4 30
(Tracy Waggott) *chsd ldrs: drvn along over 2f out: wknd over 1f out* **28/1**

0006 **9** 3 3/4 **Trulove**[90] 2657 3-8-2 **46** oh1.. NathanEvans[(5)] 3 10
(John David Riches) *hld up ins: rdn along over 2f out: wknd over 1f out* **50/1**

0500 **10** 1/2 **Another Desperado (IRE)**[13] 5354 3-8-7 **46** oh1.......... BarryMcHugh 7 9
(Rebecca Bastiman) *t.k.h: chsd wnr to over 2f out: rdn and wknd wl over 1f out* **66/1**

1m 27.67s (-1.33) **Going Correction** -0.20s/f (Firm) **10** Ran SP% **114.7**
Speed ratings (Par 98): **99,96,95,95,92 89,85,84,80,80**
CSF £35.08 CT £248.31 TOTE £6.70: £1.90, £2.00, £3.00; EX 46.50 Trifecta £281.10.
Owner Hambleton Racing Ltd XLIV **Bred** Mrs M E Slade **Trained** Hambleton, N Yorks

FOCUS
Race distance increased by 14yds. Another all-the-way winner, and he's been rated value for further.

5804 RACING UK IN HD H'CAP 5f
5:05 (5:07) (Class 6) (0-60,60) 3-Y-O+ **£2,587** (£770; £384; £192) **Stalls** High

Form RPR

5045 **1** **See Vermont**[15] 5282 8-9-5 **58**..................................(p) PaulMulrennan 8 64
(Rebecca Bastiman) *prom: effrt and rdn over 1f out: led ins fnl f: drvn out* **11/2**

0004 **2** 1/2 **Sea Of Green**[16] 5277 4-8-8 **47**...................................... BarryMcHugh 12 51
(Jim Goldie) *hld up bhd ldng gp: pushed along after 2f: drvn and hdwy over 1f out: kpt on to take 2nd nr fin* **7/1**

2412 **3** nk **Thornaby Princess**[16] 5277 5-8-11 **50**....................(p) RoystonFfrench 6 53
(Colin Teague) *prom: effrt and drvn along 2f out: kpt on fnl f: no ex and lost 2nd nr fin* **9/2**[3]

0005 **4** 1 3/4 **Amber Crystal**[7] 5582 4-8-10 **49**... TomEaves 1 46
(Linda Perratt) *wnt rt s: bhd and sn outpcd: hdwy over 1f out: kpt on fnl f: nt pce to chal* **12/1**

5266 **5** 3/4 **Chookie's Lass**[21] 5078 5-9-7 **60**....................................(p) JasonHart 13 54
(Keith Dalgleish) *led to 1/2-way: drvn and no ex fr over 1f out* **11/4**[1]

0003 **6** hd **Lowrie**[20] 5110 3-8-9 **55**...(p) NathanEvans[(5)] 9 48
(John David Riches) *w ldr: led gng wl 1/2-way: rdn and drifted rt fr over 1f out: hdd ins fnl f: sn btn* **9/1**

4440 **7** 6 **Pavers Star**[13] 5354 7-8-13 **52**..(p) JoeFanning 2 24
(Noel Wilson) *prom on outside: drvn along 1/2-way: wknd over 1f out* **7/2**[2]

00-5 **8** 27 **Dutch Dream**[118] 1839 3-9-3 **58**.. ShaneGray 3
(Linda Perratt) *s.v.s: t.o thrght* **22/1**

58.65s (-1.75) **Going Correction** -0.45s/f (Firm)
WFA 3 from 4yo+ 2lb **8** Ran SP% **117.0**
Speed ratings (Par 101): **96,95,94,91,90 90,80,37**
CSF £44.36 CT £189.06 TOTE £4.90: £1.70, £2.50, £1.70; EX 35.20 Trifecta £200.30.
Owner John Smith **Bred** Oakhill Stud **Trained** Cowthorpe, N Yorks
■ It's Time For Bed was withdrawn. Price at time of withdrawal 50-1. Rule 4 does not apply.

FOCUS
A weak sprint. The winner has been rated slightly higher than this year's previous form.
T/Plt: £36.00 to a £1 stake. Pool: £48,681.55 - 985.79 winning units T/Qpdt: £13.90 to a £1 stake. Pool: £3,255.55 - 173.00 winning units **Richard Young**

5604 WOLVERHAMPTON (A.W) (L-H)
Thursday, August 25

OFFICIAL GOING: Tapeta: standard
Wind: Light; half behind Weather: Overcast; rain from race 3

5805 GREENHOUS DAF SHREWSBURY AMATEUR RIDERS' H'CAP 1m 4f 50y (Tp)
6:15 (6:15) (Class 5) (0-70,70) 3-Y-O+ **£2,807** (£870; £435; £217) **Stalls** Low

Form RPR

6122 **1** **Duke Of Yorkshire**[24] 4934 6-10-6 **67**.....................(p) MissEEasterby[(5)] 5 72+
(Tim Easterby) *hld up in midfield: 5th and stl plenty to do whn swtchd rt over 1f out: urged along and hdwy ent fnl f: str run ins fnl f to ld towards fin* **6/4**[1]

451U **2** 3/4 **Jersey Jewel (FR)**[18] 5208 4-10-9 **70**.................[1] MissCAGreenway[(5)] 6 74
(Tom Dascombe) *pressed ldr tl led 4f out: rdn 3 l clr 2f out: drvn fnl f: hdd and no ex towards fin* **11/2**

3423 **3** 1/2 **Cool Music (IRE)**[21] 5083 6-10-1 **57**.........................(p) MissSBrotherton 8 60
(Antony Brittain) *t.k.h: chsd ldng pair: effrt over 2f out: drvn to chse wnr ent fnl f: edgd lft and kpt on same pce ins fnl f* **4/1**[3]

0006 **4** 2 1/2 **Estibdaad (IRE)**[10] 5471 6-10-6 **67**...........................(t) MissMBryant[(5)] 1 66
(Paddy Butler) *led tl 4f out: chsd ldr tl rdn and unable qck over 1f out: kpt on same pce ins fnl f* **16/1**

0654 **5** 2 **Sakhra**[20] 5100 5-9-4 **51** oh6.. MrHHunt[(5)] 4 47
(Mark Brisbourne) *hld up in midfield: 4th and effrt over 3f out: kpt on same pce and no imp fnl 2f* **33/1**

60U6 **6** 1 1/4 **Kissy Suzuki**[31] 4716 4-9-11 **60**................................. MissGDucker[(7)] 3 54+
(Hughie Morrison) *stdd s: hld up off the pce in last pair: pushed along and stl plenty to do over 2f out: sme hdwy 1f out: kpt on: nvr trbld ldrs* **3/1**[2]

001/ **7** 3 3/4 **Fujin Dancer (FR)**[588] 8162 11-11-0 **70**.......................... MissHBethell 7 58+
(Harriet Bethell) *stdd s: hld up off the pce in rr: shkn up over 1f out: edgd lft and nt clrest of runs 1f out: no imp fnl f: n.d* **22/1**

-050 **8** 1 1/4 **Powderonthebonnet (IRE)**[8] 1399 8-9-6 **55**............. MissHTLees[(7)] 2 41
(Richard Phillips) *midfield: 6th and rdn over 3f out: sn outpcd: bhd fnl f* **66/1**

2m 48.79s (7.99) **Going Correction** +0.10s/f (Slow) **8** Ran SP% **115.0**
Speed ratings (Par 103): **77,76,76,74,73 72,69,69**
CSF £10.31 CT £27.48 TOTE £2.50: £1.10, £2.40, £1.60; EX 13.00 Trifecta £28.60.
Owner Habton Farms **Bred** Redhill Bloodstock & Tweenhills Stud **Trained** Great Habton, N Yorks

FOCUS
Standard Tapeta and dry conditions ahead of the opener, a moderate amateur riders' handicap in which they went a stop-start gallop. Straightforward form.

5806 TRP HALESOWEN NURSERY H'CAP 5f 216y (Tp)
6:45 (6:46) (Class 6) (0-65,64) 2-Y-O **£2,264** (£673; £336; £168) **Stalls** Low

Form RPR

005 **1** **White Chin (IRE)**[45] 4203 2-9-7 **64**......................... RichardKingscote 10 74
(Tom Dascombe) *s.i.s: hld up in tch in last pair: c wd and effrt wl over 1f out: rdn and str run to ld jst ins fnl f: sn clr and eased towards fin* **16/1**

4543 **2** 3 1/4 **Champion Harbour (IRE)**[16] 5265 2-9-6 **63**..................... DavidNolan 8 62
(Richard Fahey) *t.k.h: hld up in tch in last quartet: effrt and swtchd rt over 1f out: hdwy to chse clr wnr over 100yds out: styd on but no threat to wnr* **6/1**[3]

044 **3** 3/4 **Dark Hero (IRE)**[85] 2786 2-9-6 **63**.......................... MichaelJMMurphy 5 60
(Charles Hills) *broke wl: sn stdd and hld up in tch in midfield: effrt 2f out: swtchd rt over 1f out: kpt on u.p ins fnl f: no threat to wnr* **8/1**

662 **4** 3/4 **Seprani**[16] 5257 2-9-7 **64** SaleemGolam 1 59
(Mrs Ilka Gansera-Leveque) *sn led: hdd after 1f and chsd ldr tl 4f out: styd chsng ldr: rdn 2f out: ev ch 1f out: styd on same pce u.p ins fnl f* **16/1**

054 **5** nse **Equity**[16] 5265 2-9-6 **63** OisinMurphy 2 58
(David Brown) *stdd after s: t.k.h: hld up in tch in midfield: effrt on inner 2f out: drvn to chse ldrs 1f out: styd on same pce ins fnl f* **11/4**[2]

0554 **6** hd **Xenon**[15] 5299 2-9-5 **62** LukeMorris 3 56
(Sir Mark Prescott Bt) *chsd ldr after 1f: rdn over 2f out: drvn and clsd over 1f out: ev ch 1f out: styd on same pce ins fnl f* **16/1**

065 **7** 1 **In The Spotlight (IRE)**[23] 4988 2-9-4 **61** ShaneKelly 4 52
(Richard Hughes) *broke in midfield: pushed up to ld after 1f: racd keenly in front and nvr totally settled: rdn wl over 1f out: drvn 1f out: sn hdd and btn: fdd fnl 100yds* **5/4**[1]

2504 **8** shd **Vinnievanbaileys**[22] 5015 2-9-4 **64** (b) JosephineGordon(3) 6 55
(Chris Dwyer) *sn dropped to last pair: effrt and swtchd rt 2f out: kpt on but no threat to ldrs* **40/1**

640 **9** 3/4 **Control Centre (IRE)**[56] 3813 2-8-11 **59** HollieDoyle(5) 9 47
(Richard Hannon) *hld up in tch in last quartet: rdn and unable over 1f out: wknd ins fnl f* **33/1**

1m 15.01s (0.51) **Going Correction** +0.10s/f (Slow) **9** Ran SP% **119.5**
Speed ratings (Par 92): **100,95,94,93,93 93,92,91,90**
CSF £112.28 CT £850.01 TOTE £16.50: £4.40, £1.50, £2.10; EX 95.60 Trifecta £1480.80.
Owner T Dascombe **Bred** Old Carhue & Graeng Bloodstock **Trained** Malpas, Cheshire

FOCUS
A weak nursery run a strong pace, which suited the ready winner.

5807 GREENHOUS DAF WOLVERHAMPTON H'CAP 5f 216y (Tp)
7:15 (7:15) (Class 6) (0-65,65) 3-Y-O+ **£2,264** (£673; £336; £168) **Stalls** Low

Form RPR

5420 **1** **Whipphound**[13] 5368 8-8-6 **50** (p) RachelRichardson(3) 6 56
(Ruth Carr) *t.k.h: chsd ldrs: hmpd after 1f: effrt over 1f out: rdn and hdwy 1f out: led 75yds out: r.o wl: rdn out* **11/1**

2262 **2** 3/4 **Jack The Laird (IRE)**[10] 5470 3-9-6 **64** (v[1]) RobertWinston 9 68
(Dean Ivory) *t.k.h: chsd ldrs and carried lft early: chsd ldr over 1f out: rdn to ld over 1f out: hdd and one pce fnl 75yds* **2/1**[1]

0403 **3** nk **Coquine**[13] 5369 3-8-9 **58** JoshDoyle(5) 8 61
(David O'Meara) *dwlt and pushed along early: rdn and hdwy over 1f out: swtchd lft ins fnl f: styd on wl towards fin* **10/1**

4423 **4** 1/2 **Only Ten Per Cent (IRE)**[13] 5368 8-9-9 **64** (v) FrederikTylicki 5 65
(J R Jenkins) *hld up in tch in midfield: effrt on inner 1f out: hdwy to chse ldrs 1f out: styd on same pce u.p fnl 100yds* **6/1**[3]

6100 **5** 1 **Storm Lightning**[6] 5605 7-9-9 **64** GeorgeBaker 4 62
(Mark Brisbourne) *bhd: hdwy 1f out: rdn ins fnl f: styd on wl fnl 100yds: nt rch ldrs* **7/1**

0544 **6** 1 **Arlecchino's Rock**[6] 5605 3-9-3 **61** (p) LiamKeniry 10 56
(Mark Usher) *w ldr and grad moving lft to inner after s: led over 4f out: rdn and hdd over 1f out: wknd fnl 100yds* **11/2**[2]

5005 **7** 2 3/4 **State Of The Union (IRE)**[17] 5236 4-9-10 **65** (t) StevieDonohoe 3 52
(Willie Musson) *dwlt: hld up in last pair: pushed along and sme hdwy over 1f out: no imp ins fnl f: nvr trbld ldrs* **18/1**

4450 **8** nk **Camdora (IRE)**[16] 5270 4-9-6 **61** TimmyMurphy 7 47
(Jamie Osborne) *hld up in tch in midfield: pushed lft and hmpd after 1f: effrt over 1f out: no imp fnl f* **7/1**

4000 **9** 3 1/4 **Seraphima**[20] 5110 6-8-2 **46** oh1 (p) NoelGarbutt(3) 12 22
(Lisa Williamson) *taken down early: hld up in last trio: swtchd rt and effrt wl over 1f out: no hdwy: wknd fnl f* **100/1**

4020 **10** 1 3/4 **Sir Geoffrey (IRE)**[16] 5277 10-9-7 **62** (b) LukeMorris 2 33
(Scott Dixon) *led tl over 4f out: chsd ldr tl over 3f out: rdn and lost pl 2f out: bhd and eased ins fnl f* **16/1**

1m 14.84s (0.34) **Going Correction** +0.10s/f (Slow)
WFA 3 from 4yo+ 3lb **10** Ran SP% **117.6**
Speed ratings (Par 101): **101,100,99,98,97 96,92,92,87,85**
CSF £33.58 CT £237.34 TOTE £11.90: £3.00, £1.60, £3.40; EX 47.10 Trifecta £981.20.
Owner Mrs Ruth A Carr **Bred** Mrs B Skinner **Trained** Huby, N Yorks
■ Stewards' Enquiry : Liam Keniry four-day ban: careless riding (Sep 8,9,11,12)

FOCUS
A low-grade sprint handicap and there was plenty of early speed, suiting those coming from behind. The runner-up has been rated just below his latest 5f form.

5808 TRP SHREWSBURY H'CAP 7f 32y (Tp)
7:45 (7:47) (Class 6) (0-65,65) 3-Y-O+ **£2,264** (£673; £336; £168) **Stalls** High

Form RPR

4045 **1** **Brick Lane**[31] 4718 3-9-2 **63** JosephineGordon(3) 5 72+
(Robyn Brisland) *mde virtually all: rdn 2f out: kpt on wl u.p fnl f: rdn out* **6/1**[3]

2063 **2** 1 3/4 **Believe It (IRE)**[26] 4876 4-9-10 **63**[1] ShaneKelly 4 70
(Richard Hughes) *chsd ldrs: effrt to chse wnr 2f out: drvn 1f out: one pce and no imp after* **11/4**[1]

413 **3** 2 1/4 **Hardy Black (IRE)**[21] 5068 5-9-11 **64** (p) LukeMorris 1 65
(Kevin Frost) *chsd ldrs: effrt in 3rd 2f out: drvn and unable qck over 1f out: 3rd and hld ins fnl f: wkng towards fin* **5/1**[2]

5004 **4** nk **Bahamian Boy**[17] 5248 3-8-11 **60** (v[1]) CharlieBennett(5) 7 58+
(Hughie Morrison) *dwlt: hld up in tch in midfield: rdn and hdwy 2f out: drvn to chse ldng pair 1f out: kpt on u.p: no threat to ldng pair* **14/1**

4400 **5** 3 **Little Indian**[9] 5509 6-9-5 **58** FrederikTylicki 9 51
(J R Jenkins) *hld up in tch in midfield: rdn and unable qck over 1f out: wknd ins fnl f* **12/1**

2035 **6** 1 3/4 **Grey Destiny**[20] 5132 6-9-5 **58** (p) DavidAllan 12 50
(Antony Brittain) *s.i.s: bhd: nt clr run over 2f out: hdwy and nt clr run on inner over 1f out: sn swtchd rt: sltly impeded jst ins fnl f: styd on fnl 100yds: nvr trbld ldrs* **17/2**

3055 **7** nk **Gavarnie Encore**[14] 5326 4-9-0 **53** KieranO'Neill 8 41
(Michael Blanshard) *stdd after s: hld up towards rr: swtchd rt and effrt 2f out: drvn over 1f out: kpt on u.p but nvr trbld ldrs* **15/2**

4350 **8** shd **Hilltop Ranger (IRE)**[27] 4844 3-9-7 **65** RichardKingscote 2 51
(Daniel Kubler) *hld up towards rr: nt clr run and swtchd rt jst over 2f out: hdwy and switching lft 1f out: styd on ins fnl f: nvr trbld ldrs* **12/1**

3605 **9** 1/2 **Fossa**[3] 5706 6-8-11 **50** WilliamCarson 10 37
(Mark Brisbourne) *dwlt: hld up in last pair: nt clr run over 2f out: swtchd rt and wd wl over 1f out: edging lft u.p 1f out: nvr trbld ldrs* **28/1**

6000 **10** 10 **Rupert Boy (IRE)**[12] 5386 3-9-2 **60** (b) DaleSwift 3 20
(Scott Dixon) *sn bustled up to press wnr on inner: rdn and lost pl rapidly 2f out: eased fnl f* **50/1**

000 **11** 8 **Baileys Perle (IRE)**[78] 3038 3-9-5 **63** (b[1]) SilvestreDeSousa 6 4
(Chris Dwyer) *in tch in midfield: rdn and lost pl over 2f out: eased fr jst over 1f out* **16/1**

520 **12** 1 1/4 **Sea Of Uncertainty**[65] 3499 3-9-4 **62** TimmyMurphy 11
(James Evans) *chsd ldrs on outer tl 4f out: sn lost pl: bhd over 1f out* **33/1**

1m 28.69s (-0.11) **Going Correction** +0.10s/f (Slow)
WFA 3 from 4yo+ 5lb **12** Ran SP% **116.2**
Speed ratings (Par 101): **104,102,99,99,95 93,93,93,92,81 72,70**
CSF £21.93 CT £89.43 TOTE £6.80: £2.10, £1.80, £1.90; EX 25.90 Trifecta £137.90.
Owner Franconson Partners **Bred** D Curran **Trained** Newmarket, Suffolk

FOCUS
A fairly weak handicap and it paid to be up with the steady pace. The first two home were well backed throughout the day. The runner-up has been rated to his best.

5809 IMPERIAL COMMERCIALS HALESOWEN DAF MAIDEN AUCTION STKS 7f 32y (Tp)
8:15 (8:17) (Class 6) 2-Y-O **£2,264** (£673; £336; £168) **Stalls** High

Form RPR

03 **1** **Let's Be Happy (IRE)**[21] 5052 2-9-0 0 ShaneKelly 4 63
(Richard Hughes) *hld up in tch in last trio: smooth hdwy on outer 3f out: trcking ldrs 2f out: rdn to ld 1f out: hrd pressed towards fin: hld on* **11/1**

4 **2** hd **Flood Defence (IRE)**[22] 5022 2-9-0 0 FergusSweeney 8 63
(Chris Wall) *hld up in tch in midfield: rdn over 2f out: hdwy u.p 1f out: str chal towards fin: hld cl home* **4/1**[2]

06 **3** 1 3/4 **All About The Pace**[51] 3986 2-9-0 0 LiamKeniry 3 58
(Mark Usher) *s.i.s: hld up in tch in last trio: hdwy to chse ldrs 2f out: swtchd lft 1f out: kpt on u.p ins fnl f: wnt 3rd towards fin* **25/1**

00 **4** hd **Tael O' Gold**[52] 3947 2-9-0 0 SilvestreDeSousa 7 58
(Iain Jardine) *sn led: drifted rt and rdn wl over 1f out: drvn and hdd 1f out: no ex and outpcd fnl 75yds* **9/1**

450 **5** 3/4 **Cape Falcone**[17] 5242 2-9-0 64[1] LukeMorris 5 56
(James Tate) *chsd ldr after 1f: rdn and ev ch 1f out: drvn and unable qck 1f out: no ex and wknd wl ins fnl f* **4/1**[2]

6 1 3/4 **Shiny** 2-9-5 0 WilliamCarson 2 57
(Jamie Osborne) *hld up in tch in midfield: nt clr run and swtchd rt over 2f out: chsng ldrs whn pushed rt and hmpd wl over 1f out: keeping on same pce whn nt clr run and swtchd rt again wl ins fnl f* **12/1**

00 **7** 3 1/2 **Nobility (IRE)**[10] 5476 2-9-5 0 DavidAllan 1 48
(Tim Easterby) *t.k.h: led: sn hdd and chsd ldng pair after 1f: rdn and struggling 2f out: sn lost pl: wknd ins fnl f* **8/1**[3]

8 5 **Shiny Line (IRE)** 2-9-0 0 JFEgan 9 31+
(John Butler) *v.s.a: rcvrd and in tch after 2f: bdly hmpd wl over 1f out: nt rcvr and n.d after* **28/1**

04 **U** **Broughtons Story**[21] 5077 2-9-5 0 StevieDonohoe 6 57+
(Willie Musson) *chsd ldng pair: pushed along whn pushed rt: clipped heels: stmbld bdly and uns rdr over 1f out* **9/4**[1]

1m 31.22s (2.42) **Going Correction** +0.10s/f (Slow) **9** Ran SP% **115.2**
Speed ratings (Par 92): **90,89,87,87,86 84,80,74,**
CSF £54.56 TOTE £11.30: £2.80, £1.60, £5.40; EX 49.60 Trifecta £652.60.
Owner Catch The Pigeon Syndicate **Bred** Cbs Bloodstock & John O' Connor **Trained** Upper Lambourn, Berkshire

FOCUS
A modest maiden in which the favourite came down on the home bend, causing interference to several runners. The fifth helps confirm this as modest form.

5810 TRP WOLVERHAMPTON H'CAP 7f 32y (Tp)
8:45 (8:47) (Class 4) (0-80,80) 3-Y-O+ **£4,690** (£1,395; £697; £348) **Stalls** High

Form RPR

1005 **1** **Arlecchino's Leap**[36] 4519 4-9-11 **79** (p) LiamKeniry 4 88
(Mark Usher) *trckd ldng trio: clsd and upside ldr on bit over 1f out: shkn up and qcknd to ld ins fnl f: sn in command: comf* **14/1**

0003 **2** 3/4 **Rosenborg Rider (IRE)**[26] 4881 3-9-0 **73** FMBerry 12 78
(Ralph Beckett) *sn chsng ldr: drvn to ld over 1f out: hdd ins fnl f: styd on same pce after* **4/1**[3]

3120 **3** 1/2 **Inexes**[34] 4608 4-9-8 **76** (p) SamJames 7 82
(Marjorie Fife) *hld up in tch in midfield: effrt to chse ldrs and nt clr run 1f out: sn swtchd rt: kpt on u.p fnl 100yds* **16/1**

1355 **4** 2 3/4 **Rocket Power**[45] 4211 3-9-5 **78** LukeMorris 6 75
(James Tate) *chsd ldrs: rdn 2f out: drvn and unable qck over 1f out: wknd ins fnl f* **3/1**[2]

1411 **5** nk **Eljaddaaf (IRE)**[31] 4714 5-9-10 **78** RobertWinston 5 79
(Dean Ivory) *hld up in tch in midfield: effrt on inner over 1f out: nt clr run and swtchd rt ins fnl f: styd on wl ins fnl f: no threat to wnr* **7/4**[1]

-220 **6** nk **Great Fun**[21] 5075 5-9-10 **78**[1] TimmyMurphy 3 78
(Michael Blake) *broke wl: stdd bk and wl in tch in midfield: effrt over 1f out: squeezed for room and hmpd 1f out: styd on ins fnl f: no threat to wnr* **33/1**

6050 **7** 2 3/4 **Pivotman**[24] 4933 8-9-1 **72** (t) RachelRichardson(3) 8 62
(Michael Easterby) *hld up in last trio: effrt wl over 1f out: kpt on but no real imp: nvr trbld ldrs* **14/1**

1003 **8** 1 3/4 **Pushaq (IRE)**[21] 5082 3-9-5 **78** (b) DanielMuscutt 10 61
(Marco Botti) *t.k.h: sn led: rdn and hdd over 1f out: sn drifted rt: wknd qckly ins fnl f* **10/1**

0100 **9** 1 1/4 **Shamlan (IRE)**[51] 3989 4-9-3 **71** (t) ShaneKelly 2 53
(Johnny Farrelly) *a towards rr: rdn and no hdwy 2f out: n.d* **14/1**

6500 **10** 8 **Moonlight Venture**[68] 3421 5-9-2 **73** (b) JosephineGordon(3) 9 34
(Conor Dore) *a bhd: n.d* **50/1**

1m 29.17s (0.37) **Going Correction** +0.10s/f (Slow)
WFA 3 from 4yo+ 5lb **10** Ran SP% **121.2**
Speed ratings (Par 105): **101,100,99,96,96 95,92,90,89,80**
CSF £72.16 CT £957.97 TOTE £16.10: £3.80, £2.10, £4.40; EX 77.30 Trifecta £621.70.
Owner K Senior **Bred** J K Beckitt & Son **Trained** Upper Lambourn, Berks

FOCUS
The feature race was a fair handicap, although a steady pace caused several hard luck stories in behind. A minor pb from the winner.

5811 IMPERIAL COMMERCIALS SERVICE & BODYSHOP MAIDEN STKS 1m 1f 103y (Tp)
9:15 (9:16) (Class 5) 3-Y-O+ **£2,911** (£866; £432; £216) **Stalls** Low

Form RPR

0 **1** **Acrux**[26] 4857 3-9-5 0 GeorgeBaker 1 84+
(David Lanigan) *hld up in tch in midfield: wnt 3rd and travelling strly over 3f out: rdn to ld ins fnl f: sn in command: pushed out: comf* **6/4**[2]

34 **2** 1 1/4 **La Contessa (IRE)**[32] 4682 3-9-0 0 DavidNolan 2 75
(Richard Fahey) *chsd ldr for 2f: chsd ldrs tl wnt 2nd again 4f out: rdn to ld 2f out: edgd lft u.p 1f out: sn hdd and one pce ins fnl f* **11/10**[1]

3405 **3** 8 **Jayjinski (IRE)**[6] 5609 3-9-5 73 ShaneKelly 5 65
(Richard Hughes) *chsd ldrs tl hdwy to ld over 6f out: rdn and hdd 2f out: 3rd and outpcd whn swtchd rt 1f out: sn wknd* **4/1**[3]

00- **4** *4 ½* **Moon Arrow (IRE)**[304] 7518 3-9-5 0 TimmyMurphy 7 56
(Michael Blake) *s.i.s: hld up in last trio: lost tch w ldng trio and swtchd rt over 2f out: wnt modest 4th wl over 1f out: no imp* **33/1**

0 **5** *12* **Rayanne**[20] 5129 3-9-0 0 PatrickMathers 9 28
(Sarah Hollinshead) *hld up in last trio: nvr on terms: rdn over 3f out: lost tch over 2f out* **50/1**

3 **6** *¾* **Hangman Jury**[6] 5608 3-9-5 0 RyanTate 6 32
(Richard Hughes) *t.k.h: hld up in tch in midfield: rdn and outpcd 3f out: sn wknd and bhd fnl 2f* **20/1**

7 *nk* **Sir Jack** 3-9-5 0 LukeMorris 8 31
(Tony Carroll) *s.i.s: t.k.h: rn green in rr: lost tch wl over 2f out: no ch and hung lft over 1f out* **8/1**

05 **8** *19* **Bettercallphoenix**[32] 4690 3-9-5 0 DavidAllan 4
(David C Griffiths) *led tl 7f out: chsd ldr tl 4f out: sn rdn and struggling: wknd wl over 2f out: t.o and eased ins fnl f* **66/1**

2m 0.88s (0.08) **Going Correction** +0.10s/f (Slow) **8** Ran SP% **129.9**
Speed ratings (Par 103): **103,101,94,90,80 79,79,62**
CSF £4.08 TOTE £2.60: £1.40, £1.10, £1.50; EX 4.70 Trifecta £11.90.
Owner Niarchos Family **Bred** Niarchos Family **Trained** Newmarket, Suffolk

FOCUS
The betting suggested it was between the first two in the market, and they came well clear of the third. It's been rated a shade more positively than might have been given the race average.
T/Jkpt: Not won. T/Plt: £100.20 to a £1 stake. Pool: £87,584.18 - 637.75 winning units T/Qpdt: £30.80 to a £1 stake. Pool: £7,972.02 - 191.02 winning units **Steve Payne**

5812 - 5813a (Foreign Racing) - See Raceform Interactive

5530 TIPPERARY (L-H)
Thursday, August 25

OFFICIAL GOING: Soft

5814a COOLMORE STUD FAIRY BRIDGE STKS (GROUP 3) (F&M) 7f 100y
5:40 (5:40) 3-Y-O+ **£28,198** (£9,080; £4,301; £1,911)

RPR

1 **Tanaza (IRE)**[39] 4435 3-9-0 105 PatSmullen 1 110+
(D K Weld, Ire) *cl up tl sn disp and led briefly: settled in 2nd tl impr gng best to ld narrowly over 1f out: rdn clr ins fnl f and styd on wl* **9/4**[2]

2 *3 ½* **Creggs Pipes (IRE)**[30] 4747 4-9-5 108 DeclanMcDonogh 5 104
(Andrew Slattery, Ire) *broke wl to ld tl sn jnd and hdd briefly: over 1 l clr at 1/2-way: pushed along over 2f out and pressed: sn rdn and hdd u.p over 1f out: no imp on wnr wl ins fnl f: kpt on same pce* **8/15**[1]

3 *9* **Lina De Vega (IRE)**[39] 4437 3-9-0 0 RonanWhelan 4 82
(P J Prendergast, Ire) *w.w bhd ldrs in 3rd: pushed along in 3rd appr st and no ex u.p fr under 2f out: one pce after* **8/1**[3]

4 *13* **World Of Good**[15] 5316 3-9-0 79 ShaneFoley 3 49
(John Joseph Murphy, Ire) *in rr thrght: pushed along appr st and sn no ex: wknd fnl 2f* **66/1**

1m 36.27s (96.27)
WFA 3 from 4yo 5lb **4** Ran SP% **108.6**
CSF £3.89 TOTE £4.00; DF 4.00 Trifecta £4.50.
Owner H H Aga Khan **Bred** His Highness The Aga Khan's Studs S C **Trained** Curragh, Co Kildare

FOCUS
The loss of Now Or Never was a blow and effectively turned it into a match. The winner was too classy for the runner-up who may have been feeling the effects of her hectic schedule. A pb from the winner.

5816a KILFRUSH STUD ABERGWAUN STKS (LISTED RACE) 5f
6:40 (6:40) 3-Y-O+
£23,860 (£7,683; £3,639; £1,617; £808; £404)

RPR

1 **Spirit Quartz (IRE)**[27] 4824 8-9-10 107 (p) ShaneFoley 1 111+
(Robert Cowell) *chsd ldrs far side early tl impr to dispute after 1f: led narrowly bef 1/2-way: rdn over 1f out and styd on wl to assert wl ins fnl f: comf* **12/1**

2 *2 ¼* **The Happy Prince (IRE)**[11] 5442 4-9-7 101 (t) SeamieHeffernan 6 100
(A P O'Brien, Ire) *chsd ldrs: 5th 1/2-way: hdwy between horses fr over 1f out: rdn into 2nd wl ins fnl f and kpt on wl: nt trble wnr* **4/1**[2]

3 *nk* **Ostatnia (IRE)**[14] 5340 4-9-2 87 (b) BillyLee 8 94
(W McCreery, Ire) *cl up early: 4th 1/2-way: rdn over 1f out and no imp on wnr wl ins fnl f: wnt 3rd clsng stages* **7/1**

4 *hd* **Gordon Lord Byron (IRE)**[18] 5217 8-10-0 114 ChrisHayes 5 105
(T Hogan, Ire) *chsd ldrs: 6th 1/2-way: sme hdwy bhd ldrs over 1f out and disp 2nd ins fnl f: no imp on wnr wl ins fnl f and dropped to 4th clsng stages* **5/1**[3]

5 *½* **Dikta Del Mar (SPA)**[20] 5135 4-9-2 82 (t) WayneLordan 2 91
(T Hogan, Ire) *edgd rt s and sltly hmpd: chsd ldrs: clsr in 3rd at 1/2-way: rdn 1 1/2f out and no imp on wnr ins fnl f: wknd into 5th clsng stages* **33/1**

6 *1 ¾* **Gracious John (IRE)**[40] 4413 3-9-5 106 DeclanMcDonogh 9 90
(David Evans) *led tl jnd after 1f: hdd narrowly bef 1/2-way: rdn over 1f out and sn wknd* **7/4**[1]

7 *1* **Byzantium**[11] 5442 4-9-2 90 (b[1]) RonanWhelan 4 82
(Edward Lynam, Ire) *bmpd sltly s and settled towards rr: last at 1/2-way: rdn under 2f out and no imp on ldrs u.p in 7th over 1f out: kpt on one pce* **20/1**

8 *10* **Stenographer (USA)**[137] 1368 3-9-5 100 KevinManning 3 51
(J S Bolger, Ire) *hmpd between horses s and settled towards rr: pushed along in 7th bef 1/2-way and sn no ex u.p: wknd to rr after 1/2-way: eased ins fnl f* **13/2**

58.7s (-0.30)
WFA 3 from 4yo+ 2lb **8** Ran SP% **114.3**
CSF £59.34 TOTE £10.60: £3.20, £1.70, £1.90; DF 64.60 Trifecta £807.30.
Owner Ecurie La Boetie **Bred** Ballygallon Stud Ltd **Trained** Six Mile Bottom, Cambs

FOCUS
A second Irish win this term for an 8yo British sprinter. The home defence was not quite equal to the task, a familiar story in Irish sprints at Listed and Group 3 level. The runner-up has been rated to his turf form, with the third to a small pb and the fifth to a similar level as she ran in this race last year.

5815 - 5818a (Foreign Racing) - See Raceform Interactive

5733 CLAIREFONTAINE (R-H)
Thursday, August 25

OFFICIAL GOING: Turf: soft

5819a PRIX LES ABAT-JOUR D'ILLUMINE (CLAIMER) (2YO COLTS & GELDINGS) (TURF) 1m
1:20 (12:00) 2-Y-O **£6,985** (£2,794; £2,095; £1,397; £698)

RPR

1 **Sunday Winner (FR)**[24] 4965 2-9-1 0 (b) StephanePasquier 9 67
(Y Gourraud, France) **6/1**[3]

2 *1* **Disco Flash (FR)**[136] 2-8-11 0 (p) TheoBachelot 3 61
(M Boutin, France) **196/10**

3 *1* **Oncle Fernand (FR)**[24] 4965 2-9-5 0 OlivierPeslier 8 66
(C Bauer, France) **11/10**[1]

4 *1 ¼* **Rinky Dink Dawn (IRE)**[20] 5141 2-8-11 0 LouisBeuzelin 2 56
(J S Moore) *racd towards rr: shkn up and clsd fr 2f out: 7th and rdn 1 1/2f out: styd on to chse ldrs 1f out: one pce fnl f: nvr on terms* **102/10**

5 *2* **Silver Top (FR)**[8] 5568 2-8-10 0 KyllanBarbaud[(8)] 5 58
(N Caullery, France) **59/10**[2]

6 *nse* **Sowgay (FR)**[55] 3871 2-9-1 0 (b) AntonioPolli 6 55
(C Plisson, France) **70/1**

7 *1 ¼* **Nudge Nudge**[32] 2-8-11 0 (b[1]) HugoJourniac[(4)] 4 52
(D Windrif, France) **103/10**

8 *3 ½* **El Pampa King (FR)**[46] 4183 2-8-11 0 (b) MaximeGuyon 1 40
(J-V Toux, France) **32/5**

9 *12* **Soldier Black (FR)** 2-9-4 0 UmbertoRispoli 7 19
(A Giorgi, Italy) **171/10**

1m 40.3s (100.30) **9** Ran SP% **119.5**
WIN (incl. 1 euro stake): 7.00. PLACES: 1.80, 3.20, 1.40. DF: 50.50. SF: 90.70.
Owner Mme S Collin, M Arias & C Maquennehan **Bred** S.C.E.A. Des Prairies, Mme C Leclerc Et Al **Trained** France

5229 FFOS LAS (L-H)
Friday, August 26

OFFICIAL GOING: Good (good to soft in places) changing to good after race 1 (2.10)
Wind: fresh across Weather: fine

5820 BRITISH STALLION STUDS EBF MAIDEN STKS (PLUS 10 RACE) 7f 80y(R)
2:10 (2:12) (Class 4) 2-Y-O **£4,528** (£1,347; £673; £336) **Stalls** Low

Form RPR

344 **1** **Our Boy (IRE)**[63] 3598 2-9-5 77 JimCrowley 10 75
(David Evans) *t.k.h early: chsd ldrs: rdn over 2f out: drvn over 1f out: stl 3rd and looked hld 75yds out: str burst to ld post* **2/1**[2]

2 *shd* **Cuttin' Edge (IRE)** 2-9-5 0 GeorgeBaker 8 75
(William Muir) *trckd ldr: rdn 2f out: led ins fnl f: ct post* **8/1**

6 **3** *1 ½* **King Of Paris**[14] 5377 2-9-5 0 ShaneKelly 6 71
(Richard Hughes) *led: rdn over 1f out: drvn and hdd ins fnl f: no ex and lost 2nd towards fin* **6/1**[3]

42 **4** *2 ¾* **Arzaak (IRE)**[18] 5229 2-9-5 0 DaneO'Neill 4 64
(Owen Burrows) *mid-div: rdn to chse ldrs 2f out: one pce and no further imp* **7/4**[1]

6 **5** *6* **Proud Show**[29] 4805 2-9-5 0 LiamKeniry 7 49
(David Dennis) *hld up towards rr: shkn up 3f out: outpcd 2f out: kpt on steadily* **33/1**

00 **6** *shd* **John T Chance (IRE)**[16] 5304 2-8-12 0 JordanUys[(7)] 3 49
(Brian Meehan) *trckd ldrs: rdn over 2f out: wknd over 1f out* **40/1**

00 **7** *1 ¼* **Harlequin Rose (IRE)**[13] 5400 2-9-0 0 MartinLane 5 41
(Mick Channon) *in rr: swtchd rt 3f out: sn rdn: modest hdwy fnl f* **33/1**

8 *1 ¼* **Harry Beau** 2-9-5 0 KieranO'Neill 9 43
(Richard Hannon) *green in paddock: s.i.s: rdn 3f out: a in rr* **11/1**

9 *1* **Zulu** 2-9-5 0 SteveDrowne 2 40
(Rod Millman) *hld up in rr: rdn 3f out: wknd 2f out* **20/1**

0 **10** *½* **Mezyan (IRE)**[25] 4951 2-9-0 0 JFEgan 1 34
(David Evans) *mid-div: rdn 2f out: wknd over 1f out* **16/1**

1m 33.11s (0.11) **Going Correction** +0.10s/f (Good) **10** Ran SP% **122.4**
Speed ratings (Par 96): **103,102,101,98,91 91,89,88,87,86**
CSF £18.94 TOTE £3.40: £1.40, £1.80, £2.20; EX 21.60 Trifecta £84.60.
Owner Walters Plant Hire & Spiers & Hartwell **Bred** Tinnakill Bloodstock & Joe Osborne **Trained** Pandy, Monmouths

FOCUS
After 2mm of rain overnight the going was good, good to soft in places. They went a steady pace in this maiden and the first four pulled clear. The winner was not quite back to his pre-race best.

5821 RUGBY BETTING AT 188BET NURSERY H'CAP 6f
2:45 (2:46) (Class 4) (0-85,85) 2-Y-O **£3,946** (£1,174; £586; £293) **Stalls** Centre

Form RPR

5221 **1** **Looting**[7] 5598 2-9-1 **79** 6ex JimCrowley 1 87
(David Brown) *mde all: rdn over 1f out: drvn out and a in command fnl f* **4/6**[1]

1U0 **2** *1 ¾* **Berkshire Boy (IRE)**[90] 2682 2-9-2 **80** LiamKeniry 3 83
(Andrew Balding) *racd keenly: hld up: clsd 3f out: shkn up and wnt 2nd 2f out: drvn appr fnl f: unable qck and hld by wnr* **7/1**[3]

61 **3** *8* **Chaplin (FR)**[18] 5229 2-9-1 **79** ShaneKelly 2 58
(Richard Hughes) *trckd ldrs: rdn 2f out: sn outpcd by ldng pair and no ch: wknd fnl f but hld on to modest 3rd* **5/2**[2]

3120 **4** *nk* **Hedging (IRE)**[36] 4553 2-8-11 **75** JohnFahy 4 53
(Eve Johnson Houghton) *trckd wnr: rdn 2f out: sn lost 2nd: wknd over 1f out* **7/1**[3]

1m 10.22s (0.22) **Going Correction** +0.10s/f (Good) **4** Ran SP% **113.6**
Speed ratings (Par 96): **102,99,89,88**
CSF £6.26 TOTE £1.60; EX 6.90 Trifecta £16.50.
Owner J C Fretwell **Bred** Dunchurch Lodge Stud Company **Trained** Averham Park, Notts

FOCUS
The going was changed to good. Not many runners, but an unexposed improver delivered in good style and the first two pulled a long way clear.

5822 HUGH JAMES MAIDEN FILLIES' STKS — 1m (R)
3:20 (3:22) (Class 4) 3-Y-O+ — **£5,175** (£1,540; £769; £384) **Stalls** Low

Form — RPR

0-0 **1** **Lady Perignon**[16] 5300 3-9-0 0 ... LiamKeniry 1 — 78+
(Andrew Balding) *mde all: shkn up and qcknd pce over 2f out: drvn clr appr fnl f: pushed out* **20/1**

3463 **2** 3 **Shadow Spirit**[10] 5527 3-9-0 73 ... JimCrowley 6 — 71
(Iain Jardine) *chsd wnr thrght: drvn 2f out: sn outpcd: kpt on to hold 2nd* **9/4**[2]

3043 **3** ½ **Apache Song**[25] 4956 3-8-9 68 ... GeorgeWood(5) 4 — 70
(Rod Millman) *trckd ldrs: drvn 2f out: one pce* **4/1**[3]

-232 **4** ½ **Dheyaa (IRE)**[23] 5038 3-9-0 70 ... (b[1]) DaneO'Neill 5 — 69
(Owen Burrows) *chsd ldrs: rdn over 2f out: one pce* **1/1**[1]

-006 **5** 7 **Tea Gown (IRE)**[30] 4777 5-9-1 67 ... MeganNicholls(5) 3 — 54
(Ed de Giles) *s.i.s: in rr: hdwy on outer over 3f out: wknd over 1f out* **10/1**

0-5 **6** 15 **Mette**[24] 4991 3-9-0 0 ... SteveDrowne 2 — 18
(Rod Millman) *hld up: rdn 3f out: wknd 2f out: t.o* **33/1**

1m 41.49s (0.49) **Going Correction** +0.10s/f (Good)
WFA 3 from 5yo 6lb — **6** Ran SP% **117.6**
Speed ratings (Par 102): **101,98,97,97,90 75**
CSF £68.34 TOTE £16.60: £6.00, £1.70; EX 61.80 Trifecta £195.90.
Owner Mrs Fitri Hay **Bred** Newsells Park Stud **Trained** Kingsclere, Hants

FOCUS
An outsider scored with authority in this maiden having enjoyed a soft lead. Some questionable types in behind and the race has been rated around the third.

5823 O'BRIEN & PARTNERS H'CAP — 1m (R)
3:55 (3:55) (Class 6) (0-65,65) 3-Y-O+ — **£2,264** (£673; £336; £168) **Stalls** Low

Form — RPR

0201 **1** **African Showgirl**[22] 5055 3-9-1 60 ... SteveDrowne 5 — 65
(George Baker) *hld up: shkn up 4f out: hdwy on outer over 2f out: drvn to ld appr fnl f: idled and rdn out* **9/2**[2]

0564 **2** ½ **Aurora Gray**[6] 5627 3-9-4 63 ... JimCrowley 3 — 67
(Hughie Morrison) *mid-div: nt clr run 3f out tl over 1f out: drvn and r.o fnl f: wnt 2nd last strides* **2/1**[1]

5651 **3** hd **Edge (IRE)**[24] 4993 5-8-6 52 ... (b) MitchGodwin(7) 2 — 58
(Bernard Llewellyn) *s.i.s: hld up: hdwy on inner 3f out: nt clr run 2f out: r.o u.p to chse wnr wl ins fnl f: lost 2nd last strides* **9/2**[2]

6636 **4** ½ **Shongololo (IRE)**[23] 5013 3-9-1 60 ... LiamKeniry 4 — 62
(Andrew Balding) *chsd ldrs: led 2f out: drvn and hdd appr fnl f: no ex and lost 2 pls fnl 75yds* **13/2**

-045 **5** 3¾ **Peppard**[16] 5308 3-9-3 62 ... MichaelJMMurphy 1 — 55
(Charles Hills) *trckd ldr: led over 2f out: sn hdd: wkng whn hmpd 1f out* **7/1**

-306 **6** 1¾ **Henry Grace (IRE)**[60] 3732 5-8-10 49 ... (b) KieranO'Neill 7 — 39
(Jimmy Fox) *led 100yds: sn in mid-div: rdn 3f out: wknd over 1f out* **14/1**

1153 **7** 24 **Trending (IRE)**[174] 832 7-9-12 65 ... (tp) GeorgeBaker 8
(Jeremy Gask) *led after 100yds: hdd over 2f out: wknd qckly: t.o* **6/1**[3]

1m 40.88s (-0.12) **Going Correction** +0.10s/f (Good)
WFA 3 from 5yo+ 6lb — **7** Ran SP% **116.5**
Speed ratings (Par 101): **104,103,103,102,99 97,73**
CSF £14.45 CT £42.71 TOTE £5.30: £2.30, £1.70; EX 14.90 Trifecta £42.00.
Owner PJL Racing 1 **Bred** Ballabeg Stables **Trained** Manton, Wilts

FOCUS
They went a steady gallop in this ordinary handicap, but an in-form runner scored in decent style from off the pace. The third helps pin the level.

5824 £25 FREE BET AT 188BET H'CAP — 1m 2f (R)
4:30 (4:31) (Class 5) (0-70,76) 3-Y-O+ — **£2,911** (£866; £432; £216) **Stalls** Low

Form — RPR

446 **1** **Red Rose Riot (IRE)**[48] 4159 3-8-5 55 ow3 ... WilliamCarson 1 — 61
(David Menuisier) *s.i.s: sn mid-div: hdwy over 2f out: rdn over 1f out: edgd lft and r.o fnl f to ld nr fin* **12/1**

6564 **2** nk **Zoffanys Pride (IRE)**[22] 5071 3-9-6 70 ... LiamKeniry 6 — 75
(Andrew Balding) *a.p: drvn 2f out: led narrowly jst ins fnl f tl hdd nr fin* **8/1**[3]

6052 **3** nk **Free Passage**[19] 5207 3-9-1 65 ... DaneO'Neill 9 — 70
(Henry Candy) *led 2f: rdn and lost 2nd over 2f out: kpt on wl u.p: ev ch ins fnl f: jst hld* **5/2**[2]

5263 **4** ½ **Wallangarra**[16] 5308 3-9-1 65 ... JimCrowley 5 — 69
(Jeremy Gask) *s.i.s: racd keenly and sn trcking ldrs: led after 2f: drvn 2f out: hdd jst ins fnl f: unable qck* **10/1**

033 **5** hd **Princess Zoffany (IRE)**[48] 4159 3-8-1 51 oh3 ... KieranO'Neill 4 — 54
(Jimmy Fox) *mid-div: pushed along and clsd 3f out: drvn over 1f out: kpt on same pce fnl f: a jst hld* **7/1**

0-02 **6** 1 **Dream Ruler**[11] 5471 5-9-4 65 ... (tp) DavidParkes(5) 2 — 66
(Jeremy Gask) *trckd ldrs: rdn over 2f out: sn sltly outpcd: kpt on towards fin* **10/1**

4556 **7** ¾ **Frivolous Prince (IRE)**[2] 5777 3-8-1 51 ... (vt) RyanPowell 10 — 51
(David Evans) *mid-div: rdn over 2f out: styd on fnl f: nvr able to chal* **16/1**

0501 **8** 4 **Intercepted**[11] 5471 3-9-12 76 6ex ... GeorgeBaker 7 — 68+
(David Lanigan) *s.s: hld up: rdn 3f out: nvr any imp* **7/4**[1]

6003 **9** ½ **Papou Tony**[16] 5302 3-9-5 69 ... SteveDrowne 8 — 60+
(George Baker) *t.k.h: rdn 3f out: a towards rr* **11/1**

006 **10** 2¼ **Yamllik**[18] 5234 4-9-2 65 ... JoshuaBryan(7) 3 — 51+
(Brian Barr) *t.k.h in rr: rdn 3f out: wknd 2f out* **25/1**

2m 11.62s (2.22) **Going Correction** +0.10s/f (Good)
WFA 3 from 4yo+ 8lb — **10** Ran SP% **126.6**
Speed ratings (Par 103): **95,94,94,94,93 93,92,89,88,87**
CSF £113.21 CT £327.10 TOTE £15.80: £4.00, £1.90, £1.50; EX 138.40 Trifecta £771.10.
Owner Clive Washbourn **Bred** Wardstown Stud Ltd **Trained** Pulborough, W Sussex

FOCUS
They went a stop-start gallop and there was a bunch finish in this handicap. The form looks limited with the field so compressed.

5825 US OPEN TENNIS AT 188BET H'CAP — 6f
5:05 (5:08) (Class 3) (0-95,95) 3-Y-O **£7,561** (£2,263; £1,131; £566; £282) **Stalls** Centre

Form — RPR

0141 **1** **Cymraeg Bounty**[20] 5182 4-9-3 88 ... LiamKeniry 12 — 97
(Iain Jardine) *chsd ldrs: drvn and hung lft over 1f out: led jst ins fnl f: r.o* **3/1**[1]

3030 **2** ½ **Sir Billy Wright (IRE)**[25] 4954 5-9-0 85 ... JimCrowley 1 — 92
(David Evans) *chsd ldrs: drvn and ev ch over 1f out: edgd rt ins fnl f: jst hld* **6/1**[3]

4133 **3** nk **Ice Age (IRE)**[11] 5488 3-8-5 78 ow1 ... JohnFahy 4 — 85
(Eve Johnson Houghton) *mid-div: nt clr run over 2f out tl swtchd rt over 1f out: r.o fnl f* **7/2**[2]

01 **4** shd **Bouclier (IRE)**[66] 3487 6-8-11 82 ... JFEgan 10 — 88
(Tony Carroll) *t.k.h: chsd ldrs: drvn and sltly outpcd 2f out: r.o ins fnl f* **3/1**[1]

1300 **5** nk **Muir Lodge**[27] 4862 5-9-7 92 ... (t) SteveDrowne 9 — 97
(George Baker) *towards rr: rdn 2f out: sn drvn: r.o ins fnl f* **14/1**

400 **6** 1 **Shore Step (IRE)**[13] 5390 6-9-6 91 ... MartinLane 11 — 93
(Mick Channon) *chsd ldr: rdn to ld wl over 1f out: hdd jst ins fnl f: no ex and lost three pls towards fin* **8/1**

620 **7** 2 **Free Zone**[11] 5488 7-9-1 86 ... (v) WilliamCarson 5 — 82
(Jamie Osborne) *led: rdn and hdd wl over 1f out: keeping on whn hmpd and carried lft ins fnl f: no ch after* **18/1**

4610 **8** nk **Russian Realm**[99] 2391 6-9-8 93 ... ShaneKelly 3 — 88
(Richard Hughes) *s.i.s: hld up: rdn over 1f out: sn edgd lft and one pce* **10/1**

5200 **9** ½ **Air Of York (IRE)**[13] 5403 4-8-5 76 oh1 ... AdamBeschizza 2 — 69
(David Evans) *chsd ldrs: drvn over 2f out: wknd over 1f out* **33/1**

150- **10** 2¾ **Sun'Aq (IRE)**[250] 8316 3-8-12 86 ... RyanPowell 7 — 70
(Sir Mark Prescott Bt) *wnt lft s: hld up: rdn and hung lft 2f out: no ch whn hmpd over 1f out* **20/1**

10-6 **11** 8 **Threave**[56] 3857 8-9-1 86 ... DaneO'Neill 8 — 45
(Laura Mongan) *wnt to post early: s.i.s: in rr: rdn and wknd 2f out* **25/1**

1m 10.1s (0.10) **Going Correction** +0.10s/f (Good)
WFA 3 from 4yo+ 3lb — **11** Ran SP% **130.2**
Speed ratings (Par 107): **103,102,101,101,101 100,97,97,96,92 82**
CSF £23.74 CT £71.79 TOTE £5.50: £2.00, £2.80, £1.70; EX 24.10 Trifecta £87.90.
Owner M Andrews **Bred** Richard Evans **Trained** Carrutherstown, D'fries & G'way

FOCUS
They went a fair pace in this good handicap and the progressive 4yo scored with a bit in hand. The form makes sense around the front five.

5826 CP HIRE H'CAP — 5f
5:40 (5:41) (Class 6) (0-65,65) 3-Y-O+ — **£2,264** (£673; £336; £168) **Stalls** Centre

Form — RPR

3016 **1** **Satchville Flyer**[11] 5475 5-9-9 64 ... JimCrowley 7 — 74
(David Evans) *hld up: shkn up 1/2-way: drvn and hdwy over 1f out: led ins fnl f: r.o wl: edgd lft nr fin* **11/4**[2]

0326 **2** 2 **Diminutive (IRE)**[38] 4484 4-8-6 47 ... (p) JFEgan 2 — 50
(Grace Harris) *s.i.s: sn chsng ldrs: drvn 2f out: r.o: outpcd by wnr fnl 110yds* **7/1**

2153 **3** nk **Go Amber Go**[16] 5282 4-8-12 58 ... GeorgeWood(5) 4 — 60
(Rod Millman) *chsd ldrs: drvn 2f out: ev ch ins fnl f: one pce* **2/1**[1]

4300 **4** 1 **Cerulean Silk**[23] 5007 6-8-5 46 oh1 ... WilliamCarson 8 — 44
(Tony Carroll) *led towards stands' side: rdn 2f out: hdd and no ex ins fnl f* **14/1**

-456 **5** 2¾ **Ryan Style (IRE)**[22] 5060 10-8-6 47 ... (p) AdamBeschizza 6 — 35
(Lisa Williamson) *s.s: in tch in rr: rdn 1/2-way: r.o fnl f: nvr able to chal* **9/1**

5010 **6** 1½ **Molly Jones**[6] 5628 7-8-11 52 ... DaneO'Neill 5 — 35
(Matthew Salaman) *prom: rdn 2f out: wknd 1f out* **10/1**

24-4 **7** ½ **Shine Likeadiamond**[148] 1167 3-9-8 65 ... GeorgeBaker 3 — 46
(Mick Channon) *prom: drvn 2f out: wknd over 1f out* **5/1**[3]

0050 **8** 3 **Bapak Bangsawan**[171] 868 6-9-0 60 ... (v) AnnStokell(5) 1 — 30
(Ann Stokell) *chsd ldrs: rdn 2f out: wknd 1f out* **14/1**

58.85s (0.55) **Going Correction** +0.10s/f (Good)
WFA 3 from 4yo+ 2lb — **8** Ran SP% **121.6**
Speed ratings (Par 101): **99,95,95,93,89 86,86,81**
CSF £24.08 CT £48.04 TOTE £3.30: £1.30, £2.40, £1.20; EX 26.40 Trifecta £105.30.
Owner A Cooke & Lynn Cullimore 1 **Bred** Newsells Park Stud **Trained** Pandy, Monmouths

FOCUS
They went a decent pace and were spread across the track in this sprint handicap. The form looks atrightforward rated around the placed horses.
T/Plt: £70.10 to a £1 stake. Pool: £60,616.47 - 630.49 winning tickets T/Qpdt: £16.60 to a £1 stake. Pool: £5,160.44 - 229.67 winning tickets **Richard Lowther**

[4862] GOODWOOD (R-H)
Friday, August 26

OFFICIAL GOING: Good (good to firm in places on round course)
Wind: Light, across Weather: Sunny, very warm

5827 NYETIMBER APPRENTICE H'CAP — 6f
5:00 (5:00) (Class 5) (0-70,65) 3-Y-O+ — **£3,234** (£962; £481; £240) **Stalls** High

Form — RPR

4056 **1** **Quite A Story**[15] 5330 4-9-6 64 ... CharlieBennett(3) 5 — 69
(Patrick Chamings) *dwlt: towards rr: prog 1/2-way: rdn to chse clr ldr 2f out: clsd to ld ins fnl f and edgd rt: jst hld on* **6/1**[3]

3630 **2** shd **Secret Witness**[59] 3743 10-9-2 57 ... (b) DanielMuscutt 1 — 62
(Ronald Harris) *in tch in chsng gp: rdn over 2f out: clsd over 1f out to chal ins fnl f and edgd rt: w wnr last 75yds: jst failed* **5/1**[2]

-062 **3** 1 **Guanabara Bay (IRE)**[22] 5088 3-9-7 65 ... [1] LouisSteward 8 — 67
(Martyn Meade) *prom in chsng gp: lost pl 2f out: renewed effrt over 1f out: tk 3rd last 100yds: styd on but nvr quite able to chal* **9/2**[1]

5341 **4** 2 **Beau Mistral (IRE)**[21] 5105 7-8-13 59 ... (b) GeorgiaCox(5) 10 — 55
(Tony Carroll) *led and sn wl clr: hung rt thrght and bdly so fr 2f out: ended against far rail: wknd and hdd ins fnl f* **8/1**

5132 **5** 1½ **Pharoh Jake**[37] 4529 8-9-9 64 ... AaronJones 9 — 55
(John Bridger) *chsd clr ldr to 2f out: fdd* **10/1**

0050 **6** nse **Lucky Di**[15] 5330 6-9-7 65 ... HectorCrouch(3) 6 — 56
(Peter Hedger) *dwlt: wl in rr and off the pce: urged along and tried to cl fr 2f out: swtchd rt jst over 1f out: one pce and no threat* **5/1**[2]

06 **7** 3 **Diamond Vine (IRE)**[59] 3743 8-8-11 52 ... (p) RobHornby 7 — 34
(Ronald Harris) *in tch in chsng gp: rdn over 2f out: wknd over 1f out* **20/1**

3222 **8** 1½ **Essaka (IRE)**[23] 5007 4-9-5 60 ... TomMarquand 2 — 38
(Tony Carroll) *slowly away: a wl in rr and nvr able to rcvr* **5/1**[2]

6066 **9** 1½ **Equal Point**[29] 4796 3-8-6 57 ... AbbieWibrew(7) 3 — 30
(William Knight) *sn outpcd in last: nvr a factor* **33/1**

0030 **10** *7* **Noble Deed**[53] [3953] 6-9-3 **63**..[1] PaddyBradley(5) 4 33
(Michael Attwater) *prom in chsng gp tl wknd 2f out* **12/1**

1m 11.45s (-0.75) **Going Correction** -0.05s/f (Good)
WFA 3 from 4yo+ 3lb **10** Ran SP% **118.1**
Speed ratings (Par 103): **103,102,101,98,96 96,92,90,88,87**
CSF £36.60 CT £153.42 TOTE £8.70: £2.30, £2.10, £2.10; EX 41.90 Trifecta £241.10.
Owner Mildmay Racing & D H Caslon **Bred** Mildmay Bloodstock Ltd **Trained** Baughurst, Hants

FOCUS
The lower bend was dolled out 5yds increasing race distances on the round course by 10yds. This ordinary sprint handicap for apprentice riders was a messy affair as they spread all over the course. The form looks limited rated through the runner-up.

5828 CHICHESTER OBSERVER MAIDEN STKS (PLUS 10 RACE) 1m
5:35 (5:35) (Class 4) 2-Y-O **£5,175** (£1,540; £769; £384) **Stalls** Low

Form RPR
34 **1** **Khalidi**[49] [4103] 2-9-5 0.. RobertHavlin 1 85+
(John Gosden) *led after 1f: mde rest: rdn and hrd pressed 2f out: edgd lft over 1f out but styd on wl* **6/5**[1]

24 **2** *2½* **Celestial Spheres (IRE)**[44] [4274] 2-9-5 0.......................... JamesDoyle 5 79
(Charlie Appleby) *led 1f: trckd wnr: clsd to chal 2f out: sn rdn: hanging lft and nt qckn over 1f out: wl hld fnl f* **11/8**[2]

4 **3** *5* **Envisaging (IRE)**[30] [4775] 2-9-5 0.. TomQueally 4 67
(James Fanshawe) *t.k.h: trckd ldng pair: clsd 2f out: sn rdn and fnd nil: wknd fnl f* **5/1**[3]

4 *67* **Rupertcambellblack (IRE)** 2-9-2 0..................... GeorgeDowning(3) 2
(Ronald Harris) *rn green in last: lost tch over 3f out: t.o* **33/1**

1m 41.22s (1.32) **Going Correction** +0.025s/f (Good) **4** Ran SP% **107.2**
Speed ratings (Par 96): **94,91,86,19**
CSF £3.11 TOTE £2.20; EX 3.50 Trifecta £4.00.
Owner Nizar Anwar **Bred** Aston House Stud **Trained** Newmarket, Suffolk

FOCUS
Add 10yds to race distance. This modest 2yo maiden was predictably tactical and has been rated around the balance of the first three, but the winner might rate a good bit higher.

5829 DOOM BAR NURSERY H'CAP 7f
6:05 (6:06) (Class 4) (0-85,78) 2-Y-O **£5,175** (£1,540; £769; £384) **Stalls** Low

Form RPR
435 **1** **Procurator (IRE)**[14] [5356] 2-9-5 **77**................................ TomMarquand 3 82
(Richard Hannon) *t.k.h: hld up in tch: trckd ldr over 2f out: rdn to ld over 1f out: edgd lft fnl f: kpt on* **3/1**[3]

61 **2** *1* **Accidental Agent**[26] [4907] 2-9-6 **78**................................ CharlesBishop 2 80
(Eve Johnson Houghton) *mde most: rdn and hdd over 1f out: hld whn nudged by wnr 75yds out* **5/2**[2]

0311 **3** *nk* **Muirsheen Durkin**[15] [5318] 2-9-6 **78**.....................(p) RichardKingscote 5 79
(Tom Dascombe) *hld up in tch: chal on outer 2f out: nt qckn over 1f out: kpt on same pce fnl f and a hld* **3/1**[3]

01 **4** *100* **Seafarer (IRE)**[15] [5325] 2-9-2 **74**.. PatDobbs 4
(Marcus Tregoning) *dwlt: sn pressed ldr: rdn 3f out: lost pl and btn over 2f out: bhd whn virtually p.u over 1f out* **9/4**[1]

1m 28.51s (1.51) **Going Correction** +0.025s/f (Good) **4** Ran SP% **109.3**
Speed ratings (Par 96): **92,90,90,**
CSF £10.57 TOTE £3.70; EX 9.50 Trifecta £24.60.
Owner J Palmer-Brown & Potensis Bloodstock Ltd **Bred** Lisieux Stud **Trained** East Everleigh, Wilts

FOCUS
Add 10yds to race distance. This nursery was a fair contest, but it was another tactical race and there was a messy finish.

5830 BUTLINS STKS (H'CAP) 2m
6:40 (6:40) (Class 5) (0-70,68) 3-Y-O **£3,234** (£962; £481; £240) **Stalls** Low

Form RPR
2413 **1** **Clear Evidence**[15] [5331] 3-9-5 **66**.. JamesDoyle 3 79
(Michael Bell) *trckd ldr: clsd to chal 2f out: pushed into ld over 1f out: rdn out* **5/4**[1]

0131 **2** *2* **Tyrell (IRE)**[29] [4810] 3-9-3 **64**............................(b) WilliamTwiston-Davies 5 75
(Alan King) *led at decent pce: rdn and pressed 2f out: hdd over 1f out: kpt on wl but safely hld* **9/4**[2]

0041 **3** *9* **Top Of The Rocks (FR)**[15] [5319] 3-8-9 **56**...........(tp) RichardKingscote 4 56
(Tom Dascombe) *t.k.h early: trckd ldrs: rdn 3f out: sn lft bhd by ldng pair* **7/1**

0220 **4** *5* **Clive Clifton (IRE)**[13] [5397] 3-8-10 **62**............................ LucyKBarry(5) 1 56
(Phil York) *hld up in tch in last pair: rdn over 3f out: sn lft bhd* **33/1**

0233 **5** *4* **Argyle (IRE)**[13] [5398] 3-9-7 **68**.. MartinDwyer 2 57
(William Muir) *stdd s: tk fierce hold in last pair: plld way through to dispute 3rd 6f out: rdn over 3f out: wknd wl over 2f out* **5/1**[3]

0400 **6** *28* **Zebedee's Son (IRE)**[13] [5399] 3-8-0 **50**......................... NoelGarbutt(3) 7
(Phil York) *in tch to over 3f out: wknd qckly: t.o* **33/1**

3m 28.25s (-0.75) **Going Correction** +0.025s/f (Good) **6** Ran SP% **110.3**
Speed ratings (Par 100): **102,101,96,94,92 78**
CSF £4.08 TOTE £2.20: £1.10, £1.70; EX 4.30 Trifecta £13.80.
Owner The Queen **Bred** The Queen **Trained** Newmarket, Suffolk

FOCUS
Add 10yds to race distance. They steadied around halfway in this modest 3yo staying handicap and the market leaders dominated. A small step forward from the winner.

5831 BREEDERS BACKING RACING EBF FILLIES' STKS (H'CAP) 1m
7:10 (7:10) (Class 3) (0-95,90) 3-Y-O+ **£9,703** (£2,887; £1,443; £721) **Stalls** Low

Form RPR
-621 **1** **Rostova (USA)**[42] [4358] 3-9-6 **90**... TedDurcan 2 102+
(Sir Michael Stoute) *hld up in 4th: prog to chse ldr wl over 1f out and sn rdn: styd on wl fnl f to ld last strides* **15/8**[2]

-221 **2** *hd* **Laugh Aloud**[53] [3958] 3-9-1 **85**...(t) JamesDoyle 4 96
(John Gosden) *led at mod pce but untrbld: wound it up fr 1/2-way: stl gng easily 2f out: rdn and more than a l ahd fnl f: edgd lft but styd on: hdd last strides* **11/8**[1]

-603 **3** *4* **Starlit Cantata**[11] [5489] 5-8-12 **79**.............................. GeorgeDowning(3) 3 81
(Eve Johnson Houghton) *stdd s: hld up in last: rdn and tried to make prog 2f out: tk 3rd fnl f but no ch of threatening ldng pair* **16/1**

4-00 **4** *1¼* **Marsh Pride**[108] [2121] 4-9-4 **82**.................................... RichardKingscote 5 81
(K R Burke) *trckd ldr: rdn over 2f out: lost 2nd and fdd wl over 1f out* **5/1**[3]

3431 **5** *2¾* **Stosur (IRE)**[19] [5190] 5-8-6 **77**..(b) DavidEgan(7) 1 69
(Gay Kelleway) *chsd ldng pair: urged along 1/2-way: dropped to last over 2f out: sn btn* **12/1**

1m 38.1s (-1.80) **Going Correction** +0.025s/f (Good)
WFA 3 from 4yo+ 6lb **5** Ran SP% **107.1**
Speed ratings (Par 104): **110,109,105,104,101**
CSF £4.54 TOTE £2.80: £1.30, £1.30; EX 3.90 Trifecta £19.50.
Owner K Abdullah **Bred** Juddmonte Farms Inc **Trained** Newmarket, Suffolk

FOCUS
Add 10yds to race distance. They went steadily in this fair fillies' handicap and two progressive sorts came clear.

5832 ULTIMATE DRIVING STKS (H'CAP) 7f
7:45 (7:46) (Class 5) (0-75,75) 3-Y-O+ **£3,234** (£962; £481; £240) **Stalls** Low

Form RPR
3246 **1** **Little Miss Kodi (IRE)**[27] [4899] 3-9-3 **71**........................... FrannyNorton 2 78
(Daniel Mark Loughnane) *chsd ldng pair: rdn to cl on inner fr 2f out: led ins fnl f: drvn out* **4/1**[2]

6041 **2** *¾* **Consulting**[23] [5027] 3-9-5 **73**.. HarryBentley 7 78
(Martyn Meade) *chsd ldr: rdn to cl fr 2f out: upsides as wnr wnt past ins fnl f: styd on* **5/1**[3]

22 **3** *1* **Baltic Prince (IRE)**[21] [5104] 6-9-2 **68**....................... GeorgeDowning(3) 4 72
(Tony Carroll) *led at str pce and spread field: rdn 2f out: hdd and no ex ins fnl f* **9/1**

3312 **4** *½* **Golden Wedding (IRE)**[36] [4557] 4-9-11 **74**..................... CharlesBishop 6 77
(Eve Johnson Houghton) *hld up in 5th: shkn up to take 4th 2f out: kpt on one pce and nvr able to rch ldrs* **3/1**[1]

0033 **5** *½* **Live Dangerously**[18] [5241] 6-9-2 **65**.................................... DannyBrock 8 66
(John Bridger) *awkward s: hld up in 7th: prog on inner 3f out: hrd rdn and kpt on one pce fnl 2f* **12/1**

3661 **6** *1¾* **Clever Bob (IRE)**[34] [4639] 3-9-4 **72**..................................(t) SamHitchcott 3 67
(Joseph Tuite) *chsd clr ldrs: rdn 3f out: lost pl 2f out: wl btn after* **6/1**

1506 **7** *4½* **Operative**[17] [5253] 3-9-0 **75**...(p) GeorgiaCox(7) 1 57
(Ed de Giles) *slowly away: t.k.h early and hld up in last: struggling fr 3f out: nvr a factor* **13/2**

353 **8** *18* **Land Of Dubai (IRE)**[15] [5327] 3-8-13 **67**.................................. FMBerry 5 1
(Clive Cox) *chsd ldng trio to 3f out: wknd qckly and wl bhd over 1f out: t.o* **12/1**

0640 **9** *17* **Palace Moon**[22] [5055] 11-8-7 **56**...(t) KierenFox 11
(Michael Attwater) *a in rr: lost tch over 2f out: t.o* **33/1**

1m 26.93s (-0.07) **Going Correction** +0.025s/f (Good)
WFA 3 from 4yo+ 5lb **9** Ran SP% **117.6**
Speed ratings (Par 103): **101,100,99,98,97 95,90,70,50**
CSF £24.88 CT £172.30 TOTE £4.90: £1.60, £1.70, £2.80; EX 28.00 Trifecta £291.40.
Owner S & A Mares **Bred** Michael O'Dwyer **Trained** Baldwin's Gate, Staffs
■ Stewards' Enquiry : George Downing two-day ban;
F M Berry jockey said filly was never travelling

FOCUS
Add 10yds to race distance. The closers struggled to land a blow in this modest handicap, but the form looks sensible through the placed horses.
T/Plt: £89.00 to a £1 stake. Pool: £50,342.83 - 412.73 winning tickets T/Qpdt: £15.00 to a £1 stake. Pool: £4,381.60 - 215.72 winning tickets **Jonathan Neesom**

5576 HAMILTON (R-H)
Friday, August 26

OFFICIAL GOING: Good to soft (good in places; 6.6)
Wind: Fresh, half behind Weather: Overcast

5833 LADBROKES NURSERY H'CAP 6f 6y
5:20 (5:21) (Class 5) (0-75,74) 2-Y-O **£3,557** (£1,058; £529; £264) **Stalls** High

Form RPR
2411 **1** **Tawny Port**[42] [4364] 2-9-6 **73**.. TomEaves 6 79
(James Given) *trckd ldrs: hdwy to ld over 1f out: rdn and r.o wl fnl f* **4/1**[1]

4341 **2** *1¾* **Trick Of The Lyte (IRE)**[14] [5352] 2-8-13 **66**......................... CamHardie 2 67
(John Quinn) *hld up on outside: hdwy to chse wnr over 1f out: kpt on same pce wl ins fnl f* **4/1**[1]

44 **3** *1¼* **Bourbonisto**[48] [4167] 2-9-0 **67**.. DougieCostello 8 64
(Ben Haslam) *dwlt: hld up: rdn and hdwy over 1f out: kpt on ins fnl f* **12/1**

344 **4** *1* **Jamacho**[41] [4379] 2-9-5 **72**.. DaleSwift 4 66
(Brian Ellison) *pressed ldr: rdn and ev ch briefly over 1f out: kpt on same pce ins fnl f* **4/1**[1]

0002 **5** *shd* **Myllachy**[4] [5712] 2-8-0 **53** oh4... DuranFentiman 7 48
(Tim Easterby) *hld up: hdwy over 2f out: rdn whn blkd over 1f out: one pce fnl f* **6/1**[2]

5112 **6** *1½* **Racemaker**[9] [5536] 2-9-7 **74**... NeilFarley 10 66
(Andrew Crook) *trckd ldrs: rdn whn nt clr run over 1f out and ins fnl f: sn no ex* **17/2**[3]

B000 **7** *4½* **Gabridan (IRE)**[29] [4804] 2-8-2 **55** ow1................................ JoeFanning 5 32
(Richard Fahey) *prom on outside: effrt and rdn over 2f out: blkd over 1f out: sn outpcd* **14/1**

2332 **8** *shd* **Decadent Times (IRE)**[51] [4000] 2-9-3 **70**............................ SamJames 9 46
(Marjorie Fife) *led tl rdn and hdd over 1f out: sn btn* **25/1**

4030 **9** *3* **Bear Essentials (IRE)**[35] [4602] 2-9-2 **69**............................ PhillipMakin 1 36
(David O'Meara) *dwlt and wnt rt s: bhd: struggling over 2f out: btn over 1f out* **10/1**

1m 13.19s (0.99) **Going Correction** +0.175s/f (Good) **9** Ran SP% **112.1**
Speed ratings (Par 94): **100,97,96,94,94 92,86,86,82**
CSF £18.66 CT £172.79 TOTE £4.70: £1.70, £1.50, £2.70; EX 18.70 Trifecta £195.00.
Owner Tawny Port Ptners & Lovely Bubbly Racing **Bred** Mrs D O'Brien **Trained** Willoughton, Lincs

FOCUS
A sound pace and this appeals as solid form for the level, the winner looking progressive and the second and third both reasonable yardsticks.

5834 WHYSETTLE IT MAIDEN STKS 1m 67y
5:55 (5:57) (Class 5) 2-Y-O **£3,881** (£1,155; £577; £288) **Stalls** Low

Form RPR
2 **1** **Now Children (IRE)**[33] [4678] 2-9-5 0...................................... TomEaves 5 85+
(Iain Jardine) *t.k.h: prom: hdwy over 2f out: shkn up to ld over 1f out: edgd rt: kpt on strly fnl f* **3/1**[2]

2 *3½* **Euro Nightmare (IRE)** 2-9-0 0.. JasonHart 6 71
(Keith Dalgleish) *trckd ldr: rdn along over 2f out: ev ch briefly over 1f out: kpt on fnl f to take 2nd nr fin: no ch w wnr* **18/1**

42 **3** *½* **Sofia's Rock (FR)**[21] [5107] 2-9-5 0.................................... JoeFanning 4 75
(Mark Johnston) *t.k.h: led to over 1f out: kpt on same pce fnl f: lost 2nd nr fin* **8/15**[1]

4 *2* **Rock N Rolla (IRE)** 2-9-5 0... PhillipMakin 2 70
(Keith Dalgleish) *trckd ldrs: effrt and pushed along 2f out: outpcd fnl f* **12/1**[3]

06 **5** *8* **Jock Talk (IRE)**[42] [4336] 2-9-5 0.................................... TadhgO'Shea 3 52
(John Patrick Shanahan, Ire) *s.i.s: hld up in tch: rdn and outpcd over 2f out: btn over 1f out* **25/1**

6 16 **Master Degree (IRE)** 2-9-5 0 DougieCostello 1 15
(K R Burke) *s.i.s: hld up: rdn and struggling over 2f out: sn btn* **16/1**
1m 48.84s (0.44) **Going Correction** +0.175s/f (Good) **6** Ran SP% **112.9**
Speed ratings (Par 94): **104,100,100,98,90 74**
CSF £48.16 TOTE £4.30: £1.80, £8.00; EX 49.40 Trifecta £77.20.
Owner Paul & Clare Rooney **Bred** Old Carhue & Graeng Bloodstock **Trained** Carrutherstown, D'fries & G'way

FOCUS
The favourite was a shade disappointing, but that's not to detract from the winner who looks potentially useful. After rail movement the actual race distance was 1m 79yds.

5835 DONNA MORTIMER BALLANTYNE TRUST, KILBRYDE HOSPICE H'CAP 1m 67y
6:25 (6:26) (Class 6) (0-60,59) 3-Y-O+ **£2,911** (£866; £432; £216) **Stalls** Low

Form RPR
0000 1 **Amy Blair**[8] 5578 3-7-13 **45** ShirleyTeasdale[(5)] 14 54
(Keith Dalgleish) *t.k.h: mde all and sn wl clr: rdn 2f out: kpt on strly fnl f: unchal* **50/1**
0455 2 2 3/4 **Opt Out**[21] 5114 6-9-7 **56** (b) PhillipMakin 1 60+
(David O'Meara) *prom chsng gp: smooth hdwy to chse (clr) wnr 2f out: rdn 1f out: sn no ex* **9/2**[2]
2605 3 2 1/4 **Incurs Four Faults**[20] 5149 5-8-13 **48** (v[1]) JasonHart 9 47
(Keith Dalgleish) *s.i.s: hld up: rdn over 2f out: hdwy over 1f out: kpt on ins fnl f: no imp* **5/1**[3]
1232 4 nk **Galilee Chapel (IRE)**[8] 5576 7-8-11 **51** (b) PhilDennis[(5)] 3 49
(Alistair Whillans) *t.k.h: cl up chsng gp: chsd (clr) wnr 3f out to 2f out: sn rdn and one pce* **9/4**[1]
4-00 5 1 1/4 **Royal Acclaim (IRE)**[27] 4895 4-9-6 **55** BarryMcHugh 5 50
(Rebecca Bastiman) *chsd (clr) wnr to 3f out: sn rdn: rallied: no ex fr over 1f out* **28/1**
0303 6 nk **Call Me Crockett (IRE)**[8] 5576 4-9-1 **50** (p) JoeFanning 8 44
(Noel Wilson) *hld up in midfield in chsng gp: rdn and effrt over 2f out: hung rt over 1f out: sn no ex* **9/1**
0652 7 1/2 **Stanlow**[17] 5252 6-9-0 **49** CamHardie 2 42
(Michael Mullineaux) *hld up: rdn over 3f out: hdwy on outside over 1f out: sn no imp* **8/1**
5436 8 shd **Munjally**[27] 4872 5-9-6 **55** (v) DougieCostello 7 48
(Patrick Holmes) *hld up: drvn and outpcd over 3f out: rallied over 1f out: sn no imp* **11/1**
6-00 9 3 1/4 **Wright Patterson (IRE)**[50] 4041 3-8-13 **54** TomEaves 6 38
(John Quinn) *in tch chsng gp: struggling over 2f out: btn over 1f out* **12/1**
0050 10 2 **Tiger's Home**[43] 4314 6-9-0 **54** KillianLeonard[(5)] 10 35
(Iain Jardine) *hld up in tch chsng gp: drvn along 3f out: wknd 2f out* **16/1**
1m 50.42s (2.02) **Going Correction** +0.175s/f (Good)
WFA 3 from 4yo+ 6lb **10** Ran SP% **114.0**
Speed ratings (Par 101): **96,93,91,90,89 89,88,88,85,83**
CSF £258.93 CT £1383.15 TOTE £36.60: £9.20, £2.50, £1.90; EX 472.10 Trifecta £1541.70.
Owner J Fyffe **Bred** Summertree Stud **Trained** Carluke, S Lanarks

FOCUS
Not the easiest race to assess, but it would appear the winner nicked it, perhaps not having to go that hard to establish a clear lead early on with the overall gallop in the main group looking fairly sedate. It was an advantage which he never really looked like relinquishing and he has been rated back to last year's best. The runner-up the only one to emerge from the pack and lay down any sort of challenge. After rail movement the actual race distance was 1m 79yds.

5836 EBF STALLIONS SCOTTISH PREMIER SERIES FILLIES' H'CAP 6f 6y
6:55 (6:57) (Class 3) (0-90,87) 3-Y-O+ **£11,644** (£3,465; £1,731; £865) **Stalls** Centre

Form RPR
2211 1 **Courier**[17] 5276 4-8-13 **81** HollieDoyle[(5)] 6 89
(Marjorie Fife) *mde all: rdn over 1f out: hld on wl fnl f* **4/1**[2]
2242 2 nk **Wowcha (IRE)**[14] 5367 3-8-9 **75** (v[1]) CamHardie 1 82
(John Quinn) *t.k.h: cl up: effrt and chsd wnr ent fnl f: kpt on: hld nr fin* **7/1**
2231 3 1 3/4 **Rose Eclair**[21] 5110 3-8-7 **73** (b) JasonHart 9 74
(Tim Easterby) *trckd wnr: rdn over 1f out: kpt on same pce ins fnl f* **10/1**
0612 4 nk **Dutch Mist**[60] 3714 3-9-7 **87** (b) TomEaves 8 87
(Kevin Ryan) *prom: rdn and effrt wl over 1f out: kpt on same pce fnl f* **6/1**[3]
1531 5 3/4 **Specialv (IRE)**[18] 5224 3-8-2 **75** (p) BenRobinson[(7)] 7 73
(Brian Ellison) *dwlt: hld up: effrt and hung lft over 1f out: kpt on fnl f: nrst fin* **7/2**[1]
2216 6 1 1/4 **Forever A Lady (IRE)**[21] 5115 3-8-12 **78** JoeFanning 3 72
(Keith Dalgleish) *hld up: rdn and hdwy over 1f out: no imp fnl f* **11/1**
-230 7 1 **Giddy**[77] 3116 3-8-12 **78** TonyHamilton 4 69
(Richard Fahey) *t.k.h: prom tl rdn and wknd ent fnl f* **7/1**
3000 8 nk **Alexandrakollontai (IRE)**[13] 5419 6-8-13 **81** (b) GarryWhillans[(5)] 2 71
(Alistair Whillans) *hld up on outside: effrt and hung rt over 1f out: sn btn* **12/1**
1602 9 3 1/2 **Classy Anne**[20] 5153 6-9-3 **80** JackGarritty 5 59
(Jim Goldie) *t.k.h: in tch: struggling wl over 1f out: sn btn* **12/1**
1m 12.85s (0.65) **Going Correction** +0.175s/f (Good)
WFA 3 from 4yo+ 3lb **9** Ran SP% **114.3**
Speed ratings (Par 104): **102,101,99,98,97 96,94,94,89**
CSF £31.74 CT £261.18 TOTE £5.80: £2.40, £2.40, £3.80; EX 38.60 Trifecta £301.30.
Owner Daniel Gath Homes Ltd **Bred** Stratford Place Stud And Watership Down **Trained** Stillington, N Yorks

FOCUS
A fairly useful fillies' sprint. The pace wasn't strong for a race of this nature, the finish dominated by those who raced prominently. The winner looks to have more to offer.

5837 LADBROKES LANARK SILVER BELL H'CAP 1m 4f 14y
7:25 (7:25) (Class 3) (0-90,87) 3-Y-O+
£16,185 (£4,846; £2,423; £1,211; £605; £304) **Stalls** High

Form RPR
0324 1 **Multellie**[20] 5157 4-9-4 **81** CamHardie 6 87
(Tim Easterby) *trckd ldrs: drvn along over 2f out: kpt on fnl f to ld cl home* **20/1**
5120 2 hd **Lord Yeats**[20] 5147 3-9-0 **87** JackGarritty 3 93
(Jedd O'Keeffe) *led: rdn 2f out: kpt on wl fnl f: hdd cl home* **9/2**[1]
4222 3 1/2 **Mukhayyam**[23] 5031 4-9-3 **80** (p) TomEaves 9 86
(Tim Easterby) *hld up: stdy hdwy whn nt clr run over 2f out: effrt and plld out over 1f out: kpt on fnl f: nrst fin* **12/1**
4120 4 nse **Renfrew Street**[70] 3347 3-8-10 **83** JoeFanning 4 88
(Mark Johnston) *pressed ldr: rdn 2f out: kpt on fnl f: hld towards fin* **15/2**[3]
2431 5 shd **Carbon Dating (IRE)**[27] 4875 4-9-6 **83** TadhgO'Shea 8 88
(John Patrick Shanahan, Ire) *hld up on outside: stdy hdwy over 2f out: rdn over 1f out: kpt on fnl f: nt pce to chal* **13/2**[2]
2331 6 1 3/4 **Salmon Sushi**[10] 5526 5-9-9 **86** 6ex JasonHart 14 88
(Tim Easterby) *dwlt: hld up: hdwy on wd outside over 2f out: sn rdn: kpt on fnl f: nt pce to chal* **8/1**
6353 7 hd **English Summer**[20] 5157 9-9-10 **87** (t) TonyHamilton 11 89
(Richard Fahey) *midfield on ins: drvn along over 2f out: hdwy over 1f out: no imp ins fnl f* **20/1**
1521 8 1/2 **Hillgrove Angel (IRE)**[38] 4491 4-8-8 **76** KillianLeonard[(5)] 5 77
(Iain Jardine) *t.k.h: trckd ldrs: effrt and ch over 1f out: no ex ins fnl f* **8/1**
4061 9 3/4 **Time Of My Life (GER)**[43] 4311 5-9-9 **86** (p) DougieCostello 1 86
(Patrick Holmes) *hld up towards rr: drvn along and outpcd over 2f out: rallied fnl f: nvr rchd ldrs* **12/1**
1100 10 hd **Indian Chief (IRE)**[26] 4919 6-9-3 **80** BarryMcHugh 2 79
(Rebecca Bastiman) *dwlt: hld up: rdn and hdwy over 1f out: no imp fnl f* **40/1**
4421 11 1/2 **Top Of The Glas (IRE)**[33] 4680 5-8-11 **81** BenRobinson[(7)] 10 79
(Brian Ellison) *in tch: drvn and outpcd 3f out: no imp fnl 2f* **9/1**
662 12 2 1/2 **Cape Of Glory (IRE)**[10] 5520 3-8-13 **86** PhillipMakin 12 80
(Keith Dalgleish) *trckd ldrs: rdn over 2f out: wknd over 1f out* **11/1**
2 13 1 1/4 **Dark Ruler (IRE)**[117] 1880 7-9-5 **82** NeilFarley 7 74
(Alan Swinbank) *midfield: rdn over 2f out: wknd wl over 1f out* **16/1**
3040 14 1 1/2 **Biff Johnson (IRE)**[41] 4406 4-8-12 **80** (v[1]) ShirleyTeasdale[(5)] 15 70
(Keith Dalgleish) *midfield: drvn and struggling over 2f out: hung rt: wknd wl over 1f out* **33/1**
2m 39.34s (0.74) **Going Correction** +0.175s/f (Good)
WFA 3 from 4yo+ 10lb **14** Ran SP% **120.0**
Speed ratings (Par 107): **104,103,103,103,103 102,102,101,101,101 100,99,98,97**
CSF £103.85 CT £1160.20 TOTE £19.10: £5.20, £2.00, £4.10; EX 143.80 Trifecta £1198.90.
Owner David Scott **Bred** Habton Farms **Trained** Great Habton, N Yorks

FOCUS
A pretty useful and competitive handicap, but the bare form has the potential to prove a little muddling, the pace being pretty sedate for a long way resulting in a bunched finish. The winner has been rated to his best. After rail movement the actual race distance was 1m4f 26yds.

5838 DOWNLOAD THE LADBROKES APP H'CAP 5f 7y
8:00 (8:00) (Class 6) (0-65,62) 3-Y-O+ **£2,911** (£866; £432; £216) **Stalls** Centre

Form RPR
6000 1 **Knockamany Bends (IRE)**[25] 4931 6-8-7 **45** [1] BarryMcHugh 8 55
(John Wainwright) *mde all: rdn along over 1f out: kpt on strly fnl f* **16/1**
2304 2 1 1/4 **Malaysian Boleh**[22] 5051 6-8-7 **52** BenRobinson[(7)] 7 57+
(Brian Ellison) *dwlt: sn pushed along in rr: hdwy and edgd lft over 1f out: kpt on to take 2nd nr fin: nt rch wnr* **15/8**[1]
3215 3 1 1/4 **Indastar**[14] 5368 6-9-7 **59** JoeFanning 9 60
(Michael Herrington) *trckd ldrs: effrt and wnt 2nd over 1f out: sn rdn: kpt on same pce ins fnl f: lost 2nd nr fin* **9/4**[2]
6006 4 4 **Mystical King**[46] 4192 6-8-7 **45** (p) CamHardie 1 31
(Linda Perratt) *in tch: sn drvn along: effrt over 1f out: no imp fnl f* **25/1**
0262 5 1 3/4 **Rock Canyon (IRE)**[8] 5582 7-9-3 **62** CliffordLee[(7)] 3 42
(Linda Perratt) *sn pushed along bhd ldng gp: effrt and rdn over 2f out: edgd rt and wknd over 1f out* **10/3**[3]
0054 6 nse **Amber Crystal**[1] 5804 4-8-11 **49** TomEaves 4 29
(Linda Perratt) *chsd wnr to over 1f out: sn rdn and wknd* **7/1**
0050 7 18 **Bannock Town**[18] 5222 5-8-2 **45** (p) PhilDennis[(5)] 6
(Linda Perratt) *chsd ldrs: drvn and outpcd 1/2-way: wknd wl over 1f out* **66/1**
1m 0.52s (0.52) **Going Correction** +0.175s/f (Good) **7** Ran SP% **112.4**
Speed ratings (Par 101): **102,100,98,91,88 88,59**
CSF £44.89 CT £96.03 TOTE £15.60: £4.90, £1.40; EX 50.90 Trifecta £120.80.
Owner D R & E E Brown **Bred** Mike Hyde **Trained** Kennythorpe, N Yorks

FOCUS
A run-of-the-mill sprint to conclude proceedings. The first three were the only ones to run anywhere near to form.
T/Plt: £1,716.90 to a £1 stake. Pool: £42,065.00 - 24.50 winning tickets T/Qpdt: £180.00 to a £1 stake. Pool: £4,548.00 - 25.26 winning tickets **Richard Young**

5363 NEWCASTLE (A.W) (L-H)
Friday, August 26

OFFICIAL GOING: Tapeta: standard
Wind: light 1/2 against Weather: fine

5839 SOLUTIONS RECRUITMENT "HANDS AND HEELS" APPRENTICE H'CAP (RACING EXCELLENCE INITIATIVE) 6f (Tp)
4:15 (4:16) (Class 6) (0-65,64) 3-Y-O+ **£2,587** (£770; £384; £192) **Stalls** Centre

Form RPR
3031 1 **Gypsy Major**[14] 5369 4-9-1 **56** (v) LewisEdmunds[(3)] 6 68
(Garry Moss) *hld up in mid-div: effrt over 2f out: 2nd over 1f out: led last 150yds: drvn out* **7/4**[2]
0113 2 3 **Sugar Town**[11] 5483 6-9-5 **57** AdamMcNamara 2 60
(Peter Niven) *led: drvn over 1f out: hdd and no ex last 150yds* **6/4**[1]
5030 3 1 1/4 **Danzeb (IRE)**[27] 4874 3-9-3 **63** LiamLewis-Salter[(5)] 4 62
(Ann Duffield) *t.k.h: trckd ldr: drvn over 2f out: kpt on same pce over 1f out* **14/1**
350- 4 1 **Life Of Fame**[305] 7516 3-9-5 **60** PatrickVaughan 7 56
(David O'Meara) *hld up in mid-div: t.k.h: effrt over 2f out: kpt on one pce* **14/1**
2565 5 1 1/4 **Goninodaethat**[18] 5225 8-8-12 **55** JamieGormley[(5)] 5 48
(Jim Goldie) *trckd ldrs: t.k.h: effrt over 2f out: one pce* **20/1**
6066 6 3 **Amis Reunis**[11] 5483 7-8-5 **46** oh1 BenSanderson[(3)] 1 30
(Colin Teague) *chsd ldrs: lost pl over 1f out* **25/1**
0236 7 1 **Cuppatee (IRE)**[14] 5369 3-9-9 **64** CameronNoble 3 45
(Ann Duffield) *n.m.r sn after s: bhd and drvn over 3f out: nvr on terms* **15/2**[3]
4000 8 10 **Rise Up Singing**[51] 4005 3-8-5 **46** oh1 DanielleMooney 8
(Colin Teague) *in last: drvn over 3f out: lost pl 2f out: sn bhd* **100/1**
1m 13.5s (1.00) **Going Correction** +0.175s/f (Slow)
WFA 3 from 4yo+ 3lb **8** Ran SP% **111.1**
Speed ratings (Par 101): **100,96,94,93,91 87,86,72**
CSF £4.36 CT £21.22 TOTE £2.60: £1.50, £1.02, £3.40; EX 4.50 Trifecta £26.00.
Owner Pinnacle Duo Partnership **Bred** Bearstone Stud Ltd **Trained** Wynyard, Stockton-On-Tees

FOCUS
There will be no speed figures at this track until there is sufficient data to calculate median times. A hands and heels handicap for apprentices featuring a progressive winner and the form looks straightforward.

5840 PARKLANDS MINI GOLF NURSERY H'CAP — 7f 14y (Tp)
4:50 (4:52) (Class 5) (0-70,70) 2-Y-O — **£3,881** (£1,155; £577; £288) **Stalls** Centre

Form — RPR

4644 **1** **Springwood (IRE)**[21] 5109 2-9-2 **70**....................(v) AdamMcNamara(5) 6 — 77
(Richard Fahey) *chsd ldrs: led over 1f out: drvn clr last 75yds* **7/1**

4434 **2** 3 ¼ **Law Power**[20] 5171 2-9-7 **70**....................[1] LukeMorris 7 — 69
(Sir Mark Prescott Bt) *dwlt: sn drvn along: hdwy to chse ldrs over 2f out: kpt on to take 2nd last 50yds* **5/2**[1]

5353 **3** ¾ **Kroy**[27] 4869 2-8-11 **60**.................... KevinStott 2 — 57
(Ollie Pears) *trckd ldrs: 2nd over 1f out: kpt on same pce* **13/2**

065 **4** ½ **Hollywood Harry (IRE)**[28] 4829 2-8-9 **58**....................[1] JoeyHaynes 1 — 54
(Keith Dalgleish) *s.i.s: hdwy to ld after 1f: hdd over 1f out: kpt on same pce* **20/1**

366 **5** ¾ **Padleyourowncanoe**[19] 5203 2-8-8 **57**.................... RoystonFfrench 8 — 51
(Daniel Mark Loughnane) *in rr and sn drvn along: hdwy over 1f out: kpt on one pce last 100yds* **20/1**

3230 **6** 1 ½ **Pulsating (IRE)**[17] 5265 2-8-12 **66**.................... RowanScott(5) 9 — 56
(Rebecca Menzies) *hld up towards rr: t.k.h: hdwy over 2f out: one pce over 1f out* **11/1**

400 **7** *hd* **Servo (IRE)**[56] 3854 2-9-0 **63**.................... SilvestreDeSousa 5 — 52
(Alan Swinbank) *hld up towards rr: t.k.h: drvn and hung lft over 2f out: chsng ldrs over 1f out: fdd clsng stages* **3/1**[2]

322 **8** 4 **Lucky Esteem**[28] 4829 2-9-7 **70**.................... GrahamLee 4 — 49
(Mark Johnston) *chsd ldrs: wknd over 1f out* **5/1**[3]

040 **9** 8 **Parkwarden (IRE)**[34] 4642 2-8-7 **56**.................... ShaneGray 3 — 14
(Chris Grant) *led 1f: carried lft over 2f out: sn lost pl and bhd* **50/1**

1m 28.85s (2.65) **Going Correction** +0.175s/f (Slow) — **9** Ran SP% **115.9**
Speed ratings (Par 94): **91,87,86,85,85 83,83,78,69**
CSF £24.41 CT £121.86 TOTE £7.60: £2.70, £1.50, £2.00; EX 30.30 Trifecta £138.50.
Owner Richard Fahey Ebor Racing Club Ltd **Bred** Con Marnane **Trained** Musley Bank, N Yorks

FOCUS
A fair nursery and although the early pace didn't appear that strong for several pulled hard, it seemed to end up a fair test. It was won by the most exposed horse in the field and the race has been rated around the placed horses.

5841 AT THE RACES H'CAP — 1m 2f 42y (Tp)
5:25 (5:29) (Class 5) (0-70,71) 3-Y-O+ — **£3,557** (£1,058; £529; £264) **Stalls** High

Form — RPR

-503 **1** **Taopix**[9] 5540 4-8-9 **51** oh3.................... JoeyHaynes 9 — 61
(Karen McLintock) *clipped heels sn after s: rr-div: effrt over 3f out: nt clr run over 1f out: styd on wl fnl 150yds: led post* **20/1**

3023 **2** *hd* **Roman De Brut (IRE)**[10] 5529 4-9-1 **62**.................... AdamMcNamara(5) 10 — 70
(Daniel Mark Loughnane) *hld up in rr: hdwy on outer over 2f out: hung lft and chsng ldr appr fnl f: led clsng stages: hdd post* **8/1**[2]

4011 **3** ½ **Cape Crystal (IRE)**[7] 5610 3-9-7 **71** 12ex....................(p) LukeMorris 5 — 78
(Sir Mark Prescott Bt) *led 1f: trckd ldrs: led 2f out: sn drvn: hdd and no ex clsng stages* **4/5**[1]

0035 **4** 1 ½ **Hernando Torres**[9] 5540 8-9-10 **69**....................(t) RachelRichardson(3) 3 — 73
(Michael Easterby) *mid-div: hdwy to trck ldrs and nt clr run over 2f out: 3rd appr fnl f: kpt on same pce* **20/1**

3665 **5** *nk* **Testa Rossa (IRE)**[18] 5228 6-8-11 **60**....................(b) LewisEdmunds(7) 12 — 64
(Jim Goldie) *mid-div: hdwy over 2f out: nt clr run over 1f out: kpt on fnl 150yds* **33/1**

652 **6** *shd* **Paddy's Rock (IRE)**[41] 4377 5-9-2 **58**.................... AndrewElliott 4 — 61
(Lynn Siddall) *mid-div: drvn 3f out: sn chsng ldrs: one pce over 1f out* **20/1**

-000 **7** 2 **Genres**[98] 2439 4-10-0 **70**.................... SilvestreDeSousa 7 — 69
(Alan Swinbank) *hmpd sn after s: hdwy on inner over 2f out: sn nt clr run: drvn to chse ldrs over 1f out: one pce* **18/1**

0050 **8** *shd* **Glasgon**[44] 4260 6-8-6 **53**.................... RowanScott(5) 13 — 52
(Ray Craggs) *chsd ldrs: drvn 3f out: one pce fnl 2f* **50/1**

6123 **8** *dht* **Gold Show**[13] 5415 7-9-7 **63**.................... KevinStott 6 — 62
(Grant Tuer) *chsd ldrs: pushed along over 5f out: one pce fnl 2f* **14/1**

36- **10** 2 **Fair Trade**[94] 3411 9-9-7 **63**....................[1] ShaneGray 8 — 59
(Wilf Storey) *s.i.s: hdwy over 2f out: nt clr run over 1f out: sn wknd* **66/1**

0352 **11** 3 ¼ **Hussar Ballad (USA)**[21] 5130 7-9-11 **67**.................... PJMcDonald 11 — 55
(Antony Brittain) *chsd ldr: led after 1f out: hdd 2f out: lost pl appr fnl f* **10/1**[3]

4461 **12** 1 ½ **Bogardus (IRE)**[17] 5264 5-8-13 **62**.................... PaulaMuir(7) 1 — 47
(Patrick Holmes) *hmpd sn after s: hld up in rr: effrt on ins over 2f out: wknd over 1f out* **10/1**[3]

-100 **13** 12 **Croft Ranger (IRE)**[93] 2576 3-8-12 **62**....................(p) GrahamLee 2 — 23
(Michael Dods) *s.i.s: drvn along: sn chsng ldrs: reminders over 3f out: lost pl over 1f out: eased whn bhd last 100yds* **33/1**

2m 10.86s (0.46) **Going Correction** +0.10s/f (Slow)
WFA 3 from 4yo+ 8lb — **13** Ran SP% **120.4**
Speed ratings (Par 103): **102,101,101,100,100 99,98,98,98,96 94,92,83**
CSF £163.12 CT £283.47 TOTE £31.40: £7.20, £2.50, £1.10; EX 285.20 Trifecta £1711.50.
Owner Roger Stockdale **Bred** Lady Jennifer Green **Trained** Ingoe, Northumberland

FOCUS
A fair gallop to this 1m2f handicap in which they bet big prices bar one. The complexion of the race changed markedly in the closing stages.

5842 DOWNLOAD THE AT THE RACES APP H'CAP — 1m 4f 98y (Tp)
6:00 (6:00) (Class 5) (0-70,70) 4-Y-O+ — **£3,881** (£1,155; £577; £288) **Stalls** High

Form — RPR

0160 **1** **Almutamarred (USA)**[13] 5392 4-8-8 **62**.................... AdamMcNamara(5) 5 — 72+
(Kevin Morgan) *hld up in rr: smooth hdwy over 4f out: cl 2nd 2f out: shkn up to ld over 1f out: drvn out clsng stages* **7/4**[1]

4565 **2** 1 **Northside Prince (IRE)**[25] 4934 10-9-0 **63**.................... SilvestreDeSousa 8 — 69
(Alan Swinbank) *trckd ldrs: chal 3f out: led over 2f out: hdd over 1f out: kpt on same pce* **3/1**[2]

0-56 **3** 11 **Toola Boola**[33] 4682 6-9-5 **68**.................... GrahamLee 1 — 57
(Jedd O'Keeffe) *chsd ldrs: drvn 6f out: lost pl over 3f out: kpt on over 1f out: tk poor 3rd nr fin* **7/1**

00 **4** *nk* **Memory Cloth**[94] 2556 9-9-7 **70**....................(p) PJMcDonald 6 — 58
(Micky Hammond) *chsd ldrs: pushed along over 3f out: modest 3rd 1f out: one pce* **9/1**

44-1 **5** 2 **Thackeray**[39] 4447 9-7-9 **51** oh4.................... PaulaMuir(7) 2 — 36
(Chris Fairhurst) *hld up in last: effrt over 3f out: kpt on fnl 2f: nvr a factor* **9/1**

0605 **6** *nk* **Celtic Power**[20] 5183 4-8-5 **61**....................[1] LewisEdmunds(7) 7 — 46
(Jim Goldie) *w ldr: led after 2f: drvn and hdd over 2f out: wknd appr fnl f* **6/1**[3]

0-00 **7** 57 **Spokesperson (USA)**[64] 3564 8-8-5 **54**....................(p) ConnorBeasley 3
(Fred Watson) *led 2f: w ldr: reminders over 5f out: lost pl over 3f out: wl bhd whn eased over 1f out: sn t.o: eventually completed* **33/1**

2m 41.0s (-0.10) **Going Correction** +0.10s/f (Slow) — **7** Ran SP% **111.1**
Speed ratings (Par 103): **104,103,96,95,94 94,56**
CSF £6.62 CT £25.86 TOTE £2.50: £1.80, £2.50; EX 7.40 Trifecta £24.80.
Owner S P Giles **Bred** Shadwell Farm LLC **Trained** Gazeley, Suffolk

FOCUS
A fair gallop to this handicap in which they finished well strung out. The first two were clear, but the form may not be anything out of the rdinary.

5843 HAPPY BIRTHDAY SAMANTHA HEATHCOTE MAIDEN STKS — 7f 14y (Tp)
6:30 (6:33) (Class 5) 3-4-Y-O — **£3,557** (£1,058; £529; £264) **Stalls** Centre

Form — RPR

1 **Visitant** 3-9-5 0.................... PatrickMathers 2 — 68
(David Thompson) *dwlt: hdwy into mid-div over 3f out: sn drvn: led 1f out: kpt on* **12/1**

0 **2** ½ **Secret Dreamer**[20] 5178 4-9-5 0.................... AdamMcNamara(5) 10 — 69
(Kevin Morgan) *hld up in rr: hdwy over 3f out: chsng ldng pair over 1f out: kpt on same pce to take 2nd nr fin* **40/1**

2230 **3** ½ **Dark Command**[20] 5151 3-9-5 65....................(p) ConnorBeasley 3 — 66
(Michael Dods) *trckd ldrs: led over 2f out: sn drvn: hdd 1f out: kpt on same pce* **1/1**[1]

02-0 **4** 3 **The Perfect Show**[20] 5169 3-9-5 70.................... LukeMorris 1 — 58
(Ed Walker) *mid-div: hdwy over 3f out: drvn to chse ldrs over 2f out: fdd fnl 75yds* **15/8**[2]

5 7 **Skadi**[104] 4-9-5 0.................... PJMcDonald 4 — 36
(Garry Moss) *sn chsng ldrs: 2nd over 2f out: wknd fnl f* **10/1**[3]

06 **6** 2 ½ **Lukoutoldmakezebak**[20] 5178 3-9-5 0.................... KevinStott 6 — 32
(James Bethell) *trckd ldrs: t.k.h: wknd 2f out* **20/1**

7 2 ¾ **Madame Bond** 4-9-5 0.................... GrahamLee 7 — 22
(Sally Hall) *s.i.s: in rr: drvn over 4f out: reminders over 3f out: hung lft: bhd fnl 3f* **25/1**

4530 **8** 6 **Smirnova (IRE)**[14] 5365 3-8-7 57.................... EvaMoscrop(7) 5 — 3
(Kenny Johnson) *led: hdd over 2f out: sn lost pl and wl bhd: t.o* **25/1**

06-0 **9** *nk* **Molivias Gem**[17] 5278 3-9-0 51.................... JoeyHaynes 8 — 3
(David Thompson) *mid-div: drvn 5f out: lost pl over 2f out: sn wl bhd: t.o* **28/1**

1m 28.23s (2.03) **Going Correction** +0.175s/f (Slow)
WFA 3 from 4yo 5lb — **9** Ran SP% **119.9**
Speed ratings (Par 103): **95,94,93,90,82 79,76,69,69**
CSF £392.21 TOTE £18.20: £3.00, £7.40, £1.10; EX 400.50 Trifecta £1550.60.
Owner N Park **Bred** Cheveley Park Stud Ltd **Trained** Bolam, Co Durham

FOCUS
Although the top rated in this maiden had a mark of 70, he ran below his best and the form may not amount to a great deal. The first four were clear and the race has been rated negatively through the third.

5844 AT THE RACES VIRGIN 565 FILLIES' H'CAP — 1m 5y (Tp)
7:00 (7:04) (Class 5) (0-75,74) 3-Y-O+ — **£3,557** (£1,058; £529; £264) **Stalls** Centre

Form — RPR

1054 **1** **Barwah (USA)**[22] 5068 5-8-10 **58**.................... AndrewMullen 5 — 69
(Peter Niven) *trckd ldng pair: 2nd over 1f out: styd on to ld towards fin* **9/4**[1]

300 **2** *nk* **Flinty Fell (IRE)**[125] 1628 3-8-10 **64**.................... GrahamGibbons 4 — 73
(Keith Dalgleish) *trckd ldr: smooth hdwy to ld over 1f out: sn drvn: hdd and no ex towards fin* **7/1**[3]

4256 **3** 6 **Page Of Wands**[14] 5365 3-8-8 **62**....................[1] ShaneGray 2 — 57
(Karen McLintock) *dwlt: sn drvn along in detached last: hdwy over 2f out: tk modest 3rd last 100yds* **12/1**

-560 **4** 5 **Gilt Edged (IRE)**[33] 4681 3-8-1 **55** oh2.................... JamesSullivan 6 — 38
(Julie Camacho) *hld up: drvn over 3f out: wknd over 1f out* **25/1**

4420 **5** ½ **Fray**[18] 5223 5-9-10 **72**.................... JoeDoyle 1 — 55
(Jim Goldie) *stdd s: hld up: hdwy over 3f out: drvn over 2f out: wknd over 1f out: n.m.r 100yds out* **3/1**[2]

4323 **6** 2 ¼ **Fidelma Moon (IRE)**[22] 5076 4-9-7 **74**.................... JordanVaughan(5) 7 — 51
(K R Burke) *led: qcknd over 2f out: hung lft: hdd & wknd over 1f out: bhd whn eased nr fin* **9/4**[1]

1m 38.5s (-0.10) **Going Correction** +0.175s/f (Slow)
WFA 3 from 4yo+ 6lb — **6** Ran SP% **110.6**
Speed ratings (Par 100): **107,106,100,95,95 92**
CSF £17.76 TOTE £2.40: £1.10, £3.30; EX 23.40 Trifecta £101.30.
Owner Keep The Faith Partnership **Bred** Shadwell Farm LLC **Trained** Barton-le-Street, N Yorks

FOCUS
A fillies' handicap and though they seemed to go a fair gallop, few got involved and the first two, who were clear, raced in second and third most of the way.

5845 AT THE RACES SKY 415 H'CAP — 7f 14y (Tp)
7:35 (7:36) (Class 5) (0-75,75) 3-Y-O+ — **£3,557** (£1,058; £529; £264) **Stalls** Centre

Form — RPR

0545 **1** **War Department (IRE)**[18] 5223 3-9-2 **70**....................(v[1]) GrahamGibbons 10 — 82+
(Keith Dalgleish) *hld up towards rr: effrt and swtchd rt 2f out: str run to ld 1f out: sn clr* **7/1**[3]

61-0 **2** 2 ¾ **Let's Twist**[14] 5367 4-9-4 **67**....................(b) ShaneGray 4 — 74
(Kristin Stubbs) *led: hdd 1f out: kpt on same pce* **33/1**

2315 **3** *hd* **Vallarta (IRE)**[18] 5224 6-9-11 **74**.................... JamesSullivan 1 — 80
(Ruth Carr) *hld up towards rr: hdwy over 2f out: chsg ldrs over 1f out: kpt on same pce* **14/1**

4653 **4** ½ **Mustaqqil (IRE)**[7] 5609 4-9-12 **75**....................(v) DanielTudhope 8 — 80
(David O'Meara) *hld up in rr: stdy hdwy over 2f out: chsng ldrs whn n.m.r over 1f out: kpt on same pce fnl f* **7/2**[1]

3623 **5** *hd* **Deansgate (IRE)**[22] 5063 3-9-0 **73**....................(e) AdamMcNamara(5) 12 — 76
(Julie Camacho) *dwlt: sn chsng ldrs: kpt on same pce fnl f* **10/1**

0621 **6** *nk* **Gun Case**[22] 5068 4-9-5 **68**....................(p) ConnorBeasley 3 — 72
(Alistair Whillans) *chsd ldrs: kpt on same pce appr fnl f* **4/1**[2]

0301 **7** 1 ¾ **Depth Charge (IRE)**[14] 5367 4-9-5 **75**....................(vt) PatrickVaughan(7) 9 — 74
(Kristin Stubbs) *chsd ldrs: edgd lft over 1f out: ended up racing far side: kpt on one pce* **7/1**[3]

0033 **8** 3 ½ **Be Kool (IRE)**[34] 4643 3-9-0 **68**.................... LukeMorris 2 — 56
(Brian Ellison) *trckd ldrs: t.k.h: drvn over 3f out: wknd appr fnl f* **7/1**[3]

1202 **9** 9 **Lucky Lodge**[32] 4714 6-9-6 **69**....................(p) SilvestreDeSousa 11 — 34
(Antony Brittain) *in rr and sn drvn along: nvr on terms* **10/1**

4624 **10** *1 ½* **Highwayman**[136] 1400 3-8-10 **64**.......... PatrickMathers 7 23
(David Thompson) *chsd ldrs: drvn 3f out: lost pl over 1f out: sn bhd* **33/1**

6002 **11** *1 ¾* **Danot (IRE)**[13] 5386 4-9-5 **68**.......... GrahamLee 13 25
(Jedd O'Keeffe) *chsd ldrs: lost pl over 1f out: sn bhd* **28/1**

0306 **12** *½* **Burning Blaze**[23] 5037 6-9-12 **75**.......... (t) BenCurtis 14 30
(Brian Ellison) *dwlt: t.k.h: sn trcking ldrs: lost pl over 1f out: sn bhd* **20/1**

04-0 **13** *½* **See The Storm**[118] 1869 8-9-9 **72**.......... PJMcDonald 6 26
(Ann Duffield) *chsd ldrs: lost pl over 1f out: sn bhd* **50/1**

1m 25.83s (-0.37) **Going Correction** +0.175s/f (Slow)
WFA 3 from 4yo+ 5lb **13** Ran SP% **120.6**
Speed ratings (Par 103): **109,105,105,105,104 104,102,98,88,86 84,83,83**
CSF £230.77 CT £3247.71 TOTE £8.90: £2.50, £8.70, £4.20; EX 313.20 Trifecta £932.00.
Owner Weldspec Glasgow Limited **Bred** Tom McDonald **Trained** Carluke, S Lanarks

FOCUS
Mainly exposed sorts in this 7f handicap in which the pace was fair and the winner scored in good style. The runner-up has been rated to his previous best.
T/Plt: £19.70 to a £1 stake. Pool: £51,197.17 - 1,896.22 winning tickets T/Qpdt: £6.30 to a £1 stake. Pool: £3,895.30 - 454.80 winning tickets **Walter Glynn**

5407 NEWMARKET (R-H)

Friday, August 26

OFFICIAL GOING: Good to firm (firm in places)
Wind: Almost nil Weather: Fine

5846 STRIDE BY TRM EBF STALLIONS MAIDEN FILLIES' STKS (PLUS 10 RACE) 7f

2:00 (2:01) (Class 4) 2-Y-O **£4,528** (£1,347; £673; £336) **Stalls** High

Form RPR

2 **1** **Spatial**[20] 5170 2-9-0 0.......... RyanMoore 6 83+
(Sir Michael Stoute) *led 1f: chsd ldr tl shkn up to ld over 1f out: r.o wl* **4/6**[1]

2 *2 ½* **Unforgettable Filly** 2-9-0 0.......... JamesDoyle 8 76+
(Hugo Palmer) *prom: pushed along 4f out: rdn and edgd rt over 1f out: r.o to go 2nd wl ins fnl f* **16/1**

3 *1* **Sobetsu** 2-9-0 0.......... WilliamBuick 5 74+
(Charlie Appleby) *prom: lost pl over 4f out: nt clr run over 2f out: hdwy over 1f out: r.o to go 3rd nr fin* **5/2**[2]

0 **4** *nk* **Flying North**[14] 5356 2-9-0 0.......... TimmyMurphy 1 73
(Richard Hannon) *hld up: hdwy over 2f out: rdn over 1f out: styd on* **20/1**

0 **5** *½* **Paradwys (IRE)**[30] 4756 2-9-0 0.......... MartinHarley 10 71
(Charles Hills) *w ldr: led 6f out: rdn and hdd over 1f out: no ex wl ins fnl f* **33/1**

5 **6** *5* **Forest Angel (IRE)**[20] 5170 2-9-0 0.......... SeanLevey 2 58
(Richard Hannon) *chsd ldrs: rdn over 2f out: wknd fnl f* **14/1**

7 *¾* **Alnasl (IRE)** 2-9-0 0.......... PaulHanagan 4 56
(Owen Burrows) *sn pushed along in rr: nvr nrr* **10/1**[3]

0 **8** *1 ¼* **Miss Sayif**[27] 4877 2-9-0 0.......... AndreaAtzeni 7 54+
(George Margarson) *hld up: nt clr run and swtchd rt over 1f out: nvr on terms* **66/1**

9 *3 ½* **Odelouca (IRE)** 2-9-0 0.......... OisinMurphy 9 43
(Brendan Powell) *prom: pushed along 1/2-way: rdn and wknd over 1f out* **50/1**

05 **10** *6* **Cambridge Favorite**[19] 5196 2-9-0 0.......... [1] SaleemGolam 3 27
(Mrs Ilka Gansera-Leveque) *broke wl: sn stdd and lost pl: rdn over 2f out: wknd over 1f out* **100/1**

1m 25.29s (-0.41) **Going Correction** +0.075s/f (Good) **10** Ran SP% **122.3**
Speed ratings (Par 93): **105,102,101,100,100 94,93,92,88,81**
CSF £15.52 TOTE £1.60: £1.02, £2.70, £1.60; EX 12.30 Trifecta £33.50.
Owner Cheveley Park Stud **Bred** Cheveley Park Stud Ltd **Trained** Newmarket, Suffolk

FOCUS
Stands Side Course used. A total of 8mm of watering took place on Tuesday, there was 2mm of rain on Wednesday and 1mm overnight, leaving the going as good to firm, firm in places (GoingStick: 8.0). This proved very straightforward for the odds-on favourite who is likely to do a good bit better.

5847 TRM GNF (GUT NUTRITION FORMULA) NURSERY H'CAP 1m

2:35 (2:35) (Class 4) (0-80,78) 2-Y-O **£4,528** (£1,347; £673) **Stalls** High

Form RPR

300 **1** **Plant Pot Power (IRE)**[14] 5356 2-9-4 **76**.......... SeanLevey 2 84
(Richard Hannon) *chsd ldr tl led 2f out: rdn over 1f out: hung lft ins fnl f: r.o wl* **9/2**[2]

31 **2** *2 ¾* **Vanity Queen**[17] 5266 2-9-5 **77**.......... AndreaAtzeni 4 78
(Luca Cumani) *hld up in tch: rdn to chse wnr over 1f out: no imp ins fnl f* **5/4**[1]

1 **3** *1* **Winston C (IRE)**[23] 5036 2-9-6 **78**.......... FrankieDettori 1 77
(Michael Bell) *led at stdy pce tl qcknd over 2f out: sn rdn and hdd 2f out: hung rt over 1f out: styd on same pce* **5/4**[1]

1m 42.9s (2.90) **Going Correction** +0.075s/f (Good) **3** Ran SP% **107.1**
Speed ratings (Par 96): **88,85,84**
CSF £9.95 TOTE £5.30; EX 8.80 Trifecta £5.70.
Owner Potensis B'Stock, J Palmer-Brown & Ptnr **Bred** Jeremy Gompertz **Trained** East Everleigh, Wilts

FOCUS
Despite only three runners, this was an interesting nursery, and there was a turn-up. The form is hard to pin down with confidence.

5848 TRM EXCELLENCE IN EQUINE NUTRITION EBF STALLIONS MAIDEN STKS (PLUS 10 RACE) 7f

3:10 (3:10) (Class 4) 2-Y-O **£4,528** (£1,347; £673; £336) **Stalls** High

Form RPR

3 **1** **Law And Order (IRE)**[15] 5332 2-9-0 0.......... MartinHarley 4 85+
(James Tate) *disp ld tl wnt on 1/2-way: rdn over 1f out: styd on wl* **15/8**[1]

2 *1 ½* **Rummani** 2-9-0 0.......... WilliamBuick 1 81+
(Charlie Appleby) *a.p: chsd wnr 2f out: sn rdn and ev ch: edgd lft and styd on same pce ins fnl f* **3/1**[3]

3 *nk* **Elucidation (IRE)** 2-9-0 0.......... TedDurcan 2 80+
(Sir Michael Stoute) *hld up: hdwy 2f out: rdn over 1f out: edgd lft: styd on* **16/1**

00 **4** *nk* **Amlad (IRE)**[37] 4533 2-9-0 0.......... JamesDoyle 3 79
(Ed Dunlop) *chsd ldrs: rdn over 1f out: kpt on* **50/1**

5 *2 ¾* **Splash Around** 2-9-0 0.......... AndreaAtzeni 6 73+
(Sir Michael Stoute) *sn pushed along in rr: rdn over 1f out: r.o ins fnl f: nt rch ldrs* **8/1**

6 *2 ¾* **Mandarin (GER)** 2-9-0 0.......... FrankieDettori 8 64+
(Marco Botti) *chsd ldrs: rdn over 1f out: edgd lft: wknd fnl f* **5/2**[2]

7 *1 ¾* **Original Choice (IRE)** 2-9-0 0.......... PatCosgrave 7 60
(William Haggas) *s.i.s: hld up: hdwy 2f out: wknd over 1f out* **16/1**

40 **8** *nk* **Nicky Baby (IRE)**[65] 3526 2-9-0 0.......... RobertWinston 12 59
(Dean Ivory) *disp ld to 1/2-way: rdn over 2f out: wknd over 1f out* **40/1**

50 **9** *hd* **Sassoferrato (IRE)**[15] 5332 2-8-11 0.......... EoinWalsh(3) 9 58
(Alan Bailey) *hld up: hdwy over 2f out: rdn and wknd over 1f out* **100/1**

60 **10** *1 ½* **Armagnac (IRE)**[14] 5371 2-9-0 0.......... OisinMurphy 5 54
(Michael Bell) *s.i.s: a in rr: rdn and wknd over 1f out* **40/1**

1m 25.16s (-0.54) **Going Correction** +0.075s/f (Good) **10** Ran SP% **119.1**
Speed ratings (Par 96): **106,104,103,103,100 97,95,94,94,93**
CSF £7.83 TOTE £2.90: £1.20, £1.80, £3.90; EX 10.40 Trifecta £74.10.
Owner Saeed Manana **Bred** Mr & Mrs Clive Martin **Trained** Newmarket, Suffolk

FOCUS
This looked a decent enough maiden and has been rated as such.

5849 HOOFMAKER BY TRM H'CAP 1m 2f

3:45 (3:47) (Class 4) (0-80,80) 3-Y-O **£5,175** (£1,540; £769; £384) **Stalls** Centre

Form RPR

-241 **1** **Exoteric**[16] 5287 3-9-5 **78**.......... WilliamBuick 2 85+
(Charles Hills) *trckd ldrs: plld hrd: rdn to go 2nd over 2f out: sn edgd lft: led u.p ins fnl f: styd on* **11/4**[2]

132 **2** *1 ½* **Tomahawk Kid**[19] 5201 3-8-13 **72**.......... JamesDoyle 6 76
(Ian Williams) *plld hrd in 2nd: jnd ldr over 7f out tl rdn and edgd lft over 2f out: rallied and ev ch ins fnl f: styd on same pce* **4/1**[3]

0632 **3** *nse* **Henry The Explorer (CAN)**[39] 4459 3-8-11 **70**.......... PatCosgrave 5 74
(Jo Hughes) *led: rdn and edgd lft over 1f out: hdd ins fnl f: styd on same pce* **14/1**

01-5 **4** *1* **Maestro Mac (IRE)**[13] 5405 3-9-6 **79**.......... AdamKirby 4 82
(Hughie Morrison) *s.i.s: hld up: pushed along over 2f out: hdwy and nt clr run over 1f out: sn rdn: kpt on* **6/1**

054 **5** *2 ½* **Mediciman**[34] 4654 3-9-4 **77**.......... MartinHarley 3 74
(Henry Candy) *chsd ldrs: rdn over 2f out: wknd ins fnl f* **9/4**[1]

2230 **6** *3 ¼* **Hepplewhite**[48] 4153 3-9-7 **80**.......... AndreaAtzeni 1 70
(Robert Eddery) *hld up: rdn over 1f out: wknd fnl f* **7/1**

2m 6.76s (1.26) **Going Correction** +0.075s/f (Good) **6** Ran SP% **110.9**
Speed ratings (Par 102): **97,95,95,94,92 90**
CSF £13.67 TOTE £2.80: £1.80, £2.30; EX 12.70 Trifecta £44.10.
Owner K Abdullah **Bred** Juddmonte Farms Ltd **Trained** Lambourn, Berks

FOCUS
They went a steady early pace and the hold-up horses were up against it.

5850 TRM MAIDEN STKS 1m

4:20 (4:21) (Class 5) 3-Y-O+ **£3,881** (£1,155; £577; £288) **Stalls** High

Form RPR

3- **1** **Qamarain (USA)**[322] 7077 3-9-0 0.......... PaulHanagan 7 75
(Brian Meehan) *mde all: set stdy pce tl qcknd 3f out: rdn and edgd rt over 1f out: edgd lft ins fnl f: r.o* **1/1**[1]

3 **2** *½* **Chiefofchiefs**[28] 4840 3-9-5 0.......... AndreaAtzeni 1 79
(Charlie Fellowes) *hld up: racd keenly: hdwy to chse wnr over 2f out: rdn over 1f out: r.o* **9/4**[2]

633 **3** *nk* **Lord Of The North (IRE)**[14] 5385 3-9-5 79.......... DarryllHolland 3 78
(Gay Kelleway) *trckd wnr 2f: remained handy: rdn over 1f out: edgd lft ins fnl f: r.o* **3/1**[3]

4 **4** *14* **Outrath (IRE)**[9] 5544 6-9-11 0.......... TimmyMurphy 5 45
(Jim Best) *prom: chsd wnr 6f out tl over 2f out: wknd over 1f out* **33/1**

6- **5** *13* **Forever Yours (IRE)**[260] 8167 3-9-5 0.......... RobertWinston 2 13
(Dean Ivory) *plld hrd and prom: rdn and hung lft 2f out: sn wknd* **33/1**

4 **6** *15* **Boru's Brook (IRE)**[4] 5709 8-9-11 0.......... JimmyQuinn 6
(Jim Best) *s.s: a in rr: lost tch fnl 3f* **66/1**

1m 40.69s (0.69) **Going Correction** +0.075s/f (Good)
WFA 3 from 6yo+ 6lb **6** Ran SP% **113.1**
Speed ratings (Par 103): **99,98,98,84,71 56**
CSF £3.57 TOTE £1.90: £1.10, £1.50; EX 4.30 Trifecta £5.00.
Owner Hamdan Al Maktoum **Bred** Shadwell Farm LLC **Trained** Manton, Wilts

FOCUS
Just a fair maiden. They went quite steady early on and the first three finished in a heap, well clear of the rest.

5851 TRM INVEST IN CALPHORMIN FILLIES' H'CAP (SUPPORTED BY THE THOROUGHBRED BREEDERS' ASSOCIATION) 1m 5f

4:55 (4:55) (Class 3) (0-95,89) 3-Y-O+ **£16,172** (£4,812; £2,405; £1,202) **Stalls** Centre

Form RPR

3411 **1** **Purple Magic**[42] 4351 3-8-8 **83**.......... EdwardGreatrex(3) 2 94+
(Michael Bell) *chsd ldr 3f: remained handy: wnt 2nd again over 3f out: swtchd lft over 2f out: rdn to ld over 1f out: styd on wl* **15/8**[1]

0-01 **2** *4* **Great And Small**[34] 4633 3-8-5 **77**.......... JimmyQuinn 1 82
(Andrew Balding) *hld up: pushed along over 2f out: hdwy over 1f out: sn rdn and edgd lft: styd on to go 2nd nr fin* **10/1**

0-05 **3** *hd* **Kiltara (IRE)**[14] 5382 4-9-12 **87**.......... AdamKirby 4 92
(Mark Johnston) *led: rdn and hdd over 1f out: no ex wl ins fnl f* **8/1**

4362 **4** *4 ½* **Perestroika**[15] 5328 4-10-0 **89**.......... FergusSweeney 3 86
(Henry Candy) *prom: rdn and nt clr run over 2f out: edgd rt over 1f out: sn wknd* **11/4**[2]

0111 **5** *2 ¼* **Lady Makfi (IRE)**[21] 5131 4-9-4 **79**.......... FrankieDettori 5 73
(Johnny Farrelly) *hld up: hdwy on outer over 2f out: rdn and hung lft over 1f out: sn wknd* **8/1**

4115 **6** *43* **Fashion Parade**[15] 5331 3-8-13 **85**.......... WilliamBuick 6 10
(Charles Hills) *prom: chsd ldr 10f out: rdn and lost 2nd over 3f out: edgd lft over 2f out: wknd wl over 1f out* **5/1**[3]

2m 42.72s (-1.28) **Going Correction** +0.075s/f (Good)
WFA 3 from 4yo 11lb **6** Ran SP% **109.4**
Speed ratings (Par 104): **106,103,103,100,99 72**
CSF £19.66 TOTE £2.50: £1.40, £4.00; EX 15.70 Trifecta £106.70.
Owner Lady Bamford **Bred** Lady Bamford **Trained** Newmarket, Suffolk

FOCUS
A good handicap won by a fast-improving filly and the placed horses showed progressive form as well.

5852 TRM-IRELAND.COM H'CAP (JOCKEY CLUB GRASSROOTS FLAT SPRINT SERIES QUALIFIER) 6f

5:30 (5:32) (Class 4) (0-85,91) 3-Y-O+ **£5,175** (£1,540; £769; £384) **Stalls** High

Form RPR

1004 **1** **Cool Bahamian (IRE)**[11] 5488 5-9-5 **83**.......... (v) EdwardGreatrex(3) 8 90
(Eve Johnson Houghton) *led at stdy pce tl qcknd 1/2-way: shkn up and hdd over 1f out: rallied to ld ins fnl f: r.o* **6/1**

0351 **2** *hd* **Reputation (IRE)**[10] 5512 3-9-13 **91** 6ex......................(v) FrankieDettori 9 97
(John Quinn) *trckd ldrs: rdn and ev ch fr over 1f out: r.o* **1/1**[1]
5630 **3** *1* **Vimy Ridge**[5] 5679 4-8-11 **75**..(p) EoinWalsh(3) 3 78
(Alan Bailey) *chsd wnr tl rdn to ld over 1f out: hdd ins fnl f: styd on same pce* **12/1**
3520 **4** *1 3/4* **Koptoon**[22] 5075 4-9-4 **79**... AdamKirby 7 77
(Jo Hughes) *prom: rdn and hung lft fr over 1f out: no ex ins fnl f* **9/2**[2]
3030 **5** *1* **Mississippi**[10] 5512 7-9-4 **79**..(p) PaulHanagan 1 74
(Paul Midgley) *broke wl: sn stdd and lost pl: rdn over 2f out: styd on: nt trble ldrs* **11/2**[3]
0145 **6** *5* **Sunraider (IRE)**[16] 5291 9-8-11 **72**.................................... MartinHarley 6 52
(Paul Midgley) *hld up: rdn over 2f out: wknd over 1f out* **16/1**

1m 12.13s (-0.37) **Going Correction** +0.075s/f (Good)
WFA 3 from 4yo+ 3lb **6** Ran SP% **111.4**
Speed ratings (Par 105): **105,104,103,101,99 93**
CSF £12.36 CT £66.09 TOTE £6.40: £2.40, £1.10; EX 10.00 Trifecta £82.00.
Owner L R Godfrey & R F Johnson Houghton **Bred** Kildaragh Stud **Trained** Blewbury, Oxon

FOCUS
They didn't go that quickly early and the pace held up in this sprint handicap. Straightforward form with the winner rated to last year's win in this race.
T/Plt: £35.10 to a £1 stake. Pool: £66,516.79 - 1,379.52 winning tickets T/Qpdt: £4.40 to a £1 stake. Pool: £4,850.71 - 808.23 winning tickets **Colin Roberts**

5726 THIRSK (L-H)
Friday, August 26

OFFICIAL GOING: Soft (7.0)
Wind: Fresh behind Weather: Cloudy with sunny periods, breezy

5853 CAPTAIN JACK SPARROW'S PIRATES DAY MAIDEN CLAIMING STKS 1m
1:50 (1:51) (Class 6) 2-Y-O **£2,587** (£770; £384; £192) **Stalls** Low

Form RPR
322 **1** **London Grammar (IRE)**[28] 4842 2-8-7 60........................ PJMcDonald 4 55
(John Quinn) *trckd ldrs: hdwy on inner and cl up 2f out: sn rdn: slt ld ent fnl f: drvn out* **6/5**[1]
052 **2** *1 1/4* **Dream On Dreamer (IRE)**[39] 4442 2-9-7 67..............[1] PaulMulrennan 2 65
(Michael Dods) *led: pushed along over 2f out: sn jnd and rdn: drvn and hdd ent fnl f: kpt on* **13/8**[2]
0532 **3** *4 1/2* **Amy Gardner**[14] 5351 2-8-4 58...................................... NathanEvans(5) 6 43
(James Given) *trckd ldrs: hdwy on outer and cl up over 2f out: rdn to chal wl over 1f out and ev ch: drvn and one pce fnl f* **11/2**[3]
00 **4** *2 1/4* **Raze Aqlaam**[37] 4524 2-8-11 0...................................... JackMitchell 5 40
(Giles Bravery) *hld up in rr: hdwy wl over 2f out: swtchd lft to inner and rdn wl over 1f out: sn drvn and no imp* **33/1**
6005 **5** *3 3/4* **Sheppard's Gift**[37] 4509 2-8-5 47........................ RachelRichardson(3) 3 29
(Tim Easterby) *trckd ldr: cl up 3f out: rdn along over 2f out: sn drvn and wknd* **25/1**
6 **6** *36* **Meadow View Girl**[17] 5250 2-7-13 0......................... SophieKilloran(7) 1
(David Flood) *in tch: pushed along over 3f out: rdn along wl over 2f out: sn outpcd and bhd fnl 2f* **66/1**

1m 46.69s (6.59) **Going Correction** +0.50s/f (Yiel) **6** Ran SP% **107.2**
Speed ratings (Par 92): **87,85,81,79,75 39**
CSF £3.00 TOTE £2.10: £1.10, £1.40; EX 3.30 Trifecta £4.40.
Owner Ross Harmon **Bred** Pier House Stud **Trained** Settrington, N Yorks

FOCUS
Following 8mm of overnight rain the going was soft. After riding in the opener Paul Mulrennan and Rachel Richardson both called the ground "soft" and PJ McDonald called it "holding". They went a fair gallop in this modest maiden claimer and the first two in the betting came clear.

5854 BRITISH STALLION STUDS EBF MAIDEN FILLIES' STKS (PLUS 10 RACE) 1m
2:20 (2:20) (Class 4) 2-Y-O **£4,269** (£1,270; £634; £317) **Stalls** Low

Form RPR
05 **1** **Anythingknappen (IRE)**[10] 5516 2-8-11 0.......... RachelRichardson(3) 7 71
(Tim Easterby) *trckd ldr: pushed along over 2f out: rdn on inner over 1f out: styd on to ld last 100yds* **16/1**
2 *1/2* **Warm Love** 2-9-0 0.. DanielTudhope 8 70+
(David O'Meara) *trckd ldrs: hdwy and cl up over 2f out: rdn to ld over 1f out: edgd lft ins fnl f: hdd and no ex last 100yds* **7/2**[3]
42 **3** *1 1/4* **Showtime Lady (IRE)**[22] 5052 2-9-0 0......................... PaulMulrennan 2 67
(Mark Johnston) *led: edgd rt home bnd: pushed along over 2f out: sn rdn: hdd over 1f out: sn drvn: kpt on same pce* **11/8**[1]
2 **4** *4 1/2* **Sue's Angel (IRE)**[16] 5290 2-9-0 0.............................. GeorgeChaloner 1 57+
(Richard Fahey) *dwlt and bhd: green and pushed along wl over 2f out: styd on appr fnl f* **9/4**[2]
00 **5** *3/4* **Silver Gleam (IRE)**[13] 5387 2-9-0 0.................................... DavidAllan 3 55
(Tim Easterby) *trckd ldrs: hdwy on wd outside and cl up 2f out: sn rdn and ev ch: hung lft over 1f out: sn wknd* **20/1**
66 **6** *nk* **Clenymistra (IRE)**[42] 4357 2-9-0 0.. LiamJones 4 55
(Marco Botti) *trckd ldrs: pushed along wl over 2f out: sn rdn and outpcd fr wl over 1f out* **33/1**

1m 47.59s (7.49) **Going Correction** +0.50s/f (Yiel) **6** Ran SP% **108.7**
Speed ratings (Par 93): **82,81,80,75,75 74**
CSF £65.85 TOTE £18.30: £6.50, £2.20; EX 70.00 Trifecta £150.20.
Owner Mrs John McEnery **Bred** Rossenarra Bloodstock Limited **Trained** Great Habton, N Yorks

FOCUS
A moderate maiden in which they went a fair pace and the first three came clear. A step forward from the winner.

5855 FOLLOW @RACING_UK ON TWITTER CLASSIFIED (S) STKS 5f
2:55 (2:55) (Class 6) 3-4-Y-O **£2,587** (£770; £384; £192) **Stalls** High

Form RPR
4050 **1** **Flowing Clarets**[23] 5032 3-8-10 72............................ GeorgeChaloner 2 68
(Richard Fahey) *cl up: chal 2f out: rdn to ld over 1f out: drvn and edgd lft ins fnl f: kpt on wl towards fin* **11/10**[1]
3015 **2** *nk* **Jaarih (IRE)**[19] 5189 4-9-6 70....................................(b[1]) PaulMulrennan 4 75
(Conor Dore) *hld up: hdwy on outer over 2f out: rdn over 1f out: ev ch ins fnl f: sn drvn and no ex towards fin* **15/8**[2]
5265 **3** *2 1/4* **Roaring Rory**[22] 5070 3-8-11 65............................(p) JacobButterfield(3) 3 63
(Ollie Pears) *cl up: led 3f out: rdn along 2f out: hdd over 1f out: sn drvn and ev ch: kpt on same pce wl ins fnl f* **8/1**
5030 **4** *7* **Cool Silk Boy (IRE)**[84] 2854 3-8-10 64.......................... AndrewMullen 6 34
(James Given) *slt ld: hdd 3f out: rdn along 1/2-way: drvn wl over 1f out: sn wknd* **13/2**[3]

1m 0.79s (1.19) **Going Correction** +0.175s/f (Good)
WFA 3 from 4yo 2lb **4** Ran SP% **106.8**
Speed ratings (Par 101): **97,96,92,81**
CSF £3.34 TOTE £1.90; EX 3.40 Trifecta £6.80.
Owner The Matthewman One Partnership **Bred** R A Fahey **Trained** Musley Bank, N Yorks

FOCUS
A lowly seller that was fought out by the front two in the market. They went a good pace and the winner has been rated just shy of her recent runs despite winning.

5856 A FOR AGENCY H'CAP 2m
3:30 (3:30) (Class 5) (0-75,75) 3-Y-O+ **£3,234** (£962; £481; £240) **Stalls** Centre

Form RPR
2305 **1** **Rock On Bollinski**[41] 4381 6-9-7 71..................................(p) BenCurtis 4 77
(Brian Ellison) *trckd ldr: cl up over 3f out: led wl over 2f out and sn rdn: drvn and hung rt wl over 1f out: carried hd high and kpt on wl u.p fnl f* **5/2**[2]
2224 **2** *1 3/4* **Wishing Well**[25] 4949 4-8-11 66.............................. CallumShepherd(5) 2 70
(Micky Hammond) *trckd ldrs: hdwy over 4f out: cl up and rdn along over 2f out: swtchd lft wl over 1f out: sn drvn and ev ch tl kpt on same pce ins fnl f* **6/1**
0245 **3** *8* **Moshe (IRE)**[22] 5061 5-9-11 75.................................... AndrewMullen 5 70
(Philip Kirby) *led: rdn along over 3f out: hdd wl over 2f out: drvn wl over 1f out: kpt on same pce* **4/1**[3]
3513 **4** *2 1/2* **Frederic**[38] 4491 5-9-8 72.. PJMcDonald 3 65
(Micky Hammond) *trckd ldng pair: effrt over 3f out: rdn along 2f out: sn drvn and one pce appr fnl f* **9/4**[1]
5432 **5** *43* **Jan Smuts (IRE)**[9] 5541 8-9-5 69...............................(tp) PaulMulrennan 1 14
(Wilf Storey) *a in rr: pushed along over 7f out: rdn 5f out: outpcd and bhd fr 3f out* **5/1**

3m 38.84s (10.54) **Going Correction** +0.50s/f (Yiel) **5** Ran SP% **110.3**
Speed ratings (Par 103): **93,92,88,86,65**
CSF £16.78 TOTE £3.90: £2.00, £3.30; EX 22.70 Trifecta £68.20.
Owner E J Worrell **Bred** Worrell, Hope, Sykes And Horsman **Trained** Norton, N Yorks

FOCUS
A moderate staying handicap in which they went a sensible gallop in the ground. The winner has been rated to his mark.

5857 THEAKSTON LIGHTFOOT H'CAP 6f
4:05 (4:06) (Class 3) (0-95,95) 3-Y-O+ **£7,762** (£2,310; £1,154; £577) **Stalls** High

Form RPR
0203 **1** **Ocean Sheridan (IRE)**[27] 4893 4-8-11 82..................... PaulMulrennan 1 93
(Michael Dods) *trckd ldrs on outer: smooth hdwy 1/2-way: led wl over 1f out: sn rdn and styd on strly* **15/2**[2]
0630 **2** *1 3/4* **Tiger Jim**[27] 4896 6-8-11 82.. JoeDoyle 2 88
(Jim Goldie) *in tch towards outer: hdwy over 2f out: chsd ldrs over 1f out: rdn to chse wnr ins fnl f: kpt on* **18/1**
-221 **3** *nk* **Magical Effect (IRE)**[28] 4845 4-8-6 77......................... JamesSullivan 17 82
(Ruth Carr) *racd towards stands' rail: towards rr: hdwy 2f out: rdn over 1f out: kpt on fnl f* **15/2**[2]
0036 **4** *1 1/4* **Eccleston**[25] 4946 5-9-6 91.......................................(v) DanielTudhope 16 95+
(David O'Meara) *racd towards stands' side: towards rr: swtchd lft and hdwy over 2f out: rdn to chse ldrs over 1f out: kpt on fnl f* **9/2**[1]
1336 **5** *2* **Intense Style (IRE)**[21] 5124 4-9-6 91.................................. DavidAllan 9 86
(Les Eyre) *in tch: hdwy 2f out: sn rdn and kpt on same pce fnl f* **8/1**[3]
3146 **6** *nk* **Escalating**[25] 4954 4-9-0 85.......................................(tp) AndrewMullen 12 79
(Michael Appleby) *dwlt: sn cl up nr stands' rail: led after 2f: hdd and cl up 1/2-way: pushed along over 2f out: rdn wl over 1f out: grad wknd* **10/1**
002 **7** *3/4* **Lucky Beggar (IRE)**[64] 3573 6-8-13 84.................................... BenCurtis 10 76
(David C Griffiths) *racd towards stands' side: cl up: led 1/2-way: rdn along and hdd 2f out: drvn over 1f out: wknd ent fnl f* **9/1**
0560 **8** *nk* **El Viento (FR)**[27] 4862 8-8-8 86..........................(v) NatalieHambling(7) 14 77
(Richard Fahey) *in tch: rdn along over 2f out: kpt on fnl f* **20/1**
-000 **9** *nk* **Magic City (IRE)**[13] 5417 7-8-7 83.............................. NathanEvans(5) 3 73
(Michael Easterby) *prom on outer: rdn along over 2f out: grad wknd* **33/1**
0030 **10** *3/4* **Khelman (IRE)**[13] 5417 6-9-0 85................................ GeorgeChaloner 6 73
(Richard Fahey) *racd towards centre: a in midfield* **25/1**
0400 **11** *1 3/4* **Holiday Magic (IRE)**[13] 5417 5-8-10 86......................... AnnaHesketh(5) 7 69
(Michael Easterby) *a towards rr* **20/1**
-100 **12** *1* **Kommander Kirkup**[11] 5479 5-8-6 82....................... CallumShepherd(5) 5 62
(John Davies) *prom on outer: rdn along over 2f out: sn drvn and wknd wl over 1f out* **33/1**
1000 **13** *2 1/4* **Blaine**[27] 4865 6-9-10 95...(b) PaulQuinn 13 68
(David Nicholls) *dwlt: a bhd* **16/1**
5013 **14** *shd* **Musharrif**[17] 5274 4-8-5 76... PatrickMathers 18 49
(Declan Carroll) *racd nr stands' rail: led 2f: cl up: rdn along 1/2-way: sn lost pl and bhd* **16/1**
1463 **15** *2 3/4* **My Name Is Rio (IRE)**[28] 4831 6-9-5 90.................(p) ConnorBeasley 15 54
(Michael Dods) *racd towards stands' side: chsd ldrs: rdn over 2f out: sn drvn and wknd* **11/1**
0000 **16** *1* **Handsome Dude**[13] 5417 4-8-13 84..........................(b) GrahamGibbons 8 45
(David Barron) *a in rr* **12/1**

1m 12.01s (-0.69) **Going Correction** +0.175s/f (Good) **16** Ran SP% **124.2**
Speed ratings (Par 107): **111,108,108,106,103 103,102,102,101,100 98,97,94,93,90 88**
CSF £127.91 CT £1102.93 TOTE £8.90: £2.20, £5.30, £2.10, £1.60; EX 166.70 Trifecta £1876.60.
Owner J Blackburn & A Turton **Bred** J Hernon **Trained** Denton, Co Durham

FOCUS
The feature race was a competitive sprint handicap in which the better ground was down the centre, counting against those drawn high on the stands' rail. The winner sets the level.

5858 HIGH DEFINITION RACING UK H'CAP (DIV I) 7f
4:40 (4:42) (Class 4) (0-80,79) 3-Y-O+ **£4,851** (£1,443; £721; £360) **Stalls** Low

Form RPR
4002 **1** **Whozthecat (IRE)**[3] 5753 9-8-10 63..............................(t) GrahamGibbons 10 71
(Declan Carroll) *mde all: rdn along 2f out: drvn over 1f out: edgd lft ins fnl f: hld on gamely* **5/1**[2]
1110 **2** *1/2* **Robero**[34] 4627 4-9-9 76.. BenCurtis 4 83
(Brian Ellison) *in tch: hdwy on inner over 3f out: cl up 2f out: rdn to chal over 1f out: sn ev ch: drvn ins fnl f: n.m.r and no ex towards fin* **5/2**[1]
6023 **3** *nse* **Signore Piccolo**[10] 5512 5-9-12 79.................................... DanielTudhope 9 86
(David O'Meara) *trckd ldrs: hdwy over 2f out: sn cl up: rdn and ev ch ent fnl f: sn drvn and kpt on* **11/2**[3]

21-0 **4** ½ **Yosemite**[38] **4496** 3-9-3 **75** DavidNolan 8 79
(Richard Fahey) *hld up in tch: hdwy on outer wl over 2f out: rdn to chal wl over 1f out: drvn ins fnl f: kpt on* **10/1**

6305 **5** 2¼ **Personal Touch**[16] **5301** 7-9-10 **77** AndrewMullen 5 77
(Michael Appleby) *trckd wnr: hdwy 3f out: cl up and rdn 2f out: drvn over 1f out: hld whn n.m.r ins fnl f* **9/1**

3436 **6** 4½ **Manatee Bay**[44] **4259** 6-9-10 **77** (v) PaulQuinn 2 66
(David Nicholls) *dwlt: a towards rr* **9/1**

0050 **7** ½ **Meshardal (GER)**[20] **5182** 6-9-6 **73** JamesSullivan 6 61
(Ruth Carr) *towards rr: sme hdwy on wd outside 3f out: rdn over 2f out: sn btn* **8/1**

6050 **8** 6 **Be Bold**[18] **5224** 4-8-10 **68** NathanEvans(5) 3 41
(Rebecca Bastiman) *a towards rr: outpcd fr over 2f out* **25/1**

31-0 **9** 1¼ **Ambriel (IRE)**[74] **3213** 3-9-6 **78** PaulMulrennan 7 45
(Michael Dods) *a towards rr* **16/1**

2000 **10** nk **Balducci**[20] **5179** 9-9-7 **74** (v) DavidAllan 1 43
(David Loughnane) *chsd ldrs: rdn along wl over 2f out: sn wknd* **20/1**

1m 28.74s (1.54) **Going Correction** +0.50s/f (Yiel)
WFA 3 from 4yo+ 5lb **10** Ran SP% **115.3**
Speed ratings (Par 105): **111,110,110,109,107 102,101,94,93,92**
CSF £17.64 CT £72.52 TOTE £5.80: £2.00, £1.40, £1.60; EX 20.70 Trifecta £90.90.

Owner Simon Bean **Bred** Liam Queally **Trained** Malton, N Yorks

FOCUS
The first division of this handicap was run in a faster time than the second. The form horses came to the fore and give it a solid look with the winner a mid 80s horse this time last year. It paid to race prominently.

5859 HIGH DEFINITION RACING UK H'CAP (DIV II) 7f
5:15 (5:15) (Class 4) (0-80,80) 3-Y-O+ **£4,851** (£1,443; £721; £360) **Stalls** Low

Form RPR
332 **1** **Run To The Hills (USA)**[38] **4477** 3-9-5 **78** DavidNolan 1 88+
(George Peckham) *trckd ldrs: hdwy on outer and cl up over 2f out: rdn to ld 1 1/2f out: kpt on wl fnl f* **4/1**[2]

5020 **2** 1¾ **King Of Swing**[11] **5482** 3-9-5 **78** AndrewMullen 9 83
(James Given) *cl up: led after 1f: rdn along and jnd over 2f out: hdd 1 1/2f out: sn drvn and kpt on same pce* **4/1**[2]

1033 **3** 3¾ **Space War**[23] **5034** 9-8-8 **67** (t) AnnaHesketh(5) 8 65
(Michael Easterby) *sn trcking ldng pair: hdwy 3f out: cl up 2f out: sn rdn and ev ch: drvn appr fnl f and sn one pce* **11/1**

2231 **4** hd **Chaplin Bay (IRE)**[22] **5075** 4-9-10 **78** JamesSullivan 2 75
(Ruth Carr) *hld up in tch: hdwy wl over 2f out: rdn wl over 1f out: drvn and one pce appr fnl f* **5/2**[1]

0010 **5** nse **Buccaneers Vault (IRE)**[20] **5179** 4-9-9 **77** (p) PaulMulrennan 5 74
(Michael Dods) *in tch: pushed along over 3f out: rdn over 2f out: sn drvn and no imp* **17/2**

0000 **6** ¾ **Comino (IRE)**[27] **4893** 5-9-6 **74** (p) KeaganLatham 7 69
(Kevin Ryan) *led 1f: chsd ldr: rdn and cl up over 2f out: drvn over 1f out: wknd appr fnl f* **8/1**

0400 **7** 5 **Compton Park**[27] **4896** 9-9-3 **76** [1] NathanEvans(5) 3 59
(Les Eyre) *hld up in rr: hdwy 3f out: rdn to chse ldrs 2f out: sn drvn and btn* **15/2**[3]

1m 29.35s (2.15) **Going Correction** +0.50s/f (Yiel)
WFA 3 from 4yo+ 5lb **7** Ran SP% **110.3**
Speed ratings (Par 105): **107,105,100,100,100 99,93**
CSF £18.79 CT £149.48 TOTE £3.30: £1.60, £2.00; EX 21.40 Trifecta £98.20.

Owner Fawzi Abdullah Nass & Justin Byrne **Bred** Dennis Rowan & Cecilia Rowan **Trained** Newmarket, Suffolk

FOCUS
The second division of this handicap was run in a slower time, but produced a more progressive winner who has more to offer. The first two came clear.

5860 PAY AND WATCH RACING UK VIA MOBILE APPRENTICE H'CAP 1m
5:50 (5:51) (Class 5) (0-70,70) 3-Y-O **£3,234** (£962; £481; £240) **Stalls** Low

Form RPR
5013 **1** **Hijran (IRE)**[2] **5759** 3-9-8 **66** (p) TimClark 8 74
(Michael Appleby) *trckd ldrs: hdwy to ld 3f out: rdn clr 2f out: edgd lft ins fnl f: kpt on* **3/1**[1]

0004 **2** 1¼ **Mon Beau Visage (IRE)**[12] **5439** 3-9-5 **69** JoshDoyle(6) 7 74
(David O'Meara) *hld up in tch: hdwy over 2f out: rdn wl over 1f out: sn chsng wnr: drvn and kpt on fnl f* **9/2**[2]

0026 **3** 2 **Quoteline Direct**[9] **5539** 3-9-2 **66** RobJFitzpatrick(6) 3 66
(Micky Hammond) *in rr: hdwy on wd outside over 2f out: rdn wl over 1f out: kpt on* **20/1**

3310 **4** hd **Bonhomie**[16] **5302** 3-9-2 **68** LuluStanford(8) 9 68
(Michael Bell) *cl up: led after 2f: hdd 3f out and sn pushed along: rdn 2f out: drvn and kpt on same pce fnl f* **5/1**[3]

0020 **5** nk **Back To Bond**[4] **5729** 3-8-13 **65** NatalieHambling(8) 1 64
(Richard Fahey) *cl up on inner: rdn along 3f out: drvn wl over 1f out: kpt on same pce* **18/1**

040 **6** 2¾ **Beverley Bullet**[4] **5732** 3-9-0 **61** NathanEvans(3) 4 54
(Les Eyre) *hld up: hdwy 3f out: rdn to chse ldrs 2f out: sn drvn and no imp* **5/1**[3]

1041 **7** 3½ **Ubla (IRE)**[16] **5302** 3-9-2 **65** (t) RhiainIngram(5) 5 49
(Gay Kelleway) *hld up: a towards rr* **8/1**

443 **8** 4½ **Pickett's Charge**[11] **5478** 3-9-12 **70** JacobButterfield 6 44
(Tony Coyle) *prom: rdn along wl over 2f out: drvn 2f out and sn wknd* **13/2**

004 **9** 14 **Glittering**[64] **3577** 3-9-2 **60** ShelleyBirkett 2 2
(James Eustace) *a towards rr* **25/1**

1m 44.52s (4.42) **Going Correction** +0.50s/f (Yiel) **9** Ran SP% **114.8**
Speed ratings (Par 100): **97,95,93,93,93 90,87,82,68**
CSF £16.27 CT £226.75 TOTE £2.90: £1.10, £1.60, £7.70; EX 21.20 Trifecta £256.30.

Owner L A Hill & C L Bacon **Bred** C Farrell **Trained** Oakham, Rutland

FOCUS
An average handicap for apprentices and they went a steady pace. The winner is possibly a shade better than the bare form.

T/Jkpt: Not won. T/Plt: £124.20 to a £1 stake. Pool: £56,907.59 - 334.43 winning tickets T/Qpdt: £18.20 to a £1 stake. Pool: £4,561.09 - 185.15 winning tickets **Joe Rowntree**

5317 BEVERLEY (R-H)
Saturday, August 27

OFFICIAL GOING: Good (7.5)
Wind: Virtually nil Weather: Grey cloud and showers

5861 GOING FOR GOLD EBF MAIDEN FILLIES' STKS (PLUS 10 RACE) 7f 100y
2:00 (2:01) (Class 4) 2-Y-O **£5,040** (£1,508; £754; £377; £188) **Stalls** Low

Form RPR
2 **1** **Peak Princess (IRE)**[28] **4885** 2-9-0 0 DaneO'Neill 4 77
(Richard Hannon) *trckd ldr: cl up over 2f out: chal wl over 1f out: sn rdn: drvn to ld ent fnl f: sn edgd lft and styd on wl towards fin* **4/6**[1]

53 **2** 2¾ **Baileys Apprentice**[17] **5290** 2-9-0 0 PaulMulrennan 7 71
(Mark Johnston) *led: pushed along over 2f out: sn jnd and rdn: drvn over 1f out: hdd ent fnl f: swtchd lft and kpt on same pce towards fin* **10/1**[3]

3 **3** nk **Show Me The Music**[14] **5387** 2-9-0 0 DavidNolan 2 70
(Richard Fahey) *trckd ldng pair: pushed along 3f out: rdn over 2f out: swtchd lft and styd on u.p ins fnl f* **2/1**[2]

63 **4** 6 **Mistress Viz (IRE)**[19] **5221** 2-9-0 0 PJMcDonald 5 56
(John Mackie) *trckd ldrs: pushed along over 3f out: rdn wl over 2f out: sn one pce* **14/1**

5 ½ **Patching** 2-9-0 0 HarryBentley 1 55
(Giles Bravery) *dwlt and in rr: rdn and hdwy over 2f out: sn no imp* **20/1**

000 **6** 6 **Beau Strata (IRE)**[40] **4451** 2-9-0 48 JamesSullivan 3 40
(Clive Mulhall) *in tch: pushed along 1/2-way: rdn wl over 2f out: sn outpcd* **100/1**

0000 **7** 3½ **Can Can Dream**[15] **5377** 2-9-0 52 [1] CamHardie 6 32
(Olly Williams) *in tch: rdn along over 3f out: sn outpcd* **100/1**

1m 32.62s (-1.18) **Going Correction** -0.275s/f (Firm) **7** Ran SP% **115.8**
Speed ratings (Par 93): **95,91,91,84,84 77,73**
CSF £9.30 TOTE £1.60: £1.10, £4.90; EX 8.90 Trifecta £14.50.
Owner Rockcliffe Stud **Bred** Roland H Alder **Trained** East Everleigh, Wilts

FOCUS
The rails were set at their widest configuration to provide fresh ground, and the jockeys indicated that it was riding on the soft side of good, following rain before racing. Two stood out on form against some low-grade rivals in this fillies' maiden, and the three market leaders came clear in the straight. The winner was firmly on top and a step forward from the second.

5862 TOTESCOOP6 RACING'S MILLIONAIRE MAKER MAIDEN STKS 5f
2:35 (2:37) (Class 4) 3-Y-O+ **£5,040** (£1,508; £754; £377; £188) **Stalls** Low

Form RPR
2522 **1** **Dance Alone**[20] **5195** 3-9-5 74 (b) TomEaves 4 74
(Kevin Ryan) *mde all: rdn wl over 1f out: drvn ins fnl f: kpt on wl last 100yds* **2/1**[2]

0 **2** 1¼ **Jabbarockie**[102] **2333** 3-9-5 0 PJMcDonald 2 70
(Paul Green) *chsd ldrs: rdn along over 2f out: hdwy ent fnl f: drvn and kpt on wl towards fin* **12/1**

6 **3** 1¼ **Young Tiger**[14] **5388** 3-9-5 0 JamesSullivan 6 65
(Tom Tate) *cl up: chal 2f out: rdn over 1f out and ev ch tl drvn ins fnl f and wknd last 100yds* **16/1**

2/ **4** 4 **Pedro Serrano (IRE)**[1450] **6015** 6-9-7 0 (e[1]) DaneO'Neill 5 51+
(Henry Candy) *blind removed late and lost several l s: sn rdn along in rr: sme hdwy wl over 1f out: n.d* **6/4**[1]

0-2 **5** 1½ **Corridor Kid (IRE)**[125] **1669** 3-9-5 75 MartinLane 1 45
(Derek Shaw) *towards rr: rdn along over 2f out: n.d* **11/4**[3]

006- **6** 1¼ **Valtashyra (IRE)**[280] **7937** 3-8-12 39 ow3 AnnStokell(5) 3 39
(Ann Stokell) *chsd ldrs: rdn along 1/2-way: sn drvn and outpcd* **125/1**

1m 2.35s (-1.15) **Going Correction** -0.225s/f (Firm)
WFA 3 from 6yo 2lb **6** Ran SP% **114.4**
Speed ratings (Par 105): **100,98,96,89,87 85**
CSF £25.19 TOTE £2.60: £1.30, £4.50; EX 23.00 Trifecta £95.50.
Owner Guy Reed Racing **Bred** Exors Of The Late G Reed **Trained** Hambleton, N Yorks

FOCUS
An ordinary sprint maiden and, with two of the three market leaders not running their races for different reasons, the form behind the winner should be treated with caution.

5863 TOTESCOOP6 BEVERLEY BULLET SPRINT STKS (LISTED RACE) 5f
3:10 (3:12) (Class 1) 3-Y-O+
£28,355 (£10,750; £5,380; £2,680; £1,345; £675) **Stalls** Low

Form RPR
5311 **1** **Alpha Delphini**[36] **4584** 5-9-0 96 [1] ConnorBeasley 4 108
(Bryan Smart) *trckd ldrs: hdwy over 1f out: rdn ins fnl f: kpt on wl to ld nr line* **13/2**[2]

2034 **2** nk **Willytheconqueror (IRE)**[21] **5143** 3-8-12 101 PhillipMakin 2 107
(William Muir) *cl up on inner: rdn to ld over 1f out: drvn ins fnl f: hdd and no ex nr line* **12/1**

036 **3** shd **Muthmir (IRE)**[29] **4824** 6-9-0 112 DaneO'Neill 7 107
(William Haggas) *in tch: hdwy over 1f out: rdn ent fnl f: styd on strly towards fin* **2/1**[1]

1412 **4** nse **Final Venture**[36] **4584** 4-9-0 100 NeilFarley 9 107
(Alan Swinbank) *stmbld s: sn slt ld: rdn 2f out: hdd over 1f out: drvn and ev ch ins fnl f: nt qckn towards fin* **8/1**

3150 **5** ½ **Mr Lupton (IRE)**[42] **4393** 3-8-12 111 BarryMcHugh 8 105
(Richard Fahey) *in tch: hdwy on outer over 1f out: rdn ent fnl f: styd on wl towards fin* **8/1**

0024 **6** shd **Line Of Reason (IRE)**[10] **5555** 6-9-0 104 MartinLane 5 107
(Paul Midgley) *in tch: hdwy on inner over 1f out: rdn and n.m.r ins fnl f: sn ev ch: drvn and no ex nr line* **8/1**

5601 **7** 1¾ **Son Of Africa**[7] **5648** 4-9-0 97 HarryBentley 6 98+
(Henry Candy) *blind removed late and dwlt: in rr: rdn along on inner 1/2-way: sme late hdwy* **14/1**

0450 **8** ¾ **Maarek**[63] **3681** 9-9-0 106 GaryHalpin 1 96+
(Miss Evanna McCutcheon, Ire) *dwlt: a towards rr* **15/2**[3]

5001 **9** 2¼ **Kingsgate Native (IRE)**[18] **5268** 11-9-0 105 (p) GrahamLee 3 88
(Robert Cowell) *chsd ldrs: rdn wl over 1f out: sn drvn and wknd ent fnl f* **20/1**

6150 **10** 1½ **Caspian Prince (IRE)**[36] **4584** 7-9-0 108 (t) BenCurtis 10 82+
(David Loughnane) *wnt lft s: a in rr* **20/1**

1m 0.89s (-2.61) **Going Correction** -0.225s/f (Firm)
WFA 3 from 4yo+ 2lb **10** Ran SP% **115.6**
Speed ratings (Par 111): **111,110,110,110,109 109,106,105,101,99**
CSF £80.72 TOTE £7.10: £2.00, £4.00, £1.20; EX 77.10 Trifecta £356.90.
Owner The Alpha Delphini Partnership **Bred** Mrs B A Matthews **Trained** Hambleton, N Yorks

FOCUS
The feature race and a contest which has been won by several top-class sprinters. It again looked a strong Listed contest and produced a thrilling finish.

5864 TOTEPOOLLIVEINFO.COM H'CAP (DIV I) 5f
3:45 (3:47) (Class 5) (0-75,83) 3-Y-O+ **£5,040** (£1,508; £754; £377; £188) **Stalls** Low

Form RPR

2313 **1** **Sandra's Secret (IRE)**[7] 5643 3-9-5 **77** NathanEvans[(5)] 3 84
(Les Eyre) *qckly away and mde all: rdn ent fnl f: sn edgd lft: drvn and hld on wl towards fin* **11/4**[1]

4131 **2** ½ **Seamster**[3] 5762 9-9-11 **83** 6ex (t) CameronNoble[(7)] 5 88
(David Loughnane) *trckd ldrs on outer: hdwy over 1f out: swtchd rt and rdn ins fnl f: kpt on wl towards fin* **11/4**[1]

6400 **3** ½ **Socialites Red**[16] 5320 3-8-13 **66** [1] BenCurtis 2 69
(Scott Dixon) *prom: effrt and ev ch over 1f out: drvn ins fnl f: kpt on* **20/1**

0053 **4** shd **One Boy (IRE)**[3] 5780 5-9-4 **69** (v) DavidNolan 11 72
(Richard Fahey) *chsd ldrs: hdwy over 1f out: rdn ent fnl f: kpt on wl towards fin* **7/1**[2]

0264 **5** nk **Flicka's Boy**[17] 5296 4-9-5 **70** (t) BarryMcHugh 1 72
(Tony Coyle) *trckd ldrs on inner: hdwy over 1f out: sn rdn and kpt on fnl f* **10/1**

5636 **6** nk **Spirit Of Wedza (IRE)**[15] 5368 4-8-9 **65** (b) JoshDoyle[(5)] 4 66
(Julie Camacho) *prom: rdn along wl over 1f out: grad wknd fnl f* **8/1**[3]

5551 **7** ¾ **Miningg old**[16] 5320 3-8-12 **68** RachelRichardson[(3)] 7 66
(Tim Easterby) *in tch: hdwy on inner over 1f out: sn rdn and kpt on fnl f* **7/1**[2]

1400 **8** ½ **Flash City (ITY)**[12] 5479 8-9-7 **72** (b) JasonHart 10 68+
(Ruth Carr) *dwlt and sltly hmpd s: sn swtchd rt and towards rr: hdwy 2f out: sn rdn and kpt on fnl f* **12/1**

4030 **9** 6 **Long Awaited (IRE)**[8] 5599 8-9-6 **71** (b) PaulMulrennan 6 46+
(Conor Dore) *a towards rr* **28/1**

-000 **10** 3¼ **Space Artist (IRE)**[18] 5274 6-9-4 **69** (vt) PhillipMakin 9 32+
(Nigel Tinkler) *a towards rr* **50/1**

0165 **11** ¾ **Round The Island**[23] 5059 3-8-9 **62** (b[1]) PaulQuinn 8 22
(Richard Whitaker) *chsd ldrs: rdn along 2f out: sn wknd* **25/1**

1m 1.76s (-1.74) **Going Correction** -0.225s/f (Firm)
WFA 3 from 4yo+ 2lb **11** Ran SP% **120.2**
Speed ratings (Par 103): **104,103,102,102,101 101,100,99,89,84 83**
CSF £9.13 CT £127.84 TOTE £3.50: £1.60, £1.50, £4.90; EX 11.30 Trifecta £196.60.
Owner Sunpak Potatoes **Bred** Tally-Ho Stud **Trained** Catwick, N Yorks

FOCUS
The first division of a competitive sprint run 0.87 sec slower than the preceding Listed contest. A minor step forward from the winner and another personal best from the second.

5865 TOTEPOOL LIVE INFO DOWNLOAD THE APP H'CAP 1m 1f 207y
4:20 (4:20) (Class 2) (0-105,102) 3-Y-O
£28,012 (£8,388; £4,194; £2,097; £1,048; £526) **Stalls** Low

Form RPR

2106 **1** **Dolphin Vista (IRE)**[40] 4448 3-9-0 **95** DavidNolan 1 102
(Richard Fahey) *trckd ldng pair on inner: hdwy wl over 1f out: rdn ins fnl f: led last 100yds: drvn and kpt on wl towards fin* **17/2**

4532 **2** hd **Mainstream**[13] 5434 3-8-12 **93** GrahamLee 7 99
(Sir Michael Stoute) *dwlt: t.k.h and trckd ldrs: hdwy over 3f out: chal on outer wl over 1f out: rdn to ld appr fnl f: sn drvn: edgd rt and hdd last 100yds: kpt on* **3/1**[1]

1230 **3** 1¾ **Ode To Evening**[7] 5651 3-9-7 **102** PaulMulrennan 6 104
(Mark Johnston) *prom: trckd ldr after 3f: hdwy 3f out: chal 2f out: sn rdn: drvn and ev ch over 1f out: kpt on same pce fnl f* **6/1**[3]

1111 **4** shd **Cote D'Azur**[11] 5520 3-8-11 **92** DavidAllan 5 96+
(Les Eyre) *hld up: hdwy over 2f out and sn trcking ldrs: effrt and nt clr run 1 1/2f out: sn swtchd lft and rdn: kpt on towards fin* **10/3**[2]

3222 **5** ½ **Haraz (IRE)**[9] 5579 3-7-13 **83** oh1 ow2 ShelleyBirkett[(3)] 8 84
(David O'Meara) *led: rdn along over 2f out: drvn and hdd appr fnl f: grad wknd* **16/1**

4404 **6** 1 **Speed Company (IRE)**[21] 5173 3-9-0 **95** JasonHart 11 94
(John Quinn) *hld up in rr: hdwy 3f out: rdn along 2f out: sn btn* **10/1**

312 **7** ¾ **His Kyllachy (IRE)**[20] 5198 3-8-0 **81** RyanPowell 4 78
(William Haggas) *chsd ldrs: rdn along over 2f out: sn drvn and grad wknd* **13/2**

000 **8** 2¾ **Bathos (IRE)**[28] 4868 3-8-5 **86** PJMcDonald 9 78
(Mark Johnston) *trckd ldrs: pushed along 3f out: rdn over 2f out: sn wknd* **10/1**

5110 **9** 10 **Another Go (IRE)**[49] 4153 3-8-5 **86** NeilFarley 3 58
(Alan Swinbank) *hld up in rr: sme hdwy on outer over 3f out: rdn along wl over 2f out: sn btn* **20/1**

2m 3.07s (-3.93) **Going Correction** -0.275s/f (Firm) **9** Ran SP% **115.1**
Speed ratings (Par 106): **104,103,102,102,101 101,100,98,90**
CSF £34.11 CT £166.95 TOTE £10.70: £3.10, £1.40, £2.10; EX 38.80 Trifecta £177.20.
Owner Y Nasib **Bred** Jim McDonald **Trained** Musley Bank, N Yorks

FOCUS
The rails were set at the widest configuration to provide fresh ground. A high-class 3yo handicap, which Mark Johnston had won three times in the last eight seasons, and the race could be worth 4lb more than rated.

5866 @TOTEPOOL FOLLOW US ON TWITTER H'CAP 7f 100y
4:55 (4:57) (Class 4) (0-85,85) 3-Y-O+
£7,470 (£2,236; £1,118; £559; £279; £140) **Stalls** Low

Form RPR

5400 **1** **Mount Tahan (IRE)**[63] 3645 4-9-8 **81** KevinStott 4 91
(Kevin Ryan) *trckd ldrs: hdwy to ld wl over 1f out: rdn ent fnl f: kpt on wl towards fin* **8/1**

255 **2** 1¾ **Alejandro (IRE)**[27] 4917 7-9-12 **85** PaulMulrennan 6 91
(David O'Meara) *hld up in tch: hdwy 2f out: rdn over 1f out: chsd wnr ent fnl f: sn drvn and no imp* **6/1**[2]

1004 **3** 1¾ **Slemy (IRE)**[10] 5538 5-9-6 **79** PJMcDonald 13 80
(Ruth Carr) *hld up in rr: hdwy over 2f out: rdn over 1f out: styd on wl fnl f: nrst fin* **22/1**

0001 **4** 1¾ **Normandy Knight**[21] 5180 4-9-1 **74** DavidNolan 5 71
(Richard Fahey) *hld up in midfield: hdwy 3f out: chsd ldrs 2f out: rdn over 1f out: sn drvn and kpt on same pce* **12/1**

004 **5** 1½ **Storm King**[21] 5180 7-9-7 **80** (p) JoeDoyle 8 73
(David C Griffiths) *chsd ldng pair: rdn along over 2f out: sn drvn and wknd* **8/1**

2211 **6** hd **Shamaheart (IRE)**[21] 5179 6-9-11 **84** (p) DavidAllan 9 77
(Geoffrey Harker) *hld up in rr: hdwy over 2f out: sn rdn and kpt on fnl f* **10/1**

2050 **7** shd **Free Code (IRE)**[14] 5389 5-9-12 **85** PhillipMakin 3 77
(David Barron) *in rr: hdwy over 2f out: sn rdn and kpt on fnl f* **10/1**

0103 **8** 1¼ **Echo Of Lightning**[24] 5033 6-8-9 **75** BenRobinson[(7)] 7 64
(Brian Ellison) *hld up: a towards rr* **16/1**

3011 **9** 2 **Sovereign Bounty**[12] 5482 4-9-8 **81** GrahamLee 11 65
(Jedd O'Keeffe) *in tch on outer: pushed along 3f out: rdn over 2f out: sn btn* **9/2**[1]

0050 **10** ¾ **Hulcolt (IRE)**[11] 5514 5-9-8 **81** JasonHart 10 63+
(Ivan Furtado) *trckd ldr: cl up 3f out: rdn along over 2f out: sn drvn and wknd wl over 1f out* **20/1**

0-01 **11** 4 **Iconic (IRE)**[79] 3061 4-9-10 **83** DaneO'Neill 12 55
(Henry Candy) *chsd ldrs: rdn along over 2f out: sn drvn and wknd over 1f out* **7/1**

3160 **12** 3½ **Spryt (IRE)**[14] 5419 4-9-3 **81** (v) JoshDoyle[(5)] 2 45+
(David O'Meara) *led: rdn along 3f out: hdd wl over 1f out: sn wknd* **13/2**[3]

1m 30.46s (-3.34) **Going Correction** -0.275s/f (Firm)
WFA 3 from 4yo+ 5lb **12** Ran SP% **121.4**
Speed ratings (Par 105): **108,106,104,102,100 100,99,98,96,95 90,86**
CSF £56.84 CT £1049.75 TOTE £9.20: £3.60, £1.70, £6.80; EX 72.40 Trifecta £2694.90 Part won..
Owner T A Rahman **Bred** S F Bloodstock **Trained** Hambleton, N Yorks
■ Swiftee was withdrawn. Price at time of withdrawal 28/1. Rule 4 does not apply.

FOCUS
The rails were set at the widest configuration to provide fresh ground. This good handicap was run in heavy rain, but the time was much faster than the juvenile contest over the trip. The winner has been rated to his best.

5867 TOTEPOOLLIVEINFO.COM H'CAP (DIV II) 5f
5:30 (5:31) (Class 5) (0-75,75) 3-Y-O+ **£5,040** (£1,508; £754; £377; £188) **Stalls** Low

Form RPR

313 **1** **Hilary J**[23] 5070 3-9-7 **74** PJMcDonald 6 86
(Ann Duffield) *mde most: rdn over 1f out: drvn out* **9/2**[1]

0000 **2** 1 **Masamah (IRE)**[35] 4632 10-9-10 **75** DavidNolan 7 83
(Richard Fahey) *cl up: rdn and ev ch over 1f out: drvn ins fnl f: kpt on same pce* **6/1**

4530 **3** 2¼ **Groundworker (IRE)**[15] 5354 5-8-12 **63** PaulMulrennan 1 63
(Paul Midgley) *hld up towards rr: gd hdwy on inner over 2f out: rdn wl over 1f out: drvn to chse ldng pair ent fnl f: sn no imp* **5/1**[2]

020U **4** nk **Mitchum**[26] 4932 7-9-5 **70** (p) DavidAllan 10 69
(Ron Barr) *hld up in rr: hdwy on outer over 1f out: sn rdn and styd on fnl f* **25/1**

0324 **5** 2½ **Razin' Hell**[23] 5060 5-9-4 **69** (v) GrahamLee 2 59
(John Balding) *chsd ldrs: rdn along wl over 1f out: sn drvn and no imp fnl f* **11/2**[3]

0330 **6** ½ **Burtonwood**[16] 5320 4-9-1 **66** (b) JoeDoyle 4 54
(Julie Camacho) *stmbld s: a towards rr* **7/1**

2216 **7** ½ **Bond Bombshell**[17] 5296 3-8-13 **71** JoshDoyle[(5)] 3 57
(David O'Meara) *chsd ldng pair: rdn along wl over 1f out: drvn and wknd appr fnl f* **15/2**

3265 **8** ½ **Maureb (IRE)**[20] 5190 4-9-9 **74** (p) BarryMcHugh 8 63
(Tony Coyle) *chsd ldrs on outer: rdn along 2f out: sn wknd* **14/1**

4355 **9** ½ **Fyrecracker (IRE)**[17] 5295 5-9-5 **70** (v[1]) KevinStott 5 53
(Grant Tuer) *chsd ldrs: rdn along 2f out: drvn over 1f out: sn wknd* **9/2**[1]

1m 2.38s (-1.12) **Going Correction** -0.225s/f (Firm)
WFA 3 from 4yo+ 2lb **9** Ran SP% **117.5**
Speed ratings (Par 103): **99,97,93,93,89 88,87,86,86**
CSF £32.16 CT £142.20 TOTE £5.20: £2.50, £1.50, £2.10; EX 20.20 Trifecta £150.30.
Owner E & R Stott **Bred** Bumble Bloodstock Ltd **Trained** Constable Burton, N Yorks

FOCUS
The second leg of this competitive sprint was run 0.62 sec slower than the first, although there had been rain in between. The first two dominated throughout.

5868 EAST GATE APPRENTICE H'CAP 1m 1f 207y
6:05 (6:05) (Class 6) (0-65,63) 4-Y-O+ **£3,234** (£962; £481; £240) **Stalls** Low

Form RPR

1541 **1** **Miningrocks (FR)**[19] 5228 4-9-4 **62** GerO'Neill[(7)] 3 75
(Declan Carroll) *mde all: clr 1/2-way: rdn wl over 1f out: styd on strly* **3/1**[1]

3513 **2** 9 **Ingleby Spring (IRE)**[14] 5392 4-9-7 **63** NatalieHambling[(5)] 9 59
(Richard Fahey) *chsd wnr: rdn over 2f out: drvn over 1f out: sn no imp* **4/1**[3]

526 **3** ½ **Paddy's Rock (IRE)**[1] 5841 5-9-7 **61** JoshDoyle[(3)] 1 56
(Lynn Siddall) *trckd ldrs: hdwy 3f out: rdn 2f out: drvn over 1f out: kpt on same pce* **7/2**[2]

2646 **4** 1 **Ferdy (IRE)**[5] 5715 7-9-5 **56** JoeDoyle 5 49
(Paul Green) *in tch: hdwy over 2f out: sn rdn and kpt on same pce* **6/1**

6534 **5** ½ **Monopoli**[11] 5513 7-8-8 **50** (p) DavidParkes[(5)] 10 42
(Ivan Furtado) *towards rr: hdwy 2f out: sn rdn and styd on wl fnl f: nrst fin* **9/1**

3012 **6** ½ **I'm Super Too (IRE)**[16] 5323 9-9-3 **57** GemmaTutty[(3)] 2 48
(Karen Tutty) *in tch: effrt and pushed along 3f out: rdn over 2f out: plugged on same pce* **5/1**

3354 **7** 13 **Make On Madam (IRE)**[18] 5276 4-9-11 **62** JacobButterfield 11 28
(Les Eyre) *t.k.h: hld up: a in rr* **12/1**

6600 **8** 11 **General Tufto**[46] 4234 11-8-1 **45** (b) BenRobinson[(7)] 6
(Charles Smith) *chsd ldng pair: rdn along over 3f out: sn lost pl and bhd* **66/1**

-660 **9** 7 **Milu Mac**[16] 5319 5-8-3 **45** RhiainIngram[(5)] 8
(Neville Bycroft) *a in rr: bhd fnl 3f* **50/1**

0000 **10** 4½ **Rosie Hall (IRE)**[2] 5800 6-8-1 **45** (v) PaulaMuir[(7)] 4
(John Wainwright) *a in rr: bhd fnl 3f* **50/1**

2m 5.96s (-1.04) **Going Correction** -0.275s/f (Firm) **10** Ran SP% **121.3**
Speed ratings (Par 101): **93,85,85,84,84 83,73,64,59,55**
CSF £15.87 CT £44.93 TOTE £4.80: £1.50, £1.70, £1.70; EX 21.00 Trifecta £60.80.
Owner Mrs Sarah Bryan **Bred** M Daguzan-Garros & Rolling Hills Farm **Trained** Malton, N Yorks

FOCUS
The rails were set at the widest configuration to provide fresh ground. A moderate apprentice handicap run in memory of the much missed Tom O'Ryan, who gained his first win as a jockey in the race back in 1972. The time was 2.89 sec slower than the earlier 3yo handicap over the trip and it became a procession in the straight.
T/Plt: £80.50 to a £1 stake. Pool: £72,231.16 - 654.39 winning tickets. T/Qpdt: £26.90 to a £1 stake. Pool: £4,972.36 - 136.60 winning tickets. **Joe Rowntree**

5827 GOODWOOD (R-H)

Saturday, August 27

OFFICIAL GOING: Good to firm (good in places; watered)

Wind: Light, across Weather: Fine, slight haze, very warm

5869 ABSOLUTE AESTHETICS MAIDEN FILLIES' STKS (PLUS 10 RACE) 6f
2:10 (2:11) (Class 4) 2-Y-O **£5,175** (£1,540; £769; £384) **Stalls** High

Form RPR

1 **Tara Celeb** 2-9-0 0 JFEgan 1 73
(Mick Channon) *slowly away: sn chsd ldrs: prog to join ldng pair over 2f out: rdn to ld ins fnl f: kpt on wl* **11/1**

63 **2** *nk* **Money In My Pocket (IRE)**[5] 5705 2-9-0 0 SeanLevey 11 72
(Richard Hannon) *led: jnd 1/2-way: rdn over 2f out: kpt on wl u.p: hdd ins fnl f: jst hld after* **11/2**

3 *1* **Bella Alissa** 2-9-0 0 AndreaAtzeni 9 71+
(Peter Chapple-Hyam) *dwlt: rn green and bdly detached in last: sed to run on 1/2-way: gd prog fr 2f out: shkn up and styd on wl to take 3rd nr fin* **8/1**

05 **4** *½* **Incentive**[44] 4287 2-9-0 0 TomQueally 5 67
(Stuart Kittow) *pressed ldr: upsides fr 1/2-way tl ins fnl f: fdd nr fin* **16/1**

5 **5** *1 ¾* **Everkyllachy (IRE)**[33] 4706 2-8-11 0 JosephineGordon(3) 10 62
(J S Moore) *chsd ldrs: shkn up and no imp fr 2f out: one pce after* **66/1**

6 *hd* **Eula Varner** 2-9-0 0 FergusSweeney 6 61
(Henry Candy) *chsd ldrs: pushed along and no imp 2f out: one pce after: bttr for r* **8/1**

7 *nk* **Glacier Point** 2-9-0 0 JohnFahy 3 60
(Clive Cox) *chsd ldrs: lost pl 1/2-way and pushed along: n.d after: kpt on ins fnl f* **16/1**

3 **8** *1 ¾* **Twilight Spirit**[19] 5229 2-9-0 0 JimCrowley 7 57
(Tony Carroll) *towards rr: prog 1/2-way: chsd ldrs 2f out and rdn: fdd fnl f* **9/2**[2]

0 **9** *½* **Curry (IRE)**[31] 4756 2-9-0 0 TimmyMurphy 4 53
(Richard Hannon) *a towards rr: no prog 2f out* **5/1**[3]

00 **10** *nk* **Seaview**[11] 5511 2-9-0 0 RenatoSouza 8 52
(Dean Ivory) *settled wl in rr: pushed along and no nticeable prog fr 2f out* **40/1**

11 *6* **Silver Mist** 2-9-0 0 TomMarquand 12 33
(Richard Hannon) *dwlt: a in rr: bhd over 1f out* **10/3**[1]

1m 11.68s (-0.52) **Going Correction** -0.175s/f (Firm) **11** Ran SP% **119.6**
Speed ratings (Par 93): **96,95,94,93,91 91,90,88,87,87 79**
CSF £71.66 TOTE £16.70: £4.20, £2.30, £2.80; EX 105.10 Trifecta £896.90.
Owner The Tara Moon Partnership I **Bred** M H And Mrs G Tourle **Trained** West Ilsley, Berks
■ Stewards' Enquiry : Sean Levey two day ban (11-12 Sep): used whip above permitted level

FOCUS
The track missed the rain overnight and the ground rode quick but safe in the opinion of jockeys involved in the first. There was fresh ground on the lower bend, and all race distances were as advertised. This wasn't a strong maiden for the course and the pace held up, but it should produce winners at the right level.

5870 PRESTIGE STKS (GROUP 3) (FILLIES) 7f
2:45 (2:45) (Class 1) 2-Y-O
£22,684 (£8,600; £4,304; £2,144; £1,076; £540) **Stalls** Low

Form RPR

6420 **1** **Kilmah**[9] 5584 2-9-0 100 FrannyNorton 9 105
(Mark Johnston) *mde all and untrbld in front: shkn up 2f out: hung lft fnl f and hrd pressed last 100yds: hld on wl* **5/1**[3]

23 **2** *nk* **Promising (IRE)**[14] 5400 2-9-0 0 SeanLevey 7 104
(Richard Hannon) *t.k.h early: hld up in last pair: prog on outer 2f out: tk 2nd jst ins fnl f: str chal last 100yds: styd on but jst hld* **4/1**[2]

1144 **3** *2 ¼* **Urban Fox**[21] 5172 2-9-0 96 MartinHarley 4 98
(James Tate) *hld up in 4th: chsd ldng pair 2f out: sn shkn up and no real imp: jst hld on for 3rd* **6/1**

1 **4** *nse* **Rich Legacy (IRE)**[15] 5371 2-9-0 0 OisinMurphy 3 99
(Ralph Beckett) *hld up in 5th: dropped to last 2f out and pushed along: no ch after: fin wl and nrly snatched 3rd* **10/3**[1]

515 **5** *nk* **Tiburtina (IRE)**[21] 5172 2-9-0 94 JimCrowley 5 97
(Sylvester Kirk) *chsd wnr: rdn and tried to chal 2f out: lost 2nd and one pce jst ins fnl f* **12/1**

10 **6** *1* **Belle Meade (IRE)**[21] 5172 2-9-0 0 PaulHanagan 1 94
(Richard Fahey) *trckd ldng pair to 2f out: steadily wknd* **9/1**

12 **7** *¾* **Grecian Light (IRE)**[21] 5172 2-9-0 0 WilliamBuick 8 92
(Charlie Appleby) *t.k.h: hld up in last pair: prog over 2f out: nt qckn and no hdwy over 1f out: wknd ins fnl f* **4/1**[2]

1m 27.08s (0.08) **Going Correction** -0.025s/f (Good) **7** Ran SP% **111.7**
Speed ratings (Par 101): **98,97,95,95,94 93,92**
CSF £23.96 TOTE £5.90: £3.10, £2.30; EX 28.80 Trifecta £104.40.
Owner Abdulla Al Mansoori **Bred** Mildmay Bloodstock Ltd **Trained** Middleham Moor, N Yorks

FOCUS
A reasonable edition of this Group 3 in which the winner set an ordinary gallop and enjoyed the extra distance. The form of the Sweet Solera Stakes didn't receive a boost.

5871 GOODWOOD REVIVAL STKS (H'CAP) 7f
3:20 (3:22) (Class 2) 3-Y-O+
£62,250 (£18,640; £9,320; £4,660; £2,330; £1,170) **Stalls** Low

Form RPR

2261 **1** **Certificate**[14] 5389 5-9-5 **103** AndreaAtzeni 6 111
(Roger Varian) *wl plcd bhd ldrs: clsd 2f out: rdn to ld jst over 1f out: hrd pressed last 100yds: hld on wl* **7/2**[1]

0200 **2** *hd* **Suzi's Connoisseur**[28] 4865 5-9-0 **98** (vt) OisinMurphy 13 105
(Stuart Williams) *hld up in last trio: sltly impeded on outer over 2f out: gd prog wl over 1f out: tk 2nd ins fnl f: str chal last 100yds: jst hld* **25/1**

2021 **3** *½* **Big Time (IRE)**[44] 4305 5-8-11 **95** (v) MartinHarley 5 103
(Kevin Ryan) *taken down early: hld up towards rr: prog and waiting for a gap 2f out: squeezed through and r.o fnl f: tk 3rd nr fin* **10/1**[3]

1530 **4** *¾* **Nuno Tristan (USA)**[14] 5418 4-8-10 **94** JFEgan 15 98
(Richard Fahey) *hld up in rr: prog on outer 2f out: rdn to chal jst ins fnl f: styd on same pce* **12/1**

0523 **5** *½* **Above The Rest (IRE)**[7] 5640 5-8-3 **92** JordanVaughan(5) 8 95
(David Barron) *hld up in rr: prog 2f out but repeatedly denied an opening tl ins fnl f: r.o but no ch to chal* **8/1**[2]

2-51 **6** *½* **Shady McCoy (USA)**[31] 4758 6-7-13 **90** MitchGodwin(7) 16 91
(Ian Williams) *hld up in midfield: shkn up on outer over 2f out: hanging but r.o fr over 1f out: styd on but nvr able to threaten* **10/1**[3]

0000 **7** *1 ¾* **That Is The Spirit**[9] 5585 5-8-9 **93** SeanLevey 4 91
(David O'Meara) *dwlt but sn rcvrd to chse ldng pair: rdn to chal over 1f out: sn nt qckn: wkng whn squeezed for room ins fnl f* **14/1**

6000 **8** *½* **Farlow (IRE)**[14] 5389 8-8-12 **96** JimmyFortune 2 91
(Richard Fahey) *rousted along to ld: hdd after 1f: led again 1/2-way to over 1f out: steadily wknd* **16/1**

0006 **9** *¾* **Rivellino**[28] 4865 6-8-9 **100** CliffordLee(7) 3 93+
(K R Burke) *wl plcd bhd ldrs: rdn and nt qckn whn cl up over 1f out: steadily fdd* **8/1**[2]

0333 **10** *½* **Rex Imperator**[14] 5417 7-8-10 **94** (p) SamJames 10 86
(David O'Meara) *stdd s: hld up in last quartet: smuggled way through on inner over 2f out: no imp on ldrs over 1f out: one pce* **14/1**

0065 **11** *½* **Intransigent**[7] 5640 7-8-10 **97** RobHornby(3) 9 88
(Andrew Balding) *wl plcd bhd ldrs: lost pl and struggling 2f out: no real hdwy after* **33/1**

0220 **12** *nse* **Heaven's Guest (IRE)**[35] 4625 6-9-2 **105** AdamMcNamara(5) 11 95
(Richard Fahey) *hld up in last trio: tried to make prog over 2f out: no hdwy over 1f out: fdd* **20/1**

-100 **13** *1* **Can't Change It (IRE)**[29] 4823 5-8-12 **96** (p) TomQueally 1 87
(David Simcock) *wl plcd bhd ldrs: prog over 2f out: rdn to ld briefly over 1f out: wkng whn squeezed for room ins fnl f* **8/1**[2]

4300 **14** *4* **Withernsea (IRE)**[28] 4865 5-8-12 **96** PaulHanagan 12 75
(Richard Fahey) *t.k.h: hld up on outer in midfield: no prog and btn whn hmpd 2f out: wknd* **14/1**

1600 **15** *2 ½* **Mister Universe**[9] 5585 4-9-2 **100** FrannyNorton 20 73
(Mark Johnston) *prom in chsng gp to 3f out: wkng whn hmpd 2f out: sn bhd* **33/1**

0000 **16** *2 ¾* **Majestic Moon (IRE)**[21] 5146 6-8-5 **94** (p) GeorgeBuckell(5) 18 57
(John Gallagher) *led after 1f to 1/2-way: lost 2nd over 2f out and wknd rapidly* **50/1**

0540 **17** *¾* **Flash Fire (IRE)**[8] 5613 4-9-10 **108** WilliamBuick 19 69
(Charlie Appleby) *a in last trio: shkn up on outer over 2f out and no prog* **16/1**

1m 25.22s (-1.78) **Going Correction** -0.025s/f (Good) **17** Ran SP% **129.6**
Speed ratings (Par 109): **109,108,108,107,106 106,104,103,102,102 101,101,100,95,93 89,89**
CSF £109.94 CT £873.96 TOTE £4.20: £1.40, £6.40, £2.90, £3.20; EX 130.40 Trifecta £1989.80.
Owner Cheveley Park Stud **Bred** Cheveley Park Stud Ltd **Trained** Newmarket, Suffolk

FOCUS
Strong handicap form with the winner recording another personal best.

5872 LEWIS BADGES 1832 MARCH STKS (LISTED RACE) 1m 6f
3:55 (3:55) (Class 1) 3-Y-O+
£28,355 (£10,750; £5,380; £2,680; £1,345; £675) **Stalls** Low

Form RPR

4220 **1** **Platitude**[31] 4753 3-8-9 103 AndreaAtzeni 4 110+
(Sir Michael Stoute) *hld up in last: prog on outer over 3f out: led 2f out: sn clr: rdn out fnl f* **13/8**[1]

0360 **2** *5* **Vive Ma Fille (GER)**[7] 5639 4-9-2 92 FrannyNorton 8 99
(Mark Johnston) *t.k.h: trckd ldng pair: led jst over 3f out to 2f out: sn outpcd by wnr: kpt on* **8/1**

1-60 **3** *7* **Mr Singh**[49] 4164 4-9-7 105 (b) FrankieDettori 1 95
(John Gosden) *t.k.h: hld up in 5th: clsd on ldrs over 3f out: outpcd fr 2f out and no ch after* **7/2**[3]

4422 **4** *1 ¾* **Zubeida**[43] 4340 3-8-4 70 KieranO'Neill 5 87
(Ismail Mohammed) *t.k.h: trckd ldr to 4f out: sn lost pl u.p and in rr: tk modest 4th nr fin* **66/1**

0160 **5** *¾* **Goldmember**[31] 4753 3-8-9 103 OisinMurphy 2 91
(David Simcock) *hld up in 4th: clsd to chal 3f out: qckly outpcd 2f out: wknd over 1f out: eased fnl f and lost 4th nr fin* **11/4**[2]

0500 **6** *3 ¾* **Glaring**[14] 5411 5-9-7 100 MartinDwyer 6 86
(Amanda Perrett) *t.k.h: hld up in last pair: rdn and making no prog whn impeded over 2f out: wknd* **16/1**

-541 **7** *13* **Flambeuse**[35] 4661 5-9-2 77 SeanLevey 9 64
(Harry Dunlop) *racd quite freely: led to jst over 3f out: wknd rapidly: t.o* **14/1**

3m 0.28s (-3.32) **Going Correction** -0.025s/f (Good)
WFA 3 from 4yo+ 12lb **7** Ran SP% **112.1**
Speed ratings (Par 111): **108,105,101,100,99 97,90**
CSF £15.03 TOTE £2.50: £1.50, £3.30; EX 13.40 Trifecta £40.00.
Owner K Abdullah **Bred** Juddmonte Farms Ltd **Trained** Newmarket, Suffolk

FOCUS
Not a strong Listed race, but a fine performance from the favourite.

5873 DOOM BAR CELEBRATION MILE (GROUP 2) 1m
4:30 (4:30) (Class 1) 3-Y-O+ **£62,040** (£23,521; £11,771; £5,863; £2,942) **Stalls** Low

Form RPR

-360 **1** **Lightning Spear**[13] 5449 5-9-4 117 OisinMurphy 2 119
(David Simcock) *hld up in last pair: effrt whn nt clr run 2f out to over 1f out: qcknd whn in the clr fnl f: led last 75yds: won gng away* **4/1**[3]

6101 **2** *1 ¾* **Zonderland**[16] 5329 3-8-12 112 FrankieDettori 5 114
(Clive Cox) *trckd clr ldr: clsd 2f out: rdn to chal fnl f: narrow ld 100yds out: sn hdd and outpcd* **11/4**[2]

00 **3** *hd* **Arod (IRE)**[13] 5449 5-9-4 114 JimmyFortune 1 114
(Peter Chapple-Hyam) *led at gd pce: 3 l ahd 1/2-way: rdn 2f out: narrowly hdd 100yds out: outpcd sn after* **10/1**

5404 **4** *3 ¼* **Toormore (IRE)**[31] 4754 5-9-7 115 WilliamBuick 3 110
(Richard Hannon) *chsd ldng pair: rdn over 2f out: wknd over 1f out* **4/1**[3]

1121 **5** *nk* **Thikriyaat (IRE)**[29] 4822 3-8-12 110 PaulHanagan 4 105
(Sir Michael Stoute) *propped s: a in last pair: pushed along by 1/2-way: rdn and btn in last over 2f out* **7/4**[1]

1m 35.96s (-3.94) **Going Correction** -0.025s/f (Good)
WFA 3 from 5yo 6lb **5** Ran SP% **112.1**
Speed ratings (Par 115): **118,116,116,112,112**
CSF £15.48 TOTE £4.50: £2.20, £1.60; EX 15.10 Trifecta £66.50.
Owner Qatar Racing Limited **Bred** Newsells Park Stud **Trained** Newmarket, Suffolk

FOCUS
A sound edition of this Group 2 prize, run at a decent gallop. The winner replicated his Queen Anne form.

5874 WHITELEY CLINIC STKS (H'CAP) 1m 1f
5:05 (5:05) (Class 3) (0-90,88) 3-Y-O+

£9,337 (£2,796; £1,398; £699; £349; £175) **Stalls** Low

Form RPR
3115 **1** **Quebee**[32] 4737 3-9-6 **87** MartinHarley 3 99+
(Clive Cox) *hld up in 6th: swtchd ins and prog to chse ldr 2f out: shkn up and clsd fnl f: led last 100yds: readily* **9/2**[2]
3312 **2** 1¼ **Dawn Mirage**[10] 5538 4-9-8 **82** WilliamBuick 9 91
(Richard Fahey) *led: committed for home jst over 2f out: drvn and hdd last 100yds: clr of rest but readily hld by wnr* **7/1**
1-46 **3** 3¾ **Red Rannagh (IRE)**[30] 4797 3-9-5 **86** (t) TomQueally 1 88+
(David Simcock) *s.s: detached in last early and then t.k.h: stl in last pair 2f out: prog on outer over 1f out: styd on to take 3rd last 100yds: no ch to threaten* **2/1**[1]
1554 **4** ½ **Pactolus (IRE)**[28] 4868 5-10-0 **88** (t) OisinMurphy 10 89
(Stuart Williams) *dwlt: hld up in last pair: prog 2f out: chsd clr ldng pair 1f out: no imp and lost 3rd last 100yds* **11/1**
0360 **5** 2½ **Shell Bay (USA)**[7] 5647 4-9-12 **86** (b) SeanLevey 6 82
(Richard Hannon) *t.k.h: hld up bhd ldrs: drvn and nt qckn over 2f out: lft bhd over 1f out: wknd ins fnl f* **16/1**
0144 **6** 4½ **Thecornishbarron (IRE)**[24] 5037 4-9-2 **76** JimmyFortune 5 63
(John Ryan) *chsd ldr to 2f out: wknd qckly* **25/1**
6061 **7** 1¼ **Illusive (IRE)**[28] 4868 5-9-10 **87** MarcMonaghan(3) 7 71
(George Scott) *chsd ldrs on outer: rdn over 2f out: wknd wl over 1f out* **6/1**[3]
4000 **8** 3¾ **Room Key**[29] 4823 4-9-11 **88** (p) EdwardGreatrex(3) 8 65
(Eve Johnson Houghton) *rousted early in rr: rdn and no prog over 2f out: sn wl btn* **14/1**
3225 **9** nse **Skeaping**[58] 3814 3-8-13 **80** KieranO'Neill 2 56
(Richard Hannon) *wl in rr: urged along 1/2-way: no prog and wl btn over 2f out* **11/1**
-102 **10** ½ **Bright Flash**[37] 4556 4-9-8 **87** HectorCrouch(5) 4 62
(David Brown) *t.k.h: trckd ldng pair to 2f out: wknd over 1f out* **14/1**

1m 54.07s (-2.23) **Going Correction** -0.025s/f (Good)
WFA 3 from 4yo+ 7lb **10** Ran SP% **118.0**
Speed ratings (Par 107): **108,106,103,103,100 96,95,92,92,91**
CSF £36.59 CT £84.06 TOTE £5.80: £2.10, £2.20, £1.20; EX 25.00 Trifecta £98.00.
Owner Martin A Collins **Bred** M A Collins **Trained** Lambourn, Berks

FOCUS
The first two finished clear in this fair handicap and the winner was impressive.

5875 GOLF ACADEMY AT GOODWOOD STKS (H'CAP) 1m 4f
5:40 (5:40) (Class 4) (0-80,80) 3-Y-O **£6,469** (£1,925; £962; £481) **Stalls** High

Form RPR
21 **1** **Guns Of Leros (USA)**[8] 5596 3-8-12 **76** HectorCrouch(5) 3 87+
(Gary Moore) *pushed up to ld and mde all: rdn 3f out: steadily drew clr fr 2f out* **5/2**[1]
0125 **2** 2¾ **Diamond Geyser (IRE)**[28] 4859 3-9-4 **77** OisinMurphy 8 84
(Luca Cumani) *sn chsd wnr: rdn 3f out: one pce and steadily outpcd fr 2f out* **11/2**[3]
0242 **3** 1¼ **Visage Blanc**[8] 5596 3-9-2 **75** JFEgan 1 80+
(Mick Channon) *hld up in tch: rdn to chse ldng pair 3f out: one pce and no imp fr 2f out* **6/1**
0355 **4** 3¾ **Bergholt (IRE)**[78] 3110 3-8-13 **72** MartinHarley 5 71+
(Philip Hide) *hld up: prog to dispute 3rd pl 3f out tl fdd over 1f out* **8/1**
4221 **5** hd **Kismet Hardy**[15] 5362 3-8-11 **75** (p) MeganNicholls(5) 2 74+
(Richard Hannon) *broke wl but stdd into rr: prog 6f out: n.m.r on inner sn after and dropped to last pair: rdn and struggling 3f out: sn no ch* **7/2**[2]
160 **6** 10 **King Of Dreams**[21] 5147 3-8-13 **77**[1] GeorgeBuckell(5) 9 60
(David Simcock) *chsd ldng pair to 3f out: wknd* **9/1**
1023 **7** 13 **Bigger And Better**[18] 5256 3-8-9 **68** SeanLevey 4 30+
(Richard Hannon) *a in last pair: rdn and struggling over 3f out: bhd whn eased ins fnl f* **8/1**

2m 38.66s (0.26) **Going Correction** -0.025s/f (Good) **7** Ran SP% **112.7**
Speed ratings (Par 102): **98,96,95,92,92 86,77**
CSF £16.03 CT £72.49 TOTE £4.00: £2.50, £2.40; EX 15.80 Trifecta £83.70.
Owner Paul Hunt **Bred** Woodcote Stud Ltd **Trained** Lower Beeding, W Sussex
■ Stewards' Enquiry : George Buckell caution: careless riding

FOCUS
Not many got into this fair handicap, which was dominated by the winner who appears to be going the right way.
T/Jkpt: Not won. T/Plt: £253.30 to a £1 stake. Pool: £134,767.00 - 388.37 winning tickets. T/Qpdt: £18.00 to a £1 stake. Pool: £10,120.86 - 415.78 winning tickets. **Jonathan Neesom**

5846 NEWMARKET (R-H)
Saturday, August 27

OFFICIAL GOING: Good to firm (watered)
Wind: Light half-against, turning fresher from race 3 Weather: Overcast

5876 EDDIE STOBART E FULFILMENT EBF STALLIONS MAIDEN STKS (PLUS 10 RACE) 6f
1:50 (1:50) (Class 4) 2-Y-O **£4,528** (£1,347; £673; £336) **Stalls** Low

Form RPR
1 **Khafoo Shememi (IRE)** 2-9-5 0 PatDobbs 3 87+
(Richard Hannon) *a.p: jnd ldrs 2f out: rdn and hung lft ins fnl f: r.o to ld nr fin* **8/1**
6 **2** nk **Mazyoun**[32] 4736 2-9-5 0 JamesDoyle 7 86
(Hugo Palmer) *s.i.s: hld up: hdwy 2f out: led over 1f out: sn rdn and hung lft: hdd nr fin* **1/2**[1]
3 1 **Al Reeh (IRE)** 2-9-5 0 RobertHavlin 5 83+
(Marco Botti) *a.p: swtchd rt over 1f out: rdn and edgd lft ins fnl f: r.o* **16/1**
33 **4** 4½ **Vaulted**[18] 5272 2-9-0 0 TonyHamilton 8 63
(Richard Fahey) *led 1f: chsd ldrs: rdn over 1f out: wknd wl ins fnl f* **9/2**[3]
222 **5** 1¼ **Mr Pocket (IRE)**[20] 5188 2-9-5 80 LukeMorris 4 64
(Paul Cole) *prom: chsd ldr 4f out tl led over 2f out: rdn and hdd over 1f out: wknd ins fnl f* **7/2**[2]
6 8 **Dolly Dimples** 2-9-0 0[1] JoeFanning 2 34
(William Jarvis) *s.i.s: hld up: shkn up and wknd over 1f out* **25/1**
6005 **7** 1¾ **Sadieroseclifford (IRE)**[7] 5631 2-9-0 62 GrahamGibbons 9 28
(Denis Quinn) *led 5f out: rdn and hdd over 2f out: wknd over 1f out* **80/1**
60 **8** 7 **Bartholomew J (IRE)**[16] 5332 2-9-2 0 SimonPearce(3) 6 11
(Lydia Pearce) *sn pushed along in rr: rdn and lost tch 1/2-way* **100/1**

1m 13.26s (0.76) **Going Correction** +0.20s/f (Good) **8** Ran SP% **130.1**
Speed ratings (Par 96): **102,101,100,94,92 81,79,70**
CSF £14.33 TOTE £13.40: £2.70, £1.10, £5.40; EX 20.40 Trifecta £181.40.
Owner Saeed Suhail **Bred** Mrs M McWey **Trained** East Everleigh, Wilts

FOCUS
Stands Side Course used. The last meeting of the year on the July course. A total of 3mm of water was put on the good to firm parts of the track and 5mm on the firm parts after racing the previous day, and the going was given as good to firm (GoingStick: 7.6). Not a bad maiden and the first three finished clear, with the winner showing a good attitude to see off the heavily backed second.

5877 FLY EASYJET FROM LONDON SOUTHEND AIRPORT NURSERY H'CAP 7f
2:25 (2:25) (Class 3) (0-95,84) 2-Y-O **£6,469** (£1,925; £962) **Stalls** Low

Form RPR
11 **1** **Rodaini (USA)**[14] 5394 2-9-6 **84** SilvestreDeSousa 4 93+
(Simon Crisford) *hld up: swtchd lft and shkn up over 2f out: hdwy to chse ldr over 1f out: rdn to ld and edgd rt wl ins fnl f: r.o: comf* **10/11**[1]
1141 **2** ½ **Clef**[14] 5407 2-8-13 **82** CallumShepherd(5) 3 86
(Richard Fahey) *sn led: rdn over 1f out: hdd wl ins fnl f: styd on same pce* **7/4**[2]
331 **3** 12 **Second Nature**[43] 4363 2-9-6 **84** LukeMorris 2 55
(James Tate) *trckd ldr: plld hrd: rdn over 2f out: lost 2nd over 1f out: wknd fnl f* **9/2**[3]

1m 27.34s (1.64) **Going Correction** +0.20s/f (Good) **3** Ran SP% **106.9**
Speed ratings (Par 98): **98,97,83**
CSF £2.75 TOTE £1.60; EX 2.40 Trifecta £2.80.
Owner Abdullah Saeed Al Naboodah **Bred** Greenwood Lodge Farm **Trained** Newmarket, Suffolk

FOCUS
Just the three runners and the early pace wasn't strong, but there was plenty to like about the way the winner ran down the leader. Even better to come from the winner with the second rated to her mark.

5878 EDDIE STOBART INDUSTRIAL SECTOR H'CAP 7f
3:00 (3:00) (Class 3) (0-90,88) 3-Y-O **£9,703** (£2,887; £1,443; £721) **Stalls** Low

Form RPR
-611 **1** **Kitaaby (IRE)**[38] 4519 3-9-2 **83** JamesDoyle 5 95
(Brian Meehan) *chsd ldr: rdn to ld over 1f out: hung lft ins fnl f: r.o* **5/1**[1]
54-1 **2** 1¼ **Shawaahid (IRE)**[19] 5246 3-9-7 **88** PatDobbs 3 97
(Richard Hannon) *led 5f: sn rdn: stl ev ch whn hmpd ins fnl f: styd on same pce* **6/1**[2]
4521 **3** 1½ **Summer Chorus**[14] 5409 3-9-3 **84** JimmyQuinn 10 89
(Andrew Balding) *hld up: plld hrd: hdwy nt clr run and swtchd lft over 1f out: sn rdn: styd on* **6/1**[2]
1502 **4** 1½ **Symbolic**[20] 5191 3-9-4 **85** RobertHavlin 1 86
(John Gosden) *racd alone on stands' side: up w ld pce: led 2f out: rdn and hdd over 1f out: hung lft and no ex ins fnl f* **7/1**[3]
105 **5** 1½ **Honiara**[45] 4271 3-9-1 **82**[1] LukeMorris 2 78
(Paul Cole) *s.i.s: hld up: drvn and swtchd rt over 2f out: nt clr run and swtchd lft over 1f out: styd on same pce fnl f* **33/1**
3431 **6** ½ **Tigerwolf (IRE)**[16] 5327 3-9-5 **86** CharlesBishop 6 81
(Mick Channon) *s.i.s: hld up: hdwy 2f out: rdn and edgd rt over 1f out: wknd ins fnl f* **6/1**[2]
0-03 **7** ¾ **Drifting Spirit (IRE)**[13] 5437 3-9-6 **87** TonyHamilton 4 81
(Richard Fahey) *hld up: pushed along over 2f out: nt clr run over 1f out: sn wknd* **12/1**
4120 **8** 3¼ **Penwortham (IRE)**[44] 4306 3-9-3 **84** JackGarritty 8 68
(Richard Fahey) *hld up: rdn over 2f out: wknd over 1f out* **10/1**
302 **9** 6 **The Commendatore**[21] 5179 3-9-0 **81** (b) GrahamGibbons 7 49
(David Barron) *trckd ldrs: racd keenly: rdn: hung rt and wknd over 1f out* **10/1**
203 **10** 29 **Midnight Macchiato (IRE)**[8] 5601 3-8-13 **80** PatCosgrave 9
(David Brown) *chsd ldrs: rdn 1/2-way: wknd wl over 2f out* **6/1**[2]

1m 26.17s (0.47) **Going Correction** +0.20s/f (Good) **10** Ran SP% **115.1**
Speed ratings (Par 104): **105,103,101,100,98 97,97,93,86,53**
CSF £34.10 CT £188.42 TOTE £5.40: £1.80, £2.50, £2.40; EX 24.50 Trifecta £174.80.
Owner Hamdan Al Maktoum **Bred** Joseph Broderick **Trained** Manton, Wilts

FOCUS
A good, competitive handicap with the front pair continuing to progress.

5879 FLY STOBART AIR H'CAP 1m 5f
3:35 (3:36) (Class 2) (0-105,100) 3-Y-O+

£28,012 (£8,388; £4,194; £2,097; £1,048; £526) **Stalls** Centre

Form RPR
1165 **1** **Yorkidding**[8] 5611 4-9-3 **93** JoeFanning 8 103
(Mark Johnston) *chsd ldrs: wnt centre and led that gp over 7f out: overall ldr over 2f out: rdn and hung lft fr over 1f out: styd on* **6/1**
1313 **2** 1¼ **Real Dominion (USA)**[21] 5147 3-8-4 **91** JimmyQuinn 13 100+
(Andrew Balding) *hld up: plld hrd: wnt prom 11f out: nt clr run and lost pl over 2f out: hdwy: hung rt and led his gp over 1f out: sn rdn: r.o: nt rch wnr* **5/2**[1]
0-06 **3** 3 **Highland Castle**[136] 1417 8-9-0 **90**[1] ShaneKelly 12 94
(David Elsworth) *hld up: hdwy over 2f out: rdn over 1f out: styd on to go 3rd wl ins fnl f* **20/1**
2342 **4** 1¼ **Masterpaver**[36] 4583 5-8-7 **83** TonyHamilton 11 85
(Richard Fahey) *s.i.s: hld up: swtchd to centre over 5f out: hdwy over 2f out: rdn and hung rt over 1f out: no ex ins fnl f* **8/1**
-020 **5** 4½ **Yarrow (IRE)**[30] 4800 4-9-10 **100** TedDurcan 10 95
(Sir Michael Stoute) *hld up: wnt centre over 7f out: hdwy u.p 2f out: wknd fnl f* **14/1**
1102 **6** 5 **Knights Table**[11] 5411 3-8-8 **95** LukeMorris 3 82
(James Tate) *prom: swtchd centre and chsd wnr over 5f out tl rdn over 2f out: wknd over 1f out* **7/2**[2]
0-14 **7** 2¾ **Great Glen**[21] 5145 4-9-3 **93** FMBerry 1 76
(Ralph Beckett) *chsd ldr: rdn and hung lft over 2f out: wknd over 1f out* **4/1**[3]
00-4 **8** 4½ **Great Hall**[14] 5411 6-9-3 **93** WilliamCarson 6 70
(Mick Quinn) *sn led: rdn: hung lft and hdd over 2f out: wknd over 1f out* **20/1**

 The Form Book, Raceform Ltd, Newbury, RG14 5SJ

200 **9** ¾ **Paddys Motorbike (IRE)**[42] 4407 4-9-0 **90**.................... PatCosgrave 5 65
(David Evans) *hld up in tch: wnt centre over 7f out: rdn over 2f out: wknd over 1f out* **20/1**

2m 47.78s (3.78) **Going Correction** +0.20s/f (Good)
WFA 3 from 4yo+ 11lb **9** Ran SP% **117.1**
Speed ratings (Par 109): **96,95,93,92,89 86,85,82,81**
CSF £21.05 CT £276.86 TOTE £5.70: £2.00, £1.50, £5.40; EX 21.50 Trifecta £277.90.
Owner Paul Robert York **Bred** Bluehills Racing Limited **Trained** Middleham Moor, N Yorks

FOCUS
A difference of opinion here as five, including the winner, came up the centre of the track in the straight, while four, including the runner-up and third, stayed more towards the stands' side. The winner posted a better effort.

5880 STOBART CLUB AND SHOP HOPEFUL STKS (LISTED RACE) 6f
4:10 (4:10) (Class 1) 3-Y-O+
£20,982 (£7,955; £3,981; £1,983; £995; £499) **Stalls** Low

Form RPR
-033 **1** **Windfast (IRE)**[28] 4887 5-9-1 106.............................. RichardKingscote 9 111
(Brian Meehan) *chsd ldrs: rdn to ld and edgd rt over 1f out: r.o* **11/1**

32 **2** *nk* **Buying Trouble (USA)**[38] 4540 3-8-8 96 ow1.................... ShaneKelly 2 106
(David Evans) *hld up: gd hdwy over 1f out: rdn and hung lft ins fnl f: r.o* **20/1**

2003 **3** 1¾ **Baccarat (IRE)**[14] 5418 7-9-1 109...................................... JamesDoyle 5 104
(Charlie Appleby) *hld up: hdwy over 2f out: rdn and ev ch over 1f out: no ex wl ins fnl f* **10/3**[2]

061 **4** *shd* **Naadirr (IRE)**[28] 4860 5-9-1 108... LukeMorris 4 104
(Marco Botti) *hld up in tch: rdn and nt clr run over 1f out: r.o wl towards fin* **7/1**

4632 **5** 1¼ **Eastern Impact (IRE)**[20] 5213 5-9-1 110.......................... JackGarritty 7 100
(Richard Fahey) *w ldrs: led wl over 1f out: sn rdn and hdd: styd on same pce fnl f* **15/8**[1]

3033 **6** ¾ **Raucous**[28] 4865 3-8-12 106...(tp) PatCosgrave 3 98
(William Haggas) *prom: rdn and ev ch over 1f out: wknd ins fnl f* **7/2**[3]

-166 **7** *hd* **Mayfair Lady**[13] 5436 3-8-7 105....................................... TonyHamilton 8 92
(Richard Fahey) *disp ld tl rdn wl over 1f out: wknd ins fnl f* **14/1**

0040 **8** 7 **B Fifty Two (IRE)**[6] 5678 7-9-1 95.........................(b) MichaelJMMurphy 1 75
(Charles Hills) *disp ld tl rdn wl over 1f out: sn wknd* **33/1**

1m 12.52s (0.02) **Going Correction** +0.20s/f (Good)
WFA 3 from 4yo+ 3lb **8** Ran SP% **115.3**
Speed ratings (Par 111): **107,106,104,104,102 101,101,91**
CSF £197.66 TOTE £13.20: £3.10, £3.50, £1.50; EX 218.20 Trifecta £3963.90 Part won..
Owner B J Meehan **Bred** Airlie Stud **Trained** Manton, Wilts

FOCUS
There was a good gallop on for this Listed sprint. The switch to sprinting seemed to suit the winner.

5881 FLY FROM LONDON SOUTHEND AIRPORT H'CAP 6f
4:45 (4:45) (Class 3) (0-90,90) 3-Y-O **£7,762** (£2,310; £1,154; £577) **Stalls** Low

Form RPR
1232 **1** **Rococoa (IRE)**[25] 4984 3-8-8 **77**.. LukeMorris 2 86
(Ed Walker) *hld up: swtchd rt and hdwy over 1f out: r.o u.p to ld post* **4/1**

-102 **2** *shd* **Mickey (IRE)**[21] 5161 3-9-4 **87**.................................(t) RichardKingscote 8 96
(Tom Dascombe) *a.p: shkn up to ld over 1f out: rdn and edgd rt ins fnl f: hdd post* **7/2**[3]

1-33 **3** 1½ **Quick Look**[15] 5372 3-8-12 **81**.................................... SilvestreDeSousa 1 85
(William Jarvis) *dwlt: hld up: hdwy u.p over 1f out: styd on same pce wl ins fnl f* **11/4**[1]

1105 **4** 1¾ **Gunmetal (IRE)**[14] 5403 3-9-5 **88**............................... MichaelJMMurphy 6 86
(Charles Hills) *w ldr: rdn: edgd lft and ev ch over 1f out: styd on same pce ins fnl f* **3/1**[2]

0050 **5** ½ **Tikthebox (IRE)**[18] 5274 3-8-2 **74**.................................... AaronJones(3) 7 71
(David Brown) *led: rdn and hdd over 1f out: nt clr run and no ex ins fnl f* **20/1**

241- **6** 1¼ **Human Nature (IRE)**[373] 5558 3-9-7 **90**........................... JamesDoyle 5 83
(Saeed bin Suroor) *plld hrd and prom: rdn over 1f out: styd on same pce* **9/1**

-000 **7** 32 **Easy Code**[11] 5512 3-8-6 **75**.. JoeFanning 3
(William Haggas) *plld hrd and prom: pushed along 1/2-way: wknd and eased wl over 1f out* **20/1**

1m 12.9s (0.40) **Going Correction** +0.20s/f (Good) **7** Ran SP% **113.4**
Speed ratings (Par 104): **105,104,102,100,99 98,55**
CSF £18.05 CT £43.18 TOTE £4.30: £2.10, £2.00; EX 17.70 Trifecta £30.50.
Owner Elaine Chivers & Merlin Racing **Bred** Tally-Ho Stud **Trained** Upper Lambourn, Berks

FOCUS
A fairly competitive handicap with the winner showing a great attitude to see off the runner-up.

5882 STOBART GROUP H'CAP 5f
5:20 (5:20) (Class 4) (0-85,85) 3-Y-O+ **£5,175** (£1,154; £1,154; £384) **Stalls** Low

Form RPR
4552 **1** **Princess Tansy**[24] 5040 4-8-5 **73**.................................... DavidEgan(7) 11 81
(Gay Kelleway) *hld up: plld hrd: hdwy 1/2-way: led over 1f out: rdn and hung lft ins fnl f: r.o* **9/1**

0126 **2** 1¼ **Ziggy Lee**[7] 5648 10-9-5 **80**...................................... RichardKingscote 6 84
(Lawrence Mullaney) *prom: rdn: edgd rt and outpcd over 1f out: r.o ins fnl f* **7/2**[1]

-610 **2** *dht* **Excellent George**[22] 5124 4-9-4 **82**................................(t) AaronJones(3) 4 86
(Stuart Williams) *prom: pushed along 1/2-way: outpcd over 1f out: r.o ins fnl f* **11/2**[2]

0224 **4** ¾ **Free To Love**[46] 4222 4-9-1 **76**.. SteveDrowne 3 77
(Charles Hills) *chsd ldrs: wnt 2nd 3f out tl rdn over 1f out: styd on same pce ins fnl f* **8/1**

2113 **5** *nk* **Justice Lady (IRE)**[28] 4861 3-9-2 **79**.................................... ShaneKelly 1 79
(David Elsworth) *hld up: plld hrd: hdwy over 1f out: no imp ins fnl f* **7/2**[1]

1300 **6** ¾ **Baileys Mirage (FR)**[39] 4475 5-9-9 **84**.................(b) SilvestreDeSousa 9 82
(Chris Dwyer) *led: shkn up and qcknd 1/2-way: rdn and hdd over 1f out: hmpd and no ex ins fnl f* **16/1**

000 **7** *nk* **Steelriver (IRE)**[21] 5182 6-9-5 **80**................................ GrahamGibbons 10 76
(David Barron) *s.i.s: hld up: r.o towards fin: nvr nrr* **8/1**

1210 **8** 1½ **Major Pusey**[54] 3956 4-9-10 **85**................................. MichaelJMMurphy 8 76
(John Gallagher) *prom: rdn over 1f out: wknd ins fnl f* **7/1**[3]

0462 **9** 1¼ **Burning Thread (IRE)**[4] 5751 9-8-11 **72**........................(b) JoeFanning 12 58
(David Elsworth) *plld hrd: trckd ldr 2f: remained handy: rdn over 1f out: hung rt and wknd ins fnl f* **12/1**

59.7s (0.60) **Going Correction** +0.20s/f (Good)
WFA 3 from 4yo+ 2lb **9** Ran SP% **118.1**
Speed ratings (Par 105): **103,101,101,99,99 98,97,95,93**
PL: £1.90 Ziggy Lee, £1.90 Excellent George; Tote Exacta: PT&EG: £41.90, PT&ZL: £29.90 CSF: PT&EG: £29.55, PT&ZL £20.78. Tricast: PT&EG&ZL: £105.63, PT&ZL&EG: £97.85 Trifecta: PT&EG&ZL: £340.40, PT&ZL&EG: £105.63 TOTE £11.10: £2.90.
Owner P Crook, G Kelleway **Bred** Minster Enterprises Ltd **Trained** Exning, Suffolk

FOCUS
An open sprint handicap rated around the balance of the principals.
T/Plt: £59.00 to a £1 stake. Pool: £110,802.00 - 1,369.67 winning tickets T/Qpdt: £18.80 to a £1 stake. Pool: £7,784.04 - 304.80 winning tickets **Colin Roberts**

5177 REDCAR (L-H)
Saturday, August 27

OFFICIAL GOING: Good to soft (good in places) changing to good to soft (soft in places) after race 5 (6.50)
Wind: Breezy, half behind Weather: Overcast

5883 RACINGUK.COM/DAYPASS H'CAP (FOR LADY AMATEUR RIDERS) 1m 2f
4:40 (4:41) (Class 5) (0-75,75) 3-Y-O+ **£2,807** (£870; £435; £217) **Stalls** Low

Form RPR
5145 **1** **San Cassiano (IRE)**[17] 5293 9-9-12 **63**.........................(b) MrsCBartley 6 69
(Ruth Carr) *pressed ldr: rdn over 2f out: edgd rt and led ins fnl f: drvn out* **10/1**

6415 **2** *nk* **Framley Garth (IRE)**[26] 4930 4-10-6 **74**...................... MissAWaugh(3) 1 79
(Patrick Holmes) *hld up in midfield: stdy hdwy over 2f out: effrt and ev ch ins fnl f: sn pressing wnr: kpt on: hld nr fin* **9/1**

2400 **3** ½ **Muqarred (USA)**[9] 5579 4-10-0 **72**........................(p) MissFMcSharry(7) 5 76
(David Loughnane) *t.k.h: led: rdn over 1f out: hdd ins fnl f: kpt on same pce* **12/1**

1221 **4** 1 **City Ground (USA)**[23] 5056 9-10-5 **70**.................... MissSBrotherton 10 72
(Michael Appleby) *prom: effrt and pushed along 2f out: kpt on same pce ins fnl f* **6/1**[3]

5502 **5** ¾ **Nelson's Bay**[2] 5800 7-9-5 **56** oh5........................... MissJoannaMason 3 57
(Wilf Storey) *dwlt: hld up: effrt against far rail 2f out: kpt on same pce ins fnl f* **9/2**[1]

6055 **6** 1½ **Bahamian C**[43] 4341 5-9-11 **67**...........................(t) MissEmilyBullock(5) 2 65
(Richard Fahey) *midfield: pushed along over 3f out: drvn and hdwy 2f out: one pce fnl f* **11/2**[2]

1646 **7** 5 **King Of The Celts (IRE)**[17] 5293 8-9-12 **68**............ MissEEasterby(5) 8 57
(Tim Easterby) *prom: hung lft and lost pl over 2f out: n.d after* **9/1**

5062 **8** ½ **Warfare**[26] 4930 7-10-5 **75**... MissHDukes(5) 9 63
(Tim Fitzgerald) *dwlt: hld up: rdn and hung lft over 2f out: sn no imp* **11/2**[2]

0661 **9** 4½ **Desert Tango**[9] 5575 3-8-11 **56**.................................. MissMMullineaux 4 36
(Michael Mullineaux) *dwlt: hld up: rdn and outpcd over 3f out: nvr on terms* **11/1**

322 **10** 14 **Flag Of Glory**[5] 5708 9-9-0 **56** oh4...............................(b) MissMEdden(5) 7 11
(Peter Hiatt) *hld up in midfield on outside: struggling over 2f out: sn btn* **14/1**

2m 6.58s (-0.52) **Going Correction** +0.10s/f (Good)
WFA 3 from 4yo+ 8lb **10** Ran SP% **115.0**
Speed ratings (Par 103): **106,105,105,104,103 102,98,98,94,83**
CSF £95.17 CT £1093.09 TOTE £13.50: £3.50, £3.50, £4.30; EX 130.50 Trifecta £2530.80 Part won..
Owner S Jackson, L Shaw, Mrs R Carr **Bred** Peter Savill **Trained** Huby, N Yorks

FOCUS
Good to soft ground, good in places after a dry day in the build up to racing. Potentially a more competitive event than many a lady amateur riders' handicap, with most of these having shown their form of late, but they went only a steady pace and few got into it. The race has been rated around the winner.

5884 BAKERS TAILORING AND FORMAL HIRE MAIDEN AUCTION STKS 6f
5:15 (5:19) (Class 5) 2-Y-O **£2,911** (£866; £432; £216) **Stalls** Centre

Form RPR
262 **1** **The Stalking Moon (IRE)**[14] 5414 2-8-12 70...................... TomEaves 3 72
(John Quinn) *prom: effrt and shkn up over 1f out: led ins fnl f: sn clr* **11/4**[1]

66 **2** 2½ **Justanotherbottle (IRE)**[13] 5433 2-9-1 0...................... DanielTudhope 6 68
(Declan Carroll) *led: rdn along wl over 1f out: hdd ins fnl f: kpt on: nt pce of wnr* **15/2**[3]

0 **3** 1¼ **Glyder**[19] 5242 2-8-6 0.. RoystonFfrench 12 55
(John Holt) *w ldrs: drvn along 2f out: kpt on same pce ins fnl f* **100/1**

0 **4** ½ **Hamba Kashe (IRE)**[14] 5414 2-9-1 0............................ DuranFentiman 1 62
(Tim Easterby) *prom: effrt and ch over 1f out: outpcd ins fnl f* **66/1**

0204 **5** 1½ **Right Action**[14] 5414 2-9-1 78...................................... PatrickMathers 4 58
(Richard Fahey) *trckd ldrs: rdn over 1f out: wknd ins fnl f* **4/1**[2]

3 **6** *nk* **Cupid's Arrow (IRE)**[75] 3216 2-9-1 0............................ JamesSullivan 10 57
(Ruth Carr) *hld up: pushed along and hdwy over 2f out: no imp fr over 1f out* **16/1**

0 **7** ¾ **Archi's Affaire**[18] 5271 2-8-13 0.................................. AndrewMullen 11 53
(Michael Dods) *s.i.s: bhd and sn pushed along: hdwy over 1f out: nvr able to chal* **33/1**

3335 **8** *hd* **Alfie's Angel (IRE)**[16] 5318 2-8-10 71.............................. PhilDennis(5) 16 54
(Bryan Smart) *midfield: drvn along 1/2-way: no imp fr 2f out* **4/1**[2]

60 **9** 2 **Bella Duchess (IRE)**[121] 1799 2-8-5 0............................ NoelGarbutt(3) 7 41
(David C Griffiths) *towards rr: drvn along 1/2-way: outpcd wl over 1f out* **100/1**

224 **10** 1 **Kody Ridge (IRE)**[52] 4022 2-9-3 74.............................. DougieCostello 20 47
(David Dennis) *prom tl rdn: edgd lft and wknd over 1f out* **11/1**

11 *hd* **Equiano Springs** 2-9-1 0... AndrewElliott 19 44
(Tom Tate) *dwlt: hld up in midfield: drvn and outpcd over 2f out: n.d after* **40/1**

12 *nk* **Man Of Verve (IRE)** 2-9-1 0.. KeaganLatham 2 44
(John Quinn) *hld up: rdn along over 2f out: wknd wl over 1f out* **25/1**

506 **13** ¾ **Silk Mill Blue**[24] 5029 2-9-1 65.................................... GeorgeChaloner 13 41
(Richard Whitaker) *sn rdn along in rr: struggling 1/2-way: nvr on terms* **14/1**

60 **14** *hd* **Breakwater Bay (IRE)**[14] 5414 2-9-3 0............................ PaddyAspell 9 43
(Tim Easterby) *chsd ldrs: lost pl over 3f out: sn struggling* **66/1**

15 *shd* **Desperados Destiny** 2-8-8 0.................................. GeorgeDowning(3) 15 36
(Ed McMahon) *sn rdn in rr: no ch fr 1/2-way* **25/1**

05 **16** 2 3/4 **Where's Stewart**[10] 5536 2-8-8 0 RowanScott(5) 17 30
(Nigel Tinkler) *bhd: drvn and outpcd over 3f out: sn btn* **66/1**

17 4 1/2 **Flashing Light** 2-8-6 0 CamHardie 18 10
(Tim Easterby) *hld up: pushed along and struggling over 3f out: sn btn* **33/1**

0 **18** 1/2 **Aegean Secret**[12] 5476 2-8-13 0 ShaneGray 14 15
(Kevin Ryan) *midfield: rdn and outpcd 1/2-way: btn fnl 2f* **50/1**

19 11 **Skellig Michael** 2-8-12 0 LouisSteward(3) 8
(Ben Haslam) *slowly away: sn lost tch: nvr on terms* **66/1**

1m 11.66s (-0.14) **Going Correction** +0.10s/f (Good) **19** Ran SP% **125.2**
Speed ratings (Par 94): **104,100,99,98,96 95,94,94,92,90 90,90,89,88,88 84,78,78,63**
CSF £21.89 TOTE £3.40: £1.60, £2.40, £21.40; EX 26.20 Trifecta £3514.80 Part won..
Owner D Ward **Bred** Norman Orminston **Trained** Settrington, N Yorks

FOCUS
Probably not so competitive a maiden auction as the size of the field might suggest, with few of these having previously shaped like imminent winners, and not many ever looked like getting involved up front. The form looks limited with the winner rated to her pre-race mark.

5885 MARKET CROSS JEWELLERS NOVICE MEDIAN AUCTION STKS 7f
5:50 (5:51) (Class 5) 2-Y-O **£2,911** (£866; £432; £216) **Stalls** Centre

Form RPR

42 **1** **Davy's Dilemma**[15] 5363 2-9-2 0 AndrewMullen 8 75
(Michael Dods) *pressed ldr: rdn 2f out: led 1f out: wandered: kpt on* **10/1**

2 1 **Subjective** 2-9-2 0 TomEaves 11 72+
(David Simcock) *dwlt: sn trckd ldrs: pushed along over 1f out: rdn ins fnl f: kpt on* **2/1**[2]

42 **3** 1/2 **Honourable**[19] 5221 2-8-11 0 PatrickMathers 2 66
(Richard Fahey) *led: racd keenly: rdn 2f out: hdd 1f out: no ex ins fnl f* **11/10**[1]

4 1 1/2 **Glorious Forever** 2-9-2 0 ThomasBrown 9 67+
(Ed Walker) *hld up: pushed along and hdwy over 2f out: wnt 4th over 1f out: kpt on* **12/1**

5 5 **Prancing Oscar (IRE)** 2-9-2 0 CamHardie 5 53
(Ben Haslam) *midfield: rdn and outpcd 3f out: nvr threatened* **33/1**

00 **6** hd **Melcano**[14] 5387 2-8-11 0 JamesSullivan 4 48
(Shaun Harris) *hld up: pushed along over 2f out: nvr threatened* **66/1**

7 1/2 **Greengairs** 2-9-2 0 ConnorBeasley 1 52
(Keith Dalgleish) *chsd ldrs: rdn over 2f out: wknd over 1f out* **33/1**

0 **8** 2 **Filudo (FR)**[70] 3382 2-9-2 0 DanielTudhope 6 46
(David O'Meara) *hld up in midfield: pushed along over 2f out: wknd over 1f out* **13/2**[3]

9 18 **Teddy Edward** 2-9-2 0 GeorgeChaloner 3
(Richard Whitaker) *s.i.s: midfield: rdn 3f out: wknd* **50/1**

1m 24.47s (-0.03) **Going Correction** +0.10s/f (Good) **9** Ran SP% **120.4**
Speed ratings (Par 94): **104,102,102,100,94 94,94,91,71**
CSF £31.41 TOTE £6.30: £2.20, £1.30, £1.10; EX 34.20 Trifecta £69.60.
Owner D Neale **Bred** Wansdyke Farms Limited **Trained** Denton, Co Durham

FOCUS
Only two of those with experience had suggested they were up to winning in this grade, but a couple of newcomers had eye-catching profiles on paper and that quartet came clear in the final furlong.

5886 PINNACLE RACING SYNDICATE SHARES AVAILABLE NOW H'CAP (PINNACLE CUP STRAIGHT MILE QUALIFIER) 1m
6:20 (6:20) (Class 4) (0-85,85) 3-Y-O+ **£6,145** (£1,828; £913; £456) **Stalls** Centre

Form RPR

6613 **1** **Fuwairt (IRE)**[25] 4976 4-9-4 **82** CameronNoble(7) 13 91
(David Loughnane) *s.i.s: hld up: pushed along and hdwy over 1f out: led ins fnl f: edgd lft: kpt on wl* **9/1**

2030 **2** 1/2 **Pumaflor (IRE)**[28] 4893 4-9-4 **75** ConnorBeasley 8 83
(Richard Whitaker) *in tch: hdwy to ld over 1f out: hung lft and hdd ins fnl f: kpt on: hld nr fin* **22/1**

1040 **3** 1 1/2 **Flyboy (IRE)**[50] 4113 3-9-4 **81** DanielTudhope 4 84
(David O'Meara) *hld up: stdy hdwy over 2f out: rdn and edgd lft over 1f out: kpt on same pce ins fnl f* **5/1**[1]

5231 **4** nk **Worlds His Oyster**[23] 5063 3-9-6 **83** (p) TomEaves 2 87
(John Quinn) *trckd ldrs: nt clr run over 2f out to over 1f out: stmbld over 1f out: sn rdn: kpt on fnl f: nt rch ldrs* **7/1**[2]

-050 **5** 3/4 **Altharoos (IRE)**[28] 4894 6-9-12 **83** DougieCostello 12 85
(Sally Hall) *hld up: stdy hdwy over 2f out: rdn and effrt over 1f out: kpt on ins fnl f: no imp* **22/1**

1260 **6** 1/2 **Qaffaal (USA)**[24] 5017 5-8-11 **73** NathanEvans(5) 17 74
(Michael Easterby) *trckd ldrs: ev ch over 1f out: sn rdn: outpcd ins fnl f* **28/1**

0420 **7** 1/2 **Hard To Handel**[21] 5180 4-9-7 **85** (p) PatrickVaughan(7) 6 85
(David O'Meara) *dwlt: hld up: rdn over 2f out: hdwy over 1f out: kpt on fnl f: nt pce to chal* **12/1**

0600 **8** 1/2 **Ingleby Angel (IRE)**[21] 5180 7-9-9 **80** RoystonFfrench 16 79
(Colin Teague) *hld up: drvn and outpcd over 2f out: n.d after* **22/1**

5216 **9** 1/2 **Eurystheus (IRE)**[30] 4808 7-9-10 **81** (tp) AndrewMullen 9 78
(Michael Appleby) *cl up: rdn over 2f out: wknd over 1f out* **12/1**

5440 **10** nk **Dark Ocean (IRE)**[33] 4717 6-9-10 **81** AndrewElliott 7 78
(Jedd O'Keeffe) *t.k.h: sn prom: effrt and ev ch over 1f out: wknd ins fnl f* **8/1**

5000 **11** 3 1/4 **Gerry The Glover (IRE)**[14] 5419 4-9-9 **80** BenCurtis 11 69
(Brian Ellison) *missed break: hld up: rdn along wl over 1f out: sn btn* **15/2**[3]

4161 **12** 4 1/2 **Victoire De Lyphar (IRE)**[33] 4704 9-9-10 **81** (e) JamesSullivan 3 60
(Ruth Carr) *cl up: rdn over 2f out: edgd lft and wknd over 1f out* **11/1**

045 **13** 4 **Indy (IRE)**[57] 3855 5-9-9 **85** PhilDennis(5) 15 55
(David Barron) *hld up in midfield: drvn and struggling over 2f out: sn btn* **25/1**

-620 **14** nk **Count Montecristo (FR)**[64] 3605 4-9-11 **82** ShaneGray 1 51
(Kevin Ryan) *led: rdn over 2f out: hdd over 1f out: sn wknd* **10/1**

1m 36.09s (-0.51) **Going Correction** +0.10s/f (Good)
WFA 3 from 4yo+ 6lb **14** Ran SP% **115.2**
Speed ratings (Par 105): **106,105,104,103,102 102,101,101,100,100 97,92,88,88**
CSF £195.72 CT £1127.41 TOTE £11.90: £3.70, £7.90, £2.30; EX 200.20 Trifecta £2331.60.
Owner Binns, Bamford, Corless & Fell **Bred** Tommy Burns **Trained** Market Drayton, Shropshire
■ Mystic Miraaj was withdrawn. Price at time of withdrawal 25/1. Rule 4 does not apply.

FOCUS
A typically open handicap with all bar one of the field split by just 4lb judged on Racing Post ratings. They went a good pace and the finish was dominated by those coming from off the pace. Those who helped force the pace are worth another chance. The winner was seemingly back to his best over a trip he has rarely raced over.

5887 RACING UK HD ON SKY432 H'CAP 7f
6:50 (6:52) (Class 6) (0-65,65) 3-Y-O+ **£2,264** (£673; £336; £168) **Stalls** Centre

Form RPR

254 **1** **Reinforced**[10] 5537 3-8-12 **56** (p) AndrewMullen 10 64
(Michael Dods) *t.k.h: cl up: led after 2f: mde rest: hrd pressed fnl f: hld on wl* **12/1**

6643 **2** nk **Desire**[18] 5276 4-9-7 **60** PatrickMathers 6 69
(Richard Fahey) *in tch: hdwy to chse wnr over 1f out: ev ch ins fnl f: kpt on u.p: hld cl home* **11/1**[3]

0U16 **3** 1 3/4 **White Flag**[18] 5276 5-9-1 **57** RachelRichardson(3) 3 61
(Tim Easterby) *hld up: pushed along 1/2-way: hdwy to chse ldrs over 1f out: kpt on same pce ins fnl f* **20/1**

5235 **4** hd **Bajan Rebel**[11] 5523 5-9-5 **63** NathanEvans(5) 19 67
(Michael Easterby) *in tch: rdn over 2f out: edgd lft: kpt on same pce ins fnl f* **14/1**

2-43 **5** 1 1/2 **Im Dapper Too**[126] 1631 5-9-4 **57** ShaneGray 5 57
(John Davies) *bhd and sn pushed along: hdwy over 1f out: kpt on ins fnl f: nrst fin* **7/1**[1]

635 **6** nse **The Big Day (IRE)**[9] 5578 3-8-8 **57** RowanScott(5) 1 55
(Nigel Tinkler) *hld up: pushed along 1/2-way: hdwy over 2f out: kpt on same pce fnl f* **14/1**

0000 **7** 1 **Shearian**[5] 5729 6-8-6 **52** (v[1]) CameronNoble(7) 15 49
(Tracy Waggott) *led 2f: cl up: rdn over 2f out: one pce fr over 1f out* **33/1**

3201 **8** nk **Caeser The Gaeser (IRE)**[10] 5535 4-9-0 **60** (p) LewisEdmunds(7) 14 56
(Nigel Tinkler) *dwlt: sn midfield: rdn over 2f out: one pce fr over 1f out* **8/1**[2]

0500 **9** 1/2 **Saltarello (IRE)**[5] 5729 4-8-12 **51** (b) CamHardie 4 46
(Marjorie Fife) *s.i.s: rdn in rr 1/2-way: sme hdwy over 1f out: kpt on: nt pce to chal* **12/1**

053 **10** 1 1/2 **Lovin' Spoonful**[31] 4766 3-9-7 **65** ConnorBeasley 13 54
(Bryan Smart) *towards rr: stmbld after 1f: sn drvn and outpcd: sme late hdwy: nvr rchd ldrs* **12/1**

0460 **11** nse **Mr Cool Cash**[21] 5151 4-9-9 **65** GeorgeDowning(3) 2 56
(Richard Guest) *hld up: shortlived effrt over 2f out: wknd over 1f out* **8/1**[2]

4464 **12** 1 **Mrs Biggs**[31] 4770 4-9-9 **62** DanielTudhope 11 50
(Declan Carroll) *chsd ldrs: lost pl over 2f out: sn btn* **8/1**[2]

-020 **13** 3/4 **No Refund (IRE)**[9] 5576 5-8-13 **52** BenCurtis 16 38
(David Loughnane) *trckd ldrs: rdn over 2f out: wknd over 1f out* **11/1**[3]

4000 **14** 2 1/4 **Clon Rocket (IRE)**[15] 5368 3-9-2 **60** RoystonFfrench 8 38
(John Holt) *in tch: drvn along 1/2-way: wknd wl over 1f out* **20/1**

5533 **15** 1/2 **Caledonia Laird**[14] 5386 5-9-12 **65** TomEaves 9 43
(Jo Hughes) *hld up: rdn over 3f out: nvr on terms* **14/1**

3356 **16** 4 1/2 **Totally Magic (IRE)**[19] 5247 4-9-7 **60** (p) GeorgeChaloner 20 26
(Richard Whitaker) *hld up: rdn over 3f out: sn btn* **20/1**

0000 **17** 21 **Clergyman**[25] 4970 4-9-11 **64** JamesSullivan 18
(Rebecca Bastiman) *bhd: drvn along 1/2-way: nvr on terms* **25/1**

1m 26.25s (1.75) **Going Correction** +0.10s/f (Good)
WFA 3 from 4yo+ 5lb **17** Ran SP% **126.6**
Speed ratings (Par 101): **94,93,91,91,89 89,88,88,87,85 85,84,83,81,80 75,51**
CSF £131.37 CT £2649.98 TOTE £15.40: £3.20, £3.30, £4.70, £2.70; EX 171.50 Trifecta £2225.80 Part won..
Owner W G McHarg & J W Stenson **Bred** Maze Rattan Limited **Trained** Denton, Co Durham

FOCUS
Plenty with chances at the weights, but also plenty of less-than-reliable sorts in a typical field for a 46-65 handicap. Few got into it and the race has been rated around the balance of the principals.

5888 RACING UK PROFITS RETURNED TO RACING H'CAP 1m 6f 19y
7:20 (7:21) (Class 6) (0-65,67) 3-Y-O **£2,264** (£673; £336; £168) **Stalls** Low

Form RPR

3005 **1** **Kazoey**[23] 5079 3-8-2 **46** oh1 DuranFentiman 1 53
(Chris Fairhurst) *mde all at stdy gallop: rdn along 2f out: hrd pressed fnl f: hld on gamely* **25/1**

6112 **2** 3/4 **High On Light**[12] 5481 3-9-6 **67** RachelRichardson(3) 4 73
(Tim Easterby) *t.k.h: prom: rdn over 2f out: hdwy to press wnr ins fnl f: kpt on: hld nr fin* **6/4**[1]

4226 **3** 2 **Becky The Thatcher**[14] 5420 3-9-2 **60** TomEaves 9 63
(Micky Hammond) *stdd in last pl: hdwy to chse wnr over 2f out to ins fnl f: kpt on same pce* **15/2**

0004 **4** 4 1/2 **Glorious Legend (IRE)**[15] 5375 3-9-2 **60** ThomasBrown 2 58
(Ed Walker) *hld up: pushed along and effrt 3f out: nt clr run briefly and outpcd 2f out: plugged on fnl f: no ch w first three* **11/4**[2]

-040 **5** 3 1/4 **Rob's Legacy**[23] 5079 3-8-2 **46** oh1 (b[1]) JamesSullivan 6 39
(Shaun Harris) *hld up: hdwy 3f out: rdn: edgd lft and wknd wl over 1f out* **50/1**

0-43 **6** 1/2 **Dream Serenade**[15] 5383 3-8-2 **46** oh1 AndrewMullen 7 39
(Michael Appleby) *t.k.h: prom: rdn 3f out: wknd 2f out* **12/1**

-641 **7** 13 **Hazely**[40] 4450 3-8-7 **51** AndrewElliott 5 27
(James Bethell) *pressed wnr: rdn over 3f out: wknd 2f out* **11/2**[3]

00-0 **8** 1/2 **Great Colaci**[16] 5322 3-8-2 **46** oh1 PatrickMathers 3 21
(Keith Reveley) *plld hrd early: trckd ldrs: struggling whn hung lft over 2f out: sn btn* **16/1**

3m 9.41s (4.71) **Going Correction** +0.10s/f (Good) **8** Ran SP% **113.2**
Speed ratings (Par 98): **90,89,88,85,84 83,76,76**
CSF £62.03 CT £326.68 TOTE £33.00: £6.90, £1.10, £3.40; EX 69.50 Trifecta £632.70.
Owner Allan Davies **Bred** Llety Farms **Trained** Middleham, N Yorks
■ Stewards' Enquiry : Rachel Richardson The Stewards held an enquiry following a report from the Starter that Rachel Richardson, the rider of HIGH ON LIGHT, had entered the wrong stall. Having heard her evidence and viewed recordings of the start they found her in breach of Rule (D)44.2 and cautioned her as to her future conduct in races.

FOCUS
After continual rain, the going was changed to good to soft, soft in places before this race. There were one or two unexposed stayers in this 3yo handicap, but it was run at just a steady pace. The winner showed improved form upped in trip on turf.

5889 HIGH DEFINITION RACING UK H'CAP 6f
7:50 (7:54) (Class 6) (0-55,60) 3-Y-O+ **£2,385** (£704; £352) **Stalls** Centre

Form RPR

0-00 **1** **Robbie Roo Roo**[10] 5554 3-8-13 **50** (vt[1]) SaleemGolam 5 60
(Mrs Ilka Gansera-Leveque) *chsd ldrs: led wl over 2f out: sn rdn: kpt on wl* **25/1**

0201 **2** 1 1/4 **Someone Exciting**[18] 5277 3-9-3 **54**............................ PatrickMathers 8 60
(David Thompson) *prom: rdn over 2f out: kpt on* **5/1**[2]
1000 **3** 3/4 **Hab Reeh**[12] 5483 8-9-6 **54**.............................(p) JamesSullivan 3 58
(Ruth Carr) *midfield towards far side: rdn and hdwy 2f out: chsd ldr over 1f out: one pce fnl f* **10/1**
6631 **4** shd **Teetotal (IRE)**[12] 5483 6-9-7 **60**.............................(b) AnnaHesketh(5) 2 64
(Nigel Tinkler) *dwlt: hld up towards far side: pushed along and hdwy over 2f out: chsd ldr over 1f out: sn rdn: one pce ins fnl f* **7/2**[1]
0054 **5** 2 3/4 **Fool's Dream**[11] 5515 3-9-0 **51**.............................(p) ConnorBeasley 14 46
(Bryan Smart) *midfield towards stands' side: rdn over 3f out: plugged on fr over 1f out: edgd lft ins fnl f: nvr threatened* **9/1**
-500 **6** 5 **Tweetheart**[18] 5276 3-9-1 **52**.............................[1] RoystonFfrench 6 32
(Ron Barr) *s.i.s: hld up: rdn 1/2-way: plugged on fr over 1f out: nvr threatened* **40/1**
6-00 **7** shd **Molivias Gem**[1] 5843 3-9-0 **51**............................ DougieCostello 11 31
(David Thompson) *chsd ldrs: rdn over 2f out: wknd over 1f out* **50/1**
0000 **8** 1 1/2 **Majestic Manannan (IRE)**[23] 5069 7-9-1 **49**............................ PaulQuinn 15 25
(David Nicholls) *prom: rdn over 2f out: wknd over 1f out* **25/1**
0003 **9** 1 **Spring Bird**[26] 4931 7-9-7 **55**............................ BenCurtis 18 28
(Alan Swinbank) *prom towards stands' side: rdn 1/2-way: wknd over 1f out* **14/1**
3004 **10** 1 3/4 **Indego Blues**[3] 5760 7-8-11 **52**.............................(p) DanielleMooney(7) 7 19
(David Nicholls) *hld up: sn pushed along: nvr threatened* **17/2**
0432 **11** 1 1/4 **Carlovian**[9] 5578 3-8-10 **50**............................ AlistairRawlinson(3) 12 14
(Christopher Kellett) *midfield: rdn 1/2-way: wknd over 1f out* **12/1**
-006 **12** 3 1/4 **Flyball**[112] 2053 4-9-6 **54**.............................[1] GrahamLee 16 8
(Kenneth Slack) *sn led: hdd 1/2-way: sn wknd* **11/2**[3]
3430 **13** 1 1/2 **Secret City (IRE)**[18] 5278 10-9-6 **54**.............................(b) DanielTudhope 19 3
(Rebecca Bastiman) *a in rr* **16/1**
0040 **14** 3 1/4 **George Bailey (IRE)**[18] 5277 4-8-13 **47**............................ TomEaves 13
(Suzzanne France) *a in rr* **33/1**

1m 14.08s (2.28) **Going Correction** +0.10s/f (Good)
WFA 3 from 4yo+ 3lb **14** Ran SP% **119.2**
Speed ratings (Par 101): **88,86,85,85,81 74,74,72,71,69 67,63,61,56**
CSF £139.73 CT £1366.35 TOTE £29.40: £7.70, £2.20, £2.20; EX 136.60 Trifecta £1377.70.
Owner Mrs I Gansera-Leveque **Bred** John James **Trained** Newmarket, Suffolk

FOCUS
Few solid propositions in a handicap less competitive than the size of the field might suggest and not many got into it. The first five came well clear and the winner has been rated back to her standout 2yo form.
T/Plt: £203.50 to a £1 stake. Pool: £54,923.88 - 196.98 winning tickets. T/Qpdt: £15.30 to a £1 stake. Pool: £6,940.76 - 334.24 winning tickets. **Richard Young & Andrew Sheret**

5484 WINDSOR (R-H)
Saturday, August 27

OFFICIAL GOING: Good to firm (good in places; watered; 8.4)
Wind: light, behind Weather: overcast, warm

5890 BATHWICK TYRES SUPPORTS HEROS MAIDEN STKS 6f
4:15 (4:18) (Class 5) 2-Y-O **£2,911** (£866; £432; £216) **Stalls** Low

Form RPR
0 **1** **Graphite Storm**[50] 4075 2-9-5 0............................ AdamKirby 13 79+
(Clive Cox) *hld up in tch in midfield: hdwy to chse ldng pair and swtchd lft over 1f out: rdn to chal ins fnl f: r.o to ld towards fin: pushed out* **10/1**
03 **2** 3/4 **Sea Shack**[32] 4736 2-9-5 0............................ JimCrowley 1 76
(William Knight) *trckd ldrs: rdn and effrt 2f out: chsd ldr wl over 1f out: drvn and styd on to chal ins fnl f: led 50yds out: hdd and no ex towards fin* **4/5**[1]
04 **3** 1 **Poetic Principle (IRE)**[24] 5008 2-9-2 0............................ JosephineGordon(3) 4 73
(J S Moore) *led: rdn 2f out: sn hung lft: hrd pressed and drvn jst ins fnl f: hdd 50yds out: no ex* **25/1**
4 7 **Desert Fox** 2-9-5 0............................ RobertWinston 12 50+
(Mike Murphy) *s.i.s: hld up in rr: pushed along and nt clr run over 1f out: sn switching rt and hdwy: kpt on to pass btn horses ins fnl f: wnt 4th towards fin: nvr trbld ldrs* **25/1**
5 1 **Delahay** 2-9-0 0............................ RyanTate 5 42
(Michael Blanshard) *in tch in midfield: rdn 1/2-way: wnt modest 4th over 1f out: no imp on ldrs: plugged on* **66/1**
0 **6** 2 **Casaclare (IRE)**[33] 4707 2-9-5 0............................ JohnFahy 14 41+
(Jonjo O'Neill) *hld up towards rr: pushed along 2f out: hdwy over 1f out: no ch but kpt on steadily ins fnl f* **50/1**
34 **7** nk **Gracious Tom (IRE)**[8] 5593 2-9-5 0............................ TomMarquand 10 40
(David Evans) *chsd ldrs: rdn 2f out: sn struggling and outpcd over 1f out: wknd ins fnl f* **7/1**[3]
8 shd **Sir Titan** 2-9-5 0............................ DannyBrock 2 40
(Marcus Tregoning) *chsd ldr: rdn over 1f out: sn hung lft and lost pl: wknd ins fnl f* **50/1**
25 **9** 4 **Sakurajima (IRE)**[29] 4837 2-9-5 0............................ WilliamTwiston-Davies 3 27
(Charles Hills) *chsd ldng trio: rdn ent fnl 2f: no rspnse and sn btn: wknd over 1f out* **9/2**[2]
0 **10** 1 **Garth Rockett**[74] 3243 2-9-5 0............................ RyanClark 15 24
(Brendan Powell) *wl in tch in midfield on outer: rdn over 2f out: struggling u.p 2f out: wknd over 1f out* **50/1**
11 3 **Orange Gin (IRE)** 2-9-5 0............................ GeorgeBaker 9 14
(Roger Charlton) *hld up in tch in midfield: pushed along 2f out: no imp and btn whn nt clrest of runs over 1f out: sn wknd* **16/1**
12 1 1/4 **Conkering Hero (IRE)** 2-9-5 0............................ SamHitchcott 6 10
(Joseph Tuite) *rn green and sn pushed along: a towards rr: wknd 2f out* **66/1**
6 **13** nk **Fausto**[39] 4479 2-9-5 0............................ FrederikTylicki 11 9
(Tom Dascombe) *hld up in tch in midfield: pushed along over 2f out: no hdwy and sn btn: wknd over 1f out* **33/1**
14 1 1/4 **Mr Scaff (IRE)** 2-9-0 0............................ GeorgeWood(5) 16
(Paul Henderson) *s.i.s: rn green: a bhd* **50/1**
15 2 3/4 **Coachella (IRE)** 2-9-5 0............................ LiamKeniry 8
(Ed de Giles) *a towards rr: rdn over 2f out: sn wknd* **33/1**

1m 13.66s (0.66) **Going Correction** -0.025s/f (Good) **15** Ran SP% **125.6**
Speed ratings (Par 94): **94,93,91,82,81 78,77,77,72,71 67,65,65,63,59**
CSF £17.91 TOTE £13.30: £3.50, £1.10, £6.60; EX 29.10 Trifecta £474.40.
Owner Mrs Olive Shaw **Bred** Mrs O A Shaw **Trained** Lambourn, Berks

FOCUS
A big field, but not much depth to this moderate maiden and the front three pulled a long way clear. The third looks the key to the form.

5891 GENTING CASINOS SOUTHERN FILLIES' H'CAP 1m 67y
4:50 (4:51) (Class 5) (0-75,79) 3-Y-O+ **£2,911** (£866; £432; £216) **Stalls** Low

Form RPR
-664 **1** **Nicarra (IRE)**[87] 2795 3-9-0 **69**............................ FergusSweeney 7 78+
(Henry Candy) *broke wl: t.k.h: chsd ldr: rdn to chal wl over 1f out: rdn to ld 1f out: sn asserted and styd on wl* **9/4**[1]
4-04 **2** 1 3/4 **Poster Girl**[99] 2431 3-9-1 **70**............................ RyanTate 2 75
(Jonathan Portman) *trckd ldng pair: swtchd lft and effrt over 1f out: drvn to chse wnr ins fnl f: styd on same pce fnl 100yds* **7/1**[3]
3202 **3** 1 **Carpe Diem Lady (IRE)**[36] 4596 3-9-5 **74**............................ AdamKirby 1 77
(Clive Cox) *sn led: rdn 2f out: drvn over 1f out: hdd ins fnl f: no ex u.p: lost 2nd and one pce fnl 150yds* **7/2**[2]
142 **4** 1/2 **Owaseyf (USA)**[10] 5551 3-9-10 **79**............................ JackMitchell 6 81
(Roger Varian) *t.k.h: hld up in tch in midfield: effrt ent fnl 2f: styd on same pce u.p fnl f* **9/4**[1]
3520 **5** 1/2 **Multigifted**[37] 4562 3-7-12 **58**............................ GeorgeWood(5) 4 59
(Michael Madgwick) *dwlt: t.k.h: hld up in tch in midfield: effrt 2f out: swtchd lft over 1f out: styd on same pce ins fnl f* **20/1**
3323 **6** 3 1/4 **Forecaster**[17] 5288 3-9-0 **69**.............................(v) JimCrowley 3 62
(Michael Bell) *t.k.h: hld up in tch in last pair: effrt 2f out: no imp u.p over 1f out: wknd ins fnl f* **8/1**
4400 **7** hd **Ixelles Diamond (IRE)**[22] 5132 5-8-7 **56**............................ TomMarquand 8 50
(Andrew Reid) *hld up in rr: effrt 2f out: no imp and edgd lft over 1f out: wknd ins fnl f* **50/1**

1m 43.33s (-1.37) **Going Correction** -0.05s/f (Good)
WFA 3 from 5yo+ 6lb **7** Ran SP% **114.1**
Speed ratings (Par 100): **104,102,101,100,100 97,96**
CSF £18.86 CT £53.04 TOTE £3.70: £2.00, £3.50; EX 20.40 Trifecta £61.90.
Owner Mrs Patricia J Burns **Bred** C J Foy **Trained** Kingston Warren, Oxon

FOCUS
Add 20yds to race distance. Not a particularly strong fillies' handicap, but one or two of these, including the winner, have the potential to do better. The balance of the placed horses sets the level.

5892 TORI "BIG 4 ALTERNATIVE" SUPPORTS HEROS H'CAP 1m 67y
5:25 (5:25) (Class 4) (0-85,85) 3-Y-O+ **£4,690** (£1,395; £697; £348) **Stalls** Low

Form RPR
1341 **1** **Wind In My Sails**[15] 5357 4-9-9 **82**............................ LiamKeniry 1 91
(Ed de Giles) *taken down early: stdd after s: hld up in tch in rr: effrt and swtchd lft over 1f out: qcknd u.p to ld wl ins fnl f: gng away at fin* **7/2**[2]
206 **2** 1 3/4 **Abareeq**[17] 5292 3-8-12 **77**............................ FrederikTylicki 7 81
(Mark Johnston) *led: rdn 2f out: drvn over 1f out: hdd and styd on same pce wl ins fnl f* **11/2**[3]
3050 **3** 1 1/4 **Athletic**[29] 4839 7-8-4 **68**.............................(v) GeorgeWood(5) 6 70
(Andrew Reid) *bmpd sn after s: hld up in tch in midfield: effrt 2f out: hdwy u.p to press ldr over 1f out: no ex and outpcd fnl 100yds* **25/1**
3344 **4** nse **Fast Dancer (IRE)**[27] 4917 4-9-7 **83**.............................(p) JosephineGordon(3) 4 85
(Joseph Tuite) *hld up in tch in midfield: effrt 2f out: hdwy u.p to press ldr 1f out: no ex jst ins fnl f: outpcd fnl 100yds* **6/1**
416 **5** 1 1/2 **Justice Smart (IRE)**[28] 4886 3-9-5 **84**............................ RyanMoore 2 82
(Sir Michael Stoute) *rdn along leaving stalls: chsd ldng pair after 1f and t.k.h: effrt 2f out: unable qck and btn 1f out: wknd ins fnl f* **9/4**[1]
5303 **6** hd **Essenaitch (IRE)**[20] 5206 3-8-10 **75**............................ JimCrowley 5 72
(David Evans) *dwlt: hld up in tch in last pair: nt clr run 2f out: swtchd rt and rdn over 1f out: styd on same pce ins fnl f* **11/2**[3]
4020 **7** nk **Fashaak (IRE)**[14] 5409 3-9-3 **82**............................ TomMarquand 8 79
(Richard Hannon) *chsd ldr: rdn over 2f out: unable qck u.p over 1f out: wknd ins fnl f* **8/1**

1m 44.58s (-0.12) **Going Correction** -0.05s/f (Good)
WFA 3 from 4yo+ 6lb **7** Ran SP% **113.0**
Speed ratings (Par 105): **98,96,95,94,93 93,92**
CSF £22.28 CT £407.03 TOTE £4.60: £2.30, £3.20; EX 23.10 Trifecta £353.30.
Owner John Manser **Bred** Meon Valley Stud **Trained** Ledbury, H'fords

FOCUS
Add 20yds to race distance. A trappy handicap run at what appeared an even gallop, but most of these were under the pump over 2f out and the winner blew them away with his turn of foot in the final furlong.

5893 WINTER HILL STKS (GROUP 3) 1m 2f 7y
6:00 (6:00) (Class 1) 3-Y-O+
£34,026 (£12,900; £6,456; £3,216; £1,614; £810) **Stalls** Centre

Form RPR
-051 **1** **Chain Of Daisies**[17] 5307 4-8-12 103............................ FergusSweeney 2 111
(Henry Candy) *mde all: stdd gallop 5f out: rdn and qcknd over 2f out: drvn over 1f out: hrd pressed ins fnl f: hld on gamely: all out* **15/2**
2101 **2** shd **Ulysses (IRE)**[31] 4753 3-8-11 111............................ RyanMoore 4 118
(Sir Michael Stoute) *hld up in tch in last pair: clsd over 2f out: rdn and hdwy to chse wnr over 1f out: ev ch and drvn ins fnl f: kpt on but a jst hld* **8/11**[1]
2305 **3** 6 **Foundation (IRE)**[21] 5159 3-8-7 110.............................(b) RobertHavlin 1 102
(John Gosden) *t.k.h: chsd ldng pair tl wnt 2nd 5f out: rdn over 2f out: lost 2nd and outpcd over 1f out: edgd lft 1f out: wknd ins fnl f* **13/2**[3]
4454 **4** 1/2 **Tony Curtis**[16] 5329 3-8-7 105............................ TomMarquand 5 101
(Richard Hannon) *stdd s: hld up in rr: clsd 1/2-way: rdn and effrt over 2f out: swtchd lft 2f out: no imp over 1f out: wknd ins fnl f* **16/1**
2612 **5** 8 **Ayrad (IRE)**[29] 4821 5-9-1 110.............................(p) AndreaAtzeni 3 86
(Roger Charlton) *chsd ldr tl 5f out: rdn over 2f out: sn lost pl: wknd over 1f out: no ch and eased ins fnl f* **4/1**[2]
-404 **6** 3 1/4 **Not So Sleepy**[46] 4253 4-9-1 102.............................(t) JimCrowley 6 80
(Hughie Morrison) *wl in tch in midfield: rdn over 2f out: sn btn and bhd over 1f out: eased fnl f* **33/1**

2m 2.58s (-6.12) **Going Correction** -0.20s/f (Firm)
WFA 3 from 4yo+ 8lb **6** Ran SP% **111.8**
Speed ratings (Par 113): **116,115,111,110,104 101**
CSF £13.46 TOTE £8.30: £3.00, £1.10; EX 12.00 Trifecta £46.90.
Owner Girsonfield Ltd **Bred** Girsonfield Ltd **Trained** Kingston Warren, Oxon

FOCUS
Add 20yds to race distance. A cracking little Group 3 contest in which the front pair came a long way clear, but not in the order expected. The winning time was less than a second off the course record despite the additional yardage.

5894 SRI LANKA AUGUST STKS (LISTED RACE) 1m 3f 135y
6:35 (6:36) (Class 1) 3-Y-O+
£20,982 (£7,955; £3,981; £1,983; £995; £499) **Stalls** Centre

Form RPR
0025 **1** **Berkshire (IRE)**29 4821 5-9-3 108....(b) JimCrowley 6 110
(Paul Cole) *mde all: racd keenly and clr after 2f: rdn over 2f out: drvn over 1f out: edgd lft u.p ins fnl f: hdd 50yds: kpt on u.p: led again last stride* **8/1**
0013 **2** *shd* **Majeed**29 4821 6-9-3 102.... FrederikTylicki 8 110
(David Simcock) *dwlt: sn detached in last: clsd 3f out: hdwy and swtchd lft over 2f out: rdn to chse wnr over 1f out: drvn and chalng ins fnl f: led 50yds out: edgd lft after and hdd last stride* **7/1**
3550 **3** *3 ¾* **Second Step (IRE)**35 4626 5-9-3 109....(b1) AndreaAtzeni 5 104
(Luca Cumani) *hld up in midfield: clsd 3f out: nt clr run 2f out tl swtchd lft ent fnl f: no ch w ldng pair: kpt on to go 3rd last strides* **7/4**1
42-0 **4** *hd* **Tashaar (IRE)**182 757 4-9-3 107.... FrankieDettori 4 104
(Richard Hannon) *hld up in midfield: clsd 3f out: nt clr run jst over 2f out tl swtchd rt over 1f out: squeezed through to chse clr ldng pair 1f out: pushed along and no imp: lost 3rd last strides* **7/2**2
1610 **5** *1 ½* **Fire Fighting (IRE)**7 5647 5-9-8 113....(b) AdamKirby 7 106
(Mark Johnston) *off the pce in last pair: rdn and hdwy over 3f out: chsng ldrs but no imp u.p over 1f out: wknd ins fnl f* **9/2**3
3223 **6** *¾* **Passover**14 5411 5-9-3 93.... LiamKeniry 3 100
(Andrew Balding) *chsd ldrs tl wnt 2nd 7f out: rdn over 2f out: lost 2nd and unable qck over 1f out: wknd ins fnl f* **20/1**
1030 **7** *6* **John Reel (FR)**7 5639 7-9-3 98.... RobertWinston 2 90
(David Evans) *chsd wnr tl 7f out: styd chsng ldrs: rdn over 2f out: drvn and unable qck 2f out: wknd over 1f out* **33/1**
-135 **8** *1 ½* **Weetles**34 4696 4-8-12 94.... RobertHavlin 1 83
(Clive Cox) *hld up off the pce in last trio: rdn 3f out: sn dropped to rr: bhd over 1f out* **16/1**

2m 23.6s (-5.90) **Going Correction** -0.20s/f (Firm) **8** Ran SP% **114.0**
Speed ratings (Par 111): **111,110,108,108,107 106,102,101**
CSF £61.73 TOTE £9.00: £2.10, £2.30, £1.30; EX 60.40 Trifecta £158.20.
Owner H R H Sultan Ahmad Shah **Bred** Newsells Park Stud **Trained** Whatcombe, Oxon

FOCUS
Add 20yds to race distance. A strongly run August Stakes with the winner tanking along early and they were well strung out from an early stage. For him to hold on after those exertions was some effort. The runner-up is the key to the level.

5895 IRISH THOROUGHBRED MARKETING SUPPORTS HEROS H'CAP 1m 3f 135y
7:05 (7:05) (Class 5) (0-70,70) 3-Y-O+ **£2,911** (£866; £432; £216) **Stalls** Centre

Form RPR
624 **1** **Officer Drivel (IRE)**14 5397 5-9-12 **68**....(v) JimCrowley 4 73
(Jim Best) *t.k.h: chsd ldr tl led 2f out: sn hrd pressed and rdn: drvn and edgd lft ins fnl f: hld on towards fin: all out* **11/4**3
4062 **2** *shd* **Not Touch**17 5287 3-9-4 **70**.... TomMarquand 5 75
(Richard Hannon) *trckd ldrs: rdn and sltly outpcd over 2f out: rallied u.p to chse ldng pair over 1f out: drvn to chal 100yds out: kpt on: jst hld* **9/4**1
2543 **3** *2* **Red Hot Chilly (IRE)**4 5746 3-9-4 **70**.... TomQueally 2 72
(Joseph Tuite) *t.k.h: hld up in tch: effrt over 2f out: sn chalng and rdn: stl ev ch tl no ex and btn 100yds out: wknd towards fin* **5/2**2
6243 **4** *2 ¾* **Megalala (IRE)**14 5399 15-8-5 **54**.... MitchGodwin(7) 3 51
(John Bridger) *led and set stdy gallop: drvn over 2f out and sn hdd: styd on same pce fr over 1f out* **14/1**
0663 **5** *2* **Perfect Rhythm**28 4880 5-8-13 **60**....1 CharlieBennett(5) 6 54
(Patrick Chamings) *stdd s: hld up in tch in last: effrt over 2f out: outpcd u.p over 1f out: wknd ins fnl f* **5/1**

2m 31.5s (2.00) **Going Correction** -0.20s/f (Firm)
WFA 3 from 5yo+ 10lb **5** Ran SP% **109.3**
Speed ratings (Par 103): **85,84,83,81,80**
CSF £9.18 TOTE £3.30: £1.70, £1.60; EX 9.50 Trifecta £16.20.
Owner A Achilleous **Bred** Patrick Keane **Trained** Lewes, E Sussex

FOCUS
Add 20yds to race distance. A modest handicap run at a steady gallop - it turned into a 4f sprint - and the time was 8 sec slower than the Listed trace over this trip 35 mins earlier. Straightforward limited form with the front three all near their respective levels.

5896 NORTH FARM STUD HOME OF HEROS CHARITY H'CAP 6f
7:35 (7:36) (Class 4) (0-80,80) 3-Y-O+ **£4,690** (£1,395; £697; £348) **Stalls** Low

Form RPR
00 **1** **Fairway To Heaven (IRE)**28 4862 7-9-7 **77**.... JimCrowley 7 86
(Michael Wigham) *stdd s: hld up in tch: effrt over 1f out: rdn and hdwy to chal 1f out: drvn to ld 100yds out: r.o* **2/1**2
0055 **2** *½* **Florencio**45 4268 3-9-6 **79**....(t) SamHitchcott 2 86
(William Muir) *chsd ldr: rdn and ev ch over 1f out: led and edgd lft jst ins fnl f: hdd 100yds: kpt on but a hld after* **10/1**
1112 **3** *1 ¾* **Inclination (IRE)**33 4708 3-9-5 **78**.... AdamKirby 5 80
(Clive Cox) *t.k.h: hld up in tch in midfield: nt clr run 2f out: gap fnlly opened ins fnl f: pushed along and kpt on to go 3rd nr fin: no threat to ldng pair* **15/8**1
6-22 **4** *½* **Joe Packet**75 3233 9-9-7 **77**.... RyanClark 9 77
(Jonathan Portman) *chsd ldrs: effrt 2f out: rdn and ev ch over 1f out: squeezed for room jst ins fnl f: no ex 100yds out: wknd towards* **5/1**3
3026 **5** *1* **Archie Stevens**180 764 6-8-3 **66**.... AledBeech(7) 1 63
(David Evans) *racd keenly: led: rdn over 1f out: hdd and no ex jst ins fnl f: wknd fnl 100yds* **20/1**
3611 **6** *1* **Secret Look**53 3985 6-9-2 **72**....(p) WilliamTwiston-Davies 3 66
(Richard Phillips) *hld up wl in tch: switching lft and nt clrest of runs over 1f out: rdn ent fnl f: no imp* **14/1**
00 **7** *¾* **Medicean El Diablo**80 3036 3-8-3 **62**.... KieranO'Neill 8 53
(Jimmy Fox) *stdd s: t.k.h: hld up in tch in rr: effrt over 1f out: sn hung lft and no imp: nvr trbld ldrs* **11/1**

1m 13.08s (0.08) **Going Correction** -0.025s/f (Good)
WFA 3 from 4yo+ 3lb **7** Ran SP% **113.6**
Speed ratings (Par 105): **98,97,95,94,93 91,90**
CSF £21.71 CT £42.01 TOTE £3.10: £1.70, £4.90; EX 24.00 Trifecta £58.40.
Owner Palatinate Thoroughbred Racing Limited **Bred** J Cullinan **Trained** Newmarket, Suffolk

FOCUS
A competitive event for the grade featuring some bang in-form sprinters, but it was won by the best handicapped horse in the race who was capable of a rating of 91 last year.

T/Plt: £60.30 to a £1 stake. Pool: £57,482.08 - 695.40 winning tickets. T/Qpdt: £9.00 to a £1 stake. Pool: £5,423.69 - 444.50 winning tickets. **Steve Payne**

5897 - 5899a (Foreign Racing) - See Raceform Interactive

4117 NAVAN (L-H)
Saturday, August 27

OFFICIAL GOING: Good

5900a LIKE NAVAN ON FACEBOOK H'CAP 1m 6f
3:50 (3:51) (45-65,65) 3-Y-O+ **£4,069** (£1,257; £595; £264; £99)

RPR
1 **Sports Barrow (IRE)**27 4922 4-9-5 **56**....(p) DeclanMcDonogh 5 63+
(Ms Sandra Hughes, Ire) *chsd ldrs: 2nd 1/2-way: disp gng wl into st and led over 3f out: drvn clr over 2f out and sn wl clr: kpt on wl ins fnl f where reduced advantage* **16/1**
2 *1 ½* **Tap Focus (IRE)**7 5664 4-9-6 **57**....(t) KevinManning 15 62+
(J S Bolger, Ire) *in tch: 7th 1/2-way: rdn under 3f out and hdwy into mod 3rd 1 1/2f out: kpt on u.p ins fnl f into nvr rnr 2nd cl home: a hld* **10/1**
3 *nk* **Creeping Ivy (IRE)**125 1682 4-8-8 **45**....1 ColmO'Donoghue 14 49
(A J Martin, Ire) *in tch: hdwy on inner over 2f out: rdn into mod 2nd over 1f out and kpt on u.p ins fnl f: dropped to 3rd cl home: a hld by wnr* **14/1**
4 *5 ½* **Shake The Bucket (IRE)**12 5496 9-8-8 **50**.... TomMadden(5) 19 46
(Niall Madden, Ire) *sn chsd ldrs: 3rd 1/2-way: rdn in 2nd over 2f out and sn no imp on wnr in mod 2nd: dropped to 4th 1 1/2f out and kpt on one pce ins fnl f to jst hold 4th* **9/2**2
5 *nse* **Ben Rumson (IRE)**14 5424 4-9-3 **54**.... BillyLee 8 50
(Timothy Doyle, Ire) *in rr of mid-div: prog fr 3f out into mod 8th over 1f out: kpt on u.p ins fnl f: jst hld for 4th: nt trble wnr* **12/1**
6 *hd* **Carpet Elegance (IRE)**37 4121 11-8-8 **48**....1 RobbieDowney(3) 1 44
(Thomas J Farrell, Ire) *chsd ldrs: 5th 1/2-way: rdn over 2f out and no imp on wnr u.p in 5th ent fnl f: kpt on one pce* **25/1**
7 *2 ½* **Seb's Choice (IRE)**378 5404 7-8-8 **45**.... LeighRoche 22 37
(Lady Jane Gillespie, Ire) *hld up: pushed along in rr of mid-div into st: rdn 3f out and sme hdwy 1 1/2f out: kpt on u.p ins fnl f* **25/1**
8 *1* **Gold Class**14 5427 5-8-7 **51**....(tp) DylanHogan(7) 13 42
(Robert Alan Hennessy, Ire) *in rr of mid-div: sme late hdwy ins fnl f: nvr nrr* **33/1**
9 *½* **Placere (IRE)**7 5664 8-8-12 **56**.... OisinOrr(7) 7 46
(Richard Brabazon, Ire) *settled bhd ldrs: pushed along under 5f out and sn lost tch: kpt on one pce fnl 2f* **4/1**1
10 *nse* **Galloping Anger**12 5493 4-9-6 **57**....(t1) ColinKeane 20 47
(Matthew J Smith, Ire) *hooded to load: towards rr: rdn 3f out and kpt on u.p on outer fr 2f out: nvr nrr* **16/1**
11 *hd* **Glacial Drift**40 4470 5-9-3 **54**....1 PatSmullen 23 44
(T J Taaffe, Ire) *chsd ldrs: 6th 1/2-way: rdn under 3f out and no imp on wnr u.p in 4th 2f out: sn wknd* **20/1**
12 *hd* **Meadow Cross (IRE)**4 2058 4-10-0 **65**....(b) SeamieHeffernan 12 54
(Denis Gerard Hogan, Ire) *mid-div: rdn in mod 9th over 2f out and sn no ex: one pce after* **12/1**
13 *¾* **Gibson Park**11 5534 3-8-7 **56**....(b) ChrisHayes 21 44
(A Oliver, Ire) *settled towards rr: sme hdwy on outer fr over 4f out: rdn in mid-div under 3f out and sn no ex: one pce fnl 2f* **7/1**3
14 *hd* **Hazariban (IRE)**8 5620 7-10-0 **65**....(tp) ShaneFoley 16 53
(Seamus Fahey, Ire) *mid-div: rdn under 3f out and sn no ex: one pce fnl 2f* **8/1**
15 *1* **Lady Argentum (IRE)**14 5424 3-7-13 **53**.... KillianLeonard(5) 2 40
(Thomas Gibney, Ire) *chsd ldrs: 4th 1/2-way: rdn in 4th into st and sn no ex: wknd over 2f out* **33/1**
16 *¾* **Blues Dancer**25 5003 4-8-8 **45**....(b) WayneLordan 6 31
(J H Culloty, Ire) *in tch: 8th 1/2-way: rdn and no ex over 2f out: sn wknd* **25/1**
17 *3* **El Dem I (IRE)**458 2624 5-8-10 **47**....(t) ConorHoban 10 28
(Michael G Cleary, Ire) *in rr: rdn into st and kpt on one pce fr 2f out* **33/1**
18 *nk* **Rightdownthemiddle (IRE)**27 4468 8-9-9 **60**.... GaryCarroll 3 41
(Michael Mulvany, Ire) *chsd ldrs early: pushed along in mid-div fr 5f out and no imp u.p 3f out: wknd over 2f out* **9/1**
19 *4 ¾* **Mrs Conn (IRE)**14 5424 5-8-8 **45**.... RoryCleary 4 19
(Thomas Cleary, Ire) *led tl jnd into st: hdd over 3f out: sn rdn and no imp on wnr: wknd in 3rd over 2f out* **20/1**
20 *2* **Sensible Girl (IRE)**497 1524 4-8-8 **45**.... MichaelHussey 11 16
(Tracey Collins, Ire) *in rr of mid-div: pushed along under 5f out and no imp u.p 3f out: wknd fnl 2f* **33/1**
21 *dist* **Montys Angel (IRE)**22 5140 6-8-8 **45**.... NGMcCullagh 9
(John C McConnell, Ire) *towards rr thrght: wknd fr over 5f out: t.o* **28/1**
P **Lexi's Red Devil (IRE)**60 3761 4-8-12 **48** ow1....(p) RonanWhelan 17
(Philip M Byrne, Ire) *mid-div: rdn over 2f out and no imp: wknd towards rr and p.u qckly ins fnl f* **25/1**

3m 7.09s (-7.91)
WFA 3 from 4yo+ 12lb **22** Ran SP% **154.8**
CSF £181.27 CT £2380.15 TOTE £16.90: £4.50, £2.90, £4.70, £1.30; DF 430.50.
Owner Mrs D T Hughes **Bred** Hugh Smith & Rossenarra Stud Bs Ltd **Trained** Kildare, Co Kildare

FOCUS
A fine piece of race-riding from the former champion here, pinching it from the front early in the straight.

5901 - 5903a (Foreign Racing) - See Raceform Interactive

2722 BADEN-BADEN (L-H)
Saturday, August 27

OFFICIAL GOING: Turf: good

5904a PREIS DER SPARKASSEN FINANZGRUPPE (EX SPRETI-RENNEN) (GROUP 3) (4YO+) (TURF) 1m 2f
4:20 (4:28) 4-Y-O+ **£23,529** (£8,823; £4,411; £2,205; £1,470)

RPR
1 **Va Bank (IRE)**27 4-9-0 0.... MartinSeidl 3 113
(M Janikowski, Poland) *settled in midfield: cl 5th and travelling strly 3f out: rdn to chal whn wnt rt wl over 1f out: sn stened and led 200yds out: drvn and r.o* **31/5**3
2 *1 ½* **Potemkin (GER)**27 4928 5-9-2 0.... EduardoPedroza 1 112
(A Wohler, Germany) *a cl up: shkn up to ld 2f out: hdd 200yds out: styd on at same pce* **9/10**1

3 6 **Felician (GER)**[41] 4438 8-8-11 0 AndraschStarke 7 95
(Ferdinand J Leve, Germany) *racd in fnl trio: gd hdwy on inner fr 2 1/2f out: chsd ldr ins last 2f: kpt on fnl f to hold 3rd but no match for front two* **175/10**

4 1/2 **Devastar (GER)**[21] 4-9-0 0 AdriedeVries 9 97
(Markus Klug, Germany) *w.w in midfield: rdn to dispute 3rd over 1 1/2f out: styd on at one pce: readily lft bhd by front two* **112/10**

5 2 1/2 **Taniya (FR)**[15] 5384 4-8-8 0 (b) AlexisBadel 8 86
(J-C Rouget, France) *t.k.h: hld up in last: hdwy over 2 1/2f out: rdn and plugged on fnl f: nt pce to be involved* **63/10**

6 nk **Quelindo (GER)**[21] 4-9-0 0 StephenHellyn 10 91
(Gabor Maronka, Hungary) *w.w in fnl trio: pushed along in last 2 1/2f out: sme late prog u.p: nvr in contention* **214/10**

7 1/2 **Palace Prince (GER)**[146] 1231 4-8-11 0 MarcLerner 4 87
(Andreas Lowe, Germany) *in tch: niggled along bef 1/2-way: plugged on at one pce* **61/10**[2]

8 1 1/2 **Wild Chief (GER)**[62] 3699 5-9-0 0 AlexanderPietsch 6 87
(J Hirschberger, Germany) *rushed up on outer to chse ldr after 2f: 2nd and rdn 2 1/2f out: dropped away u.p fr 1 1/2f out* **78/10**

9 2 1/2 **Wildpark (GER)**[41] 4438 5-9-0 0 (b) FilipMinarik 2 82
(D Moser, Germany) *led: rousted along over 2 1/2f out: hdd 2f out: grad wknd: eased ins fnl 150yds* **158/10**

2m 4.89s (-0.10) **9** Ran SP% **129.7**
WIN (incl. 10 euro stake): 72. PLACES: 19, 12, 26. SF: 179.
Owner J P Zienkiewicz **Bred** Airlie Stud **Trained** Poland

5754 DEAUVILLE (R-H)

Saturday, August 27

OFFICIAL GOING: Turf: good to soft; polytrack; standard

5905a PRIX RECONVERSION CHEVAL DE COURSE EN CHEVAL DE LOISIR (CLAIMER) (2YO) (TURF) 6f

1:05 (12:00) 2-Y-O **£8,455** (£3,382; £2,536; £1,691; £845)

RPR

1 **King Of Spades (FR)**[16] 5325 2-9-1 0 ChristopheSoumillon 5 79
(Mick Channon) *broke wl: chsd clr ldr: 2 l 2nd and rdn 2f out: no immediate imp: r.o u.p fnl f: led cl home and qckly asserted* **13/10**[1]

2 1 **Mister Art (IRE)**[36] 2-9-1 0 (b) EddyHardouin 9 76
(Matthieu Palussiere, France) **11/1**

3 3 1/2 **Glicourt (FR)**[55] 2-9-4 0 Pierre-CharlesBoudot 2 69
(P Bary, France) **23/10**[2]

4 2 **Ultimate Fight (FR)**[22] 5141 2-9-4 0 StephanePasquier 6 63
(F Monnier, France) **14/1**

5 3/4 **Miss Charlotte (IRE)**[22] 5142 2-8-3 0 MathieuPelletan(5) 4 50
(M Delcher Sanchez, France) **16/1**

6 hd **Samran Says (IRE)**[29] 4843 2-8-11 0 MickaelBarzalona 11 53
(P Monfort, France) **13/1**

6 dht **Meteorite (FR)**[40] 2-8-8 0 LudovicBoisseau(3) 1 53
(G Doleuze, France) **10/1**[3]

8 3/4 **Indian's Lad (FR)** 2-8-8 0 (p) AnthonyCrastus 12 47
(J-M Capitte, France) **31/1**

9 3 1/2 **Miss Bombay (IRE)**[34] 2-8-8 0 UmbertoRispoli 7 37
(A Giorgi, Italy) **22/1**

10 3 **Sisterleon Davis (FR)**[90] 2724 2-8-11 0 (p) AntonioPolli 10 31
(C Plisson, France) **91/1**

11 1 **Tanau (IRE)** 2-9-1 0 LouisBeuzelin 8 32
(M Delcher Sanchez, France) **92/1**

12 snk **Supercopa (SPA)**[18] 5279 2-8-3 0 JeremieCatineau(5) 3 24
(C Laffon-Parias, France) **104/1**

1m 11.21s (0.21) **12** Ran SP% **121.5**
WIN (incl. 1 euro stake): 2.30. PLACES: 1.30, 2.10, 1.40. DF: 12.40. SF: 18.50.
Owner Chris Wright & The Hon Mrs J M Corbett **Bred** E A R L Elevage Des Loges Et Al **Trained** West Ilsley, Berks

5906a PRIX RECONVERSION CHEVAL DE COURSE EN CHEVAL DE COMPLET (CONDITIONS) (4YO+) (POLYTRACK) 6f 110y

1:35 (12:00) 4-Y-O+ **£12,132** (£4,852; £3,639; £2,426; £1,213)

RPR

1 **Swift Approval (IRE)**[28] 4865 4-9-6 0 (p) StephanePasquier 3 104
(Kevin Ryan) *mde virtually all: sn led after leaving stalls: shkn up and c stands' side 2f out: drvn whn pressed wl over 1f out: hrd pressed and r.o fnl f: asserted last 50yds* **31/10**[2]

2 1/2 **Gamgoom**[13] 5453 5-9-3 0 (b[1]) EddyHardouin 1 100
(Mario Hofer, Germany) **11/1**

3 1 1/4 **Bandanetta (FR)**[55] 4-8-10 0 UmbertoRispoli 7 89
(A Bonin, France) **47/10**

4 1/2 **Super City (FR)**[232] 5-8-10 0 TheoBachelot 5 88
(S Wattel, France) **16/5**[3]

5 1 1/4 **Kenouska (FR)**[18] 4-8-10 0 Pierre-CharlesBoudot 4 84
(P Sogorb, France) **7/5**[1]

6 2 1/2 **Comedia Eria (FR)**[281] 4-8-10 0 FabriceVeron 6 77
(P Monfort, France) **18/1**

WIN (incl. 1 euro stake): 4.10. PLACES: 2.60, 4.50. SF: 25.90
Owner Middleham Park Racing XLIX **Bred** Mrs Jean Brennan **Trained** Hambleton, N Yorks

5907a PRIX RECONVERSION CHEVAL DE COURSE EN CHEVAL DE HORSE BALL (MAIDEN) (3YO) (TURF) 6f

4:50 (12:00) 3-Y-O **£9,191** (£3,676; £2,757; £1,838; £919)

RPR

1 **White Witch (USA)**[428] 3601 3-8-13 0 MickaelBarzalona 2 70
(H-A Pantall, France) *racd towards rr in stands' side gp: hdwy on inner 1 1/2f out: r.o wl fnl f: led 75yds out: sn clr* **93/10**

2 2 **Minminwin (IRE)**[18] 5280 3-8-13 0 (b[1]) ThomasHuet 11 63
(Gay Kelleway) *chsd ldr in gp of three in middle of trck: rdn to ld overall wl over 1f out: styd on u.p: hdd fnl 75yds: no ex* **33/1**

3 1 **Silent Romance (FR)**[22] 3-8-13 0 AntoineHamelin 6 60
(J E Hammond, France) **11/1**

4 1/2 **La Perle Doloise (FR)**[41] 3-8-13 0 (b) GregoryBenoist 10 58
(A Bonin, France) **28/1**

5 shd **Huda (FR)**[22] 3-8-13 0 EddyHardouin 9 58
(M Le Forestier, France) **23/1**

6 nk **Kenwana (FR)**[22] 3-8-13 0 MaximeGuyon 5 57
(P Sogorb, France) **87/10**

7 2 **Springwater (FR)**[22] 3-9-2 0 TheoBachelot 13 54
(S Wattel, France) **12/1**

8 snk **A L'Anglaise**[40] 3-8-13 0 Pierre-CharlesBoudot 1 50
(A Fabre, France) **23/5**[2]

9 1 1/4 **Bidder**[22] 3-9-2 0 VincentCheminaud 14 49
(P Bary, France) **9/5**[1]

10 snk **Vent Du Large (FR)**[59] 3-8-10 0 ClementLecoeuvre(6) 7 49
(R Chotard, France) **35/1**

11 3 1/2 **Prince Apache**[41] 4440 3-9-2 0 ChristopheSoumillon 4 38
(Andreas Lowe, Germany) **66/10**[3]

12 4 **Zaytoon (IRE)**[40] 3-9-2 0 LouisBeuzelin 8 25
(J E Hammond, France) **43/1**

13 1 3/4 **Cracker'Star (FR)**[7] 3-9-2 0 (p) FabriceVeron 3 19
(C Plisson, France) **56/1**

1m 10.96s (-0.04) **13** Ran SP% **120.1**
WIN (incl. 1 euro stake): 10.30. PLACES: 3.60, 8.70, 3.90. DF: 168.70. SF: 332.70.
Owner Godolphin SNC **Bred** Darley **Trained** France

5908 - 5912a (Foreign Racing) - See Raceform Interactive

5697 SARATOGA (R-H)

Saturday, August 27

OFFICIAL GOING: Dirt: fast; turf: firm

5913a TRAVERS STKS (GRADE 1) (3YO) (DIRT) 1m 2f (D)

10:44 (12:00) 3-Y-O **£455,782** (£156,462; £85,034; £57,823; £34,013; £23,809)

RPR

1 **Arrogate (USA)**[23] 3-9-0 0 MikeESmith 1 134+
(Bob Baffert, U.S.A) **117/10**

2 13 1/2 **American Freedom (USA)**[27] 3-9-0 0 RafaelBejarano 2 107
(Bob Baffert, U.S.A) **51/10**[2]

3 1 1/2 **Gun Runner (USA)**[27] 3-9-0 0 FlorentGeroux 13 104
(Steven Asmussen, U.S.A) **97/10**

4 3 3/4 **Gift Box (USA)**[29] 3-9-0 0 JuniorAlvarado 9 97+
(Chad C Brown, U.S.A) **178/10**

5 1 1/2 **Governor Malibu (USA)**[28] 3-9-0 0 (b) JoelRosario 4 94+
(Christophe Clement, U.S.A) **17/2**

6 1 1/2 **Connect (USA)**[29] 3-9-0 0 JohnRVelazquez 10 91
(Chad C Brown, U.S.A) **106/10**

7 hd **Creator (USA)**[28] 3-9-0 0 (b) IradOrtizJr 11 90+
(Steven Asmussen, U.S.A) **44/5**

8 2 3/4 **My Man Sam (USA)**[35] 3-9-0 0 ManuelFranco 3 85+
(Chad C Brown, U.S.A) **26/1**

9 6 1/4 **Destin (USA)**[28] 3-9-0 0 (b) JavierCastellano 8 72
(Todd Pletcher, U.S.A) **71/10**[3]

10 hd **Forever D'Oro (USA)**[29] 3-9-0 0 LuisSaez 5 72+
(Dallas Stewart, U.S.A) **76/1**

11 2 **Exaggerator (USA)**[27] 3-9-0 0 KentJDesormeaux 7 68+
(J Keith Desormeaux, U.S.A) **51/20**[1]

12 23 **Laoban (USA)**[28] 3-9-0 0 (b) JoseLOrtiz 12 22
(Eric J Guillot, U.S.A) **187/10**

13 1 1/2 **Anaximandros (USA)**[21] 3-9-0 0 (b) LeonelReyes 6 19
(Mikhail Yanakov, U.S.A) **131/1**

1m 59.36s (119.36) **13** Ran SP% **119.6**
PARI-MUTUEL (all including 2 usd stake): WIN 25.40; PLACE (1-2) 12.60, 6.70; SHOW (1-2-3) 8.40, 4.60, 6.80; SF 134.50.
Owner Juddmonte Farms Inc **Bred** Clearsky Farms **Trained** USA

FOCUS
An astonishing performance from the winner in the fastest time ever recorded in the 147-year history of the Travers.

5914a WOODFORD RESERVE BALLSTON SPA STKS (GRADE 2) (3YO+ FILLIES & MARES) (TURF) 1m 110y

11:20 (12:00) 3-Y-O+ **£149,659** (£54,421; £32,653; £16,326; £8,163; £5,442)

RPR

1 **Strike Charmer (USA)**[35] 4677 6-8-7 0 (b) JuniorAlvarado 5 110
(Mark Hennig, U.S.A) **28/1**

2 3/4 **Lady Eli (USA)**[420] 3919 4-8-9 0 IradOrtizJr 2 110
(Chad C Brown, U.S.A) **9/10**[1]

3 1/2 **Sentiero Italia (USA)**[36] 4-8-9 0 JoelRosario 4 109
(Kiaran McLaughlin, U.S.A) **77/20**[3]

4 1 **Onus (USA)**[35] 4677 4-8-7 0 JoseLOrtiz 6 105
(Claude McGaughey III, U.S.A) **98/10**

5 1/2 **Miss Temple City (USA)**[35] 4677 4-8-11 0 DraydenVanDyke 7 108
(H Graham Motion, U.S.A) **47/20**[2]

6 6 **Excilly**[21] 5185 4-8-5 0 LuisSaez 1 88
(Tom Dascombe) **46/1**

7 20 **Sympathy (USA)**[34] 4-8-5 0 AaronTGryder 3 44
(Chad C Brown, U.S.A) **75/1**

1m 38.77s (98.77) **7** Ran SP% **119.3**

Owner Courtlandt Farms **Bred** Courtlandt Farm **Trained** North America

5861 BEVERLEY (R-H)

Sunday, August 28

OFFICIAL GOING: Good to soft (soft in places; 6.7)
Wind: Virtually nil Weather: Heavy cloud

5915 JOHN JENKINS MEMORIAL CLAIMING STKS 7f 100y

1:50 (1:50) (Class 5) 3-Y-O+ **£3,780** (£1,131; £565; £283; £141) **Stalls** Low

Form RPR

2312 1 **Our Boy Jack (IRE)**[18] 5291 7-8-12 75 AdamMcNamara(5) 3 87
(Richard Fahey) *trckd ldr: cl up 1/2-way: led 3f out: rdn over 1f out: clr fnl f* **7/2**[2]

1360 **2** *4 1/2* **Layla's Hero (IRE)**[29] 4881 9-9-1 76...(v) RobertWinston 2 75
(Roger Teal) *trckd ldrs on inner: hdwy over 2f out: rdn wl over 1f out: drvn and kpt on same pce fnl f* **7/1**

110- **3** *hd* **Gramercy (IRE)**[345] 6493 9-9-5 91... TonyHamilton 7 78
(Richard Fahey) *trckd ldng pair: hdwy over 2f out: rdn wl over 1f out: drvn and kpt on same pce fnl f* **9/2**[3]

0300 **4** *1 1/2* **Fort Bastion (IRE)**[10] 5585 7-9-10 92...(b) PhillipMakin 1 80
(David O'Meara) *dwlt and in rr: hdwy wl over 2f out and sn pushed along: chsd ldrs and rdn over 1f out: sn drvn and no imp* **13/8**[1]

330 **5** *8* **Terhaal (IRE)**[13] 5482 4-9-9 75... DavidNolan 5 60
(David O'Meara) *led: pushed along and hdd 3f out: sn rdn and wknd 2f out* **9/2**[3]

0 **6** *5* **Les Darcy**[8] 5628 5-8-13 42... DavidAllan 6 38
(Ken Cunningham-Brown) *a towards rr: outpcd and bhd fnl 2f* **100/1**

1m 33.32s (-0.48) **Going Correction** +0.025s/f (Good) **6** Ran SP% **110.2**
Speed ratings (Par 103): **103,97,97,95,86 81**
CSF £25.91 TOTE £4.60: £2.70, £3.20; EX 22.10 Trifecta £59.10.

Owner Middleham Park Racing XXXVI **Bred** Mrs Ian Fox **Trained** Musley Bank, N Yorks

■ Tafahom was withdrawn. Price at time of withdrawal 16-1. Rule 4 does not apply.

FOCUS
A total of 10mm of rain since 3pm the previous day saw conditions ease to good to soft, soft in places. A fair race of its type, but just an ordinary gallop and a race in which the a couple of the market leaders disappointed. The winner matched his late 2015 form.

5916 OLD CROSSLEYANS RUGBY CLUB EBF MEDIAN AUCTION MAIDEN STKS 1m 100y
2:20 (2:20) (Class 5) 2-Y-O **£3,780** (£1,131; £565; £283) **Stalls** Low

Form RPR

53 **1** **Third Order (IRE)**[36] 4642 2-9-5 0... BenCurtis 4 75+
(K R Burke) *slt ld on outer: rdn along over 2f out: drvn over 1f out: kpt on strly fnl f* **5/1**[2]

42 **2** *4 1/2* **Maldonado (FR)**[16] 5371 2-9-5 0... MartinLane 3 66+
(Charlie Appleby) *t.k.h early: trckd ldng pair: hdwy over 2f out: rdn and edgd rt over 1f out: drvn and hung rt ent fnl f: kpt on same pce* **8/15**[1]

3 **3** *1/2* **Golconda Prince (IRE)**[26] 4966 2-9-5 0... TonyHamilton 5 65
(Richard Fahey) *hld up: effrt and sme hdwy on inner wl over 2f out: rdn wl over 1f out: kpt on same pce* **8/1**[3]

4 **4** *3/4* **Dominating (GER)**[18] 5290 2-9-5 0... JoeFanning 2 63
(Mark Johnston) *cl up on inner: effrt and ev ch over 2f out: sn rdn: drvn over 1f out: kpt on same pce* **5/1**[2]

1m 48.57s (0.97) **Going Correction** +0.025s/f (Good) **4** Ran SP% **109.7**
Speed ratings (Par 94): **96,91,91,90**
CSF £8.50 TOTE £6.70; EX 8.20 Trifecta £16.90.

Owner Clipper Logistics **Bred** John O'Connor **Trained** Middleham Moor, N Yorks

FOCUS
A fair but uncompetitive maiden in which the winner, who stepped forward again, handled the conditions much better than his rivals. The gallop was a steady one to the home turn.

5917 RACING UK HD NURSERY H'CAP 5f
2:55 (2:55) (Class 3) (0-90,86) 2-Y-O **£6,301** (£1,886; £943; £472; £235) **Stalls** Low

Form RPR

1135 **1** **Orewa (IRE)**[36] 4669 2-9-2 81... BenCurtis 3 89
(Brian Ellison) *hld up in rr: hdwy on outer to ld over 1f out: sn rdn and hung lft ins fnl f: kpt on* **7/2**[3]

362 **2** *2 1/2* **Harbour Lightning**[18] 5289 2-7-11 65 oh1... NoelGarbutt(3) 2 64
(Ann Duffield) *trckd ldrs: effrt whn nt clr run and hmpd 1 1/2f out: swtchd rt to inner and rdn: kpt on wl fnl f* **10/1**

1402 **3** *1 1/2* **Boundsy (IRE)**[36] 4629 2-8-11 76... TonyHamilton 5 70
(Richard Fahey) *trckd ldng pair: pushed along 1/2-way: rdn wl over 1f out: drvn and kpt on fnl f* **5/1**

1443 **4** *3 1/4* **Poet's Society**[23] 5113 2-9-7 86... JoeFanning 1 68
(Mark Johnston) *cl up on inner: rdn to ld and edgd lft wl over 1f out: drvn and hdd over 1f out: edgd lft and wknd fnl f* **2/1**[1]

431 **5** *9* **Sir Viktor (IRE)**[18] 5289 2-8-9 74...(v) PJMcDonald 4 24
(K R Burke) *slt ld: rdn along 2f out: sn hdd & wknd* **9/4**[2]

1m 3.49s (-0.01) **Going Correction** +0.025s/f (Good) **5** Ran SP% **112.1**
Speed ratings (Par 98): **101,97,94,89,75**
CSF £33.11 TOTE £4.50: £2.50, £4.10; EX 30.30 Trifecta £71.10.

Owner Keith Brown **Bred** Mrs C Regalado-Gonzalez **Trained** Norton, N Yorks

FOCUS
A depleted field and not much depth, but a good gallop and a useful performance from the winner, while the runner-up has been rated to her mark.

5918 BEVERLEY MIDDLE DISTANCE SERIES FINAL ROUND H'CAP 1m 4f 16y
3:30 (3:30) (Class 5) (0-75,73) 3-Y-O+ **£5,040** (£1,508; £754; £377; £188) **Stalls** Low

Form RPR

4321 **1** **Age Of Elegance (IRE)**[18] 5292 4-10-0 73...(p) PJMcDonald 6 79
(David Loughnane) *trckd ldr: hdwy 3f out: cl up over 2f out: rdn to ld over 1f out: drvn out* **11/4**[1]

3434 **2** *1/2* **Jan De Heem**[6] 5718 6-8-13 58...(p) JamesSullivan 5 63
(Tina Jackson) *hld up in rr: stdy hdwy over 3f out: trckd ldrs 2f out: effrt and n.m.r over 1f out: sn rdn: drvn and ev ch ins fnl f: kpt on* **6/1**

-045 **3** *1/2* **Best Boy**[13] 5481 4-9-1 60...(vt[1]) DavidAllan 7 64
(David C Griffiths) *led to 1/2-way: chsd ldr: hdwy to ld over 2f out: sn rdn and hdd over 1f out: drvn and ev ch ent fnl f: kpt on* **11/2**[3]

3234 **4** *1 1/2* **Brandon Castle**[29] 4888 4-9-8 72... AdamMcNamara(5) 3 74
(Simon West) *t.k.h: trckd ldrs: hdwy to ld 1/2-way and sn clr: pushed along and jnd 3f out: sn rdn and hdd over 2f out: drvn and wknd appr fnl f* **11/4**[1]

4544 **5** *7* **Yorkindred Spirit**[7] 5671 4-9-11 70...(v) JoeFanning 2 61
(Mark Johnston) *hld up in tch: hdwy over 3f out: pushed along wl over 2f out: sn rdn and btn over 1f out* **9/2**[2]

1046 **6** *18* **Skiddaw Valleys**[35] 4680 4-9-13 72... TonyHamilton 4 34
(Alan Swinbank) *in tch: pushed along 5f out: sn outpcd and bhd fnl 3f* **8/1**

2m 41.25s (1.45) **Going Correction** +0.025s/f (Good) **6** Ran SP% **112.3**
Speed ratings (Par 103): **96,95,95,94,89 77**
CSF £19.49 TOTE £3.70: £2.00, £3.20; EX 18.80 Trifecta £81.70.

Owner R G Fell **Bred** Ladyswood Stud **Trained** Market Drayton, Shropshire

FOCUS
Mainly exposed performers in a fair handicap and straightforward form. A steady gallop picked up around halfway.

5919 BEVERLEY ANNUAL BADGEHOLDERS H'CAP 1m 100y
4:05 (4:05) (Class 4) (0-80,79) 3-Y-O **£5,040** (£1,508; £754; £377; £188) **Stalls** Low

Form RPR

4242 **1** **Just Hiss**[14] 5438 3-9-5 77... DavidAllan 2 88+
(Tim Easterby) *hld up: hdwy wl over 2f out: cl up and rdn over 1f out: led jst ins fnl f: styd on strly* **7/4**[1]

5440 **2** *3 1/4* **Ninetta (IRE)**[22] 5180 3-9-7 79... PJMcDonald 4 82
(Ann Duffield) *led: rdn along over 2f out: drvn over 1f out: hdd jst ins fnl f: kpt on same pce* **5/1**[3]

0124 **3** *nse* **Arcane Dancer (IRE)**[4] 5782 3-8-6 64...(p) CamHardie 3 67
(Lawrence Mullaney) *trckd ldrs: hdwy on outer over 2f out: rdn over 1f out: sn drvn and ev ch ent fnl f: kpt on same pce* **13/2**

1501 **4** *1* **Normandie Lady**[29] 4871 3-9-1 78... AdamMcNamara(5) 5 79
(Richard Fahey) *hld up in rr: hdwy over 2f out: rdn to chse ldrs over 1f out: drvn and no imp fnl f* **2/1**[2]

5-40 **5** *6* **Cape Love (USA)**[105] 2269 3-9-2 74... DavidNolan 1 61
(David O'Meara) *trckd ldng pair on inner: pushed along wl over 2f out: rdn wl over 1f out: sn drvn and wknd* **12/1**

3505 **6** *8* **Steccando (IRE)**[24] 5063 3-9-1 73... BenCurtis 6 42
(Alan Swinbank) *cl up: rdn along 3f out: drvn 2f out: sn wknd* **16/1**

1m 47.21s (-0.39) **Going Correction** +0.025s/f (Good) **6** Ran SP% **113.3**
Speed ratings (Par 102): **102,98,98,97,91 83**
CSF £11.17 TOTE £3.00: £1.50, £2.90; EX 11.20 Trifecta £38.80.

Owner The Sandmoor Partnership **Bred** Jeremy Gompertz **Trained** Great Habton, N Yorks

FOCUS
A fair handicap run at just an ordinary gallop and a minor personal best from the winner. The field raced in the centre in the home straight.

5920 BEVERLEY LIONS H'CAP 5f
4:40 (4:41) (Class 6) (0-60,58) 3-Y-O **£2,587** (£770; £384; £192) **Stalls** Low

Form RPR

5032 **1** **David's Beauty (IRE)**[10] 5570 3-9-6 57...(p) GrahamLee 12 64
(Brian Baugh) *wnt lft s: chsd ldrs on wd outside: rdn 2f out: led ent fnl f: sn drvn: edgd rt and kpt on wl* **8/1**

0006 **2** *3/4* **Emerald Bay**[16] 5378 3-9-4 55...(v[1]) RobertWinston 1 60
(Ivan Furtado) *trckd ldrs on inner: swtchd lft and hdwy 2f out: rdn over 1f out: drvn to chal and ev ch whn hung lft jst ins fnl f: kpt on* **10/1**

3300 **3** *3/4* **Tarnend Lass**[10] 5578 3-8-10 47...(bt) JamesSullivan 11 49
(Tim Easterby) *towards rr on outer: hdwy over 2f out: rdn to chse ldrs over 1f out: drvn and n.m.r ins fnl f: kpt on wl towatrds fin* **16/1**

506 **4** *nk* **Midnight Robbery**[47] 4229 3-9-1 52... ConnorBeasley 2 53+
(Bryan Smart) *dwlt and towards rr on inner: hdwy 1/2-way: rdn wl over 1f out: styd on wl fnl f: nrst fin* **5/1**[2]

0042 **5** *1 3/4* **Chip Or Pellet**[25] 5041 3-8-5 47... RowanScott(5) 6 42
(Nigel Tinkler) *sltly hmpd s and towards rr: pushed along 1/2-way: rdn and hdwy wl over 1f out: drvn and kpt on fnl f* **4/1**[1]

0-03 **6** *shd* **Plantation (IRE)**[17] 5335 3-8-10 52... AdamMcNamara(5) 8 46
(Robert Cowell) *sltly hmpd s and towards rr: hdwy 2f out: rdn over 1f out: kpt on fnl f* **6/1**[3]

5005 **7** *1/2* **Cosmic Dust**[19] 5277 3-8-3 45... PhilDennis(5) 5 37
(Richard Whitaker) *cl up in centre: rdn 2f out: slt ld 1 1/2f out and sn drvn: hdd ent fnl f: wknd* **11/1**

0004 **8** *1 1/2* **Caymus**[51] 4096 3-9-4 55 ow2...(t) DaleSwift 9 42
(Tracy Waggott) *wnt rt s: sn prom: rdn along 2f out: sn drvn and wknd over 1f out* **20/1**

4100 **9** *6* **King's Currency**[19] 5277 3-9-7 58...(p) PJMcDonald 7 23
(Jedd O'Keeffe) *hmpd s and a in rr* **7/1**

0055 **10** *5* **Bazula (IRE)**[19] 5278 3-9-1 52...(b) JasonHart 4
(Tim Easterby) *prom: rdn along over 2f out: sn drvn and wknd* **9/1**

-605 **11** *6* **Compton Mews**[30] 4845 3-9-3 54... DavidAllan 3
(Les Eyre) *chsd ldrs towards inner: rdn along wl over 1f out: hld whn n.m.r and hmpd appr fnl f* **25/1**

0036 **12** *9* **Lowrie**[3] 5804 3-8-13 55...(p) NathanEvans(5) 10
(John David Riches) *qckly away and led on inner rail: rdn along 2f out: drvn and hdd 1 1/2f out: wknd qckly* **16/1**

1m 4.32s (0.82) **Going Correction** +0.025s/f (Good) **12** Ran SP% **122.4**
Speed ratings (Par 98): **94,92,91,91,88 88,87,84,75,67 57,43**
CSF £88.46 CT £1289.50 TOTE £10.60: £2.30, £3.60, £3.90; EX 88.60 Trifecta £2526.60.

Owner G B Hignett **Bred** Miss Sinead Looney **Trained** Audley, Staffs

FOCUS
A moderate handicap in which the gallop was sound and the winner was entitled to win off this mark. The field fanned across the course before converging towards the stands' side in the closing stages.

5921 SPONSOR OLLIE PEARS FOR THE GREAT NORTH RUN H'CAP 1m 1f 207y
5:15 (5:15) (Class 6) (0-65,65) 3-Y-O **£2,587** (£770; £384; £192) **Stalls** Low

Form RPR

0304 **1** **L'Apogee**[13] 5481 3-8-11 55...(v[1]) TonyHamilton 5 62
(Richard Fahey) *trckd ldrs: hdwy over 2f out: rdn over 1f out: led jst ins fnl f: drvn and kpt on wl* **4/1**[2]

6630 **2** *1 3/4* **Allfredandnobell (IRE)**[24] 5064 3-8-9 53... DavidAllan 2 57
(Micky Hammond) *hld up in tch: hdwy 2f out: rdn over 1f out: drvn and kpt on fnl f* **7/2**[1]

653 **3** *1/2* **Lady Canford (IRE)**[17] 5322 3-8-2 51... NathanEvans(5) 1 54
(James Bethell) *led: pushed along over 2f out: rdn over 1f out: drvn and hdd ins fnl f: kpt on same pce* **7/2**[1]

4262 **4** *2 1/2* **Lozah**[19] 5276 3-8-12 56...(tp) PJMcDonald 3 54
(David Loughnane) *hld up towards rr: swtchd wd and hdwy over 2f out: rdn and ev ch over 1f out: sn drvn and kpt on same pce* **9/2**[3]

0062 **5** *hd* **Indulgent**[12] 5517 3-8-7 51... DuranFentiman 7 49
(Tony Coyle) *trckd ldr: hdwy and cl up over 2f out: sn chal and rdn: drvn and wknd over 1f out* **11/2**

-000 **6** *1 3/4* **Triassic (IRE)**[29] 4872 3-8-11 55... JoeFanning 4 50
(Mark Johnston) *chsd ldrs: rdn along 3f out: drvn and wknd 2f out* **6/1**

0560 **7** *17* **Jon H The Lawman (IRE)**[17] 5319 3-7-13 46 oh1...(b) NoelGarbutt(3) 6 10
(Ronald Thompson) *a in rr: outpcd and bhd fr over 2f out* **25/1**

2m 8.03s (1.03) **Going Correction** +0.025s/f (Good) **7** Ran SP% **116.1**
Speed ratings (Par 98): **96,94,94,92,92 90,77**
CSF £18.95 CT £53.34 TOTE £3.60: £2.00, £2.30; EX 23.90 Trifecta £87.80.

Owner Mrs Jane Newett **Bred** Scuderia Archi Romani **Trained** Musley Bank, N Yorks

FOCUS
A low grade handicap in which the gallop was an ordinary one, but the form makes sense. The field raced in the centre in the home straight.

T/Plt: £2,069.30 to a £1 stake. Pool: £57,120.99 - 20.15 winning tickets T/Qpdt: £151.10 to a £1 stake. Pool: £4,413.02 - 21.60 winning tickets **Joe Rowntree**

5869 GOODWOOD (R-H)

Sunday, August 28

OFFICIAL GOING: Good to firm changing to good (good to firm in places on round course) after race 3 (3:10)

Wind: Fresh, half against Weather: Overcast with showers

5922 BUTLINS MAIDEN AUCTION STKS — 1m

2:05 (2:05) (Class 5) 2-Y-O — **£3,234** (£962; £481; £240) **Stalls** Low

Form — RPR

032 **1** **Carducci**[17] 5324 2-8-9 73 SeanLevey 1 — 72
(Richard Hannon) *lw: mde all: drew clr over 1f out: pushed out* **1/20**[1]

2 2 1/2 **Peloton** 2-8-4 0 KieranO'Neill 3 — 60+
(Pat Phelan) *cls cpld: chsd ldng pair: shkn up and rn green 3f out: styd on to take 2nd jst ins fnl f: unable to chal* **14/1**[2]

3 6 **Nip Down The Jug** 2-8-10 0 HarryPoulton 4 — 52
(Adam West) *leggy: athletic: t.k.h: hld up in last: prog to chse wnr over 3f out: cl up 2f out: sn rdn and wknd: lost 2nd jst ins fnl f* **40/1**[3]

00 **4** 15 **Ultimat Power (IRE)**[11] 5549 2-8-10 0 AdamBeschizza 6 — 16
(Mark Hoad) *lengthy: chsd wnr to over 3f out: wknd qckly: t.o* **66/1**

1m 44.0s (4.10) **Going Correction** +0.225s/f (Good) **4** Ran SP% **105.8**
Speed ratings (Par 94): **88,85,79,64**
CSF £1.43 TOTE £1.10; EX 1.30 Trifecta £2.10.
Owner Sultan Ali **Bred** Seamus Burns Esq **Trained** East Everleigh, Wilts

FOCUS
The track had been watered since the previous day's meeting and there were a few showers around, but the ground was given as good to firm. An uncompetitive, steadily run maiden to start and not much of a race.

5923 CHICHESTER CITY (S) STKS — 1m 3f

2:35 (2:36) (Class 4) 3-Y-O — **£6,469** (£1,925; £962; £481) **Stalls** High

Form — RPR

3024 **1** **Spinning Pearl (IRE)**[12] 5529 3-8-10 63 MartinDwyer 1 — 67
(Eve Johnson Houghton) *trckd ldng pair: gng wl whn waiting for a gap 3f out: led jst over 2f out: drvn over 1f out: kpt on wl* **7/2**[1]

2501 **2** 1 **Gabster (IRE)**[18] 5303 3-8-10 62 OisinMurphy 3 — 65
(Amanda Perrett) *trckd ldng pair: rdn to chal jst over 2f out: chsd wnr after: styd on but readily hld* **9/2**[2]

6-0 **3** 3 **Sweet Dream Lady (IRE)**[27] 4936 3-8-7 57 SamHitchcott 4 — 58
(Gary Moore) *lw: n.m.r s: t.k.h and hld up in last pair: gng wl whn waiting for a gap over 2f out: rdn and prog to take 3rd fnl f: one pce after* **12/1**

4443 **4** 1 1/2 **Harry's Endeavour**[11] 5548 3-9-1 57 (b) TimmyMurphy 5 — 63
(Daniel Kubler) *in tch disputing 5th: prog over 2f out: rdn to chse ldng pair wl over 1f out to fnl f: one pce* **8/1**[3]

0540 **5** 5 **Picture Painter (IRE)**[20] 5227 3-8-12 63 TomMarquand 2 — 52
(Jim Goldie) *in tch disputing 5th: pushed along wl over 2f out: no imp u.p wl over 1f out: fdd* **9/1**

513 **6** 1 3/4 **Becca Campbell (IRE)**[12] 5513 3-8-10 57 (p) JohnFahy 8 — 47
(Eve Johnson Houghton) *pressed ldr to over 2f out: wknd* **9/2**[2]

4312 **7** 5 **Pastoral Star**[19] 5254 3-8-10 63 JimCrowley 6 — 39
(Hughie Morrison) *led but pressed: hdd & wknd jst over 2f out* **7/2**[1]

3065 **8** 13 **Its A Sheila Thing**[23] 5100 3-8-7 51 FrannyNorton 7 — 16
(Linda Jewell) *t.k.h early: hld up in last pair: shkn up and wknd 3f out* **33/1**

2m 28.29s (1.79) **Going Correction** +0.225s/f (Good) **8** Ran SP% **112.6**
Speed ratings (Par 102): **102,101,99,98,94 93,89,80**
CSF £18.69 TOTE £3.80: £1.40, £2.00, £4.10; EX 19.90 Trifecta £144.30.The winner was bought by Phil Middleton for £14,000.
Owner Eden Racing Club **Bred** T Cahalan & D Cahalan **Trained** Blewbury, Oxon

FOCUS
Modest stuff and the 6th and 8th, while not going too fast, gave each other no peace up front. The winner has been rated to her mark.

5924 GOODWOOD "FAMOUS FOR FOOD" STKS (H'CAP) — 1m 1f 192y

3:10 (3:10) (Class 2) (0-100,99) 3-Y-O **£15,562** (£4,660; £2,330; £1,165) **Stalls** Low

Form — RPR

6003 **1** **Zhui Feng (IRE)**[9] 5699 3-9-7 **99** JimCrowley 5 — 106
(Amanda Perrett) *lw: trckd ldr: shkn up to ld wl over 1f out: drvn fnl f: jst hld on* **5/1**[3]

0-34 **2** nse **New Caledonia (IRE)**[101] 2413 3-8-10 **88** FrannyNorton 1 — 95
(Mark Johnston) *led: pushed along 3f out: hdd wl over 1f out: urged along and rallied fnl f: w wnr nr fin: jst pipped* **5/1**[3]

3-11 **3** 1/2 **You're Hired**[31] 4797 3-8-8 **86** MartinDwyer 3 — 92
(Amanda Perrett) *lw: hld up in last: prog to press ldng pair over 2f out: rdn over 1f out: wandered and nt qckn: hld after but kpt on nr fin* **6/5**[1]

3141 **4** 4 1/2 **Fidaawy**[15] 5391 3-9-2 **94** DaneO'Neill 2 — 91
(Sir Michael Stoute) *dwlt: t.k.h in 3rd: pushed along wl over 2f out: dropped to last and short of room jst over 2f out: fdd* **9/4**[2]

2m 9.97s (1.87) **Going Correction** +0.225s/f (Good) **4** Ran SP% **109.6**
Speed ratings (Par 106): **101,100,100,96**
CSF £25.58 TOTE £4.90; EX 25.20 Trifecta £33.80.
Owner John Connolly & Odile Griffith **Bred** Es Que Syndicate & Irish National Stud **Trained** Pulborough, W Sussex

FOCUS
An interesting race despite the small field and the winner and second were always forwardly placed. The form is best viewed around the trio who ran their race.

5925 GOODWOOD AMATEUR RIDER CHALLENGE H'CAP (IN MEMORY OF THE LATE GAY KINDERSLEY) — 1m 1f

3:45 (3:47) (Class 5) (0-75,75) 4-Y-O+ **£6,239** (£1,935; £967; £484) **Stalls** Low

Form — RPR

0315 **1** **Pink Ribbon (IRE)**[8] 5650 4-11-0 **68** (p) MissSBrotherton 7 — 74
(Sylvester Kirk) *mde virtually all: clr to 4f out at mod pce: hrd pressed fr 2f out: urged along and kpt fending off rivals* **3/1**[2]

11 **2** 1/2 **Pointillism**[11] 5540 4-11-2 **70** MissJWalton 9 — 75
(Iain Jardine) *trckd wnr: chal 2f out: rdn and kpt on fr over 1f out but nvr able to get upsides* **9/2**[3]

0 **3** 1/2 **Stanley (GER)**[38] 4561 5-10-13 **72** MrJJO'Neill[(5)] 4 — 76
(Jonjo O'Neill) *hld up in 4th: waiting for room over 2f out whn cl up: pushed along over 1f out and stl nt clrest of runs: styd on to take 3rd nr fin but too late to chal* **8/1**

3313 **4** 1/2 **Wordismybond**[7] 5674 7-10-11 **72** (p) MrJEPerrett[(7)] 3 — 75
(Richard Hughes) *trckd ldng pair: poised to chal on inner 2f out gng strly: shkn up over 1f out: fnd little and lost 3rd nr fin* **8/1**

2123 **5** 3 3/4 **Zephyros (GER)**[21] 5207 5-10-5 **64** [1] MissPBridgwater[(5)] 11 — 60
(David Bridgwater) *t.k.h: hld up in 7th: clsd on ldrs on outer over 2f out: rdn over 1f out: steadily fdd* **11/2**

2332 **6** 3/4 **The Gay Cavalier**[5] 5750 5-11-2 **75** (t) MrBJames[(5)] 10 — 69
(John Ryan) *hld up bhd ldrs: waiting for room over 2f out: sn pushed along: steadily fdd over 1f out* **11/4**[1]

0505 **7** 3 3/4 **Victor's Bet (SPA)**[9] 5592 7-10-4 **63** MissEllaSmith[(5)] 1 — 50+
(Ralph J Smith) *stdd s: hld up and sn wl detached in last: rapidly clsd on wd outside over 3f out: wknd 2f out* **16/1**

0-40 **8** 22 **Queen Of Norway (IRE)**[6] 5710 5-9-9 **56** oh9 [1] MissJMOlliver[(7)] 8
(Paddy Butler) *in tch to 3f out: sn wknd: t.o* **100/1**

2m 4.07s (7.77) **Going Correction** +0.225s/f (Good) **8** Ran SP% **114.3**
Speed ratings (Par 103): **74,73,73,72,69 68,65,45**
CSF £16.95 CT £96.24 TOTE £4.00: £1.50, £1.60, £2.30; EX 18.10 Trifecta £143.10.
Owner Mrs Michelle Cousins **Bred** Ann & Joe Hallinan **Trained** Upper Lambourn, Berks

FOCUS
The rain continued and the ground was changed to good, good to firm in places on the round course prior to this race. The beaten riders gave the winner, who recorded a minor personal best, too big a start and the first four raced 1-2-4-3 for much of the way.

5926 DOOM BAR SUPREME STKS (GROUP 3) — 7f

4:20 (4:21) (Class 1) 3-Y-O+

£34,026 (£12,900; £6,456; £3,216; £1,614; £810) **Stalls** Low

Form — RPR

0101 **1** **Opal Tiara (IRE)**[10] 5588 3-8-6 101 OisinMurphy 8 — 109
(Mick Channon) *swtg: trckd ldr to over 1f out: rdn and sn chalng new ldr: drvn ahd last 100yds: styd on wl* **9/1**

0016 **2** nk **Convey**[15] 5404 4-9-0 113 (p) RyanMoore 3 — 113
(Sir Michael Stoute) *lw: hld up in 5th: clsd on ldrs 2f out: rdn over 1f out: sltly awkward and nt qckn: styd on last 100yds to take 2nd nr fin* **5/2**[2]

2153 **3** nk **Jallota**[9] 5613 5-9-0 111 MartinHarley 1 — 112
(Charles Hills) *sltly impeded by ldr after 1f: racd in 3rd: squeezed between ldng pair and rdn to ld over 1f out: kpt on wl but hdd and jst outpcd last 100yds* **7/2**[3]

0002 **4** 1 1/2 **Emell**[22] 5146 6-9-0 99 (b) KieranO'Neill 2 — 108
(Richard Hannon) *chsd ldng trio: pushed along 3f out: sn lost pl: nvr able to threaten after but kpt on u.p fnl f* **25/1**

3402 **5** 1/2 **So Beloved**[9] 5613 6-9-0 112 DanielTudhope 4 — 107
(David O'Meara) *t.k.h: hld up in last: plld out wd and tried to cl 2f out: sn shkn up and looked to be hanging rt: nvr able to threaten* **11/8**[1]

0-00 **6** hd **Code Red**[97] 2546 4-9-0 108 MartinDwyer 5 — 106
(William Muir) *lw: led at gd pce: rdn and hdd over 1f out: cl up but hld whn short of room jst ins fnl f: fdd* **25/1**

1m 26.24s (-0.76) **Going Correction** +0.225s/f (Good)
WFA 3 from 4yo+ 5lb **6** Ran SP% **110.6**
Speed ratings (Par 113): **113,112,112,110,110 109**
CSF £30.76 TOTE £8.80: £3.10, £1.40; EX 30.80 Trifecta £81.40.
Owner Qatar Racing & The Sweet Partnership **Bred** Mcb Ltd & Mrs G Hedley **Trained** West Ilsley, Berks

■ Stewards' Enquiry : Martin Harley caution; careless riding
Oisin Murphy two-day ban; used whip above the permitted level (11th-12th Sept)

FOCUS
A competitive Group 3 with the winner finding more again.

5927 HARWOOD GROUP FILLIES' STKS (H'CAP) — 1m 4f

4:55 (4:55) (Class 3) (0-90,88) 3-Y-O+

£9,337 (£2,796; £1,398; £699; £349; £175) **Stalls** High

Form — RPR

-132 **1** **Colonial Classic (FR)**[16] 5382 3-9-1 **85** NickyMackay 6 — 96
(John Gosden) *mde all at variable pce: kicked on over 3f out and had rest off bridle: rdn and 2 l clr 2f out: in command after: drvn out* **4/1**

2-1 **2** 1 1/4 **Myopic**[16] 5361 3-8-13 **83** OisinMurphy 3 — 92
(Luca Cumani) *chsd wnr: cl up and pushed along over 3f out: nt qckn and edgd rt fr 2f out: kpt on fnl f but nvr able to chal after* **7/2**[3]

511 **3** 3/4 **Dawn Horizons**[39] 4501 3-9-2 **86** JimCrowley 1 — 94
(William Haggas) *str: scope: lw: trckd ldng pair: pushed along 3f out: nt qckn and no imp 2f out: kpt on fnl f* **5/2**[1]

2424 **4** 2 3/4 **Engage (IRE)**[16] 5381 3-9-4 **88** RyanMoore 4 — 91
(Sir Michael Stoute) *sn cl up: shkn up 3f out: tried to cl on inner 2f out: nt qckn and hld after: one pce* **3/1**[2]

-460 **5** 5 **Leah Freya (IRE)**[22] 5145 5-9-7 **86** PaddyBradley[(5)] 2 — 81
(Pat Phelan) *hld up in last pair: pushed along and no prog 3f out: nvr on terms after* **18/1**

21 **6** 1 1/4 **Loveable Helen (IRE)**[16] 5366 3-8-12 **82** MartinHarley 5 — 75
(Richard Fahey) *lengthy: leggy: t.k.h: hld up in last pair: rdn 3f out: wandering and no prog 2f out: wl btn after* **8/1**

2m 41.13s (2.73) **Going Correction** +0.225s/f (Good)
WFA 3 from 5yo 10lb **6** Ran SP% **112.2**
Speed ratings (Par 104): **99,98,97,95,92 91**
CSF £18.18 TOTE £4.40: £2.40, £2.20; EX 17.50 Trifecta £55.10.
Owner Merry Fox Stud Limited **Bred** Merry Fox Stud **Trained** Newmarket, Suffolk

FOCUS
Another race without much pace, the winner allowed to do her own thing in front and the runner-up in second for most of the way.

5928 MOLECOMB BLUE STKS (H'CAP) — 5f

5:30 (5:30) (Class 5) (0-70,70) 3-Y-O+ **£3,234** (£962; £481; £240) **Stalls** High

Form — RPR

1221 **1** **Babyfact**[9] 5599 5-9-7 **67** JimCrowley 6 — 74
(Malcolm Saunders) *lw: racd in centre: cl up: chal wl over 1f out: drvn to ld ins fnl f: jst hld on* **2/1**[1]

403 **2** shd **Kiringa**[42] 4426 3-8-4 **52** KieranO'Neill 11 — 59
(Robert Cowell) *lw: pressed ldr nr side: overall ldr over 1f out: drvn and hdd ins fnl f: kpt on wl nr fin: jst hld* **20/1**

0006 **3** 1/2 **Insurplus (IRE)**[15] 5386 3-9-0 **62** (v[1]) DanielTudhope 10 — 67
(Jim Goldie) *in rr nr side: wl off the pce over 1f out: r.o strly fnl f: tk 3rd nr fin and clsd on ldng pair last strides* **15/2**[2]

1346 **4** 1/2 **Captain Ryan**[25] 5007 5-8-13 **59** OisinMurphy 9 — 62
(Geoffrey Deacon) *awkward s: racd nr side: in rr: off the pce over 1f out: styd on wl fnl f: tk 4th nr fin* **12/1**

4143 **5** 3/4 **Stormflower**[27] 4952 3-9-5 **67** DannyBrock 7 — 67
(John Bridger) *overall ldr nr side to over 1f out: fdd ins fnl f* **10/1**

4365 **6** *shd* **Monumental Man**[24] 5050 7-9-5 **70**........................(p) PaddyBradley(5) 12 70
(Michael Attwater) *swtg: racd towards nr side: pressed ldrs: chal 2f out to over 1f out: steadily fdd fnl f* **8/1**[3]

50-2 **7** *6* **Dreams Of Glory**[11] 5546 8-9-9 **69**............................ RichardKingscote 3 47
(Ron Hodges) *racd in centre gp: in tch to 2f out: hanging rt and wknd over 1f out* **10/1**

0033 **8** *½* **Ask The Guru**[9] 5599 6-8-13 **59**..(p) KierenFox 1 36
(Michael Attwater) *led centre gp to 2f out: wknd over 1f out* **8/1**[3]

0040 **9** *10* **Keep It Dark**[9] 5599 7-9-4 **67**.................................... EdwardGreatrex(3) 2 8
(William Knight) *racd in centre: last of gp and struggling fr 1/2-way: nvr a factor and carried hd high fnl 2f: t.o* **8/1**[3]

P-04 **10** *9* **Bigmouth Strikes (IRE)**[22] 5168 3-9-3 **65**...................... MartinDwyer 4
(David Menuisier) *taken down early: prom in centre to 1/2-way: wknd qckly 2f out: t.o* **10/1**

58.32s (-1.88) **Going Correction** -0.30s/f (Firm)
WFA 3 from 5yo+ 2lb **10** Ran SP% **118.2**
Speed ratings (Par 103): **103,102,102,101,100 99,90,89,73,59**
CSF £48.98 CT £260.26 TOTE £3.00: £1.40, £5.50, £3.20; EX 48.50 Trifecta £501.70.
Owner Mrs Ginny Nicholas **Bred** M S Saunders And Chris Scott **Trained** Green Ore, Somerset

FOCUS

A modest but competitive sprint handicap and the winner is thriving.

T/Plt: £790.40 to a £1 stake. Pool: £77,016.87 - 71.13 winning tickets T/Qpdt: £199.60 to a £1 stake. Pool: £5,819.54 - 21.57 winning tickets **Jonathan Neesom**

5747 YARMOUTH (L-H)

Sunday, August 28

OFFICIAL GOING: Good to firm (8.0) (watered)

Wind: light, across Weather: bright spells, heavy rain race 7

5929 TOTEPOOL BETTING ON ALL UK RACING APPRENTICE H'CAP 1m 2f 23y

2:15 (2:15) (Class 5) (0-70,70) 4-Y-O+ **£4,528** (£1,347; £673; £336) **Stalls** Low

Form RPR

405 **1** **Tyrsal (IRE)**[13] 5471 5-8-10 **57**.................................... CameronNoble(3) 5 69+
(Clifford Lines) *s.i.s: hld up in rr: swtchd rt and effrt over 1f out: sn pushed into ld and wnt clr: pushed out: easily* **9/4**[1]

6110 **2** *4* **We'll Shake Hands (FR)**[15] 5392 5-9-8 **66**......................... CliffordLee 6 69
(K R Burke) *hld up in tch: hdwy to join ldrs 3f out: rdn to ld 2f out: hdd over 1f out: sn outpcd by wnr: clr 2nd and plugged on same pce fnl f* **3/1**[2]

553 **3** *3 ¼* **Maverik**[86] 2849 8-9-4 **62**..(t) MitchGodwin 4 59
(Ali Stronge) *led and set stdy gallop: rdn over 2f out: hdd 2f out: outpcd and btn over 1f out: wl hld 3rd and plugged on same pce fnl f* **9/2**[3]

6403 **4** *2 ¼* **Karam Albaari (IRE)**[71] 3403 8-9-12 **70**......................(v) GeorgeWood 1 63
(J R Jenkins) *t.k.h early: trckd ldrs: pushed along and hdwy on inner 3f out: rdn and ev ch 2f out: sn outpcd and btn over 1f out: wknd fnl f* **9/1**

20-3 **5** *½* **The Ginger Berry**[221] 256 6-8-11 **55**.......................... KillianHennessy 2 47
(Dr Jon Scargill) *chsd ldr: rdn over 2f out: sn struggling: lost pl and bhd over 1f out: wknd fnl f* **10/1**

6146 **R** **Honey Badger**[33] 4743 5-8-7 **56**...........................(b1) GabrieleMalune(5) 3
(Eugene Stanford) *ref to r* **5/1**

2m 8.99s (-1.51) **Going Correction** -0.425s/f (Firm) **6** Ran SP% **109.7**
Speed ratings (Par 103): **89,85,83,81,81**
CSF £8.73 TOTE £2.80: £1.40, £2.00; EX 8.70 Trifecta £30.20.
Owner Prima Racing Partnership **Bred** Daniel Furini **Trained** Exning, Suffolk
■ Stewards' Enquiry : Gabriele Malune two-day ban; improper riding (11th-12th Sept)

FOCUS

Moderate handicap form, the winner coming wide and from off the pace to follow up the previous season's victory in the race. The runner-up's recent form sets the level.

5930 TOTEPLACEPOT BRITISH STALLION STUDS EBF MAIDEN FILLIES' STKS (PLUS 10 RACE) 6f 3y

2:45 (2:53) (Class 4) 2-Y-O **£5,175** (£1,540; £769; £384) **Stalls** Centre

Form RPR

1 **Exmouth** 2-9-0 0.. TedDurcan 13 82+
(Sir Michael Stoute) *s.i.s: hld up in tch in rr: hdwy into midfield and travelling strly 1/2-way: swtchd rt and pushed along over 1f out: hdwy to chse ldr ins fnl f: r.o wl to ld last strides* **11/4**[2]

0 **2** *nk* **Textured (IRE)**[87] 2817 2-9-0 0................................ SilvestreDeSousa 1 80
(Sir Michael Stoute) *hld up in tch in last pair: pushed along and hdwy over 2f out: rdn to ld over 1f out: edgd rt u.p 1f out: kpt on u.p: hdd nr fin* **9/2**[3]

0 **3** *3 ¼* **Oudwood**[13] 5469 2-8-11 0.. MarcMonaghan(3) 8 70
(Hugo Palmer) *t.k.h: hld up in tch: hdwy 1/2-way: rdn and ev ch 2f out: unable qck ent fnl f: wknd ins fnl f* **16/1**

4 *½* **Alwafaa (IRE)** 2-9-0 0.. PaulHanagan 2 68
(Owen Burrows) *t.k.h: chsd ldrs: rdn to ld 2f out: sn hdd and unable qck: wknd ins fnl f* **7/4**[1]

54 **5** *2 ¾* **Alice's Dream**[70] 3433 2-9-0 0... LukeMorris 9 59
(Marco Botti) *chsd ldr: rdn and ev ent fnl 2f tl unable qck over 1f out: wknd ins fnl f* **5/1**

00 **6** *2 ½* **Pemberley House (IRE)**[18] 5298 2-9-0 0...................... TomQueally 10 51
(Paul D'Arcy) *chsd ldrs: led jst over 2f out: sn hdd and rdn: lost pl over 1f out: wknd fnl f* **50/1**

00 **7** *8* **Twaddle**[71] 3408 2-9-0 0.. RyanPowell 4 26
(Alan Coogan) *t.k.h: chsd ldrs early: steadily lost pl and bhd 1/2-way: lost tch over 1f out* **125/1**

8 *¾* **Popsilca** 2-9-0 0.. WilliamCarson 6 23
(Mick Quinn) *racd keenly: led tl hdd and rdn jst over 2f out: sn lost pl: wknd over 1f out: bhd ins fnl f* **20/1**

1m 13.34s (-1.06) **Going Correction** -0.30s/f (Firm) **8** Ran SP% **111.3**
Speed ratings (Par 93): **95,94,90,89,85 82,71,70**
CSF £14.24 TOTE £4.30: £2.00, £1.30, £4.70; EX 15.90 Trifecta £117.10.
Owner Mr & Mrs James Wigan **Bred** Mrs James Wigan & London TB Services Ltd **Trained** Newmarket, Suffolk

■ Street Jazz was withdrawn. Price at time of 9-2. Rule 4 applies to bet's placed prior to withdrawal but not to SP bets - deduction 20p in the pound. New Market formed. Geraldine was withdrawn 10-1. Rule 4 applies to all bets - deduct 5p in the pound.35

5931 TOTEQUADPOT INSURE YOUR PLACEPOT LAST FOUR NURSERY H'CAP 6f 3y

3:20 (3:27) (Class 4) (0-80,80) 2-Y-O **£5,040** (£1,508; £754; £377; £188) **Stalls** Centre

Form RPR

054 **1** **Erissimus Maximus (FR)**[15] 5395 2-8-10 **69**......... SilvestreDeSousa 10 75
(Chris Dwyer) *chsd ldr early: sn dropped into midfield: pushed along and hdwy 1/2-way: rdn to ld 2f out: hung lft fr over 1f out: hld on wl ins fnl f: rdn out* **5/1**[2]

410 **2** *½* **Jumping Around (IRE)**[29] 4884 2-9-5 **78**........................ PatCosgrave 3 82
(William Haggas) *hld up in tch: effrt over 2f out: chsd ldng pair over 1f out: rdn to chse wnr 1f out: str chal ins fnl f: kpt on but hld towards fin* **4/1**[1]

232 **3** *3 ¼* **Stanhope**[24] 5084 2-9-7 **80**.. WilliamCarson 2 74
(Mick Quinn) *t.k.h: hld up in tch in midfield: hdwy over 2f out: chsd wnr wl over 1f out: hung lft over 1f out: 3rd and unable qck 1f out: wknd wl ins fnl f* **11/2**[3]

022 **4** *1 ¾* **Happy Queen**[21] 5202 2-8-9 **68**.. TomQueally 9 56
(George Margarson) *squeezed for room leaving stalls: in tch in rr: shkn up 2f out: hdwy u.p over 1f out: kpt on same pce and no threat to ldrs ins fnl f* **8/1**

0202 **5** *nk* **Prince Of Cool**[12] 5510 2-9-7 **80**.. TomEaves 1 67
(James Given) *led tl 2f out: sn rdn and outpcd: wl hld and kpt on same pce ins fnl f* **13/2**

616 **6** *1* **Nile Empress**[30] 4843 2-9-5 **78**.. JamesDoyle 4 62
(Hugo Palmer) *hld up in tch in midfield: effrt ent fnl 2f: sn rdn and outpcd: wl hld and plugged on same pce fr over 1f out* **6/1**

521 **7** *1 ½* **Benidiction (IRE)**[59] 3820 2-8-7 **66**.................................. JoeyHaynes 6 45
(K R Burke) *t.k.h: sn chsng ldr: rdn 2f out: unable qck and losing pl whn sltly impeded over 1f out: wknd fnl f* **14/1**

2406 **8** *1 ½* **Carson City**[29] 4891 2-8-12 **71**.. LukeMorris 8 45
(Richard Fahey) *chsd ldrs: rdn ent fnl 2f: drvn and lost pl over 1f out: wknd fnl f* **15/2**

4540 **9** *17* **Snoozy Sioux (IRE)**[9] 5598 2-8-5 **64**.............................. PaulHanagan 5
(Martin Smith) *stdd and wnt rt s: hld up in rr: rdn over 2f out: sn struggling: lost tch over 1f out* **20/1**

1m 13.18s (-1.22) **Going Correction** -0.30s/f (Firm) **9** Ran SP% **114.0**
Speed ratings (Par 96): **96,95,91,88,88 86,84,82,60**
CSF £24.96 CT £113.37 TOTE £5.70: £1.80, £2.00, £1.70; EX 28.00 Trifecta £108.30.
Owner P Venner **Bred** Derek Clee **Trained** Newmarket, Suffolk

FOCUS

The front pair came clear in what was an ordinary nursery and they are clearly both ahead of their marks.

5932 TOTEEXACTA THE BETTER VALUE FORECAST H'CAP 1m 2f 23y

3:55 (3:56) (Class 2) (0-100,100) 3-Y-O+

£13,695 (£4,100; £2,050; £1,025; £512; £257) **Stalls** Low

Form RPR

-122 **1** **Rockspirit (IRE)**[50] 4153 3-8-11 **91**............................... FrankieDettori 7 100
(Marco Botti) *t.k.h: trckd ldrs: clsd to join ldrs 2f out: rdn and ev ch over 1f out: drvn to ld ins fnl f: styd on and forged ahd fnl 100yds* **4/1**[2]

-103 **2** *1* **Folkswood**[36] 4624 3-9-6 **100**.. JamesDoyle 1 107
(Charlie Appleby) *hld up in last pair: clsd as galloped slowed and swtchd rt bnd 6f out: effrt 2f out: drvn to chse ldng pair over 1f out: kpt on same pce u.p ins fnl f: wnt 2nd on post* **5/4**[1]

6441 **3** *nse* **Haalan**[16] 5382 4-9-4 **90**... LukeMorris 2 97
(James Tate) *pressed ldr tl led over 2f out: hrd pressed and drvn over 1f out: hdd ins fnl f: styd on same pce fnl 100yds: lost 2nd on post* **15/2**[3]

2311 **4** *2 ¾* **Brorocco**[17] 5333 3-8-5 **85**.. JimmyQuinn 6 87
(Andrew Balding) *s.i.s: bustled along in rr early: clsd qckly as gallop slowed and t.k.h 6f out: effrt 2f out: drvn to chse ldrs over 1f out: no imp 1f out: kpt on same pce fnl f* **4/1**[2]

1300 **5** *1 ¼* **Montsarrat (IRE)**[8] 5651 3-9-0 **94**................................... AdamKirby 5 93
(Mark Johnston) *wl in tch: nt clrest of runs over 2f out: rdn 2f out: swtchd rt and drvn over 1f out: no imp and one pce fnl f* **8/1**

3663 **6** *3 ¾* **Ansaab**[21] 5198 8-8-12 **84**... AndrewMullen 4 76
(Michael Appleby) *led: stdd gallop 1/2-way: rdn 3f out: hdd over 2f out and struggling to qckn: lost pl over 1f out: wknd ins fnl f* **25/1**

2m 3.94s (-6.56) **Going Correction** -0.425s/f (Firm)
WFA 3 from 4yo+ 8lb **6** Ran SP% **111.2**
Speed ratings (Par 109): **109,108,108,105,104 101**
CSF £9.27 CT £32.23 TOTE £5.00: £2.70, £1.20; EX 10.20 Trifecta £35.80.
Owner Giuliano Manfredini **Bred** Patrick Byrnes **Trained** Newmarket, Suffolk

FOCUS

They appeared to go a fair gallop early in what was a useful handicap, although the pace did slow past halfway. The form makes sense and has been rated positively.

5933 TOTEPOOL LIKE US ON FACEBOOK H'CAP 1m 3y

4:30 (4:30) (Class 3) (0-90,88) 3-Y-O **£8,821** (£2,640; £1,320; £660; £329) **Stalls** Centre

Form RPR

-521 **1** **Ballet Concerto**[25] 5023 3-9-1 **85**....................................... JamesDoyle 7 97+
(Sir Michael Stoute) *led for 2f: styd pressing ldr tl led again ent fnl 2f: rdn and clr over 1f out: in n.d ins fnl f: comf* **11/4**[2]

0002 **2** *3 ¾* **Top Beak (IRE)**[12] 5514 3-9-4 **88**..................................(t) AdamKirby 9 91
(Hughie Morrison) *hld up in tch: effrt ent fnl 2f: rdn to chse wnr and hung lft over 1f out: kpt on same pce and no imp ins fnl f* **6/1**

4-06 **3** *nk* **Ceaseless (IRE)**[23] 5123 4-9-7 **85**....................................... LukeMorris 1 88
(James Tate) *hld up in tch in midfield: shkn up over 2f out: drvn and unable qck over 1f out: wnt 3rd and kpt on same pce ins fnl f* **25/1**

-503 **4** *¾* **Column**[32] 4776 3-9-2 **86**... TomQueally 2 86
(James Fanshawe) *hld up in tch in rr: swtchd rt and effrt over 1f out: sn rdn: kpt on ins fnl f: no ch w wnr* **5/2**[1]

0054 **5** *½* **Faithful Creek (IRE)**[22] 5156 4-9-2 **87**.........................(tp) JordanUys(7) 5 87
(Brian Meehan) *s.i.s: t.k.h: sn rcvrd to chse ldr: led 6f out tl ent fnl 2f: sn rdn and edgd lft: unable qck over 1f out: no ch w wnr and kpt on same pce ins fnl f* **6/1**

-140 **6** *2 ½* **Arrowzone**[36] 4650 5-9-7 **88**.................................... JosephineGordon(3) 4 82
(Ivan Furtado) *t.k.h: chsd ldrs: rdn jst over 2f out: struggling to qckn whn squeezed for room ent fnl 2f: sn swtchd lft and drvn: no hdwy: wknd ins fnl f* **25/1**

1012 7 ½ **Palmerston**[16] 5376 3-8-9 **79**........................ AndrewMullen 3 74
(Michael Appleby) *stdd s: t.k.h: hld up in tch in midfield: rdn and effrt to chse ldrs 2f out: struggling to qckn whn hmpd and snatched up over 1f out: nt rcvr and wl hld after* **10/3**[3]

1m 37.74s (-2.86) **Going Correction** -0.30s/f (Firm)
WFA 3 from 4yo+ 6lb 7 Ran SP% **114.6**
Speed ratings (Par 107): **102,98,97,97,96 94,93**
CSF £19.58 CT £329.50 TOTE £3.30: £2.20, £2.60; EX 18.80 Trifecta £155.50.
Owner Saeed Suhail **Bred** Meon Valley Stud **Trained** Newmarket, Suffolk

FOCUS
No great gallop on here and the winner, racing stands' side throughout, came right away. The race has been rated around the placed horses.

5934 @TOTEPOOL FOLLOW US ON TWITTER H'CAP 7f 3y
5:05 (5:06) (Class 3) (0-95,94) 3-Y-O+ **£8,821** (£2,640; £1,320; £660; £329) **Stalls** Centre

Form RPR
0020 1 **Carnival King (IRE)**[15] 5403 4-9-3 **85**........................(b) TomQueally 4 93
(Brian Meehan) *mde all: grad moved across to r nr stands' rail: rdn wl over 1f out: kpt on wl u.p ins fnl f: edgd lft towards fin* **10/1**

2152 2 1¼ **Musdam (USA)**[36] 4662 3-8-11 **84**........................(v¹) JamesDoyle 5 87
(Sir Michael Stoute) *racd in centre: in tch in midfield overall: effrt 2f out: drvn to chse ldrs and edgd rt over 1f out: kpt on u.p ins fnl f: wnt 2nd last strides: nvr enough pce to get to wnr* **11/4**[1]

4233 3 nk **Ifwecan**[22] 5174 5-9-10 **92**........................ FrankieDettori 3 96
(Martin Smith) *racd in centre: chsd overall ldr: rdn and ev ch 2f out: unable qck 1f out: kpt on same pce ins fnl f: lost 2nd last strides* **3/1**[2]

0064 4 nse **Basil Berry**[33] 4741 5-9-12 **94**........................(b) SilvestreDeSousa 1 98
(Chris Dwyer) *stdd after s: hld up in rr and c to r nr stands' side: effrt over 2f out: drvn to chse ldrs over 1f out: kpt on same pce ins fnl f* **7/1**

0064 5 1¾ **Miracle Of Medinah**[22] 5174 5-9-9 **91**........................[1] AdamKirby 7 90
(Mark Usher) *chsd ldrs and c to r nr stands' rail: effrt ent fnl 2f: kpt on same pce u.p ins fnl f* **4/1**[3]

5230 6 2½ **Baltic Brave (IRE)**[15] 5403 5-8-10 **83**........................(t) CharlieBennett(5) 6 75
(Hughie Morrison) *chsd ldrs and c to r nr stands' rail: rdn ent 2f out: sn struggling and lost pl over 1f out: wknd ins fnl f* **8/1**

4000 7 6 **Tatlisu (IRE)**[15] 5418 6-9-11 **93**........................ PaulHanagan 2 69
(Richard Fahey) *racd in centre: stdd s: hld up in rr: rdn 2f out: sn btn: bhd and eased wl ins fnl f* **10/1**

1m 23.04s (-3.56) **Going Correction** -0.30s/f (Firm)
WFA 3 from 4yo+ 5lb 7 Ran SP% **113.5**
Speed ratings (Par 107): **108,106,106,106,104 101,94**
CSF £37.08 TOTE £13.60: £6.40, £1.70; EX 51.10 Trifecta £202.40.
Owner Phillip Gore **Bred** B Kennedy & Mrs Ann Marie Kennedy **Trained** Manton, Wilts

FOCUS
They split into two groups, albeit they ended up merging into one, with the winner, who recorded a minor personal best, racing against the stands' rail.

5935 TOTEPOOL RACING'S BIGGEST SUPPORTER APP H'CAP 7f 3y
5:40 (5:42) (Class 5) (0-70,70) 3-Y-O+ **£4,410** (£1,320; £660; £330; £164) **Stalls** Centre

Form RPR
4-26 1 **Dark Wonder (IRE)**[19] 5273 4-9-8 **66**........................ TomEaves 6 73
(Ivan Furtado) *mde all: rdn 2f out: edgd lft but hld on wl u.p ins fnl f: all out* **8/1**

0-46 2 hd **Surety (IRE)**[22] 5169 5-9-12 **70**........................ LukeMorris 10 76
(James Tate) *hld up in tch in midfield: rdn 2f out: sn drvn and sltly outpcd: rallied 1f out: str chal wl ins fnl f: jst hld* **11/2**[3]

5534 3 hd **Aberlady (USA)**[18] 5302 3-9-0 **66**........................ JosephineGordon(3) 9 69
(Sir Michael Stoute) *t.k.h: hld up in tch in midfield: effrt and switching lft over 1f out: drvn and ev ch ins fnl f: kpt on* **11/4**[1]

4014 4 1½ **Anastazia**[17] 5337 4-9-5 **70**........................ CliffordLee(7) 2 71
(Paul D'Arcy) *chsd ldrs: rdn and ev ch over 1f out: tl no ex ins fnl f: wknd towards fin* **4/1**[2]

1665 5 1¾ **Foie Gras**[16] 5367 6-9-1 **59**........................(b) SilvestreDeSousa 1 56
(Chris Dwyer) *hld up in tch in last trio: effrt 2f out: drvn over 1f out: styd on same pce ins fnl f* **14/1**

2053 6 2 **Naziba (IRE)**[17] 5330 3-9-0 **63**........................ PaulHanagan 8 52
(David Menuisier) *hld up in tch in rr: rdn over 2f out: no imp and switching lft over 1f out: kpt on but no threat to ldrs ins fnl f* **6/1**

3413 7 2 **Remember Me**[18] 5309 3-9-6 **69**........................ JamesDoyle 5 53
(Hughie Morrison) *chsd ldr: rdn ent fnl 2f: sn struggling and lost pl over 1f out: wknd ins fnl f* **4/1**[2]

0506 8 12 **U S Navy Seal (USA)**[9] 5607 4-9-7 **65**........................ TomQueally 7 18
(J R Jenkins) *hld up in rr: rdn over 2f out: sn btn: wknd over 1f out* **25/1**

1m 26.2s (-0.40) **Going Correction** -0.30s/f (Firm)
WFA 3 from 4yo+ 5lb 8 Ran SP% **118.0**
Speed ratings (Par 103): **90,89,89,87,85 83,81,67**
CSF £52.91 CT £154.56 TOTE £8.50: £2.80, £1.70, £1.90; EX 68.80 Trifecta £289.80.
Owner Mrs June Bownes **Bred** A M V Nicoll **Trained** Wiseton, Nottinghamshire

FOCUS
This was run in horrid conditions, with heavy rain having really set in. They came stands' side in what was a modest handicap run at a steady pace. A small personal best from the winner.
T/Jkpt: Not won. T/Plt: £52.80 to a £1 stake. Pool: £79,122.00 - 1,092.09 winning tickets T/Qpdt: £8.90 to a £1 stake. Pool: £6,122.13 - 507.24 winning tickets **Steve Payne**

5936 & 5938a - (Foreign Racing) - See Raceform Interactive

5682 CURRAGH (R-H)
Sunday, August 28

OFFICIAL GOING: Good (good to yielding in places)

5937a FLAME OF TARA EUROPEAN BREEDERS FUND STKS (GROUP 3) (FILLIES) 1m
2:40 (2:40) 2-Y-O

£34,705 (£11,176; £5,294; £2,352; £1,176; £588)

RPR
1 **Sea Of Grace (IRE)**[50] 4168 2-9-0 **0**........................ DeclanMcDonogh 6 104+
(John M Oxx, Ire) *w.w in rr: last at 1/2-way: gd hdwy on outer to trck ldrs over 2f out: led gng best under 2f out and rdn: hdd narrowly u.p ins fnl 150yds tl rallied wl to ld again cl home* **7/2**[2]

2 nk **Eziyra (IRE)**[33] 4745 2-9-0 **0**........................ PatSmullen 5 104+
(D K Weld, Ire) *chsd ldrs: disp 3rd at 1/2-way: impr on outer gng wl to chal: led narrowly fr 2f out tl sn hdd u.p: rallied far side to regain advantage ins fnl 150yds tl hdd again cl home* **1/1**[1]

3 3½ **Butterflies (IRE)**[36] 4670 2-9-0 **0**........................ SeamieHeffernan 7 95
(A P O'Brien, Ire) *chsd ldrs: 5th 1/2-way: tk clsr order over 2f out: sn rdn in 4th and no imp on ldrs u.p in mod 3rd ins fnl f: kpt on same pce* **7/2**[2]

4 3¼ **Legitimus (IRE)**[3] 5813 2-9-0 **90**........................ KevinManning 3 88
(J S Bolger, Ire) *led: racd keenly early: jnd bef 1/2-way: regained narrow advantage after 1/2-way: rdn and hdd fr 2f out: sn no imp on ldrs and dropped to mod 4th ins fnl f: jst hld 4th* **20/1**

5 shd **Pocketfullofdreams (FR)** 2-9-0 **0**........................ WayneLordan 1 88
(David Wachman, Ire) *hld up towards rr: 6th 1/2-way: rdn 2f out and no imp on ldrs over 1f out: kpt on ins fnl f: jst failed for mod 4th* **25/1**

6 9 **Madame Cherie (USA)**[21] 5210 2-9-0 **0**........................ ColmO'Donoghue 2 67
(Mrs John Harrington, Ire) *cl up bhd ldr early: disp 3rd at 1/2-way: rdn over 2f out and sn no ex u.p in 5th: wknd fr over 1f out* **20/1**

7 3½ **Bound (IRE)**[8] 5658 2-9-0 **0**........................ DonnachaO'Brien 4 59
(A P O'Brien, Ire) *cl up and disp bef 1/2-way: hdd narrowly after 1/2-way and pushed along in cl 2nd: sn no ex u.p and wknd fr over 2f out* **10/1**[3]

1m 37.9s (-8.10) **Going Correction** -0.775s/f (Hard) 7 Ran SP% **116.9**
Speed ratings: **109,108,105,101,101 92,89**
CSF £7.50 TOTE £4.50: £1.70, £1.60; DF 9.90 Trifecta £22.80.
Owner Sunderland Holding Inc **Bred** Mr Robert Norton **Trained** Currabeg, Co Kildare

FOCUS
Despite the official ground-description (good, good to yielding in places) the winning rider reported it as quick enough for his mount who did well to confirm previous Tipperary form with the second.

5939a SNOW FAIRY FILLIES STKS (GROUP 3) 1m 1f
3:50 (3:50) 3-Y-O+

£28,198 (£9,080; £4,301; £1,911; £955; £477)

RPR
1 **Somehow (IRE)**[26] 5002 3-9-0 **107**........................(v) SeamieHeffernan 9 114
(A P O'Brien, Ire) *s.i.s and in rr early: impr into 6th bef 1/2-way: tk clsr order on outer over 2f out where edgd sltly rt: led 1 1/2f out where edgd rt and qcknd clr: sn in command and extended advantage: easily* **5/2**[2]

2 7 **Epsom Icon**[8] 5645 3-9-3 **105**........................ RonanWhelan 1 102
(Mick Channon) *chsd ldrs: disp 3rd at 1/2-way: rdn in 3rd over 2f out and tk clsr order briefly tl sn no imp on easy wnr u.p in 2nd: kpt on same pce ins fnl f to hold mod 2nd* **10/1**

3 ½ **Skiffle**[86] 2869 3-9-0 **103**........................ WilliamBuick 5 98
(Charlie Appleby) *chsd ldrs: 5th 1/2-way: rdn into 3rd over 1f out and no imp on easy wnr: kpt on same pce ins fnl f: hld for mod 2nd* **9/4**[1]

4 2¾ **Molly Dolly (IRE)**[18] 5313 4-9-7 **96**........................ ChrisHayes 8 92
(W T Farrell, Ire) *hld up towards rr: 8th into st: hdwy on outer 2f out: sn rdn and wnt mod 4th ins fnl f: kpt on same pce: nt trble easy wnr* **25/1**

5 shd **Radiantly**[36] 4671 3-9-0 **100**........................ BillyLee 4 92
(W McCreery, Ire) *hld up: 7th 1/2-way: tk clsr order bhd ldrs far side 2f out where short of room tl swtchd lft in 7th over 1f out: rdn into mod 5th ins fnl f and kpt on same pce: nt trble easy wnr* **12/1**

6 2½ **Duchess Andorra (IRE)**[42] 4435 5-9-7 **92**........................(p) NGMcCullagh 3 87
(J P Murtagh, Ire) *trckd ldr early tl sn led: pushed along w narrow advantage over 3f out: rdn and hdd over 2f out: sn no ex and wknd* **20/1**

7 1 **Lily's Rainbow (IRE)**[33] 4747 4-9-7 **98**........................[1] WayneLordan 6 85
(Mrs Denise Foster, Ire) *hld up: 8th 1/2-way: pushed along in rr into st and no imp on ldrs: kpt on one pce into mod 7th ins fnl f* **33/1**

8 1¾ **Planchart (USA)**[31] 4812 3-9-0 **96**........................ DeclanMcDonogh 10 81
(Andrew Slattery, Ire) *broke wl to ld narrowly tl sn hdd and settled in 2nd: pushed along and impr to ld narrowly over 2f out: sn hdd u.p and hmpd 1 1/2f out: no ex and wknd qckly* **8/1**

9 1¼ **Adool (IRE)**[18] 5313 3-9-0 **102**........................ PatSmullen 7 78
(D K Weld, Ire) *chsd ldrs: disp 3rd at 1/2-way: pushed along in 4th fr 3f out tl hmpd over 2f out and lost pl: no imp after towards rr: one pce in rr ins fnl f* **4/1**[3]

1m 53.01s (-1.89) **Going Correction** +0.125s/f (Good)
WFA 3 from 4yo+ 7lb 9 Ran SP% **118.8**
Speed ratings: **113,106,106,103,103 101,100,99,98**
CSF £27.78 TOTE £2.70: £1.10, £2.60, £1.10; DF 27.50 Trifecta £83.90.
Owner Michael Tabor & Derrick Smith & Mrs John Magnier **Bred** Orpendale, Chelston & Wynatt **Trained** Cashel, Co Tipperary

FOCUS
The strength-in-depth of Aidan O'Brien's team of 3yo fillies was underlined by a comfortable win for Irish Oaks fifth Somehow. The race has been rated around the placed horses.

5940a ROUND TOWER STKS (GROUP 3) 6f
4:25 (4:25) 2-Y-O

£26,029 (£8,382; £3,970; £1,764; £882; £441)

RPR
1 **Intelligence Cross (USA)**[31] 4798 2-9-3 **108**........(t) SeamieHeffernan 6 111
(A P O'Brien, Ire) *cl up bhd ldr: cl 2nd at 1/2-way: impr travelling wl to ld nr side 1 1/2f out: sn rdn and styd on wl to extend advantage ins fnl f: easily* **11/8**[1]

2 4¼ **Holy Cat (IRE)**[17] 5339 2-9-0 **0**........................ ColinKeane 10 95
(M D O'Callaghan, Ire) *chsd ldrs: 5th 1/2-way: pushed along fr 2f out: rdn in 4th ins fnl f and clsd u.p nr side into mod 2nd fnl strides: nt trble easy wnr* **2/1**[2]

3 nk **De Boss Man (IRE)**[8] 5659 2-9-3 **0**........................ ColmO'Donoghue 2 97
(M D O'Callaghan, Ire) *chsd ldrs: 4th 1/2-way: rdn into 2nd 1f out and no imp on easy wnr: kpt on same pce ins fnl f and denied mod 2nd fnl strides* **10/1**

4 1¼ **Swish (IRE)**[8] 5661 2-9-0 **94**........................ PatSmullen 7 91
(John James Feane, Ire) *hld up towards rr: 7th 1/2-way: tk clsr order under 2f out: sn rdn in 6th and no imp on easy wnr u.p in mod 4th ins fnl f: kpt on same pce* **33/1**

5 ½ **Velveteen**[8] 5661 2-9-0 **92**........................ GaryCarroll 3 89
(G M Lyons, Ire) *broke wl to ld: narrow advantage at 1/2-way: rdn and hdd 1 1/2f out: no imp on easy wnr in 3rd jst ins fnl f: one pce clsng stages* **16/1**

6 ½ **Sportsmanship (USA)**[8] 5661 2-9-3 **97**........................ DonnachaO'Brien 8 94
(A P O'Brien, Ire) *hld up: 6th 1/2-way: pushed along fr over 2f out: rdn over 1f out where n.m.r briefly: no ex and kpt on one pce ins fnl f* **11/2**[3]

7 nk **Solar Halo (USA)**[8] 5659 2-9-0 **0**........................ BillyLee 9 87
(W McCreery, Ire) *chsd ldrs early tl dropped to 8th between horses at 1/2-way: rdn in rr over 1f out and kpt on one pce: nvr trbld ldrs* **40/1**

8 2 **Teo's Music (IRE)** 2-9-0 **0**........................ KevinManning 4 81
(J S Bolger, Ire) *w.w in rr: last at 1/2-way: swtchd rt to far side under 2f out: rdn and no imp over 1f out: kpt on one pce* **20/1**

9 2 1/2 **Mayleaf Shine (IRE)**[8] 5661 2-9-0 91 ShaneFoley 5 73
(Joseph G Murphy, Ire) *chsd ldrs: 3rd 1/2-way: rdn and no ex 2f out: wknd over 1f out* **25/1**

1m 12.06s (-3.44) **Going Correction** -0.35s/f (Firm) **9** Ran SP% **119.8**
Speed ratings: **108,102,101,100,99 98,98,95,92**
CSF £4.25 TOTE £2.30: £1.02, £1.80, £2.00; DF 5.60 Trifecta £24.80.
Owner Mrs John Magnier & Michael Tabor & Derrick Smith **Bred** Good Vibes Syndicate **Trained** Cashel, Co Tipperary

5941a TOTE IRISH CAMBRIDGESHIRE (PREMIER H'CAP) 1m

5:00 (5:00) 3-Y-O+

£43,382 (£13,970; £6,617; £2,941; £1,470; £735)

RPR

1 **Sea Wolf (IRE)**[33] 4747 4-9-5 **95** ColinKeane 23 106
(G M Lyons, Ire) *sn chsd ldrs: 6th 1/2-way: tk clsr order fr 2f out: rdn to ld over 1f out: strly pressed wl ins fnl f: kpt on wl clsng stages* **9/1**[3]

2 1/2 **Sikandarabad (IRE)**[33] 4746 3-9-0 **96** (v) PatSmullen 14 105
(D K Weld, Ire) *mid-div: tk clsr order travelling wl bhd horses under 2f out: swtchd and rdn over 1f out: prog into 2nd wl ins fnl f and kpt on wl wout matching wnr* **8/1**[2]

3 1 1/2 **Aared (IRE)**[52] 4071 4-8-8 **87** (v) GaryHalpin(3) 13 93+
(Kevin Prendergast, Ire) *hld up towards rr: hdwy nr side fr over 1f out: swtchd rt ins fnl f and r.o wl into nvr nrr 3rd cl home: nrst fin* **14/1**

4 1/2 **Hasanour (USA)**[33] 4747 6-9-11 **101** ShaneFoley 20 106
(M Halford, Ire) *mid-div: pushed along 3f out: sn rdn and clsd u.p nr side to chse ldrs in 3rd briefly wl ins fnl f: no ex clsng stages where dropped to 4th* **12/1**

5 1/2 **Dream Walker (FR)**[28] 4921 7-9-5 **95** (t) ChrisHayes 11 99
(Brian Ellison) *dwlt sltly and settled towards rr: pushed along 2f out and tk clsr order in mid-div 1f out where rdn: kpt on wl u.p ins fnl f to snatch 5th fnl stride: nrst fin* **7/1**[1]

6 shd **Texas Rock (IRE)**[13] 5492 5-8-5 **86** [1] AnaO'Brien(5) 10 90
(M C Grassick, Ire) *chsd ldrs: disp 3rd at 1/2-way: led under 2f out: sn rdn and hdd u.p over 1f out: no ex ins fnl f where dropped to 5th: denied 5th fnl stride* **28/1**

7 1 1/2 **Boomshackerlacker (IRE)**[30] 4823 6-9-11 **101** FergusSweeney 8 101
(George Baker) *mid-div: 11th 1/2-way: tk clsr order and rdn bhd ldrs 2f out: no ex far side ent fnl f: one pce wl ins fnl f* **16/1**

8 hd **Canary Row (IRE)**[28] 4921 6-8-9 **88** (v) RobbieDowney(3) 19 88
(P J Prendergast, Ire) *mid-div: tk clsr order over 1f out: rdn into 8th ins fnl f and no imp on ldrs whn rdr lost iron cl home* **18/1**

9 3/4 **Katiymann (IRE)**[32] 4782 4-8-9 **85** ConorHoban 17 83
(M Halford, Ire) *in rr of mid-div: rdn over 2f out and sme hdwy u.p nr side 1f out: short of room briefly ins fnl f: kpt on clsng stages: nvr nrr* **14/1**

10 shd **Plough Boy (IRE)**[8] 5662 5-8-3 **84** KillianLeonard(5) 16 82
(Garvan Donnelly, Ire) *cl up bhd ldrs: 5th 1/2-way: rdn 2f out and no ex u.p over 1f out: wknd ins fnl f* **33/1**

11 1 1/2 **Vastonea (IRE)**[7] 5687 8-7-8 **80** SeanDavis(10) 12 75
(Kevin Prendergast, Ire) *hld up: pushed along in rr of mid-div bef 1/2-way: no imp u.p over 1f out: kpt on ins fnl f where short of room briefly and swtchd lft: nvr nrr* **25/1**

12 3/4 **Breathe Easy (IRE)**[64] 3676 6-8-13 **89** RonanWhelan 18 82
(Gavin Cromwell, Ire) *cl up: cl 2nd at 1/2-way: rdn over 2f out and sn no ex: wknd over 1f out* **10/1**

13 nse **An Saighdiur (IRE)**[8] 5662 9-9-5 **95** 5ex (b) DeclanMcDonogh 24 88
(Andrew Slattery, Ire) *broke wl to ld: narrow advantage at 1/2-way: rdn and hdd under 2f out: wknd 1f out* **16/1**

14 1 **Beau Satchel**[29] 4899 6-8-4 **80** (t) LeighRoche 6 70
(Adrian McGuinness, Ire) *chsd ldrs early: pushed along in mid-div after 1/2-way and no ex u.p far side ent fnl f: wknd ins fnl f* **22/1**

15 hd **General Macarthur (USA)**[11] 5564 3-9-6 **102** (bt[1]) SeamieHeffernan 9 91
(A P O'Brien, Ire) *dwlt and towards rr early: rdn under 2f out and no ex in mid-div 1f out: eased wl ins fnl f* **16/1**

16 3/4 **Parish Boy**[504] 1362 4-9-11 **101** KevinManning 7 89
(J S Bolger, Ire) *s.i.s and detached in rr early: pushed along bef 1/2-way: no imp in 23rd far side over 1f out: swtchd lft and kpt on ins fnl f: nvr nrr* **16/1**

17 1/2 **Wychwood Warrior (IRE)**[11] 5564 4-9-2 **97** [1] DanielRedmond(5) 22 84
(M Halford, Ire) *sn chsd ldrs: disp 3rd at 1/2-way: pushed along over 2f out and sn no ex: wknd over 1f out* **50/1**

18 nk **Mr Right (IRE)**[14] 5444 4-8-7 **88** DonaghO'Connor(5) 2 74
(J F Levins, Ire) *in tch: 8th 1/2-way: rdn far side 2f out and sn no imp on ldrs: wknd fnl f* **25/1**

19 1 **Instant Attraction (IRE)**[74] 3273 5-9-12 **102** JackGarritty 3 86
(Jedd O'Keeffe) *chsd ldrs early: 9th 1/2-way: rdn far side 2f out and sn wknd* **16/1**

20 3/4 **Fit For The Job (IRE)**[28] 4921 4-8-10 **86** (p) WayneLordan 5 68
(David Wachman, Ire) *settled in mid-div: 15th 1/2-way: tk clsr order briefly far side 2f out: sn rdn and no ex: wknd ins fnl f* **12/1**

21 1 1/4 **Whiskey Sour (IRE)**[33] 4747 3-8-9 **91** (t) ColmO'Donoghue 15 69
(Edward Lynam, Ire) *hld up in rr of mid-div: sme hdwy nr side after 1/2-way: rdn 2f out and no ex whn eased briefly 1 1/2f out: wknd* **14/1**

22 3 **Eastern Rules (IRE)**[28] 4921 8-9-0 **97** (p) OisinOrr(7) 1 70
(M Halford, Ire) *in tch: 9th 1/2-way: rdn far side over 2f out and wknd over 1f out* **25/1**

23 2 **Cailin Mor (IRE)**[11] 5564 4-8-13 **89** (t) NGMcCullagh 4 57
(M Halford, Ire) *mid-div: rdn far side over 2f out and sn no ex: wknd over 1f out* **12/1**

24 2 **Al Mohalhal (IRE)**[56] 3928 3-9-6 **102** (p) RoryCleary 21 64
(J S Bolger, Ire) *chsd ldrs: 7th 1/2-way: sn pushed along and wknd qckly over 2f out* **33/1**

1m 37.84s (-8.16) **Going Correction** -0.775s/f (Hard)
WFA 3 from 4yo+ 6lb **24** Ran SP% **147.6**
Speed ratings: **109,108,107,106,106 106,104,104,103,103 101,101,101,100,99 99,98,98,97,96 95,92,90,88**
CSF £83.67 CT £1082.99 TOTE £12.40: £3.40, £2.10, £4.20, £4.20; DF 166.40 Trifecta £8494.20.
Owner David Spratt **Bred** Irish National Stud **Trained** Dunsany, Co Meath

FOCUS
Only three at single-figure odds in this ultra-competitive event, with two of them dominating the finish and the other in fifth. Some progressive types dominated the finish with the fourth and sixth setting the standard.

5942 - (Foreign Racing) - See Raceform Interactive

5904 BADEN-BADEN (L-H)

Sunday, August 28

OFFICIAL GOING: Turf: good

5943a GOLDENE PEITSCHE POWERED BY BURDA@TURF (GROUP 2) (3YO+) (TURF) 6f

3:40 (12:00) 3-Y-O+ **£29,411** (£11,397; £5,882; £2,941; £1,838)

RPR

1 **Donnerschlag**[91] 2722 6-9-4 0 (b) MarcLerner 14 109
(Jean-Pierre Carvalho, Germany) *broke wl and led: hdd whn c stands' side into st: rdn and regained ld wl over 1f out: r.o fnl f: fin 1st: disqualified and plcd 4th* **156/10**

2 3/4 **Markaz (IRE)**[15] 5404 4-9-4 0 (p) PaulMulrennan 12 110
(Owen Burrows) *bmpd between horses leaving stalls: sn cl up: drvn to chse ldr in centre of crse 1 1/2f out: rdn and styd on over 1f out: kpt on fnl f: nt pce of wnr: fin 2nd: awrdd the r* **7/2**[2]

3 2 **Forgino (GER)**[23] 5-9-4 0 AdriedeVries 1 110+
(T Potters, Germany) *towards rr: rdn and hdwy 2f out: styd on fnl f: nvr able to chal: fin 3rd: plcd 2nd* **84/10**

4 nk **Watchable**[43] 4393 6-9-4 0 (b) AndreasSuborics 5 109
(David O'Meara) *chsd ldr: carried stands' side into st by ldr: sn rdn and styd on fnl f: fin 4th: plcd 3rd* **107/10**

5 nk **Divine (IRE)**[30] 4824 5-9-1 0 FrederikTylicki 3 105
(Mick Channon) *racd in midfield: rdn and styd on to chse ldrs fr 1 1/2f out: one pce u.p fnl f* **19/5**[3]

6 1 **Daring Match (GER)**[35] 5-9-4 0 AlexanderPietsch 13 105
(J Hirschberger, Germany) *chsd ldr: led ent st: hdd wl over 1f out: no ex* **96/10**

7 1/2 **Son Cesio (FR)**[84] 2943 5-9-4 0 UmbertoRispoli 9 103
(H-A Pantall, France) *settled in midfield: rdn and no real imp 1 1/2f out: one pce fnl f* **21/10**[1]

8 1 **Schang (GER)**[21] 5217 3-9-1 0 FedericoBossa 6 100
(P Vovcenko, Germany) *towards rr: rdn and shortlived effrt 2f out: sn btn* **79/10**

9 2 1/4 **Mc Queen (FR)**[14] 5453 4-9-4 0 (p) StephenHellyn 7 93
(Yasmin Almenrader, Germany) *w.w in midfield: rdn and no imp 2f out: sn wknd* **246/10**

10 6 **Making Trouble (GER)**[14] 5453 4-9-4 0 FilipMinarik 4 74
(D Moser, Germany) *nvr beyond mid-div: wknd u.p ins fnl 2f* **30/1**

11 hd **Spirit Doll (HOL)**[13] 9-9-4 0 MichaelCadeddu 2 73
(Prof Dr R P Dollevoet, Holland) *a in rr: wl bhd fnl 2f* **56/1**

1m 9.43s (-0.86)
WFA 3 from 4yo+ 3lb **11** Ran SP% **130.1**
WIN (incl. 10 euro stake): 45. PLACES: 29, 30, 47. SF: 448.
Owner Gestut Hony-Hof **Bred** Jeremy Green & Sons & Brian McGrath **Trained** Germany

5944 - 5945a (Foreign Racing) - See Raceform Interactive

5905 DEAUVILLE (R-H)

Sunday, August 28

OFFICIAL GOING: Turf: good; polytrack: standard

5946a PRIX HOTEL BARRIERE LE NORMANDY DEAUVILLE (H'CAP) (3YO) (STRAIGHT) (TURF) 7f

2:30 (12:00) 3-Y-O

£20,735 (£8,382; £6,176; £3,970; £2,426; £1,544)

RPR

1 **Ella Diva (FR)**[26] 3-9-4 **0** Pierre-CharlesBoudot 9 95
(N Caullery, France) **104/10**

2 1 1/4 **Relaxed Boy (FR)**[15] 3-8-8 **0** GregoryBenoist 13 82
(P Sogorb, France) **23/1**

3 snk **Zapper Cass (FR)**[38] 3-8-11 **0** JulienAuge 6 85
(C Ferland, France) **12/1**

4 shd **Energie Green (IRE)**[15] 3-8-7 **0** AurelienLemaitre 7 80
(F Head, France) **33/1**

5 nk **London Protocol (FR)**[26] 5004 3-9-10 **0** DougieCostello 5 97
(K R Burke) *led under a t.k.h: pushed along sn after 1/2-way: rdn and kicked for home 2f out: hdd 125yds out: no ex* **77/10**[2]

6 snk **Valdaya (FR)**[59] 3-8-6 **0** AlexisBadel 4 78
(J-C Rouget, France) **79/10**[3]

7 1/2 **Siyaka (FR)** 3-8-8 **0** Francois-XavierBertras 3 79
(F Rohaut, France) **11/1**

8 3/4 **Feel Alive (FR)**[55] 3-8-6 **0** StephanePasquier 2 75
(F Rohaut, France) **9/2**[1]

9 nk **Jaaref (IRE)**[26] 3-9-3 **0** GeraldMosse 12 85
(J E Hammond, France) **9/1**

10 2 1/2 **Sas (IRE)**[26] 3-8-7 **0** (b) MickaelForest 16 68
(M Nigge, France) **34/1**

11 1 1/4 **Lady Linn (FR)**[86] 3-8-6 **0** MickaelBarzalona 8 64
(P Monfort, France) **21/1**

12 3 **Kenshaba (FR)**[17] 3-8-11 **0** (p) TheoBachelot 15 61
(M Boutin, France) **37/1**

13 nk **Shiver In The River (FR)**[55] 3-8-6 **0** (b) IoritzMendizabal 11 55
(C Botti, France) **23/1**

14 3/4 **Bobbio (FR)**[26] 3-8-7 **0** AnthonyCrastus 10 54
(N Caullery, France) **11/1**

15 3/4 **Forza Libranno (FR)**[17] 3-8-9 **0** TonyPiccone 14 54
(F Chappet, France) **12/1**

16 3 1/2 **Matey (FR)**[49] 3-9-6 **0** MaximeGuyon 1 55
(Mme Pia Brandt, France) **11/1**

1m 24.22s (-4.08) **16** Ran SP% **121.4**
WIN (incl. 1 euro stake): 11.40. PLACES: 3.90, 8.00, 4.50. DF: 149.80. SF: 254.40.
Owner Derek Ronald Lodge **Bred** Gaec Campos **Trained** France

5947a **LUCIEN BARRIERE GRAND PRIX DE DEAUVILLE (GROUP 2) (3YO+) (TURF)** **1m 4f 110y**
3:10 (12:00) 3-Y-O+ **£83,823** (£32,352; £15,441; £10,294)

RPR
1 **Savoir Vivre (IRE)**[49] 4186 3-8-6 0................................ MaximeGuyon 2 117
(Jean-Pierre Carvalho, Germany) *mde all: plld v hrd and led at mod gallop: qcknd tempo 1/2-way: kicked 6 l clr fr 3 1/2f out: sn rousted along: styd on gamely* **11/2**[3]
2 *nk* **Siljan's Saga (FR)**[56] 3936 6-9-0 0...................... Pierre-CharlesBoudot 3 114+
(J-P Gauvin, France) *hld up in 3rd: dropped to last 1/2-way: hdwy over 1 1/2f out: styd on to go 2nd 100yds out: nvr quite on terms w wnr* **8/13**[1]
3 *1 1/2* **Erupt (IRE)**[36] 4626 4-9-3 0.................................. StephanePasquier 1 115+
(F-H Graffard, France) *trckd ldr: 3rd and hrd rdn over 2f out: clsd u.p to chse ldr fr 1 1/2f out: one pce ins fnl f: lost 2nd 100yds out: no ex* **4/1**[2]
4 *10* **Garlingari (FR)**[13] 5500 5-9-6 0.........................(p) ChristopheSoumillon 4 102+
(Mme C Barande-Barbe, France) *w.w in rr: racd along on far outside bk st: rejnd main gp in 2nd over 5f out: hrd rdn and no imp 1 1/2f out: wknd appr fnl f: bhd whn eased* **11/2**[3]
2m 51.73s (5.33)
WFA 3 from 4yo+ 10lb 4 Ran SP% **112.7**
WIN (incl. 1 euro stake): 4.90. PLACES: 2.80, 2.30. SF: 17.90.
Owner Stall Ullmann **Bred** G Baron Von Ullman **Trained** Germany

5948a **PRIX QUINCEY BARRIERE (GROUP 3) (3YO+) (STRAIGHT) (TURF)** **1m (R)**
3:55 (12:00) 3-Y-O+ **£29,411** (£11,764; £8,823; £5,882; £2,941)

RPR
1 **Siyoushake (IRE)**[28] 4926 4-8-10 0.......................... StephanePasquier 4 104
(F Head, France) *settled in fnl pair on outer of stands' side gp: pushed along and hdwy on outer 2f out: rdn to ld appr 1f out: r.o and edgd lft: in command cl home* **15/8**[1]
2 *3/4* **Caointiorn (FR)**[33] 4751 5-8-13 0.................................(p) TheoBachelot 9 105
(S Wattel, France) *hld up in rr on ins rail: hdwy 3f out: drvn to chse ldr 2f out: styd on ins fnl f: wl hld by wnr* **10/1**
3 *1/2* **Waikika (FR)**[55] 3969 5-8-10 0..................................... IoritzMendizabal 2 101
(Y Barberot, France) *w.w in midfield on ins rail: nt clr run fr 2f out: angled out and in clr fnl 110yds: styd on: nrest at fin* **20/1**
4 *hd* **Maximum Aurelius (FR)**[67] 3543 3-8-10 0................ GregoryBenoist 8 105
(F-H Graffard, France) *pressed ldr on outer: rdn and nt qckn 1 1/2f out: kpt on at same pce fnl f* **7/1**[3]
5 *1* **Leader Writer (FR)**[33] 4751 4-9-0 0....................... VincentCheminaud 1 102
(H-A Pantall, France) *hld up towards rr on ins rail: rdn and no immediate imp over 1 1/2f out: styd on fnl f: nvr on terms* **18/1**
6 *snk* **Grand Vintage (FR)**[14] 5449 7-9-0 0........................ MickaelForest 5 102
(Carina Fey, France) *led stands' side gp of 7: hdd appr 1f out: grad lft bhd* **14/1**
7 *hd* **Spoil The Fun (FR)**[38] 7-9-2 0.. JulienAuge 6 103
(C Ferland, France) *cl up: swtchd outside after 2f: chsd ldr in centre of trck: styd on to chse overall ldr over 1f out: steadily dropped away* **2/1**[2]
8 *2 1/2* **Candide (FR)**[130] 1580 3-9-1 0........................... Pierre-CharlesBoudot 3 102
(A Fabre, France) *chsd ldrs on outer of stands' side gp: rdn and no imp 1 1/2f out: wknd fnl f* **15/2**
9 *3/4* **Litterature (FR)**[38] 4-8-10 0.. MaximeGuyon 7 90
(C Ferland, France) *cl up: swtchd outside after 2f and led gp of two in centre of trck: 3rd over all appr 1f out: sn btn: hld whn eased late on* **10/1**
1m 37.98s (-2.82)
WFA 3 from 4yo+ 6lb 9 Ran SP% **127.3**
WIN (incl. 1 euro stake): 2.90. PLACES: 1.60, 2.30, 3.70. DF: 12.30. SF: 21.10.
Owner Roy Racing Ltd & A Morley **Bred** Aleyrion Bloodstock Ltd **Trained** France

5949a **PRIX DE MEAUTRY BARRIERE (GROUP 3) (3YO+) (TURF)** **6f**
4:25 (12:00) 3-Y-O+ **£29,411** (£11,764; £8,823; £5,882; £2,941)

RPR
1 **Finsbury Square (IRE)**[30] 4824 4-9-5 0..........(b) ChristopheSoumillon 9 106
(F Chappet, France) *chsd ldr on outer: cl 3rd and gng v wl appr fnl f: sn drvn and r.o: led 110yds out: jst hld on* **7/1**
2 *shd* **Walec**[35] 4-9-1 0.. Pierre-CharlesBoudot 5 102
(P Sogorb, France) *w.w towards rr: last and pushed along 1/2-way: rdn and hdwy 1 1/2f out: styd on wl fnl f: jst failed* **11/1**
3 *1/2* **Lord Of The Land (IRE)**[21] 5213 5-9-1 0.....................(b) OlivierPeslier 4 100
(David O'Meara) *chsd ldr: rdn over 1f out: styd on fnl f: nt pce to chal* **9/2**[2]
4 *nk* **Silver Rainbow (IRE)**[9] 5614 4-8-11 0.......................... GeraldMosse 8 95
(Charles Hills) *led: rdn 1f out: hdd fnl 110yds: no ex* **15/8**[1]
5 *1/2* **Yakaba (FR)**[29] 4905 3-8-8 0.. MaximeGuyon 3 93
(F Head, France) *hld up in tch: hrd rdn and no imp 2f out: styd on ins fnl f: nrest at fin* **6/1**
6 *hd* **Saon Secret (FR)**[15] 6-9-1 0......................................(b) TheoBachelot 2 97
(T Castanheira, France) *w.w in rr: rdn and no imp fr 2f out: styd on fnl f: nvr in tch* **16/1**
7 *shd* **Karar**[23] 4-9-1 0..(p) GregoryBenoist 6 96
(F-H Graffard, France) *hld up towards rr: hdwy 1 1/2f out: styd on fnl f: nvr nrr* **13/2**
8 *2* **Venecia Style (FR)**[53] 4029 3-8-8 0......................... MickaelBarzalona 7 86
(P Sogorb, France) *settled in midfield: 4th and rdn over 1f out: wknd wl ins fnl f* **5/1**[3]
9 *4 1/2* **Muharaaj (IRE)**[8] 5-9-1 0..(p) AlexisBadel 1 76
(Mlle M-L Mortier, France) *cl up on inner: lost pl bef 1/2-way: hrd rdn and btn wl over 1 1/2f out* **25/1**
1m 9.71s (-1.29)
WFA 3 from 4yo+ 3lb 9 Ran SP% **127.8**
WIN (incl. 1 euro stake): 7.60. PLACES: 2.40, 3.10, 2.70. DF: 40.20. SF: 78.80.
Owner Berend Van Dalfsen **Bred** Berend Van Dalfsen **Trained** France

5098 OVREVOLL (R-H)
Sunday, August 28

OFFICIAL GOING: Turf: soft

5950a **MARIT SVEAAS MINNELOP (GROUP 3) (3YO+) (TURF)** **1m 1f**
3:35 (12:00) 3-Y-O+ **£61,349** (£19,938; £9,202; £5,521; £3,680)

RPR
1 **Brownie (FR)**[24] 5098 4-9-6 0... OliverWilson 10 106
(Bent Olsen, Denmark) **462/100**[3]
2 *3/4* **Hurricane Red (IRE)**[22] 5187 6-9-6 0......................... JacobJohansen 7 104
(Lennart Reuterskiold Jr, Sweden) **12/5**[1]
3 *nk* **Bank Of Burden (USA)**[22] 5187 9-9-4 0............ Per-AndersGraberg 13 101
(Niels Petersen, Norway) **7/2**[2]
4 *1/2* **Coprah**[26] 8-9-6 0.. NelsonDeSouza 2 102
(Cathrine Erichsen, Norway) **126/10**
5 *nk* **Bokan (FR)**[45] 4329 4-9-4 0.. Jan-ErikNeuroth 11 100
(Wido Neuroth, Norway) **181/10**
6 *2* **Fearless Hunter (GER)**[185] 721 6-9-4 0........................ CarlosLopez 4 95
(Rune Haugen) **114/10**
7 *1/2* **Rogue Runner (GER)**[22] 4-9-4 0................................. DennisSchiergen 8 94
(P Schiergen, Germany) **30/1**
8 *1 1/4* **Berling (IRE)**[22] 5187 9-9-4 0... ElioneChaves 9 92
(Jessica Long, Sweden) **102/10**
9 *1 3/4* **Quarterback (GER)**[22] 5187 4-9-6 0..............................(p) GeorgeBaker 6 90
(Rune Haugen) **7/1**
10 *1/2* **Captain Morgan (DEN)**[22] 5187 5-9-4 0............................ KevinStott 14 87
(Marc Stott, Denmark) **35/1**
11 *nse* **Captain Of Comerce (DEN)**[26] 4-9-4 0....................(b) VanessaRyall 12 87
(Jan Bjordal, Norway) **56/1**
12 *5* **Ragazzo (NOR)**[24] 5098 7-9-4 0.................................... RafaeldeOliveira 1 76
(Annike Bye Hansen, Norway) **40/1**
13 *5 1/4* **Vortex (NOR)**[45] 7-9-4 0..(b) SaleemGolam 5 65
(Rune Haugen) **25/1**
1m 50.2s (0.30) 13 Ran SP% **125.6**
Owner Lone Kaj-Nielsen **Bred** Mme Sylviane Jeffroy **Trained** Denmark

5569 CHEPSTOW (L-H)
Monday, August 29

OFFICIAL GOING: Good to soft (7.3)
Wind: slight across Weather: fine

5951 **OAKGROVE STUD SUPPORTS CHEPSTOW MENCAP EBF MEDIAN AUCTION MAIDEN FILLIES' STKS (PLUS 10 RACE)** **1m 14y**
12:30 (12:32) (Class 5) 2-Y-O **£3,881** (£1,155; £577; £288) **Stalls** Centre

Form RPR
1 **Stellar Surprise** 2-9-0 0.. OisinMurphy 2 73+
(Stuart Williams) *trckd ldng pair: plld out 2f out and sn in 2nd: shkn up to ld ins fnl f: readily* **11/8**[1]
36 2 *2* **Mia Cara**[82] 3024 2-9-0 0... ShaneKelly 5 67
(David Evans) *led: drvn over 1f out: hdd ins fnl f: hld by comfortable wnr* **3/1**[3]
640 3 *1/2* **Ok By Me (IRE)**[38] 4579 2-9-0 72... JFEgan 6 66
(David Evans) *trckd ldr: rdn over 2f out: lost 2nd over 1f out: styd on ins fnl f* **11/4**[2]
0 4 *6* **Hoover Fever**[29] 4907 2-8-7 0.. AledBeech(7) 4 53
(David Evans) *t.k.h in 4th: pushed along over 2f out: sn hld by principals: hung rt fnl f* **20/1**
06 5 *1 3/4* **Silver Chimes**[18] 5324 2-9-0 0...[1] MartinDwyer 3 49
(William Knight) *hld up: rdn over 3f out: qckly outpcd by ldrs: wknd over 1f out* **17/2**
6 *nk* **Willie's Anne (IRE)** 2-8-7 0.. TobyEley(7) 1 48
(Daniel Mark Loughnane) *s.i.s: rdn 3f out: a in rr* **25/1**
1m 38.45s (2.25) **Going Correction** +0.075s/f (Good) 6 Ran SP% **112.9**
Speed ratings (Par 91): **91,89,88,82,80 80**
CSF £5.88 TOTE £2.00: £1.30, £1.40; EX 5.30 Trifecta £10.10.
Owner J W Parry **Bred** Southcourt Stud **Trained** Newmarket, Suffolk

FOCUS
Shane Kelly described the ground as being "on the dead side of good." Probably quite a modest fillies' maiden, but the winner has more to offer. They raced under the stands' rail.

5952 **DOROTHY MORT MEMORIAL EBF MAIDEN STKS (PLUS 10 RACE)** **1m 14y**
1:00 (1:02) (Class 4) 2-Y-O **£5,175** (£1,540; £769; £384) **Stalls** Centre

Form RPR
6 1 **Hushood (IRE)**[17] 5356 2-9-0 0.. DaneO'Neill 4 79+
(Richard Hannon) *led and set stdy gallop: qcknd pce over 2f out: sn jnd: drvn ins fnl f: edgd rt and asserted fnl 110yds* **3/1**[2]
2 2 *1/2* **Good Omen**[51] 4128 2-9-0 0... PatCosgrave 6 78
(William Haggas) *pitched leaving stalls: hld up bhd ldrs: clsd 3f out: rdn to chal wnr 2f out: sn ev ch: carried rt and hld fnl 110yds* **1/2**[1]
4 3 *4 1/2* **Mashadie Boy**[27] 4975 2-9-0 0.......................................[1] LiamKeniry 7 68+
(David Simcock) *hld up: plld hrd: shkn up and hdwy into 3rd 2f out: no ch w first two but kpt on steadily* **6/1**[3]
4 *4 1/2* **Akkadian Empire** 2-9-0 0.. JFEgan 5 58
(Mick Channon) *t.k.h: cl up: rdn 3f out: sn outpcd by ldrs and hld* **20/1**
04 5 *3 3/4* **Percy Thrower (IRE)**[13] 5505 2-9-0 0.............................. SteveDrowne 3 50
(Charles Hills) *a abt same pl: shkn up over 3f out: outpcd 2f out: no ch after* **8/1**
6 *8* **Sam The Rebel** 2-9-0 0.. WilliamCarson 2 32
(Mike Hammond) *t.k.h early: prom: rdn 3f out: qckly outpcd: wknd over 1f out* **80/1**
7 *35* **Canizay (IRE)** 2-9-0 0... OisinMurphy 8
(Ronald Harris) *s.s: in rr: rdn 1/2-way: lost tch over 2f out: t.o* **50/1**
1m 38.75s (2.55) **Going Correction** +0.075s/f (Good) 7 Ran SP% **125.0**
Speed ratings (Par 96): **90,89,85,80,76 68,33**
CSF £5.43 TOTE £4.60: £1.80, £1.10; EX 6.50 Trifecta £18.50.Tally's Son was withdrawn. Price at time of withdrawal 100/1. Rule 4 does not apply
Owner Hamdan Al Maktoum **Bred** Ringfort Stud **Trained** East Everleigh, Wilts

FOCUS
Two useful types came clear in a maiden lacking depth, but the winner stepped forward from his debut. They raced centre-field.

5953 OAKGROVE STUD SUPPORTS NOAH'S ARK CHILDREN'S HOSPITAL H'CAP (DIV I) 7f 16y
1:30 (1:33) (Class 6) (0-65,70) 3-Y-O+ **£3,234** (£962; £481; £240) **Stalls** Centre

Form RPR
4002 **1** **Knight Of The Air**[9] 5627 4-9-8 **61** OisinMurphy 15 69
(Mick Channon) *hld up: clsd over 3f out: nt clr run over 2f out tl swtchd lft over 1f out: qcknd to ld ins fnl f: drvn out to hold on* **6/1**[2]
0161 **2** *nk* **Satchville Flyer**[3] 5826 5-9-10 **70** 6ex AledBeech(7) 8 78
(David Evans) *hld up: hdwy 1/2-way: nt clr run over 2f out: swtchd rt over 1f out: rdn: hung lft and r.o wl fnl f: jst hld* **7/1**[3]
4406 **3** *2* **Cascading Stars (IRE)**[16] 5393 4-9-5 **58** JFEgan 4 60
(Daniel Mark Loughnane) *prom: chal 3f out: drvn to ld over 1f out: hdd ins fnl f: one pce and lost 2nd fnl 75yds* **14/1**
0001 **4** *1 1/2* **Kaaber (USA)**[20] 5270 5-8-4 **50** (b) MitchGodwin(7) 10 48
(Roy Brotherton) *prom: rdn to ld 3f out: drvn and hdd over 1f out: no ex fnl 110yds* **10/1**
4141 **5** *shd* **Fantasy Queen**[11] 5571 3-9-6 **64** JohnFahy 1 59
(Eve Johnson Houghton) *hld up: rdn and hdwy on outer over 2f out: kpt on same pce fnl f* **5/1**[1]
0035 **6** *2* **Just Isla**[21] 5235 6-9-1 **54** (b) DanielMuscutt 2 46
(John Flint) *mid-div: clsd to chse ldrs 1/2-way: rdn 2f out: one pce fnl f* **8/1**
045 **7** *3/4* **Corella (IRE)**[23] 5168 3-8-12 **56** LukeMorris 12 44
(Clive Cox) *s.i.s: t.k.h towards rr: nt clr run 3f out to 2f out: styd on fnl f* **14/1**
0360 **8** *shd* **Oat Couture**[18] 5326 4-9-9 **62** DaneO'Neill 9 52
(Henry Candy) *s.i.s: sn mid-div: rdn over 2f out: wknd over 1f out* **9/1**
6523 **9** *2 3/4* **Aye Aye Skipper (IRE)**[18] 5326 6-9-2 **55** (p) PatCosgrave 3 37
(Ken Cunningham-Brown) *mid-div: rdn 3f out: wknd fnl f* **5/1**[1]
5006 **10** *1 1/2* **Avon Scent**[20] 5252 6-8-2 **46** oh1 (p) HollieDoyle(5) 7 24
(Christopher Mason) *chsd ldrs tl lost pl 1/2-way: no ch fnl 2f* **66/1**
-263 **11** *1 1/4* **Donttouchthechips (IRE)**[38] 4588 3-9-7 **65** TomMarquand 14 38
(Nikki Evans) *prom on stands' rail: rdn 3f out: wknd 2f out* **10/1**
/060 **12** *nk* **Ignight**[10] 5605 5-8-7 **46** oh1 JimmyQuinn 6 20
(Matthew Salaman) *in rr: rdn 3f out: wknd 2f out* **66/1**
0605 **13** *5* **Blackdown Warrior**[27] 4992 3-8-2 **46** oh1 KieranO'Neill 13 4
(Rod Millman) *chsd ldrs: rdn 3f out: wknd over 1f out* **16/1**
5006 **14** *7* **Outlaw Kate (IRE)**[21] 5235 4-8-7 **46** oh1 (v[1]) WilliamCarson 5
(Michael Mullineaux) *led: c rt to r on stands' side after 2f: rdn and hdd 3f out: wknd 2f out* **25/1**

1m 24.32s (1.12) **Going Correction** +0.075s/f (Good)
WFA 3 from 4yo+ 5lb **14** Ran SP% **125.5**
Speed ratings (Par 101): **96,95,93,91,91 89,88,88,85,83 82,81,75,67**
CSF £49.44 CT £594.03 TOTE £7.00: £2.60, £2.90, £5.40; EX 55.70 Trifecta £1097.60.
Owner Insignia Racing (Crescent) **Bred** Dulverton Equine **Trained** West Ilsley, Berks

FOCUS
Modest handicap form, but a minor personal best from the winner.

5954 OAKGROVE STUD SUPPORTS NOAH'S ARK CHILDREN'S HOSPITAL H'CAP (DIV II) 7f 16y
2:00 (2:06) (Class 6) (0-65,65) 3-Y-O+ **£3,234** (£962; £481; £240) **Stalls** Centre

Form RPR
4203 **1** **Poor Duke (IRE)**[11] 5572 6-8-10 **49** MartinDwyer 5 56
(Michael Mullineaux) *reluctant to approach stalls: towards rr: rdn over 3f out: r.o u.p on outer to ld appr fnl f: asserted nr fin* **12/1**
U522 **2** *3/4* **Wild Flower (IRE)**[7] 5710 4-8-11 **50** KieranO'Neill 3 55
(Jimmy Fox) *mid-div: rdn and swtchd lft over 2f out: ev ch ins fnl f tl no ex nr fin* **5/1**[2]
6005 **3** *1 1/4* **Suni Dancer**[25] 5055 5-8-7 **46** WilliamCarson 11 50
(Tony Carroll) *towards rr: nt clr run 2f out tl over 1f out: r.o fnl f: nvr able to chal* **20/1**
6014 **4** *1/2* **Baz's Boy**[7] 5706 3-7-12 **49** MitchGodwin(7) 1 47
(John Flint) *chsd ldrs: rdn to ld narrowly over 2f out: hdd appr fnl f: one pce* **8/1**
6440 **5** *1 1/4* **Concur (IRE)**[11] 5570 3-7-9 **46** oh1 DavidEgan(7) 4 41
(Rod Millman) *a.p: rdn and ev ch 2f out: one pce fnl f* **16/1**
5144 **6** *hd* **Hamish McGonagain**[25] 5059 3-8-13 **62** (p) DavidParkes(5) 6 56
(Jeremy Gask) *s.i.s: mid-div: rdn and hdwy 3f out: nt clr run over 1f out: styd on same pce fnl f* **14/1**
60-0 **7** *1/2* **Barista (IRE)**[136] 1456 8-9-8 **61** CharlesBishop 8 56
(Brian Forsey) *in rr: rdn over 3f out: no hdwy tl r.o fnl f* **14/1**
4232 **8** *1/2* **Harmony Bay (IRE)**[21] 5248 3-9-7 **65** LukeMorris 10 58
(Sylvester Kirk) *chsd ldrs: rdn over 3f out: drvn and one pce fnl f* **9/2**[1]
5505 **9** *2 1/2* **Jaganory (IRE)**[12] 5546 4-9-2 **55** (p) TomMarquand 15 42
(Christopher Mason) *towards rr: rdn 3f out: swtchd lft 2f out: no imp* **22/1**
5205 **10** *nse* **Waneen (IRE)**[9] 5626 3-9-6 **64** JFEgan 7 49
(Joseph Tuite) *led 1f: cl up: rdn and ev ch 2f out: wknd 1f out* **14/1**
6564 **11** *1/2* **Earthwindorfire**[45] 4369 5-9-11 **64** OisinMurphy 14 49
(Geoffrey Deacon) *cl up: rdn over 2f out: wkng whn hmpd over 1f out* **8/1**
4004 **12** *1/2* **Dandys Perier (IRE)**[27] 4992 5-8-9 **51** (p) GeorgeDowning(3) 13 35
(Ronald Harris) *prom: led after 1f tl over 2f out: wknd over 1f out* **14/1**
0114 **13** *hd* **Prince Of Cardamom (IRE)**[27] 4993 4-9-1 **59** (p) CharlieBennett(5) 12 43
(Jonathan Geake) *chsd ldrs: rdn over 3f out: wknd over 1f out* **7/1**[3]
0546 **14** *1/2* **Mostashreqah**[7] 5721 3-8-4 **48** (tp) JimmyQuinn 2 28
(Milton Bradley) *chsd ldrs: rdn and ev ch 2f out: wknd fnl f* **33/1**
00/0 **15** *22* **Alberto**[35] 4716 6-8-2 **46** oh1 MeganNicholls(5) 9
(Sarah Hollinshead) *sed awkwardly: a in rr: lost tch over 2f out: t.o* **66/1**

1m 24.17s (0.97) **Going Correction** +0.075s/f (Good)
WFA 3 from 4yo+ 5lb **15** Ran SP% **123.4**
Speed ratings (Par 101): **97,96,94,94,92 92,91,91,88,88 87,87,87,86,61**
CSF £69.52 CT £1250.24 TOTE £15.70: £4.50, £1.80, £8.80; EX 104.50 Trifecta £1906.40.
Owner Michael Mullineaux **Bred** Corrin Stud **Trained** Alpraham, Cheshire

FOCUS
The second division of this modest handicap, the time was 0.15secs quicker than the first leg. Those in behind the winner highlight the limitations of the form.

5955 OAKGROVE STUD SUPPORTS LATCH WALES H'CAP 6f 16y
2:35 (2:38) (Class 4) (0-85,85) 3-Y-O+ **£5,175** (£1,540; £769; £384) **Stalls** Centre

Form RPR
0030 **1** **Munfallet (IRE)**[16] 5417 5-9-10 **85** PatCosgrave 8 93
(David Brown) *led: rdn 2f out: hdd over 1f out: drvn to ld again wl ins fnl f* **12/1**
0302 **2** *nk* **Sir Billy Wright (IRE)**[3] 5825 5-9-10 **85** DaneO'Neill 5 92
(David Evans) *trckd wnr: drvn and ev ch over 1f out: r.o: jst hld* **9/2**[2]
2322 **3** *nk* **Pixeleen**[29] 4910 4-9-10 **85** JFEgan 3 91
(Malcolm Saunders) *chsd ldrs: led over 1f out: edgd lft u.p and hdd wl ins fnl f* **10/3**[1]
2541 **4** *1 1/4* **Gold Hunter (IRE)**[20] 5253 6-9-4 **79** (p) TomMarquand 4 81
(Steve Flook) *hld up: rdn and hdwy over 2f out: one pce fnl f* **13/2**
0013 **5** *1* **Bonjour Steve**[12] 5546 5-7-12 **66** oh3 (p) MitchGodwin(7) 10 65
(Richard Price) *chsd ldrs: rdn 2f out: nt clr run and swtchd rt over 1f out: r.o same pce fnl f* **28/1**
2132 **6** *shd* **Vincentti (IRE)**[5] 5774 6-8-10 **74** GeorgeDowning(3) 2 73+
(Ronald Harris) *dwlt: in rr: rdn 1/2-way: hdwy on outer 2f out: kpt on fnl f* **13/2**
5100 **7** *1* **Sydney Ruffdiamond**[14] 5488 4-9-9 **84** (e[1]) ShaneKelly 7 79
(Richard Hughes) *prom tl dropped towards rr after 2f: shkn up 2f out: no imp* **25/1**
4135 **8** *3/4* **Gilmer (IRE)**[20] 5253 5-8-3 **71** JoshuaBryan(7) 1 64
(Laura Young) *wnt to post early: mid-div: rdn and lost pl 3f out: wknd appr fnl f* **10/1**
6334 **9** *nk* **Nisser**[72] 3415 3-9-5 **83** OisinMurphy 9 75
(Robert Cowell) *bustled along fr stalls to chse ldrs: rdn over 2f out: wknd fnl f* **6/1**[3]
1320 **10** *3* **Cocoa Beach (IRE)**[19] 5285 3-9-3 **81** LukeMorris 6 63
(Sir Mark Prescott Bt) *t.k.h towards rr: rdn 3f out: wknd over 1f out* **9/1**

1m 11.54s (-0.46) **Going Correction** +0.075s/f (Good)
WFA 3 from 4yo+ 3lb **10** Ran SP% **116.3**
Speed ratings (Par 105): **106,105,105,103,102 102,100,99,99,95**
CSF £65.16 CT £230.24 TOTE £13.30: £2.80, £1.70, £1.70; EX 75.80 Trifecta £192.50.
Owner J C Fretwell **Bred** Miss Joann Lyons **Trained** Averham Park, Notts

FOCUS
A decent sprint that saw a really game effort from the winner. The form has been set around the runner-up.

5956 OAKGROVE STUD SUPPORTS SPARKLE&SERENNU CHILDRENS CENTRE H'CAP 1m 14y
3:10 (3:10) (Class 2) (0-105,101) 3-Y-O+ **£12,938** (£3,850; £1,924; £962) **Stalls** Centre

Form RPR
1050 **1** **Medburn Dream**[10] 5601 3-8-1 **82** oh1 JimmyQuinn 2 90
(Paul Henderson) *mde all: c over to stands' side 1/2-way: drvn over 1f out: r.o wl* **12/1**
4006 **2** *1* **Glory Awaits (IRE)**[23] 5146 6-9-6 **95** (b) ShaneKelly 7 102
(David Simcock) *hld up: racd keenly: drvn and clsd over 2f out: rdn to go 2nd ins fnl f: kpt on but hld by wnr* **15/2**
4425 **3** *1 1/2* **Peak Storm**[12] 5545 7-8-0 **82** oh6 (p) MitchGodwin(7) 8 86
(John O'Shea) *hld up: drvn over 2f out: only 8th whn swtchd rt over 1f out: r.o wl: wnt 3rd cl home* **25/1**
0456 **4** *nse* **Dessertoflife (IRE)**[33] 4757 3-9-1 **96** DaneO'Neill 5 98
(Mark Johnston) *s.i.s: towards rr: rdn 3f out: sn clsd on outer: styd on to dispute 3rd fnl f: one pce* **8/1**
5323 **5** *1/2* **Highland Colori (IRE)**[23] 5146 8-9-9 **98** (v) OisinMurphy 4 100
(Andrew Balding) *chsd ldrs: rdn 2f out: kpt on same pce: lost 2 pls nr fin* **7/1**[3]
242 **6** *1/2* **Sinfonietta (FR)**[68] 3534 4-9-1 **90** LukeMorris 9 91
(David Menuisier) *trckd ldrs: briefly in 2nd 3f out: sn rdn: wknd over 1f out* **9/4**[1]
0-03 **7** *3/4* **Persun**[71] 3438 4-8-9 **84** JFEgan 1 83
(Mick Channon) *mid-div: rdn 3f out: hdwy to dispute 2nd over 1f out: wknd ins fnl f* **8/1**
1001 **8** *hd* **Oh This Is Us (IRE)**[30] 4887 3-9-5 **100** TomMarquand 6 98
(Richard Hannon) *hld up: rdn to chse ldrs over 2f out: hung lft over 1f out: wknd fnl f* **11/2**[2]
144- **9** *7* **They Seek Him Here (IRE)**[373] 5632 3-9-6 **101** [1] PatCosgrave 3 83
(Hugo Palmer) *trckd wnr over 2f: styd prom: shkn up over 2f out and sn lost pl: wknd over 1f out* **8/1**

1m 35.95s (-0.25) **Going Correction** +0.075s/f (Good)
WFA 3 from 4yo+ 6lb **9** Ran SP% **115.3**
Speed ratings (Par 109): **104,103,101,101,100 100,99,99,92**
CSF £98.16 CT £2219.24 TOTE £15.10: £3.50, £2.20, £6.20; EX 121.60 Trifecta £1502.30.
Owner Eddie Evans **Bred** Eddie Evans **Trained** Whitsbury, Hants

FOCUS
A useful handicap with the winner resuming earlier season progress.

5957 OAKGROVE STUD SUPPORTS VELINDRE CANCER CARE APPRENTICE (S) STKS 1m 2f 36y
3:45 (3:45) (Class 6) 3-5-Y-O **£2,587** (£770; £384; £192) **Stalls** Low

Form RPR
1213 **1** **Boutan**[22] 5197 3-8-9 69 MitchGodwin(3) 2 62
(Bernard Llewellyn) *hld up in 5th: rdn over 2f out: n.m.r on ins over 1f out: styd on wl to ld fnl 75yds* **11/4**[2]
0234 **2** *1* **Rockliffe**[19] 5288 3-8-7 61 DavidEgan(5) 3 60
(Mick Channon) *t.k.h: trckd ldr: disp ld after 4f tl drvn and wnt on 2f out: hdd and no ex fnl 75yds* **9/4**[1]
3/0- **3** *1 3/4* **Istimraar (IRE)**[15] 1700 5-9-6 74 (p) CharlieBennett 4 57
(Alexandra Dunn) *led: jnd after 4f: hdd 2f out: drvn and styd on same pce: tk 3rd last strides* **14/1**
1240 **4** *nk* **Scent Of Power**[41] 4498 4-8-12 55 HollieDoyle(3) 5 52
(Barry Leavy) *t.k.h: trckd ldrs: rdn and ev ch 2f out: one pce fnl f: lost 3rd last strides* **9/4**[1]
6513 **5** *4 1/2* **Edge (IRE)**[3] 5823 5-9-6 52 (b) JordanWilliams(5) 6 53
(Bernard Llewellyn) *s.i.s: sn rcvrd to chse ldrs: drvn and ev ch 2f out: one pce whn n.m.r appr fnl f* **11/2**[3]
-065 **6** *4* **Virtual Song**[40] 4518 3-8-2 36 AledBeech(5) 1 36
(Barry Leavy) *hld up in last: rdn over 3f out: wknd 2f out* **33/1**

2m 12.75s (2.15) **Going Correction** +0.175s/f (Good)
WFA 3 from 4yo+ 8lb **6** Ran SP% **113.2**
Speed ratings (Par 101): **98,97,95,95,91 88**
CSF £9.54 TOTE £4.20: £2.10, £1.50; EX 8.90 Trifecta £52.10.
Owner Alan J Williams **Bred** Seaton Partnership **Trained** Fochriw, Caerphilly

FOCUS
They dawdled early in this seller and the fact it wasn't a proper test at the trip suited the winner. She did not need to match her recent best.

5958 OAKGROVE STUD SUPPORTS BREAST CANCER CARE CYMRU H'CAP — 1m 4f 23y
4:15 (4:18) (Class 6) (0-60,59) 3-Y-O+ — **£3,234** (£962; £481; £240) **Stalls** Low

Form — RPR

0360 **1** **Invincible Wish (IRE)**[13] 5513 4-9-9 **57** .... EoinWalsh(3) 11 — 64
(Trevor Wall) *s.s: hld up in rr: hdwy on outer over 2f out: stl plenty to do appr fnl f: r.o wl to ld fnl 75yds* **8/1**

5255 **2** 1 1/4 **Grams And Ounces**[4] 5232 9-10-0 **59** ....(t) TimmyMurphy 5 — 64
(Grace Harris) *a.p: wnt 2nd 3f out: led 2f out: sn hdd: kpt on wl u.p* **8/1**

216- **3** 3/4 **Nebula Storm (IRE)**[182] 6167 9-9-13 **58** ....(v) SteveDrowne 2 — 62
(Michael Blake) *chsd ldrs: drvn 3f out: led over 1f out: edgd rt and hdd fnl 75yds: no ex* **3/1**[1]

4153 **4** hd **Ring Eye (IRE)**[11] 5573 8-9-9 **59** .... CiaranMckee(5) 8 — 62
(John O'Shea) *hld up towards rr: hdwy 3f out: swtchd lft 2f out: styd on same pce fnl f* **11/2**[2]

5P4 **5** 2 1/2 **The Quarterjack**[28] 4950 7-9-7 **59** .... JordanWilliams(7) 10 — 58
(Ron Hodges) *hld up towards rr: hdwy over 3f out: one pce fnl f* **8/1**

0-00 **6** 1 **Work (IRE)**[34] 4740 3-8-6 **47** .... KieranO'Neill 9 — 45
(David Simcock) *hld up towards rr: clsd 4f out: rdn over 2f out: styd on same pce fnl f* **9/1**

003 **7** 1 3/4 **Keyman (IRE)**[32] 4794 3-8-6 **47** .... LukeMorris 3 — 42
(Jeremy Gask) *chsd ldrs: drvn 3f out: styd on one pce fnl 2f* **7/1**[3]

000 **8** 3/4 **Hepburn**[56] 3958 3-9-0 **55** ....[1] TomMarquand 6 — 49
(Ali Stronge) *t.k.h: chsd ldrs: rdn 3f out and sn lost pl: styd on again fnl f* **25/1**

65/5 **9** 3/4 **Another Squeeze**[22] 5208 8-9-0 **45** .... WilliamCarson 1 — 38
(Peter Hiatt) *led: rdn and hdd 2f out: nt run on: wknd fnl f* **16/1**

6500 **10** nk **Last Summer**[19] 5303 5-9-9 **57** .... RobHornby(3) 4 — 49
(Grace Harris) *s.i.s: hld up: rdn over 3f out: no ch fnl 2f* **16/1**

0044 **11** 2 **Living Leader**[10] 5592 7-9-10 **55** ....(tp) MartinDwyer 12 — 44
(Grace Harris) *t.k.h: mid-div: hdwy after 3f: drvn over 2f out: wknd over 1f out* **16/1**

500- **12** 9 **Rest Easy**[168] 4160 4-9-4 **49** .... LiamKeniry 7 — 24
(Seamus Mullins) *trckd ldr: lost 2nd 3f out: drvn and wknd 2f out* **25/1**

4000 **13** nse **Sabato (IRE)**[35] 4718 3-8-6 **52** ....(t) MeganNicholls(5) 13 — 27
(Fergal O'Brien) *s.s: a in rr* **11/1**

2m 40.79s (1.79) **Going Correction** +0.175s/f (Good)
WFA 3 from 4yo+ 10lb — **13** Ran SP% **129.9**
Speed ratings (Par 101): **101,100,99,99,97 97,96,95,95,94 93,87,87**
CSF £77.12 CT £243.12 TOTE £8.90: £2.80, £3.20, £1.60; EX 93.40 Trifecta £474.60.
Owner Michael & Lesley Wilkes **Bred** Cyril Ryan **Trained** Twitchen, Shropshire

FOCUS
A moderate handicap with the balance of the first three setting the level.
T/Plt: £403.30 to a £1 stake. Pool: £61,087.96 - 110.55 winning units T/Qpdt: £264.60 to a £1 stake. Pool: £4,398.47 - 12.3 winning units **Richard Lowther**

4784 EPSOM (L-H)
Monday, August 29

OFFICIAL GOING: Good (good to firm in places; 7.3)
Wind: light, across Weather: bright spells

5959 BRITISH STALLION STUDS EBF MEDIAN AUCTION MAIDEN STKS — 7f
2:05 (2:07) (Class 5) 2-Y-O — **£3,881** (£1,155; £577; £288) **Stalls** Low

Form — RPR

022 **1** **Hurricane Rush (IRE)**[46] 4304 2-9-5 81 .... SilvestreDeSousa 3 — 81
(Charles Hills) *dwlt and short of room leaving stalls: hld up in tch: pushed along and hdwy over 2f out: rdn to chse ldrs over 1f out: chal ins fnl f: r.o wl to ld wl ins fnl f* **11/4**[2]

3 **2** 1/2 **Firefright (IRE)**[17] 5371 2-9-5 0 .... JimCrowley 6 — 80
(Jeremy Noseda) *chsd ldng pair: clsd to join ldr ent fnl 2f: rdn to ld over 1f out: drvn 1f out: hdd and no ex wl ins fnl f* **6/5**[1]

5 **3** 1 **Vanderbilt (IRE)**[25] 5081 2-9-5 0 .... HarryBentley 7 — 77
(Martyn Meade) *in tch in midfield: effrt ent fnl 2f: hdwy and swtchd lft wl over 1f out: 3rd and kpt on same pce ins fnl f: nt that much room towards fin* **14/1**

2233 **4** 2 1/2 **Prerogative (IRE)**[23] 5171 2-9-5 82 .... SeanLevey 4 — 70
(Richard Hannon) *chsd ldr tl led over 2f out: rdn and hdd over 1f out: drvn and unable qck 1f out: wknd ins fnl f* **9/2**[3]

5 4 **Romanor** 2-9-5 0 ....[1] GeorgeBaker 8 — 59+
(Ed Walker) *s.i.s: wl off the pce in 8th: pushed along and hdwy to pass btn over 1f out: nvr trbld ldrs* **25/1**

0 **6** 3/4 **Cool Climate (IRE)**[17] 5371 2-9-5 0 .... TonyHamilton 5 — 57
(Richard Fahey) *in tch in midfield: swtchd lft and effrt ent fnl 2f: outpcd and btn over 1f out: wknd fnl f* **16/1**

4 **7** 4 **Ourmullion**[21] 5237 2-9-5 0 .... KierenFox 2 — 47
(John Best) *bustled along leaving stalls: in tch in midfield: swtchd lft and rdn over 2f out: no imp 2f out: wknd over 1f out: no ch and swtchd rt ins fnl f* **25/1**

00 **8** 3 1/4 **Aventus (IRE)**[19] 5304 2-9-5 0 .... RyanTate 1 — 38
(Richard Hughes) *led tl hdd and rdn over 2f out: sn struggling and wknd over 1f out* **66/1**

9 1 **Red Caravel (IRE)** 2-9-5 0 .... JimmyFortune 9 — 35
(Richard Hughes) *s.i.s: rn v green early and sn wl detached in last: n.d but getting the hang of things and styd on fnl f* **33/1**

1m 24.33s (1.03) **Going Correction** +0.025s/f (Good) — **9** Ran SP% **115.0**
Speed ratings (Par 94): **95,94,93,90,85 85,80,76,75**
CSF £6.14 TOTE £3.40: £1.50, £1.10, £3.80; EX 6.50 Trifecta £36.30.
Owner F Ma, R Cheung, S Tung **Bred** Gerry Flannery Developments **Trained** Lambourn, Berks

FOCUS
There were a few drizzly showers (not measurable) on Sunday, and Monday was mainly dry, so the ground was on the fast side. The rail was out 3yds from 1m to the winning post, adding 10yds to the distance of this race. They went a solid-looking gallop and the form seems at least fair.

5960 BUNBURY H'CAP (JOCKEY CLUB GRASSROOTS FLAT SPRINT SERIES QUALIFIER) — 6f
2:40 (2:40) (Class 5) (0-75,75) 3-Y-O — **£3,881** (£1,155; £577; £288) **Stalls** High

Form — RPR

6054 **1** **Ancient Astronaut**[51] 4134 3-9-3 **71** .... SilvestreDeSousa 7 — 77
(John Quinn) *t.k.h: hld up in tch in midfield: rdn ent fnl 2f: hdwy to press ldrs over 1f out: led ins fnl f: r.o wl* **4/1**[2]

4121 **2** 3/4 **Tricky Dicky**[23] 5152 3-8-10 **64** .... DuranFentiman 5 — 68
(Olly Williams) *broke wl: sn stdd to chse ldrs and t.k.h: rdn to chal over 1f out: led jst ins fnl f: sn hdd and kpt on same pce after* **6/1**

2004 **3** hd **Frenchman (FR)**[19] 5301 3-9-7 **75** .... JamesDoyle 3 — 78
(Charles Hills) *sn trcking ldr tl led wl over 1f out: sn rdn: hdd jst ins fnl f: styd on same pce fnl 100yds* **3/1**[1]

5120 **4** hd **Danecase**[25] 5075 3-9-7 **75** .... FergusSweeney 6 — 77+
(David Dennis) *hld up in tch in last pair: clsd 2f out: nt clr run and swtchd rt 1f out: hdwy u.p ins fnl f: kpt on wl: nt rch wnr* **8/1**

0136 **5** 1/2 **Pink Martini (IRE)**[17] 5379 3-9-4 **75** ....[1] JosephineGordon(3) 4 — 76
(Joseph Tuite) *hld up in tch in midfield: clsd and nt clrest of runs over 1f out: gap opened and drvn 1f out: kpt on but nvr enough pce to chal* **16/1**

12 **6** 2 **Wild Dancer**[38] 4588 3-9-0 **73** .... HectorCrouch(5) 9 — 67
(Patrick Chamings) *hld up in tch in last pair: effrt in centre over 2f out: no imp over 1f out: kpt on same pce ins fnl f: nvr trbld ldrs* **9/2**[3]

0505 **7** shd **Tikthebox (IRE)**[2] 5881 3-9-3 **74** .... AaronJones(3) 1 — 68
(David Brown) *sn led: rdn and hdd wl over 1f out: no ex over 1f out: wknd ins fnl f* **6/1**

1300 **8** 6 **In My Place**[21] 5224 3-9-2 **70** ....(b[1]) TonyHamilton 2 — 45
(Richard Fahey) *chsd ldrs: rdn over 2f out: lost pl and hung lft over 1f out: wknd fnl f* **16/1**

1m 10.47s (1.07) **Going Correction** +0.025s/f (Good) — **8** Ran SP% **114.6**
Speed ratings (Par 100): **93,92,91,91,90 88,88,80**
CSF £28.20 CT £81.43 TOTE £4.20: £1.40, £1.60, £1.60; EX 28.90 Trifecta £140.90.
Owner Harlen Ltd **Bred** D R Botterill **Trained** Settrington, N Yorks

FOCUS
This was run over 5yds further than advertised. A few of these were keen early.

5961 INDIGENOUS H'CAP — 5f
3:15 (3:16) (Class 2) (0-100,98) 3-Y-O+
£12,450 (£3,728; £1,864; £932; £466; £234) **Stalls** High

Form — RPR

4004 **1** **El Astronaute (IRE)**[9] 5657 3-8-8 **84** .... SilvestreDeSousa 9 — 93
(John Quinn) *chsd ldrs: led wl over 1f out: immediately began to hang lft: maintained advantage but hung across crse to inner rail: r.o* **11/4**[1]

0004 **2** 1/2 **Humidor (IRE)**[34] 4735 9-9-9 **97** .... FergusSweeney 8 — 104
(George Baker) *taken down early and led to post: midfield tl dropped towards rr 1/2-way: swtchd lft and effrt over 1f out: edging lft but str run ins fnl f: wnt 2nd towards fin: nvr quite getting to wnr* **5/1**[2]

3402 **3** 1/2 **Waseem Faris (IRE)**[8] 5669 7-8-12 **85** .... JosephineGordon(3) 10 — 90
(Joseph Tuite) *in tch in midfield: effrt over 1f out: sn edging lft but hdwy 1f out: styd on strly fnl 100yds: wnt 3rd nr fin: nvr quite getting to wnr* **8/1**

2060 **4** 1/2 **Hay Chewed (IRE)**[12] 5555 5-8-12 **89** .... NoelGarbutt(3) 5 — 94
(Conrad Allen) *dwlt: in last trio early: swtchd lft and hdwy 3f out: ev ch over 1f out: immediately hung lft: stl ev ch: racing on inner rail ins fnl f: keeping on same pce whn hmpd and lost 2 pls towards fin* **8/1**

-030 **5** nk **Huntsmans Close**[72] 3386 6-9-10 **98** .... JamesDoyle 2 — 103+
(Robert Cowell) *taken down early: in tch in midfield: effrt to chal over 1f out: immediately carried lft: no ex whn hmpd ins fnl f: lost 2 pls towards fin* **10/1**

6002 **6** nk **Olivia Fallow (IRE)**[5] 5780 4-8-11 **85** ....[1] MartinLane 4 — 86
(Paul Midgley) *restless in stalls: dwlt: bhd: effrt u.p over 1f out: styd nrest stands' rail and styd on ins fnl f: nt rch ldrs* **6/1**[3]

2500 **7** 1 **Union Rose**[12] 5555 4-9-6 **94** ....(p) MartinHarley 7 — 92
(Ronald Harris) *in tch in midfield: effrt over 1f out: immediately hung lft: no imp and swtchd rt 1f out: stl hanging and kpt on same pce ins fnl f* **8/1**

3001 **8** 1 1/4 **Sandfrankskipsgo**[17] 5360 7-8-12 **86** .... JimCrowley 1 — 79
(Peter Crate) *w ldr: rdn 2f out: unable qck and carried lft over 1f out: btn 1f out: wknd ins fnl f* **16/1**

0600 **9** 1 1/4 **Field Of Vision (IRE)**[9] 5657 3-9-2 **92** .... TonyHamilton 3 — 81
(Joseph Tuite) *in tch in midfield: rdn over 2f out: lost pl and swtchd lft over 1f out: sn u.p and no hdwy: wknd ins fnl f* **25/1**

0351 **10** 5 **King Crimson**[8] 5669 4-8-5 **86** 6ex .... KillianHennessy(7) 6 — 57
(Mick Channon) *led tl wl over 1f out: sn rdn and lost pl: bhd ins fnl f* **14/1**

54.65s (-1.05) **Going Correction** +0.025s/f (Good)
WFA 3 from 4yo+ 2lb — **10** Ran SP% **116.4**
Speed ratings (Par 109): **109,108,107,106,106 105,104,102,100,92**
CSF £15.97 CT £93.09 TOTE £3.60: £1.60, £2.20, £2.60; EX 17.50 Trifecta £76.70.
Owner Ross Harmon **Bred** T Jones **Trained** Settrington, N Yorks

FOCUS
An untidy affair as most of the runners either drifted or hung from the stands' side to the far side in the closing stages, perhaps following Hay Chewed, who was the first to go that way, and there was a bit of trouble late on.

5962 HENRY DORLING CONDITIONS STKS — 1m 2f 18y
3:50 (3:50) (Class 3) 3-Y-O+ — **£9,337** (£2,796; £1,398; £699) **Stalls** Low

Form — RPR

0210 **1** **Goodwood Zodiac (IRE)**[32] 4797 3-8-8 93 .... SilvestreDeSousa 5 — 106
(William Knight) *stdd and dropped in after s: hld up off the pce in last: smooth hdwy 5f out to chse ldrs 4f out: led 2f out: rdn and forged ahd over 1f out: styd on wl and a holding runner-up ins fnl f* **5/2**[2]

2450 **2** 3/4 **Maverick Wave (USA)**[72] 3383 5-9-2 107 .... JamesDoyle 2 — 104
(John Gosden) *chsd ldr: clsd to trck ldr 4f out: rdn and ev ch over 2f out: kpt on and sustained effrt u.p but a hld ins fnl f* **11/8**[1]

0000 **3** 3 **What About Carlo (FR)**[9] 5647 5-9-2 95 ....[1] JimmyFortune 3 — 98
(Eve Johnson Houghton) *hld up off the pce in 3rd: clsd to chse ldrs 4f out: swtchd rt and rdn wl over 2f out: 3rd and kpt on same pce over 1f out: eased towards fin* **7/2**[3]

6205 **4** 10 **Beach Bar (IRE)**[23] 5146 5-9-2 98 .... JimCrowley 1 — 78
(Brendan Powell) *taken down early: led and clr tl 4f out: rdn 3f out: hdd 2f out: sn btn: bhd fnl f* **5/1**

2m 7.44s (-2.26) **Going Correction** +0.025s/f (Good)
WFA 3 from 5yo 8lb — **4** Ran SP% **109.6**
Speed ratings (Par 107): **110,109,107,99**
CSF £6.44 TOTE £2.50; EX 7.20 Trifecta £12.90.
Owner Goodwood Racehorse Owners Group (22) Ltd **Bred** Kabansk Ltd & Rathbarry Stud **Trained** Patching, W Sussex

FOCUS
This was run over 20yds further than advertised. They looked to go a fair gallop despite the small field.

5963 AMATEUR DERBY (H'CAP) (FOR GENTLEMAN AMATEUR RIDERS) 1m 4f 10y
4:20 (4:28) (Class 4) (0-85,84) 4-Y-O+ **£6,239** (£1,935; £967; £484) **Stalls** Centre

Form RPR

5262 **1** **Hubertas**[66] 3602 4-11-6 **83**......(v) MrJJCodd 7 94
(John Quinn) *stdd s: hld up in last trio: clsd 3f out: rdn and wnt between rivals to ld over 1f out: styd on wl fnl f: rdn out* **3/1**[1]

0-45 **2** 3/4 **Jupiter Custos (FR)**[16] 5413 4-10-2 **68**...... MrJamesKing[(3)] 4 77
(Michael Scudamore) *hld up in tch in midfield: hdwy to chse ldrs over 2f out: rdn to ld 2f out: sn hdd: stl pressing wnr and clr 1f out: kpt on same pce ins fnl f* **16/1**

3000 **3** 6 **Eton Rambler (USA)**[33] 4752 6-11-7 **84**...... MrSWalker 10 83
(George Baker) *hld up in midfield: clsd 3f out: nt clr run and shuffled bk over 2f out: rdn and hdwy 2f out: wnt 4th and hung lft over 1f out: chsd clr ldng pair 100yds: kpt on but nvr a threat* **4/1**[3]

0063 **4** 2 **Whinging Willie (IRE)**[16] 5406 7-10-8 **76**......(v) WilliamClarke[(5)] 5 72
(Gary Moore) *t.k.h: chsd ldrs tl wnt 2nd 7f out: rdn 3f out: clsd and wl in tch whn bmpd 2f out: sn outpcd and btn 3rd 1f out: lost 3rd and wknd ins fnl f* **11/2**

1166 **5** 3 **Roy Rocket (FR)**[32] 4785 6-10-9 **72**...... MrRBirkett 2 63
(John Berry) *stdd s: hld up in rr: rdn: clsd and swtchd lft 3f out: 5th and no ex over 1f out: wknd ins fnl f* **16/1**

/000 **6** 1 1/2 **Pasaka Boy**[59] 3861 6-11-3 **83**...... MrJHarding[(3)] 8 72
(Jonathan Portman) *hld up in midfield: dropped to rr and rdn over 2f out: no ch w ldrs after: plugged on to pass btn horses ins fnl f* **8/1**

04-5 **7** 1 3/4 **Leyland (IRE)**[7] 5708 7-9-11 **65** oh12...... MrWillPettis[(5)] 9 51
(Natalie Lloyd-Beavis) *sn led and wnt clr: rdn over 2f out: hdd over 1f out and sn btn: wknd fnl f* **100/1**

5004 **8** 2 3/4 **Bohemian Rhapsody (IRE)**[20] 5262 7-10-4 **72**...... MrHHunt[(5)] 3 54
(Brendan Powell) *chsd ldr tl 7f out: styd chsng ldrs: rdn and unable qck 3f out: sn lost pl and wknd over 1f out* **14/1**

-200 **9** 1 1/4 **Diamond Joel**[9] 5642 4-11-1 **78**...... MrDHDunsdon 6 58
(Mick Channon) *stdd s: hld up in last pair: bhd 5f out: pushed along and no hdwy over 1f out: sn wknd* **20/1**

1211 **10** nse **Ickymasho**[14] 5489 4-11-7 **84**...... MrPWMullins 1 64
(Jonathan Portman) *chsd ldrs: rdn over 2f out: no rspnse and sn btn: wknd over 1f out* **7/2**[2]

2m 41.53s (2.63) **Going Correction** +0.025s/f (Good) **10** Ran SP% **117.9**
Speed ratings (Par 105): **92,91,87,86,84 83,82,80,79,79**
CSF £53.72 CT £197.60 TOTE £4.50: £2.30, £4.50, £1.20; EX 48.50 Trifecta £434.00.
Owner The Pro-Claimers **Bred** Chasemore Farm **Trained** Settrington, N Yorks

FOCUS
This was run over 20yds further than advertised. A fair handicap.

5964 STANLEY WOOTTON H'CAP 1m 2f 18y
4:55 (4:59) (Class 3) (0-90,90) 3-Y-O+
£8,715 (£2,609; £1,304; £652; £326; £163) **Stalls** Low

Form RPR

4125 **1** **Innocent Touch (IRE)**[23] 5173 5-10-0 **90**...... TonyHamilton 7 99
(Richard Fahey) *chsd ldrs: clsd to join ldrs and gng strly over 2f out: led 2f out: rdn over 1f out: kpt on and a doing enough ins fnl f: rdn out* **8/1**[3]

5434 **2** 1 **Sennockian Star**[9] 5651 6-9-7 **83**......(b) SilvestreDeSousa 2 90
(Mark Johnston) *chsd ldrs: rdn to join ldrs over 2f out: drvn and unable qck over 1f out: 3rd and one pce ins fnl f: rallied: swtchd rt wl ins fnl f: kpt on again to go 2nd nr fin* **2/1**[1]

1-01 **3** 1/2 **Interconnection**[108] 2214 5-10-0 **90**......(p) GeorgeBaker 6 96+
(Ed Vaughan) *hld up in tch: swtchd rt and effrt on outer over 2f out: rdn to chse ldrs and edging lft over 1f out: wnt 2nd 1f out: one pce and a hld after: lost 2nd nr fin* **4/1**[2]

1565 **4** 6 **Daisy Boy (IRE)**[22] 5198 5-8-12 **77**......(t) AaronJones[(3)] 3 71
(Stuart Williams) *led for 2f: chsd ldr tl over 2f out: sn outpcd: wl hld 4th and no imp over 1f out* **12/1**

4036 **5** 1 3/4 **Solo Hunter**[54] 4026 5-9-9 **88**......(b) JosephineGordon[(3)] 1 79
(Martyn Meade) *dwlt and bustled along early: hld up in tch in midfield: rdn over 2f out: sn struggling: wknd wl over 1f out* **8/1**[3]

0052 **6** 2 **Croquembouche (IRE)**[16] 5405 7-9-7 **88**...... GeorgiaCox[(5)] 4 75
(Ed de Giles) *dwlt: rdn along and rcvrd to ld 8f out: rdn and hdd 2f out: sn btn and wknd over 1f out* **9/1**

3346 **7** nk **Plutocracy (IRE)**[23] 5145 6-9-11 **87**...... WilliamTwiston-Davies 5 73
(Gary Moore) *stdd s: hld up in rr: rdn 3f out: no hdwy and bhd over 1f out* **8/1**[3]

521 **8** 3/4 **Frozen Force (IRE)**[24] 5102 3-8-13 **83**......(p) JimCrowley 8 67
(Amanda Perrett) *hld up in last pair: effrt on outer over 2f out: sn btn: bhd over 1f out* **4/1**[2]

2m 8.38s (-1.32) **Going Correction** +0.025s/f (Good)
WFA 3 from 5yo+ 8lb **8** Ran SP% **124.4**
Speed ratings (Par 107): **106,105,104,100,98 97,96,96**
CSF £26.74 CT £78.98 TOTE £6.90: £2.00, £1.60, £1.60; EX 33.20 Trifecta £119.40.
Owner Nicholas Wrigley & Kevin Hart **Bred** B Kennedy **Trained** Musley Bank, N Yorks

FOCUS
This was run over 20yds further than advertised. A decent enough handicap.

5965 ISABELLA BEETON H'CAP 1m 114y
5:25 (5:28) (Class 4) (0-80,78) 3-Y-O+ **£6,469** (£1,925; £962; £481) **Stalls** Low

Form RPR

5312 **1** **Crowning Glory (FR)**[32] 4788 3-9-6 **77**...... FMBerry 7 86
(Ralph Beckett) *sn chsng ldr: rdn to ld over 1f out: styd on wl u.p ins fnl f: rdn out* **9/2**[3]

0221 **2** 1 1/4 **Ripoll (IRE)**[13] 5525 3-9-1 **72**......(t) JimCrowley 1 78
(Sylvester Kirk) *chsd ldrs: effrt on inner over 2f out: ev ch and clr w wnr over 1f out: no ex and one pce ins fnl f* **7/1**

2530 **3** 3/4 **Stardrifter**[38] 4611 4-9-9 **73**...... TonyHamilton 5 77
(Richard Fahey) *hld up in tch in midfield: effrt whn hmpd and lost pl 2f out: swtchd rt and rallied over 1f out: wnt 3rd ins fnl f: styd on: nt rch ldrs* **16/1**

-011 **4** 3/4 **Lorelina**[32] 4788 3-8-13 **73**...... EdwardGreatrex[(3)] 9 76
(Andrew Balding) *dwlt: sn bustled along and rcvrd to chse ldrs after 1f: rdn over 2f out: hung lft and unable qck over 1f out: kpt on again and swtchd rt wl ins fnl f* **3/1**[1]

1236 **5** 3/4 **Bakht A Rawan (IRE)**[51] 4138 4-9-12 **76**...... SilvestreDeSousa 10 77
(Stuart Kittow) *stdd and dropped in after s: hld up in last trio: swtchd rt and effrt on outer over 2f out: no imp tl hdwy 1f out: kpt on ins fnl f: no threat to ldrs* **5/1**

2412 **6** hd **Feed The Goater (FR)**[35] 4709 3-9-7 **78**...... SeanLevey 2 78
(Richard Hannon) *hld up in tch in midfield: effrt and edgd lft 2f out: no imp over 1f out: kpt on same pce ins fnl f* **7/2**[2]

2156 **7** 2 3/4 **Shifting Star (IRE)**[26] 5024 11-9-8 **72**......(vt) DannyBrock 6 66
(John Bridger) *sn led: rdn and hdd over 2f out: drvn: edgd lft and outpcd over 1f out: wknd ins fnl f* **33/1**

3004 **8** 4 **Lunar Deity**[17] 5374 7-9-6 **70**...... HarryBentley 3 55
(Stuart Williams) *hld up in midfield: clsd 3f out: swtchd lft 2f out: carried lft: nt clr run and lost any ch over 1f out: pushed along and no hdwy fnl f* **16/1**

132 **9** 3 **Giovanni Di Bicci**[8] 5674 4-9-8 **72**......(t) GeorgeBaker 8 50
(Jim Boyle) *stdd s: hld up in last trio: clsd 3f out: swtchd lft and effrt 2f out: nt clr run and lost any ch over 1f out: nt pushed after* **14/1**

050- **10** 100 **The Dancing Lord**[290] 7837 7-9-3 **72**......(t[1]) HectorCrouch[(5)] 4
(Adam West) *hld up in rr: hmpd after 1f: lost tch 3f out: heavily eased fnl f: t.o* **33/1**

1m 45.99s (-0.11) **Going Correction** +0.025s/f (Good)
WFA 3 from 4yo+ 7lb **10** Ran SP% **118.9**
Speed ratings (Par 105): **101,99,99,98,97 97,95,91,89,**
CSF £36.89 CT £470.75 TOTE £5.00: £2.10, £2.20, £4.70; EX 40.00 Trifecta £658.10.
Owner The Eclipse Partnership **Bred** Car Colston Hall Stud **Trained** Kimpton, Hants

FOCUS
This was run over 20yds further than advertised. They didn't go that quick so it paid to be handy.
T/Plt: £56.10 to a £1 stake. Pool: £88,753.98 - 1154.63 winning units T/Qpdt: £30.70 to a £1 stake. Pool: £4,336.07 - 104.3 winning units **Steve Payne**

5839 NEWCASTLE (A.W) (L-H)
Monday, August 29

OFFICIAL GOING: Tapeta: standard
Wind: Fresh, half against Weather: Sunny, warm

5966 VERTEM.CO.UK/EBF IRISH STALLION FARMS MAIDEN STKS (PLUS 10 RACE) 7f 14y (Tp)
12:45 (12:47) (Class 4) 2-Y-O **£4,269** (£1,270; £634; £317) **Stalls** Centre

Form RPR

1 3/4 **Mushaireb** 2-9-5 0...... DavidNolan 9 82+
(Richard Fahey) *in tch: effrt and hdwy over 1f out: pressing wnr whn carried lft and hmpd ins fnl f: swtchd rt: kpt on fin: fin 2nd: awrdd the r* **9/2**[2]

2 **Sincil Bank (USA)** 2-9-5 0...... JoeFanning 14 82+
(David Simcock) *hld up in tch on nr side of gp: smooth hdwy to ld 2f out: drifted lft fnl f: kpt on strly: fin 1st disqualified and plcd 2nd* **3/1**[1]

3 1 1/2 **Suspect Package (USA)** 2-9-5 0...... FrederikTylicki 4 76
(James Fanshawe) *hld up: pushed along over 2f out: hdwy to chse ldng pair ins fnl f: kpt on: nt pce to chal* **9/1**

05 **4** 2 1/2 **Yarmouk (FR)**[23] 5150 2-9-5 0...... GrahamLee 6 69
(Richard Fahey) *cl up: drvn along over 2f out: checked briefly appr fnl f: kpt on same pce* **5/1**[3]

2 **5** 2 **Sugar Beach (FR)**[13] 5516 2-9-0 0...... PJMcDonald 13 59
(Ann Duffield) *midfield: drvn along over 2f out: effrt over 1f out: sn no imp* **6/1**

5 **6** 3/4 **Ladofash**[68] 3516 2-9-5 0...... BenCurtis 11 62
(K R Burke) *w ldrs tl rdn and wknd over 1f out* **9/1**

0 **7** 1 1/4 **Atrafan (IRE)**[14] 5477 2-9-5 0...... GrahamGibbons 5 58
(Alan Brown) *s.i.s: hld up: rdn over 2f out: kpt on fr over 1f out: no imp* **66/1**

00 **8** nk **Shakabula (IRE)**[25] 5067 2-9-0 0...... CallumShepherd[(5)] 10 57
(Brian Ellison) *hld up: rdn and outpcd over 3f out: rallied over 1f out: kpt on: n.d* **50/1**

9 1 **Plage Depampelonne** 2-9-0 0...... AndrewElliott 3 50
(James Bethell) *early reminders in rr: rdn and hung lft over 2f out: nvr able to chal* **33/1**

4 **10** 4 **Moonlight Blue (IRE)**[37] 4642 2-9-5 0...... PaulMulrennan 8 44
(Michael Dods) *led to over 2f out: rdn and wknd over 1f out* **7/1**

54 **11** 8 **Vocalisation (IRE)**[30] 4890 2-9-0 0...... CamHardie 7 17
(John Weymes) *t.k.h: trckd ldrs tl rdn and wknd over 2f out* **40/1**

12 5 **Balance Sheet (IRE)** 2-9-5 0...... JackGarritty 12 9
(Jedd O'Keeffe) *midfield: drvn along 1/2-way: wknd over 2f out* **22/1**

13 1/2 **With Intent** 2-9-2 0...... JacobButterfield[(3)] 2 7
(Ollie Pears) *missed break and detached: nvr on terms* **66/1**

14 8 **Kallisto Freedom (IRE)** 2-9-0 0...... AndrewMullen 1
(Philip Kirby) *prom: drvn along 1/2-way: sn lost pl and struggling* **66/1**

1m 28.88s (2.68) **Going Correction** +0.30s/f (Slow) **14** Ran SP% **122.8**
Speed ratings (Par 96): **95,96,93,90,88 87,86,85,84,79 70,65,64,55**
CSF £17.99 TOTE £4.80: £2.10, £1.80, £3.70; EX 22.60 Trifecta £203.10.
Owner Al Shaqab Racing **Bred** Lordship Stud **Trained** Musley Bank, N Yorks
■ Stewards' Enquiry : Joe Fanning two-day ban: careless riding (12-13 Sept)

FOCUS
First of eight races on the Tapeta. A wide open maiden in which the first three home were all newcomers. The original result was reversed in the stewards' room, despite the winning distance being three-quarters of a length. The fourth sets the level.

5967 VERTEMAM TWITTER BLAYDON RACE NURSERY H'CAP 1m 5y (Tp)
1:15 (1:18) (Class 2) 2-Y-O **£16,819** (£5,005; £2,501; £1,250) **Stalls** Centre

Form RPR

5116 **1** **Bongrace (IRE)**[16] 5407 2-8-4 **74**...... ShaneGray 7 80
(Kevin Ryan) *hld up: gd hdwy on nr side of gp to ld over 1f out: edgd lft: rdn and r.o wl fnl f* **20/1**

41 **2** 2 1/2 **Temerity (IRE)**[35] 4699 2-8-8 **83** ow1...... AdamMcNamara[(5)] 8 83
(Richard Fahey) *hld up in tch: hdwy nr side of gp to ld briefly 2f out: edgd lft ins fnl f: kpt on same pce* **4/1**[2]

61 **3** nk **George Reme (IRE)**[37] 4642 2-8-9 **79**...... JackGarritty 2 78
(John Quinn) *prom on far side of gp: effrt and rdn 2f out: hung rt ins fnl f: kpt on: no pce to chal* **7/1**[3]

5223 **4** 4 **Major Cornwallis (IRE)**[25] 5081 2-8-2 **72**...... PatrickMathers 4 62
(Richard Fahey) *prom: drvn and outpcd over 2f out: plugged on fnl f: kpt on: nvr rchd ldrs* **14/1**

1211 **5** 3/4 **Permian (IRE)**[13] 5519 2-9-7 **91**...... JoeFanning 1 79
(Mark Johnston) *led on far side of gp to 2f out: rdn and wknd appr fnl f* **5/2**[1]

21 **6** 2 1/2 **Roar (IRE)**[76] 3248 2-8-8 **78**............ BenCurtis 9 61
(Brian Ellison) *hld up: drvn and outpcd on nr side of gp over 3f out: no imp fr 2f out* **8/1**

013 **7** 1 **Riviere Argentee (FR)**[27] 5005 2-8-8 **85**............ CliffordLee(7) 6 65
(K R Burke) *chsd ldrs: rdn over 3f out: rallied: wknd over 1f out* **16/1**

3023 **8** 3 1/4 **Good Time Ahead (IRE)**[20] 5271 2-8-5 **75**............ AndrewMullen 5 48
(Philip Kirby) *cl up tl rdn and wknd over 1f out* **33/1**

142 **9** hd **Proud Archi (IRE)**[13] 5518 2-8-11 **81**............ PaulMulrennan 3 53
(Michael Dods) *t.k.h: cl up: rdn and ev ch over 2f out: wknd over 1f out* **4/1**[2]

1m 41.27s (2.67) **Going Correction** +0.30s/f (Slow) **9** Ran SP% **112.4**
Speed ratings (Par 100): **98,95,95,91,90 87,86,83,83**
CSF £95.43 CT £627.83 TOTE £22.90: £4.40, £1.80, £2.40; EX 120.60 Trifecta £1980.70.
Owner Bongrace Partners **Bred** Mrs Celine Collins **Trained** Hambleton, N Yorks

FOCUS
A good quality nursery featuring several promising maiden winners, but it was won by the most exposed runner in the field, which rather takes the gloss of the form. It has been rated around the placed horses.

5968 INVESTING FOR THE FUTURE H'CAP (DIV I) 6f (Tp)
1:45 (1:45) (Class 5) (0-75,76) 3-Y-O+ **£5,175** (£1,540; £769; £384) **Stalls** Centre

Form RPR

3032 **1** **Mazzini**[31] 4835 3-9-7 **75**............ FrederikTylicki 8 88+
(James Fanshawe) *hld up: pushed along and hdwy over 1f out: rdn to ld ins fnl f: kpt on wl* **2/1**[2]

3003 **2** 3/4 **Kenny The Captain (IRE)**[28] 4932 5-8-13 **67**..... RachelRichardson(3) 2 78
(Tim Easterby) *taken early to post: led: rdn and edgd rt over 1f out: hdd ins fnl f: kpt on same pce* **7/1**[3]

5451 **3** 1/2 **War Department (IRE)**[3] 5845 3-9-8 **76** 6ex............(v) GrahamGibbons 6 85
(Keith Dalgleish) *hld up in tch: pushed along over 2f out: hdwy over 1f out: effrt and ch ins fnl f: kpt on same pce* **5/4**[1]

0100 **4** 6 **Slingsby**[17] 5367 5-9-4 **69**............(b) CamHardie 4 59
(Michael Easterby) *pressed ldr: drvn along over 2f out: wknd ins fnl f* **22/1**

4010 **5** 1 1/4 **Classic Flyer**[10] 5605 4-8-12 **68**............(v) JoshDoyle(5) 5 54
(David O'Meara) *chsd ldrs: drvn along over 2f out: wknd over 1f out* **25/1**

552 **6** 1/2 **Tom Sawyer**[17] 5369 8-8-9 **65** ow1............(b) AdamMcNamara(5) 1 49
(Julie Camacho) *s.i.s: sn prom: rdn over 2f out: wknd over 1f out* **14/1**

3060 **7** hd **Burning Blaze**[3] 5845 6-9-10 **75**............ BenCurtis 3 59
(Brian Ellison) *missed break: hld up: rdn on far side of gp over 2f out: sn no imp* **25/1**

400 **8** 3/4 **Questo**[25] 5069 4-8-12 **63**............ RoystonFfrench 9 44
(Tracy Waggott) *prom: rdn along wl over 1f out: wknd fnl f* **25/1**

5000 **9** 4 1/2 **Mr Chuckles (IRE)**[54] 4007 3-8-6 **60**............ AndrewMullen 7 27
(Philip Kirby) *hld up in tch: drvn and outpcd over 2f out: sn btn* **50/1**

1200 **10** 1/2 **Oriental Splendour (IRE)**[19] 5295 4-9-7 **72**............ JamesSullivan 10 37
(Ruth Carr) *t.k.h: hld up: rdn over 1f out: sn wknd* **25/1**

1m 12.49s (-0.01) **Going Correction** +0.30s/f (Slow)
WFA 3 from 4yo+ 3lb **10** Ran SP% **118.6**
Speed ratings (Par 103): **112,111,110,102,100 100,99,98,92,92**
CSF £14.73 CT £24.55 TOTE £3.40: £1.30, £2.60, £1.10; EX 20.00 Trifecta £35.90.
Owner Mr & Mrs P Hopper, Mr & Mrs M Morris **Bred** Jan & Peter Hopper **Trained** Newmarket, Suffolk

FOCUS
Not a race of much depth and the front three, two of whom were the 'right' horses in terms of recent form, pulled nicely clear and all look capable of winning more races.

5969 INVESTING FOR THE FUTURE H'CAP (DIV II) 6f (Tp)
2:15 (2:15) (Class 5) (0-75,75) 3-Y-O+ **£5,175** (£1,540; £769; £384) **Stalls** Centre

Form RPR

0002 **1** **Master Bond**[41] 4495 7-9-9 **74**............ DavidNolan 5 82
(David O'Meara) *trckd ldrs: rdn to ld appr fnl f: kpt on wl* **5/1**[3]

3620 **2** 1 1/4 **Semana Santa**[14] 5478 3-9-6 **74**............ GrahamGibbons 7 78
(David Barron) *dwlt: hld up: rdn over 2f out: hdwy to chse wnr ins fnl f: kpt on: hld nr fin* **10/1**

253 **3** 3/4 **More Beau (USA)**[15] 5439 5-9-3 **68**............ BarryMcHugh 9 70
(David Nicholls) *t.k.h: cl up: effrt and led briefly over 1f out: rdn and no ex ins fnl f* **5/2**[1]

0036 **4** hd **Mercers Row**[7] 5714 9-8-11 **62**............ FrederikTylicki 2 63
(Michael Herrington) *hld up: rdn over 2f out: hdwy over 1f out: kpt on u.p ins fnl f* **11/1**

1121 **5** nk **Laila Honiwillow**[30] 4861 3-9-7 **75**............ JackGarritty 1 75
(Jedd O'Keeffe) *w ldr: rdn over 2f out: no ex ins fnl f* **4/1**[2]

-500 **6** 5 **Royal Mezyan (IRE)**[45] 4360 5-9-8 **73**............(e[1]) JoeFanning 6 57
(Henry Spiller) *led to over 1f out: sn rdn: wknd ins fnl f* **8/1**

0025 **7** 4 **Aprovado (IRE)**[7] 5714 4-9-4 **69**............(p) PaulMulrennan 8 40
(Michael Dods) *hld up in tch: effrt and rdn over 2f out: wknd over 1f out* **8/1**

0163 **8** 3 1/4 **Searanger (USA)**[17] 5370 3-8-13 **67**............ JoeyHaynes 3 28
(Rebecca Menzies) *prom: drvn along over 2f out: wknd over 1f out* **16/1**

0000 **9** 1 **Murdanova (IRE)**[7] 5714 3-9-0 **68**............[1] RyanPowell 4 26
(Kevin Frost) *hld up: drvn along over 2f out: hung lft and wknd wl over 1f out* **28/1**

1m 13.73s (1.23) **Going Correction** +0.30s/f (Slow)
WFA 3 from 4yo+ 3lb **9** Ran SP% **114.2**
Speed ratings (Par 103): **103,101,100,100,99 93,87,83,82**
CSF £53.06 CT £153.49 TOTE £7.00: £2.30, £2.90, £1.10; EX 48.00 Trifecta £147.60.
Owner Bonded Twentyten Partnership **Bred** Bond Thoroughbred Corporation **Trained** Upper Helmsley, N Yorks

FOCUS
An open but modest handicap and the time was over a second slower than the first division. The winner has been rated to this year's form.

5970 VERTEM MANAGEMENT H'CAP 2m 56y (Tp)
2:50 (2:50) (Class 5) (0-75,74) 4-Y-O+ **£3,881** (£1,155; £577; £288) **Stalls** Low

Form RPR

6005 **1** **Wor Lass**[12] 5541 8-8-11 **69**............ AnnaHesketh(5) 4 79+
(Susan Corbett) *prom: hdwy to ld over 2f out: sn pushed along and clr: edgd lft and kpt on wl fnl f: unchal* **14/1**

0524 **2** 6 **Next Edition (IRE)**[13] 5522 8-8-5 **63**............ PhilDennis(5) 6 66
(Philip Kirby) *stdd in last pl: smooth hdwy over 2f out: rdn to chse (clr) wnr over 1f out: sn no imp* **7/1**

4343 **3** 2 1/4 **Chebsey Beau**[25] 5061 6-9-0 **72**............ AdamMcNamara(5) 5 72
(John Quinn) *trckd ldr: rdn along over 2f out: outpcd fr over 1f out* **11/4**[2]

-633 **4** 7 **Rocktherunway (IRE)**[15] 5435 7-9-2 **69**............(p) PaulMulrennan 2 61
(Michael Dods) *t.k.h early: trckd ldrs: rdn over 2f out: wknd 2f out* **7/2**[3]

1213 **5** 1 1/4 **Megara**[197] 583 4-9-7 **74**............(p) RyanPowell 3 64
(Sir Mark Prescott Bt) *led at ordinary gallop: rdn and hdd over 2f out: wknd over 1f out* **9/4**[1]

5342 **6** 5 **Bowdler's Magic**[27] 4971 9-8-12 **65**............ PatrickMathers 1 49
(David Thompson) *s.i.s: hld up: struggling 3f out: sn wknd* **8/1**

3m 37.02s (1.82) **Going Correction** +0.20s/f (Slow) **6** Ran SP% **109.9**
Speed ratings (Par 103): **103,100,98,95,94 92**
CSF £97.66 TOTE £15.30: £6.30, £3.90; EX 81.90 Trifecta £385.80.
Owner Les Dodds **Bred** L Dodds **Trained** Otterburn, Northumberland

FOCUS
An ordinary staying handicap notable for the impressive way the winner burst clear and put the race to bed.

5971 FRESH APPROACH AT VERTEM H'CAP 1m 4f 98y (Tp)
3:25 (3:26) (Class 6) (0-60,60) 3-Y-O+ **£3,234** (£962; £481; £240) **Stalls** High

Form RPR

0445 **1** **The Resdev Way**[14] 5480 3-8-8 **50**............ BarryMcHugh 8 61
(Richard Whitaker) *hld up in midfield on outside: gd hdwy to ld 1f out: pushed out fnl f: comf* **7/1**[3]

0220 **2** 2 1/4 **Kicking The Can (IRE)**[25] 5064 5-10-0 **60**............ PatrickMathers 14 67
(David Thompson) *pressed ldr: led over 3f out to 1f out: rallied: kpt on same pce last 100yds* **11/2**[2]

0603 **3** 7 **Breton Blues**[17] 5366 6-9-5 **51**............(p) CamHardie 9 47
(Fred Watson) *hld up on outside: hdwy on outside over 2f out: chsd clr ldng pair over 1f out: kpt on same pce fnl f* **20/1**

3 **4** 3/4 **Operateur (IRE)**[58] 3901 8-9-8 **54**............ PaulMulrennan 12 49
(Ben Haslam) *prom: rdn along over 2f out: outpcd fnl f* **16/1**

5406 **5** 1 1/4 **Solid Justice (IRE)**[18] 5319 5-9-2 **48**............ JoeyHaynes 2 41
(Kenny Johnson) *dwlt: hld up: rdn along 3f out: hdwy over 1f out: kpt on fnl f: nvr able to chal* **20/1**

1560 **6** 1 1/4 **Mcvicar**[14] 5481 7-9-7 **60**............(p) PatrickVaughan(7) 5 51
(John Davies) *hld up in midfield: rdn over 2f out: kpt on fnl f: nvr able to chal* **11/1**

44-0 **7** 1 **Stamp Duty (IRE)**[25] 5064 8-8-11 **46** oh1............ JacobButterfield(3) 11 35
(Suzzanne France) *dwlt: hld up in midfield: rdn and effrt over 2f out: wknd appr fnl f* **33/1**

32-5 **8** 1 3/4 **Bold Henmie (IRE)**[16] 2343 5-9-10 **56**............(p) AndrewMullen 4 42
(Philip Kirby) *t.k.h early: in tch: rdn over 2f out: wknd over 1f out* **7/2**[1]

-266 **9** 1/2 **Highfield Lass**[21] 5228 5-8-10 **47**............ PhilDennis(5) 7 33
(Michael Dods) *t.k.h: trckd ldrs: rdn and ev ch 2f out: wknd fnl f* **7/1**[3]

5120 **10** 3/4 **Whitchurch**[14] 5481 4-9-2 **53**............(p) GarryWhillans(5) 13 37
(Philip Kirby) *hld up: hdwy on outside over 3f out: rdn over 2f out: wknd over 1f out* **11/1**

0544 **11** 5 **Latin Rebel (IRE)**[11] 5580 9-8-12 **49**............(p) AdamMcNamara(5) 6 25
(Jim Goldie) *bhd: struggling over 3f out: nvr on terms* **9/1**

0326 **12** 3/4 **Gunner Lindley (IRE)**[23] 5155 9-9-13 **59**............ GrahamLee 1 34
(Stuart Coltherd) *led to over 3f out: rdn and wknd fr 2f out* **11/1**

6000 **13** 4 1/2 **Outback Guy (IRE)**[16] 5604 3-8-5 **52**............ RowanScott(5) 10 20
(Kevin Frost) *trckd ldrs tl rdn and wknd over 2f out* **66/1**

646/ **14** 99 **Goodlukin Lucy**[864] 1567 9-8-8 **47**............ CliffordLee(7) 3
(Gemma Anderson) *t.k.h in midfield: struggling 1/2-way: lost tch fnl 4f: t.o* **25/1**

2m 43.26s (2.16) **Going Correction** +0.20s/f (Slow)
WFA 3 from 4yo+ 10lb **14** Ran SP% **121.3**
Speed ratings (Par 101): **100,98,93,93,92 91,91,89,89,89 85,85,82,16**
CSF £42.68 CT £751.78 TOTE £7.00: £2.50, £2.20, £8.40; EX 51.30 Trifecta £1517.70.
Owner Resdev **Bred** Mickley Stud **Trained** Scarcroft, W Yorks

■ Stewards' Enquiry : Joey Haynes jockey said gelding hung left in the straight
Rowan Scott three-day ban: careless riding (12-14 September)

FOCUS
A very weak handicap but the front two pulled a long way clear and the winner, a 3yo who is completely unexposed over this trip, looks one to follow.

5972 PROTECTING YOUR WEALTH CLAIMING STKS 1m 5y (Tp)
4:00 (4:00) (Class 6) 3-Y-O+ **£2,911** (£866; £432; £216) **Stalls** Centre

Form RPR

2343 **1** **Kiwi Bay**[19] 5291 11-9-11 73............ PaulMulrennan 6 78
(Michael Dods) *hld up in tch stands' side: hdwy to ld over 1f out: rdn fnl f: kpt on* **4/1**[3]

0024 **2** 1 **Inshaa**[17] 5367 4-9-5 65............(p) GrahamLee 10 70
(Michael Herrington) *led against stands' rail: rdn and hdd over 1f out: rallied: kpt on same pce towards fin* **3/1**[1]

0010 **3** 2 3/4 **Broctune Papa Gio**[17] 5367 9-8-12 65............ CliffordLee(7) 2 63
(Keith Reveley) *prom centre: effrt and rdn 2f out: kpt on same pce ins fnl f* **10/1**

050 **4** nk **Nonno Giulio (IRE)**[14] 5482 5-9-4 73............ JoshDoyle(5) 5 67
(David Loughnane) *cl up stands' side: rdn over 2f out: edgd lft and outpcd over 1f out: kpt on fnl f* **7/2**[2]

04-0 **5** 1 **Devious Spirit (IRE)**[104] 2345 4-8-12 66............ AdamMcNamara(5) 8 58
(Richard Fahey) *cl up centre: rdn over 2f out: no ex fr over 1f out* **4/1**[3]

-000 **6** 1 **Exclusive Waters (IRE)**[33] 4768 6-9-0 56............ PhilDennis(5) 1 58
(George Charlton) *in tch centre: drvn and edgd lft over 2f out: sn outpcd: no imp fr over 1f out* **20/1**

0444 **7** 2 3/4 **Border Bandit (USA)**[7] 5729 8-9-1 52............(p) RoystonFfrench 11 48
(Tracy Waggott) *dwlt: hld up in tch stands' side: rdn and hung lft 2f out: sn btn* **12/1**

1015 **8** 10 **Just Be Lucky (IRE)**[22] 5191 4-9-13 80............(p) DavidNolan 12 37
(Conor Dore) *cl up stands' side tl rdn and wknd 2f out* **7/1**

0300 **9** 21 **Bahrikate**[12] 5537 3-8-2 45............[1] JamesSullivan 9
(Michael Herrington) *cl up centre: lost pl 3f out: sn struggling: t.o* **50/1**

0040 **10** 11 **Canford Kilbey (IRE)**[17] 5355 3-8-4 46............ PatrickMathers 4
(Michael Easterby) *rrd in stalls: hld up centre: struggling over 3f out: sn lost tch: t.o* **50/1**

1m 41.66s (3.06) **Going Correction** +0.30s/f (Slow)
WFA 3 from 4yo+ 6lb **10** Ran SP% **125.2**
Speed ratings (Par 101): **96,95,92,91,90 89,87,77,56,45**
CSF £17.60 TOTE £4.40: £1.60, £1.90, £4.00; EX 15.40 Trifecta £198.90.
Owner Kiwi Racing **Bred** Templeton Stud **Trained** Denton, Co Durham

FOCUS
Mostly exposed types in this claimer and the winner is into the veteran stage of his career, but he clearly still has plenty to offer at this level. The runner-up's recent C&D form sets the level.

5973 PERFECT PARTNERSHIPS FILLIES' H'CAP — 7f 14y (Tp)
4:35 (4:36) (Class 5) (0-75,74) 3-Y-O+ **£4,851** (£1,443; £721; £360) **Stalls** Centre

Form RPR

453 **1** **Gleaming Girl**[22] 5190 4-9-4 **73** SophieKilloran(7) 6 82
(David Simcock) *dwlt: hld up: pushed along nr side of gp over 2f out: qcknd to ld over 1f out: edgd rt ins fnl f: kpt on wl* **7/1**

0541 **2** *1 ½* **Barwah (USA)**[3] 5844 5-9-2 **64** 6ex AndrewMullen 9 69
(Peter Niven) *chsd ldrs on nr side of gp: effrt and rdn over 2f out: chsd wnr ins fnl f: kpt on* **4/1**[2]

1-34 **3** *2 ¾* **Balance**[27] 4985 3-9-0 **72** AdamMcNamara(5) 3 68
(Richard Fahey) *prom: hdwy to press wnr over 1f out: one pce and lost 2nd pl ins fnl f* **4/1**[2]

0515 **4** *4 ½* **Bint Arcano (FR)**[38] 4605 3-9-4 **74** JacobButterfield(3) 5 57
(Julie Camacho) *prom: ev ch over 2f out to over 1f out: rdn and wknd ins fnl f* **12/1**

4460 **5** *7* **Cabal**[13] 5521 9-9-4 **71** (p) PhilDennis(5) 8 37
(Geoffrey Harker) *hld up in tch on nr side of gp: drvn and outpcd over 2f out: n.d after* **33/1**

5300 **6** *4 ½* **Smirnova (IRE)**[3] 5843 3-8-4 **57** JoeyHaynes 2 9
(Kenny Johnson) *hld up in tch: rdn along over 2f out: sn btn* **50/1**

0312 **7** *4 ½* **Emblaze**[7] 5717 4-9-1 **63** PaulMulrennan 10 5
(Bryan Smart) *led on nr side of gp tl edgd lft and hdd over 1f out: sn wknd* **6/1**[3]

3002 **8** *3 ½* **Flinty Fell (IRE)**[3] 5844 3-8-11 **64** GrahamGibbons 1
(Keith Dalgleish) *hld up in tch: drvn along over 2f out: sn wknd* **9/4**[1]

610 **9** *8* **Connemera Queen**[77] 3213 3-9-3 **70** PatrickMathers 7
(Tracy Waggott) *chsd ldrs on outside of gp: drvn and lost pl over 2f out: sn btn* **25/1**

645 **10** *6* **Last Star Falling (IRE)**[21] 5248 3-8-10 **63** JoeFanning 4
(Henry Spiller) *cl up on outside of gp: drvn and struggling wl over 2f out: sn wknd* **20/1**

1m 27.89s (1.69) **Going Correction** +0.30s/f (Slow)
WFA 3 from 4yo+ 5lb **10** Ran SP% **118.8**
Speed ratings (Par 100): **102,100,97,92,84 78,73,69,60,53**
CSF £34.46 CT £132.61 TOTE £8.90: £2.00, £1.20, £2.30; EX 34.30 Trifecta £145.40.
Owner Tick Tock Partnership **Bred** Rabbah Bloodstock Limited **Trained** Newmarket, Suffolk

FOCUS
Ordinary fillies' handicap form and the time was only a second or so quicker than the opening 2yo maiden.

T/Plt: £813.10 to a £1 stake. Pool: £61,154.14 - 54.9 winning units T/Qpdt: £95.20 to a £1 stake. Pool: £5,206.15, 40.46 winning units **Richard Young**

5516 RIPON (R-H)
Monday, August 29

OFFICIAL GOING: Good to soft (good in places; 7.7)
Wind: light across Weather: sunny

5974 ANDREW CAYGILL'S 60TH BIRTHDAY (S) STKS — 6f
2:10 (2:11) (Class 5) 2-Y-O **£3,067** (£905; £453) **Stalls** High

Form RPR

3033 **1** **Forster Square (IRE)**[17] 5351 2-9-2 59 PaulHanagan 1 62
(Richard Fahey) *hld up towards outer: pushed along and hdwy over 2f out: rdn to chal ent fnl f: led 110yds out: kpt on* **6/1**

6240 **2** *1 ½* **Coco La Belle (IRE)**[17] 5364 2-8-11 56 DavidAllan 6 53
(Tim Easterby) *led: rdn 2f out: edgd rt over 1f out: jnd ent fnl f: hdd 110yds out: one pce* **10/3**[3]

1644 **3** *½* **Chevalier Du Lac (IRE)**[63] 3707 2-9-7 78 JasonHart 2 61
(John Quinn) *s.i.s: hld up: pushed along and sme hdwy towards outer 2f out: swtchd lft appr fnl f: rdn and kpt on* **3/1**[2]

4644 **4** *3* **Smiley Riley (IRE)**[17] 5351 2-9-2 58 TomEaves 3 47
(Tony Coyle) *trckd ldrs: rdn over 2f out: wknd ins fnl f* **20/1**

6665 **5** *¾* **Gerrard's Return**[12] 5543 2-9-2 68 [1] RichardKingscote 8 45
(Tom Dascombe) *dwlt and stmbld sltly s: hld up: rdn over 1f out: no imp* **2/1**[1]

650 **6** *2 ½* **Gold Patch (IRE)**[20] 5271 2-8-11 57 NathanEvans(5) 5 37
(Michael Easterby) *trckd ldrs: racd keenly: rdn over 2f out: wknd appr fnl f* **16/1**

6656 **7** *1 ¼* **Lavender Skye (IRE)**[4] 5799 2-8-11 45 FrannyNorton 4 29
(K R Burke) *prom: rdn over 2f out: wknd over 1f out* **25/1**

0656 **8** *½* **Geego**[24] 5112 2-9-2 54 GeorgeChaloner 9 32
(Richard Fahey) *trckd ldrs: rdn over 2f out: wknd over 1f out* **16/1**

00 **9** *11* **Henrietta's Dream**[21] 5242 2-8-11 0 JoeDoyle 7
(John Wainwright) *s.i.s: hld up in rr: sn pushed along: bhd fr 1/2-way* **150/1**

1m 14.24s (1.24) **Going Correction** +0.075s/f (Good) **9** Ran SP% **116.7**
Speed ratings (Par 94): **94,92,91,87,86 83,81,80,66**
CSF £26.20 TOTE £9.00: £2.00, £1.10, £2.10; EX 31.20 Trifecta £74.00.
Owner Tiffin Sandwiches Limited **Bred** Thomas Jones **Trained** Musley Bank, N Yorks

FOCUS
Rail on bend from back straight to home straight dolled out by 3yds, adding 6yds to races on the round course. This was a typically weak 2yo seller rated as par for the grade.

5975 GLYNN IAN GILBERT MEMORIAL H'CAP — 1m 1f 170y
2:45 (2:46) (Class 5) (0-75,74) 3-Y-O **£3,234** (£962; £481; £240) **Stalls** Low

Form RPR

4534 **1** **Carnageo (FR)**[23] 5154 3-9-7 **74** GeorgeChaloner 2 80
(Richard Fahey) *dwlt: sn midfield towards inner: rdn over 2f out: hdwy over 1f out: led narrowly 110yds out: kpt on* **5/1**[2]

-362 **2** *nk* **Shufoog**[38] 4607 3-9-5 **72** PaulHanagan 7 77
(William Haggas) *midfield: pushed along 3f out: briefly carried lft over 2f out: rdn and hdwy 2f out: chal ins fnl f: kpt on* **7/4**[1]

10-0 **3** *nk* **Rayaa**[120] 1890 3-9-4 **71** [1] TomQueally 4 76
(John Butler) *dwlt: hld up in rr: pushed along over 2f out: gd hdwy on outside over 1f out: chal 100yds out: kpt on* **40/1**

4554 **4** *1 ½* **Ronnie Baird**[17] 5365 3-9-3 **70** (b) FrannyNorton 1 72
(Kristin Stubbs) *led: rdn whn jnd 3f out: hdd 2f out: no ex ins fnl f* **9/1**

6603 **5** *¾* **Ride The Lightning**[63] 3728 3-9-6 **73** MichaelJMMurphy 8 73
(Archie Watson) *prom: rdn to chal 3f out: led narrowly 2f out: hdd 110yds out: wknd* **8/1**

4013 **6** *6* **Airton**[17] 5365 3-9-1 **68** PJMcDonald 9 56
(James Bethell) *hld up: rdn 3f out: nvr threatened* **10/1**

2114 **7** *1* **Causey Arch (IRE)**[48] 4241 3-9-7 **74** (p) ConnorBeasley 3 60
(Michael Dods) *trckd ldrs: rdn over 3f out: wknd over 1f out* **10/1**

0032 **8** *19* **Tiga Tuan (FR)**[25] 5057 3-8-10 **63** KevinStott 6 10
(Kevin Ryan) *trckd ldrs: rdn and edgd lft over 2f out: wknd 2f out* **16/1**

3050 **9** *2* **The King's Steed**[13] 5521 3-8-5 **65** LaurenSteade(7) 5 8
(Micky Hammond) *a towards rr* **100/1**

6-14 **10** *3 ½* **Angel Grace (IRE)**[125] 1759 3-9-7 **74** AdamKirby 10 10
(David Menuisier) *trckd ldrs towards outer: rdn over 4f out: wknd over 2f out* **7/1**[3]

2m 5.0s (-0.40) **Going Correction** +0.075s/f (Good) **10** Ran SP% **114.1**
Speed ratings (Par 100): **104,103,103,102,101 96,96,80,79,76**
CSF £13.75 CT £309.01 TOTE £6.20: £1.50, £1.20, £7.30; EX 17.10 Trifecta £966.30.
Owner The Up For Anything Syndicate **Bred** Viktor Timoshenko **Trained** Musley Bank, N Yorks

FOCUS
A modest 3yo handicap with the winner rated back to his June win here. Race distance increased by 6yds.

5976 RIPON ROWELS H'CAP — 1m
3:20 (3:21) (Class 2) (0-100,99) 3-Y-O+ **£12,602** (£3,772; £1,886; £944; £470) **Stalls** Low

Form RPR

4151 **1** **Treasury Notes (IRE)**[23] 5156 4-9-10 **97** DanielTudhope 5 106
(David O'Meara) *midfield: rdn over 2f out: angled lft and hdwy on outer 2f out: r.o: led post* **4/1**[1]

1-13 **2** *shd* **Knight Owl**[66] 3623 6-9-0 **92** GeorgeWood(5) 7 100
(James Fanshawe) *dwlt sltly: sn midfield: rdn 3f out: stdy hdwy fr 2f out: edgd ahd 50yds out: kpt on: hdd post* **7/1**[3]

0220 **3** *nk* **Two For Two (IRE)**[23] 5156 8-9-5 **92** (p) PJMcDonald 11 99
(David Loughnane) *midfield towards outer: rdn and hdwy 2f out: kpt on fnl f* **12/1**

5503 **4** *¾* **Father Bertie**[23] 5180 4-8-12 **85** (tp) DavidAllan 9 90
(Tim Easterby) *led: rdn 2f out: hdd 50yds out: no ex* **8/1**

3633 **5** *½* **Rousayan (IRE)**[16] 5419 5-8-12 **88** ShelleyBirkett(3) 13 92+
(David O'Meara) *hld up: pushed along whn short of room over 2f out: hdwy over 1f out: n.m.r again appr fnl f: kpt on ins fnl f: nrst fin* **14/1**

4313 **6** *½* **Home Cummins (IRE)**[34] 4737 4-9-5 **92** (p) PaulHanagan 1 95
(Richard Fahey) *trckd ldrs: rdn over 2f out: no ex ins fnl f* **5/1**[2]

2425 **7** *½* **Dubai Dynamo**[17] 5376 11-8-8 **86** NathanEvans(5) 6 88
(Ruth Carr) *dwlt: hld up in rr: rdn over 2f out: angled lft to outer and sme hdwy over 1f out: kpt on fnl f: nvr threatened ldrs* **14/1**

4010 **8** *½* **Chevallier**[58] 3910 4-9-1 **88** MichaelJMMurphy 12 89
(Archie Watson) *prom: rdn 2f out: wknd ins fnl f* **33/1**

5400 **9** *3* **Wilde Inspiration (IRE)**[30] 4894 5-9-0 **87** ConnorBeasley 4 81
(Julie Camacho) *trckd ldrs: rdn over 2f out: wknd fnl f* **7/1**[3]

0006 **10** *5* **Finn Class (IRE)**[21] 5226 5-8-13 **86** TomEaves 3 68
(Michael Dods) *midfield on inner: rdn 3f out: wknd over 1f out* **12/1**

450 **11** *nk* **Indy (IRE)**[2] 5886 5-8-12 **85** FrannyNorton 2 67
(David Barron) *dwlt: hld up: nvr threatened* **20/1**

61-0 **12** *nk* **Newstead Abbey**[16] 5389 6-9-12 **99** PhillipMakin 8 80
(David Barron) *midfield on outside: rdn over 3f out: wknd fnl 2f* **33/1**

2000 **13** *hd* **Off Art**[23] 5156 6-9-2 **89** (p) JasonHart 14 70
(Tim Easterby) *trckd ldrs: rdn over 3f out: sn lost pl: bhd fnl 2f* **16/1**

200- **14** *10* **Tres Coronas (IRE)**[451] 2899 9-9-9 **96** TomQueally 10 54
(David Barron) *a in rr* **40/1**

1m 40.17s (-1.23) **Going Correction** +0.075s/f (Good) **14** Ran SP% **120.5**
Speed ratings (Par 109): **109,108,108,107,107 106,106,105,102,97 97,97,97,87**
CSF £30.09 CT £324.20 TOTE £4.90: £1.60, £2.40, £3.90; EX 16.70 Trifecta £344.70.
Owner T Proctor **Bred** Ammerland Verwaltung Gmbh & Co Kg **Trained** Upper Helmsley, N Yorks

FOCUS
This was highly competitive and it threw up a cracking finish. Solid form with the winner continuing to progress. Race distance increased by 6yds.

5977 LONGINES IRISH CHAMPIONS WEEKEND EBF RIPON CHAMPION TWO YRS OLD TROPHY, 2016 (LISTED RACE) — 6f
3:55 (3:56) (Class 1) 2-Y-O
£17,013 (£6,450; £3,228; £1,608; £807; £405) **Stalls** High

Form RPR

311 **1** **Alicante Dawn**[38] 4602 2-9-3 88 ConnorBeasley 1 100
(Bryan Smart) *mde all: rdn clr over 1f out: kpt on wl* **7/2**[2]

013 **2** *2 ¼* **Private Matter**[25] 5058 2-9-3 86 PaulHanagan 6 93
(Richard Fahey) *trckd ldr: rdn 2f out: kpt on* **9/1**

004 **3** *1 ¾* **Grand Coalition (IRE)**[22] 5212 2-9-3 0 DanielTudhope 2 88
(J P Murtagh, Ire) *dwlt: sn hld up iin tch on outer: rdn over 2f out: one pce: wnt 3rd towards fin* **7/1**

213 **4** *½* **Kodiline (IRE)**[45] 4352 2-9-3 96 AdamKirby 5 87
(Clive Cox) *trckd ldr: rdn over 2f out: wknd ins fnl f* **10/11**[1]

1140 **5** *½* **Kocollada (IRE)**[37] 4623 2-8-12 89 GeorgeChaloner 4 80
(Richard Fahey) *hld up in tch: rdn over 2f out: no imp* **11/2**[3]

1126 **6** *8* **Racemaker**[3] 5833 2-9-3 74 NeilFarley 7 61
(Andrew Crook) *hld up: rdn 3f out: sn wknd* **100/1**

1m 12.81s (-0.19) **Going Correction** +0.075s/f (Good) **6** Ran SP% **113.5**
Speed ratings (Par 102): **104,101,98,98,97 86**
CSF £33.27 TOTE £3.80: £1.10, £3.40; EX 16.00 Trifecta £150.30.
Owner B Smart **Bred** Natton House Thoroughbreds **Trained** Hambleton, N Yorks

FOCUS
Not a strong 2yo Listed race, but the winner was building on his impressive nursery win with the runner-up the key to the form. It was run at a routine pace and the winner dictated.

5978 BILLY NEVETT MEMORIAL H'CAP — 6f
4:30 (4:32) (Class 4) (0-80,80) 3-Y-O **£4,851** (£1,443; £721; £360) **Stalls** High

Form RPR

P003 **1** **Penny Pot Lane**[7] 5714 3-8-0 **64** NathanEvans(5) 2 74
(Richard Whitaker) *prom: rdn to ld wl over 1f out: kpt on* **7/1**

2650 **2** *¾* **Bossipop**[9] 5643 3-9-7 **80** (p) DavidAllan 8 88
(Tim Easterby) *midfield: pushed along and hdwy over 1f out: bit tight for room ent fnl f: rdn to chse wnr fnl 110yds: kpt on* **7/2**[1]

3130 **3** *1 ½* **General Alexander (IRE)**[37] 4643 3-8-12 **78** (p) BenRobinson(7) 1 81
(Brian Ellison) *prom on outer: rdn over 2f out: no ex fnl 110yds* **10/1**

0403 **4** *2* **Athollblair Boy (IRE)**[12] 5537 3-8-10 **69** TomEaves 3 66
(Nigel Tinkler) *dwlt: midfield towards outer: rdn over 2f out: one pce* **12/1**

0334 **5** *hd* **Ponty Royale (IRE)**[13] 5525 3-8-0 **62** RachelRichardson(3) 6 58
(Tim Easterby) *dwlt: hld up: rdn over 2f out: kpt on ins fnl f: nvr threatened* **8/1**

0564 **6** 1/2 **Dodgy Bob**[23] 5161 3-8-13 **79**................................(b) LewisEdmunds[(7)] 7 74
(Kevin Ryan) *midfield: rdn over 2f out: no imp* **13/2**

-066 **7** 1 1/4 **Spike (IRE)**[15] 5439 3-8-11 **70**.. PhillipMakin 5 61
(David Barron) *hld up: nvr threatened* **10/1**

-14 **8** 3/4 **Ebony N Ivory**[79] 3137 3-9-5 **78**............................... MichaelJMMurphy 4 66
(Archie Watson) *led after 1f: rdn over 2f out: hdd wl over 1f out: wknd fnl f* **5/1**[2]

5331 **9** 3 1/2 **Wilde Extravagance (IRE)**[55] 3978 3-8-11 **70**..................... JoeDoyle 9 47
(Julie Camacho) *led for 1f: trckd ldr: rdn over 2f out: wknd over 1f out* **6/1**[3]

1m 12.57s (-0.43) **Going Correction** +0.075s/f (Good) **9** Ran SP% **116.0**
Speed ratings (Par 102): **105,104,102,99,99 98,96,95,91**
CSF £31.89 CT £248.71 TOTE £6.30: £2.30, £2.00, £4.00; EX 37.40 Trifecta £416.40.
Owner A Melville **Bred** Hellwood Stud Farm & G P Clarke **Trained** Scarcroft, W Yorks

FOCUS
A modest sprint handicap where it again paid to be handy. A personal best from the winner with the runner-up rated to form.

5979 ANDY TAYLOR'S 40TH BIRTHDAY SUPPORTING SIMONONTHESTREETS.CO.UK MAIDEN STKS 1m

5:05 (5:05) (Class 5) 3-4-Y-O **£2,911** (£866; £432; £216) **Stalls** Low

Form RPR

-332 **1** **Mujaamil**[17] 5380 3-9-5 80...(b[1]) PaulHanagan 6 66+
(William Haggas) *mde all: rdn and jnd over 2f out: kpt on ins fnl f* **2/5**[1]

0004 **2** 1 3/4 **Euro Mac**[23] 5178 4-9-1 50.. NathanEvans[(5)] 5 58
(Neville Bycroft) *trckd ldr: rdn to chal strly over 2f out: one pce ins fnl f* **18/1**[3]

3 1 1/2 **Aloysius Hansom** 3-9-5 0.. TomEaves 3 59
(Kevin Ryan) *s.i.s: hld up: pushed along and hdwy over 2f out: wnt 3rd over 1f out: kpt on one pce* **9/4**[2]

0- **4** 5 **Estrella Eria (FR)**[198] 571 3-8-11 0....................... MarcMonaghan[(3)] 1 42
(George Peckham) *trckd ldr: rdn 3f out: wknd over 1f out* **20/1**

5 **5** 15 **Python**[17] 5353 4-9-11 0.. NeilFarley 4 14
(Andrew Crook) *hld up: rdn over 3f out: sn wknd* **80/1**

1m 44.34s (2.94) **Going Correction** +0.075s/f (Good)
WFA 3 from 4yo 6lb **5** Ran SP% **113.5**
Speed ratings (Par 103): **88,86,84,79,64**
CSF £10.53 TOTE £1.30: £1.02, £5.00; EX 5.20 Trifecta £9.20.
Owner Hamdan Al Maktoum **Bred** Shadwell Estate Company Limited **Trained** Newmarket, Suffolk

FOCUS
An ordinary maiden with the runner-up the key to the level. Race distance increased by 6yds.

5980 BETFAIR NOVICE FLAT AMATEUR RIDERS' H'CAP (FOR NOVICE AMATEUR RIDERS) 1m 2f 190y

5:35 (5:35) (Class 6) (0-60,57) 4-Y-O+ **£2,807** (£870; £435; £217) **Stalls** Low

Form RPR

3006 **1** **Graceful Act**[14] 5481 8-10-9 **45**.. MissEEasterby 4 51
(Ron Barr) *trckd ldrs: jnd ldr 4f out: rdn over 2f out: kpt on: led post* **9/2**[2]

3413 **2** hd **Fillydelphia (IRE)**[28] 4934 5-11-7 **57**.............................. MissAMcCain 5 63
(Patrick Holmes) *dwlt: hld up: hdwy on outer to ld over 7f out: jnd 4f out: rdn over 2f out: kpt on: hdd post* **9/2**[2]

0002 **3** 1 1/2 **Mister Marcasite**[17] 5383 6-11-3 **53**..................................... MrMEnnis 6 56
(Antony Brittain) *trckd ldrs: rdn over 2f out: one pce* **5/1**[3]

0331 **4** 1/2 **Thello**[13] 5517 4-11-7 **57**... MrBLynn 2 59
(Nigel Tinkler) *hld up in tch: hdwy on outer to trck ldrs over 3f out: rdn over 2f out: sn one pce* **13/8**[1]

0040 **5** 10 **Togetherwecan (IRE)**[21] 5228 4-11-2 **52**...........(b) MissEmmaBedford 3 36
(Mark Johnston) *hld up in tch on inner: rdn 3f out: sn wknd* **12/1**

0005 **6** 1 1/2 **Fledermaus (IRE)**[17] 5383 6-10-6 **45**...................(t) MissBJohnson[(3)] 1 26
(Tina Jackson) *s.i.s: hld up: sme hdwy on outside over 4f out: rdn over 3f out: sn wknd* **18/1**

5010 **7** 1 1/4 **Eeny Mac (IRE)**[18] 5323 9-10-12 **48**..............................(p) MrJoeWright 7 27
(John Wainwright) *led: hdd over 7f out: trckd ldr: rdn over 4f out: wknd over 2f out* **16/1**

2m 26.28s (146.28) **7** Ran SP% **110.0**
CSF £22.88 TOTE £4.60: £2.50, £2.20; EX 23.90 Trifecta £119.50.
Owner D Thomson **Bred** Mayden Stud, J A And D S Dewhurst **Trained** Seamer, N Yorks

FOCUS
A moderate handicap, confined to novice amateur riders. Race distance increased by 6yds.
T/Jkpt: £39,304.40 to a £1 stake. Pool: £58,957.00 - 1.5 winning units. T/Plt: £76.30 to a £1 stake. Pool: £79,924.82 - 764.33 winning units T/Qpdt: £41.00 to a £1 stake. Pool: £4,162.75 - 75.0 winning units **Andrew Sheret**

5981 - 5984a (Foreign Racing) - See Raceform Interactive

[5944]DEAUVILLE (R-H)

Monday, August 29

OFFICIAL GOING: Turf: good; polytrack: standard

5985a PRIX DE SAINT-PIERRE AZIF (MAIDEN) (2YO COLTS & GELDINGS) (ROUND) (TURF) 1m (R)

11:25 (12:00) 2-Y-O **£9,191** (£3,676; £2,757; £1,838; £919)

RPR

1 **Neguev (IRE)**[20] 2-9-2 0.. IoritzMendizabal 1 83
(J-C Rouget, France) **2/5**[1]

2 1/2 **Manahir (FR)** 2-9-2 0... LukasDelozier 5 82
(H-A Pantall, France) **44/5**[3]

3 3 1/2 **Nile Paris (FR)**[20] 2-9-2 0.. MickaelBarzalona 3 73
(J-P Gallorini, France) **33/1**

4 3/4 **Dolokhov**[9] 5701 2-9-2 0...(p) TonyPiccone 7 72
(J S Moore) *broke wl and led: hdd after 1f and settled in midfield: 5th and scrubbed along 2 1/2f out: chsd ldrs fr 1 1/2f out: sn lft bhd: one pce ins fnl f* **59/10**[2]

5 1/2 **Goji Berry (FR)**[18] 5348 2-9-2 0.. SebastienMaillot 2 70
(M Boutin, France) **13/1**

6 snk **Iggy Chop (FR)**[12] 5568 2-9-2 0.. VincentCheminaud 6 70
(C Boutin, France) **16/1**

7 3/4 **Lie High (FR)**[43] 2-9-2 0... OlivierPeslier 4 68
(Eric Saint-Martin, France) **28/1**

8 6 **Get Ready To Rock (IRE)** 2-8-13 0.. AntoineHamelin 8 51
(Matthieu Palussiere, France) **25/1**

1m 47.68s (6.88) **8** Ran SP% **119.4**
WIN (incl. 1 euro stake): 1.40. PLACES: 1.10, 1.60, 2.70. DF: 4.90. SF: 5.80.
Owner Daniel-Yves Treves **Bred** Earl Ecurie La Boetie **Trained** Pau, France

5986a PRIX DE PUTOT-EN-AUGE (MAIDEN) (2YO FILLIES) (ROUND) (TURF) 1m (R)

11:55 (12:00) 2-Y-O **£9,191** (£3,676; £2,757; £1,838; £919)

RPR

1 **Samuna (FR)** 2-8-10 0.. MaximeGuyon 8 74
(C Ferland, France) **3/1**[2]

2 1 **Upendi (FR)**[10] 5698 2-9-0 0... LouisBeuzelin 4 76
(Robert Collet, France) **11/2**

3 hd **Couville (FR)** 2-8-10 0... CristianDemuro 7 72
(Mme Pia Brandt, France) **4/1**[3]

4 3/4 **El Camila (FR)** 2-9-0 0... StephanePasquier 2 74
(Y Gourraud, France) **28/1**

5 3/4 **Evalya Senora (FR)**[27] 5005 2-9-0 0.............................. TheoBachelot 5 72
(Y Barberot, France) **27/10**[1]

6 snk **Copper Baked (FR)**[41] 4487 2-9-0 0............................... DougieCostello 6 72
(K R Burke) *t.k.h: chsd ldrs under restraint between horses: 5th and rdn 2f out: outpcd 1 1/2f out: kpt on ins fnl f: nt pce to get on terms* **43/5**

7 3/4 **La Berlioz (FR)**[10] 5698 2-9-0 0.. OlivierPeslier 9 70
(P De Chevigny, France) **30/1**

8 3 1/2 **Retour Gagnant (IRE)**[52] 2-8-10 0.................... EmmanuelEtienne[(4)] 10 61
(Yves de Nicolay, France) **40/1**

9 1 3/4 **Marlonne (FR)** 2-8-10 0... AlexisBadel 3 53
(H-F Devin, France) **16/1**

10 nk **Corinthe (FR)**[61] 2-9-0 0.. AntoineHamelin 1 56
(J-P Gauvin, France) **12/1**

1m 48.56s (7.76) **10** Ran SP% **120.5**
WIN (incl. 1 euro stake): 4.00. PLACES: 1.80, 1.90, 1.60. DF: 15.10. SF: 26.00.
Owner Guy Pariente **Bred** Guy Pariente Holding **Trained** France

5987a PRIX DE LA CAUVINIERE (CONDITIONS) (3YO FILLIES) (POLYTRACK) 7f 110y

12:25 (12:00) 3-Y-O **£12,500** (£5,000; £3,750; £2,500; £1,250)

RPR

1 **Yeah Baby Yeah (IRE)**[24] 5123 3-9-0 0...................... UmbertoRispoli 8 87
(Gay Kelleway) *away wl: sn stdd and w.w in last: sed to cl 2f out: nt clr run 1 1/2f out: sn rdn and r.o fnl f: led cl home* **216/10**

2 nse **Syrita (FR)**[24] 3-9-0 0.. OlivierPeslier 7 87
(M Nigge, France) **19/10**[1]

3 hd **Livinginafantasy (FR)**[27] 3-9-1 0 ow1............... ChristopheSoumillon 3 88
(S Wattel, France) **74/10**

4 hd **Grand Jete**[17] 5385 3-9-0 0... VincentCheminaud 5 86
(D Smaga, France) **39/10**[2]

5 1 3/4 **Denga (IRE)**[86] 2928 3-9-0 0... TheoBachelot 6 82
(S Wattel, France) **59/10**

6 snk **Love Street (USA)**[14] 3-8-8 0.. HugoJourniac[(6)] 2 81
(J-C Rouget, France) **47/10**[3]

7 3 1/2 **Hiort (IRE)**[28] 3-9-0 0..(p) StephanePasquier 4 73
(P Bary, France) **20/1**

8 nk **Coif (IRE)**[27] 5006 3-9-0 0.. MickaelBarzalona 1 72
(A Fabre, France) *cl up on inner: rdn to chse ldr 1 1/2f out: wknd appr fnl f* **78/10**

1m 27.51s (87.51) **8** Ran SP% **119.4**
WIN (incl. 1 euro stake): 22.60. PLACES: 4.00, 1.40, 2.30. DF: 34.70. SF: 94.20.
Owner Winterbeck Manor Stud & Sheila Bailey **Bred** Mr And Mrs P McEnery **Trained** Exning, Suffolk

5988a PRIX DE VALSEME (CLAIMER) (2YO) (YOUNG JOCKEYS & APPRENTICES) (POLYTRACK) 7f 110y

1:05 (12:00) 2-Y-O **£8,455** (£3,382; £2,536; £1,691; £845)

RPR

1 **Barbarigo (IRE)**[15] 5447 2-8-13 0.......................... NicolasLarenaudie[(5)] 11 78
(F Chappet, France) **7/2**[2]

2 1 3/4 **Zangokari (FR)**[9] 5701 2-8-11 0............................. LudovicBoisseau[(4)] 7 71
(T Lemer, France) **10/1**

3 3/4 **Ndesha (FR)** 2-8-5 0... GianniSiaffa[(6)] 5 65
(D Guillemin, France) **10/1**

4 1 3/4 **Time Sky (ITY)** 2-8-11 0.. EmmanuelEtienne[(4)] 10 65
(G Botti, France) **15/1**

5 hd **If I Say So**[12] 5568 2-9-1 0..(b) HugoJourniac[(3)] 12 68
(J S Moore) *sn led: 5 l clr appr 1/2-way: rdn 2f out: hdd over 1 1/2f out: grad dropped away fnl f* **9/5**[1]

6 1 **Chababa Rosetgri (FR)**[20] 5279 2-8-3 0.................. KyllanBarbaud[(5)] 4 55
(H De Nicolay, France) **48/1**

7 nk **Baie D'Amour (FR)**[10] 5698 2-9-1 0............................... JordanVaughan 8 61
(K R Burke) *cl up: chsd clr ldr appr 1/2-way: rdn and nt qckn fr 2f out: plugged on at one pce fnl f* **53/10**[3]

8 1 1/2 **Volstora (FR)**[10] 5698 2-8-0 0........................(b[1]) GuillaumeAmbrosioni[(8)] 3 51
(T Castanheira, France) **112/1**

9 1 1/4 **La Sarenne (FR)**[50] 4187 2-8-9 0....................................... PierreBazire[(6)] 1 55
(P Bary, France) **11/1**

10 1/2 **Daffodil Mulligan**[6] 5755 2-8-9 0..............................(p) FlorentGavilan[(4)] 9 52
(J S Moore) *t.k.h: hld up in midfield: hrd rdn and no imp fr 2f out: wknd over 1f out* **28/1**

11 1 1/2 **Prince Of Baden (IRE)** 2-8-6 0................................. ClementLecoeuvre[(5)] 2 46
(Matthieu Palussiere, France) **25/1**

12 1 3/4 **Rose Fantaisie (FR)** 2-8-8 0 ow1.................................... MlleIsisMagnin[(8)] 6 47
(J-P Gauvin, France) **36/1**

WIN (incl. 1 euro stake): 4.50. PLAC: 1.80, 3.00, 3.30. DF: 16.90. SF: 29.80

Owner Stephane Gilibert **Bred** Eledy Srl **Trained** France

5959EPSOM (L-H)

Tuesday, August 30

OFFICIAL GOING: Good (good to firm in places; 7.5)

Wind: light, across Weather: sunny and warm

5989 EBBISHAM NURSERY H'CAP 7f

2:00 (2:01) (Class 5) (0-75,74) 2-Y-O **£4,528** (£1,347; £673; £336) **Stalls** Low

Form RPR

3526 1 **Kodiac Khan (IRE)**[21] 5265 2-9-4 **74** MarcMonaghan(3) 6 79
(Hugo Palmer) *chsd ldrs: effrt 2f out: hdwy and rdn to ld over 1f out: r.o wl and drew ins fnl f: readily* **5/1**

3210 2 2 1/4 **Fair Power (IRE)**[45] 4394 2-9-0 **74** MitchGodwin(7) 4 73
(Sylvester Kirk) *t.k.h: w ldr: rdn 2f out: chsd wnr but unable qck over 1f out: styd on same pce ins fnl f* **9/2**3

3642 3 1/2 **Suffragette City (IRE)**[14] 5524 2-9-5 **72** PatDobbs 2 71
(Richard Hannon) *chsd ldrs: nt clr run and swtchd rt over 1f out: 3rd and styd on same pce ins fnl f* **3/1**2

530 4 1 3/4 **Spiritofedinburgh (IRE)**[17] 5395 2-9-4 **71** FMBerry 1 64
(Brendan Powell) *led: rdn 2f out: hdd over 1f out and sn outpcd: 4th and kpt on same pce ins fnl f* **10/1**

3001 5 nk **Ivor's Magic (IRE)**[25] 5120 2-8-3 **63** DavidEgan(7) 8 55
(David Elsworth) *hld up in tch in midfield: effrt 2f out: no imp and styd on same pce fr over 1f out: sddle slipped* **7/1**

443 6 1 **Act Of Freedom (IRE)**[22] 5237 2-9-4 **71** WilliamBuick 5 60
(Charlie Appleby) *dwlt and pushed along early: in tch in last pair: effrt on outer over 2f out: no imp: nvr trbld ldrs* **11/4**1

0454 7 1 **Kings Heart (IRE)**[11] 5598 2-8-11 **64** SteveDrowne 7 51
(Mark Usher) *stdd after s: t.k.h: hld up in last pair: effrt wl over 1f out: no imp: nvr trbld ldrs* **25/1**

405 8 7 **Cj Parker**[21] 5251 2-8-12 **65** PatCosgrave 3 33
(Jim Boyle) *dwlt: sn rcvrd and t.k.h in midfield: rdn over 2f out: lost pl and bhd over 1f out: bhd ins fnl f* **14/1**

1m 26.98s (3.68) **Going Correction** +0.075s/f (Good) **8** Ran SP% **118.6**
Speed ratings (Par 94): **81,78,77,75,75 74,73,65**
CSF £28.86 CT £80.90 TOTE £6.40: £2.00, £1.80, £1.30; EX 30.90 Trifecta £110.30.
Owner Hussain Alabbas Lootah **Bred** John P Mangan & John S Mangan **Trained** Newmarket, Suffolk

FOCUS
The going was good, good to firm in places. Rail on inner (Derby) configuration and all distances as advertised. A modest nursery to start and they went no pace, so it was crucial to be handy.

5990 BRITISH STALLION STUDS EBF MAIDEN STKS 1m 114y

2:35 (2:37) (Class 5) 2-Y-O **£3,881** (£1,155; £577; £288) **Stalls** Low

Form RPR

62 1 **Star Of The East (IRE)**[27] 5015 2-9-5 0 SilvestreDeSousa 2 83+
(Mark Johnston) *mde all: set stdy gallop tl rdn and qcknd over 3f out: clr and in command over 1f out: styd on strly: eased towards fin* **11/4**2

02 2 3 **Zymyran**[26] 5081 2-9-5 0 HarryBentley 7 74
(David Simcock) *hld up in tch in midfield: effrt over 2f out: hdwy u.p to chse clr wnr over 1f out: no imp fnl f* **5/1**3

366 3 1/2 **Oceanus (IRE)**[60] 3859 2-9-5 75 FMBerry 6 73
(Ed Dunlop) *stdd after s: hld up in rr: rdn over 2f out: wnt modest 4th 1f out: styd on ins fnl f to go 3rd wl ins fnl f: no ch w wnr* **5/1**3

4 1 3/4 **Ode To Glory** 2-9-0 0 PatCosgrave 4 64
(Rae Guest) *chsd ldng pair: rdn 3f out: chsd clr wnr but no imp 2f out: lost 2nd and styd on same pce fr over 1f out: lost 3rd wl ins fnl f* **25/1**

5 5 **Pioneering (IRE)** 2-9-5 0 WilliamBuick 5 58+
(Charlie Appleby) *sn trcking wnr: rdn over 3f out: no imp and lost 2nd 2f out: wknd over 1f out* **11/10**1

0 6 5 **Reynardo De Silver**[11] 5600 2-9-0 0 [1] HectorCrouch(5) 3 47
(Gary Moore) *stdd after s: t.k.h: hld up in last pair: rdn and dropped to last 3f out: no ch whn hung lft over 1f out* **33/1**

1m 48.07s (1.97) **Going Correction** +0.075s/f (Good) **6** Ran SP% **114.4**
Speed ratings (Par 94): **94,91,90,89,84 80**
CSF £17.10 TOTE £3.80: £2.00, £2.10; EX 13.60 Trifecta £48.70.
Owner Sheikh Hamdan bin Mohammed Al Maktoum **Bred** Darley **Trained** Middleham Moor, N Yorks

FOCUS
A modest maiden which tends to go to a 2yo with previous experience, and that was again the case. This was another slowly run affair and the winner dictated. The race has been rated around the placed horses.

5991 TERRY MILLS & JOHN AKEHURST H'CAP 6f

3:10 (3:10) (Class 3) (0-90,88) 3-Y-O+

£8,715 (£2,609; £1,304; £652; £326; £163) **Stalls** High

Form RPR

532 1 **Highland Acclaim (IRE)**[24] 5182 5-9-9 **87** HarryBentley 7 96
(David O'Meara) *chsd ldr: upsides 2f out: sn rdn: drvn ins fnl f: led wl ins fnl f: kpt on* **6/1**3

0540 2 nk **Ashpan Sam**[10] 5641 7-9-10 **88** (p) WilliamTwiston-Davies 11 96
(David W Drinkwater) *led and set str gallop: jnd and rdn 2f out: battled on gamely u.p: hdd wl ins fnl f: kpt on but hld towards fin* **8/1**

1021 3 2 1/4 **Highly Sprung (IRE)**[18] 5372 3-9-2 **83** SilvestreDeSousa 3 84+
(Mark Johnston) *dwlt: sn rcvrd and in midfield: effrt in centre 3f out: hdwy u.p over 1f out: chsd clr ldng pair ins fnl f: no imp fnl 100yds* **3/1**1

414 4 2 **Under Siege (IRE)**[25] 5103 4-8-13 **80** (t) AaronJones(3) 4 74
(Stuart Williams) *midfield: effrt over 2f out: hdwy u.p over 1f out: chsd clr ldng pair ent fnl f: 4th and kpt on same pce ins fnl f* **10/1**

0206 5 hd **Morache Music**[14] 5507 8-9-0 **83** CharlieBennett(5) 6 77
(Patrick Chamings) *off the pce in last quartet: shkn up over 2f out: styd on wl ins fnl f: nvr trbld ldrs* **16/1**

3125 6 hd **Spirit Of Zeb (IRE)**[24] 5161 4-8-13 **82** AdamMcNamara(5) 1 75
(Richard Fahey) *chsd ldrs: rdn to chse ldng pair 2f out: no imp over 1f out: lost 3rd ent fnl f: wknd ins fnl f* **7/1**

2006 7 3/4 **Papa Luigi (IRE)**[24] 5148 3-9-7 **88** PatDobbs 9 79
(Richard Hannon) *midfield: rdn 2f out: edgd lft over 1f out: swtchd rt and kpt on ins fnl f: nvr trbld ldrs* **16/1**

2526 8 1 **Foxtrot Knight**[15] 5488 4-9-3 **81** GeorgeBaker 8 69
(Ruth Carr) *stdd s: hld up off the pce in rr: effrt 2f out: sme hdwy ins fnl f: nvr trbld ldrs* **5/1**2

-162 9 1 1/4 **Happy Call**[42] 4475 3-9-1 **87** (v) GeorgeWood(5) 2 71
(Simon Crisford) *chsd ldrs tl 2f out: lost pl and hung rt over 1f out: sn wknd* **10/1**

0600 10 nk **Arctic Feeling (IRE)**[13] 5555 8-9-2 **87** NatalieHambling(7) 10 70
(Richard Fahey) *hld up off the pce in last pair: effrt 2f out: no real imp: n.d* **12/1**

0015 11 1 1/4 **Goring (GER)**[15] 5488 4-9-7 **85** JohnFahy 5 64
(Eve Johnson Houghton) *dwlt and niggled along early: off the pce in last quartet: n.d* **8/1**

1m 8.02s (-1.38) **Going Correction** +0.075s/f (Good)
WFA 3 from 4yo+ 3lb **11** Ran SP% **128.3**
Speed ratings (Par 107): **112,111,108,105,105 105,104,103,101,101 99**
CSF £58.68 CT £182.11 TOTE £7.20: £2.40, £3.90, £1.70; EX 63.80 Trifecta £284.90.
Owner Evan M Sutherland **Bred** Rathbarry Stud **Trained** Upper Helmsley, N Yorks

FOCUS
A decent sprint handicap and no hanging about this time, but despite a scorching gallop the pace held up and nothing was able to get into it from behind.

5992 JRA H'CAP 7f

3:45 (3:46) (Class 4) (0-80,80) 3-Y-O+ **£5,822** (£1,732; £865; £432) **Stalls** Low

Form RPR

0321 1 **Nouvelli Dancer (IRE)**[23] 5191 3-9-6 **79** SilvestreDeSousa 3 84
(Ivan Furtado) *mde all: rdn over 2f out: drvn over 1f out: hld on wl ins fnl f: drvn out: gamely* **11/4**1

3152 2 3/4 **Dyllan (IRE)**[20] 5284 3-8-10 **74** AdamMcNamara(5) 8 77
(Ruth Carr) *hld up in tch: effrt 2f out: hdwy to chse wnr 1f out: sn pressing wnr: kpt on but a hld by wnr* **5/1**3

320 3 1 1/2 **Giovanni Di Bicci**[1] 5965 4-9-4 **72** (t) PatCosgrave 5 73
(Jim Boyle) *s.i.s: detached in last: steadily clsd and in tch 2f out: rdn and hdwy over 1f out: edging lft and wnt 3rd ins fnl f: no imp and one pce after* **10/1**

-400 4 1 1/2 **Take A Note**[20] 5301 7-9-12 **80** (p) GeorgeBaker 7 81+
(Patrick Chamings) *hld up in tch: nt clr run over 2f out: swtchd rt and fnlly in the clr ins fnl f: styd on wl ins fnl f: unable to chal* **6/1**

0251 5 nk **Swiss Cross**[16] 5456 9-8-7 **64** (t) TimClark(3) 6 60
(Phil McEntee) *pressed ldng pair: rdn over 2f out: drvn and unable qck over 1f out: wknd wl ins fnl f* **5/1**3

2020 6 1 1/4 **Good Luck Charm**[27] 5017 7-9-3 **76** (b) HectorCrouch(5) 1 69
(Gary Moore) *dwlt: hld up in tch in rr off main gp: hdwy on inner over 2f out: rdn to chse ldrs over 1f out: no ex 1f out: wknd ins fnl f* **7/1**

3551 6 dht **Exoplanet Blue**[20] 5309 4-9-2 **75** GeorgeWood(5) 4 68
(Henry Candy) *pressed wnr: rdn over 2f out: lost 2nd 1f out and stmbld sn after: wknd ins fnl f* **4/1**2

1m 22.82s (-0.48) **Going Correction** +0.075s/f (Good)
WFA 3 from 4yo+ 5lb **7** Ran SP% **115.9**
Speed ratings (Par 105): **105,104,102,100,100 98,98**
CSF £17.26 CT £119.24 TOTE £3.30: £1.80, £3.20; EX 18.50 Trifecta £63.00.
Owner S Laffan **Bred** Colin Kennedy **Trained** Wiseton, Nottinghamshire

FOCUS
A fair handicap with a disputed lead and another powerful front-running performance. It resulted in a 1-2 for the two 3yos.

5993 WARREN H'CAP (JOCKEY CLUB GRASSROOTS FLAT MIDDLE DISTANCE SERIES QUALIFIER) 1m 4f 10y

4:20 (4:20) (Class 5) (0-70,70) 3-Y-O+ **£4,528** (£1,347; £673; £336) **Stalls** Centre

Form RPR

0321 1 **Fandango (GER)**[13] 5548 3-8-13 **70** DavidParkes(5) 3 81
(Jeremy Gask) *chsd ldng pair: effrt to chse ldr over 2f out: rdn to ld over 1f out: styd on wl and drew clr fnl f: rdn out* **6/4**2

05-3 2 4 1/2 **Alsacienne**[7] 5749 3-8-10 **62** RyanPowell 4 68
(Sir Mark Prescott Bt) *led: jnd and rdn 6f out: forged ahd again u.p over 2f out: drvn and hdd over 1f out: one pced after: eased wl ins fnl f* **1/1**1

6063 3 2 1/2 **Le Tissier**[9] 5672 3-8-7 **62** (p) RobHornby(3) 2 62
(Michael Attwater) *stdd s: hld up in rr: effrt over 3f out: 3rd but no imp on ldrs over 1f out: edgd lft ins fnl f: plugged on* **6/1**3

4040 4 12 **Deluxe**[20] 5303 4-8-12 **59** PaddyBradley(5) 1 46
(Pat Phelan) *chsd ldr tl clsd to join ldr 6f out: lost 2nd and pushed along over 2f out: sn dropped out: bhd and eased ins fnl f* **12/1**

2m 42.92s (4.02) **Going Correction** +0.075s/f (Good)
WFA 3 from 4yo 10lb **4** Ran SP% **112.0**
Speed ratings (Par 103): **89,86,84,76**
CSF £3.53 TOTE £2.30; EX 3.20 Trifecta £4.50.
Owner Anglo Australian Racing **Bred** Gestut Etzean **Trained** Stockbridge, Hants

FOCUS
A modest handicap and they dawdled to halfway.

5994 ASHTEAD H'CAP 1m 2f 18y

4:55 (4:55) (Class 5) (0-70,70) 3-Y-O+ **£4,528** (£1,347; £673; £336) **Stalls** Low

Form RPR

2141 1 **You're A Goat**[27] 5013 3-8-13 **68** HectorCrouch(5) 7 81+
(Gary Moore) *t.k.h: hld up in tch: swtchd lft and effrt to chse ldr 2f out: rdn to ld over 1f out: styd on: rdn out* **11/10**1

2616 2 1 1/2 **Barren Brook**[43] 4459 9-9-13 **69** GeorgeBaker 3 77
(Laura Mongan) *taken down early: led: rdn 2f out: hdd over 1f out: clr 2nd and styd on same pce after* **12/1**

5315 3 7 **Choral Festival**[23] 5207 10-10-0 **70** DannyBrock 5 64
(John Bridger) *chsd ldr: rdn wl over 2f out: lost 2nd and unable qck 2f out: 3rd and outpcd over 1f out: kpt on same pce after* **7/1**

050 4 1 **Celtic Ava (IRE)**[43] 4459 4-8-13 **55** JFEgan 9 47
(Pat Phelan) *hld up in 6th: effrt and swtchd lft jst over 2f out: no threat to ldrs but nt clr run over 1f out: swtchd rt wl ins fnl f: wnt 4th cl home: no ch w ldng pair* **14/1**

6054 5 nk **Farham (USA)**[27] 5028 4-9-6 **67** (p) AdamMcNamara(5) 6 58
(Richard Fahey) *chsd ldrs: rdn and unable qck over 2f out: outpcd and wl hld over 1f out: plugged on same pce after* **4/1**2

3142 6 3 1/4 **Dovil's Duel (IRE)**[41] 4531 5-9-4 **65** JordanVaughan(5) 8 50
(Tony Newcombe) *hld up in tch in midfield: effrt over 2f out: sn struggling: wknd over 1f out* **5/1**3

64P0 7 3/4 **Spiritual Star (IRE)**[33] 4784 7-9-5 **66** PaddyBradley(5) 1 49
(Lee Carter) *awkward leaving stalls and slowly away: a bhd* **25/1**

2m 9.5s (-0.20) **Going Correction** +0.075s/f (Good)
WFA 3 from 4yo+ 8lb **7** Ran SP% **115.0**
Speed ratings (Par 103): **103,101,96,95,95 92,91**
CSF £16.51 CT £66.40 TOTE £2.00: £1.30, £3.70; EX 12.40 Trifecta £48.90.
Owner Power Geneva Ltd **Bred** Mrs James Wigan **Trained** Lower Beeding, W Sussex

FOCUS
Another modest handicap and victory for the sole 3yo in the field.
T/Jkpt: £6,666.60 to a £1 stake. Pool: £10,000 - 1.5 winning units T/Plt: £60.70 to a £1 stake. Pool: £67,333.32 - 809.75 winning units T/Qpdt: £12.40 to a £1 stake. Pool: £5,198.49 - 309.73 winning units **Steve Payne**

[5922]GOODWOOD (R-H)

Tuesday, August 30

OFFICIAL GOING: Good (good to firm in places on round course; 7.6)
Wind: light breeze Weather: sunny

5995 EBF STALLIONS MAIDEN FILLIES' STKS (PLUS 10 RACE) 1m
1:50 (1:51) (Class 5) 2-Y-O **£3,234** (£962; £481; £240) **Stalls** Low

Form RPR
1 **Desert Water (IRE)** 2-9-0 0 SeanLevey 4 76+
(Richard Hannon) *athletic: in tch: hdwy 2f out: sn rdn: str run ent fnl f: led fnl 120yds: kpt on wl* **14/1**

532 2 nk **Dubara**[20] 5298 2-9-0 79 JamieSpencer 1 76+
(Luca Cumani) *cl up: nt clr run over 2f out tl swtchd lft over 1f out: r.o w ev ch ins fnl f: kpt on* **2/1**[1]

454 3 nk **Pacofilha**[8] 5722 2-9-0 0 LukeMorris 8 74
(Paul Cole) *w'like: led: rdn whn strly pressed fr 2f out: drifted lft ent fnl f: hdd fnl 120yds: kpt on but no ex* **17/2**[3]

3 4 ½ **Nathania**[24] 5170 2-9-0 0 ShaneKelly 6 75
(Richard Hughes) *str: hld up in tch: hdwy but nt clr run on rails over 2f out tl ent fnl f: sn ev ch: no ex cl home* **2/1**[1]

0 5 3¼ **Lady Valdean**[33] 4801 2-9-0 0 RenatoSouza 5 66
(Jose Santos) *racd keenly: trckd ldrs: rdn over 2f out: keeping on at same pce and hld whn short of room briefly ins fnl f* **25/1**

6 4 **Curtsy (IRE)** 2-9-0 0 JimmyFortune 7 56
(Hughie Morrison) *cmpt: in last pair but wl in tch: nudged along over 4f out: rdn over 2f out: no pce to chal: fdd ins fnl f* **12/1**

4 7 ¾ **For The Roses**[21] 5266 2-9-0 0 OisinMurphy 2 55+
(Ralph Beckett) *w'like: trckd ldr: rdn to chal over 2f out: ev ch over 1f out: wknd ins fnl f (b.b.v)* **5/1**[2]

0 8 3½ **Prairie Light**[20] 5298 2-9-0 0 TomMarquand 3 47
(Sylvester Kirk) *w'like: hung lft virtually thrght: keen early: hld up: short of room 4f out over 1f out* **66/1**

1m 41.31s (1.41) **Going Correction** -0.05s/f (Good) 8 Ran SP% **113.6**
Speed ratings (Par 91): **90,89,89,88,85 81,80,77**
CSF £41.86 TOTE £15.40: £3.80, £1.10, £2.10; EX 47.70 Trifecta £347.70.
Owner Saeed Suhail **Bred** Rabbah Bloodstock Limited **Trained** East Everleigh, Wilts
■ Stewards' Enquiry : Luke Morris jockey said the filly hung left-handed
Shane Kelly caution: careless riding
Oisin Murphy vet reported the filly had bled from the nose
Tom Marquand jockey said the filly hung left-handed

FOCUS
Race distances as advertised. A fair fillies' maiden, they went quite steady early but the winner came from last place. She looks the type to do better.

5996 LEVIN DOWN MAIDEN STKS 1m 1f 192y
2:25 (2:27) (Class 5) 3-Y-O+ **£3,234** (£962; £481; £240) **Stalls** Low

Form RPR
2 1 **Saunter (FR)**[22] 3-9-5 90 JimCrowley 1 91+
(David Menuisier) *cmpt: mde all: rdn clr over 1f out: r.o strly: comf* **7/2**[2]

2 5 **Time To Blossom** 3-9-0 0 RobertHavlin 2 74
(Simon Crisford) *athletic: s.i.s: sn rcvrd to trck wnr: rdn and ev ch over 2f out tl over 1f out: kpt on but nt pce of wnr* **4/1**[3]

3 2 **Brodie** 3-9-0 0 JamieSpencer 3 70
(Luca Cumani) *athletic: trckd ldrs: nudged along over 4f out: rdn wl over 2f out: kpt on but nt pce to threaten* **5/4**[1]

3322 4 4 **Heartstone (IRE)**[10] 5634 3-9-0 75 MichaelJMMurphy 7 62
(Charles Hills) *hld up last: hdwy over 2f out: sn rdn: wnt hld 4th over 1f out: sn hung rt: fdd fnl f* **7/1**

6344 5 5 **Silhouette (IRE)**[18] 5362 3-9-5 70 TimmyMurphy 8 57
(Daniel Kubler) *trckd ldr: rdn 3f out: wknd over 1f out* **12/1**

6 4½ **Rattle On** 3-9-5 0 SamHitchcott 6 48
(Jim Boyle) *str: last pair but in tch: outpcd over 2f out: nvr on terms: wknd over 1f out* **25/1**

B05 7 1¾ **Squire Hockey**[21] 5260 3-9-5 0 LiamKeniry 5 45
(Gary Moore) *hld up in tch: rdn wl over 2f out: sn wknd* **100/1**

3 8 1¾ **Art Of Swing (IRE)**[8] 5709 4-9-13 0 ShaneKelly 4 41
(Gary Moore) *in tch: rdn 3f out: wknd 2f out* **50/1**

2m 9.68s (1.58) **Going Correction** -0.05s/f (Good)
WFA 3 from 4yo 8lb 8 Ran SP% **113.7**
Speed ratings (Par 103): **91,87,85,82,78 74,73,71**
CSF £17.58 TOTE £3.90: £1.20, £1.50, £1.30; EX 18.80 Trifecta £46.20.
Owner Michael H Watt **Bred** S A R L Haras Du Cadran Et Al **Trained** Pulborough, W Sussex

FOCUS
Little pace on here and it paid to race handy, the winner making all.

5997 EBFSTALLIONS.COM PETER WILLETT "STALLION-RESTRICTED" CONDITIONS STKS (PLUS 10 RACE) 7f
3:00 (3:02) (Class 2) 2-Y-O **£15,562** (£4,660) **Stalls** Low

Form RPR
1 1 **Seven Heavens**[53] 4075 2-9-5 0 RobertHavlin 3 98+
(John Gosden) *str: hmpd s: tk str hold: trckd ldr: led wl over 1f out: edgd rt: sn clr: pushed out: comf* **1/10**[1]

2 2 6 **Shabeeh (IRE)**[11] 5593 2-9-1 0 FrannyNorton 2 78+
(Mark Johnston) *wnt lft s: led: rdn and hdd wl over 1f out: sn hmpd and hld: nt pce of wnr* **7/1**[2]

1m 26.73s (-0.27) **Going Correction** -0.05s/f (Good) 2 Ran SP% **103.4**
Speed ratings (Par 100): **99,92**
TOTE £1.10.
Owner K Abdullah **Bred** Cheveley Park Stud Ltd **Trained** Newmarket, Suffolk
■ Sheila's Fancy was withdrawn. Price at time of withdrawal 100/1. Rule 4 does not apply

FOCUS
Just the three declared and it was down to two after the 100-1 outsider Sheila's Fancy gave trouble and got upset in the stalls. The winner looks very useful, though, winning as he liked despite pulling hard off what was a fair pace set by the runner-up.

5998 CHARLTON HUNT NURSERY FILLIES' STKS (H'CAP) 6f
3:35 (3:35) (Class 2) 2-Y-O **£12,938** (£3,850; £1,924; £962) **Stalls** High

Form RPR
2212 1 **Paco's Angel**[31] 4884 2-8-9 79 ShaneKelly 4 88
(Richard Hughes) *athletic: lw: travelled wl: trckd ldrs: swtchd rt over 1f out: led ins fnl f: r.o wl: readily* **8/1**

223 2 1 **Miss Sugars**[31] 4884 2-8-2 75 EdwardGreatrex(3) 3 81
(David Simcock) *last pair: swtchd to center and hdwy 2f out: sn rdn: r.o chse wnr fnl 100yds: a being hld towards fin* **11/1**

1115 3 1¾ **Rajar**[18] 5359 2-9-7 91 SeanLevey 2 92
(Richard Hannon) *led: rdn over 1f out: hdd ins fnl f: no ex fnl 100ds* **4/1**[3]

4250 4 ¾ **Camargue**[10] 5638 2-9-0 84 TomMarquand 6 83
(Mark Johnston) *pressed ldr: rdn 2f out: kpt on same pce fnl f* **33/1**

11 5 nk **The Wagon Wheel (IRE)**[13] 5560 2-8-12 82 TonyHamilton 9 80
(Richard Fahey) *fly-leapt leaving stalls: in tch: rdn and hdwy over 1f out: sn hung rt: kpt on same pce fnl f* **5/2**[1]

14 6 2 **Twizzell**[109] 2219 2-8-9 79 JoeyHaynes 8 71
(K R Burke) *prom: rdn and ev ch fr 2f out tl ent fnl f: fdd fnl 120yds* **14/1**

5105 7 nk **Texas Katie**[5] 5794 2-8-1 71 LukeMorris 5 62
(Mick Channon) *cl up: nt best of runs whn rdn 2f out: flattered briefly ent fnl f: fdd fnl 120yds* **14/1**

1300 8 4½ **Sea Of Snow (USA)**[31] 4884 2-8-12 82 FrannyNorton 7 59
(Mark Johnston) *cl up: rdn 2f out: wknd jst over 1f out:* **14/1**

421 9 hd **Bee Case**[15] 5469 2-8-12 82 JimCrowley 1 59
(Hugo Palmer) *cmpt: lw: trckd ldrs: rdn over 2f out: wknd ent fnl f* **10/3**[2]

1m 10.42s (-1.78) **Going Correction** -0.05s/f (Good) 9 Ran SP% **114.0**
Speed ratings (Par 97): **109,107,105,104,103 101,100,94,94**
CSF £90.20 CT £403.67 TOTE £9.60: £2.80, £2.50, £1.50; EX 94.50 Trifecta £291.30.
Owner Biddestone Racing Partnership XVII **Bred** Biddestone Stud Ltd **Trained** Upper Lambourn, Berkshire

FOCUS
A useful fillies' nursery, the first trio home having also filled the first three places in a similar race at Newmarket last time.

5999 ROYAL SUSSEX REGIMENT STKS (H'CAP) 2m
4:10 (4:10) (Class 2) (0-105,103) 3-Y-O+ **£12,938** (£3,850; £1,924; £962) **Stalls** Low

Form RPR
2121 1 **St Michel**[24] 5176 3-8-4 93 LukeMorris 5 102+
(Sir Mark Prescott Bt) *lw: hld up bhd ldrs: smooth hdwy fr over 3f out: led jst over 2f out: sn rdn and hung lft: styd on wl to assert towards fin: drvn out* **4/5**[1]

4606 2 1½ **Oriental Fox (GER)**[10] 5655 8-10-0 103 FrannyNorton 6 107
(Mark Johnston) *led: rdn whn narrowly hdd jst over 2f out: kpt on gamely on far rails w ch fnl f: hld towards fin* **7/2**[2]

211 3 ¾ **Arty Campbell (IRE)**[13] 5553 6-8-9 84 oh2 DanielMuscutt 3 87
(Bernard Llewellyn) *trckd ldr: rdn and ev ch 2f out: carried lft over 1f out: styd on same pce fnl f* **14/1**

252 4 3 **Percy Veer**[34] 4752 4-8-8 86 EdwardGreatrex(3) 1 86
(Sylvester Kirk) *trckd ldr: rdn 3f out: styd on same pce fnl 2f* **13/2**[3]

1000 5 1 **Gang Warfare**[35] 4734 5-9-13 102 (p) RobertHavlin 4 100
(Simon Crisford) *racd in cl 4th: dropped to 5th whn sltly outpcd over 3f out: styd on fnl 2f but nvr able to get bk on terms* **8/1**

3m 29.34s (0.34) **Going Correction** -0.05s/f (Good)
WFA 3 from 4yo+ 14lb 5 Ran SP% **108.9**
Speed ratings (Par 109): **97,96,95,94,93**
CSF £3.73 TOTE £1.70: £1.10, £1.90; EX 4.10 Trifecta £20.50.
Owner J L C Pearce **Bred** J L C Pearce **Trained** Newmarket, Suffolk

FOCUS
A decent staying handicap run at a steady pace and no surprise to see it go to the progressive 3yo.

6000 GOODWOOD REVIVAL STKS (H'CAP) 6f
4:45 (4:45) (Class 4) (0-80,80) 3-Y-O+ **£6,469** (£1,925; £962; £481) **Stalls** High

Form RPR
0452 1 **Yeeoow (IRE)**[27] 5034 7-9-7 80 JoeyHaynes 1 87
(K R Burke) *pressed ldr: led wl over 1f out: drifted rt fnl f: hld on wl: rdn out* **4/1**[2]

6314 2 ¾ **Upstaging**[30] 4910 4-9-7 80 (p) LukeMorris 3 85
(Paul Cole) *slowly away: sn chsng ldrs: rdn to dispute 2nd over 1f out: kpt on but a being hld by wnr fnl f* **2/1**[1]

5-24 3 nse **Gung Ho Jack**[31] 4881 7-8-9 68 KierenFox 5 73
(John Best) *led: rdn and hdd wl over 1f out: edgd rt disputing 2nd fnl f: kpt on but no ex fnl 100yds* **4/1**[2]

0000 4 nk **Divine Call**[5] 5797 9-8-7 66 oh9 (b) FrannyNorton 2 70?
(Milton Bradley) *trckd ldrs: chalng for 2nd but nt clrest of runs fr over 1f out: kpt on wout being able to chal* **20/1**

1045 5 1¾ **Pour La Victoire (IRE)**[25] 5103 6-8-12 76 (b) GeorgiaCox(5) 6 74
(Tony Carroll) *lw: racd keenly: trckd ldrs: effrt 2f out: one pce fnl f* **4/1**[2]

6140 6 1 **Wiley Post**[30] 4910 3-9-2 78 (b) TomMarquand 4 73
(Richard Hannon) *hld up bhd ldrs: hdwy 2f out: sn rdn: fdd wl ins fnl f* **11/2**[3]

1m 11.04s (-1.16) **Going Correction** -0.05s/f (Good)
WFA 3 from 4yo+ 3lb 6 Ran SP% **113.5**
Speed ratings (Par 105): **105,104,103,103,101 99**
CSF £12.70 TOTE £4.10: £2.00, £1.70; EX 12.00 Trifecta £36.90.
Owner Ontoawinner 7 & Mrs E Burke **Bred** Arctic Tack Stud **Trained** Middleham Moor, N Yorks

FOCUS
Just a fair sprint, it paid to race on the speed.

6001 FLYING SCHOOL AT GOODWOOD STKS (H'CAP) 1m 3f
5:20 (5:20) (Class 5) (0-70,74) 4-Y-O+ **£3,234** (£962; £481; £240) **Stalls** High

Form RPR
135 1 **Hard Toffee (IRE)**[60] 3844 5-9-7 70 JimCrowley 7 77
(Conrad Allen) *lw: mde all : stuck to task v gamely whn strly chal ent fnl f: drifted lft: hld on wl: drvn rt out* **15/8**[2]

4332 2 nk **Speculator**[33] 4785 4-9-5 68 (p) JimmyFortune 6 74
(David Menuisier) *dwlt: cl up in last pair: hdwy 2f out: rdn and ev ch ent fnl f: styd on: hld cl home* **7/4**[1]

3455 3 2¾ **Solveig's Song**[15] 5489 4-9-2 65 (p) JackMitchell 1 66
(Steve Woodman) *cl up in last pair: hdwy 2f out: rdn and ev ch ent fnl f: tight for room sn after: no ex fnl 100yds* **8/1**

3053 4 ½ **Classic Mission**[13] 5547 5-9-4 67 (b) LukeMorris 4 67
(Jonathan Portman) *lw: trckd ldrs: drifted lft over 1f out: sn rdn: styd on to press for hld 3rd nring fin* **9/1**

1124 5 8 **Petrify**[30] 4913 6-8-0 56 (tp) MitchGodwin(7) 3 43
(Bernard Llewellyn) *dwlt: sn trcking ldr: rdn over 2f out: hld over 1f out: wknd ent fnl f* **11/2**[3]

2m 30.17s (3.67) **Going Correction** -0.05s/f (Good) 5 Ran SP% **107.6**
Speed ratings (Par 103): **84,83,81,81,75**
CSF £5.27 TOTE £2.70: £1.40, £1.40; EX 5.30 Trifecta £14.40.
Owner Miss Louise Allan **Bred** Marston Stud **Trained** Newmarket, Suffolk

FOCUS
Another race where they went steady and the winner showed a cracking attitude to make all.

T/Plt: £29.90 to a £1 stake. Pool: £61,479.55 - 1497.56 winning units T/Qpdt: £9.90 to a £1 stake. Pool: £4,690.43 - 350.3 winning units **Tim Mitchell**

5833 HAMILTON (R-H)

Tuesday, August 30

OFFICIAL GOING: Good to firm (7.5)

Wind: Fresh, half behind Weather: Fine

6002 ALWAYS TRYING MAIDEN STKS (PLUS 10 RACE) 6f 6y

2:15 (2:15) (Class 4) 2-Y-O **£4,204** (£1,251; £625; £312) **Stalls** High

Form RPR

3 **1** **Dakota Gold**[15] 5476 2-9-5 0 ConnorBeasley 3 77
(Michael Dods) *t.k.h: pressed ldr: rdn over 1f out: led ins fnl f: hld on wl* **17/2**

2205 **2** *shd* **In First Place**[30] 4915 2-9-5 77 JackGarritty 4 77
(Richard Fahey) *trckd ldrs: effrt and rdn over 1f out: edgd rt and chsd wnr ins fnl f: kpt on wl: jst hld* **9/2**[3]

2 **3** *nk* **Kiribati**[20] 5283 2-9-5 0 JoeFanning 2 76
(Mark Johnston) *t.k.h: led: rdn over 1f out: hdd ins fnl f: kpt on: hld nr fin* **4/1**[2]

63 **4** *nk* **Golden Apollo**[17] 5414 2-9-5 0 DavidAllan 7 75
(Tim Easterby) *sn niggled along in rr: drvn along over 2f out: hdwy fnl f: fin wl* **5/2**[1]

3 **5** *3 ¾* **X Rated (IRE)**[12] 5577 2-9-5 0 PhillipMakin 6 64
(Mark Johnston) *s.i.s: sn pushed along in rr: hdwy 2f out: no imp fnl f* **16/1**

3 **6** *½* **Pudding Chare (IRE)**[27] 5029 2-9-5 0 DavidNolan 5 62
(Richard Fahey) *chsd ldng gp: drvn and outpcd over 2f out: no imp fr over 1f out* **4/1**[2]

03 **7** *nk* **Frozen Kiss**[43] 4451 2-9-0 0 SamJames 1 57
(Bryan Smart) *t.k.h: chsd ldrs: rdn 2f out: wknd fnl f* **17/2**

1m 10.99s (-1.21) **Going Correction** -0.20s/f (Firm) **7** Ran SP% **113.7**

Speed ratings (Par 96): **100,99,99,99,94 93,93**

CSF £45.48 TOTE £9.90: £3.50, £2.60; EX 42.30 Trifecta £223.20.

Owner Doug Graham & Ron Davison **Bred** Redgate Bstock & Peter Bottowley Bstock **Trained** Denton, Co Durham

■ Stewards' Enquiry : Jack Garritty 1 day ban (13 Sep): in breach of Rule (B)45.2

FOCUS

Loop rail out 3yds adding approximately 12yds to races 3, 4, & 5. Straight dolled out from 6f to 4.5f. This threw up a bunched finish yet it wasn't a bad 2yo maiden. The riders afterwards claimed the ground was riding more like good.

6003 BESTWAY WHOLESALE MAIDEN STKS 6f 6y

2:50 (2:50) (Class 5) 3-Y-O+ **£3,881** (£1,155; £577; £288) **Stalls** High

Form RPR

0-50 **1** **Dutch Dream**[5] 5804 3-9-0 58 GrahamLee 2 49
(Linda Perratt) *squeezed out s: hld up in tch: effrt over 1f out: rdn to ld ins fnl f: kpt on wl* **14/1**[3]

23 **2** *1 ¼* **Thankyou Stars**[17] 5388 3-9-0 0 DanielTudhope 1 45
(K R Burke) *pressed ldr: rdn to ld over 1f out: hdd ins fnl f: kpt on same pce* **1/16**[1]

0064 **3** *½* **Mystical King**[4] 5838 6-9-8 40 (p) JoeDoyle 4 48
(Linda Perratt) *led: hung rt and hdd over 1f out: rallied: one pce ins fnl f* **40/1**

0500 **4** *25* **Bannock Town**[4] 5838 5-9-8 16 (p) AndrewMullen 3
(Linda Perratt) *prom tl rdn and wknd 2f out: eased whn no ch fnl f* **150/1**

40- **U** **Knotty Jack (IRE)**[284] 7919 4-9-3 0 GarryWhillans(5) 5 35
(Iain Jardine) *in tch: pushed along after 2f: 4th: rdn along and no imp whn jinked rt: sddle slipped and uns rdr over 1f out* **13/2**[2]

1m 11.25s (-0.95) **Going Correction** -0.20s/f (Firm)

WFA 3 from 4yo+ 3lb **5** Ran SP% **117.2**

Speed ratings (Par 103): **98,96,95,62,**

CSF £17.11 TOTE £23.80: £3.70, £1.02; EX 38.70 Trifecta £107.10.

Owner B Jordan **Bred** Lark Copse Ltd **Trained** East Kilbride, S Lanarks

FOCUS

This was about as uncompetitive as it gets but there was still a real turn up.

6004 DRINKS EXPRESS H'CAP 1m 1f 34y

3:25 (3:25) (Class 6) (0-60,59) 3-Y-O **£2,911** (£866; £432; £216) **Stalls** Low

Form RPR

0301 **1** **Intalza (IRE)**[8] 5715 3-9-6 58 6ex (p) JoeDoyle 6 65
(Michael Herrington) *led after 1f: mde rest: rdn 2f out: kpt on wl fnl f* **4/1**[3]

5662 **2** *¾* **Rubis**[35] 4730 3-9-2 54 JackGarritty 3 60
(Richard Fahey) *dwlt: sn prom: effrt and rdn on outside 2f out: edgd rt and chsd wnr ins fnl f: kpt on* **11/4**[1]

146 **3** *1 ¾* **Toffee Apple (IRE)**[37] 4681 3-9-7 59 JoeFanning 7 61
(Keith Dalgleish) *trckd ldrs: effrt and ev ch over 1f out: kpt on same pce fnl f* **7/2**[2]

3005 **4** *2 ¾* **Magical Lasso (IRE)**[5] 5800 3-8-10 53 (p) ShirleyTeasdale(5) 4 50
(Keith Dalgleish) *trckd ldrs: rdn over 2f out: outpcd over 1f out* **10/1**

5561 **5** *8* **Highway Robber**[22] 5227 3-9-1 53 CamHardie 1 34
(Wilf Storey) *rn in snatches: chsd ldng gp: pushed along bef 1/2-way: no imp fr 2f out* **11/2**

5034 **6** *5* **Calypso Delegator (IRE)**[37] 4681 3-8-12 50 TomEaves 8 21
(Micky Hammond) *s.i.s: bhd and sn outpcd: struggling 1/2-way: nvr on terms* **16/1**

0-52 **7** *25* **Ring Of Art**[70] 3499 3-9-6 58 ConnorBeasley 5
(Gemma Anderson) *sn outpcd in rr: drvn along 1/2-way: nvr on terms* **8/1**

1m 57.85s (-1.85) **Going Correction** -0.20s/f (Firm) **7** Ran SP% **110.4**

Speed ratings (Par 98): **100,99,97,95,88 83,61**

CSF £14.29 CT £38.14 TOTE £3.80: £2.50, £2.00; EX 15.10 Trifecta £39.70.

Owner K Fitzsimons **Bred** Patrick Ryan **Trained** Cold Kirby, N Yorks

FOCUS

A moderate 3yo handicap, rated around the runner-up. Race distance increased by 12yds.

6005 EBF STALLIONS SCOTTISH PREMIER SERIES FILLIES' H'CAP 1m 67y

4:00 (4:02) (Class 4) (0-80,79) 3-Y-O+ **£7,762** (£2,310; £1,154; £577) **Stalls** Low

Form RPR

0612 **1** **Lincoln Rocks**[17] 5415 3-9-6 79 DanielTudhope 2 87
(David O'Meara) *mde all: rdn over 1f out: hung lft ins fnl f: kpt on strly* **9/2**[2]

2513 **2** *1 ½* **Dark Intention (IRE)**[25] 5115 3-9-0 73 CamHardie 7 77
(Lawrence Mullaney) *hld up: rdn over 2f out: hdwy on outside to chse wnr ins fnl f: kpt on: nt pce to chal* **9/2**[2]

2052 **3** *¾* **Bell Heather (IRE)**[26] 5062 3-9-4 77 DavidNolan 3 79
(Richard Fahey) *in tch: rdn along over 3f out: rallied 2f out: kpt on same pce ins fnl f* **6/1**

4412 **4** *½* **Livella Fella (IRE)**[34] 4768 3-9-1 74 PhillipMakin 5 75
(Keith Dalgleish) *pressed wnr: rdn over 2f out: no ex and lost two pls ins fnl f* **11/2**[3]

0352 **5** *3 ½* **The Wee Barra (IRE)**[13] 5540 4-8-10 63 (p) JoeDoyle 6 57
(Kevin Ryan) *in tch: rdn over 2f out: hung rt: wknd over 1f out* **15/2**

1142 **6** *2* **My Lucille (IRE)**[16] 5437 3-9-5 78 DavidAllan 4 66
(Tim Easterby) *cl up: rdn along over 2f out: wknd ins fnl f* **4/1**[1]

2166 **7** *½* **Forever A Lady (IRE)**[4] 5836 3-9-5 78 JoeFanning 1 65
(Keith Dalgleish) *s.i.s: hld up bhd ldng gp: drvn along over 2f out: btn over 1f out* **15/2**

1006 **8** *2 ¼* **Dark Crystal**[6] 5779 5-9-3 70 GrahamLee 8 53
(Linda Perratt) *broke wl: sn stdd in rr: drvn along 3f out: btn fnl 2f* **40/1**

1m 45.63s (-2.77) **Going Correction** -0.20s/f (Firm)

WFA 3 from 4yo+ 6lb **8** Ran SP% **112.0**

Speed ratings (Par 102): **105,103,102,102,98 96,96,94**

CSF £23.94 CT £120.86 TOTE £5.40: £1.70, £1.60, £2.30; EX 27.20 Trifecta £169.50.

Owner Peter Smith P C Coaches Limited **Bred** James Ortega Bloodstock **Trained** Upper Helmsley, N Yorks

FOCUS

A tight fillies' handicap. There was a fair pace on, but the winner wasn't for catching. Race distance increased by 12yds.

6006 RACING UK HD ON SKY 432 H'CAP 1m 3f 14y

4:35 (4:35) (Class 5) (0-75,74) 3-Y-O+ **£3,881** (£1,155; £577; £288) **Stalls** High

Form RPR

0000 **1** **El Beau (IRE)**[24] 5180 5-9-13 73 TomEaves 3 86
(John Quinn) *trckd ldrs: smooth hdwy to ld over 1f out: pushed out ins fnl f: comf* **11/2**

5552 **2** *2* **Eez Eh (IRE)**[8] 5718 3-8-12 67 [1] ConnorBeasley 4 76
(Keith Dalgleish) *t.k.h early: chsd ldr: rdn and ev ch briefly over 1f out: sn chsng wnr: one pce fnl f: lost 2nd cl home* **15/8**[2]

0001 **3** *shd* **Calliope**[15] 5481 3-8-7 62 AndrewMullen 2 70
(Kenneth Slack) *t.k.h: hld up in tch: rdn and outpcd 3f out: rallied over 1f out: kpt on fnl f to take 2nd nr fin: no ch w wnr* **6/4**[1]

-013 **4** *9* **Chant (IRE)**[28] 4967 6-10-0 74 GrahamLee 5 67
(Ann Duffield) *led: rdn along over 2f out: hdd over 1f out: wknd fnl f* **9/2**[3]

2m 24.28s (-1.32) **Going Correction** -0.20s/f (Firm)

WFA 3 from 5yo+ 9lb **4** Ran SP% **108.3**

Speed ratings (Par 103): **96,94,94,87**

CSF £15.83 TOTE £6.80; EX 13.90 Trifecta £35.30.

Owner Highfield Racing (Camacho) **Bred** Bayview Properties Ltd **Trained** Settrington, N Yorks

FOCUS

An ordinary little handicap. It was run at a brisk early pace, but steadied leaving the far side. Race distance increased by 12yds.

6007 HIGHLAND SPRING WATER HAMILTON PARK 2-Y-O SERIES FINAL (A NURSERY H'CAP) 6f 6y

5:10 (5:11) (Class 2) 2-Y-O

£12,450 (£3,728; £1,864; £932; £466; £234) **Stalls** High

Form RPR

102 **1** **Harome (IRE)**[18] 5352 2-9-0 73 SamJames 1 80
(David Loughnane) *mde all: rdn along over 1f out: kpt on strly fnl f* **7/1**

4435 **2** *1 ¼* **Heatongrad (IRE)**[24] 5171 2-8-11 70 JackGarritty 8 73
(Richard Fahey) *trckd ldrs: effrt and pushed along 2f out: chsd wnr ins fnl f: r.o* **6/1**[3]

2122 **3** *1* **La Casa Tarifa (IRE)**[13] 5560 2-9-7 80 JoeFanning 7 80
(Mark Johnston) *trckd wnr: effrt and rdn 2f out: kpt on same pce ins fnl f* **15/8**[1]

643 **4** *nk* **Flash Of White**[37] 4678 2-9-0 73 ConnorBeasley 4 72+
(Bryan Smart) *dwlt: sn pushed along in rr: drvn and hdwy over 1f out: swtchd rt ins fnl f: r.o: no imp* **5/1**[2]

4150 **5** *1 ¾* **Reckless Serenade (IRE)**[8] 5712 2-8-8 67 AndrewMullen 5 61
(Keith Dalgleish) *in tch: effrt and drvn along 2f out: outpcd fnl f* **12/1**

5233 **6** *2* **Galahad**[47] 4315 2-8-8 67 TomEaves 2 55
(Richard Fahey) *hld up on outside: drvn and shortlived effrt wl over 1f out: btn ins fnl f* **7/1**

405 **7** *4* **Western Presence**[20] 5289 2-8-7 66 PatrickMathers 3 42
(Richard Fahey) *in tch: drvn along over 2f out: wknd over 1f out* **16/1**

0510 **8** *3 ¾* **Percy Toplis**[8] 5712 2-8-13 72 KeaganLatham 6 38
(Kevin Ryan) *in tch: rdn along over 2f out: nt clr run briefly over 1f out: sn wknd* **9/1**

1m 10.87s (-1.33) **Going Correction** -0.20s/f (Firm) **8** Ran SP% **114.3**

Speed ratings (Par 100): **100,98,97,96,94 91,86,81**

CSF £48.18 CT £110.47 TOTE £7.70: £1.90, £2.10, £1.30; EX 55.10 Trifecta £187.60.

Owner R G Fell **Bred** Limestone & Tara Studs **Trained** Market Drayton, Shropshire

FOCUS

The final of the series and it looked very competitive. It paid to be handy.

6008 RACING UK DAY PASS JUST £10 AMATEUR RIDERS' H'CAP 6f 6y

5:40 (5:40) (Class 6) (0-65,65) 4-Y-O+ **£2,807** (£870; £435; £217) **Stalls** High

Form RPR

3052 **1** **Picks Pinta**[13] 5535 5-10-9 65 (p) MrTGreenwood(5) 7 70
(John David Riches) *mde all against stands' rail: pushed along over 1f out: hld on wl fnl f* **5/2**[2]

4325 **2** *nk* **Slim Chance (IRE)**[29] 4931 7-10-3 59 (p) MissPBridgwater(5) 5 63
(Simon West) *t.k.h: pressed wnr: rdn and edgd rt 2f out: edgd lft and kpt on ins fnl f: hld nr fin* **9/1**

113 **3** *nk* **Diamonds A Dancing**[21] 5252 6-10-6 62 (be) MissAMcCain(5) 2 65+
(Donald McCain) *hld up: rdn over 2f out: hdwy over 1f out: kpt on ins fnl f: nrst fin* **6/1**

0600 **4** *nk* **Pabusar**[41] 4512 8-9-6 46 (tp) MissBeckySmith(3) 1 48
(Micky Hammond) *prom: rdn over 2f out: rallied fnl f: nrst fin* **25/1**

-305 **5** *1 ½* **Napoleon Solo**[194] 621 4-10-11 62 (e[1]) MissSBrotherton 9 60
(David Barron) *trckd ldrs: drvn along wl over 1f out: outpcd ins fnl f* **2/1**[1]

0054 **6** *2* **Pushkin Museum (IRE)**[8] 5714 5-10-5 61 MrMEnnis(5) 4 59
(Richard Fahey) *dwlt: bhd: pushed along and outpcd 1/2-way: hdwy over 1f out: nvr rchd ldrs* **5/1**[3]

3000 **7** *4 ½* **Reflation**[13] 5535 4-9-6 50 (v) MissCADods(7) 3 28
(Michael Dods) *bhd: outpcd and hung rt over 2f out: sn btn* **16/1**

1m 11.45s (-0.75) **Going Correction** -0.20s/f (Firm) **7** Ran SP% **112.6**

Speed ratings (Par 101): **97,96,96,95,93 91,85**

CSF £23.94 CT £120.15 TOTE £3.20: £1.50, £4.50; EX 20.20 Trifecta £87.20.

Owner J D Riches **Bred** Heatherwold Stud **Trained** Pilling, Lancashire

The Form Book, Raceform Ltd, Newbury, RG14 5SJ

FOCUS
A moderate sprint handicap, confined to amateur riders. The runner-up sets the level on this year's form.
T/Plt: £190.40 to a £1 stake. Pool: £44,101.21 - 169 winning units T/Qpdt: £52.30 to a £1 stake. Pool: £4,438.26 - 62.77 winning units **Richard Young**

5974 RIPON (R-H)
Tuesday, August 30

OFFICIAL GOING: Good (7.8)
Wind: light 1/2 behind Weather: fine

6009 THEAKSTONS POP-UP BEER FESTIVAL 24TH SEPTEMBER MAIDEN STKS — 6f
5:15 (5:18) (Class 5) 2-Y-O — **£3,234** (£962; £481; £240) **Stalls** High

Form — RPR

62 **1** **Colonel Frank**[26] 5077 2-9-5 0 AndreaAtzeni 1 80+
(Ed Walker) *swtchd lft after s: chsd ldrs: drvn over 1f out: styd on to ld last 75yds* **6/4**[1]

3 **2** ½ **Dawoodi**[34] 4765 2-9-5 0 JamesDoyle 4 79
(Hugo Palmer) *swtchd lft after s: led: t.k.h: drvn 1f out: hdd and no ex last 75yds* **6/4**[1]

3 7 **Buccaneers Cove (IRE)** 2-9-5 0 GeorgeChaloner 3 58+
(Richard Fahey) *dwlt: mid-div: drvn over 2f out: kpt on fnl f: tk modest 3rd nr fin* **7/1**[2]

4 ½ **Panther In Pink (IRE)** 2-9-0 0 PJMcDonald 8 51
(Ann Duffield) *chsd ldrs: kpt on one pce over 1f out* **14/1**[3]

40 **5** 1½ **Jorvik Prince**[15] 5477 2-9-5 0 ShaneGray 5 52
(Karen Tutty) *chsd ldrs: one pce over 1f out* **80/1**

6 4½ **Miss Montes** 2-9-0 0 AndrewElliott 6 33
(James Bethell) *gave problems in stalls: dwlt: in rr: hdwy and edgd rt over 2f out: wknd over 1f out* **33/1**

6 **7** ½ **I Don't Believe It**[41] 4508 2-9-5 0 PaulMulrennan 9 37
(Micky Hammond) *sn outpcd and in rr: sme hdwy over 1f out: nvr on terms* **50/1**

06 **8** 2¼ **Four Wishes**[15] 5477 2-9-5 0 JamesSullivan 7 30
(Tim Easterby) *sn outpcd and in rr* **16/1**

05 **9** 7 **Ravenoak (IRE)**[25] 5107 2-9-5 0 RichardKingscote 2 9
(Tom Dascombe) *swtchd lft after s: drvn to chse ldrs: lost pl over 1f out: eased fnl 100yds* **16/1**

1m 12.33s (-0.67) **Going Correction** -0.225s/f (Firm) **9** Ran SP% **117.1**
Speed ratings (Par 94): **95,94,85,84,82 76,75,72,63**
CSF £3.62 TOTE £2.40: £1.30, £1.10, £2.60; EX 4.60 Trifecta £15.10.
Owner Mrs Fitri Hay **Bred** Eliza Park International Pty Ltd **Trained** Upper Lambourn, Berks

FOCUS
After a couple of fair days the ground had dried out so the ground was officially good. The two Newmarket-trained contenders had shown much the best form among those with experience in this maiden, which also featured a couple of newcomers with attractive profiles on paper, and they dominated the finish. The bare form of those in behind is probably not something to get carried away with.

6010 SIS HORSES IN-RUNNING NURSERY H'CAP — 5f
5:45 (5:51) (Class 5) (0-75,74) 2-Y-O — **£3,234** (£962; £481; £240) **Stalls** High

Form — RPR

2332 **1** **Merry Banter**[25] 5125 2-9-3 70 PaulMulrennan 12 79
(Paul Midgley) *wnt rt s: led after 1f: styd on wl fnl f* **11/2**[1]

2532 **2** 1¾ **Big Lachie**[11] 5598 2-9-4 71 JamesDoyle 14 74
(Jamie Osborne) *dwlt: sn mid-div: hdwy over 2f out: chsd wnr over 1f out: no imp.* **6/1**[2]

3015 **3** 2 **Major Jumbo**[18] 5352 2-9-2 69 KevinStott 11 65
(Kevin Ryan) *wnt lft s: mid-div: hdwy over 2f out: 3rd 1f out: kpt on same pce* **8/1**

006 **4** ¾ **Mr Strutter (IRE)**[28] 4966 2-8-4 57 JamesSullivan 13 50
(John Quinn) *mid-div: drvn and outpcd over 2f out: styd on appr fnl f: tk 4th nr fin* **9/1**

366 **5** ½ **Bithynia (IRE)**[19] 5317 2-9-2 69 AndreaAtzeni 9 60
(Hugo Palmer) *mid-div: hdwy over 2f out: edgd rt and one pce fnl f* **6/1**[2]

306 **6** 1½ **My Cherry Blossom**[31] 4890 2-8-8 61 JasonHart 5 47
(Tim Easterby) *swtchd lft after s: in rr: hdwy over 1f out: kpt on* **14/1**

040 **7** 1 **Lou's Diamond**[20] 5289 2-8-6 64 NathanEvans(5) 15 46
(Michael Easterby) *mid-div: kpt on over 1f out: nvr a factor* **16/1**

1532 **8** nse **Miss Rosina (IRE)**[32] 4843 2-9-3 70 TomQueally 17 52
(George Margarson) *led 1f: chsd wnr: wknd over 1f out* **7/1**[3]

3403 **9** 1¾ **Monte Cinq (IRE)**[22] 5244 2-9-0 67 BenCurtis 4 43
(Jason Ward) *racd wd: chsd ldrs. one pce fnl 2f* **14/1**

2524 **10** nk **Sheepscar Lad (IRE)**[8] 5727 2-8-13 73 (v[1]) LewisEdmunds(7) 16 47
(Nigel Tinkler) *slowly away: kpt on over 1f out: nvr on terms* **9/1**

504 **11** 1¼ **Vaux (IRE)**[41] 4510 2-9-1 68 DougieCostello 2 38
(Ben Haslam) *in rr: swtchd wd 2f out: kpt on: nvr a factor* **40/1**

1440 **12** shd **Melaniemillie**[30] 4915 2-8-13 69 JacobButterfield(3) 8 39
(Ollie Pears) *chsd ldrs: one pce fnl 2f* **50/1**

0050 **13** 3¾ **Flying Hope (IRE)**[18] 5364 2-7-7 53 oh2 SophieKilloran(7) 10 9
(Nigel Tinkler) *chsd ldrs: lost pl over 1f out: eased clsng stages* **25/1**

604 **14** 6 **Zebedee Star**[21] 5272 2-8-11 64 ShaneGray 3
(Keith Dalgleish) *racd wd: mid-div: lost pl 2f out: eased fnl 100yds* **25/1**

58.59s (-1.41) **Going Correction** -0.225s/f (Firm) **14** Ran SP% **118.9**
Speed ratings (Par 94): **102,99,96,94,94 91,90,89,87,86 84,84,78,68**
CSF £35.72 CT £267.24 TOTE £6.50: £2.10, £2.40, £3.30; EX 35.30 Trifecta £295.30.
Owner H Thornton **Bred** Jeremy Green And Sons **Trained** Westow, N Yorks
■ Stewards' Enquiry : Nathan Evans The Starter reported that Lou's Diamond was unruly and reluctant to load. The trainer's attention was drawn to the restriction incurred under Rule (B)44 and informed that the filly could not run until the day after passing a stalls test.

FOCUS
Just four winners in the field for this 0-75 nursery, but plenty were open to improvement, with seven of them making their handicap debut. A high draw proved important.

6011 21 ENGINEER REGIMENT SAPPER H'CAP — 2m
6:15 (6:16) (Class 4) (0-85,82) 3-Y-O+ — **£4,851** (£1,443; £721; £360) **Stalls** High

Form — RPR

-411 **1** **Silva Eclipse**[54] 4033 3-8-9 77 ow1 PaulMulrennan 6 83+
(Jedd O'Keeffe) *t.k.h: w ldr: carried wd bnd after over 3f: upsides and hung rt over 3f out: led 2f out: drvn rt out* **6/5**[1]

2242 **2** 1 **Wishing Well**[4] 5856 4-8-12 66 PJMcDonald 3 71
(Micky Hammond) *trckd ldrs: lft in ld bnd after over 3f: hdd 2f out: kpt on same pce last 100yds* **11/2**[3]

3331 **3** nk **Kajaki (IRE)**[25] 5111 3-8-3 71 (p) ShaneGray 4 76
(Kevin Ryan) *drvn to ld: hung bdly lft: wd and hdd bnd after over 3f: reminders and chse ldr over 3f out: kpt on fnl f: styng on at fin* **7/2**[2]

1061 **4** 1¾ **Itlaaq**[31] 4892 10-9-9 82 (t) NathanEvans(5) 2 85
(Michael Easterby) *hld up in rr: hdwy on ins to trck ldrs whn hmpd over 2f out: kpt on same pce fnl f* **12/1**

0332 **5** 2½ **Lara Carbonara (IRE)**[12] 5580 4-9-4 72 TadhgO'Shea 5 72
(John Patrick Shanahan, Ire) *hld up: hdwy 10f out: trcking ldrs over 3f out: wknd last 100yds* **8/1**

01-0 **6** 8 **Gleese The Devil (IRE)**[10] 5642 5-9-12 80 GeorgeChaloner 1 70
(Richard Fahey) *trckd ldrs: drvn over 3f out: edgd rt over 2f out: lost pl over 1f out: bhd whn eased clsng stages* **11/1**

3m 31.91s (0.11) **Going Correction** -0.225s/f (Firm)
WFA 3 from 4yo+ 14lb **6** Ran SP% **110.2**
Speed ratings (Par 105): **90,89,89,88,87 83**
CSF £7.87 TOTE £2.00: £1.30, £2.20; EX 7.30 Trifecta £17.90.
Owner Geoff & Sandra Turnbull **Bred** R F Broad **Trained** Middleham Moor, N Yorks
■ Stewards' Enquiry : Nathan Evans jockey said the gelding was denied a clear run
Shane Gray four-day ban (13-16 Sep): used whip above permitted level

FOCUS
Not a huge turnout, but an in-form bunch assembled for this staying handicap, which was run over an extra six yards, with all bar one of the field having won or finished second last time out. As ever, it was not easy to come from behind.

6012 DAVID CHAPMAN MEMORIAL H'CAP — 5f
6:45 (6:47) (Class 3) (0-95,95) 3-Y-O+ — **£7,762** (£2,310; £1,154; £577) **Stalls** High

Form — RPR

3044 **1** **Pipers Note**[17] 5418 6-9-10 95 GeorgeChaloner 4 105
(Richard Whitaker) *chsd ldr: led over 1f out: kpt on wl* **13/2**[1]

0502 **2** ¾ **Apricot Sky**[15] 5479 6-8-5 76 BarryMcHugh 6 83
(David Nicholls) *swtchd lft after s: chsd ldrs: kpt on same pce to take 2nd last 75yds* **18/1**

1501 **3** 1¼ **Stanghow**[15] 5479 4-9-1 86 PJMcDonald 5 89
(Antony Brittain) *led: hdd over 1f out: kpt on same pce* **12/1**

0562 **4** nk **Shipyard (USA)**[10] 5648 7-9-4 89 (p) TomQueally 2 90+
(Michael Appleby) *swtchd lft after s: racd wd: mid-div: hdwy over 2f out: chsng ldrs over 1f out: kpt on same pce* **7/1**[2]

1350 **5** ½ **Avon Breeze**[17] 5417 7-9-0 90 (p[1]) NathanEvans(5) 1 90
(Richard Whitaker) *wnt rt s: sn chsng ldrs: edgd lft over 1f out: one pce* **20/1**

1656 **6** hd **Adam's Ale**[6] 5780 7-8-5 79 (b) RachelRichardson(3) 7 78
(Mark Walford) *mid-div: hdwy over 2f out: chsng ldrs over 1f out: one pce* **9/1**[3]

-465 **7** hd **Imtiyaaz (IRE)**[16] 5436 4-9-5 90 AndreaAtzeni 11 88+
(Roger Varian) *chsd ldrs: edgd rt and one pce fnl f* **7/1**[2]

0050 **8** 2 **Rita's Boy (IRE)**[31] 4873 4-8-5 76 (v) BenCurtis 13 67
(K R Burke) *mid-div: effrt over 2f out: kpt on: nvr a factor* **14/1**

5004 **9** nse **Silvanus (IRE)**[15] 5479 11-9-0 85 PaulMulrennan 3 76
(Paul Midgley) *swtchd lft s: mid-div: effrt 2f out: nvr a threat* **7/1**[2]

0450 **10** hd **Lexington Place**[17] 5390 6-9-0 85 JamesSullivan 10 75+
(Ruth Carr) *hld up towards rr: effrt over 1f out: nt clr run last 150yds: nt rcvr* **14/1**

1006 **11** 2½ **Bondi Beach Boy**[15] 5479 7-8-9 83 JacobButterfield(3) 8 64
(James Turner) *chsd ldrs: sn drvn along: lost pl over 1f out* **11/1**

4010 **12** ½ **Excessable**[10] 5657 3-8-9 82 (t) JasonHart 9 61
(Tim Easterby) *in rr: drvn 2f out: nvr on terms* **10/1**

0040 **13** 2¼ **Taexali (IRE)**[46] 4338 3-9-6 93 TadhgO'Shea 12 64
(John Patrick Shanahan, Ire) *a in rr* **11/1**

57.82s (-2.18) **Going Correction** -0.225s/f (Firm)
WFA 3 from 4yo+ 2lb **13** Ran SP% **117.6**
Speed ratings (Par 107): **108,106,104,104,103 103,102,99,99,99 95,94,90**
CSF £119.85 CT £1374.21 TOTE £7.40: £2.60, £6.20, £5.20; EX 103.30 Trifecta £1375.50.
Owner Cragg Wood Racing & Partner **Bred** Wadacre Stud **Trained** Scarcroft, W Yorks
■ Stewards' Enquiry : Andrea Atzeni The Veterinary Officer reported that Imtiyaaz was struck into its right fore.

FOCUS
This traditionally competitive 76-95 sprint looked well up to scratch, with plenty of in-form contenders and others seemingly primed for a big run, but few had the pace to get into a contest that was dominated throughout by the first three home. The race has been rated around the runner-up.

6013 SIS TRADING SERVICES FILLIES' H'CAP — 6f
7:15 (7:15) (Class 4) (0-85,82) 3-Y-O+ — **£4,851** (£1,443; £721; £360) **Stalls** High

Form — RPR

0040 **1** **Love Island**[17] 5390 7-9-5 77 [1] GeorgeChaloner 4 85
(Richard Whitaker) *mid-div: pushed along over 3f out: hdwy over 2f out: styd on fnl f: led last 75yds* **13/2**

1233 **2** ½ **Cersei**[23] 5205 3-9-2 77 (t) AndreaAtzeni 5 83
(David Simcock) *trckd ldrs: edgd rt 2f out: led narrowly 1f out: hdd and no ex last 75yds* **7/4**[1]

3444 **3** 2½ **Rural Celebration**[54] 4034 5-9-1 78 JoshDoyle(5) 1 76
(David O'Meara) *trckd ldr: led briefly over 1f out: kpt on same pce* **13/2**

4353 **4** nse **Meandmyshadow**[18] 5379 8-9-2 74 (b) BenCurtis 6 72
(Alan Brown) *led: hdd over 1f out: kpt on one pce* **6/1**[3]

6-11 **5** hd **Tanaasub (IRE)**[26] 5059 3-9-1 76 PaulMulrennan 7 73
(Robert Cowell) *trckd ldrs: effrt and edgd rt appr fnl f: kpt on same pce* **9/4**[2]

6-0 **6** 11 **Birdcage**[10] 5643 3-9-7 82 BarryMcHugh 2 44
(Richard Fahey) *dwlt: outpcd in last: lost pl over 1f out: sn wl bhd* **25/1**

1m 11.08s (-1.92) **Going Correction** -0.225s/f (Firm)
WFA 3 from 5yo+ 3lb **6** Ran SP% **111.9**
Speed ratings (Par 102): **103,102,99,98,98 84**
CSF £18.28 TOTE £7.40: £2.70, £1.20; EX 20.50 Trifecta £74.10.
Owner Nice Day Out Partnership **Bred** Hellwood Farm And J B Pemberton **Trained** Scarcroft, W Yorks

FOCUS
A really good pace for this fillies' handicap, which helped those coming from behind. The winner has a fair record here.

6014 SIS STREAM MAIDEN STKS — 1m 1f 170y
7:45 (7:46) (Class 5) 3-4-Y-O — **£3,234** (£962; £481; £240) **Stalls** Low

Form — RPR

3253 **1** **Warp Factor (IRE)**[12] 5579 3-9-3 79 TadhgO'Shea 2 76
(John Patrick Shanahan, Ire) *trckd ldrs: 2nd over 3f out: upsides 2f out: styd on to ld clsng stages* **7/4**[2]

2320 **2** 3/4 **Imperial Focus (IRE)**[39] 4611 3-9-3 78................................ JoeDoyle 3 74
(Simon Waugh) *led: jnd 2f out: hdd and no ex clsng stages* **10/3**[3]
6-22 **3** *hd* **Confident Kid**[37] 4690 3-9-3 78..[1] JamesDoyle 5 74
(Saeed bin Suroor) *trckd ldrs: t.k.h: effrt and 3rd over 3f out: sn drvn: kpt on fnl 75yds* **5/4**[1]
6 **4** *7* **Calarules**[8] 5716 3-9-0 0.. RachelRichardson[(3)] 1 60
(Tim Easterby) *dwlt: in last: sme hdwy over 3f out: outpcd fnl 2f* **50/1**
40 **5** *64* **La Salesse (FR)**[46] 4372 3-8-12 0.................................. PaulMulrennan 4
(Mark Johnston) *chsd ldr: drvn 4f out: edgd lft and lost pl over 3f out: sn bhd: t.o whn eased fnl f: eventually completed: lame* **14/1**

2m 4.55s (-0.85) **Going Correction** -0.225s/f (Firm) **5** Ran SP% **112.5**
Speed ratings (Par 103): **94,93,93,87,36**
CSF £8.17 TOTE £2.80: £1.30, £2.00; EX 6.20 Trifecta £7.90.
Owner Thistle Bloodstock Limited **Bred** Thistle Bloodstock Limited **Trained** Kells, Co Kilkenny

FOCUS
Three of these maidens were closely matched on the pick of their form, with only 1lb between the trio on BHA ratings in a contest run over an extra six yards. There was little to separate the three at the line, suggesting they probably all ran close to their marks.
T/Plt: £70.40 to a £1 stake. Pool: £76,746.79 - 794.88 winning units T/Qpdt: £28.70 to a £1 stake. Pool: £5,750.09 - 147.98 winning units **Walter Glynn**

5819 CLAIREFONTAINE (R-H)
Tuesday, August 30

OFFICIAL GOING: Turf: good

6015a PRIX DE L'ECOLE BLONDEAU (CLAIMER) (2YO) (TURF) 1m
1:20 (1:20) 2-Y-O **£9,926** (£3,970; £2,977; £1,985; £992)

RPR

1 **Florida Dream (FR)**[21] 2-9-1 0................................ StephanePasquier 4 75
(Y Gourraud, France) **33/1**
2 *snk* **Micolys (FR)**[26] 5066 2-8-13 0.. TonyPiccone 8 73
(K R Burke) **31/10**[2]
3 1/2 **Larno (FR)**[21] 5279 2-9-4 0.................................. ChristopheSoumillon 6 77
(D Prod'Homme, France) **23/10**[1]
4 *1 3/4* **Cancilla (FR)** 2-8-8 0.. MaximeGuyon 12 63
(P Sogorb, France) **78/10**
5 1/2 **Jenychope (FR)**[13] 5568 2-8-8 0..............................(p) UmbertoRispoli 9 62
(D Windrif, France) **21/1**
6 1/2 **Alfa Manifesto (FR)**[7] 5755 2-9-1 0.........................(b) AntoineHamelin 3 68
(Matthieu Palussiere, France) **12/1**
7 *hd* **Elfy James (FR)**[16] 5447 2-8-11 0.............................. HugoJourniac[(4)] 5 67
(D Windrif, France) **18/1**
8 *1* **Briseide (IRE)**[44] 2-8-11 0.. AlexisBadel 7 61
(D Zarroli, Italy) **66/10**[3]
9 *1 1/2* **Rinky Dink Dawn (IRE)**[5] 5819 2-8-11 0...................(p) LouisBeuzelin 2 57
(J S Moore) **47/1**
10 3/4 **Cima Jelois (FR)**[43] 4471 2-8-8 0...........................(p) SebastienMaillot 1 53
(Robert Collet, France) **50/1**
11 1/2 **Key Success (IRE)**[17] 5460 2-9-1 0.......................... GregoryBenoist 10 58
(Y Barberot, France) **43/5**
12 *3* **Stormberg (IRE)**[97] 2601 2-8-4 0............................ KyllanBarbaud[(7)] 11 48
(N Caullery, France) **25/1**
13 *7* **Ninian Des Aigles (FR)** 2-8-11 0............................ RonanThomas 13 31
(Mme C Barande-Barbe, France) **49/1**

1m 40.3s (100.30) **13** Ran SP% **120.0**
WIN (incl. 1 euro stake): 33.50. PLACES: 5.90, 1.80, 1.80. DF: 84.00. SF: 216.70.
Owner Yohann Gourraud **Bred** J-P Dubois **Trained** France

5623 BATH (L-H)
Wednesday, August 31

OFFICIAL GOING: Firm (good to firm in places)
Wind: Almost nil becoming fresh, against by race 4 Weather: Overcast, becoming sunny from race 4

6016 BATH FOOD FESTIVAL EUROPEAN BREEDERS' FUND NOVICE STKS 5f 161y
2:00 (2:02) (Class 5) 2-Y-O **£3,234** (£962; £481; £240) **Stalls** Centre

Form RPR

4502 **1** **Nuclear Power**[11] 5631 2-9-2 82.................................... MartinDwyer 6 83
(William Muir) *chsd ldr: led wl over 1f out: rdn clr: comf* **4/5**[1]
2 *5* **Trump's Magic (USA)** 2-9-2 0.. DaneO'Neill 1 65
(David Evans) *s.i.s: bhd tl hdwy over 1f out: chsd wnr ins fnl f: no imp* **7/1**[3]
56 **3** *2 1/4* **Imperial City (USA)**[35] 4762 2-8-11 0..................[1] MichaelJMMurphy 7 52
(Charles Hills) *in tch: drvn along 3f out: kpt on same pce* **6/1**[2]
5 **4** *shd* **Swell Hill**[134] 1543 2-8-11 0.. PatDobbs 4 52
(Richard Hannon) *chsd ldrs: lost pl and hrd rdn 2f out: kpt on ins fnl f* **10/1**
003 **5** *hd* **Fethiye Boy**[21] 5283 2-9-2 60.. LiamKeniry 2 56
(Ronald Harris) *led tl wl over 1f out: wknd fnl f* **66/1**
5 **6** *nk* **Polly's Angels (IRE)**[107] 2310 2-8-11 0.......................... ShaneKelly 9 50
(Richard Hughes) *chsd ldrs tl hung rt and wknd over 1f out* **9/1**
345 **7** *7* **Coronation Cottage**[14] 5542 2-8-11 64.............................. FMBerry 5 27
(Malcolm Saunders) *s.s: bhd: slipped over 3f out: effrt in centre over 2f out: wknd over 1f out* **12/1**

1m 11.05s (-0.15) **Going Correction** +0.025s/f (Good) **7** Ran SP% **110.6**
Speed ratings (Par 94): **102,95,92,92,91 91,82**
CSF £6.44 TOTE £1.80: £1.10, £3.70; EX 6.60 Trifecta £24.10.
Owner A A Byrne **Bred** Park Farm Racing **Trained** Lambourn, Berks

FOCUS
The going was firm, good to firm in places (GoingStick 9.1). A modest and uncompetitive novice event to start, with the hot favourite winning very much as he pleased.

6017 DRIBUILD GROUP APPRENTICE TRAINING SERIES H'CAP (BATH SUMMER SPRINT SERIES QUALIFIER) 5f 161y
2:30 (2:31) (Class 5) (0-75,75) 3-Y-O+ **£3,557** (£1,058; £529; £264) **Stalls** Centre

Form RPR

1060 **1** **Silverrica (IRE)**[21] 5305 6-9-6 **74**.................................... GeorgiaCox 8 80
(Malcolm Saunders) *stdd after s and swtchd to inner: hdwy 2f out: drvn to ld 100yds out: hld on wl* **11/2**[3]
0265 **2** 1/2 **Archie Stevens**[4] 5896 6-8-7 **66**.............................. AledBeech[(5)] 1 70
(David Evans) *led: rdn over 1f out: hdd 100yds out: r.o* **6/1**
0063 **3** *hd* **Racquet**[21] 5284 3-9-4 **75**.. HollieDoyle 6 79
(Richard Hannon) *towards rr: effrt over 1f out: r.o wl to snatch 3rd on line* **3/1**[1]
-014 **4** *hd* **Vincenzo Coccotti (USA)**[32] 4878 4-8-8 **62**.................... KevinLundie 4 65
(Ken Cunningham-Brown) *in tch: rdn to press ldrs over 1f out: r.o* **9/2**[2]
-250 **5** *1 1/2* **Go Nani Go**[21] 5284 10-9-1 **74**.................................... WilliamCox[(5)] 3 72
(Ed de Giles) *prom tl one pce ent fnl f* **16/1**
0626 **6** *nk* **Whitecrest**[10] 5669 8-9-2 **70**.. MeganNicholls 5 67
(John Spearing) *in rr: effrt over 1f out: styng on at fin* **20/1**
0-20 **7** *1 1/4* **Dreams Of Glory**[3] 5928 8-9-1 **69**................................ MitchGodwin 2 62
(Ron Hodges) *chsd ldr tl no ex over 1f out* **10/1**
053 **8** *2 1/4* **Edged Out**[21] 5285 6-9-6 **74**.. GeorgeWood 7 60
(Christopher Mason) *chsd ldrs tl wknd 1f out* **9/2**[2]

1m 11.28s (0.08) **Going Correction** +0.025s/f (Good)
WFA 3 from 4yo+ 3lb **8** Ran SP% **110.8**
Speed ratings (Par 103): **100,99,99,98,96 96,94,91**
CSF £35.73 CT £111.73 TOTE £5.00: £1.70, £2.80, £1.60; EX 35.20 Trifecta £178.80.
Owner Mrs Ginny Nicholas **Bred** Miss A R Byrne **Trained** Green Ore, Somerset

FOCUS
An ordinary apprentice sprint handicap and all eight horses were in a line across the track passing the furlong pole. The first four all ran close to their marks.

6018 MARKEL H'CAP 5f 11y
3:00 (3:00) (Class 5) (0-75,81) 3-Y-O **£3,234** (£962; £481; £240) **Stalls** Centre

Form RPR

101 **1** **Lapilli**[8] 5751 3-9-8 **81** 6ex.. GeorgiaCox[(5)] 3 91+
(William Haggas) *hld up: hdwy on bit to trck ldr 2f out: stl gng wl and chal ins fnl f: shkn up to ld nr fin* **8/15**[1]
1400 **2** *nk* **Entertaining Ben**[42] 4502 3-9-4 **72**............................ MartinDwyer 2 77
(William Muir) *led: hrd rdn fnl f: hdd and unable qck nr fin* **33/1**
4035 **3** *3* **Point Of Woods**[21] 5305 3-9-6 **74**.................................... FMBerry 4 68
(Ralph Beckett) *sn outpcd in rr: styd on u.p fr over 1f out* **4/1**[2]
1602 **4** *2* **Powerful Dream (IRE)**[42] 4502 3-9-2 **70**.......................... ShaneKelly 6 57
(Ronald Harris) *dwlt: sn disputing 3rd: hrd rdn and btn 1f out* **10/1**
5-2 **5** 3/4 **Nora Batt (IRE)**[33] 4820 3-8-10 **69**............................ GeorgeWood[(5)] 5 53
(John W Nicholson, Ire) *chsd ldr tl 2f out: rdn and btn over 1f out* **15/2**[3]

1m 1.73s (-0.77) **Going Correction** +0.025s/f (Good) **5** Ran SP% **109.0**
Speed ratings (Par 100): **107,106,101,98,97**
CSF £18.70 TOTE £1.30: £1.10, £7.80; EX 11.20 Trifecta £44.80.
Owner Sheikh Ahmed Al Maktoum **Bred** Whitsbury Manor Stud **Trained** Newmarket, Suffolk

FOCUS
A modest 3yo sprint handicap which was all about the favourite, but odds-on backers would have been nervous. The runner-up is the key to the form.

6019 EBF STALLIONS BREEDING WINNERS FILLIES' H'CAP 1m 2f 46y
3:30 (3:30) (Class 4) (0-80,80) 3-Y-O+ **£6,469** (£1,925; £962; £481) **Stalls** Low

Form RPR

0026 **1** **Sunscape (IRE)**[21] 5302 3-8-9 **71**.................................... FMBerry 5 78
(Hughie Morrison) *stdd s: hld up in 5th: hdwy to dispute ld fnl 2f: jst prevailed* **11/2**[3]
5036 **2** *hd* **Miss Minuty**[18] 5406 4-9-3 **76**.................................... GeorgeWood[(5)] 1 82
(Alexandra Dunn) *t.k.h in rr: hdwy on outer 3f out: disp ld fnl 2f: jst denied* **8/1**
54-3 **3** *1 3/4* **Canonbury (IRE)**[29] 4978 3-8-13 **75**.............................. TedDurcan 3 78
(Sir Michael Stoute) *led at modest pce for 5f: remained cl 3rd on inner: one pce fnl f* **7/4**[1]
-634 **4** *1 1/4* **Zaakhir (IRE)**[12] 5596 3-9-4 **80**.................................... DaneO'Neill 2 80
(Charles Hills) *t.k.h in 3rd: dropped to rr 4f out: rallied over 1f out: one pce* **15/8**[2]
2306 **5** *1 1/4* **Coillte Cailin (IRE)**[16] 5489 6-9-10 **78**.......................... LukeMorris 6 76
(Daniel Mark Loughnane) *in tch: chsd ldr over 4f out tl 2f out: hrd rdn and wknd over 1f out* **14/1**
2223 **6** *1 3/4* **Smart Mover (IRE)**[13] 5571 3-8-1 **70**.......................... MitchGodwin[(7)] 4 64
(Nikki Evans) *trckd ldr: led 5f out tl 2f out: n.m.r and wknd over 1f out* **28/1**

2m 10.29s (-0.71) **Going Correction** +0.025s/f (Good)
WFA 3 from 4yo+ 8lb **6** Ran SP% **107.8**
Speed ratings (Par 102): **103,102,101,100,99 98**
CSF £42.17 TOTE £6.50: £2.70, £2.70; EX 39.20 Trifecta £105.20.
Owner F Trenchard, M Morrison, D Morrison **Bred** Ballintry Stud **Trained** East Ilsley, Berks

FOCUS
A fair fillies' handicap, but rather a strange race with the pace a steady one until the outsider was sent on after half a mile. The betting was dominated by a pair of unexposed 3yos, but neither figured in the finish.

6020 ENVIRONMENTAL ESSENTIALS H'CAP 1m 2f 46y
4:00 (4:01) (Class 6) (0-55,55) 4-Y-O+ **£2,264** (£673; £336; £168) **Stalls** Low

Form RPR

0140 **1** **Eugenic**[30] 4950 5-8-10 **51**.. LuluStanford[(7)] 12 57
(Rod Millman) *mid-div: hdwy over 1f out: led ins fnl f: rdn out* **9/2**[1]
0304 **2** *nk* **Tamujin (IRE)**[11] 5625 8-9-1 **49**.................................... SamHitchcott 1 54
(Ken Cunningham-Brown) *hld up in 5th: wnt prom on inner over 2f out: kpt on fnl f* **11/2**[2]
04-6 **3** *1 1/2* **Cranwell**[21] 5308 4-9-7 **55**.. FergusSweeney 3 58
(George Baker) *disp 2nd: jnd ldr on bit 3f out: hrd rdn over 1f out: one pce* **9/2**[1]
0504 **4** 1/2 **Deftera Lad (IRE)**[27] 5080 4-8-8 **47**............................ HollieDoyle[(5)] 8 50
(Natalie Lloyd-Beavis) *bhd tl rdn and styd on fnl 2f* **9/2**[1]
5460 **5** *1* **Jackpot**[11] 5630 6-8-12 **46** oh1.......................................(p) FMBerry 6 46
(Brendan Powell) *disp 2nd: slt ld 3f out tl no ex ins fnl f* **10/1**
2024 **6** *shd* **Elle Rebelle**[9] 5708 6-9-3 **51**.. LukeMorris 4 51
(Mark Brisbourne) *dwlt: towards rr: hrd rdn 2f out: styng on at fin* **9/2**[1]

-463 **7** *shd* **Captain Oats (IRE)**[13] 5575 13-9-4 **52**.......................... TimmyMurphy 9 51
(Pam Ford) *chsd ldrs tl one pce appr fnl f* **16/1**

050- **8** *1 ¾* **Miss Dusky Diva (IRE)**[333] 6937 4-9-3 **51**....... WilliamTwiston-Davies 7 47
(David W Drinkwater) *dwlt: bhd: hdwy in centre over 2f out: rdn and btn over 1f out* **9/1**[3]

00-4 **9** *20* **Candelita**[17] 5459 9-8-12 **46** oh1..(p) ShaneKelly 2 4
(Clare Ellam) *led: sn clr: hdd & wknd 3f out: bhd and eased over 1f out* **25/1**

2m 11.26s (0.26) **Going Correction** +0.025s/f (Good) **9** Ran SP% **116.9**
Speed ratings (Par 101): **99,98,97,97,96 96,96,94,78**
CSF £29.65 CT £118.34 TOTE £5.10: £1.80, £1.70, £2.20; EX 31.80 Trifecta £217.20.
Owner Chris Scott **Bred** M S Saunders And Chris Scott **Trained** Kentisbeare, Devon

FOCUS
A moderate 46-55 handicap and not form to dwell on.

6021 SIMON "THE DADDY" AT 60 H'CAP 1m 5y
4:30 (4:30) (Class 5) (0-75,75) 3-Y-O+ **£3,234** (£962; £481; £240) **Stalls** Low

Form RPR

-111 **1** **Mia Tesoro (IRE)**[20] 5326 3-9-3 **72**....................................... ShaneKelly 3 81+
(Charlie Fellowes) *towards rr: hdwy to chse ldr 2f out: led ins fnl f: pushed out* **5/2**[1]

1016 **2** *¾* **British Embassy (IRE)**[12] 5609 4-9-5 **75**..................... JoshuaBryan(7) 5 83
(Brian Barr) *led: 10 l clr 1/2-way: hrd rdn and hdd ins fnl f: kpt on gamely* **12/1**

2325 **3** *1 ½* **The Salmon Man**[34] 4788 4-9-11 **74**...................................... TedDurcan 2 79
(Brendan Powell) *sluggish s: bhd: rdn 3f out: styd on wl fnl 2f* **3/1**[2]

5050 **4** *2 ½* **Mister Musicmaster**[19] 5357 7-9-12 **75**............................ LukeMorris 4 74
(Ron Hodges) *chsd ldrs: drvn along 2f out: styd on same pce* **16/1**

0252 **5** *1* **Marcle (IRE)**[15] 5515 3-8-11 **66**... LiamKeniry 7 62
(Ed de Giles) *chsd clr ldr tl 2f out: one pce* **11/1**

4403 **6** *shd* **Hot Mustard**[11] 5627 6-9-6 **69**.. MartinDwyer 10 65
(William Muir) *chsd ldrs: rdn over 2f out: no imp* **9/1**

0061 **7** *1 ½* **Prim And Proper**[22] 5252 5-8-13 **62**............................(b) DanielMuscutt 9 55
(John Flint) *t.k.h in rr: rdn over 2f out: nvr trbld ldrs* **14/1**

5241 **8** *2 ½* **Cosmic Storm**[12] 5592 3-9-6 **75**.. FMBerry 6 61
(Ralph Beckett) *mid-div: rdn 3f out: outpcd fnl 2f* **11/2**[3]

453 **9** *1 ¾* **Entrench**[15] 5504 3-9-5 **74**.. PatDobbs 1 56
(Amanda Perrett) *mid-div tl hrd rdn and wknd over 2f out* **10/1**

1m 40.02s (-0.78) **Going Correction** +0.025s/f (Good)
WFA 3 from 4yo+ 6lb **9** Ran SP% **116.6**
Speed ratings (Par 103): **104,103,101,99,98 98,96,94,92**
CSF £34.11 CT £94.66 TOTE £3.30: £1.70, £4.40, £1.20; EX 36.40 Trifecta £123.60.
Owner Deron Pearson **Bred** D Pearson **Trained** Newmarket, Suffolk

FOCUS
An ordinary handicap, but won by a filly on a roll and there was no messing about thanks to the runner-up. The third helps set the standard.

6022 CB PROTECTION LTD H'CAP (BATH SUMMER STAYERS' SERIES QUALIFIER) 1m 5f 22y
5:00 (5:00) (Class 6) (0-60,60) 4-Y-O+ **£2,264** (£673; £336; £168) **Stalls** High

Form RPR

6254 **1** **Captain George (IRE)**[29] 4995 5-9-4 **57**......................(v) SteveDrowne 6 62
(Michael Blake) *chsd ldrs: rdn over 2f out: styd on to ld nr fin* **12/1**

6426 **2** *nk* **Lady Hare (IRE)**[12] 5597 4-9-2 **55**.. PatDobbs 5 60
(Ken Cunningham-Brown) *led: kpt on u.p fnl f: hdd nr fin* **9/2**[2]

1261 **3** *1 ½* **Ballyfarsoon (IRE)**[10] 5680 5-9-7 **60** 6ex..........................(v) LukeMorris 7 62
(Ian Williams) *trckd ldr: rdn to chal over 1f out: one pce ins fnl f* **4/1**[1]

2230 **4** *¾* **Cape Spirit (IRE)**[7] 5777 4-8-9 **55**..........................(v) WilliamCox(7) 10 56
(Andrew Balding) *mid-div: hdwy and hrd rdn over 1f out: one pce* **10/1**

U135 **5** *½* **Dynamo (IRE)**[11] 5624 5-9-7 **60**..(t) ShaneKelly 1 60
(Richard Hughes) *prom tl one pce ent fnl f* **5/1**[3]

0540 **6** *hd* **Senor George (IRE)**[20] 5326 9-9-5 **58**................................. RyanClark 2 58
(Simon Hodgson) *towards rr tl styd on u.p fnl 2f* **20/1**

0/0- **7** *2 ¼* **Byron Blue (IRE)**[149] 145 7-8-4 **46** oh1................ EdwardGreatrex(3) 9 43
(Brian Barr) *bhd: rdn 3f out: nvr trbld ldrs* **7/1**

0426 **8** *nk* **Doctor Kehoe**[23] 5232 4-9-3 **56**...(vt) FMBerry 3 52
(David Evans) *in tch tl outpcd 2f out* **6/1**

6452 **9** *1 ¼* **Azure Amour (IRE)**[11] 5625 4-8-6 **50**.................... GeorgeWood(5) 4 44
(Rod Millman) *bhd: mod effrt in centre over 2f out: sn wknd* **7/1**

2m 53.37s (1.37) **Going Correction** +0.025s/f (Good) **9** Ran SP% **115.7**
Speed ratings (Par 101): **96,95,94,94,94 94,92,92,91**
CSF £65.37 CT £258.85 TOTE £8.20: £3.20, £2.10, £1.10; EX 70.30 Trifecta £355.00.
Owner Staverton Owners Group **Bred** Equine Associates Fr **Trained** Trowbridge, Wilts

FOCUS
A moderate staying handicap run at an ordinary pace and it paid to be handy.
T/Jkpt: £6,666.60 to a £1 stake. Pool: £10,000.00 - 1.50 winning units. T/Plt: £73.10 to a £1 stake. Pool: £62,427.26 - 622.63 winning units. T/Qpdt: £45.80 to a £1 stake. Pool: £3,626.31 - 58.5 winning units. **Lee McKenzie**

5712 CARLISLE (R-H)
Wednesday, August 31

OFFICIAL GOING: Good to soft (6.5)
Wind: Fresh, half against Weather: Overcast

6023 APOLLOBET DAILY RACING REFUNDS APPRENTICE H'CAP 5f
4:45 (4:45) (Class 6) (0-65,65) 3-Y-O+ **£2,587** (£770; £384; £192) **Stalls** Low

Form RPR

3403 **1** **Twentysvnthlancers**[32] 4855 3-9-5 **65**................ AdamMcNamara(3) 10 73
(Paul Midgley) *prom: effrt and rdn over 1f out: led ins fnl f: hld on wl cl home* **9/1**

2050 **2** *hd* **Tinsill**[13] 5582 5-8-2 **48**..(p) SophieKilloran(5) 12 55
(Nigel Tinkler) *bhd and sn outpcd: gd hdwy on wd outside over 1f out: ev ch ins fnl f: kpt on: jst hld* **10/1**

4002 **3** *½* **Gaelic Wizard (IRE)**[16] 5483 8-8-13 **60**....................(v) GemmaTutty(6) 11 65
(Karen Tutty) *bhd: rdn along over 3f out: gd hdwy over 1f out: chsd ldrs ins fnl f: kpt on fin* **12/1**

0500 **4** *2 ¾* **Bronze Beau**[13] 5582 9-9-2 **62**......................................(tp) CliffordLee(5) 5 58
(Kristin Stubbs) *led at decent gallop: rdn and edgd lft over 1f out: hdd ins fnl f: edgd rt and sn outpcd* **16/1**

3252 **5** *1 ½* **Slim Chance (IRE)**[1] 6008 7-8-13 **59**.........................(p) RowanScott(5) 4 49
(Simon West) *prom: rdn and effrt 2f out: no ex ins fnl f* **5/1**[1]

6006 **6** *hd* **Gowanless**[13] 5582 3-8-11 **60**.....................................(b) PhilDennis(6) 9 49
(Michael Dods) *wnt lft s: sn cl up: effrt and ev ch over 1f out: sn drifted lft: wknd ins fnl f* **12/1**

3556 **7** *hd* **Noodles Blue Boy**[21] 5295 10-8-13 **64**............(p) RobertDodsworth(10) 6 53
(Ollie Pears) *dwlt: bhd and rdn in rr: sme hdwy over 1f out: nvr rchd ldrs* **13/2**[2]

3550 **8** *3* **Strummer (IRE)**[14] 5537 3-9-2 **62**..................................(b) KevinStott(3) 1 40
(Kevin Ryan) *midfield: rdn along over 2f out: no imp fr over 1f out* **7/1**[3]

3165 **9** *shd* **Penny Royale**[14] 5535 4-8-12 **63**...........................(b) HannahWorrall(10) 2 41
(Tim Easterby) *sn bhd: plenty to do 1/2-way: sn pushed along and no imp* **7/1**[3]

0264 **10** *1 ½* **Tribesman**[16] 5483 3-9-2 **59**.......................................(b) JacobButterfield 8 31
(Marjorie Fife) *cl up tl rdn and wknd over 1f out* **17/2**

004 **11** *5* **Harpers Ruby**[39] 4647 6-8-5 **46** oh1.. JoeDoyle 7
(Lynn Siddall) *pressed ldr: rdn over 2f out: wknd over 1f out* **28/1**

0202 **12** *8* **Spoken Words**[22] 5278 7-8-3 **47**..............................(p) NathanEvans(3) 3
(John David Riches) *prom: rdn over 2f out: wknd wl over 1f out* **14/1**

1m 3.58s (2.78) **Going Correction** +0.625s/f (Yiel)
WFA 3 from 4yo+ 2lb **12** Ran SP% **116.0**
Speed ratings (Par 101): **102,101,100,96,94 93,93,88,88,86 78,65**
CSF £93.81 CT £747.17 TOTE £7.80: £2.90, £4.00, £3.30; EX 61.20 Trifecta £268.60.
Owner Sandfield Racing **Bred** Bucklands Farm & Stud Ltd **Trained** Westow, N Yorks

FOCUS
A low-grade sprint for apprentices featuring plenty of hard-to-win-with types. The pace was strong and the first three were clear. A minor personal best from the winner.

6024 APOLLOBET ONLINE GAMES AND CASINO MAIDEN FILLIES' STKS 1m 1f
5:20 (5:20) (Class 5) 3-Y-O+ **£3,234** (£962) **Stalls** Low

Form RPR

53- **1** **Luna Mare (IRE)**[293] 7811 3-9-0 0.................................... TonyHamilton 2 72
(Richard Fahey) *wnt lft s: mde all at stdy pce: rdn along and hrd pressed fr 2f out: edgd rt ins fnl f: kpt on wl towards fin* **6/4**[2]

5332 **2** *shd* **Golden Reign (IRE)**[9] 5709 3-9-0 74.........................(p) DanielTudhope 1 71
(William Haggas) *t.k.h early: trckd wnr: rdn to chal fr 2f out: kpt on wl fnl f: hld cl home* **1/2**[1]

2m 10.76s (13.16) **Going Correction** +0.475s/f (Yiel) **2** Ran SP% **106.7**
Speed ratings (Par 100): **60,59**
TOTE £1.50.
Owner Andrew Tinkler **Bred** Barronstown Stud **Trained** Musley Bank, N Yorks

FOCUS
A two-horse maiden run at a slow pace. Race distance increased by 16yds.

6025 APOLLOBET BET THROUGH YOUR MOBILE NOVICE AUCTION STKS 6f 195y
5:50 (5:51) (Class 5) 2-Y-O **£3,234** (£962; £481; £240) **Stalls** Low

Form RPR

32 **1** **Mister Belvedere**[51] 4188 2-9-2 0................................. PaulMulrennan 1 84+
(Michael Dods) *wnt lft s: mde all: pushed along fr over 2f out: drew clr fnl f* **5/4**[2]

1 **2** *7* **Society Red**[22] 5271 2-9-9 0... TonyHamilton 3 73
(Richard Fahey) *trckd ldr: rdn over 2f out: edgd rt and outpcd appr fnl f* **6/5**[1]

65 **3** *2 ¼* **Rita's Girl**[40] 4586 2-8-11 0.. DougieCostello 4 56
(K R Burke) *prom: drvn and outpcd over 2f out: no imp over 1f out* **9/1**[3]

0 **4** *½* **Greengairs**[4] 5885 2-9-2 0.. JasonHart 2 59
(Keith Dalgleish) *dwlt and wnt rt s: sn prom: drvn along over 2f out: wknd over 1f out* **12/1**

60 **5** *11* **Kirkby's Phantom**[38] 4678 2-8-6 0........................... NathanEvans(5) 5 25
(John David Riches) *t.k.h: hld up in tch: struggling over 2f out: btn whn hung lft over 1f out* **200/1**

1m 30.91s (3.81) **Going Correction** +0.475s/f (Yiel) **5** Ran SP% **108.1**
Speed ratings (Par 94): **97,89,86,85,73**
CSF £2.93 TOTE £2.20: £1.10, £1.30; EX 3.20 Trifecta £5.50.
Owner Allan McLuckie **Bred** Miss K Rausing **Trained** Denton, Co Durham

FOCUS
Race distance increased by 14yds. This looked a match, but not easy form to assess as the runner-up perhaps didn't show his true form.

6026 APOLLOBET FILLIES' NURSERY H'CAP 6f 195y
6:20 (6:21) (Class 5) (0-70,69) 2-Y-O **£2,911** (£866; £432; £216) **Stalls** Low

Form RPR

2432 **1** **Kilbaha Lady (IRE)**[6] 5799 2-8-6 **61**.....................(t) LewisEdmunds(7) 10 66
(Nigel Tinkler) *dwlt: hld up: rdn and gd hdwy on outside over 2f out: led appr fnl f: sn hrd pressed: hld on wl* **4/1**[1]

5526 **2** *hd* **Miss Bates**[20] 5318 2-9-2 **69**... RowanScott(5) 6 73
(Ann Duffield) *towards rr: rdn along 3f out: hdwy on outside and ev ch fnl f: kpt on: hld nr fin* **8/1**

4445 **3** *2 ½* **Bonnie Arlene (IRE)**[61] 3852 2-8-13 **61**........................... FrannyNorton 5 59
(Mark Johnston) *chsd ldrs: rdn and hdwy to ld over 2f out: hung lft: edgd rt and hdd appr fnl f: sn one pce* **7/1**[3]

056 **4** *½* **Babalugats (IRE)**[71] 3477 2-8-0 **48** oh1...................... DuranFentiman 11 44
(Tim Easterby) *hld up in tch on outside: rdn over 3f out: hdwy to chse ldrs over 1f out: one pce ins fnl f* **33/1**

035 **5** *nk* **Lucy's Law (IRE)**[30] 4943 2-8-12 **60**.................................. AndrewElliott 3 56
(Tom Tate) *t.k.h early: cl up: effrt whn nt clr run briefly over 2f out: sn rdn: kpt on same pce fnl f* **15/2**

000 **6** *6* **Cosmic Sky**[46] 4405 2-8-8 **56**.. DavidAllan 9 36
(Tim Easterby) *hld up: drvn along and outpcd 1/2-way: rallied over 1f out: kpt on: nt pce to chal* **10/1**

0044 **7** *nse* **Flawed Diamond (FR)**[25] 5165 2-8-5 **53**.......................... JoeyHaynes 8 33
(K R Burke) *t.k.h: sn midfield: drvn along over 2f out: no imp fr wl over 1f out* **13/2**[2]

460 **8** *7* **Rubiesnpearls**[39] 4663 2-8-13 **66**......................... AdamMcNamara(5) 12 27
(Richard Fahey) *hld up: rdn along over 3f out: no imp fr 2f out* **7/1**[3]

406 **9** *3 ¼* **Neigh Kid**[90] 2807 2-8-5 **53** ow2.............................. ConnorBeasley 1 6
(Keith Dalgleish) *hld up towards rr: rdn over 3f out: wknd over 1f out* **9/1**

0536 **10** *1 ½* **Quantum Field (USA)**[26] 5109 2-9-2 **64**........................ DougieCostello 7 13
(David Brown) *in tch: drvn along over 2f out: wknd 2f out* **14/1**

5004 **11** *3* **Seminole Dream (IRE)**[15] 5528 2-8-1 **48** oh3 ow1....... AndrewMullen 2 +
(Philip Kirby) *t.k.h: led: clr after 3f: hdd over 2f out: sn wknd* **20/1**

6000 **12** *13* **Queens Parade (IRE)**[19] 5364 2-8-1 **48** oh3 ow1........ PatrickMathers 4
(Sharon Watt) *cl up: drvn and struggling over 3f out: btn fnl 2f* **100/1**

1m 30.59s (3.49) **Going Correction** +0.475s/f (Yiel) **12** Ran SP% **115.7**
Speed ratings (Par 91): **99,98,95,95,95 88,88,80,76,74 71,56**
CSF £34.17 CT £220.70 TOTE £3.20: £1.50, £2.90, £2.80; EX 34.00 Trifecta £371.80.
Owner The Dapper Partnership **Bred** Helen Lyons **Trained** Langton, N Yorks

FOCUS
Race distance increased by 14yds. A modest fillies' nursery with all 12 maidens and the runner-up has been rated to her mark.. The pace was strong and the first five were clear.

6027 APOLLOBET CASHBACK IF 2ND H'CAP 6f 195y
6:50 (6:51) (Class 4) (0-80,83) 3-Y-O+ **£5,175** (£1,540; £769; £384) **Stalls** Low

Form RPR
3010 **1** **Depth Charge (IRE)**[5] 5845 4-9-7 **75**....................(vt) TonyHamilton 2 85+
(Kristin Stubbs) *dwlt: hld up: nt clr run over 2f out: effrt and hdwy over 1f out: qcknd to ld ins fnl f: idled nr fin* **12/1**
-541 **2** ½ **Bahamian Bird**[25] 5151 3-8-4 **63**.............................. PatrickMathers 8 68
(Richard Fahey) *prom: stdy hdwy gng wl over 3f out: rdn to ld over 1f out: hdd ins fnl f: kpt on* **7/1**[3]
4241 **3** *nk* **Glengarry**[7] 5782 3-9-10 **83** 6ex...................................... PhillipMakin 3 90+
(Keith Dalgleish) *awkward s: t.k.h: hld up: stdy hdwy whn nt clr run over 2f out to over 1f out: swtchd lft and kpt on wl fnl f: nrst fin* **2/1**[1]
0060 **4** ½ **My Dad Syd (USA)**[18] 5386 4-8-10 **67**.................. GeorgeDowning[(3)] 5 72
(Ian Williams) *prom: rdn over 3f out: rallied: kpt on same pce ins fnl f* **12/1**
4060 **5** ½ **Favourite Treat (USA)**[16] 5482 6-9-5 **73**..................(e) JamesSullivan 6 76
(Ruth Carr) *t.k.h: hld up: hdwy on outside over 2f out: rdn over 1f out: one pce fnl f* **16/1**
1352 **6** 1 ¾ **Like No Other**[7] 5759 3-8-12 **71**............................... GrahamGibbons 1 68
(Les Eyre) *t.k.h: hld up: rdn over 2f out: hdwy over 1f out: kpt on fnl f: nt pce to chal* **7/1**[3]
006 **7** 1 ¼ **Strong Man**[18] 5419 8-9-6 **79**..................................(b) NathanEvans[(5)] 12 75
(Michael Easterby) *t.k.h: led: rdn and hdd over 1f out: wknd ins fnl f* **16/1**
-510 **8** ½ **Royal Duchess**[44] 4443 6-9-6 **74**.. JoeDoyle 9 68
(Lucy Normile) *taken early to post: unruly in stalls: dwlt: hld up: stdy hdwy 1/2-way: effrt and cl up over 2f out: rdn and wknd over 1f out* **14/1**
3542 **9** *nk* **Relight My Fire**[15] 5521 6-9-1 **69**....................................(bt) DavidAllan 4 62
(Tim Easterby) *chsd ldr to over 3f out: rdn and wknd wl over 1f out* **6/1**[2]
045 **10** 4 **Avenue Of Stars**[51] 4193 3-9-5 **78**..............................(p) GrahamLee 7 59
(Karen McLintock) *prom: rdn along over 3f out: wknd over 2f out* **8/1**

1m 30.53s (3.43) **Going Correction** +0.475s/f (Yiel)
WFA 3 from 4yo+ 5lb **10** Ran SP% **117.5**
Speed ratings (Par 105): **99,98,98,97,96 94,93,92,92,88**
CSF £94.13 CT £245.87 TOTE £16.40: £4.70, £1.50, £2.00; EX 129.30 Trifecta £869.80.
Owner Paramount Racing III **Bred** Budget Stable **Trained** Norton, N Yorks

FOCUS
Race distance increased by 14yds. A decent gallop to this 7f handicap in which less than 2l covered the first five. The form has been rated around the runner-up and another personal best from the winner.

6028 APOLLOBET WEEKLY GOLF REFUNDS H'CAP 7f 173y
7:20 (7:21) (Class 5) (0-75,74) 3-Y-O+ **£2,911** (£866; £432; £216) **Stalls** Low

Form RPR
553 **1** **Crazy Tornado (IRE)**[9] 5717 3-8-13 **67**........................ ConnorBeasley 1 74
(Keith Dalgleish) *trckd ldrs: rdn to ld wl over 1f out: stened: hld on wl fnl f* **4/1**[2]
2006 **2** 1 **Dasheen**[20] 5322 3-8-11 **65**.. FrannyNorton 8 70
(Mark Johnston) *in tch: effrt and rdn over 2f out: chsd wnr over 1f out: edgd lft: edgd rt ins fnl f: kpt on fin* **16/1**
566 **3** 1 ½ **Auxiliary**[32] 4871 3-9-6 **74**..(p) DanielTudhope 11 75
(Patrick Holmes) *s.i.s: hld up: effrt and hdwy whn nt clr run briefly over 1f out: kpt on ins fnl f* **11/1**
51 **4** ¾ **Italian Beauty (IRE)**[47] 4348 4-9-5 **72**.................. CallumShepherd[(5)] 12 73
(Brian Ellison) *hld up: hdwy on wd outside over 2f out: rdn over 1f out: kpt on same pce ins fnl f* **7/1**[3]
3526 **5** 1 **Chiswick Bey (IRE)**[14] 5540 8-9-3 **70**................. AdamMcNamara[(5)] 13 68
(Richard Fahey) *hld up: rdn along over 2f out: hdwy over 1f out: kpt on fnl f: no imp* **9/1**
6060 **6** 4 **Rocket Ronnie (IRE)**[22] 5273 6-9-7 **69**..........................(b) GrahamLee 6 58
(Ed McMahon) *hld up midfield: rdn over 2f out: no imp fr over 1f out* **25/1**
013 **7** ¾ **McDelta**[8] 5753 6-8-10 **61**....................................(p) GeorgeDowning[(3)] 3 48
(Ian Williams) *s.i.s: hld up: hdwy on outside over 2f out: rdn and outpcd fnl f* **9/4**[1]
4104 **8** ½ **Tectonic (IRE)**[9] 5715 7-9-1 **63**......................................(v) JasonHart 2 49
(Keith Dalgleish) *hld up midfield: nt clr run briefly over 2f out: effrt over 1f out: wknd ins fnl f* **12/1**
000- **9** 4 ½ **Cara's Request (AUS)**[302] 7683 11-9-2 **64**....................... DavidAllan 4 40
(David C Griffiths) *prom tl rdn and wknd fr 2f out* **50/1**
2021 **10** 2 ½ **Talent Scout (IRE)**[21] 5291 10-8-13 **66**..................(p) GemmaTutty[(5)] 7 36
(Karen Tutty) *led: rdn and hdd wl over 1f out: sn wknd* **12/1**
1030 **11** 9 **Mercury**[22] 5273 4-8-12 **60**..(b) KevinStott 5 9
(Kevin Ryan) *midfield: drvn and lost pl 1/2-way: n.d after* **20/1**
-000 **12** 1 ¼ **Cosmic Ray**[6] 5793 4-9-10 **72**..................................(be[1]) GrahamGibbons 10 18
(Daniel Mark Loughnane) *pressed ldr tl lost pl over 2f out: btn and eased fr over 1f out* **40/1**

1m 42.95s (2.95) **Going Correction** +0.475s/f (Yiel)
WFA 3 from 4yo+ 6lb **12** Ran SP% **115.9**
Speed ratings (Par 103): **104,103,101,100,99 95,95,94,90,87 78,77**
CSF £61.51 CT £660.97 TOTE £5.00: £1.80, £5.00, £4.30; EX 73.30 Trifecta £538.10.
Owner Ken McGarrity **Bred** Celbridge Estates Ltd **Trained** Carluke, S Lanarks

FOCUS
Race distance increased by 14yds. A strong pace to this run-of-the-mill mile handicap in which the field spread out across the track. There was no obvious advantage with the winner racing towards the far side and the second near the stand-side rail.

6029 APOLLOBET HOME OF CASHBACK OFFERS H'CAP 1m 3f 39y
7:50 (7:50) (Class 6) (0-60,60) 3-Y-O+ **£2,587** (£770; £384; £192) **Stalls** High

Form RPR
6430 **1** **Canny Style**[15] 5513 3-8-9 **52**.. KevinStott 4 62
(Kevin Ryan) *plld hrd early: in tch: hdwy on wd outside and led over 1f out: styd on strly fnl f* **11/2**[3]
5536 **2** 1 ¼ **First Sargeant**[13] 5580 6-9-4 **57**.......................(p) AdamMcNamara[(5)] 10 65
(Lawrence Mullaney) *cl up: led over 2f out: edgd lft and hdd over 1f out: rallied: one pce fnl f* **6/1**
3003 **3** 8 **Moon Over Rio (IRE)**[16] 5481 5-9-12 **60**......................... GrahamLee 7 55
(Ben Haslam) *hld up: stdy hdwy on outside over 5f out: effrt and ev ch briefly over 2f out: outpcd by first two fr over 1f out* **15/2**
5324 **4** 1 ¾ **Qibtee (FR)**[19] 5383 6-9-9 **57**... DavidAllan 1 49
(Les Eyre) *prom: rdn along wl over 2f out: outpcd over 1f out* **10/1**
0056 **5** ½ **Madam Lilibet (IRE)**[17] 5435 7-9-12 **60**............................ JoeyHaynes 2 52
(Sharon Watt) *bhd and sn pushed along: struggling 1/2-way: rallied 2f out: kpt on fnl f: nrst fin* **28/1**
5-04 **6** 3 ½ **Sebastian's Wish (IRE)**[104] 2408 3-9-3 **60**.............. GeorgeChaloner 11 46
(Richard Whitaker) *s.i.s: hld up: rdn along over 3f out: btn fnl 2f* **11/1**
3222 **7** 2 **Ryan The Giant**[7] 5783 3-8-7 **50**.......................................(p) CamHardie 3 33+
(Keith Dalgleish) *s.i.s: hdwy to ld briefly over 6f out: cl up: rdn and checked over 2f out: sn wknd* **4/1**[1]
4522 **8** ¾ **Indian Giver**[32] 4872 8-9-4 **57**.....................................(p) NathanEvans[(5)] 9 39
(John David Riches) *hld up: rdn along over 3f out: btn fr 2f out* **5/1**[2]
0500 **9** 4 ½ **Glasgon**[5] 5841 6-9-0 **53**.. RowanScott[(5)] 6 27
(Ray Craggs) *hld up on ins: drvn wl over 3f out: nvr on terms* **10/1**
0350 **10** ¾ **Lean On Pete (IRE)**[16] 5481 7-9-10 **58**.....................(p) DanielTudhope 8 31
(Ollie Pears) *t.k.h early: mde most tl hdd over 2f out: sn wknd* **14/1**

2m 31.8s (8.70) **Going Correction** +0.475s/f (Yiel)
WFA 3 from 5yo+ 9lb **10** Ran SP% **114.7**
Speed ratings (Par 101): **87,86,80,79,78 76,74,74,70,70**
CSF £37.83 CT £248.06 TOTE £5.70: £1.70, £2.40, £1.80; EX 52.00 Trifecta £267.50.
Owner Hambleton Racing Ltd XXXVII **Bred** Biddestone Stud Ltd **Trained** Hambleton, N Yorks

FOCUS
Race distance increased by 16yds. A low-grade handicap featuring plenty who struggle to win. Although the early pace was ordinary, they started racing a long way out and finished well strung out. The first two, who both came towards the stand side, finished well clear. The runner-up sets the level.
T/Plt: £143.60 to a £1 stake. Pool: £44,033.32 - 223.70 winning units. T/Qpdt: £22.60 to a £1 stake. Pool: £6,718.69 - 219.50 winning units. **Richard Young**

5770 LINGFIELD (L-H)
Wednesday, August 31

OFFICIAL GOING: Good to firm (good in places; 8.1) (watered)
Wind: light, across Weather: light cloud, bright spells

6030 AABC MATERIALS CLAIMING STKS 1m 3f 106y
2:10 (2:10) (Class 6) 3-4-Y-O **£2,587** (£770; £384; £192) **Stalls** High

Form RPR
5025 **1** **Skylark Lady (IRE)**[12] 3998 3-8-12 60.................... SilvestreDeSousa 3 64
(Michael Wigham) *chsd ldr: rdn to ld 3f out: sn clr: eased wl ins fnl f* **2/7**[1]
0000 **2** 15 **Dancing Rainbow (GR)**[7] 5777 3-8-3 45..........(b) JosephineGordon[(3)] 4 32
(Amanda Perrett) *sn bustled to ld: rdn and hdd 3f out: sn outpcd and no ch w wnr: plugged on for clr 2nd* **5/1**[2]
6503 **3** 5 **Ocean Bentley (IRE)**[27] 5051 4-9-6 43..........................(b) AdamKirby 5 29
(Tony Carroll) *stdd s: t.k.h: hld up in last pair: rdn and outpcd 3f out: no ch after: wnt modest 3rd ent fnl f: plugged on* **7/1**[3]
0-00 **4** 6 **Careless Rapture**[16] 5473 3-8-3 33.........................(b) NoelGarbutt[(3)] 1 14
(Mark H Tompkins) *t.k.h: chsd ldng pair: rdn and outpcd 3f out: no ch after: wknd fnl f* **25/1**
06-0 **5** 1 ½ **Fine Share (IRE)**[232] 155 3-8-10 44.............................. DannyBrock 2 16
(John Bridger) *hld up in tch in last pair: effrt over 3f out: 3rd and outpcd 3f out: no ch after: lost 3rd ent fnl f: wknd* **25/1**

2m 33.0s (1.50) **Going Correction** -0.10s/f (Good)
WFA 3 from 4yo 9lb **5** Ran SP% **114.6**
Speed ratings (Par 101): **90,79,75,71,70**
CSF £2.47 TOTE £1.20: £1.02, £2.10; EX 2.30 Trifecta £3.80.
Owner The Gin & Tonic Partnership **Bred** David Fenlon **Trained** Newmarket, Suffolk

FOCUS
The watered ground was given as good to firm, good in places (GoingStick: 8.1). The rail on the straight course was again narrowed by 3yds on the stands' rail. With only the favourite rated higher than 45, this was a poor race and she has been rated to her previous best.

6031 HANSON REGAN 10TH BIRTHDAY MEDIAN AUCTION MAIDEN STKS 1m 3f 106y
2:40 (2:40) (Class 6) 3-4-Y-O **£2,587** (£770; £384; £192) **Stalls** High

Form RPR
0-42 **1** **Reconcilliation**[47] 4372 3-9-5 75.................................. OisinMurphy 4 82+
(Ed Vaughan) *stdd s: t.k.h: trckd ldng pair after 1f: wnt 2nd over 2f out: chal over 1f out: led 1f out: styd on and asserted ins fnl f* **4/7**[1]
5223 **2** 1 ¼ **Torquay**[14] 5550 3-9-0 72..(v[1]) JimCrowley 1 75
(Harry Dunlop) *chsd ldr tl rdn to ld over 2f out: jnd and drvn over 1f out: hdd 1f out: styd on same pce ins fnl f* **11/4**[2]
6445 **3** 15 **Pc Dixon**[11] 5623 3-9-5 75...................................... SilvestreDeSousa 2 56
(Mick Channon) *led: rdn and hdd over 2f out: sn outpcd: 3rd and wl btn over 1f out* **6/1**[3]
05 **4** 8 **Alfredo (IRE)**[22] 5255 4-10-0 0..(tp) AdamKirby 3 43
(Seamus Durack) *rn in snatches: a last pair: rdn and outpcd over 3f out: no ch fnl 3f* **33/1**
00 **5** 50 **Twilight Pursuits**[15] 5504 3-9-0 0...................................... JimmyQuinn 5
(Natalie Lloyd-Beavis) *taken down early: in tch in last pair: rdn 4f out: sn lost tch: t.o* **200/1**

2m 32.02s (0.52) **Going Correction** -0.10s/f (Good)
WFA 3 from 4yo 9lb **5** Ran SP% **108.0**
Speed ratings (Par 101): **94,93,82,76,40**
CSF £2.28 TOTE £1.40: £1.10, £1.60; EX 2.10 Trifecta £3.10.
Owner The Machell Place Partnership **Bred** Lofts Hall Stud **Trained** Newmarket, Suffolk

FOCUS
An ordinary maiden.

6032 OILFIELD OFFSHORE UNDERWRITING H'CAP 1m 2f
3:10 (3:10) (Class 4) (0-85,84) 3-Y-O **£5,175** (£1,540; £769; £384) **Stalls** Low

Form RPR
2343 **1** **Malmoosa (IRE)**[19] 5361 3-9-3 **80**.................................... PaulHanagan 4 90
(Brian Meehan) *mde all: clr and shkn up over 2f out: styd on wl u.p fr over 1f out and nvr seriously chal: eased towards fin* **5/1**[3]
21-3 **2** 1 ¾ **Wapping (USA)**[18] 5405 3-9-5 **82**................................... GeorgeBaker 1 88+
(David Lanigan) *stdd after s: hld up in last: effrt on inner ent fnl 2f: chsd wnr and hung rt wl over 1f out: wandered u.p and no imp 1f out: kpt on but nvr threatening wnr* **15/8**[1]
5210 **3** 2 ¾ **Frozen Force (IRE)**[2] 5964 3-9-6 **83**..............................(p) JimCrowley 5 84
(Amanda Perrett) *hld up in tch: effrt 3f out: no imp on wnr 2f out: wnt 3rd ent fnl f: kpt on but no threat to wnr* **6/1**
1032 **4** 3 ¾ **Al Shahaniya (IRE)**[10] 5671 3-9-6 **83**............................ FrankieDettori 8 78
(John Quinn) *styd wd early: sn chsng wnr: lost 2nd over 3f out: sn rdn and unable qck: btn over 1f out: eased wl ins fnl f* **5/2**[2]

3621 **5** *8* **California Lad**[25] 5163 3-8-13 **76**............................(v) SilvestreDeSousa 2 60
(Harry Dunlop) *t.k.h: trckd ldng pair: chsd clr wnr over 3f out: rdn and no imp over 2f out: lost 2nd and hmpd wl over 1f out: bhd 1f out: eased wl ins fnl f* **5/1**[3]

2m 9.04s (-1.46) **Going Correction** -0.10s/f (Good) **5** Ran SP% **111.0**
Speed ratings (Par 102): **101,99,97,94,88**
CSF £14.94 TOTE £5.60: £2.40, £1.50; EX 13.40 Trifecta £58.50.
Owner Hamdan Al Maktoum **Bred** Shadwell Estate Company Limited **Trained** Manton, Wilts

FOCUS
This was dominated from the front by the winner who recorded a personal best.

6033 INJURED JOCKEYS FUND NURSERY H'CAP 6f
3:40 (3:42) (Class 5) (0-70,70) 2-Y-O **£3,234** (£962; £481; £240) **Stalls** Centre

Form RPR
6351 **1** **Roys Dream**[10] 5675 2-9-3 **66** 6ex.................................... JimCrowley 11 68
(Kristin Stubbs) *wnt lft s: mde all: rdn over 1f out: edgd lft ins fnl f: hld on gamely fnl 100yds: rdn out* **7/2**[2]

4642 **2** *nk* **Princess Way (IRE)**[12] 5606 2-8-7 **56**..................... SilvestreDeSousa 10 57
(David Evans) *t.k.h early: chsd ldrs: rdn ent fnl 2f: unable qck and sltly outpcd over 1f out: rallied ins fnl f: styd on strly to press wnr towards fin: nvr quite getting to wnr* **12/1**

0002 **3** *½* **Katrine (IRE)**[9] 5707 2-9-7 **70**... PatCosgrave 7 72+
(William Knight) *stdd s: t.k.h: hld up in tch in last quartet: hmpd after 1f: swtchd lft and effrt 2f out: hdwy over 1f out: drvn to press wnr ins fnl f: kpt on but hld fnl 100yds: lost 2nd towards fin* **5/1**[3]

3456 **4** *1¼* **Peachey Carnehan**[39] 4638 2-9-4 **67**.. KierenFox 9 62
(Michael Attwater) *in tch in midfield: effrt 2f out: hdwy u.p over 1f out to chse ldrs ins fnl f: kpt on same pce fnl 100yds* **25/1**

5230 **5** *½* **Rising Eagle**[41] 4553 2-9-4 **67**... GeorgeBaker 8 61
(Charles Hills) *dwlt: racd in last pair: swtchd lft and hdwy ent fnl 2f: rdn to chse ldrs 1f out: kpt on same pce ins fnl f* **6/1**

0502 **6** *nse* **Waves (IRE)**[25] 5165 2-8-13 **62**..[1] OisinMurphy 1 56
(Eve Johnson Houghton) *stdd and dropped in bhd after s: hld up in rr: effrt over 1f out: hdwy u.p 1f out: styd on wl ins fnl f: nvr trbld ldrs* **8/1**

524 **7** *4* **One Too Many (IRE)**[20] 5317 2-9-7 **70**.............................. SeanLevey 6 51
(David Brown) *t.k.h: w ldr: rdn 2f out: no ex 1f out: lost 2nd and fdd ins fnl f* **3/1**[1]

006 **8** *1* **Makemerichjohn (IRE)**[16] 5484 2-8-5 **53** ow1........................[1] JFEgan 5 32
(David Evans) *t.k.h early: hld up in tch in last quartet: swtchd lft and effrt over 2f out: sme hdwy but hung lft wl over 1f out: swtchd rt and lost pl over 1f out: no imp and wl hld fnl f* **20/1**

052 **9** *½* **King Of Castilla**[23] 5243 2-9-1 **64**..[1] AdamKirby 2 42
(Gay Kelleway) *in tch in midfield: unable qck u.p and losing pl whn sltly hmpd over 1f out: wknd ins fnl f* **20/1**

0643 **10** *¾* **Spin Top**[14] 5543 2-9-0 **63**..(v) TomQueally 4 37
(Joseph Tuite) *chsd ldrs: rdn over 1f out: unable qck and btn 1f out: fdd ins fnl f* **10/1**

600 **11** *1* **Newz Watch**[16] 5469 2-8-13 **62**.. WilliamCarson 3 34
(Mick Quinn) *chsd ldrs: rdn ent fnl 2f: losing pl whn n.m.r over 1f out: wknd fnl f* **66/1**

1m 11.04s (-0.16) **Going Correction** -0.10s/f (Good) **11** Ran SP% **120.9**
Speed ratings (Par 94): **97,96,95,94,93 93,88,86,86,85 83**
CSF £43.98 CT £215.46 TOTE £4.90: £1.90, £3.50, £2.10; EX 53.50 Trifecta £298.90.
Owner Mrs A Pickering **Bred** Dr A Gillespie **Trained** Norton, N Yorks

FOCUS
It hasn't always been the case this summer, but the stands' rail runners held sway here.

6034 HARLEYFORD AGGREGATES MAIDEN STKS 6f
4:10 (4:13) (Class 5) 2-Y-O **£3,234** (£962; £481; £240) **Stalls** Centre

Form RPR
052 **1** **Sfumato**[21] 5304 2-9-5 78.. GeorgeBaker 8 78+
(Roger Charlton) *hld up in tch in midfield: effrt and rdn over 1f out: edgd lft but hdwy to press ldr and swtchd lft ins fnl f: led 75yds out: r.o wl and gng away at fin* **1/1**[1]

03 **2** *1½* **Darkroom Angel**[12] 5593 2-9-0 0.. AdamKirby 2 68
(Clive Cox) *chsd ldrs: rdn to press ldrs over 1f out: ev ch ins fnl f: styd on same pce and wnt 2nd towards fin* **7/1**[3]

5 **3** *½* **Sword Exceed (GER)**[116] 2038 2-9-5 0.......................... WilliamBuick 4 71
(Charlie Appleby) *wnt lft s: racd freely: led: rdn and hung lft over 1f out: hdd 75yds out: no ex: wknd and lost 2nd towards fin* **7/1**[3]

45 **4** *2¼* **Bizet (IRE)**[20] 5332 2-9-5 0... DannyBrock 1 64
(John Ryan) *in tch in midfield: rdn over 2f out: hdwy u.p to chse ldrs over 1f out: no ex 1f out: wknd ins fnl f* **12/1**

0 **5** *1½* **Wily Rumpus (IRE)**[27] 5067 2-9-5 0............................ ThomasBrown 10 59
(Ed Walker) *racd in last quartet: pushed along 2f out:hdwy and swtchd rt 1f out: kpt on ins fnl f: nvr trbld ldrs* **20/1**

6 *1¼* **The Night Before** 2-9-5 0... JoeFanning 5 56
(Robert Cowell) *chsd ldr: rdn 2f out: struggling to qckn whn sltly hmpd over 1f out: btn 1f out: fdd ins fnl f* **25/1**

5 **7** *hd* **Mercers**[22] 5258 2-9-0 0.. TomQueally 7 50
(Peter Crate) *dwlt: rn green and sn in last quartet: rdn jst over 2f out: sme hdwy and stl green over 1f out: swtchd lft ins fnl f: kpt on: nvr trbld ldrs* **66/1**

5 **8** *¾* **Lady Cleo (IRE)**[19] 5377 2-9-0 0.. OisinMurphy 3 47
(Stuart Williams) *s.i.s: t.k.h: sn rcvrd and in midfield: pushed along 2f out: kpt on ins fnl f: nvr trbld ldrs* **25/1**

60 **9** *hd* **Shadow Warrior**[20] 5332 2-9-5 0.................................... WilliamCarson 9 52
(Paul D'Arcy) *taken down early: s.i.s: bhd: sme hdwy ins fnl f: n.d* **50/1**

0 **10** *3½* **Magicinthemaking (USA)**[18] 5400 2-9-0 0........................ JimCrowley 6 39
(Jeremy Noseda) *a towards rr: pushed along 2f out: reminder and no imp over 1f out: eased ins fnl f* **5/1**[2]

64 **11** *11* **Tranquil Daze (IRE)**[16] 5484 2-9-5 0................................. SeanLevey 11 5
(David Brown) *midfield: lost pl and rdn over 2f out: bhd over 1f out* **16/1**

1m 10.25s (-0.95) **Going Correction** -0.10s/f (Good) **11** Ran SP% **121.1**
Speed ratings (Par 94): **102,100,99,96,94 92,92,91,91,86 71**
CSF £8.25 TOTE £1.70: £1.10, £2.70, £2.90; EX 8.20 Trifecta £29.40.
Owner K Abdullah **Bred** Juddmonte Farms Ltd **Trained** Beckhampton, Wilts

FOCUS
Just a fair maiden, but the winner has the ability to rate higher.

6035 OILFIELD INSURANCE AGENCIES MAIDEN AUCTION FILLIES' STKS (PLUS 10 RACE) 7f
4:40 (4:42) (Class 5) 2-Y-O **£3,881** (£1,155; £577; £288) **Stalls** Centre

Form RPR
32 **1** **Miss Icon**[18] 5395 2-8-6 0.. JimmyQuinn 1 69
(Patrick Chamings) *hld up in tch in midfield: effrt 2f out: rdn to chal 1f out: led ins fnl f: r.o wl: rdn out* **3/1**[2]

06 **2** *¾* **Captain Sue (IRE)**[14] 5549 2-8-6 0... RyanTate 2 67
(Richard Hughes) *pressed ldr: rdn and ev ch 2f out: led over 1f out: hdd and styd on same pce ins fnl f* **50/1**

060 **3** *2½* **Joyful Dream (IRE)**[26] 5142 2-8-3 0.................... JosephineGordon[(3)] 9 60
(J S Moore) *hld up in tch in midfield: effrt 2f out: hdwy and hung lft ins fnl f: styd on to snatch 3rd last stride* **12/1**

4 *shd* **Power Home (IRE)** 2-8-3 0.. PaddyPilley[(5)] 5 62
(Denis Coakley) *dwlt: hld up in tch in last trio: effrt over 2f out: rdn and hdwy over 1f out: chsd ldrs ins fnl f: tenderly handled and kpt on same pce fnl 100yds: lost 3rd last stride* **33/1**

44 **5** *2¼* **Celestation**[12] 5615 2-8-8 0.. JoeFanning 7 56
(Mark Johnston) *led: rdn 2f out: hdd over 1f out: edgd lft and lost 3rd ins fnl f: wknd fnl 100yds* **11/10**[1]

43 **6** *¾* **Affair**[69] 3555 2-8-1 0.. CharlieBennett[(5)] 4 52
(Hughie Morrison) *chsd ldrs: effrt to chal 2f out: no ex u.p ent fnl f: wkng whn swtchd lft ins fnl f* **9/2**[3]

0 **7** *1½* **Cheers All Round**[104] 2404 2-8-6 0.......................... SilvestreDeSousa 3 52
(Henry Spiller) *t.k.h: hld up in tch in midfield: nt clr run 2f out: nvr enough room after: btn whn pushed lft ins fnl f* **20/1**

8 *4½* **Implausible** 2-8-8 0.. MartinLane 6 37
(Jonathan Portman) *s.i.s: rn green in rr: swtchd lft after 3f: sme hdwy over 2f out: sn hung lft and wknd over 1f out* **20/1**

0454 **9** *5* **Surfina**[10] 5668 2-8-6 54.. DavidParkes[(5)] 8 27
(Dean Ivory) *hld up in tch in midfield: rdn and lost pl jst over 2f out: bhd fnl f* **20/1**

00 **10** *1¾* **Jenji (IRE)**[11] 5637 2-8-11 0.. JFEgan 10 22
(David Evans) *stdd s: t.k.h: hld up towards rr: rdn 2f out: sn bhd* **66/1**

1m 22.98s (-0.32) **Going Correction** -0.10s/f (Good) **10** Ran SP% **119.2**
Speed ratings (Par 91): **97,96,93,93,90 89,88,82,77,75**
CSF £153.05 TOTE £3.60: £1.50, £6.10, £2.80; EX 105.90 Trifecta £804.10.
Owner The Berks & Hants Racing Partnership **Bred** Wheelers Land Stud **Trained** Baughurst, Hants

FOCUS
With the first two drawn lowest, the stands' rail didn't appear much of an advantage in this race. The early pace wasn't strong.

6036 RETRAINING OF RACEHORSES MEDIAN AUCTION MAIDEN STKS 7f
5:15 (5:18) (Class 6) 3-5-Y-O **£3,234** (£962; £481; £240) **Stalls** Centre

Form RPR
5420 **1** **Sciarra**[42] 4517 3-8-13 67.. OisinMurphy 4 66
(Michael Bell) *chsd ldr: rdn over 2f out: drvn ent fnl f: led 50yds out and forged ahd cl home* **6/4**[1]

6600 **2** *¾* **Ten Rocks**[7] 5769 3-8-11 61... JordanUys[(7)] 6 69
(Lisa Williamson) *racd keenly: led: rdn over 1f out: hung lft ins fnl f: hdd 50yds out: no ex* **16/1**

0050 **3** *6* **Where Next**[21] 5284 3-8-13 70...................................... HectorCrouch[(7)] 9 55
(Henry Candy) *hld up in tch: effrt to chse ldrs wl over 1f out: sn hung lft and unable qck: wknd ins fnl f* **9/4**[2]

04 **4** *3¾* **Summertime Lucy (IRE)**[24] 5192 3-8-13 0....................[1] JackMitchell 5 38
(Giles Bravery) *in tch in midfield: rdn over 2f out: sn outpcd: modest 4th and plugged on same pce fnl f* **12/1**

000 **5** *hd* **Gorgeous (FR)**[7] 5766 3-8-13 0.. JFEgan 3 37
(Tony Carroll) *hld up in tch in last trio: rdn over 2f out: sn outpcd: wl hld and plugged on same pce fnl f* **50/1**

0-5 **6** *½* **Josh Perry**[14] 5544 3-9-4 0.. FrederikTylicki 1 41
(Rod Millman) *dwlt: hld up in last pair: rdn 3f out: u.p and no hdwy 2f out: wl hld and plugged on same pce fnl f* **20/1**

64 **7** *8* **Joanne Park**[18] 5388 3-8-13 0... JohnFahy 2 14
(Clive Cox) *s.i.s and rdn leaving stalls: sn rcvrd to chse ldrs after 1f and t.k.h: rdn over 2f out: drvn and btn 2f out: wknd over 1f out* **3/1**[3]

05 **8** *4½* **Sams R Man**[23] 5238 4-9-9 0.. RobertHavlin 7 9
(Linda Jewell) *chsd ldrs early: steadily lost pl and bhd 3f out: lost tch 2f out* **100/1**

1m 22.52s (-0.78) **Going Correction** -0.10s/f (Good)
WFA 3 from 4yo 5lb **8** Ran SP% **117.1**
Speed ratings (Par 101): **100,99,92,88,87 87,78,72**
CSF £28.15 TOTE £2.30: £1.10, £3.90, £1.20; EX 21.20 Trifecta £65.40.
Owner Qatar Racing Limited **Bred** Bond Thoroughbred Corporation **Trained** Newmarket, Suffolk

FOCUS
A modest maiden in which the first two came well clear.
T/Plt: £19.30 to a £1 stake. Pool: £60,596.72 - 2,282.01 winning units. T/Qpdt: £11.50 to a £1 stake. Pool: £4,832.87 - 308.60 winning units. **Steve Payne**

6037 - 6043a (Foreign Racing) - See Raceform Interactive

5734 CHELMSFORD (A.W) (L-H)
Thursday, September 1

OFFICIAL GOING: Polytrack: standard
Wind: Light, across Weather: Sunny and warm

6044 TOTEPLACEPOT SIX PLACES IN SIX RACES MAIDEN AUCTION STKS (PLUS 10 RACE) 7f (P)
5:40 (5:42) (Class 4) 2-Y-O **£5,822** (£1,732; £865; £432) **Stalls** Low

Form RPR
42 **1** **Tonahutu (IRE)**[15] 5549 2-8-10 0....................................... HarryBentley 8 71
(Ed Vaughan) *w ldrs tl trckd ldr after 2f: led wl over 1f out: sn rdn and edgd rt: kpt on ins fnl f and a doing enough* **2/1**[1]

2423 **2** *nk* **Magical Forest (IRE)**[15] 5549 2-8-8 75................(b) MarcMonaghan[(3)] 1 71
(Marco Botti) *hld up in tch in midfield: swtchd rt and hdwy u.p over 1f out: chsd ldrs over 1f out: wnt 2nd towards fin: kpt on wl but nvr quite getting to wnr* **5/2**[2]

02 **3** *½* **Getgo**[11] 5670 2-9-2 0.. MartinLane 4 75
(David Lanigan) *w ldrs tl stdd bk and in tch in midfield after 1f: effrt to chse wnr and carried rt over 1f out: kpt on same pce ins fnl f: lost 2nd towards fin* **4/1**[3]

04 **4** 3 1/4 **Charlie Rascal (FR)**[7] 5792 2-8-9 0 JosephineGordon(3) 9 62
(Peter Chapple-Hyam) *dwlt: in tch in last trio: rdn over 2f out: hdwy over 1f out: swtchd lft jst ins fnl f: 4th and no imp ins fnl f* **16/1**

05 **5** 1 1/2 **King's Coinage (IRE)**[13] 5593 2-9-4 0 LiamKeniry 3 64
(Ed Walker) *hld up in tch in midfield: nt clr run over 2f out: swtchd lft and pushed along over 1f out: hdwy to chse ldrs 1f out: sn hung rt and wknd ins fnl f* **16/1**

00 **6** 1 **Charlie Chaplin (GER)**[112] 2193 2-9-2 0 SilvestreDeSousa 5 61
(Robert Eddery) *dwlt: hld up in last trio: effrt and switching rt 2f out: sme hdwy u.p 1f out and sn swtchd lft: no imp and wl hld whn nt clrest of runs ins fnl f: eased towards fin* **9/2**

0 **7** 4 **Master Billie (IRE)**[7] 5792 2-9-3 0 SamHitchcott 7 51
(William Muir) *led after 1f: hdd and rdn wl over 1f out: unable qck u.p and btn whn hmpd jst ins fnl f: sn wknd and eased towards fin* **33/1**

0530 **8** 3 1/2 **Black Redstart**[16] 5528 2-8-6 55 LiamJones 6 29
(Alan Bailey) *broke wl: t.k.h early: sn stdd bk to chse ldrs: rdn over 2f out: lost pl u.p over 1f out: wknd fnl f* **50/1**

9 3 1/2 **Ten In The Hat (IRE)** 2-8-10 0 CharlieBennett(5) 2 28
(Shaun Harris) *dwlt: hld up in tch in rr: rdn over 2f out: sn struggling: bhd fnl f* **66/1**

1m 27.26s (0.06) **Going Correction** -0.075s/f (Stan) **9** Ran SP% **118.2**
Speed ratings (Par 97): **96,95,95,91,89 88,83,79,75**
CSF £7.34 TOTE £3.30: £1.40, £1.10, £1.70; EX 7.70 Trifecta £22.60.
Owner Ballymore Downunder Syndicate **Bred** Ringfort Stud **Trained** Newmarket, Suffolk

FOCUS
A fairly modest maiden.

6045 TOTEEXACTA FORECAST THE 1ST AND 2ND NURSERY H'CAP 1m (P)
6:10 (6:11) (Class 6) (0-65,65) 2-Y-O **£3,234** (£962; £481; £240) **Stalls** Low

Form RPR

002 **1** **Altiko Tommy (IRE)**[8] 5770 2-9-0 **58** LiamKeniry 2 61
(George Baker) *taken down early: t.k.h: hld up in tch in midfield: trckd ldrs over 2f out: shkn up to ld over 1f out: wandered rt and drvn ins fnl f: strly pressed wl ins fnl f: hld on towards fin* **7/4**[1]

000 **2** nk **Alligator**[56] 4053 2-9-0 **58** SilvestreDeSousa 3 60
(Ed Dunlop) *hld up in tch in midfield: effrt over 2f out: chsd ldrs and swtchd lft 1f out: stl edging lft but chalng wl ins fnl f: kpt on but hld towards fin* **9/4**[2]

5323 **3** 1 3/4 **Amy Gardner**[6] 5853 2-8-9 **58** NathanEvans(5) 5 56
(James Given) *chsd ldr: rdn and ev ch over 1f out: drifted rt 1f out: 3rd and outpcd fnl 100yds* **12/1**

5040 **4** 3 1/2 **Vinnievanbaileys**[7] 5806 2-9-3 **64** (b) JosephineGordon(3) 4 54
(Chris Dwyer) *sn rdn along: in tch in rr: drvn over 1f out: wnt 4th ins fnl f: no imp: nvr trbld ldrs* **7/1**

0600 **5** 7 **Heavenly Cry**[79] 3248 2-8-11 **55** DannyBrock 1 28
(Phil McEntee) *led: rdn and hdd over 1f out: sn lost pl: wknd fnl f* **33/1**

0001 **6** 17 **Ray Donovan (IRE)**[27] 5112 2-9-7 **65** JimCrowley 6
(David O'Meara) *chsd ldrs on outer: rdn 3f out: sn lost pl: bhd over 1f out: sn eased* **7/2**[3]

1m 41.25s (1.35) **Going Correction** -0.075s/f (Stan) **6** Ran SP% **112.5**
Speed ratings (Par 93): **90,89,87,84,77 60**
CSF £5.99 TOTE £2.50: £1.30, £1.70; EX 6.10 Trifecta £24.60.
Owner P Bowden **Bred** Fergus Cousins **Trained** Manton, Wilts

FOCUS
They didn't appear to go that quick early on in this nursery.

6046 TOTEQUADPOT FOUR PLACES IN FOUR RACES H'CAP (DIV I) 1m (P)
6:40 (6:42) (Class 6) (0-60,63) 3-Y-O+ **£3,234** (£962; £481; £240) **Stalls** Low

Form RPR

650 **1** **Stun Gun**[44] 4498 6-9-7 **60** (p) MartinLane 1 66
(Derek Shaw) *chsd ldrs: wnt 2nd 3f out: rdn to ld over 1f out: drvn clr 1f out: kpt on u.p and a doing enough ins fnl f* **8/1**

0-00 **2** 1 1/4 **Victoriously**[42] 4567 4-8-8 **50** (p) EoinWalsh(3) 8 53
(Andi Brown) *s.i.s: hld up in tch in last quartet: effrt u.p over 1f out: hdwy 1f out: wnt 3rd 100yds: chsd wnr wl ins fnl f: styd on wl and wnt 2nd wl ins fnl f: nvr getting to wnr* **25/1**

5060 **3** 1/2 **Dukes Meadow**[12] 5635 5-8-12 **58** RhiainIngram(7) 4 60
(Roger Ingram) *t.k.h: hld up in tch in last quartet: swtchd rt and hdwy on outer over 2f out: drvn to chse wnr 1f out: kpt on same pce after: lost 2nd wl ins fnl f* **8/1**

2454 **4** 2 **Gladys Cooper (IRE)**[13] 5610 3-8-13 **57** LiamKeniry 2 53
(Ed Walker) *in tch in midfield: effrt ent fnl 2f: chsd ldrs 1f out: no ex and styd on same pce ins fnl f* **4/1**[3]

3000 **5** 3/4 **Master Of Heaven**[80] 3236 3-9-2 **60** JackMitchell 6 54+
(Jim Boyle) *bustled along early: in tch in last quartet: rdn and effrt over 2f out: sme hdwy and swtchd rt ent fnl f: kpt on same pce ins fnl f* **7/2**[2]

0302 **6** 1 3/4 **Infiniti (IRE)**[21] 5338 3-8-13 **57** SaleemGolam 5 47
(Rae Guest) *chsd ldr tl 3f out: sn u.p and unable qck: keeping on same pce and hld whn sltly impeded jst ins fnl f: plugged on* **3/1**[1]

-601 **7** 7 **O Dee**[9] 5734 4-9-10 **63** 6ex RenatoSouza 3 37
(Jose Santos) *t.k.h: led: shkn up over 1f out: sn rdn and hdd: lost 2nd and btn 1f out: fdd ins fnl f* **5/1**

0-00 **8** 18 **Passing Dream**[33] 4882 3-8-2 **51** ow1 CharlieBennett(5) 10
(Hughie Morrison) *dwlt: swtchd rt and hdwy into midfield after 1f: rdn and struggling over 2f out: bhd over 1f out: sn eased* **25/1**

3600 **9** 22 **Captain Gerald**[19] 5399 3-8-4 **51** (p) JosephineGordon(3) 9
(John Ryan) *pushed rt sn after s: last pair after 1f: detached last and rdn 4f out: lost tch over 2f out: eased over 1f out: t.o* **16/1**

1m 39.65s (-0.25) **Going Correction** -0.075s/f (Stan)
WFA 3 from 4yo+ 5lb **9** Ran SP% **119.7**
Speed ratings (Par 101): **98,96,96,94,93 91,84,66,44**
CSF £186.17 CT £1658.97 TOTE £10.20: £2.50, £9.60, £2.40; EX 243.60 Trifecta £3387.50.
Owner John R Saville **Bred** Rothmere Bloodstock **Trained** Sproxton, Leics

FOCUS
A moderate handicap.

6047 TOTEQUADPOT FOUR PLACES IN FOUR RACES H'CAP (DIV II) 1m (P)
7:10 (7:13) (Class 6) (0-60,66) 3-Y-O+ **£3,234** (£962; £481; £240) **Stalls** Low

Form RPR

3031 **1** **German Whip**[10] 5721 3-9-3 **66** 6ex HectorCrouch(5) 3 73+
(Gary Moore) *hld up in tch in midfield: rdn and hdwy on inner over 1f out: led 100yds out: r.o wl* **2/1**[1]

0230 **2** 1 1/4 **Rosie Crowe (IRE)**[13] 5604 4-8-5 **47** JosephineGordon(3) 2 52
(Shaun Harris) *chsd ldrs: effrt jst over 2f out: rdn to chal over 1f out: led 1f out: hdd and one pced fnl 100yds* **8/1**

-000 **3** 1 **Lisala (FR)**[16] 5529 3-8-11 **58** (e[1]) MarcMonaghan(3) 10 60
(George Peckham) *sn led: rdn wl over 1f out: hdd 1f out: styd on same pce ins fnl f* **50/1**

5600 **4** 3 **Free One (IRE)**[16] 5513 4-9-2 **55** (p) SilvestreDeSousa 4 50
(Ivan Furtado) *dwlt: hld up in tch in rr: stuck bhd rivals over 2f out: hdwy u.p ent fnl f: styd on u.p to go 4th on post: nvr trbld ldrs* **6/1**[2]

4004 **5** nse **Broughtons Mystery**[31] 4936 3-8-8 **52** HarryBentley 6 46
(Willie Musson) *broke in midfield: sn pushed along and dropped to last trio after 2f: swtchd lft and hdwy u.p over 1f out: kpt on to go 4th wl ins fnl f: no threat to ldrs: lost 4th on post* **20/1**

1021 **6** 1 1/4 **Carcharias (IRE)**[14] 5572 3-8-13 **57** JimCrowley 8 48
(Ed de Giles) *chsd ldr: rdn and ev ch 2f out: unable qck and outpcd over 1f out: 4th and btn 1f out: wknd ins fnl f* **7/1**[3]

4024 **7** 2 1/4 **Bazzat (IRE)**[23] 5263 3-7-12 **49** (p) RhiainIngram(7) 5 35
(John Ryan) *in tch in midfield: unable qck u.p over 1f out: wknd ins fnl f* **9/1**

0044 **8** 5 **Bahamian Boy**[7] 5808 3-8-11 **60** (b[1]) CharlieBennett(5) 9 34
(Hughie Morrison) *s.i.s: t.k.h: hdwy to chse ldrs after 2f: effrt to press ldrs 2f out: lost pl and btn over 1f out: fdd ins fnl f* **10/1**

1230 **9** nk **Illusive Force (IRE)**[16] 5503 4-9-6 **59** (v) MartinLane 7 33
(Derek Shaw) *stdd after s: hld up in tch in rr: effrt on outer over 2f out: no imp and lost pl over 1f out: wknd fnl f* **12/1**

1m 39.57s (-0.33) **Going Correction** -0.075s/f (Stan)
WFA 3 from 4yo+ 5lb **9** Ran SP% **104.7**
Speed ratings (Par 101): **98,96,95,92,92 91,89,84,83**
CSF £14.99 CT £422.43 TOTE £2.40: £1.20, £2.60, £9.20; EX 16.50 Trifecta £760.20.
Owner G L Moore **Bred** Brightwalton Stud **Trained** Lower Beeding, W Sussex
■ Zamastar was withdrawn. Price at time of withdrawal 6-1. Rule 4 applies to all bets - deduction 10p in the pound.

FOCUS
Very marginally the quicker of the two divisions (0.08sec).

6048 TOTEPOOLLIVEINFO.COM H'CAP 1m 2f (P)
7:40 (7:42) (Class 4) (0-85,86) 3-Y-O+ **£6,469** (£1,925; £962; £481) **Stalls** Low

Form RPR

3351 **1** **Ecureuil (IRE)**[30] 4978 3-8-12 **80** JimCrowley 2 91
(Hugo Palmer) *mde all: rdn and fnd ex over 1f out: clr 1f out: kpt on u.p and a doing enough ins fnl f* **5/1**[3]

2111 **2** 3/4 **Athlon (IRE)**[10] 5724 3-9-4 **86** 6ex ShaneKelly 5 95+
(David Lanigan) *wl in tch in midfield: effrt over 2f out: 4th and hung lft over 1f out: styd on to chse wnr but stl wanting to hang lft 100yds out: kpt on but nvr getting to wnr* **5/4**[1]

0643 **3** 1 1/4 **Craftsmanship (FR)**[33] 4868 5-9-0 **82** CameronNoble(7) 7 88+
(Robert Eddery) *s.i.s: bhd and off the pce: clsd and in tch 3f out: nt clrest of runs and swtchd rt over 1f out: hdwy 1f out: styd on wl ins fnl f to go 3rd nr fin: nvr getting to wnr* **12/1**

0406 **4** 1/2 **Royal Reserve**[25] 5198 3-9-0 **82** SamHitchcott 10 87
(William Muir) *hld up in midfield rdn and effrt over 2f out: hdwy over 1f out: styd on u.p ins fnl f: wnt 4th last strides: nvr getting to wnr* **10/1**

1355 **5** nk **Demonstration (IRE)**[26] 5160 4-9-10 **85** (p) SilvestreDeSousa 3 89
(William Jarvis) *chsd wnr: rdn over 3f out: drvn and unable qck over 1f out: lost 2nd 100yds: no ex and lost 2 pls towards fin* **7/2**[2]

1335 **6** 1 3/4 **Prendergast Hill (IRE)**[14] 5574 4-9-8 **83** (p) LiamKeniry 1 84
(Ed de Giles) *t.k.h: chsd ldrs: effrt on inner over 1f out: unable qck u.p 1f out: wknd ins fnl f* **14/1**

4264 **7** 4 **Sands Chorus**[21] 5333 4-9-1 **76** LukeMorris 9 69
(James Given) *chsd ldrs on outer: rdn over 2f out: lost pl and btn over 1f out: bhd 1f out: wknd ins fnl f* **20/1**

205 **8** nk **Buckland Beau**[21] 5333 5-9-5 **80** MartinLane 4 72
(Charlie Fellowes) *stdd s: hld up in last pair: clsd over 3f out: effrt wd and wl over 1f out: no hdwy u.p over 1f out: wknd ins fnl f* **8/1**

6156 **9** 1 **Yul Finegold (IRE)**[88] 2930 6-9-1 **79** JosephineGordon(3) 6 69
(Conor Dore) *hld up in tch in midfield: effrt over 2f out: no imp over 1f out: wknd fnl f* **50/1**

2m 4.91s (-3.69) **Going Correction** -0.075s/f (Stan)
WFA 3 from 4yo+ 7lb **9** Ran SP% **124.6**
Speed ratings (Par 105): **111,110,109,109,109 107,104,104,103**
CSF £12.65 CT £77.46 TOTE £7.10: £2.20, £1.10, £3.20; EX 18.90 Trifecta £114.10.
Owner Al Asayl Bloodstock Ltd **Bred** J F Tuthill **Trained** Newmarket, Suffolk

FOCUS
A decent handicap and an all-the-way winner who improved again.

6049 @TOTEPOOLRACING WIN TICKETS ON TWITTER MAIDEN STKS 1m 5f 66y(P)
8:10 (8:11) (Class 5) 3-Y-O+ **£5,175** (£1,540; £769; £384) **Stalls** Low

Form RPR

0322 **1** **Pleasure Dome**[20] 5353 3-8-13 76 JimCrowley 1 75
(Peter Chapple-Hyam) *chsd ldr for 1f: styd handy: effrt over 2f out: ev ch u.p over 1f out: styd on u.p to ld last strides* **4/1**

-043 **2** hd **Satish**[12] 5623 3-9-4 76 (b) RobertHavlin 2 79
(John Gosden) *stdd s: hld up in tch in last: effrt on inner over 1f out: rdn to ld 150yds: sn drvn: kpt on: hdd last strides* **3/1**[3]

54 **3** 1 1/2 **Blazing Mighty**[15] 5550 3-8-10 0 JosephineGordon(3) 5 72
(Robyn Brisland) *wnt rt s: t.k.h and sn led: jnd and rdn 3f out: hdd 2f out: battled on wl u.p to ld again 1f out: sn hdd: no ex and outpcd wl ins fnl f* **20/1**

024 **4** 2 1/4 **Fashion Design (IRE)**[9] 5742 3-8-13 0 (p) TedDurcan 4 68
(Sir Michael Stoute) *chsd ldr after 1f: upsides ldr 3f out: rdn to ld 2f out: sn drvn and fnd little for press: hdd 1f out: wknd fnl 100yds* **5/2**[2]

243 **5** 2 1/2 **Rasasee (IRE)**[27] 5111 3-9-4 77 LukeMorris 3 71
(Marco Botti) *hld up in tch in 4th: rdn over 2f out: unable qck over 1f out: btn and eased ins fnl f* **9/4**[1]

2m 51.12s (-2.48) **Going Correction** -0.075s/f (Stan) **5** Ran SP% **109.1**
Speed ratings (Par 103): **104,103,102,101,100**
CSF £15.77 TOTE £4.50: £2.00, £1.30; EX 12.70 Trifecta £126.90.
Owner J G Davis **Bred** J G Davis & Star Pointe Ltd **Trained** Newmarket, Suffolk

FOCUS
Some frustrating types lined up for this maiden. Muddling form, rated around the first two.

6050 TOTEPOOLRACING FIND US ON INSTAGRAM H'CAP 1m 6f (P)
8:40 (8:40) (Class 4) (0-85,83) 3-Y-O+ **£6,469** (£1,925; £962; £481) **Stalls** Low

Form RPR

141 **1** **West Coast Flyer**[29] 5026 3-9-3 **83** JamieSpencer 6 94+
(David Simcock) *hld up in last quartet: clsd 4f out: effrt to chse ldrs over 2f out: rdn and qcknd to ld over 1f out: hung lft ins fnl f: styd on wl* **15/8**[1]

6323 **2** ½ **Graceland (FR)**[21] 5328 4-9-10 **82** LouisSteward(3) 5 92
(Michael Bell) *blind off late and s.i.s: t.k.h: hld up in last quartet: clsd 4f out: effrt over 2f out: rdn and gd hdwy over 1f out: ev ch and carried lft ins fnl f: kpt on but a hld* **14/1**

1151 **3** 1¼ **Tenzing Norgay**[12] 5633 3-9-0 **80** (p) LukeMorris 8 88
(Sir Mark Prescott Bt) *stdd s: hld up in last quartet: clsd 4f out: effrt on outer ent fnl 2f: hrd drvn to chse ldng pair 1f out: kpt on same pce ins fnl f* **3/1**[2]

100- **4** 4½ **Devon Drum**[59] 8175 8-9-6 **78** (t) AaronJones(3) 7 80
(David Brown) *hld up in midfield: effrt in 4th over 2f out: chsng ldrs and bmpd over 1f out: 4th and btn 1f out: outpcd fnl f* **33/1**

0202 **5** 6 **Sarsted**[29] 5026 4-10-0 **83** [1] JimCrowley 3 81
(Hughie Morrison) *chsd ldr tl 5f out: styd trcking ldrs: gng wl and nt clr run 2f out: shuffled bk over 1f out: swtchd rt and in the clr but any ch had gone ins fnl f: nudged along after* **5/1**[3]

31-3 **6** hd **Bellajeu**[68] 3665 4-9-9 **78** OisinMurphy 4 71
(Ralph Beckett) *t.k.h: sn led: clr after 3f: c bk to field 5f out: rdn and hdd wl over 1f out: no ex and btn 1f out: wl hld and eased ins fnl f* **8/1**

6000 **7** 1¼ **Prince Of Paris**[49] 4307 4-9-11 **80** (t) MartinLane 9 72
(Roger Ingram) *stdd after s: t.k.h: dropped in bhd after 2f: effrt 3f out: rdn and no imp 2f out: wknd over 1f out* **50/1**

3005 **8** 5 **Street Artist (IRE)**[12] 5633 6-10-0 **83** SilvestreDeSousa 1 68
(David Nicholls) *chsd ldrs: wnt 2nd 5f out: rdn and ev ch 2f out: led wl over 1f out: sn hdd and lost pl: wl hld and eased ins fnl f* **6/1**

0-06 **9** 4 **Senrima (IRE)**[47] 4396 4-9-11 **80** RobertHavlin 2 59
(Brian Meehan) *chsd ldng trio: rdn over 2f out: sn lost pl: bhd over 1f out: wknd fnl f* **9/1**

2m 59.53s (-3.67) **Going Correction** -0.075s/f (Stan)
WFA 3 from 4yo+ 11lb **9** Ran SP% **123.4**
Speed ratings (Par 105): **107,106,106,103,100 99,99,96,94**
CSF £33.86 CT £82.26 TOTE £2.60: £1.20, £3.00, £1.90; EX 21.70 Trifecta £128.10.
Owner Ali Saeed **Bred** Miss K Rausing **Trained** Newmarket, Suffolk

FOCUS
With the leader going off too quickly, this was set up for the closers. The runner-up is the key to the form.

6051 FOLLOW @CHELMSFORDCRC ON TWITTER H'CAP 6f (P)
9:10 (9:11) (Class 6) (0-65,64) 3-Y-O+ **£3,234** (£962; £481; £240) **Stalls** Centre

Form RPR

2062 **1** **Dream Dana (IRE)**[8] 5769 3-9-5 **64** TimmyMurphy 12 71
(Jamie Osborne) *chsd ldrs: effrt: swtchd lft and bmpd over 1f out: rallied u.p ins fnl f: styd on wl to ld nr fin* **12/1**

3055 **2** ½ **Costa Filey**[13] 5599 5-9-6 **63** HarryBentley 7 69
(Ed Vaughan) *t.k.h: chsd ldr: clsd and shkn to chal whn ducked rt over 1f out: rdn to ld 150yds: kpt on u.p: hdd and no ex nr fin* **9/2**[1]

2515 **3** nk **Swiss Cross**[2] 5992 9-9-4 **64** (t) TimClark(3) 4 69
(Phil McEntee) *hld up in tch in midfield: rdn and hdwy over 1f out: ev ch ins fnl f: edgd lft u.p wl ins fnl f: unable qck towards fin* **5/1**[2]

2641 **4** nk **Manipura**[12] 5636 3-8-11 **59** (p) MatthewCosham(3) 6 64
(Derek Shaw) *stdd s: hld up in rr: hdwy on inner over 1f out: drvn to press ldrs ins fnl f: n.m.r and bdly jostled wl ins fnl f: kpt on* **5/1**[2]

5460 **5** ¾ **Miss Phillyjinks (IRE)**[22] 5302 3-9-3 **62** ShaneKelly 2 63
(Paul D'Arcy) *led: clr 1/2-way: drvn and hrd pressed over 1f out: hdd 150yds out: no ex and outpcd wl ins fnl f* **10/1**

0022 **6** 1¾ **Encapsulated**[17] 5475 6-8-12 **62** RhiainIngram(7) 5 58
(Roger Ingram) *taken down early and led to post: t.k.h: in tch in midfield: swtchd rt and hdwy on outer over 2f out: kpt on same pce u.p fr over 1f out* **5/1**[2]

4060 **7** hd **Magic Strike (IRE)**[16] 5515 3-9-1 **60** (v[1]) JohnFahy 9 56
(Clive Cox) *chsd ldng trio: rdn and lost pl over 1f out: styd on same pce u.p fnl f* **11/1**

063 **8** ½ **Vale Of Flight (IRE)**[17] 5474 3-9-1 **60** JimCrowley 3 54
(Rae Guest) *hld up wl in tch in midfield: effrt to press ldrs over 1f out: no ex and short of room ins fnl f: wknd fnl 100yds* **7/1**[3]

6350 **9** 3 **Misu Pete**[13] 5605 4-9-5 **62** OisinMurphy 8 47
(Mark Usher) *dwlt: hld up in rr: swtchd rt and effrt wd bnd 2f out: no imp: nvr trbld ldrs* **10/1**

06 **10** ½ **Yasood (IRE)**[12] 5635 3-8-10 **62** GeorgiaDobie(7) 13 46
(Phil McEntee) *s.i.s: a bhd* **33/1**

006 **11** 8 **Rial (IRE)**[68] 3649 3-9-3 **62** [1] SilvestreDeSousa 1 22+
(Phil McEntee) *sn pushed along and a towards rr: bhd and eased ins fnl f* **16/1**

1m 12.76s (-0.94) **Going Correction** -0.075s/f (Stan)
WFA 3 from 4yo+ 2lb **11** Ran SP% **123.7**
Speed ratings (Par 101): **103,102,101,101,100 98,97,97,93,92 81**
CSF £68.79 CT £324.24 TOTE £11.40: £3.90, £2.20, £2.40; EX 90.20 Trifecta £354.50.
Owner J A Osborne **Bred** Ballylinch Stud **Trained** Upper Lambourn, Berks
■ Stewards' Enquiry : Tim Clark four-day ban: careless riding (15-19 Sep, 19 Sep)

FOCUS
A modest sprint handicap.
T/Plt: £50.20 to a £1 stake. Pool: £99,654.74. 1,447.15 winning tickets. T/Qpdt: £58.50 to a £1 stake. Pool: £10,229.41. 129.38 winning tickets. **Steve Payne**

5156 HAYDOCK (L-H)
Thursday, September 1

OFFICIAL GOING: Good (7.6)
Wind: Light, against Weather: Fine

6052 FREE SPINS AT 188BET CASINO MAIDEN STKS 1m 3f 200y
2:00 (2:00) (Class 5) 3-Y-O+ **£3,234** (£962; £481; £240) **Stalls** Centre

Form RPR

5 **1** **Elraazy**[93] 2767 3-9-0 0 PaulHanagan 12 85+
(John Gosden) *trckd ldrs: led wl over 1f out: rdn whn pressed ins fnl f: r.o gamely and fnd ex towards fin* **7/4**[1]

034 **2** ¾ **Queen Of The Stars**[64] 3781 3-9-0 75 JimCrowley 8 83
(William Haggas) *hld up: smooth hdwy on outer over 2f out: wnt 2nd over 1f out: str chal ins fnl f: no ex towards fin* **7/2**[3]

2 **3** 6 **Arthur Mc Bride (IRE)**[12] 5623 7-10-0 0 (t) ThomasBrown 5 79
(Nigel Twiston-Davies) *prom: w ldr after 3f: led over 3f out: rdn 2f out: hdd wl over 1f out: unable to go w front two ins fnl f: styd on same pce fnl 150yds* **7/1**

4 1¼ **Smashed (IRE)** 3-9-5 0 BenCurtis 1 77
(William Haggas) *led: rdn and hdd over 3f out: stl chsng ldrs u.p over 1f out: kpt on same pce ins fnl f* **16/1**

35 **5** 3 **Waiting For Richie**[48] 4372 3-9-5 0 JamesSullivan 2 72
(Tom Tate) *trckd ldrs: rdn 3f out: outpcd 2f out: kpt on pce but no imp ins fnl f* **100/1**

4 **6** 1¾ **Versant**[27] 5129 4-10-0 0 (t) MartinHarley 13 69
(Seamus Durack) *racd keenly on outer: prom: rdn whn chsng ldrs over 2f out: one pce fnl f* **10/1**

6 **7** 3½ **High Command (IRE)**[152] 1200 3-9-5 0 JackMitchell 7 63
(Roger Varian) *midfield: rdn 3f out: sn outpcd and n.d* **10/3**[2]

2P **8** 1 **Autumn Surprise (IRE)**[40] 4633 3-9-0 0 DavidAllan 11 57
(Tim Easterby) *hld up: pushed along over 2f out and hung lft: no imp* **25/1**

62 **9** 5 **Jonofark (IRE)**[30] 4983 3-9-5 0 PaulMulrennan 9 54
(Brian Rothwell) *racd keenly: hld up: sn in midfield: hdwy over 5f out: chsd ldrs 4f out: wknd over 2f out* **50/1**

46 **10** ½ **Lady Natasha (IRE)**[20] 5361 3-9-0 0 DougieCostello 3 48
(K R Burke) *racd keenly: prom: rdn 3f out: wknd over 2f out* **100/1**

000 **11** 1½ **Vale Of Rock (IRE)**[13] 5610 3-9-0 44 [1] AndrewMullen 4 46
(Michael Appleby) *midfield: pushed along 4f out: wknd 2f out* **200/1**

0 **12** ½ **Caracci Apache (IRE)**[35] 4792 6-10-0 0 PatDobbs 10 50
(Eve Johnson Houghton) *hld up: rdn 3f out: nvr a threat* **40/1**

13 10 **He's Magic**[32] 5-10-0 0 BarryMcHugh 6 34
(Tim Fitzgerald) *midfield: rdn and wknd over 3f out* **150/1**

2m 28.52s (-5.28) **Going Correction** -0.45s/f (Firm)
WFA 3 from 4yo+ 9lb **13** Ran SP% **120.5**
Speed ratings (Par 103): **99,98,94,93,91 90,88,87,84,83 82,82,75**
CSF £7.75 TOTE £2.60: £1.10, £1.80, £2.20; EX 9.80 Trifecta £29.70.
Owner Hamdan Al Maktoum **Bred** Shadwell Estate Company Limited **Trained** Newmarket, Suffolk

FOCUS
Good ground, the rain having missed the track. All races run over inner home straight. The opener was run over 2yds less than advertised. The first two pulled clear in this maiden, which was run at an ordinary gallop. Last year's winner added an Ascot Group 3. The form makes sense, rated around the third, fifth and sixth.

6053 188BET.CO.UK EBFSTALLIONS.COM MAIDEN STKS (PLUS 10 RACE) 6f
2:30 (2:32) (Class 4) 2-Y-O **£4,269** (£1,270; £634; £317) **Stalls** Centre

Form RPR

1 **Pennsylvania Dutch** 2-9-0 0 BenCurtis 8 81+
(William Haggas) *hld up in midfield: rdn and hdwy over 1f out: led fnl 120yds: r.o and in command nr fin* **6/1**[2]

553 **2** 1¼ **Roaring Character (IRE)**[32] 4914 2-9-0 80 RichardKingscote 7 77
(Tom Dascombe) *chsd ldr: led over 1f out: hdd fnl 120yds: no ex nr fin* **9/1**

0 **3** 1¼ **Houndstooth (IRE)**[20] 5371 2-9-0 0 DanielTudhope 6 73
(Luca Cumani) *prom: rdn and nt qckn over 1f out: styd on nr fin but nt pce of front two* **28/1**

05 **4** nse **Swag (IRE)**[19] 5410 2-9-0 0 (t) PatDobbs 10 73
(Richard Hannon) *hld up: hdwy over 2f out: swtchd lft over 1f out: chsng ldrs and cl up ins fnl f: kpt on but nt pce of ldrs* **14/1**

0 **5** ¾ **Tesko Fella (IRE)**[37] 4736 2-9-0 0 KieranO'Neill 1 71
(Richard Hannon) *chsd ldrs: rdn to chal over 1f out: kpt on same pce fnl 100yds* **16/1**

6 ½ **Somewhere Secret** 2-9-0 0 PaulMulrennan 4 69
(Robert Cowell) *racd keenly: chsd ldrs: lost pl 4f out: rallied over 1f out to chse ldrs: edgd lft ins fnl f: one pce fnl 100yds* **20/1**

7 nk **Swiss Storm** 2-9-0 0 JimCrowley 3 68+
(David Elsworth) *s.i.s: pushed along early and green: sme hdwy over 2f out: kpt on ins fnl f: nvr able to trble ldrs* **4/5**[1]

043 **8** 3¼ **Infatuated**[17] 5477 2-9-0 68 DavidAllan 9 59
(Tim Easterby) *hld up: rdn over 2f out: outpcd over 1f out: nvr a threat* **20/1**

3 **9** 1 **Coastal Cyclone**[30] 4989 2-9-0 0 MartinHarley 5 56
(Harry Dunlop) *led: rdn and hdd over 1f out: wknd fnl 100yds* **17/2**[3]

10 17 **Sheng Chi Dragon (IRE)** 2-9-0 0 DougieCostello 2 5
(K R Burke) *midfield: lost pl 4f out: u.p and outpcd after* **100/1**

1m 13.6s (-0.20) **Going Correction** -0.10s/f (Good) **10** Ran SP% **116.9**
Speed ratings (Par 97): **97,95,93,93,92 91,91,87,85,63**
CSF £55.72 TOTE £6.30: £1.70, £2.50, £4.70; EX 50.90 Trifecta £2131.00.
Owner Lael Stable **Bred** Lael Stables **Trained** Newmarket, Suffolk

FOCUS
Race distance as advertised. With the favourite disappointing this is just ordinary maiden form.

6054 188 BET EBF STALLIONS MAIDEN STKS (PLUS 10 RACE) 1m
3:00 (3:00) (Class 4) 2-Y-O **£4,269** (£1,270; £634; £317) **Stalls** Low

Form RPR

22 **1** **Star Archer**[25] 5203 2-9-0 0 JimCrowley 1 89+
(Hugo Palmer) *chsd ldrs: led over 1f out: qcknd to go clr fnl 150yds: r.o wl* **2/5**[1]

0 **2** 6 **Upgrade**[13] 5615 2-9-0 0 DougieCostello 5 75
(K R Burke) *chsd ldr: rdn and ev ch wl over 1f out: outpcd by wnr ins fnl f: sn no ch* **33/1**

0 **3** 1 **On To Victory**[33] 4866 2-9-0 0 PaulMulrennan 2 72
(Eve Johnson Houghton) *led: rdn and hdd over 1f out: kpt on same pce and no ch fnl 150yds* **16/1**

4 1 **Alqamar** 2-9-0 0 WilliamBuick 9 70+
(Charlie Appleby) *midfield on outer: lost pl 4f out: bhd: green and outpcd over 2f out: kpt on quite promisingly ins fnl f but no ch* **6/1**[2]

5 ¾ **Poseidon (IRE)** 2-9-0 0 ThomasBrown 11 68+
(Ed Walker) *in rr: hdwy on outer over 2f out: kpt on ins fnl f: nvr able to trble ldrs* **8/1**[3]

6 2½ **Katmandoo (USA)** 2-9-0 0 RichardKingscote 3 62
(Tom Dascombe) *midfield: outpcd over 2f out: one pce u.p fnl 2f* **16/1**

0 **7** ¾ **Knight Destroyer (IRE)**[56] 4040 2-9-0 0 GrahamLee 8 60
(Jonjo O'Neill) *midfield: outpcd over 2f out: green and plugged on but n.d after* **100/1**

8 nk **Inception (IRE)** 2-9-0 0 PatDobbs 12 59+
(Richard Hannon) *hld up: shkn up and sme hdwy over 2f out: one pce fnl f: nt trble ldrs* **16/1**

0 **9** 3¾ **Final Chapter**[46] 4423 2-9-0 0 DavidAllan 7 50
(Tim Easterby) *prom: wknd over 2f out: sn hung lft whn wl btn* **100/1**

10 ½ **Chocolate Box (IRE)** 2-9-0 0 DanielTudhope 4 49
(Luca Cumani) *s.i.s: midfield tl wknd over 2f out* **20/1**

11 4 **New Society (IRE)** 2-9-0 0 PJMcDonald 10 40
(James Bethell) *towards rr: rdn over 3f out: nvr a threat* **66/1**

0 **12** *26* **Bobbys Helmet (IRE)**[62] 3854 2-9-0 0 BenCurtis 6
(David C Griffiths) *midfield: rdn and wknd over 3f out* **100/1**

1m 39.41s (-4.29) **Going Correction** -0.45s/f (Firm) **12** Ran SP% **126.6**
Speed ratings (Par 97): **103,97,96,95,94 91,91,90,86,86 82,56**
CSF £34.01 TOTE £1.50: £1.02, £9.00, £3.30; EX 23.20 Trifecta £215.90.
Owner K Abdullah **Bred** Millsec Limited **Trained** Newmarket, Suffolk

FOCUS
Not many got into this maiden, which was run over 2yds shorter than advertised.

6055 US OPEN TENNIS AT 188BET H'CAP — 1m

3:30 (3:30) (Class 4) (0-80,80) 3-Y-O+ **£5,175** (£1,540; £769; £384) **Stalls** Low

Form RPR

021 **1** **Zwayyan**[23] 5260 3-9-5 **80** FrankieDettori 4 94+
(William Haggas) *midfield: hdwy over 2f out: qcknd to ld over 1f out: r.o wl fnl f and in command: eased cl home* **6/4**[1]

2106 **2** *2* **Prosecute (FR)**[48] 4358 3-9-1 **76** JimCrowley 1 84
(David Simcock) *midfield: nt clr run 2f out: effrt whn in the clr over 1f out: styd on to take 2nd ins fnl f: no imp on wnr* **17/2**

5320 **3** *1 1/2* **Bush Beauty (IRE)**[28] 5062 5-8-7 **70** SophieKilloran(7) 5 75
(Eric Alston) *hld up: hdwy whn nt clr run 2f out: plld to outer over 1f out: styd on ins fnl f wout troubling front two* **40/1**

0260 **4** *1/2* **Trinity Star (IRE)**[17] 5482 5-9-7 **77** (p) PaulMulrennan 6 81
(Michael Dods) *s.i.s: bhd: pushed along 5f out: hdwy over 1f out: styd on ins fnl f: gng on at fin but nvr gng pce to trble ldrs* **8/1**

0203 **5** *1/2* **Mr Quicksilver**[21] 5333 4-9-9 **79** (t) ThomasBrown 3 82
(Ed Walker) *s.i.s: hld up: hdwy over 2f out: effrt over 1f out: nt qckn: styd on same pce ins fnl f* **18/1**

1400 **6** *2 1/4* **Chosen Character (IRE)**[26] 5156 8-9-2 **77** (vt) AnnaHesketh(5) 11 74
(Tom Dascombe) *led: rdn over 2f out: hdd over 1f out: no ex ins fnl f: fdd fnl 150yds* **16/1**

1606 **7** *2 1/4* **Janaab (IRE)**[16] 5521 6-8-8 **67** (t) RachelRichardson(3) 2 59
(Tim Easterby) *broke wl: in tch: rdn over 2f out: outpcd over 1f out: kpt on ins fnl f: no imp* **25/1**

1302 **8** *2 3/4* **Hanseatic**[17] 5482 7-9-7 **77** JamesSullivan 9 62
(Michael Easterby) *chsd ldrs: rdn and ev ch 2f out: nt qckn over 1f out: one pce ins fnl f* **12/1**

443 **9** *3* **Dutch Artist (IRE)**[17] 5482 4-9-10 **80** GrahamGibbons 12 58
(David O'Meara) *chsd ldrs: effrt 2f out: nt qckn over 1f out: wknd ins fnl f* **15/2**[3]

3500 **10** *2* **Know Your Name**[20] 5367 5-9-0 **70** JasonHart 10 43
(Eric Alston) *chsd ldr: rdn and lost 2nd over 2f out: wknd over 1f out* **66/1**

0000 **11** *3/4* **Harry Holland**[64] 3783 4-9-6 **76** RichardKingscote 7 47
(Tom Dascombe) *hld up: pushed along over 5f out: rdn over 2f out: nvr a threat* **33/1**

2146 **12** *7* **Marbooh (IRE)**[40] 4654 3-9-5 **80** DanielTudhope 8 34
(David O'Meara) *midfield: rdn and wknd over 3f out: eased whn wl btn fnl f* **11/2**[2]

1m 39.1s (-4.60) **Going Correction** -0.45s/f (Firm) **12** Ran SP% **118.3**
WFA 3 from 4yo+ 5lb
Speed ratings (Par 105): **105,103,101,101,100 98,96,93,90,88 87,80**
CSF £14.27 CT £368.96 TOTE £2.30: £1.20, £2.70, £8.00; EX 16.90 Trifecta £256.90.
Owner Al Shaqab Racing **Bred** Newsells Park Stud & Cheveley Park Stud **Trained** Newmarket, Suffolk

FOCUS
This was run over 2yds shorter than advertised. A fair handicap, it was run at a decent pace. The 1-2 were both improved 3yos, with the form rated slightly positively.

6056 BRITISH STALLION STUDS EBF CONDITIONS STKS — 7f

4:00 (4:00) (Class 3) 3-Y-O+ **£9,703** (£2,887; £1,443; £721) **Stalls** Low

Form RPR

3326 **1** **Forge**[13] 5613 3-8-11 108 RichardKingscote 3 111
(Sir Michael Stoute) *mde all: rdn ins fnl f: kpt on wl* **15/8**[2]

5/35 **2** *1* **Muwaary**[68] 3664 5-8-12 108 PaulHanagan 8 107
(John Gosden) *racd keenly: prom: forced wd 5f out: pushed along over 2f out: wnt 2nd over 1f out: styd on ins fnl f: nvr quite on terms w wnr* **6/4**[1]

3300 **3** *2* **One Word More (IRE)**[14] 5585 6-8-12 99 DavidAllan 7 102
(Tim Easterby) *hld up: pushed along over 2f out: rdn and hdwy over 1f out: styd on ins fnl f: nt pce of front two* **9/1**

0614 **4** *3/4* **Lulu The Zulu (IRE)**[48] 4338 8-9-1 99 AndrewMullen 4 103
(Michael Appleby) *hld up: swtchd lft over 3f out: kpt on ins fnl f: nvr able to chal* **20/1**

3345 **5** *nk* **Shadow Hunter (IRE)**[75] 3392 3-8-6 92 FrannyNorton 1 95
(Hugo Palmer) *chsd ldrs: rdn and outpcd 2f out: kpt on ins fnl f* **16/1**

0623 **6** *2* **Dark Emerald (IRE)**[19] 5404 6-9-8 111 (v) GrahamLee 5 104
(Brendan Powell) *prom: wnt fairly wd 5f out: rdn and lost 2nd over 1f out: wknd fnl 100yds* **8/1**[3]

-010 **7** *4* **Amazour (IRE)**[48] 4338 4-9-5 96 WilliamBuick 2 90
(Ismail Mohammed) *hld up: rdn over 1f out: sn btn* **20/1**

1m 25.5s (-5.20) **Going Correction** -0.45s/f (Firm) course record **7** Ran SP% **111.3**
WFA 3 from 4yo+ 4lb
Speed ratings (Par 107): **111,109,107,106,106 104,99**
CSF £4.74 TOTE £2.70: £1.50, £1.50; EX 5.90 Trifecta £25.00.
Owner K Abdullah **Bred** Juddmonte Farms Ltd **Trained** Newmarket, Suffolk

FOCUS
Race run over 2yds shorter than advertised. A good conditions race in which it proved difficult to make up ground from the rear. The winner made all in new course record time. He's the type to improve further.

6057 £25 FREE BET AT 188BET H'CAP — 1m 3f 200y

4:30 (4:30) (Class 2) (0-105,102) 3-Y-O+ **£12,938** (£3,850; £1,924; £962) **Stalls** Centre

Form RPR

4040 **1** **Cymro (IRE)**[12] 5639 4-9-12 **100** RichardKingscote 5 108
(Tom Dascombe) *trckd ldrs: effrt 2f out: led over 1f out: kpt on ins fnl f: hld on gamely nr fin* **9/1**

1314 **2** *nk* **Stars Over The Sea (USA)**[13] 5611 5-10-0 **102** JoeFanning 1 109
(Mark Johnston) *led: rdn 2f out: hdd over 1f out: rallied gamely nr fin: jst hld* **2/1**[1]

5-00 **3** *1/2* **Felix Mendelssohn (IRE)**[76] 3340 5-9-8 **96** DanielTudhope 2 102
(David Simcock) *midfield: hdwy over 1f out: ev ch ins fnl f: styd on: hld nr fin* **8/1**

0000 **4** *3/4* **Beaverbrook**[26] 5173 3-8-7 **90** FrannyNorton 3 95
(Mark Johnston) *prom: rdn 2f out: checked briefly whn nt clr run ins fnl f: kpt on* **10/1**

4260 **5** *3* **Snoano**[12] 5651 4-9-6 **94** DavidAllan 6 94
(Tim Easterby) *midfield: hdwy over 3f out: rdn and ev ch over 1f out: no ex fnl 75yds* **11/2**[2]

0426 **6** *1* **Gabrial's King (IRE)**[13] 5611 7-9-2 **90** GrahamLee 7 88
(Richard Fahey) *missed break: hld up: rdn over 1f out: kpt on ins fnl f: nvr able to chal* **14/1**

2124 **7** *1/2* **Stockhill Diva**[47] 4400 6-9-5 **93** PaulMulrennan 4 90
(Brendan Powell) *missed break: hld up: hdwy over 1f out to chse ldrs: one pce ins fnl f* **25/1**

2110 **8** *2* **Ruwasi**[26] 5145 5-9-4 **92** MartinHarley 9 86
(James Tate) *hld up in rr: hdwy over 3f out: chsd ldrs wl over 1f out: wknd ins fnl f* **6/1**[3]

213- **9** *4* **Important Message**[383] 5389 4-9-8 **96** WilliamBuick 10 84
(Saeed bin Suroor) *chsd ldr over 10f out: rdn and ev ch over 2f out: wknd over 1f out* **8/1**

2m 27.77s (-6.03) **Going Correction** -0.45s/f (Firm)
WFA 3 from 4yo+ 9lb **9** Ran SP% **114.8**
Speed ratings (Par 109): **102,101,101,100,98 98,97,96,93**
CSF £27.21 CT £153.40 TOTE £10.50: £2.60, £1.40, £3.10; EX 33.10 Trifecta £282.40.
Owner D R Passant & Hefin Williams **Bred** Michael McGlynn **Trained** Malpas, Cheshire

FOCUS
Race run over 2yds shorter than advertised. A tight finish to this good handicap, in which just about all of them were in line at the two pole. The winner is rated back to his reappearance form.

6058 BEST ODDS GUARANTEED AT 188BET H'CAP (FOR GENTLEMAN AMATEUR RIDERS) — 1m 3f 200y

5:00 (5:01) (Class 5) (0-70,70) 4-Y-O+ **£2,807** (£870; £435; £217) **Stalls** Centre

Form RPR

5/22 **1** **Miss Tiger Lily**[25] 5208 6-10-10 **64** MrHHunt(5) 7 71
(Harry Dunlop) *w ldr after 1f: led 6f out: rdn 3f out: kept on gamely ins fnl f* **7/2**[1]

0250 **2** *3/4* **Sherman McCoy**[31] 4934 10-10-12 **66** MrBLynn(5) 5 71
(Marjorie Fife) *chsd ldrs: wnt 2nd 4f out: chal ins fnl f: kpt on* **8/1**

6105 **3** *1 1/4* **Diletta Tommasa (IRE)**[19] 5397 6-10-12 **61** (p) MrSWalker 6 63
(Daniel Mark Loughnane) *hld up in rr: hdwy over 2f out: swtchd lft when chasg ldrs 1f out: styd on ins fnl f: one pce towards fin* **5/1**[2]

0066 **4** *1* **Dark Amber**[28] 5096 6-10-2 **58** [1] MrJEPerrett(7) 4 59
(Brendan Powell) *hld up: rdn 2f out: hdwy to chse ldrs over 1f out: styd on same pce fnl f* **7/2**[1]

0203 **5** *2 1/4* **Correggio**[22] 5293 6-11-2 **70** MrJoeWright(5) 2 67
(Micky Hammond) *broke wl: prom: sn stdd into midfield: effrt over 2f out: plugged on ins fnl f: no imp* **5/1**[2]

6300 **6** *nk* **Zenafire**[47] 4381 7-11-1 **67** (p) MrJamesKing(3) 3 64
(Sarah Hollinshead) *midfield: hdwy over 3f out: rdn over 2f out: btn over 1f out* **7/1**[3]

2130 **7** *2 1/2* **Smoky Hill (IRE)**[28] 5053 7-11-0 **63** MrAlexEdwards 8 56
(Tony Carroll) *hld up: hdwy over 3f out: rdn and ev ch 2f out: wknd ins fnl f* **10/1**

250/ **8** *30* **Astrum**[19] 6202 6-11-2 **70** (b) MrTGillard(5) 1 15
(Donald McCain) *broke wl: led: hdd 6f out: rdn 4f out: wknd over 3f out* **22/1**

2m 30.75s (-3.05) **Going Correction** -0.45s/f (Firm) **8** Ran SP% **114.8**
Speed ratings (Par 103): **92,91,90,89,88 87,86,66**
CSF £32.21 CT £139.02 TOTE £3.80: £1.60, £3.00, £1.60; EX 35.20 Trifecta £142.10.
Owner Mr & Mrs D Hearson **Bred** Granham Farm Partnership **Trained** Lambourn, Berks
■ Stewards' Enquiry : Mr H Hunt four-day ban: use of whip (20 Sep, 3, 4, 17 Oct)

FOCUS
This was contested over 2yds shorter than advertised. A modest handicap for amateurs, and the slowest of the three C&D times. The winner has back form to suggest she can do a bit better.
T/Jkpt: £2,857.10 to a £1 stake. Pool: £10,000.00 - 3.50 winning tickets. T/Plt: £27.10 to a £1 stake. Pool: £77,589.38. 2,087.02 winning tickets. T/Qpdt: £4.40 to a £1 stake. Pool: £5,526.75. 910.05 winning tickets. **Darren Owen**

5592 SALISBURY (R-H)

Thursday, September 1

OFFICIAL GOING: Last 6f - good (good to firm in places); remainder - good to firm (8.5)
Wind: Almost nil Weather: Sunny

6059 LESTER BRUNT WEALTH MANAGEMENT EBF STALLIONS NOVICE STKS (PLUS 10 RACE) — 1m

1:40 (1:42) (Class 4) 2-Y-O **£5,822** (£1,732; £865; £432) **Stalls** High

Form RPR

0412 **1** **Salouen (IRE)**[12] 5646 2-9-8 100 TomMarquand 2 98+
(Sylvester Kirk) *trckd ldrs: shkn up over 2f out: led over 1f out: edgd lft ins fnl f where rdr dropped rein briefly: kpt on wl* **11/10**[1]

2213 **2** *1/2* **Sea Fox (IRE)**[13] 5595 2-9-5 88 JFEgan 4 94
(David Evans) *trckd ldrs: chal over 3f out: shkn up over 2f out: ev ch ins fnl f: no ex towards fin* **7/2**[3]

2221 **3** *3* **Devil's Bridge (IRE)**[20] 5363 2-9-8 85 SeanLevey 3 90
(Richard Hannon) *led at stdy pce tl qcknd whn pressed over 3f out: kpt on w narrow advantage tl hdd over 1f out: no ex fnl 120yds* **15/2**

4 *8* **Mach One** 2-9-2 0 AdamKirby 1 64+
(Clive Cox) *str: awkwardly away: racd green: last but in tch tl outpcd over 2f out: wnt 4th ins fnl f* **16/1**

321 **5** *1 1/4* **Deningy**[13] 5600 2-9-8 94 MartinLane 5 67
(Charlie Appleby) *tk str hold: trckd ldrs: effrt 2f out: wknd jst over 1f out* **3/1**[2]

1m 48.82s (5.32) **Going Correction** -0.05s/f (Good) **5** Ran SP% **112.5**
Speed ratings (Par 97): **71,70,67,59,58**
CSF £5.46 TOTE £1.80: £1.20, £1.80; EX 4.60 Trifecta £11.90.
Owner H Balasuriya **Bred** Silvercon Edgerodge Ltd **Trained** Upper Lambourn, Berks

FOCUS
Sean Levey said of the going: "It's lovely, good ground." They crawled through the early stages of this novice event.

6060 IRISH YEARLING SALES NURSERY H'CAP — 6f 212y

2:10 (2:11) (Class 5) (0-70,72) 2-Y-O **£3,234** (£962; £481; £240) **Stalls** Centre

Form RPR

6422 **1** **Princess Way (IRE)**[1] 6033 2-8-7 **56** JFEgan 1 59
(David Evans) *broke wl: led briefly: trckd ldr: pushed along over 3f out: kpt on wl to ld fnl 130yds: rdn out* **9/2**[3]

6051 **2** *1* **Inner Circle (IRE)**[7] 5796 2-9-9 **72** 6ex SeanLevey 3 72
(Richard Hannon) *trckd ldr: led narrowly over 2f out: sn rdn: hdd fnl 130yds: no ex* **5/2**[1]

000 **3** ½ **Sir Plato (IRE)**[21] 5324 2-8-8 **57** LukeMorris 2 56
(Rod Millman) *chsd ldrs: rdn 3f out: nt quite pce to chal: kpt on ins fnl f: wnt 3rd cl home* **20/1**

6430 **4** *shd* **Star Maker**[13] 5594 2-9-7 **70** OisinMurphy 7 69
(Sylvester Kirk) *swtg: sn led: rdn and narrowly hdd over 2f out: kpt on fnl f: lost 3rd cl home* **3/1**[2]

360 **5** *nk* **Fair Selene**[31] 4951 2-8-6 **60** HectorCrouch(5) 5 58+
(Heather Main) *hld up in last pair: rdn over 2f out: hdwy over 1f out: kpt on ins fnl f but nt pce to get on terms* **14/1**

3100 **6** 3 **Latest Quest (IRE)**[15] 5560 2-9-6 **69** DaneO'Neill 8 59
(Sylvester Kirk) *hld up in last trio: rdn over 2f out: nt pce to get on terms: fdd fnl 120yds* **8/1**

004 **7** 3 ½ **Intisha (IRE)**[25] 5202 2-9-4 **67** RyanTate 4 47
(Jonathan Portman) *s.i.s: sn chsng ldrs: rdn over 2f out: wknd ins fnl f* **5/1**

004P **8** 30 **Viola Park**[8] 5770 2-7-11 **49** oh4 NoelGarbutt(3) 6
(Ronald Harris) *last pair but in tch tl wknd 3f out* **40/1**

1m 29.28s (0.68) **Going Correction** -0.05s/f (Good) **8** Ran SP% **113.4**
Speed ratings (Par 95): **94,92,92,92,91 88,84,50**
CSF £15.89 CT £184.82 TOTE £4.70: £1.50, £1.50, £3.60; EX 15.40 Trifecta £216.80.
Owner Terry Reffell **Bred** Tally-Ho Stud **Trained** Pandy, Monmouths

FOCUS
A modest nursery run at a steady gallop and it paid to race handy.

6061 VIRGINIA WALWYN MEMORIAL EBF QUIDHAMPTON MAIDEN FILLIES' STKS (PLUS 10 RACE) (DIV I) 6f 212y
2:40 (2:41) (Class 3) 2-Y-O **£7,762** (£2,310; £1,154; £577) **Stalls** Centre

Form RPR

4 **1** **Poet's Vanity**[26] 5170 2-9-0 0 OisinMurphy 8 98+
(Andrew Balding) *str: sn led: qcknd pce over 3f out: travelling powerfully and clr 2f out: rdn further clr over 1f out: easily* **6/1**[3]

4 **2** 10 **Contentment**[19] 5400 2-9-0 0 PatCosgrave 6 72
(William Haggas) *str: lw: led briefly early: trckd wnr: outpcd by wnr over 2f out: no ch fr over 1f out but a holding on for 2nd* **1/2**[1]

3 ¾ **Twenty Times (IRE)** 2-9-0 0 ShaneKelly 7 68+
(Richard Hughes) *tall: hld up in last pair: rdn over 2f out: hdwy over 1f out: wnt 3rd cl home: nvr any threat* **20/1**

4 ¾ **South Sea Belle (IRE)** 2-9-0 0 JimmyFortune 2 66
(David Menuisier) *str: trckd ldrs: rdn 3f out: kpt on fnl f but nt pce to get involved* **25/1**

5 *shd* **Secret Soul** 2-9-0 0 FMBerry 5 66
(Ralph Beckett) *medium-sized: in tch: rdn 3f out: kpt on fnl f but nt pce to get involved* **3/1**[2]

6 2 ¾ **Cubswin (IRE)** 2-9-0 0[1] WilliamTwiston-Davies 3 58
(Roger Charlton) *unf: s.i.s: in tch: rdn 3f out: sn one pce* **20/1**

7 1 ¾ **Sixth Of June** 2-9-0 0 FrederikTylicki 1 54
(Rod Millman) *w'like: trckd ldrs: rdn 3f out: wknd fnl f* **50/1**

8 3 **Perla Blanca (USA)** 2-9-0 0 RoystonFfrench 9 45
(Marcus Tregoning) *lengthy: bit bkwd: s.i.s: a in last pair* **33/1**

9 4 **Fresh Fox** 2-9-0 0 LukeMorris 4 35
(Jonathan Portman) *str: s.i.s: in tch: rdn over 3f out: wknd 2f out* **33/1**

1m 29.33s (0.73) **Going Correction** -0.05s/f (Good) **9** Ran SP% **127.2**
Speed ratings (Par 96): **93,81,80,79,79 76,74,71,66**
CSF £10.00 TOTE £9.30: £1.70, £1.02, £4.30; EX 16.80 Trifecta £142.80.
Owner Mrs M E Wates **Bred** Panda Bloodstock & Trickledown Stud **Trained** Kingsclere, Hants

FOCUS
A race that can throw some smart fillies, this first division was taken apart by the impressive winner. Little got into it.

6062 VIRGINIA WALWYN MEMORIAL EBF QUIDHAMPTON MAIDEN FILLIES' STKS (PLUS 10 RACE) (DIV II) 6f 212y
3:10 (3:12) (Class 3) 2-Y-O **£7,762** (£2,310; £1,154; £577) **Stalls** Centre

Form RPR

3 **1** **Argenterie**[35] 4801 2-9-0 0 MartinDwyer 3 83+
(Marcus Tregoning) *lw: mde all: qcknd clr ent fnl f: unchal* **1/1**[1]

2 3 ¼ **Interweave** 2-9-0 0 AndreaAtzeni 6 73+
(Sir Michael Stoute) *str: scope: trckd ldrs: pushed along whn swtchd to centre over 2f out: r.o nicely to go 2nd ins fnl f: no ch w easy wnr: improve* **9/2**[3]

5 **3** 1 ¾ **Favourite Royal (IRE)**[10] 5705 2-9-0 0 RobertWinston 1 67
(Eve Johnson Houghton) *w'like: wnt lft s: chsd wnr: rdn 2f out: nt pce to get on terms: no ex whn lost 2nd ins fnl f* **20/1**

4 5 **Tazmania (IRE)** 2-9-0 0 AdamKirby 4 53+
(Clive Cox) *athletic: in tch: pushed along over 3f out: kpt on same pce fnl 2f: nvr threatened ldrs* **11/4**[2]

5 *nk* **Pussy Galore (IRE)** 2-9-0 0 SeanLevey 2 52+
(Richard Hannon) *w'like: s.i.s: sn pushed along in last pair: kpt on fr over 1f out but nvr any threat* **10/1**

6 **6** ¾ **Mystical Nelly**[33] 4885 2-9-0 0 LukeMorris 9 50
(Jonathan Portman) *str: sn chsng ldrs: rdn 3f out: wknd ent fnl f* **25/1**

5 **7** 3 **Holyroman Princess**[23] 5250 2-9-0 0 FrederikTylicki 8 42
(Rod Millman) *w'like: in last trio: nvr gng pce to get involved* **50/1**

0 **8** 14 **Tallulah Rocks**[57] 4011 2-9-0 0 RyanTate 7 4
(Jonathan Portman) *leggy: a towards rr* **50/1**

0 **9** 15 **Demi's Quest**[29] 5022 2-9-0 0 JimmyFortune 5
(Tony Carroll) *tall: racd freely: trckd wnr: rdn 3f out: hung rt and wknd jst over 2f out* **100/1**

1m 28.97s (0.37) **Going Correction** -0.05s/f (Good) **9** Ran SP% **117.5**
Speed ratings (Par 96): **95,91,89,83,83 82,78,62,45**
CSF £5.80 TOTE £1.90: £1.10, £1.40, £3.60; EX 6.70 Trifecta £31.60.
Owner Miss K Rausing **Bred** Miss K Rausing **Trained** Whitsbury, Hants

FOCUS
Division two and another taking winner, the favourite making all. The time was the quickest of the three over the trip on the day.

6063 BATHWICK TYRES DICK POOLE FILLIES' STKS (GROUP 3) 6f
3:40 (3:42) (Class 1) 2-Y-O
£24,101 (£9,137; £4,573; £2,278; £1,143; £573) **Stalls** High

Form RPR

0102 **1** **Madam Dancealot (IRE)**[19] 5416 2-9-0 91 TomQueally 5 100
(Joseph Tuite) *prom: led after 1f: kpt on strly fnl f: rdn out* **10/1**

1 **2** 1 ¼ **Mystic Dawn (IRE)**[10] 5705 2-9-0 0 FMBerry 8 96
(David Simcock) *neat: hld up but in tch: hung rt fr over 2f out: rdn and hdwy over 1f out: chsd wnr ent fnl f: kpt on but a being readily hld* **4/1**[2]

1 **3** 1 **Pellucid**[80] 3223 2-9-0 0[1] JamieSpencer 4 93
(David Simcock) *tall: scope: s.i.s: racd in last pair: pushed along whn swtchd lft 2f out: sn rdn: r.o fnl f: snatched 3rd cl home* **5/1**[3]

0363 **4** *nk* **Grizzel (IRE)**[12] 5638 2-9-0 92 SeanLevey 6 92
(Richard Hannon) *trckd wnr: rdn over 2f out: lost 2nd ent fnl f: no ex whn lost 3rd towards fin* **10/1**

21 **5** 1 ¼ **Perfect Angel (IRE)**[36] 4756 2-9-0 0 OisinMurphy 3 89
(Andrew Balding) *lw: in tch: snatched up whn briefly short of room after 1f: rdn 2f out: kpt on fnl f but nt pce to get on terms* **11/4**[1]

15 **6** 2 ¼ **Bahamadam**[12] 5632 2-9-0 83 RobertWinston 1 82
(Eve Johnson Houghton) *w'like: in tch: rdn over 2f out: nt pce to get involved: fdd fnl 100yds* **20/1**

5501 **7** 1 ¼ **Simmie (IRE)**[27] 5125 2-9-0 89 TomMarquand 2 78
(Sylvester Kirk) *in tch: hdwy over 2f out: sn rdn: wknd jst over 1f out* **22/1**

1 **8** 2 ½ **Elliptical**[27] 5119 2-9-0 0 AndreaAtzeni 7 73+
(Robert Cowell) *athletic: rrd leaving stalls: bhd: hdwy to chse ldrs wl over 3f out: sn rdn: wknd over 1f out* **13/2**

1030 **9** 1 ¼ **Dainty Dandy (IRE)**[20] 5359 2-9-0 97 LukeMorris 9 67
(Paul Cole) *racd keenly: led for 1f: trckd wnr: rdn over 2f out: sn wknd* **9/1**

1m 14.49s (-0.31) **Going Correction** -0.05s/f (Good) **9** Ran SP% **114.0**
Speed ratings (Par 102): **100,98,97,96,94 91,90,86,85**
CSF £49.13 TOTE £10.70: £2.60, £1.60, £2.20; EX 58.50 Trifecta £339.70.
Owner Mrs Olivia Hoare **Bred** Tally-Ho Stud **Trained** Lambourn, Berks

FOCUS
Not the strongest Group 3 in truth, but there were one or two nice performances.

6064 EBF STALLIONS BREEDING WINNERS "LOCHSONG" FILLIES' STKS (H'CAP) 6f
4:10 (4:10) (Class 2) (0-100,95) 3-Y-O+
£13,695 (£4,100; £2,050; £1,025; £512; £257) **Stalls** High

Form RPR

-111 **1** **Gravity Flow (IRE)**[25] 5205 3-9-2 **90** PatCosgrave 5 100
(William Haggas) *lw: a.p: rdn to ld over 1f out: kpt on wl ins fnl f: rdn out* **7/4**[1]

1054 **2** ¾ **Show Stealer**[14] 5588 3-9-3 **91** MartinDwyer 3 98
(Rae Guest) *lw: hld up bhd ldrs: hdwy 2f out: sn rdn: kpt on w ev ch ins fnl f: drifted lft fnl 100yds: no ex nring fin* **3/1**[2]

5020 **3** 1 ½ **Iseemist (IRE)**[33] 4862 5-9-9 **95** MichaelJMMurphy 9 97
(John Gallagher) *led: rdn 2f out: sn edgd lft: hdd over 1f out: kpt on but no ex ins fnl f: carried sltly lft cl home* **16/1**

041 **4** ¾ **Time To Exceed (IRE)**[19] 5388 3-7-12 **77** oh1 GeorgeWood(5) 1 77
(Henry Candy) *lw: trckd ldrs: rdn over 2f out: kpt on same pce* **7/1**

1000 **5** *nk* **Secret Hint**[28] 5098 5-9-3 **89** OisinMurphy 6 88
(Andrew Balding) *hld up bhd ldrs: rdn 2f out: kpt on ins fnl f but nt pce to get involved* **6/1**[3]

0000 **6** *nk* **Sixties Sue**[12] 5643 3-8-5 **79** ow1 JFEgan 4 77
(Mick Channon) *trckd ldrs: rdn over 2f out: kpt on same pce* **14/1**

0441 **7** 1 ¼ **Stellarta**[17] 5488 5-9-5 **91** TomMarquand 7 85
(Michael Blanshard) *hld up bhd ldrs: rdn over 2f out: sn hung lft: nvr any imp* **7/1**

1m 14.23s (-0.57) **Going Correction** -0.05s/f (Good)
WFA 3 from 5yo+ 2lb **7** Ran SP% **113.2**
Speed ratings (Par 96): **101,100,98,97,96 96,94**
CSF £6.93 CT £58.11 TOTE £2.50: £1.50, £1.90; EX 8.20 Trifecta £63.60.
Owner Sheikh Juma Dalmook Al Maktoum **Bred** Eimear Mulhern & Abbeville Stud **Trained** Newmarket, Suffolk

FOCUS
Another race where it paid to race near the speed. Fair form, the winner continuing on the upgrade.

6065 BATHWICK TYRES H'CAP 1m 4f
4:40 (4:41) (Class 4) (0-85,85) 3-Y-O+ **£5,175** (£1,540; £769; £384) **Stalls** Low

Form RPR

0333 **1** **Rydan (IRE)**[12] 5650 5-9-7 **80** (v) TomQueally 3 89
(Gary Moore) *hld up: hdwy over 2f out: rdn to ld over 1f out: drifted rt: styd on strly to assert fnl 120yds: drvn out* **8/1**

6043 **2** 2 ¼ **Plymouth Sound**[10] 5724 4-9-5 **78** (b) JohnFahy 5 84
(Eve Johnson Houghton) *mid-div: hdwy over 3f out: rdn to chal over 2f out: led wl over 1f out: sn hdd: carried rt fnl f: no ex fnl 100yds* **14/1**

5210 **3** 1 ½ **Gold Faith (IRE)**[33] 4863 3-9-3 **85** FMBerry 1 90
(Ralph Beckett) *lw: in tch: hdwy and nt clr run 2f out: sn rdn: styd on but nt pce to get on terms fnl f* **9/4**[2]

1542 **4** ½ **Sam Missile (IRE)**[56] 4044 3-9-3 **85**[1] FrederikTylicki 7 88
(James Fanshawe) *trckd ldrs: rdn over 2f out: ev ch over 1f out tl ent fnl f: kpt on same pce* **15/8**[1]

1045 **5** 3 **Genuine Approval (IRE)**[11] 5671 3-8-10 **83** GeorgeWood(5) 2 81
(Jonathan Portman) *lw: trckd ldr: led wl over 2f out: sn rdn: hdd wl over 1f out: no ex ins fnl f* **25/1**

-155 **6** ½ **Shalimah (IRE)**[35] 4785 4-8-12 **71** (v) RyanTate 8 68
(Clive Cox) *rousted along leaving stalls to ld: rdn and hdd wl over 2f out: wknd fnl f* **25/1**

6015 **7** ½ **Sunny Future (IRE)**[40] 4661 10-9-2 **75** MartinDwyer 4 71
(Malcolm Saunders) *hld up last: rdn 3f out: styd on but nt pce to get involved* **12/1**

4/04 **8** 2 ¾ **Artful Rogue (IRE)**[19] 5413 5-9-4 **77** AndreaAtzeni 6 69
(Amanda Perrett) *in tch: hdwy over 3f out: sn ev ch and rdn: looking hld whn short of room wl over 1f out: wknd fnl f* **7/1**[3]

2m 38.89s (0.89) **Going Correction** +0.225s/f (Good)
WFA 3 from 4yo+ 9lb **8** Ran SP% **111.2**
Speed ratings (Par 105): **106,104,103,103,101 100,100,98**
CSF £103.67 CT £324.52 TOTE £8.00: £2.10, £3.30, £1.10; EX 52.20 Trifecta £290.20.
Owner Jacobs Construction (Holdings) Limited **Bred** R Coffey **Trained** Lower Beeding, W Sussex

FOCUS
No great gallop on here and probably just fair form. The first three came from off the pace and the 1-2 were both potentially well treated.

6066 LITTLETON STUD RACING EXCELLENCE APPRENTICE H'CAP (WHIPS SHALL BE CARRIED BUT NOT USED) 1m
5:10 (5:12) (Class 5) (0-70,70) 3-Y-O+ **£3,234** (£962; £481; £240) **Stalls** High

Form RPR

-206 **1** **Ocean Ready (USA)**[57] 4010 3-9-2 **70** ManuelFernandes(5) 5 83+
(Sir Mark Prescott Bt) *last trio and sn pushed along: hdwy to ld over 3f out: kpt on wl fnl f: pushed out* **10/3**[1]

3-53 **2** 1 ¾ **Artists Model (IRE)**[16] 5515 3-9-0 **63** GeorgeWood 7 70
(Henry Candy) *mid-div: hdwy u.p over 2f out: chal ent fnl f: styd on but no ex fnl 100yds* **9/2**[2]

0022 **3** 2 ½ **Art Echo**[10] 5711 3-9-6 **69**................................(t) MitchGodwin 3 70
(Jonathan Portman) *mid-div: hdwy over 2f out: chsd wnr over 1f out: styd on same pce fnl f* **9/1**

0600 **4** 7 **Captain Marmalade (IRE)**[23] 5259 4-9-0 **63**.................. AledBeech[(5)] 6 49
(Jimmy Fox) *s.i.s: bhd: stdy prog fr over 2f out: wnt hld 4th ent fnl f: nvr trbld ldrs* **25/1**

1004 **5** 3 ¼ **Elegant Annie**[21] 5326 3-8-7 **56**.................................. LuluStanford 8 33
(Jonathan Portman) *in tch: rdn over 2f out: nvr threatened: wknd ent fnl f* **8/1**

0632 **6** *nk* **Indigo**[13] 5602 3-8-9 **58**...................................... MeganNicholls 9 35
(Mark Usher) *trckd ldr: rdn and ev ch over 2f out: wknd over 1f out* **12/1**

0635 **7** 1 ¼ **Indrapura (IRE)**[12] 5627 3-9-4 **70**........................(t) PatrickVaughan[(3)] 4 44
(Paul Cole) *trckd ldr: rdn over 2f out: wknd over 1f out* **12/1**

0021 **8** 3 ½ **Knight Of The Air**[3] 5953 4-9-4 **67** 6ex........................ JordanUys[(5)] 2 34
(Mick Channon) *s.i.s: last pair: midfield 3f out: effrt 2f out: wknd over 1f out:* **13/2**[3]

60-5 **9** 4 **Kylea (IRE)**[21] 5327 3-8-10 **59**.................................... HollieDoyle 10 16
(Richard Hannon) *sn led: hdd over 3f out: wknd over 2f out* **33/1**

004 **10** 10 **Faction**[45] 4458 3-9-0 **68**...[1] WilliamCox[(5)] 1 2
(Andrew Balding) *trckd ldr: pushed along over 2f out: sn wknd* **9/2**[2]

1m 42.45s (-1.05) **Going Correction** -0.05s/f (Good)
WFA 3 from 4yo 5lb **10** Ran SP% **116.1**
Speed ratings (Par 103): **103,101,98,91,88 88,86,83,79,69**
CSF £17.93 CT £123.01 TOTE £3.60: £1.80, £1.90, £2.50; EX 19.80 Trifecta £168.00.
Owner Baxter, Gregson, Jenkins & Warman **Bred** Stratford Place Stud **Trained** Newmarket, Suffolk

FOCUS
Just a modest handicap but the right horses came to the fore and the time was good. There looks more to come from the winner.
T/Plt: £17.30 to a £1 stake. Pool: £61,667.74. 2,598.72 winning tickets. T/Qpdt: £6.60 to a £1 stake. Pool: £4,406.33. 493.70 winning tickets. **Tim Mitchell**

5943 BADEN-BADEN (L-H)
Thursday, September 1

OFFICIAL GOING: Turf: good

6067a DARLEY OETTINGEN-RENNEN (GROUP 2) (3YO+) (TURF) 1m
5:25 (12:00) 3-Y-O+ **£29,411** (£11,397; £5,882; £2,941; £1,838)

RPR

1 **Pas De Deux (GER)**[46] 4438 6-9-2 0.............................. StephenHellyn 3 117
(Yasmin Almenrader, Germany) **16/5**[2]

2 5 **Degas (GER)**[53] 4185 3-8-11 0.. AdriedeVries 5 104
(Markus Klug, Germany) **6/5**[1]

3 ¾ **Drummer (GER)**[46] 4438 4-9-2 0.................................. AndraschStarke 6 103
(P Schiergen, Germany) **22/5**

4 ½ **Rosebay (GER)**[61] 3916 5-8-13 0.. MartinSeidl 2 99
(Markus Klug, Germany) **73/10**

5 1 **Ross (IRE)**[30] 4-9-2 0... DanielePorcu 4 100
(P Schiergen, Germany) **117/10**

6 7 ½ **Shy Witch (GER)**[18] 5455 3-8-8 0.. IanFerguson 1 79
(H-J Groschel, Germany) **37/10**[3]

1m 40.12s (1.01)
WFA 3 from 4yo+ 5lb **6** Ran SP% **129.0**
WIN (incl. 10 euro stake): 42. PLACES: 18, 15. SF: 131.
Owner Dirk Von Mitzlaff **Bred** Dirk Von Mitzlaff **Trained** Germany

4620 CHANTILLY (R-H)
Thursday, September 1

OFFICIAL GOING: Turf: good; polytrack: standard

6068a PRIX D'ARENBERG (GROUP 3) (2YO) (TURF) 5f
12:10 (12:00) 2-Y-O **£29,411** (£11,764; £8,823; £5,882; £2,941)

RPR

1 **Afandem (IRE)**[12] 5656 2-8-11 0.. JamesDoyle 6 107
(Hugo Palmer) **15/8**[1]

2 1 ¼ **Hargeisa (USA)**[39] 4694 2-8-11 0.......................... ChristopheSoumillon 2 103
(Mario Hofer, Germany) **7/2**[2]

3 ½ **Barroche (IRE)**[20] 5359 2-8-8 0.. GeraldMosse 3 98
(Clive Cox) **5/1**

4 *snk* **Fixette (IRE)**[32] 4925 2-8-8 0... GregoryBenoist 5 97
(F-H Graffard, France) **4/1**[3]

5 2 **Cosachope (FR)**[39] 4694 2-8-11 0............................ StephanePasquier 1 93
(P Sogorb, France) **12/1**

6 ¾ **Cheries Amours (FR)**[41] 2-8-8 0.............................. UmbertoRispoli 10 87
(T Castanheira, France) **22/1**

7 3 ½ **California Tee**[17] 5497 2-8-8 0.................................. AntoineHamelin 4 75
(Matthieu Palussiere, France) **22/1**

8 3 ½ **Ivory Choice (FR)**[17] 5497 2-8-8 0.............................. IoritzMendizabal 7 62
(F Chappet, France) **18/1**

9 3 **Westit**[11] 2-8-8 0... MaximeGuyon 9 51
(C Laffon-Parias, France) **7/1**

10 2 **Terrific Feeling (IRE)**[16] 2-8-11 0.. TonyPiccone 8 47
(Matthieu Palussiere, France) **33/1**

57.95s (-0.35) **10** Ran SP% **130.8**
WIN (incl. 1 euro stake): 2.60. PLACES: 1.50, 1.80, 2.70. DF: 7.30. SF: 11.30.
Owner Hamad Rashed Bin Ghedayer **Bred** Rabbah Bloodstock Limited **Trained** Newmarket, Suffolk

6069a PRIX DE LIANCOURT (LISTED RACE) (3YO FILLIES) (TURF) 1m 2f 110y
1:20 (12:00) 3-Y-O **£20,220** (£8,088; £6,066; £4,044; £2,022)

RPR

1 **Sweet Charity (FR)**[44] 3-8-11 0.............................. SebastienMaillot 4 100
(N Clement, France) **182/10**

2 1 **Switching (USA)**[17] 5498 3-8-11 0.............................. MickaelBarzalona 6 98
(A Fabre, France) **16/5**[2]

3 ½ **Palinodie (FR)**[25] 3-8-11 0.. GregoryBenoist 9 97
(E Leenders, France) **21/1**

4 1 ¼ **Edya**[95] 2730 3-8-11 0... UmbertoRispoli 3 95
(G Botti, France) **31/1**

5 *snk* **Fresh Strike (IRE)**[30] 5006 3-8-11 0.............................. MaximeGuyon 5 94
(F Head, France) **17/5**[3]

6 ¾ **That Which Is Not (USA)**[30] 5006 3-8-11 0........... StephanePasquier 1 93
(F-H Graffard, France) **11/5**[1]

7 2 ½ **Sagely (IRE)**[14] 5587 3-8-11 0.. JamesDoyle 2 88
(Ed Dunlop) **87/10**

8 *nk* **Bourges (FR)**[52] 3-8-11 0... CristianDemuro 7 87
(E Lellouche, France) **26/1**

9 1 ¾ **Minamya (FR)**[25] 3-8-11 0.................................... ChristopheSoumillon 8 84
(A De Royer-Dupre, France) **59/10**

2m 11.07s (2.27) **9** Ran SP% **119.2**
WIN (incl.,1 euro stake): 19.20. PLACES: 4.40, 2.10, 4.10. DF: 31.40. SF: 104.50.
Owner P A Stein, Ecurie Jml Racing Et Al **Bred** H Honore **Trained** Chantilly, France

6070a PRIX DE LA COCHERE - FONDS EUROPEEN DE L'ELEVAGE (LISTED RACE) (3YO+ FILLIES & MARES) (TURF) 1m
1:50 (12:00) 3-Y-O+ **£19,117** (£7,647; £5,735; £3,823; £1,911)

RPR

1 **Zayva (FR)**[31] 3-8-10 0 ow1............................... ChristopheSoumillon 4 103
(A De Royer-Dupre, France) **1/1**[1]

2 *nk* **Midweek**[17] 5498 3-9-0 0... VincentCheminaud 1 107
(Mme C Head-Maarek, France) **33/10**[2]

3 2 **Wanderina (IRE)**[38] 4723 3-8-9 0..................................(b) MaximeGuyon 5 97
(F Head, France) **12/1**

4 *nse* **Desert Haze**[37] 4737 3-8-9 0.. StephanePasquier 3 97
(Ralph Beckett) **15/2**[3]

5 *shd* **Rien Que Pour Toi (FR)**[23] 3-8-9 0.................................. GeraldMosse 2 97
(T Castanheira, France) **16/1**

6 1 ¼ **Prairie Pearl (FR)**[39] 4695 3-8-10 0 ow1.......................... OlivierPeslier 9 95
(H-A Pantall, France) **34/1**

7 ¾ **Dressed In Fur (IRE)**[32] 3-8-9 0.............................. MickaelBarzalona 8 92
(Mme Pia Brandt, France) **16/1**

8 *snk* **Bohemian Rhapsody (SPA)**[67] 6-9-0 0.......................... CristianDemuro 7 93
(Enrique Leon Penate, France) **10/1**

9 *nk* **Permission**[55] 4105 3-8-9 0... GregoryBenoist 6 91
(James Fanshawe) **22/1**

1m 41.6s (3.60)
WFA 3 from 6yo 5lb **9** Ran SP% **120.8**
WIN (incl. 1 euro stake): 2.00. PLACES: 1.20, 1.60, 2.10. DF: 4.10. SF: 5.00.
Owner H H Aga Khan **Bred** Hh The Aga Khan's Studs **Trained** Chantilly, France

5143 ASCOT (R-H)
Friday, September 2

OFFICIAL GOING: Straight course - good to firm (good in places; 7.9); round course - good (good to firm in places; 7.6)
Wind: Almost nil Weather: Cloudy, quite humid

6071 DARK HORSE MAIDEN AUCTION STKS (PLUS 10 RACE) 6f
2:00 (2:00) (Class 4) 2-Y-O **£6,469** (£1,925; £962; £481) **Stalls** High

Form RPR

1 **Cristal Fizz (IRE)** 2-9-0 0.. PatCosgrave 7 79+
(William Haggas) *s.s: wl in rr: stl there and waiting for room 2f out: eased to outer jst over 1f out: str run to ld last 75yds: won gng away* **16/1**

2 1 **Red Royalist** 2-9-5 0... MartinDwyer 6 81+
(Marcus Tregoning) *trckd ldrs: pushed along over 2f out: clsd to ld 1f out: styd on but hdd and outpcd last 75yds* **50/1**

3 1 ½ **Comprise** 2-9-5 0... JamieSpencer 11 76+
(Michael Bell) *hld up in rr: sltly impeded over 2f out: gd prog on wd outside to chal 1f out and w ldr: one pce last 100yds* **14/1**

4 ¾ **Redicean** 2-9-5 0... JamesDoyle 2 74
(Peter Chapple-Hyam) *wl in tch: pushed along over 2f out: styd on same pce fr over 1f out and nvr able to chal* **8/1**[3]

03 **5** *nk* **Desert Sport (USA)**[21] 5377 2-9-5 0.................................... JimCrowley 8 73
(Robert Cowell) *pressed ldr: led 2f out: hdd and outpcd 1f out* **7/1**[2]

6 *hd* **Eskimo Bay (IRE)** 2-9-5 0.. AdamKirby 10 72+
(Clive Cox) *dwlt and awkward s: wl in rr: stl there 2f out: prog on outer over 1f out: one pce and no hdwy ins fnl f* **25/1**

0023 **7** ½ **Syncopation (IRE)**[8] 5796 2-9-5 68..................................... DaneO'Neill 3 73+
(Sylvester Kirk) *hld up towards rr: nowhere to go on inner fr 2f out tl ins fnl f: r.o wl last 100yds: no ch to threaten* **8/1**[3]

06 **8** 2 ¾ **Daring Guest (IRE)**[8] 5792 2-9-5 0...................................... TomQueally 4 62
(George Margarson) *led against far rail: hdd 2f out: wknd jst over 1f out* **100/1**

00 **9** 1 **Lord Cooper**[22] 5325 2-9-5 0.......................................(t) RenatoSouza 5 59
(Jose Santos) *pressed ldng pair: rdn over 2f out: wknd over 1f out* **66/1**

3 **10** 1 ½ **Muthmira**[18] 5469 2-9-0 0.. SilvestreDeSousa 1 61+
(Simon Crisford) *trckd ldrs on inner: nt clr run fr over 2f out to 1f out then fdd tamely* **4/6**[1]

6 **11** 1 ½ **Lawfilly**[11] 5722 2-9-0 0... ShaneKelly 12 44
(Richard Hughes) *trckd ldrs to 2f out: wknd quite qckly* **40/1**

12 10 **Miriam Violet** 2-9-0 0.. RobertHavlin 9 12
(Paul Henderson) *in tch to 1/2-way: wknd over 2f out: t.o* **100/1**

1m 16.38s (1.88) **Going Correction** +0.25s/f (Good) **12** Ran SP% **119.0**
Speed ratings (Par 97): **97,95,93,92,92 92,91,87,86,84 82,69**
CSF £637.03 TOTE £12.60: £4.00, £18.50, £3.60; EX 890.90.
Owner Roberts Green Whittall-Williams Savidge **Bred** Norelands Bloodstock **Trained** Newmarket, Suffolk

FOCUS
The watered ground (4mm overnight to Tuesday morning and 4mm overnight to Wednesday morning) was given as good to firm, good in places on the Straight Course, and good, good to firm in places on the Round course (GoingStick: Straight: 7.9, Round: 7.6). The rail on the Round course was 3yds out from its innermost position from the 1m4f start, increasing to 14yds out at the home straight. The straight course had been divided in two, with a rail in the middle of the course, and the stands' side was in use for this meeting. They tacked over to race on the far rail in this opening maiden, and that resulted in one or two struggling for racing room.

6072 PETER TARRANT 50 YEARS AT ASCOT H'CAP 6f
2:35 (2:36) (Class 4) (0-80,86) 3-Y-O+ **£6,469** (£1,925; £962; £481) **Stalls** High

Form RPR

61 **1** **Boy In The Bar**[10] 5744 5-9-8 **81** 6ex..............................(b) JamesDoyle 1 92
(Ian Williams) *racd towards far side: in tch: prog over 2f out: pressed ldr over 1f out: edgd lft but drvn ahd last 75yds* **4/1**[1]

0042 **2** *nk* **Harwoods Volante (IRE)**[8] 5793 5-9-4 **77** JimCrowley 9 87
(David O'Meara) *w ldrs: led 2f out: edgd lft fnl f and hdd last 75yds* **9/2**[2]

0006 **3** *1 1/2* **Funding Deficit (IRE)**[27] 5182 6-9-0 **76** JosephineGordon(3) 14 81
(Jim Goldie) *overall ldr: hdd 2f out: kpt on same pce fnl f* **33/1**

0030 **4** *shd* **Dominium (USA)**[19] 5439 9-8-5 **69** (b) DavidParkes(5) 8 74
(Jeremy Gask) *wl in rr: rdn over 2f out: prog over 1f out: r.o wl fnl f and nrly snatched 3rd* **33/1**

2400 **5** *1* **Until Midnight (IRE)**[21] 5372 6-8-4 **70** LuluStanford(7) 7 72
(Eugene Stanford) *pressed ldrs: nt qckn 2f out: kpt on one pce fr over 1f out* **20/1**

6U5 **6** *3/4* **Fever Few**[30] 5039 7-9-0 **73** FergusSweeney 15 72
(Chris Wall) *taken down early: racd alone on nr side: wl on terms to over 1f out: one pce fnl f* **50/1**

3021 **7** *nk* **Etienne Gerard**[8] 5797 4-8-9 **75** 6ex (p) LewisEdmunds(7) 13 73
(Nigel Tinkler) *pressed ldrs to wl over 1f out: one pce* **10/1**

5204 **8** *1 1/2* **Koptoon**[7] 5852 4-9-6 **79** FMBerry 10 73
(Jo Hughes) *towards rr: rdn over 2f out: no prog tl kpt on fnl f: no ch* **14/1**

1-41 **9** *nk* **Jameerah**[29] 5078 3-9-4 **79** MartinHarley 12 72
(James Tate) *chsd ldrs: fdd jst over 1f out* **12/1**

3011 **10** *nk* **Staintondale Lass (IRE)**[9] 5774 3-9-4 **86** 6ex DavidEgan(7) 3 78
(Ed Vaughan) *towards far side and towards rr: rdn 2f out: no real prog over 1f out* **5/1**[3]

1506 **11** *1 1/2* **Bring On A Spinner**[38] 4744 3-8-4 **68** AaronJones(3) 6 55
(Stuart Williams) *a towards rr: rdn and no prog 2f out* **33/1**

0000 **12** *1* **Barnet Fair**[20] 5390 8-9-5 **78** (p) FrannyNorton 11 62
(David Nicholls) *taken down early: plld hrd: hld up: no prog 2f out: wknd fnl f* **10/1**

4642 **13** *3 3/4* **Ejbaar**[14] 5599 4-9-4 **77** RyanMoore 2 49
(Robert Cowell) *racd nrest far side: a in rr: no prog 2f out: eased whn no ch fnl f* **9/1**

0136 **14** *4 1/2* **Classic Pursuit**[17] 5512 5-8-12 **71** (p) JamieSpencer 4 28
(Ivan Furtado) *awkward s and then stdd: hld up in last: no prog 2f out: sn wknd and bhd* **16/1**

1m 14.55s (0.05) **Going Correction** +0.25s/f (Good)
WFA 3 from 4yo+ 2lb **14** Ran SP% **118.8**
Speed ratings (Par 105): **109,108,106,106,105 104,103,101,101,100 98,97,92,86**
CSF £19.84 CT £539.99 TOTE £5.10: £1.80, £1.90, £10.40; EX 25.20 Trifecta £764.20.
Owner Sovereign Racing **Bred** Brinkley Stud S R L **Trained** Portway, Worcs

FOCUS
Apart from Fever Few, who came up the stands' side, the others raced centre to far side this time. The first two built on their latest form.

6073 MILLGATE MAIDEN STKS 1m 2f
3:10 (3:10) (Class 4) 3-Y-O+ **£6,469** (£1,925; £962; £481) **Stalls** Low

Form RPR

2436 **1** **Countermeasure**[13] 5652 4-9-7 112 RyanMoore 5 87+
(Roger Charlton) *mde all: shkn up and clr 1f out: urged along and drew further away* **1/9**[1]

6323 **2** *8* **Henry The Explorer (CAN)**[7] 5849 3-9-0 70 PatCosgrave 6 74
(Jo Hughes) *chsd wnr: rdn 2f out: nt qckn over 1f out and wl hld after: 5 l bhd whn eased last 100yds* **6/1**[3]

3 *4 1/2* **Lord Marmaduke** 3-9-0 0 RobertHavlin 3 62
(Simon Crisford) *dwlt: hld up in 4th: shkn up and lft bhd over 2f out: sn tk modest 3rd: no imp after* **5/1**[2]

06 **4** *1/2* **Golden Muscade (USA)**[17] 5504 3-8-2 0 JoshuaBryan(7) 4 56
(Brian Barr) *hld up in last: shkn up and lft bhd over 2f out: rdn to take poor 4th fnl f* **50/1**

5 *2 1/2* **Threediamondrings** 3-8-11 0 JosephineGordon(3) 2 56
(Brendan Powell) *dwlt: t.k.h early: chsd ldng pair: lft bhd over 2f out: sn lost 3rd and fdd* **50/1**

2m 9.2s (1.80) **Going Correction** +0.50s/f (Yiel)
WFA 3 from 4yo 7lb **5** Ran SP% **124.9**
Speed ratings (Par 105): **112,105,102,101,99**
CSF £2.40 TOTE £1.10: £1.10, £1.90; EX 2.60 Trifecta £3.40.
Owner K Abdullah **Bred** Millsec Limited **Trained** Beckhampton, Wilts

FOCUS
Race distance increased by approximately 21yds. An uncompetitive maiden, with the favourite boasting an official mark of 112, miles clear of his rivals. The form is rated around the second.

6074 MITIE EVENTS & LEISURE H'CAP 1m 4f
3:45 (3:45) (Class 3) (0-95,90) 3-Y-O+ **£9,703** (£2,887; £1,443; £721) **Stalls** Low

Form RPR

2131 **1** **William Hunter**[29] 5053 4-9-4 **82** WilliamTwiston-Davies 8 90+
(Alan King) *trckd ldrs: gng strly over 2f out: led over 1f out: rdn and finding enough fnl f and nvr in serious danger* **5/2**[1]

1204 **2** *1 1/4* **Renfrew Street**[7] 5837 3-8-10 **83** FrannyNorton 2 87
(Mark Johnston) *led 1f: sn in 3rd: rdn and lost pl over 2f out: 5th over 1f out: styd on wl fnl f to take 2nd last strides* **5/2**[1]

24 **3** *nse* **Jacob Cats**[16] 5553 7-9-7 **85** (v) FrederikTylicki 7 89
(William Knight) *slowly away: chivvied along in detached last early: in tch but stl last 3f out: urged along on outer over 2f out: r.o fnl f and jst pipped in late swoop for 2nd* **7/1**[3]

0003 **4** *1/2* **Sunblazer (IRE)**[21] 5358 6-9-5 **90** (t) JoshuaBryan(7) 4 93
(Kim Bailey) *hld up in 6th: prog and wd bnd 3f out: chal over 2f out: nt qckn over 1f out: disp 2nd and hld after: lost pls nr fin* **6/1**[2]

4313 **5** *nk* **Dolphin Village (IRE)**[20] 5413 6-9-6 **84** DarryllHolland 6 87
(Jane Chapple-Hyam) *t.k.h: led after 1f: rdn and hdd 2f out: sn lost pl: kpt on again ins fnl f* **6/1**[2]

1056 **6** *nse* **Knight Music**[13] 5633 4-9-4 **82** JimCrowley 3 85
(Michael Attwater) *t.k.h: trckd ldr after 3f: led 2f out to over 1f out: disp 2nd and hld after: lost pl nr fin* **12/1**

-665 **7** *3 3/4* **Archangel Raphael (IRE)**[88] 2979 4-9-7 **90** HectorCrouch(5) 5 87
(Amanda Perrett) *chsd ldrs: dropped to rr 3f out: rdn and no prog over 2f out: wknd over 1f out* **14/1**

2m 36.27s (3.77) **Going Correction** +0.50s/f (Yiel)
WFA 3 from 4yo+ 9lb **7** Ran SP% **112.6**
Speed ratings (Par 107): **107,106,106,105,105 105,103**
CSF £8.16 CT £36.00 TOTE £3.20: £1.70, £1.90; EX 7.70 Trifecta £26.00.
Owner Incipe Partnership **Bred** Barbury Castle Stud **Trained** Barbury Castle, Wilts
■ Stewards' Enquiry : Joshua Bryan two-day ban: use of whip (16-17 Sep)

FOCUS
Race distance increased by approximately 21yds. They didn't go a mad gallop early and they finished in a bit of a heap, but the winner did it comfortably. The form is rateda round the third, fourth and fifth.

6075 STELLA ARTOIS H'CAP 1m (S)
4:20 (4:20) (Class 2) (0-105,104) 3-Y-O+
£18,675 (£5,592; £2,796; £1,398; £699; £351) **Stalls** High

Form RPR

3605 **1** **Aclaim (IRE)**[20] 5409 3-8-12 **97** (t) JamieSpencer 6 105+
(Martyn Meade) *hld up in last: smooth prog to trck ldng pair over 1f out: hrd rdn fnl f and r.o to ld last 50yds* **11/2**[3]

1001 **2** *3/4* **Early Morning (IRE)**[27] 5146 5-9-6 **100** AdamKirby 10 107
(Harry Dunlop) *trckd ldr: shkn up over 2f out: rdn to ld jst over 1f out: styd on but hdd and outpcd last 50yds* **9/2**[1]

21-6 **3** *3/4* **Very Talented (IRE)**[141] 1440 3-8-13 **98** JamesDoyle 2 102
(Saeed bin Suroor) *led: shkn up 2f out: rdn and hdd jst over 1f out: styd on same pce* **5/1**[2]

2536 **4** *3/4* **Truth Or Dare**[104] 2484 5-8-11 **91** MartinDwyer 12 94
(William Muir) *hld up in last trio: pushed along 2f out: rdn and styd on to take 4th ins fnl f: nvr able to threaten* **25/1**

0020 **5** *3/4* **Hors De Combat**[35] 4823 5-9-8 **102** (b[1]) OisinMurphy 9 104
(James Fanshawe) *trckd ldrs: rdn over 2f out: kpt on same pce and no imp fnl f* **5/1**[2]

5-10 **6** *1 1/4* **Balmoral Castle**[38] 4731 7-9-1 **95** RyanTate 3 94
(Jonathan Portman) *cl up: rdn over 2f out: fdd over 1f out* **8/1**

5200 **7** *2 1/2* **Grand Inquisitor**[27] 5156 4-9-0 **94** (v[1]) RyanMoore 8 87
(Sir Michael Stoute) *plld hrd: hld up and sn in last trio: rdn and no prog 2f out* **5/1**[2]

0004 **8** *1* **Bancnuanaheireann (IRE)**[27] 5146 9-8-13 **96** AlistairRawlinson(3) 1 86
(Michael Appleby) *hld up in tch: prog and wl there over 2f out: wknd over 1f out* **16/1**

112 **9** *1 3/4* **Sir Roderic (IRE)**[27] 5175 3-8-12 **97** FrederikTylicki 11 82
(Rod Millman) *t.k.h: trckd ldrs: wknd 2f out* **8/1**

1m 40.9s (0.10) **Going Correction** +0.25s/f (Good)
WFA 3 from 4yo+ 5lb **9** Ran SP% **115.5**
Speed ratings (Par 109): **109,108,107,106,106 104,102,101,99**
CSF £30.47 CT £132.80 TOTE £6.50: £2.20, £1.60, £2.10; EX 29.30 Trifecta £232.10.
Owner Canning Downs & Partner **Bred** D Farrington And Canning Downs **Trained** Newmarket, Suffolk

FOCUS
A good, competitive handicap but the pace wasn't overstrong. The form is rated around the second.

6076 CHAMPAGNE BOLLINGER CLASSIFIED STKS 1m (S)
4:55 (4:55) (Class 3) 3-Y-O+ **£9,703** (£2,887; £1,443; £721) **Stalls** High

Form RPR

4-31 **1** **Great Order (USA)**[50] 4319 3-8-12 89 JamesDoyle 7 97+
(Saeed bin Suroor) *rring as stalls opened and slowly away: in tch in last trio: pushed along and prog jst over 2f out: rdn to ld jst over 1f out: styd on wl* **5/2**[2]

1306 **2** *1 1/4* **Jacbequick**[8] 5802 5-9-3 90 (v) JimCrowley 4 95
(David O'Meara) *hld up in rr: drvn and prog wl over 1f out: styd on to take 2nd last 100yds: no imp on wnr after* **16/1**

5406 **3** *nk* **Gratzie**[20] 5396 5-9-0 90 SilvestreDeSousa 5 91
(Mick Channon) *t.k.h: prom: rdn to dispute 2nd briefly over 1f out: styd on same pce fnl f* **8/1**

0-01 **4** *nse* **Gold Sands (IRE)**[29] 5082 4-9-0 89 MartinHarley 9 91
(James Tate) *mostly chsd ldr: rdn to dispute 2nd briefly over 1f out: styd on same pce fnl f* **7/1**[3]

1200 **5** *3/4* **Pastoral Player**[20] 5403 9-8-12 89 CharlieBennett(5) 8 92
(Hughie Morrison) *hld up in last: cajoled along 2f out: prog over 1f out: pressed for a pl ins fnl f: one pce last 75yds* **20/1**

111 **6** *1/2* **Takatul (USA)**[23] 5306 3-8-12 87 DaneO'Neill 6 90
(Charles Hills) *t.k.h early: hld up in tch: shkn up 2f out: nt qckn over 1f out: kpt on same pce after* **6/4**[1]

-102 **7** *2 1/4* **Bluegrass Blues (IRE)**[16] 5545 6-8-10 88 MitchGodwin(7) 1 86
(Heather Main) *prom: drvn and lost pl 2f out: n.d fr over 1f out* **25/1**

000 **8** *2 1/2* **Red Avenger (USA)**[16] 5552 6-9-3 85 GeorgeBaker 3 80
(Gary Moore) *led: looked to be gng strly over 2f out: hdd and pushed along over 1f out: sn wknd* **16/1**

0030 **9** *10* **Directorship**[37] 4776 10-8-12 89 HectorCrouch(5) 2 56
(Patrick Chamings) *in tch on outer: shkn up 3f out: wknd 2f out* **16/1**

1m 41.21s (0.41) **Going Correction** +0.25s/f (Good)
WFA 3 from 4yo+ 5lb **9** Ran SP% **118.4**
Speed ratings (Par 107): **107,105,105,105,104 104,101,99,89**
CSF £43.20 TOTE £3.50: £1.30, £3.50, £2.40; EX 38.10 Trifecta £231.50.
Owner Godolphin **Bred** Darley **Trained** Newmarket, Suffolk

FOCUS
An interesting classified race. The winner built on his maiden form.
T/Plt: £250.40 to a £1 stake. Pool: £90,671.66 - 264.29 winning tickets T/Qpdt: £6.60 to a £1 stake. Pool: £8,972.96 - 1,003.66 winning tickets **Jonathan Neesom**

6052 HAYDOCK (L-H)
Friday, September 2

OFFICIAL GOING: Good (7.7)
Wind: Light against Weather: Overcast

6077 188BET.CO.UK EBF MAIDEN FILLIES' STKS (PLUS 10 RACE) 1m
2:10 (2:11) (Class 5) 2-Y-O **£3,234** (£962; £481; £240) **Stalls** Low

Form RPR

00 **1** **Mary Anne Evans**[24] 5266 2-9-0 0 FrankieDettori 3 73+
(John Gosden) *w ldr tl led over 3f out: shkn up over 2f out: rdn out* **3/1**[2]

0 **2** *1 1/4* **Al Nafoorah**[112] 2211 2-9-0 0 PaulMulrennan 1 70
(Ed Dunlop) *racd keenly and sn trcking ldrs: nt clr run and lost pl 3f out: hdwy over 1f out: styd on to go 2nd wl ins fnl f* **4/1**[3]

0 **3** *1/2* **Astrolabe (IRE)**[20] 5387 2-9-0 0 RichardKingscote 5 69
(Tom Dascombe) *chsd ldrs: wnt 2nd over 2f out: rdn over 1f out: styng on same pce whn rdr had whip knocked out of his hand by rival wl ins fnl f* **18/1**

4 *hd* **Canterbury Quad (FR)** 2-8-11 0 LouisSteward(3) 4 68
(Henry Spiller) *hld up: hdwy 3f out: rdn over 1f out: styd on same pce ins fnl f* **20/1**

303 **5** *8* **Helmsdale**[11] 5722 2-9-0 0 .... PatDobbs 2 49
(Richard Hannon) *led over 4f: sn rdn: wknd over 1f out* **8/11**[1]
1m 43.52s (-0.18) **Going Correction** -0.50s/f (Hard) **5** Ran SP% **112.9**
Speed ratings (Par 92): **80,78,78,78,70**
CSF £15.31 TOTE £3.70: £1.90, £2.10; EX 12.20 Trifecta £59.10.
Owner Ms Rachel D S Hood **Bred** Ms Rachel Hood **Trained** Newmarket, Suffolk

FOCUS
The inner home straight was used. Race times from Thursday suggested conditions were on the quick side of good, and there was no rain overnight. After the first Frankie Dettori said it was: "Good ground, plenty of moisture", with Thomas Brown saying: "Good ground, loose on top." Rail movements meant that this race was run over 2yds short of the advertised distance. With the favourite flopping, the form isn't worth much. The time was 5.52sec outside standard.

6078 188BET EBF MAIDEN FILLIES' STKS (PLUS 10 RACE) 6f
2:45 (2:46) (Class 5) 2-Y-O **£3,234** (£962; £481; £240) **Stalls** Centre

Form RPR
34 **1** **Moonlit Show**[25] 5242 2-8-11 0 .... EdwardGreatrex(3) 6 74
(Charlie Fellowes) *a.p: jnd ldr 5f out: rdn to ld over 1f out: flashed tail wl ins fnl f: jst hld on* **12/1**
0 **2** *nk* **Think Fashion (IRE)**[20] 5400 2-9-0 0 .... PatDobbs 7 73
(Brian Meehan) *hld up: hdwy over 1f out: sn rdn: edgd lft ins fnl f: r.o* **10/1**[3]
3 *nk* **Eartha Kitt** 2-9-0 0 .... RichardKingscote 2 72
(Tom Dascombe) *chsd ldrs: rdn and hung lft fr over 1f out: styd on* **12/5**[2]
00 **4** *2* **Foxcatcher**[20] 5400 2-9-0 0 .... JohnFahy 11 66
(Clive Cox) *led: hung lft fr over 2f out: rdn and hdd over 1f out: styd on same pce ins fnl f* **25/1**
54 **5** *1* **Outfox**[11] 5713 2-9-0 0 .... PaulMulrennan 8 64+
(Bryan Smart) *hld up: swtchd lft over 1f out: hung lft and r.o ins fnl f: nvr nrr* **33/1**
03 **6** *nk* **Vista Steppe**[30] 5022 2-9-0 0 .... SaleemGolam 9 62
(David Simcock) *hld up: hdwy 1/2-way: rdn over 1f out: hung lft and styd on same pce* **66/1**
7 *1 1/4* **Harba (IRE)** 2-9-0 0 .... FrankieDettori 5 58
(William Haggas) *trckd ldrs: racd keenly: swtchd lft over 1f out: sn hung lft: no ex ins fnl f* **11/10**[1]
8 *3 3/4* **Grey Thou Art (IRE)** 2-9-0 0 .... DanielTudhope 1 47
(Henry Candy) *hld up: hdwy on outer over 2f out: rdn and wknd over 1f out* **25/1**
9 *3 1/2* **Cool Breeze (IRE)** 2-9-0 0 .... SamHitchcott 4 37
(David Simcock) *s.i.s: sme hdwy over 2f out: wknd over 1f out* **33/1**
10 *1 1/2* **Vermilion** 2-9-0 0 .... ThomasBrown 3 32
(Ed Walker) *w ldrs: rdn over 2f out: sn wknd: fin lame* **33/1**
11 *6* **Spring Eternal** 2-9-0 0 .... PaulHanagan 10 14
(Charles Hills) *plld hrd: w ldr tl stdd after 1f: remained handy: rdn over 2f out: wknd over 1f out* **14/1**
1m 14.59s (0.79) **Going Correction** 0.0s/f (Good) **11** Ran SP% **118.5**
Speed ratings (Par 92): **94,93,93,90,89 88,87,82,77,75 67**
CSF £114.36 TOTE £13.60: £2.40, £2.60, £1.60; EX 120.80 Trifecta £722.50.
Owner Peter O'Callaghan **Bred** Belmore Lane Stud & Whitsbury Manor Stud **Trained** Newmarket, Suffolk

FOCUS
Race distance as advertised. Just fair maiden form.

6079 BANK VIEW HIRE 50TH ANNIVERSARY H'CAP 6f
3:20 (3:23) (Class 4) (0-85,85) 3-Y-O+ **£5,175** (£1,540; £769; £384) **Stalls** Centre

Form RPR
0-50 **1** **Ustinov**[27] 5161 4-9-7 **85** ....[1] DanielTudhope 15 96+
(David O'Meara) *hld up: hdwy over 2f out: rdn and r.o to ld wl ins fnl f* **8/1**
4310 **2** *3/4* **Edward Lewis**[34] 4889 3-9-2 **82** .... FrankieDettori 8 90
(John Gosden) *w ldr 1f: remained handy: rdn to chse ldr over 1f out: edgd lft and ev ch ins fnl f: styd on* **7/1**[2]
3030 **3** *3/4* **Bapak Asmara (IRE)**[34] 4896 4-9-2 **80** ....(p) ShaneGray 2 86
(Kevin Ryan) *led: rdn over 2f out: edgd rt and hdd wl ins fnl f* **25/1**
6302 **4** *1* **Tiger Jim**[7] 5857 6-9-4 **82** .... JoeDoyle 13 87+
(Jim Goldie) *mid-div: hdwy over 2f out: nt clr run and lost pl over 1f out: r.o wl towards fin* **13/2**[1]
6301 **5** *nk* **Red Tycoon (IRE)**[47] 4428 4-9-4 **82** .... PatDobbs 17 84
(David Barron) *hld up: hdwy over 1f out: r.o* **10/1**
42 **6** *3/4* **Van Gerwen**[19] 5439 3-8-3 **74** .... NathanEvans(5) 9 73
(Les Eyre) *chsd ldrs: wnt 2nd over 2f out tl rdn over 1f out: styd on same pce ins fnl f* **11/1**
0100 **7** *hd* **Pomme De Terre (IRE)**[34] 4896 4-9-5 **83** ....[1] PaulMulrennan 14 82
(Michael Dods) *hld up: rdn over 2f out: r.o ins fnl f: nvr nrr* **20/1**
0052 **8** *1/2* **Gambit**[17] 5507 3-9-2 **82** .... RichardKingscote 5 79
(Tom Dascombe) *prom: rdn over 2f out: styd on same pce ins fnl f* **15/2**[3]
1326 **9** *3/4* **Tarboosh**[43] 4569 3-9-2 **82** ....(p) PaulHanagan 12 77
(William Haggas) *hld up in tch: rdn over 1f out: no ex ins fnl f* **8/1**
0000 **10** *hd* **Patrick (IRE)**[20] 5417 4-9-7 **85** ....(p) KeaganLatham 6 79
(Richard Fahey) *prom: chsd ldr over 4f out tl rdn over 2f out: no ex ins fnl f: eased towards fin* **25/1**
4132 **11** *2* **Cosmic Chatter**[21] 5372 6-9-3 **81** ....(p) JamesSullivan 16 69
(Ruth Carr) *hld up: rdn over 2f out: nvr on terms* **7/1**[2]
1304 **12** *nk* **Lexi's Hero (IRE)**[27] 5182 8-9-5 **83** ....(v) GeorgeChaloner 1 70
(Richard Fahey) *chsd ldrs: rdn over 2f out: wknd ins fnl f* **33/1**
604- **13** *1/2* **Princess Kodia (IRE)**[323] 7235 3-8-8 **81** .... JordanUys(7) 7 66
(Brian Meehan) *mid-div: hdwy over 2f out: rdn over 1f out: wknd over 1f out* **33/1**
0000 **14** *3* **Still On Top**[20] 5409 3-8-12 **78** .... DavidAllan 11 54
(Tim Easterby) *hld up in tch: rdn whn nt clr run over 1f out: wknd fnl f* **50/1**
2630 **15** *1* **Explain**[17] 5512 4-8-13 **82** .... AnnaHesketh(5) 3 54
(Ruth Carr) *mid-div: rdn over 2f out: wknd wl over 1f out* **12/1**
5540 **16** *1/2* **Barkston Ash**[27] 5161 8-8-7 **74** ....(p) RachelRichardson(3) 4 45
(Eric Alston) *sn pushed along in rr: bhd fr 1/2-way* **16/1**
1m 13.28s (-0.52) **Going Correction** 0.0s/f (Good)
WFA 3 from 4yo+ 2lb **16** Ran SP% **123.6**
Speed ratings (Par 105): **103,102,101,99,99 98,98,97,96,96 93,93,92,88,87 86**
CSF £58.83 CT £1420.14 TOTE £8.70: £2.70, £1.20, £5.80, £2.50; EX 76.50 Trifecta £1785.20.
Owner Mrs P Good **Bred** Mrs P Good **Trained** Upper Helmsley, N Yorks

FOCUS
Race run over advertised distance. The pace was down the centre in this fair handicap, but the first three ended up on the stands' side. Sound form.

6080 US OPEN TENNIS AT 188BET H'CAP 5f
3:55 (3:57) (Class 4) (0-85,84) 3-Y-O+ **£5,175** (£1,540; £769; £384) **Stalls** Centre

Form RPR
2121 **1** **Orient Class**[24] 5269 5-8-6 **76** ow2 .... CliffordLee(7) 16 88
(Paul Midgley) *hld up: hdwy 1/2-way: hung lft over 1f out: led ins fnl f: r.o wl* **15/2**
0002 **2** *1 1/4* **Masamah (IRE)**[6] 5867 10-8-12 **75** ....(p) GeorgeChaloner 7 83
(Richard Fahey) *chsd ldrs: led 1/2-way: rdn and hdd over 1f out: styd on same pce wl ins fnl f* **8/1**
1502 **3** *3/4* **Straightothepoint**[17] 5512 4-9-4 **81** .... PaulMulrennan 3 86
(Bryan Smart) *chsd ldrs: led over 1f out: rdn and hdd ins fnl f: styd on same pce* **6/1**[2]
4612 **4** *nk* **Dynamo Walt (IRE)**[12] 5679 5-8-9 **75** ....(v) NoelGarbutt(3) 13 79
(Derek Shaw) *hld up: rdn over 1f out: r.o ins fnl f: nt rch ldrs* **16/1**
3304 **5** *nk* **Pearl Acclaim (IRE)**[9] 5780 6-9-0 **77** ....(p) PaulQuinn 9 80
(David Nicholls) *hld up: rdn: edgd lft and r.o ins fnl f: nt rch ldrs* **14/1**
0200 **6** *3/4* **Desert Ace (IRE)**[27] 5153 5-9-2 **79** ....(p) DanielTudhope 8 79
(Iain Jardine) *plld hrd and prom: rdn over 1f out: styd on same pce fnl f* **7/1**[3]
0-00 **7** *nse* **Thorntoun Lady (USA)**[9] 5780 6-8-8 **71** .... JoeDoyle 15 71
(Jim Goldie) *hld up: nt clr run over 1f out: r.o wl ins fnl f: nvr nrr* **33/1**
5022 **8** *2* **Apricot Sky**[3] 6012 6-8-8 **76** .... AnnaHesketh(5) 14 69
(David Nicholls) *chsd ldrs: rdn and edgd lft over 1f out: no ex fnl f* **9/2**[1]
0-05 **9** *nk* **Willbeme**[32] 4946 8-9-5 **82** .... DavidAllan 11 74
(Neville Bycroft) *chsd ldrs: rdn and lost pl over 1f out: nt clr run ins fnl f: styd on towards fin* **10/1**
0005 **10** *shd* **Red Stripes (USA)**[9] 5774 4-8-9 **79** ....(b) JordanUys(7) 5 70
(Lisa Williamson) *sn pushed along to chse ldrs: rdn over 1f out: wknd ins fnl f* **50/1**
-001 **11** *1/2* **Invincible Ridge (IRE)**[27] 5153 8-9-7 **84** .... NeilFarley 12 74
(Eric Alston) *prom: racd keenly: rdn and hung lft over 1f out: wknd ins fnl f* **16/1**
2206 **12** *shd* **Ballesteros**[27] 5153 7-9-4 **81** .... KeaganLatham 1 70
(Richard Fahey) *prom: rdn over 1f out: wknd ins fnl f* **28/1**
6460 **13** *3/4* **Rusty Rocket (IRE)**[24] 5274 7-9-0 **77** .... PaulHanagan 6 63
(Paul Green) *led 1f: remained handy: sn pushed along: wknd fnl f* **25/1**
0001 **14** *nk* **Bosham**[23] 5295 6-8-10 **78** ....(bt) NathanEvans(5) 4 63
(Michael Easterby) *hood removed late and s.i.s: hdwy over 3f out: rdn over 1f out: wknd ins fnl f* **16/1**
4653 **15** *nk* **Equally Fast**[12] 5669 4-9-4 **81** .... SamHitchcott 10 65
(William Muir) *pushed along early: led 4f out: hdd 1/2-way: rdn over 1f out: wknd fnl f* **12/1**
59.98s (-0.82) **Going Correction** 0.0s/f (Good) **15** Ran SP% **121.1**
Speed ratings (Par 105): **106,104,102,102,101 100,100,97,96,96 95,95,94,94,93**
CSF £64.06 CT £400.12 TOTE £8.40: £2.40, £2.90, £2.60; EX 80.40 Trifecta £965.80.
Owner F Brady,A Williams,P Lindley,S Wibberley **Bred** Frank Brady **Trained** Westow, N Yorks

FOCUS
Race run over the exact 5f. A competitive sprint handicap which, like the preceding 6f event, went to one drawn high. A clear pb from the winner, the form rated around the second and third.

6081 ACCA INSURANCE AT 188BET H'CAP 1m 2f 95y
4:30 (4:30) (Class 3) (0-95,95) 3-Y-O+ **£8,086** (£2,406; £1,202; £601) **Stalls** Centre

Form RPR
500 **1** **Lord Ben Stack (IRE)**[20] 5419 4-8-11 **87** .... CliffordLee(7) 9 98
(K R Burke) *led after 1f: clr 1/2-way: rdn over 1f out: styd on wl* **7/1**[3]
1141 **2** *1 3/4* **Muzdawaj**[20] 5405 3-9-0 **90** ....(p) PaulHanagan 3 100+
(William Haggas) *hld up: shkn up over 2f out: hdwy over 1f out: hung lft and wnt 2nd wl ins fnl f: no ch w wnr* **11/4**[2]
2304 **3** *2 1/4* **Modernism**[19] 5434 7-9-1 **84** .... GeorgeChaloner 4 87
(Richard Fahey) *hld up: rdn over 2f out: hdwy over 1f out: styd on to go 3rd nr fin* **25/1**
-1 **4** *shd* **El Vip (IRE)**[34] 4857 3-9-0 **90** .... FrankieDettori 1 93+
(Luca Cumani) *plld hrd and sn prom: chsd wnr over 3f out: rdn over 1f out: no ex ins fnl f* **11/10**[1]
0005 **5** *2 1/2* **Hit The Jackpot (IRE)**[34] 4858 7-9-12 **95** .... DanielTudhope 5 93
(David O'Meara) *hld up: rdn over 2f out: hdwy over 1f out: no ex ins fnl f* **20/1**
4406 **6** *3/4* **Silvery Moon (IRE)**[17] 5520 9-9-1 **87** .... RachelRichardson(3) 2 84
(Tim Easterby) *prom: rdn over 2f out: wknd fnl f* **40/1**
1314 **7** *2 3/4* **Grapevine (IRE)**[56] 4092 3-8-11 **87** .... RichardKingscote 6 79
(Charles Hills) *s.i.s: hld up: hdwy over 2f out: rdn over 1f out: wknd fnl f* **8/1**
1553 **8** *8* **Nayel (IRE)**[42] 4598 4-9-5 **88** ....(b) PatDobbs 7 65
(Richard Hannon) *chsd ldrs: rdn over 2f out: wknd over 1f out* **16/1**
000 **9** *1 1/4* **Capo Rosso (IRE)**[13] 5640 6-9-7 **95** .... AnnaHesketh(5) 10 69
(Tom Dascombe) *led 1f: chsd wnr tl rdn over 3f out: wknd over 1f out* **50/1**
2m 9.29s (-6.21) **Going Correction** -0.50s/f (Hard)
WFA 3 from 4yo+ 7lb **9** Ran SP% **116.8**
Speed ratings (Par 107): **104,102,100,100,98 98,95,89,88**
CSF £26.01 CT £462.14 TOTE £7.50: £2.00, £1.40, £5.30; EX 33.10 Trifecta £418.60.
Owner Owners For Owners: Lord Ben Stack **Bred** G Rollain **Trained** Middleham Moor, N Yorks

FOCUS
The winner dominated this decent handicap, which was run over 2yds shorter than advertised. The winner is rated back to his best.

6082 ASIAN H'CAP BETTING AT 188BET HANDICAP 7f
5:00 (5:01) (Class 3) (0-90,89) 3-Y-O+ **£8,086** (£2,406; £1,202; £601) **Stalls** Low

Form RPR
2044 **1** **Valley Of Fire**[20] 5403 4-9-5 **86** ....(p) DavidAllan 1 95
(William Haggas) *hld up: swtchd rt and hdwy over 2f out: rdn over 1f out: r.o to ld nr fin* **3/1**[1]
5205 **2** *shd* **Ballymore Castle (IRE)**[17] 5512 4-9-3 **84** .... GeorgeChaloner 12 92
(Richard Fahey) *hld up: hdwy over 3f out: rdn over 1f out: ev ch wl ins fnl f: r.o* **18/1**
6412 **3** *3/4* **Mishaal (IRE)**[20] 5417 6-9-6 **87** .... PaulMulrennan 9 93
(Michael Herrington) *a.p: chsd ldr over 2f out: rdn over 1f out: styd on* **10/1**
0606 **4** *nse* **He's No Saint**[17] 5514 5-9-2 **83** ....(v) DanielTudhope 8 89
(David O'Meara) *led: rdn over 1f out: hdd nr fin* **11/1**
1205 **5** *1 1/4* **George William**[14] 5601 3-9-4 **89** .... PatDobbs 3 89+
(Richard Hannon) *s.i.s: hld up: r.o ins fnl f: nt rch ldrs* **11/2**[3]

0200 **6** *hd* **Arnold Lane (IRE)**[20] 5419 7-9-5 **86**................................ CharlesBishop 2 89
(Mick Channon) *chsd ldrs: rdn over 2f out: cl up whn nt clr run and eased wl ins fnl f* **12/1**

0403 **7** *nk* **Exchequer (IRE)**[28] 5124 5-9-7 **88**.................................... KieranO'Neill 4 89
(David Brown) *prom: rdn over 1f out: styd on same pce ins fnl f* **17/2**

552 **8** *1* **Alejandro (IRE)**[6] 5866 7-9-4 **85**................................ KeaganLatham 6 83
(David O'Meara) *chsd ldr tl rdn over 2f out: no ex fnl f* **10/1**

3111 **9** *shd* **Alnashama**[17] 5514 4-9-7 **88**.. PaulHanagan 5 86
(Charles Hills) *outpcd: rdn and hung lft over 2f out: r.o ins fnl f: nvr nrr* **9/2**[2]

0500 **10** *shd* **Free Code (IRE)**[6] 5866 5-9-4 **85**.................................. FrankieDettori 10 83
(David Barron) *outpcd: rdn over 1f out: r.o ins fnl f: nvr on terms* **16/1**

1004 **11** *7* **Kalk Bay (IRE)**[20] 5389 9-8-12 **84**...........................(t) NathanEvans(5) 11 63
(Michael Easterby) *s.i.s: swtchd lft sn after s: a in rr* **20/1**

1m 25.87s (-4.83) **Going Correction** -0.50s/f (Hard)
WFA 3 from 4yo+ 4lb **11** Ran SP% **119.2**
Speed ratings (Par 107): **107,106,106,105,104 104,103,102,102,102 94**
CSF £62.23 CT £500.70 TOTE £4.40: £1.90, £4.90, £2.50; EX 79.80 Trifecta £1044.20.
Owner Sheikh Juma Dalmook Al Maktoum **Bred** Bearstone Stud Ltd **Trained** Newmarket, Suffolk

FOCUS
Race run over 2yds less than advertised. They went a good gallop in this fair handicap and nothing got involved from the rear division, although the first two came from midfield. The winner is rated close to his best.

6083 FOLLOW US ON TWITTER AT 188BET H'CAP 1m 6f
5:30 (5:31) (Class 4) (0-80,80) 3-Y-O+ **£5,175** (£1,540; £769; £384) **Stalls** Low

Form RPR

2251 **1** **Champagne Champ**[36] 4795 4-10-0 **80**........................ DanielTudhope 1 89+
(Rod Millman) *a.p: chsd ldr 12f out tl rdn to ld over 2f out: styd on wl* **3/1**[1]

6623 **2** *2 1/4* **Michael's Mount**[34] 4859 3-8-8 **71**...............................(p) DavidAllan 9 77
(Ed Dunlop) *chsd ldrs: rdn and ev ch fr over 1f out tl styd on same pce wl ins fnl f* **4/1**[3]

1315 **3** *1 1/2* **Dew Pond**[41] 4664 4-9-7 **76**.................................... RachelRichardson(3) 2 80
(Tim Easterby) *prom: racd keenly: shkn up over 1f out: styd on same pce ins fnl f* **10/1**

0520 **4** *3/4* **Snowy Dawn**[13] 5642 6-9-3 **69**...................................... AdamBeschizza 7 72
(Steph Hollinshead) *chsd ldr 2f: remained handy: rdn over 2f out: styd on same pce fnl f* **12/1**

3321 **5** *nk* **Ivanhoe**[14] 5597 6-9-2 **68**..(v) KieranO'Neill 5 71
(Michael Blanshard) *hld up: rdn over 2f out: styd on u.p ins fnl f: nvr nrr* **12/1**

2214 **6** *3/4* **Obboorr**[21] 5350 7-9-9 **75**.. PaulHanagan 12 76+
(Tim Fitzgerald) *hld up: rdn over 2f out: styd on ins fnl f: nt rch ldrs* **12/1**

0004 **7** *2 3/4* **Gabrial The Duke (IRE)**[29] 5061 6-9-7 **73**.............(v) GeorgeChaloner 6 71
(Richard Fahey) *s.i.s and pushed along in rr early: rdn over 2f out: styd on fr over 1f out: nvr on terms* **14/1**

5054 **8** *1 1/4* **Tuscan Gold**[19] 5435 9-8-11 **68**................................ RobJFitzpatrick(5) 8 64
(Micky Hammond) *hld up: rdn over 2f out: n.d* **50/1**

1056 **9** *7* **Be Perfect (USA)**[19] 5434 7-10-0 **80**........................(b) JamesSullivan 10 66
(Ruth Carr) *led: clr 12f out tl over 5f out: rdn and hdd over 2f out: wknd fnl f* **25/1**

0/04 **10** *3/4* **Great Fighter**[39] 4703 6-9-12 **78**...(p) JoeDoyle 4 63
(Jim Goldie) *hld up: hdwy 1/2-way: rdn over 3f out: wknd over 1f out* **14/1**

0640 **11** *18* **Russian Royale**[21] 5350 6-8-12 **71**................................ LaurenSteade(7) 11 31
(Micky Hammond) *hld up: hdwy 1/2-way: wknd over 2f out* **66/1**

0421 **12** *35* **Vanishing Point**[62] 3886 3-9-0 **80**..........................[1] EdwardGreatrex(3) 3
(Andrew Balding) *mid-div: pushed along at various stages: lost pl 1/2-way: wknd 3f out* **7/2**[2]

2m 56.78s (-5.22) **Going Correction** -0.50s/f (Hard)
WFA 3 from 4yo+ 11lb **12** Ran SP% **120.0**
Speed ratings (Par 105): **94,92,91,91,91 90,89,88,84,84 73,53**
CSF £14.87 CT £108.83 TOTE £4.60: £1.80, £1.40, £3.30; EX 16.80 Trifecta £108.40.
Owner Five Horses Ltd **Bred** Five Horses Ltd **Trained** Kentisbeare, Devon

FOCUS
Race run over 2yds less than advertised. This was run at a sound gallop courtesy of \bBe Perfect\p. The second and third are rated to form.
T/Jkpt: Not won. T/Plt: £289.00 to a £1 stake. Pool: £60,050.00 - 207.76 winning tickets T/Qpdt: £66.00 to a £1 stake. Pool: £5,933.00 - 89.81 winning tickets **Colin Roberts**

5763 KEMPTON (A.W) (R-H)
Friday, September 2

OFFICIAL GOING: Polytrack: standard to slow
Wind: light, across Weather: overcast

6084 32RED.COM APPRENTICE H'CAP 1m (P)
5:25 (5:26) (Class 4) (0-85,85) 3-Y-O+ **£4,690** (£1,395; £697; £348) **Stalls** Low

Form RPR

0-1 **1** **Cloudberry**[65] 3769 3-8-10 **79**... DavidEgan(5) 1 88+
(Roger Charlton) *dwlt: hld up in last trio: effrt ent fnl 2f: rdn and gd hdwy over 1f out: led ins fnl f: rn green and hung lft in front: in command and kpt on fnl 75yds* **11/2**[3]

-004 **2** *1 1/4* **Mister Music**[35] 4841 7-9-5 **78**.................................... GeorgeDowning 2 84
(Tony Carroll) *dwlt: hld up in midfield: effrt 2f out: hdwy u.p ent fnl f: styd on wl u.p fnl 150yds: wnt 2nd last strides: nvr getting to wnr* **8/1**

0644 **3** *nk* **Iberica Road (USA)**[22] 5336 3-8-2 **73**........................(t) WilliamCox(7) 5 78
(Andrew Balding) *chsd ldr for 3f: styd chsng ldrs: drvn and ev ch over 1f out tl no ex ins fnl f: sltly impeded and styd on same pce fnl 100yds: lost 2nd last strides* **25/1**

2-66 **4** *nk* **Bag Of Diamonds**[13] 5649 3-8-13 **77**.......................... TomMarquand 10 81
(Richard Hannon) *chsd ldrs: pushed along 3f out: unable qck over 1f out: rallied 1f out and battling for 2nd ins fnl f: kpt on same pce towards fin* **40/1**

0044 **5** *1* **Starboard**[26] 5191 7-9-4 **80**......................................(b[1]) GeorgeBuckell(3) 8 83
(David Simcock) *taken down early: midfield: hdwy to chse ldr 5f out: rdn to ld 2f out: drvn over 1f out: hdd ins fnl f: no ex and wknd towards fin* **20/1**

11-3 **6** *2* **Fly**[30] 5024 4-9-2 **80**.. GeorgeWood(5) 3 78
(James Fanshawe) *hld up in midfield: effrt ent fnl 2f: drvn over 1f out: styd on same pce after: nvr enough pce to threaten ldrs* **5/2**[1]

0631 **7** *1 1/4* **Tournament**[30] 5024 5-9-9 **82**.................................(t) JosephineGordon 9 77
(Seamus Durack) *s.i.s: hld up in last trio: effrt ent fnl 2f: styd on u.p ins fnl f: nvr trbld ldrs* **7/1**

1110 **8** *1/2* **Blacklister**[14] 5616 3-8-13 **82**...................................... KillianHennessy(5) 6 75
(Mick Channon) *midfield: rdn 3f out: lost pl over 2f out: no threat to ldrs and kpt on same pce fnl 2f* **33/1**

6621 **9** *3/4* **Force (IRE)**[16] 5545 3-9-3 **81**...................................... MichaelJMMurphy 7 72
(Charles Hills) *stdd after s: hld up in rr: swtchd lft and effrt over 2f out: nvr trbld ldrs* **16/1**

3000 **10** *1* **Zodiakos (IRE)**[41] 4624 3-9-7 **85**.................................. MarcMonaghan 4 73
(Hugo Palmer) *in tch in midfield: effrt 2f out: no hdwy u.p over 1f out: wknd fnl f* **7/2**[2]

2251 **11** *nk* **Lastmanlastround (IRE)**[18] 5480 3-9-0 **78**...................... RobHornby 11 66
(Rae Guest) *led: hdd and wandered lft 2f out: edging bk rt and lost pl over 1f out: sn wknd* **14/1**

1m 37.51s (-2.29) **Going Correction** 0.0s/f (Stan)
WFA 3 from 4yo+ 5lb **11** Ran SP% **116.3**
Speed ratings (Par 105): **111,109,109,109,108 106,104,104,103,102 102**
CSF £46.10 CT £1014.78 TOTE £5.50: £1.80, £3.20, £4.30; EX 57.60 Trifecta £1023.10.
Owner Beckhampton Stables Ltd **Bred** Carwell Equities Ltd **Trained** Beckhampton, Wilts

FOCUS
The going was standard to slow. They went a good pace in this interesting handicap and it set up for the closers. Fairly ordinary form, limited by the third and fourth.

6085 IRISH STALLION FARMS EBF MAIDEN STKS 1m (P)
6:00 (6:01) (Class 5) 2-Y-O **£3,234** (£962; £481; £240) **Stalls** Low

Form RPR

6 **1** **Bay Of Poets (IRE)**[48] 4379 2-9-5 0.................................. WilliamBuick 2 82+
(Charlie Appleby) *broke wl: sn restrained into midfield: clsd on inner ent fnl 2f: upsides ldr on bit ent fnl f: shkn up and qcknd to ld ins fnl f: r.o strly: easily* **2/1**[1]

43 **2** *1 3/4* **Election Day**[27] 5150 2-9-5 0... JamesDoyle 6 74
(Mark Johnston) *sn led: rdn ent fnl 2f: jnd by wnr over 1f out: hdd ins fnl f and sn brushed aside by wnr: kpt on same pce for clr 2nd after* **4/1**[2]

3 *2* **Caramuru (IRE)** 2-9-5 0... SeanLevey 9 69+
(Richard Hannon) *dwlt: steadily rcvrd and chsd ldr 5f out: rdn 3f out: drvn and outpcd 2f out: rallied u.p ent fnl f: wnt 3rd ins fnl f: kpt on same pce and no imp on ldrs* **16/1**

4 *nse* **Harbour Rock** 2-9-5 0.. JamieSpencer 1 69+
(David Simcock) *stdd s: hld up in tch towards rr: swtchd rt and hdwy wl over 1f out: no threat to ldng pair but battling for 3rd ins fnl f: kpt on* **9/2**[3]

6 **5** *nse* **Keepup Kevin**[9] 5764 2-9-2 0.. RobHornby(3) 4 69
(Pam Sly) *led early: sn hdd and chsd ldr tl 5f out: styd chsng ldrs: 3rd and unable qck w ldrs over 1f out: kpt on same pce ins fnl f* **33/1**

6 *shd* **Melodic Motion (IRE)** 2-9-0 0.. OisinMurphy 5 64+
(Ralph Beckett) *chsd ldng trio: pushed along 3f out: rdn 2f out: battling for 3rd but no threat to ldng pair ins fnl f: kpt on same pce* **6/1**

7 *6* **Desert Skyline (IRE)** 2-9-5 0... FMBerry 7 54
(David Elsworth) *in tch in last trio: rdn 1/2-way: dropped to last and struggling 3f out: n.d after* **50/1**

8 *3 3/4* **Lightly Squeeze** 2-9-5 0.................................. WilliamTwiston-Davies 8 45
(Philip Hide) *s.i.s and bustled along leaving stalls: sn t.k.h and hld up on tch in last pair: rdn over 2f out: unable qck and sn outpcd: wknd over 1f out* **6/1**

9 *1 1/4* **Hold Me Tight (IRE)** 2-9-5 0... LiamKeniry 3 42
(J S Moore) *hld up in tch in last trio: effrt ent 2f out: sn outpcd: wknd over 1f out* **100/1**

1m 40.43s (0.63) **Going Correction** 0.0s/f (Stan) **9** Ran SP% **111.9**
Speed ratings (Par 95): **96,94,92,92,92 92,86,82,81**
CSF £9.47 TOTE £2.70: £1.30, £1.50, £5.00; EX 9.20 Trifecta £48.30.
Owner Godolphin **Bred** Ammerland Verwaltung Gmbh & Co Kg **Trained** Newmarket, Suffolk

FOCUS
This didn't look very strong and the pace was steady, but the favourite was impressive under a patient ride.

6086 32RED CASINO/IRISH EBF MAIDEN STKS (DIV I) 6f (P)
6:30 (6:30) (Class 5) 2-Y-O **£3,234** (£962; £481; £240) **Stalls** Low

Form RPR

0 **1** **Hilario**[84] 3106 2-9-5 0... AndreaAtzeni 2 83+
(Charles Hills) *hld up in tch in midfield: chsng ldrs and nt clr run over 1f out: swtchd lft and hdwy ent fnl f: rdn and str chal ins fnl f: r.o wl to ld last strides* **7/2**[2]

2 *shd* **Dubai One (IRE)** 2-9-0 0.. JamesDoyle 6 78+
(Saeed bin Suroor) *trckd ldrs: effrt on inner 2f out: rdn to chal ent fnl f: led ins fnl f but immediately hrd pressed: r.o u.p: hdd last strides* **6/5**[1]

3 *2* **Etikaal** 2-9-5 0.. DaneO'Neill 9 77+
(Simon Crisford) *s.i.s: sn rcvrd and hld up in tch in midfield: rdn ent fnl 2f: unable qck and sltly outpcd over 1f out: rallied u.p ins fnl f: wnt 3rd towards fin* **6/1**[3]

46 **4** *1/2* **Hathfa (FR)**[20] 5400 2-9-0 0.. ShaneKelly 5 70
(Richard Hughes) *led: rdn wl over 1f out: hdd over 1f out: stl ev ch tl no ex ins fnl f: styd on same pce fnl 100yds: lost 3rd towards fin* **7/2**[2]

5 *3/4* **Lava Light** 2-9-0 0.. FergusSweeney 8 68+
(Henry Candy) *dwlt: t.k.h: hdwy to chse ldr over 4f out: rdn and ev ch 2f out: led over 1f out: hdd ins fnl f: no ex and sn outpcd: wknd wl ins fnl f* **33/1**

6 *3 1/4* **Ode To Paris** 2-9-5 0.. GeorgeBaker 1 63
(Ed Dunlop) *stdd after s: hld up in rr: pushed along ent fnl 2f: sme hdwy 1f out: kpt on ins fnl f: no threat to ldrs* **20/1**

6 **7** *3/4* **Red Alert**[25] 5237 2-9-5 0.. OisinMurphy 7 61
(Joseph Tuite) *stdd after s: t.k.h: hld up in tch towards rr: rdn ent fnl 2f: swtchd rt and sme hdwy 1f out: kpt on ins fnl f no threat to ldrs* **50/1**

8 *6* **Not Now Mum** 2-9-5 0.. RobertWinston 4 43
(Dean Ivory) *chsd ldr tl over 4f out: sn dropped to midfield: rdn over 2f out: edgd lft: outpcd and btn over 1f out: sn wknd* **40/1**

00 **9** *1 3/4* **Thomas Girtin (IRE)**[18] 5484 2-9-0 0........................... HectorCrouch(5) 3 38
(Gary Moore) *hld up in last trio: rdn over 2f out: sn struggling: bhd over 1f out* **100/1**

1m 14.58s (1.48) **Going Correction** 0.0s/f (Stan) **9** Ran SP% **117.3**
Speed ratings (Par 95): **90,89,87,86,85 81,80,72,69**
CSF £7.99 TOTE £4.80: £1.60, £1.10, £2.20; EX 10.20 Trifecta £43.80.
Owner Saleh Al Homaizi & Imad Al Sagar **Bred** Mrs Elizabeth Grundy **Trained** Lambourn, Berks

FOCUS
The first two had a good duel in the closing stages and pulled clear in this maiden.

6087 32RED CASINO/IRISH EBF MAIDEN STKS (DIV II) 6f (P)
7:00 (7:00) (Class 5) 2-Y-O **£3,234** (£962; £481; £240) **Stalls** Low

Form RPR
05 1 **Believable**[18] 5469 2-9-0 0 AndreaAtzeni 6 74
(Sir Michael Stoute) *mde all: rdn and qcknd ent fnl 2f: forged ahd 1f out: hld on wl whn pressed ins fnl f: rdn out* **7/4**[1]
2 ½ **Marzouq (USA)** 2-9-5 0 JFEgan 8 78+
(Jeremy Noseda) *bmpd and squeezed for room s: sn rcvrd and hld up in tch in midfield: rdn and hdwy to chse ldrs over 1f out: edgd rt ent fnl f: pressing wnr ins fnl f: kpt on* **10/1**
3 2 **Lady Capucine (FR)** 2-9-0 0 [1] MartinHarley 5 67+
(Harry Dunlop) *hld up in tch in last trio: effrt 2f out: hdwy u.p 1f out: kpt on to go 3rd ins fnl f: no threat to ldng pair* **28/1**
0 4 ¾ **Conkering Hero (IRE)**[6] 5890 2-9-5 0 OisinMurphy 3 69+
(Joseph Tuite) *chsd ldng pair: effrt 2f out: sn rdn and outpcd over 1f out: kpt on again ins fnl f* **66/1**
5 shd **Warm Words** 2-9-0 0 FMBerry 4 64+
(Ralph Beckett) *hld up in tch in midfield: effrt 2f out: chsng ldrs whn squeezed for room and lost pl ent fnl f: no threat to ldng pair but kpt on again ins fnl f* **9/4**[2]
6 ½ **Zavikon** 2-9-5 0 ShaneKelly 7 67
(Richard Hughes) *wnt lft s: sn chsng wnr: rdn and pressing wnr wl over 1f out: unable qck ent fnl f: lost 2nd ins fnl f: wknd fnl 100yds* **14/1**
0 7 2¼ **Ninety Years Young**[60] 3954 2-9-5 0 SeanLevey 9 61
(David Elsworth) *hld up in tch in last trio: effrt 2f out: sn outpcd: kpt on same pce and wl hld fr over 1f out* **16/1**
0 8 ½ **The Secrets Out**[34] 4866 2-9-5 0 AdamKirby 1 60
(Luke Dace) *stdd s: t.k.h: hld up in tch in last trio: effrt 2f out: no imp and nt clr run jst over 1f out: swtchd lft 1f out: no hdwy* **4/1**[3]

1m 14.84s (1.74) **Going Correction** 0.0s/f (Stan) **8 Ran SP% 113.7**
Speed ratings (Par 95): **88,87,84,83,83 82,79,79**
CSF £20.35 TOTE £2.30: £1.20, £1.90, £5.00; EX 15.00 Trifecta £172.40.
Owner Cheveley Park Stud **Bred** Cheveley Park Stud Ltd **Trained** Newmarket, Suffolk

FOCUS
An ordinary maiden but the winner justified support and a newcomer showed plenty of promise in second.

6088 LONGINES IRISH CHAMPIONS WEEKEND EBF FILLIES' CONDITIONS STKS (PLUS 10 RACE) 7f (P)
7:30 (7:31) (Class 3) 2-Y-O
£9,337 (£2,796; £1,398; £699; £349; £175) **Stalls** Low

Form RPR
102 1 **Soul Silver (IRE)**[13] 5632 2-9-2 85 OisinMurphy 2 89
(David Simcock) *chsd ldr: rdn 2f out: hdwy u.p to ld ins fnl f: sn in command and styd on strly: rdn out* **8/1**[3]
2 2 2 **Syndicate**[21] 5356 2-8-12 0 FMBerry 1 80
(Ralph Beckett) *led and set stdy gallop: rdn and qcknd wl over 1f out: drvn over 1f out: hdd ins fnl f: sn btn and wknd towards fin* **5/6**[1]
100 3 ½ **Nasimi**[41] 4623 2-9-2 88 WilliamBuick 3 82
(Charlie Appleby) *wnt lft s: sn rcvrd to chse ldrs: effrt 2f out: outpcd and edgd lft over 1f out: kpt on but no threat to wnr ins fnl f* **2/1**[2]
4 2¼ **Highland Pass** 2-8-12 0 LiamKeniry 5 72+
(Andrew Balding) *stdd s: t.k.h: hld up in tch in last pair: effrt and hdwy into 4th wl over 1f out: styd on same pce and no imp ins fnl f* **25/1**
5 2¼ **Prize Diva** 2-8-12 0 SeanLevey 4 66+
(David Elsworth) *hld up in tch in last pair: effrt 2f out: sn outpcd: 5th and styd on same pce fr over 1f out* **66/1**
62 6 10 **Cool Echo**[67] 3718 2-8-12 0 FrederikTylicki 6 39
(J R Jenkins) *wnt lft s: sn rcvrd and in tch in midfield: rdn over 2f out: dropped to last wl over 1f out: sn wknd* **20/1**

1m 26.99s (0.99) **Going Correction** 0.0s/f (Stan) **6 Ran SP% 109.1**
Speed ratings (Par 96): **94,91,91,88,86 74**
CSF £14.58 TOTE £6.90: £2.70, £1.10; EX 17.50 Trifecta £36.20.
Owner Qatar Racing Limited **Bred** Lisieux Stud & Irish National Stud **Trained** Newmarket, Suffolk

FOCUS
One of the leading form contenders scored with authority in this conditions event.

6089 32RED H'CAP (LONDON MIDDLE DISTANCE SERIES QUALIFIER) 1m 3f (P)
8:00 (8:00) (Class 3) (0-95,93) 3-Y-O+
£7,158 (£2,143; £1,071; £535; £267; £134) **Stalls** Low

Form RPR
-214 1 **Lord George (IRE)**[55] 4153 3-9-0 89 TomQueally 1 97+
(James Fanshawe) *hld up in tch in midfield: nt clr run ent fnl 2f: swtchd lft and hdwy over 1f out: chsd ldr 1f out: drvn to chal ins fnl f: styd on u.p to ld cl home* **7/4**[1]
4342 2 shd **Sennockian Star**[4] 5964 6-9-2 83 (v) SilvestreDeSousa 5 90
(Mark Johnston) *chsd ldr: upsides 3f out: rdn to ld ent fnl 2f: drvn over 1f out: hrd pressed ins fnl f: battled on u.p: hdd and no ex cl home* **3/1**[2]
10- 3 2 **Fergall (IRE)**[482] 1132 9-9-3 84 SteveDrowne 6 87
(Seamus Mullins) *stdd s: hld up in tch in last pair: effrt and nt clr run over 1f out: hdwy ent fnl f: wnt 3rd wl ins fnl f: kpt on* **66/1**
1-14 4 ½ **Power Game**[139] 1478 4-9-12 93 JamesDoyle 8 96
(Saeed bin Suroor) *in tch in midfield: rdn over 2f out: drvn over 1f out: kpt on same pce ins fnl f* **4/1**[3]
0603 5 4 **Blue Surf**[13] 5647 7-9-11 92 (p) MartinDwyer 7 87
(Amanda Perrett) *in tch in midfield: rdn over 2f out: drvn: unable qck and lost pl 2f out: wl and styd on same pce ins fnl f* **7/1**
20 6 ½ **Zambeasy**[21] 5358 5-9-3 84 WilliamTwiston-Davies 3 78
(Philip Hide) *led: rdn and hdd ent fnl 2f: unable qck over 1f out: wknd ins fnl f* **25/1**
060 7 1 **Storm Rock**[38] 4731 4-9-9 90 MartinHarley 4 83
(Harry Dunlop) *chsd ldrs: rdn to press ldrs ent fnl 2f: drvn and unable qck over 1f out: wknd ins fnl f* **20/1**
-220 8 7 **Glan Y Gors (IRE)**[65] 3784 4-9-7 88 JamieSpencer 2 68
(David Simcock) *stdd s: hld up in tch in rr: swtchd lft and effrt ent fnl 2f: no hdwy and sn btn: wknd fnl f* **14/1**

2m 18.11s (-3.79) **Going Correction** 0.0s/f (Stan)
WFA 3 from 4yo+ 8lb **8 Ran SP% 110.6**
Speed ratings (Par 107): **113,112,111,111,108 107,107,102**
CSF £6.48 CT £212.24 TOTE £2.60: £1.20, £1.50, £15.40; EX 7.20 Trifecta £211.50.
Owner Fred Archer Racing - Bend Or **Bred** Sarl Elevage Du Haras De Bourgeauville **Trained** Newmarket, Suffolk

FOCUS
There was an exciting finish in this good handicap. The form is rated around the second.

6090 £10 FREE BET AT 32REDSPORT.COM H'CAP 2m (P)
8:30 (8:31) (Class 5) (0-75,73) 4-Y-O+ **£2,911** (£866; £432; £216) **Stalls** Low

Form RPR
1005 1 **Fern Owl**[51] 4266 4-9-5 71 (b[1]) LiamKeniry 9 77
(Hughie Morrison) *t.k.h: hld up in tch in midfield: swtchd lft and effrt 2f out: hdwy to press ldrs 1f out: led ins fnl f: styd on: rdn out* **10/1**
4462 2 ½ **Kristjano (GER)**[24] 5262 4-9-3 69 (p) GeorgeBaker 8 74
(Chris Wall) *chsd ldr: rdn ent fnl 2f: drvn over 1f out: ev ch 1f out: styd on same pce towards fin* **9/4**[1]
3334 3 shd **Sunday Royal (FR)**[24] 5256 4-9-1 67 AdamKirby 4 72
(Harry Dunlop) *hld up in tch in last trio: hdwy u.p and switching rt over 1f out: styd on wl ins fnl f: nt quite rch ldrs* **10/1**
6-46 4 ¾ **Northern Meeting (IRE)**[38] 4501 6-9-6 72 (p) OisinMurphy 2 76
(Robert Stephens) *hld up in tch in midfield: effrt 2f out: rdn to chal over 1f out: led 1f out: drvn and hdd ins fnl f: no ex: wknd towards fin* **20/1**
/032 5 2¾ **Atalanta Bay (IRE)**[10] 5737 6-8-9 64 JosephineGordon[(3)] 1 65
(Marcus Tregoning) *t.k.h: led: rdn ent fnl 2f: hrd pressed and drvn over 1f out: hdd 1f out: no ex and wknd fnl 100yds* **4/1**[3]
P-63 6 3¼ **Meetings Man (IRE)**[30] 5035 9-9-6 72 (p) PatCosgrave 3 69
(Ali Stronge) *chsd ldrs: effrt over 2f out: drvn and pressing ldrs 2f out: no ex ent fnl f: wknd ins fnl f* **20/1**
3144 7 6 **Rainbow Pride (IRE)**[14] 5597 4-9-7 73 [1] JamieSpencer 7 65
(Sir Mark Prescott Bt) *stdd s: hld up in tch in rr: effrt over 2f out: hung rt and btn 2f out: no ch and eased ins fnl f* **7/2**[2]
220 8 4 **Hier Encore (FR)**[26] 5216 4-8-4 56 WilliamCarson 5 41
(David Menuisier) *t.k.h: hld up in tch in midfield: rdn over 3f out: lost pl u.p over 2f out: wknd over 1f out* **12/1**
3050 9 1¾ **Tobouggaloo**[14] 5597 5-9-4 70 TomQueally 6 57
(Stuart Kittow) *hld up in tch in last pair: hdwy to chse ldrs 6f out: rdn 3f out: sn drvn and lost pl ent fnl 2f: wknd over 1f out* **16/1**

3m 29.57s (-0.53) **Going Correction** 0.0s/f (Stan) **9 Ran SP% 114.3**
Speed ratings (Par 103): **101,100,100,100,98 97,94,92,91**
CSF £32.48 CT £232.56 TOTE £11.30: £2.80, £1.40, £2.90; EX 38.40 Trifecta £472.30.
Owner Sir Thomas Pilkington **Bred** Sir Thomas Pilkington **Trained** East Ilsley, Berks

FOCUS
They went a stop-start gallop and there was not much separating the first four in this staying handicap. It's hard to be positive about the form.

6091 32RED ON THE APP STORE H'CAP (JOCKEY CLUB GRASSROOTS FLAT SPRINT SERIES QUALIFIER) 6f (P)
9:00 (9:00) (Class 5) (0-70,70) 3-Y-O+ **£2,911** (£866; £432; £216) **Stalls** Low

Form RPR
1031 1 **Curious Fox**[16] 5554 3-9-1 66 WilliamCarson 7 72
(Anthony Carson) *chsd ldrs: effrt to chal over 1f out: drvn to ld ins fnl f: hdd wl ins fnl f: battled bk to ld again towards fin: gamely* **10/1**
6301 2 ½ **For Ayman**[17] 5509 5-8-12 68 (t) SeanMooney[(7)] 1 72
(Joseph Tuite) *hld up in tch in midfield: effrt 2f out: switching rt and hdwy over 1f out: rdn to chal ins fnl f: led wl ins fnl f: hdd and no ex towards fin* **5/1**[3]
0000 3 hd **Kinglami**[56] 4086 7-9-7 70 FergusSweeney 5 73
(John O'Shea) *hld up in tch in rr of main gp: hdwy u.p over 1f out: drvn and ev ch ins fnl f: unable qck towards fin* **8/1**
6131 4 hd **Helfire**[34] 4881 3-8-11 67 CharlieBennett[(5)] 2 73+
(Hughie Morrison) *taken down early: hld up in tch in midfield: effrt 2f out: chsng ldrs whn n.m.r ent fnl f: hmpd ins fnl f: squeezed between horses and r.o towards fin* **11/4**[1]
4-64 5 ½ **Many Dreams (IRE)**[43] 4563 3-8-11 65 JosephineGordon[(3)] 11 66
(Mark Usher) *led: rdn over 2f out: hung lft 2f out: hrd pressed and edgd bk rt u.p over 1f out: hdd ins fnl f: no ex and styd on same pce towards fin* **12/1**
0455 6 hd **Major Valentine**[44] 4506 4-9-0 68 CiaranMckee[(5)] 10 68
(John O'Shea) *awkward as stalls: t.k.h: sn rcvrd to chse ldrs: wnt 2nd 1/2-way tl carried rt 2f out: drvn over 1f out: stl pressing ldrs but one pced ins fnl f* **16/1**
4004 7 nse **Tagula Night (IRE)**[31] 4990 10-9-7 70 (vt) RobertWinston 9 70
(Dean Ivory) *t.k.h: chsd ldr tl 1/2-way: rdn to press ldr whn pushed lft and lost 2nd 2f out: stl pressing ldrs 1f out: styd on same pce u.p ins fnl f* **9/2**[2]
300 8 3 **Gift From God**[32] 4939 3-8-12 63 LiamKeniry 8 54
(Hugo Froud) *dwlt: hld up in last pair: effrt on inner 2f out: no imp and styd on same pce fr over 1f out* **50/1**
125 9 ¾ **Dutch Archer**[57] 4039 3-9-0 70 DavidParkes[(5)] 4 58
(Jeremy Gask) *in tch in midfield: effrt 2f out: no imp u.p and btn 1f out: wknd ins fnl f* **25/1**
4060 10 22 **Rhythm And Blues**[23] 5284 3-9-5 70 (b) AdamKirby 6
(Clive Cox) *a rr and nvr gng wl: lost tch 2f out* **11/2**

1m 12.15s (-0.95) **Going Correction** 0.0s/f (Stan)
WFA 3 from 4yo+ 2lb **10 Ran SP% 116.5**
Speed ratings (Par 103): **106,105,105,104,104 103,103,99,98,69**
CSF £59.35 CT £435.59 TOTE £11.10: £2.80, £2.00, £2.90; EX 59.50 Trifecta £439.10.
Owner Carson, Francis, Ghauri & Percy **Bred** Minster Stud **Trained** Newmarket, Suffolk

FOCUS
A competitive sprint and there was a bunch finish. The winner built on his latest C&D win.
T/Plt: £26.20 to a £1 stake. Pool: £63,798.10 - 1,771.58 winning tickets T/Qpdt: £3.50 to a £1 stake. Pool: £7,986.67 - 1,659.11 winning tickets **Steve Payne**

5798 MUSSELBURGH (R-H)
Friday, September 2

OFFICIAL GOING: Good to firm (good in places; 8.1)
Wind: fresh half against Weather: fine

6092 DONALDSON TIMBER BRITISH STALLION STUDS EBF MEDIAN AUCTION MAIDEN STKS 7f 30y
4:50 (4:50) (Class 5) 2-Y-O **£3,234** (£962; £481) **Stalls** Low

Form RPR
0 1 **Under Control (IRE)**[42] 4594 2-9-5 0 BenCurtis 2 70+
(William Haggas) *racd keenly: trckd ldr in 2nd: pushed along to chal strly wl over 1f out: carried lft appr fnl f: rdn to ld ins fnl f: edgd rt: kpt on* **4/6**[1]
0545 2 2½ **Equity**[8] 5806 2-9-5 63 TomEaves 4 63
(David Brown) *led: rdn whn jnd wl over 1f out: edgd lft appr fnl f: hdd ins fnl f: no ex fnl 75yds* **3/1**[2]

0 **3** *13* **Spin A Disc (GER)**[11] 5728 2-9-5 0 JoeFanning 3 34
(Mark Johnston) *s.i.s: hld up in 3rd: pushed along 3f out: wknd over 1f out: eased ins fnl f* **7/2**[3]

1m 32.8s (3.80) **Going Correction** -0.10s/f (Good) **3** Ran SP% **107.2**
Speed ratings (Par 95): **74,71,56**
CSF £2.88 TOTE £1.40; EX 2.90 Trifecta £2.60.
Owner D I Scott **Bred** D I Scott **Trained** Newmarket, Suffolk

FOCUS
The rail on the bottom bend had been moved out 4yds, adding 14yds to Races 1,3,4,5 & 6. The official going was good to firm, good in places. Just an ordinary maiden to start proceedings.

6093 CALA HOMES H'CAP 5f
5:20 (5:20) (Class 5) (0-75,80) 3-Y-O+ **£3,234** (£962; £481; £240) **Stalls** High

Form RPR
3126 **1** **Showdaisy**[22] 5320 3-8-13 **67** [1] PhillipMakin 4 77
(Keith Dalgleish) *mde all: rdn over 1f out: strly pressed ins fnl f: hld on wl* **5/2**[1]

0004 **2** *3/4* **Astrophysics**[15] 5582 4-9-2 **69** PaddyAspell 3 77
(Lynn Siddall) *in tch: rdn and hdwy on outer over 1f out: chal strly ins fnl f: kpt on* **9/2**[2]

3525 **3** *1* **Royal Brave (IRE)**[23] 5284 5-9-5 **72** BarryMcHugh 6 76
(Rebecca Bastiman) *trckd ldr: rdn over 1f out: bit tight for room on inner appr fnl f: kpt on fnl 110yds* **9/2**[2]

0021 **4** *1 1/2* **Master Bond**[4] 5969 7-9-8 **80** 6ex JoshDoyle(5) 2 79
(David O'Meara) *trckd ldr: rdn over 1f out: wknd ins fnl f* **5/2**[1]

6060 **5** *3/4* **Go Go Green (IRE)**[21] 5368 10-8-3 **61** ShirleyTeasdale(5) 5 57
(Jim Goldie) *hld up: rdn 2f out: nvr threatened* **11/1**[3]

0410 **6** *1/2* **Bunce (IRE)**[9] 5780 8-8-12 **65** JoeFanning 7 59
(Linda Perratt) *hld up: rdn 2f out: nvr threatened* **18/1**

59.15s (-1.25) **Going Correction** -0.10s/f (Good)
WFA 3 from 4yo+ 1lb **6** Ran SP% **107.1**
Speed ratings (Par 103): **106,104,103,100,99 98**
CSF £12.63 TOTE £3.40: £1.80, £2.50; EX 11.40 Trifecta £32.70.
Owner Ronnie Docherty & Partner **Bred** Patricia Ann Scott-Dunn **Trained** Carluke, S Lanarks

FOCUS
Race distance as advertised. A fair sprint handicap and an all-the-way winner who stepped up on even a better view of his recent form.

6094 KIER CONSTRUCTION H'CAP 1m 4f 100y
5:50 (5:50) (Class 6) (0-65,61) 3-Y-O **£2,587** (£770; £384; £192) **Stalls** Low

Form RPR
1 **Invernata (FR)**[17] 5533 3-9-7 **61** BenCurtis 4 71+
(John James Feane, Ire) *hld up: gd hdwy 3f out: pushed along to ld over 2f out: rdn and edgd rt over 1f out: kpt on wl to go clr fnl 110yds* **1/1**[1]

2220 **2** *5* **Ryan The Giant**[2] 6029 3-8-10 **50** (p) TomEaves 2 51
(Keith Dalgleish) *led: briefly pushed along over 9f out: rdn whn hdd over 2f out: short of room on rail and swtchd lft over 1f out: briefly rallied to chse wnr: one pce ins fnl f* **5/2**[2]

006 **3** *3* **King Julien (IRE)**[42] 4597 3-9-1 **55** (b[1]) PhillipMakin 1 51
(John Ryan) *in tch on outer: hdwy over 3f out: rdn to chal over 2f out: wknd ins fnl f* **18/1**

0054 **4** *1/2* **Magical Lasso (IRE)**[3] 6004 3-8-8 **53** (p) ShirleyTeasdale(5) 3 48
(Keith Dalgleish) *trckd ldrs: rdn 3f out: wknd fnl f* **6/1**[3]

00-0 **5** *65* **Baileys Galaxy (FR)**[18] 5478 3-9-6 **60** JoeFanning 5
(Mark Johnston) *prom: rdn over 3f out: wknd qckly: eased and t.o* **9/1**

2m 44.12s (2.12) **Going Correction** -0.10s/f (Good) **5** Ran SP% **108.1**
Speed ratings (Par 99): **88,84,82,82,39**
CSF £3.53 TOTE £1.90: £1.30, £1.30; EX 3.50 Trifecta £25.10.
Owner Mrs A G Kavanagh **Bred** Philippe Brosset **Trained** Curragh, Co Kildare

FOCUS
Race distance increased by 14yds. A modest handicap and not the strongest for the grade

6095 ST ANDREWS TIMBER H'CAP 1m
6:20 (6:20) (Class 5) (0-70,73) 3-Y-O+ **£3,234** (£962; £481; £240) **Stalls** Low

Form RPR
0024 **1** **Zeshov (IRE)**[10] 5753 5-9-7 **65** BarryMcHugh 1 73
(Rebecca Bastiman) *dwlt: sn midfield: hdwy 3f out: led gng wl 2f out: pushed along in narrow ld over 1f out: rdn ins fnl f: all out* **10/1**

52-2 **2** *hd* **Playtothewhistle**[28] 5114 5-9-3 **61** [1] ConnorBeasley 3 68
(Bryan Smart) *in tch: pushed along and hdwy 3f out: rdn to chal 2f out: kpt on: a jst hld* **11/4**[1]

0053 **3** *5* **Alans Pride (IRE)**[11] 5729 4-8-10 **54** oh2 (b) BenCurtis 8 50
(Michael Dods) *led: 5 l clr 5f out: reduced advantage 3f out: rdn whn hdd 2 out: wknd fnl f* **15/2**

4061 **4** *hd* **Almuhalab**[28] 5114 5-9-2 **60** (p) TomEaves 6 55
(Ruth Carr) *in tch towards outer: hdwy 3f out: rdn to chse ldrs 2f out: wknd fnl f* **9/2**[3]

3340 **5** *3 3/4* **Charles De Mille**[28] 5114 8-8-9 **58** JoshDoyle(5) 4 44
(Jedd O'Keeffe) *hld up: drvn over 2f out: nvr threatened* **14/1**

3102 **6** *2* **Whitkirk**[24] 5273 3-9-2 **65** JackGarritty 7 46
(Jedd O'Keeffe) *hld up: nvr threatened* **3/1**[2]

042 **7** *21* **Zamindo**[25] 5233 3-8-9 **58** JoeFanning 2
(Mark Johnston) *chsd clr ldr: rdn over 3f out: sn wknd* **9/1**

402- **8** *8* **Drago (IRE)**[311] 7542 4-9-10 **68** PhillipMakin 5
(David O'Meara) *tk str hold in midfield: pushed along over 3f out: sn wknd and bhd* **20/1**

1m 39.91s (-1.29) **Going Correction** -0.10s/f (Good)
WFA 3 from 4yo+ 5lb **8** Ran SP% **112.1**
Speed ratings (Par 103): **102,101,96,96,92 90,69,61**
CSF £36.28 CT £220.21 TOTE £11.50: £3.30, £1.10, £2.90; EX 36.80 Trifecta £255.90.
Owner Mrs P Bastiman **Bred** Rathbarry Stud **Trained** Cowthorpe, N Yorks

FOCUS
Race distance increased by 14yds. A modest handicap, in which the two principals pulled clear of the rest. They're rated up a bit on their recent best.

6096 EBF STALLIONS BREEDING WINNERS FILLIES' H'CAP 7f 30y
6:50 (6:51) (Class 3) (0-90,86) 3-Y-O+ **£9,703** (£2,887; £1,443; £721) **Stalls** Low

Form RPR
0520 **1** **Invoke (IRE)**[20] 5419 5-9-10 **86** PhillipMakin 2 95
(Keith Dalgleish) *mde all: sn pressed for ld but clr of rest: rdn 2f out: kpt on wl* **3/1**[3]

0000 **2** *2 3/4* **Alexandrakollontai (IRE)**[7] 5836 6-9-5 **81** (b) ConnorBeasley 5 82
(Alistair Whillans) *s.i.s: hld up in rr: rdn over 3f out: kpt on fr over 1f out: wnt 2nd ins fnl f: no threat wnr* **13/2**

2110 **3** *1 3/4* **Hawatif (IRE)**[15] 5588 3-9-6 **86** JoeFanning 4 80
(Mark Johnston) *hld up: rdn over 3f out: clsr over 2f out: one pce fr over 1f out* **9/4**[1]

3023 **4** *2 1/2* **Rose Marmara**[11] 5730 3-9-1 **81** (t) BarryMcHugh 1 68
(Brian Rothwell) *dwlt: sn chsd clr ldng pair: rdn over 2f out: wknd fnl f* **9/1**

1643 **5** *hd* **Florenza**[15] 5588 3-9-1 **81** AndrewElliott 3 68
(Chris Fairhurst) *racd keenly: pressed ldr on outer: rdn over 3f out: wknd over 1f out* **5/2**[2]

1m 28.4s (-0.60) **Going Correction** -0.10s/f (Good)
WFA 3 from 5yo+ 4lb **5** Ran SP% **107.7**
Speed ratings (Par 104): **99,95,93,91,90**
CSF £20.02 TOTE £3.20: £1.20, £3.20; EX 20.30 Trifecta £85.70.
Owner Michael Beaumont **Bred** J C Bloodstock **Trained** Carluke, S Lanarks

FOCUS
Race distance increased by 14yds. A decent handicap run at a good pace. The winner is rated similarly to when winning this last year.

6097 REALM CONSTRUCTION H'CAP 1m 6f
7:20 (7:20) (Class 5) (0-70,75) 4-Y-O+ **£3,234** (£962; £481; £240) **Stalls** Low

Form RPR
0051 **1** **Wor Lass**[4] 5970 8-9-8 **75** 6ex GarryWhillans(5) 4 88
(Susan Corbett) *in tch: hdwy 3f out: led gng wl over 2f out: pushed clr over 1f out: easily* **5/2**[2]

2114 **2** *8* **Neuf Des Coeurs**[9] 5783 5-9-6 **68** (p) PhillipMakin 1 70
(Iain Jardine) *hld up: rdn and hdwy to chse ldr 2f out: one pce and sn no ch wnr* **15/8**[1]

1434 **3** *5* **Midnight Warrior**[9] 5758 6-8-9 **57** BarryMcHugh 6 52
(Ron Barr) *trckd ldr: rdn to ld 3f out: hdd over 2f out: wknd over 1f out* **3/1**[3]

0/5- **4** *10* **Maraweh (IRE)**[38] 1198 6-9-7 **69** (p) JoeFanning 2 50
(Lucinda Russell) *in tch: lost pl and dropped to rr over 4f out: rdn over 3f out: sn btn* **11/2**

5000 **5** *5* **Danzella**[17] 5522 4-8-2 **50** oh5 (v) DuranFentiman 5 24
(Chris Fairhurst) *led: rdn whn hdd 3f out: sn wknd* **20/1**

3m 2.69s (-2.61) **Going Correction** -0.10s/f (Good) **5** Ran SP% **108.5**
Speed ratings (Par 103): **103,98,95,89,87**
CSF £7.36 TOTE £2.40: £1.50, £1.70; EX 8.50 Trifecta £17.50.
Owner Les Dodds **Bred** L Dodds **Trained** Otterburn, Northumberland

FOCUS
Race distance increased by 14yds. A modest staying handicap, in which a bang in-form mare won as she pleased. The winner is rated better than ever.

6098 JM ARCHITECTS H'CAP 5f
7:50 (7:50) (Class 6) (0-60,64) 3-Y-O+ **£2,587** (£770; £384; £192) **Stalls** High

Form RPR
4123 **1** **Thornaby Princess**[8] 5804 5-8-11 **50** (p) RoystonFfrench 4 56
(Colin Teague) *prom: rdn 2f out: rdn over 1f out: led towards fin* **11/2**

0451 **2** *nk* **See Vermont**[8] 5804 8-9-6 **64** 6ex (p) RowanScott(5) 3 69
(Rebecca Bastiman) *sn pushed along to chse ldrs: rdn 1/2-way: led appr fnl f: kpt on but hdd towards fin* **8/1**

0040 **3** *nse* **Jazz Legend (USA)**[9] 5769 3-9-6 **60** [1] PhillipMakin 2 65
(Robert Cowell) *chsd ldrs on outside: rdn 2f out: kpt on wl fnl f* **18/1**

0042 **4** *1 3/4* **Sea Of Green**[8] 5804 4-8-8 **47** BarryMcHugh 10 46
(Jim Goldie) *hld up: pushed along 1/2-way: rdn and sme hdwy over 1f out: kpt on ins fnl f: nrst fin* **9/2**[2]

4024 **5** *1 3/4* **Zebelini (IRE)**[21] 5378 4-8-5 **51** (b) RobertDodsworth(7) 8 43
(Ollie Pears) *led narrowly: rdn 1/2-way: hdd appr fnl f: hung rt and wknd ins fnl f* **11/1**

0643 **6** *1* **Mystical King**[3] 6003 6-8-9 **48** oh1 ow2 TomEaves 5 37
(Linda Perratt) *dwlt: hld up: rdn 1/2-way: nvr threatened ldrs* **20/1**

0002 **7** *2* **Windforpower (IRE)**[9] 5760 6-9-5 **58** (p) JoeFanning 9 39
(Tracy Waggott) *chsd ldrs: rdn 1/2-way: lost pl whn short of room appr fnl f: wknd* **5/1**[3]

0043 **8** *3/4* **Lorimer's Lot (IRE)**[45] 4492 5-8-12 **51** (p) JasonHart 1 30
(Mark Walford) *v.s.a: a towards rr* **10/1**

0002 **9** *nse* **Wotnot (IRE)**[26] 5200 4-9-5 **58** (v[1]) ConnorBeasley 6 40
(Bryan Smart) *pressed ldr: rdn 1/2-way: jst lost pl whn hmpd appr fnl f: sn wknd* **7/2**[1]

6-30 **10** *1 1/2* **Cheeni**[45] 4492 4-8-2 **46** oh1 ShirleyTeasdale(5) 7 19
(Jim Goldie) *dwlt: sn midfield: rdn 2f out: wknd fnl f* **33/1**

59.84s (-0.56) **Going Correction** -0.10s/f (Good)
WFA 3 from 4yo+ 1lb **10** Ran SP% **114.0**
Speed ratings (Par 101): **100,99,99,96,93 92,89,87,87,85**
CSF £47.79 CT £548.69 TOTE £7.80: £2.60, £2.50, £5.80; EX 52.10 Trifecta £489.50.
Owner Dave Scott **Bred** Dave Scott **Trained** Station Town, Co Durham

FOCUS
Race distance as advertised. A modest sprint handicap, in which the pace held up.
T/Plt: £46.50 to a £1 stake. Pool: £44,101.39 - 690.90 winning tickets T/Qpdt: £14.20 to a £1 stake. Pool: £4,747.92 - 246.78 winning tickets **Andrew Sheret**

5966 NEWCASTLE (A.W) (L-H)
Friday, September 2

OFFICIAL GOING: Tapeta: standard
Wind: fresh 1/2 against Weather: Fine

6099 WATERAID/BRITISH STALLION STUDS EBF MAIDEN STKS 6f (Tp)
1:50 (1:50) (Class 5) 2-Y-O **£3,881** (£1,155; £577; £288) **Stalls** Centre

Form RPR
0 **1** **Haworth**[18] 5476 2-9-5 0 PJMcDonald 8 71
(James Bethell) *hld up in mid-div: hdwy over 2f out: led last 150yds: drvn out* **33/1**

00 **2** *1/2* **Hotfill**[37] 4765 2-9-5 0 SamJames 7 70
(David Barron) *hld up in rr: hdwy over 1f out: styd on to take 2nd fnl strides* **50/1**

65 **3** *nk* **Fareeq**[18] 5477 2-9-5 0 GrahamGibbons 2 69
(William Haggas) *sn w ldrs: drvn over 2f out: kpt on same pce last 50yds* **9/2**[2]

2 **4** *hd* **Voice Of Truth (IRE)**[49] 4357 2-9-0 0 KevinStott 3 63
(Saeed bin Suroor) *w ldrs: led over 1f out: hdd and no ex last 150yds* **1/5**[1]

5 *2* **The Bard's Advice** 2-9-0 0 GrahamLee 1 57
(Keith Dalgleish) *hld up in mid-div: hdwy over 2f out: chsng ldrs over 1f out: fdd last 100yds* **14/1**

54 **6** ¾ **Angel Palanas**[18] 5476 2-9-5 0 DougieCostello 4 60
(K R Burke) *w ldrs: led over 2f out: hdd over 1f out: edgd rt and wknd last 150yds* **6/1**[3]
0 **7** 1½ **Oh So Dandy (IRE)**[29] 5077 2-9-5 0 MartinLane 5 56
(Derek Shaw) *mid-div: effrt over 2f out: wknd over 1f out* **100/1**
0 **8** 3¼ **Bodacious Name (IRE)**[11] 5728 2-9-5 0 CamHardie 6 46
(John Quinn) *rr-div: drvn over 2f out: lost pl over 1f out* **25/1**
0 **9** 4 **Yelow Bird**[19] 5433 2-9-5 0 ConnorBeasley 9 34
(Chris Grant) *led tl over 2f out: lost pl over 1f out* **100/1**
1m 15.24s (2.74) **Going Correction** +0.30s/f (Slow) **9** Ran SP% **133.2**
Speed ratings (Par 95): **93,92,91,91,89 88,86,81,76**
CSF £1066.13 TOTE £44.70: £4.90, £7.80, £1.50; EX 534.40 Trifecta £3259.20.
Owner Clarendon Thoroughbred Racing **Bred** R Kitching, H Mayer, M Pennell **Trained** Middleham Moor, N Yorks
FOCUS
Race distances as advertised. An uncompetitive maiden and a complete boil over, with the long odds-on favourite not even being placed. With that in mind it remains to be seen how strong the form is, but take nothing away from the winner.

6100 NORTHUMBRIAN WATER H'CAP 6f (Tp)
2:20 (2:21) (Class 6) (0-55,55) 3-Y-O+ **£3,234** (£962; £481; £240) **Stalls** Centre

Form RPR
524 **1** **Intense Starlet (IRE)**[21] 5368 5-9-6 **54** (p) SamJames 11 63
(Marjorie Fife) *mid-div: hmpd after 1f: hdwy over 2f out: styd on fnl f: led fnl strides* **7/1**
0000 **2** ½ **Reflation**[3] 6008 4-9-2 **50** (p) ConnorBeasley 4 58
(Michael Dods) *in rr:hdwy over 2f out: styd on to ld fnl 50yds: hdd fnl strides* **14/1**
0256 **3** ½ **Frangarry (IRE)**[22] 5335 4-9-6 **54** (b) GrahamGibbons 8 60
(Alan Bailey) *s.i.s: hdwy over 2f out: led briefly last 100yds: no ex* **12/1**
3000 **4** ½ **Jebel Tara**[11] 5714 11-9-7 **55** (bt) DaleSwift 7 60+
(Alistair Whillans) *led: hdd last 100yds: kpt on same pce* **12/1**
650 **5** ½ **Tell The Stars**[25] 5248 3-9-2 **52** KevinStott 2 55
(Ollie Pears) *w ldrs: hung lft over 2f out: racd far side: kpt on same pce last 100yds* **66/1**
0400 **6** 1 **George Bailey (IRE)**[6] 5889 4-8-13 **47** BarryMcHugh 10 48
(Suzzanne France) *in rr: nt clr run over 1f out: swtchd rt: styd on fnl 200yds* **66/1**
3623 **7** 1½ **Bogsnog (IRE)**[24] 5277 6-9-6 **54** TonyHamilton 13 50
(Kristin Stubbs) *w ldrs: hung lft and wknd fnl 150yds* **13/2**
0053 **8** 2½ **Sakhee's Rose**[11] 5706 6-9-6 **54** (b) GrahamLee 3 42
(Ed McMahon) *trckd ldrs: wknd appr fnl f* **9/1**
5655 **9** hd **Goninodaethat**[7] 5839 8-9-2 **55** AdamMcNamara[(5)] 6 42
(Jim Goldie) *w ldr: wknd fnl f* **16/1**
2012 **10** 2¼ **Someone Exciting**[6] 5889 3-9-4 **54** PatrickMathers 5 35
(David Thompson) *chsd ldrs: drvn over 2f out: wknd over 1f out* **11/2**[2]
0604 **11** nk **Our Place In Loule**[21] 5370 3-9-2 **52** JoeyHaynes 9 32
(Noel Wilson) *in rr: t.k.h: drvn and hdwy over 2f out: lost pl over 1f out* **25/1**
6040 **12** 1 **Stormy Art (IRE)**[8] 5803 3-9-0 **50** (b[1]) AndrewMullen 14 27
(Michael Dods) *trckd ldrs: t.k.h: wknd over 1f out* **20/1**
5060 **13** shd **Grandad Chunk (IRE)**[9] 5760 5-9-4 **52** DougieCostello 1 28
(Colin Teague) *chsd ldeers: lost pl over 1f out* **6/1**[3]
5642 **14** 11 **Decisive (IRE)**[13] 5636 4-9-7 **55** (t) LukeMorris 12
(Anthony Carson) *in rr: hmpd after 1f: drvn 3f out: sn bhd: eased over 1f out* **5/1**[1]
1m 14.05s (1.55) **Going Correction** +0.30s/f (Slow)
WFA 3 from 4yo+ 2lb **14** Ran SP% **121.7**
Speed ratings (Par 101): **101,100,99,99,98 97,95,91,91,88 88,86,86,71**
CSF £99.08 CT £1195.41 TOTE £9.00: £3.10, £5.70, £4.40; EX 155.90 Trifecta £1794.40.
Owner R W Fife **Bred** Des O'Sullivan **Trained** Stillington, N Yorks
FOCUS
A moderate 46-55 handicap and not much covering the first five at the line.

6101 FASTFLOW PIPELINE SERVICES LTD MAIDEN STKS 5f (Tp)
2:55 (2:56) (Class 5) 3-Y-O+ **£3,881** (£1,155; £577; £288) **Stalls** Centre

Form RPR
5/ **1** **Lotara**[872] 1482 4-8-10 0 AdamMcNamara[(5)] 2 63
(Jim Goldie) *hld up in rr: hdwy over 1f out: kpt on to ld last 75yds* **9/1**
4-40 **2** 1 **Shine Likeadiamond**[7] 5826 3-9-0 65 TonyHamilton 5 59
(Mick Channon) *trckd ldng pair: led 1f out: hdd and no ex last 75yds* **3/1**[2]
00 **3** ½ **Cool Angel (IRE)**[67] 3720 3-9-0 0 (b[1]) DougieCostello 4 57
(William Muir) *s.i.s: hld up in rr: hdwy over 1f out: kpt on to take 3rd last 75yds* **16/1**
26-0 **4** 1 **Lilvanita (IRE)**[23] 5295 3-8-9 64 CallumShepherd[(5)] 3 54
(Brian Ellison) *chsd ldrs: outpcd over 3f out: hdwy over 1f out: kpt on to take 4th nr fin* **13/2**
2-40 **5** ¾ **Redalani (IRE)**[22] 5320 6-9-1 49 (b) GrahamGibbons 6 51
(Alan Brown) *led: hdd 1f out: fdd clsng stages* **9/2**[3]
500 **6** 1½ **The Cheese Gang**[27] 5178 4-9-6 45 [1] JoeyHaynes 1 51?
(Susan Corbett) *mid-div: drvn and outpcd over 2f out: kpt on to chse ldrs over 1f out: wknd clsng stages* **16/1**
25 **7** 4½ **Corridor Kid (IRE)**[6] 5862 3-9-5 75 (v[1]) MartinLane 7 34
(Derek Shaw) *w ldr: wknd qckly fnl f* **15/8**[1]
1m 1.39s (1.89) **Going Correction** +0.30s/f (Slow)
WFA 3 from 4yo+ 1lb **7** Ran SP% **113.1**
Speed ratings (Par 103): **96,94,93,92,90 88,81**
CSF £35.29 TOTE £10.00: £5.50, £1.80; EX 37.60 Trifecta £468.30.
Owner Mrs Lucille Bone **Bred** Triple H Stud Ltd **Trained** Uplawmoor, E Renfrews
FOCUS
A weak maiden in which the favourite ran badly.

6102 GOWLAND & DAWSON H'CAP 2m 56y (Tp)
3:30 (3:32) (Class 6) (0-60,61) 3-Y-O+ **£3,234** (£962; £481; £240) **Stalls** Low

Form RPR
6541 **1** **Masterson (IRE)**[9] 5777 3-9-4 **61** 6ex TonyHamilton 12 68
(Mick Channon) *hld up in mid-div: hdwy over 3f out: styd on to ld 1f out: drvn out* **8/1**[3]
5565 **2** 2 **Judith Gardenier**[9] 5783 4-9-1 **45** (p) JasonHart 7 50
(Iain Jardine) *in rr: effrt over 3f out: 3rd last 100yds: 2nd post* **14/1**
4156 **3** hd **Tyrannical**[67] 3715 3-8-10 **53** LukeMorris 9 58
(Sir Mark Prescott Bt) *trckd ldrs: pushed along over 3f out: led briefly appr fnl f: kpt on same pce* **6/4**[1]
3631 **4** ½ **Question Of Faith**[11] 5726 5-9-3 **52** 6ex AdamMcNamara[(5)] 6 56
(Martin Todhunter) *s.s: in rr: hdwy over 2f out: hung lft and kpt on one pce fnl f* **4/1**[2]
0100 **5** 3 **Byronegetonefree**[41] 4645 5-9-6 **50** PatrickMathers 10 51
(Stuart Coltherd) *dwlt: in rr: hdwy on outer 6f out: chsng ldrs over 4f out: led over 2f out: hdd appr fnl f: wknd last 75yds* **20/1**
5635 **6** ¾ **No Not Yet**[27] 5155 4-9-1 **45** AndrewMullen 2 45
(Michael Dods) *hld up in rr: effrt 3f out: chsng ldrs and hung lft over 1f out: one pce* **18/1**
2024 **7** hd **Impeccability**[22] 5319 6-9-3 **47** (p) RoystonFfrench 5 46
(John Mackie) *trckd ldrs: one pce whn nt clr run over 1f out* **28/1**
0016 **8** 3½ **Lightning Steps**[17] 5522 4-9-8 **52** GrahamGibbons 13 47
(Declan Carroll) *t.k.h: trckd ldrs: wknd over 1f out* **12/1**
0/00 **9** ¾ **Hundred Acre Wood**[9] 5783 6-8-10 **45** (t) PhilDennis[(5)] 8 39
(Sandy Thomson) *mid-didivsion: hdwy 4f out: wknd over 1f out* **100/1**
0055 **10** nk **Yorkshireman (IRE)**[19] 5435 6-9-1 **45** (b) AndrewElliott 1 39
(Lynn Siddall) *in rr: drvn over 3f out: nvr on terms* **14/1**
1000 **11** 4 **Desktop**[41] 4645 4-10-0 **58** PJMcDonald 3 47
(Antony Brittain) *led 1f: chsd ldrs: led over 3f out: hdd over 2f out: wknd over 1f out: eased clsng stages* **10/1**
365/ **12** 2½ **Nay Secret**[650] 7893 8-9-4 **48** JackGarritty 4 34
(Jim Goldie) *hld up in mid-div: drvn 3f out: wknd over 1f out: eased clsng stages* **28/1**
-000 **13** 82 **Tinseltown**[14] 5607 10-8-10 **45** (p) MeganNicholls[(5)] 11
(Harriet Bethell) *led after 1f: hdd over 3f out: sn lost pl: t.o whn eased over 1f out: eventually completed* **66/1**
3m 38.18s (2.98) **Going Correction** +0.125s/f (Slow)
WFA 3 from 4yo+ 13lb **13** Ran SP% **120.6**
Speed ratings (Par 101): **97,96,95,95,94 93,93,91,91,91 89,88,47**
CSF £109.72 CT £261.04 TOTE £8.00: £2.50, £3.70, £1.20; EX 139.90 Trifecta £614.10.
Owner Box 41 Racing **Bred** Star Pointe Ltd **Trained** West Ilsley, Berks
FOCUS
A moderate staying handicap, but a fair pace thanks to the runaway leader.

6103 ESH CONSTRUCTION H'CAP 1m 4f 98y (Tp)
4:05 (4:09) (Class 6) (0-65,63) 3-Y-O+ **£3,234** (£962; £481; £240) **Stalls** High

Form RPR
4126 **1** **Falcon's Fire (IRE)**[34] 4875 3-9-2 **62** GrahamGibbons 4 74
(Keith Dalgleish) *mid-div: qcknd to ld appr fnl 2f: edgd lft over 1f out: abt 5 l clr whn eased clsng stages* **9/2**[3]
6004 **2** 2¼ **Esspeegee**[13] 5630 3-8-3 **49** oh2 [1] LukeMorris 1 52
(Alan Bailey) *trckd clr ldr: drvn over 3f out: 2nd 1f out: kpt on same pce: no ch w wnr* **9/1**
5620 **3** nk **Rockabilly Riot (IRE)**[9] 5758 6-9-3 **59** (v[1]) AdamMcNamara[(5)] 8 62
(Martin Todhunter) *in rr: drvn 5f out: hdwy over 3f out: 2nd 3f out: kpt on same pce over 1f out* **10/1**
5606 **4** 2¾ **Mcvicar**[4] 5971 7-9-9 **60** (p) GrahamLee 3 59
(John Davies) *rr-div: drvn 5f out: hdwy over 2f out: one pce* **11/1**
1264 **5** nse **Nonagon**[29] 5065 5-9-11 **62** (t) CamHardie 5 60
(Wilf Storey) *s.i.s: in rr: drvn 5f out: sme hdwy over 2f out: one pce* **16/1**
5652 **6** shd **Northside Prince (IRE)**[7] 5842 10-9-7 **63** MeganNicholls[(5)] 9 61
(Alan Swinbank) *sn mid-div: hdwy over 2f out: outpcd over 2f out: kpt on fnl f* **4/1**[2]
P-40 **7** 30 **Piper Bill**[32] 4935 5-8-7 **49** oh4 RowanScott[(5)] 2
(Jim Goldie) *chsd clr ldr: drvn over 3f out: lost pl over 1f out: sn bhd: t.o* **100/1**
5411 **8** 8 **Miningrocks (FR)**[6] 5868 4-9-4 **62** GerO'Neill[(7)] 6 +
(Declan Carroll) *t.k.h: led: wnt clr 7f out: wknd qckly and hdd appr fnl 2f: bhd whn eased appr fnl f: sn t.o: virtually p.u* **7/4**[1]
2m 41.36s (0.26) **Going Correction** +0.125s/f (Slow)
WFA 3 from 4yo+ 9lb **8** Ran SP% **108.8**
Speed ratings (Par 101): **104,102,102,100,100 100,80,75**
CSF £39.30 CT £325.64 TOTE £5.10: £1.50, £2.30, £2.80; EX 26.00 Trifecta £367.50.
Owner Ronnie Docherty **Bred** Patrick Headon **Trained** Carluke, S Lanarks
■ Silva Samourai was withdrawn. Price at time of withdrawal 14-1. Rule 4 applies to all bets - deduction 5p in the pound.
FOCUS
A modest middle-distance handicap notable for the favourite virtually bolting.

6104 STONBURY MAIDEN STKS 1m 5y (Tp)
4:35 (4:39) (Class 5) 3-Y-O+ **£3,881** (£1,155; £577; £288) **Stalls** Centre

Form RPR
6333 **1** **Lord Of The North (IRE)**[7] 5850 3-9-5 79 LukeMorris 3 79
(Gay Kelleway) *hld up in mid-div: effrt and edgd lft over 1f out: styd on to ld last 75yds: drvn out* **4/1**[3]
06 **2** 1¼ **Enmeshing**[35] 4840 3-9-5 0 DanielMuscutt 5 76+
(James Fanshawe) *trckd ldrs: effrt 2f out: edgd lft fnl 150yds: kpt on: tk 2nd post* **4/1**[3]
5 **3** shd **Westward Ho (IRE)**[34] 4895 3-9-5 0 PJMcDonald 1 76
(James Bethell) *hld up in rr: hdwy to chse ldrs over 2f out: led appr fnl f: hdd and no ex last 75yds* **8/1**
4 3 **Selection (FR)** 3-9-5 0 GrahamGibbons 2 69
(William Haggas) *sn trcking ldrs: pushed along over 3f out: led narrowly over 2f out: hdd appr fnl f: keeping on same pce whn n.m.r 100yds out: eased: will improve* **15/8**[1]
40 **5** 1½ **Ajman Prince (IRE)**[11] 5716 3-9-0 0 RowanScott[(5)] 7 65
(Alistair Whillans) *hld up in rr-div: effrt over 2f out: kpt on one pce fnl f* **100/1**
5-6 **6** ½ **Alfahad (IRE)**[119] 2008 3-9-5 0 GrahamLee 8 64
(Ed Dunlop) *trckd ldrs: t.k.h: upsides over 2f out: wknd fnl f* **3/1**[2]
6-4 **7** 5 **Three Times A Lord**[76] 3400 4-9-3 0 RPWalsh[(7)] 11 53
(Ivan Furtado) *led after 1f: hdd over 2f out: edgd lft and wknd over 1f out* **25/1**
05 **8** ½ **Bilko's Back (IRE)**[21] 5366 4-9-10 0 [1] JoeyHaynes 4 52?
(Susan Corbett) *t.k.h in rr: drvn over 3f out: lost pl over 2f out* **150/1**
9 8 **Clear Leader (USA)** 3-9-5 0 DougieCostello 9 31
(Micky Hammond) *led 1f: chsd ldrs: lost pl over 1f out: bhd whn eased clsng stages* **40/1**
10 1¼ **Clarabel** 3-9-0 0 CamHardie 6 23
(Garry Moss) *dwlt: in rr: reminders over 3f out: lost pl over 2f out: bhd whn eased clsng stages* **50/1**
1m 41.17s (2.57) **Going Correction** +0.30s/f (Slow)
WFA 3 from 4yo 5lb **10** Ran SP% **120.8**
Speed ratings (Par 103): **99,97,97,94,93 92,87,87,79,77**
CSF £20.79 TOTE £4.80: £1.60, £1.60, £3.10; EX 23.30 Trifecta £149.90.
Owner Ben Parish **Bred** J Kenny **Trained** Exning, Suffolk

FOCUS
An ordinary maiden won by the most experienced runner in the race. He's rated to form.

6105 MMB H'CAP (DIV I) 7f 14y (Tp)
5:05 (5:09) (Class 6) (0-60,60) 3-Y-O+ £3,234 (£962; £481; £240) Stalls Centre

Form RPR
6060 1 **Cool Strutter (IRE)**[21] 5368 4-9-8 **58**...............(b) SamJames 4 65
(Karen Tutty) *stdd s: hld up in rr: hdwy over 2f out: 2nd appr fnl f: kpt on to ld last 75yds* **12/1**

4360 2 ½ **Munjally**[7] 5835 5-9-5 **55**...............(b[1]) DougieCostello 6 61
(Patrick Holmes) *hld up in mid-div: hdwy over 2f out: led over 1f out: hung rt: hdd and no ex last 75yds* **11/2**[1]

0-50 3 3 **Cheeco**[148] 1295 4-8-10 **46** oh1............... LukeMorris 7 45
(Ruth Carr) *mid-div: sn pushed along: hdwy over 2f out: 3rd last 200yds: kpt on one pce* **25/1**

6000 4 1 **Thiepval**[51] 4260 4-8-7 **46** oh1............... ShelleyBirkett[(3)] 13 43
(Jason Ward) *hld up in rr: effrt and nt clr run over 2f out: 4th 1f out: one pce* **33/1**

4444 5 2¼ **Emerald Asset (IRE)**[21] 5369 3-9-0 **54**............... CamHardie 14 43
(Paul Midgley) *mid-div: effrt over 2f out: nt clr run over 1f out: kpt on* **7/1**[2]

-666 6 hd **Man Of La Mancha (IRE)**[15] 5578 3-8-8 **48**...............[1] KevinStott 12 37
(Ben Haslam) *in rr: hdwy over 2f out: chsng ldrs over 1f out: one pce* **11/2**[1]

4-00 7 4 **Clouded Gold**[49] 4370 4-8-10 **46**............... AndrewMullen 10 28
(Michael Appleby) *trckd ldrs: upsides over 1f out: sn wknd* **10/1**

3400 8 2¾ **Whispering Wolf**[29] 5069 3-8-7 **47**............... RoystonFfrench 3 20
(Suzzanne France) *trckd ldrs: drvn over 3f out: wknd appr fnl f* **28/1**

5050 9 ¾ **Steel Stockholder**[39] 4715 10-9-4 **54**............... PJMcDonald 8 28
(Antony Brittain) *ldrs: wknd over 1f out* **7/1**[2]

3520 10 9 **Ettie Hart (IRE)**[22] 5338 3-9-2 **56**............... TonyHamilton 11 7
(Mick Channon) *led: hdd over 1f out: sn wknd: eased clsng stages* **9/1**

3404 11 3½ **Riponian**[46] 4444 6-8-11 **47**...............(t) JoeyHaynes 1
(Susan Corbett) *ldrs: drvn 4f out: lost pl 2f out: sn bhd* **8/1**[3]

3050 12 nk **Miramonte Dancer (IRE)**[11] 5732 3-9-1 **60**......(v[1]) CallumShepherd[(5)] 2 2
(David C Griffiths) *ldrs: wknd and heavily eased over 1f out: sn bhd* **7/1**[2]

4000 13 4½ **My Time**[28] 5127 7-8-7 **46**...............(p[1]) TimClark[(3)] 9
(Michael Mullineaux) *in rr: sn drvn along: reminders ovcer 2f out: sn bhd* **50/1**

1000 14 12 **King's Currency**[5] 5920 3-9-4 **58**...............(b[1]) GrahamLee 5
(Jedd O'Keeffe) *ldrs: t.k.h: reminders over 3f out: hung rt and lost pl over 1f out: sn bhd: eased* **16/1**

1m 27.19s (0.99) **Going Correction** +0.30s/f (Slow)
WFA 3 from 4yo+ 4lb **14** Ran SP% **124.2**
Speed ratings (Par 101): **106,105,102,100,98 98,93,90,89,79 75,74,69,56**
CSF £76.83 CT £1664.57 TOTE £17.30: £4.30, £2.10, £7.50; EX 105.30 Trifecta £3180.50.
Owner Mrs Mary Winetroube & Thoroughbred Homes **Bred** Tally-Ho Stud **Trained** Osmotherley, N Yorks

FOCUS
The first division of a moderate handicap, with several trying a new form of headgear, and a wide-open betting market.

6106 MMB H'CAP (DIV II) 7f 14y (Tp)
5:35 (5:37) (Class 6) (0-60,61) 3-Y-O+ £3,234 (£962; £481; £240) Stalls Centre

Form RPR
5461 1 **Fine Example**[8] 5803 3-9-7 **61** 6ex...............(b) KevinStott 1 70+
(Kevin Ryan) *w ldr: led after 2f: edgd rt over 1f out: styd on wl* **3/1**[1]

0000 2 2¼ **Centre Haafhd**[11] 5729 5-8-10 **51**...............(b) AdamMcNamara[(5)] 4 54
(Jim Goldie) *chsd ldrs: 2nd 1f out: kpt on same pce* **12/1**

0244 3 hd **New Abbey Angel (IRE)**[8] 5803 3-9-6 **60**...............(p) GrahamGibbons 2 60
(Keith Dalgleish) *mid-div: hdwy over 2f out: chsng ldrs oveer 1f out: kpt on same pce* **7/2**[2]

1200 4 shd **Moi Aussie**[17] 5515 3-9-5 **59**............... GrahamLee 6 59
(Ed McMahon) *led 2f: chsd ldrs: drvn over 2f out: kpt on same pce over 1f out* **9/1**

0060 5 1½ **Prince Of Time**[44] 4516 4-8-10 **46**............... AndrewMullen 10 44
(Richard Ford) *dwlt: hdwy over 2f out: one pce over 1f out* **20/1**

4033 6 shd **Coquine**[8] 5807 3-9-1 **58**............... ShelleyBirkett[(3)] 5 54
(David O'Meara) *hld up in rr: hdwy over 2f out: one pce over 1f out* **11/2**[3]

-660 7 ½ **Bigbadboy (IRE)**[31] 4972 3-8-10 **50**............... LukeMorris 7 45
(Clive Mulhall) *chsd ldrs: one pce over 1f out* **50/1**

3560 8 1¾ **Lord Rob**[11] 5715 5-8-10 **46** oh1...............[1] PatrickMathers 12 38
(David Thompson) *dwlt: t.k.h in rr: effrt and nt clr run over 1f out: kpt on fnl f* **7/1**

51-0 9 2 **Rock Of Monaco**[17] 5525 3-9-2 **56**............... PJMcDonald 8 40
(Antony Brittain) *in rr: effrt over 2f out: nvr a factor* **14/1**

6300 10 2¾ **Saxon Gold (IRE)**[35] 4844 3-8-13 **53**............... SamJames 9 30
(John Davies) *hld up in rr: effrt over 2f out: lost pl over 1f out* **16/1**

5/60 11 1 **Tom's Anna (IRE)**[21] 5355 6-8-4 **47**............... RhiainIngram[(7)] 13 23
(Sean Regan) *chsd ldrs: drvn ove r2 f out: lost pl over 1f out* **25/1**

0460 12 1 **Cape Crusader (IRE)**[29] 5069 3-8-3 **48**...............(b[1]) PhilDennis[(5)] 11 20
(Michael Dods) *hld up in rr: hdwy over 2f out: lost pl over 1f out* **25/1**

0060 13 8 **Outlaw Kate (IRE)**[4] 5953 4-8-10 **46** oh1...............(b) CamHardie 3
(Michael Mullineaux) *chsd ldrs: drvn over 2f out: lost pl over 1f out: eased whn bhd clsng stages* . **50/1**

1m 27.4s (1.20) **Going Correction** +0.30s/f (Slow)
WFA 3 from 4yo+ 4lb **13** Ran SP% **121.7**
Speed ratings (Par 101): **105,102,102,102,100 100,99,97,95,92 91,89,80**
CSF £38.66 CT £127.98 TOTE £3.90: £1.60, £4.80, £1.40; EX 49.80 Trifecta £321.50.
Owner Hambleton Racing Ltd XLIV **Bred** Mrs M E Slade **Trained** Hambleton, N Yorks

FOCUS
The pace looked ordinary in this division and the winning time was 0.21sec slower than the first leg. Not many got into it. Ordinary form but the winner looks progressive.

T/Plt: £3,172.50 to a £1 stake. Pool: £71,491.01 - 16.45 winning tickets T/Qpdt: £66.00 to a £1 stake. Pool: £8,017.71 - 89.81 winning tickets **Walter Glynn**

2844 FONTAINEBLEAU
Friday, September 2

OFFICIAL GOING: Turf: soft

6107a GRAND PRIX DE FONTAINEBLEAU (LISTED RACE) (4YO+ FILLIES & MARES) (TURF) 1m 2f
3:00 (3:00) 4-Y-O+ £17,647 (£7,058; £5,294; £3,529; £1,764)

RPR
1 **Meliora (IRE)**[54] 4-8-13 0............... EddyHardouin 8 94
(M G Mintchev, Germany) **62/1**

2 1 **Persona Grata**[21] 5384 5-8-13 0............... StephanePasquier 1 92
(Ed Walker) **12/5**[2]

3 ¾ **Rose Rized (GER)**[26] 5219 4-8-13 0............... UmbertoRispoli 2 91
(P Schiergen, Germany) **10/1**

4 ¾ **Rosy Blush**[29] 4-8-13 0............... MaximeGuyon 3 89
(Mme Pia Brandt, France) **11/2**[3]

5 hd **Lucy The Painter (IRE)**[13] 5645 4-8-13 0............... HarryBentley 5 89
(Ed de Giles) **71/10**

6 1½ **Havre De Paix (FR)**[118] 2026 4-8-13 0............... OlivierPeslier 7 86
(David Menuisier) **26/1**

7 snk **Belle Travers**[36] 4808 4-8-13 0............... TonyPiccone 6 85
(Richard Fahey) **35/1**

8 1¼ **Deauville Shower (IRE)**[40] 4696 5-8-13 0............... VincentCheminaud 9 83
(E Libaud, France) **10/1**

9 2 **Sagaciously (IRE)**[23] 5307 4-8-13 0............... AlexisBadel 10 79
(Ed Dunlop) **11/5**[1]

10 2 **Loaves And Fishes**[21] 5384 4-8-13 0............... GeraldMosse 11 75
(David O'Meara) **17/1**

2m 0.2s (120.20) **10** Ran SP% **120.2**
WIN (incl. 1 euro stake): 62.60. PLACES: 11.40, 1.70, 3.10. DF: 105.10. SF: 329.50.
Owner Litex Commerce Ad **Bred** Litex Commerce **Trained** Germany

6071 ASCOT (R-H)
Saturday, September 3

OFFICIAL GOING: Straight course - good to firm (good in places); round course - good (good to firm in places) changing to good after race 5 (4.10)
Wind: Moderate, half behind Weather: Cloudy, rain from race 4

6108 SODEXO BRITISH STALLION STUDS EBF MAIDEN STKS (PLUS 10 RACE) 7f
2:05 (2:07) (Class 4) 2-Y-O £6,469 (£1,925; £962; £481) Stalls High

Form RPR
1 **Frontispiece** 2-9-5 0............... RyanMoore 1 79+
(Sir Michael Stoute) *trckd ldrs: pushed along and outpcd by ldng trio 2f out: styd on fr over 1f out: rdn and r.o to ld last stride* **7/1**

2 nse **Make Time (IRE)** 2-9-5 0............... WilliamCarson 6 79+
(David Menuisier) *hld up in last: gd prog jst over 2f out: clsd on ldrs fnl f: led nr fin: jst pipped last stride* **50/1**

3 3 hd **Muhajjal**[22] 5356 2-9-5 0............... PaulHanagan 13 78
(Owen Burrows) *trckd ldng pair: rdn to chal 2f out: narrow ld 1f out: kpt on u.p but hdd nr fin* **9/4**[1]

622 4 ½ **Fortune Of War**[31] 5036 2-9-5 75............... PatCosgrave 2 77
(Jane Chapple-Hyam) *trckd ldr: led narrowly 2f out: sn rdn: hdd 1f out but styd pressing new ldr tl no ex nr fin* **10/1**

5 1 **Century Dream (IRE)** 2-9-5 0............... RobertHavlin 9 74
(Simon Crisford) *trckd ldrs: pushed along and outpcd 2f out: kpt on same pce after and nvr able to chal* **6/1**[3]

6 6 nk **Zebulon (IRE)**[113] 2204 2-9-5 0............... SeanLevey 3 73
(Richard Hannon) *led to 2f out: styd w ldr: stl upsides ins fnl f: wknd last 75yds* **20/1**

7 nk **Kasperenko** 2-9-5 0............... ShaneKelly 8 73+
(David Lanigan) *settled in rr: outpcd and pushed along over 2f out: styd on wl fr over 1f out: gng on at fin* **40/1**

8 3½ **Koeman** 2-9-5 0............... CharlesBishop 11 63
(Mick Channon) *in tch in midfield but pushed along by 1/2-way: outpcd over 2f out: no imp after* **25/1**

0 9 shd **Padrinho (IRE)**[22] 5356 2-9-5 0............... KierenFox 14 63
(John Best) *wl in rr: rdn over 2f out: nvr on terms but plugged on u.p* **100/1**

6 10 2½ **Abatement**[32] 4989 2-9-5 0............... WilliamTwiston-Davies 7 56
(Roger Charlton) *hld up in rr: sme prog 2f out: no hdwy over 1f out* **7/1**

11 2 **See The Master (IRE)** 2-9-5 0............... AdamKirby 15 51
(Clive Cox) *wl in tch: shkn up 3f out: sn lost pl: btn 2f out* **9/2**[2]

12 6 **Epicurious (IRE)** 2-9-5 0............... MartinDwyer 5 35
(Brian Meehan) *dwlt: in tch in rr to over 2f out: wknd* **16/1**

13 22 **Socrates** 2-9-5 0............... LukeMorris 4
(Daniel Kubler) *dwlt: in tch to 3f out: wknd qckly: t.o* **66/1**

1m 29.06s (1.46) **Going Correction** +0.10s/f (Good) **13** Ran SP% **118.7**
Speed ratings (Par 97): **95,94,94,94,93 92,92,88,88,85 83,76,51**
CSF £332.11 TOTE £6.30: £2.50, £10.80, £1.30; EX 214.90 Trifecta £4294.80.
Owner The Queen **Bred** The Queen **Trained** Newmarket, Suffolk

FOCUS
The rail on the round course was positioned 3yds out from its innermost position from the 1m4f start increasing to 14yds out at the home straight. Increasing distances by approximately the following: Old Mile: 17yds 1m 4f & 1m 2f: 21yds. The straight course was divided in two with a rail in the middle of the course; the stands' side was used. This probably was a fair 2yo maiden, but it produced a bunched finish. Nice starts from the first two.

6109 ALBERT BARTLETT H'CAP 7f
2:40 (2:41) (Class 2) 3-Y-O+
£49,800 (£14,912; £7,456; £3,728; £1,864; £936) Stalls High

Form RPR
2113 1 **Dutch Law**[22] 5376 4-8-8 **93**............... CharlieBennett[(5)] 7 102
(Hughie Morrison) *towards rr: rdn over 3f out and looked struggling: prog on wd outside over 2f out: led u.p jst over 1f out: drvn out* **12/1**

2411 2 ½ **Firmament**[16] 5585 4-9-8 **102**............... PhillipMakin 10 110+
(David O'Meara) *hld up in midfield: trckd ldrs over 2f out: waiting for room over 1f out: r.o wl fnl f to take 2nd nr fin* **8/1**[3]

4102 **3** 3/4 **Von Blucher (IRE)**[21] 5403 3-8-12 **96**............................(t) RobertHavlin 6 100
(John Gosden) *slowly away: sn in midfield: prog 1/2-way: chal 2f out: drvn and upsides jst over 1f out: styd on same pce after* **5/1**[1]

-024 **4** hd **Squats (IRE)**[35] 4887 4-9-7 **101**.. RyanMoore 12 106+
(William Haggas) *hld up in rr: stl nrr last than first 2f out: prog over 1f out: r.o wl fnl f to take 4th last strides* **7/1**[2]

0336 **5** 1/2 **Scottish Glen**[28] 5174 10-8-10 **95**............................... HectorCrouch(5) 5 99
(Patrick Chamings) *settled towards rr: prog into midfield 2f: looked wl hld over 1f out: r.o fnl f: nrst fin* **16/1**

6053 **6** 1/2 **Charles Molson**[21] 5403 5-8-7 **94**............................(p) MitchGodwin(7) 1 96
(Patrick Chamings) *trckd ldrs: chal fr over 2f out: stl upsides jst over 1f out: one pce ins fnl f* **14/1**

6136 **7** 1/2 **Dawaa**[16] 5588 3-8-10 **94**.. PaulHanagan 18 93
(Mark Johnston) *racd towards nr side: in midfield: rdn 2f out: styd on fnl f but nvr able to threaten* **25/1**

2002 **8** 3/4 **Suzi's Connoisseur**[7] 5871 5-9-4 **101**.......................(vt) AaronJones(3) 2 100
(Stuart Williams) *hld up in rr: prog on outer over 2f out: no imp on ldrs fr over 1f out* **12/1**

2230 **9** hd **Twin Sails**[15] 5616 3-8-12 **96**..(b) SeanLevey 4 92
(Dean Ivory) *pressed ldrs: stl gng strly over 2f out: rdn wl over 1f out: nt qckn and sn lost pl* **25/1**

2155 **10** hd **Yattwee (USA)**[56] 4135 3-9-0 **105**........................... CameronNoble(7) 16 101
(Saeed bin Suroor) *trckd ldrs: shkn up over 2f out: lost pl over 1f out: n.m.r and no prog after* **8/1**[3]

1314 **11** nk **Ice Slice (IRE)**[14] 5640 5-9-0 **94**.. RyanTate 15 91
(James Eustace) *led: hrd pressed fr over 2f out: hdd & wknd jst over 1f out* **16/1**

0560 **12** 1/2 **Lincoln (IRE)**[21] 5389 5-8-8 **88**.. JFEgan 8 84
(Mick Channon) *dwlt: hld up in last trio: effrt over 2f out and sme modest hdwy: no prog over 1f out* **14/1**

0205 **13** hd **Ghalib (IRE)**[28] 5174 4-9-1 **95**.......................................(b[1]) LukeMorris 13 90
(Ed Walker) *mostly in midfield: rdn and no prog 2f out: fdd over 1f out* **25/1**

2200 **14** 3/4 **Heaven's Guest (IRE)**[7] 5871 6-9-10 **104**...................... JackGarritty 11 97
(Richard Fahey) *pressed ldrs: lost pl over 2f out: nvr much room after: wknd fnl f* **20/1**

4330 **15** hd **Muhadathat**[21] 5409 3-8-11 **95**....................................... MartinHarley 14 86
(Mark Johnston) *dwlt: mostly towards rr: rdn and no prog over 2f out* **20/1**

0350 **16** 1/2 **Jack's Revenge (IRE)**[38] 4758 8-8-6 **86**..................(bt) WilliamCarson 9 77
(George Baker) *hld up in last: shkn up and briefest of effrts over 1f out: nvr involved* **33/1**

0001 **17** 6 **Hawkeyethenoo (IRE)**[42] 4627 10-8-5 **85**........................... JoeDoyle 3 60
(Jim Goldie) *hld up towards rr on outer: stdy prog 1/2-way: cl up gng strly over 2f out: wknd sharply wl over 1f out* **20/1**

0120 **18** 4 1/2 **Bobby Wheeler (IRE)**[15] 5616 3-8-9 **93**........................... TedDurcan 17 54
(Clive Cox) *racd against nr side rail: pressed ldrs to 3f out: wknd qckly 2f out* **14/1**

1m 26.69s (-0.91) **Going Correction** +0.10s/f (Good)
WFA 3 from 4yo+ 4lb **18** Ran SP% **127.3**
Speed ratings (Par 109): **109,108,107,107,106 106,105,104,104,104 103,103,103,102,102 101,94,89**
CSF £97.23 CT £560.71 TOTE £14.70: £3.60, £2.50, £1.60, £2.10; EX 127.60 Trifecta £481.30.
Owner Raymond Tooth **Bred** Raymond Clive Tooth **Trained** East Ilsley, Berks

FOCUS
A typically strong Heritage handicap by course standards, rated around the placed horses. Another pb from the winner.

6110 APPLETISER STKS (HERITAGE H'CAP) 1m 4f
3:10 (3:11) (Class 2) 3-Y-O
£62,250 (£18,640; £9,320; £4,660; £2,330; £1,170) **Stalls** Low

Form RPR

-342 **1** **New Caledonia (IRE)**[6] 5924 3-8-7 **88**.............................. TedDurcan 11 98
(Mark Johnston) *trckd ldng trio: rdn and clsd to ld 2f out: drvn out and styd on wl* **12/1**

3541 **2** 1 1/4 **Danehill Kodiac (IRE)**[28] 5147 3-8-11 **92**......................... SeanLevey 9 100
(Richard Hannon) *settled in 6th: rdn wl over 2f out: prog after to take 2nd fnl f: styd on but no imp on wnr* **10/1**

0131 **3** 1 **Dal Harraild**[35] 4863 3-9-7 **102**.. PatCosgrave 6 108+
(William Haggas) *trckd ldng pair: wnt 2nd over 2f out and sn poised to chal gng easily: surprised by wnr sn after and nt qckn whn rdn: kpt on same pce and lost 2nd fnl f* **11/2**[2]

3421 **4** 1 **Wild Hacked (USA)**[11] 5738 3-8-8 **89**................................ LukeMorris 2 94
(Marco Botti) *chsd ldrs in 5th: rdn wl over 2f out: styd on but nvr pce to chal* **18/1**

2-13 **5** 1/2 **Stargazer (IRE)**[37] 4797 3-9-4 **99**..................................... RyanMoore 10 103+
(Sir Michael Stoute) *hld up in last trio: gng wl enough but same pl whn hmpd bnd 3f out: prog 2f out: styd on but nvr able to rch ldrs* **15/8**[1]

5110 **6** 1 1/2 **Euchen Glen**[57] 4108 3-8-4 **85**... JFEgan 3 87
(Jim Goldie) *hld up in 9th: rdn wl over 2f out: kpt on one pce after: nvr a threat* **33/1**

031 **7** 1/2 **Dance The Dream**[25] 5255 3-8-3 **84**............................. MartinDwyer 4 85
(Marcus Tregoning) *sn led and set decent pce: drvn and hdd 2f out: wknd* **16/1**

2201 **8** 2 3/4 **Gawdawpalin (IRE)**[91] 2892 3-8-3 **84**........................... KieranO'Neill 12 80
(Sylvester Kirk) *mostly in 8th: drvn and hung rt over 2f out: nt look keen and no real prog* **10/1**

5652 **9** 1 1/2 **Combative**[28] 5147 3-8-9 **90**... RobertHavlin 13 84
(Amanda Perrett) *prog fr wd draw and sn trckd ldr: drvn and lost 2nd over 2f out: wknd* **16/1**

3132 **10** nk **Real Dominion (USA)**[7] 5879 3-8-10 **94**....................... RobHornby(3) 1 88
(Andrew Balding) *dwlt: nt gng wl in last pair early: stl same pl whn hmpd bnd 3f out: no prog* **8/1**[3]

-566 **11** 1 3/4 **Paris Protocol**[56] 4131 3-8-2 **90**................................... MitchGodwin(7) 8 81
(Richard Hannon) *mostly in last: drvn and no prog 3f out* **10/1**

4200 **12** 30 **Juste Pour Nous**[28] 5147 3-8-2 **83**............................... RoystonFfrench 7 26
(Mark Johnston) *in tch in midfield but nvr gng that wl: u.p over 4f out: wknd rapidly 3f out: t.o* **66/1**

2m 32.2s (-0.30) **Going Correction** +0.225s/f (Good) **12** Ran SP% **117.7**
Speed ratings (Par 107): **110,109,108,107,107 106,106,104,103,103 101,81**
CSF £125.78 CT £742.52 TOTE £15.50: £3.70, £2.70, £2.00; EX 159.10 Trifecta £1171.90.
Owner Sheikh Hamdan bin Mohammed Al Maktoum **Bred** Darley **Trained** Middleham Moor, N Yorks

FOCUS
Race distance increaseed by 21yds. A classy 3yo handicap. They went a sound pace and the form is strong.

6111 LAVAZZA MAIDEN FILLIES' STKS (PLUS 10 RACE) 1m (R)
3:40 (3:43) (Class 4) 2-Y-O **£6,469** (£1,925; £962; £481) **Stalls** Low

Form RPR

04 **1** **Flying North**[8] 5846 2-9-0 0.. TimmyMurphy 1 75
(Richard Hannon) *mde all: set mod pce: wound up fr over 2f out: rdn out to hold on fnl f* **11/2**[3]

55 **2** 1/2 **Carol (IRE)**[35] 4885 2-9-0 0.. AdamKirby 5 74
(Ed Dunlop) *chsd wnr: rdn 2f out: clsd u.p fnl f: a jst hld* **12/1**

3 2 3/4 **Cirencester** 2-9-0 0.. RyanMoore 3 68
(Ralph Beckett) *chsd ldng pair to 2f out: rdn to go 3rd again fnl f but no real imp* **10/3**[2]

4 3/4 **Rockshine** 2-9-0 0.. SeanLevey 8 66+
(Richard Hannon) *slowly away: hld up in last: shkn up and prog on outer 2f out: styd on to take 4th ins fnl f: nrst fin* **12/1**

54 **5** 1 3/4 **Amelia Dream**[12] 5705 2-9-0 0.. JFEgan 7 62
(Mick Channon) *t.k.h: hld up in 6th: shkn up over 2f out: no real prog* **10/1**

6 1 **Nastenka** 2-9-0 0.. LukeMorris 2 60
(Ed Walker) *dwlt: hld up in 5th: rdn and outpcd 2f out: n.d after* **33/1**

7 nk **Spirit Of India** 2-9-0 0.. GrahamLee 4 59
(John Gosden) *slowly away: hld up in 7th: pushed along and no prog over 2f out: nvr a factor: kpt on nr fin* **6/4**[1]

03 **8** 3 **Robin's Purse**[10] 5772 2-9-0 0.. MartinHarley 6 53
(Charles Hills) *chsd ldng trio: drvn to take 3rd 2f out to fnl f: wknd rapidly* **10/1**

1m 45.88s (5.18) **Going Correction** +0.225s/f (Good) **8** Ran SP% **115.0**
Speed ratings (Par 94): **83,82,79,79,77 76,75,72**
CSF £67.91 TOTE £5.60: £1.60, £3.50, £1.60; EX 71.90 Trifecta £367.10.
Owner P T Tellwright **Bred** P T Tellwright **Trained** East Everleigh, Wilts

FOCUS
Race distance increaseed by 17yds. Previous experience was a big asset in this fillies' event and the first pair, both always up there, dominated. A weak race for the track.

6112 BIBENDUM WINE LTD H'CAP 6f
4:10 (4:15) (Class 2) (0-105,104) 3-Y-O+
£18,675 (£5,592; £2,796; £1,398; £699; £351) **Stalls** High

Form RPR

4441 **1** **Magnus Maximus**[13] 5678 5-9-7 **101**............................... LukeMorris 16 111
(Robyn Brisland) *racd nr side: mde all: drvn jst over 1f out: in command and styd on: unchal* **14/1**

1130 **2** 1 1/2 **Royal Birth**[17] 5555 5-8-11 **94**.......................................(t) AaronJones(3) 13 99
(Stuart Williams) *chsd ldrs nr side: urged along fr 2f out: styd on wl fnl f to take 2nd last stride* **14/1**

-230 **3** hd **Sir Robert Cheval**[35] 4865 5-9-1 **98**........................... LouisSteward(3) 8 102
(Robert Cowell) *hld up in midfield nr side: prog on outer of gp 2f out: chsd wnr 1f out: no real imp: lost 2nd last stride* **16/1**

0021 **4** shd **Normandy Barriere (IRE)**[28] 5161 4-8-4 **91**......... LewisEdmunds(7) 14 95+
(Nigel Tinkler) *racd in midfield nr side: prog 2f out: styd on fnl f: nrst fin* **7/1**[2]

2566 **5** 3/4 **Boomerang Bob (IRE)**[13] 5678 7-8-11 **91**................. WilliamCarson 17 93
(Jamie Osborne) *wl in rr nr side and wl off the pce: prog 2f out: styd on fnl f: nrst fin* **33/1**

3501 **6** nk **Kadrizzi (FR)**[28] 5148 3-9-7 **103**....................... WilliamTwiston-Davies 10 104
(Dean Ivory) *racd in midfield nr side: rdn fr 2f out: hanging bdly rt after: kpt on but nvr gng to threaten* **12/1**

0230 **7** 1/2 **Out Do**[15] 5614 7-9-10 **104**.......................................(v) JackGarritty 12 103
(David O'Meara) *hld up off the pce in rr nr side: gng wl enough over 2f out: shkn up wl over 1f out: limited rspnse* **14/1**

-501 **8** nk **Doctor Sardonicus**[39] 4741 5-8-13 **93**........................ MartinHarley 11 91
(David Simcock) *chsd wnr nr side: rdn 2f out: lost 2nd and wknd 1f out* **14/1**

0010 **9** hd **Cartmell Cleave**[14] 5648 4-8-10 **90**..................................... TedDurcan 7 87+
(Stuart Kittow) *slowly away: detached in last nr side: rdn over 2f out: r.o fnl f but all too late* **20/1**

1404 **10** 1/2 **Shamshon (IRE)**[14] 5648 5-8-10 **95**.............................. LucyKBarry(5) 15 94+
(Jamie Osborne) *stdd s: hld up wl in rr nr side and off the pce: effrt whn impeded 2f out: prog whn nt clr run ins fnl f: r.o nr fin but nvr involved* **10/1**

4611 **11** 1 1/4 **Mustallib (IRE)**[27] 5199 3-8-13 **95**.................................. PaulHanagan 1 87+
(Charles Hills) *hld up last on far side: and nvr any ch: rdn 2f out: styd on to ld gp nr fin* **9/2**[1]

3300 **12** 1/2 **Dougan**[35] 4862 4-8-12 **92**.. AdamBeschizza 6 82
(David Evans) *chsd far side ldrs: nvr any ch but led gp ins fnl f tl nr fin* **10/1**

2550 **13** hd **Rio Ronaldo (IRE)**[19] 5488 4-8-7 **87**............................. RoystonFfrench 9 77
(Mike Murphy) *t.k.h: trckd ldrs nr side: rdn and fnd nil wl over 1f out: wl btn whn impeded ins fnl f: wknd* **16/1**

0006 **14** 1/2 **Spring Loaded (IRE)**[21] 5389 4-9-2 **96**............................ SeanLevey 3 84
(Paul D'Arcy) *chsd ldr far side: led gp over 2f out: edgd lft u.p: nvr any ch and hdd in gp ins fnl f* **8/1**[3]

2000 **15** 2 3/4 **Moonraker**[21] 5418 4-9-4 **98**.. JFEgan 18 77
(Mick Channon) *chsd ldng pair nr side tl wknd over 2f out* **16/1**

012 **16** 2 **Solar Flair**[29] 5124 4-9-4 **98**... MartinDwyer 5 71
(William Knight) *led far side gp but nt on terms: hdd over 2f out: fdd* **12/1**

-000 **17** 5 **Louis The Pious**[21] 5418 8-9-2 **96**...................................(v) GrahamLee 2 53
(David O'Meara) *racd far side: in tch in gp to 2f out: wknd* **28/1**

0000 **18** 1 1/4 **Toofi (FR)**[21] 5418 5-9-5 **99**...(v) AdamKirby 4 52
(Robert Cowell) *racd far side: in tch in gp but nvr any ch: wknd 2f out* **12/1**

1m 13.53s (-0.97) **Going Correction** +0.10s/f (Good)
WFA 3 from 4yo+ 2lb **18** Ran SP% **138.5**
Speed ratings (Par 109): **110,108,107,107,106 106,105,105,104,104 102,101,101,100,97 94,87,86**
CSF £216.26 CT £3304.31 TOTE £13.80: £3.50, £3.50, £4.20, £2.10; EX 255.50 Trifecta £5350.90 Part won..
Owner Franconson Partners **Bred** St Albans Bloodstock Llp **Trained** Newmarket, Suffolk

FOCUS
A decent sprint handicap in which those drawn high held sway. The form is set around the second and third.

6113 RITZ CLUB EBF "BREEDERS SERIES" FILLIES' H'CAP 1m (S)
4:45 (4:50) (Class 2) (0-100,96) 3-Y-O+ **£19,407** (£5,775; £2,886; £1,443) **Stalls** High

Form RPR
114 **1** **Miss Carbonia (IRE)**[35] 4886 3-8-7 **82** LukeMorris 3 89
(Ismail Mohammed) *stdd s: t.k.h: hld up in tch: shkn up and prog 2f out: drvn to chal and w ldr ins fnl f: jst prevailed* **5/1**[3]
1401 **2** *nse* **Hidden Rebel**[17] 5538 4-9-1 **85** PaulHanagan 6 93
(Alistair Whillans) *trckd ldng pair: rdn to cl over 1f out: drvn to ld jst ins fnl f: edgd rt and sn jnd: jst pipped nr fin* **7/1**
1140 **3** *½* **Light And Shade**[28] 5158 4-9-12 **96** MartinHarley 2 103
(James Tate) *hld up in tch: prog 2f out: drvn to chal and w ldng pair fnl f: no ex last 50yds* **4/1**[2]
-200 **4** *1 ½* **Aljuljalah (USA)**[57] 4105 3-9-6 **95** AdamKirby 4 97
(Roger Varian) *trckd ldr: rousted to ld 2f out and sent for home: hdd and outpcd jst ins fnl f* **13/2**
5230 **5** *½* **Company Asset (IRE)**[18] 5514 3-8-5 **80** ShaneGray 1 81
(Kevin Ryan) *hld up in last pair: rdn and tried to cl on ldrs fr 2f out: nt qckn over 1f out: one pce after* **16/1**
421 **6** *1 ¼* **Labyrinth (IRE)**[32] 4991 3-8-6 **81** TedDurcan 7 79
(Sir Michael Stoute) *led: set mod pce tl after 1/2-way: hdd and shkn up 2f out: no rspnse and sn btn* **11/4**[1]
535 **7** *1 ½* **Lil Sophella (IRE)**[16] 5588 7-9-4 **88** JackGarritty 8 84
(Patrick Holmes) *hld up in last: outpcd whn sprint sed 2f out: shkn up and no prog after: nvr involved* **12/1**

1m 43.38s (2.58) **Going Correction** +0.10s/f (Good)
WFA 3 from 4yo+ 5lb **7** Ran SP% **102.7**
Speed ratings (Par 96): **91,90,90,88,88 87,85**
CSF £30.94 CT £110.50 TOTE £5.50: £2.40, £2.80; EX 33.30 Trifecta £113.50.
Owner Sheikh Juma Dalmook Al Maktoum **Bred** Mrs Elizabeth O'Leary **Trained** Newmarket, Suffolk
■ Margaret's Mission was withdrawn. Price at time of withdrawal 8-1. Rule 4 applies all bets - deduction 10p in the pound.

FOCUS
A good-quality fillies' handicap, run at a moderate tempo. The third is a decent benchmark and the winner improved back at a mile.

6114 REDCENTRIC H'CAP 5f
5:20 (5:21) (Class 3) (0-90,88) 3-Y-O+ **£9,703** (£2,887; £1,443; £721) **Stalls** High

Form RPR
2144 **1** **Dark Shot**[34] 4911 3-8-9 **80** RobHornby(3) 12 90
(Andrew Balding) *hld up in 4th nr side: waiting for an opening 2f out: squeezed through against rail fnl f: drvn and r.o wl to ld nr fin* **4/1**[1]
5313 **2** *½* **Majestic Hero (IRE)**[22] 5360 4-9-7 **88** GrahamLee 11 96
(Ronald Harris) *chsd ldr nr side tl drvn over 1f out: rallied to ld ins fnl f: styd on but hdd and outpcd nr fin* **16/1**
5141 **3** *1 ½* **Bashiba (IRE)**[21] 5390 5-8-12 **86** (t) LewisEdmunds(7) 10 89
(Nigel Tinkler) *trckd ldng pair nr side: rdn and prog to ld gp and overall ldr over 1f out: hdd and one pce ins fnl f* **6/1**[3]
0010 **4** *nk* **Sandfrankskipsgo**[5] 5961 7-9-5 **86** TedDurcan 13 88
(Peter Crate) *awkward s and slowly away: hld up in last nr side: rdn and prog over 1f out: kpt on but nvr able to chal* **25/1**
1234 **5** *1 ½* **David's Duchess (IRE)**[22] 5372 3-8-9 **77** PaulHanagan 9 73
(Richard Fahey) *hld up in last of centre gp: gd prog over 1f out: rdn to ld ins fnl f: r.o but no ch w nr side* **9/2**[2]
5000 **6** *1* **Foxy Forever (IRE)**[14] 5648 6-9-6 **87** (bt) AdamKirby 6 80
(Michael Wigham) *led nr side gp and on terms: hdd over 1f out: one pce* **16/1**
-430 **7** *nk* **Just Us Two (IRE)**[95] 2775 4-9-3 **84** MartinHarley 7 75
(Robert Cowell) *chsd ldrs in centre: rdn to ld gp briefly jst ins fnl f but already no ch: kpt on* **16/1**
0311 **8** *2 ¾* **Pine Ridge**[24] 5305 3-8-12 **80** LukeMorris 3 62
(Clive Cox) *overall ldr in centre to over 1f out: lost gp ld jst ins fnl f: wknd* **10/1**
1603 **9** *½* **Stake Acclaim (IRE)**[33] 4954 4-9-6 **87** (p) RobertWinston 5 67
(Dean Ivory) *pressed ldrs in centre to over 1f out: nt qckn and fdd fnl f* **6/1**[3]
3302 **10** *nk* **Ginzan**[24] 5305 8-8-13 **80** MartinDwyer 2 59
(Malcolm Saunders) *trckd ldrs gng easily: shkn up and fnd nil over 1f out: wknd* **20/1**
0230 **11** *3 ¾* **Dragon King (IRE)**[21] 5417 4-9-6 **87** SeanLevey 1 52
(Michael Dods) *chsd ldrs in centre: rdn 1/2-way: wknd wl over 1f out* **8/1**
3010 **12** *4* **Kibaar**[14] 5641 4-9-5 **86** (b[1]) ShaneGray 4 37
(Kevin Ryan) *pressed overall ldr in centre to wl over 1f out: wknd qckly* **14/1**

1m 0.2s (-0.30) **Going Correction** +0.10s/f (Good)
WFA 3 from 4yo+ 1lb **12** Ran SP% **119.9**
Speed ratings (Par 107): **106,105,102,102,99 98,97,93,92,92 86,79**
CSF £70.25 CT £315.75 TOTE £5.00: £1.90, £4.50, £2.60; EX 66.30 Trifecta £379.50.
Owner J C Smith **Bred** Littleton Stud **Trained** Kingsclere, Hants

FOCUS
A useful sprint, the high-drawn runners racing stands' side came out on top. The winner reversed Chepstow latest with the second.
T/Plt: £376.30 to a £1 stake. Pool: £153,816.12 - 298.32 winning tickets T/Qpdt: £126.20 to a £1 stake. Pool: £6,618.77 - 38.78 winning tickets **Jonathan Neesom**

6077 HAYDOCK (L-H)
Saturday, September 3
OFFICIAL GOING: Good to soft changing to soft after race 1 (1.50)
Wind: Light, behind Weather: Heavy rain

6115 EBF BREEDERS' SERIES 32REDSPORT.COM FILLIES' H'CAP 1m 2f 95y
1:50 (1:50) (Class 2) (0-100,97) 3-Y-O+
£18,675 (£5,592; £2,796; £1,398; £699; £351) **Stalls** Centre

Form RPR
2155 **1** **Motdaw**[38] 4757 3-8-8 **86** AlexisBadel 7 98
(Mick Channon) *racd keenly: trckd ldrs: effrt 3f out: led ins fnl f: styd on gamely: in control towards fin* **12/1**
240 **2** *½* **Rosental**[43] 4610 4-9-12 **97** AndreaAtzeni 3 108
(Luca Cumani) *trckd ldrs: travelling wl and led over 2f out: rdn over 1f out: hdd ins fnl f: kpt on: hld nr fin* **14/1**
3045 **3** *7* **Empress Ali (IRE)**[71] 3593 5-9-0 **85** AndrewElliott 9 83
(Tom Tate) *led: pushed along 3f out: hdd over 2f out: rdn and stl ev ch over 1f out: styd on same pce fnl 150yds: no ch w front two after* **12/1**
4564 **4** *2 ¼* **Dessertoflife (IRE)**[5] 5956 3-9-4 **96** FrannyNorton 4 89
(Mark Johnston) *midfield: pushed along 3f out: rdn and edgd lft whn outpcd over 1f out: kpt on ins fnl f but n.d* **13/2**[3]
3120 **5** *½* **Shafafya**[29] 5123 3-8-7 **85** [1] ChrisHayes 5 78
(Ed Dunlop) *hld up: hdwy over 3f out: rdn and ev ch 2f out: one pce fr over 1f out* **8/1**
4541 **6** *1 ½* **Zest (IRE)**[37] 4808 3-8-9 **87** TomQueally 2 77
(James Fanshawe) *hld up in rr: hdwy over 2f out: cl up chsng ldrs over 1f out: wknd ent fnl f* **5/2**[1]
2311 **7** *2* **Trainnah**[30] 5054 3-8-9 **87** (b[1]) JamieSpencer 6 73
(William Haggas) *hld up: rdn over 2f out: no imp: wl btn fnl f* **11/4**[2]
0400 **8** *4 ½* **Imshivalla (IRE)**[14] 5651 5-9-0 **90** AdamMcNamara(5) 8 67
(Richard Fahey) *racd keenly: chsd ldr tl rdn 3f out: bhd fnl f* **12/1**
4300 **9** *6* **Miss Van Gogh**[38] 4757 4-9-3 **88** TonyHamilton 1 54
(Richard Fahey) *racd keenly: hld up in midfield: pushed along and wknd 3f out: wl bhd over f out* **14/1**

2m 18.56s (3.06) **Going Correction** +0.50s/f (Yiel)
WFA 3 from 4yo+ 7lb **9** Ran SP% **116.1**
Speed ratings (Par 96): **107,106,101,99,98 97,96,92,87**
CSF £165.40 CT £2054.23 TOTE £14.90: £3.20, £3.10, £3.60; EX 164.80 Trifecta £1374.70.
Owner Derek And Jean Clee **Bred** D D & Mrs J P Clee **Trained** West Ilsley, Berks

FOCUS
All races were run over the stands' side home straight. Allowing for rail positioning on the bend the actual race distance of this was 1m2f 145yds. Torrential rain in the run up to racing, and into the afternoon, led to the ground softening significantly. A decent handicap and, having come centre-field in the straight, the front pair came clear. They were the only ones to show their form.

6116 32RED CASINO STKS (REGISTERED AS THE ASCENDANT STAKES) (LISTED RACE) 1m
2:25 (2:27) (Class 1) 2-Y-O
£14,461 (£5,482; £2,743; £1,366; £685; £344) **Stalls** Low

Form RPR
1534 **1** **Frankuus (IRE)**[21] 5401 2-9-2 95 FrannyNorton 1 100
(Mark Johnston) *sn led: rdn wl over 1f out: pressed ins fnl f: kpt on gamely* **5/1**[3]
1 **2** *¾* **Star Of Rory (IRE)**[49] 4379 2-9-2 76 RichardKingscote 3 98
(Tom Dascombe) *stdd early: hld up: rdn over 2f out: hdwy over 1f out: pressed wnr wl ins fnl f: kpt on: hld nr fin* **7/1**
1344 **3** *½* **Cunco (IRE)**[15] 5595 2-9-2 97 FrankieDettori 7 97
(John Gosden) *chsd wnr: rdn over 2f out: ev ch tl no ex nr fin* **9/4**[1]
41 **4** *¾* **Contrast (IRE)**[29] 5108 2-9-2 0 PatDobbs 6 96
(Richard Hannon) *hld up in tch: rdn and swtchd lft over 1f out to chse ldrs: kpt on same pce fnl 100yds* **10/1**
15 **5** *3 ¾* **Bahamas (IRE)**[42] 4622 2-9-2 0 DanielMuscutt 8 87
(Marco Botti) *in rr: pushed along 3f out: rdn over 2f out: no imp* **6/1**
31 **6** *7* **Red Ensign (IRE)**[18] 5505 2-9-2 0 AndreaAtzeni 2 72
(Simon Crisford) *broke wl: trckd ldrs: effrt over 2f out: wknd over 1f out* **11/4**[2]

1m 47.97s (4.27) **Going Correction** +0.65s/f (Yiel) **6** Ran SP% **110.0**
Speed ratings (Par 103): **104,103,102,102,98 91**
CSF £36.23 TOTE £6.00: £2.50, £3.00; EX 38.20 Trifecta £101.10.
Owner Hussain Lootah & Ahmad Al Shaikh **Bred** Ballylinch Stud **Trained** Middleham Moor, N Yorks

FOCUS
Allowing for rail positioning on the bend the actual race distance of this was 1m 50yds. This was always likely to prove a stern test for these juveniles with the ground having gone soft and the winner, a strong stayer at the distance, made all. He's been rated as a marginal improver.

6117 32RED MILE (REGISTERED AS THE SUPERIOR MILE STKS) (GROUP 3) 1m
3:00 (3:00) (Class 1) 3-Y-O+
£35,727 (£13,545; £6,778; £3,376; £1,694; £850) **Stalls** Low

Form RPR
021- **1** **Hathal (USA)**[351] 6502 4-9-3 111 FrankieDettori 5 117
(William Haggas) *trckd ldrs: rdn 2f out: chalng over 1f out: styd on to ld wl ins fnl f: plld out more nr fin* **11/2**[3]
-032 **2** *hd* **Mitchum Swagger**[19] 5472 4-9-3 110 GeorgeBaker 7 116
(David Lanigan) *hld up: rdn over 2f out: hdwy over 1f out: chalng wl ins fnl f: styd on: jst hld* **7/2**[2]
0162 **3** *nk* **Convey**[6] 5926 4-9-3 113 (p) AndreaAtzeni 2 115
(Sir Michael Stoute) *t.k.h: led: c wd ent st over 4f out: pressed over 2f out: hdd wl ins fnl f: kpt on but hld nr fin* **7/1**
3443 **4** *2 ¾* **Custom Cut (IRE)**[14] 5652 7-9-3 114 DanielTudhope 3 109
(David O'Meara) *chsd ldr: rdn over 2f out: ev ch over 1f out: styd on same pce ins fnl f* **10/3**[1]
-341 **5** *1* **Breton Rock (IRE)**[70] 3664 6-9-7 112 JamieSpencer 6 111
(David Simcock) *midfield: rdn over 2f out: kpt on ins fnl f: nvr able to chal* **7/2**[2]
0260 **6** *shd* **First Selection (SPA)**[55] 4185 3-8-12 109 RichardKingscote 9 105
(Simon Crisford) *chsd ldrs: rdn over 2f out: kpt on same pce fnl f* **16/1**
3544 **7** *1 ½* **Gabrial (IRE)**[14] 5652 7-9-3 113 JimmyFortune 8 103
(Richard Fahey) *racd keenly: hld up in rr: rdn over 2f out: one pce u.p ins fnl f* **12/1**
0063 **8** *2 ¾* **Tupi (IRE)**[23] 5329 4-9-3 105 FrannyNorton 4 97
(Richard Hannon) *hld up: rdn 2f out: no real imp* **25/1**

1m 47.15s (3.45) **Going Correction** +0.80s/f (Soft)
WFA 3 from 4yo+ 5lb **8** Ran SP% **112.8**
Speed ratings (Par 113): **114,113,113,110,109 109,108,105**
CSF £24.37 TOTE £5.90: £2.10, £1.50, £2.50; EX 26.40 Trifecta £96.80.
Owner Al Shaqab Racing **Bred** Tenth Street Stables Llc **Trained** Newmarket, Suffolk

FOCUS
Allowing for rail positioning on the bend the actual race distance of this was 1m 50yds. Convey led them into the straight, heading more centre-field on his own, but the remainder stayed more on the inside. Sound form, well up to scratch for the race and grade.

6118 32RED CASINO H'CAP 1m 6f
3:30 (3:31) (Class 2) (0-105,105) 3-Y-O **£38,814** (£11,550; £5,772; £2,886) **Stalls** Low

Form RPR
0212 **1** **Intense Tango**[22] 5381 5-8-5 **93** ow3 (t) CliffordLee(7) 11 103
(K R Burke) *mde all: wnt abt 5 l clr 5f out: rdn over 1f out: jst hld on fin* **12/1**

-053 **2** *hd* **Montaly**[50] [4353] 5-8-13 **94** .... OisinMurphy 5 104
(Andrew Balding) *wore hood in paddock: midfield: hdwy over 2f out: wnt 2nd jst over 1f out: styd on strly fnl 75yds: jst failed* **11/2**[2]

3/0- **3** *2 ¼* **Blue Rambler**[159] [1279] 6-9-1 **99** .... GeorgeDowning(3) 1 106
(Ian Williams) *midfield: rdn and hdwy over 2f out: styd on ins fnl f: no imp on front two towards fin* **33/1**

-201 **4** *2 ½* **Magic Circle (IRE)**[56] [4162] 4-9-2 **97** .... FMBerry 13 100+
(Ralph Beckett) *midfield: rdn and hdwy over 2f out: styd on u.p ins fnl f: no imp fnl 100yds* **9/2**[1]

434- **5** *2 ¼* **Justice Belle (IRE)**[299] [7779] 4-8-13 **94** .... ThomasBrown 15 94+
(Ed Walker) *hld up: rdn over 2f out: hdwy over 1f out: styd on ins fnl f: gng on towards fin* **22/1**

0006 **6** *½* **Suegioo (FR)**[15] [5612] 7-9-5 **105** ....(p) AdamMcNamara(5) 7 104
(Richard Fahey) *hld up: rdn over 2f out: hdwy over 1f out: styd on ins fnl f: nvr able to chal* **16/1**

1000 **7** *nk* **My Reward**[17] [5559] 4-9-0 **95** .... AndrewMullen 16 94
(Tim Easterby) *chsd ldrs: rdn over 2f out: styd on same pce u.p ins fnl f* **16/1**

2540 **8** *shd* **Gold Prince (IRE)**[15] [5611] 4-8-11 **95** .... EdwardGreatrex(3) 4 94
(Sylvester Kirk) *chsd ldrs: rdn over 2f out: cl up for press over 1f out: no ex ins fnl f: fdd fnl 100yds* **12/1**

0030 **9** *4 ½* **Angel Gabrial (IRE)**[70] [3658] 7-9-5 **100** .... TonyHamilton 3 92
(Richard Fahey) *chsd ldrs: rdn over 2f out: wknd ins fnl f* **33/1**

131 **10** *¾* **Walpole (IRE)**[25] [5275] 4-8-6 **87** .... AndreaAtzeni 6 78
(Hugo Palmer) *midfield: rdn 2f out: one pce fnl f* **11/2**[2]

3513 **11** *2 ½* **Gabrial's Star**[14] [5642] 7-8-7 **88** ....(b) FrannyNorton 2 76
(Richard Fahey) *s.i.s: hld up: u.p over 2f out: nvr a threat* **20/1**

2100 **12** *nk* **Green Light**[28] [5144] 5-8-12 **93** ....(b[1]) PatDobbs 14 80
(Ralph Beckett) *hld up in rr: hdwy 2f out: in midfield u.p over 1f out: wknd ins fnl f* **25/1**

5152 **13** *hd* **Shrewd**[14] [5655] 6-9-2 **102** .... DonaghO'Connor(5) 8 89
(Iain Jardine) *midfield: rdn and wknd over 1f out* **6/1**[3]

4620 **14** *5* **Gabrial The Hero (USA)**[14] [5639] 7-9-2 **97** ....(p) JimmyFortune 12 77
(Richard Fahey) *in tch: rdn over 3f out: wknd 2f out* **25/1**

005- **15** *3 ¼* **Excellent Result (IRE)**[343] [6749] 6-9-1 **96** ....(p) FrankieDettori 10 71
(Richard Spencer) *chsd wnr tl rdn over 2f out: wknd over 1f out* **25/1**

0000 **16** *9* **The Twisler**[14] [5655] 4-8-12 **100** .... DavidEgan(7) 9 62
(Jane Chapple-Hyam) *midfield: rdn 2f out: wknd over 1f out* **33/1**

5102 **17** *3* **Shakopee**[15] [5611] 4-9-0 **95** .... JamieSpencer 17 53
(Luca Cumani) *hld up: u.p over 2f out: nvr a threat: eased whn wl btn over 1f out* **8/1**

3m 11.68s (9.68) **Going Correction** +0.95s/f (Soft) **17** Ran SP% **131.0**
Speed ratings (Par 109): **110,109,108,107,105 105,105,105,102,102 100,100,100,97,95 90,88**
CSF £73.55 CT £2175.19 TOTE £13.80: £3.30, £2.00, £11.40, £1.40; EX 135.90 Trifecta £5348.90 Part won..

Owner Cosy Seal Racing Limited **Bred** Newsells Park Stud **Trained** Middleham Moor, N Yorks

■ Stewards' Enquiry : George Downing four-day ban; used whip above the permitted level (17th,19th-21st Sept)

Oisin Murphy two-day ban; used whip above the permitted level (17th,19th Sept)

FOCUS
Allowing for rail positioning on the bend the actual race distance of this was 1m6f 92yds. A good-quality handicap, there was a reasonable gallop on and the winner made all, skipping clear rounding the final bend and just holding on.

6119 32RED BE FRIENDLY H'CAP 5f

4:00 (4:03) (Class 2) (0-100,100) 3-Y-O+**£19,407** (£5,775; £2,886; £1,443) **Stalls** Centre

Form RPR

1055 **1** **Soie D'Leau**[14] [5648] 4-8-13 **92** .... TonyHamilton 12 101
(Kristin Stubbs) *chsd ldrs: rdn to chal over 1f out: nosed ahd fnl 75yds: kpt on gamely* **12/1**

5625 **2** *hd* **Confessional**[14] [5641] 9-8-10 **89** ....(be) CamHardie 16 97
(Tim Easterby) *hld up: rdn 2f out: hdwy over 1f out: r.o to press wnr nr fin: jst hld* **9/1**

2630 **3** *nk* **Bowson Fred**[17] [5555] 4-9-2 **100** .... NathanEvans(5) 10 107
(Michael Easterby) *prom: led over 3f out: rdn and edgd rt over 1f out: hdd narrowly fnl 75ds: kpt on* **9/1**

6200 **4** *2 ¼* **Robot Boy (IRE)**[17] [5555] 6-9-2 **95** .... FMBerry 11 94
(David Barron) *led: hdd over 3f out: remained prom: ev ch whn n.m.r and checked over 1f out: kpt on fnl 75yds but no imp on front trio* **5/1**[1]

410 **5** *nk* **Lady Macapa**[14] [5657] 3-9-0 **94** .... DanielTudhope 14 92
(William Knight) *hld up in midfield: hdwy 2f out: chsd ldrs ins fnl f: kpt on: one pce nr fin* **11/2**[2]

0 **6** *1* **Dutch Masterpiece**[39] [4735] 6-9-5 **98** .... GeorgeBaker 17 92
(Gary Moore) *stdd s: hld up: rdn over 1f out: hdwy after: styd on ins fnl f: unable to trble ldrs* **7/1**[3]

-100 **7** *3 ¼* **Tangerine Trees**[50] [4366] 11-8-8 **87** ....(v) AndrewMullen 4 69
(Michael Appleby) *prom: rdn over 2f out: styng on same pce u.p over 1f out: no ex ins fnl f* **20/1**

1055 **8** *½* **Englishman**[91] [2898] 6-8-8 **87** .... FrannyNorton 3 68
(Milton Bradley) *missed break: hld up: u.p over 1f out: no imp* **15/2**

6003 **9** *2 ¼* **Dungannon**[72] [3573] 9-8-12 **91** ....(b) OisinMurphy 1 64
(Andrew Balding) *hld up: rdn 2f out: nvr able to trble ldrs* **10/1**

0060 **10** *nk* **Stepper Point**[14] [5648] 7-8-13 **92** ....(p) SamHitchcott 15 63
(William Muir) *s.i.s: towards rr: pushed along over 2f out: nvr a threat* **20/1**

0041 **11** *4* **El Astronaute (IRE)**[5] [5961] 3-8-10 **90** 6ex .... JamieSpencer 6 62
(John Quinn) *in tch: rdn over 2f out: wknd ent fnl f* **5/1**[1]

0000 **12** *16* **Red Baron (IRE)**[39] [4735] 7-9-1 **94** .... NeilFarley 2
(Eric Alston) *prom: rdn over 2f out: sn wknd: eased whn wl btn over 1f out* **25/1**

1m 0.79s (-0.01) **Going Correction** +0.225s/f (Good)
WFA 3 from 4yo+ 1lb **12** Ran SP% **123.1**
Speed ratings (Par 109): **109,108,108,104,104 102,97,96,92,92 86,60**
CSF £116.85 CT £1053.82 TOTE £17.40: £4.20, £3.10, £3.50; EX 175.20 Trifecta £2088.40.

Owner F A T J Partnership **Bred** Mrs M Lingwood **Trained** Norton, N Yorks

■ Stewards' Enquiry : Nathan Evans caution; careless riding

FOCUS
The high-drawn runners dominated this useful sprint. The winner reversed Doncaster form with the second.

6120 32RED SPRINT CUP STKS (BRITISH CHAMPIONS SERIES) (GROUP 1) 6f

4:30 (4:34) (Class 1) 3-Y-O+

£162,190 (£61,490; £30,773; £15,329; £7,693; £3,861) **Stalls** Centre

Form RPR

1113 **1** **Quiet Reflection**[56] [4151] 3-8-12 115 .... DougieCostello 4 120
(K R Burke) *midfield: smooth hdwy fr 2f out: led appr fnl f: rdn and kpt on wl* **7/2**[1]

-101 **2** *1 ¾* **The Tin Man**[49] [4393] 4-9-3 114 .... TomQueally 6 117
(James Fanshawe) *slowly away: hld up: pushed along and gd hdwy towards outer 2f out: rdn to go 2nd ins fnl f: kpt on wl but nvr rching wnr* **6/1**[2]

2524 **3** *2 ½* **Suedois (FR)**[27] [5217] 5-9-3 115 .... DanielTudhope 7 109
(David O'Meara) *trckd ldr: rdn over 2f out: chal over 1f out: one pce fnl f* **7/1**[3]

3411 **4** *½* **Mehronissa**[20] [5436] 4-9-0 105 .... FrederikTylicki 17 104
(Ed Vaughan) *midfield: hdwy over 2f out: rdn and ev ch over 1f out: one pce fnl f* **25/1**

1505 **5** *½* **Mr Lupton (IRE)**[7] [5863] 3-9-1 111 .... JamieSpencer 12 106
(Richard Fahey) *dwlt and bmpd jst after s: hld up in rr: rdn over 2f out: kpt on ins fnl f: nvr threatened ldrs* **25/1**

/013 **6** *nse* **Jane's Memory (IRE)**[63] [3909] 4-9-0 101 .... AndreaAtzeni 1 103
(Rae Guest) *chsd ldr on outside: rdn over 2f out: one pce fnl f* **50/1**

0313 **7** *1* **Only Mine (IRE)**[91] [2923] 3-8-12 108 .... GaryCarroll 16 99
(Joseph G Murphy, Ire) *chsd ldr: rdn over 2f out: no ex fnl 110yds* **20/1**

4633 **8** *1 ¼* **Strath Burn**[25] [5268] 4-9-3 109 ....(p) OisinMurphy 10 98
(Robert Cowell) *a midfield* **25/1**

1211 **9** *3 ¾* **Dancing Star**[35] [4865] 3-8-12 108 .... FrannyNorton 3 83
(Andrew Balding) *trckd ldr: rdn over 2f out: wknd over 1f out* **7/1**[3]

6260 **10** *¾* **Kachy**[36] [4824] 3-9-1 112 .... RichardKingscote 15 84
(Tom Dascombe) *led: rdn over 2f out: hdd appr fnl f: wknd* **20/1**

-202 **11** *3 ¼* **Donjuan Triumphant (IRE)**[27] [5217] 3-9-1 114 .... AlexisBadel 11 74
(Richard Fahey) *hld up: rdn along over 3f out: nvr threatened* **7/1**[3]

3000 **12** *1 ½* **Goken (FR)**[15] [5614] 4-9-3 108 .... KevinStott 5 69
(Kevin Ryan) *hld up: nvr threatened* **22/1**

5104 **13** *½* **Gordon Lord Byron (IRE)**[9] [5816] 8-9-3 114 .... ChrisHayes 9 67
(T Hogan, Ire) *midfield: rdn over 2f out: wknd over 1f out* **22/1**

1140 **14** *11* **Magical Memory (IRE)**[56] [4151] 4-9-3 114 .... FrankieDettori 8 32
(Charles Hills) *in tch: rdn over 2f out: lost pl over 1f out: wknd and eased* **6/1**[2]

1m 13.45s (-0.35) **Going Correction** +0.375s/f (Good)
WFA 3 from 4yo+ 2lb **14** Ran SP% **120.0**
Speed ratings (Par 117): **117,114,111,110,110 109,108,106,101,100 96,94,93,79**
CSF £20.23 CT £142.80 TOTE £4.10: £2.20, £2.10, £2.60; EX 28.00 Trifecta £236.90.

Owner Ontoawinner, Strecker & Burke **Bred** Springcombe Park Stud **Trained** Middleham Moor, N Yorks

FOCUS
One key non-runner in the shape of Limato, who had been favourite in the run up to the race, but still the right horses came to the fore with Quiet Reflection impressive on her favoured soft ground. The Tin Man is rated close to form.

6121 32RED.COM H'CAP 1m 6f

5:05 (5:05) (Class 2) 3-Y-O

£28,012 (£8,388; £4,194; £2,097; £1,048; £526) **Stalls** Low

Form RPR

4161 **1** **The Graduate (IRE)**[22] [5358] 3-9-1 **84** .... OisinMurphy 7 96+
(Andrew Balding) *mde all: rdn 3f out: jnd 2f out: styd on wl: drew clr ins fnl f* **7/2**[2]

3241 **2** *4 ½* **Cosmeapolitan**[21] [5406] 3-9-7 **90** .... DougieCostello 5 95+
(Alan King) *racd keenly: hld up in tch: smooth hdwy 3f out to join ldr 2f out: rdn over 1f out: wknd ins fnl f* **7/2**[2]

6211 **3** *1 ¾* **Marmajuke Bay**[73] [3532] 3-8-10 **79** ....(p) SteveDrowne 9 82
(Mark Usher) *keen in midfield: rdn and outpcd over 3f out: swtchd lft over 2f out: styd on fr over 1f out: wnt 3rd post* **11/4**[1]

625 **4** *hd* **Togetherness (IRE)**[11] [5742] 3-8-10 **79** .... TonyHamilton 10 81
(Harry Dunlop) *trckd ldr: chal 3f out: rdn over 2f out: wknd fnl f: lost 3rd post* **25/1**

5 **5** *4 ½* **Evening Hush (IRE)**[116] [2134] 3-8-11 **80** .... JamieSpencer 4 76
(Evan Williams) *hld up: rdn 3f out: sn no imp* **7/1**[3]

2431 **6** *1 ¼* **Spinners Ball (IRE)**[21] [5397] 3-8-6 **75** ow1 .... ChrisHayes 8 69
(Sylvester Kirk) *in tch towards outer: rdn over 3f out: wknd over 1f out* **17/2**

3325 **7** *40* **October Storm**[44] [4559] 3-8-7 **76** .... AlexisBadel 2 14
(Mick Channon) *midfield towards inner: rdn 4f out: sn wknd: t.o* **10/1**

4212 **8** *2* **Space Mountain**[14] [5633] 3-8-9 **78** .... FrannyNorton 1 13
(Mark Johnston) *in tch: rdn over 3f out: sn wknd: eased fnl f* **8/1**

3m 14.52s (12.52) **Going Correction** +1.10s/f (Soft) **8** Ran SP% **118.2**
Speed ratings (Par 107): **108,105,104,104,101 101,78,77**
CSF £16.85 CT £38.47 TOTE £4.60: £1.70, £1.40, £1.30; EX 13.30 Trifecta £57.00.

Owner Mick and Janice Mariscotti **Bred** Daniel Chassagneux **Trained** Kingsclere, Hants

FOCUS
Allowing for rail positioning on the bend the actual race distance of this was 1m6f 92yds. Unsurprisingly they went steady given the conditions and it was run in a very slow time. The winner made all and was much the strongest stayer. He's on the upgrade.

T/Jkpt: Not won. T/Plt: £2,739.60,to a £1 stake. Pool of £185431.77 - 49.41 winning tickets.
T/Qpdt: £39.00 to a £1 stake. Pool of £18347.89 - 347.51 winning tickets.
Darren Owen & Andrew Sheret

[6084]KEMPTON (A.W) (R-H)

Saturday, September 3

OFFICIAL GOING: Polytrack: standard to slow

Wind: light, across Weather: overcast, rain from race 5

6122 TOTEPLACEPOT CONDITIONS STKS (PLUS 10 RACE) 7f (P)

2:10 (2:10) (Class 4) 2-Y-O **£3,946** (£1,174; £586; £293) **Stalls** Low

Form RPR

01 **1** **Sir Dancealot (IRE)**[17] 5549 2-9-2 0 JimCrowley 3 92+
(David Elsworth) *stdd s: t.k.h: hld up wl in tch: effrt on inner 2f out: hung lft but chalng over 1f out: led 1f out: forged ahd ins fnl f: in command whn edgd lft nr fin* **11/4**[2]

02 **2** *1 ½* **War Of Succession**[29] 5108 2-8-12 0 LiamKeniry 5 84
(Andrew Balding) *t.k.h: hld up wl in tch: effrt 2f out: hdwy to chal 1f out: chsd wnr and kpt in same pce ins fnl f* **16/1**

11 **3** *nk* **Fly At Dawn (USA)**[18] 5506 2-9-6 0 WilliamBuick 2 91
(Charlie Appleby) *sn w ldr tl led over 2f out: rdn 2f out: drvn and hdd 1f out: styd on same pce u.p ins fnl f* **11/2**[3]

3 **4** *½* **Parfait (IRE)**[50] 4363 2-8-12 0 JamesDoyle 4 82+
(John Gosden) *trckd ldrs on outer: effrt 2f out: drvn and ev ch 1f out: unable qck and styd on same pce ins fnl f* **10/11**[1]

01 **5** *4* **Ghayyar (IRE)**[22] 5373 2-9-2 0 TomMarquand 1 75
(Richard Hannon) *led: hdd and rdn over 2f out: drvn over 1f out: outpcd and btn 1f out: wknd ins fnl f* **11/1**

1m 26.66s (0.66) **Going Correction** +0.075s/f (Slow) **5** Ran SP% **108.7**
Speed ratings (Par 97): **99,97,96,96,91**
CSF £34.90 TOTE £3.80: £1.70, £4.00; EX 31.60 Trifecta £59.60.
Owner C Benham/ D Whitford/ L Quinn/ K Quinn **Bred** Vincent Duignan **Trained** Newmarket, Suffolk

FOCUS
The Polytrack was officially described as standard to slow. An interesting 2yo conditions event to start, won by the smart Zonderland last year, and today's winner continues to progress. They didn't go a great gallop early, with the winning time 3.06sec outside standard.

6123 TOTESCOOP6 THE MILLIONAIRE MAKER H'CAP 7f (P)

2:45 (2:45) (Class 4) (0-85,85) 3-Y-O+ **£4,690** (£1,395; £697; £348) **Stalls** Low

Form RPR

2046 **1** **Commodore (IRE)**[30] 5075 4-9-9 **84** JamesDoyle 6 93
(George Baker) *hld up in tch in midfield: effrt over 2f out: drvn and hdwy over 1f out: ev ch ins fnl f: r.o wl u.p to ld last stride* **3/1**[1]

1305 **2** *shd* **Lightning Charlie**[11] 5744 4-9-8 **83** JimCrowley 8 91
(Amanda Perrett) *t.k.h: hld up in tch in midfield: effrt 2f out: rdn to chal ent fnl f: led wl ins fnl f: r.o wl: hdd on post* **6/1**[3]

414 **3** *1* **Bahamian Dollar**[50] 4360 3-9-1 **80** JoeFanning 3 83
(James Tate) *chsd ldr: rdn to chal over 1f out: led ins fnl f: hdd wl ins fnl f: no ex and outpcd towards fin* **8/1**

4115 **4** *½* **Eljaddaaf (IRE)**[9] 5810 5-9-3 **78** RobertWinston 4 82
(Dean Ivory) *chsd ldrs: rdn ent fnl 2f: drvn and ev ch ent fnl f: no ex u.p and outpcd fnl 50yds* **5/1**[2]

2102 **5** *1 ½* **He's My Cracker**[34] 4908 3-9-2 **81** JohnFahy 2 79
(Clive Cox) *led: rdn over 2f out: drvn and hrd pressed over 1f out: hdd jst ins fnl f: no ex and wknd wl ins fnl f* **12/1**

06 **6** *nk* **Colonel Bossington (IRE)**[93] 2818 3-8-9 **74** SilvestreDeSousa 5 71
(William Knight) *chsd ldng trio: swtchd lft and effrt over 2f out: stl chsng ldrs but struggling whn qckn whn sltly hmpd 1f out: styd on same pce after* **12/1**

0015 **7** *shd* **Able Jack**[37] 4789 3-9-1 **80** (v) WilliamBuick 7 77
(Andrew Balding) *dwlt: hld up in last trio: hdwy and shifting rt over 1f out: kpt on fnl f: no threat to ldrs* **8/1**

0440 **8** *2 ½* **Harry Champion**[21] 5412 3-9-1 **80** TomMarquand 1 70
(Hugo Palmer) *hld up in tch in midfield: pushed along over 3f out: rdn over 2f out: no hdwy u.p over 1f out: one pced* **16/1**

1554 **9** *¾* **King Of Naples**[18] 5507 3-9-1 **85** GeorgeWood[(5)] 9 73
(James Fanshawe) *t.k.h: hld up in tch in midfield: rdn 2f out: drvn and no imp over 1f out: styd on same pce fnl f* **12/1**

-600 **10** *nse* **Ruban (IRE)**[78] 3358 7-8-12 **80** (t) MillyNaseb[(7)] 10 70
(Stuart Williams) *dwlt: t.k.h: hld up in last trio: effrt 2f out: rdn over 1f out: nvr trbld ldrs* **16/1**

65 **11** *3 ¼* **Show Me Again**[9] 5793 3-9-5 **84** (t) MartinLane 11 63
(David Dennis) *wnt lft s and s.i.s: hld up in rr: rdn jst over 2f out: no hdwy: n.d* **50/1**

1m 26.09s (0.09) **Going Correction** +0.075s/f (Slow)
WFA 3 from 4yo+ 4lb **11** Ran SP% **115.0**
Speed ratings (Par 105): **102,101,100,100,98 98,98,95,94,94 90**
CSF £19.93 CT £132.44 TOTE £3.40: £1.40, £2.10, £2.40; EX 18.90 Trifecta £106.10.
Owner Highclere Thoroughbred Racing - Trinity **Bred** Ringfort Stud **Trained** Manton, Wilts

FOCUS
A fair handicap, but they didn't go a great pace early and it was hard to come from behind. The winner's performance can therefore be marked up.

6124 TOTEQUADPOT SIRENIA STKS (GROUP 3) 6f (P)

3:15 (3:15) (Class 1) 2-Y-O

£23,818 (£9,030; £4,519; £2,251; £1,129; £567) **Stalls** Low

Form RPR

2123 **1** **The Last Lion (IRE)**[14] 5654 2-9-1 103 JoeFanning 7 106
(Mark Johnston) *trckd ldr: shkn up to ld over 1f out: sn rdn and qcknd clr: r.o strly: readily* **11/8**[2]

1 **2** *4* **Koropick (IRE)**[19] 5476 2-9-1 0 JimCrowley 1 94
(Hugo Palmer) *t.k.h: hld up in tch in midfield: effrt 2f out: drvn over 1f out: no ch w wnr but kpt on ins fnl f: wnt 2nd towards fin* **11/10**[1]

120 **3** *½* **Unabated (IRE)**[14] 5654 2-9-1 94 JamesDoyle 4 93
(Marco Botti) *stdd s: t.k.h: hld up in tch in midfield: effrt 2f out: drvn over 1f out: no ch w wnr but kpt on u.p: snatched 3rd on post* **10/1**[3]

3021 **4** *nse* **Queensbrydge**[14] 5632 2-8-12 82 SilvestreDeSousa 6 89
(Robyn Brisland) *led: rdn ent fnl 2f: hdd over 1f out: sn brushed aside by wnr: kpt on same pce fnl f: lost 2 pls towards fin* **20/1**

2164 **5** *1 ½* **Stop The Wages (IRE)**[16] 5583 2-8-12 81 DaneO'Neill 3 85
(Brian Meehan) *stdd s: t.k.h: hld up in tch in last pair: effrt 2f out: no ch w wnr and kpt on same pce u.p ins fnl f* **20/1**

2613 **6** *3* **Smokey Lane (IRE)**[14] 5656 2-9-1 96 ShaneKelly 8 79
(David Evans) *stdd and dropped in bhd after s: hld up in tch in last pair: hung lft bnd 4f out: rdn jst over 2f out: sn outpcd and wl hld over 1f out* **14/1**

01 **7** *nk* **Dandy Flame (IRE)**[40] 4713 2-9-1 75 (b[1]) RenatoSouza 5 78
(Jose Santos) *t.k.h: chsd ldng pair: rdn jst over 2f out: 3rd: outpcd and hung rt over 1f out: wknd fnl f* **50/1**

1m 12.7s (-0.40) **Going Correction** +0.075s/f (Slow) **7** Ran SP% **117.0**
Speed ratings (Par 105): **105,99,99,98,96 92,92**
CSF £3.27 TOTE £2.10: £1.10, £1.20; EX 3.70 Trifecta £14.10.
Owner John Brown & Megan Dennis **Bred** Barronstown Stud And Mrs T Stack **Trained** Middleham Moor, N Yorks

FOCUS
A decent renewal of the Sirenia, but the betting was dominated by two very different types, one with plenty of experience and one with potential. They eventually finished 1-2 with the streetwise performer coming out best, but it was never really a contest. The winner probably didn't need to improve.

6125 TOTESCOOP6 SEPTEMBER STKS (GROUP 3) 1m 4f (P)

3:45 (3:45) (Class 1) 3-Y-O+

£35,160 (£13,330; £6,671; £3,323; £1,667; £837) **Stalls** Low

Form RPR

2-30 **1** **Arab Spring (IRE)**[17] 5558 6-9-5 112 JimCrowley 7 116
(Sir Michael Stoute) *chsd ldr after 2f: led on bit ent fnl 2f: sn rdn and qcknd 2 l clr wl over 1f out: r.o wl and in command after: readily* **11/10**[1]

1-20 **2** *2 ¼* **Robin Of Navan (FR)**[90] 2946 3-8-10 109 SilvestreDeSousa 2 112
(Harry Dunlop) *led at v slow pce tl hdd after 1f and chsd ldng pair 10f out: nt clr run: swtchd lft and bmpd rival 2f out: sn swtchd rt and chsd wnr: kpt on u.p but no imp* **11/2**[3]

120- **3** *hd* **Sky Hunter**[305] 7697 6-9-5 115 JamesDoyle 1 112
(Saeed bin Suroor) *hld up in tch in 4th: effrt to chse ldrs whn bmpd 2f out: wnt 3rd over 1f out battling for 2nd but no imp on wnr ins fnl f: kpt on* **5/2**[2]

1660 **4** *4 ½* **Barye**[15] 5611 5-9-5 103 ShaneKelly 4 104
(Richard Hughes) *hld up in tch: rdn 2f out: sn outpcd: wl hld but kpt on ins fnl f: wnt 4th last strides* **16/1**

3000 **5** *nk* **Noble Gift**[39] 4731 6-9-5 99 CallumShepherd 5 104
(William Knight) *taken down early: stmbld s and slowly away: hdwy to ld after 1f: rdn over 2f out: hdd 2f out and immediately outpcd by wnr: wknd fnl f* **25/1**

-633 **6** *13* **Miss Marjurie (IRE)**[49] 4400 6-9-2 105 WilliamBuick 3 89
(Denis Coakley) *hld up in rr: effrt 2f out: sn outpcd and btn: bhd and heavily eased wl ins fnl f* **12/1**

2m 33.07s (-1.43) **Going Correction** +0.075s/f (Slow)
WFA 3 from 5yo+ 9lb **6** Ran SP% **109.0**
Speed ratings (Par 113): **107,105,105,102,102 93**
CSF £7.18 TOTE £2.30: £1.30, £2.40; EX 8.40 Trifecta £17.50.
Owner Ballymacoll Stud **Bred** Ballymacoll Stud Farm Ltd **Trained** Newmarket, Suffolk

FOCUS
Nothing quite of the calibre of recent winners Prince Bishop or Jack Hobbs in this season's September Stakes, but a decent line up all the same. The leader dropped anchor after hitting the front after a furlong, so this developed into something of a sprint up the home straight. Arab Spring still has some potential to progress.

6126 TOTEPOOL LONDON MILE H'CAP (SERIES FINAL) 1m (P)

4:15 (4:19) (Class 2) 3-Y-O+

£31,125 (£9,320; £4,660; £2,330; £1,165; £585) **Stalls** Low

Form RPR

-262 **1** **Afjaan (IRE)**[17] 5552 4-9-6 **94** PatCosgrave 14 106+
(William Haggas) *stdd and dropped in bhd after s: hld up in rr: clsd and nt clr run 2f out: swtchd lft and gd hdwy over 1f out: racing nr stands' rail and chsd ldrs ins fnl f: r.o wl to ld towards fin* **5/1**[2]

5006 **2** *¾* **Georgian Bay (IRE)**[17] 5552 6-8-13 **92** (v) JordanVaughan[(5)] 10 102
(K R Burke) *bustled along towards rr early: hdwy into midfield on outer 1/2-way: rdn to press ldrs 2f out: led and edgd lft over 1f out: kpt on u.p: hdd and no ex towards fin* **12/1**

1010 **3** *1* **Replenish (FR)**[17] 5552 3-8-7 **91** GeorgeWood[(5)] 7 98
(James Fanshawe) *wl in tch in midfield: effrt ent fnl 2f: hdwy u.p and hung lft over 1f out: chsd ldr ins fnl f: kpt on same pce after and lost 2nd wl ins fnl f* **8/1**

1221 **4** *2 ¼* **Dommersen (IRE)**[17] 5552 3-9-4 **97** RobertHavlin 1 99+
(John Gosden) *s.i.s: hld up in last pair: effrt on inner 2f out: gd hdwy over 1f out: chsd ldrs 1f out: no imp 150yds out: wknd towards fin* **15/8**[1]

321 **5** *½* **Wimpole Hall**[15] 5601 3-8-9 **88** (p) SilvestreDeSousa 8 88+
(William Jarvis) *t.k.h: midfield: hdwy to join ldr 1/2-way: rdn and ev ch 2f out: drvn over 1f out: no ex jst ins fnl f: wknd wl ins fnl f* **7/1**[3]

2155 **6** *¾* **Welliesinthewater (IRE)**[32] 4976 6-8-4 **81** (v) NoelGarbutt[(3)] 6 81
(Derek Shaw) *t.k.h: hld up in tch in midfield: effrt 2f out: hdwy u.p between horses 1f out: no imp ins fnl f* **40/1**

0020 **7** *nk* **Lat Hawill (IRE)**[16] 5585 5-9-10 **98** (v) PhillipMakin 5 97
(Keith Dalgleish) *s.i.s: hld up towards rr: clsd 2f out: rdn and sme hdwy whn swtchd lft over 1f out: kpt on ins fnl f: nvr trbld ldrs* **25/1**

1156 **8** *½* **Bastille Day**[38] 4776 4-9-1 **89** JimCrowley 11 87
(David Elsworth) *hld up towards rr: nt clrest of runs 2f out: swtchd lft over 1f out: kpt on ins fnl f: nvr trbld ldrs* **9/1**

1400 **9** *nk* **Cape Icon**[28] 5156 5-8-13 **87** [1] JamesDoyle 3 84
(Clive Cox) *led: rdn ent fnl 2f: hdd over 1f out and no ex 1f out: wknd ins fnl f* **14/1**

0560 **10** *½* **Jack Of Diamonds (IRE)**[17] 5552 7-8-11 **90** CallumShepherd[(5)] 9 86
(Roger Teal) *sn dropped towards rr and bustled along early: hdwy u.p and drifting rt over 1f out: no imp fnl f* **40/1**

1004 **11** *4 ½* **Cape Speed (FR)**[20] 5437 3-8-11 **90** JoeFanning 2 75
(Mark Johnston) *chsd ldr tl 1/2-way: rdn and ev ch 2f out: drvn and unable qck over 1f out: wknd qckly fnl f* **25/1**

062 **12** *2* **Abareeq**[7] 5892 3-8-10 **89** [1] DaneO'Neill 4 69
(Mark Johnston) *chsd ldrs: rdn and ducked lft 2f out: sn outpcd and btn: wknd fnl f* **20/1**

3415 **13** *1* **Secret Art (IRE)**[17] 5552 6-9-7 **95** WilliamBuick 12 74
(William Knight) *in tch in midfield on outer: rdn: lost pl and sltly impeded 2f out: bhd and n.d after* **20/1**

6023 **14** *4 ½* **Sirius Prospect (USA)**[17] 5552 8-9-7 **95** (p) RobertWinston 13 63
(Dean Ivory) *hld up in midfield: hdwy to chse ldrs 5f out: rdn and struggling to qckn whn hmpd and lost pl 2f out: bhd after* **16/1**

1m 37.91s (-1.89) **Going Correction** +0.075s/f (Slow)
WFA 3 from 4yo+ 5lb **14** Ran SP% **127.4**
Speed ratings (Par 109): **112,111,110,108,107 106,106,105,105,105 100,98,97,93**
CSF £61.46 CT £499.71 TOTE £5.10: £2.20, £3.40, £3.10; EX 83.80 Trifecta £395.50.
Owner Al Shaqab Racing **Bred** Haras Du Logis Saint Germain **Trained** Newmarket, Suffolk

FOCUS
A competitive renewal of the London Mile Final which included seven of the first nine home from the qualifier here 17 days earlier. The race had gone to a 4yo seven times in the past ten years and it did so again this time, even though there were just two from that age group in the field. The leaders may have gone off too quick as the principals came from off the pace. A smart effort from the winner.

6127 TOTEEXACTA H'CAP 2m (P)
4:50 (4:53) (Class 4) (0-80,79) 3-Y-O **£4,690** (£1,395; £697; £348) **Stalls** Low

Form | | | | RPR
1032 **1** **Blakeney Point**[38] 4778 3-9-5 **77**....(p) JamesDoyle 1 85+
(Roger Charlton) *trckd ldng pair: effrt on inner ent fnl 2f: led over 1f out: clr ins fnl f: r.o strly: rdn out* **10/3**[3]

2021 **2** *3* **Withhold**[14] 5623 3-9-7 **79**.... SilvestreDeSousa 3 83
(Charles Hills) *led: rdn over 2f out: hung lft 2f out: hdd over 1f out: styd on same pce after* **9/4**[2]

211 **3** *1 1/4* **Captain Peacock**[21] 5398 3-9-4 **76**....(v) JimCrowley 2 79
(William Knight) *hld up in tch in 4th: effrt and swtchd rt wl over 1f out: drvn to go 3rd 1f out: styd on same pce after* **6/4**[1]

0602 **4** *3/4* **Contingency**[21] 5398 3-9-0 **72**.... PatCosgrave 4 74
(Jane Chapple-Hyam) *chsd ldr: rdn and ev ch over 2f out: carried lft 2f out: 3rd and outpcd over 1f out: kpt on same pce after* **10/1**

-054 **5** *5* **McCools Gold**[17] 5548 3-8-7 **65**.... JohnFahy 5 61
(Eve Johnson Houghton) *stdd s: hld up in tch in rr: rdn over 2f out: sn btn: bhd fnl f* **14/1**

3m 33.38s (3.28) **Going Correction** +0.075s/f (Slow) **5** Ran SP% **109.6**
Speed ratings (Par 103): **94,92,91,91,89**
CSF £11.09 TOTE £3.70: £1.70, £1.50; EX 11.20 Trifecta £17.00.

Owner Axom LX **Bred** Mr & Mrs A E Pakenham **Trained** Beckhampton, Wilts

FOCUS
A fair 3yo staying handicap won by the smart Burmese last year. Three of the five runners were sired by Champs Elysees, but not the winner. They dawdled for much of the way, but the winner did it nicely.

6128 TOTETRIFECTA H'CAP (JOCKEY CLUB GRASSROOTS FLAT MIDDLE DISTANCE SERIES QUALIFIER) 1m 3f (P)
5:25 (5:27) (Class 4) (0-80,78) 3-Y-O+ **£4,690** (£1,395; £697; £348) **Stalls** Low

Form | | | | RPR
0043 **1** **Charlie Bear**[18] 5526 4-9-12 **78**.... TimmyMurphy 15 90
(Jamie Osborne) *hld up in tch in midfield: travelling strly and nt clr run over 2f out: rdn and hdwy to chse clr ldr over 1f out: styd on wl to ld ins fnl f: sn in command* **10/1**

5064 **2** *1 1/4* **Charlies Mate**[12] 5724 5-9-10 **76**.... KierenFox 2 86
(John Best) *led: rdn and kicked clr ent fnl 2f: drvn over 1f out: hdd ins fnl f: no ex* **6/1**[3]

2-34 **3** *6* **Nonios (IRE)**[26] 5231 4-9-3 **74**.... GeorgeBuckell[(5)] 12 74+
(David Simcock) *short of room leaving stalls: hld up off the pce in rr: shkn up and stl plenty to do 2f out: hdwy over 1f out: r.o wl ins fnl f: snatched 3rd last strides: nvr trbld ldrs* **11/2**[2]

1-00 **4** *nk* **Queen's Novel**[31] 5037 4-9-11 **77**.... JamesDoyle 10 76
(James Tate) *chsd ldrs: rdn ent fnl 2f: drvn and outpcd by ldng pair over 1f out: wl hld and plugged on same pce after: lost 3rd last strides* **14/1**

1000 **5** *nk* **Cat Royale (IRE)**[29] 5122 3-8-8 **73**....(p) PaddyPilley[(5)] 6 72
(Jane Chapple-Hyam) *chsd ldrs: rdn wl over 2f out: outpcd by ldng pair and btn over 1f out: battling for 3rd and plugged on same pce fnl f* **25/1**

6035 **6** *3/4* **Biotic**[14] 5649 5-9-9 **75**.... LiamKeniry 16 72
(Rod Millman) *stdd and dropped in bhd after s: hld up off the pce in rr: effrt and hdwy into midfield 2f out: no ch w ldrs but kpt on ins fnl f* **11/1**

35-0 **7** *2 1/4* **Open The Red**[35] 4868 4-9-12 **78**.... RobertHavlin 13 72
(Amanda Perrett) *hld up towards rr: effrt and hdwy into midfield 2f out: no imp over 1f out: wl hld fnl f* **8/1**

2302 **8** *3 1/2* **Desdichado**[26] 5231 4-9-12 **78**.... WilliamBuick 1 66
(Ralph Beckett) *chsd ldrs: rdn over 2f out: drvn and outpcd over 1f out: wknd 1f out: eased ins fnl f* **5/1**[1]

21-3 **9** *3/4* **Falcon's Song (USA)**[26] 5245 4-9-7 **73**.... SilvestreDeSousa 4 59
(Ismail Mohammed) *chsd ldr: rdn over 2f out: drvn and outpcd over 1f out: wknd and eased ins fnl f* **7/1**

2541 **10** *nk* **Cornelious (IRE)**[9] 5795 4-9-2 **68**....(v) DarryllHolland 7 54
(Clifford Lines) *hld up in midfield on outer: rdn over 2f out: no imp u.p wl over 1f out: sn wknd* **8/1**

0-60 **11** *3/4* **Defining Year (IRE)**[54] 4208 8-9-5 **74**....(t) TimClark[(3)] 9 59
(Hugo Froud) *dwlt: hld up towards rr: : rdn on outer 3f out: little rspnse and btn over 2f out: wknd wl over 1f out* **50/1**

5223 **12** *1 1/2* **Brasted (IRE)**[54] 4204 4-9-4 **75**.... PaddyBradley[(5)] 11 57
(Lee Carter) *wnt lft s: t.k.h: hld up in midfield: rdn over 2f out: sn struggling: wknd wl over 1f out* **33/1**

2610 **13** *1 1/2* **Glance My Way (IRE)**[15] 5603 3-9-2 **76**.... DaneO'Neill 3 55
(Richard Hannon) *dwlt: hld up in midfield: rdn over 2f out: no rspnse and sn struggling: wknd wl over 1f out* **20/1**

0050 **14** *4* **Moojaned (IRE)**[21] 5406 5-8-12 **64** oh1.... AdamBeschizza 5 37
(David Evans) *t.k.h: hld up in midfield: rdn over 2f out: sn lost pl: bhd over 1f out* **25/1**

3065 **15** *1 1/4* **Irrevocable (IRE)**[15] 5603 3-8-6 **71**.... GeorgeWood[(5)] 14 42
(Roger Charlton) *s.i.s: a bhd: rdn and no rspnse over 2f out: wl bhd over 1f out* **25/1**

2m 18.2s (-3.70) **Going Correction** +0.075s/f (Slow)
WFA 3 from 4yo+ 8lb **15** Ran SP% **126.4**
Speed ratings (Par 105): **116,115,110,110,110 109,108,105,105,104 104,103,102,99,98**
CSF £66.25 CT £377.93 TOTE £13.20: £4.20, £2.70, £2.80; EX 46.60 Trifecta £665.60.

Owner Michael Buckley **Bred** Lone Oak Stud Limited **Trained** Upper Lambourn, Berks

FOCUS
A competitive handicap to end with and the pace was solid, but the first two pulled well clear.

T/Plt: £53.50 to a £1 stake. Pool: £55,166.27 - 752.25 winning tickets T/Qpdt: £6.10 to a £1 stake. Pool: £4,754.62 - 571.50 winning tickets **Steve Payne**

5853 THIRSK (L-H)
Saturday, September 3

OFFICIAL GOING: Good to soft (good in places) changing to soft after race 1 (2.20) changing to soft (heavy in places) after race 6 (5.00)
Wind: light half-against Weather: raining

6129 LONGINES IRISH CHAMPIONS WEEKEND EBF MAIDEN STKS (PLUS 10 RACE) 7f
2:20 (2:21) (Class 4) 2-Y-O **£4,269** (£1,270; £634; £317) **Stalls** Low

Form | | | | RPR
4 **1** **Rock N Rolla (IRE)**[8] 5834 2-9-5 0.... ConnorBeasley 6 83
(Keith Dalgleish) *mde all: drvn and styd on wl fnl 2f* **5/1**[3]

2 *2* **Areen Heart (FR)** 2-9-5 0....[1] DavidNolan 8 78+
(Richard Fahey) *dwlt: sn in mid-div: swtchd rt over 2f out: edgd lft and kpt on to chse wnr fnl f* **6/1**

02 **3** *3 1/4* **Trooper's Gold**[35] 4856 2-9-5 0.... TomEaves 7 70
(Kevin Ryan) *chsd ldrs: drvn 3f out: one pce fr over 1f out* **5/1**[3]

4 *1 3/4* **Iron Islands** 2-9-5 0.... JoeyHaynes 5 66
(K R Burke) *sn chsng ldrs: drvn over 3f out: one pce over 1f out* **25/1**

36 **5** *3 1/4* **Portledge (IRE)**[15] 5615 2-9-5 0.... PJMcDonald 9 57
(James Bethell) *chsd ldrs: edgd lft and wknd over 1f out* **7/2**[2]

32 **6** *5* **Prazeres**[19] 5476 2-9-5 0.... GrahamGibbons 3 45
(William Haggas) *trckd wnr: edgd lft and wknd over 1f out* **2/1**[1]

7 *1 3/4* **Harwood** 2-9-5 0.... SamJames 10 41
(David O'Meara) *wnt rt s: in rr: sme hdwy over 3f out: lost pl 2f out* **16/1**

8 *4* **Millybond** 2-9-0 0.... PaulMulrennan 2 26
(David Brown) *in rr: bhd fnl 2f* **66/1**

0 **9** *3* **Savea (IRE)**[105] 2489 2-9-5 0.... BenCurtis 4 23
(David O'Meara) *in rr: bhd and reminders 3f out* **40/1**

00 **10** *6* **Tess Graham**[40] 4713 2-9-0 0.... PatrickMathers 1
(Sarah Hollinshead) *s.i.s: bhd fnl 2f* **100/1**

1m 32.6s (5.40) **Going Correction** +0.70s/f (Yiel) **10** Ran SP% **117.8**
Speed ratings (Par 97): **97,94,91,89,85 79,77,73,69,62**
CSF £34.68 TOTE £6.30: £2.00, £1.80, £1.70; EX 51.70 Trifecta £220.80.

Owner Weldspec Glasgow Limited **Bred** Kildaragh Stud **Trained** Carluke, S Lanarks

FOCUS
Rail movements meant distances were increased by 20yds in Races 1, 2, 4 and 7, and 30yds for Race 6. Rain fell both before and during racing and the official going was eased to good to soft. Three of the last four winners of this maiden went on to win again next time and this looked another fair renewal.

6130 MARKET CROSS JEWELLERS NURSERY H'CAP 1m
2:55 (2:55) (Class 5) (0-75,75) 2-Y-O **£3,234** (£962; £481; £240) **Stalls** Low

Form | | | | RPR
5550 **1** **Nordic Combined (IRE)**[21] 5414 2-8-5 **59**.... BenCurtis 8 68
(Brian Ellison) *in rr: bhd and reminders 4f out: hdwy on ins 3f out: led appr fnl f: swvd rt: hld on towards fin* **22/1**

1 **2** *1/2* **Reachforthestars (IRE)**[70] 3640 2-9-7 **75**.... SamJames 7 82+
(David O'Meara) *in rr: pushed along over 4f out: hdwy on wd outside over 2f out: 2nd 1f out: no ex clsng stages* **9/2**[1]

0005 **3** *4* **Reinstorm**[18] 5528 2-8-0 **54** oh1.... PatrickMathers 9 53
(Richard Fahey) *chsd ldrs: drvn over 2f out: kpt on to take 3rd nr fin* **14/1**

054 **4** *nk* **Midnight Man (FR)**[12] 5728 2-8-13 **67**.... JoeyHaynes 10 65+
(K R Burke) *mid-div: drvn over 3f out: chsng ldrs over 1f out: kpt on same pce* **5/1**[2]

4453 **5** *nk* **Tagur (IRE)**[64] 3852 2-8-13 **67**.... TomEaves 6 64
(Kevin Ryan) *chsd ldrs: one pce over 1f out* **9/1**

0522 **6** *2 1/4* **Dream On Dreamer (IRE)**[8] 5853 2-9-1 **69**....(b[1]) PaulMulrennan 1 61
(Michael Dods) *s.i.s: hdwy to ld after 1f: wandered over 1f out: sn hdd & wknd* **13/2**

055 **7** *2* **Hugging The Rails (IRE)**[48] 4423 2-8-11 **65**.... DavidAllan 3 53+
(Tim Easterby) *led early: chsd ldrs: wknd last 150yds* **17/2**

335 **8** *9* **Pantera Negra (IRE)**[35] 4856 2-8-12 **66**.... GrahamGibbons 2 34
(Ed Dunlop) *s.i.s: jnd ldr after 1f: drvn over 2f out: hung rt and lost pl over 1f out: eased clsng stages in rr: drvn 4f out: in* **7/1**

5565 **9** *7* **Mister Moosah (IRE)**[24] 5290 2-9-3 **71**.... PJMcDonald 4 24
(Micky Hammond) *in rr: effrt 3f out: lost pl wl over 1f out: bhd whn eased clsng stages* **16/1**

4336 **10** *9* **Hartswell**[14] 5637 2-9-7 **75**....(p) NickyMackay 5 8
(John Gosden) *chsd ldrs: drvn over 3f out: lost pl over 1f out: sn heavily eased* **6/1**[3]

1m 47.69s (7.59) **Going Correction** +0.925s/f (Soft) **10** Ran SP% **112.4**
Speed ratings (Par 95): **99,98,94,94,93 91,89,80,73,64**
CSF £114.33 CT £1047.76 TOTE £26.80: £5.60, £1.80, £4.90; EX 162.90 Trifecta £3187.30 Part won..

Owner Dan Gilbert **Bred** Dan Gilbert **Trained** Norton, N Yorks

■ Stewards' Enquiry : Ben Curtis four-day ban; used whip above permitted level (17th,19th, 20th,21st Sept)

FOCUS
The rail had been moved out, adding 20yds, and the ground was changed to soft. A moderate nursery run at a strong pace and the first two came clear.

6131 BARKERS OF NORTHALLERTON H'CAP (DIV I) 6f
3:25 (3:26) (Class 4) (0-80,85) 4-Y-O+ **£5,175** (£1,540; £769; £384) **Stalls** High

Form | | | | RPR
3000 **1** **Money Team (IRE)**[25] 5274 5-9-4 **77**.... GrahamGibbons 4 86
(David Barron) *trckd ldrs: 2nd appr fnl f kpt on to ld last 100yds: drvn out* **16/1**

2213 **2** *3/4* **Magical Effect (IRE)**[8] 5857 4-9-4 **77**.... JamesSullivan 5 84
(Ruth Carr) *in rr: hdwy and swtchd lft over 1f out: sn chsng ldng pair: tk 2nd nr fin* **2/1**[1]

0233 **3** *hd* **Signore Piccolo**[8] 5858 5-9-6 **79**.... DavidNolan 6 85
(David O'Meara) *trckd ldr: hung lft and led over 1f out: hdd and no ex last 100yds* **4/1**[2]

0032 **4** *2 1/2* **Kenny The Captain (IRE)**[5] 5968 5-8-10 **72**.... RachelRichardson[(3)] 8 70
(Tim Easterby) *chsd ldrs: n.m.r over 1f out: one pce* **4/1**[2]

0305 **5** *1* **Mississippi**[8] 5852 7-9-3 **76**.... PaulMulrennan 1 71
(Paul Midgley) *wnt lft s: swtchd rt after s: hdwy and nt clr run over 1f out: sn wknd* **8/1**

1000 **6** *5* **Kommander Kirkup**[8] 5857 5-9-7 **80**....(b) ConnorBeasley 9 59
(John Davies) *in rr: effrt and nt clr run on inner over 1f out: sn wknd* **22/1**

0000 **7** 2¾ **Clubland (IRE)**[9] 5797 7-8-2 **68** ow1.............................[1] KevinLundie[(7)] 2 38
(Roy Bowring) *in rr: hdwy and swtchd lft over 2f out: lost pl over 1f out* **12/1**

1312 **8** 5 **Seamster**[7] 5864 9-9-12 **85**.............................(t) PJMcDonald 7 39
(David Loughnane) *led: hdd over 1f out: sn lost pl: bhd whn eased nr fin* **15/2**[3]

1m 14.95s (2.25) **Going Correction** +0.525s/f (Yiel) **8** Ran SP% **114.1**
Speed ratings (Par 105): **106,105,104,101,100 93,89,83**
CSF £48.26 CT £158.69 TOTE £18.80: £4.20, £1.20, £1.50; EX 62.20 Trifecta £255.40.

Owner White Rose Racing **Bred** Mrs Claire Doyle **Trained** Maunby, N Yorks

FOCUS
A competitive little sprint featuring some progressive types. The action unfolded down the stands' rail and it paid to race prominently.

6132 PERSONAL TOUCHES H'CAP 1m

3:55 (3:57) (Class 3) (0-95,95) 3-Y-O **£8,086** (£2,406; £1,202; £601) **Stalls** Low

Form RPR

3-11 **1** **Murad Khan (FR)**[112] 2237 3-9-4 **92**.............................. JackMitchell 7 104
(Hugo Palmer) *led over 1f: upsides over 1f out: hung lft and led nr fin* **4/1**[3]

5211 **2** *hd* **Ballet Concerto**[6] 5933 3-9-3 **91** 6ex.......................... GrahamGibbons 8 102
(Sir Michael Stoute) *trckd ldrs: edgd lft and led over 2f out: rdn over 1f out: hdd nr fin* **5/2**[1]

6-51 **3** 7 **Michele Strogoff**[25] 5280 3-9-7 **95**.............................. ConnorBeasley 1 90
(David Loughnane) *led over 6f out: hdd and hmpd over 2f out:. one pce* **20/1**

5315 **4** 7 **Briyouni (FR)**[28] 5180 3-8-8 **82**.............................. TomEaves 6 61
(Kevin Ryan) *s.i.s: hdwy 3f out: lost pl over 1f out* **12/1**

04 **5** 1½ **High Draw (FR)**[63] 3914 3-8-9 **83**.............................. JoeyHaynes 9 58
(K R Burke) *hld up in mid-divuision: drvn over 3f out: lost pl over 1f out* **8/1**

-500 **6** ¾ **Tawdheef (IRE)**[57] 4116 3-8-13 **87**.............................(e[1]) PJMcDonald 3 61
(Simon Crisford) *rr-div: hmpd over 2f out: sn wknd* **22/1**

025 **7** 3½ **Mikmak**[47] 4448 3-9-1 **89**.............................. PaulMulrennan 4 55
(William Muir) *dwlt: hdwy to chse ldrs over 3f out: wknd over 1f out* **6/1**

4-21 **U** **In The City**[36] 4840 3-8-7 **81**.............................. BenCurtis 5
(William Haggas) *trckd ldrs: bdly hmpd on ins and uns rdr over 2f out: fatally injured* **7/2**[2]

1m 46.14s (6.04) **Going Correction** +0.925s/f (Soft) **8** Ran SP% **113.0**
Speed ratings (Par 105): **106,105,98,91,90 89,86,**
CSF £14.07 CT £173.72 TOTE £4.50: £1.70, £1.30, £4.20; EX 14.80 Trifecta £258.20.

Owner V I Araci **Bred** S C E A Haras De Manneville **Trained** Newmarket, Suffolk

FOCUS
Rail movements meant 20yds was added to the official race distance. A classy handicap featuring a number of last-time-out winners and it wasn't without drama. They went a sensible gallop in the ground, although not much got into it. The first two came clear and fought out a bobbing finish.

6133 SIMON & TOPSY BARTON H'CAP 5f

4:25 (4:31) (Class 4) (0-85,84) 3-Y-O **£5,175** (£1,540; £769; £384) **Stalls** High

Form RPR

0360 **1** **Market Choice (IRE)**[20] 5439 3-8-9 **72**.............................. PJMcDonald 7 79
(Michael Dods) *in rr: hdwy 2f out: kpt on to ld nr fin* **11/1**

211 **2** *nk* **Midnight Malibu (IRE)**[43] 4585 3-9-6 **83**.............................. DavidAllan 6 89
(Tim Easterby) *chsd ldrs: led over 1f out: hdd and no ex nr fin* **4/1**[3]

2313 **3** ¾ **Rose Eclair**[8] 5836 3-8-11 **74**.............................(b) JamesSullivan 9 77
(Tim Easterby) *mid-div: hdwy over 2f out: chsng ldrs over 1f out: kpt on same pce fnl 75yds* **8/1**

4522 **4** 1¼ **Geno (IRE)**[14] 5643 3-9-2 **79**.............................(p) TomEaves 4 78
(Kevin Ryan) *chsd ldrs: kpt on same pce appr fnl f* **11/2**

-000 **5** 1 **Ayresome Angel**[45] 4514 3-9-0 **77**.............................[1] ConnorBeasley 8 72
(Bryan Smart) *led: hung lft and hdd over 1f out: one pce* **20/1**

216 **6** 2¼ **Acclaim The Nation (IRE)**[14] 5643 3-8-12 **75**.................... JasonHart 1 62
(Eric Alston) *wnt lft s: t.k.h: sn w ldrs: wknd over 1f out: eased nr fin* **7/2**[2]

551 **7** 1½ **Swirral Edge**[12] 5730 3-9-0 **77**.............................. PaulMulrennan 10 58
(David Brown) *in rr: effrt 2f out: nvr a factor: eased nr fin* **9/4**[1]

1m 1.71s (2.11) **Going Correction** +0.525s/f (Yiel) **7** Ran SP% **112.6**
Speed ratings (Par 103): **104,103,102,100,98 95,92**
CSF £52.51 CT £373.68 TOTE £11.70: £4.40, £2.60; EX 59.80 Trifecta £414.80.

Owner Wensleydale Bacon Ltd and Rod Rider **Bred** John Hutchinson **Trained** Denton, Co Durham

FOCUS
An average sprint handicap, in which the fast pace set things up for the closers.

6134 UKINSURANCENET HAMBLETON CUP H'CAP 1m 4f

5:00 (5:00) (Class 4) (0-85,84) 3-Y-O+ **£6,469** (£1,925; £962; £481) **Stalls** High

Form RPR

0433 **1** **Tamayuz Magic (IRE)**[25] 5275 5-9-6 **78**....................(b) JamesSullivan 7 86
(Michael Easterby) . **6/1**[3]

1120 **2** *hd* **Icefall (IRE)**[14] 5653 3-9-0 **81**.............................. DavidAllan 9 88
(Tim Easterby) . **7/4**[1]

5606 **3** *hd* **Swaheen**[42] 4664 4-9-5 **82**.............................. JoshDoyle[(5)] 2 89
(Julie Camacho) . **5/1**[2]

1-04 **4** ½ **All About Time**[80] 3291 4-9-12 **84**.............................. DavidNolan 8 90
(David O'Meara) . **8/1**

1001 **5** 4½ **Play Nicely**[124] 1923 4-9-4 **76**.............................. GrahamGibbons 4 75
(David Barron) . **10/1**

0-60 **6** *shd* **Card High (IRE)**[70] 3659 6-8-12 **75**.............................(t) HollieDoyle[(5)] 5 74
(Wilf Storey) . **20/1**

00/0 **7** *hd* **Restraint Of Trade (IRE)**[15] 5611 6-9-11 **83**.............. ConnorBeasley 6 82
(Jennie Candlish) . **6/1**[3]

3135 **8** 18 **Tapis Libre**[28] 5157 8-9-8 **83**.............................. RachelRichardson[(3)] 3 53
(Jacqueline Coward) . **11/1**

2m 51.24s (15.04) **Going Correction** +0.925s/f (Soft)
WFA 3 from 4yo+ 9lb **8** Ran SP% **114.9**
Speed ratings (Par 105): **86,85,85,85,82 82,82,70**
CSF £17.03 CT £56.55 TOTE £6.40: £2.00, £1.40, £1.80; EX 19.20 Trifecta £63.30.

Owner W H & Mrs J A Tinning **Bred** Eimear Mulhern **Trained** Sheriff Hutton, N Yorks

FOCUS
An additional 30yds was added to the race distance as a result of rail movements. An average renewal of this historic handicap in which they went a slow gallop in the testing ground. The first four came clear in a tight finish.

6135 EBF STALLIONS JENNY ROBERTS ORIGINAL BRITISH MILLINERY MAIDEN FILLIES' STKS 1m

5:35 (5:37) (Class 4) 3-Y-O+ **£6,469** (£1,925; £962; £481) **Stalls** Low

Form RPR

2362 **1** **Volition (IRE)**[31] 5018 3-9-0 77.............................. GrahamGibbons 8 79+
(Sir Michael Stoute) *trckd ldr: led over 4f out: edgd lft and drvn over 1f out: hld on towards fin* **11/4**[2]

2323 **2** ¾ **Organza**[20] 5438 3-9-0 73.............................(v[1]) PaulMulrennan 1 76
(Mick Channon) *led tl over 4f out: swtchd rt over 1f out: kpt on fnl 100yds* **5/2**[1]

3 3¼ **Bybrook** 3-9-0 0.............................. SamJames 7 69+
(David Simcock) *trckd ldrs: edgd lft and outpcd over 2f out: kpt on fnl f* **4/1**[3]

4 8 **Perfectly Spirited** 3-9-0 0.............................. NickyMackay 2 50
(John Gosden) *dwlt: hld up in rr: hdwy 3f out: wknd over 1f out* **4/1**[3]

6 **5** 2¼ **Magic Mirror**[17] 5544 3-9-0 0.............................. PJMcDonald 9 45
(Mark Rimell) *trckd ldrs: drvn 3f out: wknd over 1f out* **28/1**

0-4 **6** 1¾ **Merriment**[12] 5731 3-9-0 0.............................. TomEaves 3 41
(Peter Niven) *s.i.s: in rr: brief effrt over 2f out: sn wknd* **14/1**

0 **7** 17 **Garter (IRE)**[50] 4361 3-9-0 0.............................. MichaelJMMurphy 5 2
(Charles Hills) *trckd ldrs: drvn over 3f out: lost pl 2f out: wl bhd whn eased clsng stages* **14/1**

1m 48.28s (8.18) **Going Correction** +0.925s/f (Soft)
WFA 3 from 4yo 5lb **7** Ran SP% **112.0**
Speed ratings (Par 102): **96,95,92,84,81 80,63**
CSF £9.63 TOTE £3.50: £2.10, £1.60; EX 10.90 Trifecta £30.60.

Owner Cheveley Park Stud **Bred** Doc Bloodstock **Trained** Newmarket, Suffolk

FOCUS
Rail movements resulted in the race distance being increased by 20yds. The first two home set the standard in this modest maiden. They went a fair pace in testing ground that was changed to soft (heavy in places).

6136 BARKERS OF NORTHALLERTON H'CAP (DIV II) 6f

6:05 (6:06) (Class 4) (0-80,80) 4-Y-O+ **£5,175** (£1,540; £769; £384) **Stalls** High

Form RPR

5121 **1** **Giant Spark**[63] 3907 4-9-7 **80**.............................. DavidNolan 4 94
(Paul Midgley) *trckd ldrs: led over 1f out: drvn clr* **9/4**[1]

4100 **2** 3 **Art Obsession (IRE)**[28] 5182 5-9-3 **76**.......................... JamesSullivan 3 80
(Paul Midgley) *hld up in rr: hdwy over 2f out: chsng ldrs over 1f out: tk modest 2nd nr fin* **11/2**

1203 **3** *nk* **Inexes**[9] 5810 4-9-4 **77**.............................(p) SamJames 2 80
(Marjorie Fife) *chsd ldrs: 2nd appr fnl f: kpt on same pce* **5/1**[3]

1010 **4** ½ **Royal Connoisseur (IRE)**[35] 4873 5-9-1 **74**............. GeorgeChaloner 6 75
(Richard Fahey) *chsd ldrs: drvn over 2f out: kpt on same pce over 1f out* **9/1**

2533 **5** 18 **More Beau (USA)**[5] 5969 5-8-9 **68**.............................(v[1]) BarryMcHugh 5 12
(David Nicholls) *drvn to ld: clr over 3f out: wknd and hdd over 1f out: sn bhd: eased clsng stages.* **11/4**[2]

-060 **6** 1¼ **Misu Mac**[40] 4714 6-8-7 **66** oh5.............................. AndrewElliott 1 6
(Neville Bycroft) *in rr: lost pl over 4f out: sn bhd: eased clsng stages* **33/1**

3005 **7** 1½ **Mon Brav**[20] 5439 9-8-11 **70**.............................. TomEaves 8 5
(Brian Ellison) *in rr: drvn and outpcd over 3f out: sn bhd: eased clsng stages* **8/1**

1m 16.01s (3.31) **Going Correction** +0.525s/f (Yiel) **7** Ran SP% **113.5**
Speed ratings (Par 105): **98,94,93,92,68 67,65**
CSF £14.87 CT £54.83 TOTE £2.90: £1.50, £3.00; EX 14.20 Trifecta £47.80.

Owner Frank Brady **Bred** Frank Brady **Trained** Westow, N Yorks

FOCUS
The weaker of the two divisions of this sprint handicap, but an impressive winner who struck from off a fast pace.

T/Plt: £79.90 to a £1 stake. Pool: £68,632.30 - 626.55 winning tickets T/Qpdt: £10.90 to a £1 stake. Pool: £4,084.53 - 275.40 winning tickets **Walter Glynn**

5805 WOLVERHAMPTON (A.W) (L-H)

Saturday, September 3

OFFICIAL GOING: Tapeta: standard

Wind: Fresh behind Weather: Overcast

6137 FCL GLOBAL FORWARDING MAKING LOGISTICS PERSONAL APPRENTICE H'CAP 1m 141y (Tp)

5:50 (5:50) (Class 6) (0-65,66) 3-Y-O+ **£2,587** (£770; £384; £192) **Stalls** Low

Form RPR

5244 **1** **All The Rage**[59] 4018 3-8-11 **65**.............................. ManuelFernandes[(7)] 10 75+
(Sir Mark Prescott Bt) *hmpd s: hld up: hdwy on outer over 3f out: led over 2f out: sn pushed clr: rdn out* **3/1**[1]

3000 **2** ½ **Roxie Lot**[14] 5635 4-9-4 **62**.............................(p) MeganNicholls[(3)] 9 71
(Pam Sly) *mid-div: lost pl 4f out: hdwy on outer 2f out: chsd wnr over 1f out: rdn and edgd lft ins fnl f: styd on* **12/1**

0122 **3** 3½ **Anneani (IRE)**[15] 5610 4-8-11 **59**.............................. AledBeech[(7)] 13 61
(David Evans) *hld up: nt clr run over 2f out: hdwy over 1f out: sn edgd rt: styd on to go 3rd ins fnl f: nt trble ldrs* **6/1**[3]

2323 **4** 5 **Clary (IRE)**[156] 1171 6-9-7 **65**.............................. NatalieHambling[(3)] 4 56
(James Unett) *mid-div: nt clr run and lost pl over 3f out: pushed along and hmpd over 1f out: styd on to go 4th ins fnl f* **12/1**

505 **5** ¾ **Almanack**[18] 5503 6-9-0 **62**.............................. TobyEley[(7)] 5 52
(Daniel Mark Loughnane) *hld up: pushed along over 5f out: rdn over 2f out: kpt on to go 5th nr fin* **14/1**

3205 **6** ½ **Hold Hands**[74] 3497 5-9-10 **65**.............................. DavidParkes 8 54
(Brendan Powell) *mid-div: hdwy over 3f out: rdn over 2f out: wknd fnl f* **33/1**

0021 **7** ¾ **Whozthecat (IRE)**[8] 5858 9-9-6 **66**.............................(t) GerO'Neill[(5)] 3 53+
(Declan Carroll) *led after 1f: hdd over 5f out: chsd ldr tl over 3f out: rdn and wknd over 1f out* **5/1**[2]

2033 **8** *hd* **The Dukkerer (IRE)**[30] 5085 5-9-7 **62**.............................. PhilDennis 6 49
(James Given) *prom: rdn over 2f out: wkng whn nt clr run over 1f out* **11/1**

3143 **9** 1¾ **Virile (IRE)**[15] 5605 5-9-4 **62**.............................(bt) MitchGodwin[(3)] 12 45
(Sylvester Kirk) *edgd lft s: hld up: rdn over 2f out: hung lft over 1f out: sn wknd* **11/1**

-454 **10** *1 ¼* **Assisted**[18] 5517 3-9-1 **62**...[1] ShirleyTeasdale 7 42+
(Keith Dalgleish) *led 1f: led again over 5f out: rdn and hdd over 2f out: wknd fnl f* **12/1**

0311 **11** *1 ½* **Mount Cheiron (USA)**[15] 5604 5-9-0 **58**...........(b) CallumRodriguez[(3)] 1 35+
(Richard Ford) *chsd ldrs: wnt 2nd over 3f out tl rdn over 2f out: wknd over 1f out* **8/1**

00-0 **12** *11* **Bella Blur**[236] 149 4-8-11 **55**... LuluStanford[(3)] 2 9
(Eugene Stanford) *chsd ldrs: lost pl 5f out: nt clr run over 3f out: wknd over 2f out: eased* **28/1**

1m 48.56s (-1.54) **Going Correction** -0.075s/f (Stan)
WFA 3 from 4yo+ 6lb **12** Ran SP% **119.9**
Speed ratings (Par 101): **103,102,99,95,94 93,93,93,91,90 89,79**
CSF £41.39 CT £183.72 TOTE £3.90: £1.80, £4.60, £2.10; EX 51.30 Trifecta £344.50.
Owner Denford Stud **Bred** Denford Stud Ltd **Trained** Newmarket, Suffolk

FOCUS
A modest handicap in which the pace was strong.

6138 HAPPY BIRTHDAY AMELIE CRUDDACE H'CAP 1m 141y (Tp)
6:20 (6:21) (Class 5) (0-75,75) 3-Y-O+ **£2,911** (£866; £432; £216) **Stalls** Low

Form RPR

6622 **1** **Master Gunner (USA)**[24] 5308 3-9-3 **74**.............(v[1]) RichardKingscote 3 87
(Sir Michael Stoute) *mde all: shkn up over 1f out: rdn and edgd lft ins fnl f: styd on wl* **5/4**[1]

1305 **2** *3* **Vastly (USA)**[12] 5724 7-9-5 **70**.......................................(t) SaleemGolam 2 76
(Sophie Leech) *a.p: rdn over 3f out: chsd wnr over 1f out: styd on same pce ins fnl f* **16/1**

2531 **3** *1* **Van Dyke**[15] 5608 3-8-13 **75**....................................... CharlieBennett[(5)] 11 79
(Hughie Morrison) *hld up: rdn over 2f out: hdwy over 1f out: edgd lft ins fnl f: styd on to go 3rd nr fin* **5/1**[2]

2161 **4** *nk* **Wakame (IRE)**[14] 5627 3-8-11 **71**.......................... JosephineGordon[(3)] 7 74
(Ed de Giles) *chsd wnr: rdn over 2f out: lost 2nd over 1f out: no ex ins fnl f* **11/2**[3]

1-45 **5** *1 ¾* **Al Khafji**[85] 3103 3-8-13 **75**... DavidParkes[(5)] 10 74
(Jeremy Gask) *s.i.s: hld up: rdn over 2f out: edgd lft and styd on ins fnl f: nvr nrr* **20/1**

5645 **6** *3* **Beautiful Stranger (IRE)**[10] 5779 5-9-6 **71**............(p) AndrewMullen 13 63
(Keith Dalgleish) *hld up in tch: rdn over 3f out: wknd fnl f* **22/1**

0605 **7** *½* **Idol Deputy (FR)**[26] 5246 10-9-5 **75**......................(p) RachealKneller[(5)] 1 66
(James Bennett) *chsd ldrs: rdn over 1f out: wknd fnl f* **33/1**

5052 **8** *1 ½* **The Third Man**[15] 5609 5-9-6 **71**.................................(p) ThomasBrown 4 58
(Henry Spiller) *hld up: nt clr run over 2f out: rdn and hung lft fr over 1f out: nvr on terms* **7/1**

0356 **9** *1 ¼* **Anton Chigurh**[33] 4933 7-9-1 **71**...............................(p) AnnaHesketh[(5)] 5 56
(Tom Dascombe) *trckd ldrs: racd keenly: wnt upsides over 5f out tl rdn over 3f out: wknd fnl f* **20/1**

0050 **10** *1 ½* **Symbolic Star (IRE)**[49] 4377 4-9-5 **70**........................... CamHardie 12 51
(Barry Murtagh) *hld up: rdn over 2f out: n.d* **40/1**

1000 **11** *nk* **Shamlan (IRE)**[9] 5810 4-9-0 **70**.................................(t) CiaranMckee[(5)] 8 50
(Johnny Farrelly) *s.i.s: hld up: rdn over 2f out: a in rr* **50/1**

0000 **12** *hd* **Quintus Cerialis (IRE)**[24] 5301 4-9-2 **72**.............. AdamMcNamara[(5)] 6 52
(Karen George) *hld up: rdn over 3f out: a in rr* **66/1**

-006 **13** *½* **Monsieur Chevalier (IRE)**[22] 5357 9-9-9 **74**.............. TomMarquand 9 53
(Nikki Evans) *s.i.s: drvn along over 3f out: a in rr* **40/1**

1m 47.98s (-2.12) **Going Correction** -0.075s/f (Stan)
WFA 3 from 4yo+ 6lb **13** Ran SP% **120.0**
Speed ratings (Par 103): **106,103,102,102,100 97,97,96,95,93 93,93,92**
CSF £22.31 CT £86.35 TOTE £2.00: £1.10, £3.50, £1.90; EX 18.90 Trifecta £83.60.
Owner Mrs John Magnier & Michael Tabor & Derrick Smith **Bred** Queen Of The Night Syndicate **Trained** Newmarket, Suffolk

FOCUS
A fair handicap dominated by the well-backed favourite.

6139 BET ON SLOVAKIA VS ENGLAND WITH LADBROKES NURSERY H'CAP 5f 216y (Tp)
6:50 (6:52) (Class 5) (0-75,75) 2-Y-O **£3,234** (£962; £481; £240) **Stalls** Low

Form RPR

440 **1** **Giennah (IRE)**[52] 4261 2-8-13 **74**.................................. JordanUys[(7)] 11 79
(Brian Meehan) *hld up: hdwy on outer over 2f out: shkn up to ld over 1f out: edgd lft ins fnl f: pushed out* **14/1**

0601 **2** *1* **Rose Berry**[25] 5257 2-8-11 **68**........................... JosephineGordon[(3)] 7 70
(Chris Dwyer) *hld up: hdwy over 1f out: sn rdn: r.o* **12/1**

51 **3** *1 ¼* **Just Maybe**[33] 4938 2-9-2 **70**... ShaneKelly 2 68
(Mike Murphy) *s.i.s: sn prom: rdn and swtchd rt over 1f out: edgd lft and r.o ins fnl f* **8/1**

505 **4** *½* **Oceanic (IRE)**[43] 4609 2-8-5 **59**...[1] CamHardie 8 56
(John Quinn) *s.i.s: hld up: rdn over 1f out: r.o ins fnl f: nvr nrr* **14/1**

5132 **5** *½* **Marquee Club**[17] 5543 2-9-4 **72**.................................. WilliamCarson 10 67
(Jamie Osborne) *sn led: rdn and hdd over 1f out: styd on same pce ins fnl f* **12/1**

303 **6** *1 ½* **Cajmere**[70] 3633 2-9-7 **75**.. RichardKingscote 3 66
(Tom Dascombe) *w ldr 1f: settled in disp 2nd pl: rdn over 2f out: lost 2nd over 1f out: no ex fnl f* **7/2**[1]

534 **7** *¾* **Whigwham**[37] 4804 2-8-9 **68**..................................... AdamMcNamara[(5)] 4 57
(Richard Fahey) *prom: nt clr run and lost pl 5f out: sme hdwy u.p over 1f out: no ex fnl f* **15/2**[3]

51 **8** *shd* **Ballyanna**[15] 5606 2-8-11 **65**.. DannyBrock 1 53
(David Evans) *plld hrd and prom: disp 2nd 5f out tl shkn up wl over 1f out: wknd ins fnl f* **10/1**

51 **9** *1 ¾* **Swift Mover (IRE)**[15] 5593 2-9-4 **72**................................ KieranO'Neill 5 55
(Richard Hannon) *prom: n.m.r over 3f out: rdn and edgd rt over 1f out: wknd fnl f* **7/2**[1]

044 **10** *3* **Misty Moo**[96] 2732 2-8-5 **59**.. AndrewMullen 9 33
(Michael Appleby) *s.i.s: hld up: rdn over 2f out: n.d* **40/1**

0236 **11** *1* **Lady Cristal (IRE)**[12] 5712 2-9-6 **74**............................ DougieCostello 6 45+
(K R Burke) *trckd ldrs: racd keenly: nt clr run over 2f out: wknd and eased over 1f out* **7/1**[2]

1m 14.41s (-0.09) **Going Correction** -0.075s/f (Stan) **11** Ran SP% **120.1**
Speed ratings (Par 95): **97,95,94,93,92 90,89,89,87,83 81**
CSF £174.50 CT £1477.00 TOTE £18.00: £4.50, £3.00, £2.70; EX 212.40 Trifecta £4666.10.
Owner Hamdan Al Maktoum **Bred** Shadwell Estate Company Limited **Trained** Manton, Wilts

FOCUS
A fair and competitive nursery.

6140 FCL GLOBAL FORWARDING MAKING LOGISTICS PERSONAL CLAIMING STKS 7f 32y (Tp)
7:20 (7:22) (Class 5) 3-Y-O+ **£3,234** (£962; £481; £240) **Stalls** High

Form RPR

4300 **1** **Flowers On Venus (IRE)**[19] 5488 4-9-6 87.................. DanielTudhope 3 85
(David Evans) *broke wl: sn stdd and lost pl: hdwy: nt clr run and swtchd lft over 1f out: shkn up to ld wl ins fnl f: r.o: comf* **1/1**[1]

4441 **2** *1* **Threebagsue (IRE)**[136] 1573 3-8-6 74...............(b) JosephineGordon[(3)] 7 73
(J S Moore) *a.p: chsd ldr 2f out: led over 1f out: rdn and hdd wl ins fnl f: styd on same pce* **8/1**

6100 **3** *½* **Russian Realm**[8] 5825 6-9-12 92.. ShaneKelly 5 87
(Richard Hughes) *hld up: hdwy over 1f out: rdn and ev ch wl ins fnl f: no ex nr fin* **3/1**[2]

00-0 **4** *10* **Icy Blue**[47] 4444 8-8-8 49..(e[1]) NoelGarbutt[(3)] 2 45
(Adam West) *s.i.s: hdwy u.p over 2f out: wknd fnl f* **80/1**

006 **5** *nse* **Hodgkins Trust (IRE)**[27] 5197 3-8-1 40 ow2..........(bt) MitchGodwin[(7)] 9 44
(Jeremy Gask) *chsd ldrs: wnt 2nd over 4f out tl rdn over 1f out: wknd fnl f* **100/1**

4260 **6** *7* **Bahamian Sunshine**[12] 5732 3-8-10 67................(p) RichardKingscote 1 27
(Richard Fahey) *led early: chsd ldrs: rdn over 2f out: wkng whn hung lft over 1f out* **22/1**

022 **7** *1 ¾* **Gold Flash**[26] 5246 4-9-7 74...(b) PhillipMakin 8 31
(Keith Dalgleish) *sn led: rdn and hdd over 1f out: wknd fnl f* **10/3**[3]

8 *20* **Look Who's There** 5-8-10 0.. KieranO'Neill 4
(Sarah Hollinshead) *dwlt: outpcd* **66/1**

22-4 **9** *1 ½* **Hearmenow (IRE)**[245] 16 3-8-10 73.............................(t) DannyBrock 6
(J S Moore) *hmpd s: plld hrd and sn w ldr tl settled into 2nd over 5f out: lost 2nd over 4f out: wknd over 2f out* **25/1**

1m 28.2s (-0.60) **Going Correction** -0.075s/f (Stan)
WFA 3 from 4yo+ 4lb **9** Ran SP% **121.1**
Speed ratings (Par 103): **100,98,98,86,86 78,76,53,52**
CSF £10.86 TOTE £2.00: £1.10, £2.00, £1.40; EX 13.30 Trifecta £24.90.Flowers On Venus was claimed by Mr T. Dascombe £12,000, Hodgkins Trust was claimed by Mr David Haddrell for £2,000, Russian Realm was claimed by Mr P. T. Midgley for £18,000.
Owner Shropshire Wolves **Bred** Mrs A J Donnelly **Trained** Pandy, Monmouths

FOCUS
A decent claimer and they went a proper gallop.

6141 FCL GLOBAL FORWARDING BRITISH STALLION STUDS EBF MAIDEN STKS 5f 20y (Tp)
7:50 (7:52) (Class 5) 2-Y-O **£3,234** (£962; £481; £240) **Stalls** Low

Form RPR

4 **1** **Well Done (IRE)**[43] 4580 2-9-5 0.............................. SilvestreDeSousa 7 84
(Simon Crisford) *mde all: rdn over 1f out: r.o: comf* **4/11**[1]

454 **2** *¾* **Amlak**[84] 3128 2-9-0 76... TomMarquand 10 76
(Richard Hannon) *chsd wnr: rdn over 1f out: edgd rt ins fnl f: styd on* **7/2**[2]

02 **3** *5* **Cheerful Character (IRE)**[26] 5244 2-8-9 0........... AdamMcNamara[(5)] 3 58
(Richard Fahey) *chsd ldrs: nt clr run and hung lft over 1f out: swtchd rt and styd on same pce ins fnl f: wnt 3rd nr fin* **6/1**[3]

00 **4** *½* **Miss Mayson**[43] 4586 2-9-0 0.. DannyBrock 2 57
(Roger Teal) *plld hrd and prom: rdn and edgd lft over 1f out: no ex fnl f* **25/1**

0544 **5** *2 ½* **Shadow Wing (IRE)**[36] 4842 2-8-12 58 ow3.................. AnnStokell[(5)] 8 51
(Ann Stokell) *prom: rdn over 1f out: wknd fnl f* **50/1**

00 **6** *½* **Lights**[12] 5727 2-9-0 0.. DanielTudhope 4 46
(Declan Carroll) *hld up: rdn over 1f out: wknd fnl f* **50/1**

0 **7** *3 ¾* **See You Mush**[14] 5631 2-9-5 0....................................... LemosdeSouza 1 37
(Chris Dwyer) *hld up: shkn up over 1f out: nvr on terms* **20/1**

8 *5* **With One Accord** 2-9-0 0.. KieranO'Neill 6 14
(Richard Hannon) *dwlt: outpcd* **8/1**

1m 1.12s (-0.78) **Going Correction** -0.075s/f (Stan) **8** Ran SP% **133.5**
Speed ratings (Par 95): **103,101,93,93,89 88,82,74**
CSF £2.76 TOTE £1.40: £1.10, £1.60, £1.70; EX 3.60 Trifecta £7.80.
Owner Hamad Rashed Bin Ghedayer **Bred** Kilcarn Stud **Trained** Newmarket, Suffolk

FOCUS
An uncompetitive maiden and straightforward form.

6142 LADBROKES H'CAP 1m 4f 50y (Tp)
8:20 (8:20) (Class 3) (0-95,94) 3-Y-O-**£7,246** (£2,168; £1,084; £542; £270) **Stalls** Low

Form RPR

2000 **1** **Watersmeet**[21] 5411 5-9-12 **94**.. FrannyNorton 1 103
(Mark Johnston) *chsd clr ldr: tk clsr order over 6f out: shkn up to ld over 1f out: r.o wl* **11/4**[2]

5115 **2** *1 ¾* **Nigel**[36] 4838 4-9-3 **85**... ShaneKelly 2 91
(Richard Hughes) *chsd ldrs: rdn over 1f out: r.o to go 2nd wl ins fnl f* **15/2**

2553 **3** *1 ½* **Sbraase**[14] 5633 5-9-2 **84**... LukeMorris 6 88
(James Tate) *s.i.s: hld up: hdwy over 5f out: rdn over 1f out: styd on* **9/2**[3]

620 **4** *¾* **Cape Of Glory (IRE)**[8] 5837 3-8-10 **87**...........................(v[1]) PhillipMakin 5 89
(Keith Dalgleish) *led and sn clr: c bk to the field over 6f out: rdn over 2f out: hdd over 1f out: no ex wl ins fnl f* **8/1**

/040 **5** *½* **Mijhaar**[15] 5611 8-9-11 **93**... DanielTudhope 3 95
(David O'Meara) *hld up: rdn and hung lft fr over 1f out: nt trble ldrs* **8/1**

110 **6** *hd* **Vivre Pour Vivre (IRE)**[112] 2244 3-8-10 **87**..................... JimCrowley 4 88
(Ed Dunlop) *hld up: rdn over 2f out: no imp fnl f* **2/1**[1]

000 **7** *16* **Slowfoot (GER)**[63] 3913 8-9-11 **93**.............................(v) TimmyMurphy 7 69
(Jim Best) *s.i.s: hld up: wknd 2f out* **33/1**

2m 41.67s (0.87) **Going Correction** -0.075s/f (Stan)
WFA 3 from 4yo+ 9lb **7** Ran SP% **115.1**
Speed ratings (Par 107): **94,92,91,91,91 90,80**
CSF £23.68 TOTE £3.30: £2.10, £4.10; EX 20.20 Trifecta £70.30.
Owner J Barson **Bred** Stetchworth & Middle Park Studs **Trained** Middleham Moor, N Yorks

FOCUS
A good-quality handicap and the form looks solid.

6143 DOWNLOAD THE LADBROKES APP H'CAP 1m 4f 50y (Tp)
8:50 (8:50) (Class 6) (0-60,65) 3-Y-O+ **£2,587** (£770; £384; £192) **Stalls** Low

Form RPR

005 **1** **Want The Fairytale**[17] 5550 3-9-1 **58**.................................... JohnFahy 9 64
(Clive Cox) *chsd ldrs: rdn to go 2nd over 1f out: edgd lft and styd on to ld wl ins fnl f* **10/1**

-005 **2** *1 ¼* **Fast Play (IRE)**[18] 5529 4-9-12 **60**.......................................[1] ShaneKelly 6 64
(Richard Hughes) *hld up: hdwy and nt clr run over 1f out: rdn and hung lft ins fnl f: r.o* **9/1**

6300 **3** ½ **Overlord**[14] 5625 4-9-5 **53**.....(v[1]) TomMarquand 4 56
(Mark Rimell) *chsd ldr tl led over 2f out: rdn: hdd and unable qck wl ins fnl f* **12/1**
5335 **4** *nk* **Sunshineandbubbles**[21] 5399 3-9-2 **59**.....(p) LukeMorris 10 62
(Daniel Mark Loughnane) *hld up: rdn over 2f out: hdwy over 1f out: nt clr run ins fnl f: styd on* **9/2**[2]
1540 **5** *nk* **Filament Of Gold (USA)**[15] 5610 5-9-3 **58**.....(p) MitchGodwin[(7)] 7 60
(Roy Brotherton) *hld up: rdn over 2f out: styd on fr over 1f out: nt rch ldrs* **15/2**[3]
5350 **6** ¾ **Lions Charge (USA)**[45] 4527 9-9-12 **60**.....(tp) DougieCostello 2 61
(Richard Hawker) *a.p: rdn over 1f out: styd on same pce wl ins fnl f* **28/1**
0544 **7** 3 **Heat Storm (IRE)**[11] 5739 5-8-12 **46**.....(v) RyanPowell 5 42
(James Unett) *dwlt: hld up: rdn over 2f out: nvr nrr* **25/1**
0246 **8** ¾ **Elle Rebelle**[3] 6020 6-9-2 **50**..... WilliamCarson 8 45
(Mark Brisbourne) *trckd ldrs: racd keenly: rdn over 2f out: wknd ins fnl f* **12/1**
352 **9** *nk* **Stonecoldsoba**[15] 5607 3-9-1 **58**..... JimCrowley 3 53
(David Evans) *led: rdn and hdd over 2f out: wknd fnl f* **11/10**[1]

2m 41.06s (0.26) **Going Correction** -0.075s/f (Stan)
WFA 3 from 4yo+ 9lb **9** Ran SP% **119.3**
Speed ratings (Par 101): **96,95,94,94,94 93,91,91,91**
CSF £98.96 CT £1104.05 TOTE £13.20: £3.00, £3.50, £3.90; EX 125.00 Trifecta £1578.90.
Owner Mondial Racing **Bred** Balsdon Grange Farm **Trained** Lambourn, Berks

FOCUS
Just a modest handicap.
T/Plt: £73.50 to a £1 stake. Pool: £84,341.15 - 836.55 winning tickets T/Qpdt: £15.70 to a £1 stake. Pool: £12,340.86 - 578.84 winning tickets **Colin Roberts**

6144 - 6150a (Foreign Racing) - See Raceform Interactive

6067 BADEN-BADEN (L-H)
Saturday, September 3
OFFICIAL GOING: Turf: good

6151a WACKENHUT MERCEDES BENZ STEHERPREIS (LISTED RACE) (3YO+) (TURF) 1m 6f
1:50 (12:00) 3-Y-O+ **£10,294** (£4,779; £2,205; £1,102)

RPR
1 **Weltmacht**[55] 5-9-2 0..... AdriedeVries 3 103
(Markus Klug, Germany) **33/10**[3]
2 1½ **Le Colonel (GER)**[110] 2318 4-9-3 0..... ClementL'Heureux 2 102
(A Schaerer, Switzerland) **145/10**
3 1¼ **Yorkidding**[7] 5879 4-9-0 0..... IoritzMendizabal 6 97
(Mark Johnston) **9/5**[1]
4 ½ **Botany Bay (IRE)**[17] 5559 4-9-3 0.....(b) AndraschStarke 5 99
(Charles O'Brien, Ire) **31/10**[2]
5 4¾ **Bebe Cherie (FR)**[111] 2286 4-9-2 0..... MartinSeidl 8 92
(Markus Klug, Germany) **73/10**
6 2¾ **Iraklion (GER)**[39] 4-9-3 0..... JozefBojko 4 89
(Christian Sprengel, Germany) **106/10**
7 26 **Digitalis (IRE)**[69] 3-8-6 0..... FilipMinarik 7 53
(Mario Hofer, Germany) **73/10**
8 14 **Novano (GER)**[27] 5219 4-9-5 0..... AndreasSuborics 1 35
(Waldemar Hickst, Germany) **118/10**

WIN (incl. 10 euro stake); 43. PLACES: 17, 29, 16. SF: 737
Owner Gestut Rottgen **Bred** Gestut Rottgen **Trained** Germany

6152a T VON ZASTROW STUTENPREIS (BADENER STUTENPREIS) (GROUP 2) (3YO+ FILLIES & MARES) (TURF) 1m 4f
4:25 (12:00) 3-Y-O+ **£29,411** (£11,397; £5,882; £2,941; £1,838)

RPR
1 **Parvaneh (IRE)**[27] 5220 3-8-10 0..... AnthonyCrastus 2 106+
(Waldemar Hickst, Germany) **19/5**[2]
2 2 **Kasalla (GER)**[27] 5220 3-8-10 0..... AdriedeVries 5 103+
(Markus Klug, Germany) **49/10**
3 *hd* **Techno Queen (IRE)**[27] 5218 5-9-5 0..... DanielePorcu 8 103
(T Potters, Germany) **32/5**
4 ½ **Apple Betty (IRE)**[35] 4904 3-8-10 0..... IoritzMendizabal 1 102
(J-C Rouget, France) **42/10**[3]
5 2¾ **Sarandia (GER)**[27] 5220 3-8-10 0..... AndraschStarke 3 97
(P Schiergen, Germany) **17/10**[1]
6 5 **Son Macia (GER)**[20] 5451 3-8-10 0..... FilipMinarik 6 89
(Andreas Lowe, Germany) **144/10**
7 17 **Amona (IRE)**[20] 5454 4-9-5 0..... MarcLerner 7 62
(Andreas Lowe, Germany) **18/1**
8 3 **Night Music (GER)**[27] 5220 3-8-10 0..... EduardoPedroza 4 57
(A Wohler, Germany) **84/10**

2m 32.2s (-1.26)
WFA 3 from 4yo+ 9lb **8** Ran SP% **130.0**
WIN (incl. 10 euro stake): 48. PLACES: 22, 19, 21. SF: 311.
Owner Darius Racing **Bred** Douglas Taylor **Trained** Germany

6153 - 6156a (Foreign Racing) - See Raceform Interactive

VELIEFENDI
Saturday, September 3
OFFICIAL GOING: Polytrack: standard; turf: good

6157a FRANCE GALOP - FRBC ANATOLIA TROPHY (LOCAL GROUP 2) (3YO+ NO GELDINGS) (POLYTRACK) 1m 2f (P)
6:30 (12:00) 3-Y-O+ **£84,558** (£33,823; £16,911; £8,455)

RPR
1 **Belgian Bill**[23] 5329 8-9-6 0..... FergusSweeney 2 106
(George Baker) **22/5**
2 2 **Basem**[56] 4165 5-9-6 0.....(p) MickaelBarzalona 4 102
(Saeed bin Suroor) **1/2**[2]
3 ½ **Cemcem (TUR)**[21] 5-9-6 0..... OzcanYildirim 1 101
(Metin Sacan, Turkey) **1/4**[1]
4 2½ **Payitaht (TUR)**[24] 5-9-6 0.....(t) SelimKaya 3 96
(Mehmet Tekcan, Turkey) **31/10**[3]
5 1 **Mister Strong (TUR)**[21] 4-9-6 0.....(t) BurakAverbak 5 94
(C Filiksac, Turkey) **57/10**

2m 7.53s (2.53) **5** Ran SP% **204.5**
Owner PJL, Byrne & Baker **Bred** Wickfield Stud And Hartshill Stud **Trained** Manton, Wilts

6158a ISTANBUL TROPHY (GROUP 3) (3YO+ FILLIES & MARES) (TURF) 1m
7:00 (12:00) 3-Y-O+ **£84,558** (£33,823; £16,911; £8,455)

RPR
1 **Promising Run (USA)**[36] 4822 3-8-13 0..... MickaelBarzalona 5 105
(Saeed bin Suroor) **3/20**[1]
2 ½ **Willpower (TUR)**[38] 6-9-6 0.....(t) HalisKaraca 3 107
(Ibrahim Bekirogullari, Turkey) **2/5**[2]
3 3 **Tatvan Incisi (TUR)**[17] 4-9-6 0.....(t) SelimKaya 4 100
(Ibrahim Bekirogullari, Turkey) **2/5**[2]
4 5 **Hard Baby (TUR)**[17] 5-9-6 0.....(b) OzcanYildirim 2 88
(Ibrahim Bekirogullari, Turkey) **43/20**[3]
5 2½ **Silent Cat (TUR)**[48] 3-8-13 0..... GokhanKocakaya 1 80
(S Ozolke, Turkey) **7/1**

1m 34.86s (-0.47)
WFA 3 from 4yo+ 5lb **5** Ran SP% **274.1**
Owner Godolphin **Bred** Darley **Trained** Newmarket, Suffolk

5651 YORK (L-H)
Sunday, September 4
OFFICIAL GOING: Good to soft (6.3)
Wind: moderate 1/2 against Weather: fine, showeer race 3 (3.10)

6159 JUDITH MARSHALL MEMORIAL EBF STALLIONS MAIDEN STKS (PLUS 10 RACE) 7f
2:10 (2:10) (Class 4) 2-Y-O **£7,115** (£2,117; £1,058; £529) **Stalls** Low

Form RPR
3 **1** **Zainhom (USA)**[28] 5196 2-9-5 0..... PaulHanagan 5 90+
(Sir Michael Stoute) *trckd ldrs: swtchd lft over 2f out: upsides over 1f out: drvn to ld last 150yds: styd on* **11/2**
2 2¼ **Dick Tracy (IRE)** 2-9-5 0..... TomMarquand 2 84
(Richard Hannon) *led early: trckd ldrs: upsides over 1f out: kpt on same pce: tk 2nd nr fin* **8/1**
5 **3** *nk* **First Up (IRE)**[16] 5615 2-9-5 0..... SilvestreDeSousa 4 83
(Jeremy Noseda) *t.k.h: sn led: hdd over 5f out: led 3f out: sn drvn: hdd and no ex last 150yds* **7/4**[1]
4 **4** 4 **Eynhallow**[16] 5600 2-9-5 0..... JimCrowley 7 73
(Roger Charlton) *hld up in rr: effrt over 2f out: swtchd rt over 1f out: kpt on to take modest 4th last 50yds* **7/2**[2]
526 **5** 4 **Manolito De Madrid (GER)**[36] 4866 2-9-5 71..... WilliamBuick 6 63
(Andrew Balding) *chsd ldrs: upsides and drvn over 2f out: one pce* **9/2**[3]
006 **6** 3 **Come On Percy**[20] 5476 2-9-5 70..... GeorgeChaloner 1 55
(Richard Fahey) *in rr: drvn over 2f out: lost pl over 1f out* **33/1**
7 *hd* **Dan Troop** 2-9-5 0..... TonyHamilton 3 54
(Richard Fahey) *t.k.h: sn trcking ldrs: led over 5f out: hdd 3f out: lost pl over 1f out* **22/1**
2523 **8** 2¾ **Father McKenzie**[15] 5631 2-9-5 75..... PaulMulrennan 8 47
(Mick Channon) *chsd ldrs: drvn over 2f out: lost pl over 1f out* **20/1**

1m 28.0s (2.70) **Going Correction** +0.325s/f (Good) **8** Ran SP% **115.3**
Speed ratings (Par 97): **97,94,94,89,84 81,81,78**
CSF £46.75 TOTE £6.10: £1.90, £2.70, £1.10; EX 62.40 Trifecta £171.50.
Owner Hamdan Al Maktoum **Bred** Shadwell Farm LLC **Trained** Newmarket, Suffolk

FOCUS
Rail movement reduced distances of races 2,5 & 7 by 25yds. Following 10mm of rain the previous day, the official going was good to soft. A fair maiden, but they went only a moderate pace early on and the first three came clear. They raced more towards the far side than the others. After riding in the opener Paul Hanagan called the ground "good to soft" and George Chaloner and Jim Crowley both said: "It's just on the soft side."

6160 BARKERS GARAGE STKS (H'CAP) 1m 2f 88y
2:40 (2:41) (Class 4) (0-80,80) 3-Y-O+ **£7,115** (£2,117; £1,058; £529) **Stalls** Low

Form RPR
310- **1** **Muraabit**[353] 6472 4-9-7 **80**..... ThomasBrown 15 90+
(Ismail Mohammed) *hld up in rr: hdwy over 2f out: nt clr run and swtchd rt over 1f out: styd on to ld last 50yds* **25/1**
26-2 **2** 1½ **Al Destoor**[36] 4875 6-9-2 **75**..... TomQueally 12 83+
(Jennie Candlish) *s.i.s: hld up in rr: hdwy and nt clr run over 2f out: nt clr run over 1f out: edgd rt: styd on strly to take 2nd post* **9/2**[1]
0001 **3** *shd* **El Beau (IRE)**[5] 6006 5-9-6 **79** 6ex..... TomEaves 10 86
(John Quinn) *mid-div: hdwy over 2f out: led briefly last 100yds: no ex* **5/1**[2]
3156 **4** 1 **Throckley**[20] 5482 5-9-6 **79**..... SamJames 9 84
(John Davies) *mid-div: hdwy 3f out: chsng ldrs over 1f out: kpt on same pce* **11/1**
52 **5** 1¼ **Freewheel (IRE)**[64] 3905 6-9-6 **79**..... JasonHart 1 81
(Garry Moss) *led: hdd last 100yds: fdd* **13/2**[3]
0431 **6** 1¾ **Purple Rock (IRE)**[22] 5392 4-9-6 **79**.....(t) CamHardie 4 78
(Michael Easterby) *mid-div: hdwy 3f out: hung rt over 1f out: soion wknd* **12/1**
2-00 **7** 3 **Taraz**[25] 5292 4-9-4 **77**..... DanielTudhope 16 70
(David O'Meara) *trckd ldrs: upsides over 1f out: sn wknd* **20/1**
4304 **8** *shd* **Woody Bay**[20] 5482 6-9-7 **80**..... DougieCostello 7 73
(Mark Walford) *chsd ldrs: drvn over 3f out: one pce whn sltly hmpd over 1f out: sn wknd* **16/1**
4152 **9** ¾ **Framley Garth (IRE)**[8] 5883 4-8-10 **76**..... PaulaMuir[(7)] 20 67
(Patrick Holmes) *rr-div: hdwy over 2f out: kpt on fnl f* **33/1**
5025 **10** 1¼ **Intiwin (IRE)**[25] 5292 4-8-13 **77**..... AdamMcNamara[(5)] 17 66
(Richard Fahey) *chsd ldrs: wknd over 1f out* **16/1**
4362 **11** 2¼ **Gulf Of Poets**[34] 4945 4-8-11 **75**.....(p) NathanEvans[(5)] 11 59
(Michael Easterby) *chsd ldr: wknd appr fnl f* **22/1**
0400 **12** ¾ **Biff Johnson (IRE)**[9] 5837 4-9-4 **77**.....(v) PhillipMakin 14 60
(Keith Dalgleish) *s.i.s: bhd: kpt on fnl 2f: nvr on terms* **28/1**
40 **13** 8 **Auspicion**[38] 4808 4-9-4 **77**..... JamesSullivan 19 44
(Tom Tate) *chsd ldrs: lost pl and eased over 1f out* **22/1**

5600 **14** *1½* **Shouranour (IRE)**[20] 5482 6-8-12 **76** (p) JoshDoyle(5) 5 40
(Alan Brown) *mid-div: hdwy over 2f out: lost pl over 1f out: eased clsng stages* **33/1**

0045 **15** *9* **Green Howard**[19] 5520 8-9-2 **75** JimCrowley 8 21
(Rebecca Bastiman) *in rr: brief effrt over 2f out: bhd whn eased clsng stages* **16/1**

5005 **16** *nk* **Darrington**[20] 5482 4-9-5 **78** [1] WilliamBuick 13 23
(Richard Fahey) *in rr: n.m.r bnd after 1f: sn bhd: eased clsng stages* **7/1**

1304 **17** *4* **Eastern Dragon (IRE)**[17] 5579 6-8-11 **75** GarryWhillans(5) 6 12
(Iain Jardine) *mid-div: lost pl over 2f out: bhd whn eased clsng stages* **28/1**

5266 **18** *12* **Eutropius (IRE)**[17] 5579 7-9-2 **75** SilvestreDeSousa 3
(Alan Swinbank) *sn chsng ldrs: drvn 4f out: lost pl and heavily eased over 1f out* **12/1**

2m 13.18s (0.68) **Going Correction** +0.30s/f (Good) **18** Ran SP% **132.1**
Speed ratings (Par 105): **109,107,107,106,105 104,102,102,101,100 98,98,91,90,83 83,79,70**
CSF £131.73 CT £688.36 TOTE £34.80: £7.40, £1.70, £2.00, £2.80; EX 235.90 Trifecta £2493.60.
Owner Saeed H Al Tayer **Bred** Highclere Stud **Trained** Newmarket, Suffolk

FOCUS
Rail movements meant the distance was reduced by 25yds. A competitive handicap and they went fast enough to allow the first two to be delivered from behind. The form is rated around the third and fourth.

6161 BETFRED GARROWBY STKS (LISTED RACE) 6f

3:10 (3:11) (Class 1) 3-Y-O+

£22,684 (£8,600; £4,304; £2,144; £1,076; £540) **Stalls** Centre

Form RPR

-301 **1** **Nameitwhatyoulike**[22] 5418 7-9-0 101 ConnorBeasley 3 111
(Bryan Smart) *mde all: t.k.h: drvn over 1f out: kpt on wl* **9/2**[2]

2020 **2** *1½* **Danzeno**[16] 5614 5-9-0 111 TomQueally 7 106
(Michael Appleby) *s.s: in rr: hdwy over 3f out: chsd wnr over 1f out: no imp* **1/1**[1]

5004 **3** *2* **Scrutineer (IRE)**[35] 4916 3-8-12 98 SilvestreDeSousa 6 100
(Mick Channon) *hld up towards rr: effrt over 2f out: 3rd over 1f out: kpt on same pce* **6/1**

4240 **4** *1* **Marsh Hawk**[35] 4916 4-8-9 98 TomMarquand 9 92
(Richard Hannon) *chsd ldrs: one pce over 1f out* **20/1**

2005 **5** *3* **George Dryden (IRE)**[22] 5418 4-9-0 102 PaulHanagan 8 87
(Ann Duffield) *hld up towards rr: effrt over 1f out: hung lft: nvr a threat* **11/2**[3]

0204 **6** *2¼* **Golden Amber (IRE)**[20] 5472 5-8-9 97 JimCrowley 1 75
(Dean Ivory) *dwlt: sn trcking ldrs: drvn over 2f out: wknd over 1f out* **14/1**

40 **7** *5* **Clear Spring (IRE)**[20] 5488 8-9-0 100 TomEaves 5 64
(John Spearing) *awkward to load: chsd ldrs: drvn over 2f out: lost pl over 1f out* **33/1**

1m 13.33s (1.43) **Going Correction** +0.525s/f (Yiel)
WFA 3 from 4yo+ 2lb **7** Ran SP% **112.2**
Speed ratings (Par 111): **111,109,106,105,101 98,91**
CSF £9.04 TOTE £5.00: £2.20, £1.30; EX 9.40 Trifecta £33.10.
Owner S Chappell **Bred** A E Smith And Co **Trained** Hambleton, N Yorks

FOCUS
A decent Listed sprint and they came down the middle. The winner improved again on his Ripon win.

6162 COOPERS MARQUEES IRISH STALLION FARMS EBF MAIDEN STKS (PLUS 10 RACE) 5f 89y

3:40 (3:40) (Class 3) 2-Y-O **£7,439** (£2,213; £1,106; £553) **Stalls** High

Form RPR

5 **1** **Kruger Park (IRE)**[42] 4685 2-9-5 0 TonyHamilton 8 84
(Richard Fahey) *mid-div: hdwy over 2f out: swtchd rt over 1f out: r.o to ld last 75yds* **8/1**[3]

22 **2** *½* **Her Terms**[45] 4558 2-9-0 78 WilliamTwiston-Davies 12 77
(William Haggas) *trckd ldrs: led over 1f out: hdd and no ex last 75yds* **4/1**[2]

03 **3** *2¼* **Ocelot**[13] 5727 2-9-0 0 DavidAllan 13 69
(Tim Easterby) *hld up in rr: hdwy over 2f out: kpt on fnl f: tk 3rd nr fin* **16/1**

35 **4** *nk* **Kodicat (IRE)**[88] 3024 2-9-0 0 TomEaves 6 68
(Kevin Ryan) *chsd ldrs: edgd rt and one pce fnl f* **12/1**

5 *4* **Aelius** 2-9-5 0 GrahamGibbons 7 59
(Michael Easterby) *s.s: in rr: hdwy over 1f out: edgd lft: nvr nr ldrs* **33/1**

024 **6** *1½* **Peach Pavlova (IRE)**[20] 5477 2-9-0 74 PJMcDonald 4 49
(Ann Duffield) *mid-div: hdwy over 1f out: nvr a factor* **12/1**

2050 **7** *hd* **Parys Mountain (IRE)**[18] 5560 2-9-5 78 SilvestreDeSousa 11 53
(Charles Hills) *trckd ldrs: wknd over 1f out* **7/2**[1]

06 **8** *3* **Greenview Paradise (IRE)**[19] 5516 2-9-0 0 JackGarritty 3 38
(Richard Fahey) *in rr: sn drvn along: nvr on terms* **50/1**

9 *nse* **Mezah (IRE)** 2-9-0 0 TomMarquand 5 38
(Richard Hannon) *chsd ldrs: drvn over 2f out: hung rt and lost pl over 1f out* **8/1**[3]

6555 **10** *3* **Emerald Secret (IRE)**[21] 5433 2-9-0 63 PaulMulrennan 10 27
(Paul Midgley) *led: hdd over 1f out: sn wknd* **33/1**

0 **11** *1¼* **Out Of Order (IRE)**[59] 4040 2-9-5 0 JamesSullivan 1 28
(Tim Easterby) *in rr and sn drvn along: nvr on terms* **20/1**

23 **12** *3¾* **Spinnaker Bay (IRE)**[38] 4804 2-9-0 0 JimCrowley 2 10
(William Jarvis) *chsd ldrs: lost pl over 1f out: bhd whn eased clsng stages* **7/2**[1]

1m 6.71s (2.61) **Going Correction** +0.525s/f (Yiel) **12** Ran SP% **120.5**
Speed ratings (Par 99): **100,99,95,95,88 86,86,81,81,76 74,68**
CSF £39.36 TOTE £10.80: £3.40, £1.90, £4.60; EX 41.00 Trifecta £772.60.
Owner Andrew Tinkler & Partner **Bred** Edward And Mrs S Hannigan **Trained** Musley Bank, N Yorks

FOCUS
An ordinary maiden and they went a solid pace down the middle, although the first two, who came clear, came up the stands' side. The form is straightforward and can be rated around the runner-up.

6163 FRED NOWELL MEMORIAL STKS (H'CAP) 2m 88y

4:10 (4:12) (Class 4) (0-85,84) 3-Y-O+ **£7,115** (£2,117; £1,058; £529) **Stalls** Low

Form RPR

-102 **1** **Slunovrat (FR)**[36] 4888 5-9-10 **80** PaulHanagan 3 92
(David Menuisier) *sn trcking ldrs: led over 2f out: styd on strly to forge clr last 100yds* **10/1**

2235 **2** *4* **Medina Sidonia (IRE)**[15] 5642 4-9-1 **71** (p) DavidAllan 6 78
(Tim Easterby) *in rr: hdwy to trck ldrs after 4f: led briefly 3f out: kpt on same pce fnl f* **16/1**

3211 **3** *hd* **Swashbuckle**[27] 5231 3-9-0 **83** WilliamBuick 7 90
(Andrew Balding) *sn prom: upsides 3f out: kpt on same pce fnl f* **9/4**[1]

6322 **4** *4½* **Arrowtown**[54] 4230 4-8-12 **73** NathanEvans(5) 13 74
(Michael Easterby) *hld up in rr: effrt on ins 4f out: chsng ldrs 3f out: fdd appr fnl f* **7/1**[3]

1026 **5** *5* **Bulas Belle**[24] 5321 6-9-10 **80** GrahamLee 8 75
(Grant Tuer) *trckd ldr: led over 4f out: hdd 3f out: wknd over 1f out* **20/1**

126 **6** *¾* **Ingleby Hollow**[33] 4969 4-9-10 **80** (p) DanielTudhope 10 74
(David O'Meara) *sn trcking ldrs: t.k.h: upsides 3f out: wknd over 1f out* **14/1**

10/6 **7** *nk* **Kelvingrove (IRE)**[71] 3639 6-9-8 **83** AdamMcNamara(5) 12 77
(Jonjo O'Neill) *in rr: hdwy after 4f: reminders 10f out and over 4f out: sme hdwy 3f out: nvr a factor* **25/1**

0005 **8** *2¾* **Min Alemarat (IRE)**[26] 5275 5-9-6 **79** RachelRichardson(3) 5 70
(Tim Easterby) *hld up in rr: drvn 5f out: brief effrt over 3f out: sn wknd* **14/1**

-020 **9** *½* **Waterclock (IRE)**[77] 3437 7-9-3 **73** (p) PJMcDonald 11 63
(Micky Hammond) *in rr: reminders over 9f out: sme hdwy over 2f out: nvr a factor* **25/1**

-620 **10** *½* **Cotillion**[15] 5642 10-8-10 **69** (p) GeorgeDowning(3) 2 59
(Ian Williams) *in rr: sme hdwy 3f out: nvr on terms* **25/1**

1344 **11** *17* **Touch The Sky**[23] 5358 5-10-0 **84** JimCrowley 9 53
(David Elsworth) *mid-div: effrt 3f out: lost pl and eased over 1f out: sn t.o: virtually p.u* **9/2**[2]

31 **12** *17* **Brittleton**[45] 4550 4-9-9 **79** (b) SilvestreDeSousa 1 28
(Harry Dunlop) *mid-div: effrt over 3f out: lost pl over 2f out: sn heavily eased: t.o: virtually p.u* **8/1**

6320 **13** *46* **Odeon**[16] 5611 5-9-10 **80** TomEaves 4
(James Given) *led: hdd over 4f out: sn lost pl and bhd: t.o 2f out: virtually p.u: eventually completed* **25/1**

3m 37.03s (2.53) **Going Correction** +0.30s/f (Good)
WFA 3 from 4yo+ 13lb **13** Ran SP% **121.0**
Speed ratings (Par 105): **105,103,102,100,98 97,97,96,96,95 87,78,55**
CSF £147.90 CT £482.99 TOTE £11.20: £3.00, £4.90, £1.70; EX 189.80 Trifecta £980.60.
Owner Shinco Racing Limited **Bred** Jaques & Marie-Francoise Menuisier **Trained** Pulborough, W Sussex

■ Stewards' Enquiry : Jim Crowley The Stewards held an enquiry following a report from the Starter that Jim Crowley, the rider of Touch The Sky, had entered the wrong stall. Having heard his evidence and viewed recordings of the start they found him in breach of Rule (D)44.2 and cautioned him as to his future conduct in races.

FOCUS
Rail movements meant the distance was reduced by 25yds. A fair staying handicap and they finished strung out down the middle, with the winner bounding clear. It paid to race prominently. The winner is on the upgrade.

6164 HANSON SPRINGS STKS (H'CAP) 6f

4:40 (4:41) (Class 3) (0-95,91) 3-Y-O **£9,703** (£2,887; £1,443; £721) **Stalls** Centre

Form RPR

1034 **1** **Dark Defender**[15] 5643 3-9-1 **85** (v) JimCrowley 3 93
(Keith Dalgleish) *led: hdd appr fnl f: rallied: edgd rt and kpt on to ld clsng stages* **9/2**[2]

1032 **2** *½* **Flying Pursuit**[29] 5148 3-9-7 **91** DavidAllan 7 97
(Tim Easterby) *trckd ldrs: led appr fnl f: hdd and no ex clsng stages* **11/4**[1]

4225 **3** *½* **Lagenda**[71] 3635 3-9-3 **87** (p) JoeDoyle 9 92
(Kevin Ryan) *mid-div: chsng ldrs over 1f out: n.m.r and carried rt last 150yds: kpt on towards fin* **11/2**[3]

6411 **4** *2¾* **Belledesert**[23] 5379 3-9-4 **88** RoystonFfrench 2 84
(Steph Hollinshead) *chsd ldrs: drvn over 2f out: wknd last 150yds* **9/1**

0406 **5** *½* **Paddy Power (IRE)**[22] 5409 3-8-13 **83** TonyHamilton 5 77
(Richard Fahey) *hmpd s: hld up in rr: smooth hdwy 2f out: swtchd rt over 1f out: kpt on same pce* **15/2**

2215 **6** *4½* **Laughton**[15] 5657 3-8-13 **83** ShaneGray 6 63
(Kevin Ryan) *mid-div: effrt over 2f out: lost pl over 1f out* **9/2**[2]

4010 **7** *2* **Mywayistheonlyway (IRE)**[11] 5759 3-8-12 **82** (t) KevinStott 1 56
(Grant Tuer) *mid-div: hdwy over 2f out: wknd over 1f out* **25/1**

0051 **8** *3½* **Lady Clair (IRE)**[15] 5643 3-9-0 **84** JoeyHaynes 10 46
(K R Burke) *in rr: hdwy over 2f out: lost pl over 1f out* **14/1**

10-0 **9** *6* **Silhuette (IRE)**[74] 3519 3-9-1 **85** TomEaves 4 28
(Colin Teague) *wnt rt s: in rr: brief effrt over 2f out: sn lost pl and bhd* **50/1**

1m 13.92s (2.02) **Going Correction** +0.525s/f (Yiel) **9** Ran SP% **112.7**
Speed ratings (Par 105): **107,106,105,102,101 95,92,88,80**
CSF £16.75 CT £68.02 TOTE £4.80: £1.80, £1.70, £2.10; EX 16.30 Trifecta £78.90.
Owner Prestige Thoroughbred Racing **Bred** Mrs C J Walker **Trained** Carluke, S Lanarks

FOCUS
A competitive 3yo sprint handicap in which it paid to race prominently. They finished towards the stands' side. The third helps the standard and the time was good compared to the Listed race.

6165 RACECOURSE CHALLENGE FOR CYSTIC FIBROSIS APPRENTICE STKS (H'CAP) (YORKSHIRE FUTURE STARS) 1m 4f

5:10 (5:10) (Class 4) (0-80,84) 4-Y-O+ **£7,115** (£2,117; £1,058; £529) **Stalls** Centre

Form RPR

0464 **1** **Agent Gibbs**[17] 5574 4-8-12 **76** (p) MitchGodwin(5) 6 85
(John O'Shea) *led: qcknd pce over 5f out: jnd over 1f out: fnd ex nr fin: all out* **7/1**

3234 **2** *hd* **Peterhouse (USA)**[25] 5292 4-8-10 **74** CliffordLee(5) 1 82
(Jason Ward) *hld up in rr: hdwy over 3f out: 2nd over 1f out: sn upsides: edgd lft last 100yds: jst hld* **9/1**

2223 **3** *3¾* **Mukhayyam**[9] 5837 4-9-7 **80** (p) RobHornby 10 82
(Tim Easterby) *sn trcking ldrs: chsd wnr 4f out: kpt on one pce over 1f out* **4/1**[1]

112 **4** *1½* **Pointillism**[7] 5925 4-8-8 **70** AdamMcNamara(3) 7 70
(Iain Jardine) *in rr: hdwy on ins over 2f out: 4th over 1f out: one pce* **9/2**[2]

0050 **5** *7* **Sellingallthetime (IRE)**[23] 5381 5-9-2 **75** (p) KevinStott 5 63
(Michael Appleby) *trckd ldrs: effrt 3f out: lost pl over 1f out* **13/2**[3]

0400 **6** *1½* **Dark Diamond (IRE)**[8] 5726 6-8-7 **66** oh7 (b) NoelGarbutt 8 52
(Michael Chapman) *mid-div: hdwy to chse ldrs 7f out: drvn over 4f out: lost pl over 1f out* **28/1**

40-1 **7** *4½* **Midnight Whistler (USA)**[211] 487 4-9-4 **77** [1] TomMarquand 4 56
(Martyn Meade) *trckd ldrs: t.k.h: drvn over 3f out: wknd wl over 1f out* **7/1**

1114 **8** *6* **Viserion**[64] 3905 4-9-3 **79** (p) GeorgeBuckell(3) 3 48
(David Simcock) *hld up in rr: hdwy over 3f out: lost pl wl over 1f out* **4/1**[1]

006 **9** *4* **Only Orsenfoolsies**[26] 5275 7-9-5 **78**.................. MichaelJMMurphy 12 41
(Micky Hammond) *sn chsng wnr: drvn 4f out: lost pl over 2f out* **25/1**

2m 35.86s (2.66) **Going Correction** +0.30s/f (Good) **9** Ran SP% **113.8**

Speed ratings (Par 105): **103,102,100,99,94 93,90,86,84**

CSF £66.86 CT £285.38 TOTE £7.70: £2.60, £3.00, £1.90; EX 76.90 Trifecta £285.30.

Owner The Cross Racing Club **Bred** A M Tombs **Trained** Elton, Gloucs

■ Stewards' Enquiry : Mitch Godwin four-day ban (19-22 Sep): used whip above permitted level

FOCUS

Rail movements meant the distance was reduced by 25yds. A fair apprentice handicap and the winner set a slow pace. The first two came clear of the third in fighting out a bobbing finish down the middle of the track. The form is rated around the first two.

T/Jkpt: Not won. T/Plt: £18.40 to a £1 stake. Pool of £175396.12 - 6945.25 winning tickets. T/Qpdt: £8.80 to a £1 stake. Pool of £10083.48 - 839.55 winning tickets. **Walter Glynn**

6166 - 6173a (Foreign Racing) - See Raceform Interactive

6151 BADEN-BADEN (L-H)

Sunday, September 4

OFFICIAL GOING: Turf: good

6174a STEINHOFF ZUKUNFTSRENNEN (GROUP 3) (2YO) (TURF) 7f

2:10 (12:00) 2-Y-O **£23,529** (£8,823; £4,411; £2,205; £1,470)

RPR

1 **Navarra King (IRE)**[35] 2-9-2 0.................................... AndraschStarke 4 105
(P Schiergen, Germany) **31/5**

2 *1 1/4* **Miss Infinity (IRE)**[17] 5583 2-9-1 0.................................... JoeFanning 5 101
(Mark Johnston) **23/10**[1]

3 *1 1/4* **Real Value (FR)**[44] 4620 2-9-2 0.................................... FilipMinarik 2 99
(Mario Hofer, Germany) **145/10**

4 *1 1/4* **Farshad (GER)**[34] 2-9-2 0.................................... MarvinSuerland 1 95
(Henk Grewe, Germany) **5/1**

5 *3/4* **Zaffinah (IRE)**[28] 2-8-13 0.................................... EduardoPedroza 3 90
(A Wohler, Germany) **23/5**[3]

6 *1 1/4* **Fulminato (GER)**[28] 2-9-2 0.................................... DennisSchiergen 7 90
(Andreas Lowe, Germany) **83/10**

7 *12* **Bay Of Biscaine (FR)**[36] 2-9-2 0.................................... IoritzMendizabal 8 57
(Mario Hofer, Germany) **27/10**[2]

8 *2 1/4* **Magellan (GER)**[35] 2-9-2 0.................................... MichaelCadeddu 6 51
(Jean-Pierre Carvalho, Germany) **155/10**

1m 25.35s (1.45) **8** Ran SP% **129.0**

WIN (inclk. 10 euro stake): 72. PLACES: 18, 16, 27. SF: 264.

Owner Gestut Ammerland **Bred** Gestut Ammerland **Trained** Germany

6175a LONGINES - GROSSER PREIS VON BADEN (GROUP 1) (3YO+) (TURF) 1m 4f

3:40 (12:00) 3-Y-O+ **£110,294** (£44,117; £18,382; £11,029)

RPR

1 **Iquitos (GER)**[35] 4928 4-9-6 0.................................... IanFerguson 10 116+
(H-J Groschel, Germany) **69/10**

2 *2 3/4* **Nightflower (IRE)**[21] 5454 4-9-3 0.................................... AndraschStarke 7 109
(P Schiergen, Germany) **42/10**[2]

3 *5* **Pagella (GER)**[28] 5220 3-8-8 0.................................... AlexanderPietsch 11 101
(J Hirschberger, Germany) **177/10**

4 *2 1/2* **Tiberian (FR)**[38] 4814 4-9-6 0.................................... ThierryJarnet 2 100
(Alain Couetil, France) **174/10**

5 *1/2* **Serienholde (GER)**[28] 5220 3-8-8 0.................................... EduardoPedroza 3 96
(A Wohler, Germany) **3/1**[1]

6 *1 1/4* **Meandre (FR)**[52] 4333 8-9-6 0.................................... FabriceVeron 5 97
(A Savujev, Czech Republic) **156/10**

7 *3/4* **Dylan Mouth (IRE)**[63] 3936 5-9-6 0.................................... AndreaAtzeni 4 96
(Marco Botti) **63/10**

8 *1/2* **Wasir (GER)**[22] 5428 4-9-6 0.................................... MichaelCadeddu 1 95
(A Wohler, Germany) **142/10**

9 *6 1/2* **Dschingis Secret (GER)**[56] 4186 3-8-11 0.................................... AdriedeVries 6 85
(Markus Klug, Germany) **47/10**

10 *61* **Boscaccio (GER)**[56] 4186 3-8-11 0.................................... DennisSchiergen 8
(Christian Sprengel, Germany) **23/5**[3]

2m 33.79s (0.33)

WFA 3 from 4yo+ 9lb **10** Ran SP% **129.4**

WIN (incl. 10 euro stake): 79. PLACES: 25, 20, 39. SF: 277.

Owner Stall Mulligan **Bred** Frau Dr Erika Buhmann **Trained** Germany

■ A first Group 1 win for both trainer and jockey.

FOCUS

Germany's most prestigious event, this was run in a downpour.

4330 SAINT-CLOUD (L-H)

Sunday, September 4

OFFICIAL GOING: Turf: good

6176a PRIX DE LUTECE (GROUP 3) (3YO) (TURF) 1m 7f

2:30 (12:00) 3-Y-O **£29,411** (£11,764; £8,823; £5,882; £2,941)

RPR

1 **Moonshiner (GER)**[28] 5218 3-8-11 0.................................... MaximeGuyon 2 105+
(Jean-Pierre Carvalho, Germany) **3/1**[2]

2 *1* **Dounyapour (FR)**[27] 3-8-9 0.................................... AlexisBadel 3 102
(A De Royer-Dupre, France) **15/2**

3 *1/2* **Cleonte (IRE)**[21] 5448 3-8-9 0.................................... Pierre-CharlesBoudot 4 101
(A Fabre, France) **4/5**[1]

4 *4* **Sagaroi (FR)**[99] 2712 3-8-9 0.................................... Francois-XavierBertras 1 96
(D Guillemin, France) **9/2**[3]

5 *12* **Galiteo (FR)**[65] 3-8-9 0.................................... OlivierPeslier 5 80
(Gianluca Bietolini, Italy) **16/1**

3m 14.79s (194.79) **5** Ran SP% **116.4**

WIN (incl. 1 euro stake): 3.40. PLACES: 2.30, 4.10. SF: 26.90.

Owner Stall Ullmann **Bred** Stall Ullmann **Trained** Germany

FOCUS

This event is usually run at Longchamp.

6177a PRIX LA ROCHETTE (GROUP 3) (2YO) (TURF) 7f

3:50 (12:00) 2-Y-O **£29,411** (£11,764; £8,823; £5,882; £2,941)

RPR

1 **Kontrastat (FR)**[24] 5348 2-8-11 0.................................... TheoBachelot 4 108+
(S Wattel, France) **7/1**

2 *3/4* **Mate Story (IRE)**[33] 2-8-11 0.................................... GregoryBenoist 3 106
(D Smaga, France) **5/1**[3]

3 *1 3/4* **Baileys Showgirl (FR)**[15] 5703 2-8-8 0.................................... GeraldMosse 6 98
(Mark Johnston) **13/8**[1]

4 *hd* **Body Sculpt (FR)**[29] 5186 2-8-8 0.................................... AlexisBadel 1 98
(S Kobayashi, France) **14/1**

5 *2 1/2* **Team Of Teams (USA)**[32] 5049 2-8-8 0.................................... CristianDemuro 5 91
(J-C Rouget, France) **9/4**[2]

6 *10* **Incampo (FR)**[33] 2-8-11 0.................................... MaximeGuyon 2 67
(H-A Pantall, France) **6/1**

1m 25.35s (-6.85) **6** Ran SP% **119.0**

WIN (incl. 1 euro stake): 8.20. PLACES: 3.60, 2.30. SF: 34.40.

Owner B Plainfosse & Ecurie Palos De Moguer **Bred** B Plainfosse **Trained** France

FOCUS

This event is usually run at Longchamp.

6178a PRIX DE BOULOGNE (LISTED RACE) (4YO+) (TURF) 1m 2f

5:40 (12:00) 4-Y-O+ **£19,117** (£7,647; £5,735; £3,823; £1,911)

RPR

1 **Arthenus**[20] 5500 4-9-4 0....................................(p) Pierre-CharlesBoudot 1 108
(James Fanshawe) **31/10**[2]

2 *1* **First Sitting**[29] 5173 5-9-0 0.................................... OlivierPeslier 6 102
(Chris Wall) **59/10**[3]

3 *snk* **Now We Can**[52] 4333 7-9-0 0.................................... StephanePasquier 4 102
(N Clement, France) **23/10**[1]

4 *1 1/4* **Bonusdargent (FR)**[16] 4-9-0 0.................................... MaximeGuyon 3 99
(Mme Pia Brandt, France) **9/1**

5 *3/4* **Baz (FR)**[16] 6-9-0 0....................................(p) CristianDemuro 7 98
(F-H Graffard, France) **11/1**

6 *1 1/4* **Big Blue**[28] 5218 4-9-0 0.................................... VincentCheminaud 8 95
(A Fabre, France) **31/10**[2]

7 *1* **Cash In Mind (FR)**[62] 5-9-0 0....................................(p) AurelienLemaitre 2 93
(E J O'Neill, France) **18/1**

8 *12* **Serenu (FR)**[35] 6-9-0 0.................................... TonyPiccone 5 69
(D Retif, France) **25/1**

2m 5.22s (-10.78) **8** Ran SP% **121.0**

WIN (incl. 1 euro stake): 4.10. PLACES: 1.60, 1.70, 1.40. DF: 11.70. SF: 19.40.

Owner A Coombs & J W Rowley **Bred** Brook Stud Bloodstock Ltd **Trained** Newmarket, Suffolk

6157 VELIEFENDI

Sunday, September 4

OFFICIAL GOING: Turf: good

6179a INTERNATIONAL BOSPHORUS CUP (GROUP 2) (3YO+ NO GELDINGS) (TURF) 1m 4f

2:30 (12:00) 3-Y-O+ **£132,352** (£52,941; £26,470; £13,235)

RPR

1 **Move Up**[36] 4863 3-8-10 0.................................... MickaelBarzalona 4 107
(Saeed bin Suroor) **2/5**[1]

2 *2* **Fly By Me (TUR)**[23] 6-9-6 0.................................... UgurPolat 1 105
(A Sivgin, Turkey) **2/1**[3]

3 *1* **Elbereth**[57] 4165 5-9-3 0 ow1.................................... OisinMurphy 7 100+
(Andrew Balding) **39/20**[2]

4 *1/2* **Blaze To Win (TUR)**[21] 5-9-6 0....................................(b) SelimKaya 6 103
(Aydin Kucukaksoy, Turkey) **101/20**

5 *2* **Steel Of Madrid (IRE)**[20] 5499 3-8-13 0 ow3.................................... SeanLevey 2 101
(Richard Hannon) **11/5**

6 *10* **Baybaskan (TUR)**[23] 4-9-6 0.................................... HalisKaratas 5 83
(Fehmi Demir, Turkey) **109/20**

2m 32.46s (3.66)

WFA 3 from 4yo+ 9lb **6** Ran SP% **201.9**

Owner Godolphin **Bred** The Lavington Stud **Trained** Newmarket, Suffolk

FOCUS

Not a strong Group 2 and the early pace was steady, but the winner is clearly progressive.

6180a INTERNATIONAL TRAKYA (THRACE) TROPHY (LOCAL GROUP 3) (2YO) (TURF) 6f

3:00 (12:00) 2-Y-O **£84,558** (£33,823; £16,911; £8,455)

RPR

1 **Waneta (TUR)**[22] 2-8-9 0.................................... HalisKaratas 1 90
(Z Firat, Turkey) **1/10**[1]

2 *hd* **Top Score**[37] 4825 2-9-0 0.................................... SeanLevey 4 95
(Saeed bin Suroor) **7/10**[2]

3 *2 1/2* **Best Solution (IRE)**[40] 4736 2-9-0 0.................................... MickaelBarzalona 3 87
(Saeed bin Suroor) **7/10**[2]

4 *nk* **Masham Star (IRE)**[18] 5560 2-9-0 0.................................... OisinMurphy 2 86
(Mark Johnston) **27/10**

5 *1* **Mailshot (USA)**[37] 4825 2-9-0 0.................................... HarryBentley 5 83
(Mark Johnston) **49/20**[3]

1m 10.37s (70.37) **5** Ran SP% **264.6**

Owner Murat Kadaifcioglu **Bred** Adena Springs **Trained** Turkey

6181a LONGINES INTERNATIONAL TOPKAPI TROPHY (GROUP 2) (3YO+) (TURF) 1m

3:30 (12:00) 3-Y-O+ **£198,529** (£79,411; £39,705; £19,852)

RPR

1 **Blond Me (IRE)**[15] 5645 4-9-2 0.................................... OisinMurphy 1 105
(Andrew Balding) **13/10**[2]

2 *nk* **Silent Attack**[57] 4149 3-8-13 0.................................... MickaelBarzalona 2 105+
(Saeed bin Suroor) **1/20**[1]

3 *hd* **Dayim Benim (IRE)**[21] 3-8-13 0....................(b) HalisKaratas 4 105
(Tahir Kurt, Turkey) **69/10**
4 *½* **Impulsive (TUR)**[16] 3-8-13 0.................... OzcanYildirim 6 103
(S Demiral, Turkey) **103/10**
5 *½* **Kreacher (TUR)**[21] 3-8-13 0.................... GokhanKocakaya 5 102
(S Bilgic, Turkey) **97/20**[3]
6 *nk* **Diplomat (GER)**[35] 4928 5-9-6 0.................... HarryBentley 3 105
(Mario Hofer, Germany) **49/10**

1m 36.21s (0.88)
WFA 3 from 4yo+ 5lb **6** Ran SP% **194.3**

Owner Mrs Barbara M Keller **Bred** Wardstown Stud Ltd **Trained** Kingsclere, Hants

FOCUS
The two British runners predictably came to the fore in this ordinary Group 2.

5705 BRIGHTON (L-H)

Monday, September 5

OFFICIAL GOING: Good to soft (soft in places)
Wind: virtually nil Weather: low cloud slowly clearing

6182 BRIGHTON LIONS FIREWORKS NIGHT 5TH NOV FILLIES' H'CAP 5f 213y

2:00 (2:00) (Class 5) (0-75,75) 3-Y-O+ **£2,911** (£866; £432; £216) **Stalls** Centre

Form RPR
4334 1 **Symposium**[31] 5115 3-8-13 **74**....................(p) GeorgiaCox(5) 8 83
(William Haggas) *mde all: rdn 2f out: styd on wl fnl f: rdn out* **11/4**[1]
302 2 *1* **Minminwin (IRE)**[9] 5907 3-8-5 **61** oh11....................(vt[1]) LukeMorris 3 67
(Gay Kelleway) *trckd ldng pair: effrt 2f out: hrd drvn to chse wnr jst ins fnl f: styd on same pce after* **6/1**
-005 3 *¾* **Rio's Cliffs**[52] 4360 3-9-5 **75**.................... JimCrowley 4 78
(Martyn Meade) *chsd wnr: rdn 2f out: drvn and unable qck over 1f out: 3rd and styd on same pce ins fnl f* **7/2**[2]
2451 4 *2 ¼* **Dynamic Girl (IRE)**[25] 5330 3-9-2 **72**....................(p) OisinMurphy 10 68
(Brendan Powell) *hld up in tch in last pair: effrt and swtchd lft over 1f out: no imp u.p 1f out: wknd ins fnl f* **11/4**[1]
0001 5 *¾* **Dance Band (IRE)**[75] 3527 3-8-8 **64**.................... HarryBentley 5 58
(Roger Varian) *stdd s: in tch in rr: effrt 2f out: no imp u.p 1f out: wknd ins fnl f* **9/2**[3]

1m 12.84s (2.64) **Going Correction** +0.50s/f (Yiel)
WFA 3 from 4yo 2lb **5** Ran SP% **108.0**
Speed ratings (Par 100): **102,100,99,96,95**
CSF £17.87 TOTE £3.10: £1.50, £2.90; EX 14.90 Trifecta £81.30.
Owner The Royal Ascot Racing Club **Bred** Bloomsbury Stud **Trained** Newmarket, Suffolk

FOCUS
Following a further 4mm of rain in the morning, the ground was eased to good to soft (good in places). Jim Crowley said it was "soft", and Georgia Cox "good to soft" following the opener, a moderate handicap in which the winner made all. They came middle to stands' side in the straight and the first two hailed from in-form yards. Ordinary form but a pb from the winner.

6183 BRITISH STALLION STUDS EBF MAIDEN STKS 6f 209y

2:30 (2:30) (Class 5) 2-Y-O **£3,234** (£962; £481; £240) **Stalls** Centre

Form RPR
04 1 **Colibri (IRE)**[24] 5356 2-9-5 0.................... JimCrowley 7 99+
(Hugo Palmer) *trckd ldr over 5f out: led travelling strly over 2f out: shkn up and readily wnt clr wl over 1f out: r.o strly: eased towards fin: v easily* **8/11**[1]
2 *12* **Sweet Zain (IRE)** 2-9-0 0.................... OisinMurphy 2 61
(Charlie Fellowes) *sn dropped to last pair: outpcd and rn green early: clsd and pushed lft over 3f out: rdn and chsd ldrs over 2f out: wnt 2nd wl over 1f out: no ch w wnr but plugged on for clr 2nd after* **12/1**
3 3 *4* **Endeavour (IRE)**[21] 5484 2-9-5 0.................... TimmyMurphy 4 56
(Richard Hannon) *t.k.h: chsd ldr tl over 5f out: wnt 2nd again over 2f out tl wl over 1f out: sn rdn and btn: wknd fnl f* **3/1**[2]
4 *6* **Beepeecee** 2-9-5 0.................... RyanTate 6 40
(Richard Hughes) *racd in 4th tl lost pl and short of room 3f out: effrt over 2f out: struggling and bmpd 2f out: wknd wl over 1f out* **33/1**
5 *1* **Leonidas (IRE)** 2-9-5 0.................... MartinDwyer 5 37
(Marcus Tregoning) *s.i.s: bhd and rn green early: clsd and swtchd rt over 3f out: rdn over 2f out: sn btn: hung lft and wknd over 1f out* **20/1**
0 6 *20* **Poet's Charm (IRE)**[47] 4533 2-9-5 0....................(v[1]) SilvestreDeSousa 1
(Simon Crisford) *racd freely: led: rdn and hdd over 2f out: sn dropped out and bmpd 2f out: t.o and eased ins fnl f* **6/1**[3]

1m 25.63s (2.53) **Going Correction** +0.50s/f (Yiel) **6** Ran SP% **112.6**
Speed ratings (Par 95): **105,91,86,79,78 55**
CSF £11.24 TOTE £1.40: £1.20, £3.70; EX 8.90 Trifecta £17.10.
Owner Al Asayl Bloodstock Ltd **Bred** Al Asayl Bloodstock Ltd **Trained** Newmarket, Suffolk

FOCUS
Following a further 2mm of rain, the going was changed to good to soft (soft in places). Not a strong maiden, but the last five winners all scored again later that season - three of them next time out.

6184 JASON "THE DONKEY" JONES H'CAP 6f 209y

3:00 (3:00) (Class 5) (0-75,75) 3-Y-O+ **£2,911** (£866; £432; £216) **Stalls** Centre

Form RPR
2325 1 **Pick A Little**[15] 5674 8-9-4 **69**.................... TimmyMurphy 2 75
(Michael Blake) *taken down early: midfield: swtchd rt 3f out: effrt 2f out: hdwy to chse ldr and bmpd ent fnl f: styd on wl to ld fnl 50yds: pushed out towards fin* **5/1**
3134 2 *¾* **Wordismybond**[8] 5925 7-9-0 **72**....................(p) StephenCummins(7) 4 76
(Richard Hughes) *squeezed for room: hmpd and dropped to rr sn after s: hld up in rr: swtchd rt over 2f out: hdwy to chse ldrs and edgd lft over 1f out: pressing ldrs ins fnl f: kpt on: snatched 2nd last stride* **8/1**
1112 3 *shd* **Soaring Spirits (IRE)**[15] 5673 6-9-10 **75**....................(b) RobertWinston 6 79
(Dean Ivory) *racd keenly: led and clr w rival after 1f: styd nr far rail over 2f out: rdn and forged ahd over 1f out: drvn and hrd pressed ins fnl f: hdd and no ex fnl 50yds: lost 2nd last stride* **7/2**[2]
3320 4 *7* **Sarangoo**[20] 5507 8-9-7 **72**.................... JimCrowley 3 58
(Malcolm Saunders) *midfield: effrt over 2f out: 5th and no imp u.p over 1f out: wknd fnl f* **4/1**[3]
3004 5 *nk* **Bingo George (IRE)**[14] 5711 3-8-9 **64** ow2.................... OisinMurphy 5 47
(Andrew Balding) *t.k.h: jnd wnr after 1f and sn clr of field: rdn 2f out: lost 2nd and btn jst over 1f out: wknd fnl f* **5/2**[1]

0261 6 *21* **With Approval (IRE)**[14] 5711 4-9-1 **66**....................(p) LukeMorris 7
(Laura Mongan) *chsd clr ldng pair: pushed along 4f out: drvn and lost pl ent fnl 2f: bhd and eased ins fnl f* **6/1**

1m 25.75s (2.65) **Going Correction** +0.50s/f (Yiel)
WFA 3 from 4yo+ 4lb **6** Ran SP% **112.9**
Speed ratings (Par 103): **104,103,103,95,94 70**
CSF £42.22 TOTE £6.60: £3.30, £4.30; EX 39.00 Trifecta £171.40.
Owner Mrs J M Haines **Bred** D R Tucker **Trained** Trowbridge, Wilts

FOCUS
A modest handicap and they went a good pace, which suited the closers. The winner and second have been rated close to recent form.

6185 L&S PRINTING - OFFICIAL PRINT PARTNER H'CAP 1m 3f 196y

3:30 (3:30) (Class 6) (0-60,66) 3-Y-O **£2,587** (£770; £384; £192) **Stalls** High

Form RPR
-354 1 **Buteo Bai (IRE)**[15] 5672 3-9-2 **55**.................... JimCrowley 7 63
(Lucy Wadham) *chsd ldr tl rdn to ld 2f out: asserted ins fnl f: styd on strly and gng away fnl 100yds: rdn out* **10/3**[2]
5411 2 *3 ¾* **Masterson (IRE)**[3] 6102 3-9-13 **66** 6ex.................... SilvestreDeSousa 5 68
(Mick Channon) *hld up in tch in midfield: rdn and hdwy to chal 2f out: clr w wnr over 1f out: no ex and btn ins fnl f: wknd towards fin* **2/1**[1]
006 3 *½* **Work (IRE)**[7] 5958 3-8-8 **47**.................... HarryBentley 6 49
(David Simcock) *stdd s: hld up in tch in last pair: effrt over 2f out: hdwy to chse ldng pair wl over 1f out: edgd lft and no imp 1f out: styd on same pce after* **11/2**[3]
-505 4 *13* **Permera**[54] 4273 3-9-0 **53**.................... DarryllHolland 4 35
(Mark H Tompkins) *sn bustled up to ld: clr 9f out: c to r on stands' rail 3f out: rdn and hdd 2f out: sn btn: wknd over 1f out* **6/1**
0043 5 *4* **Onehelluvatouch**[16] 5630 3-8-12 **51**.................... WilliamTwiston-Davies 3 27
(Philip Hide) *chsd ldng pair: styd on far rail 3f out: sn rdn: unable qck and btn 2f out: wknd over 1f out* **6/1**
-533 6 *nk* **Lilly Bonbon (IRE)**[14] 5708 3-9-0 **58**.................... HectorCrouch(5) 2 34
(Gary Moore) *stdd s: t.k.h: hld up in last pair: effrt over 2f out: sn struggling: wknd over 1f out* **7/1**

2m 39.53s (6.83) **Going Correction** +0.50s/f (Yiel) **6** Ran SP% **112.9**
Speed ratings (Par 99): **97,94,94,85,82 82**
CSF £10.57 TOTE £4.70: £3.40, £1.02; EX 11.80 Trifecta £50.60.
Owner Amblyn Racing **Bred** T Monaghan **Trained** Newmarket, Suffolk

FOCUS
A low-grade handicap. The six runners were all in with a chance heading into the straight, but the first three came clear of the remainder down the middle. This is rated through the second replicating his Newcastle-winning form.

6186 SUSSEX CLEANING & CARE - OFFICIAL CLEANING PARTNER H'CAP 1m 1f 209y

4:00 (4:00) (Class 5) (0-75,75) 3-Y-O+ **£2,911** (£866; £432; £216) **Stalls** High

Form RPR
2061 1 **Ocean Ready (USA)**[4] 6066 3-9-0 **70**.................... LukeMorris 3 83+
(Sir Mark Prescott Bt) *sn settled in to trck ldrs: shkn up over 3f out: clsd to ld and travelling strly ent fnl 2f: shifting rt over 1f out: in command and rousted along ins fnl f* **2/5**[1]
2155 2 *3 ½* **Lord Reason**[35] 4940 4-9-12 **75**.................... SilvestreDeSousa 8 81
(John Butler) *t.k.h: w ldrs tl stdd bk to trck ldrs after 2f: effrt to press ldrs 2f out: hmpd and squeezed for room over 1f out: sn swtchd lft and chsd wnr: hung lft u.p 1f out: btn and eased cl home* **5/1**[2]
0622 3 *6* **Not Touch**[9] 5895 3-9-1 **71**.................... TimmyMurphy 5 65
(Richard Hannon) *led: rdn and hdd ent fnl 2f: 3rd and btn over 1f out: wknd fnl f* **11/2**[3]
004 4 *9* **Tee It Up Tommo (IRE)**[15] 5674 7-9-2 **65**....................(t) HarryBentley 6 41
(Daniel Steele) *w ldr: ev ch and rdn ent fnl 2f: sltly impeded: swtchd lft and outpcd over 1f out: sn wknd* **16/1**

2m 7.78s (4.18) **Going Correction** +0.50s/f (Yiel)
WFA 3 from 4yo+ 7lb **4** Ran SP% **109.4**
Speed ratings (Par 103): **103,100,95,88**
CSF £2.87 TOTE £1.40; EX 3.10 Trifecta £4.20.
Owner Baxter, Gregson, Jenkins & Warman **Bred** Stratford Place Stud **Trained** Newmarket, Suffolk

FOCUS
A moderate handicap depleted by non-runners and the well-backed favourite took advantage. They came down the stands' side. The winner is rated to a similar level to the previous week's Salisbury success.

6187 STREAMLINE TAXIS - OFFICIAL TRANSPORT PARTNER H'CAP 7f 214y

4:30 (4:31) (Class 6) (0-60,60) 3-Y-O **£2,587** (£770; £384; £192) **Stalls** Centre

Form RPR
0004 1 **Purple Party (IRE)**[62] 3973 3-8-4 **46** oh1.................... NoelGarbutt(3) 11 53
(Gary Moore) *t.k.h: chsd ldr tl led 3f out: edgd rt over 1f out: hld on wl ins fnl f: rdn out* **9/2**[2]
606 2 *¾* **Touch Of Color**[20] 5515 3-9-1 **57**.................... JosephineGordon(3) 12 62
(Jane Chapple-Hyam) *racd in midfield: rdn 4f out: hdwy u.p over 2f out: chsng ldrs whn squeezed for room and swtchd lft ent fnl f: pressing wnr ins fnl f: unable qck wl ins fnl f* **8/1**
0240 3 *nk* **Bazzat (IRE)**[4] 6047 3-8-10 **49**....................(p) HarryBentley 6 53
(John Ryan) *chsd ldrs: effrt 2f out: drvn and clsd over 1f out: pressing ldrs ins fnl f: styd on same pce wl ins fnl f* **7/1**
4064 4 *1 ½* **The Greedy Boy**[14] 5710 3-8-10 **49**.................... SilvestreDeSousa 2 50
(Mick Channon) *wl in tch in midfield: pushed along and hdwy to press ldrs 5f out: rdn and ev ch over 2f out tl no ex jst ins fnl f: wknd fnl 100yds* **7/2**[1]
4635 5 *3 ¼* **Just Fab (IRE)**[27] 5263 3-9-2 **55**....................(bt) WilliamTwiston-Davies 5 49
(Ali Stronge) *hld up in midfield: stmbld 5f out: c to stands' side 3f out: hdwy and rdn to chse ldrs over 2f out: no ex and edgd lft over 1f out: wknd ins fnl f* **10/1**
5605 6 *1 ½* **Walking In Rhythm (IRE)**[25] 5330 3-9-7 **60**.................... TimmyMurphy 9 50
(Richard Hannon) *hld up in last trio: shkn up ent fnl 2f: rdn and hdwy into midfield over 1f out: nvr on terms w ldrs and styd on same pce ins fnl f* **9/1**
2660 7 *nk* **Buzz Lightyere**[14] 5720 3-9-4 **57**.................... KierenFox 10 46
(Michael Attwater) *chsd ldrs: reminders 4f out: drvn over 2f out: sn outpcd: wknd over 1f out* **6/1**[3]
0403 8 *11* **Burning Love (IRE)**[12] 5775 3-9-0 **53**....................(p) HarryPoulton 13 17+
(Adam West) *v awkward leaving stalls: detached in last: clsd and in tch 5f out: rdn over 2f out: sn struggling: bhd fnl f* **25/1**
-206 9 *2* **Clevedon Court**[34] 4992 3-8-10 **54**.................... HectorCrouch(5) 3 13
(Gary Moore) *t.k.h: hld up in tch in midfield: short lived effrt 2f out: sn btn: bhd fnl f* **16/1**

0060 **10** *24* **Roman Urn**[14] 5721 3-8-7 **46** oh1.................................(bt[1]) MartinDwyer 7
(Brett Johnson) *led tl rdn and hdd 3f out: lost pl 2f out: bhd and eased fnl f: t.o* **50/1**

40-0 **11** *17* **Rouge Noir**[26] 5300 3-9-2 **55**.. JimCrowley 8
(Jeremy Noseda) *dwlt: hld up in last trio: effrt jst over 2f out: no hdwy and sn btn: bhd and eased fnl f: t.o* **8/1**

1m 39.15s (3.15) **Going Correction** +0.50s/f (Yiel) **11** Ran SP% **120.2**
Speed ratings (Par 99): **104,103,102,101,98 96,96,85,83,59 42**
CSF £41.52 CT £257.63 TOTE £6.10: £2.20, £2.60, £2.50; EX 46.60 Trifecta £284.50.
Owner Mrs Mette Campbell-Andenaes **Bred** Paul Monaghan **Trained** Lower Beeding, W Sussex

FOCUS
A low-grade handicap in which they went a fair pace, and it was one of the least exposed runners who came out on top down the stands' rail. This was another bit of improvement from the winner.

6188 HARRINGTONS LETTINGS - OFFICIAL GRANDSTAND SPONSOR APPRENTICE H'CAP 7f 214y
5:00 (5:00) (Class 6) (0-60,59) 4-Y-O+ **£2,587** (£770; £384; £192) **Stalls** Centre

Form RPR

4000 **1** **World Record (IRE)**[32] 5085 6-9-5 **57**.............................. LuluStanford 4 65
(Mick Quinn) *mde all: rdn ent fnl 2f: kpt on ins fnl f: pushed along and a doing enough towards fin* **7/4**[1]

5000 **2** *nk* **Zeteah**[17] 5604 6-8-4 **45**.. MillyNaseb(3) 5 52
(Tony Carroll) *chsd ldrs: effrt to chse wnr and rdn 2f out: clr 2nd and pressing wnr 1f out: styd on towards fin but a hld* **6/1**

3336 **3** *8* **Altaira**[16] 5625 5-9-1 **53**.. RhiainIngram 3 42
(Tony Carroll) *hld up in tch in last pair: c towards stands' rail and effrt over 2f out: 3rd and no hdwy over 1f out: wknd fnl f* **3/1**[2]

5144 **4** *2 1/2* **Highlife Dancer**[12] 5776 8-9-4 **56**.............................. KillianHennessy 6 39
(Mick Channon) *chsd wnr: rdn over 2f out: lost pl and btn over 1f out: wknd fnl f* **6/1**

5600 **5** *nse* **Hawk Moth (IRE)**[42] 4715 8-9-2 **59**..........................(p) JoshuaBryan(5) 1 42
(John Spearing) *stdd s: hld up in tch in last pair: effrt 2f out: no imp over 1f out: wknd fnl f* **7/2**[3]

1m 39.88s (3.88) **Going Correction** +0.50s/f (Yiel) **5** Ran SP% **112.2**
Speed ratings (Par 101): **100,99,91,89,89**
CSF £12.68 TOTE £2.60: £1.90, £1.30; EX 13.00 Trifecta £35.40.
Owner John Quorn **Bred** Roy W Tector **Trained** Newmarket, Suffolk

FOCUS
A weak handicap lacking any worthwhile recent form and the majority came down the middle, including the first two who pulled clear. This could be rated 3-4lb higher.
T/Jkpt: £9,787.80. Pool: £19,575.68 - 2 winning units. T/Plt: £168.60 to a £1 stake. Pool: £69260.09, 299.87 winning units T/Qpdt: £74.80 to a £1 stake. Pool: £5190.91, 51.3 winning units **Steve Payne**

5890 WINDSOR (R-H)
Monday, September 5

OFFICIAL GOING: Good to soft
Wind: Almost nil Weather: Cloudy, quite humid

6189 OAKLEY COURT MAIDEN STKS 6f
2:20 (2:22) (Class 5) 2-Y-O **£3,557** (£1,058; £529; £264) **Stalls** Low

Form RPR

0 **1** **Silver Penny**[27] 5258 2-9-0 0.. PatCosgrave 1 69
(Jim Boyle) *mde virtually all and racd against rail: clr w runner-up fr 1/2-way: urged along over 2f out: narrow ld fnl f and rdn out* **20/1**

60 **2** *nk* **Red Alert**[3] 6086 2-9-5 0.. JFEgan 6 73
(Joseph Tuite) *w wnr: clr of rest fr 1/2-way: rdn and edgd lft over 1f out: stl nrly upsides ins fnl f: jst hld* **5/1**[3]

06 **3** *8* **Casaclare (IRE)**[9] 5890 2-9-5 0.................................... FergusSweeney 3 54+
(Jonjo O'Neill) *chsd ldng pair: lft bhd fr 1/2-way: no ch after but clr of rest in 3rd over 1f out* **12/1**

50 **4** *5* **Miss Reignier**[54] 4261 2-9-0 0.. DaneO'Neill 4 29
(Michael Blanshard) *sltly awkward s: in tch in rr to 1/2-way: sn no ch w ldng pair: tk poor 4th nr fin* **25/1**

334 **5** *nk* **Dontforgettocall**[119] 2104 2-9-5 71.................................... TomQueally 5 33
(Joseph Tuite) *t.k.h: trckd ldrs: outpcd 1/2-way: sn btn* **3/1**[2]

0 **6** *3 1/4* **Radar Love (IRE)**[87] 3093 2-9-0 0.................................... LiamKeniry 9 18
(J S Moore) *in tch to 1/2-way: sn no ch w ldng pair: wknd fnl f* **33/1**

06 **7** *2* **Gala Celebration (IRE)**[42] 4707 2-9-5 0................ MichaelJMMurphy 8 17
(John Gallagher) *in tch towards rr to 1/2-way: sn btn* **9/1**

8 *2 3/4* **Primadonia** 2-9-0 0.. TomMarquand 2 4+
(Richard Hannon) *slowly away: rn green and a bhd in last* **6/5**[1]

1m 13.14s (0.14) **Going Correction** -0.15s/f (Firm) **8** Ran SP% **116.4**
Speed ratings (Par 95): **93,92,81,75,74 70,67,64**
CSF £115.99 TOTE £9.30: £3.10, £2.10, £3.00; EX 79.80 Trifecta £1009.70.
Owner Inside Track Racing Club **Bred** Trickledown Stud Limited **Trained** Epsom, Surrey

FOCUS
The inner running rail was moved for the meeting as follows: Inner of straight dolled out 5yds at 6f and 2yds at the winning line. Top bend dolled out 8yds from normal inner configuration, adding 29yds to race distances of 1m plus. The going was changed to good to soft, from good, after the opener, although a couple of the jockeys felt it was "soft". Little got into this ordinary maiden, the front two always being to the fore and drawing right away.

6190 4-RAIL SERVICES H'CAP 6f
2:50 (2:52) (Class 5) (0-75,75) 3-Y-O **£3,234** (£962; £481; £240) **Stalls** Low

Form RPR

22 **1** **Sirajiah (IRE)**[28] 5238 3-9-4 **72**...(p) PatCosgrave 3 78
(William Haggas) *hld up bhd ldrs: clsd fr 2f out: drvn ahd ins fnl f: kpt on* **4/1**[1]

0351 **2** *1/2* **Equistar**[47] 4521 3-9-3 **71**...(t) FergusSweeney 6 75
(Jonathan Portman) *w ldrs thrght: drvn and upsides 1f out: jst outpcd by wnr last 100yds* **14/1**

0416 **3** *hd* **Peter Park**[34] 4985 3-8-11 **72**.................................... WilliamCox(7) 5 75
(Clive Cox) *hld up in tch: effrt and n.m.r over 1f out: got through fnl f and styd on to take 3rd last stride* **20/1**

40-4 **4** *shd* **Rosie Royce**[25] 5330 3-8-13 **67**.................................... DaneO'Neill 11 70
(Henry Candy) *w ldrs on outer: taken to far side 1/2-way: rt on terms tl no ex deep ins fnl f* **9/1**

03-5 **5** *shd* **Fashionable Spirit (IRE)**[14] 5725 3-8-9 **63**.................... AndreaAtzeni 1 65
(Amanda Perrett) *mde most: edgd off rail fr 2f out: hdd ins fnl f: jst run out of the pls nr fin* **16/1**

6210 **6** *1 1/2* **Geoff Potts (IRE)**[45] 4612 3-9-0 **73**.............................. DavidParkes(5) 4 71
(Jeremy Gask) *dwlt: hld up in last trio: drvn 2f out: kpt on but nvr able to threaten* **14/1**

4-03 **7** *nse* **In Haste (IRE)**[12] 5774 3-9-4 **72**.................................... CharlesBishop 7 69
(Eve Johnson Houghton) *w ldrs: lost pl 1/2-way and pushed along: tried to chal again over 1f out: one pce u.p* **11/2**[2]

0043 **8** *1 3/4* **Frenchman (FR)**[7] 5960 3-9-7 **75**.......................... MichaelJMMurphy 10 67
(Charles Hills) *sweating: w ldrs: lost pl 1/2-way: sn rdn: fdd over 1f out* **4/1**[1]

4013 **9** *nk* **Himalayan Queen**[20] 5525 3-8-5 **66**.......................... SophieKilloran(7) 9 57
(William Jarvis) *dwlt: hld up in last trio: nt clr run 2f out then swtchd towards far side: no prog* **11/1**

1-00 **10** *3 1/4* **Times Legacy**[74] 3580 3-9-4 **72**.................................... JimmyFortune 12 52
(Peter Chapple-Hyam) *stdd s: t.k.h and hld up in last trio: taken to far side 1/2-way: nt on terms w rival there and no prog: wknd over 1f out* **8/1**[3]

0600 **11** *13* **Peak Hill**[52] 4354 3-8-13 **67**.. JFEgan 8 6
(David Evans) *chsd ldrs but sn pushed along: wknd 1/2-way: t.o* **12/1**

1m 11.88s (-1.12) **Going Correction** -0.15s/f (Firm) **11** Ran SP% **116.5**
Speed ratings (Par 101): **101,100,100,99,99 97,97,95,95,90 73**
CSF £61.59 TOTE £4.20: £1.80, £4.20, £5.80; EX 44.60 Trifecta £1227.50.
Owner Abdulla Al Khalifa **Bred** J Hanly, T Stewart & A Stroud **Trained** Newmarket, Suffolk

FOCUS
Race distance as advertised. A modest handicap, a couple of runners headed far side in the straight but those racing more stands' side came out on top. There was a bunch for the places behind the slightly improved winner.

6191 STEVE RILEY LUTON TOWN MEMORIAL NURSERY H'CAP 1m 67y
3:20 (3:21) (Class 5) (0-75,74) 2-Y-O **£3,363** (£1,001; £500; £250) **Stalls** Low

Form RPR

0052 **1** **Quothquan (FR)**[17] 5594 2-8-6 **64**.............................. GeorgeWood(5) 2 68
(Michael Madgwick) *sweating: trckd ldr: rdn to ld wl over 1f out: kpt on wl fnl f* **7/1**[3]

0000 **2** *1 1/2* **Buskin River (IRE)**[38] 4825 2-8-4 **64**.......................... MitchGodwin(7) 4 65
(Richard Hannon) *hld up bhd ldrs: effrt whn rdr dropped whip jst over 2f out: prog to chse wnr over 1f out: urged along and kpt on but nvr able to chal* **8/1**

5121 **3** *1 1/2* **Jumping Jack (IRE)**[20] 5528 2-9-5 **72**.......................... JamieSpencer 1 70
(Richard Hughes) *led: tk field down centre by 1/2-way and to far side over 2f out: shkn up and hdd wl over 1f out: nt qckn and kpt on same pce after* **6/1**[2]

3122 **4** *1 1/4* **Mister Blue Sky (IRE)**[16] 5644 2-9-7 **74**.......................... GeorgeBaker 6 68
(Sylvester Kirk) *hld up in last: effrt over 2f out: ldrs nt stopping and no imp over 1f out* **4/5**[1]

0024 **5** *3* **Golden Guest**[28] 5239 2-9-1 **68**...(v) TomQueally 5 55
(George Margarson) *t.k.h early: hld up in tch: drvn and struggling 2f out: no ch after* **12/1**

3605 **6** *3 1/2* **At The Beach**[14] 5707 2-8-9 **62**.. KieranO'Neill 3 41
(Richard Hannon) *t.k.h early: trckd ldrs: hrd rdn and wknd 2f out* **10/1**

1m 48.69s (3.99) **Going Correction** +0.225s/f (Good) **6** Ran SP% **110.2**
Speed ratings (Par 95): **89,87,86,84,81 78**
CSF £55.56 TOTE £7.70: £3.20, £3.00; EX 52.40 Trifecta £559.70.
Owner Los Leader **Bred** Daniel Cherdo & Georges Boulard **Trained** Denmead, Hants

FOCUS
The short-price favourite disappointed in this ordinary nursery, with the field heading far side, but the winner built on his improved Salisbury form. Race distance increased by 29yds.

6192 BOODLES MAIDEN STKS 1m 3f 135y
3:50 (3:51) (Class 5) 3-Y-O **£3,557** (£1,058; £529; £264) **Stalls** Centre

Form RPR

-363 **1** **West Drive (IRE)**[75] 3508 3-9-5 80.............................(b[1]) AndreaAtzeni 1 80
(Roger Varian) *sweating: mde all: tk field to far side fr 3f out: hrd pressed and drvn 2f out: kpt on to assert fnl f* **5/4**[1]

0-62 **2** *1* **Vermeulen**[15] 5681 3-9-5 81.. RobertHavlin 4 78
(John Gosden) *trckd wnr: chal 3f out: drvn 2f out: nt qckn jst over 1f out: kpt on same pce after* **13/8**[2]

0- **3** *1/2* **Easy Gold (IRE)**[307] 7673 3-9-5 0.................................... GeorgeBaker 2 77
(Ed Walker) *settled off the pce: pushed along and adrift in 5th 4f out: edgd lft whn drvn over 2f out: r.o wl fr over 1f out: tk 3rd and gaining on front pair nr fin* **20/1**

2242 **4** *2 1/2* **Plenary (USA)**[24] 5366 3-9-5 85....................................[1] JamieSpencer 5 73
(Jeremy Noseda) *sn chsd ldng pair: hrd rdn over 3f out: no imp after but kpt on same pce: lost 3rd nr fin* **5/1**[3]

6 **5** *16* **Fastnet Monsoon (IRE)**[15] 5681 3-9-5 0......................(b[1]) AdamKirby 6 47
(Luca Cumani) *slowly away: rdn in 4th pl 5f out: sn struggling: wknd over 3f out* **16/1**

0 **6** *66* **Jamindeh**[111] 2340 3-9-5 0.. FMBerry 3
(Ian Williams) *struggling in last bef 1/2-way: t.o* **66/1**

2m 33.47s (3.97) **Going Correction** +0.225s/f (Good) **6** Ran SP% **111.3**
Speed ratings (Par 101): **95,94,94,92,81 37**
CSF £3.45 TOTE £2.50: £1.40, £1.20; EX 4.10 Trifecta £27.60.
Owner H R H Sultan Ahmad Shah **Bred** Airlie Stud **Trained** Newmarket, Suffolk

FOCUS
A fair maiden, there wasn't much pace on and the field headed far side. Race distance increased by 29yds. This has been rated cautiously.

6193 FULLER SMITH & TURNER PLC H'CAP 1m 3f 135y
4:20 (4:20) (Class 5) (0-75,75) 3-Y-O+ **£3,234** (£962; £481; £240) **Stalls** Centre

Form RPR

0001 **1** **Fire Jet (IRE)**[24] 5375 3-8-13 **71**.................................... TomQueally 7 79
(John Mackie) *trckd ldrs: pushed up to chal over 2f out towards far side: rdn to ld wl over 1f out: kpt on wl* **3/1**[2]

4233 **2** *1 1/4* **Pastoral Music**[47] 4530 3-8-9 **72**.............................. CharlieBennett(5) 6 77
(Hughie Morrison) *trckd ldrs: clsd to chal towards nr side over 2f out: on terms w wnr wl over 1f out: no ex fnl f* **8/1**

1044 **3** *1 1/4* **Chelsea's Boy (IRE)**[25] 5331 3-9-3 **75**.............................. AdamKirby 4 78
(Clive Cox) *led after 1f: rdn 3f out: hdd and nt qckn wl over 1f out: kpt on one pce fnl f* **4/1**[3]

6022 **4** *3* **Percy's Romance**[20] 5508 3-9-1 **73**.............................. AndreaAtzeni 3 71
(Sir Michael Stoute) *led at mod pce for 1f: trckd ldr: chal over 2f out: upsides wl over 1f out: hanging after and fdd fnl f* **11/8**[1]

-025 **5** *14* **Russian Bolero (GER)**[18] 342 5-9-9 **72**................(p) FergusSweeney 1 47
(David Dennis) *hld up in 5th: shkn up and no imp ldrs 3f out: wknd 2f out* **33/1**

32-3 **6** *18* **Mr Fickle (IRE)**[67] 3798 7-9-9 **72**.................................... GeorgeBaker 2 17
(Gary Moore) *hld up in last: lost tch 1/2-way: rdn and no rspnse 4f out: t.o* **8/1**

2m 32.21s (2.71) **Going Correction** +0.225s/f (Good)
WFA 3 from 4yo+ 9lb **6** Ran SP% **112.3**
Speed ratings (Par 103): **99,98,97,95,86 74**
CSF £25.86 TOTE £4.20: £2.10, £4.00; EX 22.50 Trifecta £108.70.

Owner Ladas **Bred** Ladas **Trained** Church Broughton , Derbys
FOCUS
Race distance increased by 29yds. They appeared to go a steady pace and again headed far side. Ordinary form but the winner has progressed again.

6194 FULLER SMITH & TURNER H'CAP — 1m 2f 7y
4:50 (4:50) (Class 5) (0-70,70) 3-Y-O — **£3,234** (£962; £481; £240) **Stalls** Centre

Form RPR
0365 **1** **Tom's Rock (IRE)**[47] 4530 3-9-7 **70** TomQueally 4 77
(John Butler) *hld up in midfield: clsd and swtchd to nr side over 1f out: hrd rdn and squeezed through to ld ins fnl f: styd on wl* **20/1**
300 **2** *1 ¼* **Betsalottie**[35] 4936 3-8-7 **56** DannyBrock 11 60
(John Bridger) *racd freely: led: styd against rail initially but hung lft over 2f out: sn hdd: n.m.r over 1f out: rallied to take 2nd last strides* **7/1**
5205 **3** *shd* **Multigifted**[9] 5891 3-8-5 **57** EdwardGreatrex[(3)] 2 61
(Michael Madgwick) *hld up in last pair: prog 3f out: nt clr run on inner 2f out and swtchd lft over 1f out: styd on wl to take 3rd last stride* **11/1**
5512 **4** *shd* **Fast And Hot (IRE)**[33] 5011 3-9-1 **64** (p) KieranO'Neill 7 68
(Richard Hannon) *prom: chal over 2f out: nt qckn sn after: battled for 2nd pl fnl f and kpt on* **9/2**[2]
4421 **5** *shd* **Rajadamri**[16] 5629 3-8-9 **63** GeorgeWood[(5)] 13 67
(Rod Millman) *trckd ldrs: clsd on outer 3f out: led jst over 2f out and c towards nr side rail: drvn and hdd ins fnl f: lost 3 pls nr fin* **7/1**
0045 **6** *6* **Perpetual Change (IRE)**[49] 4459 3-9-5 **68** AdamKirby 3 60
(Clive Cox) *trckd ldrs: on terms but u.p whn bmpd over 2f out: wknd over 1f out* **4/1**[1]
0620 **7** *4 ½* **Moon Over Mobay**[75] 3509 3-8-10 **59** RobertHavlin 14 42
(Michael Blanshard) *dropped to last trio and pushed along after 4f: rdn and no prog 3f out* **25/1**
0152 **8** *nk* **Port Paradise**[14] 5720 3-8-12 **68** SamuelClarke[(7)] 1 50
(William Jarvis) *t.k.h: hld up in tch: effrt 3f out: no prog 2f out: wknd* **9/1**
0340 **9** *¾* **Rock Palm (IRE)**[20] 5503 3-8-11 **60** (p) FMBerry 6 41
(Brendan Powell) *chsd ldr: rdn and sing to lose pl whn squeezed out over 2f out: wknd* **10/1**
504 **10** *20* **Heart Of Oak**[63] 3958 3-9-2 **65** JamieSpencer 8 6
(George Peckham) *hld up in last pair: rdn and no prog 3f out: eased 2f out: t.o* **6/1**[3]

2m 10.6s (1.90) **Going Correction** +0.225s/f (Good) **10** Ran SP% **113.5**
Speed ratings (Par 101): **101,100,99,99,99 94,91,91,90,74**
CSF £149.55 CT £1625.97 TOTE £12.60: £4.10, £2.40, £3.40; EX 148.40 Trifecta £4855.90.
Owner Recycled Products Limited **Bred** R G & T E Levin **Trained** Newmarket, Suffolk
FOCUS
Race distance increased by 29yds. A modest handicap, plenty had their chance. Improved form from the winner, with the third and fourth helping to set the level.

6195 BOOKER WHOLESALE H'CAP — 5f 10y
5:20 (5:22) (Class 4) (0-80,79) 3-Y-O+ — **£4,690** (£1,395; £697; £348) **Stalls** Low

Form RPR
6000 **1** **Fast Act (IRE)**[12] 5780 4-9-5 **77** KevinStott 5 87
(Kevin Ryan) *led against nr side: hung lft fr over 1f out and sn hrd pressed: jnd ins fnl f: jst prevailed* **10/1**
2364 **2** *nse* **Silken Skies (IRE)**[33] 5040 3-9-6 **79** AdamKirby 10 89
(Clive Cox) *trckd ldrs: prog to go 2nd over 1f out and sn chalng: w wnr last 100yds: jst pipped* **7/1**[3]
1332 **3** *1 ¼* **Pettochside**[52] 4355 7-9-3 **75** WilliamCarson 11 80
(John Bridger) *in tch: prog on outer 2f out: chsd ldng pair fnl f: styd on but unable to chal* **8/1**
1135 **4** *¾* **Justice Lady (IRE)**[9] 5882 3-9-6 **79** JamieSpencer 8 81+
(David Elsworth) *dwlt: hld up in last and long way off the pce: prog against nr side rail 2f out: r.o under pressed fnl f to take 4th nr fin: too much to do* **5/1**[2]
3211 **5** *¾* **May Rose (IRE)**[20] 5523 3-9-5 **78** (t) AndreaAtzeni 2 78
(Charles Hills) *trckd ldrs: rdn against nr side wl over 1f out: drifted lft after and no imp ldrs* **15/8**[1]
6400 **6** *¾* **Noble Asset**[26] 5285 5-8-11 **72** EdwardGreatrex[(3)] 7 69
(Milton Bradley) *pressed ldr to over 1f out: fdd fnl f* **25/1**
2652 **7** *nk* **Archie Stevens**[5] 6017 6-8-0 **65** AledBeech[(7)] 6 61
(David Evans) *chsd ldng pair to wl over 1f out: lost pl u.p and btn after* **11/1**
6005 **8** *3 ¼* **Taajub (IRE)**[15] 5669 9-9-5 **77** GeorgeBaker 1 61
(Peter Crate) *stdd s: hld up in last pair: effrt but hung lft towards far side fr 1/2-way: nvr on terms* **10/1**
0066 **9** *¾* **Nocturn**[12] 5774 7-9-1 **73** (p[1]) TomMarquand 9 54
(Ronald Harris) *sn pushed along to stay in tch in rr: struggling fr 1/2-way* **25/1**
2124 **10** *8* **Miracle Garden**[135] 1650 4-9-0 **79** (p) MitchGodwin[(7)] 4 32
(Roy Brotherton) *in tch to 1/2-way: sn wknd qckly: t.o* **20/1**

58.87s (-1.43) **Going Correction** -0.15s/f (Firm)
WFA 3 from 4yo+ 1lb **10** Ran SP% **114.0**
Speed ratings (Par 105): **105,104,102,101,100 99,98,93,92,79**
CSF £74.16 CT £597.57 TOTE £10.90: £3.00, £2.40, £2.50; EX 95.90 Trifecta £819.90.
Owner Hambleton Racing Ltd XXXII **Bred** Newlands House Stud **Trained** Hambleton, N Yorks
FOCUS
A pretty ordinary sprint. This was the winner's best form since his 2yo days.
T/Plt: £23,856.90 to a £1 stake. Pool: £76799.68, 2.35 winning units T/Qpdt: £115.50 to a £1 stake. Pool: £8200.91, 52.5 winning units **Jonathan Neesom**

6196 - 6199a (Foreign Racing) - See Raceform Interactive

4921 GALWAY (R-H)
Monday, September 5
OFFICIAL GOING: Soft (yielding in places)

6200a ARDILAUN HOTEL OYSTER STKS (LISTED) — 1m 4f 46y
6:35 (6:35) 3-Y-O+
£23,860 (£7,683; £3,639; £1,617; £808; £404)

RPR
1 **Almela (IRE)**[32] 5095 4-9-9 108 PatSmullen 8 108+
(D K Weld, Ire) *hld up in tch: clsr in 4th at 1/2-way: impr on outer gng wl under 3f out into 2nd over 2f out: led 1 1/2f out and rdn clr: eased cl home: easily* **8/11**[1]
2 *4 ¾* **Morga (IRE)**[15] 5689 6-9-9 94 ChrisHayes 4 97+
(Desmond McDonogh, Ire) *w.w in rr: last at 1/2-way: hdwy 3f out: nt clr run briefly on inner in 8th 2f out: gd hdwy into 3rd over 1f out: rdn into mod 2nd ins fnl f where no imp on easy wnr: kpt on wl* **10/1**
3 *2 ½* **Fact Or Folklore (IRE)**[34] 5002 4-9-9 92 BillyLee 11 93
(W McCreery, Ire) *chsd ldrs tl disp and led fr 1/2-way: rdn and strly pressed 2f out: hdd 1 1/2f out and sn no ch w easy wnr: dropped to 3rd ins fnl f and kpt on same pce* **33/1**
4 *6* **Avenante**[53] 4327 4-9-9 95 DeclanMcDonogh 3 83
(John M Oxx, Ire) *towards rr: 8th 1/2-way: hdwy to chse ldrs in 5th 2f out: rdn into 4th over 1f out and no imp on easy wnr: kpt on one pce ins fnl f* **9/1**[3]
5 *3 ½* **Glamorous Approach (IRE)**[18] 5587 3-9-0 101 KevinManning 2 78
(J S Bolger, Ire) *dwlt sltly and pushed along early: chsd ldrs: 5th fr 1/2-way: rdn in 3rd briefly fr 2f out and no imp on ldrs into st where dropped to mod 8th: kpt on one pce into mod 5th ins fnl f* **10/1**
6 *nse* **Soul Searcher (IRE)**[33] 5047 4-9-9 89 RoryCleary 7 78
(J P Murtagh, Ire) *towards rr: clsr in 7th at 1/2-way: rdn over 2f out and no imp on ldrs: kpt on one pce ins fnl f* **25/1**
7 *1* **More Mischief**[34] 5002 4-9-9 99 JoeyHaynes 9 76
(Jedd O'Keeffe) *cl up and disp briefly after 1f: 3rd 1/2-way: rdn over 2f out and sn no imp on ldrs u.p in 4th: wknd over 1f out* **10/1**
8 *¾* **Remarkable Lady (IRE)**[12] 5790 3-9-0 74 (t) ShaneFoley 5 75
(H Rogers, Ire) *wnt to post early: hld up: 9th 1/2-way: sme hdwy on outer fr over 2f out: c wd into st and sn no ex: wknd fnl f* **66/1**
9 *13* **How High The Moon (IRE)**[75] 3539 3-9-0 96 (p) SeamieHeffernan 6 54
(A P O'Brien, Ire) *hld up: 6th 1/2-way: pushed along over 3f out and wknd over 2f out* **6/1**[2]
10 *79* **Shes An Art (IRE)**[17] 5619 3-9-0 82 RonanWhelan 1
(James M Barrett, Ire) *sn led tl jnd briefly after 1f: jnd and hdd fr 1/2-way: pushed along bhd ldrs fr 3f out and wknd qckly over 2f out: eased bef st: t.o* **20/1**

2m 43.47s (163.47)
WFA 3 from 4yo+ 9lb **10** Ran SP% **122.5**
CSF £9.52 TOTE £1.70: £1.02, £2.70, £6.40; DF 10.30 Trifecta £244.00.
Owner H H Aga Khan **Bred** His Highness The Aga Khan's Studs S C **Trained** Curragh, Co Kildare
FOCUS
The Dermot Weld-trained Almela was the clear pick on official ratings and won accordingly. The front-running third has been rated to her best.

6201 - 6205a (Foreign Racing) - See Raceform Interactive

5792 LEICESTER (R-H)
Tuesday, September 6
OFFICIAL GOING: Good to soft (good in places)
Wind: Almost nil Weather: Overcast and humid

6206 BRITISH STALLION STUDS FILBERT EBF MAIDEN FILLIES' STKS (PLUS 10 RACE) — 1m 60y
2:00 (2:00) (Class 4) 2-Y-O — **£5,175** (£1,540; £769; £384) **Stalls** Low

Form RPR
1 **Coronet** 2-9-0 0 FrankieDettori 1 84+
(John Gosden) *s.i.s: hld up: swtchd lft over 2f out: hdwy sn after: shkn up to ld over 1f out: in command whn idled wl ins fnl f: pushed out: comf* **11/10**[1]
2 *½* **Alwaysandforever (IRE)** 2-9-0 0 RyanMoore 3 80+
(Luca Cumani) *chsd ldrs: shkn up to ld 2f out: hdd over 1f out: hld tl wnr idled wl ins fnl f: styd on* **5/1**[3]
3 *1* **Castellated** 2-9-0 0 TomMarquand 5 78+
(Richard Hannon) *prom: chsd ldr 6f out tl rdn over 2f out: kpt on* **9/1**
4 *2 ¼* **Agathonia (USA)** 2-9-0 0 WilliamBuick 4 73+
(Charlie Appleby) *chsd ldr 2f: remained handy: rdn over 1f out: styd on same pce fnl f* **9/1**
6 **5** *2* **Kitsey (IRE)**[31] 5170 2-9-0 0 SeanLevey 6 68
(Richard Hannon) *led at stdy pce tl qcknd 3f out: rdn and hdd 2f out: wknd ins fnl f* **16/1**
6 *10* **Struck By The Moon** 2-9-0 0 SilvestreDeSousa 2 45
(Charles Hills) *dwlt: hld up: hdwy over 3f out: rdn over 2f out: wknd over 1f out* **4/1**[2]

1m 48.7s (3.60) **Going Correction** +0.025s/f (Good) **6** Ran SP% **110.2**
Speed ratings (Par 94): **83,82,81,79,77 67**
CSF £6.65 TOTE £2.10: £1.80, £3.10; EX 6.70 Trifecta £37.70.
Owner Denford Stud **Bred** Denford Stud Ltd **Trained** Newmarket, Suffolk
FOCUS
William Buick said of the ground: "It's good to soft, holding." This had the look of a good fillies' maiden and the winner could be very smart indeed. This has been rated positively.

6207 EBF STALLIONS PRESTWOLD CONDITIONS STKS — 5f
2:30 (2:30) (Class 3) 3-Y-O+ — **£9,451** (£2,829; £1,414; £708; £352) **Stalls** High

Form RPR
0604 **1** **Hay Chewed (IRE)**[8] 5961 5-8-4 89 SilvestreDeSousa 4 101
(Conrad Allen) *mde all: shkn up 1/2-way: rdn over 1f out: r.o* **3/1**[2]
2365 **2** *1* **Ornate**[28] 5268 3-8-8 102 (t[1]) AndreaAtzeni 1 102
(William Haggas) *prom: chsd wnr 1/2-way: rdn over 1f out: edgd lft ins fnl f: styd on* **11/4**[1]
0650 **3** *2 ¼* **Burnt Sugar (IRE)**[31] 5143 4-8-4 102 (b) HollieDoyle[(5)] 7 94
(Richard Hannon) *s.i.s: in rr: pushed along 1/2-way: rdn over 1f out: r.o ins fnl f: nt rch ldrs* **9/2**
0-31 **4** *¾* **Southern Belle (IRE)**[35] 4984 3-8-3 90 TomMarquand 6 87
(Robert Cowell) *prom: rdn 1/2-way: styd on same pce fnl f* **4/1**[3]
6000 **5** *2 ½* **Field Of Vision (IRE)**[8] 5961 3-8-8 92 OisinMurphy 2 83
(Joseph Tuite) *chsd wnr tl rdn 1/2-way: wknd fnl f* **14/1**
2100 **6** *½* **Major Pusey**[10] 5882 4-8-9 85 MichaelJMMurphy 3 81
(John Gallagher) *hld up: rdn over 1f out: wknd fnl f* **28/1**
0305 **U** **Huntsmans Close**[8] 5961 6-8-9 98 AdamBeschizza 5
(Robert Cowell) *unruly in stalls: s.s and uns rdr leaving stalls* **8/1**

58.1s (-1.90) **Going Correction** -0.125s/f (Firm)
WFA 3 from 4yo+ 1lb **7** Ran SP% **111.1**
Speed ratings (Par 107): **110,108,104,103,99 98,**
CSF £10.98 TOTE £4.50: £2.40, £1.50; EX 12.60 Trifecta £45.20.
Owner John C Davies **Bred** Newlands House Stud **Trained** Newmarket, Suffolk

FOCUS
They went flying off here in what was a good little conditions sprint, but the pace held up with the winner making all.

6208 ROWLEYS PARTNERSHIP (S) STKS — 7f
3:00 (3:00) (Class 6) 2-Y-O — **£2,587** (£770; £384; £192) **Stalls** High

Form	Pos	Dist	Horse	RPR
6443	1		**Chevalier Du Lac (IRE)**[8] 5974 2-9-3 78................ SilvestreDeSousa 4 (Conor Dore) *hld up: hdwy 1/2-way: swtchd rt over 1f out: rdn to ld and hung lft wl ins fnl f: r.o* **2/1**[1]	68
0	2	1 1/4	**Shiny Line (IRE)**[12] 5809 2-8-7 0................ JFEgan 5 (John Butler) *hld up in tch: plld hrd: rdn and ev ch ins fnl f: styd on same pce* **12/1**	54
000	3	1/2	**Seaview**[10] 5869 2-8-7 54................ KieranO'Neill 6 (Dean Ivory) *chsd ldrs: rdn over 2f out: outpcd over 1f out: styd on wl towards fin* **5/2**[2]	53
3142	4	1/2	**Areyoutheway (IRE)**[35] 4982 2-9-3 66................(v) LiamJones 1 (Tom Dascombe) *w ldr tl led 1/2-way: rdn and hdd over 2f out: ev ch ins fnl f: no ex towards fin* **10/3**[3]	62
6400	5	shd	**Control Centre (IRE)**[12] 5806 2-8-12 56................ SeanLevey 3 (Richard Hannon) *chsd ldrs: led over 2f out: rdn over 1f out: hdd wl ins fnl f: nt clr run sn after: no ex* **8/1**	56
20	6	10	**Yorkshire Star (IRE)**[52] 4404 2-8-7 0................ HectorCrouch(5) 7 (Bill Turner) *sn pushed along in rr: hung rt fr over 4f out: sme hdwy 1/2-way: wknd over 2f out* **25/1**	30
0	7	1 1/4	**Shaqoos (FR)**[36] 4965 2-8-7 0................ IrineuGoncalves 9 (Jo Hughes) *hld up: sme hdwy 1/2-way: rdn over 2f out: sn wknd* **28/1**	22
040	8	8	**Jackman**[48] 4524 2-8-9 48................(p) GeorgeDowning(3) 2 (Tony Carroll) *sn pushed along in rr: wknd over 2f out* **33/1**	6
00	9	12	**Black Tie Bob (IRE)**[20] 5549 2-8-9 0................[1] JosephineGordon(3) 8 (J S Moore) *led to 1/2-way: rdn and wknd over 2f out* **66/1**	

1m 25.8s (-0.40) **Going Correction** -0.125s/f (Firm) — 9 Ran SP% **115.5**
Speed ratings (Par 93): **97,95,95,94,94 82,81,72,58**
CSF £26.08 TOTE £2.90: £1.10, £4.00, £1.30; EX 30.60 Trifecta £96.90.
Owner Mrs Jennifer Marsh **Bred** Vincent Hannon **Trained** Hubbert's Bridge, Lincs

FOCUS
A modest seller, plenty had their chance and the winner was best in at the weights.

6209 LEN CHESTERS CELEBRATION H'CAP — 1m 3f 183y
3:30 (3:30) (Class 4) (0-85,85) 3-Y-O+ — **£4,690** (£1,395; £697; £348) **Stalls** Low

Form	Pos	Dist	Horse	RPR
2455	1		**Faithful Mount**[25] 5358 7-9-8 **81**................[1] SilvestreDeSousa 3 (Ian Williams) *mde all: qcknd over 3f out: rdn over 2f out: styd on wl* **5/1**[2]	94
3412	2	3 1/4	**Rock Steady (IRE)**[29] 5240 3-9-3 **85**................ GeorgeBaker 6 (Roger Charlton) *hld up: swtchd lft and hdwy over 2f out: rdn to chse wnr and hung rt fr over 1f out: no imp ins fnl f* **7/2**[1]	94
215	3	2	**Most Celebrated (IRE)**[52] 4396 3-9-2 **84**................ JamesDoyle 4 (Saeed bin Suroor) *plld hrd and prom: rdn over 3f out: outpcd over 2f out: rallied over 1f out: styd on same pce fnl f* **7/2**[1]	89
4-36	4	3	**Al**[38] 4888 4-9-9 **82**................ AdamKirby 1 (Luca Cumani) *hld up: hdwy over 5f out: rdn over 3f out: wknd fnl f* **11/2**[3]	82
3605	5	1 1/2	**Shell Bay (USA)**[10] 5874 4-9-10 **83**................ SeanLevey 2 (Richard Hannon) *prom: chsd ldr 8f out tl rdn over 2f out: wknd over 1f out* **11/1**	80
000	6	5	**Bathos (IRE)**[10] 5865 3-9-3 **85**................ WilliamBuick 5 (Mark Johnston) *chsd wnr 4f: remained handy: rdn to go 2nd again over 2f out tl wknd over 1f out* **8/1**	74
3530	7	2 3/4	**English Summer**[11] 5837 9-9-12 **85**................(t) FMBerry 7 (Richard Fahey) *hld up: rdn and wknd over 2f out* **9/1**	70
010-	8	25	**Taskeen (IRE)**[332] 7116 3-8-13 **81**................ PaulHanagan 8 (Richard Hannon) *hld up: rdn over 3f out: sn wknd* **18/1**	26

2m 32.2s (-1.70) **Going Correction** +0.025s/f (Good)
WFA 3 from 4yo+ 9lb — 8 Ran SP% **111.2**
Speed ratings (Par 105): **106,103,102,100,99 96,94,77**
CSF £21.54 CT £65.73 TOTE £4.90: £1.80, £1.90, £1.10; EX 19.90 Trifecta £76.20.
Owner Macable Partnership **Bred** G Robinson **Trained** Portway, Worcs

FOCUS
A decent little handicap and a pb from the winner under a good front-running ride. This could be rated even higher.

6210 WEATHERBYS H'CAP — 7f
4:00 (4:01) (Class 3) (0-95,92) 3-Y-O+ — **£7,762** (£2,310; £1,154; £577) **Stalls** High

Form	Pos	Dist	Horse	RPR
1040	1		**Noble Peace**[24] 5403 3-8-9 **81**................ HarryBentley 2 (Henry Candy) *a.p: rdn to ld ins fnl f: styd on wl* **8/1**	88
411-	2	1	**In The Red (IRE)**[331] 7142 3-9-1 **87**................ TomMarquand 3 (Richard Hannon) *chsd ldr: rdn to ld over 1f out: hdd ins fnl f: styd on same pce towards fin* **16/1**	91
0042	3	1/2	**Bertiewhittle**[24] 5389 8-9-0 **87**................ RowanScott(5) 7 (David Barron) *s.i.s: hld up: rdn over 1f out: r.o to go 3rd nr fin: nt rch ldrs* **10/1**	92+
0000	4	nk	**Majestic Moon (IRE)**[10] 5871 6-9-10 **92**................ MichaelJMMurphy 6 (John Gallagher) *sn led at stdy pce: qcknd over 2f out: rdn and hdd over 1f out: no ex wl ins fnl f* **25/1**	96
3331	5	1 1/2	**Menai (IRE)**[31] 5168 3-8-6 **78** oh1................ SilvestreDeSousa 4 (Charles Hills) *hld up in tch: plld hrd: rdn over 1f out: no ex ins fnl f* **5/1**[3]	76
40-3	6	1	**Qeyaadah (IRE)**[95] 2871 3-9-5 **91**................ PaulHanagan 9 (Ed Dunlop) *plld hrd and prom: rdn over 2f out: no ex fnl f* **6/1**	86
6236	7	shd	**Archie (IRE)**[31] 5156 4-9-6 **88**................ AdamKirby 1 (Clive Cox) *hld up: rdn over 1f out: nt trble ldrs* **4/1**[2]	85
1522	8	1/2	**Musdam (USA)**[9] 5934 3-8-12 **84**................(v) RyanMoore 5 (Sir Michael Stoute) *s.i.s: hld up: nvr on terms* **9/4**[1]	78

1m 24.6s (-1.60) **Going Correction** -0.125s/f (Firm)
WFA 3 from 4yo+ 4lb — 8 Ran SP% **111.7**
Speed ratings (Par 107): **104,102,102,101,100 99,98,98**
CSF £116.42 CT £1281.19 TOTE £9.70: £2.10, £3.50, £2.80; EX 129.30 Trifecta £1782.80.
Owner One Too Many & Candy **Bred** The Pocock Family **Trained** Kingston Warren, Oxon

FOCUS
A fair handicap and career-best form from the winner and second, with the third close to form. The pace was steady.

6211 BRITISH STALLION STUDS APOLLO EBF MAIDEN STKS (PLUS 10 RACE) — 7f
4:35 (4:36) (Class 4) 2-Y-O — **£5,175** (£1,540; £769; £384) **Stalls** High

Form	Pos	Dist	Horse	RPR
3	1		**Elucidation (IRE)**[11] 5848 2-9-5 0................ TedDurcan 10 (Sir Michael Stoute) *mde all: rdn and edgd rt over 1f out: styd on wl* **4/6**[1]	85+
	2	1 3/4	**Sporting Times** 2-9-5 0................ JamesDoyle 13 (Ed Dunlop) *a.p: chsd wnr over 1f out: sn ev ch: styd on same pce ins fnl f* **66/1**	80+
6	3	6	**Presence Process**[26] 5332 2-9-5 0................ AdamKirby 3 (Luca Cumani) *prom: rdn over 2f out: wknd fnl f* **7/1**	65
	4	nk	**Adamant (GER)** 2-9-5 0................ RyanMoore 12 (Sir Michael Stoute) *s.i.s: hld up: shkn up over 2f out: styd on ins fnl f: nvr nrr* **6/1**[3]	64+
	5	1 1/2	**Al Mansor (IRE)** 2-9-5 0................ FrankieDettori 9 (Richard Hannon) *s.i.s: hdwy to chse wnr over 5f out: rdn over 2f out: lost 2nd and wknd over 1f out* **16/1**	61+
	6	3 1/4	**Jupiter Light** 2-9-5 0................ NickyMackay 2 (John Gosden) *s.i.s: hld up: racd keenly: pushed along and hdwy over 2f out: wknd over 1f out* **9/2**[2]	52
	7	1 1/4	**Quinteo (IRE)** 2-9-5 0................ FMBerry 6 (Jo Hughes) *hld up: hdwy over 2f out: rdn and wknd over 1f out* **100/1**	48
	8	nk	**Nigh Or Never (IRE)** 2-9-5 0................ LiamJones 1 (Tom Dascombe) *pushed along early in rr then plld hrd: rdn over 2f out: wknd over 1f out* **40/1**	48
	9	1	**Alemaratalyoum (IRE)** 2-9-5 0................ SilvestreDeSousa 8 (Ed Dunlop) *hld up: racd keenly: nt clr run wl over 1f out: swtchd rt: sn wknd* **12/1**	45
	10	2 3/4	**Time To Sea (IRE)** 2-9-5 0................ LiamKeniry 7 (John Butler) *hld up: rdn and n.m.r over 1f out: sn wknd* **80/1**	38

1m 24.9s (-1.30) **Going Correction** -0.125s/f (Firm) — 10 Ran SP% **124.7**
Speed ratings (Par 97): **102,100,93,92,91 87,85,85,84,81**
CSF £85.00 TOTE £1.70: £1.10, £8.80, £1.70; EX 68.40 Trifecta £371.00.
Owner Niarchos Family **Bred** Niarchos Family **Trained** Newmarket, Suffolk

FOCUS
The front pair came clear in what looked a decent maiden, even if the runner-up was a 66-1 shot. The level is a bit fluid for starters.

6212 SWAN APPRENTICE H'CAP — 1m 1f 218y
5:05 (5:05) (Class 6) (0-65,65) 4-Y-O+ — **£2,264** (£673; £336; £168) **Stalls** Low

Form	Pos	Dist	Horse	RPR
3402	1		**Stoneboat Bill**[15] 5715 4-9-0 **61**................ GerO'Neill(3) 12 (Declan Carroll) *s.i.s: hld up: hdwy and hung rt over 1f out: r.o to ld post* **3/1**[2]	67
-425	2	shd	**Inflexiball**[53] 4375 4-9-0 **58**................ CliffordLee 1 (John Mackie) *chsd ldrs: hmpd after 1f: rdn over 2f out: led over 1f out: hdd post* **7/1**[3]	64
2404	3	3/4	**Scent Of Power**[8] 5957 4-8-11 **55**................ KillianHennessy 8 (Barry Leavy) *hld up: hdwy over 2f out: rdn and ev ch ins fnl f: no ex nr fin* **16/1**	60
6553	4	2 1/4	**Master Of Song**[26] 5319 9-8-12 **56**................(p) KevinLundie 4 (Roy Bowring) *sn led: rdn and hdd over 1f out: no ex ins fnl f* **33/1**	56
051	5	shd	**Tyrsal (IRE)**[9] 5929 5-9-2 **63** 6ex................ CameronNoble(3) 3 (Clifford Lines) *s.i.s: hld up: nt clr run over 1f out: hung rt and r.o ins fnl f: nt rch ldrs* **5/2**[1]	65
0-40	6	shd	**Guantoshol (IRE)**[18] 5597 5-9-2 **65**................ JordanUys(5) 2 (Ian Williams) *hld up: hdwy: nt clr run and swtchd rt over 1f out: styd on* **18/1**	65
0431	7	1 1/2	**Roly Tricks**[13] 5776 5-9-7 **65**................ NatalieHambling 10 (Natalie Lloyd-Beavis) *hld up in tch: effrt over 2f out: styd on same pce fnl f* **14/1**	62
3605	8	1/2	**Tatawu (IRE)**[17] 5629 4-8-13 **62**................ TobyEley(5) 5 (Peter Hiatt) *chsd ldrs: rdn over 1f out: no ex ins fnl f* **9/1**	58
5345	9	5	**Monopoli**[10] 5868 7-8-7 **51** oh2................(p) MitchGodwin 6 (Ivan Furtado) *plld hrd: w ldr: rdn and ev ch over 2f out: wknd over 1f out* **9/1**	38
6560	10	hd	**L'Es Fremantle (FR)**[26] 5323 5-8-2 **51** oh6................ AledBeech(5) 11 (Michael Chapman) *hld up: hdwy over 3f out: rdn and wknd over 1f out* **66/1**	37
3353	11	1/2	**Percys Princess**[12] 5795 5-8-11 **60**................ BenRobinson(5) 7 (Michael Appleby) *w ldrs 2f: pushed along over 5f out: wknd 2f out* **10/1**	45

2m 8.1s (0.20) **Going Correction** +0.025s/f (Good) — 11 Ran SP% **117.4**
Speed ratings (Par 101): **100,99,99,97,97 97,96,95,91,91 91**
CSF £24.50 CT £291.10 TOTE £3.40: £1.50, £2.90, £4.50; EX 25.90 Trifecta £221.50.
Owner David Joseph O'Reilly **Bred** P C Hunt **Trained** Malton, N Yorks

FOCUS
Modest handicap form, but it makes sense with the front three to their pre-race marks.
T/Plt: £62.20 to a £1 stake. Pool: £75528.88, 885.77 winning units T/Qpdt: £20.00 to a £1 stake. Pool: £5939.96, 219.03 winning units **Colin Roberts**

5883 REDCAR (L-H)
Tuesday, September 6

OFFICIAL GOING: Good (good to soft in places; 7.9)
Wind: fresh 1/2 behind Weather: fine

6213 RACING UK PROFITS RETURNED TO RACING NURSERY H'CAP — 7f
1:50 (1:50) (Class 5) (0-75,75) 2-Y-O — **£2,911** (£866; £432; £216) **Stalls** Centre

Form	Pos	Dist	Horse	RPR
21	1		**Kings Gift (IRE)**[31] 5150 2-9-7 **75**................ PaulMulrennan 5 (Michael Dods) *trckd ldrs: smooth hdwy over 2f out: shkn up to ld appr fnl f: wnt clr: smoothly* **1/1**[1]	89+
2550	2	4	**Conistone**[20] 5549 2-8-12 **66**................ PJMcDonald 1 (James Bethell) *chsd ldrs: drvn over 2f out: kpt on to take modest 2nd last 75yds: no ch w wnr* **14/1**	66
5046	3	3/4	**Chickenfortea (IRE)**[25] 5364 2-8-4 **58**................ PatrickMathers 3 (Eric Alston) *t.k.h: led: drvn 2f out: hdd appr fnl f: kpt on same pce* **40/1**	56
0161	4	1 1/2	**Allux Boy (IRE)**[28] 5265 2-9-4 **72**................ AndrewMullen 4 (Nigel Tinkler) *trckd ldrs: t.k.h: kpt on one pce over 1f out* **6/1**[2]	66

300 **5** *nk* **He's A Toff (IRE)**[66] 3872 2-8-8 **62** (b) DavidAllan 8 55
(Tim Easterby) *sn detached in rr: reminders after 1f: kpt on fnl 2f: nrst fin* **11/1**

050 **6** *nk* **Heaven's Rock (IRE)**[34] 5029 2-9-6 **74** (t) RichardKingscote 2 66
(Tom Dascombe) *dwlt: sn chsng ldrs: drvn over 2f out: wknd last 75yds* **16/1**

034 **7** *1 ¾* **Inlawed**[25] 5377 2-9-0 **68** LukeMorris 7 56
(Ed Walker) *mid-div: drvn over 2f out: kpt on fnl f: nvr a factor* **8/1**

045 **8** *2* **Sheriff Garrett (IRE)**[13] 5778 2-8-11 **65** DuranFentiman 9 47
(Tim Easterby) *rr-div: drvn 3f out: sme hdwy over 1f out: nvr on terms* **33/1**

0535 **9** *1 ¾* **Our Boy John (IRE)**[32] 5109 2-8-10 **64** TonyHamilton 6 42
(Richard Fahey) *t.k.h in rr: brief effrt over 2f out: sn wknd* **7/1**[3]

1m 23.3s (-1.20) **Going Correction** -0.15s/f (Firm) **9** Ran SP% **114.2**
Speed ratings (Par 95): **100,95,94,92,92 92,90,87,85**
CSF £17.08 CT £351.70 TOTE £1.90: £1.10, £3.80, £8.30; EX 16.10 Trifecta £363.70.
Owner Geoff & Sandra Turnbull **Bred** Old Carhue & Graeng Bloodstock **Trained** Denton, Co Durham

FOCUS
The going was given as good, good to soft in places (GoingStick: 7.9) and clerk of the course Ed Gretton said: "It is softer in the back straight, it is good in the home straight. And it is only going to dry out." After riding in the opener Paddy Mathers called the ground good, PJ McDonald said "It is good, good to soft in places," Duran Fentiman said: "It is good to soft" and Richard Kingscote called it: "A bit dead." The time suggested it was no worse than good in the straight. The favourite looked in a different class to the rest in this nursery.

6214 RACING UK IN GLORIOUS HD MAIDEN AUCTION STKS 5f
2:20 (2:24) (Class 6) 2-Y-O **£2,385** (£704; £352) **Stalls** Centre

Form RPR

662 **1** **Justanotherbottle (IRE)**[10] 5884 2-9-3 67 DanielTudhope 14 72
(Declan Carroll) *hld up: hdwy to trck ldrs 2f out: styd on fnl f: led nr fin* **13/2**

322 **2** *nk* **Jeany (IRE)**[42] 4725 2-8-12 68 ConnorBeasley 7 66
(Bryan Smart) *led: drvn over 1f out: hdd and no ex nr fin* **3/1**[1]

3 **3** *1* **Lady Molly (IRE)**[12] 5798 2-8-12 0 JimCrowley 12 62
(Keith Dalgleish) *w ldrs: kpt on same pce fnl 100yds .* **6/1**[3]

0 **4** *2 ¼* **Flashing Light**[10] 5884 2-8-6 0 DuranFentiman 10 48
(Tim Easterby) *chsd ldrs: kpt on one pce fnl f* **100/1**

5 *nk* **Shannon** 2-8-6 0 LukeMorris 8 48+
(Robyn Brisland) *dwlt: rr-div: hdwy to chse ldrs over 2f out: kpt on same pce fnl f* **8/1**

03 **6** *1 ½* **Blastofmagic**[16] 5668 2-9-3 0 PhillipMakin 13 53
(David Dennis) *hld up in rr: swtchd rt and hd over 1f out: kpt on* **33/1**

46 **7** *hd* **Mere Brow**[15] 5713 2-8-6 0 [1] PJMcDonald 6 41
(Ann Duffield) *chsd ldrs: one pce over 1f out .* **4/1**[2]

2452 **8** *1 ½* **Local Artist (IRE)**[21] 5511 2-8-7 66 CallumShepherd(5) 3 42
(John Quinn) *chsd ldrs: fdd fnl 150yds* **6/1**[3]

000 **9** *½* **Nobility (IRE)**[12] 5809 2-8-13 57 DavidAllan 4 41
(Tim Easterby) *chsd ldrs: wknd last 100yds* **25/1**

0500 **10** *1 ¼* **Flying Hope (IRE)**[7] 6010 2-8-8 51 [1] AndrewMullen 2 31
(Nigel Tinkler) *chsd ldrs: wknd appr fnl f* **66/1**

0 **11** *¾* **Miss Pepper (IRE)**[15] 5727 2-8-10 0 CamHardie 15 31
(Paul Midgley) *s.i.s: swtchd lft after s: sme hdwy over 1f out: nvr a factor* **25/1**

060 **12** *1* **Mr Enthusiastic**[67] 3839 2-8-11 60 PatrickMathers 9 28
(Noel Wilson) *chsd ldrs: lost pl over 1f out* **80/1**

13 *1* **Rebel Flame** 2-8-11 0 GrahamLee 1 24
(Jedd O'Keeffe) *wnt lft s: a in rr* **28/1**

58.36s (-0.24) **Going Correction** -0.15s/f (Firm) **13** Ran SP% **115.8**
Speed ratings (Par 93): **95,94,92,89,88 86,86,83,82,80 79,78,76**
CSF £24.09 TOTE £6.80: £2.40, £1.40, £2.60; EX 24.80 Trifecta £113.40.
Owner Steve Ryan & M J Tedham **Bred** John O'Connor **Trained** Malton, N Yorks

FOCUS
A modest but fairly competitive maiden. The action developed towards the near side of the bunch. The winner confirmed his recent improvement, with the second a fair guide and this could be rated a bit higher.

6215 MARKET CROSS JEWELLERS H'CAP (DIV I) 6f
2:50 (2:52) (Class 5) (0-75,75) 3-Y-O+ **£2,911** (£866; £432; £216) **Stalls** Centre

Form RPR

0324 **1** **Kenny The Captain (IRE)**[3] 6131 5-9-1 **72** RachelRichardson(3) 9 84
(Tim Easterby) *w ldr: led 3f out: styd on wl fnl f* **9/2**[1]

3215 **2** *2* **Mr Orange (IRE)**[34] 5032 3-8-10 **66** (p) CamHardie 3 72
(Paul Midgley) *mid-div: drvn 3f out: hdwy over 1f out: kpt on to take 2nd nr fin* **6/1**[3]

2401 **3** *nk* **Enjoy Life (IRE)**[15] 5714 3-8-7 **63** JoeDoyle 1 68
(Kevin Ryan) *trckd ldrs: kpt on same pce fnl f* **5/1**[2]

4366 **4** *1 ½* **Manatee Bay**[11] 5858 6-9-7 **75** (v) FrannyNorton 5 75
(David Nicholls) *hmpd s: in rr: hdwy whn nt clr run over 1f out: swtchd rt: hung lft and kpt on fnl f: tk 4th clsng stages* **5/1**[2]

0364 **5** *¾* **Mercers Row**[8] 5969 9-8-13 **67** DanielTudhope 10 64
(Michael Herrington) *hld up in rr: hdwy to chse ldrs over 1f out: kpt on one pce* **16/1**

550 **6** *shd* **Fyrecracker (IRE)**[10] 5867 5-9-1 **69** KevinStott 2 66
(Grant Tuer) *led 3f: one pce over 1f out* **12/1**

0500 **7** *4* **Farkle Minkus**[33] 5070 3-9-1 **71** (p) JoeFanning 8 55
(Keith Dalgleish) *dwlt: a towards rr* **16/1**

0063 **8** *¾* **Insurplus (IRE)**[9] 5928 3-8-6 **62** (v) WilliamCarson 6 44
(Jim Goldie) *chsd ldrs: drvn over 2f out: lost pl over 1f out* **17/2**

4000 **9** *¾* **Questo**[8] 5968 4-8-9 **63** RoystonFfrench 7 43
(Tracy Waggott) *chsd ldrs: effrt over 2f out: wknd over 1f out* **50/1**

6242 **10** *1* **You're Cool**[28] 5269 4-8-8 **69** LewisEdmunds(7) 4 45
(John Balding) *wnt rt s: in rr: drvn and outpcd over 2f out: sme hdwy and edgd lft over 1f out: sn wknd* **11/1**

1-20 **11** *2* **Extortion**[116] 2200 3-9-5 **75** PaulMulrennan 11 45
(Bryan Smart) *t.k.h: trckd ldrs: lost pl over 1f out: bhd whn eased clsng stages* **12/1**

1m 10.0s (-1.80) **Going Correction** -0.15s/f (Firm)
WFA 3 from 4yo+ 2lb **11** Ran SP% **113.8**
Speed ratings (Par 103): **106,103,102,100,99 99,94,93,92,91 88**
CSF £30.05 CT £141.06 TOTE £4.60: £1.70, £2.40, £2.00; EX 29.50 Trifecta £115.50.
Owner Reality Partnerships V **Bred** Joe Foley & John Grimes **Trained** Great Habton, N Yorks

FOCUS
This looked pretty open on paper but the favourite made every yard for a comfortable success, stepping up on this year's form and rated to his best since his 2yo days.

6216 MARKET CROSS JEWELLERS H'CAP (DIV II) 6f
3:20 (3:20) (Class 5) (0-75,74) 3-Y-O+ **£2,911** (£866; £432; £216) **Stalls** Centre

Form RPR

0250 **1** **Aprovado (IRE)**[8] 5969 4-9-2 **69** (b[1]) ConnorBeasley 4 81
(Michael Dods) *mde all: shkn up over 1f out: sn clr* **8/1**

3153 **2** *3* **Vallarta (IRE)**[11] 5845 6-9-7 **74** JamesSullivan 9 76
(Ruth Carr) *n.m.r sn after s: hld up in rr: hdwy over 1f out: styd on to take modest 2nd last 150yds: no imp* **11/2**[2]

6202 **3** *2* **Semana Santa**[8] 5969 3-9-5 **74** GrahamGibbons 2 70
(David Barron) *chsd wnr: rdn over 1f out: kpt on same pce* **9/2**[1]

1400 **4** *½* **Eleuthera**[53] 4345 4-9-6 **73** ShaneGray 6 67
(Kevin Ryan) *trckd ldrs: t.k.h: drvn over 1f out: one pce* **10/1**

4454 **5** *½* **Perfect Words (IRE)**[13] 5762 6-8-8 **64** (p) JacobButterfield(3) 3 56
(Marjorie Fife) *chsd ldrs: drvn over 2f out: one pce over 1f out* **20/1**

4034 **6** *1 ¼* **Athollblair Boy (IRE)**[8] 5978 3-9-0 **69** TomEaves 1 57
(Nigel Tinkler) *dwlt: in rr: sme hdwy over 1f out: nvr on terms* **7/1**[3]

6054 **7** *1 ¼* **Percy's Gal**[36] 4932 5-8-7 **60** SamJames 5 44
(Karen Tutty) *chsd ldrs: drvn over 2f out: wknd last 100yds* **11/2**[2]

20U4 **8** *2* **Mitchum**[10] 5867 7-9-2 **69** (p) DavidAllan 8 47
(Ron Barr) *chsd ldrs: drvn over 2f out: lost pl over 1f out* **8/1**

2032 **9** *1 ¼* **Fujin**[14] 5736 5-8-8 **66** CharlieBennett(5) 10 40
(Shaun Harris) *chsd ldrs: edgd rt and lost pl over 1f out* **17/2**

2360 **10** *2 ¼* **Cuppatee (IRE)**[11] 5839 3-8-9 **64** [1] PJMcDonald 7 31
(Ann Duffield) *in rr: reminders after 1f: nvr on terms* **18/1**

1m 10.21s (-1.59) **Going Correction** -0.15s/f (Firm)
WFA 3 from 4yo+ 2lb **10** Ran SP% **113.3**
Speed ratings (Par 103): **104,100,97,96,96 94,92,90,88,85**
CSF £50.06 CT £227.51 TOTE £9.50: £2.60, £1.70, £2.00; EX 62.80 Trifecta £216.70.
Owner Hanson, McKiver, Percival **Bred** R N Auld **Trained** Denton, Co Durham

FOCUS
The slower of the two divisions by 0.21sec, but the winner looks back to his 3yo level.

6217 PINNACLE RACING SYNDICATE SHARES AVAILABLE H'CAP (PINNACLE CUP STRAIGHT MILE SERIES QUALIFIER) 1m
3:50 (3:53) (Class 4) (0-85,84) 3-Y-O+ **£6,469** (£1,925; £962; £481) **Stalls** Centre

Form RPR

1430 **1** **Heir To A Throne (FR)**[18] 5616 3-9-4 **83** ShaneGray 4 91
(Kevin Ryan) *chsd ldng pair: effrt over 2f out: edgd lft and styd on fnl f: led nr fin* **13/2**[2]

0515 **2** *nk* **Tadaany (IRE)**[21] 5521 4-9-5 **79** DanielTudhope 1 87
(David O'Meara) *racd alone towards far side: w ldr: led 2f out: edgd rt and hdd nr fin* **9/1**[3]

0302 **3** *¾* **Pumaflor (IRE)**[10] 5886 4-9-4 **78** [1] ConnorBeasley 8 85
(Richard Whitaker) *trckd ldrs: kpt on fnl f: no ex last 50yds* **6/1**[1]

2116 **4** *1* **Shamaheart (IRE)**[10] 5866 6-9-10 **84** (p) DavidAllan 6 88
(Geoffrey Harker) *hld up in rr: hdwy over 2f out: chsng ldrs 1f out: keeping on same pce whn hmpd 50yds out* **9/1**[3]

4000 **5** *hd* **Bahama Moon (IRE)**[38] 4894 4-9-7 **81** GrahamGibbons 5 85
(David Barron) *in rr: hdwy over 2f out: styd on wl fnl f* **10/1**

6000 **6** *nk* **Ingleby Angel (IRE)**[10] 5886 7-9-4 **78** RoystonFfrench 13 81
(Colin Teague) *chsd ldrs: drvn over 2f out: styd on fnl f* **25/1**

0505 **7** *1 ½* **Altharoos (IRE)**[10] 5886 6-9-8 **82** [1] DougieCostello 9 82
(Sally Hall) *up in rr: effrt over 3f out: kpt on fnl 2f: nvr a threat* **11/1**

5140 **8** *nk* **Lawyer (IRE)**[24] 5419 5-9-4 **78** PhillipMakin 15 77
(David Barron) *hld up towards rr: hdwy over 2f out: one pce over 1f out* **20/1**

6320 **9** *hd* **Holy Grail (IRE)**[18] 5616 3-8-10 **80** GeorgeWood(5) 12 78
(Simon West) *led: hdd 2f out: fdd appr fnl f* **20/1**

4365 **10** *shd* **Beardwood**[38] 4894 4-9-8 **82** FrannyNorton 11 80
(Mark Johnston) *mid-div: sn drvn along: reminders over 2f out: nvr a factor* **6/1**[1]

2225 **11** *2 ½* **Haraz (IRE)**[10] 5865 3-8-12 **80** ShelleyBirkett(3) 16 72
(David O'Meara) *trckd ldrs: effrt over 2f out: wknd over 1f out* **11/1**

2606 **12** *hd* **Qaffaal (USA)**[10] 5886 5-8-12 **72** CamHardie 10 64
(Michael Easterby) *trckd ldrs: effrt over 2f out: lost pl over 1f out* **25/1**

6024 **13** *½* **Abushamah (IRE)**[21] 5514 5-9-10 **84** JamesSullivan 3 75
(Ruth Carr) *trckd ldrs: effrt over 2f out: lost pl over 1f out* **11/1**

030- **14** *4* **Recently Acquired**[76] 5369 4-9-10 **84** JimCrowley 14 66
(David Loder) *in rr: drvn o ver 2f out: eased whn bhd clsng stages* **14/1**

1m 36.26s (-0.34) **Going Correction** -0.15s/f (Firm)
WFA 3 from 4yo+ 5lb **14** Ran SP% **119.9**
Speed ratings (Par 105): **95,94,93,92,92 92,90,90,90,90 87,87,87,83**
CSF £59.94 CT £370.69 TOTE £8.60: £3.30, £3.80, £1.80; EX 94.80 Trifecta £533.80.
Owner STS Racing Limited **Bred** S A R L Neustrian Associates **Trained** Hambleton, N Yorks

FOCUS
An open handicap on paper but, with the pace holding up well, few got involved. The first four have been going the right way and this has been rated positively.

6218 RACING UK DAY PASS JUST £10 MAIDEN STKS 6f
4:20 (4:21) (Class 5) 3-Y-O+ **£2,911** (£866; £432; £216) **Stalls** Centre

Form RPR

2432 **1** **Hyland Heather (IRE)**[14] 5748 3-9-0 78 [1] TonyHamilton 1 74
(Richard Fahey) *w ldrs: drvn over 2f out: led over 1f out: edgd rt: drvn out* **7/4**[1]

032 **2** *2* **Manshood (IRE)**[22] 5480 3-9-5 73 (b) DaneO'Neill 11 72
(William Haggas) *w ldr: hdd over 1f out: edgd lft: kpt on same pce* **11/4**[2]

0 **3** *1 ¾* **Andys Girl (IRE)**[135] 1669 3-8-11 0 JacobButterfield(3) 3 61
(Brian Ellison) *s.s: in rr: hdwy 2f out: edgd lft and kpt on fnl f: tk modest 23rd nr fin* **100/1**

5 **4** *1 ¾* **Skadi**[11] 5843 4-9-2 0 JasonHart 8 55
(Garry Moss) *led: hdd 3f out: kpt on one pce over 1f out* **33/1**

-020 **5** *3 ¼* **Gabbys Lad (IRE)**[21] 5515 3-9-0 48 NeilFarley 9 45
(Eric Alston) *chsd ldrs: drvn over 2f out: wknd over 1f out* **40/1**

3430 **6** *1 ¾* **Tommy G**[53] 4344 3-9-5 78 WilliamCarson 4 44
(Jim Goldie) *hld up in rr: sme hdwy over 2f out: wknd over 1f out* **4/1**[3]

02 **7** *1 ¾* **Jabbarockie**[10] 5862 3-9-5 0 PJMcDonald 2 39
(Paul Green) *hld up in rr: hdwy over 2f out: rdn and edgd lft over 1f out: sn wknd* **5/1**

-000 **8** *6* **Sunnyhills Belford**[33] 5069 3-9-0 43 PatrickMathers 5 15
(Noel Wilson) *chsd ldrs: drvn over 3f out: lost pl 2f out: bhd whn eased last 100yds* **100/1**

The Form Book, Raceform Ltd, Newbury, RG14 5SJ

9 3 1/2 **Melodya (IRE)** 3-8-9 0 .... CallumShepherd(5) 6 3
(Brian Ellison) *s.i.s: in rr: drvn and hung lft 3f out: bhd and eased over 1f out* **12/1**

1m 11.25s (-0.55) **Going Correction** -0.15s/f (Firm)
WFA 3 from 4yo 2lb **9** Ran SP% **114.7**
Speed ratings (Par 103): **97,94,92,89,85 83,80,72,68**
CSF £6.57 TOTE £2.60: £1.60, £1.20, £7.80; EX 7.40 Trifecta £153.60.

Owner Mrs H Steel **Bred** Oghill House Stud & Joseph M Burke **Trained** Musley Bank, N Yorks

FOCUS
A modest maiden.

6219 RACING UK HD ON SKY432 H'CAP — 1m 6f 19y

4:50 (4:50) (Class 6) (0-65,65) 3-Y-O+ **£2,385** (£704; £352) **Stalls** Low

Form RPR

-333 **1** **Transpennine Star**[50] 4447 3-9-3 **65** .... PaulMulrennan 6 72+
(Michael Dods) *mid-div: hdwy to trck ldrs after 4f: drvn 4f out: edgd lft and styd on fnl f: led nr fin* **2/1**[1]

6144 **2** 1/2 **Chauvelin**[15] 5726 5-9-3 **54** ....(v) AndrewMullen 8 60
(Nigel Tinkler) *mid-div: hdwy on ins over 3f out: led 1f out: no ex and hdd nr fin* **25/1**

3460 **3** 3/4 **Triple Eight (IRE)**[21] 5522 8-9-4 **60** ....(p) PhilDennis(5) 10 65
(Philip Kirby) *hld up in rr: hdwy over 3f out: led briefly over 1f out: kpt on same pce last 50yds* **22/1**

6432 **4** 3/4 **La Bacouetteuse (FR)**[13] 5781 11-9-12 **63** ....(p) DavidAllan 9 67
(Iain Jardine) *in rr: drvn over 3f out: swtchd outside over 2f out: styd on appr fnl f: keeping on wl at fin* **12/1**

3443 **5** shd **Ghostly Arc (IRE)**[19] 5580 4-9-10 **61** .... GrahamGibbons 1 66
(Noel Wilson) *led: hdd 7f out: led over 2f out: hdd over 1f out: one pce whn n.m.r nr fin* **7/1**[3]

5202 **6** nk **Monjeni**[22] 5473 3-9-0 **62** ....(p) LukeMorris 5 67
(Sir Mark Prescott Bt) *hld up towards rr: hdwy over 3f out: keeping on same pce whn hmpd and eased last 75yds* **11/2**[2]

1031 **7** 8 **Major Rowan**[33] 5065 5-9-10 **61** .... PhillipMakin 3 54
(John Davies) *hld up in rr: stdy hdwy outer 3f out: wknd and eased last 150yds* **8/1**

-563 **8** 2 1/4 **Toola Boola**[11] 5842 6-10-0 **65** .... GrahamLee 7 56
(Jedd O'Keeffe) *w ldr: led 7f out: hdd over 2f out: lost pl over 1f out* **16/1**

9 1/2 **Burnside (FR)**[127] 3-9-3 **65** .... JimCrowley 12 55
(Ian Williams) *mid-div: effrt 4f out: chsng ldrs over 2f out: lost pl over 1f out* **8/1**

3006 **10** nk **Cavalieri (IRE)**[13] 5758 6-9-4 **55** ....(p) PJMcDonald 2 45
(Philip Kirby) *chsd ldrs: lost pl over 2f out* **33/1**

5005 **11** 27 **Slipper Satin (IRE)**[10] 5522 6-9-8 **59** ....(t) JasonHart 4 13
(Simon West) *chsd ldrs: lost pl over 2f out: bhd whn eased over 1f out: virtually p.u: t.o* **16/1**

3m 4.61s (-0.09) **Going Correction** +0.05s/f (Good)
WFA 3 from 4yo+ 11lb **11** Ran SP% **114.0**
Speed ratings (Par 101): **102,101,101,100,100 100,96,94,94,94 78**
CSF £62.68 CT £853.00 TOTE £2.80: £1.40, £5.30, £6.80; EX 50.00 Trifecta £614.10.

Owner Transpennine Partnership **Bred** Dale Ablitt **Trained** Denton, Co Durham

FOCUS
The first six finished in a bit of a heap and the bare form looks limited judged through the second and fourth.

6220 RACING UK.COM APPRENTICE H'CAP — 7f

5:20 (5:22) (Class 5) (0-75,73) 3-Y-O+ **£2,911** (£866; £432; £216) **Stalls** Centre

Form RPR

0504 **1** **Nonno Giulio (IRE)**[8] 5972 5-9-11 **73** .... GeorgeBuckell 10 81
(David Loughnane) *w ldrs: led over 3f out: edgd lft fnl f: hld on clsng stages* **7/1**[3]

6235 **2** 3/4 **Deansgate (IRE)**[11] 5845 3-9-7 **73** ....(e) AdamMcNamara 2 77
(Julie Camacho) *dwlt: hld up in rr:t.k.h: hdwy over 2f out: chsd wnr last 150yds: no ex clsng stages* **7/2**[1]

4200 **3** 1 1/4 **Ravenhoe (IRE)**[16] 5677 3-9-1 **70** .... GeorgeWood(3) 3 71
(Mark Johnston) *w ldrs: kpt on same pce fnl f* **5/1**[2]

3525 **4** 1 **Popsies Joy (IRE)**[15] 5732 3-9-4 **70** ....(b[1]) CallumShepherd 8 68
(Tim Easterby) *rrd s: hld up towards rr: hdwy over 2f out: chsng ldrs appr fnl f: kpt on same pce* **8/1**

0103 **5** 1/2 **Broctune Papa Gio**[8] 5972 9-8-12 **65** .... PatrickVaughan(5) 5 64
(Keith Reveley) *chsd ldrs: kpt on same pce over 1f out* **10/1**

0150 **6** nse **First Wheat**[20] 5539 3-9-6 **72** .... NathanEvans 12 68
(Michael Easterby) *chsd ldrs: drvn over 2f out: one pce over 1f out* **12/1**

0333 **7** shd **Space War**[11] 5859 9-9-5 **67** ....(t) AnnaHesketh 4 65
(Michael Easterby) *mid-div: drvn over 2f out: sn chsng ldrs. outpcd over 1f out: kpt on clsng stages* **14/1**

403- **8** 1 3/4 **Will Mac**[308] 7677 5-9-3 **65** .... JordanVaughan 1 58
(Neville Bycroft) *chsd ldrs: reminders over 2f out: edgd rt and wknd over 1f out* **33/1**

1443 **9** nk **Rasaman (IRE)**[13] 5779 12-8-13 **66** .... LewisEdmunds(5) 7 59
(Jim Goldie) *mid-div: outpcd over 2f out: kpt on fnl f* **10/1**

020 **10** 5 **Mime Dance**[31] 5151 5-9-10 **72** ....(p) JoshDoyle 11 51
(David O'Meara) *hld up in mid-div: effrt and prom over 2f out: lost pl over 1f out* **7/1**[3]

3600 **11** 25 **Young Christian**[28] 5273 3-8-10 **65** .... RhiainIngram(3) 6
(Tom Tate) *led: hdd over 3f out: lost pl 2f out: sn eased and bhd: virtually p.u: t.o* **16/1**

1m 24.27s (-0.23) **Going Correction** -0.15s/f (Firm)
WFA 3 from 4yo+ 4lb **11** Ran SP% **116.4**
Speed ratings (Par 103): **95,94,92,91,91 90,90,88,88,82 54**
CSF £31.31 CT £137.33 TOTE £8.00: £2.80, £1.80, £1.80; EX 34.00 Trifecta £292.10.

Owner Stephen Louch **Bred** Ballygallon Stud Limited **Trained** Market Drayton, Shropshire

FOCUS
A fair handicap. The winner was back on a good mark.

T/Jkpt: Not won. T/Plt: £21.10 to a £1 stake. Pool: £81224.29, 2799.5 winning units T/Qpdt: £9.40 to a £1 stake. Pool: £5439.69, 427.42 winning units **Walter Glynn**

[6023] CARLISLE (R-H)

Wednesday, September 7

OFFICIAL GOING: Good to soft (good in places in home straight; 6.9)
Wind: Almost nil Weather: Overcast

6221 KINGMOOR PARK PROPERTIES H'CAP (JOCKEY CLUB GRASSROOTS MIDDLE DISTANCE QUALIFIER) — 1m 1f

1:50 (1:51) (Class 5) (0-70,70) 3-Y-O+ **£2,911** (£866; £432; £216) **Stalls** Low

Form RPR

5522 **1** **Eez Eh (IRE)**[8] 6006 3-9-4 **70** ....(p) ConnorBeasley 5 79
(Keith Dalgleish) *mde all: rdn 2f out: hrd pressed ins fnl f: hld on wl towards fin* **9/2**[1]

1564 **2** hd **Billy Bond**[14] 5779 4-9-4 **69** ....(v) AdamMcNamara(5) 2 77
(Richard Fahey) *in tch: effrt and hdwy over 2f out: chsd wnr over 1f out: rdn and ev ch ins fnl f: kpt on: hld nr fin* **11/1**

0510 **3** 2 3/4 **The Lynch Man**[39] 4871 3-9-3 **69** ....(v) PJMcDonald 3 71
(John Quinn) *hld up towards rr: rdn over 2f out: hdwy and edgd rt over lf out: kpt on ins fnl f: nt rch first two* **14/1**

6343 **4** hd **Remember Rocky**[16] 5715 7-9-1 **61** ....(b) DougieCostello 7 63
(Lucy Normile) *pressed ldr: rdn along over 2f out: lost 2nd over 1f out: edgd rt and one pce fnl f* **11/1**

2214 **5** 4 **City Ground (USA)**[11] 5883 9-9-7 **70** .... AlistairRawlinson(3) 1 63
(Michael Appleby) *hld up: rdn over 2f out: hdwy over 1f out: kpt on fnl f: nvr able to chal* **9/1**

3011 **6** 4 1/2 **Intalza (IRE)**[8] 6004 3-8-10 **62** 6ex........(p) PaulMulrennan 10 45
(Michael Herrington) *pressed ldrs: effrt and rdn over 2f out: wknd over 1f out* **5/1**[2]

5 **7** 1 1/4 **Ecoute (IRE)**[98] 2804 3-9-4 **70** ....[1] GrahamLee 6 51
(Kenneth Slack) *in tch: rdn over 2f out: wknd over 1f out* **7/1**[3]

-510 **8** nk **Swiss Lait**[16] 5715 5-8-13 **59** .... JackGarritty 8 39
(Patrick Holmes) *towards rr: drvn along over 2f out: wknd wl over 1f out* **33/1**

/61- **9** 2 3/4 **Baraboy (IRE)**[24] 2978 6-8-8 **61** ....(b[1]) CliffordLee(7) 9 35
(Barry Murtagh) *slowly away: hld up: hdwy on outside 3f out: edgd lft and wknd wl over 1f out* **28/1**

635 **10** 2 1/2 **Percy Verence**[32] 5178 3-8-5 **62** .... JordanVaughan(5) 12 30
(K R Burke) *hld up towards rr: rdn 3f out: struggling fnl 2f* **9/1**

1451 **11** 11 **San Cassiano (IRE)**[11] 5883 9-9-6 **66** ....(b) JamesSullivan 4 10
(Ruth Carr) *prom: rdn along over 3f out: wknd 2f out: eased whn btn fnl f* **11/1**

0504 **12** 53 **Artful Prince**[21] 5540 6-9-9 **69** ....(b) JoeDoyle 11
(James Given) *s.i.s: hld up on outside: struggling over 3f out: lost tch fnl 2f: t.o* **8/1**

1m 59.37s (1.77) **Going Correction** +0.30s/f (Good)
WFA 3 from 4yo+ 6lb **12** Ran SP% **116.5**
Speed ratings (Par 103): **104,103,101,101,97 93,92,92,89,87 77,30**
CSF £53.08 CT £643.65 TOTE £5.30: £2.00, £4.10, £5.00; EX 57.10 Trifecta £480.60.

Owner Weldspec Glasgow Limited **Bred** Moyglare Stud Farm Ltd **Trained** Carluke, S Lanarks

FOCUS
A competitive contest for the grade run at a sound pace. A pb from the winner and second, with the third to his recent form.

6222 CARRS GROUP PLC NURSERY H'CAP — 5f 193y

2:20 (2:22) (Class 5) (0-75,75) 2-Y-O **£2,911** (£866; £432; £216) **Stalls** Low

Form RPR

630 **1** **Mutahaady (IRE)**[47] 4609 2-9-1 **69** .... DougieCostello 3 73+
(K R Burke) *trckd ldrs: rdn over 2f out: swtchd lft and led ins fnl f: kpt on strly* **9/2**[1]

600 **2** 1 1/4 **Volta Do Mar (IRE)**[14] 5756 2-8-5 **59** .... BarryMcHugh 10 60+
(Richard Fahey) *bhd: drvn along 1/2-way: gd hdwy fnl f: tk 2nd cl home: nt rch wnr* **28/1**

6056 **3** hd **Dandy Place (IRE)**[16] 5728 2-9-2 **70** .... JasonHart 7 70
(Tim Easterby) *in tch on ins: rdn along and effrt wl over 1f out: kpt on fnl f: hld nr fin* **18/1**

130 **4** nk **Baltic Beau**[89] 3114 2-8-4 **58** .... PatrickMathers 2 57+
(Richard Fahey) *s.i.s: bhd and outpcd: gd hdwy on wd outside fnl f: kpt on: nvr able to chal* **16/1**

5432 **5** 1/2 **Champion Harbour (IRE)**[13] 5806 2-8-9 **63** .... JackGarritty 11 61
(Richard Fahey) *plld hrd early: cl up: led over 2f out: rdn and hdd ins fnl f: sn no ex* **9/2**[1]

0360 **6** 3/4 **La Haule Lady**[27] 5317 2-8-11 **65** .... PaulMulrennan 1 61
(Paul Midgley) *hld up: rdn along 1/2-way: hdwy and swtchd rt over 1f out: kpt on fnl f: no imp* **20/1**

4210 **7** 3 1/2 **Whiteandgold**[84] 3290 2-9-4 **72** .... ConnorBeasley 14 57
(Bryan Smart) *reluctant to enter stalls: hld up midfield on outside: effrt and hdwy 2f out: wknd ins fnl f* **12/1**

6465 **8** 3/4 **Iftitah (IRE)**[17] 5675 2-7-9 **54** oh4........ ShirleyTeasdale(5) 8 37
(George Peckham) *plld hrd early: sn chsng ldrs on outside: pressed ldr over 2f out to 1f out: sn btn and eased* **16/1**

0064 **9** 1 1/4 **Mr Strutter (IRE)**[8] 6010 2-8-3 **57** .... CamHardie 6 36
(John Quinn) *prom: rdn over 2f out: wknd appr fnl f* **9/2**[1]

3300 **10** 3/4 **Clear As A Bell (IRE)**[16] 5712 2-8-7 **64** .... RachelRichardson(3) 9 41
(Tim Easterby) *hld up on ins: rdn and struggling over 2f out: sn btn* **12/1**

0455 **11** 4 1/2 **Regal Decree**[26] 5364 2-8-1 **55** .... JamesSullivan 12 18
(Jedd O'Keeffe) *hld up midfield: drvn and outpcd 1/2-way: btn fnl 2f* **8/1**[2]

1450 **12** 6 **Fiery Character (IRE)**[18] 5638 2-9-7 **75** ....(v[1]) RichardKingscote 4 20
(Tom Dascombe) *led to over 2f out: sn rdn and wknd* **9/1**[3]

1m 15.74s (2.04) **Going Correction** +0.30s/f (Good) **12** Ran SP% **116.3**
Speed ratings (Par 95): **98,96,96,95,95 94,89,88,86,85 79,71**
CSF £144.33 CT £2089.83 TOTE £6.20: £2.50, £8.30, £8.00; EX 152.40 Trifecta £1999.40.

Owner Tim Dykes, Mrs G Buchanan & E Burke **Bred** Kevin Blake **Trained** Middleham Moor, N Yorks

FOCUS
The pace was sound for this open handicap. An improved winner.

6223 ARMSTRONG WATSON EBF MAIDEN FILLIES' STKS (PLUS 10 RACE) — 6f 195y

2:50 (2:53) (Class 5) 2-Y-O **£3,234** (£962; £481; £240) **Stalls** Low

Form RPR

2 **1** **Euro Nightmare (IRE)**[12] 5834 2-9-0 0 .... JasonHart 9 74+
(Keith Dalgleish) *pressed ldr: drvn along 3f out: led 2f out: idled and pricked ears ins fnl f: kpt on wl* **4/5**[1]

	2	3/4	**Undiscovered Angel (FR)** 2-9-0 0 .... DougieCostello 2	72+
			(K R Burke) *s.i.s: sn rcvrd and hld up bhd ldng gp: smooth hdwy over 2f out: effrt and rdn over 1f out: pressed wnr ins fnl f: kpt on* **16/1**	
3	3	nk	**Brogan**[28] 5298 2-9-0 0 .... RichardKingscote 8	71
			(Tom Dascombe) *trckd ldrs: rdn and ev ch over 1f out to ins fnl f: kpt on u.p* **7/2**[2]	
0	4	4 1/2	**Doria Road (USA)**[29] 5272 2-9-0 0 .... TomEaves 5	60
			(Kevin Ryan) *reluctant to enter stalls: trckd ldrs: rdn and edgd rt over 1f out: wknd ins fnl f* **7/1**[3]	
	5	11	**Hiawassee (USA)** 2-9-0 0 .... FrannyNorton 1	31
			(Mark Johnston) *s.i.s: rn green and sn detached: nvr on terms* **12/1**	
0	6	3 3/4	**Iron Lady (IRE)**[16] 5722 2-9-0 0 .... MartinDwyer 7	21
			(William Muir) *t.k.h: led to 2f out: rallied: wknd appr fnl f* **10/1**	

1m 30.46s (3.36) **Going Correction** +0.30s/f (Good) **6** Ran SP% **112.9**
Speed ratings (Par 92): **92,91,90,85,73 68**
CSF £15.84 TOTE £1.80: £1.40, £5.20; EX 15.80 Trifecta £39.90.
Owner J S Morrison **Bred** Miss Annmarie Burke **Trained** Carluke, S Lanarks

FOCUS
An interesting fillies' maiden run at a decent pace. The front three finished clear and the winner at least matched her debut form.

6224 LAND AND LAKES EBF MAIDEN STKS (STALLION RESTRICTED) (PLUS 10 RACE) 7f 173y

3:25 (3:25) (Class 4) 2-Y-O **£6,469** (£1,925; £962; £481) **Stalls** Low

Form				RPR
	1		**Time To Study (FR)** 2-9-5 0 .... FrannyNorton 2	83+
			(Mark Johnston) *2 handlers in paddock: mde all: shkn up 2f out: kpt on strly to draw clr fnl f: readily* **7/2**[2]	
	2	2 3/4	**Kuraka** 2-9-5 0 .... DougieCostello 1	76
			(K R Burke) *t.k.h: trckd ldrs: effrt and rdn wl over 1f out: chsd (clr) wnr ins fnl f: kpt on: no imp* **10/1**	
2	3	1 1/2	**Cuttin' Edge (IRE)**[12] 5820 2-9-5 0 .... MartinDwyer 3	73
			(William Muir) *t.k.h early: pressed ldr: rdn and ev ch over 2f out to wl over 1f out: no ex and lost 2nd pl ins fnl f* **4/9**[1]	
	4	8	**The Blues Master (IRE)** 2-9-5 0 .... JoeFanning 4	60
			(Mark Johnston) *noisy and green in paddock: prom on outside: effrt and pushed along 3f out: edgd rt and wknd over 1f out* **8/1**[3]	

1m 43.95s (3.95) **Going Correction** +0.30s/f (Good) **4** Ran SP% **111.7**
Speed ratings (Par 97): **92,89,87,79**
CSF £27.57 TOTE £4.10; EX 25.90 Trifecta £45.90.
Owner Abdulla Al Mansoori **Bred** E A R L Haras Du Quesnay **Trained** Middleham Moor, N Yorks

FOCUS
An interesting maiden despite the small field. It was run at an honest pace and the winner did it nicely. The level is fluid for starters.

6225 NORTH ASSOCIATES H'CAP 7f 173y

4:00 (4:01) (Class 3) (0-95,95) 3-Y-O+ **£7,439** (£2,213; £1,106; £553) **Stalls** Low

Form				RPR
3011	1		**Loaded (IRE)**[22] 5507 3-8-8 **87** .... RobHornby[(3)] 2	95
			(Andrew Balding) *trckd ldrs: rdn over 2f out: led ins fnl f: hld on gamely towards fin* **11/4**[1]	
1514	2	nk	**Gurkha Friend**[32] 5160 4-9-1 **86** .... DavidNolan 10	94
			(Karen McLintock) *led: rdn 2f out: hdd ins fnl f: rallied: hld nr fin* **9/1**	
5034	3	1/2	**Father Bertie**[9] 5976 4-9-0 **85** .... (tp) JasonHart 5	92
			(Tim Easterby) *trckd ldr: rdn and ev ch over 1f out: kpt on same pce wl ins fnl f* **8/1**	
-305	4	nse	**Dark Devil (IRE)**[67] 3887 3-8-7 **83** .... PatrickMathers 4	89
			(Richard Fahey) *midfield: effrt and rdn over 2f out: kpt on fnl f: nrst fin* **12/1**	
0102	5	1 3/4	**Le Chat D'Or**[51] 4448 8-9-4 **89** .... (bt) PaulMulrennan 12	92
			(Michael Dods) *hld up: stdy hdwy over 2f out: rdn over 1f out: no ex ins fnl f* **16/1**	
-002	6	hd	**Argaki (IRE)**[13] 5802 6-8-5 **81** .... ShirleyTeasdale[(5)] 3	83
			(Keith Dalgleish) *in tch: drvn along over 2f out: outpcd over 1f out: edgd lft and kpt on ins fnl f: no imp* **28/1**	
5533	7	2 3/4	**Candelisa (IRE)**[19] 5616 3-9-5 **95** .... (p) GrahamLee 8	90
			(Jedd O'Keeffe) *hld up midfield: drvn and outpcd over 2f out: rallied ins fnl f: nvr rchd ldrs* **4/1**[2]	
501P	8	3	**Edgar Balthazar**[61] 4104 4-9-3 **88** .... (p) PhillipMakin 1	77
			(Keith Dalgleish) *slowly away: hld up: rdn along wl over 2f out: sme late hdwy: nvr rchd ldrs* **11/1**	
10	9	3 1/2	**Little Lady Katie (IRE)**[25] 5419 4-8-11 **87** .... JordanVaughan[(5)] 6	68
			(K R Burke) *hld up on outside: shortlived effrt over 2f out: sn btn* **15/2**[3]	
3100	10	5	**Pintura**[38] 4921 9-9-7 **92** .... (b) DougieCostello 7	61
			(Alistair Whillans) *hld up: rdn along 3f out: sn wknd* **66/1**	
3062	S		**Jacbequick**[5] 6076 5-8-13 **89** .... (v) JoshDoyle[(5)] 11	
			(David O'Meara) *slowly away: last whn clipped heels and fell after 1f* **12/1**	

1m 40.79s (0.79) **Going Correction** +0.30s/f (Good)
WFA 3 from 4yo+ 5lb **11** Ran SP% **114.1**
Speed ratings (Par 107): **108,107,107,107,105 105,102,99,95,90**
CSF £27.16 CT £178.25 TOTE £3.60: £1.60, £2.70, £2.70; EX 31.70 Trifecta £213.10.
Owner Mr & Mrs R M Gorell **Bred** Ms Alice Fitzgerald **Trained** Kingsclere, Hants
■ Stewards' Enquiry : Patrick Mathers four-day ban: used whip above permitted level (Sep 21-23,25)
Rob Hornby two-day ban: used whip above permitted level (Sep 21-22)

FOCUS
They went a strong pace for this competitive handicap with the prominent runners always in control. A small pb from the second, with the third to his recent form.

6226 HARRISON NORTHERN LTD. H'CAP 7f 173y

4:35 (4:35) (Class 5) (0-70,72) 3-Y-O+ **£2,911** (£866; £432; £216) **Stalls** Low

Form				RPR
-435	1		**Im Dapper Too**[11] 5887 5-8-11 **57** .... SamJames 1	66
			(John Davies) *prom: rdn over 2f out: rallied and led over 1f out: hld on wl fnl f* **5/1**[2]	
4323	2	2	**Niqnaaqpaadiwaaq**[32] 5151 4-9-6 **66** .... NeilFarley 10	70
			(Eric Alston) *led: rdn and hdd over 1f out: rallied: kpt on fnl f: nt rch wnr* **6/1**[3]	
0354	3	3/4	**Hernando Torres**[12] 5841 8-9-8 **68** .... (p) CamHardie 7	70+
			(Michael Easterby) *slowly away: hld up: hdwy against far rail over 1f out: kpt on fnl f: nrst fin* **20/1**	
600	4	hd	**Tafahom (IRE)**[22] 5529 4-8-9 **60** .... (b) NathanEvans[(5)] 5	62
			(Michael Easterby) *chsd ldr: drvn over 2f out: kpt on same pce fnl f* **7/1**	
35-6	5	2	**Conry (IRE)**[68] 3849 10-9-5 **65** .... (p) PJMcDonald 8	62
			(Ian Williams) *slowly away: hld up: hdwy over 2f out: effrt whn nt clr run over 1f out to ins fnl f: no imp* **40/1**	
4604	6	1/2	**Yair Hill (IRE)**[16] 5717 8-8-10 **56** oh10 .... (p) JoeFanning 3	52
			(Thomas Cuthbert) *hld up: stdy hdwy whn nt clr run over 2f out to over 1f out: sn rdn and no imp* **80/1**	
0006	7	1 1/2	**Osteopathic Remedy (IRE)**[45] 4683 12-9-3 **63** .... (t) PhillipMakin 9	56+
			(Michael Dods) *hld up: effrt whn nt clr run over 2f out to over 1f out: sn rdn: one pce fnl f* **12/1**	
0001	8	1/2	**Bling King**[50] 4498 7-9-2 **62** .... (p) PaulMulrennan 6	53
			(Geoffrey Harker) *hld up midfield: rdn along over 3f out: wknd over 1f out* **9/1**	
624	9	nk	**Alice Thornton**[14] 5757 4-9-4 **64** .... DavidNolan 12	55
			(Martin Todhunter) *chsd ldrs: rdn along 3f out: wknd over 1f out* **22/1**	
0062	10	1 3/4	**Dasheen**[7] 6028 3-9-0 **65** .... FrannyNorton 14	51
			(Mark Johnston) *midfield on outside: rdn over 3f out: sn struggling* **3/1**[1]	
0020	11	nk	**Danot (IRE)**[12] 5845 4-9-8 **68** .... GrahamLee 11	54
			(Jedd O'Keeffe) *in tch: rdn 3f out: wknd over 1f out* **20/1**	
0465	12	3 3/4	**Tanawar (IRE)**[16] 5717 6-9-1 **61** .... (v) JamesSullivan 4	38
			(Ruth Carr) *hld up: hdwy on outside 3f out: rdn and wknd 2f out* **8/1**	

1m 41.74s (1.74) **Going Correction** +0.30s/f (Good)
WFA 3 from 4yo+ 5lb **12** Ran SP% **114.8**
Speed ratings (Par 103): **103,101,100,100,98 97,96,95,95,93 93,89**
CSF £31.40 CT £555.94 TOTE £5.70: £1.70, £2.40, £5.90; EX 44.60 Trifecta £788.10.
Owner Chris Davies & Ron Riches **Bred** Christopher T Dawson **Trained** Piercebridge, Durham

FOCUS
A fair contest for the grade run at a decent pace. The second helps set the level.

6227 BAINES WILSON LLP H'CAP 1m 6f 32y

5:05 (5:05) (Class 5) (0-75,81) 3-Y-O+ **£2,911** (£866; £432; £216) **Stalls** Low

Form				RPR
4-64	1		**Wynford (IRE)**[15] 5746 3-8-12 **67** .... RobHornby[(3)] 6	79
			(Andrew Balding) *chsd ldrs: effrt and chsd ldr over 3f out: led over 1f out: rdn clr fnl f* **5/2**[1]	
0511	2	6	**Wor Lass**[5] 6097 8-10-7 **81** 12ex .... AnnaHesketh[(5)] 5	85
			(Susan Corbett) *hld up: gd hdwy on outside to ld 4f out: sn edgd rt and kicked 3 l clr: hdd over 1f out: one pce* **11/4**[2]	
4325	3	1/2	**Jan Smuts (IRE)**[12] 5856 8-10-0 **69** .... (tp) CamHardie 4	72
			(Wilf Storey) *dwlt: hld up: drvn along 4f out: rallied 3f out: one pce fr over 1f out* **16/1**	
0-13	4	10	**Bell Weir**[21] 5541 8-10-0 **69** .... (bt) JamesSullivan 1	58
			(Dianne Sayer) *chsd ldrs: rdn and outpcd over 3f out: btn fnl 2f* **6/1**	
2230	5	44	**Love Marmalade (IRE)**[20] 5580 6-9-12 **67** .... (p) PhillipMakin 2	
			(David O'Meara) *pressed ldr: lost pl whn hmpd over 3f out: sn btn: eased over 1f out* **7/2**[3]	
041	6	24	**Another Lincolnday**[24] 5435 5-9-9 **64** .... (p) TomEaves 3	
			(Michael Herrington) *led to 4f out: rdn and wknd over 2f out: eased whn no ch fnl f* **7/1**	

3m 14.07s (6.57) **Going Correction** +0.30s/f (Good)
WFA 3 from 5yo+ 11lb **6** Ran SP% **110.1**
Speed ratings (Par 103): **93,89,89,83,58 44**
CSF £9.26 TOTE £3.20: £1.60, £1.50; EX 10.10 Trifecta £59.90.
Owner I A Balding & P Fox **Bred** Pier House Stud **Trained** Kingsclere, Hants
■ Stewards' Enquiry : Anna Hesketh two-day ban: careless riding (Sep 21-22)

FOCUS
They went an honest pace with the well-backed favourite winning easily, showing improved form. Race distance increased by 12yds.
T/Jkpt: Not won. T/Plt: £426.00 to a £1 stake. Pool: £53,080.08. 90.95 winning tickets. T/Qpdt: £27.50 to a £1 stake. Pool: £3,556.73. 95.45 winning tickets. **Richard Young**

[5386] DONCASTER (L-H)

Wednesday, September 7

OFFICIAL GOING: Good to soft (good in places; 7.2)
Wind: Virtually nil Weather: Cloudy with sunny periods

6228 IRISH STALLION FARMS EBF CONDITIONS STKS (PLUS 10 RACE) 6f

2:00 (2:00) (Class 2) 2-Y-O **£11,205** (£3,355; £1,677; £838; £419) **Stalls** Low

Form				RPR
	1		**Lost At Sea** 2-8-8 0 .... JoeyHaynes 5	99+
			(K R Burke) *rr: green and sn pushed along: rdn along 1/2-way: hdwy 2f out: drvn and cl up jst over 1f out: kpt on wl u.p to ld last 100 yds* **16/1**	
213P	2	1 1/4	**Dream Of Dreams (IRE)**[18] 5654 2-8-13 102 .... JamieSpencer 1	100
			(Kevin Ryan) *trckd ldng pair: hdwy to chse ldr over 2f out: rdn wl over 1f out: drvn and ev ch ins fnl f: kpt on same pce towards fin* **11/8**[1]	
10	3	2 1/2	**Battaash (IRE)**[85] 3247 2-8-13 0 .... DaneO'Neill 3	93+
			(Charles Hills) *plld hrd and sn led: set str pce: clr and rdn along 2f out: hung bdly rt jst over 1f out: hdd & wknd last 100 yds* **13/2**[3]	
1	4	1 3/4	**Akhlaaq**[28] 5304 2-8-13 0 .... PaulHanagan 7	87+
			(Owen Burrows) *t.k.h: trckd ldrs: hdwy on outer over 2f out: sn rdn: drvn and one pce fr over 1f out* **7/4**[2]	
4141	5	15	**Jacquard (IRE)**[49] 4508 2-8-13 87 .... JamesDoyle 2	42
			(Mark Johnston) *led early: trckd ldr: pushed along 1/2-way: rdn over 2f out and sn wknd* **9/1**	

1m 13.22s (-0.38) **Going Correction** -0.05s/f (Good) **5** Ran SP% **107.7**
Speed ratings (Par 101): **100,98,95,92,72**
CSF £37.26 TOTE £12.90: £4.90, £1.30; EX 44.70 Trifecta £174.70.
Owner Mrs Z Wentworth **Bred** P E Barrett **Trained** Middleham Moor, N Yorks

FOCUS
The ground had dried out a little from previously forecast and was good to soft, good in places (GoingStick 7.2), with clerk of the course Roderick Duncan feeling that the last 3f was pretty much good ground. Round course railed out from 1m2f to where it meets the straight, adding 3yds to the distance of race 6. An interesting conditions event to start which can go to a decent juvenile - the subsequent Group/Graded winner Barefoot Lady took it in 2010 - but this time it was a messy race. Nothing should be taken away from the winner, though. The winning time was 3.22sec outside standard and after riding in the opener Jamie Spencer said: "It is good ground," Paul Hanagan said: "It is tacky" and James Doyle said: "There is plenty of ease in it."

6229 OWLERTON GREYHOUND STADIUM-SHEFFIELD'S TOP NIGHT NURSERY H'CAP 7f

2:30 (2:30) (Class 2) 2-Y-O **£11,644** (£3,465; £1,731; £865) **Stalls** Low

Form				RPR
1	1		**Andok (IRE)**[52] 4423 2-8-10 **80** .... TonyHamilton 2	86+
			(Richard Fahey) *trckd ldrs: hdwy wl over 1f out: rdn to chal ent fnl f: sn led: drvn and kpt on wl towards fin* **13/8**[1]	

136 **2** *hd* **Appointed**[39] 4884 2-8-12 **82** ... DavidAllan 1 87+
(Tim Easterby) *rr: hdwy 2f out: swtchd rt and rdn over 1f out: styd on wl and ev ch wl ins fnl f: edgd lft towards fin: jst hld* **17/2**

2146 **3** *1* **Mutawatheb (IRE)**[21] 5560 2-9-7 **91** ... PaulHanagan 7 94
(Richard Hannon) *cl up: led 3f out: rdn wl over 1f out: hdd appr fnl f: drvn and hld whn n.m.r nr fin* **11/4**[2]

2011 **4** *nk* **Notalot (IRE)**[21] 5543 2-8-6 **81** ...(v) CallumShepherd(5) 5 83
(Michael Bell) *trckd ldng pair: hdwy over 2f out: rdn to ld jst over 1f out: drvn and hdd ins fnl f: hld whn n.m.r nr fin* **9/1**

0234 **5** *1 1/4* **Used To Be**[26] 5371 2-8-6 **76** ... JoeyHaynes 6 75
(K R Burke) *trckd ldrs: hdwy on outer over 2f out: rdn and ev ch over 1f out: drvn and kpt on same pce fnl f* **11/1**

2210 **6** *2 1/2* **Mr Hobbs**[20] 5583 2-8-10 **80** ... OisinMurphy 3 72
(Sylvester Kirk) *chsd ldrs: rdn along over 2f out: sn one pce* **7/1**[3]

0501 **7** *1/2* **Our Charlie Brown**[13] 5799 2-8-1 **71** ... DuranFentiman 4 62
(Tim Easterby) *t.k.h: led: hdd 3f out: sn rdn and wknd* **16/1**

1m 27.12s (0.82) **Going Correction** -0.05s/f (Good) **7** Ran SP% **112.0**
Speed ratings (Par 101): **93,92,91,91,89 87,86**
CSF £15.61 CT £34.92 TOTE £2.60: £1.70, £4.60; EX 18.60 Trifecta £57.10.
Owner N O'Keeffe **Bred** Leslie Laverty **Trained** Musley Bank, N Yorks

FOCUS
A decent nursery, but the early pace was steady and a few took a hold.

6230 VIP PREMIUM VAPING & E-LIQUIDS SCARBROUGH STKS (LISTED RACE) 5f

3:00 (3:00) (Class 1) 2-Y-O+
£22,684 (£8,600; £4,304; £2,144; £1,076; £540) **Stalls** Low

Form RPR

5224 **1** **Priceless**[24] 5436 3-9-7 102 ... SilvestreDeSousa 4 107+
(Clive Cox) *trckd ldng pair: hdwy 2f out: rdn to ld appr fnl f: drvn out* **4/1**[3]

3225 **2** *3/4* **Thesme**[19] 5614 4-9-8 109 ... AndreaAtzeni 6 104
(Nigel Tinkler) *cl up: led 1/2-way: rdn wl over 1f out: hdd appr fnl f: sn drvn and kpt on* **11/4**[1]

5122 **3** *shd* **Equimou**[26] 5359 2-8-0 93 ... JimmyQuinn 9 97
(Robert Eddery) *chsd ldrs: rdn along wl over 1f out: kpt on wl u.p fnl f* **7/1**

6001 **4** *2* **Demora**[145] 1453 7-9-11 99 ... AndrewMullen 10 100
(Michael Appleby) *slt ld to 1/2-way: cl up: rdn wl over 1f out: drvn and kpt on same pce fnl f* **20/1**

0400 **5** *shd* **Taexali (IRE)**[8] 6012 3-9-12 93 ... SamHitchcott 8 101
(John Patrick Shanahan, Ire) *in tch and sn rdn along: drvn 2f out: kpt on u.p fnl f: nrst fin* **66/1**

4000 **6** *shd* **Pearl Secret**[19] 5614 7-9-13 109 ... OisinMurphy 5 101
(David Barron) *hld up towards rr: hdwy wl over 1f out. sn swtchd lft and rdn: drvn ins fnl f and no imp* **3/1**[2]

5111 **7** *1 1/4* **Go On Go On Go On**[28] 5285 3-9-7 97 ... AdamKirby 11 92
(Clive Cox) *towards rr: pushed along 1/2-way: sn rdn and n.d* **7/1**

6-05 **8** *1/2* **Sunflower**[32] 5148 3-9-7 93 ... JamesDoyle 3 90
(Andrew Balding) *dwlt: a rr* **33/1**

0246 **9** *nk* **Line Of Reason (IRE)**[11] 5863 6-9-13 104 ... MartinLane 2 94
(Paul Midgley) *chsd ldrs: rdn wl over 1f out: sn drvn and wknd fnl f* **9/1**

58.85s (-1.65) **Going Correction** -0.05s/f (Good)
WFA 2 from 3yo 22lb 3 from 4yo+ 1lb **9** Ran SP% **115.9**
Speed ratings: **111,109,109,106,106 106,104,103,102**
CSF £15.23 TOTE £5.00: £1.70, £1.20, £2.80; EX 15.50 Trifecta £105.30.
Owner A D Spence **Bred** Biddestone Stud Ltd **Trained** Lambourn, Berks

FOCUS
Despite a significant late non-runner in Muthmir, this was still a competitive Listed sprint, won by the Group 1 winners Prohibit, Sole Power and Mecca's Angel in recent years. Predictably there was no hanging around, but few ever got into it. This could be 5lb higher but it has been rated cautiously.

6231 CLIPPER LOGISTICS LEGER LEGENDS CLASSIFIED STKS 1m (S)

3:35 (3:37) (Class 5) 3-Y-O+ **£6,469** (£1,925; £962; £481) **Stalls** Low

Form RPR

/00- **1** **Phosphorescence (IRE)**[427] 4018 6-11-2 70 ...(b[1]) JosephO'Brien 16 77
(George Scott) *mde all: clr and rdn over 1f out: drvn ins fnl f: styd on* **7/1**

6060 **2** *1 1/4* **Janaab (IRE)**[6] 6055 6-11-2 67 ...(t) PeterBuchanan 6 74
(Tim Easterby) *hld up: hdwy 3f out: rdn to chse ldrs wl over 1f out: kpt on fnl f* **20/1**

104 **3** *shd* **Red Charmer (IRE)**[64] 3983 6-11-2 69 ... GeorgeDuffield 9 74
(Ann Duffield) *trckd ldrs: hdwy to chse wnr 2f out: rdn over 1f out: drvn and kpt on fnl f* **20/1**

3105 **4** *1 3/4* **Bluff Crag**[38] 4909 3-10-11 70 ... RichardHughes 8 69
(Andrew Balding) *hld up in rr: hdwy 3f out: swtchd ;lft and rdn wl over 1f out: styd on fnl f* **9/4**[1]

6216 **5** *3/4* **Gun Case**[12] 5845 4-11-2 68 ...(p) LukeHarvey 7 68
(Alistair Whillans) *hld up towards rr: hdwy over 3f out: chsd ldrs 2f out and sn rdn: drvn and kpt on same pce fnl f* **33/1**

0331 **6** *2 1/2* **Pike Corner Cross (IRE)**[22] 5503 4-11-2 70 ... OlliePears 4 62
(Ed de Giles) *t.k.h early: hld up in tch: hdwy to trckd ldrs wl over 2f out: effrt wl over 1f out: sn rdn and no imp* **8/1**

0042 **7** *3/4* **Mon Beau Visage (IRE)**[12] 5860 3-10-11 70 ... GaryBardwell 10 60
(David O'Meara) *hld up: plld hrd: rapid hdwy to join ldrs and cl up after 3f: rdn along on outer over 2f out: grad wknd* **16/1**

6044 **8** *5* **Sophisticated Heir (IRE)**[52] 4427 6-11-2 70 ... TonyCulhane 5 49
(Michael Herrington) *trckd ldrs: pushed along 3f out: rdn over 2f out: grad wknd* **13/2**[3]

3202 **9** *3 1/4* **Sakhalin Star (IRE)**[44] 4702 5-11-2 67 ...(e) BillyNewnes 3 42
(Richard Guest) *t.k.h: chsd ldrs: rdn along wl over 2f out: grad wknd* **14/1**

5265 **10** *1/2* **Chiswick Bey (IRE)**[7] 6028 8-11-2 70 ... DaleGibson 11 41
(Richard Fahey) *in tch: effrt over 2f out: sn rdn and no imp* **10/1**

0131 **11** *7* **Hijran (IRE)**[12] 5860 3-10-11 70 ...(p) GayKelleway 2 23
(Michael Appleby) *dwlt: in tch on inner: rdn along over 3f out: sn wknd* **6/1**[2]

3005 **12** *2 1/4* **Stoked (IRE)**[27] 5337 4-11-2 70 ...[1] TomMcLaughlin 1 19
(Chris Dwyer) *chsd ldrs: rdn along over 3f out: sn wknd* **16/1**

5006 **13** *2 1/4* **Aldair**[26] 5375 3-10-11 68 ... TonyClark 15 13
(Richard Hannon) *awkward and dwlt s: a rr* **50/1**

-440 **14** *6* **Hammer Gun (USA)**[72] 3728 3-10-11 70 ...(v[1]) AdrianNicholls 17
(Derek Shaw) *cl up: rdn along over 3f out: sn drvn and wknd* **40/1**

1m 40.51s (1.21) **Going Correction** -0.05s/f (Good)
WFA 3 from 4yo+ 5lb **14** Ran SP% **126.4**
Speed ratings (Par 103): **91,89,89,87,87 84,83,78,75,75 68,65,63,57**
CSF £150.41 TOTE £9.00: £3.00, £4.60, £5.40; EX 198.50 Trifecta £3112.70.
Owner Niarchos Family **Bred** Niarchos Family **Trained** Newmarket, Suffolk
■ Stewards' Enquiry : Joseph O'Brien Fine: £500, used whip above permitted level

FOCUS
Probably more interest in the jockeys than the horses in this modest classified event and a timely reminder of the winning rider's talents. The winner was still below his 3yo best, with the level set around the second and third.

6232 HOWCROFT INDUSTRIAL SUPPLIES H'CAP 7f

4:10 (4:11) (Class 2) (0-100,94) 3-Y-O
£12,450 (£3,728; £1,864; £932; £466; £234) **Stalls** Low

Form RPR

5520 **1** **Stamp Hill (IRE)**[39] 4867 3-9-3 **90** ... TonyHamilton 7 96
(Richard Fahey) *hld up in rr: hdwy on outer over 2f out: chal over 1f out and sn rdn: drvn and edgd lft ins fnl f: kpt on wl to ld nr fin* **5/1**

3020 **2** *hd* **Dream Mover (IRE)**[19] 5616 3-9-3 **90** ...(t) AndreaAtzeni 1 95
(Marco Botti) *.trckd ldrs: hdwy on inner and cl up 2f out: rdn to ld ent fnl f: sn drvn: hdd and no ex nr fin* **3/1**[2]

-112 **3** *3/4* **War Glory (IRE)**[46] 4631 3-9-3 **90** ... SeanLevey 3 94
(Richard Hannon) *trckd ldrs: hdwy 2f out and sn cl up: rdn and ev ch ent fnl f: drvn and hld whn n.m.r last 50 yds* **11/4**[1]

1210 **4** *hd* **Shanghai Glory (IRE)**[25] 5389 3-9-7 **94** ... MichaelJMMurphy 6 97
(Charles Hills) *cl up on outer: led wl over 2f out: rdn wl over 1f out: hdd and drvn ent fnl f: hld whn n.m.r last 50 yds* **9/1**

0003 **5** *1 1/2* **Take The Helm**[39] 4886 3-9-0 **87** ... JimmyFortune 4 86
(Brian Meehan) *led: pushed along and hdd wl over 2f out: rdn wl over 1f out: drvn ent fnl f: one pce* **10/1**

1121 **6** *nk* **Roll On Rory**[25] 5412 3-8-13 **86** ...(v) JFEgan 5 84
(Jason Ward) *cl up: rdn along and ev ch 2f out: drvn ent fnl f: one pce* **7/2**[3]

1m 26.62s (0.32) **Going Correction** -0.05s/f (Good) **6** Ran SP% **109.6**
Speed ratings (Par 107): **96,95,94,94,92 92**
CSF £19.27 TOTE £5.10: £2.50, £1.80; EX 23.40 Trifecta £109.10.
Owner Merchants and Missionaries **Bred** Ms Ellen O'Neill **Trained** Musley Bank, N Yorks

FOCUS
A bunch finish off an ordinary pace and the field were not obviously well treated.

6233 STORY CONTRACTING-PLANT, CONSTRUCTION & RAIL CONDITIONS STKS 1m 2f 60y

4:45 (4:45) (Class 2) 3-Y-O+ **£12,450** (£3,728; £1,864; £932; £466) **Stalls** Low

Form RPR

-146 **1** **Mount Logan (IRE)**[40] 4821 5-9-8 107 ... AndreaAtzeni 2 114
(Roger Varian) *trckd ldng pair: smooth hdwy to trck ldr 2f out: shkn up and qcknd to ld 11/2f out: sn clr: readily* **13/8**[1]

60-1 **2** *6* **Landwade Lad**[30] 5240 4-9-2 92 ... OisinMurphy 4 97
(James Fanshawe) *hld up in tch: hdwy 3f out: rdn to chse wnr appr fnl f: sn drvn and no imp* **8/1**

6500 **3** *2* **Windshear**[67] 3889 5-9-2 95 ... SeanLevey 5 93
(Richard Hannon) *trckd ldr: hdwy to ld over 3f out: rdn along over 2f out: hdd 11/2f out: sn drvn and kpt on same pce* **11/1**

2025 **4** *7* **Oasis Fantasy (IRE)**[18] 5647 5-9-2 105 ...(v[1]) SilvestreDeSousa 1 80
(Ed Dunlop) *hld up and bhd: hdwy on inner 3f out: rdn along to chse ldrs over 2f out: sn drvn and one pce* **5/2**[2]

3000 **5** *17* **Revolutionist (IRE)**[18] 5647 4-9-2 105 ... JamesDoyle 3 47
(Mark Johnston) *led: rdn along and hdd over 3f out: sn drvn and wknd* **7/2**[3]

2m 8.84s (-0.56) **Going Correction** +0.20s/f (Good) **5** Ran SP% **108.3**
Speed ratings (Par 109): **110,105,103,98,84**
CSF £13.98 TOTE £2.10: £1.10, £3.60; EX 11.60 Trifecta £39.30.
Owner Sheikh Mohammed Obaid Al Maktoum **Bred** Ladyswood Stud & Canning Downs Stud Aus **Trained** Newmarket, Suffolk

FOCUS
Rail movement added 3yds to race distance. A good-quality conditions event and the winner is rated back to his best. The field made for the centre of the track on turning in.

6234 1STSECURITYSOLUTIONS.CO.UK H'CAP 5f

5:15 (5:16) (Class 4) (0-85,85) 3-Y-O+ **£7,762** (£2,310; £1,154; £577) **Stalls** Low

Form RPR

4120 **1** **Singeur (IRE)**[23] 5479 9-9-4 **82** ... DanielTudhope 10 91
(Rebecca Bastiman) *racd towards far side: rr: hdwy over 1f out: rdn and styd on strly fnl f to ld nr fin* **14/1**

0-63 **2** *hd* **Tylery Wonder (IRE)**[24] 5441 6-9-1 **79** ...(b) AdamKirby 6 87
(Paul Midgley) *overall ldr far side: rdn over 1f out: drvn and edgd rt ins fnl f: hdd and no ex nr fin: 2nd of 9 in gp* **9/2**[1]

0130 **3** *3/4* **Musharrif**[12] 5857 4-8-11 **75** ... FrederikTylicki 1 81
(Declan Carroll) *trckd ldrs far side: hdwy over 1f out: rdn and kpt on fnl f. 3rd of 9 in gp* **12/1**

1262 **4** *1* **Ziggy Lee**[11] 5882 10-8-11 **80** ... CallumShepherd(5) 4 82
(Lawrence Mullaney) *in tch far side: hdwy 2f out: rdn to chse ldrs over 1f out: kpt on fnl f: 4th of 9 in gp* **14/1**

3441 **5** *1* **Top Boy**[17] 5679 6-9-6 **84** ...(v) MartinLane 2 82
(Derek Shaw) *t.k.h: hld up in rr far side: hdwy over 1f out: sn rdn and styd on fnl f. 5th of 9 in gp* **12/1**

0040 **6** *1* **Seve**[18] 5641 4-9-7 **85** ...(t) MartinHarley 11 80
(Tom Dascombe) *led stands side gp: prom: rdn wl over 1f out: drvn and edgd lft ent fnl f: one pce. 1st of 4 in gp* **9/1**

3120 **7** *hd* **Seamster**[4] 6131 9-9-0 **85** ...(t) CameronNoble(7) 9 79
(David Loughnane) *racd towards far side: chsd ldrs: rdn along 2f out: sn wknd. 6th of 9 in gp* **10/1**

6-00 **8** *hd* **Noble Storm (USA)**[126] 1968 10-9-7 **85** ... KevinStott 3 78
(Ed McMahon) *cl up far side: rdn 2f out: sn drvn and wknd fnl f. 7th of 9 in gp* **40/1**

3131 **9** *4* **Sandra's Secret (IRE)**[11] 5864 3-9-2 **81** ... DavidAllan 5 60
(Les Eyre) *prom far side: rdn along 2f out: sn drvn and wknd. 8th of 9 in gp* **9/1**

4165 **10** *nk* **L C Saloon**[16] 5730 3-9-1 **80** ... OisinMurphy 7 58
(David C Griffiths) *cl up far side: rdn along 2f out: sn wknd. 9th of 9 in gp* **25/1**

5211 **11** *hd* **Outrage**[32] 5162 4-9-4 **82** ... DaneO'Neill 13 59
(Daniel Kubler) *racd stands side: a towards rr: 2nd of 4 in gp* **8/1**[3]

224 **12** *2* **Pea Shooter**[25] 5417 7-9-5 **83** ... SilvestreDeSousa 12 53
(Brian Ellison) *racd stands side: a rr: 3rd of 4 in gp* **5/1**[2]

-000 **13** *1 3/4* **Thorntoun Lady (USA)**[5] 6080 6-8-7 **71** oh2 ... JimmyQuinn 14 35
(Jim Goldie) *racd stands side: a rr: 4th of 4 in gp* **14/1**

59.18s (-1.32) **Going Correction** -0.05s/f (Good)
WFA 3 from 4yo+ 1lb **13** Ran SP% **116.7**
Speed ratings (Par 105): **108,107,106,104,103 101,101,101,94,94 93,90,87**
CSF £74.10 CT £819.97 TOTE £16.00: £4.70, £2.00, £3.50; EX 87.20 Trifecta £1408.80.
Owner Ms M Austerfield **Bred** Patrick Cassidy **Trained** Cowthorpe, N Yorks

FOCUS
A good sprint handicap run at a frantic pace and the field soon split into two, but the quartet who came nearside had no chance. The winner sets the level judged on his best in the past year.
T/Plt: £231.90 to a £1 stake. Pool: £121,677.38. 382.99 winning tickets. T/Qpdt: £64.10 to a £1 stake. Pool: £8,800.59. 101.50 winning tickets. **Joe Rowntree**

6122 KEMPTON (A.W) (R-H)
Wednesday, September 7

OFFICIAL GOING: Polytrack: standard to slow
Wind: Mild, behind Weather: Sunny

6235 £10 FREE BET AT 32REDSPORT.COM CLASSIFIED CLAIMING STKS 6f (P)
5:25 (5:26) (Class 5) 3-Y-O+ **£2,911** (£866; £432; £216) **Stalls** Low

Form RPR
3602 **1** **Layla's Hero (IRE)**[10] 5915 9-8-2 73..........................(v) GeorgeWood(5) 1 76
(Roger Teal) *marginal ldr: mde most: rdn jst over 2f out: kpt on wl fr over 1f out: hung lft wl ins fnl f: kpt on wl* **15/2**
0600 **2** ¾ **Brazen Spirit**[15] 5744 4-8-9 67..(v) JohnFahy 4 76
(Clive Cox) *settled in 4th on rail: rdn in 3rd 2f out: tk 2nd 1f out: kpt on tl one pce wl ins fnl f* **8/1**
5426 **3** 2 **Doctor Parkes**[19] 5599 10-8-2 72.................................... AaronJones(3) 6 65
(Stuart Williams) *hld up in 6th: rdn 2f out: nt qckn over 1f out: kpt wl ins fnl f to take 3rd nr fin* **5/2**[2]
0460 **4** ½ **Light From Mars**[25] 5408 11-9-1 72.................................(p) JimCrowley 2 74
(Ronald Harris) *disp ld: upsides over 2f out: sn rdn: kpt on one pce tl wknd fnl 110yds and lost 3rd nr fin* **9/4**[1]
0500 **5** 3 ¾ **Piazon**[44] 4714 5-8-6 68...[1] HectorCrouch(5) 7 58
(John Butler) *settled in 5th on outer: pushed along over 3f out: no imp tl sme prog over 1f out* **14/1**
6003 **6** 2 ¼ **Majestic Myles (IRE)**[14] 5773 8-8-5 72...............[1] JosephineGordon(3) 5 47
(Lee Carter) *cl up in 3rd on outer: lost pl ent st: shkn up over 2f out: sn rdn: no imp and wknd over 1f out* **5/1**[3]
5330 **7** 3 ½ **Fashionata (IRE)**[128] 1922 3-8-13 68................................. ShaneGray 12 43
(Kristin Stubbs) *s.s and carried lft s: wl in rr: no imp st* **33/1**
5000 **8** 17 **Moonlight Venture**[13] 5810 5-8-2 70...................(b) SophieKilloran(7) 10
(Conor Dore) *s.v.s: wnt lft s and carried rival: a detached in rr: eased over 2f out: t.o* **25/1**

1m 11.09s (-2.01) **Going Correction** -0.075s/f (Stan)
WFA 3 from 4yo+ 2lb **8** Ran SP% **112.3**
Speed ratings (Par 103): **110,109,106,105,100 97,93,70**
CSF £62.80 TOTE £6.20: £1.90, £2.90, £1.10; EX 52.60 Trifecta £197.00.
Owner Andrew Liddiard **Bred** Epona Bloodstock Ltd **Trained** Great Shefford, Berks

FOCUS
The going was given as standard to slow. Not a bad claimer.

6236 RACINGUK.COM/HD NURSERY H'CAP 7f (P)
5:55 (6:00) (Class 6) (0-65,65) 2-Y-O **£2,264** (£673; £252; £252) **Stalls** Low

Form RPR
1 **1** **Lord Clenaghcastle (IRE)**[17] 5668 2-9-2 65............ HectorCrouch(5) 2 71+
(Gary Moore) *settled in 3rd on rail: rdn over 2f out: led over 1f out: sn in command and drvn out fnl f* **3/1**[1]
6051 **2** 2 ¼ **Tennessee Rose (IRE)**[33] 5128 2-9-4 62.......................... LukeMorris 9 62
(Tom Dascombe) *hmpd s: sn cl up in 2nd: shkn up 3f out: rdn over 2f out: tk 2nd wl ins fnl f: kpt on* **12/1**
5601 **3** ½ **Glenys The Menace (FR)**[32] 5165 2-9-3 61..................... KierenFox 11 60+
(John Best) *reluctant to load: wnt rt s and hmpd rival: in rr: plenty to do ent st: swtchd to rail and rdn over 2f out: kpt on strly fr over 1f out to dead-heat for 3rd* **8/1**
0460 **3** dht **Restore (IRE)**[29] 5265 2-9-3 61.. PatDobbs 5 60+
(Richard Hannon) *t.k.h in mid-div: rdn over 2f out: drifted to inner over 1f out: kpt on wl ins fnl f to dead-heat for 3rd* **7/1**[3]
0015 **5** shd **Ivor's Magic (IRE)**[8] 5989 2-9-5 63.............................. JimCrowley 7 61
(David Elsworth) *settled in 4th: shkn up over 2f out: no imp tl styd on ins fnl f* **3/1**[1]
400 **6** 1 **Limelight Lady**[55] 4287 2-7-12 45..............................(b[1]) NoelGarbutt(3) 3 41
(Harry Dunlop) *settled in mid-div: niggled along ent st: rdn over 2f out: styd on one pce* **33/1**
003 **7** ¾ **Varun's Bride (IRE)**[35] 5015 2-9-0 58.............................. KieranO'Neill 6 52
(Richard Hannon) *led: shkn up over 2f out: hdd over 1f out: kpt on one pce in 2nd tl wknd fnl 100yds and lost numerous pls* **5/1**[2]
3000 **8** 3 ¼ **Royal Melody**[14] 5770 2-8-5 52............................. JosephineGordon(3) 4 37
(Heather Main) *t.k.h in last trio: rdn over 2f out: no imp fr over 1f out* **25/1**
560 **9** 2 ¾ **Son Castello (IRE)**[14] 5770 2-8-3 47.............................. NickyMackay 8 24
(Brian Meehan) *settled in 5th on outer: rdn over 2f out: one pce after* **25/1**
4050 **10** 2 **Cj Parker**[8] 5989 2-9-2 65...[1] PaddyBradley(5) 1 37
(Jim Boyle) *in last trio: rdn over 2f out: sn no imp and hld fr over 1f out* **16/1**
50U0 **11** 9 **She's Rosanna**[104] 2611 2-8-7 51.............................. RoystonFfrench 12
(Steph Hollinshead) *tk fierce hold on outer in mid-div: rdn over 2f out: sn no imp and wknd* **66/1**

1m 26.99s (0.99) **Going Correction** -0.075s/f (Stan) **11** Ran SP% **116.0**
Speed ratings (Par 93): **91,88,87,87,87 86,85,82,78,76 66**
WIN: 4.10; PL: LC 1.80, TR 2.20, GTM 1.30, R 1.10; EX: 25.00; CSF: 39.65; TC: LC-TR-GTM, 134.69, LC-TR-R 119.74; TF: LC-TR-GTM 43.30, LC-TR-R 101.40;.
Owner Michael Baldry **Bred** D McCarthy **Trained** Lower Beeding, W Sussex

FOCUS
A modest nursery - there was a lack of depth - but quite a nice performance from the winner.

6237 32RED CASINO H'CAP (DIV I) 7f (P)
6:25 (6:25) (Class 5) (0-70,69) 3-Y-O+ **£2,911** (£866; £432; £216) **Stalls** Low

Form RPR
1-02 **1** **Let's Twist**[12] 5845 4-9-9 68..(b) ShaneGray 8 80
(Kristin Stubbs) *sn clr ldr: c bk to field ent st: shkn up over 2f out: sn rdn: kpt on wl and extended advantage ins fnl f* **6/1**[3]
2340 **2** 2 **Capolavoro (FR)**[33] 5103 5-9-6 65.................................... PatCosgrave 6 71
(Robert Cowell) *settled in 2nd: upsides jst over 2f out: sn rdn: no imp on wnr ins fnl f: kpt on for 2nd* **11/2**[2]
65 **3** ½ **Frozen Lake (USA)**[25] 5386 4-9-9 68.............[1] WilliamTwiston-Davies 5 73
(Mary Hambro) *racd in 4th: pushed along ent st: ev ch over 2f out: kpt on fr over 1f out to press for 2nd ins fnl f: no ex nr fin* **6/1**[3]
1314 **4** 1 ½ **Helfire**[5] 6091 3-8-13 67... CharlieBennett(5) 4 66
(Hughie Morrison) *settled in 5th on outer: rdn and nt qckn 2f out: sme prog ins fnl f* **7/4**[1]
4526 **5** hd **Ocean Legend (IRE)**[34] 5090 11-9-3 62.............................. PatDobbs 9 62
(Tony Carroll) *settled in 3rd: rdn 2f out: outpcd over 1f out: kpt on one pce ins fnl f* **25/1**
4640 **6** hd **Miss Inga Sock (IRE)**[34] 5051 4-8-12 60............(p) GeorgeDowning(3) 3 60
(Eve Johnson Houghton) *in rr: rdn over 2f out: prog over 2f out: kpt on one pce fnl f* **16/1**
0050 **7** 1 ¾ **Freddy With A Y (IRE)**[22] 5503 6-9-0 64...................... DavidParkes(5) 1 59
(Paul Burgoyne) *in rr: rdn over 2f out: kpt on one pce fr over 1f out* **33/1**
564 **8** 1 ¼ **Nellie Deen (IRE)**[14] 5766 3-9-6 69................................. JimCrowley 2 58
(David Elsworth) *settled in 6th on rail: rdn over 2f out: sn no ex* **8/1**
2320 **9** nk **Regal Parade**[13] 5797 12-9-10 69....................................(t) LukeMorris 10 60
(Charlie Wallis) *settled in last quartet: rdn over 2f out: nt qckn and no ex fr over 1f out* **16/1**
0644 **10** nse **Zabdi**[42] 4760 3-8-13 62..[1] KierenFox 7 50
(Lee Carter) *in rr: rdn over 2f out: one pce over 1f out* **33/1**

1m 25.63s (-0.37) **Going Correction** -0.075s/f (Stan)
WFA 3 from 4yo+ 4lb **10** Ran SP% **112.9**
Speed ratings (Par 103): **99,96,96,94,94 93,91,90,90,90**
CSF £36.86 CT £204.12 TOTE £7.70: £2.30, £2.10, £1.60; EX 34.70 Trifecta £200.30.
Owner Paramount Racing II **Bred** G Reed **Trained** Norton, N Yorks

FOCUS
This was dominated from the front by the winner and few got into it. This is rated around the runner-up.

6238 32RED CASINO H'CAP (DIV II) 7f (P)
6:55 (6:55) (Class 5) (0-70,69) 3-Y-O+ **£2,911** (£866; £432; £216) **Stalls** Low

Form RPR
2000 **1** **Gulland Rock**[26] 5374 5-9-2 64.................................... LouisSteward(3) 7 73
(Anthony Carson) *mde all: shkn up over 2f out: 3 l ld 2f out: sn clr: coming bk to field wl ins fnl f but a in command* **5/1**
0036 **2** 3 ¾ **Jan Steen (IRE)**[16] 5711 3-9-6 69...................................... PatCosgrave 8 66
(Denis Coakley) *t.k.h in rr: shkn up over 2f out: in rr and nt clr run jst over 2f out: swtchd to outer and rdn 2f out: gd prog to take 2nd 1f out: nvr nrr* **5/2**[2]
3162 **3** ¾ **Fairy Mist (IRE)**[46] 4640 9-8-11 56..............................(v) WilliamCarson 2 53
(John Bridger) *settled in last trio on rail: rdn over 2f out: 4th on rail ent fnl f: tk 3rd post* **4/1**[3]
654 **4** shd **Sir Compton**[27] 5327 3-9-3 66.. TedDurcan 3 61
(Stuart Kittow) *racd in 3rd on rail: rdn along over 2f out: sn no imp on ldr: lost 2nd 1f out: one pce fnl f and lost 3rd post* **8/1**
0510 **5** 2 ¾ **Always A Dream**[22] 5515 3-8-8 64............................ SamuelClarke(7) 5 51
(Chris Wall) *racd in 4th between horses: lost pl and dropped to rr over 2f out: shuffled along on rail fr over 1f out: nvr involved* **2/1**[1]
4-00 **6** 2 ¾ **Myboydaniel**[17] 5677 4-9-6 68.. NoelGarbutt(3) 9 50
(Derek Shaw) *t.k.h in 5th on outer: prog on outer ent st: sn rdn and no imp: one pce fr over 1f out* **20/1**
1-56 **7** shd **Luath**[49] 4528 3-8-13 62..[1] NickyMackay 10 41
(Jeremy Gask) *settled in 2nd on outer: pushed along over 3f out to hold pl: rdn 3f out: sn wknd* **12/1**

1m 25.9s (-0.10) **Going Correction** -0.075s/f (Stan)
WFA 3 from 4yo+ 4lb **7** Ran SP% **122.1**
Speed ratings (Par 103): **97,92,91,91,88 85,85**
CSF £19.55 CT £57.08 TOTE £7.90: £3.50, £1.90; EX 22.60 Trifecta £118.20.
Owner W H Carson **Bred** Whitsbury Manor Stud **Trained** Newmarket, Suffolk
■ Popeswood was withdrawn. Price at time of withdrawal 20-1. Rule 4 does not apply.

FOCUS
Another all-the-way winner, and the time was 0.27sec slower than the first division.

6239 32RED.COM BREEDERS BACKING RACING EBF MAIDEN FILLIES' STKS 1m 4f (P)
7:25 (7:25) (Class 5) 3-4-Y-O **£4,204** (£1,251; £625; £312) **Stalls** Centre

Form RPR
-022 **1** **Eyeshine**[16] 5723 3-9-0 82..(p) FrankieDettori 4 89+
(John Gosden) *sn led and mde all: t.k.h: stl on bit w 3 l advantage 2f out: shkn up under 2f out: readily drew clr ins fnl f: easily* **2/5**[1]
6564 **2** 8 **Denham Sound**[29] 5267 3-9-0 70................................ FergusSweeney 5 73
(Henry Candy) *racd in 3rd on outer: rdn over 3f out: kpt on to take modest 2nd jst under 1f out: one pce after and no ch w wnr* **9/1**[3]
5 **3** 1 ¼ **Howilat (USA)**[40] 4840 3-9-0 0.. WilliamBuick 7 71
(Charlie Appleby) *settled bhd ldr: rdn along to hold tch w wnr over 3f out: lost modest 2nd jst under 1f out: one pce* **7/2**[2]
03 **4** 6 **Iconic Sky**[32] 5163 3-9-0 0... TedDurcan 2 61
(Lucy Wadham) *racd in 6th: rdn over 3f out: sn no imp: hands and heels fr over 1f out* **25/1**
40- **5** 2 ¼ **Crystalise (IRE)**[321] 7417 4-9-9 0..................................... LiamKeniry 1 58
(Robert Stephens) *racd in 5th on rail: rdn ent st: sn wknd and no imp* **100/1**
5 **6** 9 **Wink And Win (IRE)**[26] 5361 3-9-0 0................................ JimCrowley 3 43
(Charles Hills) *racd in 4th on rail: rdn along over 3f out: sn no imp and eased fnl f* **33/1**
00 **7** 45 **Imaginary**[118] 2182 3-9-0 0.. LukeMorris 8
(Heather Main) *in rr: niggled along bef 1/2-way: rdn and c v wd bnd: sn eased: t.o: lame* **100/1**

2m 31.63s (-2.87) **Going Correction** -0.075s/f (Stan)
WFA 3 from 4yo 9lb **7** Ran SP% **112.4**
Speed ratings (Par 100): **106,100,99,95,94 88,58**
CSF £4.72 TOTE £1.30: £1.10, £3.90; EX 5.10 Trifecta £8.20.
Owner Flaxman Stables Ireland Ltd & W S Farish **Bred** W S Farish **Trained** Newmarket, Suffolk

FOCUS
This proved easy enough for the favourite, who became the fourth horse on the card to make all (from five races to this point).

6240 32RED NURSERY H'CAP 1m (P)
7:55 (7:56) (Class 4) (0-85,82) 2-Y-O **£4,528** (£1,347; £673; £336) **Stalls** Low

Form RPR
422 **1** **Al Hamdany (IRE)**[22] 5505 2-9-4 79.................................. HarryBentley 5 87+
(Marco Botti) *settled in 5th: prog and shkn up in centre over 2f out: sn rdn: qcknd up and led ins fnl f: styd on wl: comf* **3/1**[1]
2234 **2** 2 ½ **Wahash (IRE)**[18] 5637 2-9-3 78..................................... FrankieDettori 8 80
(Richard Hannon) *led after 1f and sn clr ldr: 8 l clr at 1/2-way: c bk to field over 2f out: rdn over 1f out: hdd ins fnl f: one pce after* **5/1**
543 **3** ¾ **Pacofilha**[8] 5995 2-8-9 70... TomMarquand 3 70
(Paul Cole) *led for 1f: racd in 2nd after: shkn up over 2f out: rdn 2f out: kpt on ins fnl f* **9/2**[3]

6565 **4** 1 **Ocean Temptress**15 5747 2-8-3 **67** JosephineGordon(3) 1 65
(John Ryan) *settled in 4th on rail: niggled along over 3f out: rdn over 2f out: ev ch over 1f out: wknd fnl f* **40/1**

4342 **5** 1 1/4 **Law Power**12 5840 2-8-9 **70** (v1) LukeMorris 7 65
(Sir Mark Prescott Bt) *racd in 3rd on outer: rdn along 2f out: ch over 1f out: one pce and wknd ins fnl f* **4/1**2

31 **6** 2 1/2 **Gravity Wave (IRE)**27 5324 2-9-3 **78** PatDobbs 6 67
(Sylvester Kirk) *a in rr: rdn over 2f out: sn hld* **6/1**

012 **7** 9 **Northdown**22 5506 2-9-2 **77** GeorgeBaker 4 44
(David Lanigan) *a in rr: rdn over 2f out: no imp and eased fnl f* **4/1**2

1m 38.55s (-1.25) **Going Correction** -0.075s/f (Stan) **7** Ran SP% **116.6**
Speed ratings (Par 97): **103,100,99,98,97 95,86**
CSF £19.03 CT £66.62 TOTE £3.80: £2.70, £2.30; EX 17.80 Trifecta £71.10.
Owner HH Shaikh Ali Zain Alabedeen Al Khalifa **Bred** Miss Debbie Kitchin **Trained** Newmarket, Suffolk

FOCUS
The pace was quite strong and this was set up for a closer, but the leader still held on for second, and the third had led the main bunch in pursuit.

6241 RACING UK PROFITS RETURNED TO RACING H'CAP 1m (P)
8:25 (8:25) (Class 6) (0-65,65) 3-Y-O+ **£2,264** (£673; £336; £168) **Stalls** Low

Form RPR

3032 **1** **In Ken's Memory**18 5635 3-9-3 **63** JFEgan 10 69
(John Butler) *mde all: rdn over 2f out: kpt on wl ins fnl f* **10/1**3

3210 **2** 1 1/4 **Pacific Salt (IRE)**27 5322 3-9-5 **65** PatCosgrave 5 68
(Pam Sly) *settled in mid-div on rail: rdn over 2f out: kpt on wl to take 2nd nring fin* **10/1**3

-330 **3** shd **Rebel State (IRE)**22 5515 3-9-3 **63** WilliamTwiston-Davies 7 66
(Richard Spencer) *t.k.h in rr: n.m.r and gng wl over 2f out: sn rdn: 8th ent fnl f: styd on strly to take 3rd post: nvr nrr* **16/1**

6326 **4** 1/2 **Bryght Boy**22 5525 3-9-5 **65** GeorgeBaker 3 67
(Ed Walker) *settled bhd ldrs: rdn over 2f out: tk 2nd over 1f out: kpt on one pce: lost two pls nring fin* **5/1**2

0064 **5** 1 1/2 **Estibdaad (IRE)**13 5805 6-9-6 **64** (t) JosephineGordon(3) 11 63
(Paddy Butler) *settled bhd ldr on outer: rdn over 2f out: kpt on one pce fnl f* **20/1**

2441 **6** shd **All The Rage**4 6137 3-9-5 **65** LukeMorris 14 63+
(Sir Mark Prescott Bt) *t.k.h in rr: shkn up 2f out: outpcd 2f out: 10th ent fnl f: kpt on strly ins fnl f: nvr nrr* **11/10**1

044 **7** nse **Tee It Up Tommo (IRE)**2 6186 7-9-5 **65** (t) HectorCrouch(5) 4 64+
(Daniel Steele) *hld up in rr: rdn over 2f out: kpt on wl ins fnl f* **50/1**

6003 **8** nk **Swot**91 3030 4-9-7 **62** (p) JimCrowley 13 60
(Roger Teal) *settled bhd ldrs on outer: rdn in centre over 2f out: kpt on tl wknd fnl f* **14/1**

-305 **9** 4 1/2 **Matilda's Law**22 5525 3-9-2 **62** 1 TedDurcan 1 48
(Chris Wall) *settled bhd ldr on rail: rdn wl over 2f out: 4th ent fnl f: wknd qckly fnl f* **20/1**

051- **10** 1/2 **Jersey Bull (IRE)**267 8231 4-9-7 **62** LiamKeniry 2 48
(Michael Madgwick) *in rr: on rail ent st: nudged along briefly over 2f out: nvr involved* **33/1**

-655 **11** shd **Ice Alert (IRE)**16 5720 3-9-4 **64** DanielMuscutt 8 49
(John Ryan) *in rr: rdn over 2f out: sn hld* **25/1**

6004 **12** 3 1/4 **Captain Marmalade (IRE)**6 6066 4-9-8 **63** PatDobbs 6 41
(Jimmy Fox) *settled in mid-div: rdn over 2f out: sn no imp* **25/1**

0135 **13** 10 **Paladin (IRE)**63 4009 7-9-4 **64** PaddyPilley(5) 12 18
(Michael Blake) *hld up in rr on outer: rdn along over 2f out: sme prog 2f out: wknd fr over 1f out* **16/1**

060- **14** 1 1/4 **Ishikawa (IRE)**382 5636 8-9-10 **65** 1 TomMarquand 9 16
(Ali Stronge) *t.k.h in mid-div: rdn along 3f out: no imp st and eased over 1f out* **40/1**

1m 38.87s (-0.93) **Going Correction** -0.075s/f (Stan)
WFA 3 from 4yo+ 5lb **14** Ran SP% **125.5**
Speed ratings (Par 101): **101,99,99,99,97 97,97,97,92,92 92,88,78,77**
CSF £101.66 CT £1618.05 TOTE £14.10: £2.90, £3.30, £4.50; EX 149.70 Trifecta £1334.10.
Owner Greenstead Hall Racing Ltd **Bred** Greenstead Hall Racing Ltd **Trained** Newmarket, Suffolk

FOCUS
Another winner on the card to make all the running, and she posted a minor pb in the process.

6242 ROA/RACING POST OWNERS' JACKPOT H'CAP 1m 4f (P)
8:55 (8:56) (Class 5) (0-75,75) 3-Y-O **£2,911** (£866; £432; £216) **Stalls** Centre

Form RPR

0521 **1** **Rubensian**19 5607 3-9-5 **73** HarryBentley 7 86+
(David Simcock) *hld up in rr: c wd ent st: gd prog on outer over 2f out: shkn up 2f out: hung rt and led over 1f out: pushed out ins fnl f: eased nring fin* **4/6**1

0505 **2** 1 1/4 **Stamford Raffles**31 5193 3-8-6 **65** CharlieBennett(5) 3 68
(Jane Chapple-Hyam) *settled in 4th on inner: shkn up ent st: kpt on fr over 1f out: tk 2nd ins fnl f* **33/1**

5225 **3** 1/2 **Nucky Thompson**33 5111 3-9-6 **74** WilliamTwiston-Davies 8 76
(Richard Spencer) *racd in 5th: rdn along beside wnr over 2f out: sn lft bhd: kpt on one pce and lost 2nd ins fnl f* **9/2**3

0 **4** 2 3/4 **Pinwood (IRE)**14 5765 3-9-4 **72** (t) HarryPoulton 1 70
(Adam West) *reluctantly led and set sedate pce: t.k.h: qcknd 3f out: rdn over 2f out: hdd over 2f out: wknd* **25/1**

4320 **5** 3/4 **Mazalto (IRE)**25 5405 3-9-2 **75** PaddyBradley(5) 6 72
(Pat Phelan) *t.k.h bhd ldr: lost pl ent st and rdn along in rr over 2f out: one pce after* **7/2**2

3-05 **6** 3/4 **Tranquil Time**22 5527 3-9-3 **71** LukeMorris 2 69
(James Tate) *t.k.h bhd ldr: rdn along over 2f out: n.m.r and squeezed up between horses over 1f out: no ch after* **12/1**

2m 39.12s (4.62) **Going Correction** -0.075s/f (Stan) **6** Ran SP% **114.9**
Speed ratings (Par 101): **81,80,79,78,77 77**
CSF £27.47 CT £67.31 TOTE £1.90: £1.10, £10.40; EX 17.50 Trifecta £63.80.
Owner Roger & Yvonne Allsop **Bred** Cheveley Park Stud Ltd **Trained** Newmarket, Suffolk

FOCUS
They pootled along here, and the race developed into a sprint from the turn-in. The winner impressed and is progressive.
T/Plt: £97.20 to a £1 stake. Pool: £83,841.90. 629.22 winning tickets. T/Qpdt: £21.80 to a £1 stake. Pool: £9,139.77. 309.04 winning tickets. **Cathal Gahan**

6044 CHELMSFORD (A.W) (L-H)
Thursday, September 8

OFFICIAL GOING: Polytrack: standard
Wind: light, across Weather: bright spells

6243 TOTEQUADPOT RACES 3,4,5 AND 6 APPRENTICE H'CAP 1m 2f (P)
5:40 (5:40) (Class 6) (0-60,60) 3-Y-O+ **£3,234** (£962; £481; £240) **Stalls** Low

Form RPR

2621 **1** **First Summer**16 5739 4-10-0 **60** GeorgeWood 1 69
(Shaun Harris) *chsd ldrs: effrt over 2f out: rdn to chal ent fnl f: led jst ins fnl f: r.o wl and gng away at fin* **5/1**3

0623 **2** 1 3/4 **Ahraam (IRE)**20 5610 3-9-0 **56** JordanUys(3) 9 62
(Harry Whittington) *chsd ldr: rdn to chal over 2f out: led over 1f out: hdd jst ins fnl f: styd on same pce after* **8/1**

0012 **3** 3 **Boychick (IRE)**19 5630 3-8-10 **52** CameronNoble(3) 4 52
(Ed Walker) *in tch in midfield: effrt to chse ldrs over 1f out: styd on same pce ins fnl f: wnt 3rd last strides* **11/4**1

5022 **4** hd **Power Up**26 5399 5-9-9 **60** ManuelFernandes(5) 3 60
(Jane Chapple-Hyam) *led: rdn over 2f out: hdd and unable qck over 1f out: styd on same pce ins fnl f: lost 3rd last strides* **4/1**2

5044 **5** 4 1/2 **Deftera Lad (IRE)**8 6020 4-9-6 **52** KillianHennessy 6 43
(Natalie Lloyd-Beavis) *hld up in midfield: hdwy over 3f out: effrt ent fnl 2f: 5th and no imp over 1f out: wknd fnl f* **14/1**

0535 **6** 3 **Gunner Moyne**36 5021 4-10-0 **60** PaddyBradley 2 46
(Gary Moore) *hld up in last trio: hit rail over 6f out: effrt but stl plenty to wl over 1f out: no imp: wknd fnl f: n.d* **11/4**1

6000 **7** 1/2 **General Tufto**12 5868 11-8-9 **46** oh1 (b) BenRobinson(5) 5 31
(Charles Smith) *s.i.s: niggled along in last pair: rdn over 3f out: sn struggling: wknd over 1f out: n.d* **100/1**

4002 **8** 5 **Thane Of Cawdor (IRE)**16 5739 7-9-9 **60** SeanMooney(5) 7 35
(Joseph Tuite) *stdd s: hld up towards rr: effrt but stl plenty to do over 1f out: no hdwy: wknd fnl f: n.d* **14/1**

5550 **9** 8 **Rosie's Vision**21 5572 3-8-7 **46** oh1 LuluStanford 8 6
(Mark Usher) *in tch in midfield on outer: rdn over 3f out: lost pl over 2f out: bhd and eased ins fnl f* **33/1**

2m 6.99s (-1.61) **Going Correction** -0.075s/f (Stan)
WFA 3 from 4yo+ 7lb **9** Ran SP% **118.4**
Speed ratings (Par 101): **103,101,99,99,95 93,92,88,82**
CSF £45.70 CT £133.10 TOTE £6.40: £2.00, £2.70, £1.50; EX 67.30 Trifecta £212.40.
Owner Vision Bloodstock **Bred** The C H F Partnership **Trained** Carburton, Notts

FOCUS
A competitive apprentice handicap with a nice ride on the winner, who improved again.

6244 CUNNINGTONS SOLICITORS EBF MAIDEN FILLIES' STKS (PLUS 10 RACE) 6f (P)
6:10 (6:11) (Class 4) 2-Y-O **£6,469** (£1,925; £962; £481) **Stalls** Centre

Form RPR

1 **Salamah (IRE)** 2-9-0 0 SilvestreDeSousa 4 75+
(Simon Crisford) *dwlt: towards rr and rn green early: hdwy on outer 1/2-way: rdn to chse ldrs 1f out: wnt 2nd 75yds out: r.o wl to ld last strides* **5/2**2

56U **2** hd **Chica De La Noche**26 5400 2-9-0 0 NickyMackay 12 73
(Simon Dow) *chsd ldr tl rdn to ld over 1f out: wnt 2 l clr 1f out: kpt on u.p: hdd last strides* **6/1**3

50 **3** 1 3/4 **Lady Cleo (IRE)**8 6034 2-9-0 0 1 RoystonFfrench 10 68
(Stuart Williams) *stdd s: hld up in tch in midfield: swtchd rt and hdwy over 1f out: chsd ldr 1f out: kpt on same pce ins fnl f* **40/1**

036 **4** 1/2 **Twiggy**26 5410 2-8-9 66 CharlieBennett(5) 5 66
(Jane Chapple-Hyam) *short of room sn after s: hld up towards rr: shkn up over 1f out: swtchd rt 1f out: styd on wl ins fnl f: nt rch ldrs* **12/1**

5 nse **Panova** 2-9-0 0 TedDurcan 13 66+
(Sir Michael Stoute) *stdd and dropped in bhd after s: in tch towards rr: clsd and nt clr run on inner over 1f out: swtchd rt 1f out: styd on wl ins fnl f: nt rch ldrs* **7/1**

55 **6** hd **Life On Mars**15 5772 2-8-9 0 GeorgeWood(5) 1 65
(William Haggas) *chsd ldrs: rdn over 2f out: unable qck 1f out: styd on same pce ins fnl f* **6/1**3

00 **7** hd **Gaia Princess (IRE)**38 4951 2-9-0 0 FergusSweeney 6 65
(Gary Moore) *hld up in tch in midfield: effrt and hung lft over 1f out: nt clrest of runs 1f out: swtchd rt ins fnl f: kpt on towards fin* **33/1**

8 1 1/2 **Heroine Queen** 2-9-0 0 LukeMorris 9 60
(Robert Cowell) *chsd ldng trio: rdn and unable qck over 2f out: lost pl over 1f out: wknd wl ins fnl f* **20/1**

0 **9** 4 **Sweet Sienna**113 2376 2-9-0 0 RobertWinston 2 47
(Dean Ivory) *led: rdn and hdd over 1f out: no ex and lost pl 1f out: wknd ins fnl f* **33/1**

052 **10** nk **Sun Angel (IRE)**24 5484 2-9-0 77 OisinMurphy 7 48
(Henry Candy) *bustled along in midfield early: effrt over 1f out: nt clr run and no imp jst over 1f out: sn btn: wknd ins fnl f* **9/4**1

11 6 **Buena Luna** 2-9-0 0 RyanPowell 8 27
(Sir Mark Prescott Bt) *s.i.s: rn green and detached in last thrght* **50/1**

1m 13.93s (0.23) **Going Correction** -0.075s/f (Stan) **11** Ran SP% **123.1**
Speed ratings (Par 94): **95,94,92,91,91 91,91,89,83,83 75**
CSF £18.04 TOTE £4.10: £1.70, £1.70, £11.20; EX 22.00 Trifecta £1159.90.
Owner Ahmad Abdulla Al Shaikh **Bred** Rabbah Bloodstock Limited **Trained** Newmarket, Suffolk

FOCUS
An interesting and probably useful fillies' maiden won by a well-backed newcomer.

6245 TOTEQUADPOT FOUR PLACES IN FOUR RACES H'CAP 2m (P)
6:40 (6:41) (Class 6) (0-65,65) 3-Y-O+ **£3,234** (£962; £481; £240) **Stalls** Low

Form RPR

6336 **1** **Free Bounty**41 4836 3-8-7 **57** 1 SilvestreDeSousa 5 66
(Philip McBride) *stdd s: hld up in tch in last: wnt 3rd 5f out: swtchd rt and effrt wl over 1f out: chsd ldr jst over 1f out: styd on u.p to ld last strides* **3/1**3

2121 **2** 1/2 **Mystique Heights**36 5012 3-9-1 **65** (v) LukeMorris 4 73
(Sir Mark Prescott Bt) *chsd ldr: rdn to press ldr 3f out: led wl over 1f out: wnt lft u.p ins fnl f: hdd last strides* **5/6**1

6621 **3** 6 **Hiorne Tower (FR)**24 5473 5-9-9 **60** KierenFox 1 61
(John Best) *led: rdn over 2f out: c rt bnd 2f out: sn hdd: 3rd and no ex 1f out: wknd insdie fnl f* **5/2**2

4-50 4 80 **Leyland (IRE)**[10] 5963 7-8-9 **51** CharlieBennett(5) 3
(Natalie Lloyd-Beavis) *nvr travelling: chsd ldrs: drvn 6f out: dropped to last 5f out: lost tch and eased off fnl 4f* **40/1**

3m 29.14s (-0.86) **Going Correction** -0.075s/f (Stan)
WFA 3 from 4yo+ 13lb **4** Ran SP% **110.6**
Speed ratings (Par 101): **99,98,95,55**
CSF £6.15 TOTE £4.00; EX 6.40 Trifecta £6.90.
Owner Four Winds Racing & Serafino Agodino **Bred** Wood Farm Stud (Waresley) **Trained** Newmarket, Suffolk

FOCUS
A small-field staying handicap which resulted in a thrilling finish, and it could be rated a bit higher.

6246 TOTEPOOLLIVEINFO.COM FILLIES' H'CAP 1m (P)
7:10 (7:13) (Class 4) (0-85,83) 3-Y-O+ **£6,469** (£1,925; £962; £481) **Stalls** Low

Form RPR
-144 1 **Acclio (IRE)**[18] 5677 5-9-4 **80** MartinHarley 3 88
(James Tate) *in tch in midfield: rdn and qcknd to ld over 2f out: clr and drvn over 1f out: kpt on: hrd pressed but a jst holding on towards fin* **3/1**[2]

2-01 2 hd **Honorina**[23] 5504 3-8-11 **78** OisinMurphy 5 84+
(Sir Michael Stoute) *stdd s: hld up in tch in rr: effrt wl over 1f out: hdwy to chse wnr ins fnl f: r.o strly towards fin: nvr quite getting to wnr* **11/10**[1]

231- 3 1 **Farandine**[323] 7392 3-9-2 **83** LukeMorris 6 87+
(Luca Cumani) *pressed ldr tl outpcd over 2f out: edging lft u.p and rallied jst ins fnl f: kpt on ins fnl f* **6/1**

5114 4 ½ **Kylla Instinct**[16] 5743 3-9-1 **82** SilvestreDeSousa 1 85
(Philip McBride) *chsd ldng pair: nt clr run on inner and shuffled bk over 2f out: hdwy u.p over 1f out: kpt on ins fnl f* **4/1**[3]

3315 5 1½ **Sunnua (IRE)**[47] 4630 3-8-8 **80** AdamMcNamara(5) 2 79
(Richard Fahey) *led and set stdy pce tl hdd and rdn over 2f out: drvn and unable qck over 1f out: wknd ins fnl f* **8/1**

5550 6 1¾ **Ruby Wednesday**[29] 5302 3-8-2 **69** oh1 RyanPowell 7 64
(John Best) *stdd after s: hld up in tch in last pair: effrt wl over 1f out: no imp* **40/1**

1m 41.83s (1.93) **Going Correction** -0.075s/f (Stan)
WFA 3 from 5yo 5lb **6** Ran SP% **120.5**
Speed ratings (Par 102): **87,86,85,85,83 82**
CSF £7.37 TOTE £3.70: £1.80, £1.50; EX 7.90 Trifecta £36.90.
Owner Saeed Manana **Bred** E Mulryan **Trained** Newmarket, Suffolk

FOCUS
Plenty of winners on display in this interesting fillies' handicap run at a steady pace.

6247 TOTEPOOLRACING FIND US ON INSTAGRAM MAIDEN STKS 1m (P)
7:40 (7:41) (Class 5) 3-Y-O+ **£5,175** (£1,540; £769; £384) **Stalls** Low

Form RPR
0- 1 **Eltham**[434] 3813 3-8-11 0 JosephineGordon(3) 1 74+
(Robyn Brisland) *t.k.h: trckd ldng pair: rdn to chal over 1f out: led 1f out: r.o wl: rdn out* **14/1**[3]

52 2 1½ **Thundering Blue (USA)**[30] 5260 3-9-5 0 LukeMorris 3 74
(David Menuisier) *t.k.h: led tl over 2f out: rdn to ld again over 1f out: hdd 1f out: styd on same pce u.p ins fnl f* **10/11**[1]

03 3 1 **Chandon Elysees**[37] 4991 3-9-0 0 FergusSweeney 5 67
(Gary Moore) *t.k.h: hld up in tch in 5th: effrt over 1f out: kpt on ins fnl f: wnt 3rd towards fin* **40/1**

4 ¾ **Artscape** 4-9-10 0 [1] RobertWinston 6 71
(Dean Ivory) *dwlt: t.k.h: in tch in midfield: on outer: hdwy to join ldr 1/2-way: led over 2f out: rdn and hdd over 1f out: no ex ins fnl f: lost 3rd and wknd cl home* **33/1**

-243 5 nk **Divisionist**[35] 5082 3-9-5 79 TedDurcan 7 69
(Sir Michael Stoute) *t.k.h: chsd ldr tl 1/2-way: nt clrest of runs and swtchd lft over 1f out: rdn and little rspnse 1f out: wknd wl ins fnl f* **6/5**[2]

44 6 9 **Outrath (IRE)**[13] 5850 6-9-10 0 TimmyMurphy 4 49
(Jim Best) *stdd and swtchd lft after s: racd in 6th: nudged along and detached fr ldng quintet 3f out: c rt wl over 1f out: nudged along and styd on same pce after: eased towards fin* **100/1**

7 9 **Murraqib (USA)** 3-9-0 0 PaddyBradley(5) 2 26
(Brett Johnson) *dwlt: a rr: struggling over 3f out: lost tch over 1f out* **50/1**

1m 39.66s (-0.24) **Going Correction** -0.075s/f (Stan)
WFA 3 from 4yo+ 5lb **7** Ran SP% **112.8**
Speed ratings (Par 103): **98,96,95,94,94 85,76**
CSF £27.25 TOTE £14.90: £5.30, £1.30; EX 35.30 Trifecta £556.80.
Owner Franconson Partners **Bred** Mrs A R Ruggles **Trained** Newmarket, Suffolk

FOCUS
A simple-looking two-horse race beforehand; but the market got it wrong and the form looks shaky.

6248 @TOTEPOOLRACING WIN TICKETS ON TWITTER H'CAP 5f (P)
8:10 (8:10) (Class 5) (0-70,70) 3-Y-O+ **£5,175** (£1,540; £769; £384) **Stalls** Low

Form RPR
4631 1 **Verne Castle**[24] 5474 3-9-1 **68** RobHornby(3) 5 81
(Andrew Balding) *t.k.h early: sn dropped in and chsd ldng trio: clsd over 1f out: rdn to ld jst ins fnl f: sn in command: eased towards fin* **3/1**[1]

3656 2 1½ **Monumental Man**[11] 5928 7-9-7 **70** (p) LukeMorris 1 78
(Michael Attwater) *rousted along leaving stalls: chsd ldr tl led 3f out: rdn over 1f out: drvn and hrd pressed 1f out: sn hdd: kpt on same pce after* **3/1**[1]

6242 3 1½ **Innocently (IRE)**[15] 5762 5-9-6 **69** (b) MartinHarley 8 72
(David O'Meara) *broke fast: led tl 1/2-way: 3rd and no ex u.p over 1f out: styd on same pce after* **7/1**[3]

0340 4 1¼ **Lady Nayef**[35] 5078 3-9-4 **68** [1] JFEgan 3 66
(John Butler) *sn pushed along in midfield: sme hdwy u.p over 1f out: kpt on ins fnl f: nvr trbld ldrs* **7/1**[3]

2622 5 1½ **Jack The Laird (IRE)**[14] 5807 3-9-3 **67** RobertWinston 7 60
(Dean Ivory) *off the pce in last trio: c centre and effrt over 1f out: kpt on ins fnl f: nvr trbld ldrs* **4/1**[2]

2645 6 ¾ **Flicka's Boy**[12] 5864 4-9-7 **70** (t) BarryMcHugh 6 60
(Tony Coyle) *midfield: effrt 2f out: no imp u.p over 1f out: nvr trbld ldrs* **10/1**

016 7 1 **Annie Salts**[27] 5370 3-9-2 **66** [1] SilvestreDeSousa 2 52
(Chris Dwyer) *chsd ldng pair: rdn and no hdwy over 1f out: 4th and btn 1f out: wknd ins fnl f* **14/1**

0300 8 ¾ **Long Awaited (IRE)**[12] 5864 8-8-13 **69** (v) SophieKilloran(7) 4 53
(Conor Dore) *racd off the pce in last trio: effrt on inner over 1f out: no hdwy: n.d* **20/1**

040- 9 6 **Arctic Lynx (IRE)**[383] 5620 9-8-11 **65** (p) AnnStokell(5) 9 27
(Ann Stokell) *taken down early: a outpcd in rr: n.d* **40/1**

58.6s (-1.60) **Going Correction** -0.075s/f (Stan)
WFA 3 from 4yo+ 1lb **9** Ran SP% **118.0**
Speed ratings (Par 103): **109,106,104,102,99 98,97,95,86**
CSF £12.16 CT £58.43 TOTE £3.70: £1.60, £1.60, £2.90; EX 13.70 Trifecta £70.50.
Owner J C Smith **Bred** Littleton Stud **Trained** Kingsclere, Hants

FOCUS
A moderate sprint handicap run at a good clip and with a progressive winner. The race is rated around the runner-up to his recent best.

6249 WICKHAM ENGINEERING H'CAP 6f (P)
8:40 (8:41) (Class 6) (0-60,60) 3-Y-O+ **£3,234** (£962; £481; £240) **Stalls** Centre

Form RPR
0-01 1 **Quiet Warrior (IRE)**[35] 5080 5-9-3 **56** JFEgan 10 67+
(Tony Carroll) *sltly hmpd leaving stalls: t.k.h towards rr: hdwy on outer 1/2-way: rdn over 1f out: led jst ins fnl f: r.o wl* **10/3**[1]

6624 2 1½ **Poplar**[24] 5474 3-9-5 **60** MartinHarley 5 66
(Robyn Brisland) *broke fast and led: sn hdd and trckd ldrs: rdn to chal over 1f out: led 1f out: sn drvn and hdd: styd on same pce after* **6/1**[3]

3504 3 hd **Kenstone (FR)**[22] 5554 3-8-10 **51** (p) OisinMurphy 7 57
(David Dennis) *in tch in midfield: effrt in 5th ent fnl 2f: styd on u.p ins fnl f* **18/1**

533 4 1 **Cadland Lad (IRE)**[15] 5769 3-8-4 **48** [1] JosephineGordon(3) 9 50
(John Ryan) *in tch in midfield: effrt over 1f out: n.m.r 1f out: sn edging lft: kpt on u.p ins fnl f* **7/1**

4304 5 hd **Commanche**[14] 5797 7-8-10 **49** (b) SilvestreDeSousa 14 51
(Chris Dwyer) *rdn along thrght: stuck wd in midfield: drvn over 1f out: styd on ins fnl f* **5/1**[2]

0004 6 ¾ **Ershaad (IRE)**[34] 5126 4-9-0 **58** (b) CharlieBennett(5) 3 57
(Shaun Harris) *sn led: rdn over 1f out: hdd and no ex 1f out: wknd wl ins fnl f* **10/1**

5000 7 nk **Born To Finish (IRE)**[15] 5769 3-9-5 **60** (bt) MartinLane 4 58
(Jeremy Gask) *s.i.s: pushed along early: racd in last trio: clsd whn pushed rt and hmpd over 1f out: swtchd rt ins fnl f: styd on fnl 100yds* **5/1**[2]

5160 8 ½ **Le Manege Enchante (IRE)**[26] 5408 3-9-2 **60** (p) NoelGarbutt(3) 2 57
(Derek Shaw) *in tch in midfield: effrt on inner and n.m.r over 1f out: bmpd and pushed lft jst ins fnl f: styd on same pce u.p fnl 100yds* **16/1**

0330 9 ¾ **Multi Quest**[24] 5475 4-8-11 **50** (b) RobertHavlin 1 53+
(John E Long) *chsd ldrs: nt clr run over 1f out: swtchd lft and bmpd rival jst ins fnl f: stl n.m.r and lost any ch: coasted home fnl 100yds* **20/1**

4033 10 ¾ **Sacred Harp**[17] 5721 3-9-1 **59** (t) AaronJones(3) 13 51
(Stuart Williams) *sn w ldr: rdn and ev ch whn wnt lft over 1f out: no ex 1f out: wknd ins fnl f* **10/1**

5555 11 1¾ **Tilsworth Micky**[30] 5259 4-9-7 **60** FrederikTylicki 6 46
(J R Jenkins) *t.k.h: hld up in tch: sltly hmpd over 4f out: effrt over 1f out: no imp 1f out: wknd ins fnl f* **16/1**

-604 12 3 **Angel Flores (IRE)**[84] 3317 5-9-0 **53** KierenFox 12 30
(Lee Carter) *stdd and wnt lft s: a bhd* **33/1**

1m 12.23s (-1.47) **Going Correction** -0.075s/f (Stan)
WFA 3 from 4yo+ 2lb **12** Ran SP% **126.1**
Speed ratings (Par 101): **106,104,103,102,102 101,100,100,99,98 95,91**
CSF £24.67 CT £330.91 TOTE £5.60: £2.80, £2.10, £3.80; EX 25.90 Trifecta £213.90.
Owner Miss G Spence **Bred** John R Jeffers **Trained** Cropthorne, Worcs

FOCUS
A rejuvenated winner of this modest handicap, who won with something in hand. The fourth helps the opening level.
T/Plt: £130.80 to a £1 stake. Pool: £78,174.54 - 436.12 winning units. T/Qpdt: £17.70 to a £1 stake. Pool: £8,694.50 - 362.34 winning units. **Steve Payne**

5951 CHEPSTOW (L-H)
Thursday, September 8

OFFICIAL GOING: Good to soft (7.6)
Wind: slight across Weather: sunny

6250 LONGINES IRISH CHAMPIONS WEEKEND EBF MAIDEN FILLIES' STKS (PLUS 10 RACE) 7f 16y
1:45 (1:45) (Class 5) 2-Y-O **£3,557** (£1,058; £529; £264) **Stalls** Centre

Form RPR
45 1 **Miss Laila (IRE)**[23] 5524 2-9-0 0 ShaneKelly 9 72
(Richard Hughes) *flashed tail on way to s: mde all: drvn over 1f out: edgd sltly rt fnl f: jst hld on* **13/2**

46 2 nse **Washington Blue**[15] 5772 2-9-0 0 WilliamTwiston-Davies 8 72
(Clive Cox) *hld up: rdn and hdwy over 2f out: drvn and r.o fnl f: jst failed* **6/1**[3]

00 3 hd **Silver Link (IRE)**[20] 5600 2-9-0 0 SteveDrowne 3 71
(Marcus Tregoning) *chsd ldrs: clsd 3f out: rdn over 2f out: r.o wl fnl f: jst hld* **5/1**[2]

4 3½ **Eyreborn (IRE)** 2-9-0 0 RichardKingscote 2 62+
(Tom Dascombe) *s.s: in rr: rdn 1/2-way: swtchd rt over 1f out: unbalanced on trck but styd on wl fnl f: nrst fin* **20/1**

6 5 1 **Esloobaha (IRE)**[20] 5593 2-9-0 0 MichaelJMMurphy 6 60
(Charles Hills) *chsd ldrs: rdn 3f out: wknd fnl f* **8/1**

6 6 2¼ **Subatomic**[29] 5298 2-9-0 0 PatDobbs 5 59+
(Ralph Beckett) *hld up: hdwy 3f out: rdn over 2f out: sn one pce and no further imp* **7/4**[1]

0 7 1¾ **Fleeting Francesca**[17] 5722 2-9-0 0 CharlesBishop 4 49
(Chris Gordon) *t.k.h: prom: rdn and lost pl 3f out: wknd over 1f out* **200/1**

55 8 hd **Everkyllachy (IRE)**[12] 5869 2-9-0 0 DougieCostello 7 49
(J S Moore) *cl up: rdn 3f out: wknd over 1f out* **8/1**

5 9 6 **B B Queen (IRE)**[15] 5771 2-9-0 0 JohnFahy 1 33
(Clive Cox) *t.k.h: chsd ldrs tl wknd wl over 2f out: hung rt fnl 2f* **14/1**

1m 25.38s (2.18) **Going Correction** +0.125s/f (Good) **9** Ran SP% **114.8**
Speed ratings (Par 92): **92,91,91,87,86 84,82,81,74**
CSF £44.86 TOTE £5.00: £1.30, £2.30, £2.20; EX 34.80 Trifecta £313.90.
Owner Saleh Al Homaizi & Imad Al Sagar **Bred** Wicklow Bloodstock (ireland) Ltd **Trained** Upper Lambourn, Berkshire

The Form Book, Raceform Ltd, Newbury, RG14 5SJ

FOCUS
A modest fillies' maiden run at a steady pace. The level is fluid.

6251 KEITH MORGAN MOWERS MAIDEN FILLIES' STKS 7f 16y
2:15 (2:16) (Class 5) 3-Y-O+ **£2,911** (£866; £432; £216) **Stalls** Centre

Form RPR
35 **1** **Russian Finale**[25] 5438 3-9-0 0 .... RichardKingscote 1 70+
(William Haggas) *trckd ldrs: rdn and wnt 2nd over 1f out: drvn fnl f: styd on to ld nr fin* **6/5**[1]

060 **2** ½ **Canford Lilli (IRE)**[23] 5525 3-9-0 64 ....(b[1]) ShaneKelly 7 68
(Eve Johnson Houghton) *plld hrd: prom: swtchd rt to r on rail and led over 4f out: drvn appr fnl f: no ex and hdd nr fin* **14/1**

3 3¼ **Jazz Cat (IRE)** 3-9-2 0 ow2 ....[1] RyanClark 2 61
(Paul Cole) *s.i.s: hld up wl in tch: rdn over 2f out: wnt 3rd ins fnl f: one pce and hld by first two* **3/1**[3]

6-22 **4** 3 **Cinders (IRE)**[15] 5766 3-9-0 74 .... PatDobbs 5 51
(Hughie Morrison) *led over 2f: chsd ldr: rdn over 2f out: lost 2nd over 1f out: sn wknd* **9/4**[2]

0 **5** nse **Sonnentanz (IRE)**[168] 1063 3-9-0 0 .... SteveDrowne 4 51
(Daniel Kubler) *in tch in last: pushed along and outpcd 1/2-way: no imp tl styd on fnl f* **66/1**

0-00 **6** 6 **Love In The Dark**[22] 5544 3-8-9 50 ....[1] MitchGodwin(5) 3 35
(Nikki Evans) *chsd ldrs: rdn 1/2-way and sn lost pl: bhd fnl 2f* **100/1**

1m 25.07s (1.87) **Going Correction** +0.125s/f (Good) **6** Ran SP% **110.4**
Speed ratings (Par 100): **94,93,89,86,86 79**
CSF £18.78 TOTE £2.40: £1.30, £4.70; EX 14.80 Trifecta £43.30.
Owner Cheveley Park Stud **Bred** Cheveley Park Stud Ltd **Trained** Newmarket, Suffolk

FOCUS
A modest maiden that has been rated cautiously; it could be a bit better.

6252 STABLESOFT-EUROPE EQUESTRIAN SURFACES NURSERY H'CAP 5f 16y
2:50 (2:50) (Class 6) (0-60,60) 2-Y-O **£2,264** (£673; £336; £168) **Stalls** Centre

Form RPR
0620 **1** **Rebel Heart**[18] 5675 2-9-1 54 ....(v[1]) WilliamCarson 4 57
(Bill Turner) *trckd ldrs: drvn over 1f out: r.o to ld towards fin* **12/1**

035 **2** ½ **Fethiye Boy**[8] 6016 2-9-2 60 .... MitchGodwin(5) 9 61
(Ronald Harris) *racd keenly: sn led: drvn over 1f out: wandered u.p fnl f: hdd towards fin* **5/1**[3]

003 **3** ½ **The Big Short**[63] 4047 2-9-7 60 .... MichaelJMMurphy 5 59
(Charles Hills) *t.k.h: chsd ldrs: wnt 2nd after 2f: rdn and ev ch appr fnl f: edgd rt and unable qck fnl 100yds* **11/4**[1]

0650 **4** nk **In The Spotlight (IRE)**[14] 5806 2-9-6 59 .... ShaneKelly 3 57
(Richard Hughes) *chsd ldrs: pushed along over 1f out: swtchd rt ent fnl f: sn drvn: nt qckn* **7/2**[2]

340 **5** ½ **Dixie Peach**[63] 4054 2-9-5 58 ....[1] CharlesBishop 7 55+
(Eve Johnson Houghton) *wnt to post early: hld up: rdn 2f out: r.o wl fnl f* **10/1**

002 **6** 2 **Chiconomic (IRE)**[18] 5668 2-9-4 57 .... LiamJones 2 46
(Rae Guest) *in rr: rdn after 2f: styd on fnl f: nvr threatened ldrs* **10/1**

5000 **7** 1½ **Bruny Island (IRE)**[18] 5675 2-9-5 58 .... RichardKingscote 1 42
(Mark Johnston) *led early: trckd ldr tl lost 2nd after 2f: rdn 2f out: sn wknd* **7/1**

0004 **8** 1 **Miss Island Ruler**[20] 5606 2-8-8 50 ....(b) JacobButterfield(3) 6 30
(Shaun Harris) *wnt to post early: rdn over 3f out: a in rr* **66/1**

0200 **9** 7 **Kath's Boy (IRE)**[20] 5598 2-9-4 60 ....[1] GeorgeDowning(3) 8 15
(Tony Carroll) *rdn 1/2-way: a towards rr* **16/1**

1m 1.19s (1.89) **Going Correction** +0.125s/f (Good) **9** Ran SP% **111.3**
Speed ratings (Par 93): **89,88,87,86,86 82,80,78,67**
CSF £67.28 CT £209.88 TOTE £14.30: £3.50, £1.60, £1.30; EX 78.80 Trifecta £275.80.
Owner Mascalls Stud **Bred** Mascalls Stud **Trained** Sigwells, Somerset

FOCUS
Not a strong contest. It was run at an honest pace and suited those prominent.

6253 DIAMOND RACING NURSERY H'CAP 1m 14y
3:25 (3:25) (Class 6) (0-60,60) 2-Y-O **£2,264** (£673; £336; £168) **Stalls** Centre

Form RPR
0031 **1** **Madam Prancealot (IRE)**[15] 5770 2-9-3 56 .... MichaelJMMurphy 1 61
(David Evans) *led 3f: styd prom: rdn to ld again over 2f out: drvn: edgd rt and r.o fnl f* **4/1**[2]

221 **2** ½ **London Grammar (IRE)**[13] 5853 2-9-7 60 .... JackGarritty 3 64
(John Quinn) *trckd ldrs: wnt 2nd gng wl 2f out: jinked rt ent fnl f: kpt on: hld whn carried rt nr fin* **2/1**[1]

006 **3** 2¾ **Pentito Rap (USA)**[37] 4975 2-8-13 52 .... SteveDrowne 6 50
(Rod Millman) *chsd ldrs: rdn 2f out: one pce fnl f* **22/1**

3665 **4** 1¼ **Padleyourowncanoe**[13] 5840 2-9-2 55 .... DougieCostello 5 50
(Daniel Mark Loughnane) *prom: pushed along 1/2-way: drvn 3f out: styd on same pce* **6/1**[3]

006 **5** ½ **Melcano**[12] 5885 2-9-1 57 .... JacobButterfield(3) 2 51
(Shaun Harris) *wnt to post early: trckd wnr tl led after 3f: rdn and hdd over 2f out: grad wknd fnl f* **10/1**

0640 **6** nk **Battle Of Wits (IRE)**[34] 5141 2-8-6 50 .... MitchGodwin(5) 8 43
(J S Moore) *hld up: rdn and hdwy over 2f out: one pce and no imp fnl f* **20/1**

0040 **7** 1¾ **Blast Of Faith (IRE)**[17] 5719 2-9-1 54 ....[1] ShaneKelly 7 43
(Richard Hughes) *s.i.s: towards rr: rdn over 2f out: one pce and nvr any imp* **12/1**

060 **8** nk **Auric Goldfinger (IRE)**[15] 5764 2-9-7 60 .... PatDobbs 4 49
(Richard Hannon) *dwlt sltly: in rr: rdn over 2f out: no hdwy* **4/1**[2]

1m 38.71s (2.51) **Going Correction** +0.125s/f (Good) **8** Ran SP% **113.5**
Speed ratings (Par 93): **92,91,88,87,87 86,84,84**
CSF £12.23 CT £152.01 TOTE £4.00: £1.40, £1.10, £5.30; EX 9.90 Trifecta £88.10.
Owner Mrs E Evans **Bred** Martin Butler **Trained** Pandy, Monmouths

FOCUS
There was little depth to this.

6254 WATT FENCES SUPPLIES CHEPSTOW RACECOURSE H'CAP 1m 14y
4:00 (4:00) (Class 5) (0-75,74) 3-Y-O+ **£3,234** (£962; £481; £240) **Stalls** Centre

Form RPR
3124 **1** **Golden Wedding (IRE)**[13] 5832 4-9-10 74 .... CharlesBishop 6 82
(Eve Johnson Houghton) *trckd ldrs: led over 4f out: sn taken rt to r against rail: drvn over 2f out: jnd 1f out: edgd lft towards fin: hld on wl* **2/1**[1]

5016 **2** ½ **Jabbaar**[49] 4549 3-9-4 73 .... WilliamTwiston-Davies 7 79
(Owen Burrows) *hld up: rdn and hdwy 2f out: chal 1f out: kpt on u.p: jst hld* **4/1**[2]

0052 **3** 2 **Cryptic (IRE)**[29] 5302 3-9-1 70 .... ShaneKelly 2 71
(Luca Cumani) *led over 3f: styd prom: rdn 2f out: edgd rt after: kpt on same pce fnl f* **4/1**[2]

-652 **4** hd **Rahmah (IRE)**[22] 5547 4-9-3 72 .... PaddyPilley(5) 4 74
(Geoffrey Deacon) *plld hrd: prom: drvn 3f out: kpt on tl no ex fnl 100yds* **8/1**

0-00 **5** 1¾ **Barista (IRE)**[10] 5954 8-8-11 61 .... SteveDrowne 5 59
(Brian Forsey) *chsd ldrs: rdn over 2f out: hld whn nt clr run jst ins fnl f* **20/1**

50-2 **6** 2½ **Al Fatih (IRE)**[138] 1640 5-8-13 66 .... EoinWalsh(3) 3 58
(Steve Flook) *s.i.s: towards rr: rdn and hdwy over 2f out: wknd fnl f* **5/1**[3]

3540 **7** 11 **Never To Be (USA)**[48] 4589 5-8-9 62 ....(t) EdwardGreatrex(3) 1 29
(Nikki Evans) *s.i.s: sn chsng ldrs: dropped towards rr 1/2-way: drvn 3f out: wknd 1f out* **16/1**

1m 37.3s (1.10) **Going Correction** +0.125s/f (Good)
WFA 3 from 4yo+ 5lb **7** Ran SP% **111.8**
Speed ratings (Par 103): **99,98,96,96,94 92,81**
CSF £9.63 TOTE £2.80: £1.80, £2.00; EX 9.70 Trifecta £24.00.
Owner Mrs R F Johnson Houghton **Bred** Mrs R F Johnson Houghton **Trained** Blewbury, Oxon

FOCUS
A fair handicap run at a steady pace. The winner continued his good run of form with a small pb.

6255 DRIBUILD DASH (ROUND 7 OF THE CHEPSTOW SPRINT SERIES) H'CAP 6f 16y
4:35 (4:36) (Class 4) (0-85,84) 3-Y-O+ **£5,175** (£1,540; £769; £384) **Stalls** Centre

Form RPR
1326 **1** **Vincentti (IRE)**[10] 5955 6-8-11 74 .... ShaneKelly 7 82
(Ronald Harris) *dwlt then stmbld leaving stalls: bhd: 6 l adrift 1/2-way: pushed along 2f out: stl only 9th 1f out: r.o strly to ld last strides* **8/1**

0F-0 **2** ½ **Panther Patrol (IRE)**[16] 5744 6-8-9 72 .... CharlesBishop 3 78
(Eve Johnson Houghton) *trckd ldrs: shkn up to ld over 1f out: drvn fnl f: hdd last strides* **14/1**

1025 **3** ¾ **He's My Cracker**[5] 6123 3-9-2 81 .... JohnFahy 10 85
(Clive Cox) *mid-div: rdn and hdwy 2f out: chsd wnr ins fnl f: kpt on but lost 2nd cl home* **4/1**[1]

1612 **4** hd **Satchville Flyer**[10] 5953 5-8-1 71 .... AledBeech(7) 9 74
(David Evans) *wnt to post early: hld up: rdn and hdwy over 1f out: edgd lft ins fnl f: r.o* **9/2**[2]

0230 **5** 1¼ **Monarch Maid**[15] 5774 5-8-10 73 .... WilliamCarson 5 72
(Peter Hiatt) *led 3f: styd cl up: rdn 2f out: edgd rt: no ex fnl f* **10/1**

1623 **6** nse **Alizoom (IRE)**[16] 5743 3-9-5 84 .... PatDobbs 8 83
(Roger Varian) *hld up towards rr: rdn over 2f out: hdwy over 1f out: one pce fnl f* **5/1**[3]

5414 **7** ¾ **Gold Hunter (IRE)**[10] 5955 6-8-13 79 ....(p) EoinWalsh(3) 1 76
(Steve Flook) *chsd ldrs: drvn over 2f out: grad wknd fnl f* **4/1**[1]

0300 **8** 2 **Englishwoman**[39] 4910 3-8-9 74 .... MichaelJMMurphy 6 64
(David Evans) *chsd ldrs: rdn over 2f out: carried rt over 1f out: wknd fnl f* **33/1**

0135 **9** 8 **Bonjour Steve**[10] 5955 5-8-2 70 oh7 ....(p) MitchGodwin(5) 4 35
(Richard Price) *mid-div: rdn and dropped to rr over 3f out: bhd fnl 2f* **16/1**

2140 **10** 2½ **Quickaswecan**[15] 5762 5-8-4 70 ....(p) EdwardGreatrex(3) 2 27
(Milton Bradley) *cl up: led 3f out: rdn 2f out: hdd over 1f out: wknd qckly fnl f* **25/1**

1m 11.84s (-0.16) **Going Correction** +0.125s/f (Good)
WFA 3 from 5yo+ 2lb **10** Ran SP% **114.4**
Speed ratings (Par 105): **106,105,104,104,102 102,101,98,88,84**
CSF £111.17 CT £523.70 TOTE £10.00: £2.90, £4.20, £1.70; EX 104.40 Trifecta £822.90.
Owner Robert & Nina Bailey **Bred** Stephanie Hanly **Trained** Earlswood, Monmouths

FOCUS
The pace was good for this open handicap. The winner is rated to his best since his 3yo days, with the second close to last year's form.

6256 ISTADIA BIG OUTDOOR LED SCREENS H'CAP 1m 4f 23y
5:10 (5:10) (Class 6) (0-65,63) 3-Y-O+ **£2,264** (£673; £336; £168) **Stalls** Low

Form RPR
-001 **1** **Master Dancer**[37] 4995 5-9-3 58 ....(p) MitchGodwin(5) 9 68+
(Tim Vaughan) *dwlt: t.k.h and trckd ldrs after 1f: led 2f out: jinked rt 1f out: sn drvn clr: comf* **11/4**[1]

2442 **2** 4 **Fair Comment**[30] 5261 6-9-10 60 .... CharlesBishop 3 64
(Michael Blanshard) *trckd ldr: rdn over 2f out: briefly bk in 3rd 2f out: styd on same pce: no ch w wnr fnl f* **8/1**

5142 **3** ¾ **Desert Cross**[50] 4500 3-8-13 58 .... SteveDrowne 5 61
(Jonjo O'Neill) *t.k.h in mid-div: rdn and swtchd rt over 2f out: styd on: wnt 3rd 100yds out* **3/1**[2]

2552 **4** nk **Grams And Ounces**[10] 5958 9-9-9 59 ....(t) WilliamTwiston-Davies 1 61
(Grace Harris) *led and set stdy gallop: rdn and increased tempo 3f out: hdd 2f out: one pce after: lost 3rd 100yds out* **15/2**

3601 **5** 1 **Invincible Wish (IRE)**[10] 5958 4-9-10 63 6ex .... EoinWalsh(3) 6 64
(Trevor Wall) *s.s: hld up in last: hdwy 3f out: drvn over 2f out: styd on same pce fnl f and nvr able to chal* **9/2**[3]

0040 **6** 4½ **Madame Chow (IRE)**[18] 5680 3-9-3 62 .... PatDobbs 4 56
(Ralph Beckett) *trckd ldrs: rdn 3f out: wknd over 1f out* **8/1**

2536 **7** ½ **Mexican Mick**[18] 5680 7-8-11 52 .... DavidParkes(5) 2 45
(Peter Hiatt) *hld up: rdn 4f out: bhd fnl 2f* **16/1**

0132 **8** 2 **Shirataki (IRE)**[21] 5575 8-9-6 56 .... WilliamCarson 7 46
(Peter Hiatt) *s.i.s: t.k.h towards rr: rdn over 2f out: wknd over 1f out* **20/1**

2m 45.37s (6.37) **Going Correction** +0.60s/f (Yiel)
WFA 3 from 4yo+ 9lb **8** Ran SP% **114.5**
Speed ratings (Par 101): **102,99,98,98,97 94,94,93**
CSF £25.28 CT £69.37 TOTE £3.80: £1.50, £3.00, £1.20; EX 30.40 Trifecta £169.40.
Owner select-racing-club.co.uk & C Davies **Bred** D J Bloodstock, G Roddick & Wrottesley Ltd **Trained** Aberthin, Vale of Glamorgan

FOCUS
A modest contest but the winner did it nicely and this in behind help set a straightforward standard.

T/Plt: £138.80 to a £1 stake. Pool: £59,823.44 - 314.42 winning units. T/Qpdt: £13.50 to a £1 stake. Pool: £5,814.45 - 316.45 winning units. **Richard Lowther**

[6228]DONCASTER (L-H)

Thursday, September 8

OFFICIAL GOING: Good (good to soft in places) changing to good after race 3 (3.05)

Wind: fresh 1/2 against Weather: fine but breezy

6257 BRITISH STALLION STUDS "CARRIE RED" EBF FILLIES' NURSERY H'CAP 6f 110y

1:55 (1:56) (Class 2) 2-Y-O **£25,204** (£7,544; £3,772; £1,888; £940) **Stalls** Centre

Form RPR

511 **1** **Glitter Girl**[37] 4966 2-9-7 **85**........ RyanMoore 3 92
(William Haggas) *trckd ldrs: effrt over 2f out: styd on to ld last 100yds* **9/2**[1]

2133 **2** ½ **Storm Cry**[14] 5794 2-9-3 **81**........ FrannyNorton 2 86
(Mark Johnston) *led: rdn and swvd rt 1f out: wandered and hdd last 100yds: no ex* **6/1**[2]

01 **3** ½ **Fire Palace**[36] 5022 2-8-5 **76**........ CameronNoble(7) 6 80
(Robert Eddery) *mid-div: effrt over 2f out: carried rt 1f out: styd on to take 3rd nr fin* **11/1**

513 **4** ¾ **Island Vision (IRE)**[35] 5066 2-9-0 **78**........ JamieSpencer 7 80
(David Simcock) *mid-div: hdwy over 2f out: carried lft 1f out: kpt on to take 4th nr fin* **18/1**

2132 **5** ¾ **Rosabelle**[19] 5638 2-9-6 **84**........ GrahamGibbons 9 84+
(Alan Bailey) *rrd s: hdwy to chse ldrs 3f out: wknd last 100yds* **10/1**

2621 **6** ¾ **The Stalking Moon (IRE)**[12] 5884 2-8-8 **72**........ TomEaves 8 70
(John Quinn) *hld up towards rr: hdwy over 2f out: sltly hmpd 1f out: kpt on same pce* **12/1**

01 **7** 1 **Arwa (IRE)**[23] 5516 2-9-6 **84**........ AndreaAtzeni 5 79
(Charles Hills) *chsd ldrs: drvn 2f out: wknd last 100yds* **8/1**[3]

5103 **8** 1 **Seduce Me**[26] 5416 2-8-13 **82**........ JordanVaughan(5) 12 74
(K R Burke) *hld up in rr: effrt over 2f out: wknd fnl f* **8/1**[3]

661 **9** hd **Norwegian Highness (FR)**[17] 5727 2-8-9 **73**........ ShaneGray 1 65
(Kevin Ryan) *dwlt: sn trcking ldrs: fdd fnl f* **10/1**

632 **10** ½ **Money In My Pocket (IRE)**[12] 5869 2-8-6 **70**........ TomMarquand 4 60
(Richard Hannon) *chsd ldrs: drvn over 2f out: fdd fnl f* **12/1**

643 **11** 9 **Bloomin Lovely (IRE)**[19] 5637 2-8-9 **73**........ SilvestreDeSousa 10 39
(John Quinn) *in rr: drvn over 2f out: sn bhd: eased clsng stages* **9/1**

1223 **12** 6 **La Casa Tarifa (IRE)**[9] 6007 2-9-2 **80**........ JoeFanning 11 29
(Mark Johnston) *s.i.s: hdwy to chse ldrs 3f out: lost pl over 1f out: bhd whn eased clsng stages* **20/1**

1m 20.93s (1.03) **Going Correction** +0.10s/f (Good) **12** Ran SP% **116.6**
Speed ratings (Par 98): **98,97,96,96,95 94,93,92,91,91 80,74**
CSF £29.65 CT £281.09 TOTE £3.50: £1.80, £2.90, £4.60; EX 31.30 Trifecta £424.30.
Owner Cheveley Park Stud **Bred** Cheveley Park Stud Ltd **Trained** Newmarket, Suffolk

FOCUS
The round course was railed out from 1m2f until the round meets the straight. Both Andrea Atzeni and Silvestre De Sousa said the ground was "good", although Joe Fanning felt it was slightly slower. A decent fillies' nursery - traditionally strong - and the right horses came to the fore.

6258 CLUGSTON CONSTRUCTION MAY HILL STKS (GROUP 2) 1m (S)

2:30 (2:31) (Class 1) 2-Y-O

£39,697 (£15,050; £7,532; £3,752; £1,883; £945) **Stalls** Centre

Form RPR

14 **1** **Rich Legacy (IRE)**[12] 5870 2-9-0 0........ OisinMurphy 7 105
(Ralph Beckett) *trckd ldr: hdwy to ld 2f out: rdn over 1f out: hdd ins fnl f and sn drvn: rallied wl to ld again last 50 yds* **3/1**[2]

120 **2** ¾ **Grecian Light (IRE)**[12] 5870 2-9-0 97........ WilliamBuick 4 103
(Charlie Appleby) *hld up in tch: hdwy over 2f out: rdn to chal over 1f out: edgd rt and slt ld ins fnl f: sn drvn and edgd lft: hdd and no ex last 50 yds* **8/1**

1443 **3** 2 ¼ **Urban Fox**[12] 5870 2-9-0 96........ MartinHarley 8 98
(James Tate) *hld up in rr: hdwy over 2f out: rdn to chse ldng pair over 1f out: n.m.r and drvn ins fnl f: kpt on* **11/1**

12 **4** 2 ¼ **Reachforthestars (IRE)**[5] 6130 2-9-0 75........ SamJames 6 93
(David O'Meara) *hld up: hdwy on outer 3f out: rdn to chse ldrs over 1f out: drvn and kpt on same pce fnl f* **12/1**

155 **5** 1 ¼ **Tiburtina (IRE)**[12] 5870 2-9-0 94........ JamesDoyle 2 90
(Sylvester Kirk) *t.k.h: trckd ldrs: pushed along over 2f out: rdn over 1f out: drvn and kpt on same pce fnl f* **18/1**

31 **6** 1 ¼ **Blending**[40] 4885 2-9-0 85........ FrankieDettori 3 87
(John Gosden) *trckd ldrs: effrt wl over 1f out: sn rdn and btn appr fnl f* **5/2**[1]

1 **7** hd **Hidden Steps**[15] 5771 2-9-0 76........ TomQueally 9 87
(Andrew Balding) *swtchd lft s and hld up in rr: hdwy on inner 2f out: rdn to chse ldrs over 1f out: sn no imp* **11/1**

1161 **8** 2 ¾ **Bongrace (IRE)**[10] 5967 2-9-0 74........ KevinStott 5 80
(Kevin Ryan) *t.k.h: prom: pushed along 1/2-way: rdn over 3f out and sn wknd* **28/1**

4201 **9** 9 **Kilmah**[12] 5870 2-9-0 101........ FrannyNorton 1 60+
(Mark Johnston) *unruly stalls: led: pushed along 3f out: rdn and hdd 2f out: sn wknd* **9/2**[3]

1m 41.24s (1.94) **Going Correction** +0.10s/f (Good) **9** Ran SP% **115.9**
Speed ratings (Par 107): **94,93,91,88,87 86,86,83,74**
CSF £27.46 TOTE £4.00: £1.40, £2.40, £2.90; EX 27.50 Trifecta £161.90.
Owner Qatar Racing Limited **Bred** Gestut Ammerland **Trained** Kimpton, Hants

FOCUS
An ordinary May Hill on paper, but there was plenty to like about the way the winner got the job done.

6259 DFS PARK HILL STKS (GROUP 2) 1m 6f 132y

3:05 (3:07) (Class 1) 3-Y-O+

£51,039 (£19,350; £9,684; £4,824; £2,421; £1,215) **Stalls** Low

Form RPR

-240 **1** **Simple Verse (IRE)**[82] 3384 4-9-5 113........ OisinMurphy 14 113+
(Ralph Beckett) *hld up in rr: hdwy over 2f out: chsd ldr and edgd lft over 1f out: swtchd rt and styd on strly fnl 150yds: led fnl strides* **3/1**[2]

0104 **2** nk **Pretty Perfect (IRE)**[21] 5586 3-8-8 105 ow1........ SeamieHeffernan 9 113
(A P O'Brien, Ire) *w ldr: led over 3f out: over 3 l clr appr fnl f: hdd and no ex fnl strides* **13/2**

611 **3** 5 **California (IRE)**[42] 4800 4-9-5 103........ FrankieDettori 8 105
(John Gosden) *trckd ldrs: t.k.h: effrt over 2f out: 3rd over 1f out: kpt on same pce* **8/1**

1416 **4** 2 ¾ **Forever Popular (USA)**[26] 5461 4-9-5 100........ DaneO'Neill 11 101
(William Haggas) *trckd ldrs: 2nd over 2f out: kpt on one pce over 1f out* **33/1**

1121 **5** 1 **Abingdon (USA)**[21] 5587 3-8-7 107........ AndreaAtzeni 10 100
(Sir Michael Stoute) *trckd ldrs: effrt over 3f out: one pce fnl 2f* **5/2**[1]

0156 **6** 1 ¾ **Pamona (IRE)**[19] 5639 4-9-5 102........ FMBerry 7 98
(Ralph Beckett) *hld up in mid-div: hdwy over 4f out: one pce fnl 2f* **28/1**

152 **7** 5 **Tioga Pass**[42] 4800 5-9-5 101........(tp) MartinHarley 12 91
(Paul Cole) *in rr: hdwy 3f out: lost pl over 1f out* **33/1**

13-0 **8** 4 **Moderah**[131] 1855 4-9-5 103........ TomQueally 6 85
(James Fanshawe) *s.i.s: hld up in rr: reminders over 3f out: kpt on over 1f out: nvr on terms* **66/1**

1360 **9** 2 **Carnachy (IRE)**[18] 5691 4-9-5 103........ JamieSpencer 3 83
(David Simcock) *hld up in mid-div: hdwy over 2f out: lost pl over 1f out* **12/1**

3111 **10** 1 ¼ **Alyssa**[28] 5331 3-8-7 91........ SilvestreDeSousa 4 81
(Ralph Beckett) *upset in stalls: s.i.s: swtchd lft after s: in rr: pushed along 9f out: nt clr run and swtchd rt 2f out: nvr a factor: eased clsng stages* **11/2**[3]

-331 **11** 3 ¼ **Star Rider**[43] 4752 4-9-5 91........(p) JimmyFortune 2 76
(Hughie Morrison) *chsd ldrs: drvn over 3f out: sn lost pl* **50/1**

-034 **12** 1 **Mill Springs**[42] 4800 4-9-5 99........ RobertHavlin 1 75
(John Gosden) *led: drvn and hdd over 3f out: lost pl over 2f out: sn bhd* **28/1**

3m 6.08s (-1.32) **Going Correction** +0.30s/f (Good)
WFA 3 from 4yo+ 12lb **12** Ran SP% **117.3**
Speed ratings (Par 115): **115,114,112,110,110 109,106,104,103,102 100,100**
CSF £21.08 TOTE £4.00: £1.40, £2.20, £2.30; EX 25.90 Trifecta £135.00.
Owner QRL/Sheikh Suhaim Al Thani/M Al Kubaisi **Bred** Barronstown Stud **Trained** Kimpton, Hants

FOCUS
Race distance increased by 3yds. A good edition of the race, they went a decent pace and got racing a fair way out, making it a good test. Two of the three top-rated runners drew clear, with the winner doing exceptionally well to get up having met trouble, and the third helps set the level.

6260 WEATHERBYS HAMILTON £300,000 2-Y-O STKS 6f 110y

3:40 (3:44) (Class 2) 2-Y-O

£147,540 (£59,040; £29,520; £14,730; £7,380; £7,380) **Stalls** Centre

Form RPR

110 **1** **Mubtasim (IRE)**[19] 5654 2-8-9 101........ PatCosgrave 16 96+
(William Haggas) *hld up towards rr: hdwy over 2f out: styd on wl to ld last 150yds* **4/1**[1]

62 **2** 1 ¾ **Mazyoun**[12] 5876 2-8-9 0........[1] WilliamBuick 3 91
(Hugo Palmer) *chsd ldrs: hung rt and kpt on to take 2nd last 150yds: no imp* **12/1**

32 **3** ¾ **Firefright (IRE)**[10] 5959 2-8-12 0........ JamieSpencer 22 92
(Jeremy Noseda) *swtchd lft after s: hld up in rr: hdwy over 2f out: styd on wl to take 3rd clsng stages* **16/1**

1 **4** ¾ **Bamber Bridge (IRE)**[21] 5577 2-9-2 0........ PaulMulrennan 8 94
(Michael Dods) *mid-div: hdwy over 2f out: swtchd lft over 1f out: edgd rt and kpt on last 50yds tk 4th clolsing stages* **25/1**

34 **5** ¾ **Keyser Soze (IRE)**[48] 4594 2-8-9 0........ HarryBentley 14 85
(Richard Spencer) *in rr: hdwy over 2f out: chsng ldrs appr fnl f: kpt on same pce: tk 5th fnl strides* **66/1**

22 **6** 1 **Jumira Bridge**[57] 4274 2-9-2 0........ AndreaAtzeni 20 89+
(Roger Varian) *sn trcking ldrs: t.k.h: led over 1f out: hdd last 150yds: fdd* **16/1**

0231 **7** nk **Stormy Clouds (IRE)**[21] 5583 2-8-4 94........(b) KieranO'Neill 21 76+
(Richard Hannon) *sn chsng ldrs: kpt on same pce fnl f* **8/1**[3]

1534 **8** ¾ **Global Applause**[19] 5654 2-8-12 103........ RyanMoore 7 85
(Ed Dunlop) *chsd ldrs: swtchd lft over 1f out: keeping on same pce whn hmpd last 50yds* **11/2**[2]

0211 **9** 1 ¾ **Leontes**[39] 4918 2-8-9 93........ OisinMurphy 5 75
(Andrew Balding) *chsd ldrs: upsides over 1f out: one pce whn hmpd 50yds out: sn eased* **16/1**

130 **10** shd **Scofflaw**[41] 4825 2-8-12 80........ TonyHamilton 12 77
(Richard Fahey) *in rr: hdwy over 2f out: kpt on fnl f* **66/1**

130 **11** ¾ **Bohemian Flame (IRE)**[63] 4060 2-9-2 95........ PhillipMakin 9 79
(Andrew Balding) *mid-div: effrt over 2f out: one pce over 1f out* **50/1**

135 **12** 2 **Marie Of Lyon**[47] 4623 2-8-4 89........ PatrickMathers 13 62+
(Richard Fahey) *chsd ldrs: effrt over 2f out: fdd appr fnl f* **16/1**

0122 **13** 1 **Rusumaat (IRE)**[21] 5583 2-8-9 94........ PaulHanagan 18 64+
(Mark Johnston) *awkward s: sn chsng ldrs: drvn to ld over 2f out: hdd over 1f out: wknd fnl 150yds* **14/1**

1 **14** 1 ½ **Balgair**[57] 4270 2-8-12 0........ FMBerry 17 63
(Jonathan Portman) *in rr: sme hdwy over 2f out: nvr a factor* **50/1**

1024 **15** nse **Admiralty Arch**[25] 5447 2-8-9 0........ TomMarquand 15 60
(Richard Hannon) *in rr: drvn over 2f out: sme hdwy over 1f out: nvr a factor* **66/1**

301 **16** 1 **Mutawakked (IRE)**[49] 4552 2-9-2 85........ DaneO'Neill 10 64+
(Brian Meehan) *w ldrs: wknd appr fnl f* **40/1**

6100 **17** 1 ¼ **Farleigh Mac**[22] 5560 2-8-9 79........ FrannyNorton 11 54+
(Andrew Balding) *chsd ldrs: wknd over 1f out* **66/1**

6414 **18** hd **Dourado (IRE)**[19] 5644 2-9-2 78........ SeanLevey 4 60+
(Richard Hannon) *led tl over 2f out: lost pl over 1f out* **100/1**

1U02 **19** 26 **Berkshire Boy (IRE)**[13] 5821 2-8-9 80........ PJMcDonald 6
(Andrew Balding) *wnt bdly lft s: virtually ref to r: eventually set off t.o last* **80/1**

1m 19.58s (-0.32) **Going Correction** +0.10s/f (Good) **19** Ran SP% **102.8**
Speed ratings (Par 101): **105,103,102,101,100 99,98,98,96,95 95,92,91,89,89 88,87,87,57**
CSF £31.99 TOTE £4.70: £1.80, £3.50, £5.20; EX 42.40 Trifecta £511.30.
Owner Sheikh Rashid Dalmook Al Maktoum **Bred** Mrs Natasha Drennan **Trained** Newmarket, Suffolk

■ Spiritual Lady was withdrawn. Price at time of withdrawal 7/2f. Rule 4 applies to all bets - deduction 20p in the pound.

FOCUS
The usual mix of abilities on show for what was a valuable prize. They went a good pace into the headwind and the principals came from behind. The winner has been rated just below his earlier Haydock success.

6261 CROWNHOTEL-BAWTRY.COM H'CAP 1m 2f 60y
4:15 (4:16) (Class 2) (0-105,102) 3-Y-O+
£15,562 (£4,660; £2,330; £1,165; £582; £292) Stalls Low

Form RPR
1214 **1** **Central Square (IRE)**[62] 4115 4-9-6 **96**....................(b[1]) AndreaAtzeni 10 111
(Roger Varian) *trckd ldrs: hdwy over 3f out: led over 2f out: sn rdn: drvn and edgd lft ins fnl f: kpt on wl* **6/1**

3141 **2** 1 **Poet's Word (IRE)**[41] 4827 3-9-1 **98**.................................. RyanMoore 9 111
(Sir Michael Stoute) *trckd ldng pair: hdwy 3f out: cl up 2f out: sn rdn and ev ch: drvn and n.m.r ins fnl f: sn swtchd rt and kpt on* **11/8**[1]

12 **3** 3/4 **Lusory**[54] 4403 3-8-5 **88** oh1...(t) HarryBentley 8 100
(Charlie Appleby) *in tch: pushed along over 6f out: rdn along to chse ldrs 3f out: drvn wl over 1f out and ev ch: kpt on u.p fnl f* **4/1**[2]

5033 **4** 5 **Emerald (ITY)**[47] 4650 4-8-12 **88** oh1..........................(b) DanielMuscutt 7 90
(Marco Botti) *trckd ldrs: hdwy 3f out: rdn along 2f out: drvn over 1f out: kpt on same pce* **12/1**

2303 **5** 1 3/4 **Ode To Evening**[12] 5865 3-9-5 **102**.................................. JamesDoyle 5 101
(Mark Johnston) *set stdy pce: hdd 7f out and chsd ldr: rdn along over 3f out: drvn over 2f out: sn wknd* **18/1**

-164 **6** nk **Bermondsey**[19] 5647 4-9-3 **93**.. JamieSpencer 1 91
(Luca Cumani) *t.k.h: trckd ldr tl led 7f out and sn clr: pushed along over 3f out: rdn and hdd over 2f out: drvn wl over 1f out and sn wknd* **11/2**[3]

0430 **7** shd **Awake My Soul (IRE)**[19] 5651 7-9-5 **95**......................... JamesSullivan 6 93
(Tom Tate) *hld up in rr: hdwy 3f out: rdn over 2f out: sn no imp* **50/1**

0500 **8** 2 1/4 **Chancery (USA)**[19] 5651 8-9-2 **92**.................................... PhillipMakin 2 86
(David O'Meara) *a towards rr* **50/1**

0565 **9** 2 3/4 **Niceofyoutotellme**[26] 5411 7-9-3 **93**.................................. FMBerry 11 81
(Ralph Beckett) *hld up: a towards rr* **16/1**

00-0 **10** 6 **Tres Coronas (IRE)**[10] 5976 9-9-6 **96**........................ GrahamGibbons 3 73
(David Barron) *t.k.h: chsd ldrs on inner: pushed along over 4f out: sn rdn and wknd* **100/1**

2m 10.88s (1.48) **Going Correction** +0.30s/f (Good)
WFA 3 from 4yo+ 7lb **10** Ran SP% **115.5**
Speed ratings (Par 109): **106,105,104,100,99 98,98,97,94,90**
CSF £14.43 CT £37.29 TOTE £6.90: £1.60, £1.10, £1.80; EX 16.70 Trifecta £66.70.
Owner Clipper Logistics **Bred** Mrs Cherry Faeste **Trained** Newmarket, Suffolk
■ Stewards' Enquiry : Andrea Atzeni caution; careless riding

FOCUS
Race distance increased by 3yds. The right horses came clear in what looked a strong handicap and this has been rated on the positive side. They went just a steady gallop.

6262 DFS BRITISH STALLION STUDS EBF MAIDEN STKS (PLUS 10 RACE) 1m (S)
4:50 (4:53) (Class 3) 2-Y-O £9,703 (£2,887; £1,443; £721) Stalls Centre

Form RPR
2 **1** **Glencadam Glory**[27] 5373 2-9-5 0................................ FrankieDettori 5 84
(John Gosden) *swtchd rt after s: led: qcknd pce over 2f out: hdd last 150yds: styd on to ld post* **7/2**[3]

2 **2** hd **Hydroxide**[47] 4649 2-9-5 0.. JamesDoyle 7 84
(Hugo Palmer) *dwlt: hld up in rr: ducked lft over 4f out: hdwy 3f out: led narrowly last 150yds: hdd post* **2/1**[2]

3 hd **The Anvil (IRE)**[32] 5211 2-9-5 0.. RyanMoore 1 84
(A P O'Brien, Ire) *trckd ldr: drvn over 2f out: no ex nr fin* **13/8**[1]

04 **4** nk **Never Surrender (IRE)**[37] 4988 2-9-5 0....................... JamieSpencer 6 83
(Charles Hills) *n.m.r sn after s: hld up in rr: swtchd lft over 1f out: chsng ldrs last 100yds: keeping on at fin* **25/1**

5 1/2 **Okool (FR)** 2-9-5 0.. PaulHanagan 8 84+
(Owen Burrows) *trckd ldrs: drvn over 3f out: n.m.r and swtchd lft over 1f out: edgd rt and styd on wl clsng stages* **20/1**

6 3/4 **Wolf Country** 2-9-5 0... WilliamBuick 2 80
(Charlie Appleby) *trckd ldrs: effrt over 2f out: edgd lft over 1f out: kpt on same pce last 150yds: sltly hmpd nr fin* **10/1**

7 2 1/4 **Helovaplan (IRE)** 2-9-5 0... ConnorBeasley 4 75
(Bryan Smart) *dwlt: mid-div: drvn over 3f out: chsng ldrs 2f out: wknd fnl 150yds* **50/1**

8 31 **Saint Cuthberts** 2-9-5 0.. PatCosgrave 3 7
(David Brown) *mid-div: hung lft thrght: lost pl over 2f out: sn bhd: t.o whn eased fnl 100yds* **66/1**

1m 44.19s (4.89) **Going Correction** +0.10s/f (Good) **8** Ran SP% **114.8**
Speed ratings (Par 99): **79,78,78,78,77 77,74,43**
CSF £10.66 TOTE £4.50: £1.40, £1.10, £1.10; EX 11.60 Trifecta £21.20.
Owner Angus Dundee Distillers plc **Bred** D J And Mrs Deer **Trained** Newmarket, Suffolk
■ Stewards' Enquiry : Paul Hanagan caution; carless riding.

FOCUS
A good-looking maiden but the gallop was steady, controlled from the front by Frankie Dettori, and that resulted in a bunched finish and form that is hard to evaluate. Many of these could do better.

6263 LADBROKES H'CAP 6f
6:00 (6:03) (Class 3) (0-90,93) 3-Y-O+ £11,644 (£3,465; £1,731; £865) Stalls Centre

Form RPR
0000 **1** **Handsome Dude**[13] 5857 4-8-12 **81**......................(b) GrahamGibbons 10 94
(David Barron) *overall ldr: drvn clr 1f out: kpt on wl* **25/1**

3365 **2** 1 1/2 **Intense Style (IRE)**[13] 5857 4-9-7 **90**..............................(b) DavidAllan 9 97
(Les Eyre) *chsd ldrs: kpt on to take 2nd post* **10/1**

5360 **3** shd **Sakhee's Return**[26] 5389 4-8-11 **83**.............................[1] RachelRichardson(3) 12 90
(Tim Easterby) *mid-div: hdwy over 2f out: chsng ldrs over 1f out: kpt on same pce* **16/1**

1400 **4** 3/4 **Misterioso (IRE)**[18] 5678 4-9-4 **87**.................................. GeorgeBaker 5 91+
(Jamie Osborne) *hld up towards rr: smooth hdwy 2f out: sn swtchd rt: styd on wl clsng stages* **8/1**[3]

0300 **5** 3/4 **Khelman (IRE)**[13] 5857 6-9-0 **83**................................ GeorgeChaloner 15 85
(Richard Fahey) *chsd ldrs stands' side: drvn over 2f out: styd on wl fnl 150yds* **50/1**

5624 **6** nk **Shipyard (USA)**[9] 6012 7-9-6 **89**.................................(p) TomQueally 17 90
(Michael Appleby) *racd stands' side: chsd ldr: led that gp over 1f out: kpt on same pce* **4/1**[1]

1340 **7** nk **Duke Cosimo**[40] 4896 6-9-0 **83**...[1] PJMcDonald 6 83
(Michael Herrington) *chsd ldrs: kpt on wl fnl f* **20/1**

0426 **8** 1/2 **Rosie's Premiere (IRE)**[24] 5488 4-9-4 **87**....................(t) PaulHanagan 3 85
(Dean Ivory) *chsd ldrs: kpt on same pce over 1f out* **14/1**

0010 **9** 3/4 **Invincible Ridge (IRE)**[6] 6080 8-9-1 **84**.............................. NeilFarley 14 80
(Eric Alston) *chsd ldrs: one pce over 1f out* **50/1**

31- **10** 3/4 **War Whisper (IRE)**[461] 2906 3-9-4 **89**.............................. SeanLevey 19 83+
(Richard Hannon) *hld up in rr stands' side: effrt over 1f out: kpt on fnl f* **20/1**

0510 **11** nk **Links Drive Lady**[38] 4954 8-9-1 **87**................................... JackDuern(3) 1 80
(Dean Ivory) *s.i.s: hdwy over 2f out: chsng ldrs over 1f out: fdd* **50/1**

4000 **12** nk **Holiday Magic (IRE)**[13] 5857 5-8-10 **84**...................... NathanEvans(5) 4 76
(Michael Easterby) *s.i.s: hld up in rr: hdwy over 1f out: nvr a factor* **20/1**

605 **13** hd **Fendale**[26] 5417 4-9-4 **87**.. PaulMulrennan 13 78
(Michael Dods) *racd stands' side: mid-div: hdwy over 1f out: nvr a factor* **13/2**[2]

001 **14** shd **Fairway To Heaven (IRE)**[12] 5896 7-9-0 **83**................ FrankieDettori 21 74
(Michael Wigham) *chsd ldrs stands' side: one pce over 1f out* **8/1**[3]

0203 **15** 1 1/2 **Regal Dan (IRE)**[18] 5678 6-9-4 **87**...................................... SamJames 2 73
(David O'Meara) *chsd ldrs: fdd fnl f* **14/1**

0020 **16** 1 1/4 **Lucky Beggar (IRE)**[13] 5857 6-9-0 **83**................................ FMBerry 16 65
(David C Griffiths) *chsd ldrs stands' side: wknd over 1f out* **14/1**

1000 **17** 1/2 **Pomme De Terre (IRE)**[6] 6079 4-9-0 **83**......................(p) TomEaves 22 63
(Michael Dods) *rr-div: stands' side: effrt over 2f out: nvr a factor* **33/1**

5321 **18** 1 1/4 **Highland Acclaim (IRE)**[9] 5991 5-9-10 **93** 6ex.............. DavidNolan 18 69
(David O'Meara) *led stands' side gp: hdd and lost pl over 1f out* **12/1**

0301 **19** 1 3/4 **Little Palaver**[39] 4910 4-9-6 **89**... RyanTate 11 60
(Clive Cox) *chsd wnr: wknd over 1f out* **16/1**

1046 **20** 3 **Celebration**[19] 5657 3-9-3 **88**...................................(p) TonyHamilton 20 49
(Richard Fahey) *chsd ldrs stands' side: wkng whn hmpd over 1f out: sn eased* **20/1**

1m 12.95s (-0.65) **Going Correction** +0.10s/f (Good)
WFA 3 from 4yo+ 2lb **20** Ran SP% **135.8**
Speed ratings (Par 107): **108,106,105,104,103 103,103,102,101,100 100,99,99,99,97 95,94,93,90,86**
CSF £255.43 CT £4157.19 TOTE £31.10: £5.60, £3.60, £5.80, £2.70; EX 653.20 Trifecta £3909.00.
Owner W D & Mrs D A Glover **Bred** Fifehead Farms M C Denning **Trained** Maunby, N Yorks

FOCUS
A useful sprint, that split into two groups, with those down the middle emerging on top. The winner has been rated back to his best, with the second matching June's C&D success.
T/Jkpt: Not won. T/Plt: £26.80 to a £1 stake. Pool: £190,246.64 - 5,163.48 winning units. T/Qpdt: £4.90 to a £1 stake. Pool: £14,647.27 - 2,206.71 winning units. **Walter Glynn& Joe Rowntree**

5989 EPSOM (L-H)
Thursday, September 8

OFFICIAL GOING: Good (good to firm in places home straight)
Wind: Fresh, against Weather: Fine, warm

6264 BRITISH STALLION STUDS EBF MEDIAN AUCTION MAIDEN STKS 7f
2:05 (2:06) (Class 5) 2-Y-O £3,881 (£1,155; £577; £288) Stalls Low

Form RPR
422 **1** **Maldonado (FR)**[11] 5916 2-9-5 0....................................... JimCrowley 9 79
(Charlie Appleby) *pressed ldr: led 2f out: hanging lft after and drvn out but a in command* **4/7**[1]

4 **2** 1 3/4 **Akkadian Empire**[10] 5952 2-9-5 0.. JFEgan 2 74
(Mick Channon) *led: rdn and hdd 2f out: kpt on but readily hld fnl f* **10/1**[3]

3 1 1/2 **Mullarkey** 2-9-5 0.. KierenFox 7 70+
(John Best) *off the pce in midfield: 7th st: prog 3f out: rdn to chse ldng pair over 1f out: nvr able to chal but kpt on wl* **33/1**

52 **4** 2 3/4 **Emenem**[15] 5764 2-9-5 0.. NickyMackay 1 63
(Simon Dow) *prom: 5th st: chsd ldng pair 3f out to over 1f out: fdd fnl f* **5/1**[2]

5 hd **Caspian Gold (IRE)** 2-9-5 0.. BertrandFlandrin 5 62
(Richard Hughes) *off the pce in midfield: 6th st but saved grnd on inner: clsd to press for 4th fnl f: shkn up and kpt on same pce* **14/1**

20 **6** 1 1/4 **Masonic (IRE)**[22] 5549 2-9-5 0... LukeMorris 6 59
(Robyn Brisland) *prom: 4th st: drvn over 2f out: fdd over 1f out* **5/1**[2]

7 2 1/2 **Spirit Of Belle** 2-9-0 0... PaddyBradley(5) 3 52+
(Pat Phelan) *wl in rr: 8th st: shkn up over 2f out: no threat but sme late prog* **50/1**

00 **8** 2 3/4 **Equal Rights**[32] 5202 2-9-5 0... FergusSweeney 11 45
(Eve Johnson Houghton) *a in last trio: 9th st: struggling after* **25/1**

00 **9** 1 **Desidero (SPA)**[50] 4523 2-9-0 0..................................... RobertWinston 4 37
(Pat Phelan) *s.i.s: a wl in rr: last st: sn struggling* **100/1**

3 **10** 7 **Nip Down The Jug**[11] 5922 2-9-5 0................................ HarryPoulton 10 23
(Adam West) *t.k.h: prom: 3rd st: sn wknd rapidly: t.o* **50/1**

1m 25.82s (2.52) **Going Correction** +0.275s/f (Good) **10** Ran SP% **124.4**
Speed ratings (Par 95): **96,94,92,89,88 87,84,81,80,72**
CSF £8.45 TOTE £1.40: £1.10, £2.90, £7.50; EX 8.70 Trifecta £169.40.
Owner Godolphin **Bred** Snowdrop Stud Co Ltd **Trained** Newmarket, Suffolk

FOCUS
The rail was out up to 7 yards from the 1 mile marker to the winning post - adding 27 yards to all races of 1 mile +, 17 yards to 7f and 10 yards to 6f. This didn't look an overly strong juvenile maiden - the opening level is hard to pin down - and it gave the market leader a great chance to gain a first win.

6265 PINSENT MASONS H'CAP 1m 114y
2:40 (2:41) (Class 5) (0-75,75) 3-Y-O £4,528 (£1,347; £673; £336) Stalls Low

Form RPR
0330 **1** **Be Kool (IRE)**[13] 5845 3-8-6 **65**.......................(v[1]) CallumShepherd(5) 12 75
(Brian Ellison) *dwlt: wl in rr: 10th st and a long way off the pce: drvn and rapid prog on wd outside 2f out: str run fnl f to ld last strides* **16/1**

0333 **2** nk **Irish Optimism (IRE)**[15] 5782 3-9-6 **74**............................ JasonHart 3 83
(John Quinn) *trckd ldrs: 5th st: eased out and rdn over 1f out: clsd to ld ins fnl f: r.o wl but hdd last strides* **9/2**[2]

2-50 **3** 3 1/2 **Mockinbird (IRE)**[17] 5717 3-9-0 **68**......................................[1] LukeMorris 11 69
(Sir Mark Prescott Bt) *t.k.h early: trckd ldrs: 4th st: rdn to chal 2f out: led 1f out but hanging lft and briefly unbalanced: hdd and outpcd ins fnl f* **16/1**

2212 **4** 3/4 **Ripoll (IRE)**[10] 5965 3-9-1 **72**................................(t) JosephineGordon(3) 1 71
(Sylvester Kirk) *t.k.h early: trckd ldng pair: clsd to ld wl over 1f out: hdd and outpcd 1f out* **3/1**[1]

4226 **5** 1 1/2 **Ocean Eleven**[15] 5765 3-9-6 **74**... JimCrowley 10 70
(John Ryan) *chsd ldrs: 6th st: shkn up and no imp 2f out: kpt on same pce fnl f* **8/1**

0530 **6** 1 ½ **Tasteofexcellence (IRE)**[17] 5720 3-8-1 **62**................ RhiainIngram(7) 9 54
(Roger Ingram) *in tch on outer: 8th st: hanging lft fr 3f out and nvr able to make much prog: kpt on fnl f* **33/1**

6616 **7** ½ **Clever Bob (IRE)**[13] 5832 3-9-4 **72**... JFEgan 7 63
(Joseph Tuite) *led to wl over 1f out: steadily wknd* **8/1**

-451 **8** ½ **Possible Future**[32] 5193 3-9-4 **75**........................... TimClark(3) 6 65
(Ismail Mohammed) *pressed ldr to jst over 2f out: steadily wknd* **6/1**[3]

245 **9** ½ **Aid To Africa (IRE)**[18] 5681 3-9-1 **72**.......................... LouisSteward(3) 4 61
(Michael Bell) *a in midfield: 7th st: rdn and no prog over 2f out* **25/1**

01 **10** 5 **Lolwah**[80] 3464 3-9-4 **72**.. TedDurcan 8 49
(Sir Michael Stoute) *off the pce in rr: 9th st: rdn and hung lft jst over 2f out: wknd fnl f* **6/1**[3]

2343 **11** 2 ½ **Sehayli (IRE)**[38] 4939 3-9-0 **73**.................................. PaddyBradley(5) 5 45
(Lee Carter) *a wl in rr: last st: sn no ch* **20/1**

0342 **12** 13 **Harlequin Rock**[15] 5775 3-8-8 **62**.................................... MartinDwyer 2 4
(Mick Quinn) *dwlt: a wl in rr: 11th st: sn bhd: t.o* **10/1**

1m 46.76s (0.66) **Going Correction** +0.275s/f (Good) **12** Ran SP% **126.4**
Speed ratings (Par 101): **108,107,104,103,102 101,100,100,99,95 93,81**
CSF £90.54 CT £1235.71 TOTE £24.90: £5.80, £2.10, £4.70; EX 180.00 Trifecta £4363.90.
Owner Graham Brown & Brian Ellison **Bred** E Lonergan **Trained** Norton, N Yorks

FOCUS
The rail was out up to 7 yards from the 1 mile marker to the winning post, adding 27 yards to the official race distance. A competitive handicap for the level run at a decent gallop, which suited those coming off the pace. A pb from the winner and second.

6266 AMBER SCAFFOLDING HEIGHT SAFETY H'CAP 7f
3:15 (3:15) (Class 4) (0-80,78) 3-Y-O+
£7,470 (£2,236; £1,118; £559; £279; £140) **Stalls** Low

Form RPR

3204 **1** **Sarangoo**[3] 6184 8-8-13 **72**... GeorgiaCox(5) 6 82
(Malcolm Saunders) *mde all: shkn up and clr over 2f out: kpt on wl after and in no real danger: unchal* **8/1**

1203 **2** 2 **Pacolita (IRE)**[36] 5017 4-9-6 **74**... LukeMorris 9 79
(Sylvester Kirk) *t.k.h: sn chsd wnr: drvn and nt qckn over 2f out: no imp after: one pce and jst hld on for 2nd* **9/2**[2]

011 **3** shd **Cricklewood Green (USA)**[18] 5674 5-9-7 **78**...... JosephineGordon(3) 2 83+
(Sylvester Kirk) *n.m.r s: pushed along in last: drvn and prog on outer 2f out: tk 3rd ins fnl f: styd on and nrly ct runner-up* **7/2**[1]

6003 **4** 3 ¼ **Mezzotint (IRE)**[18] 5677 7-9-5 **73**..................................... JimCrowley 3 69
(Lee Carter) *chsd ldrs 5th st: chsd ldng pair wl over 2f out: sn rdn and no imp: lost 3rd ins fnl f and wknd* **6/1**

0126 **5** nk **Boycie**[26] 5412 3-9-1 **78**..(b) HollieDoyle(5) 5 72
(Richard Hannon) *chsd ldrs: 4th st: urged along over 2f out: one pce and no great prog* **8/1**

0335 **6** nk **Live Dangerously**[13] 5832 6-8-10 **64**............................... DannyBrock 8 59
(John Bridger) *towards rr: 6th st: rdn and sme prog over 2f out: disp 3rd over 1f out: wknd ins fnl f* **12/1**

0105 **7** 7 **Another Boy**[56] 4306 3-9-0 **77**...................................(p) GeorgeWood(5) 4 52
(Ralph Beckett) *chsd ldng pair: rdn and lost pl wl over 2f out: wknd qckly wl over 1f out* **12/1**

000 **8** 2 ¾ **Zacynthus (IRE)**[56] 4299 8-9-8 **76**............................... RobertWinston 1 45
(Ivan Furtado) *a in rr: 7th st: wknd over 2f out: sn bhd* **5/1**[3]

1410 **P** **Frank Bridge**[34] 5104 3-9-1 **73**..................................... FergusSweeney 7
(Eve Johnson Houghton) *lost action sn after s and p.u* **10/1**

1m 25.01s (1.71) **Going Correction** +0.275s/f (Good)
WFA 3 from 4yo+ 4lb **9** Ran SP% **118.1**
Speed ratings (Par 105): **101,98,98,94,94 94,86,83,**
CSF £44.91 CT £152.29 TOTE £11.30: £3.30, £1.80, £1.60; EX 50.90 Trifecta £257.90.
Owner M S Saunders **Bred** M S Saunders And Chris Scott **Trained** Green Ore, Somerset

FOCUS
The rail was out up to 7 yards from the 1 mile marker to the winning post, adding 17 yards to the official race distance. The winner raced prominently and was never going to be caught entering the final stages - she's been rated up slightly on this year's form, with the second to form.

6267 WINNER EVENT SERVICES JUMP JOCKEYS DERBY H'CAP (TO BE RIDDEN BY PROFESSIONAL JUMP JOCKEYS) 1m 4f 10y
3:50 (3:51) (Class 4) (0-80,80) 4-Y-O+
£7,470 (£2,236; £1,118; £559; £279; £140) **Stalls** Centre

Form RPR

433 **1** **Alberta (IRE)**[30] 5255 7-11-9 **79**...................................(v) JamieMoore 9 86
(Jim Best) *trckd ldng pair: rdn wl over 2f out: clsd to chal over 1f out: drvn ahd ins fnl f: kpt on wl* **7/1**

-452 **2** ½ **Jupiter Custos (FR)**[10] 5963 4-10-12 **68**.................. TomScudamore 1 74
(Michael Scudamore) *trckd ldrs: 4th st: rdn over 2f out: clsd to chal and upsides ins fnl f: nt qckn nr fin* **11/4**[1]

115 **3** 1 **Medburn Cutler**[42] 4795 6-11-7 **77**..............................(p) NickScholfield 2 81
(Paul Henderson) *mde most: shkn up 2f out: hdd and one pce ins fnl f* **5/1**[2]

6552 **4** nk **Lady Of Yue**[44] 4739 6-10-10 **66** oh1................................ JackQuinlan 7 69
(Eugene Stanford) *w ldr to 3f out: sn rdn: styd cl up: n.m.r between rivals over 1f out and again whn stl trying jst ins fnl f: no ex* **10/1**

105- **5** 2 ¼ **Callendula**[272] 8175 4-11-10 **80**...................................(p) JamesBanks 10 81
(Clive Cox) *hld up wl in tch: 6th st: rdn and edgd lft over 2f out: kpt on but nvr pce to rch ldrs* **14/1**

0634 **6** 2 **Whinging Willie (IRE)**[10] 5963 7-11-6 **76**....................(v) JoshuaMoore 5 75
(Gary Moore) *t.k.h early: hld up wl in tch: 7th st: shkn up and outpcd over 2f out: kpt on one pce after* **5/1**[2]

0/-0 **7** 9 **King Muro**[45] 4711 6-10-10 **66** oh1...................................(t) AlainCawley 4 56
(Fergal O'Brien) *trckd ldrs: 5th and sing to struggling st: wknd wl over 2f out* **33/1**

1202 **8** 1 ¼ **Elysian Prince**[26] 1933 5-11-7 **77**..................................(t) TrevorWhelan 3 66
(Neil King) *wl in tch in rr: 8th st: sn rdn: no prog on inner over 2f out: wknd* **6/1**[3]

0514 **9** 1 ¾ **Carthage (IRE)**[30] 5275 5-11-4 **74**................................... HenryBrooke 8 61
(Brian Ellison) *wl in tch in rr: last st: sn rdn and wknd over 2f out* **8/1**

2m 43.68s (4.78) **Going Correction** +0.275s/f (Good) **9** Ran SP% **116.6**
Speed ratings (Par 105): **95,94,94,93,92 90,84,84,82**
CSF £26.87 CT £106.68 TOTE £6.80: £1.90, £1.40, £2.00; EX 33.60 Trifecta £167.50.
Owner Allen B Pope, S&A Mares, Jamie Donnelly **Bred** Denis Fehan **Trained** Lewes, E Sussex

FOCUS
The rail was out up to 7 yards from the 1 mile marker to the winning post, adding 27 yards to the official race distance. An ordinary race but still improved Flat form from the winner.

6268 KOVARA KLADDERS H'CAP 1m 2f 18y
4:25 (4:26) (Class 5) (0-75,75) 3-Y-O **£3,881** (£1,155; £577; £288) **Stalls** Low

Form RPR

3622 **1** **Shufoog**[10] 5975 3-8-13 **72**... GeorgiaCox(5) 2 85+
(William Haggas) *hld up in rr: prog and 5th st: clsd on outer to ld 2f out: shkn up and edgd lft fr over 1f out: kpt on* **6/4**[1]

064 **2** ¾ **Street Poet (IRE)**[73] 3723 3-9-0 **71**....................... JosephineGordon(3) 4 82+
(Sir Michael Stoute) *trckd ldrs: 4th st: rdn over 2f out: chsd wnr over 1f out: styd on but nvr quite able to chal* **7/2**[3]

0351 **3** 3 ¼ **Pack It In (IRE)**[33] 5164 3-9-4 **72**..................................(b) MartinDwyer 9 76
(Brian Meehan) *trckd ldr after 2f: upsides over 2f out tl wnr wnt by sn after: lost 2nd and one pce over 1f out* **7/1**

6321 **4** ¾ **So Celebre (GER)**[29] 5308 3-9-7 **75**................................. JimCrowley 6 78
(Ian Williams) *trckd ldrs: 3rd st: cl up but rdn whn squeezed out 2f out: one pce after* **5/2**[2]

2424 **5** 7 **The Major**[32] 5193 3-9-3 **74**... LouisSteward(3) 8 63
(Michael Bell) *hld up in rr: 8th st: rdn and tried to make prog fr 3f out: nvr any imp on ldrs* **16/1**

5501 **6** 2 ½ **Adventure Zone (IRE)**[15] 5775 3-8-11 **65**.........................(v[1]) JFEgan 3 49
(Lee Carter) *mde most to 2f out: wknd* **33/1**

343 **7** 3 ¾ **Booborowie (IRE)**[27] 5380 3-9-7 **75**................................ MartinLane 7 51
(Jeremy Gask) *pressed ldr 2f: prom tl 6th and wkng st: sn no ch* **25/1**

516 **8** 2 **Petite Jack**[29] 4013 3-9-7 **75**.. JimmyQuinn 5 47
(Neil King) *rousted along early in last: a in rr: last st: sn btn* **50/1**

3650 **9** 7 **Hellavashock**[24] 5486 3-9-2 **70**.................................(b[1]) AdamBeschizza 1 28
(Giles Bravery) *a in rr: 7th st: sn rdn and wknd* **33/1**

2m 11.69s (1.99) **Going Correction** +0.275s/f (Good) **9** Ran SP% **120.9**
Speed ratings (Par 101): **103,102,99,99,93 91,88,87,81**
CSF £7.28 CT £29.21 TOTE £2.40: £1.10, £1.50, £2.50; EX 8.90 Trifecta £35.50.
Owner Hamdan Al Maktoum **Bred** Shadwell Estate Company Limited **Trained** Newmarket, Suffolk

FOCUS
The rail was out up to 7 yards from the 1 mile marker to the winning post, adding 27 yards to the official race distance. The winner and second came into this unexposed and the form is taken at face value judged around the third.

6269 ISINGLASS H'CAP 6f
5:00 (5:04) (Class 5) (0-70,70) 3-Y-O+ **£4,528** (£1,347; £673; £336) **Stalls** High

Form RPR

1003 **1** **Mad Endeavour**[14] 5797 5-9-0 **63**....................................(b) MartinLane 8 71
(Stuart Kittow) *led 1f: mostly pressed ldr after: rdn over 1f out: led ins fnl f: drvn and kpt on wl* **4/1**[1]

0420 **2** nk **Straits Of Malacca**[20] 5599 5-9-6 **69**..................................(p) JFEgan 14 76
(Simon Dow) *restless stalls: t.k.h: trckd ldrs: 5th st: effrt on outer 2f out: rdn and styd on to take 2nd nr fin* **10/1**

2111 **3** nk **Chetan**[16] 5736 4-9-7 **70**...(tp) AdamBeschizza 2 76
(Charlie Wallis) *fractious preliminaries and mounted on crse: led after 1f: mde most after: rdn and jnd 2f out: hdd and one pce ins fnl f* **5/1**[3]

0004 **4** nk **Divine Call**[9] 6000 9-8-4 **56** oh2.................................(b) NoelGarbutt(3) 16 61
(Milton Bradley) *chsd ldrs but trapped out wd early: 6th st: rdn and clsd on ldrs over 1f out: ch jst ins fnl f: nt qckn* **14/1**

325 **5** 1 ¼ **Pharoh Jake**[13] 5827 8-9-1 **64**.. DannyBrock 13 65
(John Bridger) *pressed ldrs: 3rd st: rdn to chal and upsides 2f out to 1f out: fdd nr fin* **16/1**

060 **6** ¾ **Evening Attire**[33] 5169 5-9-1 **69**.................................... HollieDoyle(5) 10 68
(William Stone) *sn in last: rdn and prog on outer fr 2f out: styd on but nvr ch to rch ldrs* **8/1**

3060 **7** 1 ½ **Hipz (IRE)**[31] 5236 5-8-5 **57**.................................(p) JosephineGordon(3) 6 51
(Laura Mongan) *in tch: 7th st: rdn to chse ldrs over 1f out: wknd fnl f* **20/1**

004 **8** 1 ¼ **Honcho (IRE)**[26] 5408 4-9-0 **63**..(v) JimCrowley 9 53
(John Ryan) *t.k.h: hld up in rr: 10th st: pushed along and no prog 2f out: styd on ins fnl f: no ch* **9/2**[2]

322 **9** ½ **Invade (IRE)**[27] 5379 4-9-1 **67**....................................(t) AaronJones(3) 12 55
(Stuart Williams) *a towards rr: 12th st: rdn and no real prog over 2f out* **9/2**[2]

0126 **10** ½ **Indus Valley (IRE)**[17] 5706 9-8-8 **60**.........................(b) NathanAlison(3) 4 47
(Lee Carter) *hld up in rr: 11th st: nudged along and no prog fr 2f out* **33/1**

5614 **11** hd **Perfect Pastime**[20] 5599 8-8-8 **64**............................... RhiainIngram(7) 11 50
(Jim Boyle) *lost pl after 1f: 9th st: pushed along and no prog over 2f out* **16/1**

3226 **12** 6 **Picansort**[34] 5105 9-8-8 **57**... JimmyQuinn 7 24
(Peter Crate) *chsd ldrs: 4th st: rdn and in tch 2f out: wknd rapidly jst over 1f out* **25/1**

6116 **13** ¾ **Secret Look**[12] 5896 6-9-7 **70**.......................................(p) MartinDwyer 3 34
(Richard Phillips) *in tch on inner: 8th st: sn lost pl and struggling: bhd over 1f out* **16/1**

1m 10.62s (1.22) **Going Correction** +0.275s/f (Good)
WFA 3 from 4yo+ 2lb **13** Ran SP% **129.1**
Speed ratings (Par 103): **102,101,101,100,99 98,96,94,93,93 92,84,83**
CSF £47.68 CT £223.46 TOTE £5.70: £2.00, £3.60, £2.20; EX 55.90 Trifecta £316.40.
Owner Reg Gifford **Bred** S R Hope **Trained** Blackborough, Devon
■ Stewards' Enquiry : Martin Lane two-day ban; used his whip above the permitted level (22nd-23rd Sept)

FOCUS
The rail was out up to 7 yards from the 1 mile marker to the winning post, adding 10 yards to the official race distance. The first and third home were first and second early on and the winner is rated back to the level of his Goodwood success.
T/Plt: £42.80 to a £1 stake. Pool: £71,163.41 - 1,211.23 winning units. T/Qpdt: £8.20 to a £1 stake. Pool: £5,397.40 - 482.19 winning units. **Jonathan Neesom**

6068 CHANTILLY (R-H)

Thursday, September 8

OFFICIAL GOING: Turf: good; polytrack: standard

6270a PRIX DES CHENES (GROUP 3) (2YO COLTS & GELDINGS) (TURF) 1m

12:10 (12:00) 2-Y-O **£29,411** (£11,764; £8,823; £5,882; £2,941)

RPR

1 **Akihiro (JPN)**[30] 2-9-2 0 MaximeGuyon 1 113+
(A Fabre, France) *hld up in midfield: angled out and rdn 2f out: hdwy to chal and led ins fnl f: sn in full control: cosily* **15/8**[1]

2 1 **High Alpha (FR)**[19] 5702 2-9-2 0 IoritzMendizabal 5 109
(Mario Hofer, Germany) *led: rdn 2f out: kpt on but reeled in and hdd fnl f: no ex w wnr after* **7/2**[3]

3 2 **National Defense**[16] 2-9-2 0 Pierre-CharlesBoudot 2 104
(Mme C Head-Maarek, France) *trckd ldr on inner: rdn and effrt 2f out: kpt on same pce and hld in 3rd fnl f* **3/1**[2]

4 1 ½ **Sea Fox (IRE)**[7] 6059 2-9-2 0 AdamKirby 4 101
(David Evans) *hld up in last: rdn 2f out: kpt on steadily but nvr any danger* **7/1**

5 4 ½ **Pazeer (FR)**[22] 5568 2-9-2 0 ChristopheSoumillon 3 90
(J-C Rouget, France) *midfield: rdn over 2f out: no ex over 1f out: wknd* **7/2**[3]

6 5 **Dolokhov**[10] 5985 2-9-2 0 (b) TonyPiccone 6 78
(J S Moore) *trckd ldr on outer: rdn early in st: no ex and wknd over 1f out: eased in last fnl f* **25/1**

1m 38.12s (0.12) **6** Ran SP% **120.6**
WIN (incl. 1 euro stake): 2.70. PLACES: 1.20, 1.90 SF: 8.40.
Owner Wertheimer & Frere **Bred** Wertheimer & Frere **Trained** Chantilly, France

6271a PRIX D'AUMALE (GROUP 3) (2YO FILLIES) (TURF) 1m

1:50 (12:00) 2-Y-O **£29,411** (£11,764; £8,823; £5,882; £2,941)

RPR

1 **Toulifaut (IRE)**[25] 5447 2-8-9 0 IoritzMendizabal 5 104
(J-C Rouget, France) *hld up in tch: rdn 2f out: r.o down outer and chal ent fnl f: sn led: asserted* **9/4**[2]

2 1 **Normandel (FR)**[20] 5698 2-8-9 0 CristianDemuro 7 102
(Mme Pia Brandt, France) *restrained early: sn midfield in tch: rdn to chal over 1f out: kpt on wout matching wnr fnl f* **4/1**

3 ½ **Asidious Alexander (IRE)**[19] 5703 2-8-9 0 MaximeGuyon 1 101
(Simon Crisford) *midfield in tch on inner: rdn 2f out: short of room on rail over 1f out: kpt on fnl f but nt able to chal: shade unlucky* **3/1**[3]

4 2 **Invincible Queen (FR)**[16] 2-8-10 0 ow1 OlivierPeslier 3 97
(F Head, France) *sn led: rdn over 1f out: hdd jst ins fnl f: no ex and wknd* **15/8**[1]

5 1 ½ **Liberale (FR)**[21] 2-8-9 0 GregoryBenoist 6 92
(J-P Gauvin, France) *sn pressing ldr on outer: rdn 2f out: no ex and btn ent fnl f: wknd* **16/1**

6 20 **Holy Makfi**[21] 2-8-9 0 MlleIsisMagnin 2 44+
(J-Y Artu, France) *stirrup leather broke and rdr lost irons s: mostly in rr and no meaningful factor: t.o in st* **25/1**

1m 40.95s (2.95) **6** Ran SP% **120.3**
WIN (incl. 1 euro stake): 3.40 PLACES: 2.00, 2.00 SF: 19.70.
Owner Andrew-James Smith **Bred** Barronstown Stud **Trained** Pau, France

6272a PRIX DU PIN (GROUP 3) (3YO+) (TURF) 7f

2:25 (12:00) 3-Y-O+ **£29,411** (£11,764; £8,823; £5,882; £2,941)

RPR

1 **Jallota**[11] 5926 5-9-1 0 ChristopheSoumillon 2 115+
(Charles Hills) *t.k.h: hld up bhd ldrs on inner: angled out and n.m.r over 2f out: drvn to chal 1 1/2f out: styd on to ld appr fnl f: sn rdn and r.o fnl f: wl on top fnl 75yds* **4/1**[3]

2 1 ¾ **Attendu (FR)**[32] 5217 3-9-2 0 MaximeGuyon 7 113
(C Laffon-Parias, France) *w.w towards rr of main gp: rdn and hdwy 1 1/2f out: chsd wnr ent fnl f: styd on: nt pce to get on terms* **3/1**[2]

3 ¾ **Karar**[11] 5949 4-9-1 0 GregoryBenoist 5 108
(F-H Graffard, France) *t.k.h: a cl up under a tight hold: riodden to chse ldrs appr fnl f: styd on at same pce u.p* **16/1**

4 ¾ **Coulsty (IRE)**[41] 4846 5-9-1 0 UmbertoRispoli 11 106
(Richard Hannon) *nvr far away: cl 3rd and rdn 2f out: styd on at same pce fnl f: nvr able to chal* **10/1**

5 ¾ **Sasparella (FR)**[95] 2945 3-8-8 0 GeraldMosse 4 99
(C Laffon-Parias, France) *chsd ldng quartet: drvn along to hold pl 1/2-way: styd on fr 1/2-way: nt muster pce to get on terms* **16/1**

6 hd **Territories (IRE)**[53] 4441 4-9-1 0 MickaelBarzalona 8 103
(A Fabre, France) *w.w in fnl trio wl off pce: tk clsr order 2f out: sn rdn and styng on whn nt clr run and lost momentum ins fnl 1 1/2f: angled out over 1f out: styd on fnl f: nvr nrr* **5/2**[1]

7 1 ½ **Blue Soave (FR)**[84] 8-9-1 0 TonyPiccone 9 99
(F Chappet, France) *chsd ldng quartet: clsd to chse ldrs bef 1/2-way: one pce u.p fnl f* **20/1**

8 1 ¼ **Noozhoh Canarias (SPA)**[45] 5-9-1 0 JoseLuisMartinez 13 96
(J A Remolina Diez, France) *led: rdn and rallied over 2f out: hdd appr fnl f: sn wknd* **33/1**

9 ¾ **Lord Of The Land (IRE)**[11] 5949 5-9-1 0 (p) DanielTudhope 10 94
(David O'Meara) *in rr of main gp: rdn on outer an no real imp 2f out: plugged on at one pce fnl f* **8/1**

10 nk **Qatar Power (FR)**[46] 4695 3-8-8 0 AurelienLemaitre 1 88
(F Head, France) *chsd ldng quartet: clsd on inner wl over 2f out: rdn and no further imp under 1 1/2f out: wknd fnl f* **16/1**

11 1 ¼ **Come Alive**[24] 5498 3-8-8 0 VincentCheminaud 14 85
(A Fabre, France) *missed break: in rr and wl off pce: sme mod later hdwy: nvr in contention* **20/1**

12 ¾ **Venecia Style (FR)**[11] 5949 3-8-8 0 CristianDemuro 3 83
(P Sogorb, France) *hld up towards rr of main gp: rdn and nt qckn under 2f out: dropped away ins fnl f* **25/1**

13 3 **Kenouska (FR)**[12] 5906 4-8-11 0 Pierre-CharlesBoudot 12 76
(P Sogorb, France) *hld up in midfield: rdn and btn appr 1 1/2f out: bhd whn eased fnl f* **25/1**

14 ½ **Black Max (FR)**[32] 5217 3-8-11 0 StephanePasquier 6 76
(H-A Pantall, France) *a in fnl trio: rdn and lost tch fr wl over 1 1/2f* **20/1**

1m 24.16s (-1.94)
WFA 3 from 4yo+ 4lb **14** Ran SP% **136.3**
WIN (incl. 1 euro stake): 3.80. PLACES: 1.70, 1.80, 2.80. DF: 8.60. SF: 12.60.
Owner Mrs Fitri Hay **Bred** Barry Walters **Trained** Lambourn, Berks

FOCUS

The winner won with a bit to spare and the second helps set the level.

6273a PRIX DES TOURELLES - FONDS EUROPEEN DE L'ELEVAGE (LISTED RACE) (3YO+ FILLIES & MARES) (TURF) 1m 4f

2:55 (12:00) 3-Y-O+ **£19,117** (£7,647; £5,735; £3,823; £1,911)

RPR

1 **Mambomiss (FR)**[26] 5461 5-9-4 0 FranckBlondel 10 98+
(D De Watrigant, France) **22/5**[3]

2 snk **Pecking Order (IRE)**[47] 4646 4-9-4 0 FrederikTylicki 3 98
(James Fanshawe) *settled in midfield: drvn to cl between horses 2f out: chsd ldr u.p 1f out: styd on to join ldr whn hdd by wnr 75yds out: unable qck* **14/1**

3 ¾ **Five Fifteen (FR)**[42] 4814 4-9-4 0 (p) EddyHardouin 5 97
(X Thomas-Demeaulte, France) **66/10**

4 nse **Sweeping Up**[40] 4883 5-9-4 0 UmbertoRispoli 4 97
(Hughie Morrison) *led: sn 2 l clr: kicked for home wl over 2f out: rallied u.p fr 1 1/2f out: hdd fnl 75yds: no ex* **12/5**[1]

5 1 **Sacrifice My Soul (IRE)**[81] 4-9-4 0 MaximeGuyon 11 95
(Mme Pia Brandt, France) **31/1**

6 snk **Notte D'Oro (IRE)**[91] 3092 4-9-4 0 MickaelBarzalona 8 95
(Mme Pia Brandt, France) **57/1**

7 snk **Pandora (IRE)**[21] 5587 4-9-4 0 DanielTudhope 9 95
(David O'Meara) *t.k.h: hld up in midfield: rdn and clsd on inner over 1 1/2f out: cl 5th and styd on fnl f: nt pce to trble ldrs* **39/10**[2]

8 snk **Mint Julep (FR)**[25] 5448 3-8-10 0 ow1 Pierre-CharlesBoudot 6 96
(F-H Graffard, France) **17/1**

9 3 **Madernia (IRE)**[21] 4-9-4 0 GeraldMosse 1 90
(C Laffon-Parias, France) **17/1**

10 4 ½ **Beshara (FR)**[18] 3-8-9 0 AlexisBadel 2 83
(A De Royer-Dupre, France) **9/1**

11 1 ¾ **Strawberry Martini**[60] 5-9-4 0 VincentCheminaud 7 80
(H-A Pantall, France) **12/1**

2m 33.7s (2.70)
WFA 3 from 4yo+ 9lb **11** Ran SP% **121.8**
WIN (incl. 1 euro stake): 5.40. PLACES: 2.00, 4.40, 2.20. DF: 41.00. SF: 76.10.
Owner Jean-Marc De Watrigant **Bred** E A R L De Beguerie **Trained** France

5637 CHESTER (L-H)

Friday, September 9

OFFICIAL GOING: Good (7.1)

Wind: fresh 1/2 behind Weather: overcast, breezy, shower race 5 (4.25)

6274 BRITISH STALLION STUDS EBF MAIDEN STKS (PLUS 10 RACE) 7f 122y

2:05 (2:06) (Class 4) 2-Y-O

£6,225 (£1,864; £932; £466; £233; £117) **Stalls** Low

Form RPR

20 1 **Max Zorin (IRE)**[21] 5615 2-8-11 0 RobHornby(3) 3 82
(Andrew Balding) *trckd ldrs: t.k.h: 2nd over 1f out: styd on to ld last 75yds* **5/4**[1]

5532 2 1 ¼ **Roaring Character (IRE)**[8] 6053 2-9-0 80 RichardKingscote 6 79
(Tom Dascombe) *trckd ldr: t.k.h: drvn over 1f out: kpt on same pce to take 2nd post* **4/1**[2]

52 3 hd **Thorndyke**[34] 5150 2-9-0 0 KevinStott 8 79
(Kevin Ryan) *swtchd lft after s: led: hdd and no ex last 75yds* **10/1**

43 4 3 ½ **Doctor Cross (IRE)**[16] 5778 2-9-0 0 DavidNolan 1 70+
(Richard Fahey) *hld up in rr: pushed along over 4f out: chsng ldrs over 2f out: one pce over 1f out* **9/2**[3]

432 5 ¾ **Election Day**[7] 6085 2-9-0 0 FrannyNorton 7 69+
(Mark Johnston) *s.i.s: hdwy over 4f out: sn pushed along: chsng ldrs over 2f out: outpcd over 1f out* **4/1**[2]

00 6 11 **Atrafan (IRE)**[11] 5966 2-9-0 0 GrahamGibbons 2 43
(Alan Brown) *s.i.s: sn outpcd and detached last: bhd fnl 2f* **66/1**

0 7 13 **Blue Rocks**[20] 5637 2-8-7 0 JordanUys(7) 4 12
(Lisa Williamson) *chsd ldrs on outer: drvn over 2f out: sn lost pl and wl bhd* **100/1**

1m 34.75s (0.95) **Going Correction** +0.20s/f (Good) **7** Ran SP% **114.2**
Speed ratings (Par 97): **103,101,101,98,97 86,73**
CSF £6.61 TOTE £2.20: £1.30, £2.00; EX 6.20 Trifecta £31.60.
Owner Chelsea Thoroughbreds - Pegasus **Bred** Tinnakill, M Sadlier & A Byrne **Trained** Kingsclere, Hants

FOCUS

Race distance increased by 13yds. The rail between the 6f and 1.5f point was moved out 3yds, increasing race 1, 2, 3 & 7 by 13yds, race 4 & 5 by 14yds and race 6 by 26yds. The official going was good. A fair maiden and not many got into it, with the first three being up there throughout. Straightforward form rated around the front three.

6275 DAYINSURE WALES RALLY GB NURSERY H'CAP 7f 2y

2:40 (2:42) (Class 4) (0-85,84) 2-Y-O

£6,225 (£1,864; £932; £466; £233; £117) **Stalls** Low

Form RPR

3202 1 **Arc Royal**[20] 5637 2-9-2 **79** RichardKingscote 3 88+
(Tom Dascombe) *mde all: drvn clr over 1f out: eased clsng stages: unchal* **5/2**[1]

540 2 4 **Herm (IRE)**[41] 4866 2-8-7 **70** SamJames 6 68
(David Evans) *chsd wnr: drvn over 2f out: kpt on same pce over 1f out* **16/1**

120 3 1 ¾ **Stoneyford Lane (IRE)**[87] 3243 2-9-4 **81** RoystonFfrench 4 74
(Steph Hollinshead) *trckd ldrs: drvn over 2f out: kpt on one pce over 1f out* **7/1**

5433 4 ½ **Cullingworth (IRE)**[63] 4090 2-9-4 **81** TonyHamilton 1 75+
(Richard Fahey) *dwlt: mid-div: outpcd whn sltly hmpd wl over 1f out: swtchd rt and styd on strly fnl 150yds:* **13/2**

634 5 2 ¾ **Amathyst**[16] 5756 2-8-6 **69** AndrewMullen 8 56
(Michael Appleby) *trckd ldrs on outer: sltly hmpd wl over 1f out: wknd fnl f* **25/1**

4111 **6** *12* **Tawny Port**[14] 5833 2-9-2 **79** TomEaves 7 31+
(James Given) *s.i.s: hld up in rr: hdwy over 2f out: bdly hmpd and lost pl wl over 1f out: nt rcvr: bhd whn eased clsng stages* **15/2**

513 **7** *5* **Morning Suit (USA)**[30] 5299 2-9-0 **77** GrahamGibbons 2 16+
(Mark Johnston) *in rr: drvn 4f out: last and outpcd whn j. faller wl over 1f out: eased clsng stages .* **5/1**[3]

541 **F** **Thomas Cranmer (USA)**[40] 4914 2-9-7 **84** FrannyNorton 5 +
(Mark Johnston) *mid-div: t.k.h: hdwy over 2f out: dispuiting 3rd whn fell wl over 1f out* **7/2**[2]

1m 28.53s (2.03) **Going Correction** +0.20s/f (Good) **8** Ran SP% **114.8**
Speed ratings (Par 97): **96,91,89,88,85 72,66,**
CSF £44.23 CT £250.00 TOTE £3.40: £1.80, £3.20, £2.00; EX 43.90 Trifecta £259.90.
Owner Satchell Moran Solicitors **Bred** D R Tucker **Trained** Malpas, Cheshire

FOCUS
Race distance increased by 13yds. A useful nursery in which there was an incident on the home bend, with a few getting hampered by the fall of Thomas Cranmer. The winner made all. The runner-up has been rated to his mark.

6276 ESL GROUP H'CAP 7f 2y
3:15 (3:21) (Class 3) (0-95,93) 3-Y-O+

£7,470 (£2,236; £1,118; £559; £279; £140) **Stalls** Low

Form RPR

1200 **1** **Penwortham (IRE)**[13] 5878 3-8-11 **82** TonyHamilton 8 94
(Richard Fahey) *rr-div: hdwy on outside over 1f out: styd on wl to ld last 50yds* **14/1**

1416 **2** *3/4* **Viscount Barfield**[21] 5616 3-9-0 **88** RobHornby(3) 3 98
(Andrew Balding) *rr-div: hdwy 2f out: styd on to ld briefly 100yds out: no ex* **5/2**[1]

0423 **3** *3* **Bertiewhittle**[3] 6210 8-9-1 **87** RowanScott(5) 6 91
(David Barron) *in rr: hdwy outer over 1f out: kpt on to take 3rd clsng stages* **7/1**[3]

4216 **4** *1 1/4* **Muntadab (IRE)**[27] 5403 4-9-12 **93** DougieCostello 1 94
(David Loughnane) *trckd ldng pair: hmpd after 1f: led over 2f out: hdd last 100yds: fdd* **7/2**[2]

1356 **5** *4* **Realize**[41] 4889 6-9-4 **85** (t) RichardKingscote 4 75
(Stuart Williams) *mid-div: chsng ldrs over 3f out: outpcd: nt clr run and swtchd lft over 1f out: kpt on one pce* **7/2**[2]

1134 **6** *1/2* **Dilgura**[69] 3895 6-8-13 **83** MatthewCosham(3) 7 71
(Stuart Kittow) *mid-div: hdwy to chse ldrs over 3f out: one pce over 1f out* **20/1**

2111 **7** *1 1/4* **Courier**[14] 5836 4-9-0 **86** NathanEvans(5) 12 71
(Marjorie Fife) *swtchd lft after s: led: hdd over 2f out: wknd fnl f* **22/1**

1103 **8** *nse* **Hawatif (IRE)**[7] 6096 3-9-1 **86** AndrewMullen 2 69
(Mark Johnston) *s.i.s: in rr: kpt on appr fnl f: nvr on terms* **12/1**

00 **9** *1 3/4* **Zaeem**[40] 4917 7-9-2 **83** (p) DavidNolan 9 63
(Ivan Furtado) *mid-div: hdwy to chse ldrs over 3f out: wknd appr fnl f* **66/1**

1116 **10** *7* **Gabrial The Tiger (IRE)**[40] 4917 4-9-2 **88** AdamMcNamara(5) 10 49
(Richard Fahey) *swtchd lft after s: w ldr: hmpd after 1f: drvn over 2f out: lost pl over 1f out: bhd whn eased clsng stages.* **16/1**

1m 26.44s (-0.06) **Going Correction** +0.20s/f (Good)
WFA 3 from 4yo+ 4lb **10** Ran SP% **116.4**
Speed ratings (Par 107): **108,107,103,102,97 97,95,95,93,85**
CSF £48.17 CT £275.77 TOTE £16.70: £4.50, £1.40, £2.20; EX 71.20 Trifecta £327.00.
Owner Richard Fahey Ebor Racing Club Ltd **Bred** Kilfeacle Stud **Trained** Musley Bank, N Yorks
■ Stewards' Enquiry : Nathan Evans three-day ban; careless riding (23rd,25th-26th Sep)

FOCUS
Race distance increased by 13yds. A useful handicap, if not the strongest for the grade, and they went a strong pace which favoured the closers. The third has been rated close to form.

6277 ALAN NEWMAN H'CAP 1m 2f 75y
3:50 (3:50) (Class 3) (0-95,92) 3-Y-O **£7,762** (£2,310; £1,154; £577) **Stalls** High

Form RPR

11 **1** **Playful Sound**[48] 4668 3-9-3 **88** GrahamGibbons 6 98+
(Sir Michael Stoute) *led: qcknd pce over 2f out: drvn over 1f out: styd on wl* **15/8**[1]

1114 **2** *1 1/4* **Cote D'Azur**[13] 5865 3-9-7 **92** DavidAllan 1 98
(Les Eyre) *trckd wnr: t.k.h: drvn over 1f out: hung lft: no real imp* **3/1**[2]

3114 **3** *nk* **Brorocco**[12] 5932 3-8-11 **85** RobHornby(3) 2 90
(Andrew Balding) *dwlt: hld up in rr: effrt 2f out: 3rd 1f out: kpt on same pce* **3/1**[2]

5420 **4** *4* **Sark (IRE)**[42] 4827 3-8-4 **75** AndrewMullen 3 72
(David Evans) *hld up: hdwy over 5f out: drvn and outpcd over 1f out: sn 4th: one pce* **10/1**

3331 **5** *1 1/2* **Toboggan's Fire**[21] 5609 3-8-2 **78** NathanEvans(5) 4 72
(Ann Duffield) *trckd ldrs: t.k.h: drvn 2f out: wknd fnl f* **12/1**

134 **6** *1 3/4* **Tukhoom (IRE)**[63] 4080 3-8-12 **83** RoystonFfrench 5 74
(Marcus Tregoning) *hekld up towards rr: hdwy to trck ldrs over 5f out: drvn over 2f out: wknd over 1f out* **8/1**[3]

2m 12.89s (1.69) **Going Correction** +0.20s/f (Good) **6** Ran SP% **112.7**
Speed ratings (Par 105): **101,100,99,96,95 93**
CSF £7.80 TOTE £2.10: £1.60, £1.60; EX 4.40 Trifecta £18.20.
Owner Newsells Park Stud **Bred** Newsells Park Stud **Trained** Newmarket, Suffolk

FOCUS
Race distance increased by 14yds. Another useful handicap, but again not the strongest for the grade, although the winner is potentially smart. It's been rated around the second and third.

6278 MBNA BORINGLY GOOD MAIDEN FILLIES' STKS 1m 2f 75y
4:25 (4:25) (Class 4) 3-Y-O+

£6,225 (£1,864; £932; £466; £233; £117) **Stalls** High

Form RPR

4-33 **1** **Canonbury (IRE)**[9] 6019 3-9-0 75 GrahamGibbons 5 75
(Sir Michael Stoute) *sn trcking ldr: led over 2f out: drvn over 2 l clr 1f out: jst hld on* **6/4**[1]

4 **2** *hd* **Flower Of Love**[24] 5504 3-9-0 0 (t) GrahamLee 3 74
(Simon Crisford) *trckd ldrs: t.k.h: effrt 3f out: 2nd 100yds out: styd on: jst denied* **7/2**[3]

52 **3** *1 1/2* **Casablanca (IRE)**[23] 5550 3-8-11 0 RobHornby(3) 7 71
(Andrew Balding) *trckd ldrs: 2nd over 1f out: kpt on same pce* **3/1**[2]

3525 **4** *2 3/4* **La Celebs Ville (IRE)**[38] 4986 3-8-9 72 (p) AnnaHesketh(5) 1 66
(Tom Dascombe) *trckd ldrs: drvn whn nt clr run over 2f out: one pce* **7/2**[3]

0050 **5** *8* **Farrah's Choice**[16] 3067 4-9-4 41 (t) TimClark(3) 4 50?
(James Grassick) *qckly away: led: hdd over 2f out: wknd fnl f* **125/1**

0- **6** *hd* **Louve Reine (FR)**[279] 8123 3-9-1 0 ow1 DougieCostello 6 50
(Daniel Mark Loughnane) *hld up in rr: pushed along 4f out: lost pl wl over 1f out: sn bhd* **50/1**

2m 13.31s (2.11) **Going Correction** +0.20s/f (Good)
WFA 3 from 4yo 7lb **6** Ran SP% **112.2**
Speed ratings (Par 102): **99,98,97,95,89 88**
CSF £7.19 TOTE £2.20: £1.10, £2.30; EX 7.30 Trifecta £14.20.
Owner Ballymacoll Stud **Bred** Ballymacoll Stud Farm Ltd **Trained** Newmarket, Suffolk

FOCUS
Race distance increased by 14yds. A fair maiden. The third has been rated close to her AW latest.

6279 EMIRATES H'CAP 1m 7f 195y
5:00 (5:00) (Class 3) (0-95,90) 3-Y-O+

£7,470 (£2,236; £1,118; £559; £279; £140) **Stalls** Low

Form RPR

5501 **1** **An Fear Ciuin (IRE)**[16] 5758 5-8-5 **74** (p) CallumRodriguez(7) 3 83
(Richard Ford) *led: sn wl clr: drvn over 2f out: stl abt 4 l clr 1f out: hld on towards fin: all out* **6/1**

31/1 **2** *1/2* **Chocala (IRE)**[20] 5642 6-9-12 **88** WilliamTwiston-Davies 4 96+
(Alan King) *chsd wnr thrght: effrt over 2f out: styd on fnl f: jst hld* **9/4**[1]

4266 **3** *6* **Gabrial's King (IRE)**[8] 6057 7-9-9 **90** AdamMcNamara(5) 2 91
(Richard Fahey) *dwlt: hld up in mid-div: hdwy 7f out: drvn over 2f out: kpt on one pce* **3/1**[2]

2210 **4** *nse* **Life Less Ordinary (IRE)**[23] 5559 4-9-12 **88** TimmyMurphy 6 89
(Jamie Osborne) *trckd ldrs: drvn over 2f out: kpt on one pce* **4/1**[3]

0004 **5** *8* **Wordiness**[20] 5642 8-9-5 **81** GrahamGibbons 7 73
(David Evans) *hld up in rr: hdwy 7f out: effrt over 2f out: wknd and eased last 100yds* **10/1**

213- **6** *15* **Borak (IRE)**[219] 6743 4-9-0 **79** RobHornby(3) 1 53
(Bernard Llewellyn) *hld up in last: drvn 5f out: sn bhd: t.o 3f out* **25/1**

0002 **7** *nk* **Norab (GER)**[40] 4912 5-9-0 **76** (p) GrahamLee 5 49
(Bernard Llewellyn) *sn chsng ldrs: pushed along 6f out: lost pl 2f out: sn bhd* **11/1**

3m 30.05s (2.05) **Going Correction** +0.20s/f (Good) **7** Ran SP% **111.3**
Speed ratings (Par 107): **102,101,98,98,94 87,87**
CSF £18.85 TOTE £7.20: £2.90, £1.70; EX 24.00 Trifecta £80.60.
Owner D M Proos **Bred** Miss S A McManus **Trained** Garstang, Lancs

FOCUS
Race distance increased by 26yds. A useful staying handicap, in which the winner was never headed after being allowed to open up a big lead. The winner has been rated similar to his latest Catterick effort.

6280 HOSPICE OF THE GOOD SHEPHERD H'CAP (FOR GENTLEMAN AMATEUR RIDERS) 7f 122y
5:30 (5:35) (Class 4) (0-80,81) 3-Y-O+

£5,996 (£1,873; £936; £468; £234; £118) **Stalls** Low

Form RPR

0400 **1** **Classic Seniority**[27] 5403 4-11-2 **80** MrBLynn(5) 2 88
(Marjorie Fife) *s.i.s: in rr: hdwy on ins 2f out: sn chsng ldrs: styd on to ld last 50yds: jst hld on* **3/1**[1]

1030 **2** *shd* **Echo Of Lightning**[13] 5866 6-11-2 **75** (p) MrSWalker 6 82
(Brian Ellison) *chsd ldrs: pushed along 3f out: 2nd over 1f out: styd on: jst denied* **4/1**[2]

0321 **3** *shd* **Character Onesie (IRE)**[17] 5750 4-10-10 **74** MrMEnnis(5) 7 81
(Richard Fahey) *mid-div: hdwy over 2f out: w ldrs whn edgd lft 75yds out: styd on: jst hld* **9/1**

2102 **4** *2 1/2* **Ralphy Boy (IRE)**[16] 5779 7-10-11 **75** MrGaryBeaumont(5) 5 76
(Alistair Whillans) *led: drvn abt 4 l clr over 1f out: edgd rt and hdd last 50yds: fdd* **10/1**

223 **5** *shd* **Baltic Prince (IRE)**[14] 5832 6-10-5 **69** MrBJames(5) 11 70
(Tony Carroll) *trckd ldrs: n.m.r 75yds out: one pce* **16/1**

0101 **6** *1 1/2* **Depth Charge (IRE)**[9] 6027 4-11-1 **81** 6ex (vt) MrBenjaminStephens(7) 1 78
(Kristin Stubbs) *hld up in rr: hdwy on ins over 1f out: kpt on: nt rchd ldrs* **6/1**[3]

2611 **7** *2* **Ellaal**[28] 5374 7-11-3 **79** MrHHunt(3) 4 71
(Ruth Carr) *in rr and sn pushed along: hdwy over 3f out: one pce fnl 2f* **7/1**

4006 **8** *5* **Chosen Character (IRE)**[8] 6055 8-11-4 **77** (vt) MrWEasterby 8 56
(Tom Dascombe) *w ldrs: wknd over 1f out* **11/1**

-506 **9** *4 1/2* **Rafaaf (IRE)**[21] 5604 8-10-6 **65** (p) MrAlexEdwards 3 33
(Richard Phillips) *in rr: drvn and sme hdwy 4f out: lost pl over 2f out: sn bhd* **33/1**

0240 **10** *shd* **Faintly (USA)**[34] 5179 5-10-8 **67** (b) MrRBirkett 10 35
(Ruth Carr) *mid-div: hdwy over 3f out: lost pl over 1f out* **14/1**

0105 **11** *20* **Joules**[29] 5336 3-10-5 **74** (t) MrWillPettis(5) 9
(Natalie Lloyd-Beavis) *s.s and wnt lft: in rr: hdwy on outer to chse ldrs over 5f out: hung rt and lost pl 2f out: sn bhd: t.o whn eased clsng stages* **33/1**

1m 36.29s (2.49) **Going Correction** +0.20s/f (Good)
WFA 3 from 4yo+ 5lb **11** Ran SP% **117.6**
Speed ratings (Par 105): **95,94,94,92,92 90,88,83,79,79 59**
CSF £14.53 CT £96.81 TOTE £4.00: £1.40, £1.80, £2.70; EX 19.80 Trifecta £174.50.
Owner Stephen Woodall **Bred** E Cantillon, D Cantillon & A Driver **Trained** Stillington, N Yorks

FOCUS
Race distance increased by 13yds. A competitive handicap for amateur riders and a thrilling finish. The winner has been rated to his best.
T/Plt: £21.60 to a £1 stake. Pool: £57380.41, 1938.24 winning units T/Qpdt: £7.10 to a £1 stake. Pool: £4522.42, 467.0 winning units **Walter Glynn**

6257 DONCASTER (L-H)
Friday, September 9

OFFICIAL GOING: Good (good to firm in places; 8.0)
Wind: Strong against Weather: Cloudy

6281 JAPAN RACING ASSOCIATION SCEPTRE STKS (GROUP 3) (F&M) 7f
1:55 (1:56) (Class 1) 3-Y-O+

£34,026 (£12,900; £6,456; £3,216; £1,614; £810) **Stalls** Centre

Form RPR

1051 **1** **Spangled**[48] 4651 4-9-2 **102** AndreaAtzeni 6 111
(Roger Varian) *hld up: hdwy on inner 2f out: rdn to chal ent fnl f: led last 100 yds: edgd lft and kpt on* **14/1**

0120 **2** nk **Mise En Rose (USA)**[25] 5498 3-8-12 105........................ WilliamBuick 7 108
(Charlie Appleby) *hld up in rr: hdwy over 2f out: chal over 1f out: rdn to take slt ld ent fnl f: sn drvn: hdd and no ex last 100 yds* **14/1**

-010 **3** 2 ¼ **Lumiere**[40] 4926 3-8-12 114.. JamesDoyle 3 102
(Mark Johnston) *trckd ldr: cl up 3f out: led wl over 1f out: sn rdn: hdd and drvn ent fnl f: kpt on same pce* **4/1**[2]

4 2 ½ **Same Jurisdiction (SAF)**[230] 5-9-2 111........................... RyanMoore 5 97
(Ed Dunlop) *trckd ldrs: hdwy over 2f out: rdn over 1f out: sn drvn and kpt on same pce* **14/1**

5433 **5** 2 ¼ **La Rioja**[26] 5436 3-8-12 104.. OisinMurphy 4 89
(Henry Candy) *trckd ldng pair: pushed along over 2f out: rdn wl over 1f out: sn wknd* **12/1**[3]

-546 **6** 3 ¼ **Maggie Pink**[33] 5190 7-9-2 96..................................... AlistairRawlinson 2 82
(Michael Appleby) *hld: pushed along wl over 2f out: rdn and hdd wl over 1f out: sn drvn and grad wknd* **100/1**

1241 **7** 10 **Nemoralia (USA)**[21] 5613 3-9-1 115............................... JamieSpencer 1 67
(Jeremy Noseda) *trckd ldrs: hdwy 3f out: cl up 2f out: rdn wl over 1f out: sn btn and eased fnl f* **4/6**[1]

1m 25.81s (-0.49) **Going Correction** -0.05s/f (Good)
WFA 3 from 4yo+ 4lb **7** Ran SP% **108.7**
Speed ratings (Par 113): **100,99,97,94,91 87,76**
CSF £162.81 TOTE £12.20: £3.80, £4.30; EX 113.90 Trifecta £486.10.
Owner Cheveley Park Stud **Bred** Cheveley Park Stud Ltd **Trained** Newmarket, Suffolk

FOCUS

The ground was changed to good, good to firm in places just before racing and clerk of the course Roderick Duncan said: "The last 2f is good to firm and the first furlong of the straight course is fairly quick." After riding in the opener Jamie Spencer said: "It is good to firm," Andrea Atzeni said: "It is on the quick side," Oisin Murphy said: "It is quicker today, proper good ground", but William Buick said: "It is a bit dead." The false rail that had been in place on the round course for the first two days was removed. This opening Group 3 wasn't particularly competitive according to the market, but in a race run at a modest gallop there was a shock result and it went to an older horse for the first time since 2005. They raced centre-to-nearside and the time was 2.81sec outside standard, though they were racing into a headwind. A length pb from the winner, with a small pb from the runner-up as well.

6282 PEPSI MAX FLYING CHILDERS STKS (GROUP 2) 5f

2:30 (2:30) (Class 1) 2-Y-O

£39,697 (£11,291; £11,291; £3,752; £1,883; £945) **Stalls** Centre

Form RPR

1100 **1** **Ardad (IRE)**[20] 5654 2-9-1 99.. FrankieDettori 10 108
(John Gosden) *hld up in rr: gd hdwy nr stands rail over 2f out: rdn to chal jst over 1f out: drvn ins fnl f: styd on to ld nr fin* **5/1**[2]

2160 **2** ¾ **Legendary Lunch (IRE)**[56] 4352 2-9-1 93........................ RyanMoore 3 105
(Richard Hannon) *hld up in rr: effrt and n.m.r wl over 1f out: sn swtchd markedly lft to outer and rdn: styd on strly fnl f* **25/1**

1231 **2** dht **The Last Lion (IRE)**[6] 6124 2-9-1 103............................. JoeFanning 11 105
(Mark Johnston) *racd towards stands rail: trckd ldrs: hdwy over 2f out: rdn to ld wl over 1f out: drvn and edgd lft ins fnl f: hdd and no ex nr fin* **11/2**[3]

5121 **4** 1 **Afandem (IRE)**[8] 6068 2-9-1 103...................................... WilliamBuick 4 101
(Hugo Palmer) *chsd ldrs: rdn along wl over 1f out: drvn and kpt on fnl f* **5/1**[2]

3310 **5** ½ **Rainbow Mist (IRE)**[22] 5583 2-9-1 95.............................. PJMcDonald 2 100
(Ann Duffield) *trckd ldrs: rdn along and outpcd 2f out: kpt on wl u.p fnl f* **50/1**

1223 **6** ½ **Equimou**[2] 6230 2-8-12 93.. AndreaAtzeni 5 95+
(Robert Eddery) *a.p: ev ch wl over 1f out: sn rdn: drvn and nt qckn wl ins fnl f* **12/1**

1150 **7** ¾ **Prince Of Lir (IRE)**[21] 5614 2-9-1 104............................... LukeMorris 7 95
(Robert Cowell) *chsd ldrs: rdn along 2f out: drvn wl over 1f out: kpt on same pce* **12/1**

3634 **8** hd **Grizzel (IRE)**[8] 6063 2-8-12 92.. SeanLevey 9 91
(Richard Hannon) *towards rr: hdwy 2f out: sn rdn and no imp* **66/1**

2115 **9** ¾ **Tis Marvellous**[19] 5690 2-9-1 0.......................................(t) AdamKirby 6 92+
(Clive Cox) *cl up: rdn and ev ch over 1f out: drvn and wknd ent fnl f* **3/1**[1]

0010 **10** 1 ½ **Yalta (IRE)**[21] 5614 2-9-1 111... JamesDoyle 8 86+
(Mark Johnston) *led: rdn along 2f out: sn hdd & wknd over 1f out* **11/2**[3]

01 **11** hd **Hit The Bid**[20] 5661 2-9-1 0.. LeighRoche 1 86
(D J Bunyan, Ire) *chsd ldrs on outer: rdn along over 1f out: wknd fnl f* **25/1**

59.19s (-1.31) **Going Correction** -0.05s/f (Good) **11** Ran SP% **115.6**
Speed ratings (Par 107): **108,106,106,105,104 103,102,102,100,98 98**
WIN: 5.80 Ardad; PL: 5.60 Legendary Lunch, 1.90 The Last Lion, 2.10 Ardad; EX: A&LL: 58.10, A&TLL 19.40; CSF: A&LL62.79, A&TL 15.52; TF: A&LL&TLL: £444.10, A&TLL&LL: 313.30; TOTE £5.80: £2.10.
Owner Abdullah Saeed Al Naboodah **Bred** Tally-Ho Stud **Trained** Newmarket, Suffolk

FOCUS

A good edition of the Flying Childers Stakes, contested by six scorers at Group level and a couple more successful in Listed company. It's not a race where the winners tend to have much longevity on the racecourse, five of the last seven having been retired at the end of their 2yo seasons. The winner and one of the dead-heaters for second came out of the highest two stalls, racing closest to the stands' rail, and the time was just 1.29sec outside standard. The fifth has been rated in line with his previous efforts at this trip, while this was a big step up from the runner-up and he might be the key to the form.

6283 LADBROKES MALLARD STKS (H'CAP) 1m 6f 132y

3:05 (3:09) (Class 2) (0-110,109) 3-Y-O+**£25,876** (£7,700; £3,848; £1,924) **Stalls** Low

Form RPR

0101 **1** **Wall Of Fire (IRE)**[20] 5653 3-8-6 **102**...............(b) JosephineGordon(3) 10 110+
(Hugo Palmer) *.hld up towards rr: hdwy over 3f out and sn pushed along rdn wl over 1f out: styd on strly ins fnl f to ld nr fin* **5/2**[1]

6205 **2** 1 ¼ **Seamour (IRE)**[20] 5655 5-9-8 **103**.......................................[1] GeorgeBaker 1 110
(Brian Ellison) *t.k.h early: trckd ldrs: smooth hdwy 3f out: led over 1f out: rdn and edgd lft ins fnl f: hdd and no ex nr fin* **8/1**

0044 **3** ½ **First Mohican**[20] 5639 8-8-12 **98**.. HollieDoyle(5) 11 104
(Alan King) *hld up in tch: hdwy 3f out: cl up 2f out: rdn and ev ch over 1f out: drvn and kpt on same pce ins fnl f* **14/1**

0-20 **4** 2 ¾ **Polarisation**[76] 3658 4-9-7 **102**...(p) WilliamBuick 4 104
(Charlie Appleby) *trckd ldrs: hdwy over 4f out: rdn to ld 2f out: drvn: edgd lft and hdd over 1f out: kpt on same pce* **12/1**

4454 **5** shd **Battersea**[20] 5655 5-9-12 **107**.. AndreaAtzeni 8 109
(Roger Varian) *trckd ldrs: hdwy on inner over 2f out: rdn wl over 1f out and ev ch: sn drvn and kpt on same pce* **5/1**[3]

0406 **6** ½ **Stipulate**[20] 5651 7-9-5 **100**... PaulHanagan 3 101
(Brian Ellison) *hld up in rr: hdwy over 3f out: chsd ldrs wl over 1f out: sn no imp* **16/1**

0010 **7** 1 ¾ **Elidor**[20] 5655 6-10-0 **109**.. SilvestreDeSousa 6 108
(Mick Channon) *hld up and bhd: sme hdwy 3f out: rdn along 2f out: n.d* **22/1**

-253 **8** 5 **Fabricate**[20] 5639 4-9-2 **97**..(p) RyanMoore 2 89+
(Michael Bell) *trckd ldrs: effrt 3f out: rdn along over 2f out: sn drvn and wknd over 1f out* **10/3**[2]

-050 **9** 4 ½ **All Talk N No Do (IRE)**[49] 4581 5-8-13 **94**...................(tp) JamesDoyle 7 80
(Seamus Durack) *led 2f: chsd ldr: led again over 3f out: rdn over 2f out: sn hdd and grad wknd* **40/1**

6062 **10** 3 ¼ **Oriental Fox (GER)**[10] 5999 8-9-8 **103**............................... JoeFanning 5 85
(Mark Johnston) *chsd ldrs: effrt and cl up on outer over 4f out: rdn along over 3f out: sn wknd* **20/1**

6520 **11** 1 ½ **Cayirli (FR)**[69] 3913 4-9-7 **102**..[1] AdamKirby 9 82
(Seamus Durack) *prom: led after 2f: rdn along over 4f out: hdd over 3f out and sn wknd* **20/1**

3m 8.92s (1.52) **Going Correction** +0.275s/f (Good)
WFA 3 from 4yo+ 12lb **11** Ran SP% **116.0**
Speed ratings (Par 109): **106,105,105,103,103 103,102,99,97,95 94**
CSF £21.34 CT £234.07 TOTE £3.60: £1.70, £2.10, £3.70; EX 21.70 Trifecta £174.50.
Owner Carmichael Jennings **Bred** B V Sangster **Trained** Newmarket, Suffolk

■ Stewards' Enquiry : Hollie Doyle two-day ban; used her whip above the permitted level (23rd, 25th Sep)

FOCUS

A warm staying handicap featuring four who ran in last month's Ebor plus the Melrose winner. They went an even pace and there was a dramatic finish, with a progressive 3yo emerging on top. Another pb from the runner-up, with the third, fourth and fifth close to form.

6284 250TH DONCASTER CUP (BRITISH CHAMPIONS SERIES) (GROUP 2) 2m 2f

3:40 (3:40) (Class 1) 3-Y-O+

£56,710 (£21,500; £10,760; £5,360; £2,690; £1,350) **Stalls** Low

Form RPR

1033 **1** **Sheikhzayedroad**[43] 4799 7-9-3 113.................................. MartinHarley 4 116
(David Simcock) *trckd ldng pair: hdwy 3f out: chsd ldr 2f out: rdn over 1f out: chal ent fnl f: sn drvn and kpt on wl to ld on line* **10/3**[2]

2361 **2** nse **Quest For More (IRE)**[21] 5612 6-9-3 114.....................(b) GeorgeBaker 7 115
(Roger Charlton) *led and sn clr: pushed along over 2f out: rdn over 1f out: jnd ent fnl f: sn drvn and kpt on gamely: hdd on line* **5/2**[1]

1211 **3** 2 ¼ **St Michel**[10] 5999 3-8-3 93...[1] LukeMorris 8 113
(Sir Mark Prescott Bt) *hld up in rr: hdwy on outer 3f out: rdn to chse ldrs whn hung lft over 1f out: drvn and kpt on fnl f* **6/1**

-545 **4** 4 **Burmese**[85] 3298 4-9-3 110...(p) WilliamBuick 3 108
(Marcus Tregoning) *trckd ldr: clsd up 4f out: rdn along wl over 2f out: drvn over 1f out: kpt on same pce* **14/1**

1114 **5** 1 ½ **Sweet Selection**[23] 5559 4-9-0 87...................................... PJMcDonald 9 103
(Hughie Morrison) *in tch: pushed along over 5f out: rdn over 3f out: sn drvn and btn* **28/1**

200 **6** 3 ¾ **Curbyourenthusiasm (IRE)**[21] 5612 5-9-3 107............ JamieSpencer 1 102
(David Simcock) *trckd ldrs: pushed along over 3f out: sn rdn and wknd* **10/1**

2105 **7** nk **Clever Cookie**[21] 5612 8-9-3 111.................................(p) DanielTudhope 5 102
(Peter Niven) *hld up towards rr: hdwy to chse ldrs 7f out: rdn along over 3f out: sn wknd* **8/1**

0-32 **8** 21 **Clondaw Warrior (IRE)**[27] 5428 9-9-3 108........................ RyanMoore 6 79
(W P Mullins, Ire) *hld up towards rr: pushed along 4f out: sn rdn and btn 3f out* **5/1**[3]

3m 52.97s (-2.03) **Going Correction** +0.275s/f (Good)
WFA 3 from 4yo+ 14lb **8** Ran SP% **112.9**
Speed ratings (Par 115): **115,114,113,112,111 109,109,100**
CSF £11.78 TOTE £3.80: £1.40, £1.30, £1.90; EX 12.10 Trifecta £55.50.
Owner Mohammed Jaber **Bred** Rabbah Bloodstock Limited **Trained** Newmarket, Suffolk

FOCUS

Not the strongest of Doncaster Cups, the likely favourite Mizzou ruled out by an abscess, but it produced a cracking finish. The runner-up set an even sort of gallop. All the first three home hung to their left in the closing stages. The level is a bit fluid, with the third and fifth rated as improving, but the winner, second and fourth fit.

6285 WEATHERBYS STALLION BOOK FLYING SCOTSMAN STKS (LISTED RACE) 7f

4:15 (4:16) (Class 1) 2-Y-O

£17,013 (£6,450; £3,228; £1,608; £807; £405) **Stalls** Centre

Form RPR

111 **1** **Rodaini (USA)**[13] 5877 2-9-0 87................................ SilvestreDeSousa 5 104
(Simon Crisford) *trckd ldrs: swtchd lft to outer and hdwy 2f out: rdn to ld over 1f out and sn edgd rt: drvn and edgd rt ins fnl f: hld on wl* **6/1**[3]

1 **2** shd **Salsabeel (IRE)**[29] 5332 2-9-0 0.. WilliamBuick 7 104
(Charlie Appleby) *t.k.h: trckd ldrs: hdwy over 2f out: rdn to chal and ev ch ent fnl f: sn drvn and kpt on* **7/2**[2]

1 **3** nse **Larchmont Lad (IRE)**[70] 3859 2-9-0 0............................... SeanLevey 6 104
(Richard Hannon) *trckd ldrs: hdwy 2f out: chal over 1f out: rdn and ev ch whn n.m.r ins fnl f: sn drvn and kpt on* **6/1**[3]

6115 **4** 3 ½ **Majoris (IRE)**[20] 5646 2-9-0 95...(t) JamesDoyle 2 95
(Hugo Palmer) *dwlt: sn trcking ldrs: cl up 1/2-way: chal 2f out:. sn rdn and n.m.r 1f out: one pce after* **8/1**

1 **5** ½ **Taamol (IRE)**[76] 3661 2-9-0 0... PaulHanagan 4 93
(Sir Michael Stoute) *t.k.h: hld up: hdwy on outer and cl up over 2f out: rdn along and hld whn n.m.r over 1f out: wknd* **7/4**[1]

512 **6** shd **Bacchus**[62] 4148 2-9-0 89.. JimmyFortune 1 93
(Brian Meehan) *set stdy pce: pushed along and qcknd 3f out: rdn 2f out: hdd and drvn over 1f out: grad wknd* **25/1**

11 **7** 3 ¼ **Senator**[23] 5536 2-9-0 0... RyanMoore 3 90
(Richard Fahey) *t.k.h: cl up on inner: pushed along whn n.m.r wl over 1f out: sn wknd and eased* **6/1**[3]

1m 27.49s (1.19) **Going Correction** -0.05s/f (Good) **7** Ran SP% **116.4**
Speed ratings (Par 103): **91,90,90,86,86 86,82**
CSF £28.07 TOTE £6.50: £2.90, £2.60; EX 38.00 Trifecta £143.20.
Owner Abdullah Saeed Al Naboodah **Bred** Greenwood Lodge Farm **Trained** Newmarket, Suffolk

FOCUS
This looked a fascinating Listed race beforehand with five of the seven runners coming into it unbeaten, but the majority of the field, including the winner, pulled hard early and with so little covering the first three home, the form doesn't look outstanding. However, a few of these are probably capable of better in a truly run race than they were able to show here and winners should still come out of this. They came towards the nearside rail. The fourth and sixth help set the level.

6286 STILL IN THE RUNNING-FM OUTSOURCE CLASSIFIED STKS 1m 2f 60y
4:50 (4:50) (Class 3) 3-Y-O+

£9,337 (£2,796; £1,398; £699; £349; £175) **Stalls** Low

Form RPR
21 **1** **Khairaat (IRE)**[47] 4690 3-8-11 85.................................... PaulHanagan 6 97+
(Sir Michael Stoute) *hld up in tch: hdwy wl over 2f out: chal jst over 1f out and sn rdn: led ins fnl f: drvn out* **6/4**[1]

0043 **2** *1* **Laurence**[41] 4858 4-9-4 85.. AdamKirby 5 92
(Luca Cumani) *trckd ldng pair: hdwy over 3f out: rdn to ld 2f out: drvn ent fnl f: hdd ins fnl f: kpt on* **6/1**

3224 **3** *1 3/4* **Rotherwick (IRE)**[46] 4710 4-9-4 85................................(t) LukeMorris 11 89
(Paul Cole) *towards rr: reminders over 4f out: hdwy 3f out: rdn wl over 1f out: styd on fnl f* **16/1**

1026 **4** *nk* **Banish (USA)**[46] 4710 3-8-11 85.................................(tp) JamesDoyle 2 88
(Hugo Palmer) *dwlt and rr: hdwy on outer 3f out: rdn along 2f out: kpt on u.p fnl f* **16/1**

4315 **5** *1* **Carbon Dating (IRE)**[14] 5837 4-9-4 83........................... PhillipMakin 10 86
(John Patrick Shanahan, Ire) *trckd ldr: cl up 1/2-way: led 3f out: rdn along and hdd 2f out: drvn over 1f out: kpt on same pce* **16/1**

4126 **6** *3/4* **Indulged**[42] 4827 3-8-9 82 ow1.. TomQueally 8 82
(James Fanshawe) *trckd ldrs on outer: hdwy 3f out: sn cl up: rdn along 2f out: drvn and wknd over 1f out* **7/2**[2]

2531 **7** *2 1/4* **Warp Factor (IRE)**[10] 6014 3-8-10 79............................. CliffordLee(7) 9 86
(John Patrick Shanahan, Ire) *led: rdn along and hdd 3f out: sn wknd* **14/1**

51-2 **8** *hd* **Winterval**[126] 2010 4-9-4 82...(b[1]) AndreaAtzeni 7 80
(Roger Varian) *. trckd ldng pair: cl up 3f out: rdn along 2f out: sn drvn and wknd over 1f out* **11/2**[3]

660- **9** *22* **Los Cerritos (SWI)**[296] 7894 4-9-4 84........................... SaleemGolam 4 36
(Sophie Leech) *rr: rdn along over 3f out: sn outpcd and bhd* **100/1**

2m 10.42s (1.02) **Going Correction** +0.275s/f (Good)
WFA 3 from 4yo 7lb **9** Ran SP% **117.2**
Speed ratings (Par 107): **106,105,103,103,102 102,100,100,82**
CSF £11.26 TOTE £2.60: £1.30, £1.90, £3.40; EX 11.80 Trifecta £71.70.
Owner Hamdan Al Maktoum **Bred** Shadwell Estate Company Limited **Trained** Newmarket, Suffolk

FOCUS
Probably a decent race of its type. Eight of the ten runnings of this event have now been won by 3yos. The bare form is ordinary rated around the third.

6287 COOPERS MARQUEES H'CAP 6f 110y
5:25 (5:27) (Class 2) (0-105,102) 3-Y-O+ **£12,938** (£3,850; £1,924; £962) **Stalls** Centre

Form RPR
0214 **1** **Normandy Barriere (IRE)**[6] 6112 4-8-13 **91**.................. AndreaAtzeni 5 103
(Nigel Tinkler) *.in tch: hdwy to chse ldrs 2f out: rdn over 1f out: chal ins fnl f: drvn and kpt on wl to ld towards fin* **11/4**[1]

0645 **2** *1/2* **Miracle Of Medinah**[12] 5934 5-8-6 **91**........................ LuluStanford(7) 9 101
(Mark Usher) *chsd ldrs: hdwy 2f out: rdn to ld 11/2f out: jnd and drvn ins fnl f: hdd and no ex towards fin* **16/1**

2613 **3** *2 3/4* **Get Knotted (IRE)**[27] 5389 4-9-4 **96**.........................(p) PaulMulrennan 10 97
(Michael Dods) *prom: cl up over 2f out: sn rdn and edgd lft: kpt on same pce* **9/2**[2]

5304 **4** *2* **Nuno Tristan (USA)**[13] 5871 4-9-2 **94**........................... JamieSpencer 7 89
(Richard Fahey) *towards rr: hdwy wl o ver 2f out: rdn wl over 1f out: kpt on: nt rch ldrs* **11/4**[1]

0040 **5** *3* **Fox Trotter (IRE)**[84] 3358 4-9-2 **94**................................. JimmyFortune 3 80
(Brian Meehan) *s.i.s and rr tl styd on fnl 2f* **20/1**

5300 **6** *1 1/2* **Lexington Times (IRE)**[125] 2033 4-9-2 **94**.................... JamesSullivan 2 76
(Ruth Carr) *dwlt and towards rr: hdwy over 2f out: sn rdn and no imp* **66/1**

6503 **7** *2 1/2* **Burnt Sugar (IRE)**[3] 6207 4-9-5 **102**...........................(bt) HollieDoyle(5) 1 76
(Richard Hannon) *prom: cl up 1/2-way: rdn to ld and edgd rt 2f out: sn drvn: hdd 11/2f out and sn wknd* **12/1**

032 **8** *2 3/4* **Northgate Lad (IRE)**[48] 4644 4-9-0 **92**............................... SeanLevey 6 58
(Brian Ellison) *cl up: rdn along whn n.m.r and hmpd 2f out: sn wknd* **10/1**

006 **9** *3/4* **Shore Step (IRE)**[14] 5825 6-8-12 **90**........................ SilvestreDeSousa 8 54
(Mick Channon) *led: rdn along whn hdd and hmpd 2f out: sn wknd* **8/1**[3]

036- **10** *8* **Sixth Sense (IRE)**[349] 6752 3-9-4 **100**............................ WilliamBuick 4 38
(Mark Johnston) *in tch: rdn along wl over 2f out: sn wknd* **20/1**

1m 17.68s (-2.22) **Going Correction** -0.05s/f (Good)
WFA 3 from 4yo+ 2lb **10** Ran SP% **116.3**
Speed ratings (Par 109): **110,109,106,104,100 98,96,92,92,82**
CSF £49.51 CT £199.70 TOTE £4.30: £1.50, £4.40, £1.70; EX 61.40 Trifecta £252.90.
Owner Eddie Carswell **Bred** Tinnakill Bloodstock & L Cantillon **Trained** Langton, N Yorks

FOCUS
A warm handicap to end with. They went a decent pace and the field finished well spread out. The winner continues to progress.
T/Plt: £1,078.70 to a £1 stake. Pool: £186070.33, 125.91 winning units T/Qpdt: £13.70 to a £1 stake. Pool: £19477.36, 1046.59 winning units **Joe Rowntree**

6059 SALISBURY (R-H)
Friday, September 9

OFFICIAL GOING: Good to soft (good in places; 7.7)
Wind: quite strong against Weather: showers

6288 BOOKER WHOLESALE MEDIAN AUCTION MAIDEN STKS 1m
4:10 (4:13) (Class 5) 2-Y-O **£3,557** (£1,058; £529; £264) **Stalls** Low

Form RPR
05 **1** **Viking Hoard (IRE)**[23] 5549 2-9-5 0............................... SamHitchcott 4 81
(Harry Dunlop) *mde all: kpt on strly: rdn out* **16/1**

2334 **2** *1* **Prerogative (IRE)**[11] 5959 2-9-5 82............................... TomMarquand 3 80
(Richard Hannon) *trckd ldrs: nt clrest of runs over 2f out: rdn over 1f: kpt on to go 2nd ins fnl f but a being hld by wnr* **2/1**[1]

3 *nk* **See Of Rome** 2-9-0 0.. GeorgeWood(5) 1 78
(Richard Hughes) *trckd ldrs: rdn to chal for 2nd over 1f out: kpt on same pce fnl f* **16/1**

0 **4** *8* **Harry Beau**[14] 5820 2-9-5 0... KieranO'Neill 10 61
(Richard Hannon) *trckd wnr: rdn over 2f out: fdd ins fnl f* **12/1**

0 **5** *1* **Red Caravel (IRE)**[11] 5959 2-8-12 0.................... StephenCummins(7) 11 59
(Richard Hughes) *mid-div: hdwy over 3f out: effrt over 2f out: fdd fnl f* **25/1**

6 *1 3/4* **Atkinson Grimshaw (FR)** 2-9-5 0.................................. DannyBrock 5 55
(Andrew Balding) *s.i.s: sn pushed along in last pair: stdy prog fnl 2f but nvr threatened to get involved* **9/2**[3]

00 **7** *1 1/2* **Maysonri**[34] 5166 2-9-2 0...(p) LouisSteward(3) 6 51
(Mark Hoad) *towards rr: rdn 3f out: nvr threatened to get on terms* **250/1**

0 **8** *nk* **Netley Abbey**[51] 4533 2-9-5 0... JohnFahy 7 51
(Harry Dunlop) *a towards rr* **50/1**

9 *3 1/4* **Peace Telegram** 2-9-0 0..[1] PaddyPilley(5) 2 44
(Michael Bell) *sn struggling: a in rr* **16/1**

30 **10** *2 1/4* **Dark Destroyer (IRE)**[22] 5583 2-9-5 0...................................... JFEgan 8 39
(Joseph Tuite) *mid-div: hdwy over 3f out: rdn to chse ldrs over 2f out: wknd over 1f out* **11/4**[2]

11 *12* **Thomas Crown (IRE)** 2-9-5 0... MartinLane 9 12
(James Tate) *chsd ldrs tl wknd over 3f out* **14/1**

1m 45.5s (2.00) **Going Correction** +0.20s/f (Good) **11** Ran SP% **116.4**
Speed ratings (Par 95): **98,97,96,88,87 85,84,84,80,78 66**
CSF £47.46 TOTE £17.30: £3.50, £1.20, £3.30; EX 66.60 Trifecta £581.90.
Owner Be Hopeful Partnership **Bred** P Monahan **Trained** Lambourn, Berks

FOCUS
This was run in a heavy rain shower in steadily worsening underfoot conditions. Something of an upset in this opener with the winner making every yard against the far rail. The first three came clear. A big step up from the winner, with the runner-up helping to set the level.

6289 BATHWICK CAR & VAN HIRE NURSERY H'CAP 6f 212y
4:45 (4:47) (Class 5) (0-75,74) 2-Y-O **£3,408** (£1,006; £503) **Stalls** Centre

Form RPR
0125 **1** **Fastnet Spin (IRE)**[21] 5594 2-9-3 **70**.......................................(v[1]) JFEgan 9 76
(David Evans) *in tch: rdn and hdwy over 3f out: chal over 1f out: led ins fnl f: r.o wl* **5/1**[2]

0230 **2** *2* **Mums The Word**[15] 5794 2-9-6 **73**............................... KieranO'Neill 8 74
(Richard Hannon) *hld up: pushed along over 3f out: hdwy over 2f out: edgd rt u.p over 1f out: r.o to go 2nd fnl 120yds: no threat to wnr* **11/1**

4233 **3** *2* **Singing Sands (IRE)**[21] 5594 2-9-7 **74**......................... OisinMurphy 7 70
(Ralph Beckett) *racd keenly: sn led: rdn over 1f out: hdd ins fnl f: no ex fnl 120yds* **5/2**[1]

031 **4** *1 1/2* **Let's Be Happy (IRE)**[15] 5809 2-9-2 **69**............................ ShaneKelly 4 61
(Richard Hughes) *trckd ldrs: rdn over 2f out: kpt on fnl f but nt pce to get on terms* **12/1**

0520 **5** *hd* **Famous Dynasty (IRE)**[17] 5740 2-9-2 **69**.......................... MartinLane 3 61
(Michael Blanshard) *pressed ldr: rdn over 2f out: hld whn sltly hmpd over 1f out: kpt on same pce* **9/1**

540 **6** *2 3/4* **Highland Dream (IRE)**[39] 4951 2-8-9 **62**.............................. JohnFahy 2 47
(Clive Cox) *in tch: hdwy over 2f out: sn rdn: fdd fnl f* **18/1**

434 **7** *nk* **Glory Of Paris (IRE)**[32] 5229 2-9-0 **72**...................... GeorgeWood(5) 10 56
(Rod Millman) *in tch: struggling 3f out: sn btn* **7/1**

444 **8** *2 1/4* **Neptunes Secret**[19] 5670 2-9-3 **70**............................... FergusSweeney 6 49
(Sylvester Kirk) *racd keenly: trckd ldrs: rdn 2f out: sn edgd rt and hld: one pce fnl f* **11/2**[3]

6044 **9** *2 1/4* **Feel The Vibes**[15] 5796 2-9-2 **69**................................... TomMarquand 5 42
(Richard Hannon) *pressed ldr: rdn over 2f out: wknd over 1f out* **17/2**

1m 29.72s (1.12) **Going Correction** +0.20s/f (Good) **9** Ran SP% **114.9**
Speed ratings (Par 95): **101,98,96,94,94 91,91,88,85**
CSF £57.94 CT £168.51 TOTE £5.30: £1.30, £4.30, £1.30; EX 54.60 Trifecta £294.90.
Owner Dukes Head Racing **Bred** Rockhart Trading Ltd **Trained** Pandy, Monmouths

FOCUS
An informative nursery, though, it was run on ground significantly softer than would have been anticipated earlier in the day. The runner-up helps set the level.

6290 BATHWICK TYRES H'CAP (DIV I) 6f
5:20 (5:20) (Class 6) (0-65,65) 3-Y-O **£2,911** (£866; £432; £216) **Stalls** Low

Form RPR
2320 **1** **Harmony Bay (IRE)**[11] 5954 3-9-7 **65**............................ TomMarquand 3 75
(Sylvester Kirk) *racd stands' side tl swtchd to center 3f out: in tch: hdwy over 3f out: rdn 2f out: led jst ins fnl f: r.o strly* **5/1**[3]

3000 **2** *3 1/4* **Nidnod**[18] 5720 3-8-7 **51** oh5... DannyBrock 2 51
(John Bridger) *racd stands' side tl swtchd to center 3f out: chsd ldr: rdn to ld jst over 1f out: hdd jst ins fnl f: kpt on but nt pce of wnr* **16/1**

4041 **3** *1/2* **Intimately**[29] 5338 3-8-5 **54**.. GeorgeWood(5) 4 53
(Jonathan Portman) *racd stands' side tl swtchd to center 3f out: s.i.s: sn mid-div: rdn 2f out: no imp tl r.o wl fnl f: clsng qckly on 2nd nring fin* **7/1**

4055 **4** *1* **Lucky Louie**[16] 5769 3-9-6 **64**...(v) FergusSweeney 1 60
(Roger Teal) *racd alone on far side: sn led and clr: swtchd to center over 3f out: rdn over 2f out: hdd jst over 1f out: no ex* **4/1**[2]

3-55 **5** *1* **Fashionable Spirit (IRE)**[4] 6190 3-9-5 **63**........................ JimCrowley 11 56
(Amanda Perrett) *racd stands' side: mid-div: rdn over 2f out: no imp tl r.o fnl f* **7/2**[1]

0400 **6** *1 1/4* **Guilded Rock**[35] 5126 3-8-7 **51** oh1................................(t) WilliamCarson 6 40
(Stuart Kittow) *racd stands' side tl swtchd to center 3f out: in tch: rdn over 2f out: sn one pce* **25/1**

0600 **7** *3/4* **Magic Strike (IRE)**[8] 6051 3-9-2 **60**.....................................(v) JohnFahy 5 47
(Clive Cox) *racd stands' side: chsd ldr: rdn over 2f out: wknd over 1f out* **9/1**

445 **8** *1/2* **Wensara Dream**[17] 5748 3-8-11 **55**............................... OisinMurphy 10 40
(Andrew Balding) *racd stands' side: last pair: rdn 2f out: little imp* **12/1**

045 **9** *hd* **Zebedee's Girl (IRE)**[22] 5571 3-8-13 **57**.. JFEgan 7 41
(David Evans) *racd stands' side: rdn over 2f out: nvr bttr than mid-div* **11/1**

0436 **10** *1 1/2* **Guapo Bay**[32] 5248 3-8-0 **51** oh2.......................................(b) TinaSmith(7) 9 31
(Richard Hannon) *awkward and hmpd leaving stalls: racd stands' side tl swtchd to center 3f out: mid-div: rdn to chse ldrs over 2f out: wknd ins fnl f* **18/1**

060 **11** *6* **Back To Love (CAN)**[16] 5766 3-8-7 **51** oh6.................... SamHitchcott 8 13
(Mark Gillard) *fly-leapt leaving stalls: racd stands' side: a towards rr* **66/1**

1m 15.38s (0.58) **Going Correction** +0.20s/f (Good) **11** Ran SP% **113.9**
Speed ratings (Par 99): **104,99,99,97,96 94,93,93,92,90 82**
CSF £79.22 CT £429.50 TOTE £5.30: £1.80, £5.50, £2.30; EX 94.00 Trifecta £585.70.
Owner M Nicolson & A Wilson **Bred** Brian Miller **Trained** Upper Lambourn, Berks

FOCUS
A moderate handicap, won decisively by the largely consistent top weight. The runner-up has been rated to the balance of her form, with the third close to his recent win.

6291 BATHWICK TYRES H'CAP (DIV II) 6f
5:50 (5:50) (Class 6) (0-65,65) 3-Y-O £2,911 (£866; £432; £216) Stalls Low

Form RPR
0032 1 **Fleeting Dream (IRE)**[20] 5626 3-9-2 **60**....................(b) PatCosgrave 3 66
(William Haggas) *in tch: swtchd rt and hdwy 3f out: led 2f out: drifted lft: r.o wl: rdn out* **11/4**[1]
000 2 2 **Flying Sakhee**[34] 5168 3-8-7 **51** oh5.................... DannyBrock 7 51
(John Bridger) *hld up: hdwy over 1f out: chalng for 2nd whn carried sltly lft ins fnl f: kpt on but nt pce of wnr fnl 120yds* **40/1**
4136 3 nk **Cooperess**[36] 5076 3-8-12 **56**....................(bt) KieranO'Neill 6 55
(Ali Stronge) *chsd ldrs: rdn 3f out: ev ch 2f out: cl 2nd whn briefly hmpd ins fnl f: no ex fnl 100yds* **6/1**[3]
2160 4 2 **Shahaama**[29] 5330 3-9-5 **63**.................... JFEgan 2 56
(Mick Channon) *stdd s: hdwy over 2f out: travelling wl enough and cl up whn nt clr run ent fnl f: kpt on but nt pce to get on terms after* **12/1**
0623 5 1 3/4 **Guanabara Bay (IRE)**[14] 5827 3-9-7 **65**.................... TomMarquand 9 53
(Martyn Meade) *trckd ldrs: rdn and edgd rt 2f out: one pce fnl f* **11/4**[1]
0144 6 2 1/2 **Baz's Boy**[11] 5954 3-8-2 **51** oh2.................... MitchGodwin(5) 4 31
(John Flint) *prom: led briefly over 2f out: sn rdn: wknd ins fnl f* **11/2**[2]
000 7 9 **Show Legend**[42] 4835 3-9-1 **62**....................(v[1]) LouisSteward(3) 10 15
(Michael Bell) *prom: led over 3f out: sn rdn: hdd over 2f out: wknd over 1f out* **9/1**
2004 8 13 **Silver Springs (IRE)**[22] 5570 3-8-11 **55**.................... JimCrowley 5
(David Evans) *led tl over 3f out: rdn over 2f out: sn wknd* **10/1**
1m 15.56s (0.76) **Going Correction** +0.20s/f (Good) 8 Ran SP% **112.2**
Speed ratings (Par 99): **102,99,98,96,93 90,78,61**
CSF £110.32 CT £610.51 TOTE £3.30: £1.30, £7.50, £2.30; EX 128.30 Trifecta £837.60.
Owner Lordship Stud **Bred** Knocktoran Stud & Kildaragh Stud **Trained** Newmarket, Suffolk
■ Stewards' Enquiry : Danny Brock caution; careless riding

FOCUS
This looked the strongest of the two divisions on paper, though it was steadily run and was marginally slower on the clock. Another step forward from the winner, with the third a bit below her form this year over further.

6292 EBF STALLIONS BREEDING WINNERS FILLIES' NURSERY H'CAP 6f
6:20 (6:20) (Class 3) (0-90,86) 2-Y-O £9,056 (£2,695; £1,346; £673) Stalls Low

Form RPR
1424 1 **Shamsaya (IRE)**[24] 5510 2-9-4 **83**.................... JimCrowley 7 93
(Simon Crisford) *trckd ldrs: shkn up to ld ent fnl f: qcknd clr fnl 140yds: readily* **10/1**
4102 2 2 1/4 **Jumping Around (IRE)**[12] 5931 2-8-13 **78**.................... PatCosgrave 2 81
(William Haggas) *trckd ldr: led wl over 2f out: rdn and hdd ent fnl f: kpt on but nt pce of wnr fnl 140yds* **11/4**[1]
14 3 3/4 **Many A Tale**[15] 5794 2-8-12 **77**.................... KieranO'Neill 6 78
(Ismail Mohammed) *hld up in tch: hdwy 2f out: ch whn rdn ent fnl f: kpt on same pce* **7/2**[2]
1050 4 shd **Texas Katie**[10] 5998 2-8-4 **69**.................... JFEgan 9 69
(Mick Channon) *hld up: hdwy over 1f out: rdn in cl 4th jst over 1f out: kpt on same pce fnl f* **7/1**
4110 5 2 3/4 **Turanga Leela**[23] 5560 2-8-13 **78**.................... ShaneKelly 4 70
(Ian Williams) *trckd ldrs: rdn 2f out: sn one pce* **10/1**
1212 6 1 **Groupie**[63] 4091 2-9-2 **86**.................... MeganNicholls(5) 5 75
(Richard Hannon) *trckd ldrs: rdn and ev ch over 1f out: wknd ent fnl f* **8/1**
1 7 1 **Santafiora**[79] 3511 2-8-8 **78**.................... GeorgeWood(5) 3 64
(Roger Charlton) *plld hrd: sn led: hdd wl over 2f out: wknd over 1 out* **13/2**[3]
242 8 3/4 **Prufrock (IRE)**[16] 5772 2-8-5 **70**.................... TomMarquand 1 54
(David Simcock) *hld up: rdn and hdwy over 2f out: wknd over 1f out* **9/1**
1m 16.32s (1.52) **Going Correction** +0.20s/f (Good) 8 Ran SP% **114.0**
Speed ratings (Par 96): **97,94,93,92,89 87,86,85**
CSF £37.54 CT £117.87 TOTE £10.10: £3.10, £1.30, £1.30; EX 36.20 Trifecta £255.10.
Owner Saeed H Al Tayer **Bred** Rabbah Bloodstock Limited **Trained** Newmarket, Suffolk

FOCUS
It's unlikely this was the strongest 0-90 ever run but it featured some largely unexposed fillies' and produced a clear-cut winner. The runner-up has been rated to her latest form.

6293 BATHWICK TYRES "PERSIAN PUNCH" CONDITIONS STKS 1m 6f 21y
6:50 (6:50) (Class 2) 3-Y-O+ £12,450 (£3,728; £1,864; £932; £466) Stalls Far side

Form RPR
0000 1 **Fun Mac (GER)**[20] 5655 5-9-2 **100**....................(t) JimCrowley 4 107
(Hughie Morrison) *trckd ldrs: carried to stands' side rails fr over 2f out: led over 1f out: drifted rt: styd on strly* **13/8**[1]
3602 2 2 **Vive Ma Fille (GER)**[13] 5872 4-8-11 **92**.................... JFEgan 6 99
(Mark Johnston) *trckd ldr: rdn to chal over 3f out: ldng whn drifted to stands side rails over 2f out: hdd over 1f out: sn hld by wnr but styd on for clr 2nd* **3/1**[2]
-063 3 10 **Highland Castle**[13] 5879 8-9-2 **90**....................(t) ShaneKelly 1 91
(David Elsworth) *hld up 5th: pushed along 5f out: racd far side and rdn over 3f out: swtchd to center over 2f out: styd on into 3rd ins fnl f: nvr threatened front pair* **6/1**
-603 4 1 1/2 **Mr Singh**[13] 5872 4-9-2 **100**....................(b) RobertHavlin 5 89
(John Gosden) *hld up 4th: hdwy over 3f out where racd center to far side: rdn to chse ldng pair over 2f out: fdd fnl f* **7/2**[3]
5006 5 7 **Glaring**[13] 5872 5-9-2 **97**.................... OisinMurphy 3 80
(Amanda Perrett) *led: racd far side fr 3f out: rdn wl over 2f out: sn hdd: wknd jst over 1f out* **8/1**
3m 4.29s (-3.11) **Going Correction** +0.025s/f (Good) 5 Ran SP% **110.7**
Speed ratings (Par 109): **109,107,102,101,97**
CSF £6.79 TOTE £2.60: £1.30, £2.30; EX 6.50 Trifecta £24.40.
Owner Mrs Angela McAlpine & Partners **Bred** Gestut Gorlsdorf **Trained** East Ilsley, Berks

FOCUS
This lacked the strength of some past renewals, though was run at a good pace and represented a proper staying test. They finished well spaced out. The runner-up has been rated to her latest effort.

6294 EBF STALLIONS MERCEDES-BENZ OF SALISBURY MAIDEN STKS 1m 1f 198y
7:20 (7:20) (Class 5) 3-Y-O £4,204 (£1,251; £625; £312) Stalls Low

Form RPR
3253 1 **Burguillos**[52] 4480 3-9-2 **80**.................... LouisSteward(3) 8 84
(Alan King) *mid-div: hdwy 2f out: rdn over 1f out: str run to ld fnl 120yds: styd on strly* **5/2**[2]
2 1 1/2 **Rock'n Gold** 3-9-5 **0**.................... PatCosgrave 2 81
(Luca Cumani) *trckd ldrs: rdn to ld 2f out: edgd lft and hdd ins fnl f: styd on but no ex* **16/1**
05-0 3 2 3/4 **Silver Ghost (IRE)**[48] 4657 3-9-0 **0**.................... PaddyPilley(5) 3 76
(Geoffrey Deacon) *trckd ldr: chal 3f out: rdn and ev ch over 1f out: styd on same pce fnl f* **80/1**
23 4 3/4 **New World Power (JPN)**[90] 3160 3-9-5 **0**.................... OisinMurphy 11 74
(Roger Varian) *hld up towards rr: hdwy 3f out: sn rdn: styd on same pce fnl 2f* **5/4**[1]
2 5 1 **Capton**[25] 5486 3-9-5 **0**.................... FergusSweeney 10 72
(Henry Candy) *trckd ldrs: rdn over 2f out: styd on same pce* **12/1**
2250 6 2 **Skeaping**[13] 5874 3-9-5 **78**.................... TomMarquand 1 68
(Richard Hannon) *led: rdn and hdd 2f out: kpt on tl no ex ins fnl f* **10/1**
4 7 4 1/2 **Transmitting**[25] 5486 3-9-5 **0**.................... JimCrowley 12 59
(Sir Michael Stoute) *hld up: rdn and sme prog into midfield over 2f out: nvr threatened: wknd fnl f* **6/1**[3]
5 8 3/4 **Threediamondrings**[7] 6073 3-9-5 **0**.................... RyanClark 6 58
(Brendan Powell) *s.i.s: sn mid-div: rdn over 2f out: nt pce to get on terms: wknd ent fnl f* **100/1**
6 9 2 1/2 **Rattle On**[10] 5996 3-9-5 **0**.................... SamHitchcott 4 53
(Jim Boyle) *a towards rr* **66/1**
10 nse **Southern States**[142] 3-9-5 **0**.................... RobertHavlin 9 52
(Lydia Richards) *s.i.s: a towards rr* **66/1**
4453 11 8 **Pc Dixon**[9] 6031 3-9-5 **73**.................... JFEgan 7 36
(Mick Channon) *racd keenly: mid-div: effrt 3f out: wknd 2f out* **33/1**
2m 13.3s (3.40) **Going Correction** +0.025s/f (Good) 11 Ran SP% **118.1**
Speed ratings (Par 101): **87,85,83,83,82 80,77,76,74,74 67**
CSF £40.80 TOTE £3.40: £1.10, £4.70, £3.30; EX 55.90 Trifecta £3092.60.
Owner Hunscote Stud **Bred** Minster Stud And Mrs H Dalgety **Trained** Barbury Castle, Wilts

FOCUS
Few could be seriously considered in this maiden. Burguillos, who set the standard on figures, opened his account. Muddling form, with the improving third the key.
T/Plt: £31.10 to a £1 stake. Pool: £54,876.01 - 1,285.46 winning tickets T/Qpdt: £11.80 to a £1 stake. Pool: £6,941.44 - 432.50 winning tickets **Tim Mitchell**

5644 SANDOWN (R-H)
Friday, September 9

OFFICIAL GOING: Good (good to firm in places)
Wind: Fresh, against Weather: Cloudy, warm

6295 BRITISH STALLION STUDS EBF MAIDEN STKS 5f 6y
1:45 (1:52) (Class 5) 2-Y-O £3,881 (£1,155; £577; £288) Stalls Low

Form RPR
5322 1 **Big Lachie**[10] 6010 2-9-5 **71**.................... PatCosgrave 6 75
(Jamie Osborne) *t.k.h: hld up in midfield on inner: rdn and prog 2f out: plld out fnl f: r.o to ld last 120yds* **5/1**[3]
2 1 **Commander Cole** 2-9-5 **0**.................... WilliamCarson 2 71
(Saeed bin Suroor) *dwlt: sn trckd ldrs on inner: wnt 2nd 2f out: led over 1f out: shkn up and edgd lft fnl f: hdd and outpcd last 120yds* **10/3**[1]
2323 3 2 1/4 **Stanhope**[12] 5931 2-9-0 **80**.................... CharlieBennett(5) 9 63+
(Mick Quinn) *mostly in last quartet: rdn 2f out: nt clrest of runs but prog over 1f out: r.o fnl f to take 3rd last stride* **7/2**[2]
4 shd **Mississippi Miss** 2-9-0 **0**.................... RobertHavlin 5 58
(Dr Jon Scargill) *fractious preliminaries: chsd ldrs: rdn 2f out: prog to take 3rd briefly nr fin: kpt on* **66/1**
6 5 nk **Eskimo Bay (IRE)**[7] 6071 2-9-5 **0**.................... TedDurcan 4 62
(Clive Cox) *pressed ldrs: rdn 2f out: lost pl over 1f out: one pce after* **7/2**[2]
56 6 nk **Polly's Angels (IRE)**[9] 6016 2-9-0 **0**.................... ShaneKelly 1 56
(Richard Hughes) *led against rail: rdn and hdd over 1f out: wknd ins fnl f* **5/1**[3]
7 3/4 **Dagonet (IRE)** 2-9-5 **0**.................... JimCrowley 10 58
(Roger Charlton) *racd on outer: in rr: effrt and rdn 2f out: no prog over 1f out* **14/1**
50 8 1 1/4 **Wild Approach (IRE)**[20] 5631 2-9-2 **0**.................... EoinWalsh(3) 8 54
(Robert Cowell) *mostly chsd ldr to 2f out: wknd qckly fnl f* **33/1**
0 9 1/2 **Orange Gin (IRE)**[13] 5890 2-9-5 **0**.................... DaneO'Neill 3 52
(Roger Charlton) *s.i.s: a wl in rr: rdn and no prog 2f out* **20/1**
4 10 nk **Geraldine (GER)**[88] 3216 2-9-0 **0**.................... HarryBentley 7 50
(Stuart Williams) *a in rr: rdn and no prog 2f out* **16/1**
11 23 **Ballysampson** 2-9-5 **0**.................... RobertWinston 12
(Roger Teal) *dwlt and wnt lft s: spd and w ldrs 2f: wknd rapidly: t.o* **66/1**
3 U **Luxford**[31] 5258 2-9-0 **0**.................... KierenFox 11
(John Best) *racd wd: in rr: no ch whn hung rt fr over 1f out: poor 11th whn jinked and uns rdr 100yds out* **50/1**
1m 2.78s (1.18) **Going Correction** +0.20s/f (Good) 12 Ran SP% **126.1**
Speed ratings (Par 95): **98,96,92,92,92 91,90,88,87,87 50,**
CSF £22.82 TOTE £5.40: £1.50, £1.50, £1.40; EX 26.10 Trifecta £73.40.
Owner A F Tait **Bred** Mrs C Lloyd **Trained** Upper Lambourn, Berks

FOCUS
The rail was at its innermost configuration other than being 2yds out around the home bend, adding 10yds to round course distances. The bare form of this opening maiden is probably just fair, but there were some promising performances.

6296 SHEPHERD COMPELLO INSURANCE BROKERS H'CAP 5f 6y
2:20 (2:26) (Class 5) (0-75,74) 3-Y-O+ £3,234 (£962; £481; £240) Stalls Low

Form RPR
530 1 **Pensax Lad (IRE)**[27] 5408 5-9-6 **73**.................... RobertWinston 10 79
(Ronald Harris) *hld up in midfield: prog over 1f out: drvn between rivals to ld ins fnl f: hrd pressed after: jst hld on* **7/1**
0152 2 hd **Jaarih (IRE)**[14] 5855 4-9-5 **72**....................(b) PatCosgrave 3 77
(Conor Dore) *s.i.s: sn in tch in midfield: rdn and clsd over 1f out: tk 2nd ins fnl f and str chal last 100yds: jst denied* **8/1**
3112 3 3/4 **John Joiner**[39] 4952 4-8-5 **63**.................... CharlieBennett(5) 11 65
(Peter Hedger) *s.i.s: hld up in last pair and off the pce: prog on outer jst over 1f out: rdn and r.o fnl f to take 3rd last strides* **8/1**
0-05 4 1/2 **Angelito**[65] 3995 7-8-8 **64**.................... EoinWalsh(3) 8 65
(Tony Newcombe) *dwlt and stdd s: hld up in last pair and off the pce: pushed along 1/2-way: prog and reminder 1f out: pushed along and r.o wl last 100yds: nrst fin but nvr cl enough to threaten* **16/1**
6024 5 nse **Billyoakes (IRE)**[19] 5673 4-9-5 **72**.................... AdamBeschizza 1 72
(Charlie Wallis) *fast away: led against rail: rdn over 1f out: hdd ins fnl f: lost pls last 100yds* **11/2**[2]

0633 **6** *hd* **Quick March**[38] 4990 3-9-5 **73** HarryBentley 4 73
(Roger Charlton) *trckd ldrs towards outer: clsd over 1f out: rdn to chal jst ins fnl f: nt qckn and lost pls last 100yds* **7/2**[1]

0601 **7** *1 1/4* **Silverrica (IRE)**[9] 6017 6-9-2 **74** GeorgiaCox(5) 9 69
(Malcolm Saunders) *chsd ldrs on outer: rdn over 2f out: nt qckn over 1f out: wl hld fnl f* **6/1**[3]

0330 **8** *1* **Ask The Guru**[12] 5928 6-8-7 **60** oh1 (p) KierenFox 2 52
(Michael Attwater) *prom on inner: rdn to chse ldr 2f out: tried to chal 1f out: wknd last 150yds* **6/1**[3]

6-06 **9** *3/4* **Dishy Guru**[23] 5546 7-8-12 **65** DaneO'Neill 5 54
(Michael Blanshard) *slowly away: sn in tch: rdn jst over 2f out: tried to make prog over 1f out: no hdwy fnl f* **33/1**

335 **10** *1 3/4* **Swanton Blue (IRE)**[42] 4820 3-8-13 **67** JimCrowley 7 50
(Ed de Giles) *pressed ldr to 2f out: lost pl u.p jst over 1f out: wknd ins fnl f* **16/1**

1m 2.09s (0.49) **Going Correction** +0.20s/f (Good)
WFA 3 from 4yo+ 1lb **10** Ran SP% **115.6**
Speed ratings (Par 103): **104,103,102,101,101 101,99,97,96,93**
CSF £61.30 CT £467.29 TOTE £8.40: £2.40, £2.70, £2.40; EX 72.70 Trifecta £648.10.
Owner S & A Mares **Bred** Seamus And James McMullan **Trained** Earlswood, Monmouths

FOCUS
A fair sprint handicap. The winner has been rated to his turf best.

6297 BREEDERS BACKING RACING EBF MAIDEN STKS 1m 14y
2:55 (2:57) (Class 5) 2-Y-O **£3,881** (£1,155; £577; £288) **Stalls** Low

Form RPR

1 **The Grape Escape (IRE)** 2-9-5 0 PatDobbs 5 80+
(Richard Hannon) *trckd ldrs: smooth prog 2f out and sn in 2nd: pushed into ld 1f out: rdn and grad asserted last 75yds* **11/4**[2]

0 **2** *nk* **Good Craic**[71] 3813 2-9-5 0 RobertHavlin 6 79
(John Gosden) *led and dictated stdy pce: shkn up 2f out: hdd 1f out: fought on wl and pressed wnr tl no ex nr fin* **9/4**[1]

3 *2* **Mister Manduro (FR)** 2-9-5 0 DaneO'Neill 7 74+
(Mark Johnston) *slowly away and awkward s: rcvrd to chse ldrs but trapped out wd: rdn 2f out: drvn into 3rd over 1f out: kpt on same pce* **8/1**

0 **4** *3/4* **Chaparrachik (IRE)**[63] 4103 2-9-5 0 FMBerry 8 72
(Amanda Perrett) *awkward s: t.k.h and trckd ldr: shkn up 2f out: sn lost 2nd and one pce* **7/1**

0 **5** *1/2* **City Limits**[24] 5505 2-9-5 0 [1] JimCrowley 2 71
(Luca Cumani) *dwlt: hld up in last trio: rdn on outer 2f out: kpt on same pce fr over 1f out* **4/1**[3]

6 *1/2* **Delannoy** 2-9-5 0 CharlesBishop 1 71
(Eve Johnson Houghton) *dwlt: hld up in last: stl there 2f out: pushed along and sme prog over 1f out: ch of 4th ins fnl f: n.m.r and eased nr fin: nt disgracd* **12/1**

02 **7** *5* **Too Many Shots**[34] 5166 2-9-5 0 KierenFox 4 58
(John Best) *in tch: rdn 2f out: wknd qckly over 1f out* **14/1**

8 *3 1/4* **Poet's Wish** 2-9-5 0 FrederikTylicki 3 50
(George Margarson) *chsd ldng pair to over 2f out: sn wknd* **33/1**

1m 46.64s (3.34) **Going Correction** +0.15s/f (Good) **8** Ran SP% **118.3**
Speed ratings (Par 95): **89,88,86,85,85 84,79,76**
CSF £9.79 TOTE £4.10: £1.50, £1.20, £2.40; EX 12.20 Trifecta £66.40.
Owner John Manley **Bred** John Manley **Trained** East Everleigh, Wilts

FOCUS
This was run over 10yds further than advertised. It's hard to get excited by the form, but there are some nice long-term projects. The opening level is fluid.

6298 FIDELITY INFORMATION SERVICES H'CAP 1m 14y
3:30 (3:31) (Class 3) (0-95,95) 3-Y-O+ **£7,439** (£2,213; £1,106; £553) **Stalls** Low

Form RPR

/02- **1** **Sacred Act**[499] 1808 5-9-4 **89** RobertHavlin 10 103+
(John Gosden) *slowly away: hld up in last: prog on inner over 2f out: gng easily but nowhere to go over 1f out to 150yds out: qcknd smartly whn in the clr to pass several rivals last 100yds: led post* **16/1**

4-12 **2** *nk* **Shawaahid (IRE)**[13] 5878 3-9-2 **92** DaneO'Neill 6 99
(Richard Hannon) *t.k.h early: trckd ldng trio: clsd fr 2f out: drvn to ld 150yds out: styd on wl but hdd post* **11/2**[3]

0152 **3** *1* **Staunch**[30] 5306 3-8-11 **87** (p) PatDobbs 8 92
(Clive Cox) *trckd ldr: rdn to ld over 1f out: hdd last 150yds: styd on same pce* **12/1**

0400 **4** *1/2* **Manson**[21] 5616 3-9-3 **93** FrederikTylicki 5 97
(Dominic Ffrench Davis) *hld up in last trio: rdn on outer over 2f out: prog over 1f out: styd on same pce u.p fnl f* **7/1**

-256 **5** *hd* **American Artist (IRE)**[102] 2752 4-9-5 **90** HarryBentley 1 94
(Roger Varian) *chsd ldng pair to wl over 1f out: styd cl up: drvn and styd on same pce fnl f* **13/2**

13-2 **6** *hd* **Haggle**[45] 4737 3-9-5 **95** JimCrowley 7 98
(Luca Cumani) *hld up in last trio: gng wl enough 2f out: shkn up and sme prog over 1f out: drvn and styd on fnl f: nvr pce to threaten* **11/4**[2]

-150 **7** *1 1/4* **Primogeniture (IRE)**[23] 5552 5-9-1 **89** [1] EdwardGreatrex(3) 9 90
(Mary Hambro) *racd on outer: chsd ldrs: rdn over 2f out: styd wl in tch tl wknd ins fnl f* **66/1**

-510 **8** *5* **Oasis Spear**[70] 3861 4-9-2 **87** TedDurcan 2 77
(Chris Wall) *trckd ldrs: shkn up 2f out: no prog over 1f out: wknd qckly fnl f* **16/1**

0501 **9** *1 1/2* **Medburn Dream**[11] 5956 3-8-11 **87** 6ex MartinDwyer 3 72
(Paul Henderson) *led: shkn up 2f out: hdd & wknd qckly over 1f out* **12/1**

0/05 **10** *14* **Quixote (GER)**[55] 4395 6-9-10 **95** FMBerry 4 49
(Tony Carroll) *hld up in 7th: rdn and no prog over 2f out: sn wknd: t.o* **2/1**[1]

1m 42.89s (-0.41) **Going Correction** +0.15s/f (Good)
WFA 3 from 4yo+ 5lb **10** Ran SP% **129.9**
Speed ratings (Par 107): **108,107,106,106,106 105,104,99,98,84**
CSF £112.96 CT £1140.24 TOTE £16.10: £4.30, £2.10, £3.50; EX 84.50 Trifecta £584.50.
Owner Lady Bamford **Bred** Lady Bamford **Trained** Newmarket, Suffolk

FOCUS
This was run over 10yds further than advertised. A decent handicap. A small pb from the third, with the fourth rated close to his C&D win.

6299 KINGSWAY CLAIMS FILLIES' H'CAP 7f 16y
4:05 (4:06) (Class 4) (0-85,81) 3-Y-O+ **£4,690** (£1,395; £697; £348) **Stalls** Low

Form RPR

255 **1** **First Experience**[19] 5677 5-8-10 **70** (v1) KierenFox 6 78
(Lee Carter) *led after 2f: mde rest: stoked up over 2f out: drvn over 1f out: hld on wl fnl f* **8/1**

416 **2** *nk* **Gale Song**[17] 5744 3-8-13 **77** HarryBentley 5 82
(Ed Walker) *hld up in midfield: plld out 2f out: rdn and prog to take 2nd 1f out: grad clsd on wnr last 100yds but a jst hld* **9/2**[2]

3201 **3** *1 3/4* **Aristocratic**[30] 5300 3-9-1 **79** TedDurcan 3 79
(Sir Michael Stoute) *led 2f: chsd wnr to 1/2-way: rdn and nt qckn 2f out: styd on same pce fr over 1f out* **5/2**[1]

2461 **4** *1 1/2* **Little Miss Kodi (IRE)**[14] 5832 3-8-12 **76** FMBerry 2 72
(Daniel Mark Loughnane) *hld up in rr: n.m.r over 2f out: drvn and kpt on to take 4th ins fnl f but n.d* **5/1**[3]

-254 **5** *3* **Russian Radiance**[174] 1003 4-9-7 **81** FrederikTylicki 1 71
(Jonathan Portman) *a in midfield: shkn up on inner 2f out: no prog over 1f out: fdd fnl f* **16/1**

6010 **6** *1 1/4* **Alyaa (IRE)**[22] 5588 3-8-11 **75** MartinDwyer 4 60
(Conrad Allen) *t.k.h: prom: trckd wnr 1/2-way: rdn 2f out: nt qckn over 1f out and sn lost 2nd: hld whn squeezed out ins fnl f: wknd* **9/2**[2]

3134 **7** *3/4* **Bay Of St Malo (IRE)**[42] 4819 3-8-12 **76** PatDobbs 9 59
(Richard Hannon) *dropped in fr wd draw and hld up in last: pushed along over 2f out: no real hdwy and nvr involved* **12/1**

4451 **8** *10* **Elusive Ellen (IRE)**[37] 5018 6-9-6 **80** (t) DaneO'Neill 7 38
(Brendan Powell) *racd wd: chsd ldrs: rdn over 2f out: wknd over 1f out: eased* **12/1**

1m 29.72s (0.22) **Going Correction** +0.15s/f (Good)
WFA 3 from 4yo+ 4lb **8** Ran SP% **114.0**
Speed ratings (Par 102): **104,103,101,99,96 95,94,82**
CSF £43.45 CT £116.14 TOTE £10.10: £2.50, £1.70, £1.20; EX 50.50 Trifecta £327.80.
Owner Clear Racing with SMD Investments **Bred** Northmore Stud **Trained** Epsom, Surrey

FOCUS
This was run over 10yds further than advertised. A fair fillies' handicap. A small pb from the runner-up.

6300 INKERMAN LONDON H'CAP 1m 14y
4:40 (4:42) (Class 4) (0-80,80) 3-Y-O+ **£4,690** (£1,395; £697; £348) **Stalls** Low

Form RPR

0-11 **1** **Cloudberry**[7] 6084 3-8-11 **79** DavidEgan(7) 3 90+
(Roger Charlton) *dwlt: sn in midfield: n.m.r briefly over 3f out: prog over 2f out to ld wl over 1f out: sn shkn up: narrowly hdd ins fnl f: rdn to ld again last 50yds* **10/11**[1]

0042 **2** *nk* **Mister Music**[7] 6084 7-9-8 **78** PatDobbs 10 87
(Tony Carroll) *hld up in midfield: stdy prog 2f out: wnt 2nd 1f out: shkn up to take narrow ld ins fnl f: drvn and hdd last 50yds* **7/1**[2]

5600 **3** *2 1/2* **Jack Of Diamonds (IRE)**[6] 6126 7-9-9 **79** RobertWinston 4 82
(Roger Teal) *s.i.s: hld up in last: stl there jst over 2f out: cajoled along and prog on outer wl over 1f out: styd on fnl f to snatch 3rd last strides* **10/1**

0602 **4** *shd* **Outback Ruler (IRE)**[20] 5649 4-9-3 **80** (p) WilliamCox(7) 12 83
(Clive Cox) *hld up wl in rr: swtchd lft over 3f out: drvn and prog 2f out: kpt on to press for 3rd nr fin* **14/1**

2113 **5** *shd* **Red Tea**[25] 5487 3-9-5 **80** AdamBeschizza 11 82
(Peter Hiatt) *trckd ldrs: prog to ld over 2f out: hdd wl over 1f out: fdd u.p fnl f* **9/1**

50-0 **6** *3 1/2* **The Dancing Lord**[11] 5965 7-9-2 **72** (t) HarryPoulton 7 66
(Adam West) *hld up in rr: wd bnd 4f out: prog to press ldrs over 2f out: wknd jst over 1f out* **66/1**

-605 **7** *3 1/2* **Postbag**[24] 5514 4-9-7 **77** DaneO'Neill 5 63
(Henry Candy) *pressed ldrs: rdn and on terms over 2f out: nt qckn over 1f out: wknd qckly fnl f* **8/1**[3]

1153 **8** *3/4* **Jazzy (IRE)**[47] 1828 3-8-12 **76** (t1) EdwardGreatrex(3) 1 60
(Martin Keighley) *led to over 2f out: sn lost pl and btn* **10/1**

1-00 **9** *1 1/4* **Graceful James (IRE)**[16] 5765 3-9-2 **77** TedDurcan 2 58
(Jimmy Fox) *chsd ldng pair to 3f out: sn lost pl and btn* **25/1**

5006 **10** *shd* **Glenalmond (IRE)**[37] 5017 4-9-2 **77** HectorCrouch(5) 9 59
(Daniel Steele) *chsd ldr to wl over 2f out: sn lost pl and btn* **25/1**

1m 43.28s (-0.02) **Going Correction** +0.15s/f (Good)
WFA 3 from 4yo+ 5lb **10** Ran SP% **120.0**
Speed ratings (Par 105): **106,105,103,103,103 99,96,95,94,93**
CSF £7.90 CT £44.37 TOTE £1.80: £1.10, £1.90, £2.50; EX 7.80 Trifecta £56.30.
Owner Beckhampton Stables Ltd **Bred** Carwell Equities Ltd **Trained** Beckhampton, Wilts

FOCUS
This was run over 10yds further than advertised. The well-handicapped winner looked to have a bit more in hand than the result suggests. The runner-up has been rated close to last year's best, with the third in line with his turf form.

6301 TELEGRAPH HILL H'CAP 1m 2f 7y
5:15 (5:23) (Class 4) (0-85,84) 3-Y-O+ **£4,690** (£1,395; £697; £348) **Stalls** Low

Form RPR

1524 **1** **Pure Fantasy**[24] 5520 3-9-3 **82** PatDobbs 8 90+
(Roger Charlton) *hld up towards rr: plenty to do whn shkn up and prog wl over 1f out: clsd to take 2nd ins fnl f: r.o wl to ld last stride* **10/1**

0224 **2** *hd* **Cape Banjo (USA)**[33] 5198 3-8-13 **78** FMBerry 13 85
(Ralph Beckett) *led: stretched on 3f out and sn had most of rivals off the bridle: drvn over 1f out: stl 2 l ahd ins fnl f: collared last stride* **16/1**

25-2 **3** *1* **Fleeting Visit**[21] 5601 3-9-2 **84** EdwardGreatrex(3) 11 89
(Eve Johnson Houghton) *sn towards rr and on outer: pushed along over 3f out: no prog tl drvn and styd on wl fr over 1f out to take 3rd nr fin* **11/4**[1]

3422 **4** *1/2* **Sennockian Star**[7] 6089 6-9-11 **83** (v) DaneO'Neill 5 87
(Mark Johnston) *chsd ldr: pushed along 3f out: rdn and no imp 2f out: stl disputing 2nd wl ins fnl f: lost pl and n.m.r nr fin* **5/1**[3]

000- **5** *shd* **Banditry (IRE)**[348] 6777 4-9-11 **83** FrederikTylicki 12 87
(Ian Williams) *stdd s and hld up in last: stl there over 2f out: taken to outer and shkn up over 1f out: r.o fnl f: clsng at fin but too much to do* **33/1**

2211 **6** *nk* **Hollywood Road (IRE)**[21] 5603 3-9-5 **84** (b) RobertWinston 1 87
(Don Cantillon) *t.k.h: prom: urged along 3f out: disp 2nd after tl wl ins fnl f: lost pls nr fin* **3/1**[2]

5142 **7** *1/2* **Compton Mill**[36] 5071 4-9-0 **77** (t) CharlieBennett(5) 6 79
(Hughie Morrison) *chsd ldrs: urged along 3f out: no imp ldrs after tl kpt on ins fnl f: nvr able to threaten* **9/1**

0240 **8** *3/4* **Fiftyshadesfreed (IRE)**[41] 4868 5-9-7 **84** (p) HectorCrouch(5) 4 85
(George Baker) *wl in tch: urged along 3f out: no imp ldrs fr 2f out: kpt on one pce after* **8/1**

6/0 **9** *1 3/4* **East India**[85] 1914 4-9-7 **79** SteveDrowne 2 76
(George Baker) *nvr beyond midfield: shkn up and lost pl over 2f out: wl in rr after: plugged on ins fnl f* **50/1**

150 **10** *3 1/4* **Youre Always Right (IRE)**[46] 4710 3-9-1 **80** TedDurcan 3 71
(Clive Cox) *chsd ldrs: rdn 3f out: lost pl over 2f out: wl btn after* **12/1**

2643 **11** *hd* **Spa's Dancer (IRE)**[77] 3621 9-9-11 **83**.................................. RyanTate 7 73
(James Eustace) *shoved along early: a in rr: shkn up and no prog 3f out* **16/1**

2m 12.39s (1.89) **Going Correction** +0.15s/f (Good)
WFA 3 from 4yo+ 7lb **11** Ran SP% **122.9**
Speed ratings (Par 105): **98,97,97,96,96 96,95,95,93,91 91**
CSF £165.46 CT £568.94 TOTE £11.90: £3.40, £4.90, £1.70; EX 151.00 Trifecta £626.20.
Owner The Queen **Bred** The Queen **Trained** Beckhampton, Wilts
■ Takbeer (66-1) was withdrawn, not under orders. Rule 4 does not apply.

FOCUS
This was run over 10yds further than advertised. Another fair handicap. The runner-up is the key to the form and has been rated as running a small pb for now. The fourth has been rated close to his recent form.
T/Jkpt: Not won. T/Plt: £49.60 to a £1 stake. Pool: £76581.27, 1126.34 winning units T/Qpdt: £14.40 to a £1 stake. Pool: £5450.71, 279.89 winning units **Jonathan Neesom**

6302 - 6309a (Foreign Racing) - See Raceform Interactive

6176 SAINT-CLOUD (L-H)
Friday, September 9

OFFICIAL GOING: Turf: good

6310a PRIX DE VELIZY (CLAIMER) (3YO) (TURF) 7f
1:00 (12:00) 3-Y-O **£9,926** (£3,970; £2,977; £1,985; £992)

RPR

1 **Ali Spirit (IRE)**[9] 3-8-11 0.. AntoineHamelin 4 78
(Matthieu Palussiere, France) **146/10**
2 *nse* **Evenchop (FR)**[92] 3-9-1 0.. EddyHardouin 7 82
(K Borgel, France) **77/10**
3 *hd* **Time Shanakill (IRE)**[9] 3-8-6 0.................................... PierreBazire[(5)] 5 77
(G Botti, France) **17/2**
4 *3/4* **Rashawn (FR)**[22] 3-9-1 0.. LukasDelozier 2 79
(H-A Pantall, France) **10/1**
5 *snk* **Bobbio (FR)**[12] 5946 3-8-4 0.. KyllanBarbaud[(7)] 8 75
(N Caullery, France) **89/10**
6 *shd* **Dylan Dancing (IRE)**[27] 3-9-4 0.......................... ChristopheSoumillon 6 82
(A Marcialis, Italy) **33/10**[1]
7 *snk* **Rip Van Suzy (IRE)**[31] 5280 3-8-8 0........................... MickaelBarzalona 3 71
(Jo Hughes) *trckd ldr: rdn to chal and upsides 2f out: kpt on and stl ev ch tl no ex wl ins fnl f* **76/10**[3]
8 *nse* **Eze**[166] 3-8-11 0.. AlexisBadel 9 74
(H-F Devin, France) **11/1**
9 *1 1/4* **Mesonera (FR)**[73] 3764 3-8-3 0............................ MathieuPelletan[(5)] 10 68
(J Parize, France) **24/1**
10 *2 1/2* **Paques Island (FR)**[57] 3-8-8 0...............................(p) RonanThomas 1 61
(J Phelippon, France) **31/1**
11 *4* **Risk Major (FR)**[6] 3-9-5 0................................. Pierre-CharlesBoudot 13 61
(J Phelippon, France) **37/10**[2]
12 *1/2* **Corroyer (IRE)**[29] 5349 3-9-2 0.............................. EmmanuelEtienne[(3)] 11 60
(F Alloncle, France) **67/1**

1m 26.05s (-6.15) **12** Ran SP% **120.7**
WIN (incl. 1 euro stake): 15.60. PLACES: 4.20, 2.30, 3.10. DF: 64.40. SF: 140.30.
Owner Z Bifov/Mrs T Marnane **Bred** Zalim Bifov **Trained** France

6016 BATH (L-H)
Saturday, September 10

OFFICIAL GOING: Good to soft (good in places; 8.2)
Wind: Light against Weather: Overcast

6311 RAINBOW CASINO TEESIDE APPRENTICE H'CAP (DIV I) 5f 161y
2:10 (2:11) (Class 6) (0-60,60) 3-Y-O+ **£2,587** (£770; £384; £192) **Stalls** Centre

Form RPR

3334 **1** **Toni's A Star**[40] 4952 4-9-4 **60**.. GeorgiaCox[(5)] 5 69
(Tony Carroll) *a.p: chsd ldr 1/2-way: led over 1f out: styd on* **3/1**[1]
5050 **2** *1/2* **Jaganory (IRE)**[12] 5954 4-8-11 **53**..............................(v) LuluStanford[(5)] 2 60
(Christopher Mason) *hld up in tch: nt clr run and pushed along 2f out: rdn to chse wnr fnl f: edgd lft: styd on* **6/1**[3]
6302 **3** *3/4* **Secret Witness**[15] 5827 10-9-7 **58**...............................(b) DanielMuscutt 8 62
(Ronald Harris) *hld up: hdwy 1/2-way: rdn over 1f out: kpt on* **3/1**[1]
0014 **4** *nse* **Kaaber (USA)**[12] 5953 5-8-8 **50**...............................(b) MitchGodwin[(5)] 1 54
(Roy Brotherton) *sn pushed along in rr: hdwy over 1f out: nt clr run and swtchd rt ins fnl f: r.o* **7/2**[2]
1000 **5** *3/4* **Triple Dream**[18] 5736 11-8-12 **49**.............................. JosephineGordon 3 50
(Milton Bradley) *led 1f: remained handy: rdn over 1/2-way: outpcd over 1f out: r.o towards fin* **9/1**
06 **6** *2 1/2* **Dark Phantom (IRE)**[39] 4993 5-8-6 **46** oh1................... PaddyPilley[(3)] 6 39
(Geoffrey Deacon) *led over 4f out: rdn and hdd over 1f out: wknd ins fnl f* **10/1**
3006 **7** *6* **Ormering**[29] 5380 3-8-6 **50**..(p) GeorgeWood[(5)] 9 23
(Roger Teal) *chsd ldrs: rdn and hung rt 1/2-way: wknd over 1f out* **16/1**
00/0 **8** *10* **Liddle Dwiggs**[23] 5572 5-8-6 **46** oh1.............................. DavidParkes[(3)] 4
(Peter Hiatt) *chsd ldrs: rdn over 2f out: wknd over 1f out* **80/1**
0-0 **9** *6* **Not My Way (IRE)**[53] 4480 3-8-11 **55**...............................(p) RhiainIngram[(5)] 7
(John O'Shea) *sn pushed along in rr: bhd fr 1/2-way* **25/1**

1m 13.8s (2.60) **Going Correction** +0.325s/f (Good)
WFA 3 from 4yo+ 2lb **9** Ran SP% **116.6**
Speed ratings (Par 101): **95,94,93,93,92 88,80,67,59**
CSF £21.78 CT £58.62 TOTE £4.20: £1.70, £1.50, £1.50; EX 27.50 Trifecta £78.50.
Owner A Star Recruitment Ltd **Bred** Paul Green **Trained** Cropthorne, Worcs

FOCUS
The ground had eased to good to soft, good in places (from good to firm) and all race distances were as advertised. A modest apprentice handicap to start featuring a couple of hardy veterans. After the race Josephine Gordon said the going was "on the good side, lovely ground." Straightforward form.

6312 RAINBOW CASINO TEESIDE APPRENTICE H'CAP (DIV II) 5f 161y
2:45 (2:45) (Class 6) (0-60,60) 3-Y-O+ **£2,587** (£770; £384; £192) **Stalls** Centre

Form RPR

0064 **1** **Burauq**[25] 5509 4-8-9 **46** oh1...................................(b) JosephineGordon 2 53
(Milton Bradley) *chsd ldrs: rdn to ld over 1f out: edgd lft: pushed out* **15/2**
6005 **2** *1 1/2* **Presto Boy**[75] 3719 4-8-5 **49**..(e[1]) NicolaCurrie[(7)] 4 51
(Richard Hughes) *chsd ldrs: lost pl over 3f out: hdwy over 1f out: chsd wnr ins fnl f: styd on same pce towards fin* **8/1**
3414 **3** *3/4* **Beau Mistral (IRE)**[15] 5827 7-9-8 **59**..............................(b) RobHornby 8 59
(Tony Carroll) *sn chsng ldrs: led over 2f out: sn hung rt: rdn and hdd over 1f out: hung lft: styd on same pce ins fnl f* **3/1**[1]
0041 **4** *shd* **Mambo Spirit (IRE)**[21] 5628 12-9-9 **60**................................ EoinWalsh 6 59+
(Tony Newcombe) *s.s: hld up: nt clr run wl over 1f out: hdwy u.p sn after: styd on: nt rch ldrs* **4/1**[3]
60 **5** *nk* **Diamond Vine (IRE)**[15] 5827 8-9-0 **51**.........................(p) LouisSteward 5 49
(Ronald Harris) *chsd ldrs: lost pl after 1f: rdn 1/2-way: r.o ins fnl f* **8/1**
-406 **6** *5* **The Reel Way (GR)**[23] 5572 5-8-6 **46**......................... HectorCrouch[(3)] 1 28
(Patrick Chamings) *s.s: rdn 1/2-way: nvr on terms* **7/2**[2]
-444 **7** *2 1/4* **Golden Rosanna**[34] 5200 3-8-4 **46** oh1......................... AnnaHesketh[(3)] 3 20
(Steph Hollinshead) *s.i.s: sn prom: led over 3f out tl wl over 2f out: wknd fnl f* **12/1**
446- **8** *nk* **Gypsy Rider**[359] 6463 7-8-12 **49**.. TimClark 9 22
(Henry Tett) *led 2f: led again wl over 2f out: sn hdd: rdn and wknd over 1f out* **12/1**

1m 14.02s (2.82) **Going Correction** +0.325s/f (Good)
WFA 3 from 4yo+ 2lb **8** Ran SP% **116.6**
Speed ratings (Par 101): **94,92,91,90,90 83,80,80**
CSF £66.42 CT £222.19 TOTE £8.10: £2.20, £3.20, £1.10; EX 90.60 Trifecta £271.60.
Owner D Smith (saul) **Bred** Kirtlington Stud Ltd **Trained** Sedbury, Gloucs

FOCUS
The winning time was 0.22sec slower than the first division. The runner-up and third help set the level.

6313 RAINBOW CASINO ABERDEEN NURSERY H'CAP 1m 5y
3:20 (3:20) (Class 6) (0-60,61) 2-Y-O **£2,264** (£673; £336; £168) **Stalls** Low

Form RPR

500 **1** **Masterofdiscovery**[22] 5600 2-9-7 **60**..............................(b[1]) JohnFahy 5 73+
(Clive Cox) *sn pushed along to chse ldr: led 6f out: rdn over 1f out: drvn clr ins fnl f* **17/2**
0003 **2** *5* **Sir Plato (IRE)**[9] 6060 2-9-4 **57**.. LukeMorris 6 57
(Rod Millman) *sn pushed along and prom: rdn over 3f out: chsd wnr and hung lft over 1f out: no ex wl ins fnl f* **9/2**[2]
0553 **3** *2 1/4* **Moneyoryourlife**[33] 5239 2-9-7 **60**.................................... PatDobbs 8 55
(Richard Hannon) *chsd ldrs: rdn over 1f out: wknd wl ins fnl f* **4/1**[1]
0005 **4** *1* **A Sure Welcome**[17] 5770 2-8-12 **54**.......................... LouisSteward[(3)] 7 47
(John Spearing) *hld up: hdwy u.p over 1f out: nt rch ldrs* **13/2**[3]
6406 **5** *3/4* **Battle Of Wits (IRE)**[2] 6253 2-8-6 **50**......................... MitchGodwin[(5)] 9 41
(J S Moore) *s.i.s: hld up: hdwy u.p over 2f out: edgd rt over 1f out: wknd fnl f* **20/1**
0536 **6** *4 1/2* **Cautious Choice (IRE)**[25] 5528 2-8-6 **45**....................[1] KieranO'Neill 12 25
(J S Moore) *chsd ldrs: rdn over 3f out: wknd fnl f* **25/1**
000 **7** *1 1/4* **Aventus (IRE)**[12] 5959 2-9-4 **57**...................................... ShaneKelly 1 35
(Richard Hughes) *hld up: rdn over 3f out: nvr on terms* **9/1**
0002 **8** *1* **Alligator**[9] 6045 2-9-5 **61**..............................(b[1]) JosephineGordon[(3)] 10 36
(Ed Dunlop) *sn led: racd keenly: hdd 6f out: hung rt 5f out: ev ch over 2f out: sn rdn: wknd fnl f* **4/1**[1]
0066 **9** *1 1/4* **Hot N Sassy (IRE)**[40] 4937 2-8-3 **45**.........................(p) NoelGarbutt[(3)] 4 17
(J S Moore) *s.i.s: hld up: rdn over 3f out: wknd over 2f out* **33/1**
0000 **10** *1/2* **On Show (IRE)**[17] 5770 2-8-1 **45**.............................(v[1]) GeorgeWood[(5)] 11 16
(David Brown) *mid-div: pushed along 6f out: rdn over 3f out: wknd over 2f out* **10/1**
000 **11** *3* **General Allenby**[63] 4154 2-8-11 **50**................................. PatCosgrave 3 14
(Henry Tett) *prom: sn pushed along: hmpd after 1f: rdn over 3f out: wknd over 2f out* **17/2**

1m 45.29s (4.49) **Going Correction** +0.325s/f (Good) **11** Ran SP% **123.2**
Speed ratings (Par 93): **90,85,82,81,81 76,75,74,73,72 69**
CSF £47.86 CT £183.13 TOTE £10.40: £3.10, £2.00, £1.80; EX 56.20 Trifecta £348.70.
Owner The Voyagers **Bred** Meon Valley Stud **Trained** Lambourn, Berks

FOCUS
A moderate nursery contested by 11 maidens, but a clear-cut winner. It's been rated around the runner-up and third.

6314 DOUBLE DIAMOND GAMING MAIDEN STKS (PLUS 10 RACE) 1m 5y
3:50 (3:55) (Class 4) 2-Y-O **£4,851** (£1,443; £721; £360) **Stalls** Low

Form RPR

22 **1** **Good Omen**[12] 5952 2-9-5 0.. PatCosgrave 6 87+
(William Haggas) *chsd ldrs: shkn up to ld and hung lft over 1f out: pushed clr: eased nr fin* **8/15**[1]
523 **2** *5* **Whip Nae Nae (IRE)**[22] 5600 2-9-5 78........................... KieranO'Neill 5 76
(Richard Hannon) *chsd ldr tl led over 2f out: rdn: edgd lft and hdd over 1f out: no ex ins fnl f: eased towards fin* **9/4**[2]
00 **3** *2 1/4* **I'Vegotthepower (IRE)**[45] 4775 2-9-5 0.....................(b) JimmyFortune 1 68
(Brian Meehan) *sn led at stdy pce: hdd over 2f out: wknd ins fnl f* **12/1**
00 **4** *2 3/4* **Raj Balaraaj (GER)**[31] 5304 2-9-5 0................................ SteveDrowne 4 62
(George Baker) *hld up: hdwy to go 4th over 2f out: nt trble ldrs* **25/1**
5 *12* **Khattar** 2-9-2 0...[1] NoelGarbutt[(3)] 7 34
(Hugo Palmer) *hld up: pushed along over 3f out: wknd over 2f out* **4/1**[3]
00 **6** *4 1/2* **The Batham Boy (IRE)**[31] 5290 2-8-12 0............................ TobyEley[(7)] 3 24
(Daniel Mark Loughnane) *hld up: rdn over 3f out: sn wknd* **66/1**
00 **7** *nk* **Chamasay**[37] 5052 2-9-2 0... JosephineGordon[(3)] 8 23+
(J S Moore) *broke wl: swvd rt after s and sn wl bhd: clsd on to the bk of the gp 6f out: wknd over 2f out* **66/1**
6 **8** *31* **Sam The Rebel**[12] 5952 2-9-5 0.. LukeMorris 2
(Mike Hammond) *trckd ldrs: racd keenly: rdn and wknd over 2f out* **50/1**

1m 45.54s (4.74) **Going Correction** +0.325s/f (Good) **8** Ran SP% **132.5**
Speed ratings (Par 97): **89,84,81,79,67 62,62,31**
CSF £2.64 TOTE £1.50: £1.10, £1.30, £2.20; EX 2.30 Trifecta £13.20.
Owner A E Oppenheimer **Bred** Hascombe And Valiant Studs **Trained** Newmarket, Suffolk

FOCUS
Only three could be seriously fancied in this maiden and the field finished well spread out. The runner-up's mark of 78 sets the benchmark. The level is a bit fluid, with the third and fourth key.

6315 RAINBOW CASINO BRISTOL H'CAP (SUMMER STAYING SERIES FINAL) 1m 5f 22y
4:25 (4:25) (Class 3) 3-Y-O+ **£12,938** (£3,850; £1,924; £962) **Stalls** High

Form RPR

5611 **1** **Rosie Royale (IRE)**[21] 5624 4-9-3 **67**............................ GeorgeWood[(5)] 9 76
(Roger Teal) *chsd ldrs: pushed along 1/2-way: led over 2f out: rdn over 1f out: styd on* **7/1**[3]
2541 **2** *2* **Captain George (IRE)**[10] 6022 5-9-2 **61**.......................(v) SteveDrowne 2 67
(Michael Blake) *chsd ldrs: rdn over 3f out: chsd wnr ins fnl f: styd on* **10/1**

0234 **3** nse **Oratorio's Joy (IRE)**21 5624 6-9-8 **67** TimmyMurphy 3 73
(Jamie Osborne) *hld up: hdwy over 2f out: rdn over 1f out: styd on* **14/1**
1112 **4** 1 3/4 **Coarse Cut (IRE)**18 5746 3-9-0 **69** (b) JohnFahy 5 72
(Eve Johnson Houghton) *sn chsng ldr: rdn over 2f out: hung lft over 1f out: no ex ins fnl f* **4/1**1
1333 **5** hd **Bernisdale**17 5232 8-8-13 **63** MitchGodwin(5) 13 66
(John Flint) *hld up: hdwy over 2f out: rdn and hung lft fr over 1f out: styd on* **20/1**
/043 **6** nk **Moss Street**21 5624 6-8-6 **51** (b) DanielMuscutt 4 54
(John Flint) *hld up in tch: rdn over 2f out: styd on same pce fnl f* **11/1**
2001 **7** 3/4 **Bob's Boy**21 5625 3-8-2 **57** (p) KieranO'Neill 12 59
(Jose Santos) *sn led: clr 11f out tl over 4f out: rdn and hdd over 2f out: styd on same pce fnl f* **5/1**2
4262 **8** 4 **Lady Hare (IRE)**10 6022 4-8-12 **57** PatDobbs 1 53
(Ken Cunningham-Brown) *mid-divison: sme hdwy u.p over 1f out: wknd fnl f* **11/1**
0-63 **9** 2 1/4 **Moon Trip**39 4995 7-8-0 **48** JosephineGordon(3) 11 40
(Geoffrey Deacon) *hld up: pushed along 10f out: rdn over 3f out: nvr on terms* **12/1**
2304 **10** 3 3/4 **Cape Spirit (IRE)**10 6022 4-8-2 **54** (v) WilliamCox(7) 10 41
(Andrew Balding) *mid-div: hdwy over 3f out: sn rdn: wknd over 1f out* **20/1**
2613 **11** shd **Ballyfarsoon (IRE)**10 6022 5-9-1 **60** (v) LukeMorris 8 46
(Ian Williams) *hld up: rdn over 3f out: a in rr* **10/1**
3115 **12** 20 **Urban Space**43 4816 10-9-5 **69** (t) HectorCrouch(5) 6 25
(John Flint) *hld up: rdn over 3f out: sn lost tch* **14/1**
0122 **13** 20 **Rum Swizzle**21 5624 4-9-10 **69** PatCosgrave 7
(Harry Dunlop) *hld up: rdn and wknd 3f out* **8/1**

2m 55.02s (3.02) **Going Correction** +0.325s/f (Good)
WFA 3 from 4yo+ 10lb **13** Ran SP% **125.7**
Speed ratings (Par 107): **103,101,101,100,100 100,99,97,96,93 93,81,69**
CSF £79.47 CT £967.84 TOTE £5.90: £3.20, £3.20, £4.50; EX 84.30 Trifecta £546.60.
Owner The Idle B's **Bred** Fergus Cousins **Trained** Great Shefford, Berks

FOCUS
A competitive final of this series as it should be for the money. Many of these were familiar to each other having met each other in the qualifiers. The pace was a decent one, but relatively few ever got into it. It's been rated slightly positively around the third.

6316 RAINBOW CASINO BIRMINGHAM H'CAP 1m 5y
4:55 (4:57) (Class 4) (0-80,80) 4-Y-O+ **£4,690** (£1,395; £697; £348) **Stalls** Low

Form RPR
0162 **1** **British Embassy (IRE)**10 6021 4-8-13 **77** HectorCrouch(5) 4 85+
(Brian Barr) *mde all: rdn and edgd rt over 1f out: styd on gamely* **5/1**3
4315 **2** 1/2 **Stosur (IRE)**15 5831 5-8-10 **76** (b) CameronNoble(7) 9 83
(Gay Kelleway) *disp 2nd tl chsd wnr 5f out: rdn and ev ch ins fnl f: nt qckn towards fin* **6/1**
4463 **3** 4 **Alcatraz (IRE)**33 5234 4-9-7 **80** SteveDrowne 8 78
(George Baker) *hld up: hdwy over 2f out: rdn over 1f out: edgd lft and styd on same pce fnl f* **9/4**1
4253 **4** 7 **Peak Storm**12 5956 7-9-6 **79** (p) LukeMorris 7 61
(John O'Shea) *chsd ldrs: rdn over 2f out: wknd fnl f* **5/1**3
2035 **5** 4 1/2 **Mr Quicksilver**9 6055 4-9-4 **77** ThomasBrown 5 48
(Ed Walker) *hld up: rdn and wknd over 1f out* **4/1**2
610 **6** nse **Lulani (IRE)**29 5357 4-9-7 **80** PatCosgrave 2 51
(Harry Dunlop) *disp 2nd 3f: chsd ldrs: rdn over 3f out: wknd over 2f out* **11/2**

1m 43.41s (2.61) **Going Correction** +0.325s/f (Good) **6** Ran SP% **113.8**
Speed ratings (Par 105): **99,98,94,87,83 82**
CSF £34.31 CT £84.79 TOTE £4.50: £1.70, £4.30; EX 43.00 Trifecta £126.50.
Owner Steven Hosie **Bred** Corduff Stud Ltd & T J Rooney **Trained** Longburton, Dorset

FOCUS
A fair handicap, but despite a good pace few ever got into it and the first two occupied those positions throughout.

6317 SEKKAI WATCHES MAIDEN STKS 5f 161y
5:30 (5:30) (Class 5) 3-Y-O+ **£3,067** (£905; £453) **Stalls** Centre

Form RPR
022 **1** **Minminwin (IRE)**5 6182 3-8-7 50 (vt) CameronNoble(7) 10 65
(Gay Kelleway) *dwlt: hld up: hdwy and hung lft over 1f out: rdn and r.o to ld towards fin* **3/1**1
3600 **2** nk **Oat Couture**12 5953 4-9-2 60 (b1) JimmyFortune 12 64
(Henry Candy) *hld up: hdwy u.p and hung lft over 1f out: ev ch wl ins fnl f: eased last strides* **9/2**3
2-0 **3** 3/4 **Zippy**112 2470 3-8-11 0 JosephineGordon(3) 8 62
(Daniel Kubler) *hld up: hdwy 2f out: nt clr run over 1f out: rdn to ld wl ins fnl f: edgd lft and hdd towards fin* **4/1**2
4 2 **Dandilion (IRE)** 3-9-0 0 1 KieranO'Neill 11 55
(Alex Hales) *trckd ldrs: led over 1f out: rdn: hung lft and hdd wl ins fnl f* **33/1**
0023 **5** 3 3/4 **Arcanista (IRE)**35 5167 3-9-0 61 (b) ShaneKelly 1 43
(Richard Hughes) *led over 4f out: rdn and hdd over 1f out: wknd ins fnl f* **9/2**3
6 3/4 **Indiana Dawn** 3-9-0 0 AdamBeschizza 4 40
(Robert Stephens) *chsd ldrs: rdn 1/2-way: wknd fnl f* **33/1**
53 **7** 1/2 **Ducissa**17 5766 3-9-0 0 LukeMorris 6 38
(Daniel Kubler) *prom: drvn along 1/2-way: wknd fnl f* **6/1**
5055 **8** 2 1/2 **Master Pekan**23 5570 3-9-0 45 MitchGodwin(5) 14 35
(Roy Brotherton) *chsd ldrs: pushed along 1/2-way: wknd over 1f out* **100/1**
00- **9** 5 **Sir Jamie**334 7166 3-9-5 0 PatDobbs 2 19
(Tony Carroll) *hld up: bhd fr 1/2-way* **20/1**
0 **10** 2 1/4 **Hellarious**49 4660 3-9-0 0 PaddyPilley(5) 3 11
(Geoffrey Deacon) *w ldrs tl rdn 1/2-way: wknd over 1f out* **50/1**
11 1 3/4 **Gold Bud** 4-9-7 0 SteveDrowne 13 5
(George Baker) *chsd ldrs: rdn 1/2-way: wknd over 1f out* **16/1**
06-6 **12** 3/4 **Valtashyra (IRE)**14 5862 3-8-10 39 ow1 1 AnnStokell(5) 9
(Ann Stokell) *racd keenly: led 1f: chsd ldrs: pushed along over 3f out: wknd 1/2-way* **200/1**
5-3 **13** 2 1/2 **Fanci That (IRE)**18 5748 3-9-0 0 PatCosgrave 7
(Rae Guest) *hld up: rdn 1/2-way: sn wknd* **14/1**
0 **14** 7 **Sense Of Snow (IRE)**28 5388 3-9-5 0 (t) SamHitchcott 5
(William Muir) *prom: lost pl after 1f: sn pushed along: wknd 1/2-way* **33/1**

1m 13.06s (1.86) **Going Correction** +0.325s/f (Good)
WFA 3 from 4yo 2lb **14** Ran SP% **125.2**
Speed ratings (Par 103): **100,99,98,95,90 89,89,85,79,76 73,72,69,60**
CSF £16.36 TOTE £4.50: £1.50, £2.60, £1.80; EX 29.30 Trifecta £144.00.
Owner Miss Gay Kelleway **Bred** P V Jackson **Trained** Exning, Suffolk

FOCUS
A modest older-horse maiden and not form to get carried away with. The runner-up has been rated to her second-place finish in this last year, with the third close to her debut 2yo form.

6318 RAINBOW CASINO CARDIFF FILLIES' H'CAP 5f 11y
6:05 (6:09) (Class 4) (0-80,80) 3-Y-O+ **£4,690** (£1,395; £697) **Stalls** Centre

Form RPR
3020 **1** **Ginzan**7 6114 8-9-7 **80** JimmyFortune 8 84
(Malcolm Saunders) *led: hdd over 3f out: led again 2f out: rdn and hdd 1f out: edgd lft and rallied u.p to ld post* **6/1**3
5521 **2** nse **Princess Tansy**14 5882 4-8-11 **77** CameronNoble(7) 4 81
(Gay Kelleway) *trckd ldrs: led 1f out: shkn up ins fnl f: edgd lft: hdd post* **5/2**1
3110 **3** 4 1/2 **Pine Ridge**7 6114 3-9-6 **80** JohnFahy 3 68
(Clive Cox) *w ldr tl led over 3f out: pushed along and hdd 2f out: wknd ins fnl f* **7/2**2

1m 3.33s (0.83) **Going Correction** +0.325s/f (Good)
WFA 3 from 4yo+ 1lb **3** Ran SP% **65.1**
Speed ratings (Par 102): **106,105,98**
CSF £6.95 TOTE £3.20; EX 5.80 Trifecta £3.70.
Owner Paul Nicholas **Bred** Hedsor Stud **Trained** Green Ore, Somerset
■ Cersei (13/8F) and Edged Out (6/1) were withdrawn. Rule 4 applies to all bets - deduction 45p in the pound.

FOCUS
This fillies' sprint handicap was hit hard by non-runners. The original field of eight was reduced to just three, with Edged Out withdrawn after pulling up on the way to post and Cersei also being withdrawn after rearing badly in the stalls. Possibly in view of what happened in the previous contest, the trio came over to race against the stands' rail. The first two have been rated to this year's form.
T/Plt: £75.20 to a £1 stake. Pool: £69,454.85 - 673.53 winning units T/Qpdt: £20.30 to a £1 stake. Pool: £3,317.97 - 120.82 winning units **Colin Roberts**

6274 CHESTER (L-H)
Saturday, September 10

OFFICIAL GOING: Good to soft (6.5)
Wind: light 1/2 against Weather: fine

6319 HOWDEN JOINERY / EBF STALLIONS MAIDEN STKS (PLUS 10 RACE) 6f 18y
1:40 (1:42) (Class 4) 2-Y-O
£6,225 (£1,864; £932; £466; £233; £117) **Stalls** Low

Form RPR
3250 **1** **Abiento (IRE)**22 5615 2-9-5 78 PatrickMathers 2 78
(Richard Fahey) *n.m.r sn after s: chsd ldrs: effrt over 1f out: hung lft and led last 100yds: drvn out* **9/4**1
644 **2** 1/2 **Glorious Artist (IRE)**38 5029 2-9-5 80 MichaelJMMurphy 3 77
(Charles Hills) *led early: chsd ldr: effrt over 1f out: upsides and hung lft 100yds out: no ex clsng stages* **9/4**1
3 1 3/4 **Unzipped** 2-8-11 0 EdwardGreatrex(3) 8 66+
(Stuart Edmunds) *mid-div: sn chsd along: hdwy over 1f out: styd on to take 3rd post* **50/1**
56 **4** nse **Ladofash**12 5966 2-9-0 0 JordanVaughan(5) 1 71+
(K R Burke) *mid-div: outpcd over 2f out: hdwy on ins over 1f out: styd on wl to take 4th post* **6/1**3
23 **5** nk **Kiribati**11 6002 2-9-5 0 MartinHarley 4 73
(Mark Johnston) *sn led: hdd 100yds out: keeping on same pce whn hmpd and eased nr fin* **11/4**2
6 **6** 2 **Performing (IRE)**17 5778 2-9-5 0 JasonHart 5 64
(John Quinn) *chsd ldrs: drvn over 2f out: one pce fnl f* **25/1**
0 **7** 1 1/4 **Pavela (IRE)**106 2637 2-9-0 0 JFEgan 9 55
(Mick Channon) *mid-div: sn pushed along: drvn over 2f out: kpt on one pce fnl f* **66/1**
006 **8** 6 **Baker Street**39 4981 2-9-5 64 RichardKingscote 6 42
(Tom Dascombe) *dwlt: in rr: outpcd over 2f out: sn bhd* **16/1**
00 **9** 1 **Av A Word**20 5676 2-9-5 0 RobertHavlin 10 39
(Daniel Kubler) *s.i.s: in rr: outpcd over 2f out: sn bhd* **50/1**

1m 17.26s (3.46) **Going Correction** +0.40s/f (Good) **9** Ran SP% **117.6**
Speed ratings (Par 97): **92,91,89,88,88 85,84,76,74**
CSF £7.54 TOTE £3.10: £1.10, £1.30, £8.30; EX 9.70 Trifecta £301.80.
Owner David Kilburn / John Nicholls Trading **Bred** Colman O'Flynn **Trained** Musley Bank, N Yorks
■ Stewards' Enquiry : Michael J M Murphy two-day ban: careless riding (Sep 25-26)

FOCUS
The rail between the 6f and 1.5f point was moved out a further 3yds after racing on Friday. This actual race distance was 6f 42yds (+24yds). The first three in the betting were drawn 2,3 and 4 and two of those battled out the finish. A minor pb from the winner. A minor pb from the winner.

6320 BETWAY H'CAP 7f 122y
2:15 (2:16) (Class 3) (0-90,89) 3-Y-O+
£12,450 (£3,728; £1,864; £932; £466; £234) **Stalls** Low

Form RPR
3020 **1** **Haley Bop (IRE)**23 5588 3-9-3 **88** JasonHart 6 100
(Mark Johnston) *chsd ldrs: drvn over 2f out: styd on to ld last 100yds* **9/1**
3000 **2** 1 1/2 **God Willing**105 2689 5-9-5 **85** PatrickMathers 8 94
(Declan Carroll) *w ldr: led 2f out: hdd and no ex last 100yds* **8/1**
0100 **3** 3 1/2 **Chevallier**12 5976 4-9-7 **87** MichaelJMMurphy 4 88
(Archie Watson) *trckd ldrs: t.k.h: kpt on same pce fnl f: tk 3rd nr fin* **8/1**
5520 **4** 1/2 **Alejandro (IRE)**8 6082 7-9-6 **86** FMBerry 1 85
(David O'Meara) *led: hdd 2f out: wknd clsng stages* **9/4**1
2-50 **5** 2 **Plough Boy (IRE)**13 5941 5-9-3 **83** MartinHarley 3 77
(Garvan Donnelly, Ire) *trckd ldrs: effrt over 2f out: kpt on same pce appr fnl f* **5/1**2
3022 **6** 3 1/4 **Sir Billy Wright (IRE)**12 5955 5-9-6 **86** RobertHavlin 12 72
(David Evans) *swtchd lft s: in rr: drvn 3f out: kpt on fnl f: nvr a factor* **8/1**
4-0 **7** 1 1/4 **Royal Shaheen (FR)**69 3-9-2 **87** RichardKingscote 9 69
(Alistair Whillans) *swtchd lft after s: mid-div: drvn 3f out: one pce fnl 2f* **25/1**
4250 **8** 3 3/4 **Dubai Dynamo**12 5976 11-9-5 **85** JamesSullivan 10 59
(Ruth Carr) *dwlt: in rr: drvn over 2f out: nvr on terms* **16/1**
5040 **9** 1/2 **Westwood Hoe**178 960 5-9-9 **89** AndrewMullen 5 61
(Tony Coyle) *mid-div: drvn 3f out: lost pl over 1f out* **14/1**

0653 **10** *14* **Steel Train (FR)**[25] 5514 5-9-2 **85** ShelleyBirkett(3) 2 22
(David O'Meara) *s.i.s: in rr: sme hdwy 3f out: lost pl over 1f out: sn bhd: eased clsng stages* **7/1**[3]

1m 35.43s (1.63) **Going Correction** +0.40s/f (Good)
WFA 3 from 4yo+ 5lb **10** Ran SP% **119.7**
Speed ratings (Par 107): **107,105,102,101,99 96,95,91,90,76**
CSF £81.03 CT £609.72 TOTE £7.40: £3.40, £2.50, £3.70; EX 90.70 Trifecta £882.00.
Owner Abdulla Al Mansoori **Bred** Mighty Universe Ltd **Trained** Middleham Moor, N Yorks

FOCUS
The rail between the 6f and 1.5f point was moved out a further 3yds after racing on Friday. This actual race distance was 7f 146yds (+24yds). Probably nothing more than a fair contest, where it paid to be reasonably prominent. The runner-up has been rated close to his reappearance form.

6321 BETWAY STAND CUP (LISTED RACE) 1m 4f 66y
2:50 (2:50) (Class 1) 3-Y-O+ **£22,684** (£8,600; £4,304; £2,144; £1,076) **Stalls** Low

Form RPR
2-13 **1** **Mountain Bell**[126] 2035 3-8-2 95 JFEgan 5 102
(Ralph Beckett) *t.k.h early: trckd ldrs: 3rd 2f out: 2nd last 100yds: styd on strly to ld nr fin* **5/2**[3]

1113 **2** *nk* **Desert Encounter (IRE)**[70] 3889 4-9-2 100 MartinHarley 4 107
(David Simcock) *stdd s: hld up in rr: hdwy on outside over 3f out: sn w ldr: led over 1f out: hdd and no ex clsng stages* **85/40**[2]

3053 **3** *1 3/4* **Foundation (IRE)**[14] 5893 3-8-8 110 ow1 [1] RobertHavlin 3 105
(John Gosden) *trckd ldr: led over 6f out: drvn and hdd over 1f out: kpt on same pce* **15/8**[1]

0300 **4** *7* **John Reel (FR)**[14] 5894 7-9-2 96 (v[1]) AndrewMullen 2 93
(David Evans) *led: hdd over 6f out: drvn over 2f out: hung rt and lost pl over 1f out* **25/1**

4046 **5** *1/2* **Not So Sleepy**[14] 5893 4-9-2 102 (t) FMBerry 6 92
(Hughie Morrison) *tk v t.k.h: trckd ldrs after 2f: wd bnd over 6f out: drvn over 2f out: lost pl 2f out* **10/1**

2m 41.84s (3.34) **Going Correction** +0.50s/f (Yiel)
WFA 3 from 4yo+ 9lb **5** Ran SP% **108.3**
Speed ratings (Par 111): **108,107,106,101,101**
CSF £7.92 TOTE £2.30: £1.10, £2.00; EX 8.00 Trifecta £10.90.
Owner Qatar Racing Limited **Bred** Theakston Stud **Trained** Kimpton, Hants

FOCUS
The rail between the 6f and 1.5f point was moved out a further 3yds after racing on Friday. This actual race distance was 1m4f 104yds (+38yds). The first three in the betting dominated the closing stages. The level is fluid.

6322 BETWAY NURSERY H'CAP 5f 110y
3:25 (3:29) (Class 3) (0-95,88) 2-Y-O
£11,205 (£3,355; £1,677; £838; £419; £210) **Stalls** Low

Form RPR
0015 **1** **Sayesse**[18] 5741 2-9-2 **83** JFEgan 2 86
(Mick Channon) *s.i.s: sn chsng ldrs: swtchd ins over 1f out: upsides fnl 150yds: edgd rt and led nr fin* **12/1**

4023 **2** *hd* **Boundsy (IRE)**[13] 5917 2-8-8 **75** PatrickMathers 10 77
(Richard Fahey) *swtchd lft after s: sn chsng ldrs: kpt on wl fnl 100yds: bmpd and tk 2nd post* **9/1**

0110 **3** *hd* **Franca Florio (IRE)**[42] 4884 2-8-5 **72** JoeDoyle 3 73
(Kevin Ryan) *s.i.s: sn trcking ldr: led narrowly last 150yds: carried rt and hdd nr fin* **5/1**[3]

021 **4** *1 3/4* **Harome (IRE)**[11] 6007 2-8-11 **78** JamesSullivan 4 74
(David Loughnane) *led: hdd last 150yds: fdd nr fin* **7/2**[2]

3010 **5** *nk* **Our Greta (IRE)**[23] 5583 2-8-4 **74** EdwardGreatrex(3) 1 69+
(Michael Appleby) *dwlt: mid-div: drvn over 2f out: kpt on same pce over 1f out* **3/1**[1]

1402 **6** *1 3/4* **Ventura Secret (IRE)**[17] 5756 2-8-11 **78** JasonHart 8 67
(Tim Easterby) *in rr: drvn over 2f out: kpt on appr fnl f: nvr a factor* **16/1**

0210 **7** *1 1/4* **Tahoo (IRE)**[29] 5359 2-9-2 **88** JordanVaughan(5) 5 73
(K R Burke) *trckd ldrs: chsng ldrs on outer whn hung rt over 1f out: wknd fnl 75yds* **6/1**

101 **8** *21* **Nayyar**[18] 5741 2-9-5 **86** MichaelJMMurphy 6
(Charles Hills) *v free to post and overshot s by over 1f: in rr: drvn over 2f out: sn lost pl: bhd whn eased fnl 100yds* **6/1**

1m 9.66s (3.46) **Going Correction** +0.50s/f (Yiel) **8** Ran SP% **116.0**
Speed ratings (Par 99): **96,95,95,93,92 90,88,60**
CSF £114.41 CT £621.05 TOTE £13.30: £3.20, £2.10, £2.00; EX 87.30 Trifecta £760.90.
Owner Lord Ilsley Racing (Steele Syndicate) **Bred** Llety Farms **Trained** West Ilsley, Berks
■ Stewards' Enquiry : J F Egan two-day ban: careless riding (Sep 25-26)
Michael J M Murphy trainer's rep said colt was unsuited by the going

FOCUS
The rail between the 6f and 1.5f point was moved out a further 3yds after racing on Friday. This actual race distance was 5f 132yds (+22yds). The winner of this nursery was more experienced than most he faced, so is a handy mark to the level achieved. The third has been rated back to form.

6323 STELLAR GROUP H'CAP 1m 2f 75y
3:55 (3:59) (Class 4) (0-80,80) 3-Y-O+
£7,470 (£2,236; £1,118; £559; £279; £140) **Stalls** High

Form RPR
3-11 **1** **Rainbow Rebel (IRE)**[17] 5779 3-9-2 **77** RichardKingscote 4 85+
(Mark Johnston) *trckd ldr: led narrowly over 1f out: hld on gamely nr fin* **5/2**[1]

-103 **2** *nk* **De Veer Cliffs (IRE)**[37] 5089 3-9-5 **80** FMBerry 3 87
(Martyn Meade) *sn chsng ldrs: no ex clsng stages* **9/2**[2]

00-5 **3** *3/4* **Fantasy Gladiator**[248] 58 10-9-10 **78** (p) AndrewMullen 6 83
(Michael Appleby) *hld up in mid-div: hdwy on ins over 1f out: kpt on same pce last 50yds* **25/1**

2344 **4** *1/2* **Brandon Castle**[13] 5918 4-9-2 **70** RobertHavlin 11 74
(Simon West) *mid-div: t.k.h: hdwy on outer over 1f out: styd on same pce towards fin* **12/1**

4404 **5** *1* **Outback Blue**[24] 5545 3-9-2 **77** (t) JFEgan 9 79
(David Evans) *s.s: hdwy over 2f out: swtchd ins over 1f out: kpt on same pce last 75yds* **11/1**

1620 **6** *3/4* **Save The Bees**[23] 5579 8-9-4 **79** (b) GerO'Neill(7) 7 80
(Declan Carroll) *trckd ldrs: kpt on same pce fnl 150yds* **11/1**

5445 **7** *1/2* **Yorkindred Spirit**[13] 5918 4-9-0 **68** (v) JasonHart 10 68
(Mark Johnston) *mid-div: hdwy on outer over 3f out: kpt on same pce fnl f* **20/1**

4003 **8** *1 1/2* **Muqarred (USA)**[14] 5883 4-9-5 **73** (p) MartinHarley 8 70
(David Loughnane) *led: hdd over 1f out: wknd last 75yds* **9/1**

/24- **9** *3* **Royal Flag**[480] 2356 6-9-11 **79** DaleSwift 5 70
(Brian Ellison) *trckd ldrs: pushed along over 3f out: wknd fnl f: eased towards fin* **5/1**[3]

0026 **10** *9* **Henshaw**[68] 3957 3-9-0 **75** [1] MichaelJMMurphy 1 48
(Charles Hills) *s.i.s: in rr: drvn over 3f out: bhd 2f out: eased clsng stages* **11/1**

2m 15.7s (4.50) **Going Correction** +0.60s/f (Yiel)
WFA 3 from 4yo+ 7lb **10** Ran SP% **114.7**
Speed ratings (Par 105): **106,105,105,104,103 103,102,101,99,92**
CSF £12.99 CT £222.52 TOTE £3.00: £1.50, £1.90, £5.30; EX 13.30 Trifecta £208.90.
Owner Owners Group 004 **Bred** Pier House Stud **Trained** Middleham Moor, N Yorks

FOCUS
The rail between the 6f and 1.5f point was moved out a further 3yds after racing on Friday. This actual race distance was 1m2f 101yds (+26yds). A smart ride by Richard Kingscote steered the market leader to victory. It's been rated around the third and fifth.

6324 CHESTERBET H'CAP 5f 16y
4:30 (4:31) (Class 4) (0-80,79) 3-Y-O+
£7,470 (£2,236; £1,118; £559; £279; £140) **Stalls** Low

Form RPR
5-02 **1** **I'll Be Good**[31] 5296 7-9-3 **75** DaleSwift 12 86
(Brian Ellison) *sn chsng ldrs on outer: led and edgd lft 1f out: styd on strly: readily* **11/1**

0220 **2** *2* **Apricot Sky**[8] 6080 6-9-7 **79** RobertHavlin 9 83
(David Nicholls) *chsd ldr: sltly hmpd 1f out: kpt on same pce* **15/2**[3]

03 **3** *shd* **Casterbridge**[57] 4345 4-9-5 **77** JasonHart 2 81
(Eric Alston) *chsd ldrs: drvn 2f out: n.m.r and swtchd rt 1f out: kpt on same pce* **4/1**[1]

0022 **4** *3/4* **Masamah (IRE)**[8] 6080 10-9-6 **78** (p) PatrickMathers 6 79+
(Richard Fahey) *s.i.s: outpcd in rr: swtchd rt appr fnl f: fin strly* **4/1**[1]

0001 **5** *nk* **Jack Luey**[48] 4691 9-9-5 **77** (b) TomEaves 8 77
(Lawrence Mullaney) *in rr: hdwy over 1f out: kpt on same pce last 100yds* **16/1**

0010 **6** *hd* **Mappin Time (IRE)**[17] 5780 8-9-5 **77** (b) AndrewMullen 1 76
(Tim Easterby) *in rr: hdwy on ins over 1f out: kpt on same pce last 100yds* **7/1**[2]

3313 **7** *hd* **Come On Dave (IRE)**[77] 3638 7-9-4 **76** (v) JFEgan 5 74
(John Butler) *sn chsng ldrs: keeping on same pce whn hung lft and hmpd 100yds out* **4/1**[1]

1001 **8** *1 1/2* **Economic Crisis (IRE)**[17] 5780 7-9-5 **77** JoeDoyle 4 70
(John David Riches) *mid-div: hdwy over 1f out: edgd rt and fdd 100yds out* **9/1**

0040 **9** *nk* **Captain Dunne (IRE)**[17] 5762 11-8-11 **69** JamesSullivan 3 61
(Tim Easterby) *led: hdd over 1f out: sn wknd* **12/1**

0150 **10** *nk* **Landing Night (IRE)**[91] 3150 4-9-1 **78** (p) JordanVaughan(5) 10 69
(Rebecca Menzies) *hld up towards rr: hdwy over 1f out: nt clr run and swtchd lft 100yds out: nvr a threat* **25/1**

1m 3.23s (2.23) **Going Correction** +0.60s/f (Yiel) **10** Ran SP% **120.0**
Speed ratings (Par 105): **106,102,102,101,100 100,100,97,97,96**
CSF £93.52 CT £405.14 TOTE £13.90: £3.20, £2.50, £1.80; EX 57.70 Trifecta £639.10.
Owner Graham Brown & Brian Ellison **Bred** Cobhall Court Stud **Trained** Norton, N Yorks

FOCUS
The rail between the 6f and 1.5f point was moved out a further 3yds after racing on Friday. This actual race distance was 5f 36yds (+20yds). A decent sprint run at a solid gallop. It's been rated around the runner-up.

6325 BETWAY STAYERS H'CAP 1m 7f 195y
5:00 (5:03) (Class 3) (0-90,84) 3-Y-O **£12,450** (£3,728; £1,864; £932) **Stalls** Low

Form RPR
0321 **1** **Blakeney Point**[7] 6127 3-9-5 **82** (p) RichardKingscote 3 91+
(Roger Charlton) *trckd ldng pair: effrt 3f out: nt clr run over 1f out: swtchd ins: sn led: styd on strly: readily* **3/1**[3]

4112 **2** *3* **Masterson (IRE)**[5] 6185 3-8-3 **66** JFEgan 4 70
(Mick Channon) *hld up in last: hdwy 3f out: chsng ldrs over 1f out: kpt on same pce to take 2nd last 50yds* **15/2**

5313 **3** *1/2* **Hereawi**[39] 4994 3-9-7 **84** FMBerry 1 87
(Ralph Beckett) *led: qcknd pce over 4f out: drvn 3f out: hdd 1f out: kpt on one pce* **15/8**[2]

4131 **4** *1 3/4* **Clear Evidence**[15] 5830 3-8-6 **72** EdwardGreatrex(3) 2 73
(Michael Bell) *trckd ldr: pushed along over 3f out: upsides over 2f out: fdd last 150yds* **13/8**[1]

3m 40.33s (12.33) **Going Correction** +0.70s/f (Yiel) **4** Ran SP% **109.6**
Speed ratings (Par 105): **97,95,95,94**
CSF £20.35 TOTE £3.70; EX 17.00 Trifecta £52.60.
Owner Axom LX **Bred** Mr & Mrs A E Pakenham **Trained** Beckhampton, Wilts

FOCUS
The rail between the 6f and 1.5f point was moved out a further 3yds after racing on Friday. This actual race distance was 2m 21yds (+46yds). Hard to think this will prove to be strong form with the two market leaders disappointing, but the winner was fairly impressive. The winner has been rated as building on his Kempton win.
T/Plt: £472.10 to a £1 stake. Pool: £83,222.59 - 128.66 winning units T/Qpdt: £143.50 to a £1 stake. Pool: £4,757.67 - 24.52 winning units **Walter Glynn**

6281 DONCASTER (L-H)
Saturday, September 10

OFFICIAL GOING: Good (good to firm in places; 8.4)
Wind: Virtually nil Weather: Grey cloud

6326 AT THE RACES CHAMPAGNE STKS (GROUP 2) (C&G) 7f
2:00 (2:00) (Class 1) 2-Y-O
£42,532 (£16,125; £8,070; £4,020; £2,017; £1,012) **Stalls** High

Form RPR
21 **1** **Rivet (IRE)**[22] 5615 2-9-0 0 AndreaAtzeni 1 114+
(William Haggas) *trckd ldng pair: swtchd lft and hdwy 2f out: rdn to chal jst over 1f out: drvn ins fnl f: led last 75 yds* **7/4**[1]

162 **2** *hd* **Thunder Snow (IRE)**[46] 4732 2-9-0 107 JamesDoyle 5 113
(Saeed bin Suroor) *cl up on inner: led 2f out: rdn over 1f out: drvn ins fnl f: hdd and no ex last 75 yds* **2/1**[2]

21 **3** *5* **D'bai (IRE)**[49] 4649 2-9-0 85 [1] WilliamBuick 3 100
(Charlie Appleby) *hld up in tch: hdwy 2f out: rdn over 1f out: drvn and kpt on same pce fnl f* **8/1**

21 **4** *nse* **Majeste**[56] 4390 2-9-0 0 .... SeanLevey 2 100
(Richard Hannon) *slt ld: pushed along and hdd 2f out: sn rdn and wknd appr fnl f* **5/1**[3]

2215 **5** *2 1/4* **Grey Britain**[21] 5654 2-9-0 100 .... JamieSpencer 6 94
(John Ryan) *in tch: pushed along over 2f out: rdn wl over 1f out: sn one pce* **12/1**

2124 **6** *4 1/2* **Tommy Taylor (USA)**[24] 5556 2-9-0 97 .... TomEaves 4 82
(Kevin Ryan) *hld up in rr: pushed along wl over 2f out: sn rdn and no hdwy* **16/1**

1m 26.63s (0.33) **Going Correction** -0.05s/f (Good) **6** Ran SP% **111.0**
Speed ratings (Par 107): **96,95,90,90,87 82**
CSF £5.39 TOTE £2.30: £1.60, £1.40; EX 5.20 Trifecta £16.70.
Owner The Starship Partnership **Bred** Des Scott **Trained** Newmarket, Suffolk

FOCUS
William Buick said of the ground: "It is good but with the recent rain it is just a bit loose on top," while James Doyle described it as "very dead." Although there was no great depth to this Group 2, the front pair, who are both smart juveniles, drew clear with the runner-up used as a reliable guide to the form. The early pace was a steady one and they raced stands' side. The level is a bit fluid, but for now the runner-up sets the level.

6327 LADBROKES PORTLAND (H'CAP) 5f 140y
2:35 (2:40) (Class 2) 3-Y-O+

£37,350 (£11,184; £5,592; £2,796; £1,398; £702) **Stalls** High

Form RPR

04U3 **1** **Captain Colby (USA)**[24] 5555 4-9-0 **95** .... (b) WilliamBuick 12 107
(Ed Walker) *trckd ldrs: pushed along over 2f out: rdn over 1f out: chal ent fnl f: drvn to ld last 100 yds: kpt on strly* **6/1**[1]

0042 **2** *1 1/2* **Humidor (IRE)**[12] 5961 9-9-3 **98** .... FergusSweeney 1 105
(George Baker) *hld up: hdwy on outer over 2f out: rdn to ld ent fnl f: drvn and hdd last 100 yds: kpt on* **20/1**

0055 **3** *1/2* **Harry Hurricane**[24] 5555 4-9-0 **95** .... RobertWinston 9 100
(George Baker) *trckd ldrs: hdwy 2f out: rdn and n.m.r over 1f out: ev ch ent fnl f: sn drvn and kpt on same pce* **10/1**

5-30 **4** *hd* **Double Up**[88] 3244 5-9-10 **105** .... (t) AndreaAtzeni 16 110
(Roger Varian) *dwlt and hld up towards rr: hdwy 1/2-way: sn in tch: swtchd rt and effrt wl over 1f out: rdn ent fnl f: kpt on* **8/1**[2]

0551 **5** *nk* **Soie D'Leau**[7] 6119 4-9-1 **96** .... TonyHamilton 14 100
(Kristin Stubbs) *cl up: led 2f out: sn rdn: drvn and hdd ent fnl f: kpt on same pce* **20/1**

1000 **6** *nk* **Hoofalong**[24] 5555 6-8-11 **97** .... (b) NathanEvans[(5)] 6 100
(Michael Easterby) *midfield: hdwy 2f out: rdn over 1f out: kpt on fnl f: nrst fin* **33/1**

3210 **7** *1/2* **Highland Acclaim (IRE)**[2] 6263 5-8-10 **91** .... SeanLevey 15 92
(David O'Meara) *chsd ldrs: rdn along 2f out: drvn and wknd fnl f* **33/1**

4040 **8** *1/2* **Shamshon (IRE)**[7] 6112 5-8-13 **94** .... JamesDoyle 17 93
(Jamie Osborne) *towards rr: hdwy 2f out: sn rdn and kpt on fnl f: nrst fin* **9/1**[3]

0441 **9** *hd* **Pipers Note**[11] 6012 6-9-4 **99** .... GeorgeChaloner 10 98
(Richard Whitaker) *cl up: rdn wl over 1f out: drvn and wknd fnl f* **20/1**

3350 **10** *hd* **Lexington Abbey**[24] 5555 5-8-13 **94** .... JamieSpencer 2 92
(Kevin Ryan) *in tch: hdwy 2f out: sn rdn and no imp fnl f* **10/1**

0026 **11** *hd* **Olivia Fallow (IRE)**[12] 5961 4-8-5 **86** .... JimmyQuinn 7 83
(Paul Midgley) *towards rr: pushed along over 2f out: sn rdn and hdwy over 1f out: chsd ldrs whn n.m.r ins fnl f: no imp* **50/1**

6252 **12** *1/2* **Confessional**[7] 6119 9-8-11 **92** .... (be) DavidAllan 19 88
(Tim Easterby) *midfield: hdwy 2f out: sn rdn and no imp* **20/1**

3202 **13** *3/4* **Related**[20] 5678 6-9-0 **95** .... (b) MartinLane 8 88
(Paul Midgley) *cl up: rdn along over 2f out: drvn wl over 1f out and grad wknd* **33/1**

2510 **14** *3/4* **Mont Kiara (FR)**[28] 5409 3-8-12 **95** .... KevinStott 4 86
(Kevin Ryan) *dwlt and rr: hdwy 1/2-way: rdn along 2f out: n.d* **20/1**

6010 **15** *nse* **Son Of Africa**[14] 5863 4-9-2 **97** .... OisinMurphy 11 88
(Henry Candy) *a towards rr* **20/1**

3220 **16** *1/2* **Red Pike (IRE)**[42] 4865 5-9-2 **97** .... ConnorBeasley 13 86
(Bryan Smart) *led: rdn along and hdd 2f out: sn drvn and wknd over 1f out* **6/1**[1]

2300 **17** *2* **Out Do**[7] 6112 7-9-8 **103** .... (v) PhillipMakin 21 85
(David O'Meara) *racd nr stands rail: in tch: effrt and swtchd lft over 1f out: sn rdn and no hdwy* **20/1**

001 **18** *3/4* **Judicial (IRE)**[21] 5641 4-9-4 **99** .... (e) GrahamLee 20 79
(Julie Camacho) *racd nr stands rail: prom: rdn along 2f out: sn drvn and wknd* **12/1**

0200 **19** *1/2* **Move In Time**[24] 5555 8-9-7 **102** .... DavidNolan 3 80
(David O'Meara) *a towards rr* **33/1**

6303 **20** *4 1/2* **Bowson Fred**[7] 6119 4-9-7 **102** .... PaulHanagan 5 65
(Michael Easterby) *dwlt a rr* **25/1**

1m 6.91s (-1.89) **Going Correction** -0.05s/f (Good)
WFA 3 from 4yo+ 2lb **20** Ran SP% **126.5**
Speed ratings (Par 109): **110,108,107,107,106 106,105,104,104,104 104,103,102,101,101 100,98,97,96,90**
CSF £124.12 CT £1235.08 TOTE £6.60: £1.90, £4.90, £2.50, £2.70; EX 130.80 Trifecta £1614.30.
Owner Lee Tze Bun Marces **Bred** Castleton Lyons & Kilboy Estate **Trained** Upper Lambourn, Berks
■ Mukaynis was withdrawn. Price at time of withdrawal 20/1. Rule 4 does not apply

FOCUS
The weights were raised a pound after The Happy Prince was rerouted to the Park Stakes. A typically competitive Portland, in which they finished in a heap behind the winner. The field split, with two runners isolated on the stands' side, then the main body of the field towards the centre, with a group of four racing a little further out. There didn't seem much in the way of an advantage and the winner came from the largest group. Straightforward form, with the winner recording a pb, the runner-up his best run of the year, and the fourth and fifth fitting.

6328 SAINT GOBAIN WEBER PARK STKS (GROUP 2) 7f
3:10 (3:14) (Class 1) 3-Y-O+

£56,710 (£21,500; £10,760; £5,360; £2,690; £1,350) **Stalls** High

Form RPR

3415 **1** **Breton Rock (IRE)**[7] 6117 6-9-4 112 .... AndreaAtzeni 8 115+
(David Simcock) *hld up in rr: hdwy over 2f out: rdn to chse ldng pair ent fnl f: sn drvn and styd on wl to ld towards fin* **7/2**[2]

4002 **2** *shd* **The Happy Prince (IRE)**[7] 6145 4-9-4 106 .... (t) SeamieHeffernan 4 114
(A P O'Brien, Ire) *prom: cl up on outer 1/2-way: led 2f out: rdn and edgd rt wl over 1f out: drvn ent fnl f: hdd and no ex towards fin* **14/1**

6024 **3** *1/2* **Adaay (IRE)**[55] 4433 4-9-4 111 .... (b[1]) PaulHanagan 3 113
(William Haggas) *hld up towards rr: hdwy on outer 2f out: rdn to chse ldrs over 1f out: drvn and ev ch ins fnl f: kpt on same pce* **4/1**[3]

5041 **4** *1* **Buckstay (IRE)**[26] 5472 6-9-4 110 .... (p) JamieSpencer 2 110
(Peter Chapple-Hyam) *trckd ldrs: hdwy to chse ldr over 1f out and sn rdn: drvn and ev ch jst ins fnl f: kpt on same pce* **9/1**

-501 **5** *1 3/4* **Richard Pankhurst**[28] 5404 4-9-7 115 .... WilliamBuick 6 109
(John Gosden) *hld up: hdwy over 2f out: rdn wl over 1f out: sn drvn and no imp fnl f* **11/4**[1]

2052 **6** *1/2* **Cougar Mountain (IRE)**[30] 5343 5-9-4 110 .... (vt[1]) DonnachaO'Brien 7 104
(A P O'Brien, Ire) *trckd ldrs on inner: pushed along over 2f out: sn rdn and wknd over 1f out* **10/1**

4044 **7** *1/2* **Toormore (IRE)**[14] 5873 5-9-7 115 .... JamesDoyle 5 106
(Richard Hannon) *led: rdn along and hdd 2f out: sn drvn and wknd* **9/2**

5045 **8** *8* **Kentuckyconnection (USA)**[48] 4688 3-9-0 105 .... (v[1]) ConnorBeasley 1 79
(Bryan Smart) *wnt lft s: sn cl up: rdn along over 2f out: sn wknd* **50/1**

1m 25.35s (-0.95) **Going Correction** -0.05s/f (Good)
WFA 3 from 4yo+ 4lb **8** Ran SP% **114.8**
Speed ratings (Par 115): **103,102,102,101,99 98,98,88**
CSF £50.32 TOTE £4.90: £1.50, £2.80, £1.60; EX 52.20 Trifecta £195.90.
Owner John Cook **Bred** George Kent **Trained** Newmarket, Suffolk

FOCUS
Racing stands' side, there was no great gallop on early in this Group 2 contest and the winner did really well to come from a poor position given how the race unfolded. The winner has been rated to his best.

6329 LADBROKES ST LEGER STKS (BRITISH CHAMPIONS SERIES) (GROUP 1) (ENTIRES COLTS & FILLIES) 1m 6f 132y
3:45 (3:49) (Class 1) 3-Y-O

£396,970 (£150,500; £75,320; £37,520; £18,830; £9,450) **Stalls** Low

Form RPR

1124 **1** **Harbour Law**[65] 4059 3-9-1 102 .... GeorgeBaker 9 116
(Laura Mongan) *hld up towards rr: hdwy 3f out: chsd ldrs 2f out: rdn to chse ldng pair and edgd lft over 1f out: drvn ins fnl f: styd on wl to ld nr fin* **22/1**

6011 **2** *3/4* **Ventura Storm (IRE)**[34] 5218 3-9-1 111 .... SilvestreDeSousa 5 115
(Richard Hannon) *trckd ldrs on inner: swtchd rt and hdwy over 2f out: sn cl up: rdn over 1f out: drvn to take slt ld jst ins fnl f: hdd and no ex nr fin* **14/1**

4412 **3** *shd* **Housesofparliament (IRE)**[24] 5557 3-9-1 113 .... (t) ColmO'Donoghue 7 115
(A P O'Brien, Ire) *trckd ldrs: hdwy on outer 3f out and sn led: jnd and rdn 2f out: drvn and hdd jst ins fnl f: kpt on gamely u.p towards fin* **7/1**[3]

2131 **4** *10* **Muntahaa (IRE)**[21] 5639 3-9-1 113 .... PaulHanagan 6 102
(John Gosden) *keen: trckd ldr tl led after 1 1/2f: pushed along over 3f out: rdn and hdd wl over 2f out: sn drvn and kpt on one pce* **4/1**[2]

115 **5** *8* **Sword Fighter (IRE)**[44] 4799 3-9-1 112 .... DonnachaO'Brien 1 92
(A P O'Brien, Ire) *led 1 1/2f: chsd ldr: rdn along and cl up over 3f out: drvn over 2f out: sn wknd* **9/1**

3304 **6** *2* **Harrison**[24] 5557 3-9-1 103 .... GrahamLee 4 89
(Mick Channon) *hld up in rr: effrt on inner whn hmpd over 3f out: bhd after* **40/1**

3022 **7** *nk* **Ormito (GER)**[28] 5402 3-9-1 102 ....[1] OisinMurphy 3 89
(Andrew Balding) *a rr* **20/1**

10 **8** *5* **The Tartan Spartan (IRE)**[85] 3341 3-9-1 96 .... PhillipMakin 8 82
(John Patrick Shanahan, Ire) *chsd ldrs: rdn along over 4f out: sn wknd* **66/1**

3321 **U** **Idaho (IRE)**[24] 5557 3-9-1 120 .... SeamieHeffernan 2
(A P O'Brien, Ire) *hld up in tch: hdwy to trck ldrs whn swtchd sltly rt, stmbld and uns rdr over 3f out* **4/6**[1]

3m 5.48s (-1.92) **Going Correction** +0.10s/f (Good) **9** Ran SP% **122.2**
Speed ratings (Par 115): **109,108,108,103,98 97,97,95,**
CSF £291.92 CT £2393.30 TOTE £29.60: £4.20, £2.70, £2.00; EX 218.60 Trifecta £2678.90.
Owner Mrs Jackie Cornwell **Bred** Hascombe And Valiant Studs **Trained** Epsom, Surrey

FOCUS
This wasn't a strong St Leger, only four of them having won a Group race and with Red Verdon a notable absentee, but it was a race of high drama with the favourite unseating early in the straight and a terrific three-way finish. They finished well strung out behind the first three in a time 2.48sec outside standard, the race having been run at what looked an even gallop. A filly won last year, but there were none involved this time.

6330 CHAMPAGNE POMMERY NURSERY H'CAP 1m (S)
4:20 (4:25) (Class 2) 2-Y-O

£11,205 (£3,355; £1,677; £838; £419; £210) **Stalls** High

Form RPR

341 **1** **Khalidi**[15] 5828 2-9-3 **85** .... AndreaAtzeni 3 90
(John Gosden) *trckd ldng pair: hdwy 2f out: rdn to ld jst over 1f out: drvn ins fnl f: kpt on strly towards fin* **5/2**[1]

4211 **2** *1 1/4* **Harbour Master**[21] 5644 2-9-7 **89** .... JamieSpencer 5 91
(Jamie Osborne) *hld up in rr: hdwy 2f out: rdn to chal ent fnl f: sn drvn and kpt on* **5/2**[1]

211 **3** *nk* **Maths Prize**[25] 5518 2-9-6 **88** ....[1] GeorgeBaker 8 89
(Roger Charlton) *hld up in rr: hdwy on outer 2f out: rdn to chse wnr ent fnl f: sn drvn and kpt on same pce towards fin* **4/1**[2]

51 **4** *2* **Mount Moriah**[17] 5764 2-8-5 **73** .... SilvestreDeSousa 9 70
(Ralph Beckett) *trckd ldng pair on inner: hdwy 2f out: rdn over 1f out: sn drvn and kpt on same pce* **13/2**

0510 **5** *1 1/4* **Arborist (IRE)**[22] 5595 2-8-7 **75** .... PaulHanagan 2 69
(Sylvester Kirk) *cl up: rdn along over 2f out: sn wknd* **12/1**

0321 **6** *3/4* **Drochaid**[36] 5107 2-8-11 **79** .... OisinMurphy 6 72+
(Andrew Balding) *led: pushed along over 2f out: rdn wl over 1f out: hdd appr fnl f: sn wknd* **6/1**[3]

1m 40.79s (1.49) **Going Correction** -0.05s/f (Good) **6** Ran SP% **112.5**
Speed ratings (Par 101): **90,88,88,86,85 84**
CSF £8.88 CT £22.47 TOTE £3.50: £1.80, £1.70; EX 9.60 Trifecta £27.30.
Owner Nizar Anwar **Bred** Aston House Stud **Trained** Newmarket, Suffolk

FOCUS
A decent nursery, despite three non-runners, and they again raced stands' side. The runner-up has been rated pretty much to his Sandown level.

6331 NAPOLEONS CASINOS & RESTAURANTS H'CAP 1m (S)
4:50 (4:51) (Class 2) (0-110,100) 3-Y-O+

£15,562 (£4,660; £2,330; £1,165; £582; £292) **Stalls** High

Form RPR

1000 **1** **Can't Change It (IRE)**[14] 5871 5-9-4 **94** .... JamieSpencer 6 102
(David Simcock) *hld up in rr: hdwy 2f out: rdn ins fnl f: styd on wl to ld towards fin* **7/1**

1502 **2** 3/4 **Banksea**[22] 5616 3-9-4 **99** AndreaAtzeni 7 105
(Luca Cumani) *trckd ldrs: hdwy over 2f out: rdn to chal over 1f out: led ent fnl f: sn drvn: hdd and no ex last 100 yds* **2/1**[1]

0000 **3** 3/4 **Dinkum Diamond (IRE)**[23] 5585 8-9-9 **99** OisinMurphy 10 104
(Henry Candy) *trckd ldrs: cl up 3f out: rdn over 1f out: drvn and ev ch ent fnl f: kpt on same pce* **12/1**

3003 **4** nk **One Word More (IRE)**[9] 6056 6-9-9 **99** DavidNolan 5 103
(Tim Easterby) *t.k.h: hld up in tch: hdwy 2f out: rdn over 1f out: drvn and kpt on fnl f* **7/1**

1211 **5** 3/4 **Breakable**[21] 5640 5-9-6 **96** DavidAllan 8 99
(Tim Easterby) *trckd ldr: led over 2f out: rdn wl over 1f out: drvn and hdd ent fnl f: grad wknd* **6/1**[3]

0-51 **6** 4 1/2 **Up In Lights (IRE)**[36] 5123 4-9-2 **92** TomQueally 1 84
(James Fanshawe) *hld up: hdwy on outer to chse ldrs 2f out: sn rdn: drvn over 1f out: sn wknd* **11/4**[2]

0500 **7** 1/2 **King's Pavilion (IRE)**[49] 4625 3-8-11 **92** NickyMackay 2 82
(Mark Johnston) *prom: cl up 1/2-way: rdn along 2f out: sn wknd* **16/1**

0-00 **8** 7 **Marcret (ITY)**[21] 5640 9-9-1 **91** GrahamLee 9 66
(Grace Harris) *sn led: rdn along and hdd over 2f out: sn wknd* **50/1**

1m 39.4s (0.10) **Going Correction** -0.05s/f (Good)
WFA 3 from 4yo+ 5lb **8** Ran SP% **114.8**
Speed ratings (Par 109): **97,96,95,95,94 89,89,82**
CSF £21.54 CT £168.80 TOTE £7.80: £2.20, £1.20, £2.70; EX 24.80 Trifecta £177.10.
Owner Mrs Fitri Hay **Bred** Peter & Hugh McCutcheon **Trained** Newmarket, Suffolk

FOCUS
A decent handicap if not particularly strong for the grade. They came down the middle. The form is set around the third to this year's form.

6332 EBF BREEDERS' SERIES FILLIES' H'CAP 1m 4f
5:25 (5:25) (Class 2) (0-100,97) 3-Y-O+
£18,675 (£5,592; £2,796; £1,398; £699; £351) **Stalls** Low

Form RPR
1-04 **1** **Bess Of Hardwick**[30] 5328 4-9-1 **86** AndreaAtzeni 5 97+
(Luca Cumani) *trckd ldrs: hdwy 3f out: narrow ld wl over 1f out: sn rdn: edgd lft and drvn ent fnl f: kpt on strly towards fin* **10/3**[1]

-053 **2** 1 3/4 **Kiltara (IRE)**[15] 5851 4-9-2 **87** OisinMurphy 2 94
(Mark Johnston) *led: pushed along over 2f out: rdn and hdd wl over 1f out: cl up and drvn whn bmpd and carried lft ent fnl f: kpt on* **11/1**

606 **3** hd **Lustrous**[50] 4610 5-9-12 **97** PhillipMakin 7 104
(David O'Meara) *hld up in rr: hdwy wl over 2f out: rdn to chse ldrs over 1f out: kpt on wl towards fin* **20/1**

-241 **4** 2 **Moorside**[38] 5025 3-9-1 **95** JamesDoyle 1 98
(Charles Hills) *trckd ldrs: hdwy over 3f out: rdn along 2f out: drvn over 1f out and sn one pce* **9/2**[3]

3-03 **5** 3/4 **Turning The Table (IRE)**[112] 2490 3-8-3 **83** oh1 NickyMackay 3 85
(David Simcock) *in tch: hdwy on inner to chse ldrs 2f out: sn rdn: drvn appr fnl f: wknd* **4/1**[2]

-306 **6** 2 **Missed Call (IRE)**[28] 5411 6-9-8 **93** TomQueally 4 92
(James Fanshawe) *hld up in rr: sme hdwy wl over 2f out: sn rdn and n.d* **6/1**

10-0 **7** 8 **Sweet P**[77] 3670 5-9-2 **87** GeorgeBaker 8 73
(Marcus Tregoning) *trckd ldr: effrt and cl up 3f out: rdn along over 2f out: drvn wl over 1f out and sn wknd* **12/1**

2042 **8** 1 **Renfrew Street**[8] 6074 3-8-3 **83** SilvestreDeSousa 6 68
(Mark Johnston) *chsd ldrs: rdn along over 3f out: sn wknd* **5/1**

2m 33.31s (-1.59) **Going Correction** +0.10s/f (Good)
WFA 3 from 4yo+ 9lb **8** Ran SP% **113.0**
Speed ratings (Par 96): **109,107,107,106,105 104,99,98**
CSF £39.36 CT £625.93 TOTE £4.40: £1.60, £3.10, £4.90; EX 39.10 Trifecta £401.00.
Owner Duke Of Devonshire **Bred** The Duke Of Devonshire **Trained** Newmarket, Suffolk

FOCUS
A useful handicap in which they appeared to go a reasonable gallop. They started off more down the centre once in line for home but some, including the winner, ended up on or towards the far rail. The runner-up has been rated as building on her back-to-form latest.

6333 HARRIET DE-VERE POWELL H'CAP 1m 4f
6:00 (6:01) (Class 2) (0-110,102) 3-Y-O+
£15,562 (£4,660; £2,330; £1,165; £582; £292) **Stalls** Low

Form RPR
14-4 **1** **Gold Trail (IRE)**[63] 4165 5-9-12 **102** JamesDoyle 3 113
(Charlie Appleby) *chsd clr ldr: tk clsr order over 3f out: led 2f out: rdn clr appr fnl f: styd on strly* **5/1**[3]

3142 **2** 5 **Stars Over The Sea (USA)**[9] 6057 5-9-12 **102** GeorgeBaker 5 105
(Mark Johnston) *led and sn wl clr: pushed along 3f out: rdn and hdd 2f out: sn drvn and kpt on u.p fnl f* **3/1**[1]

61-6 **3** 5 **Argus (IRE)**[64] 4115 4-9-1 **91** OisinMurphy 1 86
(Ralph Beckett) *trckd ldrs: pushed along 3f out: rdn 2f out: sn drvn and no imp* **3/1**[1]

003 **4** 5 **Felix Mendelssohn (IRE)**[9] 6057 5-9-5 **95** JamieSpencer 6 82
(David Simcock) *hld up: hdwy over 3f out: rdn 2f out: sn drvn and btn* **9/2**[2]

3530 **5** 2 1/2 **High Grounds (IRE)**[64] 4108 3-8-10 **95** SilvestreDeSousa 4 78
(Charles Hills) *dwlt and a rr* **9/2**[2]

6-50 **6** 13 **Ajman Bridge**[85] 3340 6-9-9 **99** [1] AndreaAtzeni 2 61
(Roger Varian) *hld up: hdwy 3f out: rdn along over 2f out: sn drvn and wknd: eased* **7/1**

2m 31.31s (-3.59) **Going Correction** +0.10s/f (Good)
WFA 3 from 4yo+ 9lb **6** Ran SP% **115.5**
Speed ratings (Par 109): **115,111,108,105,103 94**
CSF £21.03 TOTE £5.60: £2.50, £2.00; EX 21.60 Trifecta £42.60.
Owner Godolphin **Bred** Mrs S M Rogers & Sir Thomas Pilkington **Trained** Newmarket, Suffolk

FOCUS
A good handicap, but only the first two ever really got involved. They finished well spread out. The form is far from bombproof.
T/Jkpt: Not Won. T/Plt: £235.80 to a £1 stake. Pool: £188,426.1 - 583.25 winning units T/Qpdt: £79.80 to a £1 stake. Pool: £9,547.38 - 88.48 winning units **Joe Rowntree**

6030 LINGFIELD (L-H)
Saturday, September 10

OFFICIAL GOING: Good (good to firm in places) changing to good to soft after race 5 (4.10)
Wind: light to medium, behind Weather: overcast, steady rain after race 3

6334 PAUL YOUNG STAG PARTY FILLIES' H'CAP 1m 3f 106y
1:50 (1:51) (Class 5) (0-70,70) 3-Y-O+ **£3,234** (£962; £481; £240) **Stalls** High

Form RPR
3501 **1** **Corpus Chorister (FR)**[18] 5746 3-9-4 **70** MartinDwyer 7 80
(David Menuisier) *sn led and mde rest: clr 4f out: pushed along ent fnl 2f: styd on wl under hands and heels after* **9/4**[1]

2306 **2** 2 1/4 **Taurian**[31] 5294 5-9-5 **63** TomMarquand 2 69
(Ian Williams) *t.k.h early: hld up wl in tch in midfield: effrt in 3rd 3f out: rdn over 2f out: chsd wnr ins fnl f: no imp* **12/1**

3442 **3** 2 1/2 **Cacica**[25] 5529 3-9-0 **66** (b) JimCrowley 1 68
(George Scott) *led early: chsd ldr tl 8f out: wnt 2nd again over 3f out: drvn and no imp over 2f out: lost 2nd and plugged on same pce ins fnl f* **5/1**[3]

4654 **4** 2 1/2 **Princess Raihana**[18] 5749 3-9-3 **69** HarryBentley 6 67
(Marco Botti) *broke wl and pressed ldrs tl stdd into midfield after 2f: effrt in 4th over 2f out: no imp and wl hld whn drifted lft over 1f out* **11/2**

0030 **5** 5 **Sixties Love**[58] 4303 5-9-7 **65** TedDurcan 5 55
(Simon Dow) *stdd s: hld up in last pair: effrt on inner in 5th over 2f out: no imp: wknd fnl f* **25/1**

630 **6** 8 **East Coast Lady (IRE)**[57] 4356 4-9-7 **70** HollieDoyle(5) 3 46
(William Stone) *s.i.s: hld up in rr: short-lived effrt 3f out: sn btn and no ch fnl 2f* **25/1**

3152 **7** 3 **Lady Blanco (USA)**[24] 5548 3-8-11 **70** JoshuaBryan(7) 10 41
(Andrew Balding) *stdd s: t.k.h: hdwy into midfield outer after 2f: lost pl over 3f out: sn btn and no ch fnl 2f* **7/2**[2]

5463 **8** 7 **Lady Lunchalot (USA)**[17] 5776 6-9-4 **62** DaneO'Neill 4 22
(Laura Mongan) *rdn along leaving stalls: hdwy to chse ldrs after 2f: wnt 2nd 8f out tl over 3f out: sn lost pl: no ch fnl 2f* **20/1**

0034 **9** 2 **Disquotational**[33] 5245 3-9-0 **66** FrederikTylicki 8 23
(David Simcock) *stdd bk after 1f: hld up towards rr: pushed along 4f out: btn 3f out: sn lost tch* **7/1**

2m 29.93s (-1.57) **Going Correction** -0.05s/f (Good)
WFA 3 from 4yo+ 8lb **9** Ran SP% **117.7**
Speed ratings (Par 100): **103,101,99,97,94 88,86,81,79**
CSF £30.85 CT £122.44 TOTE £3.20: £1.30, £4.00, £1.90; EX 32.40 Trifecta £212.40.
Owner Clive Washbourn **Bred** Mme Elisabeth Erbeya **Trained** Pulborough, W Sussex

FOCUS
A modest fillies' handicap run at a steady pace. The runner-up has been rated a bit off, but the third to form.

6335 BANJO SERVICES H'CAP 1m 6f
2:25 (2:26) (Class 6) (0-60,62) 3-Y-O+ **£2,587** (£770; £384; £192) **Stalls** Centre

Form RPR
6442 **1** **Fearless Lad (IRE)**[28] 5397 6-9-12 **58** KierenFox 8 64
(John Best) *chsd ldrs: effrt in 3rd 2f out: kpt on u.p to chal ins fnl f: styd on wl u.p to ld towards fin* **7/2**[2]

/40- **2** nk **Londonia**[23] 2178 4-9-12 **58** (t) HarryBentley 3 65+
(Graeme McPherson) *stdd s: hld up in last trio: effrt 3f out: hdwy to chse ldrs over 1f out: wnt between rivals and ev ch ins fnl f: kpt on: wnt 2nd last strides* **8/1**

0044 **3** 1/2 **Glorious Legend (IRE)**[14] 5888 3-9-3 **60** WilliamTwiston-Davies 1 65
(Ed Walker) *chsd ldrs: wnt 2nd 3f out: rdn and ev ch over 2f out: drvn to ld over 1f out: hrd pressed ins fnl f: hdd and no ex towards fin* **3/1**[1]

5406 **4** 4 1/2 **Graceful Lady**[25] 5513 3-8-13 **56** PaoloSirigu 10 55
(Robert Eddery) *chsd ldr tl 3f out: sn rdn: unable qck over 1f out: wknd ins fnl f* **8/1**

0052 **5** 1 1/4 **Fast Play (IRE)**[7] 6143 4-10-1 **61** (p) JimCrowley 4 58
(Richard Hughes) *led: rdn and jnd over 2f out: hdd over 1f out: 4th and btn 1f out: wknd and nt given a hrd time ins fnl f* **9/2**[3]

000 **6** 7 **The Juggler**[77] 3653 3-9-0 **57** FrederikTylicki 7 45
(William Knight) *taken down early: hld up in midfield: effrt 3f out: drvn and no hdwy over 1f out: sn wknd* **6/1**

45 **7** 1 **The Quarterjack**[12] 5958 7-9-12 **58** TedDurcan 6 45
(Ron Hodges) *hld up in midfield: effrt on inner 3f out: no hdwy u.p over 1f out: sn wknd: eased wl ins fnl f* **8/1**

5434 **8** 2 **Peeps**[20] 5680 4-9-0 **53** GeorgiaDobie(7) 11 37
(Mark H Tompkins) *s.i.s: hld up in last trio: effrt over 2f out: no hdwy u.p 2f out: no ch whn short of room and eased wl ins fnl f* **20/1**

5046 **9** 23 **Star Anise (FR)**[114] 2400 5-8-9 **46** oh1 MeganNicholls(5) 9 1
(Paddy Butler) *taken down early: hld up in rr: rdn 3f out: sn btn and bhd: t.o* **66/1**

3m 12.85s (2.85) **Going Correction** -0.05s/f (Good)
WFA 3 from 4yo+ 11lb **9** Ran SP% **119.3**
Speed ratings (Par 101): **89,88,88,85,85 81,80,79,66**
CSF £32.84 CT £94.95 TOTE £4.40: £1.60, £2.70, £1.40; EX 32.60 Trifecta £201.00.
Owner Mrs Jackie Jones **Bred** Brittas House Stud & Lynch Bages & Samac **Trained** Oad Street, Kent
■ Stewards' Enquiry : Kieren Fox four-day ban: used whip above permitted level (Sep 25-28)

FOCUS
This was competitive enough for the grade. It was run at a steady pace and saw an exciting finish. The third has been rated to his best.

6336 BRITISH STALLION STUDS EBF MAIDEN FILLIES' STKS (PLUS 10 RACE) 7f 140y
3:00 (3:02) (Class 5) 2-Y-O **£3,881** (£1,155; £577; £288) **Stalls** Centre

Form RPR
2 **1** **Unforgetable Filly**[15] 5846 2-9-0 0 JimCrowley 2 89+
(Hugo Palmer) *mde all: gng best 3f out: pushed wl clr over 1f out: v easily* **4/9**[1]

44 **2** 7 **Midnight Vixen**[31] 5298 2-9-0 0 TedDurcan 1 71
(Sir Michael Stoute) *chsd wnr: rdn ent fnl 3f: unable qck and brushed aside by wnr 2f out: wl hld but clr 2nd after* **8/1**[3]

3 1 1/4 **Mouille Point** 2-9-0 0 TomMarquand 7 68
(Richard Hannon) *hld up in tch in midfield: effrt 3f out: outpcd 2f out: no ch w wnr and battling for modest 3rd 1f out: wnt 3rd last stride* **10/1**

4 shd **Crimson Lake** 2-9-0 0 HarryBentley 3 68
(David Simcock) *hld up in tch in last trio: rdn 3f out: outpcd 2f out: no ch w wnr and wnt modest 3rd 1f out: plugged on: lost 3rd last stride* **10/1**

5 ¾ **Piedita (IRE)** 2-9-0 0 .... RyanPowell 4 66
(Sir Mark Prescott Bt) *in tch in midfield: rdn ent fnl 3f out: outpcd and wnt 3rd 2f out: no ch w wnr and kpt on same pce after: lost 2 pls fnl f* **33/1**

6 3 **Kyllachys Tale (IRE)** 2-9-0 0 .... WilliamTwiston-Davies 8 59+
(Roger Teal) *t.k.h: hld up in tch in rr of main gp: swtchd lft over 2f out: sn outpcd and rdn: wknd wl over 1f out* **50/1**

04 7 8 **Satpura**[28] 5387 2-9-0 0 .... CharlesBishop 5 40
(Mick Channon) *chsd ldng pair: rdn over 2f out: sn outpcd and wknd over 1f out* **10/1**

8 6 **Jazaalah (USA)** 2-9-0 0 .... DaneO'Neill 6 26+
(Owen Burrows) *v.s.a: rn green in rr: swtchd lft 5f out: rdn over 3f out: sn btn and bhd* **9/2**[2]

1m 30.89s (-1.41) **Going Correction** -0.125s/f (Firm) **8** Ran SP% **130.7**
Speed ratings (Par 92): **102,95,93,93,92 89,81,75**
CSF £6.80 TOTE £1.40: £1.20, £1.50, £2.50; EX 5.00 Trifecta £29.70.
Owner Dr Ali Ridha **Bred** Rabbah Bloodstock Limited **Trained** Newmarket, Suffolk

FOCUS
Some powerful stables in opposition for this fillies' maiden. It's hard to pin the level, but the third, fourth and fifth will ultimately guide the true worth of the form.

6337 RECYCLE ME UK LTD H'CAP 7f 140y
3:35 (3:36) (Class 5) (0-70,71) 3-Y-O+ **£3,234** (£962; £481; £240) **Stalls** Centre

Form RPR

2060 1 **Plauseabella**[21] 5627 5-8-11 **57** .... (p) TedDurcan 3 65
(Stuart Kittow) *racd towards centre: chsd ldr: rdn and ev ch over 1f out: led ins fnl f: styd on wl: rdn out* **16/1**

462 2 1¼ **Surety (IRE)**[13] 5935 5-9-11 **71** .... JimCrowley 8 76
(James Tate) *led: rdn 2f out: drvn and edgd lft ent fnl f: hdd and styd on same pce ins fnl f* **11/4**[2]

5565 3 1 **Artful Mind**[93] 3053 3-9-0 **65** .... [1] StevieDonohoe 10 66
(Charlie Fellowes) *hld up in tch in midfield: effrt 2f out: drvn over 1f out: wnt 3rd ins fnl f: styd on same pce fnl 100yds* **5/2**[1]

-405 4 2½ **Beatbybeatbybeat**[25] 5515 3-8-12 **63** .... DaneO'Neill 5 58
(Ismail Mohammed) *chsd ldrs: rdn ent fnl 2f: unable qck u.p over 1f out: wknd ins fnl f* **7/1**

0223 5 ¾ **Art Echo**[9] 6066 3-9-4 **69** .... (t) RyanTate 11 62
(Jonathan Portman) *stdd after s: hld up in tch in rr: swtchd lft ent fnl 2f: rdn to chse ldrs over 1f out: no ex 1f out: wknd ins fnl f* **7/2**[3]

-030 6 1¾ **Courtsider**[38] 5037 4-9-7 **67** .... (b[1]) TomMarquand 2 57
(Lucy Wadham) *racd towards centre: hld up in tch: rdn over 2f out: no imp u.p over 1f out: wknd ins fnl f* **14/1**

0350 7 3½ **R Bar Open (FR)**[25] 5515 3-8-9 **63** .... [1] JackDuern[(3)] 9 43
(Dean Ivory) *hld up in tch: lost pl and rdn over 2f out: wknd over 1f out* **14/1**

125 8 14 **Dunnscotia**[42] 4881 4-9-10 **70** .... (t) WilliamCarson 4 16
(Paul Webber) *taken down early: s.i.s: t.k.h: hld up in tch: hdwy into midfield 1/2-way: rdn 3f out: sn struggling: bhd over 1f out: eased ins fnl f* **10/1**

1m 30.55s (-1.75) **Going Correction** -0.125s/f (Firm)
WFA 3 from 4yo+ 5lb **8** Ran SP% **118.3**
Speed ratings (Par 103): **103,101,100,98,97 95,92,78**
CSF £62.10 CT £154.96 TOTE £17.20: £3.90, £1.50, £1.30; EX 75.40 Trifecta £544.90.
Owner Mrs Gill Shire **Bred** West Dereham Abbey Stud **Trained** Blackborough, Devon

FOCUS
A modest handicap. The winner has been rated back to her best, with the runner-up to his latest form.

6338 BRITISH STALLION STUDS EBF CONDITIONS STKS 7f
4:10 (4:11) (Class 3) 3-Y-O+ **£9,451** (£2,829; £1,414; £708) **Stalls** Centre

Form RPR

6605 1 **Salateen**[28] 5389 4-9-2 98 .... JimCrowley 1 105
(David O'Meara) *led: rdn 2f out: hdd and bmpd 1f out: battled on wl u.p to ld again towards fin: gamely* **11/8**[1]

2004 2 ¾ **Aljuljalah (USA)**[7] 6113 3-8-7 94 .... HarryBentley 4 96
(Roger Varian) *dwlt: sn pushed up to chse wnr: rdn and ev ch 2f out: drvn to ld and edgd lft 1f out: hdd and no ex towards fin* **3/1**[3]

1504 3 11 **C Note (IRE)**[56] 4395 3-9-1 98 .... DaneO'Neill 2 74
(Martyn Meade) *chsd ldng pair: effrt over 2f out: sn struggling u.p: wknd over 1f out* **15/8**[2]

0006 4 17 **Madrinho (IRE)**[22] 5601 3-8-12 87 .... TomMarquand 3 25
(Richard Hannon) *sn rdn and struggling in rr: lost tch 2f out* **12/1**

1m 20.54s (-2.76) **Going Correction** -0.125s/f (Firm)
WFA 3 from 4yo 4lb **4** Ran SP% **109.6**
Speed ratings (Par 107): **110,109,96,77**
CSF £5.84 TOTE £2.20; EX 5.50 Trifecta £6.60.
Owner Sheikh Abdullah Almalek Alsabah **Bred** Mrs Janis Macpherson **Trained** Upper Helmsley, N Yorks

FOCUS
A fair contest despite the small field. It was run at a good pace and the front two finished clear. It's been rated around the runner-up to her recent form.

6339 RACING WELFARE H'CAP 7f
4:40 (4:41) (Class 4) (0-85,85) 3-Y-O+ **£5,175** (£1,540; £769; £384) **Stalls** Centre

Form RPR

064 1 **He's No Saint**[8] 6082 5-9-8 **83** .... (v) JimCrowley 4 92
(David O'Meara) *racd in centre: mde all: rdn wl over 1f out: styd on wl u.p ins fnl f: rdn out* **15/8**[1]

3626 2 2½ **Cincuenta Pasos (IRE)**[70] 3895 5-9-10 **85** .... DaneO'Neill 1 87
(Joseph Tuite) *racd in centre: hld up in midfield: effrt 2f out: styd on same pce u.p ins fnl f: wnt 2nd last strides* **9/2**

5011 3 nk **King Of Spin**[39] 4985 3-8-11 **76** .... (t) MartinDwyer 3 75
(William Muir) *racd in centre: chsd wnr: rdn 2f out: drvn and no imp ent fnl f: styd on same pce after: lost 2nd last strides* **7/2**[2]

1000 4 nk **Sydney Ruffdiamond**[12] 5955 4-9-1 **83** .... [1] StephenCummins[(7)] 5 83
(Richard Hughes) *racd stands' side tl wnt to centre 3f out: t.k.h: hld up in last pair: effrt over 1f out: styd on ins fnl f: no threat to wnr* **14/1**

2-04 5 1¼ **Guiding Light (IRE)**[53] 4481 4-9-1 **83** .... JoshuaBryan[(7)] 7 80
(Andrew Balding) *racd stands' side tl wnt to centre 3f out: chsd ldng pair: effrt ent fnl 2f: unable qck over 2f out: styd on same pce ins fnl f* **7/1**

0200 6 9 **Fashaak (IRE)**[14] 5892 3-9-1 **80** .... TomMarquand 6 52
(Richard Hannon) *racd stands' side tl wnt to centre 3f out: hld up in last pair: rdn 3f out: sn strugglingand wknd wl over 1f out* **4/1**[3]

1m 22.24s (-1.06) **Going Correction** -0.125s/f (Firm)
WFA 3 from 4yo+ 4lb **6** Ran SP% **114.4**
Speed ratings (Par 105): **101,98,97,97,96 85**
CSF £11.01 TOTE £2.80: £1.60, £2.50; EX 8.50 Trifecta £33.00.
Owner Peter R Ball & All About York Partners **Bred** Follow The Flag Partnership **Trained** Upper Helmsley, N Yorks

FOCUS
The going was eased to good to soft prior to the sixth. They went an honest pace for this fair handicap and those that raced up the centre filled the first three places.

6340 LAURIE GREEN MEMORIAL FILLIES' H'CAP 6f
5:15 (5:15) (Class 4) (0-85,85) 3-Y-O+ **£5,175** (£1,540; £769; £384) **Stalls** Centre

Form RPR

414 1 **Sweet Dragon Fly**[24] 5551 3-9-3 **83** .... [1] JimCrowley 3 92
(Paul Cole) *trckd ldng ldng trio: effrt to press ldrs 2f out: drvn and ev ch over 1f out: led ins fnl f: styd on strly: rdn out* **11/4**[1]

0006 2 1¼ **Sixties Sue**[9] 6064 3-8-11 **77** .... CharlesBishop 8 82
(Mick Channon) *racd nr stands' rail thrght: chsd ldr tl led 2f out: sn rdn and hrd pressed over 1f out: hdd and styd on same pce ins fnl f* **5/1**

0454 3 nk **Rebel Surge (IRE)**[28] 5396 3-9-5 **85** .... WilliamTwiston-Davies 1 89
(Richard Spencer) *hld up in last pair: swtchd lft and hdwy jst over 2f out: drvn and ev ch ent fnl f: unable qck and styd on same pce fnl 100yds* **7/1**

3512 4 3¼ **Pretty Bubbles**[26] 5488 7-9-7 **85** .... (v) FrederikTylicki 4 79
(J R Jenkins) *hld up in tch in midfield: effrt and rdn 2f out: chsd ldrs and drvn over 1f out: no imp jst ins fnl f: wknd fnl 75yds* **9/2**[3]

1365 5 2 **Pink Martini (IRE)**[12] 5960 3-8-4 **75** .... CharlieBennett[(5)] 2 62
(Joseph Tuite) *dwlt: hld up in tch in last pair: effrt jst over 2f out: drvn and no hdwy over 1f out: wknd ins fnl f* **12/1**

0004 6 1 **Souville**[18] 5744 5-9-4 **82** .... (p) TedDurcan 5 69
(Chris Wall) *led tl 2f: sn rdn and unable qck: 5th and btn 1f out: wknd ins fnl f: eased towards fin* **6/1**

1123 7 4½ **Inclination (IRE)**[14] 5896 3-8-12 **78** .... RyanTate 7 55
(Clive Cox) *chsd ldrs: rdn over 2f out: struggling to qckn and drvn wl over 1f out: sn lost pl: bhd fnl f* **4/1**[2]

1m 9.82s (-1.38) **Going Correction** -0.125s/f (Firm)
WFA 3 from 4yo+ 2lb **7** Ran SP% **116.0**
Speed ratings (Par 102): **104,102,101,97,94 93,87**
CSF £17.30 CT £86.81 TOTE £3.30: £1.50, £3.20; EX 19.80 Trifecta £88.00.
Owner Mrs Fitri Hay **Bred** Newsells Park Stud **Trained** Whatcombe, Oxon

FOCUS
A competitive fillies' handicap run at a good pace. The third has been rated to her recent best.
T/Plt: £18.00 to a £1 stake. Pool: £56,634.2 - 2294.74 winning units T/Qpdt: £7.20 to a £1 stake. Pool: £2,746.97 - 279.8 winning units **Steve Payne**

6092 MUSSELBURGH (R-H)
Saturday, September 10

OFFICIAL GOING: Good (7.1)
Wind: Almost nil Weather: Overcast, dry

6341 HANNAH FAY H'CAP 5f
4:15 (4:16) (Class 6) (0-65,68) 3-Y-O+ **£2,587** (£770; £384; £192) **Stalls** High

Form RPR

0/00 1 **Storm Trooper (IRE)**[38] 5032 5-9-5 **60** .... RoystonFfrench 4 72
(David Nicholls) *cl up: rdn over 1f out: led ins fnl f: kpt on strly* **5/1**[2]

4031 2 1¾ **Twentysvnthlancers**[10] 6023 3-9-7 **68** .... AdamMcNamara[(5)] 1 74
(Paul Midgley) *cl up on outside: rdn along 2f out: chsd wnr ins fnl f: kpt on* **9/2**[1]

4106 3 hd **Bunce (IRE)**[8] 6093 8-9-8 **63** .... PJMcDonald 3 68
(Linda Perratt) *bhd and sn outpcd: hdwy over 1f out: kpt on ins fnl f: nrst fin* **20/1**

4512 4 ¾ **See Vermont**[8] 6098 8-9-2 **64** .... (p) LewisEdmunds[(7)] 11 67
(Rebecca Bastiman) *trckd ldrs: effrt and rdn 2f out: kpt on ins fnl f* **6/1**[3]

1231 5 shd **Thornaby Princess**[8] 6098 5-8-10 **51** .... (p) CamHardie 7 53
(Colin Teague) *cl up: led over 1f out to ins fnl f: sn rdn and outpcd* **15/2**

0040 6 ½ **Caymus**[13] 5920 3-8-3 **50** .... (t) PhilDennis[(5)] 8 50
(Tracy Waggott) *hld up in tch: effrt and looking for room over 1f out: kpt on ins fnl f: no imp* **50/1**

5006 7 nk **The Cheese Gang**[8] 6101 4-8-5 **46** oh1 .... (t) JoeyHaynes 9 45
(Susan Corbett) *s.i.s: hld up: rdn and hdwy over 1f out: kpt on ins fnl f* **33/1**

0424 8 1¾ **Sea Of Green**[8] 6098 4-8-7 **48** .... BarryMcHugh 6 41
(Jim Goldie) *in tch: drvn and outpcd 2f out: no imp fnl f* **11/1**

0303 9 1¾ **Danzeb (IRE)**[15] 5839 3-9-1 **62** .... RowanScott[(5)] 5 49
(Ann Duffield) *midfield: rdn along over 2f out: edgd rt and wknd over 1f out* **14/1**

0351 10 ¾ **Run Rio Run (IRE)**[29] 5370 3-9-8 **64** .... (p) PaulMulrennan 12 48
(Michael Dods) *cl up tl rdn and wknd over 1f out* **8/1**

0430 11 1 **Lorimer's Lot (IRE)**[8] 6098 5-8-10 **51** .... (p) GrahamGibbons 13 31
(Mark Walford) *bhd: rdn along over 2f out: nvr rchd ldrs* **16/1**

3204 12 1¼ **Native Falls (IRE)**[24] 5535 5-9-8 **63** .... DougieCostello 10 39
(Alan Swinbank) *led to over 1f out: sn rdn and wknd* **14/1**

-300 13 nk **Cheeni**[8] 6098 4-8-5 **46** oh1 .... [1] DuranFentiman 2 21
(Jim Goldie) *hld up on outside: rdn over 2f out: wknd over 1f out* **66/1**

-003 14 3 **Horsforth**[39] 4968 4-9-3 **58** .... (b) JoeFanning 14 22
(Richard Guest) *midfield against stands' rail: effrt whn nt clr run over 2f out: wknd over 1f out* **15/2**

1m 0.67s (0.27) **Going Correction** +0.15s/f (Good)
WFA 3 from 4yo+ 1lb **14** Ran SP% **122.5**
Speed ratings (Par 101): **103,100,99,98,98 97,97,94,91,90 88,86,86,81**
CSF £27.43 CT £342.15 TOTE £6.30: £2.30, £2.20, £6.30; EX 31.80 Trifecta £426.70.
Owner Sporting Lives Racing **Bred** M Fahy & Rathbarry Stud **Trained** Sessay, N Yorks

FOCUS
Modest fare, but there were some decent yardsticks for the level in the shake-up and the manner in which the winner did it suggests he probably still retains most of the ability which saw him compete at a higher level earlier in his career. It's been rated around the runner-up and those close up. The runner-up and those close up set the level.

6342 EBF STALLIONS BREEDING WINNERS SCOTTISH PREMIER SERIES FILLIES' H'CAP 1m
4:45 (4:45) (Class 4) (0-85,83) 3-Y-O+ **£8,086** (£2,406; £1,202; £601) **Stalls** Low

Form RPR

-004 1 **Marsh Pride**[15] 5831 4-9-9 **80** .... PJMcDonald 4 89
(K R Burke) *pressed ldr: led over 2f out: sn hrd pressed: hld on wl fnl f* **11/4**[2]

0020 2 ¾ **Flinty Fell (IRE)**[12] 5973 3-8-5 **67** .... JoeFanning 6 73
(Keith Dalgleish) *t.k.h early: prom: hdwy over 2f out: effrt and ev ch over 1f out to ins fnl f: kpt on: hld nr fin* **9/1**

6121 **3** 3 1/4 **Lincoln Rocks**[11] 6005 3-9-7 **83** SamJames 3 82
(David O'Meara) *led to over 2f out: rallied: edgd lft and one pce fnl f* **4/1**[3]

6221 **4** 2 **Soundstrings**[17] 5757 3-8-13 **75** GrahamGibbons 5 69
(William Haggas) *s.i.s: hld up in tch on outside: stdy hdwy 1/2-way: rdn over 2f out: wknd fnl f* **15/8**[1]

1660 **5** nse **Forever A Lady (IRE)**[11] 6005 3-9-1 **77** PaulMulrennan 1 71
(Keith Dalgleish) *prom: drvn and outpcd after 3f: rallied 3f out: rdn and wknd fnl f* **11/1**

3320 **6** 13 **Quick N Quirky (IRE)**[23] 5588 3-9-6 **82** (tp) CamHardie 2 46
(Tim Easterby) *s.i.s: hld up: outpcd after 3f: struggling fr 3f out: t.o* **8/1**

1m 40.6s (-0.60) **Going Correction** +0.075s/f (Good)
WFA 3 from 4yo 5lb **6** Ran SP% **110.9**
Speed ratings (Par 102): **106,105,102,100,99 86**
CSF £25.46 TOTE £3.20: £3.00, £6.10; EX 31.50 Trifecta £150.70.
Owner John Dance **Bred** Llety Farms **Trained** Middleham Moor, N Yorks

FOCUS
A fairly useful fillies' event and there are reasons to be positive about the leading pair who pulled clear of the remainder and haven't been with their current yards long. After rail movement the actual race distance was 1m14yds. The winner has been rated back to her best.

6343 COAST TO COAST NURSERY H'CAP 5f
5:20 (5:20) (Class 5) (0-75,74) 2-Y-O **£3,234** (£962; £481; £240) **Stalls** High

Form RPR

030 **1** **Frozen Kiss**[11] 6002 2-8-10 **63** JoeFanning 12 72
(Bryan Smart) *chsd ldrs: rdn to ld 1f out: hld on wl fnl f* **13/2**

4153 **2** nk **Coolfitch (IRE)**[18] 5741 2-9-7 **74** SamJames 9 82
(David O'Meara) *in tch: effrt and rdn over 1f out: chsd wnr ins fnl f: r.o* **13/2**

0321 **3** 2 1/4 **Yorkshiredebut (IRE)**[16] 5798 2-8-12 **70** AdamMcNamara(5) 4 70
(Paul Midgley) *led: rdn and hdd 1f out: sn outpcd by first two* **9/2**[2]

4521 **4** nk **Foxy Boy**[19] 5712 2-8-12 **65** PaulMulrennan 2 64
(Michael Dods) *hld up on outside: stdy hdwy over 2f out: rdn over 1f out: one pce ins fnl f* **4/1**[1]

3066 **5** 3/4 **My Cherry Blossom**[11] 6010 2-8-3 **59** RachelRichardson(3) 5 55
(Tim Easterby) *s.i.s: t.k.h in rr: hdwy whn checked briefly over 1f out: kpt on fnl f: no imp* **10/1**

210 **6** 1/2 **Benidiction (IRE)**[13] 5931 2-8-12 **65** JoeyHaynes 3 59
(K R Burke) *cl up: rdn over 2f out: wknd fnl f* **22/1**

660 **7** 1 1/2 **Wilderswood (IRE)**[19] 5727 2-8-13 **66** PJMcDonald 8 55
(Ann Duffield) *midfield: drvn and outpcd over 2f out: n.d after* **16/1**

0000 **8** 1 1/4 **Gabridan (IRE)**[15] 5833 2-8-0 **53** oh1 CamHardie 6 37
(Richard Fahey) *bhd: rdn and struggling 1/2-way: sme late hdwy: nvr on terms* **25/1**

3041 **9** 1 **Snuggy (IRE)**[25] 5511 2-9-1 **68** GrahamGibbons 10 49
(David Barron) *cl up tl rdn and wknd over 1f out: eased whn btn ins fnl f* **11/2**[3]

1 **10** 3 1/4 **Bay Station**[30] 5317 2-9-7 **74** PaulQuinn 1 43
(David Nicholls) *dwlt: t.k.h in rr: rdn over 2f out: sn wknd: eased whn btn ins fnl f* **17/2**

602 **11** 2 **Warleggan (FR)**[52] 4526 2-8-1 **54** oh2 ow1 DuranFentiman 11 16
(Linda Perratt) *bhd: struggling over 2f out: sn btn* **66/1**

1m 0.84s (0.44) **Going Correction** +0.15s/f (Good) **11** Ran SP% **115.4**
Speed ratings (Par 95): **102,101,97,97,96 95,93,91,89,84 81**
CSF £46.50 CT £213.35 TOTE £6.70: £2.40, £1.90, £1.80; EX 60.20 Trifecta £396.20.
Owner Ceffyl Racing **Bred** Widden Stud Australia Pty Ltd **Trained** Hambleton, N Yorks

FOCUS
Fair form from the principals in this sprint nursery and there's no reason why it won't prove solid form for the level. A minor pb from the runner-up.

6344 DEUCHERS IPA H'CAP 1m 1f
5:55 (5:57) (Class 4) (0-80,84) 3-Y-O **£7,762** (£2,310; £1,154; £577) **Stalls** Low

Form RPR

2421 **1** **Just Hiss**[13] 5919 3-9-8 **84** RachelRichardson(3) 10 94
(Tim Easterby) *hld up: hdwy on outside over 2f out: sn rdn along: chsng ldr whn rdr dropped whip ins fnl f: kpt on to ld nr fin* **9/2**[2]

-003 **2** nk **Hibou**[16] 5802 3-9-4 **77**[1] PJMcDonald 8 86
(Iain Jardine) *sn pushed along in rr: hdwy over 2f out: led and hung lft ins fnl f: kpt on: hdd cl home* **3/1**[1]

5524 **3** 1 3/4 **Southern Gailes (IRE)**[18] 5738 3-9-0 **73** (t) DougieCostello 1 78
(K R Burke) *w ldr: led after 4f: rdn over 2f out: hdd ins fnl f: kpt on same pce* **10/1**

2563 **4** 3 1/4 **Page Of Wands**[15] 5844 3-8-6 **65** BarryMcHugh 4 63
(Karen McLintock) *in tch on ins: effrt and rdn over 2f out: kpt on same pce fr over 1f out* **33/1**

4152 **5** 1 3/4 **Weather Front (USA)**[61] 4199 3-9-2 **75** JoeyHaynes 2 69
(Karen McLintock) *difficult to load: hld up towards rr: hdwy over 2f out: sn rdn: wknd ins fnl f* **6/1**[3]

342 **6** 1 1/2 **La Contessa (IRE)**[16] 5811 3-8-9 **73** AdamMcNamara(5) 7 64
(Richard Fahey) *hld up towards rr: drvn and outpcd over 4f out: rallied over 1f out: kpt on ins fnl f: no imp* **7/1**

531 **7** 3 1/2 **Crazy Tornado (IRE)**[10] 6028 3-8-13 **72** JoeFanning 3 55
(Keith Dalgleish) *prom: effrt and rdn over 2f out: wknd over 1f out* **7/1**

663 **8** 1 3/4 **Auxiliary**[10] 6028 3-9-0 **73** (p) JackGarritty 6 52
(Patrick Holmes) *midfield: drvn and outpcd over 3f out: btn fnl 2f* **25/1**

2122 **9** 4 1/2 **Planetaria (IRE)**[45] 4769 3-9-7 **80** CamHardie 5 49
(Garry Moss) *led 4f: cl up: rdn over 2f out: wknd over 1f out* **14/1**

3321 **10** 3 1/4 **Mujaamil**[12] 5979 3-9-6 **79** (b) GrahamGibbons 9 41
(William Haggas) *s.i.s: hld up on outside: struggling over 3f out: sn btn* **13/2**

1m 53.93s (0.03) **Going Correction** +0.075s/f (Good) **10** Ran SP% **118.3**
Speed ratings (Par 103): **102,101,100,97,95 94,91,89,85,82**
CSF £18.71 CT £132.32 TOTE £6.00: £2.00, £1.10, £3.50; EX 19.40 Trifecta £403.90.
Owner The Sandmoor Partnership **Bred** Jeremy Gompertz **Trained** Great Habton, N Yorks

FOCUS
A fairly useful handicap which was run at a good gallop, the leading pair both coming from well off the pace. After rail movement the actual race distance was 1m1f14yds. It's been rated at face value around the third and fourth.

6345 CALEDONIAN CUP H'CAP 1m 6f
6:30 (6:30) (Class 4) (0-80,80) 3-Y-O
£11,205 (£3,355; £1,677; £838; £419; £210) **Stalls** Low

Form RPR

6515 **1** **Novalina (IRE)**[22] 5596 3-9-5 **78** GrahamGibbons 2 92+
(William Haggas) *pressed ldr: led over 2f out: drvn clr fr over 1f out* **9/4**[1]

1122 **2** 6 **High On Light**[14] 5888 3-8-5 **67** RachelRichardson(3) 1 73
(Tim Easterby) *t.k.h: hld up: hdwy over 2f out: chsd (clr) wnr over 1f out: no imp* **9/2**[3]

0436 **3** 1 1/4 **Second Serve (IRE)**[17] 5761 3-9-7 **80**[1] RoystonFfrench 5 84
(Mark Johnston) *hld up: hdwy on outside 3f out: rdn and no ex over 1f out* **5/1**

2120 **4** 16 **Space Mountain**[7] 6121 3-9-5 **78** JoeFanning 4 60
(Mark Johnston) *prom: hdwy to chse wnr over 2f out to over 1f out: sn wknd* **5/1**

2411 **5** 23 **Introductory (IRE)**[16] 5801 3-9-6 **79** PaulMulrennan 3 29
(Keith Dalgleish) *led to over 2f out: sn rdn and wknd: eased: t.o* **7/2**[2]

6404 **6** 27 **Wholesome (USA)**[17] 5761 3-9-6 **79** DougieCostello 6
(K R Burke) *trckd ldrs: struggling over 3f out: lost tch over 2f out: eased: t.o* **12/1**

3m 5.98s (0.68) **Going Correction** +0.075s/f (Good) **6** Ran SP% **112.2**
Speed ratings (Par 103): **101,97,96,87,74 59**
CSF £12.63 TOTE £2.90: £1.80, £2.50; EX 10.60 Trifecta £56.40.
Owner Messrs B Kantor & MJ Jooste **Bred** Barronstown Stud **Trained** Newmarket, Suffolk

FOCUS
Not a race with massive depth to it for the money on offer, particularly with the second favourite running so disappointingly, but the winner deserves some credit for having the rest strung out like 3m chasers in behind. After rail movement the actual race distance was 1m6f14yds. The runner-up has been rated to form, with the third close to his best.

6346 THREE HOP H'CAP 1m 4f 100y
7:00 (7:00) (Class 5) (0-75,75) 3-Y-O+ **£3,234** (£962; £481; £240) **Stalls** Low

Form RPR

1261 **1** **Falcon's Fire (IRE)**[8] 6103 3-9-0 **70** GrahamGibbons 2 79
(Keith Dalgleish) *pressed ldr: led over 2f out: rdn and hung lft over 1f out: clr ins fnl f: pushed out: comf* **6/1**[3]

1142 **2** 2 1/2 **Neuf Des Coeurs**[8] 6097 5-8-13 **67** (p) JamieGormley(7) 4 72
(Iain Jardine) *hld up: hdwy far rail wl over 1f out: chsd (clr) wnr ins fnl f: kpt on* **15/2**

2211 **3** 1/2 **Henry Smith**[64] 4099 4-9-9 **75** (be) RobJFitzpatrick(5) 8 79
(Garry Moss) *hld up: stdy hdwy to chse ldrs over 2f out: sn rdn: kpt on same pce ins fnl f* **12/5**[1]

5653 **4** hd **Gabrial The Terror (IRE)**[16] 5801 6-8-11 **58** (p) JackGarritty 5 62
(Richard Fahey) *prom: effrt and rdn over 2f out: kpt on same pce appr fnl f* **9/1**

3213 **5** 1/2 **Amirli (IRE)**[16] 5118 5-9-10 **71** (p) PJMcDonald 6 74
(Alistair Whillans) *led at ordinary gallop: rdn and hdd over 2f out: chsd wnr tl no ex ins fnl f* **7/2**[2]

4342 **6** 2 1/4 **Jan De Heem**[13] 5918 6-8-7 **59** (p) RowanScott(5) 3 58
(Tina Jackson) *stmbld sn after s: hld up: rdn over 2f out: no imp fr over 1f out* **9/1**

0000 **7** 1/2 **Genres**[15] 5841 4-9-7 **68** JoeFanning 9 67
(Alan Swinbank) *chsd ldrs: rdn over 2f out: wknd over 1f out* **9/1**

5025 **8** nse **Nelson's Bay**[14] 5883 7-8-9 **56** oh2 CamHardie 7 55
(Wilf Storey) *rrd s: hld up: rdn over 2f out: sn no imp: btn over 1f out* **20/1**

2m 47.91s (5.91) **Going Correction** +0.075s/f (Good)
WFA 3 from 4yo+ 9lb **8** Ran SP% **112.4**
Speed ratings (Par 103): **83,81,81,80,80 79,78,78**
CSF £48.10 CT £135.63 TOTE £6.50: £2.40, £2.20, £1.10; EX 24.00 Trifecta £58.40.
Owner Ronnie Docherty **Bred** Patrick Headon **Trained** Carluke, S Lanarks

FOCUS
A fair handicap featuring some in-form types. After rail movement the actual race distance was 1m4f114yds. The form is set by the second, third and fifth.

6347 VOLVO TRUCKS H'CAP 7f 30y
7:30 (7:30) (Class 6) (0-65,65) 3-Y-O+ **£2,587** (£770; £384; £192) **Stalls** Low

Form RPR

4040 **1** **Riponian**[8] 6105 6-8-10 **51** oh4 (t) JoeyHaynes 1 57
(Susan Corbett) *mde all: hrd pressed and rdn fr over 2f out: hld on gamely ins fnl f* **14/1**

2303 **2** 3/4 **Dark Command**[15] 5843 3-9-6 **65** (be[1]) PaulMulrennan 6 67
(Michael Dods) *t.k.h: hld up in tch: smooth hdwy to press ldrs over 1f out: rdn and chsd wnr ins fnl f: edgd rt: kpt on* **11/4**[1]

0002 **3** 1 1/4 **Centre Haafhd**[8] 6106 5-8-11 **52** (b) JackGarritty 3 53
(Jim Goldie) *pressed ldr: ev ch and rdn over 2f out to over 1f out: lost 2nd and one pce ins fnl f* **14/1**

6140 **4** 1/2 **Gone With The Wind (GER)**[18] 5750 5-9-7 **62** (t) BarryMcHugh 4 61
(Rebecca Bastiman) *hld up: hdwy against far rail over 2f out: effrt and rdn over 1f out: kpt on same pce ins fnl f* **12/1**

2354 **5** 1 **Bajan Rebel**[14] 5887 5-9-8 **63** CamHardie 2 60
(Michael Easterby) *t.k.h early: pressed ldrs: rdn along over 2f out: no ex ins fnl f* **9/2**[3]

0311 **6** 3 1/4 **Gypsy Major**[15] 5839 4-9-4 **64** (v) RobJFitzpatrick(5) 7 52
(Garry Moss) *blkd sn after s: sn bhd: hdwy and prom on outside over 3f out: rdn and wknd over 1f out* **7/2**[2]

0603 **7** 1 3/4 **Fire Diamond**[16] 5803 3-8-9 **54** (t) RoystonFfrench 9 35
(Tom Dascombe) *fly-jmpd s: sn prom on outside: rdn over 2f out: wknd over 1f out* **6/1**

2625 **8** 4 1/2 **Rock Canyon (IRE)**[15] 5838 7-9-9 **64** PJMcDonald 10 35
(Linda Perratt) *s.s and wl bhd: nvr on terms* **33/1**

0546 **9** 1/2 **Amber Crystal**[15] 5838 4-8-10 **51** oh3 JoeFanning 5 21
(Linda Perratt) *t.k.h: chsd ldrs tl rdn and wknd fr 2f out* **25/1**

0-51 **10** 1 1/2 **Arizona Sunrise**[139] 1667 3-9-5 **64** DougieCostello 8 28
(Tina Jackson) *chsd ldng gp: rdn and outpcd over 2f out: sn btn* **16/1**

1m 31.52s (2.52) **Going Correction** +0.075s/f (Good)
WFA 3 from 4yo+ 4lb **10** Ran SP% **115.1**
Speed ratings (Par 101): **88,87,85,85,84 80,78,73,72,70**
CSF £51.82 CT £577.72 TOTE £15.00: £4.00, £1.10, £5.10; EX 59.10 Trifecta £756.30.
Owner Girsonfield Racing Club **Bred** W B Imison **Trained** Otterburn, Northumberland
■ Stewards' Enquiry : Joey Haynes two-day ban: use of whip above permitted level (Sep 25-26)

FOCUS
A run-of-the-mill handicap to conclude things. After rail movement the actual race distance was 7f44yds. A minor pb from the winner.

T/Plt: £121.00 to a £1 stake. Pool: £52,229.07 - 314.95 winning units T/Qpdt: £8.20 to a £1 stake. Pool: £5,912.38 - 532.95 winning units **Richard Young**

6348 - 6398a (Foreign Racing) - See Raceform Interactive

5339 **LEOPARDSTOWN** (L-H)

Saturday, September 10

OFFICIAL GOING: Inner track - good (yielding in places); outer track - yielding (good in places)

6349a WILLIS TOWERS WATSON CHAMPIONS JUVENILE STKS (GROUP 3) (INNER TRACK) 1m

4:00 (4:01) 2-Y-O **£43,382** (£13,970; £6,617; £2,941; £1,470)

RPR

1 **Landfall (FR)**[20] 5684 2-9-3 0 ShaneFoley 3 110
(K J Condon, Ire) *chsd ldrs in 3rd: clsr in 2nd over 3f out: led over 1f out and rdn clr ins fnl f: styd on wl* **9/1**

2 2 ¼ **Firey Speech (USA)**[42] 4898 2-9-3 99 [1] PatSmullen 5 105
(D K Weld, Ire) *racd in rr: clsr in 4th over 3f out: kpt on wl into 2nd fnl 150yds: nt trble wnr* **7/1**[3]

3 hd **Douglas Macarthur (IRE)**[51] 4571 2-9-3 0 RyanMoore 4 105
(A P O'Brien, Ire) *led tl hdd over 1f out: no imp in 3rd fnl 150yds: kpt on same pce* **8/13**[1]

4 2 ½ **Percy (IRE)**[24] 5561 2-9-3 0 ColinKeane 2 99
(G M Lyons, Ire) *chsd ldr in 2nd: dropped to 3rd over 3f out: nt qckn in 4th over 1f out: sn one pce* **20/1**

5 ½ **Radio Silence (USA)**[20] 5683 2-9-3 107 KevinManning 1 97
(J S Bolger, Ire) *hld up in 4th: dropped to rr over 3f out: rdn and kpt on same pce fnl f* **10/3**[2]

1m 43.49s (2.29) **Going Correction** +0.325s/f (Good) 5 Ran SP% **112.3**
Speed ratings: **101,98,98,96,95**
CSF £63.09 TOTE £12.40: £3.40, £2.00; DF 52.00 Trifecta £90.20.
Owner Carl Anthony Howell & Mrs Pauline Condon & R J Con **Bred** Mme Marie-Claude Biaudis **Trained** Rathbride, Co Kildare

FOCUS
A big reputation took a knock here with the defeat of the odds-on favourite. The winner confirmed the promise of his debut win. The form will take a little time to settle.

6350a IRISH STALLION FARMS EUROPEAN BREEDERS FUND "PETINGO" H'CAP (PREMIER HANDICAP) (INNER TRACK) 1m 6f

4:35 (4:35) 3-Y-O+

£65,073 (£20,955; £9,926; £4,411; £2,205; £1,102)

RPR

1 **Quick Jack (IRE)**[21] 5655 7-9-5 **105** OisinOrr(7) 16 109+
(A J Martin, Ire) *racd in rr: clsr in mid-div over 2f out: wnt 5th 1f out: styd on strly into 2nd ins fnl 100yds: led cl home* **5/1**[2]

2 nk **Pyromaniac (IRE)**[44] 4252 6-8-8 **87** (tp) DeclanMcDonogh 3 91+
(A J Martin, Ire) *hld up: travelled wl into mid-div 3f out: wnt 3rd appr fnl f and sn led: strly pressed fnl 50yds and hdd cl home* **7/2**[1]

3 2 ¼ **Intense Tango**[7] 6118 5-8-9 **95** 5ex (t) CliffordLee(7) 6 96
(K R Burke) *led tl hdd after 2f: chsd ldr in 2nd: on terms appr fnl f: sn hdd and no ex in 3rd ins fnl 100yds* **8/1**[3]

4 ½ **Queen Alphabet (IRE)**[43] 4850 7-8-8 **87** (t) WayneLordan 1 87
(Peter Fahey, Ire) *chsd ldrs in 3rd: 4th at 1/2-way: rdn in 3rd 3f out: nt qckn in 5th ins fnl f: kpt on same pce into 4th cl home* **25/1**

5 nse **Golden Spear**[43] 4850 5-8-7 **86** RoryCleary 2 86
(A J Martin, Ire) *chsd ldrs on inner: 6th on inner 2f out: no imp ins fnl f: kpt on same pce* **8/1**[3]

6 ½ **Benkei (IRE)**[21] 5660 6-9-5 **98** [1] ChrisHayes 15 97
(H Rogers, Ire) *led after 2f: hdd 1f out and wknd fnl 100yds* **25/1**

7 1 ¼ **Le Vagabond (FR)**[23] 5591 4-9-3 **96** BillyLee 4 94
(E J O'Grady, Ire) *racd in mid-div: prog under 2f out in 8th: kpt on same pce fnl f: nvr nrr* **8/1**[3]

8 1 **Silver Concorde**[45] 3246 8-9-6 **99** LeighRoche 10 95
(D K Weld, Ire) *racd in rr: prog under 2f out: kpt on wl ins fnl f: nvr nrr* **8/1**[3]

9 3 ¼ **Radanpour (IRE)**[17] 5789 4-9-2 **95** (b[1]) PatSmullen 5 87
(D K Weld, Ire) *chsd ldrs in 4th: 5th at 1/2-way: rdn in 4th 2f out: nt qckn appr fnl f: sn one pce* **8/1**[3]

10 1 ½ **Travertine (IRE)**[43] 4850 6-9-11 **104** NiallPMadden 9 94
(Niall Madden, Ire) *hld up: pushed along over 4f out towards rr: kpt on on inner fr over 1f out: nvr on terms* **25/1**

11 hd **Renneti (FR)**[24] 5559 7-8-12 **91** KevinManning 12 80
(W P Mullins, Ire) *nvr bttr than mid-div: dropped to rr 3f out: kpt on again fnl f: nvr a threat* **12/1**

12 2 ¾ **Kalann (IRE)**[13] 4851 9-8-8 **92** (tp) KillianLeonard(5) 7 77
(Denis Gerard Hogan, Ire) *hld up towards rr: bit clsr in mid-div 4f out: nt qckn under 2f out: sn no imp* **40/1**

13 1 **Intisari (IRE)**[78] 3630 4-9-7 **100** ColinKeane 11 84
(G M Lyons, Ire) *hld up: pushed along towards rr 3f out: kpt one pce fr over 1f out: nvr on terms* **20/1**

14 2 ¾ **Avenante**[5] 6200 4-8-13 **95** GaryHalpin(3) 13 75
(John M Oxx, Ire) *racd in mid-div: clsr in 6th 5f out: rdn 3f out and wknd fr 2f out* **16/1**

15 hd **Modem**[24] 5559 6-8-6 **90** (b) TomMadden(5) 14 70
(Mrs John Harrington, Ire) *chsd ldrs: 3rd at 1/2-way: rdn 3f out and wknd under 2f out* **16/1**

16 33 **Asbury Boss (IRE)**[23] 5591 5-8-13 **92** (p) ShaneFoley 8 26
(M Halford, Ire) *racd in mid-div: pushed along 5f out: dropped to rr under 2f out and sn eased* **25/1**

3m 1.96s (0.96) **Going Correction** +0.325s/f (Good) 16 Ran SP% **136.5**
Speed ratings: **110,109,108,108,108 107,107,106,104,103 103,102,101,100,100 81**
CSF £23.57 CT £152.44 TOTE £6.00: £1.50, £1.30, £2.30, £5.80; DF 33.30 Trifecta £285.10.
Owner John Breslin **Bred** Newtown Anner Stud **Trained** Summerhill, Co. Meath

FOCUS
Having provided the winner and third in the Ebor, Tony Martin brought off another terrific feat of training with a one-two in this very valuable staying handicap. The winner, second, fourth, fifth and seventh have been rated to their marks.

6351a KPMG ENTERPRISE STKS (GROUP 3) (INNER TRACK) 1m 4f

5:05 (5:05) 3-Y-O+ **£43,382** (£13,970; £6,617; £2,941; £1,470)

RPR

1 **Zhukova (IRE)**[122] 2167 4-9-9 115 PatSmullen 3 115+
(D K Weld, Ire) *chsd ldr in 2nd: led over 1f out and sn clr: advantage reduced cl home: kpt on wl* **5/2**[2]

2 ½ **US Army Ranger (IRE)**[20] 5685 3-9-3 120 RyanMoore 2 117+
(A P O'Brien, Ire) *settled off ldrs in 3rd: niggled along in 4th under 3f out: wnt 3rd under 2f out: wnt 2nd ins fnl f: kpt on wl clsng stages to cl on wnr: nvr nrr* **8/11**[1]

3 2 **Bondi Beach (IRE)**[37] 5095 4-9-12 116 EmmetMcNamara 5 114+
(A P O'Brien, Ire) *racd in rr: prog on inner whn momentarily short of room over 1f out: swtchd rt and kpt on wl fnl f into 3rd cl home: nrst fin* **7/1**[3]

4 ¾ **Tree Of Knowledge (IRE)**[10] 6041 3-9-0 96 MichaelHussey 1 110
(A P O'Brien, Ire) *led: advantage reduced under 2f out: hdd over 1f out: kpt on same pce fnl f and dropped to 4th cl home* **33/1**

5 ¾ **Stellar Mass (IRE)**[37] 5095 3-9-3 112 KevinManning 4 112+
(J S Bolger, Ire) *settled off ldrs in 4th: pushed along under 3f out: nt qckn over 1f out and dropped to rr ins fnl f: kpt on one pce* **8/1**

2m 37.33s (2.03) **Going Correction** +0.325s/f (Good)
WFA 3 from 4yo 9lb 5 Ran SP% **113.0**
Speed ratings: **106,105,104,103,103**
CSF £4.87 TOTE £3.20: £1.60, £1.10; DF 6.40 Trifecta £14.50.
Owner Mrs C C Regalado-Gonzalez **Bred** Mrs C L Weld **Trained** Curragh, Co Kildare

FOCUS
This looked a good opportunity for the Derby runner-up, but he was outpointed by a smart and progressive four-year-old filly who may yet make her mark at the highest level.

6352a COOLMORE FASTNET ROCK MATRON STKS (GROUP 1) (OUTER TRACK) 1m

5:35 (5:35) 3-Y-O+

£151,838 (£48,897; £23,161; £10,294; £5,147; £2,573)

RPR

1 **Alice Springs (IRE)**[41] 4926 3-9-0 115 RyanMoore 7 118
(A P O'Brien, Ire) *sn settled in rr: stl last 2f out: styd on strly on outer into 4th ent fnl f: led fnl 150yds and sn clr* **5/1**[3]

2 3 ¼ **Persuasive (IRE)**[21] 5645 3-9-0 112 FrankieDettori 3 111+
(John Gosden) *hld up in 5th: pushed along under 3f out: clsr in 3rd under 2f out: led appr fnl f: hdd fnl 150yds and sn no match for wnr: kpt on same pce* **5/2**[2]

3 1 ¼ **Qemah (IRE)**[41] 4926 3-9-0 116 GregoryBenoist 5 108
(J-C Rouget, France) *bit slowly away: hld up and keen: prog on inner under 2f out into 5th: kpt on wl into 3rd ins fnl f: nvr nrr* **11/8**[1]

4 ½ **Now Or Never (IRE)**[85] 3339 3-9-0 109 ColinKeane 8 107
(M D O'Callaghan, Ire) *hld up: prog 2f out in 5th: no imp appr fnl f: kpt on same pce into 4th clsng stages: nvr nrr* **12/1**

5 1 **Hawksmoor (IRE)**[55] 4435 3-9-0 106 (b) PatSmullen 6 104+
(Hugo Palmer) *chsd ldrs in 4th: rdn over 2f out: nt qckn ins fnl f: kpt on same pce* **20/1**

6 ½ **Jet Setting (IRE)**[85] 3339 3-9-0 120 ChristopheSoumillon 1 103+
(Adrian Paul Keatley, Ire) *chsd ldrs in 3rd: travelled wl into 2nd 3f out: rdn and nt qckn ins fnl f: wknd fnl 100yds* **8/1**

7 2 ¼ **Creggs Pipes (IRE)**[16] 5814 4-9-5 107 DeclanMcDonogh 2 99+
(Andrew Slattery, Ire) *led tl hdd over 1f out: wknd fnl f* **33/1**

8 9 **Devonshire (IRE)**[55] 4435 4-9-5 109 WilliamBuick 4 78+
(W McCreery, Ire) *chsd ldr in 2nd tl 3f out: wknd qckly under 2f out: eased fnl f* **33/1**

1m 42.08s (0.88) **Going Correction** +0.60s/f (Yiel)
WFA 3 from 4yo 5lb 8 Ran SP% **116.8**
Speed ratings: **119,115,114,114,113 112,110,101**
CSF £18.00 CT £25.92 TOTE £6.90: £1.70, £1.10, £1.02; DF 21.10 Trifecta £33.70.
Owner Mrs John Magnier & Michael Tabor & Derrick Smith **Bred** Lynch - Bages & Longfield Stud **Trained** Cashel, Co Tipperary

FOCUS
A really first-rate Group 1 for fillies and mares. It produced a very emphatic winner. The standard is set by the second, fourth and fifth.

6353a CLIPPER LOGISTICS BOOMERANG STKS (GROUP 2) (OUTER TRACK) 1m

6:10 (6:10) 3-Y-O+

£86,764 (£27,941; £13,235; £5,882; £2,941; £1,470)

RPR

1 **Awtaad (IRE)**[45] 4754 3-9-6 117 [1] ChrisHayes 4 122+
(Kevin Prendergast, Ire) *chsd ldrs in 3rd: rdn in 2nd under 2f out: qcknd wl to ld ent fnl f: pushed out clsng stages* **2/1**[2]

2 1 ½ **Custom Cut (IRE)**[7] 6117 7-9-8 112 DanielTudhope 2 116
(David O'Meara) *trckd ldr in 2nd tl led 2f out and rdn clr: hdd ent fnl f and nt match wnr: kpt on same pce in 2nd* **15/2**

3 ½ **Hit It A Bomb (USA)**[30] 5343 3-9-3 116 RyanMoore 1 114+
(A P O'Brien, Ire) *hld up in 6th: last 3f out: swtchd rt and gd hdwy on outer appr fnl f: wnt 3rd ins fnl f: nvr nrr* **15/8**[1]

4 2 **Sruthan (IRE)**[39] 5000 6-9-8 110 (p) ShaneFoley 3 110
(P D Deegan, Ire) *settled off ldrs in 4th: rdn and nt qckn over 1f out: kpt on same pce fnl f* **22/1**

5 ¾ **Flight Risk (IRE)**[7] 6145 5-9-8 107 RonanWhelan 5 109
(J S Bolger, Ire) *racd in rr: sme prog under 2f out: kpt on same pce into 5th clsng stages: nvr nrr* **16/1**

6 ¾ **Gordon Lord Byron (IRE)**[7] 6120 8-9-8 113 BillyLee 6 107
(T Hogan, Ire) *led tl hdd 2f out: wknd ent fnl f* **20/1**

7 nk **Tribal Beat (IRE)**[30] 5343 3-9-3 116 (p) KevinManning 8 105
(J S Bolger, Ire) *settled in 5th: pushed along under 3f out: nt qckn over 1f out in rr: kpt on one pce* **4/1**[3]

1m 43.86s (2.66) **Going Correction** +0.60s/f (Yiel)
WFA 3 from 5yo+ 5lb 7 Ran SP% **114.9**
Speed ratings: **110,108,108,106,105 104,104**
CSF £17.56 TOTE £2.80: £1.50, £3.10; DF 15.10 Trifecta £51.00.
Owner Hamdan Al Maktoum **Bred** Shadwell Estate Company Limited **Trained** Friarstown, Co Kildare

FOCUS
A solid Group 2 event in which a Classic winner reasserted his credentials. The winner and third have been rated to their marks.

6354a QIPCO IRISH CHAMPION STKS (GROUP 1) (OUTER TRACK) 1m 2f

6:45 (6:47) 3-Y-O+

£523,897 (£174,632; £82,720; £36,764; £18,382; £9,191)

RPR

1 **Almanzor (FR)**[26] 5499 3-9-0 118 ChristopheSoumillon 10 127
(J-C Rouget, France) *racd in rr: 11th over 2f out: swtchd to outer and rapid hdwy to chse ldrs over 1f out: pressed ldr in 2nd ins fnl f: led fnl 100yds: kpt on wl* **7/1**[3]

2 ¾ **Found (IRE)**[23] 5586 4-9-4 118 .... FrankieDettori 4 123
(A P O'Brien, Ire) *hld up: towards rr: 10th over 2f out: qcknd wl over 1f out to ld ent fnl f: sn strly pressed and hdd fnl 100yds: no ex w wnr cl home* **7/1**[3]

3 2¾ **Minding (IRE)**[42] 4864 3-8-11 120 .... RyanMoore 7 117+
(A P O'Brien, Ire) *racd in mid-div whn sltly hmpd after 1f: prog on inner over 2f out in 7th: gd hdwy into 4th ent fnl f: wnt 3rd fnl 150yds: no imp on principals* **9/4**[2]

4 1¾ **New Bay**[26] 5500 4-9-7 121 .... VincentCheminaud 12 117
(A Fabre, France) *trckd ldrs in 3rd: rdn to ld over 1f out: sn pressed and hdd ent fnl f: nt qckn and sn dropped to 4th: kpt on same pce* **9/1**

5 ½ **My Dream Boat (IRE)**[70] 3912 4-9-7 122 .... AdamKirby 13 116
(Clive Cox) *hld up: prog under 2f out: 8th appr fnl f: kpt on wl into 5th cl home: nvr nrr* **33/1**

6 nk **Moonlight Magic**[20] 5685 3-9-0 111 .... KevinManning 8 115
(J S Bolger, Ire) *sn chsd ldrs in 5th: rdn in 4th under 2f out: nt qckn ins fnl f: kpt on same pce* **50/1**

7 ½ **Highland Reel (IRE)**[24] 5558 4-9-7 121 .... ColmO'Donoghue 6 114
(A P O'Brien, Ire) *trckd ldrs on inner in 4th: clsr in 2nd under 3f out: led briefly under 2f out: sn hdd and nt qckn ent fnl f: sn one pce* **10/1**

8 ¾ **Harzand (IRE)**[77] 3679 3-9-0 123 .... PatSmullen 3 112+
(D K Weld, Ire) *sn settled in 6th: pushed along over 3f out in 7th: kpt on same pce fr over 1f out: nvr on terms: struck into* **2/1**[1]

9 4½ **Hawkbill (USA)**[24] 5558 3-9-0 122 ....[1] WilliamBuick 2 103
(Charlie Appleby) *racd in mid-div: rdn in 5th over 2f out: nt qckn appr fnl f: wknd* **16/1**

10 3 **Sir Isaac Newton**[24] 5558 4-9-7 116 .... DonnachaO'Brien 5 97
(A P O'Brien, Ire) *a towards rr: rdn and sme prog under 2f out towards inner: nvr on terms* **33/1**

11 8 **Success Days (IRE)**[20] 5685 4-9-7 114 .... ShaneFoley 9 81
(K J Condon, Ire) *led and clly pressed tl hdd under 2f out: wknd qckly over 1f out: eased clsng stages* **33/1**

12 34 **Ebediyin (IRE)**[77] 3679 3-9-0 99 .... LeighRoche 11 13
(D K Weld, Ire) *sn pressed ldr in 2nd: rdn and wknd qckly to rr 2f out: sn eased* **200/1**

2m 8.93s (0.73) **Going Correction** +0.60s/f (Yiel)
WFA 3 from 4yo+ 7lb **12** Ran SP% **125.4**
Speed ratings: **121,120,118,116,116 116,115,115,111,109 102,75**
CSF £56.99 CT £149.84 TOTE £6.90: £2.80, £1.80, £1.30; DF 57.30 Trifecta £190.90.
Owner Ecurie Antonio Caro **Bred** Haras D'Etreham **Trained** Pau, France

FOCUS
A tremendous race on paper, it lived up to expectations in boiling down to a duel between a top-class three-year-old colt from France and an Irish-trained four-year-old filly who is a fine yardstick, for all her "bridesmaid" reputation. A big step up from the winner, with a small pb from the runner-up.

6355a IRISH STALLION FARMS EUROPEAN BREEDERS FUND "SOVEREIGN PATH" H'CAP (OUTER TRACK) 7f 20y
7:20 (7:21) 3-Y-0+
£65,073 (£20,955; £9,926; £4,411; £2,205; £1,102)

RPR

1 **Colour Blue (IRE)**[24] 5564 5-8-13 **91** .... BillyLee 14 102
(W McCreery, Ire) *racd in mid-div: clsr on outer 2f out: qcknd wl to ld appr fnl f and sn clr: styd on wl* **10/1**

2 3¼ **Withernsea (IRE)**[14] 5871 5-9-3 **95** .... DeclanMcDonogh 12 98
(Richard Fahey) *hld up: prog under 2f out: chsd ldr in 2nd ent fnl f: kpt on wl: nt rch wnr* **7/1**[2]

3 1 **Mizaah (IRE)**[83] 3442 3-8-9 **91** .... ChrisHayes 10 89
(Kevin Prendergast, Ire) *racd in mid-div: rdn to chse ldrs over 1f out: wnt 4th 1f out: 3rd ins fnl f but no imp on wnr fnl 100yds* **16/1**

4 2¼ **Jamesie (IRE)**[7] 6145 8-9-3 **102** ....(t) OisinOrr(7) 11 96
(David Marnane, Ire) *racd in mid-div: gd bit to do in 10th over 1f out: styd on wl fnl f into 4th cl home: nvr nrr* **25/1**

5 ½ **Reckless Endeavour (IRE)**[41] 4921 3-9-2 **98** .... ColinKeane 17 89
(G M Lyons, Ire) *chsd ldrs: clsr in 3rd 2f out and sn on terms: hdd over 1f out: no ex and dropped to 5th ins fnl f* **12/1**

6 hd **Sikandarabad (IRE)**[13] 5941 3-9-4 **100** ....(b[1]) PatSmullen 9 90
(D K Weld, Ire) *chsd ldrs in 5th: rdn and nt qckn 1f out: kpt on same ins fnl f* **5/2**[1]

7 1½ **Brazos (IRE)**[28] 5389 5-9-1 **93** ....(b) DanielTudhope 13 81
(James Tate) *racd towards rr: prog under 2f out: kpt on wl ins fnl f into 7th on line: nvr nrr* **25/1**

8 nk **Cornwallville (IRE)**[28] 5403 4-9-7 **99** ....(v) AdamKirby 16 86
(David Loughnane) *racd towards rr: prog towards outer under 2f out: kpt on wl fnl f: nvr on terms* **10/1**

9 nk **Sevenleft (IRE)**[56] 4412 3-9-0 **96** .... RonanWhelan 7 80
(Ms Sheila Lavery, Ire) *a mid-div: rdn under 2f out: kpt on same pce fr over 1f out: nvr on terms* **40/1**

10 2 **Eastern Rules (IRE)**[13] 5941 8-9-4 **96** ....(p) ShaneFoley 15 77
(M Halford, Ire) *racd in rr: kpt on wl fnl f fr over 1f out: nvr nrr* **33/1**

11 2 **Russian Soul (IRE)**[6] 6167 8-8-13 **91** .... NGMcCullagh 8 67
(M Halford, Ire) *racd in mid-div: rdn and nt qckn under 2f out: sn one pce* **40/1**

12 1¾ **Markhan (USA)**[22] 5616 3-8-11 **93** ....(t) ColmO'Donoghue 3 62
(David Marnane, Ire) *racd towards rr: kpt on one pce fr over 1f out: nvr on terms* **16/1**

13 1 **Dont Bother Me (IRE)**[30] 5343 6-9-5 **97** ....(t) WayneLordan 6 65
(Niall Moran, Ire) *chsd ldrs in 3rd: rdn in 2nd 2f out and sn on terms: hdd over 1f out and sn wknd* **33/1**

14 hd **Tony The Gent (IRE)**[22] 5618 3-8-13 **95** .... GaryCarroll 2 61
(G M Lyons, Ire) *hld up on inner: rdn under 3f out: sme prog on inner 2f out: no imp over 1f out and wknd* **8/1**[3]

15 3 **Kelinni (IRE)**[23] 5585 8-9-9 **104** .... GaryHalpin(3) 4 64
(Kevin Ryan) *led tl hdd under 2f out: wknd appr fnl f: eased clsng stages* **8/1**[3]

16 ¾ **Have A Nice Day**[21] 5662 6-9-3 **95** .... LeighRoche 1 52
(Sabrina J Harty, Ire) *chsd ldrs in 4th: clsr to dispute 2nd 3f out: nt qckn over 1f out: sn wknd and eased* **16/1**

17 12 **Time To Reason (IRE)**[21] 5662 3-9-2 **98** .... WilliamBuick 5 21
(J P Murtagh, Ire) *sn trckd ldr in 2nd: pushed along under 3f out: wknd under 2f out and eased fr 1f out* **7/1**[2]

1m 30.99s (2.29) **Going Correction** +0.60s/f (Yiel)
WFA 3 from 4yo+ 4lb **17** Ran SP% **137.8**
Speed ratings: **110,106,105,102,102 101,100,99,99,97 94,92,91,91,88 87,73**
Pick Six: Not Won - 110,861.84 carried forward to Curragh 11/09/2016. Tote Aggregates: 2015: 776,551.00, 2016: 968,877.00 CSF £83.17 CT £1165.49 TOTE £12.70: £2.60, £2.30, £3.40, £5.10; DF 128.20 Trifecta £4238.70.

Owner Garrett J Freyne **Bred** Mrs Helen Keaveney **Trained** Rathbride, Co Kildare

FOCUS
A very competitive handicap on paper, though it turned into a procession. A big step forward from the winner, with the second and third helping to set the standard.
T/Jkpt: @424.40. Pool: @284,345.00 - 468.89 winning units T/Plt: @242.00. Pool: @11,012.92 - 60.2 winning units **Alan Hewison**

5502 SAN SEBASTIAN (R-H)
Saturday, September 10

OFFICIAL GOING: Turf: soft

6356a GRAN PREMIO SAN SEBASTIAN (CONDITIONS) (3YO+) (TURF) 1m 6f
5:50 (12:00) 3-Y-0+ **£17,647** (£7,058; £3,529; £1,764)

RPR

1 **Again Charlie (FR)**[104] 3-8-7 0 .... AurelienLemaitre 10
(C Delcher-Sanchez, France) **23/5**[3]

2 ¾ **Tuvalu**[76] 4-9-4 0 .... BorjaFayosMartin 6
(J-M Osorio, Spain) **22/5**[2]

3 4¼ **Green Soldier (FR)**[873] 5-9-4 0 .... JoseLuisMartinez 9
(Ana Imaz Ceca, Spain) **67/10**

4 7 **Ziga**[76] 5-9-1 0 .... JaimeGelabert 7
(G Arizkorreta Elosegui, Spain) **92/10**

5 3½ **Rooke**[26] 5502 6-9-4 0 .... ThomasHenderson 3
(D Henderson, France) **3/1**[1]

6 ¾ **Malos Pelos (SPA)** 5-9-4 0 .... RicardoSousa 2
(J Lopez Sanchez, Spain) **63/10**

7 nk **Lateran Accord (IRE)**[26] 5502 7-9-8 0 .... VaclavJanacek 11
(G Arizkorreta Elosegui, Spain) **175/10**

8 ¾ **Sant'Alberto (ITY)**[26] 5502 8-9-4 0 ....(b) MarinoGomes 1
(D Teixeira, Spain) **30/1**

9 dist **Sureness (IRE)**[33] 5249 6-9-1 0 .... JoseLuisBorrego 4
(Charlie Mann) *settled towards front on outer: prom turning in: rdn along 2 1/2f out: unable to pick up: sn btn: t.o* **67/10**

10 dist **Tindaro (FR)**[23] 1987 9-9-4 0 ....(v) OscarUrbina 5
(Paul Webber) *towards rr early: midfield at 1/2-way: rdn along fr 3f out: unable to cl on ldrs: wl btn whn eased rt down 2f out* **81/10**

11 dist **Hurricane Volta (IRE)**[22] 5597 5-9-4 0.....(b) MlleGloriaMaderoParayre 8
(Peter Hedger) *niggled along early to ld after 2f: settled in 2nd after 3f: wknd rapidly 3f out: eased rt down* **26/1**

Owner Cuadra Bloke **Bred** Haras Du Logis Saint Germain **Trained** France

3379 TOULOUSE
Saturday, September 10

OFFICIAL GOING: Turf: good

6357a PRIX OCCITANIE (LISTED RACE) (3YO FILLIES) (TURF) 1m 2f
1:20 (12:00) 3-Y-0 **£20,220** (£8,088; £6,066; £4,044; £2,022)

RPR

1 **Not Only Florina (IRE)**[18] 3-9-0 0 .... JulienAuge 7 98+
(C Ferland, France) **13/1**

2 shd **Endless Summer (ITY)**[47] 4723 3-9-0 0 .... UmbertoRispoli 1 98
(M Guarnieri, Italy) **9/1**

3 1¼ **Al Hayyah (IRE)**[47] 4723 3-9-0 0 .... Francois-XavierBertras 5 96
(F Rohaut, France) **9/5**[1]

4 hd **Liwa Palace**[53] 3-9-0 0 .... CristianDemuro 2 95
(Rod Collet, France) **53/10**[3]

5 ½ **Elennga (FR)**[39] 5006 3-9-0 0 .... AlexisBadel 4 94
(J-C Rouget, France) **12/1**

6 nse **Magnolea (IRE)**[62] 4184 3-9-0 0 .... IoritzMendizabal 8 94
(J-C Rouget, France) **27/10**[2]

7 hd **Pure Art**[21] 5650 3-9-0 0 .... OlivierPeslier 6 94
(Ralph Beckett) *slowest away: settled towards rr on rail: effrt fr 2f out: unable to get on terms w ldrs* **61/10**

8 6½ **Secret Sense (USA)**[78] 3608 3-9-0 0 .... MickaelBarzalona 3 81
(H-A Pantall, France) **30/1**

2m 4.9s (124.90) **8** Ran SP% **120.8**
WIN (incl. 1 euro stake): 14.00. PLACES: 3.30, 2.40, 1.70. DF: 48.50. SF: 115.90.
Owner Christophe Ferland **Bred** Ecurie Des Monceaux **Trained** France

6358 - 6360a (Foreign Racing) - See Raceform Interactive

6311 BATH (L-H)
Sunday, September 11

OFFICIAL GOING: Good to soft (good in places; 7.5)
Wind: mild breeze across Weather: sunny periods

6361 SOMERSET ARMY CADET FORCE H'CAP 5f 11y
2:05 (2:06) (Class 6) (0-65,65) 3-Y-0 **£2,556** (£754; £377) **Stalls** Centre

Form RPR

2310 **1** **Secretfact**[22] 5628 3-8-8 **52** .... JimmyQuinn 9 71+
(Malcolm Saunders) *travelled strly: hld up: hdwy over 1f out: led ent fnl f: qcknd clr: easily* **4/1**[2]

4405 **2** 6 **Concur (IRE)**[13] 5954 3-8-2 **51** oh6 ....[1] GeorgeWood(5) 7 48
(Rod Millman) *chsd ldrs: rdn over 2f out: kpt on ins fnl f: wnt 2nd cl home: no ch w wnr* **8/1**

3243 **3** ½ **Andalusite**[24] 5570 3-9-2 **60** ....(p[1]) RoystonFfrench 2 55
(Ed McMahon) *prom: chal 2f out: rdn and ev ch ent fnl f: kpt on but sn outpcd by wnr* **5/2**[1]

124 **4** ½ **Tahiti One**[26] 5523 3-8-10 **54** .... FrederikTylicki 8 47
(Tony Carroll) *led: rdn and hdd ent fnl f: sn outpcd by wnr: no ex whn losing 2 pls towards fin* **13/2**

6054 **5** 1½ **Tally's Song**[22] 5628 3-8-2 **51** oh6 ....(p) MitchGodwin(5) 10 39
(Grace Harris) *prom: rdn and ev ch 2f out: hld ent fnl f: fdd* **33/1**

6612 **6** 3 **The Burnham Mare (IRE)**[34] 5230 3-9-2 **65** ....(p) HollieDoyle(5) 1 42
(J S Moore) *trckd ldrs: effrt 2f out: fdd fnl f* **6/1**[3]

1540 **7** 15 **Dominance**[33] 5269 3-9-4 **62** .... ShaneKelly 3
(Rae Guest) *chsd ldrs: rdn over 2f out: eased whn btn jst over 1f out* **9/1**

-402 **8** 3 ½ **Shine Likeadiamond**[9] 6101 3-9-5 **63**...................... SilvestreDeSousa 4
(Mick Channon) *v keen and overshot s: struggling in rr after 2f: eased whn btn fnl 2f* **6/1**[3]

1m 1.7s (-0.80) **Going Correction** +0.025s/f (Good) **8** Ran SP% **114.5**
Speed ratings (Par 99): **107,97,96,95,93 88,64,59**
CSF £35.67 CT £95.29 TOTE £3.90: £1.40, £2.90, £1.30; EX 50.10 Trifecta £277.90.
Owner Premier Conservatory Roofs **Bred** M S Saunders & D Collier **Trained** Green Ore, Somerset

FOCUS
Following a dry night the ground was the same as for the previous day's meeting - good to soft, good in places (Goingstick 7.5). Two geldings against six fillies in this modest 3yo sprint handicap and it proved one-way traffic. They came up the centre and Jimmy Quinn described the ground as "just on the slow side", while Royston Ffrench said it was "easy side of good".

6362 SOMERSET SOLDIERS' CHARITY H'CAP 2m 1f 34y
2:40 (2:40) (Class 4) (0-80,81) 4-Y-O+ **£5,175** (£1,540; £769; £384) **Stalls** Low

Form RPR

0150 **1** **Sunny Future (IRE)**[10] 6065 10-9-0 **73**...................... JimmyFortune 11 81
(Malcolm Saunders) *hld up bhd: rdn and hdwy fr 3f out: led ent fnl f: styd on wl: rdn out* **12/1**

1060 **2** ¾ **Be My Sea (IRE)**[25] 5553 5-9-4 **77**................................(p) JimmyQuinn 4 84
(Tony Carroll) *mid-div: rdn and hdwy fr 3f out: disp ld over 1f out tl ent fnl f: styd on but no ex towards fin* **5/1**[2]

3343 **3** 1 ½ **Sunday Royal (FR)**[9] 6090 4-8-8 **67**...................... MichaelJMMurphy 5 72
(Harry Dunlop) *hld up: rdn and hdwy fr 3f out: disp ld over 1f out tl ent fnl f: styd on but no ex towards fin* **9/1**

-621 **4** 6 **Kleitomachos (IRE)**[19] 5745 8-8-11 **70**.................(t) SilvestreDeSousa 7 69
(Stuart Kittow) *slowly away: sn trcking ldrs: pressed ldr 1/2-way: led over 3f out: rdn and hdd over 2f out: styd on same pce* **7/2**[1]

6306 **5** ½ **Communicator**[22] 5642 8-8-9 **75**.............................(v) JoshuaBryan(7) 12 73
(Andrew Balding) *mid-div: hdwy 3f out: sn rdn to chse ldng pair: ch over 1f out: no ex fnl f* **6/1**[3]

0133 **6** 1 ¾ **Le Rock (IRE)**[31] 5334 4-8-9 **73**.................................. MitchGodwin(5) 2 69
(J S Moore) *led: hdd over 3f out: rdn to regain ld over 2f out: hdd over 1f out: fdd fnl f* **25/1**

/514 **7** 11 **Charlie Wells (IRE)**[18] 5767 5-9-4 **77**................................ JohnFahy 9 61
(Eve Johnson Houghton) *hld up: rdn over 3f out: nvr any imp* **15/2**

4240 **8** ½ **Fitzwilly**[42] 4912 6-9-0 **73**.. GrahamLee 8 57
(Mick Channon) *trckd ldrs: rdn over 3f out: wknd over 1f out* **12/1**

3043 **9** 39 **King Calypso**[25] 5553 5-8-13 **72**......................................(v) ShaneKelly 1 13
(Denis Coakley) *in tch: rdn over 3f out: wknd over 2f out: eased* **8/1**

046 **10** 11 **See And Be Seen**[36] 5176 6-9-0 **73**..........................(p) RenatoSouza 10 2
(Sylvester Kirk) *trckd ldr tl 1/2-way: chsd ldrs: rdn wl over 3f out: sn wknd: eased* **7/1**

3m 49.92s (-1.98) **Going Correction** +0.025s/f (Good) **10** Ran SP% **117.8**
Speed ratings (Par 105): **105,104,103,101,100 100,94,94,76,71**
CSF £71.76 CT £576.89 TOTE £19.90: £5.50, £2.10, £2.80; EX 124.30 Trifecta £1801.30.
Owner M S Saunders **Bred** Mrs G Stanga **Trained** Green Ore, Somerset

FOCUS
A fair staying handicap run at an even pace and another win for a course specialist and a stable in red-hot form.

6363 CONTROL DEVELOPMENTS H'CAP (SUMMER SPRINT SERIES FINAL) 5f 161y
3:15 (3:18) (Class 3) 3-Y-O+ **£12,938** (£3,850; £1,924; £962) **Stalls** Centre

Form RPR

6343 **1** **Storm Melody**[22] 5626 3-9-4 **69**.. GrahamLee 5 81
(Jonjo O'Neill) *trckd ldrs: led pover 1f out: r.o wl: rdn out* **14/1**

6564 **2** 1 ¼ **Showmethewayavrilo**[22] 5626 3-8-13 **69**................... GeorgiaCox(5) 14 77
(Malcolm Saunders) *led: rdn and hdd over 1f out: kpt on but no ex fnl f* **8/1**

1501 **3** ¾ **Dusty Blue**[39] 5009 4-9-0 **66**..(t) EoinWalsh(3) 9 72
(Tony Carroll) *trckd ldrs: rdn over 2f out: wnt 3rd ent fnl f: kpt on* **7/1**[3]

1533 **4** 1 ¾ **Go Amber Go**[16] 5826 4-8-4 **58**..................................[1] GeorgeWood(5) 6 58
(Rod Millman) *prom: rdn to chse ldng pair 2f out: kpt on same pce fnl f* **20/1**

2220 **5** 1 **Essaka (IRE)**[16] 5827 4-8-6 **60**...................................... PaddyPilley(5) 10 56
(Tony Carroll) *mid-div: rdn over 2f out: hdwy over 1f out: kpt on same pce fnl f* **16/1**

0131 **6** 1 **Showbizzy**[22] 5626 3-9-3 **68**...(v) ShaneKelly 13 61+
(Richard Fahey) *hld up: hdwy whn nt clr run briefly 2f out: kpt on fnl f: nvr threatened* **12/1**

3261 **7** 1 **Vincentti (IRE)**[3] 6255 6-9-11 **79** 6ex........................... MitchGodwin(5) 8 69
(Ronald Harris) *hld up: hdwy over 2f out: sn rdn: no further imp fnl f* **5/1**[2]

014 **8** nk **Cherry Kool**[32] 5285 3-9-4 **72**...................................... AaronJones(3) 16 61
(Stuart Williams) *trckd ldr: rdn 2f out: wknd ins fnl f* **16/1**

2211 **9** 2 ½ **Babyfact**[14] 5928 5-9-8 **71**... JimmyFortune 12 52
(Malcolm Saunders) *hld up: hdwy whn swtchd rt 2f out: sn rdn: nt pce to get involved* **9/2**[1]

-200 **10** 1 **Dreams Of Glory**[11] 6017 8-9-5 **68**........................... FergusSweeney 11 45
(Ron Hodges) *trckd ldrs: rdn over 2f out: wknd jst over 1f out* **33/1**

1430 **11** ¾ **Virile (IRE)**[8] 6137 5-8-12 **61**..................................(bt) RobertWinston 17 36
(Sylvester Kirk) *hld up: nt clr run whn snatched up 2f out: nvr threatened to get on terms* **14/1**

0405 **12** nk **Captain Devious**[22] 5628 5-8-0 **49** oh4.........................(t) JimmyQuinn 15 23
(Grace Harris) *mid-div: rdn whn short of room briefly 2f out: wknd ent fnl f* **66/1**

0633 **13** 4 ½ **Racquet**[11] 6017 3-9-5 **75**..(b[1]) HollieDoyle(5) 3 34
(Richard Hannon) *mid-div: effrt over 2f out: wknd over 1f out* **10/1**

3464 **14** ¾ **Captain Ryan**[14] 5928 5-8-10 **59**.............................. SilvestreDeSousa 1 16
(Geoffrey Deacon) *trckd ldrs: rdn over 2f out: wknd over 1f out* **9/1**

0316 **15** 5 **Topsoil**[24] 5570 3-8-0 **51**... KieranO'Neill 7
(Ronald Harris) *plld hrd early: hld up: hdwy after 2f out: rdn over 2f out: wknd over 1f out* **25/1**

0522 **16** 3 **Catalinas Diamond (IRE)**[22] 5628 8-8-9 **56** ow2........(t) SteveDrowne 4
(Pat Murphy) *a towards rr* **20/1**

1m 10.37s (-0.83) **Going Correction** +0.025s/f (Good)
WFA 3 from 4yo+ 2lb **16** Ran SP% **128.1**
Speed ratings (Par 107): **106,104,103,101,99 98,97,96,93,91 90,90,84,83,76 72**
CSF £120.62 CT £912.40 TOTE £16.40: £3.10, £2.70, £2.60, £4.70; EX 162.10 Trifecta £794.50.

Owner P Hickey **Bred** Selwood B/S, Hoskins & Jonason **Trained** Cheltenham, Gloucs
■ Stewards' Enquiry : Jimmy Fortune caution: careless riding

FOCUS
A fiercely competitive handicap and as was the case with the stayers version the previous day, many of these had met each other in the qualifiers here during the summer. They used the whole width of the track and those that raced more towards the nearside were favoured. It was also an advantage to be handy with the winner, second and fourth always in the front rank.

6364 BOEING DEFENCE UK CONDITIONS STKS 1m 5y
3:45 (3:45) (Class 3) 3-Y-O+ **£7,762** (£2,310; £1,154; £577) **Stalls** Low

Form RPR

365 **1** **Here Comes When (IRE)**[27] 5472 6-9-2 105.................... GrahamLee 4 103
(Andrew Balding) *trckd front 3: shkn up to cl on ldr over 1f out: chal jst ins fnl f: led fnl 120yds: rdn out* **7/4**[1]

2054 **2** ¾ **Beach Bar (IRE)**[13] 5962 5-9-2 96........................... SilvestreDeSousa 5 101
(Brendan Powell) *led: pushed along to qcknd pce 4f out: 4 l clr 2f out: rdn whn jnd ent fnl f: hdd fnl 120yds: kpt on but no ex towards fin* **4/1**[3]

0024 **3** 1 ½ **Emell**[14] 5926 6-9-2 104...(p) KieranO'Neill 1 98
(Richard Hannon) *trckd ldr: rdn over 2f out: kpt on same pce* **4/1**[3]

6635 **4** 3 ¾ **Master Carpenter (IRE)**[31] 5329 5-9-2 105................. FrederikTylicki 3 89
(Rod Millman) *trckd ldr: rdn wl over 2f out: nt quite pce to chal: fdd fnl f* **9/4**[2]

1m 41.34s (0.54) **Going Correction** +0.025s/f (Good) **4** Ran SP% **107.1**
Speed ratings (Par 107): **98,97,95,92**
CSF £8.48 TOTE £2.50; EX 7.00 Trifecta £27.70.
Owner Mrs Fitri Hay **Bred** Old Carhue & Graeng Bloodstock **Trained** Kingsclere, Hants

FOCUS
A modest event of its type, with none of the quartet having won a race of any sort in nearly a year. Tactics played their part, but the right horse won.

6365 MBDA H'CAP 1m 2f 46y
4:20 (4:20) (Class 5) (0-75,75) 3-Y-O+ **£3,234** (£962; £481; £240) **Stalls** Low

Form RPR

6-35 **1** **Niblawi (IRE)**[141] 1652 4-9-10 **73**.............................. SilvestreDeSousa 8 84
(Ismail Mohammed) *trckd ldr: led over 2f out: sn rdn: hld on gamely fnl f: drvn out* **9/2**[2]

1421 **2** ¾ **Panko (IRE)**[59] 4293 3-9-0 **75**.................................. CallumShepherd(5) 3 85
(Ed de Giles) *mid-div: hdwy 3f out: rdn to chal over 1f out: styd on w ev ch tl no ex fnl 75yds* **7/1**

0-01 **3** 1 ¾ **Totally Committed**[32] 5288 3-9-2 **72**............. WilliamTwiston-Davies 11 78
(Clive Cox) *hld up towards rr: hdwy fr 3f out: rdn over 2f out: wnt 3rd over 1f out: styd on fnl f* **5/1**[3]

0235 **4** 3 ¾ **Lilbourne Prince (IRE)**[34] 5234 3-9-2 **72**................. RoystonFfrench 12 71
(David Evans) *mid-div: hdwy over 2f out: sn rdn: styd on same pce fnl f* **12/1**

6035 **5** 1 ¾ **Ride The Lightning**[13] 5975 3-9-2 **72**...................... MichaelJMMurphy 6 67
(Archie Watson) *mid-div: hdwy over 2f out: sn rdn to chse ldrs: styd on same pce fnl f* **4/1**[1]

4000 **6** 2 ½ **Berkeley Vale**[23] 5609 5-9-10 **73**................................... RobertWinston 9 63
(Roger Teal) *hld up towards rr: hdwy over 2f out: sn rdn: nvr threatened: fdd ins fnl f* **12/1**

036 **7** nk **Molten Lava (IRE)**[19] 5750 4-9-10 **73**............................. JimmyFortune 4 62
(Paul Cole) *trckd ldrs: rdn over 2f out: wknd ins fnl f* **25/1**

5 **8** 1 **Cutty Sark**[30] 5375 3-8-10 **66**... ShaneKelly 15 53
(Luca Cumani) *mid-div: hdwy over 2f out: sn rdn to chse ldrs: fdd fnl f* **12/1**

3532 **9** 1 **Chantecler**[22] 5629 5-9-9 **72**...(t) GrahamLee 1 57
(Neil Mulholland) *trckd ldr tl rdn over 2f out: wknd jst over 1f out* **8/1**

4636 **10** 17 **Touchdown Banwell (USA)**[58] 4342 3-8-7 **70**......... JoshuaBryan(7) 10 21
(Andrew Balding) *a towards rr* **16/1**

25-0 **11** 2 ¾ **Secular Society**[21] 165 6-9-10 **73**................................[1] SteveDrowne 7 19
(George Baker) *led tl rdn over 2f out: sn wknd* **50/1**

5640 **12** 10 **Isis Blue**[65] 4081 6-8-13 **67**..(p) GeorgeWood(5) 14
(Rod Millman) *a towards rr* **16/1**

0504 **13** 21 **Mister Musicmaster**[11] 6021 7-9-11 **74**..................... FergusSweeney 5
(Ron Hodges) *a towards rr: eased whn btn over 1f out* **20/1**

2m 10.76s (-0.24) **Going Correction** +0.025s/f (Good)
WFA 3 from 4yo+ 7lb **13** Ran SP% **123.9**
Speed ratings (Par 103): **101,100,99,96,94 92,92,91,90,77 74,66,50**
CSF £36.85 CT £169.35 TOTE £4.80: £1.90, £2.50, £2.10; EX 32.70 Trifecta £177.30.
Owner Sultan Ali **Bred** Rabbah Bloodstock Limited **Trained** Newmarket, Suffolk

FOCUS
A modest handicap run at just a fair pace.

6366 SERCO ARMED FORCES GOLD COVENANT CUP NURSERY H'CAP 1m 2f 46y
4:55 (4:55) (Class 5) (0-75,74) 2-Y-O **£3,234** (£962; £481; £240) **Stalls** Low

Form RPR

351 **1** **Count Calabash (IRE)**[38] 5052 2-9-7 **74**................. SilvestreDeSousa 7 83
(Paul Cole) *prom: led after 3f: styd on strly to draw clr fnl f: comf* **5/6**[1]

5401 **2** 4 **Zamadance**[20] 5719 2-8-5 **63**.. MitchGodwin(5) 3 63
(Sylvester Kirk) *trckd ldrs: wnt 2nd over 5f out: rdn over 2f out: styd on same pce fnl f* **7/1**

1242 **3** 5 **Luduamf (IRE)**[26] 5528 2-8-9 **62**.. KieranO'Neill 1 53
(Richard Hannon) *hld up last pair: wnt cl 3rd 3f out: rdn 2f out: no ex ent fnl f* **4/1**[2]

6403 **4** 10 **Ok By Me (IRE)**[13] 5951 2-9-3 **70**.. SteveDrowne 2 43
(David Evans) *s.i.s: sn trcking ldrs: rdn over 2f out: wknd over 1f out* **8/1**

0660 **5** ½ **Hot N Sassy (IRE)**[1] 6313 2-7-9 **53** oh8........................... HollieDoyle(5) 4 25
(J S Moore) *led for 3f: trckd ldrs: rdn wl over 2f out: wknd over 1f out* **50/1**

0000 **6** 37 **Devilish Guest (IRE)**[33] 5251 2-8-13 **66**............................... GrahamLee 5
(Mick Channon) *hld up last pair: rdn wl over 2f out: wknd qckly* **6/1**[3]

2m 13.41s (2.41) **Going Correction** +0.025s/f (Good) **6** Ran SP% **114.4**
Speed ratings (Par 95): **91,87,83,75,75 45**
CSF £7.79 TOTE £1.60: £1.10, £3.70; EX 8.50 Trifecta £20.10.
Owner Trish Hall & Colin Fletcher **Bred** Miss S Von Schilcher **Trained** Whatcombe, Oxon

FOCUS
This would have been quite a test for these 2yos and they finished well spread out.

6367 PRESIDENTS' RACE H'CAP 1m 5f 22y
5:30 (5:30) (Class 6) (0-65,65) 3-Y-O **£2,726** (£805; £402) **Stalls** High

Form RPR

2423 **1** **Denmead**[38] 5079 3-9-4 **62**.. RobertWinston 7 71+
(John Butler) *trckd ldr: led wl over 2f out: styd on wl: rdn out* **3/1**[2]

6026 **2** 3 ¾ **Mister Showman**[25] 5548 3-9-2 **60**............................... FergusSweeney 8 63
(Jonathan Portman) *trckd ldrs: rdn to chse wnr wl over 2f out: styd on but nt pce to mount chal* **14/1**

0251 **3** *shd* **Skylark Lady (IRE)**[11] 6030 3-9-2 **60**...................... SilvestreDeSousa 11 63
(Michael Wigham) *hld up towards rr: hdwy fr 3f out: rdn 2f out: chsd wnr over 1f out: kpt on same pce fnl f* **5/2**[1]

1 **4** *2 3/4* **Tasty Ginger (IRE)**[35] 5204 3-9-3 **61**..........................(v) FrederikTylicki 6 60
(J R Jenkins) *hld up: hdwy wl over 2f out: sn rdn: styd on same pce fr over 1f out* **7/1**

0545 **5** *2 3/4* **McCools Gold**[8] 6127 3-9-5 **63**...................................... CharlesBishop 2 58
(Eve Johnson Houghton) *trckd ldrs: rdn over 2f out: sn one pce* **6/1**

5603 **6** *1 3/4* **Sisania (IRE)**[76] 3722 3-9-1 **64**................................ HectorCrouch(5) 10 56
(Gary Moore) *mid-div: rdn and hdwy over 2f out: nvr threatened: fdd ins fnl f* **14/1**

003 **7** *18* **Pure Vanity**[26] 5508 3-9-7 **65**.............................. WilliamTwiston-Davies 5 30
(Roger Charlton) *led: rdn and hdd wl over 2f out: wknd over 1f out* **5/1**[3]

5-00 **8** *12* **Oyster Pearl (IRE)**[33] 5263 3-7-12 **49**.............................(t) WilliamCox(7) 4
(Carroll Gray) *trckd ldrs tl rdn 3f out: sn wknd* **80/1**

-050 **9** *2* **Inwithachance (IRE)**[40] 4987 3-8-2 **46** oh1..................(p) JimmyQuinn 3
(Daniel Mark Loughnane) *mid-div: rdn and wknd over 2f out* **25/1**

0045 **10** *7* **Roccor**[51] 4596 3-8-12 **61**.. MitchGodwin(5) 9
(Tim Vaughan) *a towards rr* **14/1**

2m 53.18s (1.18) **Going Correction** +0.025s/f (Good) **10** Ran SP% **122.1**
Speed ratings (Par 99): **97,94,94,92,91 90,79,71,70,66**
CSF £47.21 CT £123.65 TOTE £3.50: £1.40, £4.20, £1.60; EX 47.90 Trifecta £158.30.
Owner John O'Donnell & Noel Kelly **Bred** J O'Donnell & N Kelly **Trained** Newmarket, Suffolk

FOCUS
A moderate 3yo staying handicap with only two of these having won before and several with stamina to prove.
T/Jkpt: Not won. T/Plt: £160.10 to a £1 stake. Pool: £86,090.36 - 392.38 winning tickets T/Qpdt: £27.20 to a £1 stake. Pool: £6,023.16 - 163.35 winning tickets **Tim Mitchell**

6243 CHELMSFORD (A.W) (L-H)
Sunday, September 11

OFFICIAL GOING: Polytrack: standard
Wind: light, half behind Weather: sunny

6368 TOTEPLACEPOT RACING'S FAVOURITE BET MAIDEN STKS (PLUS 10 RACE) 7f (P)
1:45 (1:46) (Class 4) 2-Y-O **£7,115** (£2,117; £1,058; £529) **Stalls** Low

Form RPR

240 **1** **Aventinus (IRE)**[44] 4825 2-9-5 77.. JimCrowley 4 80
(Hugo Palmer) *chsd ldr tl led over 5f out: mde rest: rdn over 1f out: styd on wl fnl f: rdn out* **4/1**[3]

2 **2** *3/4* **Qatar Man (IRE)**[21] 5676 2-9-5 0...................................... HarryBentley 3 78
(Marco Botti) *hld up in tch in midfield: hdwy 2f out: chsd ldrs and rdn over 1f out: wnt 2nd and swtchd rt jst ins fnl f: styd on u.p* **2/1**[1]

55 **3** *4 1/2* **Thaaqib**[58] 4349 2-9-5 0.. PaulHanagan 1 66
(Charles Hills) *t.k.h: chsd ldrs: wnt 2nd 2f out: rdn and unable qck over 1f out: 3rd and btn jst ins fnl f: wknd fnl 100yds* **9/4**[2]

4 *3 3/4* **Elysees Palace** 2-9-5 0.. RyanPowell 10 56+
(Sir Mark Prescott Bt) *s.i.s: bhd: hdwy on outer 4f out: chsd ldrs over 2f out: outpcd and hung lft over 1f out: wknd fnl f* **50/1**

0 **5** *nse* **Jewel House**[58] 4349 2-9-5 0.. RobertHavlin 6 56
(John Gosden) *hld up in tch in midfield: effrt and hung lft over 1f out: sn outpcd: wknd fnl f* **5/1**

6 *6* **Pennington** 2-9-5 0.. PaulMulrennan 8 39
(Mark Johnston) *led tl over 5f out: chsd ldr tl rdn and lost 2nd 2f out: sn struggling: wknd over 1f out* **33/1**

7 *7* **Inscribe (USA)** 2-9-5 0... RichardKingscote 7 20
(Sir Michael Stoute) *dwlt: in tch towards rr: struggling and pushed along wl over 2f out: sn btn: bhd over 1f out* **16/1**

8 *1/2* **Distill (USA)** 2-9-5 0.. PatCosgrave 5 19
(William Haggas) *hld up in tch in midfield: rdn 2f out: sn outpcd and btn: wknd fnl f: burst blood vessel* **14/1**

0000 **9** *3 3/4* **Red Shanghai (IRE)**[48] 4712 2-8-9 46................... AdamMcNamara(5) 9 4
(Charles Smith) *chsd ldrs early: steadily lost pl and bhd 4f out: rdn over 3f out: wknd over 2f out* **100/1**

10 *2 1/2* **Lincoln Day** 2-9-5 0.. DannyBrock 2 2
(Phil McEntee) *dwlt: a in last pair: rdn over 3f out: wknd over 2f out* **66/1**

1m 26.72s (-0.48) **Going Correction** -0.075s/f (Stan) **10** Ran SP% **120.7**
Speed ratings (Par 97): **99,98,93,88,88 81,73,73,68,66**
CSF £12.82 TOTE £4.40: £1.30, £1.30, £1.30; EX 12.80 Trifecta £32.00.
Owner Seventh Lap Racing **Bred** Dr Philip J Brown **Trained** Newmarket, Suffolk

FOCUS
A valuable maiden to kick-off proceedings. The first two pulled nicely clear.

6369 TOTEEXACTA FORECAST THE 1ST AND 2ND MAIDEN AUCTION STKS 6f (P)
2:20 (2:22) (Class 5) 2-Y-O **£4,528** (£1,347; £673; £336) **Stalls** Centre

Form RPR

2 **1** **Marzouq (USA)**[9] 6087 2-9-5 0... JFEgan 7 75
(Jeremy Noseda) *hld up in tch in midfield: clsd to chse ldrs and hung rt over 1f out: drvn to press ldr 1f out: styd on to ld towards fin: hld on cl home* **11/8**[1]

454 **2** *hd* **Bizet (IRE)**[11] 6034 2-9-5 68..[1] JimCrowley 1 74
(John Ryan) *led: rdn wl over 1f out: sn drvn: kpt on u.p tl hdd towards fin: battled on but hld cl home* **5/1**[3]

53 **3** *2* **Wind In Her Sails (IRE)**[29] 5395 2-9-0 0........................ PaulHanagan 5 63
(Giles Bravery) *trckd ldrs on inner: rdn to chse ldr wl over 1f out: sn ev ch tl no ex jst ins fnl f: styd on same pce fnl 100yds* **9/2**[2]

4 **4** *nse* **Desert Fox**[15] 5890 2-9-5 0..................................... PaulMulrennan 8 68
(Mike Murphy) *stdd s: t.k.h: swtchd lft and dropped into last pair 4f out: swtchd rt and effrt wl over 1f out: styd on u.p ins fnl f* **14/1**

5 *1 3/4* **Kohinoor Diamond (IRE)** 2-9-0 0.................................. RyanPowell 2 61+
(Sir Mark Prescott Bt) *s.i.s: rn green and pushed along in rr: clsd and in tch 4f out: effrt on inner and sme hdwy over 1f out: kpt on same pce ins fnl f: eased towards fin* **50/1**

05 **6** *2* **Biologist (IRE)**[71] 3902 2-9-0 0.. PatCosgrave 6 52
(William Haggas) *chsd ldr tl wl over 1f out: unable qck and lost pl over 1f out: wknd ins fnl f* **8/1**

7 *2 1/4* **Banta Bay** 2-9-5 0.. KierenFox 9 50
(John Best) *wnt rt and sltly impeded leaving stalls: sn swtchd lft and t.k.h: in tch: effrt and unable qck over 1f out: wknd ins fnl f* **25/1**

1m 14.59s (0.89) **Going Correction** -0.075s/f (Stan) **7** Ran SP% **100.5**
Speed ratings (Par 95): **91,90,88,88,85 83,80**
CSF £6.29 TOTE £2.20: £1.40, £1.70; EX 8.10 Trifecta £17.80.
Owner Naser Buresli **Bred** Nicholas Cimino **Trained** Newmarket, Suffolk

■ Hint Of A Smile (5/1) and Huddersfilly Town (25/1) were withdrawn. Rule 4 applies to all bets - deduction 15p in the pound

FOCUS
A moderate maiden, made weaker on account of two late withdrawals. The market proved key.

6370 TOTETRIFECTA PICK THE 1,2,3 H'CAP 1m 6f (P)
2:50 (2:50) (Class 5) (0-75,72) 3-Y-O **£5,175** (£1,540; £769; £384) **Stalls** Low

Form RPR

12 **1** **Unsuspected Girl (IRE)**[18] 5763 3-8-0 **58**................ SophieKilloran(7) 1 67+
(David Simcock) *stdd s: t.k.h: hld up in tch in rr: gng wl and nt clr run over 2f out: effrt and swtchd rt 2f out: rdn to chse ldr over 1f out: hung lft and led 1f out: r.o wl* **11/4**[2]

5-33 **2** *1 3/4* **Press Gang**[118] 2300 3-9-7 **72**.. RyanTate 2 78
(James Eustace) *led: rdn and qcknd gallop over 3f out: drvn over 1f out: hdd 1f out: styd on same pce ins fnl f* **3/1**[3]

-511 **3** *3/4* **Cartwright**[20] 5718 3-9-6 **71**..[1] RyanPowell 4 76+
(Sir Mark Prescott Bt) *in tch in 4th: rdn 3f out: carried wd bnd 2f out: styd on to go 3rd ins fnl f: kpt on u.p but no threat to wnr* **6/4**[1]

6145 **4** *3 1/4* **Cold Fusion (IRE)**[26] 5508 3-9-4 **72**....................[1] JosephineGordon(3) 5 72
(Ed Vaughan) *chsd ldr: rdn over 3f out: lost 2nd and unable qck over 1f out: wknd ins fnl f* **12/1**

042 **5** *4 1/2* **Saga Sprint (IRE)**[34] 5245 3-9-7 **72**.................................... JimCrowley 3 66
(J R Jenkins) *trckd ldng pair: rdn 3f out: unable qck and lost pl over 1f out: wknd fnl f* **10/1**

3m 7.03s (3.83) **Going Correction** -0.075s/f (Stan) **5** Ran SP% **108.4**
Speed ratings (Par 101): **86,85,84,82,80**
CSF £10.89 TOTE £3.20: £1.30, £2.70; EX 11.80 Trifecta £17.90.
Owner Tick Tock Partnership **Bred** Mrs E Henry **Trained** Newmarket, Suffolk

FOCUS
A fair race for the grade with four of the five runners having won at least once from limited starts this season. They went very steadily early on and that worked against the hat-trick seeking favourite.

6371 TOTEPOOLLIVEINFO.COM H'CAP 6f (P)
3:25 (3:28) (Class 3) (0-95,95) 3-Y-O+ **£12,938** (£3,850; £1,924; £962) **Stalls** Centre

Form RPR

1303 **1** **Hakam (USA)**[62] 4199 4-8-7 **81**.. AndrewMullen 2 93+
(Michael Appleby) *hld up in midfield: short of room and edgd rt 4f out: swtchd rt and effrt 2f out: swtchd lft and hdwy over 1f out: chsd ldrs 1f out: styd on strly to ld towards fin* **7/2**[2]

-250 **2** *1/2* **Seychelloise**[28] 5441 4-9-2 **90**..(b) JimCrowley 5 100
(Sir Mark Prescott Bt) *led: rdn wl over 1f out: drvn ent fnl f: hdd and no ex towards fin* **12/1**

200 **3** *1 3/4* **Free Zone**[16] 5825 7-8-11 **85**...(v) WilliamCarson 8 89
(Jamie Osborne) *pressed ldr: rdn over 1f out: edgd rt u.p and unable qck 1f out: lost 2nd and styd on same pce ins fnl f* **25/1**

0200 **4** *2 3/4* **Primrose Valley**[29] 5390 4-9-0 **88**...............................(b) HarryBentley 10 84
(Ed Vaughan) *hld up in midfield: effrt on inner over 1f out: n.m.r 1f out: chsd ldng trio ins fnl f: kpt on but no threat to ldrs* **12/1**

3543 **5** *1 1/4* **Major Crispies**[19] 5744 5-8-5 **84**..........................(b) DavidParkes(5) 4 76
(Jeremy Gask) *chsd ldrs: rdn 2f out: hung bdly lft over 1f out: wknd ins fnl f* **12/1**

0000 **6** *1/2* **Fleckerl (IRE)**[50] 4644 6-8-12 **86**.............................(p) PaulMulrennan 3 76
(Conor Dore) *stdd s: t.k.h: hld up off the pce in last trio: rdn and hdwy over 1f out: styd on ins fnl f: nvr trbld ldrs* **33/1**

1022 **7** *1/2* **Mickey (IRE)**[15] 5881 3-9-0 **90**.................................(t) RichardKingscote 6 78
(Tom Dascombe) *chsd ldrs: 5th and rdn ent fnl 2f: sn struggling and outpcd over 1f out: wknd ins fnl f* **6/4**[1]

1404 **8** *hd* **Gentlemen**[21] 5678 5-9-4 **95**................................ JosephineGordon(3) 7 83
(Phil McEntee) *rrd as stalls opened and v.s.a: bhd: effrt and sme hdwy towards inner over 1f out: nt clr run and swtchd lft 1f out: rdn and kpt on ins fnl f: nvr trbld ldrs* **8/1**[3]

0000 **9** *1 3/4* **Secret Missile**[43] 4862 6-9-2 **90**...(b) TomQueally 1 72
(Gary Moore) *chsd ldrs: rdn and losing pl whn squeezed for room over 1f out: btn whn swtchd rt 1f out: wknd ins fnl f* **16/1**

000 **10** *2 3/4* **Steelriver (IRE)**[15] 5882 6-9-4 **92**.. PatCosgrave 11 65
(David Barron) *stdd s: hld up off the pce in last trio: effrt and hung lft over 1f out: sn rdn and no hdwy: wknd fnl f* **20/1**

-333 **11** *1/2* **Quick Look**[15] 5881 3-8-5 **81**..[1] TomMarquand 12 53
(William Jarvis) *t.k.h: hld up in midfield: hmpd and wnt sharply rt 4f out: a struggling after: rdn and no hdwy over 1f out: bhd fnl f* **10/1**

1000 **12** *8* **Zac Brown (IRE)**[99] 2903 5-9-7 **95**...................................... DavidNolan 9 41
(Charlie Wallis) *stdd s: hld up in midfield: j. path and stmbld 4f out: lost pl over 1f out: bhd and eased ins ffnl f* **28/1**

1m 11.13s (-2.57) **Going Correction** -0.075s/f (Stan)
WFA 3 from 4yo+ 2lb **12** Ran SP% **126.4**
Speed ratings (Par 107): **114,113,111,107,105 105,104,104,101,98 97,86**
CSF £46.32 CT £968.01 TOTE £4.90: £1.80, £3.30, £6.80; EX 54.50 Trifecta £889.10.
Owner The Horse Watchers **Bred** Jay W Bligh **Trained** Oakham, Rutland

FOCUS
A hotly contested sprint handicap, though very few of the runners figured.

6372 TOTEPOOLRACING FIND US ON INSTAGRAM H'CAP 1m (P)
4:00 (4:01) (Class 2) (0-100,99) 3-Y-O+ **£18,113** (£5,390; £2,693; £1,346) **Stalls** Low

Form RPR

1-40 **1** **Daily Bulletin (USA)**[23] 5601 3-8-9 **89**................................ RobertHavlin 4 102+
(John Gosden) *travelled strly: hld up in tch in midfield: clsng and switching rt 2f out: rdn to ld ent fnl f: r.o strly and drew clr: readily* **9/2**[3]

0101 **2** *3* **Huntlaw**[28] 5437 3-8-9 **89**.. PaulMulrennan 5 95
(Mark Johnston) *sn led: rdn wl over 1f out: hdd ent f: sn outpcd by wnr but battled on to hold 2nd ins fnl f* **7/1**

6131 **3** *1/2* **Fuwairt (IRE)**[15] 5886 4-8-5 **87**..................................... CameronNoble(7) 8 93+
(David Loughnane) *stdd s: hld up in rr: hdwy and v wd over 2f out: rdn to chse ldrs and edgd lft ent fnl f: styd on same pce ins fnl f* **4/1**[2]

3050 **4** *3/4* **Alfred Hutchinson**[24] 5585 8-9-10 **99**..........................(p) DavidNolan 10 103
(David O'Meara) *hld up in last trio: nt clrest of runs over 2f out: hdwy u.p over 1f out: switching lft and drvn 1f out: styd on: no threat to wnr* **20/1**

3136 **5** *1* **Home Cummins (IRE)**[13] 5976 4-8-12 **92**..........(p) AdamMcNamara(5) 2 94
(Richard Fahey) *trckd ldrs: nt clr run over 2f out: swtchd lft and effrt to chse ldrs over 1f out: fnd little for press and btn 1f out: kpt on same pce fnl f* **5/1**

0040 **6** *1 3/4* **Cape Speed (FR)**[8] 6126 3-8-7 **87**...................................... HarryBentley 11 84
(Mark Johnston) *racd in last pair: rdn over 3f out: drvn over 1f out: styd on u.p to pass btn horses ins fnl f: nvr trbld ldrs* **14/1**

-000 **7** 2 3/4 **Winklemann (IRE)**[22] 5640 4-9-2 **94**........................ MarcMonaghan(3) 7 85
(Marco Botti) *t.k.h: hld up in midfield: shifted rt and bmpd rival 6f out: effrt but no imp whn squeezed for room over 1f out: pushed along and wl hld after* **20/1**

0000 **8** *hd* **Afonso De Sousa (USA)**[22] 5651 6-9-7 **96**................... AndrewMullen 9 87
(Michael Appleby) *hld up in tch in midfield: bmpd 6f out: hdwy to chse ldrs and rdn 2f out: unable qck u.p over 1f out: wknd ins fnl f* **20/1**

1010 **9** 1 3/4 **Galvanize (USA)**[36] 5175 3-8-7 **87**...........................[1] RichardKingscote 1 73
(Sir Michael Stoute) *hld up in tch in midfield: nt clr run on inner and shuffled bk over 2f out: swtchd lft and n.m.r wl over 1f out: sn rdn and no hdwy u.p: wknd ins fnl f* **7/2**[1]

2400 **10** 7 **Unforgiving Minute**[25] 5552 5-9-1 **90**............................. SaleemGolam 6 61
(John Butler) *led early: sn hdd and chsd ldr tl lost pl qckly over 1f out: bhd and eased ins fnl f* **10/1**

1m 37.53s (-2.37) **Going Correction** -0.075s/f (Stan)
WFA 3 from 4yo+ 5lb **10** Ran SP% **119.6**
Speed ratings (Par 109): **108,105,104,103,102 101,98,98,96,89**
CSF £35.78 CT £133.75 TOTE £5.40: £2.30, £2.00, £2.40; EX 35.40 Trifecta £167.30.
Owner Godolphin **Bred** Adena Springs **Trained** Newmarket, Suffolk

FOCUS
A good feature and hard not be impressed by the way in which Daily Bulletin bounded clear.

6373 @TOTEPOOLRACING WIN TICKETS ON TWITTER H'CAP 7f (P)
4:35 (4:36) (Class 6) (0-60,60) 3-Y-O+ **£3,234** (£962; £481; £240) **Stalls** Low

Form RPR

6401 **1** **Titan Goddess**[19] 5753 4-9-2 **59**..................................... KevinLundie(7) 7 74
(Mike Murphy) *hld up in midfield: shkn up and clsd over 2f out: rdn to chse ldrs over 1f out: chal 1f out: led 100yds out: r.o wl and gng away at fin* **5/1**[3]

0004 **2** 2 1/2 **Hidden Gem**[33] 5252 3-9-5 **59**... JimCrowley 2 65
(Ed Walker) *chsd ldrs: clsd over 2f out: rdn to ld over 1f out: drvn and pressed 1f out: hdd 100yds out: sn btn: kpt on same pce for clr 2nd* **7/2**[1]

0404 **3** 4 **Onesie (IRE)**[20] 5721 3-9-4 **58**.. DanielMuscutt 8 53
(Marco Botti) *taken down early: chsd clr ldng pair: clsd over 2f out: rdn over 1f out: 3rd and unable qck 1f out: wknd ins fnl f* **4/1**[2]

0405 **4** 2 1/4 **Firgrove Bridge (IRE)**[17] 5797 4-8-12 **48**..............(p) AdamBeschizza 11 39
(Steph Hollinshead) *s.i.s: bhd: rdn and hdwy whn nt clr run and swtchd rt over 1f out: styd on u.p ins fnl f: wnt 4th last strides: nvr trbld ldrs* **9/1**

0-60 **5** *nk* **Lucia Sciarra**[96] 3003 3-8-13 **53**....................................... TomQueally 10 41
(Giles Bravery) *midfield on outer: effrt to chse ldrs ent fnl 2f out: unable qck u.p over 1f out: wknd ins fnl f* **12/1**

1543 **6** 2 **Belle Mare Plage**[35] 5195 3-9-6 **60**..............................(t) PatCosgrave 5 43
(Stuart Williams) *hld up in midfield: clsd over 2f out: swtchd lft and effrt u.p over 1f out: no imp: wknd ins fnl f* **5/1**[3]

300P **7** 5 **Kristoff (IRE)**[20] 5721 3-8-10 **50**......................................[1] RobertHavlin 1 19+
(Jim Boyle) *led and sn clr w rival: rdn and hdd over 1f out: sn dropped out: wknd fnl f* **8/1**

0425 **8** 1 1/2 **Major Muscari (IRE)**[27] 5475 8-9-7 **57**.......................(p) TomMarquand 6 24
(Shaun Harris) *dwlt and swtchd lft after s: effrt u.p over 1f out: no imp: wknd fnl f* **10/1**

0000 **9** 2 1/2 **Afkar (IRE)**[20] 5729 8-9-3 **60**..(p) RPWalsh(7) 3 20+
(Ivan Furtado) *w ldr and clr of field tl over 2f out: lost pl u.p over 1f out: wknd fnl f* **14/1**

2600 **10** *nk* **Ashford Island**[38] 5087 3-8-7 **50**.................................... NoelGarbutt(3) 9 8
(Adam West) *restless in stalls: dwlt: pushed along in rr: rdn over 2f out: swtchd rt and over 1f out: wknd fnl f* **25/1**

500- **11** 20 **Custom (IRE)**[319] 7562 3-8-12 **52**................................... PaulMulrennan 4
(Daniel O'Brien) *a towards rr: lost tch over 1f out: bhd and eased ins fnl f: t.o* **50/1**

1m 26.74s (-0.46) **Going Correction** -0.075s/f (Stan)
WFA 3 from 4yo+ 4lb **11** Ran SP% **125.9**
Speed ratings (Par 101): **99,96,91,89,88 86,80,78,76,75 52**
CSF £24.65 CT £82.37 TOTE £6.50: £2.30, £1.70, £2.10; EX 32.30 Trifecta £188.90.
Owner Phoebe's Friends **Bred** Mrs A D Bourne **Trained** Westoning, Beds

FOCUS
This took little winning.

6374 BOOK YOUR CHRISTMAS PARTY AT CHELMSFORDCITYRACECOURSE.COM H'CAP 5f (P)
5:10 (5:10) (Class 6) (0-65,64) 3-Y-O+ **£3,234** (£962; £481; £240) **Stalls** Low

Form RPR

0630 **1** **Vale Of Flight (IRE)**[10] 6051 3-9-2 **60**............................... JimCrowley 1 67
(Rae Guest) *w ldr on inner tl rdn to ld over 1f out: asserted ins fnl f: styd on: rdn out* **3/1**[1]

105 **2** 1 3/4 **Frank The Barber (IRE)**[33] 5269 4-9-2 **59**...............(t) AdamBeschizza 2 60
(Steph Hollinshead) *led: rdn 2f out: hdd over 1f out: stl ev ch tl no ex ins fnl f: flashed tail and wknd wl ins fnl f* **5/1**

4532 **3** 2 **Regal Miss**[27] 5474 4-9-4 **61**... DanielMuscutt 6 55
(Patrick Chamings) *chsd ldrs: rdn ent fnl 2f: chsd clr ldng trio jst ins fnl f: kpt on but nvr enough pce to chal* **10/3**[2]

4234 **4** *hd* **Only Ten Per Cent (IRE)**[17] 5807 8-9-4 **64**......(v) AlistairRawlinson(3) 5 57+
(J R Jenkins) *rrd as stalls opened and s.i.s: racd in last pair: hdwy u.p on inner over 1f out: kpt on ins fnl f: nvr trbld ldrs* **6/1**

1045 **5** 2 1/2 **Culloden**[18] 5762 4-9-4 **61**.. TomMarquand 3 45
(Shaun Harris) *chsd ldrs: wnt 3rd 2f out and sn swtchd rt: no imp u.p over 1f out: lost 3rd jst ins fnl f: wknd fnl 100yds* **9/2**[3]

0050 **6** 2 1/4 **State Of The Union (IRE)**[17] 5807 4-9-3 **63**........ JosephineGordon(3) 7 39
(Willie Musson) *chsd ldrs on outer tl 2f out: sn rdn and unable qck: hung lft and wknd 1f out* **8/1**

5-0 **7** 2 1/4 **Touch The Clouds**[60] 4264 5-8-7 **50** oh1.......................(b) RyanPowell 4 18
(William Stone) *s.i.s: a last pair: rdn 1/2-way: hung lft and wknd over 1f out* **11/1**

59.44s (-0.76) **Going Correction** -0.075s/f (Stan)
WFA 3 from 4yo+ 1lb **7** Ran SP% **116.7**
Speed ratings (Par 101): **103,100,97,96,92 89,85**
CSF £18.99 CT £52.52 TOTE £3.90: £2.60, £3.00; EX 25.60 Trifecta £107.10.
Owner Guy Carstairs & Sakal, Davies & Jennings **Bred** Patrick F Kelly And M J Foley **Trained** Newmarket, Suffolk

FOCUS
Very ordinary sprinting form. The first two home were dominated.
T/Plt: £46.40 to a £1 stake. Pool: £74,755.18 - 1173.87 winning units T/Qpdt: £19.40 to a £1 stake. Pool: £4,671.4 - 177.8 winning units **Steve Payne**

5820 FFOS LAS (L-H)
Sunday, September 11

OFFICIAL GOING: Soft (6.3)
Wind: fresh half across Weather: cloudy

6375 US OPEN TENNIS AT 188BET MAIDEN STKS (PLUS 10 RACE) 6f
1:55 (1:57) (Class 4) 2-Y-O **£3,946** (£1,174; £586; £293) **Stalls** Centre

Form RPR

43 **1** **Scorching Heat**[31] 5325 2-9-2 0...................................... RobHornby(3) 5 75
(Andrew Balding) *trckd ldr: shkn up to ld over 1f out: drvn fnl f: a holding runner-up* **3/1**[2]

2 **2** 3/4 **Subjective**[15] 5885 2-9-5 0.. JamieSpencer 2 73
(David Simcock) *hld up bhd ldrs: pushed along to press wnr over 1f out: rdn and ch ins fnl f: unable qck* **1/3**[1]

0 **3** 5 **Polkadot Princess (IRE)**[25] 5542 2-8-11 0.......... EdwardGreatrex(3) 10 53
(Nikki Evans) *led: rdn 2f out: hdd over 1f out: qckly outpcd by first two and no ch after* **33/1**

4 2 **Things Happen** 2-9-5 0.. JoeFanning 6 52
(David Evans) *s.i.s: chsd ldrs after 2f: outpcd 2f out: nudged along and kpt on steadily* **11/1**[3]

5 3/4 **I Wouldn't Bother** 2-9-5 0.. TimmyMurphy 7 50
(Daniel Kubler) *green in paddock: dwlt: in tch in last: rdn 2f out: kpt on same pce and nvr any ch w principals* **25/1**

1m 15.03s (5.03) **Going Correction** +0.675s/f (Yiel) **5** Ran SP% **115.1**
Speed ratings (Par 97): **93,92,85,82,81**
CSF £4.63 TOTE £3.90: £1.20, £1.10; EX 4.70 Trifecta £27.40.
Owner Qatar Racing Limited **Bred** Dukes Stud & Overbury Stallions Ltd **Trained** Kingsclere, Hants

FOCUS
The going was soft after a dry night and there was a tailwind in the straight. The jockeys said the going was "sticky" and "soft". A maiden in which the field was reduced by half due to morning withdrawals, and there was a surprise of sorts.

6376 IRISH STALLION FARMS EBF MAIDEN STKS 1m (R)
2:30 (2:30) (Class 5) 2-Y-O **£3,234** (£962; £481; £240) **Stalls** Low

Form RPR

1 **Defoe (IRE)** 2-9-5 0... AndreaAtzeni 5 72+
(Roger Varian) *hld up in share of 3rd: shkn up and hdwy 3f out: wnt 2nd 2f out: sn chal: led narrowly ins fnl f: rdn and a doing enough* **30/100**[1]

00 **2** *hd* **Bianca Minola (FR)**[19] 5740 2-9-0 0................................ MartinDwyer 3 64
(David Menuisier) *led after 1f and set modest pce: qcknd 4f out and wnt 4 l up: rdn 2f out: sn pressed: hdd ins fnl f: r.o* **11/2**[2]

3 4 **Staff College (FR)** 2-9-5 0.. FMBerry 1 60
(Henry Spiller) *broke wl: led 1f: trckd ldr and t.k.h: rdn 3f out: hung lft and lost 2nd 2f out: outpcd by first two appr fnl f* **10/1**

04 **4** 12 **Hoover Fever**[13] 5951 2-8-7 0... AledBeech(7) 2 29
(David Evans) *sed awkwardly: hld up in share of 3rd: wknd over 2f out* **8/1**[3]

1m 50.67s (9.67) **Going Correction** +0.675s/f (Yiel) **4** Ran SP% **112.5**
Speed ratings (Par 95): **78,77,73,61**
CSF £2.69 TOTE £1.20; EX 2.40 Trifecta £7.10.
Owner Sheikh Mohammed Obaid Al Maktoum **Bred** Darley **Trained** Newmarket, Suffolk

FOCUS
A small field and an uncompetitive-looking juvenile maiden, but a close finish.

6377 188BET.CO.UK NURSERY H'CAP 1m (R)
3:00 (3:00) (Class 5) (0-75,75) 2-Y-O **£2,911** (£866; £432; £216) **Stalls** Low

Form RPR

5503 **1** **Party Nights**[31] 5324 2-8-13 **67**.. JamieSpencer 5 71+
(Luca Cumani) *broke wl: hld up: hdwy over 2f out: led 2f out: shkn up 1f out: jnd ins fnl f: cleverly* **10/1**

430 **2** *shd* **Native Prospect**[53] 4533 2-9-1 **69**...................................... LiamKeniry 2 74+
(Andrew Balding) *hld up in mid-div: nt clr run over 2f out: rdn wl over 1f out: drvn and ev ch ins fnl f: jst hld* **5/1**[3]

5000 **3** 1 1/4 **Eolian**[23] 5594 2-8-8 **62**..(v[1]) MartinDwyer 4 63
(William Knight) *s.i.s and chsd along fr stalls: sn several l adrift: hdwy on outer 3f out: drvn 2f out: kpt on wl and ch ins fnl f: no ex towards fin* **8/1**

362 **4** 6 **Mia Cara**[13] 5951 2-9-3 **71**... SamHitchcott 8 59
(David Evans) *led tl rdn and hdd 2f out: kpt on u.p tl wknd fnl f* **14/1**

532 **5** 2 **Baileys Apprentice**[15] 5861 2-9-5 **73**................................ JoeFanning 6 57
(Mark Johnston) *mainly trckd ldr: rdn and ev ch 2f out: wknd appr fnl f* **7/1**

0554 **6** 1/2 **Sufrah (USA)**[23] 5594 2-9-2 **70**.......................................(v[1]) DaneO'Neill 1 53
(Brian Meehan) *chsd ldrs: rdn and nt qckn wl over 2f out: wknd over 1f out* **5/1**[3]

51 **7** 3 1/4 **Manners Please**[20] 5728 2-9-7 **75**..................................... FMBerry 3 50
(Ralph Beckett) *trckd ldrs: ev ch whn rdn over 2f out: wknd over 1f out* **4/1**[2]

4304 **8** 9 **Star Maker**[10] 6060 2-8-13 **70**.. EdwardGreatrex(3) 7 26
(Sylvester Kirk) *hld up in mid-div: hdwy 3f out: cl up but rdn whn hmpd over 2f out: nt rcvr* **3/1**[1]

1m 45.61s (4.61) **Going Correction** +0.675s/f (Yiel) **8** Ran SP% **117.7**
Speed ratings (Par 95): **103,102,101,95,93 93,89,80**
CSF £60.83 CT £427.43 TOTE £11.90: £3.50, £1.90, £3.00; EX 78.10 Trifecta £605.70.
Owner Castle Down Racing & Partners **Bred** Ed's Stud Ltd **Trained** Newmarket, Suffolk

FOCUS
This competitive little nursery was run 5.06secs faster than the preceding maiden and produced a very close finish. The market leaders disappointed.

6378 EBF STALLIONS FILLIES' H'CAP 1m 2f (R)
3:35 (3:36) (Class 4) (0-80,80) 3-Y-O+ **£6,469** (£1,925; £962; £481) **Stalls** Low

Form RPR

-431 **1** **High Hopes**[34] 5233 3-9-4 **79**... JamieSpencer 6 92+
(David Simcock) *hld up in last: smooth hdwy on outer over 2f out: led on bit 1f out: rdr barely moved: v easily* **9/2**[3]

3145 **2** 1 **St Mary'S**[19] 5738 3-9-0 **78**... RobHornby(3) 3 82
(Andrew Balding) *trckd ldng piar: drvn over 2f out: swtchd rt over 1f out: styd on to go 2nd nr fin: no ch w easy wnr* **8/1**

413 **3** *nk* **The Begum**[40] 4977 3-9-3 **78**.. FMBerry 5 81
(Ralph Beckett) *led 1f: trckd ldr: rdn to ld 2f out: hdd and unable qck 1f out: lost 2nd nr fin* **4/1**[2]

4105 **4** 1 **Ejayteekay**[37] 5123 3-8-11 **77**...................................... CharlieBennett(5) 2 78
(Hughie Morrison) *wnt to post early: hld up: rdn 3f out: sn chsng ldrs: styd on same pce u.p fnl f* **5/1**

The Form Book, Raceform Ltd, Newbury, RG14 5SJ

12 **5** *4* **Blind Faith (IRE)**[23] 5603 3-9-5 **80**................................ AndreaAtzeni 4 73
(Luca Cumani) *t.k.h: cl up: led after 1f: rdn over 2f out: sn hdd: wknd 1f out* **7/4**[1]

3151 **6** *2 1/2* **Raven Banner (IRE)**[38] 5057 3-8-10 **71**........................... JoeFanning 7 59
(Daniel Mark Loughnane) *t.k.h early: chsd ldrs: rdn over 2f out: wknd over 1f out* **7/1**

2m 17.27s (7.87) **Going Correction** +0.675s/f (Yiel) **6** Ran SP% **114.8**
Speed ratings (Par 102): **95,94,93,93,89 87**
CSF £38.95 TOTE £5.00: £2.80, £4.00; EX 43.70 Trifecta £189.80.
Owner Major M G Wyatt **Bred** Charlie Wyatt **Trained** Newmarket, Suffolk

FOCUS
A fair but tightly knit fillies' handicap, although the winner scored much more easily than the official margin suggests.

6379 188BET H'CAP 1m 4f (R)
4:10 (4:11) (Class 3) (0-95,94) 3-Y-O+ **£9,056** (£2,695; £1,346; £673) **Stalls** Low

Form RPR

-226 **1** **Monotype (IRE)**[64] 4162 4-9-8 **90**................................ AndreaAtzeni 4 101+
(Roger Varian) *chsd ldng pair: clsd over 3f out: led over 2f out: rdn and styd on wl* **9/4**[1]

0000 **2** *3* **Havana Beat (IRE)**[22] 5655 6-9-5 **94**......................(vt) LuluStanford[(7)] 6 99
(Rod Millman) *racd in 4th: rdn 3f out: wnt 2nd over 2f out: one pce after and no imp on wnr* **8/1**

0021 **3** *1 1/4* **Buonarroti (IRE)**[48] 4703 5-9-8 **90**................................ GeorgeBaker 5 93
(Declan Carroll) *hld up in 5th: rdn and hdwy over 2f out: wnt 3rd 1f out: one pce and no further imp* **3/1**[2]

6100 **4** *3 3/4* **Master Of Irony (IRE)**[22] 5651 4-9-9 **91**..........................(b[1]) FMBerry 7 88
(Ralph Beckett) *s.s: hld up in last: drvn over 2f out: styd on to go modest 4th ins fnl f but nvr cl to ldrs* **9/2**

0004 **5** *1 1/4* **Beaverbrook**[10] 6057 3-8-12 **89**.. JoeFanning 3 84
(Mark Johnston) *led early: chsd ldr: clsd over 3f out: rdn over 2f out: wknd over 1f out: lost 4th ins fnl f* **4/1**[3]

240 **6** *16* **Bazooka (IRE)**[29] 5405 5-8-12 **80** oh3.............................. MartinDwyer 2 49
(David Flood) *racd keenly and sn led: qckly 5 l clr: reduced ld 3f out: hdd over 2f out: sn wknd: eased 1f out* **25/1**

2200 **7** *47* **Glan Y Gors (IRE)**[9] 6089 4-9-3 **85**................................ JamieSpencer 1
(David Simcock) *hld up in 6th: shkn up and no rspnse 3f out: sn eased: t.o* **11/1**

2m 42.97s (5.57) **Going Correction** +0.675s/f (Yiel)
WFA 3 from 4yo+ 9lb **7** Ran SP% **117.2**
Speed ratings (Par 107): **108,106,105,102,101 91,59**
CSF £21.94 CT £55.46 TOTE £2.80: £1.60, £4.00; EX 21.30 Trifecta £77.70.
Owner Sheikh Mohammed Obaid Al Maktoum **Bred** Epona Bloodstock Ltd **Trained** Newmarket, Suffolk

FOCUS
The feature contest and a decent middle-distance handicap. They went a sound gallop and the winner scored emphatically.

6380 PETER SUTTON ON COURSE BOOKMAKERS H'CAP 1m 4f (R)
4:45 (4:45) (Class 5) (0-75,75) 3-Y-O+ **£2,911** (£866; £432; £216) **Stalls** Low

Form RPR

5111 **1** **Pacharana**[18] 5763 3-9-3 **75**.. JamieSpencer 10 84+
(Luca Cumani) *hld up towards rr: hdwy 3f out: rdn and c over to r on stands' rail 2f out: led over 1f out: styd on wl* **9/2**[3]

445 **2** *2* **Roderic's Secret (IRE)**[95] 3025 3-8-10 **68**...................... MartinDwyer 2 73
(David Menuisier) *trckd ldr: rdn and ev ch over 2f out: edgd rt over 1f out: kpt on same pce u.p* **7/1**

0500 **3** *nk* **Moojaned (IRE)**[8] 6128 5-9-4 **74**.................... KatherineGlenister[(7)] 6 79
(David Evans) *led: styd on far side and racd alone in st: pushed along over 2f out: hdd over 1f out: one pce* **14/1**

0-03 **4** *1 1/4* **Rayaa**[13] 5975 3-9-1 **73**...(t) LiamKeniry 11 76
(John Butler) *hld up: rdn and hdwy over 2f out: edgd rt over 1f out: styd on same pce* **11/4**[1]

253 **5** *1 3/4* **Knight Commander**[23] 5596 3-8-3 **68**...................... AbbieWibrew[(7)] 1 68
(William Knight) *hld up: clsd on outer 3f out: rdn and carried rt 2f out: one pce and no further imp* **13/2**

3120 **6** *5* **Blenheim Warrior**[26] 5526 4-9-8 **71**................................ AndreaAtzeni 7 63
(Richard Hughes) *mid-div: drvn 3f out: wknd wl over 1f out* **9/2**[3]

0436 **7** *2 1/2* **Rehearse (IRE)**[20] 5724 3-8-12 **73**................................ RobHornby[(3)] 8 61
(Andrew Balding) *t.k.h early: trckd ldng pair: drvn over 2f out: wknd over 1f out* **4/1**[2]

20-0 **8** *22* **Late Shipment**[50] 4634 5-9-8 **74**............................(p) EdwardGreatrex[(3)] 5 27
(Nikki Evans) *chsd ldrs: drvn over 5f out: wknd 3f out: t.o* **25/1**

2m 44.1s (6.70) **Going Correction** +0.675s/f (Yiel)
WFA 3 from 4yo+ 9lb **8** Ran SP% **119.4**
Speed ratings (Par 103): **104,102,102,101,100 97,95,80**
CSF £37.43 CT £414.97 TOTE £4.60: £1.60, £2.90, £4.00; EX 31.30 Trifecta £316.10.
Owner S Stuckey **Bred** Stuart Stuckey **Trained** Newmarket, Suffolk

FOCUS
Just a fair handicap that was run 1.13sec slower than the feature race, and won by a progressive filly.

6381 PREMIER LEAGUE BETTING AT 188BET H'CAP 5f
5:20 (5:21) (Class 6) (0-60,60) 3-Y-O+ **£2,587** (£770; £384; £192) **Stalls** Centre

Form RPR

3262 **1** **Diminutive (IRE)**[16] 5826 4-8-6 **48**............................(p) RobHornby[(3)] 6 53
(Grace Harris) *chsd ldrs: wnt 2nd 1/2-way: drvn to ld appr fnl f: sn pressed: asserted fnl 75yds* **3/1**[2]

2536 **2** *1 1/2* **Lady McGuffy (IRE)**[25] 5554 3-9-5 **59**............................(t) DaneO'Neill 4 59
(David Evans) *hld up bhd ldrs: rdn and clsd 2f out: chal 1f out tl no ex fnl 75yds* **3/1**[2]

4523 **3** *1 3/4* **Champagne Bob**[19] 5736 4-9-4 **60**........................ EdwardGreatrex[(3)] 2 53+
(Richard Price) *dwlt: in rr: rdn and nt clr run 2f out: hdwy over 1f out: r.o to go 3rd ins fnl f: clsng towards fin* **5/4**[1]

0500 **4** *2 1/2* **Bapak Bangsawan**[16] 5826 6-9-0 **58**........................(v) AnnStokell[(5)] 7 42
(Ann Stokell) *wnt to post early: led: rdn and hdd appr fnl f: wknd* **6/1**[3]

0/00 **5** *3 3/4* **Portrush Storm**[22] 5628 11-8-3 **47** oh1 ow1.............. CharlieBennett[(5)] 1 18
(Ray Peacock) *chsd ldr tl rdn and lost 2nd 1/2-way: wknd over 1f out* **25/1**

4500 **6** *8* **Majestic Girl (IRE)**[38] 5088 3-8-13 **53**........................(p) MartinDwyer 3
(Steve Flook) *srtarted slowly: sn rcvrd to chse ldrs: drvn 2f out: wknd over 1f out* **20/1**

1m 1.48s (3.18) **Going Correction** +0.675s/f (Yiel)
WFA 3 from 4yo+ 1lb **6** Ran SP% **117.3**
Speed ratings (Par 101): **101,98,95,91,85 73**
CSF £13.16 TOTE £4.90: £2.30, £2.10; EX 14.40 Trifecta £21.60.
Owner Ms Michelle Harris **Bred** Messrs D & J Fitzgerald **Trained** Shirenewton, Monmouthshire

FOCUS
A low-grade sprint handicap to end with and a couple of fillies dominated the finish.
T/Plt: £158.40 to a £1 stake. Pool: £54,972.1 - 253.32 winning units T/Qpdt: £99.00 to a £1 stake. Pool: £3,912.57 - 29.23 winning units **Richard Lowther**

[5936]CURRAGH (R-H)
Sunday, September 11

OFFICIAL GOING: Yielding (good to yielding in places on round course)

6382a IRISH STALLION FARMS EUROPEAN BREEDERS FUND "BOLD LAD" SPRINT H'CAP (PREMIER HANDICAP) 6f
2:00 (2:01) 3-Y-O+
£65,073 (£20,955; £9,926; £4,411; £2,205; £1,102)

RPR

1 **New Bidder**[29] 5390 5-9-4 **92**....................................(b) GrahamGibbons 2 100+
(David Barron) *w.w: hdwy in 10th over 1f out and r.o wl between horses ins fnl f to ld cl home* **22/1**

2 *1/2* **Intisaab**[29] 5418 5-9-8 **96**...(p) DanielTudhope 17 102
(David O'Meara) *chsd ldrs nr side: n.m.r bhd horses over 1f out: sn swtchd rt and hdwy u.p wl ins fnl f: no ch w wnr cl home where wnt 2nd* **10/3**[1]

3 *hd* **Sors (IRE)**[14] 5942 4-9-3 **96**....................................... KillianLeonard[(5)] 14 101
(Andrew Slattery, Ire) *w ldrs: cl 2nd at 1/2-way: rdn on terms over 1f out and led narrowly ins fnl f: all out wl ins fnl f and hdd cl home* **10/1**

4 *1/2* **Downforce (IRE)**[42] 4921 4-9-4 **92**.. BillyLee 4 96
(W McCreery, Ire) *w.w towards rr: hdwy far side fr 2f out to chse ldrs u.p ins fnl f: kpt on same pce: hld* **7/1**[3]

5 *nk* **Tribal Path (IRE)**[28] 5442 6-8-8 **87**......................(t) DonaghO'Connor[(5)] 5 90
(Damian Joseph English, Ire) *sn led: narrow advantage at 1/2-way: rdn and hdd over 1f out: hdd ins fnl f and no ex clsng stages where dropped to 5th* **20/1**

6 *hd* **Master Speaker (IRE)**[28] 5442 6-9-6 **94**...........(bt) ColmO'Donoghue 12 96
(Martin Hassett, Ire) *w.w: 15th at 1/2-way: sme late hdwy wl ins fnl f: nrst fin* **12/1**

7 *shd* **Captain Power (IRE)**[31] 5340 4-9-2 **93**.................. RobbieDowney[(3)] 13 95
(Edward Lynam, Ire) *hld up towards rr: 12th 1/2-way: swtchd rt under 2f out and prog on outer to chse ldrs ent fnl f: no imp on ldrs wl ins fnl f: kpt on same pce* **9/1**

8 *nk* **George Bowen (IRE)**[29] 5417 4-9-5 **93**......................(b) TonyHamilton 7 94
(Richard Fahey) *hld up: 13th 1/2-way: tk clsr order over 1f out: kpt on one pce far side ins fnl f: nvr nrr* **10/1**

9 *shd* **Split The Atom (IRE)**[28] 5441 4-8-6 **80**....................(v[1]) WayneLordan 15 81
(David Marnane, Ire) *chsd ldrs nr side: 6th 1/2-way: rdn 2f out and sn no imp on ldrs: one pce ins fnl f* **33/1**

10 *nk* **Naggers (IRE)**[43] 4873 5-8-8 **82**.. LeighRoche 16 82
(Paul Midgley) *chsd ldrs nr side: cl 3rd at 1/2-way: rdn almost on terms over 1f out and sn no ex: wknd fnl f* **7/1**[3]

11 *1/2* **Bubbly Bellini (IRE)**[14] 5942 9-8-9 **83**...............(p) DeclanMcDonogh 10 81
(Adrian McGuinness, Ire) *settled bhd ldrs: 4th 1/2-way: rdn under 2f out and no ex ins fnl f: wknd clsng stages* **14/1**

12 *hd* **Yeeoow (IRE)**[12] 6000 7-8-8 **85** 5ex.................................. JoeyHaynes[(3)] 6 82
(K R Burke) *chsd ldrs far side: 5th 1/2-way: rdn over 1f out and sn no imp on ldrs: wknd wl ins fnl f* **25/1**

13 *1 1/4* **Blairmayne (IRE)**[14] 5942 3-8-4 **80** oh3.......................... ChrisHayes 11 73
(Miss Natalia Lupini, Ire) *hld up in tch: 11th 1/2-way: rdn 2f out and sn no ex: one pce fnl f* **18/1**

14 *1 3/4* **Dark Alliance (IRE)**[14] 5942 5-8-4 **78** oh1................(tp) NGMcCullagh 18 66
(M Halford, Ire) *towards rr: rdn and no imp 2f out: one pce after* **40/1**

15 *1* **Above The Rest (IRE)**[15] 5871 5-9-4 **92**.......................... PatSmullen 8 77
(David Barron) *in tch: rdn 2f out and sn no imp: wknd fr over 1f out* **6/1**[2]

16 *2 1/4* **Dandyleekie (IRE)**[55] 4443 4-8-6 **83**........................ ShelleyBirkett[(3)] 1 60
(David O'Meara) *in tch: 10th 1/2-way: rdn over 2f out and no ex 1 1/2f out: wknd fnl f* **16/1**

17 *3 3/4* **Al Mohalhal (IRE)**[14] 5941 3-9-12 **102**......................(p) KevinManning 3 67
(J S Bolger, Ire) *chsd ldrs far side: pushed along fr 1/2-way and no ex u.p fr 2f out: wknd over 1f out* **33/1**

1m 16.32s (0.82) **Going Correction** +0.125s/f (Good)
WFA 3 from 4yo+ 2lb **17** Ran SP% **137.3**
Speed ratings: **99,98,98,97,97 96,96,96,96,95 95,94,93,90,89 86,81**
CSF £98.55 CT £871.88 TOTE £35.80: £5.00, £1.20, £2.90, £2.10; DF 215.40 Trifecta £2161.10.
Owner Mrs June Watts **Bred** West Is Best Syndicate **Trained** Maunby, N Yorks

FOCUS
A breezy afternoon, a definite ease in the ground. British-trained runners won this race in the first two editions of the Irish Champions Weekend, and it was the same story here this time, with a one-two for the visitors. A bunched finish, and the race has been rated around the balance of the first nine.

6383a MOYGLARE "JEWELS" BLANDFORD STKS (GROUP 2) (F&M) 1m 2f
2:35 (2:36) 3-Y-O+ **£86,764** (£27,941; £13,235; £5,882; £2,941)

RPR

1 **Shamreen (IRE)**[40] 5002 3-9-0 99..................................(v) PatSmullen 1 106
(D K Weld, Ire) *led: 2 l clr at 1/2-way: stl gng wl 3f out: rdn over 2f out and pressed clly: strly pressed and jnd briefly u.p ent fnl f: kpt on wl w narrow advantage wl ins fnl f to assert cl home* **2/1**[2]

2 *1/2* **Best In The World (IRE)**[40] 5002 3-9-0 108...................... RyanMoore 3 105
(A P O'Brien, Ire) *chsd ldrs: 3rd 1/2-way: pushed along into 2nd under 3f out and clsd u.p to chal on terms briefly w ev ch ent fnl f: kpt on wl wout matching wnr wl ins fnl f* **5/4**[1]

3 *3 3/4* **Santa Monica**[32] 5313 3-9-0 100...................................... FrankieDettori 5 98
(Charles O'Brien, Ire) *chsd ldrs: disp 4th at 1/2-way: pushed along into st and rdn in 4th 2f out: wnt 3rd fnl 150yds and no imp on ldrs: kpt on one pce* **6/1**[3]

4 *1/2* **Cirin Toinne (IRE)**[21] 5689 3-9-0 93.............................. KevinManning 4 97
(J S Bolger, Ire) *settled bhd ldr in 2nd: pushed along into st and sn no imp on wnr u.p in 3rd under 2f out: one pce after and dropped to 4th fnl 150yds* **6/1**[3]

5 *4 3/4* **Planchart (USA)**[14] 5939 3-9-0 96.............................. DeclanMcDonogh 6 87
(Andrew Slattery, Ire) *w.w in rr: disp 4th at 1/2-way: pushed along into st and sn no imp on ldrs u.p in rr 2f out: one pce after* **14/1**

2m 12.52s (3.22) **Going Correction** +0.20s/f (Good) **5** Ran SP% **113.0**
Speed ratings: **95,94,91,91,87**
CSF £5.07 TOTE £3.20: £1.60, £1.02; DF 5.40 Trifecta £16.30.

Owner H H Aga Khan **Bred** His Highness The Aga Khan's Studs S C **Trained** Curragh, Co Kildare

FOCUS
This looked a week Group 2 on paper, but the winner deserves plenty of credit for a battling effort. The standard is set by the second and third.

6384a DERRINSTOWN STUD FLYING FIVE STKS (GROUP 2) 5f
3:10 (3:12) 3-Y-O+

£108,455 (£34,926; £16,544; £7,352; £3,676; £1,838)

RPR

1 **Ardhoomey (IRE)**[8] 6145 4-9-4 103[1] ColinKeane 6 116
(G M Lyons, Ire) *hooded to load: w.w towards rr: hdwy gng wl under 2f out: swtchd rt to chal ins fnl f and r.o wl far side to ld clsng stages* **16/1**

2 ½ **Washington DC (IRE)**[23] 5614 3-9-3 112 (t) RyanMoore 5 114
(A P O'Brien, Ire) *w.w towards rr: hdwy 1 1/2f out: sn swtchd rt and r.o wl ins fnl f to ld ins fnl 100yds: strly pressed and hdd clsng stages: kpt on wl wout matching wnr* **9/2**[2]

3 1¾ **Iffranesia (FR)**[23] 5614 6-9-1 99 GrahamGibbons 4 105
(Robert Cowell) *chsd ldrs: rdn in 4th over 1f out and no imp on ldrs u.p in 3rd wl ins fnl f: kpt on same pce* **50/1**

4 ½ **Maarek**[15] 5863 9-9-4 106 BillyLee 2 106
(Miss Evanna McCutcheon, Ire) *hooded to load: hld up: pushed along in rr bef 1/2-way where reminders: r.o wl u.p ins fnl f into nvr nrr 4th cl home: nrst fin* **22/1**

5 ½ **In Salutem**[8] 6145 6-9-4 104 (t) ShaneFoley 12 104
(K J Condon, Ire) *w.w: tk clsr order after 1/2-way where short of room 1 1/2f out: sn swtchd lft and rdn into 6th ins fnl f: kpt on same pce clsng stages: nvr trbld ldrs* **12/1**

6 hd **Take Cover**[23] 5614 9-9-4 113 DavidAllan 3 103
(David C Griffiths) *hooded to load: broke wl to ld narrowly tl jnd bef 1/2-way: rdn w narrow advantage under 2f out: strly pressed ent fnl f and sn hdd: no ex and wknd into 6th clsng stages* **5/1**[3]

7 ½ **Sole Power**[23] 5614 9-9-4 109 PatSmullen 13 102
(Edward Lynam, Ire) *chsd ldrs nr side: disp 6th at 1/2-way: n.m.r bhd horses 1 1/2f out: swtchd rt ent fnl f and no imp on ldrs: one pce in 7th clsng stages* **8/1**

8 2 **Spirit Quartz (IRE)**[17] 5816 8-9-4 107 (p) DanielTudhope 7 94
(Robert Cowell) *cl up bhd ldr: rdn in cl 2nd 1 1/2f out and ev ch ent fnl f: sn no ex and wknd wl ins fnl f* **11/1**

9 1¼ **Cotai Glory**[23] 5614 4-9-4 112 ChrisHayes 9 90
(Charles Hills) *chsd ldrs: pushed along disputing 3rd under 2f out and no ex u.p 1f out: wknd fnl f* **11/2**

10 1¼ **Only Mine (IRE)**[8] 6120 3-9-0 107 GaryCarroll 11 82
(Joseph G Murphy, Ire) *chsd ldrs: pushed along fr 2f out and no imp on ldrs u.p ins fnl f where wnt sltly lft: sn wknd* **10/1**

11 2¾ **Dikta Del Mar (SPA)**[7] 6167 4-9-1 88 (t) WayneLordan 1 72
(T Hogan, Ire) *upset in stalls: dwlt sltly and towards rr early: 10th 1/2-way: pushed along after 1/2-way and no ex u.p over 1f out: wknd* **66/1**

12 nse **Toscanini (IRE)**[35] 5213 4-9-4 113 JamesDoyle 14 75
(M Halford, Ire) *w ldrs and disp briefly bef 1/2-way: pushed along bhd ldr after 1/2-way and wknd u.p fr over 1f out: no imp whn sltly hmpd ins fnl f* **4/1**[1]

13 1 **Gracious John (IRE)**[17] 5816 3-9-3 106 DeclanMcDonogh 8 72
(David Evans) *chsd ldrs far side: disp 6th at 1/2-way: pushed along fr 2f out and wknd 1 1/2f out* **20/1**

1m 1.54s (-1.36) **Going Correction** +0.125s/f (Good)
WFA 3 from 4yo+ 1lb **13** Ran SP% **124.9**
Speed ratings: **115,114,111,110,109 109,108,105,103,101 97,97,95**
CSF £87.92 TOTE £21.50: £4.90, £1.80, £11.20; DF 119.80 Trifecta £4945.00.

Owner Moyville Racing Syndicate **Bred** John Quinn **Trained** Dunsany, Co Meath

FOCUS
Horses drawn low ended up dominating the most important sprint in the Irish calendar. A home-trained winner, against the general trend over the past ten years, which has greatly favoured British runners. The second, third and fourth help set the standard.

6385a MOYGLARE STUD STKS (GROUP 1) (FILLIES) 7f
3:40 (3:42) 2-Y-O

£146,691 (£48,897; £23,161; £10,294; £5,147; £2,573)

RPR

1 **Intricately (IRE)**[21] 5686 2-9-0 104 DonnachaO'Brien 3 113
(Joseph Patrick O'Brien, Ire) *a.p: cl 2nd at 1/2-way: rdn 2f out and clsd u.p to ld narrowly ins fnl 150yds: jnd cl home and kpt on wl to ld on line* **25/1**

2 shd **Hydrangea (IRE)**[21] 5686 2-9-0 106 PBBeggy 1 112
(A P O'Brien, Ire) *led: narrow advantage at 1/2-way: rdn over 2f out and strly pressed: hdd narrowly ins fnl 150yds: kpt on wl far side to dispute cl home: hdd on line* **7/1**[3]

3 1¾ **Rhododendron (IRE)**[21] 5686 2-9-0 107 FrankieDettori 6 108
(A P O'Brien, Ire) *chsd ldrs: 3rd 1/2-way: rdn in 3rd 2f out and no imp on ldrs wl ins fnl f where hung rt: kpt on same pce* **5/2**[2]

4 ½ **Rehana (IRE)**[21] 5686 2-9-0 102 PatSmullen 7 107
(M Halford, Ire) *hld up bhd ldrs: racd keenly early: 5th 1/2-way: rdn in 4th 1 1/2f out and no imp on ldrs wl ins fnl f: kpt on same pce* **7/1**[3]

5 1¾ **Promise To Be True (IRE)**[52] 4573 2-9-0 0 RyanMoore 2 102
(A P O'Brien, Ire) *chsd ldrs: 4th 1/2-way: rdn in 5th over 2f out and no imp on ldrs u.p over 1f out: one pce after* **1/1**[1]

6 5½ **Brave Anna (USA)**[21] 5686 2-9-0 105 ColmO'Donoghue 4 89
(A P O'Brien, Ire) *towards rr: 6th 1/2-way: rdn and no imp 2f out* **14/1**

7 2½ **Dawn Of A New Era (IRE)** 2-9-0 0 KevinManning 5 82
(J S Bolger, Ire) *hld up in rr: last at 1/2-way: rdn and no imp 2f out* **20/1**

1m 28.5s (-2.30) **Going Correction** -0.125s/f (Firm) **7** Ran SP% **118.8**
Speed ratings: **108,107,105,105,103 97,94**
CSF £192.57 TOTE £21.20: £7.20, £2.80; DF 112.70 Trifecta £667.00.

Owner Mrs C C Regalado-Gonzalez **Bred** Whisperview Trading Ltd **Trained** Owning Hill, Co Kilkenny

FOCUS
A surprise win for a filly who had finished third behind two of these rivals in the Group 2 Debutante Stakes. The third has been rated close to her mark.

6386a GOFFS VINCENT O'BRIEN NATIONAL STKS (GROUP 1) (ENTIRE COLTS & FILLIES) 7f
4:15 (4:16) 2-Y-O

£146,691 (£48,897; £23,161; £10,294; £5,147; £2,573)

RPR

1 **Churchill (IRE)**[21] 5683 2-9-3 111 RyanMoore 5 120
(A P O'Brien, Ire) *chsd ldrs: 3rd 1/2-way: hdwy between horses to chal 2f out where sltly impeded: rdn to ld jst ins fnl f where edgd rt and styd on wl to assert wl ins fnl f: comf* **4/5**[1]

2 4¼ **Mehmas (IRE)**[45] 4798 2-9-3 0 FrankieDettori 4 109
(Richard Hannon) *hld up: clsr in 4th at 1/2-way: impr on outer to chal 2f out where edgd sltly rt: sn led narrowly tl hdd u.p jst ins fnl f: sn no imp on wnr and one pce clsng stages: jst hld 2nd* **9/4**[2]

3 nk **Lockheed**[25] 5556 2-9-3 0 PatSmullen 1 108
(William Haggas) *dwlt sltly: sn settled bhd ldr in 2nd: rdn 2f out and no imp on wnr u.p in 3rd ins fnl f: kpt on clsng stages: jst failed for 2nd* **11/1**

4 1¾ **Son Of Rest**[17] 5812 2-9-3 0 WayneLordan 7 104
(T Stack, Ire) *w.w in rr: last at 1/2-way: sme hdwy into 5th 1 1/2f out where rdn: kpt on u.p into 4th wl ins fnl f: nvr trbld ldrs* **50/1**

5 2¾ **Lancaster Bomber (USA)**[21] 5683 2-9-3 99 DonnachaO'Brien 6 97
(A P O'Brien, Ire) *broke wl to sn led: over 2 l clr at 1/2-way: reduced advantage over 2f out and hdd under 2f out: sn no ex u.p in 4th and wknd fnl f* **40/1**

6 4½ **Psychedelic Funk**[57] 4414 2-9-3 104 ColinKeane 2 86
(G M Lyons, Ire) *cl up early tl sn settled bhd ldrs: 6th 1/2-way: rdn 2f out and sn no imp on ldrs u.p in 6th: one pce after: eased wl ins fnl f* **7/1**[3]

7 4½ **Finn McCool (IRE)**[31] 5342 2-9-3 0 ColmO'Donoghue 3 75
(A P O'Brien, Ire) *chsd ldrs: 5th 1/2-way: rdn after 1/2-way and no imp in rr fr 2f out: wknd and eased fnl f* **25/1**

1m 28.28s (-2.52) **Going Correction** -0.125s/f (Firm) **7** Ran SP% **115.4**
Speed ratings: **109,104,103,101,98 93,88**
CSF £2.82 TOTE £1.80: £1.02, £1.50; DF 3.10 Trifecta £9.40.

Owner Michael Tabor & Derrick Smith & Mrs John Magnier **Bred** Liberty Bloodstock **Trained** Cashel, Co Tipperary

FOCUS
This race boasts a fine record in identifying the pick of the Ballydoyle juvenile colts in the modern era, as well as in the past. This year's winner can be rated a strong Guineas prospect for 2017. The level is a bit fluid.

6387a PALMERSTOWN HOUSE ESTATE IRISH ST. LEGER (GROUP 1) 1m 6f
4:50 (4:50) 3-Y-O+ **£167,647** (£55,882; £26,470; £11,764)

RPR

1 **Wicklow Brave**[23] 5612 7-9-11 111 FrankieDettori 2 115
(W P Mullins, Ire) *dwlt sltly and in rr briefly tl sn led and mde rest: 1 l clr at 1/2-way: stl gng wl 3f out: pushed along under 2f out: rdn over 1f out and reduced advantage ins fnl 100yds: kpt on wl clsng stages to hold on* **11/1**[3]

2 ½ **Order Of St George (IRE)**[22] 5660 4-9-11 124 RyanMoore 4 114+
(A P O'Brien, Ire) *sweated up befhand: w.w in rr of quartet: last at 1/2-way: pushed along and hdwy over 2f out into 2nd: rdn 1 1/2f out and clsd u.p to press ldr ins fnl 100yds: hld* **1/7**[1]

3 16 **Trip To Paris (IRE)**[23] 5612 5-9-11 114 (b) PatSmullen 5 92
(Ed Dunlop) *prom tl sn settled bhd ldrs in 3rd: pushed along into 2nd briefly under 3f out: sn lost pl and no imp on wnr in 3rd under 2f out: wknd 1f out* **10/1**[2]

4 ½ **Silwana (IRE)**[100] 2881 5-9-8 100 (bt[1]) ShaneFoley 6 88
(Takashi Kodama, Ire) *sn led briefly tl hdd and settled bhd ldr in 2nd: pushed along into st and sn lost pl: wknd in rr 2f out* **80/1**

3m 5.95s (-3.45) **Going Correction** +0.20s/f (Good)
WFA 3 from 4yo+ 11lb **4** Ran SP% **106.1**
Speed ratings: **117,116,107,107**
CSF £13.54 TOTE £10.00; DF 16.20 Trifecta £18.10.

Owner Wicklow Bloodstock (Ireland) Ltd **Bred** Millsec Limited **Trained** Muine Beag, Co Carlow

FOCUS
A race billed as a formality produced the shock of the season, the drama providing some compensation for a pathetic turn-out. The winner has been rated to his best.

6388a TATTERSALLS IRELAND SUPER AUCTION SALE STKS (PLUS 10 RACE) 6f 63y
5:25 (5:25) 2-Y-O

£108,823 (£42,647; £20,588; £13,235; £7,720; £4,044)

RPR

1 **Orewa (IRE)**[14] 5917 2-9-1 0 ChrisHayes 30 88
(Brian Ellison) *in tch nr side: pushed along after 1/2-way and impr to chse ldrs 1 1/2f out: clsd u.p to ld ins fnl f and styd on wl* **14/1**

2 2 **Wick Powell**[25] 5560 2-9-3 0 GrahamGibbons 25 84
(David Barron) *hld up towards rr: hdwy after 1/2-way to chse ldrs nr side ent fnl f: no imp on wnr u.p in 3rd wl ins fnl f: wnt 2nd fnl stride* **16/1**

3 nse **Medicine Jack**[35] 5212 2-9-4 107 ColinKeane 4 91+
(G M Lyons, Ire) *hld up towards rr: tk clsr order after 1/2-way: pushed along 2f out and sn n.m.r: swtchd rt in mid-div 1 1/2f out and hdwy far side into 2nd fnl 100yds: no imp on wnr cl home and denied 2nd fnl stride* **11/8**[1]

4 hd **Madam Bounska (IRE)**[18] 5784 2-8-6 72[1] GaryHalpin 28 72
(Mrs Denise Foster, Ire) *in tch: 10th 1/2-way: rdn to chse ldrs nr side over 1f out: kpt on same pce ins fnl f: nt trble wnr* **66/1**

5 hd **Fair Power (IRE)**[12] 5989 2-9-1 0 KevinManning 1 80
(Sylvester Kirk) *in tch far side: pushed along in mid-div fr 1/2-way: rdn over 2f out and sme hdwy over 1f out: kpt on wl ins fnl f: nt trble wnr* **40/1**

6 nk **Humbert (IRE)**[27] 5477 2-9-3 0[1] PatSmullen 7 82
(Hugo Palmer) *chsd ldrs: 7th 1/2-way: rdn 2f out and sme hdwy u.p ins fnl f: no imp on wnr wl ins fnl f: kpt on same pce* **9/1**[3]

7 shd **Lady In Question (IRE)**[29] 5407 2-8-12 0 TonyHamilton 12 76
(Richard Fahey) *hld up towards rr: pushed along after 1/2-way and impr into mid-div u.p ent fnl f: kpt on clsng stages: nvr nrr* **33/1**

8 ¾ **Gifted Lady (IRE)**[11] 6039 2-8-6 54 RobbieDowney 23 68
(Michael Mulvany, Ire) *mid-div: rdn 1 1/2f out and sme hdwy u.p ins fnl f where swtchd lft: kpt on clsng stages: nvr nrr* **100/1**

9 shd **Letmestopyouthere (IRE)**[25] 5560 2-9-3 0 SamJames 10 79
(David Evans) *chsd ldrs: 8th 1/2-way: rdn under 2f out and sn no ex: one pce fnl f* **40/1**

10 *shd* **Parnassian (IRE)**[20] 5713 2-9-3 0 .... DougieCostello 13 79
(K R Burke) *in tch: 10th 1/2-way: pushed along under 2f out and n.m.r over 1f out where swtchd rt: no ex u.p wl ins fnl f and one pce far side clsng stages* **6/1**[2]

11 *shd* **Mama Africa (IRE)**[20] 5712 2-8-6 0 .... MichaelHussey 2 68
(David Barron) *w.w in rr: swtchd rt after 1/2-way: sn n.m.r and swtchd lft 2f out where hdwy: kpt on same pce wl ins fnl f: nvr nrr* **50/1**

12 *1 3/4* **Diable D'Or (IRE)**[24] 5569 2-9-1 0 .... DonnachaO'Brien[(3)] 22 74
(Eve Johnson Houghton) *sn disp tl settled bhd ldr after 1f: rdn to ld briefly 1f out: sn hdd and no ex ins fnl 150yds where wknd* **20/1**

13 *3/4* **Ashurst Beacon**[28] 5433 2-9-3 0 .... RonanWhelan 18 71
(Brian Ellison) *chsd ldrs: 3rd 1/2-way: rdn in 3rd over 1f out and sn no ex: wknd fnl f* **66/1**

14 *1/2* **Madam Prancealot (IRE)**[3] 6253 2-8-10 0 .... AnaO'Brien 3 63
(David Evans) *on toes befhand: chsd ldrs far side early: pushed along in mid-div fr 1/2-way and no imp: one pce fnl 2f* **50/1**

15 *shd* **Vona (IRE)**[50] 4669 2-8-13 0 .... DanielTudhope 9 65
(Richard Fahey) *mid-div: rdn 2f out and no imp over 1f out: kpt on one pce* **25/1**

16 *shd* **Princess Way (IRE)**[10] 6060 2-8-8 0 .... TomMadden 20 60
(David Evans) *chsd ldrs and niggled along early: pushed along in 4th at 1/2-way and no ex u.p in 4th 1 1/2f out: wknd fnl f* **50/1**

17 *1/2* **Zeeyalater (IRE)**[15] 5898 2-8-11 78 .... GaryCarroll 21 61
(Ms Sheila Lavery, Ire) *hld up towards rr: sme hdwy gng wl 2f out: rdn in rr of mid-div ins fnl f and kpt on one pce* **50/1**

18 *1* **Randall Stevens (IRE)**[43] 4898 2-9-1 86 .... ColmO'Donoghue 8 63
(M D O'Callaghan, Ire) *hld up towards rr: tk clsr order in rr of mid-div 1f out: kpt on one pce ins fnl f* **14/1**

19 *1 3/4* **Miss Cogent (IRE)**[22] 5661 2-8-10 90 .... NGMcCullagh 5 53
(J P Murtagh, Ire) *towards rr: sme hdwy far side after 1/2-way: rdn under 2f out and no imp: one pce fnl f* **20/1**

20 *nk* **Sweet Zain (IRE)**[6] 6183 2-8-12 0 .... WayneLordan 27 57
(Charlie Fellowes) *chsd ldrs nr side: wknd under 2f out where n.m.r and hmpd over 1f out* **25/1**

21 *1 1/4* **High On Love (IRE)**[29] 5407 2-8-12 0 .... StevieDonohoe 19 50
(Charlie Fellowes) *chsd ldrs: 5th 1/2-way: rdn over 2f out and sn no ex: wknd 1 1/2f out* **16/1**

22 *3/4* **Mr Scaramanga**[23] 5595 2-9-5 0 .... PatDobbs 11 55
(Richard Hannon) *hooded to load: towards rr: rdn over 2f out and no imp over 1f out: kpt on one pce* **9/1**[3]

23 *3/4* **Little Nosegay (IRE)**[22] 5638 2-8-8 0 .... RoryCleary 14 42
(David Evans) *sn disp and led after 1f: extended advantage bef 1/2-way: reduced advantage 2f out and hdd u.p 1f out: wknd* **50/1**

24 *1/2* **Level Of Intensity (IRE)** 2-8-11 0 .... DonaghO'Connor[(5)] 6 48
(J S Bolger, Ire) *hld up in rr of mid-div: rdn far side over 2f out and sn no ex: wknd over 1f out* **33/1**

25 *3* **Starlite Sienna (IRE)**[26] 5524 2-8-10 0 .... DeclanMcDonogh 17 34
(Richard Fahey) *mid-div best: rdn 2f out and no ex u.p over 1f out: wknd and eased ins fnl f* **50/1**

26 *nk* **Oakledge (IRE)**[15] 5898 2-8-13 0 .... BillyLee 26 36
(W McCreery, Ire) *in tch: rdn 2f out and sn no ex: wknd and eased ins fnl f* **16/1**

27 *shd* **Makemerichjohn (IRE)**[11] 6033 2-8-13 0 .... ShaneFoley 24 35
(David Evans) *a bhd: rdn after 1/2-way and no imp: one pce fnl 2f* **100/1**

28 *2 1/4* **Elements Legacy**[32] 5297 2-8-11 0 ....(v) JoeyHaynes 15 27
(K R Burke) *in tch: pushed along in mid-div after 1/2-way and no ex: wknd over 1f out: eased ins fnl f* **66/1**

29 *1/2* **Jollydee (IRE)**[30] 5364 2-8-6 0 .... LeighRoche 29 20
(Paul Midgley) *chsd ldrs nr side: 6th 1/2-way: rdn over 2f out and sn no ex: wknd over 1f out* **100/1**

30 *4 1/4* **Bella Duchess (IRE)**[15] 5884 2-8-6 0 .... RossCoakley 16 8
(David C Griffiths) *in rr of mid-div: pushed along after 1/2-way and no imp: wknd to rr under 2f out* **100/1**

1m 20.87s (1.77) **Going Correction** +0.125s/f (Good) **30** Ran SP% **155.6**
Speed ratings: **93,90,90,90,89 89,89,88,88,87 87,85,84,83,83 83,82,81,79,78 77,76,75,74,70 70,69,66,66,60**
Pick Six. Not Won. Pool of 432,400.00 carried forward to Gowran Park on Sunday, 18th September. Tote Aggregate: 2016: 823.112.00- 2015: 626,042.00 CSF £232.79 TOTE £11.80: £3.80, £6.30, £1.70; DF 323.70 Trifecta £5558.10.
Owner Keith Brown **Bred** Mrs C Regalado-Gonzalez **Trained** Norton, N Yorks

FOCUS
A valuable sales race with limited relevance in the overall context. The one horse with high-level credentials did not get the run of the race and ended up third behind two British raiders.

6389a IRISH STALLION FARMS EUROPEAN BREEDERS FUND "NORTHFIELDS" H'CAP (PREMIER HANDICAP) 1m 2f
5:55 (6:00) 3-Y-O+
£65,073 (£20,955; £9,926; £4,411; £2,205; £1,102)

RPR

1 **Maudlin Magdalen (IRE)**[28] 5444 6-8-0 **82** .... SeanDavis[(7)] 15 86
(Donal Kinsella, Ire) *sn trckd ldr in 2nd: pushed along to chal under 2f out and led narrowly over 1f out: kpt on wl under hands and heels w narrow advantage wl ins fnl f* **25/1**

2 *hd* **Breathe Easy (IRE)**[14] 5941 6-8-10 **88** .... GaryHalpin[(3)] 14 92
(Gavin Cromwell, Ire) *sn led: rdn over 2f out and strly pressed: hdd narrowly over 1f out and kpt on wl u.p ins fnl f to strly press wnr clsng stages: jst hld* **25/1**

3 *nk* **Ringside Humour (IRE)**[28] 5444 4-9-6 **95** ....(t) KevinManning 21 98+
(J S Bolger, Ire) *chsd ldrs: 4th 1/2-way: rdn over 2f out where wandered sltly: u.p in cl 3rd ent fnl f: kpt on wl ins fnl f: hld* **20/1**

4 *nk* **Vastonea (IRE)**[14] 5941 8-8-6 **81** .... ChrisHayes 19 83+
(Kevin Prendergast, Ire) *in rr of mid-div: hdwy u.p on outer 2f out to chse ldrs ent fnl f: rdn into cl 4th wl ins fnl f and no imp on wnr clsng stages* **25/1**

5 *3/4* **Castle Guest (IRE)**[35] 5215 7-8-8 **93** ....(t) RobertSmithers[(10)] 11 94
(M Halford, Ire) *hld up towards rr early: sme hdwy after 1/2-way to chse ldrs in 5th into st: rdn 2f out and no ex between horses wl ins fnl f: kpt on same pce* **20/1**

6 *hd* **Stronger Than Me (IRE)**[28] 5444 8-9-4 **93** .... BillyLee 4 94
(W T Farrell, Ire) *hld up towards rr: hdwy over 2f out: rdn 1 1/2f out and no imp on ldrs u.p in 7th far side ins fnl f: kpt on same pce clsng stages* **16/1**

7 *hd* **Simannka (IRE)**[69] 3964 3-9-4 **100** .... LeighRoche 2 100
(D K Weld, Ire) *chsd ldrs: disp 5th at 1/2-way: rdn over 2f out and no imp on ldrs u.p in 6th ins fnl f: one pce clsng stages* **16/1**

8 *2* **Mandamus (IRE)**[91] 3203 4-9-1 **90** .... RonanWhelan 17 86
(Ms Sheila Lavery, Ire) *in rr of mid-div: sme late hdwy nr side ins fnl f: nrst fin* **33/1**

9 *nk* **Munaashid (USA)**[17] 5818 3-8-5 **90** ....(v[1]) RobbieDowney[(3)] 24 86
(D K Weld, Ire) *mid-div: 10th 1/2-way: rdn nr side under 2f out and no imp over 1f out: kpt on one pce ins fnl f* **25/1**

10 *shd* **Boherbuoy (IRE)**[45] 4811 4-9-0 **89** ....[1] WayneLordan 23 84
(David Wachman, Ire) *settled in mid-div: rdn 2f out and tk clsr order briefly over 1f out where swtchd lft: no ex ins fnl f where sltly impeded: one pce clsng stages* **9/1**

11 *shd* **Katiymann (IRE)**[14] 5941 4-8-8 **83** .... NGMcCullagh 25 78
(M Halford, Ire) *chsd ldrs: disp 5th at 1/2-way: rdn bhd ldrs under 2f out and no ex over 1f out where sltly impeded: wknd ins fnl f* **14/1**

12 *1 1/2* **Bravery (IRE)**[25] 5567 3-8-11 **98** .... AnaO'Brien[(5)] 3 90
(A P O'Brien, Ire) *in rr of mid-div: sme hdwy 2f out: rdn in mid-div over 1f out and sn no ex: one pce ins fnl f and eased clsng stages* **14/1**

13 *1/2* **Karalara (IRE)**[47] 4747 3-8-12 **94** ....(b[1]) PatSmullen 18 85
(D K Weld, Ire) *hld up in tch: 7th 1/2-way: rdn 2f out and sn no ex u.p: wknd and eased ins fnl f* **7/1**[3]

14 *1* **Whiskey Sour (IRE)**[14] 5941 3-8-8 **90** ....[1] ColmO'Donoghue 10 79
(Edward Lynam, Ire) *in tch: 9th 1/2-way: pushed along over 2f out and sltly hmpd between horses: rdn over 1f out and sn no ex: eased ins fnl 100yds* **25/1**

15 *1* **Hawke (IRE)**[28] 5444 4-9-11 **100** .... DanielTudhope 16 87
(J P Murtagh, Ire) *hld up in mid-div: swtchd rt 2f out and rdn: no imp u.p over 1f out: wknd fnl f* **16/1**

16 *hd* **Dark Red (IRE)**[22] 5651 4-9-8 **97** .... PatDobbs 9 84
(Ed Dunlop) *mid-div: 11th 1/2-way: pushed along 2f out and no imp over 1f out: wknd* **6/1**[2]

17 *nk* **Siamsaiocht (IRE)**[23] 5618 3-8-8 **90** ....(tp) RoryCleary 22 76
(J S Bolger, Ire) *mid-div: pushed along over 2f out where n.m.r bhd horses: swtchd rt under 2f out and no imp u.p over 1f out: wknd* **40/1**

18 *3/4* **Savannah Storm**[69] 3963 3-8-12 **94** .... ColinKeane 13 79
(G M Lyons, Ire) *mid-div: pushed along over 2f out and no imp over 1f out where short of room briefly: wknd and eased ins fnl f* **4/1**[1]

19 *1 3/4* **Tara Dylan (IRE)**[13] 5983 4-8-9 **84** ....(t) DeclanMcDonogh 8 65
(Thomas Mullins, Ire) *towards rr thrght: rdn over 2f out and no imp* **14/1**

20 *3 1/2* **Here For The Craic (IRE)**[8] 6148 9-8-10 **85** 5ex .... MichaelHussey 6 59
(David Kenneth Budds, Ire) *dwlt and pushed along towards rr early: rdn 2f out and no imp: one pce after* **25/1**

21 *nk* **Clonard Street**[119] 7381 4-9-2 **96** .... TomMadden[(5)] 12 70
(A J Martin, Ire) *dwlt and towards rr thrght: pushed along over 2f out and no imp: one pce fnl 2f* **25/1**

22 *3/4* **Daredevil Day (IRE)**[11] 6042 5-8-5 **85** ....(p) KillianLeonard[(5)] 7 57
(Joseph G Murphy, Ire) *s.i.s and detached in rr early: pushed along appr st and no imp: kpt on one pce fnl 2f* **20/1**

23 *9* **Diamond Rio (IRE)**[32] 5313 4-8-4 **79** oh2 ....(t) MarkGallagher 20 33
(Anthony Mullins, Ire) *dwlt and towards rr thrght: rdn over 2f out and no imp* **50/1**

24 *4 1/2* **Elusive Heights (IRE)**[65] 4123 3-9-4 **100** .... GaryCarroll 1 45
(G M Lyons, Ire) *chsd ldrs: 3rd 1/2-way: rdn and wknd fr over 2f out* **14/1**

25 *5 1/2* **Hasanour (USA)**[14] 5941 6-9-12 **101** .... ShaneFoley 5 35
(M Halford, Ire) *in tch: 8th 1/2-way: n.m.r briefly 2f out and sn lost tch: eased 1 1/2f out* **10/1**

2m 10.89s (1.59) **Going Correction** +0.20s/f (Good)
WFA 3 from 4yo+ 7lb **25** Ran SP% **158.7**
Speed ratings: **101,100,100,100,99 99,99,97,97,97 97,96,95,95,94 94,93,93,91,89 88,88,81,77,73**
CSF £595.39 CT £12021.79 TOTE £63.60: £10.50, £9.20, £4.90, £4.90; DF 2521.30.
Owner Mrs Joan Kinsella **Bred** Sweet Caroline Partnership **Trained** Dunleer, Co Louth

FOCUS
A minefield of a handicap in which the first five in a tight finish were 20-1 or bigger. It's been rated around the balance of the first seven.
T/Jkpt: Not Won. T/Plt: @5,015.10. Pool: @7,164.35 **Brian Fleming**

3448 BRO PARK (L-H)
Sunday, September 11
OFFICIAL GOING: Turf: good; dirt: standard

6390a STOCKHOLM CUP INTERNATIONAL (GROUP 3) (3YO+) (TURF) 1m 4f
4:28 (12:00) 3-Y-O+ **£64,308** (£24,115; £12,861; £7,234; £4,019)

RPR

1 **Quarterback (GER)**[14] 5950 4-9-4 0 ....(p) CarlosLopez 3 106
(Rune Haugen) *a cl up: rdn to chse ldr 2f out: led appr fnl f: drvn clr* **156/10**

2 *5* **Hurricane Red (IRE)**[14] 5950 6-9-4 0 .... JacobJohansen 8 98
(Lennart Reuterskiold Jr, Sweden) *chsd ldrs: rdn and nt qckn 2f out: styd on to go 2nd fnl stride: no ch w wnr* **152/100**[1]

3 *nse* **Icecapada (IRE)**[38] 4-9-1 0 .... ElioneChaves 2 95
(Niels Petersen, Norway) *settled in midfield: rdn to cl wl over 2 1/2f out: styd on same pce fnl f* **162/10**

4 *1 1/2* **El Abandonado (SWE)**[84] 3449 5-9-4 0 .... RafaeldeOliveira 7 96
(Maria Sandh, Sweden) *led: hdd appr fnl f: sn wknd* **110/1**

5 *1/2* **Bokan (FR)**[14] 5950 4-9-4 0 .... KevinStott 5 95
(Wido Neuroth, Norway) *w.w towards rr: tk clsr order 2f out: kpt on at same pce fnl f: n.d* **238/10**

6 *1 1/2* **Giuseppe Piazzi (IRE)**[36] 5187 4-9-4 0 .... JorgeHorcajada 1 92
(Flemming Velin, Denmark) *keen: chsd ldr: rdn and wknd wl over 1 1/2f out* **185/10**

7 *nk* **Amie Noire (GER)**[84] 3449 5-9-1 0 .... Jan-ErikNeuroth 12 89
(Wido Neuroth, Norway) *hld up in fnl pair: hdwy on outer 3f out: rdn and no further imp wl over 1 1/2f out: one pce fnl f* **13/1**

8 *nk* **Jubilance (IRE)**[36] 5187 7-9-4 0 ....(b) ShaneGray 11 91
(Bent Olsen, Denmark) *w.w in rr: rdn and kpt on fr 1 1/2f out: nvr in contention* **176/1**

9 *1* **Fields Of Athenry (IRE)**[36] 5187 4-9-4 0 .... OliverWilson 4 90
(Flemming Velin, Denmark) *prom on outer: rdn and chasded ldrs 2f out: sn wknd* **242/100**[2]

10 *2 1/2* **Bank Of Burden (USA)**[14] 5950 9-9-4 0 .... Per-AndersGraberg 9 86
(Niels Petersen, Norway) *w.w in midfield: rdn and short-lived effrt 2 1/2f out: sn btn* **15/4**[3]

11 *4* **Zen Zansai Zaid (SWE)**[234] 285 7-9-4 0........................(b) NikolajStott 6 79
(Tommy Gustafsson, Sweden) *racd towards rr of midfield: no imp u.p wl over 2f out: nvr a factor* **104/1**

12 *1 1/2* **Inaya**[36] 5187 5-9-1 0........................ NelsonDeSouza 10 74
(Jessica Long, Sweden) *midfield early: lost pl 1/2-way: bhd fnl 2f* **201/10**

Owner Team MK **Bred** Stiftung Gestut Fahrhof **Trained** Newmarket, Suffolk

6270 CHANTILLY (R-H)

Sunday, September 11

OFFICIAL GOING: Turf: good; polytrack: standard

6391a QATAR PRIX DU PETIT COUVERT (GROUP 3) (3YO+) (TURF) 5f

12:55 (12:00) 3-Y-O+ **£29,411** (£11,764; £8,823; £5,882; £2,941)

RPR

1 **Just Glamorous (IRE)**[22] 5657 3-8-13 0........... Pierre-CharlesBoudot 3 114
(Ronald Harris) *mde all: 2l clr 1/2-way: rdn 1 1/2f out: styd on wl fnl f: unchal* **16/1**

2 *3* **Marsha (IRE)**[44] 4824 3-8-9 0........................ LukeMorris 7 99+
(Sir Mark Prescott Bt) *w.w in tch: hrd rdn to chse 3l ldr fr 2f out: styd on fnl f: nvr on terms* **2/1**[1]

3 *1 1/2* **Goldream**[23] 5614 7-9-0 0........................(p) MartinHarley 4 97
(Robert Cowell) *chsd ldr: hrd rdn 2f out but no imp: one pce fnl f* **9/4**[2]

4 *1 1/2* **Spiritfix**[43] 4905 3-8-9 0........................ MaximeGuyon 11 88+
(A Fabre, France) *prom on outer: rdn and no imp 2f out: kpt on u.p fnl f: nt pce to trble ldrs* **20/1**

5 *nk* **Porthilly (FR)**[28] 5453 6-8-10 0........................ AlexisBadel 9 87
(J E Hammond, France) *chsd ldng gp towards outer: nt qckn whn asked 2f out: styd on at same pce fnl f* **33/1**

6 *3/4* **Mirza**[43] 4905 9-9-0 0........................(p) IoritzMendizabal 8 88
(Rae Guest) *cl up: nt qckn w ldrs over 2f out: sn rdn and no imp: one pce fr over 1f out* **14/1**

7 *3/4* **Gold Vibe (IRE)**[21] 3-8-13 0........................ ChristopheSoumillon 12 86
(P Bary, France) *w.w in fnl trio on inner: angled towards outer appr 2f out: styd on under hands and heels fr over 1f out: nvr nrr* **12/1**

8 *hd* **Aces (IRE)**[61] 4-9-0 0........................ GeraldMosse 10 85
(J E Hammond, France) *sn outpcd towards rr: hdwy 1 1/2f out: kpt on fnl f: nrest at fin* **40/1**

9 *1/2* **Catcall (FR)**[74] 3796 7-9-0 0........................ OlivierPeslier 5 83
(P Sogorb, France) *settled towards rr of midfield: rdn 2f out: plugged on fr wl over 1f out: nvr in contention* **8/1**[3]

10 *1/2* **Largent Du Bonheur (FR)**[43] 4905 3-8-13 0......... VincentCheminaud 6 81
(M Delzangles, France) *hld up in midfield: outpcd and rdn 2f out: sn btn* **20/1**

11 *6* **Damila (FR)**[35] 5217 3-8-13 0........................ CristianDemuro 1 60
(H-A Pantall, France) *chsd ldr on inner: outpcd and scrubbed along sn after 1/2-way: wl btn whn eased ins fnl f* **16/1**

12 *snk* **Gammarth (FR)**[74] 3796 8-9-0 0........................(b) MickaelBarzalona 13 59
(Robert Collet, France) *w.w in fnl trio: rdn and no impact after 1/2-way: n.d* **33/1**

13 *5* **Ross Castle (IRE)**[35] 5217 3-9-2 0........................(p) TonyPiccone 2 44
(Matthieu Palussiere, France) *outpcd and pushed along in rr: rdn after 1/2-way: wl bhd fnl 2f* **33/1**

56.3s (-2.00) **Going Correction** -0.075s/f (Good)
WFA 3 from 4yo+ 1lb **13** Ran SP% **122.1**
Speed ratings: **113,108,105,103,102 101,100,100,99,98 89,88,80**
WIN (incl. 1 euro stake): 20.70. PLACES: 3.40, 1.70, 1.60. DF: 31.50. SF: 71.50.
Owner Robert & Nina Bailey **Bred** Glamorous Air Partnership **Trained** Earlswood, Monmouths

FOCUS
Few got involved here, with the pace holding up, and the winner posted a big pb.

6392a QATAR PRIX NIEL (GROUP 2) (3YO COLTS & FILLIES) (TURF) 1m 4f

2:00 (12:00) 3-Y-O **£54,485** (£21,029; £10,036; £6,691; £3,345)

RPR

1 **Makahiki (JPN)**[105] 2731 3-9-2 0................ Christophe-PatriceLemaire 4 114+
(Yasuo Tomomichi, Japan) *w.w 3rd in single file field: clsd a little under 2f out: cl 3rd and shkn up 1 1/2f out: chal ins fnl f: r.o to ld 110yds out: won a shade cosily* **4/9**[1]

2 *nk* **Midterm**[122] 2190 3-9-2 0........................ VincentCheminaud 1 113
(Sir Michael Stoute) *sn led and set a stdy gallop: shkn up and qcknd tempo appr 2f out: sn rdn and hdd under 2f out: rallied u.p to press ldr 1f out: styd on gamely fnl f: got bk up for 2nd fnl strides* **11/2**[2]

3 *shd* **Doha Dream (FR)**[44] 4854 3-9-2 0........................ GregoryBenoist 2 113
(A Fabre, France) *chsd ldr: shkn up and led under 2f out: sn rdn and pressed 1f out: styd on u.p: hdd 110yds out: no ex: lost 2nd fnl strides* **6/1**[3]

4 *10* **Darabad (FR)**[20] 5733 3-9-2 0........................ ChristopheSoumillon 3 97+
(A De Royer-Dupre, France) *tk a str hold: hld up next to last: rdn and no imp wl over 1 1/2f out: lft bhd fnl f: n.d* **16/1**

5 *1 1/2* **Carzoff (FR)**[24] 3-9-2 0........................ CristianDemuro 5 94+
(Alain Couetil, France) *w.w in last: rdn and no hdwy 2f out: wl hld fnl 1 1/2f: nvr a factor* **66/1**

2m 35.84s (4.84) **Going Correction** +0.475s/f (Yiel) **5** Ran SP% **106.3**
Speed ratings: **102,101,101,95,94**
WIN (incl. 1 euro stake): 1.40. PLACES: 1.10, 1.20. SF: 4.00.
Owner Kaneko Makoto Holdings Co Ltd **Bred** Kaneko Makoto Holdings Inc **Trained** Japan

FOCUS
The gallop was steady for the 3yo colts Arc trial and it was much the slowest of the races over the trip on the card. Therefore, it's hard to know what to make of the form at this stage, although one would imagine that those connected with the first three home will be pleased with the runs of their horses with the future in mind.

6393a QATAR PRIX VERMEILLE (GROUP 1) (3YO+ FILLIES & MARES) (TURF) 1m 4f

3:10 (12:00) 3-Y-O+ **£147,051** (£58,830; £29,415; £14,694; £7,360)

RPR

1 **Left Hand**[43] 4904 3-8-8 0........................(p) MaximeGuyon 2 113+
(C Laffon-Parias, France) *w.w in tch on outer: pushed along and clsd on outer 1 1/2f out: sustained chal fr over 1f out: led fnl 50yds: readily* **7/2**[3]

2 *1/2* **Endless Time (IRE)**[24] 5586 4-9-3 0........................ MickaelBarzalona 3 112
(Charlie Appleby) *sn led: qcknd tempo ent st under 2 1/2f out: styd on u.p: hdd fnl 50yds: no ex* **10/1**

3 *3/4* **The Juliet Rose (FR)**[28] 5451 3-8-8 0................ Pierre-CharlesBoudot 6 111
(N Clement, France) *trckd ldr on outer: rdn to chse ldr 1 1/2f out: styd on fnl f: nt pce to tackle front two* **16/1**

4 *1 1/4* **Highlands Queen (FR)**[29] 5461 3-8-8 0................ StephanePasquier 4 109
(Y Gourraud, France) *w.w in fnl pair: rdn 2f out and no imp: styd on u.p fnl f: nt pce to get on terms* **10/3**[2]

5 *3/4* **Candarliya (FR)**[21] 5692 4-9-3 0........................(p) ChristopheSoumillon 1 108
(A De Royer-Dupre, France) *cl up on inner: rdn to chse ldrs 2f out: one pce u.p fnl f* **5/2**[1]

6 *1/2* **Golden Valentine (FR)**[28] 5451 3-8-8 0........................ AurelienLemaitre 5 107
(F Head, France) *hld up in fnl pair: rdn and no hdwy 2f out: kpt on fnl f: nvr threatened ldrs* **5/1**

2m 33.23s (2.23) **Going Correction** +0.475s/f (Yiel)
WFA 3 from 4yo 9lb **6** Ran SP% **105.5**
Speed ratings: **111,110,110,109,108 108**
WIN (incl. 1 euro stake): 4.50. PLACES: 2.50, 4.70. SF: 43.30.
Owner Wertheimer & Frere **Bred** Wertheimer Et Frere **Trained** Chantilly, France

FOCUS
No great pace on for this Group 1 contest and it developed into a sprint down the home straight. It's hard to think this is trustworthy form. The first two help with the standard.

6394a QATAR PRIX DU MOULIN DE LONGCHAMP (GROUP 1) (3YO+ NO GELDINGS) (TURF) 1m

3:50 (12:00) 3-Y-O+ **£189,066** (£75,639; £37,819; £18,893; £9,463)

RPR

1 **Vadamos (FR)**[28] 5449 5-9-3 0........................ VincentCheminaud 2 122
(A Fabre, France) *trckd ldr: eased to the front 2 1/2f out: nudged along and raised tempo appr 2f out: rdn and 4l clr appr fnl f: styd on wl* **3/1**[2]

2 *1 1/4* **Spectre (FR)**[28] 5449 3-8-9 0........................ Pierre-CharlesBoudot 4 115+
(M Munch, Germany) *keen: hld up in midfield: rdn to chse fr two 1 1/2f out: styd on fnl f: nt pce to trble wnr* **20/1**

3 *1 1/4* **Zelzal (FR)**[63] 4185 3-8-13 0........................ GregoryBenoist 6 116+
(J-C Rouget, France) *hld up next to last: hdwy on outer 2f out: styd on to go 3rd cl home: nvr had the pce to get involved* **13/8**[1]

4 *hd* **Zarak (FR)**[27] 5499 3-8-13 0........................ ChristopheSoumillon 3 116
(A De Royer-Dupre, France) *led: hdd 2 1/2f out: rdn to chse ld wl over 2 1/2f out: kpt on at the same pce fnl f: lost 3rd cl home* **7/2**[3]

5 *3 1/2* **Trixia (FR)**[27] 5498 3-8-9 0........................ OlivierPeslier 1 104
(A De Royer-Dupre, France) *plld v hrd early on: hld up in last: rdn and sme mod last prog: nvr in contention* **14/1**

6 *1 3/4* **Dutch Connection**[35] 5217 4-9-3 0........................ WilliamBuick 5 104+
(Charles Hills) *tk a stong hold early and nvr settled: hld up in midfield on inner: rdn and no rspnse wl over 1 1/2f out: grad ledft bhd* **8/1**

1m 38.27s (0.27) **Going Correction** +0.475s/f (Yiel)
WFA 3 from 4yo+ 5lb **6** Ran SP% **107.9**
Speed ratings: **117,115,114,114,110 109**
WIN (incl. 1 euro stake): 3.40. PLACES: 2.00, 5.90. SF: 30.70.
Owner Scea Haras De Saint Pair **Bred** Scea Haras De Saint Pair **Trained** Chantilly, France

FOCUS
This looked a quality contest on paper, but a decisive move by the winner entering the home straight proved the key to success. It's entirely possible that a few of these will prove much better by the end of the season than their efforts here suggest. The winner has been rated close to his Jacques Le Marois form.

6395a PRIX FOY (GROUP 2) (4YO+ NO GELDINGS) (TURF) 1m 4f

4:25 (12:00) 4-Y-O+ **£54,485** (£21,029; £10,036; £6,691)

RPR

1 **Silverwave (FR)**[70] 3936 4-9-2 0........................ MaximeGuyon 3 118+
(P Bary, France) *chsd ldr: drvn to ld ent fnl f: sn asserted: coasted fnl 75yds: comf* **6/4**[1]

2 *1* **Ito (GER)**[42] 4928 5-9-2 0........................ MickaelBarzalona 4 116
(Jean-Pierre Carvalho, Germany) *led: raised tempo fr 2 1/2f out: sn rdn: hdd ent fnl f: kpt on but no match for wnr* **13/2**

3 *1 3/4* **Elliptique (IRE)**[42] 4928 5-9-2 0........................ Pierre-CharlesBoudot 1 114+
(A Fabre, France) *tk a t.k.h in 3rd: nvr really settled: rdn and no immediate imp wl over 1f out: kpt on fnl f: nt trble front two* **7/2**[3]

4 *6* **One Foot In Heaven (IRE)**[70] 3936 4-9-2 0....... ChristopheSoumillon 2 105+
(A De Royer-Dupre, France) *a in rr: rdn and no hdwy 2f out: sn btn* **9/4**[2]

2m 32.28s (1.28) **Going Correction** +0.475s/f (Yiel) **4** Ran SP% **106.3**
Speed ratings: **114,113,112,108**
WIN (incl. 1 euro stake): 2.00. PLACES: 1.30, 2.80. SF: 12.00.
Owner Hspirit **Bred** Mlle M-L Collet, J Collet & Mme M Collet **Trained** Chantilly, France

FOCUS
Despite the small field, this was reasonably well run and only 3.28 seconds slower than Racing Post standard, the quickest of the three races over the trip on the card. It has, however, been a poor race for producing subsequent Arc winners.

6396a QATAR PRIX GLADIATEUR (GROUP 3) (4YO+) (TURF) 1m 7f

5:05 (12:00) 4-Y-O+ **£29,411** (£11,764; £8,823; £5,882; £2,941)

RPR

1 **Vazirabad (FR)**[70] 3936 4-9-6 0........................ ChristopheSoumillon 1 119+
(A De Royer-Dupre, France) *w.w one fr last: hdwy on outer 2 1/2f out: styd on to ld 1f out: drvn fnl f: a holding runner-up* **4/9**[1]

2 *snk* **Nahual (FR)**[24] 5-8-11 0........................(p) MaximeGuyon 6 110
(J Bertran De Balanda, France) *led: hdd 2 1/2f out but stl travelling wl: shkn up and regained ld wl over 1 1/2f out: sn hrd rdn: hdd 1f out: rallied gamely u.p* **7/1**[2]

3 *3 1/2* **Settler's Son (IRE)**[81] 3545 5-8-11 0........................ SebastienMaillot 3 105
(J Michal, France) *cl up on inner: drvn over 2f out: sn outpcd by ldrs: styd on again fnl f: nt trble front two* **20/1**

4 *1/2* **Kicky Blue (GER)**[87] 3298 6-8-10 0........................ MickaelBarzalona 4 104
(T Clout, France) *hld up in tch: rdn to chse ldrs over 2f out: outpcd wl over 1f out: kpt on at same pce* **17/2**[3]

5 *hd* **Walzertakt (GER)**[21] 5692 7-9-2 0........................ IoritzMendizabal 5 110
(Jean-Pierre Carvalho, Germany) *chsd ldr: drvn to cl over 3f out: hed 2 1/2f out: sn rdn: hdd 1 1/2f out: qckly btn* **22/1**

6 *4* **Mille Et Mille**[59] 4333 6-9-6 0........................ ThierryThulliez 2 108
(C Lerner, France) *w.w in rr: rdn and no imp fr 2f out: nvr a factor* **7/1**[2]

3m 17.96s (1.86) **Going Correction** +0.475s/f (Yiel) **6** Ran SP% **113.9**
Speed ratings: **114,113,112,111,111 109**
WIN (incl. 1 euro stake): 1.60. PLACES: 1.10, 1.40. SF: 4.20.
Owner H H Aga Khan **Bred** S C E A Haras De Son Altesse L'Aga Khan **Trained** Chantilly, France

[5695]DUSSELDORF (R-H)
Sunday, September 11

OFFICIAL GOING: Turf: good

6397a GROSSE EUROPA MEILE DES PORSCHE ZENTRUM DUSSELDORF (GROUP 3) (3YO+) (TURF) **1m**
4:25 (12:00) 3-Y-O+ **£23,529** (£8,823; £4,411; £2,205; £1,470)

RPR
1 **Noor Al Hawa (FR)**[40] 5004 3-8-11 0.......................... EduardoPedroza 3 108
(A Wohler, Germany) *keen: hld up in midfield: rdn to cl 2f out: styd on to ld 1f out: drvn clr: won easing down* **13/10**[1]
2 1 ½ **Drummer (GER)**[10] 6067 4-9-2 0.................................. AndraschStarke 4 106
(P Schiergen, Germany) *chsd ldr on outer: 8l 3rd and drvn after 1/2-way: clsd to chse ldr over 1 1/2f out: cl 3rd and hrd rdn 1f out: styd on fnl f: no match for wnr* **5/1**
3 ½ **El Loco (GER)**[21] 5696 3-8-11 0...................................... AdriedeVries 1 104
(Markus Klug, Germany) *clsed ldr on inner: led after 1/2-way and sn clr: rdn 1 1/2f out: hdd 1f out: styd on gamely fnl f* **5/2**[2]
4 ¾ **Tickle Me Blue (GER)**[21] 5696 3-8-8 0.............................. MartinSeidl 6 99
(Markus Klug, Germany) *settled next to last: hdwy on inner 2f out: cl 4th and hrd rdn 1f out: kpt on same pce fnl f* **101/10**
5 2 ¼ **Nymeria (GER)**[42] 4928 4-8-13 0............................... AndreasSuborics 5 95
(Waldemar Hickst, Germany) *w.w in fnl trio: rdn and no imp 1 1/2f out: sme late hdwy: nvr in contention* **18/5**[3]
6 1 ¼ **Gereon (GER)**[29] 8-9-2 0.. MichaelCadeddu 2 95
(C Zschache, Germany) *led: hdd after 1/2-way: chsd ldr: rdn and wknd ins last 1 1/2f* **115/10**
7 hd **Nordico (GER)**[131] 1957 5-9-2 0.......................................(p) FilipMinarik 7 95
(Mario Hofer, Germany) *w.w in rr: rdn and short-lived effrt 1 1/2f out: sn btn: nvr a factor* **202/10**

1m 37.05s (-4.11)
WFA 3 from 4yo+ 5lb **7 Ran SP% 132.2**
WIN (incl. 10 euro stake): 23. PLACES: 21, 25. SF: 150.
Owner Jaber Abdullah **Bred** Rabbah Bloodstock Limited **Trained** Germany

6398 - (Foreign Racing) - See Raceform Interactive

SEOUL (L-H)
Sunday, September 11

OFFICIAL GOING: Sand: standard

6399a KEENELAND KOREA CUP (LOCAL GRADE 1) (3YO+) (SAND) **1m 1f**
9:30 (12:00) 3-Y-O+ **£323,004** (£121,126; £80,751; £28,839; £23,071)

RPR
1 **Chrysolite (JPN)**[74] 6-9-0 0.. KanichiroFujii 3 116
(Hidetaka Otonashi, Japan) **12/5**[1]
2 6 **Kurino Star O (JPN)**[28] 6-9-0 0...................................... HideakiMiyuki 7 103
(Yoshitada Takahashi, Japan) **4/1**[3]
3 10 **Triple Nine (KOR)**[371] 4-9-0 0... PaoloAragoni 13 82
(Kim Young Kwan, Korea) **135/10**
4 4 **Power Blade (KOR)** 3-8-9 0.. KimYongGeun 16 75
(Kim Young Kwan, Korea) **59/10**
5 3 **Famous Mark (MOR)**[60] 4286 4-9-0 0................. AbderrahimFaddoul 2 68
(P Bary, France) **41/1**
6 3 **Gumpo Sky (KOR)** 5-9-0 0.. ChoiSiDae 9 61
(Sung-J Kwon, Korea) **143/1**
7 1 ½ **Wonder Bolt (USA)** 6-9-0 0... LeeChanHo 10 58
(Ji Young Hun, Korea) **56/1**
7 dht **Dynamic Dash (USA)** 4-9-0 0... LimSungSil 11 58
(Kim Byung Hak, Korea) **77/1**
9 8 **Saengil Gippeum (USA)** 3-8-9 0................................... LyuGwangHee 12 42
(Kim Gil Jung, Korea) **113/1**
10 ½ **Solar Deity (IRE)**[24] 5585 7-9-0 0.................................. DarryllHolland 8 40
(Jane Chapple-Hyam) *scrubbed along early: among backmarkers: hdwy into midfield before halfway but pushed along to do so: in final third and rdn 2 1/2f out: nvr a factor* **60/1**
11 1 ¾ **Beolmaui Kkum (USA)** 6-9-0 0.. SeoSeungUn 5 37
(Baik Kwang Yeol, Korea) **161/10**
12 ¾ **Infantry (NZ)** 4-8-13 0.. MNunes 15 34
(Hai Wang Tan, Singapore) **3/1**[2]
13 1 ½ **Mirae Yeongung (KOR)**[294] 5-9-0 0...................................... DPerovic 4 32
(M G Song, Korea) **86/1**
14 4 **Dynamic Jilju (USA)** 5-9-0 0... LimGiWon 14 24
(Kim Jeom Oh, Korea) **141/1**
15 1 ½ **Order Of The Sun (AUS)**[862] 6-9-0 0........................ ChinChuenWong 1 20
(Koh Chor Yung, Korea) **83/10**
16 2 **Need To Know (SAF)**[162] 8-9-0 0..................................... TadhgO'Shea 6 16
(A R Al Rayhi, UAE) **43/1**

1m 52.3s (112.30)
WFA 3 from 4yo+ 6lb **16 Ran SP% 125.2**

Owner U Carrot Farm **Bred** Northern Farm **Trained** Japan

WOODBINE (L-H)
Sunday, September 11

OFFICIAL GOING: Tapeta: fast

6400a ONTARIO JOCKEY CLUB STKS (LISTED RACE) (3YO+) (TAPETA) **6f (D)**
8:48 (8:48) 3-Y-O+
£29,411 (£9,803; £6,470; £2,450; £980; £588)

RPR
1 **Stacked Deck (USA)**[98] 5-8-6 0...................... RafaelManuelHernandez 7 109
(Barbara J Minshall, Canada) **9/5**[1]
2 1 ½ **Puntrooskie (USA)**[50] 5-8-8 0............................(b) EuricoRosaDaSilva 3 106
(Donald C MacRae, Canada) **2/1**[2]
3 2 ½ **Sweet Grass Creek (CAN)**[434] 4-8-6 0.................. JesseMCampbell 4 96
(Michael Keogh, Canada) **76/10**
4 ¾ **Calgary Cat (CAN)**[22] 6-8-8 0.. LuisContreras 2 96
(Kevin Attard, Canada) **4/1**[3]
5 nse **Glorious Empire (IRE)**[64] 4152 5-8-6 0............................. AlanGarcia 1 94
(Ed Walker) *racd in fnl trio: rdn and short-lived effrt wl over 1 1/2f out: sn no further imp: one pce fnl f* **43/5**
6 4 ¼ **Goodoldhockeygame (CAN)**[50] 4-8-6 0.................(b) GaryBoulanger 5 80
(Robert Tiller, Canada) **25/1**
7 ½ **Seffeara (CAN)**[673] 4-8-6 0.................................(b) Emma-JayneWilson 6 78
(Steve Owens, Canada) **32/1**

1m 8.79s (68.79) **7 Ran SP% 118.0**

Owner Bruce Lunsford **Bred** W Bruce Lunsford **Trained** Canada

[5456]LES LANDES
Sunday, September 11

OFFICIAL GOING: Turf: good to firm
Wind: Moderate, half behind away from stand Weather: Sunny and warm

6401a MILLBROOK SUMMER H'CAP SPRINT **7f**
2:30 (2:30) 3-Y-O+ **£1,780** (£640; £380)

RPR
1 **Mendacious Harpy (IRE)**[28] 5457 5-10-1 0............(p) MarcGoldstein 4 57
(George Baker) *trckd ldrs: c to stand side rail to chal 2f out: led 1f out: easily* **1/2**[1]
2 7 **Country Blue (FR)**[13] 7-10-12 0...............................(p) MattieBatchelor 3 49
(Mrs A Malzard, Jersey) *led: rdn and c stand side 2f out: hdd 1f out: no ex* **5/1**[3]
3 3 **Brown Velvet**[13] 4-8-11 0..(p) AndrewElliott 2 12
(K Kukk, Jersey) *chsd ldrs thrght: btn over 1f out* **9/1**
4 3 **Ocean Crystal**[13] 4-8-9 0... JemmaMarshall 6 2
(Mrs A Malzard, Jersey) *a bhd: btn 2f out* **9/1**
5 nk **First Cat**[13] 9-9-1 0..(p) PhilipPrince 5 7
(K Kukk, Jersey) *chsd ldrs: btn over 1f out: wknd fnl f* **11/4**[2]

Owner On The Game Partnership **Bred** Val & Angela Leeson **Trained** Manton, Wilts

6402a HUMBER RACING & BLOODSTOCK H'CAP **1m 100y**
3:05 (3:05) 3-Y-O+ **£1,780** (£640; £380)

RPR
1 **Black Night (IRE)**[72] 3918 4-10-12 0.................................. PhilipPrince 6 80
(J Moon, Jersey) *led tl 7f out then cl 2nd tl shkn up to ld again wl over 2f out: impressive* **3/1**[2]
2 4 **Aqua Ardens (GER)**[17] 5793 8-10-2 0...................(p) MattieBatchelor 2 61
(George Baker) *hld up: wnt 2nd over 2f out: kpt on: no ch w wnr* **1/2**[1]
3 6 **Benoordenhout (IRE)**[13] 5-9-0 0....................................... AndrewElliott 4 32
(T Le Brocq, Jersey) *t.k.h: trckd ldrs: kpt on one pce fr 2f out* **4/1**[3]
4 3 **Fast Freddie**[13] 12-8-5 0 oh20...(p) NoraLooby 5 16
(Mrs A Corson, Jersey) *t.k.h: led 7f out tl wl over 2f out: sn wknd* **9/1**
5 26 **Rebel Woman**[13] 10-8-5 0 oh43.....................................(v) MissMHooper 1
(Mrs A Corson, Jersey) *hld up: briefly wnt 3rd over 4f out: wknd 3f out* **25/1**

Owner Mrs Anne Moon **Bred** Manister House Stud **Trained** St-Martin, Jersey

6403a WILLIAM HILL H'CAP **1m 6f**
4:50 (4:50) 3-Y-O+ **£1,780** (£640; £380)

RPR
1 **Flutterbee**[28] 5458 4-10-12 0..(p) MattieBatchelor 3 69
(George Baker) *trckd ldrs: smooth hdwy to ld wl over 2f out: rdn clr* **4/11**[1]
2 7 **Bowl Imperior**[13] 5459 4-9-8 0... JemmaMarshall 4 41
(Mrs A Malzard, Jersey) *led tl wl over 2f out: kpt on one pce* **5/2**[2]
3 3 **Blue Sea Of Ibrox (IRE)**[13] 8-9-11 0...................................... NoraLooby 2 40
(Mrs A Corson, Jersey) *cl 2nd tl rdn and wknd fr 3f out* **7/1**[3]
P **Granit Man (FR)**[72] 4183 10-8-7 0 oh11 ow2.................. EleysaWilford 1
(J Moon, Jersey) *trckd ldrs for 5f: sddle slipped and p.u 5f out* **12/1**

Owner PJL Racing **Bred** Mill House Stud **Trained** Manton, Wilts

[6182]BRIGHTON (L-H)
Monday, September 12

OFFICIAL GOING: Good (good to soft in places; 8.4)
Wind: Fresh, against Weather: Fine and warm

6404 CALL STAR SPORTS ON 08000 521 321 MAIDEN AUCTION STKS **6f 209y**
1:50 (1:50) (Class 6) 2-Y-O **£2,264** (£673; £336; £168) **Stalls** Low

Form RPR
2220 1 **Bayston Hill**[24] 5594 2-9-1 69... DanielMuscutt 3 70
(Mark Usher) *t.k.h in 3rd: chsd ldr 3f out: led 1f out: drvn out* **7/2**[2]
0 2 shd **Otomo**[86] 3404 2-8-12 0.. WilliamTwiston-Davies 8 67
(Philip Hide) *led tl 1f out: hrd rdn: rallied wl* **20/1**
2 3 2 ¼ **Peloton**[15] 5922 2-8-6 0.. KieranO'Neill 9 55
(Pat Phelan) *dwlt: t.k.h in 4th: hrd rdn over 1f out: styd on* **5/1**
4 3 **Dancing Dragon (IRE)** 2-8-9 0... SteveDrowne 5 50
(George Baker) *pushed along towards rr tl styd on u.p fnl 2f* **9/1**
5 nk **Red Sniper (IRE)** 2-8-8 0.. MichaelJMMurphy 2 48
(Peter Chapple-Hyam) *dwlt: towards rr: rdn over 2f out: styd on fnl f* **3/1**[1]
046 6 ½ **Winning Bid**[54] 4523 2-9-0 68... JimCrowley 1 52
(Harry Dunlop) *chsd ldr tl 3f out: hrd rdn and wknd over 1f out* **9/2**[3]
40 7 hd **Pitch High (IRE)**[48] 4738 2-8-11 0.................................... AaronJones(3) 6 52
(Julia Feilden) *in tch: rdn 3f out: outpcd fnl 2f* **13/2**
00 8 8 **Cheers All Round**[12] 6035 2-8-7 0 ow1.......................... SamHitchcott 7 23
(Henry Spiller) *mid-div: rdn over 2f out: sn wknd* **20/1**
9 9 **Myhorsewithnoname (IRE)** 2-8-8 0........................ HectorCrouch(5) 4 5
(Natalie Lloyd-Beavis) *outpcd: a bhd* **66/1**

1m 23.64s (0.54) **Going Correction** -0.125s/f (Firm) **9 Ran SP% 116.4**
Speed ratings (Par 93): **91,90,88,84,84 83,83,74,64**
CSF £71.61 TOTE £3.50: £1.10, £8.20, £2.00; EX 66.60 Trifecta £326.80.
Owner High Five Racing and Partners **Bred** Selwood Bloodstock & Mrs S Read **Trained** Upper Lambourn, Berks

FOCUS
Drying ground but it was still officially on the soft side; good, good to soft in places. The rail was out between 6f & 3.5f, adding 3yds to each race distance. A modest 2yo maiden to start.

6405 GO SPORTING TICKETS & HOSPITALITY CONCIERGE APPRENTICE (S) H'CAP — 1m 1f 209y
2:20 (2:20) (Class 6) (0-60,60) 3-Y-O+ **£2,264** (£673; £336; £168) **Stalls** High

Form RPR
136 **1** **Becca Campbell (IRE)**[15] 5923 3-9-4 **57**...................(p) SophieKilloran 7 68
(Eve Johnson Houghton) *towards rr: hdwy 2f out: edgd lft and led over 1f out: sn clr* **3/1**[1]
4434 **2** 5 **Harry's Endeavour**[15] 5923 3-9-4 **57**...........................(b) GeorgeWood 4 58
(Daniel Kubler) *led for 1f: w ldrs tl outpcd by wnr fnl f* **3/1**[1]
533 **3** 2 1/4 **Maverik**[15] 5929 8-10-0 **60**..(vt[1]) MitchGodwin 5 57
(Ali Stronge) *s.s: plld hrd: hdwy to ld after 1f: hdd over 2f out: n.m.r over 1f out: no ex* **8/1**[3]
2460 **4** 1/2 **Elle Rebelle**[9] 6143 6-9-3 **49**... HollieDoyle 6 45
(Mark Brisbourne) *s.s: bhd tl rdn and r.o fnl 2f* **10/1**
014 **5** 1/2 **No No Cardinal (IRE)**[25] 5572 7-9-4 **50**.......................... KevinLundie 8 45
(Mark Gillard) *plld hrd: trckd ldrs: led over 2f out: hung lft and hdd over 1f out: wknd fnl f* **14/1**
3055 **6** 1 1/4 **Music Hall (FR)**[23] 5630 6-8-11 **46** oh1......................... MillyNaseb(3) 10 38
(Shaun Harris) *chsd ldrs tl wknd over 1f out* **16/1**
3002 **7** 6 **Ramblow**[34] 5263 3-9-6 **59**... GeorgiaCox 1 40
(William Haggas) *mid-div: hdwy and in tch whn nt clr run over 1f out: wknd fnl f* **7/2**[2]
500/ **8** 1 3/4 **Super Duplex**[702] 7115 9-9-0 **46** oh1..............................(t) RhiainIngram 3 24
(David Arbuthnot) *chsd ldrs tl outpcd 3f out* **25/1**
60-0 **9** 7 **Satin And Lace (IRE)**[233] 316 4-9-6 **55**...................... JaneElliott(3) 11 19
(Michael Madgwick) *a bhd* **66/1**
0040 **10** 8 **Capital Gearing**[95] 3080 3-9-4 **57**..................................... LuluStanford 9 6
(Henry Spiller) *towards rr: rdn 3f out: sn wl bhd* **20/1**

2m 3.29s (-0.31) **Going Correction** -0.125s/f (Firm)
WFA 3 from 4yo+ 7lb **10** Ran SP% **115.1**
Speed ratings (Par 101): **96,92,90,89,89 88,83,82,76,70**
CSF £11.51 CT £63.73 TOTE £3.60: £1.20, £1.70, £3.00; EX 13.00 Trifecta £64.00.The winner was bought in for 4,600gns.
Owner Miss E Johnson Houghton **Bred** Lynn Lodge Stud **Trained** Blewbury, Oxon
■ Stewards' Enquiry : Kevin Lundie caution: careless riding

FOCUS
This was run over 3yds further than advertised. A selling handicap and the apprentice jockeys were of limited experience, so not form to dwell on. The pace was steady through the first furlong or so, before it really picked up. The level is hard to pin down, but it's been rated a shade negatively.

6406 BIBBY FINANCIAL SERVICES REDHILL H'CAP — 1m 3f 196y
2:55 (2:55) (Class 6) (0-55,61) 3-Y-O+ **£2,587** (£770; £384; £192) **Stalls** High

Form RPR
3014 **1** **Stynes (IRE)**[19] 2634 6-9-4 **52**.......................................(t) RobHornby(3) 6 61+
(Graeme McPherson) *covered up towards rr: fnd room and hdwy over 2f out: led over 1f out: sn clr: easily* **7/1**
0350 **2** 5 **Galuppi**[34] 5261 5-9-7 **55**..(v) AlistairRawlinson(3) 4 56
(J R Jenkins) *dwlt: towards rr: hdwy and hung lft u.p 2f out: chsd wnr fnl f: no imp* **33/1**
4-63 **3** 1/2 **Cranwell**[12] 6020 4-9-9 **54**.. PatCosgrave 8 54
(George Baker) *prom: led 2f out tl over 1f out: sn outpcd by wnr* **5/1**[2]
2434 **4** hd **Megalala (IRE)**[16] 5895 15-9-4 **52**................................ AaronJones(3) 10 52
(John Bridger) *led: hrd rdn and hdd 2f out: kpt on gamely* **14/1**
0335 **5** nk **Princess Zoffany (IRE)**[17] 5824 3-8-10 **50**..................... KieranO'Neill 5 49
(Jimmy Fox) *towards rr: hdwy 2f out: no imp fnl f* **6/1**[3]
6545 **6** 1/2 **Sakhra**[18] 5805 5-9-1 **46** oh1.. RobertWinston 9 45
(Mark Brisbourne) *s.s: bhd tl styd on u.p fnl 2f* **66/1**
4506 **7** nk **Mystical Maze**[21] 5708 5-8-10 **46** oh1............................ HollieDoyle(5) 2 44
(Mark Brisbourne) *s.s: bhd: hdwy 2f out: carried lft over 1f out: no ex* **100/1**
4413 **8** 1 3/4 **Sexy Secret**[20] 5739 5-9-7 **55**..................................(p) SimonPearce(3) 11 50
(Lydia Pearce) *chsd ldr tl over 2f out: sn outpcd* **12/1**
3541 **9** 2 1/4 **Buteo Bai (IRE)**[7] 6185 3-9-7 **61** 6ex.............................. JimCrowley 3 53
(Lucy Wadham) *chsd ldrs tl outpcd 2f out* **11/8**[1]
0-03 **10** 1 3/4 **Aspasius (GER)**[41] 4993 4-9-2 **52**............................... HectorCrouch(5) 1 46
(Gary Moore) *t.k.h: trckd ldrs: hrd rdn 2f out: btn whn short of room on inner over 1f out* **11/1**
-000 **11** 3 3/4 **Rod Of Iron**[19] 5777 3-8-8 **48**.. DanielMuscutt 7 31
(Michael Madgwick) *dwlt: t.k.h: sn chsng ldrs: wknd over 2f out* **16/1**
/0-2 **12** 2 1/4 **Too Many Diamonds (IRE)**[24] 5457 5-9-2 **47**.........(tp) SteveDrowne 12 26
(Clare Ellam) *mid-div: wknd 3f out: bhd and eased fnl f* **66/1**

2m 32.97s (0.27) **Going Correction** -0.125s/f (Firm)
WFA 3 from 4yo+ 9lb **12** Ran SP% **121.0**
Speed ratings (Par 101): **94,90,90,90,90 89,89,88,86,85 83,81**
CSF £220.79 CT £1269.58 TOTE £9.60: £2.60, £9.70, £2.30; EX 257.80 Trifecta £2229.30.
Owner EPDS Racing Partnership 18 **Bred** K & D McCormack **Trained** Upper Oddington, Gloucs
■ Stewards' Enquiry : Alistair Rawlinson two-day ban: careless riding (Sep 26-27)

FOCUS
This was run over 3yds further than advertised. Straightforward low-grade handicap form.

6407 KEW ELECTRICAL BRIGHTON H'CAP — 7f 214y
3:30 (3:31) (Class 6) (0-60,60) 3-Y-O+ **£2,264** (£673; £336; £168) **Stalls** Low

Form RPR
4042 **1** **Bloodsweatandtears**[76] 3739 8-9-10 **60**............................ AmirQuinn 3 69
(William Knight) *dwlt: hld up towards rr: hdwy on outer 1/2-way: rdn and hung lft fnl 2f: r.o to ld fnl 50yds* **14/1**
4141 **2** 3/4 **Admirable Art (IRE)**[69] 3973 6-9-1 **54**...............(p) GeorgeDowning(3) 14 61
(Tony Carroll) *led tl over 1f out: kpt on wl fnl f* **9/1**
2403 **3** hd **Bazzat (IRE)**[7] 6187 3-8-5 **49** ow2..................................(p) TimClark(3) 10 55
(John Ryan) *trckd ldrs: drvn to ld ins fnl f: hdd and jst outpcd fnl 50yds* **6/1**[2]
4306 **4** 1 1/2 **Zlatan (IRE)**[21] 5720 3-9-2 **57**...(p) PatCosgrave 7 59
(Ed de Giles) *mid-div: hdwy 2f out: led over 1f out tl ins fnl f: one pce* **8/1**[3]
6-03 **5** 1/2 **Sweet Dream Lady (IRE)**[15] 5923 3-8-10 **56**.......... HectorCrouch(5) 12 57
(Gary Moore) *mid-div: nt clr run 2f out: swtchd to centre and effrt over 1f out: styd on wl fnl f* **9/1**
6005 **6** hd **Hawk Moth (IRE)**[7] 6188 8-9-9 **59**................(b) WilliamTwiston-Davies 2 61
(John Spearing) *dwlt: towards rr: n.m.r and hdwy over 1f out: styd on* **25/1**
0644 **7** 2 **The Greedy Boy**[7] 6187 3-8-8 **49**..................................... SamHitchcott 6 45
(Mick Channon) *towards rr: rdn and hdwy on inner 2f out: no ex fnl f* **11/1**
4653 **8** 1 3/4 **Pivotal Dream (IRE)**[21] 5710 3-8-1 **47**........................... HollieDoyle(5) 1 39
(Mark Brisbourne) *bhd: sme hdwy over 1f out: nvr able to chal* **12/1**
0450 **9** 1 **Corella (IRE)**[14] 5953 3-8-12 **53**......................................(b[1]) JohnFahy 11 43
(Clive Cox) *dwlt: sn chsng ldrs: drvn along and wknd 2f out* **20/1**
2434 **10** 1 **Funny Oyster (IRE)**[35] 5235 3-9-3 **58**........................(p) RobertWinston 5 51
(George Baker) *trckd ldrs tl wknd 2f out: eased whn wl btn ins fnl f* **5/1**[1]
5222 **11** 8 **Wild Flower (IRE)**[14] 5954 4-9-2 **52**...............................(p) KieranO'Neill 8 22
(Jimmy Fox) *t.k.h: mid-div tl wknd over 2f out* **8/1**[3]
463 **12** 7 **Toffee Apple (IRE)**[13] 6004 3-9-3 **58**.............................. JimCrowley 13 11
(Keith Dalgleish) *chsd ldr tl wknd over 2f out* **5/1**[1]

1m 34.29s (-1.71) **Going Correction** -0.125s/f (Firm)
WFA 3 from 4yo+ 5lb **12** Ran SP% **121.1**
Speed ratings (Par 101): **103,102,102,100,100 99,97,96,95,94 86,79**
CSF £137.33 CT £864.39 TOTE £11.40: £4.00, £3.30, £1.90; EX 67.80 Trifecta £905.90.
Owner Canisbay Bloodstock **Bred** Oakhill Stud **Trained** Patching, W Sussex

FOCUS
This was run over 3yds further than advertised. Another moderate handicap. Straightforward form in behind the winner.

6408 STARSPORTSBET.CO.UK H'CAP — 6f 209y
4:00 (4:00) (Class 6) (0-65,65) 3-Y-O+ **£2,587** (£770; £384; £192) **Stalls** Low

Form RPR
4-46 **1** **Bobby Benton (IRE)**[51] 4656 5-9-10 **65**........... WilliamTwiston-Davies 8 73
(Jim Best) *prom: led in centre 2f out: edgd lft: rdn out* **14/1**
4024 **2** 1 3/4 **Unnoticed**[20] 5736 4-9-10 **65**..(p) PatCosgrave 7 68
(Luca Cumani) *chsd ldrs: wnt cl 2nd over 1f out: unable qck ins fnl f* **11/4**[1]
0536 **3** 3/4 **Naziba (IRE)**[15] 5935 3-9-3 **62**... JimCrowley 11 61
(David Menuisier) *mid-div: hdwy over 1f out: styd on fnl f* **13/2**[3]
4360 **4** 1/2 **Port Lairge**[21] 5711 6-9-5 **60**................................(v) MichaelJMMurphy 6 60+
(John Gallagher) *dwlt: bhd tl styd on wl fnl 2f* **10/1**
1446 **5** 1 **Hamish McGonagain**[14] 5954 3-8-11 **61**...............(p) DavidParkes(5) 10 56
(Jeremy Gask) *disp ld tl 2f out: no ex fnl f* **12/1**
04 **6** 1 1/4 **The Special One (IRE)**[39] 5088 3-9-0 **59**............................. JohnFahy 1 51
(Clive Cox) *mid-div: outpcd over 2f out: styd on fnl f* **10/1**
015 **7** shd **Monsieur Valentine**[21] 5711 4-9-2 **62**........................ GeorgiaCox(5) 12 56
(Tony Carroll) *bhd: rdn over 2f out: sme late hdwy* **15/2**
6000 **8** 2 **Malvesi**[35] 5235 7-8-7 **51** oh6... NoelGarbutt(3) 4 39
(Daniel Mark Loughnane) *pushed along to chse ldrs: rdn 3f out: btn 2f out* **100/1**
0045 **9** 1 3/4 **Bingo George (IRE)**[7] 6184 3-9-0 **62**........................... RobHornby(3) 9 43
(Andrew Balding) *a in similar position: n.d fnl 2f* **9/2**[2]
-455 **10** 1 3/4 **Hereward The Wake**[33] 5288 3-9-0 **64**........................ MitchGodwin(5) 2 41
(Sylvester Kirk) *mid-div tl outpcd fnl 2f* **20/1**
2006 **11** 3/4 **Chandresh**[23] 5626 3-8-7 **52**... KieranO'Neill 3 27
(Robert Cowell) *mid-div: drvn along over 2f out: sn wknd* **20/1**
-000 **12** 3/4 **Secret Bird (IRE)**[84] 3469 4-9-2 **57**..............................[1] RobertWinston 5 32
(Dean Ivory) *disp ld tl 2f out: wknd over 1f out* **20/1**

1m 21.86s (-1.24) **Going Correction** -0.125s/f (Firm)
WFA 3 from 4yo+ 4lb **12** Ran SP% **117.8**
Speed ratings (Par 101): **102,100,99,98,97 96,95,93,91,89 88,87**
CSF £49.80 CT £285.05 TOTE £17.10: £4.90, £1.50, £2.40; EX 77.50 Trifecta £536.70.
Owner A Achilleous **Bred** Old Carhue & Graeng Bloodstock **Trained** Lewes, E Sussex

FOCUS
This was run over 3yds further than advertised. A modest race contested by some hard-to-win-with types.

6409 FOLLOW US ON TWITTER @STARSPORTS_BET H'CAP — 5f 213y
4:30 (4:30) (Class 4) (0-80,80) 3-Y-O+ **£4,690** (£1,395; £697; £348) **Stalls** Low

Form RPR
3142 **1** **Upstaging**[13] 6000 4-9-7 **80**...[1] JimCrowley 9 87
(Paul Cole) *sn prom: led 1f out: rdn out* **2/1**[1]
3320 **2** 1 **Gorokai (IRE)**[46] 4803 3-9-1 **76**......................... WilliamTwiston-Davies 1 80
(David Simcock) *t.k.h in 6th: hdwy over 1f out: r.o to take 2nd nr fin* **4/1**[3]
1123 **3** hd **Soaring Spirits (IRE)**[7] 6184 6-9-2 **75**.....................(b) RobertWinston 8 78
(Dean Ivory) *led tl 1f out: kpt on u.p* **11/4**[2]
1301 **4** 1 **Pandar**[19] 5773 7-9-7 **80**... PatCosgrave 6 80
(Michael Attwater) *chsd ldrs: effrt 2f out: one pce fnl f* **12/1**
-140 **5** 1/2 **Ebony N Ivory**[14] 5978 3-8-11 **77**..................................... GeorgiaCox(5) 2 76
(Archie Watson) *t.k.h: trckd ldrs: hrd rdn over 1f out: one pce* **8/1**
02 **6** hd **Art Collection (FR)**[61] 4268 3-9-0 **80**........................(v[1]) HectorCrouch(5) 4 78
(Gary Moore) *hld up in 5th: hrd rdn 2f out: hung bdly lft: no imp* **12/1**
04-0 **7** 4 1/2 **Princess Kodia (IRE)**[10] 6079 3-8-11 **79**....................... JordanUys(7) 3 63
(Brian Meehan) *a last: n.d fnl 2f* **16/1**

1m 9.53s (-0.67) **Going Correction** -0.125s/f (Firm)
WFA 3 from 4yo+ 2lb **7** Ran SP% **112.4**
Speed ratings (Par 105): **99,97,97,96,95 95,89**
CSF £9.92 CT £20.79 TOTE £3.00: £1.80, £2.00; EX 11.40 Trifecta £28.70.
Owner H R H Sultan Ahmad Shah **Bred** Glebe Stud **Trained** Whatcombe, Oxon

FOCUS
This was run over 3yds further than advertised. A fair sprint handicap. Pretty ordinary form, with the winner to a small pb, and the form set by the second, third and fourth.

6410 STARSPREADS.COM H'CAP — 5f 59y
5:05 (5:05) (Class 5) (0-70,70) 3-Y-O+ **£2,911** (£866; £432; £216) **Stalls** Low

Form RPR
4314 **1** **Noble Act**[20] 5751 3-9-4 **68**... JimCrowley 2 74
(Rae Guest) *mde all: hld on wl fnl f* **3/1**[2]
2402 **2** nk **Time Medicean**[21] 5706 10-8-8 **60**......................... GeorgeDowning(3) 6 65
(Tony Carroll) *sltly outpcd in 5th: hdwy over 1f out: r.o wl fnl f: clsng at fin* **5/1**
5300 **3** 1/2 **Welease Bwian (IRE)**[22] 5679 7-9-0 **70**........................(v) MillyNaseb(7) 3 73+
(Stuart Williams) *rrd s and lost 8 l: wl bhd tl gd late hdwy* **9/2**[3]
0223 **4** 1 **Indian Tinker**[20] 5751 7-9-4 **67**......................................(v) PatCosgrave 5 67
(Robert Cowell) *prom: pressed wnr 2f out tl one pce ins fnl f* **2/1**[1]
6266 **5** 1/2 **Whitecrest**[12] 6017 8-9-5 **68**............................. WilliamTwiston-Davies 7 66
(John Spearing) *chsd ldrs: rdn over 2f out: styd on fnl f* **12/1**
1500 **6** 2 1/4 **Monsieur Jamie**[58] 4389 8-9-0 **63**...............................(v) SamHitchcott 4 53
(J R Jenkins) *chsd wnr tl 2f out: btn over 1f out* **33/1**
1005 **7** 19 **Storm Lightning**[18] 5807 7-9-0 **63**.................................... KieranO'Neill 1
(Mark Brisbourne) *missed break and lost 10 l: a wl bhd* **12/1**

1m 2.05s (-0.25) **Going Correction** -0.125s/f (Firm)
WFA 3 from 7yo+ 1lb **7** Ran SP% **111.5**
Speed ratings (Par 103): **97,96,95,94,93 89,59**
CSF £17.33 TOTE £3.50: £2.10, £3.00; EX 12.90 Trifecta £76.20.
Owner C J Murfitt **Bred** Pantile Stud **Trained** Newmarket, Suffolk

FOCUS
This was run over 3yds further than advertised. This wasn't much of a race, with the 2nd and 4th winless since 2014, and the 3rd and 7th losing many lengths at the start. The runner-up helps set the standard, with the third close to his old turf best.
T/Plt: £138.00 to a £1 stake. Pool: £68961.21, 364.65 winning units T/Qpdt: £30.00 to a £1 stke. Pool: £4563.11, 112.4 winning units **Lee McKenzie**

6235 KEMPTON (A.W) (R-H)
Monday, September 12

OFFICIAL GOING: Polytrack: standard to slow
Wind: Moderate, half behind Weather: Fine, very warm

6411 APOLLOBET NEW WEBSITE H'CAP — 1m 3f (P)
2:00 (2:01) (Class 6) (0-60,60) 3-Y-O+ — **£2,264** (£673; £336; £168) — **Stalls** Low

Form — RPR

3003 **1** **Overlord**[9] 6143 4-9-5 **53**....(v) TomMarquand 5 — 61
(Mark Rimell) *settled in rr and last after 4f: pushed along 4f out: looked to be struggling 3f out: rapid prog on inner over 2f out to ld over 1f out: drvn and hld on nr fin* **8/1**[3]

6410 **2** *nk* **Iballisticvin**[23] 5625 3-8-5 **50**.... NoelGarbutt(3) 10 — 58
(Gary Moore) *trckd ldrs: rdn 3f out: prog to ld 2f out: hdd over 1f out: rallied last 100yds: jst hld* **11/2**[1]

1401 **3** *2 ¾* **Eugenic**[12] 6020 5-9-5 **53**.... FrederikTylicki 9 — 56
(Rod Millman) *hld up in midfield: rdn 3f out: prog wl over 1f out: styd on to take 3rd fnl f* **7/1**[2]

2243 **4** *¾* **Theydon Bois**[20] 5737 4-9-7 **55**....(p) JimmyQuinn 7 — 57
(Peter Charalambous) *chsd ldrs: rdn in 6th pl over 3f out: clsd over 2f out: one pce fr over 1f out* **10/1**

00-4 **5** *1 ¼* **Moon Arrow (IRE)**[18] 5811 3-9-2 **58**.... TimmyMurphy 14 — 58
(Michael Blake) *hld up in rr: rdn on outer 3f out: styd on fr over 1f out: n.d* **10/1**

6 *1 ¼* **Pension Madness (IRE)**[82] 3540 3-9-4 **60**.... DaneO'Neill 3 — 58
(Mark Usher) *prom: rdn in 5th over 3f out: clsd on ldrs over 2f out: wknd over 1f out* **33/1**

3506 **7** *1 ¾* **Lions Charge (USA)**[9] 6143 9-9-10 **58**....(tp) DougieCostello 2 — 53
(Richard Hawker) *a in midfield: pushed along by 1/2-way: u.p 4f out: one pce and no prog after* **14/1**

2350 **8** *nk* **Awesome Rock (IRE)**[19] 5777 7-8-12 **46** oh1.... RobertHavlin 4 — 41
(Roger Ingram) *hld up wl in rr: shkn up over 2f out: no real prog: nvr in it* **16/1**

0020 **9** *¾* **Thane Of Cawdor (IRE)**[4] 6243 7-9-12 **60**....(p) GeorgeBaker 11 — 53
(Joseph Tuite) *stdd s: hld up wl in rr: shkn up and no rspnse wl over 2f out* **9/1**

0015 **10** *2* **Salient**[22] 5672 12-9-5 **56**.... EdwardGreatrex(3) 8 — 46+
(Michael Attwater) *awkward s but led 2f: pressed ldr: rdn to ld over 3f out to 2f out: sn wknd* **16/1**

1004 **11** *1 ¼* **Munsarim (IRE)**[26] 5547 9-9-9 **57**....(b) KierenFox 13 — 45
(Lee Carter) *slowly away and rousted along early in last: rdn and making sme prog but nt looking enthusiastic whn nt clr run wl over 1f out: no hdwy after* **12/1**

0000 **12** *6* **Several (USA)**[105] 1182 4-9-6 **54**.... RyanPowell 1 — 33+
(Kevin Frost) *led after 2f to over 3f out: wknd qckly over 2f out* **40/1**

-456 **13** *shd* **Rennie Mackintosh (IRE)**[229] 348 4-9-8 **56**.... DannyBrock 6 — 34+
(John Bridger) *prom: chsd ldng pair after 5f to wl over 2f out: wknd qckly* **11/2**[1]

3225 **14** *11* **Whip Up A Frenzy (IRE)**[76] 3737 4-9-6 **54**.... AdamBeschizza 12 — 15
(Richard Rowe) *a wl in rr: wd bnd 9f out: wknd 3f out: t.o* **20/1**

2m 20.72s (-1.18) **Going Correction** -0.05s/f (Stan) — **14** Ran SP% **118.8**
WFA 3 from 4yo+ 8lb
Speed ratings (Par 101): **102,101,99,99,98 97,96,95,95,93 93,88,88,80**
CSF £49.81 CT £329.21 TOTE £9.60: £2.80, £2.60, £1.90; EX 70.70 Trifecta £684.90.
Owner Jack Henley **Bred** Cheveley Park Stud Ltd **Trained** Leafield, Oxon

FOCUS
The winner came from last to first in this moderate handicap. The winner has been rated to his previous winning level.

6412 APOLLOBET ONLINE CASINO & GAMES NURSERY H'CAP — 7f (P)
2:35 (2:36) (Class 6) (0-60,60) 2-Y-O — **£2,264** (£673; £336; £168) — **Stalls** Low

Form — RPR

050 **1** **Dragon Dream (IRE)**[19] 5772 2-8-9 **48**.... KierenFox 1 — 52
(Roger Ingram) *sn pushed along: chsd ldng pair to 1/2-way: drvn after: rallied on inner over 2f out: led jst over 1f out: kpt on u.p* **25/1**

0502 **2** *1* **Wentwell Yesterday (IRE)**[22] 5675 2-9-4 **57**.... WilliamCarson 14 — 61
(Jamie Osborne) *in tch in midfield: hmpd over 2f out: renewed effrt over 1f out: r.o fnl f to take 2nd last strides* **6/1**[3]

004 **3** *nk* **Ultimat Power (IRE)**[15] 5922 2-8-7 **46** ow1....(b[1]) AdamBeschizza 4 — 46
(Mark Hoad) *chsd ldrs: cl up over 2f out but hrd rdn: chsd wnr ins fnl f: no imp and lost 2nd last strides* **66/1**

0050 **4** *nk* **Sadierosesclifford (IRE)**[16] 5876 2-8-12 **58**.... CliffordLee(7) 3 — 57
(Denis Quinn) *w ldr: rdn to ld 2f out: hdd jst over 1f out: one pce and lost 2 pls ins fnl f* **5/1**[2]

6005 **5** *¾* **Heavenly Cry**[11] 6045 2-8-11 **50**....(b[1]) DannyBrock 5 — 47
(Phil McEntee) *dwlt: sn in midfield: rdn and swtchd lft 2f out: styd on fr over 1f out: nrst fin but nvr able to threaten* **33/1**

024 **6** *hd* **Acertwo**[27] 5511 2-9-7 **60**.... JFEgan 10 — 57
(Joseph Tuite) *racd wd in midfield: rdn on outer over 2f out: tried to cl over 1f out: one pce fnl f* **10/1**

600 **7** *¾* **Topmeup**[35] 5242 2-9-1 **54**.... FMBerry 12 — 49
(Stuart Edmunds) *sn in rr: drvn on inner over 2f out: kpt on one pce over 1f out: no ch* **16/1**

033 **8** *½* **Hazell Berry (IRE)**[21] 5719 2-8-11 **50**.... RobertHavlin 2 — 43
(David Evans) *mde most to 2f out: steadily wknd* **9/2**[1]

005 **9** *nk* **Henry Did It (IRE)**[19] 5764 2-9-7 **60**.... JimmyFortune 13 — 53
(Tony Carroll) *dropped in fr wd draw and hld up in last: shkn up over 2f out: taken out wd and rdn over 1f out: plugged on fnl f* **8/1**

3020 **10** *1* **Swan Serenade**[27] 5511 2-9-5 **58**.... RyanTate 6 — 48
(Jonathan Portman) *prom: chsd ldng pair over 3f out to over 2f out: wknd* **25/1**

0030 **11** *1 ¾* **Varun's Bride (IRE)**[5] 6236 2-9-5 **58**.... TomMarquand 7 — 43
(Richard Hannon) *prom: rdn 3f out: steadily wknd fr 2f out* **7/1**

2546 **12** *3 ¾* **Born To Please**[21] 5719 2-8-12 **56**.... PaddyPilley(5) 8 — 31
(Mark Usher) *a towards rr: drvn and no prog over 2f out* **16/1**

054 **13** *6* **Lemon Drop**[19] 5771 2-9-6 **59**.... AdamKirby 11 — 18
(Jim Boyle) *racd wd in rr: bhd 3f out: t.o* **6/1**[3]

000 **14** *½* **Twaddle**[15] 5930 2-8-6 **45**.... RyanPowell 9 — 3
(Alan Coogan) *sn struggling in rr: t.o* **100/1**

1m 26.98s (0.98) **Going Correction** -0.05s/f (Stan) — **14** Ran SP% **121.0**
Speed ratings (Par 93): **92,90,90,90,89 89,88,87,87,86 84,79,73,72**
CSF £165.52 CT £9768.75 TOTE £28.40: £8.50, £2.50, £10.40; EX 274.00.
Owner Drag On Funds **Bred** Pier House Stud **Trained** Epsom, Surrey
■ Stewards' Enquiry : Adam Beschizza caution: careless riding

FOCUS
A wide-open looking nursery and predictably it saw a tight finish. Ordinary form.

6413 APOLLOBET RACING REFUNDS/BRITISH STALLION STUDS EBF MAIDEN FILLIES' STKS (PLUS 10 RACE) (DIV I) — 7f (P)
3:10 (3:13) (Class 5) 2-Y-O — **£3,234** (£962; £481; £240) — **Stalls** Low

Form — RPR

4 **1** **Pichola Dance (IRE)**[65] 4147 2-9-0 0.... AndreaAtzeni 5 — 77
(Roger Varian) *a ldng trio: stoked up firmly to ld jst over 2f out: nrly 2 l clr over 1f out: pressed fnl f: kpt on wl last 100yds* **9/2**[2]

2 *¾* **Dubai Dunes** 2-9-0 0.... JamesDoyle 1 — 75+
(Saeed bin Suroor) *trckd ldrs: rdn: swtchd lft and prog 2f out: tk 2nd 1f out and looked a threat: styd on but no imp last 100yds* **6/4**[1]

3 *¾* **Ghadaayer (IRE)** 2-9-0 0.... DaneO'Neill 7 — 73+
(Sir Michael Stoute) *in tch: rdn on outer 2f out: prog over 1f out: tk 3rd fnl f: styd on but nvr able to chal* **6/1**[3]

4 *1* **Star Of Bristol (USA)** 2-9-0 0.... FMBerry 3 — 70+
(Richard Hughes) *in tch but towards rr: prog over 2f out: chsd ldrs over 1f out: kpt on same pce fnl f* **14/1**

00 **5** *1 ½* **Seyasah (IRE)**[47] 4759 2-9-0 0.... TedDurcan 10 — 66
(Chris Wall) *taken steadily towards rr: pushed along over 2f out: sme prog over 1f out: pushed along firmly and tk 5th fnl f: possible improver* **14/1**

0 **6** *2 ¼* **Modhilah (IRE)**[24] 5593 2-9-0 0.... MartinHarley 12 — 60
(Harry Dunlop) *led to jst over 2f out: lost 2nd and wknd 1f out* **25/1**

7 *2 ¾* **Melinoe** 2-9-0 0.... RyanPowell 8 — 53
(Sir Mark Prescott Bt) *slowly away: rn v green and sn virtually t.o in last: nvr a factor but kpt on quite wl fr 2f out* **33/1**

00 **8** *nk* **I Dare To Dream**[21] 5722 2-8-9 0.... CharlieBennett(5) 2 — 52
(Lisa Williamson) *slowly away: wl in rr: rdn over 2f out: nvr a factor but kpt on u.p fnl f* **200/1**

9 *hd* **Seaesta** 2-9-0 0.... FergusSweeney 6 — 51
(Laura Mongan) *difficult to load into stall: nvr beyond midfield: shkn up over 2f out: wknd over 1f out* **25/1**

10 *½* **Moonlight Silver** 2-9-0 0.... DougieCostello 11 — 50
(William Muir) *dwlt: sn chsd ldrs but racd wd: shkn up over 2f out: steadily fdd* **10/1**

0 **11** *hd* **Suraat (IRE)**[109] 2612 2-9-0 0.... RobertHavlin 9 — 49
(George Scott) *restless stalls: pressed ldr to over 2f out: wknd* **8/1**

12 *1* **Delirium (IRE)** 2-9-0 0.... FrederikTylicki 4 — 47
(Ed de Giles) *slowly away: a wl in rr: no prog fnl 2f* **40/1**

1m 26.82s (0.82) **Going Correction** -0.05s/f (Stan) — **12** Ran SP% **119.6**
Speed ratings (Par 92): **93,92,91,90,88 85,82,82,82,81 81,80**
CSF £11.21 TOTE £5.50: £1.50, £1.10, £2.10; EX 13.60 Trifecta £40.30.
Owner Merry Fox Stud Limited **Bred** Merry Fox Stud Limited **Trained** Newmarket, Suffolk

FOCUS
Time may show this to be a fair 2yo fillies' maiden. It's been rated around the race standard.

6414 APOLLOBET RACING REFUNDS/BRITISH STALLION STUDS EBF MAIDEN FILLIES' STKS (PLUS 10 RACE) (DIV II) — 7f (P)
3:45 (3:47) (Class 5) 2-Y-O — **£3,234** (£962; £481; £240) — **Stalls** Low

Form — RPR

5 **1** **Phalaborwa**[31] 5371 2-9-0 0.... FrederikTylicki 6 — 80+
(Ed Vaughan) *mde all: shkn up 2f out: 2 l ahd over 1f out: rdn and kpt on wl fnl f* **11/4**[2]

2 *¾* **Kitty Boo** 2-9-0 0.... AdamKirby 9 — 78+
(Luca Cumani) *in tch in midfield: shkn up and swtchd wd over 2f out: prog over 1f out: rdn to take 2nd last 100yds: clsd on wnr but nvr able to chal* **4/1**[3]

3 *1 ½* **Margherita** 2-9-0 0.... AndreaAtzeni 13 — 74+
(Roger Varian) *chsd wnr to 2f out: rdn and kpt on to dispute 2nd again ins fnl f: one pce last 100yds* **20/1**

4 *½* **First Dance (IRE)** 2-9-0 0.... MartinHarley 11 — 73+
(James Tate) *prom: rdn to chse wnr 2f out: no imp: lost 2nd and fdd ins fnl f* **6/1**

5 *6* **Tremendous (IRE)** 2-9-0 0.... TomMarquand 4 — 56
(Richard Hannon) *settled towards rr: pushed along and sme prog 2f out: tk modest 5th fnl f: n.d but nt disgracd* **25/1**

46 **6** *1* **Ejabah (IRE)**[30] 5395 2-9-0 0.... TedDurcan 7 — 54
(Chris Wall) *chsd ldng pair to over 2f out: wknd qckly* **16/1**

7 *2 ½* **Lady Hester (USA)** 2-9-0 0.... WilliamBuick 10 — 47
(John Gosden) *dwlt: towards rr: shkn up and rn green 3f out: no great prog and nvr a factor* **9/4**[1]

00 **8** *1 ¼* **Sweet Pursuit**[33] 5304 2-9-0 0.... RyanTate 3 — 44
(Rod Millman) *chsd ldrs tl rdn and wknd over 2f out* **50/1**

9 *2 ¼* **Medicean Ballet (IRE)** 2-9-0 0.... FergusSweeney 1 — 37
(Henry Candy) *s.v.s: mostly in last trio and nvr a factor* **33/1**

10 *¾* **Luminous** 2-9-0 0.... RobertHavlin 12 — 35
(Simon Crisford) *dwlt: in tch in midfield tl wknd over 2f out* **16/1**

11 *hd* **Newt** 2-9-0 0.... RyanPowell 8 — 35
(Sir Mark Prescott Bt) *s.i.s: rn v green and a struggling in last trio* **50/1**

12 *3* **Darcey Lou** 2-9-0 0.... KierenFox 5 — 27
(John Best) *dwlt: a in last trio: no ch over 2f out* **50/1**

1m 26.08s (0.08) **Going Correction** -0.05s/f (Stan) — **12** Ran SP% **120.9**
Speed ratings (Par 92): **97,96,94,93,87 85,83,81,79,78 77,74**
CSF £13.55 TOTE £3.70: £1.20, £1.60, £5.40; EX 19.00 Trifecta £242.40.
Owner A E Oppenheimer **Bred** Hascombe And Valiant Studs **Trained** Newmarket, Suffolk
■ Vaudieu (66-1) was withdrawn not under orders. Rule 4 does not apply.

FOCUS
This second division of the fillies' maiden saw a winning time 0.74sec quicker than the first. It's been rated around the race standard.

6415 APOLLOBET MAIDEN STKS — 1m 4f (P)
4:15 (4:17) (Class 5) 3-Y-O+ — **£2,911** (£866; £432; £216) — **Stalls** Centre

Form — RPR

1 **Musaanada** 3-9-0 0.... DaneO'Neill 10 — 74+
(William Haggas) *slowly away and shoved along early: rcvrd to chse ldng quartet after 4f: shkn up over 2f out: prog over 1f out: styd on stoutly fnl f to ld last 50yds* **2/1**[1]

0432 **2** 1 **Satish**[11] 6049 3-9-5 76..........(b) FrankieDettori 1 77
(John Gosden) *sn trckd ldng pair: chal over 2f out: chsd new ldr wl over 1f out: drvn and nrly upsides whn wnr went past 50yds out: tk 2nd again post* **5/2**[2]

2552 **3** shd **Dame Judi (IRE)**[27] 5527 3-9-0 76..........[1] RobertHavlin 4 72
(Simon Crisford) *trckd ldr: rdn to ld 2f out: edgd rt fnl f: hdd last 50yds: lost 2nd post* **10/1**

0-04 **4** 2 **Dostoyevsky (IRE)**[102] 2815 3-9-5 72.......... GeorgeBaker 6 74
(David Lanigan) *led: rdn and hdd 2f out: one pce after* **3/1**[3]

46 **5** 1 **Versant**[11] 6052 4-10-0 0..........(t[1]) MartinHarley 5 72
(Seamus Durack) *awkward and stdd s: hld up towards rr: gng bttr than many over 3f out: prog over 2f out: shkn up wl over 1f out: kpt on one pce after* **14/1**

0-0 **6** 3/4 **Mere Anarchy (IRE)**[21] 5723 5-10-0 0.......... AdamBeschizza 8 71
(Robert Stephens) *trckd ldng trio: shkn up over 2f out: hd quite high and nt qckn over 1f out: one pce* **50/1**

60 **7** 1/2 **High Command (IRE)**[11] 6052 3-9-5 0.......... AndreaAtzeni 9 70+
(Roger Varian) *hld up in 10th: pushed along over 2f out: kpt on steadily after: nrst fin: possible improver* **10/1**

00 **8** 4 **Buckle Street**[28] 5486 3-9-5 0..........[1] TomMarquand 7 64?
(Martin Keighley) *t.k.h early: hld up in midfield: rdn over 2f out: steadily wknd* **100/1**

9 10 **Warranted** 3-9-5 0.......... KierenFox 3 48
(Michael Attwater) *tk keen early but urged along in midfield by 1/2-way: lft bhd fr 3f out* **66/1**

0 **10** 3 3/4 **Mon Petite Etoile (FR)**[192] 814 3-9-0 0.......... FrederikTylicki 11 37
(David Elsworth) *a towards rr: no prog 3f out: wknd over 2f out* **66/1**

11 1/2 **Sting Jet (IRE)**[284] 7-9-7 0..........[1] LamornaBardwell[(7)] 13 41
(Seamus Mullins) *dwlt: mostly in last trio: shkn up over 3f out: no prog* **100/1**

46 **12** 8 **L Stig**[23] 5623 6-9-9 0.......... CiaranMckee[(5)] 12 28
(John O'Shea) *dwlt: a in last trio: lost tch over 3f out: sn bhd* **100/1**

46 **13** 46 **Boru's Brook (IRE)**[17] 5850 8-10-0 0.......... TimmyMurphy 2
(Jim Best) *dwlt: mostly in last: lost tch 4f out: sn t.o* **100/1**

2m 34.1s (-0.40) **Going Correction** -0.05s/f (Stan)
WFA 3 from 4yo+ 9lb 13 Ran SP% **120.7**
Speed ratings (Par 103): **99,98,98,96,96 95,95,92,86,83 83,77,47**
CSF £7.14 TOTE £2.80: £1.30, £1.30, £2.50; EX 8.40 Trifecta £39.00.
Owner Hamdan Al Maktoum **Bred** Windmill Farm Partnership **Trained** Newmarket, Suffolk

FOCUS
Straightforward maiden form. The second and third set the standard but have been rated a bit off. The form looks shaky.

6416 APOLLOBET PREMIER LEAGUE CASHBACK H'CAP 1m (P)
4:45 (4:48) (Class 4) (0-80,80) 3-Y-O+ **£4,690** (£1,395; £697; £348) **Stalls** Low

Form RPR

421 **1** **Finelcity (GER)**[33] 5301 3-9-2 77..........(v) AdamKirby 4 86
(Harry Dunlop) *led 1f: styd prom: chsd ldr 2f out: drvn ahd jst ins fnl f: styd on wl and jst clung on* **11/4**[1]

1612 **2** nse **Reaver (IRE)**[19] 5765 3-9-1 76.......... CharlesBishop 3 85+
(Eve Johnson Houghton) *hld up towards rr: prog and weaved through rival fr 2f out: 2 l down on wnr ins fnl f: r.o wl and clsd gap: jst failed* **7/2**[2]

1565 **3** 3 1/2 **Bank Of Gibraltar**[96] 3035 4-9-9 79.......... FrankieDettori 13 81
(Martin Smith) *led after 1f: drvn 2f out: hdd and outpcd jst ins fnl f: jst hld on for 3rd* **16/1**

6461 **4** hd **Fast Sprite (IRE)**[23] 5635 4-8-13 69.......... KierenFox 12 70
(John Best) *chsd ldrs on outer: rdn 2f out: styd on same pce fnl f and nrly snatched 3rd* **14/1**

1-46 **5** nse **Somethingthrilling**[65] 4160 4-9-3 80.......... JoshuaBryan[(7)] 6 81
(David Elsworth) *in tch on outer: rdn 2f out: kpt on fnl f to press for a pl nr fin* **16/1**

-646 **6** nse **Ataman (IRE)**[68] 4028 4-9-7 77..........[1] JamesDoyle 5 78
(Chris Wall) *mostly in midfield: rdn 2f out: kpt on fr over 1f out: pressed for a pl nr fin* **8/1**

122 **7** 1 1/2 **Tripartite (IRE)**[53] 4563 3-8-12 73.......... FrederikTylicki 7 70
(Jeremy Gask) *chsd ldrs: rdn wl over 2f out: tried to cl over 1f out: fdd ins fnl f* **8/1**

0030 **8** hd **Papou Tony**[17] 5824 3-8-7 68.......... TomMarquand 8 64
(George Baker) *dropped out in last: no ch whn shkn up over 2f out: sme prog over 1f out: nt clr run ins fnl f: plugged on* **16/1**

2206 **9** 1/2 **Great Fun**[18] 5810 5-9-7 77.......... TimmyMurphy 1 73
(Michael Blake) *chsd ldrs: drvn on inner 2f out: no imp over 1f out: fdd fnl f* **25/1**

0340 **10** 2 **Philadelphia (IRE)**[23] 5649 3-9-4 79.......... AndreaAtzeni 11 70
(Roger Varian) *t.k.h: prom: chsd ldr over 4f out to 2f out: wknd* **14/1**

1400 **11** 4 1/2 **Secret Glance**[27] 5507 4-9-2 72.......... AdamBeschizza 2 53
(Richard Rowe) *hld up in last pair: rdn and no prog over 2f out: wknd* **40/1**

015 **12** 54 **Ravens Quest**[46] 4793 3-9-5 80.......... GeorgeBaker 9
(Hughie Morrison) *hld up towards rr: pushed along and no prog over 2f out: sn virtually p.u* **6/1**[3]

1m 38.0s (-1.80) **Going Correction** -0.05s/f (Stan)
WFA 3 from 4yo+ 5lb 12 Ran SP% **122.7**
Speed ratings (Par 105): **107,106,103,103,103 103,101,101,100,98 94,40**
CSF £12.43 CT £136.58 TOTE £4.60: £1.70, £1.40, £4.10; EX 15.20 Trifecta £167.20.
Owner The Blue Bar Partnership **Bred** Gestut Hofgut Heymann **Trained** Lambourn, Berks

FOCUS
This competitive handicap was run at a fair pace and the first pair came clear. The third has been rated close to form.

6417 APOLLOBET BET THROUGH YOUR MOBILE H'CAP 1m 4f (P)
5:15 (5:16) (Class 4) (0-85,85) 3-Y-O **£4,690** (£1,395; £697; £348) **Stalls** Centre

Form RPR

5424 **1** **Sam Missile (IRE)**[11] 6065 3-9-7 85.......... DanielMuscutt 1 96
(James Fanshawe) *hld up in 4th: clsd gng strly over 2f out: led over 1f out but jnd: drvn and styd on wl fnl f: hld on* **4/1**[3]

2231 **2** hd **Stratum**[28] 5486 3-9-6 84.......... FrankieDettori 2 94
(John Gosden) *trckd ldng pair: pushed along over 2f out: rdn to chal and w wnr over 1f out: styd on but jst hld nr fin* **13/8**[1]

5211 **3** 1 3/4 **Rubensian**[5] 6242 3-9-1 79 6ex.......... AndreaAtzeni 3 86
(David Simcock) *sltly awkward s: hld up in last: clsd gng strly over 2f out: drvn over 1f out: styd on to take 3rd fnl f but nt pce of ldng pair* **9/4**[2]

21 **4** 1 3/4 **Scattered Stars**[20] 5742 3-9-1 79.......... WilliamBuick 5 83
(Charlie Appleby) *trckd ldr: led over 2f out: sn shkn up and those bhd travelling bttr: hdd and outpcd over 1f out* **5/1**

6314 **5** 37 **Della Valle (GER)**[41] 4977 3-9-0 78.......... TedDurcan 4 23
(Mike Murphy) *led: rdn and hdd over 2f out: sn wknd: eased fnl f* **50/1**

2m 33.12s (-1.38) **Going Correction** -0.05s/f (Stan) 5 Ran SP% **107.5**
Speed ratings (Par 103): **102,101,100,99,74**
CSF £10.43 TOTE £4.50: £1.80, £1.30; EX 11.20 Trifecta £17.50.
Owner Apple Tree Stud **Bred** Barronstown Stud **Trained** Newmarket, Suffolk

FOCUS
This fair 3yo handicap was unsurprisingly tactical. A pb from the winner, with the runner-up rated as improving as well.

6418 APOLLOBET FREE SIGN-UP BONUS H'CAP 6f (P)
5:45 (5:46) (Class 5) (0-70,70) 3-Y-O+ **£2,911** (£866; £432; £216) **Stalls** Low

Form RPR

-441 **1** **Don't Blame Me**[19] 5769 3-9-4 69.......... AdamKirby 5 77+
(Clive Cox) *pushed up to ld and mde all: rdn 2f out: edgd lft fnl f but drvn out and kpt on gamely* **7/4**[1]

-655 **2** 1 1/4 **Serradura (IRE)**[53] 4556 3-9-2 67.......... TedDurcan 4 71
(Charles Hills) *trckd ldng trio: shkn up 2f out: hanging over 1f out: clsd to take 2nd last 100yds: unable to chal* **14/1**

0003 **3** 1/2 **Kinglami**[10] 6091 7-9-7 70.......... FergusSweeney 2 72
(John O'Shea) *trckd ldng pair: wnt 2nd over 2f out: tried to chal over 1f out: hld after and lost 2nd last 100yds* **4/1**[2]

0-00 **4** nse **Dont Have It Then**[68] 4014 5-9-3 66.......... TimmyMurphy 1 68
(Willie Musson) *hld up in last trio: pushed along to cl on inner 2f out: reminder ins fnl f and kpt on to press for 3rd nr fin but nvr nr to chal* **7/1**

040 **5** 3/4 **Honcho (IRE)**[4] 6269 4-8-12 61.......... FMBerry 6 61
(John Ryan) *chsd wnr to over 2f out: sn drvn: styd cl up tl fdd ins fnl f* **5/1**[3]

3012 **6** hd **For Ayman**[10] 6091 5-8-12 68..........(t) SeanMooney[(7)] 7 67
(Joseph Tuite) *stdd s: hld up: last 1/2-way: pushed along and no prog 2f out: kpt on fnl f: nvr really involved* **6/1**

0006 **7** 1/2 **Firesnake (IRE)**[21] 5732 3-9-1 66.......... CharlesBishop 3 64
(Lisa Williamson) *restrained s: t.k.h: hld up in last tl prog on outer bnd over 3f out: rdn and nt qckn 2f out: stl ch of a pl fnl f: fdd* **25/1**

1m 12.86s (-0.24) **Going Correction** -0.05s/f (Stan)
WFA 3 from 4yo+ 2lb 7 Ran SP% **110.3**
Speed ratings (Par 103): **99,97,96,96,95 95,94**
CSF £26.05 TOTE £2.00: £1.30, £7.70; EX 21.50 Trifecta £94.20.
Owner Paul & Clare Rooney **Bred** Mickley Stud And Mick Quinn **Trained** Lambourn, Berks

FOCUS
A tight sprint handicap and there was a bunched finish. The runner-up has been rated to this year's form, with the third close to his latest.
T/Jkpt: Not Won. T/Plt: £64.80 to a £1 stake. Pool: £58540.75, 658.71 winning units T/Qpdt: £5.90 to a £1 stake. Pool: £4683.94, 581.56 winning units **Jonathan Neesom**

6137 WOLVERHAMPTON (A.W) (L-H)
Monday, September 12

OFFICIAL GOING: Tapeta: standard
Wind: light, behind Weather: overcast

6419 FCL GLOBAL FORWARDING MAKING LOGISTICS PERSONAL NURSERY H'CAP (DIV I) 5f 20y (Tp)
4:55 (4:58) (Class 6) (0-65,65) 2-Y-O **£2,587** (£770; £384; £192) **Stalls** Low

Form RPR

663 **1** **Precious Plum**[36] 5188 2-9-7 65.......... SilvestreDeSousa 5 70
(Chris Dwyer) *nt that wl away: t.k.h: hld up in midfield: rdn and hdwy over 1f out: swtchd lft 1f out: sn chalng: r.o wl u.p to ld wl ins fnl f* **5/1**[3]

306 **2** 1/2 **Coping Stone**[19] 5771 2-9-6 64.......... RichardKingscote 10 67
(David Brown) *sn pushed up to join ldr: rdn to ld over 1f out: drvn ins fnl f: hdd and one pced wl ins fnl f* **16/1**

6513 **3** 3/4 **Saxagogo**[22] 5675 2-9-4 65.......... JosephineGordon[(3)] 2 66
(George Scott) *pushed along early: sn chsng ldrs on inner: rdn 2f out: hdwy u.p to chal ins fnl f: unable qck and btn fnl 50yds* **2/1**[1]

4353 **4** 3/4 **Katebird (IRE)**[31] 5364 2-9-1 59.......... AndrewMullen 1 57
(Mark Johnston) *in tch towards rr: pushed along 3f out: hdwy to chse ldrs whn nt clrest of runs and swtchd lft jst ins fnl f: styd on same pce fnl 100yds* **8/1**

510 **5** nk **Ballyanna**[9] 6139 2-9-5 63.......... ShaneKelly 3 60
(David Evans) *trckd ldrs and travelled strly: effrt over 1f out: unable qck and styd on same pce u.p ins fnl f* **12/1**

6002 **6** 3/4 **Sheila's Return**[31] 5364 2-8-11 55.......... ConnorBeasley 6 49
(Bryan Smart) *chsd ldrs: rdn jst over 2f out: hung rt bnd 2f out: unable qck u.p over 1f out: styd on same pce ins fnl f* **7/2**[2]

5546 **7** 1 1/4 **Xenon**[18] 5806 2-9-2 60..........[1] LukeMorris 7 50
(Sir Mark Prescott Bt) *led: rdn 2f out: hdd over 1f out: wknd qckly ins fnl f* **8/1**

5445 **8** 1 **Shadow Wing (IRE)**[9] 6141 2-8-9 58 ow1.......... AnnStokell[(5)] 8 44
(Ann Stokell) *dwlt: in tch in last pair: effrt on inner over 1f out: kpt on same pce and no imp ins fnl f* **50/1**

460 **9** 1 1/2 **The Lady Hysteria (IRE)**[23] 5631 2-8-2 46 ow1.......... RoystonFfrench 4 27
(Phil McEntee) *dwlt: bhd: pushed along 3f out: no imp over 1f out: n.d* **50/1**

2344 **10** 1/2 **Climax**[31] 5352 2-9-7 65.......... PaulMulrennan 9 44
(Mark Johnston) *in tch towards rr: effrt over 1f out: no imp: wknd ins fnl f* **9/1**

1m 2.4s (0.50) **Going Correction** -0.05s/f (Stan) 10 Ran SP% **121.9**
Speed ratings (Par 93): **94,93,92,90,90 89,87,85,83,82**
CSF £85.23 CT £219.38 TOTE £7.00: £2.20, £5.10, £1.10; EX 100.60 Trifecta £477.20.
Owner Mrs Julia Hughes **Bred** Mrs J V Hughes **Trained** Newmarket, Suffolk

FOCUS
A modest nursery in which all the runners were fillies. The gallop was sound and the winner came down the centre in the straight. The second and third have been rated back to their respective pre-race levels.

6420 FCL GLOBAL FORWARDING MAKING LOGISTICS PERSONAL NURSERY H'CAP (DIV II) 5f 20y (Tp)
5:25 (5:25) (Class 6) (0-65,65) 2-Y-O **£2,587** (£770; £384; £192) **Stalls** Low

Form RPR

40 **1** **Prancelina (IRE)**[21] 5705 2-8-12 59.......... JosephineGordon[(3)] 5 62
(Phil McEntee) *chsd ldr: rdn 2f out: sn outpcd by ldr: styd on u.p to ld ins fnl f: jst hld on* **16/1**

622 **2** nse **Harbour Lightning**[15] 5917 2-9-6 64.......... PJMcDonald 7 67
(Ann Duffield) *midfield: effrt over 2f out: hdwy u.p 1f out: chsd wnr ins fnl f: styd on wl: jst hld* **9/2**[3]

033 **3** *1 ¼* **Wearethepeople**[25] 5569 2-9-7 **65**.................................... MartinDwyer 3 63
(William Muir) *off the pce in last trio: effrt and hanging lft over 2f out: stl hanging and hdwy over 1f out: hung bdly lft ins fnl f: styd on to go 3rd fnl 50yds* **9/4**[1]

0645 **4** *shd* **Tullinahoo (IRE)**[22] 5668 2-9-5 **63**.. ShaneKelly 8 61
(Denis Coakley) *s.i.s: outpcd and pushed along in rr: swtchd rt wl over 1f out: hdwy ins fnl f: styd on strly towards fin* **9/1**

006 **5** *1 ¾* **Pemberley House (IRE)**[15] 5930 2-8-13 **57**..................... TomQueally 4 48
(Paul D'Arcy) *midfield: effrt 2f out: keeping on same pce whn sltly impeded jst ins fnl f: kpt on but nvr enough pce to rch ldrs* **11/1**

0053 **6** *nk* **Roundabout Magic (IRE)**[34] 5257 2-9-7 **65**.................. NickyMackay 1 55
(Simon Dow) *taken down early: led: rdn and kicked clr wl over 1f out: drvn and tiring 1f out: hdd ins fnl f:: wknd fnl 100yds* **4/1**[2]

6604 **7** *½* **Red Savina**[31] 5364 2-8-1 **45**.. AndrewMullen 2 33
(Kevin Ryan) *chsd ldng pair tl 2f out: unable qck u.p over 1f out: no imp fnl f* **8/1**

006 **8** *hd* **Lights**[9] 6141 2-8-6 **50**... NeilFarley 6 38
(Declan Carroll) *chsd ldng trio: effrt in 3rd 2f out: unable qck over 1f out: wknd ins fnl f* **16/1**

2250 **9** *1 ¼* **Hope Against Hope (IRE)**[21] 5707 2-9-4 **62**......(b[1]) RichardKingscote 9 45
(Mark Johnston) *sn outpcd in last pair: rdn 1/2-way: sme hdwy but stl in rr whn hung bdly lft jst ins fnl f* **14/1**

1m 2.59s (0.69) **Going Correction** -0.05s/f (Stan) **9** Ran SP% **116.8**
Speed ratings (Par 93): **92,91,89,89,86 86,85,85,83**
CSF £87.53 CT £229.75 TOTE £20.40: £4.40, £2.00, £1.30; EX 98.30 Trifecta £378.30.
Owner Eventmaker Racehorses **Bred** Tally-Ho Stud **Trained** Newmarket, Suffolk

FOCUS
Division two of an ordinary nursery. The gallop was sound throughout and the winner raced just off the inside rail in the straight.

6421 FCL GLOBAL FORWARDING MAKING LOGISTICS PERSONAL MAIDEN AUCTION FILLIES' STKS (PLUS 10 RACE) 1m 141y (Tp)
5:55 (5:58) (Class 5) 2-Y-O **£3,234** (£962; £481; £240) **Stalls** Low

Form RPR

0320 **1** **Highland Lotus**[26] 5549 2-9-0 68.............................. SilvestreDeSousa 2 71
(William Haggas) *led and set stdy gallop: rdn and qcknd 2f out: 1 l clr and drvn 1f out: styd on: pressed towards fin but a holding on* **2/1**[1]

0364 **2** *hd* **Three Duchesses**[26] 5549 2-9-0 72............................... WilliamCarson 8 71
(Michael Bell) *t.k.h: chsd wnr tl stdd into 3rd over 6f out: rdn jst over 2f out: swtchd rt wl over 1f out: drvn and no imp tl str run wl ins fnl f: wnt 2nd and clsng qckly on wnr towards fin* **11/4**[2]

062 **3** *1* **Captain Sue (IRE)**[12] 6035 2-9-0 70.................................... ShaneKelly 3 68
(Richard Hughes) *t.k.h: chsd ldrs tl hdwy to press ldr over 6f out: rdn over 1f out: styd on same pce ins fnl f: lost 2nd towards fin* **4/1**[3]

0603 **4** *1 ¼* **Joyful Dream (IRE)**[12] 6035 2-8-11 66................. JosephineGordon(3) 1 66
(J S Moore) *t.k.h: chsd ldrs: stdd bk towards rr but stl wl in tch 6f out: hdwy on inner to chse ldrs 2f out: rdn and styd on same pce fr over 1f out* **8/1**

4 **5** *6* **Power Home (IRE)**[12] 6035 2-8-9 0.................................. PaddyPilley(5) 6 53
(Denis Coakley) *hld up in tch in midfield: effrt over 2f out: sn outpcd: modest 5th and no imp over 1f out* **9/2**

00 **6** *1 ¼* **Navajo Thunder (IRE)**[20] 5747 2-9-0 0......................... AndrewMullen 4 53+
(Michael Appleby) *t.k.h: hld up in tch in last pair: rdn over 3f out: outpcd and hmpd over 2f out: no ch over 1f out* **66/1**

00 **7** *11* **Mezyan (IRE)**[17] 5820 2-9-0 0... JFEgan 5 28
(David Evans) *stdd after s: t.k.h: hld up in tch in rr: swtchd rt and rdn wl over 3f out: wknd over 2f out: bhd and eased over 1f out* **28/1**

00 **8** *shd* **Cadela Rica**[67] 4064 2-9-0 0... LukeMorris 7 27
(Gay Kelleway) *t.k.h: hld up in rr: hdwy on outer 6f out: 4th and rdn 3f out: lost pl and btn 2f out: bhd and eased ins fnl f* **33/1**

1m 51.85s (1.75) **Going Correction** -0.05s/f (Stan) **8** Ran SP% **117.2**
Speed ratings (Par 92): **90,89,88,87,82 81,71,71**
CSF £7.85 TOTE £2.70: £1.10, £1.30, £1.60; EX 8.40 Trifecta £31.60.
Owner M S Bloodstock Ltd **Bred** Mike Smith **Trained** Newmarket, Suffolk
■ Stewards' Enquiry : Paddy Pilley caution: careless riding

FOCUS
Little strength in depth in just an ordinary maiden. The gallop was on the steady side to the home turn and the first four pulled clear. The winner raced centre-to-far side in the straight. It's been rated around the balance of the first four.

6422 FCL GLOBAL FORWARDING MAKING LOGISTICS PERSONAL H'CAP 2m 119y (Tp)
6:25 (6:27) (Class 6) (0-60,60) 4-Y-O+ **£2,587** (£770; £384; £192) **Stalls** Low

Form RPR

1 **Abrahams Blessing (IRE)**[74] 3829 8-8-8 **47**........... SilvestreDeSousa 1 58
(R P Burns, Ire) *hld up in midfield: clsd 5f out: swtchd rt and effrt jst over 2f out: rdn to ld over 1f out: styd on wl ins fnl f: rdn out: collapsed fatally after r* **11/2**[3]

0023 **2** *2 ¼* **Amantius**[20] 5745 7-9-7 **60**...(b) TomQueally 12 68
(Johnny Farrelly) *s.i.s and pushed along in rr: clsd and travelling wl 5f out: effrt to chse wnr and pushed along over 1f out: rdn 1f out: little rspnse and one pce after* **7/2**[1]

6-64 **3** *9* **Top Set (IRE)**[19] 5777 6-8-7 **46** oh1.........................(p) MartinDwyer 11 43
(Richard Phillips) *hld up in rr: swtchd rt and hdwy on outer 5f out: chsd ldrs 4f out: rdn to ld wl over 1f out: sn hdd: wknd fnl f* **22/1**

0256 **4** *4 ½* **Delagoa Bay (IRE)**[20] 5745 8-9-2 **58**................. JosephineGordon(3) 7 50
(Sylvester Kirk) *hld up in midfield: clsd and wl in tch 5f out: effrt over 2f out: drvn and outpcd 2f out: sn wknd* **13/2**

6-60 **5** *1 ¾* **Welsh Rebel**[55] 4483 4-8-6 **48**..................................[1] EdwardGreatrex(3) 8 38
(Nikki Evans) *lost off side cheek piece sn after s: towards rr: rdn 9f out: reminders 8f out: hdwy on outer to chse ldrs 5f out: rdn and ev ch 4f out: led 3f out tl wl over 1f out: sn wknd* **33/1**

0005 **6** *16* **Par Three (IRE)**[22] 5680 5-9-3 **56**.................................... LukeMorris 3 27
(Tony Carroll) *chsd ldrs: rdn 6f out: chsd ldr 5f out: ev ch and drvn over 3f out tl over 2f out: wknd qckly 2f out* **12/1**

0240 **7** *4 ½* **Impeccability**[10] 6102 6-8-7 **46**..................................(p) RoystonFfrench 5 11
(John Mackie) *midfield: clsd and wl in tch 5f out: rdn and struggling over 2f out: sn wknd: t.o ins fnl f* **14/1**

5652 **8** *10* **Judith Gardenier**[10] 6102 4-8-7 **46**......................................(p) JasonHart 13
(Iain Jardine) *sn chsng ldr tl led 3f out: rdn and 3f out: wknd qckly 2f out: t.o* **9/2**[2]

0640 **9** *34* **Kirkman (IRE)**[21] 5726 5-8-9 **48**.................................... WilliamCarson 6
(Peter Hiatt) *led tl rdn and hdd 6f out: dropped to rr 5f out: t.o* **10/1**

5660 **10** *11* **Ullswater (IRE)**[75] 3774 8-8-5 **49**................................(tp) PhilDennis(5) 2
(Philip Kirby) *chsd ldrs tl shuffled bk to rr and swtchd rt 4f out: sn lost tch u.p: t.o* **33/1**

5605 **11** *107* **Druot**[19] 5777 4-9-0 **53**...(b) ShaneKelly 4
(Richard Hughes) *s.i.s and rdn along early: hdwy and swtchd rt after 2f: chsd ldrs 14f out tl 7f out: sn dropped out: bhd whn swtchd rt and eased off over 5f out: t.o* **6/1**

3m 38.64s (-5.06) **Going Correction** -0.05s/f (Stan) **11** Ran SP% **117.1**
Speed ratings (Par 101): **109,107,103,101,100 93,91,86,70,65**
CSF £24.42 CT £389.76 TOTE £7.20: £2.20, £1.80, £5.30; EX 31.30 Trifecta £1247.90.
Owner Mrs Dianne Burns **Bred** Gerard Mulligan **Trained** Collinstown, Co Westmeath

FOCUS
A moderate handicap in which the gallop was sound and those held up came to the fore in the closing stages. The first two, who pulled clear in the straight, came down the centre.

6423 FCL GLOBAL FORWARDING MAKING LOGISTICS PERSONAL MAIDEN STKS 1m 1f 103y (Tp)
6:55 (6:59) (Class 5) 3-Y-O **£3,234** (£962; £481; £240) **Stalls** Low

Form RPR

1 **Wadigor** 3-9-5 0... HarryBentley 4 81+
(Roger Varian) *hld up in tch: 5th and effrt on inner 2f out: rdn to chal 1f out: led ins fnl f: rn green and hung rt in front: stened and readily asserted wl ins fnl f: gng away at fin* **5/1**[3]

303 **2** *2* **Cape Peninsular**[69] 3990 3-9-0 79..................................... LukeMorris 1 71
(James Tate) *chsd ldr: rdn and ev ch 2f out: carried wd bnd wl over 1f out: drvn to ld 1f out: hdd ins fnl f: styd on same pce after* **11/10**[1]

5535 **3** *hd* **Poet's Song (IRE)**[19] 5765 3-9-5 72................................. MartinDwyer 8 76
(Marcus Tregoning) *t.k.h: hld up in tch in midfield: effrt in 3rd over 2f out: lft w ev ch wl over 1f out: drvn and carried rt ins fnl f: styd on same pce wl ins fnl f* **11/2**

-223 **4** *1 ¾* **Confident Kid**[13] 6014 3-9-5 78..................................(p) WilliamCarson 7 73
(Saeed bin Suroor) *led: rdn ent fnl 2f: hung bdly rt bnd wl over 1f out: hdd 1f out: no ex: 4th and hld whn squeezed for room and snatched up wl ins fnl f* **9/4**[2]

33 **5** *nse* **Dubawi Hundred (IRE)**[23] 5634 3-9-5 0............................. DavidAllan 9 72
(James Tate) *hld up in tch in midfield: effrt in 4th over 2f out: pressing ldrs over 1f out: unable qck and btn whn short of room wl ins fnl f* **11/1**

0-4 **6** *19* **Demand Respect**[24] 5608 3-9-2 0............................... LouisSteward(3) 5 32
(Henry Spiller) *restless in stalls: hld up in last pair: rdn over 3f out: sn struggling: bhd fnl 2f* **66/1**

0 **7** *6* **Sir Jack**[18] 5811 3-9-5 0.. PJMcDonald 6 20
(Tony Carroll) *s.i.s: hld up in last pair: rdn 4f out: struggling 3f out: sn btn and bhd fnl 2f* **66/1**

5 **8** *4* **Sinamas (IRE)**[25] 5581 3-9-0 0... JasonHart 2 6
(Eric Alston) *chsd ldng pair tl over 3f out: sn lost pl: bhd over 1f out* **100/1**

2m 1.67s (0.87) **Going Correction** -0.05s/f (Stan) **8** Ran SP% **122.7**
Speed ratings (Par 101): **94,92,92,90,90 73,68,64**
CSF £11.89 TOTE £6.70: £2.20, £1.10, £1.60; EX 13.30 Trifecta £43.80.
Owner Sheikh Ahmed Al Maktoum **Bred** Panda Bloodstock **Trained** Newmarket, Suffolk

FOCUS
A reasonable maiden for the track and a useful looking winner. The gallop was an ordinary one and the winner edged into the centre. Muddling form, but the right horses came clear and it's been rated around the third and fifth.

6424 CHINA CASTLE H'CAP 1m 4f 50y (Tp)
7:25 (7:26) (Class 6) (0-60,60) 3-Y-O+ **£2,587** (£770; £384; £192) **Stalls** Low

Form RPR

0343 **1** **Gracesome (IRE)**[19] 5763 5-9-4 **52**................................ HarryBentley 9 61+
(Michael Blanshard) *hld up in tch towards rr: hdwy on outer over 2f out: rdn and str run to ld 1f out: sn clr: r.o wl: readily* **7/2**[2]

5406 **2** *4* **Annigoni (IRE)**[38] 5117 4-8-12 **46**..........................(p) JamesSullivan 12 49
(Ruth Carr) *in tch in midfield: rdn 3f out: hdwy u.p 1f out: styd on u.p ins fnl f: wnt 2nd wl ins fnl f: no ch w wnr* **11/1**

0005 **3** *1* **Kay Sera**[53] 4567 8-9-4 **55**.. EoinWalsh(3) 5 56
(Tony Newcombe) *stdd s: t.k.h: hld up in rr: swtchd rt and hdwy on outer over 3f out: ev ch and drvn 2f out: led ent fnl f: outpcd by wnr and styd on same pce fnl f: lost 2nd wl ins fnl f* **5/1**[3]

/50- **4** *shd* **Maid Of Tuscany (IRE)**[13] 6808 5-8-12 **51**.........(b) CharlieBennett(5) 10 52
(Alexandra Dunn) *hld up in midfield: pushed along 4f out: lost pl 3f out: switching rt 2f out: styd on wl u.p ins fnl f: no ch w wnr* **25/1**

000 **5** *hd* **Social Media**[69] 3990 3-8-12 **55**.......................... SilvestreDeSousa 4 56
(Ed Dunlop) *chsd ldr: rdn and ev ch 3f out tl outpcd by wnr and styd on same pce u.p fnl f* **7/4**[1]

253 **6** *½* **Cry Fury**[19] 5131 8-9-12 **60**.. SaleemGolam 6 62
(Sophie Leech) *stdd s: hld up in tch in last trio: nt clr run over 2f out: hdwy over 1f out: swtchd rt ins fnl f: styd on fnl 100yds: no ch w wnr* **17/2**

0000 **7** *¾* **Flying Power**[60] 4320 8-9-8 **59**............................ JacobButterfield(3) 1 58
(John Norton) *led: rdn and hrd pressed 3f out: hdd ent fnl f: sn outpcd and styd on same pce ins fnl f* **18/1**

3530 **8** *nk* **Percys Princess**[6] 6212 5-9-12 **60**..................................[1] AndrewMullen 2 60
(Michael Appleby) *chsd ldrs: nt clr run over 2f out: rdn and ev ch over 1f out tl unable qck 1f out: styd on same pce ins fnl f* **11/1**

4260 **9** *½* **Doctor Kehoe**[12] 6022 4-9-7 **55**......................................(vt) ShaneKelly 3 52
(David Evans) *hld up in tch in midfield: rdn over 2f out: unable qck u.p over 1f out: styd on same pce ins fnl f* **12/1**

536 **10** *3 ¼* **Little Choosey**[34] 5264 6-9-5 **56**......................(tp) AlistairRawlinson(3) 8 48
(Roy Bowring) *in tch in midfield: effrt over 2f out: chsng ldrs but unable qck u.p over 1f out: wknd ins fnl f* **12/1**

0005 **11** *½* **Heaven Scent**[14] 5718 3-8-12 **55**.................................(p) PJMcDonald 7 46
(Ann Duffield) *chsd ldrs: reminder 6f out: rdn 4f out: lost pl and bhd over 1f out: wknd ins fnl f* **10/1**

2m 39.86s (-0.94) **Going Correction** -0.05s/f (Stan)
WFA 3 from 4yo+ 9lb **11** Ran SP% **136.0**
Speed ratings (Par 101): **101,98,97,97,97 96,96,96,96,93 93**
CSF £49.70 CT £209.99 TOTE £5.30: £1.90, £4.00, £2.20; EX 59.20 Trifecta £351.20.
Owner W Murdoch **Bred** Simon Tindall **Trained** Upper Lambourn, Berks

FOCUS
A moderate handicap in which a fair gallop increased leaving the back straight. The easy winner came down the wide outside in the straight. A pb from the winner, but the runner-up highlights the limitations of the bare form.

6425 FCLGF.COM H'CAP 5f 20y (Tp)
7:55 (7:55) (Class 4) (0-80,80) 3-Y-O+ **£5,175** (£1,540; £769; £384) **Stalls** Low

Form RPR

0140 **1** **Oriental Relation (IRE)**[34] 5274 5-9-7 **80**........................(v) TomEaves 3 88
(James Given) *pressed ldr tl led wl over 1f out: rdn clr ent fnl f: edgd rt ins fnl f: hld on cl home* **10/1**

4006 **2** *nk* **Eternitys Gate**[22] 5679 5-9-0 **73**.............................(v) SilvestreDeSousa 8 80
(Ivan Furtado) *t.k.h: hld up in tch in midfield: swtchd rt and effrt wl over 1f out: hdwy u.p over 1f out: edgd lft and chsd wnr jst ins fnl f: styd on wl fnl 100yds: nvr quite getting to wnr* **10/3**[2]

4004 **3** *1 1/4* **Eleuthera**[6] 6216 4-9-7 **80**.............................ShaneGray 7 82
(Kevin Ryan) *dwlt and n.m.r leaving stalls: hld up in last pair: hdwy on inner and hung lft over 1f out: wnt 3rd 75yds: kpt on* **4/1**[3]

510 **4** *1/2* **Rich Again (IRE)**[22] 5679 7-9-4 **77**.............................(b) PJMcDonald 9 78
(James Bethell) *hld up in last pair: effrt over 1f out: clsd and swtchd rt jst ins fnl f: styd on wl fnl 100yds: nt rch ldrs* **3/1**[1]

4006 **5** *1 1/4* **Noble Asset**[7] 6195 5-8-10 **72**.............................EdwardGreatrex(3) 4 68
(Milton Bradley) *t.k.h: chsd ldrs: rdn over 1f out: drvn and chsd wnr briefly 1f out: wknd wl ins fnl f* **10/1**

0050 **6** *1 1/2* **Red Stripes (USA)**[10] 6080 4-9-6 **79**.............................LukeMorris 5 70
(Lisa Williamson) *in tch in midfield: rdn ent fnl 2f: swtchd rt and drvn ent fnl f: styd on same pce after* **11/1**

6400 **7** *2 3/4* **Desert Strike**[22] 5679 10-8-10 **72**.............................(p) JosephineGordon(3) 6 53
(Conor Dore) *racd wd: chsd ldrs: hung rt and rdn over 2f out: lost pl over 1f out: wknd ins fnl f* **12/1**

4002 **8** *2 3/4* **Entertaining Ben**[12] 6018 3-9-0 **74**.............................MartinDwyer 2 45
(William Muir) *led: rdn and hdd wl over 1f out: lost 2nd 1f out: sn wknd* **10/1**

5150 **9** *3/4* **Kestrel Call (IRE)**[21] 5730 3-9-1 **75**.............................(t) AndrewMullen 1 43
(Michael Appleby) *chsd ldrs: rdn and unable qck and lost pl over 1f out: wknd fnl f* **16/1**

1m 1.06s (-0.84) **Going Correction** -0.05s/f (Stan)
WFA 3 from 4yo+ 1lb **9** Ran SP% **117.3**
Speed ratings (Par 105): **104,103,101,100,98 96,91,87,86**
CSF £44.10 CT £160.23 TOTE £11.90: £3.10, £1.50, £1.80; EX 51.40 Trifecta £275.50.
Owner The Cool Silk Partnership **Bred** Brendan Laffan & Michael McCormick **Trained** Willoughton, Lincs

FOCUS
Mainly exposed sorts in a reasonable handicap. The gallop was sound throughout and the winner came down the centre. The winner has been rated to last winter's non-claiming best.

6426 FCL GLOBAL MAKING LOGISTICS PERSONAL FILLIES' H'CAP 7f 32y (Tp)
8:25 (8:27) (Class 5) (0-75,74) 3-Y-O+ **£3,234** (£962; £481; £240) **Stalls** High

Form RPR

0451 **1** **Brick Lane**[18] 5808 3-8-13 **69**.............................JosephineGordon(3) 11 79+
(Robyn Brisland) *chsd ldr tl led and travelling wl 2f out: sn rdn clr: styd on wl fnl f: eased towards fin* **7/2**[1]

1333 **2** *1* **Figurante (IRE)**[24] 5602 3-9-4 **71**.............................WilliamCarson 9 78
(Jamie Osborne) *chsd ldrs: rdn to chse wnr wl over 1f out: kpt on wl for clr 2nd but nvr able to chal wnr* **15/2**[3]

5154 **3** *2 1/4* **Bint Arcano (FR)**[14] 5973 3-9-4 **74**.............................JacobButterfield(3) 8 75
(Julie Camacho) *hld up in tch in midfield: nt clr run over 2f out: swtchd rt and hdwy over 1f out: styd on to go 3rd 75yds out: no threat to ldrs* **12/1**

0553 **4** *1 1/4* **Colourfilly**[27] 5523 4-9-4 **67**.............................(p) RichardKingscote 12 67
(Tom Dascombe) *hld up in tch in last quartet: nt clr run over 2f out: swtchd rt over 1f out: rdn and styd on wl ins fnl f: nvr trbld ldrs* **9/1**

0040 **5** *3/4* **Perfect Alchemy (IRE)**[26] 5551 5-9-6 **74**.............................CharlieBennett(5) 4 72
(Patrick Chamings) *hld up in tch in midfield: effrt over 2f out: hdwy to chse clr ldng pair 1f out: one pced and no imp after: lsot 2 pls fnl 75yds* **28/1**

3203 **6** *1* **Bush Beauty (IRE)**[11] 6055 5-8-10 **66**.............................SophieKilloran(7) 10 61
(Eric Alston) *dwlt: hld up in tch in last pair: nt clr run 2f out: swtchd rt and hdwy ent fnl f: rdn and styd on fnl 150yds: nvr trbld ldrs* **8/1**

0241 **7** *3/4* **Mallymkun**[35] 5247 4-9-3 **71**.............................JordanVaughan(5) 3 64
(K R Burke) *taken down early: hld up in tch in midfield: effrt over 2f out: no imp u.p over 1f out: styd on same pce fnl f* **15/2**[3]

2-10 **8** *1 1/4* **Doeadeer (IRE)**[89] 3284 3-9-2 **69**.............................ConnorBeasley 6 56
(Keith Dalgleish) *taken down early: racd keenly: led rdn over 2f out: hdd wl over 1f out: sn outpcd: lost 3rd 1f out: sn wknd* **20/1**

2056 **9** *2 1/4* **Hold Hands**[9] 6137 5-9-0 **63**.............................SilvestreDeSousa 1 46
(Brendan Powell) *hld up in tch in last quartet: pushed along 2f out: swtchd rt ins fnl f: nvr trbld ldrs* **11/1**

5144 **10** *3* **Magical Daze**[35] 5247 4-9-7 **70**.............................LukeMorris 2 45
(John Mackie) *chsd ldrs: rdn 3f out: unable qck and btn over 1f out: wknd ins fnl f* **13/2**[2]

-565 **11** *2* **Heart Of An Angel**[53] 4563 3-8-11 **67**.............................LouisSteward(3) 5 35
(Philip McBride) *s.i.s: a rr: n.d* **12/1**

3032 **12** *1 1/2* **Inner Knowing (IRE)**[27] 5523 3-8-10 **63**.............................(b) JoeyHaynes 7 27
(K R Burke) *t.k.h: wd in midfield: hdwy to chse ldrs after 1f: lost pl 2f out: wknd and bhd ins fnl f* **15/2**[3]

1m 27.66s (-1.14) **Going Correction** -0.05s/f (Stan)
WFA 3 from 4yo+ 4lb **12** Ran SP% **123.9**
Speed ratings (Par 100): **104,102,100,98,98 96,96,94,92,88 86,84**
CSF £30.79 CT £295.75 TOTE £4.20: £1.60, £3.20, £4.80; EX 36.50 Trifecta £505.10.
Owner Franconson Partners **Bred** D Curran **Trained** Newmarket, Suffolk

FOCUS
A fair handicap in which the gallop was reasonable. The first two pulled clear and the winner came down the centre in the straight. The winner has been rated as building on her previous C&D win, with the third a bit below her best.
T/Plt: £30.70 to a £1 stake. Pool: £75,188.13 - 1,784.64 winning tickets T/Qpdt: £8.60 to a £1 stake. Pool: £8,906.68, 758.12 winning tickets **Steve Payne**

6427 - 6431a (Foreign Racing) - See Raceform Interactive

6221 CARLISLE (R-H)
Tuesday, September 13

OFFICIAL GOING: Good to soft (soft in places; 6.5)
Wind: Almost nil Weather: Overcast

6432 APOLLOBET DAILY RACING REFUNDS H'CAP 1m 1f
4:15 (4:15) (Class 5) (0-70,70) 3-Y-O+ **£3,234** (£962; £481; £240) **Stalls** Low

Form RPR

0506 **1** **Southern Strife**[29] 5480 5-9-4 **64**.............................(b[1]) DavidAllan 4 73
(Tim Easterby) *dwlt and checked s: sn midfield: effrt and swtchd lft 2f out: led wl ins fnl f: kpt on strly* **9/1**

0535 **2** *3/4* **Taking Libertys**[57] 4446 3-9-2 **68**.............................(b) KevinStott 2 75
(Kevin Ryan) *led: rdn 2f out: edgd rt and hdd wl ins fnl f: no ex* **5/1**[2]

0556 **3** *3 1/4* **Bahamian C**[17] 5883 5-9-5 **65**.............................(t) GeorgeChaloner 9 65
(Richard Fahey) *in tch on outside: drvn along over 3f out: edgd lft 2f out: rallied: kpt on fnl f: nt rch first two* **14/1**

4021 **4** *shd* **Stoneboat Bill**[7] 6212 4-8-8 **61**.............................GerO'Neill(7) 10 61+
(Declan Carroll) *stdd s: hld up in last pl: stdy hdwy over 2f out: sn rdn: edgd rt over 1f out: kpt on wl fnl f: nrst fin* **3/1**[1]

063 **5** *1 1/4* **Mary Beale (IRE)**[56] 4477 3-9-1 **67**.............................JoeFanning 3 64
(Mark Johnston) *wnt lft s: sn pressing ldr: rdn over 2f out: edgd lft over 1f out: no ex ins fnl f* **10/1**

6222 **6** *nk* **Bit Of A Quirke**[51] 4681 3-8-8 **60**.............................JasonHart 1 57
(Mark Walford) *t.k.h: trckd ldrs: rdn over 3f out: rallied: outpcd ins fnl f* **7/1**[3]

5500 **7** *1 1/4* **Strummer (IRE)**[13] 6023 3-8-8 **60**.............................(p) JoeDoyle 12 54
(Kevin Ryan) *hld up: rdn along over 2f out: edgd rt over 1f out: no imp* **10/1**

12 **8** *nk* **Henpecked**[38] 5154 6-9-5 **70**.............................(p) GarryWhillans(5) 8 63
(Alistair Whillans) *hld up: rdn over 2f out: hdwy over 1f out: nt pce to chal* **8/1**

263 **9** *6* **Paddy's Rock (IRE)**[17] 5868 5-9-0 **60**.............................PaddyAspell 11 41
(Lynn Siddall) *hld u[: drvn along 3f out: edgd rt and wknd wl over 1f out* **14/1**

0006 **10** *1 1/2* **In Focus (IRE)**[27] 5538 5-9-5 **65**.............................NeilFarley 7 43
(Alan Swinbank) *hld up: drvn along over 3f out: btn over 1f out* **20/1**

0000 **11** *1* **Champagne Rules**[45] 4872 5-8-10 **56** oh1.............................[1] JoeyHaynes 6 32
(Sharon Watt) *hld up midfield: drvn and lost pl over 3f out: sn btn* **33/1**

0500 **12** *21* **The King's Steed**[15] 5975 3-8-4 **61**.............................RobJFitzpatrick(5) 5
(Micky Hammond) *t.k.h: trckd ldrs: lost pl over 3f out: sn lost tch: t.o* **66/1**

2m 0.48s (2.88) **Going Correction** +0.475s/f (Yiel)
WFA 3 from 4yo+ 6lb **12** Ran SP% **116.0**
Speed ratings (Par 103): **106,105,102,102,101 100,99,99,94,92 92,73**
CSF £51.48 CT £638.49 TOTE £11.40: £3.00, £2.20, £3.80; EX 70.50 Trifecta £863.70.
Owner Habton Farms **Bred** W A Tinkler **Trained** Great Habton, N Yorks

FOCUS
Bend into home Straight was out by 2yds and the bend after winning post out by 4yds. The opening race was run over 6yds further than advertised. The closers were at a real disadvantage in this ordinary handicap, and the winner showed improved form.

6433 APOLLOBET HOME OF CASHBACK OFFERS FILLIES' NOVICE STKS (PLUS 10 RACE) 7f 173y
4:45 (4:48) (Class 5) 2-Y-O **£2,911** (£866) **Stalls** Low

Form RPR

1362 **1** **Appointed**[6] 6229 2-9-4 82.............................DavidAllan 2 86+
(Tim Easterby) *mde virtually all: pushed along 2f out: kpt on strly fnl f: eased nr fin* **11/10**[1]

343 **2** *1 1/4* **Starlight Romance (IRE)**[53] 4603 2-9-0 77.............................TonyHamilton 3 77
(Richard Fahey) *t.k.h: pressed wnr: rdn and ev ch 2f out: edgd lft appr fnl f: kpt on same pce* **5/2**[2]

1m 45.89s (5.89) **Going Correction** +0.475s/f (Yiel) **2** Ran SP% **76.2**
Speed ratings (Par 92): **89,87**
TOTE £1.20.
Owner M J Macleod **Bred** Lady Jennifer Green **Trained** Great Habton, N Yorks
■ Romantic View was withdrawn. Price at time of withdrawal 5/2. Rule 4 applies to all bets - deduction 25p in the pound.

FOCUS
Add 3yds to advertised race distance. The withdrawal of Romantic View dictated this match event was tactical, but the form still looks straightforward. The winner is rated near the previous week's form, with the second improving.

6434 APOLLOBET BET ON LOTTERIES H'CAP 7f 173y
5:15 (5:15) (Class 6) (0-65,65) 3-Y-O+ **£2,911** (£866; £432; £216) **Stalls** Low

Form RPR

0002 **1** **Jordan James (IRE)**[27] 5539 3-9-4 **64**.............................DaleSwift 4 70
(Brian Ellison) *chsd clr ldng pair: rdn 3f out: hdwy to ld 1f out: edgd rt ins fnl f: kpt on* **11/4**[1]

0060 **2** *1/2* **Osteopathic Remedy (IRE)**[6] 6226 12-9-8 **63**.........(t) ConnorBeasley 6 69
(Michael Dods) *in tch: drvn and outpcd over 3f out: rallied over 1f out: chsd wnr ins fnl f: r.o* **9/2**[3]

0000 **3** *1 1/2* **Thornaby Nash**[29] 5482 5-9-10 **65**.............................(t[1]) PhillipMakin 5 67
(Colin Teague) *s.i.s: hld up: rdn and outpcd over 3f out: rallied over 1f out: kpt on fnl f: no imp* **16/1**

0500 **4** *nk* **Pivotman**[19] 5810 8-9-8 **63**.............................(bt) PaulMulrennan 2 65
(Michael Easterby) *t.k.h: led and sn clr: rdn over 2f out: hdd 1f out: sn no ex* **4/1**[2]

6046 **5** *1 1/2* **Yair Hill (IRE)**[6] 6226 8-8-10 **51** oh5.............................(p) JoeFanning 8 49
(Thomas Cuthbert) *hld up: stdy hdwy over 2f out: rdn and chsd wnr briefly ins fnl f: wknd nr fin* **17/2**

6520 **6** *6* **Stanlow**[18] 5835 6-8-10 **51** oh2.............................JoeDoyle 3 35
(Michael Mullineaux) *s.i.s: hld up: struggling 1/2-way: n.d after* **9/1**

6506 **7** *nse* **Diamond Avalanche (IRE)**[45] 4870 3-8-9 **62**.............................PaulaMuir(7) 7 45
(Patrick Holmes) *chsd clr ldr and clr of rest: rdn 3f out: hung rt and wknd 2f out* **16/1**

4-05 **8** *4 1/2* **Devious Spirit (IRE)**[15] 5972 4-9-10 **65**.............................TonyHamilton 1 39
(Richard Fahey) *hld up: drvn along over 3f out: hung rt 2f out: sn wknd* **9/2**[3]

1m 44.23s (4.23) **Going Correction** +0.475s/f (Yiel)
WFA 3 from 4yo+ 5lb **8** Ran SP% **115.3**
Speed ratings (Par 101): **97,96,95,94,93 87,87,82**
CSF £15.42 CT £164.63 TOTE £3.60: £1.10, £2.40, £5.30; EX 19.50 Trifecta £306.20.
Owner Market Avenue Racing Club Ltd **Bred** Corrin Stud **Trained** Norton, N Yorks
■ Stewards' Enquiry : Dale Swift two-day ban (27-28 Sep): used whip above permitted level

FOCUS
Add 3yds to race distance. There was a slow-motion finish to this moderate handicap.

6435 APOLLOBET ONLINE CASINO AND GAMES H'CAP 5f 193y
5:45 (5:47) (Class 5) (0-75,78) 3-Y-O+ **£3,234** (£962; £481; £240) **Stalls** Low

Form RPR

3241 **1** **Kenny The Captain (IRE)**[7] 6215 5-9-7 **78** 6ex.. RachelRichardson(3) 5 88
(Tim Easterby) *midfield on ins: drvn over 2f out: hdwy over 1f out: kpt on wl fnl f to ld towards fin* **4/1**[2]

0031 **2** *1/2* **Penny Pot Lane**[15] 5978 3-8-11 **67**.............................GeorgeChaloner 2 75
(Richard Whitaker) *trckd ldrs: rdn over 2f out: rallied and led 1f out: edgd lft ins fnl f: kpt on: hdd towards fin* **10/1**

4211 **3** *3/4* **Portland Street (IRE)**[27] 5537 3-8-11 **67**.............................(p) PaulMulrennan 7 73
(Bryan Smart) *trckd ldrs: drvn and ev ch over 1f out: edgd rt: kpt on ins fnl f: hld nr fin* **3/1**[1]

2501 **4** *nse* **Aprovado (IRE)**[7] 6216 4-9-6 **74** 6ex.............................(b) ConnorBeasley 1 79
(Michael Dods) *led: rdn 2f out: hdd 1f out: kpt on same pce* **11/1**

0541 **5** 1 3/4 **Ancient Astronaut**[15] 5960 3-9-3 **73** ... JasonHart 9 73
(John Quinn) *hld up in tch: effrt and pushed along 2f out: sn edgd lft: kpt on same pce ins fnl f* **7/1**

5000 **6** 1 1/4 **Farkle Minkus**[7] 6215 3-9-1 **71** ...(v1) JoeFanning 6 69
(Keith Dalgleish) *dwlt: hld up: pushed along over 3f out: hdwy on outside 2f out: edgd rt and no further imp ins fnl f: eased whn hld towards fin* **22/1**

6325 **7** 1 **Amood (IRE)**[45] 4889 5-9-7 **75** ...(p) PhillipMakin 4 68
(Simon West) *hld up: rdn along over 2f out: hdwy over 1f out: no imp fnl f* **10/1**

5303 **8** nk **Groundworker (IRE)**[17] 5867 5-8-8 **62** ... BarryMcHugh 10 54
(Paul Midgley) *hld up: stdy hdwy over 2f out: drvn along over 1f out: sn outpcd* **20/1**

3000 **9** 3 1/4 **In My Place**[15] 5960 3-8-13 **69** ...(b) PatrickMathers 3 50
(Richard Fahey) *s.i.s: hld up: drvn along over 2f out: hung rt and sn wknd* **40/1**

1-04 **10** 3 **Yosemite**[18] 5858 3-9-4 **74** ... TonyHamilton 12 46
(Richard Fahey) *in tch: effrt on outside over 2f out: rdn and wknd wl over 1f out* **6/1**[3]

3534 **11** 2 1/4 **Meandmyshadow**[14] 6013 8-9-5 **73** ...(b) DaleSwift 8 37
(Alan Brown) *prom tl rdn and wknd over 2f out* **16/1**

0500 **12** 10 **Lothair (IRE)**[50] 4704 7-8-7 **61** oh2 ... JoeyHaynes 11
(Alan Swinbank) *hld up on outside: drvn along over 2f out: sn wknd* **100/1**

1m 14.86s (1.16) **Going Correction** +0.325s/f (Good)
WFA 3 from 4yo+ 2lb 12 Ran SP% **116.7**
Speed ratings (Par 103): **105,104,103,103,100 99,97,97,93,89 86,72**
CSF £41.25 CT £139.07 TOTE £4.40: £1.40, £3.30, £1.60; EX 42.10 Trifecta £216.30.
Owner Reality Partnerships V **Bred** Joe Foley & John Grimes **Trained** Great Habton, N Yorks

FOCUS
A fair handicap for the class and there was a strong pace on. The winner is rated back to his best.

6436 APOLLOBET BET THROUGH YOUR MOBILE H'CAP 5f 193y
6:15 (6:16) (Class 6) (0-65,65) 3-Y-O **£2,587** (£770; £384; £192) **Stalls** Low

Form RPR

0652 **1** **Alpine Dream (IRE)**[27] 5537 3-9-5 **63** ...(b1) DavidAllan 13 69
(Tim Easterby) *dwlt: hld up: rdn over 2f out: edgd rt and hdwy over 1f out: flashed tail and led wl ins fnl f: kpt on* **7/2**[1]

0153 **2** 1 **Oasis Moon**[22] 5725 3-8-11 **55** ...(p) JoeFanning 15 58
(William Haggas) *prom: effrt and ev ch over 1f out to wl ins fnl f: kpt on* **15/2**[3]

5530 **3** 1/2 **Full Of Promise**[45] 4861 3-9-2 **60** ... DavidNolan 8 61
(Richard Fahey) *hld up: rdn over 2f out: hdwy over 1f out: ch ins fnl f: one pce nr fin* **12/1**

4320 **4** nk **Carlovian**[17] 5889 3-8-7 **51** oh1 ... NeilFarley 3 51
(Christopher Kellett) *led: rdn 2f out: hdd and no ex wl ins fnl f* **16/1**

6-01 **5** 1 3/4 **Roman Times (IRE)**[26] 5578 3-8-8 **59** ...(p) CallumRodriguez(7) 6 54
(John David Riches) *pressed ldr: drvn and ev ch over 1f out: no ex ins fnl f* **9/1**

066 **6** 1 1/4 **Lukoutoldmakezebak**[18] 5843 3-8-7 **51** oh2 ... GeorgeChaloner 10 42
(James Bethell) *prom: drvn along over 2f out: outpcd fnl f* **50/1**

-003 **7** nk **Mr Conundrum**[26] 5578 3-8-7 **51** oh4 ... JamesSullivan 2 41
(Lynn Siddall) *hld up: rdn and effrt over 2f out: no imp appr fnl f* **20/1**

4350 **8** 1 1/4 **Ss Vega**[26] 5578 3-8-7 **51** oh2 ...(p) JoeyHaynes 17 37
(James Bethell) *hld up: rdn and outpcd over 2f out: sme late hdwy: nvr on terms* **22/1**

3004 **9** 1/2 **Kirkham**[22] 5732 3-9-7 **65** ... JoeDoyle 4 49
(Julie Camacho) *blindfold slow to remove and dwlt: hld up: hdwy over 3f out: rdn and wknd wl over 1f out* **4/1**[2]

0066 **10** 3 1/2 **Gowanless**[13] 6023 3-9-0 **58** ...(b) PaulMulrennan 9 31
(Michael Dods) *dwlt: t.k.h in rr: drvn along over 2f out: sn btn* **4/1**[2]

4445 **11** 3/4 **Emerald Asset (IRE)**[11] 6105 3-8-9 **53** ... TonyHamilton 16 23
(Paul Midgley) *hld up: rdn along over 2f out: wknd over 1f out* **11/1**

5300 **12** 2 1/2 **Excellent World (IRE)**[63] 4240 3-9-2 **60** ... BarryMcHugh 7 22
(Tony Coyle) *in tch: drvn along over 2f out: sn wknd* **25/1**

1m 16.17s (2.47) **Going Correction** +0.325s/f (Good) 12 Ran SP% **120.8**
Speed ratings (Par 99): **96,94,94,93,91 89,89,87,86,82 81,77**
CSF £29.24 CT £291.29 TOTE £3.70: £1.40, £1.50, £3.50; EX 14.40 Trifecta £61.80.
Owner David & Yvonne Blunt **Bred** West Lodge Stud **Trained** Great Habton, N Yorks
■ Stewards' Enquiry : David Allan two-day ban (27-28 Sep): used whip above permitted level

FOCUS
An ordinary sprint handicap. The winner is rated back to last year's debut and those close up fit in.

6437 APOLLOBET CASHBACK IF 2ND H'CAP 6f 195y
6:45 (6:46) (Class 4) (0-80,80) 3-Y-O+ **£5,175** (£1,540; £769; £384) **Stalls** Low

Form RPR

1016 **1** **Depth Charge (IRE)**[4] 6280 4-9-2 **79** ...(vt) CliffordLee(7) 1 93
(Kristin Stubbs) *hld up on ins: gd hdwy to ld over 1f out: sn rdn and drifted lft: qcknd clr ins fnl f* **6/1**[2]

2033 **2** 4 **Inexes**[10] 6136 4-9-7 **77** ...(p) SamJames 10 81
(Marjorie Fife) *stdd and swtchd rt s: hld up: pushed along over 2f out: hdwy to chse (clr) wnr ins fnl f: kpt on* **8/1**[3]

0202 **3** nk **King Of Swing**[18] 5859 3-9-6 **80** ... PaulMulrennan 3 81
(James Given) *t.k.h: cl up: drvn along over 2f out: kpt on same pce fnl f* **11/2**[1]

2331 **4** hd **Yulong Xiongba (IRE)**[51] 4684 4-8-11 **67** ...(be) JoeDoyle 6 69
(Julie Camacho) *prom on outside: rdn over 2f out: kpt on same pce ins fnl f* **11/2**[1]

2333 **5** 1 1/2 **Signore Piccolo**[10] 6131 5-9-10 **80** ... DavidNolan 5 78
(David O'Meara) *t.k.h: hld up in tch: effrt and rdn 2f out: outpcd fnl f* **11/2**[1]

0034 **6** 1 **Fullon Clarets**[21] 5752 4-9-7 **77** ... GeorgeChaloner 4 73
(Richard Fahey) *t.k.h: trckd ldrs: rdn over 2f out: wknd over 1f out* **11/2**[1]

5646 **7** 1 3/4 **Dodgy Bob**[15] 5978 3-9-4 **78** ...(b) KevinStott 8 67
(Kevin Ryan) *t.k.h: led: pushed along and qcknd over 2f out: hdd over 1f out: sn wknd* **25/1**

0043 **8** 1/2 **Slemy (IRE)**[17] 5866 5-9-8 **78** ... JamesSullivan 7 68
(Ruth Carr) *plld hrd: hld up: rdn over 2f out: no imp fr over 1f out* **17/2**

6014 **9** 1/2 **Lido Lady (IRE)**[40] 5063 3-8-12 **72** ... JoeFanning 9 59
(Mark Johnston) *hld up: rdn whn hung rt wl over 1f out: sn wknd* **20/1**

40 **10** 1/2 **Hidden Treasures**[61] 4299 3-8-11 **71** ... TonyHamilton 2 56
(Richard Fahey) *s.i.s: sn prom: rdn along over 2f out: wknd over 1f out* **12/1**

1m 29.38s (2.28) **Going Correction** +0.475s/f (Yiel)
WFA 3 from 4yo+ 4lb 10 Ran SP% **113.8**
Speed ratings (Par 105): **105,100,100,99,98 97,95,94,93,93**
CSF £51.90 TOTE £6.30: £1.80, £2.30, £2.20; EX 62.40 Trifecta £348.20.
Owner Paramount Racing III **Bred** Budget Stable **Trained** Norton, N Yorks

FOCUS
They went just a routine pace in this modest sprint handicap. The winner has improved lately, and the 2nd, 3rd and 4th have been rated close to their recent marks.

6438 APOLLOBET WEEKLY GOLF RETURNS H'CAP 1m 6f 32y
7:15 (7:17) (Class 6) (0-65,71) 3-Y-O+ **£2,587** (£770; £384; £192) **Stalls** Low

Form RPR

3331 **1** **Transpennine Star**[7] 6219 3-9-9 **71** 6ex ... PaulMulrennan 6 80+
(Michael Dods) *t.k.h: trckd ldr: led over 2f out: rdn and drifted lft to stands' side over 1f out: kpt on strly fnl f* **2/1**[1]

3206 **2** 1 3/4 **Mikro Polemistis (IRE)**[78] 3722 3-7-13 **54** ow3 ... BenRobinson(7) 15 59
(Brian Ellison) *hld up: hdwy over 2f out: rdn over 1f out: chsd wnr against stands' rail ins fnl f: kpt on: nt pce of wnr* **8/1**[3]

5601 **3** 2 1/4 **Cosmic Tigress**[20] 5781 5-9-8 **59** ... JasonHart 5 61
(John Quinn) *t.k.h: trckd ldrs: effrt and rdn along in centre over 2f out: kpt on same pce ins fnl f* **12/1**

600/ **4** 3/4 **Marcus Antonius**[48] 1027 9-9-3 **54** ... JoeFanning 10 55
(Lucinda Russell) *t.k.h: hld up: stdy hdwy over 2f out: effrt and prom in centre over 1f out: kpt on same pce ins fnl f* **14/1**

4324 **5** 1 1/2 **La Bacouetteuse (FR)**[7] 6219 11-9-12 **63** ...(p) DavidAllan 2 62
(Iain Jardine) *hld up: rdn along over 3f out: effrt on far side of gp 2f out: kpt on fnl f: no imp* **9/1**

2645 **6** 3 **Nonagon**[11] 6103 5-9-9 **60** ...(t) KevinStott 9 55
(Wilf Storey) *dwlt: hld up: hdwy and ev ch on stands' side over 1f out: wknd ins fnl f* **22/1**

3006 **7** 1/2 **Zenafire**[12] 6058 7-10-0 **65** ...(p) PatrickMathers 13 60
(Sarah Hollinshead) *prom: effrt and cl up on outside of gp over 2f out: sn rdn: no ex appr fnl f* **11/1**

1442 **8** 1 **Chauvelin**[7] 6219 5-8-10 **54** ...(v) LewisEdmunds(7) 4 47
(Nigel Tinkler) *hld up midfield: drvn and outpcd in centre over 2f out: n.d after* **6/1**[2]

0000 **9** 1 **Ralphy Lad (IRE)**[50] 4702 5-10-0 **65** ... NeilFarley 14 57
(Alan Swinbank) *cl up: drvn along 3f out: wknd in centre over 1f out* **25/1**

0160 **10** 2 1/4 **Lightning Steps**[11] 6102 4-8-7 **51** ... GerO'Neill(7) 8 40
(Declan Carroll) *hld up towards rr: hdwy over 3f out: rdn on far side of gp 2f out: sn btn* **20/1**

4603 **11** 8 **Triple Eight (IRE)**[7] 6219 8-9-4 **60** ...(p) PhilDennis(5) 1 39
(Philip Kirby) *dwlt: hld up: hdwy over 3f out: rdn in centre over 2f out: sn wknd* **16/1**

0565 **12** 4 1/2 **Madam Lilibet (IRE)**[13] 6029 7-9-8 **59** ... JoeyHaynes 12 32
(Sharon Watt) *bhd: flashed tail and downed tools after 2f: sme hdwy over 2f out: nvr on terms* **14/1**

0003 **13** hd **Belle Peinture (FR)**[22] 5726 5-9-0 **51** oh6 ...(p) GeorgeChaloner 11 24
(Alan Lockwood) *led: rdn and hdd over 2f out: sn wknd* **80/1**

4-15 **14** 3 1/2 **Thackeray**[18] 5842 9-8-7 **51** oh4 ... PaulaMuir(7) 3 19
(Chris Fairhurst) *bhd: struggling wl over 3f out: sn btn* **25/1**

300 **15** 9 **Chiron (IRE)**[51] 4682 7-8-9 **51** oh6 ...[1] ShirleyTeasdale(5) 7 7
(Keith Dalgleish) *hld up in tch: drvn and struggling over 3f out: sn btn* **80/1**

3m 15.39s (7.89) **Going Correction** +0.475s/f (Yiel)
WFA 3 from 4yo+ 11lb 15 Ran SP% **123.2**
Speed ratings (Par 101): **96,95,93,93,92 90,90,89,89,88 83,80,80,78,73**
CSF £16.38 CT £162.08 TOTE £3.10: £1.60, £2.10, £3.50; EX 23.60 Trifecta £216.20.
Owner Transpennine Partnership **Bred** Dale Ablitt **Trained** Denton, Co Durham

FOCUS
They went a fair pace in this moderate staying handicap and the main action came down the stands' side in the home straight. The winner is on the upgrade and the second came back to form.
T/Plt: £85.10 to a £1 stake. Pool: £44,401.94 - 380.58 winning units. T/Qpdt: £14.60 to a £1 stake. Pool: £6,977.11 - 352.00 winning units. **Richard Young**

6250 CHEPSTOW (L-H)
Tuesday, September 13

OFFICIAL GOING: Good to soft changing to soft after race 1 (2.10)
Wind: slight half behind Weather: light rain

6439 SOUTH WALES IRONMEN RLFC EBF MAIDEN STKS 7f 16y
2:10 (2:12) (Class 5) 2-Y-O **£3,557** (£1,058; £529; £264) **Stalls** Centre

Form RPR

045 **1** **Trading Punches (IRE)**[29] 5484 2-9-5 0 ... JimCrowley 13 81
(David Brown) *chsd ldrs nr side but off the overall pce: rdn and hdwy over 2f out: led ent fnl f: pushed clr* **25/1**

06 **2** 5 **Pillar Of Society (IRE)**[81] 3598 2-9-5 0 ... SeanLevey 1 69
(Richard Hannon) *led one other towards far side and overall ldr: rdn 2f out and sn clr on side: kpt on tl wknd ins fnl f: jst hld 2nd* **11/1**

6423 **3** nk **Suffragette City (IRE)**[14] 5989 2-9-0 72 ... TomMarquand 15 63
(Richard Hannon) *chsd ldrs nr side but off the overall pce: rdn over 2f out: stl 5th 1f out: r.o wl: jst missed 2nd* **4/1**[3]

4 **4** nk **Hernandes (FR)**[40] 5081 2-9-5 0 ... GeorgeBaker 10 67
(Ed Walker) *led centre grp but several l off pair on far side: rdn over 2f out and briefly in 2nd: kpt on same pce: lost 3rd nr fin* **8/1**

02 **5** 1/2 **Intimate Art (IRE)**[47] 4790 2-9-5 0 ... OisinMurphy 4 66
(Andrew Balding) *racd centre tl swtchd to nr side after 1f: led gp but sme way off ldrs on far side: rdn and disp 2nd 2f out: wknd fnl f* **15/8**[1]

6 7 **It's How We Roll (IRE)** 2-9-5 0 ... MichaelJMMurphy 14 48
(Charles Hills) *racd nr side: towards rr of gp and wl off overall pce: hdwy over 3f out: rdn over 2f out: no further imp* **25/1**

4 **7** 3 3/4 **Beepeecee**[8] 6183 2-9-5 0 ... ShaneKelly 6 39
(Richard Hughes) *racd centre tl swtchd to nr side after 1f: prom in gp but sme way off overall pce: rdn over 3f out: one pce* **80/1**

8 4 **Brimham Rocks** 2-9-5 0 ... FMBerry 7 29
(Ralph Beckett) *dwlt: bhd in centre: styd on fnl f: nvr nr ldrs* **20/1**

40 **9** 2 **Skilful Lord (IRE)**[98] 2997 2-9-5 0 ... TimmyMurphy 3 24
(Stuart Kittow) *racd centre and wl off overall pce: nvr on terms* **100/1**

10 1 1/4 **Kingston Tasmania** 2-8-12 0 ... JoshuaBryan(7) 8 21
(Andrew Balding) *racd centre and wl off overall pce: rdn over 4f out: wknd over 2f out* **66/1**

3 **11** 1 1/2 **Tobrave (IRE)**[83] 3524 2-9-5 0 ... FrederikTylicki 2 17
(Roger Varian) *trckd one other towards far side and in clr 2nd overall: rdn over 2f out: sn wknd: eased over 1f out* **11/4**[2]

65 **12** 2 **Proud Show**[18] 5820 2-9-5 0 ... LiamKeniry 12 12
(David Dennis) *racd nr side: rdn 4f out: nvr on terms* **100/1**

13 shd **Turning Gold** 2-9-5 0 ... RyanPowell 11 12
(Sir Mark Prescott Bt) *s.i.s and chsd along early on nr side: a in rr* **50/1**

14 *2 1/4* **Ken's Ridge** 2-9-0 0 .... PaddyPilley(5) 9 6
(Ronald Harris) *dwlt: racd centre: sn in tch in gp but nvr on terms overall: bhd fnl 3f* **150/1**

15 *14* **Tally's Son** 2-9-0 0 .... CiaranMckee(5) 5
(Grace Harris) *wnt to post early: racd in tch in centre gp: rdn 1/2-way: wknd over 2f out* **250/1**

1m 25.64s (2.44) **Going Correction** +0.40s/f (Good) **15** Ran SP% **121.1**
Speed ratings (Par 95): **102,96,95,95,95 87,82,78,75,74 72,70,70,67,51**
CSF £269.08 TOTE £24.70: £5.20, £5.70, £1.90; EX 128.30 Trifecta £3431.50.
Owner J C Fretwell **Bred** Colin Kennedy **Trained** Averham Park, Notts

FOCUS
A moderate chase, the leaders went off pretty fast and the race set up for the winner.

6440 DRIBUILD DASH NURSERY H'CAP (FINAL ROUND OF THE CHEPSTOW SPRINT SERIES) 6f 16y
2:40 (2:40) (Class 5) (0-70,69) 2-Y-O **£3,234** (£962; £481; £240) **Stalls** Centre

Form RPR
032 **1** **Compton Lane**[92] 3231 2-9-5 **67** .... FrederikTylicki 8 75
(Rod Millman) *w ldr: led on stands' rail after 2f: rdn over 1f out: sn clr: jinked sltly wl ins fnl f: comf* **11/2**[3]

0056 **2** *2 3/4* **Apple Scruffs (IRE)**[40] 5052 2-8-10 **61** .... EdwardGreatrex(3) 11 59
(Michael Attwater) *hld up: rdn and hdwy over 2f out: wnt 2nd 1f out: styd on wl but a hld by wnr* **20/1**

0443 **3** *2 3/4* **Dark Hero (IRE)**[19] 5806 2-9-1 **63** .... OisinMurphy 10 53
(Charles Hills) *chsd ldrs: rdn over 2f out: briefly disp 2nd 1f out: hung lft and one pce fnl f* **5/1**[2]

550 **4** *nk* **Metronomic (IRE)**[60] 4336 2-9-5 **67** .... TomMarquand 4 56
(Richard Hannon) *t.k.h: chsd ldrs: pushed along 3f out: drvn whn nt clr run over 1f out: hld by ldrs and nt run on fnal f* **10/1**

300 **5** *2 1/4* **Company**[22] 5705 2-9-7 **69** .... SeanLevey 9 51
(Richard Hannon) *hld up: rdn over 2f out: sn outpcd: styd on fnl f* **10/1**

002 **6** *1/2* **Pastfact**[26] 5569 2-9-5 **67** .... JimCrowley 5 47
(Malcolm Saunders) *chsd ldrs: rdn over 2f out: briefly in 2nd over 1f out: no ex and wknd fnl f* **5/1**[2]

435 **7** *7* **Accladora**[127] 2104 2-9-4 **66** .... GeorgeBaker 6 25
(Mark Johnston) *led 2f: styd prom: rdn wl over 2f out: wknd over 1f out* **20/1**

0434 **8** *shd* **Goodwood Crusader (IRE)**[22] 5707 2-9-4 **66** .... ShaneKelly 1 25
(Richard Hughes) *prom: rdn 3f out: edgd rt and wknd over 1f out* **6/1**

0213 **9** *1* **Bobby Vee**[22] 5707 2-9-6 **68** .... RobertWinston 2 24
(Dean Ivory) *s.i.s: sn in tch on outer: rdn over 2f out: wknd appr fnl f* **3/1**[1]

4620 **10** *6* **Valley Lodge**[69] 4015 2-9-3 **65** .... FMBerry 7 3
(Julia Feilden) *s.i.s: towards rr: rdn over 3f out: wknd 2f out* **16/1**

1m 14.55s (2.55) **Going Correction** +0.45s/f (Yiel) **10** Ran SP% **121.6**
Speed ratings (Par 95): **101,97,93,93,90 89,80,80,78,70**
CSF £112.51 CT £464.61 TOTE £5.70: £1.90, £5.30, £3.70; EX 151.90 Trifecta £1260.90.
Owner The Links Partnership **Bred** Whitsbury Manor Stud & Jointsense Ltd **Trained** Kentisbeare, Devon

FOCUS
They raced stands' side in this nursery, but it didn't prove to be that competitive, with the winner racing away with it. Improvement from the winner.

6441 ULTIMATE FINANCE GROUP MAIDEN STKS 7f 16y
3:10 (3:11) (Class 5) 3-Y-O+ **£3,234** (£962; £481; £240) **Stalls** Centre

Form RPR
0202 **1** **Big Chill (IRE)**[27] 5544 4-9-4 75 .... MitchGodwin(5) 10 81
(Patrick Chamings) *trckd ldrs: chal 2f out: rdn to ld over 1f out: drvn out fnl f* **7/2**[2]

0433 **2** *3/4* **Apache Song**[18] 5822 3-9-0 68 ....[1] FrederikTylicki 6 72
(Rod Millman) *cl up: led 3f out: jnd 2f out: drvn and hdd over 1f out: styd on* **5/2**[1]

0503 **3** *7* **Where Next**[13] 6036 3-9-5 65 ....[1] DaneO'Neill 4 59
(Henry Candy) *t.k.h: prom: drvn 2f out: nt qckn and sn btn: hld mod 3rd* **10/1**[3]

03 **4** *5* **African Trader (USA)**[35] 5260 3-9-5 0 ....(t) RobertWinston 9 46
(Daniel Mark Loughnane) *chsd ldrs: rdn 3f out: wknd over 1f out: jst hld 4th* **14/1**

5 *shd* **Spanish Queen** 3-9-0 0 .... TimmyMurphy 1 41
(Mark Gillard) *qckly outpcd and wl bhd: stl last 1f out: nudged along and styd on wl past tiring rivals: jst missed 4th* **100/1**

0 **6** *3/4* **Rebel Woods (FR)**[57] 4458 3-9-5 0 .... LiamKeniry 3 44
(Geoffrey Deacon) *towards rr: rdn 1/2-way: mod hdwy over 2f out: wknd over 1f out* **100/1**

3 **7** *3/4* **Jazz Cat (IRE)**[5] 6251 3-9-0 0 ....(t) JimCrowley 7 37
(Paul Cole) *led against nr rail: rdn and hdd 3f out: wknd over 1f out* **7/2**[2]

65 **8** *1 1/2* **Magic Mirror**[10] 6135 3-9-0 0 .... TomMarquand 2 33
(Mark Rimell) *towards rr: rdn 1/2-way: edgd rt and sme hdwy 2f out: wknd 1f out* **33/1**

9 *2 1/4* **Captain Courageous (IRE)** 3-9-5 0 .... GeorgeBaker 8 32+
(Ed Walker) *dwlt: a bhd* **7/2**[2]

04 **10** *12* **Scarlet Not Blue**[36] 5233 4-9-9 0 .... SamHitchcott 5 3
(Matthew Salaman) *chsd ldrs to 1/2-way: bhd fnl 2f* **200/1**

1m 27.02s (3.82) **Going Correction** +0.45s/f (Yiel)
WFA 3 from 4yo 4lb **10** Ran SP% **116.4**
Speed ratings (Par 103): **96,95,87,81,81 80,79,77,75,61**
CSF £12.66 TOTE £3.50: £1.30, £1.50, £3.00; EX 13.10 Trifecta £57.00.
Owner Trolley Action **Bred** Corrin Stud **Trained** Baughurst, Hants

FOCUS
The front pair came clear in what was a modest maiden, with it going to one of the two older horses. The winner is rated to this year's form.

6442 DRIBUILD GROUP H'CAP 7f 16y
3:40 (3:40) (Class 4) (0-85,85) 3-Y-O+ **£4,851** (£1,443; £721; £360) **Stalls** Centre

Form RPR
6262 **1** **Cincuenta Pasos (IRE)**[3] 6339 5-9-10 **85** .... DaneO'Neill 5 93
(Joseph Tuite) *hld up last of 4 on nr side: hdwy to ld gp 3f out and cl up overall: pushed along to ld over 1f out: drvn out fnl f* **3/1**[1]

2534 **2** *1/2* **Peak Storm**[3] 6316 7-8-13 **79** ....(v) CiaranMckee(5) 3 86
(John O'Shea) *trckd ldng pair in gp of 4 far side: wnt 2nd in gp 2f out: sn edgd rt u.p: chsd wnr ins fnl f: styd on* **9/1**

1252 **3** *4 1/2* **Harlequin Striker (IRE)**[43] 4953 4-9-10 **85** .... RobertWinston 4 80
(Dean Ivory) *led gp of 4 far side and overall ldr: drvn 2f out: edgd rt and hdd over 1f out: one pce and lost 2nd ins fnl f* **7/2**[3]

6146 **4** *1 1/2* **Corporal Maddox**[19] 5793 9-9-3 **78** ....(p) OisinMurphy 1 69
(Ronald Harris) *s.i.s: last of 4 far side: drvn and clsd 3f out: one pce fnl 2f* **16/1**

0434 **5** *3 1/4* **Short Work**[37] 5206 3-9-2 **81** ....(v[1]) FMBerry 7 62
(Ralph Beckett) *led gp of 4 nr side but nt overall ldr: rdn and lost ld in gp 3f out: wknd over 1f out* **10/3**[2]

2236 **6** *8* **Smart Mover (IRE)**[13] 6019 3-8-1 **71** oh3 .... MitchGodwin(5) 6 31
(Nikki Evans) *trckd ldr in gp of 4 nr side: rdn 4f out: wknd 2f out* **28/1**

36-2 **7** *1 1/2* **Manton Grange**[48] 4766 3-8-12 **77** .... SteveDrowne 8 33
(George Baker) *trckd ldng pair in gp of 4 nr side: rdn 1/2-way: wknd over 1f out* **4/1**

50-5 **8** *2* **Caius College Girl (IRE)**[213] 558 4-8-6 **72** .... CharlieBennett(5) 2 25
(Patrick Chamings) *cl up in gp of 4 far side tl wknd over 2f out* **20/1**

1m 25.6s (2.40) **Going Correction** +0.50s/f (Yiel)
WFA 3 from 4yo+ 4lb **8** Ran SP% **114.4**
Speed ratings (Par 105): **106,105,100,98,94 85,84,81**
CSF £30.56 CT £97.60 TOTE £2.90: £1.60, £3.10, £1.40; EX 30.90 Trifecta £101.00.
Owner Mark Wellbelove **Bred** P J Gleeson **Trained** Lambourn, Berks

FOCUS
There was an even split into two groups, with the far side quartet leading early, but the winner came from those racing nearest to the stands. This fits with a better view of the winner's form, and the second is rated to form.

6443 DRIBUILD RAIL BUILDING FUTURES (S) STKS 1m 2f 36y
4:10 (4:10) (Class 6) 3-Y-O **£2,587** (£770; £384; £192) **Stalls** Low

Form RPR
6255 **1** **Monday Club**[34] 5303 3-8-7 56 .... SeanMooney(7) 1 64+
(Dominic Ffrench Davis) *trckd ldr in share of 2nd: def 2nd over 2f out: rdn to ld appr fnl f: r.o wl* **6/4**[2]

6610 **2** *7* **Desert Tango**[17] 5883 3-9-0 56 .... JimCrowley 2 52
(Michael Mullineaux) *led at stdy gallop: shkn up 2f out: drvn and hdd appr fnl f: one pce and no ch w wnr* **10/11**[1]

3 *8* **Quetzaltenango (FR)** 3-9-0 0 .... LiamKeniry 4 37
(J S Moore) *trckd ldr in share of 2nd: drvn 3f out: sn wknd and bk in 3rd* **6/1**[3]

00-0 **4** *6* **No Pleasing You (IRE)**[22] 5731 3-8-2 29 .... VictoriaWood(7) 3 21
(Bill Turner) *s.v.s and fly-jmpd leaving stalls: racd keenly and qckly in tch in last: drvn over 3f out: bhd fnl 2f* **50/1**

2m 18.32s (7.72) **Going Correction** +0.50s/f (Yiel) **4** Ran SP% **108.6**
Speed ratings (Par 99): **89,83,77,72**
CSF £3.24 TOTE £2.50; EX 3.10 Trifecta £3.20.No bid for the winner.
Owner Faber, Ffrench Davis, Head & Taylor **Bred** R F Johnson Houghton **Trained** Lambourn, Berks

FOCUS
A lowly seller, the pace was a steady one early although it did pick up from a fair way out. They finished strung out.

6444 EQUESTRIAN SURFACES LTD H'CAP 1m 2f 36y
4:40 (4:44) (Class 6) (0-65,65) 3-Y-O+ **£2,587** (£770; £384; £192) **Stalls** Low

Form RPR
6545 **1** **Collodi (GER)**[47] 3905 7-9-9 **64** .... LiamKeniry 13 76+
(Neil Mulholland) *t.k.h: trckd ldr: shkn up to ld 2f out: drvn clr fnl f: readily* **9/2**[2]

003 **2** *3* **Angelical (IRE)**[29] 5486 3-8-13 **61** .... JimCrowley 5 64
(Daniel Mark Loughnane) *trckd ldrs: drvn over 2f out: wnt 2nd over 1f out: outpcd by wnr fnl f* **8/1**

4006 **3** *1 1/4* **Sund City (FR)**[21] 5746 3-8-6 **54** .... TomMarquand 14 54
(Harry Dunlop) *led: jnd and drvn over 2f out: hdd 2f out: kpt on one pce* **11/1**

-406 **4** *1/2* **Guantoshol (IRE)**[7] 6212 5-9-7 **65** .... GeorgeDowning(3) 12 64
(Ian Williams) *dwlt: rdr briefly lost iron leaving stalls: hld up: hdwy 3f out: drvn 2f out: styd on fnl f* **8/1**

3-12 **5** *nk* **Intrigue**[40] 5065 4-9-10 **65** ....(b) DaneO'Neill 10 64
(Daniel Kubler) *chsd ldrs: drvn 2f out: kpt on same pce fnl f* **7/1**[3]

0-50 **6** *2* **Sir Pass I Am**[92] 3235 3-9-3 **65** .... OisinMurphy 8 60
(Andrew Balding) *mid-div: rdn 3f out: no real imp* **15/8**[1]

5055 **7** *1 1/2* **Oyster Card**[42] 4987 3-8-3 **51** .... AndrewMullen 9 44
(Michael Appleby) *chsd ldrs: rdn over 2f out: grad wknd over 1f out* **12/1**

-460 **8** *12* **Harikiri (IRE)**[42] 4978 3-8-13 **64** .... EdwardGreatrex(3) 1 35
(Charles Hills) *t.k.h towards rr: rdn 3f out: sme hdwy 2f out: wknd 1f out* **33/1**

2011 **9** *4* **African Showgirl**[18] 5823 3-9-2 **64** .... SteveDrowne 2 36
(George Baker) *mid-div: rdn over 3f out: wknd 2f out* **8/1**

0600 **10** *1 1/4* **Ignight**[15] 5953 5-8-10 **51** oh6 .... KieranO'Neill 4 13
(Matthew Salaman) *awkward s: hld up towards rr: drvn 3f out: wknd 2f out* **66/1**

254/ **R** **Pelham Crescent (IRE)**[1405] 7652 13-8-5 **51** oh1 .... MitchGodwin(5) 11
(Matthew Salaman) *led to s: ref to leave stalls* **66/1**

2m 15.41s (4.81) **Going Correction** +0.55s/f (Yiel)
WFA 3 from 4yo+ 7lb **11** Ran SP% **120.7**
Speed ratings (Par 101): **102,99,98,98,97 96,95,85,82,81**
CSF £41.35 CT £379.19 TOTE £5.30: £1.70, £2.70, £3.60; EX 45.00 Trifecta £482.30.
Owner T C and A Winter & Partners **Bred** Stiftung Gestut Fahrhof **Trained** Limpley Stoke, Wilts

FOCUS
They went slow early and the first three home were in the leading trio from an early stage. The winner used to be rated a lot higher.

6445 TURF SERVICES LTD H'CAP 1m 4f 23y
5:10 (5:10) (Class 4) (0-85,84) 3-Y-O+ **£4,851** (£1,443; £721; £360) **Stalls** Low

Form RPR
4641 **1** **Agent Gibbs**[9] 6165 4-8-13 **76** ....(p) MitchGodwin(5) 3 85
(John O'Shea) *wnt to post early: mde all: drvn over 2f out: styd on wl to draw clr fnl f* **9/4**[1]

3310 **2** *3 1/2* **Glens Wobbly**[26] 5574 8-8-12 **75** .... HectorCrouch(5) 2 78
(Jonathan Geake) *trckd ldrs: drvn over 3f out: wnt 2nd 1f out: qckly outpcd by wnr but kpt on u.p to hold 2nd* **18/1**

153 **3** *1/2* **Medburn Cutler**[5] 6267 6-9-5 **77** ....(p) JimCrowley 8 80
(Paul Henderson) *trckd wnr: chal over 4f out tl drvn 3f out: lost 2nd 1f out: kpt on same pce* **3/1**[2]

4120 **4** *2 1/4* **Justice Grace (IRE)**[44] 4920 3-9-3 **84** ....(v) FMBerry 1 83
(Ralph Beckett) *t.k.h in mid-div: rdn to chse ldng trio 3f out: kpt on same pce tl no ex ins fnl f* **7/1**[3]

0P **5** *4 1/2* **Manny Owens (IRE)**[44] 4920 4-9-8 **80** .... GeorgeBaker 4 72+
(Jonjo O'Neill) *hld up in last: 5 l detached 5f out: swtchd lft and hdwy over 2f out: sn drvn and no further imp: wknd ins fnl f* **20/1**

1526 **6** *nk* **Kesselring**[38] 5147 3-8-13 **80** .... TomMarquand 6 71
(Richard Hannon) *hld up towards rr: rdn over 4f out: outpcd 3f out: styd on fnl f but nvr any ch* **3/1**[2]

642 **7** *nk* **Come Back King (IRE)**[22] 5731 3-8-4 **71** .... AndrewMullen 5 62
(Michael Appleby) *chsd ldrs: rdn over 3f out: wknd 2f out* **12/1**

660- **8** *6* **Akavit (IRE)**[164] 6330 4-9-1 **73**.. LiamKeniry 7 54
(Ed de Giles) *hld up towards rr: rdn and outpcd 3f out: no ch fnl 2f* **20/1**

2m 43.52s (4.52) **Going Correction** +0.55s/f (Yiel)
WFA 3 from 4yo+ 9lb **8** Ran SP% **115.7**
Speed ratings (Par 105): **106,103,103,101,98 98,98,94**
CSF £45.20 CT £121.47 TOTE £3.80: £1.10, £4.20, £1.40; EX 41.90 Trifecta £172.20.
Owner The Cross Racing Club **Bred** A M Tombs **Trained** Elton, Gloucs

FOCUS
Add 18yds to race distance. They appeared to go a fair enough pace for what was an ordinary handicap and the winner made every yard. The winner has been rated to his latest York win.
T/Plt: £165.80 to a £1 stake. Pool: £65,034.27 - 286.2 winning units. T/Qpdt: £18.60 to a £1 stake. Pool: £5,258.86 - 208.27 winning units. **Richard Lowther**

6129 THIRSK (L-H)

Tuesday, September 13

OFFICIAL GOING: Good to firm (8.4) (watered)
Wind: light 1/2 behind Weather: sunny, very warm

6446 THIRSK RACECOURSE FANTASTIC FOR WEDDING RECEPTIONS (S) STKS 7f

2:00 (2:03) (Class 6) 2-Y-O **£2,587** (£770; £384; £192) **Stalls** Low

Form RPR

0020 **1** **Vatican Hill (IRE)**[20] 5770 2-8-9 55.......................[1] AdamMcNamara(5) 6 69+
(Richard Fahey) *s.i.s: in rr: hdwy 3f out: led over 1f out: drvn clr* **11/1**

0504 **2** *3 1/2* **Texas Katie**[4] 6292 2-9-1 67.. GrahamLee 1 60
(Mick Channon) *trckd ldrs: led briefly 2f out: kpt on same pce fnl f* **5/2**[1]

604 **3** *3 1/2* **Whitby Bay**[38] 5177 2-8-4 48....................................... NathanEvans(5) 14 45
(Michael Easterby) *in rr: hdwy to chse ldrs over 2f out: nt clr run and swtchd rt 100yds out: tk modest 3rd nr fin* **66/1**

212 **4** *1/2* **London Grammar (IRE)**[5] 6253 2-9-1 60.......................... CamHardie 13 50
(John Quinn) *mid-div: hdwy on wd outside over 2f out: kpt on to take modest 4th strides* **3/1**[2]

4431 **5** *1/2* **Chevalier Du Lac (IRE)**[7] 6208 2-9-6 74...................... PaulMulrennan 5 53
(Conor Dore) *mid-div: hdwy and hung rt over 3f out: upsides over 1f out: kpt on one pce* **5/1**

30 **6** *hd* **Best Away (FR)**[20] 5756 2-9-0 0...................................... JamesSullivan 3 47
(Ruth Carr) *s.i.s: chsng ldrs after 2f: one pce over 1f out* **33/1**

2402 **7** *7* **Coco La Belle (IRE)**[15] 5974 2-8-6 56.............. RachelRichardson(3) 12 23
(Tim Easterby) *chsd ldrs: wknd over 1f out* **9/2**[3]

00 **8** *1* **Savea (IRE)**[10] 6129 2-9-0 0.. DanielTudhope 10 25
(David O'Meara) *chsd ldrs: drvn and outpcd 3f out: lost pl over 1f out* **12/1**

0 **9** *1/2* **With Intent**[15] 5966 2-9-0 0.. PJMcDonald 2 24
(Ollie Pears) *slowly away: bhd: sme hdwy 2f out: nvr on terms* **80/1**

0455 **10** *2* **Albizu Campos**[19] 5799 2-8-9 59........................... CallumShepherd(5) 8 18
(Lawrence Mullaney) *mid-div: drvn 3f out: sn lost pl* **40/1**

0055 **11** *8* **Sheppard's Gift**[18] 5853 2-8-9 45.............................(e) DuranFentiman 7
(Tim Easterby) *w ldrs: led after 2f out: lost pl over 1f out: bhd whn eased clsng stages* **80/1**

60 **12** *1 1/4* **No Luck Penny**[43] 4943 2-8-9 0...................................... PatrickMathers 4
(Noel Wilson) *s.i.s: bhd: t.o 3f out* **100/1**

0 **13** *2 1/4* **Kallisto Freedom (IRE)**[15] 5966 2-8-4 0...................... PhilDennis(5) 11
(Philip Kirby) *t.k.h: led 2f: trckd ldrs. lost pl 2f out* **66/1**

00 **14** *2 1/4* **I Call The Shots**[76] 3772 2-8-11 0........................... JacobButterfield(3) 9
(Ollie Pears) *chsd ldrs: drvn over 4f out: lost pl over 2f out* **66/1**

1m 27.39s (0.19) **Going Correction** +0.05s/f (Good) **14** Ran SP% **117.8**
Speed ratings (Par 93): **100,96,92,91,90 90,82,81,80,78 69,68,65,62**
CSF £37.20 TOTE £12.20: £3.60, £1.40, £13.90; EX 37.20 Trifecta £1866.80.The winner was bought in for £6,500. Texas Katie was claimed by A Watson for £8,000.
Owner Merchants and Missionaries **Bred** Mrs Gillian McCalmont **Trained** Musley Bank, N Yorks

FOCUS
The watered ground (4mm Sunday night and 3mm overnight) was given as good to firm. The rail on the home (Wood) bend was dolled out around 3yds from the inside line, and the away (Stables) bend was dolled out around 4yds from the inside line, adding about 10yds to the 7f and 8f distances, and about 20yds to the 1m4f distance. An ordinary seller but the winner improved.

6447 THIRSK RACECOURSE IDEAL LOCATION FOR CONFERENCES MAIDEN AUCTION STKS (DIV I) 6f

2:30 (2:32) (Class 5) 2-Y-O **£2,911** (£866; £432; £216) **Stalls** High

Form RPR

1 **Wediddodontwe** 2-8-13 0.. DanielTudhope 1 68
(Richard Guest) *s.i.s: sn trckd ldrs: hmpd and swtchd lft over 1f out: rdn to narrowly jst ins fnl f: hdd 75yds out: kpt on: led again post* **11/4**[2]

0 **2** *nse* **Gaval**[22] 5727 2-8-12 0.. GrahamGibbons 5 67
(David Barron) *trckd ldrs: rdn 2f out: chal ent fnl f: led narrowly 75yds out: sn edgd lft: hdd post* **11/2**[3]

5 **3** *2 1/4* **Free At Last (IRE)**[28] 5511 2-8-9 0.................................. JackGarritty 6 57
(Richard Fahey) *led to post: pressed ldr: hung lft fr early stage: led wl over 1f out: sn rdn: hdd jst ins fnl f: one pce* **11/8**[1]

4 *3* **Vivardia (IRE)** 2-8-10 0.. GrahamLee 4 48
(Ben Haslam) *slowly away: hld up: pushed along 1/2-way: kpt on fr over 1f out: nvr threatened ldrs* **20/1**

0 **5** *2 1/2* **Royal Celebration**[116] 2417 2-9-1 0.............................. ConnorBeasley 2 45
(Bryan Smart) *midfield: rdn 2f out: no imp* **15/2**

0 **6** *1 1/2* **Equiano Springs**[17] 5884 2-9-0 0.................................... AndrewElliott 7 39
(Tom Tate) *led narrowly: rdn over 2f out: hdd wl over 1f out: wknd* **8/1**

7 *12* **Orientelle** 2-8-6 0... PaulQuinn 9
(Richard Whitaker) *v.s.a: a rr* **20/1**

1m 13.4s (0.70) **Going Correction** -0.05s/f (Good) **7** Ran SP% **116.6**
Speed ratings (Par 95): **93,92,89,85,82 80,64**
CSF £18.87 TOTE £2.60: £1.30, £3.50; EX 14.90 Trifecta £43.70.
Owner www.primelawns.co.uk **Bred** Mr And Mrs R Newman **Trained** Ingmanthorpe, W Yorks

FOCUS
This is rated as ordinary form.

6448 THIRSK RACECOURSE IDEAL LOCATION FOR CONFERENCES MAIDEN AUCTION STKS (DIV II) 6f

3:00 (3:00) (Class 5) 2-Y-O **£2,911** (£866; £432; £216) **Stalls** High

Form RPR

3 **1** **Anfaass (IRE)**[31] 5410 2-9-1 0... TomQueally 2 79+
(George Margarson) *hld up towards rr: hdwy and swtchd lft over 1f out: sn chsng ldr: styd on to ld last 75yds* **5/2**[2]

2022 **2** *3/4* **Lucky Mistake (IRE)**[19] 5798 2-8-13 78........................... JackGarritty 5 75
(Richard Fahey) *trckd ldrs: hung lft and led over 1f out: hdd and no ex last 75yds* **1/1**[1]

03 **3** *4* **Glyder**[17] 5884 2-8-6 0.. RoystonFfrench 7 55
(John Holt) *dwlt: sn led: hung lft and hdd over 1f out: one pce* **8/1**[3]

0 **4** *3/4* **Skellig Michael**[17] 5884 2-8-13 0.. GrahamLee 6 59
(Ben Haslam) *led early: w ldrs: one pce over 1f out* **50/1**

04 **5** *hd* **Hamba Kashe (IRE)**[17] 5884 2-8-13 0......................... DuranFentiman 9 59
(Tim Easterby) *chsd ldrs: one pce over 1f out* **10/1**

6 **6** *7* **A Bit Of Ginger**[20] 5756 2-8-7 0... PJMcDonald 1 30
(Ann Duffield) *1/2 rrd s: t.k.h: sn trcking ldrs: lost pl over 1f out: sn bhd* **12/1**

00 **7** *1 1/2* **Aegean Secret**[17] 5884 2-8-13 0... TomEaves 3 32
(Kevin Ryan) *wnt lft s: sn chsng ldrs: wknd over 1f out: sn bhd* **50/1**

36 **8** *16* **Cupid's Arrow (IRE)**[17] 5884 2-9-0 0............................ JamesSullivan 8
(Ruth Carr) *in rr: swtchd lft over 2f out: sn hung rt and lost pl: bhd whn eased* **10/1**

1m 12.55s (-0.15) **Going Correction** -0.05s/f (Good) **8** Ran SP% **119.5**
Speed ratings (Par 95): **99,98,92,91,91 82,80,58**
CSF £5.62 TOTE £4.30: £1.30, £1.10, £2.40; EX 5.80 Trifecta £24.80.
Owner Sheikh Mohamed Bin Maktoum Al Maktoum **Bred** Mrs Margaret Sinanan **Trained** Newmarket, Suffolk

FOCUS
The quicker of the two divisions by 0.85sec. The winner and second improved, and the third fits.

6449 THIRSK RACECOURSE PERFECT FOR OUTDOOR EVENTS H'CAP 6f

3:30 (3:31) (Class 3) (0-95,95) 3-Y-O+ **£7,439** (£2,213; £1,106; £553) **Stalls** High

Form RPR

U200 **1** **Mythmaker**[31] 5418 4-9-7 **95**.. TomEaves 3 104
(Bryan Smart) *swtchd lft after s: led: edgd rt 150yds out: hld on towards fin* **7/1**

3043 **2** *hd* **Vibrant Chords**[37] 5199 3-8-13 **89**....................................... GrahamLee 1 97
(Henry Candy) *trckd ldrs: effrt over 2f out: upsides over 1f out: carried lft 150yds out: no ex nr fin* **11/2**[2]

4650 **3** *3/4* **Imtiyaaz (IRE)**[14] 6012 4-9-1 **89**.................................... AndreaAtzeni 7 95
(Roger Varian) *chsd ldrs: kpt on wl last 100yds* **7/1**

000- **4** *1 1/2* **Merdon Castle (IRE)**[395] 5387 4-8-11 **85**.................(e[1]) JamesSullivan 6 86
(Ruth Carr) *mid-div: effrt over 2f out: kpt on same pce fnl f* **40/1**

100 **5** *1/2* **Udontdodou**[31] 5409 3-8-12 **88**...................................... DanielTudhope 4 88
(Richard Guest) *swtchd lft after s: hld up: swtchd outside ocver 2f out: kpt on same pce appr fnl f* **13/2**[3]

0001 **6** *3/4* **Money Team (IRE)**[10] 6131 5-8-7 **81** oh1.................... AdamBeschizza 8 78
(David Barron) *rr=div: hdwy over 2f out: nt clr run over 1f out: kpt on same pce* **12/1**

0010 **7** *shd* **Hawkeyethenoo (IRE)**[10] 6109 10-8-11 **85**...................... JackGarritty 9 82+
(Jim Goldie) *in rr: hdwy and nt clr run over 1f out: swtchd lft and styd on last 100yds* **20/1**

35-0 **8** *shd* **Twin Appeal (IRE)**[31] 5417 5-8-12 **86**...................(b) GrahamGibbons 12 83
(David Barron) *rr-div: hdwy and n.m.r over 1f out: kpt on same pce* **9/1**

4000 **9** *3 3/4* **Zanetto**[27] 5555 6-9-2 **90**...(v) PJMcDonald 2 75
(John Quinn) *mid-div: effrt over 2f out: wknd fnl f* **16/1**

5260 **10** *1 1/2* **Foxtrot Knight**[14] 5991 4-8-2 **81** oh1............................ NathanEvans(5) 10 61
(Ruth Carr) *w wnr: wknd fnl f* **8/1**

0422 **11** *1 1/2* **Harwoods Volante (IRE)**[11] 6072 5-8-7 **81**....................... SamJames 11 56
(David O'Meara) *hld up in rr: t.k.h: nvr a factor* **9/2**[1]

6500 **12** *3 3/4* **See The Sun**[31] 5417 5-9-1 **89**.. CamHardie 5 52
(Tim Easterby) *cased ldrs: wknd fnl f: eased towards fin* **40/1**

1m 11.07s (-1.63) **Going Correction** -0.05s/f (Good)
WFA 3 from 4yo+ 2lb **12** Ran SP% **116.2**
Speed ratings (Par 107): **108,107,106,104,104 103,102,102,97,95 93,88**
CSF £43.51 CT £282.49 TOTE £11.90: £3.50, £2.40, £2.20; EX 45.10 Trifecta £225.50.
Owner Crossfields Racing **Bred** Crossfields Bloodstock Ltd **Trained** Hambleton, N Yorks

FOCUS
Not a bad handicap but few got involved. A small pb from the winner.

6450 THIRSK RACECOURSE SENSATIONAL FOR DINNERS & DANCES H'CAP 1m 4f

4:00 (4:00) (Class 5) (0-70,70) 3-Y-O+ **£3,234** (£962; £481; £240) **Stalls** High

Form RPR

2233 **1** **Machine Learner**[25] 5607 3-9-0 **70**.......................(v) LouisSteward(3) 8 78
(Michael Bell) *hld up towards rr: hdwy over 3f out: nt clr run and swtchd rt over 1f out: rdn and styd on to ld last 100yds: readily* **10/3**[2]

5362 **2** *2* **First Sargeant**[13] 6029 6-8-11 **60**........................(p) AdamMcNamara(5) 4 65
(Lawrence Mullaney) *trckd ldrs: pushed along over 4f out: led narrowly over 1f out: hdd and no ex last 100yds* **6/1**

4425 **3** *hd* **The Kid**[32] 5350 5-9-12 **70**...(p) JackGarritty 9 75
(John Quinn) *mid-div: hdwy over 3f out: hung lft and upsides over 1f out: kpt on same pce last 100yds* **4/1**[3]

0136 **4** *2* **Airton**[15] 5975 3-9-1 **68**.. PJMcDonald 3 69
(James Bethell) *mid-div: drvn 3f out: chsng ldrs over 1f out: one pce* **3/1**[1]

0453 **5** *6* **Best Boy**[16] 5918 4-9-2 **60**...(vt) GrahamGibbons 7 52
(David C Griffiths) *w ldr: led over 2f out: hdd over 1f out: sn wknd* **7/1**

024 **6** *nse* **Dry Your Eyes (IRE)**[19] 5801 5-9-11 **69**............................ DanielTudhope 5 61
(David O'Meara) *hld up in rr: drvn and edgd lft over 2f out: nvr a factor* **9/1**

0-46 **7** *3 1/2* **Merriment**[10] 6135 3-8-8 **61** ow1... TomEaves 2 47
(Peter Niven) *s.s: hld up in rr: sme hdwy 3f out: hung lft and lost pl over 1f out* **20/1**

-00R **8** *3 3/4* **Rolen Sly**[103] 2836 7-8-9 **56** oh11........................... JacobButterfield(3) 1 36
(Neville Bycroft) *led: hdd over 2f out: sn lost pl: eased whn bhd clsng stages* **100/1**

2m 37.0s (0.80) **Going Correction** +0.05s/f (Good)
WFA 3 from 4yo+ 9lb **8** Ran SP% **110.6**
Speed ratings (Par 103): **99,97,97,96,92 92,89,87**
CSF £21.95 CT £76.56 TOTE £4.10: £1.20, £2.30, £1.50; EX 25.30 Trifecta £83.10.
Owner The Deflators & Partner **Bred** Bearstone Stud Ltd **Trained** Newmarket, Suffolk

FOCUS
They went a decent enough gallop in this modest affair. The form is set around the second and third, with the winner finding a bit on his recent level.

6451 2017 RACE FIXTURES AT THIRSKRACECOURSE.NET H'CAP 6f

4:30 (4:35) (Class 6) (0-65,65) 3-Y-O+ **£2,587** (£770; £384; £192) **Stalls** High

Form RPR

0023 **1** **Gaelic Wizard (IRE)**[13] 6023 8-8-11 **60**......................(v) GemmaTutty(5) 13 68
(Karen Tutty) *hld up in rr stands' side: hdwy over 1f out: styd on wl to ld last 50yds* **10/1**

2010 **2** 1 **Caeser The Gaeser (IRE)**[17] 5887 4-8-9 **60**.....(p) KieranSchofield(7) 19 65
(Nigel Tinkler) *s.i.s: in rr stands' side: hdwy over 1f out: styd on wl to take 2nd post* **17/2**

-500 **3** hd **Ki Ki**[116] 2416 4-8-11 **60**.................... PhilDennis(5) 16 64
(Bryan Smart) *swtchd rt s: mid-div: hdwy over 2f out: chsng ldrs over 1f out: edgd lft and rdr dropped whip 100yds out: kpt on same pce* **28/1**

1212 **4** nse **Tricky Dicky**[15] 5960 3-9-4 **64**.................... DuranFentiman 1 68
(Olly Williams) *chsd ldrs: led 2f out: hdd and no ex last 50yds* **11/2**[1]

0601 **5** ¾ **Cool Strutter (IRE)**[11] 6105 4-9-5 **63**..........(b) SamJames 12 65
(Karen Tutty) *rr-div: hdwy and hung lft over 1f out: kpt on wl clsng stages* **14/1**

0520 **6** ¾ **Indian Pursuit (IRE)**[27] 5537 3-9-4 **64**.......... JackGarritty 3 63
(John Quinn) *chsd ldrs: kpt on one pce fnl f* **14/1**

0004 **7** 1 ¾ **Jebel Tara**[11] 6100 11-8-10 **59**..........(bt) GeorgeBuckell(5) 17 54
(Alistair Whillans) *chsd ldrs stands' side: n.m.r: edgd lft and one pce fnl f* **7/1**[3]

0062 **8** 1 ¼ **Jacob's Pillow**[22] 5714 5-9-5 **63**.......... DanielTudhope 4 53
(Rebecca Bastiman) *chsd ldrs: fdd fnl f* **6/1**[2]

-633 **9** ½ **Cruise Tothelimit (IRE)**[20] 5762 8-9-2 **65**.......... AdamMcNamara(5) 18 53
(Patrick Morris) *led on stands' side: hdd 2f out: wknd fnl f* **8/1**

2000 **10** 1 ½ **Mustn't Grumble (IRE)**[22] 5732 3-9-2 **62**..........(p) StevieDonohoe 2 45
(Ivan Furtado) *dwlt: rr-div: sme hdwy over 1f out: nvr a factor* **33/1**

0030 **11** ½ **Horsforth**[3] 6341 4-8-9 **58**..........(b) CallumShepherd(5) 15 40
(Richard Guest) *w ldr stands' side: wknd appr fnl f* **25/1**

3116 **12** 1 **Gypsy Major**[3] 6347 4-8-13 **64**..........(v) LewisEdmunds(7) 11 42
(Garry Moss) *dwlt: rr-div: nvr a factor* **7/1**[3]

0020 **13** hd **Windforpower (IRE)**[11] 6098 6-8-11 **58**..........(p) JacobButterfield(3) 8 36
(Tracy Waggott) *mid-div: hdwy over 2f out: hmpd over 1f out: sn wknd* **33/1**

1650 **14** hd **Round The Island**[17] 5864 3-8-10 **61**..........(p) NathanEvans(5) 5 38
(Richard Whitaker) *chsd ldrs centre: rdn over 2f out: lost pl appr fnl f* **25/1**

-000 **15** ½ **French**[70] 3978 3-9-5 **65**.................... PJMcDonald 6 41
(Antony Brittain) *rr-div: hdwy over 2f out: n.m.r and swtchd lft over 1f out: sn wknd* **25/1**

6022 **16** 1 ½ **Viva Verglas (IRE)**[25] 5605 5-9-4 **62**..........(e) GrahamGibbons 9 33
(Daniel Mark Loughnane) *rrd s: a in rr* **12/1**

1m 11.48s (-1.22) **Going Correction** -0.05s/f (Good)
WFA 3 from 4yo+ 2lb **16** Ran SP% **127.3**
Speed ratings (Par 101): **106,104,104,104,103 102,100,98,97,95 95,93,93,93,92 90**
CSF £89.06 CT £1457.09 TOTE £11.00: £2.10, £2.70, £8.30, £1.70; EX 131.10 Trifecta £4214.90 Part won..
Owner Grange Park Racing (Tutty Trio) **Bred** Mrs Mary Gallagher **Trained** Osmotherley, N Yorks
■ Great Expectations was withdrawn. Price at time of withdrawal 16/1. Rule 4 does not apply.
■ Stewards' Enquiry : George Buckell jockey said the gelding was denied a clear run

FOCUS
A competitive sprint, with those drawn high and racing nearer the stands' side coming out on top. The winner has been in good form and this has been rated in keeping with his recent efforts.

6452 BREEDERS BACKING RACING EBF MAIDEN STKS 1m
5:00 (5:06) (Class 5) 3-Y-O+ **£3,881** (£1,155; £577; £288) **Stalls** Low

Form RPR

3232 **1** **Organza**[10] 6135 3-9-0 73..........(v) GrahamLee 8 77
(Mick Channon) *mde all: rdn over 1f out: kpt on wl* **7/2**[2]

63- **2** 3 ¼ **Sun Lover**[382] 5824 3-9-5 0.................... AndreaAtzeni 7 75
(Roger Varian) *racd keenly: trckd ldrs: rdn over 2f out: sn one pce in 2nd* **2/5**[1]

3 **3** 6 **Aloysius Hansom**[15] 5979 3-9-5 0.................... TomEaves 5 61
(Kevin Ryan) *s.i.s: midfield: hdwy 3f out: rdn over 2f out: edgd lft over 1f out: one pce* **5/1**[3]

/0-0 **4** 4 **Newspeak (IRE)**[22] 5716 4-9-10 40....................[1] CamHardie 4 53
(Fred Watson) *in tch: rdn over 2f out: grad wknd* **125/1**

64 **5** 5 **Calarules**[14] 6014 3-9-5 0.................... DuranFentiman 10 40
(Tim Easterby) *midfield: rdn 3f out: nvr threatened* **33/1**

0000 **6** 5 **Emilie Bronte**[32] 5370 3-9-0 47.................... AndrewElliott 9 24
(Chris Fairhurst) *racd keenly: trckd ldrs: rdn over 3f out: sn wknd* **100/1**

00- **7** ½ **Ixchell**[292] 7996 3-8-9 0.................... AdamMcNamara(5) 2 22
(Richard Fahey) *prom: rdn 3f out: sn wknd* **16/1**

8 1 ½ **Theocratic** 3-9-5 0..........(vt[1]) StevieDonohoe 11 24
(Charlie Fellowes) *s.i.s: a towards rr* **20/1**

55 **9** ½ **Python**[15] 5979 4-9-10 0.................... TomQueally 1 24
(Andrew Crook) *a rr* **100/1**

0 **P** **Melodya (IRE)**[7] 6218 3-8-9 0.................... CallumShepherd(5) 6
(Brian Ellison) *dwlt: hld up: sddle slipped 4f out and sn p.u* **40/1**

1m 40.85s (0.75) **Going Correction** +0.05s/f (Good)
WFA 3 from 4yo 5lb **10** Ran SP% **129.1**
Speed ratings (Par 103): **98,94,88,84,79 74,74,72,72,**
CSF £5.80 TOTE £3.90: £1.10, £1.10, £1.50; EX 8.40 Trifecta £18.90.
Owner Prince A A Faisal **Bred** Nawara Stud Co Ltd **Trained** West Ilsley, Berks
■ Stewards' Enquiry : Adam McNamara jockey said the filly ran too free
Andrew Elliott jockey said the filly ran too free
Callum Shepherd jockey said that his saddle slipped

FOCUS
An ordinary maiden in which the winner has been rated to form.

6453 BOOK ONLINE FOR 2017 THIRSKRACECOURSE.NET H'CAP 7f
5:30 (5:33) (Class 5) (0-70,70) 3-Y-O+ **£3,234** (£962; £481; £240) **Stalls** Low

Form RPR

05-0 **1** **Big Storm Coming**[232] 332 6-9-2 **62**.................... TomEaves 3 73
(David Brown) *trckd ldrs: nt clr run over 1f out: swtchd rt: styd on to ld last 100yds: edgd rt: drvn out* **14/1**

-261 **2** 1 **Dark Wonder (IRE)**[16] 5935 4-9-5 **68**..........(p) LouisSteward(3) 1 76
(Ivan Furtado) *s.i.s: in rr: chsng ldrs after 2f: drvn over 2f out: kpt on same pce fnl f: tk 2nd clsng stages* **7/1**[3]

0210 **3** 1 ¼ **Whozthecat (IRE)**[10] 6137 9-9-6 **66**..........(t) DanielTudhope 7 71
(Declan Carroll) *w ldr: led over 4f out: hdd and no ex last 100yds* **4/1**[1]

2020 **4** ¾ **Lucky Lodge**[18] 5845 6-9-8 **68**..........(p) PJMcDonald 2 71
(Antony Brittain) *mid-div: hdwy over 2f out: chsng ldrs over 1f out: 4th fnl strides* **20/1**

0440 **5** shd **Captain Bob (IRE)**[21] 5744 5-9-5 **70**.......... AdamMcNamara(5) 6 73
(Robert Cowell) *hld up in rr: hdwy over 2f out: kpt on one pce over 1f out* **11/2**[2]

3341 **6** 1 ¼ **Iceaxe**[22] 5732 3-9-5 **69**.................... RoystonFfrench 12 66
(John Holt) *chsd ldrs: drvn 3f out: one pce over 1f out* **15/2**

3645 **7** ¾ **Mercers Row**[7] 6215 9-9-7 **67**.................... JackGarritty 9 64
(Michael Herrington) *hld up towards rr: t.k.h: effrt over 2f out: kpt on one pce: nvr a threat* **8/1**

0620 **8** 2 **Big Amigo (IRE)**[24] 5643 3-9-4 **68**..........(e) RichardKingscote 13 58
(Tom Dascombe) *hld up in rr: sme hdwy whn nt clr run and swtchd lft over 1f out: nvr a factor* **12/1**

0-66 **9** nk **Destination Aim**[22] 5717 9-9-7 **67**.................... CamHardie 11 58
(Fred Watson) *led tl over 4f: wknd fnl f.* **33/1**

4605 **10** ¾ **Cabal**[15] 5973 9-9-10 **70**..........(v) GrahamGibbons 8 59
(Geoffrey Harker) *hld up in rr: effrt over 2f out: nvr a factor* **16/1**

043 **11** nk **Snappy Guest**[41] 5037 4-9-10 **70**..........(p) TomQueally 5 58
(George Margarson) *mid-div: drvn 3f out: nvr a factor* **10/1**

0241 **12** ½ **Pyla (IRE)**[59] 4388 4-9-9 **69**..........(p) LemosdeSouza 4 56
(Amy Murphy) *hld up in rr: sme hdwy on inner over 2f out: lost pl over 1f out* **7/1**[3]

1m 26.94s (-0.26) **Going Correction** +0.05s/f (Good)
WFA 3 from 4yo+ 4lb **12** Ran SP% **120.3**
Speed ratings (Par 103): **103,101,100,99,99 98,97,94,94,93 93,92**
CSF £110.43 CT £482.72 TOTE £19.00: £5.80, £2.20, £2.10; EX 180.40 Trifecta £1733.10.
Owner Fishlake Commercial Motors Ltd **Bred** Bearstone Stud Ltd **Trained** Averham Park, Notts

FOCUS
Fair form for the grade, rated around the front-running third. The winner has been rated to last year's form.
T/Jkpt: Not won. T/Plt: £43.30 to a £1 stake. Pool: £69,066.40 - 1,162.99 winning units. T/Qpdt: £5.90 to a £1 stake. Pool: £5,268.57 - 649.87 winning units. **Walter Glynn & Andrew Sheret**

5929 YARMOUTH (L-H)
Tuesday, September 13

OFFICIAL GOING: Good to firm (good in places; 7.8) (watered) (last race abandoned due to false ground)
Wind: light, half against Weather: sunny spells, light cloud

6454 BRITISH STALLION STUDS EBF MAIDEN FILLIES' STKS (PLUS 10 RACE) 6f 3y
2:20 (2:22) (Class 4) 2-Y-O **£4,657** (£1,386; £692; £346) **Stalls** Centre

Form RPR

30 **1** **Muthmira**[11] 6071 2-9-0 0.................... SilvestreDeSousa 9 84+
(Simon Crisford) *mde all: rdn 2f out: 2 l clr and in command 1f out: r.o wl: comf* **7/2**[2]

2 1 ¼ **Gheedaa (USA)** 2-9-0 0.................... PaulHanagan 2 80+
(William Haggas) *t.k.h: hld up in tch: shkn up and hdwy to chse ldrs over 1f out: rdn 1f out: wnt 2nd wl ins fnl f: kpt on but no threat to wnr* **7/1**

03 **3** 1 ¾ **Bouquet De Flores (USA)**[48] 4756 2-9-0 0.......... WilliamBuick 5 74
(Charlie Appleby) *t.k.h: pressed wnr: rdn 2f out: drvn and unable qck over 1f out: lost 2nd wl ins fnl f: wknd towards fin* **5/4**[1]

4 1 ½ **Always Thankful** 2-9-0 0.................... MartinHarley 7 70+
(Ismail Mohammed) *hld up in tch in midfield: effrt and pushed along over 1f out: 4th and rdn 1f out: styd on same pce after* **12/1**

5 1 ¾ **Diamond Bear (USA)** 2-9-0 0.................... LukeMorris 6 64
(Sir Mark Prescott Bt) *dwlt and pushed along leaving stalls: sn in tch in midfield: rdn over 2f out: outpcd over 1f out: wl hld and kpt on same pce fnl f* **80/1**

56U2 **6** nk **Chica De La Noche**[5] 6244 2-9-0 0.................... NickyMackay 4 63
(Simon Dow) *t.k.h: chsd ldrs: rdn over 1f out: sn lost pl and btn: wknd fnl f* **16/1**

02 **7** 1 ¾ **Textured (IRE)**[16] 5930 2-9-0 0.................... RyanMoore 1 57
(Sir Michael Stoute) *in tch in midfield: rdn 2f out: lost pl and btn over 1f out: wknd fnl f* **4/1**[3]

8 1 **Dandy Walk** 2-9-0 0.................... TedDurcan 3 54
(Chris Wall) *s.i.s: a last pair: pushed along over 1f out: sn wknd* **100/1**

0 **9** 6 **Cool Breeze (IRE)**[11] 6078 2-9-0 0.................... JamieSpencer 8 35
(David Simcock) *stdd s: hld up in rr: pushed along and hung lft over 1f out: sn btn: bhd fnl f* **66/1**

1m 11.62s (-2.78) **Going Correction** -0.525s/f (Hard) **9** Ran SP% **116.5**
Speed ratings (Par 94): **97,95,93,91,88 88,85,84,76**
CSF £28.38 TOTE £5.20: £1.50, £2.20, £1.10; EX 26.40 Trifecta £77.60.
Owner Sheikh Juma Dalmook Al Maktoum **Bred** P Finlason & Kirtlington Stud **Trained** Newmarket, Suffolk

FOCUS
The going was described as good to firm good in places after watering had taken place to maintain. A patch of false ground around the 4f marker meant the stalls were moved to the stands' side and not as advertised. An interesting maiden in which the winner posted form in keeping with her debut promise.

6455 STEPHEN WRIGHT MEMORIAL NURSERY H'CAP (FOR THE JACK LEADER CHALLENGE TROPHY) 1m 3y
2:50 (2:50) (Class 4) (0-85,84) 2-Y-O **£4,657** (£1,386; £692; £346) **Stalls** Centre

Form RPR

022 **1** **Zymyran**[14] 5990 2-8-7 **70**.................... HarryBentley 2 76
(David Simcock) *stdd after s: hld up in tch in rr: swtchd lft and clsd over 2f out: rdn to chal ent fnl f: led ins fnl f: r.o wl* **12/1**

242 **2** ¾ **Celestial Spheres (IRE)**[18] 5828 2-9-3 **80**.......... WilliamBuick 1 84
(Charlie Appleby) *in tch in midfield: rdn over 2f out: drvn and ev ch over 1f out: styd on same pce ins fnl f* **5/2**[2]

0221 **3** shd **Hurricane Rush (IRE)**[15] 5959 2-9-7 **84**.......... SilvestreDeSousa 3 88
(Charles Hills) *led: rdn 2f out: drvn and hrd pressed over 1f out: hdd and styd on same pce ins fnl f* **2/1**[1]

312 **4** 3 **Vanity Queen**[18] 5847 2-9-1 **78**.................... JamieSpencer 5 75
(Luca Cumani) *hld up in tch in last pair: nt clr run 2f out: effrt to chse ldng trio over 1f out: no imp ins fnl f* **9/2**[3]

055 **5** 7 **King's Coinage (IRE)**[12] 6044 2-8-6 **68**.................... LukeMorris 4 48
(Ed Walker) *chsd ldrs: rdn ent fnl 2f: lost pl and btn over 1f out: wknd fnl f* **16/1**

621 **6** 39 **Star Of The East (IRE)**[14] 5990 2-9-0 **77**.................... JamesDoyle 6
(Mark Johnston) *chsd ldr: rdn over 2f out: lost pl and bhd over 1f out: eased fnl f: t.o* **11/2**

1m 37.02s (-3.58) **Going Correction** -0.525s/f (Hard) **6** Ran SP% **109.0**
Speed ratings (Par 97): **96,95,95,92,85 46**
CSF £39.69 TOTE £9.30: £4.40, £1.60; EX 46.60 Trifecta £171.30.
Owner Nurlan Bizakov **Bred** Hesmonds Stud Ltd **Trained** Newmarket, Suffolk

FOCUS
Just the six runners but a competitive nursery nonetheless with two of the field holding, perhaps optimistically, Group 1 entries. The front two have been rated to their marks.

6456 DAN HAGUE RAILS BOOKMAKER H'CAP 1m 3f 104y
3:20 (3:20) (Class 2) (0-100,96) 3-Y-**£12,602** (£3,772; £1,886; £944; £470) **Stalls** Low

Form RPR
-113 **1** **You're Hired**[16] 5924 3-8-11 **86**.. RyanMoore 3 95+
(Amanda Perrett) *led for 1f: stdd and hld up in tch in 4th: pushed along and clsd to press ldrs 2f out: led 1f out: r.o wl under hands and hld ins fnl f: comf* **8/11**[1]

3440 **2** *1 1/4* **Theydon Grey**[122] 2244 3-8-7 **82**...................................... JimmyQuinn 1 89
(Peter Charalambous) *hld up in rr: nt a clr run and hmpd over 1f out: sn swtchd rt: rdn and hdwy to chse wnr 100yds out: styd on but no threat to wnr* **12/1**

4510 **3** *2 1/2* **Point Of View (IRE)**[89] 3300 3-9-0 **89**.............................. HarryBentley 5 92
(Roger Varian) *stmbld and bmpd leaving stalls: led after 2f: rdn over 2f out: hdd over 1f out: styd on same pce ins fnl f* **9/2**[2]

6151 **4** *shd* **Haddajah (IRE)**[42] 4977 3-8-12 **87**................................[1] FrankieDettori 6 90
(Sir Michael Stoute) *t.k.h: styd centre early: led after 1f tl 10f out: chsd ldr after: rdn and ev ch over 2f out: drvn over 1f out: wknd ins fnl f* **7/1**[3]

1252 **5** *1* **Diamond Geyser (IRE)**[17] 5875 3-8-2 **77**......................... LukeMorris 4 78
(Luca Cumani) *bmpd s: t.k.h: chsd ldrs after 1f: rdn over 2f out: unable qck and hmpd over 1f out: styd on same pce after* **7/1**[3]

2m 23.74s (-4.96) **Going Correction** -0.325s/f (Firm) **5** Ran SP% **108.8**
Speed ratings (Par 107): **105,104,102,102,101**
CSF £9.96 TOTE £1.50: £1.40, £4.40; EX 9.30 Trifecta £24.60.
Owner George Materna **Bred** Cheveley Park Stud Ltd **Trained** Pulborough, W Sussex

FOCUS
A race won by horses on an upward curve in recent years and there again looked to be some progressive types in action.

6457 THOMAS PRIOR MEMORIAL H'CAP 1m 6f 17y
3:50 (3:51) (Class 4) (0-80,80) 3-Y-O+ **£5,175** (£1,540; £769; £384) **Stalls** High

Form RPR
3221 **1** **Pleasure Dome**[12] 6049 3-8-12 **75**..................................... RyanMoore 2 85
(Peter Chapple-Hyam) *chsd ldr: clsd to ld over 2f out: rdn over 1f out: in command and styd on wl ins fnl f* **5/2**[1]

543 **2** *3* **Blazing Mighty**[12] 6049 3-8-3 **69**........................... JosephineGordon(3) 3 75
(Robyn Brisland) *chsd ldrs: pushed along over 3f out: chsd wnr 2f out: styd on same pce u.p fr over 1f out* **10/3**[2]

3200 **3** *3 3/4* **Odeon**[9] 6163 5-10-0 **80**.. SilvestreDeSousa 7 82
(James Given) *led: sn clr: rdn and hdd over 2f out: 3rd and one pced over 1f out: eased wl ins fnl f* **7/2**[3]

0300 **4** *9* **All The Winds (GER)**[153] 1417 11-9-8 **74**........................(t) LukeMorris 4 62
(Shaun Lycett) *racd off the pce in 5th: effrt over 3f out: nvr threatening ldrs and outpcd and btn over 2f out: modest 4th over 1f out: plugged on* **40/1**

4225 **5** *hd* **Safira Menina**[38] 5176 4-8-13 **72**............................ NatalieHambling(7) 6 60
(Martin Smith) *hld up off the pce in last pair: effrt but stl plenty to do 3f out: nvr on terms w ldrs: battling for modest 4th over 1f out: plugged on* **17/2**

2120 **6** *13* **Sandy Cove**[22] 5724 5-9-5 **71**.. RyanTate 5 40
(James Eustace) *s.i.s: a off the pce in rr: bhd fnl 2f* **6/1**

04 **7** *1/2* **Sisyphus**[33] 5321 4-9-12 **78**.. MartinHarley 1 47
(Ollie Pears) *t.k.h early: hld up in midfield: effrt 3f out: sn outpcd and btn: wknd over 2f out* **8/1**

3m 2.75s (-4.85) **Going Correction** -0.325s/f (Firm)
WFA 3 from 4yo+ 11lb **7** Ran SP% **112.2**
Speed ratings (Par 105): **100,98,96,91,90 83,83**
CSF £10.58 TOTE £2.80: £1.60, £1.90; EX 11.70 Trifecta £44.40.
Owner J G Davis **Bred** J G Davis & Star Pointe Ltd **Trained** Newmarket, Suffolk

FOCUS
The winner is rated back to her early maiden form.

6458 GREENE KING IPA CONDITIONS STKS 6f 3y
4:20 (4:20) (Class 3) 3-Y-O+ **£7,561** (£2,263; £1,131) **Stalls** Centre

Form RPR
0644 **1** **Basil Berry**[16] 5934 5-8-9 93...................................(b) SilvestreDeSousa 2 101
(Chris Dwyer) *chsd ldr tl 4f out: rdn ent fnl 2f: wnt 2nd and clsd over 1f out: led u.p 1f out: styd on and drew wl clr fnl f* **4/1**[2]

0033 **2** *6* **Baccarat (IRE)**[17] 5880 7-8-9 109.................................... WilliamBuick 4 82
(Charlie Appleby) *stdd and awkward leaving stalls: racd in 3rd tl wnt 2nd after 2f: pushed along ent fnl 2f: 3rd and swtchd rt over 1f out: sn drvn and fnd little: no ch w wnr ins fnl f: wnt 2nd 75yds out* **4/11**[1]

1404 **3** *1* **Steady Pace**[60] 4359 3-8-12 105...........................(v[1]) CameronNoble(7) 3 91
(Saeed bin Suroor) *led and set str gallop: clr after 2f: rdn over 1f out: hdd 1f out: sn btn and wknd ins fnl f* **13/2**[3]

1m 10.03s (-4.37) **Going Correction** -0.525s/f (Hard)
WFA 3 from 5yo+ 2lb **3** Ran SP% **106.6**
Speed ratings (Par 107): **108,100,98**
CSF £6.17 TOTE £4.50; EX 5.50 Trifecta £4.90.
Owner Strawberry Fields Stud **Bred** Strawberry Fields Stud **Trained** Newmarket, Suffolk

FOCUS
A disappointing turnout for this race which was dealt a further blow when Wokingham winner Outback Traveller was taken out after being found to be lame. Despite the small field they went a genuine gallop throughout. The winner has been rated to the form from this race the previous year.

6459 MOULTON NURSERIES MAIDEN STKS 6f 3y
4:50 (4:52) (Class 5) 3-Y-O+ **£3,622** (£1,078; £538; £269) **Stalls** Centre

Form RPR
6-22 **1** **Roman Holiday (IRE)**[37] 5192 3-9-0 66..........................[1] HarryBentley 1 71
(Ed Vaughan) *hld up in tch in 4th: clsd 2f out: effrt and drvn to chal over 1f out: sustained duel w rival fnl f: styd on wl to ld cl home* **3/1**[2]

2 **2** *hd* **Port Isaac (IRE)**[33] 5327 3-9-5 0....................................... MartinDwyer 4 75
(Marcus Tregoning) *t.k.h: led: rdn over 1f out: hrd pressed and edgd lft 1f out: drvn and sustained duel w wnr fnl f: hdd cl home* **10/11**[1]

6-5 **3** *3 1/4* **Forever Yours (IRE)**[18] 5850 3-9-2 0.............................. JackDuern(3) 5 65
(Dean Ivory) *t.k.h: chsd ldng pair tl 4th and sltly outpcd over 1f out: styd on same pce after: wnt 3rd wl ins fnl f* **66/1**

0/3- **4** *3 1/2* **Cockney Island**[312] 7734 4-9-2 0.................................. SilvestreDeSousa 3 49
(Philip McBride) *chsd ldr: rdn ent fnl 2f: drvn and ev ch over 1f out: no ex whn squeezed for room jst ins fnl f: wknd and lost 3rd wl ins fnl f* **7/2**[3]

5 *5* **Blynx** 3-9-0 0.. MartinHarley 2 33
(David Simcock) *dwlt and hmpd leaving stalls: in tch in rr: pushed along 1/2-way: edgd lft ent fnl 2f: wknd over 1f out* **6/1**

1m 12.78s (-1.62) **Going Correction** -0.525s/f (Hard)
WFA 3 from 4yo 2lb **5** Ran SP% **115.4**
Speed ratings (Par 103): **89,88,84,79,73**
CSF £6.54 TOTE £4.20: £2.20, £1.10; EX 6.90 Trifecta £80.00.
Owner Bloomsbury Stud **Bred** Bloomsbury Stud **Trained** Newmarket, Suffolk

FOCUS
A weak maiden and the level is fluid.

6460 TRAFALGAR RESTAURANT AT YARMOUTH H'CAP 5f 42y
(5:20) (Class 4) (0-85,) 3-Y-O+ £

T/Plt: £137.80 to a £1 stake. Pool: £60,637.75 - 321.03 winning units. T/Qpdt: £29.10 to a £1 stake. Pool: £3,261.92 - 82.70 winning units. **Steve Payne**

LAYTOWN
Tuesday, September 13

OFFICIAL GOING: Sand: standard

6461a AT THE RACES H'CAP 6f
3:05 (3:06) (50-75,75) 4-Y-O+ **£4,748** (£1,466; £694; £308; £115)

RPR
1 **My Good Brother (IRE)**[9] 6166 7-10-3 **64**........................ ColinKeane 10 76+
(T G McCourt, Ire) *chsd ldrs tl tk clsr order almost on terms fr 1/2-way: rdn to ld over 1f out and kpt on wl to assert wl ins fnl f* **11/4**[1]

2 *2 1/2* **Summersault (IRE)**[35] 5259 5-10-3 **64**......................... WilliamCarson 4 68+
(Jamie Osborne) *dwlt sltly and settled towards rr: prog after 1/2-way to chse ldrs: rdn over 1f out and kpt on wl into nvr threatening 2nd clsng stages: nt trble wnr* **5/1**[2]

3 *3/4* **Indian Landing (IRE)**[43] 4959 8-10-6 **67**...................... MichaelHussey 5 69
(Tracey Collins, Ire) *prom and led narrowly over 2f out: strly pressed and hdd over 1f out: sn no ch w wnr and dropped to 3rd clsng stages* **8/1**

4 *1 3/4* **Mr Bounty**[10] 6146 6-9-4 **54** oh2...................................... ShaneBKelly(3) 6 50
(M D O'Callaghan, Ire) *dwlt sltly and settled towards rr: pushed along fr 1/2-way and sn swtchd rt u.p in rr: r.o wl nr side ins fnl f into nvr nrr 4th: nvr trbld ldrs* **13/2**[3]

5 *3/4* **Sister Slew (IRE)**[15] 5982 6-10-5 **66**.................................. ShaneFoley 8 60
(Shane Nolan, Ire) *dwlt sltly and towards rr: pushed along fr 1/2-way and rdn nr side under 2f out: sme hdwy u.p ins fnl f: kpt on same pce: nvr trbld ldrs* **9/1**

6 *hd* **Fast In The Wind (IRE)**[9] 6166 5-10-12 **73**.................(t) RobbieColgan 3 66
(P D Deegan, Ire) *w.w towards rr far side: sme hdwy after 1/2-way: rdn under 2f out and no ex u.p in 4th briefly ins fnl f: one pce clsng stages* **7/1**

7 *1 1/2* **Zylan (IRE)**[17] 5899 4-9-12 **64**.................................. DonaghO'Connor(5) 7 52
(David Marnane, Ire) *dwlt sltly and pushed along briefly: settled towards rr tl tk clsr order after 1/2-way: sn rdn and no imp on ldrs u.p in 8th ins fnl f: kpt on one pce clsng stages* **10/1**

8 *hd* **Rigolleto (IRE)**[19] 5797 8-10-9 **70**............................ DeclanMcDonogh 9 58
(Anabel K Murphy) *chsd ldr tl disp fr 1/2-way: rdn and hdd over 2f out: sn no ex and wknd 1f out* **5/1**[2]

9 *3* **Bush Warrior (IRE)**[35] 5259 5-10-7 **68**...................... EmmetMcNamara 2 46
(Anabel K Murphy) *settled bhd ldrs: pushed along fr 1/2-way and dropped towards rr 2f out: one pce after* **12/1**

10 *15* **Faineog (IRE)**[9] 6166 5-10-9 **75**.................................. AdrianO'Shea(5) 1 5
(Mrs A M O'Shea, Ire) *wnt sltly rt s: sn led: rdn and jnd fr 1/2-way: hdd over 2f out and sn no ex: wknd: eased fnl f* **20/1**

1m 10.94s (70.94) **10** Ran SP% **128.5**
CSF £18.33 CT £108.29 TOTE £2.90: £1.40, £2.30, £2.60; DF 19.50 Trifecta £184.90.
Owner Oliver Curtis **Bred** Oghill House Stud **Trained** Stamullen, Co Meath

FOCUS
Declan McDonogh said the surface was "rattling quick" and Denis Hogan who rode the winner of the second race said something similar. For the second year stalls were in use. The winner of the opener was drawn in stall 10 and stayed wide throughout.

6462a RACING POST H'CAP 6f
3:35 (3:36) (45-65,64) 4-Y-O+ **£4,295** (£1,327; £628; £279; £104)

RPR
1 **Burren View Lady (IRE)**[17] 5899 6-11-0 **64**........................(t) DGHogan 1 72
(Denis Gerard Hogan, Ire) *sn chsd ldrs far side: impr to dispute fr 2f out: led gng best over 1f out and rdn clr: comf* **10/1**

2 *2 1/4* **War Room (IRE)**[9] 6171 7-10-9 **59**....................................... ShaneFoley 4 60
(S M Duffy, Ire) *disp early tl sn settled bhd ldrs: disp fr 2f out tl hdd over 1f out: no imp on wnr ins fnl f: kpt on same pce* **10/3**[1]

3 *nk* **Acroleina (IRE)**[17] 5899 5-9-13 **49**.........................(t) DeclanMcDonogh 8 49
(H Rogers, Ire) *dwlt sltly and settled towards rr: hdwy after 1/2-way to chse ldrs: rdn into 3rd ins fnl f and no imp on wnr: kpt on same pce* **4/1**[2]

4 *2 1/4* **Our Manekineko**[28] 5533 6-9-6 **45**..............................(t) GaryHalpin(3) 10 38+
(J A Nash, Ire) *dwlt and w.w in rr: pushed along bef 1/2-way: rdn in 9th over 2f out and r.o wl ins fnl f into nvr nrr 4th: nrst fin* **9/2**[3]

5 *3/4* **Kiss The Stars (IRE)**[9] 6166 6-10-10 **60**........................... ColinKeane 9 50
(T G McCourt, Ire) *on toes befhand: in tch: tk clsr order bef 1/2-way: rdn bhd ldrs 1 1/2f out and no ex u.p ent fnl f: one pce after* **9/2**[3]

6 *nk* **Like A Prayer**[19] 5138 5-9-4 **45**............................... DonaghO'Connor(5) 6 34
(Garvan Donnelly, Ire) *chsd ldrs: rdn in 6th over 2f out and outpcd over 1f out: no imp on wnr u.p in 7th ent fnl f: kpt on one pce* **20/1**

7 *nk* **Suburban Sky (IRE)**[20] 5788 5-9-10 **46**.....................(t) MichaelHussey 2 34
(H Rogers, Ire) *dwlt sltly: hld up in tch: rdn 2f out and sme hdwy to chse ldrs u.p far side over 1f out: no ex and one pce ins fnl f* **12/1**

8 *1* **Miss Temple (IRE)**[13] 6040 4-9-10 **46**............................. RoryCleary 5 31
(Gavin Cromwell, Ire) *disp early tl sn led: rdn and hdd under 2f out: sn no ex and wknd fr over 1f out* **12/1**

9 *2 1/2* **Athassel**[9] 6172 7-9-9 **45**...(t) WilliamCarson 7 22
(Jamie Osborne) *towards rr and pushed along early: tk clsr order nr side bef 1/2-way where rdn: sn no ex and lost tch fr over 2f out* **7/1**

10 *1 3/4* **Cliffords Reprieve**[159] 1304 8-9-9 **45**........................ EmmetMcNamara 3 17
(John Gerard Fitzgerald, Ire) *cl up: pushed along fr 1/2-way and wknd 2f out: eased in 9th wl ins fnl f* **33/1**

1m 11.0s (71.00) **10** Ran SP% **124.1**
CSF £46.30 CT £166.95 TOTE £9.10: £3.00, £1.40, £1.50; DF 62.10 Trifecta £113.60.
Owner Is That All Syndicate **Bred** L Mulryan **Trained** Cloughjordan, Co Tipperary

FOCUS
The opening winner kept wide, but this one stuck to the inner - suggesting that there was no track bias whatsoever. The winner has been rated in line with her season's best.

6463a GILNA'S COTTAGE INN MAIDEN 7f
4:05 (4:06) 4-Y-O+ **£5,200** (£1,606; £761; £338; £126)

RPR

1 **Free Running (IRE)**^{104} 2791 4-9-9 72............................ GaryHalpin$^{(3)}$ 6 61+
(John James Feane, Ire) *hld up in tch tl tk clsr order bhd ldrs in 4th bef 1/2-way: impr gng wl on outer and rdn to ld over 1f out: kpt on wl ins fnl f* **2/1**^{2}

2 3 1/4 **Approbare (IRE)**^{72} 3929 4-10-3 58....................................(t) MsKWalsh 9 57+
(T M Walsh, Ire) *w.w: clsr in 7th bef 1/2-way: pushed along and hdwy on outer fr over 2f out: rdn in 4th 1 1/2f out and r.o wl into 2nd clsng stages: nt trble wnr* **10/1**

3 1 3/4 **Snoozing Indian**^{8} 6197 4-10-3 70................................. WilliamCarson 3 52
(Jamie Osborne) *cl up and disp after 1/2-way: hdd 2f out and rdn in 2nd: no imp on wnr in 3rd ins fnl f: dropped to 4th briefly wl ins fnl f: kpt on same pce into 3rd cl home* **6/4**^{1}

4 shd **Teagan Angel (IRE)**^{97} 3049 4-9-12 66.................^{1} EmmetMcNamara 5 47
(Ms M Dowdall Blake, Ire) *sn chsd ldrs: swtchd lft fr 1/2-way and impr far side to ld fr 2f out: sn rdn and hdd u.p over 1f out: no ex and wknd into 4th ins fnl f* **12/1**

5 7 **Coral Cluster (IRE)**^{13} 6037 4-9-12 45................................ RoryCleary 4 28
(Thomas Cleary, Ire) *led narrowly tl jnd and hdd after 2f: 3rd 1/2-way: pushed along after 1/2-way and sn dropped to 5th: rdn in 6th under 2f out and no imp on ldrs: kpt on one pce in mod 5th ins fnl f* **16/1**

6 8 **Midnite Ride (IRE)**^{63} 4244 4-9-12 59................................ ShaneFoley 1 7
(Patrick Martin, Ire) *hld up in tch far side: 6th 1/2-way: pushed along after 1/2-way and no imp in mod 7th under 2f out: kpt on one pce in mod 6th ins fnl f* **16/1**

7 1 3/4 **Jackapies Bay (IRE)**^{91} 2941 8-10-3 49........................... MarkEnright 7 7
(Thomas P O'Connor, Ire) *sltly awkward s and reminders early: towards rr: pushed along in 8th bef 1/2-way and sn no imp: wknd fr over 2f out* **33/1**

8 7 **Maluhia (IRE)**^{30} 5446 4-10-3 0.. ConorHoban 2
(Kieran P Cotter, Ire) *cl up and led narrowly after 2f: jnd and hdd u.p over 2f out: sn wknd towards rr and eased fnl f* **50/1**

R **Labaik (FR)**^{125} 2151 5-10-3 0................................. DeclanMcDonogh 10
(Gordon Elliott, Ire) *ref to r* **5/1**^{3}

1m 22.38s (82.38) **9** Ran SP% **123.4**
CSF £24.73 TOTE £2.70: £1.02, £2.80, £1.10; DF 16.70 Trifecta £82.30.
Owner James Mescall & Denis P Beary **Bred** Mrs C Regalado-Gonzalez **Trained** Curragh, Co Kildare

FOCUS
A nine-runner maiden which was effectively down to eight when Labaik failed to jump with the others when the gates opened. The runner-up helps set the standard.

6464a MARQUEES NATIONWIDE CLAIMING RACE 7f
4:35 (4:36) 4-Y-O+ **£4,295** (£1,327; £628; £279; £104)

RPR

1 **Emperor Bob (IRE)**^{29} 5492 4-9-12 65................. DonaghO'Connor$^{(5)}$ 2 73+
(David Marnane, Ire) *mde all: rdn under 2f out and kpt on wl to assert ins fnl f: reduced advantage cl home: comf* **9/2**^{1}

2 2 **Rialto Magic**^{160} 1264 4-10-0 60..................................... WilliamCarson 3 63+
(Jamie Osborne) *hld up in tch: 7th 1/2-way: pushed along after 1/2-way and rdn into 2nd 1 1/2f out: no imp on wnr ent fnl f: kpt on u.p wl ins fnl f: a hld* **9/2**^{1}

3 4 **Rigid Rock (IRE)**^{20} 5786 9-10-3 59................................... ColinKeane 9 55
(Adrian McGuinness, Ire) *hld up in tch: 6th 1/2-way: rdn nr side fr 2f out and no imp u.p in 6th over 1f out: r.o into nvr threatening 3rd clsng stages: nvr trbld ldrs* **5/1**^{2}

4 1 1/4 **Kill Or Cure (IRE)**^{45} 4900 4-10-3 65................................ RoryCleary 5 52
(Gavin Cromwell, Ire) *chsd ldrs and pushed along briefly early: 3rd 1/2-way: pushed along after 1/2-way and sn no imp on wnr: u.p in 3rd ent fnl f: one pce after* **12/1**

5 1 1/2 **Jembatt (IRE)**^{45} 4899 9-10-3 64.......................................(t) ShaneFoley 4 48
(Michael Mulvany, Ire) *chsd ldrs: rdn in 4th 2f out and no imp on wnr over 1f out: one pce ins fnl f where dropped to 5th* **8/1**

6 3 1/2 **Not A Bad Oul Day (IRE)**^{24} 5663 4-10-3 60............. MichaelHussey 8 38
(Mrs D A Love, Ire) *chsd ldrs: 4th 1/2-way: rdn fr after 1/2-way and no imp on ldrs u.p in 7th under 2f out: kpt on one pce into mod 6th ins fnl f* **6/1**^{3}

7 1 1/4 **Steady Major (IRE)**^{12} 7238 4-10-0 65.......................(t) LPDempsey$^{(3)}$ 7 35
(Gordon Elliott, Ire) *s.i.s: towards rr: rdn under 3f out and no imp: one pce fnl 2f* **12/1**

8 2 3/4 **Gower Princess**^{214} 542 5-10-0 0................................ RobbieColgan 6 25
(Miss Clare Louise Cannon, Ire) *on toes befhand: v awkward and rrd s: towards rr: 8th 1/2-way: rdn and no imp fr under 2f out* **33/1**

9 2 **Dove Mountain (IRE)**^{24} 4248 5-10-3 61.............(t) DeclanMcDonogh 1 22
(Gordon Elliott, Ire) *slowly away and awkward s where reminders: towards rr early tl impr far side to chse ldrs after 1f and sn wnt 2nd: rdn over 2f out and sn no ex: wknd over 1f out* **9/2**^{1}

10 2 1/4 **Bussa**^{307} 7801 8-10-3 51..(t) ConorHoban 10 16
(S J Mahon, Ire) *awkward and rrd s where lost grnd: in rr early tl tk clsr order nr side bef 1/2-way: rdn over 2f out and sn no ex: wknd and eased fr under 2f out* **12/1**

1m 22.89s (82.89) **10** Ran SP% **122.6**
CSF £26.07 TOTE £5.20: £1.80, £1.80, £2.40; DF 24.70 Trifecta £117.20.
Owner McGettigans Management Services JLT **Bred** Simon Tindall **Trained** Bansha, Co Tipperary

FOCUS
Punters were unable to separate the front three in the betting for this 7f claimer but those who waded in on a late gamble on the eventual winner never had a moments worry.

6465a O'NEILLS SPORTS (Q.R.) H'CAP 7f
5:05 (5:05) (50-80,80) 4-Y-O+ **£5,652** (£1,746; £827; £367; £137)

RPR

1 **Korbous (IRE)**^{27} 5563 7-11-11 **73**..................................... MsKWalsh 5 76
(Richard Brabazon, Ire) *chsd ldrs: 3rd 1/2-way: impr travelling wl to chal 1 1/2f out: rdn to ld narrowly over 1f out and kpt on wl u.p ins fnl f: all out: jst* **8/1**

2 shd **Beechmount Whisper (IRE)**^{25} 5045 4-11-12 **77**..... MrSClements$^{(3)}$ 9 80+
(P J Prendergast, Ire) *hld up in tch: 7th 1/2-way: prog nr side fr 2f out to chal in cl 2nd ent fnl f: kpt on wl u.p ins fnl f to strly press wnr: jst hld* **10/1**

3 1 1/2 **Strait Of Zanzibar (USA)**^{49} 4748 7-11-13 **80**(t) MrsPaulineCondon$^{(5)}$ 2 79
(K J Condon, Ire) *chsd ldrs: 4th 1/2-way: effrt far side under 2f out: u.p in cl 3rd ent fnl f: no imp on ldrs wl ins fnl f: kpt on same pce* **6/4**^{1}

4 1/2 **Fairy Foxglove (IRE)**^{30} 5445 6-11-8 **75**....................... MrFMaguire$^{(5)}$ 3 72
(P J F Murphy, Ire) *led narrowly tl jnd briefly after 2f: sn regained advantage: narrow ld at 1/2-way: rdn and strly pressed under 2f out: sn jnd and hdd over 1f out: no ex in 4th wl ins fnl f: kpt on same pce* **4/1**^{2}

5 4 1/2 **Specific Gravity (FR)**^{9} 6172 8-11-0 **65**......................... MrDGLavery$^{(3)}$ 4 50
(Adrian McGuinness, Ire) *dwlt: sn chsd ldrs and n.m.r between horses after 2f where checked sltly: 5th 1/2-way: sme hdwy after 1/2-way bhd ldrs: rdn far side over 2f out and no ex in 5th over 1f out: one pce after* **9/1**

6 1 **Ainslie (IRE)**^{5} 6561 4-12-0 **76**...(t) MrJJCodd 10 58
(Gordon Elliott, Ire) *dismntd bef s: wnt sltly rt s and settled in rr: sme hdwy into mod 8th 1 1/2f out: kpt on into mod 6th ins fnl f: nvr involved* **12/1**

7 3/4 **Spryt (IRE)**^{17} 5866 4-11-13 **80**............................... MissKHarrington$^{(5)}$ 7 60
(Jamie Osborne) *hld up in tch: 6th 1/2-way: pushed along over 2f out and sn short of room briefly: rdn in 6th under 2f out and no imp on ldrs u.p ent fnl f: one pce after* **7/1**^{3}

8 shd **Hi Emperor (IRE)**^{24} 5662 7-11-11 **76**..............................(t) MrJJKing$^{(3)}$ 6 56
(David Marnane, Ire) *dwlt sltly and towards rr: sn swtchd rt to outer: 8th 1/2-way: rdn after 1/2-way and no imp on ldrs u.p in 7th over 1f out: one pce fnl f* **20/1**

9 8 **Jocular**^{19} 4721 5-11-8 **75**.. MrJCBarry$^{(5)}$ 1 34
(Edward U Hales, Ire) *dwlt sltly and pushed along early: impr far side to dispute briefly after 2f: sn hdd and pushed along in 2nd: wknd after 1/2-way* **16/1**

10 hd **Cyril**^{25} 3920 4-12-2 **78**.. MsNCarberry 8 36
(Gordon Elliott, Ire) *hld up towards rr: pushed along in 9th bef 1/2-way and sn no ex u.p in rr: no imp after 1/2-way* **10/1**

1m 22.97s (82.97) **10** Ran SP% **130.1**
CSF £95.08 CT £194.39 TOTE £8.60: £2.10, £3.10, £1.10; DF 91.30 Trifecta £232.20.
Owner Mrs F D McAuley **Bred** Dr F D McAuley **Trained** Curragh, Co. Kildare

FOCUS
A competitive-looking heat dominated in the market by last year's winner Strait Of Zanzibar from the Ken Condon yard. The standard is around the winner and second.

6466a HIBERNIA STEEL (Q.R.) RACE 7f
5:35 (5:36) 4-Y-O+ **£6,104** (£1,886; £893; £397; £148)

RPR

1 **Room Key**^{17} 5874 4-11-9 84.................................. MissKHarrington$^{(5)}$ 3 72+
(Jamie Osborne) *sn disp and led narrowly bef 1/2-way: pushed along and extended advantage over 2f out: sn rdn and clr ent fnl f: reduced advantage wl ins fnl f: hld on wl* **13/8**^{1}

2 1 **Dancing Noretta (IRE)**^{23} 5689 4-11-4 71......... MrsPaulineCondon$^{(5)}$ 4 64+
(K J Condon, Ire) *hld up in tch: pushed along in 5th after 1/2-way and prog bhd ldrs 1 1/2f out: rdn into 2nd 1f out and kpt on wl to press wnr clsng stages: a hld* **8/1**

3 7 **Clear Focus (IRE)**^{20} 5788 5-11-6 45.......................... MrDGLavery$^{(3)}$ 6 45
(T G McCourt, Ire) *led narrowly tl sn jnd: hdd bef 1/2-way where j. water: sn rdn in 2nd and no imp on wnr u.p in 3rd ent fnl f: one pce fnl f* **16/1**

4 1 **Noble Aussie (IRE)**^{9} 6171 5-11-5 39 ow1...................... MrJJKing$^{(3)}$ 8 41+
(Damian Joseph English, Ire) *hld up towards rr: 8th 1/2-way: short of room between horses bef 1/2-way and checked sltly: sn rdn and impr u.p into 5th under 2f out: kpt on into mod 4th cl home: nvr trbld ldrs* **25/1**

5 1/2 **Usa (IRE)**^{21} 6260 9-11-9 58.. MrFMaguire$^{(5)}$ 1 46
(S J Mahon, Ire) *s.i.s and wnt rt s: sn chsd ldrs: 4th 1/2-way: tk clsr order after 1/2-way: rdn in 2nd under 2f out and no ex over 1f out where dropped to 4th: wknd into mod 5th cl home* **4/1**^{3}

6 8 1/2 **Miro (IRE)**^{7} 245 4-11-7 73... MsNCarberry 5
(Gordon Elliott, Ire) *sn settled towards rr and pushed along after 1f: rdn and struggling bef 1/2-way: no imp and eased fr over 2f out* **3/1**^{2}

7 1/2 **The Islander (IRE)**^{49} 550 5-11-11 61.......................(t) MrSClements$^{(3)}$ 7
(Patrick Griffin, Ire) *s.i.s and towards rr early: tk clsr order in 5th bef 1/2-way: n.m.r between horses 3f out and checked sltly: sn rdn towards rr and no imp fr 2f out* **28/1**

8 3 1/2 **Fugitive Motel (IRE)**^{7} 1661 7-11-9 44.........................(t) MrJCBarry$^{(5)}$ 2
(John Gerard Fitzgerald, Ire) *cl up far side early: pushed along in 3rd bef 1/2-way and no ex u.p under 3f out where wknd* **33/1**

D 7 1/2 **Rock Lobster**^{5} 7414 4-12-0 77.......................................(t) MrJJCodd 9 26
(Gordon Elliott, Ire) *sltly awkward s where wnt rt and pushed along early: towards rr: struggling in 7th at 1/2-way: rdn and no imp 3f out: kpt on one pce in mod 6th ins fnl f: disqualified: rdr failed to weigh-in* **11/2**

1m 23.39s (83.39) **9** Ran SP% **125.7**
Tote Aggregate: 2016: 142,067.00 - 2015: 208,718.00. CSF £17.57 TOTE £2.50: £1.20, £3.20, £2.10; DF 20.90 Trifecta £192.90.
Owner Melbourne 10 Racing **Bred** R J C Wilmot-Smith **Trained** Upper Lambourn, Berks

FOCUS
Few got into this contest and those who raced up with the early pace pulled well clear towards the finish. The third and fourth limit the level.
T/Jkpt: Not won. T/Plt: @25.10. Pool: @3,097.52 - 86.21 winning units. **Brian Fleming**

6467 - 6470a (Foreign Racing) - See Raceform Interactive

^{5915}BEVERLEY (R-H)
Wednesday, September 14

OFFICIAL GOING: Good to firm (8.0)
Wind: Moderate; half behind Weather: Fine & dry

6471 TOTEPLACEPOT SIX PLACES IN SIX RACES CLAIMING STKS 5f
1:50 (1:50) (Class 6) 2-Y-O **£2,587** (£770; £384; £192) **Stalls** Low

Form RPR

6000 1 **Newgate Sioux**^{21} 5756 2-8-5 39.................................... BarryMcHugh 5 60
(Tony Coyle) *trckd ldr: cl up 2f out: rdn to chal over 1f out: kpt on to ld last 100 yds* **66/1**

4520 2 1 3/4 **Local Artist (IRE)**^{8} 6214 2-8-9 66.................................... JasonHart 7 57
(John Quinn) *trckd ldrs: hdwy 2f out: rdn over 1f out: kpt on fnl f* **5/2**^{2}

0121 3 1 1/4 **Bismarck The Flyer (IRE)**^{33} 5351 2-8-12 66........ JacobButterfield$^{(3)}$ 4 59
(Ollie Pears) *rr: pushed along 1/2-way: hdwy on outer wl over 1f out: rdn and kpt on fnl f* **9/2**^{3}

5000 4 3/4 **Flying Hope (IRE)**^{8} 6214 2-8-8 49.....................................(t) TomEaves 1 49
(Nigel Tinkler) *qckly away and led: jnd and rdn over 1f out: drvn ins fnl f: hdd & wknd last 100 yds* **18/1**

5340 5 nk **Whigwham**^{11} 6139 2-8-9 66... TonyHamilton 2 49
(Richard Fahey) *trckd ldrs on inner: hdwy to chse ldng pair over 2f out: rdn wl over 1f out: drvn and no imp appr fnl f* **10/11**^{1}

0520 6 1/2 **King Of Castilla**^{14} 6033 2-8-13 61..............................(tp) DougieCostello 6 51
(Gay Kelleway) *in tch: rdn along wl over 1f out: sn one pce* **16/1**

006 **7** *20* **Penuche**[40] 5125 2-8-5 11 NoelGarbutt(3) 3
(Derek Shaw) *chsd ldrs: rdn along bef 1/2-way: sn outpcd and bhd whn eased over 1f out* **100/1**

1m 1.5s (-2.00) **Going Correction** -0.50s/f (Hard) **7** Ran SP% **112.8**
Speed ratings (Par 93): **96,93,91,90,89 88,56**
CSF £219.79 TOTE £38.70: £12.10, £3.20; EX 270.20 Trifecta £1046.50.Newgate Sioux was claimed by J. M. Bradley for £4,000.

Owner W P S Johnson **Bred** W P S Johnson **Trained** Norton, N Yorks

FOCUS
A weak affair, but straightforward enough 2yo form. The winning time suggested lively ground.

6472 TOTEPOOL RACECOURSE CASH BACK AVAILABLE IRISH EBF MAIDEN FILLIES' STKS (PLUS 10 RACE) 7f 100y
2:25 (2:28) (Class 5) 2-Y-O **£2,456** (£2,456; £565; £283; £141) **Stalls** Low

Form RPR

223 **1** **Amabilis**[32] 5401 2-9-0 87 FMBerry 7 81
(Ralph Beckett) *trckd ldr: effrt 2f out and sn rdn: drvn ent fnl f: styd on wl towards fin to join ldr on line* **4/9**[1]

5322 **1** *dht* **Dubara**[15] 5995 2-9-0 79 DanielTudhope 3 81
(Luca Cumani) *led: pushed along over 1f out: rdn ent fnl f: kpt on: jnd on line* **5/2**[2]

3 *5* **Song Maker** 2-9-0 0 JamesDoyle 1 69+
(Charlie Appleby) *trckd ldng pair on inner: pushed along over 2f out: rdn wl over 1f out: kpt on same pce* **8/1**[3]

0 **4** *8* **Rutherford (IRE)**[36] 5272 2-9-0 0 TomEaves 2 50+
(Kevin Ryan) *in tch: pushed along and sme hdwy wl over 2f out: rdn wl over 1f out: sn one pce* **33/1**

5 *hd* **Send Up (IRE)** 2-9-0 0 RyanPowell 4 50
(Sir Mark Prescott Bt) *s.i.s: sn pushed along: green and a outpcd in rr* **50/1**

0 **6** *2* **Fully Focussed (IRE)**[91] 3283 2-9-0 0 PJMcDonald 6 45
(Ann Duffield) *chsd ldrs: rdn along over 2f out: sn drvn and wknd* **66/1**

1m 31.26s (-2.54) **Going Correction** -0.30s/f (Firm) **6** Ran SP% **115.3**
Speed ratings (Par 92): **102,102,96,87,86 84**
WIN: Amabilis 0.60, Dubara 1.80; PL: Amabilis 1.10, Dubara 1.10; EX: A/D 0.90, D/A 2.30; CSF: A/D 0.97, D/A 2.06; TF: A/D/SM 1.60, D/A/SM 3.20.

Owner Fittocks Stud **Bred** Fittocks Stud **Trained** Newmarket, Suffolk

Owner K Abdullah **Bred** Juddmonte Farms Ltd **Trained** Kimpton, Hants

■ Moll Anthony was withdrawn. Price at time of withdrawal 50-1. Rule 4 does not apply.

FOCUS
Not a bad 2yo fillies' maiden. There was a sound pace on.

6473 TOTEQUADPOT INSURE YOUR PLACEPOT LAST FOUR MAIDEN AUCTION STKS 7f 100y
3:00 (3:00) (Class 5) 2-Y-O **£3,780** (£1,131; £565; £283; £141) **Stalls** Low

Form RPR

6 **1** **Je Suis Charlie**[22] 5740 2-9-5 0 PaulMulrennan 3 73+
(Michael Bell) *towards rr: hdwy over 2f out: swtchd lft and effrt over 1f out: rdn ent fnl f: styd on to ld and edgd rt last 100 yds: kpt on* **6/4**[1]

023 **2** *hd* **Getgo**[13] 6044 2-9-5 77 (b[1]) ShaneKelly 5 73
(David Lanigan) *cl up on inner: led 1/2-way: rdn along wl over 1f out: drvn ent fnl f: edgd lft and hdd last 100 yds* **3/1**[2]

6 **3** *2 ¼* **Pepys**[84] 3516 2-9-5 0 ConnorBeasley 6 68
(Bryan Smart) *in tch: hdwy 2f out: rdn to chse ldrs over 1f out: kpt on fnl f* **6/1**[3]

4 **4** *hd* **The Blues Master (IRE)**[7] 6224 2-9-5 0 JoeFanning 7 67
(Mark Johnston) *trckd ldng pair: hdwy over 2f out: rdn to chal over 1f out: ev ch ent fnl f: hld whn n.m.r last 100 yds* **6/1**[3]

5 *2* **Glorvina (IRE)** 2-9-0 0 DanielTudhope 1 62+
(David O'Meara) *in tch on inner: effrt and nt clr run wl over 1f out: sn swtchd lft and rdn: kpt on fnl f* **25/1**

0060 **6** *¾* **Pontecarlo Boy**[34] 5318 2-9-5 51 [1] GeorgeChaloner 4 61
(Richard Whitaker) *chsd ldng pair: rdn along over 2f out: drvn wl over 1f out: grad wknd* **66/1**

7 *2 ½* **Sayif Magic** 2-9-5 0 JamesDoyle 2 55
(George Scott) *dwlt: a towards rr* **11/1**

05 **8** *nk* **Prince Of Clappers**[20] 5792 2-9-5 0 DavidAllan 8 54
(Tim Easterby) *a towards rr* **16/1**

0230 **9** *2* **Good Time Ahead (IRE)**[16] 5967 2-9-5 73 DougieCostello 9 50
(Philip Kirby) *led: hdd 1/2-way and sn pushed along: rdn over 2f out: wknd wl over 1f out* **12/1**

1m 31.36s (-2.44) **Going Correction** -0.30s/f (Firm) **9** Ran SP% **120.8**
Speed ratings (Par 95): **101,100,98,97,95 94,91,91,89**
CSF £6.35 TOTE £2.70: £1.20, £1.10, £2.40; EX 7.30 Trifecta £31.90.

Owner Mrs G Rowland-Clark & C M Budgett **Bred** Kirtlington Stud Ltd **Trained** Newmarket, Suffolk

FOCUS
An ordinary 2yo maiden. It was run at a brisk pace. The 6th showed some improvement and is the key to the level.

6474 TOTEPOOL LIVE INFO DOWNLOAD THE APP H'CAP 1m 4f 16y
3:30 (3:32) (Class 4) (0-85,83) 3-Y-O **£6,225** (£1,864; £932; £466; £233) **Stalls** Low

Form RPR

1202 **1** **Icefall (IRE)**[11] 6134 3-9-6 **82** DavidAllan 2 91
(Tim Easterby) *led 1f: trckd ldng pair on inner: hdwy over 2f out: led 11/2f out: rdn clr ent fnl f: kpt on strly* **7/2**[2]

1-54 **2** *2 ½* **Maestro Mac (IRE)**[19] 5849 3-9-2 **78** FMBerry 1 83
(Hughie Morrison) *hld up in rr: hdwy over 2f out: rdn wl over 1f out: drvn and styd on fnl f* **7/2**[2]

6003 **3** *hd* **Welford**[22] 5738 3-9-7 **83** JamesDoyle 5 88
(Mark Johnston) *led after 1f: pushed along wl over 2f out: rdn and hdd 11/2f out: drvn and kpt on u.p fnl f* **9/2**[3]

4322 **4** *¾* **Four On Eight**[21] 5768 3-9-3 **79** (v[1]) DanielTudhope 3 83
(Luca Cumani) *trckd ldrs: hdwy to chse wnr over 1f out: sn rdn: drvn and wknd ins fnl f* **6/4**[1]

3324 **5** *5* **Ice Galley (IRE)**[82] 3607 3-8-12 **74** TomEaves 4 70
(Kevin Ryan) *prom: pushed along over 2f out: rdn wl over 1f out: sn wknd* **8/1**

2m 34.72s (-5.08) **Going Correction** -0.30s/f (Firm) **5** Ran SP% **113.7**
Speed ratings (Par 103): **104,102,102,101,98**
CSF £16.27 TOTE £3.70: £2.80, £1.60; EX 13.40 Trifecta £49.00.

Owner Ryedale Partners No 10 **Bred** Victor Stud Bloodstock Ltd **Trained** Great Habton, N Yorks

FOCUS
A fair little 3yo handicap, run at a solid early pace. The winner has improved, rated around the 2nd, 3rd and 4th.

6475 @TOTEPOOLRACING WIN TICKETS ON TWITTER H'CAP (DIV I) 5f
4:05 (4:06) (Class 5) (0-75,75) 3-Y-O+ **£3,780** (£1,131; £565; £283; £141) **Stalls** Low

Form RPR

1303 **1** **Musharrif**[7] 6234 4-9-7 **75** DanielTudhope 4 85
(Declan Carroll) *prom: cl up 2f out: rdn to ld ent fnl f: kpt on strly* **15/8**[1]

4003 **2** *2* **Socialites Red**[18] 5864 3-8-11 **66** (p) DavidAllan 8 69
(Scott Dixon) *led: jnd and rdn wl over 1f out: hdd and drvn ent fnl f: kpt on* **14/1**

0000 **3** *2* **Space Artist (IRE)**[18] 5864 6-8-6 **67** (vt) KieranSchofield(7) 6 66
(Nigel Tinkler) *chsd ldrs: swtchd lft and rdn over 1f out: styd on wl towards fin* **66/1**

3306 **4** *shd* **Burtonwood**[18] 5867 4-8-11 **65** (b) JoeDoyle 7 60
(Julie Camacho) *prom: effrt and ev ch over 1f out: sn rdn and kpt on same pce fnl f* **16/1**

2000 **5** *1* **Oriental Splendour (IRE)**[16] 5968 4-9-3 **71** JamesSullivan 2 63+
(Ruth Carr) *rr: hdwy on inner 2f out: n.m.r and swtchd lft over 1f out: sn rdn and kpt on wl towards fin* **11/1**

5221 **6** *hd* **Dance Alone**[18] 5862 3-8-13 **75** (b) LewisEdmunds(7) 1 66
(Kevin Ryan) *chsd ldrs: rdn along and n.m.r over 1f out: sn drvn and no imp* **11/4**[2]

2411 **7** *½* **Salvatore Fury (IRE)**[27] 5582 6-9-5 **73** (p) GrahamLee 10 62
(Keith Dalgleish) *wnt lft s: a towards rr* **12/1**

6456 **8** *¾* **Flicka's Boy**[6] 6248 4-9-2 **70** (vt[1]) DuranFentiman 9 57
(Tony Coyle) *in tch on outer: rdn along 2f out: sn wknd* **16/1**

2160 **9** *shd* **Bond Bombshell**[18] 5867 3-8-8 **70** PatrickVaughan(7) 3 56
(David O'Meara) *chsd ldrs on inner: rdn along and n.m.r wl over 1f out: sn wknd* **14/1**

1522 **10** *10* **Jaarih (IRE)**[5] 6296 4-9-4 **72** (b) PaulMulrennan 5 22
(Conor Dore) *a towards rr* **13/2**[3]

1m 0.45s (-3.05) **Going Correction** -0.50s/f (Hard)
WFA 3 from 4yo+ 1lb **10** Ran SP% **117.4**
Speed ratings (Par 103): **104,100,97,97,95 95,94,93,93,77**
CSF £31.04 CT £1309.02 TOTE £2.80: £1.20, £3.80, £10.60; EX 32.30 Trifecta £1352.10.

Owner Ray Flegg & John Bousfield **Bred** Mr & Mrs J Davis & P Mitchell B'Stock **Trained** Malton, N Yorks

FOCUS
A modest sprint handicap. It paid to be prominent. This has been rated around the front-running 2nd to her C&D latest.

6476 @TOTEPOOLRACING WIN TICKETS ON TWITTER H'CAP (DIV II) 5f
4:40 (4:41) (Class 5) (0-75,75) 3-Y-O+ **£3,780** (£1,131; £565; £283; £141) **Stalls** Low

Form RPR

0042 **1** **Astrophysics**[12] 6093 4-9-2 **70** PaddyAspell 4 79
(Lynn Siddall) *trckd ldr: swtchd lft and hdwy wl over 1f out: sn chal: rdn to ld ent fnl f: drvn out* **6/1**

5253 **2** *1* **Royal Brave (IRE)**[12] 6093 5-9-3 **71** BarryMcHugh 3 76
(Rebecca Bastiman) *chsd ldrs: hdwy wl over 1f out: sn rdn: drvn ins fnl f: kpt on wl towards fin* **6/1**

60 **3** *1 ½* **Encantar**[27] 5582 3-8-12 **67** (v[1]) PJMcDonald 9 67
(Ann Duffield) *racd wd: cl up: rdn along and ev ch wl over 1f out: drvn and kpt on same pce fnl f* **25/1**

3060 **4** *½* **Lydia's Place**[25] 5657 3-9-6 **75** ConnorBeasley 7 73
(Richard Guest) *wnt rt s: led: rdn along and jnd over 1f out: hdd and drvn ent fnl f: wknd last 100 yds* **11/2**[3]

4000 **5** *1 ½* **Flash City (ITY)**[18] 5864 8-9-3 **71** JamesSullivan 5 64
(Ruth Carr) *dwlt and n.m.r s: towards rr: hdwy to chse ldrs over 2f out: rdn over 1f out: kpt on same pce* **7/1**

5510 **6** *¾* **Minninggold**[18] 5864 3-8-10 **68** RachelRichardson(3) 1 58
(Tim Easterby) *in tch on inner: effrt 2f out: sn rdn and no imp* **7/2**[1]

00 **7** *1* **Top Of The Bank**[25] 5657 3-9-6 **75** (b[1]) TomEaves 2 62
(Kevin Ryan) *chsd ldrs: rdn along wl over 1f out: wknd appr fnl f* **12/1**

455 **8** *3 ½* **Ruby's Day**[40] 5110 7-8-11 **65** PaulMulrennan 8 39
(David Brown) *towards rr on wd outside: pushed along bef 1/2-way: sn rdn: edgd lft and outpcd* **16/1**

2166 **9** *3 ¼* **Acclaim The Nation (IRE)**[11] 6133 3-9-4 **73** JasonHart 6 35
(Eric Alston) *sltly hmpd s and sn t.k.h: chsd ldrs: rdn along wl over 1f out and sn wknd* **4/1**[2]

1m 0.84s (-2.66) **Going Correction** -0.50s/f (Hard)
WFA 3 from 4yo+ 1lb **9** Ran SP% **116.1**
Speed ratings (Par 103): **101,99,97,96,93 92,91,85,80**
CSF £42.01 CT £845.09 TOTE £4.50: £1.80, £2.10, £5.10; EX 24.40 Trifecta £864.70.

Owner Jimmy Kay **Bred** Sarah Stoneham **Trained** Colton, N Yorks

FOCUS
This second division of the 5f handicap where again it suited those ridden handily.

6477 TOTEPOOLRACING FIND US ON INSTAGRAM MAIDEN STKS 5f
5:10 (5:11) (Class 5) 2-Y-O **£3,780** (£1,131; £565; £283; £141) **Stalls** Low

Form RPR

2426 **1** **Broadhaven Honey (IRE)**[29] 5511 2-9-0 68 GrahamLee 1 68
(Ed McMahon) *mde all: rdn over 1f out: drvn ins fnl f: kpt on wl* **3/1**[3]

05 **2** *1 ¾* **Savannah Moon (IRE)**[37] 5221 2-9-0 0 KeaganLatham 3 62
(Kevin Ryan) *towards rr: hdwy on inner 2f out: rdn over 1f out: styd on wl fnl f* **28/1**

0 **3** *nk* **Man Of Verve (IRE)**[18] 5884 2-9-5 0 TomEaves 2 66
(John Quinn) *trckd ldrs on inner: hdwy over 1f out: rdn ent fnl f: kpt on* **33/1**

53 **4** *hd* **Sword Exceed (GER)**[14] 6034 2-9-5 0 JamesDoyle 7 65
(Charlie Appleby) *cl up: rdn wl over 1f out: ev ch tl drvn ent fnl f and kpt on same pce* **7/4**[1]

5 *nk* **Pale Enchantment (IRE)** 2-9-0 0 PJMcDonald 10 59+
(Tom Dascombe) *dwlt and wnt lft s: in rr: hdwy 2f out: rdn over 1f out: kpt on fnl f: nrst fin* **33/1**

6 *½* **Spruce Lodge** 2-9-5 0 PhillipMakin 9 62
(David Barron) *dwlt and rr: hdwy wl over 1f out: sn rdn and styd on fnl f: nrst fin* **20/1**

033 **7** *nk* **Ocelot**[10] 6162 2-9-0 0 DavidAllan 6 56
(Tim Easterby) *chsd ldrs: rdn along over 1f out: grad wknd* **5/2**[2]

8 *¾* **Bearag** 2-9-0 0 DanielTudhope 5 53
(David O'Meara) *midfield: effrt 2f out: sn rdn and no imp* **9/1**

9 *¾* **Judy Woods (IRE)** 2-9-0 0 ConnorBeasley 8 51
(Bryan Smart) *a towards rr* **33/1**

00 **10** ½ **Backinanger**[30] 5477 2-9-5 0 .... KevinStott 14 54
(Kevin Ryan) *wnt lft s: a towards rr* **50/1**
11 6 **Haafhder Thought** 2-8-11 0 .... RachelRichardson(3) 13 27
(Tim Easterby) *a towards rr* **33/1**
0 **12** ½ **Equipe**[32] 5414 2-9-0 0 .... GeorgeChaloner 12 25
(Richard Whitaker) *chsd ldrs: rdn along 2f out: sn wknd* **100/1**

1m 2.19s (-1.31) **Going Correction** -0.50s/f (Hard) **12** Ran SP% **122.9**
Speed ratings (Par 95): **90,87,86,86,85 85,84,83,82,81 71,71**
CSF £90.24 TOTE £3.80: £1.40, £7.70, £6.50; EX 142.20 Trifecta £2555.10.
Owner M Doocey, S Doocey & P J Doocey **Bred** James F Hanly **Trained** Lichfield, Staffs

FOCUS
A modest 2yo maiden but it could be rated 2lb higher.

6478 COLLECT ANY TOTEPOOL WINNINGS AT BETFRED SHOPS APPRENTICE CLASSIFIED STKS — 1m 100y
5:40 (5:44) (Class 6) 3-Y-O+ **£2,587** (£577; £577; £192) **Stalls** Low

Form RPR
3440 **1** **Candesta (USA)**[102] 2899 6-8-9 51 .... LiamDoran(5) 1 54
(Julia Feilden) *trckd ldrs: hdwy over 3f out: led 2f out: rdn over 1f out: kpt on wl towards fin* **11/2**[3]
3036 **2** 1½ **Call Me Crockett (IRE)**[19] 5835 4-8-11 48 .... (p) GerO'Neill(3) 11 51
(Noel Wilson) *midfield: hdwy 3f out: chsd ldrs over 1f out: sn swtchd rt and rdn: styd on wl fnl f* **14/1**
0104 **2** dht **Wootton Vale (IRE)**[37] 5228 3-8-9 53 .... AdamMcNamara 5 50
(Richard Fahey) *prom: cl up over 3f out: rdn wl over 1f out and ev ch: drvn ins fnl f: kpt on* **11/4**[1]
600 **4** ½ **Hooks Lane**[121] 2307 4-8-9 42 .... TobyEley(5) 3 50
(Shaun Harris) *dwlt and bhd: hdwy towards outer over 2f out: rdn over 1f out: styd on strly fnl f* **33/1**
4505 **5** ½ **Pensax Lady (IRE)**[27] 5572 3-8-9 53 .... CharlieBennett 4 48
(Daniel Mark Loughnane) *in tch: hdwy on inner over 2f out: rdn to chse ldrs over 1f out: drvn and kpt on same pce fnl f* **14/1**
6356 **6** 3¾ **The Big Day (IRE)**[18] 5887 3-8-6 55 .... KieranSchofield(3) 12 39
(Nigel Tinkler) *in tch: hdwy on outer over 2f out: rdn to chse ldrs over 1f out: sn no imp* **4/1**[2]
3000 **7** ½ **Bahrikate**[16] 5972 3-8-4 40 .... AledBeech(5) 15 38
(Michael Herrington) *prom: led 3f out: sn rdn and hdd 2f out: drvn and wknd over 1f out* **33/1**
-005 **8** 1¼ **Royal Acclaim (IRE)**[19] 5835 4-8-11 53 .... LewisEdmunds(3) 16 36
(Rebecca Bastiman) *midfield: hdwy over 2f out: rdn wl over 1f out: no imp fnl f* **11/1**
/600 **9** nk **Tom's Anna (IRE)**[12] 6106 6-9-0 44 .... RhiainIngram 13 36
(Sean Regan) *a towards rr* **40/1**
0000 **10** 1 **Sunnyhills Belford**[8] 6218 3-8-9 43 .... NatalieHambling 10 33
(Noel Wilson) *chsd ldrs: rdn along over 2f out: wknd over 1f out* **50/1**
440 **11** 1¼ **Joyful Star**[67] 4144 6-9-0 55 .... CallumRodriguez 6 31
(Fred Watson) *a towards rr* **11/4**[1]
0400 **12** 13 **Robbian**[114] 2537 5-8-9 45 .... RobertDodsworth(5) 17 2
(Charles Smith) *a rr* **33/1**
00-0 **13** 35 **Lady Bacchus**[183] 948 3-8-4 43 .... (b[1]) BenRobinson(5) 2
(Richard Guest) *plld hrd: sn led and clr: hdd 3f out and wknd qckly* **25/1**

1m 45.32s (-2.28) **Going Correction** -0.30s/f (Firm)
WFA 3 from 4yo+ 5lb **13** Ran SP% **127.5**
Speed ratings (Par 101): **99,97,97,97,96 92,92,91,90,89 88,75,40**
WIN: 8.10; PL: 2.40, Wootton Vale 1.60, Call Me Crockett 3.90; EX: C/CMC 54.70, C/WV 16.30; CSF: C/CMC 39.66, C/WV 10.65; TF: C/CMC/WV 221.70, C/WV/CMC 127.50.
Owner Mrs Jo Lambert **Bred** Juddmonte Farms Inc **Trained** Exning, Suffolk
■ Euro Mac and Kopassus were withdrawn. Prices at time of withdrawal 6-1 and 9-1 respectively. Rule 4 applies to bets to board prices but not to SP bets - deduction 20p in the pound. New market formed.

FOCUS
A weak classified event, confined to apprentice riders. They went hard up front. The winner, 2nd and 4th suggest this level is sensible.
T/Plt: £54.70 to a £1 stake. Pool: £49,004.25 - 653.04 winning units T/Qpdt: £11.80 to a £1 stake. Pool: £3,814.5 - 238.50 winning units **Joe Rowntree**

6295 SANDOWN (R-H)
Wednesday, September 14

OFFICIAL GOING: Good (good to firm in places; round 7.2, sprint 7.0)
Wind: Light; against Weather: Sunny, very warm

6479 GG.CO.UK SUPPORTS THE RACEHORSE SANCTUARY H'CAP (JC GRASSROOTS FLAT SPRINT SERIES QUALIFIER) — 5f 6y
2:05 (2:06) (Class 5) (0-75,79) 3-Y-O+ **£3,234** (£962; £481; £240) **Stalls** Low

Form RPR
2203 **1** **Bahamian Sunrise**[48] 4809 4-8-11 **68** .... (p) GeorgeBuckell(5) 3 75
(John Gallagher) *lw: mde all and racd away fr rail: shkn up over 1f out: jnd ins fnl f: jst hld on* **4/1**[2]
2505 **2** shd **Go Nani Go**[14] 6017 10-9-6 **72** .... PatCosgrave 7 78
(Ed de Giles) *trckd ldrs: squeezed through to take 2nd fnl f and sn w wnr: upsides last strides: jst pipped* **14/1**
5444 **3** 1¼ **Ambitious Icarus**[74] 3907 7-9-4 **70** .... (e) RoystonFfrench 6 71
(Richard Guest) *taken down early: dwlt: in tch in rr: rdn and prog 2f out: r.o last 100yds to take 3rd last strides: nrst fin* **15/2**
0245 **4** ½ **Billyoakes (IRE)**[5] 6296 4-9-6 **72** .... AdamBeschizza 8 71
(Charlie Wallis) *trckd ldrs on outer: shkn up and no rspnse over 1f out: kpt on same pce fnl f and a hld* **9/2**[3]
0353 **5** nse **Point Of Woods**[14] 6018 3-9-5 **72** .... (b[1]) WilliamBuick 4 71
(Ralph Beckett) *lw: hld up and sn in last: rdn 2f out: styd on ins fnl f: nvr able to threaten* **4/1**[2]
4263 **6** ½ **Doctor Parkes**[7] 6235 10-9-3 **72** .... AaronJones(3) 2 69
(Stuart Williams) *racd against rail: chsd wnr: drvn over 1f out: sn lost 2nd: fdd last 100yds* **3/1**[1]
116 **7** 2 **Jumeirah Star (USA)**[29] 5523 3-8-11 **67** .... (v) EoinWalsh(3) 1 57
(Robert Cowell) *dwlt: racd against rail and in tch: rdn over 2f out: no prog over 1f out: wknd ins fnl f* **8/1**

1m 2.81s (1.21) **Going Correction** +0.35s/f (Good)
WFA 3 from 4yo+ 1lb **7** Ran SP% **112.7**
Speed ratings (Par 103): **104,103,101,101,100 100,96**
CSF £53.24 CT £399.74 TOTE £5.90: £3.00, £4.60; EX 47.90 Trifecta £388.10.
Owner Caveat Emptor Partnership **Bred** Mel Roberts & Ms Nicola Meese **Trained** Chastleton, Oxon

FOCUS
The rail on the Round Course was moved out from inner from 7f to a drop-in at 2.5f, adding 24 yards to all Round Course distances. A modest sprint that little got into. The first two have been rated to this year's form.

6480 WILLMOTT DIXON/BRITISH STALLION STUDS EBF MAIDEN STKS — 1m 14y
2:40 (2:43) (Class 5) 2-Y-O **£3,881** (£1,155; £577; £288) **Stalls** Low

Form RPR
1 **Atty Persse (IRE)** 2-9-5 0 .... GeorgeBaker 2 85+
(Roger Charlton) *str: bit bkwd: trckd ldng pair: pushed along to cl over 2f out: shkn up to take 2nd over 1f out: rdn to ld jst ins fnl f: styd on: readily* **10/11**[1]
3 **2** 1¾ **Hamada**[33] 5373 2-9-5 0 .... WilliamBuick 9 80
(Charlie Appleby) *str: lw: trckd ldr: clsd 3f out: led 2f out: rdn and hdd jst ins fnl f: styd on and clr of rest but readily hld* **10/3**[2]
65 **3** 4 **Keepup Kevin**[12] 6085 2-9-2 0 .... RobHornby(3) 3 71
(Pam Sly) *w'like: in tch disputing 5th: rdn and prog 2f out: tk 3rd fnl f: no ch w ldng pair* **16/1**
4 1 **Camerone (IRE)** 2-9-0 0 .... OisinMurphy 12 63+
(Ralph Beckett) *tall: t.k.h: hld up disputing 7th: pushed along over 2f out: prog whn impeded over 1f out: styd on ins fnl f wout posing a threat* **12/1**
5 1½ **Teodoro (IRE)** 2-9-5 0 .... RichardKingscote 10 65+
(Tom Dascombe) *leggy: in tch disputing 7th: pushed along 3f out: sme prog and shkn up 2f out: no threat but kpt on ins fnl f* **8/1**[3]
0 **6** 1¾ **Harbour Town**[63] 4270 2-9-5 0 .... DaneO'Neill 7 61
(Harry Dunlop) *led: 3 l clr 1/2-way: rdn and hdd 2f out: hanging and wknd over 1f out* **16/1**
0 **7** 2¾ **Inception (IRE)**[13] 6054 2-9-5 0 .... SeanLevey 13 55
(Richard Hannon) *w'like: in tch disputing 5th: effrt and shkn up over 2f out: hung rt over 1f out: wknd* **16/1**
0 **8** 2¼ **Lightly Squeeze**[12] 6085 2-9-5 0 .... JamieSpencer 1 50
(Philip Hide) *cmpt: slowly away: tk fierce hold early and hld up in 9th: nvr a factor but pushed along and plugged on fr 2f out* **25/1**
9 5 **Almizhar (IRE)** 2-9-5 0 .... AdamKirby 8 38+
(Ed Dunlop) *w'like: dwlt: a in last trio: no ch fnl 2f* **33/1**
0 **10** 5 **Designamento (IRE)**[29] 5505 2-9-5 0 .... LiamKeniry 5 27
(Ed de Giles) *str: slowly away: mostly in last and a wl adrift* **66/1**
00 **11** 5 **Rockaria**[48] 4786 2-9-5 0 .... FergusSweeney 4 15
(Philip Hide) *w'like: t.k.h: chsd ldng trio to wl over 2f out: wknd rapidly* **100/1**

1m 43.51s (0.21) **Going Correction** +0.125s/f (Good) **11** Ran SP% **121.2**
Speed ratings (Par 95): **103,101,97,96,94 93,90,88,83,78 73**
CSF £3.92 TOTE £2.00: £1.30, £1.20, £3.40; EX 5.30 Trifecta £33.70.
Owner B E Nielsen **Bred** Bjorn Nielsen **Trained** Beckhampton, Wilts

FOCUS
Race distance increased by 24yds. The front pair came clear in what was a fair maiden, no more, but the winner can leave this form behind.

6481 MAX PATEL WEALTH MANAGER OF CHOICE CONDITIONS STKS (PLUS 10 RACE) — 7f 16y
3:15 (3:15) (Class 3) 2-Y-O **£6,469** (£1,925; £962; £481) **Stalls** Low

Form RPR
3416 **1** **Rebel De Lope**[26] 5595 2-8-12 86 .... JamieSpencer 7 94
(Charles Hills) *trckd ldr: led 2f out: committed for home over 1f out: drvn out and styd on strly* **13/2**
1 **2** 2 **Eaton Square**[48] 4805 2-8-12 0 ....[1] RyanMoore 2 89
(John Gosden) *str: scope: hld up in 4th: waiting for a gap over 2f out: nt qckn whn wnr kicked for home over 1f out: tk 2nd fnl f: styd on but no imp* **9/4**[2]
1 **3** ½ **Khafoo Shememi (IRE)**[18] 5876 2-9-1 0 .... SeanLevey 4 91
(Richard Hannon) *str: t.k.h: trckd ldng pair: nt qckn whn wnr kicked for home over 1f out: disp 2nd fnl f: styd on same pce* **15/8**[1]
2 **4** 1 **Zefferino**[40] 5121 2-8-12 0 .... OisinMurphy 1 85+
(Roger Charlton) *athletic: lw: hld up in last: pushed along 2f out: sn outpcd and no ch after: styd on ins fnl f to take 4th last strides* **5/2**[3]
1536 **5** ½ **White Tower (IRE)**[28] 5536 2-8-12 89 .... WilliamBuick 3 84
(Mark Johnston) *led: rdn and hdd 2f out: outpcd over 1f out: one pce after* **25/1**
00 **6** 16 **Garth Rockett**[18] 5890 2-8-9 0 .... EdwardGreatrex(3) 8 42
(Brendan Powell) *in tch: rdn over 2f out: sn wknd: t.o* **100/1**

1m 31.06s (1.56) **Going Correction** +0.125s/f (Good) **6** Ran SP% **112.3**
Speed ratings (Par 99): **96,93,93,92,91 73**
CSF £21.54 TOTE £8.20: £3.20, £1.70; EX 23.70 Trifecta £47.80.
Owner P K Siu **Bred** Azienda Agricola Antonio Celli **Trained** Lambourn, Berks

FOCUS
Race distance increased by 24yds. Not much pace on for what was a decent conditions event and it paid to race handily. The winner posted an effort in keeping with his runaway Lingfield win.

6482 RACEHORSE SANCTUARY FORTUNE STKS (LISTED RACE) — 1m 14y
3:50 (3:50) (Class 1) 3-Y-O+
£20,982 (£7,955; £3,981; £1,983; £995; £499) **Stalls** Low

Form RPR
1151 **1** **Quebee**[18] 5874 3-8-8 94 .... HarryBentley 1 106
(Clive Cox) *lw: dwlt: hld up in last: pushed along whn n.m.r 3f out: drvn and prog 2f out: swtchd to inner fnl f: squeezed through to chal and r.o gamely to ld last 50yds* **16/1**
2 **2** nk **Yorker (SAF)**[25] 5652 7-9-4 116 ....[1] PatCosgrave 7 111
(William Haggas) *trckd ldr: rdn to ld over 1f out: sn hrd pressed: kpt on wl fnl f but hdd last 50yds* **6/4**[1]
/352 **3** ½ **Muwaary**[13] 6056 5-9-4 105 .... DaneO'Neill 6 110
(John Gosden) *hld up in 5th: rdn and nt qckn 2f out: looked wl hld tl styd on wl fnl f to take 3rd last strides* **9/1**
1012 **4** nk **Mustashry**[27] 5585 3-8-13 104 .... PaulHanagan 5 109
(Sir Michael Stoute) *lw: t.k.h: trckd ldng pair: swtchd towards inner over 2f out: drvn to chse ldr jst over 1f out: str chal ins fnl f: no ex and hld in cl 3rd whn short of room and dropped to 4th last strides* **3/1**[2]
-204 **5** 2¾ **Dragon Mall (USA)**[47] 4822 3-8-13 106 .... JamieSpencer 4 102
(David Simcock) *hld up in rr: rdn over 2f out: effrt to chse ldrs over 1f out: one pce fnl f* **7/1**
0411 **6** 3 **Arcanada (IRE)**[26] 5616 3-8-13 106 .... RichardKingscote 2 95
(Tom Dascombe) *swtg: led: drvn and hdd over 1f out: wknd quite qckly* **5/1**[3]

0012 **7** 1 1/4 **Early Morning (IRE)**[12] 6075 5-9-4 102 .... AdamKirby 8 95
(Harry Dunlop) *racd wd early: trckd ldng pair: wnt 2nd briefly over 1f out and tried to chal: wkng quite qckly whn short of room ins fnl f* **16/1**

6033 **8** 2 1/2 **Starlit Cantata**[19] 5831 5-8-13 78 .... JohnFahy 3 82
(Eve Johnson Houghton) *in tch in rr: shkn up 3f out: wknd fr 2f out* **100/1**

1m 42.5s (-0.80) **Going Correction** +0.125s/f (Good)
WFA 3 from 5yo+ 5lb **8** Ran SP% **116.9**
Speed ratings (Par 111): **109,108,108,107,105 102,100,98**
CSF £44.82 TOTE £17.50: £4.00, £1.20, £2.50; EX 74.20 Trifecta £852.30.
Owner Martin A Collins **Bred** M A Collins **Trained** Lambourn, Berks

FOCUS
Race distance increased by 24yds. This looked more open than the market suggested and, after going an ordinary gallop, plenty had their chance in the straight. It went to one of the outsiders, who improved again, with the second below form.

6483 SALT ISLAND MEMORIAL FILLIES' H'CAP 1m 14y
4:25 (4:28) (Class 4) (0-85,82) 3-Y-O+ **£4,690** (£1,395; £697; £348) **Stalls** Low

Form RPR

3121 **1** **Crowning Glory (FR)**[16] 5965 3-9-0 **82** .... GeorgiaCox(5) 2 90
(Ralph Beckett) *lw: wl in tch: shkn up and prog on outer to chse ldr over 1f out: rdn to ld jst ins fnl f: styd on wl* **7/2**[3]

0-01 **2** 1 **Lady Perignon**[19] 5822 3-9-0 **77** .... JamieSpencer 4 83
(Andrew Balding) *led after 2f: shkn up 2f out: hdd jst ins fnl f: styd on but readily hld after* **8/1**

6641 **3** 1 1/4 **Nicarra (IRE)**[18] 5891 3-8-11 **74** .... FergusSweeney 3 77
(Henry Candy) *t.k.h early: led 1f: sn dropped to last pair: renewed effrt and rdn 2f out: tk 3rd fnl f: kpt on but no imp ldng pair* **3/1**[2]

2221 **4** 1 **Catchment**[28] 5551 3-9-1 **78** .... RyanMoore 1 79
(Amanda Perrett) *lw: hld up in last: pushed along 2f out: sme prog on wd outside over 1f out: rdn and one pce fnl f* **8/1**

5432 **5** 1 1/4 **Ghinia (IRE)**[30] 5487 5-9-10 **82** .... AdamKirby 6 81
(Pam Sly) *cl up: chsd ldr 1/2-way: rdn over 2f out: lost 2nd over 1f out: fdd* **5/1**

3-1 **6** nk **Qamarain (USA)**[19] 5850 3-9-0 **77** .... PaulHanagan 5 74
(Brian Meehan) *t.k.h early: led after 1f tl after 2f: rdn over 2f out: effrt to dispute 2nd over 1f out: fdd sn after* **11/4**[1]

1m 43.62s (0.32) **Going Correction** +0.125s/f (Good)
WFA 3 from 5yo 5lb **6** Ran SP% **112.8**
Speed ratings (Par 102): **103,102,100,99,98 98**
CSF £30.13 TOTE £4.50: £2.30, £3.50; EX 31.00 Trifecta £111.10.
Owner The Eclipse Partnership **Bred** Car Colston Hall Stud **Trained** Kimpton, Hants

FOCUS
Race distance increased by 24yds. A fair handicap, they avoided the far rail in the straight. The winner built on her Epsom success, with the runner-up improving on her maiden win.

6484 MOLSON COORS H'CAP (JOCKEY CLUB GRASSROOTS FLAT MIDDLE DISTANCE SERIES QUALIFIER) 1m 2f 7y
5:00 (5:01) (Class 4) (0-85,85) 3-Y-O **£4,690** (£1,395; £697; £348) **Stalls** Low

Form RPR

233 **1** **Toulson**[42] 5023 3-8-12 **76** .... CharlesBishop 7 85
(Eve Johnson Houghton) *str: hld up in 6th: rdn and prog on outer over 2f out: clsd over 1f out: tk 2nd last 100yds: drvn and styd on wl to ld fnl strides* **8/1**

3012 **2** 1/2 **Bedrock**[55] 4554 3-9-4 **82** .... (p) PatCosgrave 6 90
(William Haggas) *led 2f: trckd ldr: led wl over 2f out gng strly: drvn over 1f out: hrd pressed fnl f: kpt on wl but hdd last strides* **9/2**

5232 **3** 1/2 **Both Sides**[48] 4808 3-9-7 **85** .... OisinMurphy 8 92
(Andrew Balding) *lw: trckd ldng pair: rdn to chse ldr over 2f out: clsd to chal 1f out: kpt on but lost 2nd fnl 100yds* **10/3**[1]

51-3 **4** nse **Richie McCaw**[32] 5391 3-8-13 **77** .... JamieSpencer 3 84
(Ian Williams) *hld up in last pair: rdn on outer over 2f out: no prog tl styd on fr over 1f out despite hanging: nrly snatched 3rd* **16/1**

-013 **5** 3 **Totally Committed**[3] 6365 3-8-8 **72** .... HarryBentley 1 73
(Clive Cox) *settled in 5th: rdn and no prog over 2f out: no imp ldrs after* **4/1**[3]

410- **6** 1 1/2 **Calvinist**[340] 7116 3-9-7 **85** ....[1] AdamKirby 5 85
(Brian Meehan) *dwlt: hld up in last pair: rdn over 2f out: making sme prog whn hmpd over 1f out and lost momentum: no ch after* **12/1**

2103 **7** 3 1/2 **Frozen Force (IRE)**[14] 6032 3-9-5 **83** .... (v[1]) RyanMoore 2 74
(Amanda Perrett) *trckd ldrs in 4th: rdn over 2f out: lost pl and wknd over 1f out* **12/1**

01 **8** 11 **Acrux**[20] 5811 3-9-3 **81** .... GeorgeBaker 9 50
(David Lanigan) *str: lw: t.k.h: plld way through to ld after 2f: hdd wl over 2f out and wknd: t.o* **7/2**[2]

2m 8.87s (-1.63) **Going Correction** +0.125s/f (Good) **8** Ran SP% **115.9**
Speed ratings (Par 103): **111,110,110,110,107 106,103,94**
CSF £44.37 CT £144.83 TOTE £11.80: £3.00, £1.40, £2.10; EX 51.10 Trifecta £169.00.
Owner Mrs Virginia Neale **Bred** Cherry Park Stud **Trained** Blewbury, Oxon
■ Stewards' Enquiry : Charles Bishop two-day ban: used whip above permitted level (Sep 28-29)

FOCUS
Race distance increased by 24yds. A useful 3yo handicap, the far rail was again shunned. The winner improved, with the 2nd and 3rd rated in line with a better view of their form.

6485 SILVERPEAK SYSTEMS FILLIES' H'CAP 1m 2f 7y
5:30 (5:32) (Class 5) (0-70,70) 3-Y-O+ **£3,234** (£962; £481; £240) **Stalls** Low

Form RPR

5513 **1** nse **Pina**[25] 5629 3-9-5 **68** .... GeorgeBaker 5 77+
(Roger Charlton) *in tch: rdn and prog on wd outside fr 2f out: clsd fnl f and briefly carried sltly rt: upsides last strides: jst pipped: fin 2nd: promoted to 1st* **3/1**[1]

4553 **2** **Solveig's Song**[15] 6001 4-9-6 **65** .... (p) EdwardGreatrex(3) 8 73
(Steve Woodman) *hld up wl in rr: prog on wd outside over 2f out: drvn and clsd over 1f out: edgd rt briefly but styd on u.p to ld last strides: fin 1st: disqualified and plcd 2nd* **20/1**

3551 **3** 1/2 **Perfect Quest**[36] 5254 3-9-6 **69** .... (bt) AdamKirby 11 76
(Clive Cox) *hld up in rr: prog on outer fr 3f out: rdn to ld jst over 1f out: drifted rt but kpt on: hdd last strides* **8/1**[3]

0-06 **4** 2 **Limonata (IRE)**[72] 3958 3-9-1 **64** .... HarryBentley 12 69+
(Henry Candy) *trckd ldr after 2f to 2f out: short of room sn after and lost pl: kpt on again fnl f but unable to chal* **5/1**[2]

02 **5** 1 **Patanjali (IRE)**[47] 4819 3-8-8 **57** .... JohnFahy 10 58
(Eve Johnson Houghton) *trckd ldrs on outer: clsd to take 2nd and edgd rt 2f out: rdn to ld briefly over 1f out: hung rt and wknd ins fnl f* **8/1**[3]

-236 **6** 2 **Pernickety**[41] 5089 3-9-7 **70** .... OisinMurphy 7 67
(Lucy Wadham) *hld up in last: rdn over 2f out: kpt on fr over 1f out: nvr pce to threaten* **12/1**

6313 **7** 1/2 **Rustique**[22] 5750 4-9-9 **65** .... ThomasBrown 9 61
(Ed Walker) *mde most to over 1f out: sn wknd* **9/1**

0305 **8** 1 3/4 **Pennerley**[47] 4836 3-9-1 **64** .... RyanTate 4 56
(James Eustace) *wl in tch bhd ldrs: drvn and hung rt fr 2f out: no hdwy after* **9/1**

3532 **9** 2 1/2 **Tommys Geal**[21] 5776 4-9-8 **64** .... DanielMuscutt 3 51
(Michael Madgwick) *in tch in midfield: rdn over 2f out: trying to make prog whn carried rt wl over 1f out: no hdwy after* **16/1**

3-54 **10** 5 **Nawkhatha (USA)**[43] 4978 3-9-5 **68** .... PaulHanagan 6 45
(Brian Meehan) *hld up towards rr: pushed along whn nt clr run and dropped to last wl over 2f out: no ch after* **5/1**[2]

4500 **11** 17 **Miss Fortune**[26] 5610 3-8-2 **51** oh6 .... KieranO'Neill 2
(Mark Usher) *chsd ldr 2f: styd prom tl wknd 3f out: t.o* **100/1**

2m 10.96s (0.46) **Going Correction** +0.125s/f (Good)
WFA 3 from 4yo+ 7lb **11** Ran SP% **119.9**
Speed ratings (Par 100): **102,103,102,100,100 98,98,96,94,90 77**
CSF £71.26 CT £449.00 TOTE £3.90: £1.60, £6.10, £2.50; EX 54.90 Trifecta £521.60.
Owner David & Paul Hearson **Bred** Granham Farm Partnership **Trained** Beckhampton, Wilts
■ Stewards' Enquiry : Thomas Brown caution: careless riding
Edward Greatrex caution: careless riding
John Fahy caution: careless riding

FOCUS
Race distance increased by 24yds. A modest fillies' handicap, it at least produced a good finish, with the finishers challenging wide coming to the fore. The form seems sound.
T/Jkpt: Not won. T/Plt: £110.90 to a £1 stake. Pool: £69,386.88 - 456.62 winning units T/Qpdt: £21.80 to a £1 stake. Pool: £4,749.14 - 160.68 winning units **Jonathan Neesom**

6454 YARMOUTH (L-H)
Wednesday, September 14

OFFICIAL GOING: Good to firm (good in places; 7.9) (watered) (race 6 abandoned due to false ground)
Wind: Virtually nil Weather: Sunny and hot

6486 GREENE KING IPA/BRITISH STALLION STUDS EBF MAIDEN STKS (PLUS 10 RACE) 7f 3y
2:15 (2:15) (Class 4) 2-Y-O **£4,657** (£1,386; £692; £346) **Stalls** High

Form RPR

6 **1** **Solomon's Bay (IRE)**[68] 4075 2-9-5 0 .... AndreaAtzeni 4 83
(Roger Varian) *chsd ldng trio: hdwy ent fnl 2f: rdn to chal over 1f out: led ins fnl f: styd on wl* **8/1**

32 **2** 3/4 **Calibration (IRE)**[26] 5600 2-9-5 0 .... TomMarquand 3 81
(Martyn Meade) *chsd ldr: rdn to ld over 1f out: drvn and hdd ins fnl f: styd on same pce after* **5/1**[3]

3 **3** 1/2 **Via Serendipity**[26] 5615 2-9-5 0 .... JimCrowley 1 80
(Hugo Palmer) *stdd s: hld up in tch in last trio: clsd to trck ldrs 2f out: rdn and edgd lft over 1f out: styd on same pce ins fnl f* **8/11**[1]

4 1 **Sersar** 2-9-5 0 .... SilvestreDeSousa 8 77+
(Ismail Mohammed) *in tch in last pair: swtchd lft 1/2-way: effrt 2f out: rdn and hdwy over 1f out: styd on same pce ins fnl f* **33/1**

5 1/2 **Karawaan (IRE)** 2-9-5 0 .... GrahamGibbons 6 76+
(Sir Michael Stoute) *rn green: led: rdn and hdd over 1f out: no ex u.p 1f out: styd on same pce ins fnl f* **25/1**

623 **6** 2 **Hyde Park**[68] 4103 2-9-5 87 ....[1] FrankieDettori 2 72
(John Gosden) *stdd s: hld up in tch: effrt 2f out: swtchd lft and rdn over 1f out: sn hung rt: squeezed for room and hmpd: kpt on same pce fnl f* **3/1**[2]

7 3 **Highland Cradle** 2-9-5 0 .... TedDurcan 9 62
(Sir Michael Stoute) *chsd ldng pair tl jst over 2f out: lost pl and rn green over 1f out: wknd ins fnl f* **25/1**

8 2 **Veiled Secret (IRE)** 2-9-5 0 .... LukeMorris 7 57
(Sir Mark Prescott Bt) *hld up in tch in last pair: rdn 3f out: outpcd 2f out: sn btn and wknd fnl f* **80/1**

9 1 3/4 **Sticks McKenzie** 2-9-5 0 .... MartinHarley 5 52
(Michael Bell) *hld up in tch in midfield: rdn over 2f out: sn struggling: lost pl and bhd over 1f out: wknd* **80/1**

1m 27.57s (0.97) **Going Correction** -0.25s/f (Firm) **9** Ran SP% **123.8**
Speed ratings (Par 97): **84,83,82,81,80 78,75,72,70**
CSF £48.21 TOTE £10.70: £2.30, £1.50, £1.10; EX 46.80 Trifecta £114.50.
Owner Prince A A Faisal **Bred** Nawara Stud Company Ltd S A **Trained** Newmarket, Suffolk

FOCUS
Following the problem with the wet patch of ground at around the 4f marker, the meeting had to pass a morning inspection, but as was the case on Tuesday the 5f race (which would have been the sixth contest on the card) was abandoned. The going was officially good to firm, good in places and again the stalls were on the stands' side on the straight track. Although last year's winner was sent off at 33-1, this maiden had traditionally been a good race for favourites, but the hotpot was turned over this time. After the first Frankie Dettori said: "It's much better than yesterday, it's nice ground", while Andrea Atzeni said: "It's the fast side of good." The runner-up helps set a fluid opening level.

6487 DANNY AND PEGGY WRIGHT MEMORIAL FILLIES' H'CAP (FOR THE CHALLENGE TROPHY) 6f 3y
2:50 (2:50) (Class 5) (0-75,73) 3-Y-O+ **£3,881** (£1,155; £577; £288) **Stalls** High

Form RPR

1346 **1** **Shypen**[42] 5039 3-9-4 **72** .... JimCrowley 7 81+
(George Margarson) *t.k.h: trck ldrs: nt clr run and swtchd rt over 1f out: rdn and hdwy to chal jst ins fnl f: led 50yds out: rdn out* **4/1**[2]

1620 **2** nk **Racing Angel (IRE)**[42] 5040 4-9-2 **68** .... TedDurcan 4 76
(Mick Quinn) *hld up in tch: clsd and nt clrest of runs 2f out: wnt between rivals and rdn to chal ent fnl f: drvn to ld 150yds: hdd and no ex fnl 50yds* **12/1**

2305 **3** 1 1/2 **Monarch Maid**[6] 6255 5-9-0 **73** .... LuluStanford(7) 6 76
(Peter Hiatt) *led: rdn over 1f out: hdd and unable qck 150yds out: styd on same pce after* **4/1**[2]

56-1 **4** 3 3/4 **Sakhee's Jem**[22] 5748 3-9-3 **71** .... LukeMorris 1 62
(Gay Kelleway) *hld up in tch: effrt and swtchd lft 2f out: hrd drvn to chse ldrs 1f out: no ex jst ins fnl f: wknd fnl 150yds* **13/2**[3]

635 **5** nk **Princess Momoka**[64] 4238 3-8-12 **66** .... AndreaAtzeni 3 56
(Roger Varian) *chsd ldrs: effrt over 1f out: no ex u.p 1f out: wknd ins fnl f* **4/1**[2]

6U56 **6** 2 **Fever Few**[12] 6072 7-9-5 **71** .... MartinHarley 2 55
(Chris Wall) *trckd ldrs: effrt to chse ldr 2f out: rdn and ev ch over 1f out: no ex and btn jst ins fnl f: sn wknd* **10/3**[1]

00-5 **7** 2 ½ **Baileys Pursuit**[42] 5038 4-8-10 **62**........(p) JimmyQuinn 8 38
(Christine Dunnett) *hld up in tch in last pair: effrt ent fnl 2f: no imp over 1f out: wknd fnl f* **33/1**

0502 **8** 13 **Lolita**[23] 5725 4-9-4 **70**........ FrederikTylicki 5 4
(J R Jenkins) *chsd ldr tl 2f out: sn struggling and losing pl whn sltly squeezed for room over 1f out: sn bhd and eased ins fnl f* **14/1**

1m 12.28s (-2.12) **Going Correction** -0.25s/f (Firm)
WFA 3 from 4yo+ 2lb **8** Ran SP% **113.7**
Speed ratings (Par 100): **104,103,101,96,96 93,90,72**
CSF £49.33 CT £202.47 TOTE £5.00: £1.70, £3.80, £1.50; EX 57.90 Trifecta £225.60.
Owner F Butler **Bred** F Butler **Trained** Newmarket, Suffolk

FOCUS
An ordinary fillies' sprint handicap.

6488 EBF STALLIONS JOHN MUSKER FILLIES' STKS (FOR THE JOHN MUSKER TROPHY) (LISTED RACE) 1m 2f 23y
3:25 (3:26) (Class 1) 3-Y-O+

£22,488 (£8,560; £4,284; £2,136; £1,072; £540) **Stalls** Low

Form RPR

1-11 **1** **So Mi Dar**[126] 2160 3-9-3 112........ FrankieDettori 1 118+
(John Gosden) *broke wl but stdd to trck ldng pair and travelled strly: clsd to join ldr on bit 2f out: shkn up and qcknd to ld over 1f out: in command and rdn out hands and heels ins fnl f: eased towards fin: impressive* **11/8**[1]

1315 **2** ½ **Nezwaah**[22] 5754 3-8-13 105........ AndreaAtzeni 7 111
(Roger Varian) *hld up in tch in midfield: clsd and nt clr run 2f out: rdn and hdwy to chse ldng pair over 1f out: chsd wnr jst ins fnl f: styd on u.p but nvr a serious threat to wnr* **7/1**[3]

6-20 **3** ¾ **Arabian Queen (IRE)**[102] 2894 4-9-2 115........ SilvestreDeSousa 4 106
(David Elsworth) *led: rdn over 3f out: drvn over 2f out: hdd over 1f out: kpt on u.p but comf hld in 3rd ins fnl f* **11/4**[2]

1-1 **4** 3 ¼ **Materialistic**[30] 5487 3-8-9 89........ FrederikTylicki 8 99
(Luca Cumani) *hld up in tch in midfield: swtchd rt and effrt over 2f out: rdn over 1f out: 4th and no imp fnl f* **10/1**

6211 **5** ¾ **Rostova (USA)**[19] 5831 3-8-9 97........ TedDurcan 9 98
(Sir Michael Stoute) *stdd s: hld up in tch in last pair: clsd over 2f out: nt clr run and swtchd rt over 1f out: 5th and no imp ins fnl f* **8/1**

3160 **6** 1 ¼ **We Are Ninety (IRE)**[60] 4416 3-8-13 105........ JimCrowley 6 99
(Hugo Palmer) *dwlt: hld up in tch in last pair: pushed along 4f out: swtchd rt and rdn over 2f out: no imp over 1f out: wknd fnl f* **11/1**

1403 **7** hd **Light And Shade**[11] 6113 4-9-2 97........ MartinHarley 5 95
(James Tate) *in tch in midfield: rdn ent fnl 2f out: unable qck over 1f out: wknd ins fnl f* **33/1**

0-33 **8** 2 ¾ **Maybelater**[35] 5307 4-9-2 99........ LukeMorris 2 89
(Jonathan Portman) *sn chsng ldr: clsd to press ldr and looked to be travelling wl 3f out: shkn up 2f out: rdn: little rspnse and lost pl over 1f out: wknd fnl f* **25/1**

2m 6.07s (-4.43) **Going Correction** -0.125s/f (Firm)
WFA 3 from 4yo 7lb **8** Ran SP% **116.6**
Speed ratings (Par 108): **112,111,111,108,107 106,106,104**
CSF £12.24 TOTE £2.10: £1.20, £2.10, £1.30; EX 12.50 Trifecta £38.80.
Owner Lord Lloyd-Webber **Bred** Watership Down Stud **Trained** Newmarket, Suffolk

FOCUS
A fascinating Listed contest featuring a previous Group 1 winner and an unbeaten one-time Classic hopeful returning from injury. They went an even pace and the favourite did it nicely. The form is set around the 4th, 5th and 6th and a little fluid.

6489 PARKLANDS LEISURE HOLIDAY DISTRIBUTORS H'CAP (FOR THE GOLDEN JUBILEE TROPHY) 1m 2f 23y
4:00 (4:02) (Class 3) (0-90,90) 3-Y-O+ **£7,561** (£2,263; £1,131; £566; £282) **Stalls** Low

Form RPR

3110 **1** **Al Neksh**[47] 4827 3-9-2 **87**........ FrankieDettori 4 99+
(William Haggas) *t.k.h: hld up in tch in 4th: clsd to press ldrs 2f out: rdn and chal over 1f out: led jst ins fnl f: styd on and asserted fnl 100yds: rdn out* **5/6**[1]

0-40 **2** 1 ¼ **Great Hall**[18] 5879 6-9-12 **90**........ JimCrowley 2 97
(Mick Quinn) *chsd ldng pair: effrt on inner over 1f out: nt clr run and swtchd rt jst ins fnl f: styd on to snatch 2nd last strides* **9/1**

3115 **3** hd **Absolute Zero (IRE)**[37] 5240 3-9-2 **87**........ AndreaAtzeni 3 94
(Roger Varian) *led: jnd 3f out: rdn 2f out: hdd and no ex jst ins fnl f: styd on same pce after: lost 2nd last strides* **3/1**[2]

3326 **4** 4 ½ **The Gay Cavalier**[17] 5925 5-8-7 **78**........(t) JonathanFisher[(7)] 1 76
(John Ryan) *s.i.s: bhd: clsd and in tch after 2f: rdn 2f out: sn struggling: wknd fnl f* **14/1**

0610 **5** 1 **Illusive (IRE)**[18] 5874 5-9-5 **86**........(p) MarcMonaghan[(3)] 6 82
(George Scott) *chsd ldr: upsides and rdn 3f out: unable qck and lost pl u.p over 1f out: wknd ins fnl f* **11/2**[3]

2m 7.47s (-3.03) **Going Correction** -0.125s/f (Firm)
WFA 3 from 5yo+ 7lb **5** Ran SP% **111.6**
Speed ratings (Par 107): **107,106,105,102,101**
CSF £9.34 TOTE £1.50: £1.10, £4.40; EX 10.80 Trifecta £22.10.
Owner Al Shaqab Racing **Bred** The Pocock Family **Trained** Newmarket, Suffolk

FOCUS
Not the most competitive 0-90 handicap ever run and the market spoke volumes. They only went a steady pace which didn't pick up until inside the last 3f. The winner resumed his progress and the 2nd has been rated to this year's form.

6490 SEA-DEER H'CAP 1m 3y
4:35 (4:36) (Class 4) (0-85,85) 3-Y-O+ **£5,175** (£1,540; £769; £384) **Stalls** High

Form RPR

2212 **1** **Fastnet Tempest (IRE)**[32] 5391 3-9-4 **84**........(p) FrankieDettori 6 93+
(William Haggas) *chsd ldr tl led over 2f out: rdn and asserted jst over 1f out: in command whn pricked ears and looking arnd ins fnl f: pressed wl ins fnl f: pushed along and holding chalr towards fin* **3/1**[2]

1231 **2** nk **Misty Lord (IRE)**[24] 5677 3-9-0 **80**........(t) AndreaAtzeni 1 87+
(Marco Botti) *t.k.h: hld up in tch towards rr: swtchd lft and effrt over 1f out: hdwy and rdn to chse ldrs 1f out: chalng wl ins fnl f: kpt on but hld towards fin* **15/8**[1]

5152 **3** 1 ¼ **Kestrel Dot Com**[42] 5037 4-9-5 **80**........ SilvestreDeSousa 9 85
(Chris Dwyer) *switching lft after s: t.k.h: hld up in tch: hdwy into midfield 1/2-way: rdn to chse wnr over 1f out: no imp: styd on same pce and lost 2nd ins fnl f* **7/1**[3]

0634 **4** ¾ **Destroyer**[21] 5765 3-9-0 **80**........(p) SamHitchcott 10 82
(William Muir) *t.k.h: trckd ldrs tl nt a clr run and shuffled bk over 2f out: swtchd lft ent fnl 2f: swtchd bk rt and hdwy over 1f out: kpt on u.p ins fnl f* **16/1**

1446 **5** 1 ½ **Thecornishbarron (IRE)**[18] 5874 4-9-0 **75**........ JimCrowley 7 75
(John Ryan) *t.k.h: chse ldrs: wnt 2nd jst over 2f out: rdn and unable qck over 1f out: wknd ins fnl f* **14/1**

6010 **6** 1 **Zain Emperor (IRE)**[70] 4010 3-8-13 **79**........(v) StevieDonohoe 8 75
(Charlie Fellowes) *hld up in tch in midfield: effrt over 1f out: unable qck u.p over 1f out: wknd ins fnl f* **3/1**[2]

2000 **7** 7 **Western Way (IRE)**[30] 5482 7-8-11 **72**........(p) RobertHavlin 2 52
(Don Cantillon) *taken down early: stdd s: hld up in rr: shkn up 2f out: sn bhd* **66/1**

2155 **8** 9 **Billy Roberts (IRE)**[31] 5437 3-9-1 **81**........ FrederikTylicki 3 39
(Richard Guest) *taken down early: t.k.h: led tl over 2f out: lost pl qckly and bhd over 1f out: eased ins fnl f: sddle slipped* **16/1**

1m 38.06s (-2.54) **Going Correction** -0.25s/f (Firm)
WFA 3 from 4yo+ 5lb **8** Ran SP% **117.2**
Speed ratings (Par 105): **102,101,100,99,98 97,90,81**
CSF £9.32 CT £35.72 TOTE £4.30: £1.40, £1.10, £2.20; EX 10.60 Trifecta £35.70.
Owner O T I Racing & Partner **Bred** Rockhart Trading Ltd **Trained** Newmarket, Suffolk

FOCUS
A fair handicap with the finish fought out between a couple of progressive 3yos. The 3rd and 4th help set the standard.

6491 STANLEY THREADWELL MEMORIAL H'CAP 5f 42y
(5:05) (Class 2) (0-105,) 3-Y-O+ £

6492 LA CONTINENTAL CAFE H'CAP 6f 3y
5:35 (5:38) (Class 4) (0-85,83) 3-Y-O **£5,175** (£1,540; £769; £384) **Stalls** High

Form RPR

0213 **1** **Highly Sprung (IRE)**[15] 5991 3-9-7 **83**........ SilvestreDeSousa 9 93
(Mark Johnston) *last pair and nt travelling early: swtchd lft and hdwy 2f out: str run u.p to ld 1f out: sn drew clr and r.o strly* **3/1**[2]

-314 **2** 5 **Tanasoq (IRE)**[29] 5512 3-9-3 **79**........ JimCrowley 8 73
(Owen Burrows) *hld up in tch: effrt 2f out: drvn and ev ch over 1f out: outpcd by wnr but hld on for 2nd ins fnl f* **6/1**

0650 **3** hd **Red Artist**[46] 4867 3-9-7 **83**........ RobertHavlin 7 76
(Simon Crisford) *hld up in tch in last pair: shkn up wl over 1f out: rdn and hdwy jst over 1f out: styd on and pressing for 2nd towards fin: no ch w wnr* **14/1**

0321 **4** ½ **Mazzini**[16] 5968 3-9-6 **82**........ FrederikTylicki 10 73+
(James Fanshawe) *trckd ldrs: nt clr run over 2f out: swtchd rt and fnlly in the clr 100yds out: no ch w wnr but styd on towards fin* **9/4**[1]

21 **5** ½ **Sirajiah (IRE)**[9] 6190 3-9-2 **78** 6ex........(p) AndreaAtzeni 3 68
(William Haggas) *t.k.h: hld up in tch in midfield: nt clr run over 1f out: rdn ent fnl f: styd on same pce and no ch w wnr fnl f* **5/1**[3]

0110 **6** ½ **Fang**[44] 4954 3-9-6 **82**........(t) FrankieDettori 5 70
(William Jarvis) *led: rdn over 1f out: hdd 1f out: sn outpcd and btn: plugged on same pce after* **8/1**

0613 **7** 2 ¼ **Case Key**[32] 5408 3-9-0 **76**........ AndrewMullen 1 57
(Michael Appleby) *chsd ldrs: wnt 2nd jst over 2f out: rdn and ev ch over 1f out tl no ex and btn 1f out: wknd fnl f* **14/1**

0552 **8** 17 **Florencio**[18] 5896 3-9-7 **83**........(t) SamHitchcott 4 10
(William Muir) *chsd ldr: rdn 1/2-way: lost pl ent fnl f: bhd and eased ins fnl f* **25/1**

1m 11.65s (-2.75) **Going Correction** -0.25s/f (Firm) **8** Ran SP% **115.0**
Speed ratings (Par 103): **108,101,101,100,99 99,96,73**
CSF £21.52 CT £216.27 TOTE £4.20: £1.50, £2.10, £3.50; EX 24.20 Trifecta £242.50.
Owner Douglas Livingston **Bred** Patrick J Moloney **Trained** Middleham Moor, N Yorks

FOCUS
A fair 3yo sprint handicap and the winner bolted up, but the pace looked overly strong and the level is a bit fluid.
T/Plt: £12.30 to a £1 stake. Pool: £67,270.79 - 3,960.68 winning units T/Qpdt: £2.30 to a £1 stake. Pool: £4,449.08 - 1,381.85 winning units **Steve Payne**

6493 - 6494a (Foreign Racing) - See Raceform Interactive

6467 LISTOWEL (L-H)
Wednesday, September 14

OFFICIAL GOING: Heavy

6495a EDMUND & JOSIE WHELAN MEMORIAL LISTOWEL STKS (LISTED RACE) 1m 1f
3:05 (3:05) 3-Y-O+

£21,691 (£6,985; £3,308; £1,470; £735; £367)

RPR

1 **Champagne Or Water (IRE)**[25] 5662 5-9-4 94........ BillyLee 13 96
(W McCreery, Ire) *hld up in rr of mid-div: hdwy on outer under 3f out to chse ldrs under 2f out where edgd lft: sn rdn into 2nd and clsd u.p to ld narrowly ins fnl 150yds: kpt on wl clsng stages* **8/1**

2 ½ **In My Pocket (IRE)**[43] 5000 4-9-9 102........ DeclanMcDonogh 9 100
(John M Oxx, Ire) *cl up: cl 2nd at 1/2-way: led narrowly fr 3f out: rdn 1 1/2f out and strly pressed ent fnl f: hdd narrowly ins fnl 150yds and kpt on wl wout matching wnr clsng stages* **5/1**[2]

3 ½ **Dream Walker (FR)**[17] 5941 7-9-9 95........(t) ChrisHayes 6 99+
(Brian Ellison) *settled in mid-div: pushed along into 7th over 2f out: sn rdn and hdwy on outer whn edgd sltly lft and bmpd rival over 1f out: impr into 3rd ins fnl f and r.o clsng stages: nrst fin* **11/2**[3]

4 2 ¼ **Flying Fairies (IRE)**[24] 5687 3-8-12 85........ RonanWhelan 11 89
(Joseph G Murphy, Ire) *chsd ldrs: rdn over 1f out where n.m.r and impr into 4th fnl 150yds: kpt on same pce to jst hold 4th: nvr trbld ldrs* **8/1**

5 nk **Toe The Line (IRE)**[122] 2275 7-9-4 102........ ColinKeane 4 89+
(John E Kiely, Ire) *hld up towards rr: tk clsr order on outer fr under 3f out: hdwy in 9th under 2f out and r.o wl into 5th wl ins fnl f: jst hld for 4th: nvr on terms* **5/1**[2]

6 2 **Rainfall Radar (USA)**[24] 5688 4-9-4 72........(p) ColmO'Donoghue 10 84?
(Joseph G Murphy, Ire) *chsd ldrs: 3rd 1/2-way: rdn over 2f out and no imp on ldrs u.p in 4th over 1f out: one pce after* **16/1**

7 ½ **Maneen**[24] 5685 3-9-3 99........(b[1]) PatSmullen 7 88+
(D K Weld, Ire) *dwlt sltly and pushed along early to sn chse ldrs: clsr in 4th after 1/2-way: rdn 2f out and hmpd sltly: sn edgd sltly rt and bmpd disputing 5th over 1f out: no imp in 7th after and one pce after* **4/1**[1]

8 *hd* **Flirt (IRE)**[28] 5564 3-8-12 88..(p) RoryCleary 2 83+
(David Wachman, Ire) *hld up in tch: pushed along under 3f out and n.m.r on inner bef st where checked: dropped to 10th briefly and hmpd over 1f out: kpt on again ins fnl f where hmpd between horses: nvr on terms* **25/1**

9 *2 ¼* **Just Joan (IRE)**[28] 5564 3-8-12 89.................................[1] WayneLordan 1 78
(T Stack, Ire) *towards rr for most: rdn and no imp bef st: kpt on one pce ins fnl f* **25/1**

10 *1 ¼* **Misty Millie (IRE)**[20] 5818 3-8-12 91.............................. KillianLeonard 8 76
(P Cluskey, Ire) *led narrowly: pushed along and hdd fr 3f out: dropped to 3rd u.p 1 1/2f out and no ex: wknd fnl f* **16/1**

11 *1 ½* **Stenographer (USA)**[20] 5816 3-9-3 98.......................... KevinManning 5 77
(J S Bolger, Ire) *w ldrs early: 4th 1/2-way: rdn over 2f out and no ex u.p in 6th under 2f out: sn wknd* **12/1**

12 *nk* **Island Remede**[68] 1279 5-9-4 94................................ DonnachaO'Brien 3 72
(Henry De Bromhead, Ire) *hld up in rr of mid-div early: pushed along towards rr under 3f out and no imp u.p into st: one pce fnl 2f* **16/1**

13 *2 ½* **Gallope (IRE)**[63] 4282 4-9-4 80.. ShaneFoley 12 67
(Mrs Prunella Dobbs, Ire) *a bhd: pushed along fr 3f out and no imp u.p in rr into st: one pce fnl 2f* **33/1**

2m 3.7s (123.70)
WFA 3 from 4yo+ 6lb **13** Ran SP% **126.9**
CSF £49.89 TOTE £8.20: £2.70, £1.70, £2.10; DF 55.80 Trifecta £206.20.
Owner Mrs L Scott **Bred** Guillaume De Rham & Agathe Lebailly **Trained** Rathbride, Co Kildare

FOCUS
Appreciation of the ground was key to the winner's victory, a mare who has improved a good deal too and apparently will be sold at the end of the year. The 3rd and 4th help set the standard, but the 6th is a concern.

6496 - (Foreign Racing) - See Raceform Interactive

6309 SAINT-CLOUD (L-H)
Wednesday, September 14

OFFICIAL GOING: Turf: good

6497a PRIX JOUBERT (LISTED RACE) (3YO FILLIES) (TURF) 1m 4f
3:45 (12:00) 3-Y-O **£20,220** (£8,088; £6,066; £4,044; £2,022)

RPR

1 **Alakhana (FR)**[23] 5733 3-8-13 0..................................... MaximeGuyon 1 100
(F Head, France) **11/2**

2 *shd* **Deremah (USA)**[31] 5451 3-8-13 0......................... ChristopheSoumillon 2 100
(A De Royer-Dupre, France) **49/10**[3]

3 *1 ¾* **Beraymi (IRE)**[16] 3-8-13 0... MickaelBarzalona 5 97
(A Fabre, France) *t.k.h: hld up towards rr: scrubbed along ins fnl 2 1/2f but no immediate imp: rdn and hdwy on outer under 1 1/2f out: styd on fnl f: nt rch ldrs* **53/10**

4 *snk* **Edya**[13] 6069 3-8-13 0... Pierre-CharlesBoudot 8 97
(G Botti, France) **12/1**

5 *1 ½* **Cosmica Sidera (IRE)**[41] 3-8-13 0.........................(b) GregoryBenoist 6 95
(D Smaga, France) **17/1**

6 *¾* **Do Re Mi Fa Sol (FR)**[31] 5451 3-8-13 0......................... FranckBlondel 9 93
(P Decouz, France) **18/5**[1]

7 *¾* **Myth**[43] 5006 3-8-13 0.. MarcLerner 10 92
(Waldemar Hickst, Germany) **43/1**

8 *½* **Etonnez Moi (IRE)**[186] 3-8-13 0................................ CristianDemuro 3 91
(Mme Pia Brandt, France) **57/10**

9 *2 ½* **Colonial Classic (FR)**[17] 5927 3-8-13 0......................... OlivierPeslier 4 87
(John Gosden) *sn led: shkn up and wnt for home over 2 1/2f out: hdd ins last 2f: wknd fnl f* **42/10**[2]

2m 31.32s (-9.08) **9** Ran SP% **119.6**
WIN (incl. 1 euro stake): 6.50. PLACES: 1.70, 2.00, 2.20. DF: 13.70. SF: 23.80.
Owner Wertheimer & Frere **Bred** Wertheimer & Frere **Trained** France

6498a (Foreign Racing) - See Raceform Interactive

5221 AYR (L-H)
Thursday, September 15

OFFICIAL GOING: Soft (good to soft in places; 7.5)
Wind: Light, half against Weather: Hazy, warm

6499 H&V COMMISSIONING SERVICES EBF NOVICE STKS (PLUS 10 RACE) 1m
1:30 (1:31) (Class 4) 2-Y-O **£6,469** (£1,925; £962; £481) **Stalls** Low

Form RPR

42 1 **Souter**[22] 5778 2-9-2 0.. ConnorBeasley 5 81
(Keith Dalgleish) *led: rdn 2f out: edgd lft and hdd ins fnl f: rallied gamely to ld cl home* **7/1**

321 2 *nse* **Mister Belvedere**[15] 6025 2-9-5 82.............................. PaulMulrennan 6 84
(Michael Dods) *prom: effrt and rdn wl over 1f out: led ins fnl f: edgd rt and hdd cl home* **11/4**[1]

3 *1 ¾* **Armandihan (IRE)** 2-9-2 0... TomEaves 2 77+
(Kevin Ryan) *noisy in paddock: s.i.s and t.k.h in rr: smooth hdwy over 2f out: effrt and chsd ldrs over 1f out: kpt on fnl f: impr* **7/2**[2]

61 4 *nse* **Hushood (IRE)**[17] 5952 2-9-8 79...................................... SeanLevey 1 83
(Richard Hannon) *pressed ldr: effrt and rdn over 2f out: ev ch over 1f out: kpt on same pce ins fnl f* **9/2**[3]

341 5 5 **Double Touch**[26] 5637 2-9-8 84....................................... DavidNolan 4 72
(Richard Fahey) *taken early to post: t.k.h: hld up bhd ldng gp: rdn over 2f out: no imp over 1f out: btn fnl f* **7/2**[2]

04 6 2 **Greengairs**[15] 6025 2-9-2 0... JasonHart 3 62
(Keith Dalgleish) *hld up in tch: drvn and outpcd over 2f out: btn over 1f out* **100/1**

02 7 *¾* **Upgrade**[14] 6054 2-9-2 0... DougieCostello 8 60
(K R Burke) *chsd ldrs on outside: rdn along over 2f out: wknd wl over 1f out* **9/1**

1m 44.14s (0.34) **Going Correction** 0.0s/f (Good) **7** Ran SP% **112.8**
Speed ratings (Par 97): **98,97,96,96,91 89,88**
CSF £25.82 TOTE £7.80: £3.60, £1.40; EX 29.70 Trifecta £211.10.
Owner Mrs Janis Macpherson **Bred** Rabbah Bloodstock Limited **Trained** Carluke, S Lanarks

FOCUS
The ground was officially soft, good to soft in places. Goingstick: straight course - far side and stands' side 6.9, centre 7.5; overall 7.6. The rail was on its innermost line, so all race distances as advertised. Eight of the last nine winners of this novice event had gone to a previous winner, but this time it went to a maiden. The winning time was 6.14sec outside standard and Sean Levey said: "The ground is on the soft side of good, but not too bad," Paul Mulrennan said: "It is just on the easy side" and Tom Eaves said: "It is a bit dead."

6500 HILLHOUSE QUARRY SUPPORTING THE AYRSHIRE HOSPICE H'CAP 1m
2:00 (2:00) (Class 4) (0-85,85) 3-Y-O+ **£6,469** (£1,925; £962; £481) **Stalls** Low

Form RPR

4066 1 **Silvery Moon (IRE)**[13] 6081 9-9-9 85.................................. JasonHart 4 94
(Tim Easterby) *hld up against far rail: hdwy over 2f out: swtchd lft ins fnl f: kpt on wl to ld cl home* **5/1**[1]

0343 2 *hd* **Father Bertie**[8] 6225 4-9-9 85...(tp) DavidAllan 12 93
(Tim Easterby) *cl up: rdn to ld wl over 1f out: hdd ins fnl f: rallied gamely: jst hld* **5/1**[1]

0060 3 *hd* **Finn Class (IRE)**[17] 5976 5-9-8 84............................[1] PaulMulrennan 14 92
(Michael Dods) *hld up midfield on outside: rdn and hdwy over 1f out: led ins fnl f: kpt on: hdd and no ex cl home* **16/1**

3000 4 *1 ½* **Miss Van Gogh**[12] 6115 4-9-9 85....................................... DavidNolan 7 89
(Richard Fahey) *hld up towards rr: rdn and hdwy 2f out: kpt on fnl f: nrst fin* **11/1**

3121 5 *1 ¼* **Our Boy Jack (IRE)**[18] 5915 7-9-1 82................... AdamMcNamara[(5)] 9 83
(Richard Fahey) *hld up midfield on outside: rdn over 2f out: rallied over 1f out: kpt on ins fnl f: no imp* **12/1**

2215 6 *nse* **Moonlightnavigator (USA)**[29] 5538 4-9-8 84............ DougieCostello 6 85
(John Quinn) *led: rdn and hdd wl over 1f out: rallied: no ex whn checked ins fnl f* **9/1**

060 7 *1 ¾* **Strong Man**[15] 6027 8-9-2 78.. CamHardie 3 75
(Michael Easterby) *prom:: rdn over 2f out: wknd ins fnl f* **66/1**

4200 8 *½* **Hard To Handel**[19] 5886 4-9-8 84..................................(p) PhillipMakin 1 80
(David O'Meara) *hld up midfield: rdn along over 2f out: no imp over 1f out* **17/2**[3]

5152 9 *1* **Tadaany (IRE)**[9] 6217 4-9-3 79.. DanielTudhope 2 73
(David O'Meara) *cl up: effrt and rdn 2f out: wknd ins fnl f* **6/1**[2]

0026 10 *1* **Argaki (IRE)**[8] 6225 6-9-5 81.. ConnorBeasley 10 72
(Keith Dalgleish) *trckd ldrs: drvn over 2f out: wknd over 1f out* **12/1**

1610 11 *1 ¼* **Victoire De Lyphar (IRE)**[19] 5886 9-9-5 81...............(e) JamesSullivan 8 69
(Ruth Carr) *dwlt: hld up: rdn 2f out: sn edgd lft: nvr on terms* **25/1**

0040 12 *1 ¼* **Kalk Bay (IRE)**[13] 6082 9-9-7 83..(t) TomEaves 13 69
(Michael Easterby) *missed break: hld up: rdn along over 2f out: sn btn* **66/1**

1100 13 *1 ½* **Another Go (IRE)**[19] 5865 3-9-4 85.................................. NeilFarley 11 66
(Alan Swinbank) *hld up towards rr: struggling over 2f out: sn btn* **25/1**

2305 14 *1* **Nicholas T**[38] 5226 4-9-2 78... WilliamCarson 5 58
(Jim Goldie) *dwlt: hld up: rdn over 2f out: nvr on terms* **17/2**[3]

1m 41.96s (-1.84) **Going Correction** 0.0s/f (Good)
WFA 3 from 4yo+ 5lb **14** Ran SP% **118.9**
Speed ratings (Par 105): **109,108,108,107,105 105,104,103,102,101 100,99,97,96**
CSF £27.49 CT £384.85 TOTE £7.00: £2.20, £2.20, £4.80; EX 27.90 Trifecta £469.80.
Owner C H Stevens **Bred** Colin Kennedy **Trained** Great Habton, N Yorks

FOCUS
A fair and competitive handicap and a thrilling three-way finish resulted in a 1-2 for trainer Tim Easterby. The winner has been rated to this year's form, with the 2nd helping to set the standard.

6501 BARCLAYS BANK SUPPORTING THE AYRHIRE HOSPICE H'CAP (DIV I) 7f 50y
2:35 (2:37) (Class 5) (0-75,75) 3-Y-O+ **£4,528** (£1,347; £673; £336) **Stalls** High

Form RPR

4050 1 **Sister Dude**[24] 5718 3-8-3 63.................................... JordanVaughan[(5)] 5 70
(K R Burke) *trckd ldrs: hdwy to ld over 1f out: drvn out fnl f* **12/1**

520 2 *nk* **Fire And Passion**[10] 6197 4-9-2 67...............................(b) LeighRoche 13 75
(Adrian Paul Keatley, Ire) *dwlt: hld up: hdwy on outside over 2f out: hung lft and chsd wnr over 1f out: kpt on wl towards fin* **9/1**

1-00 3 *1* **Ambriel (IRE)**[20] 5858 3-9-6 75.................................(b[1]) PaulMulrennan 4 78
(Michael Dods) *hld up midfield on outside: hdwy over 2f out: effrt and disp 2nd pl over 1f out to ins fnl f: kpt on: hld nr fin* **22/1**

4324 4 *hd* **Honeysuckle Lil (IRE)**[34] 5379 4-9-9 74........................(p) DavidAllan 10 79
(Tim Easterby) *hld up: nt clr run over 2f out: effrt and hdwy over 1f out: kpt on ins fnl f: nrst fin* **8/1**

16 5 *1 ¾* **Donnelly's Rainbow (IRE)**[55] 4605 3-9-5 74...............[1] BarryMcHugh 1 72
(Rebecca Bastiman) *hld up midfield on ins: effrt and hdwy 2f out: one pce ins fnl f* **18/1**

2346 6 *1 ¾* **Curzon Line**[43] 5033 7-9-3 68.. CamHardie 12 64
(Michael Easterby) *hld up in tch: effrt over 2f out: rdn and edgd lft over 1f out: no ex ins fnl f* **14/1**

5100 7 *1 ¼* **Royal Duchess**[15] 6027 6-9-3 73...................... AdamMcNamara[(5)] 8 66
(Lucy Normile) *taken early to post: s.i.s: hld up: rdn over 2f out: hdwy over 1f out: r.o ins fnl f: no imp* **7/1**[3]

0521 8 *½* **Novinophobia**[58] 4490 3-9-1 70.. DavidNolan 11 59
(Richard Fahey) *pressed ldr: rdn along over 2f out: wknd ins fnl f* **13/2**[2]

2231 9 *1* **Dolphin Rock**[24] 5717 9-8-8 66.........................(b) CallumRodriguez[(7)] 14 55
(Richard Ford) *led: rdn and hdd over 1f out: wknd ins fnl f* **10/1**

0066 10 *1 ¼* **Siri**[55] 4587 3-8-12 67... TomEaves 2 50
(Mick Channon) *unruly bef s: chsd ldrs: rdn over 2f out: wkng whn hmpd over 1f out* **14/1**

0343 11 *¾* **Steal The Scene (IRE)**[34] 5357 4-9-10 75......................... SeanLevey 7 58
(Richard Hannon) *hld up on ins: rdn over 2f out: wknd over 1f out* **4/1**[1]

0005 12 *1* **She's Electric (IRE)**[29] 5539 3-8-11 66......................... ConnorBeasley 6 45
(Keith Dalgleish) *s.i.s: hld up: rdn over 2f out: hung lft and sn btn* **16/1**

3165 13 *3* **Baby Ballerina**[22] 5759 3-8-8 68.........................(v[1]) CallumShepherd[(5)] 9 39
(Brian Ellison) *hld up towards rr: drvn along over 2f out: sn btn* **16/1**

1m 34.05s (0.65) **Going Correction** 0.0s/f (Good)
WFA 3 from 4yo+ 4lb **13** Ran SP% **118.4**
Speed ratings (Par 103): **96,95,94,94,92 90,88,88,87,85 84,83,80**
CSF £114.89 CT £2434.09 TOTE £16.10: £4.60, £3.40, £5.20; EX 177.40 Trifecta £3427.50.
Owner Ray Bailey **Bred** Ray Bailey **Trained** Middleham Moor, N Yorks

FOCUS
The first division of an ordinary handicap. The pace was good, but the two leaders may have done too much early. The winner built on her earlier maiden form.

6502 BARCLAYS BANK SUPPORTING THE AYRHIRE HOSPICE H'CAP (DIV II) 7f 50y

3:05 (3:08) (Class 5) (0-75,75) 3-Y-O+ **£4,528** (£1,347; £673; £336) **Stalls** High

Form				RPR
-343	**1**		**Balance**[17] 5973 3-8-10 **70**.. AdamMcNamara(5) 2 (Richard Fahey) *hld up: rdn and hdwy over 2f out: led over 1f out: sn rdn clr: kpt on wl fnl f* **4/1**[1]	80+
1532	**2**	1 ¼	**Vallarta (IRE)**[9] 6216 6-9-9 **74**.. JamesSullivan 7 (Ruth Carr) *hld up midfield on outside: rdn over 2f out: hdwy to chse wnr over 1f out: kpt on fnl f: nt pce to chal* **12/1**	81
1040	**3**	2 ¾	**Tectonic (IRE)**[15] 6028 7-8-11 **62**...............................(v) ConnorBeasley 9 (Keith Dalgleish) *prom: rdn along over 2f out: kpt on ins fnl f: nt rch first two* **28/1**	62
0060	**4**	1 ½	**Dark Crystal**[16] 6005 5-9-3 **68**... DavidNolan 13 (Linda Perratt) *hld up: rdn and hdwy over 2f out: kpt on fnl f: nrst fin* **28/1**	64
5412	**5**	¾	**Bahamian Bird**[15] 6027 3-8-11 **66**................................ PatrickMathers 4 (Richard Fahey) *chsd clr ldrs: drvn along over 2f out: kpt on same pce fnl f* **6/1**[3]	58
1506	**6**	¾	**First Wheat**[9] 6220 3-9-3 **72**.. CamHardie 12 (Michael Easterby) *s.i.s: hld up: rdn over 2f out: kpt on fnl f: no imp* **33/1**	62
022	**7**	4	**Jay Kay**[40] 5151 7-9-4 **74**.. JordanVaughan(5) 5 (K R Burke) *pressed ldr: clr of rest over 3f out: led over 2f out to over 1f out: sn wknd* **9/2**[2]	56
5244	**8**	3 ½	**Mo Henry**[38] 5224 4-8-12 **63**...(v) LeighRoche 3 (Adrian Paul Keatley, Ire) *hld up: hdwy and hung lft over 2f out: rdn and no imp over 1f out* **7/1**	36
3053	**9**	½	**American Hustle (IRE)**[22] 5757 4-8-9 **65**...........(b) CallumShepherd(5) 8 (Brian Ellison) *s.i.s: hld up: rdn and hung lft over 2f out: hdwy whn hmpd over 1f out: sn n.d* **16/1**	36
0006	**10**	6	**Comino (IRE)**[20] 5859 5-9-8 **73**.......................................(b¹) TomEaves 6 (Kevin Ryan) *led at decent gallop: clr w one other over 3f out: hdd over 2f out: wknd over 1f out* **22/1**	29
100	**11**	5	**Connemera Queen**[17] 5973 3-8-13 **68**.......................... BarryMcHugh 11 (Tracy Waggott) *hld up: drvn and struggling wl over 2f out: sn btn* **100/1**	9
-430	**12**	33	**Regal Response (IRE)**[22] 5782 3-9-4 **73**.............(b¹) PaulMulrennan 14 (Michael Dods) *prom: rdn over 2f out: sn wknd* **33/1**
-501	**U**		**Safe Voyage (IRE)**[48] 4848 3-9-6 **75**.................................... JasonHart 1 (John Quinn) *prom: rdn over 2f out: cl 5th and one pce whn sddle slipped and uns rdr over 1f out* **4/1**[1]

1m 32.66s (-0.74) **Going Correction** 0.0s/f (Good)
WFA 3 from 4yo+ 4lb **13** Ran SP% **116.7**
Speed ratings (Par 103): **104,102,99,97,96 96,91,87,86,80 74,36,**
CSF £47.44 CT £1220.32 TOTE £4.70: £1.60, £3.30, £7.30; EX 52.40 Trifecta £1281.70.
Owner Andrew Tinkler **Bred** Brook Stud Bloodstock & W A Tinkler **Trained** Musley Bank, N Yorks

FOCUS
The two leaders went off far too quick in this division, so no surprise that the winning time was 1.39sec faster than the first leg. There was a nasty incident over a furlong from home when the saddle went on one of the joint-favourites, Safe Voyage, sending his jockey crashing to the ground. Fortunately his rider was able to walk away. The winner built on her 2yo maiden win, the 2nd helping to set the standard.

6503 SCOTT BENNETT ASSOCIATES CONSULTING ENGINEERS H'CAP 1m 5f 13y

3:40 (3:40) (Class 5) (0-70,76) 3-Y-O+ **£4,528** (£1,347; £673; £336) **Stalls** Low

Form				RPR
165	**1**		**Sporty Yankee (USA)**[33] 5420 3-8-9 **66**................ JordanVaughan(5) 10 (K R Burke) *hld up: smooth hdwy 2f out: hung lft and chsd wnr appr fnl f: stened and led ins fnl f: sn clr* **9/4**[1]	80+
6334	**2**	2 ¾	**Rocktherunway (IRE)**[17] 5970 7-9-11 **67**................(b¹) ConnorBeasley 7 (Michael Dods) *dwlt: hdwy to ld after 1f: qcknd clr 3f out: rdn over 2f out: hdd ins fnl f: one pce* **11/2**[2]	75
2611	**3**	4 ½	**Falcon's Fire (IRE)**[5] 6346 3-9-10 **76** 6ex......................... PhillipMakin 8 (Keith Dalgleish) *hld up in tch: hdwy on outside to chse (clr) ldr over 2f out to over 1f out: sn outpcd* **9/4**[1]	77
1531	**4**	3 ½	**Dusky Raider (IRE)**[40] 5183 3-9-0 **66**........................(p) PaulMulrennan 11 (Michael Dods) *t.k.h early: chsd ldrs: effrt and chsd (clr) ldr over 3f out to over 2f out: wknd over 1f out* **7/1**[3]	62
2456	**5**	4 ½	**Aldreth**[34] 5350 5-9-13 **69**...(p) CamHardie 6 (Michael Easterby) *hld up: rdn and struggling 3f out: btn fnl 2f* **14/1**	58
2526	**6**	15	**Merchant Of Dubai**[22] 5783 11-9-3 **59**......................... WilliamCarson 5 (Jim Goldie) *led 1f: chsd ldr to over 3f out: rdn and wknd over 2f out* **20/1**	26
5000	**7**	14	**Ronald Gee (IRE)**[80] 3706 9-9-6 **62**.................................... TomEaves 3 (Jim Goldie) *hld up: drvn and struggling over 3f out: sn wknd* **33/1**	8
0	**8**	5	**Forcefull (IRE)**[40] 5154 3-8-13 **65**...................................... LeighRoche 4 (Adrian Paul Keatley, Ire) *dwlt: sn chsng ldrs: drvn over 3f out: wknd over 2f out* **10/1**	3

2m 58.4s (4.40) **Going Correction** 0.0s/f (Good)
WFA 3 from 5yo+ 10lb **8** Ran SP% **112.9**
Speed ratings (Par 103): **86,84,81,79,76 67,58,55**
CSF £14.76 CT £29.52 TOTE £3.20: £1.30, £1.80, £1.20; EX 15.40 Trifecta £59.50.
Owner Mrs Elaine M Burke **Bred** Brandywine Farm **Trained** Middleham Moor, N Yorks

FOCUS
A modest staying handicap run at something of a stop-start gallop, set by the 2nd, who sets the standard. The winner built on his earlier summer soft-ground form.

6504 BRITISH STALLION STUDS SCOTTISH PREMIER SERIES EBF FILLIES' H'CAP 1m 2f

4:15 (4:17) (Class 4) (0-85,81) 3-Y-O+ **£8,086** (£2,406; £1,202; £601) **Stalls** Low

Form				RPR
2-26	**1**		**Rahyah**[36] 5314 3-8-9 **69**.. LeighRoche 8 (Adrian Paul Keatley, Ire) *cl up: led after 1f and maintained ordinary gallop: styd in centre in st: rdn and edgd lft over 1f out: kpt on wl fnl f: unchal* **11/2**[2]	77
53-1	**2**	½	**Luna Mare (IRE)**[15] 6024 3-9-1 **75**...................................... DavidNolan 7 (Richard Fahey) *prom: hdwy over 2f out: rdn and outpcd over 1f out: rallied ins fnl f and wnt 2nd nr fin: a hld* **8/1**	82+
4124	**3**	½	**Livella Fella (IRE)**[16] 6005 3-9-0 **74**................................ PhillipMakin 2 (Keith Dalgleish) *led 1f: pressed wnr: drvn along over 2f out: kpt on same pce ins fnl f: lost 2nd nr fin* **9/1**	80
4522	**4**	1 ½	**Sahara (IRE)**[31] 5489 4-9-10 **77**...................................... GeorgeBaker 12 (Chris Wall) *hld up: rdn and hdwy on outside over 2f out: kpt on ins fnl f: nt pce to chal* **7/1**[3]	80+
4205	**5**	2 ½	**Fray**[20] 5844 5-9-3 **70**.. WilliamCarson 11 (Jim Goldie) *s.i.s: hld up: hdwy over 2f out: rdn and edgd lft over 1f out: sn no imp* **16/1**	68
U451	**6**	¾	**Sattelac**[52] 4702 3-8-8 **68**.. ConnorBeasley 6 (Keith Dalgleish) *restless in stalls: hld up towards rr: rdn and effrt over 2f out: wknd over 1f out* **7/2**[1]	65
1034	**7**	½	**Island Flame (IRE)**[33] 5415 3-8-12 **72**......................... PatrickMathers 1 (Richard Fahey) *midfield: drvn and effrt over 2f out: outpcd over 1f out* **9/1**	68
4-52	**8**	2 ¼	**Siren's Cove**[54] 4668 4-9-4 **76**................................ AdamMcNamara(5) 13 (Richard Fahey) *s.i.s: hld up: effrt over 2f out: rdn and no further imp over 1f out* **7/1**[3]	67
3030	**9**	4	**Heart Locket**[80] 3711 4-9-5 **72**.. CamHardie 4 (Michael Easterby) *hld up towards rr: drvn and struggling over 2f out: sn btn* **80/1**	55
236-	**10**	7	**Next Stop**[334] 7287 5-9-6 **73**.. RobertHavlin 5 (David Nicholls) *midfield: struggling over 2f out: sn wknd* **25/1**	42
1426	**11**	2 ¼	**My Lucille (IRE)**[16] 6005 3-9-4 **78**...................................... DavidAllan 3 (Tim Easterby) *chsd ldrs: rdn over 2f out: wknd wl over 1f out* **9/1**	43

2m 13.76s (1.76) **Going Correction** 0.0s/f (Good)
WFA 3 from 4yo+ 7lb **11** Ran SP% **114.7**
Speed ratings (Par 102): **92,91,91,90,88 87,87,85,82,76 74**
CSF £47.79 CT £388.90 TOTE £7.70: £2.50, £2.80, £2.50; EX 58.60 Trifecta £599.60.
Owner Equinegrowthpartners Syndicate **Bred** Horizon Bloodstock Limited **Trained** Friarstown, Co. Kildare

FOCUS
A decent prize for this fillies' handicap, but they went a modest gallop and it was crucial to be up there, with the first three always on or close to the pace. This has been rated around the 3rd.

6505 WILLIAM HILL DOONSIDE CUP STKS (LISTED RACE) 1m 2f

4:50 (4:51) (Class 1) 3-Y-O+

£36,861 (£13,975; £6,994; £3,484; £1,748; £877) **Stalls** Low

Form				RPR
/12-	**1**		**Secret Number**[313] 7759 6-9-0 109................................ DanielTudhope 3 (Saeed bin Suroor) *trckd ldrs: smooth hdwy to ld over 2f out: sn hrd pressed: rdn and styd on wl fnl f* **6/1**	112
1551	**2**	1 ¾	**Motdaw**[12] 6115 3-8-2 93.. KieranO'Neill 6 (Mick Channon) *in tch: effrt and pressed wnr wl over 1f out: kpt on ins fnl f: nt pce to chal* **20/1**	103
-201	**3**	5	**Abdon**[40] 5160 3-8-7 109... FrankieDettori 5 (Sir Michael Stoute) *s.i.s: hld up: rdn and effrt over 2f out: chsd clr ldng pair over 1f out: no imp fnl f* **9/4**[2]	99
-110	**4**	3 ½	**Maleficent Queen**[89] 3383 4-8-13 106............................... PhillipMakin 2 (Keith Dalgleish) *t.k.h: sn led: rdn and hdd over 2f out: wknd over 1f out* **9/2**[3]	90
4000	**5**	1 ½	**Imshivalla (IRE)**[12] 6115 5-8-9 88................................ PatrickMathers 10 (Richard Fahey) *chsd ldr to over 2f out: sn drvn and outpcd: btn over 1f out* **80/1**	83
-	**6**	4	**My Brother (IRE)**[43] 5046 3-8-7 85..............................1 ConnorBeasley 7 (Lee Smyth, Ire) *sn towards rr: rdn over 2f out: hung lft over 1f out: nvr on terms* **50/1**	80
1113	**7**	9	**Millefiori (IRE)**[50] 4780 4-8-9 78.......................................(p) LeighRoche 9 (Adrian Paul Keatley, Ire) *hld up: shortlived effrt over 2f out: sn btn* **40/1**	57
3232	**8**	15	**Henry The Explorer (CAN)**[13] 6073 3-8-7 70.............. JamesSullivan 8 (Jo Hughes) *early ldr: sn towards rr: struggling over 2f out: sn btn: t.o* **200/1**	32
-130	**P**		**Almodovar (IRE)**[29] 5558 4-9-0 113.................................. GeorgeBaker 4 (David Lanigan) *hld up in tch: effrt and pushed along over 2f out: wknd well over 1f out: eased, p.u and dismntd ent fnl f* **13/8**[1]

2m 9.39s (-2.61) **Going Correction** 0.0s/f (Good)
WFA 3 from 4yo+ 7lb **9** Ran SP% **112.2**
Speed ratings (Par 111): **110,108,104,101,100 97,90,78,**
CSF £101.67 TOTE £6.60: £1.90, £3.80, £1.10; EX 101.40 Trifecta £365.00.
Owner Godolphin **Bred** Darley **Trained** Newmarket, Suffolk

FOCUS
An interesting renewal of the Doonside Cup with some classy performers taking part, though a few of the others had plenty to find on these terms. Perhaps not the result many would have expected, though. The winner has been rated close to his best and the 2nd continues to progress.

6506 SM SIGNS H'CAP 5f

5:20 (5:24) (Class 5) (0-70,70) 3-Y-O+ **£4,528** (£1,347; £673; £336) **Stalls** Centre

Form				RPR
336	**1**		**Euxton**[42] 5069 4-8-7 **56** oh1...(p) KieranO'Neill 1 (Lawrence Mullaney) *wnt rt s: cl up centre: rdn and led that gp over 1f out: hrd pressed fnl f: hld on wl* **12/1**	67
3042	**2**	nse	**Malaysian Boleh**[20] 5838 6-8-7 **56** oh2......................... PatrickMathers 3 (Brian Ellison) *hld up centre: pushed along over 2f out: hdwy to press wnr over 1f out: ev ch ins fnl f: drvn and kpt on: jst hld* **11/2**[1]	67
0534	**3**	1 ½	**One Boy (IRE)**[19] 5864 5-9-6 **69**..................................... PaulMulrennan 7 (Paul Midgley) *hld up centre: rdn and hdwy over 1f out: kpt on ins fnl f: nt rch first two* **6/1**[2]	74+
1063	**4**	½	**Bunce (IRE)**[5] 6341 8-9-0 **63**.. JamesSullivan 2 (Linda Perratt) *fly-jmpd s: bhd centre: rdn and hdwy over 1f out: kpt on ins fnl f: nrst fin* **14/1**	67
2000	**5**	½	**Anieres Boy**[86] 3484 4-8-9 **58**.. CamHardie 8 (Michael Easterby) *prom centre: rdn over 2f out: kpt on same pce ins fnl f* **28/1**	60
0554	**6**	1 ¼	**Crombay (IRE)**[24] 5730 3-9-4 **68**.. DavidAllan 12 (Tim Easterby) *led main centre gp: rdn and hdd over 1f out: sn one pce* **18/1**	65
0164	**7**	½	**Addicted To Luck**[38] 5230 3-9-1 **65**.............................. RobertHavlin 6 (Jo Hughes) *prom centre: drvn along and edgd lft over 1f out: sn outpcd: n.d after* **25/1**	61
0605	**8**	hd	**Go Go Green (IRE)**[13] 6093 10-8-9 **58**........................ BarryMcHugh 4 (Jim Goldie) *dwlt: bhd centre: hdwy over 1f out: kpt on fnl f: nvr able to chal* **12/1**	53
2256	**9**	1	**Henley**[22] 5762 4-9-4 **67**.. ConnorBeasley 15 (Tracy Waggott) *pressed ldr stands' side: rdn over 2f out: wknd fnl f* **11/1**	58
3510	**10**	¾	**Show Palace**[58] 4495 3-9-2 **66**... DavidNolan 20 (Jennie Candlish) *t.k.h: led and overall ldr stands' rail to over 1f out: sn wknd* **17/2**	55
110	**11**	hd	**Spirit Of Zebedee (IRE)**[50] 4770 3-8-13 **63**...........(v¹) DougieCostello 9 (John Quinn) *prom centre: drvn along over 2f out: wknd over 1f out* **16/1**	51
6250	**12**	¾	**Rock Canyon (IRE)**[5] 6347 7-9-1 **64**................................. TomEaves 11 (Linda Perratt) *sn bhd on nr side of centre gp: rdn and hdwy over 1f out: nvr on terms* **28/1**	49

0-02 **13** *shd* **Catwilldo (IRE)**[22] 5788 6-8-12 **66**........................(b) AdamMcNamara(5) 5 51
(Garvan Donnelly, Ire) *cl up: rdn and ev ch over 1f out: wknd fnl f* **9/1**

5/1 **14** *2 3/4* **Lotara**[13] 6101 4-9-6 **69**.. WilliamCarson 16 44
(Jim Goldie) *dwlt: in tch stands' side: drvn along over 2f out: sn struggling* **25/1**

0135 **15** *2 1/2* **Star Cracker (IRE)**[31] 5479 4-9-0 **68**.................(p) CallumShepherd(5) 10 34
(Jim Goldie) *hld up midfield centre: drvn and outpcd over 2f out: sn btn* **8/1**[3]

2410 **16** *1 3/4* **Sarabi**[47] 4874 3-9-5 **69**..(p) GeorgeBaker 14 29
(Scott Dixon) *bhd on nr side of centre gp: struggling 1/2-way: nvr on terms* **16/1**

2050 **17** *2 3/4* **Crosse Fire**[25] 5678 4-9-7 **70**.....................................(p) DanielTudhope 18 20
(Scott Dixon) *prom stands' side: rdn along over 2f out: hung lft and wknd wl over 1f out* **20/1**

1630 **18** *3 3/4* **Searanger (USA)**[17] 5969 3-9-3 **67**................................ PJMcDonald 13 3
(Rebecca Menzies) *in tch centre: drvn and struggling 1/2-way: sn wknd* **40/1**

5004 **19** *20* **Bannock Town**[16] 6003 5-8-7 **56** oh11..............................(p) NeilFarley 19
(Linda Perratt) *dwlt: bhd stands' side: drvn and lost tch fr 1/2-way* **100/1**

1m 0.71s (1.31) **Going Correction** +0.35s/f (Good)
WFA 3 from 4yo+ 1lb **19** Ran SP% **131.5**
Speed ratings (Par 103): **103,102,100,99,98 96,96,95,94,93 92,91,91,86,82 80,75,69,37**
CSF £75.44 CT £458.18 TOTE £15.80: £3.80, £2.30, £2.00, £3.80; EX 138.00 Trifecta £1963.50.

Owner Mrs Tracy Nason **Bred** Highfield Farm Llp **Trained** Great Habton, N Yorks

FOCUS
A modest sprint handicap with the finish fought out between two horses out of the handicap, and another gamble landed. They raced centre-to-stands' side, but those who came nearside had no chance and the principals were all drawn low. The winner looks back to her early maiden levels.
T/Jkpt: Not won. T/Plt: £1,290.10 to a £1 stake. Pool: £85540.57, 48.4 winning units T/Qpdt: £110.30 to a £1 stake. Pool: £8051.81, 54.0 winning units **Richard Young**

6368 CHELMSFORD (A.W) (L-H)

Thursday, September 15

OFFICIAL GOING: Polytrack: standard
Wind: Light behind Weather: Fine

6507 TOTEPLACEPOT RACING'S FAVOURITE BET NURSERY H'CAP 5f (P)
5:50 (5:52) (Class 4) (0-85,83) 2-Y-O **£6,469** (£1,925; £962; £481) **Stalls** Low

Form RPR

441 **1** **Thammin**[49] 4790 2-9-2 **78**.. PaulHanagan 7 83+
(Owen Burrows) *s.i.s: hdwy over 1f out: shkn up to ld and edgd rt ins fnl f: r.o wl* **3/1**[2]

2025 **2** *1 1/4* **Prince Of Cool**[18] 5931 2-9-1 **80**........................... JosephineGordon(3) 2 80
(James Given) *led: rdn over 1f out: hdd and unable qck ins fnl f* **5/2**[1]

2120 **3** *3/4* **Lonely The Brave (IRE)**[29] 5560 2-9-6 **82**.............. RichardKingscote 5 79
(Mark Johnston) *chsd ldr: rdn over 1f out: edgd lft ins fnl f: styd on same pce* **4/1**[3]

355 **4** *1 1/4* **The Nazca Lines (IRE)**[41] 5113 2-9-4 **80**........................(v) LiamKeniry 3 72
(John Quinn) *chsd ldrs: rdn over 1f out: no ex ins fnl f* **10/1**

4545 **5** *3/4* **Lawless Louis**[30] 5510 2-9-3 **79**....................................... HarryBentley 8 69
(David O'Meara) *chsd ldrs: rdn over 1f out: styd on same pce fnl f* **8/1**

001 **6** *3/4* **Compton Poppy**[29] 5542 2-9-0 **79**........................... GeorgeDowning(3) 4 66
(Tony Carroll) *hld up: rdn: nt clr run and swtchd lft over 1f out: nt trble ldrs* **10/1**

010 **7** *4 1/2* **Dandy Flame (IRE)**[12] 6124 2-9-3 **79**.............................. RenatoSouza 1 50
(Jose Santos) *s.i.s: hld up: racd keenly: rdn over 1f out: sn wknd* **8/1**

59.9s (-0.30) **Going Correction** -0.075s/f (Stan) **7** Ran SP% **114.0**
Speed ratings (Par 97): **99,97,95,93,92 91,84**
CSF £10.88 CT £28.96 TOTE £3.60: £1.50, £2.50; EX 12.20 Trifecta £30.00.
Owner Hamdan Al Maktoum **Bred** Stratford Place Stud & Willow Bloodstock **Trained** Lambourn, Berks

FOCUS
An ordinary nursery which featured a nice performance from the winner.

6508 TOTEEXACTA FORECAST THE 1ST AND 2ND H'CAP 1m 6f (P)
6:20 (6:20) (Class 6) (0-65,63) 3-Y-O+ **£3,234** (£962; £481; £120; £120) **Stalls** Low

Form RPR

0642 **1** **Always Summer**[25] 5680 3-8-12 **61**.............................. GeorgeWood(5) 2 70+
(James Fanshawe) *chsd ldrs: n.m.r over 1f out: rdn to ld ins fnl f: r.o wl* **11/4**[2]

3361 **2** *2 3/4* **Free Bounty**[7] 6245 3-9-5 **63** 6ex.............................(t) SilvestreDeSousa 6 68
(Philip McBride) *sn led: hdd 12f out: chsd ldr tl rdn to ld and edgd lft over 1f out: sn wnt rt: hdd ins fnl f: styd on same pce* **6/4**[1]

0006 **3** *2 1/4* **Triassic (IRE)**[18] 5921 3-8-9 **53**... NickyMackay 8 56
(Mark Johnston) *led 12f out: rdn over 2f out: hdd over 1f out: no ex ins fnl f* **12/1**

4402 **4** *nse* **Whitstable Pearl (IRE)**[22] 5777 3-8-10 **54**.......................... KierenFox 4 56
(John Best) *s.s: hld up: hdwy u.p and swtchd rt over 1f out: styd on: nt rch ldrs* **4/1**[3]

5054 **4** *dht* **Permera**[10] 6185 3-8-9 **53**...[1] HarryBentley 7 55
(Mark H Tompkins) *chsd ldrs: rdn and edgd lft over 1f out: styd on same pce fnl f* **16/1**

1534 **6** *2 3/4* **Ring Eye (IRE)**[17] 5958 8-9-12 **59**.............................. FergusSweeney 1 58
(John O'Shea) *hld up: hdwy over 8f out: rdn over 1f out: wknd fnl f* **14/1**

0140 **7** *6* **Merry Dancer (IRE)**[47] 4880 4-9-8 **60**.......................... MitchGodwin(5) 3 51
(Patrick Chamings) *prom: lost pl over 8f out: rdn over 2f out: wknd over 1f out* **14/1**

200- **8** *19* **Kastela Stari**[278] 8197 9-9-1 **48**... JoeDoyle 5 14
(Tim Fitzgerald) *prom: nt clr run and lost pl after 2f: rdn over 3f out: wknd over 2f out* **40/1**

3m 5.35s (2.15) **Going Correction** -0.075s/f (Stan)
WFA 3 from 4yo+ 11lb **8** Ran SP% **116.0**
Speed ratings (Par 101): **90,88,87,87,87 85,82,71**
CSF £7.38 CT £39.92 TOTE £4.30: £1.20, £1.10, £3.40; EX 8.50 Trifecta £46.30.
Owner Dr Catherine Wills **Bred** St Clare Hall Stud **Trained** Newmarket, Suffolk

FOCUS
This modest staying handicap was steadily run and nothing got involved from the back. The time was over 14sec slower than standard.

6509 TOTETRIFECTA PICK THE 1,2,3 H'CAP 6f (P)
6:50 (6:50) (Class 6) (0-65,64) 3-Y-O+ **£3,234** (£962; £481; £240) **Stalls** Centre

Form RPR

6450 **1** **Last Star Falling (IRE)**[17] 5973 3-8-9 **58**.................(b[1]) LuluStanford(7) 1 68
(Henry Spiller) *chsd ldr tl over 4f out: remained handy: rdn to ld over 1f out: r.o* **33/1**

2050 **2** *1 1/2* **Waneen (IRE)**[17] 5954 3-9-6 **62**.............................. SilvestreDeSousa 10 67
(Joseph Tuite) *a.p: chsd ldr over 4f out: rdn and ev ch over 1f out: styd on same pce ins fnl f* **5/1**[2]

6242 **3** *2 1/4* **Poplar**[7] 6249 3-9-4 **60**.. MartinHarley 5 58
(Robyn Brisland) *led: rdn and hdd over 1f out: no ex ins fnl f* **9/4**[1]

153 **4** *3/4* **Swiss Cross**[14] 6051 9-9-7 **64**..............................(t) JosephineGordon(3) 6 60
(Phil McEntee) *mid-div: hdwy 2f out: sn rdn: styd on same pce fnl f* **5/1**[2]

0226 **5** *1* **Encapsulated**[14] 6051 6-9-1 **62**.................................... RhiainIngram(7) 9 55
(Roger Ingram) *dwlt: sn pushed along in rr: hdwy over 3f out: rdn over 1f out: no ex fnl f* **10/1**

50-4 **6** *hd* **Life Of Fame**[20] 5839 3-9-3 **59**... JimCrowley 12 51
(David O'Meara) *hld up in tch: plld hrd: lost pl over 3f out: rdn over 1f out: no imp fnl f* **11/1**

6414 **7** *3/4* **Manipura**[14] 6051 3-9-0 **59**...(p) NoelGarbutt(3) 7 49
(Derek Shaw) *hld up: rdn over 1f out: n.d* **6/1**[3]

0200 **8** *1/2* **Sir Geoffrey (IRE)**[21] 5807 10-9-6 **60**................................(p) DaleSwift 4 49
(Scott Dixon) *chsd ldrs: rdn over 2f out: wknd over 1f out* **33/1**

4201 **9** *1/2* **Whipphound**[21] 5807 8-9-0 **54**.......................................(p) PaulHanagan 3 41
(Ruth Carr) *hld up: nt clr run over 1f out: nvr on terms* **10/1**

0500 **10** *2 3/4* **Teversham**[83] 3603 3-9-7 **63**.................................. RichardKingscote 2 42
(Martin Smith) *s.i.s: hld up: nvr on terms* **11/1**

1m 12.95s (-0.75) **Going Correction** -0.075s/f (Stan)
WFA 3 from 4yo+ 2lb **10** Ran SP% **119.1**
Speed ratings (Par 101): **102,100,97,96,94 94,93,92,92,88**
CSF £195.12 CT £552.19 TOTE £30.80: £7.00, £2.30, £1.70; EX 355.20 Trifecta £3525.70.
Owner Dethrone Racing **Bred** Drumlin Bloodstock **Trained** Newmarket, Suffolk

FOCUS
The first three were always towards the fore in this moderate sprint handicap, and the hold-up horses never got into it.

6510 TOTEPOOLLIVEINFO.COM H'CAP 7f (P)
7:20 (7:20) (Class 5) (0-70,75) 3-Y-O+ **£5,175** (£1,540; £769; £384) **Stalls** Low

Form RPR

6545 **1** **Johnny B Goode (IRE)**[26] 5635 4-9-0 **63**............. SilvestreDeSousa 12 71
(Chris Dwyer) *w ldr: led over 2f out: rdn over 1f out: styd on* **8/1**[3]

4511 **2** *nk* **Brick Lane**[3] 6426 3-9-5 **75** 6ex.............................. JosephineGordon(3) 7 80
(Robyn Brisland) *sn pushed along to chse ldrs: rdn to go 2nd over 1f out: r.o* **1/1**[1]

0144 **3** *1* **Anastazia**[18] 5935 4-9-7 **70**... LukeMorris 10 74
(Paul D'Arcy) *sn pushed along in rr: hdwy over 2f out: rdn over 1f out: r.o* **8/1**[3]

1454 **4** *5* **Seek The Fair Land**[132] 2006 10-9-0 **66**..................(v) LouisSteward(3) 5 57
(Lee Carter) *hld up: hdwy over 2f out: rdn over 1f out: styd on same pce* **14/1**

5 *3* **New Record (IRE)**[114] 4-9-5 **68**.. RyanTate 6 50
(James Eustace) *mid-div: sn pushed along: rdn over 3f out: sn outpcd: styd on towards fin* **12/1**

4556 **6** *1 3/4* **Major Valentine**[13] 6091 4-8-13 **67**.............................. CiaranMckee(5) 4 45
(John O'Shea) *prom: rdn over 2f out: wknd fnl f* **16/1**

4400 **7** *2* **Daring Knight**[46] 1860 3-9-1 **68**.................................. RichardKingscote 1 38
(Martin Smith) *s.i.s: in rr: rdn over 2f out: n.d* **16/1**

0000 **8** *3/4* **Shamlan (IRE)**[12] 6138 4-9-4 **67**.....................................(tp) ShaneKelly 11 37
(Johnny Farrelly) *s.s: sn pushed along and a in rr* **20/1**

1311 **9** *3 1/2* **Not Your Call (IRE)**[31] 5475 5-9-7 **70**................................. KierenFox 3 31
(Lee Carter) *led: rdn and hdd over 2f out: wknd and eased over 1f out* **4/1**[2]

1m 25.66s (-1.54) **Going Correction** -0.075s/f (Stan)
WFA 3 from 4yo+ 4lb **9** Ran SP% **123.1**
Speed ratings (Par 103): **105,104,103,97,94 92,90,89,85**
CSF £17.55 CT £74.21 TOTE £7.50: £2.40, £1.10, £2.10; EX 22.70 Trifecta £93.80.
Owner Mrs C M Goode **Bred** Noel Brosnan **Trained** Newmarket, Suffolk

FOCUS
Another race where it proved an advantage to race prominently. The winner is rated to his Yarmouth success off the same mark, with the 2nd matching her Wolverhampton latest under a penalty and the 3rd to her recent turf form.

6511 TOTEPOOLRACING FIND US ON INSTAGRAM MAIDEN STKS 1m (P)
7:50 (7:50) (Class 5) 3-Y-O+ **£5,175** (£1,540; £769; £384) **Stalls** Low

Form RPR

4-43 **1** **Curriculum**[29] 5544 3-9-5 75.. JimCrowley 5 82+
(William Haggas) *sn chsng ldr: led 2f out: rdn clr fnl f* **5/2**[2]

2 *3 3/4* **Wealth Tax** 3-9-5 0... MartinHarley 3 73
(Ed Dunlop) *prom: chsd wnr over 1f out: styd on same pce fnl f* **25/1**

52- **3** *2* **Cat Silver**[330] 7386 3-9-5 0... TedDurcan 10 69
(Sir Michael Stoute) *hld up: hdwy over 3f out: no ex fnl f* **6/4**[1]

4 *1 1/4* **Phileas Fogg (IRE)** 3-9-2 0................................. JosephineGordon(3) 9 66
(Martyn Meade) *s.i.s: hdwy and edgd rt over 1f out: styd on: nt trble ldrs* **12/1**

4 **5** *1 1/2* **Paper Faces (USA)**[62] 4361 3-9-0 0...................................... AndreaAtzeni 8 57
(Roger Varian) *chsd ldrs: rdn over 3f out: edgd lft and wknd fnl f* **11/4**[3]

4 **6** *1 1/4* **Whispered Kiss**[23] 5735 3-9-0 0.................................. RoystonFfrench 6 55
(Mike Murphy) *hld up in tch: rdn over 2f out: wkng whn hmpd over 1f out* **33/1**

65 **7** *7* **Bemusement**[24] 5731 3-9-0 0.. RichardKingscote 7 38
(Mark Johnston) *led 6f: wknd over 1f out* **14/1**

4 **8** *14* **Zorlu (IRE)**[145] 1646 3-9-5 0... FergusSweeney 2 11
(John O'Shea) *s.i.s: a in rr: wknd over 2f out* **33/1**

000 **9** *11* **Briac (FR)**[29] 5544 5-9-10 0... TimmyMurphy 4
(Jim Best) *s.i.s: a in rr: wknd over 2f out* **100/1**

1m 39.19s (-0.71) **Going Correction** -0.075s/f (Stan)
WFA 3 from 5yo 5lb **9** Ran SP% **120.3**
Speed ratings (Par 103): **100,96,94,93,91 90,83,69,58**
CSF £66.63 TOTE £3.20: £1.10, £5.00, £1.30; EX 68.20 Trifecta £276.90.
Owner Lael Stable **Bred** Lael Stables **Trained** Newmarket, Suffolk

FOCUS
They went an ordinary gallop in what was no more than a fair maiden. The winner has been rated to a better view of his penultimate Kempton run.

6512 @TOTEPOOLRACING WIN TICKETS ON TWITTER H'CAP 1m (P)
8:20 (8:20) (Class 6) (0-60,60) 3-Y-O+ **£3,234** (£962; £481; £240) **Stalls** Low

Form RPR
1405 **1** **Theydon Thunder**[23] 5734 4-9-3 **58**............................ GeorgeWood(5) 2 66
(Peter Charalambous) *chsd ldrs: led 1f out: rdn out* **8/1**
0042 **2** 1 1/2 **Hidden Gem**[4] 6373 3-9-4 **59**............................ JimCrowley 12 62
(Ed Walker) *chsd ldrs: carried rt 2f out: rdn over 1f out: styd on same pce wl ins fnl f* **7/2**[1]
0603 **3** 1 **Dukes Meadow**[14] 6046 5-9-1 **58**............................ RhiainIngram(7) 8 60
(Roger Ingram) *mid-div: hdwy over 1f out: r.o: nt rch ldrs* **9/1**
6003 **4** 1 1/4 **Forest Lakes (IRE)**[42] 5087 3-9-5 **60**....................(p) SilvestreDeSousa 9 59
(George Scott) *prom: rdn and hung lft fr over 1f out: styd on same pce ins fnl f* **8/1**
2302 **5** 3/4 **Rosie Crowe (IRE)**[14] 6047 4-8-9 **48**.................... JosephineGordon(3) 1 45
(Shaun Harris) *chsd ldrs: rdn to ld over 1f out: sn hdd: no ex ins fnl f* **4/1**[2]
0500 **6** 2 1/2 **Scot Daddy (USA)**[37] 5264 4-9-1 **51**............................ LiamKeniry 7 42
(Denis Quinn) *hld up: hdwy over 1f out: wknd fnl f* **25/1**
2030 **7** nk **The Knave (IRE)**[33] 5386 3-9-3 **58**............................ DaleSwift 6 47
(Scott Dixon) *hld up: rdn over 1f out: nt trble ldrs* **14/1**
033 **8** 1 1/4 **Schottische**[26] 5635 6-8-12 **53**....................(p) DavidParkes(5) 3 40
(Alan Bailey) *hld up: rdn over 2f out: n.d* **16/1**
0003 **9** nse **Lisala (FR)**[14] 6047 3-8-13 **57**....................(e) MarcMonaghan(3) 13 43
(George Peckham) *led: rdn and hdd over 1f out: wknd ins fnl f* **16/1**
-000 **10** 4 **Baker**[31] 5471 4-9-10 **60**....................(bt) MartinHarley 10 38
(Robyn Brisland) *hdwy over 6f out: chsd ldr over 4f out: ev ch over 2f out: sn rdn and hung rt: wknd over 1f out* **7/1**[3]
-503 **11** 1 1/4 **Cheeco**[13] 6105 4-8-10 **46** oh1............................ LukeMorris 11 21
(Ruth Carr) *s.i.s: rdn over 2f out: nvr on terms* **20/1**
3400 **12** 1 1/2 **Mowhoob**[59] 4454 6-9-1 **51**............................ FergusSweeney 5 22
(Brian Barr) *s.i.s: nvr on terms* **12/1**
0/00 **13** 2 **Magical Peak**[137] 1892 4-8-3 **46** oh1............................ LuluStanford(7) 4 12
(John O'Shea) *hld up: n.d* **50/1**
0-04 **14** 9 **Icy Blue**[12] 6140 8-8-10 **49**....................(e) NoelGarbutt(3) 14
(Adam West) *s.i.s: hdwy 5f out: rdn over 3f out: wknd 2f out* **25/1**

1m 39.8s (-0.10) **Going Correction** -0.075s/f (Stan)
WFA 3 from 4yo+ 5lb **14** Ran SP% **127.5**
Speed ratings (Par 101): **97,95,94,93,92 90,89,88,88,84 83,81,79,70**
CSF £36.75 CT £279.05 TOTE £9.80: £3.50, £1.80, £3.30; EX 48.80 Trifecta £307.60.
Owner pcracing.co.uk **Bred** Mill Farm Stud **Trained** Newmarket, Suffolk

FOCUS
Low-grade handicap form.

6513 CHELMSFORD CITY RACECOURSE'S 100TH RACE DAY H'CAP (DIV I) 1m 2f (P)
8:50 (8:50) (Class 6) (0-60,60) 3-Y-O+ **£3,234** (£962; £481; £240) **Stalls** Low

Form RPR
542 **1** **Blushes (FR)**[38] 5241 3-9-5 **60**....................(b) JimCrowley 9 66
(Ed Dunlop) *hld up: hdwy and hmpd over 1f out: rdn to ld wl ins fnl f: r.o* **6/1**[3]
5054 **2** nk **Just Fred (IRE)**[27] 5604 3-8-3 **47**....................(p) JosephineGordon(3) 4 52
(Denis Coakley) *hmpd s: hld up: hdwy over 1f out: sn rdn: r.o* **6/1**[3]
4104 **3** 1 3/4 **Spinning Rose**[26] 5635 4-9-11 **59**............................ RobertWinston 7 61
(Dean Ivory) *led: shkn up to go clr and edgd rt over 1f out: rdn and hdd wl ins fnl f* **7/1**
006 **4** 1 1/4 **Shift On Sheila**[30] 5527 3-9-2 **60**............................ RobHornby(3) 3 60
(Pam Sly) *hld up: reminder 4f out: hdwy over 1f out: styd on same pce wl ins fnl f* **7/1**
5604 **5** 1/2 **Gilt Edged (IRE)**[20] 5844 3-8-11 **52**............................ JoeDoyle 1 52
(Julie Camacho) *hld up in tch: rdn and hmpd over 1f out: edgd lft and styd on ins fnl f* **16/1**
0465 **6** 2 1/4 **Amazing Charm**[23] 5749 4-9-12 **60**............................ LukeMorris 2 55
(James Tate) *chsd ldr over 3f: remained handy: rdn over 2f out: wknd fnl f* **3/1**[1]
0005 **7** nk **Master Of Heaven**[14] 6046 3-9-2 **57**............................[1] FergusSweeney 5 51
(Jim Boyle) *hld up: rdn over 1f out: nt trble ldrs* **9/2**[2]
-600 **8** 1 1/4 **Nutzma**[44] 4987 3-8-5 **46** oh1............................ RoystonFfrench 8 38
(Mike Murphy) *hld up: rdn over 3f out: wd over 2f out: nvr trbld ldrs* **16/1**
004 **9** 25 **Occasional Dream (IRE)**[44] 4991 3-9-5 **60**............................ TedDurcan 11 4
(Joseph Tuite) *sn prom: hung rt over 4f out: wkng whn nt clr run wl over 1f out: eased* **20/1**
060 **10** 45 **Rial (IRE)**[14] 6051 3-9-4 **59**............................ DannyBrock 6
(Phil McEntee) *prom: rdn over 3f out: wknd wl over 2f out: eased* **33/1**
1064 **P** **Ventura Falcon (IRE)**[37] 5254 3-9-1 **56**.................. SilvestreDeSousa 10
(Richard Hannon) *prom: chsd ldr over 6f out tl lost action and eased over 1f out: p.u ins fnl f* **9/1**

2m 7.35s (-1.25) **Going Correction** -0.075s/f (Stan)
WFA 3 from 4yo 7lb **11** Ran SP% **126.2**
Speed ratings (Par 101): **102,101,100,99,98 97,96,95,75,39**
CSF £45.27 CT £268.64 TOTE £6.00: £2.10, £2.10, £2.40; EX 60.80 Trifecta £335.20.
Owner The Sagacious Lot **Bred** E A R L Ecurie Villebadin **Trained** Newmarket, Suffolk

FOCUS
The first two came from the rear in this very modest handicap.

6514 CHELMSFORD CITY RACECOURSE'S 100TH RACE DAY H'CAP (DIV II) 1m 2f (P)
9:20 (9:21) (Class 6) (0-60,60) 3-Y-O+ **£3,234** (£962; £481; £240) **Stalls** Low

Form RPR
0-4 **1** **Estrella Eria (FR)**[17] 5979 3-8-5 **46** oh1............................ LukeMorris 2 59
(George Peckham) *hld up: hdwy over 1f out: rdn to ld ins fnl f: drvn out* **25/1**
6211 **2** 3 1/4 **First Summer**[7] 6243 4-9-7 **60**............................ GeorgeWood(5) 4 67
(Shaun Harris) *hld up in tch: rdn over 2f out: led and hung rt over 1f out: hdd ins fnl f: styd on same pce* **5/4**[1]
602 **3** 3/4 **Gold Return (IRE)**[41] 5132 3-9-5 **60**............................ ShaneKelly 5 65
(David Lanigan) *hld up: hdwy over 1f out: sn rdn: r.o* **7/2**[2]
0045 **4** 2 **Broughtons Mystery**[14] 6047 3-8-6 **50**.................. JosephineGordon(3) 8 52
(Willie Musson) *chsd ldrs: rdn over 2f out: styd on same pce fnl f* **12/1**
50-0 **5** 2 1/2 **General Brook (IRE)**[69] 4088 6-9-10 **58**............................ FergusSweeney 6 55
(John O'Shea) *chsd ldrs: led 8f out: rdn and hdd over 1f out: wknd ins fnl f* **8/1**
0420 **6** 1 1/2 **Zamindo**[13] 6095 3-9-2 **57**............................ RichardKingscote 7 51
(Mark Johnston) *sn led: hdd after 1f: chsd ldrs: rdn over 2f out: wknd fnl f* **12/1**
0000 **7** 2 3/4 **Baileys Perle (IRE)**[21] 5808 3-9-4 **59**............................[1] MartinHarley 10 48
(Chris Dwyer) *led after 1f: hdd 8f out: chsd ldr: rdn over 3f out: wknd fnl f* **33/1**
0-00 **8** nk **Quina Brook (IRE)**[41] 5130 3-9-5 **60**............................ JimCrowley 1 48
(Daniel Mark Loughnane) *hld up: rdn over 2f out: wknd over 1f out* **10/1**
2000 **9** nk **Clock On Tom**[89] 3401 6-9-2 **50**............................ SilvestreDeSousa 3 38
(Denis Quinn) *hld up: rdn over 2f out: wknd over 1f out* **6/1**[3]
4030 **10** 4 1/2 **Burning Love (IRE)**[10] 6187 3-8-12 **53**....................(v[1]) HarryPoulton 9 32
(Adam West) *s.s: hld up: rdn over 2f out: sn wknd* **50/1**

2m 7.64s (-0.96) **Going Correction** -0.075s/f (Stan)
WFA 3 from 4yo+ 7lb **10** Ran SP% **125.3**
Speed ratings (Par 101): **100,97,96,95,93 92,89,89,89,85**
CSF £60.38 CT £156.75 TOTE £18.90: £4.70, £1.30, £1.90; EX 52.00 Trifecta £261.60.
Owner Fawzi Abdulla Nass **Bred** D Chassagneux & E A R L Ecurie Loire **Trained** Newmarket, Suffolk

FOCUS
Very modest form, and the slower division by 0.29sec.
T/Plt: £8.60 to a £1 stake. Pool: £82,752.76 - 6975.65 winning units. T/Qpdt: £4.40 to a £1 stake. Pool: £8,959.45 - 1505.28 winning units. **Colin Roberts**

5433 PONTEFRACT (L-H)
Thursday, September 15

OFFICIAL GOING: Good to firm (good in places; 8.5)
Wind: Virtually nil Weather: Fine & dry

6515 BOOK YOUR 17TH OCTOBER TOTEPOOL PACKAGE MEDIAN AUCTION MAIDEN STKS 5f
2:20 (2:20) (Class 5) 2-Y-O **£3,234** (£962; £481; £240) **Stalls** Low

Form RPR
1 **Brian The Snail (IRE)** 2-9-5 0............................ TonyHamilton 8 85+
(Richard Fahey) *trckd ldrs: hdwy to chse ldng pair over 1f out: chal ins fnl f and sn rdn: kpt on wl to ld last 50 yds* **2/1**[1]
5230 **2** 1 **Father McKenzie**[11] 6159 2-9-5 75............................ GrahamLee 10 78
(Mick Channon) *prom: trckd ldr over 3f out: led wl over 1f out: jnd and rdn ent fnl f: sn drvn: hdd and no ex last 50 yds* **6/1**[3]
20 **3** 2 1/2 **Dundunah (USA)**[68] 4161 2-9-0 0............................ SamJames 3 64
(David O'Meara) *led: rdn along 2f out: sn hdd : drvn over 1f out: kpt on same pce* **11/4**[2]
5240 **4** 3 3/4 **Sheepscar Lad (IRE)**[16] 6010 2-8-12 71...........(v) LewisEdmunds(7) 11 56
(Nigel Tinkler) *.dwlt and t.k.h on outer: hdwy wl over 1f out: rdn and styd on fnl f* **12/1**
5 1/2 **Peace Dreamer (IRE)** 2-8-11 0............................[1] EoinWalsh(3) 2 49
(Robert Cowell) *in tch: hdwy to chse ldrs 2f out: rdn over 1f out: sn no imp* **12/1**
6 4 1/2 **Atlanta Belle (IRE)** 2-9-0 0............................ TomMarquand 7 33
(Chris Wall) *towards rr: pushed along over 2f out: sme hdwy wl over 1f out: sn rdn and no imp* **40/1**
4 **7** 1 **Jack Blane**[28] 5569 2-9-5 0............................ DaneO'Neill 6 34
(Daniel Kubler) *chsd ldrs: rdn along 2f out: sn wknd* **13/2**
00 **8** 2 **Ronnie The Rooster**[24] 5713 2-9-5 0............................ GrahamGibbons 9 27
(David Barron) *dwlt: a rr* **33/1**
5 **9** 2 1/4 **Violet Mist (IRE)**[64] 4254 2-9-0 0............................ KevinStott 5 14
(Ben Haslam) *cl up: rdn along over 2f out: wknd wl over 1f out* **66/1**
10 11 **Chillililli** 2-9-0 0............................ JoeFanning 4
(Bryan Smart) *dwlt: a outpcd in rr* **20/1**
0 **11** 4 1/2 **Sheng Chi Dragon (IRE)**[14] 6053 2-9-5 0...................(v[1]) JoeyHaynes 1
(K R Burke) *dwlt: a towards rr* **50/1**

1m 2.51s (-0.79) **Going Correction** -0.15s/f (Firm) **11** Ran SP% **116.6**
Speed ratings (Par 95): **100,98,94,88,87 80,78,75,72,54 47**
CSF £13.64 TOTE £3.10: £2.00, £2.60, £1.70; EX 11.30 Trifecta £29.10.
Owner R A Fahey **Bred** A Kirwan **Trained** Musley Bank, N Yorks

FOCUS
It was dry overnight, but watering had taken place on Monday and Wednesday (around 5mm on both days). The going was given as good to firm, good in places (GoingStick: 8.5). A fair maiden. The 2nd has to set the opening level but this might prove worth more.

6516 MATTY BOWN H'CAP (DIV I) 1m 4y
2:55 (2:55) (Class 4) (0-80,80) 3-Y-O+ **£5,175** (£1,540; £769; £384) **Stalls** Low

Form RPR
1400 **1** **Lawyer (IRE)**[9] 6217 5-9-8 **78**............................ SamJames 1 85
(David Barron) *.trckd ldrs on inner: hdwy to chse ldr 2f out: rdn over 1f out: drvn ins fnl f: styd on wl to ld last 75 yds* **7/2**[2]
0014 **2** 3/4 **Normandy Knight**[19] 5866 4-9-4 **74**............................ TonyHamilton 9 79
(Richard Fahey) *hld up towards rr: gd hdwy 3f out: chsd ldng pair over 1f out and sn rdn: drvn and ev ch wl ins fnl f: kpt on* **10/1**
1520 **3** nse **Freight Train (IRE)**[43] 5017 4-9-7 **77**....................(p) JoeFanning 2 82
(Mark Johnston) *sn led: pushed clr 2f out: rdn over 1f out: drvn and wknd ins fnl f: hdd and no ex last 75 yds* **11/4**[1]
040 **4** 7 **Zainat (IRE)**[111] 2654 3-8-13 **74**............................ JoeyHaynes 3 62
(K R Burke) *dwlt and towards rr: hdwy over 2f out: rdn along wl over 1f out: no imp* **9/2**[3]
03 **5** 2 1/4 **Stanley (GER)**[18] 5925 5-9-3 **73**............................ GrahamLee 7 57
(Jonjo O'Neill) *t.k.h and prom: grad lost pl and rr 1/2-way: swtchd to inner and hdwy wl over 2f out: rdn over 1f out: n.d* **8/1**
2160 **6** 6 **Eurystheus (IRE)**[19] 5886 7-9-10 **80**....................(tp) AndrewMullen 8 50
(Michael Appleby) *hld up: a towards rr* **14/1**
-525 **7** 16 **L'Inganno Felice (FR)**[202] 734 6-9-2 **72**............................ DaneO'Neill 6 5
(Iain Jardine) *chsd ldrs on outer: rdn along over 2f out: sn wknd* **5/1**
0036 **8** 8 **Homeland (IRE)**[51] 4727 4-9-3 **73**....................(t) KevinStott 5
(Brian Rothwell) *chsd ldr: rdn along 3f out: sn wknd* **25/1**

1m 44.15s (-1.75) **Going Correction** -0.15s/f (Firm)
WFA 3 from 4yo+ 5lb **8** Ran SP% **114.5**
Speed ratings (Par 105): **102,101,101,94,91 85,69,61**
CSF £37.83 CT £109.40 TOTE £4.40: £1.30, £2.80, £1.30; EX 36.50 Trifecta £114.90.
Owner John Knotts **Bred** Drumlin Bloodstock **Trained** Maunby, N Yorks

The Form Book, Raceform Ltd, Newbury, RG14 5SJ

FOCUS
A 1-2-3 for the rail runners, but not in the order in which they raced. The front-running 3rd is rated to form, with the 2nd to recent and the winner up slightly to better view of this year's form.

6517 BOOK YOUR CHRISTMAS PARTY HERE ON 0113 2876387 H'CAP 1m 2f 6y
3:25 (3:26) (Class 4) (0-85,85) 3-Y-O+ **£5,175** (£1,540; £769; £384) **Stalls** Low

Form RPR
0145 **1** **Mysterial**[32] 5434 6-8-10 **76**.. GerO'Neill(7) 12 84
(Declan Carroll) *chsd ldr tl led after 2f: rdn along over 2f out: drvn ins fnl f: hld on gamely* **14/1**
0015 **2** *nk* **Play Nicely**[12] 6134 4-9-3 **76**.. GrahamGibbons 7 83
(David Barron) *hld up in tch: hdwy 3f out: rdn to chse wnr ent fnl f: sn drvn to chal and ev ch tl no ex towards fin* **14/1**
3020 **3** *1 1/2* **Hanseatic**[14] 6055 7-8-13 **77**..[1] NathanEvans(5) 11 81
(Michael Easterby) *hld up towards rr: hdwy 3f out: chsd ldrs on inner and swtchd rt over 1f out: drvn and kpt on fnl f* **12/1**
614 **4** *1 1/4* **Toga Tiger (IRE)**[36] 5287 9-9-4 **77**....................................... MartinLane 2 79
(Kevin Frost) *hld up in rr: hdwy wl over 2f out: rdn over 1f out: kpt on fnl f* **10/1**
046 **5** *3/4* **Polar Forest**[75] 3905 6-9-5 **78**..(e) JoeFanning 3 78
(Richard Guest) *trckd ldrs: hdwy 4f out: rdn to chse ldng pair 2f out: drvn over 1f out and kpt on same pce* **20/1**
0013 **6** *1 3/4* **El Beau (IRE)**[11] 6160 5-9-5 **78**.. JackGarritty 9 75
(John Quinn) *midfield: effrt 3f out: sn rdn along and n.d* **6/1**[2]
0000 **7** *1/2* **Off Art**[17] 5976 6-9-9 **85**...(p) RachelRichardson(3) 10 81
(Tim Easterby) *hld up: a towards rr* **8/1**[3]
0103 **8** *4 1/2* **Plane Song (IRE)**[32] 5434 4-9-6 **79**................................ TomMarquand 5 66
(Alan Swinbank) *trckd ldrs: pushed along 3f out: rdn 2f out: sn btn* **16/1**
4400 **9** *nk* **Optima Petamus**[28] 5579 4-9-1 **74**.................................... GrahamLee 1 60
(Patrick Holmes) *led 2f: chsd ldr: rdn along over 2f out: drvn wl over 1f out: grad wknd* **10/1**
1350 **10** *17* **Tapis Libre**[12] 6134 8-9-4 **82**.. AnnaHesketh(5) 8 34
(Jacqueline Coward) *a rr* **50/1**
3421 **11** *4 1/2* **Mubajal**[26] 5634 3-9-5 **85**.. DaneO'Neill 4 28
(Owen Burrows) *t.k.h early: trckd ldrs: pushed along over 3f out: rdn wl over 2f out: sn btn* **13/8**[1]
063 **12** *9* **Berlusca (IRE)**[38] 5246 7-9-6 **84**................................ GeorgeBuckell(5) 6 9
(Lawrence Mullaney) *hld up towards rr: t.k.h and hdwy on outer to chse ldrs 6f out: rdn along over 3f out: sn wknd* **25/1**

2m 10.59s (-3.11) **Going Correction** -0.15s/f (Firm)
WFA 3 from 4yo+ 7lb **12** Ran SP% **119.2**
Speed ratings (Par 105): **106,105,104,103,102 101,101,97,97,83 80,72**
CSF £192.25 CT £2423.18 TOTE £16.80: £4.40, £4.20, £4.10; EX 161.80 Trifecta £1453.80.
Owner Mrs Sarah Bryan **Bred** Ladyswood, Canning Down & D Farrington **Trained** Malton, N Yorks

FOCUS
This was run at a decent gallop, but the leader still hung on, posting a length pb.

6518 EBF BREEDERS' SERIES FILLIES' H'CAP 6f
4:00 (4:00) (Class 2) (0-100,95) 3-Y-O+
£18,675 (£5,592; £2,796; £1,398; £699; £351) **Stalls** Low

Form RPR
6112 **1** **Kassia (IRE)**[49] 4803 3-9-6 **94**.. GrahamLee 1 104+
(Mick Channon) *trckd ldrs: swtchd lft to inner and hdwy ent fnl f: sn led: rdn out* **3/1**[1]
4410 **2** *3/4* **Stellarta**[14] 6064 5-9-5 **91**.. TomMarquand 2 98
(Michael Blanshard) *hld up towards rr: hdwy on inner 2f out: nt clr run and swtchd rt over 1f out: sn rdn and styd on wl fnl f* **7/1**
0401 **3** *3/4* **Love Island**[16] 6013 7-8-10 **82**.. GeorgeChaloner 10 87
(Richard Whitaker) *hld up towards rr: hdwy on wd outside wl over 1f out: rdn and styd on wl fnl f* **25/1**
6124 **4** *1 3/4* **Dutch Mist**[20] 5836 3-8-12 **86**...(b) DaneO'Neill 3 85
(Kevin Ryan) *hld up and bhd: hdwy wl over 1f out: sn rdn and styd on fnl f* **11/2**[3]
0203 **5** *1/2* **Iseemist (IRE)**[14] 6064 5-9-4 **95**................................ GeorgeBuckell(5) 4 94
(John Gallagher) *slt ld: hdd over 3f out: cl up: rdn along 2f out: sn drvn and grad wknd* **7/1**
2112 **6** *nk* **Midnight Malibu (IRE)**[12] 6133 3-8-8 **85**............ RachelRichardson(3) 8 81
(Tim Easterby) *cl up: led over 3f out: rdn along wl over 1f out: hdd jst ins fnl f: sn wknd* **12/1**
3512 **7** *hd* **Futoon (IRE)**[33] 5409 3-8-10 **84**.. KevinStott 5 80
(Kevin Ryan) *cl up: effrt 2f out: sn rdn and ev ch tl drvn ent fnl f and sn wknd* **8/1**
0542 **8** *4 1/2* **Show Stealer**[14] 6064 3-9-7 **95**... MartinLane 6 76
(Rae Guest) *in tch: rdn along over 2f out: sn drvn and wknd over 1f out* **5/1**[2]
-314 **9** *4* **Southern Belle (IRE)**[9] 6207 3-9-2 **90**....................... GrahamGibbons 9 59
(Robert Cowell) *chsd ldrs on outer: rdn along over 2f out: sn wknd* **10/1**

1m 15.23s (-1.67) **Going Correction** -0.15s/f (Firm)
WFA 3 from 5yo+ 2lb **9** Ran SP% **113.8**
Speed ratings (Par 96): **105,104,103,100,100 99,99,93,88**
CSF £23.85 CT £437.31 TOTE £3.70: £1.20, £3.20, £6.40; EX 25.30 Trifecta £470.80.
Owner Jon and Julia Aisbitt **Bred** Old Carhue Stud **Trained** West Ilsley, Berks

FOCUS
A decent fillies' handicap run at a good gallop, and the winner resumed her progress.

6519 ROA / RACING POST OWNERS JACKPOT H'CAP 2m 1f 22y
4:35 (4:35) (Class 5) (0-75,71) 3-Y-O+ **£3,234** (£962; £481; £240) **Stalls** Low

Form RPR
2352 **1** **Medina Sidonia (IRE)**[11] 6163 4-9-11 **71**........(p) RachelRichardson(3) 8 78
(Tim Easterby) *trckd ldrs: hdwy over 3f out: rdn along wl over 1f out: drvn on outer to chal ins fnl f: kpt on wl to ld nr line* **4/1**[2]
5113 **2** *shd* **La Fritillaire**[22] 5781 4-9-0 **57**.. AndrewMullen 9 63
(James Given) *trckd ldr: hdwy and cl up over 2f out: led wl over 1f out: sn rdn: drvn ins fnl f: hdd and no ex nr line* **12/1**
3433 **3** *1 1/2* **Chebsey Beau**[17] 5970 6-9-13 **70**.. JackGarritty 2 74
(John Quinn) *trckd ldrs on inner: hdwy 3f out: rdn wl over 1f out: drvn ent fnl f and ev ch: no ex last 50 yds* **4/1**[2]
3215 **4** *1 1/4* **Ivanhoe**[13] 6083 6-9-11 **68**...(v) DaneO'Neill 1 71
(Michael Blanshard) *hld up in rr: stdy hdwy over 4f out: chsd ldrs 2f out: sn rdn: swtchd lft and drvn ins fnl f: kpt on same pce* **7/2**[1]
2026 **5** *1 1/4* **Monjeni**[9] 6219 3-8-3 **62**..(p) RosieJessop(3) 6 65
(Sir Mark Prescott Bt) *hld up in tch: hdwy over 2f out: rdn to chse ldrs and styng on whn nt clr run and sltly hmpd ent fnl f: no imp after* **5/1**[3]
416 **6** *3 3/4* **Another Lincolnday**[8] 6227 5-9-7 **64**.............................(p) GrahamLee 3 61
(Michael Herrington) *led: pushed along and jnd over 2f out: rdn and hdd wl over 1f out: sn drvn and wknd* **8/1**
4202 **7** *4* **Riptide**[32] 5435 10-9-11 **68**.................................. WilliamTwiston-Davies 7 61
(Michael Scudamore) *hld up: effrt over 3f out: sn rdn along and n.d* **8/1**
0540 **8** *18* **Tuscan Gold**[13] 6083 9-9-3 **65**...................................(p) RobJFitzpatrick(5) 4 38
(Micky Hammond) *reminders s: rr tl t.k.h and hdwy on outer to trck ldrs after 5f: pushed along over 4f out: rdn over 3f out: sn outpcd and bhd* **20/1**

3m 45.88s (1.28) **Going Correction** -0.15s/f (Firm)
WFA 3 from 4yo+ 13lb **8** Ran SP% **113.6**
Speed ratings (Par 103): **90,89,89,88,88 86,84,75**
CSF £49.20 CT £202.34 TOTE £4.20: £1.80, £2.20, £1.80; EX 39.80 Trifecta £182.10.
Owner M Stewart **Bred** Barronstown Stud **Trained** Great Habton, N Yorks

FOCUS
The form looks ordinary, with the winner to form, the 2nd building on lower grade form, and the 3rd and 4th fitting in.

6520 WATCH RACING UK IN HD MAIDEN STKS 1m 2f 6y
5:10 (5:17) (Class 5) 3-Y-O+ **£3,234** (£962; £481; £240) **Stalls** Low

Form RPR
0342 **1** **Queen Of The Stars**[14] 6052 3-9-0 77.............. WilliamTwiston-Davies 1 79+
(William Haggas) *trckd ldng pair: hdwy to ld 2f out: sn clr: readily* **4/9**[1]
40 **2** *7* **Transmitting**[6] 6294 3-9-5 0.. JoeFanning 5 67+
(Sir Michael Stoute) *hld up towards rr: hdwy 3f out: rdn to chse ldrs wl over 1f out: sn drvn and kpt on: no ch w wnr* **9/1**[3]
3 *3/4* **Vuela** 3-8-7 0... GabrieleMalune(7) 7 61+
(Luca Cumani) *dwlt and rr: hdwy on inner 4f out: trckd ldrs whn n.m.r and swtchd rt to outer 2f out: racd wd and sn rdn: styd on fnl f* **10/1**
620 **4** *1 1/4* **Jonofark (IRE)**[14] 6052 3-9-5 0... KevinStott 2 63
(Brian Rothwell) *trckd ldrs: hdwy 3f out: rdn to chse wnr 2f out: sn rdn and kpt on one pce fnl f* **40/1**
5 *7* **Bailarico (IRE)** 3-9-5 0... MartinLane 6 52+
(Charlie Appleby) *trckd ldr: green and sn pushed along: rdn along 1/2-way: drvn over 2f out: wknd wl over 1f out* **4/1**[2]
00 **6** *7* **Serangoon**[30] 5527 3-9-0 0.. AndrewMullen 3 30
(Michael Appleby) *a towards rr: rdn along over 3f out: sn outpcd and bhd* **80/1**
0 **7** *11* **He's Magic**[14] 6052 5-9-12 0... GrahamLee 4 13
(Tim Fitzgerald) *sn led: rdn along over 3f out: hdd 2f out and sn wknd* **150/1**

2m 13.6s (-0.10) **Going Correction** -0.15s/f (Firm)
WFA 3 from 5yo 7lb **7** Ran SP% **112.7**
Speed ratings (Par 103): **94,88,87,86,81 75,66**
CSF £5.36 TOTE £1.70: £1.30, £2.50; EX 5.60 Trifecta £15.60.
Owner Normandie Stud Ltd **Bred** Normandie Stud Ltd **Trained** Newmarket, Suffolk

FOCUS
This proved straightforward enough for the favourite, who didn't need to improve.

6521 MATTY BOWN H'CAP (DIV II) 1m 4y
5:40 (5:40) (Class 4) (0-80,80) 3-Y-O+ **£5,175** (£1,540; £769; £384) **Stalls** Low

Form RPR
3332 **1** **Irish Optimism (IRE)**[7] 6265 3-8-13 **74**............................ JackGarritty 4 82+
(John Quinn) *trckd ldrs: hdwy 2f out: rdn to ld appr fnl f: drvn out* **5/4**[1]
3431 **2** *3/4* **Kiwi Bay**[17] 5972 11-9-4 **74**.. DarryllHolland 9 81
(Michael Dods) *dwlt and hld up in rr: hdwy wl over 1f out: rdn to chse wnr ins fnl f: sn drvn and kpt on wl towards fin* **14/1**
5303 **3** *2* **Stardrifter**[17] 5965 4-9-3 **73**... TonyHamilton 7 75
(Richard Fahey) *hld up: hdwy 3f out: rdn to chse ldrs over 1f out: drvn and kpt on same pce fnl f* **7/1**[3]
416 **4** *4 1/2* **La Havrese (FR)**[42] 5062 5-8-10 **66**................................... PaddyAspell 3 58
(Lynn Siddall) *hld up: hdwy wl over 2f out: rdn wl over 1f out: no imp fnl f* **33/1**
5500 **5** *1/2* **Musaaid (IRE)**[45] 4932 4-8-11 **72**................................. NathanEvans(5) 2 63
(Michael Easterby) *dwlt: sn in tch on inner: hdwy to chse ldrs over 2f out: rdn wl over 1f out: drvn and btn ent fnl f* **6/1**[2]
0500 **6** *6* **Hulcolt (IRE)**[19] 5866 5-9-3 **80**... RPWalsh(7) 5 57
(Ivan Furtado) *chsd ldng pair whn n.m.r and hmpd bnd after 1f: sn cl up: led over 3f out: rdn along 2f out: hdd over 1f out: sn drvn and wknd* **16/1**
2060 **7** *12* **Captain Revelation**[69] 4094 4-9-7 **77**................................... JoeFanning 1 27
(Tom Dascombe) *slt ld on inner: pushed along and hdd over 3f out: rdn over 2f out: drvn wl over 1f out: sn wknd* **8/1**
-000 **8** *1/2* **Taraz**[11] 6160 4-9-7 **77**... GrahamGibbons 6 25
(David O'Meara) *in tch on outer: rdn along 3f out: sn lost pl and bhd* **9/1**
002 **9** *43* **Tellovoi (IRE)**[34] 5374 8-9-5 **75**..(v) DaneO'Neill 8
(Richard Guest) *cl up on outer: pushed along 1/2-way: rdn 3f out: sn lost pl: bhd and eased fnl 2f* **16/1**

1m 43.66s (-2.24) **Going Correction** -0.15s/f (Firm)
WFA 3 from 4yo+ 5lb **9** Ran SP% **113.7**
Speed ratings (Par 105): **105,104,102,97,97 91,79,78,35**
CSF £20.75 CT £91.34 TOTE £2.20: £1.20, £2.40, £1.90; EX 17.80 Trifecta £49.20.
Owner Harlen Ltd **Bred** Cathal Ennis **Trained** Settrington, N Yorks

FOCUS
This was run at a good gallop, the front three rather taking each other on, and the time was 0.49sec quicker than the first division. The winner was well in and has been rated similar to Epsom latest, with the 2nd limiting the level.

6522 RACING UK PROFITS RETURNED TO RACING APPRENTICE H'CAP 6f
6:10 (6:12) (Class 5) (0-70,68) 3-Y-O+ **£3,234** (£962; £481; £240) **Stalls** Low

Form RPR
4600 **1** **Be Royale**[42] 5090 6-9-2 **66**..[1] BenSanderson(5) 3 76
(Michael Appleby) *in tch on inner: hdwy over 2f out: led over 1f out: rdn ins fnl f: kpt on wl towards fin* **16/1**
2152 **2** *2* **Mr Orange (IRE)**[9] 6215 3-9-2 **66**.....................(p) ManuelFernandes(3) 10 70+
(Paul Midgley) *trckd ldrs on outer: cl up 2f out: rdn over 1f out: drvn to chse wnr ins fnl f: kpt on* **11/8**[1]
0050 **3** *hd* **Mon Brav**[12] 6136 9-9-6 **68**.. BenRobinson(3) 12 71
(Brian Ellison) *rr: hdwy 2f out: rdn over 1f out: styd on: kpt on wl fnl f* **11/1**
023 **4** *3/4* **Letbygonesbeicons**[22] 5760 3-8-5 **59**......................... LiamLewis-Salter(7) 5 60
(Ann Duffield) *t.k.h: cl up: led over 2f out: rdn and hdd over 1f out: drvn ins fnl f: kpt on same pce* **10/1**[3]
0050 **5** *2 1/4* **Captain Scooby**[24] 5717 10-8-11 **63**..............................(b) LisaTodd(7) 2 56
(Richard Guest) *towards rr: hdwy 2f out: rdn to chse ldrs over 1f out: no imp ins fnl f* **16/1**
0000 **6** *3 1/2* **Clon Rocket (IRE)**[19] 5887 3-8-4 **58**..................... MeganEllingworth(7) 6 40
(John Holt) *cl up: led over 3f out: hdd and rdn over 2f out: grad wknd appr fnl f* **12/1**
-030 **7** *nk* **Jacksonfire**[37] 5270 4-8-4 **54** oh9.....................................(p) AledBeech(5) 11 35
(Michael Mullineaux) *a towards rr* **50/1**

2606 **8** ½ **Bahamian Sunshine**[12] 6140 3-8-13 **65**....................(p) HayleyIrvine(5) 4 45
(Richard Fahey) *led: hdd over 3f out: cl up on inner tl rdn over 2f out and grad wknd* **12/1**
5526 **9** ½ **Tom Sawyer**[17] 5968 8-9-5 **64**..................................(b) KieranSchofield 8 42
(Julie Camacho) *awkward s: a towards rr* **12/1**
6314 **10** 2¾ **Teetotal (IRE)**[19] 5889 6-8-12 **60**..................................(b) PaulaMuir(3) 9 29
(Nigel Tinkler) *chsd ldrs: rdn along wl over 2f out: sn wknd* **7/1**[2]

1m 16.62s (-0.28) **Going Correction** -0.15s/f (Firm)
WFA 3 from 4yo+ 2lb **10** Ran SP% **108.8**
Speed ratings (Par 103): **95,92,92,91,88 83,83,82,81,78**
CSF £33.07 CT £205.23 TOTE £17.90: £4.80, £1.10, £3.70; EX 47.40 Trifecta £314.90.
Owner Wayne Brackstone, Steve Whitear **Bred** W Brackstone & S J Whitear **Trained** Oakham, Rutland
■ Bay Mirage was withdrawn. Price at time of withdrawal 8-1. Rule 4 applies to all bets - deduction 10p in the pound.

FOCUS
A modest sprint run at a good pace, and the winner came back to form from nowhere - rated to her winter AW level.
T/Plt: £104.30 to a £1 stake. Pool: £54598.75, 381.78 winning units T/Qpdt: £46.60 to a £1 stake. Pool: £3527.68, 56.0 winning units **Joe Rowntree**

6486 YARMOUTH (L-H)
Thursday, September 15

OFFICIAL GOING: Good to firm (7.9)
Wind: light, across Weather: sunny and hot

6523 BRITISH STALLION STUDS EBF MAIDEN STKS (PLUS 10 RACE) 1m 3y
2:10 (2:10) (Class 4) 2-Y-O **£4,657** (£1,386; £692; £346) **Stalls** High

Form RPR
0 **1** **Desert Skyline (IRE)**[13] 6085 2-9-5 0.................................... FMBerry 8 80
(David Elsworth) *pressed ldng pair tl wnt 2nd 1/2-way: rdn and ev ch over 1f out: led wl ins fnl f: r.o wl* **40/1**
0 **2** 1 **Merlin**[35] 5332 2-9-5 0.. MartinHarley 5 78
(Michael Bell) *mde most: rdn over 1f out: edgd rt 1f out: hdd wl ins fnl f: no ex* **10/1**[3]
5 **3** 2¼ **Romanor**[17] 5959 2-9-5 0.. ThomasBrown 2 72
(Ed Walker) *stdd after s: t.k.h: hld up in tch in rr: hdwy 2f out: rdn over 1f out: unable qck whn sltly hmpd and swtchd lft jst ins fnl f: wknd fnl 100yds* **12/1**
5 **4** ½ **Splash Around**[20] 5848 2-9-5 0.. RyanMoore 1 71
(Sir Michael Stoute) *wl in tch in midfield: rdn over 2f out: unable qck over 1f out: styd on same pce ins fnl f* **8/15**[1]
0 **5** 1¾ **Chocolate Box (IRE)**[14] 6054 2-9-5 0................................ AdamKirby 9 67
(Luca Cumani) *w ldr tl 1/2-way: styd chsng ldrs: pushed along over 2f out: outpcd over 1f out: kpt on same pce after* **20/1**
5 **6** 1 **Pioneering (IRE)**[16] 5990 2-9-5 0...................................... WilliamBuick 4 64
(Charlie Appleby) *s.i.s: hld up in tch: rdn ent fnl 2f: no imp over 1f out: styd on same pce after* **7/2**[2]

1m 38.34s (-2.26) **Going Correction** -0.40s/f (Firm) **6** Ran SP% **111.4**
Speed ratings (Par 97): **95,94,91,91,89 88**
CSF £350.81 TOTE £20.50: £10.10, £3.50; EX 276.50 Trifecta £1614.00.
Owner C Benham/ D Whitford/ L Quinn/ K Quinn **Bred** Tinnakill Bloodstock & Cannings **Trained** Newmarket, Suffolk

FOCUS
William Buick said of the ground: "It's patchy." while Fran Berry felt it was "good." Racing stands' side in this ordinary maiden, it went to the complete outsider, who challenged nearest to the rail late on. The bare form is only ordinary but it's feasible there were some good horses on show.

6524 BRITISH STALLION STUDS/KEN LINDSAY MEMORIAL EBF MAIDEN STKS (PLUS 10 RACE) 6f 3y
2:45 (2:46) (Class 4) 2-Y-O **£4,536** (£1,357; £678; £339; £169) **Stalls** High

Form RPR
63 **1** **Battered**[54] 4663 2-9-5 0.. PatCosgrave 5 81
(William Haggas) *chsd ldrs: wnt 2nd 2f out: rdn to ld over 1f out: styd on wl fnl f: rdn out* **7/2**[2]
2 ¾ **Ekhtiyaar** 2-9-5 0... PaulHanagan 10 79+
(Roger Varian) *t.k.h: hld up in tch in midfield: hdwy 2f out: nt clr run over 1f out: rdn to press ldrs 1f out: wnt 2nd wl ins fnl f: kpt on* **7/1**
5 **3** ¾ **Nibras Again**[62] 4363 2-9-5 0.................................... SilvestreDeSousa 4 76
(Ismail Mohammed) *chsd ldrs: rdn and ev ch over 1f out: styd on same pce u.p ins fnl f* **10/1**
3 **4** nk **Al Reeh (IRE)**[19] 5876 2-9-5 0.. RyanMoore 7 79
(Marco Botti) *hld up in tch in midfield: nt clr run jst over 2f out: clsd to chse ldrs and swtchd lft 1f out: styd on same pce u.p ins fnl f* **13/8**[1]
40 **5** 7 **Zipedee**[26] 5631 2-8-11 0..................................... JosephineGordon(3) 11 48
(John Ryan) *t.k.h: chsd ldr tl 2f out: sn lost pl u.p: wl hld but plugged on fnl f* **100/1**
5 **6** nse **Shannon**[9] 6214 2-9-0 0... LukeMorris 1 48
(Robyn Brisland) *in tch in midfield: rdn 1/2-way: struggling and outpcd 2f out: wl hld whn swtchd lft 1f out: plugged on* **33/1**
0 **7** 1 **Not Now Mum**[13] 6086 2-9-5 0... RobertWinston 6 49
(Dean Ivory) *hld up in tch in rr of main gp: rdn 2f out: sn outpcd and wl btn over 1f out: plugged on* **66/1**
4 **8** 2½ **Winning Return (IRE)**[50] 4762 2-9-0 0............................ JamesDoyle 8 36
(Saeed bin Suroor) *racd freely: led: rdn and hdd over 1f out: sn wandered u.p and btn 1f out: wknd ins fnl f* **8/1**
32 **9** 9 **Dawoodi**[16] 6009 2-9-5 0..[1] JimCrowley 2 13
(Hugo Palmer) *wl in tch in midfield: lost pl and bhd 2f out: sn wknd* **9/2**[3]
00 **10** 2¾ **See You Mush**[12] 6141 2-9-5 0.................................[1] LemosdeSouza 3 4
(Chris Dwyer) *a rr: lost tch 2f out* **80/1**
11 27 **Compton Brave** 2-9-5 0... FrederikTylicki 12
(J R Jenkins) *s.i.s and wnt lft s: rn green in detached last: lost tch 1/2-way: t.o* **66/1**

1m 11.16s (-3.24) **Going Correction** -0.40s/f (Firm) **11** Ran SP% **119.4**
Speed ratings (Par 97): **105,104,103,102,93 93,91,88,76,72 36**
CSF £28.28 TOTE £4.80: £1.50, £2.40, £3.20; EX 29.20 Trifecta £256.10.
Owner B Haggas **Bred** Coln Valley Stud **Trained** Newmarket, Suffolk

FOCUS
They again headed stands' side for this fair sprint maiden, with the first four clear. The winner took a slight step forward.

6525 RACHAEL KEATLEY MEMORIAL NURSERY H'CAP 6f 3y
3:15 (3:15) (Class 4) (0-80,80) 2-Y-O **£4,536** (£1,357; £678; £339; £169) **Stalls** High

Form RPR
321 **1** **Tropical Rock**[59] 4457 2-9-4 **77**.. FMBerry 5 85+
(Ralph Beckett) *hld up in tch: nt clr run over 2f out: hdwy 2f out: rdn to ld 1f out: r.o strly and drew clr ins fnl f: readily* **7/1**
61 **2** 2½ **Hawana (USA)**[70] 4063 2-9-6 **79**...................................... JamesDoyle 6 79
(John Gosden) *chsd ldrs: effrt to chse ldr jst over 2f out: rdn and ev ch over 1f out: led ent fnl f: sn hdd: chsd wnr and r.o same pce ins fnl f* **9/2**[3]
313 **3** hd **Serengeti Sky (USA)**[26] 5644 2-9-7 **80**.........................(t) WilliamBuick 7 79
(Charlie Appleby) *in tch in last pair: rdn and hdwy 2f out: ev ch over 1f out: styd on same pce ins fnl f* **3/1**[1]
1540 **4** 2¾ **El Torito (IRE)**[29] 5560 2-9-5 **78**..................................... PatCosgrave 1 69
(Jim Boyle) *led: rdn 2f out: hdd and no ex jst over 1f out: wknd ins fnl f* **11/1**
0541 **5** 2 **Erissimus Maximus (FR)**[18] 5931 2-9-2 **75**........... SilvestreDeSousa 8 60
(Chris Dwyer) *t.k.h: pressed ldrs early: sn stdd into midfield: rdn over 2f out: no imp over 1f out* **7/1**
325 **6** ½ **Bellevarde (IRE)**[45] 4951 2-9-2 **75**.................................. TomQueally 3 58
(James Fanshawe) *in tch in midfield: clsd over 2f out: rdn and little rspnse over 1f out: sn btn: wknd fnl f* **8/1**
21 **7** 2 **Silent Assassin (IRE)**[31] 5477 2-9-3 **76**........................... JimCrowley 4 52
(Ed Walker) *chsd ldr: rdn over 2f out: sn lost pl: wl hld over 1f out: wknd fnl f* **7/2**[2]
016 **8** 18 **My Dear Baby (IRE)**[33] 5416 2-9-4 **77**................................ AdamKirby 2
(Robert Cowell) *stdd s: t.k.h: hdwy into midfield after 2f: rdn 2f out: sn btn and bhd: virtually p.u ins fnl f* **22/1**

1m 10.63s (-3.77) **Going Correction** -0.40s/f (Firm) **8** Ran SP% **114.2**
Speed ratings (Par 97): **109,105,105,101,99 98,95,71**
CSF £38.30 CT £114.59 TOTE £7.50: £1.90, £1.80, £1.40; EX 39.90 Trifecta £144.60.
Owner J C Smith **Bred** Littleton Stud **Trained** Kimpton, Hants

FOCUS
The winner came more towards the centre in this decent nursery, although the field did come stands' side. The winner built on her Yarmouth win.

6526 DAN HAGUE RAILS BOOKMAKER H'CAP 1m 6f 17y
3:50 (3:50) (Class 2) (0-100,103) 3-Y-O+ **£12,602** (£3,772; £1,886; £944; £470) **Stalls** High

Form RPR
0532 **1** **Kiltara (IRE)**[5] 6332 4-9-1 **87**....................................... SilvestreDeSousa 4 99
(Mark Johnston) *mde all: rdn and fnd ex 3f out: clr and drvn over 1f out: styd on strly: eased towards fin* **7/2**[2]
0-60 **2** 3¾ **A Soldier's Life (IRE)**[51] 4734 5-9-11 **97**.......................[1] WilliamBuick 6 103
(Charlie Appleby) *hld up in tch in last pair: shkn up 4f out: drvn ent fnl 2f: hdwy over 1f out: chsd clr wnr jst ins fnl f: styd on but no ch w wnr* **11/2**[3]
0060 **3** 2 **Dawn Missile**[27] 5611 4-9-0 **86**.. RyanMoore 5 89
(William Haggas) *hld up in tch in 5th: effrt and rdn over 2f out: chsd clr wnr over 1f out: no imp: 3rd and styd on same pce ins fnl f* **7/2**[2]
-164 **4** 1½ **Amour De Nuit (IRE)**[71] 4031 4-10-3 **103**.......................... LukeMorris 1 104
(Sir Mark Prescott Bt) *trckd ldrs: rdn over 3f out: drvn 2f out and sn outpcd: swtchd rt and kpt on same pce ins fnl f* **6/1**
-665 **5** ¾ **Noble Silk**[40] 5144 7-9-3 **89**..(v) JamieSpencer 3 89
(Lucy Wadham) *hld up in tch in midfield: effrt to chse clr ldr over 2f out: sn edging lft and no imp: lost 2nd over 1f out: hung lft and wknd ins fnl f* **8/1**
6520 **6** 4 **Combative**[12] 6110 3-8-7 **90**... JimCrowley 2 84
(Amanda Perrett) *chsd ldr: rdn 3f out: lost pl 2f over 2f out: dropped to rr over 1f out: wknd fnl f* **11/4**[1]

3m 2.98s (-4.62) **Going Correction** -0.30s/f (Firm)
WFA 3 from 4yo+ 11lb **6** Ran SP% **111.9**
Speed ratings (Par 109): **101,98,97,96,96 94**
CSF £22.26 TOTE £3.80: £1.90, £3.80; EX 19.70 Trifecta £116.20.
Owner Ballylinch Stud **Bred** Ballylinch Stud **Trained** Middleham Moor, N Yorks

FOCUS
A useful handicap, they didn't go overly fast up front and the winner made all. She posted another pb.

6527 EBF STALLIONS BREEDING WINNERS FILLIES' H'CAP 1m 3f 104y
4:25 (4:25) (Class 4) (0-80,77) 3-Y-O+ **£4,448** (£4,448; £1,019; £509) **Stalls** Low

Form RPR
3641 **1** **Taffeta Lady**[29] 5550 3-9-4 **77**.................................(v) FrederikTylicki 6 85
(Lucy Wadham) *hld up in tch: effrt to chal 2f out: sn led and bmpd over 1f out: edgd lft u.p: hdd wl ins fnl f: battled bk gamely to join ldr on post* **6/1**
5051 **1** dht **Notice (IRE)**[23] 5749 3-8-13 **72**....................................... JamieSpencer 3 80
(David Simcock) *hld up in tch in rr: hdwy over jst over 2f out: rdn to chal and edgd lft over 1f out: sustained chal and drvn to ld wl ins fnl f: kpt on: jnd on post* **4/1**[2]
2231 **3** 3 **Beauty Sleep (IRE)**[25] 5681 3-9-4 **77**............................(p) RyanMoore 4 80
(William Haggas) *chsd ldr: pushed along to join ldr over 3f out: rdn to ld over 2f out: hdd over 1f out: unable qck and short of room 1f out: kpt on same pce ins fnl f* **9/2**[3]
3352 **4** ¾ **All My Love (IRE)**[30] 5526 4-9-5 **73**................................ RobHornby(3) 1 75
(Pam Sly) *hld up in tch: clsd and nt clr run over 2f out: rdn to chal 2f out: unable qck and sltly short of room over 1f out: kpt on same pce fnl f* **8/1**
223 **5** 5 **Kath's Legacy**[25] 5671 3-9-2 **75**....................................... AdamKirby 2 69
(Ben De Haan) *chsd ldng pair: rdn to chal 2f out: unable qck and losing pl whn squeezed for room and lost pl over 1f out: wknd fnl f* **10/1**
5011 **6** 7 **Corpus Chorister (FR)**[5] 6334 3-9-3 **76** 6ex.................. MartinDwyer 5 58
(David Menuisier) *led: jnd and rdn over 3f out: hdd and drvn over 2f out: dropped to rr and wknd over 1f out* **13/8**[1]

2m 23.89s (-4.81) **Going Correction** -0.30s/f (Firm)
WFA 3 from 4yo 8lb **6** Ran SP% **110.8**
Speed ratings (Par 102): **105,105,102,102,98 93**
WIN: TL £3.50, N £2.50; PL: TL £3.40 N £2.40; EX: TL/N £18.50, N/TL £6.00; CSF: TL/N £14.42, N/TL £13.21; TF: TL/N/BS £103.20, N/TL/BS £84.20;.
Owner Anthony Rogers & Mrs Sonia Rogers **Bred** Airlie Stud & Mrs S M Rogers **Trained** Newmarket, Suffolk
Owner Mr And Mrs A E Pakenham **Bred** Mr & Mrs A E Pakenham **Trained** Newmarket, Suffolk

FOCUS
An ordinary handicap that set up for the closers. The dead-heat pair built on their recent wins.

6528 GREENE KING IPA H'CAP 1m 3f 104y
5:00 (5:01) (Class 3) (0-90,86) 3-Y-O £7,813 (£2,338; £1,169; £585) Stalls Low

Form RPR

-523 **1** **Kaatskill Nap (FR)**[77] 3809 3-9-4 **83**........ MartinDwyer 4 92
(David Menuisier) *hld up in rr: hung lft st: clsd but stl hanging over 2f out: swtchd rt and wnt between rivals to ld over 1f out: sn in command and drew wl clr fnl f: readily* **8/1**[3]

2-12 **2** 6 **Myopic**[18] 5927 3-9-5 **84**........ AdamKirby 1 84
(Luca Cumani) *led: jnd and rdn 3f out: hdd over 2f out: kpt on u.p and stl ev ch tl outpcd by wnr 1f out: plugged on to hold 2nd fnl f* **8/13**[1]

2306 **3** 2 3/4 **Hepplewhite**[20] 5849 3-8-5 **77**........ CameronNoble(7) 3 72
(Robert Eddery) *hld up in 3rd: clsd over 2f out: rdn and ev ch over 1f out: sn outpcd by wnr: wknd ins fnl f* **8/1**[3]

2114 **4** 3 1/2 **Palisade**[27] 5603 3-9-7 **86**........(v) LukeMorris 2 75
(Sir Mark Prescott Bt) *chsd ldr: clsd and upsides travelling strly 3f out: rdn to ld over 2f out: drvn and hdd over 1f out: sn btn and wknd fnl f* **7/2**[2]

2m 24.69s (-4.01) **Going Correction** -0.30s/f (Firm) **4** Ran SP% **106.4**
Speed ratings (Par 105): **102,97,95,93**
CSF £13.56 TOTE £8.00; EX 15.70 Trifecta £32.40.
Owner Clive Washbourn **Bred** Mathieu Daguzan-Garros **Trained** Pulborough, W Sussex

FOCUS
Just the four runners but they appeared to go a reasonable gallop and the winner came from last. This has been rated cautiously.

6529 DAN HAGUE FOR COMPETITIVE PRICES H'CAP 7f 3y
5:30 (5:30) (Class 3) (0-90,90) 3-Y-O £7,813 (£2,338; £1,169; £585; £291) Stalls High

Form RPR

1-50 **1** **Brave Hero**[138] 1867 3-9-3 **87**........(v1) JamesDoyle 6 99
(Saeed bin Suroor) *racd in centre: nt that wl away: racd freely and sn led gp and chsd ldrs overall: overall ldr 4f out: rdn over 1f out: clr and styd on strly ins fnl f* **10/1**

35-2 **2** 3 **Claim The Roses (USA)**[169] 1153 5-9-10 **90**........[1] FrederikTylicki 4 96
(Ed Vaughan) *racd in centre: hld up in last trio: rdn over 2f out: hdwy u.p over 1f out: styd on u.p ins fnl f: wnt 2nd last strides: no threat to wnr* **12/1**

0300 **3** nk **Plucky Dip**[40] 5174 5-9-2 **82**........ DannyBrock 5 87
(John Ryan) *racd in centre: midfield overall: rdn over 2f out: styd on u.p and 3rd overall ins fnl f: kpt on to chse clr wnr towards fin: no threat to wnr and lost 2nd last strides* **25/1**

3213 **4** 1/2 **Twin Point**[21] 5793 5-8-11 **77**........(t) StevieDonohoe 2 81
(Charlie Fellowes) *swtchd lft to r far side: overall ldr tl 4f out: chsd wnr after: rdn over 2f out: no ex u.p 1f out: wknd wl ins fnl f and lost 2 pls towards fin* **6/1**

0416 **5** 1/2 **Gothic Empire (IRE)**[64] 4263 4-9-7 **87**........ DanielMuscutt 1 89
(James Fanshawe) *racd in centre: stdd s and hld up in rr: clsd 2f out: rdn and kpt on same pce ins fnl f: nvr trbld ldrs* **9/2**[2]

0441 **6** hd **Valley Of Fire**[13] 6082 4-9-9 **89**........(v1) PatCosgrave 10 91
(William Haggas) *racd in centre: hld up in rr: effrt ent fnl 2f: rdn and hdwy over 1f out: kpt on ins fnl f: nvr trbld ldrs* **7/2**[1]

0201 **7** 3/4 **Carnival King (IRE)**[18] 5934 4-9-8 **88**........(b) TomQueally 3 88
(Brian Meehan) *wnt to r on far side sn after s: chsd overall ldr tl 4f out: styd chsng ldrs: rdn over 2f out: no ex u.p over 1f out: wknd ins fnl f* **5/1**[3]

0050 **8** 4 **Firmdecisions (IRE)**[33] 5403 6-9-5 **85**........ RobertWinston 8 74
(Dean Ivory) *racd in centre: midfield overall: rdn over 2f out: no imp u.p over 1f out: wknd ins fnl f* **20/1**

0420 **9** 1/2 **Bint Dandy (IRE)**[33] 5396 5-9-7 **87**........(b1) AdamKirby 7 75
(Chris Dwyer) *racd in centre: in tch in midfield overall: u.p over 2f out: sn no imp and lost pl over 1f out: wknd fnl f* **20/1**

-010 **10** 2 3/4 **Mamillius**[47] 4867 3-9-3 **87**........ SteveDrowne 11 65
(George Baker) *racd in centre: midfield overall: lost pl u.p ent fnl 2f: bhd over 1f out* **18/1**

3451 **11** 20 **Calvados Spirit**[23] 5743 3-8-12 **82**........ MartinDwyer 13 6
(William Muir) *racd in centre: in tch in midfield overall: lost pl and bhd 2f out: eased ins fnl f: t.o* **15/2**

1m 22.53s (-4.07) **Going Correction** -0.40s/f (Firm)
WFA 3 from 4yo+ 4lb **11** Ran SP% **118.5**
Speed ratings (Par 107): **107,103,103,102,102 101,101,96,95,92 69**
CSF £120.68 CT £2904.91 TOTE £9.10: £3.20, £3.00, £7.20; EX 107.60 Trifecta £1693.10.
Owner Godolphin **Bred** Honeypuddle Stud **Trained** Newmarket, Suffolk

FOCUS
A useful handicap. Unlike in the earlier straight course races, they shunned the stands' rail and all bar two came down the centre, with the winner racing there and building on last year's maiden win. Sound form, set around the 2nd and 3rd.
T/Plt: £7,407.20 to a £1 stake. Pool: £66462.08, 6.55 winning units T/Qpdt: £82.60 to a £1 stake. Pool: £6290.07, 56.3 winning units **Steve Payne**

6530 - 6533a (Foreign Racing) - See Raceform Interactive

6499 AYR (L-H)
Friday, September 16

OFFICIAL GOING: Good to soft (soft in places; overall 7.9; straight 7.3; sprint track: far side 7.5; centre 7.5; stands' side 6.9)
Wind: Breezy, half against Weather: Cloudy, dry

6534 AL MAKTOUM COLLEGE, DUNDEE/BRITISH STALLION STUDS EBF MAIDEN STKS (PLUS 10 RACE) (DIV I) 7f 50y
1:30 (1:30) (Class 4) 2-Y-O £6,469 (£1,925; £962; £481) Stalls High

Form RPR

42 **1** **Naval Warfare (IRE)**[59] 4479 2-9-2 0........ RobHornby(3) 10 84
(Andrew Balding) *trckd ldr: led over 3f out: rdn and 3 l clr over 1f out: hung rt ins fnl f: kpt on wl* **2/1**[1]

0 **2** 3/4 **Saint Equiano**[86] 3516 2-9-5 0........[1] PhillipMakin 7 82
(Keith Dalgleish) *hld up: hdwy and squeezed through to chse wnr over 1f out: sn rdn: kpt on fnl f: clsng at fin* **20/1**

634 **3** 2 3/4 **Golden Apollo**[17] 6002 2-9-5 78........ DavidAllan 12 75
(Tim Easterby) *hld up in tch: effrt whn nt clr run briefly over 2f out: rdn over 1f out: kpt on fnl f: nt rch first two* **6/1**[3]

4 3 1/2 **Re Run (IRE)** 2-9-5 0........ TonyHamilton 11 69+
(Richard Fahey) *t.k.h early: hld up on outside: shkn up over 2f out: hdwy over 1f out: kpt on fnl f: nt pce to chal* **9/4**[2]

002 **5** 3/4 **Hotfill**[14] 6099 2-9-5 73........ GrahamGibbons 8 65
(David Barron) *stdd s: t.k.h in rr: rdn and hdwy over 1f out: kpt on fnl f: no imp* **33/1**

53 **6** 1 1/2 **Braztime**[39] 5242 2-9-0 0........ SeanLevey 9 56
(Richard Hannon) *trckd ldrs: effrt and chsd wnr over 2f out to over 1f out: wknd ins fnl f* **9/1**

40 **7** 7 **Moonlight Blue (IRE)**[18] 5966 2-9-5 0........ ConnorBeasley 2 43
(Michael Dods) *hld up midfield: rdn along over 2f out: hung lft and wknd wl over 1f out* **14/1**

8 1 1/2 **Helm Reef (IRE)** 2-9-0 0........ PaulMulrennan 3 35
(Michael Dods) *s.i.s: hld up: pushed along and green 2f out: nvr on terms* **25/1**

0 **9** 1/2 **Giveitsomeginger**[23] 5772 2-9-0 0........ RobertHavlin 5 33
(Jo Hughes) *prom: drvn along over 2f out: sn wknd* **100/1**

10 1 3/4 **She's Zoff (IRE)** 2-9-0 0........ TomEaves 1 29
(John Quinn) *trckd ldrs: effrt and rdn over 2f out: wknd over 1f out* **11/1**

6020 **11** 40 **Warleggan (FR)**[6] 6343 2-9-5 51........(b) JamesSullivan 4
(Linda Perratt) *led: styd alone far side and hdd over 3f out: sn struggling: t.o* **250/1**

1m 35.06s (1.66) **Going Correction** +0.225s/f (Good) **11** Ran SP% **116.3**
Speed ratings (Par 97): **99,98,95,91,90 88,80,78,78,76 30**
CSF £48.74 TOTE £2.90: £1.40, £4.00, £2.10; EX 42.10 Trifecta £153.20.
Owner Qatar Racing Limited **Bred** Rathasker Stud **Trained** Kingsclere, Hants

FOCUS
The going had dried out slightly since the previous day and was now good to soft, soft in places (GoingStick - Sprint track: far side and centre 7.5, stands' side 6.9; overall 7.9). Bends out 3yds adding approx 9yds to the distance of this opening race. This was probably an ordinary maiden and all bar one shunned the inside rail on reaching the straight. The winning time was 6.76sec outside standard and after the race Phillip Makin said: "It is hard work, it is a bit tacky. It is still soft, there are not many good places."

6535 AL MAKTOUM COLLEGE, DUNDEE/BRITISH STALLION STUDS EBF MAIDEN STKS (PLUS 10 RACE) (DIV II) 7f 50y
2:00 (2:02) (Class 4) 2-Y-O £6,469 (£1,925; £962; £481) Stalls High

Form RPR

1 **Kitten's Johnstown (USA)** 2-9-5 0........ KevinStott 4 84+
(Kevin Ryan) *mde all: rdn and clr over 1f out: kpt on strly fnl f: unchal* **8/1**

2 1 1/2 **Trading Point (FR)** 2-9-5 0........ PhillipMakin 1 80+
(John Quinn) *s.i.s: hld up midfield: effrt over 2f out: rdn and chsd wnr over 1f out: kpt on ins fnl f: nt pce to chal* **7/2**[1]

62 **3** 2 **Grinty (IRE)**[25] 5713 2-9-5 0........ PaulMulrennan 2 75
(Michael Dods) *t.k.h early: trckd ldrs: effrt and chsd wnr over 2f out to over 1f out: sn no ex* **7/2**[1]

4 **4** 1 1/4 **Iron Islands**[13] 6129 2-9-5 0........ DougieCostello 6 72
(K R Burke) *hld up midfield: drvn and outpcd 3f out: rallied over 1f out: kpt on fnl f: nt pce to chal* **9/2**[2]

3340 **5** 1 1/2 **Navarone (IRE)**[25] 5713 2-9-5 78........ TonyHamilton 8 68
(Richard Fahey) *t.k.h: hld up midfield: effrt and rdn wl over 1f out: no imp fnl f* **9/1**

6 1 1/2 **Lamloom (IRE)** 2-9-5 0........ DanielTudhope 5 64
(David O'Meara) *hld up: rdn and hung lft over 2f out: rallied over 1f out: sn no imp* **18/1**

056 **7** 4 1/2 **Junoesque**[34] 5387 2-9-0 68........ MichaelJMMurphy 11 48
(John Gallagher) *trckd ldrs: rdn along over 2f out: wknd wl over 1f out* **50/1**

0 **8** 3/4 **Good Boy Jasper**[23] 5778 2-9-5 0........ GrahamLee 7 51
(Linda Perratt) *dwlt: t.k.h: hld up: drvn and outpcd 3f out: nvr on terms* **100/1**

9 nk **Devil's Guard (IRE)** 2-9-5 0........ JimCrowley 3 51
(Keith Dalgleish) *s.i.s: hld up: rdn along over 2f out: nvr on terms* **15/2**[3]

6 **10** 2 **Quiet Weekend**[41] 5150 2-9-5 0........ PJMcDonald 10 46
(James Bethell) *pressed ldr to over 2f out: rdn and wknd wl over 1f out* **14/1**

450 **11** 1 1/4 **Steel Helmet (IRE)**[55] 4642 2-9-5 66........ ChrisHayes 9 42
(Brian Ellison) *in tch on outside: drvn along 3f out: wknd 2f out* **12/1**

1m 35.7s (2.30) **Going Correction** +0.225s/f (Good) **11** Ran SP% **118.1**
Speed ratings (Par 97): **95,93,91,89,87 86,81,80,79,77 76**
CSF £36.25 TOTE £8.80: £2.40, £1.70, £2.50; EX 45.10 Trifecta £262.30.
Owner Sheikh Juma Dalmook Al Maktoum **Bred** Gallagher's Shiraz Llc **Trained** Hambleton, N Yorks

FOCUS
Rail movement added approx 9yds to race distance. The winning time was 0.64sec slower than the first division and the market got it wrong, as although a few were backed the winner wasn't one of them. The first two were both debutants and this time they all came up the centre. The winner looks a type to handle a better grade.

6536 SHADWELL STUD NURSERY H'CAP 6f
2:30 (2:33) (Class 2) 2-Y-O
£15,562 (£4,660; £2,330; £1,165; £582; £292) Stalls Centre

Form RPR

1116 **1** **Tawny Port**[7] 6275 2-9-1 **79**........ TomEaves 4 85
(James Given) *hld up in rr: n.m.r after 2f: hdwy over 2f out: pushed lft over 1f out: led last 150yds: styd on wl* **11/1**

510 **2** 3/4 **Poet's Princess**[55] 4623 2-9-3 **81**........ RobertHavlin 3 85
(Hughie Morrison) *led: hung bdly lft over 1f out: hdd and wnt rt 150yds out: styd on same pce* **9/1**

4352 **3** 1 1/2 **Heatongrad (IRE)**[17] 6007 2-8-8 **72**........ PatrickMathers 2 71
(Richard Fahey) *w ldrs: carried lft over 1f out: kpt on same pce fnl 150yds* **11/1**

2133 **4** 1/2 **Dandy Highwayman (IRE)**[35] 5352 2-9-0 **78**........ DanielTudhope 1 78
(Ollie Pears) *chsd ldrs: hmpd over 1f out: kpt on last 100yds* **8/1**[3]

2052 **5** nk **In First Place**[17] 6002 2-8-13 **77**........ TonyHamilton 5 74
(Richard Fahey) *s.i.s: hdwy over 2f out: kpt on same pce fnl f* **16/1**

01 **6** 1 1/4 **Haworth**[14] 6099 2-8-11 **75**........ PJMcDonald 12 68+
(James Bethell) *mid-div: hdwy over 2f out: kpt on same pce fnl f* **40/1**

621 **7** hd **Colonel Frank**[17] 6009 2-9-1 **79**........ JimCrowley 15 72+
(Ed Walker) *w ldrs: kpt on same pce fnl f* **9/2**[1]

1300 **8** 5 **Spin Doctor**[30] 5560 2-8-11 **80**........ AdamMcNamara(5) 9 58+
(Richard Fahey) *chsd ldrs: wknd fnl f* **22/1**

41 **9** 1 1/2 **Robben Rainbow**[34] 5414 2-9-4 **82**........ GrahamGibbons 11 55
(David Barron) *s.i.s: in rr: drvn over 2f out: sn nt clr run: weakned over 1f out* **6/1**[2]

3606 **10** shd **La Haule Lady**[9] 6222 2-8-1 **65**........ CamHardie 6 38
(Paul Midgley) *chsd ldrs: lost pl over 1f out* **66/1**

651 **11** nk **Halawain (USA)**[35] 5377 2-8-13 **77**........ PhillipMakin 7 49
(John Quinn) *hld up in rr: effrt over 2f out: wknd over 1f out* **18/1**

0100 **12** shd **Burrishoole Abbey (IRE)**[30] 5560 2-9-4 **82**........ DougieCostello 13 54
(K R Burke) *s.i.s: sme hdwy over 2f out: sn wknd* **16/1**

31 **13** 1 ¼ **Dakota Gold**[17] 6002 2-9-0 **78** ConnorBeasley 14 46
(Michael Dods) *rrd s: hld up towards rr: t.k.h: hdwy over 2f out: wknd over 1f out* **9/1**
41 **14** 1 ¾ **Rock N Rolla (IRE)**[13] 6129 2-9-7 **85** JoeFanning 10 48
(Keith Dalgleish) *chsd ldrs: drvn over 2f out: lost pl over 1f out* **6/1**[2]
5100 **15** 4 ½ **Percy Toplis**[17] 6007 2-8-6 **70** JoeDoyle 8 19
(Kevin Ryan) *chsd ldrs: weakned 2f out: eased whn bhd clsng stages* **33/1**

1m 15.33s (2.93) **Going Correction** +0.425s/f (Yiel) **15** Ran SP% **122.8**
Speed ratings (Par 101): **97,96,94,93,92 91,91,84,82,82 81,81,80,77,71**
CSF £104.97 CT £757.07 TOTE £12.50: £4.00, £3.70, £4.10; EX 146.00 Trifecta £5515.40.
Owner Tawny Port Ptners & Lovely Bubbly Racing **Bred** Mrs D O'Brien **Trained** Willoughton, Lincs

FOCUS
A warm nursery with all bar three previous winners. There was a disputed lead and the first five home started from the lowest five stalls, again suggesting that those drawn nearside were up against it. The winner is progressive and likeable.

6537 AL MAKTOUM COLLEGE, DUNDEE H'CAP 5f
3:05 (3:05) (Class 4) (0-85,85) 3-Y-O+ **£6,469** (£1,925; £962; £481) **Stalls** Centre

Form RPR
5600 **1** **Lincoln (IRE)**[13] 6109 5-9-7 **85** GrahamLee 11 96
(Mick Channon) *hld up midfield: rdn and hdwy over 1f out: led ins fnl f: kpt on strly* **11/1**
6020 **2** 1 ¾ **Classy Anne**[21] 5836 6-9-2 **80** (p) WilliamCarson 9 85
(Jim Goldie) *hld up in tch: rdn and hdwy to ld over 1f out: hdd ins fnl f: kpt on: nt pce of wnr* **28/1**
0500 **3** nse **Rita's Boy (IRE)**[17] 6012 4-8-11 **75** (v) JackGarritty 20 80
(K R Burke) *hld up midfield: rdn and effrt over 2f out: kpt on ins fnl f* **50/1**
1303 **4** hd **General Alexander (IRE)**[18] 5978 3-8-12 **77** (p) ChrisHayes 1 81
(Brian Ellison) *hld up far side: effrt and swtchd to far side of main centre gp 1/2-way: rdn and kpt on fnl f: nrst fin* **16/1**
6303 **5** nk **Vimy Ridge**[21] 5852 4-8-9 **73** (p) GrahamGibbons 15 76
(Alan Bailey) *dwlt: hld up: rdn along over 2f out: hdwy over 1f out: kpt on fnl f* **28/1**
6000 **6** ¾ **Arctic Feeling (IRE)**[17] 5991 8-9-2 **85** AdamMcNamara(5) 24 85+
(Richard Fahey) *dwlt: bhd: hdwy on nr side of centre gp over 1f out: kpt on strly fnl f: nrst fin* **12/1**
4443 **7** nse **Rural Celebration**[17] 6013 5-8-13 **77** DanielTudhope 17 77
(David O'Meara) *midfield: drvn and effrt over 2f out: kpt on same pce ins fnl f* **18/1**
3045 **7** dht **Pearl Acclaim (IRE)**[14] 6080 6-8-12 **76** (p) BarryMcHugh 2 76
(David Nicholls) *hld up in tch far side: swtchd to outside of far side gp over 2f out: rdn and one pce fnl f* **12/1**
1211 **9** ½ **Orient Class**[14] 6080 5-8-12 **83** CliffordLee(7) 5 81
(Paul Midgley) *chsd far side ldrs: rdn over 2f out: edgd rt to outside of centre gp over 1f out: kpt on same pce ins fnl f* **7/1**[2]
1442 **10** ¾ **Fumbo Jumbo (IRE)**[49] 4831 3-9-5 **84** ConnorBeasley 12 80
(Garry Moss) *prom: drvn along over 2f out: no ex ins fnl f* **12/1**
2000 **11** nk **Bogart**[70] 4112 7-9-7 **85** (p) TomEaves 8 80
(Kevin Ryan) *w ldr: rdn over 2f out: wknd ins fnl f* **20/1**
5315 **12** hd **Specialv (IRE)**[21] 5836 3-8-5 **75** (p) CallumShepherd(5) 10 69
(Brian Ellison) *bhd: rdn and effrt over 2f out: no imp fr over 1f out* **9/1**[3]
-021 **13** ½ **I'll Be Good**[6] 6324 7-9-3 **81** 6ex DaleSwift 7 73
(Brian Ellison) *gd spd far side: rdn over 2f out: no ex fr over 1f out* **13/2**[1]
5224 **14** nk **Geno (IRE)**[13] 6133 3-9-0 **79** (p) KevinStott 13 70
(Kevin Ryan) *prom: drvn along over 2f out: wknd fnl f* **18/1**
6502 **15** ½ **Bossipop**[18] 5978 3-9-1 **80** (b[1]) DavidAllan 23 69
(Tim Easterby) *hld up: rdn over 2f out: no imp fr over 1f out* **10/1**
6314 **16** ¾ **Ladweb**[41] 5153 6-9-5 **83** MichaelJMMurphy 6 69
(John Gallagher) *chsd far side ldr: drvn along over 2f out: no ex over 1f out* **12/1**
2006 **17** nk **Desert Ace (IRE)**[14] 6080 5-9-0 **78** (p) JoeFanning 19 63
(Iain Jardine) *led to over 1f out: sn rdn and wknd* **20/1**
2300 **18** hd **Dragon King (IRE)**[13] 6114 4-9-7 **85** (b[1]) PaulMulrennan 21 70
(Michael Dods) *chsd ldrs: rdn and edgd lft 2f out: wknd fnl f* **14/1**
0214 **19** ½ **Master Bond**[14] 6093 7-9-1 **79** JimCrowley 22 62
(David O'Meara) *hld up: rdn along over 2f out: nvr on terms* **33/1**
1206 **20** 1 ½ **Imperial Legend (IRE)**[70] 4100 7-8-12 **76** PaulQuinn 3 53
(David Nicholls) *dwlt: bhd far side: swtchd to main centre gp over 3f out: rdn over 2f out: nvr on terms* **50/1**
2300 **21** 3 ¾ **Giddy**[21] 5836 3-8-11 **76** TonyHamilton 16 40
(Richard Fahey) *hld up: rdn whn nt clr run briefly over 2f out: sn btn* **25/1**

1m 0.73s (1.33) **Going Correction** +0.425s/f (Yiel)
WFA 3 from 4yo+ 1lb **21** Ran SP% **134.2**
Speed ratings (Par 105): **106,103,103,102,102 101,101,101,100,99 98,98,97,96,96 94,94,94,93,90 84**
CSF £311.06 CT £14114.96 TOTE £14.80: £4.10, £7.40, £10.00, £4.50; EX 600.10 Trifecta £4260.00 Part won..
Owner Billy Parish **Bred** Tipper House Stud **Trained** West Ilsley, Berks

FOCUS
A competitive sprint handicap in which the main group came up the middle and the few who stuck closer to the far rail were at a disadvantage. The winner is rated close to this year's early best.

6538 SHADWELL STUD/EBF STALLIONS HARRY ROSEBERY STKS (LISTED RACE) 5f
3:40 (3:40) (Class 1) 2-Y-O
£28,355 (£10,750; £5,380; £2,680; £1,345; £675) **Stalls** Centre

Form RPR
2336 **1** **Clem Fandango (FR)**[29] 5584 2-8-12 92 PhillipMakin 4 100
(Keith Dalgleish) *trckd ldrs: led over 1f out: r.o strly: v readily* **11/4**[1]
16 **2** 3 ¾ **Angel Meadow**[83] 3663 2-8-12 78 PJMcDonald 3 86
(Micky Hammond) *in rr: hdwy over 2f out: chsd wnr fnl f: no imp* **40/1**
6136 **3** ½ **Smokey Lane (IRE)**[13] 6124 2-9-3 93 GrahamGibbons 9 90
(David Evans) *chsd ldrs: hung lft over 1f out: kpt on same pce last 100yds* **9/1**
1405 **4** 1 ¼ **Kocollada (IRE)**[18] 5977 2-8-12 87 GeorgeChaloner 11 80
(Richard Fahey) *chsd ldrs: drvn over 2f out: one pce over 1f out* **12/1**
1532 **5** hd **Coolfitch (IRE)**[6] 6343 2-8-12 74 SamJames 5 82+
(David O'Meara) *hld up in rr: hdwy over 2f out: nt clr run and swtchd over 1f out: kpt on same pce fnl f* **18/1**
2143 **6** ¾ **Whirl Me Round**[30] 5536 2-9-3 83 JoeDoyle 1 82
(Kevin Ryan) *chsd ldrs: drvn 2f out: one pce over 1f out* **9/1**
3212 **7** ¾ **Blue Suede (IRE)**[24] 5741 2-8-12 78 TomMarquand 2 74
(Richard Hannon) *led hdd over 1f out: sn wknd* **11/1**
2303 **8** 4 ½ **Savannah's Dream**[29] 5583 2-8-12 85 DanielTudhope 10 58
(David O'Meara) *rrd s: in rr: hdwy over 2f out: wknd appr fnl f* **13/2**[3]
2511 **9** hd **Northern Thunder (IRE)**[37] 5299 2-9-3 79 SeanLevey 8 62
(Richard Hannon) *chsd ldrs: wknd over 1f out* **14/1**
0132 **10** 5 **Private Matter**[18] 5977 2-9-3 96 TonyHamilton 6 44
(Richard Fahey) *trckd ldrs: drvn 2f out: edgd lft and sn lost pl: bhd whn eased clsng stages* **4/1**[2]
0304 **11** 8 **Just An Idea (IRE)**[32] 5497 2-9-3 88 JimCrowley 7 15
(Harry Dunlop) *in rr: sn pushed along: lost pl 2f out: bhd whn eased clsng stages* **16/1**

1m 0.72s (1.32) **Going Correction** +0.425s/f (Yiel) **11** Ran SP% **116.3**
Speed ratings (Par 103): **106,100,99,97,96 95,94,87,86,78 66**
CSF £121.36 TOTE £3.50: £1.30, £7.60, £3.20; EX 157.00 Trifecta £730.20.
Owner Middleham Park Racing LXXV **Bred** John Raw **Trained** Carluke, S Lanarks

FOCUS
This Listed contest was won by Quiet Reflection last year and this year's winner was impressive, though the poor run of the second-favourite dilutes the form to a degree. There wasn't a great deal of depth for the grade.

6539 WILLIAM HILL AYR BRONZE CUP H'CAP 6f
4:15 (4:17) (Class 2) 3-Y-O+
£18,675 (£5,592; £2,796; £1,398; £699; £351) **Stalls** Centre

Form RPR
4001 **1** **Classic Seniority**[7] 6280 4-9-4 **85** 5ex [1] DanielTudhope 5 95
(Marjorie Fife) *hld up on far side of gp: hdwy to ld over 1f out: drvn out fnl f* **20/1**
6050 **2** ½ **Fendale**[8] 6263 4-9-6 **87** [1] ConnorBeasley 7 95
(Michael Dods) *hld up: smooth hdwy over 1f out: effrt and chsd wnr ins fnl f: kpt on fin* **12/1**
3005 **3** 1 ¾ **Khelman (IRE)**[8] 6263 6-9-4 **85** GeorgeChaloner 8 87
(Richard Fahey) *bhd and sn rdn along: hdwy over 1f out: kpt on fnl f: nrst fin* **20/1**
3400 **4** nse **Duke Cosimo**[8] 6263 6-9-2 **83** (p) PJMcDonald 17 85+
(Michael Herrington) *hld up: rdn and hdwy over 1f out: kpt on ins fnl f: nt pce to chal* **10/1**
0150 **5** nk **Goring (GER)**[17] 5991 4-9-4 **85** TomMarquand 6 86
(Eve Johnson Houghton) *hld up: rdn and hdwy over 1f out: r.o ins fnl f* **25/1**
2003 **6** 1 ½ **Free Zone**[5] 6371 7-9-5 **86** (v) WilliamCarson 1 82
(Jamie Osborne) *chsd ldrs on far side of gp: effrt and ev ch over 1f out: edgd rt and no ex ins fnl f* **22/1**
2031 **7** shd **Ocean Sheridan (IRE)**[21] 5857 4-9-6 **87** 5ex PaulMulrennan 9 83
(Michael Dods) *hld up in tch: stdy hdwy whn nt clr run over 1f out: effrt whn hmpd twice ins fnl f: sn rdn and no imp* **11/2**[2]
1211 **8** 1 ½ **Giant Spark**[13] 6136 4-9-4 **85** 5ex JackGarritty 3 76
(Paul Midgley) *cl up: effrt and ev ch over 1f out: sn rdn: edgd rt and no ex ins fnl f* **7/2**[1]
0226 **9** 1 ¼ **Sir Billy Wright (IRE)**[6] 6320 5-8-11 **85** CliffordLee(7) 25 72
(David Evans) *hld up: hdwy on nr side of gp and chsng ldrs over 1f out: edgd lft and no ex ins fnl f* **20/1**
1110 **10** ½ **Courier**[7] 6276 4-9-0 **86** 5ex HollieDoyle(5) 10 72
(Marjorie Fife) *chsd ldrs: rdn over 2f out: wknd over 1f out* **28/1**
2100 **11** nk **Johnny Cavagin**[46] 4946 7-9-7 **88** (t) JimmyQuinn 11 73
(Ronald Thompson) *dwlt: hld up: stdy hdwy over 2f out: rdn and no imp over 1f out* **40/1**
1105 **12** ¾ **Anonymous Lady (IRE)**[33] 5441 4-9-5 **86** (t) ChrisHayes 24 68
(Adrian Paul Keatley, Ire) *hld up: hdwy on nr side of gp 2f out: edgd lft and no imp appr fnl f* **25/1**
2052 **13** 1 **Ballymore Castle (IRE)**[14] 6082 4-9-3 **84** PatrickMathers 21 63
(Richard Fahey) *hld up: n.m.r over 2f out: rdn whn n.m.r over 1f out: sn n.d* **14/1**
1035 **14** nk **Eastern Racer (IRE)**[54] 4689 4-9-3 **84** DaleSwift 18 62
(Brian Ellison) *prom: drvn along over 2f out: wknd over 1f out* **33/1**
1466 **15** nk **Escalating**[21] 5857 4-9-4 **85** (vt[1]) AndrewMullen 23 62
(Michael Appleby) *dwlt: bhd and sn pushed along: drvn on nr side of gp over 2f out: no imp over 1f out* **22/1**
5600 **16** hd **El Viento (FR)**[21] 5857 8-9-0 **86** (v) AdamMcNamara(5) 15 63
(Richard Fahey) *racd wout nr hind shoe: bhd and sn drvn along: nvr on terms* **33/1**
3040 **17** ¾ **Lexi's Hero (IRE)**[14] 6079 8-9-2 **83** (v) GrahamLee 14 57
(Richard Fahey) *cl up: drvn along 1/2-way: wknd over 1f out* **40/1**
0000 **18** 1 ½ **Magic City (IRE)**[21] 5857 7-8-11 **83** NathanEvans(5) 16 52
(Michael Easterby) *bhd: drvn along 1/2-way: btn over 1f out* **40/1**
5-00 **19** ½ **Twin Appeal (IRE)**[3] 6449 5-9-5 **86** (b) GrahamGibbons 13 54
(David Barron) *t.k.h: in tch: rdn over 2f out: wknd over 1f out* **18/1**
0341 **20** 1 ¾ **Dark Defender**[12] 6164 3-9-7 **90** 5ex (v) JimCrowley 4 52
(Keith Dalgleish) *chsd ldrs: ev ch briefly over 1f out: sn rdn: wknd fnl f* **8/1**[3]
0000 **21** 1 ¾ **Holiday Magic (IRE)**[8] 6263 5-9-5 **86** CamHardie 19 43
(Michael Easterby) *bhd and sn drvn along: nvr on terms* **66/1**
0200 **22** hd **Grandad's World (IRE)**[34] 5417 4-9-5 **86** TonyHamilton 20 42
(Richard Fahey) *prom: rdn over 2f out: wknd wl over 1f out* **28/1**
1000 **23** ¾ **Best Trip (IRE)**[27] 5641 9-9-6 **87** SamJames 2 41
(Marjorie Fife) *led tl rdn and hdd over 1f out: sn wknd* **28/1**
0550 **24** 1 ¼ **Englishman**[13] 6119 6-9-6 **87** JoeFanning 22 37
(Milton Bradley) *hld up on nr side of gp: effrt and rdn over 2f out: sn wknd: btn whn n.m.r ins fnl f* **25/1**

1m 14.1s (1.70) **Going Correction** +0.425s/f (Yiel)
WFA 3 from 4yo+ 2lb **24** Ran SP% **137.0**
Speed ratings (Par 109): **105,104,102,101,101 99,99,97,95,95 94,93,92,91,91 91,90,88,87,85 82,82,81,80**
CSF £213.95 CT £4883.49 TOTE £24.90: £4.80, £4.20, £7.30, £4.20; EX 394.80 Trifecta £4808.50 Part won..
Owner Stephen Woodall **Bred** E Cantillon, D Cantillon & A Driver **Trained** Stillington, N Yorks

FOCUS
A typically competitive renewal of this consolation event. The jockeys decided to spurn both rails this time and the field raced as one group up the centre. It was still an advantage to be drawn low, though. The first two were both wearing a new type of headgear for the first time. This rates a career best from the winner.

6540 BAM PROPERTIES LTD H'CAP 2m 1f 105y
4:50 (4:51) (Class 3) (0-95,90) 3-Y-O+ **£9,703** (£2,887; £1,443; £721) **Stalls** Low

Form RPR
1-14 **1** **Impulsive American**[51] 3149 4-9-0 **76** (b) JimCrowley 6 84
(David Pipe) *mid-div: trckd ldrs after 7f: upsides on bit over 2f out: led over 1f out: sn drvn: carried lft and regained ld last 50yds: drvn rt out* **5/2**[1]

0405 **2** *nk* **Mijhaar**[13] 6142 8-10-0 **90**.. DanielTudhope 2 97
(David O'Meara) *hld up in rr: smooth hdwy over 7f out: trcking ldrs over 2f out: hung lft and led narrowly last 150yds: hdd last 50yds* **8/1**

3120 **3** *½* **Always Resolute**[53] 4721 5-9-4 **80**.. ChrisHayes 3 86
(Brian Ellison) *trckd ldr: upsides after 7f: led 6f out: hdd over 1f out: crowded and kpt on same pce last 75yds* **11/2**[3]

/040 **4** *1 ½* **Great Fighter**[14] 6083 6-8-13 **75**.. WilliamCarson 9 79
(Jim Goldie) *mid-div: hdwy to chse ldrs 5f out: upsides over 2f out: one pce last 100yds* **33/1**

5130 **5** *½* **Gabrial's Star**[13] 6118 7-9-12 **88**..................................(b) GrahamLee 10 92
(Richard Fahey) *in rr: hdwy 6f out: lost pl 3f out: styd on wl fnl f: gng on at fin* **16/1**

0030 **6** *7* **Saved By The Bell (IRE)**[30] 5559 6-10-0 **90**.. SamJames 1 87
(David O'Meara) *trckd ldrs: lost pl 2f out* **18/1**

0-10 **7** *16* **Hidden Justice (IRE)**[83] 3680 7-9-13 **89**.. PhillipMakin 8 70
(John Quinn) *rr-div: hdwy 4f out: outpcd and lost pl 3f out: bhd whn eased clsng stages* **10/1**

3051 **8** *2 ½* **Rock On Bollinski**[21] 5856 6-8-12 **74**..................................(p) DavidAllan 7 52
(Brian Ellison) *in rr: drvn after 5f: chsng ldrs after 7f: 2nd 6f out: lost pl 3f out: bhd whn eased clsng stages* **4/1**[2]

5210 **9** *2 ¼* **Hillgrove Angel (IRE)**[21] 5837 4-9-0 **76**.. PJMcDonald 4 52
(Iain Jardine) *mid-div: lost pl 4f out: sn bhd: eased clsng stages* **9/1**

2213 **10** *48* **Stormin Tom (IRE)**[97] 3149 4-8-13 **78**.. RachelRichardson(3) 5 6
(Tim Easterby) *led: pushed along bnd after 5f: hdd 6f out: lost pl over 4f out: t.o 3f out: virtually p.u: eventually completed* **17/2**

4m 0.74s (5.74) **Going Correction** +0.225s/f (Good) **10** Ran SP% **118.8**
Speed ratings (Par 107): **95,94,94,93,93 90,82,81,80,58**
CSF £23.78 CT £103.51 TOTE £3.50: £1.40, £2.60, £2.30; EX 33.40 Trifecta £195.70.
Owner Mrs Jo Tracey **Bred** David Brocklehurst **Trained** Nicholashayne, Devon

FOCUS
Rail movement added approx 18yds to race distance. A decent staying handicap, but something of a stop-start pace and there were still four vying for the lead passing the furlong pole. The winner continues to progress.

6541 QTS GROUP H'CAP — 1m
5:20 (5:30) (Class 5) (0-70,71) 3-Y-O **£4,528** (£1,347; £673; £336) **Stalls** Low

Form RPR

4662 **1** **Sophie P**[23] 5782 3-9-5 **68**.. PJMcDonald 11 86
(R Mike Smith) *trckd ldrs: hdwy to ld over 2f out: sn rdn clr: unchal* **15/2**

-600 **2** *8* **Catastrophe**[30] 5540 3-9-2 **65**.. CamHardie 13 65
(John Quinn) *s.i.s: hld up: rdn and hdwy over 2f out: chsd (clr) wnr fnl f: kpt on: no imp* **16/1**

2541 **3** *½* **Reinforced**[20] 5887 3-8-11 **60**..................................(p) AndrewMullen 10 59
(Michael Dods) *led: rdn and hdd over 2f out: kpt on same pce fr over 1f out* **4/1**[1]

620 **4** *¾* **Strictly Art (IRE)**[46] 4942 3-8-13 **62**..................................(p) GrahamGibbons 7 59
(Alan Bailey) *prom: drvn along over 2f out: one pce fr over 1f out* **12/1**

6303 **5** *¾* **Primobella**[45] 4987 3-8-12 **61**.. JoeFanning 5 56
(Ed McMahon) *hld up: rdn and hdwy over 2f out: no imp fr over 1f out* **10/1**

156 **6** *2 ¼* **Maulesden May (IRE)**[93] 3285 3-9-6 **69**.. PhillipMakin 2 59
(Keith Dalgleish) *sn pushed into midfield: rdn along over 3f out: outpcd fr 2f out* **10/1**

4325 **7** *8* **Rosamaria (IRE)**[76] 3885 3-9-6 **69**.. PaulMulrennan 4 41
(Michael Dods) *hld up: drvn along and outpcd over 2f out: sn btn* **8/1**

5544 **8** *6* **Ronnie Baird**[18] 5975 3-9-6 **69**..................................(b) RobertHavlin 12 27
(Kristin Stubbs) *chsd ldr to over 3f out: rdn and wknd 2f out* **6/1**[3]

0503 **9** *1* **Firedanser**[30] 5539 3-9-6 **69**.. TonyHamilton 6 25
(Richard Fahey) *midfield: drvn along over 3f out: wknd over 2f out* **6/1**[3]

2532 **10** *5* **Al Hawraa**[23] 5757 3-9-5 **68**.. KevinStott 8 12
(Kevin Ryan) *hld up in tch: stdy hdwy over 3f out: rdn and wknd wl over 1f out* **11/2**[2]

1m 44.93s (1.13) **Going Correction** +0.225s/f (Good) **10** Ran SP% **118.6**
Speed ratings (Par 101): **103,95,94,93,93 90,82,76,75,70**
CSF £121.47 CT £441.54 TOTE £8.90: £2.90, £5.50, £1.90; EX 158.10 Trifecta £1373.80.
Owner Smith, Matheson, Stewart **Bred** New Hall Stud **Trained** Galston, E Ayrshire
■ Be Kool was withdrawn. Price at time of withdrawal 9-2. Rule 4 applies to bets placed prior to withdrawal but not to SP bets. Deduction 15p in the pound. New market formed.

FOCUS
Rail movement added approx 9yds to race distance. An ordinary handicap reduced by one when Be Kool, who was favourite at the time, was withdrawn after breaking from his stall and running loose. They came up the centre in the straight and the race ended up one-way traffic. The winner seems much improved.
T/Jkpt: Not won. T/Plt: £2,659.30 to a £1 stake. Pool: £115,262.93 - 31.64 winning tickets
T/Qpdt: £663.40 to a £1 stake. Pool: £8,248.13 - 9.20 winning tickets
Richard Young & Walter Glynn

5740 NEWBURY (L-H)
Friday, September 16

OFFICIAL GOING: Soft (heavy in places)
Wind: Moderate, against Weather: Sunny spells

6542 THATCHAM BUTCHERS EBF STALLIONS MAIDEN STKS (DIV I) (PLUS 10 RACE) — 6f 8y
1:40 (1:41) (Class 4) 2-Y-O **£5,175** (£1,540; £769; £384) **Stalls** Centre

Form RPR

1 **Musawaat** 2-9-5 0.. PaulHanagan 9 83+
(Charles Hills) *athletic: in tch: squeezed through and led over 1f out: edgd lft fnl f: hld on wl: rdn out* **6/1**

2 *hd* **Natajack** 2-9-5 0.. RichardKingscote 6 82+
(Tom Dascombe) *str: hld up: hdwy 2f out: str chal fnl f: carried lft: r.o wl* **14/1**

3 *3* **No Not Again (IRE)** 2-9-5 0.. PatDobbs 2 73
(Richard Hannon) *unf: prom: rdn 2f out: one pce appr fnl f* **12/1**

0 **4** *1* **Original Choice (IRE)**[21] 5848 2-9-5 0.. PatCosgrave 12 70
(William Haggas) *str: in tch: pushed along 3f out: styd on same pce* **2/1**[1]

5 *shd* **Trick Of The Light (IRE)** 2-9-5 0.. AndreaAtzeni 10 70
(Roger Varian) *str: bit bkwd: led tl over 1f out: no ex fnl f* **11/4**[2]

0 **6** *1 ½* **Mr Scaff (IRE)**[20] 5890 2-9-5 0.. MartinDwyer 11 66
(Paul Henderson) *tall: prom tl wknd wl over 1f out* **20/1**

7 *5* **Sonata** 2-9-0 0.. SilvestreDeSousa 3 46
(Mick Channon) *leggy: s.s: bhd: clsd on main gp and nt clr run over 2f out: sn wknd* **4/1**[3]

1m 16.35s (3.35) **Going Correction** +0.50s/f (Yiel) **7** Ran SP% **113.4**
Speed ratings (Par 97): **97,96,92,91,91 89,82**
CSF £78.86 TOTE £6.00: £2.90, £4.40; EX 50.70 Trifecta £299.70.
Owner Hamdan Al Maktoum **Bred** Lark Copse Ltd **Trained** Lambourn, Berks
■ Stewards' Enquiry : Paul Hanagan caution; careless riding

FOCUS
Horses were declared with the going good to firm, but following a deluge overnight (74mm) the meeting had to pass a morning inspection and the going has changed dramatically to soft, heavy in places. Inevitably there were stacks of non-runners. The rail was out 7yds from the 8f to 5f markers so all round course distances were 13yds longer than advertised. The first two came clear in this maiden.

6543 THATCHAM BUTCHERS EBF STALLIONS MAIDEN STKS (DIV II) (PLUS 10 RACE) — 6f 8y
2:10 (2:12) (Class 4) 2-Y-O **£5,175** (£1,540; £769; £384) **Stalls** Centre

Form RPR

1 **Executive Force** 2-9-5 0.. PatCosgrave 6 80+
(William Haggas) *str: lw: in tch: effrt 2f out: rdn to ld ins fnl f: sn clr* **2/1**[1]

2 *2 ¼* **Dark Power (IRE)** 2-9-5 0.. JohnFahy 12 73
(Clive Cox) *tall: chsd ldr: chal over 2f out: one pce fnl f* **16/1**

3 *¾* **Vigee Le Brun (IRE)** 2-9-0 0.. JimmyFortune 3 66+
(Brian Meehan) *neat: lw: stdd s: hld up in rr: rdn and r.o fnl 2f: nrest at fin* **20/1**

4 **4** *hd* **Dimitre**[37] 5304 2-9-5 0.. DaneO'Neill 4 70
(Henry Candy) *cmpt: led: rdn 2f out: hdd and one pce inisde fnl f* **5/2**[2]

024 **5** *2 ¾* **The Night Is Ours (IRE)**[87] 3507 2-8-11 0.......... JosephineGordon(3) 7 57
(J S Moore) *lw: t.k.h: trckd ldrs: rdn over 2f out: btn over 1f out* **25/1**

6 *nk* **Muscika** 2-9-5 0.. PaulHanagan 11 61
(Richard Hannon) *lengthy: str: towards rr: pushed along 3f out: nvr gng wl enough to chal* **8/1**

7 *nk* **Open Wide (USA)** 2-9-5 0.. PatDobbs 5 61
(Amanda Perrett) *tall: str: in tch tl outpcd 2f out: 6th and btn whn n.m.r over 1f out* **8/1**

50 **8** *2 ¾* **Joshlee (IRE)**[97] 3122 2-9-0 0.. ShaneKelly 9 47
(Richard Hughes) *w'like: stdd in rr s: rdn and n.d fnl 2f* **14/1**

00 **9** *8* **Orange Gin (IRE)**[7] 6295 2-9-5 0.. GeorgeBaker 1 28
(Roger Charlton) *str: t.k.h: prom tl wknd wl over 1f out* **7/1**[3]

1m 16.34s (3.34) **Going Correction** +0.50s/f (Yiel) **9** Ran SP% **117.8**
Speed ratings (Par 97): **97,94,93,92,89 88,88,84,73**
CSF £37.07 TOTE £3.00: £1.20, £3.30, £7.20; EX 22.80 Trifecta £1299.40.
Owner M J Jooste **Bred** Rabbah Bloodstock Limited **Trained** Newmarket, Suffolk

FOCUS
This was run in an almost identical time to the first division.

6544 DUBAI DUTY FREE FINEST SURPRISE H'CAP — 1m 4f 5y
2:45 (2:46) (Class 3) (0-95,94) 3-Y-O+ **£7,439** (£2,213; £1,106; £553) **Stalls** Centre

Form RPR

4605 **1** **Leah Freya (IRE)**[19] 5927 5-9-0 **82**.. SilvestreDeSousa 1 91
(Pat Phelan) *dwlt: hdwy to trck ldrs 1/2-way: led over 2f out: edgd lft ins fnl f: drvn out* **7/2**[3]

020- **2** *2 ½* **Not Never**[343] 7076 4-9-11 **93**.. RyanMoore 8 98
(Hugo Palmer) *lw: led after 2f tl over 2f out: kpt on u.p* **13/8**[1]

2010 **3** *nk* **Gawdawpalin (IRE)**[13] 6110 3-8-8 **84**.. OisinMurphy 9 89
(Sylvester Kirk) *chsd ldr after 2f tl over 2f out: styd on u.p* **2/1**[2]

005 **4** *9* **Silver Quay (IRE)**[41] 5145 4-9-5 **87**.. PatDobbs 2 78
(Richard Hannon) *s.s: hld up in 4th: dropped to last 1/2-way: rdn and n.d fnl 3f* **9/1**

0- **5** *2* **Barizan (IRE)**[496] 1551 10-8-12 **80** oh4.. FMBerry 12 68
(Brendan Powell) *bit bkwd: led for 2f: pushed along 1/2-way: in tch tl wknd over 3f out* **20/1**

2m 38.71s (3.21) **Going Correction** +0.50s/f (Yiel)
WFA 3 from 4yo+ 8lb **5** Ran SP% **108.4**
Speed ratings (Par 107): **109,107,107,101,99**
CSF £9.34 TOTE £4.90: £3.30, £1.40; EX 10.60 Trifecta £18.10.
Owner Edward Gleeson **Bred** Edward Gleeson **Trained** Epsom, Surrey

FOCUS
Race distance increased by 13yds. A host of non-runners, and only three mattered from over 3f out. The winner is rated to this year's form.

6545 DUBAI DUTY FREE H'CAP — 1m 4f 5y
3:20 (3:20) (Class 2) (0-110,102) 3-Y-O+ **£16,172** (£4,812; £2,405; £1,202) **Stalls** Centre

Form RPR

1-33 **1** **Southdown Lad (IRE)**[125] 2244 3-8-6 **90**.. SilvestreDeSousa 5 98+
(William Knight) *lw: stdd in detached last: hdwy over 2f out: led wl over 1f out: in control fnl f: rdn out* **4/1**[3]

5322 **2** *1 ¼* **Mainstream**[20] 5865 3-8-12 **96**.. RyanMoore 2 101
(Sir Michael Stoute) *t.k.h in 4th: rdn over 2f out: styd on to take 2nd ins fnl f* **3/1**[2]

3421 **3** *½* **New Caledonia (IRE)**[13] 6110 3-8-11 **95**.. WilliamBuick 3 99
(Mark Johnston) *trckd ldr: led over 3f out tl wl over 1f out: one pce* **9/2**

0401 **4** *1 ¼* **Cymro (IRE)**[15] 6057 4-9-12 **102**.. RichardKingscote 1 104
(Tom Dascombe) *handy 3rd tl outpcd and lost pl 2f out* **4/1**[3]

3-13 **5** *shd* **Who Dares Wins (IRE)**[35] 5381 4-9-4 **94**.. PatDobbs 6 96
(Alan King) *led tl over 3f out: wknd over 1f out* **11/4**[1]

2m 39.75s (4.25) **Going Correction** +0.50s/f (Yiel)
WFA 3 from 4yo+ 8lb **5** Ran SP% **109.8**
Speed ratings (Par 109): **105,104,103,103,102**
CSF £15.99 TOTE £5.10: £2.20, £1.70; EX 13.40 Trifecta £59.10.
Owner G Roddick **Bred** Barnane Stud **Trained** Patching, W Sussex

FOCUS
Race distance increased by 13yds. They went an ordinary pace here. There's more to come from the winner.

6546 HAYNES, HANSON & CLARK CONDITIONS STKS (PLUS 10 RACE) — 1m (S)
3:55 (3:56) (Class 2) 2-Y-O **£9,960** (£2,982; £1,491; £745) **Stalls** Centre

Form RPR

3 **1** **Temple Church (IRE)**[24] 5740 2-8-12 0.. JimmyFortune 3 92
(Hughie Morrison) *w'like: chsd ldr: led wl over 1f out: sn rdn clr: hld on wl nr fin* **11/2**

2 **2** *nk* **Raheen House (IRE)**[24] 5740 2-8-12 0.. RichardKingscote 8 91
(Brian Meehan) *str: gd-bodied: lw: in tch: rdn over 2f out: chsd wnr over 1f out: clsd fnl f: jst hld* **11/8**[1]

510 **3** *8* **Galactic Prince**[30] 5556 2-9-1 80 OisinMurphy 4 76
(Andrew Balding) *led tl wl over 1f out: wknd fnl f* **7/2**[3]

414 **4** *3/4* **Contrast (IRE)**[13] 6116 2-9-1 95 RyanMoore 6 75
(Richard Hannon) *str: chsd ldrs: rdn 3f out: wknd 2f out* **9/4**[2]

1m 43.5s (3.80) **Going Correction** +0.50s/f (Yiel) **4** Ran SP% **110.5**
Speed ratings (Par 101): **101,100,92,91**
CSF £13.76 TOTE £7.00; EX 15.30 Trifecta £36.70.

Owner P C J Dalby & R D Schuster **Bred** Airlie Stud **Trained** East Ilsley, Berks

FOCUS
They went steady early on but got racing plenty soon enough and the first two pulled well clear of the other pair.

6547 DUBAI DUTY FREE CUP STKS (LISTED RACE) 7f (S)
4:25 (4:26) (Class 1) 3-Y-O+

£20,982 (£7,955; £3,981; £1,983; £995; £499) **Stalls** Centre

Form RPR

6051 **1** **Aclaim (IRE)**[14] 6075 3-8-13 102 (t) JamieSpencer 12 108+
(Martyn Meade) *stdd s: hld up in rr: smooth hdwy to ld wl over 1f out: drvn clr* **4/1**[3]

1/0- **2** *1 3/4* **Fannaan (USA)**[517] 1492 4-9-2 98 PaulHanagan 1 105
(John Gosden) *lw: hld up in 6th: wnt prom 2f out: styd on same pce appr fnl f* **3/1**[2]

0002 **3** *nk* **Accession (IRE)**[41] 5174 7-9-2 98 MartinLane 5 104
(Charlie Fellowes) *in tch: outpcd 2f out: styd on fnl f* **8/1**

4025 **4** *1 1/4* **So Beloved**[19] 5926 6-9-2 112 JamesDoyle 4 101
(David O'Meara) *lw: pressed ldr: led over 2f out tl wl over 1f out: edgd rt: one pce* **5/2**[1]

0243 **5** *1* **Emell**[5] 6364 6-9-2 104 (b) KieranO'Neill 13 98
(Richard Hannon) *chsd ldrs: rdn over 2f out: one pce* **25/1**

0006 **6** *hd* **Dream Dubai**[28] 5613 3-8-13 105 OisinMurphy 2 97
(Sylvester Kirk) *prom: rdn 3f out: wknd over 1f out* **8/1**

0430 **7** *5* **Calder Prince (IRE)**[48] 4867 3-8-13 101 RichardKingscote 11 84
(Tom Dascombe) *led tl over 2f out: sn wknd* **12/1**

2400 **8** *11* **Volunteer Point (IRE)**[93] 3271 4-8-11 100 SilvestreDeSousa 9 51
(Mick Channon) *t.k.h in rr: hrd rdn and no ch fnl 2f* **8/1**

1m 27.17s (1.47) **Going Correction** +0.50s/f (Yiel)
WFA 3 from 4yo+ 3lb **8** Ran SP% **118.4**
Speed ratings (Par 111): **111,109,108,107,106 105,100,87**
CSF £17.13 TOTE £4.30: £1.50, £2.10, £2.30; EX 21.30 Trifecta £102.10.

Owner Canning Downs & Partner **Bred** D Farrington And Canning Downs **Trained** Newmarket, Suffolk

FOCUS
This looked fairly open on paper, but the winner did it well and looks progressive. The third is the key to the form.

6548 DUBAI DUTY FREE FULL OF SURPRISES EBF STALLIONS FILLIES' CONDITIONS STKS (PLUS 10 RACE) 7f (S)
5:00 (5:00) (Class 2) 2-Y-O **£9,960** (£2,982; £1,491; £745) **Stalls** Centre

Form RPR

1 **1** **Dabyah (IRE)**[69] 4147 2-9-1 0 FrankieDettori 6 95+
(John Gosden) *lw: mde all: shkn up and qcknd wl clr 1f out: easily* **1/2**[1]

0 **2** *9* **Shawami (IRE)**[118] 2467 2-8-12 0 SilvestreDeSousa 5 65
(Mick Channon) *athletic: in tch: effrt over 2f out: one pce: wnt modest 2nd ins fnl f* **8/1**[3]

3 *1* **Nancy Hart** 2-8-12 0 RichardKingscote 3 62
(Tom Dascombe) *w'like: chsd ldrs tl outpcd 2f out* **12/1**

1 **4** *1/2* **Desert Water (IRE)**[17] 5995 2-8-12 80 RyanMoore 1 61
(Richard Hannon) *trckd wnr: rdn 2f out: easily outpcd over 1f out: lost 2nd ins fnl f: fin lame* **7/2**[2]

1m 31.22s (5.52) **Going Correction** +0.50s/f (Yiel) **4** Ran SP% **107.7**
Speed ratings (Par 98): **88,77,76,76**
CSF £4.95 TOTE £1.40; EX 4.00 Trifecta £14.30.

Owner Abdullah Saeed Al Naboodah **Bred** Rabbah Bloodstock Limited **Trained** Newmarket, Suffolk

FOCUS
Curiously, of the four fillies who lined up for this conditions event three of them were sired by Sepoy. The winner outclassed the rest.

6549 BATHWICK TYRES H'CAP 1m 2f 6y
5:30 (5:33) (Class 4) (0-85,86) 3-Y-O+ **£4,690** (£1,395; £697; £348) **Stalls** Centre

Form RPR

10-1 **1** **Muraabit**[12] 6160 4-9-5 86 6ex CameronNoble(7) 4 95+
(Ismail Mohammed) *broke wl: stdd bk to 5th: hdwy and briefly nt clr run over 2f out: hung lft: r.o to ld nr fin* **11/4**[1]

6651 **2** *1/2* **Lime And Lemon (IRE)**[76] 3878 3-8-5 71 RyanTate 9 79
(Clive Cox) *sn trcking ldr: led over 3f out: hrd rdn fnl f: hdd nr fin* **9/2**[3]

0006 **3** *7* **Pasaka Boy**[18] 5963 6-9-6 80 (p) RichardKingscote 19 75
(Jonathan Portman) *chsd ldrs: hrd rdn over 2f out: one pce* **6/1**

-030 **4** *1* **Persun**[18] 5956 4-9-9 83 SilvestreDeSousa 2 76
(Mick Channon) *hld up in rr: hdwy and n.m.r 3f out: outpcd fnl 2f* **7/2**[2]

3151 **5** *1/2* **Pink Ribbon (IRE)**[19] 5925 4-8-11 71 (p) OisinMurphy 1 63
(Sylvester Kirk) *prom: rdn 4f out: wknd over 2f out* **16/1**

3013 **6** *1 3/4* **Jimenez (IRE)**[28] 5603 3-9-4 84 (p) JimmyFortune 5 73
(Brian Meehan) *sn led: hdd over 3f out: wknd 2f out* **6/1**

333 **7** *3/4* **Ardamir (FR)**[24] 5742 4-9-6 80 WilliamTwiston-Davies 15 67
(Alan King) *stdd s: hld up in 6th: rdn and n.d fnl 2f* **6/1**

2m 11.84s (3.04) **Going Correction** +0.50s/f (Yiel)
WFA 3 from 4yo+ 6lb **7** Ran SP% **115.8**
Speed ratings (Par 105): **107,106,101,100,99 98,97**
CSF £15.85 CT £68.08 TOTE £3.30: £1.90, £2.90; EX 13.70 Trifecta £73.90.

Owner Saeed H Al Tayer **Bred** Highclere Stud **Trained** Newmarket, Suffolk

FOCUS
Race distance increased by 13yds. The first two finished well clear and look nicely ahead of their marks. The winner backed up his York reappearance win.

T/Plt: £824.20 to a £1 stake. Pool: £85,674.99 - 75.88 winning tickets T/Qpdt: £50.40 to a £1 stake. Pool: £5,275.07 - 77.38 winning tickets **Lee McKenzie**

6550 - 6553a (Foreign Racing) - See Raceform Interactive

6534 AYR (L-H)
Saturday, September 17

OFFICIAL GOING: Good to soft (overall 7.8; straight average 7.6; sprint track: far side 7.8; centre 7.5; stands' side 7.6)
Wind: Light, half against Weather: Dry with sunny spells

6554 QTS/BRITISH STALLION STUDS EBF NURSERY H'CAP 1m
1:25 (1:25) (Class 2) 2-Y-O

£12,450 (£3,728; £1,864; £932; £466; £234) **Stalls** Low

Form RPR

21 **1** **Now Children (IRE)**[22] 5834 2-9-7 85 TomEaves 8 89+
(Iain Jardine) *t.k.h early: hld up: hdwy over 2f out: rdn and outpcd over 1f out: rallied u.p and led wl ins fnl f: kpt on wl* **4/1**[2]

21 **2** *1/2* **Euro Nightmare (IRE)**[10] 6223 2-8-12 76 GrahamGibbons 11 79
(Keith Dalgleish) *pressed ldr: rdn over 2f out: led over 1f out: edgd lft and hdd wl ins fnl f: kpt on* **10/1**

1 **3** *1/2* **Whatsthemessage (IRE)**[40] 5221 2-8-12 76 PhillipMakin 1 78
(Keith Dalgleish) *t.k.h: trckd ldrs: effrt and rdn 2f out: kpt on ins fnl f: hld towards fin* **8/1**

441 **4** *1/2* **Our Boy (IRE)**[22] 5820 2-8-13 77 DanielTudhope 5 78
(David Evans) *t.k.h early: led: rdn and hdd over 1f out: rallied: no ex wl ins fnl f* **7/1**[3]

421 **5** *nse* **Davy's Dilemma**[21] 5885 2-9-0 78 PaulMulrennan 9 79
(Michael Dods) *t.k.h: settled rr: rdn and hdwy 2f out: kpt on fnl f: nt pce to chal* **10/1**

0031 **6** *1/2* **Melesina (IRE)**[53] 4728 2-9-2 80 TonyHamilton 6 82
(Richard Fahey) *t.k.h: hld up towards rr: effrt whn nt clr run over 2f out: rdn and hdwy over 1f out: kpt on fnl f: no imp* **20/1**

412 **7** *5* **Temerity (IRE)**[19] 5967 2-9-2 85 AdamMcNamara(5) 10 73
(Richard Fahey) *fly-jmpd s: hld up: rdn and effrt over 2f out: hung lft and wknd over 1f out* **7/1**[3]

531 **8** *shd* **Third Order (IRE)**[20] 5916 2-8-11 75 DougieCostello 3 63
(K R Burke) *dwlt: sn midfield on ins: rdn over 2f out: wknd wl over 1f out* **7/2**[1]

613 **9** *4* **George Reme (IRE)**[19] 5967 2-9-1 79 JackGarritty 4 58
(John Quinn) *hld up in tch: rdn along over 2f out: wknd wl over 1f out* **11/1**

3444 **10** *1 1/2* **Jamacho**[22] 5833 2-8-8 72 ChrisHayes 2 47
(Brian Ellison) *t.k.h: prom: drvn along over 2f out: wknd wl over 1f out* **16/1**

051 **11** *2* **Anythingknappen (IRE)**[22] 5854 2-8-7 71 AndrewMullen 7 42
(Tim Easterby) *s.i.s: hld up: drvn and struggling over 2f out: sn btn* **33/1**

1m 44.36s (0.56) **Going Correction** +0.075s/f (Good) **11** Ran SP% **118.4**
Speed ratings (Par 101): **100,99,99,98,98 97,92,92,88,87 85**
CSF £44.26 CT £314.42 TOTE £5.40: £2.40, £2.60, £3.00; EX 28.80 Trifecta £232.90.

Owner Paul & Clare Rooney **Bred** Old Carhue & Graeng Bloodstock **Trained** Carruthterstown, D'fries & G'way

■ Stewards' Enquiry : Graham Gibbons caution: careless riding

FOCUS
It was dry overnight and the going was given as good to soft (GoingStick: Overall: 7.8; Straight Average: 7.0; Sprint Track: FS: 6.7; C: 7.4; SS: 6.7). After riding in the opener Philip Makin said: "The ground is a little bit better than yesterday" but Tom Eaves said: "It is still tacky." The rail was out 7yds on the home bend, adding approximately 21yds to distances between 7f and 1m2f, and 30yds to the 1m5f race. The stands' rail was out 3yds. A competitive nursery, with all but one of the 11 runners already successful. The early gallop wasn't that strong.

6555 WILLIAM HILL FIRTH OF CLYDE STKS (GROUP 3) (FOR THE AYRHIRE AGRICULTURAL CHALLENGE CUP) 6f
2:00 (2:00) (Class 1) 2-Y-O

£36,861 (£13,975; £6,994; £3,484; £1,748; £877) **Stalls** Centre

Form RPR

1 **1** **Delectation**[39] 5272 2-9-0 0 PaulMulrennan 13 106+
(Bryan Smart) *s.i.s: hld up in rr: swtchd lft towards far side 3f out: pushed along and gd hdwy 2f out: led ent fnl f: rdn and kpt on wl to draw clr* **11/1**

1621 **2** *2 3/4* **Rosebride**[23] 5794 2-9-0 85 TonyHamilton 6 98
(Richard Fahey) *in tch: rdn over 2f out: edgd lft over 1f out: kpt on: wnt 2nd 110yds out: no ch w wnr* **12/1**

106 **3** *1 1/4* **Belle Meade (IRE)**[21] 5870 2-9-0 92 JackGarritty 7 94
(Richard Fahey) *trckd ldrs: rdn over 2f out: outpcd and lost pl 2f out: sltl impeded and swtchd rt ent fnl f: styd on wl: wnt 3rd post* **20/1**

45 **4** *1/2* **Drumfad Bay (IRE)**[27] 5686 2-9-0 0 ColmO'Donoghue 2 93
(Mrs John Harrington, Ire) *dwlt: hld up: rdn and hdwy over 2f out: led over 1f out: hdd ent fnl f: no ex fnl 110yds* **7/1**[3]

011 **5** *1 3/4* **Partitia**[28] 5638 2-9-0 89 PatSmullen 3 88
(Sir Michael Stoute) *in tch: pushed along and hdwy over 2f out: rdn to chal over 1f out: hung lft and wknd ins fnl f* **4/1**[2]

32 **6** *nse* **Connacht Girl (IRE)**[26] 5727 2-9-0 0 DougieCostello 1 87
(K R Burke) *midfield: rdn over 2f out: one pce and nvr threatened* **33/1**

0214 **7** *nk* **Queensbrydge**[14] 6124 2-9-0 88 HarryBentley 4 86
(Robyn Brisland) *midfield: rdn and outpcd over 2f out: sltly impeded ent fnl f: one pce* **25/1**

1155 **8** *nk* **Erica Bing**[34] 5450 2-9-0 92 DavidAllan 9 86
(Jo Hughes) *led: rdn over 2f out: hdd over 1f out: sn wknd* **40/1**

204 **9** *2 1/4* **Swish (IRE)**[20] 5940 2-9-0 0 DanielTudhope 8 79
(John James Feane, Ire) *midfield: rdn over 2f out: wknd over 1f out* **12/1**

126 **10** *1 1/4* **Bletchley**[71] 4106 2-9-0 103 FMBerry 5 75+
(Ralph Beckett) *dwlt: hld up in midfield: rdn over 2f out: wknd over 1f out* **5/2**[1]

2310 **11** *4* **Stormy Clouds (IRE)**[9] 6260 2-9-0 94 (b) SeanLevey 10 63+
(Richard Hannon) *prom: rdn over 2f out: wknd over 1f out* **8/1**

4241 **12** *2 1/4* **Shamsaya (IRE)**[8] 6292 2-9-0 90 RobertHavlin 12 56+
(Simon Crisford) *trckd ldrs: rdn over 2f out: sn wknd* **9/1**

1m 14.27s (1.87) **Going Correction** +0.45s/f (Yiel) **12** Ran SP% **119.9**
Speed ratings (Par 105): **105,101,99,99,96 96,96,95,92,91 85,82**
CSF £131.27 TOTE £14.50: £4.00, £3.90, £5.30; EX 123.80 Trifecta £3177.70.

Owner Jamie Lovett **Bred** Crossfields Bloodstock Ltd **Trained** Hambleton, N Yorks

FOCUS
Not a strong Group 3, but there can be no knocking the unbeaten winner. The third and those in behind suggest the form is at least this good.

6556 WILLIAM HILL AYR SILVER CUP H'CAP 6f
2:35 (2:37) (Class 2) 3-Y-O+

£31,125 (£9,320; £4,660; £2,330; £1,165; £585) **Stalls** Centre

Form RPR

0001 **1** **Roudee**[35] 5417 4-9-9 **97**.............................. RichardKingscote 8 107
(Tom Dascombe) *chsd ldrs: rdn along 2f out: led ins fnl f: edgd lft: kpt on strly* **20/1**

6133 **2** ½ **Get Knotted (IRE)**[8] 6287 4-9-8 **96**..............(p) PaulMulrennan 9 104
(Michael Dods) *prom: rdn and hdwy over 1f out: disp ld ins fnl f: kpt on: hld nr fin* **17/2**[2]

3044 **3** hd **Nuno Tristan (USA)**[8] 6287 4-9-6 **94**.............................. JackGarritty 12 101
(Richard Fahey) *hld up: rdn and hdwy over 1f out: swtchd lft and kpt on fnl f* **12/1**[3]

0364 **4** 1 **Eccleston**[22] 5857 5-9-3 **91**..............................(v) GrahamLee 5 95
(David O'Meara) *hld up: rdn and hdwy over 1f out: kpt on ins fnl f* **14/1**

0006 **5** nse **Hoofalong**[7] 6327 6-9-4 **97**..............................(b) NathanEvans(5) 15 101
(Michael Easterby) *blindfold slow to removed and missed break: hdwy into midfield after 2f: effrt and chsd ldrs over 1f out: kpt on same pce ins fnl f* **25/1**

0000 **6** hd **Ninjago**[31] 5555 6-9-4 **92**.............................. RobertWinston 17 95
(Paul Midgley) *hld up: nt clr run over 2f out: rdn and hdwy over 1f out: kpt on fnl f: nvr able to chal* **16/1**

4630 **7** hd **My Name Is Rio (IRE)**[22] 5857 6-9-2 **90**.............................. SeanLevey 6 93
(Michael Dods) *chsd ldrs: rdn and ev ch over 1f out to ins fnl f: one pce* **50/1**

-430 **8** nk **An Saighdiur (IRE)**[20] 5941 9-9-10 **98**..............................(b) WJLee 2 100
(Andrew Slattery, Ire) *led: rdn 2f out: hdd ins fnl f: sn btn* **22/1**

0322 **9** hd **Flying Pursuit**[13] 6164 3-9-1 **91**..............................(b[1]) DavidAllan 22 92+
(Tim Easterby) *swtchd to r on nr side of main gp after 1f: hld up: rdn over 2f out: hdwy fnl f: kpt on: nrst fin* **16/1**

3652 **10** ¾ **Intense Style (IRE)**[9] 6263 4-9-3 **91**..............................(b) RobertHavlin 21 90
(Les Eyre) *swtchd lft to r on nr side of main gp over 4f out: hld up: rdn over 2f out: hdwy over 1f out: no imp fnl f* **22/1**

1222 **11** ½ **Intisaab**[6] 6382 5-9-8 **96**..............................(p) DanielTudhope 13 98+
(David O'Meara) *hld up: nt clr run over 2f out: rdn over 1f out: nvr able to chal* **5/1**[1]

2164 **12** nk **Muntadab (IRE)**[8] 6276 4-9-5 **93**.............................. PJMcDonald 20 89
(David Loughnane) *led stands' side quartet: rdn along over 2f out: kpt on fnl f: no ch w main far side gp* **25/1**

5201 **13** 1 **Stamp Hill (IRE)**[10] 6232 3-9-0 **95** 5ex.............. AdamMcNamara(5) 19 88
(Richard Fahey) *in tch on outside of stands' side gp: rdn over 2f out: no ex over 1f out* **20/1**

0000 **14** ¾ **Blaine**[22] 5857 6-9-7 **95**.............................. BarryMcHugh 18 86
(David Nicholls) *hld up: drvn along over 2f out: wknd over 1f out* **40/1**

0000 **15** ½ **George Bowen (IRE)**[6] 6382 4-9-5 **93**..............................(b) TonyHamilton 16 82
(Richard Fahey) *prom: rdn over 2f out: wknd over 1f out* **14/1**

6246 **16** ¾ **Shipyard (USA)**[9] 6263 7-9-1 **89**..............................(v[1]) AndrewMullen 4 76
(Michael Appleby) *missed break: bhd: rdn over 2f out: nvr able to chal* **14/1**

3500 **17** shd **Lexington Abbey**[7] 6327 5-9-6 **94**.............................. PatSmullen 7 80
(Kevin Ryan) *hld up midfield: effrt whn nt clr run over 2f out: lost pl over 1f out* **14/1**

3505 **18** 2 **Avon Breeze**[18] 6012 7-8-13 **90**..............................(p) RobHornby(3) 10 70
(Richard Whitaker) *bhd: rdn over 2f out: nvr on terms* **40/1**

3512 **19** shd **Reputation (IRE)**[22] 5852 3-9-1 **91**..............................(v) TomEaves 3 71
(John Quinn) *midfield: rdn along over 2f out: wknd over 1f out* **16/1**

2510 **20** ½ **Ice Lord (IRE)**[84] 3671 4-9-3 **91**.............................. JohnFahy 1 69
(Clive Cox) *hld up in tch: rdn over 2f out: wknd over 1f out* **25/1**

0001 **21** 3¾ **Handsome Dude**[9] 6263 4-9-1 **89** 5ex..............(b) GrahamGibbons 14 55
(David Barron) *chsd ldrs untiil rdn and wknd over 1f out* **25/1**

0000 **22** 2 **Louis The Pious**[14] 6112 8-8-9 **96**..............................(v) ColmO'Donoghue 11 56
(David O'Meara) *in tch: rdn over 2f out: wknd over 1f out* **20/1**

0-50 **23** 3¼ **Kickboxer (IRE)**[84] 3671 5-9-9 **97**..............................(p) HarryBentley 23 46
(Saeed bin Suroor) *chsd stands' side ldr: rdn over 2f out: sn outpcd* **20/1**

3030 **24** 29 **Mujassam**[35] 5418 4-9-6 **94**..............................(v) PhillipMakin 24
(David O'Meara) *chsd stands' side ldrs tl rdn and wknd over 2f out: t.o* **66/1**

0025 **25** 19 **Intibaah**[148] 1618 6-9-6 **94**.............................. FMBerry 25
(George Baker) *bhd stands' side: struggling over 2f out: sn wknd: t.o* **50/1**

1m 13.63s (1.23) **Going Correction** +0.45s/f (Yiel)
WFA 3 from 4yo+ 2lb **25** Ran SP% **132.6**
Speed ratings (Par 109): **109,108,108,106,106 106,106,105,105,104 103,103,102,101,100 99,99,96,96,95 90,88,83,45,19**
CSF £154.60 CT £2185.63 TOTE £20.30: £5.30, £2.90, £3.00, £3.90; EX 213.50 Trifecta £2658.90.
Owner Edwards Hughes Jenkins Roberts & Partner **Bred** Miss D Fleming **Trained** Malpas, Cheshire

FOCUS
A good quality big-field sprint handicap. They went a strong gallop, focused towards the far side rail, and five of the first eight home were drawn lower than ten, including the first, second and fourth. Sound and straightforward form, with the runner-up to a small pb and the third pretty much to form.

6557 WILLIAM HILL SUPPORTS CLIC SARGENT AYRSHIRE H'CAP 1m
3:10 (3:11) (Class 2) (0-105,101) 3-Y-O+

£15,562 (£4,660; £2,330; £1,165; £582; £292) **Stalls** Low

Form RPR

411 **1** **Morando (FR)**[98] 3130 3-9-3 **96**.............................. HarryBentley 5 109+
(Roger Varian) *in tch: pushed along and hdwy over 2f out: rdn to ld ins fnl f: kpt on wl: eased towards fin* **3/1**[1]

0201 **2** 2¼ **Haley Bop (IRE)**[7] 6320 3-9-0 **93**.............................. RichardKingscote 1 100
(Mark Johnston) *chsd clr ldr: pushed along over 2f out: led over 1f out: sn rdn: hdd ins fnl f: one pce and no ch wnr* **9/1**

3004 **3** shd **Fort Bastion (IRE)**[20] 5915 7-9-1 **90**.............................. DanielTudhope 11 97
(David O'Meara) *midfield: pushed along and hdwy over 2f out: rdn to chse ldr over 1f out: kpt on* **20/1**

-110 **4** ¾ **Garcia**[93] 3299 3-8-11 **95**.............................. AdamMcNamara(5) 10 100
(Richard Fahey) *midfield: rdn over 2f out: styd on fnl f* **10/3**[2]

1025 **5** ½ **Le Chat D'Or**[10] 6225 8-8-13 **88**..............................(bt) PaulMulrennan 14 92
(Michael Dods) *hld up in rr: pushed and stl plenty to do over 2f out: sme hdwy over 1f out: swtchd lft ent fnl f: kpt on* **22/1**

0034 **6** ½ **One Word More (IRE)**[7] 6331 6-9-9 **98**.............................. DavidAllan 9 101
(Tim Easterby) *hld up: rdn over 2f out: kpt on ins fnl f: nvr threatened* **8/1**[3]

3235 **7** ½ **Highland Colori (IRE)**[19] 5956 8-9-5 **97**..............................(v) RobHornby(3) 8 99
(Andrew Balding) *chsd ldrs: rdn over 2f out: sn one pce* **16/1**

0015 **8** shd **Another Touch**[29] 5616 3-9-2 **95**.............................. TonyHamilton 12 96
(Richard Fahey) *in tch: towards outer: rdn over 2f out: sn one pce* **11/1**

01P0 **9** 3¾ **Edgar Balthazar**[10] 6225 4-8-12 **87**..............................(p) PhillipMakin 7 80
(Keith Dalgleish) *hld up: rdn over 2f out: nvr threatened* **25/1**

0226 **10** ¾ **Bahaarah (IRE)**[42] 5175 3-9-5 **98**.............................. SeanLevey 6 89
(Richard Hannon) *hld up in midfield: rdn over 2f out: nvr threatened* **25/1**

2203 **11** nk **Two For Two (IRE)**[19] 5976 8-9-4 **93**..............................(p) PJMcDonald 2 83
(David Loughnane) *midfield towards inner: rdn 3f out: wknd over 1f out* **8/1**[3]

4600 **12** ¾ **Mohab**[28] 5651 3-9-0 **93**..............................(b[1]) TomEaves 4 82
(Kevin Ryan) *led: sn 5 l clr: rdn and reduced advantage over 1f out: wknd* **22/1**

0000 **13** 1¾ **Al Khan (IRE)**[28] 5640 7-8-13 **88**.............................. PatSmullen 13 73
(Kevin Ryan) *hld up in rr: a bhd* **33/1**

4620 **14** 4 **Sound Advice**[28] 5640 7-9-12 **101**.............................. RobertWinston 3 76
(Keith Dalgleish) *in tch: rdn 3f out: wknd over 1f out: eased fnl 110yds* **20/1**

1m 42.05s (-1.75) **Going Correction** +0.075s/f (Good)
WFA 3 from 4yo+ 4lb **14** Ran SP% **123.4**
Speed ratings (Par 109): **111,108,108,107,107 106,106,106,102,101 101,100,99,95**
CSF £27.65 CT £489.60 TOTE £3.90: £1.60, £3.10, £6.70; EX 30.20 Trifecta £605.90.
Owner H H Sheikh Mohammed Bin Khalifa Al Thani **Bred** Guy Pariente Holding Sprl **Trained** Newmarket, Suffolk

FOCUS
Race distance increased by 21yds. The early pace was steady but soon increased when the first-time blinkered Mohab shot clear. The form is set around the third and fifth, who have been rated close to their July C&D form.

6558 WILLIAM HILL AYR GOLD CUP (HERITAGE H'CAP) 6f
3:45 (3:48) (Class 2) 3-Y-O+

£124,500 (£37,280; £18,640; £9,320; £4,660; £2,340) **Stalls** Centre

Form RPR

2120 **1** **Brando**[29] 5614 4-9-10 **110**.............................. TomEaves 8 119
(Kevin Ryan) *hld up: hdwy far side of gp over 1f out: led ins fnl f: rdn and edgd rt: kpt on strly* **11/1**

1144 **2** 1¼ **Growl**[49] 4865 4-9-1 **101**.............................. GrahamLee 6 106
(Richard Fahey) *hld up in tch: hdwy and rdn over 1f out: pressed wnr ins fnl f: kpt on fin* **4/1**[1]

0121 **3** ¾ **Hoof It**[49] 4862 9-8-8 **99**.............................. NathanEvans(5) 7 102
(Michael Easterby) *chsd ldrs: rdn and ev ch over 1f out: led briefly ins fnl f: kpt on same pce towards fin* **16/1**

-560 **4** ¾ **G Force (IRE)**[14] 6145 5-9-2 **102**.............................. ChrisHayes 11 102
(Adrian Paul Keatley, Ire) *hld up midfield: rdn over 2f out: hdwy over 1f out: edgd rt and kpt on ins fnl f* **10/1**[3]

2100 **5** ¾ **Kimberella**[35] 5418 6-9-5 **105**.............................. DavidAllan 10 103
(David Nicholls) *trckd ldrs: effrt and drvn along over 2f out: no ex ins fnl f* **25/1**

1-54 **6** nk **Absolutely So (IRE)**[91] 3386 6-9-7 **110**.............................. RobHornby(3) 14 107
(Andrew Balding) *midfield: hdwy to chse ldrs over 1f out: drvn and kpt on ins fnl f* **10/1**[3]

3011 **7** hd **Nameitwhatyoulike**[13] 6161 7-9-1 **106** 5ex........... AdamMcNamara(5) 4 102
(Bryan Smart) *led: rdn 2f out: hdd ins fnl f: kpt on same pce* **8/1**[2]

-400 **8** ½ **Johnny Barnes (IRE)**[84] 3672 4-9-5 **105**.............................. RobertHavlin 18 100+
(John Gosden) *hld up: hdwy whn n.m.r briefly over 1f out and n.m.r briefly ent fnl f: no imp* **25/1**

504 **9** 1 **Aeolus**[63] 4393 5-9-2 **107**.............................. HectorCrouch(5) 19 98+
(Ed Walker) *hld up: rdn over 2f out: hdwy over 1f out: kpt on fnl f: nt pce to chal* **25/1**

0310 **10** 2½ **Perfect Pasture**[35] 5418 6-9-9 **109**..............................(v) GrahamGibbons 9 92
(Michael Easterby) *dwlt: bhd: drvn over 2f out: hdwy over 1f out: no imp* **50/1**

2303 **11** nk **Sir Robert Cheval**[14] 6112 5-8-12 **98**.............................. TonyHamilton 2 80
(Robert Cowell) *chsd ldrs: rdn and ev ch over 1f out: wknd ins fnl f* **33/1**

0040 **12** hd **Jack Dexter**[56] 4625 7-9-1 **101**.............................. FMBerry 5 83
(Jim Goldie) *in tch: rdn over 2f out: rallied over 1f out: wknd ins fnl f* **10/1**[3]

3304 **13** 2¼ **Watchable**[20] 5943 6-9-8 **108**..............................(v) DanielTudhope 3 83
(David O'Meara) *prom: rdn along over 2f out: wknd fnl f* **18/1**

0060 **14** hd **Rivellino**[21] 5871 6-9-0 **100**.............................. DougieCostello 15 74
(K R Burke) *dwlt: hld up: drvn along over 2f out: sme hdwy over 1f out: nvr rchd ldrs* **33/1**

1120 **15** ½ **Orion's Bow**[35] 5418 5-9-6 **106**.............................. BarryMcHugh 13 78
(David Nicholls) *in tch: rdn along over 2f out: wknd ins fnl f* **12/1**

0111 **16** 1¼ **Hillbilly Boy (IRE)**[48] 4916 6-9-6 **106**.............................. RichardKingscote 24 74+
(Tom Dascombe) *in tch: rdn over 2f out: wknd over 1f out* **20/1**

520- **17** ½ **Ascription (IRE)**[344] 7074 7-9-8 **108**..............................[1] PhillipMakin 1 75
(Keith Dalgleish) *missed break: bhd: rdn along over 2f out: n.d* **33/1**

3003 **18** 1 **Poyle Vinnie**[28] 5641 6-8-13 **99**.............................. AndrewMullen 23 63+
(Michael Appleby) *rrd s and slowly away: bhd: effrt whn n.m.r over 2f out: nvr on terms* **25/1**

5-20 **19** 1¾ **Flaming Spear (IRE)**[129] 2158 4-8-13 **99**.............................. RobertWinston 12 57
(Kevin Ryan) *reluctant to enter stalls: bhd: drvn along over 2f out: sn btn* **20/1**

0550 **20** ½ **Baraweez (IRE)**[31] 5555 6-9-2 **102**.............................. DaleSwift 25 58+
(Brian Ellison) *towards rr: rdn along and struggling over 2f out: sn btn* **33/1**

6144 **21** ¾ **Lulu The Zulu (IRE)**[16] 6056 8-8-13 **99**.............................. KevinStott 22 53+
(Michael Appleby) *bhd: drvn over 2f out: sn wknd* **40/1**

3310 **22** 3¾ **Glen Moss (IRE)**[29] 5613 7-9-4 **104**.............................. PaulMulrennan 17 46+
(Michael Dods) *hld up: rdn over 2f out: sn no imp: btn over 1f out* **33/1**

0-10 **23** 22 **Teruntum Star (FR)**[139] 1887 4-9-0 **100**.............................. PatSmullen 16 +
(Kevin Ryan) *midfield: struggling over 2f out: sn btn: eased over 1f out* **20/1**

1m 13.12s (0.72) **Going Correction** +0.45s/f (Yiel) **23** Ran SP% **134.3**
Speed ratings (Par 109): **113,111,110,109,108 107,107,107,105,102 101,101,98,98,97 96,95,94,91,91 90,85,55**
CSF £47.18 CT £752.09 TOTE £13.10: £2.90, £1.90, £4.00, £3.20; EX 74.00 Trifecta £1316.90.
Owner Mrs Angie Bailey **Bred** Car Colston Hall Stud **Trained** Hambleton, N Yorks

FOCUS
Following the pattern for previous races at the meeting, the main action developed centre to far side, and six of the first seven home were drawn between stalls 4 and 11. Another soild effort from the runner-up, with the third rated close to his Goodwood win.

6559 WILLIAM HILL DOWNLOAD THE APP H'CAP (REGISTERED AS THE KILKERRAN CUP) 1m 2f

4:20 (4:20) (Class 2) (0-100,98) 3-Y-O+

£15,562 (£4,660; £2,330; £1,165; £582; £292) **Stalls** Low

Form | | | | RPR
2605 **1** **Snoano**[16] 6057 4-9-4 **92** DavidAllan 11 101
(Tim Easterby) *hld up in midfield: pushed along and gd hdwy over 2f out: rdn to ld ent fnl f: kpt on* **13/2**[3]
1406 **2** ¾ **Arrowzone**[20] 5933 5-8-12 **86** (b[1]) ChrisHayes 13 94
(Ivan Furtado) *midfield towards outer: rdn over 2f out: hdwy over 1f out: kpt on fnl f: wnt 2nd post* **40/1**
0005 **3** *nse* **Imshivalla (IRE)**[2] 6505 5-8-9 **88** AdamMcNamara(5) 10 95
(Richard Fahey) *sn led: rdn 2f out: hdd ent fnl f: kpt on: lost 2nd post* **12/1**
4046 **4** ½ **Speed Company (IRE)**[21] 5865 3-8-9 **94** KillianLeonard(5) 8 100
(John Quinn) *midfield: rdn over 2f out: hdwy over 1f out: edgd lft ins fnl f: kpt on* **8/1**
5160 **5** 2 **Percy Street**[29] 5699 3-8-13 **98** JordanVaughan(5) 9 100
(K R Burke) *trckd ldr: rdn over 2f out: one pce* **7/1**
6 *shd* **Lusis Naturea**[34] 5444 5-8-12 **91** OisinOrr(5) 5 93
(Noel C Kelly, Ire) *hld up: rdn over 2f out: kpt on fnl f: nvr threatened ldrs* **20/1**
1330 **7** ¾ **Corton Lad**[63] 4407 6-8-12 **86** (tp) PhillipMakin 7 87
(Keith Dalgleish) *midfield: rdn over 2f out: one pce* **20/1**
4125 **8** 2 ¼ **Felix De Vega (IRE)**[106] 2866 4-9-0 **93** NathanEvans(5) 1 89
(Michael Easterby) *trckd ldr: rdn 3f out: wknd over 1f out* **14/1**
3656 **9** 1 ¾ **Dance King**[42] 5157 6-8-12 **86** (tp) PaulMulrennan 2 79
(Tim Easterby) *dwlt: hld up in rr: nvr threatened* **14/1**
1251 **10** *nk* **Innocent Touch (IRE)**[19] 5964 5-9-6 **94** TonyHamilton 4 86
(Richard Fahey) *midfield on inner: rdn over 2f out: wknd over 1f out* **5/1**[2]
1/24 **11** 4 ½ **Flight Officer**[49] 4858 5-9-5 **93** PatSmullen 14 76
(Saeed bin Suroor) *trckd ldr towards outer: rdn 3f out: wknd over 1f out* **9/2**[1]
0-00 **12** ¾ **Tres Coronas (IRE)**[9] 6261 9-9-2 **90** GrahamGibbons 3 72
(David Barron) *dwlt: a towards rr* **33/1**
303- **13** 3 ¾ **Esteaming**[315] 7757 6-8-13 **87** PJMcDonald 6 61
(David Barron) *hld up: rdn 3f out: sn wknd* **14/1**
44-0 **14** *hd* **They Seek Him Here (IRE)**[19] 5956 3-9-4 **98** (t) DanielTudhope 12 72
(Hugo Palmer) *trckd ldr: rdn over 3f out: wknd over 1f out* **14/1**

2m 11.77s (-0.23) **Going Correction** +0.075s/f (Good)
WFA 3 from 4yo+ 6lb **14** Ran SP% **121.1**
Speed ratings (Par 109): **103,102,102,101,100 100,99,97,96,96 92,92,89,88**
CSF £257.25 CT £3047.73 TOTE £7.50: £3.30, £10.50, £3.70; EX 276.10 Trifecta £1965.60.
Owner M J Macleod **Bred** Minster Stud **Trained** Great Habton, N Yorks

FOCUS
This was run over 21yds further than advertised. An ordinary race for the grade. Pretty straightforward form, with the winner rated back to his best.

6560 MICROTECH GROUP H'CAP 7f 50y

4:55 (4:55) (Class 3) (0-95,95) 3-Y-O+ **£9,703** (£2,887; £1,443; £721) **Stalls** High

Form | | | | RPR
0000 **1** **That Is The Spirit**[21] 5871 5-9-3 **91** DanielTudhope 7 101
(David O'Meara) *led: rdn and hdd over 1f out: rallied and regained ld ins fnl f: gamely* **6/1**[2]
4001 **2** *hd* **Mount Tahan (IRE)**[21] 5866 4-8-12 **86** KevinStott 11 95
(Kevin Ryan) *trckd ldrs: smooth hdwy to ld over 1f out: sn rdn: hdd ins fnl f: kpt on: jst hld* **8/1**[3]
3635 **3** 2 ¼ **London Protocol (FR)**[20] 5946 3-9-4 **95** (p) DougieCostello 2 97
(K R Burke) *trckd ldrs: rdn and ch over 1f out: no ex ins fnl f* **12/1**
6061 **4** 1 ¼ **Explosive Power (IRE)**[77] 3885 3-8-4 **86** JordanVaughan(5) 12 85+
(K R Burke) *hld up towards rr: rdn over 2f out: hdwy over 1f out: kpt on fnl f: no imp* **12/1**
0520 **5** *nk* **Ballymore Castle (IRE)**[1] 6539 4-8-12 **86** TonyHamilton 14 85
(Richard Fahey) *hld up: rdn along over 2f out: hdwy over 1f out: nvr able to chal* **12/1**
4233 **6** ½ **Bertiewhittle**[8] 6276 8-8-7 **86** RowanScott(5) 5 84+
(David Barron) *s.i.s: hld up: rdn over 2f out: hdwy over 1f out: kpt on fnl f: nrst fin* **8/1**[3]
0000 **7** 2 ½ **Tatlisu (IRE)**[20] 5934 6-8-12 **91** AdamMcNamara(5) 1 82
(Richard Fahey) *s.i.s: hld up: drvn along over 2f out: no imp fr over 1f out* **14/1**
5142 **8** *nk* **Gurkha Friend**[10] 6225 4-9-0 **88** GrahamLee 10 79
(Karen McLintock) *chsd wnr to over 2f out: rdn and wknd appr fnl f* **8/1**[3]
2050 **9** 1 ¼ **Ghalib (IRE)**[14] 6109 4-9-6 **94** HarryBentley 3 81
(Ed Walker) *in tch: rdn along over 3f out: wknd over 1f out* **6/1**[2]
2413 **10** *nk* **Glengarry**[17] 6027 3-8-9 **86** PhillipMakin 13 72
(Keith Dalgleish) *hld up in tch: effrt on outside over 2f out: wknd over 1f out* **4/1**[1]
320 **11** 1 ½ **Northgate Lad (IRE)**[8] 6287 4-9-3 **91** ChrisHayes 9 74
(Brian Ellison) *hld up: drvn and struggling over 2f out: sn btn* **14/1**
1-00 **12** 1 ¼ **Newstead Abbey**[19] 5976 6-9-7 **95** GrahamGibbons 8 74
(David Barron) *midfield: drvn and struggling over 2f out: sn btn* **28/1**

1m 33.05s (-0.35) **Going Correction** +0.075s/f (Good)
WFA 3 from 4yo+ 3lb **12** Ran SP% **121.8**
Speed ratings (Par 107): **105,104,102,100,100 99,97,96,95,94 93,91**
CSF £55.05 CT £577.75 TOTE £6.40: £2.00, £3.90, £3.80; EX 79.80 Trifecta £1182.10.
Owner F Gillespie **Bred** Cliveden Stud Ltd **Trained** Upper Helmsley, N Yorks

FOCUS
Race distance increased by 21yds. A decent handicap but it proved hard to make up ground. The runner-up has been rated better than ever.

6561 JORDAN ELECTRICS LTD H'CAP 1m 5f 13y

5:30 (5:32) (Class 3) (0-90,90) 3-Y-O+ **£9,703** (£2,887; £1,443; £721) **Stalls** Low

Form | | | | RPR
4041 **1** **Nietzsche**[24] 5761 3-8-10 **81** GrahamGibbons 2 89+
(Brian Ellison) *in tch: hdwy 3f out: led over 1f out: drvn and kpt on wl* **4/1**[1]
010- **2** ¾ **Major Mac**[252] 6689 4-8-9 **71** oh2 (p) RobertHavlin 9 78
(Hughie Morrison) *prom: hdwy to press ldr after 2f: led over 3f out: rdn and hung lft 2f out: hdd over 1f out: rallied: kpt on: hld cl home* **25/1**
1100 **3** 1 **Sindarban (IRE)**[29] 5611 5-10-0 **90** PhillipMakin 14 95
(Keith Dalgleish) *hld up: stdy hdwy 3f out: sn drvn along: kpt on ins fnl f: nrst fin* **10/1**
2233 **4** *nk* **Mukhayyam**[13] 6165 4-9-4 **80** (p) DavidAllan 17 84
(Tim Easterby) *midfield: effrt and hdwy 3f out: kpt on ins fnl f* **7/1**[3]
3010 **5** ¾ **Theos Lolly (IRE)**[28] 5653 3-8-9 **80** TonyHamilton 10 83
(Richard Fahey) *trckd ldrs: effrt over 2f out: rdn and ev ch over 1f out: no ex ins fnl f* **20/1**
3041 **6** 1 ½ **Trendsetter (IRE)**[31] 5541 5-9-13 **89** JackGarritty 13 90
(John Quinn) *t.k.h: midfield on outside: stdy hdwy over 2f out: rdn over 1f out: kpt on same pce* **16/1**
0206 **7** 2 ¾ **Braes Of Lochalsh**[63] 4381 5-8-13 **75** (p) DougieCostello 8 72
(Jim Goldie) *hld up: rdn and hdwy on outside over 3f out: outpcd fr 2f out* **28/1**
5112 **8** *nse* **Wor Lass**[10] 6227 8-9-3 **84** GarryWhillans(5) 3 81
(Susan Corbett) *t.k.h: hld up in tch: rdn and effrt over 2f out: wknd appr fnl f* **14/1**
4400 **9** 1 ¼ **Gworn**[23] 5802 6-8-8 **75** NathanEvans(5) 11 70
(R Mike Smith) *hld up: drvn along on outside over 3f out: sn no imp* **22/1**
13-0 **10** 8 **Classic Villager**[133] 2024 4-9-13 **89** AndrewMullen 12 72
(Michael Appleby) *prom: drvn along over 3f out: wknd over 1f out* **14/1**
0610 **11** 3 ¾ **Time Of My Life (GER)**[22] 5837 5-9-10 **86** (p) DanielTudhope 5 63
(Patrick Holmes) *hld up: drvn along over 3f out: sn outpcd: btn fnl 2f* **17/2**
0241 **12** 2 ¼ **Project Bluebook (FR)**[46] 4969 3-8-5 **81** KillianLeonard(5) 4 55
(John Quinn) *hld up: drvn along over 3f out: wknd over 2f out* **9/2**[2]
0 **13** 11 **Dark Ruler (IRE)**[22] 5837 7-9-5 **81** DaleSwift 16 38
(Alan Swinbank) *hld up: struggling over 3f out: sn btn* **33/1**
0005 **14** 4 ½ **Hernandoshideaway**[45] 5031 4-9-8 **84** [1] PaulMulrennan 7 34
(Michael Dods) *led to over 3f out: rdn and wknd 2f out: eased whn no ch fnl f* **14/1**
0034 **15** 23 **Hardstone (USA)**[31] 5541 5-9-8 **84** TomEaves 6
(Michael Dods) *pressed ldr 2f: cl up tl rdn and wknd over 3f out: t.o* **12/1**
16 57 **Captain Carleton (IRE)**[35] 5426 7-9-1 **77** ChrisHayes 1
(Adrian Paul Keatley, Ire) *dwlt: plld hrd in midfield: struggling over 3f out: sn lost pl: eased whn no ch fnl 2f* **25/1**

2m 56.35s (2.35) **Going Correction** +0.075s/f (Good)
WFA 3 from 4yo+ 9lb **16** Ran SP% **127.1**
Speed ratings (Par 107): **95,94,93,93,93 92,90,90,89,84 82,81,74,71,57 22**
CSF £117.43 CT £974.30 TOTE £4.70: £1.60, £6.30, £2.60, £2.50; EX 126.70 Trifecta £1999.50.
Owner D Gilbert, M Lawrence, A Bruce, G WIlls **Bred** West Stow Stud Ltd **Trained** Norton, N Yorks

FOCUS
Race distance increased by 30yds. They went a decent gallop and a much improved 3yo maintained his form over a slightly longer trip to get on top in the closing stages. The third has been rated close to form, with the fourth, fifth and sixth helping to set the level.
T/Jkpt: Not won. T/Plt: £1,148.00 to a £1 stake. Pool: £147,958.89 - 94.08 winning units. T/Qpdt: £86.50 to a £1 stake. Pool: £19,290.00 - 164.85 winning units. **Richard Young & Andrew Sheret**

5756 CATTERICK (L-H)

Saturday, September 17

OFFICIAL GOING: Good (7.6)
Wind: light 1/2 behind Weather: fine and sunny

6562 BRITISH STALLION STUDS EBF NOVICE STKS 5f 212y

2:25 (2:26) (Class 5) 2-Y-O **£3,234** (£962; £481; £240) **Stalls** Low

Form | | | | RPR
1544 **1** **Tibr (USA)**[64] 4352 2-9-9 92 SilvestreDeSousa 1 89
(Ed Dunlop) *trckd ldrs: 2nd over 2f out: led 1f out: pushed clr: eased towardas fin* **1/1**[1]
130 **2** 3 **Naples Bay**[50] 4825 2-9-4 80 CallumShepherd(5) 3 76
(John Quinn) *dwlt: chsd ldrs: hung rt bnd over 3f out: 3rd 1f out: kpt on to take modest 2nd clsng stages* **5/1**[3]
4315 **3** *nk* **Sir Viktor (IRE)**[20] 5917 2-9-6 74 (v) JoeyHaynes 4 72
(K R Burke) *swtchd lft after s: t.k.h: led: hdd 1f out: kpt on same pce* **11/1**
22 **4** 6 **Shabeeh (IRE)**[18] 5997 2-9-2 0 LukeMorris 2 50
(Mark Johnston) *chsd ldr: drvn 3f out: lost pl 1f out: heavily eased last 50yds* **2/1**[2]

1m 14.8s (1.20) **Going Correction** +0.275s/f (Good) **4** Ran SP% **108.3**
Speed ratings (Par 95): **103,99,98,90**
CSF £6.21 TOTE £1.70; EX 5.40 Trifecta £11.80.
Owner Abdullah Saeed Al Naboodah **Bred** Don Alberto Corporation **Trained** Newmarket, Suffolk

FOCUS
All races as advertised. Good ground going into this drawn-out eight-race card. The market leader made light of his absence to win this easily .

6563 RACING UK HD ON SKY 432 NURSERY H'CAP 7f

3:00 (3:03) (Class 4) (0-85,82) 2-Y-O **£4,528** (£1,347; £673; £336) **Stalls** Low

Form | | | | RPR
3425 **1** **Law Power**[10] 6240 2-8-8 **69** (b[1]) LukeMorris 6 76
(Sir Mark Prescott Bt) *chsd ldrs: 2nd over 4f out: led over 1f out: drvn out* **11/2**[3]
0563 **2** 2 ½ **Dandy Place (IRE)**[10] 6222 2-8-10 **71** JamesSullivan 3 71+
(Tim Easterby) *t.k.h in rr: drvn 3f out: chsng ldrs and hung lft over 1f out: kpt on to take modest 2nd nr fin* **16/1**
1266 **3** ½ **Racemaker**[19] 5977 2-8-11 **72** NeilFarley 8 71
(Andrew Crook) *led: hdd over 1f out: kpt on same pce* **33/1**
0114 **4** 1 ¾ **Notalot (IRE)**[10] 6229 2-9-4 **82** (v) LouisSteward(3) 1 76
(Michael Bell) *hld up in rr: hdwy over 3f out: 3rd over 2f out: hung rt over 1f out: kpt on one pce* **2/1**[2]
5262 **5** 1 ¾ **Miss Bates**[17] 6026 2-8-7 **73** CallumShepherd(5) 9 63
(Ann Duffield) *dwlt: in rr: hdwy on outer over 4f out: hung lft and one pce fnl 2f* **12/1**
1633 **6** 4 ½ **Tailor's Row (USA)**[48] 4915 2-9-6 **81** SilvestreDeSousa 5 59
(Mark Johnston) *trckd ldrs: t.k.h: drvn over 2f out: lost pl over 1f out: eased clsng stages* **7/4**[1]
5216 **7** 2 ½ **Geophony (IRE)**[28] 5644 2-9-0 **75** RoystonFfrench 7 46
(Mark Johnston) *in rr: t.k.h: lost pl and drvn 4f out: bhd fnl 2f* **14/1**
1250 **8** 5 **Wedding Dress**[30] 5583 2-9-1 **76** ShaneGray 4 34
(David Brown) *chsd ldrs: lost pl over 2f out: sn bhd* **16/1**

1m 28.18s (1.18) **Going Correction** +0.275s/f (Good) **8** Ran SP% **114.1**
Speed ratings (Par 97): **104,101,100,98,96 91,88,82**
CSF £85.24 CT £2646.28 TOTE £6.50: £1.60, £3.20, £5.20; EX 67.50 Trifecta £1870.40.
Owner Bluehills Racing Limited **Bred** Bluehills Racing Limited **Trained** Newmarket, Suffolk

FOCUS
A moderate race for the grade; they went a good gallop but few could get into it.

6564 RACINGUK.COM/ANYWHERE 3 DEVICES 1 PRICE NURSERY H'CAP 5f
3:35 (3:38) (Class 5) (0-75,72) 2-Y-O **£3,234** (£962; £481; £240) **Stalls** Low

Form				RPR
3615	**1**		**Four Dragons**[29] 5598 2-9-1 **66** .... LiamJones 4	69
			(Tom Dascombe) *chsd ldrs: kpt on fnl f: led nr fin* **9/1**	
0041	**2**	*nse*	**Maazel (IRE)**[73] 4015 2-9-7 **72** .... ShaneGray 9	75
			(Roger Varian) *sn detached in last: drvn over 2f out: hdwy over 1f out: styd on wl to take cl 2nd post* **5/1**[1]	
6621	**3**	*nk*	**Justanotherbottle (IRE)**[11] 6214 2-9-7 **72** .... GeorgeChaloner 11	74
			(Declan Carroll) *w ldrs: led over 1f out: hdd and no ex nr fin* **5/1**[1]	
035	**4**	*hd*	**Hot Hannah**[24] 5756 2-8-7 **63** .... PhilDennis(5) 10	64
			(Michael Dods) *rr-div: hdwy 2f out: edgd lft and kpt on wl fnl 150yds* **12/1**	
2334	**5**	*1 1/2*	**Coverham (IRE)**[27] 5675 2-8-7 **58** ....(b) CamHardie 8	54
			(James Bethell) *mid-div: drvn and outpcd over 2f out: kpt on fnl f* **9/1**	
0130	**6**	*nse*	**Mightaswellsmile**[26] 5712 2-9-3 **68** .... JamesSullivan 12	64
			(James Given) *rr-div: effrt over 2f out: kpt on same pce fnl f* **10/1**	
3320	**7**	*2 1/4*	**Decadent Times (IRE)**[22] 5833 2-9-1 **66** .... SamJames 2	55
			(Marjorie Fife) *mid-div: effrt over 2f out: one pce over 1f out* **14/1**	
3213	**8**	*2*	**Yorkshiredebut (IRE)**[7] 6343 2-9-0 **70** .... CallumShepherd(5) 5	50
			(Paul Midgley) *led over 3f out: hung lft and hdd over 1f out: sn fdd* **13/2**[3]	
3000	**9**	*1/2*	**Clear As A Bell (IRE)**[10] 6222 2-8-10 **61** .... DuranFentiman 3	40
			(Tim Easterby) *rr-div: drvn and sme hdwy over 2f out: lost pl over 1f out* **25/1**	
356	**10**	*6*	**Apamurra (USA)**[33] 5469 2-9-2 **67** .... SilvestreDeSousa 13	52
			(Mark Johnston) *chsd ldrs: wknd and heavily eased 1f out* **11/2**[2]	
5460	**11**	*2 1/4*	**Xenon**[5] 6419 2-8-9 **60** ....(p) LukeMorris 7	24
			(Sir Mark Prescott Bt) *led over 1f: lost pl over 1f out: eased clsng stages*	

1m 1.34s (1.54) **Going Correction** +0.275s/f (Good) **11** Ran SP% **117.7**
Speed ratings (Par 95): **98,97,97,97,94 94,91,87,87,77 73**
CSF £53.63 CT £259.09 TOTE £13.20: £4.10, £2.20, £3.30; EX 93.90 Trifecta £727.60.
Owner O'Halloran Owen Satchell Willcock **Bred** Grovewood Stud **Trained** Malpas, Cheshire

FOCUS
Quite a competitive little nursery in which the first four home were separated by less than 1/2l.

6565 ALI'S ANGELS BRAIN TUMOUR CHARITY H'CAP 1m 5f 175y
4:10 (4:17) (Class 4) (0-80,80) 3-Y-O+ **£5,175** (£1,540; £769; £384) **Stalls** Low

Form				RPR
0560	**1**		**Be Perfect (USA)**[15] 6083 7-9-12 **78** ....(b) JamesSullivan 6	87
			(Ruth Carr) *led early: sn settled in mid-div: hdwy 4f out: effrt on outer over 2f out: edgd lft and styd on to ld last 150yds: drvn clr* **14/1**	
3153	**2**	*2 1/2*	**Dew Pond**[15] 6083 4-9-7 **76** .... RachelRichardson(3) 3	81
			(Tim Easterby) *hld up towards rr: effrt on outer over 2f out: kpt on to take 2nd post* **3/1**[2]	
2422	**3**	*shd*	**Wishing Well**[18] 6011 4-8-10 **67** .... RobJFitzpatrick(5) 5	72
			(Micky Hammond) *hld up towards rr: hdwy over 6f out: chsng ldrs over 2f out: kpt on to same pce to take 2nd last 50yds* **16/1**	
330	**4**	*1 1/4*	**Dominada (IRE)**[29] 5611 4-9-9 **80** ....(p) CallumShepherd(5) 7	83
			(Brian Ellison) *trckd ldrs: led and hung lft over 1f out: hdd last 150yds: one pce* **9/2**[3]	
266	**5**	*1 1/2*	**Ingleby Hollow**[13] 6163 4-9-13 **79** ....(p) SamJames 2	81
			(David O'Meara) *trckd ldrs: one pce over 1f out: n.m.r on inner and eased last 50yds* **16/1**	
2203	**6**	*1*	**Isharah (USA)**[40] 5231 3-9-2 **78** .... SilvestreDeSousa 10	78
			(Mark Johnston) *hld up in rr: hdwy to join ldr after 5f: drvn over 3f out: wknd appr fnl f* **11/4**[1]	
-225	**7**	*nk*	**O'Connor's Girl**[24] 5763 3-8-5 **67** .... LukeMorris 9	66
			(Sir Mark Prescott Bt) *hld up in rr: effrt over 2f out: nvr a factor* **11/1**	
2146	**8**	*2*	**Hurry Home Poppa (IRE)**[77] 3903 6-9-3 **69** .... RoystonFfrench 4	66
			(John Mackie) *sn chsng ldrs: drvn over 2f out: wknd over 1f out* **16/1**	
2000	**9**	*1/2*	**Diamond Joel**[19] 5963 4-9-9 **75** .... JoeDoyle 1	71
			(Mick Channon) *sn led: hdd over 1f out: sn hmpd and swtchd rt: wknd fnl f* **14/1**	
4330	**10**	*5*	**Giant Redwood (IRE)**[64] 4353 4-9-8 **77** ....[1] LouisSteward(3) 8	66
			(Michael Bell) *chsd ldrs: lost pl over 1f out* **12/1**	
060	**11**	*7*	**Only Orsenfoolsies**[13] 6165 7-9-1 **74** .... LaurenSteade(7) 11	53
			(Micky Hammond) *in rr: sme hdwy outside over 5f out: lost pl over 3f out: sn bhd* **66/1**	

3m 6.32s (2.72) **Going Correction** +0.275s/f (Good)
WFA 3 from 4yo+ 10lb **11** Ran SP% **118.3**
Speed ratings (Par 105): **103,101,101,100,99 99,99,98,97,94 90**
CSF £56.20 CT £702.99 TOTE £20.30: £4.40, £1.40, £3.50; EX 95.30 Trifecta £1498.70.
Owner The Beer Stalkers & Ruth Carr **Bred** Joseph Allen **Trained** Huby, N Yorks

FOCUS
A reasonably competitive heat won in good style but the winner is an exposed handicapper and the two 3yo's didn't pull up any trees, so this wouldn't be form to get excited about. The runner-up and third have been rated to form.

6566 BAPP FOR BOLTS H'CAP (CATTERICK TWELVE FURLONG SERIES FINAL) 1m 3f 214y
4:45 (4:45) (Class 2) 3-Y-O+
£12,450 (£3,728; £1,864; £932; £466; £234) **Stalls** Centre

Form				RPR
606	**1**		**Card High (IRE)**[14] 6134 6-8-8 **73** ....(t) ShaneGray 5	81
			(Wilf Storey) *hld up in mid-div: t.k.h: effrt over 3f out: 2nd appr fnl f: led last 100yds: edgd lft: drvn out* **14/1**	
2161	**2**	*1/2*	**I Am Not Here (IRE)**[42] 5157 5-8-11 **81** .... CallumShepherd(5) 7	88
			(Brian Ellison) *wnt rt s: sn trcking ldrs: led over 2f out: hdd and no ex last 100yds* **4/1**[3]	
2621	**3**	*1 1/4*	**Hubertas**[19] 5963 4-9-10 **89** ....(v) SilvestreDeSousa 8	94
			(John Quinn) *carried rt s: swtchd lft after s: detached in last: rn in snatches: drvn over 6f out: last tl hdwy over 2f out: swtchd lft and 3rd 1f out: kpt on same pce* **11/8**[1]	
2502	**4**	*4 1/2*	**Sherman McCoy**[16] 6058 10-8-2 **67** ....(p) JamesSullivan 6	65
			(Marjorie Fife) *trckd ldr: drvn over 3f out: reminders over 2f out: wknd fnl f* **9/1**	
1422	**5**	*3*	**Wotabreeze (IRE)**[24] 5761 3-8-7 **80** .... CamHardie 3	73
			(John Quinn) *trckd ldrs: drvn over 4f out: wknd appr fnl f* **3/1**[2]	
5242	**6**	*4 1/2*	**Next Edition (IRE)**[19] 5970 8-8-1 **66** oh2 ow1........(p) JoeyHaynes 2	52
			(Philip Kirby) *hld up in mid-div: t.k.h: drvn over 4f out: outpcd over 3f out: rallied over 2f out: wknd over 1f out.* **25/1**	
	7	*1 3/4*	**Astra Hall**[121] 2399 7-8-5 **75** .... GeorgeBuckell(5) 1	58
			(Michael Appleby) *led: hdd over 2f out: wknd and eased appr fnl f* **12/1**	

2m 39.91s (1.01) **Going Correction** +0.275s/f (Good)
WFA 3 from 4yo+ 8lb **7** Ran SP% **115.3**
Speed ratings (Par 109): **107,106,105,102,100 97,96**
CSF £69.73 CT £128.98 TOTE £18.30: £6.80, £1.50; EX 102.60 Trifecta £329.40.
Owner Gremlin Racing **Bred** John Foley **Trained** Muggleswick, Co Durham

FOCUS
There didn't look to be too much depth to this feature event but it still threw up a surprise result. The winner has been rated back to a similar level to last October's C&D win.

6567 JOHN & JUDITH SANDERSON GOLDEN WEDDING ANNIVERSARY MAIDEN STKS 7f
5:20 (5:25) (Class 5) 3-4-Y-O **£3,234** (£962; £481; £240) **Stalls** Low

Form				RPR
55-4	**1**		**Masarzain (IRE)**[63] 4401 3-9-5 75........ SilvestreDeSousa 6	80+
			(Owen Burrows) *sn led: hdd after 1f: chsd ldr: kpt on to ld last 100yds: all out* **8/11**[1]	
	2	*nk*	**Strong Force** 3-9-5 0........ ShaneGray 3	79+
			(Saeed bin Suroor) *awkward s: in rr: hdwy over 2f out: 4th over 1f out: 3rd last 100yds: styd on to take 2nd last 50yds: jst hld* **11/4**[2]	
43	**3**	*2 1/2*	**Interlink (USA)**[26] 5716 3-9-5 0........ DuranFentiman 1	72
			(Tony Coyle) *chsd ldrs: led after 1f: hdd and no ex last 100yds* **16/1**	
2250	**4**	*2 3/4*	**Haraz (IRE)**[11] 6217 3-9-2 79........ ShelleyBirkett(3) 10	65
			(David O'Meara) *chsd ldrs: drvn over 2f out: one pce and hung lft over 1f out* **7/2**[3]	
33	**5**	*2 1/4*	**Captain Peaky**[26] 5731 3-9-5 0........ JoeyHaynes 5	59
			(Patrick Holmes) *led eraly: chsd ldrs: one pce fnl 2f* **14/1**	
0	**6**	*3*	**Clear Leader (USA)**[15] 6104 3-9-0 0........ CallumShepherd(5) 2	50
			(Micky Hammond) *mid-div: drvn over 3f out: one pce fnl 2f* **66/1**	
	7	*12*	**Mackiri (IRE)** 3-9-2 0........ AlistairRawlinson(3) 8	18
			(Michael Appleby) *s.i.s: towards rr: wl bhd fnl 2f* **33/1**	
00	**8**	*3 3/4*	**Mrs Frosty (IRE)**[35] 5388 3-9-0 0........ JamesSullivan 9	
			(Clive Mulhall) *in rr: wl bhd fnl 2f* **150/1**	
4005	**9**	*7*	**Vocalise**[98] 3140 3-8-9 29........ RobJFitzpatrick(5) 4	
			(Charles Smith) *chsd ldrs: lost pl over 3f out: bhd fnl 2f: eased clsng stages* **150/1**	

1m 28.9s (1.90) **Going Correction** +0.275s/f (Good) **9** Ran SP% **125.1**
Speed ratings (Par 103): **100,99,96,93,91 87,73,69,61**
CSF £3.44 TOTE £1.80: £1.10, £1.60, £3.10; EX 4.10 Trifecta £28.10.
Owner Hamdan Al Maktoum **Bred** Mrs Josephine Hughes **Trained** Lambourn, Berks

FOCUS
A weak maiden, in which the well-backed winner clung on from a horse who could easily improve past him in future. With the fourth below form the level is a bit fluid, and the race revolves around the front-running third.

6568 BOOK NOW FOR SATURDAY 15TH OCTOBER H'CAP (DIV I) 7f
5:55 (5:56) (Class 6) (0-65,63) 3-Y-O+ **£2,587** (£770; £384; £192) **Stalls** Low

Form				RPR
6432	**1**		**Desire**[21] 5887 4-9-7 **63** .... GeorgeChaloner 11	70
			(Richard Fahey) *mid-div: hdwy over 2f out: chsd ldr over 1f out: styd on to ld fnl strides .* **6/1**[2]	
0033	**2**	*hd*	**Coolcalmcollected (IRE)**[25] 5734 4-8-10 **52** .... SilvestreDeSousa 4	58
			(David Loughnane) *sn led: drvn abt 4 l clr over 2f out: hdd and no ex fnl strides* **5/2**[1]	
3055	**3**	*3/4*	**Napoleon Solo**[18] 6008 4-9-6 **62** .... JoeyHaynes 12	66
			(David Barron) *racd wd: mid-div: hdwy over 2f out: 3rd 1f out: kpt onsame pce last 50yds* **8/1**	
0060	**4**	*1*	**Flyball**[21] 5889 4-8-9 **51** ....(e[1]) CamHardie 1	53
			(Dianne Sayer) *in rr: hdwy over 2f out: n.m.r appr fnl f: styd on* **25/1**	
0300	**5**	*nk*	**Lendal Bridge**[86] 3582 5-8-8 **50** .... DuranFentiman 7	51
			(Tony Coyle) *mid-div: drvn and lost pl after 2f: hdwy on outer over 2f out: kpt on wl fnl f* **25/1**	
4640	**6**	*hd*	**Mrs Biggs**[21] 5887 4-8-11 **60** .... GerO'Neill(7) 5	60
			(Declan Carroll) *chsd ldrs: edgd rt appr fnl f: kpt on one pce* **15/2**[3]	
5600	**7**	*1 1/4*	**Lord Rob**[15] 6106 5-8-2 **49** oh4........(p) PhilDennis(5) 2	46
			(David Thompson) *chsd ldrs: 2nd over 2f out: edgd lft and wknd appr fnl f* **14/1**	
4600	**8**	*2*	**Mr Cool Cash**[21] 5887 4-9-7 **63** .... RoystonFfrench 6	55
			(Richard Guest) *chsd ldrs: drvn over 2f out: wkng whn sltly hmpd appr fnl f* **8/1**	
U163	**9**	*1 1/4*	**White Flag**[21] 5887 5-8-12 **57** .... RachelRichardson(3) 9	45
			(Tim Easterby) *in rr: last and drvn over 3f out: hdwy 2f out: kpt on: nvr a factor* **12/1**	
5654	**10**	*9*	**Dr Red Eye**[43] 5104 8-9-5 **61** ....(p) JamesSullivan 8	25
			(Scott Dixon) *led early: chsd ldrs: wknd over 1f out: bhd whn eased clsng stages* **9/1**	
3226	**11**	*3 1/2*	**Princess Peaches**[96] 3210 4-9-2 **63** ....(p) CallumShepherd(5) 13	17
			(James Bethell) *chsd ldrs: wknd and eased over 1f out* **14/1**	
-100	**12**	*1 1/2*	**Breathless**[147] 1631 4-9-6 **62** ....(t) JoeDoyle 3	12
			(Clive Mulhall) *rr-div: lost pl over 2f out: sn bhd: eased clsng stages* **40/1**	

1m 29.15s (2.15) **Going Correction** +0.275s/f (Good)
WFA 3 from 4yo+ 3lb **12** Ran SP% **118.0**
Speed ratings (Par 101): **98,97,96,95,95 95,93,91,90,79 75,74**
CSF £20.73 CT £125.00 TOTE £7.30: £2.60, £1.50, £2.50; EX 20.80 Trifecta £90.80.
Owner Peter Baldwin **Bred** Peter Baldwin **Trained** Musley Bank, N Yorks

FOCUS
A weak handicap which was very nearly stolen from the front. They finished in a bit of a heap.

6569 BOOK NOW FOR SATURDAY 15TH OCTOBER H'CAP (DIV II) 7f
6:25 (6:27) (Class 6) (0-65,65) 3-Y-O+ **£2,587** (£770; £384; £192) **Stalls** Low

Form				RPR
0132	**1**		**Mango Chutney**[26] 5732 3-9-1 **62** ....(p) SamJames 3	68
			(John Davies) *chsd ldrs: styd on appr fnl f: led fnl strides* **7/2**[1]	
4055	**2**	*nk*	**Canford Belle**[23] 5803 3-8-1 **53** .... PhilDennis(5) 8	58
			(Grant Tuer) *led early: chsd ldr: led over 1f out: hdd and no ex fnl strides* **16/1**	
004	**3**	*nse*	**Tafahom (IRE)**[10] 6226 4-9-2 **60** ....(b) CamHardie 10	66
			(Michael Easterby) *mid-div: hdwy over 2f out: edgd lft and styd on fnl f: jst hld* **15/2**[3]	
00	**4**	*1 1/2*	**Epeius (IRE)**[26] 5732 3-9-4 **65** .... GeorgeChaloner 9	66
			(Ben Haslam) *chsd ldrs: 3rd over 2f out: edgd rt over 1f out: kpt on same pce fnl f* **12/1**	
3602	**5**	*1*	**Munjally**[15] 6105 5-8-12 **56** ....(b) JoeyHaynes 14	55
			(Patrick Holmes) *towards rr: hdwy on outer over 2f out: styd on fnl f* **8/1**	

0044 **6** ½ **Kingfisher Girl**[46] 4973 3-8-5 **52** oh4 ow1 LiamJones 12 49
(Michael Appleby) *chsd ldrs: 2nd and reminders over 2f out: kpt on one pce fnl f* **33/1**
0401 **7** ¾ **Bold Spirit**[24] 5760 5-8-12 **63** (vt) GerO'Neill(7) 11 59+
(Declan Carroll) *sn led: clr over 3f out: hdd over 1f out: kpt on one pce* **9/1**
0500 **8** *nk* **Cadmium**[64] 4335 5-8-12 **61** RobJFitzpatrick(5) 5 56
(Micky Hammond) *bhd: hdwy 2f out: kpt on: nvr a factor* **20/1**
500- **9** *1* **Rosy Ryan (IRE)**[352] 6876 6-8-12 **56** JamesSullivan 13 48
(Tina Jackson) *in rr: kpt on fnl 2f: nvr a factor* **40/1**
5000 **10** *hd* **Saltarello (IRE)**[21] 5887 4-8-7 **51** oh3 (b) ShaneGray 6 43
(Marjorie Fife) *s.v.s: sme hdwy on outer over 2f out: nvr a factor* **9/1**
2000 **11** *nse* **Mr Potter**[36] 5355 3-8-7 **54** RoystonFfrench 7 45
(Richard Guest) *mid-div: drvn over 2f out: nvr nr ldrs* **16/1**
6-40 **12** *4* **Three Times A Lord**[15] 6104 4-8-12 **63** [1] RPWalsh(7) 1 44
(Ivan Furtado) *chsd ldrs: edgd lft and wknd over 1f out* **20/1**
0440 **13** *7* **Disclosure**[58] 4544 5-9-4 **62** SilvestreDeSousa 4 24
(Les Eyre) *in rr: hdwy on ins over 2f out: heavily eased last 150yds* . **6/1**[2]
0040 **14** *17* **Royal Normandy**[26] 5717 4-8-13 **62** (p) GeorgeBuckell(5) 2
(David Loughnane) *s.s: sn bhd: t.o over 2f out: heavily eased fnl f* **10/1**

1m 28.86s (1.86) **Going Correction** +0.275s/f (Good)
WFA 3 from 4yo+ 3lb **14** Ran SP% **122.8**
Speed ratings (Par 101): **100,99,99,97,96 96,95,94,93,93 93,88,80,61**
CSF £62.07 CT £419.79 TOTE £5.10: £1.80, £4.00, £2.60; EX 79.50 Trifecta £753.00.
Owner P Taylor **Bred** P Taylor **Trained** Piercebridge, Durham

FOCUS
They went a blistering gallop here and the field were well strung out by the home turn. It was set up for the closers and the most consistent horse in the field got up on the line.
T/Plt: £222.50 to a £1 stake. Pool: £54,679.45 - 179.37 winning units. T/Qpdt: £13.40 to a £1 stake. Pool: £4,478.67 - 246.10 winning units. **Walter Glynn**

6542 NEWBURY (L-H)

Saturday, September 17

OFFICIAL GOING: Good to soft (5.5)
Wind: Moderate, across away from stands Weather: Overcast

6570 WEDGEWOOD ESTATES EBF STALLIONS MAIDEN STKS (PLUS 10 RACE) (DIV I) 7f (S)

1:10 (1:13) (Class 4) 2-Y-O **£5,175** (£1,540; £769; £384) **Stalls** Centre

Form RPR
0 **1** **Swiss Storm**[16] 6053 2-9-5 0 JimCrowley 10 86+
(David Elsworth) *mde all: shkn up 2f out: edgd lft 1f out: r.o strly* **4/1**[2]
5 **2** 1 ¾ **City Of Joy**[29] 5600 2-9-5 0 RyanMoore 1 81+
(Sir Michael Stoute) *w ldrs: chal over 1f out: unable qck fnl f* **10/11**[1]
3 1 ¼ **Alfawaris** 2-9-5 0 PaulHanagan 5 77+
(Owen Burrows) *chsd ldrs: rdn over 2f out: styd on fnl f* **11/1**
0 **4** *nk* **Koeman**[14] 6108 2-9-5 0 GeorgeBaker 9 76
(Mick Channon) *w ldrs tl one pce appr fnl f* **12/1**
5 *6* **International Law** 2-9-5 0 JimmyFortune 13 60+
(Brian Meehan) *s.s: bhd: pushed along and sme hdwy 2f out: nvr rchd ldrs* **25/1**
0 **6** 2 ¼ **Perla Blanca (USA)**[16] 6061 2-9-0 0 SteveDrowne 3 50
(Marcus Tregoning) *mid-div: effrt over 2f out: sn hrd rdn and btn* **66/1**
7 ½ **Alshibaa (IRE)** 2-9-5 0 JoeFanning 11 53
(William Haggas) *dwlt: bhd tl shkn up and styd on fr over 1f out* **10/1**[3]
8 1 ½ **Casado (IRE)** 2-9-5 0 KierenFox 4 49
(John Best) *dwlt: a in similar position: rdn and no hdwy fnl 2f* **50/1**
0 **9** 2 ¾ **Silver Mist**[21] 5869 2-9-0 0 TomMarquand 8 37
(Richard Hannon) *in tch tl hrd rdn and wknd over 2f out* **25/1**
10 ½ **Nuncio** 2-9-2 0 KieranShoemark(3) 6 41
(Roger Charlton) *t.k.h: trckd ldrs: rdn over 2f out: sn wknd* **25/1**
11 ¾ **Zoffanist (IRE)** 2-9-5 0 PatDobbs 7 39
(Amanda Perrett) *a bhd* **33/1**

1m 28.83s (3.13) **Going Correction** +0.25s/f (Good) **11** Ran SP% **115.4**
Speed ratings (Par 97): **92,90,88,88,81 78,78,76,73,72 71**
CSF £7.27 TOTE £4.70: £1.40, £1.20, £2.10; EX 9.30 Trifecta £44.50.
Owner Lordship Stud & David Elsworth **Bred** Lordship Stud **Trained** Newmarket, Suffolk

FOCUS
There was 74mm of rain overnight ahead of the previous day's racing, but drying conditions since then, so good to soft ground. The rail was out 7yds from 1m to the 5f point, adding 13yds to all round course distances. The front two in this opening maiden look smart prospects.

6571 DUBAI DUTY FREE LEGACY CUP STKS (GROUP 3) (FORMERLY KNOWN AS THE ARC TRIAL) 1m 3f 5y

1:45 (1:45) (Class 1) 3-Y-O+ **£34,026** (£12,900; £6,456; £3,216; £1,614) **Stalls** Centre

Form RPR
-210 **1** **Algometer**[105] 2896 3-8-10 105 JimCrowley 3 114
(David Simcock) *hld up disputing 3rd: drvn along 3f out: led over 1f out: hung bdly lft: rdn out* **11/4**[2]
1113 **2** ¾ **Dartmouth**[56] 4626 4-9-8 119 RyanMoore 1 118
(Sir Michael Stoute) *hld up disputing 3rd: hrd rdn and n.m.r over 2f out: styd on to press wnr ins fnl f: jst hld nr fin* **13/8**[1]
2-04 **3** 2 ¼ **Tashaar (IRE)**[21] 5894 4-9-3 101 FrankieDettori 6 109
(Richard Hannon) *hld up in rr: hdwy and edgd rt fr 3f out: chal 2f out: disputing 2nd whn sltly hmpd jst ins fnl f: one pce* **15/2**
6125 **4** 3 ¼ **Ayrad (IRE)**[21] 5893 5-9-3 110 (p) AndreaAtzeni 4 103
(Roger Charlton) *led after 1f tl 4f out: hrd rdn 2f out: n.m.r and wknd over 1f out* **6/1**
-202 **5** 2 ¾ **Robin Of Navan (FR)**[14] 6125 3-8-10 109 MartinHarley 5 99
(Harry Dunlop) *led for 1f: pressed ldr tl led again 4f out: hrd rdn and wknd over 1f out* **9/2**[3]

2m 22.86s (1.66) **Going Correction** +0.25s/f (Good)
WFA 3 from 4yo+ 7lb **5** Ran SP% **109.0**
Speed ratings (Par 113): **103,102,100,98,96**
CSF £7.49 TOTE £3.60: £1.90, £1.40; EX 7.20 Trifecta £30.30.
Owner Miss K Rausing **Bred** Miss K Rausing **Trained** Newmarket, Suffolk
■ Stewards' Enquiry : Jim Crowley caution: careless riding

FOCUS
This was run over 13yds further than advertised. The 4th and 5th gave each other no peace up front, making this a good test despite the small field, and a couple of strong stayers came through to dominate the finish. The runner-up has been rated below his Hardwicke form, but the third has been rated back to form.

6572 DUBAI DUTY FREE MILL REEF STKS (GROUP 2) 6f 8y

2:15 (2:16) (Class 1) 2-Y-O

£42,532 (£16,125; £8,070; £4,020; £2,017; £1,012) **Stalls** Centre

Form RPR
2 **1** **Harry Angel (IRE)**[133] 2023 2-9-1 0 AdamKirby 1 112+
(Clive Cox) *wnt rt s: t.k.h: trckd ldrs: led over 1f out: in control fnl f: pushed out* **2/1**[1]
215 **2** 2 ½ **Perfect Angel (IRE)**[16] 6063 2-8-12 89 MartinDwyer 8 101
(Andrew Balding) *in tch: rdn and hung lft over 2f out: styd on to take 2nd nr fin* **7/1**
5340 **3** *nk* **Global Applause**[9] 6260 2-9-1 103 GeorgeBaker 4 103
(Ed Dunlop) *hmpd and stdd s: hld up in 6th: hdwy to chse wnr over 1f out: one pce: lost 2nd nr fin* **3/1**[2]
2155 **4** 2 ¾ **Grey Britain**[7] 6326 2-9-1 99 JimmyFortune 5 95
(John Ryan) *prom: rdn and lost pl over 2f out: kpt on to take 4th nr fin* **12/1**
1203 **5** *1* **Unabated (IRE)**[14] 6124 2-9-1 94 [1] AndreaAtzeni 6 92
(Marco Botti) *led tl 3f out: wknd over 1f out* **12/1**
1602 **6** ½ **Legendary Lunch (IRE)**[8] 6282 2-9-1 105 RyanMoore 7 91
(Richard Hannon) *stdd in rr s: rdn over 2f out: nvr nr ldrs* **4/1**[3]
114 **7** 1 ¼ **Sutter County**[28] 5656 2-9-1 97 JoeFanning 9 87
(Mark Johnston) *pressed ldr: led 3f out tl over 1f out: wknd fnl f* **10/1**

1m 13.18s (0.18) **Going Correction** +0.25s/f (Good) **7** Ran SP% **115.3**
Speed ratings (Par 107): **108,104,104,100,99 98,96**
CSF £17.04 TOTE £3.40: £2.00, £3.00; EX 18.50 Trifecta £78.90.
Owner Peter Ridgers **Bred** Cbs Bloodstock **Trained** Lambourn, Berks

FOCUS
An ordinary Group 2, especially with the defection of Mokarris on account of the ground, but there was plenty to like about the way the unexposed winner took it.

6573 DUBAI DUTY FREE H'CAP 1m 2f 6y

2:50 (2:51) (Class 2) (0-105,104) 3-Y-O+

£46,687 (£13,980; £6,990; £3,495; £1,747; £877) **Stalls** Centre

Form RPR
0111 **1** **Baydar**[28] 5647 3-8-12 **99** JosephineGordon(3) 2 111+
(Hugo Palmer) *mid-div on rail: pushed along over 3f out: hdwy and squeezed through fr 2f out: styd on to ld ins fnl f: rdn out* **6/1**[1]
1141 **2** ½ **Scarlet Dragon**[28] 5651 3-8-10 **99** HollieDoyle(5) 14 110
(Eve Johnson Houghton) *towards rr: hdwy 3f out: led 2f out tl ins fnl f: r.o* **10/1**
1105 **3** 1 ½ **Imperial Aviator**[31] 5557 3-8-10 **97** [1] KieranShoemark(3) 18 105
(Roger Charlton) *mid-div: hrd rdn and hdwy over 2f out: chsd ldr wl over 1f out tl ins fnl f: kpt on same pce* **8/1**[3]
0003 **4** *nk* **What About Carlo (FR)**[19] 5962 5-9-3 **95** JimmyFortune 4 102
(Eve Johnson Houghton) *bhd: hmpd on rail 7f out: gd hdwy on inner to chse ldrs over 1f out: styd on* **20/1**
1422 **5** 1 ¾ **Stars Over The Sea (USA)**[7] 6333 5-9-10 **102** GeorgeBaker 8 106
(Mark Johnston) *mid-div: hdwy to chse ldrs 2f out: styd on same pce fnl f* **10/1**
0031 **6** *1* **Zhui Feng (IRE)**[20] 5924 3-9-6 **104** 5ex PatDobbs 5 106
(Amanda Perrett) *chsd ldrs tl outpcd fnl 2f* **25/1**
5400 **7** *1* **Gold Prince (IRE)**[14] 6118 4-9-3 **95** MartinHarley 12 95
(Sylvester Kirk) *chsd ldrs tl hrd rdn and btn over 1f out* **20/1**
4224 **8** ¾ **Sennockian Star**[8] 6301 6-7-12 **83** (v) DavidEgan(7) 20 81
(Mark Johnston) *prom in chsng gp tl wknd 2f out* **33/1**
1412 **9** 1 ½ **Muzdawaj**[15] 6081 3-8-6 **90** (p) PaulHanagan 17 85
(William Haggas) *towards rr: hrd rdn 3f out: styd on fnl f* **13/2**[2]
2236 **10** 2 ½ **Passover**[21] 5894 5-8-8 **93** JoshuaBryan(7) 15 83
(Andrew Balding) *led: sn wl clr and set str pce: hdd and edgd rt 2f out: 6th and btn whn n.m.r over 1f out* **16/1**
4212 **11** *shd* **Autocratic**[71] 4108 3-8-8 **92** RyanMoore 13 82
(Sir Michael Stoute) *prom in chsng gp: wnt 2nd 3f out tl squeezed for room and wknd 2f out: eased whn btn 1f out* **6/1**[1]
120 **12** ¾ **Sir Roderic (IRE)**[15] 6075 3-8-13 **97** DanielMuscutt 7 86
(Rod Millman) *towards rr: n.m.r 7f out: n.d* **25/1**
6055 **13** ¾ **Shell Bay (USA)**[11] 6209 4-8-8 **86** TomMarquand 9 73
(Richard Hannon) *bhd: rdn over 3f out: nvr rchd ldrs* **66/1**
1646 **14** *2* **Bermondsey**[9] 6261 4-9-1 **93** AdamKirby 6 76
(Luca Cumani) *a bhd* **10/1**
140 **15** *2* **Baadi**[42] 5145 4-8-9 **87** (v) AndreaAtzeni 16 66
(Charlie Fellowes) *mid-div tl wknd 3f out* **20/1**
6226 **16** *6* **Scrutinise**[28] 5647 4-9-0 **97** GeorgeWood(5) 19 64
(Ed Dunlop) *mid-div: rdn 4f out: wknd 3f out* **20/1**
0001 **17** 3 ½ **Watersmeet**[14] 6142 5-9-7 **99** 5ex JoeFanning 3 59
(Mark Johnston) *chsd clr ldr tl wknd qckly 3f out* **50/1**
3212 **18** *24* **Goodwood Mirage (IRE)**[28] 5647 6-8-9 **90** EdwardGreatrex(3) 10
(Michael Bell) *a towards rr: rdn and n.d fnl 3f* **16/1**

2m 7.6s (-1.20) **Going Correction** +0.25s/f (Good)
WFA 3 from 4yo+ 6lb **18** Ran SP% **125.2**
Speed ratings (Par 109): **114,113,112,112,110 109,109,108,107,105 105,104,104,102,100 96,93,74**
CSF £56.33 CT £498.15 TOTE £5.40: £1.90, £2.10, £2.70, £3.90; EX 53.10 Trifecta £384.30.
Owner V I Araci **Bred** Fittocks Stud **Trained** Newmarket, Suffolk

FOCUS
This was run over 13yds further than advertised. A strong handicap run at a good gallop thanks to Passover, who soon had them well strung out. The third has been rated back to his May C&D win.

6574 DUBAI INTERNATIONAL AIRPORT WORLD TROPHY STKS (GROUP 3) 5f 34y

3:25 (3:25) (Class 1) 3-Y-O+

£34,026 (£12,900; £6,456; £3,216; £1,614; £810) **Stalls** Centre

Form RPR
0040 **1** **Cotai Glory**[6] 6384 4-9-1 112 GeorgeBaker 7 115
(Charles Hills) *prom: drvn to ld ins fnl f: hld on narrowly* **5/2**[2]
3111 **2** *shd* **Alpha Delphini**[21] 5863 5-9-1 106 (p) ConnorBeasley 8 114
(Bryan Smart) *chsd ldrs: drvn to ld 1f out: hdd ins fnl f: r.o wl* **9/2**[3]
4102 **3** 2 ¼ **Ridge Ranger (IRE)**[34] 5436 5-9-1 110 JasonHart 4 107
(Eric Alston) *led tl 1f out: hit on hd by rival's whip and no ex ins fnl f* **13/8**[1]

5010 **4** 3/4 **Spirit Quartz (IRE)**[6] 6384 8-9-1 108........................(p) JimmyFortune 11 103
(Robert Cowell) *prom: hrd rdn over 1f out: kpt on same pce* **10/1**
3620 **5** 1 **Fine Blend (IRE)**[49] 4905 3-8-11 97.............. MartinDwyer 2 97
(William Muir) *dwlt: outpcd in rr: effrt over 2f out: no imp* **25/1**
0011 **6** 5 **Boom The Groom (IRE)**[31] 5555 5-9-1 107................... AdamKirby 12 82
(Tony Carroll) *fair 5th tl wknd 2f out* **7/1**
1m 0.93s (-0.47) **Going Correction** +0.25s/f (Good)
WFA 3 from 4yo+ 1lb **6 Ran SP% 110.3**
Speed ratings (Par 113): **113,112,109,108,106 98**
CSF £13.48 TOTE £3.30: £1.60, £2.20; EX 13.50 Trifecta £27.10.
Owner Kangyu Int Racing (HK) Ltd & F Ma **Bred** Glebe Stud, J F Dean & Lady Trenchard **Trained** Lambourn, Berks

FOCUS
A quality sprint unfortunately decimated by non-runners following heavy rain two nights beforehand but the best horse in the race gained a richly deserved first win of the year. The winner has been rated close to his King's Stand form.

6575 DUBAI DUTY FREE NURSERY H'CAP 7f (S)
4:00 (4:00) (Class 3) (0-95,90) 2-Y-O
£6,225 (£1,864; £932; £466; £233; £117) **Stalls** Centre

Form RPR
01 **1** **Graphite Storm**[21] 5890 2-8-11 80..................................... RyanMoore 8 84
(Clive Cox) *hld up towards rr: hdwy 2f out: led 1f out: drvn out* **9/2**
1251 **2** 1 1/4 **Fastnet Spin (IRE)**[8] 6289 2-8-4 76..............................(v) NoelGarbutt(3) 5 77
(David Evans) *in tch: effrt over 2f out: chsd wnr fnl f: kpt on* **12/1**
41 **3** 3/4 **Shipping Forecast**[39] 5250 2-8-9 78.......................... MartinDwyer 6 77
(Brian Meehan) *w ldr tl over 1f out: kpt on u.p* **12/1**
054 **4** 1/2 **Swag (IRE)**[16] 6053 2-8-0 74..(t) HollieDoyle(5) 7 72
(Richard Hannon) *chsd ldrs: rdn 2f out: kpt on fnl f* **16/1**
321 **5** 1/2 **Novoman (IRE)**[27] 5670 2-8-9 83............................ GeorgiaCox(5) 1 79
(William Haggas) *led: hung bdly lft and hdd 1f out: no ex* **3/1[2]**
31 **6** nse **Blushing Rose**[26] 5722 2-8-9 78.................................... AndreaAtzeni 10 74+
(Sir Michael Stoute) *wnt rt s: plld hrd and stdd towards rr after 1f: rdn over 2f out: styng on at fin* **11/4[1]**
1 **7** 1 1/4 **Stellar Surprise**[19] 5951 2-8-8 77.................................. PaulHanagan 11 72+
(Stuart Williams) *dwlt: bhd: rdn 2f out: nvr able to chal* **7/2[3]**
3001 **8** 7 **Plant Pot Power (IRE)**[22] 5847 2-8-13 82.................... JimmyFortune 12 57
(Richard Hannon) *prom tl wknd 2f out* **20/1**
1m 27.81s (2.11) **Going Correction** +0.25s/f (Good) **8 Ran SP% 118.1**
Speed ratings (Par 99): **97,95,94,94,93 93,92,84**
CSF £57.76 CT £612.52 TOTE £4.60: £1.80, £2.90, £3.90; EX 74.10 Trifecta £1054.30.
Owner Mrs Olive Shaw **Bred** Mrs O A Shaw **Trained** Lambourn, Berks

FOCUS
A decent nursery handicap with seven of the remaining eight runners having won their previous race. They went a respectable gallop and the decisive winner delayed his challenge on the tacky surface.

6576 HEATHERWOLD STUD H'CAP 7f (S)
4:35 (4:36) (Class 4) (0-80,80) 3-Y-O **£4,690** (£1,395; £697; £348) **Stalls** Centre

Form RPR
2311 **1** **Aflame**[25] 5752 3-9-7 80... RyanMoore 2 94+
(Sir Michael Stoute) *prom: led 2f out: rdn clr ins fnl f* **13/8[1]**
2213 **2** 2 1/2 **Izmir (IRE)**[31] 5545 3-9-1 79...(p) GeorgiaCox(5) 3 85
(William Haggas) *hld up in 5th: rdn to chse wnr over 1f out: no imp* **5/1[2]**
2354 **3** 3/4 **Lilbourne Prince (IRE)**[6] 6365 3-8-13 72...................... SteveDrowne 9 76
(David Evans) *hld up towards rr: hrd rdn and hdwy over 1f out: r.o wl fnl f* **12/1**
5040 **4** 1/2 **See You When (IRE)**[48] 4908 3-9-0 73......................... TomMarquand 5 76
(Richard Hannon) *awkward leaving stalls: hld up in rr: hdwy over 1f out: kpt on u.p* **20/1**
126 **5** 1 1/4 **Wild Dancer**[19] 5960 3-9-0 73.. DanielMuscutt 6 72
(Patrick Chamings) *chsd ldr tl 2f out: btn over 1f out* **6/1**
3036 **6** 1 1/4 **Essenaitch (IRE)**[21] 5892 3-9-1 74................................ SaleemGolam 15 73+
(David Evans) *t.k.h: chsd ldrs tl outpcd 2f out: in rr and wl btn whn hmpd 1f out* **12/1**
6433 **7** 1/2 **Bernie's Boy**[28] 5649 3-8-13 79.................................(p) JoshuaBryan(7) 8 74
(Andrew Balding) *led tl 2f out: sn outpcd* **11/2[3]**
66 **8** 2 1/2 **Colonel Bossington (IRE)**[14] 6123 3-8-9 71...... JosephineGordon(3) 16 59
(William Knight) *hld up in rr: mod effrt over 1f out: n.d* **10/1**
1m 27.48s (1.78) **Going Correction** +0.25s/f (Good) **8 Ran SP% 113.7**
Speed ratings (Par 103): **99,96,95,94,93 91,91,88**
CSF £9.67 CT £71.08 TOTE £2.00: £1.10, £1.50, £3.60; EX 7.80 Trifecta £61.10.
Owner Lady Rothschild **Bred** Kincorth Investments Inc **Trained** Newmarket, Suffolk

FOCUS
A fair handicap won by a progressive filly. A small pb from the runner-up, while the third is a fair guide to the level.

6577 WEDGEWOOD ESTATES EBF STALLIONS MAIDEN STKS (PLUS 10 RACE) (DIV II) 7f (S)
5:05 (5:07) (Class 4) 2-Y-O **£5,175** (£1,540; £769; £384) **Stalls** Centre

Form RPR
4 **1** **Warrior's Spirit (IRE)**[58] 4552 2-9-5 0.............................. PatDobbs 7 80+
(Richard Hannon) *hld up in midfield: smooth hdwy over 1f out: rdn to ld wl ins fnl f* **11/2**
2 nk **Crystal Ocean** 2-9-5 0.. RyanMoore 5 80+
(Sir Michael Stoute) *hld up towards rr: hdwy 2f out: slt ld 1f out tl wl ins fnl f: r.o* **7/4[1]**
03 **3** hd **On To Victory**[16] 6054 2-9-5 0....................................[1] TomMarquand 8 79
(Eve Johnson Houghton) *t.k.h: prom: jnd ldrs over 1f out: hrd rdn: r.o* **16/1**
3 **4** 2 **Twenty Times (IRE)**[16] 6061 2-9-0 0.............................. ShaneKelly 9 69
(Richard Hughes) *t.k.h: trckd ldr: led 2f out tl 1f out: one pce* **16/1**
5 1 1/4 **Earthly (USA)** 2-9-5 0.. JimmyFortune 3 71+
(Ralph Beckett) *dwlt: hld up and bhd: shkn up 2f out: gng on wl at fin* **11/1**
0 **6** nk **Sir Titan**[21] 5890 2-9-5 0.. SteveDrowne 11 70
(Marcus Tregoning) *led tl 2f out: no ex fnl f* **33/1**
7 3/4 **Mafaaheem (IRE)** 2-9-5 0.. PaulHanagan 2 68
(Owen Burrows) *hld up in 6th: effrt over 2f out: btn over 1f out* **4/1[2]**
8 1 3/4 **Alwahsh (IRE)** 2-9-5 0.. StevieDonohoe 4 63
(William Haggas) *bhd: hrd rdn 3f out: nvr nr ldrs* **9/2[3]**
0 **9** 2 1/4 **Alemaratalyoum (IRE)**[11] 6211 2-9-5 0............................ AdamKirby 6 57
(Ed Dunlop) *chsd ldrs: rdn to join ldrs 2f out: wknd rapidly jst over 1f out* **18/1**
1m 29.37s (3.67) **Going Correction** +0.30s/f (Good) **9 Ran SP% 118.2**
Speed ratings (Par 97): **91,90,90,88,86 86,85,83,80**
CSF £15.92 TOTE £7.70: £2.80, £1.10, £3.30; EX 22.00 Trifecta £206.20.
Owner Pineapple Stud, Amanda Turner & Ptnr **Bred** J Fisher **Trained** East Everleigh, Wilts

FOCUS
The second division of the 7f maiden which bracketed the card was run at a decent tempo and produced a thrilling finish. The particularly well-bred runner-up displayed plenty of promise.
T/Plt: £110.70 to a £1 stake. Pool: £103,657.84 - 683.54 winning tickets T/Qpdt: £53.10 to a £1 stake. Pool: £6,843.09 - 95.34 winning tickets **Lee McKenzie**

5876 NEWMARKET (R-H)
Saturday, September 17

OFFICIAL GOING: Good (good to soft in places; 7.4)
Wind: light, half behind Weather: overcast

6578 BRITISH STALLION STUDS EBF MAIDEN FILLIES' STKS (PLUS 10 RACE) 1m
1:35 (1:35) (Class 4) 2-Y-O **£4,528** (£1,347; £673; £336) **Stalls** Centre

Form RPR
3 **1** **Sobetsu**[22] 5846 2-9-0 0.. WilliamBuick 9 99+
(Charlie Appleby) *mde virtually all: readily wnt clr ent fnl 2f: rdn and styd on strly fr over 1f out: eased cl home: impressive* **11/10[1]**
2 **2** 10 **Interweave**[16] 6062 2-9-0 0.. PatCosgrave 1 73
(Sir Michael Stoute) *hld up in tch in midfield: effrt over 2f out: chsd clr wnr 2f out: no ch w wnr and kpt on same pce after* **7/2[2]**
3 1 3/4 **God Given** 2-9-0 0.. MartinLane 4 69
(Luca Cumani) *in tch towards rr: effrt over 2f out: no ch w wnr but hdwy over: wnt 3rd ins fnl f: kpt on* **11/2[3]**
0 **4** 1/2 **Beautiful Escape (USA)**[66] 4261 2-9-0 0..................... JamesDoyle 10 68
(Saeed bin Suroor) *hld up in tch towards rr: effrt 3f out: hdwy and rn green over 2f out: sn outpcd by wnr and n.d fnl 2f: kpt on same pce after* **10/1**
5 1/2 **Perfect In Pink** 2-9-0 0... CharlesBishop 5 66+
(Mick Channon) *dwlt and bustled along leaving stalls: hld up in tch in rr: effrt over 2f out: sn outpcd by wnr: no ch but kpt on ins fnl f* **33/1**
0 **6** 3/4 **Spirit Of India**[14] 6111 2-9-0 0... NickyMackay 6 65
(John Gosden) *chsd ldrs: wnt 2nd 3f out: sn rdn: outpcd and lost 2nd 2f out: sn no ch w wnr: and plugged on same pce after: lost 3 pls ins fnl f* **10/1**
5 **7** 3/4 **Alapinta**[36] 5373 2-9-0 0.. FrederikTylicki 3 63
(Ralph Beckett) *s.i.s: in tch in rr: rdn and edgd rt over 2f out: sme hdwy but no ch w wnr over 1f out: plugged on same pce ins fnl f* **50/1**
5 **8** 2 1/2 **Pussy Galore (IRE)**[16] 6062 2-9-0 0............................ KieranO'Neill 7 57
(Richard Hannon) *racd keenly chsd wnr tl 3f out: sn struggling and losing pl qckly whn hung rt wl over 1f out: wknd fnl f* **33/1**
6 **9** 4 **Curtsy (IRE)**[18] 5995 2-9-0 0.. LiamKeniry 2 47
(Hughie Morrison) *pressed ldrs: rdn and lost pl over 2f out: bhd over 1f out* **33/1**
5 **10** 3 1/2 **Patching**[21] 5861 2-9-0 0... WilliamCarson 8 39
(Giles Bravery) *in tch towards rr: rdn and dropped to rr 3f out: bhd fnl 2f* **100/1**
1m 38.1s (-0.50) **Going Correction** +0.125s/f (Good) **10 Ran SP% 115.2**
Speed ratings (Par 94): **107,97,95,94,94 93,92,90,86,82**
CSF £4.63 TOTE £2.00: £1.20, £1.50, £1.90; EX 6.30 Trifecta £19.40.
Owner Godolphin **Bred** Darley **Trained** Newmarket, Suffolk

FOCUS
Far-side course used. Stalls: centre. A cloudy, blustery afternoon. This fillies' maiden has a rich history, the last ten runnings producing a host of subsequent Pattern-race winners, including multiple Group 1 winner Midday and 2014 Oaks heroine Taghrooda. This winner could well follow suit.

6579 NEWMARKETRACECOURSES.CO.UK H'CAP (DIV I) 7f
2:05 (2:06) (Class 4) (0-80,80) 3-Y-O+ **£5,175** (£1,540; £769; £384) **Stalls** Centre

Form RPR
2333 **1** **My Target (IRE)**[71] 4094 5-9-4 77.................................... JamesDoyle 5 87
(Michael Wigham) *hld up in tch in midfield: effrt 2f out: rdn to ld over 1f out: edgd lft and styd on wl ins fnl f: rdn out* **9/2[1]**
16 **2** 2 **Carolinae**[27] 5677 4-9-2 75.. StevieDonohoe 2 80+
(Charlie Fellowes) *trckd ldrs: wnt 2nd and travelling wl 2f out: rdn and ev ch over 1f out: chsd wnr and styd on same pce fnl f* **9/2[1]**
150/ **3** 1 1/2 **Via Via (IRE)**[819] 3448 4-9-7 80.................................... WilliamBuick 9 81
(James Tate) *dwlt and awkward leaving stalls: hld up in tch towards rr: hdwy and carried rt over 1f out: chsd ldng pair 1f out: styd on same pce ins fnl f* **9/2[1]**
1265 **4** 1 1/4 **Boycie**[9] 6266 3-9-0 76...(b) KieranO'Neill 4 72
(Richard Hannon) *chsd ldrs: rdn 3f out: unable qck and edgd rt over 1f out: styd on same pce u.p fnl f* **16/1**
2103 **5** 1 1/2 **Whozthecat (IRE)**[4] 6453 9-8-7 66..............................(t) PatrickMathers 1 59
(Declan Carroll) *racd freely: led: rdn and hrd pressed 2f out: hdd over 1f out: no ex and wknd ins fnl f* **6/1[2]**
4004 **6** 1/2 **Take A Note**[18] 5992 7-8-13 77.................................(p) CharlieBennett(5) 6 69
(Patrick Chamings) *hld up in tch in last quartet: rdn 3f out: sme hdwy over 1f out: styd on ins fnl f: nvr trbld ldrs* **16/1**
0503 **7** 1 **Athletic**[21] 5892 7-8-7 67..(v) RyanTate 3 56
(Andrew Reid) *s.i.s: hld up in last pair: shkn up over 2f out: rdn and hdwy over 1f out: kpt on ins fnl f: nvr trbld ldrs* **12/1**
0210 **8** 1 1/4 **Etienne Gerard**[15] 6072 4-8-9 75..................(p) LewisEdmunds(7) 11 61
(Nigel Tinkler) *in tch in midfield: rdn over 2f out: lost pl and btn over 1f out: wknd ins fnl f* **12/1**
0605 **9** 3 1/4 **Favourite Treat (USA)**[17] 6027 6-9-0 73...............(e) FrederikTylicki 8 50
(Ruth Carr) *hld up in tch in midfield: shkn up 2f out: rdn and no rspnse over 1f out: sn wknd* **12/1**
6000 **10** 4 **Ruban (IRE)**[14] 6123 7-8-12 78..............................(t) MillyNaseb(7) 10 44
(Stuart Williams) *hld up in last pair: rdn 1/2-way: nvr gng wl enough after: wknd over 1f out* **33/1**
4005 **11** 1/2 **Until Midnight (IRE)**[15] 6072 6-8-3 69.......................... LuluStanford(7) 7 34
(Eugene Stanford) *t.k.h: chsd ldr tl 2f out: lost pl over 1f out: fdd ins fnl f* **10/1[3]**
1m 25.39s (-0.01) **Going Correction** +0.125s/f (Good)
WFA 3 from 4yo+ 3lb **11 Ran SP% 115.7**
Speed ratings (Par 105): **105,102,101,99,97 96,96,94,91,86 85**
CSF £23.36 CT £97.86 TOTE £4.90: £1.50, £2.00, £2.50; EX 21.20 Trifecta £65.80.
Owner Tugay Akman & John B Williams **Bred** Darley **Trained** Newmarket, Suffolk

FOCUS
This looked the weaker of the two divisions. The market proved an excellent guide with the three co favourites filling the first three places. They went hard in the early stages and that benefited the winner. A turf pb from the winner.

6580 NEWMARKETRACECOURSES.CO.UK H'CAP (DIV II) 7f
2:40 (2:40) (Class 4) (0-80,80) 3-Y-O+ **£5,175** (£1,540; £769; £384) **Stalls** Centre

Form RPR
1135 **1** **Red Tea**8 6300 3-8-11 **80** LuluStanford(7) 4 89
(Peter Hiatt) *hld up in tch in last trio: effrt 2f out: rdn and hdwy to chal over 1f out: led wl ins fnl f: hld on cl home: all out* **7/2**1

606 **2** *nse* **Evening Attire**9 6269 5-8-8 **67** MartinLane 1 77
(William Stone) *led: rdn 2f out: hrd pressed and drvn over 1f out: hdd wl ins fnl f: battled on gamely towards fin: jst hld* **12/1**

126 **3** *nk* **Feed The Goater (FR)**19 5965 3-9-2 **78** TomQueally 10 86
(Richard Hannon) *hld up in tch in last trio: swtchd lft 2f out: rdn and hdwy over 1f out: ev ch 1f out: styd on wl: unable qck towards fin* **11/2**3

1113 **4** *3 1/4* **Chetan**9 6269 4-8-11 **70** (tp) AdamBeschizza 6 70
(Charlie Wallis) *taken down early: chsd ldrs: rdn and ev ch 2f out: no ex jst ins fnl f: btn whn squeezed for room and hmpd ins fnl f: wknd fnl 75yds* **9/1**

-562 **5** *4* **Song Of Norway**38 5301 5-9-2 **75** FergusSweeney 3 65
(Chris Wall) *dwlt: hld up in tch in rr: clsd and rdn ent fnl 2f: nt clrest of runs and swtchd rt and lft over 1f out: no hdwy 1f out: wknd ins fnl f* **7/1**

502 **6** *nk* **Intrude**25 5752 4-9-7 **80** PatCosgrave 5 69
(Stuart Williams) *in tch in midfield: clsd to chse ldrs and rdn 2f out: no ex and btn ent fnl f: wknd ins fnl f* **10/1**

-240 **7** *7* **Stylistik**99 3107 3-8-10 **72** KieranO'Neill 7 41
(Luke Dace) *chsd ldrs: rdn over 2f out: unable qck and lost pl over 1f out: wknd fnl f* **20/1**

4-6 **8** *3 1/4* **Il Piccolo Grande (IRE)**121 2412 3-9-3 **79** JamesDoyle 9 39
(James Tate) *chsd ldrs: rdn over 2f out: lost pl qckly 2f out: bhd over 1f out* **6/1**

0412 **9** *shd* **Consulting**22 5832 3-9-0 **76** WilliamBuick 8 36
(Martyn Meade) *chsd ldrs: rdn over 2f out: unable qck and btn over 1f out: sn wknd* **9/2**2

1m 25.42s (0.02) **Going Correction** +0.125s/f (Good)
WFA 3 from 4yo+ 3lb **9** Ran SP% **114.1**
Speed ratings (Par 105): **104,103,103,99,95 94,86,83,83**
CSF £45.84 CT £226.67 TOTE £4.90: £1.40, £3.10, £2.10; EX 58.20 Trifecta £339.20.
Owner Ken Read Shelley Tucker Jimmy Cooper **Bred** Sheikh Hamdan Bin Maktoum Al Maktoum **Trained** Hook Norton, Oxon

FOCUS
This featured some in-form horses and produced an exciting finish. It was run in a time just 0.03secs slower than the first division.

6581 CMSEVEN.COM H'CAP 1m 2f
3:15 (3:15) (Class 3) (0-95,95) 3-Y-O **£9,703** (£2,887; £1,443; £721) **Stalls** Centre

Form RPR
21 **1** **Saunter (FR)**18 5996 3-9-2 **90** MartinLane 6 104
(David Menuisier) *dwlt and rdn along leaving stalls: sn rcvrd to chse ldr: rdn and ev ch 3f out: led wl over 1f out: styd on strly and drew clr ins fnl f: eased cl home* **14/1**

411 **2** *2 3/4* **Huge Future**86 3557 3-9-7 **95** JamesDoyle 5 103
(Saeed bin Suroor) *hld up in tch in midfield: hdwy 4f out: rdn and chsd ldrs over 3f out: chsd wnr over 1f out: styd on same pce ins fnl f* **11/4**1

1143 **3** *2 3/4* **Brorocco**8 6277 3-8-11 **85** LiamKeniry 2 88
(Andrew Balding) *t.k.h: hld up in tch in midfield: shkn up and effrt over 1f out: no ch w ldrs but kpt on to pass btn horses ins fnl f: wnt 3rd wl ins fnl f* **10/1**

6116 **4** *1 3/4* **Kummiya**29 5603 3-8-12 **86** WilliamTwiston-Davies 3 85
(Roger Charlton) *hld up in tch in last trio: effrt ent fnl 2f: hdwy and drvn to chse ldrs over 1f out: no ex and btn 1f out: wknd ins fnl f* **16/1**

31- **5** *nse* **G K Chesterton (IRE)**337 7251 3-9-1 **89** WilliamBuick 4 88
(Charlie Appleby) *hld up in tch in midfield: rdn 3f out: hdwy u.p to chse ldrs over 1f out: no ex 1f out: wknd ins fnl f* **3/1**2

3631 **6** *3 3/4* **West Drive (IRE)**12 6192 3-8-8 **82** (b) FrederikTylicki 8 73
(Roger Varian) *led: rdn 3f out: hdd 2f out: lost pl u.p over 1f out: wknd ins fnl f* **8/1**

2103 **7** *1 3/4* **Wave Reviews**44 5074 3-8-10 **84** (p) PatCosgrave 7 72
(William Haggas) *broke wl: stdd to trck ldng pair: rdn 3f out: unable qck 2f out: sn wknd* **4/1**3

5416 **8** *2 1/4* **Zest (IRE)**14 6115 3-8-13 **87** TomQueally 1 70
(James Fanshawe) *s.i.s: t.k.h: hld up in tch in rr: rdn ent fnl 2f: sn btn: bhd over 1f out* **17/2**

2m 5.21s (-0.59) **Going Correction** +0.125s/f (Good) **8** Ran SP% **114.9**
Speed ratings (Par 105): **107,104,102,101,101 98,96,94**
CSF £52.91 CT £413.21 TOTE £14.00: £3.30, £1.40, £3.50; EX 61.50 Trifecta £339.10.
Owner Michael H Watt **Bred** S A R L Haras Du Cadran Et Al **Trained** Pulborough, W Sussex

FOCUS
A good quality renewal of this handicap with four of the eight runners having won last time. The runner-up has been rated in line with his handicap debut win.

6582 BETFRED CESAREWITCH TRIAL STKS (H'CAP) 2m 2f
3:50 (3:54) (Class 2) (0-105,102) 3-Y-O+
£31,125 (£9,320; £4,660; £2,330; £1,165; £585) **Stalls** Centre

Form RPR
0/05 **1** **Penglai Pavilion (USA)**77 3889 6-9-1 **93** WilliamBuick 4 104
(Charlie Appleby) *mde all: rdn and readily fnd ex 2f out: in command over 1f out: styd on strly: nvr seriously chal: eased cl home* **11/2**2

2003 **2** *3* **The Cashel Man (IRE)**31 5559 4-8-11 **89** (b1) FrederikTylicki 9 97
(David Simcock) *hld up in midfield: hmpd 4f out: effrt and rdn over 3f out: 4th 2f out: drvn to chse clr wnr over 1f out: styd on same pce ins fnl f* **11/2**2

1520 **3** *4 1/2* **Shrewd**14 6118 6-9-3 **102** CliffordLee(7) 11 105
(Iain Jardine) *chsd ldrs: 3rd and rdn over 3f out: unable qck 2f out: kpt on same pce fr over 1f out* **16/1**

400- **4** *hd* **Alton Bay (IRE)**30 5591 8-8-8 **86** (t) LiamKeniry 16 89
(Peter Fahey, Ire) *hld up towards rr: hdwy and travelling wl 5f out: swtchd rt 4f out: 4th and rdn 3f out: no imp and edging rt over 1f out: kpt on same pce after* **16/1**

2511 **5** *4 1/2* **Champagne Champ**15 6083 4-8-8 **86** MartinLane 12 84
(Rod Millman) *chsd ldrs: rdn 5f out: 5th and outpcd 2f out: btn whn hung rt over 1f out: wknd ins fnl f* **8/1**3

110 **6** *1 3/4* **Hatsaway (IRE)**31 5553 5-8-2 **80** NickyMackay 2 76
(Pat Phelan) *chsd wnr: rdn 3f out: unable qck w wnr ent fnl 2f: lost 2nd over 1f out: wknd fnl f* **40/1**

0-00 **7** *3* **Teak (IRE)**31 5559 9-8-2 **80** (p) PatrickMathers 10 73
(Ian Williams) *in tch in midfield: rdn 4f out: drvn and outpcd 3f out: no ch fnl 2f* **25/1**

4526 **8** *1* **Haines**42 5144 5-8-4 **89** WilliamCox(7) 8 81
(Andrew Balding) *t.k.h: wl in tch in midfield: drvn and unable qck over 3f out: outpcd and btn over 2f out: wknd 2f out* **16/1**

0131 **9** *3* **Oceane (FR)**31 5559 4-9-0 **92** (p) FergusSweeney 7 80
(Alan King) *hld up in tch in midfield: rdn and hdwy over 3f out: 7th and no hdwy u.p over 2f out: wknd 2f out* **5/2**1

6052 **10** *2* **Planetoid (IRE)**42 5176 8-8-6 **84** ow3 (b) SamHitchcott 1 70
(Jim Best) *hld up in last quintet: effrt 4f out: no hdwy u.p 3f out: sn wl btn* **25/1**

35-2 **11** *3* **Perceus**148 1598 4-8-8 **86** ThomasBrown 6 69
(James Eustace) *chsd ldrs: rdn 4f out: sn struggling and lost pl: wknd over 2f out* **25/1**

2113 **12** *nse* **Arty Campbell (IRE)**18 5999 6-8-6 **84** JimmyQuinn 14 67
(Bernard Llewellyn) *hld up in tch in last quintet: effrt and sme hdwy u.p over 3f out: no hdwy over 2f out: sn wknd* **33/1**

0345 **13** *3 1/4* **Air Squadron**37 5321 6-7-7 **78** SophieKilloran(7) 13 57
(Ralph Beckett) *chsd ldrs: rdn 4f out: sn lost pl: wknd over 2f out* **25/1**

5141 **14** *6* **Ravenous**36 5381 5-8-4 **82** KieranO'Neill 15 55
(Luke Dace) *hld up in tch in last quintet: effrt u.p 4f out: no imp and btn 3f out: sn wknd* **20/1**

0010 **15** *3 1/4* **Wind Place And Sho**52 4752 4-8-12 **90** RyanTate 18 59
(James Eustace) *in tch in midfield: lost pl u.p and bhd 4f out: lost tch over 2f out: t.o* **12/1**

/10- **16** *1 1/2* **Low Key (IRE)**87 7115 9-8-12 **90** (bt1) PatCosgrave 5 57
(David Pipe) *hld up in tch in last quintet: effrt and sme hdwy u.p 4f out: lost pl and btn 3f out: sn wknd: t.o* **14/1**

5-00 **17** *43* **Kalann (IRE)**7 6350 9-9-0 **92** (tp) LeighRoche 17 12
(Denis Gerard Hogan, Ire) *chsd ldrs: drvn and lost pl over 3f out: bhd and eased 2f out: t.o* **50/1**

4m 0.5s (8.50) **Going Correction** +0.125s/f (Good) **17** Ran SP% **129.9**
Speed ratings (Par 109): **86,84,82,82,80 79,78,78,76,75 74,74,73,70,68 68,49**
CSF £34.22 CT £482.19 TOTE £6.70: £1.90, £1.80, £3.50, £3.40; EX 44.60 Trifecta £224.20.
Owner Godolphin **Bred** Darley **Trained** Newmarket, Suffolk

FOCUS
A deep trial for next month's Cesarewitch and a lot to like about the performance of the formerly smart Penglai Pavilion. They finished well strung out, with many unsuited by the steady early pace.

6583 ASPALL H'CAP 6f
4:25 (4:26) (Class 4) (0-85,84) 3-Y-O+ **£6,469** (£1,925; £962; £481) **Stalls** Centre

Form RPR
4144 **1** **Under Siege (IRE)**18 5991 4-9-2 **79** (t) PatCosgrave 5 88
(Stuart Williams) *trckd ldrs: wnt 2nd and travelling wl ent fnl 2f: rdn over 1f out: drvn and led jst ins fnl f: styd on: all out cl home* **9/1**

333 **2** *hd* **Ice Age (IRE)**22 5825 3-9-1 **80** CharlesBishop 13 88
(Eve Johnson Houghton) *hld up in midfield: hdwy u.p to chse ldng pair over 1f out: styd on to chse ldr towards fin: clsng towards fin* **11/2**2

5213 **3** *3/4* **Summer Chorus**21 5878 3-9-5 **84** JimmyQuinn 12 89+
(Andrew Balding) *taken down early: dwlt: hld up in tch towards rr: effrt 2f out: hdwy u.p 1f out: styd on wl ins fnl f: wnt 3rd towards fin: nvr quite getting to ldrs* **11/2**2

3315 **4** *3/4* **Menai (IRE)**11 6210 3-8-12 **77** WilliamBuick 3 80
(Charles Hills) *led: rdn 2f out: drvn and hdd jst ins fnl f: styd on same pce u.p ins fnl f: lost 2 pls wl ins fnl f* **7/1**3

2323 **5** *1 1/4* **Compas Scoobie**77 3899 3-8-9 **74** FrederikTylicki 7 73
(Roger Varian) *stdd s: t.k.h: hld up in tch in midfield: effrt over 1f out: no imp and styd on same pce ins fnl f* **14/1**

6102 **6** *3/4* **Excellent George**21 5882 4-9-2 **82** (t) AaronJones(3) 1 78
(Stuart Williams) *racd along towards far side: in tch in midfield overall: rdn ent fnl 2f: no imp u.p over 1f out: kpt on same pce fnl f* **10/1**

0100 **7** *3/4* **Field Game**25 5744 4-8-10 **78** (t) CharlieBennett(5) 2 72
(Hughie Morrison) *hld up in tch in midfield: effrt 2f out: drvn and sme hdwy over 1f out: kpt on same pce and no imp fnl f* **12/1**

3200 **8** *nk* **Regal Parade**10 6237 12-8-7 **70** oh3 1 NickyMackay 9 63
(Charlie Wallis) *bhd: rdn over 2f out: no imp tl styd on ins fnl f: nvr trbld ldrs* **33/1**

0052 **9** *nk* **Francisco**25 5744 4-9-6 **83** KieranO'Neill 8 75
(Richard Hannon) *hld up in tch towards rr: effrt over 2f out: no imp u.p over 1f out: kpt on same pce fnl f* **9/1**

4143 **10** *1/2* **Bahamian Dollar**14 6123 3-9-1 **80** JamesDoyle 6 70
(James Tate) *chsd ldr tl 2f out: drvn and unable qck over 1f out: wknd ins fnl f* **9/2**1

0046 **11** *7* **Souville**7 6340 5-8-11 **81** SamuelClarke(7) 10 49
(Chris Wall) *t.k.h: sn chsng ldrs: rdn ent fnl 2f: little rspnse and lost pl over 1f out: wknd fnl f* **16/1**

-000 **12** *6* **Garden World (IRE)**112 2693 3-7-12 **70** KieranSchofield(7) 11 19
(Nigel Tinkler) *hld up in tch in last trio: effrt over 2f out: no hdwy: wknd over 1f out: bhd fnl f* **50/1**

1m 12.4s (0.20) **Going Correction** +0.125s/f (Good)
WFA 3 from 4yo+ 2lb **12** Ran SP% **115.7**
Speed ratings (Par 105): **103,102,101,100,99 98,97,96,96,95 86,78**
CSF £56.41 CT £305.09 TOTE £10.10: £3.00, £2.00, £1.50; EX 73.40 Trifecta £195.10.
Owner Happy Valley Racing & Breeding Limited **Bred** Irish National Stud **Trained** Newmarket, Suffolk

FOCUS
This featured some largely consistent types and represents solid form for the level. A length pb from the winner, with the fourth helping to set the standard.

6584 EBF STALLIONS BREEDING WINNERS FILLIES' H'CAP 1m 4f
5:00 (5:01) (Class 3) (0-95,91) 3-Y-O+ **£9,703** (£2,887; £1,443; £721) **Stalls** Centre

Form RPR
6111 **1** **Dubka**37 5328 3-9-6 **91** WilliamBuick 1 102+
(Sir Michael Stoute) *hld up wl in tch in last pair: clsd to trck ldrs over 3f out: rdn and ev ch 2f out: led jst over 1f out: styd on strly and drew clr u.p ins fnl f: eased cl hone* **9/4**2

3110 **2** *3 1/4* **Eager Beaver**37 5328 4-9-4 **81** SamHitchcott 5 86
(William Muir) *led: rdn ent fnl 2f: drvn and hdd jst over 1f out: no ex and outpcd ins fnl f: hld on to 2nd cl home* **20/1**

2144 **3** *nk* **Talent To Amuse (IRE)**[64] 4351 3-8-10 **81**.................. FrederikTylicki 3 86
(Roger Varian) *wl in tch in midfield: rdn over 3f out: 5th and outpcd whn hung rt wl over 1f out: rallied u.p ins fnl f: no threat to wnr but pressing for 2nd towards fin* **10/1**

51 **4** *3¼* **Elraazy**[16] 6052 3-8-9 **80**.. FrankieDettori 6 79+
(John Gosden) *trckd ldrs: wnt 2nd 5f out: rdn and ev ch over 2f out: 3rd and no ex ent fnl f: wknd ins fnl f* **1/1**[1]

1240 **5** *2* **Stockhill Diva**[16] 6057 6-9-9 **91**.................................. MitchGodwin(5) 4 87
(Brendan Powell) *t.k.h: hld up wl in tch in rr: effrt in cl 4th wl over 2f out: unable qck over 1f out: wknd ins fnl f* **16/1**

51 **6** *21* **Gala**[36] 5353 3-8-8 **79**.. NickyMackay 2 42
(John Gosden) *press ldr tl 5f out: lost pl and bhd over 3f out: wl bhd and eased over 1f out* **6/1**[3]

2m 33.32s (1.32) **Going Correction** +0.125s/f (Good)
WFA 3 from 4yo+ 8lb **6** Ran SP% **114.8**
Speed ratings (Par 104): **100,97,97,95,94 80**
CSF £41.10 TOTE £2.10: £1.10, £6.40; EX 25.10 Trifecta £105.90.
Owner Sir Evelyn De Rothschild **Bred** Southcourt Stud **Trained** Newmarket, Suffolk

FOCUS
A fascinating contest and another smooth victory from the rapidly improving Dubka. It's been rated around the runner-up.

6585 HOME OF RACING H'CAP 1m
5:35 (5:37) (Class 2) (0-100,98) 3-Y-O+ **£16,172** (£4,812; £2,405; £1,202) **Stalls** Centre

Form RPR

0002 **1** **God Willing**[7] 6320 5-8-13 **87**... FrederikTylicki 2 95
(Declan Carroll) *hld up wl in tch in last pair: hdwy and rdn over 2f out: chsd ldrs and drvn over 1f out: chal 1f out: led ins fnl f: r.o wl: rdn out* **7/1**[3]

1-41 **2** *¾* **Storm Ahead (IRE)**[87] 3534 3-8-10 **88**............................ PatCosgrave 5 95
(Marcus Tregoning) *chsd ldr: rdn 3f out: drvn and ev ch 2f out: led jst ins fnl f: hdd and styd on same pce ins fnl f* **9/2**[2]

0005 **3** *2½* **Whitman**[23] 5802 3-8-8 **86**..(b[1]) NickyMackay 10 87
(Mark Johnston) *broke fast: led and set stdy gallop. rdn and qcknd 3f out: hrd pressed and drvn 2f out: hdd jst ins fnl f: kpt on same pce after* **25/1**

2314 **4** *1* **Worlds His Oyster**[21] 5886 3-8-6 **84** oh1......................(p) JimmyQuinn 7 85+
(John Quinn) *wl in tch in midfield: rdn 3f out: struggling to qckn whn squeezed for room and hmpd jst over 2f out: rallied ins fnl f: styd on fnl 110yds: no threat to ldrs* **10/1**

0211 **5** *½* **Zwayyan**[16] 6055 3-8-10 **88**... FrankieDettori 9 86
(William Haggas) *stmbld leaving stalls: trckd ldrs: rdn 3f out: nt clr run and swtchd rt jst over 2f out: hdwy and chsng ldrs over 1f out: unable qck and edgd lft 1f out: wknd ins fnl f* **11/8**[1]

1200 **6** *4½* **Jailawi (IRE)**[30] 5585 5-9-10 **98**.. WilliamBuick 1 85
(Ismail Mohammed) *racd alone in centre: chsd ldrs: rdn 3f out: unable qck u.p 2f out: wknd fnl f* **7/1**[3]

3411 **7** *nse* **Wind In My Sails**[21] 5892 4-8-13 **87**.................................. LiamKeniry 6 74
(Ed de Giles) *taken down early: stdd s: t.k.h in rr: pushed over 2f out: nvr on terms* **14/1**

0062 **8** *1* **Glory Awaits (IRE)**[19] 5956 6-9-8 **96**............(b) WilliamTwiston-Davies 4 81
(David Simcock) *t.k.h: chsd ldrs: rdn 3f out: edgd lft and bmpd jst over 2f out: lost pl and btn over 1f out: wknd fnl f* **9/1**

1m 39.79s (1.19) **Going Correction** +0.15s/f (Good)
WFA 3 from 4yo+ 4lb **8** Ran SP% **114.9**
Speed ratings (Par 109): **100,99,96,95,95 90,90,89**
CSF £38.62 CT £749.83 TOTE £8.20: £2.20, £1.50, £6.20; EX 42.10 Trifecta £1141.10.
Owner Steven Ryan & Neil Smillie **Bred** Highbank Stud Llp **Trained** Malton, N Yorks

FOCUS
This has proved a difficult race for favourites in recent seasons and that trend continued as the well fancied Zwayyan could manage only fifth.
T/Plt: £92.90 to a £1 stake. Pool: £73,717.19 - 578.83 winning units. T/Qpdt: £39.80 to a £1 stake. Pool: £3,910.63 - 72.67 winning units. **Steve Payne**

6419 WOLVERHAMPTON (A.W) (L-H)
Saturday, September 17

OFFICIAL GOING: Tapeta: standard
Wind: Light across Weather: Fine

6586 CASH OUT AT BET365 H'CAP (DIV I) 5f 20y (Tp)
5:40 (5:40) (Class 6) (0-55,55) 3-Y-O+ **£2,587** (£770; £384; £192) **Stalls** Low

Form RPR

032 **1** **Kiringa**[20] 5928 3-9-6 **55**... JimCrowley 10 67+
(Robert Cowell) *chsd ldrs: rdn to ld ins fnl f: r.o wl* **5/2**[2]

2100 **2** *3* **Whispering Soul (IRE)**[36] 5378 3-9-6 **55**................(p) ConnorBeasley 6 56
(Brian Baugh) *disp ld: rdn and ev ch over 1f out: styd on same pce ins fnl f* **15/2**

0245 **3** *1* **Zebelini (IRE)**[15] 6098 4-9-2 **50**..................................(b) JoeFanning 5 48
(Ollie Pears) *disp ld: rdn over 1f out: hdd and no ex ins fnl f* **5/1**[3]

-405 **4** *½* **Redalani (IRE)**[15] 6101 6-9-1 **49**................................(b) PaddyAspell 3 45+
(Alan Brown) *hld up in tch: plld hrd: rdn over 1f out: edgd lft and styd on same pce ins fnl f* **16/1**

3004 **5** *½* **Cerulean Silk**[22] 5826 6-8-12 **46** oh1.............................. WilliamCarson 4 40
(Tony Carroll) *chsd ldrs: rdn and ev ch over 1f out: wknd wl ins fnl f* **10/1**

663- **6** *1¼* **Fred's Filly**[339] 7209 3-8-10 **52**..............................(b) CameronNoble(7) 11 42
(Bill Turner) *prom: rdn over 1f out: edgd lft and wknd fnl f* **28/1**

0000 **7** *¾* **Seraphima**[23] 5807 6-8-12 **46** oh1..........................(p) AdamBeschizza 2 33
(Lisa Williamson) *pushed along in rr early: hdwy u.p on inner over 1f out: wknd ins fnl f* **66/1**

0106 **8** *¾* **Molly Jones**[22] 5826 7-8-13 **52**....................................... LucyKBarry(5) 8 36
(Matthew Salaman) *s.i.s: hld up: hdwy u.p over 1f out: wknd ins fnl f* **28/1**

2563 **9** *2* **Frangarry (IRE)**[15] 6100 4-9-4 **55**..............................(b) EoinWalsh(3) 7 32+
(Alan Bailey) *s.s: bhd: effrt over 1f out: wknd fnl f* **9/4**[1]

1m 2.21s (0.31) **Going Correction** -0.025s/f (Stan)
WFA 3 from 4yo+ 1lb **9** Ran SP% **111.1**
Speed ratings (Par 101): **96,91,89,88,88 86,84,83,80**
CSF £20.13 CT £83.28 TOTE £3.40: £1.40, £2.60, £1.20; EX 18.50 Trifecta £75.30.
Owner Manor Farm Stud (rutland) **Bred** Manor Farm Stud (rutland) **Trained** Six Mile Bottom, Cambs

FOCUS
A pleasant enough, dry evening in the West Midlands for this eight-race card. Not many got into this opening division of a low-grade sprint handicap.

6587 CASH OUT AT BET365 H'CAP (DIV II) 5f 20y (Tp)
6:10 (6:11) (Class 6) (0-55,55) 3-Y-O+ **£2,587** (£770; £384; £192) **Stalls** Low

Form RPR

0040 **1** **Harpers Ruby**[17] 6023 6-9-2 **50**...................................... PaddyAspell 10 59
(Lynn Siddall) *w ldr tl led 4f out: rdn and edgd rt over 1f out: r.o* **11/1**

33-0 **2** *2½* **Wimboldsley**[33] 5470 5-9-1 **49**.............................. MichaelJMMurphy 3 49
(Scott Dixon) *led 1f: chsd wnr: rdn over 1f out: styd on same pce ins fnl f* **10/1**

1613 **3** *½* **Willow Spring**[28] 5628 4-8-10 **51**............................ CameronNoble(7) 9 49
(Conrad Allen) *hld up: hdwy 1/2-way: rdn over 1f out: styd on same pce ins fnl f* **5/1**[2]

0660 **4** *½* **Equal Point**[22] 5827 3-9-6 **55**... WilliamCarson 6 51
(William Knight) *mid-div: hdwy over 1f out: sn rdn and hung lft: styd on same pce ins fnl f* **15/2**

4440 **5** *1¼* **Golden Rosanna**[7] 6312 3-8-6 **46** oh1........................ AnnaHesketh(5) 7 38
(Steph Hollinshead) *pushed along in rr early: rdn over 1f out: r.o ins fnl f: nvr nrr* **16/1**

0-00 **6** *1½* **Camino**[26] 5725 3-9-5 **54**.. TomQueally 11 41
(Willie Musson) *chsd ldrs: hrd rdn over 1f out: hung lft and wknd wl ins fnl f* **10/1**

0400 **7** *1¾* **Simply Black (IRE)**[47] 4931 5-8-7 **46** oh1....................(p) AnnStokell(5) 5 26
(Ann Stokell) *pushed along in rr early: hdwy u.p over 1f out: wknd ins fnl f* **40/1**

6500 **8** *¾* **Eland Ally**[59] 4529 8-9-7 **55**..(p) JoeFanning 1 42+
(Anabel K Murphy) *dwlt: a in rr* **7/1**

-036 **9** *1¾* **Plantation (IRE)**[20] 5920 3-9-2 **51**..............................(v[1]) JimCrowley 8 22
(Robert Cowell) *chsd ldrs: rdn over 1f out: wknd fnl f* **11/4**[1]

50/0 **10** *3¾* **Decibelle**[44] 5080 4-8-12 **46**...[1] RyanPowell 2 4
(Barry Brennan) *pushed along in rr: rdn and wknd over 1f out* **66/1**

0026 **11** *½* **Give Us A Belle (IRE)**[33] 5470 7-9-5 **53**..............(p) AdamBeschizza 4 9
(Christine Dunnett) *prom: pushed along over 3f out: rdn 1/2-way: wknd over 1f out* **13/2**[3]

1m 1.83s (-0.07) **Going Correction** -0.025s/f (Stan)
WFA 3 from 4yo+ 1lb **11** Ran SP% **117.3**
Speed ratings (Par 101): **99,95,94,93,91 89,86,85,82,76 75**
CSF £115.83 CT £633.87 TOTE £12.80: £3.70, £3.10, £2.20; EX 118.00 Trifecta £797.20.
Owner Jimmy Kay **Bred** Select Bloodstock **Trained** Colton, N Yorks

FOCUS
Probably the weaker division of the two but a similar outcome, with few taking much of a hand and the winner again emerging from stall ten.

6588 BET365 (S) STKS 5f 216y (Tp)
6:40 (6:43) (Class 6) 2-Y-O **£2,587** (£770; £384; £192) **Stalls** Low

Form RPR

4005 **1** **Control Centre (IRE)**[11] 6208 2-9-0 59......................... TimmyMurphy 4 63
(Richard Hannon) *mid-div: sn pushed along: hdwy wl over 1f out: sn swtchd rt: rdn and r.o to ld wl ins fnl f* **6/1**

2306 **2** *1* **Pulsating (IRE)**[22] 5840 2-8-9 64.. JoeFanning 6 55
(Rebecca Menzies) *chsd ldrs: shkn up over 2f out: rdn to ld 1f out: edgd lft and hdd wl ins fnl f* **7/4**[1]

6655 **3** *3* **Gerrard's Return**[19] 5974 2-9-0 64.............................(p) JimCrowley 1 51
(Tom Dascombe) *chsd ldrs: rdn and ev ch 1f out: no ex ins fnl f* **7/2**[2]

6430 **4** *2½* **Spin Top**[17] 6033 2-9-0 61...(v) TomQueally 8 44+
(Joseph Tuite) *chsd ldr: rdn to ld over 1f out: sn edgd lft and hdd: wknd wl ins fnl f* **11/2**[3]

0 **5** *2½* **Dazacam**[32] 5524 2-8-9 0... ConnorBeasley 7 31+
(Michael Herrington) *sn led: rdn: hdd and hung lft fr over 1f out: wknd ins fnl f* **8/1**

206 **6** *1¾* **Yorkshire Star (IRE)**[11] 6208 2-9-0 52....................(b[1]) WilliamCarson 5 31
(Bill Turner) *sn outpcd: nvr nrr* **28/1**

5206 **7** *1¼* **King Of Castilla**[3] 6471 2-8-13 61....................(bt[1]) CameronNoble(7) 10 33
(Gay Kelleway) *chsd ldrs: rdn over 2f out: wknd fnl f* **10/1**

0040 **8** *2½* **Miss Island Ruler**[9] 6252 2-8-9 48.................................(b) JasonHart 2 15
(Shaun Harris) *s.i.s: outpcd* **50/1**

9 *5* **The Boys So Sharp** 2-8-9 0...................................(vt[1]) AnnaHesketh(5) 3 5
(Oliver Greenall) *s.i.s: outpcd* **40/1**

0U00 **10** *7* **She's Rosanna**[10] 6236 2-8-9 47.................................[1] AdamBeschizza 9
(Steph Hollinshead) *mid-div: rdn over 2f out: sn wknd* **100/1**

1m 14.61s (0.11) **Going Correction** -0.025s/f (Stan) **10** Ran SP% **117.3**
Speed ratings (Par 93): **98,96,92,89,86 83,82,78,72,70**
CSF £16.77 TOTE £7.50: £2.20, £1.30, £1.40; EX 20.40 Trifecta £88.10.Pulsating was bought by Ali Stronge for £6,000
Owner Simon Leech **Bred** Denis McDonnell **Trained** East Everleigh, Wilts
■ Stewards' Enquiry : Adam Beschizza caution: careless riding

FOCUS
A very moderate juvenile seller, though the pace did at least look reasonably generous.

6589 BET365.COM H'CAP 5f 216y (Tp)
7:10 (7:11) (Class 5) (0-75,75) 3-Y-O+ **£3,234** (£962; £481; £240) **Stalls** Low

Form RPR

0440 **1** **Sophisticated Heir (IRE)**[10] 6231 6-9-1 **69**..................(b) JoeFanning 7 83
(Michael Herrington) *chsd ldrs: shkn up to ld over 1f out: edgd lft ins fnl f: r.o wl* **4/1**[3]

310 **2** *4* **Kindly**[90] 3439 3-9-3 **73**... JimCrowley 1 74
(Simon Crisford) *disp ld tl rdn and hdd over 1f out: styd on same pce ins fnl f* **9/4**[1]

0000 **3** *¾* **Dark Side Dream**[152] 1528 4-9-0 **71**.................... JosephineGordon(3) 11 70
(Chris Dwyer) *disp ld: rdn and ev ch over 1f out: no ex ins fnl f* **15/2**

1000 **4** *½* **Spellmaker**[87] 3510 7-8-10 **67**... EoinWalsh(3) 3 64
(Tony Newcombe) *broke wl: sn stdd and lost pl: racd keenly: nt clr run over 2f out: hdwy over 1f out: sn rdn: styd on same pce ins fnl f* **33/1**

0611 **5** *1½* **Langley Vale**[29] 5605 7-8-6 **65**..................................(v) GeorgeWood(5) 2 57
(Roger Teal) *hld up: plld hrd: hdwy u.p over 1f out: edgd lft and styd on same pce ins fnl f* **7/2**[2]

5000 **6** *½* **Dutch Golden Age (IRE)**[24] 5774 4-9-7 **75**.................. FergusSweeney 9 66
(Gary Moore) *hld up: hdwy u.p over 1f out: wknd ins fnl f* **20/1**

0000 **7** *2½* **Clubland (IRE)**[14] 6131 7-8-9 **70**.................................. KevinLundie(7) 4 53
(Roy Bowring) *s.i.s: hdwy over 4f out: rdn over 2f out: wknd over 1f out* **9/1**

2000 **8** *2½* **Air Of York (IRE)**[22] 5825 4-8-13 **74**................................ AledBeech(7) 6 49
(David Evans) *in rr: hung rt 1/2-way: nvr on terms* **10/1**

3000 **9** 3 3/4 **Long Awaited (IRE)**[9] 6248 8-8-13 **67**........................(v) ConnorBeasley 8 30
(Conor Dore) *prom: rdn over 2f out: wknd over 1f out* **50/1**
1m 13.22s (-1.28) **Going Correction** -0.025s/f (Stan)
WFA 3 from 4yo+ 2lb **9** Ran SP% **113.5**
Speed ratings (Par 103): **107,101,100,100,98 97,94,90,85**
CSF £12.90 CT £63.27 TOTE £4.20: £1.40, £1.40, £1.90; EX 15.00 Trifecta £98.40.
Owner Darren & Annaley Yates **Bred** J S Bolger & John Corcoran **Trained** Cold Kirby, N Yorks
FOCUS
The first three home were always to the fore in this reasonable handicap for the grade. The winner has been rated to last winter's AW best.

6590 BET365 EBF MAIDEN STKS 1m 141y (Tp)
7:40 (7:40) (Class 5) 2-Y-O **£3,234** (£962; £481; £240) **Stalls** Low

Form RPR
4 **1** **Ode To Glory**[18] 5990 2-9-0 0.. MartinDwyer 3 68
(Rae Guest) *chsd ldrs: rdn over 1f out: r.o to ld nr fin* **16/1**
4 **2** *nk* **Tawfik (IRE)**[39] 5250 2-9-5 0.. JimCrowley 1 72
(Harry Dunlop) *a.p: rdn to ld wl ins fnl f: hdd nr fin* **10/1**
3 1/2 **War Chief** 2-9-5 0.. FergusSweeney 10 71+
(Alan King) *s.i.s: hld up: hdwy over 1f out: r.o wl* **14/1**
F3 **4** 1 1/2 **Paddy A (IRE)**[46] 4975 2-9-2 0................................ LouisSteward(3) 9 68
(Philip McBride) *chsd ldrs: rdn to ld and hung lft over 1f out: hdd and no ex wl ins fnl f* **4/1**[2]
0 **5** *hd* **Flauto (IRE)**[27] 5676 2-9-5 0.. PaoloSirigu 8 68
(Marco Botti) *w ldr tl led over 2f out: rdn and hdd over 1f out: edgd lft: styd on same pce ins fnl f* **33/1**
6 3 1/4 **Pathway To Freedom** 2-9-5 0.. MartinLane 5 63+
(Charlie Appleby) *dwlt: pushed along in rr early: hdwy over 2f out: rdn and edgd lft over 1f out: wknd ins fnl f* **11/8**[1]
44 **7** 1 1/4 **Dominating (GER)**[20] 5916 2-9-5 0.................................... JoeFanning 2 58
(Mark Johnston) *sn led: hdd over 2f out: wknd fnl f* **8/1**[3]
8 *hd* **Starshell (IRE)** 2-9-5 0... LukeMorris 4 58
(Sir Mark Prescott Bt) *s.i.s: sn mid-div: lost pl over 5f out: pushed along over 2f out: nt trble ldrs* **8/1**[3]
6 **9** *nse* **Willie's Anne (IRE)**[19] 5951 2-8-7 0................................ TobyEley(7) 6 53
(Daniel Mark Loughnane) *mid-div: rn green: hdwy u.p over 1f out: wknd fnl f* **100/1**
5 **10** 6 **Hiawassee (USA)**[10] 6223 2-9-0 0...................................... JasonHart 7 40
(Mark Johnston) *pushed along in rr over 6f out: rdn and wknd over 2f out* **66/1**
11 1/2 **Cape Baba** 2-9-5 0... TomMarquand 11 44
(Chris Wall) *hld up: hdwy over 4f out: wknd 2f out* **28/1**
1m 52.15s (2.05) **Going Correction** -0.025s/f (Stan) **11** Ran SP% **114.8**
Speed ratings (Par 95): **89,88,88,86,86 83,82,82,82,77 76**
CSF £158.52 TOTE £18.50: £3.70, £3.10, £3.90; EX 123.80 Trifecta £1628.50.
Owner The Reprobates **Bred** Whitsbury Manor Stud **Trained** Newmarket, Suffolk
FOCUS
Some top connections represented in this juvenile maiden, but maybe not as strong a piece of form as if might have been with none of the four market leaders making the podium.

6591 BET365 H'CAP 2m 119y (Tp)
8:10 (8:10) (Class 4) (0-85,85) 3-Y-O+ **£4,690** (£1,395; £697; £348) **Stalls** Low

Form RPR
3163 **1** **Royal Reef (IRE)**[24] 5767 4-9-3 **74**................................(v[1]) JimmyQuinn 1 87
(William Knight) *mde all: racd keenly and sn wnt clr: c bk to the field over 2f out: shkn up and wnt clr again over 1f out: unchal* **11/1**
1243 **2** 7 **Against The Odds**[24] 5761 3-9-1 **84**................................[1] JimCrowley 6 89
(Paul Cole) *chsd ldr of main gp: rdn over 3f out: styd on to go 2nd ins fnl f: no ch w wnr* **5/6**[1]
1204 **3** 3 3/4 **Space Mountain**[7] 6345 3-8-8 **77**...................................... JoeFanning 3 78
(Mark Johnston) *chsd wnr who sn wnt clr: rdn to take clsr order over 2f out: sn outpcd again: no ex and lost 2nd ins fnl f* **8/1**[3]
0045 **4** 3 3/4 **Wordiness**[8] 6279 8-9-9 **80**... MichaelJMMurphy 8 76
(David Evans) *hld up: rdn over 2f out: nvr on terms* **10/1**
1115 **5** 7 **Lady Makfi (IRE)**[22] 5851 4-9-8 **79**................................ StevieDonohoe 5 67
(Johnny Farrelly) *s.i.s: hld up: rdn over 2f out: n.d* **3/1**[2]
-060 **6** 31 **Senrima (IRE)**[16] 6050 4-9-4 **75**..[1] TomQueally 4 25
(Brian Meehan) *hld up: plld hrd: rdn over 3f out: wknd over 2f out* **25/1**
3m 40.14s (-3.56) **Going Correction** -0.025s/f (Stan)
WFA 3 from 4yo+ 12lb **6** Ran SP% **111.9**
Speed ratings (Par 105): **107,103,101,100,96 82**
CSF £20.84 CT £80.14 TOTE £11.00: £4.30, £1.10; EX 25.10 Trifecta £101.20.
Owner W J Knight **Bred** Herbertstown House Stud **Trained** Patching, W Sussex
FOCUS
The feature race of the night, stolen from the front by a crafty ride. The runner-up and third have been rated a bit below their bests.

6592 CASINO AT BET365 H'CAP 7f 32y (Tp)
8:40 (8:41) (Class 6) (0-65,70) 3-Y-O **£2,587** (£770; £384; £192) **Stalls** High

Form RPR
0604 **1** **Luang Prabang (IRE)**[24] 5769 3-9-3 **64**...................... LouisSteward(3) 2 70+
(Chris Wall) *hld up: hdwy and nt clr run over 1f out: rdn and r.o to ld wl ins fnl f* **9/2**[3]
6235 **2** 1 **Guanabara Bay (IRE)**[8] 6291 3-9-6 **64**........................ TomMarquand 11 68
(Martyn Meade) *s.i.s: hld up: shkn up and hung lft fr over 1f out: r.o ins fnl f: wnt 2nd post* **14/1**
0423 **3** *hd* **Encore Moi**[26] 5720 3-9-4 **62**...(b[1]) LukeMorris 10 66
(Marco Botti) *s.i.s: hdwy over 5f out: rdn to ld over 1f out: sn hung lft: hdd and unable qck wl ins fnl f* **9/2**[3]
2525 **4** 1 1/4 **Marcle (IRE)**[17] 6021 3-9-7 **65**...[1] JimCrowley 8 65
(Ed de Giles) *led: rdn and hdd over 1f out: carried lft and styd on same pce wl ins fnl f* **7/2**[1]
5446 **5** *hd* **Arlecchino's Rock**[23] 5807 3-9-2 **60**................................. LiamKeniry 4 60
(Mark Usher) *hld up in tch: rdn over 1f out: styd on same pce wl ins fnl f* **16/1**
4506 **6** 1 **Sexton Blake (IRE)**[39] 5259 3-9-6 **64**.......................... FergusSweeney 1 62
(Gary Moore) *hld up: hdwy: nt clr run and hung lft fr over 1f out: r.o ins fnl f: nt rch ldrs* **7/1**
6361 **7** 1 3/4 **Tulip Dress**[32] 5515 3-9-4 **62**.. KieranO'Neill 3 55
(Anthony Carson) *mid-div: rdn over 2f out: hdwy over 1f out: no ex ins fnl f* **16/1**
1040 **8** 1/2 **Broughtons Fancy**[26] 5725 3-8-12 **61**.......................... GeorgeWood(5) 6 55
(Andrew Reid) *prom: rdn over 1f out: styng on same pce whn carried lft ins fnl f* **14/1**

3201 **9** *shd* **Harmony Bay (IRE)**[8] 6290 3-9-7 **70**................................ MitchGodwin(5) 5 62
(Sylvester Kirk) *hld up: racd keenly: hdwy on outer and hung rt over 2f out: styd on same pce fr over 1f out* **4/1**[2]
0600 **10** 7 **Ginger Joe**[57] 4600 3-9-7 **65**... JoeFanning 9 40
(David Brown) *plld hrd: sn w ldr: rdn over 2f out: wknd fnl f* **33/1**
2-00 **11** 1 1/2 **Rock Warbler (IRE)**[40] 5246 3-8-13 **62**........................(t) AnnaHesketh(5) 7 33
(Oliver Greenall) *plld hrd and prom: rdn over 2f out: wknd over 1f out* **40/1**
1m 29.18s (0.38) **Going Correction** -0.025s/f (Stan) **11** Ran SP% **121.6**
Speed ratings (Par 99): **96,94,94,93,92 91,89,89,89,81 79**
CSF £68.43 CT £311.44 TOTE £6.70: £2.10, £3.70, £1.50; EX 97.60 Trifecta £598.00.
Owner Des Thurlby **Bred** Deerfield Farm **Trained** Newmarket, Suffolk
FOCUS
An ordinary 3yo event, and the winner and runner-up came very late.

6593 POKER AT BET365 H'CAP 1m 4f 50y (Tp)
9:10 (9:10) (Class 6) (0-65,64) 3-Y-O+ **£2,587** (£770; £384; £192) **Stalls** Low

Form RPR
5-32 **1** **Alsacienne**[18] 5993 3-9-2 **62**... LukeMorris 5 71
(Sir Mark Prescott Bt) *sn prom: pushed along over 3f out: rdn to chse ldr and hung lft fr over 1f out: styd on to ld nr fin* **9/4**[1]
2634 **2** 1/2 **Wallangarra**[22] 5824 3-8-13 **64**.................................. DavidParkes(5) 4 72
(Jeremy Gask) *trckd ldrs: plld hrd: wnt 2nd 10f out tl led over 2f out: rdn over 1f out: hdd nr fin* **15/2**
1223 **3** 5 **Anneani (IRE)**[14] 6137 4-9-7 **59**.. JimCrowley 6 59
(David Evans) *hld up: hdwy over 2f out: rdn over 1f out: no imp fnl f* **9/2**[3]
6-04 **4** 3/4 **Right Madam (IRE)**[51] 568 4-8-12 **50** oh2..................(p) KieranO'Neill 7 49
(Sarah Hollinshead) *hld up: rdn over 3f out: hung lft and r.o ins fnl f: nvr nrr* **66/1**
0120 **5** 1 3/4 **File Of Facts (IRE)**[31] 5548 3-8-10 **61**........................(vt) AnnaHesketh(5) 2 57
(Tom Dascombe) *led: rdn and hdd over 2f out: wknd fnl f* **14/1**
0051 **6** *nk* **Want The Fairytale**[14] 6143 3-9-2 **62**.............................. TomMarquand 1 58
(Clive Cox) *hld up: rdn over 2f out: nvr on terms* **3/1**[2]
3354 **7** 1 1/2 **Sunshineandbubbles**[14] 6143 3-8-13 **59**..........................(p) JoeFanning 8 52
(Daniel Mark Loughnane) *s.i.s: hld up: hdwy over 3f out: rdn and wknd over 1f out* **8/1**
-050 **8** 4 **Enchanted Moment**[38] 5303 4-9-2 **57**........................(p) LouisSteward(3) 9 44
(Chris Wall) *chsd ldr 2f: remained handy: rdn over 2f out: wknd over 1f out* **16/1**
000 **9** 1 **Mr Marchwood**[51] 4794 3-9-1 **61**.. LiamKeniry 3 46
(Sylvester Kirk) *hld up: rdn over 2f out: wknd wl over 1f out* **14/1**
2m 39.05s (-1.75) **Going Correction** -0.025s/f (Stan)
WFA 3 from 4yo 8lb **9** Ran SP% **117.5**
Speed ratings (Par 101): **104,103,100,99,98 98,97,94,94**
CSF £20.46 CT £71.56 TOTE £3.50: £1.40, £2.20, £1.70; EX 20.50 Trifecta £86.30.
Owner Miss K Rausing **Bred** Miss K Rausing And Mrs S M Rogers **Trained** Newmarket, Suffolk
FOCUS
A moderate middle-distance finale but one or two with the potential to improve further yet, and the initial pace appeared decent.
T/Plt: £53.20 to a £1 stake. Pool: £86,336.79 - 1184.46 winning units. T/Qpdt: £7.40 to a £1 stake. Pool: £11,383.96 - 1134.28 winning units. **Colin Roberts**

6594 - 6596a (Foreign Racing) - See Raceform Interactive

6431 MAISONS-LAFFITTE (R-H)
Saturday, September 17
OFFICIAL GOING: Turf: soft

6597a PRIX DU PRINCE D'ORANGE (GROUP 3) (3YO) (ROUND) (TURF) 1m 2f (S)
1:35 (12:00) 3-Y-O **£29,411** (£11,764; £8,823; £5,882; £2,941)

RPR
1 **Sky Kingdom (IRE)**[33] 5499 3-9-2 0................................ GeraldMosse 6 112+
(William Haggas) *a cl up on outer: shkn up to chal fr 1 1/2f out: sn rdn and sustained chal fr over 1f out: led fnl 110yds: pushed out* **17/2**
2 *snk* **Mekhtaal**[65] 4332 3-9-2 0.. ChristopheSoumillon 2 112
(J-C Rouget, France) *led: grad increased pce fr 2 1/2f out. sn rdn. hdd fnl 110yds: no ex* **8/11**[1]
3 3 **Spectroscope (USA)**[29] 5699 3-9-2 0.......................... MickaelBarzalona 3 106
(A Fabre, France) *w.w in fnl pair: last and shkn up 2f out: styd on t0 go 3rd 75yds out: nt rch ldrs* **9/1**
4 1 **Black Sea (FR)**[52] 4783 3-9-2 0.. MaximeGuyon 4 104
(A De Royer-Dupre, France) *w.w in rr: clsd to chse ldrs fr wl over 1 1/2f out: 3rd and rdn 1f out: one pce fnl f* **7/2**[2]
5 3/4 **Cohesion**[41] 5218 3-9-2 0.. VincentCheminaud 1 103
(D Smaga, France) *chsd ldrs: outpcd and pushed along 2f out: wl hld whn styd on again fnl 100yds* **14/1**
6 1/2 **Qatari Gold (USA)**[30] 3-9-2 0.. CristianDemuro 5 102
(M Delzangles, France) *keen: hld up bhd ldng pair: rdn and no imp over 1 1/2f out: lft bhd ins fnl f* **13/2**[3]
2m 10.84s (8.44) **6** Ran SP% **120.7**
WIN (incl. 1 euro stake): 15.10. PLACES: 3.40, 1.30. SF: 32.60.
Owner P Makin **Bred** Paulyn Ltd **Trained** Newmarket, Suffolk
FOCUS
The second, third and fourth have been rated to their marks.

6598a LA COUPE DE MAISONS-LAFFITTE (GROUP 3) (3YO+) (STRAIGHT) (TURF) 1m 2f (S)
2:45 (12:00) 3-Y-O+ **£29,411** (£11,764; £8,823; £5,882; £2,941)

RPR
1 **Banzari**[36] 5384 4-8-10 0.. AlexisBadel 2 110+
(H-F Devin, France) *mde all: grad upped tempo fr 3f out: shkn up and kicked for home over 1 1.2f out: rdn and r.o fnl f: cosily* **7/1**
2 1 1/2 **Ame Bleue**[27] 5691 4-8-10 0................................ Pierre-CharlesBoudot 5 106
(A Fabre, France) *trckd ldr on outer: rdn to chse ldr 1 1/2f out: styd on fnl f: nt pce of wnr* **6/4**[1]
3 1/2 **Floodlight (USA)**[46] 5004 3-8-8 0.......................... MickaelBarzalona 4 109
(A Fabre, France) *hld up bhd ldrs: rdn and nt qckn 1 1/2f out: kpt on at same pce fnl f* **7/2**[3]
4 *nk* **Now We Can**[13] 6178 7-9-0 0................................ StephanePasquier 1 108
(N Clement, France) *towards rr but in tch on inner: rdn and clsd 1 1/2f out: n.m.r ins fnl f: kpt on at same pce* **5/2**[2]
5 *snk* **Incantator (GER)**[48] 4928 4-9-0 0................................ EduardoPedroza 3 108
(A Wohler, Germany) *w.w in tch: rdn and kpt on same pce fnl f: nvr able to chal* **14/1**

The Form Book, Raceform Ltd, Newbury, RG14 5SJ

6 2 **Sussudio (FR)**163 1307 6-9-0 0 AnthonyCrastus 6 104
(Frau Hella Sauer, Germany) *w.w in rr: rdn and no imp 1 1/2f out: one pce fnl f* **9/1**

2m 9.58s (7.18)
WFA 3 from 4yo+ 6lb **6** Ran SP% **120.0**
WIN (incl. 1 euro stake): 7.90. PLACES: 3.50, 1.70. SF: 25.10.
Owner Mrs R G Hillen **Bred** New England Stud & Barton Stud **Trained** France

6599 - (Foreign Racing) - See Raceform Interactive

6400 WOODBINE (L-H)
Saturday, September 17

OFFICIAL GOING: Tapeta: fast; turf: good

6600a NORTHERN DANCER TURF STKS PRESENTED BY HPIBET (GRADE 1) (3YO+) (TURF) 1m 4f (T)
10:34 (12:00) 3-Y-O+
£88,235 (£29,411; £14,705; £7,352; £3,529; £1,764)

RPR

1 **The Pizza Man (USA)**35 5431 7-8-11 0 FlavienPrat 7 111
(Roger Brueggemann, U.S.A) *chsd ldr: rdn 2f out: styd on to ld narrowly 50yds out: drvn out* **558/100**

2 nk **Wake Forest (GER)**35 5431 6-9-0 0 IradOrtizJr 4 114+
(Chad C Brown, U.S.A) *midfield: hdwy fr 2f out: drvn over 1f out: styd on to hold ev ch wl ins fnl f: jst hld* **26/5**3

3 nk **World Approval (USA)**35 5431 4-9-0 0 (b) JulienRLeparoux 6 114
(Mark Casse, Canada) *led: set stdy pce: rdn under 2f out: hdd 50yds out: no ex clsng stages* **11/4**1

4 1 3/4 **Majeed**21 5894 6-8-7 0 JamieSpencer 3 104+
(David Simcock) *dwlt: hld up in rr: rdn 2f out: drvn and kpt on wl fnl f: nt rch ldrs* **67/10**

5 1 **Danish Dynaformer (CAN)**35 5431 4-8-9 0 (b) PatrickHusbands 8 104
(Roger L Attfield, Canada) *in tch in midfield: rdn and kpt on same pce fr 2f out: nvr able to chal* **123/20**

6 2 1/4 **Camp Creek (CAN)**27 3-8-0 0 RafaelManuelHernandez 5 100
(Rachel Halden, Canada) *hld up towards rr: rdn and unable qck 2f out: n.d* **149/10**

7 1 1/4 **Button Down**27 5-8-5 0 ow1 (b) GaryBoulanger 1 95
(Josie Carroll, Canada) *trckd ldrs: rdn and lost pl under 2f out: wknd 1f out* **37/1**

8 1 **Big Blue Kitten (USA)**98 3180 8-8-11 0 JoelRosario 2 99
(Chad C Brown, U.S.A) *hld up towards rr: dropped to rr and rdn 3f out: sn struggling* **63/20**2

2m 31.75s (2.15)
WFA 3 from 4yo+ 8lb **8** Ran SP% **118.0**
PARI-MUTUEL (all including 2 cad stake): WIN 13.10; PLACE (1-2) 5.90, 5.70; SHOW (1-2-3) 3.40, 4.50, 3.10; SF 87.40.
Owner Midwest Thoroughbreds Inc **Bred** Midwest Thoroughbreds **Trained** North America

6601a RICOH WOODBINE MILE STKS (GRADE 1) (3YO+) (TURF) 1m (T)
11:39 (12:00) 3-Y-O+
£294,117 (£117,647; £49,019; £24,509; £9,803; £4,901)

RPR

1 **Tepin (USA)**95 3242 5-8-9 0 JulienRLeparoux 8 121+
(Mark Casse, Canada) *in tch in 4th: smooth hdwy to press ldrs under 2f out: rdn to ld over 1f out: kpt on wl fnl f: rdn out* **9/20**1

2 1/2 **Tower Of Texas (CAN)**28 5-8-7 0 (b) EuricoRosaDaSilva 1 117+
(Roger L Attfield, Canada) *midfield: rdn 2f out: short of room 1 1/2f out: styd on fnl f: nt rch wnr* **239/10**

3 nk **Mutakayyef**31 5558 5-8-9 0 DaneO'Neill 2 118+
(William Haggas) *s.s: midfield: rdn 2f out: kpt on wl fnl f: nt quite able to chal* **17/5**2

4 3/4 **Full Mast (USA)**42 4-8-5 0 JoelRosario 5 113
(William Mott, U.S.A) *chsd ldr: rdn to ld under 2f out: hdd over 1f out: wknd steadily ins fnl f* **79/10**3

5 1/2 **Arod (IRE)**21 5873 5-8-7 0 OisinMurphy 3 113
(Peter Chapple-Hyam) *trckd ldrs: rdn 2f out: nt clr run and lost pl under 2f out: kpt on same pce* **189/10**

6 hd **Mr Owen (USA)**62 4441 4-8-5 0 (p) JamieSpencer 7 111
(F Rohaut, France) *hld up in rr: rdn and kpt on fr under 2f out: nt pce to chal* **42/1**

7 4 1/2 **Glenville Gardens (USA)**28 4-8-9 0 GaryBoulanger 4 105
(Sid Attard, Canada) *led: rdn and hdd under 2f out: wknd 1f out* **269/10**

8 1 1/2 **Passion For Action (CAN)**28 4-8-9 0 (b) LuisContreras 6 101
(Michael P De Paulo, Canada) *a towards rr* **56/1**

1m 34.13s (94.13) **8** Ran SP% **119.6**
PARI-MUTUEL (all including 2 cad stake): WIN 2.90; PLACE (1-2) 2.10, 10.60; SF 21.90.
Owner Robert E Masterson **Bred** Machmer Hall **Trained** North America

6602 - 6603a (Foreign Racing) - See Raceform Interactive

6037 GOWRAN PARK (R-H)
Sunday, September 18

OFFICIAL GOING: Soft changing to soft (heavy in places) after race 5 (4.20)

6604a DENNY CORDELL LAVARACK & LANWADES STUD FILLIES STKS (GROUP 3) 1m 1f 100y
3:20 (3:23) 3-Y-O+
£31,452 (£10,128; £4,797; £2,132; £1,066; £533)

RPR

1 **Duchess Andorra (IRE)**21 5939 5-9-5 92 (p) ColinKeane 1 106
(J P Murtagh, Ire) *led for nrly 2f: chsd ldr in 2nd: on terms over 3f out and sn led: strly pressed ins fnl f: kpt on wl: all out cl home* **16/1**

2 shd **Laganore (IRE)**24 5818 4-9-5 103 RonanWhelan 12 106
(A J Martin, Ire) *racd in rr tl prog under 2f out: styd on wl to press wnr in 2nd ins fnl f: kpt on wl cl home: jst hld* **8/1**

3 3/4 **Intimation**53 4757 4-9-5 90 ChrisHayes 11 104+
(Sir Michael Stoute) *hld up: clsr in mid-div 4f out: trckd ldrs in 3rd over 2f out: sn chsd ldr in 2nd: edgd lft appr fnl f where dropped to 3rd: kpt on wl clsng stages* **10/1**

4 3 1/2 **Aljazzi**43 5158 3-9-0 101 AndreaAtzeni 2 98
(Marco Botti) *hld up: towards rr at 1/2-way: prog under 2f out into 3rd: nt qckn in 4th ent fnl f: kpt on one pce* **9/2**3

5 1 **Sea Swift (IRE)**46 5046 3-9-0 96 LeighRoche 6 96
(D K Weld, Ire) *racd towards rr: prog on inner 2f out: wnt 5th appr fnl f: no ex ins fnl f: kpt on one pce* **7/2**2

6 3 1/2 **How High The Moon (IRE)**13 6200 3-9-0 96 (p) ColmO'Donoghue 3 89
(A P O'Brien, Ire) *chsd ldrs on inner: rdn and nt qckn under 2f out: sn one pce* **25/1**

7 1 **Ringside Humour (IRE)**7 6389 4-9-5 96 (t) RoryCleary 4 86
(J S Bolger, Ire) *sn chsd ldrs in 4th: rdn in 4th under 2f out: wknd appr fnl f* **12/1**

8 1 1/4 **Ibergman (IRE)**20 5983 4-9-5 90 WayneLordan 8 83
(Ms Sheila Lavery, Ire) *hld up: gd prog on outer under 2f out to chse ldrs: no imp appr fnl f: sn one pce* **33/1**

9 1 1/4 **Discipline**88 3539 3-9-0 102 [1] PatSmullen 5 82
(D K Weld, Ire) *racd in mid-div: rdn and sme prog whn short of room 2f out and swtchd lft: sn no ex* **5/2**1

10 nk **Cirin Toinne (IRE)**7 6383 3-9-0 99 KevinManning 10 81
(J S Bolger, Ire) *sn chsd ldrs in 3rd: rdn and nt qckn under 3f out: no ex whn sltly short of room 2f out* **14/1**

11 3 3/4 **Radiantly**21 5939 3-9-0 99 (b1) BillyLee 7 74
(W McCreery, Ire) *racd in mid-div: dropped towards rr 4f out: no ex over 2f out* **14/1**

12 16 **Maudlin Magdalen (IRE)**7 6389 6-9-5 86 DeclanMcDonogh 9 40
(Donal Kinsella, Ire) *trckd ldrs tl led after 2f: rdn 3f out and sn hdd: wknd qckly fr 2f out: eased* **40/1**

2m 7.34s (0.34)
WFA 3 from 4yo+ 5lb **12** Ran SP% **125.3**
CSF £144.05 TOTE £18.10: £4.30, £2.80, £2.90; DF 224.30 Trifecta £6034.70.
Owner Micheal D Ryan **Bred** M Ryan **Trained** Coolaghknock Glebe,Co Kildare

FOCUS
A gutsy performance from the winner, a mare one might have thought to fall a little bit short of winning at this level, but everything went right here. The standard is set by the second and fifth.

6605 - 6609a (Foreign Racing) - See Raceform Interactive

3699 DORTMUND (R-H)
Sunday, September 18

OFFICIAL GOING: Turf: good

6610a GROSSER PREIS VON DSW21 - 132 DEUTSCHES ST LEGER (GROUP 3) (3YO+) (TURF) 1m 6f
3:45 (12:00) 3-Y-O+ **£23,529** (£8,823; £4,411; £2,205; £1,470)

RPR

1 **Near England (IRE)**42 5220 3-8-7 0 AndreasHelfenbein 9 107+
(Markus Klug, Germany) *a cl up on outer: eased into ld appr 2f out: sn rdn and r.o: edgd lft ins fnl f: styd on wl* **98/10**

2 2 **Tellina (SAF)**176 1102 7-9-6 0 EduardoPedroza 1 107
(A Wohler, Germany) *w.w towards rr: hdwy 2f out: chsd ldr into fnl f: styd on but nt pce of wnr* **22/5**3

3 1 1/2 **Techno Queen (IRE)**15 6152 5-9-3 0 DanielePorcu 4 102
(T Potters, Germany) *w.w in fnl pair: hdwy over 1 1/2f out: chsd ldrs 1f out: nt pce to get on terms* **23/10**2

4 3/4 **Rock Of Romance (IRE)**74 4031 6-9-6 0 MarcLerner 8 104
(A Wohler, Germany) *w.w in midfield: tk clsr order 4f out: rdn to chse ldr 1 1/2f out: one pce u.p fnl f* **74/10**

5 3 1/2 **Iraklion (GER)**15 6151 4-9-6 0 MichaelCadeddu 10 99
(Christian Sprengel, Germany) *settled towards rr: rdn 2f out: styd on 1 1/2f out: kpt on til effrt petered out last 125yds* **201/10**

6 1 1/4 **Mighty Mouse (GER)**42 5219 8-9-6 0 RenePiechulek 11 97
(Annika Fust, Germany) *heald up in rr: tk clsr order on outer 1 1/2f out: kpt on wout ever getting in contention* **111/10**

7 2 **She's Gina (GER)**42 5220 3-8-7 0 MaximPecheur 3 91
(Markus Klug, Germany) *led: hdd appr 2f out: sn btn and grad dropped away* **169/10**

8 1/2 **Bebe Cherie (FR)**15 6151 4-9-3 0 CeciliaMuller 5 91
(Markus Klug, Germany) *w.w in midfield: rdn and no imp 2f out: sn btn* **29/1**

9 3 1/4 **Summershine (IRE)**29 5-9-3 0 BayarsaikhanGanbat 2 86
(Frau Anna Schleusner-Fruhriep, Germany) *outpcd early: drvn into midfield after 2 1/2f: rdn and nt qckn over 1 1/2f out: sn btn* **38/1**

10 nk **Weltmacht**15 6151 5-9-3 0 AdriedeVries 6 86
(Markus Klug, Germany) *chsd ldrs on inner: shkn up and no imp 2f out: wknd over 1f out* **19/10**1

11 9 1/2 **Buzzy (GER)**36 3-8-10 0 AntoineHamelin 7 75
(Guido Forster, Germany) *chsd ldrs on outer: lost pl 2f out: wl bhd fnl f* **42/1**

2m 56.96s (-8.54)
WFA 3 from 4yo+ 10lb **11** Ran SP% **131.3**
WIN (incl. 10 euro stake): 108. PLACES: 27, 25, 14. SF: 1,021.
Owner Gestut Wittekindshof **Bred** Gestut Wittekindshof **Trained** Germany

5696 HANOVER (L-H)
Sunday, September 18

OFFICIAL GOING: Turf: good

6611a GROSSER PREIS DER METALLBAU BURCKHARDT GMBH (LISTED RACE) (3YO+ FILLIES & MARES) (TURF) 1m
4:00 (12:00) 3-Y-O+ **£10,294** (£4,779; £2,205; £1,102)

RPR

1 **Pabouche (IRE)**28 5695 3-8-11 0 FabriceVeron 10 95
(H-A Pantall, France) *hld up in fnl pair on outer: last and rdn whn c stands' side into st over 2f out: hdwy and nt clr run 1 1/2f out: r.o un press fr over 1f out: led fnl 100yds: won gng way* **5/1**3

2 1 1/2 **Gold Sands (IRE)**16 6076 4-9-2 0 MartinHarley 3 93
(James Tate) *broke wl and led: hdd after 1f and chsd ldr: sltly impeded whn c stands' side over 2f out: hrd rdn to chal between horses 1 1/2f out: led 1f out: styd on and hdd 100yds out: no ex* **19/5**2

3 1 1/4 **Ella Diva (FR)**21 5946 3-9-1 0 FilipMinarik 7 93
(N Caullery, France) **7/2**1

4 2 **Prairie Pearl (FR)**17 6070 3-8-11 0 LukasDelozier 6 84
(H-A Pantall, France) **7/2**1

5 1 **Redenca (GER)**18 3-8-11 0 JozefBojko 8 82
(A Wohler, Germany) **79/10**

6 hd **Tendresse (GER)** 5-9-2 0 AndreasSuborics 9 83
(Henk Grewe, Germany) **96/10**

7 1 **Milenia (GER)**14 3-8-11 0 StephenHellyn 5 79
(Markus Klug, Germany) **99/10**

8 4 1/2 **Antalya (GER)**18 5-9-2 0 MartinSeidl 2 70
(Markus Klug, Germany) **6/1**

9 6 **Vanbijou (GER)**175 4-9-2 0 (p) KevinWoodburn 4 56
(Eva Fabianova, Germany) **25/1**

10 2 1/2 **Agama (GER)**329 6-9-2 0 TommasoScardino 1 50
(F Kurz, Germany) **31/1**

1m 43.2s (103.20)
WFA 3 from 4yo+ 4lb **10** Ran SP% **133.0**
WIN (incl. 10 euro stake): 60. PLACES: 21, 16, 20. SF: 273.
Owner Godolphin SNC **Bred** J Wigan & G Strawbridge **Trained** France

3701 SAN SIRO (R-H)

Sunday, September 18

OFFICIAL GOING: Turf: good to soft

6612a PREMIO FEDERICO TESIO (GROUP 2) (3YO+) (TURF) 1m 3f

4:40 (12:00) 3-Y-O+ **£44,117** (£19,411; £10,588; £5,294)

RPR

1 **Full Drago (ITY)**91 3-8-5 0 CristianDemuro 3 110
(Stefano Botti, Italy) *a cl up (front three 5l clr of rest): led 3f out: sn rdn: styd on u.p fnl 1 1/2f: a in control fnl f* **61/20**3

2 2 **Fair Mountain (GER)**42 5219 4-8-11 0 CarloFiocchi 1 105
(A Wohler, Germany) *w ldng trio: outpcd by front two 4f out: hrd rdn over 2f out: kpt on again over 1 1/2f out: styd on wl fnl f: tk 2nd cl home* **13/5**2

3 hd **Circus Couture (IRE)**91 3455 4-8-11 0 FabioBranca 2 105+
(Stefano Botti, Italy) *chsd ldng trio who were clr: smooth hdwy 2 1/2f out: rdn to chse ldr 1 1/2f out: nvr quite on terms: run flattened out fnl 75yds: lost 2nd cl home* **11/5**1

4 1 3/4 **Kloud Gate (FR)**59 4578 4-8-11 0 DarioVargiu 4 101
(Gianluca Bietolini, Italy) *w.w in fnl trio: rdn and hdwy 2f out: styd on to chse ldrs 1 1/2f out: one pce u.p fnl f* **136/10**

5 2 **Matchwinner (GER)**36 5-8-11 0 IanFerguson 5 98
(A Kleinkorres, Germany) *w.w in fnl trio: rdn and styd on fr over 1 1/2f out: nt pce to get in contention* **92/10**

6 7 **Sound Check (GER)**343 7155 3-8-5 0 AndraschStarke 6 86
(P Schiergen, Germany) *settled in midfield: no hdwy whn rowed along 2f out: sn wknd* **13/5**2

7 9 **Porsenna (IRE)**112 2729 6-8-11 0 NicolaPinna 7 69
(Stefano Botti, Italy) *missed break: w.w in rr: no imp u.p fnl 2f: n.d* **40/1**

8 5 **Victory Song (IRE)**88 3545 6-8-11 0 LucaManiezzi 8 60
(Frau S Steinberg, Germany) *sn led: hdd 3f out: rdn and wknd ins fnl 2f* **36/1**

2m 12.8s (-5.80)
WFA 3 from 4yo+ 7lb **8** Ran SP% **133.3**
WIN (incl. 1 euro stake): 4.04. PLACES: 1.47, 1.39, 1.33. DF: 7.80.
Owner Dioscuri Srl **Bred** Massimo Dragoni **Trained** Italy

6613 - (Foreign Racing) - See Raceform Interactive

6002 HAMILTON (R-H)

Monday, September 19

OFFICIAL GOING: Good to soft (soft in places; 5.7)
Wind: Light, half against Weather: Overcast

6614 RACINGUK.COM NURSERY H'CAP 6f 6y

2:20 (2:22) (Class 5) (0-75,75) 2-Y-O **£3,881** (£1,155; £577; £288) **Stalls** High

Form RPR

6301 1 **Mutahaady (IRE)**12 6222 2-8-13 **74** CliffordLee(7) 5 79+
(K R Burke) *trckd ldrs: rdn to ld over 1f out: kpt on wl fnl f* **2/1**1

054 2 1 1/4 **Yarmouk (FR)**21 5966 2-9-1 **69** GrahamLee 9 70
(Richard Fahey) *trckd ldrs: rdn: swtchd rt and chsd wnr over 1f out: kpt on same pce wl ins fnl f* **4/1**2

3511 3 3/4 **Roys Dream**19 6033 2-9-3 **71** TonyHamilton 10 70
(Kristin Stubbs) *cl up: rdn and hung rt over 1f out: kpt on same pce ins fnl f* **10/1**

6002 4 1 1/4 **Volta Do Mar (IRE)**12 6222 2-8-7 **61** BarryMcHugh 3 58+
(Richard Fahey) *sn niggled along bhd ldng gp: drvn and outpcd over 2f out: edgd lft and hdwy over 1f out: keeping on but no imp whn n.m.r towards fin* **14/1**

545 5 2 3/4 **Outfox**17 6078 2-8-13 **67** PaulMulrennan 2 54+
(Bryan Smart) *prom on outside: rdn over 2f out: wknd over 1f out* **8/1**

3412 6 1/2 **Trick Of The Lyte (IRE)**24 5833 2-8-13 **67** CamHardie 6 52
(John Quinn) *taken early to post: led: rdn and hdd over 1f out: wknd fnl f* **9/2**3

6040 7 1 **Zebedee Star**20 6010 2-8-1 **60** ShirleyTeasdale(5) 8 42
(Keith Dalgleish) *hld up bhd ldng gp: hdwy and hung rt wl over 1f out: sn wknd* **66/1**

1m 15.13s (2.93) **Going Correction** +0.475s/f (Yiel) **7** Ran SP% **99.9**
Speed ratings (Par 95): **99,97,96,94,91 90,89**
CSF £7.41 CT £36.89 TOTE £2.50: £1.60, £1.90; EX 7.90 Trifecta £47.20.
Owner Tim Dykes, Mrs G Buchanan & E Burke **Bred** Kevin Blake **Trained** Middleham Moor, N Yorks
■ Rag Tatter was withdrawn. Price at time of withdrawal 8/1. Rule 4 applies to all bets - deduction 10p in the pound

FOCUS
All distances as advertised. A fair nursery handicap. They went a respectable gallop and a winning time of over five seconds slower than standard concurred with an official going description of good to soft, soft in places. The winner continues to progress.

6615 RACING UK DAY PASS JUST £10 H'CAP (DIV I) 6f 6y

2:50 (2:51) (Class 6) (0-65,65) 3-Y-O+ **£2,911** (£866; £432; £216) **Stalls** High

Form RPR

5000 1 **Keene's Pointe**33 5535 6-9-2 **57** TonyHamilton 9 63
(Kristin Stubbs) *hld up in tch: effrt and hdwy over 1f out: rdn and kpt on wl fnl f to ld last stride* **7/2**1

00-0 2 nse **Shesnotforturning (IRE)**35 5483 6-8-9 **50**1 TomEaves 7 56
(Ben Haslam) *led rdn and hrd pressed fr over 1f out: kpt on gamely u.p fnl f: hdd last stride* **14/1**

630 3 1 1/2 **Lady Wootton**42 5225 3-8-13 **56** (v) JoeFanning 6 57
(Keith Dalgleish) *trckd ldrs: smooth hdwy and ev ch over 1f out: rdn ins fnl f: no ex whn n.m.r towards fin* **7/2**1

2500 4 3/4 **Rock Canyon (IRE)**4 6506 7-9-3 **63** NathanEvans(5) 10 62
(Linda Perratt) *hld up: rdn and hdwy 2f out: sn chsng ldrs: kpt on same pce wl ins fnl f* **7/1**3

5 3 1/2 **Spirit Be With You (IRE)**48 4997 3-9-5 **62** JoeyHaynes 8 51
(Miss Natalia Lupini, Ire) *t.k.h: hld up bhd ldng gp: drvn and outpcd over 2f out: rallied fnl f: nvr able to chal* **13/2**2

6436 6 1 **Mystical King**17 6098 6-8-5 **46** oh1 (p) JamesSullivan 5 32
(Linda Perratt) *cl up tl rdn: edgd rt and wknd over 1f out* **12/1**

0000 7 1 1/4 **Ay Up Audrey**68 4257 5-8-6 **47** oh1 ow1 BarryMcHugh 4 29
(Rebecca Bastiman) *taken early to post: t.k.h in tch: rdn over 2f out: wknd over 1f out* **25/1**

3000 8 2 1/4 **Cheeni**9 6341 4-8-5 **46** oh1 JoeDoyle 3 21
(Jim Goldie) *hld up in tch: struggling wl over 1f out: sn btn* **22/1**

0505 9 3/4 **Captain Scooby**4 6522 10-9-8 **63** (b) RoystonFfrench 1 36
(Richard Guest) *missed break: bhd: rdn along 1/2-way: nvr on terms* **7/1**3

2020 10 8 **Spoken Words**19 6023 7-8-6 **47** PatrickMathers 2
(John David Riches) *prom on outside: rdn over 2f out: wknd qckly fr over 1f out* **11/1**

1m 14.75s (2.55) **Going Correction** +0.475s/f (Yiel)
WFA 3 from 4yo+ 2lb **10** Ran SP% **113.7**
Speed ratings (Par 101): **102,101,99,98,94 92,91,88,87,76**
CSF £54.78 CT £182.15 TOTE £4.10: £1.60, £3.70, £1.40; EX 65.90 Trifecta £182.00.
Owner P A Saxton **Bred** Christopher & Annabelle Mason **Trained** Norton, N Yorks
■ Stewards' Enquiry : Tom Eaves two-day ban: use of whip (3-4 Oct)

FOCUS
A modest sprint handicap which produced a thrilling finish and it is sound form for the grade. The winner didn't quite need to match his best for the year.

6616 RACING UK DAY PASS JUST £10 H'CAP (DIV II) 6f 6y

3:20 (3:20) (Class 6) (0-65,63) 3-Y-O+ **£2,911** (£866; £432; £216) **Stalls** High

Form RPR

0002 1 **Reflation**17 6100 4-8-13 **52** (p) ConnorBeasley 10 60
(Michael Dods) *hld up: hdwy and prom over 1f out: drvn to ld wl ins fnl f: kpt on* **8/1**2

0620 2 3/4 **Jacob's Pillow**6 6451 5-9-10 **63** DanielTudhope 8 69
(Rebecca Bastiman) *led: rdn over 1f out: edgd rt and hdd wl ins fnl f: kpt on same pce* **5/2**1

2525 3 5 **Slim Chance (IRE)**19 6023 7-9-6 **59** (p) JasonHart 6 50
(Simon West) *w ldr: rdn over 2f out: outpcd by first two ins fnl f* **8/1**2

341 4 1 **Wahaab (IRE)**28 5706 5-9-10 **63** (p) PJMcDonald 9 51
(Iain Jardine) *t.k.h: hld up: rdn over and hdwy over 1f out: kpt on fnl f: nvr able to chal* **5/2**1

60 5 1 **Taffetta**57 4691 4-9-8 **61** BarryMcHugh 5 46
(Tony Coyle) *prom: rdn over 2f out: wknd fnl f* **11/1**3

0666 6 2 3/4 **Amis Reunis**24 5839 7-8-1 **45** (p) NathanEvans(5) 2 22
(Colin Teague) *chsd ldrs: rdn over 2f out: wknd over 1f out* **18/1**

5460 7 4 **Amber Crystal**9 6347 4-8-7 **46** (b) JamesSullivan 7 11
(Linda Perratt) *t.k.h: in tch: rdn over 2f out: wknd over 1f out* **18/1**

0040 8 1 3/4 **Indego Blues**23 5889 7 8 11 **50** (p) PaulMulrennan 3 9
(David Nicholls) *prom on outside tl rdn and wknd over 1f out* **14/1**

0060 9 3 **The Cheese Gang**9 6341 4-8-6 **45** (t) JoeyHaynes 4
(Susan Corbett) *hld up bhd ldng gp: drvn over 2f out: wknd wl over 1f out* **14/1**

1m 14.74s (2.54) **Going Correction** +0.475s/f (Yiel)
WFA 3 from 4yo+ 2lb **9** Ran SP% **111.6**
Speed ratings (Par 101): **102,101,94,93,91 88,82,80,76**
CSF £26.96 CT £163.35 TOTE £6.00: £2.60, £1.30, £2.20; EX 32.10 Trifecta £185.70.
Owner Mrs C E Dods **Bred** Llety Farms **Trained** Denton, Co Durham

FOCUS
The second division of a modest sprint handicap and the winning time was virtually identical. The first two were clear and the form could have been rated higher.

6617 RACING UK PROFITS RETURNED TO RACING MAIDEN STKS 1m 67y

3:50 (3:50) (Class 5) 3-4-Y-O **£3,881** (£1,155; £577; £288) **Stalls** Low

Form RPR

32-3 1 **Vizier**145 1777 3-9-5 75 DanielTudhope 3 79
(David O'Meara) *pressed ldr: led over 2f out: rdn and edgd rt over 1f out: kpt on strly fnl f* **15/8**2

- 2 2 **Shah Of Armaan (IRE)** 3-9-5 0 KevinStott 4 73
(Kevin Ryan) *t.k.h: early ldr: chsd ldrs: effrt and wnt 2nd over 1f out: rdn and kpt on same pce ins fnl f* **7/1**3

3 3 3/4 **Bybrook**16 6135 3-9-0 0 TomEaves 2 66
(David Simcock) *s.i.s: sn prom: effrt and disp 2nd pl over 1f out: rdn and kpt on one pce fnl f* **8/11**1

0 4 4 1/2 **Clarabel**17 6104 3-9-0 0 JasonHart 6 56
(Garry Moss) *sn led: rdn and hdd over 2f out: outpcd over 1f out* **100/1**

3006 5 11 **Smirnova (IRE)**21 5973 3-8-9 51 ShirleyTeasdale(5) 1 31
(Kenny Johnson) *hld up in tch: drvn and struggling over 2f out: sn btn* **66/1**

56- 6 nse **Rathvale**314 7787 3-9-0 0 PJMcDonald 5 31
(Linda Perratt) *hld up: outpcd over 3f out: btn fnl 2f* **80/1**

1m 51.39s (2.99) **Going Correction** +0.475s/f (Yiel) **6** Ran SP% **108.9**
Speed ratings (Par 103): **104,102,101,96,85 85**
CSF £13.51 TOTE £2.30: £1.60, £2.50; EX 15.50 Trifecta £17.40.
Owner Nurlan Bizakov **Bred** Hesmonds Stud Ltd **Trained** Upper Helmsley, N Yorks

FOCUS
An ordinary maiden. The tempo increased on the downhill section into the lengthy home straight and the horse with the strongest form beforehand proved a resolute winner. He's rated back to last year's AW maiden form.

6618 HOPES N DREAMS (S) STKS 1m 1f 34y
4:20 (4:20) (Class 4) 3-5-Y-O **£6,469** (£1,925; £962; £481) **Stalls** Low

Form RPR
0050 **1** **Darrington**[15] 6160 4-8-12 76.. TonyHamilton 6 64
(Richard Fahey) *t.k.h: pressed ldr: rdn and ev ch over 2f out: edgd rt and led appr fnl f: drvn out* **8/13**[1]

4540 **2** 1 ¾ **Assisted**[16] 6137 3-8-7 60..(p) JoeFanning 3 61
(Keith Dalgleish) *t.k.h: prom: smooth hdwy to ld 2f out: rdn and hdd appr fnl f: rallied: one pce last 100yds* **6/1**[2]

0003 **3** 1 ½ **Thornaby Nash**[6] 6434 5-8-12 65....................................(p[1]) TomEaves 2 57
(Colin Teague) *t.k.h: sn chsng ldrs: rdn and effrt over 2f out: kpt on ins fnl f* **13/2**[3]

56 **4** ½ **Eastern Shore (IRE)**[48] 4983 3-8-7 0................................ JoeyHaynes 5 57
(K R Burke) *led: rdn and hdd 2f out: rallied: outpcd ins fnl f* **14/1**

/0-3 **5** hd **Istimraar (IRE)**[21] 5957 5-8-7 69..............................(p) CharlieBennett[(5)] 7 56
(Alexandra Dunn) *prom on outside: effrt and rdn over 2f out: one pce over 1f out* **7/1**

050 **6** 9 **Bilko's Back (IRE)**[17] 6104 4-8-5 53..............................(t) CliffordLee[(7)] 4 38
(Susan Corbett) *hld up in last pl: struggling over 2f out: sn btn* **50/1**

2m 3.41s (3.71) **Going Correction** +0.475s/f (Yiel)
WFA 3 from 4yo+ 5lb **6** Ran SP% **110.7**
Speed ratings (Par 105): **102,100,99,98,98 90**
CSF £4.65 TOTE £1.60: £1.40, £2.40; EX 5.30 Trifecta £18.10.No bid for the winner.
Owner The G-Guck Group **Bred** Avenue Farm Stud **Trained** Musley Bank, N Yorks

FOCUS
An ordinary seller which proved a good opportunity for the clear form horse to gain a confidence boost down in grade under suitable conditions. The form jas been rated cautiously.

6619 TODAY'S RACING JUST £10 WITH RACING UK H'CAP 1m 4f 14y
4:50 (4:53) (Class 6) (0-60,59) 4-Y-O+ **£2,911** (£866; £432; £216) **Stalls** High

Form RPR
6520 **1** **Judith Gardenier**[7] 6422 4-8-8 46....................................(p) PJMcDonald 6 53
(Iain Jardine) *prom: effrt and rdn over 2f out: led wl ins fnl f: rdn out* **4/1**[1]

546/ **2** 1 **Fine Resolve**[13] 1355 7-8-12 55...........................(bt[1]) CharlieBennett[(5)] 3 60
(Alexandra Dunn) *prom: drvn and outpcd 4f out: rallied and edgd lft over 1f out: kpt on strly to take 2nd towards fin: nt rch wnr* **20/1**

0400 **3** 1 ½ **Voice From Above (IRE)**[28] 5718 7-8-13 51.............. DanielTudhope 4 54
(Patrick Holmes) *led: rdn over 2f out: hdd wl ins fnl f: one pce: lost 2nd towards fin* **5/1**[2]

0000 **4** 2 **Champagne Rules**[6] 6432 5-9-3 55................................(t) JoeyHaynes 9 55
(Sharon Watt) *dwlt: hld up: hdwy and prom over 2f out: drvn over 1f out: one pce fnl f* **12/1**

0600 **5** 1 **Adrakhan (FR)**[46] 5064 5-8-7 45.. CamHardie 2 44
(Wilf Storey) *chsd ldrs: wnt 2nd after 4f: effrt and rdn over 2f out: outpcd fnl f* **10/1**

6056 **6** 3 ¾ **Celtic Power**[24] 5842 4-9-0 59..............................(p) LewisEdmunds[(7)] 10 52
(Jim Goldie) *hld up: rdn along 3f out: plugged on fr over 1f out: no imp* **6/1**[3]

34 **7** ¾ **Operateur (IRE)**[21] 5971 8-9-0 52.................................. PaulMulrennan 8 44
(Ben Haslam) *hld up in midfield: drvn and outpcd over 2f out: n.d after* **4/1**[1]

-000 **8** 7 **Zingiber**[58] 4645 4-8-7 45... KevinStott 11 26
(Wilf Storey) *hld up: drvn and struggling over 3f out: nvr on terms* **22/1**

5440 **9** 3 ¾ **Latin Rebel (IRE)**[21] 5971 9-8-9 47....................................(p) JoeDoyle 1 23
(Jim Goldie) *hld up: stdy hdwy over 4f out: rdn and outpcd over 2f out: sn btn* **6/1**[3]

46/0 **10** 62 **Goodlukin Lucy**[21] 5971 9-8-8 46 ow1.......................... ConnorBeasley 5
(Gemma Anderson) *chsd ldr 4f: lost pl 4f out: sn struggling: btn and eased fnl 2f* **25/1**

2m 44.97s (6.37) **Going Correction** +0.475s/f (Yiel) **10** Ran SP% **115.0**
Speed ratings (Par 101): **97,96,95,94,93 90,90,85,83,41**
CSF £86.67 CT £407.72 TOTE £5.40: £1.70, £5.20, £2.20; EX 45.10 Trifecta £665.30.
Owner James A Cringan **Bred** James A Cringan **Trained** Carrutherstown, D'fries & G'way

FOCUS
A moderate middle-distance handicap. They went a respectable gallop and the form is sound enough, with a small pb from the winner.

6620 GLASVEGAS HEADLINING HERE NEXT WEEK H'CAP 1m 3f 14y
5:20 (5:20) (Class 5) (0-70,69) 3-Y-O+ **£3,881** (£1,155; £577; £288) **Stalls** High

Form RPR
4301 **1** **Canny Style**[19] 6029 3-8-8 58.. KevinStott 6 66
(Kevin Ryan) *hld up: hdwy over 3f out: rdn to ld over 1f out: r.o wl fnl f* **11/8**[1]

0403 **2** ½ **Tectonic (IRE)**[4] 6502 7-9-5 62...................................(v) ConnorBeasley 5 66
(Keith Dalgleish) *plld hrd: chsd ldr to 1/2-way: lost pl 4f out: rallied over 1f out: chsd wnr ins fnl f: kpt on* **7/2**[2]

2020 **3** nk **Sakhalin Star (IRE)**[12] 6231 5-9-10 67.....................(e) RoystonFfrench 4 71
(Richard Guest) *t.k.h: hld up in tch: effrt over 2f out: rdn and disp 2nd pl briefly ins fnl f: r.o* **6/1**

1230 **4** 1 ¾ **Gold Show**[24] 5841 7-9-5 62.. GrahamLee 2 63
(Grant Tuer) *chsd ldrs: hdwy to chse ldr over 5f out: rdn and led briefly wl over 1f out: one pce fnl f* **5/1**[3]

2000 **5** 2 ¼ **Troy Boy**[44] 5155 6-8-7 55 oh10................................(b[1]) RowanScott[(5)] 3 52
(Rebecca Bastiman) *led to 1/2-way: cl up: rdn over 2f out: outpcd over 1f out* **66/1**

0246 **6** 10 **Dry Your Eyes (IRE)**[6] 6450 5-9-12 69........................[1] DanielTudhope 1 50
(David O'Meara) *t.k.h: hld up in tch: hdwy to ld 1/2-way: rdn and hdd wl over 1f out: sn wknd and eased* **6/1**

2m 32.32s (6.72) **Going Correction** +0.475s/f (Yiel)
WFA 3 from 5yo+ 7lb **6** Ran SP% **111.1**
Speed ratings (Par 103): **94,93,93,92,90 83**
CSF £6.26 TOTE £2.00: £1.50, £1.90; EX 6.40 Trifecta £23.80.
Owner Hambleton Racing Ltd XXXVII **Bred** Biddestone Stud Ltd **Trained** Hambleton, N Yorks

FOCUS
A modest middle-distance handicap. They went a muddling gallop and the winning time was comparatively the slowest on the day. The winner can do better again.

6621 MUSIC FESTIVAL RACENIGHT FEATURING THE VIEW H'CAP 1m 67y
5:50 (5:50) (Class 6) (0-65,63) 3-Y-O+ **£2,911** (£866; £432; £216) **Stalls** Low

Form RPR
3525 **1** **The Wee Barra (IRE)**[20] 6005 4-9-3 63................(p) LewisEdmunds[(7)] 9 68
(Kevin Ryan) *trckd ldr to over 5f out: cl up: hdwy to ld over 1f out: rdn and edgd lft ins fnl f: kpt on* **5/1**[2]

6205 **2** ½ **Little Pippin**[126] 2308 3-8-8 51.. BarryMcHugh 3 55
(Tony Coyle) *hld up on ins: hdwy over 2f out: sn rdn: kpt on fnl f to take 2nd nr fin* **16/1**

0401 **3** ½ **Riponian**[9] 6347 6-9-2 55..(t) JoeyHaynes 11 58
(Susan Corbett) *led: rdn and hdd over 1f out: rallied: kpt on same pce ins fnl f* **10/1**

215 **4** nk **Ted's Brother (IRE)**[32] 5576 8-8-10 49 oh2.............(e) RoystonFfrench 2 51
(Richard Guest) *midfield: effrt over 2f out: kpt on same pce ins fnl f* **10/1**

4230 **5** nk **Big Red**[64] 4424 4-8-10 49 oh4.. TomEaves 5 50
(Rebecca Bastiman) *hld up: hdwy over 2f out: swtchd lft over 1f out: kpt on fnl f: nrst fin* **25/1**

0000 **6** ½ **Rioja Day (IRE)**[96] 3287 6-8-10 49 oh4.............................(b) JoeDoyle 10 49
(Jim Goldie) *hld up: drvn and outpcd over 3f out: rallied over 1f out: kpt on ins fnl f* **25/1**

0465 **7** ¾ **The Name's Bond**[28] 5715 4-8-10 49 oh4..................(b[1]) TonyHamilton 1 48
(Richard Fahey) *trckd ldrs: wnt 2nd over 5f out to over 2f out: drvn and outpcd fnl f* **10/1**

2443 **8** ¾ **New Abbey Angel (IRE)**[17] 6106 3-9-3 60..............(p) ConnorBeasley 4 57
(Keith Dalgleish) *hld up midfield: rdn and effrt over 2f out: no imp over 1f out* **7/2**[1]

0614 **9** 1 **Almuhalab**[17] 6095 5-9-7 60..(p) JamesSullivan 12 55
(Ruth Carr) *hld up: rdn and hdwy over 2f out: no imp fr over 1f out* **6/1**[3]

0465 **10** nk **Haymarket**[42] 5227 7-9-6 59.. PaulMulrennan 13 55
(R Mike Smith) *prom: rdn and edgd rt over 2f out: wknd over 1f out* **12/1**

0104 **11** 4 **Madam Mai Tai**[42] 5222 4-8-7 51.................................. RowanScott[(5)] 14 36
(Rebecca Bastiman) *t.k.h in rr: struggling 3f out: sn btn* **22/1**

5220 **12** 5 **Indian Giver**[19] 6029 8-9-3 56..(b) PatrickMathers 8 30
(John David Riches) *hld up midfield: drvn and outpcd over 3f out: sn btn* **15/2**

1m 52.35s (3.95) **Going Correction** +0.475s/f (Yiel)
WFA 3 from 4yo+ 4lb **12** Ran SP% **117.8**
Speed ratings (Par 101): **99,98,98,97,97 96,96,95,94,94 90,85**
CSF £79.29 CT £776.07 TOTE £7.20: £2.70, £5.90, £3.30; EX 120.40 Trifecta £783.90.
Owner Slaters Arms Racing Club **Bred** Gamra Partnership **Trained** Hambleton, N Yorks

FOCUS
A modest handicap. They went a respectable gallop and the form should stand up to scrutiny in this grade, with the placed horses close to their recent levels.
T/Plt: £54.20 to a £1 stake. Pool: £63,941.09 - 859.7 winning units T/Qpdt: £20.40 to a £1 stake. Pool: £4,843.19 - 175.6 winning units **Richard Young**

6411 KEMPTON (A.W) (R-H)
Monday, September 19

OFFICIAL GOING: Polytrack: standard to slow
Wind: light, across Weather: overcast, light rain from race 1

6622 APOLLOBET NEW WEBSITE MAIDEN STKS 5f (P)
2:10 (2:11) (Class 5) 2-Y-O **£2,911** (£866; £432; £216) **Stalls** Low

Form RPR
0 **1** **Mr Black**[28] 5727 2-9-5 0.. JamesDoyle 1 84
(George Scott) *chsd ldr: effrt to chal and clr of field over 1f out: rdn to ld 100yds out: r.o wl* **5/2**[1]

3 **2** 1 ½ **Rapid Ranger**[119] 2543 2-9-5 0.. LiamKeniry 5 79
(Gary Moore) *racd keenly: led: clr w wnr over 1f out: hdd 100yds out: styd on same pce after* **6/1**

3 1 **Kowaiyess (IRE)** 2-9-5 0.. PaulHanagan 2 77+
(Owen Burrows) *taken down early: s.i.s: off the pce in last trio: hdwy into midfield 2f out: swtchd rt over 1f out: chsd clr ldng pair 1f out: r.o strly ins fnl f: nt rch ldrs* **7/1**

6 **4** 3 ½ **Zavikon**[17] 6087 2-9-5 0... ShaneKelly 8 62
(Richard Hughes) *hld up in midfield: effrt over 1f out: wnt 4th 1f out: no imp ins fnl f: nvr trbld ldrs* **9/2**[3]

6 **5** 3 ½ **Kendamara (FR)**[53] 4804 2-9-0 0.......................... MichaelJMMurphy 7 45
(Charles Hills) *chsd ldng pair: outpcd u.p over 1f out: lost 3rd 1f out: wknd ins fnl f* **14/1**

6 **6** 1 **Supreme Power (IRE)**[30] 5631 2-9-5 0.................... SilvestreDeSousa 6 46
(Philip McBride) *hld up in midfield: no imp whn hmpd and snatched up over 1f out: swtchd lft 1f out: no ch and kpt on same pce after* **7/2**[2]

0 **7** ¾ **Miriam Violet**[17] 6071 2-9-0 0.. RobertHavlin 3 39
(Paul Henderson) *chsd ldng trio: rdn and outpcd over 1f out: wl btn and lost 4th 1f out: wknd fnl f* **150/1**

00 **8** 1 ½ **Fire Brigade**[59] 4594 2-9-5 0.. JamieSpencer 4 38
(Michael Bell) *wnt sharply lft leaving stalls and slowly away: a off the pce in last trio: n.d* **12/1**

9 nk **Orithia (USA)** 2-9-0 0.. DaneO'Neill 9 32
(Seamus Durack) *sn outpcd and off the pce in last trio: bhd fnl 2f* **22/1**

0 **10** 6 **Sea My Diamond (IRE)**[26] 5771 2-9-0 0...................... AdamBeschizza 10 10
(Mark Hoad) *midfield: rdn and losing pl over 3f out: bhd 2f out* **200/1**

59.86s (-0.64) **Going Correction** 0.0s/f (Stan) **10** Ran SP% **115.6**
Speed ratings (Par 95): **105,102,101,95,89 88,87,84,84,74**
CSF £17.73 TOTE £3.30: £1.20, £2.40, £2.20; EX 22.00 Trifecta £137.00.
Owner Mrs Michael Spencer **Bred** D J And Mrs Deer **Trained** Newmarket, Suffolk

FOCUS
Work had been done to the track in the last few days, with the BHA website three days ago stating that "50 tonnes of the original specification Clopf fibre was ameliorated into 100mm of the racing surface to rejuvenate and minimise surface kickback. In view of this the going will ride on the SLOW side, for a period of time." James Doyle said "It's riding a little bit dead but it will be alright in time", Liam Keniry said "It's riding fine, just a little bit slow that's all", while Paul Hanagan remarked "Just on the slow side but they have done a good job."A modest sprint maiden where the experienced juveniles did not set an exacting standard, but two of them fought out the finish. The winner left his debut behind.

6623 APOLLOBET RACING REFUNDS/BRITISH STALLION STUDS EBF MAIDEN STKS (PLUS 10 RACE) 1m 2f (P)

2:40 (2:40) (Class 4) 2-Y-O **£4,269** (£1,270; £634; £317) **Stalls** Low

Form RPR

1 **Percy's Word** 2-9-5 0 .... HarryBentley 4 77+
(Simon Crisford) *hld up in tch: clsd and swtchd lft over 1f out: rdn to chal ins fnl f: r.o wl to ld cl home* **20/1**

34 **2** *nk* **Spring Jig (USA)**[38] 5373 2-9-5 0 .... JimCrowley 6 77
(Hugo Palmer) *chsd ldrs after 2f: rdn to chal over 1f out: led ins fnl f: sn hrd pressed: kpt on u.p hdd cl home* **4/1**[2]

3 **3** *2* **Draw Swords**[34] 5505 2-9-5 0 .... RobertHavlin 3 73
(John Gosden) *led: rdn and hdd wl over 1f out: led again over 1f out: hdd and unable qck ins fnl f: kpt on same pce after* **5/6**[1]

3 **4** *1 3/4* **Caramuru (IRE)**[17] 6085 2-9-5 0 .... SeanLevey 2 70
(Richard Hannon) *chsd ldrs: effrt over 1f out: styd on same pce u.p ins fnl f* **11/2**[3]

04 **5** *1/2* **Chaparrachik (IRE)**[10] 6297 2-9-5 0 .... PatDobbs 7 69
(Amanda Perrett) *chsd ldr after 1f: rdn to ld wl over 1f out: sn hdd and unable qck u.p: wknd ins fnl f* **10/1**

00 **6** *6* **Netley Abbey**[10] 6288 2-9-5 0 .... PatCosgrave 5 58
(Harry Dunlop) *niggled along leaving stalls: hld up in tch: rdn over 2f out: sn struggling: wknd over 1f out* **100/1**

03 **7** *5* **Spin A Disc (GER)**[17] 6092 2-9-5 0 .... SilvestreDeSousa 1 49
(Mark Johnston) *dropped to rr after 2f and rn in snatches after: u.p and no rspnse over 2f out: bhd over 1f out* **20/1**

2m 9.76s (1.76) **Going Correction** 0.0s/f (Stan) **7** Ran SP% **109.5**
Speed ratings (Par 97): **92,91,90,88,88 83,79**
CSF £89.45 TOTE £11.10: £6.20, £2.00; EX 86.00 Trifecta £231.50.
Owner Saeed H Al Tayer **Bred** Mr & Mrs A E Pakenham **Trained** Newmarket, Suffolk

FOCUS
An interesting mile and a quarter 2yo maiden, run at a slow pace, that went to the only debutant in the field. THE form is rated tentatively.

6624 APOLLOBET/BRITISH STALLION STUDS EBF MAIDEN FILLIES' STKS (PLUS 10 RACE) (DIV I) 7f (P)

3:10 (3:12) (Class 4) 2-Y-O **£4,269** (£1,270; £634; £317) **Stalls** Low

Form RPR

42 **1** **Raven's Lady**[28] 5722 2-9-0 0 .... SilvestreDeSousa 4 83+
(Marco Botti) *mde all: pushed along and readily qcknd clr ent fnl 2f: in command after: r.o strly: easily* **5/4**[1]

4 **2** *3 1/4* **Agathonia (USA)**[13] 6206 2-9-0 0 .... WilliamBuick 3 74+
(Charlie Appleby) *midfield: effrt ent fnl 2f: chsd clr wnr jst ins fnl f: styd on wl for clr 2nd: no ch w wnr* **4/1**[2]

0 **3** *2 1/4* **Angel Of Darkness**[81] 3812 2-9-0 0 .... JamieSpencer 6 67
(Charles Hills) *wnt rt s: hld up in midfield: rdn and hdwy jst over 2f out: 3rd jst ins fnl f: kpt on same pce: no ch w wnr* **25/1**

03 **4** *2 1/4* **Oudwood**[22] 5930 2-9-0 0 .... JimCrowley 7 61
(Hugo Palmer) *chsd ldng trio: effrt ent fnl 2f: battling for placings but no ch w wnr whn edgd rt over 1f out: wknd ins fnl f* **12/1**

552 **5** *nk* **Carol (IRE)**[16] 6111 2-9-0 75 .... PatCosgrave 1 60
(Ed Dunlop) *chsd ldng pair: effrt to go 2nd ent fnl 2f: sn outpcd by wnr and wl hld over 1f out: lost 2nd jst ins fnl f: wknd* **8/1**[3]

6 *nk* **Narjes** 2-9-0 0 .... TomQueally 2 62+
(James Fanshawe) *fly.j. and wnt lft as stalls opened: slowly away and rn green in rr: pushed along and hdwy over 1f out: reminder 1f out: styd on wl ins fnl f: nvr trbld ldrs* **8/1**[3]

7 *hd* **Mawqed (IRE)** 2-9-0 0 .... PaulHanagan 9 59
(Sir Michael Stoute) *off the pce in rr: pushed along and hdwy 2f out: styd on wl ins fnl f: nvr trbld ldrs* **12/1**

8 *1/2* **Plead** 2-9-0 0 .... HarryBentley 11 58
(Roger Varian) *midfield: 6th and rdn 3f out: no imp u.p over 2f out: wl hld and plugged on same pce fnl 2f* **25/1**

5 **9** *3 1/4* **Send Up (IRE)**[5] 6472 2-9-0 0 .... LukeMorris 12 49
(Sir Mark Prescott Bt) *midfield but nvr on terms w ldrs: rdn over 2f out: no imp: wl hld and eased wl ins fnl f* **100/1**

10 *1 1/4* **Haraka (IRE)** 2-9-0 0 .... JohnFahy 10 45
(Ralph Beckett) *dwlt: rn green and a off the pce towards rr: n.d* **25/1**

00 **11** *2* **Fleeting Francesca**[11] 6250 2-9-0 0 .... AdamBeschizza 14 40
(Chris Gordon) *a off the pce towards rr: rdn and no hdwy over 2f out: n.d* **200/1**

6 **12** *1/2* **Dolly Dimples**[23] 5876 2-9-0 0 .... CharlesBishop 13 39
(William Jarvis) *t.k.h: hld up off the pce towards rr: wd bnd 3f out: no ch after* **80/1**

00 **13** *2* **Josiane (IRE)**[133] 2097 2-9-0 0 .... SeanLevey 5 33
(Richard Hannon) *chsd wnr: rdn 3f out: lost 2nd ent fnl 2f: sn dropped out: bhd ins fnl f* **80/1**

1m 26.7s (0.70) **Going Correction** 0.0s/f (Stan) **13** Ran SP% **117.5**
Speed ratings (Par 94): **96,92,89,87,86 86,86,85,81,80 78,77,75**
CSF £5.43 TOTE £2.20: £1.20, £1.60, £5.90; EX 7.10 Trifecta £90.90.
Owner Heart of the South Racing & Partner **Bred** Rabbah Bloodstock Limited **Trained** Newmarket, Suffolk

FOCUS
A maiden full of interesting raced and unraced fillies that was won in style. The winner is possibly worth more.

6625 APOLLOBET/BRITISH STALLION STUDS EBF MAIDEN FILLIES' STKS (PLUS 10 RACE) (DIV II) 7f (P)

3:40 (3:42) (Class 4) 2-Y-O **£4,269** (£1,270; £634; £317) **Stalls** Low

Form RPR

6 **1** **Belle Diva (IRE)**[40] 5304 2-9-0 0 .... SilvestreDeSousa 10 77
(Ralph Beckett) *chsd ldr: rdn to ld over 1f out: clr ins fnl f: tiring towards fin but a doing enough* **3/1**[2]

6 **2** *3/4* **Hersigh**[58] 4663 2-9-0 0 .... JamesDoyle 1 75
(Saeed bin Suroor) *chsd ldrs: rdn ent fnl 2f: hdwy to chse clr wnr 150yds: styd on wl fnl 100yds: nvr quite getting to wnr* **2/1**[1]

3 **3** *nk* **Castellated**[13] 6206 2-9-0 0 .... SeanLevey 6 74
(Richard Hannon) *chsd ldng trio: effrt ent fnl 2f: hdwy over 1f out: wnt 3rd ins fnl f: kpt on wl fnl 100yds: nvr quite getting to wnr* **9/2**[3]

4 *2 1/4* **Choumicha** 2-9-0 0 .... JimCrowley 9 68+
(Hugo Palmer) *hld up in midfield: rdn 3f out: hdwy jst over 1f out: kpt on wl ins fnl f: nvr trbld ldrs* **8/1**

0 **5** *2* **Instigation**[74] 4063 2-9-0 0 .... PatCosgrave 4 63
(Ed Dunlop) *hld up in midfield: effrt and swtchd lft over 2f out: hdwy over 1f out: kpt on steadily ins fnl f: nvr trbld ldrs* **40/1**

60 **6** *1/2* **Lawfilly**[17] 6071 2-9-0 0 .... ShaneKelly 5 61
(Richard Hughes) *led: rdn and hdd over 1f out: no ex: lost 2nd 150yds out: sn wknd* **50/1**

0 **7** *1/2* **Oh It's Saucepot**[59] 4594 2-9-0 0 .... HarryBentley 13 60
(Chris Wall) *t.k.h: hld up in midfield: rdn and effrt 2f out: kpt on steadily ins fnl f: nvr trbld ldrs* **100/1**

8 *nk* **Pyjamarama** 2-9-0 0 .... JackMitchell 3 59
(Roger Varian) *chsd ldrs: 4th and rdn over 2f out: unable qck and no imp over 1f out: wknd ins fnl f* **15/2**

9 *1 1/4* **Pobbles** 2-8-11 0 .... KieranShoemark[(3)] 2 56+
(Roger Charlton) *racd in last quartet: pushed along and sme hdwy on inner over 1f out: kpt on same pce ins fnl f: nvr trbld ldrs* **25/1**

10 *shd* **Shambra (IRE)** 2-9-0 0 .... MartinHarley 12 56
(James Tate) *hld up in rr: rdn over 2f out: sme prog over 1f out: kpt on same pce ins fnl f* **20/1**

11 *nk* **Follow Me (IRE)** 2-8-11 0 .... MarcMonaghan[(3)] 8 57+
(Hugo Palmer) *s.i.s and wnt rt s: hld up off the pce in rr: effrt and nt clr run wl over 1f out: kpt on ins fnl f: n.d* **25/1**

0 **12** *2* **Grey Thou Art (IRE)**[17] 6078 2-9-0 0 .... DaneO'Neill 7 49
(Henry Candy) *dwlt: a towards rr: rdn over 2f out: no imp: n.d* **33/1**

50 **13** *3/4* **B B Queen (IRE)**[11] 6250 2-9-0 0 .... (b[1]) JohnFahy 11 47
(Clive Cox) *in tch in midfield: rdn over 2f out: sn struggling and lost pl: bhd ins fnl f* **66/1**

1m 26.55s (0.55) **Going Correction** 0.0s/f (Stan) **13** Ran SP% **121.7**
Speed ratings (Par 94): **96,95,94,92,89 89,88,88,87,86 86,84,83**
CSF £8.82 TOTE £4.20: £1.40, £1.40, £1.60; EX 12.20 Trifecta £44.50.
Owner Qatar Racing Limited & China Horse Club **Bred** Jeremy Gompertz **Trained** Kimpton, Hants
■ Stewards' Enquiry : Martin Harley four-day ban: use of whip (3-6 Oct)

FOCUS
The second division of the maiden was well contested and was run slightly quicker than the first. The field finished quite compressed.

6626 APOLLOBET PREMIER LEAGUE CASHBACK H'CAP 1m 4f (P)

4:10 (4:10) (Class 4) (0-80,80) 3-Y-O **£4,690** (£1,395; £697; £348) **Stalls** Centre

Form RPR

3120 **1** **His Kyllachy (IRE)**[23] 5865 3-9-7 **80** .... PatCosgrave 6 86+
(William Haggas) *in tch in midfield: effrt 2f out: drvn and styd on to chal ins fnl f: kpt on to ld nr fin* **5/2**[1]

533 **2** *1/2* **Rasmee**[29] 5681 3-9-7 **80** .... (b[1]) LukeMorris 1 85
(Marco Botti) *in tch in midfield: clsd to chse ldr and swtchd rt 2f out: drvn to chal over 1f out: led 1f out: hdd and no ex towards fin* **8/1**

21 **3** *1 1/4* **Unsuspected Girl (IRE)**[8] 6370 3-8-0 **64** 6ex .... SophieKilloran[(7)] 4 70+
(David Simcock) *stdd s: wl off the pce in last: grad clsd: effrt to chse ldrs and swtchd rt 2f out: rdn and ev ch 1f out: no ex ins fnl f: wknd wl ins fnl f* **13/2**[2]

0046 **4** *2* **Ban Shoof**[39] 5333 3-9-4 **77** .... (b[1]) MartinHarley 3 77
(Ismail Mohammed) *led: rdn over 2f out: hrd pressed and drvn over 1f out: hdd 1f out: wknd ins fnl f* **7/1**[3]

4215 **5** *3 3/4* **Rajadamri**[14] 6194 3-8-1 **67** .... LuluStanford[(7)] 5 61
(Rod Millman) *hld up in last pair: swtchd lft and effrt over 2f out: 5th and no imp over 1f out: wknd ins fnl f* **12/1**

0-65 **6** *shd* **Next Train's Gone**[111] 2774 3-8-9 **68** .... RyanTate 7 62
(James Eustace) *chsd ldr tl over 2f out: sn lost pl u.p: bhd over 1f out* **9/1**

6232 **7** *4* **Michael's Mount**[17] 6083 3-9-0 **73** .... SilvestreDeSousa 2 60
(Ed Dunlop) *t.k.h: rdn and unable qck over 2f out: wknd over 1f out: bhd and eased wl ins fnl f* **5/2**[1]

2m 32.82s (-1.68) **Going Correction** 0.0s/f (Stan) **7** Ran SP% **111.8**
Speed ratings (Par 103): **105,104,103,102,100 99,97**
CSF £22.46 TOTE £2.90: £1.90, £3.00; EX 18.80 Trifecta £77.00.
Owner Sheikh Juma Dalmook Al Maktoum **Bred** Mrs D Camacho **Trained** Newmarket, Suffolk

FOCUS
A middle-distance three-year-old handicap where several had chances late on. The time was ordinary but a slightly positive view has been taken of the form.

6627 APOLLOBET BET THROUGH YOUR MOBILE H'CAP 6f (P)

4:40 (4:40) (Class 3) (0-95,95) 3-Y-O+
£7,158 (£2,143; £1,071; £535; £267; £134) **Stalls** Low

Form RPR

2502 **1** **Seychelloise**[8] 6371 4-9-2 **90** .... (b) LukeMorris 12 101
(Sir Mark Prescott Bt) *mde all and crossed to inner fr wd draw: rdn 2f out: styd on wl u.p ins fnl f: rdn out* **12/1**

6110 **2** *3/4* **Mustallib (IRE)**[16] 6112 3-9-5 **95** .... PaulHanagan 4 106+
(Charles Hills) *t.k.h: hld up in tch in midfield: effrt and switching rt over 1f out: hdwy 1f out: swtchd lft and chsd wnr 100yds out: styd on* **7/2**[1]

2020 **3** *1/2* **Related**[9] 6327 6-9-6 **94** .... (b) MartinHarley 2 101
(Paul Midgley) *t.k.h: chsd ldrs: sltly impeded after 1f: effrt u.p to chse wnr over 1f out: kpt on but a hld ins fnl f: lost 2nd 100yds out* **11/2**[3]

0100 **4** *1 3/4* **Cartmell Cleave**[16] 6112 4-9-1 **89** .... TedDurcan 1 90
(Stuart Kittow) *hld up in tch: hdwy on inner 2f out: rdn to chse ldrs over 1f out: no ex and wknd wl ins fnl f* **12/1**

0400 **5** *nk* **Shamshon (IRE)**[9] 6327 5-9-5 **93** .... JamieSpencer 6 93+
(Jamie Osborne) *hld up in midfield: nt clrest of runs 2f out: rdn and hdwy over 1f out: styd on wl u.p ins fnl f: no rch ldrs* **4/1**[2]

2300 **6** *1/2* **Alqubbah (IRE)**[101] 3116 3-9-2 **92** .... DaneO'Neill 5 92
(Ed Dunlop) *hld up in tch in midfield: effrt whn squeezed out and hmpd over 1f out: swtchd lft ent fnl f: kpt on ins fnl f: no threat to ldrs* **16/1**

3000 **7** *nse* **Dougan**[16] 6112 4-9-3 **91** .... JimCrowley 10 90+
(David Evans) *stdd s: hld up in last pair: clsd and nt clrest of runs wl over 1f out: and hdwy jst over 1f out: styd on ins fnl f: nvr trbld ldrs* **11/2**[3]

0000 **8** *3/4* **Baddilini**[29] 5678 6-8-11 **88** .... (p) JosephineGordon[(3)] 9 84
(Alan Bailey) *pressed ldr tl unable qck u.p over 1f out: wknd ins fnl f* **50/1**

2100 **9** *nk* **Highland Acclaim (IRE)**[9] 6327 5-9-3 **91** .... HarryBentley 3 86
(David O'Meara) *t.k.h: chsd ldrs: sltly impeded after 1f: rdn and unable qck wl over 1f out: wknd ins fnl f* **12/1**

00-0 **10** *1 1/4* **Picture Dealer**[29] 5678 7-8-10 **87** .... SimonPearce[(3)] 8 78
(Lydia Pearce) *dwlt: racd in last pair: effrt 2f out: no real imp: nvr trbld ldrs* **40/1**

The Form Book, Raceform Ltd, Newbury, RG14 5SJ

-0P0 **11** *3/4* **Queen's Pearl (IRE)**[65] 4398 4-9-0 **88** .... JamesDoyle 7 77
(Roger Varian) *in tch in midfield: swtchd lft and effrt over 2f out: lost pl u.p over 1f out: wknd ins fnl f* **20/1**

3005 **12** *nk* **Muir Lodge**[24] 5825 5-9-4 **92** ....(tp) PatCosgrave 11 80
(George Baker) *in tch in midfield on outer: losing pl and sltly hmpd over 2f out: bhd fnl f* **20/1**

1m 11.97s (-1.13) **Going Correction** 0.0s/f (Stan)
WFA 3 from 4yo+ 2lb **12** Ran SP% **115.9**
Speed ratings (Par 107): **107,106,105,103,102 101,101,100,100,98 97,97**
CSF £50.44 CT £266.52 TOTE £9.30: £2.90, £1.50, £2.70; EX 27.80 Trifecta £200.40.
Owner Miss K Rausing **Bred** Miss K Rausing **Trained** Newmarket, Suffolk

FOCUS
A decent Class 3 sprint that was won from the gate. The third is the best guide to the form.

6628 APOLLOBET FREE SIGN-UP BONUS H'CAP 1m (P)
5:10 (5:11) (Class 4) (0-85,84) 3-Y-O+ **£4,690** (£1,395; £697; £348) **Stalls** Low

Form RPR

1446 **1** **Mountain Rescue (IRE)**[46] 5082 4-9-7 **81** .... JamesDoyle 2 91
(Chris Wall) *led for 1f: trckd ldrs after: rdn and hdwy to ld over 1f out: styd on ins fnl f: drvn out* **11/1**

5340 **2** *1* **Sky Ship**[54] 4776 3-9-2 **80** .... TedDurcan 3 87+
(Sir Michael Stoute) *hld up wl in tch in midfield: swtchd rt and effrt over 1f out: chsd wnr ins fnl f: kpt on* **9/2**[2]

2021 **3** *1* **Ehtiraas**[28] 5731 3-9-5 **83** .... PaulHanagan 12 88
(Owen Burrows) *t.k.h: chsd ldr tl led after 1f: hdd 6f out: rdn 2f out: drvn and unable qck 1f out: 3rd and styd on same pce ins fnl f* **8/1**[3]

3616 **4** *1* **Easter Mate (IRE)**[38] 5376 3-9-1 **84** ....(p) HectorCrouch(5) 5 87
(Ralph Beckett) *t.k.h: trckd ldrs: effrt and hung rt over 1f out: styd on same pce ins fnl f* **10/1**

6122 **5** *nk* **Reaver (IRE)**[7] 6416 3-8-12 **76** .... CharlesBishop 6 78+
(Eve Johnson Houghton) *hld up in tch in midfield: effrt 2f out: rdn and hdwy over 1f out: styd on same pce ins fnl f* **7/4**[1]

3356 **6** *1* **Prendergast Hill (IRE)**[18] 6048 4-9-8 **82** ....(p) LiamKeniry 9 81
(Ed de Giles) *hld up in tch in midfield: effrt and carried rt over 1f out: kpt on same pce ins fnl f* **16/1**

4313 **7** *nk* **Torch**[40] 5306 3-9-3 **81** ....(p) SeanLevey 14 80
(Richard Hannon) *chsd ldrs tl led 6f out: rdn ent fnl 2f: hung lft and hdd over 1f out: wknd ins fnl f* **14/1**

000 **8** *nk* **Red Avenger (USA)**[17] 6076 6-9-8 **82** ....(v1) TomQueally 10 80
(Gary Moore) *t.k.h: stdd after s: hld up towards rr: effrt u.p 2f out: styd on ins fnl f: nvr trbld ldrs* **22/1**

4650 **9** *nse* **Jammy Guest (IRE)**[58] 4627 6-9-8 **82** .... JamieSpencer 13 80+
(George Margarson) *stdd s: hld up in tch in midfield: effrt 2f out: rdn and no imp over 1f out: wl hld and eased towards fin* **33/1**

6310 **10** *1 3/4* **Tournament**[17] 6084 5-9-7 **81** ....(t) ShaneKelly 8 75
(Seamus Durack) *stdd s: hld up towards rr: swtchd rt and urged along over 1f out: hung lft and no imp jst over 1f out: swtchd rt again and shkn up ins fnl f: stl wanting to hang and no imp* **14/1**

0000 **11** *5* **Prince Of Paris**[18] 6050 4-9-3 **77** ....(t) RobertHavlin 11 59
(Roger Ingram) *v.s.a: detached in last: grad rcvrd and in tch in rr 5f out: rdn over 2f out: wknd over 1f out* **50/1**

30 **12** *1* **D'Niro (IRE)**[109] 2818 3-8-6 **77** ....[1] JordanUys(7) 4 56
(Harry Dunlop) *taken down early: in tch: rdn over 2f out: sn struggling and lost pl over 1f out: wknd fnl f* **20/1**

60-0 **13** *7* **Los Cerritos (SWI)**[10] 6286 4-9-6 **80** .... SaleemGolam 1 43
(Sophie Leech) *a towards rr: rdn over 2f out: sn struggling: bhd over 1f out* **100/1**

1m 39.18s (-0.62) **Going Correction** 0.0s/f (Stan)
WFA 3 from 4yo+ 4lb **13** Ran SP% **117.3**
Speed ratings (Par 105): **103,102,101,100,99 98,98,98,98,96 91,90,83**
CSF £56.01 CT £442.83 TOTE £12.10: £4.60, £2.00, £2.00; EX 73.80 Trifecta £393.80.
Owner ValueRacingClub.co.uk **Bred** Lady Richard Wellesley **Trained** Newmarket, Suffolk

FOCUS
A competitive Class 4 handicap where it paid to be near the pace. Improvement from the winner.

6629 APOLLOBET ONLINE CASINO & GAMES H'CAP 1m (P)
5:40 (5:40) (Class 5) (0-70,70) 3-Y-O **£2,911** (£866; £432; £216) **Stalls** Low

Form RPR

0523 **1** **Cryptic (IRE)**[11] 6254 3-9-7 **70** .... PatCosgrave 4 79+
(Luca Cumani) *hld up in tch in midfield: rdn and hdwy over 1f out: chal 1f out: led and ducked rt ins fnl f: stened and styd on fnl 100yds: rdn out* **3/1**[1]

0631 **2** *1* **Broughtons Vision**[28] 5720 3-9-6 **69** .... JamesDoyle 6 75
(Willie Musson) *in tch: rdn and hdwy ent fnl 2f: drvn to over 1f out: edgd rt and hdd ins fnl f: styd on same pce fnl 100yds* **4/1**[2]

0311 **3** *3/4* **German Whip**[18] 6047 3-9-2 **70** .... HectorCrouch(5) 14 74+
(Gary Moore) *hld up in tch but stuck wd early: hdwy u.p over 1f out: chsd ldrs ins fnl f: styd on wl u.p to snatch 3rd last strides* **7/1**[3]

2331 **4** *hd* **Music Major**[49] 4936 3-8-12 **61** .... AdamBeschizza 2 65
(Michael Attwater) *dwlt: bustled along and sn rcvrd to r in midfield: rdn and hdwy to chse ldrs over 1f out: ev ch 1f out: no ex and outpcd fnl 100yds* **8/1**

3445 **5** *5* **Silhouette (IRE)**[20] 5996 3-9-7 **70** .... RichardKingscote 10 62
(Daniel Kubler) *chsd ldr: rdn and ev ch ent fnl 2f: no ex and btn ent fnl f: wknd ins fnl f* **20/1**

5640 **6** *1 1/2* **Nellie Deen (IRE)**[12] 6237 3-9-4 **67** .... SilvestreDeSousa 3 55
(David Elsworth) *s.i.s and stmbld sn after s: hld up towards rr: swtchd rt and hdwy on inner 2f out: no imp fnl f* **14/1**

0321 **7** *1* **In Ken's Memory**[12] 6241 3-9-4 **67** .... TomQueally 5 53
(John Butler) *led: rdn ent fnl 2f: hdd over 1f out: sn btn and wknd ins fnl f* **7/1**[3]

0410 **8** *hd* **Ubla (IRE)**[24] 5860 3-9-7 **70** ....(t) JamieSpencer 9 55
(Gay Kelleway) *stdd after s: hld up in rr: swtchd lft over 2f out: sme hdwy over 1f out: nvr trbld ldrs* **8/1**

5506 **9** *1/2* **Ruby Wednesday**[11] 6246 3-9-4 **67** .... KierenFox 1 51
(John Best) *chsd ldrs: swtchd rt and effrt u.p 2f out: no imp over 1f out: wknd ins fnl f* **20/1**

4053 **10** *1 1/4* **Jayjinski (IRE)**[25] 5811 3-9-7 **70** ....[1] ShaneKelly 7 51
(Richard Hughes) *hld up in tch in midfield: effrt over 1f out: sn rdn and no rspnse: wknd ins fnl f* **20/1**

2450 **11** *3/4* **Aid To Africa (IRE)**[11] 6265 3-8-13 **69** .... SophieScardifield(7) 13 48
(Michael Bell) *hld up in tch in midfield: pushed along 2f out: hung rt and no hdwy over 1f out: wknd ins fnl f* **50/1**

3430 **12** *2 1/4* **Sehayli (IRE)**[11] 6265 3-9-2 **70** .... PaddyBradley(5) 8 44
(Lee Carter) *sn dropped towards rr and nvr gng wl: bhd 1/2-way* **50/1**

240 **13** *5* **Fishergate**[28] 5720 3-8-12 **61** .... RyanPowell 12 23
(Richard Rowe) *sn dropped towards rr and pushed along: lost tch 2f out* **100/1**

1-60 **14** *103* **Davey Boy**[107] 2900 3-9-7 **70** .... MartinHarley 11
(Michael Bell) *chsd ldrs: lost pl qckly 5f out and sn hung lft: bhd and eased 3f out: t.o* **50/1**

1m 39.73s (-0.07) **Going Correction** 0.0s/f (Stan) **14** Ran SP% **120.0**
Speed ratings (Par 101): **100,99,98,98,93 91,90,89,88 87,85,80,**
CSF £13.24 CT £81.25 TOTE £4.00: £1.70, £1.60, £2.40; EX 16.90 Trifecta £102.40.
Owner Mrs Angie Silver **Bred** Old Carhue & Graeng Bloodstock **Trained** Newmarket, Suffolk

FOCUS
A competitive Class 5 where course form came to the fore. The form is rated around the third and fourth.
T/Jkpt: £70,887.90 to a £1 stake. Pool: £177,219.92 - 2.5 winning units T/Plt: £121.50 to a £1 stake. Pool: £71,487.61 - 429.4 winning units T/Qpdt: £7.30 to a £1 stake. Pool: £7,069.27 - 711.8 winning units **Steve Payne**

6206 LEICESTER (R-H)
Monday, September 19

OFFICIAL GOING: Good changing to good to soft after race 1 (2:00)
Wind: Light across Weather: Light rain

6630 ASTON FLAMVILLE FILLIES' NURSERY H'CAP 6f
2:00 (2:03) (Class 5) (0-75,74) 2-Y-O **£3,234** (£962; £481; £240) **Stalls** High

Form RPR

1 **1** **Tara Celeb**[23] 5869 2-9-6 **73** .... AndreaAtzeni 10 81+
(Mick Channon) *chsd ldrs: rdn over 1f out: r.o to ld wl ins fnl f* **11/4**[1]

13 **2** *hd* **Fields Of Song (IRE)**[26] 5756 2-9-4 **71** .... ShaneGray 12 79+
(Kevin Ryan) *w ldrs: led over 4f out: hdd 2f out: rdn over 1f out: led ins fnl f: sn hdd: r.o* **9/1**

051 **3** *2 1/2* **Believable**[17] 6087 2-9-7 **74** .... RyanMoore 5 74
(Sir Michael Stoute) *w ldrs: led 2f out: rdn over 1f out: hdd ins fnl f: no ex towards fin* **9/1**

032 **4** *3/4* **Darkroom Angel**[19] 6034 2-9-3 **70** .... AdamKirby 13 68
(Clive Cox) *racd alone towards stands' side for much of the trip: led: hdd over 4f out: remained handy: rdn over 1f out: hung rt ins fnl f: styd on* **8/1**[3]

431 **5** *1 1/2* **Fabric**[53] 4804 2-9-2 **74** .... HollieDoyle(5) 9 67
(Richard Hannon) *hld up: racd keenly: hdwy 4f out: rdn over 1f out: no ex fnl f* **10/1**

0224 **6** *1/2* **Happy Queen**[22] 5931 2-9-0 **67** .... FMBerry 3 59
(George Margarson) *chsd ldrs: rdn over 2f out: ev ch over 1f out: wknd ins fnl f* **11/1**

6216 **7** *2* **The Stalking Moon (IRE)**[11] 6257 2-9-0 **72** .... AdamMcNamara(5) 7 58
(John Quinn) *chsd ldrs: rdn over 1f out: wknd fnl f* **6/1**[2]

054 **8** *3* **Halinka (IRE)**[60] 4558 2-8-10 **70** .... CameronNoble(7) 8 47
(Roger Varian) *prom: hmpd and lost pl after 1f: n.d after* **16/1**

236 **9** *nk* **Quick Thought (IRE)**[65] 4397 2-8-12 **65** .... NickyMackay 6 41
(Dr Jon Scargill) *hld up: rdn over 2f out: a in rr* **33/1**

321 **10** *3/4* **Miss Icon**[19] 6035 2-9-6 **73** .... JimmyQuinn 4 47
(Patrick Chamings) *hld up: hdwy over 2f out: sn rdn: wknd fnl f* **10/1**

563 **11** *7* **Express (IRE)**[41] 5250 2-8-10 **63** .... KieranO'Neill 2 16
(Richard Hannon) *hld up: rdn 1/2-way: wknd over 2f out* **66/1**

1m 13.19s (0.19) **Going Correction** +0.125s/f (Good) **11** Ran SP% **108.9**
Speed ratings (Par 92): **103,102,99,98,96 95,93,89,88,87 78**
CSF £24.88 CT £175.50 TOTE £3.60: £1.70, £2.80, £2.80; EX 29.40 Trifecta £297.40.
Owner The Tara Moon Partnership I **Bred** M H And Mrs G Tourle **Trained** West Ilsley, Berks
■ Savannah Slew was withdrawn. Price at time of withdrawal 16/1 - Rule 4 does not apply.

FOCUS
The ground was good, although Andrea Atzeni said "it is good ground with just a bit of ease in places", while Shane Gray described it as "good to soft". A competitive nursery featuring four last-time-out winners and it paid to race prominently. Decent form for the grade.

6631 GOLDEN HAND (S) STKS 7f
2:30 (2:32) (Class 6) 3-Y-O **£2,587** (£770; £384; £192) **Stalls** High

Form RPR

6056 **1** **Walking In Rhythm (IRE)**[14] 6187 3-8-0 60 .... HollieDoyle(5) 12 62
(Richard Hannon) *racd towards stands' side: chsd ldrs: rdn over 1f out: styd on to ld wl ins fnl f: 1st of 5 in gp* **5/1**[2]

3026 **2** *3/4* **Infiniti (IRE)**[18] 6046 3-8-0 56 ....[1] GeorgeWood(5) 10 60
(Rae Guest) *racd towards stands' side: hld up in tch: racd keenly: rdn to ld overall over 1f out: hdd and unable qck wl ins fnl f: 2nd of 5 in gp* **3/1**[1]

6355 **3** *5* **Just Fab (IRE)**[14] 6187 3-8-5 54 ....(bt) TomMarquand 11 47
(Ali Stronge) *racd towards stands' side: chsd ldrs: rdn over 2f out: styd on same pce fr over 1f out: 3rd of 5 in gp* **12/1**

4210 **4** *3 3/4* **Mecca's Missus (IRE)**[34] 5515 3-8-9 63 ....(b) NickyMackay 8 41
(Michael Wigham) *led gp towards stands' side: overall ldr 1/2-way: rdn and hdd over 1f out: wknd ins fnl f: 4th of 5 in gp* **6/1**[3]

3566 **5** *1 3/4* **The Big Day (IRE)**[5] 6478 3-8-5 55 .... AndrewMullen 5 33+
(Nigel Tinkler) *racd centre: hmpd s: hdwy 1/2-way: rdn over 2f out: sn hung lft and outpcd: styd on towards fin: 1st of 5 in gp* **13/2**

0636 **6** *11* **Cautious Optimism**[34] 5517 3-8-10 63 .... MartinDwyer 6 9+
(William Muir) *overall ldr in centre to 1/2-way: sn rdn: hung lft and wknd over 1f out: 2nd of 5 in gp* **5/1**[2]

0205 **7** *3* **Gabbys Lad (IRE)**[13] 6218 3-8-5 48 .... NeilFarley 1 +
(Eric Alston) *racd centre chsd ldrs: stmbld after 1f: rdn over 2f out: wknd over 1f out: 3rd of 5 in gp* **25/1**

5460 **8** *8* **Mostashreqah**[21] 5954 3-8-9 45 ....(bt1) JimmyQuinn 13
(Milton Bradley) *racd towards stands' side: chsd ldrs: rdn over 2f out: wknd over 1f out: last of 5 in gp* **50/1**

000- **9** *10* **Indian Gold**[319] 7715 3-8-7 30 ....(b) NoelGarbutt(3) 3 +
(Milton Bradley) *racd centre: chsd ldrs to 1/2-way: sn wknd: 4th of 5 in gp* **200/1**

5650 **10** *16* **Heart Of An Angel**[7] 6426 3-8-2 67 ....(v1) EdwardGreatrex(3) 2 +
(Philip McBride) *s.i.s: sn pushed along in rr: hdwy over 4f out: rdn and wknd over 2f out: eased: last of 5 in gp* **6/1**[3]

1m 25.64s (-0.56) **Going Correction** +0.125s/f (Good) **10** Ran SP% **114.2**
Speed ratings (Par 99): **108,107,101,97,95 82,79,70,58,40**
CSF £19.76 TOTE £5.90: £2.00, £1.50, £3.50; EX 24.50 Trifecta £211.10.The winner was bought by Mr Frank Dronzek for 6,500gns
Owner Mrs J Wood **Bred** Moorpark Stud **Trained** East Everleigh, Wilts

FOCUS
The ground was changed to good to soft before the second race, a weak 3yo seller in which they split into two groups. Those drawn highest nearer the stands' side fared best, weakening the depth of the race further.

6632 BRITISH STALLION STUDS KEGWORTH EBF MAIDEN STKS (PLUS 10 RACE) 7f
3:00 (3:02) (Class 4) 2-Y-O **£6,469** (£1,925; £962; £481) **Stalls** High

Form RPR
1 **Emmaus (IRE)** 2-9-5 0 AndreaAtzeni 6 82+
(Roger Varian) *s.i.s: hld up: hdwy over 2f out: shkn up over 1f out: r.o to ld wl ins fnl f* **15/8**[1]
0 2 nk **Sound Bar**[31] 5600 2-9-5 0 FMBerry 8 79
(Ralph Beckett) *s.i.s: hdwy 1/2-way: rdn and hung lft over 1f out: r.o* **7/2**[2]
30 3 1 1/4 **Lualiwa**[35] 5476 2-9-5 0 ShaneGray 3 76
(Kevin Ryan) *sn prom: led wl over 1f out: sn rdn: hdd wl ins fnl f* **11/1**
63 4 2 1/4 **Presence Process**[13] 6211 2-9-5 0 MartinLane 10 70
(Luca Cumani) *racd keenly: w ldr 2f: remained handy: rdn over 2f out: no ex ins fnl f* **15/2**[3]
0 5 2 3/4 **Mystic Maeve (IRE)**[140] 1921 2-8-11 0 EdwardGreatrex(3) 2 58+
(David Loughnane) *prom: pushed along and lost pl after 1f: hdwy over 1f out: styd on* **100/1**
0 6 nk **Exspectation (IRE)**[31] 5600 2-9-5 0 TomMarquand 7 62
(Michael Blanshard) *hld up in tch: rdn over 2f out: sn outpcd: styd on ins fnl f* **100/1**
5 7 3 1/4 **Mr Maximum (USA)**[34] 5505 2-9-5 0 AdamKirby 5 54
(Harry Dunlop) *chsd ldrs: rdn and ev ch over 2f out: wknd ins fnl f* **12/1**
0636 8 7 **Permanent**[29] 5670 2-9-5 67 WilliamTwiston-Davies 9 36+
(Daniel Kubler) *led: rdn and hdd wl over 1f out: wknd fnl f* **33/1**
9 2 1/4 **Rainbow Legacy (IRE)** 2-9-5 0 RyanMoore 1 30+
(Sir Michael Stoute) *chsd ldrs: pushed along and lost pl over 5f out: wknd over 1f out* **7/2**[2]
10 13 **Jupiter Ascending** 2-9-5 0 AndrewMullen 4
(Michael Appleby) *dwlt: sn pushed along in rr: lost tch fr over 2f out* **25/1**

1m 26.9s (0.70) **Going Correction** +0.125s/f (Good) **10** Ran SP% **115.8**
Speed ratings (Par 97): **101,100,99,96,93 93,89,81,78,64**
CSF £8.17 TOTE £2.50: £1.30, £1.30, £2.60; EX 9.50 Trifecta £63.00.
Owner China Horse Club **Bred** Kilcarn Stud **Trained** Newmarket, Suffolk

FOCUS
An interesting maiden won last year by the subsequent 2,000 Guineas runner-up, Massaat, and there were a couple of well-bred newcomers. THe winner looks sure to do a good bit better.

6633 A.T. SERVICES LTD H'CAP 5f
3:30 (3:30) (Class 3) (0-95,94) 3-Y-O+ **£7,561** (£2,263; £1,131; £566; £282) **Stalls** High

Form RPR
5003 1 **Distant Past**[65] 4415 5-8-10 **83** (p) ShaneGray 16 94
(Kevin Ryan) *sn pushed along in rr: hdwy over 1f out: r.o u.p to ld nr fin* **9/1**
-102 2 1/2 **Aleef (IRE)**[51] 4889 3-8-12 **86** PhillipMakin 15 95+
(David O'Meara) *chsd ldr: rdn to ld over 1f out: hdd nr fin* **10/1**
4415 3 1 1/4 **Top Boy**[12] 6234 6-8-11 **84** (v) MartinLane 5 89
(Derek Shaw) *hld up: hdwy over 1f out: styd on to go 3rd nr fin* **14/1**
5023 4 1 1/4 **Straightothepoint**[17] 6080 4-8-8 **81** KieranO'Neill 12 81
(Bryan Smart) *chsd ldrs: rdn over 1f out: styd on same pce ins fnl f* **9/2**[1]
-000 5 1 1/4 **Noble Storm (USA)**[12] 6234 10-8-2 **82** CameronNoble(7) 3 78
(Ed McMahon) *hld up: hdwy 2f out: rdn and hung lft over 1f out: styd on same pce ins fnl f* **12/1**
1102 6 1 **Just That Lord**[112] 2751 3-8-13 **87** WilliamCarson 1 79
(Bill Turner) *led: rdn and hdd over 1f out: no ex ins fnl f* **20/1**
0030 7 nk **Dungannon**[16] 6119 9-9-0 **90** (b) RobHornby(3) 2 81
(Andrew Balding) *hld up: hdwy: nt clr run and hung rt over 1f out: nt trble ldrs* **25/1**
1603 8 1 3/4 **Seeking Magic**[30] 5648 8-9-7 **94** (t) AdamKirby 7 84
(Clive Cox) *chsd ldrs: rdn whn hmpd over 1f out: wknd ins fnl f* **11/2**[2]
5402 9 1/2 **Ashpan Sam**[20] 5991 7-9-4 **91** (p) WilliamTwiston-Davies 14 74
(David W Drinkwater) *chsd ldrs: rdn 1/2-way: wknd fnl f* **8/1**[3]
5013 10 6 **Stanghow**[20] 6012 4-8-13 **86** DavidAllan 9 47
(Antony Brittain) *chsd ldrs tl rdn and wknd over 1f out* **8/1**[3]
0600 11 6 **Stepper Point**[16] 6119 7-9-3 **90** (p) MartinDwyer 13 30
(William Muir) *chsd ldrs: rdn 1/2-way: wknd wl over 1f out* **9/1**
3132 12 6 **Majestic Hero (IRE)**[16] 6114 4-9-3 **90** TomMarquand 6 8
(Ronald Harris) *hmpd sn after s: in rr: effrt whn hmpd over 1f out: sn wknd and eased* **8/1**[3]

59.53s (-0.47) **Going Correction** +0.125s/f (Good)
WFA 3 from 4yo+ 1lb **12** Ran SP% **119.0**
Speed ratings (Par 107): **108,107,105,103,101 99,99,96,95,85 76,66**
CSF £96.26 CT £1281.80 TOTE £12.00: £3.80, £3.10, £3.50; EX 121.20 Trifecta £4970.90 Part Won..
Owner J C G Chua **Bred** J E Rose **Trained** Hambleton, N Yorks

FOCUS
A competitive sprint handicap despite four non-runners, and they set a fast pace near the stands' side, which proved an advantageous place to be. The winner and third came from the rear.

6634 BREEDERS BACKING RACING EBF MAIDEN STKS 1m 3f 183y
4:00 (4:01) (Class 5) 3-Y-O+ **£3,881** (£1,155; £577; £288) **Stalls** Low

Form RPR
3 1 **Uae Prince (IRE)**[149] 1639 3-9-5 0 AndreaAtzeni 4 95+
(Roger Varian) *trckd ldrs: racd keenly: shkn up to ld over 1f out: sn pushed clr: eased wl ins fnl f* **4/7**[1]
23 2 4 1/2 **Arthur Mc Bride (IRE)**[18] 6052 7-9-13 0 (t) WilliamTwiston-Davies 7 82
(Nigel Twiston-Davies) *led: hdd over 8f out: chsd ldr: rdn and ev ch over 1f out: no ex fnl f* **15/2**
4-33 3 3 1/4 **Lovely Story (IRE)**[47] 5025 5-9-8 92 AdamKirby 1 71
(Seamus Durack) *w ldr tl led over 8f out: rdn and hdd over 1f out: wknd ins fnl f* **11/4**[2]
0-3 4 1/2 **Easy Gold (IRE)**[14] 6192 3-9-5 0 FMBerry 3 75
(Ed Walker) *s.i.s: pushed along and wnt prom over 10f out: rdn over 3f out: wknd over 1f out* **7/1**[3]
5 2 **Flower Power**[85] 5-9-8 0 DuranFentiman 9 67
(Tony Coyle) *mid-div: hdwy 3f out: rdn and hung rt over 2f out: wknd over 1f out* **100/1**
0000 6 2 **Vale Of Rock (IRE)**[18] 6052 3-9-0 44 (p) AndrewMullen 6 64?
(Michael Appleby) *mid-div: rdn over 3f out: wkng whn nt clr run wl over 1f out* **100/1**
7 1 1/4 **Diamond Kut** 3-9-2 0 RobHornby(3) 2 67
(Andrew Balding) *s.i.s: hdwy over 5f out: rdn over 2f out: wknd wl over 1f out* **25/1**
2234 8 30 **Dubai Mission (IRE)**[104] 2999 3-9-5 76 [1] TomMarquand 8 19
(Steve Flook) *hld up: rdn and wknd over 3f out* **20/1**
0 9 22 **Kindled**[45] 5129 3-9-0 0 MartinDwyer 5
(Ed McMahon) *hld up: bhd fr 1/2-way* **100/1**

2m 34.14s (0.24) **Going Correction** +0.125s/f (Good)
WFA 3 from 5yo+ 8lb **9** Ran SP% **126.2**
Speed ratings (Par 103): **104,101,98,98,97 95,95,75,60**
CSF £6.90 TOTE £1.40: £1.10, £1.80, £1.30; EX 6.40 Trifecta £12.10.
Owner Sheikh Mohammed Obaid Al Maktoum **Bred** John Connaughton **Trained** Newmarket, Suffolk

FOCUS
A moderate maiden that revolved around the odds-on favourite, who took this by the scruff of the neck in the home straight to land a treble for Andrea Atzeni. The form isn't that solid.

6635 HIGHFIELDS FILLIES' H'CAP 1m 60y
4:30 (4:31) (Class 5) (0-75,75) 3-Y-O+ **£3,234** (£962; £481; £240) **Stalls** Low

Form RPR
-532 1 **Artists Model (IRE)**[18] 6066 3-8-10 **65** FergusSweeney 7 75+
(Henry Candy) *chsd ldrs: rdn over 2f out: led ins fnl f: edgd rt: styd on wl* **9/4**[1]
-315 2 2 1/4 **Wrapped**[27] 5743 3-9-6 **75** (p) AndreaAtzeni 9 79
(William Haggas) *s.i.s: sn prom: chsd ldr over 6f out: wnt upsides over 3f out: sn rdn: ev ch ins fnl f: styd on same pce* **9/2**[2]
0053 3 1 **Rio's Cliffs**[14] 6182 3-9-5 **74** FMBerry 1 76
(Martyn Meade) *s.i.s: sn trcking ldrs: led over 3f out: rdn over 1f out: hdd and no ex ins fnl f* **11/2**[3]
-042 4 1 3/4 **Poster Girl**[23] 5891 3-8-11 **71** GeorgeWood(5) 8 69
(Jonathan Portman) *hld up: pushed along over 3f out: hdwy u.p over 1f out: hung rt and styd on same pce ins fnl f* **11/2**[3]
3224 5 3 3/4 **Heartstone (IRE)**[20] 5996 3-9-4 **73** SteveDrowne 4 62
(Charles Hills) *hld up in tch: rdn over 2f out: wknd fnl f* **16/1**
1246 6 1/2 **Zaria**[32] 5571 5-8-7 **63** (p) HollieDoyle(5) 3 51
(Richard Price) *hld up: racd keenly: rdn over 3f out: wknd over 1f out* **20/1**
1415 7 1 3/4 **Fantasy Queen**[21] 5953 3-8-9 **64** MartinDwyer 5 48
(Eve Johnson Houghton) *hld up: pushed along 1/2-way: rdn over 2f out: wknd over 1f out* **11/2**[3]
2550 8 1 1/2 **Celtic Sixpence (IRE)**[37] 5386 8-8-12 **63** DougieCostello 2 44
(Nick Kent) *led: hdd over 3f out: rdn and wknd over 1f out* **16/1**

1m 45.77s (0.67) **Going Correction** +0.125s/f (Good)
WFA 3 from 5yo+ 4lb **8** Ran SP% **111.6**
Speed ratings (Par 100): **101,98,97,96,92 91,90,88**
CSF £11.68 CT £47.13 TOTE £3.00: £1.30, £1.70, £2.10; EX 11.60 Trifecta £48.50.
Owner Girsonfield Ltd **Bred** Summerhill Bloodstock Ltd **Trained** Kingston Warren, Oxon

FOCUS
A tight handicap in which those in behind never got involved. The first two are progressing.

6636 RACING EXCELLENCE "HANDS AND HEELS" APPRENTICE SERIES H'CAP (DIV I) 7f
5:00 (5:01) (Class 6) (0-65,65) 3-Y-O+ **£2,587** (£770; £384; £192) **Stalls** High

Form RPR
-005 1 **Barista (IRE)**[11] 6254 8-9-3 **58** HollieDoyle 2 69
(Brian Forsey) *chsd ldrs: led over 1f out: shkn up and hung lft ins fnl f: styd on* **6/1**[3]
0040 2 3 1/2 **Lunar Deity**[21] 5965 7-9-10 **65** (t) MillyNaseb 9 68
(Stuart Williams) *in tch: racd alone on stands' side tl pushed along and hung rt over 2f out: styd on same pce ins fnl f* **11/2**[2]
0045 3 hd **Elegant Annie**[18] 6066 3-8-8 **55** WilliamCox(3) 4 56
(Jonathan Portman) *led: hdd over 5f out: chsd ldrs: pushed along over 1f out: styd on same pce ins fnl f* **10/1**
0200 4 1 1/4 **No Refund (IRE)**[23] 5887 5-8-10 **51** oh1 [1] CameronNoble 1 50
(David Loughnane) *w ldr tl led over 5f out: pushed along and hdd over 1f out: no ex ins fnl f* **9/2**[1]
5233 5 1/2 **Champagne Bob**[8] 6381 4-9-2 **60** JoshuaBryan(3) 6 58+
(Richard Price) *hld up: plld hrd: pushed along over 2f out: styd on fr over 1f out: nt trble ldrs* **9/2**[1]
4054 6 1 1/4 **Firgrove Bridge (IRE)**[8] 6373 4-8-10 **54** (p) PaulaMuir(3) 3 49
(Steph Hollinshead) *chsd ldrs: pushed along over 2f out: wknd fnl f* **17/2**
0056 7 6 **Bold Grove**[67] 4289 4-8-7 **51** oh6 AledBeech(3) 5 31
(Edward Bevan) *plld hrd and prom: stmbld over 5f out: pushed along over 2f out: sn wknd* **14/1**
0006 8 4 1/2 **Pyroclastic (IRE)**[56] 4715 4-8-12 **56** (p) BenRobinson(3) 8 24
(Nick Kent) *s.i.s: hld up: racd keenly: pushed along and wknd over 2f out* **25/1**
1133 9 26 **Diamonds A Dancing**[20] 6008 6-9-7 **62** (be) AdamMcNamara 10
(Donald McCain) *chsd ldrs: pushed along and lost pl 1/2-way: sn wknd and eased* **9/2**[1]

1m 27.02s (0.82) **Going Correction** +0.125s/f (Good)
WFA 3 from 4yo+ 3lb **9** Ran SP% **114.3**
Speed ratings (Par 101): **100,96,95,94,93 92,85,80,50**
CSF £38.50 CT £325.67 TOTE £6.40: £2.70, £2.30, £3.10; EX 44.70 Trifecta £348.30.
Owner Three Oaks Racing & Mrs P Bosley **Bred** Rathasker Stud **Trained** Ash Priors, Somerset

FOCUS
The first division of a modest apprentice handicap in which they went a fair gallop. They came down the middle. The winner was back to his form of around a year ago.

6637 RACING EXCELLENCE "HANDS AND HEELS" APPRENTICE SERIES H'CAP (DIV II) 7f
5:30 (5:30) (Class 6) (0-65,65) 3-Y-O+ **£2,587** (£770; £384; £192) **Stalls** High

Form RPR
0413 1 **Intimately**[10] 6290 3-8-9 **53** GeorgeWood 8 60
(Jonathan Portman) *hld up in tch: shkn up to ld over 1f out: edgd rt ins fnl f: styd on* **9/2**[2]
2031 2 1/2 **Poor Duke (IRE)**[21] 5954 6-8-13 **54** GerO'Neill 7 61
(Michael Mullineaux) *hld up: pushed along over 2f out: hdwy over 1f out: r.o* **4/1**[1]
0001 3 1 **Gulland Rock**[12] 6238 5-9-5 **63** LiamDoran(3) 2 67
(Anthony Carson) *chsd ldrs: shkn up and ev ch over 1f out: styd on same pce ins fnl f* **4/1**[1]
0555 4 2 3/4 **Leonard Thomas**[202] 773 6-9-3 **58** AdamMcNamara 3 55
(Tony Carroll) *s.i.s: hdwy over 4f out: pushed along and ev ch over 1f out: no ex ins fnl f* **4/1**[1]

5000 **5** *nk* **Bunker Hill Lass**[25] 5797 4-8-11 **55**..........................(p) BenSanderson(3) 1 52
(Michael Appleby) *racd keenly and prom: jnd ldr over 4f out tl pushed along 2f out: no ex fnl f* **10/1**

0225 **6** *3/4* **Red Unico (IRE)**[37] 5393 4-9-3 **61**.................................. JoshuaBryan(3) 9 56
(Brian Barr) *led: pushed along and hdd over 1f out: no ex ins fnl f* **6/1**[3]

0-06 **7** *10* **The Dancing Lord**[10] 6300 7-9-10 **65**.........................(t) KieranSchofield 6 35
(Adam West) *prom: pushed along and lost pl 5f out: bhd fnl 4f* **8/1**

1m 27.69s (1.49) **Going Correction** +0.125s/f (Good)
WFA 3 from 4yo+ 3lb **7** Ran SP% **112.7**
Speed ratings (Par 101): **96,95,94,91,90 89,78**
CSF £22.03 CT £76.22 TOTE £3.80: £2.20, £2.90; EX 20.60 Trifecta £66.20.
Owner Whitcoombe Park Racing **Bred** S Emmet And Miss R Emmet **Trained** Upper Lambourn, Berks

FOCUS
The second division of this apprentice handicap in which they went a strong gallop, although the time was 0.67s slower than the first leg. The only 3yo in the race came out on top, building on his Yarmouth win.
T/Plt: £27.60 to a £1 stake. Pool: £92,629.42 - 2448.24 winning units T/Qpdt: £11.20 to a £1 stake. Pool: £8,021.73 - 526.96 winning units **Colin Roberts**

6497 SAINT-CLOUD (L-H)
Monday, September 19

OFFICIAL GOING: Turf: good to soft

6638a PRIX PHAREL (MAIDEN) (2YO COLTS & GELDINGS) (TURF) 1m
11:40 (12:00) 2-Y-0 **£9,926** (£3,970; £2,977; £1,985; £992)

RPR

1 **City Light (FR)** 2-8-11 0.. TheoBachelot 7 81
(S Wattel, France) **103/10**

2 *1 3/4* **Manahir (FR)**[21] 5985 2-9-2 0.. LukasDelozier 10 82
(H-A Pantall, France) **51/10**[2]

3 *hd* **Franked** 2-8-11 0.. VincentCheminaud 4 77
(A Fabre, France) **2/1**[1]

4 *1 1/2* **Quevillon (FR)**[31] 2-9-2 0.. CristianDemuro 11 78
(C Lerner, France) **31/5**

5 *1 3/4* **On The Sea**[51] 2-9-2 0.. ThierryThulliez 15 75
(Mme C Head-Maarek, France) **11/2**[3]

6 *shd* **Brise De Mer (FR)**[39] 5348 2-9-2 0.............................. UmbertoRispoli 12 74
(George Baker) *keen: sn pressing ldr: 2nd and rowed along 2 1/2f out: led 2f out and sn rdn: hdd appr fnl f: grad dropped away* **12/1**

7 *3* **Mybee Davis (IRE)** 2-8-6 0.. PierreBazire(5) 8 63
(G Botti, France) **45/1**

8 *2 1/2* **Heroes (FR)**[89] 2-9-2 0.. AlexisBadel 9 62
(R Chotard, France) **57/1**

9 *3/4* **Skinnydipper** 2-8-11 0...................................... Pierre-CharlesBoudot 14 56
(A Wohler, Germany) **12/1**

10 *1* **Nile Paris (FR)**[21] 5985 2-9-2 0................................. MickaelBarzalona 2 58
(J-P Gallorini, France) **23/1**

11 *1/2* **Graf (FR)** 2-8-8 0.. YoannBonnefoy(8) 5 57
(N Bellanger, France) **58/1**

12 *6* **Hell Boy (FR)**[11] 2-9-2 0.. TonyPiccone 16 44
(F-M Cottin, France) **62/1**

13 *hd* **Rhenius (FR)** 2-8-11 0.. OlivierPeslier 1 39
(M Nigge, France) **54/1**

14 *hd* **Schamberg (FR)**[27] 2-9-2 0.. ThomasHuet 13 43
(J Bertran De Balanda, France) **79/1**

15 *7* **Stormy (FR)**[94] 2-9-2 0.. AurelienLemaitre 3 28
(S Cerulis, France) **73/1**

16 *3/4* **Coco John (FR)** 2-8-6 0.. AdrienMoreau(5) 6 21
(Mlle B Renk, France) **72/1**

1m 43.29s (-4.21) **16** Ran SP% **120.4**
WIN (incl. 1 euro stake): 11.30. PLACES: 2.30, 2.00, 1.40. DF: 31.20. SF: 81.80.
Owner Ecurie Jean-Louis Bouchard **Bred** Sarl Jedburgh Stud & Mme I Corbani **Trained** France

6639a PRIX SOYA (MAIDEN) (2YO FILLIES) (TURF) 1m
12:10 (12:00) 2-Y-0 **£9,926** (£3,970; £2,977; £1,985; £992)

RPR

1 **Thais (FR)**[48] 5005 2-9-2 0.. StephanePasquier 11 81+
(P Bary, France) **2/1**[1]

2 *nk* **Normandie (GER)**[41] 2-9-2 0.. MaximeGuyon 5 80+
(Mme Pia Brandt, France) **57/10**[3]

3 *6* **Evasion Absolue (FR)**[27] 2-9-2 0................................. CristianDemuro 13 67
(E Lellouche, France) **53/1**

4 *shd* **Nile Desire**[27] 2-9-2 0.. GregoryBenoist 14 67
(D Smaga, France) **32/5**

5 *nk* **Louve Dancer (FR)** 2-9-2 0... TheoBachelot 12 66
(W Walton, France) **16/1**

6 *nk* **Belleire (FR)** 2-8-11 0.. TonyPiccone 6 61
(M Nigge, France) **15/1**

7 *1* **Venezia (SWI)**[27] 2-9-2 0... FabriceVeron 7 63
(H-A Pantall, France) **89/10**

8 *3/4* **Baileys Temptress (FR)**[31] 5698 2-9-2 0........................ GeraldMosse 8 62
(F Doumen, France) **42/1**

9 *nk* **El Camila (FR)**[21] 5986 2-9-2 0............................. Pierre-CharlesBoudot 4 61
(Y Gourraud, France) **9/1**

10 *1* **Aspirer** 2-8-11 0.. VincentCheminaud 2 54
(A Fabre, France) **51/10**[2]

11 *3* **Spunky Heart (IRE)** 2-8-11 0.. AlexisBadel 1 47
(S Kobayashi, France) **59/1**

12 *3* **Pieta (FR)**[27] 2-9-2 0.. EddyHardouin 9 46
(J-P Gallorini, France) **86/1**

13 *1 1/4* **Cote Match (FR)** 2-8-8 0.. EmmanuelEtienne(3) 3 38
(C Lerner, France) **92/1**

14 *15* **Wind In The Trees (FR)**[37] 5460 2-9-2 0..............(p) UmbertoRispoli 10 10
(George Baker) *keen: hld up towards rr: scrubbbed along 3f out and no imp: rdn 2 1/2f out: sn lost tch: eased wl over 1f out* **48/1**

1m 44.03s (-3.47) **14** Ran SP% **120.5**
WIN (incl. 1 euro stake): 3.00. PLACES: 1.30, 2.30, 8.90. DF: 9.20. SF: 14.20.
Owner Ecurie J-L Bouchard & Mme G Sandor **Bred** G Sandor & Mme G Sandor **Trained** Chantilly, France

6471 BEVERLEY (R-H)
Tuesday, September 20

OFFICIAL GOING: Good (7.3)
Wind: Light across Weather: Heavy cloud and showers

6640 PONY RACING HERE ON 2 OCTOBER EBF MAIDEN STKS 7f 100y
2:10 (2:10) (Class 5) 2-Y-0 **£3,780** (£1,131; £565; £283) **Stalls** Low

Form RPR

2 **1** **Areen Heart (FR)**[17] 6129 2-9-5 0.. GrahamLee 5 78+
(Richard Fahey) *awkward s: t.k.h: hld up: hdwy on outer over 2f out: chal and green over 1f out: rdn to ld jst ins fnl f: sn wandered and kpt on* **10/11**[1]

2 **2** *1/2* **Warm Love**[25] 5854 2-9-0 0.. DanielTudhope 2 72
(David O'Meara) *led: pushed along over 2f out: rdn over 1f out: hdd jst ins fnl f: sn drvn and kpt on wl* **6/4**[2]

3 *3/4* **Makkaar (IRE)** 2-9-5 0.. PaulHanagan 3 75
(Mark Johnston) *sn trcking ldr: effrt over 2f out: rdn along wl over 1f out: drvn and kpt on fnl f* **6/1**[3]

00 **4** *1/2* **Final Chapter**[19] 6054 2-9-5 0... DavidAllan 1 74
(Tim Easterby) *prom: rdn along 2f out: drvn over 1f out: kpt on same pce ins fnl f* **40/1**

1m 35.95s (2.15) **Going Correction** -0.125s/f (Firm) **4** Ran SP% **109.1**
Speed ratings (Par 95): **82,81,80,80**
CSF £2.58 TOTE £1.90; EX 2.40 Trifecta £3.10.
Owner Sheikh Abdullah Almalek Alsabah **Bred** S C E A Haras De La Perelle **Trained** Musley Bank, N Yorks

FOCUS
There was light drizzle since 5.45am, bringing 2.5mm of rainfall, and the going was given as good (GoingStick: 7.3). Just the four runners but a fair maiden, and the winner has clear scope to do better. The field finished compressed.

6641 BEVERLEY ANNUAL BADGEHOLDERS MAIDEN AUCTION STKS 5f
2:40 (2:40) (Class 5) 2-Y-0 **£3,780** (£1,131; £565; £283; £141) **Stalls** Low

Form RPR

1 **Reedanjas (IRE)** 2-9-0 0.. DougieCostello 1 77+
(Gay Kelleway) *cl up on inner: led 3f out: rdn clr jst over 1f out: edgd lft ins fnl f: kpt on strly* **10/1**

04 **2** *5* **Flashing Light**[14] 6214 2-9-0 0... DavidAllan 8 59
(Tim Easterby) *slt ld: hdd 3f out: cl up: rdn wl over 1f out: drvn ent fnl f: kpt on same pce* **8/1**[3]

3222 **3** *nk* **Jeany (IRE)**[14] 6214 2-9-0 67.. ConnorBeasley 7 58
(Bryan Smart) *trckd ldrs: hdwy to chse ldng pair over 1f out: sn rdn: drvn and kpt on same pce fnl f* **1/1**[1]

00 **4** *1* **Oh So Dandy (IRE)**[18] 6099 2-9-5 0...............................(v1) JasonHart 3 59
(Derek Shaw) *t.k.h: chsd ldrs on inner: rdn along wl over 2f out: drvn and one pce appr fnl f* **33/1**

5 *3/4* **Dandy Bird (IRE)** 2-9-0 0.. TomEaves 2 51+
(James Given) *rr and green: sn outpcd and bhd: rdn along 2f out: swtchd lft ent fnl f: fin strly* **20/1**

4050 **6** *3/4* **Western Presence**[21] 6007 2-9-5 63.............................. TonyHamilton 4 54
(Richard Fahey) *in tch: effrt to chse ldrs 1/2-way: rdn along wl over 1f out: sn no imp* **9/1**

66 **7** *hd* **A Bit Of Ginger**[7] 6448 2-8-9 0.. RowanScott(5) 6 48
(Ann Duffield) *in tch: pushed along 1/2-way: sn rdn and n.d* **40/1**

6222 **8** *nk* **Harbour Lightning**[8] 6420 2-9-0 64................................. GrahamLee 9 47
(Ann Duffield) *dwlt and towards rr: effrt and sme hdwy on outer over 2f out: sn rdn and btn* **7/2**[2]

00 **9** *6* **Miss Pepper (IRE)**[14] 6214 2-9-0 0.................................. PaulMulrennan 5 25
(Paul Midgley) *t.k.h: chsd ldng pair: rdn along 1/2-way: sn wknd* **66/1**

1m 3.39s (-0.11) **Going Correction** -0.125s/f (Firm) **9** Ran SP% **114.1**
Speed ratings (Par 95): **95,87,86,84,83 82,82,81,72**
CSF £81.26 TOTE £13.40: £3.40, £2.10, £1.10; EX 130.30 Trifecta £340.50.
Owner Graham Kerr **Bred** Tally-Ho Stud **Trained** Exning, Suffolk

FOCUS
A very modest maiden, but the winner, who drew clear in the closing stages, has a chance to be useful.

6642 EDDIE AND VIOLET SMITH CONDITIONS STKS 5f
3:10 (3:10) (Class 3) 3-Y-0+
£8,715 (£2,609; £1,304; £652; £326; £163) **Stalls** Low

Form RPR

1500 **1** **Caspian Prince (IRE)**[24] 5863 7-9-0 107...........................(t) TomEaves 6 113
(David Loughnane) *qckly away and mde all: rdn clr over 1f out: kpt on strly* **33/1**

3652 **2** *1 1/4* **Ornate**[14] 6207 3-8-13 100..(t) DanielTudhope 11 109
(William Haggas) *t.k.h: trckd ldrs on outer: hdwy 2f out: rdn and edgd rt ent fnl f: sn chsng wnr: drvn and no imp towards fin* **8/1**

-304 **3** *3/4* **Double Up**[10] 6327 5-9-0 105...(t) AndreaAtzeni 2 106+
(Roger Varian) *dwlt and towards rr: hdwy 2f out: chsd ldrs over 1f out and sn rdn: drvn and kpt on fnl f* **13/8**[1]

2460 **4** *hd* **Line Of Reason (IRE)**[13] 6230 6-9-3 102...................... PaulMulrennan 7 108+
(Paul Midgley) *hld up towards rr: hdwy over 1f out: sn rdn and styd on wl fnl f* **7/1**

6325 **5** *nk* **Eastern Impact (IRE)**[24] 5880 5-9-0 109...................... TonyHamilton 10 104
(Richard Fahey) *chsd ldng pair: rdn along over 1f out: drvn to chse wnr appr fnl f: grad wknd* **13/2**[3]

2200 **6** *1 1/4* **Red Pike (IRE)**[10] 6327 5-9-0 96.................................... ConnorBeasley 9 100
(Bryan Smart) *chsd ldrs: rdn along wl over 1f out: sn drvn and kpt on same pce* **9/1**

0100 **7** *1* **Son Of Africa**[10] 6327 4-9-0 97.. HarryBentley 8 96
(Henry Candy) *dwlt: a towards rr* **12/1**

000 **8** *3* **Tangerine Trees**[17] 6119 11-9-0 86...............................(v) AndrewMullen 1 85
(Michael Appleby) *dwlt: sn chsng ldrs on inner: rdn along wl over 1f out: wknd fnl f* **50/1**

6041 **9** *2 1/4* **Hay Chewed (IRE)**[14] 6207 5-8-12 97.......................... SilvestreDeSousa 4 75
(Conrad Allen) *chsd wnr: rdn wl over 1f out: drvn appr fnl f and sn wknd* **5/1**[2]

1m 1.48s (-2.02) **Going Correction** -0.125s/f (Firm)
WFA 3 from 4yo+ 1lb **9** Ran SP% **114.3**
Speed ratings (Par 107): **111,109,107,107,107 105,103,98,95**
CSF £272.26 TOTE £30.70: £7.50, £2.90, £1.10; EX 282.20 Trifecta £1029.60.
Owner Stephen Louch **Bred** Ballygallon Stud Ltd **Trained** Market Drayton, Shropshire

FOCUS
Something of a shock result, but not according to the ratings. The winner made all on a pace-favouring card and is rated to his best.

6643 ABP KEEPING BRITAIN TRADING H'CAP (DIV I) 7f 100y
3:40 (3:40) (Class 5) (0-75,75) 3-Y-O+ **£3,780** (£1,131; £565; £283; £141) **Stalls** Low

Form RPR

0241 **1** **Zeshov (IRE)**[18] 6095 5-9-2 **70**.. BarryMcHugh 5 78
(Rebecca Bastiman) *hld up in tch: hdwy 3f out: chsd ldrs 11/2f out: rdn to chal ent fnl f: sn drvn and kpt on wl to ld nr fin* **13/2**[3]

0210 **2** *shd* **Talent Scout (IRE)**[20] 6028 10-8-7 **66**.......................(p) GemmaTutty(5) 1 73
(Karen Tutty) *slt ld at gd pce: rdn wl over 1f out: jnd and drvn ent fnl f: kpt on gamely: hdd and no ex nr fin* **15/2**

2314 **3** *5* **Chaplin Bay (IRE)**[25] 5859 4-9-7 **75**.............................. JamesSullivan 2 70
(Ruth Carr) *hld up in rr: stdy hdwy on outer over 2f out: chsd ldrs over 1f out: rdn to chse ldng pair and edgd rt ent fnl f: sn drvn and kpt on same pce* **11/4**[1]

0606 **4** *shd* **Rocket Ronnie (IRE)**[20] 6028 6-8-13 **67**.........................(b) GrahamLee 7 64+
(Ed McMahon) *swtchd rt s and hld up in tch on inner: effrt and n.m.r wl over 1f out: swtchd lft and rdn ent fnl f: sn n.m.r: squeezed through and kpt on last 100 yds* **11/1**

042 **5** *nse* **Euro Mac**[22] 5979 4-8-2 **61** oh6.. NathanEvans(5) 3 55
(Neville Bycroft) *chsd ldng pair: hdwy 3f out: chsd ldr 2f out and sn rdn: drvn appr fnl f: kpt on same pce* **25/1**

5420 **6** *6* **Relight My Fire**[20] 6027 6-9-1 **69**....................................(bt) DavidAllan 10 48
(Tim Easterby) *hld up towards rr: effrt and sme hdwy over 2f out: sn rdn and n.d* **13/2**[3]

0020 **7** *3/4* **Tellovoi (IRE)**[5] 6521 8-9-7 **75**....................................(v) RoystonFfrench 4 52
(Richard Guest) *cl up: disp ld 1/2-way: rdn along over 2f out: sn drvn and wknd* **8/1**

30 **8** *nk* **Pickett's Charge**[25] 5860 3-8-12 **69**.............................. DuranFentiman 6 45
(Tony Coyle) *a towards rr* **16/1**

6534 **9** *2 1/4* **Mustaqqil (IRE)**[25] 5845 4-9-7 **75**..............................(v) DanielTudhope 9 46
(David O'Meara) *chsd ldrs: rdn along over 2f out: sn drvn and wknd wl over 1f out* **9/2**[2]

1m 32.21s (-1.59) **Going Correction** -0.125s/f (Firm)
WFA 3 from 4yo+ 3lb **9** Ran SP% **112.5**
Speed ratings (Par 103): **104,103,98,98,98 91,90,89,87**
CSF £52.51 CT £164.45 TOTE £7.30: £4.40, £2.70, £1.70; EX 68.20 Trifecta £213.60.
Owner Mrs P Bastiman **Bred** Rathbarry Stud **Trained** Cowthorpe, N Yorks

FOCUS
They went a decent early gallop and the first two finished clear, in a quicker time than the second division. The form is rated around the runner-up.

6644 ABP KEEPING BRITAIN TRADING H'CAP (DIV II) 7f 100y
4:10 (4:11) (Class 5) (0-75,75) 3-Y-O+ **£3,780** (£1,131; £565; £283; £141) **Stalls** Low

Form RPR

0420 **1** **Mon Beau Visage (IRE)**[13] 6231 3-8-13 **70**................. DanielTudhope 2 79
(David O'Meara) *t.k.h early: trckd ldrs: hdwy 2f out: chsd ldng pair over 1f out: rdn to ld ins fnl f: kpt on strly* **7/2**[2]

1024 **2** *2 1/4* **Ralphy Boy (IRE)**[11] 6280 7-9-7 **75**.............................. PaulMulrennan 1 79
(Alistair Whillans) *led: pushed along 2f out: rdn over 1f out: drvn and hdd ins fnl f: kpt on* **9/2**[3]

540 **3** *3/4* **Energia Flavio (BRZ)**[57] 4704 6-9-0 **68**............................ GrahamLee 4 70
(Richard Fahey) *hld up in tch: hdwy wl over 1f out: sn rdn: kpt on u.p fnl f* **7/1**

3540 **4** *shd* **Make On Madam (IRE)**[24] 5868 4-8-7 **61**........................... JasonHart 3 63
(Les Eyre) *chsd ldng pair: effrt 2f out: sn rdn: drvn appr fnl f: kpt on* **10/1**

0064 **5** *3/4* **Torrid**[43] 5246 5-9-1 **74**.. NathanEvans(5) 5 78+
(Michael Easterby) *hld up: hdwy on inner 2f out: chsd ldrs over 1f out: sn rdn and no imp fnl f* **10/3**[1]

2400 **6** *3/4* **Faintly (USA)**[11] 6280 5-8-11 **65**.................................(b) JamesSullivan 9 63
(Ruth Carr) *rr: hdwy over 2f out: rdn over 1f out: kpt on fnl f* **20/1**

4-00 **7** *2 1/4* **See The Storm**[25] 5845 8-9-2 **70**.............................. PJMcDonald 8 63
(Ann Duffield) *cl up: rdn to chal 2f out: drvn over 1f out: wknd fnl f* **66/1**

6001 **8** *1 1/4* **Be Royale**[5] 6522 6-8-12 **66**.......................................(t) SilvestreDeSousa 6 55
(Michael Appleby) *trckd ldrs: hdwy over 2f out: rdn along wl over 1f out: sn wknd* **11/2**

6021 **9** *nk* **Layla's Hero (IRE)**[13] 6235 9-9-7 **75**............................(v) TomMarquand 7 64
(Roger Teal) *a rr* **16/1**

1m 33.09s (-0.71) **Going Correction** -0.125s/f (Firm)
WFA 3 from 4yo+ 3lb **9** Ran SP% **112.6**
Speed ratings (Par 103): **99,96,95,95,94 93,91,89,89**
CSF £19.05 CT £101.86 TOTE £3.60: £1.60, £1.60, £2.40; EX 22.50 Trifecta £125.50.
Owner The Pink Pot Partnership LLP **Bred** Stephanie Hanly **Trained** Upper Helmsley, N Yorks

FOCUS
The slower of the two divisions by 0.88sec. The form is rated around the second.

6645 CELEBRATE CHRISTMAS AT RACECOURSE SPARKLE NIGHTS H'CAP 1m 100y
4:45 (4:45) (Class 5) (0-75,75) 3-Y-O+ **£3,780** (£1,131; £565; £283; £141) **Stalls** Low

Form RPR

2003 **1** **Ravenhoe (IRE)**[14] 6220 3-9-0 **69**.. JoeFanning 2 79
(Mark Johnston) *mde all: rdn clr wl over 1f out: styd on strly* **11/2**[3]

5222 **2** *2 1/4* **Nona Blu**[32] 5592 4-9-0 **65**.. SilvestreDeSousa 1 70
(Michael Wigham) *trckd ldrs: hdwy over 2f out and sn chsng wnr: rdn over 1f out: drvn and no imp fnl f* **11/8**[1]

0330 **3** *2 1/4* **John Caesar (IRE)**[29] 5715 5-8-12 **63**..........................(tp) PJMcDonald 5 63
(Rebecca Bastiman) *trckd ldrs on inner: pushed along and hdwy 2f out: rdn to chse ldng pair over 1f out: sn drvn and kpt on same pce* **18/1**

20-0 **4** *2 1/2* **Hungerford**[31] 5649 4-9-10 **75**.. TomMarquand 8 69
(Eve Johnson Houghton) *hld up towards rr: hdwy over 2f out: rdn along wl over 1f out: drvn over 1f out and no imp* **8/1**

03-0 **5** *nk* **Will Mac**[14] 6220 5-8-8 **62**.. JacobButterfield(3) 6 55
(Neville Bycroft) *chsd wnr: rdn along wl over 2f out: sn drvn and grad wknd* **33/1**

5642 **6** *1 1/4* **Billy Bond**[13] 6221 4-9-2 **72**...................................(v) AdamMcNamara(5) 9 62
(Richard Fahey) *in tch: pushed along 3f out: rdn over 2f out: n.d* **15/2**

0360 **7** *3* **Homeland (IRE)**[5] 6516 4-9-8 **73**.................................(t) JamesSullivan 7 56
(Brian Rothwell) *a rr* **66/1**

3620 **8** *3/4* **Gulf Of Poets**[16] 6160 4-9-4 **74**...................................... NathanEvans(5) 3 56
(Michael Easterby) *chsd ldrs on outer: pushed along wl over 2f out: sn rdn and wknd* **7/2**[2]

1m 46.57s (-1.03) **Going Correction** -0.125s/f (Firm)
WFA 3 from 4yo+ 4lb **8** Ran SP% **112.3**
Speed ratings (Par 103): **100,97,95,93,92 91,88,87**
CSF £12.96 CT £123.49 TOTE £6.50: £1.90, £1.20, £3.40; EX 15.10 Trifecta £88.00.
Owner Kingsley Park 4 - Ready To Run **Bred** Miss Linda Lyons **Trained** Middleham Moor, N Yorks

FOCUS
It proved hard to make up ground in this handicap. The winner is rated up slightly on this year's form.

6646 STEVE WALL EQUESTRIAN PHOTOGRAPHY H'CAP 1m 100y
5:15 (5:16) (Class 6) (0-65,65) 3-Y-O **£2,264** (£673; £336; £168) **Stalls** Low

Form RPR

1042 **1** **Beadlam (IRE)**[26] 5803 3-8-12 **56**........................... SilvestreDeSousa 13 67
(David Loughnane) *trckd ldr: led over 2f out: rdn clr over 1f out: kpt on strly* **10/1**[3]

0520 **2** *5* **Wayside Magic**[33] 5576 3-8-8 **52**...............................(b[1]) ConnorBeasley 8 53
(Michael Dods) *led: rdn along and hdd over 2f out: chsd wnr and drvn over 1f out: kpt on* **12/1**

0000 **3** *2* **Mr Potter**[3] 6569 3-8-10 **54**... RoystonFfrench 9 50
(Richard Guest) *trckd ldng trio: hdwy 3f out: rdn wl over 1f out: drvn appr fnl f and kpt on same pce* **20/1**

6230 **4** *hd* **Party Thyme**[29] 5720 3-9-4 **62**.. DavidAllan 7 58
(Chris Wall) *chsd ldng pair on inner: pushed along 3f out: rdn wl over 1f out: drvn over 1f out: kpt on same pce* **10/1**[3]

0263 **5** *hd* **Quoteline Direct**[25] 5860 3-9-7 **65**................................... PJMcDonald 4 60+
(Micky Hammond) *hld up: hdwy over 2f out: rdn over 1f out: styd on wl fnl f: nrst fin* **16/1**

4435 **6** *3/4* **The Excel Queen (IRE)**[77] 3982 3-9-0 **58**.................... BarryMcHugh 11 52
(Tony Coyle) *chsd ldrs: hdwy 2f out: sn rdn and no imp* **16/1**

056 **7** *1/2* **Frap**[66] 4382 3-9-1 **59**.. GrahamLee 10 52
(Richard Fahey) *midfield: hdwy over 2f out: rdn along wl over 1f out: kpt on one pce* **12/1**

1361 **8** *hd* **Becca Campbell (IRE)**[8] 6405 3-8-13 **57**................(p) TomMarquand 15 49
(Eve Johnson Houghton) *midfield: hdwy on outer over 2f out: rdn along wl over 1f out: sn one pce* **11/2**[2]

5653 **9** *hd* **Artful Mind**[10] 6337 3-9-7 **65**.. PaulMulrennan 5 57+
(Charlie Fellowes) *rr: effrt wl over 2f out: sn rdn along and nvr nr ldrs* **15/8**[1]

2624 **10** *nk* **Lozah**[23] 5921 3-8-12 **56**..(tp) SamJames 3 53+
(David Loughnane) *midfield: effrt on inner over 3f out: sn rdn along and n.d* **10/1**[3]

0060 **11** *1* **Ormering**[10] 6311 3-8-3 **47**..(p) CamHardie 1 36
(Roger Teal) *in tch on inner: rdn along wl over 2f out: wknd over 1f out* **66/1**

0000 **12** *2 1/4* **Mr Chuckles (IRE)**[22] 5968 3-8-13 **57**..........................[1] AndrewMullen 2 42+
(Philip Kirby) *a rr* **33/1**

5416 **13** *1/2* **King Oswald (USA)**[35] 5529 3-9-6 **64**................................ TomEaves 14 47+
(James Unett) *a rr* **25/1**

00-0 **14** *4* **Contendit**[119] 2553 3-8-7 **51**... JamesSullivan 6 26
(Michael Easterby) *t.k.h early: trckd ldrs: pushed along over 3f out: sn rdn and wknd* **66/1**

1m 47.25s (-0.35) **Going Correction** -0.125s/f (Firm) **14** Ran SP% **119.1**
Speed ratings (Par 99): **96,91,89,88,88 87,87,86,86 85,83,82,78**
CSF £117.12 CT £2348.77 TOTE £7.30: £3.50, £4.20, £4.90; EX 119.90 Trifecta £3160.80.
Owner R G Fell **Bred** Pipe View Stud **Trained** Market Drayton, Shropshire

FOCUS
A moderate affair, and once again it proved hard to come from off the pace. The winner has clearly improved.

6647 BRIAN AND JASON MERRINGTON MEMORIAL AMATEUR RIDERS' H'CAP 1m 1f 207y
5:45 (5:45) (Class 6) (0-60,60) 3-Y-O+ **£2,495** (£774; £386; £193) **Stalls** Low

Form RPR

3500 **1** **Lean On Pete (IRE)**[20] 6029 7-10-10 **56**....................... MissCWalton 13 64
(Ollie Pears) *mde all: rdn clr wl over 1f out: drvn out* **10/1**

6622 **2** *2* **Rubis**[21] 6004 3-9-13 **56**.. MissEmilyBullock(5) 14 60
(Richard Fahey) *trckd wnr: pushed along 2f out: rdn wl over 1f out: drvn and kpt on fnl f* **11/2**[3]

2324 **3** *nk* **Galilee Chapel (IRE)**[25] 5835 7-10-4 **55**.........(b) MrGaryBeaumont(5) 11 58+
(Alistair Whillans) *hld up towards rr: hdwy over 2f out: rdn wl over 1f out: drvn and styd on wl fnl f* **14/1**

6430 **4** *7* **Adherence**[36] 5481 3-10-1 **58**..[1] MrMEnnis(5) 7 47+
(Tony Coyle) *hld up in rr. hdwy 2f out: rdn over 1f out: swtchd lft to outer ent fnl f: kpt on* **9/1**

4043 **5** *1* **Intensified (IRE)**[26] 5800 5-10-0 **46** oh1.......................(b) MrsCBartley 12 33
(Ruth Carr) *hld up in rr: hdwy into midfield: over 3f out: rdn to chse ldrs on outer 2f out: drvn and edgd rt ent fnl f: sn no imp* **16/1**

0000 **6** *3/4* **Rainford Glory (IRE)**[70] 4234 6-10-1 **52**.................(p) MissHDukes(5) 15 38
(Tim Fitzgerald) *chsd ldrs: hdwy 3f out: rdn along to chse ldng pair wl over 1f out: wknd appr fnl f* **25/1**

3314 **7** *2 3/4* **Thello**[22] 5980 4-10-5 **56**... MrTGreenwood(5) 5 36
(Nigel Tinkler) *chsd ldrs: rdn along over 2f out: sn drvn and grad wknd* **9/2**[2]

-000 **8** *1 1/2* **Inspector Norse**[89] 3563 5-11-0 **60**..................................... MrWEasterby 9 37
(Tim Easterby) *nvr bttr than midfield* **9/1**

0023 **9** *1/2* **Mister Marcasite**[22] 5980 6-10-6 **52**........................... MissSBrotherton 3 28
(Antony Brittain) *chsd ldng pair: rdn along wl over 2f out: drvn wl over 1f out: grad wknd* **4/1**[1]

5610 **10** *1 1/2* **Gabrial's Hope (FR)**[55] 4767 7-10-9 **55**................................. MrSWalker 1 28
(Tracy Waggott) *a towards rr* **9/1**

0126 **11** *1* **I'm Super Too (IRE)**[24] 5868 9-10-11 **57**........................ MissETodd 16 28
(Karen Tutty) *trckd ldrs: hdwy over 4f out: rdn along wl over 2f out: sn wknd* **12/1**

124/ **12** *15* **Big Kenny**[787] 4657 5-10-7 **60**................................... MrTPBroughton(7) 17
(Peter Winks) *a rr* **33/1**

2m 7.63s (0.63) **Going Correction** -0.125s/f (Firm)
WFA 3 from 4yo+ 6lb **12** Ran SP% **119.7**
Speed ratings (Par 101): **92,90,90,84,83 83,80,79,79,78 77,65**
CSF £64.80 CT £785.63 TOTE £13.40: £3.10, £2.50, £3.70; EX 78.70 Trifecta £611.90.
Owner K C West **Bred** Mrs T Mahon **Trained** Norton, N Yorks

FOCUS
Once again the pace held up, with very few getting into this.
T/Jkpt: Not won. T/Plt: £22.70 to a £1 stake. Pool: £60916.97, 1957.61 winning units T/Qpdt: £9.20 to a £1 stake. Pool: £4788.48, 384.51 winning units **Joe Rowntree**

[6375]FFOS LAS (L-H)
Tuesday, September 20

OFFICIAL GOING: Good to soft (7.1)
Wind: moderate half against Weather: cloudy

6648 FELINFOEL BREWERY MAIDEN FILLIES' STKS (PLUS 10 RACE) 7f 80y(R)
3:45 (3:46) (Class 5) 2-Y-O **£3,234** (£962; £481; £240) **Stalls** Low

Form RPR
1 **Isabel De Urbina (IRE)** 2-9-0 0 FMBerry 6 75+
(Ralph Beckett) *hld up towards rr: rdn 3f out: hdwy on outer over 1f out: drvn fnl f: r.o to ld post* **10/11**[1]
33 2 nk **Brogan**[13] 6223 2-9-0 0 RichardKingscote 7 74
(Tom Dascombe) *trckd ldrs: led over 1f out: drvn and r.o fnl f: ct post* **11/4**[2]
54 3 4 ½ **Swell Hill**[20] 6016 2-9-0 0 SeanLevey 1 63
(Richard Hannon) *led narrowly: rdn over 2f out: hdd over 1f out: one pce* **14/1**
00 4 2 ¾ **Pavela (IRE)**[10] 6319 2-9-0 0 MartinDwyer 3 56
(Mick Channon) *w ldr: drvn and ev ch over 2f out: wknd fnl f* **25/1**
50 5 hd **Holyroman Princess**[19] 6062 2-9-0 0 SteveDrowne 5 55
(Rod Millman) *hld up: hung rt bnd 4f out: rdn 3f out: pushed along and styd on wl fnl f: nvr nr to chal* **50/1**
53 6 1 **Favourite Royal (IRE)**[19] 6062 2-9-0 0 CharlesBishop 8 53
(Eve Johnson Houghton) *chsd ldrs: drvn over 2f out: wknd fnl f* **5/1**[3]
03 7 3 ¼ **Polkadot Princess (IRE)**[9] 6375 2-8-11 0 EdwardGreatrex(3) 2 45
(Nikki Evans) *chsd ldrs: rdn over 2f out: wknd fnl f* **50/1**
8 5 **Dutch Cat** 2-9-0 0 JohnFahy 4 32
(Clive Cox) *s.i.s: in rr: rdn over 2f out: wknd over 1f out* **14/1**

1m 32.92s (-0.08) **Going Correction** -0.10s/f (Good) **8 Ran SP% 116.8**
Speed ratings (Par 92): **96,95,90,87,87 86,82,76**
CSF £3.59 TOTE £1.80: £1.10, £1.10, £3.10; EX 3.80 Trifecta £26.00.
Owner Merriebelle Irish Farm Limited **Bred** Merriebelle Irish Farm Ltd **Trained** Kimpton, Hants

FOCUS
After a dry day, the going remained good to soft. A modest opener but the winner, who had been well backed through the day, did well to overcome her obvious inexperience to make a winning debut.

6649 £25 FREE BET AT 188BET FILLIES' H'CAP 7f 80y(R)
4:15 (4:15) (Class 5) (0-75,75) 3-Y-O+ **£3,234** (£962; £481; £240) **Stalls** Low

Form RPR
6216 1 **Posh Bounty**[83] 3771 5-9-3 **71** FMBerry 1 79
(Joseph Tuite) *hld up in last pair: hdwy whn nt clr run over 2f out: chsd ldr appr fnl f: drvn to ld 100yds out: r.o wl* **5/1**[3]
-645 2 1 **Many Dreams (IRE)**[18] 6091 3-8-4 **64** JosephineGordon(3) 3 68
(Mark Usher) *chsd ldrs: led gng wl over 2f out: drvn over 1f out: hdd and unable qck fnl 100yds* **6/4**[1]
5516 3 3 **Exoplanet Blue**[21] 5992 4-9-2 **75** GeorgeWood(5) 7 72
(Henry Candy) *chsd ldrs: hdwy 3f out: drvn and ev ch over 2f out: hung lft and lost 2nd appr fnl f: outpcd by ldng pair fnl 100yds* **4/1**[2]
033 4 6 **Chandon Elysees**[12] 6247 3-8-13 **70** FergusSweeney 4 51
(Gary Moore) *hld up in last pair: clsd on outer over 2f out: drvn over 1f out: nt run on and sn btn* **9/1**
4016 5 13 **Dear Bruin (IRE)**[26] 5797 4-9-1 **69** (p) WilliamTwiston-Davies 2 17
(David W Drinkwater) *led 1f: styd cl up: drvn 3f out: wknd 2f out* **5/1**[3]
602 6 20 **Canford Lilli (IRE)**[12] 6251 3-9-1 **72** (b) CharlesBishop 5
(Eve Johnson Houghton) *t.k.h: hdwy to ld after 1f: rdn 3f out: hdd & wknd over 2f out: eased over 1f out: t.o* **7/1**

1m 31.57s (-1.43) **Going Correction** -0.10s/f (Good)
WFA 3 from 4yo+ 3lb **6 Ran SP% 115.8**
Speed ratings (Par 100): **104,102,99,92,77 54**
CSF £13.56 TOTE £6.40: £2.60, £1.40; EX 18.30 Trifecta £89.40.
Owner The Lamb Inn - Pethy **Bred** Mascalls Stud **Trained** Lambourn, Berks

FOCUS
A modest fillies' handicap but run at a good pace and the winner was produced late to gain her first win over the trip. She improved a little.

6650 DOWNLOAD THE APP AT 188BET MAIDEN STKS 1m (R)
4:50 (4:51) (Class 5) 3-4-Y-O **£3,234** (£962; £481; £240) **Stalls** Low

Form RPR
30 1 **Amaany**[67] 4361 3-9-0 0 DaneO'Neill 8 78+
(Charles Hills) *wnt to post early: hld up towards rr: hdwy 3f out: sn drvn: chsd ldr over 1f out: led ins fnl f: styd on wl* **5/1**[3]
2 1 **Kullu (IRE)** 3-9-0 0[1] StevieDonohoe 4 75+
(Charlie Fellowes) *s.i.s: hld up towards rr: hdwy on inner 3f out: sn drvn: swtchd rt 1f out: styd on to go 2nd 100yds out: clsng nr fin* **6/1**
3240 3 2 ½ **Ttainted Love**[74] 4081 4-9-4 77 (p) FergusSweeney 5 69
(Chris Wall) *t.k.h: trckd ldrs: rdn to ld over 1f out: hdd and no ex ins fnl f* **2/1**[2]
4332 4 2 ¼ **Apache Song**[7] 6441 3-8-11 68 (p) JosephineGordon(3) 1 64
(Rod Millman) *rousted along fr stalls to ld: drvn and hdd over 1f out: one pce and qckly btn* **6/4**[1]
00 5 5 **Garter (IRE)**[17] 6135 3-9-0 0 MichaelJMMurphy 6 52
(Charles Hills) *mid-div: hdwy to dispute 2nd over 2f out: drvn and wknd over 1f out* **33/1**
6 ¾ **Glorious Poet** 3-9-5 0 FMBerry 3 56+
(Ed Walker) *dwlt: bhd: latched on to bk of field 5f out: rdn and sme hdwy 3f out: no imp fnl 2f* **14/1**
06 7 5 **Rebel Woods (FR)**[7] 6441 3-9-5 0 JohnFahy 2 44
(Geoffrey Deacon) *chsd ldrs tl rdn and lost pl 4f out: no ch fnl 3f* **66/1**
8 8 **Bassino (USA)** 3-9-0 0 RachealKneller(5) 7 26
(James Bennett) *t.k.h: cl up: rdn and lost 2nd 3f out: wknd over 2f out* **40/1**

1m 40.38s (-0.62) **Going Correction** -0.10s/f (Good)
WFA 3 from 4yo 4lb **8 Ran SP% 117.8**
Speed ratings (Par 103): **99,98,95,93,88 87,82,74**
CSF £35.32 TOTE £5.30: £1.30, £1.90, £1.10; EX 36.90 Trifecta £86.80.
Owner Hamdan Al Maktoum **Bred** Shadwell Estate Company Limited **Trained** Lambourn, Berks

FOCUS
Not the strongest of maidens but the first two both have something to recommend them in the future. The third and fourth are both unvonvincing, however.

6651 FREE SPINS AT 188BET CASINO H'CAP 1m (R)
5:20 (5:21) (Class 6) (0-60,59) 3-Y-O+ **£2,264** (£673; £336; £168) **Stalls** Low

Form RPR
5135 1 **Edge (IRE)**[22] 5957 5-9-5 **54** (b) StevieDonohoe 5 61
(Bernard Llewellyn) *s.i.s: sn in mid-div: drvn and clsd on inner over 2f out: disp ld over 1f out: kpt on gamely to assert towards fin* **10/1**
3064 2 nk **Zlatan (IRE)**[8] 6407 3-9-4 **57** (p) DaneO'Neill 7 63
(Ed de Giles) *mid-div: hdwy over 2f out: drvn on inner to dispute ld over 1f out: ev ch tl hld towards fin* **5/1**[2]
0003 3 ¾ **Lobster Cocktail (IRE)**[47] 5080 3-9-1 **54** FMBerry 6 59
(Ed Walker) *trckd ldr: drvn over 2f out and sn lost 2nd: styd on fnl f: wnt 3rd post* **4/1**[1]
50 4 nse **Protest (IRE)**[34] 5554 3-8-8 **50** EdwardGreatrex(3) 2 55
(Sylvester Kirk) *led: drvn over 2f out: hdd over 1f out: kpt on u.p: lost 3rd post* **10/1**
6440 5 ½ **The Greedy Boy**[8] 6407 3-8-8 **47** MartinDwyer 3 50
(Mick Channon) *towards rr: drvn and hdwy 3f out: styd on u.p fnl 2f: unable to chal* **6/1**[3]
5400 6 1 **Never To Be (USA)**[12] 6254 5-9-5 **59** (vt[1]) CallumShepherd(5) 15 60
(Nikki Evans) *s.i.s: in rr: drvn 3f out: styd on fnl f* **22/1**
0- 7 hd **Worth Avenue (IRE)**[70] 4247 5-8-8 **46** JosephineGordon(3) 11 47
(W T Farrell, Ire) *wnt to post early: trckd ldrs: rdn over 2f out: kpt on same pce* **4/1**[1]
5006 8 ½ **Majestic Girl (IRE)**[9] 6381 3-8-7 **53** (p) JoshuaBryan(7) 12 53
(Steve Flook) *s.i.s: hld up towards rr: rdn and hdwy over 2f out: one pce fnl f* **50/1**
50-0 9 1 ¼ **Miss Dusky Diva (IRE)**[20] 6020 4-9-1 **50** WilliamTwiston-Davies 10 47
(David W Drinkwater) *wnt to post early: chsd ldrs: drvn over 2f out: wknd over 1f out* **14/1**
450 10 nk **Zebedee's Girl (IRE)**[11] 6290 3-9-1 **54** SteveDrowne 14 50
(David Evans) *s.i.s: in rr: drvn 2f out: modest late prog* **25/1**
0053 11 1 ¼ **Suni Dancer**[22] 5954 5-8-6 **46** MeganNicholls(5) 9 40
(Tony Carroll) *t.k.h in mid-div: effrt over 2f out: grad wknd* **7/1**
0000 12 ½ **Abertillery**[49] 4995 4-8-11 **46** CharlesBishop 13 38
(Michael Blanshard) *mid-div: rdn on outer over 2f out: sn wknd* **20/1**
-006 13 1 ½ **Love In The Dark**[12] 6251 3-8-6 **50** GeorgeWood(5) 1 39
(Nikki Evans) *trckd ldrs: drvn 3f out: sn wknd* **33/1**
-000 14 ½ **Turaathy (IRE)**[62] 4500 3-8-11 **53** EoinWalsh(3) 4 41
(Tony Newcombe) *s.i.s: rdn 3f out: a towards rr* **28/1**

1m 42.02s (1.02) **Going Correction** +0.10s/f (Good)
WFA 3 from 4yo+ 4lb **14 Ran SP% 129.6**
Speed ratings (Par 101): **98,97,96,96,96 95,95,94,93,93 91,91,89,89**
CSF £59.30 CT £245.62 TOTE £11.20: £3.70, £1.80, £1.90; EX 62.80 Trifecta £127.80.
Owner B J Llewellyn **Bred** Swordlestown Stud **Trained** Fochriw, Caerphilly

FOCUS
Low-grade fare and not so competitive as the numbers would suggest.

6652 FELINFOEL BREWERY NURSERY H'CAP 6f
5:50 (5:53) (Class 6) (0-65,65) 2-Y-O **£2,264** (£673; £336; £168) **Stalls** Centre

Form RPR
4540 1 **Kings Heart (IRE)**[21] 5989 2-9-3 **61** SteveDrowne 1 67
(Mark Usher) *hld up: drvn and gd hdwy 2f out: led 1f out: r.o wl* **9/1**
0333 2 2 ¾ **Wearethepeople**[8] 6420 2-9-2 **65** GeorgeWood(5) 5 63
(William Muir) *led 1f: trckd ldr: drvn to ld again and edgd lft 2f out: hdd 1f out: kpt on same pce* **7/2**[1]
000 3 ½ **Harlequin Rose (IRE)**[25] 5820 2-8-5 **49** (v[1]) MartinDwyer 6 45
(Mick Channon) *chsd along early to ld after 1f: drvn 1/2-way: hdd 2f out: kpt on u.p* **5/1**[3]
550 4 ½ **Everkyllachy (IRE)**[12] 6250 2-8-13 **60** JosephineGordon(3) 4 55
(J S Moore) *chsd ldrs: rdn over 2f out: styd on same pce fnl f* **7/1**
3405 5 hd **Dixie Peach**[12] 6252 2-8-13 **57** CharlesBishop 9 51
(Eve Johnson Houghton) *chsd ldrs: drvn 2f out: kpt on same pce* **9/2**[2]
0600 6 1 ¼ **Auric Goldfinger (IRE)**[12] 6253 2-9-0 **58** SeanLevey 2 48
(Richard Hannon) *s.i.s: hld up towards rr: drvn and unable qck 2f out: styd on fnl f* **8/1**
050 7 1 **Miss Salt**[32] 5606 2-8-1 **48** ow2 EdwardGreatrex(3) 3 35
(Dominic Ffrench Davis) *chsd ldrs: drvn 2f out: wknd 1f out* **28/1**
5406 8 1 ¼ **Highland Dream (IRE)**[11] 6289 2-9-2 **60** (b[1]) JohnFahy 10 44
(Clive Cox) *chsd ldrs: rdn 2f out: wknd fnl f* **8/1**
2660 9 12 **Davarde (IRE)**[34] 5543 2-9-6 **64** DaneO'Neill 8 12
(David Evans) *squeezed out s: towards rr: rdn 2f out: wknd over 1f out* **14/1**
600 10 1 ¾ **Felstead Queen**[44] 5202 2-9-2 **60** FMBerry 7
(Joseph Tuite) *wnt sltly rt leaving stalls: t.k.h towards rr: rdn over 2f out: sn wknd* **10/1**

1m 11.78s (1.78) **Going Correction** +0.30s/f (Good) **10 Ran SP% 121.0**
Speed ratings (Par 93): **100,96,95,95,94 93,91,90,74,71**
CSF £42.19 CT £186.38 TOTE £10.00: £3.70, £1.70, £2.10; EX 47.80 Trifecta £344.20.
Owner Rowdown Racing Partnership **Bred** Mrs Vera Deegan **Trained** Upper Lambourn, Berks

FOCUS
Quite an interesting race for the grade and an impressive performance from the winner, pulling clear in the final 100 yards.

6653 188BET H'CAP 5f
6:25 (6:25) (Class 4) (0-80,80) 3-Y-O+ **£5,175** (£1,540; £769; £384) **Stalls** Centre

Form RPR
6124 1 **Satchville Flyer**[12] 6255 5-9-2 **75** DaneO'Neill 6 82
(David Evans) *racd keenly: hld up: hdwy and edgd lft 2f out: drvn and r.o to ld nr fin* **3/1**[1]
0660 2 hd **Nocturn**[15] 6195 7-8-6 **70** (p) CiaranMckee(5) 3 76
(Ronald Harris) *trckd ldrs: rdn to ld appr fnl f: r.o: hdd nr fin* **11/1**
01 3 1 ¼ **Pensax Lad (IRE)**[11] 6296 5-9-3 **76** SteveDrowne 8 77
(Ronald Harris) *led: rdn over 1f out: sn hdd: unable qck* **4/1**[2]
00 4 shd **Maymyo (IRE)**[26] 5797 5-8-4 **66** oh4 EdwardGreatrex(3) 7 67
(Sylvester Kirk) *chsd ldrs tl sltly outpcd over 1f out: rdn and r.o wl fnl f: jst missed 3rd* **7/1**[3]
4234 5 1 ¾ **Head Space (IRE)**[27] 5773 8-8-4 **66** JosephineGordon(3) 1 60
(David Evans) *hld up: rdn 2f out: no imp tl r.o ins fnl f* **4/1**[2]
510 6 shd **Swirral Edge**[7] 6133 3-9-3 **77** SeanLevey 4 71
(David Brown) *hld up: drvn over 1f out: one pce and no imp* **3/1**[1]

5004 **7** 2 3/4 **Bapak Bangsawan**[9] 6381 6-8-5 **69** oh8 ow3..............(v) AnnStokell(5) 9 53
(Ann Stokell) *wnt to post early: plld hrd: cl up tl rdn over 1f out: wknd fnl f* **25/1**

59.16s (0.86) **Going Correction** +0.30s/f (Good)
WFA 3 from 4yo+ 1lb **7** Ran SP% **114.7**
Speed ratings (Par 105): **105,104,102,102,99 99,95**
CSF £36.55 CT £133.07 TOTE £4.30: £1.90, £5.80; EX 32.40 Trifecta £120.10.
Owner A Cooke & Lynn Cullimore 1 **Bred** Newsells Park Stud **Trained** Pandy, Monmouths

FOCUS
By no means strong form for the grade but the winner continued on his upward curve, registering a fifth win since joining this yard in the spring. Not too many positives from the form.

6654 188BET.CO.UK H'CAP 1m 4f (R)
6:55 (6:58) (Class 6) (0-65,65) 3-Y-O **£2,264** (£673; £336; £168) **Stalls** Low

Form RPR
0-55 **1** **Prospectus**[133] 2126 3-9-4 **62**.............................. JimmyFortune 3 70
(Hughie Morrison) *hld up: hdwy over 3f out: rdn to ld over 2f out: edgd rt over 1f out: styd on wl* **9/2**[2]
2325 **2** 3 **Nanny Makfi**[31] 5625 3-8-6 **53**.............................. JosephineGordon(3) 9 56
(Stuart Kittow) *mid-div: hdwy 4f out: drvn and ev ch over 2f out: kpt on same pce and hld by wnr fnl f* **5/2**[1]
-034 **3** 4 1/2 **Hermarna (IRE)**[54] 4794 3-9-5 **63**.............................. FMBerry 1 59
(Harry Dunlop) *chsd ldrs: led 4f out: rdn and hdd over 2f out: wkng in 3rd whn sltly hmpd over 1f out* **8/1**
5560 **4** 1/2 **Frivolous Prince (IRE)**[25] 5824 3-8-7 **51** oh2..............(vt) JohnFahy 6 47
(David Evans) *hld up: rdn over 2f out: drvn and styd on fnl f: nvr able to chal* **16/1**
0-00 **5** 1 **Incus**[70] 4233 3-8-2 **51** oh6..............................[1] GeorgeWood(5) 4 45
(Ed de Giles) *t.k.h: chsd ldrs: drvn 3f out: wknd 1f out* **50/1**
0006 **6** 2 1/4 **Rowlestonerendezvu**[76] 4025 3-8-12 **56**.............................. SteveDrowne 7 47
(Tony Carroll) *hld up towards rr: effrt on outside over 2f out: wknd fnl f* **14/1**
0460 **7** 11 **Persaverance**[50] 4942 3-9-5 **63**..............................(b[1]) FergusSweeney 5 37
(Gary Moore) *trckd ldr tl rdn and lost 2nd over 3f out: wknd 2f out* **12/1**
0523 **8** 54 **Free Passage**[25] 5824 3-9-7 **65**.............................. DaneO'Neill 2
(Henry Candy) *led tl rdn and hdd 4f out: wknd rapidly: eased over 2f out: t.o: b.b.v* **5/1**[3]

2m 36.94s (-0.46) **Going Correction** -0.125s/f (Firm) **8** Ran SP% **96.7**
Speed ratings (Par 99): **96,94,91,90,90 88,81,45**
CSF £11.41 TOTE £5.20: £1.90, £1.10, £2.30; EX 11.90 Trifecta £80.10.
Owner The Black Gold Partnership **Bred** Glebe Stud & J F Dean **Trained** East Ilsley, Berks

FOCUS
Another modest handicap but an impressive performance from the winner and the form has a solid look to it.
T/Plt: £52.60 to a £1 stake. Pool: £55,485.66 - 768.95 winning units. T/Qpdt: £20.70 to a £1 stake. Pool: £6,023.55 - 215.09 winning units. **Richard Lowther**

6334 LINGFIELD (L-H)
Tuesday, September 20

OFFICIAL GOING: Polytrack: standard
Wind: Almost nil Weather: Overcast

6655 BRITISH STALLION STUDS EBF MAIDEN STKS 1m 1y(P)
2:00 (2:00) (Class 5) 2-Y-O **£3,363** (£1,001; £500; £250) **Stalls** High

Form RPR
2342 **1** **Wahash (IRE)**[13] 6240 2-9-5 79.............................. FrankieDettori 1 85+
(Richard Hannon) *mde all: drew clr fr 2f out: easily* **4/1**[3]
22 **2** 5 **Hydroxide**[12] 6262 2-9-5 0.............................. JimCrowley 7 73
(Hugo Palmer) *dwlt: rcvrd to chse wnr on outer after 2f: rdn and nt qckn 2f out: wl hld after* **8/13**[1]
4 **3** 2 **Balashakh (USA)**[27] 5764 2-9-5 0.............................. JamieSpencer 6 68
(David Simcock) *chsd wnr 2f: sn in 4th: shkn up to take 3rd 2f out: no imp ldng pair after* **11/4**[2]
05 **4** 2 3/4 **Red Caravel (IRE)**[11] 6288 2-9-5 0.............................. ShaneKelly 2 62+
(Richard Hughes) *pushed along towards rr after 3f: gng bttr over 2f out: pushed along again and kpt on steadily to take 4th nr fin* **50/1**
3 **5** 1/2 **Mullarkey**[12] 6264 2-9-5 0.............................. KierenFox 10 63+
(John Best) *dropped in fr wd draw and hld up in last: nt clr run briefly on inner over 2f out: pushed along and prog over 1f out: reminder and 4th briefly ins fnl f: nvr really involved* **16/1**
0 **6** 2 **Hold Me Tight (IRE)**[18] 6085 2-9-5 0.............................. LiamKeniry 5 56
(J S Moore) *i tch in rr: pushed along over 2f out: sn lft bhd* **100/1**
05 **7** hd **Lady Kaviar (IRE)**[41] 5298 2-9-0 0.............................. RyanPowell 4 50
(George Margarson) *chsd ldrs: shkn up over 2f out: sn lft bhd* **33/1**
0 **7** dht **License To Thrill (USA)**[49] 4988 2-9-5 0.............................. NickyMackay 3 55
(Simon Dow) *prom: chsd ldng pair over 5f out to 2f out: wknd* **66/1**
9 5 **Bocelli** 2-9-5 0.............................. RobertHavlin 8 43+
(Simon Crisford) *dwlt: racd on outer thrght: in tch to over 2f out: sn wknd qckly* **14/1**

1m 36.84s (-1.36) **Going Correction** -0.125s/f (Stan) **9** Ran SP% **128.5**
Speed ratings (Par 95): **101,96,94,91,90 88,88,88,83**
CSF £7.68 TOTE £2.80: £1.40, £1.20, £1.40; EX 9.10 Trifecta £17.00.
Owner Al Shaqab Racing **Bred** Miss S Von Schilcher **Trained** East Everleigh, Wilts

FOCUS
A maiden lacking depth and a fine piece of judgement from the winning jockey in a race run at a modest pace. The form may not be totally reliable as a result. The second and third raced prominently too.

6656 PEARROC H'CAP (DIV I) 1m 1y(P)
2:30 (2:30) (Class 5) (0-75,75) 3-Y-O+ **£2,911** (£866; £432; £216) **Stalls** High

Form RPR
1614 **1** **Wakame (IRE)**[17] 6138 3-9-2 **71**.............................. JimCrowley 2 80
(Ed de Giles) *trckd ldrs on inner: gap appeared and led over 1f out: rdn and kpt on wl fnl f* **3/1**[2]
5026 **2** 1/2 **Wings Of Esteem (IRE)**[46] 5122 3-9-2 **71**.............................. JimmyQuinn 6 79
(Martin Smith) *t.k.h: trckd ldrs: gng strly over 2f out: effrt to chse wnr 1f out: rdn and styd on but hld nr fin* **10/1**
-416 **3** 1 3/4 **Classical Rose**[104] 3030 4-9-9 **74**.............................. FrederikTylicki 11 78
(Charlie Fellowes) *hld up towards rr: prog on inner 2f out: chsd ldng pair ins fnl f: kpt on same pce* **4/1**[3]
1560 **4** 1 **Shifting Star (IRE)**[22] 5965 11-9-5 **70**..............................(vt) WilliamCarson 3 72
(John Bridger) *led: rdn over 2f out: hdd over 1f out and wandered after: fdd* **14/1**
4P00 **5** nk **Spiritual Star (IRE)**[21] 5994 7-9-4 **74**.............................. PaddyBradley(5) 5 75
(Lee Carter) *stdd s and hld up in last: stl wl in rr over 2f out: effrt whn sltly impeded and swtchd rt 1f out: styd on but no ch to threaten* **33/1**
0360 **6** 2 **Molten Lava (IRE)**[9] 6365 4-9-4 **69**.............................. RyanClark 9 65
(Paul Cole) *chsd ldrs on outer: rdn 3f out: no prog and wl hld whn sltly impeded 1f out* **16/1**
1-30 **7** 1/2 **Falcon's Song (USA)**[17] 6128 4-9-6 **71**.............................. PatCosgrave 7 66
(Ismail Mohammed) *chsd ldr: rdn over 2f out: lost 2nd wl over 1f out: btn whn bmpd 1f out* **7/1**
6163 **8** 3/4 **Awesome Quality (USA)**[39] 5367 3-9-6 **75**.............................. LukeMorris 4 68
(James Tate) *chsd ldrs: drvn over 2f out: fading whn squeezed out 1f out* **5/2**[1]
1342 **9** 3/4 **Wordismybond**[15] 6184 7-9-0 **72**..............................(p) StephenCummins(7) 8 63
(Richard Hughes) *t.k.h: trckd ldrs: rdn over 2f out: fading whn sltly impeded 1f out* **16/1**
0056 **10** 9 **Popeswood (IRE)**[27] 5773 4-9-3 **68**..............................[1] KierenFox 10 38
(Lee Carter) *a in rr: dropped to last and struggling 1/2-way: t.o* **33/1**

1m 36.85s (-1.35) **Going Correction** -0.125s/f (Stan)
WFA 3 from 4yo+ 4lb **10** Ran SP% **119.5**
Speed ratings (Par 103): **101,100,98,97,97 95,94,94,93,84**
CSF £34.30 CT £124.77 TOTE £3.90: £1.40, £3.40, £2.50; EX 36.00 Trifecta £159.10.
Owner Simon Treacher **Bred** Tally-Ho Stud **Trained** Ledbury, H'fords

FOCUS
The first division of an ordinary handicap and quite a rough race. It was the slower division but the form looks solid enough.

6657 PEARROC H'CAP (DIV II) 1m 1y(P)
3:00 (3:00) (Class 5) (0-75,75) 3-Y-O+ **£2,911** (£866; £432; £216) **Stalls** High

Form RPR
0011 **1** **Multitask**[29] 5710 6-9-3 **73**.............................. HectorCrouch(5) 7 80
(Gary Moore) *hld up off the pce in rr gp: prog over 2f out: clsd on outer w others over 1f out: rdn to ld last 75yds: a in command after* **9/2**[3]
-542 **2** nk **Pendo**[35] 5503 5-9-5 **70**.............................. KierenFox 2 76
(John Best) *led at gd pce but pressed: rdn over 2f out: tired and pressed fnl f: hdd last 75yds: kpt on gamely to hold on for 2nd* **6/1**
3433 **3** nse **Four Poets**[28] 5752 3-9-3 **72**.............................. JamieSpencer 8 78
(David Simcock) *hld up off the pce in rr gp: prog over 2f out: clsd w others over 1f out: rdn to chal ins fnl f: nt qckn nr fin* **4/1**[2]
0452 **4** 1/2 **Dream Of Summer (IRE)**[61] 4562 3-9-6 **75**.............................. OisinMurphy 4 80
(Andrew Balding) *chsd ldng pair: rdn over 2f out: clsd 1f out and ch ins fnl f: one pce* **3/1**[1]
1340 **5** 1 **Bay Of St Malo (IRE)**[11] 6299 3-9-5 **74**.............................. KieranO'Neill 10 76+
(Richard Hannon) *hld up off the pce in rr gp: rdn over 3f out: stl in last pair and u.p over 1f out: styd on ins fnl f* **20/1**
6160 **6** nse **Clever Bob (IRE)**[12] 6265 3-8-8 **70**.............................. SeanMooney(7) 6 72
(Joseph Tuite) *chsd clr ldng quartet and wl ahd of rest: rdn over 2f out: tried to cl over 1f out: one pce after* **20/1**
3316 **7** 1 **Pike Corner Cross (IRE)**[13] 6231 4-9-7 **72**.............................. JimCrowley 9 72+
(Ed de Giles) *dropped in fr wd draw: hld up in last and wl off the pce: pushed along on inner over 2f out: kpt on fr over 1f out but nvr a threat* **4/1**[2]
2230 **8** 1 **Brasted (IRE)**[17] 6128 4-9-9 **74**..............................(t) PatCosgrave 5 71
(Lee Carter) *pressed ldr and clr of rest: lost 2nd and fdd over 1f out* **16/1**
-224 **9** 1/2 **Cinders (IRE)**[12] 6251 3-9-3 **72**.............................. PatDobbs 3 68
(Hughie Morrison) *off the pce in rr gp: rdn over 3f out: no great prog* **25/1**
026 **10** 1 **Ost Wind**[55] 4773 4-8-13 **67**.............................. RobHornby(3) 1 61
(Michael Attwater) *chsd ldng trio: rdn over 2f out: steadily wknd over 1f out* **50/1**

1m 36.52s (-1.68) **Going Correction** -0.125s/f (Stan)
WFA 3 from 4yo+ 4lb **10** Ran SP% **118.7**
Speed ratings (Par 103): **103,102,102,102,101 101,100,99,98,97**
CSF £30.56 CT £120.44 TOTE £6.00: £2.40, £1.70, £1.70; EX 35.70 Trifecta £128.50.
Owner Power Geneva Ltd **Bred** Mrs L N Harmes **Trained** Lower Beeding, W Sussex

FOCUS
They went a serious pace in this and the field was well spread out by halfway, though the principals eventually finished in a heap and it's hard to be too confident about the form. The winning time was 0.33sec quicker than the first division.

6658 DELGA PRESS/KEY PRODUCTIONS NURSERY H'CAP 5f 6y(P)
3:35 (3:36) (Class 5) (0-75,75) 2-Y-O **£2,911** (£866; £432; £216) **Stalls** High

Form RPR
6012 **1** **Rose Berry**[17] 6139 2-9-3 **71**.............................. SaleemGolam 10 77
(Chris Dwyer) *trckd ldng pair: rdn over 1f out: clsd fnl f to ld last 100yds: drvn clr* **20/1**
4542 **2** 1 1/4 **Amlak**[17] 6141 2-9-7 **75**.............................. FrankieDettori 1 76
(Richard Hannon) *led: rdn over 1f out: styd on but hdd and outpcd last 100yds* **2/1**[1]
0023 **3** 1 1/2 **Katrine (IRE)**[20] 6033 2-9-4 **72**.............................. PatCosgrave 8 68
(William Knight) *hld up in last trio: shkn up wl over 1f out: gd prog fnl f: tk 3rd nr fin but no ch to chal* **12/1**
5240 **4** 1 1/4 **One Too Many (IRE)**[20] 6033 2-9-0 **68**.............................. JimCrowley 3 59
(David Brown) *chsd ldng pair: rdn to go 2nd on inner wl over 1f out to ins fnl f: fdd* **14/1**
3006 **5** 1/2 **Grand Myla (IRE)**[29] 5705 2-9-5 **73**..............................[1] GeorgeBaker 6 62
(Gary Moore) *racd wd in midfield: rdn 2f out: nvr on terms but kpt on fnl f* **10/1**
503 **6** nse **Lady Cleo (IRE)**[12] 6244 2-9-1 **69**..............................(t) OisinMurphy 2 58
(Stuart Williams) *dwlt: sn in tch in rr: effrt on inner over 1f out: kpt on but no ch* **10/1**
0215 **7** 1/2 **Zebspear (IRE)**[46] 5125 2-9-2 **70**.............................. ShaneKelly 4 57
(Joseph Tuite) *towards rr: shkn up 2f out: kpt on same pce and nvr a threat* **33/1**
0230 **8** 3/4 **Syncopation (IRE)**[18] 6071 2-9-2 **70**.............................. PatDobbs 7 55
(Sylvester Kirk) *s.i.s: nvr gng pce to make any impact: kpt on fnl f* **7/1**[3]
3032 **9** 1 **Makman (IRE)**[57] 4712 2-9-2 **70**.............................. JamieSpencer 9 51
(Ed Dunlop) *restless stalls: s.i.s: hld up in last: brought wdst of all in st: nvr involved* **12/1**
0321 **10** nk **Compton Lane**[7] 6440 2-9-5 **73** 6ex.............................. FrederikTylicki 5 53
(Rod Millman) *chsd ldr to wl over 1f out: wknd rapidly* **11/4**[2]

58.58s (-0.22) **Going Correction** -0.125s/f (Stan) **10** Ran SP% **120.4**
Speed ratings (Par 95): **96,94,91,89,88 88,87,86,85,84**
CSF £62.23 CT £550.37 TOTE £12.20: £5.30, £1.20, £3.40; EX 94.20 Trifecta £329.10.
Owner Strawberry Fields Stud **Bred** Aljw Bloodstock **Trained** Newmarket, Suffolk

FOCUS
A modest sprint nursery and it paid to be up there.

6659 NATIONAL WINDSCREENS H'CAP 1m 7f 169y(P)
4:05 (4:06) (Class 6) (0-65,68) 3-Y-O+ **£2,264** (£673; £336; £168) **Stalls** Low

Form RPR
054 **1** **Alfredo (IRE)**[20] 6031 4-9-4 **55**....(tp) OisinMurphy 11 61
(Seamus Durack) *prom: trckd ldr after 6f: upsides 3f out: rdn to ld 2f out: pressed ins fnl f: kpt on wl* **20/1**
005 **2** ½ **Balancing Time**[107] 2929 3-8-13 **62**.... PatDobbs 4 67
(Amanda Perrett) *cl up on inner: rdn to chse wnr over 1f out: clsd and looked a threat 100yds out: kpt on but nt qckn after* **8/1**
4231 **3** 2 ¼ **Denmead**[9] 6367 3-9-5 **68** 6ex.... RobertWinston 10 70
(John Butler) *t.k.h: hld up in rr: prog on outer over 3f out: rdn to chse ldrs 2f out: nt qckn and outpcd over 1f out: tk 3rd fnl f and styd on* **11/4**[2]
1563 **4** 7 **Tyrannical**[18] 6102 3-8-5 **54**....(v[1]) LukeMorris 2 48
(Sir Mark Prescott Bt) *shkn up after s: sn hld up in rr: prog and wl in tch over 2f out: drvn and bdly outpcd sn after: tk modest 4th nr fin* **7/4**[1]
0525 **5** ¾ **Fast Play (IRE)**[10] 6335 4-9-10 **61**....(p) ShaneKelly 8 54
(Richard Hughes) *led: jnd 3f out: rdn and hdd 2f out: wknd over 1f out* **20/1**
034 **6** nk **Iconic Sky**[13] 6239 3-9-2 **65**.... JimCrowley 9 58
(Lucy Wadham) *trckd ldr 6f: styd handy: rdn and in tch over 2f out: wknd wl over 1f out* **6/1**[3]
0501 **7** 1 ¼ **Maria's Choice (IRE)**[30] 5672 7-10-0 **65**....(v) TimmyMurphy 1 56
(Jim Best) *hld up in rr: pushed along 3f out: no imp in 7th on ldng gp over 2f out* **25/1**
212- **8** 4 **Halling's Wish**[172] 5256 6-10-0 **65**.... GeorgeBaker 5 51
(Gary Moore) *stdd s: hld up in detached last: stl there over 2f out and no ch: pushed along after: nvr involved* **12/1**
406 **9** 16 **Rue Balzac (IRE)**[42] 5255 3-8-11 **60**....[1] LiamJones 3 27
(Neil King) *urged along s: in tch: drvn to press ldrs over 3f out: wknd rapidly over 2f out: t.o* **20/1**
1000 **10** 1 ½ **Lily Edge**[44] 5208 7-8-13 **50**....(v) DannyBrock 7 15
(John Bridger) *in tch: rousted along fr 7f out: wknd qckly over 2f out: t.o* **33/1**

3m 23.48s (-2.22) **Going Correction** -0.125s/f (Stan)
WFA 3 from 4yo+ 12lb **10** Ran SP% **117.2**
Speed ratings (Par 101): **100,99,98,95,94 94,93,91,83,83**
CSF £159.31 CT £586.57 TOTE £20.30: £4.80, £2.30, £1.50; EX 279.60 Trifecta £1445.60.
Owner Stephen Tucker & Keith McIntosh **Bred** Colin Kennedy **Trained** Upper Lambourn, Berkshire

FOCUS
A moderate staying handicap and not a strong pace, resulting in a few racing keenly early. The first two, both of whom were making their handicap debut, were always up there.

6660 KING AND JOHNSTON HOMES LTD H'CAP 5f 6y(P)
4:40 (4:40) (Class 6) (0-60,66) 3-Y-O+ **£2,264** (£673; £336; £168) **Stalls** High

Form RPR
4040 **1** **Zipedeedodah (IRE)**[29] 5706 4-9-5 **58**....(t) OisinMurphy 2 67
(Joseph Tuite) *trckd ldng pair on inner: wnt 2nd 2f out and sn clsd on ldr: led jst ins fnl f: drvn out* **6/1**[2]
4210 **2** 1 ½ **Red Flute**[69] 4264 4-8-13 **52**....(v) LiamKeniry 7 56
(Denis Quinn) *fast away fr wd draw and led: 2 l clr 2f out: hdd and no ex jst ins fnl f* **14/1**
0330 **3** 1 **Sacred Harp**[12] 6249 3-9-5 **59**....(t) PatCosgrave 4 59
(Stuart Williams) *chsd ldr to 2f out: one pce after* **7/1**[3]
6301 **4** ½ **Vale Of Flight (IRE)**[9] 6374 3-9-12 **66** 6ex.... JimCrowley 5 65
(Rae Guest) *towards rr: pushed along 1/2-way: kpt on fnl f to take 4th nr fin: n.d* **11/4**[1]
1052 **5** 1 **Frank The Barber (IRE)**[9] 6374 4-9-6 **59**....(t) AdamBeschizza 6 54
(Steph Hollinshead) *mostly chsd ldng trio: rdn and nt qckn wl over 1f out: lost 4th nr fin* **6/1**[2]
0546 **6** 2 **Pushkin Museum (IRE)**[21] 6008 5-9-6 **59**.... ShaneKelly 8 47
(Richard Fahey) *s.i.s: a towards rr and nvr pce to rcvr: no prog over 1f out* **11/4**[1]
4565 **7** ½ **Ryan Style (IRE)**[25] 5826 10-8-4 **46**....(p) NoelGarbutt[(3)] 1 32
(Lisa Williamson) *a in rr: pushed along after 2f: nvr pce to make prog* **33/1**
3300 **8** 3 ½ **Ask The Guru**[11] 6296 6-9-5 **58**....(p) LukeMorris 3 31
(Michael Attwater) *sn struggling in last: nvr a factor* **8/1**
63-6 **9** 6 **Fred's Filly**[3] 6586 3-8-12 **52**....(b) WilliamCarson 9 4
(Bill Turner) *spd on outer 2f: sn lost pl: t.o* **50/1**

58.88s (0.08) **Going Correction** -0.125s/f (Stan)
WFA 3 from 4yo+ 1lb **9** Ran SP% **117.1**
Speed ratings (Par 101): **94,91,90,89,87 84,83,78,68**
CSF £86.24 CT £608.61 TOTE £8.70: £2.40, £3.10, £2.40; EX 108.50 Trifecta £822.20.
Owner D M Synergy & Mark Wellbelove **Bred** Tally-Ho Stud **Trained** Lambourn, Berks

FOCUS
A moderate sprint handicap and predictably no hanging about. The first three were always up on the speed.

6661 NORMAN SMITH'S 80TH BIRTHDAY MAIDEN FILLIES' STKS 1m 2f (P)
5:10 (5:10) (Class 5) 3-Y-O+ **£2,911** (£866; £432; £216) **Stalls** Low

Form RPR
432 **1** **Entsar (IRE)**[49] 4978 3-9-0 79.... FrankieDettori 6 88+
(William Haggas) *prom: trckd ldr over 7f out: led 3f out: pushed clr over 1f out: nvr in any danger after* **8/13**[1]
3032 **2** 1 ¼ **Cape Peninsular**[8] 6423 3-9-0 79.... LukeMorris 4 85
(James Tate) *wl in tch: shkn up and prog over 2f out: chsd wnr over 1f out: drvn and cl fnl f: styd on but unable to chal* **9/2**[3]
2 **3** 4 **Time To Blossom**[21] 5996 3-9-0.... RobertHavlin 7 77
(Simon Crisford) *s.s: settled in rr: prog on outer over 3f out: chsd wnr wl over 2f out to over 1f out: fdd* **4/1**[2]
5 **4** 6 **Electrify (IRE)**[35] 5504 3-9-0 0.... JimCrowley 8 65+
(Jeremy Noseda) *hld up in last: rchd 5th over 2f out and stl gng wl: pushed along to take modest 4th over 1f out: no imp after: likely improver* **14/1**
5 **5** 3 ½ **Rianna Star**[28] 5735 3-8-9 0.... HectorCrouch[(5)] 1 58
(Gary Moore) *led 2f: styd cl up tl wknd over 2f out* **66/1**
53 **6** 6 **Howilat (USA)**[13] 6239 3-9-0 0.... MartinLane 2 46
(Charlie Appleby) *led after 2f to 3f out: wknd qckly 2f out* **8/1**
-004 **7** 7 **Hamilton Terrace**[41] 5286 3-9-0 49....[1] PatCosgrave 9 32
(Henry Candy) *racd on outer: in tch to 3f out: wknd qckly* **66/1**
8 56 **Phantomine (IRE)**[40] 4-9-6 0.... ShaneKelly 3
(Brendan Powell) *s.s: in tch to 4f out: sn wknd: virtually p.u fnl 2f* **66/1**

2m 4.46s (-2.14) **Going Correction** -0.125s/f (Stan)
WFA 3 from 4yo 6lb **8** Ran SP% **122.4**
Speed ratings (Par 100): **103,102,98,94,91 86,80,36**
CSF £4.41 TOTE £1.60: £1.20, £1.40, £1.30; EX 3.80 Trifecta £9.50.
Owner Al Shaqab Racing **Bred** Manister House Stud **Trained** Newmarket, Suffolk

FOCUS
Few could be seriously considered in this fillies' maiden. The form is rated on the positive side.

6662 INJURED JOCKEYS FUND H'CAP 1m 2f (P)
5:40 (5:41) (Class 6) (0-65,70) 3-Y-O+ **£2,911** (£866; £432; £216) **Stalls** Low

Form RPR
5451 **1** **Collodi (GER)**[7] 6444 7-10-1 **70** 6ex.... LiamKeniry 2 77
(Neil Mulholland) *trckd ldrs: rdn wl over 1f out: clsd to ld last 75yds: r.o wl and sn clr* **3/1**[1]
5124 **2** 1 ¾ **Fast And Hot (IRE)**[15] 6194 3-9-3 **64**....(p) KieranO'Neill 12 68
(Richard Hannon) *trckd ldrs on outer: chal over 3f out: led over 2f out and sn drvn: kpt on u.p but hdd and outpcd last 75yds* **10/1**
0656 **3** nk **Cliff Edge (IRE)**[84] 3738 3-9-2 **63**....(b[1]) JackMitchell 4 66
(Roger Varian) *chsd ldrs: rdn and no imp 2f out: styd on wl on wd outside fnl f to take 3rd last strides* **6/1**[2]
0645 **4** nk **Estibdaad (IRE)**[13] 6241 6-9-8 **63**....(t) MartinLane 5 66
(Paddy Butler) *disp ld to 4f out: drvn 3f out: responded wl and upsides new ldr over 2f out to over 1f out: kpt on one pce ins fnl f* **16/1**
0232 **5** shd **Roman De Brut (IRE)**[25] 5841 4-9-9 **64**.... LukeMorris 1 66
(Daniel Mark Loughnane) *wl in tch on inner: rdn over 2f out: clsd to chal over 1f out: nrly upsides ins fnl f: no ex last 75yds* **6/1**[2]
0334 **6** ½ **What A Dandy (IRE)**[16] 4527 5-9-9 **64**.... PatCosgrave 9 65
(Jim Boyle) *towards rr: shake up 3f out: prog on inner 2f out: drvn and tried to chal fnl f: one pce* **16/1**
4630 **7** 2 ¾ **Lady Lunchalot (USA)**[10] 6334 6-9-5 **60**....(p) JimCrowley 3 56
(Laura Mongan) *s.s: hld up in last pair: pushed along 3f out: kpt on steadily on inner fnl 2f but nvr cl enough to threaten* **14/1**
2334 **8** ½ **Santiburi Spring**[29] 5720 3-9-4 **65**.... KierenFox 11 60
(John Best) *dwlt: towards rr: shkn up 3f out: one pce and nvr able to make significant prog* **8/1**[3]
6550 **9** 1 ½ **Ice Alert (IRE)**[13] 6241 3-8-13 **60**....(t) DanielMuscutt 7 52
(John Ryan) *nvr bttr than midfield: n.m.r over 4f out: rdn and no prog 3f out* **33/1**
3356 **10** hd **Live Dangerously**[12] 6266 6-9-8 **63**.... WilliamCarson 14 55
(John Bridger) *stdd s fr wdst draw and hld up in last trio: rn into trble and snatched up over 2f out: nt clr run over 1f out and jst ins fnl f: nvr involved* **50/1**
002 **11** 1 ¼ **Betsalottie**[15] 6194 3-8-12 **59**.... DannyBrock 10 49
(John Bridger) *t.k.h: disp ld: led 4f out: hdd over 2f out: wknd qckly wl over 1f out* **12/1**
6021 **12** hd **Monna Valley**[38] 5399 4-9-3 **61**.... AaronJones[(3)] 6 50
(Stuart Williams) *chsd ldrs: rdn 3f out: wknd qckly 2f out* **6/1**[2]
000 **13** nk **Ixelles Diamond (IRE)**[24] 5891 5-9-0 **55**.... TomQueally 8 44
(Andrew Reid) *s.s: mostly in last pair: effrt on wd outside over 3f out: sn no prog* **66/1**
416 **14** ¾ **Embankment**[38] 5399 7-9-4 **59**.... FrederikTylicki 13 46
(Michael Attwater) *a towards rr: struggling fr 3f out* **25/1**

2m 4.76s (-1.84) **Going Correction** -0.125s/f (Stan)
WFA 3 from 4yo+ 6lb **14** Ran SP% **124.4**
Speed ratings (Par 101): **102,100,100,100,100 99,97,97,95,95 94,94,94,93**
CSF £34.57 CT £178.56 TOTE £4.00: £1.50, £4.80, £2.30; EX 47.70 Trifecta £612.60.
Owner T C and A Winter & Partners **Bred** Stiftung Gestut Fahrhof **Trained** Limpley Stoke, Wilts

FOCUS
A moderate if competitive handicap to end and another race where it paid to be prominent.
T/Plt: £138.40 to a £1 stake. Pool: £79486.74 - 419.17 winning units T/Qpdt: £50.50 to a £1 stake. Pool: £5661.28 - 82.81 winning units **Jonathan Neesom**

5995 GOODWOOD (R-H)
Wednesday, September 21

OFFICIAL GOING: Good to soft (6.6)
Wind: virtually nil Weather: sunny with cloudy periods

6663 EVE TRAKWAY EBF STALLIONS MAIDEN STKS (PLUS 10 RACE) 1m 1f
2:00 (2:01) (Class 4) 2-Y-O **£5,175** (£1,540; £769; £384) **Stalls** Low

Form RPR
2422 **1** **Celestial Spheres (IRE)**[8] 6455 2-9-5 83....[1] WilliamBuick 5 84
(Charlie Appleby) *mde all: rdn whn strly chal over 2f out: hld on to narrow advantage v gamely thrght fnl f: all out* **9/2**[3]
2 shd **Monarchs Glen** 2-9-5 0.... RobertHavlin 7 84+
(John Gosden) *qs tr: q green and noisy in prelims: trckd wnr: rdn to chal over 2f out: kpt on w ev ch thrght fnl f: jst hld* **3/1**[2]
2 **3** 1 ¾ **Dick Tracy (IRE)**[17] 6159 2-9-5 0.... PatDobbs 1 80
(Richard Hannon) *q str: trckd ldrs: rdn over 2f out: nt quite pce to chal: edgd lft and no ex fnl f* **7/4**[1]
3 **4** 2 **See Of Rome**[12] 6288 2-9-5 0.... ShaneKelly 10 76+
(Richard Hughes) *athletic: midfield: rdn over 2f out: chal for hld 4th ent fnl f: kpt on but nt pce to get involved* **10/1**
05 **5** ¾ **City Limits**[12] 6297 2-9-5 0....(t) AndreaAtzeni 8 75
(Luca Cumani) *str: scope: lw: little slowly away: sn trcking ldrs: rdn wl over 2f out: kpt on same pce* **16/1**
3 **6** 4 ½ **Sir Nigel Gresley (USA)**[63] 4533 2-9-5 0.... FergusSweeney 6 66+
(Alan King) *q tall: racd keenly: mid-div: rdn whn short of room briefly 2f out: one pce after* **7/1**
7 1 **Jukebox Jive (FR)** 2-9-5 0.... OisinMurphy 3 64
(Anthony Honeyball) *w'like: bit bkwd: s.i.s: last pair: rdn 3f out: kpt on fnl f but nt pce to get on terms* **80/1**
45 **8** 3 **Ettihadi (IRE)**[29] 5740 2-9-5 0.... JimCrowley 11 58
(Hugo Palmer) *lengthy: trckd ldrs on outer: effrt 3f out: wknd ent fnl f* **14/1**
9 2 ¾ **Sussex Ranger (USA)** 2-9-5 0.... TomQueally 4 52
(Gary Moore) *leggy: athletic: s.i.s: struggling 6f out: a in rr* **66/1**
30 **10** 11 **Nip Down The Jug**[13] 6264 2-9-5 0.... HarryPoulton 2 30
(Adam West) *s.i.s: plld hrd in mid-div: rdn 3f out: wknd over 1f out* **100/1**

1m 58.82s (2.52) **Going Correction** +0.275s/f (Good) **10** Ran SP% **117.4**
Speed ratings (Par 97): **99,98,97,95,94 90,90,87,84,75**
CSF £18.58 TOTE £5.00: £1.40, £1.50, £1.30; EX 15.70 Trifecta £35.50.
Owner Godolphin **Bred** Lane Stud Farm Ltd **Trained** Newmarket, Suffolk

FOCUS
This had the look of a decent maiden for potential middle-distance performers of next season but the fairly exposed, although useful, Godolphin colt proved good enough to hang on in front. Being prominent was an advantage, the first three always 1-2-3, and the time was 7.82 seconds slower than standard.

6664 THOROUGHBRED BREEDERS' ASSOCIATION SMALL BREEDERS' CONDITIONS STKS (PLUS 10 RACE) (COLTS/GELDINGS) 7f
2:35 (2:35) (Class 2) 2-Y-O
£15,562 (£4,660; £2,330; £1,165; £582; £292) **Stalls** Low

Form RPR
032 **1** **Sea Shack**[25] 5890 2-8-11 77 JimCrowley 1 76
(William Knight) *lw: mde all: rdn over 1f out: kpt finding whn strly pressed ins fnl f: hld on gamely: all out* **11/8**[1]
1224 **2** *shd* **Mister Blue Sky (IRE)**[16] 6191 2-9-0 74 LukeMorris 3 79
(Sylvester Kirk) *lw: trckd ldrs: rdn 2f out: str chal ins fnl f: kpt on: jst hld* **6/1**[3]
2106 **3** *3/4* **Mr Hobbs**[14] 6229 2-9-0 78 EdwardGreatrex 4 78
(Sylvester Kirk) *hld up in tch: tk clsr order on rails over 3f out: nt clrest of runs over 1f out: kpt on to hold ev ch fnl 120yds: no ex towards fin* **9/1**
4012 **4** *1 1/4* **Zamadance**[10] 6366 2-8-11 63 PatDobbs 8 71
(Sylvester Kirk) *in tch: hdwy over 3f out: effrt 2f out: nt pce to chal but kpt on to snatch 4th cl home* **50/1**
42 **5** *hd* **Akkadian Empire**[13] 6264 2-8-8 0 MartinDwyer 5 67
(Mick Channon) *swtg: trckd ldrs: upsides wnr over 4f out: rdn wl over 2f out: no ex fnl 120yds: lost 4th cl home* **8/1**
6 *3* **Pow Wow** 2-8-11 0 WilliamBuick 9 62
(Roger Charlton) *athletic: slowly away: sn pushed along in last: kpt on but nt pce to get on terms: no ex ins fnl f: rn green: encouraging* **11/1**
010 **7** *8* **Hidden Stash**[35] 5543 2-9-0 73 OisinMurphy 6 43
(Andrew Balding) *trckd wnr tl over 4f out: rdn in cl 4th 3f out: wknd over 1f out* **14/1**
0240 **8** *3 1/2* **Admiralty Arch**[13] 6260 2-9-0 88 TomMarquand 7 34
(Richard Hannon) *sn pushed along in last pair: rdn 3f out: wknd over 1f out* **4/1**[2]

1m 29.11s (2.11) **Going Correction** +0.275s/f (Good) **8** Ran SP% **114.5**
Speed ratings (Par 101): **98,97,97,95,95 91,82,78**
CSF £10.09 TOTE £2.10: £1.10, £2.00, £2.60; EX 9.80 Trifecta £42.00.
Owner Seabrook Miller **Bred** D J And Mrs Deer **Trained** Patching, W Sussex

FOCUS
A fair conditions stakes for juveniles, which looks solid enough form. The first three set the level.

6665 "NETWORK AT GOODWOOD" STKS (H'CAP) 1m 3f
3:10 (3:11) (Class 4) (0-80,79) 3-Y-O **£6,469** (£1,925; £962; £481) **Stalls** High

Form RPR
0435 **1** **Imari Kid (IRE)**[60] 4628 3-8-7 70 HectorCrouch[(5)] 7 78
(Gary Moore) *swtg: hld up last trio: hdwy over 3f out: nt clr run on rails bhd ldrs tl 2f out: led narrowly jst ins fnl f: kpt on wl: rdn out* **20/1**
11 **2** *nk* **Fadillah**[127] 2339 3-9-7 79 AndreaAtzeni 9 86+
(William Haggas) *on toes: mid-div: hdwy over 3f out: nt clr rest of runs and swtchd lft 2f out: rdn to ld briefly ent fnl f: kpt on w ev ch: hld nring fin* **4/1**[2]
4212 **3** *3/4* **Panko (IRE)**[10] 6365 3-9-3 75 JimCrowley 1 84+
(Ed de Giles) *trckd ldrs: gng wl but nt clr run over 2f out tl swtchd lft jst ins fnl f: styd on strly to go 3rd ins fnl 100yds: clsng on ldrs cl home* **5/1**[3]
-542 **4** *shd* **The Otmoor Poet**[63] 4530 3-9-3 75 FergusSweeney 2 80
(Alan King) *mid-div: hdwy and nt clr run 3f out tl swtchd lft over 1f out: styd on wl fnl f to go 4th ins fnl 120yds: clsng on ldrs cl home* **11/1**
0642 **5** *1 1/2* **Street Poet (IRE)**[13] 6268 3-9-3 75 TedDurcan 3 77
(Sir Michael Stoute) *lw: mid-div: hdwy to ld over 6f out and qcknd pce: rdn over 2f out: sn edgd sltly lft: hdd ent fnl f: no ex fnl 100yds* **4/1**[2]
0611 **6** *4* **Ocean Ready (USA)**[16] 6186 3-9-4 76 LukeMorris 5 71
(Sir Mark Prescott Bt) *trckd ldrs: pushed along over 5f out: effrt 3f out: fdd ent fnl f* **10/3**[1]
44-4 **7** *nk* **Match My Fire (IRE)**[168] 1276 3-8-10 68 FMBerry 10 63
(Ralph Beckett) *hld up last: pushed along and hdwy 2f out: swtchd lft over 1f out: sn rdn: nt pce to get involved* **8/1**
2215 **8** *3 3/4* **Kismet Hardy**[25] 5875 3-9-3 75 SeanLevey 4 63
(Richard Hannon) *led tl over 6f out: pressed ldr: rdn and ev ch over 2f out: wknd ent fnl f* **16/1**
4204 **9** *3* **Sark (IRE)**[12] 6277 3-9-2 74[1] JimmyFortune 11 56
(David Evans) *hld up towards rr: rdn over 2f out: nvr any imp: wknd over 1f out* **25/1**
04 **10** *15* **Pinwood (IRE)**[14] 6242 3-9-5 77 (t) HarryPoulton 12 32
(Adam West) *lw: racd keenly: in tch on outer: trckd ldrs over 6f out: rdn over 2f out: wknd 2f out* **100/1**

2m 30.28s (3.78) **Going Correction** +0.275s/f (Good) **10** Ran SP% **114.7**
Speed ratings (Par 103): **97,96,96,96,95 92,91,89,87,76**
CSF £95.60 CT £472.62 TOTE £24.70: £5.60, £1.40, £1.90; EX 145.50 Trifecta £1152.60.
Owner P B Moorhead **Bred** Niarchos Family **Trained** Lower Beeding, W Sussex

FOCUS
Some in-form and/or interesting types lined up for the middle-distance contest and it can produce a few winners in the short-term, although the winner was a surprise. The early gallop didn't seem overly fierce, and the time was over 9 seconds slower than standard.

6666 CRIMBOURNE STUD FOUNDATION STKS (LISTED RACE) 1m 1f 192y
3:45 (3:47) (Class 1) 3-Y-O+ **£22,684** (£8,600; £4,304; £2,144; £1,076) **Stalls** Low

Form RPR
20-3 **1** **Sky Hunter**[18] 6125 6-9-2 112 WilliamBuick 4 116
(Saeed bin Suroor) *lw: trckd ldng pair: wnt 2nd over 5f out: led gng best over 2f out: sn rdn clr and in command: readily* **5/2**[2]
3510 **2** *3 1/4* **Tullius (IRE)**[32] 5652 8-9-5 110 (v) JimmyFortune 6 113
(Andrew Balding) *hld up 5th: hdwy 3f out: rdn over 2f out: disp hld 2nd over 1f out: kpt on but nvr any threat to wnr* **7/1**[3]
1461 **3** *1 1/2* **Mount Logan (IRE)**[14] 6233 5-9-2 109 AndreaAtzeni 2 107
(Roger Varian) *little slowly away: trckd ldrs: pushed along over 3f out: rdn over 2f out: disp hld 2nd over 1f out tl ins fnl f: no ex fnl 120yds* **4/6**[1]
1402 **4** *12* **Epsom Icon**[24] 5939 3-8-8 105 OisinMurphy 1 81
(Mick Channon) *led tl rdn over 2f out: wknd over 1f out* **10/1**
-141 **5** *1* **Black Night (IRE)**[10] 6402 4-9-2 73 JoeyHaynes 3 81?
(J Moon, Jersey) *trckd ldr tl pushed along over 5f out: rdn over 2f out: sn outpcd: wknd over 1f out* **100/1**

2m 7.24s (-0.86) **Going Correction** +0.275s/f (Good)
WFA 3 from 4yo+ 6lb **5** Ran SP% **111.1**
Speed ratings (Par 111): **114,111,110,100,99**
CSF £18.90 TOTE £3.20: £1.40, £3.20; EX 18.30 Trifecta £29.60.
Owner Godolphin **Bred** Darley **Trained** Newmarket, Suffolk

FOCUS
Not for the first time on the card, the leader didn't go any great gallop early on and it turned into a sprint. The form isn't reliable whatsoever. The winner is rated close to his best.

6667 THOROUGHBRED BREEDERS' ASSOCIATION FILLIES' STKS (H'CAP) 1m 6f
4:20 (4:20) (Class 3) (0-95,91) 3-Y-O+ **£16,172** (£4,812; £2,405; £1,202) **Stalls** Low

Form RPR
1062 **1** **Daphne**[53] 4859 3-8-9 82 (p) PatCosgrave 5 90
(William Haggas) *trckd ldr: racd away fr far side rails fr over 3f out: chal 2f out: sn edgd lft: styd on wl to take v narrow advantage towards fin: hld on: all out* **5/2**[2]
3232 **2** *nse* **Graceland (FR)**[20] 6050 4-9-2 82 LouisSteward[(3)] 1 90
(Michael Bell) *s.i.s: last pair: racd away fr far side rails and hdwy fr 3f out: rdn 2f out: edging lft but ld jst over 1f out: hdd cl home: kpt on: jst hld* **9/2**[3]
4244 **3** *1* **Engage (IRE)**[24] 5927 3-9-1 88 JimCrowley 6 95
(Sir Michael Stoute) *swtg: stdd s: last: racd away fr far side rails fr over 3f out: hdwy fr wl over 2f out: chsd ldng pair jst ins fnl f: kpt on but nt quite pce to chal* **2/1**[1]
0165 **4** *2 1/2* **Elysian Fields (GR)**[41] 5328 5-10-0 91 PatDobbs 4 94
(Amanda Perrett) *on toes: led: sn clr: racd alone on far side rails fr over 3f out: rdn 2f out: edgd lft and hdd jst over 1f out: no ex ins fnl f* **10/1**
0420 **5** *1 1/4* **Renfrew Street**[11] 6332 3-8-10 83 NickyMackay 2 84
(Mark Johnston) *trckd ldrs: racd away fr far side rails and rdn 3f out: wknd fnl f* **9/1**
2120 **6** *15* **Saumur**[75] 4078 4-8-13 76 TomQueally 3 56
(Denis Coakley) *trckd ldrs: racd away fr far side rails and rdn 3f out: short of room briefly over 2f out: sn wknd* **7/1**

3m 4.96s (1.36) **Going Correction** +0.275s/f (Good)
WFA 3 from 4yo+ 10lb **6** Ran SP% **111.7**
Speed ratings (Par 104): **107,106,106,104,104 95**
CSF £13.86 TOTE £2.30: £1.80, £2.40; EX 13.10 Trifecta £27.80.
Owner The Queen **Bred** The Queen **Trained** Newmarket, Suffolk

FOCUS
Probably just an ordinary staying contest for the level, but the form seems sound.

6668 BIBENDUM STKS (H'CAP) 6f
4:55 (4:55) (Class 4) (0-80,80) 3-Y-O+ **£6,469** (£1,925; £962; £481) **Stalls** High

Form RPR
3341 **1** **Symposium**[16] 6182 3-8-11 77 (p) GeorgiaCox[(5)] 2 89
(William Haggas) *hld up in tch: hdwy over 2f out: led ins fnl f: r.o wl* **11/4**[1]
3323 **2** *1 1/4* **Pettochside**[16] 6195 7-8-13 75 JosephineGordon[(3)] 3 83
(John Bridger) *prom: led after 1f: rdn and hdd jst ins fnl f: kpt on but no ex* **3/1**[2]
F-02 **3** *2 1/2* **Panther Patrol (IRE)**[13] 6255 6-9-2 75 CharlesBishop 7 75
(Eve Johnson Houghton) *trckd ldrs: swtchd lft 2f out: sn rdn: kpt on to go 3rd fnl f but nt pce to get on terms* **11/2**[3]
3202 **4** *1 1/2* **Gorokai (IRE)**[9] 6409 3-9-1 76 JimCrowley 6 71
(David Simcock) *hld up in tch: hdwy over 2f out: sn rdn: nt quite pce to mount chal: no ex fnl 120yds* **3/1**[2]
6460 **5** *nk* **Engaging Smile**[38] 5458 4-8-7 66 oh1 JoeyHaynes 12 60
(J Moon, Jersey) *led for over 1f: prom: rdn and ev ch 2f out: sn one pce* **100/1**
0033 **6** *shd* **Kinglami**[9] 6418 7-9-0 73 (p) FergusSweeney 4 67
(John O'Shea) *trckd ldrs: rdn and ev ch 2f out: no ex fnl f* **12/1**
4202 **7** *nk* **Straits Of Malacca**[13] 6269 5-8-11 70 (p) LukeMorris 10 63
(Simon Dow) *mid-div: rdn 2f out: nt pce to get involved* **10/1**
0044 **8** *4 1/2* **Divine Call**[13] 6269 9-8-4 66 oh10 (b) NoelGarbutt[(3)] 5 45
(Milton Bradley) *squeezed up ins 1st f and dropped to last: short-lived effrt 2f out: sn btn* **20/1**

1m 11.39s (-0.81) **Going Correction** -0.25s/f (Firm)
WFA 3 from 4yo+ 2lb **8** Ran SP% **114.6**
Speed ratings (Par 105): **95,93,90,88,87 87,87,81**
CSF £11.31 CT £41.38 TOTE £3.80: £1.20, £1.50, £2.00; EX 10.00 Trifecta £28.60.
Owner The Royal Ascot Racing Club **Bred** Bloomsbury Stud **Trained** Newmarket, Suffolk

FOCUS
Four non-runners made this a bit less competitive than it had looked at the overnight stage. The fancied runners (in the betting) dominated the finish. Solid form, rated around the second.

6669 HILDON APPRENTICE STKS (H'CAP) 5f
5:25 (5:27) (Class 5) (0-75,74) 3-Y-O+ **£3,234** (£962; £481; £240) **Stalls** High

Form RPR
1435 **1** **Stormflower**[24] 5928 3-8-13 66 JosephineGordon 8 73
(John Bridger) *prom: rdn to ld over 1f out: hld on gamely whn strly pressed ins fnl f* **5/1**[2]
6520 **2** *hd* **Archie Stevens**[16] 6195 6-8-8 67 KatherineGlenister[(7)] 4 73
(David Evans) *chsd ldrs: rdn over 1f out: ev ch ins fnl f: kpt on* **11/1**
0065 **3** *1/2* **Noble Asset**[9] 6425 5-9-3 69 EdwardGreatrex 2 73
(Milton Bradley) *led: rdn and hdd jst over 1f out: kpt on w ev ch tl no ex cl home* **13/2**[3]
0552 **4** *1/2* **Costa Filey**[20] 6051 5-8-7 64[1] CameronNoble[(5)] 1 66
(Ed Vaughan) *awkwardly away: mid-div: hdwy over 2f out: rdn over 1f out: ev ch ins fnl f no ex fnl 100yds* **5/2**[1]
0050 **5** *nk* **Taajub (IRE)**[16] 6195 9-9-5 74 HectorCrouch[(3)] 6 75
(Peter Crate) *chsd ldrs tl lost pl u.p wl over 1f out: kpt on again ins fnl f but no threat* **10/1**
13 **6** *1* **Equijade**[208] 726 3-8-12 65 LouisSteward 7 63
(Robert Stephens) *mid-div: rdn over 2f out: nt pce to get on terms* **16/1**
-060 **7** *1* **Dishy Guru**[12] 6296 7-8-10 62 (v[1]) TomMarquand 3 56
(Michael Blanshard) *towards rr: effrt 2f out: fdd fnl f* **12/1**
-555 **8** *nk* **Fashionable Spirit (IRE)**[12] 6290 3-8-9 62 KieranShoemark 5 55
(Amanda Perrett) *hld up: rdn over 2f out: little imp* **8/1**
5052 **9** *1* **Go Nani Go**[7] 6479 10-9-3 72 CallumShepherd[(3)] 11 61
(Ed de Giles) *chsd ldrs: rdn 2f out: wknd jst over 1f out* **10/1**
0400 **10** *5* **Keep It Dark**[24] 5928 7-8-6 65 AbbieWibrew[(7)] 9 36
(William Knight) *awkwardly away: a towards rr* **16/1**

58.39s (-1.81) **Going Correction** -0.25s/f (Firm)
WFA 3 from 5yo+ 1lb **10** Ran SP% **115.7**
Speed ratings (Par 103): **104,103,102,102,101 100,98,97,96,88**
CSF £58.24 CT £369.65 TOTE £5.50: £2.20, £4.30, £2.60; EX 48.40 Trifecta £359.20.
Owner Mr & Mrs K Finch **Bred** R B R Burtt & D R Botterill **Trained** Liphook, Hants

FOCUS
This was between the first four in the final furlong, with the fifth picking up ground late on. Modest form for the track, rated around the second.

T/Plt: £30.70 to a £1 stake. Pool: £89,175.33. 2,117.87 winning units. T/Qpdt: £16.40 to a £1 stake. Pool: £53,52.51. 240.6 winning units. **Tim Mitchell**

6622 KEMPTON (A.W) (R-H)

Wednesday, September 21

OFFICIAL GOING: Polytrack: standard to slow

Wind: Light behind Weather: Fine

6670 RACINGUK.COM NURSERY H'CAP 7f (P)

5:40 (5:41) (Class 6) (0-65,65) 2-Y-O **£2,264** (£673; £336; £168) **Stalls** Low

Form RPR

6013 **1** **Glenys The Menace (FR)**[14] 6236 2-9-3 **61** KierenFox 1 66
(John Best) *reluctant to load: restrained bhd ldr on rail: swtchd to centre over 2f out: pushed along over 1f out: shifted sltly lft ins fnl f: kpt on wl to ld fnl stride* **6/1**

5022 **2** *shd* **Wentwell Yesterday (IRE)**[9] 6412 2-8-13 **57** WilliamCarson 3 61
(Jamie Osborne) *settled bhd ldrs: rdn over 1f out: led 1f out: kpt on wl ins fnl f: hdd fnl stride* **5/2**[1]

0021 **3** *1 1/4* **Altiko Tommy (IRE)**[20] 6045 2-9-5 **63** LiamKeniry 8 64
(George Baker) *settled in mid-div: rdn on inner over 2f out: kpt on but no threat to ldng pair* **5/1**[2]

060 **4** *shd* **Daring Guest (IRE)**[19] 6071 2-9-3 **61** AdamKirby 4 62
(George Margarson) *in rr: swtchd to outer over 2f out: rdn and stl plenty to do over 1f out: kpt on strly ins fnl f: checked sltly nring fin: nvr nrr* **11/2**[3]

0000 **5** *1/2* **Aventus (IRE)**[11] 6313 2-8-11 **55** (b[1]) ShaneKelly 7 54
(Richard Hughes) *in rr on outer: rdn over 2f out: kpt on fr over 1f out* **33/1**

0512 **6** *1 1/2* **Tennessee Rose (IRE)**[14] 6236 2-9-4 **62** RichardKingscote 2 57
(Tom Dascombe) *settled in rr: rdn on inner over 2f out: kpt on tl wknd fnl f* **8/1**

4044 **7** *1* **Primrose Place**[35] 5543 2-9-5 **63** [1] KieranO'Neill 9 56
(Richard Hannon) *cl up bhd ldrs: rdn over 2f out: one pce over 1f out* **16/1**

0504 **8** *2 3/4* **Sadierosecllfford (IRE)**[9] 6412 2-8-9 **58** GeorgeWood(5) 10 43
(Denis Quinn) *sn led: nudged along over 2f out: rdn over 1f out: hdd 1f out: wknd ins fnl f* **20/1**

5026 **9** *1 1/2* **Waves (IRE)**[21] 6033 2-9-4 **62** OisinMurphy 6 43
(Eve Johnson Houghton) *wnt to post early: in rr: prog over 2f out: rdn 2f out: kpt on wl fr over 1f out: nrst fin* **10/1**

4433 **10** *5* **Dark Hero (IRE)**[8] 6440 2-9-5 **63** MichaelJMMurphy 14 31
(Charles Hills) *pressed ldr on outer: rdn along over 2f out: sn lost pl and no imp over 2f out* **12/1**

545 **11** *2 1/4* **Alice's Dream**[24] 5930 2-9-6 **64** LiamJones 13 26
(Marco Botti) *in rr of mid-div on outer: impr position on bnd: rdn along over 2f out: one pce fr over 1f out* **20/1**

2210 **12** *2 3/4* **Princess Way (IRE)**[10] 6388 2-9-2 **60** JimmyFortune 12 14
(David Evans) *mid-div early: lost pl 1/2-way and nr rr: rdn over 2f out: sn no imp* **14/1**

550 **13** *4 1/2* **Ciel Rouge**[77] 4016 2-8-13 **57** AdamBeschizza 5
(Charlie Wallis) *settled in mid-div: rdn along over 2f out: sn lft bhd* **33/1**

1m 26.41s (0.41) **Going Correction** -0.025s/f (Stan) **13** Ran SP% **130.8**
Speed ratings (Par 93): **96,95,94,94,93 92,90,87,86,80 77,74,69**
CSF £22.47 CT £89.26 TOTE £9.50: £2.80, £1.50, £2.40; EX 28.40 Trifecta £107.10.
Owner Curtis, Malt & Jenkins **Bred** Haras D'Etreham & Georges Lugon **Trained** Oad Street, Kent

FOCUS
A clear, mild evening and, with the rejuvenated surface still bedding in, the official description of the Polytrack was once again given as standard to slow. Just a modest nursery, but the right horses came to the fore and there's no reason to suspect that the form won't hold up. The winner took a small step forward.

6671 32RED.COM MAIDEN STKS (DIV I) 7f (P)

6:10 (6:11) (Class 5) 2-Y-O **£2,911** (£866; £432; £216) **Stalls** Low

Form RPR

1 **Sultan Baybars** 2-9-5 0 AndreaAtzeni 6 82+
(Roger Varian) *carried lft s: restrained in mid-div: t.k.h bnd: shkn up 2f out and gd prog in centre ins fnl f: led nr fin: pushed out: cosily* **5/4**[1]

2 *3/4* **Cinque Port** 2-9-5 0 ShaneKelly 3 77
(Richard Hughes) *wnt lft s: sn led: rdn over 1f out: kpt on wl tl hdd nr fin* **50/1**

3 *1 1/2* **Dutch Quality** 2-9-5 0 [1] HarryBentley 2 73
(Marco Botti) *settled bhd ldr on inner: rdn 2f out: kpt on wl tl no ex ins fnl f* **8/1**

5 **4** *nk* **Al Mansor (IRE)**[15] 6211 2-9-5 0 SeanLevey 5 72
(Richard Hannon) *carried lft s: sn settled bhd ldr: rdn 2f out: kpt on* **9/2**[3]

5 *6* **Alkashaaf (USA)** 2-9-5 0 PaulHanagan 8 56
(John Gosden) *s.s: t.k.h in mid-div on outer and carried hd high: lost pl ent st: sn rdn and wknd* **7/2**[2]

6 *1 1/2* **Noble Ballad** 2-9-5 0 FMBerry 9 52
(Ralph Beckett) *s.s: sn in rr: pushed along over 2f out: sn no imp* **12/1**

7 *2 1/4* **Broughtons Admiral** 2-9-5 0 TimmyMurphy 10 46
(Willie Musson) *settled in last trio: pushed along over 2f out: sn lft bhd: pushed out after* **50/1**

8 *1 1/2* **Magdalene Fox** 2-9-5 0 GeorgeBaker 7 42
(Ed Dunlop) *settled in last trio: rdn 2f out: sn no imp* **20/1**

9 *4 1/2* **Mac's Kyllachy** 2-9-5 0 FrederikTylicki 1 30
(James Fanshawe) *settled in mid-divsion on inner: nudged along early to hold pl: rdn over 2f out: wknd qckly fr 2f out* **16/1**

1m 28.48s (2.48) **Going Correction** -0.025s/f (Stan) **9** Ran SP% **118.2**
Speed ratings (Par 95): **84,83,81,81,74 72,69,68,63**
CSF £94.03 TOTE £2.60: £1.20, £5.40, £2.40; EX 98.40 Trifecta £425.20.
Owner Nurlan Bizakov **Bred** Hesmonds Stud Ltd **Trained** Newmarket, Suffolk

FOCUS
Only one had previous experience in the first division of this maiden, and they went steady early on. That shouldn't detract from the taking performance of the winner though and the first four came clear. The winner is likely to rate a lot higher.

6672 32RED.COM MAIDEN STKS (DIV II) 7f (P)

6:40 (6:41) (Class 5) 2-Y-O **£2,911** (£866; £432; £216) **Stalls** Low

Form RPR

53 **1** **First Up (IRE)**[17] 6159 2-9-5 0 JimCrowley 4 86+
(Jeremy Noseda) *settled in cl up 4th on inner: shkn up jst over 2f out: qcknd up smartly to ld over 1f out: sn clr under hands and heels ins fnl f: impressive* **11/10**[1]

35 **2** *4 1/2* **Muzeel (IRE)**[70] 4274 2-9-5 0 PaulHanagan 10 74
(Sir Michael Stoute) *settled in 3rd on outer: rdn 2f out: kpt on to take 2nd 1f out: no ch w wnr ins fnl f* **15/8**[2]

5304 **3** *1 1/4* **Spiritofedinburgh (IRE)**[22] 5989 2-9-5 70 StevieDonohoe 2 71
(Brendan Powell) *sn led: rdn over 2f out: kpt on tl hdd and lft bhd by wnr over 1f out: lost 2nd 1f out: kpt on one pce* **14/1**

0 **4** *1* **Broughtons Knight**[93] 3463 2-9-5 0 TimmyMurphy 8 68
(Willie Musson) *settled in 6th: rdn over 2f out: lost pl 2f out: sme prog fr over 1f out* **66/1**

5 *1* **Wootyhoot (FR)** 2-9-5 0 FrederikTylicki 9 65
(James Fanshawe) *settled in 5th: rdn along turning into st: kpt on one pce tl wknd ins fnl f* **16/1**

35 **6** *hd* **Mullarkey**[1] 6655 2-9-5 0 KierenFox 6 65
(John Best) *pressed ldr: disp ld fr over 4f out: stl upsides 2f out: sn rdn and no ex: wknd ins fnl f* **14/1**

7 *3 3/4* **Solent Meads (IRE)** 2-9-5 0 RichardKingscote 1 55
(Daniel Kubler) *s.s: in last pair: struggling fr over 3f out: sn no ex* **50/1**

8 *4 1/2* **Fox King** 2-9-5 0 FMBerry 5 42
(Ralph Beckett) *in last pair: rdn along over 2f out: sn lft bhd and hld* **5/1**[3]

1m 26.59s (0.59) **Going Correction** -0.025s/f (Stan) **8** Ran SP% **121.7**
Speed ratings (Par 95): **95,89,88,87,86 85,81,76**
CSF £3.65 TOTE £2.50: £1.10, £1.30, £3.10; EX 4.10 Trifecta £18.00.
Owner S Burns, M Smyth & D Studholme **Bred** Eledy Srl **Trained** Newmarket, Suffolk

FOCUS
More experience on show than the first division and they went nearly two seconds quicker courtesy of the runaway winner. The third and sixth help to anchor the form.

6673 £10 FREE BET AT 32REDSPORT.COM MAIDEN STKS 6f (P)

7:10 (7:11) (Class 5) 2-Y-O **£2,911** (£866; £432; £216) **Stalls** Low

Form RPR

44 **1** **Glorious Rocket**[53] 4856 2-9-5 0 AdamKirby 6 78+
(Luca Cumani) *hld up under restraint in mid-divsion: rdn bhd ldrs over 2f out: str run to ld ent fnl f: pressed fnl 110yds: plld out more cl home* **7/2**[2]

3 **2** *nk* **Etikaal**[19] 6086 2-9-5 0 PaulHanagan 9 77+
(Simon Crisford) *cl up in 4th: swtchd to outer and rdn along 2f out: upsides and ev ch ent fnl f: kpt on wl to press wnr wl ins fnl f: hld fnl strides* **11/10**[1]

66 **3** *2 1/2* **Zebulon (IRE)**[18] 6108 2-9-5 0 SeanLevey 8 70
(Richard Hannon) *wnt rt s: sn chsd ldr: upsides and ev ch ent fnl f: kpt on one pce fr over 110yds out* **6/1**[3]

0 **4** *1 1/2* **Abundant Courage (IRE)**[48] 5077 2-9-5 0 JimmyFortune 5 65
(Brian Meehan) *sn led: rdn and narrow led over 1f out: hdd ent fnl f: wknd nr fin* **20/1**

6 **5** *1 3/4* **Dandy Roll (IRE)**[148] 1736 2-9-5 0 FMBerry 4 60
(Ralph Beckett) *chsd ldrs: rdn along over 2f out: upsides on inner and ev ch ent fnl f: no ex and wknd ins fnl f* **16/1**

0 **6** *nse* **Aqshion Stations**[27] 5792 2-9-5 0 ShaneKelly 3 60
(William Jarvis) *bhd ldrs in mid-div on inner: rdn along beside wnr over 2f out: kpt on one pce fr over 1f out* **66/1**

7 *shd* **Oud Metha Bridge (IRE)** 2-9-5 0 GeorgeBaker 12 59+
(Ed Dunlop) *styd wd early: sn hld up in rr: rdn along over 2f out: no imp tl kpt on again fr over 1f out* **33/1**

6 **8** *1 1/4* **Moonstone Rock**[51] 4951 2-9-0 0 FergusSweeney 2 51
(Jim Boyle) *tk fierce hold in rr: rdn 2f out on inner: sme prog fr over 1f out* **25/1**

9 *nk* **Kingofmerrows (IRE)** 2-9-5 0 JimCrowley 1 55
(David Evans) *hld up in last: rdn along ent st: sn no imp and hld* **16/1**

10 *3/4* **Al Haayelah** 2-9-0 0 [1] JackMitchell 7 48
(Roger Varian) *in rr and t.k.h: rdn along in rr over 2f whn rn green: kpt on after* **6/1**[3]

3U **11** *1 1/2* **Luxford**[12] 6295 2-9-0 0 KierenFox 11 43
(John Best) *mid-div on inner: rdn along over 2f out: wknd fr over 1f out* **66/1**

0 **12** *6* **Sixth Of June**[20] 6061 2-9-0 0 FrederikTylicki 10 25
(Rod Millman) *racd wd in mid-div: struggling ent st: sn rdn and no imp: pushed out fr over 1f out* **66/1**

1m 12.99s (-0.11) **Going Correction** -0.025s/f (Stan) **12** Ran SP% **126.2**
Speed ratings (Par 95): **99,98,95,93,90 90,90,89,88,87 85,77**
CSF £7.85 TOTE £5.10: £1.60, £1.20, £2.40; EX 10.10 Trifecta £32.30.
Owner Kangyu International Racing (HK) Limited **Bred** Whatton Manor Stud **Trained** Newmarket, Suffolk

FOCUS
Some fair types have taken this maiden in the past couple of years, but this renewal looked modest in comparison. It did, however, play host to a well-fought finish between the market principals.

6674 32RED CASINO MEDIAN AUCTION MAIDEN STKS 1m (P)

7:40 (7:43) (Class 5) 3-5-Y-O **£2,911** (£866; £432; £216) **Stalls** Low

Form RPR

30-5 **1** **Tiercel**[158] 1474 3-9-5 79 AndreaAtzeni 4 91+
(Roger Varian) *a gng wl in mid-div on rail: gd prog over 2f out: shkn up over 1f out and sn led: nudged out after: easily* **4/6**[1]

3 **2** *1 1/2* **Right Rebel**[42] 5300 4-9-1 0 EoinWalsh(3) 6 76
(Alan Bailey) *settled bhd ldr on rail: led over 2f out: sn rdn: hdd over 1f out: no ex after* **9/2**[2]

3 *1 1/4* **Issue** 3-9-0 0 [1] DanielMuscutt 8 73
(James Fanshawe) *uns rdr s: settled bhd ldrs: rdn 2f out: kpt on one pce fnl f* **9/1**

4 *7* **Loveatfirstsight** 3-9-0 0 AdamBeschizza 3 56
(Michael Attwater) *in rr: rdn 2f out: kpt on wl fr over 1f out: nvr nrr* **66/1**

5 *2 3/4* **Sovrano Dolce (IRE)** 3-8-7 0 KevinLundie(7) 14 50
(Mike Murphy) *s.s: hld up in rr and rn green: rdn 2f out: sme prog fr over 1f out* **50/1**

02 **6** *1/2* **Secret Dreamer**[26] 5843 4-9-9 0 AdamKirby 10 53
(Kevin Morgan) *sn led: hdd after 5f but remained cl up: rdn along over 2f out: kpt on one pce* **6/1**[3]

7 *1 1/2* **Lord Topper** 3-9-5 0 JimCrowley 9 50
(Charles Hills) *stater slowly: in rr: rdn over 2f out: sn hld* **10/1**

54 **8** *1/2* **Dalness Express**[69] 4310 3-9-0 0 CiaranMckee(5) 2 49
(John O'Shea) *hld up in rr: checked early: rdn over 2f out: fnd nil and kpt on one pce after* **100/1**

0 **9** *2 3/4* **Miss Geronimo**[28] 5766 4-9-4 0 SamHitchcott 13 37
(Ken Cunningham-Brown) *t.k.h: led after 5f: rdn along over 2f out and sn hdd: wknd after* **100/1**

0 **10** *1/2* **Clandon**[31] 5681 3-9-0 0 PaddyBradley(5) 11 41
(Brett Johnson) *settled in rr-div: awkward bnds: rdn over 2f out: one pce after* **100/1**

0 **11** *13* **Autumn Chorus**[42] 5300 3-9-0 0 DannyBrock 12 5
(John Bridger) *settled bhd ldrs on outer: rdn over 2f out: sn losing pl and wknd fr over 1f out* **100/1**

P **12** *29* **Royal Phoenix**[60] 4639 3-9-0 0 FergusSweeney 1
(Gary Moore) *restless in stalls: a in rr: eased over 1f out: t.o* **66/1**

1m 40.41s (0.61) **Going Correction** -0.025s/f (Stan)
WFA 3 from 4yo 4lb **12** Ran SP% **120.5**
Speed ratings (Par 103): **95,93,92,85,82 82,80,80,77,76 63,34**
CSF £4.04 TOTE £1.80: £1.10, £1.50, £2.20; EX 4.90 Trifecta £22.00.
Owner Prince A A Faisal **Bred** Nawara Stud Co Ltd **Trained** Newmarket, Suffolk
■ White Valiant was withdrawn. Price at time of withdrawal 50-1. Rule 4 does not apply.

FOCUS
No depth to this modest maiden, with the front five in the market bet to the exclusion of the rest of the field and the odds-on favourite taking it comfortably. The form is rated around the second.

6675 32RED H'CAP (LONDON MIDDLE DISTANCE SERIES QUALIFIER) 1m 3f (P)
8:10 (8:12) (Class 3) (0-95,91) 3-Y-O
£7,158 (£2,143; £1,071; £535; £267; £134) **Stalls** Low

Form RPR

0-40 **1** **Mengli Khan (IRE)**[143] 1891 3-9-7 **90** JimCrowley 6 102
(Hugo Palmer) *chsd ldr: led gng wl over 2f out: sn rdn: kpt on wl and asserted ins fnl f* **7/1**

4241 **2** *3* **Sam Missile (IRE)**[9] 6417 3-9-8 **91** 6ex DanielMuscutt 1 98
(James Fanshawe) *hld up in 7th on rail: n.m.r and rdn over 2f out: kpt on wl fr over 1f out to hold 2nd* **7/2**[3]

-463 **3** *hd* **Red Rannagh (IRE)**[25] 5874 3-9-3 **86** (t) ShaneKelly 3 92
(David Simcock) *hld up in rr: cl up in rr ent st: rdn 2f out on inner: kpt on wl over 1f out in duel for 2nd: jst hld nr fin* **11/4**[1]

5-23 **4** *3/4* **Fleeting Visit**[12] 6301 3-8-12 **84** EdwardGreatrex(3) 2 89
(Eve Johnson Houghton) *settled in 6th: nudged along 5f out to hold pl: rdn wl over 2f out: kpt on wl fr over 1f out to press for a pl: nrst fin* **8/1**

4064 **5** *3* **Royal Reserve**[20] 6048 3-8-13 **82** MartinDwyer 5 82
(William Muir) *racd in 3rd: rdn over 2f out: no ex fr over 1f out* **8/1**

1 **6** *1/2* **Flymetothestars**[232] 428 3-9-2 **85** LukeMorris 8 84
(Sir Mark Prescott Bt) *5th on outer: pushed along on bnd ent st and c wd: kpt on one pce after* **3/1**[2]

1302 **7** *1* **Goldenfield (IRE)**[29] 5738 3-8-10 **84** (p) HectorCrouch(5) 4 81
(Gary Moore) *sn led: rdn wl over 3f out: hdd over 2f out: wknd sn after* **20/1**

1 **8** *6* **Illustrissime (USA)**[41] 5349 3-9-7 **90** AdamKirby 7 77
(David Loughnane) *settled in 4th: rdn over 2f out: no ex and wknd fr over 1f out* **25/1**

2m 17.81s (-4.09) **Going Correction** -0.025s/f (Stan) **8** Ran SP% **117.2**
Speed ratings (Par 105): **113,110,110,110,107 107,106,102**
CSF £32.58 CT £84.86 TOTE £10.10: £2.70, £1.30, £1.40; EX 39.60 Trifecta £121.10.
Owner V I Araci **Bred** Ballylinch Stud **Trained** Newmarket, Suffolk

FOCUS
The feature was a decent middle-distance handicap, with the form looking right up to scratch for the grade. The first two improved.

6676 32RED ON THE APP STORE H'CAP 1m 4f (P)
8:40 (8:42) (Class 4) (0-85,83) 4-Y-O+ **£4,690** (£1,395; £697; £348) **Stalls** Centre

Form RPR

0431 **1** **Charlie Bear**[18] 6128 4-9-7 **83** TimmyMurphy 1 91
(Jamie Osborne) *settled in 3rd: shkn up over 2f out: rdn and led over 1f out: pressed ins fnl f but a doing enough: drvn out* **7/4**[1]

/040 **2** *1/2* **Artful Rogue (IRE)**[20] 6065 5-8-12 **74** JimCrowley 4 81
(Amanda Perrett) *sn led: rdn over 2f out: hdd over 1f out: kpt on again ins fnl f to take 2nd cl home* **6/1**

3135 **3** *3/4* **Dolphin Village (IRE)**[19] 6074 6-9-2 **83** CharlieBennett(5) 2 89
(Jane Chapple-Hyam) *settled in 4th on inner: rdn over 2f out: 1/2 l down on wnr ent fnl f: wknd cl home and lost 2nd nr fin* **10/1**

-343 **4** *3/4* **Nonios (IRE)**[18] 6128 4-8-12 **74** ShaneKelly 3 79
(David Simcock) *hld up in rr: rdn over 2f out: kpt on ent fnl f but nvr getting to plcd horses* **7/2**[2]

0432 **5** *2 1/4* **Plymouth Sound**[20] 6065 4-9-3 **79** (b) JohnFahy 5 80
(Eve Johnson Houghton) *hld up in 5th: rdn over 2f out: kpt on tl wknd ent fnl f* **7/1**

2025 **6** *2 1/2* **Sarsted**[20] 6050 4-9-6 **82** (p) OisinMurphy 7 79
(Hughie Morrison) *chsd ldr: shkn up on bnd ent st: sn rdn: wknd fr over 1f out* **5/1**[3]

2m 33.16s (-1.34) **Going Correction** -0.025s/f (Stan) **6** Ran SP% **111.1**
Speed ratings (Par 105): **103,102,102,101,100 98**
CSF £12.39 TOTE £2.30: £1.30, £2.80; EX 14.90 Trifecta £63.80.
Owner Michael Buckley **Bred** Lone Oak Stud Limited **Trained** Upper Lambourn, Berks

FOCUS
A fair handicap where a case could have been made for any of these. It was a bit unsatisfactory though, with a distinct lack of early pace. Ordinary form.

6677 RACING UK PROFITS RETURNED TO RACING H'CAP 6f (P)
9:10 (9:10) (Class 6) (0-60,60) 3-Y-O+ **£2,264** (£673; £336; £168) **Stalls** Low

Form RPR

3102 **1** **Assertive Agent**[47] 5105 6-9-6 **60** AdamKirby 2 66
(Tony Carroll) *hld up in mid-div: gd run up ins over 2f out: kpt on wl to ld 1f out: drvn out: jst hld on* **7/1**

0235 **2** *nse* **Arcanista (IRE)**[11] 6317 3-8-10 **59** [1] NicolaCurrie(7) 4 65
(Richard Hughes) *hld up in mid-div: rdn over 2f out: str run fr over 1f out to press wnr nring fin: jst failed* **14/1**

6002 **3** *1 1/4* **Oat Couture**[11] 6317 4-9-6 **60** (b) DaneO'Neill 3 62
(Henry Candy) *slowly away and hld up in rr: drvn along over 2f out: nt immediate rspnse tl over 1f out whn kpt on wl on outer to take 3rd post* **4/1**[2]

0003 **4** *shd* **Keiba (IRE)**[35] 5554 3-9-4 **60** (b[1]) ShaneKelly 5 62
(Gary Moore) *t.k.h bhd ldrs most of way: rdn and led briefly over 1f out: sn hdd and kpt on tl wknd wl ins fnl f: lost 3rd post* **7/2**[1]

3500 **5** *1/2* **Misu Pete**[20] 6051 4-9-6 **60** OisinMurphy 9 60
(Mark Usher) *chsd ldrs: rdn over 2f out: kpt on wl and ev ch over 1f out: hung lft and wknd wl ins fnl f* **12/1**

6266 **6** *3 1/4* **Swendab (IRE)**[44] 5236 8-8-13 **58** (v) CiaranMckee(5) 7 49+
(John O'Shea) *half-rrd leaving stalls: sn rcvrd and led: hdd over 1f out: wknd after* **10/1**

1260 **7** *3/4* **Indus Valley (IRE)**[13] 6269 9-9-5 **59** SilvestreDeSousa 8 47
(Lee Carter) *t.k.h in rr on inner: rdn bhd wnr over 2f out: kpt on one pce after* **7/2**[1]

6440 **8** *3/4* **Zabdi**[14] 6237 3-9-2 **58** KierenFox 6 44
(Lee Carter) *in rr: rdn over 2f out: sn hld* **16/1**

5054 **9** *1/2* **Whaleweigh Station**[53] 4876 5-9-6 **60** (v) IrineuGoncalves 11 45
(J R Jenkins) *sltly hmpd s: a in rr* **22/1**

003 **10** *3 1/4* **Cool Angel (IRE)**[19] 6101 3-9-4 **60** (b) MartinDwyer 10 35+
(William Muir) *pushed up fr wd draw to press ldr: rdn over 2f out: sn struggling and wknd fr over 1f out* **33/1**

2-03 **11** *1 1/2* **Zippy**[11] 6317 3-9-4 **60** RichardKingscote 12 30
(Daniel Kubler) *in rr: prog on outer and cl up by half-way: rdn 2f out: sn wknd* **9/2**[3]

1m 12.91s (-0.19) **Going Correction** -0.025s/f (Stan)
WFA 3 from 4yo+ 2lb **11** Ran SP% **131.7**
Speed ratings (Par 101): **100,99,98,98,97 93,92,91,90,86 84**
CSF £112.89 CT £374.32 TOTE £4.70: £2.50, £3.00, £1.90; EX 72.40 Trifecta £321.80.
Owner Wedgewood Estates **Bred** Miss Liza Judd **Trained** Cropthorne, Worcs

FOCUS
A mix between some older established horses and some relatively unexposed 3yos in this moderate sprint handicap. The pace rather collapsed and the winner is rated back to her best.
T/Plt: £5.20 to a £1 stake. Pool: £68,096.33. 9,486.50 winning units. T/Qpdt: £1.80 to a £1 stake. Pool: £8,421.64. 3,354.64 winning units. **Cathal Gahan**

6213 REDCAR (L-H)
Wednesday, September 21

OFFICIAL GOING: Good to firm (9.2)
Wind: Light half behind Weather: Fine & dry

6678 RACINGUK.COM/HD NURSERY H'CAP 6f
2:10 (2:10) (Class 6) (0-60,60) 2-Y-O **£2,749** (£818; £408; £204) **Stalls** Centre

Form RPR

0354 **1** **Swallow Street (IRE)**[47] 5120 2-9-4 **57** (b[1]) DanielTudhope 16 63
(Jamie Osborne) *chsd ldrs: upsides and hung lft over 1f out: kpt on to ld last 50yds* **16/1**

0463 **2** *1* **Chickenfortea (IRE)**[15] 6213 2-9-4 **57** TomEaves 18 60
(Eric Alston) *w ldrs: led over 2f out: hdd and no ex last 50yds* **12/1**

3345 **3** *2 1/2* **Coverham (IRE)**[4] 6564 2-9-5 **58** (b) PJMcDonald 3 54
(James Bethell) *chsd ldrs: drvn over 2f out: edgd rt and kpt on same pce appr fnl f* **7/2**[1]

0026 **4** *1 1/4* **Sheila's Return**[9] 6419 2-9-2 **55** ConnorBeasley 17 47
(Bryan Smart) *mid-div: hdwy over 2f out: kpt on same pce over 1f out* **12/1**

000 **5** *3/4* **Lord Cooper**[19] 6071 2-9-6 **59** (t) RenatoSouza 5 49
(Jose Santos) *mid-div: hdwy over 2f out: kpt on fnl f* **16/1**

0000 **6** *1 1/2* **Gabridan (IRE)**[11] 6343 2-8-11 **50** (b[1]) TonyHamilton 1 35
(Richard Fahey) *w ldrs: one pce over 1f out* **20/1**

465 **7** *shd* **Peny Arcade**[27] 5798 2-9-0 **58** RowanScott(5) 8 43
(Alistair Whillans) *mid-div: hdwy over 2f out: kpt on fnl f* **16/1**

045 **8** *1* **Dream Team**[30] 5728 2-9-7 **60** PaulMulrennan 7 42
(Michael Dods) *chsd ldrs: drvn over 2f out: one pce* **7/1**[2]

000 **9** *1 1/4* **Magic Journey (IRE)**[56] 4765 2-9-5 **58** CamHardie 9 36
(John Quinn) *s.i.s: sn mid-div: effrt over 2f out: nvr a factor* **16/1**

0606 **10** *2 1/4* **Pontecarlo Boy**[7] 6473 2-8-12 **51** GeorgeChaloner 20 22
(Richard Whitaker) *in rr: kpt on fnl 2f: nvr a factor* **20/1**

0000 **11** *1* **Nobility (IRE)**[15] 6214 2-9-0 **56** RachelRichardson(3) 10 24
(Tim Easterby) *chsd ldrs: drvn over 2f out: one pce* **16/1**

540 **12** *1 3/4* **Vocalisation (IRE)**[23] 5966 2-9-0 **53** SilvestreDeSousa 2 31
(John Weymes) *led: hdd over 2f out: wknd and heavily eased last 150yds* **11/1**

443 **13** *1/2* **Luv U Always**[33] 5606 2-9-1 **54** GrahamLee 19 15
(Iain Jardine) *s.i.s: in rr: sme hdwy over 1f out: nvr on terms* **14/1**

0000 **14** *nk* **Can Can Dream**[25] 5861 2-8-3 **47** NathanEvans(5) 12 8
(Olly Williams) *chsd ldrs: drvn over 2f out: lost pl over 1f out* **66/1**

050 **15** *2 1/2* **Where's Stewart**[25] 5884 2-7-13 **45** (v[1]) KieranSchofield(7) 4
(Nigel Tinkler) *s.i.s: lost pl over 2f out* **50/1**

036 **16** *1 3/4* **Blastofmagic**[15] 6214 2-9-7 **60** PhillipMakin 13 8
(David Dennis) *mid-div: drvn over 2f out: sn lost pl: eased clsng stages* **12/1**

3400 **17** *1 1/4* **Nifty Niece (IRE)**[30] 5712 2-9-3 **56** RoystonFfrench 15
(Ann Duffield) *in rr: bhd whn eased clsng stages* **25/1**

000 **18** *1 3/4* **Henrietta's Dream**[23] 5974 2-8-6 **45** [1] DuranFentiman 6
(John Wainwright) *s.i.s: a in rr: bhd whn eased clsng stages* **100/1**

4020 **19** *2 1/2* **Coco La Belle (IRE)**[8] 6446 2-9-3 **56** DavidAllan 14
(Tim Easterby) *in rr: bhd whn eased clsng stages* **10/1**[3]

1m 9.68s (-2.12) **Going Correction** -0.25s/f (Firm) **19** Ran SP% **129.1**
Speed ratings (Par 93): **104,102,99,97,96 94,94,93,91,88 87,84,84,83,80 78,76,74,70**
CSF £192.04 CT £864.99 TOTE £19.00: £3.80, £3.70, £1.50, £3.70; EX 228.90 Trifecta £2431.00.
Owner The London Partnership **Bred** R P Ryan **Trained** Upper Lambourn, Berks

FOCUS
A moderate nursery, three of the first four home came from the high numbered stalls.

6679 BRITISH STALLION STUDS EBF MAIDEN STKS (DIV I) 7f
2:45 (2:46) (Class 5) 2-Y-O **£3,234** (£962; £481; £240) **Stalls** Centre

Form RPR

642 **1** **Moi Moi Moi (IRE)**[48] 5072 2-9-5 73 JoeFanning 6 77+
(Brian Meehan) *trckd ldrs: cl up 1/2-way: led wl over 1f out: rdn and edgd lft ins fnl f: drvn out* **2/1**[1]

06 **2** *1 1/4* **Cool Climate (IRE)**[23] 5959 2-9-5 0 JackGarritty 4 73
(Richard Fahey) *cl up: led 1/2-way: pushed along over 2f out: hdd wl over 1f out: sn rdn and ev ch tl drvn and kpt on same pce ins fnl f* **7/2**[2]

3 **3** *2 1/2* **Buccaneers Cove (IRE)**[22] 6009 2-9-5 0 TonyHamilton 1 66
(Richard Fahey) *cl up: pushed along over 2f out: rdn along wl over 1f out: wknd ent fnl f* **7/2**[2]

4 *4 1/2* **Fleetfoot Jack (IRE)** 2-9-5 0 DanielTudhope 5 54+
(David O'Meara) *trckd ldrs: hdwy over 2f out: rdn over 1f out: kpt on fnl f* **11/2**[3]

0 **5** *1 1/2* **Teddy Edward**[25] 5885 2-9-5 0 [1] GeorgeChaloner 3 50
(Richard Whitaker) *trckd ldrs: pushed along 3f out: rdn 2f out: sn hung lft and wknd* **100/1**

6 *2* **Lively Lily** 2-9-0 0 PJMcDonald 2 40
(Ann Duffield) *trckd ldrs: cl up 4f out: pushed along wl over 2f out: rdn wl over 1f out: grad wknd* **14/1**

7 *1 1/4* **Lesanti** 2-9-5 0 RoystonFfrench 7 41
(Ed McMahon) *towards rr: rdn along 3f out: sn outpcd and behind* **22/1**

00 **8** *2* **Bodacious Name (IRE)**[19] 6099 2-9-5 0 JasonHart 8 36
(John Quinn) *a towards rr* **66/1**

0 **9** 4 1/2 **Shannah Bint Eric**[61] 4603 2-9-0 0 TomEaves 9 19
(Kevin Ryan) *slt ld to 1/2-way: cl up: rdn along wl over 2f out: sn wknd* **28/1**

10 4 **Siyahamba (IRE)** 2-9-5 0 ConnorBeasley 10 13
(Bryan Smart) *s.i.s: green and sn pushed along: a bhd* **14/1**

1m 22.94s (-1.56) **Going Correction** -0.25s/f (Firm) **10** Ran SP% **116.8**
Speed ratings (Par 95): **98,96,93,88,86 84,83,80,75,71**
CSF £8.77 TOTE £3.10: £1.10, £1.90, £1.70; EX 11.40 Trifecta £30.10.
Owner Sunningdale Partners **Bred** Niarchos Family **Trained** Manton, Wilts

FOCUS
The right horses came clear in what was an ordinary maiden. The first three showed improvement.

6680 WEATHERBYS "WE'VE GOT PEDIGREE" H'CAP 5f
3:20 (3:20) (Class 5) (0-70,70) 3-Y-O+ **£3,234** (£962; £481; £240) **Stalls** Centre

Form RPR

5004 **1** **Bronze Beau**[21] 6023 9-8-11 **60** (tp) ShaneGray 9 67
(Kristin Stubbs) *w ldrs: led last 100yds: drvn out* **16/1**

3510 **2** nk **Run Rio Run (IRE)**[11] 6341 3-9-0 **64** (p) ConnorBeasley 10 70
(Michael Dods) *chsd ldrs: kpt on to take 2nd nr fin* **20/1**

3404 **3** 3/4 **Lady Nayef**[13] 6248 3-9-2 **66** (t) RobertWinston 4 69
(John Butler) *w ldr: led and edgd rt over 1f out: hdd and no ex last 100yds* **14/1**

1360 **4** nk **Classic Pursuit**[19] 6072 5-9-6 **69** (p) SilvestreDeSousa 8 71
(Ivan Furtado) *sn bhd: hdwy over 1f out: swtchd rt and styd on strly* **7/1**[2]

001 **5** nk **Storm Trooper (IRE)**[11] 6341 5-9-4 **67** RoystonFfrench 15 68
(David Nicholls) *mid-div: effrt over 2f out: chsng ldrs over 1f out: kpt on wl fnl 100yds* **4/1**[1]

000 **6** 1 **Savannah Beau**[37] 5479 4-9-7 **70** (p[1]) SamJames 6 70
(Marjorie Fife) *hmpd s: in rr: hdwy over 2f out: kpt on same pce fnl f* **7/1**[2]

0400 **7** shd **Captain Dunne (IRE)**[11] 6324 11-9-0 **66** RachelRichardson(3) 5 63
(Tim Easterby) *wnt rt s: sn chsng ldrs: kpt on same pce appr fnl f* **12/1**

2433 **8** shd **Andalusite**[10] 6361 3-8-5 **60** (p) JordanVaughan(5) 11 57
(Ed McMahon) *mid-div: hdwy over 2f out: hung lft over 1f out: kpt on same pce* **9/1**

3245 **9** 1 1/4 **Razin' Hell**[25] 5867 5-9-5 **68** (v) GrahamLee 16 60+
(John Balding) *in rr: hdwy over 2f out: one pce over 1f out* **14/1**

0502 **10** 1 1/2 **Tinsill**[21] 6023 5-8-7 **56** oh6 (p) AndrewMullen 3 43
(Nigel Tinkler) *mid-div: hdwy to chse ldrs over 2f out: wknd fnl 150yds* **16/1**

5124 **11** hd **See Vermont**[11] 6341 8-9-1 **64** (p) PaulMulrennan 12 50
(Rebecca Bastiman) *in rr and sn drvn along: sme hdwy over 2f out: fdd last 100yds* **16/1**

550 **12** 1 1/4 **Ruby's Day**[7] 6476 7-9-2 **65** (v) TomEaves 2 47
(David Brown) *in rr: sme hdwy and hung bdly lft over 2f out: wknd fnl f* **33/1**

4400 **13** 3/4 **Pavers Star**[27] 5804 7-8-7 **56** oh5 (p) JoeFanning 14 35
(Noel Wilson) *chsd ldrs: wknd over 1f out* **40/1**

3046 **14** nk **Sunnyside Bob (IRE)**[63] 4521 3-9-2 **66** PJMcDonald 1 44
(Neville Bycroft) *mid-div: drvn over 2f out: nvr a threat* **33/1**

0020 **15** nk **Hit The Lights (IRE)**[38] 5439 6-8-10 **66** DanielleMooney(7) 13 43
(David Nicholls) *mid-div: drvn over 2f out: nvr a factor* **16/1**

0160 **16** hd **Annie Salts**[13] 6248 3-9-1 **65** DavidAllan 7 41
(Chris Dwyer) *led: hdd over 1f out: wknd* **25/1**

506 **17** 1 1/4 **Fyrecracker (IRE)**[15] 6215 5-9-4 **67** KevinStott 18 39
(Grant Tuer) *a towards rr* **8/1**[3]

3140 **18** 1 1/2 **A J Cook (IRE)**[37] 5483 6-8-7 **56** oh4 (p) BarryMcHugh 17 22
(Ron Barr) *s.i.s: a in rr* **33/1**

56.9s (-1.70) **Going Correction** -0.25s/f (Firm)
WFA 3 from 4yo+ 1lb **18** Ran SP% **130.5**
Speed ratings (Par 103): **103,102,101,100,100 98,98,98,96,94 93,91,90,90,89 89,87,84**
CSF £324.78 CT £4575.06 TOTE £21.80: £4.50, £5.60, £3.80, £2.60; EX 431.80.
Owner D Arundale **Bred** Meon Valley Stud **Trained** Norton, N Yorks

FOCUS
A modest but competitive sprint. The principals were always prominent.

6681 WEATHERBYS THOROUGHBRED SALES GUIDE NURSERY H'CAP 1m
3:55 (3:58) (Class 6) (0-65,65) 2-Y-O **£2,749** (£818; £408; £204) **Stalls** Centre

Form RPR

006 **1** **Crystal Dome**[31] 5676 2-9-7 **65** PaulMulrennan 14 70+
(Ed Dunlop) *hld up in rr: smooth hdwy on outer over 2f out: chal over 1f out: rdn and green ent fnl f: slt ld whn wandered bdly ins fnl f: drvn and edgd lft nr fin: kpt on* **10/1**

0053 **2** nk **Reinstorm**[18] 6130 2-8-11 **55** TonyHamilton 13 57
(Richard Fahey) *trckd ldrs: hdwy 2f out and sn cl up: rdn ent fnl f and ev ch: drvn and kpt on wl towards fin* **14/1**

0404 **3** 1 **Vinnievanbaileys**[20] 6045 2-9-2 **60** (b) SilvestreDeSousa 12 61
(Chris Dwyer) *cl up: led over 5f out: pushed along over 2f out: rdn wl over 1f out: drvn and hdd narrowly ins fnl f: hld whn n.m.r and sltly hmpd towards fin* **10/1**

006 **4** 1 1/2 **John T Chance (IRE)**[26] 5820 2-8-10 **54** JoeFanning 4 52
(Brian Meehan) *towards rr: gd hdwy on outer to chse ldrs over 3f out: rdn to chal wl over 1f out: ev ch tl drvn and kpt on same pce fnl f* **9/1**[3]

124 **5** 2 **London Grammar (IRE)**[8] 6446 2-9-6 **64** PJMcDonald 9 56
(John Quinn) *midfield: hdwy whn n.m.r and sltly hmpd 3f out: rdn to chse ldrs 2f out: sn drvn and kpt on same pce appr fnl f* **6/1**[2]

050 **6** shd **Dyna Might**[30] 5728 2-8-7 **51** AndrewMullen 6 42
(Ollie Pears) *dwlt and towards rr: pushed along over 3f out: rdn and hdwy 2f out: kpt on wl u.p fnl f* **33/1**

4405 **7** shd **Traveltalk (IRE)**[27] 5796 2-9-7 **65** (p) DaleSwift 7 56
(Brian Ellison) *cl up: rdn along wl over 1f out and ev ch tl drvn and wknd ent fnl f* **14/1**

000 **8** 1 3/4 **Hazy Manor (IRE)**[43] 5266 2-9-1 **59** GrahamGibbons 16 46
(Tom Dascombe) *slt ld : hdd over 5f out: cl up: rdn along wl over 2f out: drvn wl over 1f out: grad wknd* **28/1**

0653 **9** 1 **Lil's Affair (IRE)**[27] 5799 2-8-8 **52** ConnorBeasley 11 37
(Bryan Smart) *towards rr: hdwy 2f out: sn rdn and kpt on fnl f* **20/1**

3005 **10** 1/2 **He's A Toff (IRE)**[15] 6213 2-9-2 **60** (b) DavidAllan 10 43
(Tim Easterby) *towards rr: sme hdwy 2f out: sn rdn and plugged on fnl f* **9/2**[1]

0450 **11** 2 **Sheriff Garrett (IRE)**[15] 6213 2-9-1 **62** RachelRichardson(3) 15 41
(Tim Easterby) *chsd ldrs on outer: rdn along 3f out: sn wknd* **16/1**

0065 **12** 2 **Melcano**[13] 6253 2-8-10 **54** JamesSullivan 1 28
(Shaun Harris) *dwlt: a towards rr* **25/1**

0564 **13** 2 3/4 **Babalugats (IRE)**[21] 6026 2-8-3 **47** DuranFentiman 2 14
(Tim Easterby) *a towards rr* **14/1**

000 **14** 3 3/4 **Shadow Of Hercules (IRE)**[32] 5637 2-8-3 **47** [1] CamHardie 3 5
(Michael Mullineaux) *stmbld sltly s: sn chsng ldrs: rdn along wl over 2f out: sn wknd* **66/1**

050 **15** shd **Cambridge Favorite**[26] 5846 2-9-2 **60** (t) SaleemGolam 8 18
(Mrs Ilka Gansera-Leveque) *chsd ldrs: rdn along and n.m.r 3f out: sn lost pl and bhd* **50/1**

1m 35.9s (-0.70) **Going Correction** -0.25s/f (Firm) **15** Ran SP% **105.0**
Speed ratings (Par 93): **93,92,91,90,88 88,88,86,85,84 82,80,78,74,74**
CSF £90.97 CT £537.72 TOTE £10.60: £3.00, £4.00, £2.80; EX 104.30 Trifecta £233.40.
Owner Mrs Emma Capon & Lord Lloyd Webber **Bred** Watership Down Stud **Trained** Newmarket, Suffolk

■ Galahad and Seaview were withdrawn. Prices at time of withdrawal both 7-1. Rule 4 applies to all bets - deduction 20p in the pound.

FOCUS
A trio of the high-drawn runners came to the fore in what was a modest nursery.

6682 BRITISH STALLION STUDS EBF MAIDEN STKS (DIV II) 7f
4:30 (4:31) (Class 5) 2-Y-O **£3,234** (£962; £481; £240) **Stalls** Centre

Form RPR

1 **Forest Ranger (IRE)** 2-9-5 0 TonyHamilton 6 79+
(Richard Fahey) *hld up towards rr: hdwy over 2f out: styd on wl to ld last 100yds: comf* **9/2**[2]

225 **2** 1 **Ray's The Money (IRE)**[32] 5637 2-9-5 80 (v[1]) PaulMulrennan 7 71
(Michael Bell) *trckd ldrs: effrt over 2f out: hung lft and led appr fnl f: hdd last 100yds: kpt on same pce* **4/7**[1]

3 2 1/2 **Castle Hill Cassie (IRE)** 2-9-0 0 GrahamLee 10 60+
(Ben Haslam) *hld up towards rr: t.k.h: effrt over 2f out: kpt on same pce to take modest 3rd last 50yds* **22/1**

0 **4** 1 1/4 **Desperados Destiny**[25] 5884 2-9-5 0 KevinStott 9 61
(Ed McMahon) *w ldrs: wknd fnl f* **20/1**

6 **5** 1 1/2 **Pennington**[10] 6368 2-9-5 0 SilvestreDeSousa 5 57
(Mark Johnston) *hld up in mid-div: jnd ldrs over 3f out: led 2f out: hdd appr fnl f: wknd last 75yds* **7/1**[3]

6 3 **Ginger Love** 2-9-5 0 ConnorBeasley 2 49
(Bryan Smart) *mid-div: drvn over 3f out: chsng ldrs over 2f out: wknd appr fnl f* **14/1**

60 **7** 3/4 **I Don't Believe It**[22] 6009 2-9-5 0 PJMcDonald 3 47
(Micky Hammond) *led: hdd 2f out: wknd over 1f out* **100/1**

06 **8** 2 **Fully Focussed (IRE)**[7] 6472 2-9-0 0 RoystonFfrench 4 37
(Ann Duffield) *fly-leaped s: tk keen shold: trckd ldrs: drvn 3f out: lost pl over 1f out* **66/1**

0 **9** hd **Ten In The Hat (IRE)**[20] 6044 2-9-5 0 JamesSullivan 8 41
(Shaun Harris) *in rr: drvn 3f out: lost pl over 1f out* **125/1**

06 **10** nse **Hellomoto**[42] 5290 2-9-5 0 ShaneGray 1 41
(Kevin Ryan) *chsd ldrs: drvn 3f out: lost pl over 1f out* **14/1**

1m 25.04s (0.54) **Going Correction** -0.25s/f (Firm) **10** Ran SP% **120.1**
Speed ratings (Par 95): **86,84,82,80,78 75,74,72,72,72**
CSF £7.44 TOTE £6.90: £1.70, £1.10, £4.70; EX 8.20 Trifecta £80.70.
Owner Mrs H Steel **Bred** Yeguada De Milagro Sa **Trained** Musley Bank, N Yorks

FOCUS
The lesser of the two divisions of the 7f maiden and the time was considerably slower.

6683 WATCH RACING UK IN HD (S) STKS 1m
5:05 (5:06) (Class 5) 3-Y-O+ **£3,234** (£962; £481; £240) **Stalls** Centre

Form RPR

2650 **1** **Chiswick Bey (IRE)**[14] 6231 8-8-9 67 AdamMcNamara(5) 2 63
(Richard Fahey) *chsd ldrs: drvn over 2f out: kpt on to ld last 100yds* **14/1**

5041 **2** 1/2 **Nonno Giulio (IRE)**[15] 6220 5-9-0 77 GeorgeBuckell(5) 4 67
(David Loughnane) *stdd s: t.k.h in rr: hdwy and swtchd towards stands' side to trck ldr after 2f: led over 1f out: hung lft and hdd last 100yds: no ex* **8/1**[3]

30-0 **3** hd **Big Whiskey (IRE)**[110] 2862 6-9-0 92 SilvestreDeSousa 1 61
(David Nicholls) *trckd ldrs: drvn over 2f out: kpt on same pce last 100yds* **11/10**[1]

6000 **4** 1/2 **Spryt (IRE)**[8] 6465 4-9-5 80 (v) DanielTudhope 10 65
(Jamie Osborne) *swtchd rt s: overall ldr stands' side: hdd over 1f out: kpt on same pce last 150yds* **9/1**

4312 **5** 1 **Kiwi Bay**[6] 6521 11-9-5 74 PaulMulrennan 6 63
(Michael Dods) *hld up in rr: t.k.h: pushed along and swtchd rt towards stands' side over 3f out: chsng ldrs over 1f out: one pce* **9/4**[2]

1035 **6** 1/2 **Broctune Papa Gio**[15] 6220 9-8-12 64 CliffordLee(7) 7 62
(Keith Reveley) *chsd ldrs: one pce appr fnl f* **25/1**

0010 **7** 2 **Bling King**[14] 6226 7-9-5 61 (p) DavidAllan 9 57
(Geoffrey Harker) *chsd ldrs: one pce over 1f out* **28/1**

0-00 **8** nk **Great Colaci**[25] 5888 3-8-10 39 TonyHamilton 8 51
(Keith Reveley) *hld up in mid-div: effrt over 2f out: chsng ldrs over 1f out: one pce* **100/1**

0006 **9** 9 **Exclusive Waters (IRE)**[23] 5972 6-9-0 56 RobertWinston 3 29
(George Charlton) *chsd ldrs drvn 4f out: edgd lft over 1f out: wknd and heavily eased last 150yds* **66/1**

1m 36.37s (-0.23) **Going Correction** -0.25s/f (Firm)
WFA 3 from 4yo+ 4lb **9** Ran SP% **115.9**
Speed ratings (Par 103): **91,90,90,89,88 88,86,86,77**
CSF £115.41 TOTE £13.10: £2.80, £2.50, £1.20; EX 101.00 Trifecta £243.20.There was no bid for the winner. Big Whiskey was claimed by Miss C L Ellam for £10000. Spryt was claimed by Mr C Dore £10000.
Owner M J Macleod **Bred** Mrs Kay Egan **Trained** Musley Bank, N Yorks

FOCUS
This had the look of a reasonable seller but it went to one of the outsiders. The second and fourth raced a little away from the others early.

6684 HOLD YOUR CHRISTMAS PARTY HERE H'CAP 1m 2f
5:35 (5:36) (Class 5) (0-75,79) 3-Y-O+ **£3,234** (£962; £481; £240) **Stalls** Low

Form RPR

-351 **1** **Niblawi (IRE)**[10] 6365 4-10-0 **79** 6ex SilvestreDeSousa 4 93
(Ismail Mohammed) *chsd ldrs: niggled along over 4f out: pushed along to ld 2 1/2f out: sn rdn clr: kpt on strly* **2/1**[1]

6414 **2** 4 1/2 **San Quentin (IRE)**[39] 5392 5-9-4 **74** (b) GeorgeBuckell(5) 6 79
(David Loughnane) *hld up and bhd: hdwy over 3f out: swtchd rt to outer and rdn wl over 1f out: styd on wl fnl f* **12/1**

4132 **3** 1 1/4 **Le Deluge (FR)**[54] 4833 6-9-3 **68** (t) PJMcDonald 5 71
(Micky Hammond) *trckd ldrs on inner: hdwy over 3f out: rdn 2f out: drvn over 1f out: kpt on same pce* **11/1**[3]

0450 **4** hd **Green Howard**[17] 6160 8-9-8 **73** [1] DanielTudhope 7 75
(Rebecca Bastiman) *in tch: hdwy 4f out: chsd ldrs over 2f out: rdn to chse wnr over 1f out: drvn and kpt on same pce fnl f* **16/1**

0250 **5** ½ **Intiwin (IRE)**[17] 6160 4-9-5 **75**........ AdamMcNamara(5) 8 76
(Richard Fahey) *towards rr: hdwy over 3f out: rdn to chse ldrs whn n.m.r 2f out: drvn over 1f out and kpt on same pce* **8/1**[2]

4400 **6** 2½ **Harry Champion**[18] 6123 3-8-13 **73**........ MarcMonaghan(3) 12 69
(Hugo Palmer) *hld up in rr: hdwy 3f out: rdn wl over 1f out: sn drvn and nvr nr ldrs* **18/1**

4353 **7** nk **Jive Time**[62] 4568 3-9-3 **74**........ DavidAllan 9 70
(James Tate) *in tch: hdwy to chse ldrs over 3f out: rdn along over 2f out: drvn wl over 1f out: grad wknd* **8/1**[2]

4610 **8** nk **Bogardus (IRE)**[26] 5841 5-8-4 **62**........ PaulaMuir(7) 11 57
(Patrick Holmes) *a towards rr* **33/1**

5132 **9** 1½ **Ingleby Spring (IRE)**[25] 5868 4-8-5 **63**........ NatalieHambling(7) 14 55
(Richard Fahey) *midfield: hdwy on outer to chse ldrs over 3f out: rdn along over 2f out: sn drvn and wknd* **20/1**

1105 **10** 2¾ **Caponova (IRE)**[39] 5391 3-9-3 **74**........ GrahamGibbons 1 60
(Tom Dascombe) *prom: led over 6f out: rdn along over 3f out: hdd 2 1/2f out: drvn wl over 1f out and sn wknd* **14/1**

1035 **11** ¾ **Whozthecat (IRE)**[4] 6579 9-9-1 **66**........(t) BarryMcHugh 2 51
(Declan Carroll) *led: hdd over 6f out: chsd ldr: rdn along 3f out: sn wknd* **12/1**

465- **12** 3½ **The Osteopath (IRE)**[340] 7285 13-8-11 **62**........ ConnorBeasley 13 40
(John Davies) *a rr* **50/1**

0030 **13** 3½ **Muqarred (USA)**[11] 6323 4-9-7 **72**........(p) PaulMulrennan 3 43
(David Loughnane) *prom: rdn along over 3f out: wknd wl over 2f out* **11/1**[3]

4510 **14** 1 **San Cassiano (IRE)**[14] 6221 9-9-0 **65**........(b) JamesSullivan 10 34
(Ruth Carr) *in tch: hdwy on wd outside to chse ldrs 4f out: rdn along 3f out: sn wknd* **33/1**

2m 3.83s (-3.27) **Going Correction** -0.25s/f (Firm)
WFA 3 from 4yo+ 6lb **14** Ran SP% **118.0**
Speed ratings (Par 103): **103,99,98,98,97 95,95,95,94,91 91,88,85,84**
CSF £25.08 CT £218.93 TOTE £2.70: £1.40, £3.20, £3.10; EX 28.00 Trifecta £156.00.
Owner Sultan Ali **Bred** Rabbah Bloodstock Limited **Trained** Newmarket, Suffolk

FOCUS
A pretty ordinary handicap that was taken apart by the top one, who put in an improved run under the penalty.

6685 RACING UK DAY PASS JUST £10 H'CAP 6f
6:05 (6:07) (Class 6) (0-65,65) 3-Y-0+ **£2,749** (£818; £408; £204) **Stalls** Centre

Form RPR

0102 **1** **Caeser The Gaeser (IRE)**[8] 6451 4-9-2 **60**........(p) SilvestreDeSousa 1 67
(Nigel Tinkler) *chsd ldrs: led appr fnl f: edgd rt: fnd ex nr line* **3/1**[1]

3140 **2** hd **Teetotal (IRE)**[6] 6522 6-8-9 **60**........(v1) LewisEdmunds(7) 2 66
(Nigel Tinkler) *s.s: in rr: hdwy over 2f out: upsides last 150yds: jst hld* **14/1**

0000 **3** 1¼ **Mustn't Grumble (IRE)**[8] 6451 3-9-2 **62**........(p) TonyHamilton 13 65
(Ivan Furtado) *led tl over 3f out: chsd ldrs: kpt on same pce last 150yds* **40/1**

3345 **4** ½ **Ponty Royale (IRE)**[23] 5978 3-9-2 **62**........1 DavidAllan 17 63
(Tim Easterby) *w ldr: led over 3f out: hdd appr fnl f: kpt on same pce* **7/1**[2]

6500 **5** nk **Round The Island**[8] 6451 3-9-1 **61**........ GeorgeChaloner 14 61
(Richard Whitaker) *mid-div: hdwy over 2f out: chsng ldrs whn swtchd rt 1f out: kpt on* **33/1**

6015 **6** nk **Cool Strutter (IRE)**[8] 6451 4-9-0 **63**........(b) GemmaTutty(5) 6 62
(Karen Tutty) *in rr: hdwy over 2f out: nt clr run over 1f out: swtchd lft: kpt on* **9/1**[3]

5206 **7** shd **Indian Pursuit (IRE)**[8] 6451 3-8-13 **64**........ AdamMcNamara(5) 12 63
(John Quinn) *chsd ldrs: kpt on same pce over 1f out* **9/1**[3]

4545 **8** ½ **Perfect Words (IRE)**[15] 6216 6-9-5 **63**........(p) RobertWinston 10 61
(Marjorie Fife) *w ldrs: one pce over 1f out* **14/1**

6450 **9** 1 **Mercers Row**[8] 6453 9-9-7 **65**........ PJMcDonald 15 60
(Michael Herrington) *chsd ldrs: one pce over 1f out* **10/1**

03 **10** hd **Ypres**[40] 5354 7-9-2 **60**........ PaulMulrennan 4 56
(Jason Ward) *hld up in rr: nt clr run fr over 2f out tl swtchd lft and kpt on last 75yds* **11/1**

0100 **11** nk **Poolstock**[35] 5535 4-8-13 **57**........(v1) ConnorBeasley 20 50
(Michael Dods) *s.i.s: in rr: kpt on fnl 2f: nvr a factor* **22/1**

4400 **12** shd **Disclosure**[4] 6569 5-9-4 **62**........ JasonHart 19 56
(Les Eyre) *towards rr: hdwy over 2f out: chsng ldrs over 1f out: one pce whn hmpd 1f out* **25/1**

2005 **13** ½ **Take Charge**[45] 5195 3-9-5 **65**........ TomEaves 8 56
(David Brown) *mid-div: effrt over 2f out: nvr a factor* **33/1**

0200 **14** hd **Windforpower (IRE)**[8] 6451 6-9-0 **58**........(p) DaleSwift 11 49
(Tracy Waggott) *chsd ldrs: drvn over 3f out: one pce fnl 2f* **50/1**

-000 **15** 1 **Harbour Patrol (IRE)**[104] 3078 4-9-2 **60**........ BarryMcHugh 9 48
(Rebecca Bastiman) *mid-div: effrt over 2f out: nvr a factor* **50/1**

0060 **16** ½ **Goadby**[28] 5760 5-8-13 **57**........ RoystonFfrench 7 43
(John Holt) *w ldrs: wknd over 1f out* **33/1**

0336 **17** ¾ **Coquine**[19] 6106 3-8-13 **59**........ DanielTudhope 18 43
(David O'Meara) *slowly: a in rr* **20/1**

-006 **18** shd **Myboydaniel**[14] 6238 4-9-0 **65**........1 CliffordLee(7) 16 49
(Derek Shaw) *mid-div: drvn over 2f out: nvr a factor* **16/1**

0065 **19** 3¼ **Toledo**[28] 5760 3-8-11 **57**........ SamJames 5 31
(Marjorie Fife) *chsd ldrs: lost pl over 1f out* **33/1**

0606 **20** 1¼ **Misu Mac**[18] 6136 6-8-13 **57**........ JoeDoyle 3 27
(Neville Bycroft) *mid-div: drvn over 2f out: sn lost pl* **33/1**

1m 9.84s (-1.96) **Going Correction** -0.25s/f (Firm)
WFA 3 from 4yo+ 2lb **20** Ran SP% **128.2**
Speed ratings (Par 101): **103,102,101,100,100 99,99,98,97,97 96,96,96,95,94 93,92,92,88,86**
CSF £41.42 CT £1492.27 TOTE £4.00: £1.50, £4.20, £5.10, £3.00; EX 59.00 Trifecta £2258.80.
Owner Flying High Racing Club **Bred** Tom Foley **Trained** Langton, N Yorks

FOCUS
Pretty moderate sprinting form but it provided Nigel Tinkler with the first and second. They came out of the two lowest stalls.

T/Jkpt: Not won. T/Plt: £48.50 to a £1 stake. Pool: £69,156.08. 1,039.83 winning units. T/Qpdt: £17.60 to a £1 stake. Pool: £5,264.32, 221.2 winning units. **Walter Glynn & Joe Rowntree**

6686 - 6692a (Foreign Racing) - See Raceform Interactive

6596 MAISONS-LAFFITTE (R-H)
Wednesday, September 21

OFFICIAL GOING: Turf: good to soft

6693a PRIX BERTRAND DE TARRAGON (GROUP 3) (3YO+ FILLIES & MARES) (STRAIGHT) (TURF) 1m 1f
3:35 (12:00) 3-Y-0+ **£29,411** (£11,764; £8,823; £5,882; £2,941)

RPR

1 **Aim To Please (FR)**[37] 5498 3-8-11 0........ GeraldMosse 5 109
(F Doumen, France) *hld up in tch: rdn and hdwy 2f out: chal fnl f: styd on and led towards fin* **18/1**

2 1½ **Sayana (FR)**[31] 5691 4-9-2 0........ ChristopheSoumillon 7 105
(A De Royer-Dupre, France) *trckd ldr: rdn to chal 2f out: led over 1f out: styd on fnl f but worn down and hdd towards fin* **7/2**[2]

3 ½ **Irish Rookie (IRE)**[61] 4582 4-9-2 0........ JamieSpencer 10 104
(Martyn Meade) *trckd ldr: rdn to ld 2f out: hdd over 1f out: styd on fnl f but hld in 3rd towards fin* **9/4**[1]

4 ½ **Persona Grata**[19] 6107 5-9-2 0........ OlivierPeslier 2 103
(Ed Walker) *hld up: rdn over 2f out: styd on into 4th fnl f but nt quite able to chal* **12/1**

5 1 **Chartreuse (IRE)**[37] 5498 3-8-11 0........ ThierryJarnet 4 102
(F Head, France) *midfield in tch: rdn 2f out: kpt on same pce* **9/4**[1]

6 ½ **Game Theory (IRE)**[31] 5691 4-9-2 0........ StephanePasquier 8 100
(N Clement, France) *midfield in tch: rdn and effrt over 2f out: sn outpcd: kpt on but wl hld* **22/1**

7 ½ **Caointiorn (FR)**[24] 5948 5-9-2 0........(p) TheoBachelot 1 99
(S Wattel, France) *hld up in rr: rdn 2f out: kpt on against rail fnl f but nvr threatened* **14/1**

8 nk **Incahoots**[40] 5384 4-9-2 0........ MaximeGuyon 12 98
(F Head, France) *hld up in tch: rdn and outpcd 2f out: n.d after* **25/1**

9 3 **Double Dream (FR)**[39] 3-8-11 0........ EduardoPedroza 6 93
(A Wohler, Germany) *led: rdn and hdd 2f out: no ex fnl f: wknd* **20/1**

10 ½ **Magnanime**[37] 5498 3-8-11 0........ TonyPiccone 3 92
(F Chappet, France) *hld up: rdn over 2 out: outpcd fnl f* **28/1**

11 2 **Thank You Bye Bye (FR)**[40] 5384 4-9-2 0........ Pierre-CharlesBoudot 9 87
(J-P Gauvin, France) *hld up: rdn over 2f out: no real imp and eased whn btn fnl f* **11/1**[3]

12 dist **Besotted (IRE)**[73] 4184 3-8-11 0........ MickaelBarzalona 11
(P Sogorb, France) *midfield: wknd over 2f out and sn dropped to last: eased: t.o* **25/1**

1m 49.58s (-5.12)
WFA 3 from 4yo+ 5lb **12** Ran SP% **132.0**
WIN (incl. 1 euro stake): 15.50. PLACES: 2.80, 2.00, 1.70. DF: 44.80. SF: 117.90.
Owner J Vasicek **Bred** Haras D'Ecouves **Trained** Bouce, France

6694a PRIX ECLIPSE (GROUP 3) (2YO) (TURF) 6f (S)
4:35 (12:00) 2-Y-0 **£29,411** (£11,764; £8,823; £5,882; £2,941)

RPR

1 **Sans Equivoque (GER)**[37] 5497 2-8-8 0........ ThierryJarnet 2 101
(D Guillemin, France) *midfield in tch: rdn to chal over 1f out: r.o and led towards fin* **5/1**[2]

2 hd **King Of Spades (FR)**[25] 5905 2-8-13 0 ow2..(b1) ChristopheSoumillon 4 105
(F Vermeulen, France) *midfield in tch: rdn 2f out: chal fnl f: r.o and up for 2nd post: jst hld* **16/1**

3 hd **Fas (IRE)**[9] 6431 2-8-11 0........ MaximeGuyon 6 103
(Mme Pia Brandt, France) *sn prom: disputing 2f out: rdn to ld over 1f out: r.o but worn down and hdd towards fin: dropped to 3rd post* **5/1**[2]

4 ¾ **Spanish Fly (IRE)**[32] 5703 2-8-8 0........ GeraldMosse 7 98
(M Delcher Sanchez, France) *hld up in tch: rdn and effrt 2f out: kpt on and ev ch fnl f: jst hld towards fin* **20/1**

5 ½ **Al Johrah**[31] 5690 2-8-8 0........ GregoryBenoist 5 96
(H-F Devin, France) *pressed ldr: disputing 2f out: rdn and hdd over 1f out: no ex fnl f* **4/6**[1]

6 1¼ **Facilitate**[31] 2-8-8 0........ VincentCheminaud 3 92
(D Smaga, France) *hld up in tch: rdn over 1f out: kpt on same pce and nt able to chal* **7/1**[3]

7 3½ **Cosachope (FR)**[20] 6068 2-8-13 0........ StephanePasquier 1 87
(P Sogorb, France) *led: rdn and hdd 2f out: sn no ex: wknd and dropped to last* **18/1**

1m 11.63s (-1.77) **7** Ran SP% **121.7**
WIN (incl. 1 euro stake): 5.90. PLACES: 2.90, 5.90. SF: 93.50.
Owner Haras D'Etreham **Bred** Pontchartrain Stud Et Al **Trained** France

6695 - (Foreign Racing) - See Raceform Interactive

6507 CHELMSFORD (A.W) (L-H)
Thursday, September 22

OFFICIAL GOING: Polytrack: standard
Wind: Light behind Weather: Cloudy with sunny spells

6696 BET TOTEPLACEPOT AT TOTESPORT.COM MAIDEN AUCTION FILLIES' STKS (PLUS 10 RACE) 6f (P)
5:45 (5:45) (Class 4) 2-Y-0 **£5,175** (£1,540; £769; £384) **Stalls** Centre

Form RPR

0 **1** **Melissa Jane**[133] 2173 2-8-6 0........ HarryBentley 3 70
(Henry Spiller) *chsd ldr 2f: remained handy: wnt 2nd again over 1f out: rdn to ld ins fnl f: r.o* **7/1**

2 1 **Sea Tea Dea** 2-8-6 0........ WilliamCarson 8 67
(Anthony Carson) *hld up: hdwy over 1f out: edgd rt ins fnl f: r.o to go 2nd nr fin: nt rch wnr* **20/1**

0 **3** ¼ **Heroine Queen**[14] 6244 2-8-11 0........ JimCrowley 6 70
(Robert Cowell) *led: rdn over 1f out: hdd and unable qck ins fnl f* **3/1**[1]

06 **4** 1¼ **Radar Love (IRE)**[17] 6189 2-8-4 0........ JosephineGordon(3) 4 62
(J S Moore) *chsd ldrs: rdn over 2f out: styd on same pce ins fnl f* **66/1**

056 **5** 1¼ **Biologist (IRE)**[11] 6369 2-8-9 0........(b1) PatCosgrave 2 60
(William Haggas) *sn pushed along in mid-div: hdwy 4f out: rdn over 1f out: styd on same pce fnl f* **4/1**[2]

6 hd **Holy Roma** 2-8-8 0........ LiamJones 1 59
(William Haggas) *s.i.s: hld up: hdwy and nt clr run over 1f out: r.o: nt rch ldrs* **5/1**

The Form Book, Raceform Ltd, Newbury, RG14 5SJ

0 **7** *3* **Dandy Walk**[9] 6454 2-8-8 0 JimmyQuinn 9 50
(Chris Wall) *mid-div: racd keenly: rdn and lost pl over 2f out: n.d after* **16/1**

8 *nse* **Wouldntitbelovely (IRE)** 2-8-4 0 HollieDoyle(5) 5 51
(Richard Hughes) *s.i.s: r.o ins fnl f: nvr on terms* **14/1**

5 **9** *hd* **Kohinoor Diamond (IRE)**[11] 6369 2-8-10 0 LukeMorris 12 51
(Sir Mark Prescott Bt) *s.i.s and edgd rt s: sn pushed along: hdwy 4f out: drvn along 1/2-way: hung lft and wknd over 1f out* **9/2**[3]

0 **10** *shd* **Popsilca**[25] 5930 2-8-7 0 PaoloSirigu 11 48
(Mick Quinn) *prom: chsd ldr 4f out tl rdn over 1f out: edgd rt and wknd ins fnl f* **33/1**

11 *1 3/4* **Lauraman** 2-8-7 0 KierenFox 7 42
(Martin Smith) *prom: nt clr run and lost pl after 1f: n.d after* **20/1**

12 *1/2* **Red Guana (IRE)** 2-8-7 0 PaulHanagan 10 41
(William Jarvis) *s.i.s: a in rr* **25/1**

0 **13** *1 3/4* **Bay Of Angels (IRE)**[46] 5202 2-8-7 0 AdamBeschizza 13 36
(Stuart Williams) *s.i.s and hmpd s: sn pushed along in rr: hung rt over 4f out: wknd 2f out* **25/1**

1m 14.04s (0.34) **Going Correction** -0.10s/f (Stan) **13** Ran SP% **126.5**
Speed ratings (Par 94): **93,91,90,89,87 87,83,83,82,82 80,79,77**
CSF £149.07 TOTE £10.40: £3.00, £8.20, £1.70; EX 280.20 Trifecta £1463.30.
Owner J Gill/ H Spiller/ G Waterhouse **Bred** Whitsbury Manor Stud **Trained** Newmarket, Suffolk

FOCUS
An ordinary fillies' auction maiden. They went a decent gallop, the winner came through from a handy draw and the form appears sound.

6697 BET TOTEJACKPOT AT TOTESPORT.COM NURSERY H'CAP 6f (P)
6:15 (6:15) (Class 4) (0-85,85) 2-Y-O **£6,469** (£1,925; £962; £481) **Stalls** Centre

Form RPR

4434 **1** **Poet's Society**[25] 5917 2-9-6 **84** AndrewMullen 6 91
(Mark Johnston) *mde all: rdn over 1f out: styd on wl* **20/1**

2361 **2** *1 1/4* **Evergate**[59] 4707 2-9-7 **85** JimCrowley 3 88
(Hugo Palmer) *hld up in tch: rdn over 2f out: swtchd rt over 1f out: r.o to go 2nd nr fin: nt rch wnr* **2/1**[1]

1630 **3** *1/2* **High Acclaim (USA)**[55] 4825 2-8-11 **80** GeorgeWood(5) 1 82
(Roger Teal) *chsd ldrs: rdn to go 2nd over 1f out: edgd rt and styd on same pce ins fnl f* **9/2**[2]

0051 **4** *2 3/4* **White Chin (IRE)**[28] 5806 2-8-10 **74** RichardKingscote 2 67
(Tom Dascombe) *s.i.s: hld up: nt clr run over 1f out: r.o ins fnl f: nt rch ldrs* **8/1**

202 **5** *3/4* **Bolt Phantom (USA)**[87] 3712 2-9-0 **81** [1] AlistairRawlinson(3) 7 72
(Ismail Mohammed) *s.i.s: hld up: hdwy u.p over 1f out: nt trble ldrs* **12/1**

4210 **6** *1/2* **Bee Case**[23] 5998 2-9-1 **82** JosephineGordon(3) 10 72
(Hugo Palmer) *sn chsng ldr: rdn over 1f out: edgd lft and wknd ins fnl f* **8/1**

31 **7** *1* **The Amber Fort (USA)**[49] 5077 2-9-3 **81** RobertHavlin 11 68
(John Gosden) *s.i.s: hld up: rdn over 1f out: nt clr run wl ins fnl f: nvr trbld ldrs* **6/1**[3]

4401 **8** *1* **Giennah (IRE)**[19] 6139 2-8-9 **80** JordanUys(7) 5 64
(Brian Meehan) *s.i.s: sn prom: lost pl whn stmbld wl over 3f out: effrt over 2f out: wknd over 1f out* **11/1**

3313 **9** *4 1/2* **Second Nature**[26] 5877 2-9-4 **82** LukeMorris 4 52
(James Tate) *trckd ldrs: rdn over 2f out: wknd over 1f out* **16/1**

5210 **10** *1 1/4* **Kamra (USA)**[36] 5560 2-9-5 **83** (v) FMBerry 9 49
(Jeremy Noseda) *s.i.s: sn prom: rdn over 2f out: wknd over 1f out* **25/1**

1m 12.43s (-1.27) **Going Correction** -0.10s/f (Stan) **10** Ran SP% **118.5**
Speed ratings (Par 97): **104,102,101,98,97 96,95,93,87,86**
CSF £61.25 CT £229.76 TOTE £24.80: £6.50, £1.10, £2.50; EX 78.40 Trifecta £417.80.
Owner Sheikh Hamdan bin Mohammed Al Maktoum **Bred** Darley **Trained** Middleham Moor, N Yorks

FOCUS
A decent nursery handicap. The winner simply kept on finding off his own testing fractions.

6698 BET TOTEQUADPOT AT TOTESPORT.COM H'CAP 1m 5f 66y(P)
6:45 (6:45) (Class 6) (0-65,65) 3-Y-O **£3,234** (£962; £481; £240) **Stalls** Low

Form RPR

5052 **1** **Stamford Raffles**[15] 6242 3-9-2 **65** CharlieBennett(5) 5 74
(Jane Chapple-Hyam) *chsd ldrs: wnt 2nd over 2f out: rdn to ld over 1f out: sn hung lft: styd on wl* **5/1**[2]

4064 **2** *4 1/2* **Graceful Lady**[12] 6335 3-8-10 **54** PatCosgrave 6 57
(Robert Eddery) *hld up: hdwy over 2f out: rdn over 1f out: styd on to go 2nd post* **10/1**

-300 **3** *shd* **Purple Raven**[98] 3318 3-9-4 **65** LouisSteward(3) 2 68
(Michael Bell) *hld up: hdwy over 1f out: sn rdn: styd on same pce ins fnl f* **12/1**

0633 **4** *1/2* **Le Tissier**[23] 5993 3-9-2 **60** (p) KierenFox 1 62
(Michael Attwater) *trckd ldrs: plld hrd: wnt 2nd over 9f out tl led over 3f out: rdn and hdd over 1f out: no ex ins fnl f* **5/1**[2]

5342 **5** *2* **Iona Island**[32] 5672 3-9-7 **65** PaulHanagan 7 64
(Charles Hills) *hld up in tch: rdn over 1f out: no ex fnl f* **6/1**[3]

-436 **6** *3 1/4* **Dream Serenade**[26] 5888 3-8-2 **46** oh1 AndrewMullen 10 41
(Michael Appleby) *hld up: rdn over 3f out: nvr on terms* **50/1**

3545 **7** *1 1/2* **Regal Galaxy**[40] 5398 3-7-13 **46** oh1 NoelGarbutt(3) 9 39
(Mark H Tompkins) *s.i.s: pushed along early in rr: rdn over 2f out: nvr nrr* **50/1**

550 **8** *nk* **Motivate**[152] 1653 3-8-13 **57** LukeMorris 3 49
(Sir Mark Prescott Bt) *mid-div: hdwy over 6f out: drvn along over 3f out: wknd over 1f out* **9/2**[1]

0063 **9** *10* **Triassic (IRE)**[7] 6508 3-8-9 **53** RichardKingscote 11 31
(Mark Johnston) *led over 11f out: rdn and hdd over 3f out: wknd over 1f out* **6/1**[3]

2062 **10** *1 1/4* **Mikro Polemistis (IRE)**[9] 6438 3-8-7 **51** JimCrowley 8 28
(Brian Ellison) *s.i.s: hld up: rdn over 2f out: a in rr* **9/2**[1]

0051 **11** *shd* **Kazoey**[26] 5888 3-8-4 **48** DuranFentiman 4 24
(Chris Fairhurst) *led: hdd over 11f out: chsd ldrs: rdn over 3f out: wknd over 2f out* **25/1**

2m 54.39s (0.79) **Going Correction** -0.10s/f (Stan) **11** Ran SP% **122.8**
Speed ratings (Par 99): **93,90,90,89,88 86,85,85,79,78 78**
CSF £56.08 CT £580.56 TOTE £7.20: £2.30, £3.20, £4.80; EX 78.20 Trifecta £668.10.
Owner Mrs Charles Cyzer **Bred** C A Cyzer **Trained** Dalham, Suffolk

FOCUS
A modest 3yo staying handicap. They went a muddling gallop.

6699 BET TOTETRIFECTA AT TOTESPORT.COM H'CAP 5f (P)
7:15 (7:16) (Class 4) (0-80,80) 3-Y-O+ **£6,469** (£1,925; £962; £481) **Stalls** Low

Form RPR

6311 **1** **Verne Castle**[14] 6248 3-9-0 **74** OisinMurphy 11 85
(Andrew Balding) *sn chsng ldr: rdn to ld ins fnl f: r.o* **6/1**[3]

6562 **2** *nk* **Monumental Man**[14] 6248 7-8-11 **70** (p) KierenFox 8 80
(Michael Attwater) *sn led: rdn over 1f out: hdd ins fnl f: r.o* **8/1**

-410 **3** *3 1/4* **Jameerah**[20] 6072 3-9-5 **79** LukeMorris 1 77
(James Tate) *chsd ldrs: rdn over 1f out: no ex wl ins fnl f* **9/2**[1]

-004 **4** *1 3/4* **Immediate**[46] 5205 4-9-7 **80** StevieDonohoe 2 72+
(Robert Cowell) *s.i.s: hdwy whn hmpd wl over 3f out: styd on fr over 1f out: nt rch ldrs* **8/1**

140 **5** *1* **Cherry Kool**[11] 6363 3-9-0 **74** PatCosgrave 4 62
(Stuart Williams) *prom: racd keenly: edgd lft wl over 3f out: rdn over 1f out: no ex fnl f* **10/1**

040 **6** *1 3/4* **Krystallite**[43] 5296 3-9-5 **79** DaleSwift 12 61+
(Scott Dixon) *hld up: rdn over 1f out: nvr on terms* **50/1**

3655 **7** *1/2* **Pink Martini (IRE)**[12] 6340 3-8-11 **74** JosephineGordon(3) 5 54
(Joseph Tuite) *prom: rdn 1/2-way: wknd over 1f out* **25/1**

1364 **8** *1 1/4* **Newton's Law (IRE)**[32] 5669 5-9-4 **77** (t) TomQueally 10 53+
(Brian Meehan) *s.i.s: towards rr whn hmpd wl over 3f out: no ch after* **25/1**

3260 **9** *1/2* **Tarboosh**[20] 6079 3-9-6 **80** (b[1]) PaulHanagan 7 54+
(William Haggas) *hld up: plld hrd: hmpd wl over 3f out: nvr trbld ldrs* **5/1**[2]

0062 **10** *hd* **Eternitys Gate**[10] 6425 5-9-0 **73** (v) RobertWinston 9 46
(Ivan Furtado) *mid-div: drvn along 1/2-way: wknd over 1f out* **10/1**

0422 **11** *4 1/2* **Malaysian Boleh**[7] 6506 6-8-8 **67** JimCrowley 6 24+
(Brian Ellison) *hld up: hmpd wl over 3f out: no ch after* **7/1**

5204 **12** *1 1/2* **Sir Domino (FR)**[32] 5679 4-9-1 **74** (b) TomEaves 3 26+
(Kevin Ryan) *s.i.s: plld hrd: hdwy whn hmpd wl over 3f out: no ch after* **8/1**

58.9s (-1.30) **Going Correction** -0.10s/f (Stan)
WFA 3 from 4yo+ 1lb **12** Ran SP% **122.8**
Speed ratings (Par 105): **106,105,100,97,95 93,92,90,89,89 82,79**
CSF £54.51 CT £245.95 TOTE £6.70: £1.90, £3.50, £2.00; EX 47.30 Trifecta £286.20.
Owner J C Smith **Bred** Littleton Stud **Trained** Kingsclere, Hants
■ Stewards' Enquiry : Pat Cosgrave four-day ban; careless riding (6th, 9th-11th Oct)

FOCUS
A fairly decent sprint handicap but not many got into this contest in any meaningful way off the strong tempo with trouble in behind. The winner confirmed his latest form with the second.

6700 BET TOTEEXACTA AT TOTESPORT.COM H'CAP 1m (P)
7:45 (7:45) (Class 6) (0-65,68) 3-Y-O+ **£3,234** (£962; £481; £240) **Stalls** Low

Form RPR

0324 **1** **Celtic Artisan (IRE)**[39] 5114 5-9-1 **54** (bt) OisinMurphy 11 60
(Rebecca Menzies) *led over 6f out: rdn clr over 1f out: jst hld on* **20/1**

3303 **2** *1/2* **Rebel State (IRE)**[15] 6241 3-9-6 **63** WilliamTwiston-Davies 1 68
(Richard Spencer) *chsd ldrs: rdn to chse wnr fnl f: r.o* **4/1**[1]

5-01 **3** *shd* **Big Storm Coming**[9] 6453 6-10-1 **68** 6ex TomEaves 3 73
(David Brown) *hld up: swtchd rt and hdwy over 1f out: r.o* **5/1**[3]

2102 **4** *nk* **Pacific Salt (IRE)**[15] 6241 3-9-8 **65** PatCosgrave 9 69
(Pam Sly) *hld up in tch: plld hrd: rdn over 1f out: r.o* **6/1**

6050 **5** *1 1/2* **Tommy's Secret**[32] 5677 6-9-7 **65** CharlieBennett(5) 14 65
(Jane Chapple-Hyam) *sn pushed along and prom: chsd wnr 6f out: rdn over 2f out: edgd lft and styd on same pce ins fnl f* **14/1**

3234 **6** *1/2* **Clary (IRE)**[19] 6137 6-9-11 **64** GeorgeBaker 5 63
(James Unett) *led: hdd over 6f out: chsd ldrs: rdn over 1f out: no ex ins fnl f* **7/1**

312- **7** *5* **Thermal Column (IRE)**[290] 8134 4-9-11 **64** AndrewMullen 10 51
(Michael Appleby) *prom: rdn over 2f out: wknd over 1f out* **20/1**

3300 **8** *1/2* **Spirit Of Gondree (IRE)**[159] 1502 8-9-8 **61** (b) LukeMorris 7 47
(Milton Bradley) *hld up: sme hdwy u.p over 1f out: no ex fnl f* **33/1**

501 **9** *1 1/4* **Stun Gun**[21] 6046 6-9-7 **65** (p) CallumShepherd(5) 12 48
(Derek Shaw) *hld up: rdn over 2f out: n.d* **16/1**

4043 **10** *2* **Onesie (IRE)**[11] 6373 3-9-1 **58** DanielMuscutt 2 36
(Marco Botti) *plld hrd and prom: rdn over 2f out: wknd over 1f out* **8/1**

3400 **11** *2* **Playful Dude (USA)**[82] 3896 3-9-2 **62** JosephineGordon(3) 6 35
(Phil McEntee) *s.i.s: hld up: plld hrd: rdn over 2f out: n.d* **33/1**

-013 **12** *4 1/2* **Sober Up**[105] 3078 4-9-4 **57** (p) MartinHarley 4 20
(Ivan Furtado) *hld up: rdn over 2f out: nvr on terms* **9/2**[2]

6655 **13** *5* **Foie Gras**[25] 5935 6-9-11 **64** (p) SilvestreDeSousa 13 15
(Chris Dwyer) *hld up: shkn up over 2f out: eased over 1f out* **10/1**

1m 39.81s (-0.09) **Going Correction** -0.10s/f (Stan)
WFA 3 from 4yo+ 4lb **13** Ran SP% **129.8**
Speed ratings (Par 101): **96,95,95,95,93 93,88,87,86,84 82,77,72**
CSF £102.98 CT £499.91 TOTE £27.40: £4.90, £2.90, £3.00; EX 267.20 Trifecta £1123.40.
Owner EPDS Racing Partnership 11 **Bred** Fortbarrington Stud **Trained** Mordon, Co. Durham

FOCUS
A modest handicap. They went a muddling gallop and the winning jockey Oisin Murphy timed his front-running effort to perfection.

6701 TOTEPOOL BETTING AT TOTESPORT.COM H'CAP (DIV I) 1m 2f (P)
8:15 (8:18) (Class 5) (0-75,75) 3-Y-O+ **£5,175** (£1,540; £769; £384) **Stalls** Low

Form RPR

0113 **1** **Cape Crystal (IRE)**[27] 5841 3-9-1 **72** (p) LukeMorris 5 83+
(Sir Mark Prescott Bt) *plld hrd and prom: chsd ldr over 2f out: rdn to ld over 1f out: styd on wl* **7/4**[1]

4465 **2** *1 3/4* **Thecornishbarron (IRE)**[8] 6490 4-9-10 **75** JimCrowley 12 80
(John Ryan) *led after 1f: rdn and hdd over 1f out: styd on same pce ins fnl f* **12/1**

5 **3** *1 1/4* **New Record (IRE)**[7] 6510 4-9-3 **68** RyanTate 2 71
(James Eustace) *led 1f: chsd ldrs: rdn over 2f out: nt clr run and swtchd rt ins fnl f: styd on* **50/1**

1224 **4** *hd* **Choral Clan (IRE)**[49] 5076 5-9-7 **72** JackMitchell 10 74+
(Philip Mitchell) *hld up: hdwy over 1f out: hung lft and styd on* **11/1**

5410 **5** *2 3/4* **Cornelious (IRE)**[19] 6128 4-8-10 **68** (p) CameronNoble(7) 3 65
(Clifford Lines) *hld up: hdwy on outer 3f out: rdn over 1f out: no ex ins fnl f* **6/1**[2]

-053 **6** *1/2* **Topamichi**[77] 4050 6-9-6 **71** StevieDonohoe 8 67
(Mark H Tompkins) *prom: rdn over 1f out: no ex* **16/1**

4660 **7** *4 1/2* **The Magic Pencil (IRE)**[57] 4768 3-8-10 **67** (p) TomEaves 11 54
(Kevin Ryan) *s.i.s: hld up: styd on fr over 1f out: nvr nrr* **16/1**

4141 **8** *1/2* **Yasir (USA)**[30] 5737 8-8-9 **67** SophieKilloran(7) 6 53
(Conor Dore) *s.i.s: pushed along in rr early: nvr nr to chal* **16/1**

3554 **9** 1 ½ **Bergholt (IRE)**[26] 5875 3-8-13 **70**...................(p) WilliamTwiston-Davies 1 53
(Philip Hide) *mid-div: racd keenly: rdn over 2f out: wknd over 1f out* **7/1**[3]

333 **10** 1 ½ **Crystallographer (IRE)**[78] 4027 3-9-0 **71**.......................... ShaneKelly 7 51
(David Lanigan) *hld up in tch: rdn over 2f out: wknd over 1f out* **8/1**

0005 **11** 14 **Cat Royale (IRE)**[19] 6128 3-9-1 **72**............................(p) DarryllHolland 9 24
(Jane Chapple-Hyam) *wnt prom after 1f: chsd ldr over 7f out tl rdn over 2f out: hmpd and wknd sn after* **12/1**

64-5 **12** 19 **Commissar**[259] 88 7-9-5 **70**.................................(t) SilvestreDeSousa 4
(Mandy Rowland) *awkward leaving stalls: hld up: a in rr: wknd over 2f out: eased* **14/1**

2m 6.04s (-2.56) **Going Correction** -0.10s/f (Stan)
WFA 3 from 4yo+ 6lb 12 Ran SP% **124.3**
Speed ratings (Par 103): **106,104,103,103,101 100,97,96,95,94 83,68**
CSF £26.36 CT £829.69 TOTE £2.60: £1.30, £4.20, £9.80; EX 30.60 Trifecta £703.20.

Owner Axom LVII **Bred** Rockfield Farm **Trained** Newmarket, Suffolk

FOCUS
The first division of a fair handicap. It paid to race handily given the modest gallop and the form is rated around the second.

6702 TOTEPOOL BETTING AT TOTESPORT.COM H'CAP (DIV II) 1m 2f (P)
8:45 (8:47) (Class 5) (0-75,75) 3-Y-O+ **£5,175** (£1,540; £769; £384) **Stalls** Low

Form RPR

2265 **1** **Ocean Eleven**[14] 6265 3-9-2 **73**.. JimCrowley 3 80
(John Ryan) *mde all: rdn over 1f out: styd on* **7/1**[3]

3052 **2** 1 ¼ **Vastly (USA)**[19] 6138 7-9-6 **71**...............................(t) SaleemGolam 2 75
(Sophie Leech) *prom: rdn to chse wnr over 1f out: styd on* **10/1**

40 **3** ¾ **Bridge Of Sighs**[54] 4868 4-9-7 **72**.................................... PatCosgrave 1 75
(Martin Smith) *hld up: nt clr run over 2f out: hdwy over 1f out: sn rdn: styd on* **7/1**[3]

062 **4** hd **Enmeshing**[20] 6104 3-9-3 **74**.. DanielMuscutt 8 76+
(James Fanshawe) *hld up: hdwy and hmpd over 1f out: styd on* **6/1**[2]

4416 **5** 1 ½ **All The Rage**[15] 6241 3-8-13 **70**.. LukeMorris 5 69+
(Sir Mark Prescott Bt) *hld up in tch: cl up and rdn whn hmpd over 1f out: styd on same pce ins fnl f* **3/1**[1]

5563 **6** ½ **Rebel Lightning (IRE)**[41] 5374 3-9-1 **72**......(b) WilliamTwiston-Davies 7 70
(Richard Spencer) *chsd ldrs: rdn over 2f out: no ex ins fnl f* **7/1**[3]

4450 **7** 7 **Yorkindred Spirit**[12] 6323 4-9-1 **66**.......................(v) SilvestreDeSousa 6 50
(Mark Johnston) *hld up: rdn over 1f out: n.d* **8/1**

000 **8** 5 **Tynecastle Park**[87] 3723 3-8-9 **66**.................................... JackMitchell 4 40
(Robert Eddery) *hld up: drvn along 1/2-way: nvr on terms* **33/1**

4-33 **9** 2 ½ **Thahab Ifraj (IRE)**[41] 5375 3-8-10 **67**.............................. MartinHarley 9 51+
(Ismail Mohammed) *chsd ldrs: rdn over 2f out: cl up whn hmpd over 1f out: eased* **8/1**

0261 **10** 1 ¼ **Sunscape (IRE)**[22] 6019 3-9-4 **75**.. FMBerry 10 42
(Hughie Morrison) *sn prom: chsd wnr over 5f out tl rdn and hung rt over 1f out: sn wknd* **10/1**

0050 **11** 8 **Stoked (IRE)**[15] 6231 4-9-0 **68**............................ JosephineGordon(3) 12 19
(Chris Dwyer) *pushed along in rr early: rdn over 3f out: wknd over 2f out* **50/1**

2m 5.88s (-2.72) **Going Correction** -0.10s/f (Stan)
WFA 3 from 4yo+ 6lb 11 Ran SP% **122.1**
Speed ratings (Par 103): **106,105,104,104,103 102,97,93,91,90 83**
CSF £78.10 CT £518.98 TOTE £9.10: £2.80, £3.30, £2.30; EX 96.30 Trifecta £1248.10.

Owner W McLuskey **Bred** J C S Wilson Bloodstock **Trained** Newmarket, Suffolk

FOCUS
The second division of a fair handicap. The theme of being handy or leading off modest fractions continued as another horse successfully made all the running. The form is rated aound the first three.

6703 MLM 50 MAIDEN STKS 1m 2f (P)
9:15 (9:18) (Class 5) 3-Y-O+ **£3,881** (£1,155; £577; £288) **Stalls** Low

Form RPR

6443 **1** **Iberica Road (USA)**[20] 6084 3-9-5 73.........................(t) OisinMurphy 10 82
(Andrew Balding) *mde virtually all: rdn over 1f out: styd on* **6/1**

2 ¾ **Laqab (IRE)** 3-9-5 0.. PaulHanagan 7 81+
(Roger Varian) *s.i.s: sn mid-div: hdwy over 3f out: rdn over 1f out: edgd lft ins fnl f: r.o to go 2nd nr fin* **11/8**[1]

-622 **3** hd **Vermeulen**[17] 6192 3-9-5 81..[1] RobertHavlin 3 80
(John Gosden) *plld hrd and prom: chsd wnr over 2f out: rdn and edgd lft ins fnl f: r.o* **5/2**[2]

6- **4** 3 ¼ **Charismatic Man (IRE)**[321] 7743 3-9-5 0.............................. FMBerry 9 74+
(Ralph Beckett) *hld up: hdwy over 2f out: edgd lft fnl f: nt trble ldrs* **14/1**

0 **5** 4 **Lost The Moon**[103] 3160 3-9-0 0.................................. StevieDonohoe 1 61
(Mark H Tompkins) *prom: rdn over 2f out: wknd over 1f out* **66/1**

6 hd **Princess Nia (IRE)** 3-9-0 0.. MartinDwyer 2 60
(Brian Meehan) *mid-div: rdn over 2f out: wknd over 1f out* **28/1**

3502 **7** nk **Sacred Trust**[32] 5677 3-9-5 78.......................................(p) JimCrowley 11 65
(Hugo Palmer) *chsd wnr after 1f tl rdn over 2f out: wknd over 1f out* **7/2**[3]

0 **8** 13 **Murraqib (USA)**[14] 6247 3-9-0 0................................ PaddyBradley(5) 4 39
(Brett Johnson) *prom tl rdn and wknd over 2f out* **100/1**

00 **9** 17 **Eddy Mercs**[176] 1151 4-9-8 0................................ AlistairRawlinson(3) 8 5
(Michael Appleby) *hld up: a in rr: rdn and wknd over 2f out* **50/1**

0 **10** 3 ½ **Astrowizard**[97] 3359 3-9-2 0.. NoelGarbutt(3) 5
(Mark H Tompkins) *s.s: a in rr: rdn and wknd over 2f out* **100/1**

2m 7.26s (-1.34) **Going Correction** -0.10s/f (Stan)
WFA 3 from 4yo 6lb 10 Ran SP% **122.7**
Speed ratings (Par 103): **101,100,100,97,94 94,94,83,70,67**
CSF £15.47 TOTE £9.20: £1.90, £1.30, £1.10; EX 26.60 Trifecta £66.60.

Owner The Mucho Men Racing Partnership **Bred** Haymarket Farm Llc **Trained** Kingsclere, Hants

■ Stewards' Enquiry : Alistair Rawlinson five-day ban; used whip when out of contention (6th-10th Oct)

FOCUS
A fair maiden in which jockey Oisin Murphy completed a hat-trick on the night by stealing another race from the front through timing and sheer strength in the saddle. He built on his latest form.

T/Jkpt: Not Won. T/Plt: £159.30 to a £1 stake. Pool: £96,493.77 - 442 winning units T/Qpdt: £62.60 to a £1 stake. Pool: £11,502.79 - 135.8 winning units **Colin Roberts**

6578 NEWMARKET (R-H)
Thursday, September 22

OFFICIAL GOING: Good to firm (stands' side: 7.9, centre: 8.0, far side: 8.2)
Wind: light, half against Weather: mainly cloudy, bright spells

6704 JOHN BANKS RENAULT CAMBRIDGE EBF STALLIONS MAIDEN STKS (PLUS 10 RACE) 1m
2:00 (2:01) (Class 4) 2-Y-O **£5,175** (£1,540; £769; £384) **Stalls** High

Form RPR

1 **Eminent (IRE)** 2-9-0 0.. JimCrowley 3 84+
(Martyn Meade) *q tall: lengthy: scope: bit on the leg: hld up in tch in midfield: clsd to chse ldrs 3f out: rdn to ld over 1f out: edgd lft but r.o wl to go clr ins fnl f: readily* **6/1**

2 2 ¾ **Vantage Point (IRE)** 2-9-0 0.. RobertHavlin 10 78+
(John Gosden) *w'like: green and noisy in prelims: stdd s: hld up in tch in midfield: shkn up ent fnl 2f: rdn and hdwy over 1f out: styd on wl ins fnl f to go 2nd 50yds out: no threat to wnr* **16/1**

4 **3** ¾ **Alqamar**[21] 6054 2-9-0 0.. WilliamBuick 1 76
(Charlie Appleby) *cmpt: warm: chsd ldr: ev ch and rdn 2f out tl unable qck w wnr ent fnl f: styd on same pce after: lost 2nd 50yds out* **15/2**

4 1 ¼ **Azam** 2-9-0 0.. FrankieDettori 8 73
(John Gosden) *str: gd-bodied: lw: chsd ldrs: rdn 3f out: outpcd and swtchd lft ent fnl 2f: rallied to chse ldrs whn carried lft and hmpd over 1f out: styd on ins fnl f: no threat to wnr* **5/1**[3]

5 **5** ½ **Poseidon (IRE)**[21] 6054 2-9-0 0.. HarryBentley 2 72
(Ed Walker) *w'like: led: rdn 2f out: hdd and edgd lft u.p over 1f out: 3rd and unable qck 1f out wknd ins fnl f* **10/1**

5 **6** nse **Okool (FR)**[14] 6262 2-9-0 0.. PaulHanagan 11 77+
(Owen Burrows) *athletic: stdd s: t.k.h: hld up in tch: effrt over 2f out: hdwy to chse ldrs whn hmpd and hit rail over 1f out: nt clr run after tl pushed along and kpt on wl ins fnl f: no threat to wnr* **9/2**[2]

7 8 **Taj Mahal (IRE)**[25] 5936 2-9-0 0.................................(v[1]) RyanMoore 9 52
(A P O'Brien, Ire) *lengthy: chsd ldrs: effrt 2f out: pressing ldrs but struggling to qckn whn squeezed out and snatched up over 1f out: no ch after and eased fnl f* **9/4**[1]

8 ¾ **Beach Break** 2-9-0 0.. FMBerry 6 51
(Ralph Beckett) *medium-sized: q str: bit bkwd: in tch in midfield: outpcd and rdn 3f out: wknd over 1f out* **16/1**

9 1 **Solo Mission** 2-9-0 0.. TomQueally 5 48
(William Haggas) *athletic: bit on the leg: bmpd s: rn green and a towards rr: outpcd 3f out: bhd 2f out* **33/1**

4 **10** 1 ¾ **American Patrol (IRE)**[48] 5121 2-9-0 0.......................... OisinMurphy 4 44
(Michael Bell) *cmpt: stdd and wnt lft s: hld up in tch towards rr: rdn 3f out: sn outpcd: bhd 2f out* **100/1**

0 **11** 6 **Almizhar (IRE)**[8] 6480 2-9-0 0.. JoeFanning 7 30
(Ed Dunlop) *dwlt and short of room leaving stalls: a rr: lost tch over 2f out* **100/1**

1m 39.17s (0.57) **Going Correction** +0.05s/f (Good) 11 Ran SP% **117.4**
Speed ratings (Par 97): **99,96,95,94,93 93,85,84,83,82 76**
CSF £96.17 TOTE £9.00: £2.50, £5.90, £2.40; EX 126.90 Trifecta £1723.70.

Owner Sir Peter Vela **Bred** Premier Bloodstock **Trained** Newmarket, Suffolk

■ Stewards' Enquiry : Harry Bentley five-day ban; caused interference (6th-10th Oct)

FOCUS
Far Side Course used. Following a dry night the ground was changed to good to firm (from good the previous day) resulting in a few non-runners. Stalls: stands side except 1m4f and 2m, which were centre. The last six winners of this maiden (including the high-class Telescope in 2012) had previous racecourse experience, but this time the first two were newcomers. It was quite a rough race, with plenty of trouble against the nearside rail over a furlong from home. The pace looked just a fair one and the winning time was 4.17sec outside standard. After the race Robert Havlin said: "It's good ground", while William Buick said: "It's good to firm."

6705 TURFTRAX NURSERY H'CAP 1m
2:35 (2:35) (Class 2) 2-Y-O **£9,056** (£2,695; £1,346; £673) **Stalls** High

Form RPR

113 **1** **Fly At Dawn (USA)**[19] 6122 2-9-4 **91**.............................. WilliamBuick 9 95
(Charlie Appleby) *q str: sltly on toes: bmpd s: w ldr tl led wl over 2f out: rdn and forged ahd over 1f out: styd on wl and a doing enough fnl f: rdn out* **9/2**[3]

5232 **2** ¾ **Whip Nae Nae (IRE)**[12] 6314 2-8-5 **78**.......................... TomMarquand 3 80
(Richard Hannon) *lw: in tch in midfield: effrt 2f out: rdn and hdwy over 1f out: chsd wnr 1f out: kpt on but a hld ins fnl f* **9/1**

213 **3** 1 ¼ **Jumping Jack (IRE)**[17] 6191 2-7-7 **73** oh1...................... DavidEgan(7) 4 72
(Richard Hughes) *in tch in midfield: effrt to chse ldrs 2f out: edgd lft over 1f out: styd on same pce ins fnl f* **33/1**

411 **4** 2 ¾ **Haulani (USA)**[34] 5594 2-8-9 **82**.. PaulHanagan 2 74
(Philip Hide) *hld up in last pair: rdn 1/2-way: drvn and outpcd 3f out: rallied and swtchd lft 1f out: kpt on to pass btn horses ins fnl f: snatched 4th last stride: no threat to ldrs* **9/4**[1]

316 **5** shd **Red Ensign (IRE)**[19] 6116 2-9-3 **90**.................................. AndreaAtzeni 5 82
(Simon Crisford) *chsd ldrs: rdn and ev ch 3f out tl unable qck over 1f out: lost 2nd 1f out: wknd ins fnl f* **10/3**[2]

10 **6** 1 ¼ **Balgair**[14] 6260 2-8-8 **81** ow1.. JimCrowley 6 70
(Jonathan Portman) *led tl wl over 2f out: sn rdn and unable qck: lost pl 2f out: wknd over 1f out* **10/1**

6224 **7** 5 **Fortune Of War**[19] 6108 2-8-2 **80** ow2......................... CharlieBennett(5) 1 57
(Jane Chapple-Hyam) *in tch in midfield: rdn over 2f out: sn struggling: wknd over 1f out* **10/1**

5126 **8** 3 **Bacchus**[13] 6285 2-9-7 **94**.. JimmyFortune 7 64
(Brian Meehan) *wnt lft s: bustled along leaving stalls: in tch in midfield: effrt to chse ldrs 3f out: nt clr run over 2f out: sn struggling: bhd ins fnl f* **9/1**

1m 37.85s (-0.75) **Going Correction** +0.05s/f (Good) 8 Ran SP% **113.2**
Speed ratings (Par 101): **105,104,103,100,100 98,93,90**
CSF £42.95 CT £1181.23 TOTE £4.60: £1.30, £2.70, £3.30; EX 47.20 Trifecta £289.30.

Owner Godolphin **Bred** Darley **Trained** Newmarket, Suffolk

The Form Book, Raceform Ltd, Newbury, RG14 5SJ

FOCUS
Official figures suggested this was a useful nursery at least and the whole field remained fairly close to the stands' side. The winner grabbed the rail and raced prominently early on.

6706 THOROUGHBRED BREEDERS' ASSOCIATION SMALL BREEDERS' FILLIES' CONDITIONS STKS (PLUS 10 RACE) 7f
3:10 (3:10) (Class 2) 2-Y-O **£15,562 (**£4,660; £2,330; £1,165) **Stalls** High

Form RPR

4433 **1** **Urban Fox**[14] 6258 2-9-3 99 MartinHarley 5 97
(James Tate) *sltly on toes: stdd s: trckd ldrs: effrt 2f out: rdn to press ldr jst ins fnl f: led 100yds out: pushed out towards fin* **11/4**[2]

21 **2** *shd* **Unforgetable Filly**[12] 6336 2-9-3 0 JimCrowley 3 97
(Hugo Palmer) *q lengthy: pressed ldr: rdn to ld over 1f out: pressed and drvn jst ins fnl f: hdd 100yds out: kpt u.p towards fin* **11/10**[1]

4 **3** *1 3/4* **Highland Pass**[20] 6088 2-8-8 0 OisinMurphy 1 83
(Andrew Balding) *w'like: stdd s: hld up in tch in rr: clsd 3f out: effrt 2f out: wnt 3rd and switching rt ins fnl f: kpt on same pce fnl 100yds* **9/1**

1332 **4** *2 1/4* **Storm Cry**[14] 6257 2-9-3 84 JoeFanning 4 86
(Mark Johnston) *led: rdn ent fnl 2f: hdd over 1f out: unable qck and wknd ins fnl f* **7/2**[3]

1m 26.79s (1.39) **Going Correction** +0.05s/f (Good) **4** Ran SP% **106.5**
Speed ratings (Par 98): **94,93,91,89**
CSF £6.08 TOTE £3.20; EX 4.90 Trifecta £15.30.
Owner Saeed Manana **Bred** Mascalls Stud **Trained** Newmarket, Suffolk

FOCUS
An interesting and valuable little juvenile fillies' event. They went just an even pace despite a disputed lead.

6707 TATTERSALLS STKS (REGISTERED AS THE SOMERVILLE STAKES) (GROUP 3) (C&G) 7f
3:40 (3:41) (Class 1) 2-Y-O
£28,355 (£10,750; £5,380; £2,680; £1,345; £675) **Stalls** High

Form RPR

13 **1** **Larchmont Lad (IRE)**[13] 6285 2-9-0 0 SeanLevey 2 109
(Richard Hannon) *trckd ldrs: effrt and ev ch 2f out: drvn to ld jst ins fnl f: forged ahd wl ins fnl f: drvn out* **8/1**[3]

2 *3/4* **Whitecliffsofdover (USA)**[52] 4961 2-9-0 0 RyanMoore 5 107
(A P O'Brien, Ire) *str: pressed ldr: rdn and ev ch 2f out: drvn to ld jst over 1f out: hdd and edgd lft jst ins fnl f: styd on same pce fnl 100yds* **9/2**[2]

011 **3** *shd* **Sir Dancealot (IRE)**[19] 6122 2-9-0 92 JimCrowley 8 107+
(David Elsworth) *q str: stdd s: hld up in tch in rr: clsd and swtchd rt over 2f out: effrt to chse ldrs over 1f out: drvn and ev ch ins fnl f: changed legs and no ex wl ins fnl f: wknd cl home* **9/1**

313 **4** *1/2* **Best Solution (IRE)**[18] 6180 2-9-0 0 WilliamBuick 7 105
(Saeed bin Suroor) *in tch in midfield: clsd to trck ldrs and nt clr run 2f out: swtchd rt and effrt ent fnl f: chsd ldrs and keeping on whn pushed lft and hmpd ins fnl f: kpt on towards fin* **12/1**

31 **5** *2* **Law And Order (IRE)**[27] 5848 2-9-0 0 MartinHarley 1 100
(James Tate) *cmpt: led: rdn ent fnl 2f: drvn and hdd jst over 1f out: keeping on same pce and btn whn squeezed for room and hmpd ins fnl f: kpt on same pce after* **16/1**

31 **6** *1 1/4* **Ultimate Avenue (IRE)**[41] 5356 2-9-0 0 GeorgeBaker 6 97
(Ed Walker) *q tall: scope: t.k.h: hld up in tch in midfield: effrt and nt clr run over 1f out: effrt 1f out: sn hung rt and no imp ins fnl f* **8/1**[3]

11 **7** *4 1/2* **Escobar (IRE)**[40] 5401 2-9-0 0 FrankieDettori 3 84+
(Hugo Palmer) *q str: stdd s: hld up in tch in last pair: clsd and midfield 1/2-way: chsd ldrs and rdn 2f out: unable qck and btn ent fnl f: eased ins fnl f* **6/5**[1]

2116 **8** *hd* **Bear Valley (IRE)**[36] 5556 2-9-0 95 JoeFanning 4 84
(Mark Johnston) *in tch in midfield: lsoing pl and rdn 3f out: bhd over 1f out: wknd fnl f* **20/1**

1m 24.81s (-0.59) **Going Correction** +0.05s/f (Good) **8** Ran SP% **114.2**
Speed ratings (Par 105): **105,104,104,103,101 99,94,94**
CSF £43.62 TOTE £7.50: £2.10, £1.50, £2.50; EX 42.70 Trifecta £249.30.
Owner Michael Geoghegan **Bred** Domenico Fonzo **Trained** East Everleigh, Wilts

FOCUS
This race is best known as the Somerville Tattersall Stakes. The past ten renewals suggest a really top colt may not emerge from this, although Havana Gold went on to Group 1 success as a 3yo, but there was little doubt it was a hot race considering the recent form of these.

6708 JOCKEY CLUB ROSE BOWL (FORMERLY THE FENWOLF STKS) (LISTED RACE) 2m
4:15 (4:18) (Class 1) 3-Y-O+
£22,684 (£8,600; £4,304; £2,144; £1,076; £540) **Stalls** Centre

Form RPR

34-5 **1** **Justice Belle (IRE)**[19] 6118 4-8-12 94 FrankieDettori 4 102
(Ed Walker) *mde all: rdn jst over 2f out: hrd pressed and drvn over 1f out: styd on gamely ins fnl f: all out* **16/1**

2052 **2** *nse* **Seamour (IRE)**[13] 6283 5-9-3 104 (p) GeorgeBaker 7 107
(Brian Ellison) *stdd and dropped in bhd after s: hld up in rr: clsd over 2f out: shkn up and effrt in 4th 1f out: rdn ins fnl f: styd on to chse wnr wl ins fnl f: clsng grad cl home: jst hld* **6/4**[1]

0001 **3** *1/2* **Fun Mac (GER)**[13] 6293 5-9-3 100 (t) JimCrowley 9 106
(Hughie Morrison) *lw: styd wd: chsd ldrs: wnt 2nd and ev ch 3f out: rdn over 2f out: drvn over 1f out: kpt on but unable qck wl ins fnl f* **7/2**[2]

1605 **4** *1 1/4* **Goldmember**[26] 5872 3-8-6 103 ow1 [1] OisinMurphy 1 106
(David Simcock) *stdd s: hld up in last pair: clsd 4f out: rdn to chal over 1f out tl no ex ins fnl f: wknd wl ins fnl f* **10/1**

4164 **5** *20* **Forever Popular (USA)**[14] 6259 4-9-1 100 RyanMoore 2 79
(William Haggas) *wl in tch in midfield: rdn to chse ldrs 3f out: 5th and btn over 1f out: wknd fnl f* **7/2**[2]

26- **6** *36* **Sir Fever (URU)**[544] 1093 5-9-3 113 [1] WilliamBuick 5 38
(Charlie Appleby) *chsd wnr tl 3f out: sn rdn and lost pl: bhd 2f out: heavily eased fnl f: t.o* **7/1**[3]

3m 24.13s (-6.37) **Going Correction** +0.05s/f (Good)
WFA 3 from 4yo+ 12lb **6** Ran SP% **111.9**
Speed ratings (Par 111): **117,116,116,116,106 88**
CSF £40.55 TOTE £11.00: £3.60, £1.60; EX 47.00 Trifecta £130.30.
Owner Robert Ng **Bred** Lynch Bages Ltd & Camas Park Stud **Trained** Upper Lambourn, Berks

FOCUS
This Listed staying event was hit by four non-runners. Despite an even gallop, the first four were within a length or so of each other half a furlong from home. The winner built on her reappearance promise.

6709 WEATHERBYS GENERAL STUD BOOK H'CAP 1m 4f
4:50 (4:55) (Class 2) (0-100,95) 3-Y-O+ **£12,938 (**£3,850; £1,924; £962) **Stalls** Centre

Form RPR

314 **1** **Frontiersman**[49] 5074 3-8-13 **90** WilliamBuick 8 106+
(Charlie Appleby) *cmpt: lw: trckd ldrs: wnt 2nd and travelling strly over 2f out: led on bit over 1f out: shkn up and qcknd 1f out: sn clr and r.o strly: eased cl home: v easily* **11/8**[1]

0526 **2** *4 1/2* **Croquembouche (IRE)**[24] 5964 7-9-4 **87** LiamKeniry 2 93
(Ed de Giles) *led: rdn ent fnl 2f: drvn and jnd by cantering wnr over 1f out: hdd 1f out: no ch w wnr fnl f: kpt on to hold 2nd* **33/1**

1310 **3** *1/2* **Appeared**[124] 2487 4-9-8 **91** AndreaAtzeni 9 96+
(Roger Varian) *lw: stdd after s: t.k.h: hld up in tch in last trio: clsd to chse ldrs and rdn 2f out: wandered and unable qck jst over 1f out: no ch w wnr and kpt on same pce ins fnl f* **11/4**[2]

0231 **4** *1 1/2* **Carry Me Home**[40] 5413 3-8-10 **87** FrankieDettori 1 90
(Charles Hills) *chsd ldrs: rdn 3f out: drvn over 2f out: styd on same pce u.p fnl 2f* **7/1**[3]

102 **5** *3 3/4* **Man Look**[33] 5650 4-9-5 **88** OisinMurphy 7 85
(Andrew Balding) *lw: t.k.h: chsd ldr tl over 2f out: sn u.p and lost pl: bhd over 1f out* **12/1**

1311 **6** *nk* **William Hunter**[20] 6074 4-9-4 **87** WilliamTwiston-Davies 5 83
(Alan King) *lw: stdd after s: t.k.h: hld up in tch in last trio: clsd over 2f out: effrt and unable qck over 1f out: sn btn and wknd fnl f* **8/1**

1020 **7** *8* **Shakopee**[19] 6118 4-9-12 **95** AdamKirby 6 79
(Luca Cumani) *stdd s: hld up in tch in rr: rdn 3f out: sn struggling: bhd over 1f out* **10/1**

2m 30.33s (-1.67) **Going Correction** +0.05s/f (Good)
WFA 3 from 4yo+ 8lb **7** Ran SP% **112.1**
Speed ratings (Par 109): **107,104,103,102,100 99,94**
CSF £46.46 CT £113.08 TOTE £2.30: £1.80, £10.70; EX 42.90 Trifecta £187.00.
Owner Godolphin **Bred** Stanley Estate And Stud Co **Trained** Newmarket, Suffolk

FOCUS
This decent middle-distance handicap appeared to be run at a reasonable gallop considering the field size, and it produced an easy winner. The runner-up sets the standard.

6710 MOLSON COORS H'CAP 1m
5:20 (5:26) (Class 3) (0-95,93) 3-Y-O+ **£9,056 (**£2,695; £1,346; £673) **Stalls** High

Form RPR

1012 **1** **Huntlaw**[11] 6372 3-9-2 **89** JoeFanning 7 99
(Mark Johnston) *mde virtually all: rdn 2f out: drvn 2 l clr jst ins fnl f: hrd pressed towards fin: jst hld on* **10/1**

-311 **2** *shd* **Great Order (USA)**[20] 6076 3-9-6 **93** WilliamBuick 9 103+
(Saeed bin Suroor) *lw: dwlt: t.k.h: hld up in tch in midfield: clsd to chse ldrs 3f out: rdn and no imp over 1f out: hdwy ins fnl f: chsd wnr 100yds: styd on strly towards fin: jst failed* **7/4**[1]

1003 **3** *2 1/4* **Chevallier**[12] 6320 4-9-3 **86** FrankieDettori 8 91
(Archie Watson) *chsd ldrs: rdn and ev ch ent fnl 2f tl unable qck jst over 1f out: styd on same pce ins fnl f* **10/1**

-513 **4** *1 1/2* **Michele Strogoff**[19] 6132 3-9-6 **93** AdamKirby 4 94
(David Loughnane) *w wnr: rdn and ev ch over 2f out unable qck over 1f out: wknd ins fnl f* **9/1**

-010 **5** *2 1/4* **Iconic (IRE)**[26] 5866 4-9-0 **83** OisinMurphy 10 79
(Henry Candy) *t.k.h: pressed ldrs tl lost pl and rdn over 2f out: no imp u.p over 1f out: wknd ins fnl f* **16/1**

1006 **6** *nk* **Fieldsman (USA)**[61] 4627 4-9-6 **89** [1] TomMarquand 12 84
(George Scott) *stdd s: t.k.h: hld up in tch in midfield: effrt 2f out: no imp u.p over 1f out: wknd ins fnl f* **16/1**

215 **7** *3/4* **Wimpole Hall**[19] 6126 3-9-1 **88** (p) LiamKeniry 3 82+
(William Jarvis) *lw@ stdd s: hld up in tch: effrt 3f out: no imp 2f out: swtchd rt 1f out: kpt on same pce after* **7/1**[3]

/00- **8** *1/2* **Prince Of Johanne (IRE)**[497] 2222 10-9-7 **90** (p) ShaneKelly 1 82
(Tom Tate) *hld up in tch: hdwy 3f out: unable qck u.p over 1f out: wknd ins fnl f* **50/1**

123 **9** *5* **War Glory (IRE)**[15] 6232 3-9-3 **90** RyanMoore 6 71
(Richard Hannon) *lw: hld up wl in tch in midfield: effrt 2f out: rdn and no rspnse over 1f out: wknd ins fnl f* **9/2**[2]

0300 **10** *1 1/2* **Directorship**[20] 6076 10-9-4 **87** FergusSweeney 5 64
(Patrick Chamings) *hld up in tch: effrt 3f out: no hdwy and btn over 1f out: bhd and eased ins fnl f* **50/1**

1020 **11** *1* **Dot Green (IRE)**[34] 5616 3-8-9 **82** StevieDonohoe 2 57
(Mark H Tompkins) *in tch in midfield: effrt over 2f out: no imp u.p over 1f out: wknd fnl f: bhd and eased towards fin* **100/1**

-063 **12** *10* **Ceaseless (IRE)**[25] 5933 4-9-2 **85** MartinHarley 11 37
(James Tate) *in tch but a towards rr: rdn over 3f out: sn struggling: bhd 2f out: eased wl ins fnl f* **16/1**

1m 37.34s (-1.26) **Going Correction** +0.05s/f (Good)
WFA 3 from 4yo+ 4lb **12** Ran SP% **117.8**
Speed ratings (Par 107): **108,107,105,104,101 101,100,100,95,93 92,82**
CSF £27.46 CT £188.46 TOTE £9.90: £2.70, £1.20, £3.30; EX 33.30 Trifecta £300.00.
Owner Duke Of Roxburghe **Bred** Floors Farming **Trained** Middleham Moor, N Yorks

FOCUS
A decent handicap run at a good pace with a few vying for the lead. The winner continues to progress.

6711 NEWMARKET CHALLENGE WHIP (A H'CAP) 1m 2f
5:55 (5:56) (Class 6) (0-85,88) 3-Y-O+ **£0Stalls** High

Form RPR

152 **1** **Nigel**[19] 6142 4-9-7 **85** ShaneKelly 2 91
(Richard Hughes) *mde all: rdn 2f out: styd on wl ins fnl f: rdn out* **2/1**[2]

4322 **2** *2* **Satish**[10] 6415 3-8-6 **76** (b) FrankieDettori 3 79
(John Gosden) *swtchd rt after s: racd alone in centre: chsd wnr: rdn over 2f out: edgd lft ent fnl f: kpt on same pce ins fnl f* **5/6**[1]

1500 **3** *2 1/4* **Primogeniture (IRE)**[13] 6298 5-9-10 **88** (t) WilliamTwiston-Davies 1 86
(Mary Hambro) *hld up in tch in 3rd: effrt 2f out: unable qck u.p over 1f out: plugged on same pce ins fnl f* **7/2**[3]

2m 7.27s (1.47) **Going Correction** +0.05s/f (Good)
WFA 3 from 4yo+ 6lb **3** Ran SP% **110.1**
Speed ratings (Par 101): **96,94,92**
CSF £4.21 TOTE £2.50; EX 3.70 Trifecta £2.90.
Owner Normandie Stud Ltd **Bred** Normandie Stud Ltd **Trained** Upper Lambourn, Berkshire

FOCUS
Three runners lined up for this long-established race and it's hard to think this is form worth following. The winner is rated to his AW latest.
T/Plt: £1,462.00 to a £1 stake. Pool: £91,184.96 - 45.53 winning units T/Qpdt: £77.00 to a £1 stake. Pool: £6,647.02 - 63.85 winning units **Steve Payne**

6515 PONTEFRACT (L-H)
Thursday, September 22

OFFICIAL GOING: Good to soft (7.5)
Wind: Light behind Weather: Fine & dry

6712 EBF STALLIONS RACINGUK.COM/HD MAIDEN STKS (PLUS 10 RACE) 6f
2:20 (2:20) (Class 4) 2-Y-O **£4,528** (£1,347; £673; £336) **Stalls** Low

Form RPR
2302 **1** **Father McKenzie**[7] 6515 2-9-5 73 GrahamLee 10 78
(Mick Channon) *trckd ldng pair: hdwy to chal wl over 1f out: rdn to ld appr fnl f: kpt on strly* **5/1**[3]
2 2 ¼ **Benjamin Thomas (IRE)** 2-9-5 0 JasonHart 5 71
(John Quinn) *trckd ldrs: pushed along 2f out: rdn and hdwy over 1f out: chsd wnr ins fnl f: no imp towards fin* **10/1**
00 **3** 2 ½ **Ninety Years Young**[20] 6087 2-9-5 0 SilvestreDeSousa 13 64
(David Elsworth) *led: rdn along 11/2f out: hdd appr fnl f: sn drvn and kpt on same pce* **16/1**
4 1 ¾ **Arnold** 2-9-5 0 PaulMulrennan 6 59
(Ann Duffield) *t.k.h: hld up towards rr: hdwy over 2f out: rdn wl over 1f out: styd on fnl f: nrst fin* **9/1**
25 **5** nk **Sugar Beach (FR)**[24] 5966 2-9-0 0 PJMcDonald 1 53
(Ann Duffield) *t.k.h: in tch on inner: pushed along over 2f out: rdn to chse ldrs over 1f out: sn no imp* **7/2**[1]
0 **6** 3 ½ **Like Minds**[51] 4981 2-9-0 0 TomEaves 12 42
(David Brown) *cl up: rdn along 2f out: grad wknd* **100/1**
00 **7** 1 **Dusty Bin**[39] 5433 2-9-5 0 KevinStott 3 44
(Kevin Ryan) *midfield: effrt and sme hdwy 2f out: sn rdn and n.d* **50/1**
23 **8** 2 **Mont Royal (FR)**[31] 5713 2-9-5 0 DanielTudhope 11 38
(Ollie Pears) *hld up: effrt and sme hdwy on outer 2f out: rdn and edgd lft over 1f out: sn btn* **4/1**[2]
6 **9** 3 **Gokena (FR)**[57] 4759 2-9-0 0 ShaneGray 2 24
(Kevin Ryan) *trckd ldrs on inner: pushed along over 2f out: sn rdn and wknd* **4/1**[2]
05 **10** 1 **Wily Rumpus (IRE)**[22] 6034 2-9-5 0 ThomasBrown 9 26
(Ed Walker) *a towards rr* **16/1**
11 17 **Breathoffreshair** 2-9-5 0 RoystonFfrench 8
(Richard Guest) *dwlt: a rr: bhd fnl 2f* **25/1**
0 **12** 3 ¼ **Millybond**[19] 6129 2-9-0 0 TedDurcan 7
(David Brown) *in tch on outer: rdn along wl over 2f out: sn wknd* **100/1**

1m 18.18s (1.28) **Going Correction** +0.15s/f (Good) **12** Ran SP% **117.5**
Speed ratings (Par 97): **97,94,90,88,87 83,81,79,75,73 51,46**
CSF £52.85 TOTE £4.80: £1.70, £3.80, £4.40; EX 56.60 Trifecta £640.00.
Owner M Channon **Bred** Mike Channon Bloodstock Ltd **Trained** West Ilsley, Berks

FOCUS
After the first race Paul Mulrennan said of the ground: "It's riding slow, definitely on the easy side." It proved difficult to get into this pretty modest maiden, with the principals always well placed. The time was almost 4sec outside standard.

6713 EBF STALLIONS BREEDING WINNERS FILLIES' NURSERY H'CAP 1m 4y
2:55 (3:02) (Class 4) (0-85,83) 2-Y-O **£6,469** (£1,925; £962; £481) **Stalls** Low

Form RPR
032 **1** **Tomorrowcomes (IRE)**[30] 5747 2-8-13 75 TonyHamilton 2 78
(Richard Fahey) *trckd ldrs: hdwy 2f out: rdn ent fnl f and sn cl up: styd on wl to ld last 50 yds* **6/1**[3]
213 **2** ½ **Soldier's Girl (IRE)**[33] 5632 2-9-7 83 JamesDoyle 10 85
(Richard Hannon) *trckd ldr: hdwy and cl up 2f out: rdn to take slt ld over 1f out: drvn and edgd rt ins fnl f: hdd and no ex last 50 yds* **8/1**
003 **3** ¾ **Silver Link (IRE)**[14] 6250 2-8-10 72 SteveDrowne 9 72
(Marcus Tregoning) *dwlt: hld up in rr: rdn along and outpcd over 2f out: hdwy over 1f out: kpt on strly fnl f: tk 3rd on line* **14/1**
041 **4** shd **Nepeta (USA)**[29] 5778 2-8-9 71 SilvestreDeSousa 7 71
(Mark Johnston) *led: pushed along 2f out: rdn and hdd over 1f out: rallied and ev ch ins fnl f tl no ex last 50 yds* **5/1**[2]
1 **5** ½ **Kind Of Beauty (IRE)**[30] 5747 2-9-2 78 JackMitchell 5 77
(Hugo Palmer) *towards rr: hdwy on outer 2f out: rdn along wl over 1f out: drvn and kpt on fnl f* **7/4**[1]
604 **6** ½ **Sandwood Bay**[30] 5747 2-8-8 70 ThomasBrown 3 68
(Mark H Tompkins) *towards rr: hdwy on inner over 2f out: rdn to chse ldrs over 1f out: sn drvn and kpt on same pce* **33/1**
634 **7** 2 **Mistress Viz (IRE)**[26] 5861 2-8-3 65 JamesSullivan 4 59
(John Mackie) *trckd ldrs: effrt over 2f out: sn rdn along and wknd wl over 1f out* **33/1**
41 **8** 8 **Kiruna Peak (IRE)**[68] 4397 2-8-13 75 GrahamLee 8 51
(Mick Channon) *trckd ldrs on outer: pushed along 3f out: rdn over 2f out: sn wknd* **6/1**[3]
5502 **9** 1 ½ **Conistone**[16] 6213 2-8-3 65 CamHardie 6 38
(James Bethell) *trckd ldrs: cl up 3f out: rdn along over 2f out: sn drvn and wknd* **14/1**

1m 47.64s (1.74) **Going Correction** +0.15s/f (Good) **9** Ran SP% **111.9**
Speed ratings (Par 94): **97,96,95,95,95 94,92,84,83**
CSF £50.79 CT £640.32 TOTE £7.90: £1.60, £2.20, £3.90; EX 41.70 Trifecta £424.20.
Owner Mrs Richard Henry **Bred** Premier Bloodstock **Trained** Musley Bank, N Yorks
■ Party Nights was withdrawn. Price at time of withdrawal 3/1. Rule 4 applies to bets struck prior to board prices - deduction 25p in the pound. New market formed.

FOCUS
This was delayed by several minutes after Party Nights got loose and had to be withdrawn. They finished in a heap in this fair fillies' nursery, when again it paid to race prominently.

6714 RACING UK HD ON SKY432 H'CAP (DIV I) 6f
3:30 (3:30) (Class 4) (0-85,91) 3-Y-O+ **£5,175** (£1,540; £769; £384) **Stalls** Low

Form RPR
6001 **1** **Lincoln (IRE)**[6] 6537 5-9-13 91 6ex GrahamLee 4 99+
(Mick Channon) *trckd ldrs: hdwy on outer over 1f out: rdn ent fnl f: styd on strly to ld last 50 yds* **5/2**[1]
1320 **2** ¾ **Cosmic Chatter**[20] 6079 6-9-3 81 (p) JamesSullivan 1 87
(Ruth Carr) *trckd ldrs on inner: hdwy to chse ldr ent fnl f: sn rdn and kpt on* **7/1**
2030 **3** ¾ **Regal Dan (IRE)**[14] 6263 6-9-7 85 DanielTudhope 2 89
(David O'Meara) *led: rdn clr over 1f out: drvn ins fnl f: hdd and no ex last 50 yds* **9/2**[2]
0006 **4** ¾ **Kommander Kirkup**[19] 6131 5-9-0 78 (p) SamJames 5 79
(John Davies) *trckd ldrs: hdwy 2f out: rdn over 1f out: drvn and kpt on same pce fnl f* **33/1**
0514 **5** ½ **Gin In The Inn (IRE)**[29] 5774 3-8-12 78 TonyHamilton 12 78+
(Richard Fahey) *hld up towards rr: hdwy wl over 1f out: rdn and kpt on fnl f: nrst fin* **8/1**
040 **6** ¾ **Mass Rally (IRE)**[47] 5182 9-9-2 80 (b) PaulMulrennan 9 77
(Michael Dods) *hld up in tch: hdwy on inner over 1f out: effrt and nt clr run ent fnl f: kpt on* **16/1**
0016 **7** ½ **Money Team (IRE)**[9] 6449 5-9-2 80 GrahamGibbons 8 76
(David Barron) *trckd ldrs: hdwy 2f out: rdn over 1f out: hld whn n.m.r ins fnl f* **9/1**
5210 **8** 2 ¼ **Yeeoow (IRE)**[11] 6382 7-9-4 82 JoeyHaynes 6 70
(K R Burke) *cl up: rdn wl over 1f out: drvn appr fnl f: sn wknd* **13/2**[3]
1656 **9** nk **Brilliant Vanguard (IRE)**[29] 5759 3-9-1 81 ShaneGray 13 68
(Kevin Ryan) *a towards rr* **20/1**
0503 **10** 1 ¾ **Mon Brav**[7] 6522 9-8-0 71 oh3 BenRobinson(7) 3 53
(Brian Ellison) *a towards rr* **16/1**
450 **11** 9 **Avenue Of Stars**[22] 6027 3-8-11 77 (p) KevinStott 10 30
(Karen McLintock) *reminders s: chsd ldrs: rdn along wl over 2f out: sn wknd* **20/1**

1m 17.37s (0.47) **Going Correction** +0.15s/f (Good)
WFA 3 from 5yo+ 2lb **11** Ran SP% **117.9**
Speed ratings (Par 105): **102,101,100,99,98 97,96,93,93,90 78**
CSF £19.58 CT £75.51 TOTE £3.20: £1.40, £2.70, £1.90; EX 22.80 Trifecta £74.90.
Owner Billy Parish **Bred** Tipper House Stud **Trained** West Ilsley, Berks

FOCUS
A fair sprint handicap. The second sets the standard with the winner rated to this year's best.

6715 SIMON SCROPE DALBY SCREW-DRIVER H'CAP 1m 2f 6y
4:00 (4:00) (Class 2) (0-105,100) 3-Y-O+
£12,450 (£3,728; £1,864; £932; £466; £234) **Stalls** Low

Form RPR
124- **1** **Memorial Day (IRE)**[348] 7120 5-9-9 96 JamesDoyle 2 110
(Saeed bin Suroor) *trckd ldr: hdwy 2f out: rdn to ld 1f out: sn clr: styd on strly* **5/1**
-000 **2** 8 **Fattsota**[68] 4407 8-9-10 97 DanielTudhope 6 95
(David O'Meara) *led: rdn clr wl over 1f out: hdd 1f out: sn drvn and kpt on: no ch w wnr* **33/1**
-14 **3** 3 ½ **El Vip (IRE)**[20] 6081 3-8-11 90 JamieSpencer 1 81
(Luca Cumani) *hld up in rr: hdwy over 3f out: effrt 2f out: sn rdn: chsd ldng pair over 1f out: drvn and no imp fnl f* **15/8**[1]
1120 **4** 2 ½ **Shabbah (IRE)**[54] 4863 3-8-12 91 TedDurcan 3 77
(Sir Michael Stoute) *trckd ldrs: hdwy to chse ldng pair over 2f out: sn rdn and kpt on one pce* **7/2**[2]
3424 **5** shd **Masterpaver**[26] 5879 5-8-10 83 TonyHamilton 7 69
(Richard Fahey) *rr: hdwy over 3f out: rdn along over 2f out: plugged on: n.d* **16/1**
-115 **6** 52 **Shabeeb (USA)**[77] 4059 3-9-7 100 DaneO'Neill 4
(Roger Varian) *trckd ldrs: pushed along over 4f out: rdn along over 3f out: sn lost pl and bhd: eased fnl 2f* **4/1**[3]
3005 **7** 11 **Montsarrat (IRE)**[25] 5932 3-8-13 92 SilvestreDeSousa 5
(Mark Johnston) *chsd ldng pair on outer: pushed along over 4f out: rdn along over 3f out: sn wknd and bhd whn eased fnl 2f* **12/1**

2m 11.82s (-1.88) **Going Correction** +0.15s/f (Good)
WFA 3 from 5yo+ 6lb **7** Ran SP% **110.2**
Speed ratings (Par 109): **113,106,103,101,101 60,51**
CSF £119.27 TOTE £6.00: £2.60, £11.50; EX 151.10 Trifecta £573.00.
Owner Godolphin **Bred** Darley **Trained** Newmarket, Suffolk

FOCUS
This good handicap was run at a strong gallop, and once more those who raced up with the pace dominated. It may be prudent not to take the form of the race too literally, for all that the winner impressed.

6716 BRITISH STALLIONS STUDS EBF FRIER WOOD MAIDEN STKS (PLUS 10 RACE) 1m 4y
4:35 (4:36) (Class 4) 2-Y-O **£4,528** (£1,347; £673; £336) **Stalls** Low

Form RPR
3 **1** **Cirencester**[19] 6111 2-9-0 0 SilvestreDeSousa 5 76+
(Ralph Beckett) *mde most: rdn clr appr fnl f: styd on strly* **5/4**[1]
3663 **2** 3 ½ **Oceanus (IRE)**[23] 5990 2-9-5 75 JamesDoyle 4 73
(Ed Dunlop) *trckd ldng pair: hdwy 1/2-way and sn chsng wnr: rdn wl over 1f out: drvn and kpt on same pce fnl f* **7/2**[3]
3 **3** ¾ **Mayleen (IRE)**[100] 3248 2-9-0 0 PJMcDonald 7 66
(Ann Duffield) *hld up in tch: hdwy over 4f out: chsd ldrs over 2f out: rdn wl over 1f out: kpt on fnl f* **16/1**
434 **4** hd **Actualisation**[48] 5107 2-9-5 74 JasonHart 3 71
(John Quinn) *chsd wnr: rdn along wl over 2f out: drvn wl over 1f out: kpt on u.p fnl f* **2/1**[2]
5 2 **Avantgardist (GER)** 2-9-5 0 PaulMulrennan 1 67
(Mark Johnston) *trckd ldrs: effrt over 2f out: sn rdn and kpt on same pce* **16/1**
6 ½ **Wild Shot** 2-9-5 0 RyanTate 6 65
(James Eustace) *dwlt: t.k.h in rr: hdwy over 2f out: swtchd rt to outer and rdn wl over 1f out: sn no imp* **50/1**
7 43 **Jumbo Vee (IRE)** 2-9-5 0 DanielTudhope 2
(Declan Carroll) *a rr: rdn along over 2f out: sn outpcd and eased* **33/1**

1m 47.91s (2.01) **Going Correction** +0.15s/f (Good) **7** Ran SP% **116.7**
Speed ratings (Par 97): **95,91,90,90,88 88,45**
CSF £6.38 TOTE £2.10: £1.70, £2.00; EX 6.50 Trifecta £27.50.
Owner Robert Allcock **Bred** Bba 2010 Ltd **Trained** Kimpton, Hants

FOCUS
A very ordinary maiden in which the winner made most.

6717 RACING UK PROFITS RETURNED TO RACING H'CAP 5f
5:10 (5:10) (Class 5) (0-75,75) 3-Y-O+ **£3,234** (£962; £481; £240) **Stalls** Low

Form RPR
26 **1** **Van Gerwen**[20] 6079 3-8-13 73 NathanEvans(5) 2 83
(Les Eyre) *qckly away: mde all: rdn clr wl over 1f out: kpt on strly* **11/4**[1]
4620 **2** 2 ½ **Burning Thread (IRE)**[26] 5882 9-9-4 72 (b) SilvestreDeSousa 7 73
(David Elsworth) *hld up in rr: hdwy on inner over 1f out: rdn to chse wnr ins fnl f: sn drvn and no imp* **10/1**

3601 **3** *nk* **Market Choice (IRE)**[19] 6133 3-9-6 **75**........................ PaulMulrennan 4 75
(Michael Dods) *trckd ldrs: hdwy 2f out: rdn over 1f out: drvn and kpt on same pce fnl f* **9/2**[3]

3310 **4** *nk* **Wilde Extravagance (IRE)**[24] 5978 3-9-1 **70**........................ JoeDoyle 6 69
(Julie Camacho) *cl up on outer: effrt 2f out: sn rdn: drvn appr fnl f: kpt on same pce* **10/1**

3133 **5** *nse* **Rose Eclair**[19] 6133 3-9-5 **74**..(b) DavidAllan 1 73
(Tim Easterby) *cl up on inner: rdn along 2f out: drvn over 1f out: kpt on same pce* **3/1**[2]

0660 **6** *9* **Spike (IRE)**[24] 5978 3-8-13 **68**...................................... GrahamGibbons 3 34
(David Barron) *prom: rdn along 2f out: wknd over 1f out* **11/2**

2216 **7** *nk* **Dance Alone**[8] 6475 3-9-6 **75**..(b) ShaneGray 8 40
(Kevin Ryan) *wnt rt s: trckd ldrs: effrt 2f out: sn rdn and wknd* **10/1**

1m 4.38s (1.08) **Going Correction** +0.15s/f (Good)
WFA 3 from 5yo+ 1lb **7** Ran SP% **112.5**
Speed ratings (Par 103): **97,93,92,92,91 77,77**
CSF £29.04 CT £118.04 TOTE £4.10: £1.90, £4.40; EX 31.20 Trifecta £165.00.
Owner Sunpak Potatoes **Bred** Broughton Bloodstock **Trained** Catwick, N Yorks

FOCUS
Another race where pace held up, and not especially solid form.

6718 RACING UK HD ON SKY432 H'CAP (DIV II) 6f
5:40 (5:40) (Class 4) (0-85,89) 3-Y-O+ **£5,175** (£1,540; £769; £384) **Stalls** Low

Form RPR

2062 **1** **Captain Dion**[40] 5412 3-8-9 **75**... KevinStott 3 88
(Kevin Ryan) *slt ld on inner: rdn along over 1f out: drvn ins fnl f: hdd narrowly last 100 yds: rallied gamely to ld post* **6/1**

4220 **2** *shd* **Harwoods Volante (IRE)**[9] 6449 5-9-3 **81**.................. DanielTudhope 2 94
(David O'Meara) *trckd ldrs on inner: swtchd rt and hdwy 2f out: chal ins fnl f: rdn to take slt ld last 100 yds: hdd post* **11/2**[3]

0502 **3** *3 1/2* **Fendale**[6] 6539 4-9-7 **85**..(p) ConnorBeasley 4 87+
(Michael Dods) *trckd ldrs: pushed along and nt clr run 2f out: sn swtchd rt to outer and rdn: styd on fnl f* **7/4**[1]

1002 **4** *1* **Art Obsession (IRE)**[19] 6136 5-8-12 **76**...................... DougieCostello 12 75
(Paul Midgley) *hld up: hdwy on inner 2f out: rdn to chse ldrs over 1f out: drvn and kpt on same pce fnl f* **25/1**

5322 **5** *1 3/4* **Vallarta (IRE)**[7] 6502 6-8-10 **74**...................................... JamesSullivan 7 67
(Ruth Carr) *hld up: hdwy over 2f out: chsd ldrs wl over 1f out: sn rdn and no imp* **10/1**

6566 **6** *2 1/2* **Adam's Ale**[23] 6012 7-8-11 **78**..........................(b) RachelRichardson(3) 8 63
(Mark Walford) *chsd ldrs: rdn along 2f out: sn drvn and wknd* **14/1**

2131 **7** *3 1/4* **Highly Sprung (IRE)**[8] 6492 3-9-9 **89** 6ex............. SilvestreDeSousa 10 64
(Mark Johnston) *cl up: rdn along 2f out: sn drvn and wknd* **4/1**[2]

5100 **8** *13* **Dinneratmidnight**[124] 2476 5-9-4 **82**.......................(e) RoystonFfrench 11 15
(Richard Guest) *chsd ldrs: rdn along over 2f out: sn wknd* **40/1**

0006 **9** *4* **Canyari (IRE)**[47] 5161 5-8-12 **76**..............................(b[1]) TonyHamilton 6
(Richard Fahey) *cl up: rdn 2f out: sn wknd* **14/1**

1m 17.03s (0.13) **Going Correction** +0.15s/f (Good)
WFA 3 from 4yo+ 2lb **9** Ran SP% **114.7**
Speed ratings (Par 105): **105,104,100,98,96 93,88,71,66**
CSF £38.65 CT £81.20 TOTE £7.40: £2.00, £1.80, £1.10; EX 38.30 Trifecta £179.10.
Owner T A Rahman **Bred** Miss R J Dobson **Trained** Hambleton, N Yorks

FOCUS
The quickest of the C&D times, and once more the prominent racers were favoured. A length pb from the winner.

6719 FOLLOW @RACING_UK ON TWITTER APPRENTICE H'CAP 1m 4f 8y
6:10 (6:10) (Class 5) (0-75,81) 3-Y-O+ **£3,234** (£962; £481; £240) **Stalls** Low

Form RPR

5113 **1** **Cartwright**[11] 6370 3-8-12 **71**...............................(p) ManuelFernandes(4) 1 91
(Sir Mark Prescott Bt) *led 2f: trckd clr ldr: tk clsr oredr over 4f out: led again wl over 2f out: sn rdn clr: kpt on strly* **11/10**[1]

1111 **2** *18* **Pacharana**[11] 6380 3-9-8 **81** 6ex.......................... GabrieleMalune(4) 5 72
(Luca Cumani) *hld up: hdwy 4f out: effrt to chse clr ldng pair 3f out: rdn along over 2f out: sn wnt 2nd: kpt on: no ch w wnr* **9/4**[2]

2113 **3** *3 3/4* **Henry Smith**[12] 6346 4-9-12 **75**...............................(be) LewisEdmunds(2) 4 60
(Garry Moss) *hld up in rr: hdwy over 4f out: rdn along over 2f out: styd on fnl f: n.d* **11/2**[3]

0134 **4** *1 1/2* **Chant (IRE)**[23] 6006 6-9-13 **74**... RowanScott 7 57
(Ann Duffield) *chsd ldr: led after 2f and sn clr: pushed along 4f out: rdn 3f out: sn hdd and drvn: wknd wl over 1f out* **9/1**

00-4 **5** *20* **Sant'Elia**[150] 1711 4-8-8 **61** oh1...................................[1] GeorgiaDobie(6) 8 12
(Mark H Tompkins) *midfield: rdn along over 4f out: sn wl outpcd* **50/1**

342- **6** *15* **Royal Peculiar**[562] 838 8-9-5 **70**..............................(t) BenSanderson(4) 2
(Michael Appleby) *midfield: rdn along over 4f out: sn wl outpcd* **14/1**

0/0- **7** *21* **Storm Rider (IRE)**[486] 2560 5-9-9 **70**.......................(b) DanielleMooney 3
(David Nicholls) *.a towards rr: wl bhd fnl 3f* **33/1**

50/0 **8** *42* **Attraction Ticket**[34] 3711 7-9-0 **61** oh3...................(tp) NatalieHambling 6
(Joanne Foster) *a bhd: t.o fnl 3f* **100/1**

2m 39.85s (-0.95) **Going Correction** +0.15s/f (Good)
WFA 3 from 4yo+ 8lb **8** Ran SP% **116.3**
Speed ratings (Par 103): **109,97,94,93,80 70,56,28**
CSF £3.78 CT £8.55 TOTE £2.10: £1.10, £1.10, £1.50; EX 4.30 Trifecta £11.60.
Owner J L C Pearce **Bred** Meon Valley Stud **Trained** Newmarket, Suffolk

FOCUS
A strange race in which the winner and fourth were miles clear by halfway, and the runners finished at wide intervals. Not easy to pin down the form.
T/Plt: £626.00 to a £1 stake. Pool: £66,590.88 - 77.65 winning units T/Qpdt: £26.30 to a £1 stake. Pool: £5,808.49 - 163.21 winning units **Joe Rowntree**

6720- 6729a (Foreign Racing) - See Raceform Interactive

6115 HAYDOCK (L-H)
Friday, September 23

OFFICIAL GOING: Good (9.0)
Wind: Moderate across Weather: Fine & dry

6730 JW LEES MPA H'CAP 1m 3f 200y
1:40 (1:41) (Class 5) (0-70,76) 3-Y-O+ **£2,911** (£866; £324; £324) **Stalls** Centre

Form RPR

0060 **1** **Zenafire**[10] 6438 7-9-4 **65**..(p) JackDuern(3) 17 72
(Sarah Hollinshead) *in tch: hdwy to trck ldrs 1/2-way: effrt 3f out and sn chsng ldr: rdn to ld 11/2f out: drvn ins fnl f: hld on gamely towards fin* **28/1**

0325 **2** *nk* **Lily Trotter**[35] 5597 3-9-1 **67**..(b) OisinMurphy 5 73
(Ralph Beckett) *trckd ldng pair: pushed along 3f out: rdn and sltly outpcd 2f out: drvn and kpt on wl fnl f* **7/1**[3]

2331 **3** *nk* **Machine Learner**[10] 6450 3-9-7 **76** 6ex.....................(v) LouisSteward(3) 2 81+
(Michael Bell) *trckd ldrs on inner: effrt and n.m.r wl over 2f out: swtchd rt and hdwy wl over 1f out: sn rdn: styd on wl fnl f: nrst fin* **7/2**[1]

4555 **3** *dht* **Fastnet Blast (IRE)**[35] 5607 3-9-0 **66**.........................(b) ThomasBrown 10 71
(Ed Walker) *hld up towards rr: stdy hdwy on outer over 3f out: chsd ldrs 2f out: rdn over 1f out: drvn and ev ch ins fnl f: kpt on* **10/1**

413 **5** *3/4* **Top Of The Rocks (FR)**[28] 5830 3-8-4 **56**.....................(tp) LiamJones 15 60
(Tom Dascombe) *cl up: led after 1f: hdd after 4f and cl up tl led again 3f out: rdn along 2f out: hdd 11/2f out: sn drvn: wknd wl ins fnl f* **10/1**

1053 **6** *1/2* **Diletta Tommasa (IRE)**[22] 6058 6-9-3 **61**..............(v[1]) GrahamGibbons 4 64
(Daniel Mark Loughnane) *dwlt and towards rr: stdy hdwy on inner 4f out: pushed along 3f out: rdn wl over 1f out: kpt on fnl f: nrst fin* **16/1**

3444 **7** *1 1/4* **Brandon Castle**[13] 6323 4-9-12 **70**............................... DougieCostello 9 71+
(Simon West) *hld up in rr: hdwy over 3f out: rdn along wl over 1f out: kpt on fnl f: nrst fin* **7/1**[3]

0540 **8** *1 3/4* **Captain Swift (IRE)**[53] 4934 5-9-6 **64**................................ GrahamLee 8 62
(John Mackie) *nvr bttr than midfield* **16/1**

1601 **9** *4 1/2* **Almutamarred (USA)**[28] 5842 4-8-9 **58** oh2 ow2 AdamMcNamara(5) 12 49
(Kevin Morgan) *in tch: hdwy on outer 4f out: rdn along 3f out: drvn over 2f out: sn wknd* **7/1**[3]

0000 **10** *1/2* **Flying Power**[11] 6424 8-8-12 **59**............................... JacobButterfield(3) 7 49
(John Norton) *chsd ldrs: rdn along over 3f out: drvn 2f out: sn wknd* **40/1**

5334 **11** *1 3/4* **Merchant Of Medici**[49] 5106 9-9-1 **59**............................ JackGarritty 3 46
(Micky Hammond) *led 1f: cl up: led again after 4f: rdn along and hdd 3f out: drvn over 2f out: grad wknd* **25/1**

2335 **12** *19* **Argyle (IRE)**[28] 5830 3-9-2 **68**..............................(b[1]) SilvestreDeSousa 13 25
(William Muir) *t.k.h: cl up and j. path after 150 yds: prom: chsd ldr 7f out: rdn along over 3f out: drvn over 2f out: grad wknd* **6/1**[2]

5-62 **13** *15* **Zarawi (IRE)**[5] 5100 5-8-11 **60**..................................(b) GeorgeBuckell(5) 6
(John Gallagher) *a towards rr* **33/1**

2m 30.54s (-3.26) **Going Correction** -0.425s/f (Firm)
WFA 3 from 4yo+ 8lb **13** Ran SP% **116.6**
Speed ratings (Par 103): **93,92,92,92,92 91,90,89,86,86 85,72,62**
WIN: 39.30 Zenafire; PL: 9.60 Zenafire, 2.20 Lily Trotter, .80 Machine Learner, 2.40 Fastnet Blast; EX: 357.50; CSF: 203.67; TC: 435.80, 1058.58; TF: 974.00, 1266.20;.
Owner Robert Moseley **Bred** R J R Moseley & Mrs E Coquelin **Trained** Upper Longdon, Staffs

FOCUS
All races were run on the Inner Home Straight. Race distance reduced by 5yds. Oisin Murphy described the ground as "good" while Jack Duern felt it was on the "soft side." A modest but competitive handicap in which a few had their chance. The winner is rated back to his best form in the past year.

6731 BRITISH STALLION STUDS EBF MAIDEN STKS (PLUS 10 RACE) 6f
2:10 (2:12) (Class 4) 2-Y-O **£4,269** (£1,270; £634; £317) **Stalls** Centre

Form RPR

34 **1** **Mjjack (IRE)**[70] 4343 2-9-0 0.. JimCrowley 6 80
(K R Burke) *trckd ldrs: hdwy 2f out: rdn to ld jst ins fnl f: kpt on strly* **6/4**[1]

3 **2** *1 1/2* **Comprise**[21] 6071 2-9-0 0... PaulMulrennan 3 76
(Michael Bell) *hld up: hdwy over 2f out: rdn over 1f out: chsd wnr ins fnl f: kpt on* **9/4**[2]

0 **3** *nk* **Secret Agent**[81] 3954 2-9-0 0................................... SilvestreDeSousa 7 75
(William Muir) *led: hdd 1/2-way: rdn to ld again wl over 1f out: drvn and hdd jst ins fnl f: kpt on wl u.p towards fin* **11/1**

05 **4** *3/4* **Tesko Fella (IRE)**[22] 6053 2-9-0 0....................................... SeanLevey 4 72
(Richard Hannon) *trckd ldrs: hdwy over 2f out: rdn and ch over 1f out: drvn ent fnl f: sn edgd lft: hld whn rdr dropped whip last 50 yds* **8/1**[3]

0 **5** *2* **Dan Troop**[19] 6159 2-9-0 0... GeorgeChaloner 1 66
(Richard Fahey) *t.k.h: chsd ldrs on outer: rdn along over 2f out: wknd over 1f out* **10/1**

6 *4* **Gnaad (IRE)** 2-9-0 0.. OisinMurphy 8 54
(Robert Cowell) *wnt rt s: green and t.k.h: cl up: led 1/2-way: rdn along and hdd wl over 1f out: sn wknd* **33/1**

7 *2 1/4* **Mishari** 2-9-0 0.. RichardKingscote 2 48
(Tom Dascombe) *green and carried hd awkwardly: prom: pushed along over 2f out: sn rdn and wknd* **11/1**

1m 13.84s (0.04) **Going Correction** -0.425s/f (Firm) **7** Ran SP% **110.6**
Speed ratings (Par 97): **82,80,79,78,75 70,67**
CSF £4.61 TOTE £2.40: £1.30, £1.90; EX 5.60 Trifecta £32.10.
Owner Mrs M Gittins **Bred** Derrymore House Syndicate **Trained** Middleham Moor, N Yorks

FOCUS
Ordinary maiden form.

6732 EBF STALLIONS KENNY WASTE MANAGEMENT MAIDEN FILLIES' STKS (PLUS 10 RACE) (DIV I) 6f
2:45 (2:45) (Class 5) 2-Y-O **£3,234** (£962; £481; £240) **Stalls** Centre

Form RPR

0 **1** **Comedy School (USA)**[135] 2162 2-9-0 0................ SilvestreDeSousa 6 83
(Mark Johnston) *trckd ldrs: hdwy over 2f out: rdn to ld ent fnl f: kpt on strly towards fin* **5/2**[1]

6 **2** *2 1/2* **Star Catch**[119] 2637 2-9-0 0.. DaneO'Neill 2 76
(Charles Hills) *led: pushed along wl over 1f out: rdn: edgd lft and hdd ent fnl f: sn drvn and kpt on same pce* **5/2**[1]

30 **3** *5* **Twilight Spirit**[27] 5869 2-9-0 0.. JimCrowley 7 61
(Tony Carroll) *trckd ldrs: effrt 2f out: sn rdn and no imp* **6/1**[3]

06 **4** *5* **Poppy May (IRE)**[45] 5272 2-9-0 0.. TomEaves 1 46
(James Given) *chsd ldrs: rdn along wl over 1f out: sn wknd* **12/1**

5 *hd* **Hollywood Style** 2-9-0 0... MartinHarley 8 45
(William Knight) *wnt bdly rt s: a rr* **14/1**

6 *9* **Diamond Princess** 2-9-0 0...[1] AndrewMullen 9 18
(Michael Appleby) *bmpd s: a rr* **66/1**

0 **7** *1 1/2* **Mezah (IRE)**[19] 6162 2-9-0 0.. SeanLevey 5 13
(Richard Hannon) *chsd ldr: rdn along 2f out: sn wknd* **7/2**[2]

1m 12.51s (-1.29) **Going Correction** -0.425s/f (Firm) **7** Ran SP% **109.5**
Speed ratings (Par 92): **91,87,81,74,74 62,60**
CSF £8.03 TOTE £4.20: £2.30, £1.30; EX 10.20 Trifecta £29.10.
Owner Sheikh Hamdan bin Mohammed Al Maktoum **Bred** Darley **Trained** Middleham Moor, N Yorks

FOCUS
Division one of a fair maiden. The front pair came clear, although the time was marginally slower than the second division.

6733 EBF STALLIONS KENNY WASTE MANAGEMENT MAIDEN FILLIES' STKS (PLUS 10 RACE) (DIV II) 6f
3:20 (3:20) (Class 5) 2-Y-O **£3,234** (£962; £481; £240) **Stalls** Centre

Form RPR

4 **1** **Rosie Briar**[88] 3718 2-8-11 0.. RobHornby(3) 8 80
(Andrew Balding) *trckd ldrs: hdwy to ld over 1f out: sn rdn and kpt on wl* **7/2**[3]

2 1 1/2 **Loving** 2-9-0 0.. GrahamGibbons 5 76
(William Haggas) *trckd ldrs: swtchd rt to outer and hdwy wl over 1f out: rdn to chse wnr ent fnl f: sn drvn and no imp towards fin* **9/4**[1]

0 **3** 1 **Glacier Point**[27] 5869 2-9-0 0.. JohnFahy 2 73
(Clive Cox) *cl up: effrt over 2f out: sn rdn to dispute ld and ev ch tl drvn ent fnl f and kpt on same pce* **11/2**

523 **4** 1 **Street Jazz**[43] 5317 2-9-0 68.. TomEaves 1 70
(James Given) *led: rdn along and jnd 2f out: hdd over 1f out: kpt on same pce* **7/1**

0520 **5** shd **Sun Angel (IRE)**[15] 6244 2-9-0 77..................................... OisinMurphy 4 69
(Henry Candy) *trckd ldrs: effrt over 2f out: sn rdn and kpt on same pce fnl f* **3/1**[2]

02 **6** 5 **Shiny Line (IRE)**[17] 6208 2-9-0 0.. JFEgan 7 54
(John Butler) *cl up: rdn along over 2f out: sn wknd* **33/1**

7 3/4 **Last Word** 2-9-0 0.. ShaneKelly 3 52
(David Lanigan) *a towards rr* **25/1**

8 8 **Assertor** 2-9-0 0.. JimCrowley 9 28
(Tony Carroll) *wnt bdly rt s: green and a rr: outpcd and bhd fr wl over 1f out* **25/1**

1m 12.61s (-1.19) **Going Correction** -0.425s/f (Firm) **8** Ran SP% **116.5**
Speed ratings (Par 92): **90,88,86,85,85 78,77,66**
CSF £11.83 TOTE £5.00: £1.50, £1.20, £2.20; EX 16.20 Trifecta £68.30.
Owner Dr J A E Hobby **Bred** J A E Hobby **Trained** Kingsclere, Hants

FOCUS
A race that should produce winners and the time was fractionally quicker than division one.

6734 J W LEES BITTER 1828 NURSERY H'CAP 5f
3:55 (3:55) (Class 2) 2-Y-O **£9,056** (£2,695; £1,346; £673) **Stalls** Centre

Form RPR

3321 **1** **Merry Banter**[24] 6010 2-8-0 78.. EdwardGreatrex(3) 13 85
(Paul Midgley) *cl up centre: led 11/2f out: sn rdn: drvn ins fnl f: hld on wl towards fin* **16/1**

1601 **2** nk **Kyllang Rock (IRE)**[30] 5756 2-8-10 85................................ MartinHarley 3 91
(James Tate) *racd towards far side: trckd ldrs: hdwy 2f out: rdn over 1f out: drvn to chal ins fnl f: ev ch tl no ex towards fin* **10/1**

103 **3** 1 3/4 **Battaash (IRE)**[16] 6228 2-9-7 96... DaneO'Neill 1 96
(Charles Hills) *overall ldr towards far rail:. rdn along and edgd rt 2f out: hdd 11/2f out: sn drvn and kpt on same pce fnl f* **14/1**

2050 **4** 1 1/4 **Letmestopyouthere (IRE)**[12] 6388 2-8-8 83......................... SamJames 5 78
(David Evans) *rr: pushed along and hdwy 2f out: sn rdn: styd on strly towards far side fnl f: nrst fin* **16/1**

2211 **5** nk **Looting**[28] 5821 2-8-10 85... SeanLevey 14 79
(David Brown) *racd centre: chsd ldrs: rdn along over 2f out: kpt on same pce* **8/1**[3]

162 **6** 1 1/4 **Angel Meadow**[7] 6538 2-8-3 78.. AndrewMullen 12 68
(Micky Hammond) *racd towards stands side: towards rr: hdwy wl over 1f out: sn rdn and kpt on wl fnl f: nrst fin* **12/1**

1005 **7** 1/2 **Kachess**[34] 5638 2-8-4 79... RoystonFfrench 9 67
(Tom Dascombe) *racd centre: in tch: hdwy over 2f out: rdn to chse ldrs wl over 1f out: drvn and kpt on same pce fnl f* **16/1**

3152 **8** nse **Spiritous (USA)**[64] 4553 2-8-11 86..............................(b[1]) NickyMackay 4 74
(John Gosden) *racd towards far side: chsd ldrs: rdn along 2f out:. grad wknd* **8/1**[3]

146 **9** nk **Twizzell**[24] 5998 2-8-3 78... JoeyHaynes 15 64
(K R Burke) *racd towards stands rail: bhd: rdn along 1/2-way: hdwy over 1f out: kpt on wl towards fin* **11/1**

421 **10** 1 **Cuppacoffee (IRE)**[83] 3881 2-8-6 86................................. RowanScott(5) 6 69
(Ann Duffield) *midfield: rdn along over 2f out: n.d* **20/1**

416 **11** nse **Grey Galleon (USA)**[38] 5510 2-8-6 81.................................. JohnFahy 11 64
(Clive Cox) *s.i.s: a rr* **25/1**

6310 **12** 2 1/2 **Nautical Haven**[37] 5560 2-8-9 84... TomEaves 2 58
(Kevin Ryan) *racd towards far side: chsd ldrs: rdn along over 2f out: sn wknd* **20/1**

41 **13** 5 **Well Done (IRE)**[20] 6141 2-8-10 85............................. SilvestreDeSousa 8 41
(Simon Crisford) *racd centre: chsd ldrs: rdn over 2f out: sn wknd* **4/1**[1]

2100 **14** 4 **Naafer**[37] 5560 2-8-8 83... JimCrowley 7 24
(William Haggas) *racd centre: a towards rr* **11/2**[2]

5603 **15** 1 **Redrosezorro**[32] 5712 2-7-9 75 oh14..................................... HollieDoyle(5) 10 13
(Eric Alston) *racd towards centre. chsd ldrs: rdn along 2f out: sn drvn and wknd* **100/1**

58.62s (-2.18) **Going Correction** -0.425s/f (Firm) **15** Ran SP% **121.4**
Speed ratings (Par 101): **100,99,96,94,94 92,91,91,90,89 89,85,77,70,69**
CSF £161.18 CT £2363.41 TOTE £15.60: £3.60, £4.30, £3.70; EX 167.00 Trifecta £1442.80.
Owner H Thornton **Bred** Jeremy Green And Sons **Trained** Westow, N Yorks

FOCUS
A couple of the fancied runners disappointed in what was an open sprint.

6735 JEREMY KYLE H'CAP 1m 6f
4:30 (4:30) (Class 3) (0-95,90) 3-Y-O **£8,086** (£2,406; £1,202; £601) **Stalls** Low

Form RPR

4314 **1** **Yangtze**[34] 5633 3-9-3 81...(p) GrahamGibbons 6 92+
(Sir Michael Stoute) *prom: trckd ldr over 5f out: led 2f out: rdn over 1f out: styd on strly* **4/1**[3]

3-11 **2** 3 1/2 **Parliamentarian (IRE)**[64] 4559 3-9-12 90.............................. MartinLane 2 95+
(Charlie Appleby) *trckd ldrs: niggled along over 5f out: pushed along 4f out: rdn and hdwy 3f out: chsd wnr over 1f out: sn drvn and no imp fnl f* **11/8**[1]

113 **3** shd **Captain Peacock**[20] 6127 3-8-12 76......................................(v) JimCrowley 5 80
(William Knight) *set stdy pce: qcknd over 4f out: pushed along over 3f out: rdn and hdd 2f out: drvn over 1f out: rallied ins fnl f: kpt on* **8/1**

3210 **4** 5 **Forth Bridge**[34] 5653 3-9-10 88..[1] GeorgeBaker 7 85
(Michael Bell) *trckd ldr: pushed along 4f out: rdn 3f out: drvn 2f out and sn one pce* **8/1**

5311 **5** 7 **Proctor**[50] 5074 3-9-4 82... OisinMurphy 1 69
(Stuart Kittow) *hld up in rr: pushed along over 4f out: rdn over 3f out: sn outpcd and bhd* **11/4**[2]

3m 1.36s (-0.64) **Going Correction** -0.425s/f (Firm) **5** Ran SP% **111.0**
Speed ratings (Par 105): **84,82,81,79,75**
CSF £10.10 TOTE £4.70: £2.00, £1.20; EX 11.80 Trifecta £59.70.
Owner Philip Newton **Bred** Philip Newton **Trained** Newmarket, Suffolk

FOCUS
Race distance reduced by 5yds. A decent staying handicap, with the winner putting in an improved effort, although the pace was a steady one. The winner is rated in line with his Sandown form.

6736 GRIFFITHS AND ARMOUR H'CAP 1m
5:05 (5:06) (Class 3) (0-90,90) 3-Y-O+ **£8,086** (£2,406; £1,202; £601) **Stalls** Low

Form RPR

3023 **1** **Pumaflor (IRE)**[17] 6217 4-8-7 78....................................(p) PhilDennis(5) 11 87
(Richard Whitaker) *slt ld: hdd over 4f out: cl up: led again 2f out: rdn wl over 1f out: drvn ins fnl f: hld on gamely towards fin* **16/1**

0022 **2** hd **Top Beak (IRE)**[26] 5933 3-9-4 88..(t) JimCrowley 2 96
(Hughie Morrison) *cl up on inner: slt ld over 4f out: rdn and hdd 2f out: drvn and rallied ent fnl f: ev ch tl no ex nr fin* **7/1**[2]

3054 **3** 2 1/4 **Dark Devil (IRE)**[16] 6225 3-8-13 83...................................... JackGarritty 9 86
(Richard Fahey) *trckd ldrs: smooth hdwy on outer over 3f out: cl up 2f out: sn rdn and ev ch: drvn and kpt on same pce ins fnl f* **7/1**[2]

6335 **4** 1/2 **Rousayan (IRE)**[25] 5976 5-9-5 88.................................. ShelleyBirkett(3) 4 91+
(David O'Meara) *chsd ldrs: rdn along over 2f out: drvn over 1f out: kpt on fnl f* **8/1**[3]

5034 **5** 1/2 **Column**[26] 5933 3-8-11 86... GeorgeWood(5) 3 87
(James Fanshawe) *trckd ldrs: hdwy over 3f out: rdn along 2f out: drvn over 1f out: kpt on same pce* **4/1**[1]

4000 **6** 3/4 **Wilde Inspiration (IRE)**[25] 5976 5-8-13 84.......... AdamMcNamara(5) 5 83
(Julie Camacho) *hld up in tch: effrt wl over 2f out: sn rdn: kpt on same pce* **10/1**

00/4 **7** 3/4 **See The Rock (IRE)**[74] 4208 6-9-5 85............................... GeorgeBaker 8 82+
(Jonjo O'Neill) *hld up in rr: hdwy over 2f out: rdn wl over 1f out: styd on fnl f: nrst fin* **25/1**

0043 **8** nse **Fort Bastion (IRE)**[6] 6557 7-9-10 90................................. MartinHarley 12 87+
(David O'Meara) *hld up in rr: hdwy 2f out: sn rdn and kpt on fnl f: nrst fin* **12/1**

0461 **9** 1/2 **Commodore (IRE)**[20] 6123 4-9-7 87..................................... SteveDrowne 6 83
(George Baker) *in tch: hdwy to chse ldrs over 4f out: rdn along over 3f out: one pced fnl 2f* **14/1**

063 **10** 1 **Gratzie**[21] 6076 5-9-8 88... SilvestreDeSousa 7 82+
(Mick Channon) *dwlt and bhd: hdwy on inner 3f out: sn nt clr run and n.d* **9/1**

100 **11** nk **Little Lady Katie (IRE)**[16] 6225 4-9-1 86.................. JordanVaughan(5) 1 79
(K R Burke) *trckd ldrs on inner: effrt 3f out: rdn along over 2f out: sn drvn and wknd over 1f out* **11/1**

4165 **12** 10 **Justice Smart (IRE)**[27] 5892 3-8-13 83.................... GrahamGibbons 10 53
(Sir Michael Stoute) *prom: rdn along wl over 2f out: sn wknd* **16/1**

6003 **14** 3 **Jack Of Diamonds (IRE)**[14] 6300 7-8-11 77................ OisinMurphy 14 40
(Roger Teal) *in tch on outer: rdn along over 3f out: sn wknd* **20/1**

1m 38.72s (-4.98) **Going Correction** -0.425s/f (Firm)
WFA 3 from 4yo+ 4lb **13** Ran SP% **118.3**
Speed ratings (Par 107): **107,106,104,104,103 102,102,102,101,100 100,90,87**
CSF £122.78 CT £896.01 TOTE £16.90: £5.30, £2.30, £2.90; EX 172.70 Trifecta £1359.80.
Owner Resdev **Bred** Kevin Hannon **Trained** Scarcroft, W Yorks

FOCUS
Race distance reduced by 5yds. A useful handicap in which it very much paid to race prominent. The winner posted a pb.

6737 HAYDOCK PARK APPRENTICE H'CAP (PART OF THE RACING EXCELLENCE INITIATIVE) 1m 2f 95y
5:40 (5:43) (Class 5) (0-70,70) 3-Y-O+ **£3,234** (£962; £481; £240) **Stalls** Centre

Form RPR

4433 **1** **Hardington**[47] 5193 3-9-3 70..(v[1]) HollieDoyle(3) 6 83
(Alan King) *hld up in midfield: hdwy over 3f out: cl up 2f out: rdn over 1f out: drvn ins fnl f: styd on wl to ld towards fin* **13/2**[2]

5642 **2** nk **Zoffanys Pride (IRE)**[28] 5824 3-8-13 70............................ WilliamCox(7) 1 82
(Andrew Balding) *trckd ldr: cl up 3f out: led 2f out and sn rdn: drvn ins fnl f: hdd and no ex towards fin* **6/1**[1]

3345 **3** 4 **Torremar (FR)**[42] 5365 3-9-1 70..............................(p) LewisEdmunds(5) 15 74
(Kevin Ryan) *in tch: hdwy on outer over 4f out: trckd ldrs 3f out: effrt and cl up 2f out: sn rdn: drvn and kpt on same pce fnl f* **6/1**[1]

0230 **4** shd **Bigger And Better**[27] 5875 3-9-0 67.............................. MeganNicholls(3) 5 71
(Richard Hannon) *led: pushed along 4f out: rdn 3f out: hdd 2f out: sn drvn: grad wknd appr fnl* **12/1**

0203 **5** 4 **Sakhalin Star (IRE)**[4] 6620 5-9-9 67.............................(e) EdwardGreatrex 8 63
(Richard Guest) *hld up towards rr: hdwy 3f out: rdn along 2f out: styd on fnl f: nrst fin* **12/1**

2145 **6** 3/4 **City Ground (USA)**[16] 6221 9-9-11 69.................................. PhilDennis 9 64
(Michael Appleby) *hld up in rr: hdwy on inner 34f out: rdn along over 2f out: drvn and kpt on fnl f* **20/1**

0214 **7** 3/4 **Stoneboat Bill**[10] 6432 4-9-0 63.. GerO'Neill(5) 16 56
(Declan Carroll) *dwlt and rr: hdwy on wd outside 3f out: rdn to chse ldrs over 2f out: drvn wl over 1f out: sn one pce* **7/1**[3]

4045 **8** 1 1/4 **The Name's Paver**[30] 5782 3-8-10 60.............................. GeorgeBuckell 12 51
(Noel Wilson) *chsd ldrs: rdn along wl over 2f out: drvn and wkng whn n.m.r wl over 1f out* **20/1**

4160 **9** 1 1/4 **King Oswald (USA)**[3] 6646 3-9-0 64................................. HectorCrouch 17 53
(James Unett) *hld up: a towards rr* **28/1**

4252 **10** nse **Inflexiball**[17] 6212 4-8-12 59.. CliffordLee(3) 11 48
(John Mackie) *chsd ldng pair: rdn along over 3f out: sn wknd* **8/1**

6601 **11** 1 **Magnificent Madiba**[32] 5708 3-9-2 66...........................[1] GeorgeWood 14 53
(George Baker) *midfield: rdn along over 3f out: no hdwy* **12/1**

064- **12** 3 **Highway Code (USA)**[341] 3631 10-9-3 68.....(t) KatherineGlenister(7) 13 49
(David Evans) *a rr* **66/1**

130 **13** 6 **McDelta**[23] 6028 6-9-5 63... CallumShepherd 4 33
(Ian Williams) *a rr* **16/1**

1516 **14** 3 1/4 **Loving Your Work**[41] 5405 5-9-3 68............................ ManuelFernandes(7) 2 31
(Ken Cunningham-Brown) *trckd ldrs on inner: pushed along wl over 3f out: rdn wl over 2f out: sn wknd* **12/1**

5000 **15** 7 **Know Your Name**[22] 6055 5-9-6 67.................................... LuluStanford(3) 3 17
(Eric Alston) *t.k.h: chsd ldrs: rdn along 3f out: sn wknd* **16/1**

2m 10.2s (-5.30) **Going Correction** -0.425s/f (Firm)
WFA 3 from 4yo+ 6lb **15** Ran SP% **122.5**
Speed ratings (Par 103): **104,103,100,100,97 96,96,95,94,94 93,90,86,83,77**
CSF £43.71 CT £253.41 TOTE £6.70: £2.60, £2.40, £2.30; EX 49.20 Trifecta £141.30.

Owner The Fastnet Partnership **Bred** Litex Commerce **Trained** Barbury Castle, Wilts
FOCUS
Race distance reduced by 5yds. Not a bad little race for the grade and the 3yos dominated, with the first two clear. The winner built on his previous form.
T/Jkpt: Not Won. T/Plt: £37.80 to a £1 stake. Pool: £76486.10 - 1473.84 winning units T/Qpdt: £18.90 to a £1 stake. Pool: £4347.020 - 169.57 winning units **Joe Rowntree**

6099 NEWCASTLE (A.W) (L-H)
Friday, September 23

OFFICIAL GOING: Tapeta: standard
Wind: Breezy, across Weather: Overcast

6738 FLAME HEATING H'CAP (DIV I) 1m 4f 98y (Tp)
5:45 (5:46) (Class 6) (0-60,60) 3-Y-O+ **£2,328** (£693; £346; £173) **Stalls** High

Form RPR
1005 **1** **Byronegetonefree**[21] 6102 5-8-13 **49** .... JasonHart 9 55
(Stuart Coltherd) *led 2f: pressed ldr: regained ld 3f out: drvn along over 1f out: kpt on wl fnl f* **7/1**[3]
505 **2** 1 1/4 **Isaak (FR)**[32] 5716 3-8-11 **55** .... GrahamLee 8 59
(Donald McCain) *trckd ldrs: effrt and chsd wnr over 2f out: sn rdn: kpt on u.p ins fnl f: nt pce to chal* **25/1**
-213 **3** 3/4 **Hope Is High**[34] 5625 3-8-5 **52** .... JosephineGordon(3) 4 55
(John Berry) *trckd ldrs: effrt and rdn over 2f out: kpt on ins fnl f* **13/8**[1]
4132 **4** nk **Fillydelphia (IRE)**[25] 5980 5-9-5 **58** .... RachelRichardson(3) 2 60
(Patrick Holmes) *hld up: gd hdwy on outside 2f out: kpt on ins fnl f: nt gng pce to chal* **13/2**[2]
3426 **5** 1 1/4 **Jan De Heem**[13] 6346 6-9-9 **59** ....(p) JamesSullivan 6 59
(Tina Jackson) *t.k.h: hld up in tch: effrt and rdn over 2f out: outpcd ins fnl f* **10/1**
6033 **6** 4 **Breton Blues**[25] 5971 6-9-0 **50** ....(p) CamHardie 5 44
(Fred Watson) *t.k.h: hld up: effrt and rdn over 2f out: wknd over 1f out* **9/1**
1200 **7** 3 **Whitchurch**[25] 5971 4-9-2 **52** .... PJMcDonald 3 42
(Philip Kirby) *t.k.h in midfield: rdn along over 2f out: wknd wl over 1f out* **12/1**
4343 **8** 1/2 **Midnight Warrior**[21] 6097 6-9-6 **56** .... BarryMcHugh 7 45
(Ron Barr) *dwlt: hdwy to ld after 2f: rdn and hdd 3f out: wknd fr 2f out* **13/2**[2]
6-0 **9** 3 **Fair Trade**[17] 5841 9-9-10 **60** ....(p) ShaneGray 10 44
(Wilf Storey) *dwlt: hld up midfield on outside: rdn along over 2f out: wknd wl over 1f out* **28/1**
-006 **10** 1/2 **Come On Lulu**[32] 5726 5-8-5 **46** oh1 .... AnnaHesketh(5) 1 29
(David Thompson) *hld up on ins: drvn and outpcd over 4f out: edgd rt and wknd fr 3f out* **100/1**

2m 44.4s (3.30) **Going Correction** +0.375s/f (Slow)
WFA 3 from 4yo+ 8lb **10** Ran SP% **112.3**
Speed ratings (Par 101): **104,103,102,102,101 98,96,96,94,94**
CSF £160.04 CT £414.13 TOTE £8.60: £1.80, £7.20, £1.30; EX 170.40 Trifecta £503.50.
Owner Coltherd Conchar **Bred** Mrs A M Sturges **Trained** Selkirk, Borders
FOCUS
This was Newcastle's first meeting under lights. A modest handicap run at a steady pace. The winner is afforded a fractional pb.

6739 FLAME HEATING H'CAP (DIV II) 1m 4f 98y (Tp)
6:15 (6:16) (Class 6) (0-60,60) 3-Y-O+ **£2,328** (£693; £346; £173) **Stalls** High

Form RPR
-505 **1** **Kirtling**[29] 5795 5-9-5 **58** ....(t) EoinWalsh(3) 10 67
(Andi Brown) *missed break: hld up: hdwy on outside over 3f out: led over 2f out: sn pushed along: edgd lft ins fnl f: hld on towards fin* **20/1**
4451 **2** nk **The Resdev Way**[25] 5971 3-8-12 **56** .... BarryMcHugh 2 65
(Richard Whitaker) *plld hrd early: prom: smooth hdwy to chal over 2f out: sn rdn: kpt on ins fnl f: hld nr fin* **11/8**[1]
2202 **3** 3 1/2 **Kicking The Can (IRE)**[25] 5971 5-9-10 **60** .... LukeMorris 9 63
(David Thompson) *hld up bhd ldng gp: effrt and hdwy over 2f out: rdn and kpt on ins fnl f: nt pce to chal* **4/1**[2]
0544 **4** 3 **Magical Lasso (IRE)**[21] 6094 3-8-5 **49** ....(p) ConnorBeasley 6 47
(Keith Dalgleish) *trckd ldrs: rdn along over 2f out: outpcd wl over 1f out: kpt on ins fnl f: no imp* **11/1**
4406 **5** 1 3/4 **Perennial**[48] 5183 7-9-0 **50** ....(p) TonyHamilton 3 46
(Philip Kirby) *missed break: hld up: rdn along 3f out: sn outpcd: rallied over 1f out: kpt on ins fnl f: no imp* **12/1**
0-20 **6** 2 1/4 **Melgate Melody**[120] 2608 3-8-9 **53** .... JamesSullivan 8 45
(Michael Easterby) *led at slow gallop: rdn and hdd over 2f out: wknd over 1f out* **25/1**
4065 **7** 1 1/4 **Solid Justice (IRE)**[25] 5971 5-8-10 **46** .... PJMcDonald 5 36
(Kenny Johnson) *in tch: drvn and hung lft over 2f out: wknd over 1f out* **33/1**
006 **8** 3/4 **Applejack Lad**[50] 5065 5-9-4 **54** ....(tp) PaulMulrennan 1 43
(Michael Smith) *hld up: drvn along over 2f out: sn outpcd: n.d after* **28/1**
/23- **9** 2 3/4 **Stags Leap (IRE)**[29] 7185 9-9-2 **59** ....(p) RossTurner(7) 7 44
(Julia Brooke) *t.k.h: trckd ldrs: rdn along over 2f out: wknd over 1f out* **6/1**[3]
0065 **10** 10 **Table Manners**[50] 5064 4-9-0 **50** .... CamHardie 4 19
(Wilf Storey) *plld hrd early: trckd ldrs: rdn along over 2f out: sn wknd* **20/1**

2m 45.44s (4.34) **Going Correction** +0.375s/f (Slow)
WFA 3 from 4yo+ 8lb **10** Ran SP% **112.2**
Speed ratings (Par 101): **100,99,97,95,94 92,91,91,89,82**
CSF £43.88 CT £138.98 TOTE £21.10: £5.00, £1.10, £1.70; EX 52.60 Trifecta £299.40.
Owner Faith Hope And Charity **Bred** L P R Partnership **Trained** Newmarket, Suffolk
FOCUS
The pace was steady for this modest handicap. The winner could rate a a bit higher.

6740 TRUECO H'CAP 2m 56y (Tp)
6:45 (6:45) (Class 4) (0-85,84) 3-Y-O+ **£5,175** (£1,540; £769; £384) **Stalls** Low

Form RPR
4116 **1** **Mister Bob (GER)**[37] 5553 7-9-2 **73** ....(p) PJMcDonald 1 79
(James Bethell) *hld up in last pl: hdwy on outside to ld over 1f out: edgd lft ins fnl f: rdn out* **11/4**[2]
0136 **2** 1 3/4 **Lexi's Boy (IRE)**[37] 5541 8-9-13 **84** ....(tp) GrahamLee 5 87
(Donald McCain) *led at modest gallop: rdn and hrd pressed fr over 2f out: hdd over 1f out: plugged on fnl f: nt pce of wnr* **7/1**
2135 **3** 1/2 **Megara**[25] 5970 4-9-3 **74** ....(p) LukeMorris 4 77
(Sir Mark Prescott Bt) *sn chsng ldr: drvn and ev ch over 2f out: kpt on same pce ins fnl f* **9/4**[1]
0614 **4** 1/2 **Itlaaq**[24] 6011 10-9-11 **82** ....(t) PaulMulrennan 3 84
(Michael Easterby) *in tch: smooth hdwy and ev ch over 1f out: sn rdn: no ex ins fnl f* **5/1**
1120 **5** 6 **Wor Lass**[6] 6561 8-9-8 **84** .... GarryWhillans(5) 2 79
(Susan Corbett) *t.k.h: trckd ldrs: rdn and effrt over 2f out: wknd over 1f out* **7/2**[3]

3m 38.91s (3.71) **Going Correction** +0.375s/f (Slow) **5** Ran SP% **108.8**
Speed ratings (Par 105): **105,104,103,103,100**
CSF £19.91 TOTE £3.30: £1.80, £4.70; EX 18.10 Trifecta £46.70.
Owner Robert Gibbons **Bred** Newsells Park Stud Ltd **Trained** Middleham Moor, N Yorks
FOCUS
A fair contest despite the small field, but it was slowly run. The winner is rated back to his old best.

6741 0800 GAS REPAIR MAIDEN AUCTION STKS 1m 5y (Tp)
7:15 (7:16) (Class 5) 2-Y-O **£2,911** (£866; £432; £216) **Stalls** Centre

Form RPR
1 **Tamayef (IRE)** 2-9-2 0 .... JosephineGordon(3) 5 76+
(Hugo Palmer) *dwlt: rn green in rr: rdn and hdwy to chse ldrs over 1f out: kpt on wl fnl f to ld last stride* **17/2**
023 **2** shd **Trooper's Gold**[20] 6129 2-9-5 77 .... TomEaves 8 76
(Kevin Ryan) *cl up: rdn to ld over 1f out: kpt on wl fnl f: ct last stride* **11/4**[2]
3 3/4 **Mr Coco Bean (USA)** 2-9-5 0 .... PJMcDonald 9 74
(Ann Duffield) *hld up: rdn and hdwy over 1f out: kpt on fnl f: hld nr fin* **40/1**
5 **4** 3/4 **Glorvina (IRE)**[9] 6473 2-9-0 0 .... SilvestreDeSousa 6 68
(David O'Meara) *t.k.h: pressed ldr: led over 2f out to over 1f out: outpcd and lost 2 pls last 100yds* **5/2**[1]
434 **5** 1 **Doctor Cross (IRE)**[14] 6274 2-9-5 71 .... TonyHamilton 1 70
(Richard Fahey) *hld up: rdn and effrt 2f out: kpt on ins fnl f: nt pce to chal* **10/3**[3]
02 **6** 5 **Matthioli (FR)**[41] 5394 2-9-5 0 .... LukeMorris 2 59
(Michael Attwater) *prom: drvn along over 2f out: edgd lft and wknd wl over 1f out* **33/1**
5226 **7** 1 1/4 **Dream On Dreamer (IRE)**[20] 6130 2-9-0 67 ....(b) PaulMulrennan 4 51
(Michael Dods) *t.k.h: trckd ldrs: rdn over 2f out: wknd over 1f out* **11/2**
00 **8** 11 **Sheng Chi Dragon (IRE)**[8] 6515 2-9-5 0 ....[1] DougieCostello 7 31
(K R Burke) *led at ordinary gallop: rdn and hdd over 2f out: wknd wl over 1f out* **80/1**

1m 41.47s (2.87) **Going Correction** 0.0s/f (Stan) **8** Ran SP% **110.8**
Speed ratings (Par 95): **85,84,84,83,82 77,76,65**
CSF £30.14 TOTE £8.50: £2.40, £1.30, £3.70; EX 26.00 Trifecta £374.60.
Owner Commission Air Limited **Bred** Tally-Ho Stud **Trained** Newmarket, Suffolk
FOCUS
This was the first race run under the floodlights at Newcastle. All the field were making their AW debut for this maiden which featured runners from some powerful stables.

6742 VALOR VROOM FILLIES' H'CAP 1m 5y (Tp)
7:45 (7:45) (Class 5) (0-75,74) 3-Y-O+ **£2,911** (£866; £432; £216) **Stalls** Centre

Form RPR
3560 **1** **Totally Magic (IRE)**[27] 5887 4-8-10 **58** .... BarryMcHugh 6 66
(Richard Whitaker) *trckd ldrs: rdn to ld over 1f out: hrd pressed ins fnl f: kpt on wl* **16/1**
6554 **2** 1 1/4 **Justice Lass (IRE)**[34] 5649 3-9-7 **73** .... GrahamLee 1 78
(David Elsworth) *hld up: hdwy on far side of gp over 2f out: ev ch ins fnl f: kpt on same pce last 50yds* **8/1**
00-0 **3** 3/4 **Rosy Ryan (IRE)**[6] 6569 6-8-8 **56** .... JamesSullivan 7 59+
(Tina Jackson) *hld up: effrt whn nt clr run over 2f out to over 1f out: kpt on wl fnl f: nt rch first two* **66/1**
351 **4** 3/4 **Russian Finale**[15] 6251 3-9-8 **74** .... SilvestreDeSousa 4 76
(William Haggas) *hld up: hdwy and prom over 2f out: sn rdn: kpt on same pce fnl f* **2/1**[1]
-503 **5** 3/4 **Mockinbird (IRE)**[15] 6265 3-9-2 **68** ....(p) LukeMorris 8 68
(Sir Mark Prescott Bt) *t.k.h: trckd ldrs: drvn along over 2f out: effrt over 1f out: kpt on same pce fnl f* **8/1**
0320 **6** 6 **Tiga Tuan (FR)**[25] 5975 3-8-11 **63** .... KevinStott 3 49
(Kevin Ryan) *led: rdn and hdd over 1f out: wknd ins fnl f* **25/1**
5412 **7** 1 1/4 **Barwah (USA)**[25] 5973 5-9-3 **65** .... AndrewMullen 2 48
(Peter Niven) *hld up bhd ldng gp: rdn and outpcd over 2f out: rallied over 1f out: sn no imp* **3/1**[2]
0400 **8** shd **Haidees Reflection**[48] 5149 6-8-11 **59** ....(p) JoeDoyle 5 42
(Jim Goldie) *in tch: effrt and rdn wl over 1f out: sn outpcd: btn ins fnl f* **66/1**
9 hd **High Honcho**[85] 3835 3-9-6 **72** .... TomEaves 12 55
(John Quinn) *hld up: rdn whn nt clr run over 2f out: swtchd lft over 1f out: sn no imp: btn fnl f* **33/1**
0202 **10** 1/2 **Flinty Fell (IRE)**[13] 6342 3-9-4 **70** .... ConnorBeasley 11 51
(Keith Dalgleish) *hld up: rdn over 2f out: wknd wl over 1f out* **7/1**[3]
5254 **11** 1 **La Celebs Ville (IRE)**[14] 6278 3-9-0 **71** ....(p) AnnaHesketh(5) 9 50
(Tom Dascombe) *trckd ldr: rdn over 2f out: wknd over 1f out* **16/1**
00 **12** shd **Hidden Treasures**[10] 6437 3-9-5 **71** ....[1] TonyHamilton 10 50
(Richard Fahey) *trckd ldrs: rdn over 2f out: wknd over 1f out* **25/1**

1m 38.61s (0.01) **Going Correction** 0.0s/f (Stan)
WFA 3 from 4yo+ 4lb **12** Ran SP% **118.4**
Speed ratings (Par 100): **99,97,97,96,95 89,88,88,87,87 86,86**
CSF £132.19 CT £8081.07 TOTE £25.20: £4.30, £3.00, £14.60; EX 168.20 Trifecta £2544.50.
Owner James Marshall & Chris Marshall **Bred** G Donnelly & Ms C Clarke **Trained** Scarcroft, W Yorks
FOCUS
The pace was honest for this open handicap. Fairly ordinary form, the winner rated to her best.

6743 FLAME NURSERY H'CAP 6f (Tp)
8:15 (8:15) (Class 5) (0-75,73) 2-Y-O **£2,911** (£866; £432; £216) **Stalls** Centre

Form RPR
653 **1** **Fareeq**[21] 6099 2-9-6 **72** ....[1] SilvestreDeSousa 8 77
(William Haggas) *dwlt: hld up: hdwy on outside of gp 2f out: rdn to ld ins fnl f: kpt on wl* **5/2**[1]
6610 **2** 1/2 **Norwegian Highness (FR)**[15] 6257 2-9-7 **73** .... ShaneGray 11 76
(Kevin Ryan) *hld up: rdn and plenty to do over 1f out: gd hdwy fnl f to take 2nd nr fin* **7/1**
502 **3** shd **Elegantly Bound (IRE)**[60] 4713 2-9-0 **66** .... TomEaves 5 69
(James Given) *cl up: led gng wl over 1f out: sn rdn: hdd ins fnl f: kpt on same pce: lost 2nd nr fin* **11/1**
4564 **4** 2 **Peachey Carnehan**[23] 6033 2-9-0 **66** .... LukeMorris 9 63
(Michael Attwater) *cl up: effrt and ev ch over 1f out to ins fnl f: no ex last 100yds* **25/1**

3036 **5** *shd* **Cajmere**[20] 6139 2-9-7 **73**.. PJMcDonald 10 69
(Tom Dascombe) *pressed ldr: rdn and ev ch over 1f out: outpcd ins fnl f* **10/1**

040 **6** *shd* **Vaux (IRE)**[24] 6010 2-8-12 **64**... GrahamLee 12 60
(Ben Haslam) *hld up: rdn over 2f out: hdwy over 1f out: no imp fnl f* **40/1**

2360 **7** *hd* **Lady Cristal (IRE)**[20] 6139 2-9-6 **72**............................ DougieCostello 1 68
(K R Burke) *t.k.h: led to over 1f out: rdn and wknd ins fnl f* **20/1**

4453 **8** *½* **Bonnie Arlene (IRE)**[23] 6026 2-8-8 **60**.......................... AndrewMullen 4 54
(Mark Johnston) *trckd ldrs: drvn over 2f out: wknd over 1f out* **14/1**

054 **9** *3½* **Oceanic (IRE)**[20] 6139 2-8-7 **59**.......................................(t) CamHardie 3 43
(John Quinn) *prom: drvn along over 2f out: wknd over 1f out* **8/1**

6434 **10** *1½* **Flash Of White**[24] 6007 2-9-7 **73**................................[1] ConnorBeasley 7 52
(Bryan Smart) *plld hrd early: in tch: drvn and outpcd over 2f out: btn over 1f out* **6/1**[3]

2200 **11** *2* **Princeofthequeen (USA)**[45] 5265 2-9-5 **71**...................... SamJames 6 44
(David O'Meara) *hld up bhd ldng gp: drvn and outpcd over 2f out: sn btn* **28/1**

4325 **12** *½* **Champion Harbour (IRE)**[16] 6222 2-8-11 **63**.............. TonyHamilton 2 35
(Richard Fahey) *hld up: rdn and hung lft over 2f out: sn wknd* **5/1**[2]

1m 12.66s (0.16) **Going Correction** 0.0s/f (Stan) **12** Ran SP% **121.7**
Speed ratings (Par 95): **98,97,97,94,94 94,94,93,88,86 84,83**
CSF £19.68 CT £172.92 TOTE £3.10: £1.40, £2.70, £3.70; EX 27.20 Trifecta £155.70.
Owner Hamdan Al Maktoum **Bred** T J Cooper **Trained** Newmarket, Suffolk

FOCUS
Plenty of unexposed types in this nursery which was run at a decent pace.

6744 CASSELLIE MAIDEN STKS 5f (Tp)
8:45 (8:46) (Class 5) 3-Y-O+ **£2,911** (£866; £432; £216) **Stalls** Centre

Form RPR

1 **Nuala Tagula (IRE)**[38] 5531 3-8-9 68.................... AdamMcNamara(5) 7 62
(John Quinn) *hld up: hdwy over 1f out: rdn to ld ins fnl f: edgd lft: kpt on wl* **10/3**[2]

500 **2** *nk* **Heiba (IRE)**[108] 2999 4-9-6 72.................................. SilvestreDeSousa 10 66
(Robert Cowell) *t.k.h: in tch: hdwy to dispute ld over 1f out to ins fnl f: kpt on: hld nr fin* **15/8**[1]

5 **3** *1¼* **Eternalist**[41] 5388 3-9-0 0.. JoeDoyle 6 57
(Jim Goldie) *led: rdn 2f out: hdd ins fnl f: kpt on same pce* **9/1**

0425 **4** *1¼* **Chip Or Pellet**[26] 5920 3-9-5 47.................................. AndrewMullen 4 57
(Nigel Tinkler) *s.i.s: hld up bhd ldng gp: drvn over 2f out: kpt on fnl f: nt pce to chal* **33/1**

0320 **5** *¾* **Shesthedream (IRE)**[49] 5110 3-9-0 66............................. SamJames 9 49
(David O'Meara) *chsd ldrs: rdn along and ev ch over 1f out: kpt on same pce ins fnl f* **9/1**

0000 **6** *nk* **Questo**[17] 6215 4-9-6 59.. RoystonFfrench 1 53
(Tracy Waggott) *hld up: in tch: rdn and outpcd over 2f out: kpt on ins fnl f: no imp* **9/1**

63 **7** *1¾* **Young Tiger**[27] 5862 3-9-5 0.. JamesSullivan 2 47
(Tom Tate) *t.k.h: in tch: rdn along and edgd lft 2f out: sn outpcd* **9/2**[3]

00-0 **8** *shd* **Gettin' Lucky**[119] 2667 3-9-5 38.................................. PaulMulrennan 3 47
(John Balding) *hld up: rdn along 2f out: sn outpcd* **100/1**

54 **9** *1¼* **Skadi**[17] 6218 4-9-1 0.. JasonHart 5 37
(Garry Moss) *pressed ldr: rdn over 2f out: wknd over 1f out* **14/1**

10 *45* **Maydale** 3-9-0 0... ConnorBeasley 8
(Colin Teague) *reluctant to enter stalls: slowly away: sn t.o* **100/1**

59.04s (-0.46) **Going Correction** 0.0s/f (Stan)
WFA 3 from 4yo 1lb **10** Ran SP% **117.6**
Speed ratings (Par 103): **103,102,100,98,97 96,94,93,91,19**
CSF £10.04 TOTE £4.40: £1.70, £1.40, £2.90; EX 11.30 Trifecta £87.00.
Owner Mrs S Quinn **Bred** Miss S Von Schilcher **Trained** Settrington, N Yorks

FOCUS
A modest maiden. The fourth holds down the form, which could be rated up to 12lb better using the 1-2.

6745 ALPHA BOILERS H'CAP 5f (Tp)
9:15 (9:18) (Class 6) (0-60,60) 3-Y-O+ **£2,328** (£693; £346; £173) **Stalls** Centre

Form RPR

241 **1** **Intense Starlet (IRE)**[21] 6100 5-9-5 **58**...............................(p) SamJames 3 66
(Marjorie Fife) *hld up: rdn and hdwy over 1f out: led ins fnl f: sn hrd pressed: kpt on wl cl home* **9/2**[2]

2112 **2** *½* **Compton River**[42] 5354 4-9-6 **59**............................... PaulMulrennan 14 65
(Bryan Smart) *hld up: gd hdwy over 1f out: effrt and pressed wnr ins fnl f: kpt on: hld nr fin* **6/1**[3]

1132 **3** *1½* **Sugar Town**[28] 5839 6-8-13 **57**................................ AdamMcNamara(5) 4 58
(Peter Niven) *led at decent gallop: rdn and hdd ins fnl f: kpt on same pce* **7/2**[1]

505 **4** *nk* **Tell The Stars**[21] 6100 3-8-10 **50**.. TomEaves 10 50
(Ollie Pears) *dwlt: hld up: rdn and hdwy over 1f out: kpt on fnl f: nrst fin* **14/1**

2000 **5** *hd* **Windforpower (IRE)**[2] 6685 6-9-5 **58**...............................(v) DaleSwift 2 57
(Tracy Waggott) *in tch: drvn and edgd lft 2f out: kpt on u.p ins fnl f: nt pce to chal* **11/1**

2153 **6** *½* **Indastar**[28] 5838 6-9-6 **59**... PJMcDonald 6 56
(Michael Herrington) *trckd ldrs gng wl: smooth hdwy and poised to chal over 1f out: rdn and fnd little ins fnl f: wknd nr fin* **6/1**[3]

5550 **7** *¾* **Tilsworth Micky**[15] 6249 4-9-4 **57**................................ TonyHamilton 12 51
(J R Jenkins) *hld up: rdn and hdwy 1/2-way: no imp appr fnl f* **40/1**

04 **8** *1* **Camanche Grey (IRE)**[73] 4236 5-8-9 **48** ow1.................. GrahamLee 1 39
(Ben Haslam) *restless in stalls: bhd: drvn along over 2f out: no imp fr over 1f out* **16/1**

2316 **9** *1* **Lady Joanna Vassa (IRE)**[55] 4855 3-9-6 **60**.............. RoystonFfrench 9 47
(Richard Guest) *hld up in tch: drvn along over 1f out: wknd ins fnl f* **16/1**

0660 **10** *½* **Gowanless**[10] 6436 3-9-4 **58**................................(p) ConnorBeasley 8 43
(Michael Dods) *sn drvn along towards rr: edgd lft 1/2-way: sn n.d* **10/1**

0000 **11** *1¾* **Majestic Manannan (IRE)**[27] 5889 7-8-8 **47**..................(p) PaulQuinn 5 26
(David Nicholls) *t.k.h: cl up tl rdn and wknd over 1f out* **33/1**

0401 **12** *nk* **Harpers Ruby**[6] 6587 6-9-3 **56** 6ex............................ PaddyAspell 7 34
(Lynn Siddall) *chsd ldrs: rdn over 2f out: wknd over 1f out* **9/1**

59.01s (-0.49) **Going Correction** 0.0s/f (Stan)
WFA 3 from 4yo+ 1lb **12** Ran SP% **120.2**
Speed ratings (Par 101): **103,102,99,99,99 98,97,95,93,93 90,89**
CSF £32.25 CT £108.66 TOTE £6.00: £1.90, £2.00, £1.50; EX 33.50 Trifecta £66.90.
Owner R W Fife **Bred** Des O'Sullivan **Trained** Stillington, N Yorks

■ Clergyman was withdrawn. Price at time of withdrawal 10-1. Rule 4 applies to bet's placed prior to withdrawal, but not to SP bets - deduction 5p in the pound. New market formed.

■ Stewards' Enquiry : Dale Swift four-day ban; used whip above the permitted level and down the shoulder in the forehand (9th-12th Oct)

FOCUS
This was competitive enough for the grade.
T/Plt: £463.60 to a £1 stake. Pool: £83,750.55 - 131.85 winning tickets T/Qpdt: £140.40 to a £1 stake. Pool: £7,893.74 - 41.60 winning tickets **Richard Young**

6704 NEWMARKET (R-H)
Friday, September 23

OFFICIAL GOING: Good to firm (8.0)
Wind: light, against Weather: mainly sunny, light cloud

6746 MUHAARAR ROSEMARY STKS (LISTED RACE) (F&M) 1m
1:55 (1:56) (Class 1) 3-Y-O+
£22,684 (£8,600; £4,304; £2,144; £1,076; £540) **Stalls** Low

Form RPR

2212 **1** **Laugh Aloud**[28] 5831 3-8-12 91.....................................(t) RobertHavlin 11 111
(John Gosden) *mde all: traveling strly over 2f out: in command and rdn over 1f out: styd on wl: nvr seriously chal: rdn out* **9/1**[3]

1235 **2** *2¾* **Pirouette**[34] 5645 3-8-12 100... JimmyFortune 9 105
(Hughie Morrison) *chsd ldrs: effrt to chse clr ldr 2f out: drvn over 1f out: no imp on wnr but kpt on for clr 2nd* **8/1**[2]

-040 **3** *2* **Muffri'Ha (IRE)**[34] 5647 4-9-2 98.................................... RyanMoore 10 100
(William Haggas) *dwlt and squeezed for room leaving stalls: hld up in tch: hdwy over 2f out: rdn 2f out: wnt 3rd over 1f out: kpt on but no imp ins fnl f* **9/1**[3]

3561 **4** *½* **Promising Run (USA)**[20] 6158 3-9-1 107....................... JamesDoyle 14 102+
(Saeed bin Suroor) *hld up in tch in midfield: rdn over 2f out: sn swtchd lft: drvn an no imp over 1f out: hdwy ins fnl f: styd on fnl 100yds out: nvr trbld ldrs* **6/1**[1]

1314 **5** *½* **Desert Haze**[22] 6070 3-8-12 98.....................................[1] FrankieDettori 3 98+
(Ralph Beckett) *stdd s: hld up in rr: hdwy over 2f out: rdn 2f out: 4th 1f out: kpt on same pce ins fnl f: nvr trbld ldrs* **11/1**

-544 **6** *nk* **Molly Dolly (IRE)**[26] 5939 4-9-2 96................................ AdamKirby 1 97
(W T Farrell, Ire) *hld up in tch in last quartet: swtchd rt and effrt over 2f out: hdwy u.p over 1f out: 5th and no imp 1f out: kpt on same pce fnl f* **16/1**

7 *2* **Alnajmah**[92] 3590 3-8-12 94... PaulHanagan 15 92
(Owen Burrows) *stdd s: hld up in tch in last quartet: rdn 3f out: drvn and no imp over 1f out: wl hld but plugged on ins fnl f* **20/1**

2110 **8** *1* **September Stars (IRE)**[34] 5645 3-8-12 97........................ FMBerry 8 91+
(Ralph Beckett) *chsd wnr: rdn over 2f out: unable qck and lost 2nd 2f out: lost pl and btn over 1f out: eased wl ins fnl f* **10/1**

5535 **9** *shd* **Lucy The Painter (IRE)**[21] 6107 4-9-2 100...................... HarryBentley 2 90
(Ed de Giles) *hld up in tch: effrt over 2f out: no imp u.p over 1f out: wknd ins fnl f* **16/1**

165 **10** *1¼* **Ashadihan**[77] 4107 3-9-1 106..(p) JamieSpencer 5 92+
(Kevin Ryan) *hld up in tch in last quartet: rdn 3f out: drvn and no imp 2f out: wl hld and plugged on same pce fr over 1f out* **6/1**[1]

150 **11** *½* **Permission**[22] 6070 3-8-12 90......................................[1] DanielMuscutt 16 86
(James Fanshawe) *taken down early: stdd s: hld up in rr: effrt 2f out: sn rdn and no imp: n.d* **20/1**

5130 **12** *2¼* **Manaboo (USA)**[48] 5158 3-8-12 100.................................. WilliamBuick 4 81
(Charlie Appleby) *chsd ldrs: rdn 3f out: unable qck u.p and btn over 1f out: wl btn and eased ins fnl f* **20/1**

6050 **13** *5* **Almashooqa (AUS)**[204] 807 4-9-2 90.................................. PatSmullen 6 69
(Owen Burrows) *t.k.h: hld up in tch in midfield: rdn 3f out: sn struggling and lost pl 2f out: wknd fnl f: heavily eased towards fin* **40/1**

2321 **14** *3½* **Organza**[10] 6452 3-8-12 73..(v) FrederikTylicki 17 61
(Mick Channon) *wl in tch in midfield: rdn 3f out: sn struggling and lost pl: bhd over 1f out: eased wl ins fnl f* **100/1**

2120 **15** *2¾* **Wilamina (IRE)**[48] 5158 3-8-12 100.............................. FergusSweeney 13 55
(Martyn Meade) *chsd ldrs: rdn 3f out: lost pl over 2f out: bhd and eased wl ins fnl f* **9/1**[3]

1m 35.99s (-2.61) **Going Correction** 0.0s/f (Good)
WFA 3 from 4yo 4lb **15** Ran SP% **116.6**
Speed ratings (Par 111): **113,110,108,107,107 106,104,103,103,102 102,99,94,91,88**
CSF £70.93 TOTE £8.80: £3.10, £3.00, £3.20; EX 73.80 Trifecta £798.30.
Owner Godolphin **Bred** Darley **Trained** Newmarket, Suffolk

FOCUS
It was dry overnight and the going was given as good to firm (GoingStick: 8.0 (Stands' side 8.0; Centre 8.0; Far side 8.0). Far side course used. Stalls Far Side except 1m4f: centre. An open Listed race on paper, but a cosy and significantly improved winner. The time compared well with that of the later Group 2.

6747 PRINCESS ROYAL EBF NAYEF STKS (FORMERLY THE HARVEST STAKES) (LISTED RACE) (F&M) 1m 4f
2:30 (2:33) (Class 1) 3-Y-O+
£22,684 (£8,600; £4,304; £2,144; £1,076; £540) **Stalls** Centre

Form RPR

2-31 **1** **Journey**[118] 2690 4-9-8 114.. FrankieDettori 12 117
(John Gosden) *mde all: travelling strly over 2f out: shkn up and readily asserted over 1f out: styd on strly ins fnl f: pushed out: easily* **11/8**[1]

/155 **2** *3¼* **Lady Of Camelot (IRE)**[55] 4883 4-9-3 107.......................... RobertHavlin 6 107
(John Gosden) *hld up in tch in midfield: hdwy over 2f out: rdn to chse ldrs over 2f out: chsd clr wnr ent fnl f: kpt on for clr 2nd but no ch w wnr* **8/1**

-155 **3** *2¾* **Beautiful Romance**[55] 4864 4-9-10 112............................. WilliamBuick 3 110
(Saeed bin Suroor) *chsd wnr: rdn to press cantering wnr 3f out: unable qck over 1f out: wl hld 3rd and plugged on same pce ins fnl f* **13/2**[3]

1330 **4** *1½* **Pandora (IRE)**[15] 6273 4-9-3 99..................................... PhillipMakin 11 100
(David O'Meara) *hld up in last pair: clsd 3f out: rdn to chse ldng trio over 1f out: no imp and plugged on same pce fnl f* **16/1**

15-2 **5** *4½* **Beautiful Morning**[132] 2245 3-8-9 102.............................. HarryBentley 9 93
(Luca Cumani) *t.k.h: hld up wl in tch in midfield: effrt in 3rd 3f out: sn struggling and btn over 1f out: wknd fnl f* **3/1**[2]

316 **6** *10* **Hestina (FR)**[126] 2433 3-8-9 80.. PaulHanagan 7 77
(Peter Chapple-Hyam) *stdd s: hld up in tch in rr: effrt 3f out: drvn and no hdwy over 2f out: wl bhd over 1f out* **50/1**

3321 **7** *6* **Bocking End (IRE)**[41] 5415 3-8-9 85............................. JamieSpencer 10 67
(Michael Bell) *hld up in tch in midfield: effrt 3f out: sn u.p and struggling: wknd and bhd over 1f out* **25/1**

2150 **8** *10* **Shall We (IRE)**[69] 4400 3-8-9 105...................................... RyanMoore 1 51
(Sir Michael Stoute) *chsd ldng pair tl 3f: sooon pushed along and lost pl: bhd 2f out: sn lost tch and eased ins fnl f: t.o* **11/1**

2m 29.81s (-2.19) **Going Correction** 0.0s/f (Good)
WFA 3 from 4yo 8lb **8** Ran SP% **111.6**
Speed ratings (Par 111): **107,104,103,102,99 92,88,81**
CSF £12.65 TOTE £2.00: £1.10, £2.20, £1.70; EX 14.00 Trifecta £51.50.
Owner George Strawbridge **Bred** George Strawbridge **Trained** Newmarket, Suffolk

FOCUS
A race hit by four non-runners, though the main contenders held their ground. The 3yos had taken nine of the last ten runnings of this Listed contest, but the 4yos looked much stronger this time around and took the first four places ahead of their younger rivals, with John Gosden responsible for the front pair. The pace was sound and they came up the middle after turning in. Journey produced a smart effort and is rated to her best.

6748 SHADWELL ROCKFEL STKS (GROUP 2) (FILLIES) 7f

3:05 (3:07) (Class 1) 2-Y-O

£56,710 (£21,500; £10,760; £5,360; £2,690; £1,350) **Stalls** Low

Form RPR

1 **Spain Burg (FR)**[51] 5049 2-9-0 0...................................... FrankieDettori 8 109+
(X Thomas-Demeaulte, France) *t.k.h: hld up in tch in last trio: clsng and travelling strly whn sltly impeded over 1f out: rdn to chal 1f out: led ins fnl f: r.o strly and gng away at fin* **14/1**

113 **2** *1 ¼* **Fair Eva**[36] 5584 2-9-0 110...................................... PatSmullen 2 106
(Roger Charlton) *trckd ldr: clsd and upsides over 2f out: rdn and drifting rt wl over 1f out: drvn and led jst ins fnl f: sn hdd and styd on same pce fnl 100yds* **4/9**[1]

5152 **3** *nk* **Miss Infinity (IRE)**[19] 6174 2-9-0 101...................................... JoeFanning 3 105
(Mark Johnston) *racd keenly: led: rdn 2f out: drvn and hdd jst ins fnl f: styd on same pce fnl 100yds* **25/1**

5111 **4** *1* **Glitter Girl**[15] 6257 2-9-0 91...................................... PatCosgrave 6 102
(William Haggas) *chsd ldng pair: effrt 2f out: drvn to press ldrs over 1f out: no ex u.p ins fnl f: outpcd fnl 100yds* **8/1**[3]

1314 **5** *¾* **Nations Alexander (IRE)**[36] 5584 2-9-0 101...................................... PatDobbs 7 100
(Richard Hannon) *hld up wl in tch in midfield: effrt 2f out: drvn over 1f out: styd on same pce and no imp fnl f* **12/1**

016 **6** *2 ¾* **Perfect Madge (IRE)**[36] 5583 2-9-0 79...................................... JamesDoyle 1 93
(Kevin Ryan) *restless in stalls: hld up wl in tch in midfield: rdn 3f out: drvn and no imp over 1f out: wknd ins fnl f* **66/1**

31 **7** *¾* **Argenterie**[22] 6062 2-9-0 0...................................... MartinDwyer 5 91
(Marcus Tregoning) *dwlt and squeezed for room leaving stalls: detached in last: pushed along over 2f out: no imp and kpt on same pce after: n.d* **8/1**[3]

1 **8** *hd* **Exmouth**[26] 5930 2-9-0 0...................................... RyanMoore 4 90
(Sir Michael Stoute) *t.k.h: hld up in tch in last trio: effrt ent fnl 2f: rdn and no imp over 1f out: bhd and plugged on same pce ins fnl f* **7/1**[2]

1m 24.92s (-0.48) **Going Correction** 0.0s/f (Good) **8** Ran SP% **123.7**
Speed ratings (Par 104): **102,100,100,99,98 95,94,94**
CSF £22.58 TOTE £12.40: £2.70, £1.10, £4.40; EX 30.00 Trifecta £410.60.
Owner Roberto Cocheteux Tierno **Bred** P Perez Fernandez de la Puente **Trained** France

FOCUS
This was expected to provide Fair Eva with a good opportunity to get back on track following her York reversal, but she was turned over once again. However, it's probably wise not to underestimate the winner, who travelled best and showed a good turn of foot. Fair Eva is rated in line with her York run.

6749 SHADWELL JOEL STKS (GROUP 2) 1m

3:40 (3:40) (Class 1) 3-Y-O+

£61,813 (£23,435; £11,728; £5,842; £2,932; £1,471) **Stalls** Low

Form RPR

0526 **1** **Cougar Mountain (IRE)**[13] 6328 5-9-4 112....................(tp) RyanMoore 6 118
(A P O'Brien, Ire) *hld up in last pair: hdwy 1/2-way: rdn and chse ldr over 2f out: led over 1f out: styd on strly and drew clr ins fnl f: rdn out* **15/2**

3030 **2** *3 ¼* **Gifted Master (IRE)**[47] 5217 3-9-0 113...................................... WilliamBuick 1 111
(Hugo Palmer) *racd keenly: led and sn clr: rdn ent fnl 2f: hdd and drvn over 1f out: no ex jst ins fnl f: kpt on for clr 2nd : eased towards fin* **6/1**

1520 **3** *2 ¼* **Nathra (IRE)**[98] 3339 3-8-11 110...................................... FrankieDettori 5 102
(John Gosden) *s.i.s: hld up in rr: effrt on outer 2f: no imp and wandered over 1f out: kpt on ins fnl f: snatched 3rd last stride: no ch w ldrs* **5/2**[1]

3606 **4** *shd* **Amazing Maria (IRE)**[54] 4926 5-9-1 108...................................... JamesDoyle 2 102
(David O'Meara) *t.k.h: trckd ldng pair: rdn over 2f out: 3rd and outpcd over 1f out: wl hld and plugged on same pce ins fnl f: lost 3rd last stride* **9/2**[3]

4342 **5** *1 ¼* **Custom Cut (IRE)**[13] 6353 7-9-4 112...................................... DanielTudhope 3 102
(David O'Meara) *chsd ldr tl over 2f out: sn u.p and unable qck: 4th and wl hld 2f out: wknd ins fnl f* **9/2**[3]

3261 **6** *4 ½* **Forge**[22] 6056 3-9-0 108...................................... PatSmullen 4 95
(Sir Michael Stoute) *taken down early: stdd s: t.k.h: hld up in tch in midfield: effrt wl over 1f out: sn btn: wknd ins fnl f* **4/1**[2]

1m 36.85s (-1.75) **Going Correction** 0.0s/f (Good)
WFA 3 from 5yo+ 4lb **6** Ran SP% **111.0**
Speed ratings (Par 115): **108,104,102,102,101 96**
CSF £48.50 TOTE £9.00: £3.90, £3.30; EX 43.80 Trifecta £192.10.
Owner M Tabor/D Smith/Mrs Magnier/Mrs O'Brien **Bred** Whisperview Trading Ltd **Trained** Cashel, Co Tipperary

FOCUS
This didn't look the deepest Group 2 and not many ever really got into it, with the six runners racing closer to the far rail. Older horses had taken eight of the last ten runnings and they struck again. The winner was seemingly back to something like his best.

6750 DERRINSTOWN EBF STALLIONS MAIDEN STKS (PLUS 10 RACE) (C&G) (DIV I) 7f

4:15 (4:15) (Class 4) 2-Y-O

£5,175 (£1,540; £769; £384) **Stalls** Low

Form RPR

1 **Time Zone** 2-9-0 0...................................... JamesDoyle 5 83
(Peter Chapple-Hyam) *hld up wl in tch in midfield: clsd to join ldrs 2f out: rdn to ld over 1f out: styd on and forged ahd ins fnl f: rdn out* **14/1**

2 *1 ½* **Doctor Bartolo (IRE)** 2-9-0 0...................................... FrankieDettori 2 79
(Charles Hills) *t.k.h: w ldr tl led 3f out: rdn: hdd and hung rt over 1f out: styd on same pce ins fnl f* **10/1**

3 *2 ¼* **Red Label (IRE)** 2-9-0 0...................................... AdamKirby 10 73
(Luca Cumani) *stdd s: hld up in tch in last trio: effrt and hdwy 2f out: rdn over 1f out: kpt on ins fnl f: wnt 3rd fnl 50yds* **4/1**[3]

3 **4** *¾* **No Not Again (IRE)**[7] 6542 2-9-0 0...................................... PatDobbs 3 71
(Richard Hannon) *led tl 3f out: styd w ldr: rdn 2f out: 3rd and outpcd over 1f out: wknd ins fnl f: lost 3rd fnl 50yds* **11/4**[2]

5 *¾* **Alfarris (FR)** 2-9-0 0...................................... PaulHanagan 6 69+
(William Haggas) *s.i.s: bhd: pushed along over 2f out: hdwy into midfield and rn green over 1f out: no threat to ldrs but kpt on ins fnl f* **2/1**[1]

6 **6** *1* **Ode To Paris**[21] 6086 2-9-0 0...................................... PatCosgrave 7 66
(Ed Dunlop) *t.k.h: hld up in tch in midfield: effrt 2f out: drvn to chse ldrs but unable qck over 1f out: wknd ins fnl f* **9/1**

7 *4* **Big Sigh (IRE)** 2-9-0 0...................................... TedDurcan 9 55
(Chris Wall) *stdd s: hld up in tch in last trio: effrt 2f out: no imp and edgd rt over 1f out: wknd ins fnl f* **33/1**

8 *2* **What A Surprise (IRE)** 2-9-0 0...................................... MartinDwyer 1 50
(Conrad Allen) *dwlt: t.k.h: sn rcvrd and in tch in midfield: clsd to chse ldrs 3f out: rdn and lost pl over 1f out: wknd fnl f* **50/1**

9 *hd* **Red Emperor (IRE)** 2-9-0 0...................................... RobertHavlin 8 50
(Amanda Perrett) *hld up in tch towards rr: pushed along ent fnl 2f: sn outpcd and wl btn over 1f out* **33/1**

0 **10** *19* **Lincoln Day**[12] 6368 2-9-0 0...................................... DannyBrock 4
(Phil McEntee) *chsd ldrs: rdn over 2f out: hung lft and lost pl qckly wl over 1f out: wl bhd and eased ins fnl f* **150/1**

1m 27.46s (2.06) **Going Correction** 0.0s/f (Good) **10** Ran SP% **114.3**
Speed ratings (Par 97): **88,86,83,82,82 80,76,74,73,52**
CSF £138.20 TOTE £18.30: £4.00, £2.60, £1.60; EX 149.10 Trifecta £500.30.
Owner W Prosser **Bred** Springfield Farm Partnership **Trained** Newmarket, Suffolk

FOCUS
Usually a good maiden. They went quite steady early on and the winner quickened up well. It was the slower of the two divisions by 1.17sec. A nice debut from the winner.

6751 DERRINSTOWN EBF STALLIONS MAIDEN STKS (PLUS 10 RACE) (C&G) (DIV II) 7f

4:50 (4:50) (Class 4) 2-Y-O

£5,175 (£1,540; £769; £384) **Stalls** Low

Form RPR

33 **1** **Via Serendipity**[9] 6486 2-9-0 0...................................... RyanMoore 1 84
(Hugo Palmer) *mde all: rdn wl over 1f out: styd on wl u.p ins fnl f: rdn out* **11/8**[1]

2 *¾* **Mudallel (IRE)** 2-9-0 0...................................... JamesDoyle 5 82+
(Ed Dunlop) *t.k.h: chsd ldng trio: effrt 2f out: rdn and hdwy to chse wnr over 1f out: kpt on but a hld ins fnl f* **20/1**

5 **3** *1* **Century Dream (IRE)**[20] 6108 2-9-0 0...................................... RobertHavlin 8 79
(Simon Crisford) *chsd ldng pair: effrt 2f out: drvn over 1f out: 3rd and kpt on same pce u.p ins fnl f* **9/4**[2]

4 *3 ¼* **Sufi** 2-9-0 0...................................... PatDobbs 4 71+
(Richard Hannon) *hld up in tch towards rr: pushed long and hdwy to chse clr ldng quartet 2f out: nvr a threat but styd on steadily ins fnl f* **16/1**

5 *2 ¼* **Quloob** 2-9-0 0...................................... PaulHanagan 9 64+
(Owen Burrows) *s.i.s: in tch towards rr: pushed along and reminder 3f out: rdn and outpcd ent fnl 2f: 6th and wl hld over 1f out: kpt on same pce fnl f* **10/1**

500 **6** *shd* **Sassoferrato (IRE)**[28] 5848 2-9-0 63...................................... FMBerry 2 64
(Alan Bailey) *t.k.h: chsd wnr: rdn 2f out: lost 2nd over 1f out: 4th and btn 1f out: wknd qckly ins fnl f* **100/1**

7 *15* **Mathix (FR)** 2-9-0 0...................................... PatCosgrave 7 24
(William Haggas) *stdd s: t.k.h: hld up in tch in last pair: rdn over 2f out: sn outpcd: wknd over 1f out* **5/1**[3]

8 *3 ¼* **Dancing Alligator** 2-9-0 0...................................... FrederikTylicki 6 15
(Stuart Williams) *in tch in midfield: rdn and lost pl over 2f out: bhd over 1f out* **25/1**

9 *1* **Qatar Lion (IRE)** 2-9-0 0...................................... MartinDwyer 3 12
(Conrad Allen) *stdd strat: t.k.h: hld up in midfield: rdn over 2f out: sn lost pl: wknd over 1f out: bhd fnl f* **100/1**

1m 26.29s (0.89) **Going Correction** 0.0s/f (Good) **9** Ran SP% **115.1**
Speed ratings (Par 97): **94,93,92,88,85 85,68,64,63**
CSF £34.69 TOTE £2.10: £1.10, £3.50, £1.10; EX 24.10 Trifecta £62.20.
Owner V I Araci **Bred** R Shaykhutdinov **Trained** Newmarket, Suffolk

FOCUS
Two of the three with previous experience dominated the market in this division and they bet 10-1 bar three. The pace was decent and the winning time was 1.17sec quicker than the first leg. The sixth limits the form.

6752 MUKHADRAM GODOLPHIN STKS (LISTED RACE) 1m 4f

5:25 (5:26) (Class 1) 3-Y-O+

£22,684 (£8,600; £4,304; £2,144; £1,076; £540) **Stalls** Centre

Form RPR

1313 **1** **Dal Harraild**[20] 6110 3-8-11 104...................................... PatCosgrave 2 114
(William Haggas) *mde all: rdn ent fnl 2f: drvn and forged ahd ins fnl f: styd on strly and drew clr fnl 100yds* **9/4**[1]

1321 **2** *2 ¼* **Barsanti (IRE)**[35] 5611 4-9-5 110...................................... RyanMoore 1 110
(Roger Varian) *trckd ldng pair: wnt 2nd 3f out: rdn and ev ch 2f out tl no ex ins fnl f: kpt on same pce fnl 100yds* **3/1**[2]

-550 **3** *3 ¾* **Star Storm (IRE)**[111] 2894 4-9-5 98...................................... TomQueally 5 104
(James Fanshawe) *bmpd s: hld up in tch: clsd 3f out: 3rd and no imp u.p over 1f out: plugged on same pce fnl f* **20/1**

5503 **4** *10* **Second Step (IRE)**[27] 5894 5-9-5 108........................(b) JamieSpencer 4 88
(Luca Cumani) *dwlt and short of room leaving stalls: hld up in tch: effrt and rdn 3f out: 4th and no imp over 1f out: wknd fnl f* **9/2**[3]

5226 **5** *13* **Furia Cruzada (CHI)**[36] 5586 5-9-0 110...................................... FrankieDettori 6 71
(John Gosden) *wnt rt s: t.k.h early: hld up in tch: effrt and hung rt over 2f out: sn btn: eased ins fnl f* **13/2**

1-25 **6** *22* **Carntop**[98] 3337 3-8-11 105...................................... (b[1]) FMBerry 3 32
(Ralph Beckett) *chsd wnr tl over 2f out: sn dropped to rr and lost tch: t.o and eased ins fnl f: fin lame* **9/2**[3]

2m 30.48s (-1.52) **Going Correction** 0.0s/f (Good)
WFA 3 from 4yo+ 8lb **6** Ran SP% **110.2**
Speed ratings (Par 111): **105,103,101,94,85 71**
CSF £8.85 TOTE £3.50: £1.70, £1.40; EX 7.60 Trifecta £97.60.
Owner St Albans Bloodstock Limited **Bred** St Albans Bloodstock Llp **Trained** Newmarket, Suffolk

FOCUS
They finished well strung out in this Listed contest, which wasn't the deepest. The winner improved again.

6753 SHADWELL FARM H'CAP (SILVER CAMBRIDGESHIRE) 1m 1f
5:55 (5:59) (Class 2) 3-Y-0+

£18,675 (£5,592; £2,796; £1,398; £699; £351) **Stalls** Low

Form RPR

6313 **1** **Mithqaal (USA)**[63] 4593 3-8-3 **71** DannyBrock 18 85
(Michael Appleby) *racd in centre: chsd ldrs overall: hdwy to ld overall and travelling strly wl over 2f out: edgd rt u.p over 1f out: styd on strly ins fnl f: 1st of 11 in gp* **14/1**

1142 **2** 2 ½ **Cote D'Azur**[14] 6277 3-9-10 **92** DavidAllan 4 101
(Les Eyre) *racd far side: hld up in midfield overall: effrt over 2f out: chsd ldng pair and drvn over 1f out: kpt on same pce ins fnl f: wnt 2nd wl ins fnl f: no threat to wnr: 1st of 9 in gp* **8/1**[3]

3122 **3** 1 **Dawn Mirage**[27] 5874 4-9-9 **86** RyanMoore 1 92
(Richard Fahey) *racd far side: chsd gp ldr and prom overall: effrt to chse wnr 2f out: unable qck u.p over 1f out: kpt on same pce ins fnl f: lost 2nd wl ins fnl f: 2nd of 9 in gp* **7/1**[2]

3650 **4** ¾ **Beardwood**[17] 6217 4-9-5 **82** [1] JoeFanning 20 86
(Mark Johnston) *racd in centre: in tch in midfield overall: effrt to chse ldrs 2f out: edgd rt u.p 1f out: kpt on same pce ins fnl f: 2nd of 11 in gp* **25/1**

0432 **5** 1 ½ **Laurence**[14] 6286 4-9-8 **85** AdamKirby 15 86
(Luca Cumani) *racd in centre: in tch in midfield overall: effrt over 2f out: drvn and edgd rt ent fnl f: kpt on same pce ins fnl f: 3rd of 11 in gp* **8/1**[3]

2001 **6** ¾ **Brigliadoro (IRE)**[79] 4028 5-9-10 **87** PhillipMakin 19 87
(Philip McBride) *racd in centre: hld up in rr overall: effrt 2f out: hdwy u.p over 1f out: styd on ins fnl f: nvr threatened ldrs: 4th of 11 in gp* **20/1**

0545 **7** ½ **Faithful Creek (IRE)**[26] 5933 4-9-3 **87** JordanUys[(7)] 14 86
(Brian Meehan) *racd in centre: s.i.s: hld up in rr: rdn and hdwy ent fnl 2f: nt clrest of runs over 1f out: kpt on ins fnl f: nvr trbld ldrs: 5th of 11 in gp* **20/1**

1236 **8** 1 ½ **Giantstepsahead (IRE)**[181] 1089 7-9-10 **87** DanielMuscutt 3 82
(Alan Bailey) *racd far side: stmbld bdly s: sn rcvrd and led overall: rdn and hdd wl over 1f out: no ex u.p over 1f out: wknd ins fnl f: 3rd of 9 in gp* **66/1**

2000 **9** ½ **Hard To Handel**[8] 6500 4-9-7 **84** (p) DanielTudhope 21 78
(David O'Meara) *racd in centre: hld up towards rr overall: effrt and hdwy over 2f out: no imp u.p over 1f out: wl hld but plugged on ins fnl f: 6th of 11 in gp* **25/1**

0120 **10** 1 ¼ **Palmerston**[26] 5933 3-8-11 **79** FrederikTylicki 6 72
(Michael Appleby) *racd far side: hld up towards rr overall: rdn and hdwy ent fnl 2f: no imp over 1f out: plugged on same pce ins fnl f: 4th of 9 in gp* **14/1**

25 **11** 1 **Freewheel (IRE)**[19] 6160 6-9-2 **79** TomQueally 12 69
(Garry Moss) *racd in centre: led gp and chsd overall ldr tl 3f out: sn u.p and unable qck: wknd over 1f out: 7th of 11 in gp* **33/1**

1214 **12** shd **Briardale (IRE)**[42] 5376 4-9-7 **84** TedDurcan 17 73
(James Bethell) *racd in centre: t.k.h: hld up in tch in midfield overall: effrt over 2f out: no imp and edgd rt u.p over 1f out: wknd ins fnl f: 8th of 11 in gp* **22/1**

5203 **13** 2 ¾ **Freight Train (IRE)**[8] 6516 4-9-0 **77** (p) JamieSpencer 8 61
(Mark Johnston) *racd far side: in tch in midfield overall: rdn over 2f out: no imp over 1f out: wknd fnl f: 5th of 9 in gp* **20/1**

4054 **14** 1 ¼ **Squire**[71] 4307 5-8-12 **75** [1] RobertHavlin 13 56
(Michael Attwater) *racd in centre: stdd s: hld up in tch in midfield overall: rdn and unable qck over 2f out: sn struggling: wknd over 1f out: 9th of 11 in gp* **14/1**

1153 **15** ½ **Absolute Zero (IRE)**[9] 6489 3-9-5 **87** HarryBentley 11 68
(Roger Varian) *racd in centre: in tch in midfield overall: rdn 3f out: sn struggling and lost pl: wknd over 1f out: 10th of 11 in gp* **12/1**

6433 **16** ¾ **Craftsmanship (FR)**[22] 6048 5-8-11 **81** CameronNoble[(7)] 10 59
(Robert Eddery) *racd far side: s.i.s: in rr: clsd 1/2-way: rdn over 2f out: sn struggling: wknd over 1f out: 6th of 9 in gp* **16/1**

-401 **17** 3 ½ **Daily Bulletin (USA)**[12] 6372 3-9-11 **93** 4ex WilliamBuick 16 65
(John Gosden) *racd in centre: wl in tch in midfield overall: rdn and no hdwy ent fnl 2f: sn btn and wknd over 1f out: 11th of 11 in gp* **5/1**[1]

00 **18** 14 **Muhaafiz (IRE)**[48] 5180 4-9-6 **83** (p) PatCosgrave 2 25
(David Brown) *racd far side: in tch in midfield overall: rdn over 2f out: sn lost pl: bhd and eased over 1f out: t.o: 7th of 9 in gp* **80/1**

5311 **19** 2 **Silver Alliance**[51] 5028 8-8-11 **74** (b) AdamBeschizza 5 11
(Julia Feilden) *racd far side: restless in stalls: hld up in midfield overall: rdn 3f out: sn btn: wl bhd over 1f out: t.o: 8th of 9 in gp* **66/1**

006 **20** 72 **Bathos (IRE)**[17] 6209 3-9-3 **85** JamesDoyle 9
(Mark Johnston) *racd far side: in tch in midfield overall: rdn and lost pl over 3f out: sn bhd: eased fnl 2f: t.o* **16/1**

1m 49.77s (-1.93) **Going Correction** 0.0s/f (Good)
WFA 3 from 4yo+ 5lb **20** Ran SP% **124.3**
Speed ratings (Par 109): **108,105,104,104,102 102,101,100,100,98 98,97,95,94,93 93,90,77,75,11**
CSF £107.04 CT £889.16 TOTE £15.90: £4.20, £1.80, £1.40, £8.10; EX 145.70 Trifecta £700.40.

Owner The Horse Watchers **Bred** Extern Developments Ltd **Trained** Oakham, Rutland

FOCUS
A typically competitive seventh running of the Cambridgeshire consolation event. The field soon split into two with the larger group of 11 coming up the centre, while nine stayed far side, but with two from each flank filling the first four places there was no great bias. Improvement from the winner.
T/Plt: £85.10 to a £1 stake. Pool: £128809.66, 1104.34 winning units T/Qpdt: £22.00 to a £1 stake. Pool: £7426.64, 249.61 winning units **Steve Payne**

6754 - 6761a (Foreign Racing) - See Raceform Interactive

6319 CHESTER (L-H)
Saturday, September 24

OFFICIAL GOING: Good to soft (good in places; 6.9)
Wind: quite strong behind Weather: overcast

6762 CORBETTSPORTS MAIDEN FILLIES' STKS (PLUS 10 RACE) 7f 2y
2:30 (2:30) (Class 4) 2-Y-0

£6,225 (£1,864; £932; £466; £233; £117) **Stalls** Low

Form RPR

445 **1** **Celestation**[24] 6035 2-9-0 75 JFEgan 7 75
(Mark Johnston) *mde all: kicked clr 2f out: kpt on wl* **8/1**

42 **2** 1 ¼ **Aimez La Vie (IRE)**[31] 5771 2-9-0 0 PatrickMathers 10 72
(Richard Fahey) *in last trio on outer: pushed along early: hdwy fr over 1f out: chsd wnr fnl f: kpt on but a being hld* **6/1**

0364 **3** 2 **Twiggy**[16] 6244 2-9-0 68 GrahamGibbons 2 67
(Jane Chapple-Hyam) *trckd wnr rdn over 2f out: nt pce to chal: kpt on but no ex whn lost 2nd fnl f* **11/2**[3]

2 **4** ¾ **Undiscovered Angel (FR)**[17] 6223 2-9-0 0 DougieCostello 3 70+
(K R Burke) *s.i.s: in tch: rdn over 2f out: kpt on but nt pce to get involved* **9/4**[1]

65 **5** ½ **Kitsey (IRE)**[18] 6206 2-9-0 0 TomMarquand 1 64
(Richard Hannon) *trckd ldrs: rdn over 2f out: kpt on same pce* **8/1**

000 **6** 3 ¾ **I Dare To Dream**[12] 6413 2-8-7 56 JordanUys[(7)] 5 54
(Lisa Williamson) *in last pair: rdn over 2f out: little imp* **80/1**

464 **7** ½ **Hathfa (FR)**[22] 6086 2-9-0 74 ShaneKelly 8 53
(Richard Hughes) *trckd ldrs: rdn over 2f out: wknd over 1f out* **5/1**[2]

8 4 **Bed Of Diamonds** 2-9-0 0 HarryPoulton 6 43
(Adam West) *hld up last: struggling 3f out: wknd over 1f out* **40/1**

2333 **9** 25 **Singing Sands (IRE)**[15] 6289 2-9-0 74 JohnFahy 9
(Ralph Beckett) *cl up tl wknd over 2f out: eased whn btn* **6/1**

1m 28.45s (1.95) **Going Correction** +0.125s/f (Good) **9** Ran SP% **117.3**
Speed ratings (Par 94): **93,91,89,88,87 83,83,78,49**
CSF £56.13 TOTE £8.10: £2.00, £2.40, £2.30; EX 49.30 Trifecta £336.80.

Owner Kingsley Park 5 **Bred** The Lavington Stud **Trained** Middleham Moor, N Yorks

FOCUS
It was dry overnight and the going was given as good to soft, good in places (GoingStick: 7.2). After riding in the opener Paddy Mathers said: "It is good ground", but John Fahy said: "It is on the slow side." The rail was on the very inside so all distances were as advertised. A fair maiden.

6763 GOLDEN SQUARE SHOPPING CENTRE NURSERY H'CAP 5f 110y
3:05 (3:06) (Class 2) 2-Y-0

£12,450 (£3,728; £1,864; £932; £466; £234) **Stalls** Low

Form RPR

1325 **1** **Rosabelle**[16] 6257 2-8-11 **83** GrahamGibbons 8 89
(Alan Bailey) *mde all: kpt on strly and in command fr over 1f out: rdn out* **9/2**[3]

0416 **2** 1 ¾ **Megan Lily (IRE)**[35] 5656 2-8-5 **77** PatrickMathers 5 77
(Richard Fahey) *hmpd 1st f: chsd wnr thrght: rdn 2f out: kpt on but a being comf hld* **9/1**

3221 **3** 1 ¾ **Big Lachie**[15] 6295 2-8-5 **77** WilliamCarson 4 71+
(Jamie Osborne) *hld up in last trio: hdwy wl over 1f out: sn rdn: kpt on fnl f but nt pce to get on terms* **4/1**[2]

3110 **4** nse **Tomily (IRE)**[102] 3247 2-9-2 **93** HollieDoyle[(5)] 2 87
(Richard Hannon) *trckd ldrs: rdn 2f out: kpt on same pce fnl f* **11/4**[1]

6151 **5** 1 ½ **Four Dragons**[7] 6564 2-7-7 **72** oh3 RPWalsh[(7)] 1 61
(Tom Dascombe) *hmpd 1st f: trckd ldrs: rdn 2f out: sn one pce* **5/1**

1630 **6** nse **Super Julius**[38] 5560 2-8-11 **83** JohnFahy 9 72
(Eve Johnson Houghton) *hld up last: hdwy wl over 1f out: sn rdn and hung lft: no further imp fnl f* **8/1**

0414 **7** hd **Quench Dolly**[32] 5741 2-8-6 **78** TomMarquand 3 67
(John Gallagher) *hld up in last pair: rdn 2f out: nvr any imp on ldrs* **10/1**

546 **8** 1 **Angel Palanas**[22] 6099 2-7-8 **73** oh7 ow1 PaulaMuir[(7)] 6 58
(K R Burke) *in tch tl lost pl whn outpcd on outer 2f out: nvr bk on terms* **16/1**

1m 6.63s (0.43) **Going Correction** +0.125s/f (Good) **8** Ran SP% **117.6**
Speed ratings (Par 101): **102,99,97,97,95 95,94,93**
CSF £45.29 CT £176.66 TOTE £5.40: £1.60, £2.40, £1.40; EX 42.90 Trifecta £158.90.

Owner P T Tellwright **Bred** P T Tellwright **Trained** Newmarket, Suffolk
■ Stewards' Enquiry : Graham Gibbons caution; careless riding

FOCUS
This was dominated by the winner from the get-go.

6764 INNOSPEC H'CAP 7f 2y
3:40 (3:40) (Class 3) (0-95,94) 3-Y-0+

£12,450 (£3,728; £1,864; £932; £466; £234) **Stalls** Low

Form RPR

2350 **1** **Above The Rest (IRE)**[13] 6382 5-9-5 **92** GrahamGibbons 5 106
(David Barron) *trckd ldrs: wnt 2nd over 2f out: led over 1f out: qcknd clr: easily* **5/1**[2]

0650 **2** 7 **Intransigent**[28] 5871 7-9-4 **94** RobHornby[(3)] 7 89
(Andrew Balding) *hld up: hdwy 2f out: r.o wl to go 2nd ins fnl f but no ch w easy wnr* **9/1**

-000 **3** 2 ¼ **Newstead Abbey**[7] 6560 6-9-3 **90** TomMarquand 11 79
(David Barron) *slowly away: sn pushed along in rr: drvn 3f out: hdwy over 1f out: kpt on fnl f but nvr threatened to get on terms w front pair* **40/1**

3006 **4** 1 ¼ **Lexington Times (IRE)**[15] 6287 4-9-5 **92** JackGarritty 4 78
(Ruth Carr) *mid-div: hdwy 2f out: sn rdn: kpt on same pce fnl f (sddle slipped clsng stages)* **16/1**

5466 **5** nk **Maggie Pink**[15] 6281 7-9-3 **93** AlistairRawlinson[(3)] 12 78
(Michael Appleby) *pressed ldr: led over 2f out tl over 1f out: sn outpcd by wnr: no ex fnl f* **20/1**

1160 **6** 1 **Gabrial The Tiger (IRE)**[15] 6276 4-9-1 **88** PatrickMathers 2 70
(Richard Fahey) *led tl rdn over 2f out: chsd ldrs tl fdd ins fnl f* **7/1**

5204 **7** 1 ½ **Alejandro (IRE)**[14] 6320 7-8-12 **85** ShaneKelly 8 63
(David O'Meara) *hld up: rdn over 2f out: sme minor late prog: nvr trbld ldrs* **16/1**

6452 **8** nk **Miracle Of Medinah**[15] 6287 5-9-0 **94** LuluStanford[(7)] 3 71
(Mark Usher) *mid-div: rdn 2f out: no imp* **9/4**[1]

0004 **9** 4 **Majestic Moon (IRE)**[18] 6210 6-9-4 **91** TedDurcan 1 57
(John Gallagher) *nvr bttr than mid-div: wknd fnl f* **11/2**[3]

0000 **10** 1 ½ **Capo Rosso (IRE)**[22] 6081 6-9-2 **94** HollieDoyle[(5)] 6 56
(Tom Dascombe) *chsd ldrs for 3f: sn rdn: wknd over 1f out* **25/1**

0641 **11** 2 **He's No Saint**[14] 6339 5-9-2 **89** (v) MartinHarley 10 46
(David O'Meara) *mid-div on outer: rdn over 3f out: wknd over 1f out* **12/1**

1360 **12** 6 **Dawaa**[21] 6109 3-9-3 **93** JFEgan 9 33
(Mark Johnston) *s.i.s: rdn over 3f out: a in rr* **12/1**

1m 24.52s (-1.98) **Going Correction** +0.125s/f (Good)
WFA 3 from 4yo+ 3lb **12** Ran SP% **123.5**
Speed ratings (Par 107): **116,108,105,104,103 102,100,100,95,94 91,85**
CSF £50.73 CT £1675.84 TOTE £4.70: £2.50, £2.20, £12.10; EX 48.00 Trifecta £1052.10.

Owner Laurence O'Kane **Bred** J C Carr **Trained** Maunby, N Yorks

FOCUS
A good handicap and an impressive winner, but perhaps not form to take too literally.

6765 BET AT CORBETTSPORTS MAIDEN STKS 1m 2f 75y
4:15 (4:15) (Class 4) 3-Y-O+
£6,225 (£1,864; £932; £466; £233; £117) **Stalls** High

Form RPR
42 **1** **Flower Of Love**[15] 6278 3-9-0 0......................................(t) MartinHarley 7 78
(Simon Crisford) *trckd ldrs: wnt 2nd 3f out: hrd rdn fr wl over 1f out: str chal ent fnl f: edgd ahd cl home: drvn out* **2/1**[2]
523 **2** *nk* **Casablanca (IRE)**[15] 6278 3-8-11 74.............................. RobHornby[(3)] 1 77
(Andrew Balding) *led: rdn 2f out: narrowly hdd wl ins fnl f: no ex cl home* **11/8**[1]
0306 **3** *6* **Courtsider**[14] 6337 4-9-6 64..(v[1]) PatrickMathers 3 65
(Lucy Wadham) *s.i.s: rousted along early: in tch: wnt 3rd and drvn 3f out: one pce fnl 2f* **8/1**
3/5- **4** *13* **Deebaj (IRE)**[112] 4779 4-9-11 73.. JackGarritty 2 44
(Richard Price) *trckd ldr tl rdn over 4f out: wknd 3f out* **16/1**
5 *¾* **Cougar Kid (IRE)**[41] 5-9-8 0.......................... AlistairRawlinson[(3)] 6 43
(John O'Shea) *s.i.s: last pair: rdn over 3f out: sn btn* **18/1**
6 *hd* **Tayaar (IRE)** 3-9-5 0.. TomMarquand 5 42
(Richard Hannon) *chsd ldrs: rdn over 3f out: sn wknd* **5/1**[3]
7 *55* **Tribal Dance (IRE)**[30] 10-9-6 0.................................... CiaranMckee[(5)] 4
(John O'Shea) *slowly away: a last and sn pushed along: lost tch over 7f out: t.o* **40/1**

2m 10.59s (-0.61) **Going Correction** +0.125s/f (Good)
WFA 3 from 4yo+ 6lb **7** Ran SP% **116.8**
Speed ratings (Par 105): **107,106,101,91,90 90,46**
CSF £5.34 TOTE £1.70: £1.10, £1.40; EX 5.70 Trifecta £25.40.
Owner Mohammed Al Nabouda **Bred** Rabbah Bloodstock Limited **Trained** Newmarket, Suffolk

FOCUS
There was a good battle between the first two from the turn in here. The runner-up has been rated to her best.

6766 BOODLES H'CAP 6f 18y
4:50 (4:59) (Class 4) (0-80,81) 3-Y-O+
£6,225 (£1,864; £932; £466; £233; £117) **Stalls** Low

Form RPR
5020 **1** **Bossipop**[8] 6537 3-9-1 80..(b) RobHornby[(3)] 6 92
(Tim Easterby) *mde virtually all: r.o strly to assert ins fnl f: rdn out* **8/1**
6300 **2** *2 ¾* **Explain**[22] 6079 4-9-6 80...[1] JackGarritty 1 83+
(Ruth Carr) *hld up towards rr: hdwy 2f out: sn rdn: kpt on fnl f: snatched 2nd fnl stride* **11/2**[3]
2060 **3** *shd* **Ballesteros**[22] 6080 7-9-6 80.. ShaneKelly 4 83
(Richard Fahey) *chsd wnr: rdn to chal over 1f out tl ins fnl f: no ex fnl 120yds: lost 2nd fnl stride* **8/1**
4401 **4** *1* **Sophisticated Heir (IRE)**[7] 6589 6-9-3 77..........................(b) JFEgan 3 77
(Michael Herrington) *in tch: rdn 3f out: hdwy over 1f out: kpt on same pce fnl f* **4/1**[2]
2610 **5** *nse* **Vincentti (IRE)**[13] 6363 6-9-4 78.. MartinHarley 5 78+
(Ronald Harris) *hld up last: hdwy fr 2f out: nt clr run and swtchd lft ins fnl f: kpt on fnl 120yds but no ch* **9/1**
3031 **6** *1 ½* **Musharrif**[10] 6475 4-9-7 81.. TedDurcan 2 76
(Declan Carroll) *mid-div: rdn 3f out: hdwy 2f out: kpt on same pce fnl f* **11/4**[1]
3335 **7** *¾* **Signore Piccolo**[11] 6437 5-9-6 80.............................. GrahamGibbons 9 72
(David O'Meara) *mid-div tl lost pl over 2f out: nvr bk on terms* **9/1**
0224 **8** *1 ¾* **Masamah (IRE)**[14] 6324 10-9-3 77............................(p) PatrickMathers 7 64
(Richard Fahey) *chsd ldrs: rdn over 3f out: wknd over 1f out* **12/1**
033 **9** *¾* **Casterbridge**[14] 6324 4-9-3 77.. NeilFarley 12 61
(Eric Alston) *rrd leaving stalls: a towards rr* **25/1**
0015 **10** *¾* **Jack Luey**[14] 6324 9-8-13 76.............................(b) GeorgeDowning[(3)] 10 58
(Lawrence Mullaney) *trckd ldrs: rdn over 2f out: wknd over 1f out* **20/1**

1m 13.88s (0.08) **Going Correction** +0.125s/f (Good)
WFA 3 from 4yo+ 2lb **10** Ran SP% **120.6**
Speed ratings (Par 105): **104,100,100,98,98 96,95,93,92,91**
CSF £53.45 CT £380.06 TOTE £8.60: £2.80, £2.30, £2.60; EX 64.70 Trifecta £399.10.
Owner Ambrose Turnbull **Bred** Lady Whent **Trained** Great Habton, N Yorks

FOCUS
A competitive sprint but, not for the first time on this card, the leader proved hard to catch. The winner has been rated to the better view of his form.

6767 SAM QUEK CELEBRATORY OLYMPIC GOLD H'CAP 1m 5f 89y
5:25 (5:26) (Class 4) (0-85,85) 3-Y-O
£6,225 (£1,864; £932; £466; £233; £117) **Stalls** Low

Form RPR
2211 **1** **Pleasure Dome**[11] 6457 3-9-3 81.. TedDurcan 8 90
(Peter Chapple-Hyam) *mde all: kicked for home 3f out: in command after: comf* **4/1**[1]
1443 **2** *2 ¼* **Talent To Amuse (IRE)**[7] 6584 3-9-2 80................... GrahamGibbons 5 85
(Roger Varian) *trckd ldrs: rdn to chse wnr 2f out: styd on but a being comf hld fnl f* **4/1**[1]
1122 **3** *¾* **Masterson (IRE)**[14] 6325 3-7-11 66................................ HollieDoyle[(5)] 3 70
(Mick Channon) *hld up: hdwy over 2f out: sn rdn: wnt 3rd ent fnl f: styd on* **7/1**
4 *2 ¼* **Dino Velvet (FR)**[138] 3-9-7 85... MartinHarley 1 86
(Alan King) *trckd ldrs: rdn to chse wnr 3f out tl 2f out: styd on same pce* **11/2**[3]
3523 **5** *1* **Monaco Rose**[33] 5718 3-8-2 66.. PatrickMathers 7 65+
(Richard Fahey) *mid-div tl outpcd and dropped rr wl over 2f out: styd on fnl f but no ch w ldrs* **7/1**
0033 **6** *½* **Welford**[10] 6474 3-9-5 83..(b[1]) JFEgan 2 81
(Mark Johnston) *in tch: rdn over 2f out: nt pce to get involved* **9/2**[2]
4210 **7** *2 ¼* **Vanishing Point**[22] 6083 3-8-13 80...................................... RobHornby[(3)] 6 75
(Andrew Balding) *hmpd s: nvr really travelling: a towards rr* **10/1**
2415 **8** *14* **Monsieur Glory**[56] 4892 3-8-7 71...............................(v) TomMarquand 4 45
(Tom Dascombe) *wnt rt s: keen early: trckd wnr tl rdn over 3f out: wknd 2f out* **14/1**

2m 53.04s (0.34) **Going Correction** +0.125s/f (Good) **8** Ran SP% **114.3**
Speed ratings (Par 103): **103,101,101,99,99 98,97,88**
CSF £20.02 CT £107.24 TOTE £4.70: £1.30, £2.10, £1.90; EX 21.70 Trifecta £62.60.
Owner J G Davis **Bred** J G Davis & Star Pointe Ltd **Trained** Newmarket, Suffolk

FOCUS
Another success for a front-runner, the fourth on the card. The runner-up and third have been rated to form.

T/Plt: £95.70 to a £1 stake. Pool: £58,473.93 - 445.61 winning tickets T/Qpdt: £15.00 to a £1 stake. Pool: £3,740.97 - 183.50 winning tickets **Tim Mitchell**

6614 HAMILTON (R-H)
Saturday, September 24

OFFICIAL GOING: Soft (5.2) changing to heavy after race 2 (4.05)
Wind: Light, half behind Weather: Overcast, raining

6768 TOTEPLACEPOT NURSERY H'CAP 5f 7y
3:35 (3:35) (Class 5) (0-75,70) 2-Y-O **£3,557** (£1,058; £529; £264) **Stalls** High

Form RPR
1505 **1** **Reckless Serenade (IRE)**[25] 6007 2-8-10 64........ ShirleyTeasdale[(5)] 5 69
(Keith Dalgleish) *t.k.h: mde all against stands' rail: rdn over 1f out: kpt on strly fnl f* **7/2**[2]
106 **2** *2* **Benidiction (IRE)**[14] 6343 2-9-0 63.................................... JoeyHaynes 4 61
(K R Burke) *pressed wnr: effrt and drvn along 2f out: kpt on same pce last 100yds* **11/2**
5214 **3** *3* **Foxy Boy**[14] 6343 2-9-1 64... ConnorBeasley 1 51
(Michael Dods) *sn trcking ldrs on outside: rdn over 2f out: effrt over 1f out: wknd ins fnl f* **13/8**[1]
643 **4** *1 ¼* **Indie Rock**[67] 4494 2-9-7 70... PJMcDonald 3 53
(Mark Johnston) *in tch: outpcd and hung rt over 3f out: sn no imp: btn over 1f out* **4/1**[3]
023 **5** *4* **Cheerful Character (IRE)**[21] 6141 2-9-0 63....................... TomEaves 2 31
(Richard Fahey) *trckd ldrs tl rdn and wknd qckly wl over 1f out* **11/2**

1m 2.47s (2.47) **Going Correction** +0.35s/f (Good) **5** Ran SP% **111.1**
Speed ratings (Par 95): **94,90,86,84,77**
CSF £21.70 TOTE £4.50: £2.60, £2.40; EX 27.90 Trifecta £51.50.
Owner Weldspec Glasgow Limited **Bred** Tally-Ho Stud **Trained** Carluke, S Lanarks

FOCUS
All rails at innermost position and distances as advertised. After persistent rain prior to racing the the official going was changed to soft all over. A modest nursery and an all-the-way winner. The winner has been rated back to his pre-race level.

6769 JONATHAN LETHAM MEMORIAL H'CAP 6f 6y
4:05 (4:07) (Class 5) (0-75,73) 3-Y-O+ **£3,881** (£1,155; £577; £288) **Stalls** Centre

Form RPR
0104 **1** **Royal Connoisseur (IRE)**[21] 6136 5-9-3 73......... NatalieHambling[(7)] 8 83
(Richard Fahey) *chsd ldr: rdn and hung rt over 2f out: rallied and led over 1f out: drvn clr ins fnl f* **3/1**[1]
1350 **2** *2* **Gilmer (IRE)**[26] 5955 5-9-0 70.................................... LewisEdmunds[(7)] 7 74
(Laura Young) *bhd and sn rdn along: hdwy over 1f out: chsd wnr ins fnl f: kpt on: no imp* **9/1**[3]
5120 **3** *1 ¾* **Born Innocent (IRE)**[20] 6166 3-9-6 71........................... SamHitchcott 1 70
(John Patrick Shanahan, Ire) *chsd ldrs: rdn and ev ch briefly over 1f out: sn chsng wnr: lost 2nd and no ex ins fnl f* **12/1**
505 **4** *nk* **Pennine Warrior**[140] 2047 5-9-1 64....................................(b) DaleSwift 6 62
(Scott Dixon) *sn drvn along and outpcd towards rr: hdwy over 1f out: edgd lft and kpt on ins fnl f: no imp* **33/1**
2113 **5** *1 ¼* **Portland Street (IRE)**[11] 6435 3-9-5 70........................(p) PJMcDonald 2 64
(Bryan Smart) *prom: drvn along over 2f out: outpcd fr over 1f out* **3/1**[1]
0021 **6** *1 ¾* **Reflation**[5] 6616 4-8-9 58 6ex..................................(p) ConnorBeasley 4 47
(Michael Dods) *bhd: rdn over 3f out: shortlived effrt and edgd rt wl over 1f out: sn wknd* **5/1**[2]
0500 **7** *2* **Meshardal (GER)**[29] 5858 6-9-8 71.................................... JamesSullivan 5 54
(Ruth Carr) *dwlt: bhd: hdwy to chse ldrs wl over 1f out: wknd fnl f* **5/1**[2]
0006 **8** *5* **Farkle Minkus**[11] 6435 3-9-3 68......................................(v) TomEaves 3 36
(Keith Dalgleish) *led at decent gallop: rdn and hdd over 1f out: sn wknd* **9/1**[3]

1m 15.19s (2.99) **Going Correction** +0.60s/f (Yiel)
WFA 3 from 4yo+ 2lb **8** Ran SP% **114.0**
Speed ratings (Par 103): **104,101,99,98,96 94,91,85**
CSF £31.04 CT £283.36 TOTE £3.10: £1.90, £2.40, £2.80; EX 29.40 Trifecta £312.80.
Owner S & G Clayton, A Blower **Bred** Mrs Sheila Morrissey **Trained** Musley Bank, N Yorks

FOCUS
A fair handicap and they went a good pace in the conditions. The winner has been rated close to his old best.

6770 TOTEQUADPOT/EBF STALLIONS FLOWER OF SCOTLAND FILLIES' H'CAP 6f 6y
4:40 (4:42) (Class 3) (0-90,90) 3-Y-O+
£12,450 (£3,728; £1,864; £932; £466; £234) **Stalls** Centre

Form RPR
3244 **1** **Honeysuckle Lil (IRE)**[9] 6501 4-8-6 75...........(p) RachelRichardson[(3)] 9 84
(Tim Easterby) *hld up: hdwy nr side of gp to ld over 1f out: pushed out fnl f* **9/1**
1100 **2** *1 ¼* **Courier**[8] 6539 4-9-0 85.. RobJFitzpatrick[(5)] 7 89
(Marjorie Fife) *led tl rdn and hdd over 1f out: kpt on ins fnl f: nt pce of wnr* **9/1**
5210 **3** *shd* **Dutch Destiny**[63] 4652 3-9-8 90.. JamesSullivan 2 94
(William Haggas) *trckd ldrs: effrt and ev ch over 1f out: kpt on ins fnl f* **2/1**[1]
1244 **4** *1 ¼* **Dutch Mist**[9] 6518 3-8-11 86..................................(v[1]) LewisEdmunds[(7)] 6 86
(Kevin Ryan) *bhd: drvn and struggling 1/2-way: plenty to do over 1f out: gd hdwy fnl f: styd on strly* **7/1**[3]
2161 **5** *nk* **Posh Bounty**[4] 6649 5-8-4 77 6ex.................................. SeanMooney[(7)] 5 76
(Joseph Tuite) *trckd ldrs: drvn and outpcd over 2f out: rallied fnl f: nvr rchd ldrs* **9/1**
2422 **6** *¾* **Wowcha (IRE)**[29] 5836 3-8-11 79...(v) TomEaves 8 75
(John Quinn) *hld up in tch: rdn over 2f out: outpcd whn hung rt over 1f out: sn n.d* **4/1**[2]
3150 **7** *1 ½* **Specialv (IRE)**[8] 6537 3-8-7 75..(p) PJMcDonald 1 67
(Brian Ellison) *s.i.s: hld up: rdn and shortlived effrt over 2f out: edgd rt and no imp over 1f out* **7/1**[3]
0501 **8** *nk* **Flowing Clarets**[29] 5855 3-8-4 72.. JoeyHaynes 3 63
(Richard Fahey) *prom: drvn along over 2f out: edgd rt and wknd wl over 1f out* **14/1**
6-06 **9** *12* **Birdcage**[25] 6013 3-8-12 80..(b) ConnorBeasley 4 32
(Richard Fahey) *s.i.s: sn rcvrd and disp ld: rdn over 2f out: wknd over 1f out* **50/1**

1m 15.38s (3.18) **Going Correction** +0.60s/f (Yiel)
WFA 3 from 4yo+ 2lb **9** Ran SP% **117.0**
Speed ratings (Par 104): **102,100,100,98,98 97,95,94,78**
CSF £87.63 CT £228.12 TOTE £10.50: £2.80, £2.40, £1.50; EX 105.80 Trifecta £373.90.

Owner Ambrose Turnbull **Bred** Mrs C A Moore **Trained** Great Habton, N Yorks

FOCUS

The ground was changed to heavy before this race. A useful sprint handicap.

6771 TOTEPOOLRACING ON INSTAGRAM/ BRITISH STALLION STUDS EBF MAIDEN STKS — 1m 67y

5:15 (5:16) (Class 5) 2-Y-O — **£3,881** (£1,155; £577; £288) **Stalls** Low

Form — RPR

4325 **1** **Election Day**[15] 6274 2-9-5 74 PJMcDonald 3 — 74
(Mark Johnston) *mde all: shkn up over 2f out: rdn and drifted lft over 1f out: stened and styd on wl fnl f: unchal* **11/4**[2]

2 1 ¼ **Taxmeifyoucan (IRE)** 2-9-0 0 ShirleyTeasdale(5) 1 — 71
(Keith Dalgleish) *s.i.s: hld up in tch: outpcd and green over 3f out: rallied over 1f out: chsd wnr ins fnl f: kpt on* **16/1**

2 **3** ½ **Kuraka**[17] 6224 2-9-5 0 JoeyHaynes 2 — 70
(K R Burke) *t.k.h: pressed wnr: rdn over 2f out: edgd lft over 1f out: lost 2nd and kpt on same pce ins fnl f* **1/1**[1]

33 **4** 2 ¼ **Golconda Prince (IRE)**[27] 5916 2-9-5 0 JamesSullivan 6 — 65
(Richard Fahey) *chsd ldrs on outside: outpcd and edgd lft 3f out: rallied over 1f out: no imp fnl f* **15/2**

63 **5** ½ **Pepys**[10] 6473 2-9-5 0 ConnorBeasley 4 — 64
(Bryan Smart) *hld up in tch: drvn and outpcd 3f out: rallied wl over 1f out: sn no imp* **5/1**[3]

1m 56.33s (7.93) **Going Correction** +0.75s/f (Yiel) — **5** Ran SP% **111.0**

Speed ratings (Par 95): **90,88,88,86,85**

CSF £36.03 TOTE £2.70: £1.20, £6.50; EX 38.60 Trifecta £65.10.

Owner Sheikh Hamdan bin Mohammed Al Maktoum **Bred** Petches Farm Ltd **Trained** Middleham Moor, N Yorks

FOCUS

Just a fair maiden and another front-running winner on the card.

6772 @TOTEPOOLRACING WIN TICKETS ON TWITTER H'CAP — 1m 67y

5:50 (5:50) (Class 4) (0-80,80) 3-Y-O+ — **£7,762** (£2,310; £1,154; £577) **Stalls** Low

Form — RPR

-111 **1** **Rainbow Rebel (IRE)**[14] 6323 3-9-6 80 PJMcDonald 4 — 92+
(Mark Johnston) *led to over 4f out: w ldr: regained ld and rdn over 2f out: edgd rt and kpt on gamely fnl f* **3/1**[1]

3315 **2** 1 ¾ **Toboggan's Fire**[15] 6277 3-8-12 77 RowanScott(5) 1 — 85
(Ann Duffield) *trckd ldrs: rdn and ev ch over 2f out to over 1f out: kpt on same pce ins fnl f* **7/1**

0604 **3** 4 **Dark Crystal**[9] 6502 5-8-6 67 ow1 RobJFitzpatrick(5) 9 — 66
(Linda Perratt) *fly-jmpd s: hld up: hdwy over 3f out: rdn over 2f out: kpt on fnl f to take 3rd cl home: no ch w first two* **22/1**

3213 **4** hd **Character Onesie (IRE)**[15] 6280 4-8-13 76 NatalieHambling(7) 6 — 74
(Richard Fahey) *midfield: drvn and outpcd over 3f out: rallied over 1f out: kpt on ins fnl f: nvr able to chal* **6/1**[3]

5040 **5** shd **Mystic Miraaj**[40] 5482 4-9-4 77 (bt) RachelRichardson(3) 10 — 75
(Tim Easterby) *hld up: smooth hdwy on outside over 3f out: rdn and ev ch over 2f out to over 1f out: wknd ins fnl f: lost two pls cl home* **8/1**

0302 **6** 5 **Echo Of Lightning**[15] 6280 6-9-0 77 (p) LewisEdmunds(7) 13 — 64
(Brian Ellison) *hld up in tch: rdn and outpcd over 2f out: n.d after* **10/1**

5563 **7** 3 ¾ **Bahamian C**[11] 6432 5-8-10 66 oh3 TomEaves 12 — 44
(Richard Fahey) *bhd: detached after 3f: sme late hdwy: nvr on terms* **20/1**

310 **8** 3 ¼ **Crazy Tornado (IRE)**[14] 6344 3-8-11 71 ConnorBeasley 11 — 42
(Keith Dalgleish) *w wnr: led over 4f out to over 2f out: sn rdn and wknd* **10/1**

410 **9** 12 **Archie's Advice**[56] 4871 5-9-8 78 SamHitchcott 8 — 21
(Keith Dalgleish) *hld up towards rr: drvn and struggling over 3f out: sn btn* **10/1**

14 **10** 2 ½ **Italian Beauty (IRE)**[24] 6028 4-9-2 72 DaleSwift 5 — 9
(Brian Ellison) *in tch: nvr gng wl: struggling over 3f out: sn btn* **11/2**[2]

6110 **11** 4 **Ellaal**[15] 6280 7-9-9 79 JamesSullivan 7 — 7
(Ruth Carr) *hld up: rdn and struggling over 3f out: sn btn* **22/1**

1m 53.3s (4.90) **Going Correction** +0.75s/f (Yiel)

WFA 3 from 4yo+ 4lb — **11** Ran SP% **119.0**

Speed ratings (Par 105): **105,103,99,99,98 93,90,86,74,72 68**

CSF £23.44 CT £392.03 TOTE £3.30: £1.40, £2.20, £8.50; EX 31.50 Trifecta £501.40.

Owner Owners Group 004 **Bred** Pier House Stud **Trained** Middleham Moor, N Yorks

FOCUS

A fair and competitive handicap and a progressive winner. The runner-up has been rated as running a small pb.

6773 TOTEPOOL LIVE INFO DOWNLOAD THE APP H'CAP — 1m 5f 15y

6:20 (6:21) (Class 4) (0-80,80) 3-Y-O+ — **£7,762** (£2,310; £1,154; £577) **Stalls** Low

Form — RPR

6200 **1** **Cotillion**[20] 6163 10-8-8 67 (p) LewisEdmunds(7) 1 — 74
(Ian Williams) *hld up in tch: rdn and hung rt over 2f out: rallied over 1f out: led ins fnl f: pushed out* **11/2**

0600 **2** 1 **Only Orsenfoolsies**[7] 6565 7-9-4 70 PJMcDonald 4 — 75
(Micky Hammond) *led to over 3f out: rallied and regained ld over 1f out: hdd ins fnl f: kpt on* **10/1**

1-06 **3** ¾ **Gleese The Devil (IRE)**[25] 6011 5-9-11 77 TomEaves 2 — 81
(Richard Fahey) *in tch: rdn and outpcd over 2f out: rallied over 1f out: kpt on wl fnl f to take 3rd cl home* **8/1**

4331 **4** hd **Tamayuz Magic (IRE)**[21] 6134 5-10-0 80 (b) JamesSullivan 3 — 84
(Michael Easterby) *t.k.h: prom: lost grnd over 3f out: hdwy to chse ldrs over 1f out: kpt on same pce ins fnl f* **5/1**

3325 **5** 3 ½ **Lara Carbonara (IRE)**[25] 6011 4-9-5 71 SamHitchcott 7 — 69
(John Patrick Shanahan, Ire) *hld up: hdwy to trck ldrs over 2f out: sn rdn and edgd rt: wknd fnl f* **9/2**[3]

-313 **6** 8 **Azzir (IRE)**[75] 4190 4-9-12 78 JoeyHaynes 6 — 64
(K R Burke) *t.k.h: hld up in tch: smooth hdwy to ld over 3f out: rdn and edgd rt over 2f out: hdd over 1f out: sn wknd* **4/1**[2]

6113 **7** 1 ½ **Falcon's Fire (IRE)**[9] 6503 3-9-1 76 ConnorBeasley 5 — 60
(Keith Dalgleish) *cl up: rdn and ev ch 3f out: wknd wl over 1f out* **10/3**[1]

3m 8.32s (14.42) **Going Correction** +0.75s/f (Yiel)

WFA 3 from 4yo+ 9lb — **7** Ran SP% **113.5**

Speed ratings (Par 105): **85,84,83,83,81 76,75**

CSF £55.76 TOTE £6.20: £2.90, £4.90; EX 45.50 Trifecta £645.10.

Owner Jamie Robert Roberts **Bred** Mr & Mrs G Middlebrook **Trained** Portway, Worcs

FOCUS

A fair staying handicap and not much separated the first four home. Muddling form. The winner has been rated to his best over the past year.

6774 TOTEPOOL SUPPORTING SCOTTISH RACING H'CAP — 5f 7y

6:50 (6:50) (Class 6) (0-65,62) 3-Y-O+ — **£2,911** (£866; £432; £216) **Stalls** High

Form — RPR

4366 **1** **Mystical King**[5] 6615 6-8-7 45 (p) JoeyHaynes 6 — 52
(Linda Perratt) *mde all: rdn along 2f out: kpt on wl fnl f* **16/1**

5020 **2** 1 ½ **Tinsill**[3] 6680 5-8-6 51 (p) LewisEdmunds(7) 9 — 53
(Nigel Tinkler) *hld up: rdn and hdwy 2f out: chsd wnr ins fnl f: kpt on* **6/4**[1]

0001 **3** 2 ¼ **Knockamany Bends (IRE)**[29] 5838 6-9-1 53 (tp) PaddyAspell 5 — 47
(John Wainwright) *dwlt: sn pressing wnr: rdn and ev ch over 1f out: no ex ins fnl f* **17/2**

303 **4** ½ **Lady Wootton**[5] 6615 3-9-3 56 (v) ConnorBeasley 4 — 48
(Keith Dalgleish) *dwlt: bhd: rdn along over 2f out: hdwy over 1f out: kpt on fnl f: nt pce to chal* **3/1**[2]

5004 **5** 2 ½ **Rock Canyon (IRE)**[5] 6615 7-9-10 62 PJMcDonald 3 — 45
(Linda Perratt) *in tch: drvn and outpcd 1/2-way: no imp fr over 1f out* **9/1**

5560 **6** nk **Noodles Blue Boy**[24] 6023 10-9-10 62 TomEaves 8 — 44
(Ollie Pears) *prom: rdn along over 2f out: drifted rt over 1f out: sn wknd* **5/1**[3]

0020 **7** 2 ¼ **Lady Elizabeth (IRE)**[63] 4647 3-9-2 55 (p) DaleSwift 7 — 29
(Scott Dixon) *prom: drvn along 1/2-way: wknd over 1f out* **16/1**

0000 **8** hd **Cheeni**[5] 6615 4-8-7 45 JamesSullivan 2 — 18
(Jim Goldie) *taken early to post: s.i.s: bhd and sn struggling: nvr on terms* **25/1**

0040 **9** 17 **Bannock Town**[9] 6506 5-8-2 45 (p) ShirleyTeasdale(5) 1
(Linda Perratt) *prom: rdn over 2f out: sn struggling: lost tch fnl f* **125/1**

1m 3.47s (3.47) **Going Correction** +0.75s/f (Yiel)

WFA 3 from 4yo+ 1lb — **9** Ran SP% **118.6**

Speed ratings (Par 101): **102,99,96,95,91 90,87,86,59**

CSF £41.61 CT £236.54 TOTE £16.90: £3.60, £1.40, £2.00; EX 43.40 Trifecta £352.10.

Owner Jackton Racing Club **Bred** Miss L A Perratt **Trained** East Kilbride, S Lanarks

FOCUS

A modest sprint handicap, in which it paid to race handy. The runner-up has been rated just off his recent best.

T/Plt: £1,505.60 to a £1 stake. Pool of £35063.01 - 17.0 winning tickets. T/Qpdt: £203.60 to a £1 stake. Pool of £3825.86 - 13.90 winning tickets. **Richard Young**

6730 HAYDOCK (L-H)

Saturday, September 24

OFFICIAL GOING: Good (9.3)

Wind: Strong across Weather: Cloudy and blustery

6775 WINGATE SIGNS SUPPORTS #SUPERJOSH H'CAP — 1m 3f 200y

2:10 (2:10) (Class 3) (0-95,94) 3-Y-O+ — **£9,703** (£2,887; £1,443; £721) **Stalls** Centre

Form — RPR

001 **1** **Lord Ben Stack (IRE)**[22] 6081 4-9-7 94 CliffordLee(5) 3 — 106
(K R Burke) *mde all: rdn clr wl over 2f out: kpt on strly* **6/4**[1]

2212 **2** 1 ¾ **Rex Bell (IRE)**[94] 3532 3-8-12 88 (p) RobertHavlin 6 — 97
(John Gosden) *trckd ldrs: hdwy 3f out: rdn to chse wnr and carried hd awkwardly wl over 1f out: sn edgd lft: drvn and edgd rt ins fnl f: kpt on* **5/2**[2]

062S **3** 4 **Jacbequick**[17] 6225 5-9-8 90 JimCrowley 1 — 93
(David O'Meara) *trckd ldng pair: hdwy to chse wnr over 3f out: rdn along over 2f out: drvn wl over 1f out: kpt on same pce* **10/1**

0-45 **4** nk **Energia Fox (BRZ)**[55] 4920 6-8-13 81 TonyHamilton 2 — 83
(Richard Fahey) *hld up in tch: hdwy over 3f out: rdn along and chsd ldrs over 2f out: no imp fnl f* **14/1**

3331 **5** 8 **Rydan (IRE)**[23] 6065 5-9-3 85 (v) TomQueally 9 — 74
(Gary Moore) *dwlt: hld up in rr: hdwy over 3f out: rdn along over 2f out: n.d* **13/2**[3]

3316 **6** nk **Salmon Sushi**[29] 5837 5-9-3 85 JasonHart 5 — 74
(Tim Easterby) *hld up in rr: effrt and sme hdwy 4f out: rdn along 3f out: sn outpcd and bhd fnl 2f* **10/1**

0/00 **7** 10 **Restraint Of Trade (IRE)**[21] 6134 6-8-12 80 (v) GrahamLee 4 — 53
(Jennie Candlish) *t.k.h early: sn chsng wnr: rdn along over 4f out: sn wknd* **20/1**

500 **8** 8 **All Talk N No Do (IRE)**[15] 6283 5-9-10 92 (tp) DaneO'Neill 7 — 52
(Seamus Durack) *chsd ldrs: rdn along over 4f out: sn wknd* **20/1**

2m 27.35s (-6.45) **Going Correction** -0.425s/f (Firm)

WFA 3 from 4yo+ 8lb — **8** Ran SP% **116.3**

Speed ratings (Par 107): **104,102,100,99,94 94,87,82**

CSF £5.41 CT £23.99 TOTE £2.40: £1.10, £1.30, £2.80; EX 6.30 Trifecta £34.30.

Owner Owners For Owners: Lord Ben Stack **Bred** G Rollain **Trained** Middleham Moor, N Yorks

FOCUS

All races were run on the Inner Home Straight. Actual race distance 1m3f 195yds. Robert Havlin described the ground as being "on the easy side of good." Run at a reasonable gallop, the front pair came clear, with the favourite making all. The third has been rated close to his best.

6776 BRITISH STALLION STUDS EBF MAIDEN FILLIES' STKS (PLUS 10 RACE) — 1m

2:45 (2:46) (Class 5) 2-Y-O — **£3,234** (£962; £481; £240) **Stalls** Low

Form — RPR

1 **Fleabiscuit (IRE)** 2-9-0 0 JimCrowley 2 — 81+
(Hugo Palmer) *trckd ldrs: hdwy 2f out: led 11/2f out: shkn up ins fnl f: pushed out: readily* **5/2**[1]

2 1 **The Jean Genie** 2-9-0 0 DaneO'Neill 1 — 79
(Clive Cox) *dwlt and rr: gd hdwy on wd outside 2f out: rdn over 1f out: styd on to chse wnr ins fnl f: sn edgd lft and kpt on* **16/1**

03 **3** 2 ½ **Rickrack (IRE)**[32] 5747 2-9-0 0 MartinLane 3 — 73
(Luca Cumani) *t.k.h: trckd ldrs: hdwy to trck wnr 1/2-way: effrt and slt ld 21/2f out: sn rdn: hdd 11/2f out: sn drvn and kpt on same pce* **9/2**[3]

4 1 **Pattie** 2-9-0 0 GrahamLee 7 — 71
(Mick Channon) *towards rr: rapid hdwy on outer to join ldrs 1/2-way: pushed along 3f out: cl upo and rdn over 2f out: drvn over 1f out: kpt on same pce* **16/1**

05 **5** 1 ½ **Lady Valdean**[25] 5995 2-9-0 0 RenatoSouza 5 — 67
(Jose Santos) *t.k.h early: trckd ldrs: hdwy 3f out: rdn along 2f out: sn drvn and no imp* **33/1**

6 ½ **Duke's Girl** 2-9-0 0 [1] WilliamTwiston-Davies 4 — 66
(Michael Bell) *a towards rr* **25/1**

4 **7** 2 1/4 **Eyeborn (IRE)**[16] 6250 2-9-0 0 RichardKingscote 9 61
(Tom Dascombe) *led: pushed along over 2f out: rdn and hdd 21/2f out: sn drvn and grad wknd* **11/1**

2 **8** shd **Free To Dance (IRE)**[33] 5728 2-8-9 0 CliffordLee(5) 8 61
(K R Burke) *prom: pushed along over 3f out: rdn over 2f out: sn wknd* **3/1**[2]

4 **9** 3/4 **Rockshine**[21] 6111 2-9-0 0 SeanLevey 10 59
(Richard Hannon) *sn chsng ldr: cl up 1/2-way: rdn along wl over 2f out: drvn and wknd over 1f out* **11/2**

10 nk **Chakra** 2-9-0 0 JasonHart 6 58
(Michael Bell) *a towards rr* **66/1**

1m 40.12s (-3.58) **Going Correction** -0.425s/f (Firm) **10** Ran SP% **115.5**
Speed ratings (Par 92): **100,99,96,95,94 93,91,91,90,90**
CSF £43.26 TOTE £4.10: £1.70, £3.30, £1.50; EX 29.20 Trifecta £164.70.
Owner Lucayan Stud Ltd **Bred** Horizon Bloodstock Limited **Trained** Newmarket, Suffolk

FOCUS
Actual race distance 7f 215yds. An ordinary fillies' maiden.

6777 EBFSTALLIONS.COM MAIDEN STKS (PLUS 10 RACE) (C&G) 1m
3:20 (3:22) (Class 4) 2-Y-O **£4,269** (£1,270; £634; £317) **Stalls** Low

Form RPR

1 **Barney Roy** 2-9-0 0 SeanLevey 8 84+
(Richard Hannon) *trckd ldrs: hdwy over 1f out: swtchd lft to inner and qcknd wl to ld ins fnl f: sn clr* **9/1**

0 **2** 3 3/4 **Fujaira Bridge (IRE)**[78] 4103 2-9-0 0 AndreaAtzeni 1 75
(Roger Varian) *sn led: pushed along over 2f out: rdn over 1f out: hdd ins fnl f: kpt on same pce* **9/4**[1]

3 nk **Crowned Eagle** 2-9-0 0 RobertHavlin 9 75
(John Gosden) *hld up towards rr: hdwy 3f out: nt clr run 2f out: swtchd rt and rdn over 1f out: styd on strly fnl f* **8/1**

33 **4** 1/2 **Muhajjal**[21] 6108 2-9-0 0 DaneO'Neill 5 74
(Owen Burrows) *trckd ldng pair: hdwy over 3f out: rdn to chal 2f out and ev ch: drvn appr fnl f and kpt on same pce* **4/1**[3]

5 1 1/4 **Pincheck (IRE)** 2-9-0 0 MartinLane 2 71
(Luca Cumani) *trckd ldng pair on inner: hdwy 3f out: rdn along 2f out: drvn over 1f out: kpt on same pce* **11/1**

0 **6** 1/2 **Kasperenko**[21] 6108 2-9-0 0 TomQueally 7 70
(David Lanigan) *towards rr: hdwy wl over 2f out: sn rdn along and kpt on fnl f: nrst fin* **11/1**

6 **7** 1 1/2 **Reverend Jacobs**[36] 5600 2-9-0 0 JimCrowley 3 66
(William Haggas) *trckd ldr: cl up 3f out: rdn along over 2f out: wknd wl over 1f out* **11/4**[2]

8 4 **Lisp (IRE)** 2-9-0 0 SteveDrowne 6 57
(Charles Hills) *in tch: hdwy on outer to chse ldrs 3f out: rdn along 2f out: sn wknd* **50/1**

00 **9** 3/4 **Knight Destroyer (IRE)**[23] 6054 2-9-0 0 GrahamLee 10 55
(Jonjo O'Neill) *hld up in tch: hdwy on outer to chse ldrs 3f out: sn rdn and wknd* **50/1**

10 1/2 **Dream Machine (IRE)** 2-9-0 0 WilliamTwiston-Davies 4 54
(Michael Bell) *a towards rr* **33/1**

1m 39.8s (-3.90) **Going Correction** -0.425s/f (Firm) **10** Ran SP% **122.1**
Speed ratings (Par 97): **102,98,97,97,96 95,94,90,89,88**
CSF £30.84 TOTE £12.30: £3.00, £1.60, £2.80; EX 41.60 Trifecta £376.00.
Owner Potensis Bloodstock Limited **Bred** Eliza Park International Pty Ltd **Trained** East Everleigh, Wilts

FOCUS
Actual race distance 7f 215yds. This had the look of a decent maiden and the winner was quite impressive.

6778 ERRE INOX FOR STAINLESS WIRE H'CAP 1m
3:55 (3:57) (Class 2) (0-105,99) 3-Y-O+ **£12,938** (£3,850; £1,924; £962) **Stalls** Low

Form RPR

2305 **1** **Above N Beyond**[56] 4887 3-9-7 99 (t) RichardKingscote 2 107
(Tom Dascombe) *mde all: qcknd 2f out: rdn over 1f out: kpt on strly* **9/2**[3]

630 **2** 1 1/4 **Gratzie**[1] 6736 5-9-0 88 TonyHamilton 3 93
(Mick Channon) *hld up: hdwy over 2f out: n.m.r and swtchd lft ent fnl f: sn rdn and styd on wl towards fin* **10/1**

1314 **3** nk **Weekend Offender (FR)**[36] 5616 3-8-8 86 ShaneGray 9 93+
(Kevin Ryan) *blind removed late and slowly away: hdwy over 2f out: rdn over 1f out: styd on strly towards fin* **4/1**[2]

0661 **4** nk **Silvery Moon (IRE)**[9] 6500 9-9-0 88 JasonHart 10 91
(Tim Easterby) *prom: effrt to chal over 2f out: sn rdn and ev ch tl drvn and kpt on same pce fnl f* **12/1**

1116 **5** 3/4 **Takatul (USA)**[22] 6076 3-8-9 87 DaneO'Neill 5 88
(Charles Hills) *trckd ldrs: hdwy 3f out: ev ch 2f out: sn rdn and kpt on same pce* **9/4**[1]

3200 **6** nk **Holy Grail (IRE)**[18] 6217 3-7-10 81 oh3 SophieKilloran(7) 8 81
(Simon West) *towards rr: hdwy on outer 3f out: rdn along 2f out: sn drvn and no imp* **25/1**

36-0 **7** 2 **Sixth Sense (IRE)**[15] 6287 3-9-3 95 JimCrowley 4 91
(Mark Johnston) *cl up ev ch 2f out: sn rdn and wknd appr fnl f* **12/1**

0504 **8** 6 **Alfred Hutchinson**[13] 6372 8-9-10 98 (p) GrahamLee 6 79
(David O'Meara) *trckd ldrs: hdwy 3f out: rdn 2f out: sn btn* **14/1**

3144 **9** 7 **Worlds His Oyster**[7] 6585 3-8-5 83 CamHardie 1 47
(John Quinn) *trckd ldrs on inner: pushed along over 3f out: rdn wl over 1f out: sn wknd* **6/1**

1m 38.46s (-5.24) **Going Correction** -0.425s/f (Firm) course record
WFA 3 from 5yo+ 4lb **9** Ran SP% **118.2**
Speed ratings (Par 109): **109,107,107,107,106 106,104,98,91**
CSF £49.83 CT £198.04 TOTE £5.80: £1.90, £2.70, £1.80; EX 49.30 Trifecta £391.50.
Owner Chasemore Farm LLP & Owen Promotions Ltd **Bred** A S Denniff **Trained** Malpas, Cheshire

FOCUS
Actual race distance 7f 215yds. Useful handicap form, although they finished bunched behind the winner, who received a good ride. The winner has been rated similar to his C&D effort in May.

6779 HYDES ORIGINAL H'CAP 5f
4:30 (4:31) (Class 2) (0-105,99) 3-Y-O+
£28,012 (£8,388; £4,194; £2,097; £1,048; £526) **Stalls** Centre

Form RPR

0553 **1** **Harry Hurricane**[14] 6327 4-9-7 96 (b[1]) JimCrowley 4 105
(George Baker) *wnt rt s: trckd ldrs: hdwy wl over 1f out: rdn ent fnl f: led last 100 yds: drvn out* **5/1**[1]

4241 **2** nk **East Street Revue**[35] 5657 3-8-12 88 (b) DuranFentiman 2 96
(Tim Easterby) *chsd ldrs: hdwy and rdn over 1f out: drvn and ev ch ins fnl f: kpt on* **10/1**[3]

010 **3** 1/2 **Judicial (IRE)**[14] 6327 4-9-10 99 (e) JoeDoyle 16 105+
(Julie Camacho) *stmbld sltly s and towards rr: hdwy wl over 1f out: sn rdn and kpt on strly fnl f* **14/1**

2030 **4** nk **Gamesome (FR)**[35] 5648 5-9-4 93 DougieCostello 5 98
(Paul Midgley) *in tch: hdwy wl over 1f out: sn rdn and kpt on fnl f* **16/1**

102 **5** hd **Lightscameraction (IRE)**[35] 5641 4-9-1 97 (b) CameronNoble(7) 7 101
(Gay Kelleway) *t.k.h: led after 1f: clr 2f out: sn rdn and drifted rt to stands rail ins fnl f: hdd and no ex last 100 yds* **8/1**[2]

0011 **6** 1/2 **Lincoln (IRE)**[2] 6714 5-9-8 97 6ex GrahamLee 8 100
(Mick Channon) *towards rr: hdwy wl over 1f out sn rdn: swtchd lft jst ins fnl f: kpt on: nrst fin* **5/1**[1]

2520 **7** 1 1/2 **Confessional**[14] 6327 9-9-2 91 (be) CamHardie 14 88
(Tim Easterby) *in tch: rdn along wl over 1f out: sn drvn and kpt on same pce* **20/1**

4023 **8** 1/2 **Waseem Faris (IRE)**[26] 5961 7-8-5 85 CliffordLee(5) 3 80
(Joseph Tuite) *chsd ldrs: rdn along wl over 1f out: grad wknd* **25/1**

0422 **9** 1/2 **Humidor (IRE)**[14] 6327 9-9-10 99 FergusSweeney 15 93
(George Baker) *a towards rr* **11/1**

06 **10** 1/2 **Dutch Masterpiece**[21] 6119 6-9-1 95 (b) HectorCrouch(5) 13 87
(Gary Moore) *t.k.h: hld up: a towards rr* **11/1**

2004 **11** 3/4 **Robot Boy (IRE)**[21] 6119 6-9-6 95 ShaneGray 11 84
(David Barron) *wnt lft s: a towards rr* **11/1**

2106 **12** nk **Blithe Spirit**[35] 5641 5-9-6 95 JasonHart 9 83
(Eric Alston) *dwlt: a towards rr* **20/1**

120 **13** hd **Powerallied (IRE)**[35] 5641 3-8-6 89 SophieKilloran(7) 12 76
(Richard Fahey) *chsd ldng pair: rdn along over 2f out: sn drvn and wknd* **25/1**

0006 **14** hd **Arctic Feeling (IRE)**[8] 6537 8-8-10 85 TonyHamilton 6 72
(Richard Fahey) *dwlt: a towards rr* **20/1**

3000 **15** shd **Desert Law (IRE)**[46] 5268 8-9-6 95 MartinLane 17 81
(Paul Midgley) *led 1f: chsd ldr: rdn wl over 1f out: sn drvn and wknd appr fnl f* **20/1**

1413 **P** **Bashiba (IRE)**[21] 6114 5-8-11 86 (t) AndreaAtzeni 1
(Nigel Tinkler) *a towards rr: lost action and p.u wl over 1f out: dismntd* **12/1**

57.86s (-2.94) **Going Correction** -0.35s/f (Firm)
WFA 3 from 4yo+ 1lb **16** Ran SP% **125.5**
Speed ratings (Par 109): **109,108,107,107,106 106,103,102,102,101 100,99,99,99,98**
CSF £49.13 CT £698.78 TOTE £6.20: £1.80, £2.20, £4.00, £5.00; EX 64.10 Trifecta £1690.30.
Owner PJL Racing **Bred** Selwood Bloodstock, Hoskins & Lowry **Trained** Manton, Wilts

FOCUS
A decent sprint, the main action unfolded down the centre late on. The winner has been rated back to his best, with the runner-up recording another pb.

6780 HYDES BREWERY H'CAP 6f
5:05 (5:06) (Class 3) (0-90,90) 3-Y-O+ **£9,703** (£2,887; £1,443; £721) **Stalls** Centre

Form RPR

0362 **1** **Spring Fling**[86] 3815 5-9-6 89 DaneO'Neill 2 99+
(Henry Candy) *trckd ldrs centre: hdwy 2f out: rdn to ld jst over 1f out: sn hung bdly lft to far rail: hld on wl towards fin* **7/1**[2]

3102 **2** 1/2 **Edward Lewis**[22] 6079 3-9-1 86 RobertHavlin 15 94+
(John Gosden) *racd towards stands side: in tch: hdwy wl over 1f out and sn rdn: drvn and styng on wl whn hung bdly lft last 75 yds: jst hld hung lft last 75 yds* **11/2**[1]

2260 **3** nk **Sir Billy Wright (IRE)**[8] 6539 5-8-11 85 CliffordLee(5) 4 92
(David Evans) *racd towards centre: cl up: rdn over 1f out and ev ch tl drvn wl ins fnl f and kpt on same pce* **9/1**

5500 **4** 3/4 **Englishman**[8] 6539 6-9-2 85 RichardKingscote 16 90
(Milton Bradley) *racd nr stands rail: led 1f: cl up: rdn wl over 1f out: drvn and carried sltly lft ins fnl f: kpt on* **14/1**

0060 **5** nk **Shore Step (IRE)**[15] 6287 6-9-5 88 GrahamLee 17 92
(Mick Channon) *cl up nr stands rail: led after 1f: rdn along 2f out: sn hdd and drvn: kpt on same pce fnl f* **12/1**

4004 **6** shd **Misterioso (IRE)**[16] 6263 4-9-4 87 TimmyMurphy 3 90+
(Jamie Osborne) *racd towards far side: in tch: hdwy on wd outside 2f out: sn rdn and kpt on fnl f* **11/1**

2004 **7** nk **Primrose Valley**[13] 6371 4-9-4 87 (p) FrederikTylicki 14 89
(Ed Vaughan) *in tch nr stands rail: hdwy wl over 1f out: sn rdn and kpt on fnl f* **10/1**

4004 **8** shd **Duke Cosimo**[8] 6539 6-8-13 82 (p) JoeDoyle 5 84+
(Michael Herrington) *racd towards centre: towards rr: hdwy wl over 1f out: sn rdn and kpt on fnl f* **11/2**[1]

0-23 **9** 1/2 **Memories Galore (IRE)**[92] 3606 4-9-3 86 JimCrowley 8 86
(Harry Dunlop) *in tch centre: hdwy to chse ldrs 2f out: sn rdn and no imp fnl f* **8/1**[3]

5435 **10** 1 1/2 **Major Crispies**[13] 6371 5-8-8 82 (bt) DavidParkes(5) 1 78
(Jeremy Gask) *racd nr stands rail: a towards rr* **25/1**

5050 **11** shd **Avon Breeze**[7] 6556 7-9-2 88 (p) JacobButterfield(3) 7 83
(Richard Whitaker) *in tch centre: rdn along wl over 1f out: sn wknd* **33/1**

1030 **12** nk **Aguerooo (IRE)**[147] 1865 3-9-5 90 (p) SeanLevey 12 84
(Richard Hannon) *a towards rr nr stands rail* **25/1**

002- **13** 1/2 **Jamaican Bolt (IRE)**[322] 7754 8-9-4 87 CamHardie 6 80
(David O'Meara) *prom centre: rdn wl over 1f out: sn wknd* **14/1**

0100 **14** 1 **Hawkeyethenoo (IRE)**[11] 6449 10-9-2 85 TomQueally 11 75
(Jim Goldie) *racd towards stands rail: in tch: gd hdwy 2f out and sn cl up: rdn and ev ch over 1f out: wknd fnl f* **22/1**

3015 **15** 3/4 **Red Tycoon (IRE)**[22] 6079 4-8-13 82 ShaneGray 9 69
(David Barron) *racd nr stands rail: a towards rr* **14/1**

1m 11.85s (-1.95) **Going Correction** -0.35s/f (Firm)
WFA 3 from 4yo+ 2lb **15** Ran SP% **124.5**
Speed ratings (Par 107): **99,98,97,96,96 96,96,95,95,93 93,92,92,90,89**
CSF £44.41 CT £369.18 TOTE £8.90: £2.90, £2.30, £3.20; EX 43.30 Trifecta £323.30.
Owner Six Too Many & T A Frost **Bred** Mrs C R D Wilson **Trained** Kingston Warren, Oxon

FOCUS
They raced in two groups for 4f of the contest and the first two home ended up near both rails. The third helps set the standard.

6781 BEER STUDIO H'CAP 1m 6f
5:40 (5:42) (Class 2) (0-100,98) 3-Y-O+ **£15,202** (£4,523; £2,260; £1,130) **Stalls** Low

Form RPR

4551 **1** **Faithful Mount**[18] 6209 7-9-2 86 (p) RichardKingscote 10 95
(Ian Williams) *mde all: rdn over 2f out: drvn over 1f out: kpt on strly fnl f* **7/1**[3]

3241 **2** 1 3/4 **Multellie**[29] 5837 4-8-13 83 CamHardie 13 89
(Tim Easterby) *a chsng wnr: pushed along over 2f out: rdn wl over 1f out: drvn ins fnl f: no imp towards fin* **22/1**

0300 **3** *1* **Angel Gabrial (IRE)**[21] 6118 7-9-7 **98**........................ SophieKilloran(7) 2 103
(Richard Fahey) *in tch: hdwy on outer to trck ldrs 6f out: rdn 2f out: kpt on wl fnl f* **11/1**

12 **4** *nk* **Corinthian**[86] 3814 3-8-9 **89**..(b1) AndreaAtzeni 8 93
(Roger Varian) *trckd ldrs: pushed along 6f out: rdn along 3f out: swtchd lft to inner and drvn to chse ldrs over 1f out: kpt on* **6/4**[1]

0213 **5** *3/4* **Buonarroti (IRE)**[13] 6379 5-9-6 **90**................................ FrederikTylicki 4 93+
(Declan Carroll) *hld up in rr: hdwy on wd outside over 2f out: rdn over 1f out: styd on wl fnl f: nrst fin* **11/1**

1/12 **6** *1/2* **Chocala (IRE)**[15] 6279 6-9-8 **92**........................ WilliamTwiston-Davies 6 94+
(Alan King) *.] hld up in rr: hdwy on inner wl over 2f out: rdn wl over 1f out: kpt on fnl f: nrst fin* **9/2**[2]

13-0 **7** *2 1/4* **Important Message**[23] 6057 4-9-9 **93**............................ WilliamCarson 3 92
(Saeed bin Suroor) *trckd ldng pair: effrt 3f out: rdn along 2f out: drvn over 1f out: wknd ent fnl f* **16/1**

2663 **8** *1/2* **Gabrial's King (IRE)**[15] 6279 7-9-4 **88**.......................... TonyHamilton 11 87
(Richard Fahey) *dwlt: a towards rr* **25/1**

6063 **9** *5* **Swaheen**[21] 6134 4-9-0 **84**.. JoeDoyle 12 76
(Julie Camacho) *hld up: hdwy wl over 3f out: rdn to chse ldrs over 2f out: drvn and wknd over 1f out* **20/1**

4220 **10** *7* **Forgotten Hero (IRE)**[43] 5381 7-9-10 **94**..................(t) DougieCostello 7 76
(Kim Bailey) *hld up towards rr: hdwy on outer over 5f out: chsd ldrs over 3f out: rdn over 2f out: sn wknd* **20/1**

03-0 **11** *6* **William Of Orange**[143] 1967 5-9-10 **94**......................... TimmyMurphy 1 67
(Donald McCain) *a towards rr: outpcd and bhd fr over 2f out* **28/1**

106 **12** *21* **Vivre Pour Vivre (IRE)**[21] 6142 3-8-8 **88** ow2.................. JimCrowley 9 32
(Ed Dunlop) *chsd ldrs on outer: pushed along over 5f out: rdn wl over 3f out: sn drvn lost pl and bhd fnl 2f* **10/1**

2m 56.23s (-5.77) **Going Correction** -0.425s/f (Firm)
WFA 3 from 4yo+ 10lb **12** Ran SP% **123.5**
Speed ratings (Par 109): **99,98,97,97,96 96,95,94,92,88 84,72**
CSF £159.82 CT £1699.43 TOTE £8.60: £2.50, £8.10, £3.60; EX 190.00 Trifecta £1682.00 Part won..
Owner Macable Partnership **Bred** G Robinson **Trained** Portway, Worcs

FOCUS
Actual race distance 1m5f 215yds. A useful handicap and it paid to race handily. The fifth and sixth have been rated close to form.
T/Plt: £41.50 to a £1 stake. Pool of £82860.90 - 1454.60 winning tickets. T/Qpdt: £23.40 to a £1 stake. Pool of £4872.63 - 153.50 winning tickets. **Joe Rowntree**

6746 NEWMARKET (R-H)
Saturday, September 24

OFFICIAL GOING: Good to firm (firm in places; overall 8.3, stands' side 8.3, far side 8.4)
Wind: medium, across Weather: light cloud

6782 NEWMARKETRACECOURSES.CO.UK MAIDEN FILLIES' STKS (PLUS 10 RACE) 7f
1:50 (1:51) (Class 4) 2-Y-O **£5,175** (£1,540; £769; £384) **Stalls** Low

Form RPR

1 **Talaayeb** 2-9-0 0.. PaulMulrennan 1 90+
(Owen Burrows) *hld up in tch towards rr: stdy hdwy 1/2-way: chsd ldrs 2f out: effrt between rivals to chal whn edgd lft and struck into 1f out: led ins fnl f: r.o strly and drew clr fnl 100yds: readily* **10/1**

2 *2 1/2* **Neshmeya** 2-9-0 0.. PaulHanagan 8 80+
(Charles Hills) *hld up wl in tch in midfield: effrt to press ldrs 2f out: rdn and ev ch over 1f out tl unable qck w wnr ins fnl f: styd on same pce fnl 100yds* **7/4**[1]

50 **3** *3* **The Lacemaker**[59] 4756 2-9-0 0.................................... PatCosgrave 12 72
(Ed Dunlop) *chsd ldrs tl wnt 2nd 1/2-way: rdn and ev ch over 2f out: led over 1f out: hdd jst ins fnl f: no ex and wknd fnl 100yds* **25/1**

36 **4** *1 1/4* **Elas Ruby**[50] 5119 2-9-0 0.. JamesDoyle 14 69
(John Gosden) *led: rdn over 2f out: hdd over 1f out: 4th and struggling to qckn whn hmpd and clipped heels 1f out: sn btn and wknd ins fnl f* **8/1**

5 *1 1/2* **Crimson Rosette (IRE)** 2-9-0 0................................ StevieDonohoe 7 65+
(Charlie Fellowes) *hld up in tch in midfield: rdn and outpcd over 2f out: rallied ent fnl f: styd on steadily ins fnl f: no threat to ldrs* **14/1**

6 *nk* **Queen Of Time** 2-9-0 0.. OisinMurphy 11 64
(Henry Candy) *chsd ldng trio: effrt ent fnl 2f: sn outpcd: wl hld and plugged on same pce fr over 1f out* **25/1**

7 *5* **Meshaykh (IRE)** 2-9-0 0... FrankieDettori 6 50
(Sir Michael Stoute) *hld up in tch in midfield: cl enough and effrt ent fnl 2f: sn outpcd and struggling: wknd over 1f out* **7/1**[3]

0 **8** *6* **How's Lucy**[115] 2793 2-8-9 0.................................... CharlieBennett(5) 13 34
(Jane Chapple-Hyam) *chsd ldr tl 1/2-way: sn pushed along and lost pl 2f out: wknd over 1f out: eased wl ins fnl f* **66/1**

9 *1/2* **Smart Together (USA)** 2-9-0 0................................... NickyMackay 10 33
(John Gosden) *rn green: pushed along early: hdwy into midfield after 1f: pushed along and outpcd 3f out: no ch fnl 2f* **9/1**

10 *1/2* **Beauchamp Opal** 2-9-0 0... HarryBentley 3 32
(Charlie Fellowes) *in tch in midfield: rdn over 2f out: sn outpcd: wknd wl over 1f out* **50/1**

11 *2* **Lulu The Rocket** 2-9-0 0... FMBerry 9 26
(Peter Chapple-Hyam) *awkward leaving stalls: t.k.h: hld up towards rr: struggling 3f out: bhd fnl 2f* **66/1**

12 *2 1/2* **Ronni Layne** 2-8-11 0.. NoelGarbutt(3) 2 19
(Conrad Allen) *sn pushed along in last pair: rdn 1/2-way: bhd over 2f out* **200/1**

13 *5* **Forever Excel (IRE)** 2-9-0 0... JamieSpencer 4 6
(Charles Hills) *s.i.s: rn green in rr: lost tch over 2f out: t.o* **33/1**

14 *6* **Blue Illusion** 2-9-0 0.. WilliamBuick 5
(Charlie Appleby) *hld up in midfield: lost pl 1/2-way: sn bhd: t.o* **9/2**[2]

1m 25.59s (0.19) **Going Correction** +0.075s/f (Good) **14** Ran SP% **120.0**
Speed ratings (Par 94): **101,98,94,93,91 91,85,78,78,77 75,72,66,59**
CSF £26.64 TOTE £14.30: £3.60, £1.30, £6.50; EX 43.50 Trifecta £690.30.
Owner Hamdan Al Maktoum **Bred** Shadwell Estate Company Limited **Trained** Lambourn, Berks

FOCUS
Far Side Course used. Stalls all races Far Side. The track was not watered overnight in anticipation of a heavy dew but that didn't materialise, so the ground was changed to good to firm, firm in places prior to the first. There was a stiff breeze half into the horses' faces. This had the look of an open maiden with plenty of top stables represented but, in admittedly not many renewals, it has not produced any well-above average winners. However, that doesn't mean something isn't lurking further down the beaten runners, as Seventh Heaven, subsequently successful in Group 1 company, finished 8l fourth in 2015.

6783 JUDDMONTE ROYAL LODGE STKS (GROUP 2) (C&G) 1m
2:20 (2:22) (Class 1) 2-Y-O
£56,710 (£21,500; £8,060; £8,060; £2,690; £1,350) **Stalls** Low

Form RPR

12 **1** **Best Of Days**[38] 5556 2-9-0 0.. JamesDoyle 8 110
(Hugo Palmer) *hld up in tch in last trio: hdwy 3f out: chal 2f out: rdn to ld jst over 1f out: styd on: pressed towards fin but a lasting home: rdn out* **6/5**[1]

3 **2** *nk* **The Anvil (IRE)**[16] 6262 2-9-0 0.................................. SeamieHeffernan 3 109
(A P O'Brien, Ire) *s.i.s: hld up in tch in rr: effrt 2f out: drvn and swtchd lft over 1f out: hdwy 1f out: styd on u.p chse wnr wl ins fnl f: clsng towards fin but nvr quite getting to wnr* **25/1**

3 **3** *3/4* **Arcada (IRE)**[34] 5683 2-9-0 0....................................... DonnachaO'Brien 2 107
(Joseph Patrick O'Brien, Ire) *chsd ldr tl wl over 2f out: rdn and outpcd 2f out: rallied u.p 1f out: styd on wl ins fnl f* **12/1**

1324 **3** *dht* **Sea Fox (IRE)**[16] 6270 2-9-0 96..[1] AdamKirby 7 107
(David Evans) *pressed ldng pair: rdn to ld wl over 2f out: hdd 2f out: stl ev ch and hung rt over 1f out: chsng wnr and stl hanging 1f out: styd on same pce: lost 2nd wl ins fnl f* **16/1**

3 **5** *1 1/4* **Douglas Macarthur (IRE)**[14] 6349 2-9-0 0...................... RyanMoore 1 104
(A P O'Brien, Ire) *hld up in tch in last trio: hdwy to chse ldrs and rdn 3f out: drvn over 1f out: swtchd rt 1f out: kpt on same pce ins fnl f* **5/1**[3]

1121 **6** *1 1/4* **Montataire (IRE)**[36] 5595 2-9-0 100.................................... JoeFanning 4 101
(Mark Johnston) *led rdn and hdd wl over 1f out: stl ev ch tl no ex u.p 1f out: wknd ins fnl f* **4/1**[2]

211 **7** *3 3/4* **Kings Gift (IRE)**[18] 6213 2-9-0 92................................. PaulMulrennan 5 92
(Michael Dods) *t.k.h: hld up wl in tch in midfield: rdn and lost pl over 2f out: bhd over 1f out: wknd ins fnl f* **14/1**

61 **8** *2* **Bay Of Poets (IRE)**[22] 6085 2-9-0 0................................ WilliamBuick 6 88+
(Charlie Appleby) *stdd s: t.k.h: hld up in tch in midfield: clsd to ld and travelling strly 2f out: rdn and hdd jst over 1f out: sn btn: fdd ins fnl f* **10/1**

1m 38.98s (0.38) **Going Correction** +0.075s/f (Good) **8** Ran SP% **115.3**
Speed ratings (Par 107): **101,100,99,99,98 97,93,91**
WIN: 2.10 Best Of Days; PL: 1.30 Arcada, Best Of Days, 1.80 Sea Fox, 4.40 The Anvil; EX: 35.60; CSF: 37.52; TF: BOD&TA&A: 100.70, BOD&TA&SF 152.30.
Owner Godolphin **Bred** G Schoeningh **Trained** Newmarket, Suffolk
■ Stewards' Enquiry : James Doyle two-day ban; used whip above the permitted level (9th-10th Oct)

FOCUS
Frankel won the last running of the Royal Lodge at Ascot in 2011. The race hasn't produced a true star since, but 2014 winner Elm Park added the Racing Post Trophy while last year's runner-up, Deauville, has won a Grade 1 in the USA this season. This looked a reasonable edition of the race. They raced down the middle and the first two found cover from the headwind at the rear of the field, as well as being positioned on the stands' side of the group. It's been rated around the recent level for the race.

6784 CONNOLLY'S RED MILLS CHEVELEY PARK STKS (GROUP 1) (FILLIES) 6f
2:55 (2:55) (Class 1) 2-Y-O
£102,078 (£38,700; £19,368; £9,648; £4,842; £2,430) **Stalls** Low

Form RPR

166 **1** **Brave Anna (USA)**[13] 6385 2-9-0 0............................ SeamieHeffernan 5 112
(A P O'Brien, Ire) *dwlt: hld up in last pair: wnt 4th 1/2-way: effrt and hung rt 2f out: rdn over 1f out: styd on u.p ins fnl f: ev ch 50yds out: led last stride* **25/1**

0112 **2** *shd* **Roly Poly (USA)**[37] 5584 2-9-0 0.. RyanMoore 6 112
(A P O'Brien, Ire) *sn chsng ldr: rdn over 2f out: clsd to press ldr over 1f out: sltly outpcd ent fnl f: styd on u.p ins fnl f: led 50yds out: hdd last stride* **11/2**[3]

11 **3** *2* **Lady Aurelia (USA)**[34] 5690 2-9-0 0.............................(b) FrankieDettori 2 106
(Wesley A Ward, U.S.A) *taken down early and ponied to s: sn led and racd keenly: clr after 2f: pressed and rdn over 1f out: fnd ex for press ent fnl f: drvn ins fnl f: tired and hdd 50yds out: sn btn and eased cl home* **4/6**[1]

1311 **4** *4* **Queen Kindly**[37] 5584 2-9-0 113...................................... JamieSpencer 3 94
(Richard Fahey) *broke wl: sn stdd and racd in 3rd: rdn ent fnl 2f: no ex u.p over 1f out: wknd ins fnl f* **7/2**[2]

13 **5** *nk* **Pellucid**[23] 6063 2-9-0 0.. WilliamBuick 4 93
(David Simcock) *taken down early: hld up in rr: effrt over 2f out: no imp: wl hld and plugged on same pce fr over 1f out* **33/1**

2 **6** *3 1/2* **Holy Cat (IRE)**[27] 5940 2-9-0 0... ColinKeane 1 83
(M D O'Callaghan, Ire) *racd in midfield tl dropped to 5th 1/2-way: rdn and no imp over 2f out: wknd over 1 out* **20/1**

1m 11.92s (-0.28) **Going Correction** +0.075s/f (Good) **6** Ran SP% **109.1**
Speed ratings (Par 106): **104,103,101,95,95 90**
CSF £141.81 TOTE £26.20: £5.90, £1.70; EX 83.40 Trifecta £249.70.
Owner Mrs E M Stockwell **Bred** Mrs E Stockwell **Trained** Cashel, Co Tipperary
■ Stewards' Enquiry : Seamie Heffernan four-day ban; used whip above the permitted level (9th-12th Oct)

FOCUS
A slightly smaller field than the recent average but that didn't mean it wasn't packed with exciting juveniles. As could have been safely predicted before the off, the favourite went a good gallop once allowed to fully stride on, meaning this was a test of stamina at the trip, but while she couldn't hang on, the two Aidan O'Brien-trained fillies got down to battle out a tight finish. It was the Irish handler's first success in this contest, and the time was quicker than the Middle Park that followed it. The third has been rated a bit below her Morny form.

6785 JUDDMONTE MIDDLE PARK STKS (GROUP 1) (ENTIRE COLTS) 6f
3:30 (3:30) (Class 1) 2-Y-O
£102,078 (£38,700; £19,368; £9,648; £4,842; £2,430) **Stalls** Low

Form RPR

2312 **1** **The Last Lion (IRE)**[15] 6282 2-9-0 105.............................. JoeFanning 2 118
(Mark Johnston) *mde all: shkn up wl over 1f out: rdn and hrd pressed over 1f out: battled on gamely and a holding rival ins fnl f: rdn out* **25/1**

The Form Book, Raceform Ltd, Newbury, RG14 5SJ

1121 **2** 3/4 **Blue Point (IRE)**[35] 5654 2-9-0 115 .... WilliamBuick 5 116
(Charlie Appleby) *hld up wl in tch: nt clrest run 2f out: rdn and hdwy to chal over 1f out: clr w wnr 1f out: hrd drvn and styd on same pce ins fnl f* **11/10**[1]

2112 **3** 2 1/4 **Mehmas (IRE)**[13] 6386 2-9-0 115 .... FrankieDettori 6 109
(Richard Hannon) *s.i.s: t.k.h: hld up in tch in last trio: hdwy and switching rt 2f out: chsd ldng pair 1f out: styd on same pce u.p and no imp ins fnl f* **6/1**[2]

231 **4** 1/2 **Intelligence Cross (USA)**[27] 5940 2-9-0 0 ....(t) SeamieHeffernan 10 108
(A P O'Brien, Ire) *chsd ldrs: rdn 2f out: rdn and outpcd over 1f out: rallied and styd on ins fnl f: no threat to ldng pair* **10/1**

12 **5** 1/2 **Koropick (IRE)**[21] 6124 2-9-0 0 .... JackMitchell 4 106
(Hugo Palmer) *chsd wnr: rdn ent fnl 2f: outpcd u.p over 1f out: kpt on ins fnl f: no threat to ldng pair* **66/1**

1012 **6** hd **Mokarris (USA)**[35] 5654 2-9-0 107 .... PaulHanagan 7 105
(Simon Crisford) *t.k.h: hld up in tch: swtchd rt and effrt wl over 1f out: sme hdwy 1f out: styd on same pce ins fnl f* **7/1**[3]

6133 **7** 1 1/4 **Medicine Jack**[13] 6388 2-9-0 0 .... ColinKeane 1 102
(G M Lyons, Ire) *chsd ldrs: rdn 2f out: unable qck u.p over 1f out: wknd ins fnl f* **33/1**

4213 **8** nk **Peace Envoy (FR)**[34] 5690 2-9-0 0 .... RyanMoore 8 101
(A P O'Brien, Ire) *t.k.h: hld up in tch: effrt 2f out: rdn and sme hdwy 1f out: sn no imp: wknd ins fnl f* **9/1**

1101 **9** hd **Mubtasim (IRE)**[16] 6260 2-9-0 101 .... PatCosgrave 9 100
(William Haggas) *t.k.h: hld up in last trio: rdn 2f out: no imp and kpt on same pce ins fnl f: neevr dangerous* **10/1**

134 **10** 4 **Silver Line (IRE)**[79] 4060 2-9-0 106 .... DanielTudhope 3 88
(Saeed bin Suroor) *hld up in tch: effrt 2f out: no imp u.p over 1f out: wknd fnl f* **16/1**

1m 12.13s (-0.07) **Going Correction** +0.075s/f (Good) **10** Ran SP% **116.7**
Speed ratings (Par 109): **103,102,99,98,97 97,95,95,95,89**
CSF £52.67 CT £206.57 TOTE £16.40: £3.80, £1.30, £1.80; EX 83.70 Trifecta £336.90.
Owner John Brown & Megan Dennis **Bred** Barronstown Stud And Mrs T Stack **Trained** Middleham Moor, N Yorks

FOCUS
The Middle Park has rather lost its way in recent years, and eight of the last ten winners have failed to win another race. Star sprinter Muhaarar, however, finished third in 2014. Caravaggio was a notable absentee from this year's race, but it still looked a decent edition. The field raced towards the far side of the track and the surprise winner made all. The time was .21sec slower than Brave Anna took in the Cheveley Park. Only Dream Ahead has been rated higher than this winner in the last nine years, and the level looks pretty solid. A big pb from the winner, with the runner-up rated to his Gimcrack form and the third just off.

6786 BETFRED CAMBRIDGESHIRE (HERITAGE H'CAP) 1m 1f

4:10 (4:12) (Class 2) 3-Y-O+

£99,600 (£29,824; £14,912; £7,456; £3,728; £1,872) **Stalls** Low

Form RPR

0254 **1** **Spark Plug (IRE)**[37] 5585 5-9-4 104 ....(p) JimmyFortune 28 115
(Brian Meehan) *racd nr side: hld up in midfield overall: clsd and nt clr run over 2f out: rdn hdwy to chse ldrs over 1f out: drvn to ld ins fnl f: r.o strly and gng away at fin: 1st of 14 in gp* **12/1**

1006 **2** 2 1/4 **Carry On Deryck**[57] 4823 4-9-5 105 .... WilliamBuick 35 111
(Saeed bin Suroor) *racd nr side: in tch in midfield: clsd to press ldrs 3f out: led overall 2f out: rdn over 1f out: hdd ins fnl f: styd on same pce fnl 100yds: 2nd of 14 in gp* **20/1**

1-63 **3** 1 1/2 **Very Talented (IRE)**[22] 6075 3-8-7 98 .... KevinStott 8 102
(Saeed bin Suroor) *racd far side: wl in tch in midfield overall: clsd to chse ldrs 2f out: rdn and ev ch over 1f out: no ex and styd on same pce ins fnl f: 1st of 17 in gp* **11/1**[3]

-005 **4** 3/4 **Third Time Lucky (IRE)**[37] 5585 4-8-9 100 .... AdamMcNamara[(5)] 13 102
(Richard Fahey) *racd far side: hld up in midfield overall: effrt 2f out: hdwy u.p and nt clr run 1f out: wnt btwn horses and styd on u.p ins fnl f: wnt 4th towards fin: 2nd of 17 in gp* **14/1**

0316 **5** 1/2 **Zhui Feng (IRE)**[7] 6573 3-8-12 103 4ex .... PatDobbs 2 105
(Amanda Perrett) *racd far side: chsd gp ldrs and prom overall: rdn and ev ch 2f out: no ex jst ins fnl f: wknd wl ins fnl f: 3rd of 17 in gp* **33/1**

5200 **6** 1 1/2 **Celestial Path (IRE)**[35] 5652 4-9-4 104 ....[1] LukeMorris 32 101
(Sir Mark Prescott Bt) *racd nr side: wl in tch in midfield overall: rdn to chse ldrs 3f out: unable qck 2f out: drvn and kpt on same pce fr over 1f out: 3rd of 14 in gp* **20/1**

2403 **7** 3/4 **Erik The Red (FR)**[35] 5651 4-8-10 96 .... PaulMulrennan 23 92
(Kevin Ryan) *taken down early: racd nr side: hld up in midfield overall: effrt 2f out: hdwy and swtchd rt ent fnl f: styd on same pce u.p ins fnl f: 4th of 14 in gp* **20/1**

5141 **8** hd **Ginger Jack**[30] 5802 9-8-3 89 .... KieranO'Neill 10 84
(Garry Moss) *racd far side: chsd gp ldr and prom overall: ev ch 3f out: unable qck u.p over 1f out: btn whn edgd lft ins fnl f: 4th of 17 in gp* **50/1**

3035 **9** nse **Ode To Evening**[16] 6261 3-8-11 102 .... JoeFanning 5 98
(Mark Johnston) *racd far side: led gp and chsd ldrs overall: rdn to ld 3f out: hdd 2f out: unable qck u.p over 1f out: wknd ins fnl f: 5th of 17 in gp* **33/1**

013 **10** 1/2 **Interconnection**[26] 5964 5-8-1 90 ....(p) JosephineGordon[(3)] 34 84
(Ed Vaughan) *racd nr side: chsd gp ldr and prom: rdn and ev ch 3f out: rdn 2f out: edgd rt and unable qck over 1f out: wknd ins fnl f: 5th of 14 in gp* **20/1**

4000 **11** shd **Azraff (IRE)**[37] 5585 4-8-12 98 ....(p) AdamBeschizza 19 92
(Marco Botti) *racd far side: hld up in rr: effrt and hdwy over 2f out: drvn and no imp over 1f out: wl hld and kpt on same pce fnl f: 6th of 17 in gp* **40/1**

0034 **12** nk **Gm Hopkins**[70] 4392 5-9-12 112 .... RyanMoore 31 105+
(John Gosden) *racd nr side: rrd as stalls opened and slowly away: hld up in rr: shkn up 2f out: nt clr run over 1f out: pushed along and kpt on ins fnl f: nvr trbld ldrs: 6th of 14 in gp* **12/1**

1511 **13** 1/2 **Treasury Notes (IRE)**[26] 5976 4-9-1 101 4ex .... DanielTudhope 15 93
(David O'Meara) *racd far side: in tch in midfield overall: effrt ent fnl 2f: drvn and no imp over 1f out: wl hld and plugged on same pce ins fnl f: 7th of 17 in gp* **10/1**[2]

2565 **14** 1/2 **American Artist (IRE)**[15] 6298 4-8-4 90 .... HarryBentley 12 81
(Roger Varian) *racd far side: in tch in midfield overall: effrt 2f out: drvn and no imp over 1f out: btn whn sltly hmpd ins fnl f: wknd: 8th of 17 in gp* **20/1**

00-0 **15** nk **Bronze Angel (IRE)**[164] 1425 7-9-4 107 ....(v) LouisSteward[(3)] 24 98
(Marcus Tregoning) *racd nr side: hld up towards rr overall: rdn and no imp over 1f out: wl hld and plugged on same pce fnl f: 7th of 14 in gp* **33/1**

0254 **16** 3/4 **Oasis Fantasy (IRE)**[17] 6233 5-9-5 105 ....(b) AdamKirby 16 94
(Ed Dunlop) *racd far side: hld up towards rr overall: effrt 2f out: rdn and hdwy over 1f out: drvn and no hdwy 1f out: wknd ins fnl f: 9th of 17 in gp* **33/1**

2515 **17** nk **Educate**[35] 5652 7-9-7 112 .... GeorgeBuckell[(5)] 33 100
(Ismail Mohammed) *racd nr side: chsd gp ldrs and prom overall: ev ch 3f out: rdn and unable qck over 2f out: wknd over 1f out: 8th of 14 in gp* **33/1**

2120 **18** 1 **Goodwood Mirage (IRE)**[7] 6573 6-8-1 90 .... EdwardGreatrex[(3)] 30 76
(Michael Bell) *racd nr side: t.k.h: hld up in tch in midfield overall: effrt 2f out: no rspnse and no hdwy over 1f out: wknd ins fnl f: 9th of 14 in gp* **66/1**

5022 **19** 2 1/4 **Banksea**[14] 6331 3-8-8 99 .... JamieSpencer 14 82
(Luca Cumani) *racd far side: hld up towards rr: effrt wl over 1f out: sme hdwy over 1f out but nvr on terms w ldrs: wknd ins fnl f: 10th of 17 in gp* **9/1**[1]

0200 **20** nk **Lat Hawill (IRE)**[21] 6126 5-8-12 98 ....(v) PhillipMakin 26 79
(Keith Dalgleish) *racd nr side: in tch in midfield: rdn over 2f out: hrd drvn and no imp over 1f out: wknd ins fnl f: 10th of 14 in gp* **66/1**

4066 **21** 3/4 **Stipulate**[15] 6283 7-8-9 100 ....(p) OisinOrr[(5)] 6 79
(Brian Ellison) *racd far side: hld up in midfield overall: effrt over 2f out: drvn and no imp ent fnl f: wknd ins fnl f: 11th of 17 in gp* **20/1**

-400 **22** nk **Chil The Kite**[37] 5585 7-9-5 105 .... GeorgeBaker 3 84
(Hughie Morrison) *racd far side: hld up in rr overall: switching lft fr over 2f out: effrt u.p and no imp over 1f out: wknd ins fnl f: 12th of 17 in gp* **33/1**

-312 **23** 1 3/4 **Bravo Zolo (IRE)**[175] 1196 4-9-3 103 .... FrankieDettori 29 78
(Jeremy Noseda) *racd nr side: overall ldr tl hdd and rdn 3f out: no ex u.p over 1f out: btn and eased ins fnl f: 11th of 14 in gp* **20/1**

1560 **24** 3 **Bastille Day**[21] 6126 4-7-10 89 .... DavidEgan[(7)] 4 58
(David Elsworth) *racd far side: in tch in midfield overall: rdn over 2f out: no hdwy and wknd over 1f out: 13th of 17 in gp* **33/1**

-021 **25** 6 **Examiner (IRE)**[113] 2868 5-8-10 96 .... OisinMurphy 18 52
(Stuart Williams) *racd far side: wl in tch in midfield overall: effrt 2f out: no imp and sltly impeded over 1f out: wl btn and eased fnl f: 14th of 17 in gp* **20/1**

-132 **26** 2 **Knight Owl**[26] 5976 6-8-1 92 .... GeorgeWood[(5)] 9 44
(James Fanshawe) *racd far side: chsd ldrs overall: rdn 3f out: unable qck 2f out and sn btn: wknd over 1f out: 15th of 17 in gp* **12/1**

4012 **27** 3/4 **First Sitting**[20] 6178 5-9-6 106 .... JamesDoyle 25 56
(Chris Wall) *racd nr side: chsd gp ldrs and prom overall: drvn and ev ch 3f out: lost pl and btn over 1f out: no ch and eased ins fnl f: 12th of 14 in gp* **25/1**

1420 **28** 4 1/2 **Dark Red (IRE)**[13] 6389 4-8-11 97 .... PatCosgrave 27 38
(Ed Dunlop) *racd nr side: hld up in midfield overall: rdn 3f out: sn struggling: wknd over 1f out: 13th of 14 in gp* **40/1**

0040 **29** hd **Bancnuanaheireann (IRE)**[22] 6075 9-8-7 96 .... TimClark[(3)] 22 37
(Michael Appleby) *racd nr side: hld up in rr: effrt 3f out: sn struggling: bhd fnl 2f out: 14th of 14 in gp* **66/1**

220 **30** 23 **Master The World (IRE)**[35] 5647 5-9-8 108 ....(p) FMBerry 1
(David Elsworth) *racd far side: wl in tch in midfield overall: rdn over 2f out: no rspnse and sn btn: bhd and eased over 1f out: t.o: 16th of 17 in gp* **12/1**

-106 **31** 12 **Balmoral Castle**[22] 6075 7-8-9 95 .... RyanTate 7
(Jonathan Portman) *racd far side: in tch in midfield overall: rdn 3f and losing pl: bhd 2f out: eased fnl f: t.o: 17th of 17 in gp* **66/1**

1m 48.99s (-2.71) **Going Correction** +0.075s/f (Good)
WFA 3 from 4yo+ 5lb **31** Ran SP% **140.2**
Speed ratings (Par 109): **115,113,111,111,110 109,108,108,108,107 107,107,107,106,106 105,105,104,102,102 101,101,99,97,**
CSF £231.49 CT £2775.72 TOTE £14.70: £4.00, £4.40, £5.90, £3.70; EX 328.70 Trifecta £9155.40.
Owner J L Day **Bred** Airlie Stud **Trained** Manton, Wilts

FOCUS
The large field split into just two groups and, generally, there did not seem a great deal between them throughout the contest. Indeed, it still looked close at the furlong marker but two that stayed closest to the stands' side emerged on top from three that edged away from their bunch towards the far side. Apart from the winner, being held up in or towards rear didn't appear to be a positive. A small pb from the winner.

6787 BRITISH STALLION STUDS EBF "JERSEY LILY" FILLIES' NURSERY H'CAP 7f

4:45 (4:46) (Class 2) 2-Y-O

£18,675 (£5,592; £2,796; £1,398; £699; £351) **Stalls** Low

Form RPR

41 **1** **Pichola Dance (IRE)**[12] 6413 2-9-1 81 .... HarryBentley 11 86+
(Roger Varian) *chsd ldrs: effrt 2f out: wandered over 1f out: ev ch ins fnl f: styd on to ld wl ins fnl f: rdn out* **14/1**

233 **2** 1/2 **Harmonise**[39] 5524 2-8-4 70 .... LukeMorris 12 74
(Mick Channon) *t.k.h: hld up in tch: effrt 2f out: sltly impeded and outpcd over 1f out: rallied: edgd lft and styd on wl u.p ins fnl f: wnt 2nd last strides* **16/1**

316 **3** hd **Blushing Rose**[7] 6575 2-8-12 78 .... RyanMoore 6 81+
(Sir Michael Stoute) *.hld up in tch in rr: nt clrest of runs over 1f out: hdwy to chse ldrs and hung rt 1f out: styd on wl u.p ins fnl f: wnt 3rd last strides* **5/2**[1]

1412 **4** 1/2 **Clef**[28] 5877 2-8-11 82 .... AdamMcNamara[(5)] 9 84
(Richard Fahey) *chsd ldrs: rdn over 1f out: stl pressing ldrs but unable qck 1f out: kpt on same pce fnl 150yds* **4/1**[2]

210 **5** nk **Romantic View**[99] 3336 2-9-7 87 .... WilliamBuick 10 88
(Charlie Appleby) *led: rdn over 1f out: drvn and hrd pressed ins fnl f: hdd wl ins fnl f: no ex and wknd towards fin* **11/1**

010 **6** hd **Arwa (IRE)**[16] 6257 2-9-2 82 .... DanielTudhope 13 82
(Charles Hills) *hld up in tch: effrt over 1f out: edgd rt and styd on same pce ins fnl f* **10/1**

0440 **7** 1 **Lady In Question (IRE)**[13] 6388 2-8-11 77 .... PaulHanagan 1 75
(Richard Fahey) *hld up in tch towards rr: effrt wl over 1f out: styd on ins fnl f: nvr quite enough pce to rch ldrs* **10/1**

2230 **8** 1/2 **La Casa Tarifa (IRE)**[16] 6257 2-8-13 79 .... JoeFanning 7 75
(Mark Johnston) *hld up in tch in rr: rdn and hdwy over 1f out: styd on same pce ins fnl f* **25/1**

421 **9** 2 1/4 **Tonahutu (IRE)**[23] 6044 2-8-4 73 .... JosephineGordon[(3)] 2 63
(Ed Vaughan) *hld up in tch: effrt 2f out: no imp u.p over 1f out: wknd ins fnl f* **12/1**

3640 **10** *1 3/4* **Mama Africa (IRE)**[13] 6388 2-8-3 **69** ow1 .... MartinDwyer 8 65+
(David Barron) *hld up in tch: rdn 2f out: hdwy ent fnl f: 7th and running on whn squeezed for room: clipped heels and stmbld bdly ins fnl f: nt rcvr* **20/1**

1 **11** *nk* **Salamah (IRE)**[16] 6244 2-8-13 **79** .... FrankieDettori 4 64
(Simon Crisford) *hld up in tch: effrt 2f out: unable qck u.p over 1f out: wknd ins fnl f* **7/1**[3]

4233 **12** *hd* **Suffragette City (IRE)**[11] 6439 2-8-5 **71** .... KieranO'Neill 5 55
(Richard Hannon) *hld up wl in tch in midfield: rdn and unable qck over 1f out: sn lost pl: wknd ins fnl f* **16/1**

1m 26.01s (0.61) **Going Correction** +0.075s/f (Good) **12** Ran SP% **122.3**
Speed ratings (Par 98): **99,98,98,97,97 97,95,95,92,90 90,90**
CSF £226.10 CT £766.98 TOTE £18.30: £4.40, £6.10, £1.70; EX 403.90 Trifecta £3346.30.
Owner Merry Fox Stud Limited **Bred** Merry Fox Stud Limited **Trained** Newmarket, Suffolk

FOCUS
A decent race of its type. Most of the principals raced prominently, and the action took place towards the centre of the track.

6788 RACING UK HD H'CAP — 7f
5:20 (5:20) (Class 2) (0-105,105) 3-Y-O+ **£12,938** (£3,850; £1,924; £962) **Stalls** Low

Form RPR

6051 **1** **Salateen**[14] 6338 4-9-5 **100** .... PhillipMakin 7 108
(David O'Meara) *mde all: rdn over 1f out: hrd pressed 1f out: battled on gamely u.p: forged ahd towards fin: all out* **9/1**

-516 **2** *3/4* **Shady McCoy (USA)**[28] 5871 6-8-9 **90** .... FMBerry 1 96+
(Ian Williams) *hld up in tch: effrt nr far rail over 1f out: chsd ldrs 1f out: ev ch ins fnl f: kpt on: wnt 2nd on post* **6/1**[2]

1023 **3** *nse* **Von Blucher (IRE)**[21] 6109 3-9-0 **98** ....(t) FrankieDettori 3 103
(John Gosden) *chsd ldr: effrt over 1f out: rdn and ev ch 1f out: kpt on tl no ex and btn towards fin: lost 2nd on post* **9/4**[1]

-040 **4** *nse* **Yuften**[91] 3681 5-9-5 **100** .... GeorgeBaker 6 106+
(Roger Charlton) *hld up in tch towards rr: effrt 2f out: hdwy u.p over 1f out: styd on u.p ins fnl f: nvr quite getting to ldrs* **12/1**

0536 **5** *3/4* **Charles Molson**[21] 6109 5-8-13 **94** ....(p) PatCosgrave 5 98
(Patrick Chamings) *t.k.h: hld up in tch: effrt over 1f out: kpt on u.p ins fnl f: nvr quite enough pce to rch ldrs* **12/1**

3365 **6** *hd* **Scottish Glen**[21] 6109 10-8-9 **95** .... CharlieBennett(5) 10 98
(Patrick Chamings) *t.k.h: chsd ldrs: rdn 2f out: drvn over 1f out: kpt on ins fnl f: nvr quite enough pce to get on terms* **16/1**

0062 **7** *1 3/4* **Georgian Bay (IRE)**[21] 6126 6-8-7 **88** ....(v) HarryBentley 8 87
(K R Burke) *chsd ldrs: rdn 2f out: drvn and unable qck over 1f out: wknd ins fnl f* **12/1**

0010 **8** *3/4* **Oh This Is Us (IRE)**[26] 5956 3-9-2 **100** .... PatDobbs 11 99+
(Richard Hannon) *hld up in tch in last pair: effrt whn squeezed for room and bdly hmpd wl over 1f out: sn swtchd rt: kpt on ins fnl f but nvr any ch of getting on terms* **14/1**

31-0 **9** *1 1/2* **War Whisper (IRE)**[16] 6263 3-8-4 **88** .... KieranO'Neill 9 80
(Richard Hannon) *t.k.h: hld up in tch in midfield: rdn and unable qck whn edgd lft wl over 1f out: no imp and kpt on same pce after* **14/1**

5010 **10** *1/2* **Cornwallville (IRE)**[14] 6355 4-9-3 **98** ....(v) AdamKirby 2 89
(David Loughnane) *in tch in midfield: effrt u.p over 1f out: no imp 1f out: wknd ins fnl f* **7/1**[3]

5-26 **11** *5* **Rouleau**[226] 539 3-9-7 **105** .... WilliamBuick 12 82
(Charlie Appleby) *hld up in tch in midfield: rdn over 2f out: sn struggling: wknd over 1f out* **16/1**

0610 **12** *33* **Barracuda Boy (IRE)**[42] 5389 6-9-3 **98** .... LukeMorris 4
(Tom Dascombe) *in tch in midfield: lost pl u.p jst over 1f out: bhd over 1f out: eased: t.o* **20/1**

1m 25.24s (-0.16) **Going Correction** +0.075s/f (Good)
WFA 3 from 4yo+ 3lb **12** Ran SP% **120.5**
Speed ratings (Par 109): **103,102,102,102,101 100,98,98,96,95 90,52**
CSF £63.25 CT £168.51 TOTE £10.70: £3.30, £2.30, £1.40; EX 73.10 Trifecta £251.70.
Owner Sheikh Abdullah Almalek Alsabah **Bred** Mrs Janis Macpherson **Trained** Upper Helmsley, N Yorks

FOCUS
A good handicap, if not the strongest for the grade. The winner has been rated close to his old best, and the fifth close to this year's best, while the sixth also helps set the standard.
T/Jkpt: Not won. T/Plt: £440.20 to a £1 stake. Pool: £169,134.90 - 280.42 winning tickets T/Qpdt: £116.50 to a £1 stake. Pool: £10,931.28 - 69.42 winning tickets **Steve Payne**

6009 RIPON (R-H)

Saturday, September 24

OFFICIAL GOING: Good (good to firm in home straight)
Wind: fresh behind Weather: Overcast

6789 HUDSON FOSTER FINANCIAL SERVICES 30TH ANNIVERSARY EBF MAIDEN STKS — 6f
2:05 (2:06) (Class 5) 2-Y-O **£3,881** (£1,155; £577; £288) **Stalls** High

Form RPR

0 **1** **Uncle Charlie (IRE)**[122] 2570 2-9-5 0 .... RoystonFfrench 5 70
(Ann Duffield) *prom: rdn to ld appr fnl f: kpt on* **7/1**[3]

0 **2** *2* **Ideal Bounty (IRE)**[52] 5029 2-9-5 0 .... SilvestreDeSousa 3 64
(Andrew Crook) *hld up: pushed along and hdwy on outer over 2f out: rdn over 1f out: kpt on* **10/1**

66 **3** *nse* **Performing (IRE)**[14] 6319 2-9-5 0 .... ValdirDeSouza 8 64
(John Quinn) *led: rdn over 2f out: hdd appr fnl f: one pce* **7/1**[3]

5060 **4** *nk* **Silk Mill Blue**[28] 5884 2-9-5 62 .... GeorgeChaloner 7 63
(Richard Whitaker) *dwlt: sn chsd ldrs: rdn over 2f out: kpt on* **8/1**

05 **5** *2 3/4* **Royal Celebration**[11] 6447 2-9-0 0 .... PhilDennis(5) 2 55
(Bryan Smart) *prom: rdn over 2f out: wknd ins fnl f* **25/1**

5536 **6** *1 3/4* **Await The Storm (IRE)**[85] 3858 2-9-2 76 ....(b) MarcMonaghan(3) 4 49
(Hugo Palmer) *sn pushed along towards rr: drvn 2f out: no imp* **11/8**[1]

6 **7** *1 1/2* **Spruce Lodge**[10] 6477 2-9-5 0 .... SamJames 1 45
(David Barron) *wnt rt s: nvr bttr than midfield* **4/1**[2]

0 **8** *6* **Haafhder Thought**[10] 6477 2-9-0 0 .... DavidAllan 6 22
(Tim Easterby) *a towards rr* **33/1**

00 **9** *1* **Yelow Bird**[22] 6099 2-9-0 0 .... NathanEvans(5) 9 24
(Chris Grant) *chsd ldrs: rdn over 3f out: sn wknd* **80/1**

1m 11.45s (-1.55) **Going Correction** -0.325s/f (Firm) **9** Ran SP% **115.3**
Speed ratings (Par 95): **97,94,94,93,90 87,85,77,76**
CSF £72.23 TOTE £9.70: £1.90, £2.30, £2.40; EX 76.70 Trifecta £411.60.
Owner Mrs A McCubbin & D Barker **Bred** Knocklong House Stud **Trained** Constable Burton, N Yorks
■ Stewards' Enquiry : Valdir De Souza seven-day ban; used his whip above the permitted level (8th-14th Oct)

FOCUS
Add 6yds to all races on the Round course. An ordinary juvenile maiden. They went a decent gallop on ground officially described as good, good to firm in the home straight. The positive winning time concurred with that description and it proved hard to make up ground from off the pace.

6790 MICHAEL RABY MEMORIAL APPRENTICE H'CAP — 6f
2:40 (2:41) (Class 5) (0-70,69) 3-Y-O+ **£3,881** (£1,155; £577; £288) **Stalls** High

Form RPR

5106 **1** **Miningold**[10] 6476 3-9-6 **68** ....[1] JordanVaughan 6 75
(Tim Easterby) *prom: rdn 2f out: led appr fnl f: strly pressed ins fnl f: edgd rt: hld on wl* **10/1**

603 **2** *nk* **Encantar**[10] 6476 3-8-13 **66** ....(v) ManuelFernandes(5) 1 72
(Ann Duffield) *dwlt and carried sltly rt s: hld up in midfield on outside: rdn and gd hdwy 2f out: chal strly ins fnl f: kpt on* **11/1**

0604 **3** *nk* **My Dad Syd (USA)**[24] 6027 4-9-7 **67** ....(b[1]) PhilDennis 10 72
(Ian Williams) *led: rdn over 2f out: hdd appr fnl f: kpt on* **6/1**[3]

100 **4** *nk* **Spirit Of Zebedee (IRE)**[9] 6506 3-8-9 **62** ....(v) JoshQuinn(5) 4 66
(John Quinn) *dwlt: midfield: rdn over 2f out: hdwy over 1f out: kpt on: sltly short of room nr fin* **8/1**

1600 **5** *1 1/2* **Bond Bombshell**[10] 6475 3-9-2 **69** .... PatrickVaughan(5) 2 68
(David O'Meara) *dwlt: sn in tch: rdn over 2f out: one pce fnl f* **16/1**

4054 **6** *shd* **Never In Doubt**[31] 5759 3-9-7 **69** .... NathanEvans 3 68
(Richard Whitaker) *prom: rdn over 2f out: outpcd over 1f out* **4/1**[2]

0321 **7** *3/4* **Fleeting Dream (IRE)**[15] 6291 3-9-3 **65** ....(b) GeorgiaCox 11 62
(William Haggas) *chsd ldrs: rdn over 2f out: no imp* **9/4**[1]

0006 **8** *hd* **Clon Rocket (IRE)**[9] 6522 3-8-0 **55** .... MeganEllingworth(7) 9 51
(John Holt) *hld up: sme late hdwy: nvr threatened* **28/1**

6200 **9** *hd* **Big Amigo (IRE)**[11] 6453 3-9-3 **65** ....(e) AnnaHesketh 8 60
(Tom Dascombe) *hld up: sme late hdwy: nvr threatened* **12/1**

6552 **10** *hd* **Serradura (IRE)**[12] 6418 3-9-6 **68** ....[1] CallumShepherd 7 63
(Charles Hills) *midfield: rdn over 2f out: wknd ins fnl f* **16/1**

0606 **11** *1 1/2* **Kodimoor (IRE)**[46] 5270 3-8-4 **55** ....[1] RhiainIngram(3) 5 45
(Christopher Kellett) *midfield: rdn 1/2-way: wknd over 1f out* **66/1**

1m 11.15s (-1.85) **Going Correction** -0.325s/f (Firm)
WFA 3 from 4yo 2lb **11** Ran SP% **118.0**
Speed ratings (Par 103): **99,98,98,97,95 95,94,94,94,93 91**
CSF £115.33 CT £734.42 TOTE £8.40: £1.90, £3.00, £2.40; EX 134.80 Trifecta £1093.60 Part won..
Owner Middleham Park Racing XII & Partner **Bred** Mrs G S Rees **Trained** Great Habton, N Yorks

FOCUS
A modest apprentice riders' handicap. The third horse home set a decent gallop up the stands' rail from a favourable high draw but the bulk of the field raced more centrally. It's been rated around the second, third and fourth to this year's form.

6791 LLOYD LAND ROVER RIPON NURSERY H'CAP — 1m
3:15 (3:17) (Class 4) (0-85,85) 2-Y-O **£5,175** (£1,540; £769; £384) **Stalls** Low

Form RPR

6216 **1** **Star Of The East (IRE)**[11] 6455 2-8-13 **77** .... SilvestreDeSousa 5 84
(Mark Johnston) *trckd ldr: rdn to ld over 2f out: edgd rt over 1f out: styd on wl* **11/2**

423 **2** *3* **Honourable**[28] 5885 2-8-7 **71** .... GeorgeChaloner 4 71
(Richard Fahey) *racd keenly in tch: rdn over 1f out: wnt 2nd over 1f out: kpt on but no ch w wnr* **11/4**[2]

1420 **3** *shd* **Proud Archi (IRE)**[26] 5967 2-9-2 **80** .... AndrewMullen 1 80
(Michael Dods) *dwlt sltly: sn in tch: rdn over 2f out: kpt on* **5/1**[3]

0544 **4** *1/2* **Midnight Man (FR)**[21] 6130 2-8-2 **66** ....[1] RyanPowell 6 65
(K R Burke) *hld up: rdn 3f out: kpt on wl fnl f: nrst fin* **8/1**

5650 **5** *2 1/4* **Mister Moosah (IRE)**[21] 6130 2-8-6 **70** ow3 .... AndrewElliott 2 64
(Micky Hammond) *hld up in rr: rdn over 2f out: nvr threatened* **25/1**

4221 **6** *1 1/2* **Maldonado (FR)**[16] 6264 2-9-7 **85** ....[1] RobertWinston 8 75
(Charlie Appleby) *racd keenly: trckd ldr: led over 3f out: rdn whn hdd over 2f out: sltly hmpd on rail over 1f out: wknd* **9/4**[1]

0550 **7** *6* **Hugging The Rails (IRE)**[21] 6130 2-8-0 **64** oh2 .... PaulQuinn 9 40
(Tim Easterby) *led: rdn whn hdd over 3f out: wknd* **14/1**

1m 39.89s (-1.51) **Going Correction** -0.075s/f (Good) **7** Ran SP% **111.1**
Speed ratings (Par 97): **104,101,100,100,98 96,90**
CSF £19.77 CT £76.45 TOTE £6.40: £2.70, £2.30; EX 20.10 Trifecta £74.60.
Owner Sheikh Hamdan bin Mohammed Al Maktoum **Bred** Darley **Trained** Middleham Moor, N Yorks

FOCUS
Add 6yds to race distance. A decent nursery handicap. They went a sound pace and the form appears solid.

6792 RIPON CATHEDRAL CITY OF THE DALES H'CAP — 6f
3:50 (3:55) (Class 2) (0-105,104) 3-Y-O+
£15,562 (£4,660; £2,330; £1,165; £582; £292) **Stalls** High

Form RPR

1005 **1** **Kimberella**[7] 6558 6-9-10 **104** .... SilvestreDeSousa 10 113
(David Nicholls) *trckd ldrs: pushed along to ld ent fnl f: rdn and kpt on wl* **7/2**[1]

611 **2** *1 1/4* **Boy In The Bar**[22] 6072 5-8-1 **86** ....(b) NathanEvans(5) 9 90
(Ian Williams) *pressed ldr: rdn to ld over 1f out: hdd ent fnl f: kpt on* **7/1**[3]

3330 **3** *2 1/4* **Rex Imperator**[28] 5871 7-9-0 **94** ....(p) RonanWhelan 14 91
(David O'Meara) *in tch: rdn over 2f out: wnt 3rd jst ins fnl f: one pce* **8/1**

1660 **4** *nk* **Mayfair Lady**[28] 5880 3-9-2 **103** .... PhilDennis(5) 13 99
(Richard Fahey) *led narrowly: rdn whn hdd over 1f out: stl cl up whn but short of room on rail 1f out: no ex* **10/1**

3220 **5** *3/4* **Flying Pursuit**[7] 6556 3-8-11 **93** ....(b) DavidAllan 1 86+
(Tim Easterby) *midfield on outside: rdn over 2f out: one pce* **5/1**[2]

3031 **6** *2* **Hakam (USA)**[13] 6371 4-8-7 **87** .... AndrewMullen 7 74+
(Michael Appleby) *stmbld s: hld up: pushed along over 2f out: rdn over 2f out: one pce and nvr threatened* **7/1**[3]

3000 **7** *1 1/4* **Out Do**[14] 6327 7-9-7 **101** ....(b) LiamKeniry 11 84
(David O'Meara) *racd keenly in midfield: rdn 2f out: edgd rt over 1f out: wknd ins fnl f* **16/1**

4004 **8** *2 1/2* **Fast Track**[35] 5641 5-8-7 **87** .... DanielMuscutt 6 62
(David Barron) *midfield: rdn over 2f out: wknd over 1f out* **16/1**

6416 **9** *1 1/4* **Snap Shots (IRE)**[42] 5418 4-8-13 **93** ....(tp) BarryMcHugh 4 64
(Tom Dascombe) *dwlt: a towards rr* **9/1**

1003 **10** *1* **Russian Realm**[21] 6140 6-8-12 **92** .... RobertWinston 5 60
(Paul Midgley) *a towards rr* **20/1**

The Form Book, Raceform Ltd, Newbury, RG14 5SJ

-501 **11** 4 1/2 **Ustinov**[22] 6079 4-8-11 **91**...................................... SamJames 3 44
(David O'Meara) *midfield: rdn 1/2-way: lost pl over 2f out: wknd over 1f out* **14/1**

1m 9.43s (-3.57) **Going Correction** -0.325s/f (Firm) course record
WFA 3 from 4yo+ 2lb **11** Ran SP% **117.3**
Speed ratings (Par 109): **110,108,105,104,103 101,99,96,94,93 87**
CSF £27.67 CT £184.74 TOTE £4.30: £2.70, £2.20, £2.60; EX 30.50 Trifecta £212.60.
Owner C Titcomb **Bred** P And Mrs A G Venner **Trained** Sessay, N Yorks
■ Steve Prescott was withdrawn. Price at time of withdrawal 40/1. Rule 4 does not apply.

FOCUS
A good quality sprint handicap. They went a decent gallop up the stands' rail. The winner is better than ever and the race has been rated around the runner-up.

6793 NOEL HETHERTON MEMORIAL H'CAP 5f
4:25 (4:28) (Class 4) (0-85,85) 3-Y-O+ **£6,301** (£1,886; £943; £472; £235) **Stalls** High

Form RPR
0060 **1** **Desert Ace (IRE)**[8] 6537 5-8-12 **76**............................(p) RoystonFfrench 1 86
(Iain Jardine) *racd far side: mde all: rdn 2f out: kpt on wl* **12/1**
2202 **2** 3/4 **Apricot Sky**[14] 6324 6-9-1 **79**.. BarryMcHugh 15 86
(David Nicholls) *led stands' side: rdn 1/2-way: kpt on wl: 1st of 10 in gp* **10/1**
0060 **3** 3/4 **Bondi Beach Boy**[25] 6012 7-8-13 **82**......................... NathanEvans(5) 16 86
(James Turner) *chsd ldrs stands' side: rdn 1/2-way: kpt on: 2nd of 10 in gp* **16/1**
4430 **4** 1 **Rural Celebration**[8] 6537 5-8-12 **76**............................ RonanWhelan 18 77
(David O'Meara) *chsd ldrs stands' side: rdn 2f out: kpt on: 3rd of 10 in gp* **11/1**
1126 **5** nk **Midnight Malibu (IRE)**[9] 6518 3-9-6 **85**.............................. DavidAllan 7 85
(Tim Easterby) *chsd ldr far side: rdn 2f out: kpt on: 2nd of 8 in gp* **9/1**[3]
4013 **6** 1 **Love Island**[9] 6518 7-9-5 **83**.. GeorgeChaloner 2 79
(Richard Whitaker) *chsd ldr far side: rdn 1/2-way: one pce: 3rd of 8 in gp* **10/1**
0040 **7** nk **Silvanus (IRE)**[25] 6012 11-9-6 **84**.................................. RobertWinston 4 79
(Paul Midgley) *in tch far side: rdn 2f out: one pce: 4th of 8 in gp* **11/1**
0006 **8** 1 1/4 **Foxy Forever (IRE)**[21] 6114 6-9-6 **84**...........................(bt) LiamKeniry 13 74
(Michael Wigham) *prom stands' side: rdn 1/2-way: wknd ins fnl f: 4th of 10 in gp* **12/1**
0400 **9** 1/2 **Lexi's Hero (IRE)**[8] 6539 8-8-11 **80**..............................(v) PhilDennis(5) 5 69
(Richard Fahey) *midfield far side: rdn 2f out: one pce and nvr threatened: 5th of 8 in gp* **40/1**
4560 **10** 1/2 **Flicka's Boy**[10] 6475 4-8-4 **71** oh4................................ ShelleyBirkett(3) 9 58
(Tony Coyle) *midfield far side: rdn 1/2-way: no imp: 6th of 8 in gp* **40/1**
0100 **11** hd **Excessable**[25] 6012 3-9-1 **80**...(t) AndrewMullen 14 66
(Tim Easterby) *midfield stands' side: rdn 2f out: no imp: 5th of 10 in gp* **20/1**
1432 **12** nk **Jaywalker (IRE)**[66] 4536 5-8-10 **79**.......................... CallumShepherd(5) 8 64
(Rebecca Bastiman) *dwlt: sn swtchd lft to r stands' side: hld up on outside: rdn 1/2-way: nvr threatened: 6th of 10 in gp* **20/1**
5212 **13** 2 1/4 **Princess Tansy**[14] 6318 4-8-8 **77**................................... GeorgiaCox(5) 6 54
(Gay Kelleway) *dwlt: hld up far side: hung persistently lft fr over 1f out: nvr threatened: 7th of 8 in gp* **12/1**
0234 **14** shd **Rose Marmara**[22] 6096 3-9-0 **79**...................................(t) KeaganLatham 3 56
(Brian Rothwell) *a rr far side: last of 8 in gp* **50/1**
4065 **15** 3/4 **Paddy Power (IRE)**[20] 6164 3-8-9 **81**............................ HayleyIrvine(7) 10 55
(Richard Fahey) *s.i.s: a towards rr stands' side: 7th of 10 in gp* **8/1**[2]
0050 **16** hd **Fredricka**[40] 5479 5-9-2 **80**.. SamJames 17 53
(David Barron) *hld up stands' side: nvr threatened: 8th of 10 in gp* **25/1**
0406 **17** 4 **Seve**[17] 6234 4-9-6 **84**...(t) LiamJones 12 43
(Tom Dascombe) *s.i.s: a towards rr stands' side: 9th of 10 in gp* **9/1**[3]
466 **18** 1/2 **Discreet Hero (IRE)**[58] 4803 3-9-4 **83**...................(t) SilvestreDeSousa 11 40
(Simon Crisford) *dwlt: a towards rr stands' side: eased ins fnl f* **11/2**[1]

57.28s (-2.72) **Going Correction** -0.325s/f (Firm) course record
WFA 3 from 4yo+ 1lb **18** Ran SP% **130.5**
Speed ratings (Par 105): **108,106,105,104,103 101,101,99,98,97 97,97,93,93,92 91,85,84**
CSF £124.59 CT £2027.71 TOTE £16.70: £5.20, £3.10, £5.60, £4.10; EX 221.70 Trifecta £1855.80 Part won..
Owner Excelsior Racing Ltd **Bred** Kildaragh Stud **Trained** Carrutherstown, D'fries & G'way

FOCUS
A decent sprint handicap. They split into two distinct groups up either rail and once again it proved hard to make up ground from off the pace. It's been rated around the runner-up to the better view of this year's C&D form.

6794 THEAKSTON LEGENDARY ALES H'CAP 1m 4f 10y
5:00 (5:02) (Class 4) (0-85,83) 3-Y-O+ **£6,301** (£1,886; £943; £472; £235) **Stalls** Low

Form RPR
2334 **1** **Mukhayyam**[7] 6561 4-9-9 **80**...(p) DavidAllan 2 93
(Tim Easterby) *mde all: clr 4f out: pushed along over 2f out: 10 l clr tl eased fnl 50yds* **3/1**[2]
2342 **2** 6 **Peterhouse (USA)**[20] 6165 4-9-7 **78**..............................(p) LiamKeniry 4 80
(Jason Ward) *hld up in rr: pushed along over 3f out: styd on fr over 1f out: wnt remote 2nd 110yds out* **10/1**
2240 **3** 1 3/4 **Sennockian Star**[7] 6573 6-9-12 **83**........................(v) SilvestreDeSousa 10 83
(Mark Johnston) *chsd ldrs on outer: rdn over 4f out: sn one pce: lost modest 2nd 110yds* **4/1**[3]
0440 **4** 2 1/2 **Blue Hussar (IRE)**[36] 5611 5-9-6 **82**....................(p) CallumShepherd(5) 9 78
(Micky Hammond) *midfield: rdn over 3f out: wknd ins fnl f* **14/1**
-001 **5** 6 **Alquffaal**[89] 3715 3-9-0 **79**...(b[1]) DanielMuscutt 7 65
(Roger Varian) *midfield: pushed along 4f out: rdn over 2f out: wknd over 1f out* **11/5**[1]
3043 **6** 1 **Modernism**[22] 6081 7-9-12 **83**.. GeorgeChaloner 5 67
(Richard Fahey) *hld up: rdn over 5f out: nvr threatened* **11/1**
0505 **7** 4 **Sellingallthetime (IRE)**[20] 6165 5-9-2 **73**...................(p) AndrewMullen 8 51
(Michael Appleby) *prom: rdn over 4f out: wknd over 2f out* **22/1**
0- **8** 7 **Buyer Beware (IRE)**[22] 6910 4-9-11 **82**................................ SamJames 1 49
(Patrick Holmes) *midfield on inner: rdn over 3f out: sn wknd* **50/1**
4225 **9** 1 1/2 **Wotabreeze (IRE)**[7] 6566 3-9-1 **80**.............................. ValdirDeSouza 3 44
(John Quinn) *hld up in midfield: brief hdwy on outer over 3f out: wknd over 2f out and eased* **11/1**

2m 33.74s (-2.96) **Going Correction** -0.075s/f (Good)
WFA 3 from 4yo+ 8lb **9** Ran SP% **115.0**
Speed ratings (Par 105): **106,102,100,99,95 94,91,87,86**
CSF £32.89 CT £121.08 TOTE £3.70: £1.20, £2.30, £1.70; EX 24.40 Trifecta £95.20.
Owner T A Scothern **Bred** Mrs James Wigan **Trained** Great Habton, N Yorks

FOCUS
Add 6yds to race distance. A fairly decent middle-distance handicap. They went a decent gallop and one horse proved far superior. The winner has been rated back to something like his 3yo form, with the runner-up close to this year's form, but the level is a bit fluid.

6795 THANK YOU TO OUR GROUNDSTAFF MAIDEN STKS 1m 4f 10y
5:35 (5:38) (Class 5) 3-Y-O+ **£3,881** (£1,155; £577; £288) **Stalls** Low

Form RPR
5 **1** **Flower Power**[5] 6634 5-9-6 0.. BarryMcHugh 8 79
(Tony Coyle) *mde all: pushed along over 2f out: rdn clr over 1f out: eased towards fin* **9/1**
220 **2** 6 **Sunglider (IRE)**[112] 2909 3-9-3 79.................................. RonanWhelan 4 74
(David O'Meara) *in tch: rdn over 3f out: plugged on to go modest 2nd appr fnl f* **5/2**[2]
30 **3** 3 1/4 **Blue Jean Baby**[53] 4978 3-8-12 0............................ SilvestreDeSousa 5 64
(George Scott) *trckd ldr: rdn over 3f out: wknd appr fnl f* **11/8**[1]
2P0 **4** 1 1/4 **Autumn Surprise (IRE)**[23] 6052 3-8-12 0............................ DavidAllan 6 62
(Tim Easterby) *midfield: rdn 4f out: wknd over 1f out* **9/1**
355 **5** 7 **Waiting For Richie**[23] 6052 3-9-3 72................................ AndrewElliott 2 56
(Tom Tate) *hld up: pushed along over 5f out: a towards rr* **15/2**[3]
56 **6** nk **Wink And Win (IRE)**[17] 6239 3-8-12 0............................ RoystonFfrench 1 50
(Charles Hills) *dwlt: sn in tch: rdn 4f out: sn wknd* **25/1**
7 99 **Charamba** 3-8-12 0.. AndrewMullen 3
(James Given) *hld up: rdn over 5f out: wknd qckly and t.o* **10/1**

2m 36.17s (-0.53) **Going Correction** -0.075s/f (Good)
WFA 3 from 5yo 8lb **7** Ran SP% **115.4**
Speed ratings (Par 103): **98,94,91,91,86 86,20**
CSF £32.41 TOTE £13.10: £5.30, £2.30; EX 40.80 Trifecta £122.20.
Owner Ms Margaret Matheson **Bred** Margaret Matheson **Trained** Norton, N Yorks

FOCUS
Add 6yds to race distance. A fair middle-distance maiden. The winner dominated at his own tempo. The level is a bit fluid.
T/Plt: £987.20 to a £1 stake. Pool of £60062.20 - 44.41 winning tickets. T/Qpdt: £20.80 to a £1 stake. Pool of £4869.88 - 173.04 winning tickets. **Andrew Sheret**

6796 - (Foreign Racing) - See Raceform Interactive

3453 COLOGNE (R-H)
Saturday, September 24

OFFICIAL GOING: Turf: good

6797a PREIS DES MEDIENHAUSES DUMONT RHEINLAND - WINTERKONIGIN-TRIAL (LISTED RACE) (2YO FILLIES) (TURF) 7f 110y
3:05 (12:00) 2-Y-O **£10,294** (£4,779; £2,205; £1,102)

RPR
1 1 **Arazza (GER)** 2-9-2 0.. FilipMinarik 4 98
(J Hirschberger, Germany) *fin 2nd: awrdd r* **109/10**
2 **Tiburtina (IRE)**[16] 6258 2-9-2 0.. AndreasSuborics 6 98
(Sylvester Kirk) *mde all: rdn under 3f out: pressed fr 2f out: r.o wl fnl f but edgd lft clsng stages and hmpd rival: fin 1st: disqualified and plcd 2nd* **39/10**[3]
3 1/2 **Saloon Sold (GER)** 2-9-2 0.. AdriedeVries 3 94
(Markus Klug, Germany) **6/5**[1]
4 2 1/2 **Silver Cloud (GER)**[13] 2-9-2 0.. DanielePorcu 2 89
(S Smrczek, Germany) **139/10**
5 1/2 **Pemina (GER)** 2-9-2 0.. AlexanderPietsch 1 87
(J Hirschberger, Germany) **2/1**[2]
6 hd **Sunny Belle (IRE)** 2-8-11 0.. AndraschStarke 5 82
(P Schiergen, Germany) **54/10**

WIN (incl. 10 euro stake): 119. PLACES: 39, 31. SF: 783
Owner Gestut Auenquelle **Bred** Gestut Auenquelle **Trained** Germany

6798 - 6799a (Foreign Racing) - See Raceform Interactive

6264 EPSOM (L-H)
Sunday, September 25

OFFICIAL GOING: Good (good to soft in places; 6.4)
Wind: quite strong across Weather: sunny periods

6800 BET TOTEPLACEPOT AT TOTESPORT.COM NURSERY H'CAP 7f
2:10 (2:10) (Class 4) (0-85,85) 2-Y-O **£6,469** (£1,925; £962; £481) **Stalls** Low

Form RPR
3011 **1** **Mutahaady (IRE)**[6] 6614 2-8-11 **80** 6ex............................ CliffordLee(5) 7 84
(K R Burke) *pressed ldr: rdn over 2f out: led fnl 120yds: kpt on wl: rdn out* **3/1**[1]
0054 **2** 1/2 **Juanito Chico (IRE)**[66] 4553 2-8-6 **70**...................... SilvestreDeSousa 3 73
(William Jarvis) *racd keenly: trckd ldrs: rdn over 2f out: chal ins fnl f: kpt on* **9/2**[3]
4251 **3** hd **Law Power**[8] 6563 2-8-10 **74**..(b) LukeMorris 4 76
(Sir Mark Prescott Bt) *led: rdn 2f out: hdd fnl 120yds: kpt on but no ex cl home* **9/2**[3]
5261 **4** 3 1/4 **Kodiac Khan (IRE)**[26] 5989 2-8-13 **80**...................... MarcMonaghan(3) 1 74
(Hugo Palmer) *in tch: swtchd rt and rdn over 2f out: kpt on but nt pce to get on terms* **4/1**[2]
2100 **5** 5 **Mister Sunshine (IRE)**[71] 4394 2-9-2 **80**................................. JohnFahy 9 60
(Clive Cox) *s.i.s: towards rr: hdwy on outer over 5f out: effrt 3f out: nt pce to threaten: fdd ins fnl f* **25/1**
0122 **6** 3/4 **Assassinate (IRE)**[133] 2280 2-8-2 **73**............................ DavidEgan(7) 8 51
(Paul Cole) *cl up: hdwy over 3f out: rdn to chse ldrs over 2f out: wknd fnl f* **16/1**
4015 **7** 1 1/2 **Monoshka (IRE)**[36] 5644 2-8-13 **77**.................................. TomMarquand 2 51
(Richard Hannon) *trckd ldrs: rdn over 2f out: wknd over 1f out* **10/1**
31 **8** 10 **Sixties Habana**[108] 3075 2-8-6 **70**... JFEgan 6 17
(Pat Phelan) *last pair: rdn 3f out: wknd wl over 1f out* **25/1**
0451 **9** 1 1/2 **Trading Punches (IRE)**[12] 6439 2-9-7 **85**......................... JimCrowley 5 28
(David Brown) *last pair: rdn 3f out: wknd wl over 1f out* **8/1**

1m 24.34s (1.04) **Going Correction** +0.025s/f (Good) **9** Ran SP% **115.1**
Speed ratings (Par 97): **95,94,94,90,84 83,82,70,69**
CSF £16.49 CT £58.04 TOTE £3.90: £1.50, £1.90, £1.70; EX 21.20 Trifecta £78.90.
Owner Tim Dykes, Mrs G Buchanan & E Burke **Bred** Kevin Blake **Trained** Middleham Moor, N Yorks

FOCUS
There was 3mm of rain early in the morning and the going was given as good, good to soft in places (GoingStick: 6.4). The rail was at its innermost position (Derby configuration) and all race distances were as advertised. Not many got into this, the pace holding up pretty well. Another step forward from the winner.

6801 BET TOTEEXACTA AT TOTESPORT.COM CONDITIONS STKS (PLUS 10 RACE) 1m 114y
2:40 (2:40) (Class 3) 2-Y-O **£6,847** (£2,050; £1,025; £512; £256) **Stalls** Low

Form RPR
1402 **1** **Medieval (IRE)**[42] 5450 2-9-1 104..........(b) JimCrowley 5 101
(Paul Cole) *mde all: rdn over 2f out: kpt on strly to assert fnl f: rdn out* **11/4**[2]
1 **2** 1 3/4 **Defoe (IRE)**[14] 6376 2-8-12 0.......... AndreaAtzeni 2 94+
(Roger Varian) *little slowly away: racd in 4th: rdn over 2f out: little imp tl r.o wl ent fnl f: wnt 2nd cl home* **9/1**
201 **3** 3/4 **Max Zorin (IRE)**[16] 6274 2-9-1 83.......... JamesDoyle 4 95
(Andrew Balding) *trckd wnr: rdn over 2f out: sn hung lft: kpt chsng wnr tl no ex fnl 120yds* **7/2**[3]
100 **4** 3 1/4 **Jackhammer (IRE)**[37] 5595 2-9-1 97.......... SilvestreDeSousa 3 88+
(William Knight) *hld up 5th: rdn over 2f out: nt pce to get on terms but kpt on to go 4th cl home* **9/2**
12 **5** 1/2 **Star Of Rory (IRE)**[22] 6116 2-9-1 0.......... RichardKingscote 1 87
(Tom Dascombe) *trckd ldng pair: rdn over 2f out: nt pce to get on terms: no ex and lost 2 pls ins fnl f* **9/4**[1]

1m 47.61s (1.51) **Going Correction** +0.025s/f (Good) **5** Ran SP% **107.8**
Speed ratings (Par 99): **94,92,91,88,88**
CSF £23.35 TOTE £3.40: £1.70, £3.20; EX 19.50 Trifecta £37.80.
Owner Mrs Fitri Hay **Bred** Patrick Cassidy **Trained** Whatcombe, Oxon

FOCUS
An interesting conditions race on paper, but the winner dominated from the front. The winner has been rated to his latest French Pattern form.

6802 BET TOTEQUADPOT AT TOTESPORT.COM H'CAP 1m 2f 18y
3:15 (3:15) (Class 3) (0-95,94) 3-Y-O+ **£11,205** (£3,355; £1,677; £838; £419; £210) **Stalls** Low

Form RPR
-402 **1** **Great Hall**[11] 6489 6-9-6 **90**.......... JimCrowley 2 99
(Mick Quinn) *trckd ldrs: led gng best 3f out: qcknd clr ent fnl f: readily* **8/1**
2243 **2** 2 **Rotherwick (IRE)**[16] 6286 4-9-1 **85**..........(t) LukeMorris 9 90
(Paul Cole) *hld up last pair: hdwy over 3f out: sn rdn: chsd wnr 2f out: kpt on but a being comf hld* **13/2**
4062 **3** 1/2 **Arrowzone**[8] 6559 5-9-3 **87**..........(b) SilvestreDeSousa 4 91
(Ivan Furtado) *in tch: rdn wl over 2f out: wnt 3rd wl over 1f out: kpt on same pce fnl f* **5/1**
-144 **4** 3 3/4 **Power Game**[23] 6089 4-9-9 **93**.......... JamesDoyle 10 90
(Saeed bin Suroor) *trckd ldrs: rdn over 2f out: sn one pce* **4/1**[2]
-530 **5** hd **Mica Mika (IRE)**[32] 5790 8-8-11 **86**.......... AdamMcNamara(5) 11 82
(Richard Fahey) *hld up: rdn over 2f out: no imp tl kpt on fnl f* **12/1**
00-5 **6** nk **Banditry (IRE)**[16] 6301 4-8-13 **83**.......... FrederikTylicki 5 79
(Ian Williams) *stdd s: last: rdn and sme prog 2f out: nvr threatened to get on terms* **9/2**[3]
042 **7** 3/4 **Navajo War Dance**[48] 5226 3-8-7 **88** ow2.......... CliffordLee(5) 1 82
(K R Burke) *led: rdn and hdd 3f out: wknd fnl f* **3/1**[1]
0055 **8** 2 1/4 **Hit The Jackpot (IRE)**[23] 6081 7-9-2 **93**.......... PatrickVaughan(7) 3 83
(David O'Meara) *pressed ldr tl rdn 3f out: wknd 2f out* **16/1**

2m 7.8s (-1.90) **Going Correction** +0.025s/f (Good)
WFA 3 from 4yo+ 6lb **8** Ran SP% **117.9**
Speed ratings (Par 107): **108,106,106,103,102 102,102,100**
CSF £60.41 CT £290.42 TOTE £10.60: £3.00, £2.00, £2.00; EX 64.00 Trifecta £285.90.
Owner YNWA Partnership **Bred** Aston House Stud **Trained** Newmarket, Suffolk

FOCUS
This was run at a sound gallop and the winner did it comfortably.

6803 BET TOTETRIFECTA AT TOTESPORT.COM H'CAP 1m 114y
3:45 (3:48) (Class 3) (0-90,90) 3-Y-O **£8,715** (£2,609; £1,304; £652; £326; £163) **Stalls** Low

Form RPR
-453 **1** **Dubai Fashion (IRE)**[64] 4654 3-9-3 **86**.......... PaulHanagan 8 103
(Saeed bin Suroor) *hld up towards rr: stdy prog fr 3f out: led jst ins fnl f: kpt on wl: rdn out* **8/1**
120 **2** 2 **Blair House (IRE)**[79] 4104 3-9-7 **90**.......... JamesDoyle 1 102
(Charlie Appleby) *trckd ldrs: led 2f out: sn rdn and edgd lft: hdd jst ins fnl f: kpt on but no ex* **9/2**[2]
0114 **3** 2 3/4 **Lorelina**[27] 5965 3-8-4 **76** oh3.......... EdwardGreatrex(3) 7 82
(Andrew Balding) *mid-div: rdn and hdwy over 2f out: styd on into 3rd ent fnl f but nt pce of front pair* **5/1**[3]
45 **4** 3 **High Draw (FR)**[22] 6132 3-8-8 **82**.......... CliffordLee(5) 3 81
(K R Burke) *mid-div: hdwy over 3f out: rdn and ev ch jst over 2f out: styd on same pce* **8/1**
6164 **5** 1 1/4 **Easter Mate (IRE)**[6] 6628 3-9-1 **84**..........(b[1]) FMBerry 9 80
(Ralph Beckett) *trckd ldrs: rdn and ev ch jst over 2f out: hld over 1f out: fdd fnl f* **10/1**
5000 **6** 4 **King's Pavilion (IRE)**[15] 6331 3-9-7 **90**.......... SilvestreDeSousa 10 77
(Mark Johnston) *stdd s: last: sme minor late prog: nvr a factor* **8/1**
010 **7** 1 3/4 **Star Blaze**[106] 3156 3-8-13 **82**.......... FrederikTylicki 2 65
(Mick Channon) *chsd ldrs: rdn 3f out: sn one pce* **7/1**
1062 **8** nk **Prosecute (FR)**[24] 6055 3-8-8 **77**.......... JimCrowley 5 59
(David Simcock) *hld up towards rr: rdn over 2f out: nvr any imp* **7/2**[1]
5010 **9** 2 1/4 **Medburn Dream**[16] 6298 3-9-3 **86**.......... MartinDwyer 4 63
(Paul Henderson) *led: rdn and hdd 2f out: wknd over 1f out* **12/1**
0406 **10** 19 **Cape Speed (FR)**[14] 6372 3-9-1 **84**..........(b[1]) RichardKingscote 6 17
(Mark Johnston) *mid-div: rdn 3f out: sn wknd: eased fnl f* **33/1**

1m 44.83s (-1.27) **Going Correction** +0.025s/f (Good) **10** Ran SP% **122.6**
Speed ratings (Par 105): **106,104,101,99,98 94,92,92,90,73**
CSF £46.32 CT £209.75 TOTE £8.70: £2.60, £1.70, £2.20; EX 37.90 Trifecta £179.50.
Owner Godolphin **Bred** Hadi Al Tajir **Trained** Newmarket, Suffolk

FOCUS
The gallop picked up some way out. The first two look nicely ahead of their marks.

6804 TOTESPORT.COM APPRENTICES' DERBY H'CAP 1m 4f 10y
4:20 (4:21) (Class 4) (0-85,83) 3-Y-O+ **£7,470** (£2,236; £1,118; £559; £279; £140) **Stalls** Centre

Form RPR
211 **1** **Guns Of Leros (USA)**[29] 5875 3-9-2 **82**.......... HectorCrouch(3) 8 94
(Gary Moore) *mde all: rdn clr over 2f out: styd on strly: rdn out* **5/1**[3]
1526 **2** 3 1/4 **Thames Knight**[38] 5574 4-9-3 **79**.......... TylerSaunders(7) 11 85
(Marcus Tregoning) *trckd ldrs: rdn over 2f out: sn chsng wnr: nt pce to chal but kpt on wl for 2nd fnl f* **14/1**
4522 **3** nk **Jupiter Custos (FR)**[17] 6267 4-9-0 **72**.......... GeorgiaCox(3) 5 77
(Michael Scudamore) *trckd ldrs: rdn to dispute 2nd fr over 2f out: kpt on same pce fnl f* **10/1**
1 **4** nse **Byron Flyer**[71] 259 5-9-8 **77**.......... GeorgeDowning 6 82+
(Ian Williams) *mid-div: hdwy 3f out: sn rdn: chal for hld 2nd over 1f out: kpt on same pce fnl f* **8/1**
3211 **5** 1 1/2 **Fandango (GER)**[26] 5993 3-8-12 **78**.......... DavidParkes(3) 9 81+
(Jeremy Gask) *hld up towards rr: hdwy 2f out: sn drifted lft u.p: styd on fnl f* **8/1**
1311 **6** 3/4 **Senza Una Donna**[38] 5574 3-9-0 **80**..........(t) CharlieBennett(3) 2 82+
(Hughie Morrison) *hld up towards rr: rdn wl over 2f out: little imp tl styd on fnl f: n.d* **9/2**[2]
533 **7** 7 **Medburn Cutler**[12] 6445 6-9-7 **76**..........(p) TomMarquand 1 66
(Paul Henderson) *trckd ldrs: rdn over 2f out: wknd jst over 1f out* **20/1**
0312 **8** 8 **Pointel (FR)**[34] 5724 3-9-3 **83**.......... GeorgeWood(3) 10 61
(James Fanshawe) *mid-div: pushed along over 4f out: rdn over 3f out: nvr threatened* **4/1**[1]
5300 **9** 3 1/4 **English Summer**[19] 6209 9-9-11 **83**..........(t) AdamMcNamara(3) 4 55
(Richard Fahey) *mid-div: rdn 3f out: wknd 2f out* **10/1**
1 **10** 1 1/2 **Testimonio**[34] 5709 3-8-11 **81**.......... GabrieleMalune(7) 3 51
(Luca Cumani) *a towards rr* **10/1**
3102 **11** 3/4 **Glens Wobbly**[12] 6445 8-9-6 **75**.......... EdwardGreatrex 13 44
(Jonathan Geake) *mid-div: hdwy to trck ldr over 7f out: chal over 3f out: sn rdn: wknd over 2f out* **20/1**

2m 40.82s (1.92) **Going Correction** +0.025s/f (Good)
WFA 3 from 4yo+ 8lb **11** Ran SP% **120.5**
Speed ratings (Par 105): **94,91,91,91,90 90,85,80,77,76 76**
CSF £74.90 CT £674.77 TOTE £5.80: £2.20, £5.00, £3.20; EX 94.10 Trifecta £1023.60.
Owner Paul Hunt **Bred** Woodcote Stud Ltd **Trained** Lower Beeding, W Sussex

FOCUS
This looked open, but the winner is improving all the time and stays well, and he wasn't for catching in the straight.

6805 TOTEPOOL BETTING AT TOTESPORT.COM MAIDEN STKS 1m 2f 18y
4:55 (4:56) (Class 5) 3-Y-O **£3,881** (£1,155; £577; £288) **Stalls** Low

Form RPR
4- **1** **Squiggley**[388] 6026 3-9-0 0.......... DaneO'Neill 2 74+
(Henry Candy) *s.i.s: sn mid-div: hdwy 3f out: rdn over 2f out: styd on strly ent fnl f: edgd lft: led fnl 120yds: rdn out* **8/1**[3]
320 **2** 3/4 **Henry The Explorer (CAN)**[10] 6505 3-9-2 70..... JosephineGordon(3) 3 76
(Jo Hughes) *trckd ldrs: rdn wl over 2f out: swtchd rt jst ins fnl f: kpt on wl w wnr but a being hld* **8/1**[3]
4 **3** 1 3/4 **Aldrin (FR)**[66] 4546 3-9-5 0..........(t) JamesDoyle 4 73+
(Charlie Appleby) *in tch: hdwy to press ldr 7f out: led 3f out: sn rdn: hdd fnl 120yds: no ex* **2/1**[1]
2242 **4** 2 1/4 **Cape Banjo (USA)**[16] 6301 3-9-5 80.......... FMBerry 6 69
(Ralph Beckett) *trckd ldrs: rdn to chal wl over 2f out: hung lft: looking hld in cl 4th whn bdly hmpd and snatched up jst ins fnl f* **2/1**[1]
60 **5** 3 1/2 **Rattle On**[16] 6294 3-9-5 0.......... SamHitchcott 10 61
(Jim Boyle) *stdd s: bhd: styd on steadily fnl 2f: n.d* **100/1**
0 **6** 19 **Theocratic**[12] 6452 3-9-5 0..........(vt) StevieDonohoe 9 23
(Charlie Fellowes) *s.i.s: sn pushed along in rr: a bhd* **50/1**
50 **7** 2 1/2 **Threediamondrings**[16] 6294 3-9-5 0.......... RyanClark 8 18
(Brendan Powell) *trckd ldrs: rdn 3f out: sn wknd* **66/1**
0 **8** 2 **Dark Enemy (IRE)**[42] 5438 3-9-5 0.......... MartinDwyer 1 14
(Brendan Powell) *mid-div: rdn over 3f out: sn wknd* **66/1**
5523 **9** 11 **Dame Judi (IRE)**[13] 6415 3-9-0 75..........(p) SilvestreDeSousa 5
(Simon Crisford) *led tl 3f out: sn wknd: eased* **3/1**[2]
0 **10** 43 **Blanco (USA)**[263] 65 3-9-5 0.......... SteveDrowne 7
(George Baker) *a in rr* **50/1**

2m 11.43s (1.73) **Going Correction** +0.025s/f (Good) **10** Ran SP% **121.8**
Speed ratings (Par 101): **94,93,92,90,87 72,70,68,59,25**
CSF £70.84 TOTE £10.90: £2.50, £1.80, £1.50; EX 85.60 Trifecta £233.60.
Owner Mrs G Rowland-Clark **Bred** Mrs Gillie Rowland-Clark **Trained** Kingston Warren, Oxon

FOCUS
Just a fair maiden. The pace picked up at halfway and it paid to be ridden with a bit of patience.

6806 COLLECT TOTEPOOL WINNINGS AT BETFRED SHOPS H'CAP 7f
5:25 (5:26) (Class 4) (0-85,85) 3-Y-O+ **£6,469** (£1,925; £962; £481) **Stalls** Low

Form RPR
3500 **1** **Jack's Revenge (IRE)**[22] 6109 8-9-6 **84**..........(vt) SteveDrowne 11 93
(George Baker) *hld up towards rr: hdwy but nt clrest of runs over 1f out: str run ent fnl f: led fnl 100yds: r.o wl* **20/1**
4345 **2** 1 1/2 **Short Work**[12] 6442 3-8-12 **79**..........(b[1]) FMBerry 14 83
(Ralph Beckett) *hld up towards rr: rdn and hdwy fr 2f out: r.o wl fnl f: snatched 2nd cl home* **16/1**
1100 **3** hd **Black Bess**[41] 5488 3-9-4 **85**.......... JamesDoyle 2 88
(Jim Boyle) *pressed ldr: rdn wl over 2f out: led narrowly over 1f out: hdd fnl 100yds: kpt on but no ex* **9/2**[1]
2065 **4** nk **Morache Music**[26] 5991 8-9-3 **81**.......... DanielMuscutt 3 85
(Patrick Chamings) *trckd ldrs: rdn over 2f out: nt quite pce to mount chal: kpt on ins fnl f* **8/1**[3]
00 **5** hd **Zaeem**[16] 6276 7-9-2 **80**..........(p) SilvestreDeSousa 1 83
(Ivan Furtado) *led: rdn and strly pressed wl over 2f out: narrowly hdd over 1f out: ev ch fnl f: no ex fnl 100yds* **7/1**[2]
3444 **6** nse **Fast Dancer (IRE)**[29] 5892 4-9-4 **82**.......... TedDurcan 12 85
(Joseph Tuite) *towards rr: rdn and hdwy fr 2f out: kpt on fnl f* **8/1**[3]
0106 **7** 3/4 **Alyaa (IRE)**[16] 6299 3-8-8 **75**.......... MartinDwyer 8 75
(Conrad Allen) *trckd ldrs: rdn to chse ldng pair over 2f out: no ex ins fnl f* **10/1**
0450 **8** 1/2 **Cordite (IRE)**[44] 5357 5-8-10 **74**.......... SamHitchcott 5 74
(Jim Boyle) *in tch: rdn 3f out: kpt on same pce fnl 2f* **16/1**

5540 **9** 1 ½ **King Of Naples**[22] 6123 3-8-9 **81**.................................. GeorgeWood(5) 6 76
(James Fanshawe) *s.i.s: towards rr of midfield: rdn and sme prog over 2f out: nt pce to get on terms: fdd ins fnl f* **9/1**
2306 **10** 3 **Baltic Brave (IRE)**[28] 5934 5-8-12 **81**...................(vt¹) CharlieBennett(5) 7 68
(Hughie Morrison) *mid-div: rdn over 2f out: nvr threatened: wknd fnl f* **10/1**
0036 **11** 1 ½ **Majestic Myles (IRE)**[18] 6235 8-8-8 **75**............. JosephineGordon(3) 13 58
(Lee Carter) *mid-div on outer: c wd into st: sn rdn: nvr any imp* **33/1**
551 **12** 1 **First Experience**[16] 6299 5-8-12 **76**.................................(v) JimCrowley 9 57
(Lee Carter) *mid-div: rdn whn nt clr run over 2f out: no threat after* **8/1**³
-045 **13** shd **Guiding Light (IRE)**[15] 6339 4-8-11 **82**....................... JoshuaBryan(7) 4 62
(Andrew Balding) *trckd ldrs: rdn 3f out: wknd over 1f out* **12/1**
1220 **14** 3 **Black Caesar (IRE)**[112] 2934 5-8-7 **71** oh1................ WilliamCarson 10 43
(Philip Hide) *mid-div: rdn over 2f out: wknd over 1f out* **14/1**

1m 23.32s (0.02) **Going Correction** +0.025s/f (Good)
WFA 3 from 4yo+ 3lb **14** Ran SP% **126.0**
Speed ratings (Par 105): **100,98,98,97,97 97,96,96,94,90 89,88,87,84**
CSF £322.83 CT £1758.59 TOTE £22.40: £7.00, £3.90, £2.80; EX 344.50 Trifecta £3291.10.
Owner PJL Racing **Bred** Con Marnane **Trained** Manton, Wilts

FOCUS
The leaders were sent for home a long way out and the pace collapsed late on.
T/Jkpt: Not won. T/Plt: £274.10 to a £1 stake. Pool: £120927.21, 322.0 winning units T/Qpdt: £68.20 to a £1 stake. Pool: £9507.72, 103.1 winning units **Tim Mitchell**

6341 MUSSELBURGH (R-H)
Sunday, September 25

OFFICIAL GOING: Good (good to soft in places; 7.0)
Wind: Breezy, half against Weather: Cloudy, dry

6807 ROYAL SCOTS CLUB NURSERY H'CAP 5f
2:00 (2:02) (Class 6) (0-65,65) 2-Y-O **£2,587** (£770; £384; £192) **Stalls** High

Form RPR
0354 **1** **Hot Hannah**[8] 6564 2-9-6 **64**.. ConnorBeasley 8 70
(Michael Dods) *mde all: pushed along 2f out: edgd rt and kpt on wl fnl f* **5/2**¹
0665 **2** nk **My Cherry Blossom**[15] 6343 2-8-10 **57**.............. RachelRichardson(3) 9 62
(Tim Easterby) *blindfold slow to remove and dwlt: hld up: stdy hdwy 1/2-way: effrt and chsd wnr fnl f: edgd rt and kpt on: hld nr fin* **4/1**²
5550 **3** 3 ¾ **Emerald Secret (IRE)**[21] 6162 2-9-2 **60**.................... GrahamGibbons 5 52
(Paul Midgley) *chsd ldrs: drvn and outpcd 1/2-way: rallied to take 3rd pl towards fin: nt rch first two* **7/1**³
504 **4** ¾ **Khelly's Edge**[62] 4713 2-8-11 **55**....................................¹ JamesSullivan 3 44
(Scott Dixon) *chsd wnr: rdn 2f out: lost 2nd 1f out: sn drvn and outpcd* **20/1**
6650 **5** 1 **Zebedee Cat (IRE)**[63] 4679 2-9-5 **63**......................(v¹) DougieCostello 11 49
(Iain Jardine) *s.i.s: hld up against stands' rail: pushed along whn n.m.r over 2f out to wl over 1f out: kpt on ins fnl f: no imp* **16/1**
045 **6** nk **Not Now Nadia (IRE)**[34] 5727 2-9-2 **60**...................... PaulMulrennan 1 44+
(Michael Dods) *dwlt and bmpd s: hld up: effrt and rdn 2f out: no imp fnl f* **7/1**³
4030 **7** 1 ¼ **Monte Cinq (IRE)**[26] 6010 2-9-7 **65**..................................¹ GrahamLee 6 45
(Jason Ward) *wnt lft and bmpd rival s: bhd and sn pushed along: n.m.r and struggling over 3f out: rallied over 1f out: sn no imp* **9/1**
5400 **8** nk **Vocalisation (IRE)**[4] 6678 2-8-5 **54** ow1................ CallumShepherd(5) 4 33
(John Weymes) *hld up: effrt on outside over 2f out: hung rt over 1f out: sn btn* **20/1**
050 **9** 2 ¾ **Nyx**[42] 5433 2-8-1 **45**... RoystonFfrench 2 14
(Richard Guest) *wnt rt and bmpd rival s: in tch: hung rt thrght: rdn and drifted bdly rt over 1f out: sn btn* **20/1**
015 **10** 4 ½ **Queen Celeste (IRE)**[91] 3686 2-9-7 **65**.................. JoeFanning 10 17
(Mark Johnston) *trckd ldrs: pushed along over 2f out: wknd over 1f out* **9/1**
0060 **11** ½ **Lights**[13] 6420 2-8-5 **49**.. AndrewMullen 7
(Declan Carroll) *dwlt and bmpd s: a outpcd and bhd* **66/1**

1m 2.33s (1.93) **Going Correction** +0.225s/f (Good) **11** Ran SP% **115.2**
Speed ratings (Par 93): **93,92,86,85,83 83,81,80,76,69 68**
CSF £11.01 CT £60.90 TOTE £3.40: £1.40, £1.90, £2.90; EX 14.40 Trifecta £77.90.
Owner J A Knox and Mrs M A Knox **Bred** J A And M A Knox **Trained** Denton, Co Durham

FOCUS
The bottom bend was out 2yds, adding 7yds to races on the round course. The ground was just on the easy side. A moderate nursery to start. The runner-up has been rated back to her debut form.

6808 BREEDERS SUPPORTING RACING EBF MAIDEN STKS (PLUS 10 RACE) (SIRE-RESTRICTED RACE) 7f 30y
2:30 (2:30) (Class 4) 2-Y-O **£6,469** (£1,925; £962; £481) **Stalls** Low

Form RPR
1 **Scots Piper** 2-9-5 0.. JoeFanning 4 69+
(Mark Johnston) *mde all: shkn up 2f out: kpt on wl fnl f: comf* **5/6**¹
5300 **2** 2 ¼ **Black Redstart**[24] 6044 2-9-0 53.................................. GrahamGibbons 2 54
(Alan Bailey) *t.k.h: chsd wnr thrght: rdn over 2f out: edgd rt and one pce ins fnl f* **16/1**
3 ¾ **Nellie's Dancer** 2-9-0 0... PJMcDonald 5 52+
(Scott Dixon) *trckd ldrs: effrt and rdn over 2f out: kpt on same pce fnl f* **8/1**³
0 **4** 6 **Break The Silence**[93] 3598 2-9-5 0.............................. JamesSullivan 1 41
(Scott Dixon) *prom: reminder after 2f: rdn along over 3f out: rallied: wknd over 1f out* **16/1**
5 1 **Think So (IRE)** 2-9-5 0... PaulMulrennan 3 38+
(Mark Johnston) *s.i.s: t.k.h and rn green in tch: shortlived effrt on outside over 2f out: sn wknd* **2/1**²

1m 33.65s (4.65) **Going Correction** +0.225s/f (Good) **5** Ran SP% **110.8**
Speed ratings (Par 97): **82,79,78,71,70**
CSF £14.94 TOTE £2.10: £1.40, £3.70; EX 9.90 Trifecta £37.10.
Owner Sheikh Hamdan bin Mohammed Al Maktoum **Bred** Darley **Trained** Middleham Moor, N Yorks

FOCUS
This was run over 7yds further than advertised. The runners barely changed positions and the form of this maiden - for horses sired by a winner in excess of 9.5f - isn't worth much, but it went to a newcomer with a nice pedigree.

6809 RSP CONSULTING ENGINEERS H'CAP 5f
3:05 (3:06) (Class 5) (0-75,74) 3-Y-O+ **£3,234** (£962; £481; £240) **Stalls** Low

Form RPR
5343 **1** **One Boy (IRE)**[10] 6506 5-9-1 **68**..................................... PaulMulrennan 3 75
(Paul Midgley) *trckd ldrs: rdn to ld over 1f out: hrd pressed ins fnl f: hld on gamely towards fin* **9/2**²
3035 **2** shd **Vimy Ridge**[9] 6537 4-9-6 **73**......................................(p) GrahamGibbons 8 79
(Alan Bailey) *dwlt: bhd: gd hdwy and swtchd rt over 1f out: rdn and disp ld ins fnl f: kpt on: jst hld* **7/2**¹
2532 **3** shd **Royal Brave (IRE)**[11] 6476 5-9-4 **71**............................. DanielTudhope 4 78+
(Rebecca Bastiman) *hld up in tch: hdwy whn nt clr run fr wl over 1f out to ins fnl f: rdn and kpt on strly last 100yds: unlucky* **7/2**¹
0045 **4** 1 **Rock Canyon (IRE)**[1] 6774 7-8-9 **62**......................... GeorgeChaloner 6 64
(Linda Perratt) *s.i.s: sn pushed along in rr: hdwy over 1f out: kpt on ins fnl f* **25/1**
0006 **5** 3 ½ **Savannah Beau**[4] 6680 4-9-3 **70**.....................................(p) SamJames 1 59
(Marjorie Fife) *trckd ldrs: rdn whn n.m.r and swtchd rt appr fnl f: wknd last 150yds* **5/1**³
0005 **6** 3 ½ **Ayresome Angel**[22] 6133 3-9-6 **74**............................(p) ConnorBeasley 2 51
(Bryan Smart) *led at decent gallop: rdn and hdd over 1f out: wknd ins fnl f* **10/1**
3-66 **7** 1 ½ **Harmonic Wave (IRE)**[101] 3326 3-9-4 **72**....................... PJMcDonald 5 43
(Rebecca Menzies) *hld up in tch: rdn over 2f out: n.m.r briefly over 1f out: sn btn* **11/1**
4000 **8** 3 ½ **Captain Dunne (IRE)**[4] 6680 11-8-10 **66**............ RachelRichardson(3) 9 25
(Tim Easterby) *pressed ldr: drvn along wl over 1f out: no ex and lost pl whn hmpd and stmbld ins fnl f* **8/1**
0000 **9** 1 ¾ **Thorntoun Lady (USA)**[18] 6234 6-9-1 **68**.................... JamesSullivan 7 21
(Jim Goldie) *dwlt: bhd and outpcd: nvr on terms* **20/1**

1m 1.18s (0.78) **Going Correction** +0.225s/f (Good)
WFA 3 from 4yo+ 1lb **9** Ran SP% **116.4**
Speed ratings (Par 103): **102,101,101,100,94 88,86,80,78**
CSF £20.84 CT £61.68 TOTE £5.10: £1.80, £1.50, £1.20; EX 23.30 Trifecta £23.10.
Owner R Wardlaw **Bred** Tom Radley **Trained** Westow, N Yorks

FOCUS
A modest sprint in which the third looked the best horse in the race.

6810 ROYAL REGIMENT OF SCOTLAND H'CAP 7f 30y
3:35 (3:37) (Class 4) (0-85,85) 3-Y-O **£5,175** (£1,540; £769; £384) **Stalls** Low

Form RPR
1216 **1** **Roll On Rory**[18] 6232 3-9-7 **85**.......................................(b¹) GrahamLee 2 93
(Jason Ward) *taken early to post: mde all at decent gallop and sn clr w one other: rdn over 2f out: hld on gamely fnl f* **4/1**¹
3526 **2** 1 **Like No Other**[25] 6027 3-8-8 **72**.. PJMcDonald 5 77
(Les Eyre) *chsd clr ldng pair: effrt and chsd wnr over 1f out: kpt on ins fnl f: hld towards fin* **8/1**
1030 **3** 3 ¼ **Hawatif (IRE)**[16] 6276 3-9-6 **84**... JoeFanning 3 80
(Mark Johnston) *hld up in midfield: hdwy and pushed along over 2f out: edgd rt and no imp fnl f* **8/1**
-315 **4** 1 ½ **Prying Pandora (FR)**[73] 4318 3-9-4 **82**......................... TonyHamilton 4 74
(Richard Fahey) *hld up: rdn over 2f out: hdwy over 1f out: kpt on: nvr able to chal* **5/1**³
501U **5** 2 ¾ **Safe Voyage (IRE)**[10] 6502 3-8-11 **75**................................. JasonHart 7 60
(John Quinn) *s.i.s: hld up: effrt and hdwy whn nt clr run briefly over 2f out: hung rt over 1f out: no imp* **4/1**¹
6130 **6** 3 ¼ **Case Key**[11] 6492 3-8-12 **76**.. AndrewMullen 8 52
(Michael Appleby) *s.i.s: hld up: rdn along and edgd rt over 2f out: no imp fr over 1f out* **16/1**
0-00 **7** 6 **Silhuette (IRE)**[21] 6164 3-9-2 **80**.................................... PaulMulrennan 1 40
(Colin Teague) *prom: rdn and edgd rt over 2f out: sn wknd* **80/1**
4513 **8** ½ **War Department (IRE)**[27] 5968 3-9-2 **80**..............(v) GrahamGibbons 10 38
(Keith Dalgleish) *w wnr and clr of rest: rdn over 2f out: wknd over 1f out* **9/2**²

1m 30.29s (1.29) **Going Correction** +0.225s/f (Good) **8** Ran SP% **104.2**
Speed ratings (Par 103): **101,99,96,94,91 87,80,80**
CSF £29.52 CT £175.41 TOTE £4.30: £1.50, £3.40, £2.10; EX 32.30 Trifecta £182.50.
Owner P Adams, P Clarke, T Wickins, J Sutton **Bred** Stuart Matheson **Trained** Middleham, N Yorks
■ Dyllan was withdrawn. Price at time of withdrawal 8-1. Rule 4 applies to all bets - deduction 10p in the pound.

FOCUS
This was run over 7yds further than advertised. A fair 3yo handicap in which the winner and eighth took each other on up front, clear of the others for much of the way.

6811 EBF STALLIONS SCOTTISH PREMIER SERIES FILLIES' H'CAP 1m
4:10 (4:11) (Class 3) (0-90,88) 3-Y-O+
£15,562 (£4,660; £2,330; £1,165; £582; £292) **Stalls** Low

Form RPR
1213 **1** **Lincoln Rocks**[15] 6342 3-9-3 **83**................................... DanielTudhope 13 92
(David O'Meara) *mde all: rdn and edgd lft over 1f out: hld on wl fnl f* **9/1**
6621 **2** ½ **Sophie P**[9] 6541 3-8-9 **80**... JordanVaughan(5) 6 87
(R Mike Smith) *prom: smooth hdwy to chse wnr over 2f out: rdn and hung rt over 1f out: kpt on fnl f: hld nr fin* **7/1**³
0041 **3** 3 ½ **Marsh Pride**[15] 6342 4-9-9 **85**.. PJMcDonald 12 84
(K R Burke) *in tch on outside: drvn along and outpcd over 2f out: hung rt: rallied over 1f out: kpt on to take 3rd nr fin: nt rch first two* **9/2**¹
5132 **4** ½ **Dark Intention (IRE)**[26] 6005 3-8-7 **73**............................... CamHardie 1 71
(Lawrence Mullaney) *midfield on ins: effrt and drvn along over 2f out: rallied over 1f out: kpt on ins fnl f* **11/2**²
2334 **5** nk **Invermere**[31] 5802 3-8-12 **78**... TonyHamilton 2 75
(Richard Fahey) *trckd ldrs on ins: rdn over 2f out: hung rt ins fnl f: no ex and lost two pls towards fin* **11/2**²
0324 **6** 4 ½ **Al Shahaniya (IRE)**[25] 6032 3-9-8 **88**............................... JasonHart 9 75
(John Quinn) *hld up towards rr: drvn along 3f out: no imp fr 2f out* **14/1**
-030 **7** 3 ¾ **Drifting Spirit (IRE)**[29] 5878 3-9-4 **84**....................... GeorgeChaloner 4 62
(Richard Fahey) *hld up: rdn along over 2f out: nvr on terms* **8/1**
3206 **8** 1 **Quick N Quirky (IRE)**[15] 6342 3-9-1 **81**.........................(tp) DavidAllan 3 57
(Tim Easterby) *s.i.s: hld up: rdn on ins over 2f out: wknd over 1f out* **14/1**
0140 **9** 3 ¼ **Lido Lady (IRE)**[12] 6437 3-8-5 **71**................................... JoeFanning 14 39
(Mark Johnston) *chsd wnr to over 2f out: rdn and wknd wl over 1f out* **20/1**

402 **10** 1 ½ **Ninetta (IRE)**[28] 5919 3-8-8 **79**.. RowanScott(5) 5 44
(Ann Duffield) *s.i.s: hld up on outside: struggling wl over 2f out: sn btn* **9/1**

6605 **11** 1 ½ **Forever A Lady (IRE)**[15] 6342 3-8-9 **75**.................... DougieCostello 11 37
(Keith Dalgleish) *midfield: drvn and struggling 3f out: sn btn* **40/1**

0002 **12** 3 ¼ **Alexandrakollontai (IRE)**[23] 6096 6-9-3 **79**.............(b) ConnorBeasley 8 33
(Alistair Whillans) *dwlt: bhd: struggling over 4f out: sn btn* **14/1**

1m 41.39s (0.19) **Going Correction** +0.225s/f (Good)
WFA 3 from 4yo+ 4lb **12** Ran SP% **119.8**
Speed ratings (Par 104): **108,107,104,103,103 98,94,93,90,89 87,84**
CSF £71.49 CT £331.25 TOTE £9.90: £2.90, £2.80, £2.20; EX 86.20 Trifecta £519.70.
Owner Peter Smith P C Coaches Limited **Bred** James Ortega Bloodstock **Trained** Upper Helmsley, N Yorks

FOCUS
This was run over 7yds further than advertised. Few got into this valuable fillies' handicap - at the top of the straight the first five finishers were positioned 1st, 4th, 6th, 5th, 3rd.

6812 ROBERT PURVIS PLANT HIRE LTD H'CAP 1m 6f
4:45 (4:45) (Class 5) (0-70,69) 3-Y-0+ **£3,234** (£962; £481; £240) **Stalls** Low

Form RPR
0060 **1** **Western Prince**[87] 3824 3-9-1 **66**.................................... AndrewMullen 5 74+
(Michael Appleby) *t.k.h: hld up in tch on outside: smooth hdwy to ld over 2f out: rdn and edgd rt over 1f out: kpt on wl fnl f* **7/2**[2]

4435 **2** ¾ **Ghostly Arc (IRE)**[19] 6219 4-9-1 **61**......................... JordanVaughan(5) 4 67
(Noel Wilson) *led at modest gallop: rdn and hdd over 2f out: rallied: kpt on fnl f* **5/2**[1]

10 **3** 4 ½ **Stoneham**[32] 5758 5-9-8 **68**.. CallumShepherd(5) 1 68
(Iain Jardine) *n tch: rdn and effrt over 2f out: kpt on fnl f: nt rch first two* **4/1**[3]

3253 **4** 2 ½ **Jan Smuts (IRE)**[18] 6227 8-10-0 **69**.................................(tp) CamHardie 7 65
(Wilf Storey) *trckd ldrs: wnt 2nd 1/2-way: rdn over 2f out: outpcd fr over 1f out* **11/2**

1600 **5** 3 ¼ **Lightning Steps**[12] 6438 4-8-9 **50** oh1.......................... BarryMcHugh 3 42
(Declan Carroll) *pressed ldr to 1/2-way: drvn and outpcd over 2f out: btn over 1f out* **9/1**

0-06 **6** 3 ½ **Jonny Delta**[68] 4491 9-9-5 **60**.. PaulMulrennan 2 47
(Jim Goldie) *t.k.h: hld up: drvn along 3f out: sn no imp: btn over 1f out* **10/1**

02PR **7** 34 **Jammy Moment**[115] 2813 5-9-9 **64**................................(v[1]) PJMcDonald 9 3
(Iain Jardine) *virtually ref to r: t.o whn consented to jump off but racd keenly and tagged onto bk of pack after 3f: rdn 3f out: sn wknd: t.o* **7/1**

3m 13.18s (7.88) **Going Correction** +0.225s/f (Good)
WFA 3 from 4yo+ 10lb **7** Ran SP% **117.8**
Speed ratings (Par 103): **86,85,83,81,79 77,58**
CSF £13.33 CT £36.33 TOTE £3.80: £2.30, £2.20; EX 12.10 Trifecta £52.10.
Owner Craig Buckingham **Bred** Dayton Investments Ltd **Trained** Oakham, Rutland

FOCUS
This was run over 7yds further than advertised. A modest staying event.

6813 RACINGUK.COM/HD APPRENTICE H'CAP 5f
5:15 (5:17) (Class 6) (0-65,64) 3-Y-0+ **£2,587** (£770; £384; £192) **Stalls** Low

Form RPR
63 **1** **Longroom**[60] 4770 4-8-10 **50**.. JordanVaughan(3) 1 64+
(Noel Wilson) *cl up: led over 1f out: edgd lft and rdn clr fnl f: readily* **3/1**[1]

6050 **2** 3 ½ **Go Go Green (IRE)**[10] 6506 10-9-2 **56**.................. CallumShepherd(3) 6 57
(Jim Goldie) *dwlt: hld up: pushed along and hdwy over 1f out: chsd (clr) wnr ins fnl f: kpt on: no imp* **7/1**

0406 **3** 2 **Caymus**[15] 6341 3-8-8 **49**..(t) PhilDennis(3) 5 43
(Tracy Waggott) *t.k.h early: trckd ldrs: effrt and wnt 2nd over 1f out to ins fnl f: sn no ex* **12/1**

1240 **4** hd **See Vermont**[4] 6680 8-9-8 **64**.......................................(p) RowanScott(5) 3 57
(Rebecca Bastiman) *prom: effrt and rdn wl over 1f out: kpt on same pce fnl f* **9/2**[3]

0634 **5** ¾ **Bunce (IRE)**[10] 6506 8-9-13 **64**.. KevinStott 2 55
(Linda Perratt) *bhd and sn outpcd: hdwy over 1f out: kpt on fnl f: no imp* **13/2**

4600 **6** 3 ¼ **Amber Crystal**[6] 6616 4-7-13 **46**.......................... LeanneFerguson(10) 7 25
(Linda Perratt) *chsd ldng gp: pushed along over 2f out: wknd over 1f out* **16/1**

4000 **7** 1 ¼ **Pavers Star**[4] 6680 7-8-7 **51**..(b[1]) GerO'Neill(7) 4 26
(Noel Wilson) *t.k.h: led to over 1f out: sn rdn and wknd* **13/2**

2315 **8** 1 ¾ **Thornaby Princess**[15] 6341 5-8-11 **51**....................(p) AnnaHesketh(3) 8 19
(Colin Teague) *sn towards rr: drvn along 1/2-way: nvr on terms* **4/1**[2]

1m 1.15s (0.75) **Going Correction** +0.225s/f (Good)
WFA 3 from 4yo+ 1lb **8** Ran SP% **115.9**
Speed ratings (Par 101): **103,97,94,93,92 87,85,82**
CSF £24.89 CT £221.75 TOTE £3.80: £1.60, £2.30, £3.50; EX 22.20 Trifecta £249.90.
Owner Alderclad Ltd **Bred** Juddmonte Farms Ltd **Trained** Middleham, N Yorks

FOCUS
A moderate sprint handicap. The second and third could back this race being rated a bit higher but this looks a safe starting point.
T/Plt: £15.00 to a £1 stake. Pool: £86557.52, 4202.51 winning units T/Qpdt: £7.20 to a £1 stake. Pool: £5972.92, 610.93 winning units **Richard Young**

6814 - (Foreign Racing) - See Raceform Interactive

6720 CURRAGH (R-H)
Sunday, September 25

OFFICIAL GOING: Soft changing to heavy after race 1 (1.50)

6815a C.L. & M.F. WELD PARK STKS (GROUP 3) 7f
2:20 (2:21) 2-Y-0
£29,283 (£9,430; £4,466; £1,985; £992; £496)

RPR
1 **Eziyra (IRE)**[28] 5937 2-9-0 0...[1] PatSmullen 10 108
(D K Weld, Ire) *chsd ldrs nr side: 4th 1/2-way: hdwy gng wl to dispute over 1 1/2f out: sn led and flashed tail u.p: kpt on wl* **5/4**[1]

2 2 **Grecian Light (IRE)**[17] 6258 2-9-0 0.............................. WilliamBuick 9 103
(Charlie Appleby) *dwlt sltly: in tch: clsr in 5th 3f out: hdwy to dispute briefly u.p 1 1/2f out: no imp on wnr ins fnl f: kpt on same pce* **5/1**[2]

3 4 ¼ **Legitimus (IRE)**[28] 5937 2-9-0 0................................. RonanWhelan 6 92
(J S Bolger, Ire) *w.w down centre of trck early: clsr in 8th fr 1/2-way: rdn nr side fr 2f out and clsd u.p bhd ldrs into 4th ins fnl f: kpt on into 3rd clsng stages: nvr trbld ldrs* **16/1**

4 ½ **Tinder (IRE)**[29] 5897 2-9-0 84.................................... ColmO'Donoghue 1 91
(Mrs John Harrington, Ire) *led briefly far side tl sn settled bhd ldr: dropped to 6th at 1/2-way where tacked over: effrt 2f out: sn rdn in 3rd and no imp on wnr ins fnl f: one pce clsng stages where dropped to 4th* **25/1**

5 ¾ **Perle De La Mer (IRE)**[20] 6198 2-9-0 0.................................... BillyLee 8 89
(W McCreery, Ire) *chsd ldrs nr side early: 7th 1/2-way: swtchd over 2f out and rdn down centre of trck: no imp on ldrs u.p in 5th ent fnl f: kpt on one pce* **5/1**[2]

6 5 ½ **Dawn Of A New Era (IRE)**[14] 6385 2-9-0 0.................. KevinManning 3 76
(J S Bolger, Ire) *tacked over to nr side: chsd ldr: 2nd 1/2-way: rdn over 2f out and sn no ex: wknd under 2f out* **20/1**

7 1 ¼ **Wild Irish Rose (IRE)**[15] 6348 2-9-0 0.................................. AnaO'Brien 4 72
(A P O'Brien, Ire) *sn chsd ldrs far side early: 3rd 1/2-way: sn tacked over and rdn bhd ldrs over 2f out: wknd 1 1/2f out* **16/1**

8 1 ¼ **Nutcracker Suite (IRE)**[42] 5443 2-9-0 0............................. RyanMoore 5 69
(A P O'Brien, Ire) *chsd ldrs down centre of trck early: pushed along towards rr fr 1/2-way and no imp u.p 2f out: one pce after* **8/1**[3]

9 4 ½ **Elizabeth Browning (IRE)**[3] 6721 2-9-0 79.........(v[1]) SeamieHeffernan 2 58
(A P O'Brien, Ire) *sn led far side: clr at 1/2-way: reduced advantage fr over 2f out: jnd over 1 1/2f out and sn hdd: wknd qckly* **12/1**

10 11 **Famous Milly (IRE)**[13] 6430 2-9-0 81.................................. RoryCleary 7 31
(Gavin Cromwell, Ire) *dwlt sltly and towards rr: pushed along fr 1/2-way and sn wknd to rr* **33/1**

1m 30.36s (-0.44) **Going Correction** +0.05s/f (Good) **10** Ran SP% **119.9**
Speed ratings: **104,101,96,96,95 89,87,86,81,68**
CSF £7.59 TOTE £2.00: £1.02, £1.70, £6.20; DF 7.40 Trifecta £102.80.
Owner H H Aga Khan **Bred** His Highness The Aga Khan's Studs S C **Trained** Curragh, Co Kildare

FOCUS
Ability to handle the ground was crucial here, but Eziyra appeals as a Classic prospect for next year, with her jockey confident she will act well on good ground too. The runner-up has been rated to her May Hill form.

6816a RENAISSANCE STKS (GROUP 3) 6f
2:50 (2:51) 3-Y-0+
£26,029 (£8,382; £3,970; £1,764; £882; £441)

RPR
1 **The Happy Prince (IRE)**[15] 6328 4-9-5 112...................(t) RyanMoore 2 112
(A P O'Brien, Ire) *disp early tl sn led narrowly far side: gng wl 2f out where tacked over: pushed along over 1f out and over 1 l clr wl ins fnl f where rdn: all out clsng stages where pressed: hld on wl* **11/4**[1]

2 ¾ **Flight Risk (IRE)**[15] 6353 5-9-5 107.............................(t) KevinManning 3 110
(J S Bolger, Ire) *chsd ldrs early nr side: 2nd 1/2-way: rdn in 2nd under 2f out and no imp on wnr ent fnl f: kpt on wl clsng stages to press wnr: jst hld 2nd: a hld by wnr* **8/1**

3 nse **La Rioja**[16] 6281 3-9-0 103.. OisinMurphy 8 106
(Henry Candy) *hld up: 7th 1/2-way: n.m.r bhd horses nr side over 2f out: sn swtchd rt and pushed along to chse ldrs: rdn in 3rd ent fnl f and kpt on wl clsng stages: a hld by wnr: jst hld for 2nd* **5/1**[2]

4 4 ½ **Fort Del Oro (IRE)**[49] 5213 4-9-2 103.. BillyLee 6 92
(Edward Lynam, Ire) *hld up bhd ldrs: 5th 1/2-way: tk clsr order gng wl over 2f out: short of room and swtchd rt ins fnl f: sn no ex u.p in 4th: kpt on one pce* **5/1**[2]

5 nk **Bebhinn (USA)**[92] 3681 3-9-0 104.. ChrisHayes 9 91
(Kevin Prendergast, Ire) *dwlt sltly and settled towards rr: last at 1/2-way: sme late hdwy ins fnl f into nvr nrr 5th cl home: nrst fin* **18/1**

6 ½ **In Salutem**[14] 6384 6-9-5 104..(t) ShaneFoley 5 92
(K J Condon, Ire) *w.w towards rr: 8th 1/2-way: tk clsr order u.p over 1f out: one pce in 5th and no imp on ldrs ins fnl f: denied 5th cl home* **7/1**[3]

7 2 **Goken (FR)**[22] 6120 4-9-5 106...[1] TomEaves 4 86
(Kevin Ryan) *w.w: 6th 1/2-way: rdn bhd ldrs 2f out and sn no ex in 5th over 1f out: one pce fnl f* **14/1**

8 2 ¼ **Gordon Lord Byron (IRE)**[15] 6353 8-9-10 112............ WayneLordan 1 84
(T Hogan, Ire) *disp early far side tl sn settled bhd ldrs: 4th 1/2-way: rdn over 2f out and sn no ex: wknd over 1f out* **14/1**

9 13 **Jane's Memory (IRE)**[22] 6120 4-9-2 104............................ PatSmullen 7 34
(Rae Guest) *chsd ldrs nr side: 3rd 1/2-way: pushed along over 2f out and wknd to rr over 1f out where sltly hmpd and eased* **7/1**[3]

1m 15.91s (0.41) **Going Correction** +0.175s/f (Good)
WFA 3 from 4yo+ 2lb **9** Ran SP% **114.7**
Speed ratings: **104,103,102,96,96 95,93,90,72**
CSF £25.22 TOTE £3.60: £1.20, £2.60, £2.10; DF 24.10 Trifecta £132.60.
Owner Mrs John Magnier & Michael Tabor & Derrick Smith **Bred** Floors Farming **Trained** Cashel, Co Tipperary
■ Stewards' Enquiry : Tom Eaves caution: use of whip
Pat Smullen caution: use of whip

FOCUS
A competitive race for the grade which confirmed the winner is something of a reformed character. The first two were to the fore throughout, both handling the ground well. The second and third have been rated in line with this year's best.

6817a JUDDMONTE BERESFORD STKS (GROUP 2) 1m
3:25 (3:26) 2-Y-0
£52,058 (£16,764; £7,941; £3,529; £1,764; £882)

RPR
1 **Capri (IRE)**[51] 5136 2-9-3 108...(t) RyanMoore 7 113
(A P O'Brien, Ire) *chsd ldrs: 3rd over 3f out: tacked over into st and effrt nr side fr 2f out: rdn to ld narrowly fr 1f out and kpt on wl into to assert clsng stages* **8/11**[1]

2 ¾ **Yucatan (IRE)**[28] 5936 2-9-3 0................................. DonnachaO'Brien 2 111
(A P O'Brien, Ire) *chsd ldrs: 4th over 3f out: tacked over into st and prog between horses into 3rd under 2f out: sn rdn and clsd u.p into 2nd clsng stages: kpt on wl: a hld by wnr* **10/1**

3 ¾ **Exemplar (IRE)**[20] 6196 2-9-3 0..................................(t) SeamieHeffernan 4 110
(A P O'Brien, Ire) *trckd ldr: cl 2nd at 1/2-way: jnd into st where tacked over to nr side and led over 2f out: rdn and hdd fr 1f out and sn no imp on wnr: dropped to 3rd clsng stages* **3/1**[2]

4 16 **Eagle Spirit (IRE)**[66] 4574 2-9-3 90.. BillyLee 6 75
(Joseph Patrick O'Brien, Ire) *w.w in rr: last at 1/2-way: tacked over into st and rdn over 2f out: no imp trailing u.p 1 1/2f out: kpt on one pce into remote 4th ins fnl f* **33/1**

5 4 ½ **Latin Beat (IRE)**[31] 5812 2-9-3 93...........................(t) ColmO'Donoghue 5 65
(A P O'Brien, Ire) *broke wl and prom early tl sn sn settled towards rr: pushed along in 5th over 3f out: tacked over into st and no imp on ldrs u.p in 5th over 2f out: sn wknd* **7/1**[3]

The Form Book, Raceform Ltd, Newbury, RG14 5SJ

6 7 1/2 **Escape Clause (IRE)**[12] 6467 2-9-3 0 .... ShaneFoley 1 48
(Mrs John Harrington, Ire) *sn led: narrow advantage at 1/2-way: jnd into st where tacked over to nr side: hdd over 2f out and sn no imp on ldr: dropped to 4th under 2f out and wknd: eased ins fnl f* **20/1**

1m 45.05s (-0.95) **Going Correction** +0.05s/f (Good) **6** Ran SP% **112.2**
Speed ratings: **106,105,104,88,84 76**
CSF £9.34 TOTE £1.40: £1.02, £2.50; DF 6.30 Trifecta £9.70.
Owner Derrick Smith & Mrs John Magnier & Michael Tabor **Bred** Lynch Bages Ltd & Camas Park Stud **Trained** Cashel, Co Tipperary

FOCUS
A 16th success in this event for Aidan O'Brien, and a second six-in-a-row, the trainer having achieved the same feat between 1996 and 2001. A one-two-three into the bargain, with the odds-on favourite scoring in workmanlike fashion.

6819a MONGEY COMMUNICATIONS JOE MCGRATH H'CAP (PREMIER HANDICAP) 5f

4:30 (4:31) 3-Y-O+

£21,691 (£6,985; £3,308; £1,470; £735; £367)

RPR

1 **Tithonus (IRE)**[21] 6167 5-8-7 **80** ....(tp) GaryHalpin(3) 11 91
(Denis Gerard Hogan, Ire) *w ldrs and sn settled in 2nd: n.m.r briefly between horses over 2f out: prog to ld over 1f out where rdn: extended advantage ins fnl f: kpt on wl clsng stages where reduced ld* **12/1**

2 3/4 **Rattling Jewel**[29] 5899 4-8-6 **76** ....(p) WayneLordan 15 84
(Miss Nicole McKenna, Ire) *chsd ldrs: 5th 1/2-way: swtchd rt and rdn over 1f out: wnt 2nd u.p wl ins fnl f and kpt on wl clsng stages: a hld* **16/1**

3 1/2 **Primo Uomo (IRE)**[21] 6167 4-9-0 **84** ....(t) NGMcCullagh 4 90
(Gerard O'Leary, Ire) *mid-div: 9th 1/2-way: hdwy to chse ldrs over 1f out: r.o into 3rd wl ins fnl f and kpt on wl: nt trble wnr* **33/1**

4 1/2 **Tylery Wonder (IRE)**[18] 6234 6-8-13 **83** ....(b) PatSmullen 5 87
(Paul Midgley) *sn led: hdd u.p over 1f out and sn no imp on wnr: one pce wl ins fnl f where dropped to 4th: jst hld 4th* **7/1**[2]

5 nse **Downforce (IRE)**[14] 6382 4-9-9 **93** .... BillyLee 18 97
(W McCreery, Ire) *w.w towards rr: sme prog after 1/2-way: hdwy in 12th ent fnl f and r.o wl clsng stages: nrst fin* **6/1**[1]

6 nk **Penny Pepper (IRE)**[28] 5942 4-8-8 **85** .... DylanHogan(7) 10 88
(Kevin Prendergast, Ire) *in rr of mid-div: 13th 1/2-way: rdn after 1/2-way and sme hdwy far side ent fnl f: kpt on same pce in 6th wl ins fnl f* **20/1**

7 1 **Soie D'Leau**[15] 6327 4-9-12 **96** .... ShaneGray 17 96
(Kristin Stubbs) *mid-div: 10th 1/2-way: prog nr side to chse ldrs over 1f out: n.m.r bhd horses ins fnl f: kpt on same pce in 7th wl ins fnl f* **8/1**[3]

8 nk **Peticoatgovernment (IRE)**[28] 5942 3-9-0 **85** .... LeighRoche 12 83
(W McCreery, Ire) *mid-div: 11th 1/2-way: rdn after 1/2-way and no imp on ldrs over 1f out: sme hdwy ins fnl f: kpt on clsng stages: nvr nrr* **14/1**

9 1/2 **Master Speaker (IRE)**[14] 6382 6-9-10 **94** ....(bt) RonanWhelan 19 91
(Martin Hassett, Ire) *dwlt sltly and pushed along towards rr early: pushed along and no imp in 16th 1 1/2f out: swtchd and sme late hdwy ins fnl f: nvr nrr* **8/1**[3]

10 hd **Bainne (IRE)**[25] 6037 6-8-2 **77** .... AnaO'Brien(5) 9 73
(J F Levins, Ire) *in tch: disp 6th at 1/2-way: rdn and no ex over 1f out: sn wknd* **25/1**

11 1 **Sors (IRE)**[14] 6382 4-9-9 **98** .... KillianLeonard(5) 6 90
(Andrew Slattery, Ire) *got upset in stalls and dislodged rdr bef s: chsd ldrs: pushed along in 4th fr 1/2-way and sn no ex: wknd fnl f* **9/1**

12 1/2 **Captain Power (IRE)**[14] 6382 4-9-6 **93** .... RobbieDowney(3) 1 84
(Edward Lynam, Ire) *got upset in stalls briefly: dwlt sltly and towards rr: pushed along after 1/2-way no imp in 17th over 1f out: kpt on ins fnl f* **11/1**

13 3/4 **Shanghai Beauty (IRE)**[29] 5899 4-8-5 **82** ....(tp) AndrewBreslin(7) 2 70
(K J Condon, Ire) *in tch: disp 6th at 1/2-way: rdn 2f out and sn no ex: wknd fnl f* **16/1**

14 1 **Bubbly Bellini (IRE)**[9] 6551 9-8-11 **81** ....(p) DeclanMcDonogh 14 65
(Adrian McGuinness, Ire) *w.w towards rr: 16th at 1/2-way: rdn and no imp 1f out* **16/1**

15 hd **Athas An Bhean**[51] 5135 3-9-1 **86** .... GaryCarroll 13 70
(Adrian Paul Keatley, Ire) *in tch: 8th 1/2-way: rdn and wknd 1 1/2f out* **20/1**

16 nk **Sahreej (IRE)**[21] 6167 3-9-1 **86** ....[1] ChrisHayes 3 68
(Adrian Paul Keatley, Ire) *chsd ldrs: 3rd 1/2-way: pushed along fr 2f out and sn no ex u.p: wknd 1f out* **12/1**

17 4 1/2 **Lady Mega (IRE)**[21] 6167 5-8-13 **88** .... OisinOrr(5) 16 54
(Edward Lynam, Ire) *in rr of mid-div: 12th 1/2-way: rdn after 1/2-way and wknd 1 1/2f out* **20/1**

18 2 **Bluesbreaker (IRE)**[22] 6146 4-8-8 **78** ....(vt) RoryCleary 20 37
(Damian Joseph English, Ire) *towards rr: 15th 1/2-way: rdn and no imp in rr under 2f out* **16/1**

1m 2.6s (-0.30) **Going Correction** +0.175s/f (Good)
WFA 3 from 4yo+ 1lb **18** Ran SP% **134.0**
Speed ratings: **109,107,107,106,106 105,104,103,102,102 100,100,98,97,96 96,89,86**
CSF £192.54 CT £6283.12 TOTE £13.00: £3.00, £3.50, £9.40, £1.90; DF 253.40 Trifecta £10875.70.
Owner T & M Racing Partnership **Bred** K N Dhunjibhoy & B M Desai **Trained** Cloughjordan, Co Tipperary

FOCUS
A surprising feature of this sprint handicap was that the first three boasted winning form at Dundalk, a factor which might have been interpreted as a negative in the prevailing conditions. The standard is set around the second to the sixth.

6820a SYCAMORE LODGE EQUINE HOSPITAL LOUGHBROWN STKS (LISTED RACE) 2m

5:05 (5:06) 3-Y-O+

£20,389 (£6,566; £3,110; £1,382; £691; £345)

RPR

1 **Twilight Payment (IRE)**[36] 5660 3-8-11 108 ....(p) KevinManning 2 104+
(J S Bolger, Ire) *chsd ldrs: 4th 1/2-way: cl 3rd over 3f out: tacked over to nr side over 2f out: rdn into cl 2nd 1f out and styd on wl to ld fnl 50yds* **3/1**[2]

2 1/2 **Forgotten Rules (IRE)**[344] 7277 6-9-9 112 .... PatSmullen 6 103
(D K Weld, Ire) *hld up: 7th 1/2-way: sme hdwy on outer 4f out: gng wl in 5th 3f out: tacked over to nr side and led travelling wl fr 2f out: rdn and strly pressed ins fnl f: hdd fnl 50yds and no ex* **13/8**[1]

3 4 1/2 **Toe The Line (IRE)**[11] 6495 7-9-4 101 .... ColinKeane 9 93
(John E Kiely, Ire) *w.w: 6th 1/2-way: tk clsr order bhd ldrs under 5f out: cl 4th over 3f out: tacked over to nr side and disp over 2f out: sn hdd and no imp on ldrs u.p in 3rd fr 1f out: kpt on same pce to hold 3rd* **6/1**

4 nk **Fact Or Folklore (IRE)**[20] 6200 4-9-4 95 .... BillyLee 1 93
(W McCreery, Ire) *hooded to load: chsd ldrs: 5th 1/2-way: 6th 3f out: tacked over to nr side over 2f out: rdn into 4th under 2f out and no imp on ldrs ent fnl f: kpt on same pce clsng stages: jst hld for 3rd* **25/1**

5 1/2 **Soul Searcher (IRE)**[20] 6200 4-9-4 89 .... RoryCleary 10 92
(J P Murtagh, Ire) *broke wl to ld early tl settled towards rr after 1f: last at 1/2-way: impr into 8th fr 3f out: tacked over to nr side over 2f out: kpt on u.p into 5th ins fnl f: nvr trbld ldrs* **66/1**

6 hd **Morga (IRE)**[20] 6200 6-9-4 99 .... DeclanMcDonogh 8 92
(Desmond McDonogh, Ire) *dwlt and settled in rr: 9th 1/2-way: pushed along in 7th 3f out: tacked over to nr side over 2f out: sn rdn in 5th and no imp on ldrs u.p 1 1/2f out: kpt on one pce* **12/1**

7 9 **Benkei (IRE)**[15] 6350 6-9-9 98 ....(tp) ChrisHayes 4 87
(H Rogers, Ire) *chsd ldrs: 3rd 1/2-way: almost on terms over 3f out: tacked over to nr side over 2f out and rdn: sn no ex and wknd u.p between horses fr 2f out* **16/1**

8 9 1/2 **Jennies Jewel (IRE)**[103] 3246 9-9-4 98 .... RonanWhelan 7 72
(Jarlath P Fahey, Ire) *chsd ldrs tl impr to sn ld: jnd and hdd fr 1/2-way tl regained advantage under 5f out: pushed along over 3f out: tacked over to nr side over 2f out where jnd and hdd: wknd qckly* **5/1**[3]

9 18 **Silwana (IRE)**[14] 6387 5-9-4 97 ....(bt) ShaneFoley 3 52
(Takashi Kodama, Ire) *w.w: 8th 1/2-way: rdn and no ex 3f out: wknd: t.o* **33/1**

10 84 **Look Closer (IRE)**[39] 5562 3-8-11 81 .... LeighRoche 5
(D K Weld, Ire) *prom early and led narrowly tl sn settled bhd ldr: disp and led fr 1/2-way: pushed along and hdd fr 5f out: sn wknd and eased in rr under 4f out and t.o into st* **50/1**

3m 39.33s (6.33) **Going Correction** +0.675s/f (Yiel)
WFA 3 from 4yo+ 12lb **10** Ran SP% **117.9**
Speed ratings: **111,110,108,108,108 108,103,98,89,47**
CSF £8.15 TOTE £3.60: £1.02, £1.30, £2.00; DF 8.70 Trifecta £38.10.
Owner Godolphin **Bred** J S Bolger **Trained** Coolcullen, Co Carlow

FOCUS
A fantastic finish served up by two very good horses. The runner-up looked the likely winner for most of the race but was outbattled near the line, probably just getting caught out by the lack of a recent run.

6818 & 6821 - (Foreign Racing) - See Raceform Interactive

6797 COLOGNE (R-H)

Sunday, September 25

OFFICIAL GOING: Turf: good

6822a PREIS VON EUROPA (GROUP 1) (3YO+) (TURF) 1m 4f

3:25 (12:00) 3-Y-O+ **£73,529** (£22,058; £11,029; £5,147; £2,205)

RPR

1 **Nightflower (IRE)**[21] 6175 4-9-3 0 .... AndraschStarke 1 109
(P Schiergen, Germany) *a cl up: c stands' side into st: chsd ldrs over 1 1/2f out: styd on u.p appr 1f out: sustained run to ld fnl 50yds: won gng away* **2/1**[1]

2 3/4 **Red Cardinal (IRE)**[43] 5402 4-9-6 0 .... MarcLerner 7 111
(A Wohler, Germany) *chsd ldr: rdn to chal 1 1/2f out whn nt clr run and swtchd ins: styd on wl to ld 100yds out: hdd fnl 50yds: no ex* **128/10**

3 shd **Kasalla (GER)**[22] 6152 3-8-9 0 .... AdriedeVries 5 108
(Markus Klug, Germany) *sn led: veered lft whn rdr changed whip hand leaving bk st: rdn and rallied 1 1/2f out: hdd 100yds out: no ex* **36/5**

4 1 1/4 **Parvaneh (IRE)**[22] 6152 3-8-9 0 .... AntoineHamelin 8 106
(Waldemar Hickst, Germany) *settled in midfield: rdn 2f out and styd on: chsd ldrs 1f out: kpt on u.p fnl f* **48/10**[3]

5 1 1/2 **Iquitos (GER)**[21] 6175 4-9-6 0 .... IanFerguson 3 106
(H-J Groschel, Germany) *bmpd s and collided w rival on outer: w.w in rr: outpcd in last over 1 1/2f out: styd on wl fnl f: nvr plcd to chal* **27/10**[2]

6 2 1/4 **Elite Army**[58] 4821 5-9-6 0 .... FilipMinarik 4 103
(Saeed bin Suroor) *bdly hmpd s and adrift: sn rcvrd and moved up to chse ldr: hmpd whn ldr veered lft leaving bk st: rdn and no imp over 2f out: sn btn and grad dropped away* **119/10**

7 1 1/2 **Sirius (GER)**[84] 3934 5-9-6 0 ....(b) AndreasHelfenbein 6 100
(Andreas Lowe, Germany) *w.w towards rr: rdn and no imp over 1 1/2f out: one pce fnl f: nvr in contention* **97/10**

8 1 1/4 **Serienholde (GER)**[21] 6175 3-8-9 0 .... EduardoPedroza 2 95
(A Wohler, Germany) *wnt lft s and bmpd rival: tk a t.k.h and hld up: sn in rr: rdn and effrt over 1 1/2f out: qckly btn* **53/10**

2m 29.3s (-3.60)
WFA 3 from 4yo+ 8lb **8** Ran SP% **130.0**
WIN (incl. 10 euro stake): 30. PLACES: 12, 24, 15. SF: 332.
Owner Stall Nizza **Bred** Jurgen Imm **Trained** Germany

6612 SAN SIRO (R-H)

Sunday, September 25

OFFICIAL GOING: Turf: good

6823a PREMIO VITTORIO DI CAPUA (GROUP 1) (3YO+) (TURF) 1m

4:35 (12:00) 3-Y-O+ **£91,911** (£40,441; £22,058; £11,029)

RPR

1 **Waikika (FR)**[28] 5948 5-8-13 0 .... GeraldMosse 1 110
(Y Barberot, France) *a cl up: shkn up to press ldr fr 2f out: drvn to ld appr fnl f: r.o u.p: a holding runner-up* **13/2**

2 nk **Jallota**[17] 6272 5-9-2 0 .... JamieSpencer 4 112
(Charles Hills) *a.p: 3l 4th and travelling wl 2f out whn sltly hld up in getting a run: styd on appr 1f out: r.o u.p fnl f: nvr quite looked like collaring wnr* **226/100**[2]

3 3/4 **Kaspersky (IRE)**[70] 4438 5-9-2 0 .... UmbertoRispoli 5 110
(Endo Botti, Italy) *led: rdn whn pressed fr 2f out: hdd appriaching 1f out: styd on fnl f* **6/5**[1]

4 1/2 **Maximum Aurelius (FR)**[28] 5948 3-8-11 0 .... CristianDemuro 6 108+
(F-H Graffard, France) *hld up in fnl pair: hdwy 2f out: r.o fnl f: nrest at fin* **79/10**

5 1 1/4 **Diplomat (GER)**[21] 6181 5-9-2 0 .... CarloFiocchi 3 106
(Mario Hofer, Germany) *w.w towards rr: rdn 2 1/2f out but no immediate imp: styd on fr over 1 1/2f out: nvr nrr* **53/10**[3]

6 *3* **Basileus (IRE)**[112] 3-8-11 0 .... SilvanoMulas 7 98
(Stefano Botti, Italy) *w.w in rr: sme hdwy 1 1/2f out: kpt on at same pce fnl f: nvr in contention* **193/10**

7 *1 ¾* **Greg Pass (IRE)**[21] 4-9-2 0 .... DarioVargiu 2 95
(Il Cavallo In Testa, Italy) *chsd ldr: rdn and btn 1 1/2f out: wknd fnl f* **133/10**

8 *7* **Azzeccagarbugli (IRE)**[14] 3-8-11 0 .... FabioBranca 8 78
(Stefano Botti, Italy) *cl up on outer: rdn and nt qckn 2f out: sn btn: bhd whn eased fnl f* **189/10**

1m 34.0s (-8.10)
WFA 3 from 4yo+ 4lb **8** Ran SP% **133.5**
WIN (incl. 1 euro stake): 7.46. PLACES: 1.67, 1.36, 1.20. DF: 12.59.
Owner Philippe Bellaiche **Bred** Pontchartrain Stud **Trained** France

FOCUS
The second, third and fourth help set the standard.

6824a PREMIO ELENA E SERGIO CUMANI (GROUP 3) (3YO+ FILLIES & MARES) (TURF) 1m

5:15 (12:00) 3-Y-O+ **£25,735** (£11,323; £6,176; £3,088)

RPR

1 **Silver Step (FR)**[41] 5498 3-8-9 0 .... CristianDemuro 9 101
(Mme Pia Brandt, France) *w.w towards rr: hdwy over 1 1/2f out: styd on between horses appr 1f out: r.o wl fnl f: led 75yds out: hld on gamely* **71/20**[1]

2 *nk* **Okana**[85] 3938 3-8-9 0 .... MaximeGuyon 11 100
(C Laffon-Parias, France) *hld up towards rr: hdwy on outer under 2f out: r.o fnl f: no ex cl home* **103/20**

3 *snk* **Show Day (IRE)**[21] 3-8-9 0 .... MickaelBarzalona 7 100
(H-A Pantall, France) *hld up towards rr: pushed along over 2f out: hdwy 1 1/2f out: r.o fnl f: run flattened out cl home* **23/5**[2]

4 *1 ¼* **Signora Queen (FR)**[25] 3-8-9 0 .... DarioVargiu 8 97
(A Wohler, Germany) *w.w in midfield: tk clsr order wl over 2f out: sn chsng ldrs: rdn to chal over 1f out and sn led: kpt on at same pce u.p: hdd fnl 75yds: no ex* **32/5**

5 *1 ½* **Calantha (FR)**[21] 3-8-9 0 .... JozefBojko 1 93
(A Wohler, Germany) *cl up: chsd ldrs over 2f out: sn rdn and nt qckn: one pce fnl f* **37/4**

6 *1 ¾* **Lorenzetta (IRE)**[21] 4-9-0 0 .... MarioEsposito 2 90
(Riccardo Santini, Italy) *outpcd early and scrubbed along: sn plld way into midfield: rdn and no imp 2f out: kpt on at same pce fnl f* **146/10**

7 *nse* **Bastille (GER)**[43] 3-8-9 0 .... CarloFiocchi 3 89
(P Schiergen, Germany) *cl up: rdn and styd on the ld 1 1/2f out: sn pressed and hdd 1f out: sn btn* **128/10**

8 *2* **Rosebay (GER)**[24] 6067 5-9-0 0 .... MaximPecheur 5 86
(Markus Klug, Germany) *hld up towards rr: moved into midfield 1 1/2f out: one pce fnl f* **66/10**

9 *1 ½* **Dynamic Lips (IRE)**[35] 5695 3-8-9 0 .... UmbertoRispoli 4 81
(Andreas Lowe, Germany) *w.w towards rr: sme late prog: wl hld whn eased ins fnl f* **49/10**[3]

10 *2 ½* **Dry Your Eyes (ITY)**[119] 2730 3-8-9 0 .... FabioBranca 6 75
(Stefano Botti, Italy) *led: rdn 2f out: hdd 1 1/2f out: sn wknd* **41/5**

11 *¾* **Sognando La Cometa (IRE)**[25] 5-9-0 0 .... FedericoBossa 12 75
(P L Giannotti, Italy) *chsd ldrs: outpcd and scrubbed along 2f out: wknd over 1f out* **29/1**

12 *5* **Windy York (IRE)**[15] 3-8-9 0 .... SilvanoMulas 10 62
(Frank Turner, Italy) *towards rr on outer: rdn and btn 1 1/2f out: nvr a factor* **26/1**

1m 34.6s (-7.50)
WFA 3 from 4yo+ 4lb **12** Ran SP% **141.0**
WIN (incl. 1 euro stake): 4.57. PLACES: 1.61, 1.90, 1.94. DF: 30.32.
Owner Nils-Petter Gill **Bred** N-P Gill **Trained** France

6361 BATH (L-H)

Monday, September 26

OFFICIAL GOING: Good to soft (good in places) changing to good to soft after race 5 (4.10)
Wind: Light against Weather: Overcast

6825 ROYDS WITHY KING H'CAP 1m 5f 22y

2:10 (2:10) (Class 6) (0-60,60) 3-Y-O+ **£2,264** (£673; £336; £168) **Stalls** High

Form RPR

46/2 **1** **Fine Resolve**[7] 6619 7-9-4 **55** .... (bt) JosephineGordon(3) 9 63
(Alexandra Dunn) *mid-div: hdwy 1/2-way: shkn up to ld wl over 1f out: rdn and edgd lft ins fnl f: styd on wl: eased nr fin* **6/1**

2324 **2** *1 ¾* **Thomas Blossom (IRE)**[19] 4979 6-9-12 **60** .... (tp) JimCrowley 4 66
(Ali Stronge) *hld up: hdwy 1/2-way: rdn to chse wnr over 1f out: edgd lft and ev ch ins fnl f: styd on same pce* **5/1**[2]

50-4 **3** *1* **Maid Of Tuscany (IRE)**[14] 6424 5-8-11 **50** .... (b) CharlieBennett(5) 6 54
(Alexandra Dunn) *hld up: swtchd lft and hdwy over 1f out: r.o to go 3rd towards fin: nt rch ldrs* **14/1**

0630 **4** *1* **Shine**[38] 5597 3-9-1 **58** .... LukeMorris 8 61
(Jonathan Portman) *led: rdn and hdd wl over 1f out: no ex wl ins fnl f* **14/1**

0561 **5** *1* **DItripleseven (IRE)**[72] 4385 3-9-2 **59** .... (b[1]) ShaneKelly 2 60
(Richard Hughes) *plld hrd and prom: rdn over 1f out: styd on same pce* **4/1**[1]

4422 **6** *1 ¾* **Fair Comment**[18] 6256 6-9-12 **60** .... CharlesBishop 7 59
(Michael Blanshard) *chsd ldrs: rdn over 2f out: no ex fnl f* **11/2**[3]

2620 **7** *3 ½* **Lady Hare (IRE)**[16] 6315 4-9-9 **57** .... PatDobbs 13 51
(Ken Cunningham-Brown) *prom: chsd ldr 12f out: rdn and ev ch over 2f out: wknd fnl f* **8/1**

-220 **8** *1 ¼* **The Bay Bandit**[39] 3997 9-9-3 **51** .... (p) LiamKeniry 12 43
(Neil Mulholland) *prom: rdn over 2f out: wknd fnl f* **16/1**

5524 **9** *2 ¼* **Grams And Ounces**[18] 6256 9-9-12 **60** .... (t) StevieDonohoe 10 49
(Grace Harris) *hld up: hdwy 1/2-way: rdn over 2f out: wknd over 1f out* **10/1**

316/ **10** *2* **Soundbyte**[760] 5863 11-9-2 **50** .... (v) MichaelJMMurphy 1 36
(John Gallagher) *hld up: rdn over 3f out: wknd over 2f out* **33/1**

0-05 **11** *½* **Avocadeau (IRE)**[33] 5776 5-9-7 **55** ....[1] OisinMurphy 5 41
(Stuart Kittow) *stdd s: hld up: rdn over 3f out: sn wknd* **25/1**

2564 **12** *7* **Delagoa Bay (IRE)**[14] 6422 8-9-8 **56** .... TomMarquand 3 32
(Sylvester Kirk) *hld up: rdn over 5f out: wknd 3f out* **20/1**

2m 59.29s (7.29) **Going Correction** +0.475s/f (Yiel)
WFA 3 from 4yo+ 9lb **12** Ran SP% **117.3**
Speed ratings (Par 101): **96,94,94,93,93 92,89,89,87,86 86,81**
CSF £34.76 CT £406.63 TOTE £7.10: £3.40, £1.70, £5.10; EX 30.30 Trifecta £1172.10.
Owner West Buckland Bloodstock Ltd **Bred** Lord Blyth **Trained** West Buckland, Somerset

FOCUS
Following rain earlier in the day, the going had eased to good to soft, good in places, though the jockeys in the opener felt it was soft. A moderate staying handicap to start and they only went an ordinary pace. The runners made for the centre of the track on turning in. The race has been rated around the runner-up.

6826 M J CHURCH H'CAP 1m 5y

2:40 (2:40) (Class 6) (0-60,59) 3-Y-O+ **£2,458** (£731; £365; £182) **Stalls** Low

Form RPR

0642 **1** **Zlatan (IRE)**[6] 6651 3-9-0 **56** .... (p) JimCrowley 15 63
(Ed de Giles) *hld up in tch: chsd ldr over 1f out: sn hung lft: cajoled to ld wl ins fnl f: styd on reluctantly* **9/2**[2]

0356 **2** *hd* **Just Isla**[28] 5953 6-9-1 **53** .... (b) DanielMuscutt 2 60
(John Flint) *disp ld tl over 6f out: chsd ldr tl led over 3f out: rdn over 1f out: hung lft and hdd wl ins fnl f: kpt on* **16/1**

6406 **3** *2 ¾* **Miss Inga Sock (IRE)**[19] 6237 4-8-13 **58** .... SophieKilloran(7) 8 58
(Eve Johnson Houghton) *mid-div: pushed along over 2f out: hdwy over 1f out: sn edgd lft: styd on same pce ins fnl f* **12/1**

4300 **4** *3 ¾* **Russian Ranger (IRE)**[61] 4764 3-8-12 **59** .... (p) PaddyPilley(5) 11 51
(Jonathan Portman) *chsd ldrs: rdn over 2f out: nt clr run over 1f out: no ex ins fnl f* **25/1**

0040 **5** *½* **Captain Marmalade (IRE)**[19] 6241 4-9-7 **59** .... TimmyMurphy 16 49
(Jimmy Fox) *hld up: styd on fnl 2f: nt trble ldrs* **33/1**

062 **6** *2 ¼* **Touch Of Color**[21] 6187 3-8-9 **56** .... CharlieBennett(5) 14 41
(Jane Chapple-Hyam) *s.i.s: sn rcvrd into mid-div: hdwy u.p over 2f out: edgd lft and wknd ins fnl f* **7/1**

0040 **7** *2* **Glittering**[31] 5860 3-9-0 **56** ....[1] RyanTate 1 37
(James Eustace) *disp ld tl wnt on over 6f out: rdn and hdd over 3f out: wknd fnl f* **50/1**

6326 **8** *¾* **Indigo**[25] 6066 3-8-13 **58** .... JosephineGordon(3) 4 37
(Mark Usher) *chsd ldrs: rdn over 2f out: wknd fnl f* **11/1**

3140 **9** *1 ¼* **Miss Lillie**[14] 5085 5-9-2 **59** .... (p) GeorgeWood(5) 13 35
(Roger Teal) *hld up: hdwy over 2f out: rdn and wknd over 1f out* **16/1**

3411 **10** *5* **Mendacious Harpy (IRE)**[15] 6401 5-9-1 **53** .... (p) SteveDrowne 5 18
(George Baker) *prom: rdn over 3f out: wknd over 1f out* **6/1**[3]

5230 **11** *6* **Aye Aye Skipper (IRE)**[28] 5953 6-9-2 **54** .... PatDobbs 6 5
(Ken Cunningham-Brown) *trckd ldrs: rdn over 3f out: wknd 2f out* **14/1**

4401 **12** *2 ¼* **Candesta (USA)**[12] 6478 6-8-9 **54** .... LiamDoran(7) 9
(Julia Feilden) *hld up: rdn and wknd over 2f out* **12/1**

2233 **13** *nk* **Anneani (IRE)**[9] 6593 4-9-6 **58** .... SilvestreDeSousa 7 3
(David Evans) *hld up: pushed along over 3f out: sn wknd and eased* **4/1**[1]

5-20 **14** *11* **La Manga (IRE)**[259] 140 3-9-0 **56** .... WilliamCarson 3
(Jamie Osborne) *s.i.s: hld up: wknd 3f out* **22/1**

1m 44.46s (3.66) **Going Correction** +0.475s/f (Yiel)
WFA 3 from 4yo+ 4lb **14** Ran SP% **120.2**
Speed ratings (Par 101): **100,99,97,93,92 90,88,87,86,81 75,73,73,62**
CSF £71.49 CT £844.45 TOTE £5.60: £2.00, £6.30, £5.00; EX 105.80 Trifecta £2397.30.
Owner Gwyn Powell & Richard Meakes **Bred** Roundhill Stud **Trained** Ledbury, H'fords

FOCUS
Another moderate handicap, won by a quirky sort.

6827 CMS GROUP "BE HOPEFUL" H'CAP 1m 2f 46y

3:10 (3:10) (Class 6) (0-65,65) 3-Y-O+ **£2,264** (£673; £336; £168) **Stalls** Low

Form RPR

6400 **1** **Isis Blue**[15] 6365 6-9-8 **63** .... OisinMurphy 8 69
(Rod Millman) *a.p: chsd ldr 7f out: led over 2f out: rdn and hdd over 1f out: rallied to ld wl ins fnl f: jst hld on* **25/1**

0664 **2** *hd* **Dark Amber**[25] 6058 6-8-12 **56** .... (tp) EdwardGreatrex(3) 2 62
(Brendan Powell) *s.s: hld up: hdwy and carried rt over 1f out: edgd lft ins fnl f: r.o: nt quite rch wnr* **7/1**[3]

1242 **3** *½* **Fast And Hot (IRE)**[6] 6662 3-9-3 **64** .... (b[1]) KieranO'Neill 10 69
(Richard Hannon) *hld up: hdwy over 2f out: rdn over 1f out: ev ch wl ins fnl f: r.o* **9/2**[1]

4013 **4** *½* **Eugenic**[14] 6411 5-8-5 **53** .... LuluStanford(7) 14 57
(Rod Millman) *trckd ldrs: racd keenly: rdn to ld over 1f out: edgd lft and hdd wl ins fnl f* **10/1**

465 **5** *¾* **Daily News**[66] 4597 3-9-4 **65** .... (b[1]) AndreaAtzeni 5 68
(Roger Varian) *sn pushed along to chse ldrs: shkn up over 4f out: rdn over 2f out: edgd rt over 1f out: styng on u.p whn nt clr run towards fin* **6/1**[2]

4043 **6** *½* **Scent Of Power**[20] 6212 4-9-0 **55** .... SilvestreDeSousa 16 57
(Barry Leavy) *hld up: hdwy over 2f out: rdn over 1f out: no ex towards fin* **8/1**

0010 **7** *2 ¾* **Bob's Boy**[16] 6315 3-8-10 **57** .... (p) RenatoSouza 15 53
(Jose Santos) *sn led: rdn and hdd over 2f out: no ex wl ins fnl f* **6/1**[2]

2155 **8** *½* **Rajadamri**[7] 6626 3-8-11 **63** .... GeorgeWood(5) 3 60
(Rod Millman) *prom: rdn over 2f out: hmpd ent fnl f: no ex* **7/1**[3]

3352 **9** *11* **Golden Isles (IRE)**[39] 5571 3-8-10 **60** .... JosephineGordon(3) 6 35
(J S Moore) *hld up in tch: rdn over 3f out: wknd wl over 1f out* **14/1**

3053 **10** *13* **Evidence (FR)**[48] 5254 3-8-11 **65** .... RhiainIngram(7) 7 15
(Harry Dunlop) *prom: racd keenly: lost pl wl over 6f out: wknd over 3f out* **40/1**

0241 **11** *3* **Spinning Pearl (IRE)**[29] 5923 3-9-2 **63** .... JimCrowley 4 7
(Phil Middleton) *chsd ldr 3f: remained handy tl rdn over 2f out: wknd wl over 1f out* **8/1**

51-0 **12** *22* **Jersey Bull (IRE)**[19] 6241 4-9-7 **62** .... LiamKeniry 1
(Michael Madgwick) *s.i.s: hld up: pushed along over 4f out: wknd over 3f out* **50/1**

2m 15.07s (4.07) **Going Correction** +0.475s/f (Yiel)
WFA 3 from 4yo+ 6lb **12** Ran SP% **118.0**
Speed ratings (Par 101): **102,101,101,101,100 100,97,97,88,78 75,58**
CSF £188.68 CT £949.59 TOTE £26.00: £7.20, £2.70, £1.90; EX 272.60 Trifecta £1247.20.
Owner Cantay Racing **Bred** Mette Campbell-Andenaes **Trained** Kentisbeare, Devon

FOCUS
A modest handicap and a bunch finish. The winner didn't need to match the best of this year's form.

6828 DRIBUILD GROUP MAIDEN STKS — 1m 2f 46y
3:40 (3:40) (Class 5) 2-Y-O — **£3,234** (£962; £481; £240) **Stalls** Low

Form — RPR

342 **1** — **Spring Jig (USA)**[7] 6623 2-9-5 0 .... JimCrowley 5 — 80+
(Hugo Palmer) *hld up in tch: shkn up over 4f out: led over 1f out: edgd rt ins fnl f: pushed out* **11/8**[1]

35 **2** 1 3/4 **Jive Talking (IRE)**[65] 4642 2-8-11 0 .... LouisSteward(3) 3 — 70
(Michael Bell) *chsd ldrs: wnt 2nd over 2f out: rdn and ev ch over 1f out: styd on same pce ins fnl f* **2/1**[2]

6 **3** nk **Atkinson Grimshaw (FR)**[17] 6288 2-9-5 0 .... OisinMurphy 4 — 74
(Andrew Balding) *led: hdd over 4f out: led again over 3f out: rdn and hdd over 1f out: styd on same pce ins fnl f* **3/1**[3]

2066 **4** 18 **Yorkshire Star (IRE)**[9] 6588 2-9-5 51 ....(b) WilliamCarson 2 — 40
(Bill Turner) *chsd ldrs: led over 4f out: hdd over 3f out: sn rdn: wknd wl over 1f out: eased* **100/1**

6 **5** 11 **Rake's Progress**[100] 3404 2-9-5 0 .... LukeMorris 1 — 19
(Heather Main) *prom: pushed along over 4f out: wknd over 2f out* **16/1**

0 **6** 11 **Myhorsewithnoname (IRE)**[14] 6404 2-9-2 0 .... EoinWalsh(3) 6
(Natalie Lloyd-Beavis) *hld up: rdn over 5f out: wknd over 3f out* **100/1**

2m 14.91s (3.91) **Going Correction** +0.475s/f (Yiel) — **6** Ran SP% **108.3**
Speed ratings (Par 95): **103,101,101,86,78 69**
CSF £4.03 TOTE £2.10: £1.10, £1.90; EX 4.50 Trifecta £6.40.
Owner K Abdullah **Bred** Juddmonte Farms Inc **Trained** Newmarket, Suffolk

FOCUS
Basically a three-runner maiden. The field came closer to the stands' rail up the straight this time. There is more to come from the winner.

6829 NASH CONSULTANCY NURSERY H'CAP (DIV I) — 5f 161y
4:10 (4:10) (Class 5) (0-75,75) 2-Y-O — **£2,911** (£866; £432; £216) **Stalls** Centre

Form — RPR

1325 **1** — **Marquee Club**[23] 6139 2-9-3 **71** .... WilliamCarson 7 — 74
(Jamie Osborne) *trckd ldr: plld hrd: shkn up to ld and hung rt over 1f out: drvn out* **5/1**[3]

0412 **2** 1/2 **Maazel (IRE)**[9] 6564 2-9-7 **75** .... AndreaAtzeni 1 — 77
(Roger Varian) *hld up: hdwy u.p over 1f out: chsd wnr wl ins fnl f: r.o* **5/4**[1]

01 **3** 1/2 **Silver Penny**[21] 6189 2-8-9 **68** .... CharlieBennett(5) 5 — 68
(Jim Boyle) *chsd ldrs: led and hung rt wl over 1f out: sn rdn and hdd: styd on* **7/1**

0233 **4** 2 **Katrine (IRE)**[6] 6658 2-9-4 **72** .... JimCrowley 4 — 65
(William Knight) *hld up: hdwy 1/2-way: rdn and nt clr run 1f out: styd on same pce* **3/1**[2]

060 **5** 3/4 **Gala Celebration (IRE)**[21] 6189 2-8-10 **64** ....[1] MartinDwyer 10 — 56
(John Gallagher) *s.i.s: sn pushed along in rr: hdwy 2f out: rdn and nt clr run 1f out: styd on same pce* **33/1**

245 **6** 1/2 **The Night Is Ours (IRE)**[10] 6543 2-8-5 **62** .... JosephineGordon(3) 2 — 51
(J S Moore) *prom: pushed along 1/2-way: no ex ins fnl f* **16/1**

000 **7** nk **Gaia Princess (IRE)**[18] 6244 2-8-9 **68** .... HectorCrouch(5) 8 — 56
(Gary Moore) *racd keenly: led: rdn: hung rt and hdd wl over 1f out: no ex ins fnl f* **12/1**

2006 **8** 2 1/2 **Masquerade Bling (IRE)**[97] 3485 2-8-6 **63** .... RobHornby(3) 3 — 46
(Simon Hodgson) *sn pushed along in rr: sme hdwy whn nt clr run over 1f out: wknd ins fnl f* **33/1**

1m 12.64s (1.44) **Going Correction** +0.15s/f (Good) — **8** Ran SP% **118.1**
Speed ratings (Par 95): **96,95,94,92,91 90,89,86**
CSF £12.08 CT £43.70 TOTE £6.00: £1.90, £1.10, £3.10; EX 14.40 Trifecta £50.10.
Owner The London Partnership **Bred** Norman Court Stud, P Taplin & McB Ltd **Trained** Upper Lambourn, Berks

FOCUS
An ordinary nursery in which the runners gradually made their way right over to the stands' rail.

6830 NASH CONSULTANCY NURSERY H'CAP (DIV II) — 5f 161y
4:40 (4:40) (Class 5) (0-75,72) 2-Y-O — **£2,911** (£866; £432; £216) **Stalls** Centre

Form — RPR

3151 **1** — **Drop Kick Murphi (IRE)**[35] 5707 2-9-7 **72** .... SteveDrowne 8 — 80
(George Baker) *sn outpcd: hdwy over 1f out: rdn to ld ins fnl f: edgd lft: styd on* **7/2**[1]

004 **2** 1/2 **Foxcatcher**[24] 6078 2-9-3 **68** ....[1] JohnFahy 7 — 74
(Clive Cox) *prom: lost pl over 3f out: hdwy over 2f out: rdn over 1f out: ev ch ins fnl f: edgd lft: unable qck towards fin* **5/1**

4261 **3** 4 **Broadhaven Honey (IRE)**[12] 6477 2-9-7 **72** .... JimCrowley 5 — 65
(Ed McMahon) *w ldr tl led over 2f out: hdd & wknd ins fnl f* **9/2**[3]

3605 **4** 1/2 **Fair Selene**[25] 6060 2-8-9 **60** .... LukeMorris 9 — 51
(Heather Main) *sn pushed along in rr: hdwy u.p: nt clr run and edgd lft over 1f out: styd on same pce ins fnl f* **9/1**

054 **5** 3 1/2 **Incentive**[30] 5869 2-9-2 **67** .... LiamKeniry 2 — 47
(Stuart Kittow) *hld up: outpcd over 3f out: swtchd rt and hdwy over 1f out: wknd fnl f* **7/1**

2160 **6** 2 3/4 **Little Nosegay (IRE)**[15] 6388 2-8-7 **63** .... HollieDoyle(5) 3 — 34
(David Evans) *chsd ldrs: rdn 1/2-way: wknd ins fnl f* **6/1**

6631 **7** 4 **Precious Plum**[14] 6419 2-9-5 **70** .... SilvestreDeSousa 6 — 27
(Chris Dwyer) *prom: nt clr run and lost pl over 2f out: rdn whn nt clr run and hmpd over 1f out: sn wknd and eased* **4/1**[2]

0536 **8** 17 **Roundabout Magic (IRE)**[14] 6420 2-9-0 **65** .... NickyMackay 4
(Simon Dow) *led 3f: wknd over 1f out: eased* **16/1**

1m 11.61s (0.41) **Going Correction** +0.15s/f (Good) — **8** Ran SP% **119.7**
Speed ratings (Par 95): **103,102,97,96,91 88,82,60**
CSF £22.41 CT £81.64 TOTE £4.20: £1.20, £2.40, £2.20; EX 35.60 Trifecta £131.60.
Owner ININ Construction **Bred** Selman Tasbek **Trained** Manton, Wilts
■ Stewards' Enquiry : Nicky Mackay two-day ban: careless riding (10-11 Oct)

FOCUS
They went hard up front in this division, which played into the hands of the favourite, and the winning time was just over a second quicker than the first leg. Again they mostly came up the stands' side.

6831 THORN BAKER CONSTRUCTION RECRUITMENT CUP "HANDS AND HEELS" APPRENTICE H'CAP (RE INITIATIVE) — 5f 161y
5:10 (5:11) (Class 5) (0-75,75) 3-Y-O+ — **£2,911** (£866; £432; £216) **Stalls** Centre

Form — RPR

3512 **1** — **Equistar**[21] 6190 3-9-1 **71** ....(t) GeorgeWood 3 — 85
(Jonathan Portman) *prom: chsd ldr wl over 2f out: led over 1f out: shkn up and r.o wl: comf* **5/1**[2]

5642 **2** 3 **Showmethewayavrilo**[15] 6363 3-9-1 **71** .... CameronNoble 2 — 75
(Malcolm Saunders) *hld up: hdwy 1/2-way: pushed along to chse wnr fnl f: styd on same pce* **9/2**[1]

223 **3** 1/2 **Caitie (IRE)**[59] 4835 3-8-12 **71** ....(t) ManuelFernandes(3) 11 — 73
(Paul Cole) *hld up: swtchd lft wl over 2f out: hdwy over 1f out: styd on to go 3rd wl ins fnl f* **7/1**

6010 **4** 1 1/2 **Silverrica (IRE)**[17] 6296 6-9-7 **75** .... JaneElliott 5 — 72
(Malcolm Saunders) *led: pushed along and hdd over 1f out: no ex ins fnl f* **16/1**

0020 **5** nk **Rigolleto (IRE)**[13] 6461 8-8-12 **69** .... BenSanderson(3) 8 — 65
(Anabel K Murphy) *chsd ldrs: pushed along over 2f out: styd on same pce fnl f* **28/1**

3341 **6** shd **Toni's A Star**[16] 6311 4-8-10 **64** .... MillyNaseb 7 — 60
(Tony Carroll) *chsd ldrs: pushed along over 1f out: wknd wl ins fnl f* **11/1**

-051 **7** 3/4 **Oeil De Tigre (FR)**[96] 3510 5-9-0 **71** .... SophieRalston(3) 4 — 65
(Tony Carroll) *hld up in tch: racd keenly: pushed along and lost pl over 2f out: n.d after* **8/1**

4163 **8** hd **Peter Park**[21] 6190 3-8-13 **72** .... WilliamCox(3) 10 — 65+
(Clive Cox) *hld up: shkn up and nt clr run over 1f out: nt trble ldrs* **15/2**

3000 **9** 1 3/4 **Englishwoman**[18] 6255 3-8-13 **72** .... AledBeech(3) 13 — 59
(David Evans) *hld up: pushed along over 2f out: hdwy over 1f out: wknd ins fnl f* **25/1**

1405 **10** 1 3/4 **Ebony N Ivory**[14] 6409 3-9-2 **75** .... JoshuaBryan(3) 12 — 56
(Archie Watson) *hld up: pushed along and hdwy 2f out: wknd fnl f* **10/1**

2665 **11** 2 **Whitecrest**[14] 6410 8-8-13 **67** .... HollieDoyle 14 — 42
(John Spearing) *chsd ldrs: pushed along and lost pl over 3f out: wknd over 1f out* **20/1**

3053 **12** 2 3/4 **Monarch Maid**[12] 6487 5-9-4 **72** .... LuluStanford 15 — 38
(Peter Hiatt) *racd wd early: up w the pce: pushed along over 2f out: wknd over 1f out* **13/2**[3]

1m 11.38s (0.18) **Going Correction** +0.15s/f (Good)
WFA 3 from 4yo+ 2lb — **12** Ran SP% **118.9**
Speed ratings (Par 103): **104,100,99,97,96 96,95,95,93,90 88,84**
CSF £27.11 CT £162.46 TOTE £5.80: £2.30, £2.00, £1.90; EX 35.90 Trifecta £168.90.
Owner Mascalls Stud **Bred** Mascalls Stud **Trained** Upper Lambourn, Berks

FOCUS
An ordinary apprentices' handicap. Again they mainly came nearside, but the race ended up being dominated by those who raced more towards the centre, with the first two kept wide of their rivals early and cutting the corner as a result.

6832 BENTLEY BRISTOL H'CAP — 5f 11y
5:40 (5:44) (Class 5) (0-70,70) 3-Y-O+ — **£2,911** (£866; £432; £216) **Stalls** Centre

Form — RPR

3101 **1** — **Secretfact**[15] 6361 3-9-1 **65** .... JimmyQuinn 1 — 77+
(Malcolm Saunders) *hld up in tch: racd keenly: shkn up to ld 1f out: rdn out* **6/1**[2]

5013 **2** shd **Dusty Blue**[15] 6363 4-9-3 **66** .... TomMarquand 11 — 74
(Tony Carroll) *chsd ldrs: rdn over 1f out: r.o wl* **7/2**[1]

0321 **3** 2 1/4 **David's Beauty (IRE)**[29] 5920 3-8-11 **61** ....(p) LukeMorris 2 — 61
(Brian Baugh) *led: rdn and edgd rt over 1f out: sn hdd: styd on same pce ins fnl f* **9/1**

4640 **4** nk **Captain Ryan**[15] 6363 5-8-9 **58** .... OisinMurphy 7 — 57
(Geoffrey Deacon) *hld up: hdwy 1/2-way: rdn over 1f out: styd on same pce ins fnl f* **9/1**

4143 **5** 1 **Beau Mistral (IRE)**[16] 6312 7-8-7 **59** ....(p) GeorgeDowning(3) 9 — 54
(Tony Carroll) *stdd s: hld up: rdn and nt clr run over 1f out: r.o ins fnl f: nt rch ldrs* **12/1**

5220 **6** 3/4 **Catalinas Diamond (IRE)**[15] 6363 8-8-9 **58** oh1 ow2.(t) SteveDrowne 6 — 51
(Pat Murphy) *hld up: rdn 1/2-way: nt trble ldrs* **25/1**

2000 **7** shd **Dreams Of Glory**[15] 6363 8-9-3 **66** .... AdamBeschizza 4 — 58
(Ron Hodges) *w ldr tl pushed along 1/2-way: nt clr run over 1f out: no ex ins fnl f* **12/1**

0502 **8** 2 **Jaganory (IRE)**[16] 6311 4-8-0 **56** oh1 ....(v) LuluStanford(7) 14 — 41
(Christopher Mason) *chsd ldrs: rdn and nt clr run over 1f out: wknd ins fnl f* **12/1**

054 **9** nk **Angelito**[17] 6296 7-8-11 **63** .... EoinWalsh(3) 12 — 47
(Tony Newcombe) *in rr: pushed along over 3f out: nvr on terms* **15/2**[3]

4020 **10** 1 1/2 **Shine Likeadiamond**[15] 6361 3-8-3 **60** .... ManuelFernandes(7) 8 — 38
(Mick Channon) *in rr: pushed and hdwy over 2f out: nt clr run and wknd over 1f out* **16/1**

1m 2.41s (-0.09) **Going Correction** +0.15s/f (Good)
WFA 3 from 4yo+ 1lb — **10** Ran SP% **101.1**
Speed ratings (Par 103): **106,105,102,101,100 98,98,95,95,92**
CSF £20.59 CT £118.23 TOTE £4.50: £2.00, £1.10, £2.50; EX 16.60 Trifecta £43.20.
Owner Premier Conservatory Roofs **Bred** M S Saunders & D Collier **Trained** Green Ore, Somerset
■ Go Amber Go was withdrawn. Price at time of withdrawal 11/2. Rule 4 applies to all bets - deduction 15p in the pound.

FOCUS
A modest sprint handicap and again they came nearside.
T/Jkpt: Not won. T/Plt: £44.50 to a £1 stake. Pool: £66070.57, 1083.27 winning units T/Qpdt: £4.80 to a £1 stake. Pool: £8250.81, 1257.47 winning units **Colin Roberts**

6768 HAMILTON (R-H)
Monday, September 26

OFFICIAL GOING: Heavy (4.4)
Wind: Light, half behind Weather: Overcast

6833 TOTEPLACEPOT/BRITISH STALLION STUDS EBF MAIDEN STKS (PLUS 10 RACE) — 6f 6y
1:50 (1:50) (Class 4) 2-Y-O — **£4,269** (£1,270; £634; £317) **Stalls** High

Form — RPR

042 **1** — **Party Tiger**[45] 5377 2-9-5 73 .... TonyHamilton 7 — 73
(Richard Fahey) *pressed ldr: rdn to ld 1f out: styd on wl fnl f* **6/1**[3]

2 **2** 1 1/2 **Hee Haw (IRE)**[39] 5577 2-9-5 0 .... ConnorBeasley 8 — 69
(Keith Dalgleish) *led against stands' rail: rdn and hdd 1f out: rallied: kpt on same pce last 100yds* **7/1**

2230 **3** 1 1/2 **Perfect Symphony (IRE)**[39] 5583 2-9-5 78 .... KevinStott 4 — 64
(Kevin Ryan) *trckd ldrs on outside: drvn and effrt over 1f out: kpt on same pce ins fnl f* **9/5**[1]

4 2 1/2 **Tor** 2-9-5 0 .... JasonHart 2 — 57
(Keith Dalgleish) *dwlt: bhd and outpcd: struggling 1/2-way: hdwy fnl f: kpt on: nrst fin* **9/1**

5 *hd* **Love Power (IRE)** 2-9-5 0 .... PaulMulrennan 1 56
(Mark Johnston) *noisy in paddock: in tch: rn green and outpcd over 4f out: hdwy over 1f out: kpt on fnl f: no imp* **10/1**

6 3 ½ **Cryptonite (IRE)** 2-9-5 0 .... AndrewMullen 5 45+
(Michael Appleby) *noisy in paddock: dwlt: t.k.h and sn prom: rdn and wknd fr 2f out* **11/4**[2]

7 11 **Chinese Spirit (IRE)** 2-9-5 0 .... PJMcDonald 3 12
(R Mike Smith) *colty and v green thrght preliminaries: missed break: rn green and a struggling* **66/1**

1m 15.91s (3.71) **Going Correction** +0.525s/f (Yiel) **7** Ran SP% **109.8**
Speed ratings (Par 97): **96,94,92,88,88 83,69**
CSF £42.60 TOTE £5.40: £2.20, £3.50; EX 28.30 Trifecta £73.90.
Owner Andrew Tinkler **Bred** W A Tinkler **Trained** Musley Bank, N Yorks

FOCUS
Testing ground for a meeting that had to survive a morning inspection. The form of this opening maiden looks just fair and it has been rated around the winner.

6834 TOTEEXACTA FORECAST THE 1ST AND 2ND H'CAP (DIV I) 6f 6y
2:20 (2:22) (Class 6) (0-65,64) 3-Y-O+ **£3,234** (£962; £481; £240) **Stalls** Centre

Form RPR

5303 **1** **Full Of Promise**[13] 6436 3-8-13 **60** .... AdamMcNamara(5) 4 66
(Richard Fahey) *in tch: rdn over 3f out: rallied to chse wnr 2f out: kpt on fnl f to ld nr fin* **9/2**[3]

5253 **2** ½ **Slim Chance (IRE)**[7] 6616 7-8-12 **59** ....(v[1]) PaulaMuir(7) 7 63
(Simon West) *led: rdn over 2f out: edgd rt over 1f out: kpt on fnl f: hdd nr fin* **6/1**

0120 **3** *hd* **Someone Exciting**[24] 6100 3-9-0 **56** .... PatrickMathers 2 59
(David Thompson) *rn wout rt hind shoe: bhd: drvn and outpcd after 2f: rallied over 2f out: kpt on ins fnl f: hld nr fin* **17/2**

3414 **4** 2 ¼ **Wahaab (IRE)**[7] 6616 5-9-9 **63** ....(p) PJMcDonald 10 60
(Iain Jardine) *prom: rdn along over 2f out: outpcd appr fnl f* **7/2**[2]

0000 **5** 1 ½ **Ay Up Audrey**[7] 6615 5-8-5 **45** .... JamesSullivan 8 37
(Rebecca Bastiman) *hld up in tch: effrt and rdn over 2f out: wknd appr fnl f* **33/1**

0-02 **6** 3 **Shesnotforturning (IRE)**[7] 6615 6-8-10 **50** ....(p) TomEaves 6 33
(Ben Haslam) *chsd ldr to over 3f out: hung rt and wknd 2f out* **3/1**[1]

6330 **7** 5 **Cruise Tothelimit (IRE)**[13] 6451 8-9-10 **64** .... PaulMulrennan 9 32
(Patrick Morris) *trckd ldrs: wnt 2nd over 3f out to 2f out: sn rdn and wknd* **5/1**

1m 19.46s (7.26) **Going Correction** +1.00s/f (Soft)
WFA 3 from 5yo+ 2lb **7** Ran SP% **109.8**
Speed ratings (Par 101): **91,90,90,87,85 81,74**
CSF £28.58 CT £202.54 TOTE £4.70: £2.20, £2.70; EX 25.90 Trifecta £134.20.
Owner Richard Fahey Ebor Racing Club Ltd **Bred** Mrs Sheila Oakes **Trained** Musley Bank, N Yorks

FOCUS
A moderate sprint handicap run in awful ground.

6835 TOTEEXACTA FORECAST THE 1ST AND 2ND H'CAP (DIV II) 6f 6y
2:50 (2:51) (Class 6) (0-65,63) 3-Y-O+ **£3,234** (£962; £481; £240) **Stalls** Centre

Form RPR

0216 **1** **Reflation**[2] 6769 4-9-5 **58** 6ex ....(p) ConnorBeasley 6 67
(Michael Dods) *hld up on nr side of gp: pushed along and hdwy over 2f out: led ent fnl f: drvn clr* **4/1**[2]

6202 **2** 5 **Jacob's Pillow**[7] 6616 5-9-10 **63** .... DanielTudhope 10 57
(Rebecca Bastiman) *t.k.h: in tch: hdwy on nr side of gp and led over 2f out: rdn: edgd rt and hdd ent fnl f: kpt on: no ch w wnr* **2/1**[1]

0001 **3** 1 ¾ **Keene's Pointe**[7] 6615 6-9-10 **63** 6ex .... TonyHamilton 4 52
(Kristin Stubbs) *hld up in tch: rdn and hdwy 2f out: kpt on ins fnl f: nt pce to chal* **6/1**[3]

1604 **4** 2 ¾ **Shahaama**[17] 6291 3-9-7 **62** .... GrahamLee 1 43
(Mick Channon) *hld up on far side: stdy hdwy over 2f out: rdn and wknd appr fnl f* **8/1**

6006 **5** 1 **Amber Crystal**[1] 6813 4-8-7 **46** .... AndrewMullen 7 24
(Linda Perratt) *chsd ldrs: drvn along over 2f out: wknd fnl f* **25/1**

0003 **6** 3 **Hab Reeh**[30] 5889 8-9-1 **54** ....(p) JamesSullivan 2 23
(Ruth Carr) *hld up in tch: drvn and struggling over 2f out: n.d after* **10/1**

0030 **7** ¾ **Mr Conundrum**[13] 6436 3-8-7 **48** ow2 .... PJMcDonald 5 14
(Lynn Siddall) *dwlt: bhd: hdwy over 2f out: rdn and wknd over 1f out* **10/1**

6666 **8** ½ **Amis Reunis**[7] 6616 7-8-6 **45** .... ShaneGray 9 10
(Colin Teague) *led to over 2f out: sn rdn: wknd over 1f out* **16/1**

3661 **9** 1 ¾ **Mystical King**[2] 6774 6-8-12 **51** 6ex ....(p) JoeDoyle 3 11
(Linda Perratt) *chsd ldrs: drvn over 2f out: sn wknd: eased whn btn fnl f* **11/1**

1m 17.83s (5.63) **Going Correction** +1.00s/f (Soft)
WFA 3 from 4yo+ 2lb **9** Ran SP% **115.0**
Speed ratings (Par 101): **102,95,93,89,88 84,83,82,80**
CSF £12.33 CT £46.80 TOTE £4.20: £1.30, £1.50, £2.00; EX 14.20 Trifecta £73.20.
Owner Mrs C E Dods **Bred** Llety Farms **Trained** Denton, Co Durham

FOCUS
This second division was a weak affair and the winner has been rated back to his best.

6836 TOTEQUADPOT FOUR PLACES IN FOUR RACES CLASSIFIED CLAIMING STKS 6f 6y
3:20 (3:22) (Class 6) 3-Y-O+ **£3,234** (£962; £481; £240) **Stalls** Centre

Form RPR

3502 **1** **Gilmer (IRE)**[2] 6769 5-8-11 70 .... LewisEdmunds(7) 4 76
(Laura Young) *pressed ldr: led and rdn wl over 1f out: edgd lft ins fnl f: kpt on wl* **2/1**[1]

0000 **2** 1 ½ **In My Place**[13] 6435 3-8-8 67 ....(p) TonyHamilton 5 63
(Richard Fahey) *in tch: rdn and hung rt over 3f out: effrt over 1f out: chsd wnr ins fnl f: kpt on: no imp towards fin* **15/2**

0234 **3** 1 **Letbygonesbeicons**[11] 6522 3-8-3 58 .... RowanScott(5) 6 60
(Ann Duffield) *led to wl over 1f out: chsd wnr to ins fnl f: sn no ex* **10/3**[2]

6060 **4** *nk* **Bahamian Sunshine**[11] 6522 3-8-8 63 ....(p) PatrickMathers 7 59
(Richard Fahey) *trckd ldrs: effrt and rdn over 2f out: kpt on same pce fnl f* **6/1**

0521 **5** 6 **Picks Pinta**[27] 6008 5-8-7 66 ....(p) JordanUys(7) 2 45
(John David Riches) *dwlt: sn chsng ldrs: rdn over 2f out: wknd over 1f out* **4/1**[3]

006 **6** 12 **Be Bop Tango (FR)**[42] 5478 3-8-12 64 ....(p) DougieCostello 1 9
(K R Burke) *hld up in tch: struggling 1/2-way: lost tch fr 2f out* **14/1**

1m 18.08s (5.88) **Going Correction** +1.00s/f (Soft)
WFA 3 from 4yo+ 2lb **6** Ran SP% **109.1**
Speed ratings (Par 101): **100,98,96,96,88 72**
CSF £16.32 TOTE £3.00: £2.60, £1.70; EX 16.00 Trifecta £35.70.Gilmer was claimed by Brian Ellison for £10,000.
Owner Total Plumbing Supporters Club **Bred** Darley **Trained** Broomfield, Somerset

FOCUS
There was further rain on already testing ground. A modest claimer and low-grade form.

6837 TOTEPOOLLIVEINFO.COM/BRITISH STALLION STUDS EBF CONDITIONS STKS 6f 6y
3:50 (3:51) (Class 2) 3-Y-O+ **£16,185** (£4,846; £2,423; £1,211; £605) **Stalls** Centre

Form RPR

0043 **1** **Scrutineer (IRE)**[22] 6161 3-8-13 98 .... GrahamLee 4 106
(Mick Channon) *led 2f: pressed ldr: shkn up and regained ld over 1f out: drvn out fnl f* **3/1**[2]

0202 **2** 1 **Danzeno**[22] 6161 5-9-1 109 .... AndrewMullen 6 103
(Michael Appleby) *dwlt: sn rcvrd to chse ldr: led after 2f: rdn and hdd over 1f out: kpt on ins fnl f: nt rch wnr* **1/1**[1]

0006 **3** 4 ½ **Ninjago**[9] 6556 6-9-1 92 ....[1] PaulMulrennan 1 90
(Paul Midgley) *in tch: effrt and rdn 2f out: sn edgd rt: outpcd by first two fnl f* **7/1**

4005 **4** 3 **Taexali (IRE)**[19] 6230 3-8-13 0 .... JoeFanning 5 81
(John Patrick Shanahan, Ire) *t.k.h: trckd ldrs: pushed along over 2f out: wknd over 1f out* **10/1**

20-0 **5** 17 **Ascription (IRE)**[9] 6558 7-9-1 105 .... PhillipMakin 7 30
(Keith Dalgleish) *in tch: rdn and outpcd over 2f out: lost tch over 1f out: t.o* **6/1**[3]

1m 16.34s (4.14) **Going Correction** +1.00s/f (Soft)
WFA 3 from 5yo+ 2lb **5** Ran SP% **110.9**
Speed ratings (Par 109): **112,110,104,100,78**
CSF £6.51 TOTE £4.00: £1.80, £1.20; EX 7.00 Trifecta £24.70.
Owner Malih L Al Basti **Bred** Thomas Hassett **Trained** West Ilsley, Berks

FOCUS
The fifth straight 6f race on the card and easily the pick of them, but it only really concerned two horses.

6838 TOTETRIFECTA PICK THE 1,2,3 H'CAP 1m 67y
4:20 (4:21) (Class 5) (0-75,73) 3-Y-O+ **£3,881** (£1,155; £577; £288) **Stalls** Low

Form RPR

5352 **1** **Taking Libertys**[13] 6432 3-9-3 **70** ....(b) KevinStott 1 79
(Kevin Ryan) *missed break: sn rcvrd to chse ldrs: rdn to ld over 1f out: hung rt ins fnl f: hld on nr fin* **9/2**[1]

0206 **2** *nk* **Royal Holiday (IRE)**[56] 4930 9-9-5 **68** ....(p) SamJames 4 76
(Marjorie Fife) *led: rdn over 2f out: hdd over 1f out: rallied ins fnl f: kpt on: jst hld* **11/1**

4520 **3** ¾ **Rockwood**[56] 4930 5-9-9 **72** ....(v) GrahamLee 7 78
(Karen McLintock) *trckd ldrs: rdn over 2f out: kpt on ins fnl f* **12/1**

6043 **4** 10 **Dark Crystal**[2] 6772 5-9-3 **66** .... PaulMulrennan 10 51
(Linda Perratt) *hld up: rdn and hdwy over 2f out: plugged on fnl f: no ch w first three* **6/1**[2]

0620 **5** 2 ½ **Dasheen**[19] 6226 3-8-13 **66** .... JoeFanning 5 46
(Mark Johnston) *bhd: drvn and struggling 5f out: styd on fr over 1f out: nvr on terms* **9/1**

3040 **6** 2 ¼ **Eastern Dragon (IRE)**[22] 6160 6-9-3 **73** .... JamieGormley(7) 6 48
(Iain Jardine) *hld up: stdy hdwy over 3f out: rdn over 2f out: sn outpcd* **6/1**[2]

-050 **7** 3 ½ **Devious Spirit (IRE)**[13] 6434 4-8-13 **62** .... TonyHamilton 2 30
(Richard Fahey) *prom: drvn over 3f out: wknd fnl 2f* **16/1**

230 **8** 1 ¼ **Muroor**[58] 4871 3-9-2 **69** .... DanielTudhope 11 34
(David O'Meara) *midfield: lost grnd after 3f: rallied on outside over 2f out: sn wknd* **12/1**

1140 **9** 10 **Causey Arch (IRE)**[28] 5975 3-9-6 **73** ....(p) ConnorBeasley 9 17
(Michael Dods) *pressed ldr: rdn over 3f out: edgd both ways and wknd fr 2f out* **13/2**[3]

2310 **10** 1 ¼ **Dolphin Rock**[11] 6501 9-8-10 **66** ....(p) CallumRodriguez(7) 8 8
(Richard Ford) *in tch: drvn over 5f out: struggling fr 1/2-way: sn btn* **12/1**

2-34 **11** 7 **Cheers Buddy (IRE)**[39] 5576 8-8-10 **59** oh7 .... JackGarritty 3
(Lee Smyth, Ire) *hld up on ins: struggling over 3f out: sn wknd* **28/1**

4032 **12** 23 **Tectonic (IRE)**[7] 6620 7-8-13 **62** ....(v) JasonHart 12
(Keith Dalgleish) *stdd rr: struggling 1/2-way: sn lost tch: t.o* **10/1**

1m 56.87s (8.47) **Going Correction** +1.175s/f (Soft)
WFA 3 from 4yo+ 4lb **12** Ran SP% **119.9**
Speed ratings (Par 103): **104,103,102,92,90 88,84,83,73,72 65,42**
CSF £55.35 CT £573.16 TOTE £5.10: £2.30, £3.40, £4.00; EX 60.80 Trifecta £944.40.
Owner Hambleton Racing Ltd XXXVIII **Bred** Qatar Bloodstock Ltd **Trained** Hambleton, N Yorks

FOCUS
This was run over approximately 12yds further than advertised. The 1-2-3 raced 3-1-4 for much of the way and finished a long way clear, so few got involved.

6839 @TOTEPOOLRACING WIN TICKETS ON TWITTER APPRENTICE H'CAP 1m 1f 34y
4:55 (4:56) (Class 6) (0-60,60) 3-Y-O+ **£3,234** (£962; £481; £240) **Stalls** Low

Form RPR

0001 **1** **Amy Blair**[31] 5835 3-8-11 **50** .... ShirleyTeasdale 5 57
(Keith Dalgleish) *t.k.h early: mde all: clr to 1/2-way: rdn clr fr over 1f out: unchal* **13/2**

2420 **2** 3 **Penelope Pitstop**[17] 6307 4-9-2 **50** .... AdamMcNamara 4 50
(Lee Smyth, Ire) *chsd (clr) wnr: rdn and effrt over 2f out: one pce over 1f out* **10/3**[2]

2052 **3** 3 ¾ **Little Pippin**[7] 6621 3-8-9 **51** .... LewisEdmunds(3) 3 45
(Tony Coyle) *hld up: hdwy and prom over 3f out: rdn over 2f out: outpcd fr over 1f out* **11/4**[1]

5100 **4** 2 **Swiss Lait**[19] 6221 5-9-3 **59** .... PaulaMuir(8) 2 48+
(Patrick Holmes) *hld up in tch: rdn and outpcd 3f out: no imp fr 2f out* **16/1**

630 **5** 9 **Paddy's Rock (IRE)**[13] 6432 5-9-8 **56** .... CallumShepherd 7 27+
(Lynn Siddall) *dwlt: hld up: rdn and hdwy on outside over 3f out: rdn and wknd over 2f out* **4/1**[3]

-400 **6** 6 **Piper Bill**[24] 6103 5-8-5 **46** oh1 .... JamieGormley(7) 10 5
(Jim Goldie) *chsd ldrs: drvn and outpcd over 3f out: sn btn* **100/1**

2200 **7** 17 **Indian Giver**[7] 6621 8-9-5 **56** ....(p) JordanUys(3) 12 +
(John David Riches) *hld up: stdy hdwy 4f out: rdn and wknd over 2f out* **16/1**

2305 **8** 3 ½ **Big Red**[7] 6621 4-8-12 **46** oh1 .... RowanScott 11
(Rebecca Bastiman) *s.v.s: bucking and kicking early: t.o thrght* **6/1**

2m 12.06s (12.36) **Going Correction** +1.50s/f (Heav)
WFA 3 from 4yo+ 5lb **8** Ran SP% **110.1**
Speed ratings (Par 101): **105,102,99,97,89 83,68,65**
CSF £26.29 CT £68.13 TOTE £7.30: £1.90, £1.90, £1.10; EX 25.50 Trifecta £89.00.
Owner J Fyffe **Bred** Summertree Stud **Trained** Carluke, S Lanarks

The Form Book, Raceform Ltd, Newbury, RG14 5SJ

FOCUS
This was run over approximately 12yds further than advertised. Again it proved hard to make ground, the winner dominating and the runner-up leading the chasing pack.

6840 TOTEPOOLRACING FIND US ON INSTAGRAM H'CAP 1m 4f 14y
5:25 (5:25) (Class 5) (0-70,67) 3-Y-O+ **£3,881** (£1,155; £577; £288) **Stalls** Low

Form RPR
3342 **1** **Rockthenunway (IRE)**[11] 6503 7-10-0 **67**.................(b) ConnorBeasley 1 75
(Michael Dods) *mde all: reminders and rdn 4f out: edgd lft but kpt on strly to draw clr fr 2f out* **11/4**[1]
0162 **2** *6* **Kelvin Hall**[54] 5012 3-8-13 **60**.......................... JoeFanning 7 59
(Mark Johnston) *in tch: hdwy to chse wnr over 3f out: rdn and hung rt fr over 2f out: no imp over 1f out* **6/1**[3]
-150 **3** *8* **Thackeray**[13] 6438 9-8-2 **48** oh1.......................... PaulaMuir(7) 4 35
(Chris Fairhurst) *hld up: struggling over 4f out: rallied 2f out: tk modest 3rd ins fnl f: no ch w first two* **22/1**
3244 **4** *2* **Qibtee (FR)**[26] 6029 6-9-3 **56**.......................... PaulMulrennan 2 40
(Les Eyre) *trckd ldrs: drvn along over 3f out: outpcd over 2f out: hung rt over 1f out: sn no imp: btn fnl f* **10/1**
3165 **5** *3/4* **Young Tom**[33] 5761 3-9-3 **64**.......................... AndrewMullen 6 47
(Michael Appleby) *t.k.h early: pressed wnr to over 3f out: drvn and outpcd ins fnl f: wknd and lost two pls ins fnl f: fin tired* **11/4**[1]
6302 **6** *10* **Allfredandnobell (IRE)**[29] 5921 3-8-7 **54**.......................... PJMcDonald 3 22
(Micky Hammond) *in tch: drvn and struggling over 3f out: sn btn* **5/1**[2]
0004 **7** *25* **Champagne Rules**[7] 6619 5-8-6 **50**.................(t) PhilDennis(5) 8
(Sharon Watt) *missed break: hld up: rdn along 4f out: lost tch fr 2f out* **6/1**[3]

2m 55.53s (16.93) **Going Correction** +1.50s/f (Heav)
WFA 3 from 5yo+ 8lb **7** Ran SP% **112.0**
Speed ratings (Par 103): **103,99,93,92,91 85,68**
CSF £18.89 CT £291.54 TOTE £3.60: £1.60, £3.50; EX 11.50 Trifecta £177.30.
Owner Sedgewick,Dods,Sunley Racing Partnership **Bred** J Hanly, A Stroud And T Stewart **Trained** Denton, Co Durham

FOCUS
This was run over approximately 12yds further than advertised. All three races on the round course were won by forwardly placed runners, this one being the second to do it from the front.
T/Plt: £98.20 to a £1 stake. Pool: £70,813.06, 526.07 winning units T/Qpdt: £6.50 to a £1 stake. Pool: £6,702.21, 761.67 winning units **Richard Young**

6841a (Foreign Racing) - See Raceform Interactive

6554 AYR (L-H)
Tuesday, September 27

6842 Meeting Abandoned - waterlogged

6586 WOLVERHAMPTON (A.W) (L-H)
Tuesday, September 27

OFFICIAL GOING: Tapeta: standard
Wind: Fresh behind Weather: Cloudy with sunny spells

6850 FCL GLOBAL FORWARDING MAKING LOGISTICS PERSONAL MAIDEN STKS 7f 32y (Tp)
5:40 (5:42) (Class 5) 2-Y-O **£3,234** (£962; £481; £240) **Stalls** High

Form RPR
0 **1** **Quinteo (IRE)**[21] 6211 2-9-5 0.......................... PatCosgrave 8 71
(Jo Hughes) *sn led: hdd over 5f out: chsd ldr: rdn to ld ins fnl f: styd on* **12/1**
2 *nk* **El Cap (USA)** 2-9-5 0.......................... TedDurcan 4 70+
(Sir Michael Stoute) *sn pushed along and prom: lost pl over 4f out: rdn over 2f out: hdwy over 1f out: r.o wl* **6/1**[3]
4 **3** *nk* **Redicean**[25] 6071 2-9-5 0.......................... JamesDoyle 1 70
(Peter Chapple-Hyam) *w ldr tl over 5f out: remained handy: rdn over 2f out: r.o* **8/15**[1]
4 *1/2* **Gmaash** 2-8-11 0.......................... EdwardGreatrex(3) 10 63+
(Saeed bin Suroor) *hdwy to ld over 5f out: rdn and hdd ins fnl f: no ex nr fin* **4/1**[2]
5 *2 1/4* **Mamdood (IRE)** 2-9-5 0.......................... PaulHanagan 9 63
(Richard Hannon) *s.i.s: hdwy over 4f out: rdn over 1f out: edgd lft and styd on same pce fnl f* **12/1**
6 *11* **Spello (IRE)** 2-9-5 0.......................... DannyBrock 3 36
(John Ryan) *prom tl rdn and wknd over 2f out* **50/1**
0 **7** *1 1/4* **French Silver (FR)**[42] 5524 2-8-11 0.......................... GeorgeDowning(3) 5 28
(Tony Carroll) *s.i.s: rdn and wknd over 2f out* **80/1**
8 *18* **See You After (IRE)** 2-9-5 0.......................... LukeMorris 6
(Sir Mark Prescott Bt) *s.i.s: sn pushed along and a in rr: rdn and wknd over 2f out* **18/1**

1m 28.45s (-0.35) **Going Correction** -0.10s/f (Stan) **8** Ran SP% **123.4**
Speed ratings (Par 95): **98,97,97,96,94 81,80,59**
CSF £87.78 TOTE £17.70: £2.50, £1.20, £1.10; EX 124.50 Trifecta £309.90.
Owner Richard and Nicola Hunt & Jo Hughes **Bred** Platasava Partnership **Trained** Lambourn, Berks

FOCUS
A bit of a punt was landed in this maiden, but the form looks fluid.

6851 WILLIAM BEARDSHAW "NOT FORGOTTEN" MEMORIAL FILLIES' H'CAP 7f 32y (Tp)
6:10 (6:11) (Class 5) (0-70,70) 3-Y-O+ **£3,234** (£962; £481; £240) **Stalls** High

Form RPR
0400 **1** **Arize (IRE)**[67] 4604 3-9-0 **63**.......................... PatCosgrave 3 70
(David Brown) *mde all: rdn over 1f out: edgd rt ins fnl f: styd on u.p* **50/1**
220 **2** *1* **Invade (IRE)**[19] 6269 4-9-4 **67**.................(t) AaronJones(3) 2 72
(Stuart Williams) *chsd ldrs: rdn to chse wnr ins fnl f: styd on* **12/1**
6041 **3** *shd* **Luang Prabang (IRE)**[10] 6592 3-9-2 **68**.......................... LouisSteward(3) 7 75+
(Chris Wall) *awkward leaving stalls: hld up: shkn up over 2f out: hdwy over 1f out: rdn and r.o wl towards fin* **4/1**[1]
-223 **4** *nk* **Polymnia**[36] 5711 3-9-1 **69**.......................... HollieDoyle(5) 5 72
(Richard Hannon) *plld hrd and prom: rdn over 2f out: styd on* **14/1**
4013 **5** *nse* **Enjoy Life (IRE)**[21] 6215 3-9-0 **63**.......................... SilvestreDeSousa 4 66
(Kevin Ryan) *chsd wnr: rdn over 2f out: styd on* **4/1**[1]
5343 **6** *3/4* **Aberlady (USA)**[30] 5935 3-9-4 **67**.......................... TedDurcan 9 68+
(Sir Michael Stoute) *hld up: racd keenly: hdwy and swtchd lft over 1f out: styd on* **7/1**[2]
1443 **7** *hd* **Anastazia**[12] 6510 4-9-10 **70**.......................... LukeMorris 12 71+
(Paul D'Arcy) *hld up: rdn over 2f out: hdwy over 1f out: styd on: nt rch ldrs* **10/1**
3144 **8** *1/2* **Helfire**[20] 6237 3-8-13 **67**.......................... CharlieBennett(5) 10 66
(Hughie Morrison) *chsd ldrs: rdn over 2f out: styd on same pce ins fnl f* **17/2**
2036 **9** *1 1/4* **Bush Beauty (IRE)**[15] 6426 5-8-10 **63**.......................... SophieKilloran(7) 1 59
(Eric Alston) *mid-div: hdwy over 1f out: no ex ins fnl f* **8/1**[3]
0015 **10** *1/2* **Dance Band (IRE)**[22] 6182 3-9-1 **64**.......................... HarryBentley 6 58
(Roger Varian) *hld up: rdn 1/2-way: hung lft over 1f out: nvr on terms* **17/2**
0-05 **11** *1 3/4* **Prisom (IRE)**[98] 3496 3-9-0 **63**.......................... TomMarquand 8 52
(Gay Kelleway) *s.i.s: hld up: hdwy over 1f out: wknd ins fnl f* **40/1**
100 **12** *11* **Doeadeer (IRE)**[15] 6426 3-9-3 **66**..........................[1] JimCrowley 11 26
(Keith Dalgleish) *hld up: rdn over 2f out: sn wknd and eased* **28/1**

1m 27.96s (-0.84) **Going Correction** -0.10s/f (Stan)
WFA 3 from 4yo+ 3lb **12** Ran SP% **116.0**
Speed ratings (Par 100): **100,98,98,98,98 97,97,96,95,94 92,80**
CSF £553.61 CT £2991.06 TOTE £46.30: £13.40, £4.60, £1.50; EX 943.40 Trifecta £6540.00.
Owner Mrs Sandra Brown & Mrs Ann Harrison **Bred** Peter Onslow & T Whelan **Trained** Averham Park, Notts

FOCUS
A modest fillies' handicap dictated by the winner from the front. The winner was down to a fair mark on her best form.

6852 FCL GLOBAL FORWARDING MAKING LOGISTICS PERSONAL H'CAP (DIV I) 5f 216y (Tp)
6:40 (6:41) (Class 6) (0-55,55) 3-Y-O+ **£2,587** (£770; £288; £288) **Stalls** Low

Form RPR
-001 **1** **Robbie Roo Roo**[31] 5889 3-9-5 **55**.................(vt) SaleemGolam 8 63
(Mrs Ilka Gansera-Leveque) *sn chsng ldrs: rdn to ld ins fnl f: r.o* **9/2**[1]
-000 **2** *1/2* **Rock Warbler (IRE)**[10] 6592 3-9-5 **55**.................(t[1]) PaulHanagan 6 62+
(Oliver Greenall) *s.i.s: hld up: nt clr run over 1f out: shkn up and r.o wl ins fnl f: nt rch wnr* **16/1**
2010 **3** *3/4* **Whipphound**[12] 6509 8-9-6 **54**.................(p) JamesSullivan 13 58
(Ruth Carr) *sn chsng ldr: led wl over 1f out: rdn and hdd ins fnl f: styd on same pce* **9/1**[3]
2300 **3** *dht* **Krazy Paving**[73] 4389 4-8-10 **51**.................(b) JoshuaBryan(7) 7 55
(Anabel K Murphy) *mid-div: hdwy over 1f out: r.o: nt rch ldrs* **8/1**[2]
6253 **5** *1 1/4* **Dream Ally (IRE)**[53] 5127 6-9-7 **55**.................(be) LukeMorris 9 55
(John Weymes) *broke wl and led: lost pl: sn stdd but remained handy: rdn over 2f out: edgd rt ins fnl f: styd on u.p* **9/2**[1]
1002 **6** *1 3/4* **Whispering Soul (IRE)**[10] 6586 3-9-5 **55**.................(p) PatCosgrave 1 50
(Brian Baugh) *plld hrd and prom: rdn over 1f out: swvd lft and no ex ins fnl f* **9/2**[1]
3160 **7** *hd* **Topsoil**[16] 6363 3-8-8 **49**.......................... CiaranMckee(5) 10 43
(Ronald Harris) *s.s: hld up: racd keenly: rdn over 1f out: nt clr run ins fnl f: nvr nrr* **16/1**
0350 **8** *shd* **Bushwise (IRE)**[81] 4085 3-8-8 **47**.................(p) JosephineGordon(3) 3 41
(Milton Bradley) *s.i.s: sn rcvrd into mid-div: hdwy over 1f out: styd on same pce ins fnl f* **9/1**[3]
4000 **9** *1 3/4* **Whispering Wolf**[25] 6105 3-8-8 **47**.......................... JacobButterfield(3) 5 36
(Suzzanne France) *prom: rdn over 2f out: wknd ins fnl f* **28/1**
0040 **10** *nse* **Magic Garden (IRE)**[38] 5628 3-9-2 **52**.................(t) RyanTate 11 40
(Jonathan Portman) *sn pushed along in rr: nvr on terms* **10/1**
605 **11** *1/2* **Diamond Vine (IRE)**[17] 6312 8-9-2 **50**.................(p) ShaneKelly 2 37
(Ronald Harris) *s.i.s: sn pushed along and a in rr* **9/1**[3]
2050 **12** *1/2* **Gabbys Lad (IRE)**[8] 6631 3-8-12 **48**.......................... NeilFarley 12 33
(Eric Alston) *led: rdn and hdd wl over 1f out: wknd fnl f* **33/1**

1m 14.6s (0.10) **Going Correction** -0.10s/f (Stan)
WFA 3 from 4yo+ 2lb **12** Ran SP% **122.9**
Speed ratings (Par 101): **95,94,93,93,91 89,89,88,86,86 85,85**
WIN: 5.80 Robbie Roo Roo; PL: 1.60 Whipphound, 4.40 Rock Warbler, 2.40 Robbie Roo Roo, 1.80 Krazy Paving; EX: 63.10; CSF: 86.59; TC: 287.58, 324.29; TF: 340.70, 254.30;.
Owner Mrs I Gansera-Leveque **Bred** John James **Trained** Newmarket, Suffolk

FOCUS
A moderate heat, but the winner looks progressive.

6853 FCL GLOBAL FORWARDING MAKING LOGISTICS PERSONAL H'CAP (DIV II) 5f 216y (Tp)
7:10 (7:12) (Class 6) (0-55,55) 3-Y-O+ **£1,678** (£1,678; £384; £192) **Stalls** Low

Form RPR
6604 **1** **Equal Point**[10] 6587 3-9-4 **54**.......................... JimCrowley 8 61
(William Knight) *chsd ldrs: rdn to ld and hung lft ins fnl f: jnd towards fin* **9/1**[3]
0144 **1** *dht* **Kaaber (USA)**[17] 6311 5-9-2 **50**.................(b) TomMarquand 6 57
(Roy Brotherton) *chsd ldrs: rdn and edgd lft ins fnl f: r.o to join wnr towards fin* **16/1**
6050 **3** *1 1/2* **Fossa**[33] 5808 6-8-8 **47**.......................... CharlieBennett(5) 11 50
(Mark Brisbourne) *hld up: hdwy over 1f out: r.o to go 3rd nr fin* **25/1**
0332 **4** *nk* **Coolcalmcollected (IRE)**[10] 6568 4-9-6 **54**.........(p) SilvestreDeSousa 5 56
(David Loughnane) *sn w ldr: led 2f out: rdn over 1f out: hdd and edgd lft ins fnl f: styd on same pce* **7/4**[1]
2145 **5** *1 3/4* **Wedgewood Estates**[51] 5194 5-9-7 **55**.......................... AdamKirby 7 55
(Tony Carroll) *prom: lost pl after 1f: hdwy whn nt clr run and swtchd rt 1f out: r.o: nt rch ldrs* **9/2**[2]
0000 **6** *1/2* **Top Cop**[75] 4290 7-8-12 **46** oh1.................(p) ShaneKelly 4 41
(Ronald Harris) *mid-div: racd keenly: hdwy over 1f out: styd on same pce ins fnl f* **18/1**
066 **7** *1/2* **Dark Phantom (IRE)**[17] 6311 5-8-7 **46** oh1..................[1] PaddyPilley(5) 2 40
(Geoffrey Deacon) *sn led: rdn and hdd 2f out: carried lft and no ex ins fnl f* **25/1**
5000 **8** *1* **Eland Ally**[10] 6587 8-8-12 **53**.................(v) JoshuaBryan(7) 10 44
(Anabel K Murphy) *hld up: rdn over 2f out: r.o ins fnl f: nvr nrr* **50/1**
2300 **9** *hd* **Secret Interlude (IRE)**[41] 5554 3-8-11 **52**.................. LucyKBarry(5) 12 42
(Jamie Osborne) *in tch but sn pushed along: lost pl after 1f: n.d after* **16/1**
0530 **10** *1/2* **Sakhee's Rose**[25] 6100 6-9-2 **53**.................(b) RobHornby(3) 1 45
(Ed McMahon) *hld up: hdwy over 1f out: styng on whn nt clr run ins fnl f: nt rcvr* **10/1**
5043 **11** *nk* **Kenstone (FR)**[19] 6249 3-9-1 **51**.................(p) LukeMorris 13 39
(David Dennis) *sn chsng ldrs: rdn over 2f out: wknd fnl f* **14/1**

0641 **12** *1* **Burauq**[17] 6312 4-9-0 **51** (b) JosephineGordon(3) 9 36
(Milton Bradley) *chsd ldrs: lost pl over 4f out: rdn over 2f out: wknd over 1f out* **10/1**

1m 13.63s (-0.87) **Going Correction** -0.10s/f (Stan)
WFA 3 from 4yo+ 2lb **12** Ran SP% **116.1**
Speed ratings (Par 101): **101,101,99,98,96 95,94,93,93,92 92,90**
WIN: EQ £3.70, K £8.50; PL: EQ £2.30, K £5.10 EX: EQ/K £30.50; K/EQ £86.20 CSF: EQ/K £68.99, K/EQ £73.54; TC: EQ/K/F £1,739.53, K/EQ/F £1805.90; TF: EQ/K/F £1,622.00, K/EQ/F £2,024.40;.
Owner Angmering Park Thoroughbreds III et al **Bred** Mrs Susan Cole & Miss Lesley McGrath **Trained** Patching, W Sussex
Owner Jeremy Holt **Bred** Shadwell Farm LLC **Trained** Elmley Castle, Worcs

FOCUS
The first two raced alongside each other behind the leaders and finished in similar style, and the judge couldn't split them at the line. It was the quicker of the two divisions by 0.97sec. Ordinary form.

6854 FCLGF.COM H'CAP 1m 5f 194y (Tp)
7:40 (7:40) (Class 4) (0-85,85) 3-Y-O+ **£5,175** (£1,540; £769; £384) **Stalls** Low

Form RPR
1631 **1** **Royal Reef (IRE)**[10] 6591 4-9-9 **80** (v) JimmyQuinn 5 87+
(William Knight) *chsd ldr: rdn to ld over 1f out: styd on u.p: edgd lft nr fin* **3/1**[2]

340 **2** *1* **Marshall Aid (IRE)**[36] 5724 3-8-0 **67** oh1 KieranO'Neill 2 72
(Mark Usher) *chsd ldrs: rdn over 3f out: styd on to go 2nd nr fin* **16/1**

-364 **3** *½* **Al**[21] 6209 4-9-9 **80** AdamKirby 7 88+
(Luca Cumani) *hld up: rdn over 3f out: hdwy over 1f out: hung lft ins fnl f: styd on to go 3rd post* **11/4**[1]

460 **4** *shd* **Plutocracy (IRE)**[29] 5964 6-10-0 **85** (p) SaleemGolam 1 89
(Gary Moore) *led at stdy pce: qcknd over 3f out: rdn and hdd over 1f out: no ex towards fin* **8/1**

5601 **5** *4* **Be Perfect (USA)**[10] 6565 7-9-10 **81** (b) JamesSullivan 3 80
(Ruth Carr) *hld up in tch: rdn over 2f out: no ex ins fnl f* **7/1**

5533 **6** *3* **Sbraase**[24] 6142 5-9-12 **83** MartinHarley 9 77
(James Tate) *s.i.s: hld up: sme hdwy u.p over 1f out: wknd ins fnl f* **5/1**[3]

00-4 **7** *1 ¼* **Devon Drum**[26] 6050 8-9-5 **76** (t) PatCosgrave 6 69
(David Brown) *prom: pushed along over 6f out: rdn over 4f out: wknd over 1f out* **17/2**

2660 **8** *18* **Eutropius (IRE)**[23] 6160 7-9-2 **73** SilvestreDeSousa 10 40
(Alan Swinbank) *s.i.s: hld up: rdn and wknd over 2f out* **14/1**

2m 58.92s (-5.88) **Going Correction** -0.10s/f (Stan)
WFA 3 from 4yo+ 10lb **8** Ran SP% **115.0**
Speed ratings (Par 105): **112,111,111,111,108 107,106,96**
CSF £48.87 CT £145.93 TOTE £3.70: £1.30, £4.00, £1.50; EX 48.50 Trifecta £242.80.
Owner W J Knight **Bred** Herbertstown House Stud **Trained** Patching, W Sussex

FOCUS
A fair handicap with the principals always handy.

6855 FCL GLOBAL FORWARDING MAKING LOGISTICS PERSONAL MEDIAN AUCTION MAIDEN STKS 1m 141y (Tp)
8:10 (8:10) (Class 6) 3-5-Y-O **£2,587** (£770; £384; £192) **Stalls** Low

Form RPR
4455 **1** **Silhouette (IRE)**[8] 6629 3-9-5 70 RichardKingscote 5 74
(Daniel Kubler) *edgd rt s: chsd ldrs: wnt 2nd over 3f out: led over 2f out: rdn over 1f out: all out* **15/8**[2]

0232 **2** *hd* **Best Laid Plans**[39] 5608 3-9-0 71 [1] LukeMorris 1 68
(James Tate) *prom: rdn over 2f out: chsd wnr over 1f out: hung lft ins fnl f: r.o u.p* **10/11**[1]

6002 **3** *8* **Ten Rocks**[27] 6036 3-8-12 64 JordanUys(7) 6 54
(Lisa Williamson) *hmpd s: led after 1f: rdn and hdd over 2f out: wknd ins fnl f* **12/1**

5 **4** *2 ¾* **Annoushka**[46] 5380 3-9-0 0 (t) SaleemGolam 3 43
(Mrs Ilka Gansera-Leveque) *hld up: hdwy on outer over 2f out: sn rdn and wknd* **11/1**[3]

5000 **5** *1 ¼* **Miss Fortune**[13] 6485 3-9-0 43 KieranO'Neill 4 40
(Mark Usher) *s.i.s: hld up: hdwy wl over 1f out: sn rdn: edgd lft and wknd* **100/1**

6 *6* **Poetic Queen (IRE)** 3-9-0 0 JasonHart 2 26
(Eric Alston) *sn led: hdd over 7f out: chsd ldr tl over 3f out: rdn and wknd over 1f out* **16/1**

1m 48.51s (-1.59) **Going Correction** -0.10s/f (Stan) **6** Ran SP% **110.1**
Speed ratings (Par 101): **103,102,95,93,92 86**
CSF £3.72 TOTE £3.50: £1.50, £1.10; EX 4.10 Trifecta £12.10.
Owner Titan Assets **Bred** Oghill House Stud **Trained** Lambourn, Berks

FOCUS
This looked a two-horse race on paper and sure enough they had it between them from the top of the straight. A muddling race and weak form.

6856 FCLGF.COM FILLIES' H'CAP 1m 1f 103y (Tp)
8:40 (8:40) (Class 5) (0-75,78) 3-Y-O+ **£3,234** (£962; £481; £240) **Stalls** Low

Form RPR
1411 **1** **You're A Goat**[28] 5994 3-9-6 **74** AdamKirby 6 84+
(Gary Moore) *hld up: hdwy u.p over 1f out: hung lft and led wl ins fnl f: drvn out* **9/4**[1]

0262 **2** *nk* **Wings Of Esteem (IRE)**[7] 6656 3-9-3 **71** JimmyQuinn 1 79
(Martin Smith) *hld up in tch: shkn up to ld over 1f out: rdn and hdd wl ins fnl f: r.o* **3/1**[2]

004 **3** *3* **Pray For Paris**[36] 5723 3-9-0 **71** JosephineGordon(3) 3 73+
(Martyn Meade) *s.i.s and sn pushed along in rr: rdn over 2f out: r.o ins fnl f: wnt 3rd post* **11/2**[3]

1243 **4** *hd* **Livella Fella (IRE)**[12] 6504 3-9-7 **75** PhillipMakin 8 76
(Keith Dalgleish) *led: rdn over 2f out: hdd over 1f out: no ex ins fnl f* **7/1**

4632 **5** *nse* **Shadow Spirit**[32] 5822 3-9-2 **70** JimCrowley 5 71
(Iain Jardine) *prom: rdn over 2f out: styng on same pce whn nt clr run ins fnl f* **17/2**

-056 **6** *3 ¾* **Tranquil Time**[20] 6242 3-9-1 **69** MartinHarley 7 62
(James Tate) *chsd ldr: rdn over 2f out: wknd ins fnl f* **9/1**

0030 **7** *6* **So Much Fun (IRE)**[42] 5525 3-9-1 **69** SilvestreDeSousa 2 50
(Ismail Mohammed) *chsd ldrs: rdn over 2f out: wknd fnl f* **8/1**

1m 59.58s (-1.22) **Going Correction** -0.10s/f (Stan) **7** Ran SP% **115.3**
Speed ratings (Par 100): **101,100,98,97,97 94,89**
CSF £9.33 CT £31.98 TOTE £3.20: £1.80, £1.70; EX 10.10 Trifecta £51.90.
Owner Power Geneva Ltd **Bred** Mrs James Wigan **Trained** Lower Beeding, W Sussex
■ Stewards' Enquiry : Adam Kirby two-day ban (11-12 Oct): used whip without giving time to respond

FOCUS
The first three home raced in the last three places for most of the race. The winner continues to progress.

6857 PERSONAL LOGISTICS FROM FCL GLOBAL FORWARDING H'CAP 1m 4f 103y (Tp)
9:10 (9:10) (Class 6) (0-60,60) 3-Y-O+ **£2,587** (£770; £384; £192) **Stalls** Low

Form RPR
5500 **1** **Ice Alert (IRE)**[7] 6662 3-9-5 **60** AdamKirby 2 71+
(John Ryan) *chsd ldrs: rdn to ld over 1f out: drvn clr fnl f: eased nr fin* **6/1**[2]

0064 **2** *5* **Shift On Sheila**[12] 6513 3-9-0 **58** RobHornby(3) 7 59
(Pam Sly) *chsd ldr tl led over 2f out: rdn and hdd over 1f out: no ex ins fnl f* **13/2**[3]

0005 **3** *shd* **Cahar Fad (IRE)**[39] 5610 4-9-0 **50** (bt) AdamBeschizza 3 50
(Steph Hollinshead) *chsd ldrs: rdn over 2f out: styd on same pce fnl f* **6/1**[2]

5055 **4** *1 ¼* **Pensax Lady (IRE)**[13] 6478 3-8-9 **50** LukeMorris 6 48+
(Daniel Mark Loughnane) *hld up in tch: rdn over 2f out: styd on same pce fnl f* **5/1**[1]

0400 **5** *¾* **Ferryview Place**[55] 5011 7-8-8 **51** (p) LukeCatton(7) 13 47+
(Ian Williams) *hld up: rdn over 2f out: nt trble ldrs* **8/1**

0600 **6** *¾* **Ormering**[7] 6646 3-8-6 **47** (p) KieranO'Neill 5 43
(Roger Teal) *plld hrd and prom: rdn over 1f out: wknd ins fnl f* **33/1**

4-00 **7** *nk* **Stamp Duty (IRE)**[29] 5971 8-8-7 **46** oh1 JacobButterfield(3) 9 42+
(Suzzanne France) *hld up: rdn whn hmpd over 1f out: n.d* **16/1**

5333 **8** *hd* **Maverik**[15] 6405 8-9-8 **58** (vt) PatCosgrave 12 52+
(Ali Stronge) *s.i.s: hld up: rdn over 1f out: nvr on terms* **7/1**

3110 **9** *hd* **Mount Cheiron (USA)**[24] 6137 5-9-1 **58** (p) CallumRodriguez(7) 1 53+
(Richard Ford) *s.i.s: hld up: nt clr run over 2f out: hdwy over 1f out: no ex fnl f* **10/1**

0450 **10** *nk* **Roccor**[16] 6367 3-9-2 **57** TomMarquand 8 51+
(Tim Vaughan) *hld up: rdn over 2f out: n.d* **28/1**

0502 **11** *nk* **Zamastar**[39] 5604 5-8-12 **51** (p) EdwardGreatrex(3) 11 43+
(Brendan Powell) *hld up: rdn over 2f out: hung lft over 1f out: n.d* **15/2**

300 **12** *4 ½* **Embroidery (IRE)**[42] 5504 3-9-3 **58** MartinHarley 10 43
(Harry Dunlop) *led: rdn and hdd over 2f out: wknd fnl f* **33/1**

2m 0.76s (-0.04) **Going Correction** -0.10s/f (Stan)
WFA 3 from 4yo+ 5lb **12** Ran SP% **118.3**
Speed ratings (Par 101): **96,91,91,90,89 89,88,88,88,88 87,83**
CSF £43.88 CT £244.63 TOTE £7.10: £3.00, £1.90, £2.20; EX 47.00 Trifecta £326.90.
Owner Miss Hannah Marie Turner **Bred** Ballyhane Stud **Trained** Newmarket, Suffolk

FOCUS
A moderate affair, but it was won in some style and the winner looks well ahead of his mark.
T/Jkpt: Not won. T/Plt: £169.00 to a £1 stake. Pool: £103,717.79 - 447.93 winning units. T/Qpdt: £38.40 to a £1 stake. Pool: £10,549.93 - 201.18 winning units. **Colin Roberts**

6858 - 6859a (Foreign Racing) - See Raceform Interactive

4176 FAIRYHOUSE (R-H)
Tuesday, September 27

OFFICIAL GOING: Soft to heavy

6860a BLENHEIM STKS (LISTED) 6f
3:20 (3:20) 2-Y-O
£21,691 (£6,985; £3,308; £1,470; £735; £367)

RPR
1 **Moonlit Show**[25] 6078 2-8-12 0 BillyLee 6 98
(Charlie Fellowes) *mde all: pushed along to extend advantage over 2f out: clr appr fnl f: kpt on wl: advantage reduced cl home* **6/1**

2 *1 ¾* **Born To Be (IRE)**[56] 4996 2-9-3 0 DeclanMcDonogh 5 98+
(John M Oxx, Ire) *hld up in 4th: pushed along and nt qckn under 2f out in 5th: kpt on wl into 2nd fnl 150yds: clsd on wnr at fin but nvr on terms* **5/2**[1]

3 *1 ¼* **Istan**[72] 4432 2-9-3 93 SeamieHeffernan 2 94
(A P O'Brien, Ire) *hld up in 5th: sme prog on inner 2f out in 4th: wnt 3rd whn short of room and swtchd lft over 1f out: kpt on wl ins fnl f: nvr nrr* **9/2**[3]

4 *3* **Brooklyn's Rose (IRE)**[37] 5686 2-8-12 97 ColinKeane 3 80
(G M Lyons, Ire) *chsd ldrs in 3rd: rdn and no imp under 2f out: kpt on one pce ins fnl f in 4th* **3/1**[2]

5 *¾* **Mack Attack**[27] 6038 2-9-3 0 GaryCarroll 1 83
(G M Lyons, Ire) *chsd ldr in 2nd: rdn and nt qckn under 2f out: no ex ins fnl f: wknd* **5/1**

6 *3 ¾* **Giselle's Charm (IRE)**[38] 5661 2-8-12 90 PatSmullen 7 76
(M D O'Callaghan, Ire) *in rr thrght: sme prog under 2f out: no imp appr fnl f: eased clsng stages* **8/1**

1m 18.45s (5.95) **6** Ran SP% **113.8**
CSF £21.81 TOTE £7.50: £3.60, £1.60; DF 25.70 Trifecta £109.70.
Owner Peter O'Callaghan **Bred** Belmore Lane Stud & Whitsbury Manor Stud **Trained** Newmarket, Suffolk

FOCUS
The absence of Leo Minor because of the ground was a blow. Three of these were rated 90 or higher, but it was not the strongest renewal. The winner got an easy lead and won comfortably.

6861 - 6864a (Foreign Racing) - See Raceform Interactive

6670 KEMPTON (A.W) (R-H)
Wednesday, September 28

OFFICIAL GOING: Polytrack: standard to slow
Wind: Moderate, across Weather: Fine but cloudy, warm

6865 RACINGUK.COM H'CAP 5f (P)
5:40 (5:40) (Class 7) (0-50,50) 3-Y-O+ **£1,940** (£577; £288; £144) **Stalls** Low

Form RPR
4060 **1** **Westbourne Grove (USA)**[48] 5338 3-9-6 **50** (t[1]) RobertWinston 8 56
(John Butler) *taken down early: awkward s: chsd ldrs but had to r wd: stoke up fr 2f out: prog to chse ldr ins fnl f: styd on to ld last strides* **10/3**[1]

2453 **2** *½* **Zebelini (IRE)**[11] 6586 4-9-6 **49** (b) JoeFanning 3 53
(Ollie Pears) *mde most: drew 2 l clr wl over 1f out: looked likely to hold on fnl f: wilted last 100yds and hdd fnl strides* **7/2**[2]

0060 **3** *1* **Chandresh**[16] 6408 3-9-5 **49** (v[1]) KieranO'Neill 6 49
(Robert Cowell) *chsd ldrs: rdn over 1f out: styd on fnl f to take 2nd nr fin* **14/1**

0002 **4** *shd* **Nidnod**[19] 6290 3-9-5 **49** FrederikTylicki 5 49
(John Bridger) *in tch in midfield: nt clr run over 1f out to ins fnl f: styd on nr fin and nrly tk 3rd* **6/1**[3]

 The Form Book, Raceform Ltd, Newbury, RG14 5SJ

0044 **5** ½ **Hurricane Alert**[48] 5335 4-9-6 **49**........................ ShaneKelly 1 47
(Mark Hoad) *taken down early: awkward s: chsd ldng pair: rdn over 1f out: disp 2nd ins fnl f: one pce* **6/1**[3]

0052 **6** *shd* **Edith Weston**[47] 5378 3-9-1 **48**........................(p) AaronJones(3) 10 46
(Robert Cowell) *slowly away: hld up in last: wd bnd 2f out and lost tch: urged along and kpt on fnl f: no ch* **10/1**

0006 **7** ¾ **Top Cop**[1] 6853 7-8-11 **45**........................(p) CiaranMckee(5) 4 40
(Ronald Harris) *dwlt: mostly in last pair: shoved along and no prog 2f out: kpt on ins fnl f* **6/1**[3]

0260 **8** *nk* **Give Us A Belle (IRE)**[11] 6587 7-9-2 **50**........................(v) PaddyPilley(5) 9 44
(Christine Dunnett) *rousted fr wd draw to chse ldr: rdn 2f out: lost 2nd ins fnl f: wknd qckly last 75yds* **20/1**

5-00 **9** *nk* **Touch The Clouds**[17] 6374 5-9-4 **47**........................(b) TimmyMurphy 2 40
(William Stone) *dwlt: a in rr: rdn 2f out: no prog* **10/1**

1m 0.91s (0.41) **Going Correction** 0.0s/f (Stan)
WFA 3 from 4yo+ 1lb **9** Ran SP% **117.8**
Speed ratings (Par 97): **96,95,93,93,92 92,91,90,90**
CSF £15.54 CT £145.38 TOTE £4.40: £1.70, £1.40, £4.40; EX 21.10 Trifecta £282.50.
Owner K Quinn/ C Benham **Bred** Richard Alexander Sanders **Trained** Newmarket, Suffolk

FOCUS
A low-grade sprint with the winner rated back to his early season figure over this trip.

6866 32RED.COM/BRITISH STALLION STUDS EBF MAIDEN FILLIES' STKS (PLUS 10 RACE) (DIV I) 6f (P)
6:10 (6:13) (Class 5) 2-Y-O **£3,234** (£962; £481; £240) **Stalls** Low

Form RPR

4 **1** **Magical Dreamer (IRE)**[83] 4063 2-9-0 0........................ TomQueally 5 76
(James Fanshawe) *much tail swishing: trckd ldrs: tk 2nd on inner 2f out: pushed into ld over 1f out: nrly a l ahd 75yds out: idled and jst hld on* **7/4**[1]

0 **2** *hd* **Parlance (IRE)**[119] 2793 2-9-0 0........................ RyanMoore 7 75+
(Sir Michael Stoute) *trckd ldr: urged along over 2f out: sn lost 2nd: no imp tl styd on ins fnl f: tk 2nd again nr fin and clsd on wnr qckly* **11/4**[2]

6 **3** ½ **Atlanta Belle (IRE)**[13] 6515 2-9-0 0........................ SteveDrowne 6 74
(Chris Wall) *racd freely: led: rdn and hdd over 1f out: kpt on wl but lost 2nd nr fin* **20/1**

5 **4** 1½ **Lava Light**[26] 6086 2-9-0 0........................ HarryBentley 9 69
(Henry Candy) *trckd ldrs: cl 4th 2f out: shkn up and no imp over 1f out: one pce after* **6/1**

5 *shd* **Circulate** 2-9-0 0........................ PatCosgrave 10 69+
(William Haggas) *racd on outer: trckd ldrs: outpcd 2f out: shkn up and kpt on again fnl f* **10/1**

6 *nse* **Dommyah** 2-9-0 0........................ AndreaAtzeni 11 69
(Roger Varian) *nt that wl away but sn in midfield: sme prog 2f out: no hdwy over 1f out: kpt on fnl f* **5/1**[3]

7 3½ **Magique Touch** 2-8-11 0........................ KieranShoemark(3) 12 57+
(Roger Charlton) *stdd s fr wdst draw: hld up in last: pushed along and sme prog over 2f out: nvr on terms and no hdwy over 1f out* **20/1**

8 ½ **Island Cloud** 2-9-0 0........................ DougieCostello 8 56+
(Heather Main) *dwlt: wl in rr: wd in st: kpt on one pce fnl 2f: n.d* **40/1**

0 **9** 3½ **Darcey Lou**[16] 6414 2-9-0 0........................ RobertWinston 1 45
(John Best) *bmpd after 100yds: in tch tl wknd over 2f out* **50/1**

00 **10** *nk* **Bay Of Angels (IRE)**[6] 6696 2-9-0 0........................ FrederikTylicki 4 44
(Stuart Williams) *in tch in midfield tl wknd over 2f out* **33/1**

0 **11** ¾ **Glam'Selle**[42] 5542 2-8-9 0........................ CiaranMckee(5) 2 41
(Ronald Harris) *a in rr: no ch fnl 2f* **50/1**

1m 15.02s (1.92) **Going Correction** 0.0s/f (Stan) **11** Ran SP% **121.9**
Speed ratings (Par 92): **87,86,86,84,83 83,79,78,73,73 72**
CSF £6.32 TOTE £2.80: £1.50, £1.40, £4.90; EX 8.00 Trifecta £86.10.
Owner Fred Archer Racing - Ladylove **Bred** Rockfield Farm **Trained** Newmarket, Suffolk

FOCUS
They didn't go much of a gallop here and it was difficult to make any significant ground from off the pace.

6867 32RED.COM/BRITISH STALLION STUDS EBF MAIDEN FILLIES' STKS (PLUS 10 RACE) (DIV II) 6f (P)
6:40 (6:44) (Class 5) 2-Y-O **£3,234** (£962; £481; £240) **Stalls** Low

Form RPR

2 **1** **Dubai One (IRE)**[26] 6086 2-9-0 0........................ WilliamBuick 5 83+
(Saeed bin Suroor) *mde all at gd pce: pushed along over 2f out: edgd sltly lft fr over 1f out: a in command and pushed out fnl f* **4/5**[1]

5 **2** ¾ **Panova**[20] 6244 2-9-0 0........................ RyanMoore 4 80
(Sir Michael Stoute) *trckd ldng pair: shkn up 2f out: styd on to take 2nd ins fnl f: nvr really able to threaten wnr* **5/2**[2]

4 **3** ¾ **Alwafaa (IRE)**[31] 5930 2-9-0 0........................ PaulHanagan 10 77
(Owen Burrows) *t.k.h early: trckd wnr: shkn up over 1f out: kpt on but lost 2nd ins fnl f* **7/1**[3]

4 3½ **Tundra** 2-9-0 0........................ AndreaAtzeni 9 66+
(Roger Varian) *jst in tch disputing 7th: pushed along over 2f out: kpt on steadily to take 4th ins fnl f: no threat to ldng trio* **8/1**

5 1 **Bombay Dream** 2-9-0 0........................ PatCosgrave 12 63+
(William Haggas) *in tch in 6th: pushed along over 2f out: kpt on one pce after: nt disgracd* **20/1**

0 **6** ¾ **Odelouca (IRE)**[33] 5846 2-9-0 0........................ FMBerry 6 60
(Brendan Powell) *reluctant to enter stall: jst in tch disputing 7th: pushed along over 2f out: no threat but kpt on fr over 1f out* **50/1**

40 **7** ¾ **Geraldine (GER)**[19] 6295 2-9-0 0........................ FrederikTylicki 3 58
(Stuart Williams) *chsd ldrs in 5th: pushed along over 2f out: nvr on terms but kpt on same pce over 1f out* **33/1**

8 *nse* **Kath's Legend** 2-9-0 0........................ RyanTate 8 58
(Ben De Haan) *difficult to load into stall: chsd ldng trio: no imp over 2f out: lost 4th and fdd jst over 1f out* **66/1**

9 13 **Forest Steps (IRE)** 2-9-0 0........................ LiamKeniry 7 16
(J S Moore) *rn green and sn detached: t.o* **100/1**

0 **10** 1½ **Venetian Proposal (IRE)**[58] 4951 2-9-0 0........................ HarryBentley 11 11
(Zoe Davison) *dwlt: a detached in rr: t.o* **100/1**

00 **11** ½ **Demi's Quest**[27] 6062 2-9-0 0........................ TomQueally 1 10
(Tony Carroll) *hld up and sn wl detached in 11th: nvr in it and no ch whn reminders 2f out: t.o* **100/1**

12 1¾ **Diptych (USA)** 2-9-0 0........................ RyanPowell 2
(Sir Mark Prescott Bt) *slowly away: rn green and wl detached in last: t.o* **66/1**

1m 13.02s (-0.08) **Going Correction** 0.0s/f (Stan) **12** Ran SP% **123.4**
Speed ratings (Par 92): **100,99,98,93,92 91,90,89,72,70 69,67**
CSF £2.91 TOTE £1.70: £1.10, £1.10, £2.10; EX 3.40 Trifecta £8.60.
Owner Godolphin **Bred** Darley **Trained** Newmarket, Suffolk

FOCUS
As with the first division, few got into it, but this looked a stronger race, they went a better early gallop and the first three drew right away, clocking a time 2sec quicker than the preceding division. The first five finished in betting order.

6868 32RED CASINO NOVICE STKS (PLUS 10 RACE) 1m (P)
7:10 (7:11) (Class 4) 2-Y-O **£3,946** (£1,174; £586; £293) **Stalls** Low

Form RPR

210 **1** **Total Star**[39] 5646 2-9-8 90........................ RyanMoore 3 91
(Luca Cumani) *mde all: committed for home over 2f out: rdn and 3 l ahd over 1f out: ld dwindled fnl f but nvr in real danger* **6/4**[1]

14 **2** ¾ **Euginio (IRE)**[45] 5450 2-9-8 0........................ AndreaAtzeni 1 89
(Richard Hannon) *tried to match strides w wnr early but sn settled in 2nd: shkn up and nt qckn over 2f out: 3 l down over 1f out: grad clsd fnl f but nvr able to threaten seriously* **6/4**[1]

1004 **3** 6 **Jackhammer (IRE)**[3] 6801 2-9-8 97........................ GeorgeBaker 4 78
(William Knight) *hld up in last pair: shkn up and nt qckn over 2f out: no imp ldng pair over 1f out: fdd fnl f* **3/1**[2]

00 **4** 2½ **The Secrets Out**[26] 6087 2-9-2 0........................ KieranO'Neill 2 63
(Luke Dace) *in tch in last pair: rdn over 2f out: wknd over 1f out* **33/1**[3]

1m 39.57s (-0.23) **Going Correction** 0.0s/f (Stan) **4** Ran SP% **107.9**
Speed ratings (Par 97): **101,100,94,91**
CSF £4.01 TOTE £2.30; EX 4.50 Trifecta £4.70.
Owner Fittocks Stud **Bred** Fittocks Stud **Trained** Newmarket, Suffolk

FOCUS
Another race in which the pace held up.

6869 100% PROFIT BOOST AT 32REDSPORT.COM NURSERY H'CAP 7f (P)
7:40 (7:40) (Class 3) (0-90,89) 2-Y-O **£6,225** (£1,864; £932; £466; £233) **Stalls** Low

Form RPR

21 **1** **Timeless Flight**[81] 4161 2-9-2 **84**........................(t) WilliamBuick 3 86+
(Charlie Appleby) *dwlt: racd in last and pushed along at times: quick move on inner 2f out: rdn to ld jst over 1f out: edgd lft after: hrd pressed fnl f and drvn out to hold on* **6/5**[1]

401 **2** *nk* **Aventinus (IRE)**[17] 6368 2-8-13 **81**........................ JimCrowley 6 82
(Hugo Palmer) *trckd ldr: shkn up to chal over 1f out: pressed wnr fnl f: styd on but jst hld* **11/4**[2]

2243 **3** ½ **Tafaakhor (IRE)**[55] 5077 2-9-0 **82**........................ PaulHanagan 5 82
(Richard Hannon) *settled in 4th: pushed along over 2f out and sn dropped to last: effrt again to take 3rd ins fnl f: clsd on ldng pair nr fin* **8/1**

6442 **4** 1¼ **Glorious Artist (IRE)**[18] 6319 2-8-10 **78**........................ FMBerry 2 75
(Charles Hills) *t.k.h: hld up in 3rd: rdn to chal over 1f out: hanging and hld whn short of room briefly 1f out: fdd* **5/1**[3]

4105 **5** 1¾ **Aardwolf (USA)**[46] 5416 2-9-7 **89**........................ JoeFanning 1 81
(Mark Johnston) *t.k.h: led: hld together tl hdd and reminder jst over 1f out: sltly short of room sn after: fdd tamely* **8/1**

1m 26.15s (0.15) **Going Correction** 0.0s/f (Stan) **5** Ran SP% **111.0**
Speed ratings (Par 99): **99,98,98,96,94**
CSF £4.78 TOTE £2.00: £1.20, £1.50; EX 4.20 Trifecta £18.50.
Owner Godolphin **Bred** Kassala Limited **Trained** Newmarket, Suffolk

FOCUS
A small field but an interesting nursery with the winner overcoming a track bias towards front-runners.

6870 32RED H'CAP (LONDON MIDDLE DISTANCE SERIES QUALIFIER) 1m 3f (P)
8:10 (8:12) (Class 4) (0-85,85) 3-Y-O+ **£4,690** (£1,395; £697; £348) **Stalls** Low

Form RPR

0264 **1** **Banish (USA)**[19] 6286 3-9-5 **85**........................(bt[1]) JimCrowley 9 97
(Hugo Palmer) *hld up in last pair: stl there over 2f out: rapid prog and wdst of all sn after: hanging fr over 1f out but clsd qckly and drvn to ld last 75yds* **6/1**

/00- **2** ½ **Mohatem (USA)**[501] 2278 4-9-5 **78**........................ PaulHanagan 8 89
(Owen Burrows) *trckd ldrs: wnt 2nd over 3f out: led over 2f out and sn rdn: hrd pressed over 1f out: kpt on wl but hdd and outpcd last 75yds* **9/2**[2]

0642 **3** 1¼ **Charlies Mate**[25] 6128 5-9-6 **79**........................ GeorgeBaker 3 88
(John Best) *wl plcd bhd fast pce: prog to trck ldr jst over 2f out: chal over 1f out: nt qckn and hld fnl f: sn lost 2nd* **5/2**[1]

1266 **4** 4 **Indulged**[19] 6286 3-9-2 **82**........................ TomQueally 11 84
(James Fanshawe) *hld up wl in rr: pushed along over 3f out: brought wd and rapid prog to dispute 3rd 2f out: hanging and fnd nil over 1f out: fdd* **6/1**

0356 **5** 1¾ **Biotic**[25] 6128 5-9-1 **74**........................(t) FrederikTylicki 13 73
(Rod Millman) *dwlt: hld up in last pair: tried to make prog on inner but nowhere to go wl over 2f out: hdwy wl over 1f out but kpt on at same pce after* **14/1**

2116 **6** *shd* **Hollywood Road (IRE)**[19] 6301 3-9-3 **83**........................(b) FMBerry 4 82
(Don Cantillon) *wl in tch in midfield: prog 3f out: chsd ldng pair 2f out: wknd fnl f* **5/1**[3]

2400 **7** 2 **Fiftyshadesfreed (IRE)**[19] 6301 5-9-9 **82**........................(p) LiamKeniry 7 78
(George Baker) *hld up in rr: effrt and nt clr run briefly over 2f out: sme hdwy over 1f out: no prog after* **25/1**

0464 **8** 1 **Ban Shoof**[9] 6626 3-8-11 **77**........................(v[1]) TomMarquand 5 71
(Ismail Mohammed) *in tch in midfield: prog to chse ldrs 2f out: sn rdn and wknd over 1f out* **16/1**

0334 **9** *nse* **Ladurelli (IRE)**[56] 5026 4-9-7 **80**........................(b[1]) LukeMorris 10 74
(Paul Cole) *hld up wl in rr: nt clr run over 2f out: prog on inner and drvn wl over 1f out: wknd fnl f* **8/1**

0455 **10** 5 **Genuine Approval (IRE)**[27] 6065 3-8-10 **81**........................ GeorgeWood(5) 2 66
(Jonathan Portman) *chsd ldrs: pushed along over 4f out: lost pl fr 3f out: sn in rr* **33/1**

/10- **11** 1 **Song Light**[284] 5162 6-9-2 **75**........................ SteveDrowne 1 59
(Seamus Mullins) *dwlt: hld up in rr: effrt on inner and hmpd 3f out: no ch after* **33/1**

12 1¼ **Takbeer (IRE)**[344] 4-9-5 **83**........................(p) CallumShepherd(5) 6 65
(Nikki Evans) *chsd ldng pair to wl over 2f out: wknd qckly* **50/1**

-123 **13** 12 **Dune Dancer (IRE)**[35] 5768 3-9-1 **81**........................[1] ShaneKelly 12 42
(David Lanigan) *chsd ldr at fast pce tl lost pl qckly fr 3f out* **8/1**

000- **14** 26 **George Guru**[408] 5446 9-9-4 **77**........................(b) DannyBrock 14
(John Bridger) *fast away fr wdst draw: led at furious pce: hdd and stopped to nthing over 2f out: sn t.o* **66/1**

2m 17.62s (-4.28) **Going Correction** 0.0s/f (Stan)
WFA 3 from 4yo+ 7lb **14** Ran SP% **139.9**
Speed ratings (Par 105): **115,114,113,110,109 109,108,107,107,103 102,101,93,74**
CSF £37.85 CT £92.89 TOTE £7.20: £2.60, £2.80, £1.60; EX 53.20 Trifecta £207.10.
Owner HighclereThoroughbredRacing-Smart Strike **Bred** Nicole Gunther **Trained** Newmarket, Suffolk

FOCUS
This was run at a good gallop.

6871 32RED ON THE APP STORE H'CAP 1m 3f (P)
8:40 (8:42) (Class 6) (0-60,60) 3-Y-0+ **£2,264** (£673; £336; £168) **Stalls** Low

Form RPR
4102 **1** **Iballisticvin**[16] 6411 3-8-13 **54** JimCrowley 12 62
(Gary Moore) *trckd ldr to 5f out and again 3f out: led 2f out and drvn for home: styd on wl whn pressed fnl f* **5/2**[1]
3431 **2** *1* **Gracesome (IRE)**[16] 6424 5-9-11 **59** HarryBentley 3 66
(Michael Blanshard) *prom: rdn over 2f out: chsd wnr over 1f out: styd on wl but a hld* **7/1**[3]
0224 **3** *3* **Power Up**[20] 6243 5-9-7 **60** CharlieBennett(5) 2 62
(Jane Chapple-Hyam) *prom: rdn over 2f out: tk 3rd 1f out: styd on but outpcd by ldng pair* **14/1**
0031 **4** *2 1/4* **Overlord**[16] 6411 4-9-11 **59** (v) TomMarquand 7 57
(Mark Rimell) *slowly away: towards rr: rdn and prog over 2f out: kpt on to take 4th fnl f but readily outpcd* **8/1**
4024 **5** *1 1/2* **Whitstable Pearl (IRE)**[13] 6508 3-8-10 **54** EdwardGreatrex(3) 6 50
(John Best) *wl in tch in midfield: rdn and prog on inner over 2f out: chsd ldrs over 1f out: wknd fnl f* **8/1**
0-45 **6** *3/4* **Moon Arrow (IRE)**[16] 6411 3-9-1 **56** TimmyMurphy 1 51
(Michael Blake) *led: rdn and hdd 2f out: lost 2nd over 1f out and wknd* **7/1**[3]
406 **7** *hd* **Senor George (IRE)**[28] 6022 9-9-8 **56** RyanClark 4 50
(Simon Hodgson) *wl in tch in midfield: rdn over 2f out: no prog and wl btn over 1f out* **33/1**
0200 **8** *2 1/4* **Thane Of Cawdor (IRE)**[16] 6411 7-9-11 **59** GeorgeBaker 11 50+
(Joseph Tuite) *hld up in last in steadily run event: modest prog over 2f out into midfield over 1f out: no ch to threaten* **16/1**
6 **9** *1* **Pension Madness (IRE)**[16] 6411 3-9-3 **58** [1] LiamKeniry 5 47
(Mark Usher) *t.k.h: hld up in midfield: rdn and no prog over 2f out: wknd over 1f out* **33/1**
0-22 **10** *3/4* **Tingo In The Tale (IRE)**[49] 5303 7-9-10 **58** SaleemGolam 14 46+
(Sophie Leech) *hld up in last trio: sme prog 1/2-way: dropped to rr and pushed along over 2f out: nvr involved* **12/1**
504 **11** *1/2* **Celtic Ava (IRE)**[29] 5994 4-9-6 **59** PaddyBradley(5) 13 46+
(Pat Phelan) *stdd s: hld up in last trio: pushed along over 2f out: no great prog and nvr involved* **25/1**
2053 **12** *2* **Multigifted**[23] 6194 3-8-11 **57** GeorgeWood(5) 8 41+
(Michael Madgwick) *hld up in midfield: sddle slipped and t.k.h after 4f: prog on wd outside to go 2nd 5f out to 3f out: sn wknd* **6/1**[2]
5336 **13** *1/2* **Lilly Bonbon (IRE)**[23] 6185 3-8-10 **56** HectorCrouch(5) 9 39
(Gary Moore) *nvr bttr than midfield: rdn and struggling over 2f out: sn no ch* **25/1**

2m 23.33s (1.43) **Going Correction** 0.0s/f (Stan)
WFA 3 from 4yo+ 7lb **13** Ran SP% **123.9**
Speed ratings (Par 101): **94,93,91,89,88 87,87,86,85,84 84,82,82**
CSF £19.54 CT £211.70 TOTE £3.00: £1.30, £2.90, £5.10; EX 18.20 Trifecta £177.00.
Owner Scuderia Vita Bella **Bred** Houghton-Barrons Partnership **Trained** Lower Beeding, W Sussex

FOCUS
A moderate affair in which it paid to race handily. The winner seems to be on the upgrade.

6872 RACING UK PROFITS RETURNED TO RACING H'CAP 7f (P)
9:10 (9:11) (Class 6) (0-65,65) 3-Y-0+ **£2,264** (£673; £336; £168) **Stalls** Low

Form RPR
133 **1** **Hardy Black (IRE)**[34] 5808 5-9-5 **64** (p) LukeMorris 9 72
(Kevin Frost) *trckd ldrs: prog to take 2nd over 2f out gng easily: led wl over 1f out: sn rdn: kpt on wl enough fnl f* **8/1**
3402 **2** *1* **Capolavoro (FR)**[21] 6237 5-9-6 **65** PatCosgrave 10 70
(Robert Cowell) *trckd ldrs: rdn over 2f out: prog to chse wnr over 1f out: kpt on wl but nvr able to chal seriously* **7/2**[2]
0502 **3** *2 1/2* **Veeraya**[48] 5337 6-9-3 **62** (t) AdamBeschizza 3 61
(Julia Feilden) *towards rr: rdn and prog on inner over 2f out: styd on same pce to take 3rd ins fnl f* **10/1**
0610 **4** *3/4* **Prim And Proper**[28] 6021 5-9-3 **62** (b) DanielMuscutt 2 59
(John Flint) *dwlt: wl in rr: prog 2f out: rdn and styd on to take 4th nr fin: no ch to threaten* **16/1**
5330 **5** *1* **Caledonia Laird**[32] 5887 5-9-6 **65** JoeyHaynes 4 59
(Jo Hughes) *chsd ldrs: urged along on inner fr over 2f out: kpt on one pce* **12/1**
0660 **6** *nk* **Dark Forest**[61] 4835 3-9-0 **65** LouisSteward(3) 5 57
(Simon West) *chsd ldr to over 2f out: sn lost pl: one pce fnl f* **12/1**
1534 **7** *1 1/2* **Swiss Cross**[13] 6509 9-9-2 **64** (t) JosephineGordon(3) 1 53
(Phil McEntee) *led: rdn and hdd wl over 1f out: wknd fnl f* **12/1**
5254 **8** *1 3/4* **Marcle (IRE)**[11] 6592 3-9-2 **64** (p) JimCrowley 7 47
(Ed de Giles) *buried away in midfield: rdn and no prog over 2f out* **3/1**[1]
5030 **9** *1 1/4* **Athletic**[11] 6579 7-9-0 **64** (v) GeorgeWood(5) 6 45
(Andrew Reid) *dwlt: rousted along in last pair: effrt on wd outside over 2f out: no great prog* **6/1**[3]
0000 **10** *1 3/4* **Shamlan (IRE)**[13] 6510 4-9-6 **65** (t) StevieDonohoe 12 41
(Johnny Farrelly) *sn detached in last: wl bhd and drvn over 2f out: suddenly r.o fnl f and fin w a flourish* **25/1**
0130 **11** *1* **Himalayan Queen**[23] 6190 3-8-10 **65** SophieKilloran(7) 11 37
(William Jarvis) *dwlt: hld up wl in rr: nudged along over 2f out: no real prog* **14/1**
3413 **12** *1 1/4* **Bridge Builder**[133] 2380 6-9-6 **65** (e[1]) CharlesBishop 14 35
(Peter Hedger) *trapped out wd: chsd ldng pair to 3f out: wknd* **10/1**
4544 **13** *1 1/4* **Seek The Fair Land**[13] 6510 10-9-6 **65** (v) AmirQuinn 13 32
(Lee Carter) *trapped out wd in midfield: wknd over 2f out* **20/1**
1350 **14** *1 1/4* **Paladin (IRE)**[21] 6241 7-8-13 **63** PaddyPilley(5) 8 26
(Michael Blake) *nvr bttr than midfield: wknd 2f out* **20/1**

1m 25.99s (-0.01) **Going Correction** 0.0s/f (Stan)
WFA 3 from 4yo+ 3lb **14** Ran SP% **139.8**
Speed ratings (Par 101): **100,98,96,95,94 93,91,89,88,86 85,83,82,81**
CSF £41.13 CT £319.85 TOTE £11.20: £3.20, £1.60, £3.40; EX 41.80 Trifecta £250.30.
Owner Blue Grey Chevron Racing **Bred** A M V Nicoll **Trained** Market Drayton, Shropshire

FOCUS
A modest handicap, but the first two pulled a little way clear of the rest and the form looks straightforward.
T/Plt: £16.80 to a £1 stake. Pool: £79,073.91. 3,416.87 winning units. T/Qpdt: £5.80 to a £1 stake. Pool: £9,730.25. 1,240.44 winning units. **Jonathan Neesom**

5377 NOTTINGHAM (L-H)
Wednesday, September 28

OFFICIAL GOING: Good (7.6)
Wind: Moderate against Weather: Cloudy

6873 GOLDENSHEAF DINABF SLIP ANCHOR MAIDEN STKS 5f 13y
2:00 (2:02) (Class 5) 2-Y-O **£3,234** (£962; £481; £240) **Stalls** Centre

Form RPR
5 **1** **Trick Of The Light (IRE)**[12] 6542 2-9-5 0 JackMitchell 5 75+
(Roger Varian) *trckd ldrs: swtchd lft and hdwy over 1f out: rdn to chal ins fnl f and rdr lost whip: styd on wl to ld nr line* **6/1**
602 **2** *shd* **Red Alert**[23] 6189 2-9-5 73 RobertHavlin 4 73
(Joseph Tuite) *prom: cl up 1/2-way: rdn to ld 1f out: drvn ins fnl f: hdd and no ex nr line* **20/1**
0 **3** *1 1/2* **Dagonet (IRE)**[19] 6295 2-9-5 0 [1] FMBerry 3 68+
(Roger Charlton) *towards rr: hdwy over 2f out: rdn to chse ldrs over 1f out: kpt on wl* **14/1**
60 **4** *3/4* **Jet Setter (IRE)**[121] 2732 2-8-12 0 [1] JordanUys(7) 8 65
(Brian Meehan) *wnt rt s and rr: swtchd lft and rdn wl over 1f out: styd on wl fnl f: nrst fin* **100/1**
22 **5** *hd* **Her Terms**[24] 6162 2-9-0 78 WilliamTwiston-Davies 6 59
(William Haggas) *wnt lft s: cl up: slt ld 2f out and sn rdn: hdd and drvn 1f out: kpt on same pce* **3/1**[3]
2 **6** *4* **Commander Cole**[19] 6295 2-9-5 0 KevinStott 14 50
(Saeed bin Suroor) *led: pushed along 1/2-way: hdd 2f out: sn rdn and grad wknd* **5/2**[1]
7 *1* **Majestic Stone (IRE)** 2-9-5 0 PaulMulrennan 11 46
(Robert Cowell) *trckd ldrs: rdn along over 2f out: sn wknd* **33/1**
00 **8** *nk* **Equipe**[14] 6477 2-9-0 0 GeorgeChaloner 10 40
(Richard Whitaker) *dwlt and rr: rdn: swtchd lft and sme hdwy wl over 1f out: n.d* **200/1**
06 **9** *6* **Lady Gwhinnyvere (IRE)**[38] 5668 2-9-0 0 TomQueally 7 19
(John Spearing) *a towards rr* **200/1**
10 *1* **Wind Of Heaven (IRE)** 2-9-0 0 FergusSweeney 9 15
(Henry Candy) *a towards rr* **25/1**
00 **11** *1/2* **Sweet Sienna**[20] 6244 2-9-0 0 GrahamLee 2 13
(Dean Ivory) *racd wd: a towards rr* **100/1**
033 **12** *2 1/4* **Bouquet De Flores (USA)**[15] 6454 2-9-0 78 JamesDoyle 12 5+
(Charlie Appleby) *cl up: rdn along over 2f out: sn lost pl: eased appr fnl f* **11/4**[2]

1m 1.65s (0.15) **Going Correction** +0.05s/f (Good) **12** Ran SP% **115.7**
Speed ratings (Par 95): **100,99,97,96,95 89,87,87,77,76 75,71**
CSF £115.43 TOTE £6.70: £2.20, £4.00, £4.50; EX 104.80 Trifecta £1136.50.
Owner Jon Collins & Chris Fahy **Bred** Forenaghts Stud Farm Ltd **Trained** Newmarket, Suffolk

FOCUS
Outer track used, all distances as advertised. Good ground, although James Doyle said it was "on the easy side" in the back straight after riding in the second race. A fair sprint maiden that should produce winners. They raced stands' side.

6874 BATTERBOYS MILE EBF OH SO SHARP MAIDEN FILLIES' STKS (PLUS 10 RACE) 1m 75y
2:30 (2:30) (Class 5) 2-Y-O **£3,234** (£962; £481; £240) **Stalls** Centre

Form RPR
1 **Dowayla (IRE)** 2-9-0 0 JamesDoyle 5 85+
(Saeed bin Suroor) *cl up: led 21/2f out: rdn clr over 1f out: kpt on strly* **2/1**[1]
0 **2** *1 1/2* **Counterweight (IRE)**[43] 5524 2-9-0 0 RichardKingscote 8 80+
(Sir Michael Stoute) *sn slt ld: hdd after 2: c lose up: rdn over 2f out: drvn over 1f out: kpt on wl u.p towards fin* **20/1**
3 *nk* **Whispering Bell (IRE)** 2-9-0 0 RobertHavlin 4 79+
(John Gosden) *trckd ldrs: hdwy wl over 2f out: rdn over 1f out: chse wnr ins fnl f: kpt on* **7/2**[3]
4 *2 3/4* **Mistress Quickly (IRE)** 2-9-0 0 FMBerry 6 73+
(Ralph Beckett) *dwlt and rr: hdwy over 3f out: chsd ldrs 2f out: sn rdn and no imp appr fnl f* **9/4**[2]
5 **5** *4 1/2* **Devoran**[46] 5387 2-9-0 0 WilliamTwiston-Davies 2 62+
(Alan King) *towards rr: hdwy 3f out: rdn along 2f out: styd on appr fnl f: nrst fin* **16/1**
6 **6** *1 1/2* **Nastenka**[25] 6111 2-9-0 0 GrahamLee 9 59
(Ed Walker) *trckd ldrs: hdwy on outer and cl up over 3f out: rdn along 2f out: sn wknd* **12/1**
0 **7** *3 1/2* **Penny Green**[118] 2817 2-9-0 0 RyanTate 3 51
(James Eustace) *trckd ldrs on inner: pushed along over 3f out: rdn wl over 2f out: sn wknd* **25/1**
05 **8** *10* **Mystic Maeve (IRE)**[9] 6632 2-9-0 0 SilvestreDeSousa 1 28
(Roger Fell) *cl up on inner: led after 2f: rdn along over 3f out: hdd 21/2f out: sn drvn and wknd* **20/1**
9 *6* **Noreena** 2-9-0 0 TomQueally 7 14
(Paul D'Arcy) *rr: sme hdwy on wd outside over 3f out: sn rdn along: outpcd and bhd* **50/1**

1m 46.84s (-2.16) **Going Correction** -0.25s/f (Firm) **9** Ran SP% **115.2**
Speed ratings (Par 92): **100,98,98,95,90 89,85,75,69**
CSF £46.69 TOTE £2.70: £1.40, £5.20, £1.40; EX 40.00 Trifecta £173.60.
Owner Godolphin **Bred** Darley **Trained** Newmarket, Suffolk

FOCUS
This had the look of a decent fillies' maiden and the first four are worth keeping on side.

6875 GEORGES KITCHEN NOTTINGHAM NURSERY H'CAP 1m 2f 50y
3:00 (3:00) (Class 5) (0-75,74) 2-Y-O **£2,911** (£866; £432; £216) **Stalls** Low

Form RPR
644 **1** **Outre Mer (IRE)**[67] 4649 2-9-7 **74** JamesDoyle 1 88+
(John Gosden) *hld up in tch: smooth hdwy to trck ldrs over 3f out: chal 2f out: rdn to ld jst over 1f out and sn edgd: led: sn clr: kpt on strly* **7/2**[2]
514 **2** *7* **Mount Moriah**[18] 6330 2-9-6 **73** FMBerry 11 73
(Ralph Beckett) *a cl up: effrt 3f out: rdn to ld 2f out: hdd jst over 1f out: sn drvn and kpt on: no ch w wnr* **11/4**[1]
5325 **3** *3 1/4* **Baileys Apprentice**[17] 6377 2-9-4 **71** SilvestreDeSousa 3 65
(Mark Johnston) *cl up on inner: led after 1f: rdn along 3f out: hdd and drvn 2f out: kpt on same pce appr fnl f* **8/1**
060 **4** *3/4* **Kozier (GER)**[36] 5740 2-8-2 **60** HollieDoyle(5) 8 52+
(Alan King) *dwlt and rr: hdwy on inner 3f out: rdn along 2f out: kpt on appr fnl f* **8/1**

5433 **5** *nk* **Pacofilha**[21] 6240 2-9-4 **71**..............................[1] GrahamLee 6 63
(Paul Cole) *trckd ldrs: hdwy to chse ldng pair 3f out: rdn along 2f out: sn drvn and kpt on one pce* **6/1**[3]

5001 **6** *7* **Masterofdiscovery**[18] 6313 2-9-6 **73**..............................(b) JohnFahy 7 52
(Clive Cox) *hld up: hdwy on wd outside over 3f out: sn chsng ldrs: rdn 2f out and sn wknd* **10/1**

0054 **7** *6* **A Sure Welcome**[18] 6313 2-8-0 **53** oh1.............................. NickyMackay 4 20
(John Spearing) *trckd ldrs on inner: hdwy over 3f out: rdn along over 2f out: sn drvn and wknd* **33/1**

5025 **8** *3/4* **Phoenix Dawn**[68] 4595 2-9-1 **68**.............................. MartinDwyer 10 34
(Brendan Powell) *a towards rr* **33/1**

6034 **9** *2* **Joyful Dream (IRE)**[16] 6421 2-9-0 **67**.............................. RyanPowell 5 29
(J S Moore) *t.k.h: in tch: rdn along over 3f out: sn wknd* **50/1**

045 **10** *1 1/2* **Percy Thrower (IRE)**[30] 5952 2-9-2 **69**.............................. MichaelJMMurphy 9 28
(Charles Hills) *a towards rr* **10/1**

4006 **11** *43* **Limelight Lady**[21] 6236 2-7-11 **53** oh8..............................(b) NoelGarbutt[(3)] 12
(Harry Dunlop) *led 1f: cl up: rdn along over 4f out: sn wknd* **100/1**

2m 10.38s (-3.92) **Going Correction** -0.25s/f (Firm) 2y crse rec **11** Ran SP% **112.4**
Speed ratings (Par 95): **105,99,96,96,95 90,85,84,83,82 47**
CSF £12.55 CT £68.84 TOTE £3.90: £1.60, £1.50, £3.00; EX 13.80 Trifecta £66.80.
Owner Godolphin **Bred** Darley **Trained** Newmarket, Suffolk

FOCUS
An ordinary nursery that was taken apart by the top weight.

6876 KFE SCHOOL OF FRYING EXCELLENCE H'CAP (THE JOCKEY CLUB GRASSROOTS MIDDLE DISTANCE SERIES FINAL) 1m 2f 50y

3:30 (3:31) (Class 3) 3-Y-O+

£15,562 (£4,660; £2,330; £1,165; £582; £292) **Stalls** Low

Form RPR

6206 **1** **Save The Bees**[18] 6323 8-9-0 **78**..............................(b) PhilDennis[(5)] 6 86
(Declan Carroll) *sn led: rdn along over 2f out: drvn over 1f out: hld on gamely towards fin* **33/1**

1420 **2** *nk* **Compton Mill**[19] 6301 4-8-13 **77**..............................(t) CharlieBennett[(5)] 5 84
(Hughie Morrison) *trckd ldng pair: hdwy to chal over 2f out: rdn over 1f out: drvn and ev ch ins fnl f: kpt on* **9/1**[3]

0122 **3** *1 1/2* **Bedrock**[14] 6484 3-9-4 **83**..............................(p) SilvestreDeSousa 13 87
(William Haggas) *hld up in midfield: hdwy over 3f out: chsd ldrs 2f out and sn rdn: drvn and kpt on fnl f* **7/4**[1]

1612 **4** *hd* **I Am Not Here (IRE)**[11] 6566 5-9-10 **83**.............................. JamesDoyle 3 87
(Brian Ellison) *hld up towards rr: hdwy over 3f out: swtchd rt chsd ldrs 2f out: sn rdn: drvn and kpt on fnl f: nrst fin* **7/2**[2]

4105 **5** *nse* **Cornelious (IRE)**[6] 6701 4-8-9 **68**.............................. AdamBeschizza 7 72
(Clifford Lines) *trckd ldrs: hdwy to chse ldng pair over 2f out: sn rdn: drvn over 1f out: kpt on same pce* **20/1**

1606 **6** *nk* **Eurystheus (IRE)**[13] 6516 7-9-6 **79**..............................(tp) AndrewMullen 10 82
(Michael Appleby) *in tch: hdwy on inner 3f out: rdn along 2f out: drvn over 1f out: kpt on: nrst fin* **25/1**

153 **7** *4* **Choral Festival**[29] 5994 10-8-11 **70**.............................. DannyBrock 1 65
(John Bridger) *dwlt and rr: sme hdwy 3f out: rdn 2f out: n.d* **33/1**

2200 **8** *nk* **Cottesloe (IRE)**[12] 5574 7-9-2 **75**..............................(b) WilliamTwiston-Davies 4 70
(John Berry) *towards rr: sme hdwy wl over 2f out: sn rdn and n.d* **20/1**

1050 **9** *nse* **Caponova (IRE)**[7] 6684 3-8-9 **74**.............................. RichardKingscote 14 69
(Tom Dascombe) *rr: sme hdwy 3f out: rdn along 2f out: n.d* **25/1**

5426 **10** *2 3/4* **Trulee Scrumptious**[38] 5671 7-8-6 **65**..............................(v) JimmyQuinn 8 54
(Peter Charalambous) *trckd wnr: cl up over 3f out: sn rdn and wknd fnl 2f* **20/1**

1520 **11** *3 1/2* **Framley Garth (IRE)**[24] 6160 4-9-2 **75**.............................. DanielTudhope 11 57
(Patrick Holmes) *nvr bttr than midfield* **16/1**

465 **12** *1/2* **Polar Forest**[13] 6517 6-9-4 **77**..............................(e) ConnorBeasley 9 58
(Richard Guest) *in tch: hdwy over 3f out: rdn along over 2f out: sn drvn and wknd* **16/1**

6131 **13** *1 3/4* **Lord Franklin**[41] 5579 7-9-10 **83**.............................. NeilFarley 16 61
(Eric Alston) *led early: trckd ldrs: effrt 3f out: sn rdn and wknd 2f out* **12/1**

3145 **14** *11* **Della Valle (GER)**[16] 6417 3-8-13 **78**.............................. TedDurcan 15 34
(Mike Murphy) *a towards rr* **50/1**

5040 **15** *16* **Artful Prince**[21] 6221 6-8-10 **69**..............................(b) TomEaves 12
(James Given) *midfield: hdwy over 4f out: rdn along 3f out: sn drvn and wknd* **33/1**

2m 10.07s (-4.23) **Going Correction** -0.25s/f (Firm)
WFA 3 from 4yo+ 6lb **15** Ran SP% **120.8**
Speed ratings (Par 107): **106,105,104,104,104 104,100,100,100,98 95,95,93,85,72**
CSF £274.22 CT £812.15 TOTE £42.90: £9.90, £3.80, £1.10; EX 247.00 Trifecta £661.90.
Owner Steve Ryan **Bred** S P Ryan **Trained** Malton, N Yorks

FOCUS
They appeared to go a decent clip in this fair handicap, but still little got into it with the winner making all.

6877 T. QUALITY - YOUR FOODSERVICE SOLUTION H'CAP 1m 75y

4:05 (4:07) (Class 4) (0-85,85) 3-Y-O **£4,690** (£1,395; £697; £348) **Stalls** Centre

Form RPR

1322 **1** **Tomahawk Kid**[33] 5849 3-8-9 **73**.............................. RobertHavlin 10 84
(Ian Williams) *t.k.h: trckd ldrs: hdwy to ld 2f out: rdn clr over 1f out: drvn out* **9/1**[3]

6210 **2** *1 3/4* **Force (IRE)**[26] 6084 3-9-3 **81**.............................. JamesDoyle 4 87
(Charles Hills) *t.k.h: slt ld: pushed along 3f out: rdn and hdd 2f out: drvn over 1f out: kpt on u.p fnl f* **16/1**

4-00 **3** *1 1/2* **Royal Shaheen (FR)**[18] 6320 3-9-7 **85**.............................. PaulMulrennan 3 88
(Alistair Whillans) *plld hrd: trckd ldrs on inner: over 2f out: rdn wl over 1f out: kpt on* **33/1**

0403 **4** *shd* **Flyboy (IRE)**[32] 5886 3-9-3 **81**.............................. DanielTudhope 9 83+
(David O'Meara) *dwlt and hld up in rr: swtchd rt to outer and hdwy 2f out: rdn over 1f out: styd on wl fnl f: nrst fin* **6/1**[2]

61 **5** *1* **Timeless Art (IRE)**[102] 3389 3-9-0 **78**.............................. JoeyHaynes 11 78
(K R Burke) *t.k.h: hld up in rr: hdwy on outer over 3f out: rdn along to chse ldrs 2f out: drvn over 1f out: kpt on same pce* **6/1**[2]

1310 **6** *1 3/4* **Hijran (IRE)**[21] 6231 3-8-4 **71** oh1..............................(p) TimClark[(3)] 13 67
(Michael Appleby) *cl up: rdn along over 2f out: drvn over 1f out: wknd fnl f* **25/1**

1320 **7** *1/2* **Thaqaffa (IRE)**[40] 5601 3-9-0 **81**.............................. LouisSteward[(3)] 1 76
(Marcus Tregoning) *plld hrd: trckd ldrs: hdwy over 3f out: rdn over 2f out: sn drvn and one pce* **10/1**

545 **8** *1 1/4* **Mediciman**[33] 5849 3-8-12 **76**.............................. FergusSweeney 12 68
(Henry Candy) *hld up: hdwy on outer and in tch 1/2-way: effrt 3f out: rdn to chse ldrs 2f out: sn drvn and wknd* **10/1**

6221 **9** *1* **Master Gunner (USA)**[25] 6138 3-9-3 **81**..............................(v) RichardKingscote 8 71
(Sir Michael Stoute) *dwlt: sn trcking ldrs: effrt and pushed along 3f out: rdn over 2f out: sn drvn and btn* **3/1**[1]

3433 **10** *12* **Al Nasser Alwashik**[68] 4607 3-8-9 **73**.............................. SilvestreDeSousa 6 60
(Roger Fell) *rr: rdn along over 3f out: sn outpcd* **6/1**[2]

1m 45.35s (-3.65) **Going Correction** -0.25s/f (Firm) **10** Ran SP% **108.7**
Speed ratings (Par 103): **108,106,104,104,103 101,101,100,99,87**
CSF £129.25 CT £4144.56 TOTE £7.40: £2.10, £4.80, £7.20; EX 135.50 Trifecta £4676.20.
Owner Phil Mousley **Bred** Phil Mousley **Trained** Portway, Worcs
■ Le Roi Du Temps (16-1) and North Creek were withdrawn. Rule 4 does not apply.

FOCUS
An ordinary handicap and it again paid to race handy.

6878 KFE 20TH ANNIVERSARY CELEBRATION H'CAP (THE JOCKEY CLUB GRASSROOTS SPRINT SERIES FINAL) 6f 15y

4:40 (4:43) (Class 3) 3-Y-O+

£15,562 (£4,660; £2,330; £1,165; £582; £292) **Stalls** Centre

Form RPR

0101 **1** **Syrian Pearl**[46] 5408 5-9-1 **82**.............................. TedDurcan 2 92
(Chris Wall) *hld up towards rr: gd hdwy on wd outside 2f out: rdn to chal ins fnl f: led last 50 yds* **12/1**

6521 **2** *nk* **Alpine Dream (IRE)**[15] 6436 3-8-0 **69** oh3..............................(b) CamHardie 6 78
(Tim Easterby) *trckd ldrs: hdwy 2f out: rdn to ld ent fnl f: sn drvn and edgd lft: hdd and no ex last 50 yds* **25/1**

0455 **3** *1 1/2* **Pour La Victoire (IRE)**[29] 6000 6-8-8 **75**..............................(b) JoeyHaynes 5 79
(Tony Carroll) *rr pushed along and hdwy over 2f out: rdn over 1f out: styd on strly fnl f* **20/1**

204 **4** *1 1/2* **Danecase**[30] 5960 3-8-6 **75**.............................. MartinDwyer 1 74
(David Dennis) *chsd ldrs: effrt 2f out: rdn and ch over 1f out: drvn and kpt on same pce fnl f* **14/1**

1135 **5** *1 1/4* **Guishan**[54] 5124 6-9-7 **91**.............................. TimClark[(3)] 9 86
(Michael Appleby) *sn led: rdn along 2f out: sn hdd and drvn: grad wknd* **12/1**

2040 **6** *hd* **Koptoon**[26] 6072 4-8-11 **78**..............................(p) AndrewMullen 13 73+
(Jo Hughes) *towards rr: hdwy 2f out: sn rdn: kpt on wl fnl f: nrst fin* **20/1**

0312 **7** *1* **Penny Pot Lane**[15] 6435 3-7-11 **71**.............................. NathanEvans[(5)] 3 63
(Richard Whitaker) *cl up: rdn to take slt wl over 1f out: drvn and hdd ent fnl f: grad wknd* **7/1**[2]

4405 **8** *nk* **Captain Bob (IRE)**[15] 6453 5-8-2 **69**..............................(v[1]) JamesSullivan 4 60
(Robert Cowell) *chsd ldrs: effrt and ev ch 2f out: sn rdn and one pce ent fnl f* **12/1**

5415 **9** *1* **Ancient Astronaut**[15] 6435 3-8-4 **73**.............................. SilvestreDeSousa 8 65+
(John Quinn) *dwlt and towards rr: swtchd lft and hdwy 2f out: sn rdn and keeping on whn n.m.r over 1f out: one pce after* **4/1**[1]

0041 **10** *3/4* **Cool Bahamian (IRE)**[33] 5852 5-9-1 **85**..............................(v) EdwardGreatrex[(3)] 17 70+
(Eve Johnson Houghton) *towards rr: hdwy towards stands rail 2f out: sn rdn and kpt on fnl f* **17/2**[3]

4114 **11** *2 1/4* **Belledesert**[24] 6164 3-9-5 **88**.............................. AdamBeschizza 16 66+
(Steph Hollinshead) *prom on outer: rdn along 2f out: grad wknd* **10/1**

0520 **12** *1 1/2* **Go Nani Go**[7] 6669 10-8-6 **73**.............................. ShaneGray 11 46
(Ed de Giles) *a towards rr* **33/1**

4443 **13** *1* **Ambitious Icarus**[14] 6479 7-8-2 **69**..............................(e) PatrickMathers 14 39
(Richard Guest) *in tch: rdn along 2f out: sn wknd* **16/1**

430 **14** *2 1/2* **Frenchman (FR)**[23] 6190 3-8-6 **75**.............................. JimmyQuinn 12 37
(Charles Hills) *prom: rdn along over 2f out: sn wknd* **14/1**

0311 **15** *1/2* **Curious Fox**[26] 6091 3-7-11 **69** oh1.............................. NoelGarbutt[(3)] 7 29
(Anthony Carson) *chsd ldrs: rdn along 2f out: drvn and wknd over 1f out* **20/1**

5524 **16** *1/2* **Costa Filey**[7] 6669 5-8-0 **67** oh3..............................(p) NickyMackay 10 26
(Ed Vaughan) *a towards rr* **25/1**

2110 **17** *nk* **Outrage**[21] 6234 4-9-1 **82**.............................. RichardKingscote 15 40
(Daniel Kubler) *prom: rdn along over 2f out: sn wknd* **14/1**

1m 13.89s (-0.81) **Going Correction** +0.05s/f (Good)
WFA 3 from 4yo+ 2lb **17** Ran SP% **126.0**
Speed ratings (Par 107): **107,106,104,102,100 100,99,98,97,96 93,91,90,86,86 85,85**
CSF £297.99 CT £3196.62 TOTE £11.60: £3.00, £5.10, £3.40, £4.10; EX 382.20.
Owner The Clodhoppers **Bred** Jeremy Green And Sons **Trained** Newmarket, Suffolk

FOCUS
A decent little sprint, the main action unfolding down the centre.

6879 CF GROUP FINANCE FOR BUSINESS H'CAP 5f 13y

5:10 (5:14) (Class 5) (0-75,75) 3-Y-O+ **£2,911** (£866; £432; £216) **Stalls** Centre

Form RPR

03-3 **1** **Mysterious Glance**[100] 3471 3-9-0 **69**.............................. KevinStott 2 78
(Ed McMahon) *chsd ldrs: led 2f out: drvn out* **16/1**

5220 **2** *1/2* **Jaarih (IRE)**[14] 6475 4-9-6 **74**..............................(b) PaulMulrennan 10 81
(Conor Dore) *mid-div: hdwy and nt clr run 2f out: chsng ldrs 1f out: wandered fnl f: kpt on same pce to take 2nd towards fin* **12/1**

2454 **3** *1/2* **Billyoakes (IRE)**[14] 6479 4-9-3 **71**..............................[1] RichardKingscote 15 76+
(Charlie Wallis) *n.m.r s: in rr: hdwy 2f out: styd on fnl 100yds: tk 3rd nr fin* **7/1**[3]

/3-4 **4** *3/4* **Cockney Island**[15] 6459 4-9-4 **72**.............................. SilvestreDeSousa 12 75+
(Philip McBride) *swvd rt s: in rr: hdwy and n.m.r over 1f out: kpt on* **14/1**

4166 **5** *nse* **Rainbow Orse**[55] 5050 4-9-4 **72**..............................(p) DanielTudhope 8 75
(Robert Cowell) *chsd ldrs: kpt on on same pce fnl f* **7/1**[3]

0-44 **6** *3/4* **Rosie Royce**[23] 6190 3-8-12 **67**.............................. FergusSweeney 3 67
(Henry Candy) *chsd ldrs: kpt on same pce fnl f* **5/1**[2]

0506 **7** *shd* **Red Stripes (USA)**[16] 6425 4-9-0 **75**..............................(b) JordanUys[(7)] 1 74
(Lisa Williamson) *sn chsng ldrs: hung bdly lft 2f out: kpt on same pce fnl f* **11/1**

2234 **8** *3/4* **Indian Tinker**[16] 6410 7-8-13 **67**..............................(p) JamesDoyle 7 64
(Robert Cowell) *chsd ldrs: hung lft over 1f out: kpt on one pce* **9/2**[1]

6126 **9** *3/4* **The Burnham Mare (IRE)**[17] 6361 3-8-5 **65**..............................(p) HollieDoyle[(5)] 16 59
(J S Moore) *in rr: sme hdwy over 1f out: nvr a factor* **25/1**

0000 **10** *nse* **Evanescent (IRE)**[88] 3892 7-9-3 **74**.............................. GeorgeDowning[(3)] 14 68
(Tony Carroll) *in rr: sme hdwy over 1f out: nvr a factor* **12/1**

0003 **11** *1* **Space Artist (IRE)**[14] 6475 6-8-12 **66**..............................(vt) TomEaves 13 56
(Nigel Tinkler) *wnt rt s: a towards rr* **20/1**

0020 **12** *2* **Entertaining Ben**[16] 6425 3-9-4 **73**.............................. MartinDwyer 6 56
(William Muir) *led: hdd 2f out: sn wknd* **12/1**

250 **13** *1 3/4* **Corridor Kid (IRE)**[26] 6101 3-9-6 **75**..............................(v) MartinLane 11 52
(Derek Shaw) *in rr: lost pl over 1f out* **50/1**

1600 **14** 3 1/4 **Roy's Legacy**[76] 4295 7-8-3 **64**............ TobyEley(7) 9 29
(Shaun Harris) *mid-div: lost pl 2f out: eased clsng stages* **33/1**

1m 0.97s (-0.53) **Going Correction** +0.05s/f (Good)
WFA 3 from 4yo+ 1lb **14** Ran SP% **117.3**
Speed ratings (Par 103): **106,105,104,103,103 101,101,100,99,99 97,94,91,86**
CSF £183.54 CT £1510.45 TOTE £18.10: £5.10, £3.70, £3.00; EX 205.70 Trifecta £2522.20.
Owner S L Edwards **Bred** The Lavington Stud **Trained** Lichfield, Staffs

FOCUS
Plenty had their chance in this modest sprint.
T/Jkpt: Not won. T/Plt: £1,361.30 to a £1 stake. Pool: £81682.18, 43.8 winning units T/Qpdt: £62.60 to a £1 stake. Pool: £7536.36, 89.0 winning units **Joe Rowntree & Walter Glynn**

6288 SALISBURY (R-H)
Wednesday, September 28

OFFICIAL GOING: Soft (6.1)
Wind: mild breeze against Weather: sunny periods

6880 WILKINS KENNEDY BRITISH STALLION STUDS EBF MAIDEN STKS (PLUS 10 RACE) (DIV I) 6f 212y
1:50 (1:51) (Class 4) 2-Y-O **£4,528** (£1,347; £673; £336) **Stalls** Low

Form RPR
2 **1** **Make Time (IRE)**[25] 6108 2-9-5 0............ JimmyFortune 7 95+
(David Menuisier) *travelled wl: prom: led over 2f out: kicked clr ent fnl f: comf* **3/1**[2]
2 5 **Swiftsure (IRE)** 2-9-5 0............ RyanMoore 5 83
(Sir Michael Stoute) *mid-div: pushed along and hdwy over 2f out: chsd wnr jst over 1f out: kpt on but nt pce to get on terms* **6/1**[3]
3 nk **Anythingtoday (IRE)** 2-9-5 0............ JimCrowley 13 82
(Hugo Palmer) *s.i.s: bhd: stdy prog fr over 3f out: rdn over 1f out: kpt on to go 3rd ent fnl f: chal for 2nd fnl 120yds* **10/1**
20 **4** 3 1/2 **Dance Teacher (IRE)**[40] 5615 2-9-0 0............ PatDobbs 9 68
(Ralph Beckett) *mid-div: hdwy over 2f out: sn rdn: kpt on same pce fr over 1f out* **8/1**
5 1 1/4 **Ajman King (IRE)** 2-9-5 0............ AndreaAtzeni 10 73+
(Roger Varian) *mid-div: rdn and sme prog over 3f out: nvr threatened ldrs: one pce fnl 2f* **10/1**
0 **6** 2 3/4 **Medicean Ballet (IRE)**[16] 6414 2-9-0 0............ DaneO'Neill 11 58
(Henry Candy) *trckd ldrs: rdn wl over 2f out: sn one pce* **80/1**
0 **7** 1 1/4 **Open Wide (USA)**[12] 6543 2-9-5 0............ AdamKirby 2 60
(Amanda Perrett) *led: rdn and hdd over 2f out: kpt pressing ldrs tl wknd ent fnl f* **25/1**
34 **8** hd **Parfait (IRE)**[25] 6122 2-9-5 0............ WilliamBuick 4 59
(John Gosden) *wnt rt s: trckd ldrs: swtchd rt over 2f out: sn rdn: nt pce to chal: wknd ent fnl f* **15/8**[1]
5 **9** 3 1/2 **Caspian Gold (IRE)**[20] 6264 2-9-5 0............ ShaneKelly 6 51
(Richard Hughes) *a towards rr* **25/1**
00 **10** 1 3/4 **Sixth Of June**[7] 6673 2-9-0 0............ FrederikTylicki 8 41
(Rod Millman) *mid-div: rdn wl over 2f out: wknd over 1f out* **250/1**
11 9 **Mr Mac** 2-9-5 0............ SteveDrowne 3 24
(Peter Hedger) *mid-div tl over 3f out: wknd over 1f out* **200/1**
12 5 **Morello (IRE)** 2-9-0 0............ MartinHarley 12 6
(Henry Candy) *a towards rr* **33/1**

1m 31.43s (2.83) **Going Correction** +0.60s/f (Yiel) **12** Ran SP% **116.1**
Speed ratings (Par 97): **107,101,100,96,95 92,90,90,86,84 74,68**
CSF £20.00 TOTE £3.70: £1.50, £2.00, £3.40; EX 21.20 Trifecta £194.10.
Owner Gail Brown Racing (vii) **Bred** Kildaragh Stud **Trained** Pulborough, W Sussex

FOCUS
The ground was officially soft. The 1m juvenile maiden which would have opened the card had been abandoned due to patches of unstable ground between the 7f and 1m starts. The first division of an interesting maiden, but it was taken apart by the winner. The jockeys reported conditions as between heavy and very hard work.

6881 WILKINS KENNEDY BRITISH STALLION STUDS EBF MAIDEN STKS (PLUS 10 RACE) (DIV II) 6f 212y
2:20 (2:22) (Class 4) 2-Y-O **£4,528** (£1,347; £673; £336) **Stalls** Low

Form RPR
34 **1** **Mucho Applause (IRE)**[79] 4203 2-9-5 0............ OisinMurphy 12 81+
(Andrew Balding) *.trckd ldr: led over 2f out: sn rdn: kpt on strly fnl 120yds: readily* **7/1**
6 **2** 2 **Redgrave (IRE)**[86] 3954 2-9-5 0............ WilliamBuick 10 76
(Charles Hills) *in tch: rdn and hdwy over 1f out: chsd wnr ent fnl f: wandered sltly u.p: no ex fnl 120yds* **11/4**[1]
6 **3** 3 **Eula Varner**[32] 5869 2-9-0 0............ DaneO'Neill 4 63
(Henry Candy) *trckd ldrs: rdn to chse wnr 2f out tl ent fnl f: kpt on same pce* **12/1**
4 1 1/2 **Hajjam** 2-9-5 0............ MartinHarley 5 64+
(William Knight) *mid-div: rdn 3f out: hdwy over 1f out: kpt on nicely to go 4th ins fnl f* **40/1**
44 **5** 1 1/2 **Hernandes (FR)**[15] 6439 2-9-5 0............ GeorgeBaker 6 60
(Ed Walker) *led: rdn and hdd over 2f out: no ex ins fnl f* **17/2**
6 2 1/4 **Sable Island (IRE)** 2-9-5 0............ RyanMoore 14 54+
(Sir Michael Stoute) *towards rr: stdy prog fr 3f out: kpt on fnl f but nt pce to get involved* **12/1**
7 1/2 **Clemento (IRE)** 2-9-5 0............ AndreaAtzeni 2 53+
(Richard Hughes) *rdn over 2f out: nvr bttr than mid-div* **10/1**
6 **8** 3 3/4 **Delannoy**[19] 6297 2-9-5 0............ CharlesBishop 3 43
(Eve Johnson Houghton) *mid-div: pushed along over 4f out: nvr any imp* **11/1**
04 **9** 3/4 **Conkering Hero (IRE)**[26] 6087 2-9-5 0............ LiamKeniry 1 41
(Joseph Tuite) *a mid-div* **66/1**
562 **10** 1 1/4 **Mr Tyrrell (IRE)**[52] 5196 2-9-5 80............ SeanLevey 7 38+
(Richard Hannon) *slowly into strifde: sn in tch: effrt over 2f out: nvr threatened: wknd over 1f out* **6/1**[3]
04 **11** 3/4 **Koeman**[11] 6570 2-9-5 0............ JimCrowley 11 36+
(Mick Channon) *mid-div: hdwy over 3f out: sn rdn: wknd over 1f out* **11/2**[2]
12 nk **Beaconsfield** 2-9-5 0............ JimmyFortune 13 35
(Hughie Morrison) *stdd s: a towards rr* **50/1**
0 **13** 2 1/2 **Brimham Rocks**[15] 6439 2-9-5 0............ PatDobbs 8 29
(Ralph Beckett) *a towards rr* **33/1**
14 9 **Paco Dawn** 2-9-0 0............ ShaneKelly 9
(Philip Hide) *s.i.s: a towards rr* **100/1**

1m 32.48s (3.88) **Going Correction** +0.60s/f (Yiel) **14** Ran SP% **122.0**
Speed ratings (Par 97): **101,98,95,93,91 89,88,84,83,82 81,80,78,67**
CSF £26.32 TOTE £8.20: £2.70, £2.20, £4.50; EX 30.80 Trifecta £615.70.
Owner Transatlantic Racing **Bred** Pediment Syndicate **Trained** Kingsclere, Hants

FOCUS
This looked the weaker division and the winning time was just over a second slower than the first leg. It paid to be up with the pace.

6882 BATHWICK TYRES CONDITIONS STKS (PLUS 10 RACE) 6f
2:50 (2:50) (Class 2) 2-Y-O **£9,703** (£2,887; £1,443; £721) **Stalls** Low

Form RPR
1363 **1** **Smokey Lane (IRE)**[12] 6538 2-9-2 92............ AdamKirby 4 94
(David Evans) *trckd ldrs: rdn over 2f out: chal jst over 1f out: led ins fnl f: kpt on strly* **3/1**[2]
13 **2** 1 1/4 **Eqtiraan (IRE)**[39] 5646 2-9-2 0............ PaulHanagan 1 90
(Richard Hannon) *led: rdn whn strly chal over 1f out: edgd lft and hdd ins fnl f: no ex* **1/2**[1]
156 **3** 6 **Bahamadam**[27] 6063 2-8-11 83............ RobertWinston 5 67
(Eve Johnson Houghton) *trckd ldr: rdn 2f out: nt quite pce to mount chal: wknd fnl f* **13/2**[3]
02 **4** 10 **Shawami (IRE)**[12] 6548 2-8-7 0............ AndreaAtzeni 2 33
(Mick Channon) *chsd ldrs: rdn over 2f out: wknd over 1f out* **20/1**

1m 17.87s (3.07) **Going Correction** +0.60s/f (Yiel) **4** Ran SP% **109.8**
Speed ratings (Par 101): **103,101,93,80**
CSF £5.09 TOTE £4.40; EX 5.60 Trifecta £8.30.
Owner Walters Plant Hire P T Civil Engineering **Bred** Miss Philippa Proctor Quinn **Trained** Pandy, Monmouths

FOCUS
An interesting little conditions event in which odds-on backers got their fingers burnt. The winner has been rated back to his best.

6883 ALFORD INVESTMENTS LTD H'CAP 6f
3:20 (3:20) (Class 4) (0-85,85) 3-Y-O+ **£5,175** (£1,540; £769; £384) **Stalls** Low

Form RPR
3232 **1** **Pettochside**[7] 6668 7-8-8 **75**............ JosephineGordon(3) 5 82
(John Bridger) *mde all: drvn and strly chal fr over 2f out: hld on v gamely fnl f: all out* **4/1**[2]
3052 **2** nk **Lightning Charlie**[25] 6123 4-9-4 **85**............ KieranShoemark(3) 2 91
(Amanda Perrett) *in tch: hdwy over 2f out: rdn to chal wl over 1f out: kpt on w ev ch fnl f: hld nring fin* **9/1**
6236 **3** 1/2 **Alizoom (IRE)**[20] 6255 3-9-4 **84**............ HarryBentley 4 88
(Roger Varian) *trckd ldrs: rdn over 2f out: kpt on fnl f* **8/1**
4625 **4** nk **Hope Cove**[69] 4569 3-9-3 **83**............ GeorgeBaker 3 86+
(Ed Walker) *hld up: hdwy but nt clrest of runs 2f out: sn rdn to chse ldrs: kpt on ins fnl f* **17/2**
1505 **5** 1 **Goring (GER)**[12] 6539 4-9-6 **84**............ TomMarquand 9 84
(Eve Johnson Houghton) *trckd ldrs: rdn over 2f out: kpt on same pce* **7/1**[3]
0010 **6** 2 1/4 **Fairway To Heaven (IRE)**[20] 6263 7-9-5 **83**............ JimCrowley 6 76
(Michael Wigham) *s.i.s: last trio: rdn whn swtchd lft 2f out: kpt on fnl f but nt pce to make any imp* **9/1**
0062 **7** 6 **Sixties Sue**[18] 6340 3-8-12 **78**............ LukeMorris 1 52
(Mick Channon) *disp ld tl rdn over 2f out: wknd over 1f out* **9/1**
6010 **8** 1/2 **Nightingale Valley**[76] 4291 3-8-10 **76**............ OisinMurphy 7 48
(Stuart Kittow) *hld up last pair: struggling 3f out: wknd over 1f out* **20/1**
2441 **9** 3 1/2 **Foresight (FR)**[60] 4870 3-8-12 **78**............ JamieSpencer 8 39
(David Simcock) *hld up: struggling over 3f out: sn btn* **11/4**[1]

1m 17.39s (2.59) **Going Correction** +0.60s/f (Yiel)
WFA 3 from 4yo+ 2lb **9** Ran SP% **115.6**
Speed ratings (Par 105): **106,105,104,104,103 100,92,91,86**
CSF £39.72 CT £275.24 TOTE £5.00: £1.60, £2.80, £3.00; EX 41.00 Trifecta £123.80.
Owner P Cook **Bred** New Hall Stud **Trained** Liphook, Hants

FOCUS
A fair sprint handicap with not much covering the first five at the line.

6884 WEATHERBYS HAMILTON H'CAP 1m 1f 198y
3:55 (3:55) (Class 2) (0-105,105) 3-Y-O+
£12,450 (£3,728; £1,864; £932; £466; £234) **Stalls** Low

Form RPR
600 **1** **Storm Rock**[26] 6089 4-8-10 **87**............ HarryBentley 8 98
(Harry Dunlop) *mid-div: hdwy whn nt clr run over 3f out: swtchd lft and gd prog over 2f out: led over 1f out: styd on wl fnl 120yds: rdn out* **8/1**
0-12 **2** 1 3/4 **Landwade Lad**[21] 6233 4-9-1 **92**............ OisinMurphy 9 99
(James Fanshawe) *wnt lft s: mid-div: rdn and hdwy over 3f out: chal over 1f out: styd on but no ex fnl 120yds* **9/2**[2]
-605 **3** 1 1/4 **Captain Morley**[101] 3436 5-9-8 **99**............ JamieSpencer 3 104
(David Simcock) *mid-div: rdn and hdwy fr wl over 2f out: wnt 3rd ins fnl f: styd on but nvr trbld ldrs* **8/1**
0542 **4** 1/2 **Beach Bar (IRE)**[17] 6364 5-9-2 **96**............ JosephineGordon(3) 4 100
(Brendan Powell) *led: clr after 2f: reduced advantage and rdn 3f out: hdd over 1f out: no ex fnl f* **10/1**
1414 **5** 1 1/2 **Fidaawy**[31] 5924 3-8-11 **94**............ DaneO'Neill 5 95
(Sir Michael Stoute) *trckd ldrs: rdn wl over 2f out: sn one pce* **4/1**[1]
6354 **6** nk **Master Carpenter (IRE)**[17] 6364 5-9-4 **102**............ LuluStanford(7) 1 102
(Rod Millman) *chsd clr ldr: clsd on ldr 3f out: sn rdn: one pce fnl 2f* **7/1**
5003 **7** 9 **Windshear**[21] 6233 5-9-2 **93**............ SeanLevey 2 75
(Richard Hannon) *chsd clr ldr tl rdn over 3f out: wknd 2f out* **7/1**
001 **8** 29 **Zamperini (IRE)**[89] 3861 4-8-12 **89**............ JimCrowley 6 13
(Mike Murphy) *hld up: rdn over 3f out: sn wknd: eased over 1f out* **6/1**[3]
5602 **9** 8 **Captain Cat (IRE)**[95] 3672 7-10-0 **105**............ AdamKirby 7 13
(Tony Carroll) *hld up: rdn 3f out: nvr any imp: wknd 2f out: eased* **16/1**

2m 12.63s (2.73) **Going Correction** +0.525s/f (Yiel)
WFA 3 from 4yo+ 6lb **9** Ran SP% **114.7**
Speed ratings (Par 109): **110,108,107,107,106 105,98,75,68**
CSF £43.55 CT £299.21 TOTE £11.60: £3.10, £2.10, £2.50; EX 58.30 Trifecta £427.00.
Owner Malcolm & Alicia Aldis **Bred** Kempsons Stud **Trained** Lambourn, Berks

FOCUS
A warm handicap and a strong pace thanks to the fourth horse. The field were soon well spread out and it became a war of attrition.

6885 BATHWICK TYRES H'CAP (DIV I) 1m 6f 21y
4:30 (4:31) (Class 5) (0-75,75) 3-Y-O+ **£3,234** (£962; £481; £240) **Stalls** Far side

Form RPR
1-36 **1** **Bellajeu**[27] 6050 4-10-0 **75**............ OisinMurphy 3 83
(Ralph Beckett) *trckd ldr: led over 2f out: styd on wl: rdn out* **13/2**
6024 **2** 1 1/4 **Contingency**[25] 6127 3-9-0 **71**............ JimmyFortune 10 77
(Jane Chapple-Hyam) *trckd ldrs: rdn w ev ch fr 2f out: styd on but no ex nring fin* **14/1**

/221 **3** *nk* **Miss Tiger Lily**[27] 6058 6-9-6 **67** .... JimCrowley 8 73
(Harry Dunlop) *led: rdn and hdd over 2f out: kpt chsng wnr disputing 2nd: styd on fnl f* **9/2**[3]
1015 **4** *2 3/4* **Onorina (IRE)**[46] 5406 4-9-9 **70** .... SamHitchcott 7 72
(Jim Boyle) *racd keenly: in tch: rdn over 3f out: styd on same pce fnl 2f* **20/1**
2154 **5** *3/4* **Ivanhoe**[13] 6519 6-9-7 **68** .... (v) DaneO'Neill 6 69
(Michael Blanshard) *mid-div tl lost pl 4f out: rdn and prog over 2f out: styd on same pce fnl f* **7/1**
535 **6** *2 1/4* **Knight Commander**[17] 6380 3-8-10 **67** .... LukeMorris 12 65
(William Knight) *hld up last pair: rdn and hdwy 3f out: nt pce to get on terms: fdd fnl 120yds* **4/1**[2]
3543 **7** *12* **Lilbourne Prince (IRE)**[11] 6576 3-9-2 **73** ow1 .... AdamKirby 5 54
(David Evans) *hld up: effrt and sme prog 3f out: wknd over 1f out* **7/1**
3511 **8** *2* **Hearty (IRE)**[97] 3570 3-8-8 **65** .... (p) JamieSpencer 1 43
(Jeremy Noseda) *in tch: hdwy over 3f out: sn rdn: wknd 2f out* **3/1**[1]
3/06 **9** *4 1/2* **Daliance (IRE)**[119] 2805 7-9-8 **69** .... (v) TomMarquand 2 41
(Noel Williams) *mid-div tl rdn over 5f out: sn bhd* **50/1**

3m 18.5s (11.10) **Going Correction** +0.525s/f (Yiel)
WFA 3 from 4yo+ 10lb **9** Ran SP% **114.9**
Speed ratings (Par 103): **89,88,88,86,86 84,77,76,74**
CSF £91.29 CT £450.97 TOTE £6.90: £2.30, £4.10, £1.60; EX 94.30 Trifecta £739.50.
Owner QRL/Sheikh Suhaim Al Thani/M Al Kubaisi **Bred** Windymains Farm Ltd **Trained** Kimpton, Hants

FOCUS
The first division of a modest staying handicap and not many got into it, with the 1-2-3 racing 2-3-1 for much of the journey. This was one for the girls with the four fillies and mares filling the first four places.

6886 BATHWICK TYRES H'CAP (DIV II) 1m 6f 21y
5:00 (5:00) (Class 5) (0-75,75) 3-Y-O+ **£3,234** (£962; £481; £240) **Stalls** Far side

Form RPR
0443 **1** **Glorious Legend (IRE)**[18] 6335 3-8-4 **61** .... TomMarquand 6 71
(Ed Walker) *mde virtually all: styd on wl: drvn out* **7/1**[3]
1440 **2** *2 1/4* **Rainbow Pride (IRE)**[26] 6090 4-9-12 **73** .... LukeMorris 3 80
(Sir Mark Prescott Bt) *trckd ldrs: rdn to chse wnr over 2f out: drifted to far rails and hld over 1f out: styd on same pce* **14/1**
-641 **3** *3 1/2* **Wynford (IRE)**[21] 6227 3-9-1 **75** .... RobHornby(3) 2 77
(Andrew Balding) *mid-div: rdn 3f out: wnt 3rd over 1f out: styd on same pce fnl f* **11/4**[2]
3205 **4** *2 3/4* **Mazalto (IRE)**[21] 6242 3-9-2 **73** .... JamieSpencer 9 71
(Pat Phelan) *hld up: swtchd to center and stdy prog u.p fr over 3f out: wnt hld 4th over 1f out: nvr threatened ldrs* **12/1**
465 **5** *8* **Versant**[16] 6415 4-9-10 **71** .... (t) MartinHarley 11 58
(Seamus Durack) *racd keenly: trckd ldrs after 1f: rdn over 3f out: wknd over 1f out* **8/1**
452 **6** *3 1/4* **Roderic's Secret (IRE)**[17] 6380 3-8-12 **69** .... JimCrowley 4 52
(David Menuisier) *trckd wnr after 1f: rdn over 3f out: wknd over 1f out* **2/1**[1]
1150 **7** *2 1/2* **Urban Space**[18] 6315 10-9-7 **68** .... (t) DanielMuscutt 7 47
(John Flint) *in tch: effrt over 3f out: wknd over 1f out* **28/1**
6004 **8** *35* **Astrosecret**[35] 5763 3-8-9 **66** .... StevieDonohoe 5
(Mark H Tompkins) *mid-div: rdn over 4f out: wknd 3f out: eased* **25/1**
2232 **9** *1/2* **Torquay**[28] 6031 3-9-1 **72** .... (v) SamHitchcott 10
(Harry Dunlop) *struggling over 4f out: a in rr: eased* **12/1**
2-36 **10** *82* **Mr Fickle (IRE)**[23] 6193 7-9-8 **69** .... GeorgeBaker 1
(Gary Moore) *lft at s: sauntered rnd in own time: a wl bhd* **20/1**

3m 13.61s (6.21) **Going Correction** +0.525s/f (Yiel)
WFA 3 from 4yo+ 10lb **10** Ran SP% **117.7**
Speed ratings (Par 103): **103,101,99,98,93 91,90,70,70,23**
CSF £97.12 CT £336.32 TOTE £9.50: £2.70, £3.90, £1.70; EX 76.30 Trifecta £292.40.
Owner Kangyu International Racing (HK) Limited **Bred** Greenwood Lodge Farm Inc **Trained** Upper Lambourn, Berks

FOCUS
A shambolic start to the second division of this staying handicap, which saw Mr Fickle immediately tailed off and a few soon pulling furiously for their heads. The field finished well spread out and again it paid to be up there.
T/Plt: £898.40 to a £1 stake. Pool: £61847.49, 50.25 winning units T/Qpdt: £89.00 to a £1 stake. Pool: £4428.58, 36.82 winning units **Tim Mitchell**

6404 BRIGHTON (L-H)
Thursday, September 29

OFFICIAL GOING: Good to firm
Wind: Fresh, against Weather: Overcast

6887 ROA/RACING POST OWNERS JACKPOT NURSERY H'CAP 5f 59y
1:50 (1:51) (Class 6) (0-60,58) 2-Y-O **£2,587** (£770; £384; £192) **Stalls** Low

Form RPR
0003 **1** **Harlequin Rose (IRE)**[9] 6652 2-8-12 **49** .... (v) SilvestreDeSousa 4 54
(Mick Channon) *dwlt: towards rr: rdn 3f out: hdwy and hung lft to ins rail over 1f out: r.o to ld fnl 50yds* **11/4**[1]
033 **2** *1* **Glyder**[16] 6448 2-9-5 **56** .... AdamKirby 2 57
(John Holt) *led: hrd rdn fnl f: hdd and one pce fnl 50yds* **10/3**[2]
6201 **3** *1/2* **Rebel Heart**[21] 6252 2-9-7 **58** .... (v) WilliamCarson 3 57
(Bill Turner) *prom: chsd wnr 2f out: one pce ins fnl f: lost 2nd fnl 75yds* **6/1**
404 **4** *3 1/2* **Ginger Truffle**[55] 5099 2-8-13 **55** .... PaddyBradley(5) 8 42
(Brett Johnson) *chsd ldr tl 2f out: wknd fnl f* **20/1**
4450 **5** *nk* **Shadow Wing (IRE)**[17] 6419 2-8-13 **55** .... AnnStokell(5) 7 41
(Ann Stokell) *dwlt: bhd tl styd on fr over 1f out* **50/1**
405 **6** *1/2* **Zipedee**[14] 6524 2-9-3 **54** .... JimCrowley 5 38
(John Ryan) *in tch: rdn and carried lft over 1f out: no ex fnl f* **4/1**[3]
5660 **7** *4* **Hi There Silver (IRE)**[36] 5770 2-8-11 **53** .... (v[1]) GeorgeWood(5) 1 22
(Michael Madgwick) *in tch: hrd rdn 3f out: sn wknd* **25/1**
0500 **8** *3 1/2* **Miss Salt**[9] 6652 2-8-6 **46** .... EdwardGreatrex(3) 6 3
(Dominic Ffrench Davis) *a bhd* **20/1**

1m 3.5s (1.20) **Going Correction** +0.15s/f (Good) **8** Ran SP% **99.4**
Speed ratings (Par 93): **96,94,93,88,87 86,80,74**
CSF £8.42 CT £28.93 TOTE £3.60: £1.20, £1.30, £1.90; EX 9.30 Trifecta £25.60.
Owner Harlequin Direct Ltd **Bred** Langton Stud **Trained** West Ilsley, Berks
■ Nuptials was withdrawn. Price at time of withdrawal 5/1. Rule 4 applies to all bets - deduction 15p in the pound.

FOCUS
A lowly nursery and the picture changed late on. The second and third are rated near their pre-race marks.

6888 IRISH STALLION FARMS EBF MEDIAN AUCTION MAIDEN STKS 6f 209y
2:20 (2:22) (Class 5) 2-Y-O **£3,697** (£1,100; £549; £274) **Stalls** Low

Form RPR
1 **Come On Come On (IRE)** 2-9-5 0 .... AdamKirby 1 78+
(Clive Cox) *s.i.s: rn green in rr: hdwy and hung lft fr 2f out: r.o to ld fnl 75yds: pushed out* **9/2**[3]
425 **2** *3/4* **Akkadian Empire**[8] 6664 2-9-5 0 .... SilvestreDeSousa 2 74
(Mick Channon) *dwlt: sn slt ld on inner: kicked on 2f out: hdd and one pce fnl 75yds* **15/8**[1]
3 **3** *1/2* **Miss Fay (IRE)**[36] 5771 2-9-0 0 .... MartinHarley 10 68
(Michael Bell) *cl up: rdn to chse ldr wl over 1f out: kpt on same pce* **5/1**
054 **4** *2 1/2* **Tesko Fella (IRE)**[6] 6731 2-9-5 0 .... KieranO'Neill 6 66
(Richard Hannon) *t.k.h towards rr: hdwy and carried lft over 1f out: styd on same pce* **7/2**[2]
603 **5** *3 1/2* **Rock On Dandy (FR)**[54] 5166 2-9-5 67 .... (b) JimCrowley 11 56
(Harry Dunlop) *dwlt: hld up in 6th: rdn 3f out: btn 2f out* **14/1**
2305 **6** *1/2* **Rising Eagle**[29] 6033 2-9-5 67 .... MichaelJMMurphy 5 55
(Charles Hills) *t.k.h: chsd ldr tl outpcd fnl 2f* **7/1**
40 **7** *3 1/4* **Beepeecee**[16] 6439 2-9-5 0 .... ShaneKelly 4 46
(Richard Hughes) *chsd ldrs: rdn 3f out: wknd 2f out* **33/1**
05 **8** *nk* **Take This Waltz**[55] 5099 2-9-0 0 .... WilliamCarson 7 41
(Bill Turner) *pressed ldr tl 2f out: hrd rdn and wknd over 1f out* **100/1**
0 **9** *1 1/2* **Kingston Tasmania**[16] 6439 2-8-12 0 .... JoshuaBryan(7) 8 41
(Andrew Balding) *a towards rr* **33/1**

1m 24.3s (1.20) **Going Correction** +0.15s/f (Good) **9** Ran SP% **117.9**
Speed ratings (Par 95): **99,98,97,94,90 90,86,86,84**
CSF £13.56 TOTE £5.50: £2.20, £1.20, £1.50; EX 16.40 Trifecta £64.40.
Owner Paul & Clare Rooney **Bred** Razza Pallorsi Snc **Trained** Lambourn, Berks

FOCUS
A modest maiden. The winner came from last place and the form is rated around the second.

6889 HERBERT WILLIAM HALL MEMORIAL H'CAP 1m 1f 209y
2:50 (2:50) (Class 5) (0-75,75) 4-Y-O+ **£3,557** (£1,058; £529; £264) **Stalls** High

Form RPR
403 **1** **Bridge Of Sighs**[7] 6702 4-9-4 **72** .... PatCosgrave 4 80
(Martin Smith) *hld up towards rr: hdwy 2f out: r.o to ld fnl 75yds: rdn out* **3/1**[1]
2645 **2** *nk* **Gannicus**[48] 5374 5-8-13 **67** .... (tp) MartinDwyer 10 74
(Brendan Powell) *trckd ldr: led and hung lft over 1f out: hdd fnl 75yds: kpt on* **11/1**
6/00 **3** *1 3/4* **East India**[20] 6301 4-9-7 **75** .... SteveDrowne 12 79
(George Baker) *mid-div tl rdn and styd on wl fnl 2f* **8/1**
5-00 **4** *1 1/4* **Secular Society**[11] 6365 6-9-1 **69** .... (t) LiamKeniry 11 70
(George Baker) *led tl over 1f out: no ex fnl f* **25/1**
4550 **5** *1 1/2* **Top Diktat**[73] 4459 8-8-11 **70** .... HectorCrouch(5) 6 68+
(Gary Moore) *bhd tl rdn and styd on fnl 2f* **12/1**
5531 **6** *3 3/4* **Solveig's Song**[15] 6485 4-8-10 **67** .... (p) EdwardGreatrex(3) 9 58
(Steve Woodman) *towards rr: rdn and hdwy over 1f out: nvr able to chal* **7/1**[3]
5040 **7** *2* **Mister Musicmaster**[18] 6365 7-9-2 **70** .... JimCrowley 5 57
(Ron Hodges) *prom tl wknd over 1f out* **14/1**
1552 **8** *6* **Lord Reason**[24] 6186 4-9-7 **75** .... SilvestreDeSousa 7 50
(John Butler) *t.k.h: chsd ldrs tl wknd qckly over 1f out: eased ins fnl f* **10/3**[2]
6162 **9** *5* **Barren Brook**[30] 5994 9-9-3 **71** .... GeorgeBaker 1 36
(Laura Mongan) *stdd s: plld hrd: hdwy into midfield after 2f out: wknd qckly 2f out* **9/1**
5003 **10** *3 1/4* **Moojaned (IRE)**[18] 6380 5-9-6 **74** .... AdamKirby 2 32
(David Evans) *t.k.h in midfield: wknd over 2f out* **7/1**[3]

2m 5.57s (1.97) **Going Correction** +0.15s/f (Good) **10** Ran SP% **120.7**
Speed ratings (Par 103): **98,97,96,95,94 91,89,84,80,78**
CSF £38.47 CT £247.73 TOTE £3.90: £1.80, £3.10, £2.90; EX 37.00 Trifecta £331.40.
Owner SN Racing VI **Bred** S Nunn **Trained** Newmarket, Suffolk

FOCUS
A modest handicap. The winner resumed his earlier progress.

6890 PARK LANE GROUP H'CAP (DIV I) 1m 1f 209y
3:25 (3:25) (Class 6) (0-55,55) 3-Y-O+ **£2,587** (£770; £384; £192) **Stalls** High

Form RPR
0436 **1** **Moss Street**[19] 6315 6-9-3 **50** .... (bt) DanielMuscutt 6 60
(John Flint) *s.i.s: hld up towards rr: hdwy over 2f out: drvn to ld ins fnl f* **8/1**
0041 **2** *nk* **Purple Party (IRE)**[24] 6187 3-8-5 **47** .... NoelGarbutt(3) 5 56
(Gary Moore) *plld hrd: prom: led over 2f out tl ins fnl f: kpt on wl* **5/2**[1]
0-33 **3** *2* **Smiley Bagel (IRE)**[156] 1740 3-8-12 **51** .... RichardKingscote 9 56+
(Ed Walker) *towards rr: rdn over 2f out: hung lft over 1f out: styd on wl fnl f* **7/2**[2]
2113 **4** *2* **Barnaby Brook (CAN)**[117] 2899 6-9-8 **55** .... (b) MartinHarley 7 56
(Robyn Brisland) *t.k.h: trckd ldrs: rdn over 2f out: one pce appr fnl f* **6/1**[3]
4560 **5** *3/4* **Rennie Mackintosh (IRE)**[17] 6411 4-9-8 **55** .... DannyBrock 10 55
(John Bridger) *chsd ldrs: drvn along over 2f out: one pce* **12/1**
-633 **6** *3 3/4* **Cranwell**[17] 6406 4-9-7 **54** .... PatCosgrave 11 47
(George Baker) *t.k.h towards rr: hrd rdn 2f out: n.d* **8/1**
7 *2 1/2* **Light Of The Moon (IRE)**[41] 5565 5-8-13 **46** oh1 .... (t) JFEgan 8 34
(David Evans) *bhd: hrd rdn 3f out: nvr rchd ldrs* **40/1**
4605 **8** *1 3/4* **Jackpot**[29] 6020 6-8-6 **46** oh1 .... (p) LuluStanford(7) 1 31
(Brendan Powell) *chsd ldrs: led after 3f tl over 2f out: wknd over 1f out* **33/1**
0050 **9** *2 1/4* **Master Of Heaven**[14] 6513 3-9-1 **54** .... (v[1]) FergusSweeney 3 35
(Jim Boyle) *chsd ldrs tl wknd over 2f out* **14/1**
00-0 **10** *1 1/2* **Maer Rocks (IRE)**[118] 2851 3-8-11 **50** .... JimCrowley 4 30
(Marcus Tregoning) *led for 3f: chsd ldrs tl n.m.r and wknd wl over 1f out* **7/1**

2m 5.18s (1.58) **Going Correction** +0.15s/f (Good)
WFA 3 from 4yo+ 6lb **10** Ran SP% **119.5**
Speed ratings (Par 101): **99,98,97,95,94 91,89,88,86,85**
CSF £29.05 CT £85.87 TOTE £8.00: £2.80, £1.60, £1.60; EX 38.20 Trifecta £177.60.
Owner Burnham P & D ltd **Bred** Redland Bloodstock Limited **Trained** Kenfig Hill, Bridgend
■ Stewards' Enquiry : Noel Garbutt two-day ban; used his whip above the permitted level (13th-14th Oct)
Fergus Sweeney jockey said that the gelding hung left-handed

FOCUS
Lowly handicap form but a decent race for the grade.

6891 PARK LANE GROUP H'CAP (DIV II) 1m 1f 209y
4:00 (4:00) (Class 6) (0-55,55) 3-Y-O+ **£2,587** (£770; £384; £192) **Stalls** High

Form RPR

0435 **1** **Onehelluvatouch**[24] 6185 3-8-11 **50**....(b[1]) JimCrowley 2 61+
(Philip Hide) *hld up: hdwy over 2f out: led wl over 1f out: rdn clr: edgd lft: comf* **3/1**[2]

1444 **2** *5* **Highlife Dancer**[24] 6188 8-9-8 **55**.... SilvestreDeSousa 8 57
(Mick Channon) *chsd ldrs: rdn 2f out: wnt 2nd 1f out: no ch w wnr* **9/2**[3]

3440 **3** *1* **Top Pocket**[25] 4992 4-9-0 **47**.... DanielMuscutt 10 49
(Michael Madgwick) *bhd: nt clr run 2f out: styd on wl fr over 1f out* **7/1**

4344 **4** *1 1/4* **Megalala (IRE)**[17] 6406 15-9-5 **52**.... DannyBrock 4 49
(John Bridger) *led tl wl over 1f out: kpt on same pce* **6/1**

00/0 **5** *nk* **Jenny Sparks**[38] 5710 5-8-13 **46** oh1.... HarryPoulton 9 43
(Sheena West) *bhd: rdn and hdwy over 1f out: styd on same pce* **50/1**

-033 **6** *2* **Hermosa Vaquera (IRE)**[36] 5777 6-8-13 **51**....(tp) HectorCrouch[(5)] 5 46
(Gary Moore) *prom: rdn 3f out: 4th and btn whn squeezed out ins fnl f* **11/4**[1]

0000 **7** *3 1/2* **Abertillery**[9] 6651 4-8-13 **46**.... TomMarquand 3 32
(Michael Blanshard) *bhd: effrt and hrd rdn over 2f out: nvr able to chal* **14/1**

00P0 **8** *1* **Kristoff (IRE)**[18] 6373 3-8-8 **47**....(p) SamHitchcott 7 31
(Jim Boyle) *in tch: rdn to chse ldrs over 2f out: wknd over 1f out* **25/1**

5/50 **9** *13* **Another Squeeze**[31] 5958 8-8-13 **46** oh1.... LiamKeniry 11 6
(Peter Hiatt) *prom tl wknd and n.m.r over 2f out* **12/1**

0-00 **10** *22* **Spice Boat**[103] 3401 4-8-8 **46** oh1.... MeganNicholls[(5)] 6
(Paddy Butler) *trckd ldrs tl wknd over 2f out* **66/1**

2m 4.96s (1.36) **Going Correction** +0.15s/f (Good)
WFA 3 from 4yo+ 6lb **10** Ran SP% **118.3**
Speed ratings (Par 101): **100,96,95,94,93 92,89,88,78,60**
CSF £17.10 CT £88.11 TOTE £3.40: £1.70, £1.90, £2.70; EX 18.50 Trifecta £128.30.
Owner Heart Of The South Racing **Bred** Soft Touch Syndicate **Trained** Findon, W Sussex

■ Stewards' Enquiry : Harry Poulton £140 fine; arrived in the Parade Ring after the signal to mount had been given

FOCUS
Division two of a lowly handicap and it was won in dominant fashion. The winner recorded a pb.

6892 VEOLIA RECYCLING H'CAP 1m 3f 196y
4:30 (4:32) (Class 5) (0-75,75) 4-Y-O+ **£3,557** (£1,058; £529; £264) **Stalls** High

Form RPR

6346 **1** **Whinging Willie (IRE)**[21] 6267 7-9-0 **73**....(v) HectorCrouch[(5)] 6 82
(Gary Moore) *t.k.h towards rr: hdwy to ld 2f out: hld on wl fnl f* **9/2**[3]

5-00 **2** *3/4* **Open The Red**[26] 6128 4-9-7 **75**.... JimCrowley 8 83
(Amanda Perrett) *in tch: drvn to chal whn hung lft over 1f out: no ex nr fin* **9/4**[1]

2100 **3** *8* **Longside**[51] 5267 4-9-2 **70**.... RyanTate 5 65
(James Eustace) *chsd ldrs tl outpcd fnl 2f* **20/1**

5654 **4** *1* **Daisy Boy (IRE)**[31] 5964 5-9-4 **75**....(t) AaronJones[(3)] 1 69
(Stuart Williams) *led tl outpcd 2f out* **3/1**[2]

-636 **5** *3 1/4* **Meetings Man (IRE)**[27] 6090 9-9-2 **70**....(p) AdamKirby 3 58
(Ali Stronge) *pressed ldr tl rdn and lost pl 2f out: passed btn horses fnl f* **12/1**

1665 **6** *1* **Roy Rocket (FR)**[31] 5963 6-9-2 **70**.... DanielMuscutt 2 57
(John Berry) *towards rr: sme hdwy 2f out: sn wknd* **8/1**

2255 **7** *1/2* **Safira Menina**[16] 6457 4-8-9 **70**.... NatalieHambling[(7)] 9 56
(Martin Smith) *dwlt: bhd: sme hdwy on inner 2f out: sn wknd* **8/1**

0534 **8** *nk* **Classic Mission**[30] 6001 5-8-5 **66**....(b) Pierre-LouisJamin[(7)] 4 52
(Jonathan Portman) *s.s: sn chsng ldrs: hrd rdn over 2f out: wknd over 1f out* **16/1**

0305 **9** *12* **Sixties Love**[19] 6334 5-8-8 **62**.... KieranO'Neill 7 28
(Simon Dow) *s.s: towards rr: hdwy 1/2-way: wknd over 2f out* **20/1**

2m 33.03s (0.33) **Going Correction** +0.15s/f (Good) **9** Ran SP% **119.3**
Speed ratings (Par 103): **104,103,98,97,95 94,94,94,86**
CSF £15.60 CT £180.69 TOTE £6.10: £1.80, £1.40, £4.10; EX 16.70 Trifecta £195.60.
Owner P B Moorhead **Bred** Joe Rogers **Trained** Lower Beeding, W Sussex

FOCUS
The front pair, both challenging centre-field, came right away in what was an ordinary handicap. The winner is rated around his recent form rather than his early-season peak.

6893 FROSTS CARS FILLIES' H'CAP 7f 214y
5:05 (5:05) (Class 5) (0-75,75) 3-Y-O+ **£3,557** (£1,058; £529; £264) **Stalls** Low

Form RPR

3152 **1** **Wrapped**[10] 6635 3-9-3 **75**....(p) GeorgiaCox[(5)] 2 83+
(William Haggas) *s.s: towards rr: hdwy 2f out: led and edgd rt over 1f out: edgd lft ins fnl f: all out* **10/3**[1]

023 **2** *nk* **Carpe Diem Lady (IRE)**[33] 5891 3-9-7 **74**....(b[1]) AdamKirby 8 79
(Clive Cox) *led: hrd rdn and hdd over 1f out: hung lft ins fnl f: rallied wl nr fin* **9/2**

1054 **3** *1 1/4* **Ejayteekay**[18] 6378 3-9-8 **75**.... JimCrowley 9 79+
(Hughie Morrison) *towards rr: hdwy to press wnr whn nt clr run over 1f out: swtchd lft and nt clr run ins fnl f: kpt on* **4/1**[3]

4600 **4** *4 1/2* **Harikiri (IRE)**[16] 6444 3-8-0 **60**.... CameronNoble[(7)] 7 52
(Charles Hills) *s.s: bhd: hdwy over 1f out: no imp fnl f* **33/1**

3405 **5** *2* **Bay Of St Malo (IRE)**[9] 6657 3-9-7 **74**.... KieranO'Neill 1 61
(Richard Hannon) *chsd ldrs tl wknd over 1f out* **8/1**

3104 **6** *1 1/2* **Bonhomie**[34] 5860 3-8-13 **66**.... MartinHarley 10 50
(Michael Bell) *in tch: effrt and hung lft fr 2f out: wknd over 1f out* **8/1**

3-45 **7** *13* **My Favourite Thing**[121] 2783 3-9-6 **73**.... HarryBentley 3 27
(Roger Varian) *chsd ldrs tl wknd over 2f out* **7/2**[2]

0601 **8** *21* **Plauseabella**[19] 6337 5-8-11 **60**....(p) MartinDwyer 4
(Stuart Kittow) *chsd ldr tl wknd and n.m.r over 2f out* **10/1**

1m 35.42s (-0.58) **Going Correction** +0.15s/f (Good)
WFA 3 from 5yo+ 4lb **8** Ran SP% **117.7**
Speed ratings (Par 100): **108,107,106,101,99 98,85,64**
CSF £19.32 CT £62.41 TOTE £3.90: £1.20, £1.70, £1.60; EX 15.50 Trifecta £43.40.
Owner Cheveley Park Stud **Bred** Whatton Manor Stud **Trained** Newmarket, Suffolk

FOCUS
A fair fillies' handicap run at a decent pace. The form is set around the second.

6894 ROCS ELECTRICAL H'CAP 5f 213y
5:35 (5:35) (Class 6) (0-60,60) 3-Y-O+ **£2,587** (£770; £384; £192) **Stalls** Low

Form RPR

4300 **1** **Virile (IRE)**[18] 6363 5-9-5 **58**....(bt) GeorgeBaker 9 66
(Sylvester Kirk) *s.s: t.k.h and hld up in last: rapid hdwy over 1f out: str run to ld fnl 50yds* **4/1**[1]

4066 **2** *1 3/4* **The Reel Way (GR)**[19] 6312 5-8-7 **46** oh1.... JimmyQuinn 4 49
(Patrick Chamings) *in tch: chal 2f out: hrd rdn and ev ch ins fnl f: outpcd fnl 50yds* **14/1**

6410 **3** *nse* **Burauq**[2] 6853 4-8-12 **51**....(b) RichardKingscote 1 54
(Milton Bradley) *towards rr: hdwy 2f out: led over 1f out: hrd rdn fnl f: hdd and one pce fnl 50yds* **8/1**

0005 **4** *nk* **Triple Dream**[19] 6311 11-8-2 **48**.... LuluStanford[(7)] 8 50
(Milton Bradley) *led tl over 1f out: kpt on u.p* **12/1**

1623 **5** *1 3/4* **Fairy Mist (IRE)**[22] 6238 9-9-3 **56**....(v) DannyBrock 3 52
(John Bridger) *outpcd in rr tl styd on fr over 1f out* **5/1**[3]

0600 **6** *hd* **Hipz (IRE)**[21] 6269 5-9-2 **55**....(p) LiamKeniry 7 51
(Laura Mongan) *mid-div: rdn 2f out: kpt on fnl f* **9/1**

1004 **7** *1/2* **Noverre To Go (IRE)**[43] 5546 10-9-7 **60**....(p) TomMarquand 12 54
(Ronald Harris) *dwlt: sn chsng ldrs on outer: hrd rdn 2f out: hung lft: btn over 1f out* **10/1**

0600 **8** *2* **Goadby**[8] 6685 5-9-4 **57**.... MichaelJMMurphy 2 45
(John Holt) *stmbld s: chsd ldr tl wknd over 1f out* **12/1**

6000 **9** *1 1/4* **Magic Strike (IRE)**[20] 6290 3-9-2 **57**....(b) AdamKirby 11 42
(Clive Cox) *prom tl wknd over 1f out* **9/2**[2]

1446 **10** *nk* **Baz's Boy**[20] 6291 3-8-4 **48**.... NoelGarbutt[(3)] 6 32
(John Flint) *mid-div: pushed along 1/2-way: outpcd fnl 2f* **8/1**

60-0 **11** *3 1/2* **Kylies Wild Card**[87] 3953 4-8-3 **47**.... MeganNicholls[(5)] 5 20
(Simon Hodgson) *outpcd towards rr: rdn and n.d fnl 2f* **33/1**

1m 11.04s (0.84) **Going Correction** +0.15s/f (Good)
WFA 3 from 4yo+ 2lb **11** Ran SP% **121.2**
Speed ratings (Par 101): **100,97,97,97,94 94,93,91,89,89 84**
CSF £63.07 CT £445.12 TOTE £4.30: £2.20, £4.10, £2.50; EX 57.80 Trifecta £545.40.
Owner Gerry Dolan **Bred** B Holland, S Hillen & J Cullinan **Trained** Upper Lambourn, Berks

FOCUS
Another race on the day that went to a closer. The form makes sense.
T/Jkpt: Not won. T/Plt: £26.00 to a £1 stake. Pool: £89408.18, 2507.91 winning units T/Qpdt: £13.00 to a £1 stake. Pool: £6515.67, 369.6 winning units **Lee McKenzie**

6696 CHELMSFORD (A.W) (L-H)
Thursday, September 29

OFFICIAL GOING: Polytrack: standard
Wind: light to medium, half behind Weather: dry

6895 TOTEPLACEPOT NURSERY H'CAP (DIV I) 6f (P)
5:40 (5:41) (Class 6) (0-60,63) 2-Y-O **£3,234** (£962; £481; £240) **Stalls** Centre

Form RPR

4650 **1** **Iftitah (IRE)**[22] 6222 2-8-11 **50**....[1] StevieDonohoe 9 63
(George Peckham) *bhd: hdwy between horses to chse clr ldng pair over 1f out: str run to ld ins fnl f: sn clr: readily* **7/1**[3]

3541 **2** *4 1/2* **Swallow Street (IRE)**[8] 6678 2-9-10 **63** 6ex....(b) WilliamCarson 5 62
(Jamie Osborne) *chsd ldr: effrt to chse ldr over 2f out: ev ch ent fnl f: chsd wnr and kpt on same pce ins fnl f* **11/8**[1]

0055 **3** *1 1/2* **Heavenly Cry**[17] 6412 2-8-7 **49**....(b) JosephineGordon[(3)] 2 44
(Phil McEntee) *taken down early: led: rdn over 1f out: wandered and hdd ins fnl f: sn btn and wknd wl ins fnl f* **8/1**

0440 **4** *1 1/4* **Misty Moo**[26] 6139 2-9-4 **57**.... AndrewMullen 3 48
(Michael Appleby) *midfield: effrt in 4th whn hung rt over 1f out: nvr on terms w ldrs but kpt on ins fnl f* **16/1**

0026 **5** *1* **Chiconomic (IRE)**[21] 6252 2-9-3 **56**....(b[1]) LiamJones 7 44
(Rae Guest) *midfield and sn pushed along: no imp whn pushed rt over 1f out: plugged on but wl hld after* **12/1**

000 **6** *2 3/4* **Rockaria**[15] 6480 2-8-6 **45**.... KierenFox 6 25
(Philip Hide) *broke wl to chse ldrs but wd: rdn and lost pl over 4f out: hung rt and dropped to rr 3f out: no ch over 1f out* **12/1**

5040 **7** *1 1/4* **Sadieroseclifford (IRE)**[8] 6670 2-9-2 **60**.... CliffordLee[(5)] 8 36
(Denis Quinn) *racd in last pair: effrt and swtchd rt over 1f out: no imp: nvr trbld ldrs* **6/1**[2]

4540 **8** *2 3/4* **Surfina**[29] 6035 2-8-11 **53**....(b[1]) JackDuern[(3)] 1 21
(Dean Ivory) *chsd ldrs: wnt 2nd over 3f out tl over 2f out: lost pl over 1f out: wknd fnl f* **12/1**

000 **9** *1 1/4* **See You Mush**[14] 6524 2-9-6 **59**....(b[1]) LemosdeSouza 4 23
(Chris Dwyer) *t.k.h: chsd ldr tl over 3f out: steadily lost pl: nudged rt over 1f out: sn wknd* **8/1**

1m 13.78s (0.08) **Going Correction** -0.125s/f (Stan) **9** Ran SP% **120.1**
Speed ratings (Par 93): **94,88,86,84,83 79,77,74,72**
CSF £17.75 CT £84.20 TOTE £9.30: £4.10, £1.02, £2.60; EX 21.30 Trifecta £149.00.
Owner Fawzi Abdulla Nass **Bred** Palmerston Bloodstock Ltd **Trained** Newmarket, Suffolk

FOCUS
The first division of a mainly moderate handicap was run at a fair tempo and the pace rather collapsed. The winner left his earlier form behind.

6896 TOTEPLACEPOT NURSERY H'CAP (DIV II) 6f (P)
6:10 (6:12) (Class 6) (0-60,60) 2-Y-O **£3,234** (£962; £481; £240) **Stalls** Centre

Form RPR

0246 **1** **Acertwo**[17] 6412 2-9-1 **59**.... CliffordLee[(5)] 7 66
(Joseph Tuite) *in tch in midfield: effrt ent fnl 2f: swtchd lft and hdwy over 1f out: chsd clr ldr jst ins fnl f: clsng and swtchd rt ins fnl f: styd on to ld cl home* **2/1**[2]

0006 **2** *1/2* **Gabridan (IRE)**[8] 6678 2-8-11 **50**....(v[1]) GeorgeChaloner 5 55
(Richard Fahey) *led: rdn and kicked clr over 1f out: drvn and tiring ins fnl f: hdd cl home* **8/1**

0300 **3** *5* **Varun's Bride (IRE)**[17] 6412 2-9-1 **54**.... PatDobbs 3 44
(Richard Hannon) *hld up in tch in midfield: effrt jst over 2f out: swtchd lft and no imp over 1f out: no threat to ldng pair and kpt on same pce ins fnl f: snatched 3rd last stride* **5/1**[3]

5500 **4** *shd* **Ciel Rouge**[8] 6670 2-9-4 **57**.... KierenFox 4 47
(Charlie Wallis) *chsd ldr: rdn over 2f out: chsd clr ldr and edgd rt over 1f out: 3rd and kpt on same pce ins fnl f* **20/1**

0033 **5** *7* **The Big Short**[21] 6252 2-9-7 **60** JamesDoyle 6 29
(Charles Hills) *restless in stalls: chsd ldr: effrt over 2f out: little rspnse to press and btn over 1f out: wknd ins fnl f* **15/8**[1]

0000 **6** *2 1/2* **Red Shanghai (IRE)**[18] 6368 2-7-13 **45** AledBeech(7) 9 6
(Charles Smith) *a in last pair: rdn over 3f out: struggling 2f out: sn bhd* **66/1**

5030 **7** *10* **Secret Ballerina**[70] 4564 2-8-11 **53** (b[1]) ShelleyBirkett(3) 1
(Julia Feilden) *a in last pair: rdn over 3f out: sn struggling: bhd over 1f out* **25/1**

1m 13.99s (0.29) **Going Correction** -0.125s/f (Stan) **7** Ran SP% **106.0**
Speed ratings (Par 93): **93,92,85,85,76 72,59**
CSF £14.74 CT £50.51 TOTE £3.20: £1.70, £2.80; EX 19.00 Trifecta £55.30.
Owner B R Tregurtha **Bred** Mickley Stud & J Kent **Trained** Lambourn, Berks
■ Best Away was withdrawn. Price at time of withdrawal 6/1. Rule 4 applies to all bets - deduct 10p in the pound.

FOCUS
The second division of the 6f nursery was run in a time marginally slower than the first. Hardly anything got into the race. The first two came clear and the form is weak.

6897 TOTEEXACTA MAIDEN FILLIES' STKS (PLUS 10 RACE) 7f (P)
6:40 (6:46) (Class 4) 2-Y-O **£5,175** (£1,540; £769; £192; £192) **Stalls** Low

Form RPR

1 **Ebbesbourne (IRE)** 2-9-0 0 TedDurcan 14 77+
(Sir Michael Stoute) *stdd s: swtchd lft and hld up in tch in last trio: shkn up and gd hdwy on inner over 1f out: led 100yds out: r.o wl* **14/1**

2 *nk* **Hyper Dream (IRE)** 2-9-0 0 JimCrowley 6 76+
(Hugo Palmer) *dwlt: sn in tch in midfield: swtchd rt and hdwy over 1f out: ev ch ins fnl f: kpt on but a jst hld* **6/5**[1]

6U26 **3** *3/4* **Chica De La Noche**[16] 6454 2-9-0 77 NickyMackay 12 74
(Simon Dow) *hld up in tch in midfield: rdn over 2f out: hdwy u.p over 1f out: ev ch ins fnl f: styd on same pce towards fin* **12/1**

4 *2* **Nostalgie** 2-9-0 0 PatCosgrave 13 69
(Rae Guest) *dwlt: pushed along: in tch in last trio: outpcd and wd bnd 2f out: swtchd rt over 1f out: styd on wl ins fnl f* **33/1**

0 **4** *dht* **Pyjamarama**[10] 6625 2-9-0 0 JackMitchell 3 69
(Roger Varian) *led: rdn ent fnl 2f: hdd ent fnl f: outpcd fnl 100yds* **8/1**

6 *shd* **Rosemay (FR)** 2-9-0 0 RobertHavlin 4 68
(Simon Crisford) *w ldr: rdn ent fnl 2f: drvn over 1f out: sn led: hdd and no ex fnl 100yds* **7/1**[3]

50 **7** *1* **Pussy Galore (IRE)**[12] 6578 2-9-0 0 PatDobbs 2 66
(Richard Hannon) *in tch in midfield: effrt and swtchd rt over 1f out: sn drvn and unable qck: kpt on same pce ins fnl f* **33/1**

0 **8** *1/2* **Plead**[10] 6624 2-9-0 0 StevieDonohoe 9 64
(Roger Varian) *hld up in tch in midfield: effrt over 1f out: swtchd lft ent fnl f: kpt on same pce fnl 150yds* **12/1**

5 **9** *1/2* **Diamond Bear (USA)**[16] 6454 2-9-0 0 RyanPowell 7 63
(Sir Mark Prescott Bt) *chsd ldrs: rdn and struggling to qckn whn nt clrest of runs wl over 1f out: sn outpcd and styd on same pce ins fnl f* **25/1**

56 **10** *2* **Every Nice Girl (USA)**[37] 5747 2-9-0 0 TomQueally 10 58
(Marco Botti) *stdd s: hld up in tch towards rr: wd and lost pl bnd 2f out: shkn up over 1f out: reminder 1f out: kpt on same pce ins fnl f* **50/1**

4 **11** *5* **Star Of Bristol (USA)**[17] 6413 2-9-0 0 ShaneKelly 5 44
(Richard Hughes) *chsd ldng pair: rdn 3f out: swtchd rt wl over 1f out: sn outpcd and lost pl: wknd ins fnl f* **6/1**[2]

12 *3 3/4* **Embleton** 2-9-0 0 KierenFox 1 34
(Charlie Wallis) *dwlt: hld up in tch towards rr: rdn and unable qck wl over 1f out: sn lost pl: bhd ins fnl f* **66/1**

1m 27.2s **Going Correction** -0.125s/f (Stan) **12** Ran SP% **118.6**
Speed ratings (Par 94): **95,94,93,91,91 91,90,89,89,86 81,76**
CSF £30.21 TOTE £14.70: £3.10, £1.10, £2.70; EX 40.20 Trifecta £332.40.
Owner James Wigan **Bred** J Wigan & London Thoroughbred Services **Trained** Newmarket, Suffolk
■ Jazaalah was withdrawn. Price at time of withdrawal 16/1. Rule 4 does not apply.

FOCUS
Probably just a fair race of its type, and the winner got a clear passage up the inside as all her rivals edged towards the middle of the track. The race is rated around the third's recent course form.

6898 TOTEQUADPOT NURSERY H'CAP 1m (P)
7:10 (7:14) (Class 5) (0-75,73) 2-Y-O **£4,528** (£1,347; £673; £336) **Stalls** Low

Form RPR

01 **1** **Under Control (IRE)**[27] 6092 2-9-4 **70** PatCosgrave 4 75+
(William Haggas) *stdd s: t.k.h: hld up in tch in midfield: clsd and nt clr run over 1f out: swtchd lft jst ins fnl f: sn rdn and hdwy to ld 75yds out: r.o wl: rdn out* **5/2**[1]

206 **2** *1/2* **Masonic (IRE)**[21] 6264 2-8-13 **68** JosephineGordon(3) 3 71
(Robyn Brisland) *t.k.h: chsd ldr early: stdd bk into midfield after 1f: effrt to press ldrs over 1f out: styd on to chse wnr wl ins fnl f: kpt on* **7/1**

133 **3** *3/4* **Jumping Jack (IRE)**[7] 6705 2-9-6 **72** ShaneKelly 6 73
(Richard Hughes) *jnd ldr after 1f: rdn 2f out: drvn jst over 1f out: stl ev ch tl unable qck and styd on same pce fnl 75yds* **4/1**[3]

5031 **4** *nk* **Party Nights**[18] 6377 2-9-7 **73** JimCrowley 1 73
(Luca Cumani) *led: rdn 2f out: drvn jst ins fnl f: hdd and no ex fnl 75yds* **7/2**[2]

505 **5** *1/2* **Rita's Man (IRE)**[63] 4790 2-9-1 **67** PatDobbs 2 66
(Richard Hannon) *hld up in tch in midfield: clsd to chse ldrs and swtchd lft over 1f out: styd on same pce u.p ins fnl f* **12/1**

653 **6** *2 1/2* **Keepup Kevin**[15] 6480 2-9-2 **71** RobHornby(3) 7 64
(Pam Sly) *hld up in tch in last pair: effrt wl over 1f out: no imp and edgd lft ent fnl f: kpt on same pce after* **9/2**

1654 **7** *39* **Fancy Day (IRE)**[56] 5066 2-9-3 **69** JamesDoyle 5
(Mark Johnston) *chsd ldrs: rdn over 3f out: lost pl u.p over 2f out: bhd and eased over 1f out: t.o* **20/1**

1m 39.85s (-0.05) **Going Correction** -0.125s/f (Stan) **7** Ran SP% **113.9**
Speed ratings (Par 95): **95,94,93,93,92 90,51**
CSF £20.41 TOTE £2.80: £1.90, £3.80; EX 24.80 Trifecta £93.20.
Owner D I Scott **Bred** D I Scott **Trained** Newmarket, Suffolk

FOCUS
The early gallop didn't look overly strong so the winner did well to come from off the gallop. Most of these ran to their recent form.

6899 TOTEPOOLLIVEINFO.COM H'CAP 1m (P)
7:40 (7:45) (Class 4) (0-80,80) 3-Y-O+ **£6,469** (£1,925; £962; £481) **Stalls** Low

Form RPR

263 **1** **Feed The Goater (FR)**[12] 6580 3-9-5 **79** JamesDoyle 4 89+
(Richard Hannon) *in tch in midfield: rdn over 2f out: hdwy u.p over 1f out: str run to ld wl ins fnl f: sn in command: eased cl home* **10/3**[1]

-021 **2** *1 1/4* **Let's Twist**[22] 6237 4-9-3 **73** (b) ShaneGray 10 80
(Kristin Stubbs) *sn led: rdn 2f out: drvn over 1f out: kpt on wl u.p tl hdd and one pced wl ins fnl f* **8/1**

6344 **3** *1/2* **Destroyer**[15] 6490 3-9-2 **79** (p) RobHornby(3) 2 85
(William Muir) *trckd ldrs: swtchd lft and effrt over 1f out: rdn and ev ch ins fnl f: unable qck and styd on same pce fnl 100yds* **7/1**[3]

3152 **4** *1* **Stosur (IRE)**[19] 6316 5-9-5 **78** (b) JosephineGordon(3) 1 82
(Gay Kelleway) *chsd ldr: rdn and ev ch over 1f out tl no ex u.p ins fnl f: wknd towards fin* **8/1**

0034 **5** *nk* **Mezzotint (IRE)**[21] 6266 7-9-10 **80** JimCrowley 3 83
(Lee Carter) *hld up in tch in midfield: swtchd lft and effrt on inner over 1f out: drvn and ev ch ins fnl f tl no ex and wknd towards fin* **10/1**

6312 **6** *hd* **Broughtons Vision**[10] 6629 3-8-9 **69** StevieDonohoe 5 71
(Willie Musson) *hld up in tch in midfield: effrt wl over 1f out: styd on same pce u.p ins fnl f* **6/1**[2]

6-12 **7** *1 3/4* **Ritasun (FR)**[241] 421 3-9-4 **78** (p) PatDobbs 9 76
(Richard Hannon) *stdd s: hld up in tch in midfield: effrt over 2f out: no imp and styd on same pce ins fnl f* **16/1**

0032 **8** *shd* **Rosenborg Rider (IRE)**[35] 5810 3-9-2 **76** (b[1]) FMBerry 7 74
(Ralph Beckett) *chsd ldrs: effrt and drvn over 1f out: no ex ins fnl f: wknd fnl 100yds* **6/1**[2]

650 **9** *1 1/2* **Show Me Again**[26] 6123 3-9-5 **79** [1] MartinLane 14 74
(David Dennis) *stdd s: hld up in rr: rdn 2f out: sme hdwy and edging rt over 1f out: no imp ins fnl f: nvr trbld ldrs* **66/1**

0-53 **10** *2 1/2* **Fantasy Gladiator**[19] 6323 10-9-8 **78** (p) AndrewMullen 12 67
(Michael Appleby) *hld up in last pair: effrt u.p over 1f out: no imp: nvr trbld ldrs* **33/1**

134- **11** *2* **Manolito**[307] 8017 4-8-12 **73** CharlieBennett(5) 13 57
(Hughie Morrison) *stdd s: hld up in tch towards rr: effrt 2f out: no imp u.p over 1f out: wknd ins fnl f* **25/1**

2340 **12** *13* **Dubai Mission (IRE)**[10] 6634 3-9-2 **76** (t[1]) TimmyMurphy 8 30
(Steve Flook) *in tch in midfield: rdn and lost pl over 2f out: bhd over 1f out* **50/1**

1523 **13** *10* **Kestrel Dot Com**[15] 6490 4-9-10 **80** SilvestreDeSousa 6 11
(Chris Dwyer) *stuck wd: midfield tl dropped to rr and rdn over 3f out: drvn and no rspnse 2f out: bhd and eased ins fnl f* **7/1**[3]

1m 38.52s (-1.38) **Going Correction** -0.125s/f (Stan)
WFA 3 from 4yo+ 4lb **13** Ran SP% **124.1**
Speed ratings (Par 105): **101,99,99,98,97 97,96,95,94,91 89,76,66**
CSF £30.86 CT £189.52 TOTE £3.80: £2.00, £2.90, £3.50; EX 28.00 Trifecta £219.90.
Owner Middleham Park Racing LXXI **Bred** Haras Du Mezeray **Trained** East Everleigh, Wilts

FOCUS
Plenty of these held a chance inside the final furlong, so this may not be strong form. It's set around the third and fourth.

6900 ATTOTEPOOLRACING WIN TICKETS ON TWITTER H'CAP 1m (P)
8:10 (8:13) (Class 6) (0-55,55) 3-Y-O+ **£3,234** (£962; £481; £240) **Stalls** Low

Form RPR

4033 **1** **Bazzat (IRE)**[17] 6407 3-8-12 **50** (p) JimCrowley 2 55
(John Ryan) *trckd ldrs: effrt to chal over 1f out: sustained duel u.p w rival fr 1f out: kpt in to ld last stride* **2/1**[1]

0040 **2** *shd* **Lmntrix**[48] 5380 4-9-7 **55** PatCosgrave 13 60
(George Margarson) *pressed ldr tl led over 2f out: rdn over 1f out: sustained duel w wnr after: kpt on wl: hdd last stride* **33/1**

0060 **3** *nk* **Majestic Girl (IRE)**[9] 6651 3-8-4 **49** (p) JoshuaBryan(7) 6 54
(Steve Flook) *s.i.s: hld up towards rr: effrt and swtchd rt over 2f out: clsd and swtchd rt jst over 1f out: r.o strly ins fnl f* **33/1**

0056 **4** *3/4* **Secret Lightning (FR)**[38] 5729 4-9-1 **52** AlistairRawlinson(3) 5 54
(Michael Appleby) *chsd ldrs: effrt to press ldrs over 1f out: styd on same pce u.p ins fnl f* **8/1**

4650 **5** *hd* **The Name's Bond**[10] 6621 4-8-12 **46** oh1 (v[1]) GeorgeChaloner 8 48
(Richard Fahey) *hld up in tch in midfield: effrt over 1f out: chsd ldrs jst ins fnl f: nt clrest of runs and styd on same pce ins fnl f* **14/1**

-002 **6** *hd* **Victoriously**[28] 6046 4-9-0 **51** (p) EoinWalsh(3) 9 52
(Andi Brown) *hld up in tch in midfield: shkn up 1/2-way: effrt and swtchd rt over 1f out: styd on u.p ins fnl f: nt rch ldrs* **5/1**[3]

0550 **7** *1 1/4* **Oyster Card**[16] 6444 3-8-11 **49** AndrewMullen 1 47
(Michael Appleby) *chsd ldrs: effrt towards inner over 1f out: stl pressing ldrs but unable qck ent fnl f: styd on same pce ins fnl f* **7/2**[2]

0556 **8** *1* **Music Hall (FR)**[17] 6405 6-8-7 **46** oh1 CharlieBennett(5) 16 42
(Shaun Harris) *stdd and dropped in after s: effrt over 1f out: kpt on ins fnl f: nvr threatened ldrs* **20/1**

-300 **9** *nk* **Officer In Command (USA)**[71] 4516 10-9-1 **49** (tp) LiamJones 11 44
(Alan Bailey) *in tch in midfield: effrt over 1f out: styd on same pce and no imp ins fnl f* **25/1**

0040 **10** *1 1/4* **Poetic Guest**[59] 4936 3-9-3 **55** TomQueally 3 47
(George Margarson) *hld up in tch in midfield: effrt u.p over 1f out: drvn and no imp 1f out: wknd ins fnl f* **16/1**

044 **11** *3 3/4* **Summertime Lucy (IRE)**[29] 6036 3-9-3 **55** [1] JackMitchell 12 38
(Giles Bravery) *in tch towards rr: hdwy over 1f out: no imp u.p 1f out: wknd ins fnl f* **25/1**

0600 **12** *8* **Royal Mighty**[40] 5630 3-8-8 **46** oh1 [1] NickyMackay 4 10
(Jane Chapple-Hyam) *led tl over 2f out: lost pl u.p over 1f out: btn and eased ins fnl f* **50/1**

066 **13** *2* **Skiff**[75] 4384 4-9-3 **51** FMBerry 10 10
(Brendan Powell) *in tch towards rr tl over 2f out: sn bhd* **10/1**

14 *19* **Northern Bay (GER)**[29] 6-8-13 **52** (t) CliffordLee(5) 15
(Keith Reveley) *midfield but stuck wd: rdn and lost pl over 3f out: bhd 2f out: sn lost tch: t.o* **25/1**

1m 40.3s (0.40) **Going Correction** -0.125s/f (Stan)
WFA 3 from 4yo+ 4lb **14** Ran SP% **129.1**
Speed ratings (Par 101): **93,92,92,91,91 91,90,89,88,87 83,75,73,54**
CSF £93.53 CT £1878.62 TOTE £2.80: £1.30, £6.90, £14.70; EX 83.00 Trifecta £1671.20.
Owner John Stocker **Bred** Ballyhane Stud **Trained** Newmarket, Suffolk

FOCUS
This didn't look a strong race before the off and it was taken by an exposed maiden from a gelding who'd shown little previously, but was carrying top weight. The second is the best guide.

6901 TOTEPOOL LIKE US ON FACEBOOK FILLIES' H'CAP 1m 2f (P)
8:40 (8:44) (Class 5) (0-70,70) 3-Y-O+ **£5,175** (£1,540; £769; £384) **Stalls** Low

Form RPR

6544 **1** **Princess Raihana**[19] 6334 3-9-2 **68** HarryBentley 3 75
(Marco Botti) *mde all: rdn clr over 1f out: pressed wl ins fnl f: kpt on and a doing enough towards fin* **9/2**[2]

3236 **2** *hd* **Forecaster**[33] 5891 3-9-2 **68**.....(v) AdamKirby 2 74
(Michael Bell) *hld up in tch in midfield: nt clr run over 2f out: swtchd rt and hdwy over 1f out: chsd clr wnr 1f out: styd on to press wnr wl ins fnl f: hld towards fin* **9/1**

306 **3** *2 ½* **East Coast Lady (IRE)**[19] 6334 4-9-7 **67**..... MartinLane 7 68
(William Stone) *fly j. as stalls opened and slowly away: hld up in rr: hdwy on inner over 1f out: kpt on wl to go 3rd wl ins fnl f* **33/1**

03 **4** *1* **Tenerezza (IRE)**[55] 5130 3-9-0 **66**..... ShaneKelly 5 65
(David Lanigan) *in tch in midfield: effrt to chse ldng pair: over 2f out: styd on same pce fr 1f out: lost 3rd wl ins fnl f* **9/2**[2]

05 **5** *2 ¾* **Medicean Queen (IRE)**[37] 5737 5-8-13 **62**.....[1] JosephineGordon(3) 1 56
(Phil McEntee) *chsd ldrs tl wnt 2nd 3f out: sn u.p and unable qck: lost 2nd 1f out: wknd ins fnl f* **50/1**

-613 **6** *1* **Mercy Me**[103] 3402 4-9-7 **67**..... RyanPowell 11 59
(John Ryan) *hld up in tch in last quartet: effrt and wnt rt over 1f out: hdwy u.p and hung lft over 1f out: no imp ins fnl f* **25/1**

0002 **7** *¾* **Roxie Lot**[26] 6137 4-9-2 **65**..... RobHornby(3) 9 55
(Pam Sly) *hld up in tch in last pair: effrt wd and then pushed even wdr bnd 2f out: sme hdwy and edging lft ins fnl f: nvr trbld ldrs* **14/1**

5421 **8** *hd* **Blushes (FR)**[14] 6513 3-8-11 **63**.....(v[1]) JimCrowley 4 53
(Ed Dunlop) *hld up in last trio: nt clr run over 2f out: swtchd rt and hdwy over 1f out: drvn 1f out: styd on same pce and no imp ins fnl f* **5/2**[1]

5642 **9** *3 ¼* **Aurora Gray**[34] 5823 3-8-12 **64**..... JimmyFortune 8 47
(Hughie Morrison) *hld up in tch in midfield: effrt 2f out: no hdwy and btn over 1f out: eased ins fnl f* **8/1**

2366 **10** *3 ¾* **Pernickety**[15] 6485 3-9-2 **68**.....[1] SilvestreDeSousa 6 44
(Lucy Wadham) *t.k.h: chsd ldrs: rdn and finding little whn pushed rt over 1f out: sn btn and eased fnl f* **6/1**[3]

046 **11** *18* **Poppy Time**[37] 5742 3-9-4 **70**..... RyanTate 12 10
(James Eustace) *t.k.h: in tch: hdwy to chse ldrs 7f out: rdn over 3f out: lost pl and bhd 2f out: eased over 1f out* **50/1**

0514 **12** *6* **Pivotal Flame (IRE)**[40] 5629 3-9-4 **70**.....(p) MartinHarley 10
(James Tate) *chsd ldr tl 3f out: sn u.p and lost pl: bhd and eased over 1f out* **10/1**

2m 5.31s (-3.29) **Going Correction** -0.125s/f (Stan)
WFA 3 from 4yo+ 6lb **12** Ran SP% **126.8**
Speed ratings (Par 100): **108,107,105,105,102 102,101,101,98,95 81,76**
CSF £46.95 CT £1229.85 TOTE £6.60: £2.80, £3.40, £10.10; EX 50.80 Trifecta £937.90.
Owner Classic Racing (Raihana) I **Bred** Essafinaat **Trained** Newmarket, Suffolk

■ Stewards' Enquiry : Ryan Tate £140 fine; trainer arrived at the start with the incorrect number cloth.

Martin Harley £140 fine; trainer arrived at the start with the incorrect number cloth.

FOCUS
A competitive handicap for fillies and mares, but pretty modest form rated around the second.

6902 CHELMSFORDCITYRACECOURSE.COM H'CAP 6f (P)
9:10 (9:13) (Class 7) (0-50,56) 3-Y-O+ **£3,234** (£962; £481; £240) **Stalls** Centre

Form RPR

3045 **1** **Commanche**[21] 6249 7-9-5 **48**.....(b) SilvestreDeSousa 11 55
(Chris Dwyer) *sn rdn along: chsd ldr: rdn to ld over 1f out and sn drvn clr: kpt on u.p* **7/2**[1]

5334 **2** *½* **Cadland Lad (IRE)**[21] 6249 3-9-2 **47**.....(vt[1]) JimCrowley 10 52
(John Ryan) *hld up in tch towards rr: clsd and nt clr run wl over 1f out: hdwy jst over 1f out: str run to chse wnr wl ins fnl f: r.o: nvr quite getting to wnr* **7/2**[1]

4000 **3** *1 ¼* **Simply Black (IRE)**[12] 6587 5-8-11 **45**.....(p) AnnStokell(5) 1 46
(Ann Stokell) *taken down early: in tch in midfield: swtchd rt and hdwy over 1f out: chsd wnr 1f out: kpt on: lost 2nd wl ins fnl f* **100/1**

5650 **4** *1 ¼* **Ryan Style (IRE)**[9] 6660 10-8-10 **46**.....(p) JordanUys(7) 6 44
(Lisa Williamson) *dwlt and bustled along early: hld up towards rr: hdwy on inner over 1f out: kpt on ins fnl f: nvr rchd ldrs* **33/1**

4360 **5** *¾* **Guapo Bay**[20] 6290 3-8-12 **48**.....(b) MeganNicholls(5) 2 43
(Richard Hannon) *hld up in last pair: hdwy over 1f out: rdn and styd on same pce fnl f* **14/1**

0601 **6** *½* **Westbourne Grove (USA)**[1] 6865 3-9-11 **56** 6ex.....(t) AdamKirby 4 50
(John Butler) *taken down early: in tch in midfield: nt clr run over 2f out: hdwy u.p 1f out: kpt on same pce ins fnl f* **7/2**[1]

605 **7** *¾* **Lucia Sciarra**[18] 6373 3-9-2 **50**.....[1] JosephineGordon(3) 7 42
(Giles Bravery) *in tch in midfield: effrt 2f out: styd on ins fnl f: nvr trbld ldrs* **9/1**[3]

-660 **8** *1* **Noneedtotellme (IRE)**[49] 5338 3-8-11 **45**.....(v) RobHornby(3) 14 34
(James Unett) *in rr: effrt on outer bnd 2f out: kpt on ins fnl f: nvr trbld ldrs* **50/1**

-064 **9** *6* **Cytringan**[51] 5260 3-9-2 **50**.....[1] SimonPearce(3) 12 21
(Lydia Pearce) *bmpd s: sn chsd ldrs: rdn and unable qck over 1f out: wknd fnl f* **16/1**

3300 **10** *2* **Multi Quest**[21] 6249 4-9-7 **50**.....(b) RobertHavlin 9 15
(John E Long) *led: rdn ent fnl 2f: hdd over 1f out: sn btn: wknd qckly ins fnl f* **10/1**

5000 **11** *½* **Romancingthestone**[38] 5721 3-9-2 **47**.....(p) DarryllHolland 8 10
(Karen George) *midfield but stuck wd: no imp over 1f out: sn wknd* **40/1**

060- **12** *2 ¼* **Bedazzling Lady (IRE)**[288] 8243 3-9-5 **50**..... PatCosgrave 13 6
(Robert Eddery) *bmpd s: a towards rr: no imp over 1f out: sn wknd* **20/1**

6040 **13** *nk* **Angel Flores (IRE)**[21] 6249 5-9-6 **49**..... KierenFox 5 4
(Lee Carter) *in tch in midfield: rdn and unable qck over 2f out: no imp and drifted rt wl over 1f out: sn wknd: fin lame* **6/1**[2]

002 **14** *5* **Betty Boo (IRE)**[92] 3777 6-9-0 **48**..... CharlieBennett(5) 3
(Shaun Harris) *chsd ldrs: rdn 2f out: unable qck and sn wknd* **20/1**

1m 12.75s (-0.95) **Going Correction** -0.125s/f (Stan)
WFA 3 from 4yo+ 2lb **14** Ran SP% **130.4**
Speed ratings (Par 97): **101,100,98,97,96 95,94,93,85,82 81,78,78,71**
CSF £15.20 CT £1136.73 TOTE £4.50: £1.80, £1.70, £22.60; EX 16.10 Trifecta £827.80.
Owner M M Foulger **Bred** Paramount Bloodstock **Trained** Newmarket, Suffolk

FOCUS
Probably a fair contest for the level, although the run of the third is a way of limiting it. The winner did not need to match this summer's best.

T/Plt: £75.10 to a £1 stake. Pool of £83288.83 - 809.40 winning tickets. T/Qpdt: £13.50 to a £1 stake. Pool of £9875.60 - 537.62 winning tickets. **Steve Payne**

6738 NEWCASTLE (A.W) (L-H)
Thursday, September 29

OFFICIAL GOING: Tapeta: standard
Wind: Fairly strong, half against Weather: Cloudy, bright

6903 PERFECT IMAGE NURSERY H'CAP 1m 5y (Tp)
2:10 (2:10) (Class 4) (0-80,78) 2-Y-O **£5,175** (£1,540; £769; £384) **Stalls** Centre

Form RPR

0221 **1** **Zymyran**[16] 6455 2-9-4 **75**..... JamieSpencer 3 84+
(David Simcock) *s.i.s: hld up in last pl: smooth hdwy over 1f out: shkn up to ld ins fnl f: sn clr: readily* **11/10**[1]

2234 **2** *3 ¾* **Major Cornwallis (IRE)**[31] 5967 2-8-13 **70**..... TonyHamilton 7 70
(Richard Fahey) *in tch: rdn and hdwy over 1f out: wnt 2nd ins fnl f: no ch w ready wnr* **11/1**

3652 **3** *1 ½* **Book Of Poetry (IRE)**[54] 5171 2-8-11 **68**..... JoeFanning 5 65+
(Mark Johnston) *led at ordinary gallop: rdn and qcknd 2f out: hdd ins fnl f: kpt on same pce* **12/1**

5010 **4** *½* **Our Charlie Brown**[22] 6229 2-9-0 **71**..... DavidAllan 6 67+
(Tim Easterby) *pressed ldr: drvn over 2f out: lost 2nd and no ex ins fnl f* **9/1**

4215 **5** *10* **Davy's Dilemma**[12] 6554 2-9-7 **78**..... PaulMulrennan 2 52
(Michael Dods) *t.k.h: trckd ldrs tl rdn and wknd 2f out* **11/4**[2]

6441 **6** *½* **Springwood (IRE)**[34] 5840 2-9-1 **77**.....(v) AdamMcNamara(5) 4 50
(Richard Fahey) *chsd ldrs: drvn along over 2f out: sn wknd* **8/1**[3]

1m 44.16s (5.56) **Going Correction** +0.525s/f (Slow) **6** Ran SP% **111.4**
Speed ratings (Par 97): **93,89,87,87,77 76**
CSF £14.15 TOTE £2.00: £1.30, £3.10; EX 14.40 Trifecta £105.00.
Owner Nurlan Bizakov **Bred** Hesmonds Stud Ltd **Trained** Newmarket, Suffolk

FOCUS
The track had had routine gallop-mastering since the last meeting, but the clerk of the course said: "It is going to be slow today as they are racing into a strong headwind." A fair staying nursery to start and indeed it did look very hard work for these youngsters, despite a modest pace. Joe Fanning and Tony Hamilton said that the first half of the race was fine, but once they went past the trees around 3.5f out the wind kicked in and it was really hard work. It may have been significant that the first two came from behind, having got shelter from the wind, but the winner was still impressive. He might have been slightly flattered though.

6904 MICROSOFT/IRISH STALLION FARMS EBF MAIDEN STKS 7f 14y (Tp)
2:40 (2:40) (Class 5) 2-Y-O **£3,881** (£1,155; £577; £288) **Stalls** Centre

Form RPR

1 **1** **Sincil Bank (USA)**[31] 5966 2-9-5 0..... JamieSpencer 1 82
(David Simcock) *hld up in tch: stdy hdwy over 2f out: shkn up to ld over 1f out: pushed out: comf* **8/11**[1]

0 **2** *3 ½* **Farook (IRE)**[103] 3408 2-9-5 0..... PaulHanagan 5 73+
(Charles Hills) *early ldr: trckd ldr: rdn to ld briefly over 1f out: kpt on fnl f: nt pce of wnr* **7/1**[3]

3 *nk* **Valley Of Rocks (IRE)** 2-9-5 0..... JoeFanning 2 73+
(Mark Johnston) *dwlt: t.k.h and sn led: rdn and hdd over 1f out: kpt on same pce fnl f* **20/1**

460 **4** *5* **Starlite Sienna (IRE)**[18] 6388 2-9-0 0..... TonyHamilton 7 55
(Richard Fahey) *prom: drvn and outpcd over 2f out: n.d after* **25/1**

3 **5** *½* **Suspect Package (USA)**[31] 5966 2-9-5 0..... FrederikTylicki 3 59
(James Fanshawe) *trckd ldrs: rdn over 2f out: wknd over 1f out* **5/2**[2]

0 **6** *6* **Veiled Secret (IRE)**[15] 6486 2-9-5 0..... LukeMorris 4 44
(Sir Mark Prescott Bt) *hld up: rdn and struggling 3f out: sn btn* **40/1**

7 *1* **Shackles** 2-9-5 0..... PJMcDonald 6 41
(Alistair Whillans) *hld up: drvn and outpcd over 2f out: sn wknd* **150/1**

1m 30.78s (4.58) **Going Correction** +0.525s/f (Slow) **7** Ran SP% **110.7**
Speed ratings (Par 95): **94,90,89,83,83 76,75**
CSF £5.96 TOTE £1.60: £1.20, £3.00; EX 5.90 Trifecta £39.50.
Owner Never Say Die Partnership **Bred** John T L Jones III **Trained** Newmarket, Suffolk

FOCUS
A maiden lacking depth and the pattern of the race was similar to the opener, in that the favourite probably had the ideal trip in the conditions. The second and third are the keys to the form.

6905 ALAN SHEARER FOUNDATION MAIDEN STKS 7f 14y (Tp)
3:15 (3:18) (Class 5) 3-Y-O+ **£3,881** (£1,155; £577; £288) **Stalls** Centre

Form RPR

63-2 **1** **Sun Lover**[16] 6452 3-9-5 85..... AndreaAtzeni 4 86
(Roger Varian) *mde all: rdn along 2f out: hld on wl fnl f* **1/1**[1]

2 *½* **Barjeel (USA)** 3-9-5 0..... PaulHanagan 3 84
(William Haggas) *s.i.s: hld up in tch: hdwy to chse wnr over 2f out: shkn up and kpt on fnl f: hld nr fin* **5/4**[2]

3 **3** *9* **New Signal**[45] 5480 3-9-5 0..... DanielTudhope 6 59
(David O'Meara) *t.k.h: trckd ldr to over 2f out: rdn and sn outpcd by first two* **11/2**[3]

0P **4** *9* **Melodya (IRE)**[16] 6452 3-8-11 0..... JacobButterfield(3) 1 30
(Brian Ellison) *in tch: drvn and struggling wl over 2f out: sn btn* **150/1**

0600 **5** *3 ¼* **Justice Pleasing**[56] 5068 3-9-5 60.....[1] PJMcDonald 2 26
(Roger Fell) *trckd ldrs tl rdn and wknd fr 2f out* **80/1**

1m 29.91s (3.71) **Going Correction** +0.525s/f (Slow)
WFA 3 from 5yo 3lb **5** Ran SP% **111.7**
Speed ratings (Par 103): **99,98,88,77,74**
CSF £2.58 TOTE £1.90: £1.10, £1.30; EX 2.80 Trifecta £3.60.
Owner Sheikh Mohammed Obaid Al Maktoum **Bred** Lofts Hall Stud, B Sangster & St Albans
Trained Newmarket, Suffolk

FOCUS
Basically just a three-runner older-horse maiden and the finish was dominated by the big two in the market. The winner set a good standard on his second 2yo run.

6906 ALTERYX H'CAP 2m 56y (Tp)
3:50 (3:50) (Class 5) (0-75,73) 3-Y-O+ **£3,881** (£1,155; £577; £288) **Stalls** Low

Form RPR

1131 **1** **Cartwright**[7] 6719 3-9-2 **73**.....(p) LukeMorris 6 79+
(Sir Mark Prescott Bt) *hld up in tch: niggled over 4f out: hdwy to ld over 1f out: drvn and hung rt ins fnl f: styd on wl* **4/9**[1]

1314 **2** *1 ½* **Clear Evidence**[19] 6325 3-8-10 **72**..... AdamMcNamara(5) 2 76
(Michael Bell) *trckd ldrs: effrt whn nt clr run over 2f out: rallied to chse wnr fnl f: kpt on: hld towards fin* **11/4**[2]

5204 **3** *1 ½* **Snowy Dawn**[27] 6083 6-9-10 **69**..... AdamBeschizza 3 71
(Steph Hollinshead) *trckd ldr: led over 2f out to over 1f out: kpt on same pce fnl f* **11/1**[3]

2534 **4** *nk* **Jan Smuts (IRE)**[4] 6812 8-9-3 **62**....(tp) CamHardie 5 63
(Wilf Storey) *prom: stdy hdwy over 2f out: sn rdn: kpt on same pce fnl f* **25/1**

166 **5** *37* **Another Lincolnday**[14] 6519 5-9-4 **63**....(p) TomEaves 1 20
(Michael Herrington) *led at modest gallop: rdn and hdd over 2f out: wknd and drifted rt wl over 1f out: eased whn no ch fnl f* **25/1**

3m 36.9s (1.70) **Going Correction** +0.20s/f (Slow)
WFA 3 from 5yo+ 12lb **5** Ran SP% **111.9**
Speed ratings (Par 103): **103,102,101,101,82**
CSF £2.00 TOTE £1.40: £1.10, £1.50; EX 1.90 Trifecta £4.00.
Owner J L C Pearce **Bred** Meon Valley Stud **Trained** Newmarket, Suffolk

FOCUS
A modest staying handicap with a very lopsided look to it. The pace was ordinary and the order didn't change for the first 1m4f. Rather muddling form, with the winner better than this.

6907 QLIK H'CAP 1m 5y (Tp)
4:20 (4:21) (Class 5) (0-70,76) 3-Y-O+ **£3,881** (£1,155; £577; £288) **Stalls** Centre

Form RPR

6060 **1** **Qaffaal (USA)**[23] 6217 5-9-9 **69**.... GrahamGibbons 10 80
(Michael Easterby) *hld up midfield: hdwy to ld over 1f out: sn hrd pressed: hld on gamely towards fin* **10/3**[1]

4201 **2** *nk* **Mon Beau Visage (IRE)**[9] 6644 3-9-12 **76** 6ex.... DanielTudhope 9 86
(David O'Meara) *hld up: smooth hdwy over 2f out: chal over 1f out to ins fnl f: kpt on: hld towards fin* **11/2**[2]

2165 **3** *1 3/4* **Gun Case**[22] 6231 4-9-8 **68**....(p) DougieCostello 11 74
(Alistair Whillans) *hld up: hdwy over 2f out: rdn and edgd lft over 1f out: kpt on ins fnl f: nt rch first two* **11/2**[2]

0602 **4** *1 1/4* **Janaab (IRE)**[22] 6231 6-9-6 **69**....(t) RachelRichardson(3) 2 72
(Tim Easterby) *prom: drvn along 3f out: rallied and ev ch over 1f out: kpt on same pce ins fnl f* **8/1**

6336 **5** *1 1/4* **Cliff (IRE)**[49] 5323 6-8-11 **64**.... LewisEdmunds(7) 7 64
(Nigel Tinkler) *prom: drvn along over 2f out: ev ch briefly over 1f out: outpcd fnl f* **10/1**

335 **6** *4* **Captain Peaky**[12] 6567 3-9-1 **65**.... JackGarritty 8 56
(Patrick Holmes) *hld up: rdn and hdwy over 2f out: outpcd appr fnl f* **25/1**

2102 **7** *nk* **Talent Scout (IRE)**[9] 6643 10-9-1 **66**....(p) GemmaTutty(5) 1 56
(Karen Tutty) *led tl rdn and hdd over 1f out: sn btn* **12/1**

043 **8** *3/4* **Red Charmer (IRE)**[22] 6231 6-9-9 **69**.... PJMcDonald 3 58
(Ann Duffield) *hld up midfield: hdwy over 2f out: rdn and wknd over 1f out* **12/1**

5250 **9** *1 1/2* **L'Inganno Felice (FR)**[14] 6516 6-9-10 **70**.... DavidAllan 12 55
(Iain Jardine) *hld up: hdwy over 2f out: rdn and wknd over 1f out* **13/2**[3]

5330 **10** *9* **Avalanche Express**[66] 4717 4-9-10 **70**....[1] GrahamLee 14 34
(William Muir) *racd alone stands' side: in tch: rdn along over 2f out: wknd wl over 1f out* **14/1**

02-0 **11** *7* **Drago (IRE)**[27] 6095 4-9-8 **68**.... PhillipMakin 6 30
(David O'Meara) *cl up: drvn along over 2f out: wknd wl over 1f out* **40/1**

1000 **12** *1 1/4* **Breathless**[12] 6568 4-9-5 **65**....(t) PaulMulrennan 5 24
(Clive Mulhall) *prom: drvn along over 2f out: sn lost pl* **100/1**

01/0 **13** *1/2* **Fujin Dancer (FR)**[35] 5805 11-9-7 **67**.... TomEaves 4 25
(Harriet Bethell) *hld up: drvn and struggling over 2f out: sn btn* **66/1**

1m 42.01s (3.41) **Going Correction** +0.525s/f (Slow)
WFA 3 from 4yo+ 4lb **13** Ran SP% **118.2**
Speed ratings (Par 103): **103,102,100,99,98 94,94,93,91,82 81,80,80**
CSF £20.10 CT £93.49 TOTE £4.20: £1.30, £2.10, £2.60; EX 24.60 Trifecta £168.30.
Owner T Calam & P Holdsworth **Bred** Shadwell Farm LLC **Trained** Sheriff Hutton, N Yorks

FOCUS
An ordinary handicap, but another winning favourite. All bar one raced centre-to-far side and the race unfolded more towards the inside. The first three all came from off the pace. The winner can probably do better still on the AW.

6908 EXTREME FILLIES' H'CAP 7f 14y (Tp)
4:55 (4:55) (Class 5) (0-75,73) 3-Y-O+ **£3,881** (£1,155; £577; £288) **Stalls** Centre

Form RPR

2214 **1** **Soundstrings**[19] 6342 3-9-6 **72**....[1] GrahamGibbons 5 81+
(William Haggas) *dwlt: hld up: hdwy far side of gp over 2f out: rdn to ld over 1f out: kpt on strly fnl f* **3/1**[1]

4125 **2** *1 3/4* **Bahamian Bird**[14] 6502 3-9-0 **66**.... TonyHamilton 3 70
(Richard Fahey) *trckd ldrs: hdwy to ld briefly over 1f out: drvn and kpt on ins fnl f: nt rch wnr* **8/1**

4201 **3** *1 3/4* **Sciarra**[29] 6036 3-9-1 **67**....[1] OisinMurphy 2 66+
(Michael Bell) *dwlt: hld up: rdn and outpcd wl over 1f out: rallied fnl f: tk 3rd towards fin: nt rch first two* **9/1**

0025 **4** *1/2* **Isntshesomething**[51] 5276 4-8-5 **54** oh2....(p) JoeFanning 8 53
(Richard Guest) *prom: effrt and cl up over 1f out: kpt on same pce ins fnl f* **33/1**

03 **5** *3/4* **Who's Shirl**[84] 4043 10-8-8 **57** ow1.... AndrewElliott 1 54
(Chris Fairhurst) *hld up: rdn and edgd towards stands' rail over 2f out: rallied over 1f out: kpt on fnl f: nt pce to chal* **22/1**

5254 **6** *1/2* **Popsies Joy (IRE)**[23] 6220 3-9-2 **68**....(b) DuranFentiman 10 63
(Tim Easterby) *hld up: rdn over 2f out: hdwy towards stands' rail over 1f out: kpt on fnl f: no imp* **11/1**

5340 **7** *1/2* **Meandmyshadow**[16] 6435 8-9-8 **71**....(b) DaleSwift 6 65
(Alan Brown) *led: rdn over 2f out: hdd over 1f out: sn wknd* **33/1**

4120 **8** *3 1/2* **Barwah (USA)**[6] 6742 5-8-11 **65**.... NathanEvans(5) 4 50
(Peter Niven) *hld up: effrt and rdn over 2f out: edgd lft and wknd over 1f out* **7/2**[2]

0422 **9** *3* **Hidden Gem**[14] 6512 3-8-8 **60**.... LukeMorris 11 36
(Ed Walker) *hld up in tch: drvn and outpcd over 2f out: wknd over 1f out* **7/1**[3]

2650 **10** *3 3/4* **Maureb (IRE)**[33] 5867 4-9-3 **73**....(p) LewisEdmunds(7) 9 40
(Tony Coyle) *in tch: drvn along over 2f out: wknd wl over 1f out* **20/1**

0421 **11** *6* **Beadlam (IRE)**[9] 6646 3-8-10 **62** 6ex.... PJMcDonald 7 11
(Roger Fell) *cl up: rdn along 3f out: wknd wl over 1f out* **10/1**

1m 28.86s (2.66) **Going Correction** +0.525s/f (Slow)
WFA 3 from 4yo+ 3lb **11** Ran SP% **113.2**
Speed ratings (Par 100): **105,103,101,100,99 99,98,94,91,86 79**
CSF £24.71 CT £189.36 TOTE £3.60: £1.50, £3.00, £2.70; EX 26.90 Trifecta £210.50.
Owner Lael Stable **Bred** S Boucheron **Trained** Newmarket, Suffolk

FOCUS
An ordinary fillies' handicap. This was another race where those who raced centre-to-far side were favoured and more misery for the Newcastle bookmakers. The winner is only rated to form.

6909 AMAZON WEB SERVICES H'CAP (DIV I) 5f (Tp)
5:25 (5:27) (Class 6) (0-60,64) 3-Y-O+ **£3,234** (£962; £481; £240) **Stalls** Centre

Form RPR

4254 **1** **Chip Or Pellet**[6] 6744 3-8-7 **47**.... TomEaves 10 57+
(Nigel Tinkler) *hld up: hdwy on nr side of gp to ld appr fnl f: rdn and edgd lft ins fnl f: kpt on wl* **9/1**

0525 **2** *2* **Frank The Barber (IRE)**[9] 6660 4-9-6 **59**....(t) AdamBeschizza 6 62
(Steph Hollinshead) *led: rdn and hdd appr fnl f: rallied: kpt on fnl f: nt pce of wnr* **10/1**

0005 **3** *nse* **Windforpower (IRE)**[6] 6745 6-9-4 **57**....(p) DaleSwift 5 60
(Tracy Waggott) *trckd ldrs: drvn along over 2f out: kpt on u.p ins fnl f* **12/1**

0-46 **4** *nse* **Life Of Fame**[14] 6509 3-9-3 **57**.... DanielTudhope 7 60
(David O'Meara) *dwlt: hld up in tch: hdwy and ev ch over 1f out: kpt on same pce ins fnl f* **7/1**[3]

411 **5** *3 1/2* **Intense Starlet (IRE)**[6] 6745 5-9-11 **64** 6ex....(p) SamJames 2 54
(Marjorie Fife) *hld up: rdn and effrt 2f out: no imp fnl f* **11/4**[1]

0040 **6** *hd* **Jebel Tara**[16] 6451 11-9-1 **54**....(bt) KevinStott 8 43+
(Alistair Whillans) *rrd and lost grnd s: bhd and outpcd: hdwy fnl f: kpt on: nvr able to chal* **10/1**

4500 **7** *1/2* **Mercers Row**[8] 6685 9-9-7 **60**.... FrederikTylicki 3 48
(Michael Herrington) *hld up midfield: stdy hdwy over 2f out: rdn wl over 1f out: sn outpcd* **7/2**[2]

0050 **8** *2* **Cosmic Dust**[32] 5920 3-8-1 **46** oh1.... NathanEvans(5) 9 26
(Richard Whitaker) *cl up: rdn over 2f out: wknd over 1f out* **14/1**

5050 **9** *1/2* **Captain Scooby**[10] 6615 10-8-13 **52**....(b) JoeFanning 4 31
(Richard Guest) *dwlt: bhd: drvn along over 2f out: sn no imp* **22/1**

0020 **10** *hd* **Wotnot (IRE)**[27] 6098 4-9-5 **58**....(p) ConnorBeasley 1 36
(Bryan Smart) *trckd ldrs: rdn over 2f out: wknd over 1f out* **11/1**

1m 2.05s (2.55) **Going Correction** +0.525s/f (Slow)
WFA 3 from 4yo+ 1lb **10** Ran SP% **116.6**
Speed ratings (Par 101): **100,96,96,96,91 90,89,86,85,85**
CSF £95.28 CT £1110.09 TOTE £8.90: £2.70, £2.60, £3.90; EX 52.40 Trifecta £707.80.
Owner S Duncan **Bred** L T Roberts **Trained** Langton, N Yorks

FOCUS
The first division of a moderate sprint handicap and some respite for the bookmakers. The pace was strong and those that came up the centre were favoured this time. The winner has clearly improved.

6910 AMAZON WEB SERVICES H'CAP (DIV II) 5f (Tp)
5:55 (5:58) (Class 6) (0-60,60) 3-Y-O+ **£3,234** (£962; £481; £240) **Stalls** Centre

Form RPR

0300 **1** **Horsforth**[16] 6451 4-9-3 **56**....(b) JoeFanning 8 65
(Richard Guest) *trckd ldrs: smooth hdwy to ld over 1f out: sn rdn and qcknd: kpt on wl fnl f* **20/1**

3030 **2** *1/2* **Groundworker (IRE)**[16] 6435 5-9-7 **60**....(t) PaulMulrennan 6 67
(Paul Midgley) *hld up: smooth hdwy whn nt clr run over 2f out: effrt and chsd wnr over 1f out: kpt on fnl f: hld towards fin* **7/2**[2]

0006 **3** *1 3/4* **Questo**[6] 6744 4-9-6 **59**.... ConnorBeasley 3 60
(Tracy Waggott) *in tch: effrt and swtchd lft over 1f out: kpt on ins fnl f* **11/2**

30 **4** *1 1/4* **Ypres**[8] 6685 7-9-2 **55**....(p) LukeMorris 2 51
(Jason Ward) *bhd and sn pushed along: drvn and hdwy over 1f out: hung lft ins fnl f: one pce* **3/1**[1]

0000 **5** *2 3/4* **Clergyman**[33] 5887 4-9-5 **58**.... BarryMcHugh 4 44
(Rebecca Bastiman) *prom on outside: drvn along over 2f out: ev ch briefly over 1f out: wknd ins fnl f* **6/1**

1536 **6** *5* **Indastar**[6] 6745 6-9-6 **59**....(b[1]) PJMcDonald 5 27
(Michael Herrington) *trckd ldrs: shkn up and ev ch over 1f out: rdn and wknd qckly fnl f* **4/1**[3]

4010 **7** *2 1/2* **Under Approval**[58] 4968 5-8-8 **52**....(b) GemmaTutty(5) 1 11
(Karen Tutty) *bhd on outside: drvn along 1/2-way: sn no imp: btn fnl f* **14/1**

0360 **8** *1/2* **Lowrie**[32] 5920 3-8-7 **52**.... NathanEvans(5) 7 10
(John David Riches) *walked to s: led: rdn and hdd over 1f out: sn wknd* **33/1**

060/ **9** *nse* **On The High Tops (IRE)**[702] 7519 8-8-8 **47** oh1 ow1.(p) AndrewElliott 9 4
(Colin Teague) *w ldr: drvn along over 2f out: wknd wl over 1f out* **150/1**

1m 0.76s (1.26) **Going Correction** +0.525s/f (Slow)
WFA 3 from 4yo+ 1lb **9** Ran SP% **111.9**
Speed ratings (Par 101): **110,109,106,104,100 92,88,87,87**
CSF £85.43 CT £448.62 TOTE £12.30: £4.20, £1.40, £2.60; EX 79.30 Trifecta £2271.50.
Owner Morecool Racing **Bred** Laundry Cottage Stud Farm **Trained** Ingmanthorpe, W Yorks

FOCUS
They raced more towards the nearside this time and the winning time was 1.29sec quicker than the first division. The form is rated around the first pair.
T/Plt: £7.80 to a £1 stake. Pool: £61456.5, 5702.76 winning units T/Qpdt: £3.90 to a £1 stake. Pool: £5560.21, 1033.64 winning units **Richard Young**

4220 COMPIEGNE (L-H)
Thursday, September 29

OFFICIAL GOING: Turf: soft

6911a PRIX DE MELICOCQ (CONDITIONS) (3YO COLTS & GELDINGS) (TURF) 7f
12:10 (12:00) 3-Y-O **£10,661** (£4,264; £3,198; £2,132; £1,066)

RPR

1 **Pirate's Cove (IRE)**[29] 3-8-2 0....(b) NicolasBarzalona(7) 6 88
(A Fabre, France) **22/5**[3]

2 *1 1/2* **Post Var (FR)**[17] 3-9-0 0.... TheoBachelot 4 89
(S Wattel, France) **7/5**[1]

3 *snk* **Shabbab (FR)**[45] 3-9-0 0.... GregoryBenoist 3 89
(H-F Devin, France) **131/10**

4 *1 3/4* **Gymkhana**[151] 3-9-0 0.... VincentCheminaud 2 84
(D Smaga, France) **3/1**[2]

5 *snk* **Lefortovo (FR)**[111] 3120 3-9-0 0.... ChristopheSoumillon 5 84
(Jo Hughes) **49/10**

6 *7* **Risk Major (FR)**[20] 6310 3-9-0 0.... Pierre-CharlesBoudot 7 65
(J Phelippon, France) **166/10**

7 3 1/2 **Ali Spirit (IRE)**[20] 6310 3-9-0 0 .... AntoineHamelin 1 55
(Matthieu Palussiere, France) **186/10**

1m 27.22s (87.22) **7** Ran SP% **120.0**
PARI-MUTUEL (all including 1 euro stake): WIN 5.40; PLACE 2.00, 1.50; DF SF 14.80.
Owner Godolphin SNC **Bred** Darley **Trained** Chantilly, France

6912a PRIX DE JANVILLE (H'CAP) (3YO FILLIES) (TURF) 7f
1:50 (12:00) 3-Y-O **£11,029** (£4,411; £3,308; £2,205; £1,102)

RPR

1 **Blonville (FR)**[12] 3-9-2 0 .... SebastienMaillot 8 85
(Robert Collet, France) **91/10**

2 nk **Greenshoe (IRE)**[12] 3-8-13 0 .... ChristopheSoumillon 2 81
(F-H Graffard, France) **7/2**[1]

3 3/4 **Silk Words**[26] 3-9-4 0 .... LukasDelozier 3 84
(H-A Pantall, France) **134/10**

4 3/4 **Des Annees Folles (FR)**[32] 3-8-11 0 .... (p) TheoBachelot 10 75
(P Adda, France) **223/10**

5 snk **Blessed Silence (FR)**[127] 2602 3-9-2 0 .... OlivierPeslier 17 80
(J-M Beguigne, France) **186/10**

6 3/4 **Dervahel (FR)**[12] 3-8-11 0 .... ThierryThulliez 9 73
(Mme C Barande-Barbe, France) **63/10**[3]

7 3/4 **Strategic Blue (FR)**[32] 3-8-10 0 .... EddyHardouin 11 69
(T Clout, France) **106/10**

8 nk **Touch Of Real (FR)**[40] 3-9-3 0 .... TonyPiccone 7 76
(M Boutin, France) **29/1**

9 1 1/2 **Zenani (FR)**[42] 3-8-10 0 .... Pierre-CharlesBoudot 6 65
(A Fabre, France) **119/10**

10 3/4 **Mesonera (FR)**[20] 6310 3-8-10 0 .... AntoineHamelin 1 63
(J Parize, France) **237/10**

11 1 1/4 **Energie Green (IRE)**[32] 5946 3-9-4 0 .... AurelienLemaitre 4 67
(F Head, France) **54/10**[2]

12 1 1/2 **Rip Van Suzy (IRE)**[20] 6310 3-9-1 0 .... UmbertoRispoli 16 60
(Jo Hughes) **139/10**

13 1 1/4 **Gamoudiya (FR)**[12] 3-8-7 0 .... (p) JeromeMoutard(3) 15 52
(T Castanheira, France) **51/1**

14 snk **My Girl Market (FR)**[40] 3-8-11 0 .... GregoryBenoist 13 52
(J Reynier, France) **136/10**

15 nse **Kenshaba (FR)**[32] 5946 3-9-2 0 .... VincentCheminaud 5 57
(M Boutin, France) **38/1**

1m 26.93s (86.93) **15** Ran SP% **119.6**
PARI-MUTUEL (all including 1 euro stake): WIN 10.10; PLACE 3.40, 2.10, 4.90; DF 19.10; SF 55.40.
Owner David Dahan **Bred** Franklin Finance S.A. **Trained** Chantilly, France

6913 - (Foreign Racing) - See Raceform Interactive

6108 ASCOT (R-H)
Friday, September 30

OFFICIAL GOING: Good
Wind: Light, against Weather: Fine

6914 VEOLIA H'CAP 7f
2:00 (2:00) (Class 4) (0-85,85) 3-Y-O+ **£6,469** (£1,925; £962; £481) **Stalls** High

Form RPR

4165 1 **Gothic Empire (IRE)**[15] 6529 4-9-7 **85** .... DanielMuscutt 9 94
(James Fanshawe) *dwlt: settled in midfield: stdy prog over 2f out: rdn over 1f out: drvn to ld ins fnl 100yds out: edgd lft but styd on* **8/1**

6530 2 nk **Steel Train (FR)**[20] 6320 5-9-7 **85** .... DanielTudhope 17 93
(David O'Meara) *settled in midfield: stdy prog 2f out: swtchd rt over 1f out: drvn to ld ins fnl f: hdd 100yds out: styd on* **16/1**

3565 3 2 **Realize**[21] 6276 6-9-5 **83** .... (t) OisinMurphy 8 86
(Stuart Williams) *hld up in rr: stl in last trio whn swtchd towards nr side wl over 1f out: drvn and r.o fnl f to take 3rd last stride* **8/1**

-465 4 shd **Somethingthrilling**[18] 6416 4-8-8 **79** .... JoshuaBryan(7) 18 81
(David Elsworth) *racd against nr side thrght: mde most: drvn and edgd rt over 1f out: hdd and one pce ins fnl f* **14/1**

000 5 1 **Free Code (IRE)**[28] 6082 5-9-5 **83** .... GrahamGibbons 7 83
(David Barron) *towards rr: rdn over 2f out: styd on fr over 1f out: nrst fin* **14/1**

0165 6 3/4 **Lyfka**[48] 5396 4-9-6 **84** .... (tp) MartinHarley 16 82
(Paul Cole) *led main gp in centre and on terms w overall ldr to 2f out: fdd ins fnl f* **25/1**

0006 7 hd **Fleckerl (IRE)**[19] 6371 6-9-4 **85** .... (p) LouisSteward(3) 13 82
(Conor Dore) *dwlt: wl in rr: rdn over 2f out: prog over 1f out: styd on but unable to threaten* **50/1**

3331 8 hd **My Target (IRE)**[13] 6579 5-9-5 **83** .... AdamKirby 11 80
(Michael Wigham) *chsd ldrs: rdn over 2f out: kpt on same pce u.p and n.d* **9/2**[1]

0000 9 3/4 **Holiday Magic (IRE)**[14] 6539 5-9-2 **80** .... JamieSpencer 14 75
(Michael Easterby) *hld up wl in rr: shkn up 2f out: kpt on fr over 1f out: nt pce to rch ldrs* **10/1**

0011 10 1/2 **Red Paladin (IRE)**[36] 5793 6-9-2 **80** .... (p) ShaneKelly 1 73
(Kristin Stubbs) *hld up in last: effrt over 2f out: sme prog over 1f out: keeping on but no ch whn short of room 50yds out* **20/1**

1351 11 1 1/2 **Red Tea**[13] 6580 3-8-9 **83** .... LuluStanford(7) 5 71
(Peter Hiatt) *w ldrs: rdn and losing pl whn crowded over 1f out: fdd* **7/1**[3]

113 12 2 1/4 **Cricklewood Green (USA)**[22] 6266 5-9-1 **79** .... RyanMoore 4 62
(Sylvester Kirk) *nvr bttr than midfield: rdn wl over 2f out: no prog* **6/1**[2]

0051 13 nk **Arlecchino's Leap**[36] 5810 4-9-5 **83** .... (p) LiamKeniry 2 65
(Mark Usher) *chsd ldrs: rdn and already lost pl whn short of room over 1f out: fdd* **25/1**

1346 14 nse **Dilgura**[21] 6276 6-9-1 **82** ....[1] MatthewCosham(3) 10 64
(Stuart Kittow) *prom: rdn and sing to lose pl whn bmpd over 1f out: wknd* **20/1**

4140 15 2 1/2 **Gold Hunter (IRE)**[22] 6255 6-9-0 **78** .... (p) TomMarquand 6 53
(Steve Flook) *hld up in rr: effrt on outer of gp over 2f out: no prog and wknd over 1f out* **25/1**

3000 16 18 **Shyron**[111] 3163 5-9-1 **79** .... TomQueally 3 6
(George Margarson) *dwlt: hld up in rr: effrt on outer of gp over 2f out: wknd qckly over 1f out: t.o* **25/1**

1m 26.66s (-0.94) **Going Correction** +0.025s/f (Good)
WFA 3 from 4yo+ 3lb **16** Ran SP% **122.4**
Speed ratings (Par 105): **106,105,103,103,102 101,101,100,99,99 97,95,94,94,91 71**
CSF £117.07 CT £1115.09 TOTE £8.80: £2.50, £4.30, £2.90, £4.00; EX 211.80 Trifecta £1170.10.
Owner Hamen Fan **Bred** Michael O'Mahony **Trained** Newmarket, Suffolk
■ Stewards' Enquiry : Daniel Tudhope caution; careless riding.
Daniel Muscutt caution; careless riding.

FOCUS
The going was officially good (GoingStick: straight 8.4, round 7.6). Rail on round course out 3yds from innermost position from the 1m4f start, increasing to 14yds out at the home straight. Straight course divided into two with a rail in the middle of the course. Stands' side used for this meeting. A competitive handicap to start and they went a solid pace, with the winning time only just over a second outside standard. The main action unfolded more towards the nearside. The winner is rated back to his Yarmouth form.

6915 GALLIARD HOMES WILLOW FOUNDATION EBF STALLIONS CLASSIFIED STKS 1m (S)
2:35 (2:38) (Class 3) 3-Y-O+ **£9,703** (£2,887; £1,443; £721) **Stalls** High

Form RPR

512 1 **Raising Sand**[54] 5206 4-9-3 89 .... GeorgeBaker 14 97
(Jamie Osborne) *hld up in rr: prog nr side fr 2f out: drvn to ld ins fnl f: r.o wl* **6/1**[3]

0016 2 3/4 **Brigliadoro (IRE)**[7] 6753 5-9-3 87 .... SilvestreDeSousa 6 95
(Philip McBride) *dwlt: hld up in last: stdy prog on wd outside fr 1/2-way: led wl over 1f out: drvn and hdd ins fnl f: styd on* **11/2**[2]

4160 3 3/4 **Zest (IRE)**[13] 6581 3-8-10 87 ....[1] TomQueally 11 90
(James Fanshawe) *stdd s: t.k.h: hld up bhd ldrs: lost pl 2f out: rdn and sltly awkward over 1f out: r.o wl fnl f nr side and tk 3rd last 75yds: gaining at fin* **16/1**

2121 4 1 1/2 **Fastnet Tempest (IRE)**[16] 6490 3-8-13 88 .... (p) FrankieDettori 12 90
(William Haggas) *trckd ldrs: drvn to chal on nr side 2f out: nrly upsides 1f out: one pce after and lost 3rd last 75yds* **9/2**[1]

3354 5 2 1/4 **Rousayan (IRE)**[7] 6736 5-9-3 88 .... DanielTudhope 9 85
(David O'Meara) *stdd s: hld up in rr: effrt over 2f out: prog over 1f out: rdn and kpt on but nvr pce to threaten* **13/2**

11-2 6 nse **In The Red (IRE)**[24] 6210 3-8-13 88 .... PatDobbs 10 85
(Richard Hannon) *pressed ldrs: chal and upsides 2f out: fdd jst over 1f out* **10/1**

5364 7 3/4 **Truth Or Dare**[28] 6075 5-8-12 90 .... GeorgeWood(5) 2 83
(William Muir) *hld up towards rr: trckd ldrs 2f out: taken to outer and shkn up over 1f out: one pce after* **11/1**

1164 8 3 **Kummiya**[13] 6581 3-8-10 86 .... KieranShoemark(3) 3 76+
(Roger Charlton) *t.k.h: trckd ldrs: chal 2f out: wknd over 1f out* **10/1**

355 9 nk **Margaret's Mission (IRE)**[69] 4644 5-9-0 85 .... MartinHarley 1 72
(Jim Goldie) *hld up in last pair: shkn up over 2f out: modest late prog but nvr any ch* **20/1**

2621 10 2 **Cincuenta Pasos (IRE)**[17] 6442 5-9-3 89 .... DaneO'Neill 7 71
(Joseph Tuite) *towards rr: effrt whn nt clr run wl over 1f out and dropped to last: no ch after* **20/1**

2005 11 1 **Pastoral Player**[28] 6076 9-8-12 88 .... CharlieBennett(5) 5 68
(Hughie Morrison) *stdd s: hld up in rr: shkn up and no prog 2f out* **20/1**

1020 12 1 **Bluegrass Blues (IRE)**[28] 6076 6-9-3 88 .... TomMarquand 8 66
(Heather Main) *pressed ldr: upsides 2f out: sn wknd* **50/1**

2010 13 1 3/4 **Carnival King (IRE)**[15] 6529 4-9-3 88 .... (v[1]) JimmyFortune 13 62
(Brian Meehan) *led: rdn and hdd wl over 1f out: wknd qckly* **14/1**

515- 14 4 **Haaf A Sixpence**[335] 7632 7-9-3 87 .... FMBerry 4 53
(Ralph Beckett) *awkward s: t.k.h: hld up bhd ldrs: chal 2f out: wknd rapidly over 1f out* **25/1**

1m 41.05s (0.25) **Going Correction** +0.025s/f (Good)
WFA 3 from 4yo+ 4lb **14** Ran SP% **120.3**
Speed ratings (Par 107): **99,98,97,96,93 93,92,89,89,87 86,85,83,79**
CSF £35.82 TOTE £7.20: £2.40, £2.10, £5.20; EX 44.90 Trifecta £1057.90.
Owner Nick Bradley Racing 22 & Partner **Bred** Meon Valley Stud **Trained** Upper Lambourn, Berks

FOCUS
A tight classified event, but this time the pace was ordinary and a few took a hold. Again the action unfolded towards the nearside. The winner continues to progress.

6916 ORIGINAL HARROGATE WATER H'CAP 6f
3:10 (3:10) (Class 2) (0-105,103) 3-Y-O
£18,675 (£5,592; £2,796; £1,398; £699; £351) **Stalls** High

Form RPR

3411 1 **Symposium**[9] 6668 3-7-13 **84** 6ex .... (p) JosephineGordon(3) 11 94
(William Haggas) *trckd ldrs: wnt 2nd over 1f out: drvn to chal ins fnl f: styd on wl to ld last strides* **8/1**

6522 2 hd **Ornate**[10] 6642 3-9-4 **100** .... (t) RyanMoore 1 109
(William Haggas) *led and sn 2 l ahd: rdn over 1f out: kpt on wl u.p but hdd last strides* **5/1**[3]

3214 3 2 **Mazzini**[16] 6492 3-7-11 **84** oh2 .... GeorgeWood(5) 4 87
(James Fanshawe) *awkward s: hld up in rr: prog over 2f out: tk 3rd jst over 1f out: cl enough ins fnl f: one pce last 100yds* **9/2**[2]

0510 4 2 **Ower Fly**[48] 5403 3-8-0 **87** .... HollieDoyle(5) 3 83
(Richard Hannon) *chsd ldr to over 1f out: sn btn but hld on for 4th* **50/1**

5016 5 1/2 **Kadrizzi (FR)**[27] 6112 3-9-7 **103** .... RobertWinston 6 98
(Dean Ivory) *bmpd s: towards rr: rdn over 2f out: nt qckn over 1f out: one pce and nvr on terms* **6/1**

1-00 6 nk **War Whisper (IRE)**[6] 6788 3-8-6 **88** .... TomMarquand 7 82
(Richard Hannon) *wnt rt s: in rr: rdn 2f out: one pce and nvr any imp ldrs* **20/1**

0432 7 shd **Vibrant Chords**[17] 6449 3-8-9 **91** .... HarryBentley 5 84
(Henry Candy) *towards rr: sme prog over 2f out: sn rdn: fdd over 1f out* **3/1**[1]

5100 8 1 1/2 **Mont Kiara (FR)**[20] 6327 3-8-12 **94** .... JamieSpencer 2 83
(Kevin Ryan) *v awkward s and slowly away: hld up in last: pushed along and effrt whn rn into trble jst over 1f out: modest hdwy after* **8/1**

-050 9 1 3/4 **Sunflower**[23] 6230 3-8-10 **92** .... OisinMurphy 10 75
(Andrew Balding) *t.k.h: trckd ldrs: wknd wl over 1f out* **20/1**

1310 10 6 **Highly Sprung (IRE)**[8] 6718 3-8-11 **93** .... SilvestreDeSousa 8 57
(Mark Johnston) *chsd ldrs tl wknd 2f out: eased fnl f* **8/1**

1m 13.09s (-1.41) **Going Correction** +0.025s/f (Good) **10** Ran SP% **119.0**
Speed ratings (Par 107): **110,109,107,104,103 103,103,101,98,90**
CSF £47.63 CT £211.82 TOTE £7.20: £2.30, £1.90, £2.20; EX 24.70 Trifecta £68.90.
Owner The Royal Ascot Racing Club **Bred** Bloomsbury Stud **Trained** Newmarket, Suffolk

FOCUS
A warm 3yo sprint handicap which has been won by some decent performers in recent seasons, not least the smart The Tin Man last year. Few got into this, though, and it resulted in a 1-2 for trainer William Haggas. The winner is still progressing.

6917 LONDONMETRIC NOEL MURLESS STKS (LISTED RACE) 1m 6f
3:45 (3:45) (Class 1) 3-Y-O
£20,982 (£7,955; £3,981; £1,983; £995; £499) **Stalls** Low

Form RPR
1110 **1** **Alyssa**[22] 6259 3-8-10 91 .... FMBerry 7 102
(Ralph Beckett) *t.k.h: sn trckd ldng pair: pushed along 3f out: rdn to ld 2f out: jnd on both sides over 1f out: battled on wl and jst prevailed* **8/1**
5210 **2** *nse* **Fireglow**[43] 5586 3-8-13 104 .... WilliamBuick 3 105
(Mark Johnston) *in tch: pushed along 3f out: prog on outer over 2f out: rdn to press wnr over 1f out: upsides after and gd battle fnl f: jst denied* **6/1**[3]
2201 **3** *1 1/4* **Platitude**[34] 5872 3-9-4 108 .... RyanMoore 2 108
(Sir Michael Stoute) *in tch: shkn up and prog to press wnr wl over 1f out: upsides after tl no ex last 100yds* **6/4**[1]
-012 **4** *6* **Great And Small**[35] 5851 3-8-10 77 .... OisinMurphy 4 92
(Andrew Balding) *hld up in last pair: rdn and no prog over 2f out: tk modest 4th last stride* **33/1**
5151 **5** *hd* **Novalina (IRE)**[20] 6345 3-8-10 86 .... GrahamGibbons 6 92
(William Haggas) *led: jnd 3f out: hdd 2f out: sn fdd* **16/1**
100 **6** *1 3/4* **The Tartan Spartan (IRE)**[20] 6329 3-9-1 94 .... TadhgO'Shea 5 94
(John Patrick Shanahan, Ire) *n.m.r s and hld up in last pair: effrt on inner over 2f out: wknd over 1f out* **33/1**
7 *3 1/2* **Aydoun (IRE)**[15] 6532 3-9-1 0 .... PatSmullen 1 89
(D K Weld, Ire) *trckd ldr: chal and upsides 3f out to 2f out: sn wknd: eased* **2/1**[2]

3m 3.59s (2.59) **Going Correction** +0.425s/f (Yiel) **7** Ran SP% **110.5**
Speed ratings (Par 109): **109,108,108,104,104 103,101**
CSF £50.55 TOTE £9.50: £3.00, £3.00; EX 50.20 Trifecta £99.90.
Owner Miss K Rausing **Bred** Miss K Rausing **Trained** Kimpton, Hants

FOCUS
Rail movement added 30yds to race distance. This 3yo Listed staying event has been won by some smart performers since moving from Newmarket in 2011, including the top-class hurdler Nichols Canyon in 2013 and Big Orange two years ago. The betting for this year's race was dominated by a pair of geldings, but it produced a thrilling finish between two fillies. The pace was by no means strong. The form makes sense aside from the winner.

6918 TROY ASSET MANAGEMENT H'CAP 7f
4:20 (4:20) (Class 3) (0-95,95) 3-Y-O **£8,409** (£2,502; £1,250; £625) **Stalls** High

Form RPR
5220 **1** **Musdam (USA)**[24] 6210 3-8-10 84 .... GrahamGibbons 9 95
(Sir Michael Stoute) *racd towards nr side early: hld up: rdn jst over 2f out: brought bk to nr side and prog over 1f out: drvn to ld jst ins fnl f: r.o wl* **12/1**
-020 **2** *1 1/4* **Albernathy**[90] 3908 3-8-13 87 .... MartinLane 10 95
(Charlie Appleby) *racd towards nr side early: prom: rdn 2f out: brought towards nr side again and led jst over 1f out: hanging and hdd jst ins fnl f: kpt on same pce* **14/1**
460 **3** *3 1/4* **Palawan**[48] 5403 3-9-3 91 .... SeanLevey 11 90
(Richard Hannon) *hld up and racd towards nr side early: rdn and last over 2f out: styd towards nr side and kpt on wl over 1f out to take 3rd ins fnl f* **22/1**
-501 **4** *1/2* **Brave Hero**[15] 6529 3-9-4 95 .... (b[1]) EdwardGreatrex(3) 13 93
(Saeed bin Suroor) *racd towards far side early: overall ldr: rdn and hung rt to far side fr 2f out: hdd & wknd jst over 1f out* **7/2**[1]
2312 **5** *3* **Misty Lord (IRE)**[16] 6490 3-8-9 83 .... (t) HarryBentley 7 73
(Marco Botti) *racd towards far side: hld up: effrt over 2f out: one pce and nvr able to threaten ldrs* **5/1**[3]
2201 **6** *3/4* **Fighting Temeraire (IRE)**[62] 4886 3-9-5 93 .... RobertWinston 5 81
(Dean Ivory) *chsd ldrs towards far side: rdn over 2f out: n.m.r sn after: one pce and lost grnd fr over 1f out* **13/2**
-134 **7** *1/2* **Hornsby**[62] 4867 3-9-6 94 .... WilliamBuick 1 80
(Charlie Appleby) *s.s: racd towards far side: sn in tch: prog and cl up over 2f out: wknd over 1f out* **4/1**[2]
0035 **8** *1 1/4* **Take The Helm**[23] 6232 3-8-12 86 .... JimmyFortune 6 69
(Brian Meehan) *hld up in last towards far side: taken to rail and sme prog 2f out: shkn up and wknd over 1f out: eased* **25/1**
0401 **8** *dht* **Noble Peace**[24] 6210 3-8-11 85 .... DaneO'Neill 3 68
(Henry Candy) *led gp towards far side: on terms 2f out: sn wknd* **14/1**
162 **10** *1/2* **Gale Song**[21] 6299 3-8-4 81 .... JosephineGordon(3) 8 62
(Ed Walker) *t.k.h: prom and racd towards nr side early: wknd 2f out* **9/1**
0614 **11** *10* **Explosive Power (IRE)**[13] 6560 3-8-7 86 .... JordanVaughan(5) 4 40
(K R Burke) *racd towards far side: chsd ldrs: rdn and lost pl over 2f out: wknd: t.o* **14/1**

1m 27.01s (-0.59) **Going Correction** +0.025s/f (Good) **11** Ran SP% **118.1**
Speed ratings (Par 105): **104,102,98,98,94 94,93,92,92,91 80**
CSF £168.96 CT £2242.87 TOTE £14.30: £3.30, £4.20, £7.20; EX 155.50 Trifecta £6236.80.
Owner Saeed Suhail **Bred** Timothy S O'Toole **Trained** Newmarket, Suffolk

FOCUS
A decent 3yo handicap, but a big track bias. The field split into two early with six going far side, but five came more towards the nearside and that group produced the first four home. The form may not be solid as a result. The first two finished clear though and have not had many chances.

6919 IRON STAND GORDON CARTER H'CAP 2m
4:55 (4:55) (Class 3) (0-95,92) 3-Y-O+ **£8,409** (£2,502; £1,250; £625) **Stalls** Low

Form RPR
2104 **1** **Life Less Ordinary (IRE)**[21] 6279 4-9-9 87 .... JamieSpencer 2 96
(Jamie Osborne) *hld up in 8th: stdy prog over 2f out to chse ldr over 1f out: cajoled along and clsd to ld ins fnl f: styd on wl* **4/1**[2]
6655 **2** *1 1/2* **Noble Silk**[15] 6526 7-9-6 87 .... (v) JosephineGordon(3) 8 94
(Lucy Wadham) *rousted along early to trck ldr: led over 2f out and committed for home: styd on but hdd and outpcd ins fnl f* **8/1**
0-3 **3** *1 1/2* **Golden Doyen (GER)**[41] 1598 5-9-1 79 .... WilliamTwiston-Davies 6 84
(Philip Hobbs) *rousted along early to chse ldng pair: rdn over 3f out: tk 2nd briefly wl over 1f out: one pce fnl f* **7/2**[1]
1130 **4** *3/4* **Arty Campbell (IRE)**[13] 6582 6-9-5 83 .... StevieDonohoe 7 87
(Bernard Llewellyn) *hld up in 8th: rdn over 2f out: prog over 1f out: styd on to take 4th ins fnl f: nt pce to threaten* **20/1**
24 **5** *1 1/2* **Percy Veer**[31] 5999 4-9-2 85 .... MitchGodwin(5) 10 88
(Sylvester Kirk) *hld up in 7th: rdn and prog to chse ldrs 2f out: no imp over 1f out: one pce after* **12/1**
4052 **6** *1 1/4* **Mijhaar**[14] 6540 8-10-0 92 .... (v) DanielTudhope 4 93
(David O'Meara) *stdd s: hld up in last pair: rdn over 2f out: swtchd ins and kpt on fr over 1f out: nvr any ch* **8/1**
1320 **7** *1 1/4* **Rideonastar (IRE)**[97] 3670 5-9-7 85 .... MartinDwyer 11 85
(Brendan Powell) *chsd ldrs in 5th: rdn and tried to cl over 2f out: no imp over 1f out: fdd* **20/1**
000 **8** *3 3/4* **Teak (IRE)**[13] 6582 9-8-13 77 .... (v) FMBerry 5 72
(Ian Williams) *chsd ldng trio to jst over 2f out: wknd* **13/2**[3]
0454 **9** *1 1/2* **Wordiness**[13] 6591 8-9-1 79 .... MichaelJMMurphy 12 72
(David Evans) *led at gd pce to over 2f out: wknd* **33/1**
0034 **10** *7* **Sunblazer (IRE)**[28] 6074 6-9-11 89 .... (t) GeorgeBaker 1 74
(Kim Bailey) *hld up in 10th: pushed along over 2f out: no prog and nvr involved* **10/1**
6650 **11** *3/4* **Archangel Raphael (IRE)**[28] 6074 4-9-8 86 .... PatDobbs 3 70
(Amanda Perrett) *chsd ldrs in 6th: lost pl jst over 2f out: sn wknd* **33/1**
1106 **12** *2 3/4* **Hatsaway (IRE)**[13] 6582 5-9-1 79 .... JFEgan 9 60
(Pat Phelan) *hld up in last: rdn and no prog over 2f out: wknd over 1f out* **12/1**

3m 32.37s (3.37) **Going Correction** +0.425s/f (Yiel) **12** Ran SP% **117.7**
Speed ratings (Par 107): **108,107,106,106,105 104,104,102,101,98 97,96**
CSF £33.85 CT £121.81 TOTE £4.40: £1.90, £2.70, £1.80; EX 41.20 Trifecta £178.10.
Owner Michael Buckley & Mrs Karima Burman **Bred** Aidan Sexton **Trained** Upper Lambourn, Berks

FOCUS
Rail movement added 30yds to race distance. A decent handicap which had been won by the classy stayers Quest For More and Burmese in the last two runnings. The 3yo generation had won five of the last seven runnings, but none from that age group were present this year. They only went an ordinary pace, so not the strongest test of stamina at the trip. The second helps with the standard.
T/Jkpt: Not won. T/Plt: £7,215.20 to a £1 stake. Pool: £146677.42, 14.84 winning units T/Qpdt: £238.20 to a £1 stake. Pool: £11485.08, 35.67 winning units **Jonathan Neesom**

6903 NEWCASTLE (A.W) (L-H)
Friday, September 30

OFFICIAL GOING: Tapeta: standard
Wind: Fresh, half against Weather: Fine, dry

6920 VERTEM.CO.UK H'CAP 1m 4f 98y (Tp)
5:20 (5:20) (Class 6) (0-60,60) 3-Y-O+ **£2,264** (£673; £336; £168) **Stalls** High

Form RPR
4512 **1** **The Resdev Way**[7] 6739 3-9-0 56 .... BarryMcHugh 4 70+
(Richard Whitaker) *prom: smooth hdwy to ld over 2f out: sn qcknd clr on bridle: shkn up briefly last 100yds: readily* **6/4**[1]
5031 **2** *2* **Taopix**[35] 5841 4-9-6 54 .... JoeyHaynes 14 63
(Karen McLintock) *dwlt: hld up: hdwy on outside over 2f out: chsd (clr) wnr over 1f out: kpt on to pull clr of rest fnl f: no ch w ready wnr* **4/1**[2]
3460 **3** *8* **Kerry Icon**[43] 5576 3-8-4 46 oh1 .... AndrewMullen 10 43
(Iain Jardine) *midfield: rdn along over 3f out: rallied and edgd lft over 2f out: kpt on fnl f: nt rch first two* **20/1**
6100 **4** *1* **Gabrial's Hope (FR)**[10] 6647 7-9-7 55 .... DaleSwift 5 51
(Tracy Waggott) *missed break: hld up: rdn and effrt over 2f out: kpt on fnl f: n.d* **50/1**
0000 **5** *1/2* **Zingiber**[11] 6619 4-8-12 46 oh1 .... CamHardie 8 41
(Wilf Storey) *hld up midfield: stdy hdwy over 3f out: drvn and effrt over 2f out: outpcd over 1f out* **100/1**
0051 **6** *1 1/2* **Byronegetonefree**[7] 6738 5-9-7 55 6ex .... JasonHart 7 48
(Stuart Coltherd) *led 3f: cl up: drvn along and chsd wnr over 2f out to over 1f out: edgd lft and wknd fnl f* **6/1**[3]
3540 **7** *2 1/4* **Sunshineandbubbles**[13] 6593 3-9-1 57 .... LukeMorris 13 46
(Daniel Mark Loughnane) *midfield: drvn and outpcd over 3f out: rallied whn hmpd wl over 1f out: sn no imp* **11/1**
5266 **8** *nse* **Merchant Of Dubai**[15] 6503 11-9-1 56 .... (b[1]) LewisEdmunds(7) 2 45
(Jim Goldie) *in tch on ins: rdn along over 3f out: wknd fr 2f out* **22/1**
5444 **9** *2 3/4* **Magical Lasso (IRE)**[7] 6739 3-8-7 49 .... (p) ConnorBeasley 12 34
(Keith Dalgleish) *in tch: hdwy to ld after 3f: rdn and hdd over 2f out: wknd over 1f out* **11/1**
0336 **10** *6* **Breton Blues**[7] 6738 6-9-2 50 .... GrahamLee 9 26
(Fred Watson) *prom: rdn over 2f out: sn wknd* **16/1**
0000 **11** *6* **Ronald Gee (IRE)**[15] 6503 9-9-6 59 .... AdamMcNamara(5) 1 26
(Jim Goldie) *hld up: struggling over 3f out: nvr on terms* **50/1**
0060 **12** *99* **Applejack Lad**[7] 6739 5-9-6 54 .... (tp) PaulMulrennan 11
(Michael Smith) *cl up: lost pl and struggling over 2f out: btn whn bdly hmpd wl over 1f out: eased* **50/1**
0-05 **U** **Baileys Galaxy (FR)**[28] 6094 3-8-13 55 .... JoeFanning 3
(Mark Johnston) *dwlt: hld up towards rr: stdy hdwy whn nt clr run briefly over 2f out: shkn up bhd ldng sextet whn crowded, stmbld and uns rdr wl over 1f out* **20/1**

2m 40.55s (-0.55) **Going Correction** +0.025s/f (Slow)
WFA 3 from 4yo+ 8lb **13** Ran SP% **117.6**
Speed ratings (Par 101): **102,100,95,94,94 93,91,91,89,85 81,15,**
CSF £6.16 CT £84.80 TOTE £2.20: £1.10, £2.20, £6.60; EX 8.70 Trifecta £136.00.
Owner Resdev **Bred** Mickley Stud **Trained** Scarcroft, W Yorks

FOCUS
Three recent course winners in a typical 46-60 handicap featuring the usual number who were hard to fancy on current form but it turned into a one-horse race. Decent efforts fro the grade from the first two.

6921 PROTECTING YOUR WEALTH H'CAP 1m 2f 42y (Tp)
5:50 (5:53) (Class 6) (0-65,65) 3-Y-O+ **£2,264** (£673; £336; £168) **Stalls** High

Form RPR
6 **1** **Bollihope**[66] 4730 4-9-3 58 .... JasonHart 10 66
(Richard Guest) *t.k.h: hld up in tch: smooth hdwy over 2f out: shkn up to ld over 1f out: sn hrd pressed: styd on wl u.p fnl f* **20/1**
6655 **2** *1 1/4* **Testa Rossa (IRE)**[35] 5841 6-8-12 60 .... (b) LewisEdmunds(7) 13 66
(Jim Goldie) *hld up: hdwy on outside over 2f out: effrt and pressed wnr over 1f out: kpt on same pce last 100yds* **12/1**
2325 **3** *3 1/4* **Roman De Brut (IRE)**[10] 6662 4-9-9 64 .... LukeMorris 14 64
(Daniel Mark Loughnane) *hld up: rdn and hdwy over 2f out: prom whn hung lft over 1f out: kpt on same pce ins fnl f* **9/2**[3]
6563 **4** *nk* **Cliff Edge (IRE)**[10] 6662 3-9-2 63 .... (b) JackMitchell 5 62+
(Roger Varian) *trckd ldr: effrt and ev ch over 2f out to over 1f out: edgd lft and kpt on same pce fnl f* **11/4**[1]
405 **5** *1 1/4* **Ajman Prince (IRE)**[28] 6104 3-8-13 65 .... RowanScott(5) 11 62
(Alistair Whillans) *s.i.s: hld up: rdn over 2f out: hdwy over 1f out: kpt on fnl f: no imp* **16/1**

0050 **6** *3/4* **She's Electric (IRE)**[15] **6501** 3-9-1 **62**........................(p) ConnorBeasley 6 58
(Keith Dalgleish) *t.k.h: hld up midfield: rdn and effrt over 2f out: hung lft and no imp over 1f out* **33/1**

12-0 **7** *3* **Thermal Column (IRE)**[8] **6700** 4-9-9 **64**........................ AndrewMullen 4 54
(Michael Appleby) *trckd ldrs: effrt over 2f out: edgd lft u.p wl over 1f out: sn wknd* **12/1**

643 **8** *1* **Best Tamayuz**[56] **5102** 5-9-10 **65**... BenCurtis 2 54+
(Scott Dixon) *led: jnd over 2f out: rdn and hdd over 1f out: sn wknd* **12/1**

0000 **9** *1 1/4* **Arantes**[24] **5715** 5-9-1 **56**..(p) PJMcDonald 12 42
(R Mike Smith) *hld up towards rr: drvn along wl over 2f out: sn no imp* **33/1**

-125 **10** *3* **Intrigue**[17] **6444** 4-9-10 **65**..(b) JimCrowley 3 46+
(Daniel Kubler) *s.i.s: hld up midfield: effrt and swtchd lft over 2f out: keeping on but no imp whn hmpd over 1f out: sn btn and eased* **7/2**[2]

0033 **11** *12* **Thornaby Nash**[11] **6618** 5-9-10 **65**.......................................[1] TomEaves 1 24
(Colin Teague) *prom tl rdn and wknd over 2f out* **33/1**

0500 **12** *nk* **Symbolic Star (IRE)**[27] **6138** 4-9-10 **65**..........................(b[1]) GrahamLee 7 24
(Barry Murtagh) *s.i.s: hld up: drvn along over 2f out: sn btn* **20/1**

0250 **13** *4* **Nelson's Bay**[20] **6346** 7-8-13 **54**... CamHardie 8 6
(Wilf Storey) *t.k.h: hld up on ins: shortlived effrt over 2f out: wknd wl over 1f out: eased fnl f* **20/1**

2m 10.16s (-0.24) **Going Correction** +0.025s/f (Slow)
WFA 3 from 4yo+ 6lb **13** Ran SP% **119.1**
Speed ratings (Par 101): **101,100,97,97,96 95,93,92,91,88 79,79,75**
CSF £222.79 CT £1273.47 TOTE £16.10: £5.30, £3.50, £1.80; EX 239.00 Trifecta £1849.30.
Owner Alfa Site Services Ltd **Bred** Minster Stud And Mrs H Dalgety **Trained** Ingmanthorpe, W Yorks

FOCUS
Few of these had been shaping like imminent handicap winners and this was not a strong contest for a 51-65 but they went a good pace. Probably just modest form.

6922 @VERTEMAM FOLLOW US ON TWITTER FILLIES' H'CAP 1m 2f 42y (Tp)
6:20 (6:21) (Class 5) (0-75,74) 3-Y-O+ **£3,234** (£962; £481; £240) **Stalls** High

Form RPR

0340 **1** **Island Flame (IRE)**[15] **6504** 3-9-2 **70**............................ PatrickMathers 5 80
(Richard Fahey) *hld up in tch: effrt and rdn over 2f out: hdwy over 1f out: led wl ins fnl f: edgd lft: hld on wl* **8/1**

4165 **2** *hd* **All The Rage**[8] **6702** 3-9-2 **70**.. LukeMorris 7 79
(Sir Mark Prescott Bt) *hld up: smooth hdwy on outside over 2f out: led over 1f out: sn rdn: hdd wl ins fnl f: kpt on: jst hld* **2/1**[1]

1222 **3** *4* **High On Light**[20] **6345** 3-8-10 **67**.......................... RachelRichardson(3) 6 68
(Tim Easterby) *trckd ldr: led gng wl over 2f out: rdn and hdd over 1f out: outpcd by first two ins fnl f* **5/1**[3]

0300 **4** *2 1/2* **Heart Locket**[15] **6504** 4-9-4 **71**..................................(b) NathanEvans(5) 8 67
(Michael Easterby) *prom: effrt whn edgd lft and n.m.r 2f out: rdn and outpcd fr over 1f out* **11/1**

4345 **5** *3* **Sepal (USA)**[65] **4761** 3-9-6 **74**... JimCrowley 1 64
(Charles Hills) *trckd ldrs on ins: rdn and lost pl over 2f out: n.d after* **4/1**[2]

4164 **6** *3/4* **La Havrese (FR)**[15] **6521** 5-9-3 **65**.................................... PaddyAspell 3 54
(Lynn Siddall) *hld up on ins: drvn along and outpcd over 2f out: sn no imp* **18/1**

0235 **7** *14* **Malhama**[114] **3042** 3-9-3 **71**.. PaulHanagan 9 32
(Roger Varian) *t.k.h early: led at stdy pce: rdn and hdd over 2f out: wknd over 1f out: eased whn btn ins fnl f* **5/1**[3]

2m 10.67s (0.27) **Going Correction** +0.025s/f (Slow)
WFA 3 from 4yo+ 6lb **7** Ran SP% **111.4**
Speed ratings (Par 100): **99,98,95,93,91 90,79**
CSF £23.17 CT £86.16 TOTE £10.30: £4.50, £1.70; EX 30.00 Trifecta £94.10.
Owner Northumbria Leisure Ltd **Bred** Christopher Maye **Trained** Musley Bank, N Yorks

FOCUS
Only a few of these fillies had solid chances at the weights judged on recent form, in a handicap weakened by the three withdrawals. They went only a steady pace and several raced keenly.

6923 PERFECT PARTNERSHIPS NURSERY H'CAP 1m 5y (Tp)
6:50 (6:50) (Class 6) (0-65,64) 2-Y-O **£2,264** (£673; £336; £168) **Stalls** Centre

Form RPR

0355 **1** **Lucy's Law (IRE)**[30] **6026** 2-9-2 **59**.................................. AndrewElliott 5 67
(Tom Tate) *s.i.s: hld up: hdwy nr side of gp to ld over 1f out: edgd lft ins fnl f: pushed out* **14/1**

5002 **2** *1 1/2* **Snookered (IRE)**[36] **5796** 2-8-9 **52**................................ TonyHamilton 2 57
(Richard Fahey) *hld up: rdn over 2f out: hdwy to press wnr 1f out: kpt on ins fnl f: no imp towards fin* **6/1**[2]

4043 **3** *1 3/4* **Vinnievanbaileys**[9] **6681** 2-9-3 **60**....................................(b) DavidAllan 9 61
(Chris Dwyer) *mde most tl rdn and hdd over 1f out: kpt on same pce ins fnl f* **8/1**

0124 **4** *3/4* **Zamadance**[9] **6664** 2-9-5 **62**.. JimCrowley 6 61
(Sylvester Kirk) *cl up: rdn over 2f out: ev ch over 1f out: no ex ins fnl f* **15/8**[1]

000 **5** *nk* **Cliff Bay (IRE)**[81] **4188** 2-8-13 **56**.................................. ConnorBeasley 1 55
(Keith Dalgleish) *t.k.h: prom on far side of gp: rdn and hung lft over 1f out: kpt on ins fnl f: no imp* **10/1**

440 **6** *1 3/4* **Dominating (GER)**[13] **6590** 2-9-5 **62**................................ JoeFanning 4 57
(Mark Johnston) *cl up: drvn along over 2f out: wknd ins fnl f* **8/1**

500 **7** *1* **Spanish Beauty**[52] **5271** 2-8-8 **54**........................... JacobButterfield(3) 7 47
(Ollie Pears) *hld up bhd ldng gp: drvn along over 2f out: no imp fr over 1f out* **50/1**

0000 **8** *1/2* **On Show (IRE)**[20] **6313** 2-8-2 **45**... LukeMorris 8 37
(David Brown) *prom: drvn and outpcd over 2f out: n.d after* **16/1**

5054 **9** *1 1/4* **Belle's Angel (IRE)**[39] **5719** 2-8-6 **49**............................... PaulHanagan 3 38
(Ann Duffield) *trckd ldrs: drvn and lost pl over 2f out: sn btn* **16/1**

3323 **10** *3 1/4* **Bridal March**[56] **5112** 2-9-7 **64**................................ SilvestreDeSousa 10 46
(Mark Johnston) *t.k.h prom on nr side of gp: rdn over 2f out: wknd over 1f out* **13/2**[3]

1m 40.93s (2.33) **Going Correction** -0.075s/f (Stan) **10** Ran SP% **114.1**
Speed ratings (Par 93): **85,83,81,81,80 78,77,77,76,72**
CSF £93.61 CT £745.60 TOTE £13.70: £4.30, £2.40, £3.00; EX 97.20 Trifecta £414.60.
Owner Ms Fionnuala Cassidy **Bred** Lady Richard Wellesley **Trained** Tadcaster, N Yorks

FOCUS
Only one previous winner but several of the runners in this low-grade nursery were open to improvement. Though they went only a steady pace to halfway this is a stiff mile for a two-year-old and the finish was fought out by two who came from well off the pace.

6924 VERTEM MANAGEMENT/BRITISH STALLIONS STUDS EBF MAIDEN STKS 1m 5y (Tp)
7:20 (7:21) (Class 5) 2-Y-O **£3,557** (£1,058; £529; £264) **Stalls** Centre

Form RPR

6 **1** **Mandarin (GER)**[35] **5848** 2-9-5 0.............................. SilvestreDeSousa 7 85+
(Marco Botti) *mde all: rdn clr 2f out: eased cl home* **10/11**[1]

2 *3 3/4* **Cool Team (IRE)** 2-9-5 0...[1] JimCrowley 2 77+
(Hugo Palmer) *hld up: pushed along over 2f out: hdwy to chse (clr) wnr ins fnl f: kpt on: no imp* **10/1**

033 **3** *2 1/4* **Glendun (USA)**[40] **5670** 2-9-5 74...................................... PaulMulrennan 3 72
(Brian Meehan) *plld hrd early: chsd wnr: rdn over 2f out: lost 2nd and outpcd ins fnl f* **13/2**[3]

6 **4** *1 3/4* **Pathway To Freedom**[13] **6590** 2-9-5 0............................ JamesDoyle 11 68
(Charlie Appleby) *racd nr side of gp: prom: effrt and disp 2nd pl over 1f out to ins fnl f: sn outpcd* **5/2**[2]

5 *2* **Rosarno (IRE)** 2-9-5 0... PaulHanagan 5 64+
(Charles Hills) *hld up: shkn up over 2f out: hdwy over 1f out: edgd lft and kpt on fnl f: nvr nrr* **20/1**

6 *6* **La Vie En Rose** 2-9-0 0.. JoeFanning 9 46
(Mark Johnston) *cl up: rdn over 2f out: edgd lft and wknd over 1f out* **25/1**

0 **7** *3/4* **Starshell (IRE)**[13] **6590** 2-9-5 0.. LukeMorris 8 49
(Sir Mark Prescott Bt) *hld up: pushed along and outpcd 3f out: sme late hdwy: nvr on terms* **25/1**

0 **8** *1/2* **Siyahamba (IRE)**[9] **6679** 2-9-5 0.................................. ConnorBeasley 6 48
(Bryan Smart) *trckd ldrs: drvn and outpcd over 2f out: sn wknd* **125/1**

9 *1 1/2* **Little Kingdom (IRE)** 2-8-9 0... PhilDennis(5) 4 40
(Tracy Waggott) *s.i.s: hld up: rdn over 2f out: btn over 1f out* **200/1**

0 **10** *10* **New Society (IRE)**[29] **6054** 2-9-5 0.................................... PJMcDonald 1 23
(James Bethell) *in tch on outside: drvn and struggling wl over 2f out: sn wknd* **33/1**

0 **11** *4* **Thenewsfromspain (IRE)**[77] **4363** 2-9-5 0................. AndrewMullen 10 14
(Ollie Pears) *hld up: rdn and struggling over 2f out: sn btn* **200/1**

1m 39.12s (0.52) **Going Correction** -0.075s/f (Stan) **11** Ran SP% **120.6**
Speed ratings (Par 95): **94,90,88,86,84 78,77,77,75,65 61**
CSF £11.75 TOTE £1.90: £1.10, £2.70, £1.80; EX 14.50 Trifecta £57.60.
Owner Sheikh Mohammed Bin Khalifa Al Maktoum **Bred** Dr K Schulte **Trained** Newmarket, Suffolk

FOCUS
The field for this maiden was much longer on potential than proven form but there were some encouraging performances and it may turn out to e a fair race. A likeable effort from the winner.

6925 FRESH APPROACH/EBFSTALLIONS.COM MAIDEN FILLIES' STKS (PLUS 10 RACE) 6f (Tp)
7:50 (7:53) (Class 5) 2-Y-O **£3,557** (£1,058; £529; £264) **Stalls** Centre

Form RPR

1 **Castleacre** 2-9-0 0.. JimCrowley 11 80+
(Hugo Palmer) *wore hood in paddock: cl up on nr side of gp: led over 3f out: rdn and qcknd clr fnl f: comf* **6/4**[1]

5 **2** *4 1/2* **Dandy Bird (IRE)**[10] **6641** 2-9-0 0...................................... TomEaves 7 67
(James Given) *led to over 3f out: disp ld to over 1f out: kpt on fnl f: nt pce of wnr* **40/1**

4 **3** *1 3/4* **Ocean Princess (IRE)**[106] **3321** 2-9-0 0.......................... PaulMulrennan 8 61
(Michael Dods) *hld up: shkn up and hdwy nr side of gp over 1f out: kpt on to take 3rd pl wl ins fnl f: nvr nrr* **16/1**

0 **4** *hd* **Bearag**[16] **6477** 2-9-0 0.. PhillipMakin 3 61
(David O'Meara) *prom on far side of gp: drvn along over 2f out: kpt on ins fnl f: nt rch first three* **33/1**

0 **5** *1/2* **Al Haayelah**[9] **6673** 2-9-0 0.. JackMitchell 14 59
(Roger Varian) *hld up midfield on nr side of gp: effrt and rdn over 2f out: no imp fr over 1f out* **14/1**[3]

05 **6** *3/4* **Dazacam**[13] **6588** 2-9-0 0.. DougieCostello 1 57
(Michael Herrington) *hld up on far side of gp: rdn and effrt over 2f out: one pce fr over 1f out* **100/1**

7 *nk* **Marseille (IRE)** 2-9-0 0.. JoeDoyle 13 56
(Julie Camacho) *missed break: t.k.h in rr: shkn up and hdwy over 1f out: no imp fnl f* **22/1**

43 **8** *hd* **Best Bid (IRE)**[134] **2404** 2-9-0 0.. JasonHart 12 56
(John Quinn) *hld up bhd ldng gp: rdn along over 2f out: no imp fr over 1f out* **25/1**

0 **9** *2 1/2* **Chillililli**[15] **6515** 2-9-0 0.. ConnorBeasley 10 48
(Bryan Smart) *w ldrs: rdn over 2f out: wknd ins fnl f* **100/1**

0 **10** *1 1/2* **She's Zoff (IRE)**[14] **6534** 2-9-0 0... CamHardie 6 44
(John Quinn) *t.k.h: in tch: drvn over 2f out: wknd over 1f out* **40/1**

11 *1/2* **Remal Dubai (USA)** 2-9-0 0... JamesDoyle 5 42
(Saeed bin Suroor) *s.i.s: t.k.h and sn prom: rdn over 2f out: wknd over 1f out* **13/8**[2]

4 **12** *nk* **Cool Run Girl (IRE)**[43] **5577** 2-9-0 0................................... DavidAllan 2 41
(Iain Jardine) *hld up: rdn over 2f out: nvr on terms* **20/1**

13 *1/2* **Miss Quick** 2-9-0 0.. PJMcDonald 4 40
(Ann Duffield) *in tch: drvn along over 2f out: wknd over 1f out* **33/1**

0 **14** *3* **Tilly Devine**[46] **5469** 2-9-0 0.. LukeMorris 9 31
(Scott Dixon) *prom: drvn and lost pl over 3f out: btn fnl 2f* **100/1**

1m 12.09s (-0.41) **Going Correction** -0.075s/f (Stan) **14** Ran SP% **117.3**
Speed ratings (Par 92): **99,93,90,90,89 88,88,88,84,82 82,81,81,77**
CSF £75.15 TOTE £2.50: £1.20, £8.70, £3.90; EX 67.00 Trifecta £600.00.
Owner Saeed Manana **Bred** Rabbah Bloodstock Limited **Trained** Newmarket, Suffolk

FOCUS
A couple of interesting newcomers in a maiden lacking a contender with outstanding claims on form - they were the only pair not to start at double-figure odds and with one of then not living up to market expectations it is not easy to judge the merit of this race. The winner can improve on the bare form.

6926 INVESTING FOR THE FUTURE H'CAP (DIV I) 5f (Tp)
8:20 (8:23) (Class 4) (0-85,85) 3-Y-O+ **£4,851** (£1,443; £721; £360) **Stalls** Centre

Form RPR

104 **1** **Rich Again (IRE)**[18] **6425** 7-8-12 **76**..............................(b) PJMcDonald 7 85
(James Bethell) *s.i.s: bhd and pushed along: hdwy over 1f out: led ins fnl f: edgd rt: kpt on wl* **17/2**

2624 **2** *3/4* **Ziggy Lee**[23] **6234** 10-8-11 **80**...................................... AdamMcNamara(5) 5 86
(Lawrence Mullaney) *bhd: rdn along after 2f: hdwy over 1f out: swtchd rt and chsd wnr wl ins fnl f: r.o* **12/1**

4300 **3** 1/2 **Just Us Two (IRE)**[27] 6114 4-9-5 **83**...............................[1] JamesDoyle 10 88
(Robert Cowell) *in tch: effrt and rdn 2f out: wnt 2nd briefly ins fnl f: kpt on same pce nr fin* **10/1**

0601 **4** 1 1/4 **Desert Ace (IRE)**[6] 6793 5-8-13 **82** 6ex........................(p) CliffordLee[(5)] 9 82
(Iain Jardine) *cl up: rdn to ld over 1f out: hdd ins fnl f: kpt on same pce* **5/1**[1]

0603 **5** 1 **Bondi Beach Boy**[6] 6793 7-8-13 **82**............................. NathanEvans[(5)] 1 78
(James Turner) *in tch on far side of gp: drvn along over 2f out: rallied over 1f out: kpt on same pce ins fnl f* **7/1**[3]

0005 **6** nse **Noble Storm (USA)**[11] 6633 10-8-11 **82**.................. CameronNoble[(7)] 3 78
(Ed McMahon) *led at decent gallop: rdn and hdd over 1f out: wknd ins fnl f* **12/1**

0105 **7** shd **Buccaneers Vault (IRE)**[35] 5859 4-8-13 **77**...........(p) ConnorBeasley 12 73
(Michael Dods) *bhd and sn pushed along towards nr side of gp: hdwy over 1f out: r.o ins fnl f: nrst fin* **20/1**

3200 **8** 2 1/2 **Cocoa Beach (IRE)**[32] 5955 3-9-2 **81**.............................. LukeMorris 11 68
(Sir Mark Prescott Bt) *towards rr: drvn along after 2f: sn no imp* **11/2**[2]

2115 **9** 1/2 **May Rose (IRE)**[25] 6195 3-8-13 **78**..................................(t) JimCrowley 2 63
(Charles Hills) *t.k.h: in tch towards far side of gp: effrt and rdn over 1f out: wknd fnl f* **5/1**[1]

0500 **10** 1 1/4 **Crosse Fire**[15] 6506 4-9-7 **85**.. DaleSwift 13 66
(Scott Dixon) *bhd and sn rdn on nr side of gp: no imp fr 2f out* **50/1**

4336 **11** hd **Appleberry (IRE)**[85] 4034 4-8-12 **76**.............................. AndrewMullen 4 56
(Michael Appleby) *prom: drvn and outpcd over 2f out: sn wknd* **25/1**

1310 **12** 2 1/4 **Sandra's Secret (IRE)**[23] 6234 3-9-1 **80**............................. DavidAllan 6 52
(Les Eyre) *cl up: rdn over 2f out: wknd over 1f out* **9/1**

58.48s (-1.02) **Going Correction** -0.075s/f (Stan)
WFA 3 from 4yo+ 1lb **12** Ran SP% **116.8**
Speed ratings (Par 105): **105,103,103,101,99 99,99,95,94,92 92,88**
CSF £102.19 CT £1038.39 TOTE £10.30: £1.60, £3.70, £3.10; EX 106.50 Trifecta £1494.30.
Owner Richard T Vickers **Bred** Mrs Sandra Maye **Trained** Middleham Moor, N Yorks

FOCUS
Some formerly fair sprinters who were well handicapped plus a handful of obviously in-form contenders made this a potentially competitive 71-85. They went a good pace, which suited the first two home.

6927 INVESTING FOR THE FUTURE H'CAP (DIV II) 5f (Tp)
8:50 (8:50) (Class 4) (0-85,85) 3-Y-O+ **£4,851** (£1,443; £721; £360) **Stalls** Centre

Form RPR

5014 **1** **Aprovado (IRE)**[17] 6435 4-8-13 **77**...........................(b) ConnorBeasley 11 85
(Michael Dods) *pressed ldr: led 2f out: drvn out fnl f* **10/1**

035 **2** 1/2 **Rosina**[37] 5780 3-9-1 **80**.. PJMcDonald 2 86
(Ann Duffield) *hld up on far side of gp: rdn and hdwy over 1f out: chsd wnr ins fnl f: kpt on* **7/1**

2040 **3** 3/4 **Sir Domino (FR)**[8] 6699 4-8-10 **74**................................(b) GrahamLee 10 77
(Kevin Ryan) *hld up in tch: smooth hdwy over 2f out: rdn to chse wnr over 1f out to ins fnl f: one pce towards fin* **10/1**

0230 **4** 1 3/4 **First Bombardment**[40] 5679 3-8-13 **78**............................ PhillipMakin 6 75
(David O'Meara) *hld up in tch: drvn along over 2f out: rallied over 1f out: kpt on same pce ins fnl f* **6/1**[3]

0025 **5** 1 1/4 **Elusivity (IRE)**[40] 5679 8-9-4 **82**.................................(p) PaulMulrennan 4 75
(Conor Dore) *led tl rdn and hdd 2f out: rallied: wknd ins fnl f* **14/1**

3202 **6** 1 3/4 **Cosmic Chatter**[8] 6714 6-9-3 **81**..............................(p) JamesSullivan 12 67
(Ruth Carr) *anticipated s and dwlt: bhd and outpcd: kpt on fnl f: nvr able to chal* **9/2**[2]

1401 **7** nk **Oriental Relation (IRE)**[18] 6425 5-9-5 **83**......................(v) TomEaves 13 68
(James Given) *chsd ldrs: rdn 2f out: wknd ins fnl f* **13/2**

1500 **8** 1 3/4 **Landing Night (IRE)**[20] 6324 4-8-13 **77**.....................(p) JoeyHaynes 8 56
(Rebecca Menzies) *t.k.h: hld up in tch: rdn over 2f out: wknd over 1f out* **16/1**

3006 **9** 7 **Baileys Mirage (FR)**[34] 5882 5-9-5 **83**..................(b) SilvestreDeSousa 9 37
(Chris Dwyer) *chsd ldrs: rdn along over 2f out: wknd over 1f out: eased whn no ch wl ins fnl f* **3/1**[1]

58.46s (-1.04) **Going Correction** -0.075s/f (Stan)
WFA 3 from 4yo+ 1lb **9** Ran SP% **114.0**
Speed ratings (Par 105): **105,104,103,100,98 95,94,92,80**
CSF £76.84 CT £724.47 TOTE £8.80: £2.60, £1.80, £3.30; EX 83.40 Trifecta £1113.30.
Owner Hanson, McKiver, Percival **Bred** R N Auld **Trained** Denton, Co Durham

FOCUS
Seemingly the less competitive of the two divisions, with no fewer than five withdrawals, and the first five came clear.
T/Plt: £81.90 to a £1 stake. Pool: £76,374.35 - 680.07 winning tickets T/Qpdt: £20.50 to a £1 stake. Pool: £8,284.47 - 298.54 winning tickets **Richard Young**

6928 - 6931a (Foreign Racing) - See Raceform Interactive

6754 DUNDALK (A.W) (L-H)
Friday, September 30

OFFICIAL GOING: Polytrack: standard

6932a TEXT YOUR BET TO PADDY POWER ON 51465 DIAMOND STKS (GROUP 3) 1m 2f 150y(P)
7:35 (7:37) 3-Y-O+
£27,352 (£8,823; £4,191; £1,875; £948; £485)

RPR

1 **Long Island Sound (USA)**[48] 5429 3-9-3 108....(vt[1]) SeamieHeffernan 2 108
(A P O'Brien, Ire) *led and sn clr: advantage reduced 3f out: hung rt 2f out: strly pressed ent fnl f and hdd: rallied wl to ld cl home* **4/5**[1]

2 nk **Battalion (IRE)**[41] 5651 6-9-8 104..................................(p) PatCosgrave 4 105
(William Haggas) *settled off ldrs in 4th: wnt 3rd 4f out: clsr on inner over 1f out: led ins fnl f: strly rdn and hdd cl home* **6/1**[3]

3 1/2 **Hawke (IRE)**[19] 6389 4-9-8 100.. BillyLee 5 104+
(J P Murtagh, Ire) *racd towards rr: prog to chse ldng trio in 4th under 2f out: kpt on wl on outer into 3rd cl home: nrst fin* **7/1**

4 hd **Qatari Hunter (IRE)**[65] 4753 3-9-3 107.......................... KevinManning 1 106
(J S Bolger, Ire) *sn chsd clr ldr in 2nd: clsr 3f out: dropped to 3rd ins fnl f: kpt on same pce and dropped to 4th cl home* **7/2**[2]

5 5 1/2 **Poitin**[47] 5444 6-9-5 84... RobbieDowney 3 90
(Keith Henry Clarke, Ire) *racd in mid-div: pushed along in 5th 3f out: no imp under 2f out: kpt on one pce fnl f* **33/1**

6 6 **Tennessee Wildcat (IRE)**[78] 4326 6-9-8 102.................... ColinKeane 8 81
(G M Lyons, Ire) *sn mid-div: niggled along 3f out in 6th: rdn and nt qckn under 2f out: sn no ex* **14/1**

7 14 **Cruiseliner (BRZ)**[397] 5-9-5 104.. ShaneFoley 7 51
(Takashi Kodama, Ire) *chsd ldrs in 3rd: dropped to 4th 4f out: rdn and nt qckn 2f out: wknd qckly over 1f out: eased clsng stages* **50/1**

8 4 3/4 **Remarkable Lady (IRE)**[25] 6200 3-9-0 75......................(t) ChrisHayes 6 44
(H Rogers, Ire) *a towards rr: qckly dropped to rr and detached under 3f out: no ex: eased clsng stages* **100/1**

2m 14.5s (134.50)
WFA 3 from 4yo+ 7lb **8** Ran SP% **117.1**
CSF £6.53 TOTE £1.80: £1.02, £2.30, £2.20; DF 8.30 Trifecta £26.70.
Owner Derrick Smith & Mrs John Magnier & Michael Tabor & **Bred** Edward A Cox Jr **Trained** Cashel, Co Tipperary

FOCUS
A Group Three contest with quite a few high-class operators on the scoresheet over the years and it boasted a multitude of International form for punters to sink their teeth into.

6933 - 6936a (Foreign Racing) - See Raceform Interactive

6728 SAINT-CLOUD (L-H)
Friday, September 30

OFFICIAL GOING: Turf: good

6937a PRIX KANTAR (MAIDEN) (2YO FILLIES) (TURF) 7f
1:15 (12:00) 2-Y-O **£9,926** (£3,970; £2,977; £1,985; £992)

RPR

1 **Beauty Of Love** 2-8-11 0... MickaelBarzalona 3 81
(Mme Pia Brandt, France) **186/10**

2 1 3/4 **Followmeifucan (IRE)**[21] 6309 2-9-2 0........................ ThierryThulliez 5 81
(C Lerner, France) **81/10**

3 2 1/2 **Grande Bleue (IRE)**[18] 2-9-2 0...................................... MaximeGuyon 9 74
(C Laffon-Parias, France) **11/5**[1]

4 shd **Pink Paint (FR)**[84] 2-9-2 0... OlivierPeslier 10 74
(M Delcher Sanchez, France) **41/1**

5 snk **La Breviere**[22] 2-9-2 0.. ChristopheSoumillon 8 74
(F Chappet, France) **29/1**

6 snk **Gold Sister (FR)**[38] 2-9-2 0.. IoritzMendizabal 1 73
(F Chappet, France) **14/1**

7 1 **Sunderia (FR)**[44] 5568 2-9-2 0.. AnthonyCrastus 11 70
(Mme S Allouche, France) **67/10**

8 1/2 **Louversey** 2-9-2 0.. CristianDemuro 12 69
(P Sogorb, France) **54/10**[2]

9 1 3/4 **Lady Capucine (FR)**[28] 6087 2-9-2 0.......................... AntoineHamelin 6 64
(Harry Dunlop) *hld up bhd ldng gp: 6l 5th and scrubbed along 3f out: edgd rt over 2f out: sn rdn and no imp: one pce fnl f* **12/1**

10 4 1/2 **Panameras (FR)**[22] 2-9-2 0... GeraldMosse 4 52
(T Castanheira, France) **14/1**

11 1 1/2 **Dallas Affair** 2-8-11 0.. ThierryJarnet 7 43
(F Head, France) **6/1**[3]

12 2 **Villa Salaria (FR)** 2-8-11 0... UmbertoRispoli 2 38
(G Doleuze, France) **32/1**

1m 26.32s (-5.88) **12** Ran SP% **120.0**
WIN (incl. 1 euro stake): 19.60. PLACES: 4.50, 2.90, 1.70. DF: 90.70. SF: 261.40.
Owner Ecurie Des Charmes **Bred** Haras D'Etreham **Trained** France

6938a PRIX DE CARRIERES-SOUS-POISSY (CLAIMER) (4YO+) (TURF) 1m 7f
4:00 (12:00) 4-Y-O+ **£6,985** (£2,794; £2,095; £1,397; £698)

RPR

1 **Lady Zinaad (GER)**[337] 6-8-0 0......................... ClementLecoeuvre[(8)] 12 62
(E Lellouche, France) **9/5**[1]

2 1 1/2 **Le Rock (IRE)**[19] 6362 4-9-8 0.................................... IoritzMendizabal 10 74
(J S Moore) *led after 1f: set stdy pce: niggled along and wound up tempo more than 2 1/2f out: sn rdn: hdd 2f out: styd on u.p: nt pce of wnr* **12/1**

3 3/4 **Penardini (USA)**[1059] 7-8-11 0................................ StephanePasquier 9 62
(Y Gourraud, France) **23/1**

4 shd **Stock Exchange (FR)**[42] 5700 9-8-8 0........................... JeromeCabre 8 59
(J-F Doucet, France) **10/1**

5 snk **Tony's Power**[29] 9-9-2 0...................................(b) ChristopheSoumillon 1 67
(A Marcialis, Italy) **5/1**[2]

6 2 **Enfin Seuls (FR)**[11] 5-9-2 0... GeraldMosse 4 64
(Yves de Nicolay, France) **10/1**

7 1 1/4 **Mumgala (FR)**[18] 6-9-6 0... MickaelBarzalona 11 66
(F Vermeulen, France) **31/5**[3]

8 1 3/4 **Funky Mary (GER)**[42] 5700 7-9-2 0...........................(b) RonanThomas 3 60
(C Plisson, France) **10/1**

9 1 1/4 **Becquarius (FR)**[26] 6-9-1 0.. AntoineHamelin 6 58
(Eric Saint-Martin, France) **32/1**

10 4 1/2 **Wolverine (FR)**[40] 9-8-11 0....................................(p) UmbertoRispoli 7 48
(H Billot, France) **14/1**

11 6 **Aussi Celebre (IRE)**[293] 7-8-11 0.........................(p) AnthonyCrastus 5 40
(Mlle I Essig, France) **41/1**

12 shd **Pink Courageous (FR)**[500] 5-8-13 0..............(p) Jean-BaptisteHamel 2 42
(B Legros, France) **33/1**

WIN (incl. 1 euro stake): 2.80. Places: 1.80, 3.30, 5.60. DF: 22.10. SF: 31.00.
Owner Gerard Augustin-Normand **Bred** Stall Parthenaue **Trained** Lamorlaye, France

6914 ASCOT (R-H)
Saturday, October 1

OFFICIAL GOING: Good to soft changing to soft after race 1 (2.00)
Wind: Moderate, across Weather: Fine but cloudy, heavy shower race 3

6939 TOTEPOOL EBF STALLIONS BREEDING WINNERS OCTOBER STKS (LISTED RACE) (F&M) 7f
2:00 (2:00) (Class 1) 3-Y-O+
£22,684 (£8,600; £4,304; £2,144; £1,076; £540) **Stalls** High

Form RPR

1321 **1** **Eternally**[49] 5396 3-8-12 100.. FrankieDettori 15 105+
(John Gosden) *racd freely: mde virtually all towards nr side: shkn up and decisive advantage 2f out: styd on wl* **11/4**[1]

-304 **2** 2 1/4 **Robanne**[119] 2928 3-8-12 98..................................... GrahamGibbons 10 99
(William Knight) *chsd wnr towards nr side: def 2nd overall over 1f out: kpt on but no imp* **14/1**

112 **3** ¾ **Battlement**[55] 5205 3-8-12 89.. JimmyFortune 2 97
(Roger Charlton) *hld up in rr towards far side: prog against far rail over 2f out: chsd ldrs over 1f out: styd on but nvr able to chal* **12/1**

021 **4** ½ **Yeah Baby Yeah (IRE)**[33] 5987 3-8-12 87.................(p) TonyHamilton 4 96
(Gay Kelleway) *hld up in last far side: gd prog over 2f out: chsd ldrs fnl f: styd on but unable to chal* **66/1**

-541 **5** 1½ **Colour Blue (IRE)**[21] 6355 5-9-0 98.. WJLee 9 93
(W McCreery, Ire) *pressed ldr towards far side: carried lft 2f out: one pce over 1f out* **8/1**[3]

2310 **6** 1 **Delve (IRE)**[71] 4582 3-8-12 87.. JamieSpencer 6 89
(Sir Michael Stoute) *hld up in rr towards far side: virtually last whn nt clr run briefly 2f out: prog over 1f out: kpt on but no ch* **20/1**

21 **7** 1¼ **Dazzling Rose**[78] 4361 3-8-12 88.. RobertHavlin 8 86
(John Gosden) *led gp towards far side and on terms w wnr to over 2f out: hung lft 2f out: sn btn* **10/1**

5205 **8** ½ **Make Fast**[91] 3911 3-8-12 97.. OisinMurphy 1 84
(Andrew Balding) *pressed ldrs towards far side: on terms over 2f out: wknd over 1f out* **20/1**

3455 **9** nk **Shadow Hunter (IRE)**[30] 6056 3-8-12 92........................ ShaneKelly 7 83
(Hugo Palmer) *chsd ldrs towards far side: rdn over 2f out: no prog and btn over 1f out* **33/1**

6503 **10** 1 **Imtiyaaz (IRE)**[18] 6449 4-9-0 90.. AdamKirby 14 82
(Roger Varian) *hld up towards nr side: rdn 2f out: no significant prog* **20/1**

0524 **11** 2¼ **Mix And Mingle (IRE)**[42] 5645 3-8-12 100........................ TedDurcan 3 75
(Chris Wall) *in tch gp towards far side: rdn over 2f out: wknd wl over 1f out* **8/1**[3]

5113 **12** ½ **Namhroodah (IRE)**[64] 4826 4-9-0 102........................ MartinHarley 12 74
(James Tate) *dwlt: sn prom nr side: wknd u.p 2f out* **9/2**[2]

4000 **13** nk **Volunteer Point (IRE)**[15] 6547 4-9-0 98........................ GrahamLee 13 73
(Mick Channon) *t.k.h: hld up towards nr side: shkn up and no great prog whn nt clr run briefly 2f out: wknd* **50/1**

0260 **14** hd **Black Cherry**[42] 5645 4-9-0 99.. SeanLevey 5 73
(Richard Hannon) *chsd ldrs towards far side tl wknd 2f out* **14/1**

162 **15** nk **Carolinae**[14] 6579 4-9-0 76.. StevieDonohoe 17 72
(Charlie Fellowes) *hld up towards nr side: shkn up and no prog 2f out* **33/1**

1m 28.43s (0.83) **Going Correction** +0.325s/f (Good)
WFA 3 from 4yo+ 2lb **15** Ran SP% **120.8**
Speed ratings (Par 111): **108,105,104,104,102 101,99,99,98,97 95,94,94,93,93**
CSF £39.56 TOTE £3.40: £1.40, £4.70, £3.90; EX 45.50 Trifecta £759.10.
Owner Cheveley Park Stud **Bred** Cheveley Park Stud Ltd **Trained** Newmarket, Suffolk

FOCUS
Following the rain leading up to the meeting the going had eased to good to soft. Rail on round course out 3yds from innermost position from the 1m4f start, increasing to 14yds out at the home straight. Straight course divided into two with a rail in the middle of the course. Stands' side used for this meeting. The 3yos had dominated this race until the 4yo Pelerin took it last year, but they were back on track this time, providing the first four home. The field soon split with the first two racing in the nearside group, but the third and fourth raced far side. A winning time 2.83sec outside standard suggested the ground wasn't that bad, but the ground was changed to soft after the race. The runner-up helps with the standard and the form could be rated a bit higher.

6940 GIGASET CUMBERLAND LODGE STKS (GROUP 3) 1m 4f
2:30 (2:30) (Class 1) 3-Y-O+

£34,026 (£12,900; £6,456; £3,216; £1,614; £810) **Stalls** Low

Form RPR

-131 **1** **Move Up**[27] 6179 3-8-13 107.. WilliamBuick 3 116
(Saeed bin Suroor) *trckd ldr: shkn up to ld wl over 1f out: sn jnd: gd battle after: drvn and jst asserted last 50yds* **5/1**

-301 **2** nk **Arab Spring (IRE)**[28] 6125 6-9-4 113........................ JamieSpencer 1 114
(Sir Michael Stoute) *trckd ldng pair: shkn up to join wnr over 1f out: gd battle after and stl upsides 75yds out: no ex after* **7/2**[1]

5311 **3** 1¾ **Kings Fete**[49] 5402 5-9-4 112.. TedDurcan 4 111
(Sir Michael Stoute) *led: shkn up and hdd wl over 1f out: nt qckn: kpt on same pce* **4/1**[2]

2366 **4** shd **Western Hymn**[70] 4626 5-9-1 115........................ FrankieDettori 2 108
(John Gosden) *trckd ldng trio: urged along fr 2f out but no imp: kpt on to press for 3rd nr fin* **9/2**[3]

5022 **5** 4½ **Duretto**[42] 5639 4-9-1 100.. JimmyFortune 6 101
(Andrew Balding) *awkward to post: hld up in 7th: rdn over 2f out: kpt on one pce to take modest 5th fnl f* **10/1**

2265 **6** 1 **Sumbal (IRE)**[118] 2947 4-9-1 110........................ OisinMurphy 7 99
(David Simcock) *in tch in 6th: shkn up and no prog 2f out: wl btn after* **15/2**

1415 **7** 1½ **Black Night (IRE)**[10] 6666 4-9-1 73........................ TonyHamilton 8 97?
(J Moon, Jersey) *mostly in last pair: rdn and no prog over 2f out: kpt on u.p to pass two rivals fnl f* **100/1**

5503 **8** 3¼ **Star Storm (IRE)**[8] 6752 4-9-1 98.. TomQueally 5 92
(James Fanshawe) *chsd ldrs in 5th: rdn over 2f out: wknd over 1f out* **10/1**

2101 **9** 3½ **Goodwood Zodiac (IRE)**[33] 5962 3-8-8 100............ GrahamGibbons 9 86
(William Knight) *a in last pair: rdn and no prog over 2f out* **14/1**

2m 37.93s (5.43) **Going Correction** +0.725s/f (Yiel)
WFA 3 from 4yo+ 7lb **9** Ran SP% **114.7**
Speed ratings (Par 113): **110,109,108,108,105 104,103,101,99**
CSF £22.69 TOTE £4.90: £1.80, £1.60, £1.60; EX 20.40 Trifecta £55.80.
Owner Godolphin **Bred** The Lavington Stud **Trained** Newmarket, Suffolk

FOCUS
Rail movement added 21yds to race distance. A well up-to-scratch renewal of the Cumberland Lodge with the ground now officially soft, but the early pace wasn't that strong and a couple took a grip, while the principals were always up there. The form reads well enough amongst the principals.

6941 JOHN GUEST BENGOUGH STKS (GROUP 3) 6f
3:05 (3:06) (Class 1) 3-Y-O+

£39,697 (£15,050; £7,532; £3,752; £1,883; £945) **Stalls** High

Form RPR

111- **1** **Shalaa (IRE)**[371] 6764 3-9-1 121........................ FrankieDettori 10 115+
(John Gosden) *racd quite freely: mde all: hrd pressed jst over 1f out: urged along strly but wout use of whip: hld on wl* **7/4**[1]

4114 **2** nk **Mehronissa**[28] 6120 4-8-13 105........................ FrederikTylicki 3 111
(Ed Vaughan) *t.k.h: trckd ldrs: wnt 2nd wl over 1f out: str chal fnl f: kpt on wl but a jst hld* **8/1**

0336 **3** 1½ **Raucous**[35] 5880 3-9-1 105..(tp) JimmyFortune 4 109
(William Haggas) *dwlt: hld up in last: rdn over 2f out: prog on outer over 1f out: styd on to take 3rd ins fnl f: no threat* **10/1**

1510 **4** nk **Don't Touch**[84] 4151 4-9-2 112.. TonyHamilton 6 108
(Richard Fahey) *settled towards rr: shkn up and prog 2f out: rdn to dispute 3rd 1f out: kpt on same pce after* **5/1**[2]

0010 **5** 1¾ **Outback Traveller (IRE)**[84] 4166 5-9-2 108................. MartinHarley 1 103
(Robert Cowell) *hld up: stdy prog over 2f out gng wl: shkn up and fnd nil over 1f out: wl btn after* **14/1**

-101 **6** 3¼ **Mobsta (IRE)**[133] 2495 4-9-8 109.. GrahamLee 9 98
(Mick Channon) *chsd ldrs: shoved along sn after 1/2-way: lost pl 2f out: wknd* **14/1**

1023 **7** ½ **Ridge Ranger (IRE)**[14] 6574 5-9-3 110........................ ShaneKelly 2 92
(Eric Alston) *pressed wnr to wl over 1f out: sn wknd* **11/1**

14 **8** ½ **Naadirr (IRE)**[35] 5880 5-9-2 107..(p) AdamKirby 7 89
(Marco Botti) *towards rr against rail: shkn up 2f out: hanging bdly and no prog* **7/1**[3]

6330 **9** 2¾ **Strath Burn**[28] 6120 4-9-2 107..(p) OisinMurphy 8 80
(Robert Cowell) *trckd ldng pair: looked poised to chal 2f out: sn shkn up and wknd: eased fnl f* **10/1**

1m 14.32s (-0.18) **Going Correction** +0.325s/f (Good)
WFA 3 from 4yo+ 1lb **9** Ran SP% **116.5**
Speed ratings (Par 113): **114,113,111,111,108 104,103,103,99**
CSF £16.59 TOTE £2.30: £1.50, £2.60, £3.50; EX 11.60 Trifecta £76.80.
Owner Al Shaqab Racing **Bred** Mogeely Stud **Trained** Newmarket, Suffolk

FOCUS
It started to rain again before this race. A fascinating Group 3 sprint with all the attention surrounding one horse, and he didn't disappoint. Shalla has been rated a length or so below his 2yo best on the bare form.

6942 TOTESCOOP6 CHALLENGE CUP (HERITAGE H'CAP) 7f
3:40 (3:43) (Class 2) 3-Y-O+

£112,050 (£33,552; £16,776; £8,388; £4,194; £2,106) **Stalls** High

Form RPR

1214 **1** **Librisa Breeze**[43] 5613 4-9-9 108........................ RobertWinston 16 117+
(Dean Ivory) *hld up towards rr: gng easily but nowhere to go fr 2f out tl last 150yds: tremendous burst whn in the clr and stormed into the ld fnl strides* **11/2**[1]

4112 **2** ½ **Firmament**[28] 6109 4-9-7 106.. DanielTudhope 8 113
(David O'Meara) *cl up: gng easily over 2f out: led over 1f out: sn rdn: hrd pressed ins fnl f: kpt on wl but hdd and outpcd last strides* **8/1**

0244 **3** hd **Squats (IRE)**[28] 6109 4-8-13 103........................ GeorgiaCox(5) 11 109
(William Haggas) *hld up towards rr: prog over 2f out: nt clr run briefly over 1f out: drvn to chal ins fnl f: nrly upsides nr fin but then jst outpcd* **12/1**

2220 **4** ½ **Intisaab**[14] 6556 5-8-11 99..(p) ShelleyBirkett(3) 10 104+
(David O'Meara) *t.k.h early: prom: nt clr run fr 2f out: rdn and styd on fnl f but wnr stl overtk him* **28/1**

0414 **5** ¾ **Buckstay (IRE)**[21] 6328 6-9-10 109........................(p) JamieSpencer 12 112
(Peter Chapple-Hyam) *dwlt: hld up wl in rr: shkn up over 2f out: styd on steadily fr over 1f out but nvr quite cl enough to chal* **12/1**

1442 **6** shd **Growl**[14] 6558 4-9-5 104.. GrahamLee 3 106
(Richard Fahey) *trckd ldrs: drvn to ld briefly wl over 1f out: one pce fnl f* **10/1**

2621 **7** nse **Afjaan (IRE)**[28] 6126 4-9-2 101.. FrankieDettori 7 103
(William Haggas) *hld up towards rr: prog on outer over 2f out: tried to cl on ldrs and ended up on far side fnl f: kpt on but nt quite pce to chal* **15/2**[3]

5023 **8** nse **Doncha (IRE)**[64] 4823 5-9-1 100.. AdamKirby 4 102
(Robert Eddery) *in tch in midfield on outer: prog over 2f out: rdn to chal wl over 1f out: ended up towards far side and kpt on same pce fnl f* **8/1**

0066 **9** nk **Dream Dubai**[15] 6547 3-9-2 103........................ FrederikTylicki 2 103
(Sylvester Kirk) *in tch in midfield on outer: rdn to chal 2f out: one pce fr jst over 1f out* **25/1**

0412 **10** nk **Right Touch**[42] 5640 6-9-3 102.. TonyHamilton 14 103
(Richard Fahey) *trckd ldrs: shkn up 2f out: steadily outpcd fnl f* **20/1**

1131 **11** ½ **Dutch Law**[28] 6109 4-8-9 99.. CharlieBennett(5) 5 98
(Hughie Morrison) *towards rr: taken to outer and stoked up over 3f out: prog and upsides ldr 2f out to over 1f out: no ex fnl f* **14/1**

1125 **12** shd **Remarkable**[108] 3269 3-9-4 105..(b) RobertHavlin 13 103
(John Gosden) *hld up in rr: tried to make prog fr over 2f out but only styd on at same pce* **6/1**[2]

2000 **13** nk **Heaven's Guest (IRE)**[28] 6109 6-9-3 102........................ MartinHarley 9 100
(Richard Fahey) *trckd ldrs: rdn and fnd little 2f out: sn btn* **20/1**

-014 **14** ¾ **Coprah**[20] 8-9-6 105..(t) MartinLane 15 101
(Cathrine Erichsen, Norway) *w ldr: led briefly 2f out: wknd fnl f* **100/1**

0020 **15** 1 **Suzi's Connoisseur**[28] 6109 5-9-2 101........................(vt) OisinMurphy 18 95
(Stuart Williams) *hld up towards rr: nt clr run over 2f out to over 1f out: no real prog whn in the clr fnl f* **20/1**

5030 **16** 1 **Burnt Sugar (IRE)**[22] 6287 4-9-0 99..(b) SeanLevey 6 90
(Richard Hannon) *dwlt: hld up wl in rr: effrt on wd outside 2f out: wknd jst over 1f out* **33/1**

0100 **17** ¾ **Cornwallville (IRE)**[7] 6788 4-8-13 98........................ ShaneKelly 1 87
(Roger Fell) *plld hrd early and hld up in last pair: rdn and no prog over 2f out* **66/1**

3040 **18** 5 **Watchable**[14] 6558 6-9-6 105..(p) GrahamGibbons 17 81
(David O'Meara) *led against nr side rail to 2f out: wknd qckly* **33/1**

1m 28.35s (0.75) **Going Correction** +0.325s/f (Good)
WFA 3 from 4yo+ 2lb **18** Ran SP% **124.7**
Speed ratings (Par 109): **108,107,107,106,105 105,105,105,105,104 104,104,103,102,101 100,99,94**
CSF £42.82 CT £538.43 TOTE £6.00: £2.10, £2.10, £2.70, £6.70; EX 37.80 Trifecta £685.20.
Owner Tony Bloom **Bred** Newsells Park Stud **Trained** Radlett, Herts

FOCUS
A fiendishly competitive handicap as it should be for the money. The field raced as one group close to the nearside rail, though they finished spread out across the track. You won't see many races won with such a dramatic late turn of foot as this. The first ten were covered by around 3l.

6943 ASCOT AND CAMRA 10TH ANNIVERSARY ROUS STKS (LISTED RACE) 5f
4:15 (4:17) (Class 1) 3-Y-O+

£25,519 (£9,675; £4,842; £2,412; £1,210; £607) **Stalls** High

Form RPR

1-52 **1** **Easy Road**[20] 6-9-0 106..(t) WilliamBuick 10 111
(Cathrine Erichsen, Norway) *chsd ldrs but sn pushed along: rdn to take 2nd over 1f out: hanging whn chalng after: drvn to take narrow ld 100yds out: hld on* **9/2**[3]

6656 **2** *shd* **Medicean Man**[45] 5555 10-9-0 102....................(tp) MartinLane 8 110
(Jeremy Gask) *chsd ldrs: rdn 2f out: clsd fnl f: tk 2nd last 50yds and chal: jst denied* **14/1**

4056 **3** *hd* **Mirza**[20] 6391 9-9-0 102....................(p) MartinHarley 7 109
(Rae Guest) *w ldr: led 1/2-way: rdn over 1f out: narrowly hdd 100yds out: kpt on but lost 2nd last 50yds* **16/1**

0342 **4** *1 1/4* **Willytheconqueror (IRE)**[35] 5863 3-9-0 105.......... SamHitchcott 11 105
(William Muir) *in tch: rdn 2f out: styd on to take 4th fnl f: nvr able to chal* **8/1**

0400 **5** *1 1/2* **Sole Power**[20] 6384 9-9-0 108.......... JamieSpencer 6 99
(Edward Lynam, Ire) *stdd and awkward s: hld up in last trio: shkn up 2f out: one pce and unable to cl on ldrs* **3/1**[1]

4603 **6** *1/2* **Iffranesia (FR)**[20] 6384 6-8-9 103.......... GrahamGibbons 13 92
(Robert Cowell) *s.s: sn in tch in last pair: rdn over 1f out: kpt on but no ch* **8/1**

0051 **7** *nk* **Kimberella**[7] 6792 6-9-0 109.......... BarryMcHugh 2 96
(David Nicholls) *racd on wd outside: led to 1/2-way: wknd over 1f out* **4/1**[2]

6205 **8** *3/4* **Fine Blend (IRE)**[14] 6574 3-8-9 97.......... GrahamLee 12 89
(William Muir) *sn in last pair: rdn and no prog wl over 1f out* **16/1**

0-00 **9** *1/2* **Polybius**[98] 3655 5-9-0 105.......... TedDurcan 9 92
(David Lanigan) *in tch: rdn and nt qckn 2f out: no prog after* **9/1**

2035 **10** *1 3/4* **Iseemist (IRE)**[16] 6518 5-8-9 94.......... MichaelJMMurphy 3 80
(John Gallagher) *racd on outer: pressed ldrs to 2f out: sn wknd* **25/1**

1m 0.96s (0.46) **Going Correction** +0.325s/f (Good) **10** Ran SP% **117.7**
Speed ratings (Par 111): **109,108,108,106,104 103,102,101,100,98**
CSF £66.17 TOTE £4.80: £1.70, £4.30, £5.70; EX 62.90 Trifecta £1318.90.
Owner Stall Easy Road **Bred** Michael E Broughton **Trained** Norway

FOCUS
A competitive Listed sprint run at a good pace in the conditions and again the nearside was the place to be. Pretty ordinary orm for the grade, the ageing second and third helping the standard.

6944 MCGEE GROUP JOINING JACK H'CAP 5f
4:50 (4:52) (Class 3) (0-95,94) 3-Y-O+ **£12,938** (£3,850; £1,924; £962) **Stalls** High

Form RPR

4005 **1** **Shamshon (IRE)**[12] 6627 5-9-5 **92**.......... JamieSpencer 14 101
(Jamie Osborne) *stdd s: hld up wl in rr: shkn up over 1f out: drvn and gd prog fnl f: r.o to ld post* **5/1**[1]

060 **2** *shd* **Dutch Masterpiece**[7] 6779 6-9-1 **93**..........(b) HectorCrouch(5) 13 102
(Gary Moore) *dwlt: hld up in midfield: prog over 1f out: led jst ins fnl f and looked sure to win: hanging bdly rt last 100yds: hdd post* **8/1**

0031 **3** *nk* **Distant Past**[12] 6633 5-9-1 **88**..........(p) ShaneGray 12 96
(Kevin Ryan) *prom: rdn 2f out: drvn to chal 1f out: chsd ldr sn after: styd on but lost 2nd nr fin* **13/2**[3]

6300 **4** *1/2* **My Name Is Rio (IRE)**[14] 6556 6-9-2 **89**..........(p) SeanLevey 5 95
(Michael Dods) *taken down early: in tch in midfield: rdn over 1f out: styd on fnl f: nrst fin* **14/1**

2460 **5** *nk* **Shipyard (USA)**[14] 6556 7-9-0 **87**.......... FrederikTylicki 7 92
(Michael Appleby) *taken down early: pressed ldrs: drvn to chal over 1f out: one pce last 150yds* **6/1**[2]

1100 **6** *1* **A Momentofmadness**[65] 4803 3-9-2 **89**.......... SteveDrowne 6 91
(Charles Hills) *taken down early: pressed ldr: disp ld 1/2-way to jst ins fnl f: no ex* **33/1**

0460 **7** *nse* **Celebration**[23] 6263 3-9-0 **87**..........(p) TonyHamilton 15 89
(Richard Fahey) *chsd ldrs: rdn and nt qckn over 1f out: one pce after* **16/1**

1006 **8** *nk* **Major Pusey**[25] 6207 4-8-11 **84**.......... MichaelJMMurphy 3 84
(John Gallagher) *hld up wl in rr: prog on outer of gp over 1f out: kpt on fnl f but nvr pce to chal* **33/1**

5500 **9** *1/2* **Rio Ronaldo (IRE)**[28] 6112 4-8-13 **86**.......... RobertWinston 8 84
(Mike Murphy) *dwlt: wl in rr: cajoled along fr 2f out: kpt on one pce and no ch* **8/1**

1320 **10** *3/4* **Majestic Hero (IRE)**[12] 6633 4-9-3 **90**.......... GrahamLee 1 85
(Ronald Harris) *pressed ldrs: rdn wl over 1f out: wknd ins fnl f* **20/1**

0230 **11** *hd* **Waseem Faris (IRE)**[7] 6779 7-8-12 **85**.......... WilliamBuick 11 80
(Joseph Tuite) *led: jnd 2f out: disp after tl hdd & wknd jst ins fnl f* **16/1**

6440 **12** *1/2* **Another Wise Kid (IRE)**[70] 4667 8-9-7 **94**.......... MartinHarley 16 87
(Paul Midgley) *racd towards nr side: a in rr: struggling 2f out: one pce after* **16/1**

4153 **13** *3/4* **Top Boy**[12] 6633 6-8-11 **84**..........(v) MartinLane 2 74
(Derek Shaw) *chsd ldrs: lost pl and rdn 2f out: fdd* **16/1**

0005 **14** *8* **Field Of Vision (IRE)**[25] 6207 3-8-7 **87**.......... SeanMooney(7) 17 49
(Joseph Tuite) *racd alone against nr side rail: sn struggling* **25/1**

0300 **15** *3/4* **Dungannon**[12] 6633 9-9-1 **88**..........(b) OisinMurphy 4 47
(Andrew Balding) *mostly in last: wknd over 1f out* **12/1**

5000 **16** *32* **Union Rose**[33] 5961 4-9-6 **93**..........(p) AdamKirby 10
(Ronald Harris) *a in rr: wknd qckly 2f out: virtually p.u fnl f* **8/1**

1m 1.1s (0.60) **Going Correction** +0.325s/f (Good) **16** Ran SP% **130.0**
Speed ratings (Par 107): **108,107,107,106,106 104,104,103,103,101 101,100,99,86,85 34**
CSF £45.06 CT £221.71 TOTE £5.30: £1.80, £2.40, £1.90, £3.60; EX 29.80 Trifecta £82.60.
Owner Michael Buckley **Bred** Stonethorn Stud Farms Ltd **Trained** Upper Lambourn, Berks

FOCUS
A decent sprint handicap contested by 16 geldings, including the last two winners of the race. Despite all the evidence of the two-day meeting here, all bar one of these raced up the centre early, but the winner was switched to the nearside for his effort and that almost certainly made the difference. Several had a chance passing the furlong pole and this is straightforward form.
T/Jkpt: Not won. T/Plt: £110.10 to a £1 stake. Pool: £206,669.84 - 1370.24 winning units T/Qpdt: £38.40 to a £1 stake. Pool: £12,318.79 - 237.08 winning units **Jonathan Neesom**

6782 NEWMARKET (R-H)
Saturday, October 1

OFFICIAL GOING: Good to firm (firm in places) changing to good to firm after race 1 (1.45)
Wind: light, half behind Weather: showers

6945 NKT FINANCIAL SOLUTIONS LTD EBF STALLIONS MAIDEN STKS (PLUS 10 RACE) 1m
1:45 (1:46) (Class 4) 2-Y-O **£4,528** (£1,347; £673; £336) **Stalls** Low

Form RPR

35 **1** **Via Egnatia (USA)**[77] 4390 2-9-5 0.......... RobertTart 2 95
(John Gosden) *mde all: rdn and qcknd clr 2f out: in n.d 1f out: eased towards fin: easily* **9/2**[3]

044 **2** *7* **Never Surrender (IRE)**[23] 6262 2-9-5 82.......... SilvestreDeSousa 10 78
(Charles Hills) *t.k.h: chsd ldng pair: chsd wnr 3f out: rdn and hung rt ent fnl 2f out: no ch w wnr but kpt on for clr 2nd after* **3/1**[2]

3 *6* **Pivoine (IRE)** 2-9-5 0.......... RyanMoore 4 64+
(Sir Michael Stoute) *chsd ldng trio: effrt in 3rd 2f out: sn outpcd and wl btn over 1f out: plugged on* **9/4**[1]

0 **4** *3 3/4* **Zoffanist (IRE)**[14] 6570 2-9-5 0.......... MartinDwyer 7 55
(Amanda Perrett) *chsd wnr tl 3f out: 4th and outpcd whn edgd lft 2f out: sn wknd* **33/1**

5 *hd* **Bedouin (IRE)** 2-9-5 0..........(b[1]) AndreaAtzeni 9 54
(Luca Cumani) *sn bustled along in midfield: lost pl and u.p 1/2-way: rallied 3f out: outpcd and btn 2f out: sn wknd* **8/1**

6 *3 3/4* **Jive Factor (USA)** 2-9-5 0.......... PaulMulrennan 3 45
(Ed Dunlop) *stdd after s: hld up in tch in last pair: sme hdwy 1/2-way: rdn over 2f out: sn btn: wknd 2f out* **12/1**

7 *2* **Moon Idol** 2-9-5 0.......... TomMarquand 6 41
(Richard Hannon) *in tch in midfield: lost pl and rdn 3f out: sn btn and bhd 2f out* **7/1**

8 *27* **Abouttimeyoutoldme** 2-9-5 0.......... FMBerry 1
(Ralph Beckett) *s.i.s: a rr: swtchd rt and rdn over 3f out: lost tch over 2f out: t.o* **20/1**

1m 38.17s (-0.43) **Going Correction** +0.15s/f (Good) **8** Ran SP% **113.0**
Speed ratings (Par 97): **108,101,95,91,91 87,85,58**
CSF £17.94 TOTE £5.30: £1.50, £1.30, £1.20; EX 15.40 Trifecta £36.90.
Owner K Abdullah **Bred** Juddmonte Farms Inc **Trained** Newmarket, Suffolk

FOCUS
Stands' side course used. Stalls on far side except 1m4f, centre. The re-positioning of the bend into the home straight increased the distance of the 1m4f handicap by 3yds. There was 2.2mm of rain on Thursday, it was dry on Friday and overnight, and race day was rainy, with reportedly 3mm falling before this opener. All that considered, credit to the clerk of the course for letting the ground quicken up, with the meeting kicking off on good to firm, firm in places, before being downgraded to just good to firm following this opener. There was a smart-looking winner.

6946 BRITISH EBF FILLIES' SERIES SPRINT H'CAP 6f
2:15 (2:16) (Class 2) 3-Y-O+
£31,125 (£9,320; £4,660; £2,330; £1,165; £585) **Stalls** Low

Form RPR

2133 **1** **Summer Chorus**[14] 6583 3-9-0 **84**.......... JimmyQuinn 9 92+
(Andrew Balding) *taken down early: hld up in tch in midfield: nt clr run ent fnl 2f: hdwy u.p over 1f out: chsd ldrs ins fnl f: styd on strly towards fin: led last stride* **9/2**[2]

3223 **2** *shd* **Pixeleen**[33] 5955 4-9-2 **85**.......... JFEgan 2 92
(Malcolm Saunders) *taken down early: chsd ldrs: effrt over 1f out: rdn to ld 1f out: drvn ins fnl f: kpt on: hdd last stride* **4/1**[1]

4141 **3** *nk* **Sweet Dragon Fly**[21] 6340 3-8-12 **87**..........(t) GeorgeWood(5) 10 93
(Paul Cole) *trckd ldrs: effrt to chse ldrs 2f out: drvn and ev ch jst ins fnl f: kpt on wl* **6/1**

4102 **4** *1* **Stellarta**[16] 6518 5-9-10 **93**.......... TomMarquand 5 96+
(Michael Blanshard) *hld up in tch in last pair: nt clr run 2f out: rdn and effrt over 1f out: hdwy whn squeezed for room ins fnl f: swtchd rt and styd on wl towards fin: nt rch ldrs* **11/1**

0221 **5** *nk* **Minminwin (IRE)**[21] 6317 3-7-11 **70** oh9..........(vt) JosephineGordon(3) 8 72
(Gay Kelleway) *dwlt: hld up in tch towards rr: effrt over 1f out: hdwy ins fnl f: styd on wl fnl 100yds: nt rch ldrs* **28/1**

0201 **6** *nk* **Ginzan**[21] 6318 8-8-12 **81**.......... MartinDwyer 11 82
(Malcolm Saunders) *chsd ldrs: effrt 2f out: stl pressing ldrs but unable qck 1f out: styd on same pce ins fnl f* **25/1**

6202 **7** *1/2* **Racing Angel (IRE)**[17] 6487 4-7-8 **70**.......... DavidEgan(7) 14 69
(Mick Quinn) *t.k.h: hld up in tch in midfield: effrt 2f out: n.m.r ins fnl f: styd on same pce fnl 100yds* **11/1**

0620 **8** *3/4* **Sixties Sue**[3] 6883 3-8-8 **78**.......... SilvestreDeSousa 1 75
(Mick Channon) *stdd s: hld up in tch: hdwy u.p to chse ldrs over 1f out: drvn and no imp jst ins fnl f: wknd towards fin* **8/1**

1213 **9** *1* **Emerald Loch**[60] 4984 3-8-9 **79**..........(p) FMBerry 3 73
(Ralph Beckett) *hld up in tch in midfield: nt clr run jst over 2f out: effrt over 1f out: styd on same pce and no imp ins fnl f* **14/1**

200 **10** *5* **Calypso Choir**[39] 5744 3-8-8 **81**.......... EdwardGreatrex(3) 7 59
(Sylvester Kirk) *led: rdn 2f out: hdd 1f out: wkng whn squeezed for room ins fnl f: wknd fnl 100yds* **20/1**

3141 **11** *1 1/4* **Noble Act**[19] 6410 3-7-12 **71**.......... NoelGarbutt(3) 12 45
(Rae Guest) *hld up in tch in midfield: rdn 2f out: sn lost pl and bhd over 1f out: wknd fnl f* **20/1**

2345 **12** *1 1/4* **David's Duchess (IRE)**[28] 6114 3-8-7 **77**.......... PaulHanagan 6 47
(Richard Fahey) *chsd ldrs: rdn 2f out: sn lost pl and btn: bhd ins fnl f* **11/2**[3]

1m 12.13s (-0.07) **Going Correction** +0.15s/f (Good)
WFA 3 from 4yo+ 1lb **12** Ran SP% **119.1**
Speed ratings (Par 96): **106,105,105,104,103 103,102,101,100,93 92,90**
CSF £21.62 CT £112.33 TOTE £5.40: £1.70, £2.30, £2.10; EX 23.30 Trifecta £78.80.
Owner Sheikh Juma Dalmook Al Maktoum **Bred** Genesis Green Stud Ltd And Thurso Ltd **Trained** Kingsclere, Hants

FOCUS
This fillies' sprint handicap was competitive.

6947 BRITISH EBF PROMOTING FILLIES' SERIES H'CAP 1m
2:50 (2:50) (Class 2) 3-Y-O+
£31,125 (£9,320; £4,660; £2,330; £1,165; £585) **Stalls** Low

Form RPR

0403 **1** **Muffri'Ha (IRE)**[8] 6746 4-9-10 **98**.......... PatCosgrave 6 110
(William Haggas) *chsd ldr tl led 3f out: rdn and wnt clr w rival over 1f out: styd on strly and asserted ins fnl f: rdn out* **11/2**[1]

1211 **2** *1 3/4* **Crowning Glory (FR)**[17] 6483 3-8-10 **87**.......... FMBerry 3 95
(Ralph Beckett) *hld up in tch in midfield: hdwy to chse ldrs 3f out: wnt clr w wnr and shkn up over 1f out: rdn 1f out: styd on same pce and btn 100yds out* **6/1**[2]

3-16 **3** *2* **Qamarain (USA)**[17] 6483 3-7-7 **77** oh1.......... DavidEgan(7) 4 80
(Brian Meehan) *hld up wl in tch in midfield: clsd to chse ldrs 3f out: rdn and outpcd 2f out: n.m.r over 1f out: rallied ins fnl f: styd on wl fnl 100yds: wnt 3rd towards fin* **10/1**

3400 **4** *1* **Sharaakah (IRE)**[44] 5588 3-9-3 **94**.......... RyanMoore 7 95
(Ed Dunlop) *hld up in tch in last trio: effrt 2f out: rdn and hdwy over 1f out: chsd clr ldng pair 1f out: styd on same pce ins fnl f: lost 3rd towards fin* **9/1**

2131 **5** ½ **Lincoln Rocks**[6] 6811 3-8-12 **89** 6ex ColmO'Donoghue 14 89
(David O'Meara) *hld up in tch in midfield: effrt 2f out: no imp over 1f out: ket on ins fnl f: nvr threatened ldrs* **8/1**

0330 **6** 1 **Starlit Cantata**[17] 6482 5-8-1 **78** EdwardGreatrex(3) 2 76
(Eve Johnson Houghton) *hld up in tch in rr: hdwy over 2f out: rdn to chse ldng pair but unable qck over 1f out: lost 3rd 1f out: wknd ins fnl f* **20/1**

302 **7** 1¾ **Gratzie**[7] 6778 5-9-0 **88** SilvestreDeSousa 5 82
(Mick Channon) *stdd s: hld up in tch in rr: clsd and nt clrest of runs 2f out: sme hdwy u.p over 1f out: kpt on but no threat to ldrs ins fnl f* **7/1**[3]

2012 **8** 1¼ **Haley Bop (IRE)**[14] 6557 3-9-3 **94** JoeFanning 1 85
(Mark Johnston) *led tl 3f out: sn rdn: lost pl and btn over 1f out: wknd ins fnl f* **8/1**

31-3 **9** 1 **Farandine**[23] 6246 3-8-7 **84** TomMarquand 9 72
(Luca Cumani) *in tch in midfield: rdn over 2f out: sn lost pl: wl hld whn wnt rt over 1f out: wknd ins fnl f* **10/1**

4216 **10** 3¼ **Labyrinth (IRE)**[28] 6113 3-8-4 **81** JimmyQuinn 12 62
(Sir Michael Stoute) *stdd s: t.k.h: hld up in tch: hdwy 3f out: sn rdn: lost pl and btn over 1f out: wknd ins fnl f: eased towards fin* **14/1**

4200 **11** 3 **Bint Dandy (IRE)**[16] 6529 5-8-6 **83** (b) JosephineGordon(3) 10 57
(Chris Dwyer) *chsd ldrs tl rdn and lost pl jst over 2f out: wl hld and edgd rt over 1f out: wknd ins fnl f: eased towards fin* **20/1**

13-0 **12** hd **Fourth Way (IRE)**[172] 1396 3-9-2 **93** AndreaAtzeni 11 67
(Roger Varian) *chsd ldrs tl over 2f out: sn lost pl: bhd and eased wl ins fnl f* **8/1**

1m 37.87s (-0.73) **Going Correction** +0.15s/f (Good)
WFA 3 from 4yo+ 3lb **12** Ran SP% **119.9**
Speed ratings (Par 96): **109,107,105,104,103 102,101,99,98,95 92,92**
CSF £38.15 CT £321.45 TOTE £6.00: £2.00, £1.90, £4.00; EX 39.60 Trifecta £741.70.
Owner Sheikh Juma Dalmook Al Maktoum **Bred** Lodge Park Stud **Trained** Newmarket, Suffolk

FOCUS
A decent fillies' handicap and a smart performance from the top weight.

6948 BRITISH STALLION STUDS EBF FILLIES' SERIES MIDDLE DISTANCE H'CAP 1m 2f
3:25 (3:26) (Class 2) 3-Y-O+

£31,125 (£9,320; £4,660; £2,330; £1,165; £585) **Stalls** Low

Form RPR

0215 **1** **Sharja Queen**[52] 5307 3-9-5 **102** AndreaAtzeni 3 112
(Roger Varian) *hld up in tch in midfield: hdwy 3f out: rdn to chse ldr 2f out: sn chalng: led ins fnl f: styd on strly: rdn out* **6/1**[3]

3431 **2** 1¼ **Malmoosa (IRE)**[31] 6032 3-8-4 **87** PaulHanagan 5 94
(Brian Meehan) *led: rdn 2f out: drvn and hrd pressed over 1f out: hdd and styd on same pce ins fnl f* **5/1**[2]

3-26 **3** 1¾ **Haggle**[22] 6298 3-8-12 **95** PatCosgrave 6 99
(Luca Cumani) *in tch in midfield: effrt 3f out: wnt 2nd briefly over 2f out: 3rd and styd on same pce ins fnl f* **4/1**[1]

0304 **4** ¾ **Persun**[15] 6549 4-8-4 **82** SilvestreDeSousa 7 84
(Mick Channon) *t.k.h: hld up in tch in midfield: effrt 3f out: hdwy u.p 2f out: 4th and kpt on same pce ins fnl f* **9/1**

5644 **5** 1¼ **Dessertoflife (IRE)**[28] 6115 3-8-12 **95** JoeFanning 9 95
(Mark Johnston) *chsd ldrs: rdn to chse ldr 3f out tl over 2f out: outpcd over 1f out: wknd ins fnl f* **14/1**

5241 **6** 1½ **Pure Fantasy**[22] 6301 3-7-9 **85** DavidEgan(7) 8 82
(Roger Charlton) *t.k.h: hld up in tch in last trio: effrt 3f out: no imp u.p over 1f out: wknd ins fnl f* **7/1**

1205 **7** 1¾ **Shafafya**[28] 6115 3-8-1 **84** JimmyQuinn 11 77
(Ed Dunlop) *stdd s: t.k.h: hld up in tch in last trio: effrt 3f out: no imp u.p wl over 1f out: wknd ins fnl f* **16/1**

6344 **8** 5 **Zaakhir (IRE)**[31] 6019 3-7-11 **83** oh5 JosephineGordon(3) 4 66
(Charles Hills) *t.k.h: chsd ldr tl 3f out: lost pl u.p over 2f out: wknd over 1f out* **16/1**

5120 **9** 6 **Sagaciously (IRE)**[29] 6107 4-9-10 **102** RyanMoore 12 73
(Ed Dunlop) *stdd s: hld up in tch in last trio: effrt ent fnl 2f: no prog and sn btn: bhd and eased ins fnl f* **6/1**[3]

1215 **10** nk **Sightline**[70] 4668 3-8-5 **88** JohnFahy 1 58
(Ralph Beckett) *hld up in tch: pushed along and hdwy 4f out: rdn and lost pl qckly over 2f out: bhd over 1f out* **12/1**

2m 5.44s (-0.36) **Going Correction** +0.15s/f (Good)
WFA 3 from 4yo+ 5lb **10** Ran SP% **113.9**
Speed ratings (Par 96): **107,106,104,104,103 101,100,96,91,91**
CSF £35.17 CT £133.67 TOTE £6.00: £2.20, £1.60, £1.40; EX 34.20 Trifecta £225.60.
Owner Sheikh Mohammed Obaid Al Maktoum **Bred** Darley **Trained** Newmarket, Suffolk

FOCUS
Another good fillies' handicap.

6949 KINGDOM OF BAHRAIN SUN CHARIOT STKS (BRITISH CHAMPIONS SERIES) (GROUP 1) (F&M) 1m
4:00 (4:00) (Class 1) 3-Y-O+

£141,775 (£53,750; £26,900; £13,400; £6,725; £3,375) **Stalls** Low

Form RPR

3101 **1** **Alice Springs (IRE)**[21] 6352 3-9-0 118 RyanMoore 7 118
(A P O'Brien, Ire) *trckd ldng trio: angled out and clsd over 2f out: led wl over 1f out: sn rdn: styd on strly ins fnl f: rdn out* **13/8**[1]

1334 **2** ¾ **Always Smile (IRE)**[64] 4826 4-9-3 110 AndreaAtzeni 9 116
(Saeed bin Suroor) *trckd ldr: clsd and upsides travelling strly over 2f out: rdn and ev ch wl over 1f out: edgd rt 1f out: kpt on u.p but nvr quite matching pce of wnr ins fnl f* **7/1**

-253 **3** 1 **Ervedya (FR)**[48] 5449 4-9-3 113 [1] Christophe-PatriceLemaire 1 114
(J-C Rouget, France) *trckd ldng pair: effrt over 1f out: switching lft and kpt on ins fnl f* **4/1**[3]

-451 **4** 1¾ **Siyoushake (IRE)**[34] 5948 4-9-3 107 AurelienLemaitre 2 110
(F Head, France) *stdd after s: hld up in tch in rr: effrt 2f out: hdwy ent fnl f: styd on u.p fnl 100yds: nvr threatened ldrs* **20/1**

0433 **5** ¾ **Irish Rookie (IRE)**[10] 6693 4-9-3 107 ColmO'Donoghue 6 108
(Martyn Meade) *hld up in tch in midfield: n.m.r ent fnl 2f: effrt u.p over 1f out: styd on same pce and no imp fnl f* **16/1**

-203 **6** ½ **Arabian Queen (IRE)**[17] 6488 4-9-3 114 SilvestreDeSousa 4 107
(David Elsworth) *led: jnd and rdn over 2f out: hdd and unable qck wl over 1f out: hld and styd on same pce ins fnl f* **10/1**

132 **7** 3½ **Volta (FR)**[62] 4926 3-9-0 113 [1] Pierre-CharlesBoudot 3 99
(F-H Graffard, France) *dwlt: hld up in tch in midfield: effrt ent fnl 2f: no imp and outpcd over 1f out: wknd ins fnl f* **7/2**[2]

4024 **8** 2¼ **Epsom Icon**[10] 6666 3-9-0 105 JFEgan 8 94
(Mick Channon) *stdd after s: hld up in tch: effrt 2f out: sn drvn and no imp: wknd ins fnl f* **100/1**

1m 37.46s (-1.14) **Going Correction** +0.15s/f (Good)
WFA 3 from 4yo+ 3lb **8** Ran SP% **113.5**
Speed ratings (Par 117): **111,110,109,107,106 106,102,100**
CSF £13.70 CT £38.86 TOTE £1.90: £1.10, £2.00, £1.50; EX 10.10 Trifecta £45.60.
Owner Mrs John Magnier & Michael Tabor & Derrick Smith **Bred** Lynch - Bages & Longfield Stud **Trained** Cashel, Co Tipperary

FOCUS
This was a solid if unspectacular running of the Sun Chariot - high-class South African mare Smart Call would have been an intriguing runner, but she was taken out due to lameness - and few got involved off what looked just an ordinary pace.

6950 £150,000 TATTERSALLS OCTOBER AUCTION STKS 6f
4:35 (4:37) (Class 2) 2-Y-O

£81,165 (£33,210; £14,775; £7,365; £3,690; £1,470) **Stalls** Low

Form RPR

612 **1** **Accidental Agent**[36] 5829 2-8-9 79 CharlesBishop 30 87
(Eve Johnson Houghton) *racd nr side: stdd s: hld up in rr: swtchd lft and gd hdwy over 1f out: led ins fnl f: r.o strly: rdn out: 1st of 15 in gp* **14/1**

5010 **2** 1 **Simmie (IRE)**[30] 6063 2-8-2 86 JimmyQuinn 19 77
(Sylvester Kirk) *racd nr side: chsd ldrs: rdn to ld overall 2f out: drvn over 1f out: hdd and styd on same pce ins fnl f: 2nd of 11 in gp* **14/1**

2 **3** 1 **Red Royalist**[29] 6071 2-8-9 0 MartinDwyer 25 81+
(Marcus Tregoning) *racd nr side: stdd s: hld up in rr: swtchd rt and effrt 2f out: hdwy u.p 1f out: styd on strly ins fnl f: nt rch ldrs: 3rd of 15 in gp* **20/1**

1030 **4** nk **Seduce Me**[23] 6257 2-8-4 80 [1] JoeyHaynes 2 75
(K R Burke) *racd far side: in tch in midfield: hdwy u.p over 1f out: chsd ldrs overall 1f out: styd on same pce ins fnl f: 1st of 11 in gp* **10/1**

310 **5** nk **Dakota Gold**[15] 6536 2-8-11 77 ConnorBeasley 4 81
(Michael Dods) *racd far side: trckd gp ldrs and in tch overall: effrt u.p to ld gp and chse overall ldrs over 1f out: styd on same pce ins fnl f: 2nd of 11 in gp* **50/1**

12 **6** 1¼ **Society Red**[31] 6025 2-8-7 79 PaulHanagan 1 73
(Richard Fahey) *racd far side: hld up in tch in midfield overall: effrt over 1f out: swtchd lft ins fnl f: kpt on wout threatening ldrs: 3rd of 11 in gp* **12/1**

345 **7** nk **Keyser Soze (IRE)**[23] 6260 2-8-13 85 AndreaAtzeni 10 78
(Richard Spencer) *racd far side: dwlt: hld up in rr: effrt over 2f out: edgd lft u.p over 1f out: styd on same pce ins fnl f: 4th of 11 in gp* **8/1**[3]

0321 **8** ¾ **Sea Shack**[10] 6664 2-9-1 77 RyanMoore 5 77
(William Knight) *racd far side: chsd gp ldrs and in tch overall: effrt 2f out: styd on same pce ins fnl f: 5th of 11 in gp* **7/1**[2]

53 **9** shd **Nibras Again**[16] 6524 2-8-11 0 SilvestreDeSousa 14 73
(Ismail Mohammed) *racd nr side: stdd s: t.k.h: hld up in midfield overall: effrt and hdwy over 1f out: no imp ins fnl f: wknd towards fin: 4th of 15 in gp* **10/1**

0232 **10** nk **Boundsy (IRE)**[21] 6322 2-8-7 77 JohnFahy 13 68
(Richard Fahey) *racd nr side: in tch in midfield overall: effrt 2f out: unable qck over 1f out: styd on same pce ins fnl f: 5th of 15 in gp* **33/1**

43 **11** hd **Vote**[46] 5511 2-8-2 0 DannyBrock 9 62
(James Eustace) *racd far side: led gp and chsd ldrs overall: rdn 2f out: unable qck over 1f out: wknd ins fnl f: 6th of 11 in gp* **50/1**

3440 **12** ½ **Climax**[19] 6419 2-8-4 62 JoeFanning 21 63
(Mark Johnston) *racd nr side: chsd overall ldr tl 2f out: sn u.p and unable qck: wknd ins fnl f: 6th of 15 in gp* **50/1**

14 **13** 1½ **Bamber Bridge (IRE)**[23] 6260 2-9-1 0 PaulMulrennan 16 69
(Michael Dods) *racd nr side: dwlt: sn in tch in midfield: effrt and n.m.r ent fnl 2f: no imp over 1f out: kpt on same pce ins fnl f: 7th of 15 in gp* **9/4**[1]

2201 **14** nk **Bayston Hill**[19] 6404 2-8-7 70 DanielMuscutt 27 60
(Mark Usher) *racd nr side: hld up in midfield overall: effrt jst over 2f out: no imp over 1f out: wknd ins fnl f: 8th of 15 in gp* **66/1**

2062 **14** dht **Masonic (IRE)**[2] 6898 2-8-7 67 JosephineGordon 6 60
(Robyn Brisland) *racd far side: chsd ldrs and in tch overall: effrt ent fnl 2f: no imp over 1f out: wknd ins fnl f: 7th of 11 in gp* **50/1**

56 **16** hd **Shannon**[16] 6524 2-8-2 0 JaneElliott 20 54
(Robyn Brisland) *racd nr side: in tch in midfield overall: rdn and unable qck over 1f out: wknd ins fnl f: 9th of 15 in gp* **100/1**

0151 **17** 1½ **Sayesse**[21] 6322 2-8-11 87 JFEgan 17 59
(Mick Channon) *racd nr side: hld up in tch in midfield overall: effrt 2f out: unable qck and lost pl over 1f out: wknd ins fnl f: 10th of 15 in gp* **16/1**

3062 **18** ¾ **Coping Stone**[19] 6419 2-8-6 66 AaronJones 26 51
(David Brown) *racd nr side: broke wl but sn midfield: rdn 2f out: no rspnse and lost pl over 1f out: wknd ins fnl f: 11th of 15 in gp* **100/1**

02 **19** ½ **Gaval**[18] 6447 2-8-7 0 LiamJones 23 51
(David Barron) *racd nr side: in tch in midfield overall: nt clr run 2f out: rdn and sme hdwy over 1f out: kpt on same pce ins fnl f: 12th of 15 in gp* **50/1**

1050 **20** 1½ **Stringybark Creek**[109] 3247 2-8-9 80 FMBerry 18 48
(Mick Channon) *racd nr side: in tch in midfield overall: rdn over 2f out: lost pl and btn over 1f out: wknd ins fnl f: 13th of 15 in gp* **50/1**

0222 **21** nk **Lucky Mistake (IRE)**[18] 6448 2-8-7 75 PatrickMathers 11 45
(Richard Fahey) *racd far side: in tch in midfield: rdn over 2f out: outpcd 2f out: wknd ins fnl f* **33/1**

0400 **22** nk **Miss Island Ruler**[14] 6588 2-8-3 46 ow1 PaddyPilley 22 40
(Shaun Harris) *racd nr side: wl in tch in midfield overall: rdn jst over 2f out: lost pl over 1f out: sn wknd: 14th of 15 in gp* **200/1**

1006 **23** hd **Latest Quest (IRE)**[30] 6060 2-8-9 66 FergusSweeney 24 45
(Sylvester Kirk) *racd nr side: sn led overall and clr 1/2-way: rdn and hdd 2f out: sn btn: wknd fnl f: 15th of 15 in gp* **100/1**

0265 **24** 2½ **Chiconomic (IRE)**[2] 6895 2-8-2 56 (b) NoelGarbutt 12 30
(Rae Guest) *taken down early: racd far side: swtchd rt after s: t.k.h and hld up in midfield overall: rdn over 2f out: sn lost pl: bhd over 1f out: 9th of 11 in gp* **100/1**

0060 **25** 1 **Masquerade Bling (IRE)**[5] 6829 2-8-2 63 SimonPearce 8 27
(Simon Hodgson) *racd far side: hld up in tch in midfield overall: rdn over 2f out: sn struggling: bhd fnl f: 10th of 11 in gp* **100/1**

004 **26** 5 **Tael O' Gold**[37] 5809 2-8-2 63 DavidEgan 15 11
(Iain Jardine) *racd far side: chsd ldrs tl over 2f out: sn lost pl and unbalanced over 1f out: bhd fnl f: 11th of 11 in gp* **100/1**

1m 12.41s (0.21) **Going Correction** +0.15s/f (Good) **26** Ran SP% **129.8**
Speed ratings (Par 101): **104,102,101,100,100 98,98,97,97,96 96,96,94,93,93 93,91,90,89,87 87,86,86,83,81 75**
CSF £176.77 TOTE £16.30: £4.80, £5.40, £5.90; EX 232.90 Trifecta £3479.50 Part Won..
Owner Mrs R F Johnson Houghton **Bred** Mrs R F Johnson Houghton **Trained** Blewbury, Oxon

FOCUS
Typically muddling big-field sales race form. The almost side-on camera angle, just before halfway, showed the nearside bunch with a significant advantage over the far-side group, and that's where the first three finishers raced.

6951 EBF FILLIES' SERIES #THISFILLYCAN H'CAP 1m 4f
5:10 (5:13) (Class 2) 3-Y-O+
£31,125 (£9,320; £4,660; £2,330; £1,165; £585) **Stalls** Centre

Form RPR
1654 **1** **Elysian Fields (GR)**[10] 6667 5-8-12 **90** KieranShoemark(3) 3 101
(Amanda Perrett) *hld up in tch in midfield: clsd to trck ldrs 4f out: led 2f out and sn rdn clr: edgd lft and pressed ins fnl f: kpt on: rdn out* **8/1**
00-0 **2** ¾ **Groovejet**[273] 19 5-9-4 **93** FMBerry 1 102
(Richard Spencer) *hld up in rr: smooth hdwy over 2f out: chsd wnr over 1f out: rdn 1f out: pressing wnr and carried lft ins fnl f: kpt on but a hld* **50/1**
063 **3** 7 **Lustrous**[21] 6332 5-9-10 **99** SilvestreDeSousa 10 97
(David O'Meara) *hld up in tch: effrt 3f out: chsd ldrs and drvn over 1f out: 3rd and no imp 1f out: wknd ins fnl f* **4/1**[3]
1452 **4** 2½ **St Mary'S**[20] 6378 3-8-1 **83** oh4 ow1 DannyBrock 2 77
(Andrew Balding) *t.k.h: chsd ldr tl 6f out: styd prom: rdn and ev ch briefly jst over 2f out: 4th and btn 1f out: wknd fnl f* **16/1**
-035 **5** 4½ **Turning The Table (IRE)**[21] 6332 3-7-7 **82** DavidEgan(7) 5 68
(David Simcock) *stdd s: t.k.h: hld up in last pair: hdwy to chse ldr 6f out: led 5f out: hdd and hung lft 2f out: btn over 1f out: wknd fnl f* **10/3**[2]
1102 **6** ¾ **Eager Beaver**[14] 6584 4-8-6 **81** MartinDwyer 8 66
(William Muir) *led tl 5f out: chsd ldr: rdn 3f out: unable qck and lost pl 2f out: wknd fnl f* **8/1**
3210 **7** 10 **Colonial Classic (FR)**[17] 6497 3-8-7 **89** JimmyQuinn 6 58
(John Gosden) *t.k.h: hld up in tch in midfield: u.p and no rspnse over 2f out: wknd 2f out* **3/1**[1]
4133 **8** 2 **The Begum**[20] 6378 3-7-12 **83** oh4 ow1 JosephineGordon(3) 7 49
(Ralph Beckett) *t.k.h: hld up in tch: effrt 3f out: hung lft and btn jst over 2f out: sn wknd* **10/1**
3-12 **9** ½ **Luna Mare (IRE)**[16] 6504 3-8-0 **82** oh4 PatrickMathers 9 47
(Richard Fahey) *in tch in midfield: rdn 1/2-way: lost pl and bhd 3f out: sn wknd* **10/1**

2m 31.89s (-0.11) **Going Correction** +0.175s/f (Good)
WFA 3 from 4yo+ 7lb **9** Ran SP% **116.3**
Speed ratings (Par 96): **107,106,101,100,97 96,90,88,88**
CSF £306.49 CT £1828.50 TOTE £9.80: £2.60, £9.70, £1.70; EX 286.50 Trifecta £2895.40.
Owner Mrs Alexandra J Chandris **Bred** Queensway S A **Trained** Pulborough, W Sussex

FOCUS
This was run over an additional 3yds. An ordinary race of its type.
T/Plt: £75.90 to a £1 stake. Pool: £129,010.64 - 1,239.93 winning tickets T/Qpdt: £34.40 to a £1 stake. Pool: £8,075.37 - 173.45 winning tickets **Steve Payne**

6678 REDCAR (L-H)
Saturday, October 1

OFFICIAL GOING: Good to firm (8.9)
Wind: moderate 1/2 against Weather: overcast

6952 RACINGUK.COM/DAYPASS EBF STALLIONS MAIDEN STKS 7f
2:10 (2:12) (Class 5) 2-Y-O **£3,234** (£962; £481; £240) **Stalls** Centre

Form RPR
52 **1** **City Of Joy**[14] 6570 2-9-5 0 JimCrowley 10 81+
(Sir Michael Stoute) *n.m.r sn after s: hld up in mid-div: hdwy over 2f out: drvn to chal appr fnl f: styd on to ld clsng stages* **4/7**[1]
2 ½ **Archer's Arrow (USA)** 2-9-5 0 JamesDoyle 11 79
(Saeed bin Suroor) *w ldrs: led over 2f out: hdd and no ex clsng stages* **6/1**[3]
4 **3** 1¼ **Sersar**[17] 6486 2-9-0 0 GeorgeBuckell(5) 8 76+
(Ismail Mohammed) *n.m.r and carried rt s: hld up in last: swtchd rt over 4f out: hdwy to chse ldrs over 1f out: edgd lft: kpt on same pce* **4/1**[2]
4 1 **Baashiq (IRE)** 2-9-5 0 DaneO'Neill 1 73
(Roger Varian) *hld up in rr: swtchd rt after 1f: hdwy over 2f out: chsng ldrs over 1f out: edgd lft and kpt on same pce* **7/1**
5 ¾ **Powerful Love (IRE)** 2-9-5 0 JasonHart 2 71
(Mark Johnston) *mid-div: hdwy 3f out: sn outpcd: kpt on appr fnl f* **25/1**
6 1 **True Romance (IRE)** 2-9-5 0 TomEaves 4 69
(James Given) *chsd ldrs: drvn 3f out: one pce over 1f out* **100/1**
7 4½ **Pindaric**[84] 4168 2-9-5 0 CamHardie 9 56
(Alan Lockwood) *led: hdd over 2f out: lost pl over 1f out* **66/1**
8 ½ **Sunset Sally (IRE)** 2-9-0 0 DougieCostello 7 50
(John Quinn) *wnt rt s: in rr: drvn and outpcd over 2f out: sme hdwy appr fnl f: nvr a factor* **66/1**
9 1¾ **Port Master** 2-9-5 0 PJMcDonald 3 50
(Ann Duffield) *trckd ldrs: t.k.h: drvn over 2f out: lost pl over 1f out* **66/1**
0 **10** shd **Turning Gold**[18] 6439 2-9-5 0 RyanPowell 6 50
(Sir Mark Prescott Bt) *wnt rt s: chsd ldrs: drvn 3f out: lost pl over 1f out* **200/1**
6 **11** 1¼ **Lively Lily**[10] 6679 2-8-9 0 RowanScott(5) 12 42
(Ann Duffield) *sn trcking ldrs: wknd over 1f out* **66/1**

1m 26.71s (2.21) **Going Correction** -0.025s/f (Good) **11** Ran SP% **121.7**
Speed ratings (Par 95): **86,85,84,82,82 80,75,75,73,73 71**
CSF £4.96 TOTE £1.50: £1.10, £2.00, £1.10; EX 5.80 Trifecta £10.30.
Owner Saeed Suhail **Bred** Hascombe And Valiant Studs **Trained** Newmarket, Suffolk

FOCUS
A cool, sunny afternoon for the feature meeting of Redcar's season. This informative maiden was fought out by the first three in the market. The pace was ordinary and some of these may have been flattered. The winner has the scope to do significantly better.

6953 RACING UK IN GLORIOUS HD (S) STKS 1m 2f
2:40 (2:43) (Class 5) 3-5-Y-O **£3,234** (£962; £481; £240) **Stalls** Low

Form RPR
3140 **1** **Thello**[11] 6647 4-9-1 55 LewisEdmunds(7) 6 65
(Nigel Tinkler) *hld up in tch: stdy hdwy 3f out: swtchd rt and chsd ldng pair wl over 1f out: sn rdn and edgd lft: drvn to chal ins fnl f: styd on wl to ld last 50 yds* **15/2**
4110 **2** 1¼ **Miningrocks (FR)**[29] 6103 4-9-3 71 [1] PhilDennis(5) 8 63
(Declan Carroll) *led: pushed along 3f out: jnd and rdn 2f out: drvn over 1f out: hdd and no ex last 50 yds* **4/1**[2]
2660 **3** nk **Highfield Lass**[33] 5971 5-8-12 45 AndrewMullen 3 52
(Michael Dods) *trckd ldrs: hdwy 3f out: cl up 2f out: rdn to chal over 1f out: drvn and ev ch whn edgd lft ins fnl f: no ex last 50 yds* **10/1**
0506 **4** 6 **Nonchalant**[15] 4768 5-9-3 69 JimCrowley 4 45
(David O'Meara) *hld up: hdwy on outer 3f out: chsd ldrs 2f out and sn rdn: drvn over 1f out and sn one pce* **6/5**[1]
3156 **5** 8 **Ronya (IRE)**[37] 5800 5-9-3 59 JasonHart 2 29
(Tracy Waggott) *chsd ldr: hdwy over 3f out: rdn along over 2f out: sn drvn and wknd* **5/1**[3]
0005 **6** 4 **Kantara Castle (IRE)**[46] 5513 5-8-12 43 (tp) CliffordLee(5) 7 21
(John Mackie) *rr: hdwy over 4f out: pushed along over 3f out: rdn wl over 2f out and nvr a factor* **28/1**
-000 **7** nk **Great Colaci**[10] 6683 3-8-12 39 TomEaves 5 20
(Keith Reveley) *chsd ldng pair: rdn along over 3f out: sn wknd* **50/1**
0000 **8** 5 **Sunnyhills Belford**[17] 6478 3-8-2 40 ow2 DanielleMooney(7) 1 7
(Noel Wilson) *chsd ldrs: rdn along 4f out: sn wknd* **150/1**
4602 **9** 1¾ **Bertha Burnett (IRE)**[40] 5729 5-8-12 49 JamesSullivan 9 2
(Brian Rothwell) *rr and sn rdn along: a outpcd and bhd* **20/1**

2m 4.03s (-3.07) **Going Correction** -0.25s/f (Firm)
WFA 3 from 4yo+ 5lb **9** Ran SP% **113.8**
Speed ratings (Par 103): **102,101,100,95,89 86,86,82,80**
CSF £35.88 TOTE £8.90: £1.90, £1.50, £3.00; EX 36.90 Trifecta £248.00.The winner was brought in by Mr James Gaffney for £8,000
Owner Y T Szeto **Bred** Mickley Stud & Mr W T Whittle **Trained** Langton, N Yorks

FOCUS
This seller lacked depth and, with the 45-rated Highfield Lass filling a close-up third, it's unlikely this took too much winning.

6954 TOTEPOOL TWO-YEAR-OLD TROPHY STKS (LISTED RACE) 6f
3:15 (3:16) (Class 1) 2-Y-O
£110,414 (£41,860; £15,692; £15,692; £5,237; £2,628) **Stalls** Centre

Form RPR
2202 **1** **Wick Powell**[20] 6388 2-8-3 85 AndrewMullen 8 84
(David Barron) *mde all: rdn over 1f out: kpt on wl clsng stages* **12/1**
1436 **2** nk **Whirl Me Round**[15] 6538 2-8-6 83 JoeDoyle 1 86
(Kevin Ryan) *hld up in rr: hdwy over 2f out: chsng ldrs over 1f out: hung lerft and kpt on to take 2nd nr fin* **20/1**
115 **3** hd **The Wagon Wheel (IRE)**[32] 5998 2-8-11 82 JackGarritty 5 90
(Richard Fahey) *w ldrs: drvn over 1f out: no ex clsng stages* **13/2**[3]
622 **3** dht **Mazyoun**[23] 6260 2-8-12 92 (b[1]) JimCrowley 18 91
(Hugo Palmer) *hld up: hdwy and n.m.r over 1f out: styd on fnl f: keeping on at fin* **7/2**[1]
4400 **5** 1½ **Lady In Question (IRE)**[7] 6787 2-8-4 76 CamHardie 3 79
(Richard Fahey) *s.i.s: in rr: hdwy over 2f out: hmpd 1f out: kpt on same pce* **33/1**
5455 **6** 1¾ **Lawless Louis**[16] 6507 2-8-12 76 PhillipMakin 4 81
(David O'Meara) *chsd ldrs: edgd rt 1f out: kpt on one pce* **80/1**
5632 **7** nk **Dandy Place (IRE)**[14] 6563 2-8-12 71 JamesSullivan 6 80?
(Tim Easterby) *towards rr: hdwy over 2f out: kpt on one pce fnl f* **100/1**
3105 **8** ¾ **Rainbow Mist (IRE)**[22] 6282 2-8-9 100 PJMcDonald 7 75
(Ann Duffield) *trckd ldrs: t.k.h: effrt over 1f out: edgd rt: one pce* **7/1**
3511 **9** ½ **Orewa (IRE)**[20] 6388 2-9-0 90 ChrisHayes 11 78
(Brian Ellison) *chsd ldrs: drvn 2f out: one pce whn hung rt 1f out* **12/1**
2504 **10** nk **Camargue**[32] 5998 2-8-11 82 JasonHart 2 77
(Mark Johnston) *chsd ldrs: one pce whn nt clr run 1f out* **50/1**
3621 **11** nse **Appointed**[18] 6433 2-8-1 85 DuranFentiman 16 64
(Tim Easterby) *chsd ldrs: one pce fnl 2f* **16/1**
2156 **12** ½ **Medici Banchiere**[42] 5654 2-9-0 99 DougieCostello 13 75
(K R Burke) *chsd ldrs: one pce over 1f out* **11/2**[2]
2501 **13** 1¼ **Abiento (IRE)**[21] 6319 2-8-12 80 GeorgeChaloner 12 72
(Richard Fahey) *in rr: sme hdwy over 2f out: no imp whn hmpd 1f out* **28/1**
4026 **14** ½ **Ventura Secret (IRE)**[21] 6322 2-8-9 76 DavidAllan 14 65
(Tim Easterby) *rr-div: sme hdwy and edgd rt over 1f out: nvr a factor* **66/1**
2150 **15** 1½ **Repton (IRE)**[42] 5646 2-8-12 103 JamesDoyle 15 63
(Richard Hannon) *rr-div: sn drvn along: nvr a factor* **11/2**[2]
4440 **16** ½ **Jamacho**[14] 6554 2-8-9 69 KevinStott 9 59
(Brian Ellison) *mid-div: effrt over 2f out: n.m.r and lost pl 1f out* **150/1**
1161 **17** 6 **Tawny Port**[15] 6536 2-8-12 85 TomEaves 19 42
(James Given) *mid-div: hdwy over 2f out: lost pl over 1f out* **20/1**
320 **18** 1¾ **Dawoodi**[16] 6524 2-9-2 77 JackMitchell 17 41+
(Hugo Palmer) *chsd ldrs: wknd 2f out: bhd whn eased clsng stages* **66/1**
5455 **19** 20 **Outfox**[12] 6614 2-8-9 65 SamJames 23 +
(Bryan Smart) *detached in rr: hmpd over 1f out: eased* **100/1**
1250 **U** **Lexington Sky (IRE)**[49] 5407 2-8-11 77 KieranO'Neill 22
(Richard Hannon) *rr-div: effrt over 2f out: no imp whn n.m.r: wnt lft, stmbld and uns rdr over 1f out* **100/1**

1m 11.16s (-0.64) **Going Correction** -0.025s/f (Good) **20** Ran SP% **125.8**
Speed ratings (Par 103): **103,102,102,102,100 98,97,96,96,95 95,95,93,92,90 90,82,79,53,**
PLACES: M £0.90, WW £1.60. TRIFECTA: WP-WMR-M £833.90, WP-WMR-WW £1,034.00. CSF £243.28 TOTE £14.10: £4.10, £6.60; EX 276.20 TRIFECTA Part Won..
Owner Miss N J Barron **Bred** Usk Valley Stud, Mr Martin Graham **Trained** Maunby, N Yorks
■ Stewards' Enquiry : David Allan seven-day ban: careless riding (15- 21 Oct)

FOCUS
A substandard renewal of this valuable 2yo contest with only two of the field rated in excess of 100. It was a dramatic race and produced an exciting finish, but the form can't really be rated any higher.

6955 TOTESCOOP6 EBF STALLIONS GUISBOROUGH STKS (LISTED RACE) 7f
3:50 (3:52) (Class 1) 3-Y-O+
£22,684 (£8,600; £4,304; £2,144; £1,076; £540) **Stalls** Centre

Form RPR
223- **1** **Latharnach (USA)**[428] 4816 4-9-0 113 JamesDoyle 5 116+
(Charlie Appleby) *trckd ldng pair: hdwy to ld wl over 1f out: jnd and drvn ins fnl f: kpt on wl towards fin* **5/2**[1]
611 **2** ½ **Certificate**[35] 5871 5-9-0 108 JackMitchell 6 114
(Roger Varian) *trckd ldrs: hdwy on inner 2f out: chsd wnr over 1f out: rdn to chal ins fnl f: drvn and ev ch tl no ex towards fin* **3/1**[2]
0254 **3** 1½ **So Beloved**[15] 6547 6-9-3 111 PhillipMakin 3 113
(David O'Meara) *dwlt: t.k.h and hld up in rr: hdwy on outer 2f out: rdn to chal and ev ch ent fnl f: sn drvn and edgd bdly lft: kpt on same pce* **6/1**
2222 **4** 3¼ **Sovereign Debt (IRE)**[76] 4433 7-9-0 113 ChrisHayes 7 101
(David Nicholls) *cl up effrt 2f out and ev ch: rdn wl over 1f out: drvn and kpt on same pce fnl f* **4/1**[3]

1623 **5** ½ **Convey**[28] 6117 4-9-3 112 (p) JimCrowley 2 103
(Sir Michael Stoute) *led: pushed along over 2f out: rdn and hdd wl over 1f out: sn drvn and grad wknd* **4/1**[3]

4060 **6** ½ **Gordon Lord Byron (IRE)**[6] 6816 8-9-7 112 DougieCostello 8 105
(T Hogan, Ire) *trckd ldrs: hdwy 3f out and sn cl up: rdn along wl over 1f out: wknd appr fnl f* **22/1**

1m 23.23s (-1.27) **Going Correction** -0.025s/f (Good) **6** Ran SP% **112.2**
Speed ratings (Par 111): **106,105,103,100,99 98**
CSF £10.26 TOTE £3.40: £1.90, £2.00; EX 11.20 Trifecta £63.20.
Owner Godolphin **Bred** Darley **Trained** Newmarket, Suffolk

FOCUS
A strong race for the grade and much to like about the performance of Latharnach, who made light of his 428-day absence. He's rated to form. The first three came feom the back.

6956 PINNACLE CUP STRAIGHT-MILE SERIES FINAL H'CAP 1m
4:25 (4:26) (Class 2) 3-Y-O+
£12,450 (£3,728; £1,864; £932; £466; £234) **Stalls** Centre

Form RPR

3432 **1** **Father Bertie**[16] 6500 4-9-10 **87** (tp) DavidAllan 2 97
(Tim Easterby) *racd alone towards far side: edgd lft and racd far side 4f out: overall ldr over 2f out: drvn out* **4/1**[1]

1223 **2** 1 **Dawn Mirage**[8] 6753 4-9-5 **87** AdamMcNamara(5) 15 95
(Richard Fahey) *swtchd lft sn after s: sn trcking ldrs: swtchd rt over 1f out: hung lft and styd on to take 2nd clsng stages* **9/2**[2]

1220 **3** 1½ **Planetaria (IRE)**[21] 6344 3-9-0 **80** JasonHart 5 84
(Garry Moss) *overall ldr centre: drvn and hdd over 2f out: kpt on same pce fnl f* **16/1**

0231 **4** 1 **Pumaflor (IRE)**[8] 6736 4-9-0 **82** (p) PhilDennis(5) 9 84
(Richard Whitaker) *chsd ldrs: drvn over 2f out: kpt on same pce over 1f out* **8/1**

1164 **5** ¾ **Shamaheart (IRE)**[25] 6217 6-9-7 **84** (p) KevinStott 10 84
(Geoffrey Harker) *hld up in mid-div: effrt over 2f out: edgd lft and kpt on same pce fnl f* **18/1**

0142 **6** 1¾ **Normandy Knight**[16] 6516 4-8-12 **75** JackGarritty 6 71
(Richard Fahey) *chsd ldrs: hung lft and fdd fnl 150yds* **15/2**

0240 **7** ½ **Abushamah (IRE)**[25] 6217 5-9-6 **83** JamesSullivan 1 78
(Ruth Carr) *hld up towards rr: hdwy and edgd lft over 2f out: sn chsng ldrs: wknd fnl f* **20/1**

1313 **8** ½ **Fuwairt (IRE)**[20] 6372 4-9-3 **87** CameronNoble(7) 8 81
(Roger Fell) *gave problems in stalls: hld up towards rr: hdwy 3f out: upsides over 1f out: edgd lft and wknd fnl 150yds* **12/1**

4001 **9** ½ **Lawyer (IRE)**[16] 6516 5-9-4 **81** SamJames 7 74
(David Barron) *mid-div: pushed along over 3f out: wknd over 1f out* **20/1**

6504 **10** 4½ **Beardwood**[8] 6753 4-9-4 **81** (p) PJMcDonald 11 63
(Mark Johnston) *sn drvn along in rr: nvr on terms* **7/1**[3]

5050 **11** 1¼ **Altharoos (IRE)**[25] 6217 6-9-3 **80** DougieCostello 13 60
(Sally Hall) *hld up towards rr: effrt over 2f out: lost pl over 1f out* **20/1**

2060 **12** *hd* **Quick N Quirky (IRE)**[6] 6811 3-9-1 **81** (bt) AndrewMullen 4 60
(Tim Easterby) *trckd ldrs: effrt over 2f out: wknd over 1f out* **25/1**

0006 **13** 6 **Ingleby Angel (IRE)**[25] 6217 7-9-0 **77** TomEaves 14 42
(Colin Teague) *mid-div: drvn over 3f out: bhd fnl 2f: eased clsng stages* **33/1**

2333 **14** 12 **Arithmetic (IRE)**[50] 5362 3-8-3 **69** KieranO'Neill 12 7
(Charles Hills) *mid-div: drvn over 3f out: lost pl 2f out: bhd whn eased clsng stages* **16/1**

2006 **15** 6 **Holy Grail (IRE)**[7] 6778 3-8-5 **78** SophieKilloran(7) 16 2
(Simon West) *bhd: drvn over 3f out: eased clsng stages* **25/1**

1m 36.08s (-0.52) **Going Correction** -0.025s/f (Good)
WFA 3 from 4yo+ 3lb **15** Ran SP% **123.2**
Speed ratings (Par 109): **101,100,98,97,96 95,94,94,93,89 87,87,81,69,63**
CSF £19.14 CT £275.49 TOTE £6.10: £2.60, £1.50, £4.70; EX 16.70 Trifecta £485.90.
Owner John R Saville **Bred** Bambi Bloodstock **Trained** Great Habton, N Yorks

FOCUS
This was hugely competitive and represents rock solid handicap form.

6957 MARKET CROSS JEWELLERS H'CAP 1m 2f
5:00 (5:04) (Class 4) (0-85,84) 3-Y-O+ **£4,851** (£1,443; £721; £360) **Stalls** Low

Form RPR

0032 **1** **Hibou**[21] 6344 3-9-0 **79** (b) TomEaves 8 95+
(Iain Jardine) *hld up towards rr: smooth hdwy 4f out: trckd ldrs over 2f out: swtchd rt and effrt on bit to chal over 1f out: shkn up to ld jst ins fnl f: readily* **11/2**[3]

3211 **2** 2½ **Age Of Elegance (IRE)**[34] 5918 4-8-9 **76** (p) CameronNoble(7) 7 84
(Roger Fell) *trckd ldrs: hdwy 3f out: rdn to ld 2f out: jnd and drvn jst iover 1f out: hdd jst ins fnl f: kpt on* **20/1**

50 **3** 3¼ **Freewheel (IRE)**[8] 6753 6-9-4 **78** JasonHart 4 79
(Garry Moss) *trckd ldr: hdwy over 3f out: led wl over 2f out: hdd and rdn 2f out: sn drvn and kpt on same pce* **6/1**

2500 **4** ¾ **Dubai Dynamo**[21] 6320 11-9-10 **84** JamesSullivan 11 84
(Ruth Carr) *hld up and bhd: hdwy 3f out: rdn wl over 1f out: styd on fnl f: nrst fin* **33/1**

4034 **5** *hd* **Flyboy (IRE)**[3] 6877 3-9-2 **81** PhillipMakin 5 80
(David O'Meara) *in tch: hdwy over 4f out: trckd ldrs 3f out: rdn 2f out: sn drvn and kpt on same pce* **7/2**[1]

0105 **6** 3¾ **Theos Lolly (IRE)**[14] 6561 3-8-10 **80** AdamMcNamara(5) 10 72
(Richard Fahey) *in tch: pushed along over 3f out: rdn wl over 2f out: sn wknd* **7/2**[1]

24-0 **7** ½ **Royal Flag**[21] 6323 6-9-3 **77** [1] CamHardie 13 68
(Brian Ellison) *a towards rr* **33/1**

1451 **8** ¾ **Mysterial**[16] 6517 6-9-0 **79** PhilDennis(5) 6 68
(Declan Carroll) *led: rdn along over 3f out: hdd wl over 2f out: sn wknd* **11/1**

0000 **9** *nk* **Off Art**[16] 6517 6-9-6 **83** (p) RachelRichardson(3) 1 72
(Tim Easterby) *trckd ldng pair: pushed along over 3f out: rdn wl over 2f out: sn drvn and wknd* **4/1**[2]

16-0 **10** 8 **Daleelak (IRE)**[158] 1750 3-8-10 **75** PJMcDonald 12 48
(Mark Johnston) *in tch: rdn along on outer 4f out: sn drvn: outpcd and bhd* **50/1**

2m 3.05s (-4.05) **Going Correction** -0.25s/f (Firm)
WFA 3 from 4yo+ 5lb **10** Ran SP% **115.1**
Speed ratings (Par 105): **106,104,101,100,100 97,97,96,96,90**
CSF £109.06 CT £680.92 TOTE £7.30: £2.40, £3.30, £2.80; EX 82.00 Trifecta £955.50.
Owner Tapas Partnership **Bred** Darley **Trained** Carrutherstown, D'fries & G'way

FOCUS
A competitive handicap, in which the winner could not have been more impressive.

6958 WATCH RACING UK ANYWHERE H'CAP (DIV I) 5f
5:35 (5:36) (Class 5) (0-70,70) 3-Y-O+ **£3,234** (£962; £481; £240) **Stalls** Centre

Form RPR

6005 **1** **Bond Bombshell**[7] 6790 3-8-12 **68** PatrickVaughan(7) 4 78
(David O'Meara) *dwlt: effrt over 2f out: edgd lft: led over 1f out: drvn out* **12/1**

0312 **2** 1¼ **Twentysvnthlancers**[21] 6341 3-9-1 **69** CliffordLee(5) 8 74
(Paul Midgley) *hmpd s: in rr: hdwy over 1f out: styd on to take 2nd post* **7/2**[1]

0005 **3** *shd* **Flash City (ITY)**[17] 6476 8-9-7 **70** JamesSullivan 1 74
(Ruth Carr) *wnt rt s: hld up in rr: hdwy over 1f out: kpt on to take 2nd last 75yds: styd on same pce* **6/1**

0321 **4** 1¾ **Kiringa**[14] 6586 3-8-13 **62** KieranO'Neill 6 60
(Robert Cowell) *chsd ldrs: upsides over 1f out: kpt on one pce* **8/1**

0030 **5** *nse* **Space Artist (IRE)**[3] 6879 6-8-10 **66** (v) LewisEdmunds(7) 2 63
(Nigel Tinkler) *gave problems in stalls: hmpd s: in rr: hdwy over 1f out: kpt on one pce* **10/1**

0200 **6** ½ **Hit The Lights (IRE)**[10] 6680 6-8-9 **65** DanielleMooney(7) 3 60
(David Nicholls) *chsd ldrs: upsides over 1f out: one pce* **18/1**

3001 **7** *shd* **Horsforth**[2] 6910 4-8-13 **62** 6ex (b) JasonHart 9 57
(Richard Guest) *wnt lft s: mid-div: effrt over 2f out: one pce over 1f out* **14/1**

5102 **8** ½ **Run Rio Run (IRE)**[10] 6680 3-9-3 **66** (p) TomEaves 5 60
(Michael Dods) *led: hdd over 1f out: fdd fnl 150yds* **10/1**

5546 **9** ½ **Crombay (IRE)**[16] 6506 3-9-4 **67** DavidAllan 7 63+
(Tim Easterby) *chsd ldrs: wknd appr fnl f: hmpd and eased clsng stages* **5/1**[2]

4220 **10** ¾ **Malaysian Boleh**[9] 6699 6-8-11 **60** PJMcDonald 11 56+
(Brian Ellison) *in rr: sn pushed along: nvr on terms: hmpd clsng stages* **11/2**[3]

58.2s (-0.40) **Going Correction** -0.025s/f (Good) **10** Ran SP% **117.5**
Speed ratings (Par 103): **102,100,99,97,96 96,96,95,94,93**
CSF £54.26 CT £290.97 TOTE £12.90: £3.70, £1.70, £2.60; EX 73.30 Trifecta £355.30.
Owner Trendy Ladies **Bred** Mrs P M A Avison **Trained** Upper Helmsley, N Yorks

FOCUS
A fair sprint handicap, in which it paid to race towards the far rail.

6959 WATCH RACING UK ANYWHERE H'CAP (DIV II) 5f
6:05 (6:05) (Class 5) (0-70,70) 3-Y-O+ **£3,234** (£962; £481; £240) **Stalls** Centre

Form RPR

2222 **1** **Fruit Salad**[40] 5730 3-9-2 **70** [1] NathanEvans(5) 6 80
(James Bethell) *chsd ldrs: effrt over 2f out: led appr fnl f: drvn out* **11/2**

015 **2** 1¼ **Storm Trooper (IRE)**[10] 6680 5-9-4 **67** DavidAllan 7 72
(David Nicholls) *chsd ldrs: drvn over 2f out: kpt on same pce fnl 150yds: tk 2nd post* **13/8**[1]

0041 **3** *nse* **Bronze Beau**[10] 6680 9-9-0 **63** (tp) JamesSullivan 5 67
(Kristin Stubbs) *chsd ldr: kpt on same pce fnl 150yds: tk 3rd post* **8/1**

2423 **4** *nse* **Innocently (IRE)**[23] 6248 5-9-5 **68** (v) PhillipMakin 4 72
(David O'Meara) *swtchd lft after s: led: hdd appr fnl f: kpt on same pce* **5/1**[3]

6300 **5** 1¾ **Searanger (USA)**[16] 6506 3-9-3 **66** DougieCostello 3 65
(Rebecca Menzies) *wnt rt s: hdwy to chse ldrs over 3f out: wknd clsng stages* **33/1**

1316 **6** *shd* **Showbizzy**[20] 6363 3-9-0 **68** (v) AdamMcNamara(5) 10 66
(Richard Fahey) *wnt rt s: hld up: swtchd lft over 3f out: effrt and swtchd rt over 1f out: kpt on one pce* **9/2**[2]

6600 **7** 1¾ **Gowanless**[8] 6745 3-8-7 **56** oh1 (p) AndrewMullen 8 48
(Michael Dods) *chsd ldrs: one pce fnl 2f* **16/1**

0005 **8** 2¾ **Anieres Boy**[16] 6506 4-8-8 **57** CamHardie 9 38
(Michael Easterby) *sn chsng ldrs: drvn over 2f out: lost pl over 1f out* **14/1**

58.0s (-0.60) **Going Correction** -0.025s/f (Good) **8** Ran SP% **114.9**
Speed ratings (Par 103): **103,101,100,100,98 97,95,90**
CSF £14.96 CT £71.10 TOTE £5.20: £1.60, £1.40, £2.40; EX 18.50 Trifecta £113.30.
Owner Clarendon Thoroughbred Racing **Bred** Mrs James Bethell **Trained** Middleham Moor, N Yorks
■ Stewards' Enquiry : Nathan Evans two-day ban: use of whip (16-17 October)

FOCUS
As with the first division, this far side was the place to be.
T/Plt: £53.80 to a £1 stake. Pool: £72,669.99 - 985.59 winning units T/Qpdt: £25.70 to a £1 stake. Pool: £4,559.76 - 130.93 winning units **Walter Glynn & Joe Rowntree**

6850 WOLVERHAMPTON (A.W) (L-H)
Saturday, October 1

OFFICIAL GOING: Tapeta: standard
Wind: Light against Weather: Overcast

6960 LADBROKES MAIDEN FILLIES' STKS 7f 32y (Tp)
5:40 (5:41) (Class 5) 3-Y-O+ **£2,911** (£866; £432; £216) **Stalls** High

Form RPR

4 **1** **Perfectly Spirited**[28] 6135 3-9-0 0 NickyMackay 10 82+
(John Gosden) *prom: racd keenly: wnt 2nd 6f out tl led over 2f out: shkn up over 1f out: r.o: comf* **9/2**[3]

42- **2** 2¼ **Peaceful Journey**[290] 8253 3-8-11 0 [1] MarcMonaghan(3) 1 71
(Marco Botti) *trckd ldrs: plld hrd: rdn to chse wnr and hung lft ins fnl f: styd on same pce* **11/4**[2]

600 **3** 1 **Caledonia Duchess**[51] 5330 3-9-0 62 IrineuGoncalves 11 68
(Jo Hughes) *wnt prom after 1f: rdn over 2f out: hung lft over 1f out: styd on* **16/1**

45 **4** 1¾ **Paper Faces (USA)**[16] 6511 3-9-0 0 StevieDonohoe 6 63+
(Roger Varian) *broke wl: lost pl after 1f: shkn up over 2f out: r.o ins fnl f* **5/1**

530 **5** *nse* **Ducissa**[21] 6317 3-9-0 67 [1] TomQueally 2 63
(Daniel Kubler) *hld up in tch: rdn over 2f out: styd on same pce fr over 1f out* **25/1**

-035 **6** ½ **Welsh Rose**[45] 5551 3-8-9 74 [1] GeorgeWood(5) 4 62
(Ed de Giles) *plld hrd: led 6f out: hdd over 2f out: wknd ins fnl f* **2/1**[1]

03 **7** 1¼ **Andys Girl (IRE)**[25] 6218 3-9-0 0 BenCurtis 9 58+
(Brian Ellison) *s.i.s: hld up: rdn over 2f out: nvr on terms* **33/1**

8 3½ **Polish Empress** 3-9-0 0 TomMarquand 8 49
(William Muir) *s.i.s: hld up: pushed along 1/2-way: n.d* **33/1**

The Form Book, Raceform Ltd, Newbury, RG14 5SJ

0 **9** 2 1/4 **Race Time (USA)**[87] 3996 3-9-0 0 .... WilliamTwiston-Davies 7 43
(Seamus Durack) *hld up: a in rr* **40/1**

5 **10** 6 **Blynx**[18] 6459 3-9-0 0 .... SaleemGolam 3 27
(David Simcock) *led 1f: chsd ldrs: rdn 1/2-way: wknd over 2f out* **50/1**

1m 29.14s (0.34) **Going Correction** -0.05s/f (Stan) **10** Ran SP% **114.9**
Speed ratings (Par 100): **96,93,92,90,90 89,88,84,81,74**
CSF £16.23 TOTE £5.00: £1.50, £2.40, £3.30; EX 21.70 Trifecta £267.60.
Owner Helena Springfield Ltd **Bred** Meon Valley Stud **Trained** Newmarket, Suffolk

FOCUS
An ordinary fillies' maiden. They went a respectable gallop on standard Tapeta and the winner found significant improvement from her turf debut the previous month for a leading yard.

6961 LADBROKES (S) STKS 7f 32y (Tp)
6:10 (6:11) (Class 6) 2-Y-O **£2,264** (£673; £336; £168) **Stalls** High

Form RPR

450 **1** **Alice's Dream**[10] 6670 2-8-1 62 .... GeorgeWood(5) 2 59
(Marco Botti) *chsd ldrs: rdn to ld over 1f out: sn hung rt: jst hld on* **8/1**

0051 **2** nk **Control Centre (IRE)**[14] 6588 2-9-2 65 .... TomMarquand 7 68
(Richard Hannon) *mid-div: rdn over 2f out: hdwy over 1f out: chsd wnr and hung lft ins fnl f: r.o* **11/4**[1]

6553 **3** 3/4 **Gerrard's Return**[14] 6588 2-8-11 61 .... RichardKingscote 11 61
(Tom Dascombe) *hld up: hdwy over 1f out: rdn and edgd rt ins fnl f: r.o* **13/2**

4315 **4** 2 1/2 **Chevalier Du Lac (IRE)**[18] 6446 2-9-7 70 .... LiamKeniry 1 66
(Conor Dore) *led: led: rdn and hdd over 1f out: nt clr run sn after: no ex ins fnl f* **9/1**

004 **5** 1 1/4 **Pavela (IRE)**[11] 6648 2-8-6 59 .... RyanTate 10 47
(Mick Channon) *chsd ldrs: rdn over 2f out: no ex ins fnl f* **9/2**[3]

0565 **6** hd **Biologist (IRE)**[9] 6696 2-8-6 65 ....(b) BenCurtis 3 47
(William Haggas) *prom: rdn 1/2-way: styd on same pce fr over 1f out* **7/2**[2]

4065 **7** 2 **Battle Of Wits (IRE)**[21] 6313 2-8-11 47 .... JimCrowley 5 47
(J S Moore) *hld up: hdwy over 2f out: rdn over 1f out: wknd ins fnl f* **16/1**

0600 **8** 2 3/4 **Makemerichjohn (IRE)**[20] 6388 2-8-11 51 ....(t) TomQueally 6 40
(David Evans) *chsd ldr tl rdn 2f out: wknd ins fnl f* **40/1**

5366 **9** 1 1/4 **Cautious Choice (IRE)**[21] 6313 2-8-1 42 ....(p) HollieDoyle(5) 4 32
(J S Moore) *s.i.s: sn pushed along in rr: hdwy over 1f out: sn rdn: wknd fnl f* **50/1**

0 **10** 10 **The Boys So Sharp**[14] 6588 2-8-6 0 ....(vt) AnnaHesketh(5) 9 13
(Oliver Greenall) *hld up: rdn and wknd 1/2-way* **100/1**

1m 28.99s (0.19) **Going Correction** -0.05s/f (Stan) **10** Ran SP% **112.8**
Speed ratings (Par 93): **96,95,94,91,90 90,88,84,83,72**
CSF £29.12 TOTE £10.00: £3.00, £1.50, £2.50; EX 36.80 Trifecta £206.70.Control Centre was brought in by Mrs Marjorie Fife for £6,000
Owner HH Shaikh Nader Mohamed Al Khalifa **Bred** Giles Wates **Trained** Newmarket, Suffolk

FOCUS
A modest juvenile seller. The winning filly got the run of the race from a good draw and her slight progression proved good enough. Par form for the grade.

6962 LADBROKES H'CAP 5f 216y (Tp)
6:40 (6:41) (Class 3) (0-95,95) 3-Y-O+ **£7,246** (£2,168; £1,084; £542; £270) **Stalls** Low

Form RPR

0000 **1** **Dougan**[12] 6627 4-9-2 90 .... JimCrowley 8 103
(David Evans) *mid-div: hdwy over 2f out: shkn up up to ld and edgd lft ins fnl f: r.o wl* **5/1**[2]

416 **2** 2 **Clear Water (IRE)**[85] 4104 3-8-12 90 .... EdwardGreatrex(3) 1 97
(Saeed bin Suroor) *mid-div: hdwy and nt clr run wl over 1f out: sn rdn: styd on same pce wl ins fnl f* **3/1**[1]

6030 **3** 1 1/4 **Seeking Magic**[12] 6633 8-9-4 92 ....(t) RyanTate 7 95
(Clive Cox) *led 5f out: rdn over 1f out: edgd rt and hdd ins fnl f: styd on same pce* **13/2**[3]

0300 **4** shd **Aguerooo (IRE)**[7] 6780 3-9-4 93 ....(p) TomMarquand 12 96
(Richard Hannon) *hld up: rdn over 1f out: r.o ins fnl f: nt rch ldrs* **33/1**

3001 **5** nk **Flowers On Venus (IRE)**[28] 6140 4-8-13 87 .... RichardKingscote 3 89
(Tom Dascombe) *prom: shkn up over 1f out: edgd lft ins fnl f: styd on* **3/1**[1]

5665 **6** nk **Boomerang Bob (IRE)**[28] 6112 7-9-2 90 .... WilliamCarson 13 91
(Jamie Osborne) *hld up: rdn over 1f out: r.o ins fnl f: nvr nrr* **10/1**

5010 **7** 3/4 **Ustinov**[7] 6792 4-9-3 91 .... LiamKeniry 9 89
(David O'Meara) *hld up: nt clr run and swtchd lft ins fnl f: r.o: nt rch ldrs* **10/1**

4554 **8** hd **Sir Dudley (IRE)**[61] 4947 3-8-6 84 ....(b) JosephineGordon(3) 5 82
(James Given) *chsd ldrs: rdn over 1f out: no ex ins fnl f* **16/1**

00-4 **9** 1 1/2 **Merdon Castle (IRE)**[18] 6449 4-9-7 95 ....(e) BenCurtis 11 88
(Ruth Carr) *s.i.s: nvr nrr* **33/1**

1000 **10** nk **Johnny Cavagin**[15] 6539 7-8-13 87 ....(t) JimmyQuinn 2 79
(Ronald Thompson) *hld up: effrt over 1f out: nt clr run ent fnl f: n.d* **33/1**

0000 **11** 2 **Secret Missile**[20] 6371 6-9-0 88 ....(b) TomQueally 4 74
(Gary Moore) *led 1f: chsd ldr tl rdn over 2f out: wknd fnl f* **40/1**

2640 **12** 1 1/4 **Suqoor**[42] 5657 3-9-5 94 ....(b[1]) SilvestreDeSousa 6 76
(Chris Dwyer) *chsd ldrs: rdn over 2f out: wknd fnl f* **14/1**

1m 12.6s (-1.90) **Going Correction** -0.05s/f (Stan) course record
WFA 3 from 4yo+ 1lb **12** Ran SP% **122.0**
Speed ratings (Par 107): **110,107,105,105,105 104,103,103,101,101 98,96**
CSF £20.40 CT £103.68 TOTE £7.10: £2.70, £1.40, £2.20; EX 26.80 Trifecta £131.10.
Owner Shropshire Wolves **Bred** Glebe Stud, J F Dean & Lady Trenchard **Trained** Pandy, Monmouths

FOCUS
The feature contest was a good sprint handicap. They went a contested gallop and the form makes sense.

6963 LADBROKES NURSERY H'CAP 1m 141y (Tp)
7:10 (7:10) (Class 6) (0-65,65) 2-Y-O **£2,264** (£673; £336; £168) **Stalls** Low

Form RPR

0064 **1** **John T Chance (IRE)**[10] 6681 2-8-10 54 ....[1] JimCrowley 2 59
(Brian Meehan) *led 1f: chsd ldr: rdn to ld ins fnl f: r.o* **3/1**[1]

5126 **2** 1 3/4 **Tennessee Rose (IRE)**[10] 6670 2-9-3 61 .... RichardKingscote 8 62
(Tom Dascombe) *led at stdy pce after 1f: qcknd over 2f out: rdn over 1f out: edgd lft and hdd ins fnl f: styd on same pce* **17/2**

0020 **3** 1 1/2 **Alligator**[21] 6313 2-9-3 61 .... TomQueally 1 59
(Ed Dunlop) *chsd ldrs: rdn over 2f out: no ex ins fnl f* **8/1**[3]

0506 **4** hd **Dyna Might**[10] 6681 2-8-5 49 .... JimmyQuinn 3 46
(Ollie Pears) *s.i.s: sn prom: rdn over 1f out: styd on* **20/1**

4603 **5** 1 **Restore (IRE)**[24] 6236 2-9-2 60 .... TomMarquand 5 55+
(Richard Hannon) *prom: hmpd and lost pl over 7f out: hdwy u.p over 1f out: nt trble ldrs* **13/2**[2]

4350 **6** 3/4 **Accladora**[18] 6440 2-9-5 63 .... SilvestreDeSousa 13 57+
(Mark Johnston) *s.i.s: hld up: hdwy over 1f out: nvr nrr* **20/1**

065 **7** hd **Silver Chimes**[33] 5951 2-8-8 55 .... JosephineGordon(3) 4 48
(William Knight) *plld hrd and prom: rdn over 1f out: no ex ins fnl f* **16/1**

666 **8** hd **Clenymistra (IRE)**[36] 5854 2-8-9 56 ....[1] MarcMonaghan(3) 9 49+
(Marco Botti) *s.i.s: hld up: rdn over 1f out: nvr nrr* **22/1**

0555 **9** 1/2 **King's Coinage (IRE)**[18] 6455 2-9-7 65 .... WilliamTwiston-Davies 10 57+
(Ed Walker) *hld up: rdn over 2f out: n.d* **17/2**

0222 **10** 1 **Wentwell Yesterday (IRE)**[10] 6670 2-9-3 61 .... WilliamCarson 7 51+
(Jamie Osborne) *hld up in tch: plld hrd: rdn over 2f out: wknd ins fnl f* **3/1**[1]

000 **11** 4 **Hollow Crown**[52] 5304 2-8-4 53 .... GeorgeWood(5) 11 34+
(Denis Coakley) *hld up: rdn over 2f out: nvr on terms* **50/1**

330 **12** 3 1/4 **Hazell Berry (IRE)**[19] 6412 2-8-5 49 ....(v[1]) BenCurtis 6 24
(David Evans) *prom: racd keenly and forced to r wd: rdn and wknd over 2f out* **16/1**

1m 51.54s (1.44) **Going Correction** -0.05s/f (Stan) **12** Ran SP% **123.1**
Speed ratings (Par 93): **91,89,88,87,87 86,86,86,85,84 81,78**
CSF £29.55 CT £196.72 TOTE £4.80: £1.60, £2.60, £2.20; EX 38.00 Trifecta £272.20.
Owner Barton Farm Partners **Bred** Mountarmstrong Stud **Trained** Manton, Wilts

FOCUS
A modest nursery handicap. They went a muddling gallop and it paid to race prominently. The form is rated around the second and third.

6964 LADBROKES FILLIES' H'CAP 1m 141y (Tp)
7:40 (7:40) (Class 4) (0-85,85) 3-Y-O+ **£4,690** (£1,395; £697; £348) **Stalls** Low

Form RPR

3241 **1** **Mukaabra**[38] 5765 3-9-4 83 ....(p) JoeFanning 6 91+
(James Tate) *a.p: rdn to ld ins fnl f: r.o* **9/4**[1]

1111 **2** 1 1/2 **Mia Tesoro (IRE)**[31] 6021 3-8-12 77 .... StevieDonohoe 2 82
(Charlie Fellowes) *trckd ldrs: racd keenly: rdn over 1f out: r.o to go 2nd nr fin* **10/1**

3621 **3** 1/2 **Volition (IRE)**[28] 6135 3-8-12 77 .... GrahamGibbons 3 81
(Sir Michael Stoute) *sn led: rdn over 1f out: hdd ins fnl f: styd on same pce* **8/1**

01-0 **4** 1/2 **City Chic (USA)**[57] 5123 3-9-6 85 .... MartinLane 5 88
(Charlie Appleby) *hld up: rdn and hung lft fr over 1f out: r.o towards fin: nvr nrr* **4/1**[2]

3211 **5** 3/4 **Nouvelli Dancer (IRE)**[32] 5992 3-9-4 83 .... OisinMurphy 7 84
(Ivan Furtado) *chsd ldr: rdn over 1f out: no ex ins fnl f* **10/1**

5020 **6** 1 1/4 **Mustique (IRE)**[44] 5588 3-8-12 77 .... SilvestreDeSousa 9 75
(Richard Fahey) *hld up: rdn and hung lft fr over 1f out: nvr trbld ldrs* **6/1**

2132 **7** 4 1/2 **Izmir (IRE)**[14] 6576 3-9-1 80 ....(p) JimCrowley 4 68
(William Haggas) *hld up: rdn over 1f out: wknd fnl f* **9/2**[3]

1m 47.47s (-2.63) **Going Correction** -0.05s/f (Stan) **7** Ran SP% **112.5**
Speed ratings (Par 102): **109,107,107,106,106 105,101**
CSF £24.80 CT £150.90 TOTE £3.10: £1.40, £3.00; EX 14.90 Trifecta £131.20.
Owner Sheikh Juma Dalmook Al Maktoum **Bred** Biddestone Stud Ltd **Trained** Newmarket, Suffolk

FOCUS
A decent fillies' handicap. They went a proper gallop and the winner confirmed the positive impression when landing a third victory of the year at Kempton in August.

6965 DOWNLOAD THE LADBROKES APP H'CAP 1m 4f 50y (Tp)
8:10 (8:11) (Class 5) (0-70,70) 3-Y-O+ **£2,911** (£866; £432; £216) **Stalls** Low

Form RPR

4423 **1** **Cacica**[21] 6334 3-8-13 66 ....(b) SilvestreDeSousa 11 75
(George Scott) *chsd ldr tl over 9f out: remained handy: led over 3f out: rdn over 1f out: styd on u.p* **3/1**[2]

0536 **2** 1 1/2 **Diletta Tommasa (IRE)**[8] 6730 6-8-8 61 ....(v) TobyEley(7) 6 67
(Daniel Mark Loughnane) *hld up: hdwy over 5f out: chsd wnr over 2f out: rdn over 1f out: styd on* **25/1**

0355 **3** 1 1/2 **Ride The Lightning**[20] 6365 3-9-3 70 .... OisinMurphy 9 74
(Archie Watson) *prom: rdn over 2f out: styd on same pce wl ins fnl f* **13/8**[1]

1410 **4** 6 **Yasir (USA)**[9] 6701 8-9-7 67 .... MartinLane 1 61
(Conor Dore) *hld up: hdwy over 3f out: rdn over 1f out: wknd fnl f* **14/1**

4500 **5** 9 **Yorkindred Spirit**[9] 6702 4-9-3 63 ....(v) JoeFanning 5 43
(Mark Johnston) *s.i.s and pushed along in rr early: effrt on outer over 2f out: nvr on terms: eased whn btn fnl f* **13/2**[3]

050- **6** 5 **Gambol (FR)**[113] 4134 6-9-7 70 .... GeorgeDowning(3) 2 42
(Ian Williams) *hld up: rdn over 3f out: n.d* **22/1**

040 **7** 2 1/2 **Pinwood (IRE)**[10] 6665 3-9-3 70 ....(t) TomQueally 4 38
(Adam West) *prom tl rdn and wknd over 3f out* **66/1**

60-0 **8** 7 **Akavit (IRE)**[18] 6445 4-9-10 70 .... JimCrowley 8 26
(Ed de Giles) *led: hdd over 9f out: chsd ldr tl rdn over 3f out: nt clr run and wknd over 2f out* **9/1**

0030 **9** nk **Moojaned (IRE)**[2] 6889 5-9-0 60 .... GrahamGibbons 10 16
(David Evans) *plld hrd and prom: led over 9f out: hdd over 3f out: wknd over 2f out* **11/1**

4034 **10** 2 **Karam Albaari (IRE)**[34] 5929 8-9-5 68 ....(v) AlistairRawlinson(3) 3 21
(J R Jenkins) *hld up: lost pl 5f out: wknd over 2f out* **28/1**

2m 37.07s (-3.73) **Going Correction** -0.05s/f (Stan)
WFA 3 from 4yo+ 7lb **10** Ran SP% **114.6**
Speed ratings (Par 103): **110,109,108,104,98 94,93,88,88,86**
CSF £79.27 CT £159.63 TOTE £4.10: £1.50, £4.60, £1.20; EX 48.80 Trifecta £379.50.
Owner Black Cat Partnership **Bred** J M Beever **Trained** Newmarket, Suffolk

FOCUS
A modest middle-distance handicap. They went a decent gallop and the form should stand up to close scrutiny.

6966 CASHOUT AVAILABLE ON THE APP AT LADBROKES H'CAP (DIV I) 1m 103y (Tp)
8:40 (8:40) (Class 6) (0-55,56) 3-Y-O **£2,264** (£673; £336; £168) **Stalls** Low

Form RPR

504 **1** **Protest (IRE)**[11] 6651 3-8-11 50 .... MitchGodwin(5) 2 57
(Sylvester Kirk) *led: hdd 8f out: chsd ldr tl led again over 2f out: rdn over 1f out: styd on* **9/2**[3]

4544 **2** 1 1/4 **Gladys Cooper (IRE)**[30] 6046 3-9-7 55 .... JimCrowley 6 60
(Ed Walker) *prom: chsd wnr 2f out: rdn over 1f out: styd on* **13/8**[1]

5604 **3** 2 **Frivolous Prince (IRE)**[11] 6654 3-9-0 48 ....(vt) GrahamGibbons 5 50
(David Evans) *hld up: pushed along and hdwy 2f out: rdn over 1f out: styd on same pce wl ins fnl f* **5/2**[2]

6530 **4** 3/4 **Pivotal Dream (IRE)**[19] 6407 3-8-7 46 .... CharlieBennett(5) 7 46
(Mark Brisbourne) *hld up: pushed along and hdwy on outer over 1f out: rdn and edgd lft ins fnl f: nt trble ldrs* **8/1**

00-0 **5** 2 3/4 **Bassett Bleu**[54] 5228 3-8-7 46 oh1 ....(b[1]) ShirleyTeasdale(5) 8 41
(Iain Jardine) *hld up: rdn over 3f out: styd on ins fnl f: nvr on terms* **33/1**

650 **6** *2 ½* **Magic Mirror**[18] 6441 3-9-3 **51** .... TomMarquand 3 41
(Mark Rimell) *chsd ldrs: rdn over 2f out: wknd over 1f out* **20/1**

0006 **7** *8* **Icons Image**[53] 5263 3-8-13 **47** .... DanielMuscutt 1 22
(Alan Bailey) *pushed along early: led 8f out: rdn and hdd over 2f out: wknd over 1f out* **14/1**

006 **8** *1 ½* **Somepink (IRE)**[176] 1324 3-8-5 **46** oh1 .... TobyEley(7) 10 18
(Daniel Mark Loughnane) *s.i.s: a in rr: rdn over 2f out: wknd wl over 1f out* **50/1**

2m 1.18s (0.38) **Going Correction** -0.05s/f (Stan) **8** Ran SP% **112.3**
Speed ratings (Par 99): **96,94,93,92,90 87,80,79**
CSF £11.74 CT £21.12 TOTE £5.90: £1.20, £1.30, £1.70; EX 13.40 Trifecta £29.30.
Owner Sylvester Kirk **Bred** Paget Bloodstock & Eadling Farm **Trained** Upper Lambourn, Berks

FOCUS
The first division of a moderate 3yo handicap. Once again it paid to race handily off an ordinary pace. Not much to dwell on behind the first two.

6967 CASHOUT AVAILABLE ON THE APP AT LADBROKES H'CAP (DIV II) 1m 1f 103y (Tp)

9:10 (9:10) (Class 6) (0-55,54) 3-Y-O **£2,264** (£673; £336; £168) **Stalls** Low

Form RPR

0554 **1** **Pensax Lady (IRE)**[4] 6857 3-9-3 **50** .... GrahamGibbons 7 55
(Daniel Mark Loughnane) *chsd ldr: rdn to ld ins fnl f: edgd lft: styd on* **4/1**[3]

0542 **2** *¾* **Just Fred (IRE)**[16] 6513 3-9-2 **49** .... (p) OisinMurphy 9 53
(Denis Coakley) *trckd ldrs: racd keenly: rdn over 1f out: edgd lft ins fnl f: r.o* **7/4**[1]

000 **3** *nk* **Monologue (IRE)**[84] 4156 3-9-3 **50** .... TomMarquand 2 53+
(Simon Hodgson) *hld up: rdn over 2f out: hdwy over 1f out: r.o* **25/1**

050 **4** *1* **Thatsthewaytodoit (IRE)**[68] 4718 3-9-2 **54** .... CharlieBennett(5) 6 55+
(Daniel Mark Loughnane) *hld up in tch: rdn over 2f out: r.o* **33/1**

4405 **5** *shd* **The Greedy Boy**[11] 6651 3-8-13 **46** .... SilvestreDeSousa 1 47
(Mick Channon) *chsd ldrs: rdn over 1f out: styd on same pce ins fnl f* **15/8**[2]

0-56 **6** *nse* **Josh Perry**[31] 6036 3-9-0 **47** .... JimCrowley 4 48
(Rod Millman) *led: rdn over 2f out: hdd ins fnl f: styd on same pce* **9/1**

006 **7** *1 ½* **Olympus Mons (FR)**[56] 5181 3-8-12 **45** .... LiamKeniry 3 45
(Jo Hughes) *hld up: plld hrd: hdwy and nt clr run over 1f out: sn rdn and hung lft: styd on same pce ins fnl f* **40/1**

0000 **8** *1 ¼* **Sakhastic**[79] 4316 3-8-12 **45** .... TomQueally 5 41
(John Mackie) *hld up: rdn over 1f out: nvr trbld ldrs* **20/1**

-006 **9** *10* **Blue Jay (FR)**[80] 4275 3-9-0 **47** .... (t) JimmyQuinn 8 24
(Ronald Thompson) *hld up: rdn over 2f out: wknd over 1f out* **50/1**

2m 4.71s (3.91) **Going Correction** -0.05s/f (Stan) **9** Ran SP% **117.1**
Speed ratings (Par 99): **80,79,79,78,78 78,76,75,66**
CSF £11.04 CT £153.68 TOTE £5.50: £1.50, £1.10, £5.00; EX 13.40 Trifecta £158.30.
Owner S & A Mares **Bred** Select Bloodstock & Melchior Bloodstock **Trained** Baldwin's Gate, Staffs

FOCUS
The second division of a moderate 3yo handicap. The winning time was nearly four seconds slower off a sedate gallop. The winner is rated near her best.
T/Plt: £48.30 to a £1 stake. Pool: £93,596.49 - 1412.25 winning units T/Qpdt: £10.60 to a £1 stake. Pool: £10,762.31 - 750.45 winning units **Colin Roberts**

6968 - 6970a (Foreign Racing) - See Raceform Interactive

6391 CHANTILLY (R-H)

Saturday, October 1

OFFICIAL GOING: Turf: good; polytrack: standard
Meeting transferred from Longchamp

6971a QATAR PRIX CHAUDENAY (GROUP 2) (3YO) (TURF) 1m 7f

1:00 (12:00) 3-Y-O **£83,823** (£32,352; £15,441; £10,294; £5,147)

RPR

1 **Doha Dream (FR)**[20] 6392 3-9-2 0 .... GregoryBenoist 5 108
(A Fabre, France) *a cl up: shkn up to chal on outer 2f out: led approching 1 1/2f out: sn rdn: r.o gamely u.p fnl f* **11/10**[1]

2 *shd* **Moonshiner (GER)**[27] 6176 3-9-2 0 .... MaximeGuyon 3 108
(Jean-Pierre Carvalho, Germany) *w.w next to last: moved up qckly on outer to trck ldr fr 1/2-way: rdn to chal between horses 1 1/2f out: sustained run u.p fnl f: nvr quite jnd wnr* **2/1**[2]

3 *8* **Marmelo**[48] 5448 3-9-2 0 .... UmbertoRispoli 1 98
(Hughie Morrison) *led: shkn up and raised tempo 3f out: pressed fr 2 1/2f out: rdn and rallied whn hdd appr 1 1/2f out: lft bhd by front two fnl f: kpt on for 3rd* **11/1**[3]

4 *3* **Peribsen (IRE)**[48] 5448 3-9-2 0 .... GeraldMosse 6 94
(F Head, France) *hld up in tch: rdn and nt qckn wl over 1 1/2f out: plugged on at one pce* **11/1**[3]

5 *3 ½* **Gontchar (FR)**[34] 3-9-2 0 .... CristianDemuro 2 89
(A Savujev, Czech Republic) *trckd ldrs: dropped next to last 1/2-way: rowed along 4f out and no imp: grad dropped away* **25/1**

6 *dist* **Minamya (FR)**[30] 6069 3-8-13 0 .... ChristopheSoumillon 4
(A De Royer-Dupre, France) *rrd as stalls opened and slowly away: a in rr: rdn and no imp 2 1/2f out: sn wknd: t.o* **11/1**[3]

3m 12.58s (-3.52) **Going Correction** +0.15s/f (Good) **6** Ran SP% **109.8**
Speed ratings: **115,114,110,109,107**
WIN (incl. 1 euro stake): 1.90. PLACES: 1.20, 1.40. SF: 3.80.
Owner Al Shaqab Racing **Bred** Ecurie Haras Bouquetot Sas **Trained** Chantilly, France

6972a QATAR PRIX DE ROYALLIEU (GROUP 2) (3YO+ FILLIES & MARES) (TURF) 1m 4f

1:35 (12:00) 3-Y-O+ **£104,779** (£40,441; £19,301; £12,867; £6,433)

RPR

1 **The Juliet Rose (FR)**[20] 6393 3-8-7 0 .... StephanePasquier 6 113+
(N Clement, France) *mde all: rdn and rallied over 2f out: styd on strly fr 1 1/2f out: drew clr fnl f* **15/8**[2]

2 *3* **Almela (IRE)**[26] 6200 4-9-1 0 .... PatSmullen 3 109
(D K Weld, Ire) *a cl up: shkn up to press ldr 3f out: rdn and styd on over 1 1/2f out: nt match wnr fnl f* **11/8**[1]

3 *4* **Sotteville (FR)**[48] 5451 3-8-7 0 .... CristianDemuro 1 102+
(J-C Rouget, France) *w.w towards rr: rdn over 2f out and no immediate imp: styd on ins fnl f: wnt 3rd 100yds out: no ch w front two* **7/1**[3]

4 *2* **Mango Tango (FR)**[49] 5461 3-8-7 0 .... LouisBeuzelin 2 98
(P Bary, France) *trckd ldr: rdn to chse ldng pair over 1 1/2f out: grad lft bhd fnl f: lost 3rd 100yds out and wknd* **8/1**

5 *4* **Impressionist (IRE)**[48] 5451 3-8-7 0 .... VincentCheminaud 5 92
(A Fabre, France) *w.w in rr: rdn and no hdwy over 2f out: bhd fnl f* **12/1**

6 *3* **Gambissara (FR)**[63] 4904 3-8-7 0 .... AndraschStarke 4 87
(Lennart Hammer-Hansen, Germany) *w.w in fnl pair: last and rdn 2 1/2f out: nvr trbld ldrs* **33/1**

2m 31.14s (0.14) **Going Correction** +0.375s/f (Good)
WFA 3 from 4yo 7lb **6** Ran SP% **111.1**
Speed ratings: **114,112,109,108,105 103**
WIN (incl. 1 euro stake): 2.60. PLACES: 1.40, 1.50. SF: 6.60.
Owner Mayfair Speculators Sarl & Equifrance Holdings **Bred** Guy Heald **Trained** Chantilly, France

FOCUS
The placed horses set the standard and a personal best from the winner.

6973a QATAR PRIX DOLLAR (GROUP 2) (3YO+) (TURF) 1m 2f

2:50 (12:00) 3-Y-O+ **£83,823** (£32,352; £15,441; £10,294; £5,147)

RPR

1 **Potemkin (GER)**[35] 5904 5-9-0 0 .... EduardoPedroza 4 113
(A Wohler, Germany) *prom on outer: drvn to chse ldng trio over 1 1/2f out: styd on u.p to ld 110yds out: sn clr* **15/2**[3]

2 *1 ¾* **Heshem (IRE)**[47] 5499 3-9-0 0 .... GregoryBenoist 1 114
(C Ferland, France) *a cl up: shkn up and chal ldrs fr 2f out: rdn and styd on to ld 1f out: hdd 110yds out: kpt on at same pce* **9/1**

3 *nk* **Zarak (FR)**[20] 6394 3-8-9 0 .... ChristopheSoumillon 8 108+
(A De Royer-Dupre, France) *w.w in fnl trio: swtchd outside and hdwy 2f out: styd on u.p fnl f: nt pce to chal* **1/1**[1]

4 *hd* **Alignement**[43] 5699 3-8-9 0 .... MaximeGuyon 7 108+
(C Laffon-Parias, France) *hld up in midfield on outer: scrubbed along 2 1/2f out: 5th and hrd rdn 1 1/2f out: kpt on ins fnl f: nvr quite on terms* **10/1**

5 *nse* **Yorker (SAF)**[17] 6482 7-9-0 0 .... PStrydom 5 108
(William Haggas) *led: hdd 1 1/2f out: rallied u.p: one pce fnl f* **5/1**[2]

6 *1 ¾* **Flanders Flame**[41] 3-8-9 0 .... RicardoSousa 3 104
(Helder Pereira, Spain) *chse ldr: rdn to chal 2f out: led narrowly 1 1/2f out: hdd 1f out: plugged on at one pce* **40/1**

7 *¾* **Arthenus**[27] 6178 4-9-0 0 .... (p) VincentCheminaud 2 103
(James Fanshawe) *w.w in midfield on inner: rdn to chse ldrs fr 2f out: nvr able to chal: wknd ins fnl f* **14/1**

8 *shd* **Meandre (FR)**[7] 8-9-0 0 .... CristianDemuro 9 103
(A Savujev, Czech Republic) *w.w in rr: no hdwy tl styd on ins fnl f: nrest at fin* **33/1**

9 *8* **Free Port Lux**[101] 3544 5-9-0 0 .... MickaelBarzalona 6 87
(F Head, France) *hld up in fnl trio: rdn 2f out and no imp: lost tch fnl f* **16/1**

2m 6.54s (1.74) **Going Correction** +0.60s/f (Yiel)
WFA 3 from 4yo+ 5lb **9** Ran SP% **115.5**
Speed ratings: **117,115,115,115,115 113,113,113,106**
WIN (incl. 1 euro stake): 8.50. PLACES: 1.70, 1.60, 1.10. DF: 26.30. SF: 59.20.
Owner Klaus Allofs & Stiftung Gestut Fahrhof **Bred** Siftung Gestut Fahrhof **Trained** Germany

6974a QATAR PRIX DU CADRAN (GROUP 1) (4YO+) (TURF) 2m 4f 110y

3:25 (12:00) 4-Y-O+ **£126,044** (£50,426; £25,213; £12,595; £6,308)

RPR

1 **Quest For More (IRE)**[22] 6284 6-9-2 0 .... (b) GeorgeBaker 8 117+
(Roger Charlton) *hld up in fnl trio: last at 1/2-way: hdwy on outer over 2 1/2f out: rdn and styd on wl appr fnl f: grad gained on ldr: led 50yds out: all out* **7/2**[2]

2 *snk* **Vazirabad (FR)**[20] 6396 4-9-2 0 .... ChristopheSoumillon 11 117
(A De Royer-Dupre, France) *w.w in fnl pair: stdy hdwy fr 3f out: 6th and styng on 2f out: led appr fnl f: styd on u.p: hdd 50yds out: no ex* **6/5**[1]

3 *5* **Nearly Caught (IRE)**[41] 5692 6-9-2 0 .... UmbertoRispoli 6 112
(Hughie Morrison) *led: hdd wl bef 1/2-way: remained prom: rdn to chal fr 2f out: styd on u.p fnl f: nt pce of front two* **6/1**[3]

4 *1* **Trip To Rhodos (FR)**[41] 5692 7-9-2 0 .... CristianDemuro 2 111
(Pavel Tuma, Czech Republic) *hld up in midfield on inner: 6th and styng on whn n.m.r over 1f out: swtchd outside and styd on fnl f: nt pce to get on terms* **25/1**

5 *snk* **Mille Et Mille**[20] 6396 6-9-2 0 .... ThierryThulliez 9 111
(C Lerner, France) *w.w in midfield: moved up to join ldrs after 3f: led bef 1/2-way: hdd 2f out: kpt on at one pce* **16/1**

6 *shd* **Nahual (FR)**[20] 6396 5-9-2 0 .... (p) MaximeGuyon 12 111
(J Bertran De Balanda, France) *cl up: drvn to ld 2f out: hdd appr fnl f: one pce u.p* **16/1**

7 *4* **Burmese**[22] 6284 4-9-2 0 .... (b) PatSmullen 4 107
(Marcus Tregoning) *w.w in rr: stdy hdwy on outer fr 1/2-way: rdn to chse ldrs whn jinked rt 2f out: no further imp fr 1 1/2f out: sn wknd* **16/1**

8 *12* **Cayirli (FR)**[22] 6283 4-9-2 0 .... OlivierPeslier 5 95
(Seamus Durack) *hld up towards rr: tk clsr order 3 1/2f out: sn rdn: wknd fnl 1 1/2f and lost tch* **66/1**

9 *4* **Kicky Blue (GER)**[20] 6396 6-8-13 0 .... MickaelBarzalona 7 88
(T Clout, France) *chsd ldrs: rdn and no imp over 1 1/2f out: sn btn: bhd whn eased over 1f out* **33/1**

10 *4* **Amour De Nuit (IRE)**[16] 6526 4-9-2 0 .... LukeMorris 3 87
(Sir Mark Prescott Bt) *hld up in midfield: no imp u.str.p 2f out: sn lost tch* **33/1**

11 *10* **Fly With Me (FR)**[41] 5692 6-9-2 0 .... (b) StephanePasquier 1 77
(E Libaud, France) *prom on inner: lost pl 3f out: wkng whn n.m.r 1 1/2f out: sn wl btn* **33/1**

12 *20* **Autor (IRE)**[27] 6-9-2 0 .... GregoryBenoist 10 57
(Z Koplik, Czech Republic) *cl up: outpcd and drvn wl over 3f out: lost tch 2f out: t.o* **50/1**

4m 23.57s (263.57) **12** Ran SP% **115.7**
WIN (incl. 1 euro stake): 5.90. PLACES: 1.70, 1.20, 1.40. DF: 6.20. SF: 15.30.
Owner H R H Sultan Ahmad Shah **Bred** Epona Bloodstock Ltd **Trained** Beckhampton, Wilts

FOCUS
The fifth, who won this last year, helps with the form.

6975a QATAR PRIX DANIEL WILDENSTEIN (GROUP 2) (3YO+) (TURF) 1m

4:12 (12:00) 3-Y-O+ **£83,823** (£32,352; £15,441; £10,294; £5,147)

RPR

1 **Taareef (USA)**[47] 5499 3-8-11 0 .... IoritzMendizabal 2 113+
(J-C Rouget, France) *plld early: nvr really settled: a cl up: drvn to chal 2f out: led 1 1/2f out: styd on and rdn clr fnl f* **9/2**

2 *1 ¾* **Hello My Love (FR)**[20] 5-9-1 0 .... EddyHardouin 5 109
(Carina Fey, France) *keen: led under a tight hold: rdn whn pressed 2f out: hdd 1 1/2f out: kpt on gamely u.p fnl f to hold 2nd* **33/1**

3 *snk* **Moonlight Magic**[21] 6354 3-8-11 0................................(p) KevinManning 7 108+
(J S Bolger, Ire) *a cl up: rdn to chse ldr 2f out: nt qckn u.p: styd on ins fnl f: nvr on terms* **3/1**[2]

4 *½* **Wireless (FR)**[48] 5-9-1 0.. TheoBachelot 1 108
(V Luka Jr, Czech Republic) *hld up in fnl pair: tk clsr order over 2f out: rdn and no real imp 1 1/2f out: styd on u.p fnl f: nt pce to chal* **25/1**

5 *¾* **Zayva (FR)**[30] 6070 3-8-9 0 ow1.......................... ChristopheSoumillon 6 103
(A De Royer-Dupre, France) *w.w in rr: styd on ins fnl f: nvr in contention* **4/1**[3]

6 *nk* **Dicton**[48] 5449 3-8-11 0.. OlivierPeslier 3 104
(Gianluca Bietolini, Italy) *w.w in tch: rdn and no imp fr 2f out: one pce fnl f* **2/1**[1]

7 *1 ¾* **Sasparella (FR)**[23] 6272 3-8-8 0.................................. MaximeGuyon 4 97
(C Laffon-Parias, France) *tk a str hold: w.w towards rr: rdn 2f out: no real imp: kpt on at same pce* **16/1**

1m 43.19s (5.19) **Going Correction** +1.05s/f (Soft)
WFA 3 from 5yo 3lb **7** Ran SP% **109.2**
Speed ratings: **116,114,114,113,112 112,110**
WIN (incl. 1 euro stake): 4.60. PLACES: 2.70, 6.00. SF: 60.70.
Owner Hamdan Al Maktoum **Bred** Dixiana Farms Llc **Trained** Pau, France

FOCUS
This developed into a sprint up the home straight.

6976 - 6982a (Foreign Racing) - See Raceform Interactive

5812 TIPPERARY (L-H)
Sunday, October 2

OFFICIAL GOING: Flat & chase courses - soft to heavy; hurdle course - soft (yielding to soft in places)

6983a COOLMORE STUD HOME OF CHAMPIONS CONCORDE STKS (GROUP 3) 7f 100y
2:10 (2:12) 3-Y-O+
£29,283 (£9,430; £4,466; £1,985; £992; £496)

RPR

1 **Jet Setting (IRE)**[22] 6352 3-9-7 119.................................... ShaneFoley 7 120+
(Adrian Paul Keatley, Ire) *cl up bhd ldr and disp ld after 2f: gng best into st where led narrowly: rdn clr over 1f out and styd on strly: eased cl home: easily* **7/4**[1]

2 *6 ½* **Joailliere (IRE)**[168] 1509 4-9-2 98.. LeighRoche 5 98+
(D K Weld, Ire) *w.w and sn settled towards rr: 7th 1/2-way: rdn into 5th 2f out and clsd u.p into mod 2nd wl ins fnl f: kpt on wl wout ever troubling easy wnr* **14/1**

3 *1 ¼* **Sruthan (IRE)**[22] 6353 6-9-5 110.......................................(p) ChrisHayes 2 98
(P D Deegan, Ire) *chsd ldrs early: 8th 1/2-way: rdn into 6th under 2f and clsd u.p ins fnl f between horses into mod 3rd clsng stages: nt trble easy wnr* **6/1**[3]

4 *½* **Flight Risk (IRE)**[7] 6816 5-9-5 108................................(t) RonanWhelan 8 97
(J S Bolger, Ire) *hld up in tch: pushed along in 4th fr 1/2-way and no imp on easy wnr u.p in 3rd ent fnl f: one pce ins fnl f* **6/1**[3]

5 *1 ½* **Creggs Pipes (IRE)**[22] 6352 4-9-2 106..................... DeclanMcDonogh 3 90
(Andrew Slattery, Ire) *broke wl to ld tl jnd and disp ld after 2f: pushed along and hdd narrowly into st: sn no imp on easy wnr u.p in 2nd: wknd ins fnl f* **7/1**

6 *1 ½* **Erysimum (IRE)**[46] 5564 3-9-0 93... BillyLee 10 85
(W McCreery, Ire) *hld up in tch tl tk clsr order in 3rd after 2f: dropped to 5th at 1/2-way: rdn and no imp on ldrs under 2f out: one pce after* **12/1**

7 *½* **Dolce Strega (IRE)**[99] 3682 3-9-3 100................................ WayneLordan 6 87
(W McCreery, Ire) *dwlt sltly and settled in rr: last at 1/2-way: rdn and no imp u.p in 9th under 2f out: kpt on one pce ins fnl f* **20/1**

8 *3 ¾* **Pacodali (IRE)**[14] 6609 3-9-3 94.......................................(p) ColinKeane 9 78
(J P Murtagh, Ire) *towards rr: clsr in 6th at 1/2-way: rdn in 8th 2f out and sn no ex: one pce after* **16/1**

9 *11* **The Happy Prince (IRE)**[7] 6816 4-9-8 112............(t) DonnachaO'Brien 4 54
(A P O'Brien, Ire) *chsd ldrs: 3rd 1/2-way: rdn into st and sn no imp on easy wnr u.p in 4th: eased fr 1f out* **5/1**[2]

10 *15* **Cailin Mor (IRE)**[35] 5941 4-9-2 92................................(t) NGMcCullagh 1 11
(M Halford, Ire) *dwlt sltly and pushed along towards rr early: sn chsd ldrs and disp 3rd briefly: dropped to rr bef 1/2-way: rdn and no imp fr 1/2-way: wknd and eased fnl 2f* **50/1**

1m 41.56s (101.56)
WFA 3 from 4yo+ 2lb **10** Ran SP% **121.1**
CSF £31.53 TOTE £2.40: £1.02, £4.90, £1.90; DF 38.40 Trifecta £262.50.
Owner China Horse Club International Ltd **Bred** P Kelly **Trained** Friarstown, Co. Kildare

FOCUS
A very impressive performance by the winner on her favoured softer ground. She proves time and time again, that, given her preferred conditions, she is a very classy individual. The time was good comapared with the handicap.

6984a THETOTE.COM H'CAP 7f 100y
2:45 (2:46) (60-100,99) 3-Y-O+ **£10,852** (£3,352; £1,588; £705; £264)

RPR

1 **Downforce (IRE)**[7] 6819 4-9-8 **93**.. BillyLee 2 101
(W McCreery, Ire) *chsd ldrs: 5th 1/2-way: travelling wl over 2f out and smooth hdwy to ld over 1f out: sn rdn and pressed wl ins fnl f: kpt on wl u.p clsng stages: all out* **2/1**[1]

2 *nk* **Master Speaker (IRE)**[7] 6819 6-9-9 **94**..................(t) ColmO'Donoghue 9 101
(Martin Hassett, Ire) *w.w towards rr: hdwy in 10th over 2f out to chse ldrs over 1f out: rdn into 2nd wl ins fnl f where edgd sltly lft and pressed wnr: jst hld* **10/1**

3 *1* **Mizaah (IRE)**[22] 6355 3-9-5 **92**.. ChrisHayes 12 96
(Kevin Prendergast, Ire) *mid-div: tk clsr order fr 1/2-way and impr to chse ldrs under 2f out: sn rdn and clsd u.p into 2nd ins fnl f where pressed wnr briefly: no ex in 3rd cl home where short of room and checked* **6/1**[2]

4 *3* **Canary Row (IRE)**[16] 6551 6-9-2 **90**............................(v) GaryHalpin[(3)] 1 87
(P J Prendergast, Ire) *chsd ldrs: 4th 1/2-way: rdn 2f out and no imp on wnr u.p in 4th ins fnl f: kpt on one pce* **10/1**

5 *1* **Military Angel (USA)**[46] 5564 4-9-11 **99**...................... ShaneBKelly[(3)] 8 94
(M D O'Callaghan, Ire) *mid-div: pushed along fr 1/2-way and no imp on ldrs into st: kpt on u.p into mod 5th wl ins fnl f: nvr trbld ldrs* **20/1**

6 *1 ¼* **Bubbly Bellini (IRE)**[7] 6819 9-8-4 **80**..................(p) KillianLeonard[(5)] 13 72
(Adrian McGuinness, Ire) *chsd ldrs: cl 3rd at 1/2-way: led narrowly over 2f out: sn rdn and hdd u.p over 1f out: wknd* **14/1**

7 *nse* **Tribal Path (IRE)**[16] 6551 6-8-12 **88**......................(t) DonaghO'Connor[(5)] 3 80
(Damian Joseph English, Ire) *broke wl to ld: narrow advantage at 1/2-way: rdn and hdd over 2f out: sn no ex u.p and wknd 1f out* **8/1**[3]

8 *½* **Severus (GER)**[68] 4748 6-8-4 **75**..................................... WayneLordan 5 65
(Des Donovan, Ire) *hld up towards rr: impr into 7th after 1/2-way: sn pushed along and no ex u.p over 2f out: one pce after* **12/1**

9 *1* **Best Not Argue (IRE)**[105] 3444 4-8-4 **75**......................... NGMcCullagh 7 63
(John Joseph Murphy, Ire) *settled in rr: pushed along in 12th fr 3f out and no imp into st: kpt on one pce fnl 2f* **20/1**

10 *nk* **Beau Satchel**[7] 6821 6-8-8 **79**..(t) LeighRoche 10 66
(Adrian McGuinness, Ire) *hld up: rdn in 11th fr 1/2-way and no imp into st: one pce fnl 2f* **10/1**

11 *1 ¾* **An Saighdiur (IRE)**[15] 6556 9-9-12 **97**.................... DeclanMcDonogh 4 80
(Andrew Slattery, Ire) *settled bhd ldr: cl 2nd at 1/2-way: brought wd into st and rdn: sn no ex and wknd fr under 2f out* **16/1**

12 *9* **Enough Is Enough (IRE)**[14] 6607 9-8-4 **75** oh9................ RoryCleary 6 35
(P Meany, Ire) *towards rr thrght: rdn and no imp fr 1/2-way: wknd under 3f out* **50/1**

13 *6* **Seanie (IRE)**[16] 6551 7-9-2 **92**...(t) OisinOrr[(5)] 14 37
(David Marnane, Ire) *chsd ldrs: pushed along in 6th after 1/2-way and lost pl u.p under 3f out: wknd* **16/1**

1m 43.24s (103.24)
WFA 3 from 4yo+ 2lb **13** Ran SP% **123.6**
CSF £23.03 CT £113.63 TOTE £2.90: £1.50, £3.20, £1.80; DF 27.30 Trifecta £161.50.
Owner Donal Finnan **Bred** P Burns **Trained** Rathbride, Co Kildare

FOCUS
Just a neck separated the first two past the post, and a stewards' inquiry was called after the winner seemed to edge right close to the winning line. It wasn't deemed significant enough by the stewards to reverse placings.

6985 - (Foreign Racing) - See Raceform Interactive

6971 CHANTILLY (R-H)
Sunday, October 2

OFFICIAL GOING: Turf: good
Meeting transferred from Longchamp

6986a TOTAL PRIX MARCEL BOUSSAC - CRITERIUM DES POULICHES (GROUP 1) (2YO FILLIES) (TURF) 1m
1:10 (12:00) 2-Y-O **£126,044** (£50,426; £25,213; £12,595; £6,308)

RPR

1 **Wuheida**[57] 5170 2-8-11 0.. WilliamBuick 2 113
(Charlie Appleby) *chsd ldrs early: sn cl up on outer: virtually jnd ldr 3f out: niggled along 2f out and sltly outpcd wl over 1 1/2f out: sn rdn and styd on wl fnl f: led last 125yds: drvn out* **10/1**

2 *¾* **Promise To Be True (IRE)**[21] 6385 2-8-11 0.................. RyanMoore 8 111
(A P O'Brien, Ire) *a in ldng quartet: 3rd and drvn 2f out: r.o u.p fnl f: small fly jump as wnr crossed in front 150yds out: kpt on strly to go 2nd cl home* **7/2**[2]

3 *snk* **Dabyah (IRE)**[16] 6548 2-8-11 0...................................... FrankieDettori 10 111
(John Gosden) *led: virtually jnd 3f out: shkn up and kicked for home wl over 1 1/2f out: styd on u.p: hdd 125yds out: no ex* **3/1**[1]

4 *¾* **Senga (USA)**[23] 6309 2-8-11 0.................................. StephanePasquier 4 109+
(P Bary, France) *v keen: hld up in fnl pair on inner: angled out and n.m.r appr 1 1/2f out: sn rdn and wnt between horses: gd hdwy wl over 1f out: styd on strly fnl f: nrest at fin* **16/1**

5 *2* **Cavale Doree (FR)**[43] 5703 2-8-11 0.................. Pierre-CharlesBoudot 9 104
(C Ferland, France) *tk a str hold: hld up towards rr: rowed along 2f out: sn hrd rdn and hdd on fr over 1f out: nt pce to get on terms* **7/1**[3]

6 *1 ¾* **First Of Spring (IRE)**[45] 2-8-11 0.................. ChristopheSoumillon 3 100
(J-C Rouget, France) *chsd ldng gp: rdn and nt qckn 1 1/2f out: one pce fnl f* **8/1**

7 *½* **Normandel (FR)**[24] 6271 2-8-11 0................................ CristianDemuro 7 99
(Mme Pia Brandt, France) *towards rr: tk clsr order on inner over 2f out: sn rdn and nt qckn: kpt on at same pce* **20/1**

8 *½* **Toulifaut (IRE)**[24] 6271 2-8-11 0................................ IoritzMendizabal 11 104+
(J-C Rouget, France) *v keen: hld up in midfield: hemmed in fr wl over 2 1/2f out: angled out and shkn up but nt clr run 2f out: stdd and wnt for gap whn squeezed out and stmbld appr fnl f: nt rcvr* **7/2**[2]

9 *2 ½* **Elegante Bere (FR)**[43] 5702 2-8-11 0................................ ThierryJarnet 1 92
(D Guillemin, France) *w.w in midfield on inner: 6th and rdn 2f out but no imp: wknd ins fnl f* **100/1**

10 *1 ¼* **Baileys Showgirl (FR)**[28] 6177 2-8-11 0.......................... JoeFanning 5 89
(Mark Johnston) *sweated up: fly j. leaving stalls: settled in fnl pair: short-lived effrt on outer 2f out: sn btn* **50/1**

11 *2 ½* **Body Sculpt (FR)**[28] 6177 2-8-11 0.................................. AlexisBadel 6 83
(S Kobayashi, France) *keen: trckd ldr on inner: cl 4th and pushed along 2f out: wknd fnl 1 1/2f* **100/1**

1m 35.85s (-2.15) **Going Correction** -0.10s/f (Good) **11** Ran SP% **116.7**
Speed ratings: **106,105,105,104,102 100,100,99,97,95 93**
WIN (incl. 1 euro stake): 10.80. PLACES: 2.90, 1.90, 2.00. DF: 26.30. SF: 48.60.
Owner Godolphin **Bred** Darley **Trained** Newmarket, Suffolk

FOCUS
With Longchamp undergoing an extensive two-year renovation the Arc meeting was moved North of Paris to Chantilly, the home of the largest training centre in Europe. The ground was in decent nick and very close to the official description.\n\x\x This looked a very strong Marcel Boussac on paper, and the form has initially been treated as fluid. However, the principals controlled the pace and those waited with stood no chance.

6987a QATAR PRIX JEAN-LUC LAGARDERE (GRAND CRITERIUM) (GROUP 1) (2YO COLTS & FILLIES) (TURF) 1m
1:45 (12:00) 2-Y-O **£147,051** (£58,830; £29,415; £14,694; £7,360)

RPR

1 **National Defense**[24] 6270 2-9-0 0........................ Pierre-CharlesBoudot 2 119+
(Mme C Head-Maarek, France) *mde all: led under a tight hold: shkn up and qcknd clr under 1 1/2f out: drvn out fnl f: v readily* **5/1**[3]

2 *4 ½* **Salouen (IRE)**[31] 6059 2-9-0 0... MaximeGuyon 1 108
(Sylvester Kirk) *a little slow to stride early and rowed along to chse ldrs: 4l 3rd and rdn 1 1/2f out: styd on u.p fr over 1f out: grad reeled in eventual 3rd to go 2nd 100yds out: no ch w wnr* **8/1**

3 *snk* **Whitecliffsofdover (USA)**[10] 6707 2-9-0 0........................ RyanMoore 3 108
(A P O'Brien, Ire) *chsd ldr: drvn to try and chal over 2f out: nvr quite upsides and outpcd whn ldr qcknd 1 1/2f out: styd on at same pce u.p: lost 2nd fnl 100yds* **2/1**[1]

4 2 **Kontrastat (FR)**[28] 6177 2-9-0 0 TheoBachelot 5 103
(S Wattel, France) *hld up in rr: clsng on inner whn swtchd outside 2f out: kpt on at same pce fnl f: nvr trbld ldrs* **9/4**[2]

5 2 ½ **King Of Spades (FR)**[11] 6694 2-9-0 0 (b) ChristopheSoumillon 4 97
(F Vermeulen, France) *settled towards rr: rdn and edgd lft 2f out: sn btn* **25/1**

6 1 ¾ **Thais (FR)**[13] 6639 2-8-10 0 StephanePasquier 6 89
(P Bary, France) *w.w towards rr on outer: drvn 2f out but no real imp: bhd ins fnl 1 1/2f* **14/1**

7 1 ½ **Utah (IRE)**[38] 5813 2-9-0 0 SeamieHeffernan 7 89+
(A P O'Brien, Ire) *chsd ldrs on outer: stmbld 3 1/2f out: struggling u.p fnl 2 1/2f: bhd last 1 1/2f* **12/1**

1m 35.53s (-2.47) **Going Correction** -0.10s/f (Good) 7 Ran SP% **110.1**
Speed ratings: **108,103,103,101,98 97,95**
WIN (incl. 1 euro stake): 5.30. PLACES: 3.00, 4.10. SF: 38.20.
Owner Sun Bloodstock Sarl **Bred** Ecurie Des Monceaux & Meridian International Sarl **Trained** Chantilly, France

FOCUS
A weak edition of this prestigious 2yo event. There was a fair pace on but again it paid to be handy as the winner dominated. A fine effort from National Defense but the second and third hold down the form a little.

6988a PRIX DE L'OPERA LONGINES (GROUP 1) (3YO+ FILLIES & MARES) (TURF) 1m 2f

2:20 (12:00) 3-Y-O+ **£168,058** (£67,235; £33,617; £16,794; £8,411)

RPR

1 **Speedy Boarding**[42] 5691 4-9-2 0 FrederikTylicki 6 116
(James Fanshawe) *w.w in tch on outer: steadily clsd to join ldr 3f out: shkn up 2f out and led 1 1/2f out: sn rdn to maintain narrow ld: hdd 100yds out: r.o gamely u.p to get bk up fnl strides* **11/2**[2]

2 shd **Pleascach (IRE)**[386] 6337 4-9-2 0 KevinManning 5 116
(J S Bolger, Ire) *pressed ldr on outer: led after nrly 3f: jnd by eventual wnr 3f out: sn rowed along and hdd 1 1/2f out: rdn and rallied bravely u.p: r.o and led again 100yds out: hdd fnl strides* **6/1**[3]

3 ½ **So Mi Dar**[18] 6488 3-8-11 0 FrankieDettori 2 115+
(John Gosden) *keen early: hld up in tch on inner: drvn and nt qckn 2f out: nt clr run and angled out appr fnl 1 1/2f: began to stay on appr 1f out: kpt on wl fnl f but nt pce to reel in front two* **4/6**[1]

4 3 ½ **Jemayel (IRE)**[40] 5754 3-8-11 0 GregoryBenoist 7 108
(J-C Rouget, France) *led: hdd after 3f: remained prom: 4th and rdn over 1f out: styd on at same pce* **15/2**

5 1 **Royal Solitaire (IRE)**[42] 5691 4-9-2 0 AndraschStarke 4 106+
(P Schiergen, Germany) *hld up in fnl pair on outer: 6th and scrubbed along over 2f out: sn rdn and no imp: plugged on u.p fnl f: nvr in contention* **20/1**

6 1 ¼ **Sea Front (FR)**[42] 5691 5-9-2 0 Pierre-CharlesBoudot 1 104
(E Libaud, France) *settled twowards rr: rdn and no hdwy 2f out: wknd ins fnl f* **40/1**

7 nk **Pagella (GER)**[28] 6175 3-8-11 0 AlexanderPietsch 3 103
(J Hirschberger, Germany) *w.w in fnl pair on inner: rdn and no imp 2f out: wl hld fr over 1f out* **40/1**

2m 2.03s (-2.77) **Going Correction** -0.10s/f (Good)
WFA 3 from 4yo+ 5lb 7 Ran SP% **111.1**
Speed ratings: **107,106,106,103,102 101,101**
WIN (incl. 1 euro stake): 5.80. PLACES: 3.20, 3.70. SF: 33.50.
Owner Helena Springfield Ltd **Bred** Meon Valley Stud **Trained** Newmarket, Suffolk

FOCUS
Numerically the smallest Prix de l'Opera since 2006, but it still featured three individual Group 1 winners. Once again those racing on the pace held sway.

6989a QATAR PRIX DE L'ARC DE TRIOMPHE (GROUP 1) (3YO+ NO GELDINGS) (TURF) 1m 4f

3:05 (12:00) 3-Y-O£**2,100,735** (£840,441; £420,220; £209,926; £105,147)

RPR

1 **Found (IRE)**[22] 6354 4-9-2 0 RyanMoore 12 124
(A P O'Brien, Ire) *midfield: rdn and gd hdwy fr 2 1/2f out: led under 2f out: r.o wl: drvn out* **6/1**[3]

2 1 ¾ **Highland Reel (IRE)**[22] 6354 4-9-5 0 SeamieHeffernan 11 124
(A P O'Brien, Ire) *trckd ldrs: rdn 3f out: wnt 2nd 1f out: styd on: no imp on wnr* **20/1**

3 1 ½ **Order Of St George (IRE)**[21] 6387 4-9-5 0 FrankieDettori 16 122
(A P O'Brien, Ire) *racd away fr main gp first 3f: chsd ldr after: rdn 3f out: sltly outpcd and short of room 2f out: kpt on fnl f* **14/1**

4 ¾ **Siljan's Saga (FR)**[35] 5947 6-9-2 0 Pierre-CharlesBoudot 3 118
(J-P Gauvin, France) *towards rr of midfield: hdwy fr 2 1/2f out: rdn over 2f out: kpt on wl but nvr able to chal* **100/1**

5 2 ½ **Postponed (IRE)**[46] 5558 5-9-5 0 AndreaAtzeni 7 117
(Roger Varian) *trckd ldrs: rdn 2 1/2f out: lost pl over 1f out: wknd fnl f* **15/8**[1]

6 nse **One Foot In Heaven (IRE)**[21] 6395 4-9-5 0 CristianDemuro 9 117
(A De Royer-Dupre, France) *s.s: in rr: rdn and styd on fr 3f out: nvr able to chal* **100/1**

7 snk **New Bay**[22] 6354 4-9-5 0 VincentCheminaud 8 116
(A Fabre, France) *towards rr: rdn and hdwy on outer fr 3f out: drvn 1 1/2f out: kpt on but nvr in contention* **12/1**

8 1 ½ **Savoir Vivre (IRE)**[35] 5947 3-8-11 0 FrederikTylicki 10 113
(Jean-Pierre Carvalho, Germany) *s.s: in rr: rdn 3f out: kpt on fr 2f out: nvr a factor* **40/1**

9 1 ¾ **Harzand (IRE)**[22] 6354 3-8-11 0 PatSmullen 6 110
(D K Weld, Ire) *midfield: rdn and unable qck 3f out: squeezed between two rivals 2 1/2f out: plugged on* **11/2**[2]

10 2 **Vedevani (FR)**[18] 6498 3-8-11 0 AlexisBadel 1 107
(A De Royer-Dupre, France) *led: rdn clr 3f out: hdd under 2f out: hmpd 1 1/2f out: sn wl btn* **250/1**

11 7 **Talismanic**[18] 6498 3-8-11 0 MickaelBarzalona 5 96
(A Fabre, France) *a towards rr* **40/1**

12 1 **Left Hand**[21] 6393 3-8-8 0 (p) MaximeGuyon 15 91
(C Laffon-Parias, France) *midfield: rdn 2 1/2f out: lost pl under 2f out: sn btn* **16/1**

13 ¾ **Silverwave (FR)**[21] 6395 4-9-5 0 ChristopheSoumillon 4 94
(P Bary, France) *midfield: rdn and unable qck 2 1/2f out: wknd 1 1/2f out* **16/1**

14 3 **Makahiki (JPN)**[21] 6392 3-8-11 0 Christophe-PatriceLemaire 14 88
(Yasuo Tomomichi, Japan) *midfield on outer: rdn and lost pl 2 1/2f: sn btn* **13/2**

15 1 ¼ **Migwar (IRE)**[23] 4-9-5 0 OlivierPeslier 13 87
(F Head, France) *towards rr of midfield: hmpd under 3f out: sn rdn and struggling* **100/1**

16 1 ¼ **The Grey Gatsby (IRE)**[46] 5558 5-9-5 0 (p) JamesDoyle 2 85
(Kevin Ryan) *trckd ldrs: rdn 3 1/2f out: lost pl 2 1/2f out: sn wl btn* **50/1**

2m 23.61s (-7.39) **Going Correction** -0.10s/f (Good)
WFA 3 from 4yo+ 7lb 16 Ran SP% **118.9**
Speed ratings: **120,118,117,117,115 115,115,114,113,112 107,106,106,104,103 102**
WIN (incl. 1 euro stake): 10.60. PLACES: 3.60, 7.60, 4.80. DF: 109.00. SF: 176.80.
Owner Michael Tabor & Derrick Smith & Mrs John Magnier **Bred** Roncon, Wynatt & Chelston **Trained** Cashel, Co Tipperary

FOCUS
Run away from its usual home of Longchamp, it perhaps wasn't a vintage edition of the race, but the form is solid, with King George and Ascot Gold Cup winners chasing home the remarkably consistent and high-class winner, and it also produced one of the great training performances, with Aidan O'Brien responsible for saddling the first three home. Although run at a good gallop, little got involved from the rear, and older horses wiped the floor with the Classic generation.

6990a QATAR PRIX DE L'ABBAYE DE LONGCHAMP (GROUP 1) (2YO+) (TURF) 5f

4:35 (12:00) 2-Y-O+ **£147,051** (£58,830; £29,415; £14,694; £7,360)

RPR

1 **Marsha (IRE)**[21] 6391 3-9-7 0 LukeMorris 12 114
(Sir Mark Prescott Bt) *in tch in midfield: rdn 2f out: styd on wl to ld 75yds out: drvn out* **16/1**

2 ¾ **Washington DC (IRE)**[21] 6384 3-9-11 0 RyanMoore 15 115
(A P O'Brien, Ire) *towards rr: rdn and hdwy on outer fr over 1f out: styd on wl fnl f: nt rch wnr* **10/1**

3 shd **Mecca's Angel (IRE)**[44] 5614 5-9-7 0 PaulMulrennan 7 110+
(Michael Dods) *chsd ldrs: rdn 2f out: led 1 1/2f out: hdd 75yds out: no ex cl home* **6/4**[1]

4 ¾ **Finsbury Square (IRE)**[35] 5949 4-9-11 0 (b) ChristopheSoumillon 17 111
(F Chappet, France) *midfield on outer: drvn and hdwy fr 1f out: r.o wl: nt quite able to chal* **50/1**

5 1 **Son Cesio (FR)**[35] 5943 5-9-11 0 VincentCheminaud 10 107
(H-A Pantall, France) *towards rr: rdn and kpt on wl fr under 2f out: nrst fin* **25/1**

6 snk **Duke Of Firenze**[46] 5555 7-9-11 0 DavidAllan 16 107
(David C Griffiths) *dwlt: towards rr: rdn and kpt on fr under 2f out: nvr able to chal* **50/1**

7 shd **Profitable (IRE)**[44] 5614 4-9-11 0 AdamKirby 11 106
(Clive Cox) *in tch: rdn and hdwy fr 2f out: ev ch 1f out: wknd last 100yds* **13/2**[3]

8 1 **Line Of Reason (IRE)**[12] 6642 6-9-11 0 MartinLane 9 103
(Paul Midgley) *towards rr of midfield: rdn 3f out: kpt on steadily fnl f: nvr a factor* **66/1**

9 hd **Ardad (IRE)**[23] 6282 2-8-7 0 RobertHavlin 5 97
(John Gosden) *midfield: rdn and unable qck 1 1/2f out: wknd steadily ins fnl f* **10/1**

10 hd **Cotai Glory**[15] 6574 4-9-11 0 GeorgeBaker 14 101
(Charles Hills) *trckd ldrs on outer: rdn 2f out: ev ch over 1f out: wkng whn hmpd ins fnl f: sn btn* **20/1**

11 ¾ **Porthilly (FR)**[21] 6391 6-9-7 0 GeraldMosse 1 95
(J E Hammond, France) *trckd ldrs: rdn 2f out: wknd 1f out: eased clsng stages* **100/1**

12 snk **Maarek**[21] 6384 9-9-11 0 SeamieHeffernan 6 98
(Miss Evanna McCutcheon, Ire) *s.s: pushed along towards rr thrght: nvr a factor* **66/1**

13 nk **Harry Hurricane**[8] 6779 4-9-11 0 (b) UmbertoRispoli 4 97
(George Baker) *in tch in midfield: pushed along 2f out: rdn and lost pl over 1f out* **40/1**

14 shd **Goldream**[21] 6391 7-9-11 0 (p) MartinHarley 3 97
(Robert Cowell) *prom: rdn 2f out: lost pl 1f out: wknd fnl f* **14/1**

15 3 ½ **Take Cover**[21] 6384 9-9-11 0 FMBerry 13 84
(David C Griffiths) *s.v.s: a bhd* **20/1**

16 3 **Just Glamorous (IRE)**[21] 6391 3-9-11 0 Pierre-CharlesBoudot 2 74
(Ronald Harris) *led: rdn 2f out: hdd 1 /2f out: wknd qckly: eased* **11/2**[2]

17 1 ¼ **Eskimo Point (IRE)**[14] 4-9-11 0 TonyPiccone 8 69
(Mario Hofer, Germany) *prom: pushed along and lost pl 2 1/2f out: sn wl btn* **80/1**

57.27s (-1.03) **Going Correction** +0.225s/f (Good) 17 Ran SP% **124.4**
Speed ratings: **117,115,115,114,112 112,112,110,110,110 109,108,108,108,102 97,95**
WIN (incl. 1 euro stake): 24.40. PLACES: 4.90, 3.20, 1.60. DF: 134.20. SF: 190.50.
Owner Elite Racing Club **Bred** Elite Racing Club **Trained** Newmarket, Suffolk

FOCUS
Bit of a turn-up here, with two of the 3yos (only three in the field) coming to the fore late on down the outside, with the favourite unable to quicken. The pace was strong.

6991a QATAR PRIX DE LA FORET (GROUP 1) (3YO+) (TURF) 7f

5:15 (12:00) 3-Y-O+ **£126,044** (£50,426; £25,213; £12,595; £6,308)

RPR

1 **Limato (IRE)**[44] 5614 4-9-2 0 HarryBentley 1 126+
(Henry Candy) *trckd ldrs: hdwy to ld under 2f out: sn rdn: drew clr fnl f: comf* **8/11**[1]

2 3 **Karar**[24] 6272 4-9-2 0 GregoryBenoist 12 117
(F-H Graffard, France) *led: rdn over 2f out: hdd under 2f out: no ch w wnr after bef styd on gamely to hold 2nd* **40/1**

3 ½ **Suedois (FR)**[29] 6120 5-9-2 0 DanielTudhope 10 116
(David O'Meara) *in tch: rdn over 2f out: drvn 1f out: kpt on and pressed 2nd thrght fnl f: no ch w wnr* **8/1**[3]

4 ¾ **Jimmy Two Times (FR)**[56] 5217 3-9-0 0 VincentCheminaud 6 113
(A Fabre, France) *in tch: rdn and kpt on same pce fr 2f out: nvr able to chal* **6/1**[2]

5 ½ **Attendu (FR)**[24] 6272 3-9-0 0 MaximeGuyon 7 111
(C Laffon-Parias, France) *midfield: rdn over 2f out: kpt on steadily: nvr able to chal* **12/1**

6 3 ½ **Birchwood (IRE)**[44] 5613 3-9-0 0 JamesDoyle 9 102
(Richard Fahey) *chsd ldr: rdn over 2f out: ev ch under 2f out: wknd 1f out* **25/1**

7 snk **Harry's Son (AUS)**[190] 1106 5-9-2 0 PStrydom 4 102
(C Alonso Pena, Spain) *dwlt: towards rr: rdn and kpt on same pce fr 2f out: nvr a factor* **50/1**

8 shd **Coulsty (IRE)**[24] 6272 5-9-2 0 SeanLevey 2 102
(Richard Hannon) *midfield: rdn over 2f out: drvn and outpcd 1 1/2f out: no hdwy fnl f* **40/1**

9 6 **Same Jurisdiction (SAF)**[23] 6281 5-8-13 0 WilliamBuick 3 83
(Ed Dunlop) *a towards rr* **33/1**

10 1 ½ **Trixia (FR)**[21] 6394 3-8-10 0 OlivierPeslier 5 77
(A De Royer-Dupre, France) *dwlt: towards rr of midfield: rdn and no hdwy 2f out: wknd 1f out* **12/1**

11 5 **Moon Trouble (IRE)**[61] 5004 3-9-0 0 MickaelBarzalona 8 67
(F Head, France) *dwlt: a in rr* **33/1**

1m 21.83s (-4.27) **Going Correction** -0.10s/f (Good)
WFA 3 from 4yo+ 2lb **11** Ran SP% **115.3**
Speed ratings: **120,116,116,115,114 110,110,110,103,101 96**
WIN (incl. 1 euro stake): 1.80. PLACES: 1.30, 3.60, 2.00. DF: 24.90. SF: 33.90.
Owner Paul G Jacobs **Bred** Seamus Phelan **Trained** Kingston Warren, Oxon

FOCUS
A race that revolved around Limato and he didn't disappoint. He's rated to his mark.

6397 DUSSELDORF (R-H)
Sunday, October 2

OFFICIAL GOING: Turf: good

6992a GROSSER PREIS DER LANDESHAUPTSTADT DUSSELDORF (GROUP 3) (3YO+) (TURF) 1m 110y
4:20 (12:00) 3-Y-O+ **£23,529** (£8,823; £4,411; £2,205; £1,470)

RPR

1 **Noor Al Hawa (FR)**[21] 6397 3-9-1 0 EduardoPedroza 6 110
(A Wohler, Germany) *hld up in midfield: rdn and styd on 1 1/2f out: r.o fnl f to ld last 100yds: drvn out* **3/5**[1]

2 ¾ **Degas (GER)**[31] 6067 3-8-13 0 AdriedeVries 1 106
(Markus Klug, Germany) *hld up in midfield on inner: followed eventual wnr fr 1 1/2f out: styd on u.p fnl f: a being hld* **13/5**[2]

3 1 ¼ **Nordico (GER)**[21] 6397 5-9-2 0 (p) StephenHellyn 8 101
(Mario Hofer, Germany) *led: sn 3l clr: pushed along 1 1/2f out: styd on at same pce u.p fnl f: hdd 100yds out: no ex* **163/10**

4 1 ¼ **Kenrivash (FR)**[119] 2949 3-8-9 0 NormanRichter 4 97
(Henk Grewe, Germany) *plld v hrd early on: hld up in 3rd: rdn and drifted lft under 2f out: kpt on at same pce* **32/1**

5 1 ¾ **Nymeria (GER)**[21] 6397 4-8-13 0 RonanThomas 3 92
(Waldemar Hickst, Germany) *w.w towards rr: rdn and effrt 1 1/2f out: kpt on ins fnl f: nvr trbld ldrs* **73/10**[3]

6 1 **Sussudio (FR)**[15] 6598 6-9-2 0 FilipMinarik 5 92
(Frau Hella Sauer, Germany) *settled towards rr on outer: rdn and no imp 2f out: kpt on u.p fnl f: nvr in contention* **104/10**

7 ¾ **Dhaba (GER)**[56] 5220 3-8-9 0 AndreasHelfenbein 7 89
(Markus Klug, Germany) *keen: hld up in rr: sme mod late prog: nvr a factor* **132/10**

8 3 ½ **Wildpark (GER)**[36] 5904 5-9-2 0 (b) IanFerguson 2 83
(D Moser, Germany) *chsd ldr on inner: rdn and no imp wl over 1 1/2f out: sn wknd* **185/10**

1m 45.2s (-2.38)
WFA 3 from 4yo+ 3lb **8** Ran SP% **132.1**
WIN (incl. 10 euro stake): 16. PLACES: 11,11, 19. SF: 22..
Owner Jaber Abdullah **Bred** Rabbah Bloodstock Limited **Trained** Germany

6993 - 7002a (Foreign Racing) - See Raceform Interactive

6712 PONTEFRACT (L-H)
Monday, October 3

OFFICIAL GOING: Good to soft (good in places) (7.9)
Wind: Light half against Weather: Fine & dry

7003 RACINGUK.COM/BRITISH STALLION STUDS EBF MAIDEN STKS (PLUS 10 RACE) 1m 2f 6y
2:00 (2:01) (Class 4) 2-Y-O **£4,528** (£1,347; £673; £336) **Stalls** Low

Form RPR

32 1 **Hamada**[19] 6480 2-9-5 0 WilliamBuick 2 83
(Charlie Appleby) *mde all: rdn clr wl over 1f out: unchal* **1/2**[1]

5 2 6 **Avantgardist (GER)**[11] 6716 2-9-5 0 JoeFanning 3 70
(Mark Johnston) *dwlt and awkward s: towards rr: hdwy 1/2-way: chsd ldrs over 2f out: rdn along wl over 1f out: kpt on wl fnl f* **10/1**[3]

3 nk **Physicist (IRE)** 2-9-5 0[1] LukeMorris 9 70
(Paul Cole) *prom: trckd wnr after 3f: pushed along 3f out: rdn 2f out: sn drvn and kpt on same pce* **25/1**

4344 4 4 ½ **Actualisation**[11] 6716 2-9-5 73 (v[1]) JasonHart 8 62
(John Quinn) *t.k.h: trckd ldng pair: pushed along 2f out: rdn wl over 1f out: no imp* **14/1**

5 2 ½ **Eagle's Stare (IRE)** 2-9-5 0 DanielTudhope 6 57
(Saeed bin Suroor) *in tch: hdwy to trck ldrs 4f out: rdn along over 2f out: kpt on same pce* **13/2**[2]

33 6 1 ¾ **Mayleen (IRE)**[11] 6716 2-9-0 0 GrahamLee 7 49
(Ann Duffield) *t.k.h: hld up towards rr: effrt and sme hdwy over 3f out: rdn along over 2f out: n.d* **12/1**

44 7 ½ **The Blues Master (IRE)**[19] 6473 2-9-5 0 SilvestreDeSousa 5 53
(Mark Johnston) *a rr* **12/1**

2300 8 1 **Good Time Ahead (IRE)**[19] 6473 2-9-5 71 PJMcDonald 4 51
(Philip Kirby) *a rr* **40/1**

6 9 20 **Master Degree (IRE)**[38] 5834 2-9-5 0 DougieCostello 1 15
(K R Burke) *trckd wnr on inner: pushed along 3f out: rdn over 2f out: sn drvna nd wknd* **50/1**

2m 15.8s (2.10) **Going Correction** +0.10s/f (Good) **9** Ran SP% **119.4**
Speed ratings (Par 97): **95,90,89,86,84 82,82,81,65**
CSF £6.95 TOTE £1.30: £1.10, £3.40, £4.90; EX 7.10 Trifecta £67.40.
Owner Godolphin **Bred** Darley **Trained** Newmarket, Suffolk

FOCUS
It was dry overnight and the going was given as good to soft, good in places (GoingStick: 7.9), but after the first race most of the riders said it was either 'soft' or 'good to soft at best.' This proved very straightforward for the odds-on favourite.

7004 RACING UK CLUB DAY 17TH OCTOBER NURSERY H'CAP 6f
2:30 (2:30) (Class 4) (0-85,85) 2-Y-O **£4,528** (£1,347; £673; £336) **Stalls** Low

Form RPR

6303 1 **High Acclaim (USA)**[11] 6697 2-9-2 80 DanielTudhope 9 89
(Roger Teal) *cl up: led over 2f out: rdn clr ent fnl f: drvn and hld on wl towards fin* **9/1**

3215 2 hd **Novoman (IRE)**[16] 6575 2-9-5 83 PatCosgrave 13 92+
(William Haggas) *rr: effrt whn nt clr run and hmpd over 1f out: rdn and styng on whn n.m.r jst ins fnl f: fin strly: jst failed* **15/2**

3523 3 3 ½ **Heatongrad (IRE)**[17] 6536 2-8-8 72 TonyHamilton 5 70
(Richard Fahey) *hld up: hdwy on outer wl over 1f out: sn rdn and styd on wl fnl f* **13/2**[3]

0542 4 ½ **Yarmouk (FR)**[14] 6614 2-8-6 70 PaulHanagan 8 66
(Richard Fahey) *in tch: hdwy 2f out: rdn over 1f out: styd on fnl f* **7/1**

44 5 ½ **Kreb's Cycle (IRE)**[51] 5416 2-9-7 85 SilvestreDeSousa 11 80
(Richard Hannon) *chsd ldrs on outer: rdn wl over 1f out: drvn and kpt on same pce fnl f* **11/1**

5401 6 1 ¼ **Kings Heart (IRE)**[13] 6652 2-8-4 68 TomMarquand 6 59
(Mark Usher) *dwlt and towards rr: hdwy on inner wl over 1f out: sn rdn and styng on whn n.m.r ins fnl f: nrst fin* **16/1**

3021 7 ½ **Father McKenzie**[11] 6712 2-8-11 75 GrahamLee 4 64
(Mick Channon) *slt ld: pushed along 3f out: hdd narrowly over 2f out and sn rdn drvn ent fnl f: grad wknd* **7/2**[1]

623 8 1 ½ **Grinty (IRE)**[17] 6535 2-8-11 75 PaulMulrennan 1 60
(Michael Dods) *midfield: hdwy to chse ldrs over 2f out: sn rdn and wkng whn n.m.r and sltly hmpd over 1f out* **11/2**[2]

0330 9 shd **Ocelot**[19] 6477 2-8-8 72 DavidAllan 10 56
(Tim Easterby) *a towards rr* **33/1**

0105 10 1 **Our Greta (IRE)**[23] 6322 2-8-10 74 BenCurtis 7 55
(Michael Appleby) *chsd ldrs: rdn along over 2f out: sn wknd* **16/1**

1203 11 1 ½ **Stoneyford Lane (IRE)**[24] 6275 2-9-1 79 RoystonFfrench 2 56
(Steph Hollinshead) *cl up on inner: rdn along wl over 2f out: sn drvn and wknd* **10/1**

1m 18.57s (1.67) **Going Correction** +0.10s/f (Good) **11** Ran SP% **117.3**
Speed ratings (Par 97): **92,91,87,86,85 84,83,81,81,79 77**
CSF £74.75 CT £481.43 TOTE £10.40: £3.60, £2.20, £2.60; EX 84.40 Trifecta £1471.80.
Owner Excel Racing **Bred** Regis Farms Lp **Trained** Great Shefford, Berks
■ Stewards' Enquiry : Tom Marquand caution: careless riding

FOCUS
The leaders went off pretty quick here and the winner deserves credit for hanging on, for all that the runner-up was unlucky not win.

7005 TRADEWAY SHIPPING PETER KIRKHAM RETIRING H'CAP 1m 4y
3:00 (3:00) (Class 3) (0-95,91) 3-Y-O
£9,337 (£2,796; £1,398; £699; £349; £175) **Stalls** Low

Form RPR

1202 1 **Blair House (IRE)**[8] 6803 3-9-6 90 (b[1]) WilliamBuick 7 100+
(Charlie Appleby) *hld up in rr: hdwy on wd outside 2f out: rdn to chal jst over 1f out: led jst ins fnl f: kpt on strly* **9/4**[1]

1111 2 ¾ **Rainbow Rebel (IRE)**[9] 6772 3-9-2 86 JoeFanning 9 94
(Mark Johnston) *trckd ldr: hdwy and cl up over 2f out: rdn and led briefly appr fnl f: sn hdd and drvn: kpt on wl towards fin* **6/1**

10 3 ½ **Illustrissime (USA)**[12] 6675 3-9-3 87 DanielTudhope 1 94
(Roger Fell) *hld up in tch: effrt on inner and nt clr run over 2f out: sn swtchd rt and hdwy wl over 1f out: rdn ent fnl f: kpt on wl* **25/1**

1-26 4 3 ¼ **In The Red (IRE)**[3] 6915 3-9-4 88 TomMarquand 5 87
(Richard Hannon) *trckd ldng pair: pushed along wl over 2f out: rdn wl over 1f out: hld whn n.m.r and hmpd jst ins fnl f* **11/2**[3]

1346 5 hd **Tukhoom (IRE)**[24] 6277 3-8-11 81 PaulHanagan 3 80
(Marcus Tregoning) *hld up in rr: hdwy over 4f out: rdn along over 2f out: drvn to chse ldrs wl over 1f out: no imp* **13/2**

2604 6 2 ½ **Lazzam**[62] 4976 3-9-7 91 LukeMorris 2 84
(Marco Botti) *a towards rr* **9/2**[2]

0053 7 nk **Whitman**[16] 6585 3-9-1 85 (b) SilvestreDeSousa 8 77
(Mark Johnston) *sn led: rdn along over 2f out: drvn and hdd jst over 1f out: sn wknd* **12/1**

3154 8 ½ **Briyouni (FR)**[30] 6132 3-8-11 81 KevinStott 6 72
(Kevin Ryan) *trckd ldrs: hdwy over 3f out: prom and rdn 2f out: sn drvn and wknd appr fnl f* **11/1**

1m 45.22s (-0.68) **Going Correction** +0.10s/f (Good) **8** Ran SP% **111.8**
Speed ratings (Par 105): **107,106,105,102,102 99,99,99**
CSF £15.24 CT £256.36 TOTE £3.20: £1.50, £1.50, £5.70; EX 9.90 Trifecta £141.80.
Owner Godolphin **Bred** Darley **Trained** Newmarket, Suffolk

FOCUS
A decent handicap run at a sound gallop. A small pb from the runner-up.

7006 RACING UK HD BLUFF COVE H'CAP (ROUND 7 OF THE PONTEFRACT STAYERS CHAMPIONSHIP 2016) 2m 1f 216y
3:30 (3:30) (Class 5) (0-75,75) 3-Y-O+ **£3,234** (£962; £481; £240) **Stalls** Low

Form RPR

1132 1 **La Fritillaire**[18] 6519 4-8-11 58 AndrewMullen 8 65
(James Given) *trckd ldr: hdwy to ld over 3f out: jnd and rdn wl over 1f out: drvn and hdd narrowly ins fnl f: rallied gamely to ld again towards fin* **14/1**

44-1 2 hd **Leoncavallo (IRE)**[72] 4637 4-9-10 71 WilliamBuick 9 78
(Charlie Appleby) *trckd ldrs: hdwy over 4f out: cl up over 2f out: chal wl over 1f out and sn rdn: drvn to take slt advantage ins fnl f: hdd and no ex towards fin* **2/1**[1]

2020 3 2 **Riptide**[18] 6519 10-9-6 67 DougieCostello 2 72
(Michael Scudamore) *reminders s and towards rr: hdwy over 3f out: rdn along and styd on along inner 2f out: sn chsng ldng pair: drvn and kpt on fnl f* **14/1**

4112 4 shd **Duke Of Diamonds**[53] 5334 4-9-10 74 ShelleyBirkett[(3)] 7 79
(Julia Feilden) *trckd ldrs: hdwy over 3f out: rdn 2f out: sn drvn and kpt on same pce* **10/1**

0265 5 3 **Monjeni**[18] 6519 3-8-2 61 (v) LukeMorris 3 63
(Sir Mark Prescott Bt) *trckd ldrs: hdwy over 3f out: rdn to chse ldng pair 2f out: sn drvn and one pce appr fnl f* **4/1**[2]

5400 6 1 **Tuscan Gold**[18] 6519 9-9-1 62 (p) PJMcDonald 4 62
(Micky Hammond) *a towards rr* **33/1**

3521 7 ½ **Medina Sidonia (IRE)**[18] 6519 4-9-9 73 (p) RachelRichardson[(3)] 6 73
(Tim Easterby) *trckd ldng pair: effrt 3f out and sn rdn along: drvn over 2f out and sn wknd* **5/1**[3]

5650 8 1 ½ **Madam Lilibet (IRE)**[20] 6438 7-8-10 57 JoeyHaynes 5 55
(Sharon Watt) *reminders s and rr: rn in snatches: hdwy over 4f out: rdn to chse ldrs over 2f out: sn drvn and wknd over 1f out* **25/1**

3300 9 61 **Giant Redwood (IRE)**[16] 6565 4-10-0 75 (p) SilvestreDeSousa 1 6
(Michael Bell) *led: rdn along and hdd over 3f out: sn wknd* **13/2**

4m 3.43s (7.23) **Going Correction** +0.10s/f (Good)
WFA 3 from 4yo+ 12lb **9** Ran SP% **112.5**
Speed ratings (Par 103): **87,86,86,85,84 84,83,83,56**
CSF £41.10 CT £408.77 TOTE £12.30: £3.40, £1.10, £4.80; EX 47.50 Trifecta £703.90.
Owner Ingram Racing **Bred** Mrs P M Ignarski **Trained** Willoughton, Lincs
■ Stewards' Enquiry : William Buick two-day ban: used whip above permitted level (Oct 17-18)

FOCUS
A modest staying handicap. The third helps with setting the level.

7007 BOOK YOUR CHRISTMAS PARTY ON 0113 287 6387 H'CAP (DIV I) 1m 4y

4:00 (4:00) (Class 5) (0-75,75) 3-Y-O+ **£3,234** (£962; £481; £240) **Stalls** Low

Form RPR

6000 **1** **Shouranour (IRE)**[29] 6160 6-9-7 **75**..........................(b) DanielTudhope 3 84
(Alan Brown) *trckd ldng pair: hdwy on inner 2f out: swtchd rt and rdn to ld over 1f out: drvn ins fnl f: hld on wl towards fin* **4/1**[1]

2640 **2** *nk* **Sands Chorus**[32] 6048 4-9-6 **74**.............................. PaulMulrennan 6 82
(James Given) *led: rdn 2f out: hdd over 1f out: sn drvn: rallied ins fnl f: kpt on wl towards fin* **4/1**[1]

4330 **3** *shd* **Al Nasser Alwashik**[5] 6877 3-9-2 **73**...................... SilvestreDeSousa 2 81
(Roger Fell) *trckd ldrs: hdwy 2f out: chsd ldng pair over 1f out: sn rdn: drvn ins fnl f: styd on wl strly towards fin* **6/1**[2]

3303 **4** *8* **John Caesar (IRE)**[13] 6645 5-8-8 **62**.............................(tp) LukeMorris 4 52
(Rebecca Bastiman) *dwlt and towards rr: hdwy into midfield 1/2-way: rdn along to chse ldrs 2f out: drvn and no imp over 1f out* **14/1**

2035 **5** *1 ½* **Sakhalin Star (IRE)**[10] 6737 5-8-13 **67**.....................(e) ConnorBeasley 8 53
(Richard Guest) *chsd ldrs: rdn along over 2f out: drvn wl over 1f out: grad wknd* **12/1**

3253 **6** *nk* **The Salmon Man**[33] 6021 4-9-5 **73**............................[1] DougieCostello 9 59
(Brendan Powell) *dwlt and rr: hdwy on inner over 2f out: sn rdn and styd on fnl f: nrst fin* **10/1**

4351 **7** *2* **Im Dapper Too**[26] 6226 5-8-7 **61**....................................... SamJames 13 42
(John Davies) *in tch: pushed along over 3f out: rdn over 2f out: sn drvn and no hdwy* **6/1**[2]

5601 **8** *1 ½* **Totally Magic (IRE)**[10] 6742 4-8-7 **61**........................... BarryMcHugh 5 38
(Richard Whitaker) *dwlt: a rr* **7/1**[3]

0242 **9** *1 ¼* **Ralphy Boy (IRE)**[13] 6644 7-9-7 **75**............................... PJMcDonald 10 50
(Alistair Whillans) *sn chsng ldr: rdn along over 2f out: sn drvn and grad wknd* **10/1**

-510 **10** *3 ¼* **Arizona Sunrise**[23] 6347 3-8-7 **64**................................. JamesSullivan 7 31
(Tina Jackson) *midfield: rdn along over 3f out: sn outpcd* **50/1**

36-0 **11** *17* **Next Stop**[18] 6504 5-9-3 **71**.. JoeFanning 12
(David Nicholls) *midfield: rdn along 3f out: sn outpcd and bhd* **20/1**

1m 45.66s (-0.24) **Going Correction** +0.10s/f (Good)
WFA 3 from 4yo+ 3lb **11** Ran SP% **120.3**
Speed ratings (Par 103): **105,104,104,96,95 94,92,91,90,86 69**
CSF £19.50 CT £97.38 TOTE £5.30: £1.90, £2.00, £2.30; EX 27.20 Trifecta £125.90.
Owner David Lumley **Bred** His Highness The Aga Khan's Studs S C **Trained** Yedingham, N Yorks

FOCUS
There was a good finish to this handicap, the first three pulling well clear of the rest. The first two were both well treated on their C&D form earlier this year and have been rated back to that level.

7008 RACING UK PROFITS RETURNED TO RACING H'CAP 1m 4f 8y

4:30 (4:30) (Class 5) (0-70,70) 3-Y-O **£3,234** (£962; £481; £240) **Stalls** Low

Form RPR

4006 **1** **Harry Champion**[12] 6684 3-9-4 **70**........................... MarcMonaghan[(3)] 7 78
(Hugo Palmer) *trckd ldr: pushed along over 2f out: rdn over 1f out: drvn ent fnl f: styd on wl u.p to ld nr fin* **6/1**

1622 **2** *hd* **Kelvin Hall**[7] 6840 3-8-11 **60**... JoeFanning 10 67
(Mark Johnston) *led: rdn clr wl over 1f out: drvn ins fnl f: wknd and hdd towards fin* **8/1**

4304 **3** *¾* **Adherence**[13] 6647 3-8-8 **57**..(p) BarryMcHugh 2 63
(Tony Coyle) *trckd ldrs: hdwy 2f out: sn chsng ldng pair: rdn over 1f out: drvn and edgd lft ins fnl f: styd on wl towards fin* **10/1**

3426 **4** *5* **La Contessa (IRE)**[23] 6344 3-9-1 **69**.................... AdamMcNamara[(5)] 8 67
(Richard Fahey) *in tch: hdwy 3f out: rdn along 2f out: sn drvn and no imp* **4/1**[2]

3453 **5** *3 ¼* **Torremar (FR)**[10] 6737 3-9-7 **70**.......................................(p) KevinStott 3 63
(Kevin Ryan) *towards rr: hdwy on outer over 3f out: rdn along 2f out: sn drvn and n.d* **11/4**[1]

5422 **6** *1 ¼* **Mamoo**[39] 5795 3-8-10 **59**...[1] MartinDwyer 5 50
(Mike Murphy) *trckd ldr: rdn along over 2f out: sn drvn and wknd* **5/1**[3]

645 **7** *1 ¾* **Calarules**[20] 6452 3-8-11 **60**.. DavidAllan 9 48
(Tim Easterby) *a rr* **16/1**

40 **8** *35* **Aislabie (FR)**[71] 4682 3-9-4 **67**.. JasonHart 6
(Mark Walford) *in tch: rdn along over 4f out: wknd 3f out: sn bhd and eased* **12/1**

2m 40.88s (0.08) **Going Correction** +0.10s/f (Good) **8** Ran SP% **111.4**
Speed ratings (Par 101): **103,102,102,99,96 96,94,71**
CSF £49.75 CT £458.07 TOTE £8.20: £2.30, £1.90, £2.60; EX 51.00 Trifecta £1161.50.
Owner Raymond Tooth **Bred** Raymond Clive Tooth **Trained** Newmarket, Suffolk
■ Stewards' Enquiry : Marc Monaghan two-day ban: used whip above permitted level (Oct 17-18)
Kevin Stott three-day ban: careless riding (Oct 17-19)

FOCUS
A modest handicap. The first three raced on the rail most of the way into the straight. The runner-up sets the standard, while the third has been rated to form.

7009 BUY YOUR 2017 ANNUAL BADGE TODAY MAIDEN STKS 1m 4y

5:00 (5:01) (Class 5) 3-Y-O+ **£3,234** (£962; £481; £240) **Stalls** Low

Form RPR

2 **1** **Kullu (IRE)**[13] 6650 3-9-0 0... StevieDonohoe 10 72+
(Charlie Fellowes) *mde all: rdn wl over 1f out: drvn ins fnl f: kpt on wl towards fin* **6/1**

2 *1 ½* **First Voyage (IRE)** 3-9-5 0... WilliamBuick 2 74+
(Charlie Appleby) *dwlt and towards rr: stdy hdwy on outer 1/2-way: effrt over 2f out: rdn to chal over 1f out: drvn and ev ch ins fnl f: kpt on* **11/10**[1]

4 **3** *½* **Selection (FR)**[31] 6104 3-9-5 0.. PatCosgrave 5 72+
(William Haggas) *trckd ldng pair on inner: effrt wl over 1f out and sn nt clr run: rdn and n.m.r ins fnl f: kpt on towards fin* **4/1**[2]

-006 **4** *nk* **Frankster (FR)**[42] 5731 3-9-5 67.................................(t) PJMcDonald 6 72
(Micky Hammond) *trckd ldrs: hdwy wl over 1f out: sn rdn: drvn and ch ent fnl f: kpt on* **80/1**

-2 **5** *1 ¼* **Shah Of Armaan (IRE)**[14] 6617 3-9-5 0............................. KevinStott 1 69
(Kevin Ryan) *trckd ldrs: effrt and n.m.r over 1f out: swtchd rt and rdn ent fnl f: kpt on* **9/2**[3]

0 **6** *nk* **Spinart**[50] 5438 3-9-0 0... CallumShepherd[(5)] 8 68
(Pam Sly) *trckd ldrs: hdwy wl over 1f out: sn rdn and kpt on towards fin* **14/1**

0 **7** *1 ½* **Captain Courageous (IRE)**[20] 6441 3-9-5 0.............. ThomasBrown 4 65+
(Ed Walker) *towards rr: hdwy and in tch over 2f out: rdn over 1f out: kpt on fnl f: nrst fin* **40/1**

2435 **8** *1 ¼* **Divisionist**[25] 6247 3-9-5 78... GrahamGibbons 9 62
(Sir Michael Stoute) *trckd wnr: effrt 2f out: sn rdn along: drvn ent fnl f: wknd* **12/1**

06 **9** *76* **Jamindeh**[28] 6192 3-9-5 0... GrahamLee 3
(Ian Williams) *dwlt and rr: rdn along and outpcd 3f out:. sn bhd and eased* **100/1**

1m 48.37s (2.47) **Going Correction** +0.10s/f (Good)
WFA 3 from 6yo 3lb **9** Ran SP% **119.1**
Speed ratings (Par 103): **91,89,89,88,87 87,85,84,8**
CSF £13.45 TOTE £7.10: £1.70, £1.10, £1.50; EX 22.30 Trifecta £70.30.
Owner A E Oppenheimer **Bred** Hascombe Stud **Trained** Newmarket, Suffolk

FOCUS
A fair maiden but much the slowest of the four C&D races. The sixth has been rated close to his debut C&D run.

7010 BOOK YOUR CHRISTMAS PARTY ON 0113 287 6387 H'CAP (DIV II) 1m 4y

5:30 (5:31) (Class 5) (0-75,75) 3-Y-O+ **£3,234** (£962; £481; £240) **Stalls** Low

Form RPR

6000 **1** **Mr Cool Cash**[16] 6568 4-8-7 **61**... JoeFanning 2 71
(Richard Guest) *cl up: led wl over 1f out: rdn clr appr fnl f: kpt on strly* **7/1**

4504 **2** *2 ¼* **Green Howard**[12] 6684 8-9-4 **72**.................................(t) DanielTudhope 3 77+
(Rebecca Bastiman) *hld up towards rr: hdwy on inner over 2f out: rdn over 1f out: chsd wnr ins fnl f: kpt on* **9/2**[2]

6501 **3** *2* **Chiswick Bey (IRE)**[12] 6683 8-8-13 **72**................. AdamMcNamara[(5)] 4 72
(Richard Fahey) *rr: hdwy 2f out: rdn over 1f out: sn swtchd rt and styd on wl fnl f: nrst fin* **12/1**

3232 **4** *2* **Niqnaaqpaadiwaaq**[26] 6226 4-8-12 **66**.................................. NeilFarley 7 62
(Eric Alston) *wnt rt s: led: rdn along and hdd wl over 1f out: sn drvn and kpt on same pce* **6/1**[3]

4006 **5** *5* **Faintly (USA)**[13] 6644 5-8-10 **64**...............................(b) JamesSullivan 12 48+
(Ruth Carr) *bhd: hdwy over 2f out: swtchd rt to outer wl over 1f out: sn rdn and styd on wl fnl f: nrst fin* **50/1**

4000 **6** *1 ½* **Optima Petamus**[18] 6517 4-9-3 **71**....................................... GrahamLee 6 52
(Patrick Holmes) *trckd ldrs: hdwy over 2f out: rdn wl over 1f out: sn drvn and kpt on same pce* **14/1**

0602 **7** *shd* **Osteopathic Remedy (IRE)**[20] 6434 12-8-11 **65**...(t) ConnorBeasley 14 45
(Michael Dods) *towards rr: hdwy over 2f out: rdn wl over 1f out: kpt on appr fnl f: nrst fin* **25/1**

0645 **8** *¾* **Torrid**[13] 6644 5-9-1 **74**... NathanEvans[(5)] 5 53+
(Michael Easterby) *hld up: hdwy over 2f out: rdn and n.m.r wl over 1f out: n.d* **7/2**[1]

3236 **9** *5* **Fidelma Moon (IRE)**[38] 5844 4-9-0 **73**.................. JordanVaughan[(5)] 11 40
(K R Burke) *chsd ldrs: rdn along 2f out: sn drvn and wknd over 1f out* **16/1**

2635 **10** *½* **Quoteline Direct**[13] 6646 3-8-7 **64**.................................... PJMcDonald 9 30
(Micky Hammond) *a towards rr* **25/1**

500 **11** *2 ¼* **Win Lose Draw (IRE)**[192] 1079 4-8-8 **62**....................... AndrewMullen 8 23
(Michael Appleby) *hmpd s: midfield: effrt whn n.m.r and sltly hmpd jst over 2f out: n.d* **25/1**

13 **12** *1 ¾* **Uncle Dermot (IRE)**[95] 3802 8-9-2 **70**............................... MartinDwyer 1 27
(Brendan Powell) *chsd ldrs on inner: rdn along 2f out: sn drvn and wknd over 1f over 1f out* **9/1**

4206 **13** *¾* **Relight My Fire**[13] 6643 6-8-11 **68**..................(bt) RachelRichardson[(3)] 13 23
(Tim Easterby) *chsd ldrs: rdn along over 2f out: sn wknd* **25/1**

00 **14** *13* **Auspicion**[29] 6160 4-9-7 **75**...(b) AndrewElliott 10
(Tom Tate) *prom on outer: rdn along over 2f out: sn wknd* **14/1**

1m 46.75s (0.85) **Going Correction** +0.10s/f (Good)
WFA 3 from 4yo+ 3lb **14** Ran SP% **121.4**
Speed ratings (Par 103): **99,96,94,92,87 86,86,85,80,79 77,75,75,62**
CSF £36.43 CT £301.73 TOTE £8.70: £2.90, £2.10, £4.00; EX 48.40 Trifecta £573.60.
Owner I Lawson **Bred** T G Holdcroft **Trained** Ingmanthorpe, W Yorks
■ Stewards' Enquiry : James Sullivan caution: careless riding

FOCUS
The winner and fourth poached a lead off the turn while the rest got stuck behind weakening horses. The second and third finished fast but the race was already over. The time was 1.09sec slower than the first division. The winner has been rated to form.
T/Jkpt: Not won. T/Plt: £76.90 to a £1 stake. Pool: £76344.94, 724.14 winning units. T/Qpdt: £21.50 to a £1 stake. Pool: £6846.64, 234.59 winning units. **Joe Rowntree**

6189 WINDSOR (R-H)

Monday, October 3

OFFICIAL GOING: Good to soft (good in places) (7.5)
Wind: Almost nil Weather: Glorious autumn day

7011 DENNING LEGAL MAIDEN STKS 6f

1:50 (1:53) (Class 5) 3-Y-O+ **£2,911** (£866; £432; £216) **Stalls** Low

Form RPR

1 **Santorini (IRE)** 3-9-5 0.. DaneO'Neill 8 72+
(Henry Candy) *chsd ldrs: pushed along on outer to cl fr over 2f out: shkn up to ld ins fnl f: styd on: readily* **7/2**[1]

40 **2** *1* **Bella's Venture**[142] 2234 3-9-0 0........................... MichaelJMMurphy 16 64
(John Gallagher) *w ldrs: rdn to ld 1f out: hdd ins fnl f: styd on but readily hld* **5/1**[3]

3 *1* **Hurricane Rock** 3-9-5 0.. JFEgan 1 66+
(Simon Dow) *settled in midfield: shkn up over 2f out: gd prog jst over 1f out: styd on to take 3rd on outer last strides* **20/1**

0 **4** *nse* **Q Cee**[66] 4840 3-9-5 0.. FMBerry 6 66
(Eugene Stanford) *towards rr: prog into midfield on inner over 2f out: shkn up and styd on wl fnl f to press for 3rd last strides* **28/1**

6 **5** *½* **Indiana Dawn**[23] 6317 3-9-0 0..................................... AdamBeschizza 9 59
(Robert Stephens) *green to post: w ldrs: shkn up wl over 1f out: kpt on same pce fnl f* **12/1**

0 **6** *½* **Gold Bud**[23] 6317 4-9-6 0... SteveDrowne 4 62
(George Baker) *trckd ldrs: stmbld sltly over 3f out: prog to go 2nd over 2f out: chal wl over 1f out: no ex ins fnl f* **16/1**

6026 **7** *shd* **Canford Lilli (IRE)**[13] 6649 3-9-0 72..............................(b) ShaneKelly 3 57
(Eve Johnson Houghton) *racd against rail: mde most: rdn and hdd 1f out: nt qckn and lost pls last 100yds* **7/2**[1]

0 **8** *7* **Notoursortdear**[75] 4521 4-9-1 0.. TomQueally 15 35
(John Gallagher) *nvr bttr than midfield on outer: shkn up over 2f out: lft bhd over 1f out* **20/1**

9 *1 ½* **Degas Bronze** 3-9-0 0... FergusSweeney 11 30
(Gary Moore) *dwlt: struggling in rr 1/2-way: modest late prog* **4/1**[2]

10 *nse* **Secret Striker** 4-9-1 0 SamHitchcott 13 30
(Ken Cunningham-Brown) *v.s.a and lost at least 10 l: ct up at bk of field after 2f: nvr a factor but passed a few late on* **33/1**

00 11 *1/2* **Hellarious**[23] 6317 3-9-5 0 TimmyMurphy 10 33
(Geoffrey Deacon) *settled in midfield: gng bttr than many 3f out: rdn and wknd 2f out* **66/1**

00 12 *3 1/2* **Autumn Chorus**[12] 6674 3-9-0 0 DannyBrock 5 17
(John Bridger) *pressed ldrs but sn pushed along: wknd qckly wl over 1f out* **200/1**

13 *2 1/2* **Monsieur Paddy** 3-9-2 0 GeorgeDowning(3) 2 14
(Tony Carroll) *dwlt: a wl in rr: rn green over 2f out: nvr a factor* **16/1**

P0 14 *4 1/2* **Royal Phoenix**[12] 6674 3-8-9 0 HectorCrouch(5) 7
(Gary Moore) *sn struggling in rr: bhd fnl 2f* **100/1**

15 *1 1/2* **Little Lizzie** 3-9-0 0 MartinLane 14
(Paddy Butler) *a wl in rr: last and struggling 1/2-way* **66/1**

16 *21* **Blue Mischief** 5-9-6 0 DanielMuscutt 12
(Miss Joey Ellis) *gd spd to chse ldr to over 2f out: rn v green and hanging bdly after: wknd rapidly and virtually p.u nr fin* **66/1**

1m 14.24s (1.24) **Going Correction** +0.10s/f (Good)
WFA 3 from 4yo+ 1lb **16** Ran SP% **122.4**
Speed ratings (Par 103): **95,93,92,92,91 90,90,81,79,79 78,74,70,64,62 34**
CSF £19.43 TOTE £4.00: £1.90, £2.20, £6.30; EX 20.70 Trifecta £236.30.
Owner One Too Many Partners **Bred** Knocktoran Stud **Trained** Kingston Warren, Oxon

FOCUS
The inner of the straight was dolled out 5yds at 6f and 2yds at the winning line, and the top bend was out 10yds from normal inner configuration, adding 36yds to race distances of 1m-plus. It was dry overnight and a dry but cool day, and the ground was given as just on the slow side. A modest-looking sprint maiden to begin. It's been nominally rated around the runner-up to her debut figure.

7012 BRITISH STALLION STUDS EBF MAIDEN STKS (DIV I) 1m 67y
2:20 (2:21) (Class 5) 2-Y-O **£3,234** (£962; £481; £240) **Stalls** Low

Form RPR

4 1 **Glorious Forever**[37] 5885 2-9-5 0 GeorgeBaker 9 78
(Ed Walker) *mde virtually all: stretched on over 3f out: stl gng easily over 2f out: pressed and shkn up over 1f out: gd battle after and jst asserted last 50yds* **13/8**[1]

05 2 *nk* **Jewel House**[22] 6368 2-9-5 0 FrankieDettori 8 77
(John Gosden) *trckd wnr 2f: settled in 3rd: sltly outpcd over 3f out: clsd to take 2nd again wl over 1f out and sn chalng: gd battle and w wnr tl nt qckn last 50yds* **4/1**[3]

06 3 *2* **Kasperenko**[9] 6777 2-9-5 0 ShaneKelly 10 73
(David Lanigan) *s.i.s: rcvrd to chse wnr after 2f tl wl over 1f out: one pce after* **3/1**[2]

4 *3 3/4* **Ahlan Bil Zain (FR)** 2-9-5 0 JimCrowley 2 64+
(David Simcock) *settled in midfield: outpcd over 3f out: shkn up to take modest 4th wl over 1f out: kpt on but no ch* **8/1**

5 *4 1/2* **Arab Moon** 2-9-5 0 MartinHarley 1 54
(William Knight) *nvr bttr than midfield: outpcd over 3f out: no imp ldrs aft* **25/1**

65 6 *1 1/4* **Rake's Progress**[7] 6828 2-9-2 0 JosephineGordon(3) 7 51
(Heather Main) *chsd ldrs: urged along and outpcd over 3f out: nvr on terms after* **80/1**

04 6 *dht* **Harry Beau**[24] 6288 2-9-5 0 PatDobbs 6 51
(Richard Hannon) *chsd ldrs: outpcd in 4th and pushed along over 3f out: steadily fdd* **16/1**

8 *1 1/4* **Cape Cruiser (USA)** 2-9-5 0 FMBerry 11 48
(Ralph Beckett) *dwlt: mostly in last pair: struggling fr 1/2-way: sn no ch: kpt on fnl f* **20/1**

60 9 *3/4* **Amadeus Rox (FR)**[41] 5740 2-9-5 0 WilliamTwiston-Davies 3 46
(Alan King) *nvr bttr than midfield: rn green and dropped to rr over 3f out: sn no ch* **25/1**

0 10 *5* **Poet's Wish**[24] 6297 2-9-5 0 TomQueally 4 35+
(George Margarson) *dwlt: mostly in last pair and rn green: nvr a factor* **40/1**

11 *1/2* **Sallee** 2-8-9 0 CiaranMckee(5) 5 29
(Adrian Wintle) *slowly away: mostly in last trio and rn green: nvr a factor* **150/1**

1m 45.18s (0.48) **Going Correction** +0.025s/f (Good) **11** Ran SP% **116.9**
Speed ratings (Par 95): **98,97,95,91,87 86,86,84,84,79 78**
CSF £7.62 TOTE £2.70: £1.10, £1.30, £1.20; EX 8.40 Trifecta £17.80.
Owner Kangyu International Racing (HK) Limited **Bred** Miss K Rausing **Trained** Upper Lambourn, Berks

FOCUS
This was run over 36yds further than advertised. The first three finishers filled the top three spots for most of the way, with the winner just about making all.

7013 BRITISH STALLION STUDS EBF MAIDEN STKS (DIV II) 1m 67y
2:50 (2:50) (Class 5) 2-Y-O **£3,234** (£962; £481; £240) **Stalls** Low

Form RPR

4 1 **Adamant (GER)**[27] 6211 2-9-5 0 RyanMoore 6 76
(Sir Michael Stoute) *mde all: racd against rail in st: hrd pressed 2f out: drvn over 1f out: styd on wl* **7/4**[1]

2 *1 1/4* **Munawer** 2-9-5 0 FrankieDettori 1 73+
(Hugo Palmer) *trckd ldrs: pushed along and lost pl sltly on inner over 2f out: renewed effrt over 1f out: chsd wnr ins fnl f: styd on but no imp* **7/1**

3 *1 3/4* **High Commander** 2-9-5 0 OisinMurphy 9 69+
(Andrew Balding) *nt that wl away but pushed up to trck wnr: rdn to chal 2f out: hld 1f out: one pce and sn lost 2nd* **25/1**

4 *1* **Another Eclipse (IRE)** 2-9-5 0 (b[1]) JimCrowley 4 67+
(David Simcock) *s.i.s: wl off the pce in 9th early: pushed along and stl wl in rr over 2f out: reminders over 1f out: styd on wl to snatch 4th nr fin* **20/1**

5 5 *shd* **Earthly (USA)**[16] 6577 2-9-5 0 FMBerry 2 67
(Ralph Beckett) *plld hrd early: trckd ldrs: tried to chal 2f out: nt qckn over 1f out: one pce after* **9/4**[2]

0 6 *hd* **Spirit Of Belle**[25] 6264 2-9-5 0 JFEgan 8 66
(Pat Phelan) *settled in rr: pushed along over 3f out: prog on wd outside over 2f out: nt qckn over 1f out: one pce after* **80/1**

7 *1* **Dubawi Prince** 2-9-5 0 AndreaAtzeni 3 64
(Roger Varian) *trckd ldrs: shkn up and tried to chal fr 2f out: lost pl jst over 1f out: kpt on again nr fin* **6/1**[3]

0 8 *nk* **Leapt**[45] 5600 2-9-5 0 GeorgeBaker 7 63+
(Roger Charlton) *hld up in midfield: prog on outer over 2f out: rdn and hld whn short of room over 1f out: fdd* **7/1**

6 9 *hd* **It's How We Roll (IRE)**[20] 6439 2-9-5 0 MichaelJMMurphy 5 63
(Charles Hills) *jst in tch in midfield: rdn over 3f out: prog over 2f out: tried to cl on ldrs over 1f out: wknd ins fnl f* **40/1**

10 *7* **Any Questions** 2-9-5 0 MartinHarley 10 47
(William Knight) *slowly away: rn green and mostly in last: brief effrt over 3f out: wknd over 2f out* **50/1**

1m 46.71s (2.01) **Going Correction** +0.025s/f (Good) **10** Ran SP% **120.7**
Speed ratings (Par 95): **90,88,87,86,85 85,84,84,84,77**
CSF £14.75 TOTE £2.20: £1.10, £3.00, £5.80; EX 14.90 Trifecta £127.90.
Owner Highclere Thoroughbred Racing - Tennyson **Bred** Mark Johnston Racing Ltd **Trained** Newmarket, Suffolk

FOCUS
This was run over 36yds further than advertised. Like the first leg, a front-running winner. The race average is helpful for setting the opening level.

7014 WAYNE STEWART 60TH BIRTHDAY CLAIMING STKS 1m 2f 7y
3:20 (3:20) (Class 5) 3-4-Y-O **£2,911** (£866; £432; £216) **Stalls** Centre

Form RPR

2506 1 **Skeaping**[24] 6294 3-9-3 77 (b[1]) PatDobbs 1 78
(Richard Hannon) *trckd ldr: led over 3f out: cruised clr against nr side rail fr over 2f out: easily* **2/1**[2]

1454 2 *5* **Cold Fusion (IRE)**[22] 6370 3-8-1 70 (p) JosephineGordon(3) 6 53
(Ed Vaughan) *chsd ldrs: pushed along over 3f out: outpcd and rdn over 2f out: kpt on to take 2nd last 100yds: no ch* **13/8**[1]

3 3 *hd* **Quetzaltenango (FR)**[20] 6443 3-8-4 0 HollieDoyle(5) 5 58
(J S Moore) *dwlt: bhd in last early: prog 1/2-way: chsd wnr 3f out but sn lft bhd: no ch after: lost 2nd last 100yds* **50/1**

2131 4 *4* **Boutan**[35] 5957 3-8-5 69 MitchGodwin(5) 3 51
(Bernard Llewellyn) *chsd clr ldrs: rdn over 3f out: effrt to dispute 2nd over 2f out: hanging u.str.p over 1f out: wknd* **5/2**[3]

5016 5 *6* **Adventure Zone (IRE)**[25] 6268 3-8-7 60 (b) KierenFox 4 36
(Lee Carter) *rousted to ld and set gd pce: hdd over 3f out: sn wknd* **20/1**

05 6 *2 3/4* **Rayanne**[39] 5811 3-8-3 0 KieranO'Neill 8 26
(Sarah Hollinshead) *a in last pair: struggling and rdn 4f out: sn no ch* **66/1**

2m 8.23s (-0.47) **Going Correction** +0.025s/f (Good) **6** Ran SP% **108.2**
Speed ratings (Par 103): **102,98,97,94,89 87**
CSF £5.17 TOTE £3.10: £1.20, £1.20; EX 6.20 Trifecta £75.00.Skeaping was claimed by M. Mckay for £16000. Cold Fusion was claimed by D.J. Flood £8000.
Owner Pall Mall Partners **Bred** Dunchurch Lodge Stud Company **Trained** East Everleigh, Wilts

FOCUS
This was run over 36yds further than advertised. A useful winner for the grade. The easy winner has been rated close to the balance of his form.

7015 ADAMSON CONSTRUCTION H'CAP 1m 3f 135y
3:50 (3:50) (Class 3) (0-90,90) 3-Y-O+ **£7,439** (£2,213; £1,106; £553) **Stalls** Centre

Form RPR

4214 1 **Wild Hacked (USA)**[30] 6110 3-9-4 **89** HarryBentley 5 101+
(Marco Botti) *trckd ldrs: nt clr run against rail jst over 2f out and again over 1f out: squeezed through and shkn up to ld ins fnl f: cleverly* **3/1**[1]

2312 2 *1/2* **Stratum**[21] 6417 3-9-2 **87** FrankieDettori 3 97
(John Gosden) *trckd ldr: led over 2f out: drvn over 1f out: hdd ins fnl f: r.o but safely hld* **7/2**[2]

1112 3 *3 3/4* **Athlon (IRE)**[32] 6048 3-9-5 **90** GeorgeBaker 9 94
(David Lanigan) *hld up in midfield: smooth prog over 2f out to chse ldng pair over 1f out: sn rdn and nt qckn: lost grnd fnl f* **9/2**[3]

3511 4 *3/4* **Niblawi (IRE)**[12] 6684 4-9-5 **88** HectorCrouch(5) 7 91
(Ismail Mohammed) *hld up in midfield: pushed along 3f out: nowhere to go fr 2f out tl swtchd sharply lft over 1f out: rdn and styd on but no ch to threaten* **10/1**

1004 5 *3/4* **Master Of Irony (IRE)**[22] 6379 4-9-11 **89** (b) OisinMurphy 15 91
(Ralph Beckett) *slowly away: hld up in last pair: shkn up 3f out: rdn and sme prog on wd outside whn carried lft over 1f out: kpt on but nvr able to threaten* **10/1**

5262 6 *hd* **Thames Knight**[8] 6804 4-8-8 **79** TylerSaunders(7) 8 80
(Marcus Tregoning) *hld up in last quartet: pushed along 4f out: kpt on quite wl fr 2f out: nrst fin* **25/1**

1410 7 *1* **Ravenous**[16] 6582 5-9-4 **82** KieranO'Neill 2 82
(Luke Dace) *dwlt: qckly rcvrd to press ldng pair: rdn 3f out: wknd 2f out* **20/1**

06 8 *1 1/2* **Zambeasy**[31] 6089 5-9-4 **82** WilliamTwiston-Davies 16 79
(Philip Hide) *led at str pce: hdd & wknd over 2f out* **25/1**

054 9 *3* **Silver Quay (IRE)**[17] 6544 4-9-7 **85** PatDobbs 6 77
(Richard Hannon) *hld up in last pair: shkn up 3f out: no real prog and nvr a factor* **40/1**

10/ 10 *nk* **Wrangler**[786] 5164 5-9-11 **89** RyanMoore 13 81
(William Haggas) *hld up in rr: rdn over 2f out: no great prog whn carried lft over 1f out: no ch after* **12/1**

5103 11 *11* **Point Of View (IRE)**[20] 6456 3-9-3 **88** AndreaAtzeni 10 62
(Roger Varian) *chsd ldrs: rdn wl over 2f out: wknd qckly wl over 1f out: eased* **10/1**

-333 12 *19* **Lovely Story (IRE)**[14] 6634 5-9-11 **89** [1] DaneO'Neill 14 33
(Seamus Durack) *slowly away: rcvrd into midfield after 2f: rdn and wknd over 3f out: t.o* **33/1**

2m 27.48s (-2.02) **Going Correction** +0.025s/f (Good)
WFA 3 from 4yo+ 7lb **12** Ran SP% **118.2**
Speed ratings (Par 107): **107,106,104,103,103 103,102,101,99,99 91,79**
CSF £12.27 CT £46.87 TOTE £3.70: £1.60, £1.90, £2.10; EX 15.90 Trifecta £40.90.
Owner Khalid Bin Ali Al Khalifa **Bred** Moyglare Stud **Trained** Newmarket, Suffolk
■ Stewards' Enquiry : Hector Crouch two-day ban: careless riding (Oct 17-18)

FOCUS
This was run over 36yds further than advertised. A decent handicap, but few got involved. The fourth has been rated close to his Redcar win.

7016 RUTLAND PARTNERS NURSERY H'CAP 1m 67y
4:20 (4:26) (Class 4) (0-85,82) 2-Y-O **£3,946** (£1,174; £586; £293) **Stalls** Low

Form RPR

010 1 **Geneva Convention (IRE)**[67] 4802 2-9-5 **80** RyanMoore 2 84
(Richard Hannon) *led 2f: pressed ldr: led against rail over 2f out: rdn over 1f out: drvn out fnl f and kpt on wl* **4/1**[2]

322 2 *1/2* **Calibration (IRE)**[19] 6486 2-9-7 **82** JimCrowley 3 85
(Martyn Meade) *hld up in rr: prog towards outer over 2f out: rdn over 1f out: tk 2nd ins fnl f: styd on but jst hld* **2/1**[1]

0521 3 *1 3/4* **Quothquan (FR)**[28] 6191 2-8-2 **68** GeorgeWood(5) 6 67
(Michael Madgwick) *t.k.h early: hld up in tch: prog on outer over 2f out: rdn and tried to cl over 1f out: kpt on same pce fnl f* **16/1**

10 **4** *nk* **Stellar Surprise**[16] 6575 2-9-1 **76**.................... OisinMurphy 1 74
(Stuart Williams) *trckd ldrs: prog to chse wnr wl over 1f out: sn rdn: hanging and fnd nil: lost 2nd and fdd ins fnl f* **4/1**[2]

0033 **5** *1 3/4* **Silver Link (IRE)**[11] 6713 2-8-12 **73**.................... SteveDrowne 9 67
(Marcus Tregoning) *slowly away: hld up in last: looking for a gap over 2f out: shkn up and prog to take 5th over 1f out: no imp after* **8/1**[3]

5205 **6** *3/4* **Famous Dynasty (IRE)**[24] 6289 2-8-6 **67**.................... KieranO'Neill 8 59
(Michael Blanshard) *hld up in rr: shkn up over 2f out: kpt on same pce fr over 1f out: n.d* **33/1**

040 **7** *shd* **City Dreamer (IRE)**[41] 5740 2-8-9 **70**.................... FergusSweeney 7 62
(Alan King) *hld up towards rr: rdn over 2f out: one pce and no threat fr over 1f out* **14/1**

624 **8** *5* **Mia Cara**[22] 6377 2-8-8 **69**.................... JFEgan 5 50
(David Evans) *plld hrd: trckd ldrs: rdn and lost pl 2f out: eased whn no ch fnl f* **25/1**

1025 **9** *3 3/4* **Fair Power (IRE)**[22] 6388 2-8-12 **78**.................... MitchGodwin[(5)] 4 50
(Sylvester Kirk) *t.k.h: trckd ldrs: wknd 2f out* **17/2**

510 **10** *13* **Manners Please**[22] 6377 2-8-11 **72**.................... FMBerry 10 14
(Ralph Beckett) *tk fierce hold: plld way through to ld after 2f: hdd over 2f out: wknd rapidly: t.o* **25/1**

1m 44.69s (-0.01) **Going Correction** +0.025s/f (Good) **10** Ran SP% **118.2**
Speed ratings (Par 97): **101,100,98,98,96 95,95,90,87,74**
CSF £12.30 CT £116.18 TOTE £4.20: £1.70, £1.20, £3.30; EX 11.80 Trifecta £76.20.
Owner Mrs J K Powell, W Drew and Partner **Bred** Stonecross Stud **Trained** East Everleigh, Wilts

FOCUS
This was run over 36yds further than advertised. A fair nursery. The runner-up has been rated as stepping up on his maiden form.

7017 HYTERA TWO-WAY RADIO H'CAP — 1m 67y
4:50 (4:53) (Class 4) (0-85,84) 3-Y-O+ **£4,690** (£1,395; £697; £348) **Stalls** Low

Form RPR

0-51 **1** **Tiercel**[12] 6674 3-9-2 **82**.................... AndreaAtzeni 14 93+
(Roger Varian) *hld up in last quintet and off the pce: stdy prog on outer over 2f out: rdn to ld last 75yds: hld on* **3/1**[1]

6024 **2** *hd* **Outback Ruler (IRE)**[24] 6300 4-9-2 **79**....................(p) OisinMurphy 12 87
(Clive Cox) *hld up in 8th: prog on outer over 2f out: rdn to ld ins fnl f: hdd last 75yds: kpt on: jst hld* **9/1**

1241 **3** *3/4* **Golden Wedding (IRE)**[25] 6254 4-9-0 **77**.................... CharlesBishop 3 83
(Eve Johnson Houghton) *trckd ldrs in 5th: wnt 2nd wl over 2f out: rdn to ld over 1f out: hdd ins fnl f: kpt on* **8/1**

604 **4** *1 1/2* **Fire Ship**[56] 5234 7-9-3 **80**....................(v) JimCrowley 4 83
(William Knight) *chsd ldrs in 7th: rdn and kpt on fnl 2f: nrst fin but unable to threaten* **5/1**[3]

4325 **5** *1 3/4* **Ghinia (IRE)**[19] 6483 5-9-0 **80**.................... RobHornby[(3)] 13 79
(Pam Sly) *won battle for ld fr wd draw and set gd pce: drvn and hdd over 1f out: steadily fdd* **9/1**

0004 **6** *shd* **Sydney Ruffdiamond**[23] 6339 4-9-5 **82**....................[1] ShaneKelly 7 81
(Richard Hughes) *hld up in rr quintet and off the pce: prog over 2f out: kpt on fr over 1f out: nvr pce to rch ldrs* **5/1**[3]

2523 **7** *4* **Harlequin Striker (IRE)**[20] 6442 4-9-7 **84**.................... JFEgan 6 73
(Dean Ivory) *trckd ldng trio: on terms and rdn 2f out: nt qckn and lost pl over 1f out: fdd* **10/1**

3000 **8** *1 1/2* **Directorship**[11] 6710 10-9-6 **83**.................... FergusSweeney 9 69
(Patrick Chamings) *hld up in rr quintet and off the pce: effrt over 3f out: nvr able to make significant prog* **33/1**

3542 **9** *2 1/4* **Aqua Ardens (GER)**[22] 6402 8-8-13 **76**.................... SteveDrowne 1 57
(George Baker) *hld up in last quintet and off the pce: shkn up 3f out: no rspnse and sn btn* **25/1**

414- **10** *3/4* **Hells Babe**[338] 7631 3-9-3 **83**.................... FMBerry 10 62
(Jonjo O'Neill) *fractious preliminaries: chsd ldrs in 6th: gng wl enough 3f out: rdn and fnd nil 2f out: wknd* **50/1**

3402 **11** *9* **Sky Ship**[14] 6628 3-9-2 **82**....................[1] RyanMoore 8 40
(Sir Michael Stoute) *hld up in last quintet and off the pce: sme prog over 2f out but sn u.p and only modest hdwy: nvr on terms and eased fnl f* **7/2**[2]

1302 **12** *shd* **Double Czech (IRE)**[95] 3802 5-8-7 **75**.................... MitchGodwin[(5)] 2 33
(Patrick Chamings) *t.k.h: pressed ldng pair tl wknd rapidly over 2f out* **20/1**

0150 **13** *3/4* **Just Be Lucky (IRE)**[35] 5972 4-9-0 **77**....................(p) MartinHarley 11 33
(Conor Dore) *chsd ldr to wl over 2f out: wknd rapidly* **66/1**

1m 43.67s (-1.03) **Going Correction** +0.025s/f (Good)
WFA 3 from 4yo+ 3lb **13** Ran SP% **121.1**
Speed ratings (Par 105): **106,105,105,103,101 101,97,96,93,93 84,84,83**
CSF £29.19 CT £209.23 TOTE £3.90: £1.60, £2.80, £2.90; EX 34.30 Trifecta £186.10.
Owner Prince A A Faisal **Bred** Nawara Stud Co Ltd **Trained** Newmarket, Suffolk

FOCUS
This was run over 36yds further than advertised. A competitive handicap. The runner-up has been rated to form.

7018 BEST PARTIES EVER STKS (AN AMATEUR RIDERS' H'CAP) — 5f 10y
5:20 (5:21) (Class 6) (0-65,65) 3-Y-O+ **£2,183** (£677; £338; £169) **Stalls** Low

Form RPR

5630 **1** **Frangarry (IRE)**[16] 6586 4-9-11 **55**....................(b) MissJCooley[(7)] 16 62
(Alan Bailey) *prom: led in centre over 1f out: in command after: pushed out and ld dwindled nr fin but nvr in danger* **20/1**

2345 **2** *3/4* **Head Space (IRE)**[13] 6653 8-10-9 **65**.................... MissEMacKenzie[(5)] 13 69
(David Evans) *sn detached in last: rapid prog over 1f out: r.o to take 2nd nr fin: nt rch wnr* **14/1**

1435 **3** *3/4* **Beau Mistral (IRE)**[7] 6832 7-10-1 **59**....................(b) MrGGilbertson[(7)] 14 61
(Tony Carroll) *led in centre to over 1f out: hld by wnr after: lost 2nd nr fin* **11/1**

4022 **4** *nk* **Time Medicean**[21] 6410 10-10-4 **62**.................... MissSAColl[(7)] 6 63
(Tony Carroll) *towards rr: prog over 1f out: styd on fnl f and nrly snatched 3rd* **8/1**

0401 **5** *nk* **Zipedeedodah (IRE)**[13] 6660 4-10-6 **64**....................(t) MrsCPownall[(7)] 4 63
(Joseph Tuite) *prom: urged along fr 2f out: ch of a pl fnl f: kpt on* **12/1**

U356 **6** *2* **Quality Art (USA)**[75] 4529 8-10-4 **60**.................... MissPBridgwater[(5)] 12 52
(Simon Hodgson) *towards rr on wd outside: kpt on fr over 1f out: n.d* **33/1**

5334 **7** *shd* **Go Amber Go**[22] 6363 4-10-6 **57**.................... MrPMillman 5 49
(Rod Millman) *towards rr: shkn up and one pce fr over 1f out: no imp ldrs* **11/2**[1]

0144 **8** *3/4* **Vincenzo Coccotti (USA)**[33] 6017 4-10-4 **62**.................... MrRWithey[(7)] 15 51
(Ken Cunningham-Brown) *s.i.s: in tch in midfield: rdn 2f out: no prog over 1f out: fdd* **7/1**[3]

2006 **9** *1/2* **Excellent Aim**[62] 4980 9-10-6 **62**.................... MissKMargarson[(5)] 8 49
(George Margarson) *hld up wl in* **50/1**

0106 **10** *1/2* **Coiste Bodhar (IRE)**[65] 4874 5-10-8 **64**.................... MrKLocking[(5)] 3 50
(Scott Dixon) **14/1**

255 **11** *1/2* **Pharoh Jake**[25] 6269 8-10-5 **63**.................... MissTannyaBagoban[(7)] 1 47
(John Bridger) **10/1**

2000 **12** *1 1/4* **Sir Geoffrey (IRE)**[18] 6509 10-10-3 **54**....................(b) MrSWalker 11 33
(Scott Dixon) **10/1**

2336 **13** *shd* **Limerick Lord (IRE)**[41] 5734 4-10-5 **56**....................(p) MrRBirkett 2 35
(Julia Feilden) **6/1**[2]

4120 **14** *1* **Oscars Journey**[52] 5369 6-10-7 **65**....................(v) MrSSayers[(7)] 10 40
(J R Jenkins) **10/1**

1m 0.5s (0.20) **Going Correction** +0.10s/f (Good) **14** Ran SP% **119.6**
Speed ratings (Par 101): **102,100,99,99,98 95,95,94,93,92 91,89,89,87**
CSF £271.29 CT £1956.11 TOTE £23.40: £7.20, £3.80, £4.20; EX 459.00 Trifecta £6035.30.
Owner Dr S P Hargreaves **Bred** Carrigbeg Stud & David Powell **Trained** Newmarket, Suffolk
■ Jess Cooley's first winner.

FOCUS
For the first time on this eight-race card - in the finale - the runners shunned the near rail, racing more up the middle, and the finish was dominated by high-drawn runners. The first two dictate a straightforward level.
T/Plt: £8.10 to a £1 stake. Pool: £76530.93, 6876.85 winning units. T/Qpdt: £4.60 to a £1 stake. Pool: £6455.59, 1028.77 winning units. **Jonathan Neesom**

7019 - 7026a (Foreign Racing) - See Raceform Interactive

6822 COLOGNE (R-H)
Monday, October 3

OFFICIAL GOING: Turf: good

7027a BHF-BANK HERBSTPREIS (LISTED RACE) (3YO+) (TURF) — 7f
2:55 (12:00) 3-Y-O+ **£10,294** (£4,779; £2,205; £1,102)

RPR

1 **Swift Approval (IRE)**[37] 5906 4-9-0 0....................(p) AndreasSuborics 7 102
(Kevin Ryan) *mde all: led: pressed thrght: 1l clr and rdn turning for home: edgd lft into centre of crse 2 1/2f out: styd on gamely u.p fnl f: jst hld on* **69/10**

2 *hd* **Antalya (GER)**[15] 6611 5-8-10 0.................... AdriedeVries 12 97
(Markus Klug, Germany) **179/10**

3 *nk* **Shining Emerald**[22] 5-9-6 0.................... JozefBojko 5 106
(A Wohler, Germany) **7/5**[1]

4 *1/2* **Schang (GER)**[36] 5943 3-9-4 0.................... FilipMinarik 1 104
(P Vovcenko, Germany) **4/1**[2]

5 *1/2* **Making Trouble (GER)**[36] 5943 4-9-0 0.................... OliverWilson 11 97
(D Moser, Germany) **47/1**

6 *1 1/4* **Donna Doria (GER)**[22] 3-8-8 0.................... MaximPecheur 8 89
(J Hirschberger, Germany) **50/1**

7 *hd* **Mc Queen (FR)**[36] 5943 4-9-3 0.................... StephenHellyn 10 97
(Yasmin Almenrader, Germany) **27/1**

8 *hd* **Guavia (GER)**[22] 4-8-10 0.................... AndraschStarke 2 89
(P Schiergen, Germany) **43/5**

9 *hd* **Forgino (GER)**[36] 5943 5-9-3 0.................... DanielePorcu 6 95
(T Potters, Germany) **22/5**[3]

10 *1/2* **Princess Asta (FR)**[22] 3-8-11 0....................(b) KoenClijmans 9 89
(Mario Hofer, Germany) **238/10**

11 *hd* **Schutzenpost (GER)**[43] 5695 4-9-0 0.................... MichaelCadeddu 4 91
(J Hirschberger, Germany) **234/10**

12 *3/4* **Lovemedo (FR)**[33] 4-8-10 0.................... LukasDelozier 3 85
(H-A Pantall, France) **179/10**

WIN (incl. 10 euro stake): 79. PLACES: 30, 28, 15. SF: 1,555.
Owner Middleham Park Racing XLIX **Bred** Mrs Jean Brennan **Trained** Hambleton, N Yorks

5453 HOPPEGARTEN (R-H)
Monday, October 3

OFFICIAL GOING: Turf: good

7028a PFERDEWETTEN.DE 26 PREIS DER DEUTSCHEN EINHEIT (GROUP 3) (3YO+) (TURF) — 1m 2f
3:50 (12:00) 3-Y-O+ **£33,088** (£11,764; £5,147; £3,308; £1,838)

RPR

1 **Devastar (GER)**[37] 5904 4-9-4 0.................... MartinSeidl 1 106
(Markus Klug, Germany) *chsd ldng pair: rowed along in pursuit of clr ldr over 2f out: r.o u.p fnl f: grad reeled in ldr to get up fnl strides* **10/1**

2 *1/2* **Capitano (GER)**[43] 5696 3-9-0 0.................... AlexanderPietsch 7 106
(J Hirschberger, Germany) *led: kicked 3l clr over 2f out: sn rdn and responded: styd on fnl f: hdd fnl strides* **74/10**[2]

3 *3/4* **Global Storm (GER)** 3-9-0 0.................... BauyrzhanMurzabayev 6 105
(R Dzubasz, Germany) *a cl up: sltly outpcd 2f out: sn rdn and no immediate imp: styd on fr over 1f out: nt pce to chal* **153/10**

4 *nk* **Brisanto**[49] 5500 4-9-4 0.................... IanFerguson 8 103
(M G Mintchev, Germany) *trckd ldr on outer: nt qckn whn tempo increased over 2f out: styd on appr fnl f: nvr quite on terms* **9/1**[3]

5 *nk* **Wai Key Star (GER)**[43] 5696 3-9-0 0.................... EduardoPedroza 3 103
(A Wohler, Germany) *w.w in midfield: crept on to heels of ldrs 3f out: rdn and no imp over 2f out: styd on fnl f: nvr nrr* **2/5**[1]

6 *3/4* **Palace Prince (GER)**[37] 5904 4-9-4 0.................... AndreasHelfenbein 5 101
(Andreas Lowe, Germany) *hld up towards rr: rdn and hdwy over 1 1/2f out: kpt on ins fnl f: nt pce to trble ldrs* **99/10**

7 *1/2* **Palang (USA)**[83] 4253 4-9-4 0.................... DarioVargiu 4 100
(Andreas Lowe, Germany) *w.w in midfield: rdn and kpt on at same pce fnl 1 1/2f* **231/10**

8 *1* **Bravo Girl (FR)**[106] 4-9-1 0.................... MarcLerner 9 95
(Waldemar Hickst, Germany) *w.w in rr: outpcd and adrift 3 1/2f out: rdn and clsd 2f out: kpt on fnl f wout ever being in contention* **223/10**

9 *2 1/2* **Apoleon (GER)**[58] 6-9-4 0.................... RobinWeber 2 93
(Frau Anna Schleusner-Fruhriep, Germany) *settled in fnl pair: no hdwy u.p over 2f out: plugged on at one pce* **204/10**

2m 7.0s (0.30)
WFA 3 from 4yo+ 5lb **9** Ran SP% **130.8**
WIN (incl. 10 euro stake): 110. PLACES: 28, 24, 27. SF: 577.
Owner Gestut Park Wiedingen **Bred** Gestut Park Wiedingen **Trained** Germany

6693 MAISONS-LAFFITTE (R-H)

Monday, October 3

OFFICIAL GOING: Turf: good

7029a PRIX CHARLES LAFFITTE (LISTED RACE) (3YO FILLIES) (TURF) 1m 2f 110y

3:05 (12:00) 3-Y-0 **£20,220** (£8,088; £6,066; £4,044; £2,022)

RPR

1 **Palinodie (FR)**[32] 6069 3-9-0 0 Pierre-CharlesBoudot 1 105+
(E Leenders, France) **83/10**[3]

2 1/2 **Switching (USA)**[32] 6069 3-9-0 0 MickaelBarzalona 10 104
(A Fabre, France) *hld up in midfield on outer: moved on to heels of ldng trio under a tight hold wl bef 1/2-way: qcknd to ld 1 1/2f out: drvn and styd on fnl f: hdd 75yds out: no ex* **33/10**[2]

3 2 **Deremah (USA)**[19] 6497 3-9-0 0 ChristopheSoumillon 6 100
(A De Royer-Dupre, France) **17/10**[1]

4 nk **Lily Passion**[24] 3-9-0 0 RonanThomas 9 100
(P Bary, France) **11/1**

5 hd **Etonnez Moi (IRE)**[19] 6497 3-9-0 0 GregoryBenoist 2 99
(Mme Pia Brandt, France) **11/1**

6 2 1/2 **Very Dashing**[54] 5307 3-9-0 0 FrederikTylicki 11 94
(Luca Cumani) *settled in fnl quartet on outer: next to last and scrubbed along 2f out: styd on fr 1 1/2f out: run flattened out ins fnl f: nvr in contention* **12/1**

7 snk **Fresh Strike (IRE)**[32] 6069 3-9-0 0 MaximeGuyon 8 94
(F Head, France) **12/1**

8 1 1/2 **Olala (GER)**[29] 3-9-0 0 AntoineHamelin 4 91
(M Figge, Germany) **14/1**

9 1 3/4 **Restiana (FR)**[112] 3241 3-9-3 0 (b) JulienAuge 3 91
(P Sogorb, France) **30/1**

10 1 3/4 **Edya**[19] 6497 3-9-0 0 (p) CristianDemuro 5 84
(G Botti, France) **18/1**

2m 11.6s (131.60) **10** Ran SP% **118.3**

WIN (incl. 1 euro stake): 9.30. PLACES: 1.70, 1.40, 1.40. DF: 11.80. SF: 41.60.

Owner Douglas McMillan **Bred** Ecurie Maulepaire **Trained** France

7030a PRIX DE BONNEVAL (LISTED RACE) (3YO+) (TURF) 5f 110y

4:05 (12:00) 3-Y-0+ **£19,117** (£7,647; £5,735; £3,823; £1,911)

RPR

1 **The Right Man**[57] 5217 4-9-0 0 Francois-XavierBertras 11 106+
(D Guillemin, France) **39/10**[2]

2 1 3/4 **Spirit Quartz (IRE)**[16] 6574 8-9-6 0 (p) ChristopheSoumillon 7 106
(Robert Cowell) *sn led: swtchd ins to stands' rail after 1 1/2f: rdn and hdd wl over 1 1/2f out: styd on same pce fnl f* **57/10**[3]

3 nk **Spiritfix**[22] 6391 3-8-10 0 MaximeGuyon 4 96
(A Fabre, France) **32/5**

4 1/2 **Saon Secret (FR)**[21] 6-9-0 0 (b) UmbertoRispoli 10 97
(T Castanheira, France) **11/1**

5 1 1/4 **Immediate**[11] 6699 4-8-10 0 VincentCheminaud 6 89
(Robert Cowell) *w.w in rr: rdn and n.m.r 1/2-way: drvn and styd on fr 1f out: nrest at fin* **34/1**

6 3/4 **Largent Du Bonheur (FR)**[22] 6391 3-9-0 0 ThierryThulliez 5 92
(M Delzangles, France) **18/1**

7 shd **Blue Soave (FR)**[25] 6272 8-9-0 0 TonyPiccone 12 90
(F Chappet, France) **15/1**

8 snk **Walec**[36] 5949 4-9-4 0 Pierre-CharlesBoudot 3 94
(P Sogorb, France) **12/5**[1]

9 1/2 **Royal Prize**[32] 6-9-0 0 (b) AlexisBadel 2 88
(Mme M Bollack-Badel, France) **9/1**

10 nk **Pupa Di Saronno (FR)**[65] 4905 5-8-10 0 CristianDemuro 9 83
(H-A Pantall, France) **19/1**

11 snk **Yakaba (FR)**[36] 5949 3-8-10 0 AurelienLemaitre 1 84
(F Head, France) **22/1**

1m 5.0s (-2.30) **11** Ran SP% **120.3**

WIN (incl. 1 euro stake): 4.90. Places: 1.90, 2.60, 2.40. DF: 18.00. SF: 22.50..

Owner Pegase Bloodstock **Bred** Mme D Wigan **Trained** France

7031 - (Foreign Racing) - See Raceform Interactive

6887 BRIGHTON (L-H)

Tuesday, October 4

OFFICIAL GOING: Good (8.1)

Wind: Fresh, across towards stand Weather: Sunny

7032 GREENEKING.CO.UK MAIDEN AUCTION STKS 6f 209y

2:10 (2:14) (Class 5) 2-Y-0 **£3,234** (£962; £481; £240) **Stalls** Centre

Form RPR

0232 1 **Getgo**[20] 6473 2-9-0 75 (b) ShaneKelly 8 75
(David Lanigan) *sn in tch: wnt 2nd over 2f out: rdn to ld 1f out: in control fnl 50yds* **1/1**[1]

02 2 nk **Otomo**[22] 6404 2-8-10 0 SilvestreDeSousa 1 68
(Philip Hide) *led tl 1f out: kpt on u.p: hld nr fin* **2/1**[2]

063 3 8 **All About The Pace**[40] 5809 2-8-4 64 KieranO'Neill 5 41
(Mark Usher) *in tch: rdn over 2f out: sn outpcd* **10/1**[3]

4 shd **Fox Mint** 2-8-9 0 ow1 AdamBeschizza 4 45
(Stuart Williams) *dwlt: outpcd: bhd tl styd on fnl 2f* **25/1**

0 5 3 1/2 **Wouldntitbelovely (IRE)**[12] 6696 2-8-9 0 RyanTate 2 36
(Richard Hughes) *prom tl hrd rdn and wknd wl over 1f out* **16/1**

0 6 1 1/2 **Sayif Magic**[20] 6473 2-8-13 0 TomMarquand 3 36
(George Scott) *sn chsng ldr: wknd over 2f out* **12/1**

0 7 3 1/2 **Banta Bay**[23] 6369 2-8-11 0 KierenFox 7 24
(John Best) *outpcd: sn bhd* **22/1**

1m 22.22s (-0.88) **Going Correction** -0.15s/f (Firm) **7** Ran SP% **114.2**

Speed ratings (Par 95): **99,98,89,89,85 83,79**

CSF £3.13 TOTE £1.70: £1.10, £1.60; EX 3.40 Trifecta £9.80.

Owner The Getgo Partnership **Bred** Cheveley Park Stud Ltd **Trained** Newmarket, Suffolk

■ Champagne Reign was withdrawn. Price at time of withdrawal 33/1. Rule 4 does not apply

FOCUS

The going was officially good (GoingStick 8.1) and the winning rider in the opener described it as "lovely good ground". Rail dolled out between the 6f and 2.5f markers, adding 4yds to all race distances. A moderate maiden auction to start in which they bet 10-1 bar two. There was a delay to the start when Champagne Reign got rid of her rider and ran loose all the way around the track. The big two in the market fought out the finish and came clear of the rest. The runner-up has been rated similar to his level here last time.

7033 ALAN BLAIR CELEBRATION OF LIFE NURSERY H'CAP 6f 209y

2:40 (2:43) (Class 5) (0-75,75) 2-Y-0 **£3,234** (£962; £481; £240) **Stalls** Centre

Form RPR

0542 1 **Juanito Chico (IRE)**[9] 6800 2-9-2 70[1] SilvestreDeSousa 10 75
(William Jarvis) *dwlt: sn rcvrd and led: mde rest: rdn and hld on wl fnl 2f* **5/2**[1]

0512 2 1/2 **Inner Circle (IRE)**[33] 6060 2-9-5 73 PatDobbs 7 77
(Richard Hannon) *chsd wnr: kpt on u.p fnl 2f: a hld* **14/1**

11 3 2 3/4 **Lord Clenaghcastle (IRE)**[27] 6236 2-9-0 73 HectorCrouch(5) 2 69
(Gary Moore) *hld up in 6th: rdn 2f out: styd on fnl f* **8/1**

2315 4 nk **Tap Tap Boom**[68] 4802 2-9-5 73 SteveDrowne 8 68
(George Baker) *chsd ldrs: rdn 2f out: one pce* **6/1**[3]

0544 5 1/2 **Swag (IRE)**[17] 6575 2-9-5 73 (t) TomMarquand 5 67
(Richard Hannon) *prom: hrd rdn over 1f out: one pce* **8/1**

532 6 1 **Challow (IRE)**[57] 5239 2-9-3 71 (b[1]) LiamKeniry 9 62
(Sylvester Kirk) *dwlt: hld up in 7th on outer: rdn 2f out: nvr able to chal* **8/1**

613 7 1/2 **Chaplin (FR)**[39] 5821 2-9-7 75 ShaneKelly 4 68
(Richard Hughes) *hld up in rr: nt clr run 2f out: fnd gap and effrt over 1f out: nvr rchd ldrs* **14/1**

1204 8 shd **Hedging (IRE)**[39] 5821 2-9-4 72 JimCrowley 1 62
(Eve Johnson Houghton) *in tch: outpcd 2f out: sn btn* **14/1**

2513 9 2 1/4 **Law Power**[9] 6800 2-9-6 74 (b) RyanPowell 3 66
(Sir Mark Prescott Bt) *s.i.s: bhd: sme hdwy into midfield whn hmpd on rail ins fnl f: eased* **9/2**[2]

1m 22.32s (-0.78) **Going Correction** -0.15s/f (Firm) **9** Ran SP% **114.4**

Speed ratings (Par 95): **98,97,94,93,93 92,91,91,88**

CSF £39.58 CT £246.05 TOTE £3.20: £1.40, £3.60, £2.40; EX 39.00 Trifecta £159.00.

Owner Tony Verrier **Bred** Miss Catherine Monaghan **Trained** Newmarket, Suffolk

FOCUS

Rail movement added 4yds to race distance. An ordinary nursery and a race where few got into it, with the first two holding those positions virtually throughout. The front two have been rated as taking a step forward.

7034 BRITISH STALLION STUDS EBF MAIDEN STKS 7f 214y

3:10 (3:11) (Class 5) 2-Y-0 **£3,557** (£1,058; £529; £264) **Stalls** Centre

Form RPR

4 1 **Camerone (IRE)**[20] 6480 2-9-0 0 FMBerry 1 70+
(Ralph Beckett) *broke wl: sn stdd bk to 5th: drvn along over 2f out: styd on to ld fnl 50yds* **11/4**[2]

4 2 1/2 **Harbour Rock**[32] 6085 2-9-5 0 OisinMurphy 5 74
(David Simcock) *chsd ldr after 2f: carried rt over 2f out: led over 1f out: hung lft: hdd and outpcd fnl 50yds* **3/1**[3]

53 3 1 1/4 **Vanderbilt (IRE)**[36] 5959 2-9-5 0 JimCrowley 6 73
(Martyn Meade) *hanging lft early: sn led: edgd rt over 2f out: hdd and edgd lft over 1f out: jst hld whn n.m.r ins fnl f* **7/4**[1]

53 4 1 1/2 **Romanor**[19] 6523 2-9-5 0 GeorgeBaker 2 68
(Ed Walker) *dwlt: hld up in rr: rdn over 2f out: styd on fr over 1f out* **8/1**

05 5 hd **Chocolate Box (IRE)**[19] 6523 2-9-5 0 PatCosgrave 4 67
(Luca Cumani) *cl up tl hrd rdn and btn 2f out* **16/1**

5 6 7 **Khattar**[24] 6314 2-9-5 0 (t) DaneO'Neill 3 51
(Hugo Palmer) *dwlt: sn prom: wknd 2f out* **14/1**

1m 35.43s (-0.57) **Going Correction** -0.15s/f (Firm) **6** Ran SP% **111.7**

Speed ratings (Par 95): **96,95,94,92,92 85**

CSF £11.28 TOTE £3.70: £2.00, £1.80; EX 14.50 Trifecta £34.40.

Owner H H Sheikh Mohammed Bin Khalifa Al Thani **Bred** Al Shahania Stud **Trained** Kimpton, Hants

■ Stewards' Enquiry : Oisin Murphy caution: careless riding

FOCUS

Rail movement added 4yds to race distance. Quite an interesting little staying maiden. The level is fluid, but the third has been rated a bit below form.

7035 BRIGHTON RACES OKTOBERFEST 13TH OCT H'CAP (DIV I) 7f 214y

3:40 (3:40) (Class 6) (0-65,65) 3-Y-0+ **£2,587** (£770; £384; £192) **Stalls** Centre

Form RPR

4054 1 **Beatbybeatbybeat**[24] 6337 3-9-0 61 (v[1]) SilvestreDeSousa 7 71+
(Ismail Mohammed) *prom: led 2f out: rdn clr 1f out: comf* **7/2**[1]

1351 2 3 3/4 **Edge (IRE)**[14] 6651 5-8-12 56 (b) WilliamTwiston-Davies 9 59
(Bernard Llewellyn) *hld up towards rr: n.m.r over 2f out: hdwy over 1f out: r.o to take 2nd ins fnl f* **5/1**[3]

3640 3 2 **Wasseem (IRE)**[91] 3982 3-9-4 65 (tp) MartinHarley 8 62
(Simon Crisford) *led tl 2f out: wknd fnl f* **9/1**

0110 4 2 1/4 **African Showgirl**[21] 6444 3-9-3 64 SteveDrowne 6 56
(George Baker) *bhd: rdn over 3f out: styd on fr over 1f out* **7/1**

3314 5 1 1/2 **Music Major**[15] 6629 3-9-2 63 AdamBeschizza 10 51
(Michael Attwater) *in tch tl outpcd 2f out* **9/2**[2]

2304 6 nk **Party Thyme**[14] 6646 3-8-11 61 LouisSteward(3) 2 48
(Chris Wall) *chsd wnr tl 2f out: sn wknd* **7/1**

440 7 nse **Tee It Up Tommo (IRE)**[27] 6241 7-9-0 63 (t) HectorCrouch(5) 4 50
(Daniel Steele) *t.k.h in rr: rdn 3f out: n.d* **11/1**

0000 8 2 **Mr Marchwood**[17] 6593 3-8-8 55 (b[1]) LiamKeniry 3 38
(Sylvester Kirk) *rdn early: sn in midfield: hrd rdn and wknd 2f out* **16/1**

1140 9 1 **Prince Of Cardamom (IRE)**[36] 5954 4-9-1 59 (p) RyanTate 1 39
(Jonathan Geake) *chsd ldrs tl wknd 2f out* **8/1**

1m 34.33s (-1.67) **Going Correction** -0.15s/f (Firm)

WFA 3 from 4yo+ 3lb **9** Ran SP% **117.4**

Speed ratings (Par 101): **102,98,96,94,93 92,92,90,89**

CSF £21.34 CT £146.31 TOTE £3.90: £1.50, £1.90, £3.50; EX 16.30 Trifecta £77.50.

Owner Saif Ali & Saeed H Al Tayer **Bred** Rabbah Bloodstock Limited **Trained** Newmarket, Suffolk

FOCUS

Rail movement added 4yds to race distance. A moderate handicap. The winner has been rated back to the level he was at when winning this race last year.

7036 BRIGHTON RACES OKTOBERFEST 13TH OCT H'CAP (DIV II) 7f 214y

4:10 (4:10) (Class 6) (0-65,64) 3-Y-0+ **£2,587** (£770; £384; £192) **Stalls** Centre

Form RPR

0111 1 **Multitask**[14] 6657 6-9-1 63 HectorCrouch(5) 1 72
(Gary Moore) *t.k.h and restrained: mde all: rdn and hld on wl fnl 2f* **5/4**[1]

6421 **2** 1/2 **Zlatan (IRE)**8 6826 3-9-4 64 6ex....(p) JimCrowley 4 72
(Ed de Giles) *cl up: chsd wnr over 1f out: hung bdly lft: unable qck fnl 100yds* **7/2**2

0421 **3** 2 1/2 **Bloodsweatandtears**22 6407 8-9-5 62.... AmirQuinn 10 64
(William Knight) *dwlt: towards rr: hdwy 2f out: hung lft: styd on to take 3rd ins fnl f* **5/1**3

5033 **4** 2 1/4 **Where Next**21 6441 3-9-2 62....(p) DaneO'Neill 8 59
(Henry Candy) *plld hrd early: chsd wnr tl outpcd and hung lft over 1f out* **16/1**

0056 **5** 2 3/4 **Hawk Moth (IRE)**22 6407 8-9-0 57....(b) WilliamTwiston-Davies 6 48
(John Spearing) *dwlt: bhd: rdn 2f out: sme late hdwy* **16/1**

4550 **6** hd **Hereward The Wake**22 6408 3-8-11 62.... MitchGodwin(5) 9 52
(Sylvester Kirk) *prom: lost pl and towards rr over 3f out: styd on same pce u.p fnl 2f* **25/1**

6235 **7** 2 **Fairy Mist (IRE)**5 6894 9-8-13 56....(b) DannyBrock 2 42
(John Bridger) *prom tl wknd 2f out* **14/1**

0660 **8** 4 1/2 **Siri**19 6501 3-9-4 64.... CharlesBishop 3 39
(Mick Channon) *a bhd* **14/1**

0002 **9** 1/2 **Zeteah**29 6188 6-8-0 50 oh4.... MillyNaseb(7) 5 24
(Tony Carroll) *mid-div tl wknd over 2f out* **14/1**

1m 34.31s (-1.69) **Going Correction** -0.15s/f (Firm)
WFA 3 from 4yo+ 3lb **9** Ran SP% **118.9**
Speed ratings (Par 101): **102,101,99,96,94 93,91,87,86**
CSF £5.76 CT £16.80 TOTE £2.50: £1.30, £1.10, £1.80; EX 8.00 Trifecta £16.10.
Owner Power Geneva Ltd **Bred** Mrs L N Harmes **Trained** Lower Beeding, W Sussex

FOCUS
Rail movement added 4yds to race distance. Three dominated the market in this division and they finished 1-2-3. The winning time was almost identical to the first leg.

7037 GIN & JAZZ CHRISTMAS PARTY NIGHTS H'CAP 1m 1f 209y
4:40 (4:40) (Class 6) (0-65,65) 3-Y-O+ **£2,587** (£770; £384; £192) **Stalls** High

Form RPR

3610 **1** **Becca Campbell (IRE)**14 6646 3-8-12 63....(p) HollieDoyle(5) 1 72
(Eve Johnson Houghton) *hld up in rr: hdwy 3f out: led 1f out: drvn out* **9/2**3

5010 **2** 3 **Maria's Choice (IRE)**14 6659 7-9-9 64....(v) CharlesBishop 3 67
(Jim Best) *chsd ldrs: wnt 2nd 1f out: kpt on same pce* **14/1**

000- **3** 3 1/2 **Meddlesome**384 6429 3-9-2 62.... RyanPowell 11 58
(Sir Mark Prescott Bt) *prom: drvn along and lost pl over 3f out: styd on fnl f* **14/1**

3560 **4** 2 **Live Dangerously**14 6662 6-9-7 62.... DannyBrock 8 55+
(John Bridger) *t.k.h: chsd ldr: led after 3f and set str pce: hdd & wknd 1f out* **6/1**

66-4 **5** 3/4 **Mr Rock (IRE)**78 4459 5-9-10 65....(p) PatCosgrave 7 56
(George Baker) *towards rr: sme hdwy on inner 2f out: no further prog* **3/1**1

5640 **6** hd **Earthwindorfire**36 5954 5-9-3 63....1 PaddyPilley(5) 2 54
(Geoffrey Deacon) *led for 3f: chsd ldr after: rdn 4f out: wknd over 1f out* **9/1**

5050 **7** 1/2 **Victor's Bet (SPA)**37 5925 7-9-6 61.... WilliamTwiston-Davies 10 51
(Ralph J Smith) *dwlt: bhd: drvn along over 2f out: nvr rchd ldrs* **20/1**

5306 **8** 1 **Tasteofexcellence (IRE)**26 6265 3-9-0 60.... SteveDrowne 5 48
(Roger Ingram) *a towards rr* **12/1**

3120 **9** 5 **Pastoral Star**37 5923 3-9-3 63.... JimCrowley 6 41
(Jim Boyle) *mid-div tl wknd over 2f out* **12/1**

4064 **10** 20 **Guantoshol (IRE)**21 6444 5-9-8 63.... RobertWinston 4 3
(Ian Williams) *s.s: sn in midfield: wknd over 2f out* **4/1**2

2m 0.71s (-2.89) **Going Correction** -0.15s/f (Firm)
WFA 3 from 5yo+ 5lb **10** Ran SP% **120.9**
Speed ratings (Par 101): **105,102,99,98,97 97,97,96,92,76**
CSF £68.18 CT £832.34 TOTE £5.40: £1.40, £5.10, £3.30; EX 110.10 Trifecta £2585.50 Part Won..
Owner Miss E Johnson Houghton **Bred** Lynn Lodge Stud **Trained** Blewbury, Oxon

FOCUS
Rail movement added 4yds to race distance. Another moderate handicap in which the leaders looked to go off too quick. The runner-up has been rated to his turf form earlier this year.

7038 FRIGHT FESTIVAL 29TH OCT H'CAP 5f 213y
5:10 (5:10) (Class 6) (0-60,64) 3-Y-O+ **£2,587** (£770; £384; £192) **Stalls** Centre

Form RPR

2205 **1** **Essaka (IRE)**23 6363 4-9-5 58.... JimCrowley 6 65
(Tony Carroll) *dwlt: t.k.h and sn in midfield: hdwy 2f out: led 1f out: rdn out* **7/2**1

3001 **2** hd **Virile (IRE)**5 6894 5-9-6 64 6ex....(bt) MitchGodwin(5) 10 70
(Sylvester Kirk) *dwlt: hld up in rr: swtchd wd and gd hdwy over 1f out: chal ins fnl f: r.o* **4/1**2

4330 **3** 1 3/4 **Andalusite**13 6680 3-9-4 58....(p) RoystonFfrench 7 59
(Ed McMahon) *chsd ldrs: outpcd 2f out: styd on fnl f* **7/1**

-030 **4** 1/2 **Zippy**13 6677 3-9-4 58.... SteveDrowne 11 57
(Daniel Kubler) *mid-div tl styd on fnl 2f* **14/1**

4465 **5** 2 1/4 **Arlecchino's Rock**17 6592 3-9-5 59....(p) DannyBrock 4 52+
(Mark Usher) *led at gd pce tl 1f out: wknd ins fnl f* **6/1**

0600 **6** 1 1/4 **Back To Love (CAN)**25 6290 3-7-13 46 oh1....1 MillyNaseb(7) 13 35
(Mark Gillard) *towards rr tl rdn and styd on fnl 2f* **66/1**

6404 **7** shd **Captain Ryan**8 6832 5-9-0 58.... PaddyPilley(5) 12 46
(Geoffrey Deacon) *in tch: chal 2f out: wknd fnl f* **12/1**

1324 **8** 1 1/2 **Valmina**36 9-9-2 60....(t) HectorCrouch(5) 2 44
(Philip Hide) *towards rr: sme hdwy 2f out: hrd rdn and no ex fnl f* **14/1**

0023 **9** shd **Oat Couture**13 6677 4-9-7 60....(b) DaneO'Neill 3 44
(Henry Candy) *chsd ldr tl wknd over 1f out* **5/1**3

0-00 **10** 1 1/4 **Kylies Wild Card**5 6894 4-8-8 47....1 KieranO'Neill 1 27
(Simon Hodgson) *prom tl wknd wl over 1f out* **66/1**

0034 **11** 1 1/2 **Keiba (IRE)**13 6677 3-9-6 60....(v1) LiamKeniry 5 35
(Gary Moore) *mid-div tl wknd over 1f out* **10/1**

640 **12** 2 3/4 **Joanne Park**34 6036 3-9-4 58.... JohnFahy 8 25
(Clive Cox) *outpcd: a bhd* **16/1**

1m 9.83s (-0.37) **Going Correction** -0.15s/f (Firm)
WFA 3 from 4yo+ 1lb **12** Ran SP% **124.7**
Speed ratings (Par 101): **96,95,93,92,89 88,87,85,85,84 82,78**
CSF £18.26 CT £96.92 TOTE £5.30: £2.10, £1.80, £2.40; EX 21.50 Trifecta £140.00.
Owner Mrs J Carrington **Bred** Dream Vision Partnership **Trained** Cropthorne, Worcs

FOCUS
Rail movement added 4yds to race distance. A moderate sprint handicap in which they went a searching pace. Straightforward form.

7039 ANTIQUES & COLLECTABLES FAIR 6TH NOV "HANDS AND HEELS" APPRENTICE SERIES H'CAP 1m 3f 196y
5:45 (5:45) (Class 6) (0-55,60) 3-Y-O+ **£2,587** (£770; £384; £192) **Stalls** High

Form RPR

1021 **1** **Iballisticvin**6 6871 3-9-5 60 6ex.... JoshuaBryan 5 66
(Gary Moore) *mid-div: rdn over 2f out: styd on to ld over 1f out: hld on wl fnl f* **7/5**1

5533 **2** nk **Little Orchid**62 5016 3-8-6 50.... LiamDoran(3) 8 56
(Julia Feilden) *s.s: bhd: hdwy wl over 1f out: chal ins fnl f: r.o* **12/1**

50-3 **3** 1/2 **Helium (FR)**155 1450 11-9-3 51.... JordanUys 6 56+
(Alexandra Dunn) *towards rr: hdwy over 1f out: pressed ldrs ins fnl f: r.o* **5/1**2

4442 **4** 6 **Highlife Dancer**5 6891 8-9-7 55.... HollieDoyle 2 50
(Mick Channon) *prom tl outpcd fnl 2f* **7/1**3

465 **5** hd **Surprise Us**47 5575 9-8-7 46 oh1....(p1) LiamLewis-Salter(5) 9 41
(Mark Gillard) *led tl over 1f out: sn wknd* **50/1**

0 **6** 1 **Madness Light (FR)**64 4950 7-8-12 46 oh1.... KieranSchofield 4 39
(Daniel Steele) *dwlt: hdwy 8f out: pressed ldr 5f out tl wknd 2f out* **66/1**

3430 **7** 1/2 **Vedani (IRE)**90 4023 7-9-6 54.... TobyEley 1 46
(Tony Carroll) *dwlt: sn prom: wknd 2f out* **8/1**

2435 **8** 2 1/2 **Dellbuoy**64 4950 7-9-0 51.... SophieRalston(3) 7 44
(Pat Phelan) *mid-div: effrt over 2f out: no ex fnl f* **8/1**

0150 **9** 2 1/2 **Salient**22 6411 12-9-7 55.... CameronNoble 11 39
(Michael Attwater) *prom on outer tl wknd 2f out* **33/1**

030 **10** 38 **Keyman (IRE)**36 5958 3-8-5 46 oh1....1 MitchGodwin 10
(Jeremy Gask) *nvr gng wl: sn wl bhd: t.o and eased fnl 3f* **10/1**

2m 34.35s (1.65) **Going Correction** -0.15s/f (Firm)
WFA 3 from 6yo+ 7lb **10** Ran SP% **116.2**
Speed ratings (Par 101): **88,87,87,83,83 82,82,80,79,53**
CSF £20.18 CT £69.08 TOTE £2.30: £1.10, £3.40, £1.70; EX 20.20 Trifecta £114.70.
Owner Scuderia Vita Bella **Bred** Houghton-Barrons Partnership **Trained** Lower Beeding, W Sussex

FOCUS
Rail movement added 4yds to race distance. A very moderate 46-55 "hands and heels" apprentice handicap and the pace looked ordinary, with all bar one still in a heap coming to the last furlong. The second and third help with the opening level.
T/Plt: £23.70 to a £1 stake. Pool: £69,695.13 - 2145.68 winning units T/Qpdt: £14.50 to a £1 stake. Pool: £5,007.97 - 255.14 winning units **Lee McKenzie**

6562 CATTERICK (L-H)
Tuesday, October 4

OFFICIAL GOING: Good to soft (soft in places; 7.1)
Wind: Moderate behind Weather: Fine & dry

7040 IRISH STALLION FARMS EBF MAIDEN STKS 5f
2:00 (2:02) (Class 5) 2-Y-O **£3,234** (£962; £481; £240) **Stalls** Low

Form RPR

0 **1** **Wadood (IRE)**71 4713 2-9-5 0.... LukeMorris 5 76
(Robert Cowell) *mde all: rdn over 1f out: drvn ins fnl f: kpt on wl towards fin* **11/2**3

334 **2** 1/2 **Vaulted**38 5876 2-9-0 72.... TonyHamilton 6 69
(Richard Fahey) *chsd ldrs and sn pushed along: hdwy 2f out: rdn to chal ins fnl f: kpt on* **5/6**1

33 **3** 1 3/4 **Lady Molly (IRE)**28 6214 2-9-0 0.... PhillipMakin 7 62
(Keith Dalgleish) *cl up: disp ld wl over 1f out: sn rdn and ev ch: drvn ins fnl f: kpt on same pce* **3/1**2

4 1 3/4 **Flame Of Hope (IRE)** 2-9-0 0.... GrahamGibbons 4 56
(David Barron) *trckd ldrs: hdwy and cl up over 2f out: rdn over 1f out: grad wknd fnl f* **14/1**

04 **5** 3 3/4 **Skellig Michael**21 6448 2-9-5 0.... GrahamLee 1 48
(Ben Haslam) *towards rr: rdn along over 2f out: nvr nr ldrs* **22/1**

0 **6** 1 **Desert Gift (IRE)**45 5631 2-9-0 0.... KevinStott 3 39
(Robert Cowell) *sltly hmpd s and rr: pushed along over 2f out: sn rdn and n.d* **14/1**

0400 **7** 3 1/2 **Sadieroseclifford (IRE)**5 6895 2-9-0 59.... JoeyHaynes 2 26
(Denis Quinn) *chsd ldrs: rdn along over 2f out: sn wknd* **40/1**

8 2 1/4 **Fairy Lock (IRE)** 2-9-0 0.... SamJames 8 18
(David Barron) *dwlt and wnt rt s: a rr* **40/1**

1m 1.52s (1.72) **Going Correction** +0.275s/f (Good) **8** Ran SP% **117.5**
Speed ratings (Par 95): **97,96,93,90,84 83,77,73**
CSF £10.69 TOTE £5.30: £1.40, £1.10, £1.40; EX 11.80 Trifecta £27.60.
Owner Abdulla Al Mansoori **Bred** Mrs Teresa Thornton **Trained** Six Mile Bottom, Cambs

FOCUS
All distances as advertised. The right horses came to the fore in what was a modest maiden. The third and sixth offer perspective to the level.

7041 RACING TO SCHOOL NURSERY H'CAP 5f 212y
2:30 (2:31) (Class 6) (0-65,65) 2-Y-O **£2,587** (£770; £384; £192) **Stalls** Low

Form RPR

4050 **1** **Traveltalk (IRE)**13 6681 2-9-5 63....(p) BenCurtis 10 67
(Brian Ellison) *hld up: pushed along 1/2-way: rdn and hdwy over 2f out: drvn to chse ldng pair and edgd lft ins fnl f: kpt on strly to ld nr fin* **15/2**

360 **2** nk **Cupid's Arrow (IRE)**21 6448 2-9-3 61.... JamesSullivan 4 64
(Ruth Carr) *midfield: gd hdwy wl over 2f out: led 11/2f out: clr ent fnl f: drvn and wknd last 100 yds: hdd nr fin* **14/1**

0031 **3** 2 3/4 **Harlequin Rose (IRE)**5 6887 2-8-11 55 6ex....(v) LukeMorris 2 50
(Mick Channon) *trckd ldng pair on inner: chsd ldr 11/2f out and sn rdn: drvn ins fnl f: kpt on same pce* **9/2**2

0036 **4** 1 1/4 **Breaking Free**66 4869 2-8-12 56.... CamHardie 9 47
(John Quinn) *rr: hdwy wl over 2f out: sn swtchd rt to outer and rdn: styd on wl fnl f: nrst fin* **16/1**

003 **5** nk **Ninety Years Young**12 6712 2-9-5 63.... GrahamLee 5 53
(David Elsworth) *prom: effrt and cl up 2f out: sn rdn and wknd over 1f out* **3/1**1

005 **6** 5 **Silver Gleam (IRE)**39 5854 2-8-13 60.... RachelRichardson(3) 6 35
(Tim Easterby) *sn outpcd and bhd: hdwy wl over 2f out: rdn wl over 1f out: kpt on fnl f: nrst fin* **14/1**

005 **7** shd **Dreamorchid (IRE)**50 5476 2-9-2 60.... DavidAllan 8 35
(Tim Easterby) *midfield: pushed along and hdwy over 2f out: rdn wl over 1f out: kpt on same pce* **10/1**

5452 **8** *nse* **Equity**[32] 6092 2-9-4 **62** PhillipMakin 7 37
(David Brown) *dwlt and towards rr: hdwy over 2f out: sn rdn and n.d* **5/1**[3]

660 **9** *1* **A Bit Of Ginger**[14] 6641 2-9-0 **58** PJMcDonald 3 30+
(Ann Duffield) *chsd ldrs: rdn along wl over 2f out: sn wknd* **16/1**

0150 **10** *2 1/4* **Queen Celeste (IRE)**[9] 6807 2-9-7 **65** (b[1]) PaulMulrennan 1 30+
(Mark Johnston) *led: rdn along 2f out: hdd 11/2f out: sn drvn and wknd* **40/1**

4400 **11** *2* **Melaniemillie**[35] 6010 2-9-7 **65** AndrewMullen 11 24+
(Ollie Pears) *chsd ldrs: rdn along over 2f out: sn drvn and wknd* **20/1**

1m 17.02s (3.42) **Going Correction** +0.525s/f (Yiel) **11** Ran SP% **113.0**
Speed ratings (Par 93): **98,97,93,92,91 85,85,85,83,80 78**
CSF £103.07 CT £536.32 TOTE £8.00: £2.50, £3.80, £1.90; EX 127.90 Trifecta £915.70.
Owner John James & Brian Ellison **Bred** Denis Noonan **Trained** Norton, N Yorks

FOCUS
Moderate nursery form, they went a good gallop and the closers were favoured. A small step forward from the runner-up.

7042 WATCH ON 3 DEVICES RACING UK.COM/ANYWHERE NURSERY H'CAP 7f

3:00 (3:02) (Class 3) (0-95,95) 2-Y-O **£7,470** (£2,236; £1,118; £559; £279) **Stalls** Low

Form RPR

0525 **1** **In First Place**[18] 6536 2-8-2 **76** PatrickMathers 3 80
(Richard Fahey) *sn pushed along in rr: hdwy over 2f out and sn rdn: drvn to chal ins fnl f: styng on whn edgd lft last 50 yds: led nr fin* **9/2**[3]

0644 **2** *1 1/4* **Masham Star (IRE)**[30] 6180 2-8-13 **87** PaulMulrennan 1 88
(Mark Johnston) *trckd ldr: hdwy to ld wl over 1f out: sn rdn: drvn ins fnl f: hdd and no ex towards fin* **9/2**[3]

1032 **3** *nk* **Top Score**[30] 6180 2-9-7 **95** (p) KevinStott 4 95
(Saeed bin Suroor) *trckd ldng pair: effrt over 2f out and sn rdn along: drvn over 1f out: keeping on u.p whn n.m.r and sltly hmpd last 50 yds* **13/8**[1]

13 **4** *4* **Whatsthemessage (IRE)**[17] 6554 2-8-4 **78** LukeMorris 2 68
(Keith Dalgleish) *trckd ldrs: pushed along 3f out: rdn over 2f out: sn drvn and one pce* **3/1**[2]

3153 **5** *3 1/4* **Sir Viktor (IRE)**[17] 6562 2-8-1 **75** ow1 (v) JoeyHaynes 5 57+
(K R Burke) *led: rdn along over 2f out: hdd wl over 1f out: sn drvn and wknd* **9/1**

1m 30.06s (3.06) **Going Correction** +0.525s/f (Yiel) **5** Ran SP% **109.5**
Speed ratings (Par 99): **103,101,101,96,92**
CSF £23.41 TOTE £4.50: £3.40, £3.20; EX 24.90 Trifecta £71.70.
Owner CBWS & Partner **Bred** Trebles Holford Farm Thoroughbreds **Trained** Musley Bank, N Yorks

FOCUS
A decent little nursery, the outsider of the field went charging off and the race set up for the winner, who came from off the pace.

7043 SPONSOR GRANT TUER'S MARATHON RUNNING H'CAP 1m 3f 214y

3:30 (3:34) (Class 5) (0-75,75) 3-Y-O+ **£3,234** (£962; £481; £240) **Stalls** Centre

Form RPR

1133 **1** **Henry Smith**[12] 6719 4-9-7 **75** (be) AdamMcNamara[(5)] 9 86+
(Garry Moss) *prom: led 2f out: sn rdn clr: kpt on strly* **17/2**[3]

2304 **2** *3 3/4* **Gold Show**[15] 6620 7-8-12 **61** JackGarritty 6 66
(Grant Tuer) *trckd ldrs: hdwy on inner 3f out: rdn to chse wnr wl over 1f out: drvn and no imp fnl f* **14/1**

1-60 **3** *1 1/4* **Status Quo (IRE)**[109] 3355 3-9-4 **74** [1] LukeMorris 7 77
(Sir Mark Prescott Bt) *hld up towards rr: hdwy 4f out: rdn to chse ldrs wl over 1f out: drvn and kpt on fnl f* **12/1**

5024 **4** *1* **Sherman McCoy**[17] 6566 10-9-3 **66** JamesSullivan 5 67
(Marjorie Fife) *trckd ldrs: hdwy over 3f out: rdn along over 2f out: sn drvn and kpt on same pce* **10/1**

-006 **5** *1* **Cloud Monkey (IRE)**[18] 4044 6-9-8 **71** DavidNolan 11 71
(Martin Todhunter) *in tch: hdwy over 3f out: chsd ldrs 2f out: sn rdn and kpt on same pce* **16/1**

0 **6** *3 1/2* **Astra Hall**[17] 6566 7-9-8 **74** AlistairRawlinson[(3)] 2 68
(Michael Appleby) *in tch: effrt and sme hdwy on inner 3f out: rdn along over 2f out: n.d* **22/1**

5061 **7** *1 1/2* **Southern Strife**[21] 6432 5-9-6 **69** (b) DavidAllan 1 61
(Tim Easterby) *hld up towards rr: hdwy over 4f out: rdn along and outpcd over 3f out: sme hdwy fnl 2f: n.d* **2/1**[1]

4010 **8** *6* **Shalamzar (FR)**[116] 3117 7-9-4 **72** RobJFitzpatrick[(5)] 10 54
(Micky Hammond) *hld up: a towards rr* **66/1**

2035 **9** *8* **Correggio**[33] 6058 6-9-5 **68** PJMcDonald 3 37
(Micky Hammond) *trckd ldrs: hdwy 4f out: led 3f out: rdn and hdd 2f out: drvn and wknd over 1f out* **12/1**

233- **10** *5* **Take Two**[576] 558 7-9-7 **73** JosephineGordon[(3)] 8 34
(Alex Hales) *awkward s and dwlt: a towards rr* **20/1**

3245 **11** *5* **Ice Galley (IRE)**[20] 6474 3-9-1 **71** KevinStott 12 24
(Kevin Ryan) *led: pushed along over 4f out: rdn and hdd 3f out: sn wknd* **4/1**[2]

043 **12** *39* **Jessica Jo (IRE)**[118] 3019 3-8-12 **68** PaulMulrennan 13
(Mark Johnston) *trckd ldr: cl up 1/2-way: rdn along over 3f out: sn wknd* **25/1**

610- **13** *99* **Spifer (IRE)**[128] 5777 8-9-7 **70** GrahamLee 4
(Julia Brooke) *a rr: rdn along and bhd 1/2-way: t.o fr over 4f out* **33/1**

2m 43.88s (4.98) **Going Correction** +0.525s/f (Yiel)
WFA 3 from 4yo+ 7lb **13** Ran SP% **118.3**
Speed ratings (Par 103): **104,101,100,100,99 97,96,92,86,83 80,54,**
CSF £111.77 CT £1432.66 TOTE £7.70: £1.50, £4.90, £4.30; EX 152.40 Trifecta £1611.20 Part Won..
Owner Pinnacle Duo Partnership **Bred** M Pennell **Trained** Wynyard, Stockton-On-Tees

FOCUS
Not many got into this, with the winner assuming control early in the straight. The runner-up has been rated to form.

7044 SKYRAM H'CAP (DIV I) 1m 5f 175y

4:00 (4:04) (Class 6) (0-60,61) 3-Y-O+ **£2,587** (£770; £384; £192) **Stalls** Low

Form RPR

6/21 **1** **Fine Resolve**[8] 6825 7-9-10 **61** 6ex (bt) JosephineGordon[(3)] 8 68+
(Alexandra Dunn) *led: hdd over 5f out: cl up: led again 2f out: sn rdn clr: kpt on strly* **11/4**[1]

4265 **2** *2 1/2* **Jan De Heem**[11] 6738 6-9-10 **58** JamesSullivan 10 61
(Tina Jackson) *hld up in rr: gd hdwy on wd outside over 2f out: rdn to chse ldrs over 1f out: drvn to chse wnr and hung lft ins fnl f: kpt on* **14/1**

0060 **3** *1 1/2* **Come On Lulu**[11] 6738 5-8-12 **46** oh1 PatrickMathers 6 47
(David Thompson) *trckd ldrs: hdwy 3f out: rdn 2f out: sn drvn and kpt on fnl f* **150/1**

432/ **4** *nk* **Miss Tree**[142] 5-9-2 **50** JackGarritty 7 50
(John Quinn) *t.k.h: trckd ldrs: hdwy to ld over 5f out: rdn along and hdd 2f out: sn drvn and kpt on same pce* **11/4**[1]

6030 **5** *1 1/4* **Triple Eight (IRE)**[21] 6438 8-9-12 **60** PhillipMakin 11 58
(Philip Kirby) *midfield: hdwy over 3f out: rdn to chse ldrs 2f out: sn drvn and kpt on* **20/1**

4065 **6** *1* **Perennial**[11] 6739 7-8-9 **48** (p) GarryWhillans[(5)] 1 45
(Philip Kirby) *dwlt and bhd: hdwy over 4f out: chsd ldrs over 2f out: rdn wl over 1f out: kpt on same pce* **12/1**[3]

6005 **7** *nk* **Adrakhan (FR)**[15] 6619 5-8-12 **46** oh1 CamHardie 12 42
(Wilf Storey) *towards rr: hdwy wl over 2f out: sn rdn: kpt on fnl f: nrst fin* **28/1**

6203 **8** *1 1/2* **Rockabilly Riot (IRE)**[32] 6103 6-9-6 **59** (v) AdamMcNamara[(5)] 3 53
(Martin Todhunter) *prom: cl up 3f out: rdn 2f out: sn drvn and wknd* **10/1**[2]

4420 **9** *3 3/4* **Chauvelin**[21] 6438 5-9-7 **55** (v) AndrewMullen 5 43
(Nigel Tinkler) *in tch: rdn along 4f out: wknd 3f out* **10/1**[2]

5360 **10** *1 1/2* **Mexican Mick**[26] 6256 7-9-2 **50** LukeMorris 9 35
(Peter Hiatt) *trckd ldrs: cl up 1/2-way: rdn along 4f out: wknd 3f out* **20/1**

6005 **11** *1 1/2* **Lightning Steps**[9] 6812 4-9-1 **49** TonyHamilton 13 32
(Declan Carroll) *a towards rr* **14/1**

0346 **12** *14* **Calypso Delegator (IRE)**[35] 6004 3-8-6 **49** PJMcDonald 4 9
(Micky Hammond) *chsd ldrs: rdn along over 5f out: sn wknd* **10/1**[2]

3m 14.26s (10.66) **Going Correction** +0.525s/f (Yiel)
WFA 3 from 4yo+ 9lb **12** Ran SP% **115.3**
Speed ratings (Par 101): **90,88,87,87,86 86,86,85,83,82 81,73**
CSF £42.87 CT £4554.82 TOTE £3.60: £1.40, £3.90, £19.90; EX 33.20 Trifecta £1466.00.
Owner West Buckland Bloodstock Ltd **Bred** Lord Blyth **Trained** West Buckland, Somerset

FOCUS
Moderate handicap form. The runner-up, third and seventh help set the opening level.

7045 SKYRAM H'CAP (DIV II) 1m 5f 175y

4:30 (4:33) (Class 6) (0-60,60) 3-Y-O+ **£2,587** (£770; £384; £192) **Stalls** Low

Form RPR

0-43 **1** **Maid Of Tuscany (IRE)**[8] 6825 5-8-13 **50** (b) JosephineGordon[(3)] 4 56
(Alexandra Dunn) *hld up in rr: hdwy over 3f out: rdn to chse ldrs over 1f out: swtchd lft jst ins fnl f: sn drvn and styd on wl to ld last 75 yds* **11/2**[2]

4366 **2** *3/4* **Dream Serenade**[12] 6698 3-8-3 **46** oh1 AndrewMullen 5 51
(Michael Appleby) *trckd ldrs: hdwy and cl up 5f out: led over 3f out: rdn 2f out: jnd and drvn over 1f out: hdd and no ex last 75 yds* **28/1**

1354 **3** *3/4* **Saint Thomas (IRE)**[40] 5795 9-9-9 **57** GrahamGibbons 7 61
(John Mackie) *hld up towards rr: hdwy 4f out: chsd ldrs over 2f out: rdn to chal over 1f out: sn drvn and ev ch tl no ex last 75 yds* **25/1**

0620 **4** *6* **Mikro Polemistis (IRE)**[12] 6698 3-9-1 **58** BenCurtis 10 52
(Brian Ellison) *hld up: gd hdwy on outer over 4f out: cl up 3f out: rdn 2f out: drvn over 1f out and sn one pce* **8/1**

0060 **5** *1* **Cavalieri (IRE)**[28] 6219 6-9-4 **52** [1] PhillipMakin 9 44
(Philip Kirby) *hld up in rr: hdwy over 3f out: chsd ldrs on outer 2f out: rdn and no imp appr fnl f* **33/1**

6013 **6** *6* **Cosmic Tigress**[21] 6438 5-9-11 **59** JasonHart 13 42
(John Quinn) *trckd ldrs: hdwy 4f out: rdn to chse eladers over 2f out: drvn wl over 1f out: kpt on one pce* **7/1**

4062 **7** *6* **Annigoni (IRE)**[22] 6424 4-8-12 **46** (p) JamesSullivan 3 19
(Ruth Carr) *midfield: hdwy 4f out: rdn along 3f out: sn drvn and n.d* **10/1**

1324 **8** *nk* **Fillydelphia (IRE)**[11] 6738 5-9-7 **58** RachelRichardson[(3)] 11 31
(Patrick Holmes) *trckd ldrs: hdwy 4f out: cl up 3f out: rdn over 2f out: sn drvn and wknd* **10/1**

3622 **9** *6* **First Sargeant**[21] 6450 6-9-7 **60** (p) AdamMcNamara[(5)] 6 23
(Lawrence Mullaney) *hld up: a towards rr* **13/2**[3]

5634 **10** *2 3/4* **Tyrannical**[14] 6659 3-8-11 **54** (v) LukeMorris 2 13
(Sir Mark Prescott Bt) *trckd ldrs: pushed along 4f out: rdn 3f out: sn wknd* **9/2**[1]

2263 **11** *3 1/2* **Becky The Thatcher**[38] 5888 3-9-2 **59** PJMcDonald 1 12
(Micky Hammond) *trckd ldrs: pushed along 5f out: sn rdn and wknd* **11/2**[2]

0065 **12** *18* **Smirnova (IRE)**[15] 6617 3-8-8 **51** JoeyHaynes 8
(Kenny Johnson) *cl up: led over 5f out: rdn along and hdd over 3f out: sn wknd* **100/1**

00R0 **13** *40* **Rolen Sly**[21] 6450 7-8-9 **46** oh1 JacobButterfield[(3)] 12
(Neville Bycroft) *led: hdd 5f out: sn lost pl and bhd* **80/1**

3m 11.58s (7.98) **Going Correction** +0.525s/f (Yiel)
WFA 3 from 4yo+ 9lb **13** Ran SP% **116.5**
Speed ratings (Par 101): **98,97,97,93,93 89,86,86,82,81 79,68,45**
CSF £157.69 CT £3507.82 TOTE £5.90: £2.40, £8.70, £7.40; EX 179.20 Trifecta £2379.60.
Owner Qdos Racing **Bred** Cora Srl **Trained** West Buckland, Somerset

FOCUS
The front three came clear in what looked the lesser of the two divisions. A minor pb from the runner-up, with the third just off his recent best.

7046 RACING AGAIN SATURDAY 15TH OCTOBER AMATEUR RIDERS' H'CAP 5f

5:00 (5:03) (Class 6) (0-55,54) 3-Y-O+ **£2,495** (£774; £386; £193) **Stalls** Low

Form RPR

3450 **1** **Very First Blade**[50] 5483 7-10-3 **48** (be) MrLewisStones[(5)] 14 55
(Michael Mullineaux) *chsd ldrs: hdwy on outer 2f out: rdn to chal ent fnl f and ev ch: sn drvn and kpt on wl to ld nr line* **33/1**

0103 **2** *hd* **Whipphound**[7] 6852 8-10-13 **53** (p) MissSBrotherton 4 59
(Ruth Carr) *trckd ldrs: nt clr run and swtchd rt to outer jst ins fnl f: sn rdn and fin strly* **5/1**[2]

631 **3** *hd* **Longroom**[9] 6813 4-10-10 **50** MrSWalker 15 56
(Noel Wilson) *cl up: slt ld wl over 1f out: sn rdn: drvn and edgd lft ins fnl f: hdd and no ex nr line* **11/8**[1]

6060 **4** *1 1/4* **Kodimoor (IRE)**[10] 6790 3-10-6 **51** (bt) MrMEnnis[(5)] 2 53
(Christopher Kellett) *chsd ldrs: hdwy 2f out: rdn over 1f out: drvn and kpt on fnl f* **33/1**

0446 **5** *1* **Kingfisher Girl**[17] 6569 3-10-2 **47** MrJJO'Neill[(5)] 9 45
(Michael Appleby) *chsd ldrs on inner: rdn along and hdwy over 1f out: kpt on same pce fnl f* **16/1**

0000 **6** *3/4* **Sir Geoffrey (IRE)**[1] 7018 10-10-9 **54** (b) MrKLocking[(5)] 6 49
(Scott Dixon) *cl up: rdn along over 2f out: drvn and ev ch over 1f out: kpt on same pce fnl f* **9/1**

0500 **7** *1/2* **Red Forever**[50] 5483 5-10-2 **45** MissHelenCuthbert[(3)] 8 38
(Thomas Cuthbert) *trckd ldrs: swtchd rt and rdn ent fnl f: kpt on same pce* **33/1**

1400 **8** *1 1/4* **A J Cook (IRE)**[13] 6680 6-10-7 **52** MissEmilyBullock[(5)] 10 40
(Ron Barr) *chsd ldrs: lost pl after 1f and towards rr 1/2-way: swtchd rt to outer and rdn 2f out: styd on fnl f* **18/1**

6660 **9** *2* **Amis Reunis**[8] 6835 7-10-0 **45**..(p) MrBLynn(5) 13 26
(Colin Teague) *t.k.h: chsd ldrs: rdn along over 2f out: sn wknd* **40/1**

020 **10** *1 ½* **Betty Boo (IRE)**[5] 6902 6-10-8 **48**.................................... MrsCBartley 11 24
(Shaun Harris) *a towards rr* **20/1**

4532 **11** *shd* **Zebelini (IRE)**[6] 6865 4-10-9 **49**......................................(b) MissCWalton 3 28
(Ollie Pears) *led: rdn along 1/2-way: hdd wl over 1f out: wkng whn hmpd appr fnl f* **8/1**[3]

6004 **12** *1 ¼* **Pabusar**[35] 6008 8-10-3 **46**....................................(tp) MissBeckySmith(3) 1 17
(Micky Hammond) *a towards rr* **16/1**

0000 **13** *2* **Eland Ally**[7] 6853 8-10-13 **53**.................................(b) MissJoannaMason 5 17
(Anabel K Murphy) *dwlt: a rr* **28/1**

0100 **14** *3* **Under Approval**[5] 6910 5-10-12 **52**..................................(b) MissETodd 12 5
(Karen Tutty) *a outpcd in rr* **33/1**

3-60 **15** *9* **Fred's Filly**[14] 6660 3-10-1 **48**....................................(b) MissPSkipper(7) 7
(Bill Turner) *chsd ldrs: rdn along bef 1/2-way: sn lost pl and bhd* **80/1**

1m 2.21s (2.41) **Going Correction** +0.275s/f (Good) **15** Ran SP% **120.6**
Speed ratings (Par 101): **91,90,90,88,86 85,84,82,79,77 77,75,71,67,52**
CSF £180.39 CT £402.55 TOTE £51.50: £7.90, £1.70, £1.40; EX 318.40 Trifecta £1370.20.
Owner Ogwen Valley Racing **Bred** L R Owen **Trained** Alpraham, Cheshire

FOCUS
A bit of a turn up here, one of the outsiders edging it. Straightforward form rated around the first two.

T/Jkpt: Not Won. T/Plt: £1,227.20 to a £1 stake. Pool: £57,681.28 - 34.31 winning units T/Qpdt: £262.40 to a £1 stake. Pool: £3,298.47 - 9.3 winning units **Joe Rowntree**

6865 KEMPTON (A.W) (R-H)
Tuesday, October 4

OFFICIAL GOING: Polytrack: standard to slow
Wind: Fresh, half behind Weather: Fine

7047 RACING UK.COM NURSERY H'CAP 7f (P)
5:40 (5:40) (Class 6) (0-60,60) 2-Y-O **£2,264** (£673; £336; £168) **Stalls** Low

Form RPR

0501 **1** **Dragon Dream (IRE)**[22] 6412 2-9-0 **53**................................ KierenFox 8 57
(Roger Ingram) *chsd ldrs: outpcd and rdn 2f out: styd on wl fr over 1f out to ld last 60yds* **8/1**

6006 **2** *¾* **Auric Goldfinger (IRE)**[14] 6652 2-9-3 **56**........................... SeanLevey 7 58
(Richard Hannon) *prom: trckd ldr 4f out: chal over 2f out and sn clr of rest: jst getting up whn wnr thrust past 60yds out* **10/1**

6054 **3** *nk* **Fair Selene**[8] 6830 2-9-7 **60**..[1] OisinMurphy 12 61
(Heather Main) *spd fr wd draw and sn led: kicked for home whn pressed over 2f out: kpt on but hdd and dropped to 3rd last 60yds* **10/1**

3534 **4** *½* **Katebird (IRE)**[22] 6419 2-9-5 **58**................................ SilvestreDeSousa 2 58
(Mark Johnston) *hld up in rr: outpcd over 2f out: drvn and prog wl over 1f out: styd on to take 4th last strides* **9/2**[2]

000 **5** *nk* **Fleeting Francesca**[15] 6624 2-9-0 **53**........................... WilliamCarson 9 52
(Chris Gordon) *chsd ldr 3f: racd in 3rd after: outpcd 2f out: tried to cl again fr over 1f out but lost 2 pls ins fnl f* **50/1**

0440 **6** *1* **Primrose Place**[13] 6670 2-9-7 **60**......................................(t) PatDobbs 1 56
(Richard Hannon) *hld up in midfield: outpcd over 2f out: rdn and kpt on fr over 1f out: no ch to threaten* **11/2**[3]

5504 **7** *1 ¼* **Everkyllachy (IRE)**[14] 6652 2-9-6 **59**....................[1] MichaelJMMurphy 4 52
(J S Moore) *in tch in midfield: outpcd over 2f out: n.d after: plugged on fnl f* **20/1**

0050 **8** *½* **Henry Did It (IRE)**[22] 6412 2-9-6 **59**............................... JimmyFortune 6 51
(Tony Carroll) *racd wd towards rr: outpcd and rdn over 2f out: no ch after: plugged on* **8/1**

0005 **9** *1 ¼* **Aventus (IRE)**[13] 6670 2-9-2 **55**..(b) ShaneKelly 5 43
(Richard Hughes) *rrd s and slowly away: mostly in last trio: rdn over 2f out: no great hdwy* **4/1**[1]

000 **10** *½* **Orange Gin (IRE)**[18] 6543 2-9-6 **59**.............................. GeorgeBaker 10 46
(Roger Charlton) *chsd ldrs: outpcd over 2f out: wknd over 1f out* **11/1**

2000 **11** *2 ¾* **Kath's Boy (IRE)**[26] 6252 2-9-0 **56**......................... GeorgeDowning(3) 13 35
(Tony Carroll) *dropped in fr wd draw and hld up in last: rdn and no ch over 2f out* **80/1**

0562 **12** *1 ½* **Apple Scruffs (IRE)**[21] 6440 2-9-4 **60**..................... EdwardGreatrex(3) 3 35
(Michael Attwater) *plld hrd early: hld up towards rr: struggling over 2f out: sn wknd* **11/1**

1m 27.73s (1.73) **Going Correction** 0.0s/f (Stan) **12** Ran SP% **118.6**
Speed ratings (Par 93): **90,89,88,88,87 86,85,84,83,82 79,77**
CSF £84.36 CT £815.86 TOTE £8.00: £2.40, £3.60, £3.40; EX 121.60 Trifecta £851.40.
Owner Drag On Funds **Bred** Pier House Stud **Trained** Epsom, Surrey

FOCUS
A moderate nursery in which it paid to race fairly handily. Another step forward from the winner, with the runner-up rated back to his previous course form.

7048 RACING UK PROFITS RETURNED TO RACING H'CAP 1m (P)
6:10 (6:10) (Class 6) (0-60,63) 3-Y-O+ **£2,264** (£673; £336; £168) **Stalls** Low

Form RPR

4654 **1** **Check 'Em Tuesday (IRE)**[60] 5132 3-9-4 **60**...................... DaleSwift 2 66
(Daniel Mark Loughnane) *trckd ldrs: prog to ld 2f out: hrd rdn and edgd lft after: kpt on* **8/1**

3000 **2** *1 ¾* **Spirit Of Gondree (IRE)**[12] 6700 8-9-7 **60**..........(b) RichardKingscote 1 62
(Milton Bradley) *slowly away: hld up in rr: prog over 2f out: rdn to take 2nd jst 1f out: rdn awkwardly and nt qckn after* **10/1**

0216 **3** *1* **Carcharias (IRE)**[33] 6047 3-9-1 **57**................................. OisinMurphy 3 56
(Ed de Giles) *prom: rdn over 2f out: tried to cl over 1f out and sn disp 2nd briefly: one pce* **9/2**[2]

265 **4** *¾* **Ocean Legend (IRE)**[27] 6237 11-9-4 **60**.................. GeorgeDowning(3) 7 58+
(Tony Carroll) *trckd ldrs: shkn up on outer jst over 2f out: clsd to dispute 2nd 1f out: nt qckn and safely hld after* **8/1**

0000 **5** *1* **Afkar (IRE)**[23] 6373 8-8-11 **57**..(p) RPWalsh(7) 4 52
(Ivan Furtado) *led: rdn and hdd 2f out: steadily fdd fnl f* **20/1**

4005 **6** *¾* **Little Indian**[40] 5808 6-9-3 **56**................................... SilvestreDeSousa 5 49
(J R Jenkins) *towards rr: rdn and in tch w ldrs over 1f out: no imp after* **7/1**[3]

2600 **7** *1* **Indus Valley (IRE)**[13] 6677 9-9-4 **57**........................(b) StevieDonohoe 10 48
(Lee Carter) *hld up in rr: rdn and no prog over 2f out: one pce after* **25/1**

6004 **8** *½* **Harikiri (IRE)**[5] 6893 3-8-13 **60**................................ MeganNicholls(5) 14 50
(Charles Hills) *slowly away: rapid hdwy to trck ldr: lost 2nd over 2f out: fdd* **16/1**

-505 **9** *10* **Red Ruffian (IRE)**[200] 979 3-9-1 **60**............................ JackDuern(3) 11 26
(Dean Ivory) *chsd ldrs: rdn 1/2-way: wknd over 2f out: sn bhd* **16/1**

0600 **10** *24* **Aegean Boy**[61] 5088 3-9-2 **58**..[1] WilliamCarson 9
(John Bridger) *slowly away: a in last pair: wknd 3f out: t.o* **40/1**

5001 **P** **Ice Alert (IRE)**[7] 6857 3-9-7 **63** 6ex.. FMBerry 8
(John Ryan) *pushed along and dropped to rr after 2f: p.u after 3f: dismntd* **2/1**[1]

1m 40.5s (0.70) **Going Correction** 0.0s/f (Stan)
WFA 3 from 5yo+ 3lb **11** Ran SP% **118.1**
Speed ratings (Par 101): **96,94,93,92,91 90,89,89,79,55**
CSF £83.60 CT £327.08 TOTE £9.90: £2.60, £3.60, £1.70; EX 110.00 Trifecta £672.30.
Owner David Slater **Bred** Owen Flood **Trained** Baldwin's Gate, Staffs

■ Mistymoistymorning was withdrawn. Price at time of withdrawal 33/1. Rule 4 does not apply

FOCUS
A moderate heat. A small step up from the winner.

7049 32REDSPORT.COM MAIDEN FILLIES' STKS (PLUS 10 RACE) (DIV I) 1m (P)
6:40 (6:40) (Class 5) 2-Y-O **£2,911** (£866; £432; £216) **Stalls** Low

Form RPR

0 **1** **Illaunmore (USA)**[122] 2885 2-9-0 0.......................... RichardKingscote 8 79
(John Gosden) *trckd ldr after 2f: pushed into ld over 1f out: sn pressed: shkn up and styd on wl fnl f* **9/1**

3 **2** *¾* **Song Maker**[20] 6472 2-9-0 0..................................... WilliamBuick 2 77
(Charlie Appleby) *led to over 6f out: sn in 3rd: pushed along over 2f out: clsd to chal jst over 1f out: pressed wnr after: styd on but hld last 75yds* **3/1**[2]

3 *½* **Great Court (IRE)** 2-9-0 0... OisinMurphy 7 76+
(Luca Cumani) *slowly away: mostly in last pair: pushed along wl over 2f out: modest prog over 1f out: shkn up and styd on wl fnl f to take 3rd last strides* **16/1**

22 **4** *nk* **Syndicate**[32] 6088 2-9-0 0... FMBerry 4 75
(Ralph Beckett) *t.k.h early: trckd ldrs: cl up gng strly 2f out: shkn up and nt qckn over 1f out: wl hld after: lost 3rd last strides* **11/10**[1]

6 **5** *¾* **Seyadah**[62] 5036 2-9-0 0.. HarryBentley 1 73
(Marco Botti) *chsd ldrs: shkn up over 2f out: effrt over 1f out: kpt on same pce fnl f* **9/1**

00 **6** *1 ¼* **Ashazuri**[60] 5119 2-9-0 0... MartinHarley 5 70
(Jonathan Portman) *dwlt: in rr: pushed along and effrt to chse ldrs 2f out: no imp after: fdd fnl f* **66/1**

02 **7** *1* **Al Nafoorah**[32] 6077 2-9-0 0.. PatCosgrave 3 68
(Ed Dunlop) *led over 6f out at decent pce: rdn and hdd over 1f out: wknd* **7/1**[3]

0 **8** *1 ¾* **Newt**[22] 6414 2-9-0 0... RyanPowell 6 64
(Sir Mark Prescott Bt) *urged along early in last trio: shkn up 3f out whn hanging and stl green: no prog but lost no further grnd* **66/1**

60 **9** *2 ¾* **Toy Theatre**[119] 2990 2-9-0 0..................................... SilvestreDeSousa 10 57
(Mark Johnston) *sn hld up in 6th: shkn up and no prog over 2f out: wknd over 1f out* **25/1**

1m 39.46s (-0.34) **Going Correction** 0.0s/f (Stan) **9** Ran SP% **117.8**
Speed ratings (Par 92): **101,100,99,99,98 97,96,94,91**
CSF £36.73 TOTE £11.10: £2.30, £1.40, £3.80; EX 41.50 Trifecta £536.80.
Owner Chasemore Farm **Bred** Chasemore Farm **Trained** Newmarket, Suffolk

FOCUS
A fair maiden. The level is a bit fluid.

7050 32REDSPORT.COM MAIDEN FILLIES' STKS (PLUS 10 RACE) (DIV II) 1m (P)
7:10 (7:11) (Class 5) 2-Y-O **£2,911** (£866; £432; £216) **Stalls** Low

Form RPR

1 **Assanilka (FR)** 2-9-0 0.. RichardKingscote 7 79+
(Harry Dunlop) *dwlt: hld up in last pair: gng easily but stl there over 2f out: prog over 1f out: shkn up and str run fnl f to snatch unlikely win last strides* **50/1**

42 **2** *nk* **Agathonia (USA)**[15] 6624 2-9-0 0................................ WilliamBuick 8 78
(Charlie Appleby) *trckd ldr: pushed into ld 2f out: rdn over 1f out: at least 2 l ahd ins fnl f: styd on but hdd last strides* **2/1**[2]

3 *3 ¼* **High Laugh (IRE)** 2-9-0 0... DanielMuscutt 3 70
(Marco Botti) *trckd ldrs: pushed along over 2f out: styd on to dispute 2nd ins fnl f: outpcd after* **25/1**

5 **4** *1* **Secret Soul**[33] 6061 2-9-0 0... FMBerry 1 68
(Ralph Beckett) *led: shkn up and hdd 2f out: no ch w wnr 1f out and sn lost 2 pls* **7/2**[3]

5 *½* **Penny Red** 2-9-0 0.. MartinHarley 2 67
(William Knight) *settled in last trio: pushed along over 2f out: nvr a threat but kpt on quite steadily fr over 1f out* **33/1**

6 *¾* **Erinyes (IRE)** 2-9-0 0.. OisinMurphy 6 65
(Archie Watson) *mostly in midfield: rn green and outpcd over 2f out: n.d but kpt on fnl f* **50/1**

2 **7** *hd* **Dubai Dunes**[22] 6413 2-9-0 0... JimCrowley 10 65
(Saeed bin Suroor) *racd wd: chsd ldrs: shkn up over 2f out: nt qckn wl over 1f out: wknd fnl f* **6/4**[1]

5 **8** *5* **Piedita (IRE)**[24] 6336 2-9-0 0... RyanPowell 9 53+
(Sir Mark Prescott Bt) *completely missed the break and lft abt 12 l: mostly in last: pushed along 3f out: passed a couple fnl f* **66/1**

20 **9** *3 ½* **Sweet Zain (IRE)**[23] 6388 2-9-0 0................................ StevieDonohoe 5 44
(Charlie Fellowes) *prom to 1/2-way: shkn up 3f out: sn wknd qckly* **12/1**

50 **10** *4 ½* **Hiawassee (USA)**[17] 6590 2-9-0 0.............................. SilvestreDeSousa 4 33
(Mark Johnston) *nvr bttr than midfield: rdn wl over 2f out: sn wknd and eased* **33/1**

1m 39.4s (-0.40) **Going Correction** 0.0s/f (Stan) **10** Ran SP% **118.4**
Speed ratings (Par 92): **102,101,98,97,96 96,96,91,87,83**
CSF £148.50 TOTE £45.20: £9.10, £1.20, £6.10; EX 295.40 Trifecta £5108.90.
Owner The Three Musketeers **Bred** Jean-Michel Queron **Trained** Lambourn, Berks

FOCUS
There was a shock result to this maiden, but there's plenty to like about the winner. It was marginally the quicker of the two divisions. The level is fluid, but the winner could be good (has a 100-rated sibling).

7051 100% PROFIT BOOST AT 32REDSPORT.COM H'CAP 1m (P)
7:40 (7:40) (Class 5) (0-75,75) 3-Y-O+ **£2,911** (£866; £432; £216) **Stalls** Low

Form RPR

5231 **1** **Cryptic (IRE)**[15] 6629 3-9-2 **75**...................................... PatCosgrave 5 84
(Luca Cumani) *hld up bhd ldrs: prog to go 2nd 2f out: rdn to chal over 1f out: led ins fnl f: edgd lft and drvn out* **15/8**[1]

5313 **2** *½* **Van Dyke**[31] 6138 3-8-11 **75**................................... CharlieBennett(5) 2 83
(Hughie Morrison) *pushed up to go prom: chsd ldr 3f out: led over 2f out: drvn and hdd ins fnl f: styd on* **5/1**[2]

0060 **3** 1 1/4 **Glenalmond (IRE)**[25] 6300 4-8-12 **73**......................(p) HectorCrouch(5) 3 78
(Daniel Steele) *stdd s: hld up in last: shkn up and prog 2f out: drvn and styd on to take 3rd nr fin: no ch to chal* **40/1**
5340 **4** 1/2 **Mustaqqil (IRE)**[14] 6643 4-9-5 **75**............................(b) DanielTudhope 11 79
(David O'Meara) *hld up in last trio: pushed along and gd prog on inner fr 2f out: chsd ldng pair and rdn 1f out: no imp after: lost 3rd nr fin* **8/1**
P005 **5** 1 1/4 **Spiritual Star (IRE)**[14] 6656 7-8-13 **74** ow1................ PaddyBradley(5) 1 75
(Lee Carter) *hld up in midfield: rdn 2f out: prog to take 3rd briefly jst over 1f out: one pce after* **20/1**
2654 **6** 1/2 **Boycie**[17] 6579 3-9-2 **75**...(b) KieranO'Neill 9 75
(Richard Hannon) *t.k.h: hld up in midfield: rdn 2f out: n.m.r over 1f out: styd on same pce and n.d* **16/1**
3600 **7** 1 1/2 **Karnage (IRE)**[82] 4288 4-9-2 **72**..(b) AdamKirby 8 68
(Daniel Kubler) *settled in rr: rdn and no prog wl over 2f out: no ch after: plugged on fnl f* **20/1**
0031 **8** 3 1/2 **Ravenhoe (IRE)**[14] 6645 3-9-2 **75**.............................. SilvestreDeSousa 7 63
(Mark Johnston) *chsd ldrs: pushed along 1/2-way: lost pl and struggling u.p over 2f out* **8/1**
0220 **9** 1 1/4 **Gold Flash**[31] 6140 4-9-4 **74**.......................................(p) JimmyFortune 12 59
(Keith Dalgleish) *t.k.h: chsd ldr to 3f out: sn btn: wknd over 1f out* **25/1**
0000 **10** 1 **Harry Holland**[33] 6055 4-9-2 **72**................................ RichardKingscote 6 54
(Tom Dascombe) *led to over 2f out: sn wknd* **10/1**
0162 **11** shd **Jabbaar**[26] 6254 3-9-2 **75**..(b1) DaneO'Neill 4 57
(Owen Burrows) *dwlt: pushed up to go prom: rdn on wd outside 3f out: wknd* **6/1**[3]

1m 38.66s (-1.14) **Going Correction** 0.0s/f (Stan)
WFA 3 from 4yo+ 3lb **11** Ran SP% **118.7**
Speed ratings (Par 103): **105,104,103,102,101 101,99,96,94,93 93**
CSF £10.30 CT £283.13 TOTE £2.90: £1.40, £2.00, £9.40; EX 12.90 Trifecta £428.40.
Owner Mrs Angie Silver **Bred** Old Carhue & Graeng Bloodstock **Trained** Newmarket, Suffolk

FOCUS
A couple of the 3yos had this between them from over a furlong out. The runner-up has been rated as running a pb in line with the better view of his form.

7052 32RED ON THE APP STORE MAIDEN STKS 1m 4f (P)
8:10 (8:12) (Class 5) 3-Y-O+ **£2,911** (£866; £432; £216) **Stalls** Low

Form RPR
342 **1** **Mazaz (IRE)**[124] 2816 3-9-5 88.....................................(t) FrankieDettori 10 74+
(John Gosden) *led after 1f tl after 2f: trckd ldr: led wl over 2f out: pushed along and sn clr* **2/9**[1]
04- **2** 2 **Cry Wolf**[304] 8123 3-9-5 0.. TimmyMurphy 9 69
(James Evans) *led 1f: sn settled bk towards midfield: nudged along and gd prog over 2f out: chsd wnr over 1f out: no ch to chal but styd on quite wl* **10/1**[3]
25 **3** 3 1/4 **Capton**[25] 6294 3-9-5 0.. DaneO'Neill 1 64
(Henry Candy) *t.k.h: hld up in midfield: shkn up and prog over 2f out to take 3rd fnl f: no ch w ldng pair* **5/1**[2]
30 **4** 4 1/2 **Art Of Swing (IRE)**[35] 5996 4-9-12 0.............................. GeorgeBaker 8 57
(Gary Moore) *hld up in rr: pushed along and prog over 2f out: nvr on terms but kpt on steadily fr over 1f out* **20/1**
0 **5** nk **Warranted**[22] 6415 3-9-5 0... KierenFox 2 56
(Michael Attwater) *dwlt: wl in rr: shkn up 3f out: kpt on same pce fr 2f out: n.d* **33/1**
6 2 **Kerrera** 3-9-0 0... WilliamCarson 3 48
(Paul Webber) *towards rr: prog 1/2-way: effrt to chse wnr over 2f out to over 1f out: wknd qckly* **25/1**
06 **7** 3/4 **Theocratic**[9] 6805 3-9-5 0..(vt) StevieDonohoe 4 52
(Charlie Fellowes) *in tch in midfield: rdn and no prog over 2f out: no ch after* **33/1**
00 **8** 1 1/2 **Angel Of Light (IRE)**[161] 1739 4-9-7 0..................... IrineuGoncalves 13 44
(Jo Hughes) *trckd ldrs: shuffled along on inner and wknd fr 2f out* **66/1**
9 nse **Ravenswood** 3-9-5 0... RichardKingscote 11 49
(Jonathan Portman) *dwlt: wl in rr: rdn 3f out: no significant hdwy* **12/1**
00 **10** 5 **Murraqib (USA)**[12] 6703 3-9-0 0............................... PaddyBradley(5) 7 41
(Brett Johnson) *dwlt: a in rr: no ch over 2f out* **100/1**
460 **11** 4 **Boru's Brook (IRE)**[22] 6415 8-9-12 0.............. WilliamTwiston-Davies 5 35
(Jim Best) *slowly away: a in rr: rdn and no prog over 2f out* **66/1**
12 1 **Jackblack**[329] 4-9-12 0.. JimmyQuinn 6 33
(Patrick Chamings) *chsd ldrs tl wknd qckly over 2f out* **50/1**
00- **13** 9 **Stimulator**[347] 7429 3-9-5 0...[1] CharlesBishop 14 19
(Chris Gordon) *stdd s: plld hrd and rushed through to ld after 2f: hdd & wknd rapidly wl over 2f out* **66/1**

2m 36.57s (2.07) **Going Correction** 0.0s/f (Stan)
WFA 3 from 4yo+ 7lb **13** Ran SP% **137.2**
Speed ratings (Par 103): **93,91,89,86,86 84,84,83,83,80 77,76,70**
CSF £4.86 TOTE £1.20: £1.10, £2.80, £1.50; EX 6.80 Trifecta £14.10.
Owner Al Shaqab Racing **Bred** Knighton Hse, Eadling Farm & Marengo **Trained** Newmarket, Suffolk
■ The Banshee was withdrawn. Price at time of withdrawal 100/1. Rule 4 does not apply.

FOCUS
The pace slowed right down in the back straight, before picking up again from the turn in. Muddling form.

7053 32RED H'CAP 1m 4f (P)
8:40 (8:41) (Class 4) (0-80,80) 3-Y-O+ **£4,690** (£1,395; £697; £348) **Stalls** Low

Form RPR
2525 **1** **Diamond Geyser (IRE)**[21] 6456 3-8-13 **76**...................... PatCosgrave 6 89
(Luca Cumani) *trckd ldrs: shkn up over 2f out: c to nr side and led wl over 1f out: pushed along and drew rt away after* **3/1**[1]
63- **2** 6 **Majrooh (IRE)**[234] 575 4-9-10 **80**.......................................[1] HarryBentley 9 83
(George Peckham) *hld up bhd ldrs: quick move to dispute ld 1/2-way: drvn to ld briefly 2f out: no ch w wnr fr over 1f out* **7/2**[3]
05-5 **3** 1 3/4 **Callendula**[26] 6267 4-9-8 **78**......................................(p) AdamKirby 3 78
(Clive Cox) *hld up in tch: gng strly over 3f out: rdn over 2f out: kpt on to take 3rd over 1f out: no ch* **12/1**
0402 **4** 1 1/2 **Artful Rogue (IRE)**[13] 6676 5-9-5 **75**.............................(b1) JimCrowley 2 73
(Amanda Perrett) *led at mod pce: qcknd whn jnd 1/2-way: drvn and hdd 2f out: fdd* **10/3**[2]
4655 **5** 2 **Versant**[6] 6886 4-9-1 **71**...(t) OisinMurphy 4 66
(Seamus Durack) *dwlt: hld up in last and detached early: effrt over 2f out: sn no imp ldrs* **8/1**
-113 **6** 1 1/2 **The New Pharaoh (IRE)**[95] 3862 5-9-6 **76**...................... GeorgeBaker 7 68
(Chris Wall) *hld up in rr: nudged along fr 3f out: v modest prog and nvr in it* **13/2**
0063 **7** 1/2 **Pasaka Boy**[18] 6549 6-9-7 **77**...................................... RichardKingscote 1 68
(Jonathan Portman) *prom: rdn 3f out: wknd 2f out* **9/1**
6-06 **8** 9 **Prairie Town (IRE)**[157] 1873 5-8-8 **67**...................... GeorgeDowning(3) 5 44
(Tony Carroll) *in tch: rdn once pce lifted 1/2-way: struggling in rr over 2f out* **40/1**
156- **9** 16 **St Saviour**[184] 7172 4-9-9 **79**............................... WilliamTwiston-Davies 8 60
(Philip Hobbs) *prom: rdn over 3f out: wknd over 2f out: sn eased and t.o* **16/1**

2m 32.93s (-1.57) **Going Correction** 0.0s/f (Stan)
WFA 3 from 4yo+ 7lb **9** Ran SP% **120.8**
Speed ratings (Par 105): **81,77,75,74,73 72,72,66,55**
CSF £14.44 CT £112.95 TOTE £4.00: £1.40, £2.20, £2.50; EX 20.60 Trifecta £127.90.
Owner Leonidas Marinopoulos **Bred** Mount Coote Stud, Richard Pegum & M Bell Racing **Trained** Newmarket, Suffolk

FOCUS
A fair handicap and an impressive winner. The runner-up has been rated to form.

7054 32RED.COM H'CAP 6f (P)
9:10 (9:11) (Class 4) (0-85,85) 3-Y-O+ **£4,690** (£1,395; £697; £348) **Stalls** Low

Form RPR
1421 **1** **Upstaging**[22] 6409 4-9-5 **83**.. JimCrowley 6 96
(Paul Cole) *mde all: rdn 2f out and edgd lft after: pressed fnl f but styd on strly* **4/1**[3]
2202 **2** 3/4 **Harwoods Volante (IRE)**[12] 6718 5-9-6 **84**..............(p) DanielTudhope 5 95
(David O'Meara) *t.k.h early: trckd wnr 2f: styd cl up: wnt 2nd again wl over 1f out: drvn to chal and styd on but a hld* **9/2**
-230 **3** 3 **Memories Galore (IRE)**[10] 6780 4-9-7 **85**......................... AdamKirby 1 86+
(Harry Dunlop) *trckd ldng trio: rdn 2f out: tk 3rd over 1f out and cl enough: outpcd fnl f* **11/4**[1]
6503 **4** 3/4 **Red Artist**[20] 6492 3-9-3 **82**....................................... SilvestreDeSousa 10 81
(Simon Crisford) *trckd wnr after 2f to wl over 1f out: nt qckn and hld after: outpcd fnl f* **7/2**[2]
4200 **5** 2 1/2 **Captain Lars (SAF)**[49] 5507 7-8-8 **75**.........................(p) NoelGarbutt(3) 8 66
(Derek Shaw) *in tch: wd bnd 3f out and sn outpcd: tk modest 5th 1f out: no imp after* **66/1**
4510 **6** hd **Elusive Ellen (IRE)**[25] 6299 6-9-2 **80**..............................(t) ShaneKelly 12 70+
(Brendan Powell) *racd wd in rr: outpcd over 2f out: modest late hdwy* **33/1**
3340 **7** 1 1/4 **Nisser**[36] 5955 3-9-2 **81**.. HarryBentley 9 67
(Robert Cowell) *a towards rr: outpcd and rdn over 2f out: no real prog* **12/1**
4110 **8** nk **Salvatore Fury (IRE)**[20] 6475 6-9-4 **82**..........................(p) JimmyFortune 2 67
(Keith Dalgleish) *nvr beyond midfield: outpcd over 2f out: no ch after* **25/1**
5124 **9** hd **Pretty Bubbles**[24] 6340 7-9-6 **84**.................................(v) FrederikTylicki 4 69
(J R Jenkins) *plld hrd early: chsd ldrs: outpcd over 2f out: wknd fnl f* **16/1**
2043 **10** 4 1/2 **Borough Boy (IRE)**[153] 1958 6-8-11 **80**...................(v) HectorCrouch(5) 3 50
(Derek Shaw) *hld up in last: pushed along over 2f out: no prog* **33/1**
5363 **R** **Bahamian Heights**[44] 5679 5-8-13 **77**.............................. PatCosgrave 7
(Robert Cowell) *ref to r: tk no part* **14/1**

1m 11.6s (-1.50) **Going Correction** 0.0s/f (Stan)
WFA 3 from 4yo+ 1lb **11** Ran SP% **118.5**
Speed ratings (Par 105): **110,109,105,104,100 100,98,98,98,92**
CSF £21.90 CT £59.27 TOTE £4.90: £1.60, £1.90, £1.50; EX 24.00 Trifecta £86.40.
Owner H R H Sultan Ahmad Shah **Bred** Glebe Stud **Trained** Whatcombe, Oxon

FOCUS
The first four in the betting raced in the first four places from early on and the positions hadn't changed much at the finish. The runner-up has been rated similar to his previous two starts over this C&D.
T/Plt: £378.00 to a £1 stake. Pool: £79,680.63 - 153.84 winning units T/Qpdt: £14.00 to a £1 stake. Pool: £11,832.89 - 621.89 winning units **Jonathan Neesom**

6630 LEICESTER (R-H)
Tuesday, October 4

OFFICIAL GOING: Good to soft (good in places; 7.2)
Wind: Fresh behind Weather: Fine

7055 BRITISH STALLION STUDS EBF MAIDEN FILLIES' STKS (PLUS 10 RACE) (DIV I) 7f
2:20 (2:20) (Class 4) 2-Y-O **£6,469** (£1,925; £962; £481) **Stalls** High

Form RPR
4 **1** **Choumicha**[15] 6625 2-9-0 0... AndreaAtzeni 6 74
(Hugo Palmer) *led 1f: remained handy: rdn to chse ldr over 1f out: led ins fnl f: r.o* **9/4**[1]
04 **2** nk **Rutherford (IRE)**[20] 6472 2-9-0 0... ShaneGray 1 73
(Kevin Ryan) *led 6f out: rdn over 1f out: hdd ins fnl f: r.o* **50/1**
3 3 1/2 **Italian Heiress** 2-9-0 0.. AdamKirby 10 65
(Clive Cox) *hld up: hdwy 4f out: pushed along 1/2-way: outpcd wl over 1f out: edgd rt and styd on ins fnl f* **9/2**[3]
4 1/2 **Yellowhammer** 2-8-11 0...................................... KieranShoemark(3) 4 63+
(Roger Charlton) *hld up: pushed along and hdwy over 2f out: styd on same pce ins fnl f* **22/1**
5 3/4 **Parisienne Rose (IRE)** 2-9-0 0..................................... RobertHavlin 9 62
(Simon Crisford) *chsd ldrs: rdn over 1f out: nt clr run ins fnl f: styd on same pce* **10/3**[2]
6 hd **Aqdameya (IRE)** 2-9-0 0... JoeFanning 7 61
(Mark Johnston) *w ldr 1f: racd in 2nd pl tl rdn over 1f out: edgd rt and wknd ins fnl f* **22/1**
7 nk **Ettu** 2-9-0 0... JamieSpencer 8 60
(Jeremy Noseda) *hld up: pushed along over 1f out: nt clr and styd on ins fnl f: nt rch ldrs* **20/1**
6 **8** 1/2 **Kyllachys Tale (IRE)**[24] 6336 2-8-9 0............................ GeorgeWood(5) 11 59
(Roger Teal) *s.i.s: hld up: rdn over 2f out: nt trble ldrs* **100/1**
9 1 3/4 **Freediver** 2-9-0 0.. TedDurcan 5 55
(Sir Michael Stoute) *s.i.s: sn rcvrd into mid-div: pushed along 1/2-way: wknd over 1f out* **7/1**
10 nk **Sulafah (IRE)** 2-9-0 0.. PaulHanagan 2 54
(Roger Varian) *hld up: pushed along 1/2-way: sme hdwy over 1f out: wknd ins fnl f* **17/2**
0 **11** 2 **Last Word**[11] 6733 2-9-0 0.. TomQueally 3 49
(David Lanigan) *s.i.s: rdn over 2f out: a in rr* **100/1**

1m 25.06s (-1.14) **Going Correction** -0.075s/f (Good) **11** Ran SP% **112.5**
Speed ratings (Par 94): **103,102,98,98,97 97,96,96,94,93 91**
CSF £140.35 TOTE £3.00: £1.30, £7.60, £2.20; EX 63.10 Trifecta £760.00.
Owner Saleh Al Homaizi & Imad Al Sagar **Bred** Pantile Stud **Trained** Newmarket, Suffolk

FOCUS
Andrea Atzeni described the ground as "tacky" after winning the first. Some decent fillies have won this maiden in recent seasons, and Star Of Seville, third in 2014, went on to win the French Oaks. They raced down the centre. The first two finished clear, with the time 2.36sec outside standard and 0.59sec quicker than the second division.

7056 BRITISH STALLION STUDS EBF MAIDEN FILLIES' STKS (PLUS 10 RACE) (DIV II) 7f
2:50 (2:51) (Class 4) 2-Y-O **£6,469** (£1,925; £962; £481) **Stalls** High

Form RPR
66 **1** **Subatomic**[26] 6250 2-9-0 0 JamesDoyle 4 79
(Ralph Beckett) *sn w ldr: pushed along 1/2-way: led 2f out: sn rdn: styd on wl* **10/1**
2 3 1/2 **Scarlet Thrush (IRE)** 2-9-0 0 HarryBentley 5 70
(Marco Botti) *prom: lost pl 4f out: hdwy over 1f out: r.o to go 2nd wl ins fnl f* **28/1**
0 **3** 1 1/4 **Moondust (IRE)**[136] 2467 2-9-0 0 RobertHavlin 9 67
(John Gosden) *led 5f: sn rdn: no ex ins fnl f* **3/1**[2]
3 **4** 1/2 **Unzipped**[24] 6319 2-9-0 0 StevieDonohoe 7 66
(Stuart Edmunds) *chsd ldrs: rdn over 1f out: styd on same pce* **7/1**[3]
5 2 1/4 **Dariga** 2-9-0 0 AndreaAtzeni 2 60
(Roger Varian) *edgd rt s: hld up: pushed along and hdwy over 2f out: rdn over 1f out: wknd ins fnl f* **16/1**
6 1 1/4 **Set In Stone (IRE)** 2-9-0 0 TadhgO'Shea 10 57
(John Patrick Shanahan, Ire) *in rr: rdn over 2f out: swtchd rt and styd on ins fnl f: nt trble ldrs* **66/1**
0 **7** 4 **Delirium (IRE)**[22] 6413 2-9-0 0 FrederikTylicki 1 47
(Ed de Giles) *hmpd s: styd on ins fnl f: nvr nrr* **100/1**
3 **8** 3 1/2 **Ghadaayer (IRE)**[22] 6413 2-9-0 0 PaulHanagan 3 39
(Sir Michael Stoute) *prom: pushed along 1/2-way: rdn over 2f out: wknd fnl f* **1/1**[1]
9 2 1/2 **Mordoree (IRE)** 2-9-0 0 AdamKirby 8 32
(Clive Cox) *chsd ldrs: rdn 1/2-way: wknd over 1f out* **25/1**
10 3 3/4 **Shiloh** 2-9-0 0 MartinLane 6 23
(Simon Crisford) *s.i.s: a in rr: bhd fnl 4f* **25/1**

1m 25.65s (-0.55) **Going Correction** -0.075s/f (Good) **10** Ran SP% **116.1**
Speed ratings (Par 94): **100,96,94,94,91 90,85,81,78,74**
CSF £247.44 TOTE £12.00: £2.80, £6.90, £1.10; EX 225.80 Trifecta £3951.10 Part Won..
Owner Qatar Racing Limited **Bred** Stratford Place Stud **Trained** Kimpton, Hants

FOCUS
This looked the weaker division, and the time was slightly slower than that of division one. Again they raced down the middle of the track. The opening level is fluid.

7057 STOAT (S) STKS 1m 1f 218y
3:20 (3:20) (Class 6) 3-Y-O **£2,587** (£770; £384; £192) **Stalls** Low

Form RPR
2300 **1** **Muroor**[8] 6838 3-8-11 69 JamieSpencer 5 60
(David O'Meara) *chsd ldr: rdn to ld and hung lft 2f out: hdd 1f out: carried rt wl ins fnl f: styd on to ld post* **2/1**[1]
2551 **2** nse **Monday Club**[21] 6443 3-8-8 57 SeanMooney(7) 3 64
(Dominic Ffrench Davis) *hld up in tch: nt clr run over 2f out: carried lft fr over 1f out: led 1f out: hung rt wl ins fnl f: hdd post* **10/3**[2]
4010 **3** 8 **Jocks Wa Hae (IRE)**[47] 5580 3-9-5 61 TadhgO'Shea 1 54
(John Patrick Shanahan, Ire) *s.i.s: pushed along at times in rr: rdn 1/2-way: hdwy over 1f out: wknd ins fnl f* **7/2**[3]
0 **4** 3/4 **Burnside (FR)**[28] 6219 3-8-11 65 (v[1]) RobertHavlin 7 45
(Ian Williams) *s.i.s and wnt lft s: sn prom: rdn and hung lft over 2f out: wknd over 1f out* **7/1**
0040 **5** 6 **Occasional Dream (IRE)**[19] 6513 3-8-6 56 JFEgan 4 29
(Joseph Tuite) *chsd ldrs: rdn over 3f out: wknd over 1f out* **8/1**
4000 **6** 1 **Playful Dude (USA)**[12] 6700 3-8-6 60 GeorgeWood(5) 2 32
(Phil McEntee) *led: clr 1/2-way tl over 3f out: rdn and hung lft fr over 2f out: sn hdd: wknd over 1f out* **33/1**
500 **7** 3 **Zebedee's Girl (IRE)**[14] 6651 3-8-3 52 (b[1]) NoelGarbutt(3) 6 22
(David Evans) *hld up: rdn over 3f out: sn lost tch* **20/1**

2m 8.53s (0.63) **Going Correction** -0.075s/f (Good) **7** Ran SP% **109.9**
Speed ratings (Par 99): **94,93,87,86,82 81,78**
CSF £8.05 TOTE £2.80: £1.60, £2.00; EX 8.90 Trifecta £16.70.No bid for the winner.
Owner Hambleton Racing XLVII **Bred** Shadwell Estate Company Limited **Trained** Upper Helmsley, N Yorks
■ Stewards' Enquiry : Sean Mooney caution: careless riding

FOCUS
There was a false rail from the top of the hill in the back straight all the way to the winning line, increasing all distances on the round course by approximately 17yds. An ordinary seller. The first two, who finished clear, came over to the stands' side as they locked horns before drifting back into the centre of the track late on. The winner has been rated 9lb off this year's best.

7058 SQUIRREL H'CAP 1m 3f 183y
3:50 (3:50) (Class 2) (0-110,102) 3£16,762 (£4,715; £2,357; £1,180; £587) **Stalls** Low

Form RPR
2530 **1** **Fabricate**[25] 6283 4-9-3 97 (p) AdamKirby 1 104
(Michael Bell) *hld up in tch: shkn up over 5f out: nt clr run over 2f out: rdn to ld ins fnl f: all out* **9/2**[2]
2360 **2** shd **Passover**[17] 6573 5-8-13 96 RobHornby(3) 3 102
(Andrew Balding) *hld up: hdwy to ld 2f out: rdn and hdd ins fnl f: styd on* **8/1**
1000 **3** 1 1/2 **Tawdeea**[45] 5655 4-9-8 102 DanielTudhope 5 106
(David O'Meara) *hld up: hdwy 2f out: chsd ldr over 1f out: sn rdn: ev ch ins fnl f: edgd rt: no ex towards fin* **8/1**
4225 **4** 7 **Stars Over The Sea (USA)**[17] 6573 5-9-8 102 JoeFanning 4 94
(Mark Johnston) *chsd ldrs: wnt 2nd over 7f out: rdn over 2f out: wknd over 1f out* **5/1**[3]
21-0 **5** 2 3/4 **Classic Collection**[164] 1629 4-9-4 98 JamesDoyle 7 86
(Saeed bin Suroor) *s.i.s: hdwy 9f out: rdn over 2f out: wknd over 1f out* **15/2**
0005 **6** nk **Noble Gift**[31] 6125 6-9-0 99 CallumShepherd(5) 8 87
(William Knight) *w ldr tl wnt on over 10f out: edgd rt over 7f out: rdn and hdd 2f out: wknd fnl f* **16/1**
5511 **7** 8 **Faithful Mount**[10] 6781 7-8-11 96 (p) NathanEvans(5) 2 71
(Ian Williams) *led: hdd over 10f out: chsd ldr tl nt clr run over 7f out: remained handy: rdn over 2f out: wknd wl over 1f out* **8/1**
2261 **P** **Monotype (IRE)**[23] 6379 4-9-2 96 AndreaAtzeni 6
(Roger Varian) *hld up: pushed along over 5f out: reminders over 4f out: sn eased and p.u* **5/2**[1]

2m 29.85s (-4.05) **Going Correction** -0.075s/f (Good) **8** Ran SP% **114.4**
Speed ratings (Par 109): **110,109,108,104,102 102,96,**
CSF £39.87 CT £278.47 TOTE £4.70: £1.80, £2.70, £2.40; EX 43.90 Trifecta £466.20.
Owner The Queen **Bred** The Queen **Trained** Newmarket, Suffolk

FOCUS
Add 17yds to advertised race distance. A worthwhile prize and a good handicap. The leaders went off too fast and the first three, who finished clear, were all held up. The first three have been rated close to their marks.

7059 RED DEER H'CAP 6f
4:20 (4:22) (Class 5) (0-70,70) 3-Y-O+ **£3,234** (£962; £481; £240) **Stalls** High

Form RPR
062 **1** **Evening Attire**[17] 6580 5-9-7 70 MartinLane 9 78
(William Stone) *w ldrs: led over 3f out: rdn over 1f out: edgd lft ins fnl f: all out* **9/1**[2]
1522 **2** nse **Mr Orange (IRE)**[19] 6522 3-8-12 67 (p) CliffordLee(5) 16 75
(Paul Midgley) *hld up: hdwy 1/2-way: rdn over 1f out: ev ch ins fnl f: r.o* **13/2**[1]
1021 **3** hd **Caeser The Gaeser (IRE)**[13] 6685 4-9-0 63 (p) JoeFanning 8 70
(Nigel Tinkler) *a.p: rdn over 1f out: ev ch ins fnl f: r.o* **14/1**
5335 **4** 1/2 **More Beau (USA)**[31] 6136 5-9-4 67 BarryMcHugh 2 73
(David Nicholls) *s.i.s: hld up: hdwy over 1f out: rdn and hung lft ins fnl f: r.o* **25/1**
0554 **5** 2 1/4 **Lucky Louie**[25] 6290 3-8-8 63 [1] GeorgeWood(5) 14 62
(Roger Teal) *mid-div: rdn 1/2-way: hdwy over 1f out: styd on* **16/1**
0242 **6** nk **Unnoticed**[22] 6408 4-9-2 65 (b[1]) AndreaAtzeni 11 63
(Luca Cumani) *chsd ldrs: rdn over 1f out: edgd rt and no ex ins fnl f* **13/2**[1]
0105 **7** 3/4 **Classic Flyer**[36] 5968 4-9-4 67 (v) DanielTudhope 4 62
(David O'Meara) *prom: rdn over 1f out: styd on same pce ins fnl f* **33/1**
3032 **8** nse **Dark Command**[24] 6347 3-9-3 67 (be) ConnorBeasley 13 62
(Michael Dods) *s.i.s: sn pushed along in rr: rdn over 2f out: r.o ins fnl f: nvr nrr* **10/1**[3]
1203 **9** 1/2 **Born Innocent (IRE)**[10] 6769 3-9-6 70 TadhgO'Shea 7 63
(John Patrick Shanahan, Ire) *led: hdd over 3f out: remained handy: rdn and edgd lft over 1f out: no ex ins fnl f* **22/1**
2000 **10** nk **Regal Parade**[17] 6583 12-9-4 67 (tp) PaulHanagan 12 59
(Charlie Wallis) *chsd ldrs: rdn and nt clr run over 1f out: eased whn btn ins fnl f* **20/1**
1402 **11** 1 **Teetotal (IRE)**[13] 6685 6-8-7 63 (v) LewisEdmunds(7) 1 52
(Nigel Tinkler) *hld up: rdn over 1f out: kpt on ins fnl f: nt trble ldrs* **16/1**
-004 **12** shd **Dont Have It Then**[22] 6418 5-9-0 63 TomQueally 15 52
(Henry Spiller) *in rr and pushed along over 3f out: styd on ins fnl f: nvr nrr* **11/1**
3240 **13** 3/4 **Kingthistle**[74] 4612 3-9-4 68 JamesDoyle 6 55
(Ian Williams) *mid-div: rdn 1/2-way: nvr on terms* **10/1**[3]
0044 **14** 3/4 **Refuse Colette (IRE)**[62] 5038 7-9-2 65 PaoloSirigu 5 49
(Mick Quinn) *mid-div: rdn and swtchd rt over 1f out: n.d* **40/1**
4000 **15** 1 **Harwoods Star (IRE)**[87] 4155 6-9-0 63 JFEgan 18 44
(John Butler) *s.i.s: a in rr* **33/1**
0031 **16** 1 3/4 **Mad Endeavour**[26] 6269 5-9-2 65 (b) MartinDwyer 3 40
(Stuart Kittow) *racd alone towards far side: w ldrs: rdn over 2f out: wknd over 1f out* **10/1**[3]
U566 **17** nk **Fever Few**[20] 6487 7-9-6 69 TedDurcan 10 43
(Chris Wall) *mid-div: rdn over 2f out: eased whn btn ins fnl f* **18/1**
1160 **18** 6 **Secret Look**[26] 6269 6-9-5 68 (p) TimmyMurphy 17 23
(Richard Phillips) *hld up: a in rr* **80/1**

1m 12.06s (-0.94) **Going Correction** -0.075s/f (Good)
WFA 3 from 4yo+ 1lb **18** Ran SP% **118.5**
Speed ratings (Par 103): **103,102,102,102,99 98,97,97,96,96 95,95,94,93,91 89,88,80**
CSF £58.41 CT £847.70 TOTE £10.10: £2.80, £1.90, £3.00, £3.80; EX 80.30 Trifecta £1725.00.
Owner Miss Caroline Scott **Bred** Howard Barton Stud **Trained** West Wickham, Cambs

FOCUS
A tight finish to this moderate sprint handicap. Another small pb from the runner-up, and a small step forward from the third.

7060 BROCK HILL BADGER H'CAP 1m 3f 183y
4:50 (4:53) (Class 4) (0-85,83) 3-Y-O **£5,175** (£1,540; £769; £384) **Stalls** Low

Form RPR
0310 **1** **Dance The Dream**[31] 6110 3-9-6 82 MartinDwyer 3 96+
(Marcus Tregoning) *chsd ldrs: led 2f out: rdn clr fnl f* **5/1**[1]
3166 **2** 4 **Hestina (FR)**[11] 6747 3-9-4 80 AndreaAtzeni 11 87+
(Peter Chapple-Hyam) *hld up: hdwy over 2f out: nt clr run and swtchd lft over 1f out: styd on to go 2nd post: no ch w wnr* **12/1**
3120 **3** nk **Pointel (FR)**[9] 6804 3-9-7 83 FrederikTylicki 13 89
(James Fanshawe) *mid-div: hdwy over 6f out: rdn over 2f out: chsd wnr ins fnl f: no imp: lost 2nd post* **7/1**[3]
0011 **4** 3 1/2 **Fire Jet (IRE)**[29] 6193 3-9-1 77 TomQueally 10 78
(John Mackie) *prom: lost pl over 6f out: sn pushed along: hdwy over 3f out: rdn to chse wnr over 1f out tl hung rt and wknd ins fnl f* **10/1**
0116 **5** 1 1/2 **Corpus Chorister (FR)**[19] 6527 3-9-2 78 RobertHavlin 6 76
(David Menuisier) *sn led: rdn and hdd 2f out: nt clr run over 1f out: wknd fnl f* **14/1**
0443 **6** 1 1/2 **Chelsea's Boy (IRE)**[29] 6193 3-8-13 75 TedDurcan 9 71
(Clive Cox) *hld up: rdn over 3f out: hung rt fr over 1f out: styd on ins fnl f: nvr nrr* **16/1**
5310 **7** nk **Warp Factor (IRE)**[25] 6286 3-9-4 80 TadhgO'Shea 4 75
(John Patrick Shanahan, Ire) *prom: rdn over 3f out: wknd over 1f out* **8/1**
5642 **8** 1 1/4 **Denham Sound**[27] 6239 3-8-3 70 GeorgeWood(5) 7 63
(Henry Candy) *hld up: rdn and hung rt over 2f out: nvr on terms* **14/1**
-160 **9** 1 1/2 **Walsingham Grange (USA)**[144] 2224 3-8-10 75 RobHornby(3) 1 66
(Pam Sly) *hld up: rdn over 2f out: sn wknd* **12/1**
-542 **10** 8 **Maestro Mac (IRE)**[20] 6474 3-9-2 78 JamesDoyle 2 67
(Hughie Morrison) *prom: chsd ldr over 3f out tl rdn over 2f out: wknd over 1f out: eased* **11/2**[2]
2000 **11** 17 **Juste Pour Nous**[31] 6110 3-9-5 81 JoeFanning 12 32
(Mark Johnston) *chsd ldr tl rdn over 3f out: wknd over 2f out* **25/1**
6254 **12** 6 **Togetherness (IRE)**[31] 6121 3-9-3 79 JamieSpencer 8 20
(Harry Dunlop) *hld up: rdn over 3f out: sn lost tch* **22/1**
14 **13** nk **Pumblechook**[66] 4859 3-9-3 79 DougieCostello 5 20
(Lucy Wadham) *s.i.s: hld up: rdn and wknd over 2f out* **12/1**

2m 30.76s (-3.14) **Going Correction** -0.075s/f (Good) **13** Ran SP% **115.2**
Speed ratings (Par 103): **107,104,104,101,100 99,99,98,97,92 81,77,76**
CSF £62.13 CT £420.24 TOTE £5.60: £2.30, £3.50, £2.60; EX 62.90 Trifecta £303.30.
Owner Mrs Hugh Dalgety **Bred** Minster Stud And Mrs H Dalgety **Trained** Whitsbury, Hants

FOCUS
Add 17yds to advertised race distance. A fair handicap run at a decent pace. The third has been rated to his penultimate AW form.

7061 BREEDERS BACKING RACING EBF DORMOUSE MAIDEN STKS 7f

5:20 (5:20) (Class 5) 3-Y-O+ **£4,528** (£1,347; £673; £336) **Stalls** High

Form RPR

1 **Team Talk** 3-9-5 0 .... [1] FrederikTylicki 7 94+
(Saeed bin Suroor) *s.s: hld up: hdwy over 2f out: shkn up to ld over 1f out: c readily clr fnl f* **1/2**[1]

523- 2 6 **Rockley Point**[318] 7945 3-9-0 75 .... CliffordLee[(5)] 2 76
(Paul D'Arcy) *led: rdn and hdd over 1f out: outpcd fnl f* **13/2**[3]

2 3 4 ½ **James The Elder (IRE)**[64] 4939 3-9-5 0 .... TimmyMurphy 1 64
(Seamus Durack) *w ldr tl nt clr run after 1f: remained handy: wnt 2nd again over 2f out tl rdn over 1f out: sn wknd* **5/1**[2]

4 9 **Ross Raith Rover** 3-9-5 0 .... AndreaAtzeni 4 40
(Robert Eddery) *sn pushed along in rr: nvr on terms* **12/1**

5 ¾ **Samphire Coast** 3-9-2 0 .... NoelGarbutt[(3)] 5 38
(Derek Shaw) *hld up: rdn 1/2-way: n.d* **100/1**

6 4 **Mindy Pendance (IRE)** 3-9-0 0 .... TadhgO'Shea 3 22
(John Patrick Shanahan, Ire) *s.i.s: hdwy to chse ldr and edgd lft 6f out: rdn 1/2-way: hung rt fr over 2f out: sn wknd* **25/1**

1m 24.22s (-1.98) **Going Correction** -0.075s/f (Good) **6** Ran SP% **109.2**
Speed ratings (Par 103): **108,101,96,85,84 80**
CSF £4.02 TOTE £1.40: £1.20, £1.70; EX 3.30 Trifecta £7.20.
Owner Godolphin **Bred** Darley **Trained** Newmarket, Suffolk

FOCUS
A weak, late-season maiden. The runner-up will give a guide to the true level in due course.

7062 LEVERET APPRENTICE H'CAP 7f

5:50 (5:52) (Class 6) (0-60,60) 3-Y-O+ **£2,587** (£770; £384; £192) **Stalls** High

Form RPR

4011 1 **Titan Goddess**[23] 6373 4-9-2 **56** .... KevinLundie[(3)] 15 74+
(Mike Murphy) *hld up: hdwy over 2f out: led and edgd lft over 1f out: r.o wl* **5/1**[1]

0262 2 7 **Infiniti (IRE)**[15] 6631 3-9-5 **58** .... (p) CallumShepherd 4 58
(Rae Guest) *s.i.s: hld up: hdwy over 2f out: rdn and ev ch over 1f out: styd on same pce fnl f* **5/1**[1]

6406 3 nk **Mrs Biggs**[17] 6568 4-9-8 **59** .... PhilDennis 17 59
(Declan Carroll) *led: hdd over 4f out: remained handy: rdn and ev ch over 1f out: edgd rt and styd on same pce fnl f* **9/1**

4131 4 1 ¼ **Intimately**[15] 6637 3-9-4 **57** .... GeorgeWood 8 53
(Jonathan Portman) *s.i.s: hld up: hdwy over 2f out: rdn and ev ch over 1f out: no ex ins fnl f* **8/1**[3]

5554 5 nk **Leonard Thomas**[15] 6637 6-9-4 **55** .... GeorgeBuckell 2 51
(Tony Carroll) *sn pushed along in rr: rdn over 1f out: r.o ins fnl f: nrst fin* **9/1**

4063 6 ½ **Miss Inga Sock (IRE)**[8] 6826 4-9-4 **58** .... SophieKilloran[(3)] 16 53
(Eve Johnson Houghton) *mid-div: rdn over 1f out: edgd rt and styd on ins fnl f: nt trble ldrs* **7/1**[2]

5000 7 ½ **Teversham**[19] 6509 3-9-0 **56** .... NatalieHambling[(5)] 14 48
(Martin Smith) *w ldr tl led over 4f out: rdn and hdd over 2f out: ev ch over 1f out: no ex ins fnl f* **50/1**

0453 8 nse **Elegant Annie**[15] 6636 3-8-11 **55** .... Pierre-LouisJamin[(5)] 12 47
(Jonathan Portman) *chsd ldrs: rdn and swtchd rt over 1f out: no ex fnl f* **10/1**

0005 9 1 ¼ **Bunker Hill Lass**[15] 6637 4-9-2 **53** .... (p) AnnaHesketh 13 43
(Michael Appleby) *prom: pushed along and lost pl over 4f out: n.d after* **25/1**

1322 10 1 ½ **Deben**[53] 5355 3-9-1 **59** .... LewisEdmunds[(5)] 7 44
(Kevin Ryan) *chsd ldrs: led over 2f out: hdd over 1f out: sn wknd* **8/1**[3]

0010 11 1 ¾ **Zebs Lad (IRE)**[88] 4088 4-9-4 **60** .... (p) PatrickVaughan[(5)] 6 42
(Nikki Evans) *w ldrs: rdn over 2f out: wknd over 1f out* **33/1**

5105 12 shd **Always A Dream**[27] 6238 3-9-0 **58** .... SamuelClarke[(5)] 9 39
(Chris Wall) *mid-div: rdn over 2f out: n.d* **12/1**

635 13 12 **Humour (IRE)**[151] 2013 5-9-7 **58** .... DavidParkes 11 10
(Christine Dunnett) *hld up: hdwy over 2f out: rdn and wknd over 1f out* **33/1**

0060 14 1 **Myboydaniel**[13] 6685 4-9-6 **60** .... (t[1]) CliffordLee[(3)] 3 9
(Derek Shaw) *chsd ldrs: rdn over 2f out: wknd over 1f out* **25/1**

1m 24.4s (-1.80) **Going Correction** -0.075s/f (Good)
WFA 3 from 4yo+ 2lb **14** Ran SP% **120.4**
Speed ratings (Par 101): **107,99,98,97,96 96,95,95,94,92 90,90,76,75**
CSF £26.72 CT £229.59 TOTE £4.70: £1.90, £2.90, £3.40; EX 29.70 Trifecta £225.30.
Owner Phoebe's Friends **Bred** Mrs A D Bourne **Trained** Westoning, Beds
■ Stewards' Enquiry : Sophie Killoran caution: careless riding

FOCUS
This moderate apprentice handicap was taken apart by the winner. The winner has been rated to her recent level.
T/Plt: £211.10 to a £1 stake. Pool: £71,616.1 - 247.65 winning units T/Qpdt: £24.80 to a £1 stake. Pool: £7,001.25 - 208.4 winning units **Colin Roberts**

7047 KEMPTON (A.W) (R-H)

Wednesday, October 5

OFFICIAL GOING: Polytrack: standard to slow

7063 100% PROFIT BOOST AT 32REDSPORT.COM MEDIAN AUCTION MAIDEN STKS 1m 3f (P)

5:20 (5:20) (Class 5) 3-5-Y-O **£2,911** (£866; £432; £216) **Stalls** Low

Form RPR

2332 1 **Pastoral Music**[30] 6193 3-9-5 74 .... RyanMoore 4 81
(Hughie Morrison) *settled in 4th: shkn up and angled out ent st: drvn over 1f out and sn led: clr fnl f where kpt up to work: pushed out* **9/2**[2]

24 2 2 ½ **Regicide (IRE)**[139] 2414 3-9-5 0 .... TomQueally 2 77
(James Fanshawe) *hld up in 5th: stl in rr on inner ent st: nt clr run tl swtchd to outer over 1f out: chsd wnr over 1f out where rn green: shuffled along ins fnl f: b.b.v* **1/2**[1]

0 3 1 ¾ **Lord Topper**[14] 6674 3-9-5 0 .... JimCrowley 8 74
(Charles Hills) *encouraged leaving stalls: chsd ldr on outer: rdn wl over 2f out: kpt on tl wknd ins fnl f* **25/1**

4360 4 4 **Rehearse (IRE)**[24] 6380 3-9-5 72 .... WilliamBuick 1 67
(Andrew Balding) *t.k.h on rail bhd ldr: stl keen ent st: swtchd to rail and rdn 2f out: one pce after* **5/1**[3]

3430 5 8 **Booborowie (IRE)**[27] 6268 3-9-5 73 .... MartinLane 7 53
(Jeremy Gask) *sn led: rdn over 2f out: hdd over 1f out: wknd* **25/1**

403- 6 nk **Bowsers Bold**[489] 2857 5-9-4 60 .... RhiainIngram[(7)] 3 53
(Roger Ingram) *t.k.h: in last quartet: rdn ent st: sn hld and one pce after* **66/1**

050 7 52 **Sams R Man**[35] 6036 4-9-8 35 .... GeorgeDowning[(3)] 6
(Linda Jewell) *hld up in last: reminders 1/2-way: rdn 4f out: lost tch ent st: t.o* **200/1**

2m 22.43s (0.53) **Going Correction** 0.0s/f (Stan)
WFA 3 from 4yo+ 6lb **7** Ran SP% **111.2**
Speed ratings (Par 103): **98,96,94,92,86 85,48**
CSF £6.85 TOTE £4.90: £1.70, £1.10; EX 6.80 Trifecta £38.50.
Owner MNC Racing **Bred** Melksham Craic **Trained** East Ilsley, Berks

FOCUS
Chilly and breezy conditions for this eight-race twilight fixture. There wasn't much obvious strength in depth to this opening, and two of the three market leaders failed to give their very best.

7064 32RED/BRITISH STALLION STUDS EBF MAIDEN STKS (DIV I) 7f (P)

5:50 (5:51) (Class 5) 2-Y-O **£3,234** (£962; £481; £240) **Stalls** Low

Form RPR

4 1 **Intrepidly (USA)**[55] 5332 2-9-5 0 .... RyanMoore 8 82+
(Jeremy Noseda) *hld up in mid-div: rdn along in centre over 2f out: picked up wl fr over 1f out to ld fnl 75yds: gng away at fin* **2/1**[2]

4 2 1 ¾ **Sheikspear**[64] 4981 2-9-5 0 .... JFEgan 3 77
(Joseph Tuite) *wl away and settled bhd ldr: drvn along wl over 2f out: led 2f out: kpt finding tl hdd & wknd fnl 75yds* **25/1**

34 3 ¾ **Al Reeh (IRE)**[20] 6524 2-9-5 0 .... GeorgeBaker 5 75
(Marco Botti) *settled in 3rd on outside: travelling best ent 2f out: rdn over 1f out: nt qckn and pushed out ins fnl f* **6/5**[1]

54 4 4 ½ **Al Mansor (IRE)**[14] 6671 2-9-5 0 .... FrankieDettori 2 63
(Richard Hannon) *settled in 4th on rail: rdn jst over 2f out: kpt on and ev ch over 1f out: sn lft bhd and one pce* **7/1**[3]

5 1 ½ **Call Me Grumpy (IRE)** 2-9-5 0 .... HarryBentley 9 59+
(Roger Varian) *hld up in mid-div: prog ent st: shkn up alongside wnr over 2f out: nt qckn: but kpt on nicely under hands and heels* **20/1**

6 hd **Zamalight** 2-9-5 0 .... JimCrowley 6 59+
(Amanda Perrett) *in last quartet: rdn along ent st: rdn over 2f out: sn hld* **25/1**

7 ½ **Azaly (IRE)** 2-9-5 0 .... PaulHanagan 4 57
(Owen Burrows) *in last three: drvn along on inner ent st: briefly r.o bef wknd fr over 1f out* **20/1**

2 8 2 ¼ **Cinque Port**[14] 6671 2-9-5 0 .... ShaneKelly 10 51
(Richard Hughes) *sn led at gd gallop: drvn 2f out and sn hdd: 5th ent fnl f: wknd and eased* **10/1**

60 9 3 ½ **Pass The Cristal (IRE)**[74] 4659 2-9-5 0 .... SamHitchcott 7 42
(William Muir) *awkward s: mid-div: rdn 3f out: sn no ex* **66/1**

40 10 1 ¾ **Ourmullion**[37] 5959 2-9-5 0 .... KierenFox 11 37
(John Best) *a in rr: rdn over 3f out: no imp after* **66/1**

0 11 19 **See You After (IRE)**[8] 6850 2-9-5 0 .... LukeMorris 1
(Sir Mark Prescott Bt) *settled in mid-div: rdn along over 4f: wknd qckly* **200/1**

1m 25.09s (-0.91) **Going Correction** 0.0s/f (Stan) **11** Ran SP% **121.1**
Speed ratings (Par 95): **105,103,102,97,95 95,94,91,87,85 64**
CSF £57.28 TOTE £3.30: £1.40, £5.60, £1.30; EX 72.30 Trifecta £165.00.
Owner The Honorable Earle Mack & T Hind Racing **Bred** WinStar Farm LLC **Trained** Newmarket, Suffolk

FOCUS
Plenty of good yards represented in division one of the juvenile maiden, and a decent pace from the outset had the field stretched before halfway. A much improved run from the winner, with the second also taking a nice step forward. The third and fourth have been rated as a good few lengths below form.

7065 32RED/BRITISH STALLION STUDS EBF MAIDEN STKS (DIV II) 7f (P)

6:20 (6:24) (Class 5) 2-Y-O **£3,234** (£962; £481; £240) **Stalls** Low

Form RPR

025 1 **Intimate Art (IRE)**[22] 6439 2-9-5 79 .... JimCrowley 11 80
(Andrew Balding) *sn c across and led: shkn up 2f out: pressed by runner-up 1f out: asserted fnl 100yds* **7/1**

2 1 ¼ **Radjash** 2-9-5 0 .... WilliamBuick 1 77
(Charlie Appleby) *settled in 3rd on rail: shkn up 2f out: upsides and ev ch 1f: no ex fnl 100yds* **6/4**[1]

3 2 ½ **Teqany (IRE)** 2-9-5 0 .... PaulHanagan 4 70
(Owen Burrows) *stdd leaving stalls: rn green in 4th on outer: swtchd to outer and shkn up 2f out: sn carried hd high: got the hang of things fnl f and tk 3rd post* **6/1**[3]

4 hd **Habbad (FR)** 2-9-5 0 .... FrankieDettori 8 69
(Richard Hannon) *cl up on outer: shkn up 2f out to chse wnr: lft bhd jst over 1f out: lost 3rd cl home* **10/1**

5 1 ½ **Meteoric Riser (USA)** 2-9-5 0 .... ShaneKelly 5 65
(Richard Hughes) *racd in 4th on inner: shkn up over 2f out and sn ct on heels: shuffled along after and hld 5th post* **50/1**

6 nk **Esprit De Corps** 2-9-5 0 .... GeorgeBaker 9 64+
(Roger Charlton) *hld up in mid-div: shkn up in centre 2f out: hung lft over 1f out: stened up and kpt on under hands and heels to press for 5th fin: nvr nrr* **14/1**

7 2 ½ **Melting Dew** 2-9-5 0 .... RyanMoore 7 58
(Sir Michael Stoute) *racd green in rr-div: rdn along to hold pl on bnd 4f out: kpt on one pce after* **9/2**[2]

60 8 nk **Tis Wonderful (IRE)**[54] 5356 2-9-5 0 .... JohnFahy 10 57
(Clive Cox) *in rr: rdn over 2f out: briefly r.o tl wknd fr 1f out* **16/1**

9 3 ¼ **Punkawallah** 2-9-5 0 .... RichardKingscote 3 48
(Tom Dascombe) *in rr: struggling over 3f out* **12/1**

0 10 hd **Broughtons Admiral**[14] 6671 2-9-5 0 .... TomQueally 2 48
(Henry Spiller) *in rr: rdn along over 3f out: wknd over 1f out* **66/1**

1m 26.89s (0.89) **Going Correction** 0.0s/f (Stan) **10** Ran SP% **117.8**
Speed ratings (Par 95): **94,92,89,89,87 87,84,84,80,80**
CSF £18.02 TOTE £6.70: £1.60, £1.20, £2.10; EX 20.00 Trifecta £81.20.
Owner Thurloe Thoroughbreds XXXIX **Bred** Mrs Clodagh McStay **Trained** Kingsclere, Hants

FOCUS
The slightly more competitive of the two divisions judged on the market, but despite another reasonable-looking early tempo a winning time 1.8 seconds slower than division one. The winner has been rated back to his previous best.

7066 32RED.COM H'CAP 7f (P)
6:50 (6:51) (Class 4) (0-80,80) 3-Y-O+ **£4,690** (£1,395; £697; £348) **Stalls** Low

Form RPR
124 **1** **Ripoll (IRE)**[27] 6265 3-8-7 **73**......(t) MitchGodwin[(5)] 12 81+
(Sylvester Kirk) *wnt lft s and banged into rival: hld up in rr: stl last turning in: travelling strly and swtchd to nrside rail over 1f out: rdn and flew home to get up post* **14/1**
4333 **2** ½ **Four Poets**[15] 6657 3-8-11 **72**...... SilvestreDeSousa 10 79
(David Simcock) *hld up bhd ldrs: rdn 2f out: led over 1f out: kpt on wl gng hd-to-hd w eventual 3rd fnl f: nabbed cl home* **11/2**[3]
4120 **3** nk **Consulting**[18] 6580 3-9-1 **76**...... HarryBentley 1 82
(Martyn Meade) *bhd ldrs on rail: rdn along over 2f out: gng hd-to-hd w runner-up fr 1f out to fin: no ex fnl strides* **5/1**[2]
6500 **4** 1 **Jammy Guest (IRE)**[16] 6628 6-9-7 **80**...... JimCrowley 5 84
(George Margarson) *hld up in rr: prog over 2f out: rdn over 1f out: kpt on wl ins fnl f* **17/2**
5-41 **5** ½ **Masarzain (IRE)**[18] 6567 3-9-4 **79**...... PaulHanagan 9 81
(Owen Burrows) *settled bhd ldrs: pressed ldr after 3f: kpt on* **7/1**
4604 **6** ½ **Light From Mars**[28] 6235 11-8-13 **72**......(p) ShaneKelly 2 74
(Ronald Harris) *mid-div on inner: rdn 2f out: kpt on one pce* **33/1**
622 **7** nse **Surety (IRE)**[25] 6337 5-9-1 **74**...... LukeMorris 11 76
(James Tate) *plld way to front after 2f: rdn 2f out: hdd but kpt on tl wknd wl ins fnl f* **14/1**
6 **8** hd **Art Collection (FR)**[23] 6409 3-9-3 **78**......(b) GeorgeBaker 13 78
(Gary Moore) *banged into s: sn settled in mid-div on outer: prog out wd over 2f out: sn rdn and kpt on one pce* **40/1**
0000 **9** hd **Ruban (IRE)**[18] 6579 7-9-2 **75**......(t) PatCosgrave 3 76
(Stuart Williams) *hld up in rr: plenty to do 2f out: nt clr run over 1f out: picked up wl under hands and heels ins fnl f: nvr nrr* **20/1**
-165 **10** ½ **Showing Off (IRE)**[53] 5412 3-9-4 **79**...... DaneO'Neill 4 77
(Henry Candy) *mid-div on outer under restraint: rdn over 2f out: one pce after* **7/2**[1]
0332 **11** 1 **Inexes**[22] 6437 4-9-4 **77**......(p) SamJames 6 78+
(Marjorie Fife) *hld up in rr: rdn over 2f out: nt clr run 1f out and again 1f out: eased fnl 100yds fnl f* **8/1**
5653 **12** ½ **Bank Of Gibraltar**[23] 6416 4-9-6 **79**...... JimmyQuinn 8 74
(Martin Smith) *t.k.h bhd ldrs early: prom on outer after: rdn 2f out: wknd fr over 1f out: eased nr fin* **12/1**
0600 **13** 1 **Captain Revelation**[20] 6521 4-9-7 **80**...... RichardKingscote 7 72
(Tom Dascombe) *led early: hdd after 2f: settled bhd ldrs after: rdn over 2f out: no ex fr 1f out and wknd* **40/1**
0004 **14** nk **Spryt (IRE)**[14] 6683 4-9-5 **78**......(v) MartinHarley 14 70
(Conor Dore) *hld up in rr: rdn over 2f out: sn hld* **100/1**
1m 25.36s (-0.64) **Going Correction** 0.0s/f (Stan)
WFA 3 from 4yo+ 2lb **14** Ran SP% **123.0**
Speed ratings (Par 105): **103,102,102,100,100 99,99,99,99,98 97,97,95,95**
CSF £87.88 CT £464.42 TOTE £13.80: £4.00, £2.00, £2.80; EX 85.10 Trifecta £729.70.
Owner D Harding, C Conroy & P Reglar **Bred** Mrs Bridget Delaney **Trained** Upper Lambourn, Berks
FOCUS
A tight handicap for the grade, and an audacious victory grabbed in the dying strides.

7067 32RED ON THE APP STORE H'CAP (LONDON MIDDLE DISTANCE SERIES QUALIFIER) 1m 3f (P)
7:20 (7:21) (Class 4) (0-85,85) 3-Y-O+ **£4,690** (£1,395; £697; £348) **Stalls** Low

Form RPR
6116 **1** **Ocean Ready (USA)**[14] 6665 3-8-9 **76**......[1] LukeMorris 5 84+
(Sir Mark Prescott Bt) *hld up: nudged along leaving stalls to sit handy on outer of ldr: nudged along to hold pl bnd: bussled along after: strly rdn in line of four jst over 1f out: led 1f out: on top ins fnl f: gng on at fin* **5/1**[3]
4122 **2** ½ **Rock Steady (IRE)**[29] 6209 3-9-4 **85**......[1] GeorgeBaker 2 92+
(Roger Charlton) *hld up in 5th on inner: rdn over 2f out: ev ch in line of four 1f out: kpt on: but no ch w wnr* **6/4**[1]
1156 **3** ¾ **Fashion Parade**[40] 5851 3-9-2 **83**...... SilvestreDeSousa 8 89
(Charles Hills) *hld up in 6th on outer: rdn over 2f out: gd prog on outer fr 1f out to take 3rd fnl 100yds* **20/1**
2123 **4** ¾ **Panko (IRE)**[14] 6665 3-8-11 **78**...... JimCrowley 6 82
(Ed de Giles) *sn led: rdn over 2f out: hdd 1f out: one pce after and lost 3rd fnl 100yds* **5/1**[3]
2432 **5** 1 ½ **Rotherwick (IRE)**[10] 6802 4-9-10 **85**......(t) MartinHarley 3 87
(Paul Cole) *settled in 3rd on inner: rdn over 2f out: ev ch upsides in line of four 1f out: wknd fnl f* **8/1**
-055 **6** 1 ½ **River Dart (IRE)**[62] 5071 4-9-2 **77**...... RoystonFfrench 4 76
(Marcus Tregoning) *settled in 4th on outer: rdn 2f out: lft bhd fr over 1f out* **12/1**
1206 **7** ½ **Saumur**[14] 6667 4-9-0 **75**...... TomQueally 7 74
(Denis Coakley) *in rr: c wd st: rdn over 2f out: kpt on tl wknd fnl f* **33/1**
4402 **8** nse **Theydon Grey**[22] 6456 3-9-4 **85**...... JimmyQuinn 1 83
(Peter Charalambous) *in rr and t.k.h: rdn 2f out: no ex fr 1f out* **4/1**[2]
2m 20.7s (-1.20) **Going Correction** 0.0s/f (Stan)
WFA 3 from 4yo 6lb **8** Ran SP% **119.8**
Speed ratings (Par 105): **104,103,103,102,101 100,100,99**
CSF £13.63 CT £142.90 TOTE £7.30: £2.20, £1.30, £3.40; EX 21.00 Trifecta £234.40.
Owner Baxter, Gregson, Jenkins & Warman **Bred** Stratford Place Stud **Trained** Newmarket, Suffolk
FOCUS
A finish dominated by two runners sporting first-time cheekpieces.

7068 EBFSTALLIONS.COM CONDITIONS STKS 6f (P)
7:50 (7:52) (Class 3) 3-Y-O+
£10,271 (£3,075; £1,537; £768; £384; £193) **Stalls** Low

Form RPR
330 **1** **Lord Of The Land (IRE)**[27] 6272 5-9-2 102......(v) DanielTudhope 6 106
(David O'Meara) *hmpd s: settled in 3rd on outer: rdn and led over 1f out: kpt on wl ins fnl f: pushed out* **9/2**[2]
4450 **2** 1 ¼ **Dhahmaan (IRE)**[90] 4062 3-9-1 98......(b[1]) HarryBentley 1 102
(Marco Botti) *hld up in 7th on rail: rdn over 2f out: kpt on wl fr over 1f out: but nvr getting to wnr* **7/1**[3]
0100 **3** 1 **Amazour (IRE)**[34] 6056 4-9-2 96...... MartinHarley 5 99+
(Ismail Mohammed) *squeezed out s: in rr: prog in centre fr over 2f out tl rdn jst over 1f out: tk 3rd fnl 100yds* **12/1**
6441 **4** ¾ **Basil Berry**[22] 6458 5-9-5 98......(b) SilvestreDeSousa 4 99
(Chris Dwyer) *hmpd s: sn settled in 6th on outer: rdn 2f out kpt on one pce tl prog ins fnl f* **7/1**[3]
-616 **5** ½ **Taneen (USA)**[90] 4062 3-9-1 101...... PaulHanagan 2 95
(Roger Varian) *5th on rail: rdn over 1f out on inner: ev ch 1f out: wknd and lost two plcd fnl 100yds* **5/4**[1]
0600 **6** 1 **Rivellino**[18] 6558 6-9-9 98...... DougieCostello 3 99
(K R Burke) *wnt lft s: rdn along over 3f out: prog fnl f: eased last strides* **14/1**
305U **7** 3 ¼ **Huntsmans Close**[29] 6207 6-8-13 98...... EoinWalsh[(3)] 7 81
(Robert Cowell) *t.k.h and sn grabbed rail in disp ld: 1 l ldr at 1/2-way: rdn 2f out and hdd over 1f out: wknd fnl f* **33/1**
0040 **8** 1 ½ **Chookie Royale**[83] 4299 8-9-7 106......(p) PhillipMakin 8 81
(Keith Dalgleish) *sn pressed ldr on outer: clr 2nd at 1/2-way: rdn over 2f out: steadily wknd fr over 1f out* **10/1**
1m 11.02s (-2.08) **Going Correction** 0.0s/f (Stan)
WFA 3 from 4yo+ 1lb **8** Ran SP% **114.0**
Speed ratings (Par 107): **113,111,110,109,108 107,102,100**
CSF £35.46 TOTE £4.80: £1.90, £1.80, £3.60; EX 36.80 Trifecta £143.00.
Owner George Turner **Bred** Ammerland Verwaltung Gmbh **Trained** Upper Helmsley, N Yorks
FOCUS
A fair conditions event, in which the early pace was contested.

7069 32RED CASINO H'CAP 6f (P)
8:20 (8:20) (Class 6) (0-65,65) 3-Y-O+ **£2,264** (£673; £336; £168) **Stalls** Low

Form RPR
3635 **1** **He's My Boy (IRE)**[43] 5750 5-9-6 **65**......(v) TomQueally 7 74
(James Fanshawe) *in last quarter on inner: swtchd for ins run and rapid prog to ld 1f out: pushed out fnl f: comf* **4/1**[2]
0502 **2** 1 ½ **Waneen (IRE)**[20] 6509 3-9-4 **64**...... JFEgan 11 67
(Joseph Tuite) *racd freely in 2nd on outer: rdn and led 2f out: hdd 1f out: kpt on to hold 2nd in duel ins fnl f* **13/2**
2344 **3** hd **Only Ten Per Cent (IRE)**[24] 6374 8-9-4 **63**...... FrederikTylicki 3 65
(J R Jenkins) *racd freely in 2nd on outer: settled in 4th on outer: rdn 2f out: kpt on wl in duel for 2nd: jst hld* **6/1**
4 **4** 1 ½ **Maymyo (IRE)**[15] 6653 5-9-1 **65**......(t) MitchGodwin[(5)] 1 62
(Sylvester Kirk) *5th on inner: rdn 2f out: kpt on one pce* **9/2**[3]
0215 **5** ¾ **Mossy's Lodge**[201] 978 3-9-1 **64**...... LouisSteward[(3)] 10 59
(Anthony Carson) *in rr: rdn on inner 2f out: kpt on one pce* **14/1**
0003 **6** ¾ **Mustn't Grumble (IRE)**[14] 6685 3-9-2 **62**......(p) SilvestreDeSousa 2 55
(Ivan Furtado) *3rd on inner: rdn 2f out: sn one pce* **7/2**[1]
-000 **7** 2 **Cloak And Degas (IRE)**[140] 2379 4-9-3 **62**......(v) LukeMorris 4 49
(Tim McCarthy) *led: rdn and hdd 2f out: wknd steadily fr over 1f out* **20/1**
3323 **8** 6 **Royal Rettie**[244] 442 4-9-2 **61**...... MartinLane 8 30
(Paddy Butler) *hld up in last trio: rdn 2f out: no ex* **20/1**
0000 **9** 4 ½ **Balliol**[41] 5797 4-9-3 **62**......[1] JimCrowley 9 17
(Ronald Harris) *hld up in rr: t.k.h: plld way through pack on outer on bnd to dispute ld ent st: wknd qckly over 1f out* **10/1**
1m 13.12s (0.02) **Going Correction** 0.0s/f (Stan)
WFA 3 from 4yo+ 1lb **9** Ran SP% **113.3**
Speed ratings (Par 101): **99,97,96,94,93 92,90,82,76**
CSF £29.53 CT £152.12 TOTE £4.90: £1.80, £2.90, £2.10; EX 31.40 Trifecta £120.50.
Owner P S Ryan **Bred** Rossenarra Bloodstock Limited **Trained** Newmarket, Suffolk
FOCUS
Competitive but moderate fare, and a winning time perhaps unsurprisingly over two seconds slower than that of the 102-rated Lord Of The Land half an hour earlier. The second and third set a straightforward level.

7070 RACING UK PROFITS RETURNED TO RACING H'CAP 7f (P)
8:50 (8:51) (Class 6) (0-55,55) 3-Y-O+ **£2,264** (£673; £336; £168) **Stalls** Low

Form RPR
005 **1** **Garter (IRE)**[15] 6650 3-9-5 **55**...... MichaelJMMurphy 7 63
(Charles Hills) *covered up in rr-div: pushed along over 2f out and swtchd to centre: gd prog fr over 1f out to ld ins fnl f: pushed out* **12/1**
3562 **2** 1 ¾ **Just Isla**[9] 6826 6-9-5 **53**......(b) DanielMuscutt 12 57
(John Flint) *settled bhd ldrs: rdn 2f out: chd clr ldr over 1f out: tk 2nd ins fnl fnl f: but no ch w wnr* **6/1**[3]
0400 **3** nk **Capital Gearing**[23] 6405 3-9-4 **54**......(b) SilvestreDeSousa 10 56
(Henry Spiller) *hld up in rr: nt clr run 2f out: sn clr and rdn: kpt on wl fr over 1f out: nvr nrr* **20/1**
0051 **4** ¾ **Barista (IRE)**[16] 6636 8-9-2 **55**...... HollieDoyle[(5)] 5 56
(Brian Forsey) *mid-div on inner: niggled bnd: taken off rail and rdn over 2f out: kpt on* **9/2**[2]
4400 **5** shd **Zabdi**[14] 6677 3-9-5 **55**...... KierenFox 6 55
(Lee Carter) *led on outer: rdn over 2f out and 1 l up over 1f out: hdd ins fnl f where one pce* **8/1**
3553 **6** shd **Just Fab (IRE)**[16] 6631 3-9-2 **52**......(bt) JimCrowley 11 52
(Ali Stronge) *restrained bhd ldrs on inner: rdn over 2f out: kpt on one pce* **8/1**
4000 **7** 1 ½ **Makhfar (IRE)**[97] 3821 5-9-5 **53**......(v) PatCosgrave 4 52
(Kevin Morgan) *slowly away: hld up in last: shkn up over 2f out: stdy run fr over 1f out: eased nring line* **7/2**[1]
0550 **8** 1 ¼ **Gavarnie Encore**[41] 5808 4-9-3 **51**...... TomMarquand 2 44
(Michael Blanshard) *in rr on inner: nudged along early: lost pl ent st: rdn along over 2f out:* **9/2**[2]
000 **9** 2 **Welsh Inlet (IRE)**[50] 5503 8-9-3 **51**...... DannyBrock 9 39
(John Bridger) *mid-div on outer: sltly hmpd early: lost pl ent st: rdn over 2f out: son hld* **14/1**
0240 **10** 2 ½ **Lutine Charlie (IRE)**[44] 5710 9-9-2 **50**......(v[1]) TomQueally 1 31
(Emma Owen) *disp ld on inner: pushed along ent st: sn rdn: lost pl fr 2f out: wknd and hands and heels fr over 1f out* **20/1**
0000 **11** 3 **Bubbly Bailey**[50] 5509 6-9-7 **55**......(v) FrederikTylicki 8 28
(J R Jenkins) *mid-div on outer: niggled along over 2f out: sn no ex* **33/1**
0445 **12** 1 ½ **Deftera Lad (IRE)**[27] 6243 4-9-0 **51**......(b[1]) EoinWalsh[(3)] 14 20
(Natalie Lloyd-Beavis) *awkward leaving stalls: mid-divisn on outer: mde grnd bnd: pushed along ent st: wknd fr over 1f out* **20/1**
1m 25.77s (-0.23) **Going Correction** 0.0s/f (Stan)
WFA 3 from 4yo+ 2lb **12** Ran SP% **126.7**
Speed ratings (Par 101): **101,99,98,97,97 97,95,94,92,89 85,84**
CSF £83.68 CT £1487.89 TOTE £17.70: £5.10, £2.90, £5.20; EX 81.40 Trifecta £747.50.
Owner Highclere Thoroughbred Racing (Walpole) **Bred** Herbertstown House Stud **Trained** Lambourn, Berks
FOCUS
A pretty moderate finale, and the slowest of the three races over the 7f trip on the evening, but the winner can progress. The runner-up has been rated close to her recent good run at Bath.
T/Plt: £28.90 to a £1 stake. Pool: £87,783.72 - 2214.18 winning tickets T/Qpdt: £19.30 to a £1 stake. Pool: £10,995.25 - 421.46 winning tickets **Cathal Gahan**

[6873]NOTTINGHAM (L-H)

Wednesday, October 5

OFFICIAL GOING: Good to soft (6.7)

Wind: fresh behind Weather: Cloudy

7071 £10 FREE AT 32RED.COM EBF MAIDEN STKS (DIV I) 6f 15y

1:30 (1:32) (Class 5) 2-Y-O **£3,234** (£962; £481; £240) **Stalls** Centre

Form RPR

1 **Dreamfield** 2-9-5 0 ... JamesDoyle 11 99+
(John Gosden) *mde all: qcknd clr over 1f out: v readily* **4/5**[1]

2 *8* **Sitar** 2-9-0 0 ... FrederikTylicki 4 67
(James Fanshawe) *in tch: hdwy over 2f out: rdn along to chse ldng trio over 1f out: styd on wl fnl f: tk 2nd nr fin* **25/1**

03 3 *nk* **Houndstooth (IRE)**[34] 6053 2-9-5 0 ... DanielTudhope 7 71
(Luca Cumani) *trckd wnr: shkn up over 2f out: sn rdn: drvn and kpt on same pce fnl f* **7/2**[2]

4 *3/4* **Queens Royale** 2-9-0 0 ... LukeMorris 1 64
(Michael Appleby) *chsd ldrs on outer: rdn along over 2f out: kpt on same pce appr fnl f* **66/1**

36 5 *1 1/4* **Plato's Kode (IRE)**[92] 3971 2-9-5 0 ... OisinMurphy 10 65
(Seamus Durack) *racd towards stands rail: chsd ldrs: rdn along over 2f out: kpt on same pce* **14/1**

626 6 *1 1/2* **Cool Echo**[33] 6088 2-9-0 78 ... TomMarquand 2 56
(J R Jenkins) *prom: pushed along 1/2-way: sn rdn and grad wknd* **16/1**

7 *nk* **Harvest Wind (IRE)** 2-9-5 0 ... AdamKirby 3 60+
(Clive Cox) *dwlt: green and outpcd in rr: sme hdwy 2f out: kpt on: nrst fin* **10/1**[3]

005 8 *1 3/4* **Seyasah (IRE)**[23] 6413 2-9-0 71 ... TedDurcan 6 55+
(Chris Wall) *in tch: rdn along wl over 2f out: n.d* **14/1**

0 9 *11* **Coachella (IRE)**[39] 5890 2-9-5 0 ... ShaneGray 8 21
(Ed de Giles) *in tch: rdn along 1/2-way: sn outpcd* **66/1**

0 10 *2 1/2* **Breathoffreshair**[13] 6712 2-9-5 0 ... ConnorBeasley 5 14
(Richard Guest) *a rr: bhd fr 1/2-way* **150/1**

1m 13.14s (-1.56) **Going Correction** -0.45s/f (Firm) **10** Ran SP% **113.6**
Speed ratings (Par 95): **92,81,80,79,78 76,75,73,58,55**
CSF £29.62 TOTE £1.80: £1.10, £5.90, £1.10; EX 18.60 Trifecta £75.40.
Owner Godolphin **Bred** Meon Valley Stud **Trained** Newmarket, Suffolk

FOCUS
A breezy day and the ground had dried out slightly, with the going now officially good to soft all over (from good to soft, soft in places). Outer track used. Rail out 2yds on home bend, adding 6yds to race distances on the round course. The betting for the first division of this juvenile maiden was dominated by two horses, one a beautifully bred newcomer and the other with form on the board, while they bet 10-1 bar the pair. They raced centre-to-nearside and the winner could hardly have been more impressive. The winning time was 2.54sec outside standard and James Doyle felt the going was "genuine good to soft ground and quite dead." The hugely impressive winner has been given a three-figure rating, with the form straightforward in behind.

7072 £10 FREE AT 32RED.COM EBF MAIDEN STKS (DIV II) 6f 15y

2:00 (2:01) (Class 5) 2-Y-O **£3,234** (£962; £481; £240) **Stalls** Centre

Form RPR

2 1 **Dark Power (IRE)**[19] 6543 2-9-5 0 ... AdamKirby 6 75
(Clive Cox) *led 11/2f: trckd ldr: hdwy to chal wl over 1f out: rdn ent fnl f: slt ld last 10 yds: kpt on* **1/1**[1]

062 2 *shd* **Pillar Of Society (IRE)**[22] 6439 2-9-5 77 ... SeanLevey 3 75
(Richard Hannon) *cl up: led over 4f out: pushed along wl over 1f out: sn jnd and rdn: drvn ins fnl f: hdd narrowly last 100 yds: kpt on wl* **5/1**[2]

3 *4* **Harvest Moon** 2-9-0 0 ... TonyHamilton 1 58+
(Richard Fahey) *trckd ldrs: pushed along 2f out: sn rdn and kpt on same pce fnl f* **16/1**

4 *2 3/4* **Dream Reversion** 2-9-5 0 ... RichardKingscote 2 54+
(Tom Dascombe) *trckd ldrs: pushed along: green and sltly outpcd wl over 2f out: rdn wl over 1f out: styd on fnl f* **14/1**

0 5 *1 3/4* **Sonata**[19] 6542 2-9-0 0 ... SilvestreDeSousa 7 44
(Mick Channon) *towards rr: hdwy on outer 1/2-way: rdn along to chse ldrs 2f out: kpt on fnl f: nrst fin* **16/1**

5 6 *1 1/2* **I Wouldn't Bother**[24] 6375 2-9-5 0 ... TimmyMurphy 8 45+
(Daniel Kubler) *rr: hdwy over 2f out: sn rdn and no imp* **66/1**

4 7 *nk* **Arnold**[13] 6712 2-9-5 0 ... PaulMulrennan 10 44
(Ann Duffield) *trckd ldrs: hdwy to chse ldng pair 1/2-way: rdn along 2f out: grad wknd* **6/1**[3]

66 8 *2 3/4* **Ode To Paris**[12] 6750 2-9-5 0 ... AndreaAtzeni 9 36
(Ed Dunlop) *trckd ldrs: pushed along wl over 2f out: sn rdn and grad wknd* **9/1**

9 *14* **Katie's Surprise (IRE)** 2-9-0 0 ... LiamKeniry 4
(John Butler) *dwlt: a rr* **66/1**

0 10 *5* **Compton Brave**[20] 6524 2-9-5 0 ... FrederikTylicki 5
(J R Jenkins) *t.k.h: chsd ldrs: rdn along 1/2-way: sn lost pl and bhd* **100/1**

1m 13.62s (-1.08) **Going Correction** -0.45s/f (Firm) **10** Ran SP% **113.4**
Speed ratings (Par 95): **89,88,83,79,77 75,75,71,52,46**
CSF £5.81 TOTE £1.80: £1.10, £1.80, £3.70; EX 6.70 Trifecta £39.20.
Owner Alan G Craddock **Bred** Guy O'Callaghan **Trained** Lambourn, Berks

FOCUS
No exciting debutant in this division and the form horses dominated both the race and the finish. The winning time was nearly half a second slower than the first leg. The winner has been rated as replicating his debut effort.

7073 32RED CASINO NURSERY H'CAP 5f 13y

2:30 (2:36) (Class 4) (0-85,85) 2-Y-O **£3,946** (£1,174; £586; £293) **Stalls** Centre

Form RPR

3560 1 **Awesome Allan (IRE)**[50] 5510 2-8-13 77 ...[1] JimCrowley 13 81
(David Evans) *chsd ldrs: hdwy 2f out: rdn to ld ent fnl f: sn drvn and edgd lft: kpt on wl towards fin* **20/1**

1105 2 *nk* **Turanga Leela**[26] 6292 2-8-13 77 ... SilvestreDeSousa 10 80
(Ian Williams) *sn led: rdn along 2f out: hdd ent fnl f: sn drvn and kpt on wl u.p towards fin* **7/1**

5325 3 *nk* **Coolfitch (IRE)**[19] 6538 2-9-2 80 ... DanielTudhope 7 82
(David O'Meara) *trckd ldrs: hdwy over 2f out: sn trcking ldng pair: cl up and rdn ent fnl f: ev ch: drvn and no ex last 50 yds* **6/1**[3]

2120 4 *2* **Blue Suede (IRE)**[19] 6538 2-9-0 78 ... SeanLevey 5 73
(Richard Hannon) *cl up: rdn along 2f out: ev ch tl drvn over 1f out and kpt on same pce* **13/2**

1520 5 *1 1/4* **Spiritous (USA)**[12] 6734 2-9-7 85 ...(p) JamesDoyle 9 75
(John Gosden) *dwlt and towards rr: pushed along and hdwy 1/2-way: swtchd rt and rdn wl over 1f out: kpt on fnl f: nrst fin* **3/1**[1]

3000 6 *1 1/4* **Spin Doctor**[19] 6536 2-8-13 77 ... TonyHamilton 3 63
(Richard Fahey) *towards rr: hdwy over 2f out: sn rdn and no imp fr over 1f out* **12/1**

4010 7 *1* **Diable D'Or (IRE)**[24] 6388 2-9-0 81 ... EdwardGreatrex[(3)] 1 63
(Eve Johnson Houghton) *in tch on wd outside: rdn along to chse ldrs 2f out: wknd over 1f out* **5/1**[2]

210 8 *2 1/2* **Cuppacoffee (IRE)**[12] 6734 2-9-2 85 ... RowanScott[(5)] 4 58
(Ann Duffield) *midfield: rdn along 1/2-way: n.d* **10/1**

0320 9 *hd* **Makman (IRE)**[15] 6658 2-8-4 68 ... LukeMorris 11 40
(Ed Dunlop) *wnt lft s: chsd ldrs: rdn along 2f out: sn wknd* **50/1**

004 10 *nk* **Oh So Dandy (IRE)**[15] 6641 2-7-12 65 ...(v) NoelGarbutt[(3)] 2 36
(Derek Shaw) *dwlt: a rr* **100/1**

1203 11 *3 3/4* **Lonely The Brave (IRE)**[20] 6507 2-9-3 81 ... JoeFanning 12 39
(Mark Johnston) *midfield: rdn along over 2f out: sn wknd* **16/1**

0540 12 *1 1/2* **Halinka (IRE)**[16] 6630 2-7-10 67 ... DavidEgan[(7)] 14 19
(Roger Varian) *a towards rr* **20/1**

59.5s (-2.00) **Going Correction** -0.45s/f (Firm) **12** Ran SP% **116.9**
Speed ratings (Par 97): **98,97,97,93,91 89,88,84,83,83 77,75**
CSF £148.07 CT £975.02 TOTE £22.20: £6.20, £2.70, £1.90; EX 178.20 Trifecta £1709.90.
Owner Walters Plant Hire Ltd **Bred** D G Iceton **Trained** Pandy, Monmouths

FOCUS
A fair sprint nursery reduced by one when Northern Thunder was withdrawn after getting out under his stall and running loose. They came up the centre pf the track and very few ever got into this, with the principals up there from the start.

7074 EBF STALLIONS 32RED CASINO OATH MAIDEN STKS (STALLION-RESTRICTED) (PLUS 10 RACE) 1m 75y

3:00 (3:03) (Class 4) 2-Y-O **£6,469** (£1,925; £962; £481) **Stalls** Centre

Form RPR

52 1 **Contrapposto (IRE)**[47] 5615 2-9-5 0 ... MartinDwyer 5 86+
(David Menuisier) *cl up: led over 4f out: rdn wl over 1f out: kpt on strly* **5/2**[2]

2 *2 1/4* **Al Zaman (IRE)** 2-9-5 0 ... SilvestreDeSousa 9 81+
(Simon Crisford) *dwlt and rr: gd hdwy on wd outside wl over 2f out: chsd ldrs over 1f out: styd on wl fnl f: tk 2nd nr fin* **25/1**

222 3 *nk* **Hydroxide**[15] 6655 2-9-5 83 ...[1] JimCrowley 6 80
(Hugo Palmer) *trckd ldrs: hdwy to trck wnr 4f out: effrt and cl up 2f out: sn rdn: drvn over 1f out: kpt on same pce* **9/4**[1]

4 *1 1/4* **Jake's Hill** 2-9-5 0 ... CharlesBishop 7 78
(Eve Johnson Houghton) *dwlt and rr: hdwy on inner 3f out: rdn over 2f out: drvn and kpt on wl fnl f* **50/1**

5 *3/4* **Stradivarius (IRE)** 2-9-5 0 ... RobertHavlin 12 76+
(John Gosden) *trckd ldrs: hdwy to chse ldng pair over 3f out: rdn along 2f out: kpt on same pce* **3/1**[3]

24 6 *4 1/2* **Fields Of Fortune**[43] 5740 2-9-5 0 ... TomMarquand 2 66
(Richard Hannon) *in tch: hdwy 3f out: rdn along over 2f out: n.d* **6/1**

7 *2 1/2* **Star Story** 2-9-0 0 ... OisinMurphy 1 56
(Ralph Beckett) *trckd ldrs: pushed along 3f out: rdn along 2f out: grad wknd* **16/1**

04 8 *9* **Mungo Madness**[63] 5036 2-9-2 0 ... ShelleyBirkett[(3)] 4 41
(Julia Feilden) *led: hdd over 4f out: chsd ldng pair: rdn along 3f out: wknd fnl 2f* **50/1**

0 9 *15* **Jumbo Vee (IRE)**[13] 6716 2-9-5 0 ... DanielTudhope 11 8
(Declan Carroll) *a towards rr: rdn along over 3f out: sn outpcd and bhd* **100/1**

1m 46.77s (-2.23) **Going Correction** -0.30s/f (Firm) **9** Ran SP% **113.3**
Speed ratings (Par 97): **99,96,96,95,94 89,87,78,63**
CSF £62.32 TOTE £4.40: £1.70, £2.70, £1.20; EX 47.20 Trifecta £144.60.
Owner Clive Washbourn **Bred** Gerard & Anne Corry **Trained** Pulborough, W Sussex

FOCUS
Rail movement added 6yds to race distance. An interesting maiden which resulted in a 1-2 for the sire Cacique and another boost for the form of York's Convivial Maiden. A small step forward from the winner.

7075 EBF STALLIONS 32RED.COM NURSERY H'CAP 1m 1f

3:30 (3:32) (Class 3) (0-90,85) 2-Y-O **£9,703** (£2,887; £1,443; £721) **Stalls** Low

Form RPR

6441 1 **Outre Mer (IRE)**[7] 6875 2-9-2 80 6ex ... JamesDoyle 7 90+
(John Gosden) *trckd ldrs: hdwy and cl up over 6f out: led wl over 4f out: pushed along over 2f out: rdn over 1f out: kpt on strly* **10/11**[1]

2213 2 *2 1/2* **Devil's Bridge (IRE)**[34] 6059 2-9-7 85 ... SilvestreDeSousa 1 90
(Richard Hannon) *trckd ldrs: swtchd lft to inner over 3f out: hdwy to chal 2f out and sn rdn: drvn ent fnl f: kpt on* **5/1**[2]

0321 3 *nk* **Tomorrowcomes (IRE)**[13] 6713 2-9-1 79 ... TonyHamilton 3 83
(Richard Fahey) *trckd ldrs: hdwy 3f out: rdn along 2f out: sn drvn and kpt on* **16/1**

5103 4 *4 1/2* **Galactic Prince**[19] 6546 2-9-2 80 ... OisinMurphy 5 75
(Andrew Balding) *hld up in rr: hdwy 4f out: rdn along 2f out: styd on fnl f: nrst fin* **9/1**

410 5 *1 1/2* **Kiruna Peak (IRE)**[13] 6713 2-8-10 74 ... GrahamLee 2 66
(Mick Channon) *hld up: hdwy over 2f out: sn rdn along and n.d* **50/1**

414 6 *5* **Our Boy (IRE)**[18] 6554 2-8-13 77 ... DanielTudhope 6 59
(David Evans) *trckd ldrs: hdwy over 3f out: rdn over 2f out: sn drvn and wknd* **7/1**[3]

051 7 *9* **Viking Hoard (IRE)**[26] 6288 2-9-3 81 ... AdamKirby 4 45
(Harry Dunlop) *led: hdd wl over 4f out: rdn along over 3f out: sn drvn and wknd* **9/1**

1m 55.56s (-2.04) **Going Correction** -0.30s/f (Firm) **7** Ran SP% **109.4**
Speed ratings (Par 99): **97,94,94,90,89 84,76**
CSF £5.10 TOTE £1.70: £1.20, £2.20; EX 5.70 Trifecta £22.20.
Owner Godolphin **Bred** Darley **Trained** Newmarket, Suffolk

FOCUS
Rail movement added 6yds to race distance. A decent staying nursery and a good test in the conditions, but it all revolved around one horse and he did all that was necessary. The first two are ahead of their marks.

7076 32RED ON THE APP STORE H'CAP 1m 75y

4:00 (4:01) (Class 5) (0-73,73) 3-Y-O+ **£3,067** (£905; £453) **Stalls** Centre

Form RPR

035 1 **Stanley (GER)**[20] 6516 5-9-6 72 ... GrahamLee 13 81
(Jonjo O'Neill) *chsd ldrs: led over 1f out: drvn out* **12/1**

2612 **2** 1 1/4 **Dark Wonder (IRE)**[22] 6453 4-9-5 **71**....................(p) SilvestreDeSousa 3 77
(Ivan Furtado) *chsd ldrs: led after 1f: hdd over 1f out: styd on same pce: sddle slipped* **7/1**[2]

5066 **3** 1/2 **First Wheat**[20] 6502 3-8-10 **70**.................................... NathanEvans(5) 15 75
(Michael Easterby) *hld up in rr: hdwy on ins over 3f out: 3rd over 1f out: kpt on same pce* **14/1**

0404 **4** 1 1/4 **See You When (IRE)**[18] 6576 3-9-2 **71**........................ TomMarquand 2 73
(Richard Hannon) *s.i.s: in rr: hdwy over 3f out: 4th over 2f out: kpt on same pce over 1f out* **14/1**

0006 **5** 1 1/2 **Berkeley Vale**[24] 6365 5-9-5 **71**.. JackMitchell 6 70
(Roger Teal) *led 1f: chsd ldrs: one pce fnl 2f* **7/1**[2]

524 **6** nk **Rahmah (IRE)**[27] 6254 4-9-6 **72**.................................. TimmyMurphy 12 70
(Geoffrey Deacon) *wnt lft s: trckd ldrs on outer: hmpd bnd over 5f out: one pce fnl 2f* **25/1**

6426 **7** 1 1/2 **Billy Bond**[15] 6645 4-9-1 **72**.................................(v) AdamMcNamara(5) 9 67
(Richard Fahey) *mid-div: effrt over 3f out: one pce fnl 2f* **12/1**

630 **8** 3 3/4 **Auxiliary**[25] 6344 3-9-3 **72**..(p) JamesSullivan 10 58
(Patrick Holmes) *hmpd s: hld up in rr: hdwy on ins over 2f out: nvr a factor* **25/1**

203 **9** 1 **Major Assault**[65] 4953 3-9-4 **73**... AdamKirby 1 57
(Clive Cox) *trckd ldrs: t.k.h: effrt over 2f out: one pce* **8/1**[3]

-044 **10** 2 **Inn The Bull (GER)**[56] 5306 3-9-2 **71**.............. FergusSweeney 16 50
(Alan King) *mid-div: sme hdwy over 2f out: nvr on terms* **14/1**

1054 **11** 1 3/4 **Bluff Crag**[28] 6231 3-9-1 **70**..(b[1]) OisinMurphy 8 45
(Andrew Balding) *trckd ldrs: t.k.h: wkng whn stmbld 2f out: sn eased* **4/1**[1]

0026 **12** nse **Dora's Field (IRE)**[79] 4462 3-9-3 **72**............................... AndreaAtzeni 4 47
(Ed Dunlop) *mid-div: pushed along over 5f out: nvr a factor* **11/1**

0430 **13** 2 **Snappy Guest**[22] 6453 4-9-3 **69**.................................. JamieSpencer 11 39
(George Margarson) *hmpd s: hld up in rr: nvr on terms* **14/1**

0050 **14** 2 1/4 **St Patrick's Day (IRE)**[72] 4717 4-9-4 **70**..................(v) FrederikTylicki 17 35
(J R Jenkins) *s.i.s: hld up: a towards rr: eased clsng stages* **33/1**

0200 **15** 2 **Red Cossack (CAN)**[103] 3612 5-9-4 **70**......................(t) WilliamCarson 5 30
(Paul Webber) *mid-div: lost pl over 2f out: bhd whn eased clsng stages* **100/1**

0060 **16** 1/2 **Monsieur Chevalier (IRE)**[32] 6138 9-8-13 **70**...(b) CallumShepherd(5) 7 29
(Nikki Evans) *s.i.s: a in rr: bhd whn eased clsng stages* **66/1**

1m 45.77s (-3.23) **Going Correction** -0.30s/f (Firm)
WFA 3 from 4yo+ 3lb **16** Ran SP% **119.6**
Speed ratings (Par 103): **104,102,102,101,99 99,97,93,92,90 89,89,87,84,82 82**
CSF £88.22 CT £1254.88 TOTE £12.90: £3.10, £2.20, £4.50, £4.10; EX 77.00 Trifecta £4413.10.

Owner Paul & Clare Rooney **Bred** Gestut Hof Ittlingen **Trained** Cheltenham, Gloucs

FOCUS
Rail movement added 6yds to race distance. An ordinary handicap, but despite the large field this was dominated by those up with the pace as the front pair held the first two positions almost throughout, though in reverse order.

7077 32RED.COM H'CAP 1m 2f 50y
4:30 (4:30) (Class 4) (0-85,85) 3-Y-O+ **£4,690** (£1,395; £697; £348) **Stalls** Low

Form RPR

6-22 **1** **Al Destoor**[31] 6160 6-9-3 **78**... DavidNolan 9 87+
(Jennie Candlish) *hld in midfield: hdwy over 3f out: chsd ldrs 2f out: rdn and n.m.r jst ins fnl f: sn swtchd rt and styd on strly to ld towards fin* **4/1**[2]

2300 **2** 1 **Zzoro (IRE)**[68] 4827 3-9-3 **83**.. PatDobbs 1 90
(Amanda Perrett) *sn led: pushed along over 2f out: rdn wl over 1f out: drvn ins fnl f: hdd and no ex towards fin* **14/1**

2531 **3** 1/2 **Burguillos**[26] 6294 3-9-2 **82**............................... WilliamTwiston-Davies 8 88
(Alan King) *t.k.h: trckd ldr: hdwy 3f out: sn cl up: rdn to chal wl over 1f out: drvn and ev ch ins fnl f: kpt on same pce towards fin* **5/1**[3]

2331 **4** 3/4 **Toulson**[21] 6484 3-8-12 **78**.. CharlesBishop 3 83
(Eve Johnson Houghton) *trckd ldrs: effrt wl over 2f out: rdn over 1f out: drvn ent fnl f: kpt on same pce* **11/4**[1]

4500 **5** 3/4 **Indy (IRE)**[37] 5976 5-9-3 **78**.. GrahamGibbons 6 83
(David Barron) *trckd ldrs: hdwy 3f out: rdn over 1f out: styng on and ev ch whn nt clr run and hmpd jst ins fnl f: nt rcvr* **25/1**

0203 **6** 2 **Hanseatic**[20] 6517 7-8-11 **77**....................................(p) NathanEvans(5) 7 76
(Michael Easterby) *midfield: hdwy on inner 3f out: chsd ldrs 2f out: sn rdn: drvn and kpt on same pce fnl f* **16/1**

0256 **7** 1/2 **Sarsted**[14] 6676 4-9-1 **76**... OisinMurphy 15 74
(Hughie Morrison) *prom: effrt on outer wl over 2f out: rdn wl over 1f out: sn drvn and no imp* **12/1**

5224 **8** 3 3/4 **Sahara (IRE)**[20] 6504 4-9-2 **77**... TedDurcan 5 68
(Chris Wall) *chsd ldrs: rdn along wl over 2f out: sn no imp* **16/1**

3020 **9** 1/2 **Desdichado**[32] 6128 4-8-12 **78**.................................. HectorCrouch(5) 13 68
(Ralph Beckett) *a towards rr* **14/1**

-000 **10** 3/4 **Tres Coronas (IRE)**[18] 6559 9-9-10 **85**...................... PaulMulrennan 16 73
(David Barron) *a towards rr* **50/1**

0P5 **11** 1 3/4 **Manny Owens (IRE)**[22] 6445 4-9-1 **76**...........................(t) GrahamLee 12 61
(Jonjo O'Neill) *a towards rr* **50/1**

1032 **12** 9 **De Veer Cliffs (IRE)**[25] 6323 3-9-2 **82**.......................... JamieSpencer 14 49
(Martyn Meade) *chsd ldrs: hdwy on outer over 3f out: rdn wl over 2f out: sn drvn and wknd* **8/1**

03-0 **13** nk **Esteaming**[18] 6559 6-9-10 **85**.. AndrewMullen 4 51
(David Barron) *chsd ldrs: rdn along over 3f out: sn drvn and wknd* **20/1**

2m 13.41s (-0.89) **Going Correction** -0.30s/f (Firm)
WFA 3 from 4yo+ 5lb **13** Ran SP% **119.8**
Speed ratings (Par 105): **91,90,89,89,88 87,86,83,83,82 81,74,73**
CSF £56.90 CT £288.72 TOTE £5.30: £2.50, £5.10, £1.80; EX 78.60 Trifecta £436.30.
Owner Glen's Fools 2 **Bred** Richard Moses Bloodstock **Trained** Basford Green, Staffs

FOCUS
Rail movement added 6yds to race distance. A fair handicap and another race favouring those ridden handily, which makes the winner's performance more meritorious.

7078 32REDSPORT.COM APPRENTICE H'CAP 1m 2f 50y
5:00 (5:01) (Class 5) (0-70,70) 3-Y-O+ **£2,911** (£866; £432; £108; £108) **Stalls** Low

Form RPR

5004 **1** **Pivotman**[22] 6434 8-9-2 **63**..(bt) NathanEvans(3) 2 70
(Michael Easterby) *mde virtually all: edgd lft over 1f out: drvn rt out* **7/1**[3]

2140 **2** 1/2 **Stoneboat Bill**[12] 6737 4-9-1 **62**.. PhilDennis(3) 6 68+
(Declan Carroll) *hld up towards rr: hdwy over 2f out: 3rd over 1f out: kpt on to take 2nd nr fin* **6/1**[2]

-436 **3** nk **Maroc**[77] 4530 3-9-0 **70**...(t) ManuelFernandes(7) 11 75+
(Paul Cole) *trckd ldrs: t.k.h: 2nd over 3f out: hung lft over 1f out: swtchd rt and kpt on same pce last 75yds* **7/1**[3]

5150 **4** 2 **Hydrant**[56] 5293 10-8-13 **64**... LisaTodd(7) 9 65
(Richard Guest) *mid-div: hdwy over 3f out: kpt on same pce appr fnl f* **20/1**

515 **4** dht **Tyrsal (IRE)**[29] 6212 5-9-1 **64**.................................... CameronNoble(5) 10 65+
(Clifford Lines) *s.s: hld up in rr: hdwy over 2f out: kpt on same pce fnl f* **8/1**

1456 **6** 1 **City Ground (USA)**[12] 6737 9-9-10 **68**.................... AlistairRawlinson 16 67+
(Michael Appleby) *stdd s: hld up in rr: hdwy over 3f out: kpt on one pce over 1f out* **14/1**

6002 **7** nk **Catastrophe**[19] 6541 3-8-11 **65**.. JoshQuinn(5) 1 63
(John Quinn) *s.i.s: drvn along to sn chse ldrs: one pce fnl 2f* **9/1**

1426 **8** 1 **Dovil's Duel (IRE)**[36] 5994 5-9-4 **65**........................ JordanVaughan(3) 13 61
(Tony Newcombe) *chsd ldrs: one pce fnl 2f* **12/1**

6220 **9** hd **First Sargeant**[1] 7045 6-8-13 **60**.........................(p) AdamMcNamara(3) 4 56
(Lawrence Mullaney) *s.i.s: sn drvn along in rr: hdwy over 2f out: nvr a threat* **11/2**[1]

0046 **10** 1 1/2 **Distant High**[66] 4913 5-8-13 **60**...............................(p) GeorgeWood(3) 14 53
(Richard Price) *mid-div: effrt over 3f out: nvr a factor* **33/1**

0220 **11** 13 **Handheld**[44] 5729 9-9-5 **63**...(p) ShelleyBirkett 3 30
(Julia Feilden) *trckd ldrs: lost pl over 2f out: sn bhd: eased clsng stages* **10/1**

3-05 **12** 9 **Will Mac**[15] 6645 5-9-2 **60**... JacobButterfield 5 9
(Neville Bycroft) *s.i.s: mid-div after 3f: lost pl 2f out: bhd whn eased clsng stages* **33/1**

-600 **13** 6 **Davey Boy**[16] 6629 3-8-11 **67**................................ SophieScardifield(7) 12 4
(Michael Bell) *racd wd: chsd ldrs: lost pl over 2f out: bhd whn eased clsng stages* **50/1**

40 **14** nk **Albert Boy (IRE)**[51] 5471 3-9-6 **69**............................ JosephineGordon 7 5
(Scott Dixon) *w ldrs: lost pl over 2f out: bhd whn eased clsng stages* **16/1**

2m 13.68s (-0.62) **Going Correction** -0.30s/f (Firm)
WFA 3 from 4yo+ 5lb **14** Ran SP% **117.7**
Speed ratings (Par 103): **90,89,89,87,87 86,86,85,85,84 74,66,62,61**
CSF £45.73 CT £308.94 TOTE £8.00: £3.10, £1.90, £3.50; EX 35.60 Trifecta £551.80.
Owner K Wreglesworth **Bred** Cheveley Park Stud Ltd **Trained** Sheriff Hutton, N Yorks

FOCUS
Rail movement added 6yds to race distance. A modest apprentice handicap to end with and more evidence, were it needed, that being on the sharp end was an advantage.
T/Jkpt: Part won. £10,000 - 0.5 winning units. T/Plt: £22.60 to a £1 stake. Pool: £70,539.68 - 2268.63 winning units. T/Qpdt: £15.00 to a £1 stake. Pool: £5,260.92 - 259.03 winning units.
Joe Rowntreee & Walter Glynn

7079- 7085a (Foreign Racing) - See Raceform Interactive

6937 SAINT-CLOUD (L-H)
Wednesday, October 5

OFFICIAL GOING: Turf: good

7086a PRIX THOMAS BRYON (GROUP 3) (2YO) (TURF) 7f
12:25 (12:00) 2-Y-O **£29,411** (£11,764; £8,823; £5,882; £2,941)

RPR

1 **Mate Story (IRE)**[31] 6177 2-8-11 0........................ ChristopheSoumillon 3 109
(D Smaga, France) *mde all: qcknd in st and r.o strly: eased towards fin: cosily* **9/2**

2 1 **Dame Du Roi (IRE)**[23] 6431 2-8-8 0........................... AurelienLemaitre 1 103
(F Head, France) *a.p: angled out and rdn 2f out: kpt on and wnt 2nd towards fin: no match for wnr and flattered by proximity* **12/5**[2]

3 1/2 **North Thunder (FR)**[23] 6431 2-8-11 0......................... GregoryBenoist 6 105
(A Fabre, France) *trckd wnr: rdn and effrt 2f out: kpt on but sn hld: lost 2nd towards fin* **39/10**[3]

4 2 1/2 **Greyway (FR)**[32] 2-8-11 0... IoritzMendizabal 4 98
(J-M Lefebvre, France) *restrained and hld up: rdn over 1f out: styd on into 4th but n.d* **22/1**

5 3 **Ajmal (IRE)**[23] 2-8-11 0... Pierre-CharlesBoudot 5 90+
(A Fabre, France) *midfield: rdn for effrt whn veered sharply rt over 1f out: unrideable after and jst hld on for 5th* **7/5**[1]

6 hd **Holy Makfi**[27] 6271 2-8-8 0... StephanePasquier 2 87
(J-Y Artu, France) *midfield: rdn 2f out: outpcd and btn fnl f* **46/1**

7 shd **Savile Row (FR)**[18] 2-8-11 0.. EddyHardouin 8 89
(Frau Erika Mader, Germany) *hld up in rr: rdn over 2f out: no imp and nvr threatened* **77/1**

8 2 1/2 **Neelanjali (FR)**[60] 5186 2-8-8 0.................................... AnthonyCrastus 7 80
(N Caullery, France) *midfield: rdn early in st: outpcd and btn fnl 2f: wknd: dropped to last towards fin* **49/1**

1m 27.91s (-4.29) **8** Ran SP% **119.4**
WIN (incl. 2 euro stake): 5.50. Places: 1.50, 1.50, 1.60. DF: 8.50. SF: 16.30..
Owner Aleyrion Bloodstock Ltd **Bred** Aleyrion Bloodstock & J E Dubois **Trained** Lamorlaye, France

7087a PRIX DAHLIA - FONDS EUROPEEN DE L'ELEVAGE (LISTED RACE) (4YO+ FILLIES & MARES) (TURF) 1m 2f
1:05 (12:00) 4-Y-O+ **£17,647** (£7,058; £5,294; £3,529; £1,764)

RPR

1 **Rosental**[32] 6115 4-8-11 0.. Pierre-CharlesBoudot 5 99
(Luca Cumani) *a little keen: restrained in share of 2nd on outer: drvn over 2f out: sustained chal fr wl over 1f out: led fnl 100yds: rdn out* **27/10**[1]

2 hd **Game Theory (IRE)**[14] 6693 4-9-2 0.......................... StephanePasquier 3 104
(N Clement, France) **19/5**[3]

3 1 1/2 **Madernia (IRE)**[27] 6273 4-8-11 0.. OlivierPeslier 1 96
(C Laffon-Parias, France) **18/1**

4 1/2 **Spring Leaf (FR)**[11] 6798 4-8-11 0.. ThierryJarnet 6 95
(A De Royer-Dupre, France) **10/1**

5 3/4 **Johara (IRE)**[54] 5384 5-8-11 0.. AlexisBadel 7 94
(H-F Devin, France) **14/5**[2]

6 snk **Rosy Blush**[33] 6107 4-8-11 0.............................. ChristopheSoumillon 4 93
(Mme Pia Brandt, France) **39/10**

7 3/4 **Stone Roses (FR)**[129] 2727 4-8-11 0........................... MickaelBarzalona 2 92
(F Head, France) **22/1**

8 nk **Weetles**[39] 5894 4-8-11 0.. GeraldMosse 8 91
(Clive Cox) *keen: hld up in midfield on outer: 4th and scrubbed along to hold pl 2 1/2f out: grad dropped way fr wl over 1f out* **17/1**

2m 9.75s (-6.25) **8** Ran SP% **118.8**
WIN (incl. 1 euro stake): 3.70. Places: 1.80, 2.00, 4.20. DF: 11.60. SF: 20.10..
Owner P Stokes & S Krase **Bred** Darley **Trained** Newmarket, Suffolk

7088a PRIX SCARAMOUCHE (LISTED RACE) (3YO+) (TURF) 1m 6f
1:35 (12:00) 3-Y-O+ £19,117 (£7,647; £5,735; £3,823; £1,911)

RPR
1 **She Is No Lady**[46] 5655 4-9-1 0 FMBerry 6 97
(Ralph Beckett) *a cl up: slighly impeded over 4f out: cl 3rd and shkn up over 2 1/2f out: rdn to chse ldr 2f out: styd on wl fnl f: led fnl strides* **6/4**[1]
2 hd **Sacrifice My Soul (IRE)**[27] 6273 4-9-1 0 MickaelBarzalona 8 97
(Mme Pia Brandt, France) **21/1**
3 3/4 **Iraklion (GER)**[17] 6610 4-9-4 0 MichaelCadeddu 3 99
(Christian Sprengel, Germany) **54/1**
4 3/4 **Amirant (GER)**[30] 6203 8-9-4 0 Pierre-CharlesBoudot 7 98
(E Leenders, France) **74/10**
5 snk **Dalshand (FR)**[22] 3-8-9 0 AlexisBadel 10 98
(A De Royer-Dupre, France) **71/10**[3]
6 2 **Saane (FR)**[30] 6203 5-9-4 0 TonyPiccone 2 95
(G Taupin, France) **10/1**
7 hd **Settler's Son (IRE)**[24] 6396 5-9-6 0 SebastienMaillot 1 97
(J Michal, France) **47/10**[2]
8 4 **Leomar (GER)**[44] 5733 3-8-9 0 AntoineHamelin 4 89
(M Figge, Germany) **28/1**
9 4 **Swordshire (GER)**[21] 5-9-4 0 UmbertoRispoli 9 83
(Werner Glanz, Germany) **10/1**
10 12 **Fixed Rate**[52] 5448 3-8-9 0 VincentCheminaud 5 67
(D Smaga, France) **9/1**

3m 4.71s (-7.49)
WFA 3 from 4yo+ 9lb **10** Ran SP% **119.8**
WIN (incl. 1 euro stake): 2.50. Places: 1.50, 5.10, 9.90. DF: 30.60. SF: 39.30..
Owner D & J Newell **Bred** Derek & Judith Newell **Trained** Kimpton, Hants

7089 - (Foreign Racing) - See Raceform Interactive

6554 AYR (L-H)
Thursday, October 6

OFFICIAL GOING: Soft (good to soft in places; 7.2)
Wind: Breezy, half behind Weather: Sunny

7090 BEN MAIDEN STKS 6f
1:40 (1:40) (Class 5) 2-Y-O £3,234 (£962; £481; £240) Stalls High

Form RPR
02 1 **Saint Equiano**[20] 6534 2-9-5 0 PhillipMakin 3 83+
(Keith Dalgleish) *wore hood in paddock: t.k.h early: mde all: qcknd clr wl over 1f out: sn shkn up: eased last 100yds: readily* **2/1**[2]
23 2 2 3/4 **Midaawi (IRE)**[71] 4762 2-9-5 0 ShaneGray 5 69
(Kevin Ryan) *taken early to post: prom: rdn 2f out: rallied to take 2nd pl 1f out: kpt on fin: flattered by proximity to eased-down wnr* **7/2**[3]
4 3 2 1/4 **Things Happen**[25] 6375 2-9-5 0 SamJames 7 62
(David Evans) *dwlt: hld up in tch: rdn and outpcd over 2f out: rallied fnl f: kpt on: nvr able to chal* **40/1**
4 4 hd **Vivardia (IRE)**[23] 6447 2-9-0 0 GrahamLee 4 56
(Ben Haslam) *chsd ldrs: drvn and outpcd over 2f out: rallied fnl f: kpt on: no imp* **33/1**
3422 5 1 3/4 **Full Intention**[68] 4890 2-9-5 88 RichardKingscote 6 56
(Tom Dascombe) *chsd wnr: rdn 2f out: edgd lft and lost 2nd 1f out: wknd last 150yds* **5/4**[1]
6 21 **Golconda King (IRE)** 2-9-5 0 TonyHamilton 1
(Richard Fahey) *dwlt: bhd and green: struggling over 3f out: sn lost tch: t.o* **16/1**
7 4 1/2 **Enlighten Me (IRE)** 2-9-0 0 JoeyHaynes 2
(Philip Kirby) *missed break: bhd and green: struggling fr 1/2-way: t.o* **100/1**

1m 14.26s (1.86) **Going Correction** +0.25s/f (Good) **7** Ran SP% **112.3**
Speed ratings (Par 95): **97,93,90,90,87 59,53**
CSF £9.04 TOTE £2.50: £1.10, £3.50; EX 9.10 Trifecta £125.60.
Owner Paul & Clare Rooney **Bred** Usk Valley Stud **Trained** Carluke, S Lanarks

FOCUS
The ground was drying out all the time and was now soft, good to soft in places. The original 1m and 1m2f races on the card were abandoned due to waterlogging and replaced with 5f and 6f handicaps, meaning all races on the card were over an extended 7f or less. Rail in 9yds, adding 27yds to 7f races. Not a bad little maiden to start, with a few of these having shown decent ability, but the winner was out on his own. A winning time 4.26sec outside standard suggested the ground still had some ease in it.

7091 TENNENT'S NURSERY H'CAP 6f
2:10 (2:10) (Class 5) (0-75,72) 2-Y-O £3,234 (£962; £481; £240) Stalls High

Form RPR
6345 1 **Amathyst**[27] 6275 2-9-1 66 AndrewMullen 1 69
(Michael Appleby) *chsd ldr: drvn along 2f out: led ins fnl f: edgd rt: drvn out* **4/1**[2]
5051 2 1 1/4 **Reckless Serenade (IRE)**[12] 6768 2-9-0 70 ShirleyTeasdale[(5)] 5 69
(Keith Dalgleish) *t.k.h early: led: rdn over 1f out: hdd ins fnl f: kpt on* **5/1**
6320 3 1 1/4 **Dandy Place (IRE)**[5] 6954 2-9-6 71 JamesSullivan 2 67
(Tim Easterby) *hld up: hdwy on outside over 2f out: effrt and cl up over 1f out: kpt on same pce ins fnl f* **11/4**[1]
2226 4 1 3/4 **Bazwind (IRE)**[59] 5229 2-9-4 69 SamJames 3 59
(David Evans) *dwlt: in tch: drvn and outpcd over 2f out: rallied over 1f out: kpt on fnl f: no imp* **17/2**
300 5 8 **Bear Essentials (IRE)**[41] 5833 2-9-1 66 (v[1]) DanielTudhope 7 32
(David O'Meara) *trckd ldrs: rdn over 2f out: wknd over 1f out* **12/1**
235 6 1 1/4 **Quiet Moment (IRE)**[54] 5414 2-9-2 67 GrahamLee 8 30
(Ben Haslam) *hld up in tch: drvn and struggling over 2f out: edgd lft and sn btn* **10/1**
6000 7 2 1/4 **Jollydee (IRE)**[25] 6388 2-8-4 55 CamHardie 4 11
(Paul Midgley) *dwlt: hld up: rdn over 2f out: wknd wl over 1f out* **25/1**
0365 8 9 **Cajmere**[13] 6743 2-9-7 72 [1] RichardKingscote 6
(Tom Dascombe) *dwlt: sn in tch: lost pl 1/2-way: sn struggling* **9/2**[3]

1m 14.52s (2.12) **Going Correction** +0.25s/f (Good) **8** Ran SP% **112.7**
Speed ratings (Par 95): **95,93,91,89,78 77,74,62**
CSF £23.51 CT £62.78 TOTE £4.70: £1.80, £1.70, £1.20; EX 24.10 Trifecta £110.40.
Owner C L Bacon **Bred** J W Mitchell **Trained** Oakham, Rutland

FOCUS
A modest nursery with only one of these having hit the target before. Not many got into it and the winning time was 0.26sec slower than the opening maiden. The runner-up has been rated to her Hamilton win.

7092 HAIG CLUB CLUBMAN H'CAP 6f
2:40 (2:42) (Class 6) (0-65,65) 3-Y-O+ £2,587 (£770; £384; £192) Stalls High

Form RPR
6550 1 **Goninodaethat**[34] 6100 8-8-4 53 NathanEvans[(5)] 1 61
(Jim Goldie) *mde all: sn 2 l clr: rdn and qcknd over 1f out: kpt on wl fnl f* **7/1**
4144 2 1 **Wahaab (IRE)**[10] 6834 5-8-12 63 (p) LewisEdmunds[(7)] 5 68
(Iain Jardine) *hld up midfield: rdn over 2f out: hdwy over 1f out: kpt on to take 2nd towards fin: nt rch wnr* **6/1**
0454 3 3/4 **Rock Canyon (IRE)**[11] 6809 7-9-3 61 GrahamLee 3 64
(Linda Perratt) *prom: effrt and rdn 2f out: chsd wnr ins fnl f: no ex and lost 2nd towards fin* **10/1**
2161 4 1 1/4 **Reflation**[10] 6835 4-9-4 62 6ex (p) ConnorBeasley 7 61+
(Michael Dods) *hld up: drvn along over 2f out: hdwy over 1f out: kpt on fnl f: nvr able to chal* **7/2**[2]
004 5 1 **Spirit Of Zebedee (IRE)**[12] 6790 3-9-3 62 (v) PJMcDonald 8 58
(John Quinn) *in tch: hdwy to chse wnr over 2f out: rdn and hung lft over 1f out: lost 2nd ins fnl f: sn btn* **11/2**[3]
0005 6 2 1/2 **Ay Up Audrey**[10] 6834 5-8-7 51 oh6 BarryMcHugh 11 40+
(Rebecca Bastiman) *hld up: rdn over 2f out: kpt on fnl f: nvr able to chal* **40/1**
0065 7 3/4 **Amber Crystal**[10] 6835 4-8-7 51 oh6 AndrewMullen 2 37
(Linda Perratt) *prom: effrt and rdn 2f out: wknd ent fnl f* **25/1**
3452 8 1 1/2 **Head Space (IRE)**[3] 7018 8-9-7 65 DanielTudhope 13 47+
(David Evans) *dwlt: hld up: rdn over 2f out: nvr on terms* **3/1**[1]
0500 9 2 **Captain Scooby**[7] 6909 10-9-3 61 (b) JoeFanning 9 42+
(Richard Guest) *dwlt: bhd: drvn along over 2f out: sn btn* **18/1**
0036 10 2 **Hab Reeh**[10] 6835 8-8-10 54 (p) JamesSullivan 12 24+
(Ruth Carr) *bhd and sn drvn along: nvr on terms* **14/1**
0000 11 1 3/4 **Jessie Allan (IRE)**[71] 4771 5-8-0 51 oh6 JamieGormley[(7)] 10 16
(Jim Goldie) *chsd wnr to over 2f out: rdn and wknd wl over 1f out* **100/1**

1m 13.49s (1.09) **Going Correction** +0.25s/f (Good)
WFA 3 from 4yo+ 1lb **11** Ran SP% **117.7**
Speed ratings (Par 101): **102,100,99,98,96 93,92,90,87,85 82**
CSF £48.17 CT £330.31 TOTE £8.10: £2.90, £1.90, £3.30; EX 67.20 Trifecta £768.60.
Owner G E Adams & J S Goldie **Bred** W G H Barrons **Trained** Uplawmoor, E Renfrews

FOCUS
A moderate sprint handicap and unlike in the first two races, the runners made straight for the far rail despite stalls being on the stands' side. This was another race where it paid to be handy. The runner-up has been rated close to her recent best.

7093 WHYTE & MACKAY H'CAP 5f
3:15 (3:15) (Class 6) (0-65,65) 3-Y-O+ £2,587 (£770; £384; £192) Stalls High

Form RPR
05 1 **Taffetta**[17] 6616 4-9-0 58 BarryMcHugh 5 68+
(Tony Coyle) *awkward s: hld up: hdwy on far side of gp and edgd lft over 1f out: led ins fnl f: r.o strly* **15/2**[3]
2022 2 1 1/4 **Jacob's Pillow**[10] 6835 5-9-7 65 DanielTudhope 4 70
(Rebecca Bastiman) *cl up: led over 2f out: rdn over 1f out: hdd ins fnl f: kpt on towards fin* **11/4**[1]
2532 3 1 1/2 **Slim Chance (IRE)**[10] 6834 7-8-7 58 (v) PaulaMuir[(7)] 1 58
(Simon West) *trckd ldrs: drvn along 2f out: kpt on same pce ins fnl f* **7/1**[2]
6345 4 1/2 **Bunce (IRE)**[11] 6813 8-9-6 64 PJMcDonald 7 62+
(Linda Perratt) *bhd: rdn over 2f out: hdwy fnl f: nvr able to chal* **9/1**
0040 5 3/4 **Bapak Bangsawan**[16] 6653 6-8-6 55 (v) AnnStokell[(5)] 10 50
(Ann Stokell) *led to over 2f out: rallied: drvn and outpcd ins fnl f* **28/1**
0000 6 hd **Cheeni**[12] 6774 4-8-2 51 oh6 (p) NathanEvans[(5)] 9 45
(Jim Goldie) *in tch: rdn along 2f out: no ex fnl f* **100/1**
5000 7 1/2 **Mercers Row**[7] 6909 9-9-5 63 DavidNolan 2 56
(Michael Herrington) *hld up in tch: rdn along over 1f out: no imp fnl f* **8/1**
3160 8 3/4 **Lady Joanna Vassa (IRE)**[13] 6745 3-9-1 59 ConnorBeasley 8 50
(Richard Guest) *cl up: rdn over 2f out: wknd ent fnl f* **7/1**[2]
0502 9 nse **Go Go Green (IRE)**[11] 6813 10-8-7 56 CallumShepherd[(5)] 6 46
(Jim Goldie) *dwlt: sn midfield: drvn and outpcd over 2f out: no imp over 1f out* **7/1**[2]
0030 10 4 **Spring Bird**[40] 5889 7-8-10 54 JoeFanning 13 29+
(Alan Swinbank) *in tch on nr side of gp: drvn along over 2f out: sn wknd* **20/1**
0406 11 1/2 **Jebel Tara**[7] 6909 11-8-13 57 (bt) DaleSwift 3 31
(Alistair Whillans) *bhd: drvn and outpcd over 3f out: hung lft and btn over 1f out* **11/1**
6610 12 6 **Mystical King**[10] 6835 6-8-7 51 oh2 (p) JoeyHaynes 12 3+
(Linda Perratt) *bhd on nr side of gp: struggling wl over 2f out: sn btn* **25/1**
400 13 31 **Bannock Town**[12] 6774 5-8-7 51 oh6 (p) AndrewMullen 11 +
(Linda Perratt) *bhd on nr side of gp: struggling 1/2-way: sn lost tch: t.o* **250/1**

1m 0.3s (0.90) **Going Correction** +0.25s/f (Good) **13** Ran SP% **118.8**
Speed ratings (Par 101): **102,100,97,96,95 94,93,93,86 86,76,26**
CSF £27.05 CT £141.83 TOTE £9.00: £3.20, £1.40, £2.60; EX 37.10 Trifecta £254.40.
Owner Mrs Heather Raw **Bred** Heather Raw **Trained** Norton, N Yorks

FOCUS
Another moderate sprint handicap and despite what happened in the previous race, the runners came up the middle, though the winner ended up against the far rail and was the only one to go there. It's been rated around the runner-up and fifth.

7094 ROA/RACING POST OWNERS' JACKPOT H'CAP 6f
3:50 (3:50) (Class 4) (0-85,84) 3-Y-O+ £5,175 (£1,540; £769; £384) Stalls High

Form RPR
0110 1 **Naggers (IRE)**[25] 6382 5-9-4 81 RobertWinston 1 91
(Paul Midgley) *hld up on far side of gp: stdy hdwy 1/2-way: trcking ldrs and shkn up over 1f out: drvn and kpt on wl to ld cl home* **7/2**[1]
3024 2 nse **Tiger Jim**[34] 6079 6-8-13 83 LewisEdmunds[(7)] 3 92
(Jim Goldie) *trckd ldrs on far side of gp: rdn to ld over 1f out: kpt on wl fnl f: hdd cl home* **11/2**[2]
2411 3 3 1/2 **Kenny The Captain (IRE)**[23] 6435 5-9-4 84 RachelRichardson[(3)] 12 82
(Tim Easterby) *trckd ldrs: rdn along over 2f out: kpt on ins fnl f: nt rch first two* **10/1**
160 4 nse **Dandyleekie (IRE)**[25] 6382 4-9-4 81 DanielTudhope 11 79
(David O'Meara) *hld up midfield on nr side of gp: rdn and effrt 2f out: kpt on ins fnl f: nt pce to chal* **9/1**

330 **5** 2 **Casterbridge**[12] 6766 4-8-13 **76**.. JasonHart 4 67
(Eric Alston) *disp ld to over 1f out: rdn and wknd ins fnl f* **16/1**

1350 **6** ½ **Star Cracker (IRE)**[21] 6506 4-8-2 **70** oh3.................... NathanEvans(5) 2 60
(Jim Goldie) *mde most to over 1f out: drvn and wknd ins fnl f* **25/1**

1256 **7** 1 **Spirit Of Zeb (IRE)**[37] 5991 4-8-12 **80**.................. AdamMcNamara(5) 5 66
(Richard Fahey) *trckd ldrs: rdn: edgd rt and outpcd over 1f out: n.d after* **9/1**

406 **8** 4 **Mass Rally (IRE)**[14] 6714 9-9-1 **78**............................(b) PaulMulrennan 8 52
(Michael Dods) *dwlt: hld up: hdwy on far side of gp over 1f out: nvr able to chal* **14/1**

0000 **9** nk **Pomme De Terre (IRE)**[28] 6263 4-9-4 **81**.................(p) ConnorBeasley 7 54
(Michael Dods) *towards rr: drvn along over 2f out: no imp fr over 1f out* **16/1**

0040 **10** ½ **Duke Cosimo**[12] 6780 6-9-4 **81**....................................(p) PJMcDonald 10 52
(Michael Herrington) *dwlt: hld up: rdn over 2f out: nvr a factor* **8/1**[3]

0064 **11** nk **Kommander Kirkup**[14] 6714 5-9-0 **77**............................(p) SamJames 14 47
(John Davies) *hld up on nr side of gp: rdn and edgd lft over 2f out: sn outpcd: btn over 1f out* **28/1**

3002 **12** nk **Explain**[12] 6766 4-9-3 **80**..(p) JamesSullivan 13 49
(Ruth Carr) *hld up on nr side: rdn over 2f out: sn btn* **18/1**

4660 **13** 1½ **Escalating**[20] 6539 4-9-5 **82**..(tp) AndrewMullen 9 46
(Michael Appleby) *dwlt: sn drvn along in rr: no ch fr 1/2-way* **16/1**

1000 **14** 7 **Dinneratmidnight**[14] 6718 5-9-3 **80**..................................(e) JoeFanning 6 22
(Richard Guest) *midifield: rdn and outpcd over 2f out: sn btn* **25/1**

1m 12.71s (0.31) **Going Correction** +0.25s/f (Good) **14** Ran SP% **118.5**
Speed ratings (Par 105): **107,106,102,102,99 98,97,92,91,91 90,90,88,79**
CSF £20.11 CT £182.49 TOTE £4.60: £1.60, £2.50, £2.60; EX 20.30 Trifecta £108.00.
Owner Taylor's Bloodstock Ltd **Bred** Azienda Agricola Rosati Colarieti **Trained** Westow, N Yorks

FOCUS
A fair sprint handicap in which they raced centre-to-far side and the two market leaders pulled clear, providing a thrilling finish. Pace held out and the winner resumed his progress.

7095 CRABBIES H'CAP 7f 50y
4:25 (4:26) (Class 3) (0-95,93) 3-Y-O+ **£7,762** (£2,310; £1,154; £577) **Stalls** High

Form RPR

2156 **1** **Moonlightnavigator (USA)**[21] 6500 4-9-0 **83**............ DougieCostello 3 93
(John Quinn) *trckd ldrs: effrt and rdn over 1f out: led ins fnl f: kpt on strly* **6/1**[3]

2603 **2** 1½ **Sir Billy Wright (IRE)**[12] 6780 5-8-12 **86**........................ CliffordLee(5) 9 92
(David Evans) *trckd ldrs gng wl: shkn up to ld over 1f out: drvn and hdd ins fnl f: kpt on: hld nr fin* **9/1**

6010 **3** nk **Lavetta**[75] 4644 4-9-0 **83**.. JoeFanning 1 88
(Alan Swinbank) *plld hrd in midfield: effrt and rdn 2f out: kpt on ins fnl f: nrst fin* **22/1**

5205 **4** 2¼ **Ballymore Castle (IRE)**[19] 6560 4-9-2 **85**..................... TonyHamilton 8 84
(Richard Fahey) *t.k.h: prom: drvn along 2f out: kpt on same pce ins fnl f* **10/1**

0012 **5** ¾ **Mount Tahan (IRE)**[19] 6560 4-9-8 **91**................................. KevinStott 11 89+
(Kevin Ryan) *hld up: rdn over 2f out: angled rt and hdwy over 1f out: carried hd high and edgd lft ins fnl f: kpt on: no imp* **11/2**[2]

1520 **6** 2¼ **Tadaany (IRE)**[21] 6500 4-8-13 **82** ow1........................... DanielTudhope 10 74
(David O'Meara) *mde most tl rdn and hdd over 1f out: rdn and wknd ins fnl f* **9/1**

0400 **7** 3¼ **Westwood Hoe**[26] 6320 5-9-4 **87**...(p) BenCurtis 7 70
(Tony Coyle) *disp ld to over 2f out: sn rdn: wknd fnl f* **20/1**

0030 **8** ½ **Russian Realm**[12] 6792 6-9-8 **91**.................................. RobertWinston 4 73
(Paul Midgley) *hld up: pushed along over 2f out: sn no imp* **20/1**

0064 **9** 2 **Lexington Times (IRE)**[12] 6764 4-9-7 **90**..................... JamesSullivan 2 67
(Ruth Carr) *slowly away: bhd: pushed along over 2f out: nvr on terms* **25/1**

321 **10** 1½ **Run To The Hills (USA)**[41] 5859 3-8-10 **86**......... AdamMcNamara(5) 5 58
(George Peckham) *hld up: drvn along over 3f out: edgd lft over 2f out: sn btn* **11/4**[1]

0003 **11** 6 **Newstead Abbey**[12] 6764 6-9-5 **88**.......................... GrahamGibbons 13 45
(David Barron) *midfield: drvn and outpcd over 2f out: sn btn* **18/1**

1P00 **12** 1 **Edgar Balthazar**[19] 6557 4-8-12 **86**....................(p) ShirleyTeasdale(5) 14 41
(Keith Dalgleish) *slowly away: bhd: struggling over 3f out: nvr on terms* **40/1**

1640 **13** ½ **Muntadab (IRE)**[19] 6556 4-9-10 **93**................................ PJMcDonald 12 46
(Roger Fell) *in tch: rdn over 2f out: wknd wl over 1f out* **9/1**

1m 34.45s (1.05) **Going Correction** +0.35s/f (Good)
WFA 3 from 4yo+ 2lb **13** Ran SP% **120.8**
Speed ratings (Par 107): **108,106,105,103,102 99,96,95,93,91 84,83,83**
CSF £54.94 CT £1162.64 TOTE £6.90: £2.40, £2.70, £5.20; EX 59.60 Trifecta £686.90.
Owner Malcolm Walker **Bred** Highfield Farm **Trained** Settrington, N Yorks

FOCUS
Rail movement added 27yds to race distance. A decent handicap, but again it was important to be handy with the front pair tracking the pace throughout. The winner is rated back to his old best.

7096 STRATHMORE H'CAP (DIV I) 7f 50y
5:00 (5:02) (Class 6) (0-60,60) 3-Y-O+ **£2,587** (£770; £384; £192) **Stalls** High

Form RPR

5413 **1** **Reinforced**[20] 6541 3-9-5 **60**...(p) AndrewMullen 6 68
(Michael Dods) *mde all: rdn over 1f out: hrd pressed ins fnl f: hld on gamely towards fin* **3/1**[1]

4063 **2** ¾ **Cascading Stars (IRE)**[38] 5953 4-9-6 **59**.................. GrahamGibbons 1 66
(Daniel Mark Loughnane) *hld up in tch: hdwy 2f out: rdn to dispute ld ins fnl f: kpt on: hld nr fin* **11/1**

6240 **3** 1¾ **Alice Thornton**[29] 6226 4-9-7 **60**.. DavidNolan 4 63
(Martin Todhunter) *hld up in midfield: stdy hdwy over 2f out: effrt and rdn over 1f out: kpt on fnl f: nt rch first two* **14/1**

4552 **4** 1 **Opt Out**[41] 5835 6-9-3 **56**..(b) DanielTudhope 7 57
(David O'Meara) *hld up: hdwy over 2f out: kpt on ins fnl f: nt pce to chal* **6/1**[2]

5202 **5** 7 **Wayside Magic**[16] 6646 3-8-11 **52**...............................(b) ConnorBeasley 5 34
(Michael Dods) *chsd ldrs: drvn along over 3f out: wknd over 1f out* **15/2**[3]

0000 **6** 2 **Mr Chuckles (IRE)**[16] 6646 3-8-8 **54**..............................(p) PhilDennis(5) 8 31
(Philip Kirby) *hld up towards rr: rdn along over 3f out: kpt on fnl f: nvr able to chal* **25/1**

4430 **7** hd **New Abbey Angel (IRE)**[17] 6621 3-9-5 **60**....................(v1) PhillipMakin 9 37
(Keith Dalgleish) *pressed wnr: rdn and hung lft over 2f out: wknd over 1f out* **8/1**

00-0 **8** 1¾ **Ixchell**[23] 6452 3-8-5 **46** oh1... PatrickMathers 10 18
(Richard Fahey) *prom: drvn along 3f out: wknd over 1f out* **20/1**

4006 **9** 1¼ **Piper Bill**[10] 6839 5-8-2 **46** oh1...................................(v1) NathanEvans(5) 14 16
(Jim Goldie) *slowly away: t.k.h in rr: rdn over 2f out: nvr on terms* **100/1**

4446 **10** 2 **The Armed Man**[55] 5367 3-9-2 **57**.................................. AndrewElliott 11 21
(Chris Fairhurst) *midfield: rdn over 2f out: sn lost pl and struggling* **9/1**

5000 **11** 8 **The King's Steed**[23] 6432 3-9-4 **59**.................................. PJMcDonald 2 3
(Micky Hammond) *hld up towards rr: struggling over 3f out: sn btn* **66/1**

06-6 **12** 10 **Granite City Doc**[165] 1667 3-8-11 **52**.......................... DougieCostello 13
(Lucy Normile) *towards rr: struggling over 3f out: sn btn* **50/1**

3005 **13** 4½ **Lendal Bridge**[19] 6568 5-8-10 **49**..(p) BenCurtis 12
(Tony Coyle) *towards rr: struggling 1/2-way: sn btn* **10/1**

0403 **14** 10 **Ginger Charlie**[45] 5732 3-8-9 **50**.................................... JamesSullivan 3
(Ruth Carr) *slowly away: bhd: struggling 1/2-way: wknd* **11/1**

1m 35.75s (2.35) **Going Correction** +0.35s/f (Good)
WFA 3 from 4yo+ 2lb **14** Ran SP% **117.6**
Speed ratings (Par 101): **100,99,97,96,88 85,85,83,82,79 70,59,54,42**
CSF £34.64 CT £405.69 TOTE £4.40: £1.70, £3.00, £5.10; EX 35.40 Trifecta £323.80.
Owner W G McHarg & J W Stenson **Bred** Maze Rattan Limited **Trained** Denton, Co Durham

FOCUS
Rail movement added 27yds to race distance. The first division of a moderate handicap and the first four pulled well clear. The winner has been rated to his recent form.

7097 STRATHMORE H'CAP (DIV II) 7f 50y
5:30 (5:33) (Class 6) (0-60,60) 3-Y-O+ **£2,587** (£770; £384; £192) **Stalls** High

Form RPR

0006 **1** **Rioja Day (IRE)**[17] 6621 6-8-2 **46** oh1.......................(b) NathanEvans(5) 2 57
(Jim Goldie) *mde all: drvn clr over 1f out: unchal* **13/2**[2]

1000 **2** 4½ **Poolstock**[15] 6685 4-9-2 **55**.......................................(v) PaulMulrennan 11 55
(Michael Dods) *t.k.h: hld up: hdwy over 2f out: rdn and chsd (clr) wnr ins fnl f: kpt on: no imp* **9/1**

0604 **3** 2¼ **Flyball**[19] 6568 4-8-11 **50**...(e) CamHardie 1 44
(Dianne Sayer) *trckd ldrs: wnt 2nd over 3f out: effrt and rdn over 2f out: one pce and lost 2nd ins fnl f* **17/2**[3]

4650 **4** ½ **Tanawar (IRE)**[29] 6226 6-9-6 **59**..................................(p) JamesSullivan 5 52
(Ruth Carr) *in tch: effrt and rdn over 2f out: no imp fr over 1f out* **6/1**[1]

6240 **5** 1½ **Lozah**[16] 6646 3-9-1 **56**..(tp) TonyHamilton 6 44
(Roger Fell) *hld up midfield: rdn and effrt over 2f out: edgd lft and outpcd over 2f out* **10/1**

4000 **6** 2½ **Haidees Reflection**[13] 6742 6-8-11 **57**..............(b1) LewisEdmunds(7) 13 40
(Jim Goldie) *s.i.s: hld up: rdn over 2f out: hdwy over 1f out: kpt on fnl f: no imp* **18/1**

2154 **7** 1¼ **Ted's Brother (IRE)**[17] 6621 8-8-10 **49**..........................(b) JoeFanning 8 29
(Richard Guest) *hld up midfield: stdy hdwy over 2f out: rdn and edgd lft over 1f out: sn wknd* **13/2**[2]

1040 **8** 1½ **Madam Mai Tai**[17] 6621 4-8-6 **50**................................ RowanScott(5) 4 26
(Rebecca Bastiman) *hld up towards rr: drvn along over 2f out: nvr rchd ldrs* **10/1**

1000 **9** 10 **Croft Ranger (IRE)**[41] 5841 3-9-5 **60**......................(p) ConnorBeasley 3 10
(Michael Dods) *chsd wnr to over 3f out: rdn and wknd fr 2f out* **12/1**

5000 **10** hd **Cadmium**[19] 6569 5-9-6 **59**..(p) PJMcDonald 12 10
(Micky Hammond) *towards rr: drvn along over 4f out: nvr on terms* **18/1**

4600 **11** 8 **Wishing Tree**[49] 5578 3-8-9 **50**.. BenCurtis 10
(Brian Ellison) *prom: drvn and struggling 3f out: sn btn* **9/1**

56-6 **12** 13 **Rathvale**[17] 6617 3-8-10 **51**.. BarryMcHugh 9
(Linda Perratt) *s.i.s: bhd: struggling over 3f out: sn btn* **80/1**

-000 **13** 7 **Molivias Gem**[40] 5889 3-8-5 **46** oh1............................. PatrickMathers 7
(David Thompson) *trckd ldrs: struggling over 3f out: sn btn* **40/1**

4630 **P** **Toffee Apple (IRE)**[24] 6407 3-8-12 **58**.................... ShirleyTeasdale(5) 14
(Keith Dalgleish) *midfield on outside: lost pl over 3f out: sn lost tch and eased: p.u and dismntd ins fnl f* **12/1**

1m 36.06s (2.66) **Going Correction** +0.35s/f (Good)
WFA 3 from 4yo+ 2lb **14** Ran SP% **119.2**
Speed ratings (Par 101): **98,92,90,89,88 85,83,82,70,70 61,46,38,**
CSF £63.35 CT £519.99 TOTE £7.10: £2.90, £3.60, £2.70; EX 82.90 Trifecta £1392.00.
Owner Ayrshire Racing & Partner **Bred** Mrs Eleanor Commins **Trained** Uplawmoor, E Renfrews

FOCUS
Rail movement added 27yds to race distance. This division was wide open according to the market and another all-the-way winner. The winning time was 0.31sec slower than the first leg. The race has been rated conservatively given the conditions.
T/Jkpt: Not Won. T/Plt: £186.90 to a £1 stake. Pool: £74058.31, 289.2 winning units. T/Qpdt: £65.70 to a £1 stake. Pool: £6771.65, 76.26 winning units. **Richard Young**

6895 CHELMSFORD (A.W) (L-H)
Thursday, October 6

OFFICIAL GOING: Polytrack: standard
Wind: medium, half against Weather: dry, light cloud

7098 TOTEPOOL LIVE INFO DOWNLOAD THE APP CLAIMING STKS 7f (P)
5:55 (5:55) (Class 5) 2-Y-O **£3,557** (£1,058; £529; £264) **Stalls** Low

Form RPR

3100 **1** **Franceleya (IRE)**[42] 5794 2-8-4 69.............................. GeorgeWood(5) 2 68
(Marco Botti) *trckd ldrs: effrt to chse ldr wl over 1f out: drvn to chal jst ins fnl f: led wl ins fnl f: styd on* **13/8**[1]

5366 **2** ½ **Await The Storm (IRE)**[12] 6789 2-8-11 75.......... JosephineGordon(3) 1 72
(Hugo Palmer) *led: rdn wl over 1f out: clr w wnr jst over 1f out: hdd and styd on same pce wl ins fnl f* **5/2**[2]

0340 **3** 5 **Joyful Dream (IRE)**[8] 6875 2-8-7 67.................................... LukeMorris 5 51
(J S Moore) *broke wl: stdd and chsd ldrs: effrt jst over 2f out: outpcd and hung lft over 1f out: wl hld 3rd and plugged on same pce ins fnl f* **5/1**

500 **4** hd **Pussy Galore (IRE)**[7] 6897 2-8-9 0.............................. TomMarquand 3 53
(Richard Hannon) *midfield: rdn 5f out: sn struggling and detached fr ldng quartet: no threat to ldrs after: plugged on ins fnl f* **7/2**[3]

0500 **5** 1¼ **Cj Parker**[29] 6236 2-8-3 60...(be1) WilliamCarson 4 43
(Jim Boyle) *dwlt: sn rcvrd to chse ldr: wnt rt and lost 2nd wl over 1f out: awkward hd carriage u.p and sn outpcd: wknd ins fnl f* **20/1**

06 **6** 2½ **Gog Elles (IRE)**[61] 5166 2-8-2 0.................................... MitchGodwin(5) 6 40
(J S Moore) *a off the pce in last pair: n.d* **40/1**

004 **7** 22 **Raze Aqlaam**[41] 5853 2-8-7 46.. JackMitchell 8
(Giles Bravery) *s.i.s: a off the pce: bhd and eased ins fnl f* **50/1**

1m 27.54s (0.34) **Going Correction** -0.10s/f (Stan) **7** Ran SP% **114.7**
Speed ratings (Par 95): **94,93,87,87,86 83,58**
CSF £5.95 TOTE £2.50: £1.80, £1.30; EX 5.70 Trifecta £17.10.
Owner Isa Al-Khalifa **Bred** Tally-Ho Stud **Trained** Newmarket, Suffolk

The Form Book, Raceform Ltd, Newbury, RG14 5SJ

FOCUS
The first two pulled away in the closing stages of this claimer. The runner-up helps guide the level.

7099 BRITISH STALLION STUDS EBF MAIDEN FILLIES' STKS (PLUS 10 RACE) 6f (P)
6:25 (6:27) (Class 5) 2-Y-O **£3,881** (£1,155; £577; £288) **Stalls** Centre

Form RPR

1 **Really Special** 2-9-0 0 .... JimCrowley 7 84+
(Saeed bin Suroor) *t.k.h: hld up in tch in midfield: short of room and shuffled bk to last quartet 5f out: nt clr run over 1f out: swtchd lft and hdwy ent fnl f: str run to ld wl ins fnl f: sn in command: impressive* **5/1**

434 **2** 2 **Island In The Sky (IRE)**[50] 5542 2-9-0 75 .... OisinMurphy 6 75
(David Simcock) *t.k.h: chsd ldr: rdn to ld wl over 1f out: kpt on wl u.p tl hdd and outpcd by wnr wl ins fnl f* **6/1**

3 1 1/4 **Gorgeous Noora (IRE)** 2-9-0 0 .... AndreaAtzeni 4 71+
(Luca Cumani) *hld up wl in tch in midfield: effrt to chse ldr over 1f out tl ins fnl f: styd on same pce after* **11/4**[1]

4 **4** 1 **Mississippi Miss**[27] 6295 2-9-0 0 .... RobertHavlin 2 69
(Dr Jon Scargill) *hld up in tch in midfield: nt clr run over 2f out: rdn and hdwy jst over 1f out: styd on ins fnl f* **20/1**

4 **5** shd **Always Thankful**[23] 6454 2-9-0 0 .... MartinHarley 1 68
(Ismail Mohammed) *chsd ldrs: effrt and swtchd lft over 1f out: styd on same pce ins fnl f* **7/2**[3]

6 3 3/4 **Killermont Street (IRE)** 2-9-0 0 .... SilvestreDeSousa 11 57+
(Mark Johnston) *chsd ldrs: effrt: rn green and unable qck over 1f out: wknd ins fnl f* **3/1**[2]

7 nse **Paquita Bailarina** 2-9-0 0 .... TomEaves 8 57
(James Given) *hld up in last quartet: swtchd rt over 1f out: hdwy 1f out: styd on ins fnl f: nvr trbld ldrs* **50/1**

0 **8** 5 **Embleton**[7] 6897 2-9-0 0 .... AdamBeschizza 10 42
(Charlie Wallis) *t.k.h: hld up in tch in midfield: swtchd rt and effrt over 1f out: sn outpcd: wknd ins fnl f* **100/1**

05 **9** 3 1/2 **Instigation**[17] 6625 2-9-0 0 .... FMBerry 9 31
(Ed Dunlop) *s.i.s and bustled along early: hdwy on outer 3f out: sn rdn: lost pl over 1f out: wknd fnl f* **25/1**

3U0 **10** 2 **Luxford**[15] 6673 2-9-0 0 .... KierenFox 3 25
(John Best) *led tl wl over 1f out: sn lost pl and wknd* **50/1**

0 **11** 3 **Buena Luna**[28] 6244 2-9-0 0 .... LukeMorris 12 16+
(Sir Mark Prescott Bt) *awkward as stalls opened and s.i.s: sn bustled along: a towards rr: rdn over 2f out: wknd over 1f out* **50/1**

12 10 **Lily Cliff** 2-9-0 0 .... TomQueally 5
(Paul D'Arcy) *s.i.s: bhd: hung rt bnd over 3f out: lost tch over 1f out* **50/1**

1m 13.19s (-0.51) **Going Correction** -0.10s/f (Stan) **12** Ran SP% **122.3**
Speed ratings (Par 92): **99,96,94,93,93 88,88,81,76,74 70,56**
CSF £34.44 TOTE £4.90: £1.70, £1.80, £1.80; EX 23.20 Trifecta £77.50.
Owner Godolphin **Bred** Darley **Trained** Newmarket, Suffolk

FOCUS
A fair maiden. The runner-up guides the opening level.

7100 TOTEPOOL RACECOURSE CASH BACK AVAILABLE MAIDEN STKS 1m (P)
6:55 (6:58) (Class 5) 2-Y-O **£3,234** (£962; £481; £240) **Stalls** Low

Form RPR

62 **1** **Hersigh**[17] 6625 2-9-0 0 .... SilvestreDeSousa 3 75
(Saeed bin Suroor) *led: rdn over 1f out: hld on wl u.p ins fnl f: rdn out* **11/8**[1]

3342 **2** nk **Prerogative (IRE)**[27] 6288 2-9-5 80 ....[1] SeanLevey 4 79
(Richard Hannon) *in tch in midfield: hdwy to chse ldng pair 3f out: drvn to press wnr 1f out: kpt on u.p: hld towards fin* **5/1**[3]

3 1 **Zumurudee (USA)** 2-9-5 0 .... RyanMoore 8 77+
(Marco Botti) *chsd ldr: rdn and ev ch over 1f out: lost 2nd but stl ev ch 1f out: hit on nose by rivals whip and styd on same pce ins fnl f* **2/1**[2]

6 **4** 2 1/2 **Wild Shot**[14] 6716 2-9-5 0 .... RyanTate 7 71
(James Eustace) *in tch in last pair: effrt in 4th and rdn over 2f out: no imp and styd on same pce fr over 1f out* **33/1**

05 **5** 7 **Flauto (IRE)**[19] 6590 2-9-5 0 .... LukeMorris 6 54
(Marco Botti) *in tch in midfield: effrt in 5th over 2f out: no imp and wl hld over 1f out: wknd ins fnl f* **25/1**

6 22 **Daily Trader** 2-9-5 0 .... WilliamBuick 5
(John Gosden) *dwlt: rn green in rr and sn niggled along: rdn over 3f out: c wd and lost tch 2f out: t.o and eased fnl f* **6/1**

0 **7** 7 **Jupiter Ascending**[17] 6632 2-9-5 0 .... OisinMurphy 1
(Michael Appleby) *t.k.h: sn trcking ldrs: rdn 3f out: sn lost pl: lost tch wl over 1f out: eased ins fnl f: t.o* **66/1**

1m 40.24s (0.34) **Going Correction** -0.10s/f (Stan) **7** Ran SP% **114.7**
Speed ratings (Par 95): **94,93,92,90,83 61,54**
CSF £8.91 TOTE £2.40: £1.50, £1.90; EX 7.40 Trifecta £17.40.
Owner Godolphin **Bred** Darley **Trained** Newmarket, Suffolk

FOCUS
The winner proved tough in front in this maiden. The runner-up limits the form.

7101 TOTEPOOL RACING'S BIGGEST SUPPORTER CONDITIONS STKS 1m 2f (P)
7:25 (7:28) (Class 3) 3-Y-O+ **£9,703** (£2,887; £1,443; £721) **Stalls** Low

Form RPR

1221 **1** **Rockspirit (IRE)**[39] 5932 3-8-12 96 .... AndreaAtzeni 6 107
(Marco Botti) *stdd s: hld up in tch in rr: clsd over 2f out: swtchd rt and effrt over 1f out: rdn to chse ldr jst ins fnl f: r.o wl u.p to ld last stride* **9/2**[3]

-052 **2** shd **Basem**[33] 6157 5-9-0 110 .... EdwardGreatrex(3) 1 107
(Saeed bin Suroor) *awkward as stalls opened and s.i.s: in tch: wnt 3rd 5f out: effrt to chse ldr 2f out: drvn to ld 1f out: kpt on u.p: hdd last stride* **15/8**[1]

41-2 **3** 3 **Mustajeer**[177] 1395 3-8-12 98 .... PaulHanagan 4 101
(Owen Burrows) *led: rdn ent fnl 2f: hdd 1f out: no ex and outpcd fnl 100yds: eased cl home* **5/1**

4544 **4** 4 1/2 **Tony Curtis**[40] 5893 3-8-12 105 .... SeanLevey 3 92
(Richard Hannon) *chsd ldr tl over 1f out: unable qck u.p and btn 4th 1f out: wknd ins fnl f* **5/1**

4010 **5** 22 **Daily Bulletin (USA)**[13] 6753 3-8-12 98 .... WilliamBuick 5 48
(John Gosden) *chsd ldrs tl 5f out: rdn 3f out: sn dropped to rr and btn whn c wd bnd 2f out: bhd and eased ins fnl f* **3/1**[2]

2m 4.17s (-4.43) **Going Correction** -0.10s/f (Stan)
WFA 3 from 5yo 5lb **5** Ran SP% **111.3**
Speed ratings (Par 107): **113,112,110,106,89**
CSF £13.54 TOTE £4.20: £2.50, £1.40; EX 12.00 Trifecta £44.40.
Owner Giuliano Manfredini **Bred** Patrick Byrnes **Trained** Newmarket, Suffolk

FOCUS
A decent contest, and an improving winner. The form is rated around the third.

7102 "TOTEPOOL" WIN TICKETS ON FACEBOOK MAIDEN STKS 1m 2f (P)
7:55 (7:57) (Class 5) 3-4-Y-O **£4,204** (£1,251; £625; £312) **Stalls** Low

Form RPR

2 **1** **Strong Force**[19] 6567 3-9-5 0 .... OisinMurphy 7 90+
(Saeed bin Suroor) *mde all: set stdy gallop tl rdn and qcknd 2f out: r.o wl and a holding runner up ins fnl f* **9/4**[1]

2 1 1/4 **Alf Guineas (IRE)** 3-9-0 0 .... TomQueally 9 82+
(John Gosden) *stdd s: hld up in tch in last pair: hdwy on outer 3f out: chsd wnr and rdn over 1f out: clr 2nd and kpt on same pce ins fnl f* **20/1**

4-24 **3** 4 **Statuesque**[93] 3990 3-9-0 81 .... RyanMoore 3 74
(Sir Michael Stoute) *chsd wnr tl over 1f out: unable qck u.p jst over 1f out: outpcd ins fnl f* **9/4**[1]

2 **4** 1 1/4 **Rock'n Gold**[27] 6294 3-9-5 0 .... ShaneKelly 5 76
(Luca Cumani) *hld up in tch in midfield: effrt and hung lft over 1f out: unable qck and outpcd jst over 1f out: kpt on same pce fnl f* **7/2**[2]

5 shd **St Malo (USA)** 3-9-5 0 .... AndreaAtzeni 6 76
(Roger Varian) *hld up in tch in midfield: effrt on inner over 1f out: unable qck and btn 1f out: kpt on same pce after* **10/1**

522 **6** 3 **Thundering Blue (USA)**[28] 6247 3-9-5 78 .... JimCrowley 1 70
(David Menuisier) *t.k.h: chsd ldrs: rdn and unable qck over 1f out: sn btn and wknd ins fnl f* **8/1**[3]

05 **7** 1/2 **Lost The Moon**[14] 6703 3-9-0 0 .... StevieDonohoe 4 64
(Mark H Tompkins) *stdd s: hld up in tch in rr: rdn and outpcd 2f out: wl hld and plugged on same pce fr over 1f out* **100/1**

4 **8** 21 **Phileas Fogg (IRE)**[21] 6511 3-9-2 0 .... JosephineGordon(3) 2 27
(Martyn Meade) *taken down early: chsd ldrs tl 1/2-way: rdn and lost pl over 2f out: bhd and eased ins fnl f* **14/1**

2m 8.27s (-0.33) **Going Correction** -0.10s/f (Stan) **8** Ran SP% **116.4**
Speed ratings (Par 103): **97,96,92,91,91 89,88,72**
CSF £51.69 TOTE £3.50: £1.30, £4.30, £1.20; EX 52.90 Trifecta £205.10.
Owner Godolphin **Bred** Hascombe And Valiant Studs **Trained** Newmarket, Suffolk

FOCUS
This was steadily run and dominated from the front, but the runner-up posted a very encouraging debut. The form is rated close to face value.

7103 @TOTEPOOLRACING FOLLOW US ON TWITTER H'CAP 1m 2f (P)
8:25 (8:29) (Class 6) (0-55,56) 3-Y-O+ **£2,911** (£866; £432; £216) **Stalls** Low

Form RPR

0-41 **1** **Estrella Eria (FR)**[21] 6514 3-9-0 **53** .... LukeMorris 12 63+
(George Peckham) *hld up in tch in midfield: hdwy over 2f out: rdn to chse ldr over 1f out: led ins fnl f: r.o wl* **7/2**[1]

4351 **2** 1 1/2 **Onehelluvatouch**[7] 6891 3-9-3 **56** 6ex ....(b) JimCrowley 11 63
(Philip Hide) *hld up in tch in midfield: clsd to chse ldrs over 2f out: rdn to ld over 1f out: hdd ins fnl f: styd on same pce after* **4/1**[2]

5500 **3** 2 3/4 **Oyster Card**[7] 6900 3-8-7 **49** .... TimClark(3) 7 52
(Michael Appleby) *chsd ldrs: nt clr run over 2f out: effrt u.p to press ldrs over 1f out: 3rd and styd on same pce ins fnl f* **8/1**[3]

6045 **4** 3/4 **Gilt Edged (IRE)**[21] 6513 3-8-11 **50** .... JoeDoyle 15 50
(Julie Camacho) *stdd s: hld up in rr: rdn and hdwy over 1f out: r.o ins fnl f: nt rch ldrs* **16/1**

0-05 **5** 6 **General Brook (IRE)**[21] 6514 6-9-7 **55** .... FergusSweeney 1 44
(John O'Shea) *led: rdn 2f out: hdd over 1f out: sn btn and wknd ins fnl f* **14/1**

0-00 **6** 1 1/4 **Dusty Raven**[114] 3256 3-9-2 **55** .... LiamKeniry 2 42
(Neil Mulholland) *hld up in tch in last trio: swtchd lft and sme hdwy over 1f out: no imp 1f out: wknd ins fnl f* **20/1**

5440 **7** 3/4 **Heat Storm (IRE)**[33] 6143 5-8-12 **46** oh1 ....(v) RyanPowell 6 31
(James Unett) *s.i.s and rdn along early: in tch in last trio: rdn and sme hdwy over 1f out: no imp 1f out: wknd ins fnl f* **33/1**

0040 **8** 1 **Munsarim (IRE)**[24] 6411 9-9-7 **55** ....(v) KierenFox 4 38
(Lee Carter) *hld up in tch in last trio: hdwy 4f out: rdn to chse ldrs over 2f out: struggling and lost pl over 1f out: wknd fnl f* **12/1**

0402 **9** 8 **Lmntrix**[7] 6900 4-9-7 **55** .... FMBerry 14 23
(George Margarson) *chsd ldrs: lost pl u.p over 1f out: sn wknd* **9/1**

4032 **10** 1/2 **Understory (USA)**[110] 3401 9-9-4 **52** .... RyanTate 10 19
(Tim McCarthy) *chsd ldrs: outpcd u.p and drifted rt over 1f out: wknd fnl f* **16/1**

50-0 **11** 3/4 **King Of Cornwall (IRE)**[48] 5610 3-8-12 **51** ....(t) ShaneKelly 3 17
(David Lanigan) *hld up in tch in midfield: shuffled bk 3f out: rdn and no hdwy over 1f out: bhd ins fnl f* **7/2**[1]

5560 **12** 6 **Music Hall (FR)**[7] 6900 6-8-7 **46** oh1 .... CharlieBennett(5) 5
(Shaun Harris) *chsd ldrs tl lost pl over 2f out: bhd fnl f* **16/1**

2m 6.84s (-1.76) **Going Correction** -0.10s/f (Stan)
WFA 3 from 4yo+ 5lb **12** Ran SP% **125.3**
Speed ratings (Par 101): **103,101,99,99,94 93,92,91,85,85 84,79**
CSF £18.34 CT £110.39 TOTE £4.60: £1.60, £1.40, £3.50; EX 18.40 Trifecta £216.90.
Owner Fawzi Abdulla Nass **Bred** D Chassagneux & E A R L Ecurie Loire **Trained** Newmarket, Suffolk

FOCUS
This was run at a good gallop and it looks sound form for the grade. It's been rated quite positively, with the runner-up and third fitting, and the first two a little clear of the third and fourth.

7104 TOTEPOOL COLLECT YOUR WINNINGS AT BETFRED SHOPS H'CAP 2m (P)
8:55 (8:58) (Class 6) (0-65,65) 3-Y-O+ **£3,234** (£962; £481; £240) **Stalls** Low

Form RPR

656 **1** **Next Train's Gone**[17] 6626 3-9-3 **65** .... RyanTate 6 71
(James Eustace) *hld up in tch in last pair: hdwy 6f out: rdn to chse leasers 2f out: wnt 2nd and edgd lft over 1f out: upsides ins fnl f: styd on wl to ld 50yds out* **3/1**[2]

3612 **2** 3/4 **Free Bounty**[21] 6508 3-9-2 **64** ....(t) SilvestreDeSousa 4 69
(Philip McBride) *led: rdn ent fnl 2f: drvn and jnd ins fnl f: hdd and no ex fnl 50yds* **6/4**[1]

0550 **3** 2 1/2 **Shrubland**[66] 4942 3-8-6 **54** ....(b) TomMarquand 1 57
(Ed Walker) *hld up in tch in midfield: nt clr run wl over 1f out: hdwy 1f out: chse clr ldng pair jst ins fnl f: styd on but nvr threatening ldrs* **8/1**

3003 **4** 4 **Purple Raven**[14] 6698 3-9-0 **65** .... LouisSteward(3) 8 62
(Michael Bell) *stdd s: hld up in tch in rr: clsd 3f out: effrt 2f out: wnt 3rd briefly 1f out: 4th and no imp ins fnl f* **6/1**[3]

3500 **5** 3 1/4 **Awesome Rock (IRE)**[24] 6411 7-8-9 **46** oh1 .... RobertHavlin 7 39
(Roger Ingram) *hld up in tch in rr: hdwy into midfield 4f out: nt clr run and swtchd rt over 1f out: sn rdn and no imp: wknd ins fnl f* **25/1**

2250 **6** 2½ **O'Connor's Girl**[19] 6565 3-9-3 **65** LukeMorris 5 55
(Sir Mark Prescott Bt) *t.k.h: chsd ldr: rdn over 2f out: lost 2nd and btn over 1f out: wknd ins fnl f* **3/1**[2]

0630 **7** 5 **Triassic (IRE)**[14] 6698 3-8-3 **51** NickyMackay 3 35
(Mark Johnston) *chsd ldrs: unable qck u.p over 1f out: sn btn and wknd fnl f* **16/1**

0-45 **8** 26 **Sant'Elia**[14] 6719 4-9-4 **55** StevieDonohoe 2 8
(Mark H Tompkins) *rn in snatches: in tch in midfield: rdn and lost pl 6f out: lost tch and eased over 1f out: t.o* **50/1**

3m 29.55s (-0.45) **Going Correction** -0.10s/f (Stan)
WFA 3 from 4yo+ 11lb **8** Ran SP% **127.1**
Speed ratings (Par 101): **97,96,95,93,91 90,88,75**
CSF £8.98 CT £35.32 TOTE £4.60: £1.70, £1.10, £2.90; EX 10.40 Trifecta £95.90.
Owner Harold Nass **Bred** Rockville Pike Partnership **Trained** Newmarket, Suffolk

FOCUS
A fairly modest staying handicap. The third, fourth and fifth were not definite stayers and this form will take a while to work out.
T/Plt: £10.70 to a £1 stake. Pool: £91,688.04. 6,213.01 winning units. T/Qpdt: £4.10 to a £1 stake. Pool: £9,520.64. 1,690.35 winning units. **Steve Payne**

6920 NEWCASTLE (A.W) (L-H)

Friday, October 7

OFFICIAL GOING: Tapeta: standard
Wind: Light, half behind Weather: Overcast races 1-2

7105 DSE H'CAP 1m 4f 98y (Tp)

5:40 (5:41) (Class 6) (0-65,65) 3-Y-O+ **£2,264** (£673; £336; £168) **Stalls** High

Form RPR

040- **1** **Lugano**[317] 7980 3-9-2 **60** LukeMorris 9 65+
(Sir Mark Prescott Bt) *t.k.h early: prom: outpcd and rn green over 2f out: rallied over 1f out: led wl ins fnl f to ld cl home* **7/2**[2]

4055 **2** hd **Ajman Prince (IRE)**[7] 6921 3-9-7 **65** JoeDoyle 10 70
(Alistair Whillans) *hld up: hdwy on outside over 2f out: chsd ldr and hung lft u.p over 1f out: led wl ins fnl f: kpt on: hdd cl home* **7/1**[3]

5051 **3** 1¼ **Kirtling**[14] 6739 5-9-9 **63** (t) EoinWalsh(3) 7 66
(Andi Brown) *missed break: hld up: hld up: hdwy on outside to ld over 3f out: rdn over 2f out: edgd lft fr over 1f out: hdd and no ex wl ins fnl f* **7/1**[3]

066/ **4** 1 **Up Ten Down Two (IRE)**[1104] 6877 7-9-4 **58** RachelRichardson(3) 6 60
(Michael Easterby) *t.k.h: cl up: rdn and outpcd over 2f out: rallied fnl f: kpt on: no imp* **20/1**

0312 **5** 2¾ **Taopix**[7] 6920 4-9-3 **54** JoeyHaynes 2 51
(Karen McLintock) *t.k.h: in tch: hdwy to chse ldr over 2f out: hung lft and lost 2nd over 1f out: wknd ins fnl f* **6/4**[1]

1004 **6** 1¼ **Gabrial's Hope (FR)**[7] 6920 7-9-3 **54** DaleSwift 4 50
(Tracy Waggott) *s.s: bhd: rdn over 2f out: sme late hdwy: nvr on terms* **28/1**

0545 **7** 2¼ **Loose Ends**[102] 3722 3-9-2 **60** DougieCostello 1 52
(David Simcock) *hld up bhd ldng gp on ins: drvn along 3f out: no imp fr 2f out* **28/1**

4003 **8** 1 **Voice From Above (IRE)**[18] 6619 7-8-6 **50** PaulaMuir(7) 8 41
(Patrick Holmes) *chsd ldrs tl rdn and wknd over 2f out* **40/1**

-046 **9** 9 **Sebastian's Wish (IRE)**[37] 6029 3-8-12 **56** TedDurcan 11 33
(Richard Whitaker) *led at modest gallop: rdn and hdd over 3f out: wknd 2f out* **17/2**

0056 **10** 4½ **Fledermaus (IRE)**[39] 5980 6-8-9 **46** oh1 (t) JamesSullivan 5 16
(Tina Jackson) *t.k.h: hld up: struggling over 2f out: sn btn* **125/1**

0506 **11** 20 **Bilko's Back (IRE)**[18] 6618 4-8-11 **53** (t) GarryWhillans(5) 3
(Susan Corbett) *cl up on ins tl rdn and wknd 3f out: t.o* **200/1**

2m 40.49s (-0.61) **Going Correction** +0.025s/f (Slow)
WFA 3 from 4yo+ 7lb **11** Ran SP% **113.1**
Speed ratings (Par 101): **103,102,102,101,99 98,97,96,90,87 74**
CSF £25.02 CT £160.32 TOTE £3.60: £1.60, £1.90, £2.60; EX 27.20 Trifecta £134.80.
Owner J L C Pearce **Bred** Lordship Stud **Trained** Newmarket, Suffolk
■ Stewards' Enquiry : Joe Doyle seven-day ban; used his whip above the permitted level (21st-22nd, 24th-27th Oct)

FOCUS
A modest handicap run at a steady pace, with the winner swooping late. He has clear scope to do better over further.

7106 MALONE & SONS MAIDEN STKS 1m 4f 98y (Tp)

6:10 (6:10) (Class 5) 3-Y-O+ **£2,911** (£866; £432; £216) **Stalls** High

Form RPR

5332 **1** **Rasmee**[18] 6626 3-9-5 82 [1] LukeMorris 4 87
(Marco Botti) *dwlt: t.k.h in tch: hdwy to ld over 2f out: hung lft and sn rdn clr: kpt on wl fnl f: unchal* **7/4**[2]

30 **2** 2¾ **Song Of Namibia (IRE)**[83] 4401 5-9-12 0 TedDurcan 3 84+
(Sir Michael Stoute) *t.k.h: hld up: nt clr run 3f out: sn swtchd lft and chsd clr ldng pair: shkn up and hdwy to chse (clr) wnr ins fnl f: kpt on: nvr nr to chal: improve* **4/1**[3]

23-2 **3** 5 **Paris Magic**[151] 2098 3-9-5 85 [1] JackMitchell 6 74
(Hugo Palmer) *t.k.h: pressed ldr: led over 3f out to over 2f out: chsd (clr) wnr tl wknd ins fnl f* **11/10**[1]

4-00 **4** 13 **Royal Flag**[6] 6957 6-9-12 77 (p) DaleSwift 2 53
(Brian Ellison) *chsd ldrs: drvn and outpcd 3f out: n.d after* **33/1**

00 **5** 3¼ **Kindled**[18] 6634 3-9-0 0 PaulMulrennan 5 43
(Ed McMahon) *led at modest gallop: rdn and hdd over 3f out: wknd 2f out* **250/1**

00 **6** 8 **He's Magic**[22] 6520 5-9-12 0 JamesSullivan 1 35
(Tim Fitzgerald) *hld up in tch: struggling wl over 3f out: sn btn* **250/1**

7 ¾ **First Of Never (IRE)**[94] 10-9-12 0 PaddyAspell 7 34
(Lynn Siddall) *missed break: hld up: drvn and outpcd wl over 2f out: sn wknd* **500/1**

2m 40.9s (-0.20) **Going Correction** +0.025s/f (Slow)
WFA 3 from 5yo+ 7lb **7** Ran SP% **107.9**
Speed ratings (Par 103): **101,99,95,87,85 79,79**
CSF £7.93 TOTE £2.60: £2.10, £1.80; EX 9.20 Trifecta £12.90.
Owner Sheikh Mohammed Bin Khalifa Al Maktoum **Bred** Essafinaat **Trained** Newmarket, Suffolk

FOCUS
The three market leaders pulled clear in this older-horse maiden. The winner is rated to a better view of his handicap latest.

7107 GUTHRIE FINANCIAL PLANNING SERVICES MAIDEN AUCTION FILLIES' STKS (PLUS 10 RACE) 1m 5y (Tp)

6:40 (6:41) (Class 5) 2-Y-O **£2,911** (£866; £432; £216) **Stalls** Centre

Form RPR

3642 **1** **Three Duchesses**[25] 6421 2-8-6 72 LuluStanford(7) 5 71
(Michael Bell) *t.k.h early: hld up bhd ldng gp: hdwy and swtchd rt over 2f out: led appr fnl f: sn hung lft: rdn out* **11/8**[1]

2 ¾ **White Chocolate (IRE)** 2-9-0 0 DougieCostello 7 70
(David Simcock) *hld up in tch: hdwy over 2f out: effrt and chal over 1f out: hung lft ins fnl f: kpt on: hld nr fin* **6/1**[3]

3 **3** 1¼ **Nellie's Dancer**[12] 6808 2-8-10 0 PJMcDonald 6 63
(Scott Dixon) *led: rdn and hdd appr fnl f: carried lft ins fnl f: kpt on same pce* **16/1**

42 **4** nk **Flood Defence (IRE)**[43] 5809 2-8-10 0 TedDurcan 4 66
(Chris Wall) *trckd ldrs: wnt 2nd over 2f out: rdn and jst outpcd whn hmpd appr fnl f: rallied ins fnl f: kpt on* **9/4**[2]

5 7 **Lady Freyja** 2-8-12 0 StevieDonohoe 1 49
(John Ryan) *pressed ldr to over 2f out: drvn and wknd over 1f out* **14/1**

0 **6** 2¾ **Orientelle**[24] 6447 2-8-9 0 (b[1]) GeorgeChaloner 3 39
(Richard Whitaker) *t.k.h: hld up in tch: drvn over 2f out: wknd wl over 1f out* **100/1**

7 2 **Haldaw** 2-9-0 0 LukeMorris 2 40
(Mick Channon) *prom on far side of gp tl rdn and wknd over 2f out* **9/1**

1m 40.28s (1.68) **Going Correction** -0.175s/f (Stan) **7** Ran SP% **110.7**
Speed ratings (Par 92): **84,83,82,81,74 71,69**
CSF £9.59 TOTE £2.20: £1.20, £3.10; EX 10.40 Trifecta £67.90.
Owner Hon James Broughton **Bred** Barton Stud **Trained** Newmarket, Suffolk
■ Stewards' Enquiry : Dougie Costello caution; careless riding

FOCUS
A fair maiden with a couple worth noting in behind.

7108 DOWNLOAD THE AT THE RACES APP H'CAP 1m 5y (Tp)

7:10 (7:10) (Class 4) (0-85,84) 3-Y-O+ **£4,690** (£1,395; £697; £348) **Stalls** Centre

Form RPR

0110 **1** **Red Paladin (IRE)**[7] 6914 6-9-3 **80** (p) TonyHamilton 7 88
(Kristin Stubbs) *s.i.s: hld up: rdn over 2f out: hdwy nr side of gp over 1f out: led ins fnl f: kpt on wl* **10/1**

2140 **2** nk **Briardale (IRE)**[14] 6753 4-9-7 **84** PJMcDonald 6 91
(James Bethell) *hld up midfield: hdwy over 2f out: drvn and ev ch ins fnl f: kpt on: hld nr fin* **4/1**[1]

0000 **3** nk **Mont Ras (IRE)**[43] 5802 9-9-6 **83** ConnorBeasley 11 90
(Roger Fell) *led at ordinary gallop: rdn and hdd over 1f out: rallied and ch ins fnl f: kpt on* **22/1**

4020 **4** nk **Sky Ship**[4] 7017 3-9-2 **82** (p) GrahamGibbons 4 88
(Sir Michael Stoute) *hld up midfield: hdwy on far side of gp to chse ldrs over 1f out: effrt and ch ins fnl f: kpt on* **5/1**[3]

6110 **5** 1¼ **Imperial State**[62] 5179 3-9-1 **84** (t) LouisSteward(3) 13 87
(George Scott) *hld up: hdwy nr side of gp to ld over 1f out: hdd ins fnl f: sn no ex* **14/1**

0020 **6** shd **Alexandrakollontai (IRE)**[12] 6811 6-9-2 **79** (b) PaulMulrennan 3 82
(Alistair Whillans) *hld up: rdn over 2f out: hdwy far side of gp over 1f out: kpt on fnl f: nt pce to chal* **50/1**

2305 **7** ¾ **Company Asset (IRE)**[34] 6113 3-8-13 **79** GrahamLee 9 80
(Kevin Ryan) *s.i.s: hld up: rdn over 2f out: hdwy over 1f out: kpt on fnl f: no imp* **18/1**

263 **8** ¾ **North Creek**[44] 5765 3-9-0 **80** TedDurcan 5 79
(Chris Wall) *trckd ldrs: rdn over 2f out: outpcd fr over 1f out* **9/2**[2]

0260 **9** 1¼ **Argaki (IRE)**[22] 6500 6-8-11 **79** ShirleyTeasdale(5) 14 76
(Keith Dalgleish) *t.k.h: cl up on nr side of gp tl rdn and wknd over 1f out* **33/1**

503 **10** 1¾ **Freewheel (IRE)**[6] 6957 6-9-1 **78** LukeMorris 10 71
(Garry Moss) *trckd ldrs: rdn over 2f out: wknd over 1f out* **7/1**

0000 **11** hd **Hard To Handel**[14] 6753 4-9-4 **81** (v[1]) DavidNolan 2 73
(David O'Meara) *hld up: rdn on far side of gp over 2f out: btn over 1f out* **5/1**[3]

1100 **12** 10 **Ellaal**[13] 6772 7-9-1 **78** JamesSullivan 8 47
(Ruth Carr) *cl up tl rdn and wknd over 2f out* **66/1**

5006 **13** 1¼ **Hulcolt (IRE)**[22] 6521 5-9-1 **78** (b[1]) DaleSwift 12 44
(Ivan Furtado) *t.k.h: prom: drifted rt to stands' rail after 3f: rdn and wknd fr over 2f out* **33/1**

1m 36.54s (-2.06) **Going Correction** -0.175s/f (Stan) course record
WFA 3 from 4yo+ 3lb **13** Ran SP% **118.7**
Speed ratings (Par 105): **103,102,102,102,100 100,100,99,98,96 96,86,84**
CSF £47.48 CT £878.59 TOTE £11.80: £4.00, £2.00, £6.40; EX 57.30 Trifecta £1591.90.
Owner K Stubbs, Dr Grieve, T Baker & Clark **Bred** Noel O'Callaghan **Trained** Norton, N Yorks

FOCUS
A decent, open-looking handicap and a tight four-way finish. A surprise pb from the winner.

7109 FOLLOW AT THE RACES ON TWITTER NURSERY H'CAP (DIV I) 7f 14y (Tp)

7:40 (7:56) (Class 6) (0-65,65) 2-Y-O **£2,264** (£673; £336; £168) **Stalls** Centre

Form RPR

6501 **1** **Iftitah (IRE)**[8] 6895 2-8-12 **56** 6ex (t) StevieDonohoe 12 65
(George Peckham) *hld up: hdwy nr side of gp to ld appr fnl f: rdn clr* **2/1**[1]

4535 **2** 2¾ **Tagur (IRE)**[34] 6130 2-9-7 **65** [1] TomEaves 9 67
(Kevin Ryan) *led: rdn 2f out: hdd appr fnl f: kpt on: nt pce of wnr* **9/1**

1304 **3** 1 **Baltic Beau**[30] 6222 2-9-0 **58** TonyHamilton 1 57
(Richard Fahey) *s.i.s: hld up: rdn and hdwy on nr side of gp 2f out: hung lft: kpt on fnl f: nvr able to chal* **7/2**[2]

006 **4** nk **Atrafan (IRE)**[28] 6274 2-9-3 **61** GrahamGibbons 11 60
(Alan Brown) *pressed ldr: rdn over 2f out: kpt on same pce fnl f* **14/1**

6530 **5** hd **Lil's Affair (IRE)**[16] 6681 2-8-6 **50** ow1 [1] ConnorBeasley 7 48+
(Bryan Smart) *hld up bhd ldng gp: rdn and outpcd over 2f out: rallied on far side of gp over 1f out: kpt on: no ch w nr side ldrs* **11/1**

0604 **6** 1¼ **Silk Mill Blue**[13] 6789 2-9-7 **65** GeorgeChaloner 5 60
(Richard Whitaker) *hld up bhd ldng gp: rdn over 2f out: hdwy over 1f out: sn no imp* **13/2**[3]

6043 **7** ½ **Whitby Bay**[24] 6446 2-8-2 **51** NathanEvans(5) 10 45
(Michael Easterby) *chsd ldrs: drvn and outpcd over 2f out: n.d after* **25/1**

5350 **8** 2 **Our Boy John (IRE)**[31] 6213 2-9-0 **63** AdamMcNamara(5) 8 51
(Richard Fahey) *trckd ldrs: rdn over 2f out: wknd over 1f out* **22/1**

6060 **9** nk **La Haule Lady**[21] 6536 2-9-5 **63** DougieCostello 2 51
(Paul Midgley) *hld up on far side of gp: shortlived effrt 2f out: sn btn* **66/1**

5644 **10** *nk* **Peachey Carnehan**[14] 6743 2-9-7 **65**.............................. LukeMorris 4 52
(Michael Attwater) *cl up: rdn over 2f out: wknd over 1f out* **16/1**

000 **11** *3 ¼* **Shakabula (IRE)**[39] 5966 2-9-4 **62**.............................. BenCurtis 3 40
(Brian Ellison) *s.i.s: hld up: drvn and outpcd over 2f out: sn btn* **10/1**

0000 **12** *8* **Bruny Island (IRE)**[29] 6252 2-8-11 **55**.............................. PaulMulrennan 6 13
(Mark Johnston) *plld hrd: cl up tl rdn and lost pl over 2f out: sn btn* **50/1**

1m 25.57s (-0.63) **Going Correction** -0.175s/f (Stan) **12** Ran SP% **115.1**
Speed ratings (Par 93): **96,92,91,91,91 89,89,86,86,86 82,73**
CSF £19.00 CT £60.47 TOTE £2.80: £1.30, £3.10, £2.10; EX 19.60 Trifecta £69.60.
Owner Fawzi Abdulla Nass **Bred** Palmerston Bloodstock Ltd **Trained** Newmarket, Suffolk

FOCUS
A clear-cut winner in the first division of a modest nursery.

7110 FOLLOW AT THE RACES ON TWITTER NURSERY H'CAP (DIV II) 7f 14y (Tp)
8:10 (8:24) (Class 6) (0-65,65) 2-Y-O **£2,264** (£673; £336; £168) **Stalls** Centre

Form RPR

000 **1** **Ronnie The Rooster**[22] 6515 2-8-12 **56**.............................. GrahamGibbons 11 60+
(David Barron) *hld up on nr side of gp: effrt and rn green over 2f out: rallied and led ins fnl f: kpt on* **11/2**[2]

0264 **2** *nk* **Sheila's Return**[16] 6678 2-8-9 **53**.............................. ConnorBeasley 4 56
(Bryan Smart) *led: rdn over 1f out: edgd rt and hdd ins fnl f: kpt on fin* **4/1**[1]

3506 **3** *1* **Accladora**[6] 6963 2-9-5 **63**.............................. PJMcDonald 1 63
(Mark Johnston) *t.k.h: w ldr: rdn 2f out: ev ch tl no ex ins fnl f* **8/1**

0450 **4** *nk* **Dream Team**[16] 6678 2-9-0 **58**..............................[1] PaulMulrennan 9 58
(Michael Dods) *prom: rdn along 2f out: kpt on same pce fnl f* **8/1**

560 **5** *½* **Royal Cosmic**[46] 5727 2-9-1 **59**.............................. TonyHamilton 6 57
(Richard Fahey) *hld up bhd ldg gp: pushed along and outpcd over 2f out: rallied on far side of gp over 1f out: no imp* **12/1**

6060 **6** *1 ¾* **Pontecarlo Boy**[16] 6678 2-8-8 **52** ow1..............................(p) GeorgeChaloner 3 46
(Richard Whitaker) *prom: drvn over 2f out: rallied: outpcd fnl f* **14/1**

1213 **7** *hd* **Bismarck The Flyer (IRE)**[23] 6471 2-9-4 **65**.......... JacobButterfield[(3)] 2 58
(Ollie Pears) *cl up on far side of gp: rdn over 2f out: btn fnl f* **13/2**[3]

005 **8** *1* **Chalieb**[59] 5272 2-9-4 **62**.............................. TomEaves 10 53
(Nigel Tinkler) *stdd s: hld up: rdn and outpcd over 2f out: kpt on ins fnl f: nvr able to chal* **7/1**

0040 **9** *½* **Tael O' Gold**[6] 6950 2-8-12 **63**.............................. LewisEdmunds[(7)] 7 52
(Iain Jardine) *hld up: rdn and outpcd over 2f out: btn whn edgd lft over 1f out* **20/1**

4600 **10** *1 ¼* **Rubiesnpearls**[37] 6026 2-8-13 **62**.............................. AdamMcNamara[(5)] 5 48
(Richard Fahey) *chsd ldrs: drvn and outpcd over 2f out: sn btn* **20/1**

1440 **11** *5* **Hi Milady (IRE)**[43] 5796 2-9-7 **65**.............................. LiamKeniry 8 38
(Dominic Ffrench Davis) *hld up: rdn and struggling over 2f out: sn btn* **14/1**

1m 26.68s (0.48) **Going Correction** -0.175s/f (Stan) **11** Ran SP% **114.0**
Speed ratings (Par 93): **90,89,88,88,87 85,85,84,83,82 76**
CSF £26.81 CT £175.04 TOTE £6.50: £2.40, £1.60, £3.00; EX 25.10 Trifecta £204.10.
Owner Ron Hull **Bred** Richard Kent & Robert Percival **Trained** Maunby, N Yorks

FOCUS
The second division of a modest nursery and the time was 1.11sec slower than the first leg.

7111 AT THE RACES SKY 415 H'CAP 7f 14y (Tp)
8:40 (8:54) (Class 5) (0-75,75) 3-Y-O **£2,911** (£866; £432; £216) **Stalls** Centre

Form RPR

2012 **1** **Mon Beau Visage (IRE)**[8] 6907 3-9-7 **75**..............(p) GrahamGibbons 12 83+
(David O'Meara) *stdd s: t.k.h in rr: rdn and hdwy over 1f out: kpt on wl u.p to ld cl home* **2/1**[1]

0346 **2** *shd* **Athollblair Boy (IRE)**[31] 6216 3-8-7 **68**.............................. LewisEdmunds[(7)] 5 75
(Nigel Tinkler) *in tch: hdwy on far side of gp to ld over 1f out: kpt on wl fnl f: hdd cl home* **10/1**[3]

2352 **3** *1 ¼* **Deansgate (IRE)**[31] 6220 3-9-1 **74**..............(e) AdamMcNamara[(5)] 13 78
(Julie Camacho) *s.i.s: hld up: gd hdwy on nr side of gp to ld briefly over 1f out: hung lft: kpt on same pce last 75yds* **7/2**[2]

1235 **4** *hd* **Inaam (IRE)**[162] 1809 3-9-3 **71**.............................. TonyHamilton 1 74
(Richard Fahey) *hld up on far side of gp: hdwy and cl up over 1f out: rdn and kpt on same pce wl ins fnl f* **16/1**

4300 **5** *6* **Regal Response (IRE)**[22] 6502 3-9-5 **73**..............(b) PaulMulrennan 10 60
(Michael Dods) *in tch: rdn over 2f out: outpcd by ldng quartet fr over 1f out* **16/1**

004 **6** *2 ½* **Epeius (IRE)**[20] 6569 3-8-10 **64**..............................[1] GrahamLee 6 44
(Ben Haslam) *hld up: rdn and outpcd over 2f out: rallied over 1f out: kpt on fnl f: nvr able to chal* **12/1**

6556 **7** *5* **Furiant**[44] 5782 3-9-1 **69**.............................. PJMcDonald 2 36
(Mark Johnston) *prom on far side of gp: drvn over 2f out: wknd wl over 1f out* **16/1**

1400 **8** *shd* **Causey Arch (IRE)**[11] 6838 3-9-5 **73**..............(p) ConnorBeasley 8 39
(Michael Dods) *disp ld to over 1f out: sn rdn and wknd* **25/1**

3416 **9** *½* **Iceaxe**[24] 6453 3-9-1 **69**.............................. RoystonFfrench 9 34
(John Holt) *chsd ldrs on nr side of gp: rdn over 2f out: sn wknd* **14/1**

0546 **10** *2 ¼* **Never In Doubt**[13] 6790 3-9-0 **68**.............................. GeorgeChaloner 3 27
(Richard Whitaker) *cl up: rdn and edgd lft over 2f out: wknd over 1f out* **12/1**

0 **11** *2 ¾* **High Honcho**[14] 6742 3-9-2 **70**..............(vt[1]) TomEaves 11 22
(John Quinn) *prom on nr side of gp: drvn over 2f out: sn wknd* **66/1**

500 **12** *¾* **Avenue Of Stars**[15] 6714 3-9-7 **75**..............(v) DavidNolan 7 24
(Karen McLintock) *mde most tl hdd over 1f out: sn wknd* **12/1**

1m 24.5s (-1.70) **Going Correction** -0.175s/f (Stan) **12** Ran SP% **117.4**
Speed ratings (Par 101): **102,101,100,100,93 90,84,84,84,81 78,77**
CSF £22.78 CT £68.67 TOTE £2.40: £1.30, £2.60, £1.30; EX 26.90 Trifecta £185.30.
Owner The Pink Pot Partnership LLP **Bred** Stephanie Hanly **Trained** Upper Helmsley, N Yorks

FOCUS
A fair handicap in which the first four pulled clear of the rest. The form is rated around the second and third.

7112 WATCH TODAYS REPLAYS ON THE ATR APP H'CAP 5f (Tp)
9:10 (9:22) (Class 4) (0-80,82) 3-Y-O+ **£4,690** (£1,395; £697; £348) **Stalls** Centre

Form RPR

2304 **1** **First Bombardment**[7] 6927 3-9-4 **78**.............................. GrahamGibbons 14 87
(David O'Meara) *pressed ldr: clr of rest w one other over 1f out: shkn up to ld ins fnl f: kpt on wl* **8/1**

5106 **2** *1* **New Road Side**[46] 5730 3-9-2 **76**..............(v) ConnorBeasley 6 81
(Richard Guest) *t.k.h early: led: clr w wnr over 1f out: hdd ins fnl f: kpt on same pce* **40/1**

0500 **3** *2 ¼* **Fredricka**[13] 6793 5-9-3 **77**.............................. JasonHart 8 73+
(David Barron) *towards rr: rdn after 2f: hdwy nr side of gp to chse clr ldng pair over 1f out: kpt on fnl f: no imp* **10/1**

1041 **4** *hd* **Rich Again (IRE)**[7] 6926 7-9-8 **82** 6ex..............(b) PJMcDonald 12 77+
(James Bethell) *bhd: rdn over 2f out: hdwy nr side of gp over 1f out: kpt on: no imp* **3/1**[1]

4300 **5** *¾* **Something Lucky (IRE)**[62] 5153 4-9-3 **77**..............(p) ShaneGray 11 69+
(Kristin Stubbs) *s.i.s: hld up: hdwy whn nt clr run briefly wl over 1f out: kpt on fnl f: no imp* **16/1**

6014 **6** *1 ¾* **Desert Ace (IRE)**[7] 6926 5-9-6 **80**..............(p) RoystonFfrench 13 66
(Iain Jardine) *in tch on nr side of gp: hdwy to chse clr ldng pair briefly over 1f out: sn rdn and outpcd* **9/2**[3]

50 **7** *hd* **Willbeme**[35] 6080 8-9-3 **80**.............................. JacobButterfield[(3)] 1 65
(Neville Bycroft) *chsd ldrs on far side of gp: rdn over 1f out: wknd over 1f out* **28/1**

0300 **8** *2 ¼* **Soul Brother (IRE)**[53] 5479 5-9-4 **78**..............(b) DavidAllan 5 55
(Tim Easterby) *dwlt: hld up: pushed along 2f out: sn no imp* **22/1**

6000 **9** *shd* **Stocking**[128] 2787 4-9-4 **78**.............................. PaulMulrennan 4 55
(Bryan Smart) *hld up bhd ldrs on far side of gp: rdn and flashed tail fr over 2f out: wknd over 1f out* **33/1**

0043 **10** *hd* **Eleuthera**[25] 6425 4-9-5 **79**.............................. TomEaves 9 55
(Kevin Ryan) *chsd ldrs: rdn over 2f out: edgd lft and wknd over 1f out* **7/2**[2]

0020 **11** *nk* **Emjayem**[93] 3995 6-9-4 **78**.............................. KevinStott 2 53
(Ed McMahon) *t.k.h: chsd ldrs tl rdn and wknd wl over 1f out* **25/1**

3055 **12** *4 ½* **Personal Touch**[42] 5858 7-8-12 **79**..............(p) NatalieHambling[(7)] 10 38
(Michael Appleby) *hld up in tch: drvn and struggling over 2f out: btn over 1f out* **11/1**

5- **13** *7* **Rocking Rudolph (USA)**[409] 5724 3-9-5 **79**.............................. GrahamLee 7 14
(Robert Cowell) *chsd ldrs to 1/2-way: sn rdn and wknd* **16/1**

57.83s (-1.67) **Going Correction** -0.175s/f (Stan) course record **13** Ran SP% **122.7**
Speed ratings (Par 105): **106,104,100,100,99 96,96,92,92,92 91,84,73**
CSF £310.53 CT £3339.53 TOTE £9.30: £2.50, £9.30, £3.80; EX 327.10 Trifecta £2190.90.
Owner Northern Hart Racing & Partner **Bred** Habton Farms **Trained** Upper Helmsley, N Yorks

FOCUS
A decent sprint handicap and, unlike several other races on the card, the speed held up with very few getting into it. The winner is rated up a bit on his previous best.
T/Plt: £145.30 to a £1 stake. Pool: £88,303.93 - 443.36 winning tickets T/Qpdt: £13.80 to a £1 stake. Pool: £10,059.15 - 538.04 winning tickets **Richard Young**

[6945]NEWMARKET (R-H)
Friday, October 7

OFFICIAL GOING: Good to firm (good in places; 8.0)
Wind: light, half against Weather: light drizzle before racing, clearing to bright spells

7113 NEWMARKET ACADEMY GODOLPHIN BEACON PROJECT CORNWALLIS STKS (GROUP 3) 5f
1:35 (1:36) (Class 1) 2-Y-O
£45,368 (£17,200; £8,608; £4,288; £2,152; £1,080) **Stalls** High

Form RPR

1111 **1** **Mrs Danvers**[56] 5359 2-8-12 104.............................. RichardKingscote 11 106
(Jonathan Portman) *trckd ldrs tl wnt 2nd over 1f out: pushed into ld 1f out: in command and r.o wl ins fnl f: pushed out: comf* **2/1**[1]

3361 **2** *1 ½* **Clem Fandango (FR)**[21] 6538 2-8-12 99.............................. PhillipMakin 7 100
(Keith Dalgleish) *hld up in tch in midfield: pushed along over 1f out: hdwy u.p ins fnl f: wnt 2nd towards fin: no threat to wnr* **15/2**

1033 **3** *½* **Battaash (IRE)**[14] 6734 2-9-1 96.............................. PaulHanagan 10 101
(Charles Hills) *t.k.h: wnt rt s and hung rt thrght: led: rdn over 1f out: hdd 1f out: kpt on same pce ins fnl f: lost 2nd towards fin* **9/1**

1214 **4** *1* **Afandem (IRE)**[28] 6282 2-9-4 107.............................. JamesDoyle 4 100
(Hugo Palmer) *chsd ldrs: effrt over 1f out: edgd lft u.p and unable qck 1f out: kpt on same pce ins fnl f* **4/1**[2]

5021 **5** *hd* **Nuclear Power**[37] 6016 2-9-1 82.............................. MartinDwyer 5 99
(William Muir) *hld up in tch in midfield: effrt over 1f out: nt clr run jst ins fnl f: gap opened 100yds out: styd on wl towards fin: no threat to wnr* **25/1**

0100 **6** *1* **Yalta (IRE)**[28] 6282 2-9-4 108.............................. WilliamBuick 1 96
(Mark Johnston) *racd towards centre thrght: chsd ldr tl unable qck u.p over 1f out: wknd ins fnl f* **13/2**

25 **7** *2 ¼* **Courage Under Fire (USA)**[16] 6688 2-9-1 0..............(t) RyanMoore 6 85
(A P O'Brien, Ire) *awkward leaving stalls: hld up in rr: effrt 2f out: no imp and styd on same pce fr over 1f out* **5/1**[3]

1510 **8** *½* **Sayesse**[6] 6950 2-9-1 87.............................. JFEgan 3 83
(Mick Channon) *dwlt and niggled along in last trio: no hdwy 2f out: wl hld and styd on same pce after* **40/1**

0121 **9** *11* **Rose Berry**[17] 6658 2-8-12 77.............................. SilvestreDeSousa 8 41
(Chris Dwyer) *bmpd s: a last trio: rdn 2f out: sn btn and bhd over 1f out: wknd* **50/1**

58.69s (-0.41) **Going Correction** +0.15s/f (Good) 2y crse rec **9** Ran SP% **113.3**
Speed ratings (Par 105): **109,106,105,104,103 102,98,97,80**
CSF £17.15 TOTE £2.40: £1.20, £2.80, £3.30; EX 14.00 Trifecta £88.10.
Owner Turf Club 2014 **Bred** M A Burton & Connie Hopper **Trained** Upper Lambourn, Berks

FOCUS
Stands' side course used. Stalls: 1m4f centre, remainder stands' side. The watered ground (3mm applied to the straight on Wednesday) was given as good to firm, good in places (GoingStick: 8.0). The Cornwallis Stakes has been hugely boosted by subsequent Group 1 exploits of last year's winner Quiet Reflection. It was strongly run this year, with riders shunning the near rail, and resulted in a new 2yo course record on the quick going. Fillies have now taken the last three editions. The form has been rated at the lower end of recent renewals.

7114 VISIONSPORT.COM OH SO SHARP STKS (GROUP 3) (FILLIES) 7f
2:05 (2:06) (Class 1) 2-Y-O
£45,368 (£17,200; £8,608; £4,288; £2,152; £1,080) **Stalls** High

Form RPR

41 **1** **Poet's Vanity**[36] 6061 2-9-0 0.............................. OisinMurphy 11 106
(Andrew Balding) *t.k.h: chsd ldr tl led wl over 1f out: drvn and hld on wl ins fnl f: rdn out* **13/2**[3]

1114 **2** *1* **Glitter Girl**[14] 6748 2-9-0 101.............................. RyanMoore 4 103
(William Haggas) *chsd ldrs: effrt to chal wl over 1f out: drvn 1f out: styd on same pce ins fnl f* **8/1**

212 **3** *1* **Unforgetable Filly**[15] 6706 2-9-0 94.............................. JimCrowley 6 100
(Hugo Palmer) *hld up in tch: clsd and nt clr run 2f out: rdn and hdwy over 1f out: chsd ldrs and kpt on same pce ins fnl f* **10/1**

2121 **4** ¾ **Paco's Angel**[38] 5998 2-9-0 86 ShaneKelly 8 98
(Richard Hughes) *hld up in tch in midfield: effrt over 1f out: kpt on same pce u.p ins fnl f* **16/1**

5 ½ **Double Lady (FR)**[25] 2-9-0 0 Pierre-CharlesBoudot 7 97+
(A Fabre, France) *stdd after s: hld up in tch in last trio: swtchd lft and clsd 2f out: rdn and hdwy over 1f out: styd on same pce and no imp ins fnl f* **3/1**[1]

12 **6** 2 **Mystic Dawn (IRE)**[36] 6063 2-9-0 0 MartinHarley 2 92
(David Simcock) *in tch in midfield: effrt u.p over 1f out: no imp 1f out: wknd ins fnl f* **10/1**

1523 **7** 1½ **Miss Infinity (IRE)**[14] 6748 2-9-0 103 JoeFanning 1 87
(Mark Johnston) *led and set stdy gallop: hdd and rdn wl over 1f out: no ex over 1f out: wknd ins fnl f* **10/1**

2126 **8** 1¾ **Groupie**[28] 6292 2-9-0 85 SeanLevey 9 83
(Richard Hannon) *stdd after s: hld up in tch in rr: effrt 2f out: no imp and edgd lft over 1f out: wknd ins fnl f* **66/1**

421 **9** 1¾ **Raven's Lady**[18] 6624 2-9-0 85 SilvestreDeSousa 13 78
(Marco Botti) *t.k.h: chsd ldng trio: rdn 2f out: unable qck and lost pl over 1f out: wknd ins fnl f* **16/1**

411 **10** 2 **Pichola Dance (IRE)**[13] 6787 2-9-0 85 AndreaAtzeni 10 73
(Roger Varian) *t.k.h: hld up in tch: effrt 2f out: no imp whn squeezed for room and hmpd over 1f out: wknd ins fnl f* **20/1**

0123 **11** 2 **Asidious Alexander (IRE)**[29] 6271 2-9-0 0 FrankieDettori 5 67
(Simon Crisford) *in tch in midfield: effrt u.p wl over 1f out: no imp and lost pl 1f out: wknd ins fnl f* **14/1**

2022 **12** 3¼ **Grecian Light (IRE)**[12] 6815 2-9-0 103 WilliamBuick 12 58+
(Charlie Appleby) *stdd and swtchd rt after s: hld up in tch in last trio: hdwy int midfield 3f out: lost pl and unbalanced on downhill run wl over 1f out: rdn and no hdwy over 1f out: bhd and eased wl ins fnl f* **5/1**[2]

1m 25.47s (0.07) **Going Correction** +0.15s/f (Good) **12** Ran SP% **118.1**
Speed ratings (Par 102): **105,103,102,101,101 99,97,95,93,91 88,85**
CSF £57.53 TOTE £7.60: £2.40, £3.00, £3.40; EX 45.20 Trifecta £879.00.
Owner Mrs M E Wates **Bred** Panda Bloodstock & Trickledown Stud **Trained** Kingsclere, Hants

FOCUS
With the ground riding quick and the early pace a modest one, it very much paid to be up there. This is rated the third best Oh So Sharp Stakes of the last 15 years and could feasilby be up to 5lb better. The runner-up basically repeated her Rockfel form.

7115 DUBAI 100 CHALLENGE STKS (GROUP 2) 7f
2:40 (2:41) (Class 1) 3-Y-O+

£92,720 (£35,152; £17,592; £8,763; £4,398; £2,207) **Stalls** High

Form RPR

0511 **1** **Aclaim (IRE)**[21] 6547 3-9-1 105 (t) FrankieDettori 8 115
(Martyn Meade) *hld up in tch and travelled wl: effrt over 1f out: led ins fnl f: r.o wl* **6/1**[2]

0103 **2** 1 **Lumiere**[28] 6281 3-8-12 114 JamesDoyle 5 109
(Mark Johnston) *led: rdn over 1f out: hdd and one pced ins fnl f* **8/1**

3312 **3** ½ **Jallota**[12] 6823 5-9-3 111 JamieSpencer 7 112
(Charles Hills) *chsd ldrs: effrt over 1f out: pressed ldrs and drvn 1f out: kpt on same pce ins fnl f* **10/1**

112 **4** ½ **Certificate**[6] 6955 5-9-3 108 AndreaAtzeni 3 111
(Roger Varian) *chsd ldrs: effrt over 1f out: kpt on same pce ins fnl f* **8/1**

5261 **5** 1 **Cougar Mountain (IRE)**[14] 6749 5-9-6 115 (tp) RyanMoore 4 111
(A P O'Brien, Ire) *in tch: effrt to chse ldrs and drvn over 1f out: no imp ins fnl f* **10/3**[1]

5015 **6** nk **Richard Pankhurst**[27] 6328 4-9-6 115 WilliamBuick 2 110+
(John Gosden) *hld up in tch: effrt over 1f out: kpt on ins fnl f: nvr threatened ldrs* **7/1**[3]

1011 **7** 1¼ **Opal Tiara (IRE)**[40] 5926 3-8-12 109 OisinMurphy 11 101+
(Mick Channon) *hld up in tch: effrt and edging rt over 1f out: nt clr run wl ins fnl f: nvr trbld ldrs* **16/1**

12-1 **8** 1½ **Tasleet**[174] 1477 3-9-1 110 PaulHanagan 12 99
(William Haggas) *in tch in midfield: unable qck and drifted rt over 1f out: wknd ins fnl f* **12/1**

0302 **9** 2½ **Gifted Master (IRE)**[14] 6749 3-9-1 113 JimCrowley 9 92
(Hugo Palmer) *chsd ldr tl lost pl over 1f out: wknd ins fnl f* **6/1**[2]

2543 **10** 2¾ **So Beloved**[6] 6955 6-9-3 111 PhillipMakin 6 86
(David O'Meara) *restless in stalls: s.i.s: hld up in rr: rdn 2f out: sn btn* **20/1**

006 **11** 1¼ **Code Red**[40] 5926 4-9-3 106 MartinDwyer 1 82
(William Muir) *in tch in midfield: rdn over 2f out: lost pl and btn over 1f out: wknd fnl f* **66/1**

2606 **12** shd **First Selection (SPA)**[34] 6117 3-9-1 106 SilvestreDeSousa 10 81
(Simon Crisford) *stdd s: t.k.h: hld up in rr: effrt over 2f out: sn struggling: wknd fnl f* **25/1**

1m 23.92s (-1.48) **Going Correction** +0.15s/f (Good)
WFA 3 from 4yo+ 2lb **12** Ran SP% **119.1**
Speed ratings (Par 115): **114,112,112,111,110 110,108,107,104,101 99,99**
CSF £52.63 TOTE £7.20: £1.80, £3.40, £3.90; EX 72.30 Trifecta £389.60.
Owner Canning Downs & Partner **Bred** D Farrington And Canning Downs **Trained** Newmarket, Suffolk

FOCUS
Another highly competitive running of this Group 2 prize. They split into two groups before merging inside the final furlong and went a solid pace. Aclaim progressed again and the third sets the level.

7116 DUBAI FILLIES' MILE (GROUP 1) 1m
3:10 (3:13) (Class 1) 2-Y-O

£302,689 (£114,756; £57,431; £28,609; £14,357; £7,205) **Stalls** High

Form RPR

113 **1** **Rhododendron (IRE)**[26] 6385 2-9-0 0 RyanMoore 4 117
(A P O'Brien, Ire) *broke wl: stdd and hld up in tch in rr: smooth hdwy over 2f out: pushed into ld wl over 1f out: clr 1f out: r.o wl: comf* **5/2**[1]

22 **2** 2¼ **Hydrangea (IRE)**[26] 6385 2-9-0 0 SeamieHeffernan 8 112
(A P O'Brien, Ire) *racd in stands side pair: pressed ldrs overall: rdn over 2f out: led 2f out: sn hdd: clr 2nd and kpt on same pce fnl f* **4/1**[2]

4331 **3** 6 **Urban Fox**[15] 6706 2-9-0 99 MartinHarley 7 98
(James Tate) *racd in nr side pair: stdd s: hld up in tch in rr: effrt 2f out: chsd clr ldng pair jst over 1f out: no imp* **40/1**

141 **4** 3¾ **Rich Legacy (IRE)**[29] 6258 2-9-0 105 OisinMurphy 3 90
(Ralph Beckett) *t.k.h: led for 2f: pressed ldr after: rdn and ev ch over 2f out tl unable qck wl over 1f out: sn btn: wknd fnl f* **10/1**

31 **5** 3 **Sobetsu**[20] 6578 2-9-0 0 WilliamBuick 6 83
(Charlie Appleby) *hld up in tch in midfield: rdn over 2f out: no rspnse and sn struggling: wl btn over 1f out: wknd* **5/2**[1]

21 **6** 6 **Spatial**[42] 5846 2-9-0 0 AndreaAtzeni 5 69
(Sir Michael Stoute) *t.k.h: chsd ldrs tl led after 2f: rdn and hdd 2f out: sn btn: wknd over 1f out* **6/1**[3]

1 **7** ½ **Fleabiscuit (IRE)**[13] 6776 2-9-0 0 JimCrowley 2 68
(Hugo Palmer) *hld up in tch: effrt over 2f out: sn struggling and lost pl: bhd over 1f out* **16/1**

10 **8** 1¾ **Easy Victory**[62] 5172 2-9-0 0 FrederikTylicki 1 64
(Saeed bin Suroor) *hld up in tch towards rr: hdwy 1/2-way: rdn over 2f out: sn lost pl: wknd over 1f out* **20/1**

1m 37.73s (-0.87) **Going Correction** +0.15s/f (Good) **8** Ran SP% **113.6**
Speed ratings (Par 106): **110,107,101,98,95 89,88,86**
CSF £12.51 CT £310.39 TOTE £3.30: £1.30, £1.40, £6.70; EX 9.70 Trifecta £122.90.
Owner Mrs John Magnier & Michael Tabor & Derrick Smith **Bred** Orpendale, Chelston & Wynatt **Trained** Cashel, Co Tipperary

FOCUS
Some promising fillies lined up for this Group 1 and they went a good gallop. As a result they finished well spread out, and the impressive winner moved to the top of the ante post Guineas market. Aidan O'Brien, who sent out a 1-2, was winning the race for the fourth time in the last ten years, and for the third year in succession. Rhododendron is rated 2lb shy of Minding, with Hydrangea running to her mark.

7117 GODOLPHIN FLYING START OLD ROWLEY CUP (HERITAGE H'CAP) 1m 4f
3:45 (3:53) (Class 2) 3-Y-O

£87,150 (£26,096; £13,048; £6,524; £3,262; £1,638) **Stalls** Centre

Form RPR

1412 **1** **Scarlet Dragon**[20] 6573 3-8-12 103 HollieDoyle[(5)] 17 112+
(Eve Johnson Houghton) *t.k.h: hld up in tch towards rr: hdwy and squeezed through 2f out: rdn to chal 1f out: led 100yds out: r.o strly* **8/1**[3]

4213 **2** 1¾ **New Caledonia (IRE)**[21] 6545 3-8-9 95 WilliamBuick 2 101
(Mark Johnston) *chsd ldrs tl hdwy to ld wl over 2f out: rdn 2f out: kpt on gamely u.p tl hdd and outpcd fnl 100yds* **6/1**[2]

5412 **3** shd **Danehill Kodiac (IRE)**[34] 6110 3-8-9 95 SeanLevey 5 101
(Richard Hannon) *chsd ldrs: effrt to press ldrs 3f out: ev ch and drvn 2f out: no ex and outpcd fnl 100yds* **8/1**[3]

1312 **4** nse **Sixties Groove (IRE)**[70] 4827 3-8-4 90 (p) SilvestreDeSousa 12 96+
(Jeremy Noseda) *t.k.h: hld up in tch towards rr: nt clr run and swtchd lft ent fnl 2f: hdwy u.p over 1f out: styd on strly ins fnl f: nt rch ldrs* **9/1**

1320 **5** nk **Real Dominion (USA)**[34] 6110 3-8-8 94 OisinMurphy 6 99
(Andrew Balding) *hld up in tch towards rr: hdwy and nt clrest of runs wl over 1f out: chsd ldrs 1f out: kpt on ins fnl f* **14/1**

2103 **6** ¾ **Gold Faith (IRE)**[36] 6065 3-8-0 86 oh1 JimmyQuinn 8 90
(Ralph Beckett) *hld up in tch in midfield: effrt to chse ldrs 3f out: ev ch u.p over 1f out tl no ex ins fnl f: wknd towards fin* **20/1**

4655 **7** ¾ **Steel Of Madrid (IRE)**[33] 6179 3-9-7 107 RyanMoore 1 110
(Richard Hannon) *hld up in tch in midfield: effrt over 2f out: hdwy to chse ldrs and drvn ent fnl f: no ex ins fnl f: wknd towards fin* **20/1**

211 **8** ½ **Saunter (FR)**[20] 6581 3-8-13 99 JimCrowley 3 101
(David Menuisier) *hld up in tch in midfield: hdwy over 2f out: rdn and ev ch over 1f out tl no ex ins fnl f: wknd wl ins fnl f* **7/2**[1]

2412 **9** 1¾ **Cosmeapolitan**[34] 6121 3-8-6 92 JohnFahy 10 91
(Alan King) *stdd s: hld up in tch in rr: swtchd lft and hdwy over 2f out: rdn to chse ldrs over 1f out: no ex 1f out: wknd ins fnl f* **14/1**

0103 **10** ½ **Gawdawpalin (IRE)**[21] 6544 3-8-0 86 oh2 KieranO'Neill 7 84
(Sylvester Kirk) *in tch in midfield: rdn 3f out: outpcd and lost pl 2f out: n.d and kpt on same pce fr over 1f out* **25/1**

5231 **11** nk **Kaatskill Nap (FR)**[22] 6528 3-8-6 92 MartinDwyer 4 90
(David Menuisier) *stdd s: hld up in tch in rr: effrt over 2f out: no imp and hung lft wl over 1f out: kpt on same pce after* **20/1**

-234 **12** hd **Fleeting Visit**[16] 6675 3-7-7 86 oh2[1] SophieKilloran[(7)] 14 84
(Eve Johnson Houghton) *hld up in tch in midfield: lost pl and towards rr whn sltly impeded over 2f out: edging rt but kpt on ins fnl f: no threat to ldrs* **25/1**

2641 **13** 2¾ **Banish (USA)**[9] 6870 3-8-2 91 6ex (bt) JosephineGordon[(3)] 15 84
(Hugo Palmer) *t.k.h: hld up in tch in midfield: rdn over 2f out: losing pl whn squeezed for room and hmpd wl over 1f out: n.d after* **20/1**

5321 **14** hd **Sir Valentine (GER)**[46] 5723 3-8-2 88 DannyBrock 11 81
(Alan King) *t.k.h: chsd ldr: rdn and ev ch 3f out tl lost pl ent fnl 2f: btn and hung rt over 1f out: wknd ins fnl f* **12/1**

0121 **15** 7 **Manjaam (IRE)**[90] 4131 3-8-9 95 FrankieDettori 18 77
(Ed Dunlop) *t.k.h: chsd ldrs: rdn 3f out: lost pl and edgd rt 2f out: bhd ins fnl f* **16/1**

1202 **16** 8 **Lord Yeats**[42] 5837 3-8-2 88 PaulHanagan 9 57
(Jedd O'Keeffe) *t.k.h: led tl wl over 2f out: sn lost pl: bhd and eased fnl f* **33/1**

2m 34.23s (2.23) **Going Correction** +0.40s/f (Good) **16** Ran SP% **125.3**
Speed ratings (Par 107): **108,106,106,106,106 106,105,105,104,103 103,103,101,101,96 91**
CSF £50.75 CT £411.26 TOTE £9.00: £2.00, £2.20, £2.30, £2.50; EX 75.60 Trifecta £305.10.
Owner HP Racing Scarlet Dragon **Bred** Usk Valley Stud **Trained** Blewbury, Oxon

FOCUS
Add 12yds to advertised race distance. A line-up befitting the outstanding prize money on offer. It was a sound test and the form is straightforward amongst the first seven or so.

7118 VISIONSPORT.COM MAIDEN FILLIES' STKS (PLUS 10 RACE) 7f
4:20 (4:26) (Class 2) 2-Y-O **£16,172** (£4,812; £2,405; £1,202) **Stalls** High

Form RPR

1 **Astronomy's Choice** 2-9-0 0 FrankieDettori 4 84+
(John Gosden) *dwlt: hld up in tch in last trio: rdn over 2f out: hdwy over 1f out: chalng jst ins fnl f: led and rn green wl ins fnl f: eased cl home* **8/1**

4 **2** ½ **First Dance (IRE)**[25] 6414 2-9-0 0 MartinHarley 10 80
(James Tate) *in tch in midfield: clsd 2f out: rdn to ld over 1f out: hdd and styd in same pce wl ins fnl f* **12/1**

64 **3** 3 **Heavenly Angel**[63] 5119 2-9-0 0 SeanLevey 9 72
(Richard Hannon) *chsd ldr tl led ent fnl 2f: hdd over 1f out: no ex and styd on same pce ins fnl f* **20/1**

4 nk **Alouja (IRE)** 2-9-0 0 JimCrowley 7 71+
(Hugo Palmer) *dwlt: hld up in tch in last trio: rdn over 2f out: no imp and stmbld over 1f out: hdwy ins fnl f: kpt on fnl 100yds: no threat to ldrs* **3/1**[1]

05 **5** ½ **Paradwys (IRE)**[42] 5846 2-9-0 0 JamesDoyle 1 70
(Charles Hills) *led tl ent fnl 2f: sn rdn and stl ev ch tl no ex ins fnl f: kpt on same pce after* **20/1**

6 ½ **Dream Of Joy (IRE)** 2-9-0 0 AndreaAtzeni 3 69+
(Roger Varian) *hld up in tch in midfield: effrt whn rn green and unable qck over 1f out: nt clr run and swtchd lft ins fnl f: n.m.r and kpt on same pce fnl 100yds* **25/1**

43 **7** *nse* **Highland Pass**[15] 6706 2-9-0 0.. OisinMurphy 5 68+
(Andrew Balding) *chsd ldng pair: rdn 2f out: unable qck and outpcd whn swtchd rt 1f out: kpt on same pce after* **7/2**[2]

3 **8** *½* **Vigee Le Brun (IRE)**[21] 6543 2-9-0 0.............................. MartinDwyer 6 67+
(Brian Meehan) *stdd after s: hld up in tch in last trio: rdn over 2f out: no imp: no threat to ldrs but sme hdwy whn nt clr run jst ins fnl f: n.m.r and kpt on same pce fnl 100yds* **8/1**

9 *2 ½* **Fashion Theory** 2-9-0 0.. WilliamBuick 2 63+
(Charlie Appleby) *hld up in tch in midfield: pushed along and unable qck in dip whn sltly impeded over 1f out: btn and hung rt 1f out: eased wl ins fnl f* **9/2**[3]

10 *2 ¼* **Mittens** 2-9-0 0.. RyanMoore 8 54
(Sir Michael Stoute) *t.k.h: hld up in tch in midfield: effrt 2f out: unable qck and lost pl over 1f out: wknd fnl f* **11/1**

1m 25.87s (0.47) **Going Correction** +0.15s/f (Good) **10** Ran SP% **117.0**
Speed ratings (Par 98): **103,102,99,98,98 97,97,96,94,91**
CSF £95.97 TOTE £9.30: £3.00, £3.50, £4.80; EX 90.50 Trifecta £1202.60.
Owner R J H Geffen **Bred** R J H Geffen **Trained** Newmarket, Suffolk

FOCUS
This maiden should throw up a few winners, without the bare form being worth much more.

7119 DUBAI BUSINESS INTERNSHIPS PRIDE STKS (FORMERLY SEVERALS STAKES) (LISTED RACE) (F&M) 1m 2f

4:50 (4:58) (Class 1) 3-Y-O+

£28,355 (£10,750; £5,380; £2,680; £1,345; £675) **Stalls** High

Form RPR

042 **1** **Laganore (IRE)**[19] 6604 4-9-3 101.. JimCrowley 8 111
(A J Martin, Ire) *stdd s: hld up in rr: shkn up and hdwy over 1f out: led jst ins fnl f: r.o strly: comf* **13/2**

1552 **2** *4* **Lady Of Camelot (IRE)**[14] 6747 4-9-3 107..................... FrankieDettori 5 103
(John Gosden) *hld up in tch in last trio: hdwy jst over 2f out: rdn to press ldrs over 1f out: kpt on to go 2nd towards fin: no ch w wnr* **9/4**[1]

2410 **3** *¾* **Pure Art**[27] 6357 3-8-12 92.. FMBerry 1 101
(Ralph Beckett) *chsd ldr tl led 2f out: sn drvn: hdd jst ins fnl f: sn outpcd and kpt on same pce after: lost 2nd towards fin* **25/1**

1511 **4** *¾* **Quebee**[23] 6482 3-9-1 102.. AdamKirby 2 103
(Clive Cox) *hld up in tch: effrt 2f out: rdn and hdwy to chal over 1f out: kpt on same pce ins fnl f* **5/1**[3]

16-1 **5** *nk* **Dawn Of Hope (IRE)**[163] 1771 3-8-12 97........................ AndreaAtzeni 3 99
(Roger Varian) *in tch: effrt to chse ldrs 3f out: ev ch u.p wl over 1f out: kpt on same pce ins fnl f* **12/1**

0 **6** *4 ½* **Alnajmah**[14] 6746 3-8-12 94... PaulHanagan 7 90
(Owen Burrows) *led tl 2f out: edgd rt and btn over 1f out: wknd ins fnl f* **33/1**

1-14 **7** *3* **Materialistic**[23] 6488 3-8-12 98..................................... FrederikTylicki 9 84
(Luca Cumani) *chsd ldrs: rdn over 2f out: unable qck and lost pl over 1f out: wknd fnl f* **9/1**

111 **8** *2 ½* **Playful Sound**[28] 6277 3-8-12 93... RyanMoore 4 79
(Sir Michael Stoute) *chsd ldrs tl over 2f out: sn struggling and lost pl: bhd fnl f* **11/4**[2]

0-1 **P** **Eltham**[29] 6247 3-8-12 77.. JosephineGordon 6
(Robyn Brisland) *hld up in tch in midfield: rdn and lost pl over 2f out: bhd and eased over 1f out: p.u and dismntd nr fin* **66/1**

2m 4.46s (-1.34) **Going Correction** +0.15s/f (Good)
WFA 3 from 4yo 5lb **9** Ran SP% **113.4**
Speed ratings (Par 111): **111,107,107,106,106 102,100,98,**
CSF £20.84 TOTE £6.80: £1.80, £1.10, £5.90; EX 21.70 Trifecta £272.30.
Owner Newtown Anner Stud Farm Ltd **Bred** Newtown Anner Stud Farm Ltd **Trained** Summerhill, Co. Meath

FOCUS
This fillies' Listed race was run at a fair pace and it can be rated around the runner-up. The winner continues to progress.
T/Plt: £493.90 to a £1 stake. Pool: £156089.23, 230.67 winning units. T/Qpdt: £87.10 to a £1 stake. Pool: £11895.72, 101.02 winning units. **Steve Payne**

6159 YORK (L-H)

Friday, October 7

OFFICIAL GOING: Good (good to firm in places; 7.0)
Wind: moderate 1/2 against Weather: Overcast, rain last 2

7120 TSG PAUL BEIOLEY MEMORIAL STKS (NURSERY H'CAP) 6f

1:45 (1:46) (Class 3) (0-95,91) 2-Y-O **£9,703** (£2,887; £1,443; £721) **Stalls** Centre

Form RPR

01 **1** **Comedy School (USA)**[14] 6732 2-8-8 78........................ PJMcDonald 2 91
(Mark Johnston) *racd towards far side: trckd ldrs: hdwy over 2f out: led wl over 1f out and sn rdn: drvn and clr whn hung rt ins fnl f: styd on wl* **8/1**[3]

631 **2** *3 ¼* **Battered**[22] 6524 2-8-11 81... BenCurtis 6 84
(William Haggas) *trckd ldrs towards far side: hdwy over 2f out: rdn to chal and ev ch over 1f out: drvn and edgd lft ins fnl f: kpt on* **5/2**[1]

1104 **3** *nk* **Tomily (IRE)**[13] 6763 2-9-7 91.. TomMarquand 11 93
(Richard Hannon) *racd towards stands rail: trckd ldrs: hdwy 2f out: rdn over 1f out: kpt on wl fnl f* **20/1**

554 **4** *1* **The Nazca Lines (IRE)**[22] 6507 2-8-8 78.......................... JasonHart 3 77
(John Quinn) *racd towards far side: led: rdn along over 2f out: hdd wl over 1f out: sn drvn and kpt on same pce* **50/1**

2213 **5** *hd* **Big Lachie**[13] 6763 2-8-6 76.. GrahamGibbons 9 76
(Jamie Osborne) *towards rr: hdwy 2f out: sn rdn: n.m.r over 1f out: styd on wl fnl f* **16/1**

2021 **6** *¾* **Arc Royal**[28] 6275 2-8-11 86..................................... AnnaHesketh(5) 12 83+
(Tom Dascombe) *racd towards stands side: in tch: hdwy 2f out: rdn and edgd lft over 1f out: sn drvn and kpt on* **20/1**

613 **7** *nk* **Lanjano**[52] 5510 2-8-9 79.. KevinStott 16 75
(Kevin Ryan) *racd towards stands side: prom: cl up 1/2-way: rdn along over 2f out: drvn and wknd over 1f out: hung rt ins fnl f* **16/1**

4122 **8** *½* **Maazel (IRE)**[11] 6829 2-7-12 75.................................... DavidEgan(7) 8 69
(Roger Varian) *in tch towards far side: hdwy 12f out: sn rdn and kpt on same pce* **16/1**

1144 **9** *nk* **Notalot (IRE)**[20] 6563 2-8-5 82..................................(v) LuluStanford(7) 15 77
(Michael Bell) *in tch towards stands side: hdwy 2f out: rdn and n.m.r over 1f out: sltly hmpd and swtchd lft ent fnl f: sn drvn and kpt on* **20/1**

4054 **10** *½* **Kocollada (IRE)**[21] 6538 2-8-10 85......................... AdamMcNamara(5) 5 77
(Richard Fahey) *awkward s: sn chsng ldrs towards far side: rdn along 2f out: grad wknd* **12/1**

016 **11** *shd* **Haworth**[21] 6536 2-7-13 74... GeorgeWood(5) 1 65
(James Bethell) *racd towards far side: towards rr: hdwy on wd outside over 2f out: sn rdn and n.d* **12/1**

0504 **12** *¾* **Letmestopyouthere (IRE)**[14] 6734 2-8-12 82................. SamJames 18 71
(David Evans) *racd towards stands rail: a towards rr* **20/1**

1300 **13** *hd* **Scofflaw**[29] 6260 2-8-9 79.. TonyHamilton 17 68
(Richard Fahey) *racd towards stands side: a towards rr* **16/1**

6102 **14** *1 ½* **Norwegian Highness (FR)**[14] 6743 2-8-5 75................. ShaneGray 14 59
(Kevin Ryan) *dwlt: a towards rr* **20/1**

3612 **15** *3* **Evergate**[15] 6697 2-9-2 86... JackMitchell 7 61
(Hugo Palmer) *racd towards centre: chsd ldrs: rdn along over 2f out: sn drvn and wknd* **9/2**[2]

612 **16** *¾* **Baby Gal**[115] 3254 2-8-1 76... NathanEvans(5) 13 49
(Giles Bravery) *racd towards stands side: midfield: rdn along over 2f out: sn wknd* **20/1**

1334 **17** *hd* **Dandy Highwayman (IRE)**[21] 6536 2-8-8 78............. AndrewMullen 10 50
(Ollie Pears) *racd towards centre: in tch: rdn along over 2f out: sn wknd* **20/1**

1m 11.34s (-0.56) **Going Correction** 0.0s/f (Good) **17** Ran SP% **132.1**
Speed ratings (Par 99): **103,98,98,96,96 95,95,94,94,93 93,92,92,90,86 85,84**
CSF £26.20 CT £434.94 TOTE £9.00: £2.30, £1.40, £4.40, £10.70; EX 27.80 Trifecta £1289.40.
Owner Sheikh Hamdan bin Mohammed Al Maktoum **Bred** Darley **Trained** Middleham Moor, N Yorks

FOCUS
The ground had eased slightly and was now good, good to firm in places (from good to firm, good in places). After riding in the opener Adam McNamara and Tony Hamilton called the ground good, but Kevin Stott said: "It is just a touch on the soft side", while P J McDonald said: "It is definitely on the easy side." Rail around home bend from 9f out to entrance to home straight on inside of established racing line, reducing the distance of the 1m races by 24yds and the 1m6f race by 42yds. A decent and competitive nursery to start and they split into two early, but the groups eventually merged. Those that raced more far side just seemed to have the edge and the winning time was 1.34sec outside standard. The race should definitely produce winners. Comedy School produced a nice step up on his maiden win.

7121 STANJAMES.COM BET ON YOUR MOBILE STKS (H'CAP) 1m

2:20 (2:21) (Class 2) (0-100,100) 4-Y-O+

£18,675 (£5,592; £2,796; £1,398; £699; £351) **Stalls** Low

Form RPR

2350 **1** **Highland Colori (IRE)**[20] 6557 8-9-2 95........................(b[1]) LiamKeniry 14 103
(Andrew Balding) *hld up in mid-div: hdwy over 3f out: chsd ldrs 2f out: led last 150yds: hld on nr fin* **22/1**

1365 **2** *hd* **Home Cummins (IRE)**[26] 6372 4-8-12 91...................(p) JackGarritty 15 99
(Richard Fahey) *trckd ldrs: brought wd over 3f out: 3rd 1f out: tk 2nd clsng stages: kpt on* **12/1**

0003 **3** *1 ½* **Dinkum Diamond (IRE)**[27] 6331 8-9-0 98.............. HectorCrouch(5) 12 102
(Henry Candy) *rr-div: hdwy on outer over 2f out: styd on to take 3rd nr fin* **16/1**

3140 **4** *shd* **Ice Slice (IRE)**[34] 6109 5-9-1 94.. RyanTate 11 98
(James Eustace) *led: hdd last 150yds: fdd nr fin* **10/1**

2030 **5** *2 ¼* **Two For Two (IRE)**[20] 6557 8-8-13 92........................... PJMcDonald 16 91
(Roger Fell) *prom: drvn over 2f out: styd on one pce* **33/1**

0346 **6** *¾* **One Word More (IRE)**[20] 6557 6-9-1 97.......... RachelRichardson(3) 20 94
(Tim Easterby) *s.i.s: in rr: hdwy over 2f out: keeping on at fin* **10/1**

0000 **7** *nk* **Afonso De Sousa (USA)**[26] 6372 6-8-13 92..........(p) AndrewMullen 19 88
(Michael Appleby) *hld up towards rr: hdwy over 2f out: kpt on fnl f* **66/1**

0213 **8** *½* **Big Time (IRE)**[41] 5871 5-9-5 98.......................................(v) KevinStott 7 93
(Kevin Ryan) *hld up in mid-div: hdwy to chse ldrs over 2f out: one pce* **11/2**[1]

5162 **9** *shd* **Shady McCoy (USA)**[13] 6788 6-8-12 91..................... RobertWinston 17 89+
(Ian Williams) *s.i.s: swtchd lft after s: in rr: hdwy over 2f out: swtchd lft and kpt on last 150yds* **9/1**[3]

0430 **10** *hd* **Fort Bastion (IRE)**[14] 6736 7-8-11 90................................ SamJames 4 84
(David O'Meara) *chsd ldrs: edgd lft and one pce fnl f* **14/1**

0021 **11** *1 ¼* **God Willing**[20] 6585 5-8-13 92.. TonyHamilton 13 84
(Declan Carroll) *chsd ldrs: brought wd over 3f out: wknd over 1f out* **8/1**[2]

1060 **12** *1 ¾* **Balmoral Castle**[13] 6786 7-8-9 93.............................. GeorgeWood(5) 8 81
(Jonathan Portman) *mid-div: drvn 3f out: nvr a threat* **20/1**

-100 **13** *hd* **Keystroke**[81] 4448 4-9-2 95.. TomQueally 18 82
(Jeremy Noseda) *s.i.s: in rr: sme hdwy over 2f out: nvr a factor* **14/1**

6200 **14** *1 ¼* **Sound Advice**[20] 6557 7-9-2 100.................................. CliffordLee(5) 9 84
(Keith Dalgleish) *t.k.h: trckd ldrs: 2nd over 6f out: wknd over 1f out* **25/1**

5040 **15** *½* **Alfred Hutchinson**[13] 6778 8-9-3 96............................(p) DavidNolan 10 79
(David O'Meara) *prom: hdwy to chse ldrs over 2f out: wknd over 1f out* **16/1**

62S3 **16** *½* **Jacbequick**[13] 6775 5-8-11 90.....................................(b[1]) PaulMulrennan 3 72
(David O'Meara) *s.i.s: a towards rr* **16/1**

150 **17** *7* **Secret Art (IRE)**[34] 6126 6-9-1 94.............................. GrahamGibbons 2 60
(William Knight) *prom: chsng ldrs over 2f out: sn wknd: bhd whn eased clsng stages* **14/1**

5-22 **18** *2 ¼* **Claim The Roses (USA)**[22] 6529 5-8-12 91............(t) FergusSweeney 6 52
(Ed Vaughan) *in rr: eased whn bhd clsng stages* **12/1**

6410 **19** *2 ¼* **He's No Saint**[13] 6764 5-8-10 89......................................(v) GrahamLee 1 44
(David O'Meara) *dwlt: sn hld up in mid-div: hdwy to chse ldrs over 2f out: sn wknd: bhd whn eased clsng stages* **20/1**

1m 37.5s (-1.50) **Going Correction** +0.05s/f (Good) **19** Ran SP% **129.9**
Speed ratings (Par 109): **109,108,107,107,104 104,103,103,103,103 101,100,99,98,98 97,90,88,86**
CSF £260.21 CT £4348.83 TOTE £32.00: £5.70, £2.80, £4.20, £2.50; EX 422.50 Trifecta £4801.80.
Owner Evan M Sutherland **Bred** Rathbarry Stud **Trained** Kingsclere, Hants

FOCUS
Rail movement reduced race distance by 24yds. A warm handicap, but the early pace didn't look that strong and they spread right out across the track after turning in. The winner found a bit on this year's form.

7122 JWPCREERS SUPPORTING LORD MAYOR'S CHARITIES EBF STALLIONS MAIDEN STKS (PLUS 10 RACE) 5f 89y

2:50 (2:51) (Class 3) 2-Y-O **£7,762** (£2,310; £1,154; £577) **Stalls** Centre

Form RPR

0 **1** **Carlton Frankie**[147] 2219 2-9-0 0.. CamHardie 3 76+
(Michael Easterby) *qckly away: mde all: rdn wl over 1f out: drvn and edgd rt ins fnl f: jst hld on* **14/1**

0 **2** *nse* **Kingofmerrows (IRE)**[16] 6673 2-9-5 0 SamJames 10 81
(David Evans) *trckd ldrs on outer: hdwy over 2f out: rdn along over 1f out: sn chal: drvn and ev ch whn bmpd sltly ins fnl f: styd on wl towards fin: jst failed* **20/1**

3 *2* **The Feathered Nest (IRE)** 2-9-0 0 TonyHamilton 11 69+
(Richard Fahey) *hld up: hdwy over 2f out: rdn to chal over 1f out: ev ch whn edgd rt ins fnl f: sn drvn and kpt on* **5/2**[1]

25 **4** *1/2* **Her Terms**[9] 6873 2-9-0 78 WilliamTwiston-Davies 5 67
(William Haggas) *trckd ldrs: hdwy 2f out: rdn and ev ch over 1f out: drvn and kpt on same pce fnl f* **3/1**[2]

354 **5** *1* **Kodicat (IRE)**[33] 6162 2-9-0 71 TomEaves 1 64
(Kevin Ryan) *trckd ldrs: effrt to chse wnr wl over 1f out: sn rdn and wknd ins fnl f* **7/1**

6 *hd* **Glorious Politics** 2-9-5 0 GrahamGibbons 12 68+
(David Barron) *hld up towards rr: hdwy 2f out: styd on fnl f: nrst fin* **9/2**[3]

2404 **7** *shd* **Sheepscar Lad (IRE)**[22] 6515 2-8-12 68 (v) LewisEdmunds(7) 13 68
(Nigel Tinkler) *stdd s and sn swtchd lft: towards rr: swtchd lft to outer and hdwy 2f out: sn rdn: styd on fnl f: nrst fin* **25/1**

04 **8** *3 1/2* **Abundant Courage (IRE)**[16] 6673 2-9-5 0 JimmyFortune 6 55
(Brian Meehan) *chsd wnr: rdn along 2f out: drvn over 1f out: grad wknd* **20/1**

54 **9** *1 1/4* **Can't Do Spells**[51] 5536 2-9-5 0 DavidAllan 8 51
(Tim Easterby) *trckd ldrs: hdwy over 2f out: rdn wl over 1f out: sn wknd* **16/1**

0 **10** *1* **Pavers Pride**[53] 5477 2-9-5 0 PatrickMathers 2 47
(Noel Wilson) *dwlt: sn chsng ldrs: rdn along over 2f out: sn wknd* **66/1**

6 **11** *3* **The Night Before**[37] 6034 2-9-5 0 RobertWinston 7 37
(Robert Cowell) *chsd wnr: rdn along over 2f out: sn drvn and wknd* **14/1**

12 *11* **Chaucer's Tale** 2-9-0 0 NathanEvans(5) 9
(Michael Easterby) *dwlt: a rr: bhd fr 1/2-way* **50/1**

13 *6* **Mr Hill** 2-9-5 0 BarryMcHugh 4
(Rebecca Bastiman) *towards rr: hmpd after 1f: bhd fr 1/2-way* **50/1**

1m 4.33s (0.23) **Going Correction** 0.0s/f (Good) **13** Ran SP% **122.3**
Speed ratings (Par 99): **98,97,94,93,92 92,91,86,84,82 77,60,50**
CSF £273.61 TOTE £15.60: £4.40, £6.90, £1.60; EX 433.40 Trifecta £5420.50.
Owner B Padgett S Hollings S Hull & D Fielding **Bred** D Curran **Trained** Sheriff Hutton, N Yorks

FOCUS
Not the strongest maiden York will ever stage.

7123 STANJAMES.COM STKS (H'CAP) 1m 6f
3:25 (3:31) (Class 2) (0-105,104) 3-Y-O
£31,125 (£9,320; £4,660; £2,330; £1,165; £585) **Stalls** Low

Form RPR
10-6 **1** **Calvinist**[23] 6484 3-8-2 85 (t) KierenFox 6 95
(Brian Meehan) *trckd ldrs: drvn over 3f out: led over 2f out: all out* **16/1**

3364 **2** *hd* **Master Blueyes (IRE)**[48] 5653 3-8-1 84 AndrewMullen 5 93
(Alan King) *trckd ldrs: effrt 3f out: upsides over 2f out: jst hld* **9/2**[1]

3141 **3** *1/2* **Yangtze**[14] 6735 3-8-6 89 ow1 (p) GrahamGibbons 8 98
(Sir Michael Stoute) *hld up in mid-div: stdy hdwy over 2f out: rdr dropped whip appr fnl f: styd on wl: gng on and tk 3rd nr fin* **7/1**

2311 **4** *1 1/4* **Cape Cova (IRE)**[69] 4859 3-8-4 87 NickyMackay 7 94
(John Gosden) *hld up in rr: t.k.h: effrt 3f out: kpt on same pce fnl f: tk 4th nr fin* **6/1**[2]

2115 **5** *1 1/2* **Fandango (GER)**[12] 6804 3-8-0 83 oh5 RyanPowell 12 88
(Jeremy Gask) *chsd ldrs: drvn and hung lft over 3f out: one pce appr fnl f* **50/1**

3211 **6** *shd* **Blakeney Point**[27] 6325 3-8-1 89 (p) GeorgiaCox(5) 1 94
(Roger Charlton) *hld up in mid-div: hdwy over 3f out: upsides 2f out: kpt on one pce over 1f out* **14/1**

2102 **7** *4 1/2* **Fireglow**[7] 6917 3-9-7 104 PaulMulrennan 2 102
(Mark Johnston) *sn led: drvn over 3f out: hung lft and hdd over 2f out: wknd over 1f out* **10/1**

8 *1/2* **Landsman (IRE)**[55] 5425 3-8-2 85 TomMarquand 4 83
(A J Martin, Ire) *mid-div: drvn over 3f out: one pce fnl 2f* **14/1**

1611 **9** *4 1/2* **The Graduate (IRE)**[34] 6121 3-8-4 90 EdwardGreatrex(3) 3 81
(Andrew Balding) *mid-div: effrt over 3f out: wknd over 1f out* **9/1**

124 **10** *nk* **Corinthian**[13] 6781 3-8-6 89 MartinLane 9 80
(Roger Varian) *in rr: sn drvn along: hdwy over 3f out: hung lft over 2f out: lost pl over 1f out* **10/1**

2432 **11** *1 1/2* **Against The Odds**[20] 6591 3-7-8 84 DavidEgan(7) 11 73
(Paul Cole) *rr-div: hdwy over 3f out: hmpd over 2f out: lost pl over 1f out* **16/1**

411 **12** *2 3/4* **West Coast Flyer**[36] 6050 3-8-7 90 FergusSweeney 13 75
(David Simcock) *hld up in rr: hdwy over 3f out: edgd lft and wknd over 1f out* **25/1**

111 **13** *5* **Guns Of Leros (USA)**[12] 6804 3-7-11 83 oh1 NoelGarbutt(3) 14 61
(Gary Moore) *swtchd lft sn after sn: sn chsng ldrs: drvn over 3f out: lost pl over 2f out: bhd whn eased clsng stages* **13/2**[3]

2021 **14** *8* **Icefall (IRE)**[23] 6474 3-8-4 87 CamHardie 10 54
(Tim Easterby) *led early: sn mid-div: drvn over 3f out: lost pl over 1f out: bhd whn eased clsng stages* **33/1**

2m 58.08s (-2.12) **Going Correction** +0.05s/f (Good) **14** Ran SP% **120.3**
Speed ratings (Par 107): **108,107,107,106,106 105,103,103,100,100 99,97,95,90**
CSF £85.30 CT £567.80 TOTE £21.00: £6.20, £2.10, £2.70; EX 128.50 Trifecta £983.90.
Owner Manton Thoroughbreds **Bred** Fonthill Stud **Trained** Manton, Wilts

■ Stewards' Enquiry : Kieren Fox four-day ban; used his whip above the permitted level (21st, 24th-26th Oct)

FOCUS
Rail movement reduced race distance by 42yds. A decent 3yo staying handicap - something of a mini-Melrose - but rather a lopsided one with the top weight conceding upwards of a stone to the rest. The pace was solid thanks to a disputed lead and the whole field came up the centre in the straight. A clear pb from the winner.

7124 PARSONAGE HOTEL AND CLOISTERS SPA STKS (H'CAP) 5f
3:55 (3:58) (Class 3) (0-95,93) 3-Y-O+ **£12,938** (£3,850; £1,924; £962) **Stalls** Centre

Form RPR
0040 **1** **Robot Boy (IRE)**[13] 6779 6-9-7 93 GrahamGibbons 2 102
(David Barron) *racd towards far side: trckd ldrs: smooth hdwy to ld wl over 1f out: rdn ent fnl f: drvn out* **9/1**

0100 **2** *nk* **Kibaar**[34] 6114 4-8-13 85 (p) KevinStott 14 93
(Kevin Ryan) *trckd ldrs towards nr side: hdwy over 2f out: rdn and edgd lft wl over 1f out: chse wnr ins fnl f: drvn and kpt on wl towards fin* **40/1**

4420 **3** *3/4* **Fumbo Jumbo (IRE)**[21] 6537 3-8-12 84 TomMarquand 8 90
(Garry Moss) *in tch centre: pushed along over 2f out: rdn wl over 1f out: styd on appr fnl f* **20/1**

0000 **4** *1/2* **Bogart**[21] 6537 7-8-11 83 (p) TomEaves 17 87
(Kevin Ryan) *prom nr stands rail: cl up 1/2-way: rdn wl over 1f out: ev ch: drvn ins fnl f: kpt on* **16/1**

4605 **5** *hd* **Shipyard (USA)**[6] 6944 7-9-1 87 BenCurtis 3 90
(Michael Appleby) *racd towards far side: in tch: hdwy over 2f out: chsd ldrs over 1f out: sn rdn and kpt on* **6/1**[2]

1201 **6** *nk* **Singeur (IRE)**[30] 6234 9-9-1 87 PJMcDonald 15 89
(Rebecca Bastiman) *rr nr stands rail: hdwy wl over 1f out: swtchd rt and rdn ent fnl f: styd on wl towards fin* **33/1**

3004 **6** *dht* **My Name Is Rio (IRE)**[6] 6944 6-9-3 89 (p) ConnorBeasley 4 91
(Michael Dods) *racd towards far side: rr: hdwy 2f out: sn rdn and styd on fnl f* **12/1**

2412 **8** *nk* **East Street Revue**[13] 6779 3-9-4 90 (b) DuranFentiman 10 92
(Tim Easterby) *racd centre: hld up towards rr: hdwy wl over 1f out: sn rdn and kpt on fnl f* **8/1**

0-52 **9** *1/2* **Love On The Rocks (IRE)**[48] 5657 3-8-12 84 MichaelJMMurphy 16 84
(Charles Hills) *racd nr stands rail: cl up:. disp ld 1/2-way: rdn along wl over 1f out: drvn appr fnl f and grad wknd* **16/1**

2300 **10** *1/2* **Waseem Faris (IRE)**[6] 6944 7-8-8 85 CliffordLee(5) 19 82
(Joseph Tuite) *chsd ldrs nr stands rails: rdn along 2f out: sn drvn and wknd* **28/1**

1060 **11** *nk* **Blithe Spirit**[13] 6779 5-9-7 93 JasonHart 6 89
(Eric Alston) *racd towards far side: led: rdn along 2f out: sn hdd and drvn: wknd ent fnl f* **25/1**

413P **12** *nk* **Bashiba (IRE)**[13] 6779 5-8-7 86 (t) LewisEdmunds(7) 18 81
(Nigel Tinkler) *racd nr stands rail: towards rr: hdwy 2f out: rdn to chse ldrs over 1f out: wknd fnl f* **20/1**

3200 **13** *3/4* **Majestic Hero (IRE)**[6] 6944 4-9-4 90 GrahamLee 13 82
(Ronald Harris) *racd centre: in tch: rdn along over 2f out: sn wknd* **33/1**

6324 **14** *nk* **Tylery Wonder (IRE)**[12] 6819 6-8-11 83 (b) RobertWinston 5 74
(Paul Midgley) *hld up towards rr far side: sme hdwy over 2f out: sn rdn along and n.d* **7/1**[3]

0060 **15** *nk* **Arctic Feeling (IRE)**[13] 6779 8-8-11 83 GeorgeChaloner 20 73
(Richard Fahey) *a towards rr stands side* **33/1**

0000 **16** *3/4* **Desert Law (IRE)**[13] 6779 8-9-7 93 MartinLane 9 80
(Paul Midgley) *hld up towards rr centre: sme hdwy 2f out: sn rdn and btn* **20/1**

0000 **17** *2 3/4* **Best Trip (IRE)**[21] 6539 9-8-13 85 (b[1]) SamJames 1 62
(Marjorie Fife) *racd towards far side: cl up: disp ld 1/2-way: rdn along 2f out: sn drvn and wknd* **33/1**

1265 **18** *1 1/4* **Midnight Malibu (IRE)**[13] 6793 3-8-12 84 DavidAllan 12 58
(Tim Easterby) *chsd ldrs centre: rdn along over 2f out: sn wknd* **16/1**

1022 **19** *2* **Aleef (IRE)**[18] 6633 3-9-4 90 JackGarritty 7 57
(David O'Meara) *racd towards far side: chsd ldrs: rdn along over 2f out: sn wknd* **11/4**[1]

58.26s (-1.04) **Going Correction** 0.0s/f (Good) **19** Ran SP% **135.7**
Speed ratings (Par 107): **108,107,106,105,105 104,104,104,103,102 102,101,100,100,99 98,93,91,88**
CSF £352.21 CT £7105.24 TOTE £11.90: £3.10, £12.00, £4.70, £4.30; EX 662.10.
Owner Laurence O'Kane & Paul Murphy **Bred** Corduff Stud Ltd **Trained** Maunby, N Yorks

FOCUS
An ultra-competitive sprint handicap and there seemed no great track bias. Pretty straightforward form, the winner's best since last summer.

7125 ELEVATOR COMPANY MAIDEN AUCTION STKS (PLUS 10 RACE) 1m
4:30 (4:34) (Class 3) 2-Y-O **£7,762** (£2,310; £1,154; £577) **Stalls** Low

Form RPR
22 **1** **Raheen House (IRE)**[21] 6546 2-9-3 0 JimmyFortune 14 86+
(Brian Meehan) *trckd ldr: led over 1f out: drvn out* **4/7**[1]

4302 **2** *1 3/4* **Native Prospect**[26] 6377 2-9-1 73 LiamKeniry 2 78
(Andrew Balding) *led: hdd over 1f out: styd on same pce* **6/1**[2]

3 *3 1/2* **Lord Commander** 2-9-3 0 TonyHamilton 13 72+
(Richard Fahey) *mid-div hdwy over 3f out: chsng ldrs over 1f out: kpt on same pce: tk modest 3rd post* **12/1**[3]

4 *shd* **Crushed (IRE)** 2-8-11 0 BenCurtis 7 66
(William Haggas) *trckd ldrs: t.k.h: one pce over 1f out* **20/1**

5 *1 1/2* **Auberge Du Lac (IRE)** 2-9-1 0 FergusSweeney 3 66+
(David Simcock) *hld up in rr: hdwy over 2f out: kpt on one pce over 1f out* **25/1**

6 *4 1/2* **Mirzam (IRE)** 2-8-12 0 GrahamLee 10 53
(Mick Channon) *chsd ldrs: wknd over 1f out* **16/1**

033 **7** *3/4* **On To Victory**[20] 6577 2-8-13 77 TomMarquand 6 52
(Eve Johnson Houghton) *mid-div: t.k.h: effrt over 3f out: wknd over 1f out* **6/1**[2]

8 *nk* **Cornerstone Lad** 2-8-11 0 JackGarritty 11 50
(Micky Hammond) *s.s: hld up in rr: sme hdwy over 2f out: nvr a factor* **100/1**

0 **9** *hd* **Follow Me (IRE)**[18] 6625 2-8-7 0 MarcMonaghan(3) 8 48
(Hugo Palmer) *chsd ldrs: wknd over 1f out* **28/1**

10 *nk* **Meyandi** 2-9-0 0 EdwardGreatrex(3) 4 54
(Andrew Balding) *in rr: drvn over 2f out: nvr on terms* **25/1**

11 *6* **Regal Mirage (IRE)** 2-8-13 0 DavidAllan 15 37
(Tim Easterby) *s.i.s: in rr: bhd fnl 2f* **66/1**

0 **12** *4 1/2* **Casado (IRE)**[20] 6570 2-9-1 0 KierenFox 9 28
(John Best) *mid-div: drvn and lost pl 2f out* **100/1**

13 *9* **Unonothinjonsnow** 2-8-13 0 ConnorBeasley 5 6
(Richard Guest) *mid-div: drvn over 3f out: lost pl 2f out: bhd whn eased clsng stages* **50/1**

1m 39.56s (0.56) **Going Correction** +0.05s/f (Good) **13** Ran SP% **127.1**
Speed ratings (Par 99): **99,97,93,93,92 87,86,86,86,86 80,75,66**
CSF £4.38 TOTE £1.60: £1.10, £1.80, £2.60; EX 5.60 Trifecta £29.10.
Owner J L Day **Bred** Sunderland Holdings Inc **Trained** Manton, Wilts

FOCUS
Rail movement reduced race distance by 24yds. An uncompetitive maiden despite the numbers and few got into it, with it proving all very straightforward for the hot favourite.

7126 RACING UK HD ON SKY432 APPRENTICE STKS (H'CAP) 7f
5:00 (5:05) (Class 4) (0-85,85) 3-Y-O+ **£7,762** (£2,310; £1,154; £577) **Stalls** Low

Form RPR
2336 **1** **Bertiewhittle**[20] 6560 8-9-6 85 RowanScott(3) 15 96
(David Barron) *in rr: hdwy on outside over 2f out: styd on to ld last 50yds* **9/1**[3]

-000 **2** *nk* **Twin Appeal (IRE)**[21] 6539 5-9-7 83 (b) HectorCrouch 12 93
(David Barron) *hld up in rr: smooth hdwy 3f out: sn led: hdd and no ex last 50yds* **12/1**

1000 **3** *1 1/2* **Hawkeyethenoo (IRE)**[13] 6780 10-9-2 **83**............. LewisEdmunds(5) 10 89
(Jim Goldie) *in rr: hdwy on outer over 2f out: rdr dropped whip appr fnl f: kpt on* **16/1**
6212 **4** *1 3/4* **Sophie P**[12] 6811 3-9-2 **80**.. DavidParkes 13 80
(R Mike Smith) *mid-div: hdwy over 2f out: kpt on one pce over 1f out* **10/1**
05 **5** *1 1/2* **Zaeem**[12] 6806 7-9-1 **80**.......................................(p) MeganNicholls(3) 9 77
(Ivan Furtado) *mid-div: kpt on fnl 2f: nvr trbld ldrs* **16/1**
-040 **6** *2 1/4* **Desert Ruler**[149] 2161 3-9-1 **79**................................. CallumShepherd 18 69
(Jedd O'Keeffe) *chsd ldrs outer: one pce fnl 2f* **40/1**
2560 **7** *1 1/4* **Boots And Spurs**[69] 4894 7-9-4 **80**..............................(v) GeorgeWood 7 68
(Scott Dixon) *chsd ldrs: fdd over 1f out* **11/1**
0500 **8** *hd* **Avon Breeze**[13] 6780 7-9-9 **85**... PhilDennis 20 72
(Richard Whitaker) *hld up towards rr: hdwy on outer over 2f out: fdd over 1f out* **40/1**
0053 **9** *3 1/2* **Khelman (IRE)**[21] 6539 6-9-8 **84**............................. AdamMcNamara 11 62
(Richard Fahey) *mid-div: drvn over 3f out: chsng ldrs over 2f out: lost pl over 1f out: eased last 75yds* **8/1**[2]
0000 **10** *1 3/4* **Magic City (IRE)**[21] 6539 7-9-2 **78**.................................. NathanEvans 1 51
(Michael Easterby) *chsd ldrs: lost pl over 1f out* **4/1**[1]
3225 **11** *nk* **Vallarta (IRE)**[15] 6718 6-8-12 **77**.............................. CliffordLee(3) 4 49
(Ruth Carr) *trckd ldr: led over 3f out: hdd over 2f out: lost pl over 1f out* **12/1**
1002 **12** *4* **Courier**[13] 6770 4-9-9 **85**..(p) RobJFitzpatrick 17 47
(Marjorie Fife) *chsd ldrs: wknd over 1f out: eased clsng stages* **20/1**
0412 **13** *nk* **Nonno Giulio (IRE)**[16] 6683 5-9-1 **77**........................... GeorgeBuckell 3 38
(Roger Fell) *s.i.s: soo n chsng ldrs: drvn over 2f out: lost pl over 1f out* **25/1**
0303 **14** *3/4* **Regal Dan (IRE)**[15] 6714 6-9-4 **85**......................... PatrickVaughan(5) 19 44
(David O'Meara) *chsd ldrs outer: lost pl over 1f out* **20/1**
0400 **15** *2 1/4* **Kalk Bay (IRE)**[22] 6500 9-9-3 **82**.....................(t) DanielleMooney(3) 8 35
(Michael Easterby) *s.v.s and reluctant: nvr on terms* **25/1**
314- **16** *2 3/4* **Tafteesh (IRE)**[319] 7955 3-9-1 **79**.................................... AnnaHesketh 5 23
(Michael Easterby) *chsd ldrs: lost pl over 2f out* **40/1**
2441 **17** *shd* **Honeysuckle Lil (IRE)**[13] 6770 4-9-3 **79**.................(p) JordanVaughan 2 24
(Tim Easterby) *mid-div: effrt over 2f out: sn wknd* **16/1**
-000 **18** *3 1/2* **Silhuette (IRE)**[12] 6810 3-8-13 **80**........................ NatalieHambling(3) 14 15
(Colin Teague) *led tl over 3f out: lost pl over 2f out: bhd whn eased clsng stages* **66/1**
430 **19** *1 1/4* **Dutch Artist (IRE)**[36] 6055 4-9-0 **79**........................[1] MitchGodwin(3) 16 11
(David O'Meara) *chsd ldrs: lost pl 2f out: bhd whn eased clsng stages* **25/1**

1m 24.73s (-0.57) **Going Correction** +0.05s/f (Good)
WFA 3 from 4yo+ 2lb **19** Ran SP% **121.4**
Speed ratings (Par 105): **105,104,102,100,99 96,95,95,91,89 88,84,83,82,80 77,77,73,71**
CSF £82.84 CT £1102.09 TOTE £9.80: £2.60, £3.60, £3.10, £2.60; EX 122.30 Trifecta £403.30.
Owner JKB Racing & Partners **Bred** E Dafydd **Trained** Maunby, N Yorks
■ Steel Train was withdrawn. Price at time of withdrawal 9/2. Rule 4 applies to all bets - deduction 15p in the pound.

FOCUS
A competitive apprentice handicap, though weakened slightly when the fancied Steel Train was withdrawn at the start. The leaders looked to go off much too fast, though, with the first three right out the back early. It provided a 1-2 for trainer David Barron. The winner is rated similarly to when winning this last year.
T/Jkpt: Not Won. T/Plt: £829.30 to a £1 stake. Pool: £134704.33, 118.57 winning units. T/Qpdt: £170.40 to a £1 stake. Pool: £9536.24, 41.4 winning units. **Walter Glynn & Joe Rowntree**

7128 - 7129a (Foreign Racing) - See Raceform Interactive

6928 DUNDALK (A.W) (L-H)
Friday, October 7

OFFICIAL GOING: Polytrack: standard

7130a IRISH STALLION FARMS EUROPEAN BREEDERS FUND STAR APPEAL STKS (LISTED RACE) 7f (P)
7:00 (7:01) 2-Y-O
£23,860 (£7,683; £3,639; £1,617; £808; £404)

RPR

1 **Ambassadorial (USA)**[33] 6168 2-9-3 .... ShaneFoley 2 105+
(M Halford, Ire) *bit slowly away: hld up: prog under 2f out: almost on terms 1f out and sn led: styd on wl to draw clr clsng stages* **4/1**[3]
2 *1 1/2* **Executive Force**[21] 6543 2-9-3 .... PatCosgrave 6 101
(William Haggas) *chsd ldrs in 4th: rdn to press ldr in 2nd over 1f out and sn on terms: hdd ent fnl f: no ex w wnr clsng stages in 2nd* **2/1**[1]
3 *3* **Leo Minor (USA)**[48] 5661 2-9-3 98........................ DonnachaO'Brien 5 93
(A P O'Brien, Ire) *sn pressed ldr in 2nd: led over 1f out tl hdd ent fnl f where dropped to 3rd: kpt on same pce* **7/2**[2]
4 *shd* **Oh Grace (IRE)**[47] 5686 2-8-12 94..............................(p) KevinManning 4 88
(J S Bolger, Ire) *sn led narrowly: hdd over 1f out: no imp fnl 100yds: kpt on same pce in 4th* **25/1**
5 *1 1/2* **Confrontational (IRE)**[67] 4957 2-9-3 87.................. ColmO'Donoghue 3 89
(John Joseph Murphy, Ire) *racd towards rr: prog on inner over 1f out: swtchd rt ins fnl f: kpt on wl: nvr nrr* **50/1**
6 *1/2* **Rebel De Lope**[23] 6481 2-9-3 .... ChrisHayes 1 87
(Charles Hills) *chsd ldrs in 3rd on inner tl rdn under 2f out: nt qckn appr fnl f: wknd* **4/1**[3]
7 *2 1/2* **Grand Coalition (IRE)**[39] 5977 2-9-3 92.......................... PatSmullen 7 80
(J P Murtagh, Ire) *hld up: rdn and no imp appr fnl f: kpt on one pce : nvr on terms* **20/1**
8 *3 3/4* **King Electric (IRE)**[78] 4574 2-9-3 102...........................(b[1]) ColinKeane 8 70
(G M Lyons, Ire) *chsd ldrs on outer: rdn and nt qckn under 2f out: sn wknd* **6/1**
9 *8 1/2* **Low Latency**[12] 6814 2-9-3 .... LeighRoche 10 47
(D J Bunyan, Ire) *stmbld after 100yds and qckly dropped to rr: sme prog 1/2-way: rdn and no imp over 1f out: sn eased* **33/1**

1m 23.7s (83.70) **9** Ran SP% **123.4**
CSF £12.95 TOTE £4.90: £1.40, £1.30, £1.80; DF 14.90 Trifecta £65.90.
Owner Godolphin **Bred** Darley **Trained** Doneany, Co Kildare

FOCUS
There have been some top-class winners of this race and on the back of another competitive heat, the winner can be expected to keep the flag flying.

7131 - 7135a (Foreign Racing) - See Raceform Interactive

7029 MAISONS-LAFFITTE (R-H)
Friday, October 7

OFFICIAL GOING: Turf: good

7136a PRIX DE PORT-MARLY (CLAIMER) (2YO) (TURF) 6f 110y
12:40 (12:00) 2-Y-O **£9,926** (£3,970; £2,977; £1,985; £992)

RPR

1 **Bocca De La Verita (FR)**[16] 2-8-8 0............................. ThierryThulliez 3 76
(C Lerner, France) **11/5**[2]
2 *shd* **Douceur D'Antan (FR)**[45] 5755 2-8-13 0....................... MaximeGuyon 2 81
(K Borgel, France) **11/5**[2]
3 *nk* **Dolokhov**[29] 6270 2-8-11 0...(p) TonyPiccone 1 78
(J S Moore) *led single file field: drvn whn pressed fr under 2f out: hdd ent fnl f: rallied u.p: no ex cl home* **8/5**[1]
4 *5* **La Dame En Rouge (FR)**[81] 2-8-8 0...........................(p) MickaelForest 4 61
(M Pimbonnet, France) **83/10**[3]
5 *1 3/4* **Private Money (FR)** 2-8-9 0.............................. ClementLecoeuvre(6) 5 63
(J-M Lefebvre, France) **12/1**

1m 25.07s (85.07) **5** Ran SP% **119.4**
WIN (incl. 1 euro stake): 3.20. PLACES: 1.60, 1.60. SF: 6.90.
Owner Nicolas Saltiel **Bred** Ecurie La Vallee Martigny **Trained** France

7137a PRIX LE FABULEUX (LISTED RACE) (3YO) (STRAIGHT) (TURF) 1m 1f
1:40 (12:00) 3-Y-O **£20,220** (£8,088; £6,066; £4,044; £2,022)

RPR

1 **Kourkan (FR)**[20] 6596 3-9-0 0.............................. ChristopheSoumillon 7 108+
(J-M Beguigne, France) *w.w in fnl pair: hdwy ins fnl 2f: drvn to chse ldr under 1 1/2f out: rdn and chal wl ins fnl f: led fnl 110yds: rdn out* **17/5**[3]
2 *nk* **Robin Of Navan (FR)**[20] 6571 3-9-0 0............................ TonyPiccone 3 107
(Harry Dunlop) *racd a little keenly: trckd ldr: shkn up and qcknd to ld wl over 1 1/2f out: rdn and edgd lft appr 1f out and again ins fnl f: hdd 110yds out: kpt on* **21/10**[1]
3 *3/4* **Spectroscope (USA)**[20] 6597 3-9-0 0..................... MickaelBarzalona 1 105
(A Fabre, France) *w.w towards rr wl in tch: clsd over 1 1/2f out: sn rdn to chse ldrs: carried sltly lft by ldr appr 1f out and again ins fnl f: styd on wout ever being quite on terms* **27/10**[2]
4 *1 3/4* **Gianyar (FR)**[27] 6358 3-9-0 0.. GregoryBenoist 4 101
(E Lellouche, France) **20/1**
5 *3/4* **Zhui Feng (IRE)**[13] 6786 3-9-0 0....................................... OlivierPeslier 2 100
(Amanda Perrett) *led: drvn 2f out: hdd wl over 1 1/2f out: edgd rt wl over 1f out: one pce u.p fnl f* **54/10**
6 *nk* **Le Juge (IRE)**[83] 4422 3-9-0 0... MaximeGuyon 5 99
(A Fabre, France) **12/1**
7 *3 1/2* **Jorvick (USA)**[49] 5699 3-9-0 0...............................(b) VincentCheminaud 6 92
(D Smaga, France) **11/1**

1m 51.26s (-3.44) **7** Ran SP% **118.4**
WIN (incl. 1 euro stake): 4.40. PLACES: 1.90, 1.80. SF: 19.50.
Owner Suc. Henri De La Chauvelais **Bred** Mme H De La Chauvelais **Trained** France

7105 NEWCASTLE (A.W) (L-H)
Saturday, October 8

OFFICIAL GOING: Tapeta: standard
Wind: Almost nil Weather: Cloudy races 1-2

7138 JPS H'CAP 2m 56y (Tp)
5:40 (5:42) (Class 6) (0-65,63) 3-Y-O+ **£2,911** (£866; £432; £216) **Stalls** Low

Form RPR

6410 **1** **Hazely**[42] 5888 3-8-0 **51**.. GeorgeWood(5) 5 60
(James Bethell) *led 2f: trckd ldrs: effrt and regained ld appr fnl f: hrd pressed and edgd rt u.p ins fnl f: hld on wl* **7/2**[1]
6526 **2** *nk* **Northside Prince (IRE)**[36] 6103 10-10-0 **63**.................. BenCurtis 12 71
(Alan Swinbank) *in tch: smooth hdwy to ld over 2f out: rdn and hdd appr fnl f: drvn and styd w wnr: kpt on fnl f: jst hld* **13/2**[2]
5344 **3** *5* **Jan Smuts (IRE)**[9] 6906 8-9-12 **61**..............................(tp) CamHardie 6 63
(Wilf Storey) *hld up midfield: rdn over 2f out: hdwy to chse clr ldng pair ent fnl f: kpt on: no imp* **17/2**
2340 **4** *1 1/2* **Ellerina**[167] 1665 4-8-12 **47**....................................... DuranFentiman 11 47
(Chris Fairhurst) *plld hrd: sn chsng ldr: rdn and ev ch over 2f out: outpcd fnl f* **25/1**
0-30 **5** *1/2* **Omid**[37] 2089 8-8-10 **52**..(tp) CameronNoble(7) 3 52
(Kenneth Slack) *s.i.s: sn pushed along in rr: hdwy to press ldr after 6f: rdn and ev ch over 2f out: outpcd over 1f out: n.d after* **12/1**
5500 **6** *1/2* **Motivate**[16] 6698 3-8-9 **55**.. RyanPowell 13 54
(Sir Mark Prescott Bt) *t.k.h: hld up midfield: drvn along and effrt over 2f out: edgd rt and outpcd over 1f out* **7/2**[1]
2426 **7** *3/4* **Next Edition (IRE)**[21] 6566 8-9-11 **63**................(p) JacobButterfield(3) 10 61
(Philip Kirby) *slowly away: hld up : rdn and effrt on outside over 2f out: nvr rchd ldrs* **16/1**
0605 **8** *nk* **Cavalieri (IRE)**[4] 7045 6-9-13 **62**.....................................(tp) JasonHart 7 60
(Philip Kirby) *t.k.h: hld up midfield: rdn over 2f out: outpcd fr over 1f out* **7/1**[3]
0656 **9** *1 1/2* **Perennial**[4] 7044 7-8-6 **48**...(p) PaulaMuir(7) 9 44
(Philip Kirby) *missed break: hld up: rdn and hd high over 2f out: sn n.d* **9/1**
3245 **10** *1 1/4* **La Bacouetteuse (FR)**[25] 6438 11-9-8 **62**.............(p) GarryWhillans(5) 1 56
(Iain Jardine) *s.i.s: sn pushed along in rr: effrt and drvn 3f out: wknd 2f out* **16/1**
6206 **11** *23* **Symbolist (IRE)**[131] 2746 4-9-11 **60**.............................(v) PaddyAspell 2 27
(John Norton) *in tch: rdn over 4f out: wknd over 2f out* **50/1**
00-2 **12** *9* **Strobe**[33] 5118 12-8-11 **46**...(p) JoeDoyle 8
(Lucy Normile) *led after 2f: rdn and hdd over 2f out: sn wknd* **16/1**

3m 34.24s (-0.96) **Going Correction** -0.075s/f (Stan)
WFA 3 from 4yo+ 11lb **12** Ran SP% **122.0**
Speed ratings (Par 101): **99,98,96,95,95 95,94,94,93,93 81,77**
CSF £26.64 CT £185.62 TOTE £3.80: £1.90, £2.00, £3.10; EX 27.00 Trifecta £154.00.
Owner Clarendon Thoroughbred Racing **Bred** Whitley Stud **Trained** Middleham Moor, N Yorks

FOCUS
A moderate handicap. The first two left the rest behind inside the last 2f.

7139 CCF H'CAP — 1m 4f 98y (Tp)
6:10 (6:11) (Class 4) (0-85,88) 3-Y-O+ **£5,175** (£1,540; £769; £384) **Stalls** High

Form RPR
16 **1** **Flymetothestars**[17] 6675 3-9-3 **83** RyanPowell 4 96+
(Sir Mark Prescott Bt) *t.k.h early: chsd ldrs on outside: hdwy to ld 2f out: sn rdn and edgd lft: kpt on strly fnl f: eased last 50yds* **1/1**[1]
-044 **2** *1 1/2* **All About Time**[35] 6134 4-9-11 **84** DavidNolan 8 90
(David O'Meara) *hld up in tch: effrt over 2f out: rdn and hung lft over 1f out: chsd wnr ins fnl f: kpt on: nt pce to chal* **9/1**[3]
2146 **3** *1 1/4* **Obboorr**[36] 6083 7-9-1 **74** JoeDoyle 7 78
(Tim Fitzgerald) *dwlt: hld up: rdn along 3f out: hdwy and edgd lft wl over 1f out: kpt on fnl f: nrst fin* **12/1**
3300 **4** *nk* **Corton Lad**[21] 6559 6-9-12 **85** (tp) ConnorBeasley 1 88
(Keith Dalgleish) *trckd ldrs: drvn along over 2f out: kpt on same pce fr over 1f out* **9/1**[3]
6015 **5** *shd* **Be Perfect (USA)**[11] 6854 7-9-8 **81** (b) JackGarritty 3 84
(Ruth Carr) *t.k.h: cl up: led over 3f out to 2f out: sn rdn: outpcd ins fnl f* **6/1**[2]
-520 **6** *2* **Siren's Cove**[23] 6504 4-8-10 **76** CameronNoble(7) 2 76
(Kenneth Slack) *hld up in tch: rdn over 2f out: no imp fr over 1f out* **10/1**
4142 **7** *4 1/2* **San Quentin (IRE)**[17] 6684 5-9-1 **74** (b) BenCurtis 6 67
(Roger Fell) *missed break: hld up: shortlived effrt over 2f out: sn btn* **16/1**
4205 **8** *8* **Renfrew Street**[17] 6667 3-9-2 **82** PaulMulrennan 9 62
(Mark Johnston) *led: rdn and hdd over 3f out: wknd over 2f out* **12/1**

2m 38.06s (-3.04) **Going Correction** -0.075s/f (Stan)
WFA 3 from 4yo+ 7lb **8** Ran SP% **114.6**
Speed ratings (Par 105): **107,106,105,104,104 103,100,95**
CSF £10.96 CT £69.87 TOTE £2.00: £1.20, £3.00, £1.60; EX 12.10 Trifecta £93.90.
Owner Lady Bamford **Bred** Lady Bamford **Trained** Newmarket, Suffolk

FOCUS
There was a comfortable win for the unexposed favourite in this fair middle-distance contest.

7140 OFFICE GLASS PARTITIONS NORTHERN LTD NURSERY H'CAP — 1m 5y (Tp)
6:45 (6:45) (Class 5) (0-75,73) 2-Y-O **£2,911** (£866; £432; £216) **Stalls** Centre

Form RPR
044 **1** **Rashford's Double (IRE)**[45] 5778 2-8-9 **66** AdamMcNamara(5) 1 70+
(Richard Fahey) *hld up: stdy hdwy far side of gp over 2f out: rdn to ld appr fnl f: edgd lft: kpt on strly* **5/2**[1]
0414 **2** *1 3/4* **Nepeta (USA)**[16] 6713 2-9-5 **71** AndrewMullen 7 71
(Mark Johnston) *led at ordinary gallop: rdn and hdd over 2f out: rallied ins fnl f: wnt 2nd towards fin: nt rch wnr* **5/1**[3]
3201 **3** *hd* **Highland Lotus**[26] 6421 2-9-7 **73** (p) BenCurtis 3 73
(William Haggas) *pressed ldr: led gng wl over 2f out: rdn and hdd appr fnl f: kpt on tl no ex and lost 2nd nr fin* **5/1**[3]
0061 **4** *shd* **Crystal Dome**[17] 6681 2-9-7 **73** PaulMulrennan 5 74
(Ed Dunlop) *stdd in last pl: stdy hdwy over 2f out: effrt and rdn over 1f out: edgd lft ins fnl f: kpt on* **3/1**[2]
564 **5** *2* **Ladofash**[28] 6319 2-9-1 **72** JordanVaughan(5) 4 66
(K R Burke) *in tch: rdn over 2f out: outpcd over 1f out: kpt on fnl f: no imp* **6/1**
560 **6** *1/2* **Inglorious**[47] 5713 2-9-1 **67** [1] ConnorBeasley 2 60
(Keith Dalgleish) *t.k.h: cl up: rdn and ev ch briefly over 2f out: wknd over 1f out* **14/1**
6430 **7** *2 1/4* **Bloomin Lovely (IRE)**[30] 6257 2-9-7 **73** JasonHart 6 61
(John Quinn) *t.k.h: prom: rdn over 2f out: wknd over 1f out* **16/1**

1m 41.24s (2.64) **Going Correction** -0.10s/f (Stan) **7** Ran SP% **113.7**
Speed ratings (Par 95): **82,80,80,79,77 77,75**
CSF £15.21 TOTE £3.40: £1.80, £3.10; EX 15.90 Trifecta £78.90.
Owner Middleham Park Racing XC **Bred** Manister House Stud **Trained** Musley Bank, N Yorks

FOCUS
Luck in running played a part in the result of this nursery.

7141 JPS CEILINGS H'CAP — 1m 5y (Tp)
7:15 (7:15) (Class 5) (0-75,75) 3-Y-O+ **£3,234** (£962; £481; £240) **Stalls** Centre

Form RPR
0406 **1** **Eastern Dragon (IRE)**[12] 6838 6-8-11 **72** [1] LewisEdmunds(7) 6 82
(Iain Jardine) *hld up: hdwy on far side of gp over 2f out: led ins fnl f: styd on strly* **33/1**
042 **2** *2* **So It's War (FR)**[122] 3013 5-9-3 **71** (p) ConnorBeasley 11 76
(Keith Dalgleish) *cl up: rdn and led over 1f out: hdd ins fnl f: kpt on same pce* **20/1**
1525 **3** *1 1/2* **Weather Front (USA)**[28] 6344 3-9-4 **75** JoeyHaynes 8 77
(Karen McLintock) *s.i.s: hld up: rdn and hdwy over 2f out: chsd ldrs over 1f out: one pce ins fnl f* **11/1**
3143 **4** *nk* **Chaplin Bay (IRE)**[18] 6643 4-9-7 **75** JackGarritty 9 76
(Ruth Carr) *hld up midfield: hdwy and prom 2f out: kpt on same pce ins fnl f* **11/1**
0212 **5** *1* **Let's Twist**[9] 6899 4-9-6 **74** (b) ShaneGray 10 73
(Kristin Stubbs) *w ldr: led over 2f out to over 1f out: rdn and nt qckn fnl f* **4/1**[2]
0200 **6** *3 3/4* **Tellovoi (IRE)**[18] 6643 8-9-1 **74** (v) AdamMcNamara(5) 14 64
(Richard Guest) *racd alone stands' rail: swtchd to nr side of gp after 3f: drvn over 2f out: rallied: outpcd fnl f* **50/1**
-545 **7** *1/2* **Zabeel Star (IRE)**[56] 5392 4-9-2 **73** RobHornby(3) 7 62
(Graeme McPherson) *bhd: drvn and outpcd over 3f out: kpt on fnl f: nvr able to chal* **9/2**[3]
3404 **8** *1/2* **Mustaqqil (IRE)**[4] 7051 4-9-7 **75** (b) DavidNolan 4 63
(David O'Meara) *hld up in tch: hdwy to chse ldrs over 1f out: rdn and wknd ins fnl f* **6/1**
3543 **9** *1 3/4* **Hernando Torres**[31] 6226 8-9-0 **68** (p) AndrewMullen 2 52
(Michael Easterby) *prom on far side of gp: rdn over 2f out: wknd over 1f out* **16/1**
0400 **10** *1 1/2* **Royal Normandy**[21] 6569 4-9-4 **72** (p) BenCurtis 1 53
(Roger Fell) *led on far side of gp to over 2f out: rdn and wknd over 1f out* **100/1**
4000 **11** *3 1/2* **Gworn**[21] 6561 6-9-5 **73** JasonHart 13 46
(R Mike Smith) *hld up in tch on nr side of gp: drvn and struggling 3f out: btn fnl 2f* **20/1**
0624 **12** *7* **Enmeshing**[16] 6702 3-9-3 **74** [1] DanielMuscutt 12 30
(James Fanshawe) *hld up: rdn and outpcd over 2f out: sn btn* **10/3**[1]
300- **13** *36* **Star Focus (IRE)**[391] 6364 3-9-4 **75** PaulMulrennan 3
(Mark Johnston) *plld hrd: hld up on far side of gp: struggling 3f out: lost tch fnl 2f* **50/1**
0600 **P** **Strong Man**[23] 6500 8-9-7 **75** CamHardie 5
(Michael Easterby) *chsd ldrs: drvn and outpcd over 2f out: sn wknd: lost tch and p.u ins fnl f* **25/1**

1m 37.41s (-1.19) **Going Correction** -0.10s/f (Stan)
WFA 3 from 4yo+ 3lb **14** Ran SP% **119.3**
Speed ratings (Par 103): **101,99,97,97,96 92,91,91,89,88 84,77,41,**
CSF £550.76 CT £7513.95 TOTE £26.40: £7.10, £5.90, £3.40; EX 426.80 Trifecta £4262.30.
Owner George Brian Davidson **Bred** James Mahon **Trained** Carrutherstown, D'fries & G'way

FOCUS
Fair handicap form.

7142 ROCKFON MAIDEN STKS — 6f (Tp)
7:45 (7:46) (Class 5) 2-Y-O **£2,911** (£866; £432; £216) **Stalls** Centre

Form RPR
5 **1** **El Hombre**[86] 4308 2-9-0 0 ShirleyTeasdale(5) 3 76
(Keith Dalgleish) *t.k.h: cl up on far side of gp: rdn and led over 1f out: edgd lft ins fnl f: kpt on wl towards fin* **25/1**
035 **2** *1 1/2* **Desert Sport (USA)**[36] 6071 2-9-0 73 AdamMcNamara(5) 6 71
(Robert Cowell) *w ldr: led over 2f out: edgd lft and hdd over 1f out: chsd wnr: kpt on same pce wl ins fnl f* **7/2**[2]
3 *hd* **Chipping (IRE)** 2-9-5 0 ConnorBeasley 12 70
(Michael Dods) *hld up in tch on nr side of gp: pushed along 3f out: hdwy and prom over 1f out: edgd lft: kpt on ins fnl f* **5/4**[1]
4 *3/4* **Ascot Day (IRE)** 2-9-5 0 SaleemGolam 2 70
(David Simcock) *prom on far side of gp: effrt and disp 2nd pl over 1f out: half a l down and keeping on whn hmpd ins fnl f: nt rcvr* **4/1**[3]
0 **5** *1 1/2* **Judy Woods (IRE)**[24] 6477 2-9-0 0 PaulMulrennan 7 59
(Bryan Smart) *hld up: pushed along and hdwy over 1f out: kpt on fnl f: nvr able to chal* **25/1**
5 **6** *3 1/4* **Stubytuesday**[144] 2344 2-9-5 0 CamHardie 11 54
(Michael Easterby) *bhd: drvn and outpcd over 3f out: rallied over 1f out: kpt on: nvr able to chal* **33/1**
006 **7** *2* **Eldorado Creek (IRE)**[89] 4188 2-9-5 76 TonyHamilton 4 48
(Richard Fahey) *in tch: drvn over 2f out: wknd wl over 1f out* **5/1**
0 **8** *2 1/4* **Rebel Flame**[32] 6214 2-9-5 0 JackGarritty 10 41
(Jedd O'Keeffe) *cl up on nr side of gp: rdn 3f out: wknd over 1f out* **100/1**
9 *1 1/2* **Red Douglas** 2-9-5 0 BenCurtis 5 37
(Scott Dixon) *s.i.s: bhd on far side of gp: struggling over 2f out: sn btn* **50/1**
00 **10** *2 3/4* **Ten In The Hat (IRE)**[17] 6682 2-9-0 0 PaddyPilley(5) 8 28
(Shaun Harris) *hld up in tch: rdn over 2f out: wknd wl over 1f out* **150/1**
00 **11** *6* **Millybond**[16] 6712 2-9-0 0 TomEaves 9 5
(David Brown) *led to over 2f out: sn rdn and wknd* **150/1**
12 *5* **Stretewise (IRE)** 2-9-0 0 JasonHart 1
(Jason Ward) *v s.i.s: sn wl bhd: nvr on terms* **100/1**

1m 11.79s (-0.71) **Going Correction** -0.10s/f (Stan) **12** Ran SP% **119.2**
Speed ratings (Par 95): **100,98,97,96,94 90,87,84,82,79 71,64**
CSF £109.75 TOTE £21.40: £4.50, £1.20, £1.50; EX 103.70 Trifecta £497.10.
Owner Weldspec Glasgow Limited **Bred** Mrs J McMahon **Trained** Carluke, S Lanarks
■ Stewards' Enquiry : Saleem Golam five-day ban; careless riding (22nd,24th-27th Oct)

FOCUS
An ordinary maiden.

7143 HADLEY STEEL FRAMING NURSERY H'CAP — 6f (Tp)
8:15 (8:15) (Class 6) (0-65,65) 2-Y-O **£2,911** (£866; £432; £216) **Stalls** Centre

Form RPR
0400 **1** **Lou's Diamond**[39] 6010 2-8-13 **62** NathanEvans(5) 2 66
(Michael Easterby) *mde virtually all: drvn 2f out: hld on wl towards fin* **20/1**
0506 **2** *shd* **Western Presence**[18] 6641 2-9-3 **61** TonyHamilton 3 65
(Richard Fahey) *hld up: hdwy far side of gp to chse ldrs over 1f out: rdn and kpt on fnl f: tk 2nd cl home: jst hld* **20/1**
3062 **3** *hd* **Pulsating (IRE)**[21] 6588 2-8-12 **61** CliffordLee(5) 14 64
(Ali Stronge) *prom on nr side of gp: hdwy and ev ch over 1f out: sn rdn: kpt on fnl f: no ex and lost 2nd nr fin* **9/1**
5133 **4** *2 3/4* **Saxagogo**[26] 6419 2-9-2 **65** AdamMcNamara(5) 1 60
(George Scott) *hld up: rdn and hdwy nr side of gp wl over 1f out: kpt on fnl f: nvr able to chal* **7/2**[1]
3332 **5** *1 1/2* **Wearethepeople**[18] 6652 2-9-2 **65** GeorgeWood(5) 12 55
(William Muir) *disp ld to over 1f out: rdn and no ex ins fnl f* **7/1**[3]
00 **6** *1/2* **Mary Brady**[60] 5257 2-9-5 **63** DavidNolan 4 52
(David O'Meara) *in tch on far side of gp: rdn over 2f out: rallied: kpt on same pce fnl f* **33/1**
3560 **7** *hd* **Apamurra (USA)**[21] 6564 2-9-7 **65** PaulMulrennan 6 53
(Mark Johnston) *hld up: drvn on far side of gp over 2f out: rallied over 1f out: no imp fnl f* **20/1**
0406 **8** *1 1/4* **Vaux (IRE)**[15] 6743 2-9-4 **62** CamHardie 11 47
(Ben Haslam) *hld up: rdn over 2f out: edgd lft and hdwy over 1f out: kpt on: nt pce to chal* **16/1**
540 **9** *1 1/4* **Oceanic (IRE)**[15] 6743 2-9-0 **58** (t[1]) JackGarritty 9 39
(John Quinn) *dwlt: hld up: rdn along over 2f out: sn no imp* **11/1**
2143 **10** *3/4* **Foxy Boy**[14] 6768 2-9-5 **63** ConnorBeasley 13 42
(Michael Dods) *prom on nr side of gp: drvn over 2f out: wknd over 1f out* **8/1**
6624 **11** *4* **Seprani**[44] 5806 2-9-4 **62** DanielMuscutt 7 29
(Marco Botti) *midfield: rdn over 2f out: sn no imp: btn over 1f out* **4/1**[2]
5202 **12** *1* **Local Artist (IRE)**[24] 6471 2-9-5 **63** JasonHart 5 27
(John Quinn) *prom: drvn and struggling over 2f out: sn btn* **16/1**
0235 **13** *3/4* **Cheerful Character (IRE)**[14] 6768 2-9-2 **60** GeorgeChaloner 8 21
(Richard Fahey) *prom: rdn over 2f out: wknd wl over 1f out* **14/1**
5360 **14** *2* **Quantum Field (USA)**[38] 6026 2-9-4 **62** TomEaves 10 17
(David Brown) *swtchd to r stands' rail sn after s: bhd: rdn and struggling 1/2-way: sn btn* **20/1**

1m 12.04s (-0.46) **Going Correction** -0.10s/f (Stan) **14** Ran SP% **124.6**
Speed ratings (Par 93): **99,98,98,94,92 92,92,90,88,87 82,81,80,77**
CSF £361.73 CT £3936.69 TOTE £24.30: £6.10, £5.90, £3.20; EX 466.90 Trifecta £4239.70.
Owner K Wreglesworth & D Scott **Bred** M W Easterby **Trained** Sheriff Hutton, N Yorks

FOCUS
A competitive nursery.

7144 JPS STEEL FRAME STRUCTURES APPRENTICE H'CAP (DIV I) — 6f (Tp)
8:45 (8:47) (Class 6) (0-60,60) 3-Y-O+ **£2,264** (£673; £336; £168) **Stalls** Centre

Form RPR
5005 **1** **Round The Island**[17] 6685 3-9-3 **59** NathanEvans(3) 3 65
(Richard Whitaker) *pressed ldr: rdn and led 2f out: hrd pressed fnl f: hld on gamely cl home* **5/1**[1]

The Form Book, Raceform Ltd, Newbury, RG14 5SJ

5500 **2** *shd* **Gold Beau (FR)**[82] 4454 6-9-2 **59**.....(p) GerO'Neill(5) 10 65
(Kristin Stubbs) *bhd: rdn and hdwy on nr side of gp to press wnr over 1f out: ev ch ins fnl f: kpt on: jst hld* **6/1**[3]

3-02 **3** *hd* **Wimboldsley**[21] 6587 5-8-11 **49**..... MichaelJMMurphy 4 54
(Scott Dixon) *taken down early and walked to s: hld up: rdn and hdwy on nr side of gp over 1f out: kpt on fnl f: jst hld* **12/1**

0156 **4** *2* **Cool Strutter (IRE)**[17] 6685 4-9-5 **60**.....(b) GemmaTutty(3) 11 61
(Karen Tutty) *taken early to post: hld up: pushed along and hdwy over 2f out: rdn and kpt on same pce ins fnl f* **11/2**[2]

054 **5** *½* **Tell The Stars**[15] 6745 3-8-10 **49**..... JacobButterfield 12 47
(Ollie Pears) *in tch on nr side of gp: pushed along over 2f out: effrt and edgd lft wl over 1f out: outpcd ins fnl f* **8/1**

0254 **6** *3* **Isntshesomething**[9] 6908 4-9-0 **52**.....(p) ShelleyBirkett 5 41
(Richard Guest) *in tch: rdn over 2f out: edgd lft and outpcd over 1f out: btn fnl f* **6/1**[3]

2120 **7** *½* **Fortinbrass (IRE)**[99] 3843 6-9-2 **59**..... LewisEdmunds(5) 1 46
(John Balding) *prom on far side of gp: rdn over 2f out: outpcd over 1f out: sn btn* **8/1**

0545 **8** *1¼* **Fool's Dream**[42] 5889 3-8-8 **50**.....(p) PhilDennis(3) 2 33
(Bryan Smart) *hld up: hdwy over 2f out: rdn and wknd wl over 1f out* **12/1**

0000 **9** *¾* **Pavers Star**[13] 6813 7-8-5 **46** oh1.....[1] JordanVaughan(3) 9 27
(Noel Wilson) *led tl rdn and hdd 2f out: sn wknd* **20/1**

5660 **10** *½* **Circuitous**[52] 5535 8-8-12 **53**.....(v) ShirleyTeasdale(3) 8 33
(Keith Dalgleish) *chsd ldrs: drvn and outpcd over 2f out: sn btn* **14/1**

0046 **11** *1* **Ershaad (IRE)**[30] 6249 4-9-1 **56**..... PaddyPilley(3) 7 33
(Shaun Harris) *s.i.s: sn prom: drvn over 2f out: sn lost pl and struggling* **11/1**

1m 12.16s (-0.34) **Going Correction** -0.10s/f (Stan)
WFA 3 from 4yo+ 1lb **11** Ran SP% **118.0**
Speed ratings (Par 101): **98,97,97,94,94 90,89,87,86,86 84**
CSF £34.68 CT £351.11 TOTE £6.60: £2.40, £2.10, £3.50; EX 41.00 Trifecta £554.50.
Owner Robin Dollar & David Horner **Bred** R Dollar, T Adams & G F Pemberton **Trained** Scarcroft, W Yorks
■ The Cheese Gang was withdrawn. Price at time of withdrawal 33/1. Rule 4 does not apply

FOCUS
A moderate sprint. Bar the winner, those who raced close to the pace dropped away.

7145 JPS STEEL FRAME STRUCTURES APPRENTICE H'CAP (DIV II) 6f (Tp)
9:15 (9:16) (Class 6) (0-60,60) 3-Y-O+ **£2,264** (£673; £336; £168) **Stalls** Centre

Form RPR

0002 **1** **Rock Warbler (IRE)**[11] 6852 3-9-4 **57**.....(t) KevinStott 6 66
(Oliver Greenall) *hld up: gd hdwy on nr side of gp over 1f out: edgd lft and led ins fnl f: pushed out* **5/2**[1]

3030 **2** *¾* **Danzeb (IRE)**[28] 6341 3-9-2 **60**..... RowanScott(5) 1 67
(Ann Duffield) *in tch: hdwy far side of gp to ld over 2f out: rdn over 1f out: hdd ins fnl f: kpt on: hld nr fin* **6/1**[3]

2535 **3** *4* **Dream Ally (IRE)**[11] 6852 6-8-11 **54**.....(be) CliffordLee(5) 8 49
(John Weymes) *in tch: rdn over 2f out: effrt and chsd ldng pair appr fnl f: outpcd fnl 100yds* **9/2**[2]

5000 **4** *1½* **Captain Scooby**[2] 7092 10-8-5 **50** ow1.....(b) LisaTodd(7) 4 40
(Richard Guest) *hld up: hdwy on far side of gp and cl up over 2f out: wknd ins fnl f* **16/1**

0040 **5** *1¾* **Blackasyourhat (IRE)**[49] 5636 4-8-3 **46** oh1.....(t) RhiainIngram(5) 5 31
(Michael Attwater) *hld up: rdn and hdwy 1/2-way: wknd over 1f out* **33/1**

4000 **6** *1* **Cadeaux Pearl**[80] 4516 8-8-11 **49**.....(b) MichaelJMMurphy 3 31
(Scott Dixon) *chsd ldrs: rdn over 2f out: wknd over 1f out* **16/1**

0500 **7** *¾* **Cosmic Dust**[9] 6909 3-8-4 **46** oh1..... NathanEvans(3) 9 26
(Richard Whitaker) *cl up: rdn over 2f out: wknd over 1f out* **10/1**

0040 **8** *½* **Pabusar**[4] 7046 8-8-7 **46** ow2.....(tp) RobJFitzpatrick(3) 10 26
(Micky Hammond) *s.i.s: bhd and pushed along: nvr on terms* **20/1**

0060 **9** *1¼* **Clon Rocket (IRE)**[14] 6790 3-8-7 **53**.....[1] MeganEllingworth(7) 11 26
(John Holt) *led to over 2f out: rdn and wknd over 1f out* **7/1**

6-04 **10** *2* **Lilvanita (IRE)**[36] 6101 3-9-4 **60**..... CallumShepherd(3) 7 27
(Brian Ellison) *in tch: drvn and struggling over 2f out: sn btn* **25/1**

0362 **11** *hd* **Call Me Crockett (IRE)**[24] 6478 4-8-10 **51**.....(p) JordanVaughan(3) 12 17
(Noel Wilson) *prom on nr side of gp: drvn along over 2f out: sn wknd* **7/1**

1m 12.18s (-0.32) **Going Correction** -0.10s/f (Stan)
WFA 3 from 4yo+ 1lb **11** Ran SP% **118.4**
Speed ratings (Par 101): **98,97,91,89,87 86,85,84,82,79 79**
CSF £17.05 CT £66.63 TOTE £4.00: £1.50, £2.60, £1.90; EX 19.50 Trifecta £67.60.
Owner R A Royle & S Evason **Bred** Sir E J Loder **Trained** Oldcastle Heath, Cheshire
■ Stewards' Enquiry : Rob J Fitzpatrick one-day ban; weighed out heavy (24th Oct)

FOCUS
The winning time was almost identical to the first division.
T/Plt: £1,536.30 to a £1 stake. Pool: £78,290.49 - 37.2 winning units T/Qpdt: £295.60 to a £1 stake. Pool: £11,026.43 - 27.6 winning units **Richard Young**

7113 NEWMARKET (R-H)
Saturday, October 8

OFFICIAL GOING: Good (good to firm in places; 7.7)
Wind: light, half behind Weather: overcast

7146 VISIONSPORT.COM EBF STALLIONS BOADICEA FILLIES' STKS (LISTED RACE) 6f
1:45 (1:45) (Class 1) 3-Y-O+
£28,355 (£10,750; £5,380; £2,680; £1,345; £675) **Stalls** High

Form RPR

1121 **1** **Kassia (IRE)**[23] 6518 3-9-0 99..... GrahamLee 10 109
(Mick Channon) *racd in stands' side trio: last of trio but midfield overall: swtchd rt and rdn to cl over 1f out: wnt 2nd ent fnl f: chal ins fnl f: styd on wl to ld towards fin: 1st of 3 in trio* **15/2**

1111 **2** *hd* **Gravity Flow (IRE)**[37] 6064 3-9-0 99..... PatCosgrave 12 108
(William Haggas) *racd in stands' side trio: led and clr overall ldr: rdn over 1f out: drvn and hrd pressed ins fnl f: hdd towards fin: 2nd of 3 in gp* **4/1**[2]

1202 **3** *4* **Mise En Rose (USA)**[29] 6281 3-9-0 106.....[1] WilliamBuick 2 96+
(Charlie Appleby) *racd in centre: s.i.s: hld up towards rr: hdwy over 2f out: rdn over 1f out: styd on to 3rd wl ins fnl f: no threat to ldng pair: 1st of 10 in gp* **7/2**[1]

3621 **4** *½* **Spring Fling**[14] 6780 5-9-1 93..... AdamKirby 5 94+
(Henry Candy) *racd in centre: hld up in rr: effrt over 1f out: styd on wl ins fnl f: no threat to ldrs: 2nd of 10 in gp* **8/1**

4111 **5** *nk* **Symposium**[8] 6916 3-9-0 90.....(p) RyanMoore 3 93
(William Haggas) *racd in centre: midfield overall: rdn 2f out: hdwy ins fnl f: styd on u.p: nvr threatened ldrs: 3rd of 10 in gp* **7/1**[3]

5030 **6** *¾* **Imtiyaaz (IRE)**[7] 6939 4-9-1 89..... AndreaAtzeni 1 91
(Roger Varian) *racd in centre: prom in gp but nt on terms w overall ldr: rdn to ld gp 2f out: kpt on same pce ins fnl f: nvr trbld ldrs: 4th of 10 in gp* **16/1**

5120 **7** *nk* **Futoon (IRE)**[23] 6518 3-9-0 84..... SilvestreDeSousa 13 90
(Kevin Ryan) *racd in stands' side trio: chsd overall ldr: rdn wl over 1f out: lost 2nd and btn ent fnl f: wknd wl ins fnl f: 3rd of 3 in gp* **25/1**

2232 **8** *1½* **Pixeleen**[7] 6946 4-9-1 86..... JimmyFortune 11 85
(Malcolm Saunders) *taken down early: racd in centre: t.k.h: prom in gp but nt on terms w overall ldrs: effrt 2f out: no imp over 1f out: wknd ins fnl f: 5th of 10 in gp* **12/1**

1024 **9** *½* **Stellarta**[7] 6946 5-9-1 93..... TomMarquand 9 83
(Michael Blanshard) *racd in centre: hld up in midfield: rdn over 2f out: no imp: kpt on same pce fr over 1f out: 6th of 10 in gp* **20/1**

1413 **10** *3½* **Sweet Dragon Fly**[7] 6946 3-9-0 87.....(t) JamieSpencer 7 72
(Paul Cole) *racd in centre: broke fast: led gp but nt on terms w overall ldr: lost gp ld and rdn 2f out: sn lost pl: wknd fnl f: 7th of 10 in gp* **9/1**

1140 **11** *1* **Belledesert**[10] 6878 3-9-0 86..... AdamBeschizza 6 69
(Steph Hollinshead) *racd in centre: hld up in rr: rdn over 2f out: sn btn: bhd over 1f out: 8th of 10 in gp* **66/1**

0005 **12** *½* **Secret Hint**[37] 6064 5-9-1 88..... OisinMurphy 8 67
(Andrew Balding) *racd in centre: midfield: shkn up over 1f out: sn btn: wknd fnl f: 9th of 10 in gp* **25/1**

4514 **13** *2¾* **Dynamic Girl (IRE)**[33] 6182 3-9-0 72.....(p) FMBerry 4 58
(Brendan Powell) *racd in centre: hld up in rr: rdn 2f out: sn struggling: bhd over 1f out: sddle slipped: 10th of 10 in gp* **200/1**

1m 11.04s (-1.16) **Going Correction** 0.0s/f (Good)
WFA 3 from 4yo+ 1lb **13** Ran SP% **115.6**
Speed ratings (Par 108): **107,106,101,100,100 99,98,96,96,91 90,89,85**
CSF £34.49 TOTE £7.40: £2.90, £1.70, £1.60; EX 31.20 Trifecta £61.50.
Owner Jon and Julia Aisbitt **Bred** Old Carhue Stud **Trained** West Ilsley, Berks

FOCUS
Stands' side used. Stalls on stands' side except 2m2f - centre. There was 3mm of water applied to the straight on Wednesday, and after 1.2mm of rain following Friday's card plus overnight into Saturday, the ground had eased to good, good to firm in places. The majority of these raced towards the middle of the track, but three runners stayed near side, soon holding a significant advantage, they included the first two home. A bit muddling then, although the one-two pulled a long way clear of the other runner on their side and are improving. The form could be rated higher at face value.

7147 DUBAI BUSINESS INTERNSHIPS FILLIES' NURSERY H'CAP 7f
2:20 (2:21) (Class 2) 2-Y-O
£24,900 (£7,456; £3,728; £1,864; £932; £468) **Stalls** High

Form RPR

5134 **1** **Island Vision (IRE)**[30] 6257 2-8-12 **78**..... JimCrowley 16 87
(David Simcock) *hld up in midfield: hdwy u.p over 1f out: chsd ldr ins fnl f: styd on wl to ld 50yds out: rdn out* **11/1**

041 **2** *1* **Flying North**[35] 6111 2-8-11 **77**..... TimmyMurphy 14 83+
(Richard Hannon) *wnt lft s: sn rcvrd to chse ldrs: led ent fnl 2f: rdn jst over 1f out: hdd 50yds out: kpt on same pce after* **14/1**

422 **3** *1½* **Aimez La Vie (IRE)**[14] 6762 2-8-6 **72**..... PatrickMathers 15 74
(Richard Fahey) *in tch in midfield: effrt u.p over 1f out: chsd ldr jst over 1f out tl ins fnl f: 3rd and styd on same pce ins fnl f* **10/1**

013 **4** *1* **Fire Palace**[30] 6257 2-8-12 **78**..... AndreaAtzeni 7 78+
(Robert Eddery) *t.k.h: wl in tch in midfield: hdwy and drvn to chse ldrs over 1f out: no ex 1f out: wknd wl ins fnl f* **8/1**[2]

2231 **5** *shd* **Amabilis**[24] 6472 2-9-5 **85**..... FMBerry 10 84+
(Ralph Beckett) *s.i.s: in tch towards rr: effrt 2f out: nt clr run wl over 1f out: hdwy jst over 1f out: drvn and swtchd rt ins fnl f: styd on fnl 100yds: nvr gng to rch ldrs* **7/1**[1]

0304 **6** *1½* **Seduce Me**[7] 6950 2-9-0 **80**.....(p) PJMcDonald 12 75
(K R Burke) *chsd ldrs: rdn to chse ldr ent fnl 2f tl unable qck over 1f out: wknd ins fnl f* **14/1**

4232 **7** *1¼* **Honourable**[14] 6791 2-8-5 **71**..... PaulHanagan 9 63
(Richard Fahey) *broke wl restrained to chse ldrs and t.k.h: chsd ldrs: rdn and unable qck over 1f out: btn whn hmpd ins fnl f: wknd fnl 75yds* **16/1**

2332 **8** *¾* **Harmonise**[14] 6787 2-8-6 **72**..... LukeMorris 11 62
(Mick Channon) *in tch in midfield: effrt u.p and switching rt over 1f out: no imp 1f out: wknd ins fnl f* **9/1**[3]

5414 **9** *3¾* **Night Law**[49] 5638 2-8-12 **78**.....[1] OisinMurphy 4 58+
(Andrew Balding) *in tch towards rr: pushed along 2f out: no imp tl sme hdwy and swtchd lft ins fnl f: kpt on to pass btn horses fnl 100yds: nvr trbld ldrs* **20/1**

102 **10** *½* **Parsnip (IRE)**[44] 5794 2-9-0 **80**.....(t) JamieSpencer 6 58
(Michael Bell) *s.i.s: hld up in tch in rr: effrt over 1f out: sn u.p and no imp: nvr trbld ldrs* **8/1**[2]

2360 **11** *1¾* **Quick Thought (IRE)**[19] 6630 2-8-0 **66** oh4.....[1] NickyMackay 3 44+
(Dr Jon Scargill) *hld up in tch in rr: pushed along 2f out: unbalanced and no hdwy over 1f out: no ch whn squeezed for room and hmpd ins fnl f* **66/1**

020 **12** *nk* **Textured (IRE)**[25] 6454 2-8-12 **78**..... RyanMoore 17 51
(Sir Michael Stoute) *in tch in midfield: lost pl and rdn over 2f out: wknd over 1f out* **20/1**

0520 **13** *1* **High On Love (IRE)**[27] 6388 2-9-4 **84**.....[1] StevieDonohoe 13 54
(Charlie Fellowes) *led tl rdn and hdd jst over 2f out: sn struggling: wknd over 1f out* **33/1**

11 **14** *½* **Tara Celeb**[19] 6630 2-8-13 **79**..... GrahamLee 1 48+
(Mick Channon) *wnt rt s: hld up in tch towards rr: rdn and sme hdwy over 1f out: nvr threatened ldrs: wknd ins fnl f: burst blood vessel* **8/1**[2]

2105 **15** *nse* **Romantic View**[14] 6787 2-9-7 **87**..... WilliamBuick 8 56+
(Charlie Appleby) *chsd ldrs: cl 4th and rdn over 2f out: unbalanced and no hdwy wl over 1f out: sn lost pl: btn and eased ins fnl f* **10/1**

2512 **16** *21* **Fastnet Spin (IRE)**[21] 6575 2-8-12 **78**.....(v) JFEgan 5
(David Evans) *in tch in midfield: rdn over 3f out: no imp over 2f out: btn and eased over 1f out: t.o* **16/1**

1m 25.01s (-0.39) **Going Correction** 0.0s/f (Good) **16** Ran SP% **121.4**
Speed ratings (Par 98): **102,100,99,98,97 96,94,93,89,89 87,86,85,84,84 60**
CSF £149.43 CT £1016.27 TOTE £12.50: £2.70, £3.50, £2.60, £2.10; EX 207.10 Trifecta £1355.10.
Owner Sheikh Juma Dalmook Al Maktoum **Bred** Black Crow Syndicate **Trained** Newmarket, Suffolk
■ Stewards' Enquiry : J F Egan two-day ban; careless riding (24th-25th Oct)

FOCUS
Near side had been the place to be in the opening 6f Listed race, so that's where they all raced this time and a high draw was helpful, with the 1-2-3 drawn 16-14-15. The third looks the best guide.

7148 DUBAI 100 AUTUMN STKS (GROUP 3) 1m
2:55 (2:55) (Class 1) 2-Y-O

£45,368 (£17,200; £8,608; £4,288; £2,152; £1,080) **Stalls** High

Form RPR

3134 **1** **Best Solution (IRE)**[16] 6707 2-9-1 102 WilliamCarson 3 111
(Saeed bin Suroor) *chsd ldr: clsd and upsides travelling best 2f out: rdn to ld over 1f out: edgd lft 1f out: styd on: drvn out* **12/1**

31 **2** 2 **Zainhom (USA)**[34] 6159 2-9-1 0 PaulHanagan 1 106+
(Sir Michael Stoute) *stdd s: hld up in last pair: clsd and nt clr run 2f out: swtchd lft and hdwy over 1f out: chsd wnr ins fnl f: styd on same pce fnl 100yds* **16/1**

32 **3** 2 **The Anvil (IRE)**[14] 6783 2-9-1 0 RyanMoore 8 102
(A P O'Brien, Ire) *hld up in tch in midfield: effrt ent fnl 2f out: drvn over 1f out: wnt 3rd ins fnl f: kpt on same pce after* **11/4**[1]

1216 **4** 1 ¾ **Montataire (IRE)**[14] 6783 2-9-1 100 WilliamBuick 4 98
(Mark Johnston) *led: jnd and rdn 2f out: hdd over 1f out: struggling to qckn whn sltly impeded 1f out: lost 2nd ins fnl f: wknd fnl 100yds: eased nr fin* **8/1**

2133 **5** 2 ¼ **Lockheed**[27] 6386 2-9-1 108 FrankieDettori 9 93+
(William Haggas) *t.k.h: chsd ldrs: effrt and hung rt jst over 2f out: stl hanging and no imp over 1f out: wknd ins fnl f* **9/2**[2]

3243 **6** 1 ½ **Sea Fox (IRE)**[14] 6783 2-9-1 106 (t) AdamKirby 2 89
(David Evans) *wl in tch in midfield: effrt and hung rt over 2f out: no imp and stl hanging over 1f out: wknd fnl f* **14/1**

1314 **7** 1 **Pleaseletmewin (IRE)**[74] 4732 2-9-1 104 FMBerry 10 87
(Ralph Beckett) *t.k.h: chsd ldrs: rdn 3f out: unable qck u.p and lost pl 2f out: wknd over 1f out* **8/1**

315 **8** 4 **Law And Order (IRE)**[16] 6707 2-9-1 99 MartinHarley 7 78
(James Tate) *half rrd as stalls opened and s.i.s: hld up in tch: effrt 2f out: no imp whn sltly impeded over 1f out: sn btn and wknd fnl f* **16/1**

1111 **9** 10 **Rodaini (USA)**[29] 6285 2-9-1 105 SilvestreDeSousa 6 55+
(Simon Crisford) *dwlt: hld up in tch in rr: nt clr run 2f out: pushed along whn stmbld bdly wl over 1f out: nt rcvr and no imp after: eased ins fnl f* **5/1**[3]

61 **10** 4 ½ **Solomon's Bay (IRE)**[24] 6486 2-9-1 0 AndreaAtzeni 5 44+
(Roger Varian) *t.k.h: hld up in tch in midfield: effrt and bmpd over 2f out: no imp u.p and bmpd again over 1f out: sn btn: eased ins fnl f* **16/1**

1m 37.15s (-1.45) **Going Correction** 0.0s/f (Good) **10** Ran SP% **115.7**
Speed ratings (Par 105): **107,105,103,101,99 97,96,92,82,78**
CSF £185.34 TOTE £17.30: £4.20, £3.80, £1.40; EX 236.80 Trifecta £2394.90.
Owner Godolphin **Bred** Cecil And Martin McCracken **Trained** Newmarket, Suffolk

FOCUS
On a card full of decent races, this one is bang up there for producing at least smart 3yo performers, with Kite Wood, Trading Leather and Kingston Hill taking the prize in the previous decade among other classy types. Order Of St George could finish only fifth in 2014. By this stage of the afternoon, all of the field headed down the stands' rail early and that was clearly the best place to be. Quite a positive view has been taken of the bare form.

7149 DUBAI DEWHURST STKS (GROUP 1) (ENTIRE COLTS & FILLIES) 7f
3:30 (3:32) (Class 1) 2-Y-O

£283,550 (£107,500; £53,800; £26,800; £13,450; £6,750) **Stalls** High

Form RPR

1111 **1** **Churchill (IRE)**[27] 6386 2-9-1 0 RyanMoore 3 120+
(A P O'Brien, Ire) *t.k.h early: hld up in tch in midfield: nt clr run and swtchd rt over 1f out: rdn and hdwy to ld jst ins fnl f: styd on strly: rdn out* **8/11**[1]

45 **2** 1 ¼ **Lancaster Bomber (USA)**[27] 6386 2-9-1 0 ColmO'Donoghue 2 115
(A P O'Brien, Ire) *led: rdn 2f out: edgd rt over 1f out: hdd jst ins fnl f: 3rd and onepced 100yds out: kpt on to go 2nd again nr fin: no threat to wnr* **66/1**

1212 **3** ½ **Blue Point (IRE)**[14] 6785 2-9-1 115 WilliamBuick 4 114
(Charlie Appleby) *stdd s: hld up in tch: effrt and hdwy over 1f out: rdn and chal 1f out: nt match pce of wnr and btn 100yds out: lost 2nd nr fin* **8/1**

1622 **4** nk **Thunder Snow (IRE)**[28] 6326 2-9-1 113 JimCrowley 1 113
(Saeed bin Suroor) *chsd ldrs: ev ch 2f out tl unable qck u.p jst ins fnl f: styd on same pce fnl 150yds* **16/1**

211 **5** 1 ½ **Rivet (IRE)**[28] 6326 2-9-1 114 AndreaAtzeni 5 109
(William Haggas) *hld up in tch in midfield: rdn over 2f out: no imp and swtchd rt jst ins fnl f: styd on same pce and no threat to ldrs ins fnl f* **11/1**

111 **6** ¾ **South Seas (IRE)**[49] 5646 2-9-1 106 OisinMurphy 6 107
(Andrew Balding) *chsd ldr: rdn and ev ch 2f out tl no ex jst ins fnl f: wknd fnl 100yds* **15/2**[3]

11 **7** 1 **Seven Heavens**[39] 5997 2-9-1 0 FrankieDettori 7 104
(John Gosden) *stdd s: plld hrd and hld up in tch in rr: effrt over 1f out: no imp and styd on same pce ins fnl f* **7/1**[2]

1m 23.8s (-1.60) **Going Correction** 0.0s/f (Good) **7** Ran SP% **109.0**
Speed ratings (Par 109): **109,107,107,106,104 104,102**
CSF £48.58 TOTE £1.60: £1.10, £9.70; EX 39.60 Trifecta £214.40.
Owner Michael Tabor & Derrick Smith & Mrs John Magnier **Bred** Liberty Bloodstock **Trained** Cashel, Co Tipperary

FOCUS
Despite the near rail having looked the place to be in the first three races, only the rank outsider was positioned against the fence this time, and having been allowed an uncontested lead to boot he rallied for second after looking likely to drop away. He's probably best ignored when assessing this form, although he is well bred and represents top connections. Churchill is the type to do just enough, which tempers his rating.

7150 BETFRED CESAREWITCH (HERITAGE H'CAP) 2m 2f
4:10 (4:18) (Class 2) 3-Y-O+

£155,625 (£46,600; £23,300; £11,650; £5,825; £2,925) **Stalls** Centre

Form RPR

1145 **1** **Sweet Selection**[29] 6284 4-8-8 87 SilvestreDeSousa 23 98
(Hughie Morrison) *chsd ldrs tl rdn to ld over 2f out: styd on strly fr over 1f out: rdn out* **7/1**[2]

0443 **2** 3 **First Mohican**[29] 6283 8-9-0 98 HollieDoyle(5) 16 106
(Alan King) *stdd s: hld up in rr: hdwy over 4f out: rdn to chse ldrs 2f out: chsd wnr jst over 1f out: kpt on same pce ins fnl f* **50/1**

2125 **3** 1 ¼ **Sea Of Heaven (IRE)**[49] 5639 4-9-1 94 AndreaAtzeni 1 101+
(Sir Mark Prescott Bt) *hld up in tch in midfield: hdwy to chse ldrs 5f out: rdn to chse wnr 2f out: sn drvn and no imp: 3rd and kpt on same pce fnl f* **8/1**[3]

0032 **4** ½ **The Cashel Man (IRE)**[21] 6582 4-8-10 89 (b) WilliamBuick 8 95+
(David Simcock) *hld up in rr: rdn and effrt 3f out: hdwy u.p over 1f out: styd on wl ins fnl f: wnt 4th towards fin: no threat to ldrs* **9/1**

0-15 **5** 2 **Golden Spear**[28] 6350 5-8-7 86 (t) TomMarquand 15 90+
(A J Martin, Ire) *hld up in midfield: rdn 3f out: hdwy over 1f out: kpt on ins fnl f: wnt 5th nr fin: nvr trbld ldrs* **16/1**

/0-3 **6** ¾ **Blue Rambler**[35] 6118 6-9-3 99 GeorgeDowning(3) 4 102
(Ian Williams) *t.k.h: chsd ldrs tl led over 3f out: hdd over 2f out: 4th and outpcd over 1f out: wknd ins fnl f: lost 2 pls towards fin* **16/1**

513 **7** ¾ **Yorkidding**[35] 6151 4-9-5 98 AdamKirby 34 100
(Mark Johnston) *hld up towards rr: pushed along 8f out: hdwy u.p over 2f out: kpt on ins fnl f: nvr threatened ldrs* **40/1**

3310 **8** 1 **Star Rider**[30] 6259 4-8-12 91 (p) JimmyFortune 27 92
(Hughie Morrison) *in tch in midfield: clsd and rdn in 4th 3f out: drvn and outpcd ent fnl 2f: wknd ins fnl f* **33/1**

0500 **9** 1 ¼ **Grumeti**[105] 3657 8-8-6 85 MartinLane 7 85
(Alan King) *in tch in midfield: rdn 6f out: drvn 3f out: plugged on same pce after and no threat to ldrs after* **25/1**

-063 **10** 1 **Moonmeister (IRE)**[20] 6608 5-8-7 86 (t) MickaelBarzalona 25 85
(A J Martin, Ire) *in tch in midfield: effrt 3f out: unable qck u.p 2f out: wknd fnl f* **25/1**

1203 **11** 1 ½ **Always Resolute**[22] 6540 5-8-1 80 JimmyQuinn 36 77
(Brian Ellison) *hld up in tch in midfield: effrt u.p 3f out: no imp and btn over 1f out: btn whn short of room ent fnl f: wknd ins fnl f* **50/1**

5203 **12** 1 **Shrewd**[21] 6582 6-9-4 102 DonaghO'Connor(5) 28 98
(Iain Jardine) *hld up in tch in midfield: rdn 3f out: sme modest hdwy over 1f out: plugged on fnl f: nvr trbld ldrs* **40/1**

000 **13** nk **Teak (IRE)**[8] 6919 9-8-1 80 (v) KieranO'Neill 31 76
(Ian Williams) *chsd ldr tl over 3f out: sn u.p and lost pl: wl hld and plugged on same pce u.p fr over 1f out* **100/1**

1305 **14** 2 ¾ **Gabrial's Star**[22] 6540 7-8-9 88 (b) PatDobbs 22 81
(Richard Fahey) *hld up in midfield: pushed along and no imp over 1f out: plugged on to pass btn horses 1f out: nvr trbld ldrs* **100/1**

3003 **15** shd **Angel Gabrial (IRE)**[14] 6781 7-9-7 100 FMBerry 11 92
(Richard Fahey) *hld up in tch: effrt to chse ldrs and rdn over 2f out: drvn and btn over 1f out: wknd and eased ins fnl f* **33/1**

0422 **16** ¾ **Nakeeta**[52] 5559 5-9-6 99 PJMcDonald 21 91+
(Iain Jardine) *hld up in tch in midfield: hdwy to chse ldrs 4f out: rdn over 2f out: sn btn and wknd over 1f out* **20/1**

2113 **17** 1 ¾ **St Michel**[29] 6284 3-8-6 97 4ex (p) LukeMorris 32 91+
(Sir Mark Prescott Bt) *t.k.h: wl in tch in midfield: clsd to chse ldrs 8f out: ev ch and stl on bit 3f out: rdn over 2f out: unable qck and btn over 1f out: wknd and eased ins fnl f* **13/2**[1]

0110 **18** 8 **Mistiroc**[49] 5639 5-9-3 96 (v) MartinHarley 12 77
(John Quinn) *t.k.h: hld up in tch in midfield: rdn over 2f out: sn btn and wknd over 1f out* **50/1**

0000 **19** 6 **The Twisler**[35] 6118 4-9-2 100 CharlieBennett(5) 10 74
(Jane Chapple-Hyam) *hld up in tch towards rr: hmpd over 5f out: effrt over 2f out: no imp and wl hld whn swtchd lft over 1f out: no ch and eased ins fnl f: t.o* **100/1**

0013 **20** 1 ½ **Fun Mac (GER)**[16] 6708 5-9-11 104 4ex (t) JimCrowley 33 77
(Hughie Morrison) *chsd ldrs tl rdn and lost pl over 3f out: bhd 2f out: eased ins fnl f: t.o* **33/1**

6200 **21** 1 ½ **Gabrial The Hero (USA)**[35] 6118 7-9-4 97 PaulHanagan 19 68
(Richard Fahey) *hld up in midfield: lost pl and towards rr whn rdn 3f out: no imp and wl btn over 1f out: eased ins fnl f: t.o* **66/1**

160/ **22** 1 **Ennistown**[40] 7718 6-9-7 100 (t) RyanMoore 29 70
(David Pipe) *stdd s: hld up in rr: hmpd after 2f: short-lived effrt 3f out: eased fnl 2f: t.o* **20/1**

1 **23** ¾ **Starchitect (IRE)**[133] 2699 5-8-10 89 (bt) JamieSpencer 26 58
(David Pipe) *led tl rdn and hdd over 2f out: dropped out qckly over 2f out: eased over 1f out: t.o* **13/2**[1]

0340 **24** 1 ¾ **Mill Springs**[30] 6259 4-9-6 99 FrankieDettori 17 66
(John Gosden) *hld up in tch in midfield: lost pl qckly and rdn 3f out: bhd and eased eased wl over 1f out: t.o* **25/1**

0100 **25** 3 ½ **Wind Place And Sho**[21] 6582 4-8-11 90 RyanTate 14 53
(James Eustace) *hld up in tch in midfield: effrt over 2f out: no hdwy and btn whn hung rt 2f out: sn wknd and eased ins fnl f: t.o* **66/1**

2300 **26** 2 **Modem**[28] 6350 6-8-11 90 (b) ColmO'Donoghue 2 51
(Mrs John Harrington, Ire) *chsd ldrs tl lost pl over 4f out: bhd and eased over 1f out: t.o* **40/1**

0002 **27** 4 **Havana Beat (IRE)**[27] 6379 6-9-1 94 (vt) RobertWinston 35 51
(Rod Millman) *hld up towards rr: short-lived effrt over 2f out: sn wl btn: eased wl over 1f out: t.o* **25/1**

0620 **28** ½ **Oriental Fox (GER)**[29] 6283 8-9-10 103 JoeFanning 6 59
(Mark Johnston) *hld up in midfield: rdn 3f out: sn lost pl and wl btn: eased wl over 1f out: t.o* **16/1**

0000 **29** 12 **My Reward**[35] 6118 4-9-2 95 GrahamLee 20 38
(Tim Easterby) *restless in stalls: hld up in tch in midfield: rdn 3f out: sn lost pl and wl btn: eased over 1f out: t.o* **66/1**

050- **30** 10 **Graasten (GER)**[7] 4-8-5 84 AdamBeschizza 13 16
(Gary Moore) *t.k.h: chsd ldrs tl lost pl 4f out: bhd and eased 2f out: t.o* **50/1**

6051 **P** **Leah Freya (IRE)**[22] 6544 5-8-11 90 4ex JFEgan 5
(Pat Phelan) *hld up in tch in midfield: lost action and p.u over 5f out: fatally injured* **66/1**

500 **P** **The Minch (IRE)**[91] 4164 5-8-13 92 WilliamCarson 9
(Jim Goldie) *hld up in tch: lost pl over 3f out: bhd whn lost action and p.u over 1f out: dismntd* **33/1**

3000 **U** **Seismos (IRE)**[49] 5655 8-9-6 102 MarcMonaghan(3) 18
(Marco Botti) *hld up towards rr: clipped heels, stmbld and uns rdr after 2f* **50/1**

3m 53.41s (1.41) **Going Correction** +0.35s/f (Good)
WFA 3 from 4yo+ 12lb **33** Ran SP% **140.7**
Speed ratings (Par 109): **110,108,108,107,107 106,106,105,105,104 104,103,103,102,102 102,101,97,95,94 93,93,92,92,90 8**
CSF £338.77 CT £2942.83 TOTE £8.50: £2.60, £9.50, £2.90, £2.90; EX 555.50 Trifecta £3065.30.
Owner Paul Brocklehurst **Bred** S A Douch **Trained** East Ilsley, Berks

FOCUS

A terrific handicap full of horses easy to make a case for, even though the trip is one that very few stay properly on the Flat. Indeed, dual-purpose types had a good recent record. The previous four winners went off at 66-1, 66-1, 10-1 and 50-1, illustrating perfectly how open the race generally is and there were umpteen angles to explore in this renewal including runners being really well-in considering their future marks or those who'd got on to a handy official rating - it turned out that one of those 'chucked in' proved much too strong. Seismos unshipped his rider early and steadily made his way to the front of the pack, possibly aiding the winner in the latter stages. The runner-up is the best guide to the form.

7151 GODOLPHIN FLYING START ZETLAND STKS (LISTED RACE) 1m 2f

4:45 (4:57) (Class 1) 2-Y-O

£28,355 (£10,750; £5,380; £2,680; £1,345; £675) **Stalls** High

Form RPR

1 **1** **Coronet**[32] 6206 2-8-11 0.......... FrankieDettori 3 96+
(John Gosden) *s.s: hld up off the pce in last trio: stdy prog on outer over 3f out: clsng whn bmpd over 1f out: shkn up to ld ins fnl f: kpt on wl and a holding on* **3/1**[1]

3443 **2** *nk* **Cunco (IRE)**[35] 6116 2-9-2 97.......... RobertHavlin 10 100
(John Gosden) *trckd ldrs: wnt 2nd over 2f out and sn pressed ldr: upsides 1f out: jst outpcd by wnr but styd on nr fin* **11/1**

2115 **3** *1/2* **Permian (IRE)**[40] 5967 2-9-2 91.......... JoeFanning 4 99
(Mark Johnston) *trckd ldr: led over 2f out: hrd pressed over 1f out: hdd ins fnl f: kpt on wl* **20/1**

4 *3 3/4* **Wings Of Eagles (FR)**[51] 5589 2-9-2 0.......... RyanMoore 9 92+
(A P O'Brien, Ire) *hld up off the pce in last trio: prog 3f out: shkn up and hanging 2f out: trying to cl whn nt clr run briefly over 1f out: tk 4th fnl f but no ch* **10/1**

1131 **5** *3/4* **Fly At Dawn (USA)**[16] 6705 2-9-2 98.......... WilliamBuick 11 91
(Charlie Appleby) *trckd ldrs: rdn and cl up over 2f out tl fdd jst over 1f out* **6/1**[3]

221 **6** *1 1/4* **Star Archer**[37] 6054 2-9-2 90.......... JimCrowley 13 89
(Hugo Palmer) *t.k.h: hld up in midfield: rdn to cl on ldrs over 2f out: wandered over 1f out and sn btn: wknd fnl f* **10/3**[2]

142 **7** *1/2* **Euginio (IRE)**[10] 6868 2-9-2 0.......... SeanLevey 12 88
(Richard Hannon) *trckd ldrs: rdn over 2f out: sn lost pl: steadily wknd over 1f out* **33/1**

43 **8** *1 1/2* **Redicean**[11] 6850 2-9-2 0.......... JimmyFortune 7 85
(Peter Chapple-Hyam) *hld up in last and long way off the pce: sme prog over 2f out: reminder wl over 1f out: nvr on terms but kpt on and nt disgracd* **33/1**

31 **9** *15* **Genetics (FR)**[46] 5740 2-9-2 85.......... OisinMurphy 1 58
(Andrew Balding) *t.k.h: racd on outer and prom: rdn and wknd over 3f out: t.o* **8/1**

0106 **10** *1 1/4* **Arwa (IRE)**[14] 6787 2-8-11 82.......... TomMarquand 8 51
(Charles Hills) *racd on outer: hld up: rdn over 3f out: sn struggling: t.o* **66/1**

12 **11** *2* **Defoe (IRE)**[13] 6801 2-9-2 0.......... AndreaAtzeni 6 52+
(Roger Varian) *racd on outer: in tch to over 3f out: sn wknd: eased over 1f out: t.o* **9/1**

1160 **12** *4* **Bear Valley (IRE)**[16] 6707 2-9-2 93.......... SilvestreDeSousa 5 45+
(Mark Johnston) *led against rail to over 2f out: wknd qckly: heavily eased fnl f: t.o* **16/1**

2m 2.89s (-2.91) **Going Correction** 0.0s/f (Good) 2y crse rec **12** Ran SP% **118.9**
Speed ratings (Par 103): **111,110,110,107,106 105,105,104,92,91 89,86**
CSF £35.68 TOTE £3.90: £2.00, £3.00, £6.50; EX 37.50 Trifecta £1039.80.
Owner Denford Stud **Bred** Denford Stud Ltd **Trained** Newmarket, Suffolk

FOCUS

This event used to be run at the end of October. Again, limited interest from the jockeys in the seemingly favoured near rail. There were plenty of appealing types in this and John Gosden had the one-two, with the winner looking really promising. A pb from the runner-up.

7152 GODOLPHIN STUD AND STABLE STAFF AWARDS DARLEY STKS (GROUP 3) 1m 1f

5:20 (5:34) (Class 1) 3-Y-O+

£45,368 (£17,200; £8,608; £4,288; £2,152; £1,080) **Stalls** High

Form RPR

4031 **1** **Muffri'Ha (IRE)**[7] 6947 4-9-0 105.......... PatCosgrave 6 112
(William Haggas) *t.k.h early: chsd ldr for 2f: styd handy: effrt to chal between horses over 1f out: sn led: styd on strly to assert 100yds out: rdn out* **8/1**

0062 **2** *1 1/2* **Carry On Deryck**[14] 6786 4-9-3 109.......... JimCrowley 3 111
(Saeed bin Suroor) *chsd ldrs tl wnt 2nd after 2f: rdn and ev ch over 1f out tl no ex ins fnl f: outpcd fnl 100yds* **3/1**[2]

421- **3** *1 1/2* **Johannes Vermeer (IRE)**[342] 7665 3-8-13 113..........[1] RyanMoore 1 109
(A P O'Brien, Ire) *stdd s: hld up in tch in midfield: effrt to press ldrs and rdn over 1f out: styd on same pce u.p ins fnl f* **5/2**[1]

2013 **4** *1* **Abdon**[23] 6505 3-8-13 109.......... FrankieDettori 8 107
(Sir Michael Stoute) *t.k.h: hld up in tch in midfield: nt clr run 2f out: effrt to chse ldrs over 1f out: no imp u.p ins fnl f: wknd fnl 75yds* **7/2**[3]

0130 **5** *1/2* **Light Up Our World (IRE)**[54] 5498 3-8-10 103.......... PatDobbs 4 103
(Richard Hannon) *hld up in tch in midfield: effrt 2f out: unable qck and outpcd over 1f out: hld and styd on same pce ins fnl f* **22/1**

6 *shd* **Ancient History (IRE)**[12] 3-8-13 96.......... MickaelBarzalona 5 105
(A Fabre, France) *stdd s: hld up in tch: effrt 2f out: no imp u.p over 1f out: kpt on wl ins fnl f: nvr threatened ldrs* **11/1**

3425 **7** *1* **Custom Cut (IRE)**[15] 6749 7-9-3 112.......... AdamKirby 2 102
(David O'Meara) *led: rdn ent fnl 2f: hdd over 1f out: wknd ins fnl f* **9/1**

2064 **8** *8* **Big Baz (IRE)**[197] 1068 6-9-3 108.......... GrahamLee 7 85
(William Muir) *stdd s: hld up in tch in rr: shkn up 2f out: sn btn: wknd fnl f* **16/1**

1m 51.71s (0.01) **Going Correction** 0.0s/f (Good)
WFA 3 from 4yo+ 4lb **8** Ran SP% **115.5**
Speed ratings (Par 113): **99,97,96,95,95 94,94,86**
CSF £32.62 TOTE £9.20: £2.10, £1.40, £1.30; EX 30.90 Trifecta £167.60.
Owner Sheikh Juma Dalmook Al Maktoum **Bred** Lodge Park Stud **Trained** Newmarket, Suffolk

FOCUS

An ordinary running of this Group 3 and the near rail was again helpful. The winner and second backed up their latest handicap form.

T/Jkpt: Not Won. T/Plt: £84.50 to a £1 stake. Pool: £208,733.66 - 1802.65 winning units T/Qpdt: £19.50 to a £1 stake. Pool: £14,113.01 - 535.4 winning units **Steve Payne & Jonathan Neesom**

7120 YORK (L-H)

Saturday, October 8

OFFICIAL GOING: Good (good to firm in places; 6.9)

Wind: light 1/2 against Weather: fine, sunny intervals

7153 CORAL STKS (H'CAP) 1m

2:00 (2:01) (Class 2) (0-100,94) 3-Y-O

£21,787 (£6,524; £3,262; £1,631; £815; £409) **Stalls** Low

Form RPR

3143 **1** **Weekend Offender (FR)**[14] 6778 3-8-13 **86**.......... TomEaves 5 94+
(Kevin Ryan) *trckd ldrs: hdwy over 2f out: led 11/2f out: rdn and hung lft jst ins fnl f: sn drvn: kpt on wl towards fin* **5/1**[1]

0150 **2** *nk* **Another Touch**[21] 6557 3-9-7 **94**.......... TonyHamilton 4 101
(Richard Fahey) *hld up towards rr: hdwy over 2f out: swtchd lft and effrt over 1f out: rdn to chal ins fnl f: sn drvn and ev ch tl no ex nr fin* **8/1**

4211 **3** *nk* **Just Hiss**[28] 6344 3-9-0 **87**.......... DavidAllan 10 93+
(Tim Easterby) *hld up in rr: hdwy wl over 2f out: chsd ldrs over 1f out: rdn and edgd lft ins fnl f: sn drvn and kpt on* **7/1**[3]

-412 **4** *1 1/4* **Storm Ahead (IRE)**[21] 6585 3-9-5 **92**.......... RoystonFfrench 1 95
(Marcus Tregoning) *trckd ldrs on inner: hdwy 2f out: chal over 1f out: sn rdn and ev ch: drvn and kpt on same pce fnl f* **7/1**[3]

2016 **5** *1/2* **Fighting Temeraire (IRE)**[8] 6918 3-9-6 **93**.......... FrederikTylicki 8 98+
(Dean Ivory) *t.k.h early: hld up in tch: hdwy 2f out: rdn to chse ldrs whn n.m.r and hmpd jst ins fnl f: nt rcvr* **10/1**

-310 **6** *3/4* **Alyday**[84] 4391 3-8-9 **82**.......... TedDurcan 6 83
(Sir Michael Stoute) *trckd ldrs: hdwy over 2f out: rdn wl over 1f out: kpt on same pce* **16/1**

3131 **7** *shd* **Mithqaal (USA)**[15] 6753 3-8-8 **81**.......... AndrewMullen 9 81
(Michael Appleby) *trckd ldrs on outer: pushed along wl over 2f out: rdn wl over 1f out: no imp* **5/1**[1]

-122 **8** *1 3/4* **Shawaahid (IRE)**[29] 6298 3-9-7 **94**.......... DaneO'Neill 7 91
(Richard Hannon) *t.k.h: trckd ldng pair on outer: pushed along over 2f out: rdn wl over 1f out: sn one pce* **6/1**[2]

0136 **9** *3 1/4* **Jimenez (IRE)**[22] 6549 3-8-10 **83**..........(p) PaulMulrennan 3 75
(Brian Meehan) *keen: cl up: slt ld over 4f out: rdn along over 2f out: drvn and hdd 11/2f out: sn wknd* **10/1**

0620 **10** *3/4* **Prosecute (FR)**[13] 6803 3-8-4 **80** oh3.......... EdwardGreatrex[(3)] 11 67
(David Simcock) *dwlt and swtchd lft s: plld hrd and hld up in rr: swtchd rt and hdwy 2f out: sn rdn and hung bdly rt ent fnl f: nvr a factor* **33/1**

0006 **11** *1/2* **King's Pavilion (IRE)**[13] 6803 3-9-1 **88**.......... JamesDoyle 2 81
(Mark Johnston) *slt ld: hdd over 4f out: cl up: and rdn along over 2f out: drvn wl over 1f out: wkng and hld whn hmpd* **20/1**

1m 38.99s (-0.01) **Going Correction** +0.075s/f (Good) **11** Ran SP% **115.5**
Speed ratings (Par 107): **103,102,102,101,100 99,99,98,94,94 93**
CSF £43.87 CT £285.75 TOTE £4.90: £1.90, £2.60, £2.50; EX 48.90 Trifecta £316.50.
Owner Matt & Lauren Morgan **Bred** Mathieu Daguzan-Garros Et Al **Trained** Hambleton, N Yorks

FOCUS

The ground was officially good, good to firm in places and clerk of the course William Derby said: "We had 4mm of rain on Friday but it has been dry since and the forecast is for it to stay dry this afternoon." After riding in the opener Tom Eaves said the ground good, while Ted Durcan said: "There is no firm in it, it is definitely on the easy side" and Dane O'Neill reported: "It is a bit sticky." This was a highly competitive opener. It saw a messy finish after a routine pace, but the form is strong for the class. Race distance reduced by 25yds.

7154 DOWNLOAD THE CORAL APP STKS (H'CAP) 1m 2f 88y

2:35 (2:35) (Class 2) (0-110,104) 3-Y-O+

£21,787 (£6,524; £3,262; £1,631; £815; £409) **Stalls** Low

Form RPR

2120 **1** **Autocratic**[21] 6573 3-8-13 **96**.......... TedDurcan 8 108
(Sir Michael Stoute) *trckd ldrs: hdwy on inner to ld 2f out: sn rdn clr: drvn ins fnl f: kpt on wl towards fin* **11/2**

3112 **2** *1* **Great Order (USA)**[16] 6710 3-9-1 **98**.......... KevinStott 2 108
(Saeed bin Suroor) *t.k.h: trckd ldrs: hdwy on outer over 2f out: rdn to chse wnr ent fnl f and sn edgd lft: sn drvn and ev ch tl kpt on same pce towards fin* **3/1**[1]

2141 **3** *3 1/2* **Central Square (IRE)**[30] 6261 4-9-12 **104**..........(b) PaulMulrennan 7 107
(Roger Varian) *dwlt and hld up in rr: hdwy over 2f out: rdn over 1f out: kpt on fnl f: nrst fin* **4/1**[2]

1422 **4** *hd* **Cote D'Azur**[15] 6753 3-8-13 **96**.......... DavidAllan 1 99
(Les Eyre) *t.k.h: trck ldng pair: hdwy and cl up over 2f out: rdn over 1f out: drvn and wknd fnl f* **5/1**[3]

1061 **5** *2 1/2* **Dolphin Vista (IRE)**[42] 5865 3-9-2 **99**.......... DavidNolan 6 97
(Richard Fahey) *trckd ldr: hdwy and cl up 3f out: rdn along over 2f out: drvn and wknd over 1f out* **9/1**

0002 **6** *3/4* **Fattsota**[16] 6715 8-9-5 **97**.......... JamesDoyle 9 94
(David O'Meara) *set stdy pce: pushed along and qcknd over 3f out: rdn and hdd 2f out: sn drvn and wknd* **14/1**

5000 **7** *1* **Chancery (USA)**[30] 6261 8-9-4 **96**.......... JackGarritty 3 91
(David O'Meara) *in tch: pushed along 3f out: rdn over 2f out: sn btn* **25/1**

6051 **8** *1/2* **Snoano**[21] 6559 4-9-1 **96**.......... RachelRichardson[(3)] 10 90
(Tim Easterby) *dwlt: sn in tch: pushed along wl over 2f out: sn rdn and wknd* **10/1**

2540 **9** *3* **Oasis Fantasy (IRE)**[14] 6786 5-9-7 **104**..........(b) AdamMcNamara[(5)] 5 92
(Ed Dunlop) *dwlt and rr: effrt 3f out: rdn along over 2f out: nvr a factor* **16/1**

2m 11.12s (-1.38) **Going Correction** +0.075s/f (Good)
WFA 3 from 4yo+ 5lb **9** Ran SP% **112.5**
Speed ratings (Par 109): **108,107,104,104,102 101,100,100,98**
CSF £21.65 CT £71.94 TOTE £5.40: £1.90, £1.50, £1.80; EX 20.00 Trifecta £102.00.
Owner Cheveley Park Stud **Bred** Cheveley Park Stud Ltd **Trained** Newmarket, Suffolk

FOCUS

Race distance reduced by 25yds. They went a sound enough pace in this decent handicap and two smart 3yos came clear.

7155 CORAL.CO.UK ROCKINGHAM STKS (LISTED RACE) 6f

3:10 (3:12) (Class 1) 2-Y-O

£28,355 (£10,750; £5,380; £2,680; £1,345; £337) **Stalls** Centre

Form RPR

0113 **1** **Sir Dancealot (IRE)**[16] 6707 2-9-1 103.......... ShaneKelly 13 107+
(David Elsworth) *stdd and swtchd lft s: hld up and bhd: hdwy on bit whn n.m.r and swtchd lft wl over 1f out: smooth hdwy to chal ins fnl f: rdn to ld last 100 yds* **6/1**[2]

13P2 **2** 3/4 **Dream Of Dreams (IRE)**[31] 6228 2-9-1 102........................ KevinStott 6 105
(Kevin Ryan) *led: jnd and rdn over 2f out: drvn over 1f out: hdd last 100 yds: kpt on* **8/1**[3]

2152 **3** 1/2 **Perfect Angel (IRE)**[21] 6572 2-8-10 100.......................... MartinDwyer 3 98
(Andrew Balding) *cl up: chal over 2f out: sn disp ld: rdn over 1f out: drvn and ev ch ins fnl f: edgd lft and no ex last 100 yds* **9/2**[1]

3 **4** 2 1/4 **De Boss Man (IRE)**[41] 5940 2-9-1 0........................ GrahamGibbons 10 97
(M D O'Callaghan, Ire) *chsd ldrs: pushed along 2f out: sn swtchd rt and rdn: kpt on same pce fnl f* **12/1**

1340 **5** 1/2 **Silver Line (IRE)**[14] 6785 2-9-1 106.............................. JamesDoyle 11 95
(Saeed bin Suroor) *chsd ldrs on outer: rdn along wl over 1f out: sn drvn and kpt on same pce* **6/1**[2]

5441 **6** 1 1/4 **Tibr (USA)**[21] 6562 2-9-1 92.. FrederikTylicki 9 91
(Ed Dunlop) *towards rr: hdwy over 2f out: sn rdn: drvn and kpt on fnl f* **33/1**

1 **6** dht **Lost At Sea**[31] 6228 2-9-1 0.. JoeyHaynes 12 91
(K R Burke) *towards rr: hdwy on outer over 2f out: sn rdn: drvn and kpt on fnl f* **6/1**[2]

3631 **8** 1/2 **Smokey Lane (IRE)**[10] 6882 2-9-1 95................................ SamJames 7 90
(David Evans) *trckd ldrs: hdwy 2f out: rdn over 1f out: wknd fnl f* **20/1**

2140 **9** 2 1/4 **Queensbrydge**[21] 6555 2-8-10 87................................... AndrewMullen 8 78
(Robyn Brisland) *a towards rr* **50/1**

1 **10** 1 1/2 **Ernststavroblofeld (USA)**[65] 5084 2-9-1 0................ PaulMulrennan 5 79
(Martyn Meade) *chsd ldrs: rdn along over 2f out: sn wknd* **10/1**

6212 **11** 1/2 **Rosebride**[21] 6555 2-8-10 95.. TonyHamilton 4 72
(Richard Fahey) *a towards rr* **14/1**

21 **12** 10 **Rich And Famous (USA)**[56] 5410 2-9-1 0.............. RichardKingscote 1 47
(Mark Johnston) *chsd ldrs: rdn along over 2f out: sn wknd* **6/1**[2]

1m 12.15s (0.25) **Going Correction** +0.15s/f (Good) **12** Ran SP% **119.5**
Speed ratings (Par 103): **104,103,102,99,98 97,97,96,93,91 90,77**
CSF £52.91 TOTE £7.00: £2.10, £3.30, £1.80; EX 61.40 Trifecta £324.00.
Owner C Benham/ D Whitford/ L Quinn/ K Quinn **Bred** Vincent Duignan **Trained** Newmarket, Suffolk

■ Stewards' Enquiry : Graham Gibbons caution; entered the wrong stall

FOCUS
They went a decent pace in this 2yo Listed sprint and the right horses fought it out. It's usually a strong race for the grade.

7156 CORAL SPRINT TROPHY (H'CAP) 6f
3:45 (3:48) (Class 2) (0-105,102) 3-Y-O+

£62,250 (£18,640; £9,320; £4,660; £2,330; £1,170) **Stalls** Centre

Form RPR

2204 **1** **Intisaab**[7] 6942 5-9-6 **100**...(p) ShelleyBirkett(3) 15 110
(David O'Meara) *hld up towards rr: hdwy over 2f out: styd on wl fnl f: led nr fin* **14/1**

5000 **2** nk **Lexington Abbey**[21] 6556 5-9-1 **92**.................................(b[1]) KevinStott 3 101
(Kevin Ryan) *overall ldr far side: edgd rt fnl f: hdd and no ex nr fin* **12/1**

1213 **3** 1 3/4 **Hoof It**[21] 6558 9-9-4 **100**... NathanEvans(5) 20 103
(Michael Easterby) *racd stands' side: chsd ldrs: edgd rt over 1f out: kpt on to take 3rd nr fin* **14/1**

4410 **4** 1/2 **Pipers Note**[28] 6327 6-9-8 **99**.. JamesSullivan 13 101
(Ruth Carr) *chsd ldrs: edgd rt over 1f out: kpt on wl* **33/1**

2006 **5** nk **Red Pike (IRE)**[18] 6642 5-9-4 **95**................................... ConnorBeasley 8 96
(Bryan Smart) *w ldrs: kpt on same pce fnl f: hmpd 100yds out* **12/1**

0000 **6** hd **George Bowen (IRE)**[21] 6556 4-9-1 **92**........................ TonyHamilton 19 92+
(Richard Fahey) *s.i.s: in rr stands' side: hdwy over 2f out: hmpd and swtchd lft 1f out: kpt on wl* **25/1**

0065 **7** nk **Hoofalong**[21] 6556 6-9-6 **97**..(b) PhillipMakin 14 96
(Michael Easterby) *gave problems loading: in rr: hdwy over 1f out: styng on at fin* **25/1**

0011 **8** 1 **Roudee**[21] 6556 4-9-10 **101**.. RichardKingscote 18 97
(Tom Dascombe) *chsd ldrs stands' side: hdwy over 1f out: keeping on at fin* **20/1**

0063 **9** shd **Ninjago**[12] 6837 6-9-1 **92**... DougieCostello 10 88
(Paul Midgley) *s.i.s: hld up towards rr: hdwy over 1f out: keeping on at fin* **20/1**

1332 **10** 3/4 **Get Knotted (IRE)**[21] 6556 4-9-7 **98**..........................(p) PaulMulrennan 6 91
(Michael Dods) *chsd ldrs: one pce over 1f out* **6/1**[2]

6604 **11** 3/4 **Mayfair Lady**[14] 6792 3-9-5 **102**........................... AdamMcNamara(5) 17 93
(Richard Fahey) *racd stands' side: mid-div: kpt on fnl f: nvr a factor* **22/1**

4160 **11** dht **Snap Shots (IRE)**[14] 6792 4-9-1 **92**...........................(p) BarryMcHugh 12 83
(Tony Coyle) *s.i.s: in rr: sme hdwy over 1f out: nvr a factor* **33/1**

2001 **13** 3/4 **Mythmaker**[25] 6449 4-9-6 **97**... TomEaves 7 86
(Bryan Smart) *w ldrs: wknd fnl 150yds* **16/1**

3030 **14** 3/4 **Sir Robert Cheval**[21] 6558 5-9-5 **99**......................... LouisSteward(3) 16 85
(Robert Cowell) *mid-div: effrt over 2f out: one pce* **33/1**

0030 **15** shd **Poyle Vinnie**[21] 6558 6-9-8 **99**.................................... AndrewMullen 4 85
(Michael Appleby) *mid-div: hdwy to chse ldrs over 1f out: wknd last 150yds* **25/1**

2141 **16** nk **Normandy Barriere (IRE)**[29] 6287 4-8-12 **96**......... LewisEdmunds(7) 9 81
(Nigel Tinkler) *towards rr: hdwy over 1f out: nvr a factor* **7/1**[3]

0-66 **17** 3/4 **Orvar (IRE)**[149] 2192 3-9-4 **96**.. JamesDoyle 2 78
(Robert Cowell) *chsd ldrs towards far side: wknd 1f out* **33/1**

-100 **18** 4 1/2 **Teruntum Star (FR)**[21] 6558 4-9-7 **98**........................(b[1]) ShaneGray 11 66
(Kevin Ryan) *w ldrs: wknd appr fnl f: eased clsng stages* **33/1**

0200 **19** 1/2 **Suzi's Connoisseur**[7] 6942 5-9-8 **99**........................(v) FrederikTylicki 5 65
(Stuart Williams) *mid-div towards far side: lost pl over 1f out: eased clsng stages* **16/1**

4U31 **20** 6 **Captain Colby (USA)**[28] 6327 4-9-10 **101**..................(b) GeorgeBaker 1 48
(Ed Walker) *chsd ldrs far side: drvn over 2f out: wknd and heavily eased 1f out* **3/1**[1]

1m 11.24s (-0.66) **Going Correction** +0.15s/f (Good)
WFA 3 from 4yo+ 1lb **20** Ran SP% **132.4**
Speed ratings (Par 109): **110,109,107,106,106 105,105,104,104,103 102,102,101,100,99 99,98,92,91,83**
CSF £156.84 CT £2447.56 TOTE £16.80: £3.50, £4.00, £1.90, £7.40; EX 273.70 Trifecta £5214.00.
Owner Stuart Graham **Bred** Shadwell Estate Company Limited **Trained** Upper Helmsley, N Yorks

■ Stewards' Enquiry : Nathan Evans two-day ban; careless riding (24th-25th Oct)
Kevin Stott caution; careless riding
Shelley Birkett two-day ban; used her whip above the permitted level (24th-25th Oct)

FOCUS
A highly competitive sprint handicap. The main action came down the centre.

7157 CORAL.CO.UK EBF STALLIONS MAIDEN STKS (PLUS 10 RACE) 7f
4:20 (4:26) (Class 3) 2-Y-O **£9,703** (£2,887; £1,443; £721) **Stalls** Low

Form RPR

43 **1** **Gulliver**[149] 2193 2-9-5 0..(bt[1]) JamesDoyle 1 84
(Hugo Palmer) *trckd ldrs: cl up 1/2-way: led over 2f out: rdn clr over 1f out: edgd lft ins fnl f: kpt on* **4/1**[2]

2 1 **Dubai Horizon (IRE)** 2-9-5 0.. KevinStott 7 81+
(Saeed bin Suroor) *in tch: pushed along 3f out: hdwy 2f out: rdn over 1f out: chsd wnr: green and edgd lft ins fnl f: kpt on* **4/1**[2]

3 2 **Mojito (IRE)** 2-9-5 0.. GeorgeBaker 9 76+
(William Haggas) *rr: hdwy on wd outside over 2f out: rdn over 1f out: styd on strly fnl f* **3/1**[1]

3 **4** 1 **Nancy Hart**[22] 6548 2-9-0 0.. RichardKingscote 11 69
(Tom Dascombe) *led: pushed along and hdd over 2f out: sn rdn: drvn and kpt on same pce fnl f* **20/1**

5 1 3/4 **Tai Sing Yeh (IRE)** 2-9-5 0..................................... MichaelJMMurphy 3 70+
(Charles Hills) *towards rr: gd hdwy whn nt clr run and hmpd over 1f out: sn swtchd lft and kpt on wl fnl f* **20/1**

32 **6** 1/2 **Etikaal**[17] 6673 2-9-5 0... DaneO'Neill 4 68
(Simon Crisford) *trckd ldrs: hdwy over 2f out: rdn wl over 1f out: grad wknd* **3/1**[1]

7 1/2 **Mulzim** 2-9-5 0... FrederikTylicki 8 66
(Ed Dunlop) *chsd ldrs: rdn along 2f out: wknd over 1f out* **20/1**

64 **8** nse **Tawaafoq**[56] 5410 2-9-5 0... TomEaves 5 66
(Richard Hannon) *prom: cl up over 2f out: rdn along wl over 1f out: grad wknd* **12/1**[3]

5 **9** 1/2 **Aelius**[34] 6162 2-9-5 0.. GrahamGibbons 6 65
(Michael Easterby) *dwlt and rr: pushed along wl over 2f out: sn rdn and kpt on appr fnl f* **16/1**

0 **10** 4 **Fox King**[17] 6672 2-9-5 0.. JohnFahy 12 55
(Ralph Beckett) *chsd ldrs: rdn along 3f out: sn wknd* **33/1**

33 **11** 1/2 **Buccaneers Cove (IRE)**[17] 6679 2-9-5 0.................. TonyHamilton 13 53
(Richard Fahey) *chsd ldrs on outer: rdn along wl over 2f out: sn wknd* **16/1**

12 3 **Spirit Of Rome (IRE)** 2-9-0 0...................................... DougieCostello 2 41
(James Bethell) *dwlt: a rr* **33/1**

4 **13** 1/2 **Fleetfoot Jack (IRE)**[17] 6679 2-9-5 0.............................. PhillipMakin 10 44
(David O'Meara) *a towards rr* **22/1**

1m 26.4s (1.10) **Going Correction** +0.15s/f (Good) **13** Ran SP% **134.0**
Speed ratings (Par 99): **99,97,95,94,92 91,91,91,90,86 85,82,81**
CSF £20.99 TOTE £4.50: £1.70, £2.40, £1.70; EX 24.00 Trifecta £38.50.
Owner Saleh Al Homaizi & Imad Al Sagar **Bred** S A Douch **Trained** Newmarket, Suffolk

FOCUS
A 2yo maiden that ought to produce plenty of future winners.

7158 CORAL STAYERS STKS (H'CAP) 2m 88y
4:55 (4:55) (Class 4) (0-85,84) 4-Y-O+ **£9,703** (£2,887; £1,443; £721) **Stalls** Low

Form RPR

-063 **1** **Gleese The Devil (IRE)**[14] 6773 5-9-0 **77**.................. GeorgeChaloner 7 86
(Richard Fahey) *in tch: hdwy over 4f out: cl up 3f out: rdn and slt ld 11/2f out: drvn ent fnl f: kpt on gamely towards fin* **11/2**[2]

4565 **2** nk **Aldreth**[23] 6503 5-7-13 **67**..(b) NathanEvans(5) 11 76
(Michael Easterby) *in tch: hdwy over 4f out: slt ld 3f out: sn jnd and rdn: hdd narrowly 11/2f out: drvn to dispute ld ent fnl f: ev ch tl no ex towards fin* **10/1**

0603 **3** 4 1/2 **Dawn Missile**[23] 6526 4-9-7 **84**.. GeorgeBaker 4 87+
(William Haggas) *hld up and bhd: hdwy over 3f out: chsd ldrs 2f out: sn rdn and kpt on fnl f* **15/8**[1]

2130 **4** 1 1/4 **Stormin Tom (IRE)**[22] 6540 4-8-12 **78**................ RachelRichardson(3) 6 80
(Tim Easterby) *trckd ldng pair: hdwy and cl up over 3f out: chsd ldng pair over 2f out and sn rdn: drvn over 1f out: kpt on same pce* **12/1**

6144 **5** 9 **Itlaaq**[15] 6740 10-8-11 **81**.......................................(t) DanielleMooney(7) 12 72
(Michael Easterby) *hld up and bhd: hdwy over 4f out: rdn along to chse ldrs over 2f out: sn drvn and no imp* **12/1**

2003 **6** 2 1/4 **Odeon**[25] 6457 5-9-2 **79**.. TomEaves 10 67
(James Given) *trckd ldrs: hdwy over 4f out: cl up 3f out: sn rdn and btn* **16/1**

0311 **7** 4 1/2 **Bertie Moon**[20] 5334 6-9-2 **84**.......................................(p) CliffordLee(5) 3 67
(Lydia Pearce) *trckd ldr: hdwy over 4f out: cl up over 3f out: sn rdn along and wknd* **8/1**

4540 **8** shd **Wordiness**[8] 6919 8-9-0 **77**.. MichaelJMMurphy 8 60
(David Evans) *led: rdn along 4f out: hdd 3f out and sn wknd* **14/1**

0200 **9** 2 **Waterclock (IRE)**[34] 6163 7-8-7 **70**..................................(p) JoeyHaynes 5 50
(Micky Hammond) *reminders after s and sn bhd: effrt 5f out: sn drvn along nvr a factor* **20/1**

0520 **10** 1 **Planetoid (IRE)**[21] 6582 8-9-4 **81**................................(b) DougieCostello 1 60
(Jim Best) *a towards rr: outpcd and bhd fnl 3f* **16/1**

51 **11** 11 **Flower Power**[14] 6795 5-9-2 **79**..................................... BarryMcHugh 2 45
(Tony Coyle) *a towards rr: outpcd and bhd fnl 3f* **7/1**[3]

3m 33.24s (-1.26) **Going Correction** +0.075s/f (Good) **11** Ran SP% **121.4**
Speed ratings (Par 105): **106,105,103,102,98 97,95,95,94,93 88**
CSF £61.65 CT £143.28 TOTE £6.30: £2.10, £3.60, £1.20; EX 73.10 Trifecta £381.10.
Owner Dr Marwan Koukash **Bred** K And Mrs Cullen **Trained** Musley Bank, N Yorks

■ Stewards' Enquiry : Nathan Evans two-day ban; used whip in the incorrect place (26th-27th Oct)

FOCUS
Race distance reduced by 25yds. They didn't hang about in this modest staying handicap and only two mattered inside the final furlong.

7159 COLDSTREAM GUARDS ASSOCIATION CUP (H'CAP) 1m 2f 88y
5:30 (5:31) (Class 4) (0-85,89) 3-Y-O+ **£9,703** (£2,887; £1,443; £721) **Stalls** Low

Form RPR

062 **1** **Novelty Seeker (USA)**[92] 4113 7-9-6 **81**.................. GrahamGibbons 10 93
(Michael Easterby) *trckd ldrs: led over 3f out: hung lft 1f out: drvn rt out* **20/1**

0413 **2** 2 1/4 **Marsh Pride**[13] 6811 4-9-5 **85**... CliffordLee(5) 3 92
(K R Burke) *hld up in mid-div: t.k.h: hdwy 3f out: kpt on to take 2nd last 75yds* **6/1**[2]

0321 **3** 1 1/4 **Hibou**[7] 6957 3-9-9 **89**...(b) TomEaves 13 94+
(Iain Jardine) *hld up towards rr: stdy hdwy over 3f out: 2nd over 1f out: n.m.r and swtchd rt 1f out: kpt on same pce* **4/1**[1]

1-34 **4** 1 3/4 **Richie McCaw**[24] 6484 3-8-11 **77**................................... JamesDoyle 19 78
(Ian Williams) *swtchd lft after s: chsd ldrs: 2nd and drvn 3f out: kpt on one pce over 1f out* **4/1**[1]

3033 **5** *1* **Stardrifter**[23] 6521 4-8-11 **72**.. GeorgeChaloner 8 71
(Richard Fahey) *mid-div: effrt over 3f out: kpt on same pce fnl f* **16/1**

6560 **6** *1* **Dance King**[21] 6559 6-9-7 **85**........................(tp) RachelRichardson(3) 17 82
(Tim Easterby) *s.i.s: in rr: kpt on fnl 2f: nvr a factor* **14/1**

5341 **7** *1 ¾* **Carnageo (FR)**[40] 5975 3-8-11 **77**.................................. TonyHamilton 6 71
(Richard Fahey) *chsd ldrs: drvn 3f out: one pce and edgd rt over 1f out* **9/1**[3]

6066 **8** *nk* **Eurystheus (IRE)**[10] 6876 7-9-4 **79**..........................(tp) FrederikTylicki 15 72
(Michael Appleby) *chsd ldrs: drvn 3f out: one pce* **33/1**

4045 **9** *¾* **Outback Blue**[28] 6323 3-8-10 **76**..(t) ShaneKelly 7 67
(David Evans) *hld up in rr: effrt over 3f out: kpt on one pce: nvr a factor* **14/1**

0000 **10** *2 ½* **Off Art**[7] 6957 6-9-3 **78**...(p) DavidAllan 4 64
(Tim Easterby) *chsd ldrs: wknd over 1f out* **12/1**

2505 **11** *3* **Intiwin (IRE)**[17] 6684 4-8-12 **73**...................................... BarryMcHugh 18 53
(Richard Fahey) *mid-div: effrt 3f out: wknd appr fnl f* **20/1**

4316 **12** *nse* **Purple Rock (IRE)**[34] 6160 4-8-13 **79**.....................(t) NathanEvans(5) 14 59
(Michael Easterby) *trckd ldrs: effrt 3f out: lost pl over 1f out* **14/1**

5004 **13** *4 ½* **Dubai Dynamo**[7] 6957 11-9-8 **83**................................ JamesSullivan 12 54
(Ruth Carr) *s.i.s: a towards rr* **33/1**

2202 **14** *3 ¾* **Sunglider (IRE)**[14] 6795 3-8-11 **77**.................................. PhillipMakin 1 41
(David O'Meara) *hld up towards rr: sme hdwy over 3f out: lost pl over 1f out* **25/1**

2061 **15** *nk* **Save The Bees**[10] 6876 8-9-2 **82**...................................(b) PhilDennis(5) 9 45
(Declan Carroll) *led: styd far side over 4f out: hdd over 3f out: wknd over 2f out* **20/1**

3500 **16** *2* **Tapis Libre**[23] 6517 8-9-1 **81**.. MeganNicholls(5) 2 40
(Jacqueline Coward) *detached in last: pushed along 6f out: nvr on terms* **50/1**

43-5 **17** *3* **Cadeau Magnifique**[51] 5579 4-8-8 **76**..................... NatalieHambling(7) 5 29
(Richard Fahey) *in rr: sme hdwy over 3f out: lost pl 2f out* **14/1**

0630 **18** *26* **Berlusca (IRE)**[23] 6517 7-9-4 **84**.......................... CallumShepherd(5) 11
(Lawrence Mullaney) *s.i.s: rapid hdwy on wd outside after 2f: 2nd and hung rt over 6f out: lost placxe 3f out: bhd whn heavily eased over 1f out: eventually completed: t.o.* **66/1**

2m 10.52s (-1.98) **Going Correction** +0.075s/f (Good)
WFA 3 from 4yo+ 5lb **18 Ran SP% 132.0**
Speed ratings (Par 105): **110,108,107,105,105 104,102,102,101,99 97,97,93,90,90 89,86,65**
CSF £134.56 CT £604.54 TOTE £28.20: £4.80, £2.10, £1.80, £1.50; EX 223.40 Trifecta £2197.30 Part Won..
Owner B Padgett **Bred** Darley **Trained** Sheriff Hutton, N Yorks

FOCUS
Race distance reduced by 25yds. This fair handicap was run at a sound pace and the principals came clear.
T/Plt: £57.90 to a £1 stake. Pool: £119,686.0 - 2066.83 winning units T/Qpdt: £27.80 to a £1 stake. Pool: £6,928.0 - 248.66 winning units **Joe Rowntree & Walter Glynn**

7160 - 7167a (Foreign Racing) - See Raceform Interactive

6986 CHANTILLY (R-H)
Saturday, October 8

OFFICIAL GOING: Turf: good; polytrack: standard

7168a PRIX DU PASSAGE (CONDITIONS) (3YO) (POLYTRACK) 1m 110y
1:05 (12:00) 3-Y-O **£10,661** (£4,264; £3,198; £2,132; £1,066)

RPR

1 **Atlantic Sun**[54] 5472 3-9-4 0.................................. GregoryBenoist 1 99
(Richard Hannon) **33/10**[3]

2 *snk* **Secret Existence (IRE)**[46] 3-8-6 0.......................... IoritzMendizabal 4 87
(F Chappet, France) **7/5**[1]

3 *snk* **Never Caught (USA)**[187] 1240 3-8-9 0........................ MaximeGuyon 2 90
(A Fabre, France) **33/10**[3]

4 *¾* **Onlyjim (FR)**[21] 6596 3-8-9 0.. CristianDemuro 3 88
(P Bary, France) **13/5**[2]

5 *6* **Miss Terre (FR)**[297] 3-8-6 0... AurelienLemaitre 6 72
(F-X De Chevigny, France) **31/1**

WIN (incl. 1 euro stake): 4.30. PLACES: 1.80, 1.30. SF: 9.30
Trained East Everleigh, Wilts **Bred** D J Weston **Owner** Middleham Park Racing XLV

7169a PRIX DE CONDE (GROUP 3) (2YO) (TURF) 1m 1f
2:45 (12:00) 2-Y-O **£29,411** (£11,764; £8,823; £5,882; £2,941)

RPR

1 **Frankuus (IRE)**[35] 6116 2-8-11 0................................ IoritzMendizabal 3 103
(Mark Johnston) **42/10**[3]

2 *nk* **Prinz Hlodowig (FR)**[34] 2-8-11 0............................ VincentCheminaud 5 102
(M Delzangles, France) **11/1**

3 *shd* **Waldgeist**[30] 2-8-11 0.. Pierre-CharlesBoudot 1 102
(A Fabre, France) **6/5**[1]

4 *4* **High Alpha (FR)**[30] 6270 2-8-11 0.............................. ChristopheSoumillon 4 94
(Mario Hofer, Germany) **6/4**[2]

5 *2 ½* **Upendi (FR)**[20] 2-8-8 0... GregoryBenoist 2 86
(Robert Collet, France) **16/1**

1m 51.62s (0.52) **5 Ran SP% 118.9**
WIN (incl. 1 euro stake): 5.20. PLACES: 3.10, 4.70. SF: 34.10.
Owner Hussain Lootah & Ahmad Al Shaikh **Bred** Ballylinch Stud **Trained** Middleham Moor, N Yorks

7170a CRITERIUM DE VITESSE (LISTED RACE) (2YO) (TURF) 5f
3:15 (12:00) 2-Y-O **£23,897** (£9,558; £7,169; £4,779; £2,389)

RPR

1 **Becquamis (FR)**[54] 5497 2-8-13 0.................................. AntoineWerle 6 98
(T Lemer, France) **164/10**

2 *¾* **Hyper Hyper**[26] 6431 2-8-13 0.............................. ChristopheSoumillon 3 95
(Mario Hofer, Germany) **66/10**[3]

3 *shd* **Megan Lily (IRE)**[14] 6763 2-8-9 0................................. ThierryJarnet 5 91
(Richard Fahey) **15/1**

4 *snk* **Rainbow Mist (IRE)**[7] 6954 2-8-13 0........................... GeraldMosse 11 94
(Ann Duffield) **14/5**[1]

5 *1 ¾* **Vona (IRE)**[27] 6388 2-9-0 0.................................... Pierre-CharlesBoudot 7 89
(Richard Fahey) **47/10**[2]

6 *1 ¼* **Creme De Cremes (FR)**[18] 2-8-9 0......................(b[1]) AntoineHamelin 12 80
(Matthieu Palussiere, France) **45/1**

7 *nk* **Mister Art (IRE)**[18] 2-8-13 0...................................(b) EddyHardouin 9 83
(Matthieu Palussiere, France) **9/1**

8 *1 ½* **Cheries Amours (FR)**[5] 2-8-9 0.................................... MaximeGuyon 8 73
(T Castanheira, France) **10/1**

9 *¾* **Star Washwasha (IRE)**[26] 2-8-9 0............................ AurelienLemaitre 1 70
(E J O'Neill, France) **18/1**

10 *¾* **Morigane Forlonge (FR)**[18] 2-8-9 0......................(p) CristianDemuro 2 68
(A Giorgi, Italy) **16/1**

11 *2 ½* **Hamadryade**[17] 2-8-9 0... TonyPiccone 4 59
(F Chappet, France) **18/1**

12 *2 ½* **Nofoemaypass (FR)**[51] 2-8-13 0.................................. AlexisBadel 10 54
(H-F Devin, France) **67/10**

57.79s (-0.51) **12 Ran SP% 119.7**
WIN (incl. 1 euro stake): 17.40. PLACES: 5.60, 2.70, 4.00. DF: 73.80. SF: 171.40.
Owner Mme Virginie Becquart **Bred** B Becquart, R Schlienger, P Schlienger & J-P Mesna **Trained** France

7135 KEENELAND (L-H)
Saturday, October 8

OFFICIAL GOING: Dirt: fast; turf: firm

7171a FIRST LADY STKS (GRADE 1) (3YO+ FILLIES & MARES) (TURF) 1m
9:35 (12:00) 3-Y-O+

£163,265 (£54,421; £27,210; £13,605; £8,163; £1,088)

RPR

1 **Photo Call (IRE)**[35] 5-8-12 0................................ KentJDesormeaux 10 115+
(Todd Pletcher, U.S.A) **30/1**

2 *2 ¾* **Tepin (USA)**[21] 6601 5-8-12 0....................................... JulienRLeparoux 2 119+
(Mark Casse, Canada) **2/5**[1]

3 *3 ½* **Celestine (USA)**[119] 3178 4-8-12 0................................ JuniorAlvarado 8 111+
(William Mott, U.S.A) **33/10**[2]

4 *3* **Nemoralia (USA)**[29] 6281 3-8-9 0....................................... JoeBravo 5 104+
(Jeremy Noseda) **176/10**

5 *½* **She's Not Here (USA)**[35] 5-8-12 0...........................(b) JoseLezcano 1 103+
(Victoria H Oliver, U.S.A) **83/1**

6 *1 ¼* **Cash Control (USA)**[35] 5-8-12 0............................. ShaunBridgmohan 3 100+
(Brad H Cox, U.S.A) **47/1**

7 *2* **Onus (USA)**[28] 4-8-12 0.. JoseLOrtiz 9 95+
(Claude McGaughey III, U.S.A) **158/10**[3]

8 *½* **Now Or Never (IRE)**[28] 6352 3-8-9 0.................................. LuisSaez 4 94+
(M D O'Callaghan, Ire) **222/10**

9 *1 ½* **Secret Someone (USA)**[35] 5-8-12 0............................. RobbyAlbarado 7 91+
(Michael Stidham, U.S.A) **49/1**

10 *7 ¾* **Mississippi Delta (USA)**[27] 4-8-12 0............................ CoreyJLanerie 6 73+
(Mark Casse, Canada) **71/1**

1m 35.62s (95.62)
WFA 3 from 4yo+ 3lb **10 Ran SP% 120.2**
PARI-MUTUEL (all including 2 usd stake): WIN 61.40; PLACE (1-2) 10.60, 2.20; SHOW (1-2-3) 5.60, 2.10, 2.40; SF 184.80.
Owner Teresa Viola Racing Stables **Bred** Mrs Evie Stockwell **Trained** USA

7172a SHADWELL TURF MILE STKS (GRADE 1) (3YO+) (TURF) 1m
10:45 (12:00) 3-Y-O+

£408,163 (£136,054; £68,027; £34,013; £20,408; £2,268)

RPR

1 **Miss Temple City (USA)**[42] 5914 4-8-11 0........................ EdgarSPrado 7 112
(H Graham Motion, U.S.A) **77/10**[3]

2 *hd* **Ironicus (USA)**[119] 3180 5-9-0 0....................................... JoseLOrtiz 8 115+
(Claude McGaughey III, U.S.A) **3/1**[1]

3 *½* **Tourist (USA)**[49] 5-9-0 0...(b) JoseLezcano 10 114
(William Mott, U.S.A) **26/5**[2]

4 *1* **Mondialiste (IRE)**[56] 5431 6-9-0 0................................. DanielTudhope 4 112
(David O'Meara) **3/1**[1]

5 *½* **Kasaqui (ARG)**[56] 5431 6-9-0 0.................................... RobbyAlbarado 6 110
(Ignacio Correas IV, U.S.A) **153/10**

6 *nse* **Pleuven (FR)**[33] 5-9-0 0.. CoreyJLanerie 2 110
(Philip A Sims, U.S.A) **63/1**

7 *hd* **Ring Weekend (USA)**[33] 5-9-0 0...........................(b) JuniorAlvarado 9 110
(H Graham Motion, U.S.A) **99/10**

8 *1* **What A View (USA)**[182] 5-9-0 0.......................(b) KentJDesormeaux 11 108
(Kenneth D Black, U.S.A) **41/5**

9 *1* **Grand Arch (USA)**[49] 7-9-0 0.. LuisSaez 5 105
(Brian A Lynch, Canada) **111/10**

10 *4 ¾* **Tower Of Texas (CAN)**[21] 6601 5-9-0 0.................(b) JulienRLeparoux 3 94
(Roger L Attfield, Canada) **194/10**

11 *7* **Triple Threat (FR)**[97] 6-9-0 0.......................................(b) PacoLopez 1 78
(William Mott, U.S.A) **54/1**

1m 37.04s (97.04) **11 Ran SP% 120.3**
PARI-MUTUEL (all including 2 usd stake): WIN 17.40; PLACE (1-2) 8.20, 4.60; SHOW (1-2-3) 5.40, 3.00, 4.00; SF 90.40.
Owner The Club Racing Llc, Allen Rosenblum & Sagamore Fa **Bred** Bobfeld Bloodstock **Trained** USA

7173 - 7182a (Foreign Racing) - See Raceform Interactive

6663 GOODWOOD (R-H)
Sunday, October 9

OFFICIAL GOING: Good (good to soft in places; 7.2)
Wind: Light, half behind Weather: Cloudy

7183 EVE TRAKWAY ALDERBROOK STKS (H'CAP) (TO BE RIDDEN BY PROFESSIONAL NATIONAL HUNT JOCKEYS) 2m
2:00 (2:00) (Class 4) (0-80,79) 4-Y-O+ **£6,469** (£1,925; £962; £481) **Stalls** Low

Form RPR

232 **1** **Arthur Mc Bride (IRE)**[20] 6634 7-11-12 **79**...................(t) DaveCrosse 14 88
(Nigel Twiston-Davies) *trckd ldr after 4f and sn upsides: led over 4f out: sn kicked for home and 3 l clr: drvn 2f out: stl 3 l up ins fnl f: jst hld on* **7/1**[2]

10/4 **2** *hd* **Harry Hunt**[142] 922 9-11-11 **78**.. KielanWoods 2 86
(Graeme McPherson) *wl in tch: prog 4f out: rdn 3f out: tk 3rd 2f out and 2nd jst ins fnl f whn 3 l down: clsd towards fin: jst failed* **16/1**

10-2 **3** 3 1/4 **Major Mac**[22] 6561 4-11-7 **74**..........(p) TomO'Brien 5 78
(Hughie Morrison) *cl up: chsd wnr over 3f out and sn rdn: no imp and lost 2nd jst ins fnl f: one pce* **9/2**[1]

0602 **4** 1 **Be My Sea (IRE)**[28] 6362 5-11-12 **79**..........(p) GavinSheehan 3 82
(Tony Carroll) *s.i.s: sn settled in midfield: rdn on outer 3f out: kpt on fnl 2f but nvr able to chal* **9/2**[1]

0-31 **5** 1 3/4 **Guards Chapel**[124] 1450 8-11-0 **67**..........(v) AndrewGlassonbury 12 68
(Gary Moore) *s.i.s: hld up in last trio: prog over 4f out: rdn 3f out: tried to cl 2f out but one pce after* **33/1**

1445 **6** 3/4 **Voice Control (IRE)**[47] 5745 4-11-3 **70**.......... MarcGoldstein 13 70
(Laura Mongan) *hld up in midfield: rdn on outer over 3f out: trying to cl over 1f out but hanging rt: one pce after* **28/1**

0-5 **7** shd **Barizan (IRE)**[23] 6544 10-11-7 **74**..........(v) AdamWedge 8 74
(Brendan Powell) *hld up towards rr: rdn over 3f out: kpt on one pce fr over 2f out: n.d* **25/1**

-360 **8** 1 1/2 **Mr Fickle (IRE)**[11] 6886 7-11-2 **69**..........(v) JoshuaMoore 9 67
(Gary Moore) *hld up in last: nt gng wl fr 1/2-way: effrt u.p on outer over 3f out: plugged on but nvr a real threat* **10/1**[3]

1665 **9** 5 **Atalan**[61] 5267 4-11-1 **68**.......... JakeGreenall 11 60
(Hughie Morrison) *sn hld up in midfield: rdn over 3f out: no prog 2f out: wknd over 1f out* **12/1**

325 **10** 6 **Starcrossed**[95] 4012 4-11-0 **67**..........(b) DavidBass 6 52
(Eve Johnson Houghton) *hld up in rr: prog over 5f out: rchd midfield and rdn 3f out: wknd 2f out* **14/1**

1353 **11** 4 1/2 **Megara**[16] 6740 4-11-6 **73**..........(v[1]) MichealNolan 16 52
(Sir Mark Prescott Bt) *pressed ldrs to 3f out: wknd qckly and eased* **14/1**

115- **12** 8 **Night Generation (GER)**[63] 7250 4-11-10 **77**..........(p) TomCannon 10 47
(Chris Gordon) *pressed ldr 4f: pushed along and lost pl 6f out: wknd over 3f out: t.o* **25/1**

003/ **13** nk **Carry On Sydney**[152] 7431 6-11-8 **75**.......... LeightonAspell 15 44
(Oliver Sherwood) *hld up in last trio: rdn and lost tch 4f out: t.o* **20/1**

6111 **14** 3/4 **Rosie Royale (IRE)**[29] 6315 4-11-5 **72**.......... RichieMcLernon 7 40
(Roger Teal) *nvr bttr than midfield: dropped to rr 6f out: struggling 4f out: t.o* **12/1**

215- **15** 8 **Bold Runner**[163] 7474 5-11-8 **75**..........(p) TrevorWhelan 4 34
(Jose Santos) *led but pressed: hdd over 4f out: wknd qckly over 3f out: eased and t.o* **7/1**[2]

3m 33.74s (4.74) **Going Correction** +0.05s/f (Good) **15** Ran SP% **123.9**
Speed ratings (Par 105): **90,89,88,87,86 86,86,85,83,80 77,73,73,73,69**
CSF £108.27 CT £571.32 TOTE £7.60: £2.90, £4.80, £2.30; EX 111.80 Trifecta £723.80.
Owner John Gaughan & Rob Rexton **Bred** Pat Kinsella **Trained** Naunton, Gloucs

FOCUS
Race distances as advertised. The going was described as good, good to soft in places with a GoingStick reading of 7.2. It had been dry since 9pm the previous night after 2.5mm of rain fell at the track during the day. A wide open race for jump jockeys in which seven of the 15 runners had finished in the first three on their most recent starts. They went a good gallop form the off and very few were able to get competitive, with those who raced up with pace filling the places.

7184 EVE TRAKWAY MAIDEN AUCTION STKS 6f
2:35 (2:36) (Class 5) 2-Y-O £5,175 (£1,540; £769; £384) **Stalls** High

Form RPR

1 **Gold Award (IRE)** 2-8-10 0.......... SilvestreDeSousa 10 73+
(Mick Channon) *in tch: rdn and prog wl over 1f out: chsd ldr ins fnl f: drvn and r.o to ld last 75yds: won gng away* **10/1**

454 **2** 1 **Black Bubba (IRE)**[73] 4790 2-8-11 66.......... JFEgan 9 71
(David Evans) *led: pressed over 1f out: edgd rt but kpt on wl: hdd and outpcd last 75yds* **20/1**

6 **3** 2 **Liberatum**[132] 2748 2-8-12 0..........[1] JimCrowley 8 66
(Hugo Palmer) *cl up: trckd ldr 2f out: rdn to chal over 1f out: btn off and lost 2nd ins fnl f: one pce* **9/2**[3]

34 **4** 1 1/2 **No Not Again (IRE)**[16] 6750 2-8-13 0.......... PatDobbs 7 63
(Richard Hannon) *trckd ldrs: chsd ldng pair wl over 1f out: sn shkn up and ot qckn: lost 3rd and outpcd fnl f* **11/4**[1]

5 1 **Ferocity (IRE)** 2-8-3 0.......... DavidEgan[(7)] 6 57
(Robyn Brisland) *t.k.h: hld up in tch: outpcd and rdn 2f out: rn green after but kpt on fnl f* **9/1**

533 **6** 4 **Wind In Her Sails (IRE)**[28] 6369 2-8-7 73.......... PaulHanagan 1 42
(Giles Bravery) *chsd ldr to 2f out: wknd over 1f out* **3/1**[2]

50 **7** 1 1/4 **Kohinoor Diamond (IRE)**[17] 6696 2-8-8 0.......... LukeMorris 3 39
(Sir Mark Prescott Bt) *in tch: shkn up 2f out: wknd over 1f out* **25/1**

8 1 1/4 **Bahamian Paradise** 2-8-6 0.......... JohnFahy 2 33
(Hughie Morrison) *swvd bdly rt s: detached in last pair: nvr a factor* **25/1**

44 **9** 3 1/2 **Desert Fox**[28] 6369 2-8-10 0.......... ShaneGray 5 27
(Mike Murphy) *t.k.h and hld up in tch: stmbld sltly after 100yds: pushed along and wknd qckly wl over 1f out: eased* **6/1**

10 4 **Sniper Viper** 2-8-4 0..........(b[1]) KieranO'Neill 4 9
(Daniel Kubler) *rn v green and sn wl detached in last: nvr a factor* **66/1**

1m 12.41s (0.21) **Going Correction** -0.075s/f (Good) **10** Ran SP% **117.2**
Speed ratings (Par 95): **95,93,91,89,87 82,80,79,74,69**
CSF £190.03 TOTE £10.10: £2.60, £4.20, £1.80; EX 139.80 Trifecta £552.20.
Owner Insignia Racing (Medallion) **Bred** Airlie Stud **Trained** West Ilsley, Berks

FOCUS
A modest maiden for the track.

7185 IRISH STALLION FARMS EBF NURSERY STKS (H'CAP) 7f
3:10 (3:11) (Class 4) (0-85,85) 2-Y-O £6,469 (£1,925; £962; £481) **Stalls** Low

Form RPR

210 **1** **Colonel Frank**[23] 6536 2-9-1 **79**.......... JimCrowley 2 84
(Ed Walker) *t.k.h: pressed ldr: clr of rest 2f out: rdn to ld 1f out and hanging rt: 2 l ahd 75yds out: hld on* **10/3**[2]

6531 **2** 3/4 **Fareeq**[16] 6743 2-8-12 **76**..........(t) PaulHanagan 8 79
(William Haggas) *dwlt: settled in last: rdn over 2f out and no prog: stl last whn taken to wd outside over 1f out: rapid prog fnl f: tk 3rd last 75yds and clsd on wnr fin* **8/1**

356 **3** 1 **Mullarkey**[18] 6672 2-8-7 **71**.......... KierenFox 7 71
(John Best) *racd wd: towards rr: rdn 2f out: prog jst over 1f out: styd on wl fnl f to take 3rd nr fin* **33/1**

132 **4** 1/2 **Fields Of Song (IRE)**[20] 6630 2-8-12 **76**.......... ShaneGray 3 75
(Kevin Ryan) *led: pressed by wnr 2f out but clr of rest: hdd 1f out and impeded sn after: kpt on but lost 2 pls last 75yds* **9/2**[3]

4351 **5** nk **Procurator (IRE)**[44] 5829 2-9-4 **82**.......... SeanLevey 4 80
(Richard Hannon) *hld up in tch: waiting for a run over 2f out: rdn and prog to chse ldng pair jst ins fnl f: kpt on wl but lost 2 pls last 75yds* **3/1**[1]

3415 **6** 3/4 **Double Touch**[24] 6499 2-9-7 **85**.......... DavidNolan 5 81
(Richard Fahey) *wl in tch: rdn and prom in chsng gp 2f out: no imp after: one pce* **8/1**

1063 **7** 3/4 **Mr Hobbs**[18] 6664 2-8-8 **77**.......... MitchGodwin[(5)] 9 71
(Sylvester Kirk) *t.k.h: hld up towards rr: gd run through on inner over 2f out and prog to chse ldng pair over 1f out: no imp and fdd fnl f* **12/1**

0324 **8** nk **Darkroom Angel**[20] 6630 2-8-5 **69**.......... LukeMorris 10 62
(Clive Cox) *nvr bttr than midfield: rdn 2f out: n.m.r after but kpt on at same pce* **20/1**

250U **9** 1/2 **Lexington Sky (IRE)**[8] 6954 2-8-13 **77**.......... KieranO'Neill 1 69
(Richard Hannon) *t.k.h: trckd ldng pair: outpcd 2f out: lost 3rd over 1f out: fdd* **33/1**

4106 **10** 1 1/2 **Whiteley (IRE)**[51] 5598 2-8-1 **65**.......... JimmyQuinn 11 53
(Mick Channon) *stdd s and hld up fr wd draw: tried to make prog on inner 2f out: one pce and no real hdwy* **40/1**

10 **11** 3/4 **Santafiora**[30] 6292 2-8-9 **76**..........[1] KieranShoemark[(3)] 13 62
(Roger Charlton) *stdd s and dropped in fr wd draw: t.k.h in rr: shkn up over 2f out: nvr much room but nt gng wl enough to pose a threat* **25/1**

5402 **12** 3/4 **Herm (IRE)**[30] 6275 2-8-7 **71** ow2.......... JFEgan 12 55
(David Evans) *racd wd: nvr beyond midfield: struggling 2f out: wknd* **25/1**

606 **13** 7 **Lawfilly**[20] 6625 2-7-9 **66**.......... DavidEgan[(7)] 6 31
(Richard Hughes) *t.k.h: chsd ldrs: lost pl 2f out: racd in wayward fashion and wknd qckly fnl f* **20/1**

1m 28.07s (1.07) **Going Correction** +0.05s/f (Good) **13** Ran SP% **121.7**
Speed ratings (Par 97): **95,94,93,92,92 91,90,90,89,87 86,86,78**
CSF £27.78 CT £792.44 TOTE £4.20: £1.70, £2.70, £9.30; EX 33.70 Trifecta £449.20.
Owner Mrs Fitri Hay **Bred** Eliza Park International Pty Ltd **Trained** Upper Lambourn, Berks

FOCUS
A good race for the grade and one which could produce a few winners in time.

7186 "HAPPY BIRTHDAY TONY PANNETT" STKS (H'CAP) 6f
3:45 (3:45) (Class 3) (0-95,95) 3-Y-O+ £9,703 (£2,887; £1,443; £721) **Stalls** High

Form RPR

4105 **1** **Lady Macapa**[36] 6119 3-9-5 **94**.......... JimCrowley 8 104
(William Knight) *mde all in centre: def advantage fr 4f out: rdn over 1f out: hrd pressed fnl f: kpt on gamely* **14/1**

0522 **2** 3/4 **Lightning Charlie**[11] 6883 4-8-9 **86**.......... KieranShoemark[(3)] 1 94
(Amanda Perrett) *hld up towards rr: prog 1/2-way: rdn to go 2nd over 1f out: chal ins fnl f: kpt on but hld nr fin* **7/1**[3]

332 **3** 1/2 **Ice Age (IRE)**[22] 6583 3-8-4 **82**.......... EdwardGreatrex[(3)] 4 88
(Eve Johnson Houghton) *hld up towards rr: prog over 2f out: chsd ldng pair over 1f out: styd on but nvr able to chal* **6/1**[2]

112 **4** 1/2 **Boy In The Bar**[15] 6792 5-9-0 **88**..........(v[1]) SilvestreDeSousa 9 93
(Ian Williams) *prom: rdn to chse wnr over 2f out: no imp and lost 2nd over 1f out: kpt on* **4/1**[1]

0050 **5** 1 **Joey's Destiny (IRE)**[127] 2898 6-9-0 **88**.......... SteveDrowne 5 90
(George Baker) *towards rr: nt clr run briefly over 2f out: rdn and kpt on fr over 1f out: nvr able to threaten* **14/1**

5365 **6** nk **Charles Molson**[15] 6788 5-9-0 **93**..........(p) MitchGodwin[(5)] 15 94
(Patrick Chamings) *swtchd to r in centre after 150yds: in midfield after: rdn and no prog 2f out: kpt on fnl f: nrst fin* **10/1**

2000 **7** 1 1/4 **Grandad's World (IRE)**[23] 6539 4-8-10 **84**.......... PaulHanagan 12 81
(Richard Fahey) *chsd wnr in centre to over 2f out: steadily lost pl* **16/1**

4260 **8** nse **Rosie's Premiere (IRE)**[31] 6263 4-8-12 **86**..........(bt[1]) RobertWinston 2 82
(Dean Ivory) *dwlt: wl in rr: rdn over 2f out: one pce and no imp ldrs over 1f out* **10/1**

0116 **9** 1/2 **Lincoln (IRE)**[15] 6779 5-9-7 **95**.......... GrahamLee 13 90
(Mick Channon) *hld up towards rr: rdn and no real prog 2f out: kpt on one pce after* **8/1**

5100 **10** 2 **Links Drive Lady**[31] 6263 8-8-9 **86**.......... JackDuern[(3)] 6 74
(Dean Ivory) *dwlt: a in rr: rdn and no real prog 2f out* **33/1**

1004 **11** nk **Cartmell Cleave**[20] 6627 4-9-0 **88**.......... TedDurcan 3 76
(Stuart Kittow) *dwlt: wl in rr: rdn over 2f out: no great prog and nvr on terms* **10/1**

3010 **12** nk **Little Palaver**[31] 6263 4-9-1 **89**.......... AdamKirby 14 76
(Clive Cox) *led pair on nr side but nt on terms: n.d over 1f out* **25/1**

3100 **13** 2 **Highly Sprung (IRE)**[9] 6916 3-9-1 **90**.......... JoeFanning 16 70
(Mark Johnston) *chsd rival nr side: nvr on terms w main gp* **25/1**

5004 **14** 3 **Englishman**[15] 6780 6-8-11 **85**.......... LukeMorris 11 56
(Milton Bradley) *prom in chsng gp to 2f out: wknd* **16/1**

5100 **15** 5 **Ice Lord (IRE)**[22] 6556 4-9-2 **90**..........(b[1]) JohnFahy 10 45
(Clive Cox) *prom in chsng gp to 1/2-way: lost pl qckly over 2f out: bhd fnl f* **25/1**

1m 10.53s (-1.67) **Going Correction** -0.075s/f (Good)
WFA 3 from 4yo+ 1lb **15** Ran SP% **124.7**
Speed ratings (Par 107): **108,107,106,105,104 103,102,102,101,98 98,98,95,91,84**
CSF £107.58 CT £684.25 TOTE £15.20: £4.30, £2.80, £2.50; EX 161.00 Trifecta £823.40.
Owner Fromthestables.com Racing V **Bred** Peter Winkworth **Trained** Patching, W Sussex
■ Stewards' Enquiry : Paul Hanagan two-day ban: used whip above permitted level (Oct 24-25)

FOCUS
A whole host of in-form runners clashed in this fiercely competitive sprint, where those who raced towards the far side came out on top.

7187 HILDON WATER IRISH EBF MAIDEN STKS (PLUS 10 RACE) 1m 1f
4:20 (4:20) (Class 4) 2-Y-O £6,469 (£1,925; £962; £481) **Stalls** Low

Form RPR

2 **1** **Monarchs Glen**[18] 6663 2-9-5 0.......... FrankieDettori 1 85+
(John Gosden) *led after 1f then t.k.h: clr over 2f out: pushed along fr over 1f out: nvr in serious danger after* **1/3**[1]

2 1 1/4 **Pealer (GER)** 2-9-5 0.......... RobertHavlin 10 83+
(John Gosden) *hld up in 6th and off the pce: prog over 2f out gng wl: chsd clr wnr over 1f out: shkn up and clsd fnl f but nvr able to chal* **10/1**

3 4 1/2 **Count Octave** 2-9-5 0.......... OisinMurphy 7 74
(Andrew Balding) *t.k.h early: trckd ldng pair after 3f: shkn up to dispute 2nd briefly over 1f out: outpcd after: jst hld on for 3rd* **4/1**[2]

4 nk **Really Super** 2-9-0 0.......... FMBerry 5 68
(Ralph Beckett) *hld up in last pair and wl off the pce: pushed along and sme prog over 2f out: styd on wl fnl f and nrly snatched 3rd* **20/1**

4 **5** 5 **Mach One**[38] 6059 2-9-5 0.......... AdamKirby 9 63
(Clive Cox) *rn green early and rousted to chse wnr after 1f: rdn 3f out: lost 2nd and wknd over 1f out* **9/1**[3]

6 2 3/4 **Nobleman (GER)** 2-9-5 0.......... JimmyFortune 2 57
(Hughie Morrison) *hld up off the pce in 6th: briefly threatened to cl over 2f out: wknd over 1f out* **33/1**

06 **7** 1/2 **Reynardo De Silver**[40] 5990 2-9-2 0..........(p) HectorCrouch[(3)] 6 56
(Gary Moore) *led 1f: styd cl up tl wknd 2f out* **100/1**

8 4 1/2 **Tomsamcharlie** 2-9-5 0.......... TimmyMurphy 11 47
(Gary Moore) *sn in last: lost tch 1/2-way and virtually t.o: passed two eased rivals fnl f* **50/1**

9 *8* **Black Prince (FR)** 2-9-5 0... JFEgan 3 31
(Anthony Honeyball) *a in rr: rdn 4f out: sn no ch: eased over 1f out: t.o* **25/1**

10 *9* **Magic Beans** 2-9-5 0... JimCrowley 4 13
(Hughie Morrison) *a in rr: rdn wl over 3f out: sn no ch: eased over 1f out: t.o* **16/1**

1m 56.73s (0.43) **Going Correction** +0.05s/f (Good) **10** Ran SP% **134.5**
Speed ratings (Par 97): **100,98,94,94,90 87,87,83,76,68**
CSF £6.70 TOTE £1.30: £1.10, £2.70, £1.50; EX 7.30 Trifecta £16.30.
Owner K Abdullah **Bred** Juddmonte Farms Ltd **Trained** Newmarket, Suffolk

FOCUS
An informative maiden featuring a couple of potentially useful performers.

7188 GOODWOOD RACEHORSE OWNERS GROUP STKS (H'CAP) 1m 4f
4:50 (4:52) (Class 2) (0-100,96) 3-Y-O+ **£19,407** (£5,775; £2,886; £1,443) **Stalls** High

Form RPR

0010 **1** **Soldier In Action (FR)**[71] 4863 3-9-5 **94**......................... JoeFanning 10 108
(Mark Johnston) *trckd ldng pair: led over 2f out: urged along and steadily drew rt away fr over 1f out* **12/1**

231 **2** *6* **Higher Power**[109] 3525 4-9-0 **87**......................... GeorgeWood(5) 9 93
(James Fanshawe) *hld up disputing 7th: effrt on inner whn nt clr run briefly wl over 2f out: hdwy wl over 1f out: r.o fnl f to take 2nd last stride* **13/2**

4053 **3** *shd* **Pinzolo**[79] 4583 5-9-11 **93**......................... SilvestreDeSousa 2 97
(Ismail Mohammed) *trckd ldng pair: chal over 2f out: chsd wnr after: hanging and lft bhd over 1f out: fdd fnl f and lost 2nd last stride* **8/1**

-401 **4** *1 ½* **Mengli Khan (IRE)**[18] 6675 3-9-7 **96**......................... JimCrowley 5 98
(Hugo Palmer) *trckd ldr: led over 3f out to over 2f out: qckly outpcd: steadily fdd over 1f out* **11/4**[1]

331 **5** *½* **Southdown Lad (IRE)**[23] 6545 3-9-5 **94**......................... MartinHarley 1 95
(William Knight) *hld up disputing 5th: gng wl enough over 3f out: rdn and nt qckn over 2f out: ch of a pl 1f out: one pce after* **5/1**[3]

2122 **6** *1 ¼* **Rex Bell (IRE)**[15] 6775 3-9-2 **91**.........................(p) FrankieDettori 8 90
(John Gosden) *hld up disputing 7th: rdn over 3f out: sme prog u.p 2f out and ch of a pl 1f out: fdd* **7/2**[2]

3066 **7** *11* **Missed Call (IRE)**[29] 6332 6-9-8 **90**......................... FrederikTylicki 3 71
(James Fanshawe) *hld up disputing 5th: rdn over 3f out: sn btn: bhd over 1f out* **14/1**

43 **8** *1 ¼* **Jacob Cats**[37] 6074 7-9-3 **85**.........................(v) KierenFox 11 64
(William Knight) *s.s: wl bhd in last early and tk little interest: nvr a factor* **33/1**

/240 **9** *27* **Flight Officer**[22] 6559 5-9-9 **91**......................... OisinMurphy 4 27
(Saeed bin Suroor) *led to over 3f out: wknd rapidly and eased: t.o* **20/1**

2m 36.41s (-1.99) **Going Correction** +0.05s/f (Good)
WFA 3 from 4yo+ 7lb **9** Ran SP% **112.1**
Speed ratings (Par 109): **108,104,103,102,102 101,94,93,75**
CSF £84.22 CT £662.17 TOTE £14.50: £3.60, £2.00, £2.50; EX 91.20 Trifecta £516.50.
Owner A D Spence **Bred** Randolf Peters **Trained** Middleham Moor, N Yorks

FOCUS
With three last-time-out winners and a trio of horses who had made the frame on their last outing, this race looked like it would take plenty of winning but in the end it was all one-way traffic.

7189 SEASON FINALE STKS (H'CAP) 1m
5:20 (5:20) (Class 4) (0-85,85) 3-Y-O+ **£6,469** (£1,925; £962; £481) **Stalls** Low

Form RPR

0543 **1** **Dark Devil (IRE)**[16] 6736 3-9-2 **83**......................... DavidNolan 12 90
(Richard Fahey) *wl plcd bhd ldr: wnt 2nd 2f out: rdn to chal over 1f out: pressed ldr after: led last 100yds: drvn and hld on wl* **6/1**[2]

4446 **2** *nk* **Fast Dancer (IRE)**[14] 6806 4-9-4 **82**......................... JFEgan 8 88
(Joseph Tuite) *hld up towards rr: rdn and gd prog on wd outside jst over 2f out: hung rt over 1f out but sn rdn to ld: narrowly hdd last 100yds: nt qckn after* **12/1**

2102 **3** *1 ¼* **Force (IRE)**[11] 6877 3-9-2 **83**......................... FrankieDettori 13 86
(Charles Hills) *t.k.h: in tch on outer: prog 2f out: hmpd over 1f out: renewed effrt to chse ldng pair ins fnl f: kpt on but nvr cl enough to chal* **12/1**

500 **4** *nk* **Czech It Out (IRE)**[74] 4758 6-9-7 **85**......................... JimCrowley 3 87
(Amanda Perrett) *wl plcd on inner: rdn 2f out: kpt on to take 4th ins fnl f but nvr pce to chal* **4/1**[1]

0366 **5** *1 ½* **Essenaitch (IRE)**[22] 6576 3-7-12 **72**......................... DavidEgan(7) 1 71
(David Evans) *racd freely: led at decent pce: hdd over 1f out: fdd fnl f* **11/1**

0422 **6** *1* **Mister Music**[30] 6300 7-9-3 **81**......................... PatDobbs 11 78
(Tony Carroll) *hld up in last: limited prog over 2f out: nt clr run briefly over 1f out: rdn and kpt on fnl f: nrst fin but no ch* **7/1**[3]

1225 **7** *nk* **Reaver (IRE)**[20] 6628 3-9-1 **82**......................... CharlesBishop 7 78
(Eve Johnson Houghton) *hld up wl in rr: prog over 2f out to chse ldrs over 1f out: rdn and no imp after: fdd last 100yds* **10/1**

-511 **8** *¾* **Unison (IRE)**[50] 5649 6-9-1 **79**......................... SilvestreDeSousa 2 73
(Jeremy Scott) *chsd ldr: rdn 3f out: lost 2nd 2f out: cl up but hld whn hmpd over 1f out: one pce after* **4/1**[1]

0450 **9** *2 ¾* **Guiding Light (IRE)**[14] 6806 4-9-2 **80**.........................(b[1]) OisinMurphy 14 68
(Andrew Balding) *racd on outer: cl up: shkn up whn short of room briefly over 2f out: n.d after: fdd fnl f* **40/1**

0645 **10** *5* **Royal Reserve**[18] 6675 3-8-12 **79**......................... MartinDwyer 6 55
(William Muir) *nvr bttr than midfield: rdn and no prog over 2f out: sn wknd* **14/1**

0000 **11** *hd* **Red Avenger (USA)**[20] 6628 6-9-1 **79**.........................(v) JimmyFortune 4 55
(Gary Moore) *awkward s and slowly away: sn in tch: rdn on inner over 2f out: wknd wl over 1f out* **11/1**

2021 **12** *1 ½* **Big Chill (IRE)**[26] 6441 4-8-6 **75**......................... MitchGodwin(5) 5 48
(Patrick Chamings) *chsd ldrs: rdn wl over 2f out: losing pl whn bdly hmpd over 1f out: wknd and eased* **16/1**

4000 **13** *3 ¾* **Secret Glance**[27] 6416 4-9-2 **80**......................... AdamBeschizza 10 44
(Richard Rowe) *a in rr: shkn up and no prog 3f out: sn struggling* **66/1**

1m 39.4s (-0.50) **Going Correction** +0.05s/f (Good)
WFA 3 from 4yo+ 3lb **13** Ran SP% **124.4**
Speed ratings (Par 105): **104,103,102,102,100 99,99,98,95,90 90,89,85**
CSF £79.62 CT £858.66 TOTE £7.70: £2.70, £3.50, £2.80; EX 93.80 Trifecta £624.10.
Owner Arnold, Leitao, Woodward & Wrigley **Bred** Yeomanstown Stud **Trained** Musley Bank, N Yorks

■ Stewards' Enquiry : J F Egan two-day ban: careless riding (Oct 26-27)

FOCUS
An open finale.
T/Jkpt: Not Won. T/Plt: £434.50 to a £1 stake. Pool: £122548.86, 205.88 winning units. T/Qpdt: £46.80 to a £1 stake. Pool: £11819.87, 186.7 winning units. **Jonathan Neesom**

7190 - (Foreign Racing) - See Raceform Interactive

6814 CURRAGH (R-H)
Sunday, October 9

OFFICIAL GOING: Straight course - good to yielding; round course - good

7191a ELMER HANNON TRAVEL WATERFORD TESTIMONIAL STKS (LISTED RACE) 6f
2:40 (2:40) 3-Y-O+

£19,522 (£6,286; £2,977; £1,323; £661; £330)

RPR

1 **Shanghai Glory (IRE)**[32] 6232 3-9-5 94......................... WilliamBuick 2 105
(Charles Hills) *broke wl to ld narrowly tl sn hdd and settled bhd ldrs: hdwy far side to ld over 1f out and sn edgd sltly lft u.p: kpt on wl* **14/1**

2 *1* **Master Speaker (IRE)**[7] 6984 6-9-6 97.................(bt) ColmO'Donoghue 4 102+
(Martin Hassett, Ire) *w.w: 11th 1/2-way: rdn 1 1/2f out and r.o wl ins fnl f into nvr nrr 2nd on line: nt trble wnr* **12/1**

3 *hd* **Bebhinn (USA)**[14] 6816 3-9-0 102......................... ChrisHayes 3 96
(Kevin Prendergast, Ire) *mid-div: pushed along after 1/2-way and prog far side u.p over 1f out to chse ldrs: rdn into 2nd wl ins fnl f and no imp on wnr clsng stages: denied 2nd on line* **11/1**

4 *hd* **G Force (IRE)**[22] 6558 5-9-6 101......................... PatSmullen 14 101
(Adrian Paul Keatley, Ire) *chsd ldrs: cl 4th at 1/2-way: impr to chal 1 1/2f out: no imp on wnr u.p in 2nd ins fnl f: no ex clsng stages where dropped to 4th* **10/3**[1]

5 *½* **Byzantium**[45] 5816 4-9-1 88.........................(v[1]) RobbieDowney 1 94
(Edward Lynam, Ire) *dwlt sltly and towards rr: hdwy far side after 1/2-way: rdn under 2f out and clsd u.p ins fnl f: nvr trbld ldrs* **50/1**

6 *shd* **Nameitwhatyoulike**[22] 6558 7-9-7 107......................... ConnorBeasley 8 102
(Bryan Smart) *sn disp and led narrowly after 1f: rdn under 2f out and hdd between horses over 1f out: sn sltly hmpd and no ex bhd ldrs ins fnl f: one pce clsng stages* **11/2**[3]

7 *½* **Fort Del Oro (IRE)**[14] 6816 4-9-4 103......................... BillyLee 9 95
(Edward Lynam, Ire) *chsd ldrs: disp 5th at 1/2-way: gng wl bhd ldrs after 1/2-way: swtchd lft under 2f out and sn tk clsr order: rdn in 5th ins fnl f and sn no ex: one pce clsng stages* **7/2**[2]

8 *nk* **In Salutem**[14] 6816 6-9-6 104.........................(t) ShaneFoley 12 96
(K J Condon, Ire) *in tch: 8th 1/2-way: pushed along under 2f out: rdn over 1f out and nt clr run ins fnl f: eased clsng stages* **8/1**

9 *1 ¼* **Flight Risk (IRE)**[7] 6983 5-9-6 108.........................(t) KevinManning 7 92
(J S Bolger, Ire) *chsd ldrs: disp 2nd at 1/2-way: rdn 2f out and sn short of room: swtchd lft bhd ldrs over 1f out and nt clr run briefly: one pce after and eased in 8th clsng stages* **6/1**

10 *3 ½* **Peticoatgovernment (IRE)**[14] 6819 3-9-0 84.................. LeighRoche 5 76
(W McCreery, Ire) *settled in rr: pushed along after 1/2-way and sme hdwy u.p into 10th over 1f out: one pce fnl f* **33/1**

11 *1 ¼* **Time To Reason (IRE)**[9] 6931 3-9-5 97......................... ColinKeane 11 77
(J P Murtagh, Ire) *in tch: 7th 1/2-way: rdn nr side under 2f out and no imp ent fnl f: wknd* **25/1**

12 *1* **Peacehaven (IRE)**[42] 5942 4-9-1 79.........................(t) NGMcCullagh 6 69
(J P Murtagh, Ire) *towards rr thrght: rdn under 2f out and no imp ent fnl f* **50/1**

13 *2 ¼* **Tribal Path (IRE)**[7] 6984 6-9-6 87.........................(t) RoryCleary 10 67
(Damian Joseph English, Ire) *cl up: disp cl 2nd and pushed along at 1/2-way: rdn and wknd over 2f out* **33/1**

14 *1 ½* **Miss Elizabeth (IRE)**[147] 2272 3-9-0 97......................... WayneLordan 13 57
(Edward Lynam, Ire) *mid-div: pushed along fr 1/2-way and wknd to rr under 2f out* **25/1**

1m 14.21s (-1.29) **Going Correction** -0.125s/f (Firm)
WFA 3 from 4yo+ 1lb **14** Ran SP% **126.3**
Speed ratings: **103,101,101,101,100 100,99,99,97,92 91,89,86,84**
CSF £168.93 TOTE £16.80: £2.60, £4.10, £3.90; DF 234.20 Trifecta £3176.80.
Owner Kangyu Int Racing (HK) Ltd & F Ma **Bred** Owenstown Stud **Trained** Lambourn, Berks

FOCUS
Another valuable Irish sprint for export here, with victory going to a 94-rated British-trained handicapper. The second and fourth help with the standard.

7193a STAFFORDSTOWN STUD STKS (LISTED RACE) (FILLIES) 1m
3:50 (3:50) 2-Y-O

£20,389 (£6,566; £3,110; £1,382; £691; £345)

RPR

1 **Calare (IRE)**[50] 5703 2-9-0 0......................... JamesDoyle 1 98
(Charlie Appleby) *chsd ldrs: 3rd 1/2-way: rdn over 2f out where bmpd sltly: nt clr run over 1f out and swtchd lft in 3rd: clsd u.p ins fnl f where looked rt briefly to ld cl home where edgd sltly rt* **8/1**

2 *¾* **Bound (IRE)**[21] 6602 2-9-0 84......................... ColmO'Donoghue 8 96
(A P O'Brien, Ire) *sn led on outer: narrow advantage at 1/2-way: over 1 l clr 3f out: rdn over 2f out and sn strly pressed: jnd and hdd under 2f out: regained ld wl ins fnl f tl hdd cl home* **8/1**

3 *¾* **Queen Anne's Lace (USA)**[21] 6602 2-9-0 0......................... PatSmullen 6 96
(D K Weld, Ire) *chsd ldrs: 4th 1/2-way: gng wl bhd ldrs into st and impr on outer into 2nd 2f out where edgd sltly rt: sn rdn to ld narrowly tl hdd ins fnl f: no ex in 3rd cl home where sltly hmpd* **11/8**[1]

4 *3* **Kazimiera**[79] 4579 2-9-0 0......................... WilliamBuick 2 88
(Charlie Appleby) *disp early tl sn settled bhd ldr: cl 2nd at 1/2-way: pushed along 3f out and sltly hmpd between horses 2f out: sn rdn in 4th and no imp on ldrs ins fnl f: kpt on one pce* **7/2**[3]

5 *2 ½* **Butterflies (IRE)**[42] 5937 2-9-0 99......................... DonnachaO'Brien 4 82
(A P O'Brien, Ire) *disp early tl sn settled bhd ldrs: 5th 1/2-way: rdn in 5th over 2f out and sn no ex: one pce fnl f* **3/1**[2]

6 *1 ¾* **Chelsea Corsage (IRE)**[9] 6930 2-9-0 76......................... ChrisHayes 7 78
(A Oliver, Ire) *towards rr: 6th 1/2-way: rdn in 6th over 2f out and no imp on ldrs: one pce after* **66/1**

7 *16* **Rooney O'Mara**[6] 7019 2-9-0 0......................... NGMcCullagh 3 41
(W M Roper, Ire) *in rr thrght: pushed along fr 1/2-way and no imp into st: nvr a factor* **80/1**

1m 44.95s (-1.05) **Going Correction** -0.175s/f (Firm) **7** Ran SP% **114.3**
Speed ratings: **98,97,96,93,91 89,73**
CSF £67.77 TOTE £10.90: £2.90, £3.80; DF 70.30 Trifecta £198.60.
Owner Godolphin **Bred** Darley **Trained** Newmarket, Suffolk

FOCUS
Nothing special about this Listed event which was contested by four previous winners and three maidens. The most memorable incident came early in the final furlong when the winner. Calare appeared to snap at Queen Anne's Lace before edging right and going on about her business.

7195a TOTE IRISH CESAREWITCH (PREMIER H'CAP) 2m
4:55 (4:55) 3-Y-0+

£43,382 (£13,970; £6,617; £2,941; £1,470; £735)

RPR

1 **Laws Of Spin (IRE)**[66] 5094 3-8-6 **89**.....(t) ChrisHayes 97
(W P Mullins, Ire) *chsd ldrs: 5th 3f out: impr to chal u.p in 2nd over 1f out: led 1f out and kpt on wl ins fnl f* **7/1**[2]

2 1 1/4 **Cradle Mountain (IRE)**[7] 4771 4-9-0 **89**.....(tp) DonnachaO'Brien(3) 96
(Joseph Patrick O'Brien, Ire) *towards rr and pushed along early: reminders after 1/2-way: clsr in 11th 3f out: clsd u.p to chse ldrs in 5th over 1f out and r.o wl into 2nd wl ins fnl f: nvr on terms* **16/1**

3 1/2 **Swamp Fox (IRE)**[26] 4721 4-8-13 **85**.....(b) WayneLordan 91
(Joseph G Murphy, Ire) *in tch: tk clsr order 4f out: cl 4th 3f out and impr travelling wl to ld over 2f out: sn rdn and strly pressed: hdd 1f out and no imp on wnr wl ins fnl f where dropped to 3rd* **7/1**[2]

4 2 3/4 **Artful Artist (IRE)**[52] 5591 7-8-12 **84**.....(t) ShaneFoley 87
(A J Martin, Ire) *mid-div: 10th 3f out: prog fr 2f out to chse ldrs u.p in 6th ent fnl f: kpt on ins fnl f: nvr trbld ldrs* **12/1**

5 nk **Jennies Jewel (IRE)**[14] 6820 9-9-12 **98**..... RonanWhelan 101
(Jarlath P Fahey, Ire) *sn led tl hdd bef 1/2-way: pushed along appr st to regain narrow advantage 3f out: rdn and hdd over 2f out and no imp on ldrs u.p in 5th 1f out: kpt on same pce* **14/1**

6 nk **Rashaan (IRE)**[26] 6043 4-8-12 **84**..... NGMcCullagh 87
(Colin Kidd, Ire) *chsd ldrs: cl 3rd 3f out: rdn 2f out and no ex u.p in 4th 1f out: one pce after* **16/1**

7 3 **Pyromaniac (IRE)**[29] 6350 6-9-1 **92**.....(tp) OisinOrr(5) 91
(A J Martin, Ire) *w.w towards rr early: gng wl in 7th fr 3f out: rdn under 2f out and u.p in 6th over 1f out: one pce fnl f* **6/1**[1]

8 1 3/4 **Benkei (IRE)**[14] 6820 6-9-11 **97**.....(t) KevinManning 95
(H Rogers, Ire) *hld up towards rr: sme late hdwy fr over 2f out into mod 9th over 1f out: kpt on one pce* **25/1**

9 nk **Alton Bay (IRE)**[22] 6582 8-9-0 **86**.....(t) LiamKeniry 83
(Peter Fahey, Ire) *lost grnd s and in rr: last at 1/2-way: gng wl towards rr into st: sme hdwy 2f out into 10th over 1f out: kpt on one pce* **12/1**

10 shd **Synopsis**[14] 6818 4-8-7 **79**.....(t) ConorHoban 76
(G M Lyons, Ire) *mid-div: pushed along in 9th 3f out and sn no ex: one pce fnl 2f* **33/1**

11 1 3/4 **Water Sprite (IRE)**[11] 5426 5-8-0 **79**.....(t) SeanDavis(7) 74
(Gordon Elliott, Ire) *lost grnd s and in rr: sltly hmpd after 1f: sltly hmpd again on inner at 1/2-way: sme hdwy fr over 2f out into mod 12th over 1f out: kpt on one pce ins fnl f* **12/1**

12 2 **Prickly (IRE)**[7] 5620 6-8-6 **83**..... KillianLeonard(5) 76
(E J O'Grady, Ire) *hld up in tch: tk clsr order bhd ldrs 4f out: 6th 3f out: rdn and wknd 2f out* **25/1**

13 1/2 **Automated**[30] 6308 5-7-11 **79**.....[1] DannySheehy(10) 71
(Gordon Elliott, Ire) *mid-div on outer: pushed along into st and sn no ex: one pce fnl 2f* **10/1**[3]

14 14 **Slunovrat (FR)**[35] 6163 5-9-2 **88**..... ColinKeane 65
(David Menuisier) *cl up and settled bhd ldr in 2nd tl led bef 1/2-way: narrow advantage 4f out: hdd 3f out and sn no ex u.p: wknd fr over 2f out* **12/1**

15 1 **Kashmiri Sunset**[33] 7124 5-8-10 **82**.....[1] MichaelHussey 58
(Gordon Elliott, Ire) *hld up: pushed along towards rr bef 1/2-way and no imp into st: one pce fnl 2f* **25/1**

16 4 1/4 **Theos Well**[14] 6818 8-9-0 **86**..... ColmO'Donoghue 57
(Michael Winters, Ire) *chsd ldrs: pushed along in 8th fr 3f out and sn no ex: wknd under 2f out* **10/1**[3]

17 1 **Eshtiaal (USA)**[53] 5559 6-9-5 **91**.....(tp) DeclanMcDonogh 61
(Gordon Elliott, Ire) *chsd ldrs: rdn and wknd 4f out: eased over 2f out* **16/1**

18 50 **Udogo**[14] 6818 5-8-3 **80**..... AnaO'Brien(5)
(Joseph Patrick O'Brien, Ire) *hld up: tk clsr order bhd ldrs bef 1/2-way: pushed along in 4th fr 4f out and sn lost pl: wknd into st and sn eased: t.o* **33/1**

19 12 **Magnolia Rose (IRE)**[43] 5901 3-8-11 **94**..... PatSmullen
(D K Weld, Ire) *mid-div: pushed along into st and no imp: wknd and eased over 2f out: t.o* **6/1**[1]

P **Papa's Way (IRE)**[24] 6533 6-8-11 **83**.....(bt[1]) RoryCleary
(P D Deegan, Ire) *w ldrs tl p.u qckly after 1f* **33/1**

3m 29.4s (103.40) **Going Correction** +0.275s/f (Good)
WFA 3 from 4yo+ 11lb **20** Ran SP% **147.2**
Speed ratings: **109,108,108,106,106 106,104,104,103,103 103,102,101,94,94 92,91,66,60,**
CSF £126.61 CT £858.66 TOTE £7.20: £1.60, £3.40, £1.90, £5.10; DF 201.80 Trifecta £5052.00.
Owner Hourihane/O'Brien Partnership **Bred** Ballylinch Stud **Trained** Muine Beag, Co Carlow

FOCUS
A competitive renewal of the historic handicap was captured by Willie Mullins for the second year in succession. The three-year-old winner can probably emulate his principal victims by becoming a useful dual-purpose type.

7196a BROWN PANTHER STKS (LISTED RACE) 1m 4f
5:25 (5:27) 3-Y-0+

£19,522 (£6,286; £2,977; £1,323; £661; £330)

RPR

1 **Alveena (IRE)**[72] 4850 4-9-2 98..... PatSmullen 7 95+
(D K Weld, Ire) *w.w: 6th 1/2-way: tk clsr order bhd ldrs in 5th fr 2f out: r.o wl u.p on outer ins fnl f to ld fnl strides* **11/4**[2]

2 nk **Hibiscus (IRE)**[17] 6722 3-8-9 81..... MichaelHussey 1 95+
(A P O'Brien, Ire) *hld up bhd ldrs: 4th 1/2-way: tk clsr order bhd ldrs on inner 2f out: sn sltly hmpd: kpt on wl in 4th ins fnl f into nvr nrr 3rd on line: nrst fin: promoted to 2nd following enquiry* **14/1**

3 1/2 **Soul Searcher (IRE)**[14] 6820 4-9-2 96..... RoryCleary 2 94
(J P Murtagh, Ire) *chsd ldrs: 3rd 1/2-way: rdn to ld over 1f out where edgd sltly rt: all out wl ins fnl f and hdd fnl strides: demoted to 3rd following enquiry* **11/1**

4 nse **Bravery (IRE)**[16] 6760 3-9-0 94..... DonnachaO'Brien 3 99+
(A P O'Brien, Ire) *w.w: last at 1/2-way: tk clsr order bhd ldrs on inner fr 2f out: short of room briefly tl sn rdn and r.o wl ins fnl f into cl 3rd: hld by wnr fnl strides and denied 3rd on line* **11/1**

5 2 1/2 **Xebec (USA)**[46] 5790 4-9-7 90.....(b) DeclanMcDonogh 5 95
(John M Oxx, Ire) *hooded to load: led: 3 l clr at 1/2-way: reduced advantage into st: rdn 2f out and hdd u.p over 1f out: sn no ex in 2nd and wknd into 5th ins fnl f* **12/1**

6 3/4 **How High The Moon (IRE)**[21] 6604 3-8-9 94..... ColmO'Donoghue 4 84
(A P O'Brien, Ire) *chsd ldr: racd keenly early: 2nd 1/2-way: rdn in 2nd 2f out and no ex u.p in 3rd whn sltly hmpd over 1f out: wknd into 6th ins fnl f* **9/1**[3]

7 5 **Stellar Mass (IRE)**[29] 6351 3-9-5 112..... KevinManning 6 86
(J S Bolger, Ire) *hld up bhd ldrs: 5th 1/2-way: pushed along in 4th appr st and sn no ex u.p in 5th over 2f out: sn wknd to rr and eased fnl f* **1/1**[1]

2m 38.83s (0.33) **Going Correction** +0.275s/f (Good)
WFA 3 from 4yo 7lb **7** Ran SP% **117.7**
Speed ratings: **109,108,108,108,106 104,100**
Pick Six. Not Won. Pool of 26,578.00 carried forward to Sunday 16th October. Tote Aggregate: 2016: 277,865.00 - 2015: 272,497.00. CSF £40.58 TOTE £3.00: £1.50, £4.30; DF 43.50 Trifecta £271.90.
Owner H H Aga Khan **Bred** His Highness The Aga Khan's Studs Sc **Trained** Curragh, Co Kildare
■ Stewards' Enquiry : Rory Cleary one-day ban: careless riding (TBC)

FOCUS
Not a particularly strong race for this level, and the trainers involved with the first three (all fillies) are entitled to be satisfied by the outcome, though Johnny Murtagh may have some reservations following the alteration of placings involving second and third.
T/Jkpt: Not Won. T/Plt: @6,377.97. Pool: @2,232.20 **Brian Fleming**

7194 - 7199a (Foreign Racing) - See Raceform Interactive

7098 CHELMSFORD (A.W) (L-H)
Monday, October 10

OFFICIAL GOING: Polytrack: standard
Wind: light, against Weather: mainly dry, shower before racing

7200 BET TOTEPLACEPOT AT TOTESPORT.COM APPRENTICE H'CAP (DIV I) 6f (P)
4:55 (4:56) (Class 6) (0-60,60) 3-Y-0+ **£2,911** (£866; £432; £216) **Stalls** Centre

Form RPR

0050 1 **Anieres Boy**[9] 6959 4-9-4 **55**..... NathanEvans(3) 2 61
(Michael Easterby) *mde all: rdn over 1f out: edgd lft u.p: hld on towards fin* **4/1**[2]

0430 2 shd **Kenstone (FR)**[13] 6853 3-8-12 **50**.....(p) CallumShepherd(3) 9 56
(David Dennis) *hld up in tch in midfield: effrt to chse wnr and carried lft over 1f out: ev ch ins fnl f: kpt on: jst hld towards fin* **12/1**

5550 3 2 **Fashionable Spirit (IRE)**[19] 6669 3-9-11 **60**.....(b[1]) KieranShoemark 1 59
(Amanda Perrett) *s.i.s: in tch in rr of main gp: hdwy to chse ldrs over 1f out: wnt 3rd wl ins fnl f: kpt on but no threat to ldng pair* **4/1**[2]

2352 4 2 **Arcanista (IRE)**[19] 6677 3-9-1 **60**.....(tp) NicolaCurrie(10) 3 53
(Richard Hughes) *chsd ldrs: effrt over 1f out: unable qck 1f out: lost 3rd and wknd wl ins fnl f* **3/1**[1]

3303 5 3 1/2 **Sacred Harp**[20] 6660 3-9-6 **58**.....(t) AaronJones(3) 6 40
(Stuart Williams) *chsd ldr: hung rt bnd 4f out tl 2f out: lost pl over 1f out: wknd ins fnl f* **5/1**[3]

6504 6 1 1/2 **Ryan Style (IRE)**[11] 6902 10-8-12 **46** oh1.....(p) MichaelJMMurphy 8 23
(Lisa Williamson) *dwlt: rcvrd to chse ldrs after 2f: rdn wl over 1f out: sn outpcd: wknd fnl f* **20/1**

3360 7 1/2 **Limerick Lord (IRE)**[7] 7018 4-8-12 **56**.....(p) LiamDoran(10) 7 31
(Julia Feilden) *taken down early: in tch in midfield: rdn over 1f out: sn outpcd: wknd fnl f* **7/1**

06 8 7 **Les Darcy**[43] 5915 5-8-7 **46** oh1..... MeganNicholls(5) 5
(Ken Cunningham-Brown) *sn dropped to rr: rdn over 2f out: wknd over 1f out: bhd fnl f* **12/1**

1m 12.2s (-1.50) **Going Correction** -0.275s/f (Stan)
WFA 3 from 4yo+ 1lb **8** Ran SP% **114.3**
Speed ratings (Par 101): **99,98,96,93,88 86,86,76**
CSF £49.88 CT £204.57 TOTE £3.90: £1.60, £3.20, £1.70; EX 43.20 Trifecta £362.20.
Owner M W Easterby **Bred** Az Agr Rosati Colarieti Antonio **Trained** Sheriff Hutton, N Yorks

FOCUS
The track was gallop master finished to two inches. A low-grade apprentice sprint handicap with a thrilling finish. The winner is rated back to his previos best.

7201 BET TOTEPLACEPOT AT TOTESPORT.COM APPRENTICE H'CAP (DIV II) 6f (P)
5:25 (5:28) (Class 6) (0-60,60) 3-Y-0+ **£2,911** (£866; £432; £216) **Stalls** Centre

Form RPR

040 1 **Silver Springs (IRE)**[31] 6291 3-9-4 **58**..... RhiainIngram(5) 4 63
(David Evans) *led for 1f: styd pressing ldr: rdn to ld 1f out: sn hrd pressed: hld on wl towards fin: rdn out* **12/1**

6420 2 hd **Decisive (IRE)**[38] 6100 4-9-7 **55**.....[1] LouisSteward 1 59
(Anthony Carson) *hld up in tch: effrt to chse ldrs and swtchd rt over 1f out: rdn to chal jst ins fnl f: kpt on but hld towards fin* **9/4**[2]

3342 3 3/4 **Cadland Lad (IRE)**[11] 6902 3-8-11 **49**.....(vt) PaddyPilley(3) 7 51
(John Ryan) *hld up in tch in rr: effrt over 1f out: chsd ldrs and hung lft ins fnl f: kpt on but nvr quite getting to ldng pair* **7/4**[1]

054 4 3 1/4 **Sharp Boy (IRE)**[48] 5748 3-9-5 **57**.....[1] AaronJones(3) 8 49
(Stuart Williams) *dwlt and bustled along leaving stalls: hdwy to ld after 1f: rdn over 1f out: hdd 1f out: no ex: wknd fnl 100yds* **6/1**

2423 5 4 **Poplar**[25] 6509 3-9-8 **60**.....[1] CallumShepherd(3) 9 39
(Robyn Brisland) *in tch: outpcd u.p over 1f out: wknd fnl f* **7/2**[3]

0000 6 2 3/4 **Fearless Poppy**[60] 5338 3-8-8 **46** oh1.....(v[1]) NathanEvans(3) 6 16
(Christine Dunnett) *in tch: short of room and swtchd lft over 1f out: sn outpcd: wknd fnl f* **50/1**

1m 12.41s (-1.29) **Going Correction** -0.275s/f (Stan)
WFA 3 from 4yo+ 1lb **6** Ran SP% **113.3**
Speed ratings (Par 101): **97,96,95,91,86 82**
CSF £39.90 CT £71.52 TOTE £9.50: £3.60, £1.80; EX 46.60 Trifecta £116.10.
Owner Dukes Head Racing **Bred** Golden Vale Stud **Trained** Pandy, Monmouths
■ Bemusement was withdrawn not under orders. Rule 4 applies to board prices prior to withdrawal - deduction 10p in the pound. New market formed.

The Form Book, Raceform Ltd, Newbury, RG14 5SJ

FOCUS
The second division of a low-grade apprentice sprint handicap saw another tight finish. Weak form, the winner back towards his better efforts this year.

7202 BET TOTEJACKPOT AT TOTESPORT.COM H'CAP 5f (P)
5:55 (5:57) (Class 4) (0-85,84) 3-Y-O+ **£4,851** (£1,443; £721; £360) **Stalls** Low

Form				RPR
0001	**1**		**Fast Act (IRE)**[35] 6195 4-9-4 **81** KevinStott 9 (Kevin Ryan) *mde all: shkn up ent fnl f: rdn: kpt on and a doing enough ins fnl f* **10/1**	90
1530	**2**	½	**Top Boy**[9] 6944 6-9-7 **84** (v) MartinLane 5 (Derek Shaw) *chsd ldrs: effrt over 1f out: swtchd lft and chsd wnr jst ins fnl f: styd on wl but nvr quite getting to wnr* **3/1**[2]	91
3003	**3**	1 ½	**Just Us Two (IRE)**[10] 6926 4-9-6 **83** (p) SilvestreDeSousa 2 (Robert Cowell) *in tch in midfield: effrt over 1f out: chsd ldrs 1f out: edgd lft and kpt on same pce ins fnl f* **11/4**[1]	85
6124	**4**	½	**Dynamo Walt (IRE)**[38] 6080 5-9-2 **82** (v) NoelGarbutt(3) 1 (Derek Shaw) *chsd ldrs: effrt over 1f out: kpt on same pce ins fnl f* **6/1**[3]	82
160	**5**	½	**Olympic Runner**[74] 4803 3-8-12 **80** [1] GeorgiaCox(5) 4 (William Haggas) *in tch in midfield: squeezed for room and swtchd rt over 5f out: hung rt and wd in midfield after: rdn over 1f out: kpt on ins fnl f: nvr enough pce to threaten ldrs* **8/1**	79+
333	**6**	nse	**Flying Bear (IRE)**[65] 5162 5-9-1 **78** FrederikTylicki 11 (Jeremy Gask) *hld up in tch in last quartet: rdn and hdwy ent fnl f: styd on fnl 100yds: nt rch ldrs* **14/1**	76
5060	**7**	1	**Red Stripes (USA)**[12] 6879 4-8-10 **73** (v) MichaelJMMurphy 6 (Lisa Williamson) *chsd wnr: rdn over 1f out: unable qck and lost 2nd jst ins fnl f: wknd fnl 100yds* **10/1**	67
0255	**8**	½	**Elusivity (IRE)**[10] 6927 8-9-3 **80** (p) DavidNolan 10 (Conor Dore) *chsd ldrs: rdn and unable qck over 1f out: wknd ins fnl f* **33/1**	72
0060	**9**	nk	**Foxy Forever (IRE)**[16] 6793 6-9-3 **80** (t) ConnorBeasley 12 (Michael Wigham) *stdd s: hld up in last pair: effrt and n.m.r jst over 1f out: sme hdwy ins fnl f: nvr trbld ldrs* **7/1**	71
5000	**10**	hd	**Crosse Fire**[10] 6926 4-9-3 **80** BenCurtis 3 (Scott Dixon) *awkward as stalls opened and s.i.s: a rr: rdn wl over 1f out: kpt on but nvr trbld ldrs* **33/1**	71
2202	**11**	3 ½	**Jaarih (IRE)**[12] 6879 4-8-13 **76** (b) AdamBeschizza 7 (Conor Dore) *hld up in last quartet: effrt wl over 1f out: sn struggling: bhd ins fnl f* **25/1**	54

58.75s (-1.45) **Going Correction** -0.275s/f (Stan) **11** Ran SP% **124.1**
Speed ratings (Par 105): **100,99,96,96,95 95,93,92,92,91 86**
CSF £41.78 CT £111.53 TOTE £12.90: £3.70, £1.60, £1.60; EX 60.80 Trifecta £287.40.
Owner Hambleton Racing Ltd XXXII **Bred** Newlands House Stud **Trained** Hambleton, N Yorks

FOCUS
A typical Chelmsford 5f handicap, where the winner was always in front. He still has mileage on his 2yo form.

7203 BET TOTEQUADPOT AT TOTESPORT.COM H'CAP 7f (P)
6:25 (6:28) (Class 5) (0-70,70) 3-Y-O+ **£3,234** (£962; £481; £240) **Stalls** Low

Form				RPR
4233	**1**		**Encore Moi**[23] 6592 3-8-11 **62** (b) AndreaAtzeni 4 (Marco Botti) *trckd ldrs: gng wl whn nt clr run over 1f out: swtchd rt and wnt 2nd wl over 1f out: rdn to ld jst over 1f out: sn hrd pressed: hdd wl ins fnl f: battled on to ld again on post* **4/1**[2]	71
4130	**2**	nse	**Remember Me**[43] 5935 3-9-3 **68** JimCrowley 11 (Hughie Morrison) *in tch in midfield: effrt to chse ldrs over 1f out: rdn and str chal 1f out: led wl ins fnl f: hdd on post* **20/1**	77
0632	**3**	2	**Believe It (IRE)**[46] 5808 4-8-10 **66** (p) StephenCummins(7) 2 (Richard Hughes) *dwlt and bustled along leaving stalls: sn rcvrd and in tch in midfield: effrt to chse ldrs over 1f out: kpt on to go 3rd wl ins fnl f* **7/1**[3]	70
4611	**4**	½	**Fine Example**[38] 6106 3-9-2 **67** (b) KevinStott 1 (Kevin Ryan) *led: rdn over 1f out: drvn and hdd jst over 1f out: no ex u.p ins fnl f: outpcd fnl 100yds* **11/4**[1]	69
561	**5**	¾	**Quite A Story**[45] 5827 4-8-12 **66** CharlieBennett(5) 6 (Patrick Chamings) *taken down early: hld up in tch in midfield: nt clr run and swtchd rt over 1f out: hdwy and edgd rt 1f out: styd on ins fnl f: no threat to ldrs* **14/1**	67
653	**6**	1 ½	**Frozen Lake (USA)**[33] 6237 4-9-0 **68** (bt) GeorgeWood(5) 12 (Mary Hambro) *chsd ldrs on outer: hung rt 4f out: pressing ldrs and rdn over 2f out: unable qck over 1f out: wknd ins fnl f* **7/1**[3]	65
0362	**7**	¾	**Jan Steen (IRE)**[33] 6238 3-9-4 **69** SilvestreDeSousa 13 (Denis Coakley) *hld up in tch in midfield: effrt over 1f out: carried rt and sltly impeded 1f out: pushed along and no imp ins fnl f* **10/1**	63
6064	**8**	¾	**Palpitation (IRE)**[52] 5609 3-8-9 **67** TomDonoghue(7) 7 (David Brown) *pressed ldr tl rdn and unable qck over 1f out: btn and lost pl 1f out: wknd ins fnl f* **20/1**	59
012	**9**	1 ½	**Desert River (IRE)**[60] 5336 3-8-7 **65** GeorgiaDobie(7) 15 (Mark H Tompkins) *s.i.s: hld up in rr: effrt over 1f out: sme modest hdwy ins fnl f: nvr trbld ldrs* **20/1**	53
1643	**10**	1	**Star Of The Stage**[55] 5503 4-9-7 **70** (p) AdamBeschizza 3 (Julia Feilden) *hld up in tch in midfield: rdn over 2f out: no imp whn sltly hmpd and swtchd rt ent fnl f: wknd ins fnl f* **9/1**	56
0000	**11**	1 ¼	**Wink Oliver**[136] 2635 4-9-4 **67** (p) MartinLane 8 (David Dennis) *dwlt: hld up in rr: effrt jst over 1f out: no imp: n.d* **20/1**	50
2540	**12**	2 ¾	**Marcle (IRE)**[12] 6872 3-8-12 **63** (p) ShaneGray 10 (Ed de Giles) *pressed ldrs early: sn settled bk to chse ldrs: rdn and lost pl over 1f out: bhd whn edgd lft 1f out: wknd ins fnl f* **16/1**	37

1m 24.58s (-2.62) **Going Correction** -0.275s/f (Stan)
WFA 3 from 4yo+ 2lb **12** Ran SP% **122.4**
Speed ratings (Par 103): **103,102,100,100,99 97,96,95,94,92 91,88**
CSF £88.60 CT £541.75 TOTE £4.90: £1.90, £4.30, £2.80; EX 55.70 Trifecta £887.90.
Owner Scuderia Vittadini Srl **Bred** Scuderia Vittadini Srl **Trained** Newmarket, Suffolk

FOCUS
A competitive Class 5 handicap run at a good pace and won by the narrowest of margins. The form seems sound.

7204 BET TOTEEXACTA AT TOTESPORT.COM H'CAP 1m (P)
6:55 (6:55) (Class 4) (0-80,80) 3-Y-O+ **£4,851** (£1,443; £721; £360) **Stalls** Low

Form				RPR
6141	**1**		**Wakame (IRE)**[20] 6656 3-9-0 **76** JimCrowley 9 (Ed de Giles) *pressed ldr tl rdn to ld over 1f out: kpt on wl u.p ins fnl f: rdn out* **7/2**[2]	81
-435	**2**	1 ¼	**Topology**[83] 4481 3-9-1 **77** JFEgan 6 (Joseph Tuite) *chsd ldrs: effrt over 1f out: sn drvn: kpt on u.p wl ins fnl f: wnt 2nd last strides* **10/1**	79
125	**3**	shd	**Blind Faith (IRE)**[29] 6378 3-9-3 **79** AdamKirby 5 (Luca Cumani) *hld up wl in tch in midfield: effrt and drvn over 1f out: kpt on u.p fnl 100yds: wnt 3rd last strides* **3/1**[1]	81
0016	**4**	hd	**Ilzam (IRE)**[63] 5246 3-9-3 **79** (t) AndreaAtzeni 2 (Marco Botti) *taken down early: hld up in tch in last pair: clsd over 1f out: nt clr run and swtchd lft 1f out: chsng ldr u.p but stl nt clrest of runs ins fnl f: kpt on u.p* **9/2**[3]	82
5112	**5**	shd	**Brick Lane**[25] 6510 3-8-10 **77** CallumShepherd(5) 1 (Robyn Brisland) *t.k.h: led: rdn and hdd over 1f out: kpt on same pce u.p ins fnl f: lost 3 pls cl home* **3/1**[1]	78
0-10	**6**	6	**Muthraab Aldaar (IRE)**[170] 1636 3-8-12 **74** WilliamCarson 3 (Jim Boyle) *sn dropped to rr: swtchd rt and effrt over 1f out: sn struggling: wknd ins fnl f* **16/1**	61
0450	**7**	3 ¾	**Outback Blue**[2] 7159 3-9-0 **76** (t) ShaneKelly 7 (David Evans) *sn chsng ldrs on outer: rdn over 2f out: lost pl u.p over 1f out: wknd ins fnl f* **8/1**	54

1m 37.59s (-2.31) **Going Correction** -0.275s/f (Stan) **7** Ran SP% **116.5**
Speed ratings (Par 105): **100,98,98,98,98 92,88**
CSF £38.19 CT £117.12 TOTE £3.90: £2.20, £5.50; EX 43.30 Trifecta £154.20.
Owner Simon Treacher **Bred** Tally-Ho Stud **Trained** Ledbury, H'fords

FOCUS
A competitive Class 4 handicap featuring a masterclass from the soon-to-be champion jockey. A muddling race which has been rated a bit cautiously.

7205 TOTEPOOL SUPPORTING WORLD MENTAL HEALTH DAY FILLIES' H'CAP 1m 2f (P)
7:25 (7:27) (Class 5) (0-75,74) 3-Y-O+ **£3,234** (£962; £481; £240) **Stalls** Low

Form				RPR
6136	**1**		**Mercy Me**[11] 6901 4-9-3 **67** AdamKirby 9 (John Ryan) *hld up in tch in midfield: chsd ldrs 4f out: rdn to ld jst over 1f out: kpt on ins fnl f: rdn out* **12/1**	74
213	**2**	¾	**Unsuspected Girl (IRE)**[21] 6626 3-8-4 **66** SophieKilloran(7) 10 (David Simcock) *stdd and swtchd lft after s: hld up in last pair: clsd and nt clr run over 1f out: gap opened and hdwy ins fnl f: chsd ldrs and swtchd lft wl ins fnl f: r.o to go 2nd last strides* **8/1**	74+
1652	**3**	nk	**All The Rage**[10] 6922 3-9-5 **74** LukeMorris 7 (Sir Mark Prescott Bt) *s.i.s: hld up in tch in last trio: swtchd rt and effrt over 1f out: hdwy to chse wnr and drvn ins fnl f: kpt on: lost 2nd last strides* **9/2**[2]	79
3004	**4**	1 ¾	**Heart Locket**[10] 6922 4-9-3 **70** (b) NathanEvans(3) 2 (Michael Easterby) *in tch in midfield: effrt over 1f out: swtchd rt and kpt on same pce ins fnl f* **12/1**	71
4231	**5**	2	**Cacica**[9] 6965 3-9-2 **71** (b) SilvestreDeSousa 8 (George Scott) *chsd ldr tl rdn to ld over 1f out: sn hdd: unable qck and hld whn hmpd wl ins fnl f: eased off towards fin* **3/1**[1]	70
046	**6**	nk	**Sleeplessinseattle**[97] 3990 3-8-13 **68** FrederikTylicki 4 (James Fanshawe) *led: hdd and rdn over 1f out: unable qck and btn jst ins fnl f: wl hld and eased towards fin* **6/1**[3]	66
3063	**7**	hd	**East Coast Lady (IRE)**[11] 6901 4-9-3 **67** MartinLane 3 (William Stone) *s.i.s: t.k.h: hld up in tch in last pair: effrt over 1f out: no imp u.p and styd on same pce ins fnl f* **8/1**	63
1400	**8**	2 ¼	**Lido Lady (IRE)**[15] 6811 3-9-0 **69** JimCrowley 1 (Mark Johnston) *chsd ldrs tl unable qck and lost pl over 1f out: wknd ins fnl f* **20/1**	61
3322	**9**	4 ½	**Golden Reign (IRE)**[40] 6024 3-9-5 **74** BenCurtis 6 (William Haggas) *in tch in midfield: carried rt 6f out: rdn 3f out: sn struggling and lost pl over 1f out: bhd ins fnl f* **10/1**	57
500	**P**		**Tangba**[103] 3781 3-9-2 **71** AndreaAtzeni 5 (Roger Varian) *wl in tch in midfield: reminder and rdn over 7f out: wnt rt and eased 6f out: p.u and dismntd 4f out* **8/1**

2m 4.74s (-3.86) **Going Correction** -0.275s/f (Stan)
WFA 3 from 4yo 5lb **10** Ran SP% **120.0**
Speed ratings (Par 100): **104,103,103,101,100 99,99,97,94,**
CSF £107.37 CT £506.85 TOTE £11.50: £3.00, £2.10, £2.10; EX 92.90 Trifecta £338.00.
Owner G Smith-Bernal & A Dee **Bred** Aston Mullins Stud **Trained** Newmarket, Suffolk

FOCUS
A competitive fillies' handicap seemingly run at a slow pace resulting in a messy finish. The winner was close to her early 3yo form.

7206 TOTEPOOL BETTING AT BETFRED.COM H'CAP 6f (P)
7:55 (7:57) (Class 4) (0-85,85) 3-Y-O+ **£4,851** (£1,443; £721; £360) **Stalls** Centre

Form				RPR
4103	**1**		**Jameerah**[18] 6699 3-8-13 **78** LukeMorris 1 (James Tate) *travelled strly: chsd ldr: clsd and stl on bit over 1f out: shkn up to ld jst ins fnl f: r.o: rdn out* **4/1**[2]	87
0450	**2**	1 ½	**Pearl Acclaim (IRE)**[24] 6537 6-8-11 **75** (p) SilvestreDeSousa 2 (David Nicholls) *t.k.h: hld up in midfield: effrt over 1f out: drvn to chse wnr 150yds out: kpt on same pce after* **5/1**[3]	79
1134	**3**	shd	**Chetan**[23] 6580 4-8-10 **74** (tp) AdamBeschizza 11 (Charlie Wallis) *taken down early: hld up in tch: rdn and swtchd rt over 1f out: styd on wl u.p fnl 100yds* **14/1**	78
0124	**4**	nse	**Merhoob (IRE)**[66] 5124 4-9-7 **85** JimCrowley 3 (John Ryan) *s.i.s: bhd: hdwy on inner over 1f out: styng on whn swtchd rt ins fnl f: kpt on wl towards fin: no threat to wnr* **9/4**[1]	89+
5520	**5**	½	**Florencio**[26] 6492 3-9-1 **85** (t) GeorgeWood(5) 12 (William Muir) *midfield on outer: rdn 1/2-way: hdwy u.p ins fnl f: styd on wl fnl 100yds* **20/1**	87
0006	**6**	½	**Dutch Golden Age (IRE)**[23] 6589 4-8-6 **73** HectorCrouch(3) 6 (Gary Moore) *hld up in tch in midfield: effrt over 1f out: swtchd rt 1f out: styd on same pce ins fnl f: eased towards fin* **33/1**	73
04	**7**	nk	**Dominium (USA)**[38] 6072 9-8-11 **75** (b) FrederikTylicki 5 (Jeremy Gask) *hld up in tch in midfield: effrt u.p over 1f out: styd on same pce ins fnl f* **14/1**	74
6300	**8**	2 ¼	**Irish Eclare (IRE)**[58] 5412 3-8-13 **78** MichaelJMMurphy 7 (Charles Hills) *dwlt: bhd: rdn over 2f out: sme hdwy ins fnl f: nvr trbld ldrs* **12/1**	70
3510	**9**	1 ½	**King Crimson**[42] 5961 4-9-4 **82** AdamKirby 4 (John Butler) *led: rdn over 1f out: hdd jst ins fnl f: sn btn and wknd fnl 100yds* **16/1**	69
0406	**10**	2 ½	**Koptoon**[12] 6878 4-9-4 **82** (p) DavidNolan 8 (Jo Hughes) *dwlt: hld up towards rr: effrt over 1f out: no imp: eased wl ins fnl f* **8/1**	61

0036 **11** *2 ½* **Free Zone**[24] 6539 7-9-7 **85**..(v) WilliamCarson 10 77
(Jamie Osborne) *chsd ldrs: rdn and unable qck 2f out: lost pl and btn whn squeezed for room and hmpd 1f out: eased ins fnl f* **7/1**

1m 10.9s (-2.80) **Going Correction** -0.275s/f (Stan)
WFA 3 from 4yo+ 1lb **11** Ran SP% **125.7**
Speed ratings (Par 105): **107,105,104,104,104 103,103,100,98,94 91**
CSF £26.34 CT £271.03 TOTE £4.80: £1.50, £1.90, £2.90; EX 28.30 Trifecta £215.40.
Owner Saeed Manana **Bred** Rabbah Bloodstock Limited **Trained** Newmarket, Suffolk

FOCUS
A competitive Class 4 sprint won in taking style, the winner resuming her progress. The second was close to form.

7207 BOOK YOUR CHRISTMAS PARTY AT CCR MAIDEN STKS 6f (P)
8:25 (8:27) (Class 5) 3-Y-O+ **£4,204** (£1,251; £625; £312) **Stalls** Centre

Form RPR
433 **1** **Interlink (USA)**[23] 6567 3-9-5 74.. BenCurtis 1 78
(Tony Coyle) *mde all: rdn over 1f out: r.o wl and drew clr ins fnl f: comf* **7/4**[1]

20-0 **2** *5* **Equinette (IRE)**[124] 3036 3-9-0 69.................................... JimCrowley 2 57
(Amanda Perrett) *wnt rt s: chsd wnr thrght: rdn over 1f out: unable qck and outpcd fnl f: plugged on for clr 2nd* **7/2**[3]

3 *3 ¾* **La Fortuna** 3-9-0 0.. AdamBeschizza 4 45
(Charlie Wallis) *v.s.a: rn green and off the pce in rr: rdn and wnt between rivals over 1f out: wnt 3rd jst over 1f out: nvr on terms w ldrs* **25/1**

4 *2 ½* **Arctic Angel (IRE)** 3-9-5 0... FrederikTylicki 6 42
(James Fanshawe) *wnt rt s: off the pce in 4th: pushed along to go 3rd over 2f out: no imp and lost 3rd jst over 1f out* **5/2**[2]

5 *5* **Noblewoman** 3-8-11 0.. KieranShoemark(3) 3 30
(Roger Charlton) *wnt sharply rt leaving stalls: chsd clr ldng pair: rdn and lost 3rd over 2f out: dropped to last over 1f out: wknd fnl f* **4/1**

1m 11.48s (-2.22) **Going Correction** -0.275s/f (Stan) **5** Ran SP% **111.0**
Speed ratings (Par 103): **103,96,91,88,81**
CSF £8.29 TOTE £2.80: £2.00, £1.70; EX 8.00 Trifecta £59.30.
Owner Craig Buckingham **Bred** R S Evans **Trained** Norton, N Yorks
■ Samphire Coast was withdrawn. Price at time of withdrawal 33/1. Rule 4 does not apply

FOCUS
A modest maiden dominated by the two with racecourse experience. The time wasn't bad compared with the earlier handicap.
T/Jkpt: Not Won. T/Plt: £585.80 to a £1 stake. Pool: £79,086.99 - 98.55 winning units T/Qpdt: £21.90 to a £1 stake. Pool: £11,898.3 - 402.0 winning units **Steve Payne**

6880 SALISBURY (R-H)
Monday, October 10

OFFICIAL GOING: Good to soft (soft in places; 7.3)
Wind: almost nil Weather: sunny periods

7208 BATHWICK CAR & VAN HIRE MAIDEN AUCTION STKS (DIV I) 6f 212y
1:50 (1:52) (Class 5) 2-Y-O **£3,557** (£1,058; £529; £264) **Stalls** Low

Form RPR
3 **1** **War Chief**[23] 6590 2-9-0 0... JimmyFortune 7 80+
(Alan King) *s.i.s: last pair: smooth hdwy fr over 3f out: led jst over 1f out: pushed clr: easily* **5/4**[1]

2 *5* **Bataka** 2-8-5 0... JosephineGordon(3) 10 60+
(Harry Dunlop) *wnt lft s: sn pushed along in last pair: stdy hdwy fr 2f out: r.o wl ins fnl f: wnt 2nd cl home: no ch w wnr* **16/1**

06 **3** *½* **Exspectation (IRE)**[21] 6632 2-8-13 0............................. RobertHavlin 8 63
(Michael Blanshard) *trckd ldrs: rdn over 2f out: kpt on ins fnl f: wnt 2nd briefly fnl 75yds* **10/1**

4 *1 ¾* **Eburaci (IRE)** 2-9-1 0.. TomQueally 4 61
(Charlie Fellowes) *in last trio: rdn and stdy prog fr 2f out: r.o fnl f: snatched 4th fnl strides* **8/1**

6 **5** *nk* **Holy Roma**[18] 6696 2-8-9 0... PaulHanagan 5 54
(William Haggas) *trckd ldrs: rdn to ld 2f out: hdd jst over 1f out: fdd ins fnl f* **7/2**[2]

000 **6** *3 ¼* **Desidero (SPA)**[32] 6264 2-8-8 0...................................... KieranO'Neill 9 45
(Pat Phelan) *hld up: rdn and sme prog over 2f out: nvr trbld ldrs: one pce fnl f* **150/1**

000 **7** *1 ¼* **Chamasay**[30] 6314 2-8-11 0.. DannyBrock 3 45
(J S Moore) *prom: rdn over 2f out: sn carried lft and hld: wknd ins fnl f* **125/1**

62 **8** *nse* **Stevie Brown**[62] 5271 2-8-11 0... OisinMurphy 1 45
(David Brown) *led: rdn and hdd 2f out: drifted lft: wknd ins fnl f* **9/2**[3]

9 *8* **Everlasting Sea** 2-8-6 0... RobHornby(3) 2 23
(Stuart Kittow) *in tch: rdn over 3f out: wknd 2f out* **33/1**

1m 31.47s (2.87) **Going Correction** +0.35s/f (Good) **9** Ran SP% **115.3**
Speed ratings (Par 95): **97,91,90,88,88 84,83,83,74**
CSF £25.41 TOTE £2.40: £1.20, £5.80, £2.40; EX 24.40 Trifecta £149.80.
Owner Alan King **Bred** Duggan Bloodstock **Trained** Barbury Castle, Wilts

FOCUS
Rail erected up to 20ft off the permanent far-side rail up the last 7f. This was an ordinary 2yo maiden. Afterwards winning rider Jimmy Fortune said the going was "pretty tacky."

7209 BATHWICK CAR & VAN HIRE MAIDEN AUCTION STKS (DIV II) 6f 212y
2:20 (2:24) (Class 5) 2-Y-O **£3,557** (£1,058; £529; £264) **Stalls** Low

Form RPR
1 **Billesdon Bess** 2-8-6 0... TomMarquand 2 71+
(Richard Hannon) *trckd ldrs: led over 1f out: kpt on wl: rdn out* **25/1**

23 **2** *1 ½* **Peloton**[28] 6404 2-8-6 0.. KieranO'Neill 1 67
(Pat Phelan) *led: rdn 2f out: hdd over 1f out: kpt on same pce fnl f* **12/1**

6 **3** *3* **Narjes**[21] 6624 2-8-10 0.. TomQueally 4 64
(James Fanshawe) *slowly away: racd keenly in last pair: hdwy over 2f out: wnt 3rd and rdn over 1f out: drifted rt: kpt on same pce* **2/1**[1]

04 **4** *nk* **Broughtons Knight**[19] 6672 2-9-1 0............................ TimmyMurphy 7 68
(Henry Spiller) *hld up: rdn and hdwy fr over 1f out: wnt 4th ins fnl f: kpt on but no ch w ldrs* **14/1**

002 **5** *4 ½* **Bianca Minola (FR)**[29] 6376 2-8-7 0.............................. PaulHanagan 5 49
(David Menuisier) *trckd ldrs: rdn over 2f out: fdd fnl f* **5/1**[3]

6 **6** *2 ¾* **Noble Ballad**[19] 6671 2-8-11 0.. FMBerry 10 46
(Ralph Beckett) *towards rr: rdn 3f out: little imp* **10/1**

5 **7** *hd* **Red Sniper (IRE)**[28] 6404 2-8-4 0......................... JosephineGordon(3) 8 41
(Peter Chapple-Hyam) *mid-div: rdn wl over 2f out: wknd over 1f out* **11/1**

33 **8** *½* **Golden Eye**[91] 4209 2-8-11 0.. OisinMurphy 3 44
(Sylvester Kirk) *mid-div: rdn and hdwy to chse ldrs 2f out: wknd ent fnl f* **9/1**

06 **9** *19* **Harbour Town**[26] 6480 2-8-13 0................................. RichardKingscote 6
(Harry Dunlop) *in tch: rdn 3f out: wknd 2f out* **9/2**[2]

0 **10** *1 ¼* **Wind Of Heaven (IRE)**[12] 6873 2-8-5 0.......................... RobHornby(3) 9
(Henry Candy) *trckd ldr: rdn over 3f out: wknd over 2f out* **50/1**

1m 29.83s (1.23) **Going Correction** +0.35s/f (Good) **10** Ran SP% **115.8**
Speed ratings (Par 95): **106,104,100,100,95 92,92,91,69,68**
CSF £292.93 TOTE £16.90: £4.90, £3.20, £1.60; EX 139.90 Trifecta £828.50.
Owner Pall Mall Partners **Bred** Stowell Hill Partners **Trained** East Everleigh, Wilts

FOCUS
The second division of the modest 7f 2yo maiden. The first pair were always up there and the winning time was 1.64secs quicker than the opener. Ordinary form.

7210 BATHWICK TYRES BRITISH STALLION STUDS EBF MAIDEN FILLIES' STKS (PLUS 10 RACE) 6f 212y
2:50 (2:52) (Class 5) 2-Y-O **£3,557** (£1,058; £529; £264) **Stalls** Low

Form RPR
1 **Icespire** 2-9-0 0..[1] RobertHavlin 1 83+
(John Gosden) *s.i.s: towards rr: smooth hdwy fr 3f out: led ent fnl f: rdn clr: comf* **6/4**[1]

3 **2** *4* **Mouille Point**[30] 6336 2-9-0 0... SeanLevey 8 72
(Richard Hannon) *cl up: rdn and ev ch briefly over 1f out: sn hld: kpt on but nt pce of wnr* **5/1**[3]

4 **3** *nk* **Crimson Lake**[30] 6336 2-9-0 0... OisinMurphy 6 71
(David Simcock) *in tch: rdn to chse ldrs 2f out: kpt on ins fnl f* **5/1**[3]

0 **4** *2 ½* **Haraka (IRE)**[21] 6624 2-9-0 0.................................... RichardKingscote 2 65
(Ralph Beckett) *mid-div: rdn over 1f out: kpt on to go 4th ins fnl f but nt pce to get on terms* **11/1**

5 **5** *½* **Warm Words**[38] 6087 2-9-0 0.. FMBerry 9 64
(Ralph Beckett) *trckd ldr: led over 2f out: sn rdn: hdd ent fnl f: wknd fnl 120yds* **9/2**[2]

030 **6** *4 ½* **Polkadot Princess (IRE)**[20] 6648 2-8-11 58........ JosephineGordon(3) 3 53
(Nikki Evans) *trckd ldr: nt clr run briefly over 2f out: sn rdn: wknd ent fnl f* **100/1**

60 **7** *4* **Curtsy (IRE)**[23] 6578 2-9-0 0....................................... TomMarquand 11 43
(Hughie Morrison) *a towards rr* **33/1**

8 *1* **White Mischief (IRE)** 2-9-0 0... PatDobbs 10 40
(Richard Hannon) *a towards rr* **8/1**

0 **9** *hd* **Morello (IRE)**[12] 6880 2-9-0 0.. JimmyFortune 4 40
(Henry Candy) *a towards rr* **40/1**

00 **10** *8* **Miriam Violet**[21] 6622 2-9-0 0.. PaulHanagan 7 20
(Paul Henderson) *led: rdn and hdd over 2f out: wknd over 1f out* **150/1**

1m 30.44s (1.84) **Going Correction** +0.35s/f (Good) **10** Ran SP% **118.0**
Speed ratings (Par 92): **103,98,98,95,94 89,84,83,83,74**
CSF £9.34 TOTE £2.50: £1.10, £2.00, £1.70; EX 9.10 Trifecta £16.80.
Owner K Abdullah **Bred** Juddmonte Farms Ltd **Trained** Newmarket, Suffolk

FOCUS
The winner is a nice prospect but the bare form looks quite ordinary in behind.

7211 BATHWICK TYRES H'CAP (DIV I) 6f 212y
3:20 (3:21) (Class 6) (0-60,60) 3-Y-O+ **£2,911** (£866; £432; £216) **Stalls** Low

Form RPR
3324 **1** **Coolcalmcollected (IRE)**[13] 6853 4-9-1 **54**................(p) PaulHanagan 8 61
(David Loughnane) *mde all: kpt on gamely fnl f: rdn out* **5/2**[1]

4052 **2** *¾* **Concur (IRE)**[29] 6361 3-8-5 **46**.......................................(tp) KieranO'Neill 7 50
(Rod Millman) *trckd ldrs: pushed along over 4f out: rdn 3f out: kpt on ins fnl f: wnt 2nd fnl 140yds: hld nring fin* **7/1**

0405 **3** *¾* **Captain Marmalade (IRE)**[14] 6826 4-9-4 **57**................ TimmyMurphy 2 60
(Jimmy Fox) *hld up: hdwy on far rails fr over 2f out: rdn over 1f out: kpt on to go 3rd fnl 130yds* **6/1**[3]

4340 **4** *1 ½* **Funny Oyster (IRE)**[28] 6407 3-9-2 **57**.......................(v[1]) TomMarquand 1 55
(George Baker) *prom: rdn and ev ch over 2f out tl edgd rt over 1f out: no ex fnl f* **5/1**[2]

4066 **5** *½* **Natalia**[59] 5383 7-8-4 **46** oh1..[1] RobHornby(3) 12 44
(Sarah Hollinshead) *hld up towards rr: rdn 2f out: no real imp tl r.o wl fnl f: nvr threatened* **11/1**

4006 **6** *1 ¼* **Guilded Rock**[31] 6290 3-8-7 **48**..................................(bt[1]) DannyBrock 11 42
(Stuart Kittow) *mid-div: rdn and sme prog 3f out: nt pce t get on terms: no ex fnl 120yds* **16/1**

0-50 **7** *3 ¼* **Kylea (IRE)**[39] 6066 3-9-0 **55**.. PatDobbs 3 41
(Richard Hannon) *bmpd leaving stalls: mid-div: rdn 2f out: nvr threatened: wknd fnl f* **16/1**

6160 **8** *1* **Arctic Flower (IRE)**[49] 5721 3-8-10 **54**............... JosephineGordon(3) 10 37
(John Bridger) *chsd ldrs: rdn over 2f out: wknd fnl f* **14/1**

2300 **9** *7* **Aye Aye Skipper (IRE)**[14] 6826 6-8-11 **50**.................(p) SamHitchcott 9 17
(Ken Cunningham-Brown) *in last trio: rdn over 2f out: nvr threatened: wknd jst over 1f out* **10/1**

0100 **10** *14* **Zebs Lad (IRE)**[6] 7062 4-9-7 **60**......................................(p) OisinMurphy 5
(Nikki Evans) *mid-div: rdn wl over 2f out: wknd over 1f out* **12/1**

1m 31.42s (2.82) **Going Correction** +0.35s/f (Good)
WFA 3 from 4yo+ 2lb **10** Ran SP% **115.6**
Speed ratings (Par 101): **97,96,95,93,93 91,87,86,78,62**
CSF £19.83 CT £95.08 TOTE £3.60: £1.60, £2.60, £2.30; EX 20.40 Trifecta £132.90.
Owner From The Front Racing **Bred** The Kathryn Stud **Trained** Market Drayton, Shropshire

FOCUS
A very moderate handicap which saw a slow-motion finish.

7212 BATHWICK TYRES H'CAP (DIV II) 6f 212y
3:50 (3:50) (Class 6) (0-60,60) 3-Y-O+ **£2,911** (£866; £432; £216) **Stalls** Low

Form RPR
2004 **1** **No Refund (IRE)**[21] 6636 5-8-10 **49**...............................(p) PaulHanagan 2 57
(David Loughnane) *mde all: kpt on strly fnl f: rdn out* **5/1**[3]

1363 **2** *3* **Cooperess**[31] 6291 3-9-1 **56**..(bt) FMBerry 12 56
(Ali Stronge) *mid-div: rdn and hdwy over 1f out: wnt 2nd fnl 120yds: kpt on but no further imp on wnr* **11/2**

0636 **3** *2 ¼* **Miss Inga Sock (IRE)**[6] 7062 4-9-1 **57**...............(v[1]) GeorgeDowning(3) 4 52
(Eve Johnson Houghton) *mid-div: hdwy over 2f out: sn rdn: ch wl over 1f out: kpt on same pce fnl f* **9/2**[2]

1606 **4** *½* **Trust Me Boy**[108] 3624 8-8-9 **48** ow2................................ RobertHavlin 11 42
(John E Long) *trckd ldrs: rdn over 2f out: chalng for 2nd whn hung baldy rt jst over 1f out: no ex fnl 120yds* **12/1**

3605 **5** *2* **Guapo Bay**[11] 6902 3-8-6 **47**..(b) KieranO'Neill 8 35
(Richard Hannon) *trckd ldrs: rdn over 2f out: hld whn sltly hmpd over 1f out: kpt on same pce* **20/1**

6364 **6** *shd* **Shongololo (IRE)**[45] 5823 3-9-5 **60**..................................[1] OisinMurphy 3 47
(Andrew Balding) *trckd ldrs: rdn over 2f out: nt pce to mount chal* **4/1**[1]

440 **7** ½ **Living Leader**[42] 5958 7-8-10 **52**....(bt) RobHornby(3) 7 39
(Grace Harris) *s.i.s: last pair: hdwy over 2f out: sn rdn: hld in 5th whn hmpd ins fnl f* **20/1**

3000 **8** 2¼ **Gift From God**[38] 6091 3-9-5 **60**....[1] SamHitchcott 10 41
(Hugo Froud) *hld up bhd : rdn wl over 1f out: little imp* **25/1**

0-00 **9** 1¼ **Maer Rocks (IRE)**[11] 6890 3-8-7 **48**....[1] TomMarquand 6 25
(Marcus Tregoning) *mid-div: rdn over 2f out: wknd fnl f* **25/1**

0-43 **10** nk **Locommotion**[63] 5233 4-8-13 **55**.... JosephineGordon(3) 1 33
(Matthew Salaman) *trckd ldrs: rdn over 2f out: tight for room over 1f out: wknd fnl f* **9/1**

0000 **11** 13 **Romancingthestone**[11] 6902 3-7-12 **46** oh1....(v[1]) MillyNaseb(7) 5
(Karen George) *mid-div: rdn 3f out: wknd over 1f out* **100/1**

0002 **12** 1¾ **Flying Sakhee**[31] 6291 3-8-11 **52**.... DannyBrock 9
(John Bridger) *mid-div: rdn 3f out: wknd over 1f out* **10/1**

1m 31.08s (2.48) **Going Correction** +0.35s/f (Good)
WFA 3 from 4yo+ 2lb **12** Ran SP% **115.2**
Speed ratings (Par 101): **99,95,93,92,90 90,89,86,85,85 70,68**
CSF £29.25 CT £133.69 TOTE £6.50: £2.10, £1.90, £1.80; EX 38.20 Trifecta £164.60.
Owner Macguire's Bloodstock Ltd **Bred** Bricklow Stud **Trained** Market Drayton, Shropshire

FOCUS
The second division of the moderate 7f handicap. The first pair raced down the middle and there aren't many positives to take from those behind the winner.

7213 EBF STALLIONS BATHWICK TYRES CONDITIONS STKS 6f 212y
4:20 (4:20) (Class 3) 3-Y-0+ **£9,056** (£2,695; £1,346; £673) **Stalls** Low

Form RPR

11-6 **1** **Crazy Horse**[148] 2283 3-9-5 107.... RobertHavlin 3 115
(John Gosden) *hld up: hdwy over 2f out: rdn to chal over 1f out: led fnl 130yds: r.o wl* **11/4**[2]

200- **2** ¾ **Estidhkaar (IRE)**[421] 5431 4-9-2 110.... PaulHanagan 6 109
(Richard Hannon) *led: rdn whn chal over 1f out: hdd fnl 130yds: no ex towards fin* **11/4**[2]

-546 **3** 3¾ **Absolutely So (IRE)**[23] 6558 6-9-7 109.... OisinMurphy 4 104
(Andrew Balding) *racd keenly trcking ldrs: rdn and ev ch over 1f out: no ex fnl 120yds* **15/8**[1]

042- **4** 1¾ **Kool Kompany (IRE)**[135] 4-9-7 105.... SeanLevey 5 100
(Richard Hannon) *trckd ldr: rdn 2f out: kpt on same pce* **11/1**[3]

2311 **5** 2¾ **Baron Bolt**[47] 5759 3-9-0 93.... JimmyFortune 1 87
(Paul Cole) *broke wl: sn stdd bk into last pair: hdwy over 2f out: effrt over 1f out: fdd ins fnl f* **14/1**

4300 **6** nk **Calder Prince (IRE)**[24] 6547 3-9-0 99.... RichardKingscote 7 86
(Tom Dascombe) *trckd ldrs: rdn over 2f out: sn outpcd: kpt on again but no threat fnl f* **16/1**

0100 **7** 6 **Medburn Dream**[15] 6803 3-9-0 85.... PatDobbs 8 70
(Paul Henderson) *trckd ldrs: rdn over 2f out: wknd over 1f out* **66/1**

1m 28.87s (0.27) **Going Correction** +0.35s/f (Good)
WFA 3 from 4yo+ 2lb **7** Ran SP% **110.5**
Speed ratings (Par 107): **112,111,106,104,101 101,94**
CSF £9.98 TOTE £3.40: £2.00, £1.50; EX 11.20 Trifecta £23.10.
Owner Ms Rachel D S Hood **Bred** Rachel D S Hood **Trained** Newmarket, Suffolk

FOCUS
A decent conditions event and solid form, with a smart effort from the unexposed winner.

7214 BATHWICKCARANDVANHIRE.CO.UK H'CAP 1m 1f 198y
4:50 (4:53) (Class 5) (0-70,70) 3-Y-0 **£3,234** (£962; £481; £240) **Stalls** Low

Form RPR

2304 **1** **Bigger And Better**[17] 6737 3-9-4 **67**.... SeanLevey 4 76
(Richard Hannon) *mid-div: hdwy 3f out: rdn to ld over 1f out: styd on wl* **5/1**[2]

4363 **2** 1 **Maroc**[5] 7078 3-9-7 **70**....(t) JimmyFortune 10 77
(Paul Cole) *led: rdn 3f out: hdd over 1f out: styd on gamely but a being hld fnl f* **7/1**

4-40 **3** 1¼ **Match My Fire (IRE)**[19] 6665 3-9-4 **67**.... FMBerry 3 71
(Ralph Beckett) *in tch: rdn to chse ldrs over 2f out: styd on same pce ins fnl f* **9/2**[1]

402 **4** ½ **Transmitting**[25] 6520 3-9-4 **67**.... RobertHavlin 11 70
(Sir Michael Stoute) *s.i.s: towards rr: hdwy fr 2f out: rdn over 1f out: styd on fnl f but nt pce to get on terms* **9/1**

3050 **5** 1 **Pennerley**[26] 6485 3-8-13 **62**.... ThomasBrown 6 63
(James Eustace) *mid-div: rdn and hdwy over 1f out where nt clrest of runs: styng on ins fnl f but hld whn nt clr run towards fin* **16/1**

-040 **6** nk **Kuantan**[109] 3558 3-9-4 **67**....(b[1]) GeorgeBaker 9 67
(Roger Charlton) *hld up bhd: rdn over 2f out: hdwy over 1f out: styd on same pce fnl f: nvr trbld ldrs* **6/1**[3]

-466 **7** 3 **Combe Hay (FR)**[100] 3894 3-9-3 **69**.... JosephineGordon(3) 1 63
(Henry Spiller) *trckd ldrs: rdn and ev ch 2f out: wknd ins fnl f* **20/1**

53-3 **8** hd **Hairdryer**[192] 1185 3-9-7 **70**.... OisinMurphy 12 64
(Andrew Balding) *mid-div: hdwy over 2f out: sn rdn: chsd ldrs over 1f out: fdd fnl 120yds* **6/1**[3]

5634 **9** 2¼ **Cliff Edge (IRE)**[10] 6921 3-8-13 **62**....[1] PaulHanagan 8 52
(Roger Varian) *rdn over 2f out: nvr bttr than mid-div* **10/1**

0456 **10** 1¼ **Perpetual Change (IRE)**[35] 6194 3-9-3 **66**.... PatDobbs 5 53
(Clive Cox) *trckd ldr: rdn 3f out: wknd over 1f out* **16/1**

605 **11** 3¼ **Rattle On**[15] 6805 3-8-13 **62**.... SamHitchcott 7 43
(Jim Boyle) *mid-div: sme hdwy u.p over 2f out: nvr threatened: wknd over 1f out* **14/1**

0425 **12** 7 **Saga Sprint (IRE)**[29] 6370 3-9-7 **70**.... TomMarquand 2 37
(J R Jenkins) *in tch: rdn 3f out: wknd over 1f out* **33/1**

2m 11.72s (1.82) **Going Correction** +0.35s/f (Good) **12** Ran SP% **121.1**
Speed ratings (Par 101): **106,105,104,103,103 102,100,100,98,97 94,89**
CSF £40.99 CT £172.75 TOTE £7.10: £2.40, £2.50, £2.20; EX 35.70 Trifecta £201.80.
Owner Carmichael Pryde **Bred** Cheveley Park Stud Ltd **Trained** East Everleigh, Wilts

FOCUS
They went a routine pace in this modest handicap and the main action was again near the stands' side. The winner built on his latest back-to-form effort.

7215 BATHWICK TYRES "SEASON FINALE" H'CAP 1m 6f 21y
5:20 (5:22) (Class 3) (0-95,93) 3-Y-0+ **£8,086** (£2,406; £1,202; £601) **Stalls** Far side

Form RPR

5115 **1** **Champagne Champ**[23] 6582 4-9-7 **86**.... RichardKingscote 7 96
(Rod Millman) *a.p: rdn to ld over 2f out: edgd lft over 1f out: styd on wl: rdn out* **12/1**

20-2 **2** 1 **Not Never**[24] 6544 4-9-11 **93**.... JosephineGordon(3) 9 101
(Hugo Palmer) *trckd ldrs: rdn to chse wnr whn swtchd rt over 1f out: styd on but a being hld* **7/1**

242 **3** 1¾ **Endless Acres (IRE)**[89] 4265 3-8-6 **80**....(v[1]) TomMarquand 5 86
(Charlie Fellowes) *mid-div: rdn and hdwy whn swtchd rt over 1f out: styd on fnl f: wnt 3rd fnl 120yds* **10/1**

2111 **4** 3 **Pleasure Dome**[16] 6767 3-8-13 **87**.... JimmyFortune 12 88
(Peter Chapple-Hyam) *led: rdn and hdd over 2f out: styd on same pce* **11/1**

1-63 **5** ½ **Argus (IRE)**[30] 6333 4-9-11 **90**.... OisinMurphy 11 91
(Ralph Beckett) *mid-div: hdwy 3f out: sn swtchd rt: rdn 2f out: chsd ldng pair over 1f out tl no ex fnl 140yds* **8/1**

-112 **6** 4½ **Parliamentarian (IRE)**[17] 6735 3-9-2 **90**.... GeorgeBaker 10 84
(Charlie Appleby) *in tch: hdwy 3f out: sn rdn: chsng ldrs whn swtchd rt over 1f out: wknd ins fnl f* **4/1**[1]

2113 **7** nk **Marmajuke Bay**[37] 6121 3-8-5 **79**....(p) PaulHanagan 8 73
(Mark Usher) *hld up towards rr: rdn and hdwy over 2f out: nvr threatened: wknd ins fnl f* **11/2**[3]

5424 **8** ¾ **The Otmoor Poet**[19] 6665 3-7-12 **77**.... HollieDoyle(5) 2 70
(Alan King) *hld up towards rr: hdwy over 2f out: effrt over 1f out: wknd ins fnl f* **5/1**[2]

-125 **9** hd **Jack Bear**[24] 5381 5-8-11 **79**.... RobHornby(3) 4 72
(Harry Whittington) *mid-div: rdn over 2f out: wknd ent fnl f* **16/1**

3200 **10** shd **Rideonastar (IRE)**[10] 6919 5-9-4 **83**.... PatDobbs 1 75
(Brendan Powell) *in tch: rdn 3f out: wknd over 1f out* **25/1**

1000 **11** 8 **Green Light**[37] 6118 5-9-13 **92**....(b) FMBerry 3 73
(Ralph Beckett) *a towards rr* **25/1**

3m 9.96s (2.56) **Going Correction** +0.35s/f (Good)
WFA 3 from 4yo+ 9lb **11** Ran SP% **114.4**
Speed ratings (Par 107): **106,105,104,102,102 99,99,99,99,99 94**
CSF £90.96 CT £870.20 TOTE £11.60: £3.10, £2.60, £3.70; EX 97.20 Trifecta £1436.30.
Owner Five Horses Ltd **Bred** Five Horses Ltd **Trained** Kentisbeare, Devon

FOCUS
A fair staying handicap in which it proved hard to make up ground. The winner continued his recent progress.
T/Plt: £20.10 to a £1 stake. Pool: £52,823.17 - 1912.03 winning units. T/Qpdt: £5.40 to a £1 stake. Pool: £3,382.27 - 459.79 winning units. **Tim Mitchell**

7011 WINDSOR (R-H)
Monday, October 10

OFFICIAL GOING: Good to firm (good in places; 8.8)
Wind: Moderate, behind Weather: Fine but cloudy

7216 BRITISH STALLION STUDS EBF MAIDEN STKS 6f
1:30 (1:31) (Class 5) 2-Y-0 **£3,234** (£962; £481; £240) **Stalls** Low

Form RPR

00 **1** **Open Wide (USA)**[12] 6880 2-9-5 0.... PaulMulrennan 9 77+
(Amanda Perrett) *hld up in rr: prog on outer fr 1/2-way: clsd on ldrs over 1f out and rdn: led last 75yds: won gng away* **10/1**

5 **2** 1 **Rebecca Rocks**[125] 2990 2-9-0 0.... FergusSweeney 10 69
(Henry Candy) *pressed ldrs on outer: led over 1f out and crossed to rail: drvn fnl f: hdd and outpcd last 75yds* **8/1**

3 1¼ **Founding Father (FR)** 2-9-5 0.... MartinHarley 4 70
(James Tate) *cl up: rdn to ld 2f out to over 1f out: one pce after* **5/2**[1]

0 **4** 2½ **Magique Touch**[12] 6866 2-8-11 0.... KieranShoemark(3) 8 58
(Roger Charlton) *in tch on outer: effrt over 2f out: outpcd fr over 1f out: kpt on* **25/1**

60 **5** ½ **Moonstone Rock**[19] 6673 2-9-0 0.... LiamKeniry 2 56+
(Jim Boyle) *hld up in 9th: nudged along over 2f out: reminder over 1f out: gd prog fnl f: r.o wl nr fin: likely improver* **50/1**

40 **6** ½ **Star Stream**[52] 5615 2-9-5 0.... MartinDwyer 7 60
(Marcus Tregoning) *pressed ldrs: upsides over 2f out: wknd over 1f out* **4/1**[3]

4 **7** ¾ **Vibes (IRE)**[60] 5324 2-9-5 0.... WilliamCarson 1 57
(Jamie Osborne) *stdd sn after s: hld up in detached last: pushed along over 2f out: stl looked green but kpt on fnl f: do bttr* **7/1**

0 **8** 1¾ **Orithia (USA)**[21] 6622 2-9-0 0.... JimCrowley 5 47
(Seamus Durack) *mde most to 2f out: wknd over 1f out* **25/1**

2 **9** 1 **Trump's Magic (USA)**[40] 6016 2-9-5 0.... AdamKirby 6 52
(David Evans) *trckd ldrs: shkn up 2f out: wknd tamely over 1f out* **11/4**[2]

10 8 **Wedgewood Wonder** 2-9-0 0.... JFEgan 3 20
(Tony Carroll) *t.k.h: hld up towards rr and rn green: wknd over 2f out: sn bhd* **100/1**

1m 11.25s (-1.75) **Going Correction** -0.20s/f (Firm) **10** Ran SP% **118.6**
Speed ratings (Par 95): **103,101,100,96,96 95,94,92,90,80**
CSF £85.61 TOTE £16.20: £4.20, £2.40, £2.00; EX 123.50 Trifecta £702.80.
Owner George Materna & John McInerney **Bred** Moyglare Stud **Trained** Pulborough, W Sussex

FOCUS
There hadn't been much rain over the previous few days but 3mm of selective watering had taken place on Saturday, leaving the going as good to firm, good in places (GoingStick: 8.8). The inner running rail had been moved to provide fresh racing lines for this meeting - the inner of the straight was dolled out 13yds at 6f and 5yds at the winning line, and the top bend was dolled out 4yds from its normal inner configuration, adding 20yds to race distances of 1m+. No more than a fair maiden, but the winner may have more to offer.

7217 BERKSHIRE COLLEGE OF AGRICULTURE NURSERY H'CAP 5f 10y
2:00 (2:03) (Class 5) (0-75,75) 2-Y-0 **£2,911** (£866; £432; £216) **Stalls** Low

Form RPR

2613 **1** **Broadhaven Honey (IRE)**[14] 6830 2-9-4 **72**.... JimCrowley 11 77
(Ed McMahon) *racd in centre: mde all: drvn over 1f out: hld on wl fnl f* **7/1**[2]

315 **2** ½ **Fabric**[21] 6630 2-9-4 **72**.... TedDurcan 14 75
(Richard Hannon) *racd in centre: trckd ldrs: prog to take 2nd 2f out: drvn to chal fnl f: kpt on but a hld* **15/2**[3]

230 **3** ¾ **Spinnaker Bay (IRE)**[36] 6162 2-8-13 **72**.... AdamMcNamara(5) 16 72
(William Jarvis) *racd in centre: chsd ldrs: rdn 2f out: styd on fnl f: nvr quite able to chal* **16/1**

0500 **4** hd **Parys Mountain (IRE)**[36] 6162 2-9-7 **75**.... SteveDrowne 7 75
(Charles Hills) *t.k.h: hld up in rr: prog towards centre 2f out: styd on ins fnl f: nrst fin* **17/2**

51 **5** nk **Trick Of The Light (IRE)**[12] 6873 2-9-7 **75**.... JackMitchell 1 74+
(Roger Varian) *racd against nr side: on terms w overall ldrs in centre to 2f out: kpt on against last 100yds* **2/1**[1]

5036 **6** hd **Lady Cleo (IRE)**[20] 6658 2-8-13 **67**....(t) MartinHarley 15 65
(Stuart Williams) *racd in centre: hld up: effrt on wd outside 2f out: kpt on fnl f: nrst fin* **33/1**

3251 **7** *nk* **Marquee Club**[14] 6829 2-9-7 **75** WilliamCarson 8 72
(Jamie Osborne) *racd towards nr side: on terms w overall ldrs in centre: stl nrly upsides over 1f out: one pce after* **17/2**
5360 **8** *1 1/4* **Roundabout Magic (IRE)**[14] 6830 2-8-9 **63** NickyMackay 9 55
(Simon Dow) *s.s: mostly in last tl styd on u.p fr 2f out: nvr able to rch ldrs* **66/1**
510 **9** *shd* **Swift Mover (IRE)**[37] 6139 2-8-13 **72** HollieDoyle(5) 4 64
(Richard Hannon) *awkward to post: racd towards nr side: nvr bttr than midfield: kpt on fnl f but nt pce to threaten* **16/1**
4440 **10** *2 1/4* **Neptunes Secret**[31] 6289 2-8-12 **69** EdwardGreatrex(3) 5 53
(Sylvester Kirk) *hld up in rr: rdn over 2f out: fnd little and nvr a threat* **25/1**
2150 **11** *3/4* **Zebspear (IRE)**[20] 6658 2-9-1 **69** JFEgan 6 50
(Joseph Tuite) *spd towards nr side 3f: fdd fnl f* **25/1**
0026 **12** *nk* **Pastfact**[27] 6440 2-8-8 **67** GeorgiaCox(5) 3 47
(Malcolm Saunders) *t.k.h: hld up in rr and racd towards nr side: no prog over 1f out* **12/1**
3210 **13** *1/2* **Compton Lane**[20] 6658 2-9-7 **75** FrederikTylicki 12 53
(Rod Millman) *racd in centre: pressed wnr to 2f out: sn wknd* **14/1**
566 **14** *2 1/2* **Polly's Angels (IRE)**[31] 6295 2-8-11 **65** ShaneKelly 13 34
(Richard Hughes) *chsd ldrs in centre: hanging and wknd over 1f out: eased* **33/1**
0060 **15** *10* **Latest Quest (IRE)**[9] 6950 2-8-6 **65** MitchGodwin(5) 2
(Sylvester Kirk) *racd towards nr side: struggling in rr bef 1/2-way: t.o* **40/1**

59.78s (-0.52) **Going Correction** -0.20s/f (Firm) **15** Ran SP% **122.3**
Speed ratings (Par 95): **96,95,94,93,93 92,92,90,90,86 85,84,84,80,64**
CSF £55.47 CT £828.71 TOTE £6.00: £1.60, £2.40, £5.10; EX 57.60 Trifecta £391.30.
Owner M Doocey, S Doocey & P J Doocey **Bred** James F Hanly **Trained** Lichfield, Staffs

FOCUS
The race developed up the centre and those drawn high came to the fore. A tight finish and the form looks sensible rated around the principals.

7218 WINDSOR VEHICLE LEASING MAIDEN STKS (DIV I) 1m 67y
2:30 (2:31) (Class 5) 3-Y-O+ **£2,911** (£866; £432; £216) **Stalls** Low

Form RPR
0-4 **1** **Eljeemi (IRE)**[123] 3066 3-9-5 0 JimCrowley 1 84
(William Haggas) *mde all: gng best over 2f out: drvn over 1f out against nr side rail: styd on wl: unchal* **3/1**[2]
2 **2** *2 1/4* **First Voyage (IRE)**[7] 7009 3-9-5 0 AdamKirby 2 79
(Charlie Appleby) *chsd wnr: shkn up over 2f out: tried to cl over 1f out u.p: no impresson fnl f* **6/4**[1]
6 **3** *1 3/4* **Commodity (IRE)**[181] 1397 3-9-5 0 TedDurcan 3 75
(Sir Michael Stoute) *trckd ldng pair: pushed along over 2f out: shkn up and kpt on same pce fr over 1f out: no imp* **3/1**[2]
3 **4** *3/4* **Singapore Sling**[112] 3464 3-9-5 0 FrederikTylicki 10 73
(James Fanshawe) *trckd ldng pair: pushed along over 2f out: shkn up disputing 3rd fr over 1f out: no imp* **5/1**[3]
60 **5** *7* **Saleh (IRE)**[54] 5544 3-9-0 0 (e[1]) PaddyBradley(5) 4 57
(Lee Carter) *hld up off the pce disputing 7th: gng bttr than sme 3f out: rdn over 2f out: tk modest 5th wl over 1f out: no ch* **50/1**
6 **6** *1 1/4* **Princess Nia (IRE)**[18] 6703 3-9-0 0 (b[1]) MartinDwyer 5 49
(Brian Meehan) *sn detached in last pair: urged along bef 1/2-way: plugged on fr over 2f out: nvr a factor* **33/1**
46 **7** *3/4* **Whispered Kiss**[25] 6511 3-9-0 0 GrahamLee 8 47
(Mike Murphy) *plld hrd early: hld up disputing 5th: steadily wknd over 2f out* **50/1**
00 **8** *9* **Millady Percy**[259] 331 3-8-9 0 MitchGodwin(5) 9 27
(Roy Brotherton) *t.k.h early: hld up disputing 5th: wknd wl over 2f out* **100/1**
5 **9** *5* **Cougar Kid (IRE)**[16] 6765 5-9-8 0 FergusSweeney 6 20
(John O'Shea) *sn detached in last: nvr a factor and a bhd* **66/1**
0 **10** *27* **Martyna**[147] 2312 3-9-0 0 WilliamCarson 7
(John Spearing) *dwlt: disp 7th and nvr on terms: wknd over 2f out: t.o* **100/1**

1m 41.97s (-2.73) **Going Correction** -0.25s/f (Firm)
WFA 3 from 5yo 3lb **10** Ran SP% **117.0**
Speed ratings (Par 103): **103,100,99,98,91 90,89,80,75,48**
CSF £7.86 TOTE £4.40: £1.50, £1.10, £1.20; EX 8.70 Trifecta £22.10.
Owner Sheikh Ahmed Al Maktoum **Bred** Hascombe And Valiant Studs **Trained** Newmarket, Suffolk

FOCUS
Race distance increased by 20yds. The positions changed very little in this maiden, the winner controlling things from the front. The first three all built on previous efforts.

7219 WINDSOR VEHICLE LEASING MAIDEN STKS (DIV II) 1m 67y
3:00 (3:03) (Class 5) 3-Y-O+ **£2,911** (£866; £432; £216) **Stalls** Low

Form RPR
36/ **1** **Archery Peak**[737] 6928 4-9-8 0 AdamKirby 3 84+
(Luca Cumani) *trckd ldng pair: shkn up over 2f out: clsd on outer over 1f out: led ins fnl f: r.o wl and sn clr* **1/1**[1]
5353 **2** *3* **Poet's Song (IRE)**[28] 6423 3-9-5 75 MartinDwyer 6 77
(Marcus Tregoning) *trckd ldr: shkn up over 2f out: clsd to ld over 1f out: hdd ins fnl f and sn outpcd* **2/1**[2]
54 **3** *3* **Electrify (IRE)**[20] 6661 3-9-0 0 JimCrowley 10 66
(Jeremy Noseda) *led: gng bttr than chalrs over 2f out: shkn up and hdd over 1f out: sn btn and only jst clung on for 3rd* **7/2**[3]
5 **4** *shd* **Sovrano Dolce (IRE)**[19] 6674 3-8-7 0 KevinLundie(7) 1 65
(Mike Murphy) *chsd ldrs in 5th: pushed along to take 4th over 2f out: rdn over 1f out: styd on ins fnl f: nrly snatched 3rd* **22/1**
5 *11* **Piccola Poppy** 3-9-0 0 WilliamCarson 5 40
(John Bridger) *mostly in 6th: rdn over 3f out: sn no ch* **33/1**
00 **6** *1 1/4* **Dark Enemy (IRE)**[15] 6805 3-9-2 0 EdwardGreatrex(3) 9 42
(Brendan Powell) *towards rr and nvr gng wl: u.p bef 1/2-way: nvr a factor* **66/1**
00 **7** *3/4* **Jaunty Joh (IRE)**[125] 2999 3-9-0 0 FergusSweeney 7 35
(Henry Candy) *chsd clr ldng trio to over 2f out: wknd* **20/1**
40 **8** *13* **Zorlu (IRE)**[25] 6511 3-9-0 0 CiaranMckee(5) 8 11
(John O'Shea) *v awkward s: a wl bhd: t.o* **66/1**
5 **9** *3 1/2* **Spanish Queen**[27] 6441 3-9-0 0 JohnFahy 2
(Mark Gillard) *sn in last pair and bhd: urged along bef 1/2-way: t.o* **33/1**
10 *4* **Masked Bandit** 3-9-5 0 JFEgan 4
(Simon Dow) *slowly away: plld hrd in rr: wd bnd over 5f out: wknd over 3f out: t.o* **33/1**

1m 42.61s (-2.09) **Going Correction** -0.25s/f (Firm)
WFA 3 from 4yo 3lb **10** Ran SP% **126.5**
Speed ratings (Par 103): **100,97,94,93,82 81,80,67,64,60**
CSF £3.35 TOTE £2.00: £1.10, £1.10, £1.50; EX 3.40 Trifecta £6.80.
Owner Jon S Kelly **Bred** Lofts Hall Stud, B Sangster & St Albans **Trained** Newmarket, Suffolk

FOCUS
Race distance increased by 20yds. This was run in a time 0.64sec slower than the first division. The winner has clear potential to do better, the second setting the standard.

7220 EQUESTRIAN SURFACES FILLIES' H'CAP 1m 67y
3:30 (3:30) (Class 4) (0-80,79) 3-Y-O+ **£4,690** (£1,395; £697; £348) **Stalls** Low

Form RPR
3345 **1** **Invermere**[15] 6811 3-8-11 **77** AdamMcNamara(5) 7 83
(Richard Fahey) *hld up in midfield: prog in centre of the crse over 2f out: rdn to ld jst over 1f out: drvn and hld on ins fnl f* **5/1**[3]
6413 **2** *1/2* **Nicarra (IRE)**[26] 6483 3-8-13 **74** FergusSweeney 4 79
(Henry Candy) *mde most: racd against nr side in st: hrd pressed 2f out: hdd jst over 1f out: kpt on wl nr fin* **7/2**[1]
232 **3** *shd* **Carpe Diem Lady (IRE)**[11] 6893 3-9-1 **76** (b) AdamKirby 1 81
(Clive Cox) *rousted to go prom fr s: plld off rail and rdn over 2f out: chal over 1f out: kpt on but a jst hld* **9/2**[2]
0543 **4** *1* **Ejayteekay**[11] 6893 3-8-8 **74** GeorgeWood(5) 9 79+
(Hughie Morrison) *hld up in last trio: pushed along and prog against rail over 2f out: trying to cl whn nt clr run 1f out: kpt on but nt rcvr* **5/1**[3]
2403 **5** *1/2* **Ttainted Love**[20] 6650 4-9-5 **77** (p) TedDurcan 10 79
(Chris Wall) *t.k.h early: hld up in last trio: sme prog on outer over 2f out: rdn and kpt on fnl f but too late to chal* **10/1**
3210 **6** *1 1/2* **Organza**[17] 6746 3-9-0 **75** (v) GrahamLee 8 73
(Mick Channon) *w ldr tl fdd u.p wl over 1f out* **16/1**
0424 **7** *1/2* **Poster Girl**[21] 6635 3-8-5 **71** MitchGodwin(5) 12 68
(Jonathan Portman) *dwlt: hld up in last trio: brought wd in st: tried to cl on ldrs fr 2f out but kpt on at same pce* **12/1**
046 **8** *1 1/4* **Malmostosa**[54] 5551 3-9-2 **77** (b[1]) MartinHarley 2 71
(Marco Botti) *hld up in midfield: swtchd off rail and shkn up 2f out: nt qckn and no imp ldrs after* **16/1**
0-26 **9** *10* **Giveaway Glance**[81] 4556 3-9-4 **79** JimCrowley 6 50
(Alan King) *t.k.h: cl up tl wknd qckly jst over 2f out* **7/1**
003 **10** *28* **Ambriel (IRE)**[25] 6501 3-9-1 **76** (b) PaulMulrennan 11
(Michael Dods) *t.k.h: pressed ldrs: wknd rapidly wl over 2f out: t.o* **20/1**
2400 **11** *69* **Stylistik**[23] 6580 3-8-5 **69** EdwardGreatrex(3) 5
(Luke Dace) *hld up in last trio: bdly squeezed for room against rail over 4f out: lost tch and sn virtually p.u* **33/1**

1m 41.74s (-2.96) **Going Correction** -0.25s/f (Firm)
WFA 3 from 4yo+ 3lb **11** Ran SP% **122.5**
Speed ratings (Par 102): **104,103,103,102,101 100,99,98,88,60**
CSF £23.90 CT £89.01 TOTE £5.20: £2.10, £1.40, £1.90; EX 27.20 Trifecta £178.40.
Owner Mcculloch Bloodstock Ltd **Bred** The Lavington Stud **Trained** Musley Bank, N Yorks

FOCUS
Race distance increased by 20yds. A tight handicap which was sound run, and straightforward form.

7221 MPM FLOORING LTD H'CAP 6f
4:00 (4:00) (Class 4) (0-80,80) 3-Y-O+ **£4,690** (£1,395; £697; £348) **Stalls** Low

Form RPR
3154 **1** **Menai (IRE)**[23] 6583 3-9-3 **77** SteveDrowne 16 92
(Charles Hills) *a gng wl: sn trckd ldr: led 2f out: shkn up and drew clr: comf* **6/1**[2]
5121 **2** *4* **Equistar**[14] 6831 3-9-1 **80** (t) GeorgeWood(5) 15 82
(Jonathan Portman) *led against rail: rdn and hdd 2f out: sn no ch w wnr but hld on for 2nd* **6/1**[2]
0342 **3** *1/2* **Anonymous John (IRE)**[47] 5773 4-9-6 **79** JFEgan 5 80
(Dominic Ffrench Davis) *chsd ldng pair: pushed along 1/2-way: one pce u.p fnl 2f but kpt on* **14/1**
-224 **4** *shd* **Joe Packet**[44] 5896 9-8-11 **77** Pierre-LouisJamin(7) 7 77
(Jonathan Portman) *settled in midfield: rdn on outer 2f out: styd on fnl f: nrly snatched 3rd* **20/1**
6105 **5** *3/4* **Vincentti (IRE)**[16] 6766 6-9-5 **78** ShaneKelly 6 76
(Ronald Harris) *in tch in midfield: drvn 2f out: kpt on fnl f to press for a pl nr fin* **12/1**
0520 **6** *nk* **Gambit**[38] 6079 3-9-6 **80** MartinHarley 3 77
(Tom Dascombe) *chsd ldng pair: rdn 2f out: one pce after and no imp* **7/1**[3]
3014 **7** *1/2* **Pandar**[28] 6409 7-9-7 **80** FrederikTylicki 12 75
(Michael Attwater) *hld up in last trio: rdn on outer 2f out: kpt on fnl f but nvr able to threaten* **25/1**
6011 **8** *1* **Upavon**[50] 5673 6-9-7 **80** (t) JackMitchell 1 72+
(Stuart Williams) *dwlt: hld up in last trio: stl there 2f out: pushed along and beginning to run on whn nt clr run jst ins fnl f: kpt on but nvr involved* **7/1**[3]
0060 **9** *nk* **Fleckerl (IRE)**[10] 6914 6-9-7 **80** (p) PaulMulrennan 4 71
(Conor Dore) *dwlt: hld up in last trio: pushed along 2f out: nvr in it but kpt on last 100yds* **9/1**
5145 **10** *1 1/2* **Gin In The Inn (IRE)**[18] 6714 3-8-12 **77** AdamMcNamara(5) 10 63
(Richard Fahey) *chsd ldng pair: rdn and no imp jst over 2f out: wknd jst over 1f out* **3/1**[1]
6200 **11** *1 1/2* **Sixties Sue**[9] 6946 3-9-2 **76** GrahamLee 14 58
(Mick Channon) *a towards rr on outer: rdn and no prog 2f out* **12/1**
4-00 **12** *6* **Princess Kodia (IRE)**[28] 6409 3-8-8 **75** JordanUys(7) 8 37
(Brian Meehan) *free to post: dwlt: rcvrd and in tch on outer after 2f: wknd 2f out: sn bhd* **40/1**

1m 10.97s (-2.03) **Going Correction** -0.20s/f (Firm)
WFA 3 from 4yo+ 1lb **12** Ran SP% **121.7**
Speed ratings (Par 105): **105,99,99,98,97 97,96,95,95,93 91,83**
CSF £42.15 CT £501.81 TOTE £8.60: £2.40, £2.80, £3.80; EX 52.30 Trifecta £470.00.
Owner Julie Martin & David R Martin & Partner **Bred** Yeomanstown Stud **Trained** Lambourn, Berks

FOCUS
They didn't go that quick early on and it paid to race handily (first two were drawn wide but crossed over to race stands' side), but nevertheless it was still a good effort from the winner to pull clear. It was a surprise step forward from him.

7222 CHATTERBOX TWO-WAY RADIO "CONFINED" H'CAP 1m 2f 7y
4:30 (4:30) (Class 4) (0-85,82) 3-Y-O+ **£4,690** (£1,395; £697; £348) **Stalls** Centre

Form RPR
5040 **1** **Beardwood**[9] 6956 4-9-10 **80** (p) AdamKirby 5 89
(Mark Johnston) *hld up in midfield: prog on outer 3f out: rdn to ld over 1f out: kpt on fnl f and a holding runner-up* **6/1**[3]
2540 **2** *1/2* **Priors Brook**[93] 4138 5-9-5 **75** LiamKeniry 3 83
(Andrew Balding) *trckd ldrs: clsd to ld wl over 1f out: sn hdd: pressed wnr after but nt qckn and hld ins fnl f* **7/1**

2403 **3** 1 1/2 **Sennockian Star**[16] **6794** 6-9-12 **82**...........................(v) PaulMulrennan 4 87
(Mark Johnston) *led 1f: chsd ldr: led again 3f out and sn rdn: hdd and nt qckn wl over 1f out: kpt on again ins fnl f* **4/1**[2]

3306 **4** 2 1/2 **Starlit Cantata**[9] **6947** 5-9-7 **77**.. JohnFahy 2 77
(Eve Johnson Houghton) *in tch in midfield: rdn and effrt 2f out: drvn and no imp over 1f out: fdd ins fnl f* **12/1**

3044 **5** nk **Persun**[9] **6948** 4-9-11 **81**.. GrahamLee 8 80
(Mick Channon) *chsd ldrs: pushed along 3f out: nt qckn wl over 1f out: one pce after* **7/1**

5540 **6** 2 **Bergholt (IRE)**[18] **6701** 3-8-3 **67**...........................(v[1]) EdwardGreatrex(3) 7 62
(Philip Hide) *led after 1f: drvn and hdd 3f out: lost 2nd 2f out against rail and fdd* **14/1**

3432 **7** 6 **Melabi (IRE)**[66] **5102** 3-8-9 **77**.................................. CallumRodriguez(7) 1 60
(Richard Ford) *hld up in last trio: pushed along 3f out: no prog and btn 2f out* **12/1**

6466 **8** 4 **Ataman (IRE)**[28] **6416** 4-9-6 **76**...(t) TedDurcan 6 51
(Chris Wall) *hld up in last: rdn and no prog over 2f out: wl btn after* **7/1**

0000 **9** 2 1/4 **Zodiakos (IRE)**[38] **6084** 3-9-7 **82**... JimCrowley 9 53
(Hugo Palmer) *chsd ldng pair to 1/2-way: rdn 3f out and sn lost pl: wknd and bhd over 1f out* **7/2**[1]

2m 4.7s (-4.00) **Going Correction** -0.25s/f (Firm)
WFA 3 from 4yo+ 5lb **9** Ran SP% **116.1**
Speed ratings (Par 105): **106,105,104,102,102 100,95,92,90**
CSF £47.68 CT £188.74 TOTE £6.40: £2.10, £2.70, £1.80; EX 25.50 Trifecta £242.10.
Owner A D Spence & M B Spence **Bred** Kirtlington Stud Ltd **Trained** Middleham Moor, N Yorks

FOCUS
Race distance increased by 20yds. A 'confined' handicap for horses who have not won for a year, so probably not form to be too positive about. It does read as sound, however.

7223 MOULDEN MARKETING H'CAP 1m 3f 135y
5:00 (5:00) (Class 5) (0-70,70) 3-Y-O **£2,911** (£866; £432; £216) **Stalls** Centre

Form RPR

3-00 **1** **Velvet Revolution**[157] **2012** 3-9-4 **67**................................ MartinHarley 10 77
(Marco Botti) *hld up in rr: prog over 3f out: rdn to chse ldr 2f out: clsd over 1f out: drvn into narrow ld last 75yds: jst hld on* **17/2**

1312 **2** nse **Tyrell (IRE)**[45] **5830** 3-9-4 **67**..(b) FergusSweeney 8 77
(Alan King) *led at gd pce: stretched on 4f out and had most in trble: drvn over 2f out: narrowly hdd 75yds out: kpt on wl: jst failed* **9/4**[1]

-506 **3** 4 **Sir Pass I Am**[27] **6444** 3-8-11 **63**............................... EdwardGreatrex(3) 5 66
(Andrew Balding) *settled towards rr: rdn and struggling 4f out: kpt on fr over 2f out to take 3rd fnl f* **10/3**[2]

1223 **4** 5 **Masterson (IRE)**[16] **6767** 3-9-3 **66**....................................... GrahamLee 4 61
(Mick Channon) *mostly chsd ldr: rdn over 3f out: no imp and lost 2nd 2f out: fdd and lost 3rd fnl f* **8/1**

6614 **5** 5 **Midnight Mood**[69] **4987** 3-8-11 **60**.. LiamKeniry 1 47
(Dominic Ffrench Davis) *in tch: shkn up and effrt over 3f out: no prog and btn 2f out: wknd* **10/1**

0 **6** 3 1/2 **Light Of Air (FR)**[113] **3453** 3-9-4 **70**............................ HectorCrouch(3) 9 51
(Gary Moore) *hld up in rr: pushed along and reminder 4f out: no prog 3f out: fdd* **16/1**

000 **7** 28 **Ma Peek (USA)**[121] **3160** 3-9-6 **69**................................[1] PaulMulrennan 7 4
(Brian Meehan) *disp 2nd pl to 1/2-way: rdn 4f out: wknd qckly over 2f out: t.o* **6/1**[3]

-405 **8** 12 **Sayedaati Saadati (IRE)**[101] **3841** 3-8-13 **62**..............[1] SaleemGolam 2
(John Butler) *sn wl detached in last: t.o fr 1/2-way* **66/1**

0-30 **9** 4 **Sennockian Song**[107] **3636** 3-9-4 **67**.................................. JimCrowley 6
(Mark Johnston) *disp 2nd pl for 5f: lost pl and struggling over 4f out: t.o* **10/1**

2m 26.78s (-2.72) **Going Correction** -0.25s/f (Firm) **9** Ran SP% **115.3**
Speed ratings (Par 101): **99,98,96,92,89 87,68,60,57**
CSF £27.94 CT £78.03 TOTE £13.60: £3.30, £1.40, £1.50; EX 41.10 Trifecta £231.70.
Owner Heart of the South Racing & Partner **Bred** Newsells Park Stud **Trained** Newmarket, Suffolk

FOCUS
Race distance increased by 20yds. This was run at a good gallop and the first two finished nicely clear. The winner belatedly built on his debut promise and the form should work out.
T/Plt: £68.50 to a £1 stake. Pool: £71,903.71 - 765.19 winning units. T/Qpdt: £4.30 to a £1 stake. Pool: £6,748.29 - 1153.77 winning units. **Jonathan Neesom**

6523 YARMOUTH (L-H)
Monday, October 10

OFFICIAL GOING: Good changing to good to soft after race 1 (2.10) changing to soft after race 2 (2.40)
Wind: breezy Weather: very changeable with showers; 12 degrees

7224 BRITISH STALLION STUDS EBF MAIDEN STKS (PLUS 10 RACE) 6f 3y
2:10 (2:13) (Class 4) 2-Y-O **£4,657** (£1,386; £692; £346) **Stalls** Centre

Form RPR

2 **1** **Ekhtiyaar**[25] **6524** 2-9-5 0.. DaneO'Neill 3 85+
(Roger Varian) *mde all: pushed clr 2f out: easily* **30/100**[1]

03 **2** 3 1/2 **Secret Agent**[17] **6731** 2-9-5 0.. RyanMoore 9 72+
(William Muir) *chsd wnr: drvn 2f out: kpt on same pce and a hld after* **4/1**[2]

50 **3** 3 **King Of Nepal**[87] **4349** 2-9-5 0...................................... GrahamGibbons 1 63
(Henry Candy) *v keen chsng ldrs: 3rd and rdn 2f out: one pce and wl hld after* **12/1**[3]

60 **4** 2 3/4 **Tea El Tee (IRE)**[59] **5371** 2-9-5 0.. LukeMorris 7 55
(Gay Kelleway) *racd keenly: cl up tl drvn over 2f out: sn btn and hanging lft* **50/1**

06 **5** 4 1/2 **Aqshion Stations**[19] **6673** 2-9-5 0.. JoeFanning 2 41
(William Jarvis) *plld hrd: cl up tl drvn and fdd over 2f out* **40/1**

6 1/2 **Verdi (IRE)** 2-9-5 0.. StevieDonohoe 6 40
(John Ryan) *towards rr: rdn and fdd over 2f out* **28/1**

7 1 3/4 **Proud Kate** 2-9-0 0.. AdamBeschizza 8 30
(Christine Dunnett) *last away: sn pushed along and outpcd: struggling 1/2-way* **100/1**

1m 12.48s (-1.92) **Going Correction** -0.375s/f (Firm) **7** Ran SP% **113.5**
Speed ratings (Par 97): **97,92,88,84,78 78,75**
CSF £1.77 TOTE £1.20: £1.10, £1.30; EX 1.90 Trifecta £5.80.
Owner Hamdan Al Maktoum **Bred** James Ortega Bloodstock **Trained** Newmarket, Suffolk

FOCUS
There was 7mm of rain overnight and further rain around during the day, but there was no problem with the wet patch which blighted the September Festival, so the runners were able to use the whole of the straight track rather than avoiding the area at the 5f pole. The going was changed to good to soft, soft in places following this opener. The order in this maiden didn't change much and the form is rated around the first two.

7225 EBF STALLIONS MAIDEN STKS (PLUS 10 RACE) (DIV I) 1m 3y
2:40 (2:41) (Class 4) 2-Y-O **£4,657** (£1,386; £692; £346) **Stalls** Centre

Form RPR

6 **1** **Wolf Country**[32] **6262** 2-9-5 0.. WilliamBuick 5 88+
(Charlie Appleby) *mde all and travelled strly: pushed clr 2f out: v comf* **4/5**[1]

2 3 1/2 **Dhajeej (IRE)** 2-9-5 0... DaneO'Neill 3 80+
(Roger Varian) *cl up: chsd wnr after 2f: rdn over 2f out: no imp after but kpt on nicely: promising* **16/1**

3 3 1/2 **American History (USA)** 2-9-5 0.................................... FrankieDettori 7 75+
(John Gosden) *towards rr: stdy prog fr 1/2-way: sn pushed along: last of three who wnt clr 2f out: kpt on same pce after* **7/2**[2]

4 5 **Blushing Red (FR)** 2-9-5 0... LukeMorris 9 62
(Ed Dunlop) *last after 2f: pushed along to go mod 4th 2f out: nvr nr ldrs* **40/1**

5 4 **Medicean Dream (IRE)** 2-9-5 0... JamieSpencer 8 53
(Luca Cumani) *midfield: rdn and outpcd wl over 2f out* **20/1**

0 **6** 3 1/4 **Solo Mission**[18] **6704** 2-9-5 0.. GrahamGibbons 4 46
(William Haggas) *chsd ldrs: rdn wl over 3f out: struggling over 2f out: t.o* **11/2**[3]

7 4 **Desert Grey (IRE)** 2-9-5 0... AndreaAtzeni 2 37
(Roger Varian) *prom: rdn after 2f: lost pl and struggling over 2f out: t.o over 1f out* **16/1**

0 **8** 5 **Sticks McKenzie**[26] **6486** 2-9-5 0.. JoeFanning 6 26
(Michael Bell) *chsd ldrs: rdn wl over 3f out: sn wknd: t.o fnl 2f* **40/1**

9 35 **Here I Go Again (IRE)** 2-9-5 0.................................. AdamBeschizza 1
(Christine Dunnett) *slowly away: plld hrd sn pressing ldrs: rdn and wknd 1/2-way: t.o over 3f out* **150/1**

1m 36.58s (-4.02) **Going Correction** -0.375s/f (Firm) **9** Ran SP% **115.2**
Speed ratings (Par 97): **105,101,98,93,89 85,81,76,41**
CSF £16.04 TOTE £1.90: £1.10, £2.60, £1.90; EX 14.60 Trifecta £61.40.
Owner Godolphin **Bred** Stiftung Gestut Fahrhof **Trained** Newmarket, Suffolk

FOCUS
There was another going change following this race, conditions easing again to soft all over. The winner put his experience to good use and looked promising, with the next four, who came home at fair intervals, all newcomers. The first two were in those positions throughout.

7226 EBF STALLIONS MAIDEN STKS (PLUS 10 RACE) (DIV II) 1m 3y
3:10 (3:12) (Class 4) 2-Y-O **£4,657** (£1,386; £692; £346) **Stalls** Centre

Form RPR

1 **Fierce Impact (JPN)** 2-9-5 0.. JamieSpencer 6 76+
(David Simcock) *cl up and gng strly: effrt to ld over 2f out: rdn and wl in command fnl f* **14/1**

0 **2** 1 3/4 **Casina Di Notte (IRE)**[47] **5764** 2-9-5 0......................(b[1]) DanielMuscutt 3 72
(Marco Botti) *led: drvn and hdd over 2f out: sn lost pl* **50/1**

3 1/2 **Tamleek (USA)** 2-9-5 0.. RyanMoore 4 71+
(Saeed bin Suroor) *missed break: last early: stdy prog over 2f out: styd on ins fnl f: too much to do: b.b.v* **3/1**[2]

5 **4** 1 3/4 **Alfarris (FR)**[17] **6750** 2-9-5 0.. DaneO'Neill 7 67+
(William Haggas) *missed break: bhd: prog over 2f out: rdn and no imp ins fnl f: too much to do* **7/4**[1]

5 3/4 **Joshua Reynolds** 2-9-5 0... FrankieDettori 2 66
(John Gosden) *nvr bttr than midfield: pushed along and btn over 1f out: will do bttr* **4/1**[3]

6 1/2 **Daira Prince (IRE)** 2-9-5 0.. AndreaAtzeni 1 64
(Roger Varian) *towards rr: rdn and effrt over 2f out: no ch w ldrs over 1f out* **8/1**

7 shd **Envoy** 2-9-5 0.. RyanTate 5 64
(James Eustace) *pressed ldr tl rdn and no ex over 2f out* **66/1**

0 **8** nk **Mukallaf (IRE)**[105] **3730** 2-9-5 0...................................... WilliamBuick 9 64
(Roger Varian) *prom: rdn 2f out: no ex over 1f out* **14/1**

6 **9** 2 3/4 **Jive Factor (USA)**[9] **6945** 2-9-5 0.. JoeFanning 8 58+
(Ed Dunlop) *racd keenly: chsd ldrs tl rdn and wknd 2f out* **40/1**

1m 38.49s (-2.11) **Going Correction** -0.175s/f (Firm) **9** Ran SP% **111.7**
Speed ratings (Par 97): **103,101,100,99,98 97,97,97,94**
CSF £498.73 TOTE £15.40: £2.70, £4.60, £1.30; EX 441.00 Trifecta £4720.30.
Owner Qatar Racing Limited **Bred** Keiai Orthopedic Appliance Co Ltd **Trained** Newmarket, Suffolk

FOCUS
The bare form doesn't look anything out of the ordinary, but there were some likely improvers among them. They finished compressed.

7227 CUSTOM KITCHENS, BEDROOMS AND LIVING AT LOWESTOFT H'CAP 1m 3y
3:40 (3:42) (Class 5) (0-75,74) 3-Y-O+ **£2,911** (£866; £432; £216) **Stalls** Centre

Form RPR

5422 **1** **Pendo**[20] **6657** 5-9-3 **70**.. KierenFox 4 80
(John Best) *taken down early: mde all: drvn 1f out: styd on gamely to hold chalrs after* **8/1**

6402 **2** 1 1/4 **Sands Chorus**[7] **7007** 4-9-7 **74**.. TomEaves 12 81
(James Given) *prom: rdn over 2f out: sn outpcd in 4th: rallied ins fnl f: wnt 2nd cl home: nt rch wnr* **10/3**[1]

3651 **3** 1/2 **Tom's Rock (IRE)**[35] **6194** 3-9-3 **73**............................... RobertWinston 7 79
(John Butler) *cl up: rdn and ev ch 1f out: nt qckn fnl 120yds and lost 2nd after* **5/1**[3]

6-00 **4** 1 3/4 **Daleelak (IRE)**[9] **6957** 3-9-0 **70**... JoeFanning 3 72
(Mark Johnston) *prom: rdn 2f out: ev ch over 1f out: hung rt and kpt on same pce after* **40/1**

3106 **5** 2 **Hijran (IRE)**[12] **6877** 3-9-0 **70**......................................(p) AndrewMullen 11 67
(Michael Appleby) *pressed ldrs: drvn over 2f out: styd on same pce and btn over 1f out* **16/1**

6064 **6** 2 **Rocket Ronnie (IRE)**[20] **6643** 6-9-0 **67**.........................(b) JimmyQuinn 10 60
(Ed McMahon) *plld v hrd in rr: rdn and sme prog over 1f out: no ch w ldrs* **18/1**

5163 **7** 4 **Exoplanet Blue**[20] **6649** 4-9-7 **74**.. DaneO'Neill 14 57
(Henry Candy) *racd alone stands side: chsd ldrs: rdn over 2f out: sn btn* **22/1**

5542 **8** 1 1/2 **Justice Lass (IRE)**[17] **6742** 3-9-3 **73**................................. RyanMoore 13 53
(David Elsworth) *rdn and struggling in rr wl over 2f out* **4/1**[2]

4500 **9** 1 1/2 **Aid To Africa (IRE)**[21] 6629 3-8-4 **67** .... LuluStanford(7) 9 44
(Michael Bell) *sn detached last and rdn and labouring* **33/1**

6530 **10** *hd* **Artful Mind**[20] 6646 3-8-9 **65** .... StevieDonohoe 8 41
(Charlie Fellowes) *cl up tl rdn and lost pl wl over 2f out* **9/1**

5042 **11** *16* **Green Howard**[7] 7010 8-9-5 **72** .... (t) LukeMorris 2 11
(Rebecca Bastiman) *hrd drvn and struggling over 3f out: t.o* **6/1**

1m 38.35s (-2.25) **Going Correction** -0.175s/f (Firm)
WFA 3 from 4yo+ 3lb **11** Ran SP% **116.0**
Speed ratings (Par 103): **104,102,102,100,98 96,92,91,89,89 73**
CSF £33.70 CT £151.31 TOTE £8.60: £2.50, £1.80, £2.20; EX 35.20 Trifecta £251.20.
Owner Brett Hopson **Bred** Miss Sue Parkinson **Trained** Oad Street, Kent

FOCUS
An ordinary handicap. The winner improved again.

7228 INSPECTION VERIFICATION BUREAU NURSERY H'CAP 7f 3y
4:10 (4:12) (Class 5) (0-70,69) 2-Y-O **£3,040** (£904; £452; £226) **Stalls** Centre

Form RPR

2500 **1** **Hope Against Hope (IRE)**[28] 6420 2-8-11 **59** .... JoeFanning 11 63
(Mark Johnston) *cl up early: lost pl and bhd 1/2-way: renewed effrt over 2f out: rdn and swtchd to stands' rails 1f out: swooped late to pass duelling ldrs and get up nr fin* **50/1**

5042 **2** 1/2 **Texas Katie**[27] 6446 2-9-6 **68** .... [1] LukeMorris 3 71
(Archie Watson) *w ldr: slt advantage but drvn and hanging fire fr 1f out: hdd cl home* **11/2**[2]

5006 **3** *shd* **Sassoferrato (IRE)**[17] 6751 2-9-2 **64** .... GrahamGibbons 8 67
(Alan Bailey) *disp ld: drvn 1f out: ev ch tl nt qckn fnl 50yds* **6/1**[3]

556 **4** 1 1/2 **Life On Mars**[32] 6244 2-9-4 **66** .... RyanMoore 10 65
(William Haggas) *a cl up: rdn over 1f out: no ex ins fnl f* **9/2**[1]

034 **5** 1/2 **Oudwood**[21] 6624 2-9-4 **69** .... MarcMonaghan(3) 13 67
(Hugo Palmer) *t.k.h: chsd ldrs: rdn 2f out: one pce over 1f out* **10/1**

020 **6** 1 1/4 **Too Many Shots**[31] 6297 2-9-5 **67** .... KierenFox 7 62
(John Best) *bhd: rdn and effrt 2f out: no ex over 1f out* **16/1**

000 **7** *nse* **Fire Brigade**[21] 6622 2-8-11 **59** .... JamieSpencer 4 54
(Michael Bell) *uns rdr at s and rn loose briefly: missed break: sn rdn along: nvr trbld ldrs* **7/1**

2100 **8** 3/4 **Princess Way (IRE)**[19] 6670 2-8-12 **60** .... JimmyQuinn 12 53
(David Evans) *prom: drvn over 2f out: no ex over 1f out* **14/1**

4016 **9** *1* **Kings Heart (IRE)**[7] 7004 2-9-6 **68** .... RobertWinston 1 58
(Mark Usher) *last after 2f: rdn and hdwy over 2f out but nvr gng wl enough: btn over 1f out* **6/1**[3]

024 **10** *4* **Shawami (IRE)**[12] 6882 2-9-1 **63** .... DaneO'Neill 2 43
(Mick Channon) *cl up: rdn 2f out: wknd over 1f out* **16/1**

663 **11** *4* **Performing (IRE)**[16] 6789 2-9-4 **66** .... TomEaves 6 36
(John Quinn) *nvr bttr than midfield: rdn over 2f out: sn btn* **8/1**

1m 25.55s (-1.05) **Going Correction** -0.175s/f (Firm) **11** Ran SP% **115.2**
Speed ratings (Par 95): **99,98,98,96,96 94,94,93,92,87 83**
CSF £302.89 CT £1956.00 TOTE £25.40: £6.80, £1.80, £2.70; EX 193.80 Trifecta £3036.10.
Owner Thurloe XXXI and Stuart & Ross Counsell **Bred** E Browne **Trained** Middleham Moor, N Yorks

FOCUS
A modest nursery. The third and fourth help with the level.

7229 TRAFALGAR RESTAURANT AT YARMOUTH H'CAP 1m 2f 23y
4:40 (4:41) (Class 4) (0-80,82) 3-Y-O+ **£4,690** (£1,395; £697; £348) **Stalls** Low

Form RPR

2651 **1** **Ocean Eleven**[18] 6702 3-9-1 **76** .... StevieDonohoe 2 83
(John Ryan) *mde all: rdn 2f out: kpt finding plenty fnl f: readily* **9/1**

3214 **2** 1 1/4 **So Celebre (GER)**[32] 6268 3-9-0 **75** .... WilliamBuick 11 79
(Ian Williams) *pressed wnr: rdn 3f out: lost 2nd 1f out and hld by wnr after: regained 2nd fnl 50yds* **3/1**[1]

-230 **3** 1/2 **Blaze Of Hearts (IRE)**[47] 5765 3-9-3 **78** .... RobertWinston 5 81
(Dean Ivory) *chsd ldrs: rdn 2f out: wnt 2nd 1f out: no imp on wnr and lost 2nd cl home* **12/1**

0152 **4** 1/2 **Play Nicely**[25] 6517 4-9-8 **78** .... GrahamGibbons 6 80
(David Barron) *a abt same pl: rdn 3f out: nt qckn over 1f out* **5/1**[3]

031 **5** *1* **Bridge Of Sighs**[11] 6889 4-9-6 **76** .... DanielMuscutt 1 76+
(Martin Smith) *hld up towards rr: effrt 2f out: n.m.r on far rails over 1f out: rdn and nt get in a blow after* **9/1**

5450 **6** *shd* **Mediciman**[12] 6877 3-8-13 **74** .... [1] DaneO'Neill 4 74+
(Henry Candy) *missed break: bhd: sme prog fnl 2f: nt rch ldrs* **13/2**

52-3 **7** *nk* **Cat Silver**[25] 6511 3-9-1 **76** .... RyanMoore 10 75
(Sir Michael Stoute) *t.k.h: trckd ldrs tl 3f out: kpt on same pce after* **9/2**[2]

-530 **8** *1* **Fantasy Gladiator**[11] 6899 10-9-7 **77** .... (p) AndrewMullen 9 74
(Michael Appleby) *towards rr: rdn over 3f out: one pced fnl 2f* **28/1**

335 **9** *12* **Dubawi Hundred (IRE)**[28] 6423 3-8-11 **72** .... JamieSpencer 7 45
(James Tate) *sn last: brief effrt 4f out but sn racing awkwardly: wl bhd fnl 2f* **10/1**

2m 11.1s (0.60) **Going Correction** +0.20s/f (Good)
WFA 3 from 4yo+ 5lb **9** Ran SP% **113.4**
Speed ratings (Par 105): **105,104,103,103,102 102,102,101,91**
CSF £35.54 CT £327.45 TOTE £11.60: £2.80, £1.60, £3.70; EX 39.70 Trifecta £434.50.
Owner W McLuskey **Bred** J C S Wilson Bloodstock **Trained** Newmarket, Suffolk

FOCUS
It proved hard to make up ground, with the 1-2 racing in that order for most of the way. The winner confirmed his improved latest start.

7230 BURLINGTON PALM HOTEL OF YARMOUTH H'CAP 1m 2f 23y
5:10 (5:11) (Class 6) (0-60,60) 3-Y-O **£2,264** (£673; £336; £168) **Stalls** Low

Form RPR

3035 **1** **Primobella**[24] 6541 3-9-7 **60** .... JoeFanning 10 67
(Ed McMahon) *prom: led 2f out: ears pricked and gng wl 1f out: rdn and hld on wl fnl f* **4/1**[1]

2220 **2** 3/4 **Go On Gal (IRE)**[51] 5630 3-8-11 **53** .... ShelleyBirkett(3) 8 59
(Julia Feilden) *hld up: stdy prog 3f out: n.m.r: rdn to chse wnr over 1f out: kpt on steadily but a hld* **9/2**[2]

0034 **3** 4 1/2 **Forest Lakes (IRE)**[25] 6512 3-9-6 **59** .... (p) JamieSpencer 12 57
(George Scott) *midfeld: effrt to trck ldrs 3f out: sn rdn: nt qckn over 1f out* **15/2**

6000 **4** 3 1/4 **Nutzma**[25] 6513 3-8-7 **46** oh1 .... AndrewMullen 3 38
(Mike Murphy) *bhd: sme hdwy fnl 2f: tk poor 4th ins fnl f* **20/1**

0000 **5** 1 3/4 **Let There Be Light**[68] 5041 3-9-4 **57** .... RyanPowell 2 46
(Gay Kelleway) *chsd ldrs: rdn 3f out: no ch w ldrs fnl 2f* **40/1**

0100 **6** 4 1/2 **Bob's Boy**[14] 6827 3-9-4 **57** .... (p) RenatoSouza 9 37
(Jose Santos) *rdn and prom: wknd over 2f out* **9/2**[2]

0020 **7** *nse* **Ramblow**[28] 6405 3-9-3 **56** .... [1] GrahamGibbons 4 36
(William Haggas) *prom: led 3f out: rdn and hdd 2f out: sn lost pl* **5/1**[3]

0-00 **8** *shd* **Little Lotte (IRE)**[36] 2300 3-9-1 **54** .... DougieCostello 5 34
(Tom Gretton) *midfield: rdn 3f out: sn outpcd: plodded on* **40/1**

3500 **9** *33* **R Bar Open (FR)**[30] 6337 3-9-7 **60** .... (p) RobertWinston 7
(Dean Ivory) *led at fast pce tl hdd 3f out: dropped out rapidly: t.o and eased* **18/1**

0000 **10** 2 1/2 **Russian Rascal**[91] 4210 3-8-7 **46** oh1 .... JimmyQuinn 6
(Clive Drew) *t.k.h: chsd ldrs tl dropped to rr 4f out: t.o 2f out: eased* **66/1**

0440 **11** *10* **Summertime Lucy (IRE)**[11] 6900 3-8-4 **50** .... (bt[1]) LuluStanford(7) 1
(Giles Bravery) *drvn and rdn and nvr travelling in last pair: t.o 3f out: eased* **40/1**

063 **12** 3 3/4 **King Julien (IRE)**[8] 6094 3-8-11 **50** .... (t) StevieDonohoe 11
(John Ryan) *missed break: rdn and nvr travelling in last pair: t.o and eased 4f out* **15/2**

2m 11.46s (0.96) **Going Correction** +0.20s/f (Good) **12** Ran SP% **115.4**
Speed ratings (Par 99): **104,103,99,97,95 92,92,92,65,63 55,52**
CSF £20.20 CT £129.24 TOTE £4.50: £1.50, £2.10, £2.80; EX 21.00 Trifecta £100.60.
Owner Dalwhinnie Racing **Bred** Dalwhinnie Bloodstock **Trained** Lichfield, Staffs

FOCUS
The ground had unexpectedly softened by now. A moderate handicap. The first two finished clear and are given a bit of credit.

7231 NORWICH AIRPORT H'CAP 1m 3f 104y
5:40 (5:40) (Class 6) (0-55,55) 3-Y-O+ **£2,264** (£673; £336; £168) **Stalls** Low

Form RPR

3236 **1** **Chestnut Storm (IRE)**[67] 5079 3-9-1 **55** .... TomEaves 9 63
(Ed Dunlop) *towards rr: drvn and plenty to do over 3f out: stdy prog after: led over 1f out: styd on steadily whn holding rivals after* **10/1**

4130 **2** *2* **Sexy Secret**[28] 6406 5-9-4 **55** .... (p) SimonPearce(3) 2 60
(Lydia Pearce) *led 4f: 2nd tl led again over 2f out: pushed along and hdd over 1f out: kpt on gamely but hld by wnr fnl f* **10/1**

006 **3** 1 3/4 **The Juggler**[30] 6335 3-9-0 **54** .... JimmyQuinn 3 56
(William Knight) *prom: 3rd and rdn over 4f out: nt qckn over 1f out* **7/1**[3]

60 **4** *1* **Pension Madness (IRE)**[12] 6871 3-8-8 **55** .... LuluStanford(7) 12 55
(Mark Usher) *chsd ldrs: rdn over 2f out: one pce over 1f out* **14/1**

U500 **5** 1/2 **Topalova**[51] 5630 3-8-12 **52** .... [1] StevieDonohoe 11 51
(Mark H Tompkins) *bhd: rdn and hdwy on outer fnl 2f: styd on but nvr got in a blow* **18/1**

4424 **6** 1 1/2 **Highlife Dancer**[6] 7039 8-9-7 **55** .... DaneO'Neill 8 52
(Mick Channon) *a abt same pl: rdn over 2f out: sn no imp* **11/2**[2]

0006 **7** *nk* **Vale Of Rock (IRE)**[21] 6634 3-8-12 **52** .... (p) AndrewMullen 4 48
(Michael Appleby) *chsd ldrs fr 1/2-way: rdn 3f out: plugged on and no imp fnl 2f* **7/1**[3]

6043 **8** 1 3/4 **Frivolous Prince (IRE)**[9] 6966 3-8-0 **47** .... (vt) AledBeech(7) 7 40
(David Evans) *midfiield: rdn 3f out: no imp or danger after* **5/1**[1]

0005 **9** 3/4 **Troy Boy**[21] 6620 6-8-7 **46** oh1 .... RowanScott(5) 14 38
(Rebecca Bastiman) *bhd early: nvr trbld ldrs* **25/1**

0454 **10** *shd* **Broughtons Mystery**[25] 6514 3-8-6 **46** oh1 .... JoeFanning 6 38
(Henry Spiller) *nvr bttr than midfield: struggling 3f out* **8/1**

0000 **11** *7* **Clock On Tom**[25] 6514 6-8-10 **47** .... TimClark(3) 13 28
(Denis Quinn) *a struggling in rr and racing awkwardly* **22/1**

4400 **12** 3 1/4 **Heat Storm (IRE)**[4] 7103 5-8-12 **46** oh1 .... (v) GrahamGibbons 10 21
(James Unett) *racd wd: bhd early: rdn to ld after 4f: hdd over 2f out: dropped out qckly: t.o* **11/1**

6000 **13** *29* **Ashford Island**[29] 6373 3-8-1 **48** .... KieranSchofield(7) 1
(Adam West) *chsd ldrs: rdn 5f out: lost pl tamely: t.o fnl 3f* **50/1**

2m 32.12s (3.42) **Going Correction** +0.20s/f (Good)
WFA 3 from 5yo+ 6lb **13** Ran SP% **116.8**
Speed ratings (Par 101): **95,93,92,91,91 90,89,88,88,87 82,80,59**
CSF £101.74 CT £751.20 TOTE £8.40: £2.90, £3.70, £2.70; EX 68.50 Trifecta £388.10.
Owner Jimmy Strauss & Sir Anthony Page-Wood **Bred** Grange & Manister House Studs **Trained** Newmarket, Suffolk

FOCUS
A lowly handicap run on ground that had eased unexpectedly. The second and third set the level.
T/Plt: £67.30 to a £1 stake. Pool: £66,608.17 - 722.0 winning units. T/Qpdt: £66.70 to a £1 stake. Pool: £4,096.85 - 45.4 winning units. **Iain Mackenzie**

7232 - 7238a (Foreign Racing) - See Raceform Interactive

7055 LEICESTER (R-H)
Tuesday, October 11

OFFICIAL GOING: Straight course - good to firm; round course - good (good to firm in places)
Wind: Light across Weather: Cloudy

7239 BRITISH STALLION STUDS EBF MAIDEN STKS (PLUS 10 RACE) 1m 60y
2:10 (2:14) (Class 4) 2-Y-O **£5,175** (£1,540; £769; £384) **Stalls** Low

Form RPR

3 **1** **Red Label (IRE)**[18] 6750 2-9-5 0 .... AdamKirby 6 78+
(Luca Cumani) *a.p: shkn up over 3f out: chsd ldr 2f out: sn edgd rt: rdn to ld 1f out: styd on* **5/1**[2]

35 **2** 1 1/4 **X Rated (IRE)**[42] 6002 2-9-5 0 .... SilvestreDeSousa 4 76
(Mark Johnston) *led: rdn over 2f out: edgd lft and hdd 1f out: styd on same pce ins fnl f* **40/1**

02 **3** 3 1/2 **Fujaira Bridge (IRE)**[17] 6777 2-9-5 0 .... AndreaAtzeni 3 68
(Roger Varian) *racd keenly: trckd ldr 2f: remained handy: rdn over 2f out: styd on same pce fnl f* **4/1**[1]

4 3/4 **Special Relation (IRE)** 2-9-5 0 .... RobertHavlin 8 66+
(Hughie Morrison) *s.i.s: hdwy over 5f out: shkn up over 2f out: styd on towards fin* **100/1**

5 **5** *1* **Quloob**[18] 6751 2-9-5 0 .... PaulHanagan 7 64
(Owen Burrows) *chsd ldrs: wnt 2nd 6f out: rdn and lost 2nd 2f out: n.m.r sn after: styd on same pce fr over 1f out* **16/1**[3]

6 *1* **First Nation** 2-9-5 0 .... WilliamBuick 1 62+
(Charlie Appleby) *prom: lost pl 6f out: hdwy over 2f out: no ex fnl f* **16/1**[3]

7 *11* **Star Of Doha** 2-9-0 0 .... FMBerry 10 32+
(Ralph Beckett) *hld up: racd keenly: shkn up over 2f out: sn wknd* **25/1**

8 *9* **King's Shadow (USA)** 2-9-5 0 .... MartinLane 2 18
(Saeed bin Suroor) *hld up: pushed along 1/2-way: wknd over 2f out* **16/1**[3]

9 1 1/4 **Red Bordeaux (FR)** 2-9-2 0 .... GeorgeDowning(3) 9 15
(Tony Carroll) *s.i.s: rn green in rr: wknd over 2f out* **250/1**

1m 45.63s (0.53) **Going Correction** +0.025s/f (Good) **9** Ran SP% **62.0**
Speed ratings (Par 97): **98,96,93,92,91 90,79,70,69**
CSF £54.50 TOTE £3.10: £1.80, £5.00, £1.10; EX 48.60 Trifecta £149.40.
Owner Jon S Kelly **Bred** Rabbah Bloodstock Limited **Trained** Newmarket, Suffolk
■ Azam was withdrawn. Price at time of withdrawal EvensF. Rule 4 applies to all bets - deduct 45p in the pound.

FOCUS
There was a false rail from the top of the hill on the back straight all the way to the winning line, increasing all distances on the round course by approx 17yds. Paul Hanagan described the ground as being: "On the slow side." A fair maiden that was blown wide open after the short-price Azam favourite had to be withdrawn. The front pair came clear, with the winner overcoming market weakness. He has obvious scope to build on this form.

7240 WHISSENDINE (S) STKS — 7f
2:40 (2:42) (Class 6) 3-4-Y-O **£2,587** (£770; £384; £192) **Stalls** High

Form / RPR

5636 **1** **Rebel Lightning (IRE)**[19] 6702 3-8-10 70................(b) JamieSpencer 10 — 73
(Richard Spencer) *trckd ldr stands' side tl merged w centre gp over 4f out: led overall over 1f out: edgd rt and c clr ins fnl f* **5/2**[1]

2622 **2** 2 1/4 **Infiniti (IRE)**[7] 7062 3-8-0 58....................................(p) GeorgeWood(5) 12 — 60
(Rae Guest) *racd stands' side tl gp merged w centre over 4f out: hld up in tch: rdn over 1f out: edgd rt and r.o to go 2nd nr fin: nt trble wnr* **3/1**[2]

2035 **3** 3/4 **Doctor Bong**[49] 5752 4-8-6 71 ow1..........................(b) JoshuaBryan(7) 16 — 65
(Andrew Balding) *led stands' side gp tl merged w centre over 4f out: up w the pce: overall ldr over 2f out: tl rdn over 1f out: edgd rt and styd on same pce fnl f* **7/2**[3]

0300 **4** 4 **Jacksonfire**[26] 6522 4-9-1 43 ow3...................................(p) RobertTart 5 — 56
(Michael Mullineaux) *w ldrs in centre to 1/2-way: rdn over 2f out: wknd ins fnl f* **66/1**

0002 **5** shd **In My Place**[15] 6836 3-9-4 65......................................(p) TonyHamilton 13 — 60
(Richard Fahey) *racd stands' side tl merged w centre gp over 4f out: chsd ldrs: rdn over 2f out: wknd ins fnl f* **12/1**

0416 **6** 3/4 **Castlerea Tess**[61] 5338 3-8-9 49..................................... PaulHanagan 1 — 49
(Sarah Hollinshead) *overall ldr in centre tl rdn and hdd over 2f out: wknd ins fnl f* **33/1**

00 **7** nk **Sir Jack**[29] 6423 3-8-10 0... AdamBeschizza 4 — 49
(Tony Carroll) *racd centre: sn pushed along in rr: hdwy u.p over 1f out: nvr on terms* **100/1**

2220 **8** 1/2 **Wild Flower (IRE)**[29] 6407 4-8-7 51.................................. KieranO'Neill 9 — 44
(Jimmy Fox) *racd stands' side tl merged w centre gp over 4f out: hld up: plld hrd: rdn over 2f out: n.d* **16/1**

0600 **9** 2 1/2 **Myboydaniel**[7] 7062 4-8-12 60.....................................(p1) MartinLane 11 — 42
(Derek Shaw) *racd stands' side tl merged w centre gp over 4f out: stdd s: hld up: rdn over 2f out: nvr on terms* **66/1**

1134 **10** 1 1/2 **Imperial Link**[88] 4335 4-8-10 61.................................. CiaranMckee(5) 14 — 41
(John O'Shea) *racd stands' side tl merged w centre gp over 4f out: hld up: rdn over 2f out: n.d* **28/1**

1500 **11** 1 3/4 **Just Be Lucky (IRE)**[8] 7017 4-9-10 77..................(b) SilvestreDeSousa 3 — 45
(Conor Dore) *racd centre: hld up: hdwy 1/2-way: rdn and wknd over 1f out* **10/1**

16-6 **12** 3 3/4 **Q Ten Girl (IRE)**[274] 147 3-8-5 65.............................(v) AndrewMullen 2 — 17
(James Unett) *w ldrs in centre to 1/2-way: rdn and wknd over 1f out* **50/1**

06 **13** 5 **Moving Robe (IRE)**[113] 3473 3-8-2 0........................... NoelGarbutt(3) 7 — 4
(Conrad Allen) *racd keenly: w ldrs in centre to 1/2-way: rdn over 2f out: sn wknd* **25/1**

/000 **14** 3 **Magical Peak**[26] 6512 4-8-4 40.............................. EdwardGreatrex(3) 15
(John O'Shea) *racd stands' side tl merged w centre gp over 4f out: s.i.s: sn prom: rdn and wknd over 2f out* **150/1**

1m 25.02s (-1.18) **Going Correction** -0.075s/f (Good)
WFA 3 from 4yo 2lb **14** Ran SP% **115.3**
Speed ratings (Par 101): **103,100,99,95,94 94,93,93,90,88 86,82,76,73**
CSF £8.84 TOTE £3.40: £1.40, £1.50, £1.50; EX 10.50 Trifecta £32.40.There was no bid for the winner. Doctor Bong was claimed by Miss G. Harris for £7000.
Owner Rebel Racing III **Bred** Thomas Hassett **Trained** Newmarket, Suffolk

FOCUS
Race distance as advertised. The right horses came to the fore in this big-field seller. The second and fourth set the level.

7241 WREAKE H'CAP — 7f
3:10 (3:11) (Class 2) (0-110,100) 3£15,752 (£4,715; £2,357; £1,180; £587) **Stalls** High

Form / RPR

5043 **1** **C Note (IRE)**[31] 6338 3-9-2 **97**.......................................(b1) JimCrowley 4 — 104
(Martyn Meade) *trckd ldrs: led wl over 1f out: drvn out: edgd rt towards fin* **4/1**[3]

6502 **2** 1 1/4 **Intransigent**[17] 6764 7-9-3 **94**... OisinMurphy 3 — 101
(Andrew Balding) *chsd ldrs: pushed along 3f out: sn lost pl: rallied over 1f out: chsd wnr fnl f: sn rdn and ev ch: unable qck towards fin* **6/1**

0023 **3** 2 3/4 **Accession (IRE)**[25] 6547 7-9-7 **100**.................................... MartinLane 2 — 98
(Charlie Fellowes) *chsd ldrs: led over 2f out: rdn: edgd lft and hdd wl over 1f out: rdr dropped nrside rein ent fnl f: no ex* **4/1**[3]

0001 **4** 7 **Can't Change It (IRE)**[31] 6331 5-9-4 **97**........................ JamieSpencer 5 — 84
(David Simcock) *s.i.s: hld up: hdwy u.p over 1f out: eased whn btn ins fnl f* **9/4**[1]

4665 **5** nk **Maggie Pink**[17] 6764 7-9-0 **91**.............................. AlistairRawlinson(3) 1 — 74
(Michael Appleby) *w ldr tl led over 4f out: rdn and hdd over 2f out: wknd over 1f out* **25/1**

0001 **6** 14 **That Is The Spirit**[24] 6560 5-9-4 **97**.............................. DanielTudhope 6 — 37
(David O'Meara) *led: hdd over 4f out: remained w ldrs tl rdn over 2f out: wknd over 1f out: eased* **7/2**[2]

1m 22.87s (-3.33) **Going Correction** -0.075s/f (Good)
WFA 3 from 5yo+ 2lb **6** Ran SP% **111.1**
Speed ratings (Par 109): **116,114,111,103,103 87**
CSF £26.60 TOTE £3.70: £1.50, £2.50; EX 24.70 Trifecta £63.90.
Owner Richard Barnes **Bred** Mountarmstrong Stud **Trained** Newmarket, Suffolk

FOCUS
Race distance as advertised. A good little handicap that went to the only 3yo in the field. The market leaders both disappointed.

7242 SIS AUTUMN SPRINT H'CAP — 5f
3:45 (3:45) (Class 2) (0-110,107) 3-Y-O+
£15,562 (£4,660; £2,330; £1,165; £582; £292) **Stalls** High

Form / RPR

0563 **1** **Mirza**[10] 6943 9-9-4 **104**...(p) MartinHarley 7 — 112
(Rae Guest) *hld up: swtchd rt and hdwy over 1f out: rdn and r.o to ld towards fin* **9/1**

25 **2** 1/2 **Lightscameraction (IRE)**[17] 6779 4-8-11 **97**............(p) JamieSpencer 6 — 103
(Gay Kelleway) *sn trcking ldr: led over 1f out: rdn and hung rt fnl f: hdd towards fin* **4/1**[1]

4220 **3** 1 1/2 **Humidor (IRE)**[17] 6779 9-8-13 **99**................................. FergusSweeney 1 — 100
(George Baker) *hld up: pushed along and hdwy over 1f out: edgd rt ins fnl f: no ex towards fin* **14/1**

0001 **4** nk **Dougan**[10] 6962 4-8-10 **93**... JimCrowley 2 — 96
(David Evans) *sn prom: rdn and ev ch over 1f out: cl 2nd whn carried rt ins fnl f: hmpd wl ins fnl f: styd on same pce* **4/1**[1]

0300 **5** 1 **Poyle Vinnie**[3] 7156 6-8-13 **99**..................................[1] FrederikTylicki 4 — 95
(Michael Appleby) *chsd ldrs: rdn and ev ch over 1f out: hung rt and no ex ins fnl f* **5/1**[2]

0116 **6** 1 1/4 **Boom The Groom (IRE)**[24] 6574 5-9-7 **107**...................... AdamKirby 5 — 99
(Tony Carroll) *chsd ldrs: rdn over 2f out: styd on same pce fnl f* **6/1**[3]

51-0 **7** 3 **Kasbah (IRE)**[107] 3696 4-8-10 **92**......................................[1] AndreaAtzeni 8 — 77
(Robert Cowell) *chsd ldrs: nt clr run and lost pl 4f out: rdn over 2f out: wknd fnl f* **10/1**

0410 **8** 3 1/4 **Hay Chewed (IRE)**[21] 6642 5-8-11 **97**...................... SilvestreDeSousa 3 — 66
(Conrad Allen) *sn led and crossed over to stands' side rail: rdn over 2f out: hdd over 1f out: wknd fnl f* **6/1**[3]

58.49s (-1.51) **Going Correction** -0.075s/f (Good) **8** Ran SP% **111.0**
Speed ratings (Par 109): **109,108,105,105,103 101,96,91**
CSF £42.19 CT £487.98 TOTE £11.60: £3.30, £1.50, £3.30; EX 43.50 Trifecta £515.30.
Owner C J Mills **Bred** C J Mills **Trained** Newmarket, Suffolk
■ Stewards' Enquiry : Jamie Spencer caution: careless riding

FOCUS
Race distance as advertised. A decent sprint run at a strong pace. The winner is rated pretty much back to his old best.

7243 EBFSTALLIONS.COM REFERENCE POINT MAIDEN STKS (STALLION-RESTRICTED) (PLUS 10 RACE) — 7f
4:15 (4:15) (Class 4) 2-Y-O **£6,469** (£1,925; £962; £481) **Stalls** High

Form / RPR

1 **Utmost (USA)** 2-9-0 0.. RobertHavlin 4 — 83+
(John Gosden) *hld up in tch: shkn up to ld 1f out: edgd rt: r.o: comf* **11/4**[1]

2 1 **Cape Byron** 2-9-0 0.. AndreaAtzeni 5 — 80+
(Roger Varian) *hld up: swtchd lft and hdwy over 2f out: rdn to ld over 1f out: sn hdd: edgd rt and styd on same pce wl ins fnl f* **12/1**

3 **3** 2 1/4 **Makkaar (IRE)**[21] 6640 2-9-0 0.. PaulHanagan 3 — 74
(Mark Johnston) *led: rdn and hdd over 2f out: kpt on ins fnl f* **12/1**

3 **4** 1 1/2 **Valley Of Rocks (IRE)**[12] 6904 2-9-0 0.................... SilvestreDeSousa 2 — 70
(Mark Johnston) *s.i.s: hld up: plld hrd: hdwy to join ldr 1/2-way: led over 2f out: rdn and hdd over 1f out: no ex wl ins fnl f* **8/1**[3]

62 **5** 2 **Redgrave (IRE)**[13] 6881 2-9-0 0.. JimCrowley 1 — 65
(Charles Hills) *prom: racd keenly: rdn over 1f out: no ex ins fnl f* **11/4**[1]

5 **6** shd **Leonidas (IRE)**[36] 6183 2-9-0 0.. SteveDrowne 8 — 64+
(Marcus Tregoning) *hld up: pushed along over 2f out: sme hdwy over 1f out: styd on same pce fnl f* **80/1**

44 **7** 1 3/4 **Eynhallow**[37] 6159 2-9-0 0.. JamieSpencer 7 — 60
(Roger Charlton) *w ldr 3f: remained handy tl lost pl wl over 1f out* **4/1**[2]

8 1 **Amakhala (USA)** 2-9-0 0.. WilliamBuick 6 — 57
(Charlie Appleby) *s.i.s: hung rt and rn green in rr: effrt over 1f out: wknd fnl f* **10/1**

1m 25.8s (-0.40) **Going Correction** -0.075s/f (Good) **8** Ran SP% **110.2**
Speed ratings (Par 97): **99,97,95,93,91 91,89,88**
CSF £34.41 TOTE £3.30: £1.50, £2.80, £3.40; EX 33.40 Trifecta £260.20.
Owner George Strawbridge **Bred** George Strawbridge Jr **Trained** Newmarket, Suffolk

FOCUS
Race distance as advertised. Two of the newcomers dominated this maiden. The winner looks a lovely recruit.

7244 FOSSE WAY NURSERY H'CAP — 1m 60y
4:45 (4:45) (Class 6) (0-60,60) 2-Y-O **£2,587** (£770; £384; £192) **Stalls** Low

Form / RPR

0022 **1** **Snookered (IRE)**[11] 6923 2-9-4 **57**.................................. TonyHamilton 4 — 60
(Richard Fahey) *mde all: rdn over 1f out: styd on* **7/2**[2]

4530 **2** 1/2 **Bonnie Arlene (IRE)**[18] 6743 2-9-6 **59**..................... SilvestreDeSousa 2 — 63+
(Mark Johnston) *hld up in tch: nt clr run and swtchd lft over 1f out: r.o to go 2nd nr fin* **3/1**[1]

5533 **3** 3/4 **Moneyoryourlife**[31] 6313 2-9-5 **58**.. PatDobbs 1 — 58
(Richard Hannon) *a.p: chsd wnr and swtchd lft over 1f out: sn rdn: styd on* **5/1**[3]

404 **4** 1 **Misty Moo**[12] 6895 2-8-11 **55**.. HollieDoyle(5) 7 — 54
(Michael Appleby) *hld up: nt clr run over 2f out: hdwy over 1f out: styd on* **16/1**

000 **5** 2 3/4 **Maysonri**[32] 6288 2-9-4 **57**.. AdamBeschizza 6 — 48
(Mark Hoad) *s.i.s: hld up: rdn over 1f out: r.o ins fnl f: nvr nrr* **100/1**

050 **6** 2 1/2 **Mystic Maeve (IRE)**[13] 6874 2-9-7 **60**................................ AdamKirby 3 — 46
(Roger Fell) *hld up in tch: reminder over 5f out: rdn over 2f out: wknd ins fnl f* **25/1**

0000 **7** 1/2 **Hazy Manor (IRE)**[20] 6681 2-9-3 **56**........................[1] RichardKingscote 9 — 40
(Tom Dascombe) *chsd wnr tl rdn over 1f out: wknd ins fnl f* **9/1**

6000 **8** 1/2 **Topmeup**[29] 6412 2-9-1 **54**... StevieDonohoe 5 — 37
(Stuart Edmunds) *awkward leaving stalls: hld up: rdn over 3f out: nvr trbld ldrs* **10/1**

0500 **9** 3/4 **Henry Did It (IRE)**[7] 7047 2-9-6 **59**...................................... JimCrowley 8 — 41
(Tony Carroll) *hld up: nvr on terms* **13/2**

650 **10** 1 **Proud Show**[28] 6439 2-9-1 **54**... MartinLane 10 — 33
(David Dennis) *prom: rdn over 2f out: wknd over 1f out* **16/1**

1m 48.75s (3.65) **Going Correction** +0.025s/f (Good) **10** Ran SP% **112.9**
Speed ratings (Par 93): **82,81,80,79,77 74,74,73,72,71**
CSF £13.88 CT £50.46 TOTE £3.70: £1.80, £1.40, £1.50; EX 10.50 Trifecta £32.90.
Owner Kristian Strangeway **Bred** Michael Burke **Trained** Musley Bank, N Yorks

FOCUS
Race distance increased by 17yds. A moderate nursery, with the winner making all. He built on his Newcastle run.

7245 STEWARDS H'CAP (DIV I) — 1m 1f 218y
5:15 (5:15) (Class 5) (0-75,75) 3-Y-O+ **£3,234** (£962; £481; £240) **Stalls** Low

Form / RPR

5106 **1** **Van Huysen (IRE)**[56] 5526 4-9-8 **73**................................. OisinMurphy 10 — 81
(Dominic Ffrench Davis) *a.p: chsd ldr 7f out: wnt upsides over 4f out tl led over 1f out: sn rdn and edgd rt: styd on* **8/1**

0500 **2** 3/4 **Caponova (IRE)**[13] 6876 3-9-2 **72**........................ RichardKingscote 1 — 79
(Tom Dascombe) *s.i.s: hld up: hdwy 2f out: rdn to chse wnr and hung rt over 1f out: kpt on* **12/1**

0-26 **3** 3 1/2 **Al Fatih (IRE)**[33] 6254 5-9-1 **66**.................................. TomMarquand 4 — 66
(Steve Flook) *towards rr: hdwy 6f out: rdn over 3f out: styd on to go 3rd wl ins fnl f* **16/1**

0000 **4** 1 1/2 **Taraz**[26] 6521 4-9-7 **72**.. DanielTudhope 3 — 69
(David O'Meara) *led: jnd over 4f out: rdn and hdd over 1f out: no ex ins fnl f* **5/1**[3]

0-10 **5** *hd* **Midnight Whistler (USA)**[37] 6165 4-9-10 **75**..........(p) FergusSweeney 6 71
(Martyn Meade) *chsd ldr 3f: remained handy: rdn over 2f out: styd on same pce fr over 1f out* **8/1**
6101 **6** *nk* **Becca Campbell (IRE)**[7] 7037 3-8-8 **69** 6ex...............(p) HollieDoyle(5) 5 65
(Eve Johnson Houghton) *hld up: rdn over 2f out: hung rt fnl f: styd on same pce* **7/2**[2]
0355 **7** *2 ¾* **Mr Quicksilver**[31] 6316 4-9-10 **75**.................................(t) ThomasBrown 2 65
(Ed Walker) *hld up in tch: rdn over 2f out: wknd over 1f out* **10/1**
3202 **8** *¾* **Henry The Explorer (CAN)**[16] 6805 3-9-0 **70**......... SilvestreDeSousa 8 59
(Jo Hughes) *plld hrd and prom: stdd and lost pl over 6f out: hdwy over 2f out: sn rdn: wkng whn nt clr run fnl f* **9/4**[1]

2m 7.47s (-0.43) **Going Correction** +0.025s/f (Good)
WFA 3 from 4yo+ 5lb **8** Ran SP% **114.5**
Speed ratings (Par 103): **102,101,98,97,97 97,94,94**
CSF £96.72 CT £1491.17 TOTE £8.60: £2.70, £2.90, £4.20; EX 92.90 Trifecta £800.90.
Owner Prof C D Green **Bred** Prof C Green **Trained** Lambourn, Berks

FOCUS
Race distance increased by 17yds. The first leg of an ordinary handicap, the fancied runners disappointed. A turf best from the winner and close to his AW form.

7246 STEWARDS H'CAP (DIV II) 1m 1f 218y
5:50 (5:50) (Class 5) (0-75,75) 3-Y-O+ **£3,234** (£962; £481; £240) **Stalls** Low

Form RPR
3303 **1** **Al Nasser Alwashik**[8] 7007 3-9-2 **72**........................ SilvestreDeSousa 1 84
(Roger Fell) *chsd ldrs: chal over 1f out: rdn and hung lft ins fnl f: styd on to ld towards fin* **4/1**[3]
5321 **2** *nk* **Artists Model (IRE)**[22] 6635 3-9-1 **71**................................. DaneO'Neill 5 82
(Henry Candy) *chsd ldr tl rdn to ld over 1f out: edgd rt ins fnl f: hdd towards fin* **7/4**[1]
/003 **3** *2* **East India**[12] 6889 4-9-10 **75**... SteveDrowne 3 82
(George Baker) *hld up: hdwy and swtchd rt over 2f out: rdn over 1f out: styd on* **10/1**
0135 **4** *4* **Totally Committed**[27] 6484 3-9-3 **73**.................................. AdamKirby 9 72
(Clive Cox) *hld up: nt clr run and swtchd rt over 2f out: rdn: swtchd lft and hdwy over 1f out: nt trble ldrs* **10/3**[2]
650 **5** *1 ¼* **Polar Forest**[13] 6876 6-9-6 **74**...............................(e) GeorgeDowning(3) 2 71
(Richard Guest) *led: rdn and hdd over 1f out: wknd ins fnl f* **20/1**
6215 **6** *7* **California Lad**[41] 6032 3-9-5 **75**..(v) JimCrowley 6 58
(Harry Dunlop) *prom: racd keenly: rdn over 2f out: wknd over 1f out* **9/1**
4400 **7** *7* **Hammer Gun (USA)**[34] 6231 3-8-11 **67**............................. MartinLane 4 36
(Derek Shaw) *s.i.s: pushed along 1/2-way: a bhd* **66/1**
2112 **8** *4* **First Summer**[26] 6514 4-8-9 **65**.................................... GeorgeWood(5) 10 26
(Shaun Harris) *hld up: hdwy u.p over 2f out: wknd over 1f out* **25/1**
04-0 **9** *4 ½* **Never Give In**[109] 3609 3-9-0 **70**................................. FergusSweeney 7 22
(K R Burke) *hld up: plld hrd: hdwy 8f out: rdn and wknd over 2f out* **25/1**

2m 6.96s (-0.94) **Going Correction** +0.025s/f (Good)
WFA 3 from 4yo+ 5lb **9** Ran SP% **112.5**
Speed ratings (Par 103): **104,103,102,98,97 92,86,83,79**
CSF £10.59 CT £62.03 TOTE £3.60: £1.10, £1.40, £3.50; EX 15.00 Trifecta £64.00.
Owner R G Fell **Bred** Rabbah Bloodstock Limited **Trained** Nawton, N Yorks

FOCUS
Race distance increased by 17yds. Run at a good gallop, the front pair enjoyed a good tussle and the form looks sound. It was the quicker division by half a second and the form looks sound.
T/Plt: £42.00 to a £1 stake. Pool: £80209.33 - 1391.09 winning units T/Qpdt: £25.50 to a £1 stake. Pool: £4394.62 - 127.37 winning units. **Colin Roberts**

6807 MUSSELBURGH (R-H)
Tuesday, October 11

OFFICIAL GOING: Good (good to firm in places) changing to good after race 1 (1.50)
Wind: Breezy, half behind Weather: Overcast, raining races 1-2

7247 WWW.MACBETSPORTS.CO.UK MAIDEN STKS 1m
1:50 (1:51) (Class 5) 2-Y-O **£3,234** (£962; £481; £240) **Stalls** Low

Form RPR
4 **1** **Tor**[15] 6833 2-9-5 0... JasonHart 6 79+
(Keith Dalgleish) *trckd ldr: led over 2f out: rdn and edgd lft over 1f out: edgd rt and drew clr ins fnl f* **4/1**[3]
5 **2** *3 ¾* **Powerful Love (IRE)**[10] 6952 2-9-5 0........................... PaulMulrennan 1 70
(Mark Johnston) *noisy in paddock: dwlt: hld up on ins: effrt and swtchd rt 3f out: sn pushed along: kpt on fnl f to take 2nd cl home: no ch w wnr* **3/1**[1]
3 **3** *½* **Mr Coco Bean (USA)**[18] 6741 2-9-5 0.............................. PJMcDonald 2 69
(Ann Duffield) *prom: effrt and chsd wnr over 1f out: kpt on same pce fnl f: lost 2nd nr fin* **7/2**[2]
00 **4** *6* **Good Boy Jasper**[25] 6535 2-9-5 0.................................... DavidNolan 9 55
(Linda Perratt) *led to over 2f out: chsd wnr to over 1f out: kpt on same pce fnl f* **100/1**
6 **5** *1 ½* **Lamloom (IRE)**[25] 6535 2-9-5 0...................................... PhillipMakin 7 52
(David O'Meara) *plld hrd early: chsd ldrs: effrt over 2f out: drifted lft over 1f out: sn wknd* **3/1**[1]
6 *1 ¾* **Four Kingdoms (IRE)** 2-9-5 0.. DougieCostello 5 48
(K R Burke) *s.i.s: sn pushed along bhd ldng quartet: drvn and outpcd 1/2-way: n.d after* **16/1**
7 *shd* **Dirty Randy (IRE)** 2-9-0 0... ShirleyTeasdale(5) 8 47
(Keith Dalgleish) *broke wl but sn lost pl and in rr after 1f: drvn along over 3f out: nvr on terms* **25/1**
8 *5* **Addicted To You (IRE)** 2-9-5 0... JoeFanning 3 36
(Mark Johnston) *s.i.s: hld up: pushed along and effrt on outside over 3f out: rdn and wknd fr 2f out* **7/1**

1m 40.9s (-0.30) **Going Correction** -0.10s/f (Good) **8** Ran SP% **115.4**
Speed ratings (Par 95): **97,93,92,86,85 83,83,78**
CSF £16.63 TOTE £5.10: £1.80, £1.80, £1.30; EX 19.40 Trifecta £45.30.
Owner I Wilson **Bred** Iain Wilson **Trained** Carluke, S Lanarks

FOCUS
Following 2mm of overnight rain the going had eased slightly to good, good to firm in places (from good to firm, good in places). Stands' bend out by 2.5yds and bottom bend out by 2yds, adding 7yds to 7f and 1m races and 13yds to 1m4f and 2m races. An ordinary maiden to start and a tight betting heat. The field were well spread out from an early stage and the winning time was 2.4sec outside standard. On the ground Joe Fanning said: "It's good to soft and if we get much more rain it will be soft", Phillip Makin said: "It's loose on top and perhaps still good underneath", while winning rider Jason Hart said: "It's on the easy side of good." The winner built on his debut promise.

7248 BEST ODDS GUARANTEED ALL RACES AT MACBET MAIDEN STKS 5f
2:20 (2:21) (Class 5) 2-Y-O **£3,234** (£962; £481; £240) **Stalls** High

Form RPR
0260 **1** **Computable**[54] 5583 2-9-5 79.. DavidAllan 6 80+
(Tim Easterby) *plld hrd early: trckd ldrs: rdn to ld ins fnl f: kpt on strly* **5/2**[2]
235 **2** *2 ¼* **Kiribati**[31] 6319 2-9-5 75.. JoeFanning 4 72
(Mark Johnston) *wnt lft s: led: rdn over 1f out: hung rt and hdd ins fnl f: kpt on same pce* **2/1**[1]
246 **3** *3 ¼* **Peach Pavlova (IRE)**[37] 6162 2-8-9 71..................... RowanScott(5) 7 55
(Ann Duffield) *trckd ldrs: rdn over 1f out: hung rt and sn outpcd by ldng pair* **6/1**
540 **4** *1* **Ashurst Beacon**[30] 6388 2-9-5 0.. BenCurtis 2 57
(Brian Ellison) *cl up: drvn along over 2f out: no ex fr over 1f out* **15/2**
40 **5** *½* **Cool Run Girl (IRE)**[11] 6925 2-9-0 0................................. PJMcDonald 3 50
(Iain Jardine) *in tch: rdn along 1/2-way: no imp fr over 1f out* **40/1**
22 **6** *½* **Hee Haw (IRE)**[15] 6833 2-9-5 0...................................... PhillipMakin 1 53
(Keith Dalgleish) *prom on outside: rdn over 2f out: wknd over 1f out* **5/1**[3]
00 **7** *5* **Filudo (FR)**[45] 5885 2-9-5 0.. GrahamGibbons 5 35
(David O'Meara) *dwlt and hmpd s: bhd and sn outpcd: no ch fr 1/2-way* **20/1**

59.57s (-0.83) **Going Correction** -0.10s/f (Good) **7** Ran SP% **111.8**
Speed ratings (Par 95): **102,98,93,91,90 90,82**
CSF £7.54 TOTE £3.70: £1.90, £1.10; EX 8.40 Trifecta £37.90.
Owner B Guerin, Mrs E J Wills & Habton Farms **Bred** Whitsbury Manor Stud **Trained** Great Habton, N Yorks

FOCUS
The going was changed to good all over before this race. A modest sprint maiden but the winner has definite scope to progress at three.

7249 EASTLOTHIAN.ORG H'CAP 1m 4f 100y
2:50 (2:50) (Class 6) (0-65,65) 3-Y-O+ **£3,234** (£962; £481; £240) **Stalls** Low

Form RPR
3011 **1** **Canny Style**[22] 6620 3-9-1 **61**.. KevinStott 3 71
(Kevin Ryan) *sn trcking ldrs on ins: smooth hdwy to ld over 2f out: rdn over 1f out: edgd rt and kpt on wl fnl f* **5/1**[3]
6222 **2** *½* **Kelvin Hall**[8] 7008 3-9-0 **60**... JoeFanning 1 68
(Mark Johnston) *pressed ldr: led over 3f out to over 2f out: styd upsides wnr: kpt on ins fnl f: no ex last 50yds* **9/4**[1]
2305 **3** *5* **Love Marmalade (IRE)**[34] 6227 6-9-12 **65**.................(p) PhillipMakin 2 65
(David O'Meara) *prom: effrt and rdn over 2f out: outpcd by first two fnl f* **7/1**
4650 **4** *1 ½* **Haymarket**[22] 6621 7-9-4 **57**.. DavidAllan 6 55
(R Mike Smith) *hld up in tch on outside: drvn and outpcd over 2f out: n.d after* **10/1**
00-3 **5** *8* **Meddlesome**[7] 7037 3-9-2 **62**..[1] LukeMorris 4 48
(Sir Mark Prescott Bt) *sn bhd and nvr gng wl: shortlived effrt wl over 2f out: sn btn* **5/2**[2]
0011 **6** *3* **Amy Blair**[15] 6839 3-8-5 **56**... ShirleyTeasdale(5) 5 37
(Keith Dalgleish) *t.k.h: led to over 3f out: rdna nd wknd over 2f out* **7/1**

2m 42.63s (0.63) **Going Correction** -0.10s/f (Good)
WFA 3 from 6yo+ 7lb **6** Ran SP% **110.1**
Speed ratings (Par 101): **93,92,89,88,83 81**
CSF £16.01 TOTE £5.20: £2.70, £1.30; EX 9.80 Trifecta £36.10.
Owner Hambleton Racing Ltd XXXVII **Bred** Biddestone Stud Ltd **Trained** Hambleton, N Yorks

FOCUS
Rail movement added 13yds to race distance. A moderate middle-distance handicap, though two of the six runners were bidding for a hat-trick. The pace was solid enough and the winner continues to thrive.

7250 BREEDERS BACKING RACING FLYING SCOTSMAN EBF CONDITIONS STKS 5f
3:20 (3:21) (Class 3) 3-Y-O+ **£9,056** (£2,695; £1,346; £673) **Stalls** High

Form RPR
5001 **1** **Caspian Prince (IRE)**[21] 6642 7-9-7 107...................(t) ConnorBeasley 3 106
(Roger Fell) *mde all: sn crossed to stands' rail: rdn and edgd rt over 1f out: kpt on wl fnl f* **4/1**[3]
6411 **2** *1 ¼* **Glenrowan Rose (IRE)**[149] 2267 3-9-4 95......................... PhillipMakin 2 100
(Keith Dalgleish) *pressed wnr: effrt and drvn along wl over 1f out: kpt on ins fnl f: nt pce of wnr* **16/1**
0304 **3** *nk* **Gamesome (FR)**[17] 6779 5-9-4 93.................................. PaulMulrennan 7 98
(Paul Midgley) *sn trcking ldrs against stands' rail: rdn along 2f out: kpt on ins fnl f* **4/1**[3]
0510 **4** *nk* **Kimberella**[10] 6943 6-9-4 109... JoeFanning 5 97
(David Nicholls) *hld up in tch on outside: effrt and rdn wl over 1f out: kpt on same pce last 100yds* **9/4**[1]
0054 **5** *hd* **Taexali (IRE)**[15] 6837 3-9-4 94.................................(v[1]) GrahamGibbons 6 97
(John Patrick Shanahan, Ire) *trckd ldrs: rdn and sltly outpcd over 1f out: rallied ent fnl f: sn no imp* **18/1**
0526 **6** *1 ½* **Duke Of Firenze**[9] 6990 7-9-4 103.. DavidAllan 4 91
(David C Griffiths) *hld up on outside: stdy hdwy 1/2-way: effrt and rdn over 1f out: wknd ins fnl f* **5/2**[2]

58.54s (-1.86) **Going Correction** -0.10s/f (Good) **6** Ran SP% **110.5**
Speed ratings (Par 107): **110,108,107,107,106 104**
CSF £55.05 TOTE £6.60: £2.60, £6.00; EX 44.30 Trifecta £154.70.
Owner Stephen Louch **Bred** Ballygallon Stud Ltd **Trained** Nawton, N Yorks
■ Roger Fell's first winner.

FOCUS
An interesting conditions sprint run at a strong pace, but the order barely changed during the contest. There was a bunch finish and the form is rated around the third.

7251 RURAL INSURANCE H'CAP 2m
3:55 (3:55) (Class 5) (0-75,75) 3-Y-O+ **£3,234** (£962; £481; £240) **Stalls** High

Form RPR
2450 **1** **La Bacouetteuse (FR)**[3] 7138 11-9-1 **62**.........................(b) DavidAllan 6 72
(Iain Jardine) *bhd and sn pushed along: drvn 1/2-way: gd hdwy over 2f out: led ins fnl f: sn clr* **8/1**

3421 **2** *3 ¾* **Rocktherunway (IRE)**[15] 6840 7-9-11 **72**.................(b) ConnorBeasley 1 77
(Michael Dods) *cl up: led over 3f out: rdn over 1f out: hdd ins fnl f: kpt on same pce* **11/2**[2]

3255 **3** *3 ½* **Lara Carbonara (IRE)**[17] 6773 4-9-10 **71**.................. GrahamGibbons 9 72
(John Patrick Shanahan, Ire) *dwlt and swtchd rt s: hld up: hdwy on outside over 2f out: sn rdn: plugged on fnl f: no imp* **9/1**

-603 **4** *nse* **Status Quo (IRE)**[7] 7043 3-9-2 **74**..................................(p) LukeMorris 4 75
(Sir Mark Prescott Bt) *t.k.h early: trckd ldrs: rdn and chsd ldr over 2f out: hung rt u.p and lost 2nd over 1f out: sn no ex* **5/2**[1]

03 **5** *3 ¼* **Stoneham**[16] 6812 5-9-0 **68**.. LewisEdmunds(7) 5 65
(Iain Jardine) *tk t.k.h early: hld up: effrt and pushed along over 2f out: sn no imp* **9/1**

6 *4 ½* **Gladiator King (IRE)**[268] 7495 7-9-2 **63**...........................(t) GrahamLee 2 54
(A J Martin, Ire) *hld up midfield: stdy hdwy over 4f out: drvn over 2f out: edgd rt and wknd wl over 1f out* **8/1**

-066 **7** *1 ¾* **Jonny Delta**[16] 6812 9-8-6 **56**.......................................[1] NathanEvans(3) 3 45
(Jim Goldie) *cl up: led after 2f to over 3f out: rdn and wknd over 2f out* **25/1**

1130 **8** *2 ¼* **Falcon's Fire (IRE)**[17] 6773 3-9-3 **75**.......................... PhillipMakin 8 62
(Keith Dalgleish) *hld up in tch: rdn whn nt clr run briefly over 2f out: sn wknd* **17/2**

4352 **9** *45* **Ghostly Arc (IRE)**[16] 6812 4-8-11 **63**....................... JordanVaughan(5) 7
(Noel Wilson) *led 2f: cl up tl rdn and wknd over 3f out: lost tch fnl 2f: t.o* **7/1**[3]

3m 30.03s (-3.47) **Going Correction** -0.10s/f (Good)
WFA 3 from 4yo+ 11lb **9** Ran SP% **113.1**
Speed ratings (Par 103): **104,102,100,100,98 96,95,94,71**
CSF £50.34 CT £403.25 TOTE £10.30: £2.60, £2.00, £2.40; EX 66.00 Trifecta £545.40.
Owner Miss S A Booth **Bred** Sarl Classic Breeding & Maria R Mendes **Trained** Carruthertown, D'fries & G'way

FOCUS
Rail movement added 13yds to race distance. A modest staying handicap, but an amazing performance from the winner. He's rated close to last year's best.

7252 RACING UK HD H'CAP 5f
4:25 (4:25) (Class 5) (0-75,75) 3-Y-O+ **£3,234** (£962; £481; £240) **Stalls** High

Form RPR

1261 **1** **Showdaisy**[39] 6093 3-9-5 **73**..(p) PhillipMakin 1 85+
(Keith Dalgleish) *mde all: sn crossed to stands' rail: rdn over 1f out: kpt on strly fnl f: unchal* **8/1**[3]

1122 **2** *2 ¼* **Compton River**[18] 6745 4-8-10 **64**............................... ConnorBeasley 7 67
(Bryan Smart) *chsd ldrs: effrt and wnt 2nd 1/2-way: kpt on ins fnl f: nt pce to chal* **17/2**

5000 **3** *¾* **Landing Night (IRE)**[11] 6927 4-9-7 **75**...........................[1] PJMcDonald 6 75
(Rebecca Menzies) *in tch on outside: effrt and cl up over 1f out: kpt on same pce ins fnl f* **22/1**

3431 **4** *shd* **One Boy (IRE)**[16] 6809 5-9-2 **70**................................... PaulMulrennan 11 70
(Paul Midgley) *in tch: drvn and effrt 2f out: kpt on ins fnl f: nvr able to chal* **5/1**[1]

3454 **5** *hd* **Bunce (IRE)**[5] 7093 8-8-9 **63**.. GrahamLee 10 62
(Linda Perratt) *hld up midfield: rdn along 2f out: kpt on fnl f: nvr rchd ldrs* **28/1**

1061 **6** *1 ¼* **Mininggold**[17] 6790 3-8-13 **70**..........................(b[1]) RachelRichardson(3) 4 66
(Tim Easterby) *prom: effrt and rdn 2f out: kpt on same pce ins fnl f* **16/1**

0053 **7** *1* **Flash City (ITY)**[10] 6958 8-9-2 **70**.................................. JamesSullivan 8 61
(Ruth Carr) *hld up: rdn along 1/2-way: kpt on fnl f: n.d* **10/1**

0150 **8** *½* **Jack Luey**[17] 6766 9-9-6 **74**...(b) JasonHart 9 63
(Lawrence Mullaney) *chsd wnr to 1/2-way: rdn and no ex fr over 1f out* **11/1**

0152 **9** *¾* **Storm Trooper (IRE)**[10] 6959 5-8-13 **67**........................ BarryMcHugh 14 58+
(David Nicholls) *midfield on stands' rail: rdn over 2f out: no imp whn hmpd ins fnl f* **13/2**[2]

2060 **10** *¾* **Imperial Legend (IRE)**[25] 6537 7-9-6 **74**............................ PaulQuinn 3 58
(David Nicholls) *dwlt: bhd and drvn along 1/2-way: nvr rchd ldrs* **25/1**

0051 **11** *¾* **Bond Bombshell**[10] 6958 3-8-12 **73**....................... PatrickVaughan(7) 12 55
(David O'Meara) *dwlt: bhd: drvn along 1/2-way: sn btn* **16/1**

3506 **12** *1* **Star Cracker (IRE)**[5] 7094 4-8-10 **67**.......................(p) NathanEvans(3) 2 45
(Jim Goldie) *hld up: rdn along on outside over 2f out: sn btn* **10/1**

2030 **13** *½* **Born Innocent (IRE)**[7] 7059 3-9-2 **70**......................... GrahamGibbons 13 47
(John Patrick Shanahan, Ire) *rrd as stalls opened and slowly away: a struggling in rr* **10/1**

3166 **14** *hd* **Showbizzy**[10] 6959 3-8-9 **68**.................................(v) AdamMcNamara(5) 5 44
(Richard Fahey) *dwlt: bhd and sn rdn along: no ch fr 1/2-way* **14/1**

59.1s (-1.30) **Going Correction** -0.10s/f (Good) **14** Ran SP% **117.3**
Speed ratings (Par 103): **106,102,101,101,100 98,97,96,95,93 92,91,90,90**
CSF £70.65 CT £1479.29 TOTE £6.70: £2.80, £3.50, £8.50; EX 58.10 Trifecta £1207.50.
Owner Ronnie Docherty & Partner **Bred** Patricia Ann Scott-Dunn **Trained** Carluke, S Lanarks

FOCUS
A modest sprint handicap, but a competitive one and a smart performance from the winner, who posted another clear pb.

7253 RACING UK PROFITS RETURNED TO RACING H'CAP (DIV I) 7f 30y
4:55 (4:56) (Class 6) (0-65,67) 3-Y-O+ **£3,234** (£962; £481; £240) **Stalls** Low

Form RPR

5524 **1** **Opt Out**[5] 7096 6-8-13 **56**...(v) PhillipMakin 2 63
(David O'Meara) *prom: shkn up over 2f out: effrt and swtchd lft over 1f out: led wl ins fnl f: rdn out* **4/1**[3]

0553 **2** *½* **Napoleon Solo**[24] 6568 4-9-5 **62**.............................. GrahamGibbons 4 68
(David Barron) *pressed ldr: led after 3f: rdn along 2f out: hdd wl ins fnl f: kpt on* **5/2**[1]

4010 **3** *nk* **Bold Spirit**[24] 6569 5-9-0 **62**..(t) PhilDennis(5) 9 67
(Declan Carroll) *trckd ldrs: wnt 2nd after 3f: ev ch gng wl over 2f out: rdn over 1f out: kpt on same pce wl ins fnl f* **12/1**

0530 **4** *3 ¼* **Lovin' Spoonful**[45] 5887 3-9-4 **63**............................... ConnorBeasley 8 59
(Bryan Smart) *in tch: rdn along over 2f out: kpt on same pce over 1f out* **12/1**

0001 **5** *3 ½* **Mr Cool Cash**[8] 7010 4-9-10 **67** 6ex..................................... JoeFanning 1 55
(Richard Guest) *led 3f: trckd ldrs: rdn and edgd lft over 1f out: sn wknd* **3/1**[2]

5060 **6** *1 ¾* **Diamond Avalanche (IRE)**[28] 6434 3-9-0 **59**.................... GrahamLee 7 42
(Patrick Holmes) *midfield: drvn and outpcd over 2f out: n.d after* **50/1**

2410 **7** *1 ¾* **Mallymkun**[29] 6426 4-9-2 **64**................................... JordanVaughan(5) 3 43
(K R Burke) *s.i.s: hld up: rdn and hdwy wl over 1f out: sn no imp* **8/1**

4013 **8** *3 ¾* **Riponian**[22] 6621 6-8-12 **55**...(t) JoeyHaynes 10 25
(Susan Corbett) *in tch on outside: effrt and rdn over 2f out: edgd rt and wknd wl over 1f out* **12/1**

0330 **9** *¾* **Thornaby Nash**[11] 6921 5-9-6 **63**...............................(p) PaulMulrennan 6 31
(Colin Teague) *bhd: struggling over 4f out: nvr on terms* **25/1**

6-60 **10** *1 ¾* **Rathvale**[5] 7097 3-8-6 **51**... JamesSullivan 5 14
(Linda Perratt) *s.i.s: bhd: struggling 3f out: sn btn* **100/1**

000 **11** *24* **Bannock Town**[5] 7093 5-8-4 **50** oh5.........................(p) NathanEvans(3) 11
(Linda Perratt) *hld up: rdn along over 3f out: lost tch fr over 2f out: t.o* **200/1**

1m 28.47s (-0.53) **Going Correction** -0.10s/f (Good)
WFA 3 from 4yo+ 2lb **11** Ran SP% **115.1**
Speed ratings (Par 101): **99,98,98,94,90 88,86,82,81,79 51**
CSF £13.88 CT £110.03 TOTE £4.70: £1.50, £1.40, £3.40; EX 12.50 Trifecta £109.00.
Owner Akela Construction Ltd **Bred** Darley **Trained** Upper Helmsley, N Yorks

FOCUS
Rail movement added 7yds to race distance. The first division of a moderate handicap that included the winners of both divisions of this race last year. They finished first and third here and this was a race few ever got into despite a disputed lead. Straightforward form.

7254 RACING UK PROFITS RETURNED TO RACING H'CAP (DIV II) 7f 30y
5:25 (5:25) (Class 6) (0-65,65) 3-Y-O+ **£3,234** (£962; £481; £240) **Stalls** Low

Form RPR

6600 **1** **Circuitous**[3] 7144 8-8-7 **56**...............................(v) ShirleyTeasdale(5) 4 62
(Keith Dalgleish) *pressed ldr: led over 2f out: hld on wl u.p fnl f* **22/1**

0424 **2** *¾* **Oak Bluffs (IRE)**[162] 1925 5-9-2 **65**......................... AdamMcNamara(5) 2 69
(Richard Fahey) *t.k.h: trckd ldrs: effrt over 2f out: chsd wnr over 1f out: kpt on fnl f: hld nr fin* **13/2**[3]

1442 **3** *nk* **Wahaab (IRE)**[5] 7092 5-8-12 **63**.............................(p) LewisEdmunds(7) 5 67
(Iain Jardine) *hld up in tch: effrt and pushed along over 1f out: n.m.r briefly ins fnl f: swtchd lft and kpt on wl nr fin* **3/1**[2]

0043 **4** *¾* **Tafahom (IRE)**[24] 6569 4-9-1 **62**..............................(b) NathanEvans(3) 3 64
(Michael Easterby) *s.i.s: hld up: rdn and hdwy against far rail over 2f out: kpt on ins fnl f: no imp* **11/4**[1]

0465 **5** *¾* **Yair Hill (IRE)**[28] 6434 8-8-7 **51** oh4.................................(p) JoeFanning 1 54+
(Thomas Cuthbert) *t.k.h: hld up: stdy hdwy whn nt clr run over 1f out: sn rdn: kpt on fnl f: nrst fin* **20/1**

0450 **6** *shd* **The Name's Paver**[18] 6737 3-8-12 **58**.......................... DougieCostello 8 56
(Noel Wilson) *chsd ldrs: drvn and outpcd over 2f out: rallied over 1f out: kpt on fnl f: no imp* **12/1**

0434 **7** *1 ½* **Dark Crystal**[15] 6838 5-9-7 **65**.. DavidNolan 7 61
(Linda Perratt) *trckd ldrs: drvn over 2f out: wknd over 1f out* **9/1**

1243 **8** *1 ¾* **Arcane Dancer (IRE)**[44] 5919 3-9-4 **64**..........................(p) JasonHart 10 54
(Lawrence Mullaney) *midfield: drvn and outpcd 3f out: n.d after* **13/2**[3]

00-0 **9** *hd* **Cara's Request (AUS)**[41] 6028 11-9-1 **59**......................... DavidAllan 6 50
(David C Griffiths) *led: rdn and hdd over 2f out: chsd wnr to over 1f out: wknd ins fnl f* **33/1**

0650 **10** *3* **Amber Crystal**[5] 7092 4-8-7 **51** oh6................................ JamesSullivan 9 34
(Linda Perratt) *missed break: bhd: drvn on outside over 2f out: sn btn* **66/1**

0023 **11** *2 ¾* **Centre Haafhd**[31] 6347 5-8-7 **51**......................................(b) PJMcDonald 11 27
(Jim Goldie) *chsd ldrs: drvn along over 2f out: wknd over 1f out* **16/1**

1m 29.24s (0.24) **Going Correction** -0.10s/f (Good)
WFA 3 from 4yo+ 2lb **11** Ran SP% **115.5**
Speed ratings (Par 101): **94,93,92,91,91 90,89,87,87,83 80**
CSF £151.33 CT £561.17 TOTE £28.70: £5.20, £2.20, £1.70; EX 131.40 Trifecta £1657.30.
Owner Alison Walker Sarah Cousins **Bred** Deepwood Farm Stud **Trained** Carluke, S Lanarks

FOCUS
Rail movement added 13yds to race distance. The last Flat race of the year in Scotland for which the winning time was 0.77sec slower than the first division. The second and third help with the level.
T/Plt: £174.00 to a £1 stake. Pool: £52392.82 - 219.79 winning units T/Qpdt: £57.50 to a £1 stake. Pool: £2728.32 - 35.10 winning units **Richard Young**

6960 WOLVERHAMPTON (A.W) (L-H)
Tuesday, October 11

OFFICIAL GOING: Tapeta: standard
Wind: light, half against Weather: dry

7255 NTM FINLAND APPRENTICE H'CAP 5f 216y (Tp)
5:45 (5:45) (Class 6) (0-65,65) 3-Y-O+ **£2,846** (£847; £423; £211) **Stalls** Low

Form RPR

1440 **1** **Vincenzo Coccotti (USA)**[8] 7018 4-8-13 **62**........... HectorCrouch(3) 11 70+
(Ken Cunningham-Brown) *stdd after s: hld up towards rr: clsd and swtchd lft 1f out: hdwy to chse ldr ins fnl f: r.o wl u.p to ld towards fin* **9/1**[3]

5340 **2** *½* **Swiss Cross**[13] 6872 9-9-2 **62**....................................[1] JosephineGordon 4 69
(Phil McEntee) *chsd ldrs: effrt to chal over 1f out: drvn to ld jst ins fnl f: hdd and no ex towards fin* **7/1**[2]

0060 **3** *1 ¼* **Firesnake (IRE)**[29] 6418 3-8-9 **63**..................................... JordanUys(7) 6 66
(Lisa Williamson) *awkward leaving stalls: hld up towards rr: hdwy and swtchd rt 1f out: r.o strly fnl 100yds: nt rch ldrs* **22/1**

0012 **4** *½* **Virile (IRE)**[7] 7038 5-8-12 **63**....................................(bt) MitchGodwin(5) 7 64
(Sylvester Kirk) *hld up in tch in midfield: nt clr run and shuffled bk over 2f out: hdwy towards inner to chse ldrs 1f out: slty impeded and styd on same pce ins fnl f* **11/4**[1]

0032 **5** *½* **Socialites Red**[27] 6475 3-9-3 **64**..........................(p) MichaelJMMurphy 2 64
(Scott Dixon) *chsd ldr: rdn over 1f out: unable qck u.p jst ins fnl f: one pce fnl 100yds* **9/1**[3]

1300 **6** *½* **Himalayan Queen**[13] 6872 3-8-11 **63**......................... SophieKilloran(5) 10 61
(William Jarvis) *s.i.s: hld up in rr: hdwy on inner over 1f out: nt clr run and swtchd rt ins fnl f: kpt on: nvr trbld ldrs* **12/1**

0505 **7** *nse* **Mighty Zip (USA)**[139] 2571 4-9-2 **65**....................(p) CharlieBennett(3) 12 63
(Lisa Williamson) *taken down early: led and crossed to inner: rdn over 1f out: hdd and no ex jst ins fnl f: wknd fnl 75yds* **50/1**

0365 **8** *½* **Loumarin (IRE)**[63] 5270 4-8-11 **64**............................ BenSanderson(7) 1 61
(Michael Appleby) *t.k.h: hld up in tch in midfield: nt clrest of runs over 1f out: kpt on ins fnl f: no threat to ldrs* **16/1**

4501 **9** *nk* **Last Star Falling (IRE)**[26] 6509 3-8-12 **64**..............(b) LuluStanford(5) 13 60
(Henry Spiller) *hld up towards rr: effrt on outer bnd 2f out: styd on same pce ins fnl f: nvr trbld ldrs* **10/1**

115 **10** *¾* **Intense Starlet (IRE)**[12] 6909 5-9-1 **64**..............(p) RobJFitzpatrick(3) 3 57
(Marjorie Fife) *t.k.h: hld up in tch in midfield: n.m.r 2f out: effrt jst over 1f out: styd on same pce ins fnl f* **7/1**[2]

0600 **11** *2 ¾* **Lackaday**[59] 5386 4-9-0 **63**.....................................(p) CallumShepherd(3) 8 48
(Mark Walford) *chsd ldrs: rdn 2f out: sn struggling and lost pl over 1f out: wknd ins fnl f* **11/1**

446 **12** *12* **Pearly Queen**[62] 5300 3-9-4 **65**........................ JackDuern 5 14
(Dean Ivory) *chsd ldrs: rdn 1/2-way: lost pl 2f out: bhd and eased ins fnl f* **12/1**

1m 13.47s (-1.03) **Going Correction** -0.175s/f (Stan)
WFA 3 from 4yo+ 1lb **12** Ran SP% **116.7**
Speed ratings (Par 101): **99,98,96,96,95 94,94,93,93,92 88,72**
CSF £69.57 CT £1370.09 TOTE £9.90: £3.60, £2.00, £7.90; EX 80.70 Trifecta £2552.70.
Owner David Henery **Bred** Gainesway Thoroughbreds Ltd Et Al **Trained** Danebury, Hants
■ Stewards' Enquiry : Hector Crouch caution: careless riding

FOCUS
An ordinary sprint handicap, confined to apprentice riders. The winner is better than the bare form, the second and third helping with the level.

7256 NTM SCANDINAVIA CLASSIFIED STKS 1m 1f 103y (Tp)
6:15 (6:16) (Class 6) 3-Y-O+ **£2,846** (£847; £423; £211) **Stalls** Low

Form RPR
041 **1** **Protest (IRE)**[10] 6966 3-8-7 54........................ MitchGodwin(5) 4 59
(Sylvester Kirk) *sn led and mde rest: rdn over 1f out: hrd pressed and hld on wl fnl 75yds out: rdn out* **5/2**[1]

0500 **2** *½* **Enchanted Moment**[24] 6593 4-8-13 54..................(p) LouisSteward(3) 7 57
(Chris Wall) *chsd ldrs: rdn wl over 1f out: chsd wnr and edgd sltly lft jst ins fnl f: ev ch wl ins fnl f: hld towards fin* **14/1**

533 **3** *nk* **Lady Canford (IRE)**[44] 5921 3-8-9 51.................. JosephineGordon(3) 6 57+
(James Bethell) *hld up in midfield: effrt 2f out: rdn and hdwy over 1f out: ev ch wl ins fnl f: hld towards fin* **5/1**[2]

1042 **4** *½* **Wootton Vale (IRE)**[27] 6478 3-8-12 52........................ JackGarritty 2 57
(Richard Fahey) *chsd ldrs: effrt 2f out: styd on u.p and ev ch wl ins fnl f: unable qck towards fin* **8/1**[3]

0033 **5** *½* **Lobster Cocktail (IRE)**[21] 6651 3-8-12 54.....................[1] ShaneKelly 13 56
(Ed Walker) *hld up in tch in midfield: swtchd rt and effrt 2f out: hdwy 1f out: kpt on u.p: nvr quite getting to ldrs* **5/1**[2]

5541 **6** *4 ½* **Pensax Lady (IRE)**[10] 6967 3-8-12 53........................ RobertWinston 11 47
(Daniel Mark Loughnane) *sn chsng wnr: rdn 2f out: unable qck and lost 2nd whn hmpd jst ins fnl f: sn wknd* **10/1**

6102 **7** *1* **Desert Tango**[28] 6443 3-9-0 53 ow2........................ RobertTart 8 47
(Michael Mullineaux) *stdd s: hld in in last quartet: sme hdwy u.p into midfield over 1f out: no imp ins fnl f* **14/1**

0060 **8** *1 ¼* **Olympus Mons (FR)**[10] 6967 3-8-12 40........................ LiamKeniry 1 43
(Jo Hughes) *stdd s: t.k.h: hld up in last quartet: effrt on inner over 1f out: no imp ins fnl f: n.d* **33/1**

5-54 **9** *1* **Black Hole Sun**[262] 318 4-9-2 55........................ WilliamCarson 5 40
(Tony Carroll) *hld up in tch in midfield: u.p over 3f out: no imp and btn over 1f out: wknd ins fnl f* **40/1**

0000 **10** *hd* **Serendib's Glory (IRE)**[61] 5338 3-8-9 54................(p) ShelleyBirkett(3) 3 40
(Julia Feilden) *wl in tch in midfield: rdn over 2f out: struggling and lost pl over 1f out: wknd fnl f* **50/1**

4440 **11** *4* **Magical Lasso (IRE)**[11] 6920 3-8-12 47........................(p) TomEaves 12 33
(Keith Dalgleish) *in tch in midfield: rdn 4f out: wknd 2f out* **33/1**

2662 **12** *2* **Lynngale**[167] 1791 5-9-2 55........................ ShaneGray 10 28
(Kristin Stubbs) *hld up in tch: effrt wd bnd 2f out: sn btn and wknd* **9/1**

0300 **13** *29* **Burning Love (IRE)**[26] 6514 3-8-5 46..................(v) KieranSchofield(7) 9
(Adam West) *v.s.a and wnt sharply lft leaving stalls: grad rcvrd and tagged onto bk of field over 6f out: rdn over 2f out: sn lost tch: t.o* **100/1**

1m 59.61s (-1.19) **Going Correction** -0.175s/f (Stan)
WFA 3 from 4yo+ 4lb **13** Ran SP% **116.7**
Speed ratings (Par 101): **98,97,97,96,96 92,91,90,89,89 85,84,58**
CSF £38.86 TOTE £3.30: £1.80, £2.90, £3.10; EX 47.70 Trifecta £362.30.
Owner Sylvester Kirk **Bred** Paget Bloodstock & Eadling Farm **Trained** Upper Lambourn, Berks

FOCUS
A moderate classified event. The form is straightforward if ordinary, the winner getting a softish lead.

7257 NTM GB H'CAP 1m 1f 103y (Tp)
6:45 (6:45) (Class 6) (0-65,64) 3-Y-O+ **£2,846** (£847; £423; £211) **Stalls** Low

Form RPR
2000 **1** **Thane Of Cawdor (IRE)**[13] 6871 7-8-13 **58**......... JosephineGordon(3) 9 65
(Joseph Tuite) *hld up in tch in midfield: hdwy on outer 2f out: chsd ldrs over 1f out: led ins fnl f: kpt on: rdn out* **22/1**

1402 **2** *nk* **Stoneboat Bill**[6] 7078 4-9-6 **62**........................ FrederikTylicki 2 69
(Declan Carroll) *stdd s: hld up in last pair: clsd and nt clrest of runs over 1f out: hdwy 1f out: chsd wnr wl ins fnl f: r.o wl: nvr quite getting to wnr* **11/4**[2]

1043 **3** *1 ¼* **Spinning Rose**[26] 6513 4-9-2 **58**........................ RobertWinston 3 62
(Dean Ivory) *t.k.h: chsd ldrs: wnt 2nd over 6f out tl rdn to ld over 1f out: hdd ins fnl f: no ex and one pced after* **15/2**[3]

2520 **4** *1* **Inflexiball**[18] 6737 4-8-11 **58**........................ CliffordLee(5) 7 60
(John Mackie) *in tch in midfield: n.m.r wl over 1f out tl hdwy jst ins fnl f: styd on u.p fnl 100yds: no threat to ldrs* **10/1**

3032 **5** *½* **Rebel State (IRE)**[19] 6700 3-9-4 **64**........................ JamieSpencer 8 67
(Richard Spencer) *hld up in tch in midfield: clsd to chse ldrs and nt clr run over 1f out: swtchd lft and rdn 1f out: styd on same pce fnl 100yds* **9/4**[1]

0210 **6** *¾* **Monna Valley**[21] 6662 4-9-2 **61**........................ AaronJones(3) 11 61
(Stuart Williams) *hld up in tch in last quartet: effrt on outer wl over 1f out: styd on ins fnl f: nvr trbld ldrs* **17/2**

5040 **7** *½* **Heart Of Oak**[36] 6194 3-9-1 **64**........................(vt[1]) MarcMonaghan(3) 12 64
(George Peckham) *chsd ldrs: rdn 2f out: unable qck over 1f out: wknd ins fnl f* **20/1**

0560 **8** *nse* **Hold Hands**[29] 6426 5-9-4 **60**........................ FMBerry 13 59
(Brendan Powell) *s.i.s: hld up in tch in last trio: shkn up and effrt over 1f out: no imp ins fnl f: nvr trbld ldrs* **40/1**

430 **9** *¾* **Best Tamayuz**[11] 6921 5-9-6 **62**........................ MichaelJMMurphy 4 59
(Scott Dixon) *led after 1f out: rdn and hdd over 1f out: wknd ins fnl f* **16/1**

1/00 **10** *¾* **Fujin Dancer (FR)**[12] 6907 11-9-3 **62**................. JacobButterfield(3) 10 58
(Harriet Bethell) *s.i.s: in tch in rr: swtchd lft and rdn over 1f out: no imp: nvr trbld ldrs* **40/1**

060 **11** *1* **Yamllik**[46] 5824 4-9-3 **62**........................(p) HectorCrouch(3) 1 56
(Brian Barr) *t.k.h: led for 1f out: chsd ldrs after tl unable qck u.p over 1f out: wknd ins fnl f* **20/1**

1m 59.46s (-1.34) **Going Correction** -0.175s/f (Stan)
WFA 3 from 4yo+ 4lb **11** Ran SP% **113.4**
Speed ratings (Par 101): **98,97,96,95,95 94,94,94,93,92 91**
CSF £75.37 CT £508.64 TOTE £29.30: £5.50, £2.00, £2.10; EX 106.40 Trifecta £563.10.
Owner Alan & Christine Bright **Bred** Balmerino Bldstock & Newsells Park Stud **Trained** Lambourn, Berks

FOCUS
This weak handicap was a muddling affair. Straightforward form. The winner is a likeable type in this grade.

7258 NTM GERMANY NURSERY H'CAP 5f 20y (Tp)
7:15 (7:15) (Class 4) (0-85,81) 2-Y-O **£5,433** (£1,617; £808; £404) **Stalls** Low

Form RPR
6310 **1** **Precious Plum**[15] 6830 2-8-10 **70**........................ SilvestreDeSousa 9 77
(Chris Dwyer) *chsd ldr: drvn to ld 1f out: hld on wl u.p towards fin: drvn out* **17/2**

3253 **2** *½* **Coolfitch (IRE)**[6] 7073 2-9-6 **80**........................ DanielTudhope 8 86
(David O'Meara) *hld up in tch in midfield: effrt over 1f out: rdn to chse wnr ins fnl f: r.o wl: hld towards fin* **10/3**[2]

2365 **3** *3* **Sheila's Palace**[54] 5569 2-7-12 **63**........................ HollieDoyle(5) 7 57
(J S Moore) *chsd ldrs: effrt over 1f out: edgd rt 1f out: kpt on same pce ins fnl f: wnt 3rd last strides* **33/1**

0100 **4** *hd* **Dandy Flame (IRE)**[26] 6507 2-9-1 **75**........................ RenatoSouza 5 68
(Jose Santos) *in tch in midfield: swtchd lft and effrt ent fnl f: kpt on same pce fnl 150yds* **33/1**

01 **5** *shd* **Mr Black**[22] 6622 2-9-5 **79**........................ JamieSpencer 4 75+
(George Scott) *dwlt and squeezed for room leaving stalls: hld up in last pair: swtchd rt and effrt wl over 1f out: swtchd lft jst ins fnl f: kpt on but no threat to ldrs* **11/8**[1]

2025 **6** *nse* **Gerrard's Fur Coat**[80] 4629 2-8-13 **73**................... RichardKingscote 10 66
(Tom Dascombe) *led: rdn over 1f out: hdd 1f out: 3rd and btn ins fnl f: wknd and lost 3 pls last strides* **40/1**

5040 **7** *1 ¼* **Camargue**[10] 6954 2-9-6 **80**........................ FMBerry 1 68
(Mark Johnston) *chsd ldrs: rdn 2f out: unable qck u.p over 1f out: wknd ins fnl f* **9/2**[3]

0500 **8** *3 ¾* **Stringybark Creek**[10] 6950 2-9-4 **78**........................ CharlesBishop 2 53
(Mick Channon) *sn pushed along in midfield: rdn and btn over 1f out: wknd fnl f* **12/1**

4010 **9** *3* **Secret Potion**[52] 5656 2-9-3 **77**........................ ShaneKelly 6 41
(Ronald Harris) *t.k.h to post: t.k.h: wl in tch in midfield: lost pl and nt pushed 2f out: hld onto and wl btn over 1f out: sddle slipped* **28/1**

401 **10** *1* **Prancelina (IRE)**[29] 6420 2-8-0 **63**................... JosephineGordon(3) 3 23
(Phil McEntee) *dwlt and short of room leaving stalls: a rr: swtchd rt and effrt over 1f out: no hdwy: bhd fnl f* **20/1**

1m 0.76s (-1.14) **Going Correction** -0.175s/f (Stan) 2y crse rec **10** Ran SP% **118.1**
Speed ratings (Par 97): **102,101,96,96,95 95,93,87,83,81**
CSF £35.47 CT £716.98 TOTE £11.90: £2.20, £1.70, £7.60; EX 48.00 Trifecta £894.80.
Owner Mrs Julia Hughes **Bred** Mrs J V Hughes **Trained** Newmarket, Suffolk

FOCUS
This modest nursery was run at a frantic pace. Good efforts from the first two to come clear.

7259 NTM EAST EBF STALLIONS MEDIAN AUCTION MAIDEN STKS 5f 216y (Tp)
7:45 (7:49) (Class 5) 2-Y-O **£3,557** (£1,058; £529; £264) **Stalls** Low

Form RPR
04 **1** **Desperados Destiny**[20] 6682 2-9-2 0........................ RobHornby(3) 9 74+
(Ed McMahon) *chsd ldr for 1f out: styd handy: effrt and lft in ld jst over 1f out: sustained duel w runner up fnl f: r.o and a jst doing enough: rdn out* **6/1**[2]

22 **2** *nk* **Subjective**[30] 6375 2-9-5 0........................ JamieSpencer 11 73+
(David Simcock) *pushed along leaving stalls: in tch in midfield: effrt and lft w ev ch jst over 1f out: sustained duel w wnr fnl f: r.o but a jst hld* **2/5**[1]

00 **3** *6* **Blue Rocks**[32] 6274 2-8-12 0........................ JordanUys(7) 3 55
(Lisa Williamson) *uns rdr gng to post: chsd ldrs: effrt and swtchd rt over 1f out: outpcd by ldng pair 1f out: wnt modest 3rd wl ins fnl f: kpt on* **100/1**

4 *shd* **Must Be Amazing** 2-9-0 0........................ MartinLane 7 50+
(Jeremy Gask) *dwlt and pushed along early: hdwy after 2f: 6th and rdn 2f out: no ch w ldng pair but battling for modest 3rd wl ins fnl f: kpt on* **33/1**

5 *3* **Jessiboo (IRE)** 2-9-0 0........................ RichardKingscote 12 41
(Tom Dascombe) *led: hung bdly lft and hdd jst over 1f out: wknd ins fnl f* **14/1**

6 *½* **Four Candles (IRE)** 2-9-5 0........................ SilvestreDeSousa 2 44+
(Philip McBride) *in tch in midfield: nt clr run and shuffled bk towards rr 2f out: rdn and sme hdwy 1f out: kpt on but no ch w ldrs* **11/1**

05 **7** *¾* **Impassioned**[64] 5242 2-9-0 0........................ RyanPowell 1 37+
(Sir Mark Prescott Bt) *bustled along leaving stalls: pressed ldr after 1f: rdn and ev ch 2f out: squeezed for room and bdly hmpd over 1f out: nt rcvr: swtchd rt 1f out: no hdwy after* **15/2**[3]

00 **8** *1 ¼* **Glam'Selle**[13] 6866 2-9-0 0........................ LiamKeniry 4 33
(Ronald Harris) *t.k.h: hld up towards rr: swtchd rt and effrt over 1f out: sn btn and wknd fnl f* **100/1**

50 **9** *nk* **Caspian Gold (IRE)**[13] 6880 2-9-5 0........................ ShaneKelly 8 37
(Richard Hughes) *dwlt: sn outpcd and detached in last: clsd 1/2-way: edgd lft and wknd over 1f out* **14/1**

00 **10** *9* **Lincoln Day**[18] 6750 2-9-5 0........................ DannyBrock 5 10
(Phil McEntee) *midfield: rdn 4f out: lost pl u.p 2f out: bhd fnl f* **80/1**

60 **11** *8* **Sam The Rebel**[31] 6314 2-9-5 0........................ WilliamCarson 6
(Mike Hammond) *a towards rr: wd bnd 2f out: sn bhd* **80/1**

1m 13.28s (-1.22) **Going Correction** -0.175s/f (Stan) **11** Ran SP% **126.5**
Speed ratings (Par 95): **101,100,92,92,88 87,86,85,84,72 62**
CSF £9.46 TOTE £9.80: £2.00, £1.02, £26.60; EX 15.00 Trifecta £1069.50.
Owner William Arblaster **Bred** William Arblaster **Trained** Lichfield, Staffs

FOCUS
An ordinary 2yo maiden.

7260 NTM EUROPE H'CAP (DIV I) 7f 32y (Tp)
8:15 (8:16) (Class 6) (0-60,60) 3-Y-O+ **£2,846** (£847; £423; £211) **Stalls** High

Form RPR
2256 **1** **Red Unico (IRE)**[22] 6637 4-9-0 **60**........................ JoshuaBryan(7) 12 67
(Brian Barr) *racd keenly: sn chsng ldr: rdn to ld jst over 1f out: drvn and hrd pressed towards fin: hld on: all out* **7/1**

406 **2** *nk* **Beverley Bullet**[46] 5860 3-9-2 **57**........................ RobertWinston 3 63
(Les Eyre) *chsd ldrs: effrt over 1f out: swtchd rt and chsd wnr 100yds: kpt on u.p: nvr quite getting to wnr* **9/2**[1]

4650 **3** *1 ½* **Great Expectations**[63] 5259 8-9-5 **58**..................(vt) FrederikTylicki 4 61
(J R Jenkins) *jostling sn after s: trckd ldrs: effrt in 3rd over 1f out: styd on same pce u.p ins fnl f* **10/1**

1106 **4** *½* **Free To Roam (IRE)**[133] 2784 3-8-9 **53**.............. JosephineGordon(3) 6 54
(Philip McBride) *jostling sn after s: hld up in midfield: rdn over 2f out: hdwy over 1f out: chsd ldrs and swtchd rt ins fnl f: kpt on same pce towards fin* **5/1**[2]

5005 **5** *3/4* **Misu Pete**[20] 6677 4-8-13 **59**........ LuluStanford(7) 7 59
(Mark Usher) *hld up in midfield: clsd and rdn over 1f out: kpt on same pce ins fnl f* **13/2**

/46- **6** *2 1/4* **McCarthy Mor (IRE)**[294] 8346 5-8-7 **49**........(v) RobHornby(3) 8 43
(Mandy Rowland) *taken down early: dwlt: off the pce in last pair: rdn and hdwy over 1f out: styd on ins fnl f: nvr trbld ldrs* **22/1**

0130 **7** *3 1/4* **Sober Up**[19] 6700 4-9-4 **57**........(p) SilvestreDeSousa 2 43
(Ivan Furtado) *led: rdn hdd over 1f out: wknd ins fnl f* **11/2**[3]

200 **8** *2 1/4* **Sea Of Uncertainty**[47] 5808 3-9-0 **58**........ HectorCrouch(3) 5 38
(James Evans) *jostling sn after s: hld up in midfield: rdn over 2f out: sn struggling: wknd over 1f out* **33/1**

0-00 **9** *1 1/2* **Contendit**[21] 6646 3-8-8 **49**........ CamHardie 11 25
(Michael Easterby) *nvr travelling and a towards rr: wknd over 1f out* **50/1**

-006 **10** *12* **Synodic (USA)**[106] 3724 4-9-7 **60**........(bt[1]) JackMitchell 1 8
(Seamus Durack) *s.i.s: off the pce in rr: effrt u.p 2f out: sn lost tch* **8/1**

0060 **11** *1/2* **Pyroclastic (IRE)**[22] 6636 4-9-0 **53**........(b) RobertTart 10
(Nick Kent) *in tch in midfield: rdn 3f out: sn struggling: wknd over 1f out* **16/1**

1m 28.04s (-0.76) **Going Correction** -0.175s/f (Stan)
WFA 3 from 4yo+ 2lb **11** Ran SP% **111.4**
Speed ratings (Par 101): **97,96,94,94,93 90,87,84,82,69 68**
CSF £35.67 CT £311.82 TOTE £6.70: £2.10, £2.20, £3.10; EX 42.20 Trifecta £650.50.
Owner The Golden Horse Racing Club **Bred** E O'Gorman **Trained** Longburton, Dorset

FOCUS
They went hard up front in this wide-open looking handicap. Ordinary form.

7261 NTM EUROPE H'CAP (DIV II) 7f 32y (Tp)
8:45 (8:45) (Class 6) (0-60,60) 3-Y-O+ **£2,846** (£847; £423; £211) **Stalls** High

Form RPR

0564 **1** **Secret Lightning (FR)**[12] 6900 4-8-8 **50**........ AlistairRawlinson(3) 5 56
(Michael Appleby) *hld up in tch in midfield: nt clr run over 2f out tl hdwy over 1f out: chsd wnr 1f out: r.o wl u.p to ld cl home* **8/1**

02 **2** *nk* **For Shia And Lula (IRE)**[49] 5734 7-9-3 **59**........ JosephineGordon(3) 8 64
(Daniel Mark Loughnane) *chsd ldr tl over 5f out: styd chsng ldrs: effrt and rdn to ld over 1f out: drvn ins fnl f: kpt on: hdd cl home* **6/1**[2]

-050 **3** *1 1/4* **Prisom (IRE)**[14] 6851 3-9-3 **58**........ TomMarquand 11 60
(Gay Kelleway) *stdd s: hld up in tch in last trio: nt clr run 2f out: hdwy u.p 1f out: sn chsng ldng pair: styd on same pce fnl 100yds* **16/1**

4063 **4** *1* **Mrs Biggs**[7] 7062 4-9-6 **59**........ TomEaves 12 59
(Declan Carroll) *taken down early: chsd ldrs: ev ch 2f out: sn rdn and unable qck: styd on same pce ins fnl f* **5/1**[1]

0503 **5** *1 3/4* **Fossa**[14] 6853 6-8-3 **47**........ CharlieBennett(5) 3 42
(Mark Brisbourne) *stdd s: hld up in tch in last trio: nt clr run 2f out: effrt 1f out: edging lft and kpt on ins fnl f: nvr threatened ldrs* **15/2**

2004 **6** *hd* **Moi Aussie**[39] 6106 3-9-4 **59**........ MartinDwyer 9 53
(Ed McMahon) *t.k.h: hld up in midfield on outer: hdwy to chse ldr over 5f out: led over 2f out: rdn and hdd over 1f out: wknd ins fnl f* **7/1**[3]

3204 **7** *1* **Carlovian**[28] 6436 3-8-7 **48**........ KieranO'Neill 7 40
(Christopher Kellett) *t.k.h: hld up in tch in midfield: nt clr run over 2f out: hdwy to chse ldrs and drvn over 1f out: unable qck: wknd ins fnl f* **16/1**

3220 **8** *hd* **Deben**[7] 7062 3-9-4 **59**........ JoeDoyle 6 50
(Kevin Ryan) *t.k.h: hld up in tch in midfield: swtchd rt 4f out: effrt u.p over 1f out: no imp: wknd ins fnl f* **7/1**[3]

0056 **9** *nk* **Little Indian**[7] 7048 6-9-3 **56**........ FrederikTylicki 1 47
(J R Jenkins) *chsd ldrs: nt clr run and shuffled bk 2f out: tried to rally over 1f out: kpt on same pce fnl f* **17/2**

0000 **10** *8* **Rupert Boy (IRE)**[47] 5808 3-9-0 **55**........(b) MichaelJMMurphy 2 26
(Scott Dixon) *sn led: hdd and rdn over 2f out: lost pl 2f out: wknd fnl f* **33/1**

4000 **F** **Disclosure**[20] 6685 5-9-7 **60**........ RobertWinston 10
(Les Eyre) *t.k.h: hld up in tch in last trio: stmbld and fell over 2f out* **8/1**

1m 27.91s (-0.89) **Going Correction** -0.175s/f (Stan)
WFA 3 from 4yo+ 2lb **11** Ran SP% **115.2**
Speed ratings (Par 101): **98,97,96,95,93 92,91,91,91,82**
CSF £54.24 CT £765.43 TOTE £10.30: £3.40, £2.20, £4.50; EX 69.70 Trifecta £1110.50.
Owner Mick Appleby Racing **Bred** Jeffrey Colin Smith **Trained** Oakham, Rutland

FOCUS
This second division of the moderate 7f handicap was run at a decent pace. Straightforward form, and the winner should be competitive off a small rise.

7262 NTM RUSSIA H'CAP 1m 4f 50y (Tp)
9:15 (9:16) (Class 7) (0-50,50) 3-Y-O+ **£2,264** (£673; £336; £168) **Stalls** Low

Form RPR

2060 **1** **Ali Bin Nayef**[23] 5749 4-9-6 **49**........ SilvestreDeSousa 5 56
(Michael Wigham) *hld up in tch in midfield: effrt 2f out: hdwy u.p to chal jst ins fnl f: led 75yds out: rdn out* **7/2**[2]

3352 **2** *1* **Mrs Burbidge**[23] 1322 6-9-6 **49**........(tp) LiamKeniry 11 54
(Neil Mulholland) *trckd ldrs: rdn to ld over 1f out: drvn and hdd 75yds out: styd on same pce after* **5/2**[1]

-643 **3** *1 3/4* **Top Set (IRE)**[29] 6422 6-9-2 **45**........(p) TimmyMurphy 2 48
(Richard Phillips) *hld up in tch: effrt and hdwy over 1f out: kpt on ins fnl f: nvr enough pce to rch ldrs* **12/1**

-044 **4** *2 1/2* **Right Madam (IRE)**[24] 6593 4-9-5 **48**........(p) KieranO'Neill 6 47
(Sarah Hollinshead) *sn bhd: pushed along 8f out: clsd and in tch 4f out: rdn and hdwy over 2f out: styd on ins fnl f: nvr trbld ldrs* **8/1**[3]

3450 **5** *1 1/4* **Monopoli**[35] 6212 7-8-12 **48**........(p) RPWalsh(7) 7 45
(Ivan Furtado) *t.k.h: hld up wl in tch in midfield: stl travelling wl over 2f out: nt clr run over 1f out tl swtchd rt ins fnl f: kpt on but no threat to ldrs* **16/1**

6004 **6** *3/4* **Hooks Lane**[27] 6478 4-9-7 **50**........ StevieDonohoe 4 45
(Shaun Harris) *racd in last pair: 10th and rdn 6f out: hdwy ent fnl f: styd on to pass btn horses ins fnl f: nvr trbld ldrs* **20/1**

2202 **7** *3/4* **Ryan The Giant**[39] 6094 3-9-0 **50**........(p) TomEaves 8 44
(Keith Dalgleish) *led: rdn over 3f out: drvn and hdd over 1f out: lost pl over 1f out: wknd ins fnl f* **7/2**[2]

0400 **8** *1/2* **Street Art (IRE)**[62] 5303 4-8-13 **49**........ KevinLundie(7) 3 42
(Mike Murphy) *hld up towards rr: effrt on inner over 1f out: kpt on same pce ins fnl f: nvr trbld ldrs* **22/1**

03 **9** *hd* **Willshebetrying**[97] 4019 5-9-2 **45**........(v) WilliamTwiston-Davies 1 38
(Jim Best) *chsd ldrs tl wnt 2nd over 6f out: rdn and ev ch over 2f out tl unable qck and btn over 1f out: wknd ins fnl f* **22/1**

5206 **10** *5* **Stanlow**[9] 6434 6-9-5 **48**........(v) RobertTart 12 33
(Michael Mullineaux) *hld up in last trio: clsd 4f out: effrt u.p on outer over 2f out: sn btn and wknd over 1f out* **25/1**

0-20 **11** *nse* **Too Many Diamonds (IRE)**[29] 6406 5-8-11 **45**........(tp) PaddyPilley(5) 9 30
(Clare Ellam) *chsd ldr tl over 6f out: styd prom: rdn over 2f out: wknd over 1f out* **66/1**

2m 39.98s (-0.82) **Going Correction** -0.175s/f (Stan)
WFA 3 from 4yo+ 7lb **11** Ran SP% **116.5**
Speed ratings (Par 97): **95,94,93,91,90 90,89,89,89,85 85**
CSF £11.53 CT £93.42 TOTE £4.10: £1.80, £1.40, £3.30; EX 16.00 Trifecta £187.20.
Owner P J Edwards & M Wigham **Bred** Sheikh Hamdan Bin Maktoum Al Maktoum **Trained** Newmarket, Suffolk

FOCUS
This bottom-drawer handicap was run at a solid pace. The form is rated around the consistent second.
T/Plt: £383.90 to a £1 stake. Pool of £93854.33 - 178.45 winning tickets. T/Qpdt: £21.90 to a £1 stake. Pool of £12530.64 - 422.28 winning tickets. **Steve Payne**

2712 BORDEAUX LE BOUSCAT (R-H)
Tuesday, October 11

OFFICIAL GOING: Turf: good to soft

7263a GRAND CRITERIUM DE BORDEAUX - PRIX DU HONG KONG JOCKEY CLUB (LISTED RACE) (2YO) (TURF) 1m
11:55 (12:00) 2-Y-O **£23,897** (£9,558; £7,169; £4,779; £2,389)

RPR

1 **Brametot (IRE)**[52] 5702 2-8-11 0........ CristianDemuro 4 97
(J-C Rouget, France) **7/10**[1]

2 *1 1/2* **Samuna (FR)**[43] 5986 2-8-8 0........ JulienAuge 3 91
(C Ferland, France) **41/10**[3]

3 *3* **Moi Moi Moi (IRE)**[20] 6679 2-8-11 0........ IoritzMendizabal 5 87
(Brian Meehan) *disp on outer: rdn and hdd 2f out: no ex w front pair fnl f but sme rally and bk up for 3rd cl home* **17/2**

4 *nk* **Skyron (FR)** 2-8-8 0........ AlexandreGavilan 1 83
(D Guillemin, France) **3/1**[2]

5 *7 1/2* **Numeration (FR)**[12] 6913 2-8-8 0........ MlleAdelineMerou 2 66
(B De Montzey, France) **24/1**

1m 41.31s (101.31) **5** Ran SP% **118.0**
WIN (incl. 1 euro stake): 1.70. PLACES: 1.20, 1.90. SF: 4.30.
Owner G Augustin-Normand & Mme E Vidal **Bred** H Cardemil **Trained** Pau, France

7264 - (Foreign Racing) - See Raceform Interactive

7086 SAINT-CLOUD (L-H)
Tuesday, October 11

OFFICIAL GOING: Turf: good

7265a PRIX DE BUZENVAL (CLAIMER) (3YO) (TURF) 1m 4f
2:55 (12:00) 3-Y-O **£6,985** (£2,794; £2,095; £1,397; £698)

RPR

1 **Texada**[9] 3-8-8 0........ StephaneBreux 9 61
(F-H Graffard, France) **27/10**[1]

2 *hd* **Last Tango (FR)**[27] 3-8-11 0........ VincentVion 6 64
(Alain Couetil, France) **41/10**[2]

3 *1 3/4* **Larox (GER)**[150] 3-8-8 0........ YohannBourgois 12 58
(C Von Der Recke, Germany) **15/1**

4 *2* **Love Moon (FR)**[197] 3-8-11 0........ SylvainRuis 5 58
(J Phelippon, France) **41/5**

5 *1 1/2* **First Conde (FR)**[305] 3-9-4 0........ JeremyCrocquevieille 10 63
(M Nigge, France) **12/1**

6 *1* **Illyrio (IRE)**[26] 3-9-1 0........ FrankPanicucci 3 58
(J Phelippon, France) **9/1**

7 *1 1/2* **Waldenon (FR)**[24] 3-9-1 0........(p) NathanKasztelan 1 56
(S Jesus, France) **16/1**

8 *3* **Porte Joie (GER)**[125] 3-8-11 0........(p) ValentinGambart 14 47
(E Lellouche, France) **10/1**

9 *1 1/2* **Quetzaltenango (FR)**[8] 7014 3-8-11 0........ LouisBeuzelin 11 44
(J S Moore) *prom: rdn into st and sn outpcd: wknd fnl f* **63/10**[3]

10 *1 1/2* **Stormy Angel (FR)**[81] 3-8-11 0........ AntonioPolli 13 42
(Andrew Hollinshead, France) **67/1**

11 *5* **Cevedale (FR)**[34] 3-8-11 0........ MlleMargotRomary 8 34
(Mlle B Renk, France) **93/1**

12 *1 3/4* **Chantegrive (FR)**[84] 3-8-11 0........ MlleSophieChuette 2 31
(Adrien Desespringalle, France) **107/1**

13 *1/2* **Minabest (FR)**[82] 3-8-8 0........ JimmyTastayre 7 27
(Robert Collet, France) **53/1**

14 *dist* **Super Dream (FR)**[218] 3-9-4 0........ MllePaulineDominois 4
(Louis Baudron, France) **22/1**

2m 38.98s (-1.42) **14** Ran SP% **119.8**
WIN (incl. 1 euro stake): 3.70. PLACES: 1.60, 1.70, 3.40. DF: 7.00. SF: 13.20.
Owner Ecurie Mathieu Offenstadt **Bred** Juddmonte Farms Ltd **Trained** France

7174 SANTA ANITA (L-H)
Tuesday, October 11

OFFICIAL GOING: Turf: firm

7266a ZUMA BEACH STKS (LISTED RACE) (2YO) (TURF) 1m (T)
12:30 (12:00) 2-Y-O
£40,816 (£13,605; £8,163; £4,081; £1,360; £234)

RPR

1 **Big Score (USA)**[37] 2-8-8 0........ FlavienPrat 11 108
(Tim Yakteen, U.S.A) **48/10**[3]

2 *3 1/4* **Sonic Boom (USA)** 2-8-6 0........ BrianJosephHernandezJr 10 99
(Ian Wilkes, U.S.A) **43/10**[2]

3 *1/2* **Ventry Bay (USA)** 2-8-6 0........(b) FlorentGeroux 12 97
(Wesley A Ward, U.S.A) **123/10**

4 *nse* **Harbour Master**[31] 6330 2-8-6 0........ MikeESmith 9 97
(Jamie Osborne) **67/10**

5 *hd* **Oopper Wallah (USA)** 2-8-6 0..............................(b) NorbertoArroyoJr 2 97
(Peter Miller, U.S.A) **25/1**
6 *1 1/4* **Offshore (USA)** 2-8-8 0.. KentJDesormeaux 1 96
(Neil Drysdale, U.S.A) **193/10**
7 *1/2* **Billy Big (IRE)**[37] 2-8-8 0.......................................(b) SantiagoGonzalez 6 95
(Philip D'Amato, U.S.A) **28/1**
8 *2 3/4* **Bowies Hero (USA)**[37] 2-8-10 0...............................(b) RafaelBejarano 7 90
(Philip D'Amato, U.S.A) **21/10**[1]
9 *hd* **Riser (USA)** 2-8-6 0...(b) GaryStevens 3 86
(Blaine Wright, U.S.A) **77/10**
10 *1/2* **Colonel Samsen (USA)**[26] 2-8-6 0..........................(b) VictorEspinoza 5 85
(Eoin Harty, U.S.A) **29/1**
11 *nk* **Secret House (USA)**[58] 2-8-6 0.. TylerBaze 8 84
(Doug O'Neill, U.S.A) **44/1**
12 *5 3/4* **Sorry Erik (USA)** 2-8-6 0... MarioGutierrez 4 71
(Doug O'Neill, U.S.A) **77/1**

1m 33.56s (-0.31) **12** Ran SP% **119.4**

Owner George Krikorian **Bred** George Krikorian **Trained** USA

6825 BATH (L-H)

Wednesday, October 12

OFFICIAL GOING: Good to firm (good in places; 8.8)

Wind: moderate across Weather: cloudy with sunny periods

7267 ROA/RACING POST, OWNERS' JACKPOT H'CAP (DIV I) 5f 161y

1:30 (1:30) (Class 5) (0-75,75) 3-Y-O+ **£4,204** (£1,251; £625; £312) **Stalls** Centre

Form RPR

1265 **1** **Wild Dancer**[25] 6576 3-8-13 **71**.................................. HectorCrouch(3) 10 79
(Patrick Chamings) *mid-div: swtchd to center over 2f out: hdwy over 1f out: led ent fnl f: r.o wl: pushed out* **8/1**

0440 **2** *1* **Divine Call**[21] 6668 9-8-7 **61** oh5......................................(b) JoeFanning 7 66
(Milton Bradley) *s.i.s: last trio: hdwy 2f out: swtchd rt over 1f out: r.o ins fnl f but a being hld* **20/1**

3535 **3** *1/2* **Point Of Woods**[28] 6479 3-9-1 **70**...(b) FMBerry 8 73
(Ralph Beckett) *in last trio: swtchd to center over 2f out: hdwy wl over 1f out: kpt on ins fnl f* **8/1**

-023 **4** *3/4* **Panther Patrol (IRE)**[21] 6668 6-9-7 **75**........................ CharlesBishop 11 76
(Eve Johnson Houghton) *mid-div: hdwy 2f out: rdn over 1f out: kpt on same pce fnl f* **9/2**[1]

6115 **5** *1 1/4* **Langley Vale**[25] 6589 7-8-11 **65**.......................................(v) JackMitchell 6 61
(Roger Teal) *racd keenly trcking ldrs: rdn 2f out: kpt on same pce fnl f* **12/1**

6602 **6** *nse* **Nocturn**[22] 6653 7-9-0 **73**..(p) CiaranMckee(5) 2 69
(Ronald Harris) *trckd ldrs: rdn whn ev ch ent fnl f: kpt on same pce* **16/1**

0126 **7** *1* **For Ayman**[30] 6418 5-8-7 **68**..(t) SeanMooney(7) 4 61
(Joseph Tuite) *mid-div: rdn over 2f out: kpt on ins fnl f but nt pce to get involved* **14/1**

0000 **8** *nk* **Air Of York (IRE)**[25] 6589 4-8-11 **72**................................ AledBeech(7) 5 64
(David Evans) *mid-div: hdwy over 2f out: sn rdn and hung rt: one pce fnl f* **20/1**

2666 **9** *nse* **Swendab (IRE)**[21] 6677 8-8-8 **67**............................(b) MitchGodwin(5) 12 59
(John O'Shea) *prom: led over 2f out: sn rdn: hdd ent fnl f: fdd fnl 120yds* **40/1**

4553 **10** *1 1/2* **Pour La Victoire (IRE)**[14] 6878 6-9-7 **75**........................(b) LukeMorris 9 62
(Tony Carroll) *dwlt: a towards rr* **5/1**[2]

2110 **11** *shd* **Babyfact**[31] 6363 5-9-3 **71**.. JimmyFortune 3 58
(Malcolm Saunders) *mid-div: hdwy over 2f out: sn rdn: fdd ins fnl f* **11/2**[3]

0530 **12** *4* **Monarch Maid**[16] 6831 5-8-10 **71**................................. LuluStanford(7) 1 44
(Peter Hiatt) *led tl rdn over 2f out: wknd fnl f* **8/1**

1m 10.7s (-0.50) **Going Correction** -0.125s/f (Firm)
WFA 3 from 4yo+ 1lb **12** Ran SP% **115.8**
Speed ratings (Par 103): **98,96,96,95,93 93,91,91,91,89 89,84**
CSF £157.13 CT £1319.14 TOTE £7.80: £2.70, £6.80, £2.80; EX 217.10 Trifecta £764.20 Part won..
Owner The Foxford House Partnership **Bred** Wheelers Land Stud **Trained** Baughurst, Hants

FOCUS

Race distances as advertised. Bath's last fixture of the season and after winning the first Hector Crouch reported that the ground was "mainly good ground, with a few quicker patches." The first division of a run-of-the-mill sprint handicap where the first three all challenged down the centre of the course. It was 0.85sec slower than division two and the form is just ordinary.

7268 ROA/RACING POST, OWNERS' JACKPOT H'CAP (DIV II) 5f 161y

2:00 (2:00) (Class 5) (0-75,75) 3-Y-O+ **£4,204** (£1,251; £625; £312) **Stalls** Centre

Form RPR

6202 **1** **Burning Thread (IRE)**[20] 6717 9-9-4 **72**...........................(b) FMBerry 12 84
(David Elsworth) *towards rr: hdwy over 2f out: led over 1f out: rdn clr fnl f: readily* **10/1**

6422 **2** *2 1/2* **Showmethewayavrilo**[16] 6831 3-8-13 **71**............. JosephineGordon(3) 9 75+
(Malcolm Saunders) *a.p: rdn and ev ch over 1f out: kpt on but nt pce of ready wnr fnl f* **7/2**[1]

013 **3** *3/4* **Pensax Lad (IRE)**[22] 6653 5-9-7 **75**............................ RobertWinston 10 77
(Ronald Harris) *awkwardly away: last pair: rdn and hdwy fr jst over 2f out: wnt 3rd ent fnl f: kpt on* **12/1**

0334 **4** *3/4* **Indian Affair**[63] 5284 6-8-11 **65**..(bt) LukeMorris 8 64
(Milton Bradley) *trckd ldrs: rdn over 2f out: kpt on fnl f but nt pce to get on terms* **14/1**

5202 **5** *3/4* **Archie Stevens**[21] 6669 6-9-0 **68**... JFEgan 7 65
(David Evans) *led: rdn and hdd over 1f out: no ex fnl f* **12/1**

0132 **6** *3/4* **Dusty Blue**[16] 6832 4-9-0 **71**.. GeorgeDowning(3) 1 65
(Tony Carroll) *mid-div: rdn over 1f out: little imp* **8/1**[3]

2524 **7** *1 3/4* **Jack Nevison**[63] 5305 3-9-6 **75**.. DaneO'Neill 2 63
(Henry Candy) *mid-div: hdwy over 2f out: sn rdn: nvr threatened: fdd fnl f* **4/1**[2]

6002 **8** *1/2* **Brazen Spirit**[35] 6235 4-8-13 **67**..(v) JohnFahy 3 54
(Clive Cox) *s.i.s: swtchd rt over 1f out: a towards rr* **10/1**

330 **9** *3/4* **Racquet**[31] 6363 3-9-5 **74**..(b) SeanLevey 5 58
(Richard Hannon) *mid-div: effrt 2f out: wknd ins fnl f* **10/1**

5050 **10** *3 1/4* **Tikthebox (IRE)**[44] 5960 3-9-2 **71**.. JoeFanning 4 44
(David Brown) *wnt to s early: trckd ldrs: rdn and losing pl whn hmpd over 1f out: wknd* **10/1**

5020 **11** *2 1/2* **Jaganory (IRE)**[16] 6832 4-8-2 **61** oh6.....................(v) MitchGodwin(5) 11 26
(Christopher Mason) *sn outpcd: a in rr* **66/1**

1400 **12** *6* **Quickaswecan**[34] 6255 5-8-11 **68**.......................(p) EdwardGreatrex(3) 6 13
(Milton Bradley) *little slowly away: sn pressing ldr: rdn over 2f out: wknd over 1f out* **40/1**

1m 9.85s (-1.35) **Going Correction** -0.125s/f (Firm)
WFA 3 from 4yo+ 1lb **12** Ran SP% **115.7**
Speed ratings (Par 103): **104,100,99,98,97 96,94,93,92,88 85,77**
CSF £43.73 CT £346.52 TOTE £13.70: £3.80, £1.20, £4.00; EX 50.10 Trifecta £434.60.
Owner D R C Elsworth **Bred** James Lombard **Trained** Newmarket, Suffolk

FOCUS

The centre of the track was once again the place to be in the second division of a modest sprint handicap, with the first three home drawn 12, 9 and 10 respectively. They went 0.85sec quicker than the first division. The winner was back to last year's form.

7269 LDF/EBF STALLIONS MAIDEN STKS 5f 11y

2:30 (2:31) (Class 5) 2-Y-O **£3,881** (£1,155; £577; £288) **Stalls** Centre

Form RPR

222 **1** **Tschierschen (IRE)**[56] 5542 2-9-0 74............................ PatCosgrave 10 72
(William Haggas) *chsd ldr: pushed along over 2f out: rdn whn swtchd rt over 1f out: kpt on wl to ld fnl 75yds: hld on: rdn out* **9/4**[2]

3 **2** *shd* **Kowaiyess (IRE)**[23] 6622 2-9-5 0.. DaneO'Neill 8 77
(Owen Burrows) *s.i.s and wnt rt: sn rcvrd to trck ldrs: rdn 2f out: chal wl ins fnl f: kpt on: jst hld* **6/4**[1]

352 **3** *3/4* **Fethiye Boy**[34] 6252 2-9-5 62... ShaneKelly 4 74
(Ronald Harris) *led at decent pce: rdn 2f out: no ex whn hdd fnl 75yds* **20/1**

6022 **4** *1 3/4* **Red Alert**[14] 6873 2-9-5 74... JFEgan 7 68
(Joseph Tuite) *chsd ldrs: rdn over 2f out: no ex fnl 120yds* **7/2**[3]

5 **5** *4 1/2* **Pale Enchantment (IRE)**[28] 6477 2-9-0 0.............. RichardKingscote 5 46
(Tom Dascombe) *mid-div: outpcd wl over 2f out: kpt on ins fnl f but nt pce to get involved* **8/1**

06 **6** *nse* **Like Minds**[20] 6712 2-9-0 0.. JoeFanning 3 46
(David Brown) *mid-div: outpcd wl over 2f out: kpt on again fnl f but nvr threatened to get involved* **50/1**

7 *3* **Angelical Eve (IRE)** 2-9-0 0.. LiamKeniry 2 35
(George Baker) *outpcd in last pair: sme hdwy 2f out: nvr threatened to get involved* **25/1**

0 **8** *2 3/4* **Tally's Son**[29] 6439 2-9-5 0... DougieCostello 1 31
(Grace Harris) *mid-div: rdn wl over 2f out: nvr gng pce to get on terms* **200/1**

9 *14* **Paco Lady** 2-9-0 0... LukeMorris 6
(Ivan Furtado) *sn outpcd: a in rr* **40/1**

1m 1.99s (-0.51) **Going Correction** -0.125s/f (Firm) **9** Ran SP% **117.6**
Speed ratings (Par 95): **99,98,97,94,87 87,82,78,55**
CSF £5.90 TOTE £2.80: £1.10, £1.10, £5.40; EX 5.90 Trifecta £53.00.
Owner China Horse Club **Bred** Corduff Stud & T J Rooney **Trained** Newmarket, Suffolk

FOCUS

A close finish to this modest end-of-season maiden, with the front two in the market taking a long time to pick up the 62-rated third. The winner didn't have to improve.

7270 GOLDEN HOOVES H'CAP 2m 1f 34y

3:05 (3:06) (Class 5) (0-70,70) 3-Y-O+ **£4,528** (£1,347; £673; £336) **Stalls** Centre

Form RPR

5455 **1** **McCools Gold**[31] 6367 3-8-8 **61**.......................................(p[1]) JohnFahy 1 67
(Eve Johnson Houghton) *trckd ldrs: led over 7f out and qcknd pce: rdn over 3f out: a holding on fnl f: styd on gamely* **12/1**

050 **2** *3/4* **Endive**[71] 4979 4-9-5 **61**...[1] PatCosgrave 12 67+
(Robert Stephens) *in last trio: hdwy over 3f out: sn rdn: styd on fnl 2f: edging lft but fin strly: wnt 2nd towards fin* **20/1**

505 **3** *hd* **Coeur De Lion**[68] 5129 3-9-3 **70**.................................. FergusSweeney 7 75+
(Alan King) *mid-div: rdn whn outpcd 3f out: hdwy fr 2f out: styd on fnl f: n.m.r fnl 100yds but squeezed through to go 3rd towards fin* **9/2**[2]

5615 **4** *1 1/4* **Dltripleseven (IRE)**[16] 6825 3-8-3 **59**.................. JosephineGordon(3) 2 63
(Richard Hughes) *mid-div: led chsng gp in 4th 7f out: clsd on ldrs 3f out: sn drvn: chsd wnr ent fnl f: no ex whn losing 2 pls cl home* **5/1**[3]

3252 **5** *2* **Lily Trotter**[19] 6730 3-9-1 **68**..(b) FMBerry 6 70
(Ralph Beckett) *trckd ldrs: rdn to chse wnr over 3f out: nt quite pce to mount chal: hld in 5th whn squeezed out towards fin* **6/1**

23 **6** *2 3/4* **For Goodness Sake (IRE)**[18] 5262 4-9-8 **67**......(p) EdwardGreatrex(3) 8 66
(Warren Greatrex) *led tl 7f out: trckd wnr: rdn wl over 2f out: fdd ins fnl f* **7/1**

5001 **7** *4 1/2* **Danglydontask**[55] 5573 5-9-5 **61**......................................(b) LukeMorris 5 55
(David Arbuthnot) *s.i.s: last pair: sme prog u.p 4f out: styd on fnl 2f but nvr threatened to get on terms* **11/1**

5346 **8** *28* **Ring Eye (IRE)**[27] 6508 8-8-11 **58**..............................[1] CiaranMckee(5) 10 21
(John O'Shea) *a towards rr* **33/1**

3433 **9** *1 1/4* **Sunday Royal (FR)**[31] 6362 4-9-12 **68**.................................. JamesDoyle 4 30
(Harry Dunlop) *mid-div: dropped rr whn outpcd 5f out: nvr bk on terms: eased ent fnl f* **3/1**[1]

6400 **10** *6* **Kirkman (IRE)**[30] 6422 5-8-9 **51** oh3..................................[1] JoeFanning 11 6
(Peter Hiatt) *trckd ldrs tl over 6f out: dropped to rr over 4f out: eased fnl f* **33/1**

1500 **11** *24* **Urban Space**[14] 6886 10-9-11 **67**..................................(t) DanielMuscutt 3
(John Flint) *.towards rr: sme prog u.p over 3f out: nvr threatened to get involved: wknd over 2f out: eased* **20/1**

3m 50.82s (-1.08) **Going Correction** +0.15s/f (Good)
WFA 3 from 4yo+ 11lb **11** Ran SP% **118.1**
Speed ratings (Par 103): **108,107,107,106,106 104,102,89,88,86 74**
CSF £230.75 CT £1243.03 TOTE £14.90: £2.80, £10.60, £1.70; EX 443.90 Trifecta £1288.30 Part won..
Owner Ms Caroline Rowland **Bred** Ms Caroline Rowland **Trained** Blewbury, Oxon

FOCUS

Plenty of these trying a marathon trip for the first time, but just modest form. The race was the scene of a superb piece of race riding from John Fahy on the winner. The form is rated a bit cautiously.

7271 BRITISH STALLION STUDS EBF BECKFORD FILLIES' STKS (LISTED RACE) 1m 6f

3:40 (3:41) (Class 1) 3-Y-O+

£22,684 (£8,600; £4,304; £2,144; £1,076; £540) **Stalls** Centre

Form RPR

4230 **1** **Twitch (IRE)**[55] 5587 4-9-7 100..(p) JamesDoyle 4 100
(Hugo Palmer) *mid-div: rdn and hdwy over 2f out: drifted rt over 1f out: led ins fnl f: r.o wl* **12/1**

6022 **2** ½ **Vive Ma Fille (GER)**[33] 6293 4-9-7 93 JFEgan 8 99
(Mark Johnston) *trckd ldrs: led over 2f out: sn rdn: hdd ins fnl f: styd on but no ex* **16/1**

1-16 **3** ¾ **Anzhelika (IRE)**[55] 5587 4-9-7 93 JimmyFortune 9 98
(David Lanigan) *s.i.s: towards rr: swtchd to center and hdwy over 2f: sn drvn to chse ldrs: nvr quite ev ch but styd on wl fnl f* **16/1**

4111 **4** nk **Purple Magic**[47] 5851 3-8-12 94 JamieSpencer 6 98
(Michael Bell) *hld up towards rr: hdwy fr 4f out: drvn over 2f out: drifted lft whn chsng ldrs over 1f out: styd on fnl f* **11/2**[2]

1111 **5** ¾ **Dubka**[25] 6584 3-8-12 99 RyanMoore 5 96+
(Sir Michael Stoute) *mid-div: rdn and hdwy on far rails fr 3f out: ch over 1f out: styd on same pce fnl f* **6/4**[1]

2414 **6** 1 **Moorside**[32] 6332 3-8-12 95 SteveDrowne 7 95
(Charles Hills) *trckd ldrs: rdn and ev ch over 2f out: no ex fnl f* **25/1**

520 **7** 2¼ **Tioga Pass**[34] 6259 5-9-7 101 (p) LukeMorris 12 92
(Paul Cole) *s.i.s: towards rr: rdn 3f out: styd on same pce fnl 2f: nvr threatened* **20/1**

30 **8** 1¾ **Tiptree (IRE)**[55] 5587 3-8-12 98 ShaneKelly 3 89
(Luca Cumani) *rdn over 2f out: drifted lft over 1f out: nvr bttr than mid-div* **25/1**

633 **9** 3 **Lustrous**[11] 6951 5-9-7 99 RichardKingscote 13 85
(David O'Meara) *prom: rdn and ev ch 3f out: wknd over 1f out* **18/1**

6541 **10** 1¾ **Elysian Fields (GR)**[11] 6951 5-9-7 96 FMBerry 14 83
(Amanda Perrett) *s.i.s: towards rr: hdwy over 5f out on outer: chal wl over 2f out: sn rdn: wknd over 1f out* **11/1**

5321 **11** 1 **Kiltara (IRE)**[27] 6526 4-9-7 93 JoeFanning 1 81
(Mark Johnston) *led tl rdn over 2f out: sn hld: wknd fnl f* **10/1**[3]

4224 **12** 2 **Zubeida**[46] 5872 3-8-12 70 KieranO'Neill 11 79
(Ismail Mohammed) *trckd ldrs: rdn over 3f out: wknd over 2f out* **100/1**

1213 **13** 9 **Intense Tango**[32] 6350 5-9-7 99 (t) CliffordLee 10 66
(K R Burke) *mid-div tl rdn over 3f out: sn bhd* **12/1**

3m 2.66s (-1.14) **Going Correction** +0.15s/f (Good)
WFA 3 from 4yo+ 9lb **13** Ran SP% **118.7**
Speed ratings (Par 108): **109,108,108,108,107 107,105,104,103,102 101,100,95**
CSF £180.67 TOTE £16.70: £3.40, £4.30, £4.70; EX 193.80 Trifecta £2018.80 Part won..
Owner The Dukes of Roxburghe & Devonshire **Bred** Floors Farming & The Duke Of Devonshire **Trained** Newmarket, Suffolk
■ Stewards' Enquiry : James Doyle two-day ban: used whip above permitted level (Oct 26-27)

FOCUS
The inaugural running of this Listed race attracted a good-sized field and resulted in form that looks up to scratch for this level. The winner is rated to form, with the runner-up the key.

7272 JANET DENNING FIFEHEAD FARMS MEMORIAL FILLIES' H'CAP 1m 5y
4:10 (4:12) (Class 5) (0-70,69) 3-Y-O+ **£4,204** (£1,251; £625; £312) **Stalls** Low

Form RPR

0541 **1** **Beatbybeatbybeat**[8] 7035 3-9-2 67 6ex (v) JamesDoyle 10 74+
(Ismail Mohammed) *trckd ldrs: led over 1f out: drifted lft fnl f: kpt on wl: drvn out* **3/1**[1]

2234 **2** 1 **Polymnia**[15] 6851 3-8-13 69 MeganNicholls[(5)] 2 73
(Richard Hannon) *hld up: hdwy in center fr 2f out: rdn to chse wnr ins fnl f: no ex towards fin* **10/1**

3324 **3** 1 **Apache Song**[22] 6650 3-9-4 69 (p) LuluStanford 5 71
(Rod Millman) *trckd ldrs: rdn 2f out: ch over 1f out: kpt on same pce fnl f* **17/2**

2346 **4** 1¼ **Clary (IRE)**[20] 6700 6-8-11 62 HectorCrouch[(3)] 3 61
(James Unett) *mid-div: hdwy over 2f out: sn rdn to chse ldrs: kpt on same pce fnl f* **20/1**

6642 **5** 1 **Dark Amber**[16] 6827 6-8-6 57 (tp) EdwardGreatrex[(3)] 4 57+
(Brendan Powell) *slowly into strdie: towards rr: rdn and hdwy whn nt clr run and snatched up on stands' side rails 2f out: kpt on but no ch after* **7/1**[2]

50 **6** ½ **Cutty Sark**[31] 6365 3-8-12 63 JamieSpencer 9 61+
(Luca Cumani) *in tch: hdwy over 2f out: travelling wl enough whn nt clr run and snatched up on stands' side rails over 1f out: kpt on but no ch after* **10/1**

106 **7** ¾ **Saint Helena (IRE)**[53] 5627 8-9-7 69 (b) FMBerry 6 63
(Mark Gillard) *s.i.s: towards rr: effrt into midfield 2f out: one pce fnl f* **14/1**

0040 **8** ¾ **Harikiri (IRE)**[8] 7048 3-8-5 56 JimmyQuinn 1 48
(Charles Hills) *towards rr: hdwy 2f out: sn rdn: short of room jst over 1f out : hld after* **22/1**

2366 **9** nk **Smart Mover (IRE)**[29] 6442 3-8-12 68 CallumShepherd[(5)] 12 60
(Nikki Evans) *trckd ldr: rdn over 2f out: ev ch over 1f out: fdd fnl f* **66/1**

3210 **10** nse **In Ken's Memory**[23] 6629 3-9-2 67 JFEgan 7 58
(John Butler) *led: rdn whn drifted rt 2f out: hdd over 1f out: wknd ins fnl f* **8/1**[3]

5320 **11** 2½ **Tommys Geal**[28] 6485 4-9-1 63 DanielMuscutt 8 49
(Michael Madgwick) *mid-div: rdn over 2f out: wknd ent fnl f* **25/1**

1m 41.69s (0.89) **Going Correction** +0.15s/f (Good)
WFA 3 from 4yo+ 3lb **11** Ran SP% **98.4**
Speed ratings (Par 100): **101,100,99,97,96 96,95,94,94,94 91**
CSF £21.89 CT £139.63 TOTE £2.70: £1.20, £3.10, £2.40; EX 22.60 Trifecta £95.50.Simply Me was withdrawn. Price at time of withdrawal 5-1. Rule 4 applies to all bets - dedcution 15p in the pound.
Owner Saif Ali & Saeed H Al Tayer **Bred** Rabbah Bloodstock Limited **Trained** Newmarket, Suffolk

FOCUS
No depth to this modest fillies' handicap and with Simply Me being forced to withdraw after arriving at the start without the declared cheekpieces, this became even more straightforward for the winner, backing up her Brighton win of eight days earlier. The field raced on the stands' side.

7273 WILTSHIRE HEIGHTS/EBF STALLIONS MAIDEN STKS 1m 2f 46y
4:45 (4:45) (Class 5) 2-Y-O **£3,881** (£1,155; £577; £288) **Stalls** Low

Form RPR

33 **1** **Castellated**[23] 6625 2-9-0 0 SeanLevey 5 77+
(Richard Hannon) *trckd ldrs: rdn for str chal fr 2f out: kpt on: won on nod* **7/2**[2]

2 **2** nse **Vantage Point (IRE)**[20] 6704 2-9-5 0 RyanMoore 6 82
(John Gosden) *hld up but wl in tch: hdwy over 2f out: sn rdn to chal: tk narrow advantage over 1f out: kpt on: lost on nod* **2/5**[1]

0 **3** 1½ **Jukebox Jive (FR)**[21] 6663 2-9-5 0 JFEgan 3 79
(Anthony Honeyball) *led: rdn whn strly pressed fr over 2f out: narrowly hdd over 1f out: stl ev ch ins fnl f: no ex towards fin* **25/1**

36 **4** 3½ **Sir Nigel Gresley (USA)**[21] 6663 2-9-5 0 FergusSweeney 1 72
(Alan King) *racd keenly trcking ldrs: effrt over 2f out: kpt on same pce fnl f* **10/1**[3]

06 **5** 11 **Hold Me Tight (IRE)**[22] 6655 2-9-5 0 LiamKeniry 4 52
(J S Moore) *pressed ldr: rdn and ev ch 2f out: hld whn edgd rt over 1f out: wknd fnl f* **100/1**

6 13 **Kenyan (FR)** 2-9-2 0 JosephineGordon[(3)] 2 27
(Seamus Durack) *s.i.s: in last pair but wl in tch: rdn 3f out: sn hld: wknd over 1f out* **33/1**

2m 13.32s (2.32) **Going Correction** +0.15s/f (Good) **6** Ran SP% **110.5**
Speed ratings (Par 95): **96,95,94,91,83 72**
CSF £5.15 TOTE £4.00: £1.40, £1.10; EX 5.60 Trifecta £30.20.
Owner Cheveley Park Stud **Bred** Cheveley Park Stud Ltd **Trained** East Everleigh, Wilts
■ Stewards' Enquiry : Ryan Moore two-day ban: used whip above permitted level (Oct 26-27)

FOCUS
The two that dominated the betting fought out a close finish, with the filly just coming out best and claiming the spoils. They are rated near their respective pre-race marks.

7274 CULLODEN H'CAP 1m 3f 144y
5:15 (5:15) (Class 5) (0-70,70) 3-Y-O+ **£3,557** (£1,058; £529; £264) **Stalls** Low

Form RPR

5230 **1** **Free Passage**[22] 6654 3-9-0 65 DaneO'Neill 16 74+
(Henry Candy) *mid-div: hdwy over 2f out: sn rdn: str run fnl f: led towards fin: rdn out* **11/1**

4150 **2** 1¼ **Monsieur Glory**[18] 6767 3-9-4 69 (p) RichardKingscote 15 76
(Tom Dascombe) *trckd ldrs: led over 2f out: sn rdn: kpt on but no ex whn hdd towards fin* **10/1**

3062 **3** 1¼ **Taurian**[32] 6334 5-9-7 65 JamesDoyle 8 70
(Ian Williams) *trckd ldrs: rdn for str chal over 2f out: stl ev ch ins fnl f: no ex towards fin* **7/1**[2]

0315 **4** ½ **Mystikana**[77] 4778 3-9-4 69 (b) JimmyFortune 9 73
(Marcus Tregoning) *hld up towards rr: hdwy fr over 2f out: rdn and ev ch over 1f out: styd on same pce fnl f* **8/1**[3]

0601 **5** 2¼ **Zenafire**[19] 6730 7-9-6 67 (p) JackDuern[(3)] 4 67
(Sarah Hollinshead) *mid-div: hdwy over 4f out: rdn and ev ch over 1f out: styd on same pce fnl f* **11/1**

1556 **6** 1¾ **Shalimah (IRE)**[41] 6065 4-9-11 69 (v) JohnFahy 5 67
(Clive Cox) *mid-div: rdn over 2f out: styd on same pce* **12/1**

4253 **7** 4½ **The Kid**[29] 6450 5-9-12 70 DougieCostello 12 60
(John Quinn) *in tch: rdn over 2f out: nt pce to mount chal: fdd ins fnl f* **8/1**[3]

5412 **8** 1 **Captain George (IRE)**[32] 6315 5-9-0 63 (v) MitchGodwin[(5)] 14 51
(Michael Blake) *chsd ldrs: rdn 3f out: sn one pce* **8/1**[3]

1300 **9** 4 **Smoky Hill (IRE)**[41] 6058 7-9-0 61 GeorgeDowning[(3)] 1 43
(Tony Carroll) *sn pushed along towards rr: nvr any imp on ldrs* **33/1**

1520 **10** 18 **Lady Blanco (USA)**[32] 6334 3-9-5 70 JamieSpencer 6 22+
(Andrew Balding) *mid-div: rdn over 2f out: sn btn: eased over 1f out* **5/1**[1]

6320 **11** ½ **Hurricane Volta (IRE)**[32] 6356 5-9-9 67 (b) CharlesBishop 2 18
(Peter Hedger) *led tl over 2f out: sn wknd* **14/1**

4006 **12** 6 **Never To Be (USA)**[22] 6651 5-8-8 57 (bt[1]) CallumShepherd[(5)] 10
(Nikki Evans) *a towards rr: eased whn btn over 1f out* **50/1**

100- **13** 2½ **Ayla's Emperor**[99] 7797 7-9-2 60 (p) DanielMuscutt 7
(John Flint) *mid-div tl wknd wl over 2f out: eased over 1f out* **10/1**

0-00 **P** **Akavit (IRE)**[11] 6965 4-9-9 67 (p) FMBerry 11
(Ed de Giles) *trckd ldrs tl lost pl qckly 5f out: p.u 3f out* **14/1**

2m 31.86s (1.26) **Going Correction** +0.15s/f (Good)
WFA 3 from 4yo+ 7lb **14** Ran SP% **123.3**
Speed ratings (Par 103): **101,100,99,99,97 96,93,92,90,78 77,73,72,**
CSF £119.53 CT £842.12 TOTE £14.90: £5.80, £3.20, £2.50; EX 140.60 Trifecta £961.30 Part won..
Owner The Earl Cadogan **Bred** The Earl Cadogan **Trained** Kingston Warren, Oxon

FOCUS
A modest handicap and the market gave an insight into just how wide open this race was. They finished well strung out and the form looks sound.
T/Plt: £650.50 to a £1 stake. Pool: £72,269.57 - 81.09 winning units. T/Qpdt: £54.40 to a £1 stake. Pool: £7,153.47 - 97.30 winning units. **Tim Mitchell**

7063 KEMPTON (A.W) (R-H)
Wednesday, October 12

OFFICIAL GOING: Polytrack: standard to slow
Wind: Moderate, half behind Weather: Fine but cloudy

7275 RACING UK NURSERY H'CAP 5f (P)
5:20 (5:36) (Class 6) (0-60,60) 2-Y-O **£2,264** (£673; £336; £168) **Stalls** Low

Form RPR

6056 **1** **At The Beach**[37] 6191 2-9-5 58 TimmyMurphy 1 62
(Richard Hannon) *chsd ldr: chal jst over 1f out: styd on to ld last 75yds* **7/2**[2]

004 **2** ¾ **Miss Mayson**[39] 6141 2-9-5 58 SilvestreDeSousa 3 59
(Roger Teal) *led: rdn over 1f out: kpt on tl hdd and no ex last 75yds* **3/1**[1]

4304 **3** ¾ **Spin Top**[25] 6588 2-9-6 59 (v) TomMarquand 9 57
(Joseph Tuite) *chsd ldrs in 5th: sltly wd and a little outpcd 2f out: styd on fr over 1f out: tk 3rd last stride* **10/1**

5400 **4** hd **Snoozy Sioux (IRE)**[45] 5931 2-9-4 60 TimClark[(3)] 5 58
(Martin Smith) *cl up: chsd ldng pair 2f out: cl enough over 1f out: fnd little after: lost 3rd last stride* **10/1**

400 **5** hd **Geraldine (GER)**[14] 6867 2-9-0 56 AaronJones[(3)] 7 53
(Stuart Williams) *towards rr: urged along 1/2-way: styd on fr over 1f out: nrst fin* **11/2**[3]

0005 **6** 1½ **Lord Cooper**[21] 6678 2-8-11 57 [1] SeanMooney[(7)] 10 48
(Jose Santos) *trapped out wd: towards rr: effrt wl over 1f out: one pce and nvr able to rch ldrs* **13/2**

0360 **7** 3¾ **Blastofmagic**[21] 6678 2-9-4 57 MartinLane 8 35
(David Dennis) *chsd ldng pair to 2f out: wknd qckly fnl f* **12/1**

4000 **8** shd **Sadieroseclifford (IRE)**[8] 7040 2-8-12 58 PatrickVaughan[(7)] 4 36
(Denis Quinn) *dwlt: a in rr: no ch over 1f out* **20/1**

0006 **9** 1¾ **I Dare To Dream**[18] 6762 2-8-10 56 JordanUys[(7)] 6 27
(Lisa Williamson) *s.s then veered lft: wl bhd in last: brief effrt 2f out: hung lft over 1f out and no prog* **40/1**

500 **10** 3¼ **B B Queen (IRE)**[23] 6625 2-9-1 54 (b) SamHitchcott 2 14
(Clive Cox) *sn urged along towards rr: nvr a factor: wknd wl over 1f out* **14/1**

59.73s (-0.77) **Going Correction** -0.075s/f (Stan) **10** Ran SP% **115.7**
Speed ratings (Par 93): **103,101,100,100,99 97,91,91,88,83**
CSF £14.30 CT £96.42 TOTE £4.30: £1.30, £1.70, £2.10; EX 18.80 Trifecta £86.10.
Owner Dick Hitchcock Alan King Norman Woodcock **Bred** Whitley Stud **Trained** East Everleigh, Wilts

FOCUS
There was a delay of around 15mins prior to this weak nursery debut to late arrival of an ambulance. The winner bounced back to form.

7276 32RED CASINO H'CAP 5f (P)
5:55 (6:02) (Class 6) (0-55,55) 3-Y-0+ **£2,264** (£673; £336; £168) **Stalls** Low

Form RPR
3000 **1** **Ask The Guru**^{22} 6660 6-9-7 **55**....(p) KierenFox 9 62
(Michael Attwater) *chsd ldng trio: clsd on outer over 1f out: led last 150yds: rdn and kpt on wl* **8/1**
6133 **2** *1* **Willow Spring**^{25} 6587 4-9-0 **51**.... NoelGarbutt$^{(3)}$ 1 54
(Conrad Allen) *taken down early: t.k.h: trckd ldng pair: tk 2nd over 1f out: chalng and upsides whn wnr wnt by 150yds out: kpt on same pce* **12/1**
5-30 **3** *1½* **Fanci That (IRE)**^{32} 6317 3-9-5 **53**.... JimCrowley 3 54+
(Rae Guest) *dwlt: hld up in 8th and wl off the pce: shkn up over 1f out: squeezed through and r.o fnl f to take 3rd last stride: too late to chal* **7/1**
6016 **4** *shd* **Westbourne Grove (USA)**^{13} 6902 3-9-5 **53**....(t) TomMarquand 8 52
(John Butler) *dwlt: outpcd in last: u.p bef 1/2-way: no prog tl styd on wl fr over 1f out: nrly snatched 3rd* **9/2**^{2}
2621 **5** *nk* **Diminutive (IRE)**^{31} 6381 4-8-12 **49**....(p) RobHornby$^{(3)}$ 5 46
(Grace Harris) *racd on outer: off the pce in midfield: shkn up 1/2-way: kpt on fr over 1f out: nrst fin* **10/1**
244 **6** *½* **Tahiti One**^{31} 6361 3-9-6 **54**.... SilvestreDeSousa 4 50
(Tony Carroll) *chsd ldng quartet but nt on terms: rdn 1/2-way: kpt on fr over 1f out: unable to threaten* **4/1**^{1}
2102 **7** *nse* **Red Flute**^{22} 6660 4-9-2 **53**.... TimClark$^{(3)}$ 6 48
(Denis Quinn) *fast away: led: rdn over 1f out: hdd & wknd 150yds out* **6/1**^{3}
2206 **8** *½* **Catalinas Diamond (IRE)**^{16} 6832 8-9-4 **52**....(t) SamHitchcott 10 45
(Pat Murphy) *outpcd and forced to r wd in rr: kpt on fnl f: no ch* **25/1**
4010 **9** *1½* **Harpers Ruby**^{19} 6745 6-9-7 **55**.... PaddyAspell 7 42
(Lynn Siddall) *chsd ldr to over 1f out: wknd qckly* **14/1**
0000 **10** *3½* **Bubbly Bailey**^{7} 7070 6-9-7 **55**....(b) OisinMurphy 2 30
(J R Jenkins) *off the pce in midfield and sn urged along: wknd 2f out* **12/1**

59.74s (-0.76) **Going Correction** -0.075s/f (Stan) **10** Ran SP% **111.1**
Speed ratings (Par 101): **103,101,99,98,98 97,97,96,94,88**
CSF £94.12 CT £697.15 TOTE £11.40: £2.80, £3.80, £3.10; EX 118.30 Trifecta £877.90.
Owner Canisbay Bloodstock **Bred** Redmyre Bloodstock & Tweenhills Stud **Trained** Epsom, Surrey

FOCUS
A moderate sprint handicap, and typical form for the grade.

7277 32RED ON THE APP STORE MAIDEN FILLIES' STKS (PLUS 10 RACE) (DIV I) 7f (P)
6:25 (6:28) (Class 5) 2-Y-0 **£2,911** (£866; £432; £216) **Stalls** Low

Form RPR
U263 **1** **Chica De La Noche**^{13} 6897 2-9-0 76.... NickyMackay 3 76
(Simon Dow) *wl in tch: prog 2f out: led 1f out: pushed along firmly and kpt on wl* **5/1**^{3}
2 *¾* **Fairy Lights** 2-9-0 0.... AndreaAtzeni 6 74
(Roger Varian) *chsd ldrs: clsd 2f out: rdn to chal over 1f out: chsd wnr ins fnl f: styd on same pce* **7/2**^{2}
0 **3** *1¼* **Island Cloud**^{14} 6866 2-9-0 0.... OisinMurphy 8 71
(Heather Main) *t.k.h: trckd ldr: shkn up to ld 2f out: rdn and hdd 1f out: one pce* **25/1**
2 **4** *¾* **Hyper Dream (IRE)**^{13} 6897 2-9-0 0.... JimCrowley 1 69
(Hugo Palmer) *hld up in 6th: shkn up over 2f out and no real prog: kpt on to take 4th fnl f: n.d* **4/11**^{1}
5 *3* **Cheerfilly (IRE)** 2-9-0 0.... TomMarquand 9 60
(Tom Dascombe) *racd on outer in rr: urged along fr 1/2-way: no prog tl kpt on to take 5th fnl f* **25/1**
6 *3½* **Persephone (IRE)** 2-9-0 0.... LukeMorris 5 51
(Paul Cole) *t.k.h: led to 2f out: wknd qckly over 1f out* **12/1**
0 **7** *¾* **Dutch Cat**^{22} 6648 2-9-0 0.... SamHitchcott 4 49
(Clive Cox) *chsd ldng pair tl wknd fr 2f out* **50/1**
0 **8** *2* **Paco Dawn**^{14} 6881 2-9-0 0.... WilliamTwiston-Davies 7 44
(Philip Hide) *dwlt: a in rr: rdn and no prog over 2f out: wknd over 1f out* **50/1**
00 **9** *½* **Venetian Proposal (IRE)**^{14} 6867 2-8-11 0.... RobHornby$^{(3)}$ 2 42
(Zoe Davison) *a in last: nvr a factor* **100/1**

1m 27.33s (1.33) **Going Correction** -0.075s/f (Stan) **9** Ran SP% **132.5**
Speed ratings (Par 92): **89,88,86,85,82 78,77,75,74**
CSF £25.60 TOTE £9.90: £1.50, £1.30, £5.30; EX 37.60 Trifecta £293.10.
Owner Robert Moss **Bred** Horizon Bloodstock Limited **Trained** Ashtead, Surrey

FOCUS
A modest 2yo fillies' maiden, rated around the experienced winner who was entitled to win one of these.

7278 32RED ON THE APP STORE MAIDEN FILLIES' STKS (PLUS 10 RACE) (DIV II) 7f (P)
6:55 (6:57) (Class 5) 2-Y-0 **£2,911** (£866; £432; £216) **Stalls** Low

Form RPR
1 **Tribute Act** 2-9-0 0.... FrederikTylicki 8 72+
(James Fanshawe) *dwlt: sn in 6th: pushed along over 2f out: rdn and prog on outer over 1f out: led jst ins fnl f: pushed out after* **13/2**
2 *¾* **Golden Nectar** 2-9-0 0.... JimCrowley 3 70+
(Laura Mongan) *in tch in midfield: shkn up on inner over 2f out: prog over 1f out: rdn and r.o to take 2nd last 75yds* **20/1**
3 *nse* **Shaaqaaf (IRE)** 2-9-0 0.... PaulHanagan 1 70+
(John Gosden) *s.i.s and rn green in last: stl last over 2f out: urged along and prog over 1f out: r.o ins fnl f: nrly snatched 2nd* **7/4**^{1}
06 **4** *¾* **Odelouca (IRE)**^{14} 6867 2-9-0 0.... OisinMurphy 9 68
(Brendan Powell) *t.k.h: pressed ldr: protracted battle fr 3f out and narrow ld over 1f out: hdd and no ex jst ins fnl f* **20/1**
5 **5** *1* **Circulate**^{14} 6866 2-9-0 0.... PatCosgrave 6 65
(William Haggas) *led but pressed: battled w chalr fr 3f out: narrowly hdd over 1f out: fdd ins fnl f: hmpd last strides* **9/4**^{2}
6 *½* **Ambrosia** 2-9-0 0.... AndreaAtzeni 7 64+
(Roger Varian) *dwlt: racd in last trio: pushed along over 2f out: rn green and no prog tl kpt on fnl f* **4/1**^{3}
0 **7** *1* **Diptych (USA)**^{14} 6867 2-9-0 0.... LukeMorris 4 61
(Sir Mark Prescott Bt) *chsd ldrs: pushed along over 2f out: no imp over 1f out: fdd fnl f* **100/1**
60 **8** *1* **Dolly Dimples**^{23} 6624 2-9-0 0.... SilvestreDeSousa 5 59
(William Jarvis) *chsd ldrs: rdn over 2f out: no imp over 1f out: wknd fnl f* **25/1**
9 *3¾* **Nargiza (USA)** 2-8-11 0.... LouisSteward$^{(3)}$ 2 48
(Chris Wall) *a in last trio: pushed along and no prog over 2f out: wknd over 1f out* **20/1**

1m 27.31s (1.31) **Going Correction** -0.075s/f (Stan) **9** Ran SP% **119.6**
Speed ratings (Par 92): **89,88,88,87,86 85,84,83,78**
CSF £123.11 TOTE £8.00: £1.60, £4.40, £1.40; EX 186.40 Trifecta £859.70.
Owner Elite Racing Club **Bred** Elite Racing Club **Trained** Newmarket, Suffolk

FOCUS
This second division of the 7f fillies' maiden was run at a routine pace. The field finished compressed and this isn't form to take literally.

7279 32RED.COM MAIDEN FILLIES' STKS (PLUS 10 RACE) 6f (P)
7:25 (7:25) (Class 5) 2-Y-0 **£2,911** (£866; £432; £216) **Stalls** Low

Form RPR
2 **1** **Gheedaa (USA)**^{29} 6454 2-9-0 0.... PaulHanagan 2 76+
(William Haggas) *t.k.h: mde all: hld together tl pressed over 1f out: shkn up and sn asserted: pushed out: readily* **8/13**^{1}
4 **2** *2* **Tundra**^{14} 6867 2-9-0 0.... AndreaAtzeni 1 69
(Roger Varian) *cl up: wnt 2nd 2f out and sn chalng: qckly put in pl by wnr jst over 1f out: styd on* **5/2**^{2}
3 *1½* **Qatari Riyals (IRE)** 2-9-0 0.... SeanLevey 6 64+
(Richard Hannon) *pressed ldrs: lost pl sltly over 2f out: effrt again and rdn wl over 1f out: kpt on to win battle for 3rd* **14/1**
0 **4** *nse* **Guiding Star**^{60} 5400 2-9-0 0.... OisinMurphy 4 64
(Henry Candy) *hld up in 5th: pushed along and clsd 2f out: shkn up over 1f out: kpt on to battle for 3rd fnl f* **10/1**^{3}
5 *3¾* **Parisian Chic (IRE)** 2-8-7 0.... GabrieleMalune$^{(7)}$ 3 53
(Luca Cumani) *mostly in last pair: shkn up and no prog over 2f out: no ch after* **33/1**
06 **6** *2¼* **Iron Lady (IRE)**^{35} 6223 2-9-0 0....^{1} MartinDwyer 7 46
(William Muir) *t.k.h: racd on outer: chsd wnr to 2f out: sn wknd* **66/1**
0 **7** *2* **Kokanee Creek**^{97} 4054 2-9-0 0.... SteveDrowne 5 40
(Mark Usher) *mostly in last: shkn up and no prog over 2f out* **100/1**

1m 12.59s (-0.51) **Going Correction** -0.075s/f (Stan) **7** Ran SP% **111.7**
Speed ratings (Par 92): **100,97,95,95,90 87,84**
CSF £2.19 TOTE £1.50: £1.10, £1.40; EX 2.70 Trifecta £9.20.
Owner Hamdan Al Maktoum **Bred** Shadwell Farm LLC **Trained** Newmarket, Suffolk

FOCUS
An above-average little fillies' sprint maiden. The winner possibly didn't need to replicate her debut form.

7280 MATILDA FLORENCE MAIDEN STKS 1m 4f (P)
7:55 (7:57) (Class 5) 3-5-Y-0 **£2,911** (£866; £432; £216) **Stalls** Low

Form RPR
6223 **1** **Vermeulen**^{20} 6703 3-9-5 78.... RobertHavlin 12 85
(John Gosden) *trckd ldr after 2f: rdn to ld wl over 1f out and sent for home: hung rt sn after: drvn out and kpt on* **4/1**^{2}
5 **2** *nk* **St Malo (USA)**^{6} 7102 3-9-5 0.... AndreaAtzeni 5 84
(Roger Varian) *trckd ldng pair after 2f: rdn over 2f out: tk 2nd on inner jst over 1f out: a hld but clsd gap nr fin* **13/2**
5224 **3** *¾* **Mahfooz (IRE)**^{88} 4384 3-9-5 78.... PaulHanagan 3 82+
(Charles Hills) *t.k.h: hld up in 9th: sme prog 2f out: rdn over 1f out: styd on wl after: tk 3rd and clsng nr fin* **8/1**
3 **4** *¾* **Brodie**^{43} 5996 3-9-0 0.... JimCrowley 10 76
(Luca Cumani) *trckd ldrs: rdn and nt qckn over 2f out: sn outpcd: styd on again fr over 1f out: nrst fin* **11/4**^{1}
5232 **5** *¾* **Casablanca (IRE)**^{18} 6765 3-9-0 74.... OisinMurphy 7 75
(Andrew Balding) *t.k.h early: trckd ldr 2f: styd in tch: rdn and nt qckn over 2f out: kpt on same pce fr over 1f out* **6/1**^{3}
3330 **6** *½* **Lovely Story (IRE)**^{9} 7015 5-9-7 89.... SeanLevey 4 74
(Seamus Durack) *t.k.h: led: tried to kick for home over 2f out: hdd wl over 1f out: wknd fnl f* **12/1**
04-2 **7** *4* **Cry Wolf**^{8} 7052 3-9-5 0.... TimmyMurphy 11 73
(James Evans) *in tch: prog over 3f out: cl enough over 2f out: shkn up and wknd over 1f out* **16/1**
2424 **8** *4* **Plenary (USA)**^{37} 6192 3-9-5 75....(p) RyanMoore 8 66
(Jeremy Noseda) *hld up in last quartet: rdn 2f out: one pce and nvr nr ldrs* **7/1**
9 *½* **Dinsdale** 3-9-5 0.... WilliamTwiston-Davies 9 66
(Michael Scudamore) *s.s: mostly in last quartet: rdn wl over 3f out: nvr a real factor* **33/1**
40- **10** *¾* **Boethius**^{296} 8323 3-9-0 0.... MitchGodwin$^{(5)}$ 2 64
(Tim Vaughan) *stdd s: hld up in last quartet: rdn 2f out: no great prog after* **100/1**
000 **11** *5* **Nightswift**^{70} 5023 4-9-9 0.... HectorCrouch$^{(3)}$ 6 56
(James Evans) *in tch in midfield: pushed along over 3f out: wknd over 2f out* **200/1**
00 **12** *8* **Astrowizard**^{20} 6703 3-9-5 0.... StevieDonohoe 13 44
(Mark H Tompkins) *a in last pair: t.o* **200/1**
0000 **13** *4½* **Briac (FR)**^{27} 6511 5-9-12 0.... JimmyQuinn 1 36
(Jim Best) *dwlt: sn in 8th: rdn and wknd wl over 2f out: t.o* **100/1**

2m 33.86s (-0.64) **Going Correction** -0.075s/f (Stan)
WFA 3 from 4yo+ 7lb **13** Ran SP% **117.4**
Speed ratings (Par 103): **99,98,98,97,97 96,94,91,91,90 87,82,79**
CSF £29.67 TOTE £5.50: £1.90, £1.40, £2.90; EX 34.50 Trifecta £313.00.
Owner Emma Capon & Mrs Simon Marsh **Bred** Watership Down Stud **Trained** Newmarket, Suffolk

FOCUS
It paid to be handy in this competitive middle-distance maiden, which was steadily run.

7281 32RED/STALLIONS BREEDING WINNERS EBF FILLIES' H'CAP 7f (P)
8:25 (8:25) (Class 4) (0-85,83) 3-Y-0+ **£6,469** (£1,925; £962; £481) **Stalls** Low

Form RPR
1421 **1** **Coronation Day**^{58} 5478 3-9-1 **79**.... DavidAllan 11 86
(James Tate) *plld hrd early: pressed ldr: led wl over 1f out but pressed: drvn to assert 150yds out: jst hld on* **14/1**
2013 **2** *hd* **Aristocratic**^{33} 6299 3-9-1 **79**....^{1} RyanMoore 7 85
(Sir Michael Stoute) *pushed along early but showed no zest and sn in last: flat out 3f out and no prog: stl last over 1f out: rdr persisted and fnlly r.o strly fnl f: tk 2nd nr fin and jst failed* **11/4**^{2}
2214 **3** *nk* **Catchment**^{28} 6483 3-9-0 **78**.... JimCrowley 2 83
(Amanda Perrett) *trckd ldng pair: chal on inner over 1f out: w wnr tl 150yds: nt qckn and dropped to 3rd last strides* **9/4**^{1}
4614 **4** *1¼* **Little Miss Kodi (IRE)**^{33} 6299 3-8-12 **76**.... LukeMorris 9 78
(Daniel Mark Loughnane) *trckd ldng trio: hanging whn asked for effrt wl over 1f out: one pce after and nvr threatened* **14/1**

24 **5** *shd* **Owaseyf (USA)**[46] 5891 3-9-1 **79** AndreaAtzeni 1 80
(Roger Varian) *hld up in tch: effrt on inner 2f out: one pce and no imp over 1f out* **7/2**[3]

0010 **6** *3/4* **Be Royale**[22] 6644 6-8-11 **73** PaulHanagan 5 73
(Michael Appleby) *led: rdn and hdd wl over 1f out: fdd and lost pls fnl f* **25/1**

1656 **7** *3/4* **Lyfka**[12] 6914 4-9-7 **83** (tp) SilvestreDeSousa 6 81
(Paul Cole) *dwlt: t.k.h: hld up in last pair: pushed along 2f out: drvn 1f out and no rspnse* **8/1**

0-14 **8** *1 3/4* **Out Of The Dark (IRE)**[124] 3107 3-9-5 **83** TomMarquand 3 76
(Richard Hannon) *hld up in tch: rdn over 2f out: hanging over 1f out and no prog* **12/1**

1m 24.6s (-1.40) **Going Correction** -0.075s/f (Stan)
WFA 3 from 4yo+ 2lb **8** Ran SP% **115.6**
Speed ratings (Par 102): **105,104,104,103,102 102,101,99**
CSF £53.23 CT £123.10 TOTE £11.60: £2.90, £1.50, £1.40; EX 39.10 Trifecta £125.70.
Owner James Tate Racing Limited **Bred** Whitsbury Manor Stud **Trained** Newmarket, Suffolk

FOCUS
A fair fillies' handicap, run at a modest pace.

7282 100% PROFIT BOOST AT 32REDSPORT.COM CLASSIFIED STKS 1m (P)
8:55 (8:56) (Class 6) 3-Y-O+ **£2,264** (£673; £336; £168) **Stalls** Low

Form RPR

0331 **1** **Bazzat (IRE)**[13] 6900 3-9-2 52 (p) JimCrowley 6 60
(John Ryan) *trckd ldr: drvn to ld over 2f out and committed for home: styd on wl and in command fnl f* **4/1**[2]

4450 **2** *2 1/4* **Deftera Lad (IRE)**[7] 7070 4-9-5 51 JimmyQuinn 14 55
(Natalie Lloyd-Beavis) *dropped in fr wd draw: hld up in last pair and wl bhd: gd prog on inner over 2f out: chsd wnr jst over 1f out: styd on but no imp* **50/1**

0000 **3** *2 1/4* **Mr Marchwood**[8] 7035 3-9-2 55 LiamKeniry 1 50
(Sylvester Kirk) *trckd ldrs: rdn over 2f out: nvr able to chal but kpt on to take 3rd fnl f* **16/1**

0-06 **4** *3/4* **Purple Belle**[49] 5766 3-8-11 40 HollieDoyle(5) 10 48
(Jimmy Fox) *urged along in rr bef 1/2-way: sme prog u.p 2f out: styd on fnl f to take 4th nr fin* **66/1**

-030 **5** *shd* **Santadelacruze**[70] 5019 7-9-5 52 (b) AdamBeschizza 4 48
(Mark Hoad) *settled in midfield: hrd rdn over 2f out: kpt on fr over 1f out: nvr pce to threaten* **20/1**

4003 **6** *3/4* **Capital Gearing**[7] 7070 3-9-2 54 (b) SilvestreDeSousa 3 46
(Henry Spiller) *led at gd pce: rdn and hdd over 2f out: lost 2nd jst over 1f out: fdd* **9/2**[3]

0051 **7** *nk* **Garter (IRE)**[7] 7070 3-9-8 55 MichaelJMMurphy 5 51+
(Charles Hills) *trckd ldrs: rdn over 2f out: effrt to dispute 2nd over 1f out: wknd ins fnl f* **15/8**[1]

-000 **8** *1 3/4* **Glorious Dancer**[98] 4009 4-9-5 54 (p) KierenFox 7 41
(Lee Carter) *t.k.h: hld up towards rr and racd on outer: shkn up over 2f out: no great prog* **9/1**

6600 **9** *1* **Buzz Lightyere**[37] 6187 3-9-2 55 [1] LukeMorris 9 38
(Michael Attwater) *in tch in midfield: rdn and no prog over 2f out: steadily fdd* **9/1**

4500 **10** *2 3/4* **Roccor**[15] 6857 3-8-11 55 MitchGodwin(5) 12 32
(Tim Vaughan) *a in rr: wdst of all in st and no prog* **25/1**

5605 **11** *1* **Rennie Mackintosh (IRE)**[13] 6890 4-9-5 53 TomMarquand 13 29
(John Bridger) *chsd ldrs: drvn over 2f out: wknd over 2f out* **20/1**

056- **12** *34* **New Look (IRE)**[297] 8314 6-9-5 53 SeanLevey 8
(Ralph J Smith) *in tch tl wknd rapidly wl over 2f out: t.o* **20/1**

/0-P **13** *48* **Dutchartcollector**[280] 55 5-9-5 55 (p) RyanTate 11
(Tim McCarthy) *slowly away: nvr gng wl and t.o bef 1/2-way* **50/1**

1m 38.74s (-1.06) **Going Correction** -0.075s/f (Stan)
WFA 3 from 4yo+ 3lb **13** Ran SP% **122.4**
Speed ratings (Par 101): **102,99,97,96,96 95,95,93,92,90 89,55,7**
CSF £204.34 TOTE £5.50: £1.70, £13.40, £4.40; EX 175.70 Trifecta £1900.80.
Owner John Stocker **Bred** Ballyhane Stud **Trained** Newmarket, Suffolk

FOCUS
A weak handicap, run at a sound pace.
T/Plt: £238.30 to a £1 stake. Pool: £76,394.39 - 233.95 winning units. T/Qpdt: £34.20 to a £1 stake. Pool: £9,097.23 - 196.35 winning units. **Jonathan Neesom**

7071 NOTTINGHAM (L-H)
Wednesday, October 12

OFFICIAL GOING: Good to soft (soft in places; 6.9) changing to soft after race 2 (2.10)
Wind: Moderate behind Weather: Heavy cloud and showers

7283 KIER CONSTRUCTION CENTRAL NOTTINGHAM EBF MAIDEN STKS 1m 75y
1:40 (1:41) (Class 5) 2-Y-O **£3,234** (£962; £481; £240) **Stalls** Centre

Form RPR

53 **1** **Century Dream (IRE)**[19] 6751 2-9-5 0 RobertHavlin 3 87
(Simon Crisford) *mde all: rdn wl over 1f out: drvn ins fnl f: kpt on strly* **8/1**

5 **2** *3/4* **Ajman King (IRE)**[14] 6880 2-9-5 0 AndreaAtzeni 8 85
(Roger Varian) *t.k.h: trckd ldrs on outer: hdwy 3f out: effrt 2f out: rdn to chse wnr ent fnl f: sn drvn and ev ch tl no ex last 75 yds* **5/1**[3]

3 **3** *3 1/4* **Crowned Eagle**[18] 6777 2-9-5 0 FrankieDettori 12 78+
(John Gosden) *trckd ldrs: hdwy over 3f out: rdn along 2f out and sn sltly outpcd: kpt on u.p fnl f: tk 3rd nr fin* **2/1**[1]

23 **4** *hd* **Dick Tracy (IRE)**[21] 6663 2-9-5 0 PatDobbs 10 78
(Richard Hannon) *trckd wnr: cl up 3f out: rdn along wl over 1f out: drvn appr fnl f and grad wknd: lost 3rd nr fin* **3/1**[2]

5 *8* **Working Class** 2-9-5 0 JimCrowley 4 60
(Peter Chapple-Hyam) *in tch on inner: hdwy over 3f out: sn pushed along: rdn along over 2f out: sn no imp* **20/1**

6 *3 1/4* **Music Seeker (IRE)** 2-9-5 0 RyanTate 6 53
(James Eustace) *chsd ldrs 2f: in tch: rdn along over 2f out: n.d* **100/1**

7 *7* **Just In Time** 2-9-0 0 HollieDoyle(5) 7 38
(Alan King) *a towards rr* **66/1**

5 **8** *3/4* **Pincheck (IRE)**[18] 6777 2-9-5 0 DanielTudhope 9 36
(Luca Cumani) *trckd ldng pair: pushed along on inner over 3f out: rdn along wl over 2f out: sn wknd* **11/2**

9 *1/2* **Scoones** 2-9-5 0 FrederikTylicki 2 35
(James Fanshawe) *towards rr: sme hdwy and in tch over 3f out: rdn along: outpcd and bhd fr over 2f out* **16/1**

00 **10** *23* **Designamento (IRE)**[28] 6480 2-9-5 0 ShaneGray 5
(Ed de Giles) *a rr: outpcd and bhd fnl 3f* **200/1**

60 **11** *nk* **Copa Beech**[89] 4371 2-9-2 0 RobHornby(3) 11
(Olly Williams) *a towards rr: outpcd and bhd fnl 3f* **200/1**

12 *3 1/2* **Hediddodinthe (IRE)** 2-9-5 0 ConnorBeasley 1
(Richard Guest) *dwlt: a bhd* **100/1**

1m 47.3s (-1.70) **Going Correction** -0.25s/f (Firm) **12** Ran SP% **116.6**
Speed ratings (Par 95): **98,97,94,93,85 82,75,74,74,51 51,47**
CSF £46.31 TOTE £9.40: £2.40, £1.70, £1.10; EX 58.50 Trifecta £289.00.
Owner Abdullah Saeed Belhab **Bred** Rabbah Bloodstock Limited **Trained** Newmarket, Suffolk

FOCUS
The going had eased to good to soft all over following a sharp shower before racing. Outer track in use. Rail out 4yds on home bend, adding 12yds to race distances on the round course. Nine of the last ten winners of this maiden had previous experience and those with form on the board dominated again, with the field finishing well spread out. The time was exactly five seconds outside standard, suggesting the rain had got in. A step up from the winner.

7284 KIER CONSTRUCTION CENTRAL EBF MAIDEN FILLIES' STKS (PLUS 10 RACE) (DIV I) 1m 75y
2:10 (2:11) (Class 5) 2-Y-O **£3,234** (£962; £481; £240) **Stalls** Centre

Form RPR

1 **Tansholpan** 2-9-0 0 AndreaAtzeni 2 80+
(Roger Varian) *dwlt: t.k.h and towards rr: hdwy on inner 5f out: sn trcking ldrs: hdwy and cl up 2f out: sn rdn: drvn ins fnl f: kpt on wl to ld towards fin* **14/1**

6 **2** *3/4* **Melodic Motion (IRE)**[40] 6085 2-9-0 0 OisinMurphy 8 78
(Ralph Beckett) *trckd ldrs: cl up after 2f: led 3f out: rdn 2f out: hdd over 1f out: drvn and led again ins fnl f: hdd and no ex towards fin* **4/1**[2]

3 *1/2* **Sea Tide** 2-9-0 0 JimCrowley 1 77+
(Hugo Palmer) *trckd ldrs: smooth hdwy on outer over 3f out: cl up over 2f out: led wl over 1f out: green and sn rdn: hdd ins fnl f: kpt on same pce* **7/4**[1]

40 **4** *5* **Rockshine**[18] 6776 2-9-0 0 PatDobbs 11 66
(Richard Hannon) *led 2f:. prom: rdn along 3f out: drvn 2f out: kpt on same pce* **10/1**[3]

5 *shd* **Mubhirah** 2-9-0 0 PaulHanagan 9 66+
(John Gosden) *dwlt and rr: hdwy wl over 2f : green and pushed along wl over 1f out: kpt on fnl f: nrst fin* **4/1**[2]

0 **6** *4 1/2* **Beauchamp Opal**[18] 6782 2-9-0 0 StevieDonohoe 3 56
(Charlie Fellowes) *towards rr: hdwy on outer over 3f out: rdn along over 2f out: plugged on: n.d* **50/1**

6 **7** *nk* **La Vie En Rose**[12] 6924 2-9-0 0 AndrewMullen 5 55
(Mark Johnston) *in tch: rdn along 3f out: sn no imp* **25/1**

0 **8** *4* **Let's Sway**[63] 5298 2-9-0 0 PaulMulrennan 7 47
(Martyn Meade) *cl up: led after 2f: rdn along and hdd 3f out: sn wknd* **14/1**

9 *2 1/4* **Duchess Of Fife** 2-9-0 0 MartinHarley 10 42
(William Knight) *a rr* **33/1**

40 **10** *3* **Eyreborn (IRE)**[18] 6776 2-9-0 0 PJMcDonald 4 35
(Tom Dascombe) *a towards rr* **20/1**

11 *3* **Cribbs Causeway (IRE)** 2-8-11 0 KieranShoemark(3) 6 29
(Roger Charlton) *a rr* **25/1**

1m 49.18s (0.18) **Going Correction** -0.15s/f (Firm) **11** Ran SP% **116.1**
Speed ratings (Par 92): **93,92,91,86,86 82,81,77,75,72 69**
CSF £64.46 TOTE £17.90: £2.90, £1.30, £1.20; EX 110.20 Trifecta £315.90.
Owner Nurlan Bizakov **Bred** Hesmonds Stud Ltd **Trained** Newmarket, Suffolk

FOCUS
Rail movement added 12yds to the race distance. An interesting fillies' maiden won by the smart Architecture last year. Those with previous experience didn't set too high a standard and a newcomer duly won, though not one many would have expected. Again they finished well spread out, the first three clear.

7285 KIER CONSTRUCTION CENTRAL EBF MAIDEN FILLIES' STKS (PLUS 10 RACE) (DIV II) 1m 75y
2:40 (2:41) (Class 5) 2-Y-O **£3,234** (£962; £481; £240) **Stalls** Centre

Form RPR

4 **1** **Horseplay**[82] 4579 2-9-0 0 OisinMurphy 9 95+
(Andrew Balding) *trckd ldr: cl up 5f out: led jst over 2f out: sn rdn wl clr: easily* **15/8**[1]

00 **2** *13* **Plead**[13] 6897 2-9-0 0 AndreaAtzeni 7 66
(Roger Varian) *led: rdn along 3f out: hdd over 2f out: sn drvn and kpt on same pce* **11/2**[3]

3 *2* **Lassana Angel** 2-9-0 0 [1] WilliamTwiston-Davies 1 64+
(Roger Charlton) *rr: hdwy wl over 2f out: rdn wl over 1f out: styd ion fnl f: nrst fin* **28/1**

4 *nk* **So Sleek** 2-9-0 0 DanielTudhope 2 61+
(Luca Cumani) *trckd ldng pair: effrt over 3f out: rdn along over 2f out: sn one pce* **7/1**

5 *2 3/4* **Lenoire** 2-9-0 0 FrankieDettori 6 55
(John Gosden) *trckd ldrs on outer: effrt over 3f out and sn pushed along: rdn over 2f out: sn wknd* **9/4**[2]

6 *1 1/4* **Doreen** 2-9-0 0 TedDurcan 8 52
(Sir Michael Stoute) *trckd ldrs on inner: pushed along wl over 3f out: rdn wl over 2f out: sn wknd* **16/1**

7 *4 1/2* **Inchikhan** 2-9-0 0 FrederikTylicki 3 42
(James Fanshawe) *dwlt: a rr* **16/1**

8 *hd* **Legalized** 2-9-0 0 TomEaves 4 42
(James Given) *dwlt: a rr* **40/1**

6 **9** *11* **Diamond Princess**[19] 6732 2-9-0 0 AndrewMullen 5 18
(Michael Appleby) *chsd ldrs: rdn along over 4f out: sn wknd* **100/1**

1m 48.21s (-0.79) **Going Correction** -0.05s/f (Good) **9** Ran SP% **112.1**
Speed ratings (Par 92): **101,88,86,85,82 81,77,77,66**
CSF £12.11 TOTE £2.80: £1.30, £1.30, £7.90; EX 12.30 Trifecta £181.40.
Owner Cliveden Stud **Bred** Cliveden Stud **Trained** Kingsclere, Hants

FOCUS

Rail movement added 12yds to the race distance. The ground was changed to soft before this race. Even less previous experience on show in this division, but two of the three to have run before dominated the contest throughout, and that eventually become one. The winning time was almost a second quicker than the first leg, which is impressive considering the ground had continued to ease. The winner looks a smart filly.

7286 KIER CONSTRUCTION NURSERY H'CAP 1m 75y

3:15 (3:16) (Class 5) (0-70,70) 2-Y-O **£2,911** (£866; £432; £216) **Stalls** Centre

Form RPR

5344 **1** **Katebird (IRE)**[8] 7047 2-8-9 **58**.................................... AndrewMullen 10 65+
(Mark Johnston) *hld up: rdn and hdwy on outside over 2f out: led appr fnl f: edgd lft ins fnl f: kpt on strly last 100yds* **7/1**[3]

055 **2** 1 ¾ **Lady Valdean**[18] 6776 2-9-6 **69**.................................... RenatoSouza 11 72
(Jose Santos) *w ldr: led over 3f out: sn rdn: hung lft and hdd appr fnl f: rallied: kpt on same pce last 100yds* **20/1**

4335 **3** 2 ½ **Pacofilha**[14] 6875 2-9-1 **69**.................................... GeorgeWood(5) 17 67
(Paul Cole) *prom: effrt and rdn over 2f out: ev ch over 1f out: no ex ins fnl f* **5/1**[1]

0003 **4** 1 ¾ **Eolian**[31] 6377 2-9-0 **63**....................................(v) MartinHarley 15 57
(William Knight) *s.i.s: sn pushed along in rr: drvn over 3f out: hdwy and hung lft over 1f out: kpt on fnl f: nrst fin* **6/1**[2]

0533 **5** shd **Tigerfish (IRE)**[49] 5770 2-8-0 **49** oh1 ow3.................. NathanEvans(3) 13 45
(William Stone) *hld up: rdn and hdwy over 2f out: effrt and ev ch briefly over 1f out: no ex ins fnl f* **25/1**

543 **6** shd **Swell Hill**[22] 6648 2-9-2 **65**.................................... PatDobbs 6 58
(Richard Hannon) *hld up in tch on ins: shuffled bk bhd wkng rival over 4f out: rallied over 2f out: sn drvn: no imp over 1f out* **16/1**

5504 **7** 1 ¾ **Metronomic (IRE)**[29] 6440 2-8-10 **64**.............................. HollieDoyle(5) 8 53
(Richard Hannon) *hld up: effrt and rdn 3f out: outpcd wl over 1f out* **8/1**

635 **8** ½ **Pepys**[18] 6771 2-9-6 **69**.................................... ConnorBeasley 4 57
(Bryan Smart) *dwlt: sn led: rdn and hdd over 3f out: rallied: wknd wl over 1f out* **12/1**

250 **9** ¾ **Sakurajima (IRE)**[46] 5890 2-9-7 **70**.............................. DanielTudhope 7 57
(Charles Hills) *hld up: rdn and effrt on outside over 2f out: hung lft and sn no imp* **11/1**

3110 **10** nk **Madam Prancealot (IRE)**[31] 6388 2-9-0 **63**........... MichaelJMMurphy 5 49
(David Evans) *early ldr: prom: effrt and rdn 3f out: wknd 2f out* **6/1**[2]

600 **11** 10 **Armagnac (IRE)**[47] 5848 2-9-4 **67**.............................. WilliamCarson 12 31
(Michael Bell) *hld up midfield: outpcd and hung lft over 2f out: sn wknd* **14/1**

6046 **12** ½ **Sandwood Bay**[20] 6713 2-9-6 **69**.............................. StevieDonohoe 16 32
(Mark H Tompkins) *dwlt: sn trcking ldrs on outside: rdn over 3f out: wknd over 2f out* **20/1**

400 **13** 4 ½ **Pitch High (IRE)**[30] 6404 2-9-0 **66**.............................. ShelleyBirkett(3) 14 19
(Julia Feilden) *t.k.h in midfield: drvn along over 3f out: wknd over 2f out* **33/1**

3230 **14** 4 ½ **Bridal March**[12] 6923 2-8-13 **62**.................................... PJMcDonald 3 5
(Mark Johnston) *in tch on ins: outpcd over 4f out: wknd fr 3f out* **16/1**

1m 49.2s (0.20) **Going Correction** +0.05s/f (Good) **14** Ran SP% **119.6**
Speed ratings (Par 95): **101,99,96,95,94 94,93,92,91,91 81,81,76,72**
CSF £144.83 CT £789.64 TOTE £4.80: £1.60, £6.90, £3.20; EX 149.20 Trifecta £1141.30 Part won..
Owner J David Abell **Bred** Peter Grimes & The Late Jackie Grimes **Trained** Middleham Moor, N Yorks

FOCUS

Rail movement added 12yds to the race distance. An ordinary staying nursery and quite a test for these 2yos in the conditions. They went a fair pace in the circumstances and the winner took this purely through stamina, building on her latest effort.

7287 KIER LIVING H'CAP 1m 2f 50y

3:50 (3:50) (Class 3) (0-95,95) 3-Y-O+

£7,470 (£2,236; £1,118; £559; £279; £140) **Stalls** Low

Form RPR

4021 **1** **Great Hall**[17] 6802 6-9-10 **95**.................................... JimCrowley 13 108
(Mick Quinn) *hld up in rr: stdy hdwy on outer 4f out: trckd ldrs over 2f out: rdn to ld 1 1/2f out: sn hung lft: drvn clr: styd on wl* **5/1**[2]

1112 **2** 3 ¼ **Rainbow Rebel (IRE)**[9] 7005 3-8-10 **86**.......................... PJMcDonald 6 93
(Mark Johnston) *hld up in midfield: hdwy on outer 3f out: rdn to chse wnr ent fnl f: sn drvn and no imp* **4/1**[1]

0005 **3** 1 **Bahama Moon (IRE)**[36] 6217 4-8-10 **81**.................... GrahamGibbons 9 86
(David Barron) *hld up towards rr: hdwy into midfield 1/2-way: effrt to chse ldrs 2f out: sn rdn: drvn and kpt on fnl f* **7/1**

0222 **4** 1 ½ **Top Beak (IRE)**[19] 6736 3-9-1 **91**....................................(t) RobertHavlin 4 93
(Hughie Morrison) *trckd ldrs: hdwy and cl up over 3f out: chal over 2f out: sn rdn and ev ch: drvn wl over 1f out and kpt on same pce* **11/2**[3]

0623 **5** ¾ **Arrowzone**[17] 6802 5-9-2 **87**....................................(b) DavidAllan 3 87
(Ivan Furtado) *pushed along after s and sn in tch: hdwy over 3f out: rdn along over 2f out: drvn over 1f out: kpt on* **12/1**

0550 **6** 1 ½ **Hit The Jackpot (IRE)**[17] 6802 7-9-5 **90**....................... DanielTudhope 1 87
(David O'Meara) *trckd ldrs: hdwy on inner 4f out: cl up 3f out: sn led and rdn: drvn and hdd wl over 1f out: grad wknd* **14/1**

0334 **7** ½ **Emerald (ITY)**[34] 6261 4-9-2 **87**....................................(b) HarryBentley 12 83
(Marco Botti) *hld up in rr: hdwy on inner 3f out: rdn along over 2f out: sn drvn and no imp* **5/1**[2]

420 **8** 2 ½ **Navajo War Dance**[17] 6802 3-8-9 **85**.............................. JoeyHaynes 11 76
(K R Burke) *chsd ldrs on outer: hdwy over 3f out: rdn along wl over 2f out: sn drvn and one pce* **16/1**

230- **9** 5 **Mezajy (IRE)**[371] 7035 4-8-11 **82**.................................... PaulMulrennan 8 63
(Ed Walker) *trckd ldrs: hdwy over 3f out: rdn along wl over 2f out: sn wknd* **25/1**

1420 **10** ½ **Gurkha Friend**[25] 6560 4-9-3 **88**.................................... DavidNolan 5 68
(Karen McLintock) *slt ld: hdd and cl up over 6f out: rdn to ld again briefly 3f out: sn hdd and drvn: grad wknd* **16/1**

5100 **11** 10 **Oasis Spear**[33] 6298 4-9-1 **86**.................................... TedDurcan 7 46
(Chris Wall) *sn cl up: led over 6f out: rdn along and hdd 3f out: sn wknd* **25/1**

1310 **12** 44 **Lord Franklin**[14] 6876 7-8-7 **83**.................................... PhilDennis(5) 10
(Eric Alston) *prom: rdn along over 4f out: sn wknd* **25/1**

2m 13.7s (-0.60) **Going Correction** +0.15s/f (Good)
WFA 3 from 4yo+ 5lb **12** Ran SP% **118.9**
Speed ratings (Par 107): **108,105,104,103,102 101,101,99,95,94 86,51**
CSF £24.73 CT £137.35 TOTE £6.30: £2.30, £1.30, £2.70; EX 16.60 Trifecta £226.30.
Owner YNWA Partnership **Bred** Aston House Stud **Trained** Newmarket, Suffolk

FOCUS

Rail movement added 12yds to the race distance. A decent handicap in which they went a sensible pace and shunned the inside rail up the straight. The first three came from the back and the form could rate higher at face value.

7288 KIER IN PARTNERSHIP WITH ALZHEIMERS SOCIETY H'CAP (DIV I) 5f 13y

4:20 (4:21) (Class 4) (0-85,85) 3-Y-O+ **£4,690** (£1,395; £697; £348) **Stalls** High

Form RPR

1062 **1** **New Road Side**[5] 7112 3-8-12 **76**..............................(v) ConnorBeasley 1 84
(Richard Guest) *mde all: rdn over 1f out: hrd pressed fnl f: hld on gamely towards fin* **8/1**

2110 **2** hd **Orient Class**[26] 6537 5-9-0 **83**.............................. AdamMcNamara(5) 4 89
(Paul Midgley) *chsd ldng gp on outside: hdwy 2f out: rdn and ev ch ins fnl f: kpt on: hld nr fin* **9/2**[1]

31 **3** hd **Hilary J**[46] 5867 3-9-3 **81**.................................... PJMcDonald 2 88
(Ann Duffield) *chsd ldrs: effrt and wnt 2nd 2f out: drvn and ev ch ins fnl f: kpt on: hld towards fin* **6/1**[3]

2221 **4** nk **Fruit Salad**[11] 6959 3-8-7 **74**..............................(p) NathanEvans(3) 3 79+
(James Bethell) *dwlt: bhd and sn outpcd: plenty to do 1/2-way: gd hdwy fnl f: fin strly* **5/1**[2]

55 **5** 1 ¼ **Diamond Lady**[71] 4984 5-8-13 **82**.............................. HollieDoyle(5) 12 82
(William Stone) *chsd ldng gp: rdn along over 2f out: kpt on fnl f: nvr able to chal* **11/1**

2022 **6** nk **Apricot Sky**[18] 6793 6-9-3 **81**.................................... BarryMcHugh 9 80
(David Nicholls) *chsd wnr to 2f out: sn rdn and hung lft: kpt on same pce fnl f* **9/2**[1]

0000 **7** 2 ½ **Zac Brown (IRE)**[31] 6371 5-9-2 **80**..............................[1] DanielTudhope 6 70
(Charlie Wallis) *t.k.h: cl up: rdn and outpcd over 2f out: n.d after* **22/1**

2500 **8** ¾ **Dominate**[102] 3892 6-9-1 **79**..............................[1] TedDurcan 5 66
(George Scott) *bhd and nvr gng wl: no ch fr 1/2-way* **14/1**

1241 **9** shd **Satchville Flyer**[22] 6653 5-9-0 **78**.......................... MichaelJMMurphy 8 65
(David Evans) *dwlt: bhd and drvn along: nvr on terms* **16/1**

0056 **10** shd **Noble Storm (USA)**[12] 6926 10-8-9 **80**.................[1] CameronNoble(7) 11 66
(Ed McMahon) *trckd ldrs: rdn over 2f out: hung lft and wknd over 1f out* **8/1**

1m 0.12s (-1.38) **Going Correction** -0.125s/f (Firm) **10** Ran SP% **114.8**
Speed ratings (Par 105): **106,105,105,104,102 102,98,97,97,96**
CSF £43.19 CT £198.47 TOTE £8.40: £3.40, £1.20, £2.60; EX 58.00 Trifecta £398.20.
Owner Morecool Racing **Bred** Highclere Stud **Trained** Ingmanthorpe, W Yorks

FOCUS

A fair sprint handicap in which the runners raced centre to nearside. It produced a game front-running performance from the winner. The bare form is ordinary.

7289 KIER IN PARTNERSHIP WITH ALZHEIMERS SOCIETY H'CAP (DIV II) 5f 13y

4:55 (4:58) (Class 4) (0-85,84) 3-Y-O+ **£4,690** (£1,395; £697; £348) **Stalls** High

Form RPR

3360 **1** **Appleberry (IRE)**[12] 6926 4-8-13 **76**..............................[1] AndrewMullen 4 85
(Michael Appleby) *chsd ldrs: hdwy over 1f out: rdn jst over 1f out: chal ent fnl f: drvn to ld last 100 yds* **25/1**

3642 **2** ½ **Silken Skies (IRE)**[37] 6195 3-8-12 **82**.......................... WilliamCox(7) 7 90
(Clive Cox) *trckd ldrs: hdwy wl over 1f out: sn rdn: styd on wl fnl f* **6/1**[2]

2240 **3** 1 ¼ **Geno (IRE)**[26] 6537 3-9-1 **78**....................................(p) TomEaves 10 82
(Kevin Ryan) *cl up on outer: effrt to chal over 1f out: sn rdn and ev ch tl drvn ins fnl f and kpt on same pce towards fin* **8/1**

0650 **4** nk **Paddy Power (IRE)**[18] 6793 3-9-1 **78**.............................. TonyHamilton 5 81
(Richard Fahey) *sn cl up: led wl over 1f out: jnd and rdn ent fnl f: sn drvn: hdd and kpt on same pce last 100 yds* **7/1**[3]

4430 **5** 1 **Ambitious Icarus**[14] 6878 7-8-7 **70** oh3..........................(e) ShaneGray 8 68
(Richard Guest) *awkward s and rr: rdn along and hdwy 2f out: drvn over 1f out: styd on wl fnl f: nrst fin* **14/1**

0060 **6** shd **Major Pusey**[11] 6944 4-9-5 **82**.............................. MichaelJMMurphy 1 80
(John Gallagher) *cl up on wd outside: effrt 2f out: sn rdn and wknd appr fnl f* **8/1**

0200 **7** ½ **Lucky Beggar (IRE)**[34] 6263 6-9-4 **81**..........................(p[1]) DavidAllan 13 77
(David C Griffiths) *towards rr: rdn along over 2f out: kpt on fnl f* **7/1**[3]

5003 **8** 1 ½ **Rita's Boy (IRE)**[26] 6537 4-8-13 **76**..............................(v) BenCurtis 3 66
(K R Burke) *prom: cl up over 2f out: sn rdn and wknd over 1f out* **9/2**[1]

0100 **9** 1 ½ **Invincible Ridge (IRE)**[34] 6263 8-9-1 **83**.................... PhilDennis(5) 6 68
(Eric Alston) *towards rr. rdn along over 2f out: sn drvn and n.d* **10/1**

21-0 **10** 5 **Swiss Affair**[158] 2042 4-9-7 **84**..............................[1] GrahamGibbons 9 51
(Robert Cowell) *led: rdn along over 2f out: hdd wl over 1f out and sn wknd* **25/1**

1m 0.1s (-1.40) **Going Correction** -0.125s/f (Firm) **10** Ran SP% **103.1**
Speed ratings (Par 105): **106,105,103,102,101 100,100,97,95,87**
CSF £135.68 CT £995.84 TOTE £31.10: £5.30, £2.00, £2.60; EX 175.50 Trifecta £1501.40 Prat won..
Owner M J Golding, T Pryke, M Appleby **Bred** Doc Bloodstock **Trained** Oakham, Rutland

■ Aprovade was withdrawn. price at time of withdrawal 6-1. Rule 4 applies to all bets - deduction 10p in the poound.

FOCUS

The field was reduced by one when Aprovado was withdrawn after breaking out from his stall. The winning time was a fraction quicker than division one. Pretty straightforward form.

7290 KIER CENTRAL WITH THE EAR FOUNDATION H'CAP 5f 13y

5:25 (5:26) (Class 6) (0-65,65) 3-Y-O+ **£2,264** (£673; £336; £168) **Stalls** High

Form RPR

1060 **1** **Coiste Bodhar (IRE)**[9] 7018 5-8-13 **64**.................... NatalieHambling(7) 1 73
(Scott Dixon) *mde all at decent gallop: drvn along 2f out: drew clr fnl f* **20/1**

051 **2** 2 ¾ **Taffetta**[6] 7093 4-9-6 **64** 6ex.................................... BarryMcHugh 15 63+
(Tony Coyle) *dwlt and hmpd s: bhd: rdn along 1/2-way: gd hdwy to chse (clr) wnr wl ins fnl f: kpt on: nt pce to chal* **7/1**[3]

0010 **3** ¾ **Horsforth**[11] 6958 4-9-0 **58**....................................(b) ConnorBeasley 2 54
(Richard Guest) *prom: drvn and chsd wnr over 1f out to wl ins fnl f: kpt on same pce* **14/1**

0334 **4** nk **Where Next**[8] 7036 3-9-4 **62**.................................... HarryBentley 14 58
(Henry Candy) *hld up midfield: pushed along over 2f out: hdwy and edgd lft over 1f out: kpt on: nt pce to chal* **11/2**[1]

0302 **5** nk **Groundworker (IRE)**[13] 6910 5-9-2 **60**....................(t) PaulMulrennan 17 54
(Paul Midgley) *hld up in tch: pushed along and effrt over 1f out: edgd lft: kpt on same pce ins fnl f* **6/1**[2]

4000 **6** 1 **Keep It Dark**[21] 6669 7-9-5 **63**....................................(p) MartinHarley 9 54
(William Knight) *bhd and sn pushed along: hdwy over 1f out: kpt on fnl f: nvr able to chal* **14/1**

4353 **7** *1* **Beau Mistral (IRE)**[9] 7018 7-9-0 **58**..........................(b) WilliamCarson 12 45
(Tony Carroll) *chsd ldrs: rdn over 2f out: hung lft over 1f out: btn ins fnl f* **16/1**

2006 **8** *shd* **Hit The Lights (IRE)**[11] 6958 6-9-4 **62**................................ PaulQuinn 16 49
(David Nicholls) *prom: rdn over 2f out: wknd over 1f out* **12/1**

1350 **9** *hd* **Bonjour Steve**[34] 6255 5-8-13 **62**..........................(p) AdamMcNamara(5) 3 48
(Richard Price) *towards rr: drvn and hdwy over 2f out: no further imp over 1f out* **12/1**

303 **10** *1/2* **Prigsnov Dancer (IRE)**[61] 5378 11-8-7 **56**.................... PaddyPilley(5) 8 40
(John Balding) *sn pushed along in rr: drvn along 1/2-way: nvr rchd ldrs* **20/1**

0413 **11** *2* **Bronze Beau**[11] 6959 9-9-5 **63**..................................(tp) ShaneGray 13 40
(Kristin Stubbs) *chsd wnr tl rdn and wknd over 1f out* **12/1**

0011 **12** *3/4* **Robbie Roo Roo**[15] 6852 3-9-0 **58**..............................(vt) SaleemGolam 5 33
(Mrs Ilka Gansera-Leveque) *towards rr: drvn along 1/2-way: nvr on terms* **10/1**

0501 **13** *3 1/4* **Anieres Boy**[2] 7200 4-8-8 **55**.. NathanEvans(3) 6 18
(Michael Easterby) *rrd and lost grnd s: a outpcd and bhd* **11/2**[1]

6000 **14** *3/4* **Roy's Legacy**[14] 6879 7-8-11 **62**.. TobyEley(7) 4 22
(Shaun Harris) *towards rr: drvn along 1/2-way: sn btn* **50/1**

1m 0.27s (-1.23) **Going Correction** -0.125s/f (Firm) **14** Ran SP% **120.4**
Speed ratings (Par 101): **104,99,98,97,97 95,94,94,93,92 89,88,83,82**
CSF £151.50 CT £2104.21 TOTE £27.00: £8.40, £2.30, £5.50; EX 166.30 TRIFECTA Not won..
Owner Yvonne Lowe & W A Robinson **Bred** C Amerian **Trained** Babworth, Notts

FOCUS
A moderate sprint handicap and there was only one horse in it from some way out. He produced a pb.
T/Jkpt: Not Won. T/Plt: £36.10 to a £1 stake. Pool: £64,050.62 - 1291.85 winning units. T/Qpdt: £11.40 to a £1 stake. Pool: £4,984.35 - 323.32 winning units. **Joe Rowntree & Richard Young**

7168 CHANTILLY (R-H)
Wednesday, October 12

OFFICIAL GOING: Turf: good; polytrack: standard

7291a PRIX DES TERROIRS DE FRANCE (MAIDEN) (UNRACED 2YO) (TURF) 6f
11:55 (12:00) 2-Y-O **£9,926** (£3,970; £2,977; £1,985; £992)

RPR

1 **Charm Appeal (FR)** 2-8-13 0.. AlexisBadel 8 79
(H-F Devin, France) **5/2**[1]

2 *snk* **Precieuse (IRE)** 2-8-13 0.................................. Pierre-CharlesBoudot 1 79
(F Chappet, France) **31/5**

3 *2* **Etoile Bere (FR)** 2-8-13 0... StephanePasquier 6 73
(N Clement, France) **32/5**

4 *1 1/2* **Bijin (FR)** 2-8-13 0.. LukasDelozier 3 68
(H-A Pantall, France) **74/10**

5 *1 1/2* **Kings Academy** 2-9-2 0.. ChristopheSoumillon 5 67
(Paul Cole) *led: rdn whn pressed ins last 1 1/2f: hdd over 1f out: grad lft bhd fnl f* **9/2**[3]

6 *3* **Spanish History (USA)** 2-9-2 0............................. MickaelBarzalona 7 58
(A Fabre, France) *w.w towards rr: rdn and short-lived effrt 1 1/2f out: sn btn and wl hld fnl f* **13/5**[2]

7 *2 1/2* **Crystal Bleu** 2-8-13 0... LouisBeuzelin 2 47
(Miss V Haigh, France) **51/1**

8 *20* **Warcraft (FR)** 2-9-2 0..(p) AurelienLemaitre 4
(Mlle V Dissaux, France) **30/1**

1m 12.7s (1.30) **8** Ran SP% **119.0**
WIN (incl. 1 euro stake): 3.50. PLACES: 1.60, 1.90, 2.30. DF: 11.80. SF: 20.10..
Owner Mrs R G Hillen **Bred** East Bloodstock Ltd **Trained** France

7292a PRIX DU RANELAGH (LISTED RACE) (3YO+) (TURF) 1m
12:25 (12:00) 3-Y-O+ **£19,117** (£7,647; £5,735; £3,823; £1,911)

RPR

1 **Bravo Zolo (IRE)**[18] 6786 4-9-3 0.......................... ChristopheSoumillon 3 104
(Jeremy Noseda) *mde all: pressed for ld early: kicked for home over 1 1/2f out: drvn out fnl f: readily* **16/5**[1]

2 *snk* **Qurbaan (USA)**[32] 6358 3-9-0 0........................ Francois-XavierBertras 4 104+
(F Rohaut, France) **9/2**

3 *1 1/4* **Dhevanafushi**[32] 6358 3-9-0 0................................... MickaelBarzalona 1 101
(H-A Pantall, France) **33/10**[2]

4 *1/2* **Grand Vintage (FR)**[18] 6798 7-9-3 0.............................. MickaelForest 5 100
(Carina Fey, France) **11/1**

5 *1 3/4* **Campillo (FR)**[108] 7-9-3 0.................................. Pierre-CharlesBoudot 6 96
(J Phelippon, France) **39/10**[3]

6 *2* **Boxeur (IRE)**[32] 6358 3-9-0 0.. MaximeGuyon 9 91
(F Rossi, France) **10/1**

7 *snk* **Kenrivash (FR)**[10] 6992 3-8-10 0.................................. CristianDemuro 8 87
(Henk Grewe, Germany) **11/1**

8 *3* **Bohemian Rapsody (FR)**[37] 6203 6-9-0 0................ IoritzMendizabal 7 81
(Enrique Leon Penate, France) **17/1**

9 *1/2* **Stillman (FR)**[78] 4751 5-9-6 0...(b) OlivierPeslier 2 86
(P Khozian, France) **20/1**

1m 37.06s (-0.94)
WFA 3 from 4yo+ 3lb **9** Ran SP% **119.7**
WIN (incl. 1 euro stake): 4.20. PLACES: 1.60, 1.60, 1.60. DF: 11.00. SF: 17.10..
Owner Marc Keller **Bred** Tipper House Stud **Trained** Newmarket, Suffolk

7293a PRIX DE L'ALLEE CAMELIA (CLAIMER) (2YO COLTS & GELDINGS) (POLYTRACK) 7f
1:05 (12:00) 2-Y-O **£8,455** (£3,382; £2,536; £1,691; £845)

RPR

1 **Dolokhov**[5] 7136 2-9-4 0..(p) TonyPiccone 5 81+
(J S Moore) *w.w in fnl pair: hdwy over 2f out: chsd ldr fr 1 1/2f out: styd on strly to ld 1f out: sn clr: v comf* **19/10**[2]

2 *3 1/2* **If I Say So**[44] 5988 2-9-1 0...(b) IoritzMendizabal 2 69
(J S Moore) *led: rdn whn pressed under 2f out: hdd 1f out: no match for wnr: kpt on at same pce fnl f* **39/10**[3]

3 *3/4* **Sunday Winner (FR)**[28] 2-9-1 0............................(b) StephanePasquier 4 67
(Y Gourraud, France) **71/10**

4 *1 1/4* **Barbarigo (IRE)**[44] 5988 2-9-0 0............................ NicolasLarenaudie(5) 1 67
(F Chappet, France) **17/10**[1]

5 *2* **Zanzari (FR)**[133] 2-8-11 0.. RonanThomas 7 54
(C Boutin, France) **13/1**

6 *4* **Silver Poker (FR)**[33] 6309 2-9-1 0........................ ThibaultSpeicher(3) 3 50
(D Chenu, France) **41/1**

7 *snk* **Rinky Dink Dawn (IRE)**[43] 6015 2-8-11 0.................... EddyHardouin 6 43
(R Schoof, Belgium) **22/1**

Owner Mrs T Burns & J S Moore **Bred** Lady Legard & Sir Tatton Sykes **Trained** Upper Lambourn, Berks

7294a PRIX DE L'ALLEE DURBAR (CLAIMER) (2YO FILLIES) (POLYTRACK) 7f
1:35 (12:00) 2-Y-O **£8,455** (£3,382; £2,536; £1,691; £845)

RPR

1 **Touching The Sky (IRE)**[104] 2-9-4 0.................. ChristopheSoumillon 2 77
(Alex Fracas, France) **31/10**[2]

2 *3* **Incantu (IRE)**[64] 5279 2-9-4 0...(b) TonyPiccone 9 69
(F Chappet, France) **12/1**

3 *3/4* **Ekatea (FR)** 2-8-11 0... FrankPanicucci 8 60
(C Laffon-Parias, France) **19/1**

4 *1 1/2* **Sea Of Lights (GER)** 2-8-11 0................................. SebastienMaillot 6 56
(N Clement, France) **19/1**

5 *1* **Joyful Dream (IRE)**[6] 7098 2-8-11 0.............................. MickaelBerto 4 53
(J S Moore) *chsd ldr: led briefly 1/2-way: sn hdd and remained 2nd: rdn and nt qckn over 1 1/2f out: sn outpcd by ldrs: one pce fnl f* **9/1**

6 *snk* **Briseide (IRE)**[43] 6015 2-8-11 0................................... CristianDemuro 3 53
(D Zarroli, Italy) **54/10**

7 *snk* **Vixenta (FR)**[21] 2-9-4 0... IoritzMendizabal 7 59
(Eric Saint-Martin, France) **19/1**

8 *nk* **Tawaret (FR)**[50] 5755 2-9-3 0..........................(p) ClementLecoeuvre(5) 5 63
(Mme M-C Naim, France) **23/10**[1]

9 *15* **Sirma Traou Land (FR)**[50] 5755 2-8-10 0............ JeremieCatineau(6) 1 16
(B De Montzey, France) **5/1**[3]

WIN (incl. 1 euro stake): 4.10. PLACES: 2.10, 3.60, 4.10. DF: 21.80. SF: 35.10.
Owner Jose-Manuel Garcia-Sahagun **Bred** Ecurie Haras Du Cadran, Ecurie Patrick Klein & A G **Trained** France

7295a PRIX DES ALLEES CAVALIERES (CLAIMER) (4YO+) (AMATEUR LADY RIDERS) (POLYTRACK) 1m 1f
2:05 (12:00) 4-Y-O+ **£5,882** (£2,352; £1,764; £1,176; £588)

RPR

1 **Babel Ouest (FR)**[50] 8-9-13 0................................ MlleBarbaraGuenet 8 70
(W Mongil, Germany) **41/10**[2]

2 *1 1/2* **Appiano (FR)**[123] 5-9-3 0...............................(p) MlleTracyMenuet(4) 5 61
(W Menuet, France) **16/1**

3 *3 1/2* **Hey Joe (FR)**[68] 4-9-0 0....................................(b) MllePerrineCheyer(4) 1 51
(J-Y Artu, France) **21/1**

4 *3/4* **Go Parti (FR)**[142] 6-9-11 0.. MlleMarieRollando 10 56
(Alex Fracas, France) **11/1**

5 *3/4* **I Fight For Kisses (GER)**[20] 8-9-4 0.......................... FrauBeritWeber 6 48
(Carina Fey, France) **6/4**[1]

6 *1 1/4* **Sheila's Buddy**[111] 3557 7-9-7 0............................ MlleDianaLopezLeret 4 48
(J S Moore) *hld up towards rr: in fnl trio and pushed along 2f out: styd on u.p fnl 1 1/2f out: n.d* **9/1**

7 *nk* **Zitat (GER)** 4-9-1 0... FrauLarissaBiess 7 41
(Waldemar Hickst, Germany) **17/1**

8 *snk* **Mahajanga (FR)**[42] 6-9-1 0..........................(b) MlleBlancheDeGranvilliers 3 41
(B Legros, France) **48/1**

9 *4* **Chinese Soldier (FR)**[68] 4-9-0 0.................. MlleSaraVermeersch(4) 11 36
(Stijn Derycke, Belgium) **56/1**

10 *3 1/2* **Tostaky Blue (FR)**[82] 7-9-3 0..............(p) MlleCharlotteRinckenbach(4) 12 31
(A Spanu, France) **15/1**

11 *3 1/2* **Salar Glorious**[82] 7-9-4 0.. MissMelaniePlat 2 21
(A Marcialis, Italy) **53/10**[3]

12 *dist* **Monsea (IRE)**[223] 5-9-0 0.. MlleKatiaSegains(4) 9
(Mlle M Henry, France) **88/1**

WIN (incl. 1 euro stake): 5.10. PLACES: 2.50, 5.40, 6.30. DF: 38.70. SF: 64.10.
Owner Galopp-Club Rhein-Main **Bred** Mme M A Leray **Trained** Germany

7032 BRIGHTON (L-H)
Thursday, October 13

OFFICIAL GOING: Good (good to firm in places)
Wind: Fresh, across towards stand Weather: Cloudy

7296 CALL STAR SPORTS ON 08000 521 321 / EBF MAIDEN STKS 5f 213y
1:30 (1:30) (Class 5) 2-Y-O **£3,881** (£1,155; £577; £288) **Stalls** Centre

Form RPR

4 **1** **Gmaash**[16] 6850 2-9-0 0... JimCrowley 7 67
(Saeed bin Suroor) *hdwy to press ldrs after 2f: led 3f out: drvn along fnl f: jst hld on* **6/5**[1]

5 **2** *shd* **Desert Mark (IRE)**[132] 2847 2-9-5 0............................... TomMarquand 4 72
(Richard Hannon) *chsd ldrs: effrt 2f out: r.o wl fnl f: jst failed* **5/1**[3]

5 **3** *2 1/2* **Peace Dreamer (IRE)**[28] 6515 2-9-0 0............................... LukeMorris 5 60
(Robert Cowell) *pushed along in 5th after 2f: styd alone on far rail in st: chsd wnr 2f out tl ins fnl f: one pce* **9/1**

05 **4** *8* **Sonata**[8] 7072 2-9-0 0.. SilvestreDeSousa 2 36
(Mick Channon) *chsd ldr tl 1/2-way: btn over 2f out* **14/1**

326 **5** *1 1/2* **Prazeres**[40] 6129 2-9-5 **75**.. PatCosgrave 1 36
(William Haggas) *led tl 3f out: wknd 2f out* **9/4**[2]

4505 **6** *8* **Shadow Wing (IRE)**[14] 6887 2-8-9 **53**.............................. AnnStokell(5) 6 7
(Ann Stokell) *plld hrd early: sn lost pl and bhd* **100/1**

1m 9.3s (-0.90) **Going Correction** -0.175s/f (Firm) **6** Ran SP% **110.5**
Speed ratings (Par 95): **99,98,95,84,82 72**
CSF £7.51 TOTE £1.90: £1.10, £2.50; EX 7.50 Trifecta £35.30.
Owner Godolphin **Bred** Darley **Trained** Newmarket, Suffolk

FOCUS
The going was good, good to firm in places (watered). Rail out between the 6f and 3.5f markers, adding 3.8yds to all race distances. A moderate and uncompetitive maiden to start in which they used the full width of the track after the cutaway, with the first two coming more nearside. The winning time was just 0.6sec outside standard, with the winning rider describing the ground as good to firm.

7297 STARSPORTSBET.CO.UK EBF MEDIAN AUCTION MAIDEN STKS 7f 214y
2:00 (2:00) (Class 5) 2-Y-O **£3,234** (£962; £481; £240) **Stalls** Centre

Form RPR
50 **1** **Diamond Bear (USA)**[14] 6897 2-9-0 0 .... LukeMorris 8 74
(Sir Mark Prescott Bt) *w ldr: rdn to ld over 1f out: hung lft: drvn out* **8/1**
4252 **2** *1 3/4* **Akkadian Empire**[14] 6888 2-9-5 75 .... SilvestreDeSousa 4 75
(Mick Channon) *led tl 3f out: chsd wnr ins fnl f: one pce* **5/2**[2]
333 **3** *2 1/2* **Glendun (USA)**[13] 6924 2-9-5 74 .... JimCrowley 1 69
(Brian Meehan) *chsd ldrs: led 3f out tl over 1f out: no ex fnl f* **9/4**[1]
5 **4** *1* **Mamdood (IRE)**[16] 6850 2-9-5 0 .... PaulHanagan 5 67+
(Richard Hannon) *hld up in 6th: pushed along 3f out: hdwy 2f out: one pce appr fnl f* **7/2**[3]
0 **5** *6* **Shambra (IRE)**[24] 6625 2-9-0 0 .... MartinHarley 3 48
(James Tate) *t.k.h: in tch: rdn 4f out: wknd wl over 1f out* **14/1**
65 **6** *3 3/4* **Esloobaha (IRE)**[35] 6250 2-9-0 0 .... MichaelJMMurphy 7 40
(Charles Hills) *prom: rdn 4f out: wknd wl over 1f out* **20/1**
7 *nk* **Maori Bob (IRE)** 2-9-5 0 .... WilliamCarson 2 44
(Michael Bell) *outpcd: sn bhd* **17/2**
00 **8** *3* **Kingston Tasmania**[14] 6888 2-9-5 0 .... OisinMurphy 6 37
(Andrew Balding) *towards rr: rdn 5f out: n.d fnl 3f* **50/1**
0 **9** *8* **Chakra**[19] 6776 2-8-11 0 .... LouisSteward(3) 9 14
(Michael Bell) *outpcd: sn wl bhd* **33/1**

1m 33.55s (-2.45) **Going Correction** -0.175s/f (Firm) **9** Ran SP% **119.5**
Speed ratings (Par 95): **105,103,100,99,93 90,89,86,78**
CSF £28.97 TOTE £11.10: £2.40, £1.10, £1.90; EX 32.60 Trifecta £125.80.
Owner Donald R Dizney **Bred** Donald R Dizney Llc **Trained** Newmarket, Suffolk

FOCUS
Rail movement added 3.8yds to race distance. A modest maiden with the betting dominated by the pair with the best form and most experience. It looked initially as though they would stay in the centre of the track after the cutaway, but they ended up drifting to the inside rail.

7298 BRIGHTON & HOVE ALBION SUPPORTING AITC H'CAP (DIV I) 7f 214y
2:30 (2:30) (Class 6) (0-60,60) 3-Y-O+ **£2,911** (£866; £432; £216) **Stalls** Centre

Form RPR
1412 **1** **Admirable Art (IRE)**[31] 6407 6-9-2 55 ....(p) AdamKirby 2 65
(Tony Carroll) *mde virtually all: jnd by runner-up over 2f out: drvn ahd ins fnl f: gamely* **9/2**[2]
0111 **2** *2* **Titan Goddess**[9] 7062 4-8-10 56 .... KevinLundie(7) 11 61
(Mike Murphy) *mid-div: hdwy to join wnr over 2f out: unable qck ins fnl f* **1/1**[1]
0404 **3** *3 3/4* **Deluxe**[44] 5993 4-8-13 57 .... PaddyBradley(5) 9 54
(Pat Phelan) *towards rr: hdwy over 2f out: one pce appr fnl f* **14/1**
0001 **4** *3/4* **World Record (IRE)**[38] 6188 6-9-6 59 .... JimCrowley 6 54
(Mick Quinn) *pressed wnr tl over 2f out: sn outpcd* **9/2**[2]
2400 **5** *nse* **Lutine Charlie (IRE)**[8] 7070 9-8-11 50 ....(p) LukeMorris 8 45
(Emma Owen) *mid-div: rdn over 2f out: styd on fnl f* **25/1**
0626 **6** *1* **Touch Of Color**[17] 6826 3-8-9 56 .... CharlieBennett(5) 1 49
(Jane Chapple-Hyam) *prom: sltly lost pl 4f out: rallied over 1f out: no ex fnl f* **10/1**[3]
3050 **7** *4 1/2* **Big Red**[17] 6839 4-8-7 46 oh1 .... BarryMcHugh 5 28
(Rebecca Bastiman) *s.s: a towards rr: n.d fnl 3f* **25/1**
000 **8** *1* **Signal Hill (IRE)**[99] 3996 3-9-4 60 .... OisinMurphy 3 40
(Andrew Balding) *chsd ldrs tl wknd over 2f out* **14/1**
5200 **9** *2 3/4* **Ettie Hart (IRE)**[41] 6105 3-8-6 55 .... KillianHennessy(7) 7 29
(Mick Channon) *chsd ldrs tl wknd over 2f out* **20/1**
660 **10** *4 1/2* **Dark Phantom (IRE)**[16] 6853 5-8-3 47 oh1 ow1 ....(p) PaddyPilley(5) 10 10
(Geoffrey Deacon) *dwlt: a bhd* **66/1**
0300 **11** *5* **Ron's Ballad**[100] 3973 3-8-4 46 oh1 .... KieranO'Neill 4
(Michael Madgwick) *dwlt: a bhd* **66/1**

1m 33.33s (-2.67) **Going Correction** -0.175s/f (Firm)
WFA 3 from 4yo+ 3lb **11** Ran SP% **124.2**
Speed ratings (Par 101): **106,104,100,99,99 98,93,92,90,85 80**
CSF £9.48 CT £63.37 TOTE £5.60: £1.70, £1.10, £2.50; EX 12.00 Trifecta £116.70.
Owner D Morgan **Bred** Longview Stud & Bloodstock Ltd **Trained** Cropthorne, Worcs

FOCUS
Rail movement added 3.8yds to race distance. The first division of a moderate handicap with a rather lopsided betting market. This time the runners stayed centre to nearside after the cutaway and the first two came clear.

7299 BRIGHTON & HOVE ALBION SUPPORTING AITC H'CAP (DIV II) 7f 214y
3:05 (3:05) (Class 6) (0-60,58) 3-Y-O+ **£2,911** (£866; £432; £216) **Stalls** Centre

Form RPR
2163 **1** **Carcharias (IRE)**[9] 7048 3-9-3 57 .... JimCrowley 9 64
(Ed de Giles) *mde all: drvn clr ins fnl f: styd on wl* **2/1**[1]
0565 **2** *3 1/2* **Hawk Moth (IRE)**[9] 7036 8-9-6 57 ....(p) LukeMorris 4 56
(John Spearing) *dwlt: bhd: rdn and hdwy over 1f out: styd on to take 2nd nr fin* **6/1**[3]
3512 **3** *hd* **Edge (IRE)**[9] 7035 5-9-5 56 ....(b) StevieDonohoe 10 54
(Bernard Llewellyn) *dwlt: towards rr: hdwy 2f out: briefly wnt 2nd wl ins fnl f: styd on* **9/4**[2]
0050 **4** *3/4* **Bunker Hill Lass**[9] 7062 4-8-11 53 ....(p) AnnaHesketh(5) 3 50
(Michael Appleby) *prom: chsd wnr 2f out tl wl ins fnl f: one pce* **8/1**
00-0 **5** *1/2* **Sir Jamie**[33] 6317 3-8-5 45 .... TomMarquand 5 41
(Tony Carroll) *in tch: outpcd and struggling 3f out: styd on fr over 1f out* **20/1**
2350 **6** *3 1/2* **Fairy Mist (IRE)**[9] 7036 9-9-4 55 ....(b) WilliamCarson 6 43
(John Bridger) *in tch: outpcd 2f out: btn whn n.m.r and swtchd lft over 1f out* **9/1**
0F50 **7** *hd* **Machiavelian Storm (IRE)**[71] 3021 4-8-8 45 .... KieranO'Neill 1 32
(Richard Mitchell) *chsd wnr tl outpcd 2f out* **33/1**
0050 **8** *7* **Royal Acclaim (IRE)**[29] 6478 4-8-13 50 ....(b[1]) BarryMcHugh 7 21
(Rebecca Bastiman) *prom tl wknd 2f out* **10/1**

1m 33.77s (-2.23) **Going Correction** -0.175s/f (Firm)
WFA 3 from 4yo+ 3lb **8** Ran SP% **116.3**
Speed ratings (Par 101): **104,100,100,99,99 95,95,88**
CSF £14.97 CT £28.95 TOTE £2.60: £1.10, £1.60, £1.30; EX 14.40 Trifecta £31.40.
Owner Boardman, Golder, Sercombe & Viall I **Bred** Mrs Helen Walsh **Trained** Ledbury, H'fords

FOCUS
Rail movement added 3.8yds to race distance. Again they stayed nearside after the cutaway and it resulted in another all-the-way winner. The winning time was 0.44sec slower than the first division.

7300 ALBION IN THE COMMUNITY CHARITY H'CAP 1m 1f 209y
3:40 (3:40) (Class 6) (0-60,60) 3-Y-O+ **£2,911** (£866; £432; £216) **Stalls** High

Form RPR
3330 **1** **Maverik**[16] 6857 8-9-8 55 ....[1] TomMarquand 2 62
(Ali Stronge) *mde all: hrd rdn over 2f out: hld on wl* **6/1**
4361 **2** *1 1/4* **Moss Street**[14] 6890 6-9-8 55 ....(bt) DanielMuscutt 6 60
(John Flint) *s.i.s: hld up in 6th: hdwy 2f out: chsd wnr fnl f: styd on* **2/1**[1]
0050 **3** *1 1/4* **Troy Boy**[3] 7231 6-8-12 45 ....(b) BarryMcHugh 8 48
(Rebecca Bastiman) *sn rdn up to press wnr: one pce fnl f* **10/1**
0530 **4** *1 1/4* **Multigifted**[15] 6871 3-9-5 57 .... JimCrowley 5 57
(Michael Madgwick) *towards rr: rdn 4f out: styd on fr over 1f out* **4/1**[3]
5442 **5** *hd* **Gladys Cooper (IRE)**[12] 6966 3-9-4 56 .... LukeMorris 1 56
(Ed Walker) *prom: hrd rdn over 1f out: no ex fnl f* **7/2**[2]
1100 **6** *2 1/4* **Mount Cheiron (USA)**[16] 6857 5-9-3 57 ....(v) CallumRodriguez(7) 4 53
(Richard Ford) *in tch: rdn to chse ldrs 2f out: wknd fnl f* **10/1**
0660 **7** *60* **Skiff**[14] 6900 4-8-13 46 ....[1] FMBerry 7
(Brendan Powell) *in tch: wknd over 3f out: sn bhd: eased fnl 2f* **14/1**

2m 1.51s (-2.09) **Going Correction** -0.175s/f (Firm)
WFA 3 from 4yo+ 5lb **7** Ran SP% **114.7**
Speed ratings (Par 101): **101,100,99,98,97 96,48**
CSF £18.58 CT £118.22 TOTE £8.10: £3.20, £1.70; EX 24.10 Trifecta £127.20.
Owner Stuart Leigh & Margaret Kidger **Bred** J G Davis & Star Pointe Ltd **Trained** Eastbury, Berks

FOCUS
Rail movement added 3.8yds to race distance. Another moderate handicap and yet another race where the winner was left alone in front. Again they mainly stayed nearside.

7301 ALBIONINTHECOMMUNITY.ORG.UK H'CAP 6f 209y
4:15 (4:15) (Class 5) (0-75,75) 3-Y-O+ **£3,234** (£962; £481; £240) **Stalls** Centre

Form RPR
0000 **1** **Evanescent (IRE)**[15] 6879 7-9-0 71 .... GeorgeDowning(3) 4 79
(Tony Carroll) *mde all: hld on wl fnl f* **12/1**
0533 **2** *1/2* **Rio's Cliffs**[24] 6635 3-9-4 74 .... FMBerry 8 80
(Martyn Meade) *chsd ldrs: rdn over 2f out: r.o wl to take 2nd nr fin* **5/1**[1]
5035 **3** *nk* **Mockinbird (IRE)**[20] 6742 3-8-11 67 ....(v[1]) LukeMorris 9 72
(Sir Mark Prescott Bt) *pressed wnr: hung lft over 1f out: kpt on u.p: lost 2nd nr fin* **5/1**[1]
-030 **4** *nk* **In Haste (IRE)**[38] 6190 3-9-0 70 ....[1] ShaneKelly 5 74
(Eve Johnson Houghton) *cl up: pressed ldrs 2f out: kpt on u.p* **7/1**[2]
2200 **5** *3/4* **Black Caesar (IRE)**[18] 6806 5-9-1 69 .... WilliamTwiston-Davies 12 72
(Philip Hide) *prom: drvn to chal 2f out: one pce ins fnl f* **11/1**
2044 **6** *1/2* **Danecase**[15] 6878 3-9-4 74 .... FergusSweeney 11 75
(David Dennis) *dwlt: sn in midfield: rdn over 2f out: styd on fnl f* **7/1**[2]
0224 **7** *nk* **Time Medicean**[10] 7018 10-8-8 62 .... WilliamCarson 10 63
(Tony Carroll) *dwlt: towards rr: rdn 3f out: nrest at fin* **20/1**
0206 **8** *hd* **Good Luck Charm**[44] 5992 7-9-4 75 ....(b) HectorCrouch(3) 14 76
(Gary Moore) *dwlt: bhd tl styd on fr over 1f out* **12/1**
402 **9** *1 1/2* **Lunar Deity**[24] 6636 7-8-11 65 .... OisinMurphy 1 62
(Stuart Williams) *dwlt: sn in midfield: effrt 2f out: no imp over 1f out* **7/1**[2]
3640 **10** *2 1/4* **Newton's Law (IRE)**[21] 6699 5-9-0 75 ....(tp) JordanUys(7) 13 66
(Brian Meehan) *bhd: sme hdwy on inner over 1f out: sn fdd* **14/1**
0046 **11** *9* **Take A Note**[26] 6579 7-9-2 75 ....(p) MitchGodwin(5) 3 41
(Patrick Chamings) *a towards rr: n.d fnl 3f* **10/1**
0-00 **12** *3 1/4* **Los Cerritos (SWI)**[24] 6628 4-9-2 70 .... SaleemGolam 6 27
(Sophie Leech) *chsd ldrs tl wknd over 2f out* **66/1**
3251 **13** *34* **Pick A Little**[38] 6184 8-9-3 71 .... TimmyMurphy 2
(Michael Blake) *v.s.a: a wl bhd: eased over 2f out* **8/1**[3]

1m 21.87s (-1.23) **Going Correction** -0.175s/f (Firm)
WFA 3 from 4yo+ 2lb **13** Ran SP% **127.7**
Speed ratings (Par 103): **100,99,99,98,97 97,96,96,95,92 82,78,39**
CSF £75.91 CT £355.35 TOTE £25.70: £6.10, £2.60, £1.60; EX 170.60 Trifecta £1694.50.
Owner A W Carroll **Bred** Oliver Donlon **Trained** Cropthorne, Worcs

FOCUS
Rail movement added 3.8yds to race distance. A modest handicap and they finished in a bit of a heap. Again it was crucial to be handy with the winner making nearly all and most of the other principals racing handily. This time the runners tended to edge down the camber towards the inside late on.

7302 AITC GIVING PEOPLE A CHANCE H'CAP 5f 213y
4:50 (4:50) (Class 6) (0-55,55) 3-Y-O+ **£2,911** (£866; £432; £216) **Stalls** Centre

Form RPR
0530 **1** **Suni Dancer**[23] 6651 5-8-9 46 .... GeorgeDowning(3) 10 54
(Tony Carroll) *towards rr: sltly hmpd over 4f out: hdwy on outer 2f out: led 1f out: rdn out* **8/1**
6000 **2** *1* **National Service (USA)**[50] 5760 5-8-13 54 ....(tp) CallumRodriguez(7) 11 59+
(Richard Ford) *dwlt: hdwy 1/2-way: led briefly over 1f out: kpt on u.p* **9/1**
4103 **3** *1 1/2* **Buraug**[14] 6894 4-8-10 51 ....(b) LuluStanford(7) 2 52
(Milton Bradley) *chsd ldrs: drvn to chal 1f out: one pce* **6/1**[3]
0662 **4** *1/2* **The Reel Way (GR)**[14] 6894 5-8-12 46 .... JimmyQuinn 4 45
(Patrick Chamings) *led tl over 1f out: one pce* **5/1**[2]
0040 **5** *1* **Justice (IRE)**[196] 1164 3-8-11 46 oh1 .... RenatoSouza 16 42
(Jose Santos) *prom: hrd rdn over 1f out: no ex fnl f* **33/1**
005- **6** *nk* **Oddsocks (IRE)**[316] 8075 4-8-12 46 oh1 .... WilliamCarson 15 41
(Tony Carroll) *in tch: pushed along and squeezed for room over 2f out: styd on fnl f* **25/1**
0060 **7** *3/4* **Top Cop**[15] 6865 7-8-12 46 oh1 ....(p) OisinMurphy 3 39
(Ronald Harris) *chsd ldrs: one pce fnl 2f* **12/1**
0003 **8** *3/4* **Simply Black (IRE)**[14] 6902 5-8-8 47 oh1 ow1 ....(p) AnnStokell(5) 12 38
(Ann Stokell) *chsd ldrs tl squeezed for room 2f out* **20/1**
2260 **9** *2 1/4* **Picansort**[35] 6269 9-9-7 55 ....(b) ShaneKelly 8 39
(Peter Crate) *in tch: effrt 2f out: wknd over 1f out* **9/1**
3500 **10** *1 1/2* **Bushwise (IRE)**[16] 6852 3-9-6 55 ....(p) LukeMorris 6 34
(Milton Bradley) *prom tl ran and squeezed out 2f out* **20/1**
0056 **11** *1* **Ay Up Audrey**[7] 7092 5-8-12 46 oh1 ....(b[1]) BarryMcHugh 7 22
(Rebecca Bastiman) *dwlt: sn in midfield: rdn and btn 2f out* **16/1**
46-0 **12** *nk* **Gypsy Rider**[33] 6312 7-8-10 47 .... TimClark(3) 5 22
(Henry Tett) *sn outpcd towards rr* **16/1**
3500 **13** *7* **Arizona Snow**[101] 3953 4-9-4 52 ....(p) TomMarquand 9 6
(Ronald Harris) *a bhd* **14/1**
6006 **14** *5* **Back To Love (CAN)**[9] 7038 3-8-11 46 oh1 .... FMBerry 1
(Mark Gillard) *prom tl bdly hmpd on rail over 4f out: lost pl: sn bhd* **20/1**

The Form Book, Raceform Ltd, Newbury, RG14 5SJ

6006 **15** 3¾ **Hipz (IRE)**[14] 6894 5-9-5 **53**..(p) JimCrowley 13
(Laura Mongan) *v.s.a: a t.o* **4/1**[1]

1m 10.1s (-0.10) **Going Correction** -0.175s/f (Firm)
WFA 3 from 4yo+ 1lb **15** Ran SP% **129.3**
Speed ratings (Par 101): **93,91,89,89,87 87,86,85,82,80 78,78,69,62,57**
CSF £77.25 CT £489.84 TOTE £13.80: £4.20, £3.80, £2.50; EX 113.90 Trifecta £1532.40.
Owner Ian Furlong **Bred** Mickley Stud And Mr G A Greaves **Trained** Cropthorne, Worcs

FOCUS
Rail movement added 3.8yds to race distance. A moderate sprint handicap and again most of the principals were up there, which makes the winner's performance all the more creditable.

7303 SUPPORT ALBION IN THE COMMUNITY TODAY H'CAP 5f 59y
5:20 (5:20) (Class 5) (0-75,73) 3-Y-O+ **£3,234** (£962; £481; £240) **Stalls** Centre

Form RPR
2031 **1** **Bahamian Sunrise**[29] 6479 4-9-4 **70**........................(p) FergusSweeney 10 78
(John Gallagher) *w ldr at str pce: led 2f out: hld on wl* **7/1**[3]
0505 **2** ½ **Taajub (IRE)**[22] 6669 9-9-4 **73**.. HectorCrouch(3) 9 79
(Peter Crate) *mid-div: hdwy on inner to chal 1f out: r.o* **7/1**[3]
34 **3** *hd* **One Big Surprise**[52] 5725 4-9-4 **70**..................................(p) ShaneKelly 4 75
(Richard Hughes) *off the pce in 5th: r.o wl fr over 1f out: clsng at fin* **11/2**[1]
3003 **4** ¾ **Welease Bwian (IRE)**[31] 6410 7-8-11 **70**...................... MillyNaseb(7) 11 73
(Stuart Williams) *outpcd towards rr: gd late hdwy* **8/1**
6550 **5** *1* **Pink Martini (IRE)**[21] 6699 3-9-6 **72**..............................(t) OisinMurphy 8 72
(Joseph Tuite) *outpcd towards rr: r.o fr over 1f out: nrest at fin* **13/2**[2]
0653 **6** *2* **Noble Asset**[22] 6669 5-9-0 **69**.................................... EdwardGreatrex(3) 6 61
(Milton Bradley) *led at str pce tl 2f out: no ex 1f out* **13/2**[2]
6650 **7** ¾ **Whitecrest**[17] 6831 8-8-13 **65**.. TomMarquand 3 55
(John Spearing) *outpcd towards rr tl styd on fr over 1f out* **22/1**
6444 **8** *nk* **Desert Command**[123] 3193 6-9-7 **73**...............................(p) LukeMorris 1 62
(Robert Cowell) *chsd clr ldrs in 3rd tl fdd fnl 2f* **9/1**
5200 **9** *1* **Go Nani Go**[15] 6878 10-9-0 **71**.. GeorgiaCox(5) 7 56
(Ed de Giles) *outpcd towards rr: sme hdwy 2f out: no imp fnl f* **12/1**
3014 **10** 2½ **Vale Of Flight (IRE)**[23] 6660 3-9-0 **66**.............................. JimCrowley 2 43
(Rae Guest) *dwlt: sn rcvrd but off the pce in 4th: wknd 2f out* **7/1**[3]
540 **11** *11* **Angelito**[17] 6832 7-8-8 **63** ow1.. TimClark(3) 5 1
(Tony Newcombe) *s.s: outpcd: sn wl bhd* **12/1**

1m 1.71s (-0.59) **Going Correction** -0.175s/f (Firm) **11** Ran SP% **120.4**
Speed ratings (Par 103): **97,96,95,94,93 89,88,88,86,82 65**
CSF £56.78 CT £299.72 TOTE £7.70: £3.00, £2.70, £2.40; EX 60.50 Trifecta £1076.90.
Owner Caveat Emptor Partnership **Bred** Mel Roberts & Ms Nicola Meese **Trained** Chastleton, Oxon

FOCUS
Rail movement added 3.8yds to race distance. An ordinary if wide open sprint handicap and they went hard up front, but the winner was on the pace throughout. They certainly used the full width of the track in the second half of the contest.
T/Jkpt: Not Won. T/Plt: £10.10 to a £1 stake. Pool: £67894.21, 4886.67 winning units T/Qpdt: £4.60 to a £1 stake. Pool: £5275.15, 832.3 winning units **Lee McKenzie**

7200 CHELMSFORD (A.W) (L-H)
Thursday, October 13

OFFICIAL GOING: Polytrack: standard
Wind: light, half against Weather: dry

7304 BET TOTEPLACEPOT AT BETFRED.COM MAIDEN AUCTION STKS 1m (P)
5:50 (5:50) (Class 5) 2-Y-O **£3,557** (£1,058; £529; £264) **Stalls** Low

Form RPR
02 **1** **Claire's Secret**[49] 5792 2-8-7 0.................................... SilvestreDeSousa 2 66
(Philip McBride) *mde all: rdn over 1f out: styd on and a doing enough ins fnl f: rdn out* **1/1**[1]
0620 **2** ½ **Masonic (IRE)**[12] 6950 2-8-8 72............................ JosephineGordon(3) 6 69
(Robyn Brisland) *trckd ldng pair: wnt 2nd 2f out: sn drvn and unable qck: styd on u.p fnl 100yds: nvr enough pce to get to wnr* **5/4**[2]
0466 **3** *13* **Winning Bid**[31] 6404 2-8-13 66...................................(v[1]) PatCosgrave 1 40
(Harry Dunlop) *trckd wnr tl 2f out: sn u.p and btn 3rd over 1f out: fdd fnl f* **5/1**[3]
00 **4** *4* **Wind In The Trees (FR)**[24] 6639 2-8-10 0..................... SteveDrowne 4 27
(George Baker) *bmpd leaving stalls: sn detached in last: nvr on terms* **33/1**

1m 41.43s (1.53) **Going Correction** -0.125s/f (Stan) **4** Ran SP% **114.1**
Speed ratings (Par 95): **87,86,73,69**
CSF £2.77 TOTE £2.20; EX 2.60 Trifecta £3.50.
Owner Howard J Cooke **Bred** M C Humby **Trained** Newmarket, Suffolk

FOCUS
The track was power harrowed to four inches and gallop master finished to two inches. A weak juvenile maiden in which the form can be rated around the runner-up.

7305 BET TOTEJACKPOT AT BETFRED.COM NURSERY H'CAP 6f (P)
6:20 (6:20) (Class 4) (0-85,85) 2-Y-O **£4,204** (£1,251; £625; £312) **Stalls** Centre

Form RPR
0514 **1** **White Chin (IRE)**[21] 6697 2-8-9 **73**............................ RichardKingscote 2 83
(Tom Dascombe) *hld up in tch: hdwy and swtchd rt over 1f out: chsd wnr 1f out: chal and hung lft ins fnl f: led 100yds: stl hanging but r.o wl* **6/1**[3]
21 **2** *2* **Dubai One (IRE)**[15] 6867 2-9-1 **79**.. AndreaAtzeni 1 83
(Saeed bin Suroor) *broke wl: stdd to trck ldrs: swtchd rt and jnd ldrs over 1f out: sn rdn and qcknd to ld: hdd 100yds out: nt match pce of wnr but kpt on for clr 2nd* **2/1**[1]
441 **3** *4* **Glorious Rocket**[22] 6673 2-9-2 **80**.. AdamKirby 9 72
(Luca Cumani) *hld up in tch towards rr: hdwy on outer over 1f out: hung lft 1f out: wnt 3rd ins fnl f: kpt on but no threat to ldng pair* **7/1**
31 **4** 2¼ **Maakaasib**[86] 4473 2-9-7 **85**.. RobertHavlin 3 70
(Simon Crisford) *sn led: rdn and hdd over 1f out: unable qck and btn 3rd 1f out: wknd ins fnl f* **10/3**[2]
221 **5** 1¾ **Zamjar**[98] 4047 2-9-4 **82**.. FrankieDettori 8 62
(Ed Dunlop) *pressed ldr tl rdn and unable qck over 1f out: wknd fnl f* **8/1**
6510 **6** *nk* **Halawain (USA)**[27] 6536 2-8-12 **76**.................................... PatCosgrave 6 55
(John Quinn) *t.k.h: hld up in tch towards rr: effrt over 1f out: outpcd 1f out: wl hld and styd on same pce fnl f* **33/1**
445 **7** *nse* **Kreb's Cycle (IRE)**[10] 7004 2-9-7 **85**.............................. KieranO'Neill 5 64
(Richard Hannon) *racd in last pair: effrt u.p on inner over 1f out: no imp ins fnl f: nvr threatened ldrs* **14/1**
166 **8** 1¾ **Nile Empress**[46] 5931 2-8-9 **76**............................ JosephineGordon(3) 10 50
(Hugo Palmer) *chsd ldrs: effrt and unable qck over 1f out: wknd fnl f* **33/1**
01 **9** *1* **Melissa Jane**[21] 6696 2-8-7 **71**.................................. SilvestreDeSousa 4 42
(Henry Spiller) *chsd ldrs: rdn and lost pl over 1f out: wknd fnl f* **8/1**
4542 **10** 1¾ **Bizet (IRE)**[32] 6369 2-8-11 **75**..(p) StevieDonohoe 7 40
(John Ryan) *bhd: swtchd rt and effrt over 1f out: no imp: n.d* **25/1**
5240 **11** 4½ **Logi (IRE)**[77] 4802 2-9-0 **78**.. SeanLevey 12 30
(Richard Hannon) *pressed ldrs: losing pl u.p whn short of room over 1f out: wknd fnl f* **25/1**

1m 12.46s (-1.24) **Going Correction** -0.125s/f (Stan) **11** Ran SP% **125.7**
Speed ratings (Par 97): **103,100,95,92,89 89,89,86,85,83 77**
CSF £19.06 CT £91.95 TOTE £7.40: £2.90, £1.50, £2.60; EX 29.20 Trifecta £221.20.
Owner T Dascombe **Bred** Old Carhue & Graeng Bloodstock **Trained** Malpas, Cheshire

FOCUS
A competitive nursery featuring a handful of last-time-out maiden winners, and while they didn't go a breakneck pace, none of the trio that set the pace were placed. It paid to be drawn low.

7306 BET TOTEQUADPOT AT BETFRED.COM MAIDEN STKS (DIV I) 7f (P)
6:50 (6:53) (Class 5) 2-Y-O **£3,881** (£1,155; £577; £288) **Stalls** Low

Form RPR
553 **1** **Thaaqib**[32] 6368 2-9-5 77.. PaulHanagan 6 77
(Charles Hills) *chsd ldr: clsd and upsides 2f out: rdn over 1f out: led and edgd lft ins fnl f: kpt on: rdn out* **5/1**[3]
2025 **2** ½ **Bolt Phantom (USA)**[21] 6697 2-9-5 79..................(p) SilvestreDeSousa 4 76
(Ismail Mohammed) *chsd ldrs: 3rd whn edgd lft u.p and outpcd over 1f out: rallied ins fnl f: swtchd rt and styd on to go 2nd towards fin: nvr quite getting to wnr* **3/1**[2]
2240 **3** ½ **Fortune Of War**[21] 6705 2-9-0 77................................ CharlieBennett(5) 5 74
(Jane Chapple-Hyam) *led: rdn and jnd ent fnl 2f: hdd 1f out and carried lft ins fnl f: wknd and lost 2nd towards fin* **10/1**
4 2¾ **Blue On Blue (USA)** 2-9-5 0..[1] FrankieDettori 1 67
(John Gosden) *s.i.s: towards rr: clsd and in tch in midfield 4f out: rdn 3f out: modest 5th 1f out: kpt on steadily ins fnl f: nvr threatened ldrs* **11/10**[1]
06 **5** *2* **Veiled Secret (IRE)**[14] 6904 2-9-5 0.................................. RyanPowell 2 61
(Sir Mark Prescott Bt) *dwlt and niggled along in rr: hdwy 1f out: styd on to pass btn horses ins fnl f: nvr trbld ldrs* **100/1**
0 **6** ½ **Sliceoflife**[166] 1850 2-9-5 0.. AndreaAtzeni 10 60
(Marco Botti) *chsd ldrs tl unable qck over 1f out: wknd ins fnl f* **25/1**
7 1¼ **Sureyoutoldme (IRE)** 2-9-5 0.. SeanLevey 9 57
(Richard Hannon) *s.i.s: hld up in last trio: swtchd rt and effrt over 1f out: kpt on same pce after: nvr trbld ldrs* **25/1**
F34 **8** ¾ **Paddy A (IRE)**[26] 6590 2-9-0 0.. CliffordLee(5) 8 55
(Philip McBride) *midfield: rdn and hung lft over 1f out: no hdwy and wknd fnl f* **20/1**
00 **9** *34* **Jupiter Ascending**[7] 7100 2-9-5 0.................................. AndrewMullen 7
(Michael Appleby) *in tch in midfield: u.p and losing pl 3f out: bhd over 1f out: t.o* **100/1**

1m 27.04s (-0.16) **Going Correction** -0.125s/f (Stan) **9** Ran SP% **112.8**
Speed ratings (Par 95): **95,94,93,90,88 87,86,85,46**
CSF £18.01 TOTE £5.50: £1.20, £1.30, £2.70; EX 14.50 Trifecta £68.60.
Owner Hamdan Al Maktoum **Bred** Panda Bloodstock **Trained** Lambourn, Berks
■ Solajan was withdrawn. Price at time of withdrawal 14/1. Rule 4 applies to all bets - deduct 5p in the pound.

FOCUS
A moderate juvenile maiden that fell to the horse with the best form. They went a sedate pace.

7307 BET TOTEQUADPOT AT BETFRED.COM MAIDEN STKS (DIV II) 7f (P)
7:20 (7:22) (Class 5) 2-Y-O **£3,881** (£1,155; £577; £288) **Stalls** Low

Form RPR
24 **1** **Voice Of Truth (IRE)**[41] 6099 2-9-0 0...................... SilvestreDeSousa 6 76
(Saeed bin Suroor) *chsd ldr: rdn to chal over 1f out: drvn to ld 1f out: kpt on: drvn out* **9/4**[1]
2 *nk* **Cliffs Of Capri** 2-9-5 0.. FrankieDettori 3 80
(Simon Crisford) *sn dropped to rr: nt clr run wl over 1f out: swtchd rt ent fnl f: hdwy between horses jst ins fnl f: r.o wl to go 2nd towards fin: nvr quite getting to wnr* **11/2**[3]
0 **3** ¾ **Oud Metha Bridge (IRE)**[22] 6673 2-9-5 0........................ PatCosgrave 1 78
(Ed Dunlop) *in tch in last pair: swtchd rt and hung lft over 1f out: hdwy 1f out: edgd lft but r.o wl ins fnl f: wnt 3rd towards fin* **20/1**
44 **4** *1* **Asaas (USA)**[90] 4349 2-9-5 0...(b[1]) AndreaAtzeni 9 75
(Roger Varian) *chsd ldrs tl led 5f out: drvn and hdd over 1f out: styd on same pce ins fnl f: lost 2 pls towards fin* **9/4**[1]
6 **5** ½ **Muscika**[27] 6543 2-9-5 0.. PaulHanagan 2 74
(Richard Hannon) *hld up in tch in midfield: effrt to chse ldrs and edgd lft over 1f out: stl edging lft and styd on same pce ins fnl f* **8/1**
3 **6** *5* **Dutch Quality**[22] 6671 2-9-5 0.. HarryBentley 5 61
(Marco Botti) *in tch in midfield: effrt in 4th jst over 2f out: unable qck u.p over 1f out: wknd ins fnl f* **9/2**[2]
0 **7** *2* **Magdalene Fox**[22] 6671 2-9-5 0.. MartinHarley 7 55
(Ed Dunlop) *chsd ldrs: rdn 3f out: unable qck and lost pl jst over 1f out: wknd ins fnl f* **66/1**
8 *6* **Torqit (IRE)** 2-9-5 0.. DannyBrock 4 39
(John Ryan) *in tch in last trio: rdn 2f out: sn struggling and hung lft: wknd fnl f* **33/1**

1m 26.26s (-0.94) **Going Correction** -0.125s/f (Stan) **8** Ran SP% **115.4**
Speed ratings (Par 95): **100,99,98,97,97 91,89,82**
CSF £15.29 TOTE £2.90: £1.10, £2.40, £4.20; EX 16.30 Trifecta £170.00.
Owner Godolphin **Bred** Darley **Trained** Newmarket, Suffolk

FOCUS
The second division of this moderate maiden was run in a 0.78s faster time.

7308 BET TOTEEXACTA AT BETFRED.COM H'CAP 7f (P)
7:50 (7:51) (Class 4) (0-85,85) 3-Y-O+ **£5,175** (£1,540; £769; £384) **Stalls** Low

Form RPR
0500 **1** **Firmdecisions (IRE)**[28] 6529 6-9-4 **82**............................ PatCosgrave 10 90+
(Dean Ivory) *hld up in tch in last quartet: effrt over 1f out: hdwy 1f out: str run ins fnl f to ld last strides* **12/1**
2040 **2** *hd* **Alejandro (IRE)**[19] 6764 7-9-5 **83**.. DavidNolan 3 90
(David O'Meara) *chsd ldrs: effrt and swtchd rt over 1f out: drvn and ev ch ins fnl f: styd on to ld cl home: hdd last strides* **8/1**
0000 **3** *nk* **Baddilini**[24] 6627 6-9-2 **85**..(p) PaddyPilley(5) 1 91
(Alan Bailey) *led: rdn over 1f out: battled on wl u.p tl hdd and lost 2 pls last strides* **16/1**
0001 **4** *nk* **Room Key**[30] 6466 4-9-1 **84**.. HollieDoyle(5) 8 89
(Eve Johnson Houghton) *chsd ldrs: effrt to chse ldr jst over 2f out: ev ch fnl f: kpt on but unable qck towards fin* **12/1**
3003 **5** 1¾ **Plucky Dip**[28] 6529 5-9-4 **82**.. DannyBrock 6 83
(John Ryan) *chsd ldrs: effrt ent fnl 2f: styd on same pce ins fnl f* **7/1**[3]

1556 **6** ¾ **Welliesinthewater (IRE)**[40] 6126 6-9-2 **80**..................(v) MartinLane 12 79
(Derek Shaw) *hld up in tch in last quartet: effrt over 1f out: hdwy whn nt clr run and swtchd rt ins fnl f: styd on towards fin: nt rch ldrs* **8/1**

5262 **7** ¾ **Like No Other**[18] 6810 3-9-2 **82**.. DavidAllan 7 78
(Les Eyre) *hld up in tch last quartet: nt clrest of runs 2f out: effrt over 1f out: kpt on ins fnl f: no threat to ldrs* **10/1**

2134 **8** *nse* **Twin Point**[28] 6529 5-8-13 **77**......................................(t) StevieDonohoe 5 73
(Charlie Fellowes) *in tch in midfield: effrt over 1f out unable qck and styd on same pce ins fnl f* **5/1**[1]

5004 **9** *1* **Jammy Guest (IRE)**[8] 7066 6-9-2 **80**................................ AdamKirby 9 74
(George Margarson) *s.i.s: bhd: clsd onto bk of field 1/2-way: rdn and hdwy over 1f out: no imp ins fnl f* **8/1**

45 **10** *1 ¾* **Storm King**[47] 5866 7-9-1 **79**...................................(p) MartinHarley 2 68
(David C Griffiths) *chsd ldr tl over 2f out: edgd rt and rdn wl over 1f out: wknd ins fnl f* **8/1**

1306 **11** *11* **Case Key**[18] 6810 3-8-9 **75**..[1] AndrewMullen 4 33
(Michael Appleby) *in tch in midfield: rdn over 2f out: lost pl and btn over 1f out: bhd and eased ins fnl f* **33/1**

3000 **12** *17* **Irish Eclare (IRE)**[3] 7206 3-8-12 **78**....................... SilvestreDeSousa 14
(Charles Hills) *dwlt: sn in tch in midfield: pushed along 1/2-way: lost pl and bhd 2f out: lost tch and eased fnl f: t.o* **6/1**[2]

030- **13** *17* **Starfield**[497] 2861 7-9-4 **85**..(v) RobHornby(3) 13
(Mandy Rowland) *in tch in midfield on outer: rdn and struggling 2f out: sn lost pl: bhd and eased fnl f: t.o* **50/1**

1m 25.15s (-2.05) **Going Correction** -0.125s/f (Stan)
WFA 3 from 4yo+ 2lb **13** Ran SP% **123.2**
Speed ratings (Par 105): **106,105,105,105,103 102,101,101,100,98 85,66,46**
CSF £108.08 CT £1616.76 TOTE £15.10: £4.10, £3.20, £5.00; EX 114.60 Trifecta £2107.40.
Owner White Bear Racing **Bred** Thomas O'Meara **Trained** Radlett, Herts

FOCUS
An average handicap and they went a moderate gallop, resulting in a bunched finish. It was an advantage to race prominently.

7309 BET TOTETRIFECTA AT BETFRED.COM H'CAP 2m (P)
8:20 (8:21) (Class 6) (0-60,60) 3-Y-O **£3,234** (£962; £481; £240) **Stalls** Low

Form RPR

063 **1** **Work (IRE)**[38] 6185 3-8-7 **46**... HarryBentley 1 53
(David Simcock) *hld up in midfield and travelled wl: swtchd rt and effrt wl over 1f out: rdn to ld over 1f out: styd on wl ins fnl f: rdn out* **8/1**

5503 **2** *3 ½* **Shrubland**[7] 7104 3-9-1 **54**...................................(b) SilvestreDeSousa 10 57
(Ed Walker) *chsd ldrs tl wnt 2nd after 4f: led over 2f out: drvn and hdd over 1f out: kpt on same pce ins fnl f* **7/2**[1]

0-01 **3** *shd* **Madame Claud**[113] 3509 3-9-7 **60**.................... WilliamTwiston-Davies 5 63
(Hughie Morrison) *dwlt: hld up in tch in rr: travelling wl and stuck bhd horses over 2f out: effrt over 1f out: plugged on same pce ins fnl f* **4/1**[2]

6334 **4** *shd* **Le Tissier**[21] 6698 3-9-7 **60**..(p) KierenFox 3 63
(Michael Attwater) *t.k.h: chsd ldr for 4f: styd chsng ldrs: rdn to go 2nd over 2f out tl unable qck over 1f out: kpt on same pce ins fnl f* **9/1**

2513 **5** *1 ½* **Skylark Lady (IRE)**[11] 6367 3-9-7 **60**................................ AdamKirby 4 61
(Michael Wigham) *dwlt: in tch in midfield: rdn 6f out: drvn to chse ldrs over 2f out: unable qck over 1f out: kpt on same pce ins fnl f* **9/2**[3]

0500 **6** *12* **Master Of Heaven**[14] 6890 3-8-13 **52**..........................(p) PatCosgrave 7 38
(Jim Boyle) *t.k.h: hld up in tch in last pair: rdn and effrt over 2f out: no imp and btn over 1f out: wknd fnl f* **16/1**

0544 **7** *4 ½* **Permera**[28] 6508 3-8-12 **51**.. StevieDonohoe 6 32
(Mark H Tompkins) *broke wl: stdd bk and in tch in midfield: effrt to chse ldrs over 2f out: no ex and lost pl over 1f out: wknd fnl f* **20/1**

135 **8** *11* **Top Of The Rocks (FR)**[20] 6730 3-9-3 **56**..........(tp) RichardKingscote 8 24
(Tom Dascombe) *sn led: rdn 4f out: hdd over 2f out: sn bhd* **7/1**

0642 **P** **Graceful Lady**[21] 6698 3-9-2 **55**....................................... AndreaAtzeni 9
(Robert Eddery) *t.k.h: chsd ldrs: shkn up 4f out: sn lost pl and eased: t.o and p.u jst ins fnl f* **8/1**

3m 31.67s (1.67) **Going Correction** -0.125s/f (Stan) **9** Ran SP% **115.8**
Speed ratings (Par 99): **90,88,88,88,87 81,79,73,**
CSF £36.26 CT £130.30 TOTE £10.80: £2.30, £1.60, £2.00; EX 46.40 Trifecta £321.10.
Owner Andrew Whitlock Racing Ltd **Bred** T Jones **Trained** Newmarket, Suffolk

FOCUS
A weak staying handicap in which they went only a moderate gallop.

7310 TOTEPOOL BETTING AT BETFRED.COM H'CAP 1m (P)
8:50 (8:51) (Class 6) (0-65,65) 3-Y-O+ **£3,234** (£962; £481; £240) **Stalls** Low

Form RPR

6550 **1** **Foie Gras**[21] 6700 6-9-4 **62**.....................................(p) SilvestreDeSousa 7 70
(Chris Dwyer) *hld up in tch in last quartet: effrt and swtchd lft over 1f out: hdwy u.p to chse ldrs 1f out: r.o to ld wl ins fnl f: rdn out* **14/1**

0505 **2** ¾ **Tommy's Secret**[21] 6700 6-9-0 **63**.......................... CharlieBennett(5) 1 69
(Jane Chapple-Hyam) *broke wl: stdd to chse ldrs: effrt to chal over 1f out: rdn to ld 1f out: drvn ins fnl f: hdd and one pced wl ins fnl f* **5/2**[1]

1134 **3** *2* **Barnaby Brook (CAN)**[14] 6890 6-8-12 **63**............(b) SamuelClarke(7) 14 65
(Robyn Brisland) *midfield and stuck wd: hdwy to chse ldrs 4f out: rdn over 1f out: kpt on same pce ins fnl f* **6/1**[3]

0102 **4** ¾ **Polar Kite (IRE)**[155] 2153 8-9-4 **65**.............................. RobHornby(3) 6 65
(Michael Attwater) *hld up in tch in midfield: effrt over 1f out: kpt on same pce ins fnl f* **20/1**

6033 **5** *nk* **Dukes Meadow**[28] 6512 5-8-7 **58**................................ RhiainIngram(7) 8 57
(Roger Ingram) *chsd ldrs: effrt over 1f out: unable qck 1f out: styd on same pce after* **10/1**

5010 **6** *nk* **Stun Gun**[21] 6700 6-9-6 **64**...(p) MartinLane 4 63
(Derek Shaw) *led: rdn over 1f out: hdd 1f out: no ex and wknd wl ins fnl f* **8/1**

060 **7** *2 ¾* **Yasood (IRE)**[11] 6051 3-8-12 **62**........................[1] JosephineGordon(3) 12 54
(Phil McEntee) *hld up in midfield: rdn ent fnl 2f: edgd lft u.p over 1f out: no imp fnl f* **50/1**

6621 **8** ½ **Rock Icon**[68] 5167 3-9-0 **61**... JimmyQuinn 11 52
(Patrick Chamings) *hld up in tch in midfield: swtchd rt and effrt u.p over 1f out: no imp: wl hld and kpt on same pce fnl f* **8/1**

350- **9** *2* **Caledonian Gold**[353] 7507 3-8-10 **62**............................. CliffordLee(5) 3 48
(Paul D'Arcy) *taken down early: t.k.h: chsd ldrs tl unable qck and outpcd over 1f out: wknd ins fnl f* **20/1**

0140 **10** *1* **The Happy Hammer (IRE)**[89] 4388 10-9-0 **65**......... LuluStanford(7) 10 49
(Eugene Stanford) *hld up in tch in last quartet: rdn and sme hdwy whn nt clr run: hmpd and swtchd rt over 1f out: no imp and wl hld fnl f* **20/1**

002- **11** *5* **Battle Of Bosworth (IRE)**[399] 6236 3-9-1 **62**............(b[1]) MartinHarley 2 35
(Paul Cole) *in tch in midfield: lost pl u.p and btn over 1f out: wknd fnl f* **5/1**[2]

-406 **12** *1* **Bukle (IRE)**[76] 4818 3-9-4 **65**... AdamKirby 5 35
(Rod Millman) *pressed ldr tl lost pl qckly over 1f out: fdd ins fnl f* **11/1**

2400 **13** *5* **Fishergate**[24] 6629 3-8-10 **57**...................................... RyanPowell 9 16
(Richard Rowe) *s.i.s: a bhd* **66/1**

2250 **14** *2* **Whip Up A Frenzy (IRE)**[31] 6411 4-8-8 **52**.............. AdamBeschizza 13 6
(Richard Rowe) *s.i.s: a bhd* **33/1**

1m 39.17s (-0.73) **Going Correction** -0.125s/f (Stan)
WFA 3 from 4yo+ 3lb **14** Ran SP% **126.5**
Speed ratings (Par 101): **98,97,95,94,94 93,91,90,88,87 82,81,76,74**
CSF £47.94 CT £256.27 TOTE £16.90: £4.60, £1.80, £2.10; EX 69.80 Trifecta £466.00.
Owner Mrs Shelley Dwyer **Bred** Sir Eric Parker **Trained** Newmarket, Suffolk

FOCUS
A moderate handicap in which they went a good gallop.

7311 BOOK YOUR CHRISTMAS PARTY AT CCR MAIDEN STKS 7f (P)
9:20 (9:22) (Class 5) 3-Y-O+ **£3,234** (£962; £481; £240) **Stalls** Low

Form RPR

23-2 **1** **Rockley Point**[9] 7061 3-9-0 75.. CliffordLee(5) 2 75
(Paul D'Arcy) *mde all: rdn over 1f out: styd on wl ins fnl f: rdn out* **6/1**[2]

2 **2** ¾ **Wealth Tax**[28] 6511 3-9-5 0... MartinHarley 10 73
(Ed Dunlop) *hld up in tch in midfield: rdn and hdwy over 1f out: styd on u.p ins fnl f: wnt 2nd last strides: nvr getting to wnr* **6/1**[2]

4 **3** *nk* **Loveatfirstsight**[22] 6674 3-9-0 0................................ AdamBeschizza 8 67
(Michael Attwater) *hld up wl in tch in midfield: hdwy u.p over 1f out: chsd wnr ins fnl f: kpt on but nvr getting to wnr: lost 2nd last strides* **40/1**

2 **4** *1 ¼* **Barjeel (USA)**[14] 6905 3-9-5 0...................................... PaulHanagan 6 69
(William Haggas) *hld up in tch in midfield: rdn over 1f out: styd on same pce and nvr getting on terms w wnr ins fnl f* **1/2**[1]

30 **5** *1 ¾* **Jazz Cat (IRE)**[30] 6441 3-9-0 0..............................[1] SilvestreDeSousa 1 59
(Paul Cole) *chsd ldrs: effrt to chse clr wnr over 1f out: kpt on same pce and no imp: lost 2nd ins fnl f: wknd towards fin* **16/1**

00 **6** *2 ¾* **Captain Courageous (IRE)**[10] 7009 3-9-5 0.............. ThomasBrown 4 57+
(Ed Walker) *s.i.s: wl off the pce in rr: hdwy over 1f out: swtchd lft and pushed along 1f out: r.o wl ins fnl f: nvr trbld ldrs* **16/1**

4 **7** *1 ¼* **Ross Raith Rover**[9] 7061 3-9-5 0.................................. JackMitchell 3 53
(Robert Eddery) *in tch in midfield: rdn 3f out: sn outpcd: wl hld and kpt on same pce fr over 1f out* **25/1**

8 *3* **Spring Of Hope** 3-9-5 0.. RobertHavlin 5 45
(Simon Crisford) *chsd wnr: rdn and lost 2nd over 1f out: sn btn and wknd fnl f* **9/1**[3]

0-0 **9** *5* **Wild Bloom**[187] 1337 3-9-0 0.. HarryBentley 11 27
(Ed Vaughan) *midfield but nvr on terms w ldrs: effrt and no hdwy over 1f out: wl hld and eased ins fnl f* **40/1**

05 **10** *3 ¾* **Sonnentanz (IRE)**[35] 6251 3-9-0 0................................ SteveDrowne 13 17
(Daniel Kubler) *a off the pce towards rr: rdn 2f out: no hdwy* **100/1**

11 *1 ½* **Pleadings (USA)** 3-9-5 0... KierenFox 14 17
(Charlie Wallis) *s.i.s: rn green and a rr* **50/1**

12 *3 ¼* **Annabella** 3-9-0 0... RyanTate 12 4
(Tim McCarthy) *v.s.a: n.d* **100/1**

0 **13** *2 ½* **Stylish Queen**[260] 352 3-8-11 0............................... SimonPearce(3) 15
(Lydia Pearce) *sn bhd: n.d* **200/1**

00- **14** *19* **Nofizzophobia**[334] 7861 3-9-0 0...................................... MartinLane 7
(Derek Shaw) *a towards rr: hung rt and eased 2f out: t.o* **150/1**

1m 25.44s (-1.76) **Going Correction** -0.125s/f (Stan) **14** Ran SP% **130.8**
Speed ratings (Par 103): **105,104,103,102,100 97,95,92,86,82 80,76,74,52**
CSF £44.90 TOTE £8.80: £2.20, £2.00, £4.00; EX 70.50 Trifecta £374.00.
Owner Rowley Racing **Bred** Newsells Park Stud **Trained** Newmarket, Suffolk

FOCUS
An average maiden, but the odds-on favourite disappointed and there was a surprise winner.
T/Plt: £323.60 to a £1 stake. Pool of £93740.65 - 211.45 winning tickets. T/Qpdt: £63.60 to a £1 stake. Pool of £11494.80 - 133.66 winning tickets. **Steve Payne**

6913 LYON PARILLY (R-H)
Thursday, October 13

OFFICIAL GOING: Turf: good to soft

7312a PRIX ANDRE BABOIN - GRAND PRIX DES PROVINCES (GROUP 3) (3YO+) (TURF) 1m 2f
1:20 (12:00) 3-Y-O+ **£29,411** (£11,764; £8,823; £5,882; £2,941)

RPR

1 **Subway Dancer (IRE)**[14] 4-9-0 0..................................... RadekKoplik 4 106
(Z Koplik, Czech Republic) *sn led and mde rest: rdn over 2f out: styd on wl against rail and asserted: comf* **113/10**

2 *3 ½* **Master's Spirit (IRE)**[9] 5-9-0 0.................................... FranckBlondel 1 99+
(J Reynier, France) *hld up in midfield: rdn into st: wnt 2nd over 1f out: styd on wl enough fnl f but no real imp on wnr* **37/10**[3]

3 *snk* **Alakhana (FR)**[29] 6497 3-8-6 0....................................... MaximeGuyon 3 96+
(F Head, France) *midfield: rdn and outpcd into st: rallied u.p and styd on into 3rd fnl f but no threat to wnr* **5/2**[1]

4 *3 ½* **Johara (IRE)**[8] 7087 5-8-10 0... AlexisBadel 2 88+
(H-F Devin, France) *trckd wnr: rdn into st: sn outpcd: no ex and fdd into 4th fnl f* **12/1**

5 *1* **Baz (FR)**[19] 6798 6-9-0 0....................................(b) Pierre-CharlesBoudot 5 90+
(F-H Graffard, France) *s.i.s and hld up: rdn into st: plugged on wout ever threatening* **47/10**

6 *1 ½* **Bonusdargent (FR)**[19] 6798 4-9-0 0.......................... MickaelBarzalona 6 87
(Mme Pia Brandt, France) *trckd wnr: rdn and outpcd early in st: sn wknd* **17/5**[2]

7 *3 ½* **Khaleesy (IRE)**[60] 5451 3-8-6 0...................................... GregoryBenoist 7 77
(F Rohaut, France) *hld up: rdn in last 2f out: no imp and sn btn* **73/10**

2m 14.87s (134.87)
WFA 3 from 4yo+ 5lb **7** Ran SP% **118.0**
WIN (incl. 1 euro stake): 12.30. PLACES: 4.30., 2.40. SF: 48.00.
Owner Bonanza **Bred** Haras De Saint Pair **Trained** Czech Republic

6775 HAYDOCK (L-H)

Friday, October 14

OFFICIAL GOING: Good (9.1)

Wind: Moderate half behind Weather: Cloudy

7313 ST HELENS STAR NURSERY H'CAP 5f

1:30 (1:30) (Class 5) (0-75,75) 2-Y-O **£3,234** (£962; £481; £240) **Stalls** Centre

Form RPR

1515 **1** **Four Dragons**[20] 6763 2-9-1 **69** RichardKingscote 7 75
(Tom Dascombe) *cl up: chal over 2f out: led over 1f out and sn rdn: edgd lft ins fnl f: kpt pon wl towards fin* **5/1**[2]

0210 **2** 3/4 **Father McKenzie**[11] 7004 2-9-7 **75** TonyHamilton 2 78
(Mick Channon) *trckd ldrs: hdwy over 2f out: rdn to chal over 1f out: ev ch and drvn ins fnl f: kpt on same pce towards fin* **9/2**[1]

5234 **3** 1 1/4 **Street Jazz**[21] 6733 2-9-0 **68** TomEaves 6 67
(James Given) *slt ld: rdn along wl over 1f out: sn hdd and drvn: ev ch tl kpt on same pce ins fnl f* **8/1**

3541 **4** 1/2 **Hot Hannah**[19] 6807 2-9-2 **70** ConnorBeasley 1 67
(Michael Dods) *cl up: rdn along wl over 1f out: sn drvn and wknd ins fnl f* **13/2**

1062 **5** shd **Benidiction (IRE)**[20] 6768 2-8-9 **63** JasonHart 8 59
(K R Burke) *towards rr: hdwy and in tch 1/2-way: chsd ldrs 11/2f out: sn rdn and kpt on fnl f* **14/1**

1306 **6** 1 3/4 **Mightaswellsmile**[27] 6564 2-8-12 **66** JamesSullivan 3 56
(James Given) *in tch: rdn along over 2f out: sn one pce* **10/1**

6652 **7** nk **My Cherry Blossom**[19] 6807 2-8-8 **62** DavidAllan 11 51
(Tim Easterby) *wnt bdly rt s and rr: hdwy on outer 1/2-way: swtchd lft and rdn to chse ldrs wl over 1f out: sn wknd* **13/2**

6030 **8** 1 **Redrosezorro**[21] 6734 2-8-7 **61** NeilFarley 10 46
(Eric Alston) *in tch on outer: rdn along over 2f out: grad wknd* **25/1**

0035 **9** 1 **Ninety Years Young**[10] 7041 2-8-9 **63** OisinMurphy 9 45
(David Elsworth) *a rr* **6/1**[3]

1606 **10** 1 3/4 **Little Nosegay (IRE)**[18] 6830 2-8-7 **61** JFEgan 5 36
(David Evans) *chsd ldrs: rdn along over 2f out: drvn wl over 1f out: sn wknd* **16/1**

58.51s (-2.29) **Going Correction** -0.375s/f (Firm) 2y crse rec **10** Ran SP% **112.4**
Speed ratings (Par 95): **103,101,99,99,98 96,95,93,92,89**
CSF £26.67 CT £174.43 TOTE £5.20: £1.60, £2.10, £3.30; EX 27.50 Trifecta £102.20.
Owner O'Halloran Owen Satchell Willcock **Bred** Grovewood Stud **Trained** Malpas, Cheshire

FOCUS

Good ground which hadn't been watered. After riding in the opener Jason Hart, John Egan, Tom Eaves and Tony Hamilton all agreed that the ground was 'good'. The inner home straight was used. An ordinary sprint nursery, but it was run in a two-year-old track record time. However it is worth bearing in mind that juveniles rarely get the chance to race on decent ground at this stage of the season, when they are three months older, stronger and faster than their summer selves and therefore capable of quicker times.

7314 DAVID SMITH TRAVEL MAIDEN FILLIES' STKS (PLUS 10 RACE) 6f

2:00 (2:03) (Class 5) 2-Y-O **£3,234** (£962; £481; £240) **Stalls** Centre

Form RPR

3 **1** **Eartha Kitt**[42] 6078 2-9-0 0 RichardKingscote 11 84
(Tom Dascombe) *prom: hdwy and cl up over 2f out: chal over 1f out: rdn to ld ins fnl f: edgd lft and kpt on wl* **5/2**[1]

2 3/4 **Cashla Bay** 2-9-0 0 FrankieDettori 10 82
(John Gosden) *trckd ldrs: hdwy over 2f out and sn cl up: rdn over 1f out: sn chal and ev ch: drvn and edgd lft ins fnl f: no ex towards fin* **10/3**[2]

3 1 3/4 **Classical Times** 2-9-0 0 JamesDoyle 1 77
(Peter Chapple-Hyam) *trckd ldrs: hdwy over 2f out: rdn to chal over 1f out: ev ch ent fnl f: kpt on same pce* **16/1**

03 **4** 1 1/4 **Glacier Point**[21] 6733 2-9-0 0 JohnFahy 7 73
(Clive Cox) *led 2f: cl up: rdn to ld again 11/2f out: drvn and hdd ins fnl f: grad wknd* **10/1**

50 **5** 1 1/4 **Sparkle**[70] 5119 2-9-0 0 GrahamGibbons 12 69
(Ed Dunlop) *midfield: hdwy 2f out: sn rdn and styd on wl fnl f: nrst fin* **25/1**

6 **6** 1 **Queen Of Time**[20] 6782 2-9-0 0 DaneO'Neill 3 66
(Henry Candy) *chsd ldrs: rdn along 2f out: drvn over 1f out: grad wknd* **9/2**[3]

5 **7** 1/2 **Bombay Dream**[16] 6867 2-9-0 0 PatCosgrave 5 65
(William Haggas) *t.k.h: trck ldr: led after 2f: rdn along 2f out: hdd 11/2f out: sn wknd* **6/1**

8 3 3/4 **Chicago Star** 2-9-0 0 TonyHamilton 6 53
(Mick Channon) *t.k.h: trckd ldrs: pushed along over 2f out: sn rdn and wknd* **66/1**

9 3 3/4 **Rely On Me (IRE)** 2-9-0 0 OisinMurphy 9 42
(Andrew Balding) *dwlt and rr: hdwy on outer and in tch over 2f out: rdn wl over 1f out: sn wknd* **14/1**

10 3 **Sherbert** 2-9-0 0 SeanLevey 8 33
(Richard Hannon) *a towards rr* **40/1**

11 2 1/2 **Nuzha** 2-9-0 0 JFEgan 13 26
(David Evans) *in tch: rdn along over 2f out: sn wknd* **100/1**

0 **12** 4 1/2 **Kulgri**[66] 5272 2-9-0 0 TomEaves 4 12
(Kevin Ryan) *a towards rr* **100/1**

1m 10.73s (-3.07) **Going Correction** -0.375s/f (Firm) 2y crse rec **12** Ran SP% **115.5**
Speed ratings (Par 92): **105,104,101,100,98 97,96,91,86,82 79,73**
CSF £10.05 TOTE £3.80: £1.50, £1.80, £3.10; EX 12.10 Trifecta £93.90.
Owner Chasemore Farm **Bred** Chasemore Farm **Trained** Malpas, Cheshire

FOCUS

This maiden should produce winners.

7315 CRISPY COD KNOWSLEY ROAD H'CAP 6f

2:35 (2:35) (Class 3) (0-95,92) 3-Y-O+ **£7,439** (£2,213; £1,106; £553) **Stalls** Centre

Form RPR

0301 **1** **Munfallet (IRE)**[46] 5955 5-9-2 **87** PatCosgrave 11 96
(David Brown) *led and sn clr: pushed along 2f out: rdn over 1f out: hdd ins fnl f: sn drvn and rallied gamely to ld on line* **18/1**

0000 **2** shd **Blaine**[27] 6556 6-9-7 **92** (b) TomEaves 14 101
(David Nicholls) *trckd ldrs. cl up 2f out: chal over 1f out: rdn to ld ins fnl f: sn drvn: hdd on line* **33/1**

5023 **3** 1/2 **Fendale**[22] 6718 4-9-4 **89** (p) ConnorBeasley 9 96
(Michael Dods) *trckd ldrs: hdwy 2f out and sn cl up: rdn to chal ent fnl f: ev ch tl drvn and no ex towards fin* **7/1**[2]

4400 **4** 1 1/2 **Another Wise Kid (IRE)**[13] 6944 8-9-6 **91** OisinMurphy 12 93
(Paul Midgley) *chsd wnr: hdwy 2f out: rdn over 1f out and ev ch tl drvn and kpt on same pce ins fnl f* **25/1**

6656 **5** nk **Boomerang Bob (IRE)**[13] 6962 7-9-4 **89** WilliamCarson 10 90
(Jamie Osborne) *in tch: hdwy 2f out: chsd ldrs and n.m.r over 1f out: swtchd rt and drvn ins fnl f: kpt on* **12/1**

2205 **6** 3/4 **Flying Pursuit**[20] 6792 3-9-6 **92** (b) DavidAllan 7 91
(Tim Easterby) *trckd ldrs: hdwy on outer 2f out: sn rdn and ev ch: wknd ins fnl f* **7/1**[2]

1022 **7** nk **Edward Lewis**[20] 6780 3-9-3 **89** FrankieDettori 16 87
(John Gosden) *trckd ldrs: pushed along wl over 1f out: rdn and n.m.r ent fnl f: sn drvn and no imp* **11/4**[1]

1-40 **8** 1/2 **Quatrieme Ami**[55] 5657 3-9-5 **91** ShaneKelly 1 87
(Philip McBride) *nvr bttr than midfield* **33/1**

0000 **9** 2 **Tatlisu (IRE)**[27] 6560 6-9-4 **89** TonyHamilton 15 79
(Richard Fahey) *a towards rr* **20/1**

3644 **10** nse **Eccleston**[27] 6556 5-9-6 **91** (p) GrahamGibbons 4 81
(David O'Meara) *chsd ldrs: rdn along 2f out: sn wknd* **8/1**[3]

000- **11** 1 **Wentworth Falls**[548] 1424 4-9-4 **89** JamesSullivan 5 76
(Geoffrey Harker) *a towards rr* **100/1**

6210 **12** nk **Cincuenta Pasos (IRE)**[14] 6915 5-9-4 **89** DaneO'Neill 8 75
(Joseph Tuite) *a towards rr* **25/1**

6520 **13** shd **Intense Style (IRE)**[27] 6556 4-9-6 **91** (b) RobertHavlin 17 76
(Les Eyre) *chsd ldrs: rdn along 2f out: sn wknd* **10/1**

0100 **14** 1/2 **Ustinov**[13] 6962 4-9-6 **91** DanielTudhope 13 75
(David O'Meara) *hld up: a rr* **10/1**

3410 **15** 14 **Dark Defender**[28] 6539 3-9-2 **88** (v) JoeFanning 3 27
(Keith Dalgleish) *in tch on outer: rdn along over 2f out: sn wknd* **16/1**

1m 10.24s (-3.56) **Going Correction** -0.375s/f (Firm)
WFA 3 from 4yo+ 1lb **15** Ran SP% **119.1**
Speed ratings (Par 107): **108,107,107,105,104 103,103,102,100,100 98,98,98,97,78**
CSF £530.41 CT £4497.66 TOTE £20.50: £6.30, £8.00, £2.30; EX 587.90 Trifecta £5221.60.
Owner J C Fretwell **Bred** Miss Joann Lyons **Trained** Averham Park, Notts

FOCUS

A competitive sprint handicap in which the main action took place towards the stands' side. The time was 0.76sec below standard, suggesting the ground is on the quick side. The pace held out and the third helps with the standard.

7316 DAVID SMITH FAMOUS CHRISTMAS PARTIES H'CAP 1m

3:10 (3:10) (Class 3) (0-95,92) 3-Y-O+ **£7,439** (£2,213; £1,106; £553) **Stalls** Low

Form RPR

21 **1** **Raising Sand**[14] 6915 4-9-7 **92** FrankieDettori 6 100+
(Jamie Osborne) *trckd ldrs: hdwy 2f out: rdn over 1f out: drvn ins fnl f: styd on wl to ld nr fin* **5/2**[1]

3545 **2** nk **Rousayan (IRE)**[14] 6915 5-9-2 **87** DanielTudhope 4 94
(David O'Meara) *trckd ldrs: hdwy over 2f out: led wl over 1f out: drvn ins fnl f: hdd and no ex towards fin* **9/2**[2]

0000 **3** 1/2 **Al Khan (IRE)**[27] 6557 7-9-1 **86** TomEaves 5 92
(Kevin Ryan) *midfield: hdwy 2f out: rdn over 1f out: drvn and styd on wl fnl f* **40/1**

4321 **4** 3/4 **Father Bertie**[13] 6956 4-9-7 **92** (tp) DavidAllan 7 96
(Tim Easterby) *trckd ldng pair: hdwy and cl upo 2f out: rdn over 1f out: drvn ent fnl f: kpt on wl u.p* **5/1**[3]

0000 **5** shd **Capo Rosso (IRE)**[20] 6764 6-9-6 **91** RichardKingscote 9 95
(Tom Dascombe) *led: pushed along over 2f out: rdn wl over 1f out: sn hdd and drvn: grad wknd fnl f* **14/1**

0405 **6** hd **Fox Trotter (IRE)**[35] 6287 4-9-7 **92** JamesDoyle 2 95
(Brian Meehan) *trckd ldrs: hdwy 3f out: rdn along 2f out: deriven over 1f out: kpt on* **10/1**

020 **7** 3/4 **Gratzie**[13] 6947 5-9-3 **88** OisinMurphy 10 92+
(Mick Channon) *dwlt and rr: hdwy over 2f out: sn rdn: kpt on fnl f: nrst fin* **12/1**

5001 **8** 1/2 **Jack's Revenge (IRE)**[19] 6806 8-9-4 **89** (vt) SteveDrowne 8 90
(George Baker) *a towards rr* **20/1**

0255 **9** 3/4 **Le Chat D'Or**[27] 6557 8-9-3 **88** (bt) ConnorBeasley 1 87
(Michael Dods) *in tch on inner: hdwy to chse ldrs 3f out: rdn along 2f out: sn wknd* **16/1**

0305 **10** 1/2 **Two For Two (IRE)**[7] 7121 8-9-7 **92** (p) TonyHamilton 11 90
(Roger Fell) *a towards rr* **14/1**

1410 **11** 1 **Ginger Jack**[20] 6786 9-9-4 **89** JasonHart 13 84
(Garry Moss) *trckd ldr: hdwy and cl up 3f out: rdn along 2f out: sn drvn and wknd over 1f out* **12/1**

350 **12** 8 **Lil Sophella (IRE)**[41] 6113 7-8-9 **87** PaulaMuir(7) 12 64
(Patrick Holmes) *a rr* **40/1**

00-0 **13** 7 **Prince Of Johanne (IRE)**[22] 6710 10-9-3 **88** (p) ShaneKelly 3 49
(Tom Tate) *midfield: pushed along 3f out: sn rdn and wknd* **25/1**

1m 38.67s (-5.03) **Going Correction** -0.425s/f (Firm) **13** Ran SP% **120.6**
Speed ratings (Par 107): **108,107,107,106,106 106,105,104,104,103 102,94,87**
CSF £12.39 CT £361.18 TOTE £3.30: £1.40, £2.00, £9.60; EX 16.00 Trifecta £795.40.
Owner Nick Bradley Racing 22 & Partner **Bred** Meon Valley Stud **Trained** Upper Lambourn, Berks

■ Stewards' Enquiry : Daniel Tudhope four-day ban; used his whip above the permitted level and down the shoulder in the forehand position (28th Nov-1st Nov)

FOCUS

Add 1 yard to race distance. Another quickish time for this fair handicap, in which the pace held up. There was something of a bunch finish and the winner continues to progress.

7317 ST HELENS WINDOWS EBF MAIDEN STKS (PLUS10 RACE) (DIV I) 1m

3:45 (3:47) (Class 4) 2-Y-O **£4,269** (£1,270; £634; £317) **Stalls** Low

Form RPR

2 **1** **Trading Point (FR)**[28] 6535 2-9-5 0 PhillipMakin 4 80
(John Quinn) *trckd ldr: led after 2f: pushed along 2f out: rdn clr ent fnl f: kpt on* **4/1**[2]

2 3/4 **Materialist** 2-9-5 0 AndreaAtzeni 6 78
(Roger Varian) *t.k.h: trckd ldng trio: hdwy over 2f out: effrt and green over 1f out: sn rdn to chse wnr ins fnl f: kpt on wl towards fin* **9/1**

3 **3** 1 3/4 **High Commander**[11] 7013 2-9-5 0 OisinMurphy 8 74
(Andrew Balding) *prom: trckd wnr after 2f: effrt and cl up over 2f out: rdn wl over 1f out: drvn ent fnl f: kpt on same pce* **13/2**[3]

4 1/2 **Weekender** 2-9-5 0 FrankieDettori 3 73
(John Gosden) *dwlt and rr: hdwy 1/2-way: trckd ldrs 3f out: shkn up 2f out: rdn: green and edgd lft over 1f out: kpt on same pce* **1/1**[1]

5 1 3/4 **Muqaatil (USA)** 2-9-5 0 DaneO'Neill 2 69
(Richard Hannon) *led 2f: trckd ldrs on inner: pushed along 3f out: rdn 2f out: sn no imp* **14/1**

6 *nse* **Breanski** 2-9-5 0 DanielTudhope 1 69
(David O'Meara) *in tch: pushed along 3f out: rdn over 2f out: n.d* **33/1**

7 *1 3/4* **Desert Dream** 2-9-5 0 TedDurcan 7 65
(Sir Michael Stoute) *a towards rr* **14/1**

8 *15* **Legato (IRE)** 2-9-5 0 RichardKingscote 9 30
(Tom Dascombe) *a rr: rdn along 1/2-way: sn outpcd and bhd fnl 3f* **33/1**

1m 40.42s (-3.28) **Going Correction** -0.425s/f (Firm) **8** Ran SP% **112.5**
Speed ratings (Par 97): **99,98,96,96,94 94,92,77**
CSF £37.95 TOTE £4.40: £1.30, £1.60, £1.60; EX 32.20 Trifecta £101.70.
Owner Sheikh Abdullah Almalek Alsabah **Bred** Gerard Ferron **Trained** Settrington, N Yorks
■ Zacchetto was withdrawn. Price at time of withdrawal 50/1. Rule 4 does not apply.

FOCUS
Add 1 yard to race distance. This looked the warmer of the two divisions on paper.

7318 ST HELENS WINDOWS EBF MAIDEN STKS (PLUS10 RACE) (DIV II) 1m
4:20 (4:20) (Class 4) 2-Y-O **£4,269** (£1,270; £634; £317) **Stalls** Low

Form RPR

1 **Eldritch (IRE)** 2-9-5 0 FrankieDettori 3 71+
(John Gosden) *trckd ldrs: n.m.r wl over 1f out: effrt and nt clr run appr fnl f: sn swtchd rt and rdn styd on strly to ld last 100 yds* **2/1**[1]

0 **2** *1* **Dubawi Prince**[11] 7013 2-9-5 0 AndreaAtzeni 7 69
(Roger Varian) *trckd ldrs: niggled along 3f out: pushed along 2f out: nt clr run and swtchd rt ent fnl f: sn rdn and kpt on wl towards fin* **11/4**[2]

0 **3** *nse* **Beaconsfield**[16] 6881 2-9-5 0 LiamKeniry 5 69
(Hughie Morrison) *hld up towards rr: hdwy on wd outside over 2f out: rdn over 1f out: styd on strly fnl f* **25/1**

0 **4** *nk* **Lisp (IRE)**[20] 6777 2-9-5 0 SteveDrowne 8 68
(Charles Hills) *prom: trckd ldrs after 2f: cl up over 2f out: rdn wl over 1f out: drvn and kpt on wl fnl f* **16/1**

65 **5** *nk* **Pennington**[23] 6682 2-9-5 0 JamesDoyle 4 68
(Mark Johnston) *led: pushed along over 2f out: rdn wl over 1f out: drvn ent fnl f: hdd and no ex last 100 yds* **11/1**

6 *1 3/4* **Nathan Mayer** 2-9-5 0 TedDurcan 2 63
(Sir Michael Stoute) *prom: rdn along over 2f out: drvn wl over 1f out: kpt on same pce* **6/1**[3]

6 **7** *2 3/4* **True Romance (IRE)**[13] 6952 2-9-5 0 TomEaves 9 57
(James Given) *trckd ldrs: hdwy on outer 3f out: rdn wl over 1f out: sn drvn and edgd lft: wknd fnl f* **12/1**

8 *19* **Le Pinchy (GER)** 2-9-5 0 RichardKingscote 1 13
(Tom Dascombe) *a rr: outpcd and bhd fnl 3f* **18/1**

9 *shd* **Nick Vedder** 2-9-5 0 DougieCostello 6 13
(K R Burke) *a rr: outpcd and bhd fnl 3f* **12/1**

1m 41.66s (-2.04) **Going Correction** -0.425s/f (Firm) **9** Ran SP% **113.0**
Speed ratings (Par 97): **93,92,91,91,91 89,86,67,67**
CSF £7.21 TOTE £2.50: £1.10, £1.50, £6.30; EX 8.00 Trifecta £93.10.
Owner George Strawbridge **Bred** Macha Bloodstock & Ptn **Trained** Newmarket, Suffolk

FOCUS
Add 1 yard to race distance. This was the slower division by 1.4sec, and they finished in a heap. The form looks less than solid, but it was still a nice performance from the winner.

7319 THREE SISTERS NURSERY H'CAP 7f
4:55 (4:56) (Class 5) (0-75,75) 2-Y-O **£3,234** (£962; £481; £240) **Stalls** Low

Form RPR

332 **1** **Brogan**[24] 6648 2-9-6 **74** RichardKingscote 3 77
(Tom Dascombe) *led: rdn along 2f out: drvn and hdd ent fnl f: sn lft in ld and kpt on wl towards fin* **5/1**[1]

5300 **2** *1/2* **Juan Horsepower**[97] 4128 2-9-5 **73** TomMarquand 5 75
(Richard Hannon) *trckd ldr: cl up over 2f out: rdn to chal over 1f out: drvn and ev ch ins fnl f: no ex towards fin* **20/1**

062 **3** *2* **Cool Climate (IRE)**[23] 6679 2-9-3 **71** GeorgeChaloner 2 68
(Richard Fahey) *trckd ldrs on inner: hdwy over 2f out: rdn wl over 1f out: drvn and kpt on fnl f* **6/1**[2]

326 **4** *3/4* **Challow (IRE)**[10] 7033 2-9-3 **71** LiamKeniry 8 66
(Sylvester Kirk) *towards rr: hdwy 3f out: rdn to chse ldrs over 1f out: kpt on same pce* **12/1**

6040 **5** *3* **Ingleby Mackenzie**[97] 4148 2-9-2 **70** OisinMurphy 7 57
(Mick Channon) *hld up towards rr: hdwy over 2f out: sn rdn and no imp appr fnl f* **33/1**

2264 **6** *3/4* **Bazwind (IRE)**[8] 7091 2-9-1 **69** JFEgan 6 54
(David Evans) *prom: rdn along over 2f out: drvn over 1f out: sn wknd* **20/1**

0025 **7** *1* **Hotfill**[28] 6534 2-9-2 **70** GrahamGibbons 10 52
(David Barron) *swtchd lft s and rr: sme hdwy 2f out: rdn along and keeping on whn hmpd jst ins fnl f: nt rcvr* **8/1**

0544 **8** *1* **Tesko Fella (IRE)**[15] 6888 2-9-3 **71** SeanLevey 9 51
(Richard Hannon) *a rr* **12/1**

5233 **9** *1* **Heatongrad (IRE)**[11] 7004 2-9-4 **72** TonyHamilton 11 49
(Richard Fahey) *a towards rr* **8/1**

6632 **10** *10* **Oceanus (IRE)**[22] 6716 2-9-7 **75** AndreaAtzeni 4 26
(Ed Dunlop) *t.k.h: trckd ldrs: hdwy on outer 3f out: rdn along 2f out: sn drvn and wknd* **7/1**[3]

2663 **11** *9* **Racemaker**[27] 6563 2-9-2 **70** NeilFarley 12
(Andrew Crook) *a towards rr: hmpd jst ins fnl f* **28/1**

4036 **P** **Dusker (USA)**[77] 4825 2-9-3 **71** JamesDoyle 1
(Mark Johnston) *trckd ldrs: hdwy to trck ldng pair over 2f out: rdn and slt ld ent fnl f: sn lost action and p.u: fatally injured* **5/1**[1]

1m 27.2s (-3.50) **Going Correction** -0.425s/f (Firm) 2y crse rec **12** Ran SP% **113.6**
Speed ratings (Par 95): **103,102,100,99,95 95,93,92,91,80 69,**
CSF £106.51 CT £609.27 TOTE £5.70: £2.00, £6.60, £2.10; EX 96.40 Trifecta £232.10.
Owner Chasemore Farm **Bred** Chasemore Farm Llp **Trained** Malpas, Cheshire

FOCUS
Add 1 yard to race distance. The order didn't change much in this modest nursery, which was marred by the sad injury to Dusker. He hampered several struggling opponents as he was pulled up.

7320 RAINHILL WINDOWS H'CAP 2m 45y
5:30 (5:31) (Class 4) (0-85,84) 3-Y-O+ **£4,690** (£1,395; £697; £348) **Stalls** Low

Form RPR

0212 **1** **Withhold**[41] 6127 3-8-13 **80** [1] SteveDrowne 11 88
(Charles Hills) *mde all: rdn clr jst over 1f out: drvn out* **7/1**[3]

356 **2** *3/4* **London Prize**[105] 3845 5-8-13 **72** GeorgeDowning[(3)] 5 79+
(Ian Williams) *s.i.s and bhd: hdwy on wd outside 2f out: rdn over 1f out: drvn to chse wnr and edgd lft ins fnl f: styd on wl towards fin* **9/1**

0000 **3** *2 1/4* **Aramist (IRE)**[97] 4162 6-9-10 **80** JoeFanning 9 84
(Alan Swinbank) *hld up in rr: hdwy on outer over 2f out: rdn over 1f out: drvn and styd on wl towards fin* **14/1**

6413 **4** *hd* **Wynford (IRE)**[16] 6886 3-8-8 **75** OisinMurphy 14 79
(Andrew Balding) *a cl up: rdn along over 2f out: drvn over 1f out: kpt on same pce fnl f* **9/2**[2]

0051 **5** *shd* **Fern Owl**[42] 6090 4-9-3 **73** (b) LiamKeniry 2 77
(Hughie Morrison) *hld up in midfield: hdwy 3f out: rdn along 2f out chsd ldrs over 1f out: kpt on fnl f* **20/1**

6014 **6** *2 3/4* **Aristocles (IRE)**[45] 3615 3-8-2 **72** (p) EdwardGreatrex[(3)] 7 73
(Stuart Edmunds) *chsd ldng pair on inner: pushed along 3f out: rdn 2f out: drvn over 1f out: kpt on same pce* **25/1**

0265 **7** *3 1/2* **Bulas Belle**[40] 6163 6-9-9 **79** DougieCostello 8 75
(Grant Tuer) *trckd ldng pair: pushed along over 3f out: rdn 2f out: sn drvn and wknd* **28/1**

4432 **8** *1 1/2* **Talent To Amuse (IRE)**[20] 6767 3-9-0 **81** AndreaAtzeni 12 76
(Roger Varian) *hld up in rr: gd hdwy wl over 2f out: in tch and styng on whn n.m.r and hmpd over 1f out: nt rcvr* **11/4**[1]

0631 **9** *3 1/4* **Gleese The Devil (IRE)**[6] 7158 5-9-13 **83** 6ex GeorgeChaloner 10 74
(Richard Fahey) *chsd ldrs on outer: hdwy over 3f out: rdn along over 2f out: sn drvn and wknd over 1f out* **7/1**[3]

3210 **10** *1 3/4* **Injam (IRE)**[55] 5653 3-9-3 **84** TomEaves 4 73
(Jedd O'Keeffe) *trckd ldrs: hdwy over 3f out:. rdn along wl over 2f out: sn wknd* **15/2**

665 **11** *14* **Ingleby Hollow**[27] 6565 4-9-8 **78** (p) DanielTudhope 3 50
(David O'Meara) *in tch on inner: hdwy over 3f out: rdn along over 2f out: sn wknd* **14/1**

310 **12** *9* **Brittleton**[40] 6163 4-9-9 **79** (v) JamesDoyle 1 40
(Harry Dunlop) *a towards rr* **20/1**

3m 28.7s (-5.60) **Going Correction** -0.425s/f (Firm)
WFA 3 from 4yo+ 11lb **12** Ran SP% **121.8**
Speed ratings (Par 105): **97,96,95,95,95 93,92,91,89,88 81,77**
CSF £66.59 CT £874.28 TOTE £7.40: £2.10, £3.70, £4.30; EX 89.50 Trifecta £1214.30.
Owner K Abdullah **Bred** Millsec Limited **Trained** Lambourn, Berks
■ Mister Bob was withdrawn. Price at time of withdrawal 10/1. Rule 4 does not apply.

FOCUS
The winner set an ordinary gallop in what was just a fair staying handicap. The winner is accorded a pb.
T/Jkpt: £27,361.60. Pool: £27,361.60, 1 winning unit T/Plt: £151.50 to a £1 stake. Pool: £77855.58, 375.07 winning units T/Qpdt: £42.10 to a £1 stake. Pool: £7012.55, 123.06 winning units **Joe Rowntree**

7138 NEWCASTLE (A.W) (L-H)
Friday, October 14

OFFICIAL GOING: Tapeta: standard
Wind: Almost nil Weather: Dull races 1-2, showers

7321 ESH CHARITABLE TRUST H'CAP 1m 4f 98y (Tp)
5:50 (5:53) (Class 5) (0-70,70) 3-Y-O+ **£3,234** (£962; £481; £240) **Stalls** High

Form RPR

0552 **1** **Ajman Prince (IRE)**[7] 7105 3-8-7 **63** RowanScott[(5)] 3 74
(Alistair Whillans) *hld up midfield: stdy hdwy whn nt clr run briefly over 2f out: effrt and chsng ldrs whn swtchd lft and nt clr run over 1f out: led ins fnl f: kpt on strly* **6/1**[3]

1364 **2** *2 1/2* **Airton**[31] 6450 3-8-13 **67** JosephineGordon[(3)] 9 74
(James Bethell) *hld up in tch: hdwy to ld over 2f out: sn hrd pressed: hdd ins fnl f: kpt on same pce* **5/1**[2]

600 **3** *1 3/4* **High Command (IRE)**[32] 6415 3-9-4 **69** HarryBentley 6 73
(Roger Varian) *hld up: hdwy on outside to dispute ld 2f out to ins fnl f: outpcd last 100yds* **4/1**[1]

4104 **4** *3* **Yasir (USA)**[13] 6965 8-9-8 **66** PaulMulrennan 11 65
(Conor Dore) *hld up: rdn and hdwy 2f out: kpt on same pce last 100yds* **40/1**

5553 **5** *3 1/4* **Fastnet Blast (IRE)**[21] 6730 3-9-2 **67** (b) LukeMorris 12 60
(Ed Walker) *hld up: hdwy and prom wl over 1f out: rdn and wknd ins fnl f* **8/1**

1323 **6** *6* **Le Deluge (FR)**[23] 6684 6-9-4 **67** (t) RobJFitzpatrick[(5)] 1 51
(Micky Hammond) *t.k.h: hld up on ins: drvn over 2f out: wknd over 1f out* **20/1**

3042 **7** *2 3/4* **Gold Show**[10] 7043 7-9-0 **61** JacobButterfield[(3)] 10 40
(Grant Tuer) *w ldr 5f: cl up: rdn over 2f out: sn wknd* **12/1**

-551 **8** *nk* **Prospectus**[24] 6654 3-9-4 **69** MartinLane 2 48
(Hughie Morrison) *prom on ins: rdn over 3f out: wknd fr 2f out* **4/1**[1]

2500 **9** *1/2* **L'Inganno Felice (FR)**[15] 6907 6-9-11 **69** (v[1]) PJMcDonald 5 47
(Iain Jardine) *plld hrd: hld up in tch: hdwy to ld after 5f: hdd over 2f out: sn btn* **11/1**

2030 **10** *1 3/4* **Rockabilly Riot (IRE)**[10] 7044 6-9-1 **59** (p) DavidNolan 7 34
(Martin Todhunter) *dwlt: hld up: rdn along 3f out: sn n.d: btn over 1f out* **33/1**

6002 **11** *65* **Only Orsenfoolsies**[20] 6773 7-9-7 **70** CallumShepherd[(5)] 4
(Micky Hammond) *led 5f: cl up: tl rdn and wknd fr 3f out: eased whn no ch fnl 2f* **12/1**

2m 36.76s (-4.34) **Going Correction** -0.125s/f (Stan) course record
WFA 3 from 4yo+ 7lb **11** Ran SP% **115.9**
Speed ratings (Par 103): **109,107,106,104,101 97,95,95,95,94 50**
CSF £34.79 CT £134.90 TOTE £6.20: £1.80, £2.20, £2.00; EX 38.70 Trifecta £282.90.
Owner J D Wright **Bred** Darley **Trained** Newmill-On-Slitrig, Borders

FOCUS
After rain and with cooler temperatures clerk of the course James Armstrong predicted that the Tapeta surface would ride faster than has been the case during the summer. This was a 56-70 handicap featuring five relatively unexposed three-year-olds who filled the top five spots in the market. The pace was decent and the hold-up horses dominated the finish.

7322 MEDIAWORKS NURSERY H'CAP 1m 5y (Tp)
6:20 (6:21) (Class 4) (0-85,84) 2-Y-O **£4,010** (£1,193; £596; £298) **Stalls** Centre

Form RPR

3251 **1** **Election Day**[20] 6771 2-8-13 **76** PJMcDonald 4 79
(Mark Johnston) *prom: smooth hdwy to ld 2f out: rdn and drifted lft ins fnl f: kpt on strly* **5/1**[3]

4120 **2** *1 1/2* **Temerity (IRE)**[27] 6554 2-9-2 **84** AdamMcNamara[(5)] 5 84
(Richard Fahey) *t.k.h: cl up: ev ch over 2f out to over 1f out: sn chsng wnr: one pce last 100yds* **11/2**

114 **3** *3/4* **Haulani (USA)**[22] 6705 2-9-5 **82** WilliamTwiston-Davies 6 80
(Philip Hide) *in tch: effrt and angled lft over 2f out: effrt and drvn over 1f out: kpt on ins fnl f* **11/4**[1]

1 **4** *3 1/4* **Tamayef (IRE)**[21] 6741 2-9-0 **80**...[1] JosephineGordon(3) 3 71
(Hugo Palmer) *dwlt: t.k.h and sn cl up: ev ch over 2f out: rdn and outpcd over 1f out: n.d after* **3/1**[2]

523 **5** *shd* **Thorndyke**[35] 6274 2-9-0 **77**... KevinStott 1 68
(Kevin Ryan) *t.k.h: led at stdy pce: rdn and hdd 2f out: wknd ins fnl f* **3/1**[2]

1m 38.47s (-0.13) **Going Correction** -0.125s/f (Stan) **5** Ran SP% **108.7**
Speed ratings (Par 97): **95,93,92,89,89**
CSF £29.34 TOTE £6.30: £2.70, £2.30; EX 31.70 Trifecta £87.80.
Owner Sheikh Hamdan bin Mohammed Al Maktoum **Bred** Petches Farm Ltd **Trained** Middleham Moor, N Yorks

FOCUS
A five-runner nursery but four were previous winners. After a steady first couple of furlongs the pace was solid though curiously the whole field drifted over to the far rail.

7323 SMART FIX H'CAP 7f 14y (Tp)
6:50 (6:51) (Class 6) (0-60,66) 3-Y-O+ **£2,264** (£673; £336; £168) **Stalls** Centre

Form RPR

2403 **1** **Alice Thornton**[8] 7096 4-9-7 **60**... DavidNolan 14 74
(Martin Todhunter) *prom: hdwy to ld 2f out: drvn clr fnl f: eased nr fin* **7/1**[3]

0002 **2** *5* **Poolstock**[8] 7097 4-9-2 **55**...(b) PaulMulrennan 3 55
(Michael Dods) *hld up: hdwy to chse wnr over 1f out: rdn and kpt on same pce ins fnl f* **9/1**

035 **3** *2 1/4* **Who's Shirl**[15] 6908 10-9-2 **55**... AndrewElliott 5 49
(Chris Fairhurst) *bhd and sn pushed along: plenty to do 1/2-way: gd hdwy nr side of gp over 1f out: edgd rt and kpt on fnl f: nt rch far side ldrs* **17/2**

3360 **4** *3/4* **Coquine**[23] 6685 3-9-2 **57**... HarryBentley 7 48
(David O'Meara) *hld up: smooth hdwy and prom over 2f out: effrt and rdn over 1f out: kpt on same pce ins fnl f* **10/1**

1564 **5** *2 1/2* **Cool Strutter (IRE)**[6] 7144 4-9-2 **60**...(b) GemmaTutty(5) 2 46
(Karen Tutty) *taken early to post: in tch on far side of gp: pushed along whn hmpd and lost pl over 2f out: rallied ins fnl f: no imp* **11/2**[2]

0300 **6** *hd* **The Knave (IRE)**[29] 6512 3-9-1 **56**...(p) BenCurtis 10 40
(Scott Dixon) *cl up on far side of gp: rdn over 2f out: checked appr fnl f: sn btn* **16/1**

2640 **7** *shd* **Tribesman**[44] 6023 3-8-13 **57**... JacobButterfield(3) 9 41
(Marjorie Fife) *hld up bhd ldng gp: effrt on nr side of gp over 2f out: no imp over 1f out* **20/1**

4131 **8** *nk* **Reinforced**[8] 7096 3-9-11 **66** 6ex...(p) AndrewMullen 6 49
(Michael Dods) *led: edgd towards far side over 3f out: rdn and hdd over 1f out: wknd fnl f* **3/1**[1]

-501 **9** *3 1/2* **Dutch Dream**[45] 6003 3-8-12 **58**... AdamMcNamara(5) 12 33
(Linda Perratt) *s.i.s: bhd: hdwy on nr side of gp over 2f out: sn rdn: no further imp over 1f out: sn btn* **33/1**

4060 **10** *nk* **Jebel Tara**[8] 7093 11-9-1 **54**...(bt) DaleSwift 8 29
(Alistair Whillans) *prom: rdn and lost pl over 2f out: sn btn* **16/1**

500- **11** *3/4* **Boboli Gardens**[385] 6714 6-8-9 **53**... GarryWhillans(5) 13 26
(Susan Corbett) *hld up: rdn and hdwy over 2f out: wknd over 1f out* **50/1**

425 **12** *nk* **Euro Mac**[24] 6643 4-8-13 **55**... NathanEvans(3) 11 27
(Neville Bycroft) *cl up on nr side of gp: rdn over 2f out: wknd over 1f out* **8/1**

0-04 **13** *1/2* **Newspeak (IRE)**[31] 6452 4-9-0 **53**...(p) CamHardie 4 24
(Fred Watson) *prom: drvn and lost pl over 3f out: sn struggling* **28/1**

1-00 **14** *25* **Rock Of Monaco**[42] 6106 3-9-1 **56**...[1] WilliamTwiston-Davies 1
(Antony Brittain) *s.i.s: bhd and sn struggling: no ch fr 1/2-way: btn and eased fnl 2f* **25/1**

1m 24.48s (-1.72) **Going Correction** -0.125s/f (Stan) course record
WFA 3 from 4yo+ 2lb **14** Ran SP% **122.3**
Speed ratings (Par 101): **104,98,95,94,92 91,91,91,87,86 86,85,85,56**
CSF £65.63 CT £570.61 TOTE £7.00: £2.80, £2.30, £3.30; EX 68.50 Trifecta £489.60.
Owner Javas Charvers **Bred** Dunchurch Lodge Stud Co **Trained** Orton, Cumbria

FOCUS
A low-grade handicap with most hard-to-win-with sorts and not many coming into it in much form. The pace was fair and there was a runaway winner who like the second raced towards the far side rail.

7324 MGF 35TH ANNIVERSARY H'CAP (DIV I) 6f (Tp)
7:20 (7:21) (Class 5) (0-75,75) 3-Y-O+ **£2,911** (£866; £432; £216) **Stalls** Centre

Form RPR

300 **1** **Frenchman (FR)**[16] 6878 3-9-4 **73**...[1] LukeMorris 6 82
(Charles Hills) *trckd ldrs: rdn to ld appr fnl f: edgd rt ins fnl f: drvn out* **13/2**[3]

3664 **2** *3/4* **Manatee Bay**[38] 6215 6-9-6 **74**...(v) AndrewMullen 1 81+
(David Nicholls) *s.i.s: hld up: rdn and gd hdwy appr fnl f: kpt on to take 2nd last 30yds* **8/1**

3400 **3** *nk* **Meandmyshadow**[15] 6908 8-9-2 **70**...(b) DaleSwift 12 76
(Alan Brown) *spd stands' side: rdn and hung lft over 2f out: outpcd over 1f out: rallied ins fnl f: kpt on* **12/1**

2060 **4** *1/2* **Indian Pursuit (IRE)**[23] 6685 3-8-7 **62**... CamHardie 11 66
(John Quinn) *cl up stands' side: carried lft over 2f out: hdwy to ld briefly over 1f out: kpt on same pce ins fnl f* **16/1**

1252 **5** *1/2* **Bahamian Bird**[15] 6908 3-8-9 **69**... AdamMcNamara(5) 7 71
(Richard Fahey) *trckd ldrs: rdn along and outpcd wl over 1f out: kpt on ins fnl f* **3/1**[1]

2160 **6** *1 1/4* **Dance Alone**[22] 6717 3-9-5 **74**...(b) KevinStott 5 72
(Kevin Ryan) *led: rdn and hdd over 1f out: rallied: no ex ins fnl f* **12/1**

2100 **7** *1/2* **Etienne Gerard**[27] 6579 4-8-13 **74**...(p) LewisEdmunds(7) 8 71
(Nigel Tinkler) *in tch: effrt and rdn over 2f out: no imp over 1f out* **6/1**[2]

5005 **8** *1 1/2* **Musaaid (IRE)**[29] 6521 4-8-12 **69**... NathanEvans(3) 4 61
(Michael Easterby) *t.k.h: cl up: rdn over 2f out: outpcd appr fnl f* **6/1**[2]

1050 **9** *1/2* **Classic Flyer**[10] 7059 4-9-0 **68** ow1...(v) DavidNolan 9 58
(David O'Meara) *hld up bhd ldng gp: rdn over 2f out: no imp over 1f out* **16/1**

1160 **10** *3 1/4* **Gypsy Major**[31] 6451 4-8-10 **64**...(v) JasonHart 2 44
(Garry Moss) *s.i.s: hld up: hdwy over 2f out: wknd over 1f out* **8/1**

0600 **11** *1* **Wilsons Ruby (IRE)**[63] 5354 3-8-7 **62**... SamJames 10 39
(Marjorie Fife) *taken early to post: prom stands' side: carried lft over 2f out: rdn and wknd over 1f out* **50/1**

1100 **12** *4 1/2* **Point North (IRE)**[95] 4211 9-9-7 **75**...(b) PaulMulrennan 3 37
(John Balding) *hld up: drvn and outpcd over 2f out: sn btn* **33/1**

1m 11.04s (-1.46) **Going Correction** -0.125s/f (Stan)
WFA 3 from 4yo+ 1lb **12** Ran SP% **121.2**
Speed ratings (Par 103): **104,103,102,101,101 99,98,96,96,91 90,84**
CSF £59.16 CT £632.03 TOTE £4.70: £2.70, £2.10, £3.90; EX 31.50 Trifecta £663.00.
Owner Kennet Valley Thoroughbreds V **Bred** S C E A Ecurie De Montfort & K Morice **Trained** Lambourn, Berks

FOCUS
A fair sprint handicap. Although the three highest drawn raced stands' side initially they edged over to the others soon after halfway and there didn't appear to be any draw bias.

7325 MGF 35TH ANNIVERSARY H'CAP (DIV II) 6f (Tp)
7:50 (7:50) (Class 5) (0-75,75) 3-Y-O+ **£2,911** (£866; £432; £216) **Stalls** Centre

Form RPR

1004 **1** **Slingsby**[46] 5968 5-8-11 **68**...(b) NathanEvans(3) 9 77
(Michael Easterby) *mde all: rdn 2f out: hld on wl fnl f* **7/1**[3]

0003 **2** *1* **Dark Side Dream**[27] 6589 4-8-13 **70**... JosephineGordon(3) 8 76
(Chris Dwyer) *pressed wnr: effrt and ev ch over 1f out: kpt on ins fnl f: hld last 75yds* **7/1**[3]

0024 **3** *1/2* **Art Obsession (IRE)**[22] 6718 5-9-7 **75**... DavidNolan 10 79
(Paul Midgley) *hld up in tch: drvn over 2f out: rallied and chsd ldrs over 1f out: kpt on same pce ins fnl f* **7/2**[1]

2200 **4** *1/2* **Malaysian Boleh**[13] 6958 6-9-1 **69**... BenCurtis 2 72
(Brian Ellison) *s.i.s: hld up: rdn and hdwy over 1f out: edgd lft and kpt on ins fnl f: nt pce to chal* **12/1**

1215 **5** *nse* **Laila Honiwillow**[46] 5969 3-9-6 **75**... JackGarritty 6 77
(Jedd O'Keeffe) *chsd ldrs: drvn along 2f out: kpt on same pce ins fnl f* **8/1**

2000 **6** *hd* **Big Amigo (IRE)**[20] 6790 3-8-8 **63**... LukeMorris 11 65
(Tom Dascombe) *s.i.s: hld up: rdn and hdwy 2f out: kpt on ins fnl f: nt pce to chal* **11/1**

032 **7** *hd* **Encantar**[20] 6790 3-8-12 **67**...(v) PJMcDonald 4 68
(Ann Duffield) *hld up bhd ldng gp: drvn along over 2f out: kpt on same pce fnl f* **8/1**

-040 **8** *1* **Yosemite**[31] 6435 3-9-0 **74**... AdamMcNamara(5) 3 72
(Richard Fahey) *hld up: rdn along over 2f out: edgd lft over 1f out: wknd ins fnl f* **9/1**

0204 **9** *1/2* **Lucky Lodge**[31] 6453 6-9-0 **68**...(v[1]) WilliamTwiston-Davies 7 64
(Antony Brittain) *prom: drvn over 2f out: wknd over 1f out* **13/2**[2]

016- **10** *1 1/4* **Ad Vitam (IRE)**[314] 8119 8-8-7 **61**...(bt) BarryMcHugh 1 53
(Suzzanne France) *t.k.h: cl up: rdn and outpcd over 2f out: wknd over 1f out* **50/1**

6013 **11** *2 1/2* **Market Choice (IRE)**[22] 6717 3-9-5 **74**... PaulMulrennan 5 58
(Michael Dods) *t.k.h: in tch: rdn over 2f out: sn struggling: btn fnl f* **11/1**

1m 10.78s (-1.72) **Going Correction** -0.125s/f (Stan)
WFA 3 from 4yo+ 1lb **11** Ran SP% **119.1**
Speed ratings (Par 103): **106,104,104,103,103 103,102,101,100,99 95**
CSF £56.13 CT £179.59 TOTE £9.30: £3.10, £3.10, £1.80; EX 64.00 Trifecta £397.00.
Owner S Hull, B Hoggarth & Mrs C Mason **Bred** R H Mason **Trained** Sheriff Hutton, N Yorks

FOCUS
A 61-75 handicap run at a fair gallop. The first two were up there throughout but it was something of a bunch finish with just over two lengths covering the first seven home so the form is unlikely to be anything special.

7326 JEWSONS DURHAM FILLIES' H'CAP 1m 5y (Tp)
8:20 (8:21) (Class 5) (0-75,75) 3-Y-O+ **£3,234** (£962; £481; £240) **Stalls** Centre

Form RPR

6010 **1** **Totally Magic (IRE)**[11] 7007 4-8-7 **61**... BarryMcHugh 4 69
(Richard Whitaker) *mde virtually all: set stdy pce: rdn and qcknd 2f out: kpt on wl fnl f* **3/1**[1]

2245 **2** *1 3/4* **Heartstone (IRE)**[25] 6635 3-8-10 **70**... JosephineGordon(3) 6 73
(Charles Hills) *pressed wnr: effrt and drvn along 2f out: edgd lft ins fnl f: kpt on same pce last 100yds* **9/2**

2430 **3** *nse* **Arcane Dancer (IRE)**[3] 7254 3-8-4 **64**...(p) NathanEvans(3) 5 67
(Lawrence Mullaney) *trckd ldrs: drvn over 2f out: rallied over 1f out: kpt on ins fnl f* **4/1**[3]

454 **4** *2 3/4* **Paper Faces (USA)**[13] 6960 3-8-8 **65**... HarryBentley 7 62
(Roger Varian) *hld up: drvn and outpcd 3f out: hung lft: rallied over 1f out: kpt on: nvr able to chal* **9/2**

1646 **5** *shd* **La Havrese (FR)**[14] 6922 5-8-10 **64**... PaddyAspell 1 60
(Lynn Siddall) *t.k.h: prom: rdn over 2f out: outpcd fr over 1f out* **16/1**

0206 **6** *2 1/2* **Mustique (IRE)**[13] 6964 3-9-4 **75**... DavidNolan 2 66
(Richard Fahey) *t.k.h: trckd ldrs: rdn over 2f out: wknd over 1f out* **7/2**[2]

000- **7** *hd* **Percy's Lass**[477] 3558 4-8-7 **61** oh6... BenCurtis 3 51
(Brian Ellison) *hld up beihnd ldng gp: drvn and outpcd over 2f out: btn over 1f out* **33/1**

1m 38.26s (-0.34) **Going Correction** -0.125s/f (Stan)
WFA 3 from 4yo+ 3lb **7** Ran SP% **112.4**
Speed ratings (Par 100): **96,94,94,91,91 88,88**
CSF £16.20 TOTE £3.40: £2.00, £2.50; EX 20.00 Trifecta £55.60.
Owner James Marshall & Chris Marshall **Bred** G Donnelly & Ms C Clarke **Trained** Scarcroft, W Yorks

FOCUS
A mile handicap for fillies and mares rated 61-75. The pace was moderate, the winner was gifted a soft lead and the form may prove unreliable.

7327 SOLUTION GROUP DESIGN PARTNERS OF KINGS MEDIAN AUCTION MAIDEN STKS 1m 5y (Tp)
8:50 (8:51) (Class 5) 3-5-Y-O **£3,234** (£962; £481; £240) **Stalls** Centre

Form RPR

32 **1** **Right Rebel**[23] 6674 4-9-0 0... JosephineGordon(3) 3 74+
(Alan Bailey) *t.k.h early: w ldr: led over 2f out: shkn up and qcknd over 1f out: pushed out fnl f: comf* **6/4**[1]

2322 **2** *3/4* **Best Laid Plans**[17] 6855 3-9-0 70... LukeMorris 1 71
(James Tate) *t.k.h: led at modest gallop: rdn and hdd over 2f out: hung lft over 1f out: rallied ins fnl f: kpt on: hld towards fin* **6/4**[1]

3356 **3** *5* **Captain Peaky**[15] 6907 3-9-5 62... JackGarritty 5 64
(Patrick Holmes) *trckd ldrs: rdn over 2f out: outpcd by first two fr over 1f out* **6/1**[2]

4 *hd* **Einstein** 3-9-5 0...[1] SaleemGolam 2 63
(Mrs Ilka Gansera-Leveque) *s.s: t.k.h and sn tagged onto bk of gp: stdy hdwy over 4f out: rdn and outpcd over 2f out: no imp over 1f out* **7/1**[3]

-050 **5** *5* **Will Mac**[9] 7078 5-9-5 60...[1] NathanEvans(3) 4 52
(Neville Bycroft) *prom: drvn and outpcd over 4f out: n.d after* **20/1**

0006 **6** *2* **Emilie Bronte**[31] 6452 3-9-0 42... AndrewElliott 6 42
(Chris Fairhurst) *hld up: drvn and struggling 1/2-way: sn btn* **66/1**

1m 38.74s (0.14) **Going Correction** -0.125s/f (Stan)
WFA 3 from 4yo+ 3lb **6** Ran SP% **113.0**
Speed ratings (Par 103): **94,93,88,88,83 81**
CSF £3.88 TOTE £2.20: £1.10, £1.30; EX 5.30 Trifecta £7.50.
Owner Barber Hood Bloodstock **Bred** Racing To The Maxx **Trained** Newmarket, Suffolk

FOCUS
A median auction event in which the top-rated runner was 70 and they bet double figure prices bar the front two. The pace was just fair and the first two both took a fair grip.

7328 COREPEOPLE CUP MAIDEN AUCTION STKS — 7f 14y (Tp)
9:20 (9:25) (Class 6) 2-Y-O — **£2,264** (£673; £336; £168) **Stalls** Centre

Form — RPR

0232 **1** **Trooper's Gold**[21] 6741 2-9-5 77 .... TomEaves 1 — 79
(Kevin Ryan) *in tch: smooth hdwy to ld over 1f out: shkn up and sn clr: readily* **2/1**[2]

5 **2** 3 ¼ **Nature Boy (IRE)**[115] 3495 2-9-5 0 .... PaulMulrennan 4 — 71
(Peter Chapple-Hyam) *t.k.h: pressed ldr: rdn and led briefly over 1f out: edgd lft and kpt on fnl f: no ch w wnr* **10/3**[3]

5322 **3** ¾ **Roaring Character (IRE)**[35] 6274 2-9-5 78 .... LukeMorris 6 — 69
(Tom Dascombe) *prom: rdn over 2f out: hdwy and edgd lft over 1f out: kpt on same pce ins fnl f* **6/4**[1]

53 **4** 5 **Free At Last (IRE)**[31] 6447 2-9-0 0 .... DavidNolan 2 — 52
(Richard Fahey) *led: crossed to stands' rail over 5f out: rdn and hdd over 1f out: sn wknd* **8/1**

05 **5** 1 **Teddy Edward**[23] 6679 2-9-5 0 .... (t) GeorgeChaloner 5 — 54
(Richard Whitaker) *hld up in tch: drvn along over 2f out: wknd over 1f out* **50/1**

6 ½ **Musico (IRE)** 2-9-5 0 .... JoeyHaynes 3 — 53
(Patrick Holmes) *dwlt: hld up: hdwy and pushed along 3f out: wknd 2f out* **33/1**

7 1 ¾ **Arabela Dawn (IRE)** 2-9-0 0 .... DougieCostello 8 — 43
(John Quinn) *s.i.s: hld up: shkn up briefly over 1f out: sn n.d: btn fnl f* **33/1**

1m 26.62s (0.42) **Going Correction** -0.125s/f (Stan) — **7** Ran SP% **115.4**
Speed ratings (Par 93): **92,88,87,81,80 80,78**
CSF £9.24 TOTE £2.60: £1.50, £2.00; EX 11.00 Trifecta £23.60.
Owner Jaber Abdullah **Bred** Rabbah Bloodstock Limited **Trained** Hambleton, N Yorks
■ Scarpash was withdrawn. Price at time of withdrawal 33/1. Rule 4 does not apply.

FOCUS
Probably just an ordinary juvenile maiden run at moderate gallop, but quite an impressive winner. The forst three finished clear.
T/Plt: £305.30 to a £1 stake. Pool: £96,0464.21 - 230.61 winning tickets T/Qpdt: £48.00 to a £1 stake. Pool: £9,866.92 - 151.95 winning tickets **Richard Young**

6952 REDCAR (L-H)
Friday, October 14

OFFICIAL GOING: Good to soft (good in places) changing to good to soft after race 1 (1.45)
Wind: fresh 1/2 behind Weather: overcast and chilly

7329 RACINGUK.COM/DAYPASS BRITISH STALLION STUDS EBF MAIDEN STKS — 1m
1:45 (1:49) (Class 5) 2-Y-O — **£3,234** (£962; £481; £240) **Stalls** Centre

Form — RPR

4 **1** **Baashiq (IRE)**[13] 6952 2-9-5 0 .... PaulHanagan 9 — 82
(Roger Varian) *wnt rt s: led: hdd narrowly 1f out: kpt on to ld fnl strides* **9/2**[2]

2 hd **Maghfoor** 2-9-5 0 .... SilvestreDeSousa 3 — 82
(Saeed bin Suroor) *chsd ldrs: drvn over 2f out: led narrowly 1f out: hdd and no ex fnl strides* **11/2**[3]

3 **3** 3 ¼ **Armandihan (IRE)**[29] 6499 2-9-5 0 .... KevinStott 8 — 74
(Kevin Ryan) *chsd ldrs: drvn and hung lft over 2f out: swtchd lft over 1f out: kpt on same pce* **15/8**[1]

4 1 ¼ **The Grey Warrior (IRE)** 2-9-5 0 .... GrahamLee 1 — 72
(Kevin Ryan) *chsd ldrs: drvn 4f out: hung lft over 2f out: carried lft over 1f out: swtchd rt and one pce* **25/1**

5 4 **Wordsearch (USA)** 2-9-5 0 .... JimCrowley 2 — 63
(Hugo Palmer) *chsd ldrs: drvn 3f out: wknd over 1f out* **8/1**

6 2 **Dal Riata (IRE)** 2-9-0 0 .... PJMcDonald 10 — 53
(Mark Johnston) *carried rt s: sn chsng ldrs: drvn 3f out: wknd over 1f out* **33/1**

2 **7** 2 ½ **Taxmeifyoucan (IRE)**[20] 6771 2-9-0 0 .... ShirleyTeasdale(5) 11 — 53
(Keith Dalgleish) *wnt rt s: mid-div: drvn 3f out: sn hung bdly lft and lost pl: no threat after* **10/1**

0 **8** ¾ **Helovaplan (IRE)**[36] 6262 2-9-5 0 .... BenCurtis 6 — 51
(Bryan Smart) *mid-div: sn drvn along: hdwy to chse ldrs 3f out: lost pl over 1f out* **9/1**

23 **9** 2 **Kuraka**[20] 6771 2-9-5 0 .... JoeyHaynes 4 — 47
(K R Burke) *chsd ldrs: drvn 3f out: lost pl over 1f out* **8/1**

0 **10** 24 **Saint Cuthberts**[36] 6262 2-9-5 0 .... ShaneGray 7
(David Brown) *detached in last: sn drvn along: reminders and hung lft over 3f out: sn bhd: t.o whn eased* **100/1**

1m 39.51s (2.91) **Going Correction** +0.275s/f (Good) — **10** Ran SP% **117.4**
Speed ratings (Par 95): **96,95,92,91,87 85,82,82,80,56**
CSF £29.34 TOTE £6.70: £2.10, £1.90, £1.10; EX 28.00 Trifecta £61.90.
Owner Hamdan Al Maktoum **Bred** Shadwell Estate Company Limited **Trained** Newmarket, Suffolk

FOCUS
With 11mm of rain falling in the previous 24 hours, the going was officially described as good to soft, good in places after the runners were declared on good to firm, good in places. A strong maiden for the track, featuring several well-bred newcomers and the already proven favourite. The first two pulled clear and fought out an exciting finish.

7330 WATCH RACING UK TODAY JUST £10 CLAIMING STKS — 7f
2:15 (2:15) (Class 6) 2-Y-O — **£2,587** (£770; £384; £192) **Stalls** Centre

Form — RPR

0024 **1** **Volta Do Mar (IRE)**[25] 6614 2-8-4 61 ow2 .... PatrickMathers 8 — 62
(Richard Fahey) *rr-div: drvn and hdwy over 2f out: styd on fnl f: led post* **6/1**

0045 **2** nse **Pavela (IRE)**[13] 6961 2-7-13 58 .... NathanEvans(3) 2 — 60
(Mick Channon) *led 1f: w ldr: led over 1f out: hdd post* **14/1**

3210 **3** ½ **Springforth**[84] 4602 2-8-11 67 .... PaulHanagan 1 — 68
(Richard Fahey) *chsd ldrs: upsides over 1f out: no ex clsng stages* **13/2**

3154 **4** 2 ½ **Chevalier Du Lac (IRE)**[13] 6961 2-8-5 67 .... SilvestreDeSousa 6 — 56
(Conor Dore) *hld up towards rr: t.k.h: effrt and hung bdly lft over 2f out: upsides over 1f out: fdd last 100yds* **9/2**[2]

3043 **5** 2 ¼ **Baltic Beau**[7] 7109 2-8-5 58 .... BarryMcHugh 9 — 50
(Richard Fahey) *dwlt: reminders sn after s: in rr: kpt on appr fnl f* **11/2**[3]

056 **6** 1 **Dazacam**[14] 6925 2-8-0 60 ow1 .... AaronJones(3) 10 — 45
(Michael Herrington) *t.k.h: led after 1f: hdd over 1f out: sn wknd* **28/1**

0 **7** 2 ¼ **Little Kingdom (IRE)**[14] 6924 2-8-0 0 .... AndrewMullen 12 — 36
(Tracy Waggott) *s.i.s: in rr: hdwy to chse ldrs 3f out: wknd over 1f out* **100/1**

430 **8** 1 ½ **Best Bid (IRE)**[14] 6925 2-8-6 62 .... BenCurtis 11 — 38
(John Quinn) *mid-div: effrt 3f out: lost pl over 1f out* **14/1**

1245 **9** 2 ¾ **London Grammar (IRE)**[23] 6681 2-8-0 62 .... CamHardie 7 — 25
(John Quinn) *chsd ldrs: drvn over 2f out: lost pl over 1f out* **6/1**

3662 **10** 1 ¼ **Await The Storm (IRE)**[8] 7098 2-9-1 75 .... JimCrowley 4 — 37
(Hugo Palmer) *chsd ldrs: rdn over 2f out: lost pl over 1f out* **4/1**[1]

0050 **11** ½ **Dreamorchid (IRE)**[10] 7041 2-8-2 60 .... DuranFentiman 3 — 23
(Tim Easterby) *trckd ldrs: wknd 2f out* **40/1**

1m 26.39s (1.89) **Going Correction** +0.275s/f (Good) — **11** Ran SP% **115.7**
Speed ratings (Par 93): **100,99,99,96,93 92,90,88,85,83 83**
CSF £83.83 TOTE £7.30: £2.30, £5.20, £2.20; EX 123.90 Trifecta £1892.60.
Owner McGrath, Taylor, Trevitt **Bred** Jim McGrath **Trained** Musley Bank, N Yorks

FOCUS
An ordinary claimer and a suspicion that many of these failed to handle the rain-softened conditions.

7331 MARKET CROSS JEWELLERS EBFSTALLIONS.COM MAIDEN STKS — 6f
2:50 (2:52) (Class 5) 2-Y-O — **£3,234** (£962; £481; £240) **Stalls** Centre

Form — RPR

1 **Khamaary (IRE)** 2-9-0 0 .... PaulHanagan 10 — 69
(Mark Johnston) *chsd ldrs: 2nd 1f out: edgd lft and styd on to ld fnl strides* **3/1**[2]

3665 **2** nk **Bithynia (IRE)**[45] 6010 2-9-0 67 .... JimCrowley 1 — 68
(Hugo Palmer) *led: t.k.h: drvn over 1f out: no ex and hdd fnl strides* **4/1**[3]

4 **3** 3 **Dream Reversion**[9] 7072 2-9-5 0 .... PJMcDonald 2 — 64
(Tom Dascombe) *chsd ldrs: drvn and hung lft over 1f out: kpt on same pce* **6/1**

6 **4** nk **Somewhere Secret**[43] 6053 2-9-5 0 .... SilvestreDeSousa 11 — 63
(Robert Cowell) *hld up towards rr: effrt over 2f out: chsng ldrs over 1f out: kpt on same pce* **11/4**[1]

6 **5** 2 ¾ **Cryptonite (IRE)**[18] 6833 2-9-5 0 .... BenCurtis 9 — 55
(Michael Appleby) *chsd ldrs: drvn over 2f out: edgd lft over 1f out: one pce* **4/1**[3]

0 **6** 2 ¼ **Pindaric**[13] 6952 2-9-5 0 .... CamHardie 8 — 48
(Alan Lockwood) *dwlt: in rr: drvn over 3f out: edgd lft over 1f out: nvr a factor* **40/1**

60 **7** 1 ¾ **Gokena (FR)**[22] 6712 2-9-0 0 .... [1] KevinStott 7 — 38
(Kevin Ryan) *t.k.h: sn trcking ldrs: hung lft and wknd over 1f out* **16/1**

000 **8** 4 ½ **Equipe**[16] 6873 2-8-11 48 .... NathanEvans(3) 6 — 24
(Richard Whitaker) *chsd ldrs: wknd over 1f out* **100/1**

9 9 **Ching Ching Lor (IRE)** 2-9-5 0 .... PaulMulrennan 3 — 2
(Declan Carroll) *sn chsng ldrs: lost pl over 3f out: sn bhd* **33/1**

0 **10** 1 ¾ **Mr Hill**[7] 7122 2-9-5 0 .... BarryMcHugh 4
(Rebecca Bastiman) *mid-div: drvn over 3f out: lost pl over 2f out: bhd whn eased clsng stages* **100/1**

11 13 **Bun An Churraigh** 2-9-5 0 .... GrahamLee 5
(Michael Mullineaux) *chsd ldrs: hung lft and lost pl over 3f out: sn wl bhd* **50/1**

1m 13.07s (1.27) **Going Correction** +0.275s/f (Good) — **11** Ran SP% **121.2**
Speed ratings (Par 95): **102,101,97,97,93 90,88,82,70,67 50**
CSF £15.77 TOTE £4.20: £1.70, £2.20, £2.50; EX 16.30 Trifecta £82.90.
Owner Hamdan Al Maktoum **Bred** Shadwell Estate Company Limited **Trained** Middleham Moor, N Yorks

FOCUS
A weak maiden, in which the runner-up set only a modest standard.

7332 SAM HALL MEMORIAL H'CAP — 1m 6f 19y
3:25 (3:26) (Class 5) (0-75,76) 3-Y-O+ — **£3,234** (£962; £481; £240) **Stalls** Low

Form — RPR

4223 **1** **Wishing Well**[27] 6565 4-9-1 **67** .... CallumShepherd(5) 2 — 76
(Micky Hammond) *trckd ldrs: effrt on inner over 3f out: led over 1f out: drvn clr* **10/1**

51 **2** 2 ½ **Sporty Yankee (USA)**[29] 6503 3-9-5 **75** .... JoeyHaynes 7 — 81
(K R Burke) *hld up towards rr: hdwy 7f out: trcking ldrs over 3f out: hung lft over 1f out: kpt on to take 2nd last 150yds* **4/1**[2]

1460 **3** 1 ¼ **Hurry Home Poppa (IRE)**[27] 6565 6-9-7 **68** .... GrahamLee 9 — 72
(John Mackie) *mid-div: pushed along 6f out: hdwy over 2f out: swtchd lft over 1f out: kpt on to take 3rd last 100yds* **18/1**

3250 **4** 1 ½ **October Storm**[41] 6121 3-9-4 **74** .... PaulHanagan 12 — 76
(Mick Channon) *hld up in rr: drvn 6f out: hdwy over 2f out: kpt on to take 4th clsng stages* **11/1**

4431 **5** 1 **Glorious Legend (IRE)**[16] 6886 3-8-11 **67** .... ThomasBrown 10 — 67
(Ed Walker) *led after 2f: hdd over 1f out: fdd last 150yds* **3/1**[1]

0466 **6** 3 ¼ **Skiddaw Valleys**[47] 5918 4-9-9 **70** .... SilvestreDeSousa 3 — 66
(Alan Swinbank) *led 2f: chsd ldrs: drvn over 3f out: one pce fnl 2f* **10/1**

5630 **7** 1 ½ **Toola Boola**[38] 6219 6-9-1 **62** .... JackGarritty 6 — 56
(Jedd O'Keeffe) *trckd ldrs: effrt over 2f out: one pce* **50/1**

3405 **8** ¾ **Carpe Vita (IRE)**[66] 5262 4-9-8 **69** .... DavidNolan 1 — 62
(David O'Meara) *rr-div: hdwy 7f out: trcking ldrs over 3f out: rdr dropped whip over 1f out: one pce* **12/1**

0510 **9** 11 **Rock On Bollinski**[28] 6540 6-9-13 **74** .... (p) BenCurtis 4 — 51
(Brian Ellison) *s.s and sn given reminders: detached in last: reminders over 4f out: nvr on terms: eased clsng stages* **9/1**

0061 **10** 1 ¼ **Harry Champion**[11] 7008 3-9-3 **76** 6ex .... MarcMonaghan(3) 11 — 51
(Hugo Palmer) *trckd ldrs: effrt over 2f out: lost pl over 1f out: eased whn bhd clsng stages* **9/2**[3]

0-40 **11** 2 ½ **Devon Drum**[17] 6854 8-9-13 **74** .... JimCrowley 5 — 46
(David Brown) *mid-div: drvn over 3f out: lost pl 2f out: sn heavily eased* **16/1**

3m 5.87s (1.17) **Going Correction** +0.20s/f (Good)
WFA 3 from 4yo+ 9lb — **11** Ran SP% **120.5**
Speed ratings (Par 103): **104,102,101,101,100 98,97,97,91,90 88**
CSF £51.07 CT £730.60 TOTE £9.80: £2.90, £1.90, £4.60; EX 57.60 Trifecta £560.70.
Owner The Pennies Dropped Partnership **Bred** D Hudson-Wood **Trained** Middleham, N Yorks

FOCUS
This featured five last-time-out winners and represents a decent level of form for the grade.

7333 RACING UK IN GLORIOUS HD H'CAP (DIV I) 7f
4:00 (4:00) (Class 5) (0-70,70) 3-Y-O+ £3,234 (£962; £481; £240) Stalls Centre

Form RPR
1653 **1** **Gun Case**[15] 6907 4-9-4 67........(p) PaulHanagan 11 75
(Alistair Whillans) *in rr: outpcd in last and edgd lft over 3f out: hdwy over 2f out: chsng ldrs over 1f out: led 1f out: hld on towards fin.* **9/2**[3]
0021 **2** *nk* **Jordan James (IRE)**[31] 6434 3-9-2 67........ DaleSwift 1 73
(Brian Ellison) *chsd ldrs: led briefly over 1f out: kpt on towards fin* **9/1**
0040 **3** *1* **Kirkham**[31] 6436 3-9-0 65........ JoeDoyle 5 68
(Julie Camacho) *hld up in mid-div: smooth hdwy to trck ldrs over 1f out: rdn and kpt on same pce fnl f* **16/1**
6043 **4** *1* **My Dad Syd (USA)**[20] 6790 4-9-4 67........(v[1]) SilvestreDeSousa 6 69
(Ian Williams) *mid-div: hdwy over 2f out: kpt on same pce over 1f out* **7/2**[2]
030 **5** *2 3/4* **Firedanser**[28] 6541 3-8-11 67........ AdamMcNamara[(5)] 4 60
(Richard Fahey) *chsd ldrs: one pce over 1f out* **9/1**
6100 **6** *7* **Bay Mirage (IRE)**[58] 5537 3-9-1 66........(p) KevinStott 9 40
(Kevin Ryan) *carried rt s: rr-div: drvn and sme hdwy over 2f out: lost pl over 1f out* **33/1**
-000 **7** *nse* **Ivors Involvement (IRE)**[109] 3717 4-8-11 60........(e) CamHardie 2 35
(Tina Jackson) *t.k.h: led after 1f: hdd over 1f out: sn wknd* **66/1**
5500 **8** *nk* **Celtic Sixpence (IRE)**[25] 6635 8-8-12 61........ JackGarritty 7 35
(Nick Kent) *led 1f: chsd ldrs: lost pl over 1f out* **14/1**
0200 **9** *1 1/2* **Danot (IRE)**[37] 6226 4-9-3 66........ GrahamLee 12 36
(Jedd O'Keeffe) *in rr: drvn 3f out: nvr on terms* **22/1**
013 **10** *5* **Big Storm Coming**[22] 6700 6-9-6 69........ JimCrowley 10 26
(David Brown) *carried rt s: in rr: hdwy over 3f out: lost pl over 1f out: eased clsng stages* **3/1**[1]
0130 **11** *14* **Riponian**[3] 7253 6-8-7 56 oh1........(t) JoeyHaynes 3
(Susan Corbett) *wnt rt s: chsd ldrs: drvn 4f out: sn lost pl and bhd: eased clsng stages* **20/1**
3005 **12** *1/2* **Regal Response (IRE)**[7] 7111 3-9-5 70........[1] PaulMulrennan 8
(Michael Dods) *wnt rt s: chsd ldrs: reminders over 3f out: nt run on and lost pl over 1f out: sn heavily eased* **16/1**

1m 26.02s (1.52) **Going Correction** +0.275s/f (Good)
WFA 3 from 4yo+ 2lb **12** Ran SP% **117.4**
Speed ratings (Par 103): **102,101,100,99,96 88,88,87,86,80 64,63**
CSF £42.27 CT £607.33 TOTE £5.30: £1.60, £2.90, £5.00; EX 47.20 Trifecta £448.90.
Owner A C Whillans **Bred** Mildmay Bloodstock Ltd **Trained** Newmill-On-Slitrig, Borders

FOCUS
This looked the weaker of the two divisions on paper.

7334 RACING UK IN GLORIOUS HD H'CAP (DIV II) 7f
4:35 (4:35) (Class 5) (0-70,69) 3-Y-O+ £3,234 (£962; £481; £240) Stalls Centre

Form RPR
0135 **1** **Enjoy Life (IRE)**[17] 6851 3-8-13 63........[1] KevinStott 7 75
(Kevin Ryan) *led 1f: trckd ldrs: led 3f out: hdd appr fnl f: styd on to ld again nr fin* **9/2**[3]
1203 **2** *nk* **Someone Exciting**[18] 6834 3-8-6 56........ PatrickMathers 2 67
(David Thompson) *in rr: hdwy over 3f out: sn chsng ldrs: led appr fnl f: hdd nr fin* **12/1**
4321 **3** *2* **Desire**[27] 6568 4-8-13 66........ AdamMcNamara[(5)] 8 73
(Richard Fahey) *chsd ldrs: hung lft over 1f out: kpt on same pce* **6/1**
3365 **4** *2 1/4* **Cliff (IRE)**[15] 6907 6-8-7 62........ LewisEdmunds[(7)] 6 63
(Nigel Tinkler) *in rr: hdwy over 2f out: kpt on same pce fnl f* **7/2**[2]
0500 **5** *1 1/4* **Be Bold**[49] 5858 4-9-4 66........ BarryMcHugh 3 63
(Rebecca Bastiman) *mid-div: hdwy to chse ldrs over 2f out: one pce over 1f out* **20/1**
1321 **6** *2 3/4* **Mango Chutney**[27] 6569 3-9-1 65........(p) SamJames 12 54
(John Davies) *mid-div: effrt over 2f out: one pce* **10/1**
3314 **7** *2* **Yulong Xiongba (IRE)**[31] 6437 4-9-5 67........(be) JoeDoyle 1 51
(Julie Camacho) *trckd ldrs: effrt over 2f out: wknd over 1f out* **10/3**[1]
1614 **8** *3 1/4* **Reflation**[8] 7092 4-8-12 65........(p) PhilDennis[(5)] 5 41
(Michael Dods) *hld up in rr: effrt over 2f out: nvr a factor* **16/1**
3330 **9** *7* **Space War**[38] 6220 9-8-12 65........(t) AnnaHesketh[(5)] 11 22
(Michael Easterby) *in rr: edgd rt over 2f out: sn lost pl: bhd whn eased clsng stages* **25/1**
4400 **10** *3 1/2* **Fly True**[76] 4861 3-8-12 62........[1] JimCrowley 10 8
(Jeremy Gask) *s.i.s: t.k.h: hdwy to ld after 2f: hdd 3f out: sn lost pl: bhd whn eased clsng stages* **16/1**
3600 **11** *3/4* **Homeland (IRE)**[24] 6645 4-9-6 68........(bt[1]) AndrewMullen 4 13
(Brian Rothwell) *awkward s: w ldr: led after 1f: hdd aftr 2f: lost pl 2f out: sn bhd: eased clsng stages* **50/1**

1m 26.08s (1.58) **Going Correction** +0.275s/f (Good)
WFA 3 from 4yo+ 2lb **11** Ran SP% **116.9**
Speed ratings (Par 103): **101,100,98,95,94 91,88,85,77,73 72**
CSF £55.64 CT £335.49 TOTE £5.00: £1.80, £3.90, £2.00; EX 64.10 Trifecta £509.10.
Owner CN Farm Limited **Bred** E Puerari & Mme D Ades-Hazan **Trained** Hambleton, N Yorks

FOCUS
A modest 3yo handicap, in which many struggled in the conditions. It was run in a very similar time to that of the first division.

7335 RACING UK HD ON SKY432 MAIDEN STKS 6f
5:05 (5:12) (Class 5) 3-Y-O+ £3,234 (£962; £481; £240) Stalls Centre

Form RPR
0502 **1** **Gabrielle**[112] 3625 3-9-0 74........ SilvestreDeSousa 2 71
(Ed Dunlop) *s.i.s: drvn 4f out: chsng ldrs over 2f out: led over 1f out: kpt on* **13/8**[1]
5460 **2** *1 3/4* **Never In Doubt**[7] 7111 3-9-2 68........ NathanEvans[(3)] 4 70
(Richard Whitaker) *trckd ldr: edgd lft over 1f out: kpt on same pce to take 2nd last 75yds* **5/2**[2]
3205 **3** *3/4* **Shesthedream (IRE)**[21] 6744 3-9-0 65........ SamJames 1 63
(David O'Meara) *led: hdd over 1f out: one pce* **7/1**
4 *nk* **Blue Cliffs (IRE)** 3-9-5 0........ AndrewMullen 3 67
(Michael Appleby) *s.s: hdwy to chse ldrs after 2f: 2nd 2f out: one pce appr fnl f* **9/2**[3]
2334 **5** *9* **Cee Jay**[188] 1337 3-9-5 70........ GrahamLee 6 38
(Robert Cowell) *racd isolated towards stands' side: outpcd over 3f out: lost pl 2f out: bhd whn eased clsng stages* **6/1**

1m 14.26s (2.46) **Going Correction** +0.275s/f (Good)
WFA 3 from 4yo 1lb **5** Ran SP% **111.6**
Speed ratings (Par 103): **94,91,90,90,78**
CSF £6.05 TOTE £1.70: £1.10, £2.70; EX 5.80 Trifecta £18.20.
Owner The Belfour Partnership **Bred** Farmers Hill Stud **Trained** Newmarket, Suffolk

■ Pound Note was withdrawn. Price at time of withdrawal 50/1. Rule 4 does not apply.

FOCUS
This was weak and and took little winning.

7336 RACINGUK.COM/HD H'CAP (FOR LADY AMATEUR RIDERS) 1m 2f
5:35 (5:35) (Class 6) (0-65,65) 3-Y-O+ £2,634 (£810; £405) Stalls Low

Form RPR
3243 **1** **Galilee Chapel (IRE)**[24] 6647 7-9-8 55........(b) MissKBryson[(3)] 12 62
(Alistair Whillans) *hld up towards rr: hdwy to trck ldrs over 3f out: styd on fnl f: led fnl strides* **12/1**
5251 **2** *hd* **The Wee Barra (IRE)**[25] 6621 4-10-0 65........(p) MissHTLees[(7)] 10 72
(Kevin Ryan) *chsd ldrs: upsides over 2f out: led last 100yds: hdd fnl strides* **10/1**
5630 **3** *1 1/4* **Bahamian C**[20] 6772 5-10-0 63........ MissEmilyBullock[(5)] 2 67
(Richard Fahey) *trckd ldrs: led narrowly over 1f out: hdd and no ex last 100yds* **7/2**[1]
3034 **4** *2 1/4* **John Caesar (IRE)**[11] 7007 5-10-4 62........(tp) MrsCBartley 9 62
(Rebecca Bastiman) *s.i.s: in rr: hdwy over 3f out: one pce over 1f out* **16/1**
300 **5** *2 3/4* **McDelta**[21] 6737 6-10-5 63........ MissSBrotherton 6 58
(Ian Williams) *mid-div: effrt over 3f out: one pce fnl 2f* **7/2**[1]
356 **6** *hd* **The Excel Queen (IRE)**[24] 6646 3-9-3 57........ MissHDukes[(5)] 8 52
(Tony Coyle) *chsd ldrs: effrt on inner 3f out: one pce fnl 2f* **10/1**
-206 **7** *1/2* **Melgate Melody**[21] 6739 3-9-3 52........ MissJoannaMason 1 46
(Michael Easterby) *led 3f: chsd ldrs: led over 2f out: hdd over 1f out: fdd clsng stages* **8/1**[3]
5001 **8** *6* **Lean On Pete (IRE)**[24] 6647 7-10-2 60........ MissCWalton 7 43
(Ollie Pears) *w ldr: led after 3f: hdd over 2f out: wkng whn n.m.r on inner over 1f out* **7/1**[2]
3340 **9** *5* **Merchant Of Medici**[21] 6730 9-9-10 57........ MissBeckySmith[(3)] 11 31
(Micky Hammond) *mid-div: hdwy 4f out: lost pl over 1f out* **16/1**
1004 **10** *1 3/4* **Swiss Lait**[18] 6839 5-9-11 58........ MissAWaugh[(3)] 4 29
(Patrick Holmes) *s.i.s: in rr: swtchd rt 4f out: brife effrt over 2f out: sn wknd* **22/1**
5615 **11** *15* **Highway Robber**[45] 6004 3-9-4 56 ow3........ MissHelenCuthbert[(3)] 13
(Wilf Storey) *rr-div: sme hdwy 7f out: bhd fnl 3f: eased clsng stages* **16/1**
6350 **12** *2 3/4* **Percy Verence**[37] 6221 3-9-6 60........[1] MissKMargarson[(5)] 15
(K R Burke) *ldrs: lost pl 3f out: sn bhd: eased clsng stages* **25/1**
6030 **13** *18* **Diamond Runner (IRE)**[56] 5604 4-9-5 54....(p) MissEmmaBedford[(5)] 14
(John Norton) *ldrs: lost pl over 3f out: bhd whn eased over 1f out: t.o* **25/1**

2m 9.67s (2.57) **Going Correction** +0.20s/f (Good)
WFA 3 from 4yo+ 5lb **13** Ran SP% **123.6**
Speed ratings (Par 101): **97,96,95,94,91 91,91,86,82,81 69,66,52**
CSF £128.08 CT £516.71 TOTE £6.70: £3.80, £3.20, £1.40; EX 98.40 Trifecta £688.20.
Owner A C Whillans **Bred** Tally-Ho Stud **Trained** Newmill-On-Slitrig, Borders

FOCUS
Few got involved in this low-grade handicap for lady amateur riders.
T/Plt: £156.90 to a £1 stake. Pool: £62,599.33 - 291.14 winning units T/Qpdt: £29.50 to a £1 stake. Pool: £4,863.00 - 121.85 winning units **Walter Glynn**

7337 - 7338a (Foreign Racing) - See Raceform Interactive

7127 DUNDALK (A.W) (L-H)
Friday, October 14

OFFICIAL GOING: Polytrack: standard

7339a IRISHINJUREDJOCKEYS.COM APPRENTICE H'CAP 7f (P)
6:35 (6:38) 3-Y-O+ £4,748 (£1,466; £694; £308; £115)

RPR
1 **Appointment Only**[21] 6756 3-9-0 67........ ETDaly[(4)] 8 71
(John Joseph Murphy, Ire) *racd in mid-div on outer: clsr in 4th 3f out: rdn under 2f out: chsd clr ldr in 2nd ent fnl f: styd on wl between horses to ld cl home* **25/1**
2 *hd* **Dark Alliance (IRE)**[33] 6382 5-9-11 76........(t) RobertSmithers[(4)] 9 80
(M Halford, Ire) *racd towards rr: prog under 2f out: wnt 3rd ent fnl f: styd on wl to press ldrs in 3rd fnl 100yds: wnt 2nd cl home* **6/1**[3]
3 *hd* **Fairy Foxglove (IRE)**[31] 6465 6-10-0 75........ AnaO'Brien 6 78
(P J F Murphy, Ire) *sn chsd ldr in 2nd: travelled wl to ld 2f out and clr appr fnl f: strly pressed and hdd fnl 50yds: dropped to 3rd cl home* **10/1**
4 *1 3/4* **Murmuration (IRE)**[14] 6928 3-9-4 67........ DanielRedmond 5 65
(Brendan W Duke, Ire) *racd in mid-div: rdn under 2f out: wnt 6th ent fnl f: kpt on wl into 4th cl home: nt rch ldng trio* **40/1**
5 *nk* **Star Links (USA)**[210] 986 10-8-1 52........(b) DannySheehy[(4)] 10 50+
(S Donohoe, Ire) *hld up towards outer: 10th at 1/2-way: prog over 1f out: kpt on wl into 5th cl home: nvr nrr* **25/1**
6 *hd* **Hollybrowne (IRE)**[21] 6756 3-9-5 68........ TomMadden 2 64
(John James Feane, Ire) *led for 1f: chsd ldrs in 4th on inner: rdn and nt qckn under 2f out: 4th ent fnl f: no ex fnl 100yds* **10/1**
6 *dht* **Arbourfield (IRE)**[21] 6757 4-9-1 62........(v) KillianLeonard 12 59
(Mrs Prunella Dobbs, Ire) *racd in mid-div: pushed along 3f out: chsd ldrs in 5th under 2f out: nt qckn ins fnl f: kpt on one pce* **7/1**
8 *1 1/4* **Yamato (IRE)**[39] 6197 3-9-10 73........ ConorMcGovern 3 66
(M Halford, Ire) *racd in mid-div: rdn under 2f out: sme prog whn bit short of room over 1f out: kpt on same pce ins fnl f: nvr on terms* **9/2**[1]
9 *nk* **More Than Munny (USA)**[94] 4245 3-9-13 76........ OisinOrr 4 68
(J P Murtagh, Ire) *hld up: 12th at 1/2-way: prog over 1f out: kpt on same pce fnl f: nvr nrr* **10/1**
10 *1/2* **Tennesse Waltz (IRE)**[70] 5133 5-8-2 51........ AndrewBreslin[(2)] 14 43
(David Marnane, Ire) *hld up towards rr: swtchd wd 2f out: kpt on one pce fr over 1f out: nvr nrr* **20/1**
11 *1 3/4* **Black Agnes (IRE)**[7] 7132 3-9-2 67........(b) DylanHogan[(2)] 13 53
(Lee Smyth, Ire) *broke wl and tacked across to ld after 1f: hdd 2f out and wknd fnl f* **8/1**
12 *1/2* **Spirit Be With You (IRE)**[22] 6725 3-8-9 60........ SeanDavis[(2)] 11 45
(Miss Natalia Lupini, Ire) *hld up: towards rr at 1/2-way: rdn along in rr 2f out: kpt on one pce fr 1f out: nvr on terms* **50/1**
13 *3/4* **Nona Blu**[24] 6645 4-9-9 70........ DonaghO'Connor 7 54
(Michael Wigham) *t.k.h to chse ldrs in 3rd: rdn and nt qckn under 2f out: sn wknd* **6/1**[3]
14 *nse* **Indian Landing (IRE)**[31] 6461 8-8-12 66........ KillianGallagher[(7)] 1 50
(Tracey Collins, Ire) *racd in mid-div: sme prog towards inner over 1f out: no imp ins fnl f* **5/1**[2]

1m 25.35s (85.35)
WFA 3 from 4yo+ 2lb **14** Ran SP% **131.2**
CSF £175.76 CT £1660.19 TOTE £46.20: £9.30, £2.40, £3.10; DF 368.40 Trifecta £2153.40.

Owner Armada Racing Partnership **Bred** Miss A Gibson Fleming **Trained** Upton, Co Cork

FOCUS

A driving finish inside the final furlong, the winner proving nicely handicapped on his first start in the grade.

7337 - 7341a (Foreign Racing) - See Raceform Interactive

7342a CARLINGFORD STKS (LISTED RACE) 1m 2f 150y(P)

8:05 (8:05) 3-Y-0+

£19,522 (£6,286; £2,977; £1,323; £661; £330)

RPR

1 **Hawke (IRE)**[14] 6932 4-9-7 103 PatSmullen 7 106+
(J P Murtagh, Ire) *hld up: travelled wl to take clsr order 2f out: led appr fnl f and sn rdn clr: kpt on wl clsng stages* **5/4**[1]

2 1 ¾ **Elusive Heights (IRE)**[21] 6760 3-9-2 100 ColinKeane 8 104+
(G M Lyons, Ire) *racd in rr: travelled wl to cl over 1f out: rdn to chse ldr in 2nd ent fnl f: kpt on wl: nt rch wnr* **4/1**[3]

3 1 ½ **Tennessee Wildcat (IRE)**[14] 6932 6-9-7 101 GaryCarroll 2 100
(G M Lyons, Ire) *hld up towards rr: prog on inner under 2f out: chsd ldrs in 3rd ent fnl f: no imp fnl 100yds: kpt on same pce* **16/1**

4 4 ½ **St Gallen (IRE)**[58] 5566 3-9-2 93 [1] DeclanMcDonogh 4 92
(John Joseph Murphy, Ire) *trckd ldr in 2nd: rdn over 2f out: nt qckn over 1f out in 5th: sn one pce in 4th* **10/1**

5 nse **Mandatario**[57] 5591 5-9-7 96 (t) KevinManning 5 91
(J S Bolger, Ire) *chsd ldrs: rdn 2f out: nt qckn appr fnl f in 6th: kpt on one pce* **14/1**

6 3 ¼ **Chilli Spice (IRE)**[14] 6933 3-8-11 91 NGMcCullagh 1 81
(J P Murtagh, Ire) *led tl hdd appr fnl f: sn wknd* **14/1**

7 ½ **Spruce Meadows (IRE)**[14] 6933 3-9-2 91 (p) ChrisHayes 3 85
(John James Feane, Ire) *chsd ldrs on inner in 3rd: rdn and nt qckn under 2f out: wknd qckly fr 1f out* **7/2**[2]

8 31 **Highly Toxic (IRE)**[26] 6608 5-9-7 89 (v) LeighRoche 6 23
(Patrick J Flynn, Ire) *racd in mid-div on outer: clsr in 4th after 4f: rdn and no imp under 2f out: sn eased* **50/1**

2m 12.35s (132.35)
WFA 3 from 4yo+ 6lb **8** Ran SP% **116.9**
CSF £6.64 TOTE £2.20: £1.02, £1.20, £2.60; DF 6.70 Trifecta £34.90.
Owner Ballygallon Stud Limited **Bred** Ballygallon Stud Limited **Trained** Coolaghknock Glebe,Co Kildare

FOCUS

An impressive performance from the winner, a horse that clearly loves this surface and looks a horse that can hold his own in Group company.

7343 - 7344a (Foreign Racing) - See Raceform Interactive

7136 MAISONS-LAFFITTE (R-H)

Friday, October 14

OFFICIAL GOING: Turf: good to soft

7345a PRIX DEEP ROOTS (MAIDEN) (2YO COLTS & GELDINGS) (ROUND) (TURF) 1m (S)

12:45 (12:00) 2-Y-0 **£9,926** (£3,970; £2,977; £1,985; £992)

RPR

1 **Mankib**[18] 2-9-2 0 AurelienLemaitre 4 78
(F Head, France) **9/5**[1]

2 ½ **Rayon Vert (FR)**[36] 2-9-2 0 VincentCheminaud 9 77
(H-A Pantall, France) **47/10**[3]

3 hd **Staff College (FR)**[33] 6376 2-9-2 0 ChristopheSoumillon 5 76
(Henry Spiller) *sn led: kicked for home over 2 1/2f out: 2l clr and hrd rdn 1 1/2f out: styd on u.p: hdd fnl strides and lost 2nd post* **9/1**

4 1 ¾ **Haky (IRE)**[21] 2-9-2 0 ThierryJarnet 1 73
(J E Hammond, France) **54/10**

5 1 ½ **Galipad** 2-8-11 0 MaximeGuyon 3 64
(A Fabre, France) **12/5**[2]

6 7 **Nile Paris (FR)**[25] 6638 2-9-2 0 EddyHardouin 8 54
(J-P Gallorini, France) **62/1**

7 12 **Alsylal Dolois (FR)**[14] 2-8-8 0 ClementLecoeuvre(8) 7 28
(A Bonin, France) **32/1**

8 ½ **L'Amour Du Risk (FR)** 2-9-2 0 MickaelBarzalona 6 26
(J-P Gallorini, France) **17/1**

1m 42.6s (0.30) **8** Ran SP% **118.5**
WIN (incl. 1 euro stake): 1.90 (Mankib coupled with Haky). PLACES: 1.20, 1.50, 1.90. DF: 6.10. SF: 9.80.
Owner Hamdan Al Maktoum **Bred** Shadwell Estate Company Limited **Trained** France

7346a PRIX BANSHEE (MAIDEN) (2YO FILLIES) (ROUND) (TURF) 1m (S)

1:15 (12:00) 2-Y-0 **£9,926** (£3,970; £2,977; £1,985; £992)

RPR

1 **Normandie (GER)**[25] 6639 2-9-2 0 MaximeGuyon 7 80
(Mme Pia Brandt, France) **6/5**[1]

2 2 ½ **Pink Paint (FR)**[14] 6937 2-9-2 0 OlivierPeslier 10 75
(M Delcher Sanchez, France) **12/1**

3 ¾ **Canterbury Quad (FR)**[42] 6077 2-9-2 0 ChristopheSoumillon 9 73
(Henry Spiller) *settled in rr fr wd draw: hdwy fr last over 2f out: rdn and styd on appr fnl f: kpt on u.p but nt pce to get on terms: run flattened out last 100yds* **14/1**

4 1 ½ **Overview** 2-8-11 0 VincentCheminaud 5 65
(A Fabre, France) **37/10**[2]

5 5 **Zouk (FR)**[52] 2-9-2 0 LouisBeuzelin 8 59
(P Bary, France) **32/1**

6 2 ½ **Marchantie (FR)**[18] 2-9-2 0 StephanePasquier 6 53
(Y Gourraud, France) **69/10**

7 15 **Roman Beauty (FR)**[105] 2-9-2 0 (p) Pierre-CharlesBoudot 1 20
(D Prod'Homme, France) **67/10**[3]

8 2 **Nile Desire**[25] 6639 2-9-2 0 GregoryBenoist 2 16
(D Smaga, France) **10/1**

9 nse **Kallipso (FR)**[36] 2-8-10 0 KyllanBarbaud(6) 4 16
(A Junk, France) **95/1**

1m 43.08s (0.78) **9** Ran SP% **119.9**
WIN (incl. 1 euro stake): 2.20. PLACES: 1.30, 2.40, 3.10. DF: 11.00. SF: 17.00.
Owner Laurent Dassault **Bred** Gestut Wittekindshof **Trained** France

7347a CRITERIUM DE MAISONS-LAFFITTE (GROUP 2) (2YO) (TURF) 6f (S)

1:45 (12:00) 2-Y-0 **£79,632** (£30,735; £14,669; £9,779; £4,889)

RPR

1 **Sans Equivoque (GER)**[23] 6694 2-8-13 0 ThierryJarnet 8 108
(D Guillemin, France) *w.w in rr: hdwy on outer over 1 1/2f out: rdn to chal ent fnl f: r.o u.p: led 100yds out: all out* **3/1**[2]

2 hd **Boos (FR)**[24] 2-8-13 0 CristianDemuro 1 107
(P Sogorb, France) *w.w in fnl pair: drvn to cl over 1 1/2f out: chsd ldrs ent fnl f: styd on u.p: jst hld* **56/10**

3 1 **Nations Alexander (IRE)**[21] 6748 2-8-13 0 PatDobbs 2 104
(Richard Hannon) *cl up on inner: rdn to chal under 1 1/2f out: led 1f out: hdd fnl 100yds: no ex* **53/10**[3]

4 1 ¼ **Fas (IRE)**[23] 6694 2-9-2 0 MaximeGuyon 7 103
(Mme Pia Brandt, France) *keen: chsd ldng pair: drvn 2f out: ev ch over 1f out: one pce u.p fnl f* **63/10**

5 snk **King Of Spades (FR)**[12] 6987 2-9-2 0 (b) ChristopheSoumillon 6 103
(F Vermeulen, France) *sn chsng ldrs: outpcd and drvn 1/2-way: hrd rdn over 1f out: styd on u.p last 100yds: nvr on terms* **8/1**

6 ¾ **Stop The Wages (IRE)**[41] 6124 2-8-13 0 MickaelBarzalona 4 98
(Brian Meehan) *led: hdd 1f out: one pce u.p fnl f* **28/1**

7 6 **Koropick (IRE)**[20] 6785 2-9-2 0 JackMitchell 9 83
(Hugo Palmer) *keen: pressed ldr on outer: rdn to hold pl under 2f out: wknd appr fnl f* **19/10**[1]

1m 12.78s (-0.62) **7** Ran SP% **118.8**
WIN (incl. 1 euro stake): 4.00. PLACES: 1.50, 1.90, 1.80. DF: 10.60. SF: 17.60.
Owner Sun Bloodstock Sarl **Bred** Pontchartrain Stud Et Al **Trained** France

FOCUS

Not a strong race for the level, even before two key non-runners.

7348a PRIX DE SAINT-CYR (LISTED RACE) (3YO FILLIES) (STRAIGHT) (TURF) 7f (S)

2:15 (12:00) 3-Y-0 **£20,220** (£8,088; £6,066; £4,044; £2,022)

RPR

1 **Pas De Soucis (IRE)**[15] 3-8-10 0 RonanThomas 5 100
(Robert Collet, France) **69/10**[3]

2 ¾ **Sasparella (FR)**[13] 6975 3-8-10 0 MaximeGuyon 7 98
(C Laffon-Parias, France) **41/5**

3 snk **Qatar Power (FR)**[36] 6272 3-9-0 0 (b[1]) OlivierPeslier 1 101
(F Head, France) **11/1**

4 snk **Robanne**[13] 6939 3-8-11 0 ow1 ChristopheSoumillon 9 98
(William Knight) *w.w in tch in gp of 6 towards centre of trck: drvn 2f out: chsd ldrs appr 1f out: styd on same pce fnl f* **3/1**[1]

5 ½ **Pietrafiore (IRE)**[33] 3-8-10 0 LukasDelozier 4 96
(H-A Pantall, France) *w.w towards rr of stands' side gp of 7: rdn 2f and tk clsr order: styd on same pce fnl f: nvr on terms* **50/1**

6 nk **Syrita (FR)**[32] 3-8-10 0 AntoineHamelin 11 95
(M Nigge, France) **13/1**

7 nk **Blossomtime**[22] 6728 3-8-10 0 MickaelBarzalona 10 94
(H-A Pantall, France) *cl up in gp of 6 towards centre of trck: pushed along to overall 2f out: hdd appr fnl f: grad lft bhd* **11/1**

8 hd **Spiga (IRE)**[22] 6728 3-8-10 0 Pierre-CharlesBoudot 13 93
(A Fabre, France) **12/1**

9 nk **Yeah Baby Yeah (IRE)**[13] 6939 3-8-10 0 (p) UmbertoRispoli 1 93
(Gay Kelleway) *in rr of gp of 7 on stands' side: rdn and no imp wl over 1 1/2f out: styd on fnl f: nrest at fin* **24/1**

10 4 **Ella Diva (FR)**[26] 6611 3-8-10 0 GregoryBenoist 2 82
(N Caullery, France) **36/1**

11 nk **Pop By (USA)**[44] 3-8-10 0 StephanePasquier 3 81
(F-H Graffard, France) **37/1**

12 ½ **Midweek**[43] 6070 3-9-0 0 VincentCheminaud 8 84
(Mme C Head-Maarek, France) **7/2**[2]

13 4 **Villebaudon (FR)**[15] 3-8-10 0 CristianDemuro 6 69
(C Ferland, France) **15/1**

1m 26.5s (-1.50) **13** Ran SP% **119.8**
WIN (incl. 1 euro stake): 7.90. PLACES: 2.50, 2.80, 3.60. DF: 39.00. SF: 82.00.
Owner Mme Anne-Marie Hayes **Bred** Knocktoran & Ballantines Racing Stud Ltd **Trained** Chantilly, France

6939 ASCOT (R-H)

Saturday, October 15

OFFICIAL GOING: Good

Wind: Light, half behind Weather: Fine but cloudy

7349 QIPCO BRITISH CHAMPIONS LONG DISTANCE CUP (GROUP 2) 2m

1:25 (1:26) (Class 1) 3-Y-0+

£198,485 (£75,250; £37,660; £18,760; £9,415; £4,725) **Stalls** Low

Form RPR

0331 1 **Sheikhzayedroad**[36] 6284 7-9-7 115 MartinHarley 3 117
(David Simcock) *trckd ldng pair: rdn 2f out and carried hd awkwardly: clsd over 1f out: drvn ahd last 110yds: styd on stoutly* **11/1**

6121 2 ½ **Quest For More (IRE)**[14] 6974 6-9-7 118 (b) GeorgeBaker 6 116
(Roger Charlton) *t.k.h: trckd ldr: shkn up to chal 2f out: upsides fnl f but wnr wnt past 110yds out: styd on* **9/1**

2401 3 ½ **Simple Verse (IRE)**[37] 6259 4-9-4 113 OisinMurphy 4 113
(Ralph Beckett) *trckd ldng trio: rdn 3f out: styd on fr 2f out: tk 3rd cl home but nvr quite able to chal* **6/1**[2]

1123 4 ½ **Order Of St George (IRE)**[13] 6989 4-9-7 120 RyanMoore 9 115
(A P O'Brien, Ire) *sweating: sn in 6th: rdn wl over 2f out and no prog: styd on fr over 1f out: tk 4th cl home and nrst fin but nvr able to threaten* **4/6**[1]

3113 5 ¾ **Nearly Caught (IRE)**[14] 6974 6-9-7 113 UmbertoRispoli 1 114
(Hughie Morrison) *led: semt for home 3f out: drvn 2f out: hdd and fdd last 110yds* **25/1**

101- 6 3 ½ **Litigant**[343] 7757 8-9-7 112 JamesDoyle 5 110
(Joseph Tuite) *chsd ldrs in 5th: drvn 3f out: no imp 2f out: fdd* **20/1**

50-2 7 hd **Forgotten Rules (IRE)**[20] 6820 6-9-7 112 PatSmullen 8 110
(D K Weld, Ire) *hld up in 8th: plenty to do whn pce lifted 3f out: shkn up and no prog over 2f out* **8/1**[3]

0066 8 ¾ **Suegioo (FR)**[42] 6118 7-9-7 104 (p) PaulHanagan 2 109
(Richard Fahey) *settled in last pair: rdn and struggling over 3f out: no prog after* **66/1**

6510 **9** *nk* **Sandro Botticelli (IRE)**[79] 4799 4-9-7 107....................(p) FrankieDettori 7 109
(John Ryan) *a in last pair: rdn and struggling over 3f out* **50/1**

4000 **10** *1 ¼* **Gold Prince (IRE)**[28] 6573 4-9-7 93.................................. AdamKirby 10 107?
(Sylvester Kirk) *sn in 7th: rdn and no prog 3f out: wknd wl over 1f out* **100/1**

3m 31.52s (2.52) **Going Correction** +0.15s/f (Good) **10** Ran SP% **116.8**
Speed ratings (Par 115): **99,98,98,98,97 96,96,95,95,94**
CSF £98.65 CT £655.78 TOTE £12.70: £2.40, £2.40, £1.80; EX 81.80 Trifecta £365.80.
Owner Mohammed Jaber **Bred** Rabbah Bloodstock Limited **Trained** Newmarket, Suffolk

FOCUS
The Straight Course was divided into two with a rail in the middle of the course. The rail on the Round Course was at its innermost position so distances are as advertised. Pat Smullen described the going as "lovely good ground", although Martin Harley felt it was "on the slow side" and Oisin Murphy felt it may have been "a bit quicker" than good, so differing reports. End of a long season for many of these classy stayers, they soon steadied the reasonable early gallop and it certainly paid to race prominently. The Doncaster Cup 1-2 again came to the fore, filling the same positions here ahead of the front pair in the betting. A small pb from Sheikhzayedroad.

7350 QIPCO BRITISH CHAMPIONS SPRINT STKS (GROUP 1) 6f
2:00 (2:02) (Class 1) 3-Y-O+

£340,260 (£129,000; £64,560; £32,160; £16,140; £8,100) **Stalls** Centre

Form RPR

1012 **1** **The Tin Man**[42] 6120 4-9-2 115.. TomQueally 3 121
(James Fanshawe) *hld up in last of trio towards far side and off the pce: clsd fr 2f out: rdn to ld 110yds out: styd on wl* **13/2**

4426 **2** *1* **Growl**[14] 6942 4-9-2 104...[1] GrahamLee 8 118
(Richard Fahey) *hld up in midfield of gp towards nr side: rdn and prog and moved towards far side over 1f out: styd on to take 2nd last strides* **50/1**

1201 **3** *shd* **Brando**[28] 6558 4-9-2 116... TomEaves 7 118
(Kevin Ryan) *travelled wl: hld up towards rr of nr side gp: rdn and prog to ld gp over 1f out but several l bhd overall ldr: styd on wl fnl f to take 3rd last strides* **14/1**

1531 **4** *½* **Signs Of Blessing (IRE)**[69] 5217 5-9-2 117........... StephanePasquier 2 116
(F Rohaut, France) *wl away: overall ldr towards far side: clr and rdn wl over 1f out: fdd and hdd 110yds out* **9/1**

5104 **5** *shd* **Don't Touch**[14] 6941 4-9-2 110.....................................(v[1]) TonyHamilton 1 116
(Richard Fahey) *chsd overall ldr towards far side: rdn 2f out: grad clsd fnl f but lost pls nr fin* **33/1**

2141 **6** *1 ½* **Librisa Breeze**[14] 6942 4-9-2 113.................................. RobertWinston 6 111
(Dean Ivory) *racd towards nr side: hld up in last trio: rdn 2f out: styd on fr over 1f out: nrst fin but n.d* **6/1[3]**

1131 **7** *1 ¼* **Quiet Reflection**[42] 6120 3-8-12 116........................... DougieCostello 9 104
(K R Burke) *trckd ldrs nr side: shkn up 2f out: nt qckn wl over 1f out: steadily fdd* **4/1[1]**

0400 **8** *¾* **Jack Dexter**[28] 6558 7-9-2 99... DanielTudhope 4 105
(Jim Goldie) *racd towards nr side: hld up in last trio: rdn over 2f out: styd on same pce fr over 1f out: nvr able to rch ldrs* **100/1**

5055 **9** *1 ½* **Mr Lupton (IRE)**[42] 6120 3-9-1 109................................ JamieSpencer 5 100
(Richard Fahey) *racd towards nr side: sn in last: rdn and kpt on fr over 1f out: no ch* **33/1**

11-1 **10** *¾* **Shalaa (IRE)**[14] 6941 3-9-1 121....................................... FrankieDettori 10 98
(John Gosden) *led gp towards nr side but nt on terms w overall ldr: hdd in gp over 1f out and wknd* **4/1[1]**

-510 **11** *5* **Twilight Son**[98] 4151 4-9-2 117.. RyanMoore 11 82
(Henry Candy) *trckd ldrs nr side: shkn up 2f out: no prog and sn btn: wknd over 1f out* **5/1[2]**

0113 **12** *nk* **Mecca's Angel (IRE)**[13] 6990 5-8-13 122.................. PaulMulrennan 14 78
(Michael Dods) *racd clst to nr side rail: chsd ldrs: rdn and struggling 2f out: sn wknd* **8/1**

2020 **13** *3 ¼* **Donjuan Triumphant (IRE)**[42] 6120 3-9-1 114.............. AlexisBadel 13 70
(Richard Fahey) *chsd ldrs towards nr side tl wknd qckly 2f out* **40/1**

1m 12.15s (-2.35) **Going Correction** +0.15s/f (Good)
WFA 3 from 4yo+ 1lb **13** Ran SP% **123.3**
Speed ratings (Par 117): **121,119,119,118,118 116,115,114,112,111 104,104,99**
CSF £315.78 CT £4383.09 TOTE £8.20: £2.30, £10.30, £4.10; EX 365.00 Trifecta £12278.90.
Owner Fred Archer Racing - Ormonde **Bred** Mrs Elizabeth Grundy **Trained** Newmarket, Suffolk
■ Mobsta was withdrawn. Price at time of withdrawal 66-1. Rule 4 does not apply.
■ Stewards' Enquiry : Stephane Pasquier trainer brought an unallowable substance into the stables and also an allowable substance but without permission. They interviewed the trainer, the Veterinary Officer and two Equine Welfare and Integrity Officers. Having heard their evidence, the Stewards referred the matter to the Head Office of the British Horseracing Authority under Rule (G)2.6.1.

FOCUS
The absence of Limato was a shame, but still a race worthy of the name featuring five individual Group 1 winners. The field split into two early with the main group racing more towards the nearside, while three came up the middle and they finished first, fourth and fifth. With a couple of handicappers (albeit very good ones) finishing in the places and several of the big names disappointing, it would be easy to downgrade the form, but despite what looked a far-from-breakneck early pace they they dipped 0.45sec under standard time, so the winner still deserves all the plaudits. The field was reduced by one when Mobsta was withdrawn after getting upset in the stalls. The Tin Man is an up-to-scratch winner, wth Growl a big improver.

7351 QIPCO BRITISH CHAMPIONS FILLIES & MARES STKS (GROUP 1) 1m 4f
2:35 (2:35) (Class 1) 3-Y-O+

£340,260 (£129,000; £64,560; £32,160; £16,140; £8,100) **Stalls** Low

Form RPR

-311 **1** **Journey**[22] 6747 4-9-5 115.. FrankieDettori 11 121
(John Gosden) *trckd clr ldr: pushed along to cl fr 2f out: shkn up to ld jst over 1f out: stormed clr: impressive* **4/1[2]**

1511 **2** *4* **Speedy Boarding**[13] 6988 4-9-5 115............................ FrederikTylicki 12 115
(James Fanshawe) *wl in tch: swtchd lft and rdn 2f out: prog to chse ldg pair wl over 1f out: styd on to take 2nd last 110yds: no ch w wnr* **14/1**

4423 **3** *nk* **Queen's Trust**[58] 5586 3-8-12 112.................................... AndreaAtzeni 3 114+
(Sir Michael Stoute) *nt that wl away and in rr: nt clr run over 2f out: drvn and gd prog wl over 1f out: styd on wl to take 3rd last 50yds and pressed runner-up nr fin* **11/1**

1042 **4** *1* **Pretty Perfect (IRE)**[37] 6259 3-8-12 111.................... SeamieHeffernan 8 112
(A P O'Brien, Ire) *led: clr after 4f: reeled in fr 2f out: hdd jst over 1f out: no ch w wnr and lost 2 pls last 100yds* **14/1**

1611 **5** *shd* **Seventh Heaven (IRE)**[58] 5586 3-8-12 119.................... RyanMoore 13 112+
(A P O'Brien, Ire) *swtchd fr wd draw: tried to burrow way through on inner early but stl towards rr: rdn over 2f out: kpt on fr over 1f out: nrst fin but n.d* **5/4[1]**

2023 **6** *½* **Architecture (IRE)**[69] 5220 3-8-12 112.................................. JamesDoyle 4 111+
(Hugo Palmer) *bmpd abt in midfield after 2f: stYd in tch: rdn and tried to cl on ldrs over 2f out: kpt on but nvr able to threaten* **16/1**

-111 **7** *9* **Zhukova (IRE)**[35] 6351 4-9-5 115...[1] PatSmullen 1 97
(D K Weld, Ire) *prom in chsng gp: chsd ldng pair briefly 2f out: wknd qckly jst over 1f out* **7/1[3]**

3100 **8** *nk* **Even Song (IRE)**[58] 5586 3-8-12 110............................ JamieSpencer 2 96
(A P O'Brien, Ire) *in tch in midfield: rdn and effrt whn nudged 2f out: no prog over 1f out: wknd* **22/1**

1104 **9** *1 ¼* **Maleficent Queen**[30] 6505 4-9-5 105.................................[1] PhillipMakin 6 94
(Keith Dalgleish) *dwlt: racd in last pair: drvn 3f out: no great prog over 2f out: sn no ch* **66/1**

4210 **10** *nk* **Bocca Baciata (IRE)**[55] 5691 4-9-5 111................. StephanePasquier 10 94
(Mrs John Harrington, Ire) *trapped out wd and tk fierce hold early: towards rr: rdn wl over 2f out and no prog* **50/1**

5614 **11** *¾* **Promising Run (USA)**[22] 6746 3-8-12 106........................ JimCrowley 5 92
(Saeed bin Suroor) *prom in chsng gp tl wknd jst over 2f out* **50/1**

6113 **12** *½* **California (IRE)**[37] 6259 4-9-5 103.................................... RobertHavlin 7 92
(John Gosden) *prom in chsng gp but trapped out wd: wkng whn nudged 2f out* **40/1**

2515 **13** *7* **Bateel (IRE)**[55] 5691 4-9-5 104.. WilliamBuick 9 80
(David Simcock) *hld up in last pair fr wd draw: rdn and no prog 3f out: sn no ch* **25/1**

2m 28.41s (-4.09) **Going Correction** +0.15s/f (Good)
WFA 3 from 4yo 7lb **13** Ran SP% **120.5**
Speed ratings (Par 117): **119,116,116,115,115 115,109,108,108,107 107,107,102**
CSF £55.19 CT £583.15 TOTE £5.20: £1.60, £3.10, £3.10; EX 64.60 Trifecta £682.10.
Owner George Strawbridge **Bred** George Strawbridge **Trained** Newmarket, Suffolk

FOCUS
A good edition of this, it was a bit of a rough race and the Ballydoyle pacemaker opened up a clear lead, but a clear-cut and impressive winner emerged. The form makes sense.

7352 QUEEN ELIZABETH II STKS (GROUP 1) (SPONSORED BY QIPCO) 1m (S)
3:10 (3:12) (Class 1) 3-Y-O+

£656,432 (£248,867; £124,549; £62,043; £31,137; £15,626) **Stalls** Centre

Form RPR

1113 **1** **Minding (IRE)**[35] 6354 3-8-12 120...................................... RyanMoore 8 123+
(A P O'Brien, Ire) *trckd ldng pair in centre: shkn up and clsd to ld overall jst over 2f out: rdn and asserted over 1f out: ld dwindled nr fin but a in charge* **7/4[1]**

3131 **2** *½* **Ribchester (IRE)**[62] 5449 3-9-1 121.................................. WilliamBuick 2 124
(Richard Fahey) *t.k.h: trckd overall ldr in centre: clsd smoothly to chal jst over 2f out: sn rdn and nt qckn w wnr: styd on to cl last 150yds: a hld* **7/2[2]**

3601 **3** *1* **Lightning Spear**[49] 5873 5-9-4 117.................................. OisinMurphy 7 122
(David Simcock) *hld up in last pair nr side: prog wl over 1f out and swtchd towards centre: chsd ldng pair jst over 1f out: styd on same pce after* **9/1**

1301 **4** *2 ¼* **Awtaad (IRE)**[35] 6353 3-9-1 118.....................................(t) ChrisHayes 12 117
(Kevin Prendergast, Ire) *hld up in midfield nr side: rdn to cl whn bmpd wl over 1f out: edgd rt after but kpt on in 4th pl fnl f: no imp ldrs* **15/2**

2120 **5** *3 ¼* **Galileo Gold**[62] 5449 3-9-1 122.. FrankieDettori 9 109
(Hugo Palmer) *t.k.h: trckd ldr nr side: shkn up to chal whn bmpd wl over 1f out: carried rt sn after: fdd fnl f* **11/2[3]**

1020 **6** *½* **Stormy Antarctic**[62] 5449 3-9-1 114................................. GeorgeBaker 5 108
(Ed Walker) *stdd s: hld up in last of centre gp: effrt and sme prog on far side over 2f out: no hdwy over 1f out: kpt on same pce after* **40/1**

0243 **7** *1 ¾* **Adaay (IRE)**[35] 6328 4-9-4 111....................................(bt) PaulHanagan 11 104
(William Haggas) *racd nr side: hld up in midfield: drvn and no prog over 2f out: kpt on one pce over 1f out* **66/1**

21-1 **8** *¾* **Hathal (USA)**[42] 6117 4-9-4 113....................................(p) PatCosgrave 10 102
(William Haggas) *hld up bhd ldrs nr side: effrt and in tch 2f out: wknd over 1f out* **25/1**

1-33 **9** *nk* **Hit It A Bomb (USA)**[35] 6353 3-9-1 113.................. SeamieHeffernan 4 101
(A P O'Brien, Ire) *stdd s: hld up in 4th of centre gp: rdn and no prog over 2f out: wl btn over 1f out* **18/1**

4151 **10** *2* **Breton Rock (IRE)**[35] 6328 6-9-4 113............................. AndreaAtzeni 6 97
(David Simcock) *stdd s: hld up in last pl nr side: no prog 2f out: nvr a factor* **40/1**

1661 **11** *hd* **Jet Setting (IRE)**[13] 6983 3-8-12 120................................ ShaneFoley 13 93
(Adrian Paul Keatley, Ire) *led nr side gp and on terms to over 2f out: lost gp ld and wknd wl over 1f out* **25/1**

0322 **12** *3 ¾* **Mitchum Swagger**[42] 6117 4-9-4 112............................ JamieSpencer 3 88
(David Lanigan) *stdd s: hld up in 5th of centre gp: rdn and no prog over 2f out: wl btn whn eased fnl f* **33/1**

-000 **13** *10* **Barchan (USA)**[123] 3242 4-9-4 80...................................... JamesDoyle 1 65
(Roger Varian) *overall ldr in centre: hdd & wknd jst over 2f out: eased over 1f out* **150/1**

1m 38.53s (-2.27) **Going Correction** +0.15s/f (Good)
WFA 3 from 4yo+ 3lb **13** Ran SP% **118.7**
Speed ratings (Par 117): **117,116,115,113,110 109,107,107,106,104 104,100,90**
CSF £6.94 CT £45.11 TOTE £2.60: £1.40, £1.60, £2.40; EX 9.60 Trifecta £64.00.
Owner Derrick Smith & Mrs John Magnier & Michael Tabor **Bred** Orpendale, Chelston & Wynatt **Trained** Cashel, Co Tipperary
■ Stewards' Enquiry : James Doyle caution; guilty of failing to take all reasonable and permissible measures to obtain the best possible placing.

FOCUS
A cracking renewal of this Championship event, with Minding rated well up to standard. All that was really missing was a top-class older miler, such as a Solow, and five of the seven 3yos were officially rated higher than any of their elders. The field split into two fairly equal groups early with the first two coming up the centre, but although the third and fourth horses raced in the nearside group early, they both edged right towards the centre late on. The pace was solid and this was another race to dip inside standard, this time by 0.27sec.

7353 QIPCO CHAMPION STKS (BRITISH CHAMPIONS MIDDLE DISTANCE) (GROUP 1) 1m 2f
3:45 (3:49) (Class 1) 3-Y-O+

£737,230 (£279,500; £139,880; £69,680; £34,970; £17,550) **Stalls** Low

Form RPR

1111 **1** **Almanzor (FR)**[35] 6354 3-9-0 127.......................... ChristopheSoumillon 1 129+
(J-C Rouget, France) *dwlt: sn rcvrd into 5th on inner: plld off rail and prog over 2f out: shkn up to ld over 1f out: r.o strly: won decisively* **11/8[1]**

2221 **2** *2* **Found (IRE)**[13] 6989 4-9-2 123.. RyanMoore 11 122
(A P O'Brien, Ire) *hld up towards rr: prog jst over 2f out: chsd wnr jst over 1f out: r.o wl but readily hld* **5/2[2]**

13-P **3** *1 ¾* **Jack Hobbs**[168] 1863 4-9-5 123 .... WilliamBuick 9 122+
(John Gosden) *hld up in last trio: rdn and gd prog on outer fr 2f out: styd on to take 3rd wl ins fnl f: no ch w ldng pair* **7/1**[3]

5155 **4** *1 ¼* **My Dream Boat (IRE)**[35] 6354 4-9-5 122 .... AdamKirby 3 119
(Clive Cox) *wl in rr: stl in last pair and rdn 2f out: styd on fnl f to take 4th last stride: no ch* **20/1**

260 **5** *hd* **The Grey Gatsby (IRE)**[13] 6989 5-9-5 113 .... JamesDoyle 8 119
(Kevin Ryan) *trapped out wd but chsd ldrs: prog and rdn to ld jst over 2f out: hdd and outpcd over 1f out: fdd ins fnl f: lost 4th last stride* **33/1**

114- **6** *1* **Racing History (IRE)**[364] 7281 4-9-5 117 .... SilvestreDeSousa 5 117
(Saeed bin Suroor) *t.k.h: trckd ldr: chal over 2f out: sn outpcd and btn: fdd* **16/1**

-152 **7** *shd* **Midterm**[34] 6392 3-9-0 113 .... AndreaAtzeni 6 117
(Sir Michael Stoute) *t.k.h: trckd ldrs: lost pl and rdn 2f out: n.d after: kpt on nr fin* **12/1**

1242 **8** *nk* **US Army Ranger (IRE)**[35] 6351 3-9-0 119 .... SeamieHeffernan 2 116
(A P O'Brien, Ire) *trckd ldng pair: lost pl and outpcd jst over 2f out: tried to rally fnl f but no ch: one pce after* **7/1**[3]

5440 **9** *1 ¼* **Gabrial (IRE)**[42] 6117 7-9-5 110 .... JimmyFortune 7 114
(Richard Fahey) *slowly away: hld up in last pair: rdn and no prog over 2f out: kpt on same pce after* **66/1**

4502 **10** *nk* **Maverick Wave (USA)**[47] 5962 5-9-5 102 .... RobertHavlin 4 113
(John Gosden) *mde most: upped the pce fr 4f out: hdd & wknd jst over 2f out* **100/1**

2m 5.94s (-1.46) **Going Correction** +0.15s/f (Good)
WFA 3 from 4yo+ 5lb **10** Ran SP% **119.4**
Speed ratings (Par 117): **111,109,108,107,106 106,105,105,104,104**
CSF £4.82 CT £17.58 TOTE £2.20: £1.20, £1.30, £2.00; EX 4.80 Trifecta £20.70.
Owner Ecurie Antonio Caro **Bred** Haras D'Etreham **Trained** Pau, France
■ Stewards' Enquiry : James Doyle two-day ban; used his whip above the permitted level (29th-30th Oct)

FOCUS
A pair of top-notchers took centre stage here and, despite them going no great gallop, it's solid Group 1 form, with a repeat of the Irish Champion Stakes result. The field finished slightly compressed though, and the form could easily be rated a length higher. Last year's winner Fascinating Rock was taken out because of the ground.

7354 BALMORAL H'CAP (SPONSORED BY QIPCO) 1m (S)
4:25 (4:27) (Class 2) 3-Y-O+
£155,625 (£46,600; £23,300; £11,650; £5,825; £2,925) **Stalls** Centre

Form RPR

0404 **1** **Yuften**[21] 6788 5-9-1 **101** .... AndreaAtzeni 1 110
(Roger Charlton) *hld up in midfield far side: stdy prog against rail 2f out: led jst over 1f out: hung lft fnl f but styd on wl* **12/1**

1250 **2** *1* **Remarkable**[14] 6942 3-9-0 **103** .... (b) RobertHavlin 9 110
(John Gosden) *trckd ldrs far side: rdn to chse wnr fnl f: hung lft and styd on: no imp last 100yds* **12/1**

1122 **3** *½* **Firmament**[14] 6942 4-9-8 **108** .... DanielTudhope 16 114
(David O'Meara) *swtchd to r far side: hld up towards rr: swtchd bk to centre and effrt 2f out: squeezed through rivals 1f out: r.o to take 3rd last strides* **7/1**[2]

6210 **4** *hd* **Afjaan (IRE)**[14] 6942 4-8-13 **99** .... FrankieDettori 12 105+
(William Haggas) *hld up in rr far side: prog over 1f out: nt clrest of runs but styd on wl fnl f to take 4th last strides* **8/1**

0054 **5** *hd* **Third Time Lucky (IRE)**[21] 6786 4-8-10 **101** .... AdamMcNamara[(5)] 21 106
(Richard Fahey) *trckd ldrs in centre gp of six: clsd 2f out: drvn and styng on whn carried lft ins fnl f: lost pl nr fin* **8/1**

3501 **6** *½* **Highland Colori (IRE)**[8] 7121 8-9-1 **101** 6ex .... (b) LiamKeniry 6 105
(Andrew Balding) *overall ldr far side to jst over 1f out: one pce fnl f* **40/1**

4111 **7** *hd* **Morando (FR)**[28] 6557 3-9-1 **104** .... HarryBentley 3 109+
(Roger Varian) *hld up in midfield far side: pushed along and nt clr run wl over 1f out tl ins fnl f: r.o last 100yds but no ch* **5/1**[1]

2435 **8** *1* **Emell**[29] 6547 6-9-2 **102** .... (b) KieranO'Neill 2 103
(Richard Hannon) *pressed overall ldr far side to over 1f out: fdd last 100yds* **50/1**

0230 **9** *nse* **Donncha (IRE)**[14] 6942 5-9-0 **100** .... PatSmullen 15 103+
(Robert Eddery) *trckd ldrs far side: rdn over 1f out: stl pressing for a pl whn squeezed out last 100yds and eased* **10/1**

651 **10** *nk* **Here Comes When (IRE)**[34] 6364 6-9-5 **105** .... JamieSpencer 14 105
(Andrew Balding) *awkward s and slowly away: hld up in last of far side gp: stl wl in rr and nt clr run over 1f out: styd on ins fnl f but too late to threaten* **25/1**

-201 **11** *hd* **Sea Wolf (IRE)**[48] 5941 4-9-2 **102** .... ColinKeane 19 102
(G M Lyons, Ire) *led centre gp of six and on terms to 2f out: lost ld and fdd over 1f out* **12/1**

2200 **12** *hd* **Master The World (IRE)**[21] 6786 5-9-8 **108** .... (p) PatDobbs 5 107
(David Elsworth) *dwlt: nvr on terms w ldrs far side: drvn over 2f out: keeping on but no ch whn impeded ins fnl f* **25/1**

1655 **12** *dht* **Zhui Feng (IRE)**[8] 7137 3-8-13 **102** .... JimCrowley 17 101
(Amanda Perrett) *pressed ldr in centre gp of six: upsides 2f out: one pce fr over 1f out* **16/1**

5102 **14** *1 ¾* **Tullius (IRE)**[24] 6666 8-9-10 **110** .... (v) JimmyFortune 7 113+
(Andrew Balding) *cl up far side: rdn over 1f out: stl pressing ldrs whn bdly hmpd jst ins fnl f: nt rcvr and no ch after* **25/1**

0340 **15** *1 ¾* **Gm Hopkins**[21] 6786 5-9-10 **110** .... RyanMoore 8 101
(John Gosden) *hld up wl in rr far side: shkn up and no rspnse 2f out* **15/2**[3]

0-00 **16** *hd* **Bronze Angel (IRE)**[21] 6786 7-9-2 **105** .... (b) LouisSteward[(3)] 22 96
(Marcus Tregoning) *racd in centre gp of six: struggling and u.p 2f out* **33/1**

10-0 **17** *½* **Mutarakez (IRE)**[196] 1196 4-9-0 **100** ....[1] PaulHanagan 10 90
(Brian Meehan) *dwlt: hld up towards rr far side: drvn and no prog 2f out* **14/1**

4000 **18** *4 ½* **Chil The Kite**[21] 6786 7-9-2 **102** .... GeorgeBaker 20 81
(Hughie Morrison) *stdd s: hld up in last of centre gp of six: a bhd* **25/1**

153 **19** *5* **Dream Walker (FR)**[31] 6495 7-9-1 **101** .... (t) ChrisHayes 23 69
(Brian Ellison) *chsd ldrs in centre gp of six: wknd 2f out* **50/1**

1m 39.7s (-1.10) **Going Correction** +0.15s/f (Good)
WFA 3 from 4yo+ 3lb **19** Ran SP% **132.6**
Speed ratings (Par 109): **111,110,109,109,109 108,108,107,107,107 106,106,106,104,103 102,102,97,92**
CSF £146.47 CT £1142.73 TOTE £13.10: £3.30, £3.70, £2.30, £2.20; EX 237.20 Trifecta £2881.60.
Owner Saleh Al Homaizi & Imad Al Sagar **Bred** Saleh Al Homaizi & Imad Al Sagar **Trained** Beckhampton, Wilts
■ Stewards' Enquiry : Liam Keniry two-day ban; careless riding (29th-31st Oct)

FOCUS
A red-hot handicap as it should be for such a whopping purse, with only one of the 19 runners not boasting a three-figure rating. A smaller group of six came centre to nearside while the larger group raced more towards the far side, and again that was the place to be. There was all sorts of trouble inside the last 2f as room got tight, not least with the winner hanging away to his left after hitting the front and causing problems for quite a few.
T/Jkpt: Not won. T/Plt: £230.90 to a £1 stake. Pool: £365,550.12 - 1,155.44 winning tickets T/Qpdt: £11.60 to a £1 stake. Pool: £26,515.92 - 1,690.09 winning tickets **Jonathan Neesom**

[7040]CATTERICK (L-H)
Saturday, October 15

OFFICIAL GOING: Soft (6.4)
Wind: Moderate half behind Weather: Cloudy

7355 TOTEPLACEPOT MEDIAN AUCTION MAIDEN STKS 5f 212y
1:45 (1:48) (Class 6) 2-Y-O **£3,234** (£962; £481; £240) **Stalls** Low

Form RPR

03 **1** **Man Of Verve (IRE)**[31] 6477 2-9-5 0 .... JasonHart 9 78
(John Quinn) *led: hdd 2f out and sn pushed along: cl up and rdn over 1f out: drvn and rallied ins fnl f: led last 50 yds* **12/1**

023 **2** *½* **Rag Tatter**[66] 5289 2-9-5 75 .... KevinStott 6 77
(Kevin Ryan) *trckd wnr: cl up 1/2-way: led 2f out: rdn over 1f out: drvn ins fnl f: hdd and no ex last 50 yds* **10/3**[3]

5 **3** *6* **Love Power (IRE)**[19] 6833 2-9-5 0 .... JoeFanning 4 59
(Mark Johnston) *trckd ldng pair: pushed along over 2f out: rdn wl over 1f out: sn no imp* **3/1**[2]

40 **4** *2* **Arnold**[10] 7072 2-9-0 0 .... RowanScott[(5)] 1 53
(Ann Duffield) *hld up towards rr: hdwy on inner 2f out: swtchd rt and rdn over 1f out: kpt on same pce* **10/1**

3342 **5** *nk* **Vaulted**[11] 7040 2-9-0 71 ....[1] GeorgeChaloner 3 47
(Richard Fahey) *towards rr: hdwy over 2f out: rdn along wl over 1f out: sn no imp* **13/8**[1]

6 *4* **Baby Helmet** 2-9-5 0 .... TomMarquand 5 40
(Robert Cowell) *a towards rr* **14/1**

00 **7** *2 ¼* **Kallisto Freedom (IRE)**[32] 6446 2-9-0 0 .... AndrewMullen 7 28
(Philip Kirby) *chsd ldrs: rdn along over 2f out: sn wknd* **200/1**

8 *10* **Slave To Freedom** 2-9-0 0 .... PJMcDonald 8
(Ann Duffield) *dwlt and wnt rt s: a rr* **33/1**

1m 17.47s (3.87) **Going Correction** +0.60s/f (Yiel) **8** Ran SP% **113.1**
Speed ratings (Par 93): **98,97,89,86,86 80,77,64**
CSF £50.71 TOTE £10.00: £2.50, £1.20, £1.40; EX 53.70 Trifecta £220.40.
Owner The Splash Of Verve Partnership **Bred** P O'Donnell **Trained** Settrington, N Yorks

FOCUS
Race distance increased by 6yds. The ground was officially soft and clerk of the course Fiona Needham said: "It was good last weekend but we have had 18mm of rain since last Sunday." After riding in the opener Jason Hart and Kevin Stott called the ground soft, George Chaloner described it is very soft and Joe Fanning reckoned it was heavy. A fair maiden and few got into it, with the first two up there throughout.

7356 TOTESCOOP6 THE MILLIONAIRE MAKER MAIDEN FILLIES' STKS (PLUS 10 RACE) 7f
2:20 (2:25) (Class 5) 2-Y-O **£3,881** (£1,155; £577; £288) **Stalls** Low

Form RPR

1 **Ce La Vie** 2-9-0 0 .... ConnorBeasley 2 80+
(Keith Dalgleish) *trckd ldrs: green and pushed along 3f out: hdwy 2f out: rdn to chse ldng pair over 1f out: styd on wl to ld last 100 yds* **9/2**[2]

3432 **2** *2 ¼* **Starlight Romance (IRE)**[32] 6433 2-9-0 76 .... DavidNolan 3 74
(Richard Fahey) *trckd ldr: hdwy 2f out: rdn to chal over 1f out: led ent fnl f: sn drvn: hdd last 100 yds: kpt on same pce* **1/1**[1]

3300 **3** *2 ½* **Ocelot**[12] 7004 2-9-0 69 .... AndrewMullen 1 68
(Tim Easterby) *trckd ldng pair on inner: pushed along wl over 2f out: rdn wl over 1f out: sn drvn and kpt on same pce* **8/1**[3]

4 *nk* **Echoism (IRE)** 2-9-0 0 .... JoeFanning 5 67
(Mark Johnston) *sn led: pushed along over 2f out: jnd and rdn over 1f out: hdd ent fnl f: grad wknd* **9/2**[2]

0 **5** *10* **Enlighten Me (IRE)**[9] 7090 2-9-0 0 .... JoeyHaynes 8 42
(Philip Kirby) *dwlt and towards rr: hdwy and in tch 3f out: sn rdn: outpcd and bhd fnl 2f* **100/1**

6 *4 ½* **Safwah (IRE)** 2-9-0 0 .... JackGarritty 4 31
(John Quinn) *rr: pushed along 1/2-way: rdn wl over 2f out: sn outpcd and bhd* **9/1**

1m 32.28s (5.28) **Going Correction** +0.65s/f (Yiel) **6** Ran SP% **108.5**
Speed ratings (Par 92): **95,92,89,89,77 72**
CSF £8.80 TOTE £4.90: £2.00, £1.20; EX 10.30 Trifecta £31.50.
Owner Weldspec Glasgow Limited **Bred** Natton House Thoroughbreds & Mark Woodall **Trained** Carluke, S Lanarks

FOCUS
Race distance increased by 6yds. A fair maiden won in good style by a newcomer.

7357 TOTEPOOLLIVEINFO.COM CLAIMING STKS 1m 3f 214y
2:55 (2:55) (Class 6) 3-Y-O+ **£2,587** (£770; £384; £192) **Stalls** Low

Form RPR

0416 **1** **Trendsetter (IRE)**[28] 6561 5-9-12 89 .... (p) JackGarritty 4 90+
(John Quinn) *trckd ldng pair: hdwy on bit 2f out: shkn up to ld jst ins fnl f: rdn out* **9/4**[2]

06 **2** *4* **Astra Hall**[11] 7043 7-9-5 72 .... AndrewMullen 2 75
(Michael Appleby) *trckd ldr: hdwy to ld 2f out: sn rdn: drvn and hdd jst ins fnl f: kpt on same pce* **9/1**

5011 **3** *6* **An Fear Ciuin (IRE)**[36] 6279 5-9-1 80 .... (p) CallumRodriguez[(7)] 3 68
(Richard Ford) *led: pushed along and hdd 2f out: cl up and rdn over 1f out: drvn and one pce fnl f* **3/1**[3]

3000 **4** *¾* **English Summer**[20] 6804 9-9-5 81 .... (t) DavidNolan 1 64
(Richard Fahey) *hld up in tch: hdwy 3f out: sn niggled along: rdn to chse ldrs over 1f out: sn drvn and no imp* **2/1**[1]

000 **5** *7* **Biff Johnson (IRE)**[41] 6160 4-9-1 75 .... (p) ShirleyTeasdale[(5)] 5 54
(Keith Dalgleish) *trckd ldng pair: pushed along 3f out: rdn over 2f out: sn outpcd* **9/1**

2m 48.23s (9.33) **Going Correction** +0.70s/f (Yiel) **5** Ran SP% **109.1**
Speed ratings (Par 101): **96,93,89,88,84**
CSF £19.96 TOTE £2.70: £1.60, £4.10; EX 27.60 Trifecta £50.90.Trendsetter was claimed by M. D. Hammond for £16000.
Owner Maxilead Limited **Bred** Denis McDonnell **Trained** Settrington, N Yorks

FOCUS
Race distance increased by 6yds. A decent claimer and an easy winner.

7358 TOTESCOOP6 CATTERICK DASH H'CAP 5f
3:30 (3:30) (Class 2) (0-100,99) 3-Y-O+
£15,562 (£4,660; £2,330; £1,165; £582; £292) **Stalls** Low

Form RPR
0310 **1** **Ocean Sheridan (IRE)**[29] 6539 4-8-9 **87**.................... ConnorBeasley 14 95
(Michael Dods) *prom nr stands rail: hdwy over 1f out: swtchd lft and rdn to chal ent fnl f: drvn and kpt on to ld nr fin* **6/1**[2]
5200 **2** *nk* **Confessional**[21] 6779 9-8-12 **90**....................................(be) CamHardie 11 97
(Tim Easterby) *prom nr stands rail: rdn to chal over 1f out: drvn to ld wl ins fnl f: hdd and no ex nr fin 2nd of 5 in gp* **25/1**
0220 **3** *nk* **Aleef (IRE)**[8] 7124 3-8-12 **90**.................................... GrahamGibbons 12 97
(David O'Meara) *led stands side gp: overall ldr 1/2-way: rdn over 1f out: drvn and hdd ins fnl f: kpt on 3rd of 5 in gp* **14/1**
1005 **4** 4 ½ **Udontdodou**[32] 6449 3-8-9 **87**.................................... JoeFanning 13 78
(Richard Guest) *dwlt: trckd ldrs stands side: cl up 1/2-way: rdn along wl over 1f out: sn drvn and kpt on same pce 4th of 5 in gp* **5/1**[1]
0210 **5** ½ **I'll Be Good**[29] 6537 7-8-0 **85** oh3.................................. BenRobinson[(3)] 5 73+
(Brian Ellison) *.qckly away and overall ldr nr far rail: hdd 1/2-way: cl up and rdn wl over 1f out: kpt on same pce fnl f 1st of 8 in gp* **28/1**
0313 **6** 1 ¼ **Distant Past**[14] 6944 5-8-11 **89**...(p) ShaneGray 2 72
(Kevin Ryan) *cared towards centre: hdwy to chse ldrs over 2f out: sn rdn and no imp. 2nd of 8 in gp* **6/1**[2]
3041 **7** 3 ½ **First Bombardment**[8] 7112 3-8-4 **85** oh2.................. ShelleyBirkett[(3)] 10 57
(David O'Meara) *cl up nr stands rail: rdn along 2f out: grad wknd 5th of 5 in gp* **33/1**
3140 **8** ½ **Ladweb**[29] 6537 6-8-7 **85** oh2.. BenCurtis 6 54
(John Gallagher) *racd towards centre: prom: rdn wl over 1f out: sn drvn and grad wknd. 3rd of 8 in gp* **20/1**
4104 **9** 1 ½ **Pipers Note**[7] 7156 6-9-7 **99**... JamesSullivan 7 63
(Ruth Carr) *hld up: hdwy towards centre 1/2-way: rdn wl over 1f out: sn no imp. 4th of 8 in gp* **7/1**[3]
0000 **10** 1 ¼ **Desert Law (IRE)**[8] 7124 8-8-6 **91**...........................[1] LewisEdmunds[(7)] 4 50
(Paul Midgley) *racd towards far side: bhd fr 1/2-way: 5th of 8 in gp* **14/1**
4203 **11** ½ **Fumbo Jumbo (IRE)**[8] 7124 3-8-7 **85** oh1.................... TomMarquand 3 43
(Garry Moss) *a towards rr far side: 6th of 8 in gp* **12/1**
3240 **12** 1 **Tylery Wonder (IRE)**[8] 7124 6-8-4 **85** oh2..............(b) NathanEvans[(3)] 9 39
(Paul Midgley) *racd towards centre: prom: rdn along 1/2-way: sn wknd. 7th of 8 in gp* **9/1**
0014 **13** 1 **Demora**[38] 6230 7-9-4 **99**.. AlistairRawlinson[(3)] 8 49
(Michael Appleby) *cl up towards far side: rdn along over 2f out: sn wknd. 8th of 8 in gp* **8/1**

1m 0.52s (0.72) **Going Correction** +0.375s/f (Good) **13** Ran SP% **114.9**
Speed ratings (Par 109): **109,108,108,100,100 98,92,91,89,87 86,84,83**
CSF £150.73 CT £1320.87 TOTE £5.60: £2.40, £6.70, £5.20; EX 121.00 Trifecta £2149.30.
Owner J Blackburn & A Turton **Bred** J Hernon **Trained** Denton, Co Durham

FOCUS
A competitive sprint handicap, in which they went a good pace, but the draw played a big part, with the first four home taking advantage of a double-figure berth and racing close to the favoured stands' rail.

7359 TOTEEXACTA H'CAP 1m 3f 214y
4:05 (4:05) (Class 4) (0-80,83) 3-Y-O+ **£6,469** (£1,925; £962; £481) **Stalls** Low

Form RPR
3313 **1** **Machine Learner**[22] 6730 3-8-13 **77**.....................(v) EdwardGreatrex[(3)] 2 86
(Michael Bell) *hld up and bhd: gd hdwy on wd outside 2f out: str run to chal ins fnl f: rdn to ld last 75 yds: kpt on strly* **13/2**[2]
3314 **2** 1 ½ **Tamayuz Magic (IRE)**[21] 6773 5-9-9 **80**...................(b) NathanEvans[(3)] 1 87
(Michael Easterby) *led: hdd 1/2-way: cl up and led again over 3f out: rdn clr wl over 1f out: drvn ent fnl f: hdd last 75 yds: kpt on* **8/1**[3]
1331 **3** *hd* **Henry Smith**[11] 7043 4-9-8 **83**........................(be) LewisEdmunds[(7)] 7 90
(Garry Moss) *dwlt and hld up in rr: stdy hdwy 3f out: chsd ldr over 1f out: sn rdn: swtchd rt and drvn ins fnl f: kpt on* **5/1**[1]
061 **4** 4 ½ **Card High (IRE)**[28] 6566 6-9-9 **77**......................................(t) ShaneGray 9 76
(Wilf Storey) *hld up towards rr: hdwy 4f out: chsd ldrs 2f out: sn rdn and kpt on same pce* **16/1**
2112 **5** 2 ¼ **Age Of Elegance (IRE)**[14] 6957 4-9-9 **77**..............(p) GrahamGibbons 6 73
(Roger Fell) *trckd ldng pair: hdwy over 3f out: chsd ldr over 2f out: sn rdn: drvn wl over 1f out: grad wknd* **8/1**[3]
0610 **6** 3 **Southern Strife**[11] 7043 5-9-1 **69**....................................(b) CamHardie 11 60
(Tim Easterby) *midfield: hdwy to trck ldrs over 4f out: pushed along wl over 2f out: sn rdn and plugged on one pce* **16/1**
00-0 **7** 9 **Seagull Star**[58] 5579 5-9-9 **77**..[1] ConnorBeasley 3 54
(Keith Dalgleish) *trckd ldrs: hdwy to chse ldr 3f out: rdn over 2f out: sn drvn and wknd* **12/1**
4404 **8** 4 ½ **Blue Hussar (IRE)**[21] 6794 5-9-12 **80**..............................(p) PJMcDonald 13 49
(Micky Hammond) *a towards rr* **12/1**
-454 **9** 2 **Energia Fox (BRZ)**[21] 6775 6-9-11 **79**........................ GeorgeChaloner 12 45
(Richard Fahey) *sn cl up: led 1/2-way: rdn along and hdd over 3f out: sn drvn and wknd* **9/1**
5200 **10** 1 ½ **Framley Garth (IRE)**[17] 6876 4-8-13 **74**........................... PaulaMuir[(7)] 4 38
(Patrick Holmes) *a towards rr* **50/1**
2040 **11** 2 ½ **Busy Street**[62] 5434 4-9-9 **77**.. BenCurtis 8 37
(Alan Swinbank) *chsd ldrs: rdn along wl over 3f out: sn wknd* **11/1**
1056 **12** 32 **Theos Lolly (IRE)**[14] 6957 3-9-4 **79**.................................. DavidNolan 10
(Richard Fahey) *trckwed ldrs: rdn along over 4f out: sn wknd* **5/1**[1]

2m 48.74s (9.84) **Going Correction** +0.80s/f (Soft)
WFA 3 from 4yo+ 7lb **12** Ran SP% **116.3**
Speed ratings (Par 105): **99,98,97,94,93 91,85,82,81,80 78,57**
CSF £56.62 CT £282.93 TOTE £5.90: £2.00, £2.90, £2.70; EX 44.90 Trifecta £195.80.
Owner The Deflators & Partner **Bred** Bearstone Stud Ltd **Trained** Newmarket, Suffolk

FOCUS
Race distance increased by 6yds. A useful, competitive looking handicap, in which the front three were clear of the rest.

7360 TOTETRIFECTA H'CAP 7f
4:40 (4:40) (Class 4) (0-80,80) 3-Y-O+ **£6,469** (£1,925; £962; £481) **Stalls** Low

Form RPR
0001 **1** **Shouranour (IRE)**[12] 7007 6-9-0 **78**.............................(b) JoshDoyle[(5)] 15 86
(Alan Brown) *cl up on outer: led after 2f: c wd towards stands rail home turn: rdn wl over 1f out: drvn ins fnl f: hld on wl towards fin* **11/1**
0405 **2** *hd* **Mystic Miraaj**[21] 6772 4-9-4 **77**...................................(bt) DuranFentiman 9 84
(Tim Easterby) *hld up towards rr: stdy hdwy 2f out: chsd ldrs and rdn over 1f out: drvn to chal ins fnl f: ev ch tl no ex nr fin* **9/1**
3152 **3** 1 ¼ **Toboggan's Fire**[21] 6772 3-9-4 **79**.................................. PJMcDonald 13 82
(Ann Duffield) *chsd ldrs: cl up and wd st: rdn wl over 1f out: drvn ent fnl f: kpt on* **8/1**[2]
000 **4** *hd* **Showboating (IRE)**[93] 4299 8-8-9 **75**..................... LewisEdmunds[(7)] 10 79
(John Balding) *hld up in rr: hdwy on outer 1/2-way: chsd ldrs and wd st to stands rail: rdn along wl over 1f out: drvn and kpt on fnl f* **18/1**
1434 **5** 1 ½ **Chaplin Bay (IRE)**[7] 7141 4-9-1 **74**.............................. JamesSullivan 4 74
(Ruth Carr) *hld up in rr: hdwy 2f out: rdn over 1f out: chsd ldrs ins fnl f: no imp towards fin* **8/1**[2]
3155 **6** 1 ¾ **Sunnua (IRE)**[37] 6246 3-9-5 **80**..................................... PatrickMathers 11 74
(Richard Fahey) *towards rr: hdwy over 2f out: sn rdn and kpt on* **9/1**
220 **7** *nk* **Jay Kay**[30] 6502 7-9-1 **74**.. JoeyHaynes 12 68
(K R Burke) *in tch on inner: rdn along 2f out: drvn over 1f out: sn one pce* **25/1**
0346 **8** ½ **Fullon Clarets**[32] 6437 4-9-4 **77**................................(p) GeorgeChaloner 7 70
(Richard Fahey) *chsd ldng pair: rdn along wl over 1f out: drvn over 1f out: grad wknd* **10/1**
0121 **9** 1 **Mon Beau Visage (IRE)**[8] 7111 3-9-4 **79**...............(p) GrahamGibbons 2 69
(David O'Meara) *towards rr: sme hdwy wl over 1f out: n.d* **17/2**[3]
3350 **10** 2 ½ **Signore Piccolo**[21] 6766 5-9-5 **78**...................................... DavidNolan 14 62
(David O'Meara) *chsd ldrs: wd st: rdn along 2f out: wknd over 1f out* **9/1**
0621 **11** *hd* **Captain Dion**[23] 6718 3-9-4 **79**... KevinStott 3 62
(Kevin Ryan) *slt ld 2f: cl up on inner: styd towards far side st: rdn 2f out and grad wknd* **9/2**[1]
0024 **12** 1 **English Hero**[92] 4344 3-8-13 **74**...................................... AndrewMullen 6 54
(John Mackie) *a towards rr* **33/1**
020 **13** 2 ½ **Ninetta (IRE)**[20] 6811 3-8-13 **79**.................................. RowanScott[(5)] 8 52
(Ann Duffield) *in tch whn n.m.r and lost pl after 2f: rr after* **25/1**
6460 **14** 1 ¾ **Dodgy Bob**[32] 6437 3-9-2 **77**..(p) ShaneGray 1 46
(Kevin Ryan) *chsd ldrs on inner: rdn along over 3f out: sn wknd* **28/1**

1m 31.91s (4.91) **Going Correction** +0.85s/f (Soft)
WFA 3 from 4yo+ 2lb **14** Ran SP% **117.7**
Speed ratings (Par 105): **105,104,103,103,101 99,99,98,97,94 94,93,90,88**
CSF £99.71 CT £864.84 TOTE £18.10: £5.10, £4.00, £3.00; EX 151.70 Trifecta £1424.70.
Owner David Lumley **Bred** His Highness The Aga Khan's Studs S C **Trained** Yedingham, N Yorks
■ Stewards' Enquiry : Duran Fentiman two-day ban; used whip above the permitted level (29th,31st Oct)

FOCUS
Race distance increased by 6yds. Another competitive handicap run at a good pace.

7361 @TOTEPOOL FOLLOW US ON TWITTER APPRENTICE H'CAP (GO RACING IN YORKSHIRE FUTURE STARS SERIES) 1m 5f 175y
5:15 (5:15) (Class 6) (0-60,67) 3-Y-O+ **£3,234** (£962; £481; £240) **Stalls** Low

Form RPR
32/4 **1** **Miss Tree**[11] 7044 5-8-13 **50**... JoshQuinn[(5)] 9 57
(John Quinn) *cl up: led after 3f: rdn clr wl over 2f out: drvn and kpt on wl fnl f* **9/2**[2]
2652 **2** ½ **Jan De Heem**[11] 7044 6-9-10 **59**.................................. RowanScott[(3)] 3 65
(Tina Jackson) *hld up in rr: stdy hdwy over 3f out: chsd wnr wl over 1f out: sn rdn: styd on wl fnl f* **9/2**[2]
0050 **3** 8 **Adrakhan (FR)**[11] 7044 5-8-11 **46** oh1..................... LewisEdmunds[(3)] 6 41
(Wilf Storey) *trckd ldrs: rdn along 3f out: drvn wl over 1f out: plugged on one pce* **8/1**
/211 **4** 1 ½ **Fine Resolve**[11] 7044 7-10-7 **67**...............................(bt) CharlieBennett 5 60
(Alexandra Dunn) *led 3f: chsd wnr: rdn along over 2f out: drvn wl over 1f out: grad wknd* **9/4**[1]
00/4 **5** ¾ **Marcus Antonius**[24] 6438 9-9-0 **53**............................ NicolaCurrie[(7)] 8 45
(Lucinda Russell) *hld up and bhd: sme hdwy over 3f out: sn rdn along and nvr a factor* **10/1**
3543 **6** *shd* **Saint Thomas (IRE)**[11] 7045 9-9-13 **59**........................... JoshDoyle 2 51
(John Mackie) *hld up: hdwy to chse ldrs over 4f out: rdn along over 2f out: sn drvn and wknd* **7/1**[3]
0030 **7** 42 **Voice From Above (IRE)**[8] 7105 7-8-12 **49**..................(p) PaulaMuir[(5)] 1
(Patrick Holmes) *chsd ldrs: rdn along over 5f out: sn outpcd and bhd whn eased fnl 2f* **12/1**
0603 **8** 8 **Come On Lulu**[11] 7044 5-9-0 **46**.. PhilDennis 4
(David Thompson) *prom: pushed along 6f out: rdn along and outpcd over 4f out: bhd whn eased fnl 2f* **20/1**
0061 **9** 29 **Graceful Act**[47] 5980 8-9-1 **47**.. ShirleyTeasdale 7
(Ron Barr) *a rr: outpcd and bhd fnl 3f* **25/1**

3m 18.15s (14.55) **Going Correction** +0.90s/f (Soft) **9** Ran SP% **116.1**
Speed ratings (Par 101): **94,93,89,88,87 87,63,59,42**
CSF £25.25 CT £157.64 TOTE £5.50: £1.90, £2.40, £4.60; EX 29.60 Trifecta £384.90.
Owner Trainers House Enterprises Ltd **Bred** Trainers House Enterprises Limited **Trained** Settrington, N Yorks
■ Stewards' Enquiry : Charlie Bennett caution; careless riding
Rowan Scott four-day ban; used whip above the permitted level (29th,31st Oct, 2nd,4th Nov)

FOCUS
Only a modest staying handicap.
T/Plt: £230.50 to a £1 stake. Pool of £64305.39 - 203.60 winning tickets. T/Qpdt: £54.50 to a £1 stake. Pool of £3795.71 - 51.50 winning tickets. **Joe Rowntree**

7255 WOLVERHAMPTON (A.W) (L-H)
Saturday, October 15

OFFICIAL GOING: Tapeta: standard
Wind: Light against Weather: Showers

7362 FCL GLOBAL FORWARDING MAKING LOGISTICS PERSONAL MAIDEN STKS 5f 20y (Tp)
5:45 (5:46) (Class 5) 3-Y-O+ **£3,234** (£962; £481; £240) **Stalls** Low

Form RPR
022 **1** **Waneen (IRE)**[10] 7069 3-9-5 64.. JFEgan 6 68
(Joseph Tuite) *led 1f: trckd ldrs: swtchd rt wl over 1f out: rdn to ld 1f out: drvn out* **5/2**[1]
5002 **2** *hd* **Heiba (IRE)**[22] 6744 4-9-5 71... PatCosgrave 3 66
(Robert Cowell) *a.p: rdn over 1f out: r.o* **5/2**[1]
53 **3** 1 ¼ **Eternalist**[22] 6744 3-9-0 0.. JoeDoyle 9 58
(Jim Goldie) *led 4f out: rdn and hdd 1f out: styd on same pce wl ins fnl f* **8/1**[3]
0200 **4** ¾ **Shine Likeadiamond**[19] 6832 3-9-0 57......................... PaulMulrennan 7 55
(Mick Channon) *prom: chsd ldr over 3f out: rdn and ev ch over 1f out: no ex ins fnl f* **20/1**

04 **5** 1 ¼ **Q Cee**[12] 7011 3-9-5 0 FMBerry 4 56+
(Eugene Stanford) *hld up: pushed along on outer 1/2-way: hdwy over 1f out: r.o: nt rch ldrs* **9/1**
2-04 **6** shd **The Perfect Show**[50] 5843 3-9-5 65 (b[1]) LukeMorris 1 55
(Ed Walker) *s.i.s: pushed along in rr early: hdwy over 1f out: sn rdn: styd on same pce ins fnl f* **11/2**[2]
06 **7** 2 ½ **Gold Bud**[12] 7011 4-9-5 0 SteveDrowne 10 45
(George Baker) *hld up in tch: rdn: edgd lft and wknd ins fnl f* **18/1**
0545 **8** ½ **Tally's Song**[34] 6361 3-9-0 42 (p) StevieDonohoe 2 39
(Grace Harris) *prom: rdn over 2f out: wknd fnl f* **100/1**
65 **9** 3 ¼ **Indiana Dawn**[12] 7011 3-9-0 0 [1] AdamBeschizza 5 28
(Robert Stephens) *s.i.s: pushed along 1/2-way: effrt over 1f out: wknd fnl f* **12/1**
6534 **10** 8 **Matilda Gleam**[179] 1554 3-8-9 54 GeorgeWood[(5)] 11
(Lisa Williamson) *plld hrd and prom: rdn 1/2-way: wknd over 1f out* **50/1**
4050 **11** 2 ¼ **Captain Devious**[34] 6363 5-9-5 44 (t) TimmyMurphy 8
(Grace Harris) *hld up: pushed along 3f out: wknd 1/2-way* **100/1**
1m 1.25s (-0.65) **Going Correction** -0.175s/f (Stan) **11** Ran SP% **115.3**
Speed ratings (Par 103): **98,97,95,94,92 92,88,87,82,69 65**
CSF £7.66 TOTE £3.50: £1.30, £1.30, £2.40; EX 11.40 Trifecta £54.90.
Owner Stewart Brown **Bred** Roundhill Stud **Trained** Lambourn, Berks

FOCUS
A routine maiden, but the less exposed runners have some potential in similar company.

7363 FCL GLOBAL FORWARDING MAKING LOGISTICS PERSONAL FILLIES' H'CAP (DIV I) 5f 216y (Tp)
6:15 (6:15) (Class 5) (0-75,75) 3-Y-O+ **£3,234** (£962; £481; £240) **Stalls** Low

Form RPR
3461 **1** **Shypen**[31] 6487 3-8-13 75 JaneElliott[(7)] 6 85
(George Margarson) *trckd ldrs: racd keenly: shkn up to ld ins fnl f: rdn out* **5/1**
3102 **2** 2 **Kindly**[28] 6589 3-9-4 73 MartinLane 5 77
(Simon Crisford) *sn led: hdd over 4f out: chsd ldr tl rdn to ld 1f out: edgd lft and hdd ins fnl f: styd on same pce* **7/2**[1]
1335 **3** ¾ **Rose Eclair**[23] 6717 3-9-4 73 (b) JasonHart 4 75
(Tim Easterby) *hld up in tch: rdn and edgd lft over 1f out: styd on u.p to go 3rd nr fin* **14/1**
3031 **4** nk **Full Of Promise**[19] 6834 3-8-7 62 BarryMcHugh 1 63
(Richard Fahey) *hld up: pushed along and hdwy over 2f out: rdn over 1f out: styd on* **14/1**
5534 **5** 1 **Colourfilly**[33] 6426 4-8-13 67 (p) RichardKingscote 2 64
(Tom Dascombe) *hld up: hdwy and nt clr run over 1f out: styd on same pce wl ins fnl f* **4/1**[2]
3045 **6** ½ **Penny Dreadful**[79] 4787 4-9-2 70 (p) LukeMorris 8 66
(Scott Dixon) *chsd ldrs: led over 4f out: rdn and hdd 1f out: no ex ins fnl f* **25/1**
4222 **7** 1 ½ **Tigserin (IRE)**[72] 5078 3-9-1 70 JackMitchell 3 61
(Giles Bravery) *led early: chsd ldrs: rdn over 2f out: edgd lft over 1f out: wknd ins fnl f* **9/2**[3]
3-44 **8** 2 **Cockney Island**[17] 6879 4-9-3 71 FMBerry 9 56
(Philip McBride) *hld up: rdn and hung lft over 1f out: nvr on terms* **11/1**
3210 **9** 18 **Fleeting Dream (IRE)**[21] 6790 3-8-10 65 (b) PatCosgrave 7
(William Haggas) *hood removed late: s.s and a bhd* **6/1**
1m 12.99s (-1.51) **Going Correction** -0.175s/f (Stan)
WFA 3 from 4yo 1lb **9** Ran SP% **116.9**
Speed ratings (Par 100): **103,100,99,98,97 96,94,92,68**
CSF £23.18 CT £231.50 TOTE £2.20: £1.10, £1.40, £3.40; EX 11.50 Trifecta £120.70.
Owner F Butler **Bred** F Butler **Trained** Newmarket, Suffolk

FOCUS
A middling race of its type, run at an untesting pace for 6f until they quickened 2f out.

7364 FCL GLOBAL FORWARDING MAKING LOGISTICS PERSONAL FILLIES' H'CAP (DIV II) 5f 216y (Tp)
6:45 (6:47) (Class 5) (0-75,74) 3-Y-O+ **£3,234** (£962; £481; £240) **Stalls** Low

Form RPR
30-0 **1** **Kashtan**[66] 5305 3-9-3 71 RichardKingscote 7 80
(Harry Dunlop) *mde virtually all: rdn over 1f out: styd on u.p* **16/1**
215 **2** 1 ¼ **Sirajiah (IRE)**[31] 6492 3-9-6 74 (p) PatCosgrave 4 79+
(William Haggas) *hld up: hdwy over 1f out: rdn and edgd lft ins fnl f: r.o to go 2nd nr fin: nt rch wnr* **9/4**[1]
4304 **3** nk **Rural Celebration**[21] 6793 5-9-0 74 PatrickVaughan[(7)] 6 78
(David O'Meara) *chsd ldrs: wnt 2nd over 3f out: rdn and edgd lft over 1f out: styd on same pce wl ins fnl f: lost 2nd nr fin* **5/1**[3]
3120 **4** 1 ½ **Penny Pot Lane**[17] 6878 3-9-2 70 PaulMulrennan 1 69
(Richard Whitaker) *prom: rdn over 2f out: styd on same pce ins fnl f* **9/2**[2]
6044 **5** 1 ½ **Shahaama**[19] 6835 3-8-7 61 JFEgan 2 55
(Mick Channon) *prom: rdn 1/2-way: no ex ins fnl f* **10/1**
0506 **6** 1 ¾ **Lucky Di**[50] 5827 6-9-4 71 CharlesBishop 8 60
(Peter Hedger) *hld up: rdn over 1f out: nvr nrr* **11/1**
6-14 **7** hd **Sakhee's Jem**[31] 6487 3-9-1 69 LukeMorris 3 57
(Gay Kelleway) *hld up: rdn over 2f out: nvr on terms* **8/1**
5520 **8** 2 ¾ **Serradura (IRE)**[21] 6790 3-8-13 67 (p) FMBerry 5 46
(Charles Hills) *s.i.s: hld up: rdn and hung rt over 1f out: no ch whn wnt lft ins fnl f* **10/1**
1640 **9** 21 **Addicted To Luck**[30] 6506 3-8-10 64 JoeDoyle 9
(Jo Hughes) *chsd wnr over 2f: sn rdn: wknd over 2f out* **20/1**
1m 13.18s (-1.32) **Going Correction** -0.175s/f (Stan)
WFA 3 from 5yo+ 1lb **9** Ran SP% **113.9**
Speed ratings (Par 100): **101,99,98,96,94 92,92,88,60**
CSF £51.53 CT £213.07 TOTE £16.90: £3.80, £1.40, £2.10; EX 63.80 Trifecta £286.30.
Owner The Late C Whitaker, Gehring & Partners **Bred** R, J D & M R Bromley Gardner **Trained** Lambourn, Berks

FOCUS
This was run at a better pace than Division I, but the winner made all and can be rated a little higher for that.

7365 FCL GLOBAL FORWARDING MAKING LOGISTICS PERSONAL H'CAP 1m 4f 50y (Tp)
7:15 (7:16) (Class 3) (0-95,95) 3-Y-O **£7,246** (£2,168; £1,084; £542; £270) **Stalls** Low

Form RPR
0200 **1** **Shakopee**[23] 6709 4-9-9 92 MartinLane 7 102
(Luca Cumani) *trckd ldrs: racd keenly: led over 1f out: rdn and edgd lft ins fnl f: jst hld on* **10/1**
-140 **2** hd **Great Glen**[49] 5879 4-9-8 91 FMBerry 5 101+
(Ralph Beckett) *hld up in tch: rdn over 1f out: chsd wnr and edgd lft ins fnl f: r.o* **9/2**[2]
5114 **3** 1 ½ **Niblawi (IRE)**[12] 7015 4-9-5 88 LukeMorris 1 95
(Ismail Mohammed) *hld up: hdwy 2f out: rdn over 1f out: edgd lft ins fnl f: styd on* **11/2**[3]
2260 **4** 3 ½ **Scrutinise**[28] 6573 4-9-12 95 PatCosgrave 3 97
(Ed Dunlop) *hld up: hdwy 2f out: rdn over 1f out: no ex ins fnl f* **8/1**
455- **5** 2 **High Admiral**[388] 6649 4-8-9 81 oh2 RobHornby[(3)] 4 79
(Andrew Balding) *s.i.s: hld up: nt clr run and swtchd rt over 1f out: styd on ins fnl f: nvr nrr* **25/1**
3166 **6** ¾ **Salmon Sushi**[21] 6775 5-9-4 87 JasonHart 9 84
(Tim Easterby) *hld up: rdn on outer over 1f out: nvr on terms* **11/1**
0340 **7** 2 ¼ **Hardstone (USA)**[28] 6561 5-9-0 83 (t) PaulMulrennan 8 76
(Michael Dods) *chsd ldrs: led 2f out: rdn and hdd over 1f out: wknd fnl f* **16/1**
6445 **8** 8 **Dessertoflife (IRE)**[14] 6948 3-9-2 92 JoeFanning 10 72
(Mark Johnston) *s.i.s: sn prom: lost pl 8f out: hdwy over 3f out: rdn over 2f out: wknd wl over 1f out* **13/2**
2443 **9** 5 **Engage (IRE)**[24] 6667 3-8-12 88 [1] RichardKingscote 6 60
(Sir Michael Stoute) *led: hdd 10f out: remained w ldr: ev ch over 2f out: sn pushed along: wknd over 1f out* **10/3**[1]
5262 **10** 9 **Croquembouche (IRE)**[23] 6709 7-8-13 87 GeorgiaCox[(5)] 11 45
(Ed de Giles) *chsd ldrs: led 10f out: rdn and hdd 2f out: edgd lft and wknd over 1f out* **18/1**
2m 35.12s (-5.68) **Going Correction** -0.175s/f (Stan)
WFA 3 from 4yo+ 7lb **10** Ran SP% **113.5**
Speed ratings (Par 107): **111,110,109,107,106 105,104,98,95,89**
CSF £53.13 CT £274.56 TOTE £12.10: £3.60, £2.10, £1.50; EX 73.70 Trifecta £437.10.
Owner Kangyu International Racing (HK) Limited **Bred** Fittocks Stud **Trained** Newmarket, Suffolk

FOCUS
A competitive and good-quality handicap, though few of the runners came into it in top form. The pace was slack until quickening 2f out.

7366 CONTACT US AT FCLGF.COM EBF MAIDEN STKS 1m 141y (Tp)
7:45 (7:45) (Class 5) 2-Y-O **£3,234** (£962; £481; £240) **Stalls** Low

Form RPR
2 **1** **Munawer**[12] 7013 2-9-2 0 MarcMonaghan[(3)] 1 73
(Hugo Palmer) *trckd ldrs: shkn up over 2f out: rdn to ld wl ins fnl f: styd on* **8/11**[1]
0000 **2** 1 ¼ **Royal Melody**[38] 6236 2-9-0 48 [1] JackMitchell 2 65
(Heather Main) *led: rdn and hung rt fr over 1f out: hdd and unable qck wl ins fnl f* **66/1**
020 **3** ¾ **Upgrade**[30] 6499 2-9-5 75 DougieCostello 8 69
(K R Burke) *chsd ldr: rdn over 2f out: nt clr run over 1f out: edgd lft ins fnl f: kpt on* **7/2**[2]
0 **4** 1 ¾ **Punkawallah**[10] 7065 2-9-5 0 RichardKingscote 3 65
(Tom Dascombe) *hld up: pushed along 1/2-way: styd on appr fnl f: nt trble ldrs* **4/1**[3]
00 **5** 6 **Starshell (IRE)**[15] 6924 2-9-5 0 LukeMorris 5 53
(Sir Mark Prescott Bt) *hld up: shkn up over 2f out: sn outpcd* **6/1**
60 **6** 3 ½ **Willie's Anne (IRE)**[28] 6590 2-9-0 0 JoeFanning 7 40
(Daniel Mark Loughnane) *s.i.s: hld up: rdn over 2f out: nvr nrr* **33/1**
60 **7** nk **Master Degree (IRE)**[12] 7003 2-9-0 0 CliffordLee[(5)] 4 45
(K R Burke) *plld hrd and prom: rdn over 2f out: wknd over 1f out* **50/1**
8 7 **Dragonite (IRE)** 2-9-5 0 StevieDonohoe 6 30
(Daniel Mark Loughnane) *s.i.s: hld up: rdn and wknd over 2f out* **20/1**
1m 49.9s (-0.20) **Going Correction** -0.175s/f (Stan) **8** Ran SP% **125.6**
Speed ratings (Par 95): **93,91,91,89,84 81,80,74**
CSF £90.37 TOTE £1.70: £1.10, £10.40, £1.60; EX 60.70 Trifecta £232.80.
Owner Al Shaqab Racing **Bred** Cheveley Park Stud Ltd **Trained** Newmarket, Suffolk

FOCUS
This looked a modest maiden, with the runner-up holding down the form and the winner running below his potential. They went a solid gallop after turning into the back straight.

7367 FCLGF.COM H'CAP 2m 119y (Tp)
8:15 (8:17) (Class 6) (0-60,59) 3-Y-O+ **£2,587** (£770; £384; £192) **Stalls** Low

Form RPR
0541 **1** **Alfredo (IRE)**[25] 6659 4-10-0 59 (tp) SeanLevey 6 75
(Seamus Durack) *chsd ldr wnt clr 10f out: tk clsr order 6f out: led over 3f out: rdn clr fr over 2f out: easily* **2/1**[1]
0136 **2** 12 **Cosmic Tigress**[11] 7045 5-9-13 58 JasonHart 10 59
(John Quinn) *hld up: hdwy and nt clr run over 3f out: rdn over 2f out: sn outpcd: wnt 2nd nr fin: no ch w wnr* **7/1**[3]
5456 **3** nse **Sakhra**[33] 6406 5-9-0 45 GrahamGibbons 13 46
(Mark Brisbourne) *hld up: hdwy 12f out: rdn over 2f out: sn outpcd* **25/1**
0500 **4** hd **Powderonthebonnet (IRE)**[27] 5805 8-9-5 50 JoeDoyle 8 51
(Richard Phillips) *chsd ldrs: rdn over 3f out: outpcd fr over 2f out* **16/1**
5640 **5** ¾ **Delagoa Bay (IRE)**[19] 6825 8-9-4 54 MitchGodwin[(5)] 2 54
(Sylvester Kirk) *hld up: nt clr run over 2f out: nvr nrr* **16/1**
0/53 **6** nk **Tamarillo Grove (IRE)**[85] 4592 9-9-13 58 (t) SaleemGolam 1 57
(Sophie Leech) *mid-div: rdn and nt clr run over 2f out: nvr on terms* **15/2**
0000 **7** 2 ¾ **Flying Power**[22] 6730 8-9-7 55 (p) JacobButterfield[(3)] 11 51
(John Norton) *led: wnt clr 10f out tl 6f out: hdd over 3f out: sn rdn: wknd over 1f out* **12/1**
0305 **8** 3 ¾ **Sixties Idol**[84] 4636 3-8-8 50 JFEgan 12 42
(Mick Channon) *hld up: rdn over 3f out: hung lft over 1f out: n.d* **14/1**
-620 **9** 4 **Zarawi (IRE)**[22] 6730 5-9-13 58 (p) LukeMorris 7 45
(John Gallagher) *prom: rdn over 3f out: wknd over 2f out* **33/1**
-431 **10** 7 **Maid Of Tuscany (IRE)**[11] 7045 5-9-5 55 (b) CharlieBennett[(5)] 9 33
(Alexandra Dunn) *hld up: hdwy 10f out: rdn and wknd over 2f out* **9/2**[2]
00-0 **11** 1 ¾ **Kastela Stari**[30] 6508 9-9-0 45 JamesSullivan 5 21
(Tim Fitzgerald) *hld up: rdn over 2f out: a in rr* **40/1**
4-60 **12** 14 **Lacey**[159] 2105 7-9-10 58 (b) RobHornby[(3)] 4 18
(Sarah Hollinshead) *s.i.s: hld up: rdn over 3f out: sn wknd* **25/1**
3404 **P** **Ellerina**[7] 7138 4-9-1 46 DuranFentiman 3
(Chris Fairhurst) *chsd ldrs: lost pl 12f out: wknd over 10f out: p.u over 7f out* **9/1**
3m 37.0s (-6.70) **Going Correction** -0.175s/f (Stan)
WFA 3 from 4yo+ 11lb **13** Ran SP% **125.0**
Speed ratings (Par 101): **108,102,102,102,101 101,100,98,96,93 92,86,**
CSF £16.19 CT £289.45 TOTE £2.90: £1.10, £3.00, £8.00; EX 20.80 Trifecta £546.80.
Owner Stephen Tucker & Keith McIntosh **Bred** Colin Kennedy **Trained** Upper Lambourn, Berkshire

The Form Book, Raceform Ltd, Newbury, RG14 5SJ

FOCUS
A generally moderate contest with the winner proving to be a different class from his rivals. The runners were soon strung out by nearly 20 lengths, but the gallop slowed significantly with a circuit left until the winner went for home 3f out.

7368 FCL GLOBAL FORWARDING H'CAP 1m 141y (Tp)
8:45 (8:47) (Class 6) (0-65,66) 3-Y-O+ **£2,587** (£577; £577; £192) **Stalls** Low

Form RPR
405 **1** **Mercifilly (FR)**[66] 5302 3-9-3 **63**............................(t) RichardKingscote 6 69
(Ed Walker) *sn led: hdd over 4f out: chsd ldr tl led again over 1f out: rdn out* **9/2**[1]
330 **2** *nk* **Anneani (IRE)**[19] 6826 4-9-2 **58**............................ JFEgan 12 62
(David Evans) *chsd ldrs: rdn over 2f out: r.o* **15/2**[3]
300- **2** *dht* **Oregon Gift**[285] 7008 4-9-6 **62**............................ BenCurtis 11 66
(Brian Ellison) *prom: chsd wnr 6f out tl led over 4f out: rdn and hdd over 1f out: r.o* **14/1**
0020 **4** *1 3/4* **Catastrophe**[10] 7078 3-9-4 **64**............................ CamHardie 9 65
(John Quinn) *hld up in tch: rdn and nt clr run over 1f out: styd on* **15/2**[3]
3305 **5** *nse* **Caledonia Laird**[17] 6872 5-9-7 **63**............................ JoeyHaynes 8 63
(Jo Hughes) *hld up: hdwy over 1f out: styd on: nt trble ldrs* **10/1**
5004 **6** *1 1/4* **Sooqaan**[82] 4715 5-9-7 **63**............................ PatCosgrave 5 61
(Antony Brittain) *chsd ldrs: rdn over 1f out: no ex wl ins fnl f* **13/2**[2]
2-00 **7** *nk* **Drago (IRE)**[16] 6907 4-9-8 **64**............................ JoeFanning 4 61
(David O'Meara) *hmpd s: hdwy over 6f out: rdn over 1f out: no ex ins fnl f* **11/1**
0065 **8** *1 1/4* **Faintly (USA)**[12] 7010 5-9-6 **62**............................(b) JamesSullivan 7 56
(Ruth Carr) *hld up: hdwy over 1f out: sn rdn: wknd wl ins fnl f* **9/1**
0002 **9** *1/2* **Spirit Of Gondree (IRE)**[11] 7048 8-9-5 **61**............................(b) LukeMorris 13 54
(Milton Bradley) *hld up: hdwy over 1f out: no ex ins fnl f* **16/1**
6541 **10** *nk* **Check 'Em Tuesday (IRE)**[11] 7048 3-9-6 **66**............................ DaleSwift 10 60
(Daniel Mark Loughnane) *hld up in tch: racd keenly: rdn over 2f out: wknd ins fnl f* **13/2**[2]
11 *15* **Coillte Mach**[203] 1097 3-8-10 **63**............................ TobyEley(7) 2 25+
(Daniel Mark Loughnane) *broke out of stalls early: wnt rt and sn bhd* **66/1**
0000 **12** *4 1/2* **Shamlan (IRE)**[17] 6872 4-9-7 **63**............................(tp) StevieDonohoe 1 15
(Johnny Farrelly) *s.i.s: a bhd* **18/1**
000- **13** *3/4* **Air Of Glory (IRE)**[348] 5376 6-9-4 **60**............................ DougieCostello 3 11+
(John Spearing) *hmpd s: plld hrd and sn prom: n.m.r and lost pl 7f out: rdn and wknd over 2f out* **66/1**

1m 48.94s (-1.16) **Going Correction** -0.175s/f (Stan)
WFA 3 from 4yo+ 4lb **13** Ran SP% **116.6**
Speed ratings (Par 101): **98,97,97,96,96 95,94,93,93,92 79,75,74**
WIN: £5.30, PLACES: Anneani: £2.50,Oregon Gift: £5.20, Mercifilly £1.90 EX: M/OG £52.00, M/A £21.50; CSF: M/OG £34.02, M/A £18.10; TRICAST: M/OG/A £239.28, M/A/OG £225.79; TRIFECTA: M/OG/A £462.30, M/A/OG£425.30;.

Owner Laurence Bellman **Bred** E A R L Haras Du Cadran & A Gilibert **Trained** Upper Lambourn, Berks

FOCUS
A medium tempo suited those who raced handily in this routine handicap. Even though the stalls were flipped open by one of the runners, he was well beaten and the result was allowed to stand.

7369 PERSONAL LOGISTICS FROM FCL GLOBAL FORWARDING H'CAP 1m 103y (Tp)
9:15 (9:20) (Class 6) (0-52,52) 3-Y-O+ **£2,587** (£770; £384; £192) **Stalls** Low

Form RPR
006 **1** **Mr Frankie**[117] 3476 5-9-6 **52**............................(p) JoeDoyle 4 60+
(Richard Phillips) *led 1f: chsd ldrs: led over 1f out: rdn and edgd lft ins fnl f: jst hld on* **7/2**[1]
0026 **2** *nk* **Victoriously**[16] 6900 4-9-4 **50**............................(p) MartinLane 6 57
(Andi Brown) *prom: lost pl over 3f out: hdwy over 1f out: r.o* **11/2**
5060 **3** *2 1/4* **Rafaaf (IRE)**[36] 6280 8-9-4 **50**............................(p) GrahamGibbons 7 53
(Richard Phillips) *hld up: hdwy over 1f out: styd on same pce ins fnl f* **22/1**
0006 **4** *1 3/4* **Rainford Glory (IRE)**[25] 6647 6-9-4 **50**............................(p) BarryMcHugh 1 50
(Tim Fitzgerald) *prom: rdn over 1f out: styd on same pce fnl f* **18/1**
0066 **5** *shd* **Rowlestonerendezvu**[25] 6654 3-9-2 **52**............................ LukeMorris 11 53
(Tony Carroll) *s.i.s: hld up: hdwy over 2f out: rdn over 1f out: no ex ins fnl f* **4/1**[2]
2000 **6** *3/4* **Whitchurch**[22] 6738 4-9-5 **51**............................ DougieCostello 5 49
(Philip Kirby) *hld up: hdwy over 3f out: chsd ldr over 2f out: led wl over 1f out: sn rdn and hdd: wknd ins fnl f* **25/1**
0053 **7** *hd* **Cahar Fad (IRE)**[18] 6857 4-9-4 **50**............................(bt) AdamBeschizza 12 48
(Steph Hollinshead) *hld up: hdwy and nt clr run over 1f out: nt trble ldrs* **8/1**
501 **8** *1 1/4* **Outlaw Torn (IRE)**[65] 5323 7-9-5 **51**............................(e) JoeFanning 8 46
(Richard Guest) *chsd ldrs: rdn over 1f out: wknd ins fnl f* **5/1**[3]
0000 **9** *nk* **Saltarello (IRE)**[28] 6569 4-9-2 **48**............................ SamJames 9 43
(Marjorie Fife) *s.i.s: nvr on terms* **12/1**
4005 **10** *nk* **Ferryview Place**[18] 6857 7-9-1 **50**............................(p) GeorgeDowning(3) 2 44
(Ian Williams) *s.s: a in rr* **10/1**
0230 **11** *1 3/4* **Mister Marcasite**[25] 6647 6-9-5 **51**............................ PatCosgrave 13 42
(Antony Brittain) *led after 1f: rdn and hdd wl over 1f out: wknd ins fnl f* **10/1**
0400 **12** *20* **Glittering**[19] 6826 3-9-2 **52**............................(p) RyanTate 10 6
(James Eustace) *chsd ldrs: wnt 2nd over 7f out: rdn over 3f out: nt clr run over 2f out: sn wknd* **22/1**

1m 59.77s (-1.03) **Going Correction** -0.175s/f (Stan)
WFA 3 from 4yo+ 4lb **12** Ran SP% **129.1**
Speed ratings (Par 101): **97,96,94,93,93 92,92,91,90,90 89,71**
CSF £24.47 CT £393.96 TOTE £5.80: £2.10, £2.50, £4.20; EX 29.40 Trifecta £450.20.

Owner Richard Phillips **Bred** S G Martin **Trained** Adlestrop, Gloucs

■ Boychick was withdrawn. Price at time of withdrawal 3/1. Rule 4 applies to bets struck prior to withdrawal but not to SP bets - deduct 25p in the pound. New market formed.

FOCUS
This modest handicap was run at a routine tempo.
T/Plt: £11.00 to a £1 stake. Pool of £99593.62 - 6583.55 winning tickets. T/Qpdt: £5.10 to a £1 stake. Pool of £9837.11 - 1426.42 winning tickets. **Colin Roberts**

7370 - 7371a (Foreign Racing) - See Raceform Interactive

4996 CORK (R-H)
Saturday, October 15

OFFICIAL GOING: Good to yielding

7372a CORKRACECOURSE.IE NAVIGATION STKS (LISTED RACE) 1m 100y
2:50 (2:51) 3-Y-O+
£19,522 (£6,286; £2,977; £1,323; £661; £330)

RPR
1 **Brendan Brackan (IRE)**[74] 5000 7-9-7 103............................ GaryCarroll 5 107
(G M Lyons, Ire) *sn led and clr: shkn up to extend advantage 3f out to 6l: styd on wl ins fnl f* **9/2**
2 *3 1/2* **Black Hawk War (USA)**[7] 7162 3-9-4 99............................(t) DonnachaO'Brien 8 99+
(A P O'Brien, Ire) *chsd ldrs in 3rd: wnt 2nd at 1/2-way: no imp on ldr 2f out: rdn and kpt on same pce fnl f: nvr on terms* **2/1**[1]
3 *1 1/2* **Tipstaff**[10] 7085 3-9-4 0............................ KevinManning 6 96+
(J S Bolger, Ire) *hld up in 5th: pushed along in modest 3rd over 3f out: no imp appr fnl f: kpt on same pce: nvr nrr* **7/2**[3]
4 *3 1/4* **Sruthan (IRE)**[13] 6983 6-9-10 109............................(p) DeclanMcDonogh 2 92
(P D Deegan, Ire) *settled off ldrs in 4th: 5th at 1/2-way: rdn and no imp 3f out: wnt 4th under 2f out: kpt on one pce fnl f: nvr nrr* **5/2**[2]
5 *8 1/2* **Just Joan (IRE)**[31] 6495 3-8-13 89............................ WayneLordan 3 65
(T Stack, Ire) *chsd ldr in 2nd to 1/2-way: rdn and no imp 3f out in 4th: wknd* **25/1**
6 *18* **Sas (IRE)**[48] 5946 3-8-13 77............................(bt) NGMcCullagh 1 26
(Denis W Cullen, Ire) *slowly away: racd towards rr thrght: nvr a factor* **100/1**
7 *14* **Kalisma (IRE)**[27] 6608 3-8-13 88............................ LeighRoche 7
(D K Weld, Ire) *sn in rr: nvr a factor eased fr under 2f out* **16/1**

1m 54.12s (114.12)
WFA 3 from 5yo+ 3lb **7** Ran SP% **113.0**
CSF £13.61 TOTE £7.90: £2.10, £1.30; DF 17.40.
Owner David Spratt & Sean Jones **Bred** Anamoine Ltd **Trained** Dunsany, Co Meath

FOCUS
A repeat victory in this race for this grand old servant as none of his rivals could land a blow.

7373 - 7377a (Foreign Racing) - See Raceform Interactive

7179 CAULFIELD (R-H)
Saturday, October 15

OFFICIAL GOING: Turf: good

7378a BMW CAULFIELD CUP (GROUP 1 H'CAP) (3YO+) (TURF) 1m 4f
6:30 (12:00) 3-Y-O+
£940,594 (£210,396; £111,386; £61,881; £49,504; £37,128)

RPR
1 **Jameka (AUS)**[13] 6996 4-8-4 **0**............................ NicholasHall 11 115+
(Ciaron Maher, Australia) **16/5**[1]
2 *3* **Scottish (IRE)**[56] 5652 4-8-9 **0**............................ KerrinMcEvoy 6 113
(Charlie Appleby) **6/1**[3]
3 *3/4* **Exosphere**[59] 5558 4-8-10 **0**............................ DamienOliver 3 113+
(Lee & Anthony Freedman, Australia) **14/1**
4 *1/2* **Almoonqith (USA)**[13] 6994 6-8-7 **0**............................(b) MichaelWalker 2 110+
(David A & B Hayes & Tom Dabernig, Australia) **70/1**
5 *3/4* **Real Love (AUS)**[15] 6-8-4 **0**............................(t) CraigAWilliams 9 105
(Darren Weir, Australia) **11/2**[2]
6 *nk* **Our Ivanhowe (GER)**[13] 6996 6-8-13 **0**............................(bt) DwayneDunn 5 113
(Lee & Anthony Freedman, Australia) **20/1**
7 *1 1/4* **Sir Isaac Newton**[35] 6354 4-8-9 **0**............................ ColmO'Donoghue 8 107
(A P O'Brien, Ire) **15/1**
8 *nk* **Vengeur Masque (IRE)**[13] 6994 4-7-13 **0**............................ PatrickMoloney 15 97
(Michael Moroney, Australia) **100/1**
9 *1/2* **De Little Engine (AUS)**[13] 6996 6-7-13 **0**............................ BenEThompson 12 96
(Danny O'Brien, Australia) **60/1**
10 *shd* **Sir John Hawkwood (IRE)**[14] 6978 7-8-6 **0**............................(t) BlakeSpriggs 4 103
(John P Thompson, Australia) **12/1**
11 *hd* **Preferment (NZ)**[13] 6996 5-9-0 **0**............................(tp) HughBowman 13 111
(Chris Waller, Australia) **25/1**
12 *hd* **Tally (AUS)**[13] 6996 4-8-5 **0**............................(b) BrentonAvdulla 16 103
(J O'Shea, Australia) **18/1**
13 *1 1/4* **Articus (FR)**[76] 4928 4-8-5 **0**............................ ZacPurton 10 99
(A Wohler, Germany) **17/2**
14 *1 3/4* **Pemberley (NZ)**[7] 5-7-13 **0**............................(bt) BenAllen 14 90
(Ciaron Maher, Australia) **30/1**
15 *shd* **Sacred Master (NZ)**[14] 6978 5-8-3 **0** ow1............................(p) TommyBerry 7 94
(Chris Waller, Australia) **13/1**
16 *1* **Go Dreaming (AUS)**[15] 7-7-13 **0**............................ KatelynMallyon 1 89
(Grant Kluske, Australia) **100/1**

2m 28.88s (148.88) **16** Ran SP% **113.9**

Owner C L Maher, Mrs J M McKenna Et Al **Bred** Gilgai Farm **Trained** Australia

FOCUS
This didn't look a particularly strong Caulfield Cup on paper, if competitive as always. After the dash to the first bend the pace slowed up dramatically and a lot of these pulled for their heads. It proved very difficult to get involved from off the gallop and there were a number who found trouble as the field bunched going into the home turn.

7197 KEENELAND (L-H)

Saturday, October 15

OFFICIAL GOING: Turf: firm

7379a QUEEN ELIZABETH II CHALLENGE CUP STKS PRESENTED BY LANE'S END (GRADE 1) (3YO FILLIES) (TURF) 1m 1f (T)

10:30 (12:00) 3-Y-O

£204,081 (£68,027; £34,013; £17,006; £10,204; £2,268)

RPR

1 **Time And Motion (USA)**[55] 5697 3-8-9 0 JohnRVelazquez 6 106
(James J Toner, U.S.A) **3/1**[2]

2 *hd* **Harmonize (USA)**[55] 5693 3-8-9 0 (b) JunierAlvarado 4 106+
(William Mott, U.S.A) **107/10**

3 *nse* **Hawksmoor (IRE)**[35] 6352 3-8-9 0 (b) CoreyJLanerie 5 106
(Hugo Palmer) **106/10**

4 *4 ¾* **On Leave (USA)**[28] 6595 3-8-9 0 JoseLOrtiz 2 96
(Claude McGaughey III, U.S.A) **31/10**[3]

5 *½* **Mokat (USA)**[55] 5693 3-8-9 0 KentJDesormeaux 8 95
(Richard Baltas, U.S.A) **117/10**

6 *nk* **Stays In Vegas (USA)**[55] 5693 3-8-9 0 FlavienPrat 3 94
(Jerry Hollendorfer, U.S.A) **142/10**

7 *5* **Catch A Glimpse (USA)**[55] 5697 3-8-9 0 FlorentGeroux 1 84
(Mark Casse, Canada) **17/10**[1]

8 *3 ½* **Queen Caroline (USA)**[38] 3-8-9 0 AlexCintron 7 76
(Michael Matz, U.S.A) **48/1**

1m 50.24s (0.44) **8** Ran SP% **120.1**

PARI-MUTUEL (all including 2 usd stake): WIN 8.00; PLACE (1-2) 4.60, 8.40; SHOW (1-2-3) 3.80, 5.20, 7.20; SF 65.40.

Owner Phillips Racing Partnership **Bred** Phillips Racing Partnership **Trained** USA

7321 NEWCASTLE (A.W) (L-H)

Sunday, October 16

OFFICIAL GOING: Tapeta: standard

Wind: Light, half against Weather: Overcast

7380 EQUINEPRODUCTS-UKLTD.COM/EBF MAIDEN FILLIES' STKS (PLUS 10 RACE) 6f (Tp)

2:15 (2:21) (Class 4) 2-Y-O **£4,528** (£1,347; £673; £336) **Stalls** Centre

Form RPR

52 **1** **Panova**[18] 6867 2-9-0 0 TedDurcan 5 79
(Sir Michael Stoute) *pressed ldr: rdn to ld over 1f out: hrd pressed ins fnl f: kpt on wl towards fin* **8/11**[1]

2 *¾* **Dealer's Choice (IRE)** 2-9-0 0 JackMitchell 7 77
(Roger Varian) *t.k.h: prom: effrt and chsd wnr over 1f out: edgd lft: ev ch and rdn ins fnl f: kpt on: hld nr fin* **25/1**

04 **3** *5* **Bearag**[16] 6925 2-9-0 0 DanielTudhope 6 62
(David O'Meara) *prom: drvn and outpcd over 2f out: rallied fnl f: kpt on: nt rch first two* **10/1**[3]

43 **4** *hd* **Ocean Princess (IRE)**[16] 6925 2-9-0 0 PaulMulrennan 14 61
(Michael Dods) *trckd ldrs: effrt and rdn 2f out: outpcd ins fnl f* **10/1**[3]

0 **5** *2* **Royal Icon**[125] 3223 2-9-0 0 KevinStott 11 55
(Kevin Ryan) *hld up: effrt and pushed along over 2f out: no imp fr over 1f out* **80/1**

52 **6** *1 ¼* **Dandy Bird (IRE)**[16] 6925 2-9-0 0 TomEaves 12 51
(James Given) *led tl rdn and hdd over 1f out: outpcd ins fnl f* **10/1**[3]

00 **7** *2 ¼* **She's Zoff (IRE)**[16] 6925 2-9-0 0 CamHardie 13 45
(John Quinn) *hld up: rdn and outpcd over 2f out: n.d after* **125/1**

000 **8** *2 ¾* **Cheers All Round**[34] 6404 2-8-11 0 JosephineGordon(3) 3 36
(Henry Spiller) *prom: drvn and outpcd over 2f out: sn btn* **100/1**

03 **9** *1 ¼* **Moondust (IRE)**[12] 7056 2-9-0 0 RobertHavlin 2 33
(John Gosden) *cl up: rdn along 3f out: edgd lft and wknd 2f out* **11/4**[2]

60 **10** *½* **Babouska**[109] 3772 2-8-11 0 NathanEvans(3) 1 31
(Michael Easterby) *hld up: drvn and struggling over 3f out: btn fnl 2f* **150/1**

60 **11** *1 ½* **Lively Lily**[15] 6952 2-8-9 0 RowanScott(5) 9 27
(Ann Duffield) *s.i.s: hld up: pushed along over 3f out: sn btn* **100/1**

1m 10.65s (-1.85) **Going Correction** -0.425s/f (Stan) **11** Ran SP% **120.4**

Speed ratings (Par 94): **95,94,87,87,84 82,79,76,74,73 71**

CSF £29.69 TOTE £1.70: £1.10, £3.70, £2.60; EX 16.40 Trifecta £107.10.

Owner Cheveley Park Stud **Bred** Cheveley Park Stud Ltd **Trained** Newmarket, Suffolk

FOCUS

A routine fillies' maiden, though a few had already shown ability. Four of these met over C&D last month and the 2-3-4-10 from there finished 6-4-3-7 here. The first two pulled right away.

7381 PREMIER E BY EQUINE PRODUCTS UK LTD/EBF MAIDEN STKS (PLUS 10 RACE) 5f (Tp)

2:45 (2:47) (Class 4) 2-Y-O **£4,528** (£1,347; £673; £336) **Stalls** Centre

Form RPR

2303 **1** **Perfect Symphony (IRE)**[20] 6833 2-9-5 75 KevinStott 9 76
(Kevin Ryan) *hld up: rdn and hdwy over 1f out: kpt on wl fnl f to ld nr fin* **2/1**[1]

0300 **2** *nk* **Monte Cinq (IRE)**[21] 6807 2-9-5 62 BenCurtis 2 75
(Jason Ward) *led: rdn wl over 1f out: kpt on fnl f: hdd nr fin* **28/1**

23 **3** *¾* **Hamidans Girl (IRE)**[61] 5516 2-9-0 0 PhillipMakin 7 67
(Keith Dalgleish) *t.k.h: trckd ldrs: effrt and pressed wnr over 1f out to ins fnl f: kpt on same pce towards fin* **11/4**[2]

36 **4** *1 ¾* **Pudding Chare (IRE)**[47] 6002 2-9-5 0 TonyHamilton 1 66
(Richard Fahey) *prom: rdn over 2f out: kpt on ins fnl f: nt pce to chal* **11/2**[3]

0332 **5** *nk* **Glyder**[17] 6887 2-9-0 58 PatrickMathers 6 60
(John Holt) *hld up in tch: rdn and effrt over 2f out: kpt on same pce ins fnl f* **16/1**

653 **6** *2* **Love Oasis**[79] 4832 2-9-0 68 JoeFanning 10 53
(Mark Johnston) *hld up in tch: effrt and pushed along 2f out: no imp fnl f* **10/1**

02 **7** *shd* **Ideal Bounty (IRE)**[22] 6789 2-9-5 0 NeilFarley 4 57
(Andrew Crook) *pressed ldr tl rdn and wknd over 1f out* **25/1**

65 **8** *¾* **Dandy Roll (IRE)**[25] 6673 2-9-5 0 GeorgeBaker 5 55
(Ralph Beckett) *prom: effrt and rdn over 2f out: wknd over 1f out* **13/2**

00 **9** *4 ½* **Chillilili**[16] 6925 2-9-0 0 ConnorBeasley 8 33
(Bryan Smart) *prom: rdn over 2f out: wknd over 1f out* **100/1**

50 **10** *1 ½* **Violet Mist (IRE)**[31] 6515 2-9-0 0 GrahamLee 3 28
(Ben Haslam) *s.i.s: bhd: struggling 1/2-way: edgd lft and sn btn* **200/1**

58.37s (-1.13) **Going Correction** -0.425s/f (Stan) **10** Ran SP% **112.5**

Speed ratings (Par 97): **92,91,90,87,87 83,83,82,75,72**

CSF £64.58 TOTE £3.00: £1.30, £6.10, £1.50; EX 48.80 Trifecta £228.00.

Owner Hambleton Racing Ltd XLVI **Bred** Ballyhane Stud **Trained** Hambleton, N Yorks

FOCUS

A modest sprint maiden.

7382 SELENAVITE E THE ULTIMATE VITAMIN & MINERAL SUPPLEMENT H'CAP 2m 56y (Tp)

3:20 (3:20) (Class 5) (0-70,69) 3-Y-O+ **£3,234** (£962; £481; £240) **Stalls** Low

Form RPR

6421 **1** **Always Summer**[31] 6508 3-8-11 **67** GeorgeWood(5) 7 80
(James Fanshawe) *hld up in tch: shkn up and hdwy on outside to ld 2f out: sn rdn clr: readily* **2/1**[2]

-321 **2** *4* **Alsacienne**[29] 6593 3-9-4 **69** LukeMorris 3 77
(Sir Mark Prescott Bt) *prom: pushed along over 4f out: hdwy to ld briefly over 2f out: rdn and hung lft over 1f out: kpt on same pce: eased whn hld ins fnl f* **11/8**[1]

3443 **3** *6* **Jan Smuts (IRE)**[8] 7138 8-9-5 **60** (tp) CamHardie 4 61
(Wilf Storey) *prom: hdwy to chse ldr after 4f: led over 3f out to over 2f out: edgd lft and outpcd wl over 1f out* **12/1**

0046 **4** *5* **Gabrial's Hope (FR)**[9] 7105 7-8-12 **53** BenCurtis 6 48
(Tracy Waggott) *dwlt: hld up: drvn along over 4f out: sn outpcd: no imp fr 2f out* **16/1**

6-P5 **5** *2 ¼* **Front Five (IRE)**[122] 3302 4-9-12 **67** RobertHavlin 5 59
(Martin Bosley) *led to over 3f out: rdn and wknd over 2f out* **14/1**

2023 **6** *16* **Kicking The Can (IRE)**[23] 6739 5-9-5 **60** PatrickMathers 8 33
(David Thompson) *t.k.h: trckd ldr 4f: cl up tl rdn and wknd over 2f out* **7/1**[3]

3m 34.08s (-1.12) **Going Correction** -0.20s/f (Stan)

WFA 3 from 4yo+ 10lb **6** Ran SP% **108.2**

Speed ratings (Par 103): **94,92,89,86,85 77**

CSF £4.69 CT £17.48 TOTE £2.80: £1.50, £1.40; EX 5.30 Trifecta £20.00.

Owner Dr Catherine Wills **Bred** St Clare Hall Stud **Trained** Newmarket, Suffolk

FOCUS

An ordinary staying handicap and not the greatest test of stamina with the early pace a modest one. It always seemed likely to be dominated by the two 3yo fillies with similar profiles, though one proved far too good for the other.

7383 RESTORELYTE BY EQUINE PRODUCTS UK LTD H'CAP 1m 2f 42y (Tp)

3:50 (3:50) (Class 3) (0-95,94) 3-Y-O+ **£7,762** (£2,310; £1,154; £577) **Stalls** High

Form RPR

1144 **1** **Palisade**[31] 6528 3-8-6 **84** (b) LukeMorris 12 96
(Sir Mark Prescott Bt) *hld up: smooth hdwy over 2f out: rdn to ld over 1f out: styd on wl u.p ins fnl f* **17/2**

4531 **2** *½* **Dubai Fashion (IRE)**[21] 6803 3-9-1 **93** PaulHanagan 1 104
(Saeed bin Suroor) *in tch: smooth hdwy to ld over 2f out: rdn and hdd over 1f out: rallied: kpt on ins fnl f: hld towards fin* **5/2**[1]

103 **3** *1 ¼* **Replenish (FR)**[43] 6126 3-9-1 **93** FrederikTylicki 3 101
(James Fanshawe) *hld up midfield: stdy hdwy and prom wl over 1f out: sn rdn: hung lft ins fnl f: kpt on same pce* **4/1**[2]

6460 **4** *shd* **Bermondsey**[29] 6573 4-9-4 **91** JamieSpencer 8 99
(Luca Cumani) *s.i.s: hld up: hdwy and in tch over 1f out: drvn and kpt on ins fnl f* **7/1**

134 **5** *8* **Michele Strogoff**[24] 6710 3-9-0 **92** ConnorBeasley 11 84
(Roger Fell) *trckd ldr: led briefly over 2f out: rdn and hung lft over 1f out: wknd fnl f* **20/1**

1003 **6** *6* **Sindarban (IRE)**[29] 6561 5-9-4 **91** PhillipMakin 9 71
(Keith Dalgleish) *hld up: effrt and pushed along over 2f out: wknd wl over 1f out* **13/2**[3]

0000 **7** *3 ½* **Chancery (USA)**[8] 7154 8-9-2 **89** (p) DanielTudhope 7 62
(David O'Meara) *hld up: rdn along over 2f out: sn outpcd: btn over 1f out* **22/1**

1250 **8** *1* **Felix De Vega (IRE)**[29] 6559 4-9-2 **92** NathanEvans(3) 4 63
(Michael Easterby) *prom: rdn over 4f out: wknd over 2f out* **14/1**

3555 **9** *1* **Demonstration (IRE)**[45] 6048 4-8-11 **84** (p) JoeFanning 6 53
(William Jarvis) *led: rdn and hdd over 2f out: wknd wl over 1f out* **17/2**

2116 **10** *27* **Faiseur De Miracle**[156] 2199 4-9-7 **94** GrahamLee 2 9
(Micky Hammond) *trckd ldrs tl rdn and wknd fr 3f out: t.o* **40/1**

2m 4.88s (-5.52) **Going Correction** -0.20s/f (Stan) course record

WFA 3 from 4yo+ 5lb **10** Ran SP% **113.7**

Speed ratings (Par 107): **114,113,112,112,106 101,98,97,96,75**

CSF £28.57 CT £98.94 TOTE £9.00: £2.50, £1.50, £1.40; EX 31.10 Trifecta £103.20.

Owner Cheveley Park Stud **Bred** Cheveley Park Stud Ltd **Trained** Newmarket, Suffolk

FOCUS

A decent handicap run at a solid pace and another race dominated by the 3yos. The first four pulled miles clear and the form should stand up.

7384 HAEMAVITE B PLUS BY EQUINE PRODUCTS UK LTD MAIDEN STKS 1m 2f 42y (Tp)

4:25 (4:26) (Class 5) 3-Y-O **£3,234** (£962; £481; £240) **Stalls** High

Form RPR

2 **1** **Laqab (IRE)**[24] 6703 3-9-5 0 DaneO'Neill 7 86+
(Roger Varian) *hld up: stdy hdwy on outside over 2f out: shkn up and led 1f out: drvn and edgd lft: kpt on wl* **5/2**[2]

5 **2** *nk* **Dharoos (IRE)**[121] 3359 3-9-5 0 PaulHanagan 4 85+
(John Gosden) *hld up in tch: rdn over 3f out: rallied and led 2f out: hdd 1f out: kpt on fnl f: hld nr fin* **2/1**[1]

40 **3** *1 ¾* **Stanley**[107] 3845 3-9-5 0 JamieSpencer 3 81
(Luca Cumani) *trckd ldrs: smooth hdwy to dispute ld over 2f out to wl over 1f out: kpt on ins fnl f* **4/1**[3]

4 *4 ½* **Mutadaffeq (IRE)**[114] 3632 3-9-5 80 DanielTudhope 2 72
(David O'Meara) *trckd ldrs: rdn over 2f out: outpcd over 1f out: btn fnl f* **16/1**

6 **5** *nk* **Dubawi Fifty**[183] 1479 3-9-5 0 GrahamLee 1 71
(Karen McLintock) *s.i.s: hld up: rdn and outpcd over 2f out: rallied over 1f out: no imp fnl f* **200/1**

-044 **6** *1* **Dostoyevsky (IRE)**[34] 6415 3-9-5 72 GeorgeBaker 9 69
(David Lanigan) *t.k.h: hld up: rdn and hung lft 2f out: sn no imp* **8/1**

43 **7** ¾ **Selection (FR)**[13] 7009 3-9-5 0 .... GrahamGibbons 10 68
(William Haggas) *cl up: led 3f out to 2f out: sn rdn and wknd* **7/1**

6 **8** 15 **Glorious Poet**[26] 6650 3-9-5 0 .... LukeMorris 8 38
(Ed Walker) *t.k.h: led after 2f: rdn and hdd 3f out: wknd 2f out* **66/1**

4 **9** 1 **Vernatti**[94] 4319 3-8-11 0 .... RobHornby(3) 6 31
(Pam Sly) *led 2f: cl up tl rdn and wknd over 2f out* **25/1**

2m 7.13s (-3.27) **Going Correction** -0.20s/f (Stan) **9** Ran SP% **117.2**
Speed ratings (Par 101): **105,104,103,99,99 98,98,86,85**
CSF £8.01 TOTE £3.00: £1.20, £1.60, £1.40; EX 8.70 Trifecta £23.90.
Owner Hamdan Al Maktoum **Bred** Shadwell Estate Company Limited **Trained** Newmarket, Suffolk

FOCUS
An uncompetitive 3yo maiden in which the front three came clear. It resulted in a 1-2 for owner Hamdan Al Maktoum and the winning time was 2.25sec slower than the preceding 0-95 handicap.

7385 EQUINE PRODUCTS UK LTD PIONEERING NEW FRONTIERS H'CAP — 1m 4f 98y (Tp)

5:00 (5:00) (Class 5) (0-70,70) 3-Y-O+ **£3,234** (£962; £481; £240) **Stalls** High

Form RPR

5121 **1** **The Resdev Way**[16] 6920 3-9-2 **67** .... BarryMcHugh 5 79+
(Richard Whitaker) *trckd ldrs: clr w two others ent st: led gng wl 2f out: sn rdn clr: eased wl ins fnl f* **2/1**[1]

1665 **2** ¾ **Another Lincolnday**[17] 6906 5-9-3 **61** ....[1] TomEaves 10 66
(Michael Herrington) *dwlt: hld up: rdn over 2f out: gd hdwy over 1f out: kpt on wl to take 2nd nr fin: flattered by proximity to eased-down wnr* **50/1**

0320 **3** nk **Tectonic (IRE)**[20] 6838 7-9-5 **63** ....(v) ConnorBeasley 12 67
(Keith Dalgleish) *stdd s: hld up: rdn over 2f out: gd hdwy over 1f out: chsd wnr ins fnl f: no ex and lost 2nd pl cl home* **33/1**

5064 **4** 2¼ **Nonchalant**[15] 6953 5-9-7 **65** ....(b) DanielTudhope 9 66
(David O'Meara) *led at reasonable gallop: clr w two others ent st: hdd 2f out: no ex and lost 2nd pl ins fnl f* **8/1**

0454 **5** 2¼ **Perceysvivace**[93] 4375 3-8-8 **59** .... TonyHamilton 3 56
(Richard Fahey) *in tch: hdwy to chse clr ldng trio over 3f out: sn rdn: hung lft and no imp over 1f out* **9/1**

043 **6** nse **Notion Of Beauty (USA)**[65] 5353 3-9-0 **65** .... DougieCostello 8 62
(K R Burke) *midfield on outside: rdn over 3f out: plugged on same pce fnl 2f* **25/1**

630P **7** 3 **Toffee Apple (IRE)**[10] 7097 3-8-2 **58** .... ShirleyTeasdale(5) 4 50
(Keith Dalgleish) *pressed ldr: clr w two others ent st: rdn and wknd 2f out* **40/1**

/00- **8** 3¾ **Precision Strike**[560] 1198 6-9-11 **69** .... GeorgeChaloner 6 55
(Richard Whitaker) *hld up: nt clr run 3f out: swtchd rt and sn rdn: nvr able to chal* **66/1**

6010 **9** 4 **Almutamarred (USA)**[23] 6730 4-9-3 **66** .... AdamMcNamara(5) 11 46
(Kevin Morgan) *hld up: rdn over 2f out: hung lft and sn struggling* **16/5**[2]

0430 **10** 5 **Jessica Jo (IRE)**[12] 7043 3-9-0 **65** .... JasonHart 7 37
(Mark Johnston) *dwlt: sn: midfield: struggling over 3f out: btn fnl 2f* **50/1**

2222 **11** 20 **Kelvin Hall**[5] 7249 3-9-4 **69** .... JoeFanning 2 9
(Mark Johnston) *cl up tl rdn and wknd over 3f out: eased whn no ch fnl 2f* **7/2**[3]

2m 38.78s (-2.32) **Going Correction** -0.20s/f (Stan)
WFA 3 from 4yo+ 7lb **11** Ran SP% **115.1**
Speed ratings (Par 103): **99,98,98,96,95 95,93,90,88,84 71**
CSF £127.29 CT £2537.62 TOTE £2.80: £1.80, £12.60, £3.30; EX 119.80 Trifecta £1890.10.
Owner Resdev **Bred** Mickley Stud **Trained** Scarcroft, W Yorks

FOCUS
A modest handicap with the winner in a completely different league. The pace was good and they were soon well spread out.

7386 EQUINE PRODUCTS UK LTD- YOUR HORSE DESERVE THE BEST H'CAP — 5f (Tp)

5:30 (5:31) (Class 5) (0-75,75) 3-Y-O+ **£3,105** (£924; £461; £230) **Stalls** Centre

Form RPR

5006 **1** **Royal Mezyan (IRE)**[48] 5969 5-9-0 **71** .... JosephineGordon(3) 3 81
(Henry Spiller) *in tch centre: hdwy to ld over 1f out: rdn and edgd lft ins fnl f: kpt on wl* **12/1**

0620 **2** ¾ **Eternitys Gate**[24] 6699 5-9-7 **75** ....(v) TomEaves 9 82+
(Ivan Furtado) *hld up towards stands' side: rdn and hdwy over 1f out: kpt on to take 2nd towards fin: nt rch far side wnr* **9/1**

2560 **3** ¾ **Henley**[31] 6506 4-8-12 **66** .... ConnorBeasley 2 71
(Tracy Waggott) *cl up far side: wnt 2nd over 2f out: rdn and kpt on fnl f: no ex and lost 2nd nr fin* **11/1**

0421 **4** ¾ **Astrophysics**[32] 6476 4-9-5 **73** .... PaddyAspell 5 75
(Lynn Siddall) *in tch centre: rdn along over 2f out: edgd rt over 1f out: kpt on same pce fnl f* **11/2**[2]

5600 **5** 1 **Flicka's Boy**[22] 6793 4-8-13 **67** .... BarryMcHugh 6 65
(Tony Coyle) *taken early to post: hld up centre: rdn and hdwy over 1f out: no imp ins fnl f* **10/1**

0403 **6** ½ **Sir Domino (FR)**[16] 6927 4-9-5 **73** ....(p) KevinStott 10 70+
(Kevin Ryan) *hld up centre: rdn and hdwy over 1f out: kpt on fnl f: nvr able to chal* **3/1**[1]

6-11 **7** 1¼ **China Excels**[159] 2120 9-8-12 **69** .... RobHornby(3) 4 61
(Mandy Rowland) *led towards far side: rdn and hdd over 1f out: wknd ins fnl f* **28/1**

1020 **8** 1 **Run Rio Run (IRE)**[15] 6958 3-8-12 **66** ....(p) PaulMulrennan 14 55
(Michael Dods) *in tch towards stands side: rdn 1/2-way: outpcd over 1f out* **11/1**

5450 **9** ½ **Perfect Words (IRE)**[25] 6685 6-8-8 **62** ....(p) SamJames 12 49
(Marjorie Fife) *in tch: rdn over 2f out: wknd over 1f out* **28/1**

0051 **10** ½ **Round The Island**[8] 7144 3-8-4 **61** .... NathanEvans(3) 13 47
(Richard Whitaker) *dwlt: hld up stands' side: rdn and shortlived effrt over 2f out: no further imp over 1f out* **7/1**[3]

1-00 **11** 1 **Vroom (IRE)**[206] 1060 3-9-6 **74** .... DougieCostello 7 56
(Gay Kelleway) *prom centre: rdn over 2f out: wknd over 1f out* **25/1**

30-3 **12** 2¼ **Teajan (IRE)**[173] 1753 3-9-4 **72** .... LukeMorris 8 46
(James Tate) *hld up centre: drvn along over 2f out: nvr on terms* **12/1**

0405 **13** ½ **Bapak Bangsawan**[10] 7093 6-8-7 **66** ow1 ....(v) AnnStokell(5) 1 37
(Ann Stokell) *w ldr far side to 1/2-way: rdn and wknd wl over 1f out* **50/1**

58.41s (-1.09) **Going Correction** -0.425s/f (Stan) **13** Ran SP% **116.7**
Speed ratings (Par 103): **91,89,88,87,85 85,83,81,80,79 78,74,73**
CSF £109.01 CT £1266.98 TOTE £12.40: £4.80, £4.40, £4.80; EX 139.20 Trifecta £1197.60.
Owner Peter-Robert Spiller **Bred** Mark Salmon **Trained** Newmarket, Suffolk

FOCUS
An ordinary sprint handicap with the main action unfolding centre-to-far side.
T/Jkpt: £1,732.40. Pool: £14,726 - 8.50 winning units. T/Plt: £5.60 to a £1 stake. Pool: £111,617.29 -14,320.63 winning units. T/Qpdt: £3.50 to a £1 stake. Pool: £8,879.29 - 1849.86 winning units. **Richard Young**

6686 NAAS (L-H)
Sunday, October 16

OFFICIAL GOING: Soft to heavy

7387a TIFRUMS EUROPEAN BREEDERS FUND (C & G) MAIDEN (PLUS 10 RACE) — 6f

2:05 (2:05) 2-Y-O **£7,009** (£2,165; £1,025; £455; £170)

RPR

1 **Spirit Of Valor (USA)**[7] 7190 2-9-2 0 ....(t) DonnachaO'Brien(3) 4 85
(A P O'Brien, Ire) *cl up bhd ldr in 2nd: rdn to ld over 1f out: wandered sltly ins fnl f and kpt on wl u.p to assert clsng stages* **8/13**[1]

2 ¾ **Imagine If (IRE)**[113] 3675 2-9-5 0 .... ColinKeane 1 83
(G M Lyons, Ire) *led far side gp: rdn and hdd over 1f out: no imp on wnr wl ins fnl f: kpt on same pce to jst hold 2nd* **7/2**[2]

3 hd **Invincible Ryker (IRE)** 2-9-5 0 .... ShaneFoley 7 82
(M Halford, Ire) *bmpd sltly s: chsd ldrs far side gp: rdn over 1f out and no imp on wnr u.p in 3rd wl ins fnl f: kpt on clsng stages: jst hld for 2nd* **10/1**

4 1½ **Guardia Svizzera (IRE)** 2-9-5 0 .... DeclanMcDonogh 2 78+
(John M Oxx, Ire) *chsd ldrs far side gp: rdn bhd ldrs over 1f out and no imp u.p in 4th wl ins fnl f: kpt on same pce* **20/1**

5 9 **Arizona State (USA)** 2-9-5 0 ....[1] SeamieHeffernan 12 57+
(A P O'Brien, Ire) *dwlt sltly: chsd ldrs nr side gp: sme hdwy in 6th over 2f out: no imp on ldrs in mod 5th over 1f out: kpt on one pce ins fnl f* **8/1**[3]

6 9½ **Acclamatio (IRE)**[67] 5310 2-9-5 0 .... MichaelHussey 5 22
(A J Martin, Ire) *chsd ldrs far side gp: rdn in 5th 2f out and sn no imp on ldrs: one pce in mod 6th fr 1 1/2f out* **33/1**

7 5½ **Great Uncle (IRE)** 2-9-5 0 .... KevinManning 8 6+
(J S Bolger, Ire) *prom nr side gp early: rdn and wknd fr 1/2-way* **12/1**

8 4½ **Michaels Boots** 2-9-0 0 .... KillianLeonard(5) 9
(Des Donovan, Ire) *prom nr side gp early tl tacked over to far side gp after 2f: sn pushed along and no imp towards rr fr 1/2-way: wknd* **50/1**

9 25 **Whosasking (IRE)** 2-9-5 0 .... BillyLee 6
(A J Martin, Ire) *wnt sltly rt s and sltly bmpd rival: towards rr far side gp: rdn and wknd fr 1/2-way: t.o* **66/1**

1m 19.97s (6.77) **9** Ran SP% **123.2**
CSF £3.23 TOTE £1.50: £1.02, £1.80, £3.40; DF 3.50 Trifecta £13.90.
Owner Stonestreet Stables, LLC & Mrs John Magnier & Mich **Bred** Nursery Place **Trained** Cashel

FOCUS
The soft ground posed as an inconvenience to the long odds-on favourite but he still got the job done and probably possesses a fair bit more natural talent than today's rivals do.

7388 - 7390a (Foreign Racing) - See Raceform Interactive

7391a HOSPITALITY AT NAAS H'CAP — 7f

4:20 (4:20) 3-Y-O+ **£4,522** (£1,397; £661; £294; £110)

RPR

1 **Snoozing Indian**[13] 7021 4-9-7 **68** .... WayneLordan 12 74
(T J O'Mara, Ire) *chsd ldrs: pushed along fr 3f out: sn rdn and clsd u.p in 3rd 1 1/2f out to ld narrowly ins fnl 100yds: all out clsng stages: hld on wl* **10/1**

2 hd **Ecoeye**[13] 7021 4-9-11 **72** .... ConnorKing 10 77
(Augustine Leahy, Ire) *prom tl sn settled bhd ldr: 2nd 1/2-way: led over 2f out: rdn over 1f out and sn strly pressed: hdd narrowly ins fnl 100yds and kpt on wl clsng stages: jst hld* **5/1**[1]

3 1¾ **Feeling Easy (IRE)**[6] 7233 4-9-6 **74** .... DenisLinehan(7) 13 74+
(Anthony Mulholland, Ire) *mid-div: hdwy on outer fr under 2f out to chse ldrs in 5th ent fnl f: kpt on u.p into 3rd clsng stages: nvr trbld ldrs* **10/1**

4 ¾ **Severus (GER)**[14] 6984 6-9-9 **75** .... KillianLeonard(5) 3 73
(Des Donovan, Ire) *sn chsd ldrs: rdn bhd ldrs 2f out and u.p in 4th over 1f out: kpt on same pce ins fnl f* **12/1**

5 nk **Teagan Angel (IRE)**[6] 7234 4-8-6 **63** ....(t) DannySheehy(10) 15 60+
(Ms M Dowdall Blake, Ire) *chsd ldrs: gng wl bhd ldrs over 2f out: sn rdn in 6th and no imp on ldrs ins fnl f: kpt on same pce* **14/1**

6 ½ **William Ashford (IRE)**[8] 7163 4-9-2 **68** ....(p) TomMadden(5) 8 64
(J C Hayden, Ire) *w.w towards rr: prog after 1/2-way to chse ldrs in 8th 1 1/2f out: kpt on same pce ins fnl f: nvr trbld ldrs* **5/1**[1]

7 2¼ **Heavy Weight (IRE)**[303] 8293 7-9-6 **67** ....(t) RonanWhelan 14 57
(J S Bolger, Ire) *hld up towards rr: sme hdwy on outer fr 2f out: rdn briefly in 11th over 1f out and kpt on into 7th clsng stages: nvr nrr* **10/1**

8 ½ **Mzuri (IRE)**[7] 7194 4-9-8 **69** ....[1] SeamieHeffernan 6 58
(Ms Sheila Lavery, Ire) *towards rr and pushed along early: pushed along into st and no imp: sme late hdwy on outer ins fnl f: nvr nrr* **8/1**[2]

9 ¾ **Seaforth (IRE)**[78] 4899 4-9-4 **65** ....(b) ColinKeane 2 52
(John Joseph Murphy, Ire) *dwlt and towards rr: no imp in 14th over 1f out: sme late hdwy ins fnl f: nvr nrr* **16/1**

10 ½ **Chillie Billie**[13] 7022 7-8-13 **63** .... RossCoakley(3) 1 48
(J Larkin, Ire) *chsd ldrs: 3rd 1/2-way: tk clsr order bhd ldr and rdn in 2nd 1 1/2f out: no ex u.p in 3rd 1f out and sn wknd* **16/1**

11 nk **Atlas (IRE)**[42] 6170 3-9-7 **73** ....(v) ShaneBKelly(3) 16 56
(M D O'Callaghan, Ire) *chsd ldrs: rdn over 2f out and sn no imp on ldrs u.p in 9th: one pce fnl f* **10/1**

12 nk **Saxum (FR)**[11] 7079 3-8-6 **58** ....(t) RobbieDowney(3) 5 41
(Edward Lynam, Ire) *in rr of mid-div for most: rdn over 2f out and no imp* **25/1**

13 hd **Stamp Of Authority (IRE)**[13] 7021 4-8-9 **63** ....(t) DylanHogan(7) 11 46
(T G McCourt, Ire) *in rr of mid-div: tk clsr order after 1/2-way: rdn bhd ldrs far side under 2f out where n.m.r briefly and sn no ex: wknd wl ins fnl f* **9/1**[3]

14 4½ **Cresendo (IRE)**[41] 6197 3-8-11 **60** ....(p) KevinManning 7 30
(J S Bolger, Ire) *mid-div: sme hdwy after 1/2-way to chse ldrs: rdn in 5th under 2f out and sn no ex: wknd and eased ins fnl f* **16/1**

15 hd **Lady Ranger (IRE)**[24] 6727 5-9-2 **63** .... ConorHoban 9 33
(Peter McCreery, Ire) *dwlt and towards rr thrght: pushed along bef 1/2-way and no imp into st* **20/1**

16 8½ **Peremptory (IRE)**[24] 6727 4-8-12 **59** ....[1] RoryCleary 4 6
(M A Gunn, Ire) *sn led: sn led clr at 1/2-way: rdn and hdd over 2f out: sn wknd* **40/1**

1m 32.22s (4.72)
WFA 3 from 4yo+ 2lb **16** Ran SP% **133.9**
CSF £63.82 CT £545.01 TOTE £13.20: £3.00, £1.20, £2.40, £3.20; DF 90.90.
Owner Miss R Hickey **Bred** George Strawbridge **Trained** Fethard, Co Tipperary

7392a **CLODOVIL EUROPEAN BREEDERS FUND GARNET STKS (LISTED RACE) (F&M)** **1m**
4:55 (4:56) 3-Y-O+
£24,944 (£8,033; £3,805; £1,691; £845; £422)

RPR

1 **Intimation**28 6604 4-9-3 100 ColinKeane 3 110+
(Sir Michael Stoute) *chsd ldrs: hdwy travelling wl into st to ld far side over 2f out: rdn over 1f out and pressed briefly: styd on wl ins fnl f to extend advantage: comf* **3/1**2

2 4 **Rose De Pierre (IRE)**75 5000 3-9-3 103 PatSmullen 1 102
(D K Weld, Ire) *dwlt sltly and settled in mid-div early: hdwy gng wl in 11th into st into 2nd 1 1/2f out: sn rdn and pressed wnr briefly: no imp on wnr ins fnl f: kpt on same pce* **1/1**1

3 2 **Flying Fairies (IRE)**32 6495 3-9-0 92 GaryCarroll 10 94
(Joseph G Murphy, Ire) *mid-div early: 10th into st: sn pushed along and rdn into 7th over 1f out: clsd u.p ins fnl f into nvr nrr 3rd : nt trble easy wnr* **16/1**

4 ½ **Ibergman (IRE)**28 6604 4-9-3 90 WayneLordan 18 94
(Ms Sheila Lavery, Ire) *mid-div: tk clsr order nr side 2f out: sn rdn and no imp on easy wnr u.p in 3rd ent fnl f: kpt on same pce and dropped to 4th clsng stages* **33/1**

5 ½ **How High The Moon (IRE)**7 7196 3-9-0 92 (v1) SeamieHeffernan 8 92
(A P O'Brien, Ire) *hld up in tch: impr bhd ldrs under 2f out: sn rdn disputing 3rd and no ex ent fnl f: kpt on one pce in 5th wl ins fnl f* **16/1**

6 1 **Penny Pepper (IRE)**21 6819 4-9-3 85 GaryHalpin 11 91
(Kevin Prendergast, Ire) *in rr of mid-div: sme hdwy between horses 1 1/2f out: rdn in mod 8th over 1f out and no imp on wnr in mod 6th far side wl ins fnl f: kpt on one pce* **28/1**

7 2¾ **Glamorous Approach (IRE)**41 6200 3-9-0 99 KevinManning 19 83
(J S Bolger, Ire) *tacked over to sn chse ldrs: rdn 2f out and sn no imp on easy wnr u.p in 6th: one pce fnl f* **11/1**3

8 2 **Military Angel (USA)**14 6984 4-9-3 97 ShaneBKelly 2 80
(M D O'Callaghan, Ire) *mid-div: pushed along and sme hdwy bhd ldrs 2f out: sn rdn disputing 3rd and no ex over 1f out: wknd ins fnl f* **25/1**

9 7 **Granny May (IRE)**6 7233 4-9-3 70 RobbieDowney 15 64
(John James Feane, Ire) *in rr of mid-div early: rdn towards rr over 2f out and no imp: kpt on one pce ins fnl f* **100/1**

10 nk **Flirt (IRE)**32 6495 3-9-0 88 (p) RoryCleary 14 62
(David Wachman, Ire) *w ldrs and disp fr bef 1/2-way: rdn and hdd over 2f out: sn wknd* **40/1**

11 5 **Lily's Rainbow (IRE)**49 5939 4-9-6 96 (p) LeighRoche 7 55
(Mrs Denise Foster, Ire) *sn led narrowly tl jnd after 1f: sn hdd and dropped to cl 4th after 1/2-way: rdn bhd ldrs over 2f out and sn no ex: wknd 1 1/2f out* **25/1**

12 1¾ **Cool Thunder (IRE)**105 3928 3-9-0 98 ChrisHayes 4 47
(Kevin Prendergast, Ire) *in rr of mid-div: tk clsr order after 1/2-way: rdn 2f out and sn no ex: wknd over 1f out* **12/1**

13 4½ **Planchart (USA)**35 6383 3-9-3 96 (b1) DeclanMcDonogh 9 39
(Andrew Slattery, Ire) *w ldrs and disp after 1f: rdn and hdd over 2f out and sn no ex whn short of room between horses: wknd 1 1/2f out* **16/1**

14 2¾ **Millefiori (IRE)**31 6505 4-9-3 78 (p) MichaelHussey 13 31
(Adrian Paul Keatley, Ire) *chsd ldrs: pushed along in 6th bef st and sn no ex: wknd over 2f out* **50/1**

1m 46.07s (6.07)
WFA 3 from 4yo 3lb **14** Ran SP% **128.1**
CSF £6.35 TOTE £3.30: £1.60, £1.02, £5.10; DF 8.80 Trifecta £116.50.
Owner Cheveley Park Stud **Bred** Cheveley Park Stud Ltd **Trained** Newmarket, Suffolk

FOCUS
A runaway performance from the winner who excelled in the conditions.

7393a **ANJAAL EUROPEAN BREEDERS FUND BLUEBELL STKS (LISTED RACE) (F&M)** **1m 4f**
5:25 (5:28) 3-Y-O+
£24,944 (£8,033; £3,805; £1,691; £845; £422)

RPR

1 **Toe The Line (IRE)**21 6820 7-9-7 101 ColinKeane 4 99+
(John E Kiely, Ire) *chsd ldrs early: 8th 1/2-way: prog fr over 2f out: sn rdn and clsd u.p into 3rd ent fnl f: styd on wl to ld ins fnl 100yds* **9/2**2

2 1 **Shall We (IRE)**23 6747 3-9-0 102 ChrisHayes 1 97
(Sir Michael Stoute) *hooded to load: sn led tl hdd after 1f and settled bhd ldrs: prog gng wl to ld over 2f out: rdn 1 1/2f out and sn wandered sltly: edgd sltly rt wl ins fnl f and sn hdd: no ex clsng stages* **6/1**3

3 1 **Sea Swift (IRE)**28 6604 3-9-0 94 PatSmullen 12 95
(D K Weld, Ire) *in rr of mid-div: 11th 1/2-way: hdwy on outer fr under 4f out: rdn 2f out and clsd u.p into cl 2nd ins fnl f: sltly hmpd wl ins fnl f and no ex in 3rd clsng stages* **9/2**2

4 2¼ **Dew Line (IRE)**11 7084 4-9-7 72 LeighRoche 5 92?
(Michael Mulvany, Ire) *chsd ldrs: 4th 1/2-way: rdn far side over 2f out and no imp on ldrs u.p in 4th wl ins fnl f: kpt on same pce* **66/1**

5 2½ **Island Remede**32 6495 5-9-7 92 WayneLordan 7 88
(Henry De Bromhead, Ire) *cl up and led after 1f: rdn and hdd over 2f out: no ex over 1f out where sltly hmpd: one pce in 5th wl ins fnl f* **25/1**

6 nk **Hibiscus (IRE)**7 7196 3-9-0 95 DonnachaO'Brien 6 87
(A P O'Brien, Ire) *settled in rr of mid-div: sme hdwy far side 2f out: u.p in 6th ent fnl f and sn no imp on ldrs: kpt on same pce* **11/4**1

7 4¾ **Eavesdrop (IRE)**6 7236 3-9-0 75 1 SeamieHeffernan 15 80
(A P O'Brien, Ire) *hld up: 10th 1/2-way: rdn and no imp over 2f out: mod 10th over 1f out: kpt on u.p ins fnl f: nvr nrr* **25/1**

8 ¾ **Fact Or Folklore (IRE)**21 6820 4-9-7 96 BillyLee 10 79
(W McCreery, Ire) *hooded to load: w.w towards rr: gd hdwy fr 1/2-way to chse ldrs on outer in 4th bef st: rdn under 3f out and sn no ex: one pce fnl 2f* **8/1**

9 1¾ **Avenante**36 6350 4-9-7 94 GaryHalpin 2 76
(John M Oxx, Ire) *hld up bhd ldrs in 6th: rdn far side over 2f out and no imp on ldrs u.p in 7th over 1f out: wknd* **16/1**

10 2¼ **Soul Searcher (IRE)**7 7196 4-9-7 95 RoryCleary 16 72
(J P Murtagh, Ire) *hld up in tch: 7th 1/2-way: rdn over 2f out and sn no ex: one pce fnl 2f* **12/1**

11 13 **Uninhibited (IRE)**67 5313 3-9-0 88 DeclanMcDonogh 8 51
(Charles O'Brien, Ire) *hld up bhd ldrs in 5th: rdn far side over 2f out and wknd over 1f out* **25/1**

12 3¼ **Tara Dylan (IRE)**35 6389 4-9-7 84 (t) GaryCarroll 13 46
(Thomas Mullins, Ire) *dwlt sltly and towards rr: rdn and no imp detached 4f out: one pce fnl 2f* **33/1**

13 15 **An Cailin Orga (IRE)**92 4416 3-9-0 89 KevinManning 11 22
(J S Bolger, Ire) *mid-div: 9th 1/2-way: rdn and no imp under 3f out: wknd and eased fnl 2f: t.o* **12/1**

14 2½ **Alyssum (IRE)**6 7236 3-9-0 0 RonanWhelan 9 18
(J S Bolger, Ire) *chsd ldrs tl impr into 2nd after 1f: rdn over 3f out and sn wknd: eased fr over 1f out: t.o* **33/1**

15 4½ **Ruth Melody (IRE)**268 299 4-9-7 0 ShaneBKelly 14 11
(Lee Smyth, Ire) *towards rr: pushed along bef 1/2-way and no imp trailing and detached in rr over 4f out: eased fnl 2f: t.o* **100/1**

2m 46.05s (166.05)
WFA 3 from 4yo+ 7lb **15** Ran SP% **129.6**
CSF £32.20 TOTE £5.20: £2.00, £2.20, £2.10; DF 38.30 Trifecta £120.00.
Owner Lillingston Family **Bred** A Lillingston **Trained** Dungarvan, Co Waterford

FOCUS
A deserving win for an admirable mare who has bumped her head against some good horses in recent months.

7394 - (Foreign Racing) - See Raceform Interactive

6390 BRO PARK (L-H)
Sunday, October 16

OFFICIAL GOING: Turf: good to soft

7395a **COOLMORE MATCHMAKER STKS (LISTED RACE) (3YO+ FILLIES & MARES) (TURF)** **1m 2f 110y**
2:30 (12:00) 3-Y-O+ **£24,115** (£8,038; £4,019; £2,411; £1,607)

RPR

1 **Amie Noire (GER)**35 6390 5-9-4 0 Jan-ErikNeuroth 4 97
(Wido Neuroth, Norway) **13/10**1

2 1½ **Icecapada (IRE)**35 6390 4-9-4 0 ElioneChaves 5 94
(Niels Petersen, Norway) **13/10**1

3 nk **Shalalee (SWE)**707 4-9-4 0 JacobJohansen 1 93
(Wido Neuroth, Norway) **167/20**

4 nse **Brandybend (IRE)**103 3979 4-9-4 0 DanielMuscutt 2 93
(Marco Botti) *chsd ldrs: rdn and kpt on on fnl f: nvr quite on terms* **59/10**2

5 8 **Zarzuela (DEN)**35 6-9-4 0 (p) Per-AndersGraberg 3 78
(Niels Petersen, Norway) **68/10**3

Owner Stall Perlen **Bred** Gestut Zoppenbroich **Trained** Norway

7291 CHANTILLY (R-H)
Sunday, October 16

OFFICIAL GOING: Turf: soft; polytrack: standard

7396a **PRIX DU CONSEIL DE PARIS (GROUP 2) (3YO+) (TURF)** **1m 4f**
2:45 (12:00) 3-Y-O+ **£54,485** (£21,029; £10,036; £6,691; £3,345)

RPR

1 **One Foot In Heaven (IRE)**14 6989 4-9-6 0 ChristopheSoumillon 3 114+
(A De Royer-Dupre, France) *w.w in middle of main pack chsng clr ldr: grad clsd fr 3f out: sustained chal fr over 1f out: styd on wl u.p: led fnl 75yds: hld on gamely* **4/6**1

2 snk **Tiberian (FR)**42 6175 4-9-2 0 ThierryJarnet 6 110
(Alain Couetil, France) *cl up in main gp bhd clr ldr: hdwy fr 3f out: led 1 1/2f out: styd on u.p: hdd fnl 75yds: rallied gamely* **15/2**

3 5 **Now We Can**29 6598 7-9-2 0 Pierre-CharlesBoudot 4 103
(N Clement, France) *settled in fnl pair: styd on u.p over 2f out: chsd ldng pair 1f out: kpt on at one pce* **9/2**3

4 5 **Sacrifice My Soul (IRE)**11 7088 4-8-13 0 MaximeGuyon 2 92
(Mme Pia Brandt, France) *chsd clr ldr: led ent fnl 2f: sn rdn hdd 1 1/2f out: wknd fnl f* **18/1**

5 10 **Berkshire (IRE)**50 5894 5-9-2 0 (b) OlivierPeslier 5 78
(Paul Cole) *broke wl and led: sn 15l or more clr: floundering whn hdd ent fnl 2f: wknd* **7/2**2

6 1 **Casino (FR)**12 4-9-2 0 EddyHardouin 1 76
(P Khozian, France) *w.w in rr: lost tch fr 1/2-way: nvr involved* **50/1**

2m 29.63s (-1.37) **6** Ran SP% **119.4**
WIN (incl. 1 euro stake): 1.80 (One Foot In Heaven coupled with Sacrifice My Soul). PLACES: 1.40, 2.20. SF: 7.00.
Owner Fair Salinia Ltd **Bred** Craigavon Agro Ltd **Trained** Chantilly, France

7397a **PRIX CASIMIR DELAMARRE (LISTED RACE) (3YO+ FILLIES & MARES) (TURF)** **1m 1f**
3:15 (12:00) 3-Y-O+
£19,117 (£7,647; £5,735; £3,823; £955; £955)

RPR

1 **Rostova (USA)**32 6488 3-8-11 0 VincentCheminaud 5 101+
(Sir Michael Stoute) *w.w in midfield: 5th and nudged along on outer 2 1/2f out: rdn and grad reeled in ldr fr 1 1/2f out: led fnl 110yds: asserted cl home* **74/10**

2 ½ **Magnolea (IRE)**36 6357 3-8-13 0 ow2 ChristopheSoumillon 7 102
(J-C Rouget, France) **59/10**3

3 nk **That Which Is Not (USA)**45 6069 3-8-11 0 Pierre-CharlesBoudot 6 99
(F-H Graffard, France) **33/10**1

4 snk **Havre De Paix (FR)**44 6107 4-9-1 0 OlivierPeslier 1 99
(David Menuisier) *led: kicked nrly 3l clr wl over 1 1/2f out: sn rdn and labouring ent fnl f: hdd last 110yds: rallied gamely* **30/1**

5 snk **Golden Stunner (IRE)**71 5158 3-8-11 0 FMBerry 12 99
(Ralph Beckett) *w.w towards rr: hdwy u.p on outer 1 1/2f out: styd on fnl f: nvr nrr* **10/1**

5 dht **Saimaa (IRE)**24 6728 3-8-11 0 GregoryBenoist 8 99
(H-F Devin, France) **11/2**2

7 1 **Spring Leaf (FR)**11 7087 4-9-1 0 ThierryJarnet 10 97
(A De Royer-Dupre, France) **11/1**

8 3 **La Patria**24 6728 3-8-11 0 MickaelBarzalona 2 90
(A Fabre, France) *w.w towards rr: hdwy 2f out: 5th and rdn ent fnl 1 1/2f: one pce last f* **31/5**

9 2 1/2 **Maisons (FR)**[59] 3-8-11 0 ClementLecoeuvre 4 85
(E Lellouche, France) **14/1**
10 4 1/2 **Coisa Boa (IRE)**[63] 4-9-1 0 AntoineHamelin 11 76
(J E Hammond, France) **22/1**
11 3 1/2 **Classe Vendome (FR)**[123] 3274 3-8-11 0 EddyHardouin 3 68
(P Sogorb, France) **27/1**
12 1 3/4 **Toinette (IRE)**[42] 3-8-11 0 MaximeGuyon 9 65
(H-A Pantall, France) **19/1**

1m 48.86s (-2.24)
WFA 3 from 4yo 4lb 12 Ran SP% **119.2**
WIN (incl. 1 euro stake): 8.40. PLACES: 2.50, 2.20, 1.80. DF: 26.10. SF: 66.80.
Owner K Abdullah **Bred** Juddmonte Farms Inc **Trained** Newmarket, Suffolk

7398a PRIX DE LA VIEILLE ROUTE (CLAIMER) (4YO+) (TURF) 5f
4:15 (12:00) 4-Y-O+ **£6,985** (£2,794; £2,095; £1,397; £698)

RPR

1 **King David (FR)**[34] 8-9-1 0 TheoBachelot 6 68
(M Boutin, France) **77/10**
2 2 **Sunset Sail (IRE)**[167] 4-8-11 0 GregoryBenoist 4 57
(Gerald Geisler, Germany) **16/1**
3 snk **Secly (IRE)**[25] 5-9-6 0 (b) ChristopheSoumillon 12 65
(F Chappet, France) **31/5**[3]
4 shd **Thorpe Bay**[329] 7-9-2 0 MaximeGuyon 10 61
(P G Van Kempen, Holland) **32/5**
5 nse **Princess Tansy**[22] 6793 4-9-2 0 (p) Pierre-CharlesBoudot 7 61
(Gay Kelleway) *chsd ldrs in main gp on stands' side (two racd alone on far side): drvn and styd on to ld over 1f out: hdd fnl 100yds: dropped three pls cl home* **29/10**[1]
6 nk **Xenophanes (IRE)**[25] 6-9-1 0 KorentinNaimi(7) 11 66
(M Boutin, France) **8/1**
7 1/2 **Rhythm Of Life (GER)**[108] 7-8-11 0 (b) AntonioPolli 3 53
(G Bernaud, Belgium) **17/1**
8 1 3/4 **Bellcanto (GER)**[84] 4-9-6 0 MickaelBarzalona 8 56
(S Smrczek, Germany) **41/10**[2]
9 3/4 **Spirit Of Teofilo (FR)**[139] 6-9-2 0 RaphaelMarchelli 1 49
(D De Waele, France) **18/1**
10 snk **Renounce (FR)**[20] 5-9-6 0 (b) EddyHardouin 5 53
(D De Waele, France) **18/1**
11 1 1/4 **Zalkaya (FR)**[20] 4-9-1 0 DavidBreux 9 43
(Mlle S Sine, France) **105/1**
12 8 **Lovemie (FR)** 4-8-5 0 LudovicBoisseau(3) 2 7
(M Baudy, France) **127/1**

59.2s (0.90) 12 Ran SP% **118.9**
WIN (incl. 1 euro stake): 8.70. PLACES: 2.50, 4.60, 2.70. DF: 60.40. SF: 159.40.
Owner Jean-Pierre Vanden Heede **Bred** Mrs K Sundgren **Trained** France

7027 COLOGNE (R-H)
Sunday, October 16

OFFICIAL GOING: Turf: good

7399a PREIS DES WINTERFAVORITEN (GROUP 3) (2YO) (TURF) 1m
3:10 (12:00) 2-Y-O
£62,500 (£22,794; £15,073; £7,573; £4,044; £1,985)

RPR

1 **Langtang (GER)** 2-9-2 0 JozefBojko 2 104
(A Wohler, Germany) *a cl up: drvn to ld under 1 1/2f out: styd on wl fnl f: asserted last 110yds* **21/10**[1]
2 2 **Fulminato (GER)**[42] 6174 2-9-2 0 DennisSchiergen 1 99
(Andreas Lowe, Germany) *cl up on inner: lost pl 3 1/2f out: rdn and styd on again 2 1/2f out: chsd ldr u.p fnl f: wl hld last 110yds* **147/10**
3 1 1/2 **Real Value (FR)**[42] 6174 2-9-2 0 StephenHellyn 5 96
(Mario Hofer, Germany) *chsd ldrs: sltly outpcd and rdn 2f out: styd on fnl f: nt pce to get on terms* **5/1**[3]
4 1 1/4 **Ming Jung (FR)** 2-9-2 0 MartinSeidl 3 93
(Markus Klug, Germany) *pushed along towards rr early on: sn settled in fnl trio: rdn and styd on wl over 1f out: nvr nrr* **127/10**
5 nk **Colomano** 2-9-2 0 AdriedeVries 9 92
(Markus Klug, Germany) *in rr: hdwy on outer 1/2-way: styd on u.p fnl f: n.d* **29/10**[2]
6 nk **Empire Of The Star (FR)** 2-9-2 0 MarcLerner 7 92
(A Wohler, Germany) *broke wl and led: hdd after 1 1/2f and chsd ldr: no imp u.p over 1 1/2f out: one pce fnl f* **74/10**
7 2 **Sant Angelo (GER)** 2-9-2 0 TonyPiccone 4 87
(Henk Grewe, Germany) *led after 1 1/2f: pressed fr over 3f out: hdd 1 1/2f out: wknd* **27/1**
8 6 1/2 **Ardashir (USA)** 2-9-2 0 AndreasSuborics 6 72
(Andreas Lowe, Germany) *slow to stride and rowed along: sn settled towards rr: rdn and short-lived effrt wl over 2f out: sn btn* **56/10**
9 2 1/2 **Enjoy Vijay (GER)** 2-9-2 0 AndraschStarke 8 66
(P Schiergen, Germany) *chsd ldrs on outer: pressed ldr over 3f out: wknd u.p fr 1 1/2f out* **77/10**

1m 33.86s (-4.53) 9 Ran SP% **130.4**
WIN (incl. 10 euro stake): 31. PLACES: 17, 40, 23. SF: 490.
Owner Klaus Allofs & Stiftung Gestut Fahrhof **Bred** Stiftung Gestut Fahrhof **Trained** Germany

7198 SAN SIRO (R-H)
Sunday, October 16

OFFICIAL GOING: Turf: good

7400a PREMIO DEL PIAZZALE (GROUP 3) (3YO+) (TURF) 1m 1f
2:10 (12:00) 3-Y-O+ **£21,691** (£9,544; £5,205; £2,602)

RPR

1 **Voice Of Love (IRE)**[21] 3-8-9 0 CristianDemuro 9 108
(Stefano Botti, Italy) *mde all: scrubbed along 2f out and responded: rdn over 1f out: styd on strly fnl f: unchal* **3/4**[1]
2 1 1/2 **Circus Couture (IRE)**[28] 6612 4-9-0 0 FabioBranca 1 105
(Stefano Botti, Italy) *a cl up: trckd ldr travelling wl 3f out: rdn 2f out and no real imp: kpt on at same pce fnl f: jst hld 2nd* **3/4**[1]
3 hd **Diplomat (GER)**[21] 6823 5-9-2 0 FilipMinarik 3 107
(Mario Hofer, Germany) *v keen early: hld up in tch on outer: drvn 4f out: chsd ldng pair fr 1 1/2f out: styd on fnl f: jst missed 2nd* **43/20**[2]
4 nk **Felician (GER)**[50] 5904 8-8-11 0 MichaelCadeddu 5 101
(Ferdinand J Leve, Germany) *hld up in fnl pair: rdn and clsd under 2f out: styd on fnl f: nt pce to get on terms* **53/10**
5 1 1/2 **Brex Drago (ITY)**[14] 4-8-11 0 SilvanoMulas 2 98
(Stefano Botti, Italy) *settled in midfield on inner: drvn 3 1/2f out: rdn and nt qckn 2f out: kpt on at same pce: nvr trbld ldrs* **111/10**
6 shd **Greg Pass (IRE)**[21] 6823 4-9-0 0 DarioVargiu 7 101
(Il Cavallo In Testa, Italy) *keen: chsd ldr: rdn and nt qckn w ldrs 2f out: grad dropped away fnl f* **19/4**[3]
7 hd **Berling (IRE)**[49] 5950 9-8-11 0 OisinMurphy 4 98
(Jessica Long, Sweden) *settled towards rr: rdn and clsd a little 2f out: kpt on fnl f: nvr in contention* **166/10**
8 nk **Rogue Runner (GER)**[49] 5950 4-8-11 0 CarloFiocchi 8 97
(P Schiergen, Germany) *w.w in midfield on outer: no real imp u.p 2f out: kpt on at one pce: n.d* **43/20**[2]
9 dist **Pepparone (IRE)**[1113] 6-8-11 0 NicolaPinna 6
(Silvia Casati, Italy) *w.w in rr: rdn and no imp 2 1/2f out: bhd whn eased ins fnl f* **164/10**

1m 51.6s (-6.30)
WFA 3 from 4yo+ 4lb 9 Ran SP% **230.7**
WIN (incl. 1 euro stake): 1.77 (Voice Of Love coupled with Circus Couture). PLACES: 1.82, 1.21, 1.65. DF: 5.37.
Owner Scuderia Effevi SRL **Bred** Massimo Parri **Trained** Italy

7401a GRAN CRITERIUM (GROUP 2) (2YO COLTS & FILLIES) (TURF) 7f 110y
3:20 (12:00) 2-Y-O **£91,911** (£40,441; £22,058; £11,029)

RPR

1 **Skarino Gold (GER)**[54] 2-8-11 0 MichaelCadeddu 3 109
(Jean-Pierre Carvalho, Germany) *a cl up: drvn to chal 2f out: styd on u.p to ld over 1f out: dug in to go clr: wl on top at fin* **123/10**
2 2 1/2 **Bahamas (IRE)**[43] 6116 2-8-11 0 FrankieDettori 1 103
(Marco Botti) *settled in fnl trio: 5th and drvn along 3f out: stl struggling to get on terms 2f out: styd on u.p fnl f: wnt 2nd fnl strides: nvr trbld wnr* **11/4**[3]
3 shd **Amyntas (ITY)** 2-8-11 0 CristianDemuro 6 103
(Stefano Botti, Italy) *chsd ldrs: rdn and ev ch 2f out: styd on to chse ldr over 1f out: kpt on at same pce fnl f: lost 2nd fnl strides* **7/2**
4 2 **Sun Devil (ITY)**[35] 2-8-11 0 FabioBranca 7 98
(Stefano Botti, Italy) *chsd ldrs: rdn to ld 2f out: hdd over 1f out: sn wknd* **49/20**[2]
5 hd **Biz Power (IRE)**[21] 2-8-11 0 SilvanoMulas 2 98
(Stefano Botti, Italy) *w.w in rr: hdwy on outside 1 1/2f out: styd on u.p fnl f: nvr nrr* **8/5**[1]
6 6 **Aethos (IRE)**[35] 2-8-11 0 DarioVargiu 5 84
(Stefano Botti, Italy) *wnt rt s: led: drvn for home 3f out: hdd 2f out: sn btn* **8/5**[1]
7 dist **A Magic Man (IRE)**[28] 2-8-11 0 UmbertoRispoli 4
(Henk Grewe, Germany) *hld up in fnl trio: last and drvn along 3f out: no imp appr 2f out: sn t.o* **148/10**

1m 33.0s (-2.50) 7 Ran SP% **168.6**
WIN (incl. 1 euro stake): 13.34. PLACES: 5.09, 2.45. DF: 21.57.
Owner Phoenix Stable **Bred** Mme C Post-Schultzke **Trained** Germany

FOCUS
This event has lost its Group 1 status.

7402a PREMIO JOCKEY CLUB (GROUP 1) (3YO+) (TURF) 1m 4f
3:55 (12:00) 3-Y-O+ **£91,911** (£40,441; £22,058; £11,029)

RPR

1 **Ventura Storm (IRE)**[36] 6329 3-8-13 0 CristianDemuro 2 114
(Richard Hannon) *a cl up: niggled along to press ldr wl over 3f out: styd on to join ldr 2f out: led narrowly 1 1/2f out: hdd over 1f out: rallied gamely to regain ld 120yds out and wnt a half-l up: all out* **6/5**[1]
2 nk **Full Drago (ITY)**[28] 6612 3-8-13 0 UmbertoRispoli 5 114
(Stefano Botti, Italy) *led: drvn whn pressed more than 3f out: hdd narrowly 1 1/2f out: rallied to regain ld over 1f out: hdd fnl 120yds: kpt on bravely u.p* **758/100**
3 2 3/4 **Elbereth**[42] 6179 5-9-1 0 OisinMurphy 4 105
(Andrew Balding) *w.w towards rr: hdwy on outer more than 2 1/2f out: chsd ldng pair u.p wl over 1f out: styd on at same pce fnl f* **93/10**
4 2 3/4 **Arab Spring (IRE)**[15] 6940 6-9-4 0 FrankieDettori 3 103
(Sir Michael Stoute) *w.w in fnl trio: tk clsr order after 1/2-way: chsd ldrs fr 1 1/2f out: no ex fnl f* **53/20**[2]
5 1/2 **Kloud Gate (FR)**[28] 6612 4-9-4 0 DarioVargiu 6 102
(Gianluca Bietolini, Italy) *settled in rr: rdn to dispute 4th 1 1/2f out: kpt on u.p: nt pce to get on terms* **32/1**
6 8 **Guignol (GER)**[63] 5454 4-9-4 0 FilipMinarik 1 90
(Jean-Pierre Carvalho, Germany) *chsd ldr on inner: outpcd and drvn 3f out: wl hld fnl 1 1/2f* **5/1**[3]
7 nk **Dylan Mouth (IRE)**[42] 6175 5-9-4 0 FabioBranca 7 89
(Marco Botti) *keen: hld up in tch on outer: rdn and no imp over 2f out: wknd fr 1 1/2f out* **51/10**

2m 29.2s (-2.30)
WFA 3 from 4yo+ 7lb 7 Ran SP% **130.3**
WIN (incl. 1 euro stake): 2.22. PLACES: 1.57, 2.65. DF: 9.30.
Owner Middleham Park Racing LXXII **Bred** Laurence Kennedy **Trained** East Everleigh, Wilts

[6613] WOODBINE (L-H)

Sunday, October 16

OFFICIAL GOING: Tapeta: fast; turf: firm

7403a NEARCTIC STKS (GRADE 2) (3YO+) (TURF) 6f

8:48 (12:00) 3-Y-O+

£88,235 (£29,411; £17,647; £7,352; £3,529; £1,470)

RPR

1 **Calgary Cat (CAN)**[35] 6400 6-8-5 0 .... LuisContreras 7 109
(Kevin Attard, Canada) **16/1**

2 *hd* **Stacked Deck (USA)**[35] 6400 5-8-7 0 .... RafaelManuelHernandez 4 111
(Barbara J Minshall, Canada) **91/20**[3]

3 *hd* **Conquest Enforcer (CAN)**[35] 3-8-4 0 .... JavierCastellano 6 108
(Mark Casse, Canada) **37/20**[1]

4 *3/4* **Full Mast (USA)**[29] 6601 4-8-5 0 .... JoelRosario 2 106
(William Mott, U.S.A) **23/10**[2]

5 *1 1/4* **Springhouse (CAN)**[15] 3-8-4 0 .... DJMoran 3 102
(Michael Keogh, Canada) **59/1**

6 *1 1/4* **Divine (IRE)**[49] 5943 5-8-4 0 .... AlexisBadel 1 97
(Mick Channon) **15/2**

7 *hd* **Passion For Action (CAN)**[29] 6601 4-8-9 0 ......(b) EuricoRosaDaSilva 5 101
(Michael P De Paulo, Canada) **15/2**

8 *1 3/4* **Expected Ruler (USA)**[22] 3-8-4 0 ....(b) FlorentGeroux 8 91
(Liam D Benson, U.S.A) **27/1**

1m 8.32s (68.32)
WFA 3 from 4yo+ 1lb **8** Ran SP% **118.1**

Owner Stephen Chesney & Cory S Hoffman **Bred** WinStar Farm LLC **Trained** Canada

7404a E. P. TAYLOR STKS PRESENTED BY HPIBET (GRADE 1) (3YO+ FILLIES & MARES) (TURF) 1m 2f (T)

9:56 (12:00) 3-Y-O+

£147,058 (£49,019; £24,509; £12,254; £4,901; £2,450)

RPR

1 **Al's Gal (USA)**[31] 5-8-12 0 .... FlorentGeroux 7 108
(Michael J Maker, U.S.A) **123/20**

2 *nse* **Suffused**[43] 4-8-12 0 .... JoseLOrtiz 4 108+
(William Mott, U.S.A) **74/10**

3 *1/2* **Banzari**[29] 6598 4-8-12 0 .... AlexisBadel 6 107
(H-F Devin, France) **213/10**

4 *hd* **Guapaza (CHI)**[43] 5-8-12 0 .... JavierCastellano 10 107+
(Chad C Brown, U.S.A) **17/1**

5 *1/2* **Rainha Da Bateria (USA)**[29] 4-8-12 0 ....(b) JulienRLeparoux 5 106
(Chad C Brown, U.S.A) **11/2**[2]

6 *nk* **Swiss Range**[78] 4864 3-8-7 0 .... JoelRosario 1 105
(John Gosden) **57/10**[3]

7 *1/2* **Nezwaah**[32] 6488 3-8-7 0 .... AndreaAtzeni 11 104
(Roger Varian) **79/10**

8 *1/2* **Parvaneh (IRE)**[21] 6822 3-8-7 0 .... FlavienPrat 2 103
(Waldemar Hickst, Germany) **178/10**

9 *hd* **Tuttipaesi (IRE)**[36] 6-8-12 0 .... ChristopherPDeCarlo 12 103
(William Mott, U.S.A) **29/1**

10 *nse* **Strut The Course (CAN)**[29] 6-8-12 0 .... RafaelManuelHernandez 8 103
(Barbara J Minshall, Canada) **32/1**

11 *1* **Aim To Please (FR)**[25] 6693 3-8-7 0 .... GeraldMosse 9 101
(F Doumen, France) **218/10**

12 *1 1/4* **Best In The World (IRE)**[35] 6383 3-8-7 0 .... RyanMoore 3 98
(A P O'Brien, Ire) **31/10**[1]

2m 1.6s (-2.42)
WFA 3 from 4yo+ 5lb **12** Ran SP% **117.9**
PARI-MUTUEL (all including 2 cad stake): WIN 14.30; PLACE (1-2) 6.90, 7.70; SHOW (1-2-3) 4.50, 5.60, 10.40; SF 78.20.
Owner Kenneth L & Sarah K Ramsey **Bred** Malone Racing Llc **Trained** USA

7405a PATTISON CANADIAN INTERNATIONAL STKS (GRADE 1) (3YO+) (TURF) 1m 4f (T)

10:40 (12:00) 3-Y-O+

£294,117 (£98,039; £49,019; £24,509; £9,803; £5,882)

RPR

1 **Erupt (IRE)**[49] 5947 4-9-0 0 .... StephanePasquier 8 116+
(F-H Graffard, France) **122/10**

2 *1* **Dartmouth**[29] 6571 4-9-0 0 .... WilliamBuick 5 114+
(Sir Michael Stoute) **67/20**[2]

3 *1/2* **Wake Forest (GER)**[29] 6600 6-9-0 0 .... JavierCastellano 6 114+
(Chad C Brown, U.S.A) **10/1**

4 *1/2* **The Pizza Man (USA)**[29] 6600 7-9-0 0 .... FlavienPrat 4 113+
(Roger Brueggemann, U.S.A) **91/10**

5 *1/2* **Idaho (IRE)**[36] 6329 3-8-7 0 .... RyanMoore 3 112+
(A P O'Brien, Ire) **7/5**[1]

6 *nk* **Danish Dynaformer (CAN)**[29] 6600 4-9-0 0 ....(b) JoelRosario 1 112+
(Roger L Attfield, Canada) **34/1**

7 *1/2* **Taghleeb (USA)**[21] 5-9-0 0 ....(b) FlorentGeroux 7 111+
(Michael J Maker, U.S.A) **56/1**

8 *nse* **World Approval (USA)**[29] 6600 4-9-0 0 ....(b) JulienRLeparoux 2 111
(Mark Casse, Canada) **129/10**

9 *3/4* **Protectionist (GER)**[63] 5454 6-9-0 0 .... AndreaAtzeni 9 109
(A Wohler, Germany) **58/10**[3]

2m 30.87s (1.27)
WFA 3 from 4yo+ 7lb **9** Ran SP% **117.7**
PARI-MUTUEL (all including 2 cad stake): WIN 26.30; PLACE (1-2) 9.50, 4.70; SHOW (1-2-3) 5.60, 3.50, 5.10; SF 77.60.
Owner Niarchos Family **Bred** Niarchos Family **Trained** France

FOCUS
This was only steadily run.

[7003] PONTEFRACT (L-H)

Monday, October 17

OFFICIAL GOING: Soft (7.3)
Wind: Moderate half behind Weather: Sunny and showers

7406 BET TOTEPLACEPOT AT TOTESPORT.COM NURSERY H'CAP 1m 4y

2:10 (2:12) (Class 5) (0-75,74) 2-Y-O **£3,234** (£962; £481; £240) **Stalls** Low

Form RPR

5142 1 **Mount Moriah**[19] 6875 2-9-6 **73** .... FMBerry 6 80
(Ralph Beckett) *trckd ldng pair: hdwy on outer 2f out: led wl over 1f out: sn rdn clr and edgd lft: drvn and hung bdly rt ins fnl f: jst hld on* **10/3**[1]

0335 2 *shd* **Silver Link (IRE)**[14] 7016 2-9-5 **72** .... SteveDrowne 1 79
(Marcus Tregoning) *trckd ldrs on inner: effrt 2f out and sn n.m.r: swtchd rt over 1f out and rdn to chse wnr ins fnl f: styng on and ev ch whn carried rt 100 yds out: drvn and kpt on strly: jst failed* **10/3**[1]

3444 3 *7* **Actualisation**[14] 7003 2-9-6 **73** ....(v) JasonHart 11 65
(John Quinn) *trckd ldr: effrt over 2f out: rdn along wl over 1f out: drvn and kpt on same pce fnl f* **18/1**

2625 4 *1 1/4* **Miss Bates**[30] 6563 2-9-5 **72** .... GrahamLee 4 61+
(Ann Duffield) *dwlt and rr: hdwy over 2f out: rdn wl over 1f out: kpt on fnl f: nrst fin* **14/1**

0314 5 *3/4* **Party Nights**[18] 6898 2-9-7 **74** .... JamieSpencer 5 62
(Luca Cumani) *trckd ldrs: hdwy over 2f out: rdn along wl over 1f out: sn drvn and one pce* **9/2**[2]

066 6 *1/2* **Poetic Force (IRE)**[78] 4907 2-8-13 **66** ....[1] JimCrowley 10 53
(Jonathan Portman) *rr: hdwy 3f out: effrt on outer wl over 1f out: sn rdn and no imp fnl f* **12/1**

0614 7 *3 1/4* **Crystal Dome**[9] 7140 2-9-6 **73** .... PaulMulrennan 3 53
(Ed Dunlop) *in tch: hdwy 3f out: rdn along 2f out: sn drvn and n.d* **13/2**[3]

3253 8 *3/4* **Baileys Apprentice**[19] 6875 2-9-2 **69** .... JoeFanning 8 47
(Mark Johnston) *led: rdn along over 2f out: hdd wl over 1f out: grad wknd* **14/1**

3000 9 *2* **Good Time Ahead (IRE)**[14] 7003 2-9-1 **68** .... JoeyHaynes 2 42
(Philip Kirby) *a towards rr* **50/1**

5645 10 *9* **Ladofash**[9] 7140 2-9-2 **69** .... PJMcDonald 7 24
(K R Burke) *chsd ldrs: rdn along 3f out: sn drvn and wknd* **16/1**

1m 49.97s (4.07) **Going Correction** +0.625s/f (Yiel) **10** Ran SP% **111.8**
Speed ratings (Par 95): **104,103,96,95,94 94,91,90,88,79**
CSF £13.28 CT £170.27 TOTE £3.30: £1.40, £1.90, £4.80; EX 13.20 Trifecta £170.80.
Owner Norman Brunskill **Bred** Lady Bland And Newsells Park Stud Ltd **Trained** Kimpton, Hants

FOCUS
A total of 27mm of rain had fallen over the previous seven days, but it had been dry since midday on Sunday. The going was given as soft (GoingStick: 7.3). The bend between 3f and 2f was dolled out 3yds, adding approximately 4yds to all race distances. The first two came clear in this nursery but the winner had to survive a stewards' inquiry.

7407 BET TOTEEXACTA AT TOTESPORT.COM MAIDEN AUCTION STKS 6f

2:40 (2:43) (Class 5) 2-Y-O **£3,234** (£962; £481; £240) **Stalls** Low

Form RPR

2220 1 **Lucky Mistake (IRE)**[16] 6950 2-8-13 72 .... TonyHamilton 5 75
(Richard Fahey) *cl up: led over 2f out: rdn clr over 1f out: drvn ins fnl f: hld on wl* **7/2**[2]

2 2 *hd* **Benjamin Thomas (IRE)**[25] 6712 2-9-0 0 .... JasonHart 2 75
(John Quinn) *prom: chsd wnr wl over 1f out: rdn and hdwy to chal ins fnl f: sn drvn and ev ch: no ex towards fin* **8/11**[1]

0 3 *8* **Red Guana (IRE)**[25] 6696 2-8-7 0 .... JoeFanning 8 44
(William Jarvis) *dwlt and towards rr: hdwy 3f out: chsd ldrs 2f out: sn rdn and no imp fnl f* **33/1**

0 4 *1 1/4* **Paquita Bailarina**[11] 7099 2-8-6 0 .... AndrewMullen 4 40
(James Given) *trckd ldrs: hdwy wl over 1f out: sn rdn: kpt on fnl f* **14/1**

4040 5 *hd* **Sheepscar Lad (IRE)**[10] 7122 2-8-10 68 ....(v) LewisEdmunds[(7)] 3 50
(Nigel Tinkler) *trckd ldrs on inner: effrt and nt clr run 2f out: nt clr run and hmpd over 1f out: kpt on fnl f* **5/1**[3]

06 6 *9* **Orientelle**[10] 7107 2-8-6 0 .... CamHardie 6 12
(Richard Whitaker) *in tch: hdwy to chse ldrs over 2f out: rdn wl over 1f out: grad wknd* **80/1**

0 7 *1* **Unonothinjonsnow**[10] 7125 2-8-11 0 .... JacobButterfield[(3)] 9 17
(Richard Guest) *a towards rr* **80/1**

8 *2 3/4* **Sussex Girl** 2-8-4 0 .... JosephineGordon[(3)] 1 2
(John Berry) *slt ld: pushed along 3f out: rdn and hdd over 2f out: sn drvn and wknd* **25/1**

04U 9 *4* **Broughtons Story**[53] 5809 2-8-13 0 .... TimmyMurphy 10
(Henry Spiller) *a towards rr* **14/1**

1m 20.16s (3.26) **Going Correction** +0.625s/f (Yiel) **9** Ran SP% **119.4**
Speed ratings (Par 95): **103,102,92,90,90 78,76,73,67**
CSF £6.53 TOTE £4.00: £1.10, £1.10, £6.80; EX 7.50 Trifecta £127.20.
Owner The Musley Bank Partnership & Partner **Bred** Gerald & Bernie Colclough **Trained** Musley Bank, N Yorks

FOCUS
Race distance increased by approximately 4yds. The first two pulled well clear, and there was a lot to like about the way the winner dug in. He has been rated to the balance of this year's form.

7408 BET TOTEQUADPOT AT TOTESPORT.COM H'CAP (DIV I) 1m 2f 6y

3:10 (3:12) (Class 4) (0-85,85) 3-Y-O+ **£5,175** (£1,540; £769; £384) **Stalls** Low

Form RPR

0453 1 **Empress Ali (IRE)**[44] 6115 5-9-9 **84** .... JamesSullivan 1 94
(Tom Tate) *trckd ldng pair: pushed along on inner over 2f out: swtchd rt and rdn to ld wl over 1f out: clr ent fnl f: sn drvn and kpt on strly* **5/1**[2]

0136 2 *3 1/4* **El Beau (IRE)**[32] 6517 5-8-13 **81** .... JoshQuinn[(7)] 5 85
(John Quinn) *trckd ldrs: hdwy 2f out: rdn over 1f out: chsd wnr ins fnl f: sn drvn and no imp towards fin* **10/1**

2360 3 *1 1/4* **Giantstepsahead (IRE)**[24] 6753 7-9-10 **85** .... DanielMuscutt 2 86
(Alan Bailey) *led: pushed along over 2f out: hdd and rdn over 1f out: drvn ent fnl f: kpt on* **9/2**[1]

0501 4 *hd* **Darrington**[28] 6618 4-9-1 **76** .... TonyHamilton 9 77
(Kristin Stubbs) *trckd ldrs: effrt on outer over 2f out: rdn wl over 1f out: drvn and kpt on same pce fnl f* **16/1**

5005 5 *1/2* **Indy (IRE)**[12] 7077 5-8-12 **78** .... CliffordLee[(5)] 6 78
(David Barron) *in tch: effrt on inner over 2f out: rdn to chse ldrs over 1f out: drvn and kpt on same pce fnl f* **9/2**[1]

0000 6 *nk* **Tres Coronas (IRE)**[12] 7077 9-9-5 **80** .... GrahamGibbons 10 79
(David Barron) *hld up in rr: hdwy over 2f out: swtchd rt to outer wl over 1f out: sn rdn: kpt on same pce fnl f* **20/1**

2036 **6** *dht* **Hanseatic**[12] 7077 7-9-2 **77** CamHardie 3 76
(Michael Easterby) *hld up in tch: hdwy on inner over 2f out: sn rdn to chse ldrs: drvn and kpt on same pce fnl f* **11/1**

1000 **8** *4½* **Indian Chief (IRE)**[52] 5837 6-9-2 **77** BarryMcHugh 4 67
(Rebecca Bastiman) *hld up in rr: hdwy 3f out: rdn along 2f out: sn drvn and n.d* **14/1**

526 **9** *13* **Roderic's Secret (IRE)**[19] 6886 3-8-5 **71** oh2 ShaneGray 11 35
(David Menuisier) *a rr* **25/1**

54 **10** *¾* **High Draw (FR)**[22] 6803 3-9-0 **80** DougieCostello 13 43
(K R Burke) *trckd ldr: cl up 1/2-way: rdn along 3f out: drvn wl over 1f out: sn wknd* **20/1**

060 **11** *1¼* **Vivre Pour Vivre (IRE)**[23] 6781 3-9-5 **85** JimCrowley 7 45
(Ed Dunlop) *a towards rr* **14/1**

5203 **12** *3* **Rockwood**[21] 6838 5-8-12 **73** (v) GrahamLee 8 27
(Karen McLintock) *in tch: hdwy to chse ldrs 3f out: rdn along 2f out: sn drvn and wknd* **16/1**

6425 **13** *19* **Street Poet (IRE)**[26] 6665 3-8-9 **75** (v[1]) TedDurcan 12
(Sir Michael Stoute) *midfield: pushed along 3f out: sn rdn and wknd* **7/1**[3]

2m 18.4s (4.70) **Going Correction** +0.625s/f (Yiel)
WFA 3 from 4yo+ 5lb **13** Ran SP% **121.4**
Speed ratings (Par 105): **106,103,102,102,101 101,101,98,87,87 86,83,68**
CSF £53.73 CT £246.50 TOTE £5.80: £2.00, £4.00, £2.20; EX 65.40 Trifecta £381.40.
Owner T T Racing **Bred** Denis McDonnell **Trained** Tadcaster, N Yorks

FOCUS
Race distance increased by approximately 4yds. A pretty open handicap. The winner looked better than ever, rated around the runner-up to his recent form.

7409 EBF STALLIONS BET TOTETRIFECTA AT TOTESPORT.COM SILVER TANKARD STKS (LISTED RACE) 1m 4y
3:40 (3:42) (Class 1) 2-Y-O
£19,848 (£7,525; £3,766; £1,876; £941; £472) **Stalls** Low

Form RPR

213 **1** **D'bai (IRE)**[37] 6326 2-9-3 103 (p) WilliamBuick 1 100
(Charlie Appleby) *trckd ldrs: effrt and swtchd rt wl over 1f out: rdn to ld and edgd lft ins fnl f: drvn and hung rt 100 yds: out: drvn and kpt on* **9/4**[1]

4221 **2** *hd* **Al Hamdany (IRE)**[40] 6240 2-9-3 88 GrahamLee 3 100
(Marco Botti) *hld up: gd hdwy on outer 2f out: chal ent fnl f and ev ch whn hmpd 100 yds out: kpt on* **14/1**

1 **3** *1½* **Forest Ranger (IRE)**[26] 6682 2-9-3 0 TonyHamilton 8 96
(Richard Fahey) *hld up: hdwy over 2f out: rdn over 1f out: kpt on fnl f* **12/1**

221 **4** *6* **Good Omen**[37] 6314 2-9-3 92 PatCosgrave 7 83
(William Haggas) *trckd ldng pair: cl up over 2f out: rdn and led briefly jst over 1f out: drvn and hdd ent fnl f: kpt on same pce* **9/2**[2]

1126 **5** *2¼* **Monticello (IRE)**[58] 5646 2-9-3 92 JoeFanning 4 78
(Mark Johnston) *led: rdn along over 2f out: drvn wl over 1f out: hdd appr fnl f: wknd* **6/1**

212 **6** *8* **Euro Nightmare (IRE)**[30] 6554 2-8-12 78 JasonHart 2 56
(Keith Dalgleish) *cl up on inner: rdn along 3f out: wknd over 2f out* **11/1**

124 **7** *3¾* **Reachforthestars (IRE)**[39] 6258 2-8-12 95 DanielTudhope 6 47
(David O'Meara) *in tch: hdwy on outer to trck ldrs over 2f out: effrt whn bmpd wl over 1f out: sn rdn and btn* **7/1**

1 **8** *12* **Dowayla (IRE)**[19] 6874 2-8-12 0 JimCrowley 5 21
(Saeed bin Suroor) *trckd ldrs: pushed along 3f out: rdn over 2f out: sn wknd* **11/2**[3]

1m 49.66s (3.76) **Going Correction** +0.625s/f (Yiel) **8** Ran SP% **113.8**
Speed ratings (Par 103): **106,105,104,98,96 88,84,72**
CSF £35.76 TOTE £2.60: £1.10, £3.70, £4.20; EX 30.10 Trifecta £250.90.
Owner Godolphin **Bred** Lodge Park Stud **Trained** Newmarket, Suffolk

FOCUS
Race distance increased by approximately 4yds. The pace seemed to pick up from a fair way out, which might explain why the two at the back stayed on to be second and third. The winner has been rated in line with his Doncaster form.

7410 TOTEPOOLRACING WIN TICKETS ON FACEBOOK MAIDEN STKS 1m 4f 8y
4:10 (4:13) (Class 5) 3-Y-O+ **£3,234** (£962; £481; £240) **Stalls** Low

Form RPR

2 **1** **Timekeeping (IRE)**[173] 1784 3-9-2 0 JosephineGordon(3) 1 90
(Saeed bin Suroor) *trckd ldrs: hdwy over 3f out: sn chsng ldr: rdn to chal over 1f out: drvn and styd on to ld ins fnl f* **15/8**[1]

-252 **2** *3¾* **Admiral's Sunset**[130] 3063 3-9-0 73 JimCrowley 3 80
(Hughie Morrison) *led: pushed along 3f out: rdn wl over 1f out: drvn and hdd ins fnl f: kpt on same pce towards fin* **5/2**[2]

23 **3** *22* **Time To Blossom**[27] 6661 3-9-0 0 RobertHavlin 6 45
(Simon Crisford) *in tch: hdwy to trck ldrs over 4f out: effrt 3f out and sn rdn along: drvn 2f out and plugged on one pce* **8/1**[3]

5 **4** *11* **Bailarico (IRE)**[32] 6520 3-9-5 0 (b[1]) WilliamBuick 10 32
(Charlie Appleby) *towards rr: reminders after 3f: pushed along 1/2-way: rdn along 4f out: nvr a factor* **10/1**

0 **5** *2¾* **Mackiri (IRE)**[30] 6567 3-9-5 0 BenCurtis 2 28
(Michael Appleby) *towards rr: sme hdwy 4f out: sn rdn along: nvr a factor* **50/1**

360/ **6** *63* **Star Of Namibia (IRE)**[788] 5600 6-9-12 52 TomEaves 7
(Michael Mullineaux) *a rr: outpcd and bhd fnl 3f* **150/1**

7 *3* **Mighty Minks** 4-9-4 0 AlistairRawlinson(3) 5
(Michael Appleby) *dwlt: a rr: outpcd and bhd fnl 3f* **66/1**

6 **8** *hd* **Poetic Queen (IRE)**[20] 6855 3-9-0 0 JasonHart 4
(Eric Alston) *trckd ldr: pushed along 1/2-way: rdn over 4f out: sn lost pl and bhd* **100/1**

2 **9** *2¼* **Alf Guineas (IRE)**[11] 7102 3-9-0 0 TomQueally 8
(John Gosden) *racd wd: prom: chsd ldr 5f out: rdn along 4f out: wknd qckly 3f out: sn bhd and eased* **5/2**[2]

2m 43.4s (2.60) **Going Correction** +0.625s/f (Yiel)
WFA 3 from 4yo+ 7lb **9** Ran SP% **117.2**
Speed ratings (Par 103): **116,113,98,91,89 47,45,45,44**
CSF £6.98 TOTE £2.80: £1.20, £1.30, £1.70; EX 7.70 Trifecta £34.10.
Owner Godolphin **Bred** Darley **Trained** Newmarket, Suffolk

FOCUS
Race distance increased by approximately 4yds. This was run at a demanding gallop given the conditions and proved a real test of stamina. They finished strung out in behind. This has been rated around the front-running 2nd.

7411 TOTEPOOL PHIL BULL TROPHY CONDITIONS STKS (ROUND 8 OF THE PONTEFRACT STAYERS CHAMPIONSHIP 2016) 2m 1f 216y
4:40 (4:41) (Class 3) 3-Y-O+ **£7,762** (£2,310; £1,154; £577) **Stalls** Low

Form RPR

6200 **1** **Oriental Fox (GER)**[9] 7150 8-9-2 103 JoeFanning 7 107
(Mark Johnston) *trckd ldr: led 10f out: rdn clr 2f out: styd on strly* **11/2**[3]

4540 **2** *3* **Burmese**[16] 6974 4-9-2 110 (p) WilliamBuick 4 104
(Marcus Tregoning) *trckd ldrs: hdwy to chse wnr over 2f out: rdn wl over 1f out: drvn and no imp fnl f* **5/6**[1]

0130 **3** *5* **Fun Mac (GER)**[9] 7150 5-9-5 102 (t) CharlieBennett(5) 1 107
(Hughie Morrison) *hld up in rr: hdwy over 4f out: rdn along to chse ldng pair 2f out: sn drvn and kpt on same pce* **4/1**[2]

2000 **4** *4½* **Cayirli (FR)**[16] 6974 4-9-2 100 TimmyMurphy 8 95
(Seamus Durack) *trckd ldrs on inner: pushed along over 3f out: rdn over 1f out: plugged on one pce* **12/1**

0526 **5** *9* **Mijhaar**[17] 6919 8-9-2 92 DanielTudhope 5 86
(David O'Meara) *hld up in rr: hdwy on outer 5f out in tch 4f out: rdn along 3f out: sn drvn and outpcd* **9/1**

6 *10* **Foxcub (IRE)**[168] 8-9-2 0 JamieSpencer 2 76
(Tom Symonds) *led: hdd 10f out: cl up: rdn along 4f out: drvn 3f out: sn wknd* **22/1**

0203 **7** *14* **Riptide**[14] 7006 10-9-2 67 DougieCostello 6 62
(Michael Scudamore) *trckd ldrs: pushed along over 4f out: sn rdn: outpcd and bhd fr over 2f out* **100/1**

4m 13.73s (17.53) **Going Correction** +0.625s/f (Yiel) **7** Ran SP% **113.0**
Speed ratings (Par 107): **86,84,82,80,76 72,65**
CSF £10.25 TOTE £6.30: £3.00, £1.10; EX 10.90 Trifecta £35.60.
Owner Markus Graff **Bred** Gestut Auenquelle **Trained** Middleham Moor, N Yorks

FOCUS
Race distance increased by approximately 4yds. They didn't go a mad gallop early on, and this has been rated around the 1st and 3rd to this year's form.

7412 BET TOTEQUADPOT AT TOTESPORT.COM H'CAP (DIV II) 1m 2f 6y
5:10 (5:14) (Class 4) (0-85,85) 3-Y-O+ **£5,175** (£1,540; £769; £384) **Stalls** Low

Form RPR

0053 **1** **Bahama Moon (IRE)**[5] 7287 4-9-6 **81** GrahamGibbons 2 93
(David Barron) *hld up in tch: smooth hdwy over 2f out: led wl over 1f out: sn rdn clr: styd on strly* **5/2**[1]

-221 **2** *2½* **Al Destoor**[12] 7077 6-9-7 **82** DavidNolan 8 89
(Jennie Candlish) *hld up towards rr: hdwy over 2f out: rdn over 1f out: chsd wnr fnl f: sn drvn and no imp* **3/1**[2]

-040 **3** *7* **Woodacre**[164] 2017 9-8-11 **72** GeorgeChaloner 10 65
(Richard Whitaker) *trckd ldrs on inner: hdwy over 2f out: rdn over 1f out: kpt on same pce fnl f* **22/1**

3136 **4** *1½* **Azzir (IRE)**[23] 6773 4-8-11 **77** CliffordLee(5) 1 67
(K R Burke) *prom: trckd ldr 4f out: rdn along 2f out: drvn and one pce fr over 1f out* **15/2**

0036 **5** *3¼* **Odeon**[9] 7158 5-9-2 **77** TomEaves 4 61
(James Given) *led: rdn along over 2f out: hdd and drvn wl over 1f out: grad wknd* **16/1**

140 **6** *13* **Angel Grace (IRE)**[49] 5975 3-8-8 **74** ShaneGray 6 32
(David Menuisier) *trckd ldrs: effrt over 2f out: rdn along wl over 1f out: sn one pce* **20/1**

1564 **7** *2½* **Throckley**[43] 6160 5-9-4 **79** SamJames 9 32
(John Davies) *nvr bttr than midfield* **6/1**[3]

6200 **8** *12* **Gulf Of Poets**[27] 6645 4-8-12 **73** CamHardie 7 2
(Michael Easterby) *midfield on outer: pushed along over 4f out: rdn over 3f out: sn wknd* **50/1**

1 **9** *10* **Sabre Squadron (IRE)**[147] 2541 3-9-0 **80** JamieSpencer 12
(Peter Chapple-Hyam) *hld up: a rr* **13/2**

1000 **10** *shd* **Another Go (IRE)**[32] 6500 3-9-2 **82** BenCurtis 11
(Alan Swinbank) *nvr bttr than midfield* **50/1**

3-00 **11** *1* **Classic Villager**[30] 6561 4-9-10 **85** AndrewMullen 5
(Michael Appleby) *trckd ldr: cl up 5f out: rdn along 4f out: sn wknd* **14/1**

2m 19.48s (5.78) **Going Correction** +0.625s/f (Yiel)
WFA 3 from 4yo+ 5lb **11** Ran SP% **118.5**
Speed ratings (Par 105): **101,99,93,92,89 79,77,67,59,59 58**
CSF £9.60 CT £131.32 TOTE £3.70: £1.70, £1.50, £7.80; EX 13.70 Trifecta £247.90.
Owner Pryde, Van Der Hoeven & Beaumont **Bred** Ammerland Verwaltung Gmbh & Co Kg **Trained** Maunby, N Yorks
■ Invictus was withdrawn. Price at time of withdrawal 12/1. Rule 4 applies to bets struck prior to withdrawal but not to SP bets - deduct 5p in the pound. New market formed.

FOCUS
Race distance increased by approximately 4yds. They shunned the inside rail but four of the first five still raced for the most part on the inside of the pack. The winner's earlier defeat of Treasury Notes worked out well enough and he is rated back to that sort of form.

7413 TOTEPOOLRACING FIND US ON INSTAGRAM H'CAP 5f
5:40 (5:41) (Class 4) (0-85,85) 3-Y-O+ **£5,175** (£1,540; £769; £384) **Stalls** Low

Form RPR

2026 **1** **Cosmic Chatter**[17] 6927 6-9-3 **81** (p) JamesSullivan 2 90
(Ruth Carr) *in tch: hdwy 2f out: swtchd rt and rdn over 1f out: styd on strly fnl f: led last 50 yds* **12/1**

2105 **2** *1¼* **I'll Be Good**[2] 7358 7-9-4 **82** BenCurtis 11 86+
(Brian Ellison) *qckly away and led: rdn clr wl over 1f out: drvn ins fnl f: hdd and no ex last 50 yds* **11/2**[1]

0603 **3** *¾* **Ballesteros**[23] 6766 7-9-1 **79** GeorgeChaloner 1 80
(Richard Fahey) *trckd ldrs on inner: hdwy 2f out: rdn to chse ldr ent fnl f: sn drvn and kpt on* **9/1**

0600 **4** *hd* **Arctic Feeling (IRE)**[10] 7124 8-8-12 **81** AdamMcNamara(5) 12 82+
(Richard Fahey) *towards rr: hdwy on wd outside wl over 1f out: sn rdn and styd on wl fnl f: nrst fin* **6/1**[2]

4150 **5** *1¼* **Ancient Astronaut**[19] 6878 3-8-8 **72** CamHardie 3 69
(John Quinn) *dwlt and towards rr: hdwy 2f out: sn rdn: styd on fnl f: nrst fin* **12/1**

305 **6** *1½* **Casterbridge**[11] 7094 4-8-10 **74** JasonHart 4 65
(Eric Alston) *chsd ldr: rdn along 2f out: drvn over 1f out: grad wknd fnl f* **10/1**

5000 **7** *3¼* **Avon Breeze**[10] 7126 7-9-7 **85** (p) DavidNolan 10 64
(Richard Whitaker) *towards rr: hdwy on outer 2f out: rdn over 1f out: no imp fnl f* **10/1**

0430 **8** 1 **Eleuthera**[10] 7112 4-8-7 **71**........[1] ShaneGray 7 46
(Kevin Ryan) *chsd ldrs: rdn along and n.m.r wl over 1f out: sn drvn and one pce* **20/1**

0000 **9** 1 3/4 **Patrick (IRE)**[45] 6079 4-9-5 **83**........ TonyHamilton 8 52
(Richard Fahey) *dwlt: a towards rr* **14/1**

0400 **10** 1 3/4 **Silvanus (IRE)**[23] 6793 11-9-4 **82**........ PaulMulrennan 5 45
(Paul Midgley) *midfield: effrt and sme hdwy wl over 1f out: sn rdn and n.d* **9/1**

2400 **11** 2 **Tylery Wonder (IRE)**[2] 7358 6-9-5 **83**........(b) GrahamGibbons 14 39
(Paul Midgley) *prom: rdn along over 2f out: sn wknd* **10/1**

1665 **12** 1/2 **Rainbow Orse**[19] 6879 4-8-4 **71**........(p) AaronJones(3) 6 25
(Robert Cowell) *chsd ldrs: rdn along over 2f out: sn wknd* **22/1**

000 **13** 1 3/4 **Tangerine Trees**[27] 6642 11-9-7 **85**........ TomEaves 13 32
(Michael Appleby) *prom: rdn along over 2f out: sn wknd* **25/1**

261 **14** 15 **Van Gerwen**[25] 6717 3-9-3 **81**........ JoeFanning 9
(Les Eyre) *towards rr: rdn along over 2f out: sn outpcd and bhd whn eased over 1f out* **8/1**[3]

1m 5.57s (2.27) **Going Correction** +0.625s/f (Yiel) **14** Ran SP% **123.1**
Speed ratings (Par 105): **106,104,102,102,100 98,92,91,88,85 82,81,78,54**
CSF £76.34 CT £656.61 TOTE £16.20: £4.00, £2.50, £3.40; EX 117.30 Trifecta £3196.40.
Owner Grange Park Racing VII **Bred** Harrowgate Bloodstock Ltd **Trained** Huby, N Yorks

FOCUS
Race distance increased by approximately 4yds. This was run at a good gallop and set up for a closer, and the winner has been rated back to last year's form.
T/Plt: £17.20 to a £1 stake. Pool: £74099.17, 3131.98 winning units. T/Qpdt: £8.40 to a £1 stake. Pool: £5515.77, 484.34 winning units. **Joe Rowntree**

7216 WINDSOR (R-H)

Monday, October 17

OFFICIAL GOING: Soft (good to soft in places in final 3f; 6.9)
Wind: Moderate, behind Weather: Fine but cloudy

7414 SKY BET MEDIAN AUCTION MAIDEN STKS 5f 10y

1:50 (1:53) (Class 5) 2-Y-O **£2,911** (£866; £432; £216) **Stalls** Low

Form RPR

0042 **1** **Foxcatcher**[21] 6830 2-9-0 72........(b[1]) AdamKirby 4 72
(Clive Cox) *trckd ldng pair: shkn up and clsd to ld jst over 1f out: styd on wl* **4/7**[1]

50 **2** 2 1/2 **Mercers**[47] 6034 2-9-0 0........ ShaneKelly 14 63
(Peter Crate) *stdd s fr wd draw: hld up but sn in 6th: prog on outer 2f out: rdn to take 2nd fnl f: no imp on wnr but kpt on* **33/1**

5 **3** 1 3/4 **Oh Geno**[70] 5229 2-9-5 0........ DaneO'Neill 9 62
(Richard Spencer) *sn pushed along in rr: styd on u.p fr 2f out to take 3rd wl ins fnl f* **7/2**[2]

000 **4** 1 **Glam'Selle**[6] 7259 2-9-0 0........ LiamKeniry 12 53
(Ronald Harris) *pressed ldr: led briefly over 1f out: hanging lft and fdd fnl f* **66/1**

00 **5** 2 1/2 **Popsilca**[25] 6696 2-9-0 0........ WilliamCarson 10 44
(Mick Quinn) *led against rail to over 1f out: wknd* **50/1**

0 **6** 1 **Majestic Stone (IRE)**[19] 6873 2-9-5 0........ LukeMorris 1 46
(Robert Cowell) *sn rdn and struggling to go the pce: nvr a factor* **8/1**

50 **7** 1 3/4 **Dangerous Ends**[101] 4075 2-9-5 0........ JFEgan 7 39
(Brett Johnson) *s.i.s: sn rdn in rr: nvr on terms* **16/1**

00 **8** nse **Compton Brave**[12] 7072 2-9-5 0........ FrederikTylicki 8 39
(J R Jenkins) *settled in rr: shkn up and no prog 2f out* **66/1**

9 shd **Vicky Park** 2-9-0 0........ RobertWinston 6 34
(Dean Ivory) *chsd ldrs: rdn 2f out: wknd qckly over 1f out* **7/1**[3]

10 12 **Secret Storm** 2-9-5 0........ TomMarquand 2
(J R Jenkins) *restless stalls: s.i.s: a bhd: t.o* **50/1**

59.34s (-0.96) **Going Correction** -0.10s/f (Good) **10** Ran SP% **125.2**
Speed ratings (Par 95): **103,99,96,94,90 89,86,86,85,66**
CSF £37.35 TOTE £1.40: £1.10, £5.50, £1.60; EX 23.40 Trifecta £78.20.
Owner C J Harper **Bred** Whitsbury Manor Stud **Trained** Lambourn, Berks

FOCUS
All inner running rail had been moved as follows: Home straight at normal inner configuration, thus making the home straight maximum width. Top bend was dolled out 7yds from normal inner configuration, adding 23yds to race distances of 1m plus. 24mm of rain since Saturday, although Adam Kirby felt it wasn't too bad, saying: "it's more good to soft - there is very little soft out there." A pretty weak maiden in which the winner confirmed her recent improvement.

7415 SKY BET CLASSIFIED CLAIMING STKS 6f

2:20 (2:21) (Class 5) 3-Y-O+ **£2,911** (£866; £432; £216) **Stalls** Low

Form RPR

5010 **1** **Flowing Clarets**[23] 6770 3-8-6 69........ PatrickMathers 2 74
(Richard Fahey) *trckd ldrs against rail: chal over 1f out but sn hanging lft: drvn to ld fnl f: styd on wl nr fin* **7/1**[2]

5140 **2** 1 1/4 **Dynamic Girl (IRE)**[9] 7146 3-8-8 72........(p) JFEgan 1 72
(Brendan Powell) *led against nr side rail: hanging bdly lft fr wl over 1f out: hdd fnl f: kpt on* **9/1**

300 **3** nse **Racquet**[5] 7268 3-8-7 74........(b) HollieDoyle(5) 5 76
(Richard Hannon) *trckd ldng pair: chal on outer wl over 1f out: sltly impeded sn after: kpt on fnl f* **14/1**

5430 **4** 1/2 **Lilbourne Prince (IRE)**[19] 6885 3-8-10 72........ LiamKeniry 7 72
(David Evans) *in rr: rdn and no prog 2f out: kpt on towards nr side fnl f: nrst fin* **12/1**

0001 **5** 1/2 **Evanescent (IRE)**[4] 7301 7-8-13 71........ RobertWinston 10 75
(Tony Carroll) *in tch: effrt on outer 2f out: trying to chal whn sltly impeded jst over 1f out: one pce after* **9/4**[1]

4365 **6** nk **Fantasy Justifier (IRE)**[76] 4990 5-8-11 69........ OisinMurphy 9 70
(Ronald Harris) *hld up in last and detached: rdn and no prog over 2f out: kpt on against nr side rail fnl f* **10/1**

6026 **7** 1 1/4 **Nocturn**[5] 7267 7-8-8 73........(p) ShaneKelly 12 63
(Ronald Harris) *racd wdst of all: effrt and drvn 2f out: no prog over 1f out: fdd* **8/1**[3]

233 **8** 1/2 **Caitie (IRE)**[21] 6831 3-9-1 71........(t) LukeMorris 8 69
(Paul Cole) *sn pushed along in rr: rdn and no prog 2f out* **7/1**[2]

0060 **9** 1 **Canyari (IRE)**[25] 6718 5-8-10 73........ JackGarritty 3 60
(Richard Fahey) *pressed ldr to 2f out: sn lost pl and btn* **8/1**[3]

1m 11.89s (-1.11) **Going Correction** -0.10s/f (Good)
WFA 3 from 5yo+ 1lb **9** Ran SP% **111.4**
Speed ratings (Par 103): **103,101,101,100,99 99,97,97,95**
CSF £64.53 TOTE £6.80: £2.00, £2.80, £4.30; EX 60.60 Trifecta £1372.40.Flowing Clarets was claimed by J. J. Bridger for £6,000.
Owner The Matthewman One Partnership **Bred** R A Fahey **Trained** Musley Bank, N Yorks

FOCUS
Race distance as advertised. An open claimer and little got into it. It has been rated around the 2nd and 3rd.

7416 BEST OF LUCK SUKEY SHERRITT NURSERY H'CAP 1m 67y

2:50 (2:50) (Class 4) (0-85,80) 2-Y-O **£3,946** (£1,174; £586; £293) **Stalls** Low

Form RPR

0250 **1** **Phoenix Dawn**[19] 6875 2-8-6 **65**........[1] MartinDwyer 6 66
(Brendan Powell) *led: hung bdly lft bnd over 5f out: urged along and reminders over 4f out: attacked on all sides 2f out: hdd fnl f: kpt on to ld again last 75yds* **12/1**

3113 **2** nk **Muirsheen Durkin**[52] 5829 2-9-7 **80**........(p) RichardKingscote 7 80
(Tom Dascombe) *trckd wnr: shkn up to chal 2f out: disp narrow ld fnl f: hdd and nt qckn last 75yds* **11/8**[1]

140 **3** nse **Funky Footsteps (IRE)**[79] 4884 2-9-0 **73**........ CharlesBishop 5 73
(Eve Johnson Houghton) *hld up in last: clsd on outer over 2f out: shkn up to chal wl over 1f out: disp narrow ld fnl f: hdd and nt qckn last 75yds* **11/4**[3]

5120 **4** hd **Fastnet Spin (IRE)**[9] 7147 2-9-5 **78**........ AdamKirby 1 78
(David Evans) *hld up in 3rd: rdn over 2f out: chal on nr side wl over 1f out: nt qckn fnl f: kpt on* **5/2**[2]

1m 48.74s (4.04) **Going Correction** +0.05s/f (Good) **4** Ran SP% **105.0**
Speed ratings (Par 97): **81,80,80,80**
CSF £27.49 TOTE £11.30; EX 21.30 Trifecta £63.30.
Owner Winterbeck Manor Stud **Bred** Winterbeck Manor Stud **Trained** Upper Lambourn, Berks

FOCUS
Race distance increased by 23yds. A steady early pace resulted in the four being in a row inside the final furlong and it was the complete outsider who emerged on top. It's hard to rate this race much higher.

7417 WALL TO WALL COMMUNICATIONS LTD H'CAP 1m 67y

3:20 (3:21) (Class 5) (0-70,70) 3-Y-O+ **£2,911** (£866; £432; £216) **Stalls** Low

Form RPR

4212 **1** **Zlatan (IRE)**[13] 7036 3-9-2 **68**........(p) DaneO'Neill 3 78
(Ed de Giles) *hld up in midfield gng wl: stdy prog and shkn up to chse ldr over 1f out: chal fnl f: rdn to ld last 120yds: r.o* **5/1**[1]

1606 **2** 1/2 **Clever Bob (IRE)**[27] 6657 3-9-3 **69**........ OisinMurphy 6 78
(Joseph Tuite) *trckd ldng pair: rdn to ld wl over 1f out: styd on but hdd and hld last 120yds* **11/2**[2]

5604 **3** 7 **Shifting Star (IRE)**[27] 6656 11-9-6 **69**........(vt) WilliamCarson 4 63
(John Bridger) *led 1f: taken wd to centre of crse and led over 3f out to 2f out: no ch w ldng pair after but clr of rest* **5/1**[1]

4341 **4** 5 **Lord Of The Storm**[98] 4200 8-9-4 **67**........ KierenFox 2 49
(Michael Attwater) *hld up in last trio: rdn and sme prog over 2f out: tk modest 4th fnl f: no ch* **14/1**

4036 **5** 1 **Hot Mustard**[47] 6021 6-9-4 **67**........ MartinDwyer 8 47
(William Muir) *t.k.h: hld up in midfield: rdn over 2f out and tried to cl on ldrs: wknd over 1f out* **13/2**

2235 **6** 3/4 **Baltic Prince (IRE)**[38] 6280 6-9-5 **68**........ TomMarquand 1 46
(Tony Carroll) *nipped through on inner and led after 1f: hdd over 3f out: led again nr side 2f out: sn hdd & wknd* **8/1**

3066 **7** shd **Bond Trader**[109] 3816 3-9-3 **69**........ AdamKirby 14 46
(Clive Cox) *nvr beyond midfield: rdn and no prog over 2f out* **9/1**

0065 **8** 8 **Berkeley Vale**[12] 7076 5-9-6 **69**........(v) JackMitchell 9 29
(Roger Teal) *racd in 8th: pushed along 1/2-way: no prog: t.o* **6/1**[3]

12- **9** 1 3/4 **Cahala Dancer (IRE)**[412] 5969 8-8-13 **65**........(t) NoelGarbutt(3) 12 21
(Adam West) *hld up in last: shkn up and no prog 3f out: t.o* **33/1**

30 **10** 1 **Uncle Dermot (IRE)**[14] 7010 8-9-6 **69**........ LiamKeniry 13 22
(Brendan Powell) *taken down early: chsd ldrs: reminders 1/2-way: wknd over 2f out: t.o* **25/1**

4300 **11** 3/4 **Snappy Guest**[12] 7076 4-9-4 **67**........(v[1]) JFEgan 11 19
(George Margarson) *a in rr: t.o* **14/1**

1m 43.36s (-1.34) **Going Correction** +0.05s/f (Good)
WFA 3 from 4yo+ 3lb **11** Ran SP% **117.6**
Speed ratings (Par 103): **108,107,100,95,94 93,93,85,83,82 82**
CSF £32.10 CT £146.01 TOTE £5.40: £2.10, £2.00, £2.20; EX 37.60 Trifecta £193.10.
Owner Gwyn Powell & Richard Meakes **Bred** Roundhill Stud **Trained** Ledbury, H'fords

FOCUS
Race distance increased by 23yds. Two of the 3yos dominated this modest handicap.

7418 IVOR LAWS MEMORIAL H'CAP (DIV I) 1m 2f 7y

3:50 (3:50) (Class 4) (0-85,85) 3-Y-O+ **£4,690** (£1,395; £697; £348) **Stalls** Centre

Form RPR

2411 **1** **Exoteric**[52] 5849 3-9-2 **82**........ RichardKingscote 6 93+
(Charles Hills) *hld up in 7th: prog nr side over 2f out: shkn up to ld jst over 1f out: r.o wl and sn clr* **9/4**[1]

4500 **2** 3 **Cordite (IRE)**[22] 6806 5-8-11 **72**........ SamHitchcott 8 77
(Jim Boyle) *t.k.h: trckd ldrs: styd nr side in st: rdn over 2f out: tried to chal over 1f out but wnr sn wnt past: styd on to snatch 2nd* **20/1**

1234 **3** nk **Panko (IRE)**[12] 7067 3-8-11 **77**........ DaneO'Neill 2 81
(Ed de Giles) *cl up: prog on outer over 2f out: rdn to ld briefly over 1f out: sn no ch w wnr and jst lost out in r for 2nd* **3/1**[2]

4330 **4** 1 1/4 **Craftsmanship (FR)**[24] 6753 5-8-13 **81**........ CameronNoble(7) 3 83
(Robert Eddery) *dwlt: hld up in last: rdn and gd prog on wd outside fr 3f out to chal wl over 1f out: no ch w wnr fnl f and one pce* **7/1**

06 **5** 3 1/4 **Bazooka (IRE)**[36] 6379 5-9-0 **75**........ RobertWinston 1 69
(David Flood) *hld up in 8th: shkn up 3f out: no imp ldrs 2f out: fdd* **16/1**

130 **6** 1/2 **Torch**[28] 6628 3-9-0 **80**........(p) SeanLevey 9 73
(Richard Hannon) *prom: drvn 3f out: lost pl 2f out: steadily fdd* **6/1**[3]

1515 **7** shd **Pink Ribbon (IRE)**[31] 6549 4-8-5 **71**........(p) MitchGodwin(5) 4 64
(Sylvester Kirk) *t.k.h: trckd ldr: rdn to chal fr 3f out: edgd towards outer after: lost 2nd and btn 2f out: wknd* **16/1**

4000 **8** 1 3/4 **Fiftyshadesfreed (IRE)**[19] 6870 5-9-5 **80**........(p) LiamKeniry 11 70
(George Baker) *trckd ldrs: shkn up on outer 3f out: no prog 2f out: sn wknd* **10/1**

0300 **9** 3/4 **Moojaned (IRE)**[16] 6965 5-8-5 **73**........ KatherineGlenister(7) 7 61
(David Evans) *led: edgd towards centre fr 3f out: hdd over 1f out: short of room briefly and wknd* **16/1**

2m 7.7s (-1.00) **Going Correction** +0.05s/f (Good)
WFA 3 from 4yo+ 5lb **9** Ran SP% **114.1**
Speed ratings (Par 105): **106,103,103,102,99 98,98,97,96**
CSF £49.13 CT £137.20 TOTE £2.40: £1.20, £6.00, £1.50; EX 47.60 Trifecta £264.50.
Owner K Abdullah **Bred** Juddmonte Farms Ltd **Trained** Lambourn, Berks

FOCUS
Race distance increased by 23yds. A fair handicap taken in good style by the favourite, who was completing a hat-trick. This could be rated 3lb to 4lb higher judged on the 2nd to 4th.

7419 IVOR LAWS MEMORIAL H'CAP (DIV II) 1m 2f 7y
4:20 (4:20) (Class 4) (0-85,84) 3-Y-O+ **£4,690** (£1,395; £697; £348) **Stalls** Centre

Form RPR
1366 **1** **Inniscastle Lad**[58] 6569 4-9-5 **79**....(b) AdamKirby 7 86
(Stuart Williams) *mde all: sent for home 3f out: styd against nr side rail after: drvn over 2f out: hld on wl* **10/1**
4325 **2** ¾ **Rotherwick (IRE)**[12] 7067 4-9-10 **84**....(t) LukeMorris 5 89
(Paul Cole) *hld up in 5th: stoked up over 3f out: drvn to chse wnr over 1f out: grad narrowed the gap but a hld* **2/1**[2]
6512 **3** 1 **Lime And Lemon (IRE)**[31] 6549 3-8-11 **76**.... OisinMurphy 11 79
(Clive Cox) *hld up in 4th: effrt out wd over 2f out: disp 2nd over 1f out: kpt on same pce after* **6/4**[1]
5014 **4** 2¼ **Normandie Lady**[50] 5919 3-8-13 **78**.... JackGarritty 3 77
(Richard Fahey) *hld up in last: gng wl whn tried to make prog on outer wl over 2f out: no hdwy and swtchd bk towards inner over 1f out: kpt on but no ch* **11/2**[3]
-120 **5** 3 **Ritasun (FR)**[18] 6899 3-8-13 **78**....(p) KieranO'Neill 1 71
(Richard Hannon) *chsd ldng pair: drvn to chse wnr over 2f out: nt qckn and lost 2nd over 1f out: wknd* **9/1**
5-03 **6** 1¼ **Silver Ghost (IRE)**[38] 6294 3-8-4 **74**.... PaddyPilley[(5)] 10 64
(Geoffrey Deacon) *chsd wnr: rdn and edgd lft towards centre fr 3f out: lost 2nd over 2f out: wknd over 1f out* **16/1**

2m 8.23s (-0.47) **Going Correction** +0.05s/f (Good)
WFA 3 from 4yo 5lb **6** Ran SP% **113.7**
Speed ratings (Par 105): **103,102,101,99,97 96**
CSF £31.07 CT £47.58 TOTE £9.50: £4.20, £1.70; EX 21.40 Trifecta £66.40.
Owner Happy Valley Racing & Breeding Limited **Bred** G Doyle & Lord Margadale **Trained** Newmarket, Suffolk

FOCUS
Race distance increased by 23yds. An old school Windsor race, with the winner making all and racing against the stands' rail in the straight. He has been rated to a better view of his summer form for his previous yard.

7420 BEN WOOLLACOTT MEMORIAL H'CAP 5f 10y
4:50 (4:55) (Class 5) (0-70,76) 3-Y-O+ **£2,911** (£866; £432; £216) **Stalls** Low

Form RPR
0000 **1** **Dreams Of Glory**[21] 6832 8-8-12 **64**.... EdwardGreatrex[(3)] 3 70
(Ron Hodges) *chsd ldrs: rdn 2f out: clsd over 1f out: racd nrest to rail and styd on to ld last 100yds* **8/1**
4351 **2** nk **Stormflower**[26] 6669 3-9-5 **68**.... DannyBrock 8 73
(John Bridger) *checked over bef r: chsd ldrs: rdn 2f out: tried to chal 1f out: kpt on but jst outpcd by wnr* **5/1**[2]
3336 **3** nk **Flying Bear (IRE)**[7] 7202 5-9-6 **69**.... MartinLane 12 72
(Jeremy Gask) *chsd ldrs: rdn 1/2-way: kpt on u.p fr over 1f out: tk 3rd nr fin* **5/1**[2]
6105 **4** ½ **Fine 'n Dandy (IRE)**[55] 5751 5-9-6 **69**....(t) FrederikTylicki 11 71
(J R Jenkins) *led but away fr nr side rail: drvn over 1f out: hdd & wknd last 100yds* **25/1**
-446 **5** nk **Rosie Royce**[19] 6879 3-9-3 **66**.... DaneO'Neill 13 68
(Henry Candy) *in tch: rdn on outer of gp over 2f out: tried to cl u.p over 1f out: kpt on* **5/1**[2]
4305 **6** 1¼ **Ambitious Icarus**[5] 7289 7-9-4 **67**....(e) LiamKeniry 2 63
(Richard Guest) *hld up in rr: rdn 2f out: plugged on same pce fr over 1f out: n.d* **5/2**[1]
2200 **7** 1¾ **Mossgo (IRE)**[128] 3159 6-9-5 **68**....(t) KierenFox 14 58
(John Best) *fast away: disp ld on outer tl taken to r against far side rail 1/2-way: nt on terms fr over 1f out* **25/1**
4043 **8** 3¼ **Lady Nayef**[26] 6680 3-9-3 **66**....(t) JFEgan 16 45
(John Butler) *racd on outer: struggling to keep in tch fr 1/2-way: wknd over 1f out* **7/1**[3]
6613 **9** 3 **Evening Starlight**[152] 2373 3-9-3 **66**.... LukeMorris 5 34
(Ron Hodges) *rdn and struggling in last 1/2-way: sn no ch* **25/1**

1m 0.3s **Going Correction** -0.10s/f (Good) **9** Ran SP% **113.7**
Speed ratings (Par 103): **96,95,95,94,93 91,88,83,78**
CSF £43.60 CT £189.70 TOTE £9.90: £2.60, £2.10, £1.90; EX 54.70 Trifecta £456.50.
Owner P E Axon **Bred** P E Axon **Trained** Charlton Mackrell, Somerset
■ Perfect Pastime was withdrawn. Price at time of withdrawal 14/1. Rule 4 applies to all bets - deduction 5p in the pound.

FOCUS
Race distance as advertised. A moderate sprint, the winner repeating last year's victory in the race. This has been rated around the 2nd.

7421 RJ CLYDE BUILDERS AMATEUR H'CAP (FOR GENTLEMAN AMATEUR RIDERS) 1m 3f 135y
5:20 (5:21) (Class 6) (0-65,65) 3-Y-O+ **£2,183** (£677; £338; £169) **Stalls** Centre

Form RPR
5255 **1** **Fast Play (IRE)**[27] 6659 4-11-3 **60**....(b[1]) MrJEPerrett[(7)] 6 66
(Richard Hughes) *slowly away: detached in last: long way adrift 1/2-way: prog over 4f out: clsng qckly whn hung bdly lft fr 2f out and ended against far rail: r.o to ld last 100yds: sn clr* **10/1**
1006 **2** 2¼ **Bob's Boy**[7] 7230 3-10-9 **57**....(b[1]) MrWillPettis[(5)] 3 60
(Jose Santos) *racd freely: led and clr: rdn over 3f out and stl clr: unchal on nr side but hdd and outpcd by far side wnr last 100yds* **6/1**
3612 **3** 3½ **Moss Street**[4] 7300 6-11-0 **55**....(bt) MrRichardPatrick[(5)] 8 52
(John Flint) *in tch: rdn to go 3rd 3f out: kpt on u.p but nvr able to chal* **9/2**[2]
-504 **4** 2 **Leyland (IRE)**[39] 6245 7-10-11 **47**....(b) MrFTett 12 41
(Natalie Lloyd-Beavis) *chsd clr ldr: wl ahd of rest 4f out: no imp over 2f out: fdd over 1f out* **33/1**
356 **5** 2¾ **Knight Commander**[19] 6885 3-11-3 **65**.... MrJDoe[(5)] 2 55
(William Knight) *in tch: prog to chse ldng pair after 5f: rdn and no imp 3f out: sn wknd* **7/2**[1]
1423 **6** 3½ **Desert Cross**[17] 6256 3-10-10 **58**.... MrJJO'Neill[(5)] 13 42
(Jonjo O'Neill) *in tch: rdn and no imp 3f out: wknd 2f out* **5/1**[3]
000/ **7** 15 **Amadiva (IRE)**[856] 3229 5-10-10 **46** oh1....[1] MrZBaker 1 7
(Martin Bosley) *chsd ldrs: struggling over 4f out: sn wl bhd* **66/1**
0063 **8** 2 **Sund City (FR)**[34] 6444 3-10-10 **53**.... MrMLegg 5 11
(Harry Dunlop) *in tch to 1/2-way: struggling in rr over 4f out: sn wl bhd* **15/2**
6010 **9** 22 **Magnificent Madiba**[24] 6737 3-11-8 **65**.... MrSWalker 7
(George Baker) *in tch in rr to 5f out: sn t.o* **5/1**[3]
0066 **10** nk **Rail Dancer**[118] 3498 4-11-4 **57**.... MrDavidTurner[(3)] 9
(Richard Rowe) *in tch to 1/2-way: wknd 5f out: t.o* **33/1**
3060 **11** 19 **Silver Lining (IRE)**[153] 2323 4-10-12 **53**....(t) MrSeanHoulihan[(5)] 4
(Mark Hoad) *a in rr: struggling 5f out: sn t.o* **50/1**

2m 33.67s (4.17) **Going Correction** +0.05s/f (Good)
WFA 3 from 4yo+ 7lb **11** Ran SP% **118.2**
Speed ratings (Par 101): **88,86,84,82,81 78,68,67,52,52 39**
CSF £67.81 CT £313.25 TOTE £12.80: £3.20, £2.60, £1.80; EX 109.30 Trifecta £633.90.
Owner Boyd Mortimer Terry Wellard Partners **Bred** Fintan Walsh **Trained** Upper Lambourn, Berkshire

FOCUS
Race distance increased by 23yds. The field was soon strung out, thanks to the runner-up, and little got into it. This has been rated around the 2nd and 3rd.
T/Jkpt: Not Won. T/Plt: £762.80 to a £1 stake. Pool: £74455.54, 71.25 winning units. T/Qpdt: £137.40 to a £1 stake. Pool: £6075.96, 32.7 winning units. **Jonathan Neesom**

5985 DEAUVILLE (R-H)
Monday, October 17

OFFICIAL GOING: Polytrack: standard

7422a PRIX DES GLAIEULS (CLAIMER) (2YO COLTS & GELDINGS) (POLYTRACK) 6f 110y
11:25 (12:00) 2-Y-O **£6,985** (£2,794; £2,095; £1,397; £698)

RPR
1 **If I Say So**[5] 7293 2-9-1 0....(b) IoritzMendizabal 6 73
(J S Moore) **1/1**[1]
2 3 **Dubai Knights (IRE)**[35] 2-8-11 0....(p) TheoBachelot 4 61
(P Monfort, France) **131/10**
3 nk **Le Candidat (FR)** 2-8-9 0.... HugoJourniac[(6)] 2 64
(J-C Rouget, France) **56/10**
4 1¾ **Costa Esmeralda (FR)** 2-9-8 0.... Roberto-CarlosMontenegro 1 66
(J A Remolina Diez, France) **4/1**[3]
5 ½ **Zanzari (FR)**[5] 7293 2-8-10 0....(p) TomLefranc[(8)] 3 60
(C Boutin, France) **218/10**
6 12 **Forty Foot (IRE)**[60] 2-9-3 0....(b) JeromeMoutard[(5)] 5 31
(T Castanheira, France) **33/10**[2]
\n\x\x PARI-MUTUEL (all including 1 euro stake): WIN 2.00; PLACE 1.70, 4.20; SF
Owner D G Pryde & J S Moore **Bred** Llety Farms **Trained** Upper Lambourn, Berks

7275 KEMPTON (A.W) (R-H)
Tuesday, October 18

OFFICIAL GOING: Polytrack: standard to slow
Wind: light, across Weather: dry

7423 RACINGUK.COM/HD NURSERY H'CAP 7f (P)
5:40 (5:44) (Class 6) (0-60,60) 2-Y-O **£2,264** (£673; £336; £168) **Stalls** Low

Form RPR
0540 **1** **A Sure Welcome**[20] 6875 2-8-10 **49**....[1] TomMarquand 1 53
(John Spearing) *in tch in midfield: effrt over 2f out: chal over 1f out: led jst ins fnl f: hld on wl u.p: all out* **12/1**
050 **2** hd **Deleyll**[67] 5377 2-8-9 **53**....(b[1]) GeorgiaCox[(5)] 4 56+
(William Haggas) *hld up in last quartet: rdn over 2f out: hdwy to chse ldrs 1f out: ev ch ins fnl f: kpt on wl: wnt 2nd last strides* **7/2**[2]
5011 **3** nk **Dragon Dream (IRE)**[14] 7047 2-9-5 **58**.... KierenFox 3 61
(Roger Ingram) *led for 2f: styd chsng ldr: rdn ent fnl 2f: ev ch over 1f out: kpt on u.p: unable qck wl ins fnl f* **9/4**[1]
0600 **4** 1¼ **Masquerade Bling (IRE)**[17] 6950 2-9-7 **60**.... GeorgeBaker 14 59
(Simon Hodgson) *stdd s and dropped in bhd: hld up in rr: effrt ent fnl 2f: rdn and hdwy over 1f out: styd on wl ins fnl f: nt rch ldrs* **25/1**
6035 **5** 1 **Restore (IRE)**[17] 6963 2-9-6 **59**.... SeanLevey 10 56+
(Richard Hannon) *chsd ldr tl led 5f out: rdn and veered bdly lft 2f out shifting bk rt and jnd over 1f out: hdd 1f out: wknd ins fnl f* **4/1**[3]
0000 **6** ¾ **Bruny Island (IRE)**[11] 7109 2-8-11 **50**.... RichardKingscote 5 45
(Mark Johnston) *t.k.h: hld up in tch in midfield: effrt 2f out: fnd little for press over 1f out: plugged on same pce fnl f* **20/1**
0313 **7** 6 **Harlequin Rose (IRE)**[14] 7041 2-9-1 **54**....(v) GrahamLee 6 33
(Mick Channon) *chsd ldrs: rdn over 2f out: outpcd and btn over 1f out: wknd fnl f* **8/1**
0650 **8** 7 **Silver Chimes**[17] 6963 2-8-13 **52**.... JimCrowley 8 13
(William Knight) *t.k.h: hld up in tch in midfield: outpcd and rdn 2f out: sn wknd* **10/1**
504 **9** 5 **Miss Reignier**[43] 6189 2-9-1 **54**.... DaneO'Neill 7 2
(Michael Blanshard) *dwlt: hld up in tch in last quartet: effrt 2f out: no imp and sn wknd* **40/1**
6600 **10** 2¾ **Hi There Silver (IRE)**[19] 6887 2-8-5 **49**.... GeorgeWood[(5)] 9
(Michael Madgwick) *in tch in midfield: lost pl and bhd over 2f out: wknd 2f out* **40/1**
4306 **11** 6 **Crystal Secret**[55] 5770 2-9-1 **54**.... DannyBrock 11
(John Bridger) *taken down early: chsd ldrs on outer tl rdn and lost pl 3f out: bhd over 1f out* **25/1**

1m 27.79s (1.79) **Going Correction** +0.075s/f (Slow) **11** Ran SP% **118.2**
Speed ratings (Par 93): **92,91,91,90,88 88,81,73,67,64 57**
CSF £51.05 CT £131.59 TOTE £14.80: £4.20, £1.90, £1.50; EX 80.80 Trifecta £301.20.
Owner Kinnersley Partnership 3 **Bred** Richard Evans Bloodstock **Trained** Kinnersley, Worcs
■ Take This Waltz was withdrawn. Price at time of withdrawal 66/1. Rule 4 does not apply.

FOCUS
A moderate nursery. Those hugging the rail into the straight dominated. The winner has been rated to his pre-race best.

7424 32RED.COM MAIDEN STKS 6f (P)
6:10 (6:16) (Class 5) 2-Y-O **£2,911** (£866; £432; £216) **Stalls** Low

Form RPR
03 **1** **Dagonet (IRE)**[20] 6873 2-9-5 0....(t) GeorgeBaker 8 83+
(Roger Charlton) *chsd ldr tl led gng strly over 1f out: pushed along and in command fnl f: comf* **9/4**[1]
530 **2** 1¼ **Nibras Again**[17] 6950 2-9-5 76.... KieranO'Neill 9 73
(Ismail Mohammed) *chsd ldrs: rdn and swtchd lft over 1f out: chsd wnr ins fnl f: no imp and one pced after* **11/4**[2]

3 1 **Ripp Orf (IRE)** 2-9-5 0.. SeanLevey 4 70+
(David Elsworth) *t.k.h: hld up in tch in last trio: swtchd rt 2f out: gd hdwy on inner over 1f out: wnt 3rd ins fnl f: kpt on wl but no threat to wnr* **11/2**[3]

50 **4** 1 ½ **Mr Maximum (USA)**[29] [6632] 2-9-5 0............................ RichardKingscote 3 66
(Harry Dunlop) *chsd ldrs: shkn up over 1f out: rdn and kpt on same pce ins fnl f* **33/1**

5 hd **Modern Life (IRE)** 2-9-5 0.. FrederikTylicki 6 65+
(David Elsworth) *rn green: in tch in midfield: rdn 2f out: no threat to wnr but kpt on ins fnl f* **40/1**

6 **6** 1 ½ **Aqdameya (IRE)**[14] [7055] 2-9-0 0.. DaneO'Neill 1 55
(Mark Johnston) *led: rdn and hdd over 1f out: no ex u.p: lost 2nd ins fnl f: wknd fnl 100yds* **7/1**

56 **7** hd **I Wouldn't Bother**[13] [7072] 2-9-5 0..................................... GrahamLee 2 61
(Daniel Kubler) *in tch in midfield: nt clr run over 1f out: pushed along and kpt on same pce ins fnl f: nvr trbld ldrs* **100/1**

40 **8** ½ **Vibes (IRE)**[8] [7216] 2-9-5 0... WilliamCarson 10 58+
(Jamie Osborne) *stdd s: hld up in tch in last trio: pushed along over 1f out: no imp: nvr trbld ldrs* **16/1**

00 **9** 1 **Inception (IRE)**[34] [6480] 2-9-5 0...................................... TomMarquand 7 55
(Richard Hannon) *t.k.h: chsd ldrs: rdn 2f out: sn lost pl: wknd ins fnl f* **16/1**

06 **10** 1 ½ **Singula**[96] [4287] 2-9-5 0.. FergusSweeney 5 51
(Alan King) *t.k.h: hld up in tch in rr: pushed along over 1f out: no imp: n.d* **7/1**

1m 15.28s (2.18) **Going Correction** +0.075s/f (Slow) **10** Ran SP% **116.0**
Speed ratings (Par 95): **88,86,85,83,82 80,80,79,78,76**
CSF £8.32 TOTE £3.10: £1.40, £1.40, £2.20; EX 9.20 Trifecta £42.30.
Owner Michael Pescod **Bred** Patrick Cummins **Trained** Beckhampton, Wilts

FOCUS
A fair maiden and a cosy winner. The runner-up is rated to the balance of his form.

7425 RACING UK HD H'CAP 1m 4f (P)
6:40 (6:43) (Class 6) (0-65,65) 3-Y-O **£2,264** (£673; £336; £168) **Stalls** Low

Form RPR

3340 **1** **Santiburi Spring**[28] [6662] 3-9-6 **64**.. KierenFox 4 70
(John Best) *in tch in midfield: rdn and swtchd lft over 2f out: hdwy u.p over 1f out: led ins fnl f: styd on: rdn out* **8/1**

6420 **2** ¾ **Aurora Gray**[19] [6901] 3-9-6 **64**.. JimmyFortune 6 68
(Hughie Morrison) *squeezed for room leaving stalls: hld up in rr: swtchd lft and rdn over 2f out: hdwy 1f out: styd on wl ins fnl f: wnt 2nd wl ins fnl f: nvr quite getting to wnr* **16/1**

0506 **3** hd **Alcanar (USA)**[94] [4385] 3-9-4 **62**.................................... WilliamCarson 5 65
(Tony Carroll) *hld up in tch towards rr: effrt ent fnl 2f: swtchd lft and hdwy over 1f out: kpt on wl ins fnl f* **20/1**

6340 **4** 1 ½ **Cliff Edge (IRE)**[8] [7214] 3-9-4 **62**..(b) FMBerry 7 63
(Roger Varian) *in tch in last trio: reminder 4f out: rdn 3f out: hdwy u.p 1f out: styd on ins fnl f: wnt 4th nr fin: nvr trbld ldrs* **4/1**[2]

5110 **5** ½ **Hearty (IRE)**[20] [6885] 3-9-7 **65**..(p) JimCrowley 10 65+
(Jeremy Noseda) *dwlt and pushed along early: in rr: hdwy into midfield 7f out: wnt cl 2nd 3f out: rdn to ld 2f out: hdd and no ex ins fnl f: wknd fnl 75yds* **13/2**[3]

3425 **6** 1 **Iona Island**[26] [6698] 3-9-6 **64**.. RichardKingscote 8 63
(Charles Hills) *chsd ldrs: rdn ent fnl 2f: sn chalng tl no ex ins fnl f: wknd fnl 100yds* **7/1**

0 **7** nk **Southern States**[39] [6294] 3-9-7 **65**.................................. CharlesBishop 9 63
(Lydia Richards) *in tch in midfield: rdn 3f out: unable qck u.p and kpt on same pce fr over 1f out* **66/1**

-333 **8** 1 ¼ **Smiley Bagel (IRE)**[19] [6890] 3-8-7 **51**............................ TomMarquand 1 47
(Ed Walker) *in tch in midfield: effrt over 2f out: unable qck u.p over 1f out: wknd ins fnl f* **7/2**[1]

020 **9** nk **Betsalottie**[28] [6662] 3-8-13 **57**.. DannyBrock 3 53
(John Bridger) *chsd ldrs: effrt u.p ent fnl 2f: stl pressing ldrs but unable qck 1f out: wknd ins fnl f* **16/1**

0343 **10** shd **Hermarna (IRE)**[28] [6654] 3-9-3 **61**.................................... PatCosgrave 2 57
(Harry Dunlop) *led: rdn 2f out: hdd over 1f out: stl pressing ldrs 1f out: sn btn and wknd ins fnl f* **8/1**

0034 **11** 93 **Purple Raven**[12] [7104] 3-9-4 **65**.................................. LouisSteward(3) 11
(Michael Bell) *chsd ldr tl 3f out: sn rdn and lost pl: bhd and eased 2f out: t.o* **12/1**

2m 34.99s (0.49) **Going Correction** +0.075s/f (Slow) **11** Ran SP% **116.0**
Speed ratings (Par 99): **101,100,100,99,99 98,98,97,97,97 35**
CSF £126.43 CT £2450.94 TOTE £9.80: £3.00, £4.70, £6.40; EX 101.40 Trifecta £1509.80.
Owner Paine, Hill, Young & Mair **Bred** John Best **Trained** Oad Street, Kent

FOCUS
Something of a pace collapse here, with those at the back early on taking charge late.

7426 32RED CASINO H'CAP (DIV I) 1m (P)
7:10 (7:13) (Class 6) (0-55,60) 3-Y-O+ **£2,264** (£673; £336; £168) **Stalls** Low

Form RPR

4010 **1** **Candesta (USA)**[22] [6826] 6-9-6 **54**.. GeorgeBaker 5 62
(Julia Feilden) *chsd ldrs and travelled strly: wnt 2nd 2f out: led over 1f out: sn rdn clr: eased towards fin: comf* **6/1**

0514 **2** 2 **Barista (IRE)**[13] [7070] 8-9-2 **55**.. HollieDoyle(5) 2 58
(Brian Forsey) *in tch in midfield: rdn over 1f out: styd on to chse clr wnr 100yds out: kpt on but no threat to wnr* **11/2**[3]

0134 **3** 1 ¼ **Eugenic**[22] [6827] 5-8-12 **53**.. LuluStanford(7) 3 53
(Rod Millman) *hld up in rr: swtchd lft over 2f out: rdn and hdwy on outer 1f out: styd on wl ins fnl f: wnt 3rd last strides: no threat to ldrs* **3/1**[1]

00 **4** nk **Welsh Inlet (IRE)**[13] [7070] 8-9-0 **48**................................ WilliamCarson 9 47
(John Bridger) *chsd ldrs: effrt ent fnl 2f: wnt 3rd but nt on terms w ldrs 1f out: kpt on same pce fnl f* **20/1**

1540 **5** ¾ **Ted's Brother (IRE)**[12] [7097] 8-9-1 **49**..........................(e) GrahamLee 13 47
(Richard Guest) *hld up in midfield: effrt 2f out: sme hdwy over 1f out: kpt on but no threat to ldrs ins fnl f* **20/1**

3241 **6** 2 ½ **Coolcalmcollected (IRE)**[8] [7211] 4-9-7 **60** 6ex.....(p) GeorgeWood(5) 10 52
(David Loughnane) *rdr slow removing hood and dwlt: pushed along early: hdwy to ld 6f out: rdn and hdd over 1f out: sn outpcd: lost 2nd and wknd ins fnl f* **5/1**[2]

4110 **7** 1 **Mendacious Harpy (IRE)**[22] [6826] 5-9-5 **53**..................(p) LiamKeniry 7 42
(George Baker) *hld up in tch in midfield: effrt 2f out: no imp fr over 1f out: nvr trbld ldrs* **8/1**

0020 **8** 2 ¼ **Zeteah**[14] [7036] 6-8-12 **46**.. TomMarquand 8 30
(Tony Carroll) *s.i.s: hld up in last trio: effrt 2f out: no imp: n.d* **25/1**

6000 **9** 1 ¾ **Captain Gerald**[47] [6046] 3-8-13 **50**..............................(p) JimCrowley 11 29
(John Ryan) *led for 2f: chsd ldr tl 2f out: 3rd and outpcd over 1f out: wknd fnl f* **8/1**

000/ **10** 1 ½ **Frankie**[728] [7346] 5-9-3 **51**.. SeanLevey 1 27
(Jimmy Fox) *hld up in last trio: effrt and sme hdwy 2f out: no imp over 1f out: nvr trbld ldrs* **66/1**

6050 **11** 13 **Jackpot**[19] [6890] 6-8-12 **46** oh1......................................(p) MartinDwyer 12
(Brendan Powell) *chsd ldrs tl over 2f out: sn u.p and lost pl: bhd and eased ins fnl f* **20/1**

060- **12** 3 ¾ **Milly Royale**[320] [8095] 4-8-12 **46** oh1............................... KieranO'Neill 14
(Michael Blanshard) *midfield: rdn and lost pl over 2f out: bhd and eased ins fnl f* **100/1**

1m 40.01s (0.21) **Going Correction** +0.075s/f (Slow)
WFA 3 from 4yo+ 3lb **12** Ran SP% **114.2**
Speed ratings (Par 101): **101,99,97,97,96 94,93,90,89,87 74,70**
CSF £33.92 CT £111.91 TOTE £7.10: £2.00, £2.10, £1.40; EX 43.80 Trifecta £149.10.
Owner Mrs Jo Lambert **Bred** Juddmonte Farms Inc **Trained** Exning, Suffolk

FOCUS
An ordinary handicap. The winner has been rated to his best 2015 mark.

7427 32RED CASINO H'CAP (DIV II) 1m (P)
7:40 (7:41) (Class 6) (0-55,58) 3-Y-O+ **£2,264** (£673; £336; £168) **Stalls** Low

Form RPR

3311 **1** **Bazzat (IRE)**[6] [7282] 3-9-8 **58** 6ex...................................(p) JimCrowley 11 67
(John Ryan) *nt that wl away: hdwy to chse ldr after 2f tl led over 2f out: sn rdn: styd on wl and asserted ins fnl f: rdn out* **9/4**[1]

3066 **2** 1 ¼ **Henry Grace (IRE)**[53] [5823] 5-8-9 **47**...........................(b) HollieDoyle(5) 1 54
(Jimmy Fox) *in tch in midfield: hdwy over 2f out: rdn to chal 2f out tl no ex ins fnl f: outpcd fnl 100yds* **15/2**[2]

412 **3** 1 **Purple Party (IRE)**[19] [6890] 3-8-12 **51**........................ HectorCrouch(3) 6 55+
(Gary Moore) *hld up in tch towards rr: clsd and swtchd lft over 1f out: hdwy u.p 1f out: styd in wl ins fnl f: wnt 3rd last strides: nt rch ldrs* **9/4**[1]

4005 **4** hd **Lutine Charlie (IRE)**[5] [7298] 9-9-1 **48**..............................(p) TomQueally 8 52
(Emma Owen) *t.k.h: chsd ldrs: effrt over 1f out: styd on same pce ins fnl f: lost 3rd last strides* **16/1**

5500 **5** nk **Gavarnie Encore**[13] [7070] 4-9-3 **50**..................................[1] KieranO'Neill 9 55
(Michael Blanshard) *in tch in midfield: nt clr run and swtchd lft over 1f out: hdwy 1f out: styd on ins fnl f: nt rch ldrs* **12/1**[3]

0560 **6** 1 ¾ **Little Indian**[7] [7261] 6-9-7 **54**.. FrederikTylicki 4 53
(J R Jenkins) *in tch in midfield: rdn to chse ldrs 2f out: no imp over 1f out: wknd ins fnl f* **16/1**

0-60 **7** 1 ¾ **Pintle's Image**[96] [4289] 4-8-12 **45**.................................... WilliamCarson 2 40
(John Spearing) *chsd ldr for 2f: styd prom: rdn 2f out: unable qck over 1f out: wknd ins fnl f: eased towards fin* **66/1**

0350 **8** shd **West Leake (IRE)**[132] [3030] 10-9-6 **53**.............................. LiamKeniry 10 48
(Paul Burgoyne) *stdd s: hld up in last trio: shkn up and hdwy over 1f out: no hdwy 1f out: eased wl ins fnl f* **25/1**

0605 **9** 2 **Prince Of Time**[46] [6106] 4-8-5 **45**........................... CallumRodriguez(7) 14 35
(Richard Ford) *dwlt: hdwy to chse ldrs after 2f: rdn and unable qck over 1f out: wknd ins fnl f* **25/1**

-006 **10** ¾ **Camino**[31] [6587] 3-9-2 **52**.. JimmyFortune 7 39
(Henry Spiller) *hld up in last trio: swtchd rt and hdwy 2f out: no imp 1f out: wknd ins fnl f* **25/1**

4500 **11** hd **Play The Blues (IRE)**[90] [4505] 9-8-10 **46**.....................(t) RobHornby(3) 13 34
(Henry Tett) *stdd s: hld up in rr: swtchd lft over 2f out: rdn and no hdwy over 1f out: n.d* **50/1**

065 **12** 6 **Hodgkins Trust (IRE)**[45] [6140] 3-8-9 **45**.......................... TomMarquand 5 17
(Julia Feilden) *led: rdn and hdd 2f over 2f out: lost pl qckly over 1f out: wknd fnl f* **33/1**

0030 **13** 2 **Bennelong**[118] [3522] 10-9-7 **54**...(b) AmirQuinn 3 22
(Lee Carter) *in tch in midfield: lost pl and drvn 2f out: sn bhd* **16/1**

1m 40.26s (0.46) **Going Correction** +0.075s/f (Slow)
WFA 3 from 4yo+ 3lb **13** Ran SP% **116.6**
Speed ratings (Par 101): **100,98,97,97,97 95,93,93,91,90 90,84,82**
CSF £18.12 CT £43.50 TOTE £3.00: £1.20, £2.60, £1.30; EX 23.30 Trifecta £93.10.
Owner John Stocker **Bred** Ballyhane Stud **Trained** Newmarket, Suffolk

FOCUS
The slower of the two divisions by 0.25sec. Another pb from the winner.

7428 32RED H'CAP 1m (P)
8:10 (8:11) (Class 4) (0-85,85) 3-Y-O+ **£4,690** (£1,395; £697; £348) **Stalls** Low

Form RPR

0200 **1** **Bluegrass Blues (IRE)**[18] [6915] 6-9-4 **85**..................... HectorCrouch(3) 8 93+
(Heather Main) *hld up in tch in last trio: rdn and hdwy over 1f out: styd on wl ins fnl f to ld last strides* **11/1**

4461 **2** nk **Mountain Rescue (IRE)**[29] [6628] 4-9-7 **85**...................... TomMarquand 1 92
(Chris Wall) *chsd ldrs: rdn to chal 2f out: led ent fnl f: kpt on u.p: hdd last strides* **11/2**[3]

2311 **3** 1 **Cryptic (IRE)**[14] [7051] 3-8-12 **79**.. PatCosgrave 10 82
(Luca Cumani) *chsd ldng trio: rdn 2f out: hdwy u.p 1f out: kpt on wl ins fnl f* **11/4**[2]

0345 **4** 1 ¾ **Column**[25] [6736] 3-9-4 **85**.. FrederikTylicki 11 84
(James Fanshawe) *chsd ldr tl 2f out: kpt on same pce u.p fr over 1f out* **9/4**[1]

1030 **5** ½ **Frozen Force (IRE)**[34] [6484] 3-9-1 **82**............................(v) JimCrowley 9 80
(Amanda Perrett) *led: rdn and jnd 2f out: drvn and hdd ent fnl f: lost 2nd 100yds out: wknd towards fin* **8/1**

4250 **6** 1 **Franco's Secret**[59] [5650] 5-9-4 **82**..............................(p) CharlesBishop 6 78
(Peter Hedger) *dwlt: hld up in tch in last trio: effrt on inner 2f out: kpt on same pce and no imp ins fnl f* **10/1**

0000 **7** ½ **Prince Of Paris**[29] [6628] 4-8-13 **77**.................................... DaneO'Neill 2 72
(Roger Ingram) *dwlt: in tch in midfield: effrt 2f out: kpt on same pce ins fnl f* **33/1**

4400 **8** 1 ¾ **Dark Ocean (IRE)**[52] [5886] 6-9-1 **79**.................................... GrahamLee 3 70
(Jedd O'Keeffe) *in tch in midfield: effrt ent fnl 2f: lost pl and btn over 1f out: wknd ins fnl f* **20/1**

04-2 **9** 1 ¼ **Best Example (USA)**[274] [240] 4-9-4 **85**..................... ShelleyBirkett(3) 7 73
(Julia Feilden) *hld up in last pair: rdn wl over 1f out: no hdwy: nvr trbld ldrs* **20/1**

4000 **10** 1 ¾ **Stylistik**[8] [7220] 3-8-8 **75**.. KieranO'Neill 5 58
(Luke Dace) *in tch in midfield: rdn 3f out: lost pl and bhd 2f out: n.d after* **66/1**

1m 38.52s (-1.28) **Going Correction** +0.075s/f (Slow)
WFA 3 from 4yo+ 3lb **10** Ran SP% **115.3**
Speed ratings (Par 105): **109,108,107,105,105 104,103,102,100,99**
CSF £66.50 CT £220.00 TOTE £15.90: £3.30, £1.80, £1.40; EX 80.50 Trifecta £489.50.
Owner Marcus Scott Russell & Sam Thomasson **Bred** Yeomanstown Stud **Trained** Kingston Lisle, Oxon

FOCUS
Not a bad handicap, and a good performance from the winner to get up from where he raced. This has been rated around the 2nd and 3rd.

7429 32RED ON THE APP STORE H'CAP 1m 3f (P)
8:40 (8:42) (Class 5) (0-70,70) 3-Y-O+ **£2,911** (£866; £432; £216) **Stalls** Low

Form RPR

3553 **1** **Ride The Lightning**[17] 6965 3-9-3 **70**................................ JimCrowley 3 77+
(Archie Watson) *chsd ldr tl rdn to ld 2f out: styd on wl fnl f: rdn out* **9/4**[1]

-026 **2** *1 ¼* **Dream Ruler**[53] 5824 5-9-6 **67**........................(tp) GeorgeBaker 8 72
(Jeremy Gask) *chsd ldng trio: effrt 2f out: rdn and no imp over 1f out: hdwy to chse wnr 100yds out: no imp* **8/1**

246 **3** *¾* **Rahmah (IRE)**[13] 7076 4-9-9 **70**.................................... FrederikTylicki 2 74
(Geoffrey Deacon) *chsd ldrs: effrt u.p over 1f out: chsd wnr 1f out: no imp: lost 2nd and one pce fnl 100yds* **20/1**

3154 **4** *½* **Mystikana**[6] 7274 3-9-2 **69**..(b) JimmyFortune 9 72+
(Marcus Tregoning) *hld up in midfield: effrt u.p over 1f out: hdwy 1f out: styd on wl ins fnl f: nt rch ldrs* **7/2**[2]

5505 **5** *½* **Top Diktat**[19] 6889 8-9-5 **69**...................................... HectorCrouch(3) 13 71
(Gary Moore) *in tch in midfield: swtchd lft and effrt jst over 2f out: kpt on u.p ins fnl f* **6/1**[3]

0-35 **6** *nk* **The Ginger Berry**[51] 5929 6-9-0 **66**........................ GeorgeWood(5) 6 67
(Dr Jon Scargill) *t.k.h: hld up in tch in midfield: swtchd rt and hdwy on inner 2f out: chsd ldrs and drvn 1f out: kpt on same pce ins fnl f* **20/1**

1530 **7** *½* **Trending (IRE)**[53] 5823 7-9-1 **67**..........................(t) MitchGodwin(5) 4 67
(Jeremy Gask) *wl in tch in midfield: swtchd rt and effrt 2f out: drvn and styd on same pce fr over 1f out* **25/1**

1003 **8** *nk* **Longside**[19] 6892 4-9-7 **68**... ThomasBrown 1 68
(James Eustace) *led: rdn and hdd 2f out: unable qck over 1f out: lost 2nd and wknd fnl 100yds* **25/1**

5160 **9** *¾* **Loving Your Work**[25] 6737 5-9-7 **68**............................ PatCosgrave 11 68
(Ken Cunningham-Brown) *hld up in tch in midfield: clsd and nt clr run over 1f out: swtchd lft and hdwy ent fnl f: nt clr run again and no hdwy ins fnl f: eased towards fin* **28/1**

1530 **10** *1 ¼* **Choral Festival**[20] 6876 10-9-7 **68**............................... WilliamCarson 5 66
(John Bridger) *in tch in midfield: effrt 2f out: nt clr run: hmpd and swtchd lft over 1f out: no imp: wknd ins fnl f* **50/1**

1306 **11** *1 ¾* **Bamako Du Chatelet (FR)**[89] 4551 5-9-4 **65**........... TomMarquand 10 58
(Ian Williams) *hld up in tch in last quartet: effrt 2f out: no imp over 1f out: wknd ins fnl f* **20/1**

6635 **12** *3 ½* **Perfect Rhythm**[52] 5895 5-8-13 **65**.......................... CharlieBennett(5) 14 52
(Patrick Chamings) *stdd s: hld up in tch in last quartet: effrt 2f out: sn btn* **40/1**

6656 **13** *1 ¼* **Roy Rocket (FR)**[19] 6892 6-9-4 **68**.......................... ShelleyBirkett(3) 12 53
(John Berry) *stdd s: hld up in rr: swtchd lft and effrt over 2f out: no hdwy: n.d* **66/1**

6555 **14** *16* **Versant**[14] 7053 4-9-7 **68**..(t) DaneO'Neill 7 24
(Seamus Durack) *stdd s: plld hrd: hld up in tch in last quartet: effrt over 2f out: sn btn: bhd and eased ins fnl f* **7/1**

2m 22.37s (0.47) **Going Correction** +0.075s/f (Slow)
WFA 3 from 4yo+ 6lb **14** Ran SP% **122.2**
Speed ratings (Par 103): **101,100,99,99,98 98,98,98,97,96 95,92,91,80**
CSF £18.22 CT £301.75 TOTE £3.10: £1.30, £2.70, £5.20; EX 22.30 Trifecta £200.00.
Owner The Ride The Lightning Partnership **Bred** Usk Valley Stud **Trained** Upper Lambourn, West Berks
■ Stewards' Enquiry : Mitch Godwin caution: careless riding

FOCUS
The pace steadied down the back and it didn't hurt to be prominent here, with the first three home always in the first four. The level is set around the placed horses.

7430 100% PROFIT BOOST AT 32REDSPORT.COM H'CAP 6f (P)
9:10 (9:12) (Class 5) (0-70,70) 3-Y-O+ **£2,911** (£866; £432; £216) **Stalls** Low

Form RPR

-221 **1** **Roman Holiday (IRE)**[35] 6459 3-9-2 **69**..................(p) FrederikTylicki 3 81+
(Ed Vaughan) *chsd ldrs: rdn to ld ent fnl f: r.o wl and drew clr ins fnl f: comf* **7/2**[2]

1260 **2** *2 ½* **For Ayman**[6] 7267 5-8-9 **68**..(t) SeanMooney(7) 2 72
(Joseph Tuite) *hld up in tch in midfield: swtchd rt and hdwy over 1f out: chsd wnr ins fnl f: no imp* **5/1**[3]

2020 **3** *shd* **Straits Of Malacca**[27] 6668 5-9-4 **70**......................(p) JimCrowley 6 74
(Simon Dow) *chsd ldrs: effrt over 1f out: no threat to wnr but kpt on ins fnl f* **11/2**

2636 **4** *½* **Doctor Parkes**[34] 6479 10-9-4 **70**.................................. PatCosgrave 12 72
(Stuart Williams) *hld up in tch in midfield: rdn and hdwy over 1f out: styd on ins fnl f* **10/1**

6306 **5** *1 ½* **Heartsong (IRE)**[74] 5103 7-9-2 **68**......................... MichaelJMMurphy 1 65
(John Gallagher) *led: rdn 2f out: hdd ent fnl f: sn outpcd: lost 2nd and wknd ins fnl f* **20/1**

0336 **6** *nk* **Kinglami**[27] 6668 7-8-13 **70**.....................................(p) MitchGodwin(5) 11 66
(John O'Shea) *hld in tch in last trio: rdn and hdwy over 1f out: no imp and kpt on same pce ins fnl f* **14/1**

3604 **7** *shd* **Classic Pursuit**[27] 6680 5-9-3 **69**............................(p) FergusSweeney 7 65
(Ivan Furtado) *hld up in tch: effrt 2f out: no imp over 1f out: kpt on same pce ins fnl f* **10/1**

0-50 **8** *½* **Caius College Girl (IRE)**[35] 6442 4-8-11 **68**........... CharlieBennett(5) 5 62
(Natalie Lloyd-Beavis) *in tch in midfield: effrt towards inner 2f out: no imp over 1f out: styd on same pce fnl f* **66/1**

0205 **9** *shd* **Rigolleto (IRE)**[22] 6831 8-8-9 **68**.................................... JoshuaBryan(7) 9 62
(Anabel K Murphy) *chsd ldr: rdn and ev ch 2f out tl unable qck ent fnl f: wknd ins fnl f* **16/1**

6000 **10** *4* **Musical Taste**[89] 4563 3-8-12 **70**.............................. PaddyBradley(5) 10 51
(Pat Phelan) *in tch in last trio: effrt u.p 2f out: no imp over 1f out: wknd ins fnl f* **100/1**

6351 **11** *hd* **He's My Boy (IRE)**[13] 7069 5-9-4 **70**..............................(v) TomQueally 8 51+
(James Fanshawe) *restless in stalls: s.i.s: bhd: effrt 2f out: no imp and wl hld whn edgd rt ins fnl f* **3/1**[1]

1m 12.96s (-0.14) **Going Correction** +0.075s/f (Slow)
WFA 3 from 4yo+ 1lb **11** Ran SP% **117.2**
Speed ratings (Par 103): **103,99,99,98,96 96,96,95,95,90 89**
CSF £21.12 CT £95.03 TOTE £3.70: £1.80, £2.10, £2.30; EX 21.20 Trifecta £169.50.
Owner Bloomsbury Stud **Bred** Bloomsbury Stud **Trained** Newmarket, Suffolk

FOCUS
A modest sprint won by the least-exposed runner in the line-up. Straightforward form rated around the 2nd and 3rd.
T/Plt: £33.00 to a £1 stake. Pool: £77,218.50 - 1704.34 winning units. T/Qpdt: £23.80 to a £1 stake. Pool: £8,016.18 - 248.85 winning units. **Steve Payne**

7380 NEWCASTLE (A.W) (L-H)
Tuesday, October 18

OFFICIAL GOING: Tapeta: standard
Wind: Almost nil Weather: Cloudy

7431 PARKLANDS MINI GOLF TEAM BUILDING EVENTS MAIDEN AUCTION STKS 1m 5y (Tp)
2:00 (2:00) (Class 6) 2-Y-O **£2,587** (£770; £384; £192) **Stalls** Centre

Form RPR

4 **1** **Ahlan Bil Zain (FR)**[15] 7012 2-9-5 0................................ OisinMurphy 5 75
(David Simcock) *t.k.h: trckd ldrs: hdwy to ld over 1f out: drvn and kpt on wl fnl f* **11/8**[1]

3 **2** *nk* **Mister Manduro (FR)**[39] 6297 2-9-5 0.............................. JoeFanning 7 74
(Mark Johnston) *led at ordinary gallop: rdn and hdd over 1f out: rallied: kpt on: hld nr fin* **6/4**[2]

0 **3** *2 ¼* **Somnambulist**[99] 4188 2-9-5 0..[1] JasonHart 2 69
(Keith Dalgleish) *taken early to post: sn pressing ldr: rdn over 2f out: lost 2nd over 1f out: kpt on same pce fnl f* **8/1**[3]

4 *4* **Sabador (FR)** 2-9-5 0.. HarryBentley 4 60
(Ed Walker) *s.i.s: hld up in tch: smooth hdwy on outside over 3f out: effrt and rdn 2f out: outpcd fnl f* **9/1**

00 **5** *¾* **Siyahamba (IRE)**[18] 6924 2-9-5 0................................. ConnorBeasley 3 59
(Bryan Smart) *trckd ldrs: rdn over 2f out: wknd fr over 1f out* **100/1**

0 **6** *1* **Dirty Randy (IRE)**[7] 7247 2-9-0 0......................... ShirleyTeasdale(5) 6 56
(Keith Dalgleish) *hld up in tch: rdn and outpcd over 2f out: btn over 1f out* **50/1**

0506 **7** *1* **Mystic Maeve (IRE)**[7] 7244 2-9-0 60...........................[1] TonyHamilton 8 49
(Roger Fell) *prom: drvn along over 2f out: wknd over 1f out* **22/1**

1m 40.2s (1.60) **Going Correction** -0.025s/f (Stan) **7** Ran SP% **110.5**
Speed ratings (Par 93): **91,90,88,84,83 82,81**
CSF £3.39 TOTE £2.10: £1.30, £1.20; EX 4.30 Trifecta £14.00.
Owner Ahmad Abdulla Al Shaikh **Bred** E A R L Haras Saint James **Trained** Newmarket, Suffolk

FOCUS
A fair maiden, in which the pace was steady, and it proved a lively betting heat.

7432 @NEWCASTLERACES FOLLOW US ON TWITTER MAIDEN STKS 7f 14y (Tp)
2:30 (2:30) (Class 5) 2-Y-O **£3,557** (£1,058; £529; £264) **Stalls** Centre

Form RPR

26 **1** **Commander Cole**[20] 6873 2-9-5 0.................................[1] OisinMurphy 8 90+
(Saeed bin Suroor) *prom: hdwy to ld 2f out: drvn clr appr fnl f: edgd lft: kpt on strly: eased towards fin* **7/2**[3]

4 **2** *6* **Re Run (IRE)**[32] 6534 2-9-5 0.. TonyHamilton 5 74+
(Richard Fahey) *hld up: stdy hdwy over 2f out: drvn and swtchd rt over 1f out: chsd (clr) wnr ins fnl f: kpt on: no imp* **3/1**[2]

232 **3** *2* **Midaawi (IRE)**[12] 7090 2-9-5 73.. ShaneGray 2 69
(Kevin Ryan) *t.k.h early: led: rdn and hdd 2f out: chsd wnr to ins fnl f: no ex* **8/1**

3 **4** *3 ½* **Anythingtoday (IRE)**[20] 6880 2-9-5 0....................... GrahamGibbons 11 60
(Hugo Palmer) *sn trcking ldr: effrt and disp 2nd pl over 1f out to ins fnl f: wknd last 75yds* **7/4**[1]

5 *shd* **Alfred Richardson** 2-9-5 0.. SamJames 6 60+
(John Davies) *s.i.s: hld up: hdwy and green over 1f out: kpt on ins fnl f: no imp* **150/1**

5 **6** *½* **Call Me Grumpy (IRE)**[13] 7064 2-9-5 0........................ HarryBentley 3 59
(Roger Varian) *hld up: stdy hdwy to chse ldrs over 2f out: rdn and edgd lft over 1f out: wknd ins fnl f* **11/2**

7 *5* **Titi Makfi** 2-9-0 0... JoeFanning 10 41
(Mark Johnston) *prom: drvn along over 2f out: wknd wl over 1f out* **20/1**

8 *shd* **You Look Different** 2-9-0 0... CamHardie 1 41
(Antony Brittain) *s.i.s: hld up: rdn over 2f out: wknd over 1f out* **100/1**

0 **9** *nk* **Shackles**[19] 6904 2-9-5 0... PJMcDonald 4 45
(Alistair Whillans) *hld up: drvn and struggling over 2f out: sn btn* **100/1**

0 **10** *4 ½* **American Craftsman (IRE)**[73] 5150 2-9-5 0.............. PaulMulrennan 9 34
(Jedd O'Keeffe) *chsd ldrs: drvn over 3f out: wknd over 2f out* **100/1**

0 **11** *1 ¾* **Balance Sheet (IRE)**[50] 5966 2-9-5 0........................... JackGarritty 7 30
(Jedd O'Keeffe) *cl up tl rdn and struggling fr 3f out* **100/1**

1m 25.5s (-0.70) **Going Correction** -0.025s/f (Stan) **11** Ran SP% **119.5**
Speed ratings (Par 95): **103,96,93,89,89 89,83,83,83,77 75**
CSF £14.58 TOTE £6.70: £1.50, £1.90, £2.80; EX 17.60 Trifecta £73.70.
Owner Godolphin **Bred** Usk Valley Stud **Trained** Newmarket, Suffolk
■ Stewards' Enquiry : Cam Hardie caution: careless riding

FOCUS
An interesting maiden with the future in mind and the winner won as he pleased.

7433 PARKLANDS DRIVING RANGE H'CAP (DIV I) 6f (Tp)
3:00 (3:00) (Class 4) (0-80,83) 3-Y-O+ **£5,175** (£1,540; £769; £384) **Stalls** Centre

Form RPR

4320 **1** **Jaywalker (IRE)**[24] 6793 5-9-6 **79**.................................. PJMcDonald 11 89
(Rebecca Bastiman) *mde all: drvn along wl over 1f out: hld on wl fnl f* **16/1**

3000 **2** *½* **Soul Brother (IRE)**[11] 7112 5-9-2 **75**....................(b) GrahamGibbons 7 83
(Tim Easterby) *hld up: hdwy over 1f out: rdn to chse wnr ins fnl f: kpt on: hld towards fin* **40/1**

6642 **3** *½* **Manatee Bay**[4] 7324 6-9-1 **74**.......................................(v) BarryMcHugh 4 81
(David Nicholls) *hld up: hdwy to press wnr over 1f out to ins fnl f: sn rdn and no ex* **3/1**[1]

0063 **4** *2 ¾* **Funding Deficit (IRE)**[46] 6072 6-9-3 **76**........................ OisinMurphy 5 74
(Jim Goldie) *hld up: pushed along and hdwy over 1f out: kpt on fnl f: no imp* **14/1**

604 **5** *1 ½* **Dandyleekie (IRE)**[12] 7094 4-9-7 **80**......................... DanielTudhope 3 73
(David O'Meara) *hld up: pushed along over 2f out: hdwy over 1f out: kpt on fnl f: no imp* **9/2**[2]

4014 **6** *shd* **Sophisticated Heir (IRE)**[24] 6766 6-9-4 **77**..............(b) JoeFanning 10 70
(Michael Herrington) *chsd ldrs: rdn over 2f out: effrt over 1f out: wknd ins fnl f* **5/1**[3]

3142 **7** *1* **Tanasoq (IRE)**[34] 6492 3-9-5 **79**...................................[1] PaulMulrennan 1 69
(Owen Burrows) *w wnr: rdn over 2f out: wknd fnl f* **11/2**

0640 **8** *1* **Kommander Kirkup**[12] 7094 5-9-2 **75**...........................(p) SamJames 6 61
(John Davies) *chsd ldrs: drvn over 2f out: wknd over 1f out* **25/1**

5130 **9** *½* **War Department (IRE)**[23] 6810 3-9-1 **80**...........(v) ShirleyTeasdale(5) 9 65
(Keith Dalgleish) *s.i.s: hld up: effrt over 2f out: outpcd over 1f out* **7/1**

00 **10** *5* **Willbeme**[11] 7112 8-9-1 **77**.. NathanEvans(3) 12 46
(Neville Bycroft) *chsd ldrs tl rdn and wknd 2f out* **25/1**

-540 **11** *2 1/4* **Shootingsta (IRE)**[80] 4893 4-9-6 **79**..........................(p) ConnorBeasley 2 41
(Bryan Smart) *hld up in tch: rdn and hung lft over 2f out: sn wknd* **10/1**

1m 11.91s (-0.59) **Going Correction** -0.025s/f (Stan)
WFA 3 from 4yo+ 1lb **11** Ran SP% **119.5**
Speed ratings (Par 105): **102,101,100,97,95 94,93,92,91,84 81**
CSF £543.23 CT £2470.50 TOTE £23.70: £6.00, £10.30, £1.30; EX 503.00 Trifecta £3874.70.
Owner Ms M Austerfield **Bred** Kilfrush Stud **Trained** Cowthorpe, N Yorks

FOCUS
A decent, competitive looking sprint handicap and the winner was up there throughout. Straightforward form, rated around the 3rd.

7434 PARKLANDS DRIVING RANGE H'CAP (DIV II) 6f (Tp)
3:30 (3:30) (Class 4) (0-80,80) 3-Y-O+ **£5,175** (£1,540; £769; £384) **Stalls** Centre

Form RPR
2-14 **1** **Spanish City**[115] 3644 3-9-2 **76**.. HarryBentley 9 90+
(Roger Varian) *hld up: nt clr run briefly over 1f out: shkn up and qcknd to ld ins fnl f: nudged out: comf* **7/2**[1]

1050 **2** *nk* **Buccaneers Vault (IRE)**[18] 6926 4-9-4 **77**...............(p) ConnorBeasley 1 87
(Michael Dods) *prom: smooth hdwy to ld over 1f out: sn rdn: hdd ins fnl f: kpt on but comf hld by wnr* **11/1**

0400 **3** *4* **Duke Cosimo**[12] 7094 6-9-7 **80**....................................... PJMcDonald 11 77
(Michael Herrington) *dwlt: hld up: hdwy to trck ldrs over 1f out: rdn and outpcd by first two ins fnl f* **9/2**[2]

2140 **4** *3/4* **Master Bond**[32] 6537 7-9-5 **78**....................................... DanielTudhope 8 73
(David O'Meara) *prom: hdwy and ev ch over 1f out: drvn and outpcd ins fnl f* **8/1**

0550 **5** *1* **Personal Touch**[11] 7112 7-9-1 **77**.......................... AlistairRawlinson(3) 6 69
(Michael Appleby) *pressed ldr: led over 2f out to over 1f out: sn no ex* **22/1**

0160 **6** *nse* **Money Team (IRE)**[26] 6714 5-9-1 **79**.............................. CliffordLee(5) 4 70
(David Barron) *hld up: rdn and effrt over 1f out: no imp fnl f* **5/1**[3]

3450 **7** *3/4* **David's Duchess (IRE)**[17] 6946 3-8-10 **75**......... AdamMcNamara(5) 10 64
(Richard Fahey) *hld up in tch: hdwy and rdn over 1f out: hmpd ins fnl f: sn btn* **10/1**

4502 **8** *2 3/4* **Pearl Acclaim (IRE)**[8] 7206 6-9-2 **75**..........................(p) BarryMcHugh 3 55
(David Nicholls) *plld hrd: chsd ldrs: rdn and outpcd whn hmpd over 1f out: sn btn* **5/1**[3]

4410 **9** *3 3/4* **Honeysuckle Lil (IRE)**[11] 7126 4-9-6 **79**..........................(p) JasonHart 2 47
(Tim Easterby) *led to over 2f out: rdn and wknd over 1f out* **12/1**

1m 11.27s (-1.23) **Going Correction** -0.025s/f (Stan)
WFA 3 from 4yo+ 1lb **9** Ran SP% **114.3**
Speed ratings (Par 105): **107,106,101,100,98 98,97,94,89**
CSF £42.44 CT £176.11 TOTE £4.50: £1.70, £4.10, £1.70; EX 46.50 Trifecta £321.30.
Owner Merry Fox Stud Limited **Bred** Merry Fox Stud Limited **Trained** Newmarket, Suffolk
■ Stewards' Enquiry : Harry Bentley two-day ban: careless riding (Nov 1-2)

FOCUS
The second division of a decent handicap was run in a marginally quicker time than the first leg. The unexposed winner was quite impressive in overcoming trouble and there was a pb from the 2nd.

7435 ATR H'CAP 1m 2f 42y (Tp)
4:00 (4:00) (Class 5) (0-70,70) 3-Y-O+ **£3,557** (£1,058; £529; £264) **Stalls** High

Form RPR
61 **1** **Bollihope**[18] 6921 4-9-3 **63**... ConnorBeasley 12 70
(Richard Guest) *hld up on outside: stdy hdwy over 2f out: rdn to ld over 1f out: kpt on wl fnl f* **11/4**[1]

6325 **2** *1/2* **Shadow Spirit**[21] 6856 3-8-12 **70**.............................. LewisEdmunds(7) 7 76
(Iain Jardine) *hld up midfield: effrt and pushed along over 1f out: rdn to chse wnr ins fnl f: kpt on* **11/2**[2]

20 **3** *3/4* **Henpecked**[35] 6432 6-9-5 **70**..................................(p) GarryWhillans(5) 10 74
(Alistair Whillans) *t.k.h: hld up: stdy hdwy whn nt clr run over 2f out: drvn over 1f out: angled rt and kpt on fnl f: nrst fin* **12/1**

566 **4** *3/4* **Maulesden May (IRE)**[32] 6541 3-9-3 **68**..........................[1] PhillipMakin 6 71
(Keith Dalgleish) *pressed ldr: led gng wl 3f out: rdn and hdd over 1f out: chsd wnr to ins fnl f: one pce* **12/1**

5103 **5** *hd* **The Lynch Man**[41] 6221 3-9-2 **67**..................................(v) PJMcDonald 5 69
(John Quinn) *tk keen hold: trckd ldrs: hdwy and ev ch over 1f out: no ex ins fnl f* **6/1**[3]

300 **6** *shd* **Pickett's Charge**[28] 6643 3-9-2 **67**.................................. BarryMcHugh 9 69
(Tony Coyle) *hld up midfield: stdy hdwy over 2f out: rdn and ev ch over 1f out: no ex ins fnl f* **16/1**

300 **7** *shd* **Auxiliary**[13] 7076 3-9-4 **69**..(p) DanielTudhope 13 71
(Patrick Holmes) *hld up: stdy hdwy over 2f out: rdn over 1f out: swtchd lft ins fnl f: kpt on* **12/1**

2-00 **8** *1 1/4* **Thermal Column (IRE)**[18] 6921 4-8-13 **62**......... AlistairRawlinson(3) 11 61
(Michael Appleby) *hld up in tch: stdy hdwy to trck ldrs over 2f out: rdn over 1f out: no ex ins fnl f* **12/1**

3520 **9** *nk* **Hussar Ballad (USA)**[53] 5841 7-9-7 **67**............................ CamHardie 14 66
(Antony Brittain) *hld up: pushed along and effrt 2f out: kpt on fnl f: nvr able to chal* **25/1**

3206 **10** *3 3/4* **Tiga Tuan (FR)**[25] 6742 3-8-11 **62**...................................... ShaneGray 2 53
(Kevin Ryan) *t.k.h: trckd ldrs: rdn over 2f out: wknd over 1f out* **20/1**

11 *1 3/4* **Bromance**[52] 5903 3-9-1 **66**.. TomEaves 1 54
(Peter Niven) *hld up midfield: rdn over 2f out: wknd over 1f out* **10/1**

2055 **12** *1 1/2* **Fray**[33] 6504 5-9-9 **69**.. PaulMulrennan 4 54
(Jim Goldie) *s.i.s: hld up: rdn and outpcd over 2f out: sn btn* **11/1**

4000 **13** *6* **Royal Normandy**[10] 7141 4-9-8 **68**....................................(p) BenCurtis 3 41
(Roger Fell) *led to 3f out: rallied: rdn and wknd over 1f out* **28/1**

2m 10.65s (0.25) **Going Correction** +0.075s/f (Slow)
WFA 3 from 4yo+ 5lb **13** Ran SP% **122.5**
Speed ratings (Par 103): **102,101,101,100,100 100,100,99,98,95 94,93,88**
CSF £16.61 CT £162.67 TOTE £2.80: £1.10, £2.70, £3.80; EX 15.80 Trifecta £71.70.
Owner Alfa Site Services Ltd **Bred** Minster Stud And Mrs H Dalgety **Trained** Ingmanthorpe, W Yorks

FOCUS
An ordinary handicap and they finished in a bit of a heap.

7436 ATR CLASSIFIED STKS 1m 5y (Tp)
4:30 (4:30) (Class 5) 3-Y-O+ **£2,911** (£866; £432; £216) **Stalls** Centre

Form RPR
5243 **1** **Southern Gailes (IRE)**[38] 6344 3-8-11 75............(t) JordanVaughan(5) 9 83
(K R Burke) *cl up stands' side gp: hdwy and overall ldr over 2f out: rdn and drifted lft to far side ins fnl f: kpt on wl* **9/2**[2]

0420 **2** *1 1/2* **Green Howard**[8] 7227 8-9-5 72....................................... DanielTudhope 2 81
(Rebecca Bastiman) *hld up far side gp: effrt and hdwy over 1f out: chsd wnr ins fnl f: kpt on* **14/1**

1426 **3** *3/4* **Normandy Knight**[17] 6956 4-9-5 74.............................. TonyHamilton 13 79
(Richard Fahey) *trckd ldrs stands' side: smooth hdwy 2f out: rdn and carried lft over 1f out: kpt on ins fnl f* **10/1**

0000 **4** *hd* **Magic City (IRE)**[11] 7126 7-9-2 75................................ NathanEvans(3) 6 78
(Michael Easterby) *cl up far side gp: rdn and sltly outpcd over 2f out: rallied appr fnl f: one pce last 100yds* **13/2**[3]

0422 **5** *1* **So It's War (FR)**[10] 7141 5-9-5 72...............................(p) ConnorBeasley 1 76
(Keith Dalgleish) *hld up in tch far side gp: hdwy and cl up over 1f out: drvn and no ex ins fnl f* **9/2**[2]

0060 **6** *3/4* **Ingleby Angel (IRE)**[17] 6956 7-9-5 75........................ GrahamGibbons 12 74
(Colin Teague) *cl up nr side gp: drvn over 2f out: rallied: edgd lft over 1f out: outpcd ins fnl f* **20/1**

5253 **7** *1 3/4* **Weather Front (USA)**[10] 7141 3-9-2 74.......................... DavidNolan 10 69
(Karen McLintock) *slowly away: hld up nr side gp: rdn over 2f out: hdwy over 1f out: no imp fnl f* **4/1**[1]

6000 **8** *1/2* **Karnage (IRE)**[14] 7051 4-9-5 71....................................(b) OisinMurphy 5 69
(Daniel Kubler) *hld up far side gp: drvn and outpcd over 2f out: kpt on fnl f: no imp* **20/1**

6122 **9** *1 1/4* **Dark Wonder (IRE)**[13] 7076 4-9-5 72..................................(p) TomEaves 4 69+
(Ivan Furtado) *led far side gp tl wnr wnt on over 2f out: rdn and outpcd whn hmpd over 1f out: sn btn* **12/1**

1215 **10** *4 1/2* **Our Boy Jack (IRE)**[33] 6500 7-9-0 75................... AdamMcNamara(5) 3 56
(Richard Fahey) *chsd ldrs in far side gp: drvn along and outpcd over 2f out: btn over 1f out* **12/1**

0040 **11** *7* **Spryt (IRE)**[13] 7066 4-9-5 74...(v) PaulMulrennan 11 40
(Conor Dore) *chsd ldrs in nr side of gp: drvn and outpcd over 2f out: sn wknd* **40/1**

2420 **12** *3 1/4* **Ralphy Boy (IRE)**[15] 7007 7-9-5 75.............................. PJMcDonald 7 32
(Alistair Whillans) *led nr side gp to over 2f out: sn rdn and wknd* **22/1**

5146 **13** *2 3/4* **Clayton Hall (IRE)**[88] 4607 3-9-2 75.............................. BarryMcHugh 8 25
(John Wainwright) *cl up far side gp: drvn over 3f out: struggling fnl 2f* **50/1**

1m 39.5s (0.90) **Going Correction** -0.025s/f (Stan)
WFA 3 from 4yo+ 3lb **13** Ran SP% **119.1**
Speed ratings (Par 103): **94,92,91,91,90 89,88,87,86,81 74,71,68**
CSF £60.61 TOTE £6.10: £1.80, £5.00, £3.20; EX 84.90 Trifecta £993.20.
Owner PalatinateRacing Chandler Westwood Bryce **Bred** Sean Finnegan **Trained** Middleham Moor, N Yorks
■ Stewards' Enquiry : Jordan Vaughan caution: careless riding

FOCUS
Straightforward form; a pb from the winner, with the level set around the 3rd and 5th.

7437 ATTHERACES.COM FILLIES' H'CAP 5f (Tp)
5:00 (5:02) (Class 5) (0-75,79) 3-Y-O+ **£3,557** (£1,058; £529; £264) **Stalls** Centre

Form RPR
3043 **1** **Rural Celebration**[3] 7364 5-9-7 **74**............................(v) DanielTudhope 7 87
(David O'Meara) *pressed ldr in centre of gp: rdn to ld over 1f out: kpt on strly to draw clr ins fnl f* **15/8**[1]

2611 **2** *3* **Showdaisy**[7] 7252 3-9-12 **79** 6ex....................................(p) PhillipMakin 11 83
(Keith Dalgleish) *led on nr side of gp: rdn and hdd over 1f out: kpt on same pce ins fnl f* **10/3**[2]

4100 **3** *1 1/4* **Sarabi**[33] 6506 3-9-2 **69**...[1] BenCurtis 8 68
(Scott Dixon) *prom on nr side of gp: drvn along 1/2-way: effrt over 1 out: kpt on same pce ins fnl f* **20/1**

512 **4** *1* **Taffetta**[6] 7290 4-8-10 **63**.. BarryMcHugh 9 57
(Tony Coyle) *sn pushed along in rr on nr side of gp: drvn 1/2-way: hdwy wl over 1f out: kpt on fnl f: no imp* **8/1**

6355 **5** *1 3/4* **Princess Momoka**[34] 6487 3-8-12 **65**.............................. HarryBentley 5 54
(Roger Varian) *hld up in tch in centre of gp: effrt and rdn wl over 1f out: no imp fnl f* **13/2**[3]

0000 **6** *1/2* **Thorntoun Lady (USA)**[23] 6809 6-8-12 **65**.................. OisinMurphy 10 51
(Jim Goldie) *dwlt: outpcd and bhd on nr side of gp: hdwy over 1f out: kpt on fnl f: nvr able to chal* **25/1**

6060 **7** *2* **Misu Mac**[27] 6685 6-8-6 **62**.. NathanEvans(3) 3 41
(Neville Bycroft) *bhd and sn outpcd in centre of gp: struggling 1/2-way: sme late hdwy: nvr on terms* **40/1**

-660 **8** *1/2* **Harmonic Wave (IRE)**[23] 6809 3-9-3 **70**........................ PJMcDonald 2 48
(Rebecca Menzies) *hld up towards far side of gp: rdn along and hdwy over 1f out: wknd ins fnl f* **33/1**

4-00 **9** *nk* **Richter Scale (IRE)**[70] 5274 3-9-5 **72**........................ PaulMulrennan 6 49
(Michael Dods) *cl up in centre of gp: rdn over 2f out: wknd over 1f out* **14/1**

0056 **10** *2 1/4* **Ayresome Angel**[23] 6809 3-9-3 **70**.............................(p) ConnorBeasley 4 39
(Bryan Smart) *in tch on far side of gp: drvn over 2f out: sn wknd* **11/1**

5460 **11** *1 1/4* **Crombay (IRE)**[17] 6958 3-8-12 **65**.. JasonHart 1 30
(Tim Easterby) *hld up on far side of gp: rdn and hung lft over 2f out: sn wknd* **25/1**

58.51s (-0.99) **Going Correction** -0.025s/f (Stan) **11** Ran SP% **115.1**
Speed ratings (Par 100): **106,101,99,97,94 94,90,90,89,85 83**
CSF £6.95 CT £90.81 TOTE £2.10: £1.10, £1.70, £4.80; EX 8.90 Trifecta £113.30.
Owner Hambleton Racing Ltd - Two Chances **Bred** J A And M A Knox **Trained** Upper Helmsley, N Yorks

FOCUS
The two market leaders came to the fore in a fair sprint handicap and this could prove a bit better than it has been rated.

7438 ATTHERACES VIRGIN 535 APPRENTICE H'CAP 1m 4f 98y (Tp)
5:30 (5:30) (Class 6) (0-60,58) 3-Y-O+ **£2,264** (£673; £336; £168) **Stalls** High

Form RPR
0-05 **1** **Bassett Bleu**[17] 6966 3-7-13 **45**..............................(b) JamieGormley(7) 9 49
(Iain Jardine) *hld up on outside: hdwy over 2f out: rdn to ld ins fnl f: edgd lft and kpt on wl cl home* **14/1**

0460 **2** *3/4* **Sebastian's Wish (IRE)**[11] 7105 3-8-13 **52**............(b[1]) LewisEdmunds 6 55
(Richard Whitaker) *t.k.h: led at modest gallop: rdn and hrd pressed fr 2f out: hdd ins fnl f: edgd rt: kpt on* **11/2**[2]

5000 **3** *3/4* **Glasgon**[48] 6029 6-9-4 **50**..[1] RowanScott 4 52
(Ray Craggs) *in tch: effrt over 2f out: sn pushed along: kpt on ins fnl f* **7/1**

0060 **4** *2 1/2* **Exclusive Waters (IRE)**[27] 6683 6-9-9 **55**.................. NatalieHambling 3 53
(George Charlton) *dwlt: plld hrd towards rr: outpcd 3f out: rallied over 1f out: kpt on fnl f: nt pce to chal* **16/1**

4603 **5** *1* **Kerry Icon**[18] 6920 3-8-6 **45**.. RhiainIngram 11 42
(Iain Jardine) *t.k.h early: trckd ldrs: effrt and disp ld over 1f out: rdn and no ex ins fnl f* **5/1**[1]

6043 **6** *3/4* **Flyball**[12] 7097 4-8-12 **49**...(e) TobyEley(5) 8 44
(Dianne Sayer) *fly-jmpd s: hld up: shkn up and effrt over 2f out: no imp fr over 1f out* **8/1**

0005 **7** *1* **Zingiber**[18] 6920 4-8-13 **45** .... MeganNicholls 7 39
(Wilf Storey) *pressed ldr: rdn and ev ch over 2f out: edgd lft and wknd over 1f out* **10/1**

3240 **8** *1 1/4* **Fillydelphia (IRE)**[14] 7045 5-9-7 **58** .... PaulaMuir(5) 5 50
(Patrick Holmes) *hld up: hdwy on wd outside and prom over 2f out: rdn and wknd over 1f out* **6/1**[3]

5450 **9** *4* **Loose Ends**[11] 7105 3-9-4 **57** ....[1] SophieKilloran 2 43
(David Simcock) *t.k.h: hld up on ins: pushed along and outpcd over 2f out: btn over 1f out* **11/2**[2]

0000 **10** *18* **Ronald Gee (IRE)**[18] 6920 9-9-9 **55** .... CliffordLee 10 14
(Jim Goldie) *dwlt: hld up: drvn and outpcd wl over 2f out: sn btn* **20/1**

6/00 **11** *16* **Norfolk Sound**[146] 2573 5-8-10 **45** ....(t) PatrickVaughan(3) 1
(Stuart Coltherd) *cl up tl rdn and wknd 3f out* **25/1**

2m 41.64s (0.54) **Going Correction** +0.075s/f (Slow)
WFA 3 from 4yo+ 7lb **11** Ran SP% **115.6**
Speed ratings (Par 101): **101,100,100,98,97 97,96,95,93,81 70**
CSF £87.69 CT £593.35 TOTE £19.60: £4.80, £2.50, £3.30; EX 120.80 Trifecta £1346.00.
Owner The Cosmic Cases **Bred** The Cosmic Cases **Trained** Carrutherstown, D'fries & G'way

FOCUS
A moderate apprentice handicap and a surprise winner. Not a race to be positive about.
T/Plt: £194.80 to a £1 stake. Pool: £60882.95, 228.06 winning units. T/Qpdt: £45.90 to a £1 stake. Pool: £5294.06, 85.2 winning units. **Richard Young**

7224 YARMOUTH (L-H)
Tuesday, October 18

OFFICIAL GOING: Good to soft (good in places) changing to soft after race 1 (1:50) (5:20 abandoned due to lack of medical cover)
Wind: Fresh across Weather: Cloudy with sunny spells

7439 BRITISH STALLION STUDS EBF FILLIES' MAIDEN STKS (PLUS 10 RACE) 6f 3y
1:50 (1:54) (Class 4) 2-Y-O **£4,657** (£1,386; £692; £346) **Stalls** Centre

Form RPR

2 **1** **Loving**[25] 6733 2-9-0 0 .... RyanMoore 9 76+
(William Haggas) *trckd ldrs: racd keenly: shkn up to ld over 1f out: r.o wl* **13/8**[1]

233 **2** *1 1/2* **Coral Sea**[62] 5542 2-9-0 74 .... JamesDoyle 4 72
(Charles Hills) *chsd ldrs: rdn over 2f out: ev ch over 1f out: styd on same pce ins fnl f* **17/2**

3 *nk* **Wurood** 2-9-0 0 .... PaulHanagan 1 71+
(William Haggas) *s.i.s: hdwy over 2f out: ev ch over 1f out: styd on same pce ins fnl f* **17/2**

055 **4** *nk* **Paradwys (IRE)**[11] 7118 2-9-0 76 .... SteveDrowne 5 70
(Charles Hills) *led: rdn and hdd over 1f out: no ex wl ins fnl f* **7/1**[3]

05 **5** *9* **Al Haayelah**[18] 6925 2-9-0 0 .... AndreaAtzeni 10 43
(Roger Varian) *unruly to post: chsd ldr tl pushed along over 2f out: edgd lft and wknd over 1f out* **16/1**

6 *nk* **Denver Spirit (IRE)** 2-9-0 0 .... ShaneKelly 7 42+
(Luca Cumani) *mid-div: rdn over 2f out: wknd wl over 1f out* **20/1**

00 **7** *2 1/2* **Buena Luna**[12] 7099 2-9-0 0 .... LukeMorris 2 34
(Sir Mark Prescott Bt) *towards rr: pushed along over 3f out: wknd over 2f out* **250/1**

2 **8** *nse* **Bequia (IRE)**[74] 5119 2-9-0 0 .... JamieSpencer 6 34
(Martyn Meade) *s.i.s: hld up: wknd over 2f out* **3/1**[2]

0 **9** *1 3/4* **Proud Kate**[8] 7224 2-9-0 0 .... AdamBeschizza 3 29
(Christine Dunnett) *s.s: a in rr: rdn and wknd over 2f out* **250/1**

10 *1* **Highland Clearance (FR)** 2-8-11 0 .... JosephineGordon(3) 8 26
(Giles Bravery) *mid-div: rdn and wknd over 2f out* **100/1**

11 *3 3/4* **Moll Anthony (IRE)** 2-9-0 0 .... RobertHavlin 11 15
(Peter Chapple-Hyam) *s.i.s: towards rr: pushed along over 3f out: wknd over 2f out* **66/1**

1m 12.13s (-2.27) **Going Correction** -0.30s/f (Firm) **11** Ran SP% **110.6**
Speed ratings (Par 94): **103,101,100,100,88 87,84,84,82,80 75**
CSF £15.07 TOTE £2.20: £1.30, £2.30, £2.20; EX 14.00 Trifecta £54.30.
Owner Cheveley Park Stud **Bred** Cheveley Park Stud Ltd **Trained** Newmarket, Suffolk

FOCUS
Robert Havlin described the ground as "very soft." The first four came clear in what was a fair maiden, and the 2nd and 4th offer some perspective.

7440 "GREAT TIMES BRITANNIA AND WELLINGTON PIERS" NURSERY H'CAP 6f 3y
2:20 (2:24) (Class 5) (0-75,75) 2-Y-O **£3,040** (£904; £452; £226) **Stalls** Centre

Form RPR

310 **1** **Savannah Slew**[54] 5794 2-9-6 **74** ....[1] LukeMorris 5 81
(James Given) *hld up: pushed along over 2f out: hdwy over 1f out: rdn to ld ins fnl f: r.o* **11/1**

0421 **2** *1 1/2* **Party Tiger**[22] 6833 2-9-5 **73** .... GeorgeChaloner 2 76
(Richard Fahey) *hld up in tch: shkn up to ld over 1f out: rdn and hdd ins fnl f: styd on same pce* **7/2**[1]

5415 **3** *1/2* **Erissimus Maximus (FR)**[33] 6525 2-9-6 **74** .... MartinHarley 4 75
(Chris Dwyer) *led: rdn and hdd over 1f out: styd on same pce ins fnl f* **5/1**[2]

5113 **4** *1 1/2* **Roys Dream**[29] 6614 2-9-3 **71** .... ShaneKelly 1 68
(Kristin Stubbs) *chsd ldrs: wnt 2nd over 2f out: rdn and ev ch over 1f out: no ex ins fnl f* **12/1**

3451 **5** *1/2* **Amathyst**[12] 7091 2-9-3 **71** .... AndrewMullen 10 66
(Michael Appleby) *chsd ldrs: rdn over 1f out: styd on same pce fnl f* **6/1**[3]

430 **6** *1/2* **Vote**[17] 6950 2-9-2 **70** .... RyanTate 6 64
(James Eustace) *plld hrd and prom: rdn over 2f out: no ex ins fnl f* **9/1**

240 **7** *1* **Mia Cara**[15] 7016 2-8-12 **66** .... MichaelJMMurphy 3 57
(David Evans) *prom: lost pl over 3f out: rdn over 1f out: styd on same pce* **18/1**

036 **8** *1* **Vista Steppe**[46] 6078 2-8-12 **66** .... JamieSpencer 8 57
(David Simcock) *s.i.s: hld up: shkn up over 2f out: nvr on terms* **7/1**

604 **9** *1 1/4* **Jet Setter (IRE)**[20] 6873 2-9-0 **68** .... RyanMoore 9 52
(Brian Meehan) *s.i.s: hld up: rdn over 1f out: no rspnse* **8/1**

1235 **10** *23* **Who Told Jo Jo (IRE)**[129] 3128 2-9-7 **75** .... JFEgan 7
(Bill Turner) *w ldr tl hung lft over 2f out: sn rdn: wknd and eased over 1f out* **25/1**

1m 12.28s (-2.12) **Going Correction** -0.30s/f (Firm) **10** Ran SP% **111.9**
Speed ratings (Par 95): **102,100,99,97,96 96,94,93,91,61**
CSF £47.37 CT £217.39 TOTE £13.10: £3.70, £1.50, £2.30; EX 57.40 Trifecta £350.00.
Owner Dachel Stud **Bred** Dachel Stud **Trained** Willoughton, Lincs

FOCUS
The ground was changed to soft prior to this race. A modest nursery.

7441 BREEDERS BACKING RACING EBF MAIDEN FILLIES' STKS (PLUS 10 RACE) 1m 3y
2:50 (2:53) (Class 4) 2-Y-O **£4,657** (£1,386; £692; £346) **Stalls** Low

Form RPR

1 **Shutter Speed** 2-9-0 0 .... FrankieDettori 7 80+
(John Gosden) *a.p: chsd ldr over 1f out: shkn up: edgd lft and r.o to ld wl ins fnl f* **5/1**[3]

32 **2** *nk* **Song Maker**[14] 7049 2-9-0 0 .... JamesDoyle 10 79
(Charlie Appleby) *led: rdn over 1f out: edgd lft and hdd wl ins fnl f* **8/1**

3 **3** *3* **God Given**[31] 6578 2-9-0 0 .... JamieSpencer 14 72
(Luca Cumani) *stmbld sn after s: hld up in tch: rdn over 2f out: styd on same pce fnl f: wnt 3rd nr fin* **4/1**[2]

2 **4** *nk* **Neshmeya**[24] 6782 2-9-0 0 .... PaulHanagan 2 72+
(Charles Hills) *w ldrs: swtchd rt to chse ldr over 2f out: rdn over 1f out: no ex ins fnl f* **15/8**[1]

5 *3 1/4* **Coconut Creme** 2-9-0 0 .... AndreaAtzeni 3 65+
(William Haggas) *hld up: hdwy over 2f out: rdn over 1f out: wknd ins fnl f* **12/1**

6 *3 1/2* **Hertford Dancer** 2-9-0 0 .... RobertHavlin 12 57
(John Gosden) *mid-div: pushed along: hdwy and swtchd rt over 2f out: rdn: edgd lft and wknd over 1f out* **33/1**

50 **7** *3 1/4* **Piedita (IRE)**[14] 7050 2-9-0 0 .... LukeMorris 11 50
(Sir Mark Prescott Bt) *hld up: hdwy over 2f out: wknd over 1f out* **150/1**

0 **8** *1 1/4* **Lulu The Rocket**[24] 6782 2-9-0 0 .... MartinHarley 15 47
(Peter Chapple-Hyam) *mid-div: effrt whn hmpd over 2f out: sn wknd* **150/1**

02 **9** *shd* **Counterweight (IRE)**[20] 6874 2-9-0 0 .... RyanMoore 5 47
(Sir Michael Stoute) *w ldr 3f: sn pushed along: wknd over 1f out* **7/1**

10 *1 1/2* **Seventii** 2-9-0 0 .... JFEgan 8 43
(Robert Eddery) *hld up: hdwy over 2f out: wknd over 1f out* **150/1**

11 *nk* **Fortia** 2-9-0 0 .... PatCosgrave 13 43
(William Haggas) *s.i.s: in rr: rdn over 2f out: wknd wl over 1f out* **40/1**

00 **12** *1* **Penny Green**[20] 6874 2-9-0 0 .... RyanTate 4 41
(James Eustace) *chsd ldrs: hmpd over 3f out: wknd wl over 2f out* **200/1**

13 *1 1/2* **Lagertha (IRE)** 2-8-11 0 .... JosephineGordon(3) 9 37
(Hugo Palmer) *s.i.s: in rr: pushed along over 4f out: wknd over 2f out* **66/1**

0 **14** *49* **Lily Cliff**[12] 7099 2-9-0 0 .... RobertWinston 16
(Paul D'Arcy) *chsd ldr tl rdn over 3f out: wknd over 2f out* **200/1**

1m 37.64s (-2.96) **Going Correction** -0.30s/f (Firm) **14** Ran SP% **112.6**
Speed ratings (Par 94): **102,101,98,98,95 91,88,87,87,85 85,84,82,33**
CSF £41.17 TOTE £6.20: £2.30, £2.20, £1.60; EX 39.10 Trifecta £279.40.
Owner K Abdullah **Bred** Juddmonte Farms Ltd **Trained** Newmarket, Suffolk

FOCUS
The front pair, both representing top connections, drew clear late on in what looked a decent maiden. There was a minor pb from the 2nd, with the 3rd fitting.

7442 INJURED JOCKEYS FUND H'CAP 7f 3y
3:20 (3:22) (Class 6) (0-65,65) 3-Y-O+ **£2,264** (£673; £336; £168) **Stalls** Centre

Form RPR

0500 **1** **Stoked (IRE)**[26] 6702 4-8-13 **64** .... MillyNaseb(7) 3 72
(Chris Dwyer) *chsd ldrs: led over 1f out: rdn out* **9/1**

5545 **2** *1/2* **Leonard Thomas**[14] 7062 6-8-10 **54** ....(p) JoeyHaynes 2 61
(Tony Carroll) *in rr: pushed along 1/2-way: hdwy 2f out: sn rdn: r.o to 2nd wl ins fnl f: nt rch wnr* **8/1**[3]

3604 **3** *3/4* **Port Lairge**[36] 6408 6-9-1 **59** ....(v) MichaelJMMurphy 5 64
(John Gallagher) *chsd ldr tl led over 2f out: rdn and hdd over 1f out: styd on same pce wl ins fnl f* **15/2**[2]

4-20 **4** *2* **Dose**[235] 725 3-9-2 **62** .... GeorgeChaloner 10 61
(Richard Fahey) *hld up: swtchd rt and hdwy u.p over 1f out: edgd lft ins fnl f: nt rch ldrs* **9/1**

6064 **5** *6* **Trust Me Boy**[8] 7212 8-8-9 **53** oh5 ow2 .... RobertHavlin 9 38
(John E Long) *prom on stands' side rail: lost pl over 4f out: n.d after* **12/1**

0000 **6** *1* **Regal Parade**[14] 7059 12-9-7 **65** ....(tp) AdamBeschizza 6 47
(Charlie Wallis) *chsd ldrs: rdn over 2f out: wknd over 1f out* **8/1**[3]

50-0 **7** *3/4* **Caledonian Gold**[5] 7310 3-9-2 **62** .... LukeMorris 4 44
(Paul D'Arcy) *hld up: pushed along 1/2-way: nt clr run over 2f out: sme hdwy u.p over 1f out: sn wknd* **18/1**

6503 **8** *2* **Great Expectations**[7] 7260 8-9-3 **61** ....(vt) PaulHanagan 13 37
(J R Jenkins) *hld up: hdwy 1/2-way: rdn and wknd over 1f out* **8/1**[3]

0440 **9** *3 1/2* **Refuse Colette (IRE)**[14] 7059 7-9-4 **62** .... ShaneKelly 7 29
(Mick Quinn) *led over 4f: rdn and wknd over 1f out* **9/1**

2352 **10** *1 1/2* **Guanabara Bay (IRE)**[31] 6592 3-9-5 **65** ....(p) JamieSpencer 1 27+
(Martyn Meade) *hld up: hdwy over 2f out: wknd and eased over 1f out* **10/3**[1]

-300 **11** *nse* **Heathfield Park (IRE)**[112] 3735 3-8-5 **51** oh1 .... AndrewMullen 11 13
(William Stone) *sn outpcd: no ch whn hung lft over 2f out* **33/1**

4460 **12** *3 3/4* **Pearly Queen**[7] 7255 3-9-0 **63** .... JackDuern(3) 8 16
(Dean Ivory) *chsd ldrs: rdn 1/2-way: hung lft and wknd over 2f out* **33/1**

1m 25.7s (-0.90) **Going Correction** -0.30s/f (Firm)
WFA 3 from 4yo+ 2lb **12** Ran SP% **117.0**
Speed ratings (Par 101): **93,92,91,89,82 81,80,78,74,72 72,68**
CSF £78.15 CT £567.46 TOTE £15.00: £4.60, £3.30, £2.60; EX 112.70 Trifecta £1001.00.
Owner Mrs Shelley Dwyer **Bred** Es Que Syndicate **Trained** Newmarket, Suffolk

FOCUS
Moderate handicap form but the 2nd and 3rd make sense at this level.

7443 OPTIMIST DESIGN LTD H'CAP 6f 3y
3:50 (3:51) (Class 4) (0-85,84) 3-Y-O+ **£4,690** (£1,395; £697; £348) **Stalls** Centre

Form RPR

2022 **1** **Harwoods Volante (IRE)**[14] 7054 5-9-7 **84** .... FrankieDettori 2 94
(David O'Meara) *hld up: hdwy over 2f out: shkn up to ld wl ins fnl f: r.o: comf* **8/1**[3]

4113 **2** *3/4* **Kenny The Captain (IRE)**[12] 7094 5-9-3 **83** ..... RachelRichardson(3) 14 90
(Tim Easterby) *led: shkn up over 1f out: hdd and unable qck wl ins fnl f* **10/1**

1541 **3** *1 1/4* **Menai (IRE)**[8] 7221 3-9-5 **83** 6ex .... SteveDrowne 8 86
(Charles Hills) *chsd ldr: rdn and ev ch over 1f out: styd on same pce ins fnl f* **11/2**[1]

3330 **4** *1/2* **Quick Look**[37] 6371 3-9-3 **81** .... PaulHanagan 6 82
(William Jarvis) *hld up in tch: shkn up over 2f out: rdn ins fnl f: styd on* **14/1**

6254 **5** *3/4* **Hope Cove**[20] 6883 3-9-5 **83** ....(p) LukeMorris 1 82
(Ed Walker) *hld up: pushed along and hdwy over 2f out: rdn over 1f out: hung lft ins fnl f: styd on same pce* **12/1**

5021 **6** ½ **Gilmer (IRE)**[22] 6836 5-8-5 **71** JosephineGordon(3) 4 68
(Brian Ellison) *chsd ldrs: pushed along over 3f out: no ex wl ins fnl f* **9/1**

352 **7** 2½ **Vimy Ridge**[23] 6809 4-8-6 **74** (v¹) MitchGodwin(5) 12 63
(Alan Bailey) *chsd ldrs: ev ch over 2f out: rdn and edgd lft over 1f out: wknd ins fnl f* **16/1**

21- **8** 2¾ **Tailwind**[320] 8090 3-9-2 **80** AndreaAtzeni 10 60
(Roger Varian) *hld up: shkn up over 2f out: nvr on terms* **11/2**[1]

0-40 **9** 4½ **Merdon Castle (IRE)**[17] 6962 4-9-7 **84** (e) JamesSullivan 5 50
(Ruth Carr) *hld up: swtchd rt over 3f out: rdn and wknd over 2f out* **33/1**

0430 **10** 2 **Borough Boy (IRE)**[14] 7054 6-9-2 **79** (v) MartinLane 9 38
(Derek Shaw) *hld up: rdn and wknd over 2f out* **100/1**

1- **11** 1 **Saucy Spirit**[355] 7578 3-9-3 **81** RyanMoore 11 37
(Hughie Morrison) *hld up: shkn up over 2f out: sn wknd* **16/1**

5000 **12** 99 **Rio Ronaldo (IRE)**[17] 6944 4-9-7 **84** JamieSpencer 7
(Mike Murphy) *s.s and hmpd sn after s: c home in own time* **6/1**[2]

1 **U** **Santorini (IRE)**[15] 7011 3-8-11 **75** MartinHarley 3
(Henry Candy) *swvd rt and uns rdr sn after s* **8/1**[3]

1m 11.66s (-2.74) **Going Correction** -0.30s/f (Firm)
WFA 3 from 4yo+ 1lb **13** Ran SP% **116.4**
Speed ratings (Par 105): **106,105,103,102,101 101,97,94,88,85 84, ,**
CSF £83.43 CT £497.07 TOTE £8.60: £2.80, £3.30, £2.10; EX 98.80 Trifecta £331.50.
Owner Great Northern Partnership **Bred** Gerry And John Rowley **Trained** Upper Helmsley, N Yorks

FOCUS
A decent little handicap, with the winner pretty much back to his best and a small pb from the 2nd.

7444 LA CONTINENTAL CAFE IN YARMOUTH H'CAP (DIV I) 6f 3y
4:20 (4:20) (Class 6) (0-60,60) 3-Y-O+ **£2,264** (£673; £336; £168) **Stalls** Centre

Form RPR

4000 **1** **Robbian**[34] 6478 5-8-0 **46** oh1 RPWalsh(7) 5 55
(Charles Smith) *a.p: chsd ldr over 4f out: led over 2f out: rdn out* **33/1**

0013 **2** ¾ **Keene's Pointe**[22] 6835 6-9-6 **59** ShaneKelly 4 66
(Kristin Stubbs) *hld up: hdwy 2f out: rdn to chse wnr ins fnl f: unable qck towards fin* **9/2**[3]

0-06 **3** nk **Caribbean Spring (IRE)**[89] 4570 3-8-10 **57** JaneElliott(7) 3 63
(George Margarson) *chsd ldrs: shkn up over 1f out: r.o* **10/1**

1032 **4** 1½ **Whipphound**[14] 7046 8-9-2 **55** (p) JamesSullivan 2 56
(Ruth Carr) *chsd ldrs: rdn over 1f out: no ex ins fnl f* **4/1**[2]

5000 **5** 2½ **Zebedee's Girl (IRE)**[14] 7057 3-8-7 **50** JosephineGordon(3) 6 44
(David Evans) *hmpd after 1f: sn pushed along in rr: hdwy over 2f out: rdn over 1f out: no ex fnl f* **8/1**

1223 **6** ¾ **Colourbearer (IRE)**[140] 2765 9-8-8 **47** (t) LukeMorris 11 39
(Charlie Wallis) *led over 3f: rdn over 1f out: no ex fnl f* **5/1**

0000 **7** 2 **Harwoods Star (IRE)**[14] 7059 6-9-7 **60** (v) JFEgan 7 46
(John Butler) *hld up: nt clr run wl over 1f out: sn rdn: nvr trbld ldrs* **10/3**[1]

0006 **8** ¾ **Fearless Poppy**[8] 7201 3-8-7 **47** oh1 ow1 (v) AdamBeschizza 9 30
(Christine Dunnett) *chsd ldr tl over 4f out: remained handy: rdn over 2f out: wknd over 1f out* **50/1**

0-64 **9** 15 **Palmina**[222] 885 3-8-13 **56** JackDuern(3) 1
(Dean Ivory) *prom on outer: rdn over 3f out: wknd over 1f out* **16/1**

5006 **10** 15 **Monsieur Jamie**[36] 6410 8-9-7 **60** (v) PaulHanagan 10
(J R Jenkins) *hld up in tch: lost pl over 3f out: rdn and wknd over 2f out* **16/1**

1m 14.07s (-0.33) **Going Correction** -0.30s/f (Firm)
WFA 3 from 5yo+ 1lb **10** Ran SP% **114.8**
Speed ratings (Par 101): **90,89,88,86,83 82,79,78,58,38**
CSF £173.75 CT £1624.26 TOTE £40.70: £8.40, £1.50, £3.20; EX 214.90 Trifecta £2237.30.
Owner Rob Lewin **Bred** John Starbuck **Trained** Temple Bruer, Lincs

FOCUS
Racing stands' side, it paid to race handy in division one of this sprint.

7445 LA CONTINENTAL CAFE IN YARMOUTH H'CAP (DIV II) 6f 3y
4:50 (5:05) (Class 6) (0-60,60) 3-Y-O+ **£2,264** (£673; £336; £168) **Stalls** Centre

Form RPR

0304 **1** **Zippy**[14] 7038 3-8-13 **56** JosephineGordon(3) 11 63
(Daniel Kubler) *wnt rt s: sn chsng ldrs: led over 1f out: rdn out* **9/4**[1]

3000 **2** hd **Multi Quest**[19] 6902 4-8-9 **48** (b) RobertHavlin 10 54
(John E Long) *chsd ldrs: ev ch fr over 1f out: rdn ins fnl f: nt qckn nr fin* **7/1**

60-0 **3** 1¾ **Bedazzling Lady (IRE)**[19] 6902 3-8-7 **47** JFEgan 1 48+
(Robert Eddery) *chsd ldrs: led over 2f out: rdn and hdd over 1f out: styd on same pce ins fnl f* **20/1**

5500 **4** 1¾ **Tilsworth Micky**[25] 6745 4-9-2 **55** PaulHanagan 5 51
(J R Jenkins) *hld up in tch: racd keenly: lost pl over 2f out: rallied over 1f out: styd on same pce ins fnl f* **6/1**[3]

0110 **5** 1 **Robbie Roo Roo**[6] 7290 3-9-4 **58** (vt) SaleemGolam 6 51
(Mrs Ilka Gansera-Leveque) *wnt rt s: plld hrd and sn prom: lost pl over 4f out: rdn over 2f out: styd on ins fnl f* **9/2**[2]

0506 **6** 1½ **State Of The Union (IRE)**[37] 6374 4-9-6 **59** (vt) StevieDonohoe 3 47
(Henry Spiller) *prom: rdn over 1f out: wknd fnl f* **12/1**

000 **7** 2½ **Touch The Clouds**[20] 6865 5-8-7 **46** oh1 (tp) AndrewMullen 4 27
(William Stone) *sn led: hdd over 2f out: rdn and wknd over 1f out* **12/1**

0004 **8** 6 **Captain Scooby**[10] 7145 10-9-5 **58** (b) GeorgeChaloner 2 21
(Richard Guest) *chsd ldrs: rdn over 2f out: wknd over 1f out* **9/1**

0050 **9** 3¾ **Vocalise**[31] 6567 3-7-13 **46** oh1 RPWalsh(7) 9
(Charles Smith) *s.s and hmpd sn after s: a bhd* **66/1**

350 **U** **Humour (IRE)**[14] 7062 5-8-11 **55** (b¹) DavidParkes(5) 8
(Christine Dunnett) *hmpd and uns rdr leaving stalls* **12/1**

1m 13.66s (-0.74) **Going Correction** -0.30s/f (Firm)
WFA 3 from 4yo+ 1lb **10** Ran SP% **115.1**
Speed ratings (Par 101): **92,91,89,87,85 83,80,72,67,**
CSF £17.99 CT £255.89 TOTE £3.00: £1.40, £3.00, £4.90; EX 15.60 Trifecta £256.40.
Owner Selwood Bloodstock Ltd **Bred** Honeypuddle Stud **Trained** Lambourn, Berks
■ Baileys Pursuit was withdrawn. Price at time of withdrawal 16/1. Rule 4 does not apply.

FOCUS
They raced centre-field this time and it looked stronger than the first leg.

7446 NORFOLK CHAMBER OF COMMERCE H'CAP 1m 3f 104y
(5:20) (Class 5) (0-75,) 3-Y-O+ £

T/Jkpt: Not Won. T/Plt: £211.00 to a £1 stake. Pool: £78640.75, 271.99 winning units. T/Qpdt: £45.70 to a £1 stake. Pool: £6091.15, 98.55 winning units. **Colin Roberts**

7453a (Foreign Racing) - See Raceform Interactive

7422 DEAUVILLE (R-H)
Tuesday, October 18

OFFICIAL GOING: Polytrack: standard, turf: good

7454a PRIX DE LA GOUSSERIE (CONDITIONS) (2YO) (POLYTRACK) 7f 110y
11:10 (11:10) 2-Y-O **£9,558** (£3,823; £2,867; £1,911; £955)

RPR

1 **Fils De L'Air (FR)**[22] 2-9-4 0 Pierre-CharlesBoudot 4 89
(P Sogorb, France) **29/10**[2]

2 snk **Rip (FR)** 2-9-2 0 ChristopheSoumillon 1 87
(F Rossi, France) **21/10**[1]

3 4½ **Vue Du Ciel (FR)**[60] 5698 2-8-10 0 IoritzMendizabal 7 70
(J-C Rouget, France) **31/10**[3]

4 ½ **Fleurdelune (FR)**[107] 2-8-5 0 ClementLecoeuvre(5) 9 69
(M Delaplace, France) **44/5**

5 1¼ **Zahiria (FR)**[129] 3182 2-8-10 0 AntoineHamelin 2 66
(P Adda, France) **40/1**

6 nk **Rock On Dandy (FR)**[19] 6888 2-8-11 0 TonyPiccone 3 66
(Harry Dunlop) *midfield in tch on outer: rdn and effrt into st: sn outpcd and btn: wknd* **56/10**

7 hd **Saranne My Love (FR)** 2-8-10 0 JulienAuge 5 65
(P Monfort, France) **39/1**

8 shd **Silk Of Rio (FR)** 2-9-1 0 (p) StephanePasquier 6 69
(Y Gourraud, France) **24/1**

9 ¾ **Blusterysky (FR)**[15] 2-8-11 0 CristianDemuro 8 64
(M Narduzzi, Italy) **31/1**

WIN (incl. 1 euro stake): 3.90. PLACES: 1.20, 1.20, 1.20. DF: 5.20. SF: 10.40
Owner Ecurie Normandie Pur Sang **Bred** S Springer **Trained** France

7455a PRIX DES MARGUERITES (CLAIMER) (2YO FILLIES) (POLYTRACK) 6f 110y
12:10 (12:10) 2-Y-O **£6,985** (£2,794; £2,095; £1,397; £698)

RPR

1 **Tiger's Nest (ITY)** 2-9-1 0 ChristopheSoumillon 4 73
(Simone Brogi, France) **6/4**[1]

2 3 **Mad Rose (IRE)** 2-9-1 0 MickaelBarzalona 11 64
(J Reynier, France) **14/1**

3 ¾ **Samran Says (IRE)**[27] 2-8-11 0 JulienAuge 12 58
(P Monfort, France) **68/1**

4 nk **Meteorite (FR)**[22] 2-9-1 0 UmbertoRispoli 8 61
(G Doleuze, France) **28/1**

5 1 **Miss Charlotte (IRE)**[7] 2-8-9 0 NicolasBarzalona(6) 13 58
(F Vermeulen, France) **54/10**[2]

6 nk **Radar Love (IRE)**[26] 6696 2-9-1 0 TonyPiccone 9 58
(J S Moore) *trckd ldr: rdn to chal 2f out: upsides and ev ch ent fnl f: sn no ex: wknd* **9/1**[3]

7 1¼ **Cydalise (FR)** 2-9-1 0 SebastienMartino 14 54
(H-A Pantall, France) **17/1**

8 shd **Key Success (IRE)**[49] 6015 2-8-11 0 (b¹) GregoryBenoist 3 50
(Y Barberot, France) **9/1**[3]

9 snk **La Surfeuse (FR)**[190] 2-8-11 0 LudovicBoisseau(4) 5 53
(T Lemer, France) **16/1**

10 1¼ **The Night Is Ours (IRE)**[22] 6829 2-9-1 0 ThierryJarnet 1 50
(J S Moore) *prom: rdn over 1f out: nt qckn* **12/1**

11 ½ **Royale Wave (FR)** 2-8-11 0 (b) IoritzMendizabal 6 44
(Mario Hofer, Germany) **45/1**

12 3 **Ngendha (FR)**[18] 2-8-4 0 KyllanBarbaud(7) 10 36
(N Caullery, France) **16/1**

13 ¾ **Retour Gagnant (IRE)**[15] 2-8-11 0 (b¹) TristanNormand 2 34
(Yves de Nicolay, France) **87/1**

14 1 **Eblouis Moi (FR)**[142] 2724 2-9-4 0 CristianDemuro 7 38
(A Giorgi, Italy) **42/1**

15 5 **Cholpon Ata (FR)**[15] 2-9-1 0 AurelienLemaitre 15 21
(Mme P Butel, France) **64/1**

WIN (incl. 1 euro stake): 2.50. PLACES: 1.50, 3.80, 12.40. DF: 18.50. SF: 26.00
Owner Louis-Armand Jolly **Bred** Azienda Agricola Luciani Loreto **Trained** France

7456a PRIX VULCAIN (LISTED RACE) (3YO) (TURF) 1m 4f 110y
1:50 (1:50) 3-Y-O **£20,220** (£8,088; £6,066; £4,044; £2,022)

RPR

1 **Maniaco**[26] 6729 3-9-0 0 MaximeGuyon 9 102+
(A Fabre, France) **29/10**[1]

2 1¼ **Marmelo**[17] 6971 3-9-0 0 UmbertoRispoli 7 98
(Hughie Morrison) *led: rdn and qcknd 2f out: clr ent fnl f: kpt on but reeled in and hdd nring fin: no ex* **49/10**[3]

3 1½ **San Salvador (GER)**[121] 3453 3-9-0 0 MarcLerner 3 96
(Andreas Lowe, Germany) **58/1**

4 ½ **Happy Approach (FR)**[77] 5006 3-8-10 0 AntoineHamelin 11 91+
(M Nigge, France) **18/1**

5 ½ **Carzoff (FR)**[37] 6392 3-9-0 0 ThierryJarnet 8 94+
(Alain Couetil, France) **33/1**

6 snk **Federico**[114] 3-9-0 0 IoritzMendizabal 10 94
(J-C Rouget, France) **12/1**

7 ¾ **Al Haram (FR)**[34] 6498 3-9-0 0 GregoryBenoist 6 93
(E Lellouche, France) **31/10**[2]

8 2 **Wind Of Change (GER)**[34] 6498 3-9-0 0 Pierre-CharlesBoudot 14 90
(Jean-Pierre Carvalho, Germany) **10/1**

9 hd **Lord George (IRE)**[46] 6089 3-9-0 0 TomQueally 1 89
(James Fanshawe) *midfield on inner: rdn into st: outpce fnl 2f* **66/1**

10 snk **Phedre**[115] 3-8-10 0 TheoBachelot 4 85
(S Wattel, France) **31/1**

11 2½ **Sagaroi (FR)**[44] 6176 3-9-3 0 Francois-XavierBertras 12 88
(D Guillemin, France) **11/1**

12 7 **Shalakar (FR)**[65] 5448 3-9-0 0 ChristopheSoumillon 13 74
(M Delzangles, France) **16/1**

2m 39.68s (-6.72) **12** Ran SP% **119.3**
WIN (incl. 1 euro stake): 3.90. PLACES: 2.00, 2.10, 11.40. DF: 10.30. SF: 19.50.
Owner Wertheimer & Frere **Bred** Wertheimer & Frere **Trained** Chantilly, France

7423 KEMPTON (A.W) (R-H)

Wednesday, October 19

OFFICIAL GOING: Polytrack: standard to slow

Weather: Cold, cloudy

7457 100% PROFIT BOOST AT 32REDSPORT.COM H'CAP 1m (P)

5:50 (5:50) (Class 5) (0-75,75) 3-Y-O+ **£2,911** (£866; £432; £216) **Stalls** Low

Form RPR

4524 **1** **Dream Of Summer (IRE)**[29] 6657 3-9-1 **75** RobHornby(3) 8 86
(Andrew Balding) *settled in 3rd bhd clr ldr: rdn over 2f out: led 2f out: kpt on wl fr over 1f out: drvn out fnl f* **9/2**[2]

0055 **2** 2 **Spiritual Star (IRE)**[15] 7051 7-8-12 **71** PaddyBradley(5) 6 78
(Lee Carter) *mid-div: tk clsr order over 2f out: rdn jst over 1f out: kpt on in centre fr 1f out: styd on wl ins fnl f but no ch w wnr* **8/1**

0540 **3** 1 1/4 **Squire**[26] 6753 5-9-6 **74** (t) LukeMorris 11 78
(Michael Attwater) *settled bhd ldrs: rdn along over 2f out: kpt on* **10/1**

2244 **4** 1 1/2 **Choral Clan (IRE)**[27] 6701 5-9-4 **72** JackMitchell 4 73
(Philip Mitchell) *settled in 4th on inner: rdn over 2f out: hemmed in whn trying to angle to centre over 1f out: kpt on fnl f* **11/1**

3160 **5** 1/2 **Pike Corner Cross (IRE)**[29] 6657 4-9-4 **72** HarryBentley 14 72+
(Ed de Giles) *in rr: prog on inner over 2f out: prog over 1f out* **8/1**

0000 **6** 1 1/4 **Ruban (IRE)**[14] 7066 7-9-2 **73** (t) AaronJones(3) 5 70
(Stuart Williams) *settled in rr-div: rdn 2f out: kpt on* **6/1**[3]

1111 **7** 1 3/4 **Multitask**[15] 7036 6-9-4 **75** HectorCrouch(3) 1 70+
(Gary Moore) *hld up in mid-div on inner: gng wl whn nt clr run over 2f out: swtchd to centre over 1f out: nt qckn and one pce after* **7/2**[1]

3-05 **8** 3/4 **Camakasi (IRE)**[13] 4520 5-9-7 **75** (t) TomMarquand 10 66
(Ali Stronge) *missed break: pushed up to settle in rr: rdn 2f out: kpt on one pce* **50/1**

2006 **9** 1 3/4 **Tellovoi (IRE)**[11] 7141 8-9-4 **72** (v) JFEgan 3 59
(Richard Guest) *sn led: 6 l advantage at 1/2-way: commited for home ent st where 10 l ldr: pack clsd wl over 2f out: hdd & wknd fr 2f out* **20/1**

0603 **10** 1 1/4 **Glenalmond (IRE)**[15] 7051 4-9-5 **73** (p) GeorgeBaker 9 57
(Daniel Steele) *in rr: suffled along on outer ent st: prog past btn horses fr over 1f out* **7/1**

0500 **11** 1 1/2 **St Patrick's Day (IRE)**[14] 7076 4-9-5 **73** (v) FrederikTylicki 7 54
(J R Jenkins) *a in rr: effrt over 2f out: no imp after* **66/1**

652 **12** 1/2 **Thecornishbarron (IRE)**[27] 6701 4-9-7 **75** JimmyFortune 12 54
(John Ryan) *racd wd in bhd ldrs: rdn over 2f out: sn no imp and wknd* **14/1**

060 **13** 8 **The Dancing Lord**[30] 6637 7-9-2 **70** (t) HarryPoulton 13 31
(Adam West) *hld up in rr: rdn ent st: sn hld* **100/1**

1000 **14** 7 **Mr Christopher (IRE)**[106] 3989 4-9-6 **74** RichardKingscote 2 19
(Tom Dascombe) *settled in 2nd bhd clr ldr: rdn over 2f out on inner: stl there u.p over 1f out: wknd qckly and eased fnl f* **25/1**

1m 38.0s (-1.80) **Going Correction** 0.0s/f (Stan)
WFA 3 from 4yo+ 3lb **14** Ran SP% **126.6**
Speed ratings (Par 103): **109,107,105,104,103 102,100,100,98,97 95,95,87,80**
CSF £41.20 CT £357.78 TOTE £5.40: £1.90, £3.30, £4.80; EX 72.90 Trifecta £915.80.
Owner Happy Valley Racing & Breeding Limited **Bred** Llang Bloodstock **Trained** Kingsclere, Hants

FOCUS
A fair handicap opened the card, with the Polytrack still given an official description of Standard To Slow. Tellovoi tore off in front and was largely ignored, but even the chasing pack went a good pace. A pb from the winner.

7458 32RED/BRITISH STALLION STUDS EBF MAIDEN STKS 1m (P)

6:20 (6:20) (Class 5) 2-Y-O **£3,234** (£962; £481; £240) **Stalls** Low

Form RPR

3 **1** **Pivoine (IRE)**[18] 6945 2-9-5 0 TedDurcan 6 79+
(Sir Michael Stoute) *disp ld tl 3f whn settled bhd ldr on inner: swtchd to inner rail and rdn 2f out: kpt on wl to ld jst ins fnl f: in n.d and eased cl home: comf* **5/2**[2]

2 **2** 2 1/2 **Archer's Arrow (USA)**[18] 6952 2-9-2 0 JosephineGordon(3) 9 73
(Saeed bin Suroor) *t.k.h early bhd ldrs: gng wl and nursed into ld 2f out: sn rdn and hdd jst ins fnl f: wandered sltly u.p but kpt on to hold 2nd* **1/2**[1]

06 **3** 1 **Spirit Of Belle**[16] 7013 2-9-5 0 JFEgan 1 70
(Pat Phelan) *settled in mid-div: pushed along on outer to make prog bnd: rdn and upsides ldrs ent st: stl there over 1f out: kpt on one pce ins fnl f* **12/1**

0 **4** 1 **Duchess Of Fife**[7] 7284 2-9-0 0 LukeMorris 4 63+
(William Knight) *s.i.s: hld up in mid-div: pushed along ent st: hrd rdn over 2f out: 4th last and plenty to do over 1f out: kpt on nicely under hands and heels fr 1f out: nvr nrr* **33/1**

04 **5** 4 **Zoffanist (IRE)**[18] 6945 2-9-5 0 MartinDwyer 10 59
(Amanda Perrett) *disp ld early: sn outrt ldr: rdn and hdd 2f out: sn one pce and wknd ins fnl f* **9/1**[3]

0 **6** 1 1/4 **Mr Mac**[21] 6880 2-9-5 0 CharlesBishop 5 56
(Peter Hedger) *settled in 4th on inner: rdn over 2f out: sn no imp* **66/1**

0 **7** 2 1/4 **Magic Beans**[10] 7187 2-9-5 0 LiamKeniry 3 51
(Hughie Morrison) *in rr: rdn over 2f out: sn lft bhd: hands and heels after* **33/1**

8 1 1/4 **Sheltered Waters** 2-9-0 0 ShaneKelly 2 43
(Eve Johnson Houghton) *s.i.s: in rr: rdn along on inner over 2f out: lft bhd over 1f out* **20/1**

0 **9** 21 **Abouttimeyoutoldme**[18] 6945 2-9-5 0 RichardKingscote 8
(Ralph Beckett) *in rr on outer: rdn over 2f out: no rspnse and sn lft bhd: t.o* **20/1**

1m 40.08s (0.28) **Going Correction** 0.0s/f (Stan) **9** Ran SP% **129.8**
Speed ratings (Par 95): **98,95,94,93,89 88,86,84,63**
CSF £4.46 TOTE £3.30: £1.10, £1.10, £3.10; EX 4.80 Trifecta £19.30.
Owner Ballymacoll Stud **Bred** Ballymacoll Stud Farm Ltd **Trained** Newmarket, Suffolk

FOCUS
The market was dominated by the two horses who fought out the finish in a race that changed complexion markedly in the straight. A fluid starting point as far as ratings go.

7459 32RED CASINO MEDIAN AUCTION MAIDEN STKS 6f (P)

6:50 (6:51) (Class 5) 3-4-Y-O **£2,911** (£866; £432; £216) **Stalls** Low

Form RPR

3235 **1** **Compas Scoobie**[32] 6583 3-9-5 73 HarryBentley 4 77+
(Roger Varian) *covered up in mid-divsion: nt clr run and angled out to centre over 1f out: in clr on outer jst over 1f out: qcknd past ldng trio to ld cl home: cosily* **7/4**[1]

22 **2** 3/4 **Port Isaac (IRE)**[36] 6459 3-9-5 0 MartinDwyer 7 74
(Marcus Tregoning) *pressed ldr and t.k.h: led 3f out: narrow ld whn rdn 2f out: nk and nk w 4th ins fnl f: kpt on but hdd cl home* **7/4**[1]

2240 **3** hd **Cinders (IRE)**[29] 6657 3-9-0 69 JimmyFortune 5 69
(Hughie Morrison) *settled in 3rd: rdn 2f out: kpt on wl and almost on terms over 1f out: ev ch fnl f: kpt on* **11/2**[2]

23 **4** hd **James The Elder (IRE)**[15] 7061 3-9-5 0 GeorgeBaker 10 73
(Seamus Durack) *sn led: hdd 3f out but remained pressing ldr: rdn 2f: nk and nk w runner-up wl ins fnl f: wknd last strides* **8/1**[3]

00 **5** 3 **Notoursortdear**[16] 7011 4-9-1 0 MichaelJMMurphy 3 60
(John Gallagher) *hld up in mid-div: rdn 2f out: kpt on one pce* **50/1**

6 1 **Beauden Barrett** 3-9-5 0 MartinLane 6 62
(Jeremy Gask) *hld up bhd ldrs: rdn 2f out: one pce after* **16/1**

00 **7** 4 1/2 **Blanco (USA)**[24] 6805 3-9-5 0 (t) SteveDrowne 1 50
(George Baker) *in rr: rdn 2f out: one pce after* **66/1**

0-6 **8** 1 1/4 **Pacabag**[252] 516 3-9-0 0 CharlesBishop 8 42
(Peter Hedger) *s.i.s: hld up in rr: rdn over 2f out: no imp* **66/1**

9 2 1/4 **Scribner Creek (IRE)** 3-9-5 0 DaleSwift 11 41
(Daniel Mark Loughnane) *half-rrd s: t.k.h in rr: rdn 2f out: no ex fr over 1f out* **25/1**

10 1 **Rigsby** 3-9-5 0 LukeMorris 2 38
(Zoe Davison) *s.s: wanting to run lft and pushed rival after 1f: rapid prog under restraint out wd: wnt to nrside rail ent st: sn wknd* **100/1**

000 **11** 24 **Autumn Chorus**[16] 7011 3-9-0 33 DannyBrock 9
(John Bridger) *s.s: pushed wd by rival wanting to go lft after 1f: sn hld up in rr: rdn over 2f out: sn no imp and eased fr over 1f out* **150/1**

1m 13.38s (0.28) **Going Correction** 0.0s/f (Stan)
WFA 3 from 4yo 1lb **11** Ran SP% **115.5**
Speed ratings (Par 103): **98,97,96,96,92 91,85,83,80,79 47**
CSF £4.36 TOTE £2.90: £1.20, £1.20, £1.60; EX 5.90 Trifecta £16.30.
Owner Michael Hill **Bred** Aston Mullins Stud **Trained** Newmarket, Suffolk

FOCUS
A bunched finish to a muddling maiden, and it has been rated around the 3rd and 4th for now.

7460 32RED ON THE APP STORE NURSERY H'CAP 7f (P)

7:20 (7:20) (Class 4) (0-85,80) 2-Y-O **£4,528** (£1,347; £673; £336) **Stalls** Low

Form RPR

0010 **1** **Plant Pot Power (IRE)**[32] 6575 2-9-2 **80** HollieDoyle(5) 8 85+
(Richard Hannon) *hld up in rr: prog on heels of ldrs 2f out: daring run between horses wl over 1f out: rdn and ducked rt to ins over 1f out: sn stened up under rt-hand drive and led 1f out: pushed out wl ins fnl f: easily* **10/1**

5421 **2** 2 **Juanito Chico (IRE)**[15] 7033 2-9-4 **77** MartinDwyer 5 77
(William Jarvis) *settled in last on inner: gd prog ent st: rdn 2f out w clr run up inner: rapid prog and sn led: kpt on tl hdd 1f out: one pce after* **4/1**[3]

1065 **3** 3 **Nibras Bounty (IRE)**[72] 5239 2-9-3 **76** SeanLevey 3 68
(Richard Hannon) *pressed ldr early tl settled in 2nd after 3f: rdn and led 2f out: hdd over 1f out: kpt on one pce* **8/1**

01 **4** 3/4 **Hajaj (IRE)**[59] 5676 2-9-5 **78** StevieDonohoe 6 68
(Charlie Fellowes) *settled prom on outer: rdn 2f out: sn hld* **7/2**[2]

004 **5** 1 **The Secrets Out**[21] 6868 2-8-6 **65** KieranO'Neill 2 52
(Luke Dace) *settled in 3rd: rdn 2f out: one pce after* **20/1**

31 **6** 3 **Anfaass (IRE)**[36] 6448 2-9-4 **77** PatCosgrave 7 60
(George Margarson) *in rr: nt clr run twice over 1f out: no imp after* **3/1**[1]

413 **7** nk **Shipping Forecast**[32] 6575 2-9-5 **78** JimmyFortune 4 57
(Brian Meehan) *wnt lft s: t.k.h: sn in mid-div: rdn 2f out: no imp* **4/1**[3]

310 **8** 5 **Sixties Habana**[24] 6800 2-8-8 **67** JFEgan 1 33
(Pat Phelan) *t.k.h in ld: rdn over 2f out: sn hdd: wknd and eased fnl f* **40/1**

1m 25.83s (-0.17) **Going Correction** 0.0s/f (Stan) **8** Ran SP% **114.6**
Speed ratings (Par 97): **100,97,94,93,92 88,88,82**
CSF £49.85 CT £342.96 TOTE £12.40: £2.90, £1.60, £2.60; EX 49.50 Trifecta £321.40.
Owner Potensis B'Stock, J Palmer-Brown & Ptnr **Bred** Jeremy Gompertz **Trained** East Everleigh, Wilts

FOCUS
Despite the fact only one of these was proven on the Polytrack it still looked like a fair race of its type.

7461 32RED.COM H'CAP (DIV I) 7f (P)

7:50 (7:50) (Class 4) (0-85,85) 3-Y-O+ **£4,690** (£1,395; £697; £348) **Stalls** Low

Form RPR

5104 **1** **Ower Fly**[19] 6916 3-9-0 **85** HollieDoyle(5) 4 92
(Richard Hannon) *prom on outer: rdn along 3f out: kpt on wl to ld 1f out: kpt up to work ins fnl f: a doing enough* **9/1**

2413 **2** 1/2 **Golden Wedding (IRE)**[16] 7017 4-9-0 **78** CharlesBishop 9 85
(Eve Johnson Houghton) *hld up in mid-div: taken up on outer over 2f out: rdn 2f out: kpt on wl ins fnl f to grab 2nd cl home* **9/2**[2]

0046 **3** hd **Sydney Ruffdiamond**[16] 7017 4-9-3 **81** (tp) ShaneKelly 11 87
(Richard Hughes) *racd in 2nd: rdn 2f out: kpt on wl and upsides wnr ent fnl f: lost 2nd cl home* **10/1**

6560 **4** nk **Brilliant Vanguard (IRE)**[27] 6714 3-8-13 **79** ShaneGray 13 84+
(Kevin Ryan) *hld up in rr-div: rdn and gd prog fr over 1f out: kpt on wl fnl f: nvr nrr* **16/1**

5205 **5** 3/4 **Florencio**[9] 7206 3-9-0 **85** (t) GeorgeWood(5) 3 88
(William Muir) *settled bhd ldr: rdn over 3f out: one pce after* **4/1**[1]

1340 **6** 1/2 **Presumido (IRE)**[154] 2378 6-9-4 **82** NickyMackay 5 84
(Simon Dow) *settled in mid-div: rdn over 2f out: modest prog after* **20/1**

130 **7** 1/2 **Cricklewood Green (USA)**[19] 6914 5-8-10 **79** MitchGodwin(5) 8 80
(Sylvester Kirk) *in rr: rdn on inner over 2f out: no qckn fr over 1f out* **10/1**

0654 **8** 1/2 **Morache Music**[24] 6806 8-8-12 **81** CharlieBennett(5) 10 81
(Patrick Chamings) *in rr-div: rdn over 2f out: picked up fr 1f out: nvr nrr* **9/1**

2005 **9** 1/2 **Captain Lars (SAF)**[15] 7054 7-8-6 **73** (p) NoelGarbutt(3) 7 71
(Derek Shaw) *sn led: clr ldr ent st hdd 1f out: wknd qckly fnl f* **20/1**

3620 **10** 3/4 **Jan Steen (IRE)**[9] 7203 3-8-5 **71** oh2 LukeMorris 12 66
(Denis Coakley) *hld up in mid-div: rdn over 2f out: kpt on tl wknd fnl f* **20/1**

5226 **11** 2 **Thundering Blue (USA)**[13] 7102 3-8-10 **76** (v[1]) MartinDwyer 6 66
(David Menuisier) *in rr: rdn 2f out: no imp* **8/1**[3]

3400 **12** 1 1/4 **Nisser**[15] 7054 3-8-12 **78** JimCrowley 2 64
(Robert Cowell) *settled bhd ldrs: rdn 2f out: wknd fr over 1f out* **8/1**[3]

6100 **13** 2 1/2 **Yourartisonfire**[67] 5419 6-9-4 **82** (p) LiamKeniry 1 63
(Lisa Williamson) *in rr: rdn 2f out: sn hld* **50/1**

1m 24.84s (-1.16) **Going Correction** 0.0s/f (Stan)
WFA 3 from 4yo+ 2lb **13** Ran SP% **120.7**
Speed ratings (Par 105): **106,105,105,104,104 103,102,102,101,100 98,97,94**
CSF £47.24 CT £437.59 TOTE £9.30: £2.50, £1.70, £4.60; EX 47.90 Trifecta £658.30.
Owner Green Pastures Farm **Bred** Green Pastures Farm **Trained** East Everleigh, Wilts

FOCUS
A pb from the winner.

7462 32RED.COM H'CAP (DIV II) 7f (P)
8:20 (8:20) (Class 4) (0-85,84) 3-Y-O+ **£4,690** (£1,395; £697; £348) **Stalls** Low

Form RPR

4211 **1** **Finelcity (GER)**^{37} 6416 3-9-5 **84**....(v) JimCrowley 11 93+
(Harry Dunlop) *sn led: rdn over 1f out: kpt on wl ins fnl f* **3/1**^{1}

0035 **2** ¾ **Plucky Dip**^{6} 7308 5-9-5 **82**.... DannyBrock 1 89
(John Ryan) *settled in 3rd: rdn over 1f out: kpt on wl ins fnl f: nt get to wnr* **6/1**^{3}

3001 **3** *nk* **Frenchman (FR)**^{5} 7324 3-9-0 **79** 6ex.... LukeMorris 3 84
(Charles Hills) *settled bhd ldrs on outer: rdn 2f out: kpt on to press for 2nd nring fin* **8/1**

0402 **4** 1 ½ **Alejandro (IRE)**^{6} 7308 7-9-6 **83**.... DavidNolan 5 85
(David O'Meara) *settled in 4th: rdn 2f out: kpt on one pce fnl f* **15/2**

0040 **5** ¾ **Jammy Guest (IRE)**^{6} 7308 6-9-2 **79**.... JFEgan 7 79+
(George Margarson) *s.s: in rr: rdn along on inner 2f out: kpt on tl wknd ins fnl f* **12/1**

0203 **6** *nse* **Straits Of Malacca**^{1} 7430 5-8-4 **70**....(p) JosephineGordon$^{(3)}$ 8 70
(Simon Dow) *settled in 2nd and t.k.h: stl prom and rdn over 1f out: wknd fnl f* **33/1**

-160 **7** *hd* **House Of Commons (IRE)**^{56} 5765 3-8-12 **77**....(b^{1}) OisinMurphy 4 75
(Paul Cole) *settled in mid-div: rdn over 1f out: nt qckn ins fnl f* **9/1**

4130 **8** *nse* **Jordan Sport**^{123} 3414 3-9-5 **84**....^{1} GeorgeBaker 10 82+
(David Simcock) *in rr: rdn w plenty to do over 1f out: kpt on nicely fr 1f out: nvr nrr* **6/1**^{3}

241 **9** 1 ¾ **Ripoll (IRE)**^{14} 7066 3-8-8 **78**.... MitchGodwin$^{(5)}$ 6 71
(Sylvester Kirk) *rn wout tongue tie: in rr on outer: rdn over 1f out: sn no imp* **11/2**^{2}

-140 **10** 4 **Out Of The Dark (IRE)**^{7} 7281 3-9-4 **83**.... SeanLevey 2 66
(Richard Hannon) *in rr-div on inner: rdn over 1f out: wknd qckly fr 1f out* **33/1**

1m 25.3s (-0.70) **Going Correction** 0.0s/f (Stan)
WFA 3 from 5yo+ 2lb **10** Ran SP% **115.4**
Speed ratings (Par 105): **104,103,102,101,100 100,99,99,97,93**
CSF £20.54 CT £130.56 TOTE £3.50: £1.80, £3.00, £2.50; EX 23.60 Trifecta £193.50.
Owner The Blue Bar Partnership **Bred** Gestut Hofgut Heymann **Trained** Lambourn, Berks

FOCUS
Half a second slower than the first division. Not much early pace, winner soon in front from wide draw and had the run of things, finding plenty though and well worth another pb. The 2nd sets the level.

7463 RACING UK IN GLORIOUS HD CLASSIFIED STKS 7f (P)
8:50 (8:51) (Class 6) 3-Y-O+ **£2,264** (£673; £336; £168) **Stalls** Low

Form RPR

3000 **1** **Dark Confidant (IRE)**^{78} 4973 3-9-5 54.... DavidNolan 4 61
(Richard Fahey) *hld up in mid-div: rdn in centre over 2f out: kpt on wl to ld wl ins fnl f: on top cl home* **10/1**

5536 **2** 1 ½ **Just Fab (IRE)**^{14} 7070 3-9-5 51....(bt) JimCrowley 1 57
(Ali Stronge) *hld up in mid-div on inner: rdn over 2f out: led over 1f out: hdd wl ins fnl f: kpt on but no ch w wnr* **9/2**^{2}

4502 **3** 2 **Deftera Lad (IRE)**^{7} 7282 4-9-7 50.... JimmyQuinn 3 53
(Natalie Lloyd-Beavis) *hld up in rr: shkn up over 2f out: gd prog past horses in centre: rdn 1f out: kpt on wl to grab 3rd post* **8/1**^{3}

0552 **4** *hd* **Canford Belle**^{32} 6569 3-9-0 55.... PhilDennis$^{(5)}$ 5 51
(Grant Tuer) *settled bhd ldrs on inner: rdn 2f out: led over 1f out: hdd 1f out: stuck on but lost 3rd post* **8/1**^{3}

0003 **5** *nse* **Mr Marchwood**^{7} 7282 3-9-5 50.... LiamKeniry 7 51
(Sylvester Kirk) *promenant on outer: rdn over 2f out: wdst over 1f out: shuffled along ins fnl f: nrst fin* **8/1**^{3}

00 **6** ½ **Home Again**^{58} 5721 3-9-5 54.... KierenFox 9 50
(Lee Carter) *racd in 3rd: rdn over 2f out: nt qckn: kpt on one pce tl wknd fnl f* **9/2**^{2}

-063 **7** *nk* **Color Force (IRE)**^{69} 5338 3-9-5 52.... LukeMorris 6 49
(Gay Kelleway) *settled bhd ldrs on inner. rdn 2f out: one pce after* **3/1**^{1}

540 **8** ½ **Dalness Express**^{28} 6674 3-9-0 49.... CiaranMckee$^{(5)}$ 8 48
(John O'Shea) *s.s: in rr: rdn over 2f out: kpt on* **33/1**

0000 **9** *nk* **Rupert Boy (IRE)**^{8} 7261 3-8-12 55....(b) NatalieHambling$^{(7)}$ 10 47
(Scott Dixon) *sn led: rdn over 2f out: hdd over 1f out: wknd after* **40/1**

0360 **10** ½ **Plantation (IRE)**^{32} 6587 3-9-5 51.... PatCosgrave 14 46
(Robert Cowell) *in rr-div and t.k.h: rdn 2f out and sn ct on heels: kpt on one pce tl wknd ins fnl f* **33/1**

4005 **11** 1 ¾ **Zabdi**^{14} 7070 3-9-0 54.... PaddyBradley$^{(5)}$ 11 41
(Lee Carter) *in rr: rdn over 2f out: nt qckn and no imp after* **20/1**

4450 **12** 1 ¼ **Wensara Dream**^{40} 6290 3-9-5 52.... OisinMurphy 2 38
(Andrew Balding) *s.s: a in rr* **14/1**

0-00 **13** 2 ¾ **Miss Dusky Diva (IRE)**^{29} 6651 4-9-7 48.... WilliamCarson 13 32
(David W Drinkwater) *a in rr* **40/1**

1m 26.72s (0.72) **Going Correction** 0.0s/f (Stan)
WFA 3 from 4yo 2lb **13** Ran SP% **126.0**
Speed ratings (Par 101): **95,93,91,90,90 90,89,89,88,88 86,84,81**
CSF £55.06 TOTE £10.00: £2.60, £2.10, £3.00; EX 56.60 Trifecta £483.20.
Owner D I Perry **Bred** Rabbah Bloodstock Limited **Trained** Musley Bank, N Yorks

FOCUS
Only two of these had previously managed to win a race and this is ordinary form.

7464 RACINGUK.COM H'CAP 1m 3f (P)
9:20 (9:21) (Class 6) (0-55,55) 3-Y-O+ **£2,264** (£673; £336; £168) **Stalls** Low

Form RPR

0400 **1** **Munsarim (IRE)**^{13} 7103 9-9-2 **55**....(b) PaddyBradley$^{(5)}$ 14 61
(Lee Carter) *hld up in rr: gd prog on inner fr wl over 2f out: rdn 2f out: kpt on wl to ld fnl 110yds: rdn out* **12/1**

4403 **2** *hd* **Top Pocket**^{20} 6891 4-9-3 **51**.... DanielMuscutt 11 58
(Michael Madgwick) *hld up in rr-div: trapped on heels over 2f out: squeezed between horses and rdn 2f out: kpt on wl fnl f to take 2nd: nr fin* **16/1**

0335 **3** ½ **Lobster Cocktail (IRE)**^{8} 7256 3-9-0 **54**....^{1} LukeMorris 1 59+
(Ed Walker) *settled bhd ldrs on inner: gng wl wnt rdn 2f out: led over 1f out: kpt on wl ins fnl f tl hdd last 110yds and lost 2nd nr fin* **11/4**^{1}

5422 **4** ¾ **Just Fred (IRE)**^{18} 6967 3-8-10 **50**....(p) OisinMurphy 4 54
(Denis Coakley) *t.k.h in mid-div on inner: gng wl whn c to center and rdn wl over 1f out: one pce fnl f* **5/1**^{2}

060 **5** *nk* **Senor George (IRE)**^{21} 6871 9-9-6 **54**.... GeorgeBaker 2 57
(Simon Hodgson) *covered up in mid-div: dropped to 3rd last ent st: smooth prog fr over 2f out: rdn jst under 2f out: kpt on wl* **6/1**^{3}

3502 **6** 1 **Galuppi**^{37} 6406 5-9-4 **55**....(v) AlistairRawlinson$^{(3)}$ 5 57
(J R Jenkins) *mid-div on inner under restraint: rdn over 2f out: kpt on wl fr over 1f out: nvr nrr* **20/1**

0630 **7** *shd* **Sund City (FR)**^{2} 7421 3-8-13 **53**.... TomMarquand 3 54
(Harry Dunlop) *sn led: rdn over 2f out: hdd over 1f out: wknd ins fnl f* **11/1**

0-40 **8** 3 **Trust The Man (IRE)**^{116} 3652 3-9-1 **55**.... NickyMackay 6 52
(Simon Dow) *restless in stalls and completely missed break: rdn along over 2f out: stl last over 1f out: kpt on nicely fnl f* **50/1**

5003 **9** ½ **Oyster Card**^{13} 7103 3-8-9 **49**.... AndrewMullen 9 45
(Michael Appleby) *mid-div on outer: rdn over 2f out: nt qckn: kpt on again fnl f* **6/1**^{3}

5006 **10** ¾ **Master Of Heaven**^{6} 7309 3-8-12 **52**....^{1} PatCosgrave 13 47
(Jim Boyle) *settled in rr-div on outer: angled wd ent st: sn rdn: one pce after* **14/1**

3444 **11** *nse* **Megalala (IRE)**^{20} 6891 15-9-3 **51**.... DannyBrock 7 46
(John Bridger) *settled in mid-div: rdn over 2f out: no prog after and wknd fnl f* **16/1**

1500 **12** 2 **Salient**^{15} 7039 12-9-5 **53**.... KierenFox 12 44
(Michael Attwater) *pushed up to press ldr early: rdn ent st: kpt plugging away tl wknd over 1f out* **16/1**

6000 **13** 2 **Buzz Lightyere**^{7} 7282 3-9-1 **55**....(p) SteveDrowne 10 43
(Michael Attwater) *settled in mid-div: rdn over 2f out: no ex fr over 1f out* **25/1**

6050 **14** *hd* **Rennie Mackintosh (IRE)**^{7} 7282 4-9-5 **53**.... WilliamCarson 8 41
(John Bridger) *settled bhd ldrs on outer: rdn wl over 2f out: no imp and steadily wknd* **25/1**

2m 23.04s (1.14) **Going Correction** 0.0s/f (Stan)
WFA 3 from 4yo+ 6lb **14** Ran SP% **126.7**
Speed ratings (Par 101): **95,94,94,93,93 93,92,90,90,89 89,88,86,86**
CSF £191.94 CT £692.91 TOTE £21.40: £5.60, £4.00, £1.80; EX 270.60 Trifecta £646.20.
Owner Wackey Racers Harefield **Bred** Shadwell Estate Company Limited **Trained** Epsom, Surrey

FOCUS
Moderate form.
T/Jkpt: Not Won. T/Plt: £116.90 to a £1 stake. Pool: £64,369.0 - 550.4 winning tickets T/Qpdt: £32.50 to a £1 stake. Pool: £9,408.21 - 214 winning units **Cathal Gahan**

7146 NEWMARKET (R-H)
Wednesday, October 19

OFFICIAL GOING: Good to soft (7.3)
Wind: light, half behind Weather: overcast

7465 DISCOVERNEWMARKET.CO.UK MEDIAN AUCTION MAIDEN FILLIES' STKS (PLUS 10 RACE) (DIV I) 7f
1:30 (1:31) (Class 5) 2-Y-O **£3,881** (£1,155; £577; £288) **Stalls** Low

Form RPR

2 **1** **White Chocolate (IRE)**^{12} 7107 2-9-0 0.... JamieSpencer 10 77+
(David Simcock) *str: hld up in tch midfield: clsd to press ldrs 3f out: rdn over 1f out: pushed along hands and heels ins fnl f: r.o to ld nr fin* **7/2**^{1}

2 *hd* **Curlew River** 2-9-0 0.... WilliamBuick 8 77+
(Mark Johnston) *tall: scope: w ldrs: rdn and ev ch 3f out: led 2f out: edgd rt u.p ins fnl f: styd on: hdd nr fin* **7/1**

4 **3** 1 ½ **Nostalgie**^{20} 6897 2-9-0 0.... JimCrowley 6 73
(Rae Guest) *unf: wnt lft s: sn pressing ldr: rdn and ev ch over 2f out: carried sltly rt ins fnl f: no ex and wknd fnl 75yds* **4/1**^{2}

5 **4** 3 ½ **Dariga**^{15} 7056 2-9-0 0.... AndreaAtzeni 1 64+
(Roger Varian) *w'like: sn led: rdn over 2f out: hdd 2f out: 4th and outpcd over 1f out: wknd ins fnl f* **13/2**^{3}

5 4 **Paradise Cove** 2-9-0 0.... PatCosgrave 7 54+
(William Haggas) *str: s.i.s: in tch in rr: rdn ent fnl 2f: hdwy into 5th and edgd rt over 1f out: no imp and styd on same pce ins fnl f* **7/1**

6 1 ¼ **Kassandra (IRE)** 2-9-0 0.... SeanLevey 9 51
(Richard Hannon) *athletic: dwlt and pushed along early: in tch towards rr: hdwy to chse ldrs 3f out: sn rdn and outpcd 2f out: wknd over 1f out* **4/1**^{2}

0 **7** *hd* **Ronni Layne**^{25} 6782 2-9-0 0.... FMBerry 3 50
(Conrad Allen) *lengthy: dwlt: t.k.h: hld up in tch in midfield: rdn over 2f out: sn outpcd: wknd over 1f out* **100/1**

8 3 **Angel In Disguise (IRE)** 2-9-0 0.... TomQueally 4 43
(Philip McBride) *leggy: stdd s: t.k.h: hld up in tch in midfield: rdn over 2f out: sn struggling: wknd over 1f out* **16/1**

9 4 ½ **Autumn Glow** 2-9-0 0.... DanielMuscutt 5 32
(Miss Joey Ellis) *cmpt: bit bkwd: t.k.h: hld up in tch in midfield: rdn over 2f out: sn outpcd and btn whn unbalanced and stmbld over 1f out: sn wknd* **100/1**

5 **10** 7 **Hollywood Style**^{26} 6732 2-9-0 0.... MartinHarley 2 14
(William Knight) *lean: chsd ldrs: rdn 3f out: sn outpcd and bhd 2f out: wknd* **22/1**

1m 25.99s (0.59) **Going Correction** 0.0s/f (Good) **10** Ran SP% **112.8**
Speed ratings (Par 92): **96,95,94,90,85 84,83,80,75,67**
CSF £27.11 TOTE £3.10: £1.50, £2.20, £1.80; EX 26.50 Trifecta £115.20.
Owner The Rumble Racing Club **Bred** Scuderia Waldeck Srl **Trained** Newmarket, Suffolk

FOCUS
Stands' side course used. Stalls: far side. Following 6mm of rain on Sunday and a further 5mm on Tuesday and overnight, the going was given as good to soft (GoingStick: 7.9). A tailwind carried them home. The first three came clear in this fillies' maiden. A mixed standard so a fluid starting point ratings-wise.

7466 DISCOVERNEWMARKET.CO.UK MEDIAN AUCTION MAIDEN FILLIES' STKS (PLUS 10 RACE) (DIV II) 7f
2:00 (2:04) (Class 5) 2-Y-O **£3,881** (£1,155; £577; £288) **Stalls** Low

Form RPR

06 **1** **Medicean Ballet (IRE)**^{21} 6880 2-9-0 0.... DaneO'Neill 4 75
(Henry Candy) *str: in tch in midfield: rdn 3f out: hdwy and drvn to chse ldrs over 1f out: swtchd rt 1f out: led ins fnl f: styd on wl: rdn out* **6/1**

0 **2** 1 ¼ **Sulafah (IRE)**^{15} 7055 2-9-0 0....^{1} PaulHanagan 7 72
(Roger Varian) *str: w ldr: rdn and ev ch 2f out: led over 1f out: hdd ins fnl f: styd on same pce fnl 100yds* **5/1**

3 ¾ **Passcode** 2-9-0 0.... OisinMurphy 10 70
(Andrew Balding) *str: wnt lft s: in tch in midfield: effrt over 2f out: rdn to chse ldrs and swtchd rt jst over 1f out: swtchd lft and wnt 3rd 100yds out: styd on* **3/1**^{1}

4 3 **Babamunchkin** 2-9-0 0.... JamesDoyle 9 63+
(Michael Bell) *str: lw: sn led: rdn over 2f out: drvn and hdd over 1f out: no ex ins fnl f: wknd fnl 100yds* **9/2**^{3}

5 6 **Camaradorie (IRE)** 2-8-11 0 SimonPearce(3) 1 48+
(Lydia Pearce) *broke wl: sn stdd and wl in tch: effrt ent fnl 2f: 5th and outpcd over 1f out: wknd ins fnl f* **33/1**

6 5 **Diamante (IRE)** 2-9-0 0 TomQueally 3 35
(Daniel Kubler) *in tch towards rr: pushed along and rn green over 2f out: sn outpcd and wl hld after* **12/1**

50 7 ¾ **Alapinta**[32] 6578 2-9-0 0 FMBerry 6 33
(Ralph Beckett) *athletic: s.i.s: hld up in rr: effrt over 2f out: sn pushed along and outpcd: wknd 2f out* **4/1**[2]

8 1 **Lady Of York** 2-9-0 0 ShaneKelly 2 31
(Alan Bailey) *lengthy: pressed ldr pair: rdn 3f out: sn lost pl and wknd 2f out* **20/1**

9 17 **Raspberry Princess** 2-9-0 0 PatCosgrave 5
(Stuart Williams) *cmpt: bit bkwd: in tch towards rr: pushed along 3f out: sn struggling and bhd 2f out: eased ins fnl f* **14/1**

1m 26.53s (1.13) **Going Correction** 0.0s/f (Good) **9** Ran SP% **116.2**
Speed ratings (Par 92): **93,91,90,87,80 74,73,72,53**
CSF £36.28 TOTE £7.10: £2.20, £1.90, £1.30; EX 39.10 Trifecta £230.70.
Owner Simon Broke And Partners **Bred** New Line Stud Ltd **Trained** Kingston Warren, Oxon

FOCUS
This looked the weaker of the two divisions and the time was slower by 0.54sec, but again the level is fluid.

7467 NEWMARKET EQUINE SECURITY NURSERY H'CAP 7f
2:30 (2:36) (Class 5) (0-75,75) 2-Y-O **£3,881** (£1,155; £577; £288) **Stalls** Low

Form RPR

3154 1 **Tap Tap Boom**[15] 7033 2-9-4 **72** SteveDrowne 16 77
(George Baker) *led tl 3f out: styd w ldrs: rdn 2f out: led again jst ins fnl f: styd on u.p: rdn out* **9/1**

0422 2 ½ **Texas Katie**[9] 7228 2-9-0 **68** (p[1]) LukeMorris 11 72
(Archie Watson) *w ldrs tl led 3f out: drvn and hdd wl over 1f out: stl ev ch after: unable qck wl ins fnl f* **9/1**

3040 3 ½ **Star Maker**[38] 6377 2-8-10 **69** MitchGodwin(5) 4 72
(Sylvester Kirk) *lw: hld up in tch in last trio: swtchd rt and hdwy over 2f out: chsd ldrs and drvn 1f out: kpt on u.p ins fnl f* **20/1**

5004 4 ¾ **Parys Mountain (IRE)**[9] 7217 2-9-7 **75** WilliamBuick 15 76
(Charles Hills) *t.k.h: chsd ldrs: rdn and unable qck over 1f out: rallied ins fnl f: styd on u.p fnl 100yds* **8/1**[3]

4140 5 hd **Dourado (IRE)**[41] 6260 2-9-7 **75** SeanLevey 8 75
(Richard Hannon) *hld up in tch in midfield: effrt 2f out: drvn over 1f out: kpt on u.p ins fnl f* **6/1**[1]

2330 6 nk **Suffragette City (IRE)**[25] 6787 2-9-2 **70** JamesDoyle 14 69
(Richard Hannon) *w ldrs: rdn to ld wl over 1f out: hdd jst ins fnl f: no ex u.p: wknd towards fin* **12/1**

3563 7 ½ **Mullarkey**[10] 7185 2-9-3 **71** KierenFox 6 69
(John Best) *cmpt: wl in tch in midfield: effrt over 1f out: styd on same pce u.p ins fnl f* **8/1**[3]

365 8 1 ¾ **Plato's Kode (IRE)**[14] 7071 2-8-12 **66** OisinMurphy 1 60
(Seamus Durack) *w'like: t.k.h: hld up in tch in last pair: effrt 3f out: hdwy over 1f out: kpt on ins fnl f: nvr trbld ldrs* **12/1**

634 9 nk **Elementary**[76] 5084 2-9-3 **71** [1] RyanMoore 3 64
(Michael Bell) *tall: in tch in midfield: rdn over 2f out: unable qck u.p and outpcd over 1f out: styd on same pce ins fnl f* **12/1**

01 10 2 ½ **Uncle Charlie (IRE)**[25] 6789 2-9-3 **71** GrahamLee 13 58+
(Ann Duffield) *unf: stmbld bdly sn after leaving stalls: sn chsng ldrs and t.k.h: chsd ldrs: rdn and lost pl ent fnl 2f: wknd fnl f* **11/1**

034 11 nk **Miss Anticipation (IRE)**[64] 5516 2-9-6 **74** GeorgeBaker 9 60
(Roger Charlton) *leggy: stdd s: t.k.h: hld up in tch in rr: shkn up whn nt clr run and swtchd lft over 1f out: no imp after: nvr trbld ldrs* **20/1**

2013 12 4 **Highland Lotus**[11] 7140 2-9-5 **73** PatCosgrave 5 49
(William Haggas) *in tch in midfield: rdn ent fnl 2f: sn struggling and lost pl 2f out: wknd fnl f* **16/1**

634 13 6 **Presence Process**[30] 6632 2-9-4 **72** AndreaAtzeni 12 33
(Luca Cumani) *str: free to post: in tch in midfield: rdn 3f out: struggling u.p and edgd rt over 1f out: bhd fnl f* **7/1**[2]

1m 25.77s (0.37) **Going Correction** 0.0s/f (Good) **13** Ran SP% **115.8**
Speed ratings (Par 95): **97,96,95,95,94 94,93,91,91,88 88,83,76**
CSF £84.91 CT £1612.21 TOTE £11.50: £3.30, £3.40, £6.70; EX 74.30 Trifecta £1422.00.
Owner Steve & Jolene De'Lemos **Bred** London Thoroughbred Services Ltd **Trained** Manton, Wilts

FOCUS
The early gallop wasn't strong and, with the pace holding up well, few got into it.

7468 NEWMARKETRACECOURSES.CO.UK MAIDEN STKS (PLUS 10 RACE) 7f
3:05 (3:10) (Class 4) 2-Y-O **£4,528** (£1,347; £673; £336) **Stalls** Low

Form RPR

2 1 **Cape Byron**[8] 7243 2-9-0 0 AndreaAtzeni 1 86+
(Roger Varian) *str: lw: hld up in tch in midfield and travelled strly: clsd over 2f out: pushed along and qcknd to ld over 1f out: clr and r.o wl ins fnl f: pushed out: comf* **3/1**[2]

2 2 ½ **Manchego** 2-9-0 0 JimCrowley 4 77
(Hugo Palmer) *str: lw: chsd ldrs: clsd and jnd ldrs 3f out tl led 2f out: sn rdn: hdd and drvn and unable qck over 1f out: styd on same pce ins fnl f* **8/1**[3]

2 3 1 ¼ **Rummani**[54] 5848 2-9-0 0 WilliamBuick 2 74
(Charlie Appleby) *racd keenly: led tl 3f out: stl ev ch tl unable qck u.p over 1f out: styd on same pce ins fnl f* **10/11**[1]

02 4 nk **Farook (IRE)**[20] 6904 2-9-0 0 DaneO'Neill 10 73
(Charles Hills) *str: lw: dwlt: sn in tch in midfield: hdwy to chse ldrs 3f out: ev ch and rdn 2f out: unable qck over 1f out: one pced ins fnl f* **14/1**

3 5 nk **Teqany (IRE)**[14] 7065 2-9-0 0 PaulHanagan 7 72
(Owen Burrows) *str: w ldr tl led 3f out: rdn and hdd 2f out: unable qck and outpcd over 1f out: plugged on same pce ins fnl f* **10/1**

6 hd **Volatile** 2-9-0 0 MartinHarley 3 72
(James Tate) *str: bit bkwd: in tch in midfield: clsd over 2f out: pushed along and no imp over 1f out: keeping on same pce whn n.m.r wl ins fnl f* **33/1**

7 1 ½ **Revel** 2-9-0 0 OisinMurphy 12 68
(Stuart Williams) *stdd and swtchd rt s: hld up in tch in last quartet: swtchd rt and rdn jst over 2f out: 7th and no imp over 1f out: kpt on same pce after* **100/1**

8 1 ¼ **Paradise Lake (IRE)** 2-9-0 0 RyanMoore 14 65
(Sir Michael Stoute) *athletic: lengthy: stdd s: hld up in tch in rr: rdn 3f out: sme hdwy 2f out: no imp over 1f out: no threat to ldrs but kpt on fnl 100yds* **14/1**

9 1 ¼ **Medalla De Oro** 2-9-0 0 LukeMorris 11 62
(Peter Chapple-Hyam) *athletic: bit bkwd: squeezed for room leaving stalls: in tch towards rr: effrt u.p over 2f out: no imp and outpcd over 1f out: wknd ins fnl f* **50/1**

10 hd **Enhancement (IRE)** 2-9-0 0 SeanLevey 13 61
(Richard Hannon) *cmpt: stdd s: hld up in tch in last quartet: hdwy 3f out: rdn and no imp over 1f out: wknd ins fnl f* **33/1**

11 3 ¾ **Treagus** 2-9-0 0 StevieDonohoe 9 52
(Charlie Fellowes) *leggy: bit bkwd: in tch in midfield: rdn 3f out: lost pl and bhd 2f out: son wknd* **100/1**

12 1 ¼ **Widnes** 2-9-0 0 LiamJones 5 49
(Alan Bailey) *leggy: in tch in midfield: rdn 3f out: sn lost pl and bhd 2f oit: sn wknd* **100/1**

13 13 **Pushjockeypush** 2-9-0 0 SteveDrowne 8 16
(Stuart Williams) *tall: s.i.s: a towards rr: rdn 3f out: sn struggling and bhd 2f out* **100/1**

1m 25.54s (0.14) **Going Correction** 0.0s/f (Good) **13** Ran SP% **122.7**
Speed ratings (Par 97): **99,96,94,94,94 93,92,90,89,89 84,83,68**
CSF £27.70 TOTE £4.00: £1.30, £2.70, £1.10; EX 34.60 Trifecta £68.50.
Owner Sheikh Mohammed Obaid Al Maktoum **Bred** Darley **Trained** Newmarket, Suffolk
■ Canadian Royal was withdrawn. Price at time of withdrawal 100/1. Rule 4 does not apply.

FOCUS
This looked a good maiden on paper, and it was the quickest of the first four races on the card.

7469 AR LEGAL HOUGHTON CONDITIONS STKS (PLUS 10 RACE) 7f
3:40 (3:40) (Class 2) 2-Y-O **£9,056** (£2,695; £1,346; £673) **Stalls** Low

Form RPR

1 1 **Dreamfield**[14] 7071 2-9-2 0 JamesDoyle 3 99
(John Gosden) *str: t.k.h: sn led: jnd 2f out: wandered lft and rdn over 1f out: sustained duel w runner up ins fnl f: hld on wl u.p* **2/5**[1]

0323 2 shd **Top Score**[15] 7042 2-9-2 94 JimCrowley 2 99
(Saeed bin Suroor) *trckd ldrs: effrt wl over 1f out: swtchd rt ent fnl f: str chal and sustained duel w wnr ins fnl f: r.o: jst hld* **7/2**[2]

11 3 1 ¾ **Sincil Bank (USA)**[20] 6904 2-9-2 82 JamieSpencer 5 94
(David Simcock) *tall: scope: racd in centre tl 1/2-way: chsd ldr: effrt and ev ch 2f out tl unable qck 1f out: 3rd and styd on same pce ins fnl f* **7/1**[3]

110 4 4 **Parnassian (IRE)**[38] 6388 2-9-2 0 DougieCostello 1 84
(K R Burke) *cmpt: hld up in tch in 4th: effrt 2f out: no imp over 1f out: wknd and ins fnl f* **16/1**

04 5 11 **Justice Frederick (IRE)**[75] 5108 2-9-2 0 TomQueally 4 57
(Paul D'Arcy) *racd in centre tl 1/2-way: s.i.s: a rr: rdn over 2f out: bhd over 1f out* **50/1**

1m 25.19s (-0.21) **Going Correction** 0.0s/f (Good) **5** Ran SP% **114.0**
Speed ratings (Par 101): **101,100,98,94,81**
CSF £2.33 TOTE £1.30: £1.10, £1.60; EX 2.50 Trifecta £5.00.
Owner Godolphin **Bred** Meon Valley Stud **Trained** Newmarket, Suffolk

FOCUS
John Gosden had won this the previous two years and was represented by a hot favourite this time around, but he made hard work of landing the odds. Unsurprisingly, it was the quickest of the five races run over the trip on the card. The level is a bit fluid but the winner was no better than on his debut.

7470 BREEDERS SUPPORTING RACING EBF MAIDEN STKS (STALLION-RESTRICTED) (PLUS 10 RACE) 1m
4:15 (4:16) (Class 4) 2-Y-O **£6,469** (£1,925; £962; £481) **Stalls** Low

Form RPR

1 **Cracksman** 2-9-5 0 RobertHavlin 1 91+
(John Gosden) *athletic: hld up in tch towards rr: hdwy 3f out: rdn and ev ch over 1f out: led ins fnl f: r.o wl* **9/2**[3]

2 1 ¼ **Wild Tempest** 2-9-5 0 WilliamBuick 11 88+
(Charlie Appleby) *lengthy: pushed lft s: sn rcvrd and chsd ldr: led 2f out: sn pushed along: rn green and hung rt: rdn and hdd ins fnl f: styd on same pce after* **12/1**

3 3 2 ¾ **Alfawaris**[32] 6570 2-9-5 0 PaulHanagan 4 82
(Owen Burrows) *tall: lengthy: lw: led: hdd and rdn 2f out: carried rt and unable qck over 1f out: 3rd and kpt on same pce ins fnl f* **9/4**[1]

5 4 2 **Stradivarius (IRE)**[14] 7074 2-9-5 0 FrankieDettori 2 77
(John Gosden) *athletic: chsd ldrs: rdn over 2f out: outpcd u.p over 1f out: wl hld and kpt on same pce ins fnl f* **3/1**[2]

5 2 ½ **Fibonacci** 2-9-5 0 JimCrowley 7 71
(Hugo Palmer) *str: lengthy: lw: chsd ldrs: rdn over 2f out: outpcd and btn whn carried rt over 1f out: wknd ins fnl f* **11/2**

5 6 nk **Bedouin (IRE)**[18] 6945 2-9-5 0 (b) PatCosgrave 10 71
(Luca Cumani) *str: wnt lft s: t.k.h: hld up in tch: effrt 2f out: edgd rt u.p and no imp over 1f out: wknd ins fnl f* **16/1**

7 3 ½ **Almoreb (IRE)** 2-9-5 0 DaneO'Neill 8 63
(Richard Hannon) *athletic: in tch: rdn over 2f out: sn struggling and outpcd: wknd over 1f out* **20/1**

0 8 13 **Desert Grey (IRE)**[9] 7225 2-9-5 0 AndreaAtzeni 6 33
(Roger Varian) *str: in tch in midfield: rdn and lost pl over 2f out: sn bhd and lost tch over 1f out* **25/1**

9 ½ **Our Cilla** 2-8-11 0 ShelleyBirkett(3) 9 27
(Julia Feilden) *leggy: in tch towards rr: rdn over 2f out: sn btn: lost tch over 1f out* **100/1**

10 33 **Abacus** 2-9-5 0 JamieSpencer 3
(Michael Bell) *str: bit bkwd: s.i.s: rn green and a detached in last: lost tch over 2f out: eased fnl f: t.o* **33/1**

1m 37.68s (-0.92) **Going Correction** 0.0s/f (Good) **10** Ran SP% **115.4**
Speed ratings (Par 97): **104,102,100,98,95 95,91,78,78,45**
CSF £53.31 TOTE £5.70: £1.60, £3.10, £1.70; EX 54.90 Trifecta £170.70.
Owner A E Oppenheimer **Bred** Hascombe And Valiant Studs **Trained** Newmarket, Suffolk

FOCUS
A good maiden, and the first two in particular look promising types for next season.

7471 RACING UK HD NURSERY H'CAP 1m 1f
4:50 (4:52) (Class 4) (0-85,83) 2-Y-O **£4,528** (£1,347; £673; £336) **Stalls** Low

Form RPR

01 1 **Desert Skyline (IRE)**[34] 6523 2-9-7 **83** FMBerry 5 92+
(David Elsworth) *athletic: hld up in tch: clsd to chal wl over 1f out: rdn to ld jst ins fnl f: r.o strly to draw clr fnl 100yds: comf* **13/2**

015 2 3 ½ **Ghayyar (IRE)**[46] 6122 2-9-7 **83** FrankieDettori 1 85
(Richard Hannon) *led and set stdy gallop: rdn and qcknd 2f out: drvn over 1f out: hdd jst ins fnl f: outpcd by wnr but kpt on for clr 2nd* **4/1**[1]

61 **3** *2* **Je Suis Charlie**[35] 6473 2-8-13 **75**................................ JamieSpencer 6 73
(Michael Bell) *str: stdd s: t.k.h: hld up in tch: hdwy 5f out: chsd ldrs and rdn 2f out: unable qck over 1f out: styd on same pce fnl f: wnt 3rd and eased wl ins fnl f* **5/1**[2]

621 **4** *1 ¼* **Hersigh**[13] 7100 2-9-2 **78**.. JamesDoyle 4 74
(Saeed bin Suroor) *t.k.h: chsd ldrs: rdn and ev ch 2f out tl no ex jst ins fnl f: wknd fnl 100yds* **4/1**[1]

41 **5** *2 ¾* **Ode To Glory**[32] 6590 2-8-7 **69**.. AndreaAtzeni 2 59
(Rae Guest) *athletic: t.k.h: chsd ldrs: rdn ent fnl 2f: unable qck and outpcd over 1f out: wknd ins fnl f* **10/1**

3421 **6** *2 ¾* **Spring Jig (USA)**[23] 6828 2-9-6 **82**..............................(b[1]) JimCrowley 3 67
(Hugo Palmer) *t.k.h: chsd ldrs: hdwy to join ldr 4f out: rdn and outpcd ent fnl 2f: wknd over 1f out* **11/2**[3]

61 **7** *2 ½* **First Quest (USA)**[76] 5073 2-9-2 **78**................................... RyanMoore 8 58
(Ed Dunlop) *hld up in tch in rr: effrt 3f out: sn rdn and no imp: wknd over 1f out* **6/1**

040 **8** *26* **Mungo Madness**[14] 7074 2-8-5 **70**............................. ShelleyBirkett(3) 7
(Julia Feilden) *in tch towards rr: rdn 3f out: sn struggling and bhd: lost tch over 1f out: eased ins fnl f: t.o* **33/1**

1m 52.11s (0.41) **Going Correction** 0.0s/f (Good) **8** Ran SP% **111.7**
Speed ratings (Par 97): **98,94,93,92,89 87,84,61**
CSF £31.08 CT £139.08 TOTE £7.60: £2.60, £1.70, £1.60; EX 27.40 Trifecta £212.00.
Owner C Benham/ D Whitford/ L Quinn/ K Quinn **Bred** Tinnakill Bloodstock & Cannings **Trained** Newmarket, Suffolk

FOCUS
An open nursery and the winner is improving fast. The form should be at least this good looking at the 2nd-4th.

7472 HOME OF RACING FILLIES' H'CAP 1m
5:20 (5:21) (Class 2) (0-100,93) 3-Y-O+ **£12,938** (£3,850; £1,924; £962) **Stalls** Low

Form RPR

0103 **1** **Lavetta**[13] 7095 4-9-0 **83**... JoeFanning 2 91+
(Alan Swinbank) *taken down early: t.k.h: chsd ldrs: wnt 2nd 1/2-way: upsides ldr over 2f out: rdn to ld over 1f out: hld on wl u.p ins fnl f: wnt lft cl hone* **11/2**[2]

000 **2** *nk* **Little Lady Katie (IRE)**[26] 6736 4-8-10 **84**.............. JordanVaughan(5) 5 91
(K R Burke) *led: rdn 2f out: hdd over 1f out: stl ev ch and kpt on wl u.p ins fnl f: keeping on same pce and hld whn carried lft cl hone* **7/1**

4004 **3** *¾* **Sharaakah (IRE)**[18] 6947 3-9-7 **93**................................... JamesDoyle 3 97
(Ed Dunlop) *t.k.h: chsd ldr tl 1/2-way: rdn 2f out: drvn over 1f out: kpt on same pce ins fnl f* **7/2**[1]

550 **4** *1* **Margaret's Mission (IRE)**[19] 6915 5-9-0 **83**................... MartinHarley 4 86
(Jim Goldie) *stdd s: t.k.h: hld up in tch in midfield: effrt 2f out: chsd ldrs and drvn 1f out: styd on same pce ins fnl f* **8/1**

-516 **5** *½* **Up In Lights (IRE)**[39] 6331 4-9-9 **92**................................. TomQueally 9 94+
(James Fanshawe) *stdd and dropped in after s: hld up in tch in rr: effrt 2f out: drvn over 1f out: kpt on ins fnl f: nvr enough pce to get involved* **7/2**[1]

0206 **6** *½* **Alexandrakollontai (IRE)**[12] 7108 6-8-9 **78**..............(b) JamesSullivan 8 79
(Alistair Whillans) *hld up in tch: pushed along 3f out: rdn over 2f out: kpt on u.p ins fnl f: nvr enough pce to get on terms* **25/1**

3-00 **7** *1* **Fourth Way (IRE)**[18] 6947 3-9-4 **90**.................................. OisinMurphy 1 87+
(Roger Varian) *hld up in tch in last pair: ome hdwy u.p over 1f out: kpt on same pce and no imp ins fnl f* **11/1**

500 **8** *½* **Lil Sophella (IRE)**[5] 7316 7-9-4 **87**................................. JackGarritty 7 84
(Patrick Holmes) *lw: t.k.h: hld up in tch in midfield: rdn ent fnl 2f: unable qck and lost pl over 1f out: kpt on same pce fnl f* **25/1**

4012 **9** *2 ¾* **Hidden Rebel**[46] 6113 4-9-4 **87**...................................... PaulMulrennan 6 78
(Alistair Whillans) *restless in stalls: in tch and flashing tail at times: rdn ent fnl 2f: unable qck and lost pl over 1f out: wknd and flashed tail ins fnl f* **6/1**[3]

1m 40.01s (1.41) **Going Correction** 0.0s/f (Good)
WFA 3 from 4yo+ 3lb **9** Ran SP% **113.8**
Speed ratings (Par 96): **92,91,90,89,89 88,87,87,84**
CSF £42.89 CT £151.53 TOTE £6.40: £2.10, £2.50, £1.50; EX 50.10 Trifecta £272.70.
Owner Guy Reed Racing **Bred** G Reed **Trained** Melsonby, N Yorks

FOCUS
The pace held up in this fillies' handicap and few got involved. A small pb from the winner.
T/Plt: £17.90 to a £1 stake. Pool: £64,787.42 - 2641.59 winning units. T/Qpdt: £8.20 to a £1 stake. Pool: £6,022.11 - 537.46 winning units. **Steve Payne**

7473 - (Foreign Racing) - See Raceform Interactive

7079 NAVAN (L-H)
Wednesday, October 19
OFFICIAL GOING: Yielding to soft

7474a WWW.NAVANRACECOURSE.IE H'CAP 5f
2:35 (2:36) (45-75,71) 3-Y-O+ **£4,522** (£1,397; £661; £294; £110)

RPR

1 **One Boy (IRE)**[8] 7252 5-10-0 **71**... PatSmullen 8 83
(Paul Midgley) *chsd ldrs: clsr in 3rd fr 1/2-way and impr on outer to ld narrowly 1f out: rdn and kpt on wl u.p ins fnl f* **11/2**[1]

2 *½* **Doonard Prince (IRE)**[9] 7234 7-9-3 **60**.........................(b) ShaneFoley 5 70
(Ross O'Sullivan, Ire) *disp early tl sn settled bhd ldr: 2nd 1/2-way: impr to ld 2f out: rdn and hdd narrowly 1f out: kpt on wl wout matching wnr ins fnl f* **13/2**[3]

3 *2* **Mo Henry**[34] 6502 4-8-9 **62**....................................(v) DannySheehy(10) 11 65
(Adrian Paul Keatley, Ire) *chsd ldrs: rdn into 3rd jst ins fnl f and no imp on ldrs clsng stages: kpt on same pce* **12/1**

4 *1 ¾* **Enter The Red (IRE)**[22] 6861 7-9-9 **71**......................(b) TomMadden(5) 9 68
(Aidan Anthony Howard, Ire) *chsd ldrs: rdn in 6th over 1f out and no imp on ldrs u.p in 4th ins fnl f: kpt on same pce* **8/1**

5 *¾* **Roryslittlesister (IRE)**[9] 7234 6-7-11 **47** oh2.........(t) AndrewBreslin(7) 2 41
(S M Duffy, Ire) *mid-div: sme hdwy far side after 1/2-way: rdn to dispute 5th 1f out and sn no imp on ldrs: kpt on one pce ins fnl f* **25/1**

6 *nk* **Suburban Sky (IRE)**[14] 7080 5-7-11 **47** oh2............(bt) SeanDavis(7) 10 40
(H Rogers, Ire) *mid-div: sme hdwy on outer after 1/2-way: no imp on ldrs u.p in 6th wl ins fnl f: kpt on one pce* **12/1**

7 *½* **Count Of Carabass (IRE)**[11] 7163 5-9-3 **60**..................(p) ChrisHayes 1 51
(Miss Hilary McLoughlin, Ire) *chsd ldrs: rdn in 4th 2f out and no imp on ldrs over 1f out: one pce fnl f* **7/1**

8 *1 ¾* **Future Icon**[14] 7080 4-9-7 **69**... AnaO'Brien(5) 6 54
(Edward Lynam, Ire) *mid-div: rdn in 9th over 1f out and no imp: kpt on one pce* **6/1**[2]

9 *nk* **Botanical Lady (IRE)**[16] 7023 5-9-4 **61**....................... WayneLordan 14 45
(H Rogers, Ire) *hld up: rdn and no imp in 10th over 1f out: kpt on one pce* **10/1**

10 *¾* **Battleroftheboyne (IRE)**[10] 7192 7-9-10 **67**........... DeclanMcDonogh 4 48
(Eamonn O'Connell, Ire) *disp early tl sn led narrowly: rdn and hdd 2f out: no ex u.p in 2nd 1 1/2f out and sn wknd* **7/1**

11 *1 ¾* **Art World (IRE)**[14] 7080 4-7-11 **47** oh2.....................(t) DamienMelia(7) 13 22
(James Coyle, Ire) *hld up: rdn in rr after 1/2-way and sme hdwy into mod 11th ins fnl f: kpt on one pce* **20/1**

12 *2 ¾* **Affinia Fifty (IRE)**[12] 7132 6-8-4 **47** oh2............................ RoryCleary 12 12
(Thomas Gibney, Ire) *w ldrs: pushed along in 3rd bef 1/2-way and sn no ex: wknd fnl 2f* **66/1**

13 *nk* **Love Is All Around (IRE)**[14] 7080 3-8-6 **49**...............(b) ConorHoban 15 14
(Dermot Anthony McLoughlin, Ire) *towards rr: pushed along after 1/2-way and no imp u.p in 13th 1 1/2f out: one pce* **66/1**

14 *nse* **Little Cupcake**[89] 4619 5-8-10 **53**...................................[1] RonanWhelan 3 17
(Paul W Flynn, Ire) *dwlt sltly: sn settled in rr of mid-div: rdn under 2f out and sn no imp u.p towards rr: one pce fnl f* **25/1**

P **Periwig (IRE)**[14] 7079 3-9-3 **65**..[1] OisinOrr(5) 7
(Edward Lynam, Ire) *dwlt and sltly awkward s: towards rr: eased after 1/2-way and p.u under 2f out* **20/1**

1m 3.97s (-2.83) **15** Ran SP% **123.8**
CSF £38.06 CT £432.69 TOTE £5.60: £1.60, £2.50, £5.80; DF 33.30 Trifecta £643.10.
Owner R Wardlaw **Bred** Tom Radley **Trained** Westow, N Yorks

FOCUS
Plenty of familiar faces in this 45-75 sprint. The front two pulled clear inside the final furlong. They did not hang about despite the conditions.

7475a COME RACING AGAIN SUNDAY 13TH NOVEMBER H'CAP 5f 182y
3:10 (3:10) 3-Y-O+ **£7,235** (£2,235; £1,058; £470; £176)

RPR

1 **Giant Spark**[33] 6539 4-9-10 **89**.. PatSmullen 9 98
(Paul Midgley) *sn led: narrow advantage at 1/2-way: rdn and hdd 1 1/2f out: remained prom and regained advantage fnl 150yds: styd on wl to assert clsng stages* **3/1**[1]

2 *1 ¼* **Rattling Jewel**[10] 7192 4-8-13 **78**................................(p) WayneLordan 1 83
(Miss Nicole McKenna, Ire) *wnt lft s: sn chsd ldrs: clsr in 2nd bef 1/2-way: rdn to ld narrowly 1 1/2f out tl hdd u.p fnl 150yds: no imp on wnr clsng stages* **5/1**[3]

3 *nk* **Shanghai Beauty (IRE)**[10] 7192 4-8-9 **81**............(tp) AndrewBreslin(7) 7 85
(K J Condon, Ire) *chsd ldrs: tk clsr order over 1f out: sn rdn and disp 2nd ent fnl f: no imp on wnr u.p in 3rd wl ins fnl f: kpt on same pce: jst hld 3rd* **12/1**

4 *nse* **Fair Game (IRE)**[16] 7021 3-9-0 **79**...................................(p) BillyLee 6 84
(E J O'Grady, Ire) *prom tl sn settled bhd ldr: 3rd 1/2-way: rdn bhd ldrs 1 1/2f out and no imp on wnr u.p in 4th wl ins fnl f: kpt on same pce: jst hld for 3rd* **10/1**

5 *½* **Captain Power (IRE)**[24] 6819 4-9-11 **93**................. RobbieDowney(3) 4 95
(Edward Lynam, Ire) *in rr: pushed along fr 1/2-way and sme hdwy u.p nr side ins fnl f to chse ldrs in 5th: nvr on terms* **4/1**[2]

6 *½* **Ducky Mallon (IRE)**[10] 7192 5-9-1 **80**.....................(t) SeamieHeffernan 3 81
(Donal Kinsella, Ire) *hld up in tch: rdn in 7th 1 1/2f out and no imp on ldrs wl ins fnl f where wnt 6th: nvr on terms* **5/1**[3]

7 *hd* **Geological (IRE)**[5] 7233 4-9-0 **79**...................................... RoryCleary 5 79
(Damian Joseph English, Ire) *towards rr: 8th 1/2-way: rdn in 8th under 2f out and no imp on ldrs in 7th wl ins fnl f: kpt on same pce* **16/1**

8 *½* **Louis Leroy (IRE)**[9] 7234 4-8-5 **70**................................(vt) LeighRoche 8 68
(Edward Lynam, Ire) *w.w towards rr: 7th 1/2-way: hdwy bhd ldrs 1 1/2f out: rdn in 5th ins fnl f and sn no ex: wknd towards rr clsng stages* **9/1**

9 *¾* **Bubbly Bellini (IRE)**[17] 6984 9-8-13 **78**...............(p) DeclanMcDonogh 2 74
(Adrian McGuinness, Ire) *settled bhd ldrs: tk clsr order bhd ldrs far side at 1/2-way: rdn disputing 3rd 1 1/2f out and sn no ex: wknd to rr ins fnl f* **7/1**

1m 14.92s (0.32)
WFA 3 from 4yo+ 1lb **9** Ran SP% **123.5**
CSF £19.68 CT £165.49 TOTE £2.40: £1.40, £2.10, £4.50; DF 22.90 Trifecta £221.40.
Owner Frank Brady **Bred** Frank Brady **Trained** Westow, N Yorks

FOCUS
A decent quality sprint handicap for the time of year. The winner, sent off favourite, looked in deep trouble at the halfway mark and traded at 49-1 for a small sum. A pb from the winner.

7476 - 7479a (Foreign Racing) - See Raceform Interactive

7454 DEAUVILLE (R-H)
Wednesday, October 19
OFFICIAL GOING: Polytrack: standard; turf: good

7480a PRIX DES RESERVOIRS (GROUP 3) (2YO FILLIES) (ROUND) (TURF) 1m (R)
12:25 (12:25) 2-Y-O **£29,411** (£11,764; £8,823; £5,882; £2,941)

RPR

1 **Melesina (IRE)**[32] 6554 2-8-10 0...................................... ThierryJarnet 6 103
(Richard Fahey) *midfield in tch: rdn to chal 2f out: led ins fnl f: kpt on wl* **14/1**[3]

2 *1 ¼* **Turf Laurel (IRE)**[41] 2-8-10 0... AlexisBadel 8 100
(S Kobayashi, France) *led: rdn and strly pressed 2f out: kpt on but hdd ins fnl f: no ex w wnr after* **22/1**

3 *1 ½* **Onthemoonagain (FR)**[46] 2-8-10 0................. Jean-BernardEyquem 5 96
(J-C Rouget, France) *hld up in midfield: rdn 2f out: kpt on but nt pce to chal: up for 3rd fnl strides* **5/2**[1]

4 *hd* **Invincible Queen (FR)**[41] 6271 2-8-10 0.............................. OlivierPeslier 3 96
(F Head, France) *midfield on inner: angled out and rdn early in st: kpt on but nt pce to chal: lost 3rd fnl strides* **3/1**[2]

5 *1 ¼* **Assanilka (FR)**[15] 7050 2-8-10 0.......................... Pierre-CharlesBoudot 1 93
(Harry Dunlop) *sn prom on inner: rdn and effrt 2f out: nt qckn fnl f and fdd into 5th towards fin* **5/2**[1]

6 *2* **Vadsariya (FR)**[60] 5702 2-8-11 0 ow1................. ChristopheSoumillon 4 90
(A De Royer-Dupre, France) *hld up and sn in rr: pushed along to try and cl in st: outpcd and nvr on terms* **3/1**[2]

7 *¾* **Barlongueta (IRE)**[24] 2-8-10 0................................ VincentCheminaud 7 87
(M Delcher Sanchez, France) *trckd ldr: rdn and v brief effrt 2f out: sn no ex and btn: wknd* **28/1**

8 *9* **Holy Makfi**[14] 7086 2-8-10 0.. MlleIsisMagnin 2 66
(J-Y Artu, France) *hld up: a in rr: bhd and wl btn fnl f* **33/1**

1m 40.68s (-0.12) **8** Ran SP% **124.5**
PARI-MUTUEL (all including 1 euro stake): WIN 27.10; PLACE 4.10, 2.80, 1.70; DF 74.00; SF 204.20.

Owner Nick Bradley Racing (Lastroseofsummer) **Bred** Duggan Bloodstock **Trained** Musley Bank, N Yorks

GEELONG (L-H)
Wednesday, October 19

OFFICIAL GOING: Turf: good

7481a BET365 GEELONG CUP (GROUP 3 H'CAP) (3YO+) (TURF) 1m 4f
6:00 (6:00) 3-Y-O+

£89,108 (£26,732; £13,366; £6,683; £3,712; £2,970)

RPR

1 **Qewy (IRE)**[85] 4734 6-8-7 **0** KerrinMcEvoy 6 106
(Charlie Appleby) **3/1**[2]

2 *hd* **Grey Lion (IRE)**[59] 5692 4-8-9 **0** KatelynMallyon 8 108
(Matt Cumani, Australia) **11/2**

3 *3/4* **Oceanographer**[60] 5655 4-8-7 **0** BenMelham 5 106+
(Charlie Appleby) **19/10**[1]

4 *2* **Kinema (IRE)**[60] 5655 5-8-7 **0** (t) CraigNewitt 1 101
(Chris Waller, Australia) **17/2**

5 *2 1/2* **Swacadelic (GER)**[17] 6994 5-8-8 **0** ow1 (b) MichaelWalker 7 98+
(Aaron Purcell, Australia) **20/1**

6 *shd* **All I Survey (AUS)**[7] 5-8-7 **0** (v) MichaelDee 4 97
(Pat Carey, Australia) **15/1**

7 *3/4* **Lucques (AUS)**[17] 6994 5-8-7 **0** (v) DamianLane 3 96
(Mathew Ellerton & Simon Zahra, Australia) **5/1**[3]

8 *7* **Wells (AUS)**[59] 9-8-7 **0** BenAllen 2 85
(Kathryn Durden, Australia) **40/1**

2m 28.98s (148.98) **8** Ran SP% **115.5**

Owner Godolphin **Bred** Darley **Trained** Newmarket, Suffolk

7304 CHELMSFORD (A.W) (L-H)
Thursday, October 20

OFFICIAL GOING: Polytrack: standard
Wind: light, across Weather: dry

7482 TOTEPLACEPOT NURSERY H'CAP 1m 2f (P)
5:45 (5:47) (Class 6) (0-65,65) 2-Y-O **£2,911** (£866; £432; £216) **Stalls** Low

Form RPR

3441 **1** **Katebird (IRE)**[8] 7286 2-9-6 **64** 6ex AndrewMullen 2 70
(Mark Johnston) *hld up wl in tch in midfield: gng wl but nt clr run over 2f out: trcking ldrs over 1f out: gap opened and qcknd to ld 150yds: r.o wl: readily* **9/2**[2]

6660 **2** *1 1/4* **Clenymistra (IRE)**[19] 6963 2-8-9 **53** (p) LukeMorris 6 57
(Marco Botti) *in tch in midfield: effrt over 1f out: drvn and styd on ins fnl f: chsd wnr wl ins fnl f: r.o for clr 2nd but no threat to wnr* **16/1**

5004 **3** *1 1/2* **Pussy Galore (IRE)**[14] 7098 2-9-7 **65** SeanLevey 5 66
(Richard Hannon) *stdd s: hld up in last quartet: effrt and swtchd sharply rt over 1f out: hdwy 1f out: kpt on ins fnl f: wnt 3rd towards fin: nvr threatened ldrs* **14/1**

0641 **4** *3/4* **John T Chance (IRE)**[19] 6963 2-9-2 **60** (p) JimCrowley 8 60
(Brian Meehan) *chsd ldr: ev ch 2f out: rdn to ld over 1f out: drvn and hdd 150yds: no ex: wknd towards fin* **7/2**[1]

0433 **5** *hd* **Vinnievanbaileys**[20] 6923 2-9-4 **62** [1] MartinHarley 1 61
(Chris Dwyer) *chsd ldrs: rdn and edgd lft over 1f out: stl pressing ldrs but unable qck u.p 1f out: wknd towards fin* **10/1**

0000 **6** *1* **Topmeup**[9] 7244 2-8-10 **54** JFEgan 7 51
(Stuart Edmunds) *dwlt: hld up towards rr: effrt over 1f out: swtchd rt and clsd 1f out: nt clr run briefly ins fnl f: styd on wl fnl 100yds: nvr trbld ldrs* **25/1**

1244 **7** *1/2* **Zamadance**[20] 6923 2-9-2 **65** MitchGodwin[(5)] 4 62
(Sylvester Kirk) *t.k.h: hld up in tch in midfield: effrt over 1f out: kpt on ins fnl f: nvr enough pce to threaten ldrs* **6/1**[3]

050 **8** *1 1/4* **Ravenoak (IRE)**[51] 6009 2-8-4 **48** WilliamCarson 11 42
(Tom Dascombe) *swtchd lft after s: chsd ldrs: rdn ent fnl 2f: unable qck over 1f out: wknd ins fnl f* **33/1**

0660 **9** *1/2* **Crucial Moment**[80] 4937 2-8-12 **61** GeorgeWood[(5)] 9 54
(Bill Turner) *awkward and wnt rt leaving stalls: in tch in midfield: effrt whn pushed rt and impeded over 1f out: no imp and styd on same pce after* **25/1**

400 **10** *1* **Speciale Di Giorno (IRE)**[58] 5747 2-9-0 **58** AndreaAtzeni 3 50
(Marco Botti) *sn led: rdn 2f out: hdd and no ex over 1f out: wknd fnl f* **7/1**

026 **11** *1 3/4* **Matthioli (FR)**[27] 6741 2-9-4 **62** KierenFox 12 50
(Michael Attwater) *s.i.s: hld in rr: rdn over 2f out: swtchd rt and no imp u.p over 1f out: n.d* **33/1**

0203 **12** *7* **Alligator**[19] 6963 2-9-3 **61** RyanMoore 13 37
(Ed Dunlop) *hld up in tch in last pair: effrt whn nt clr run and swtchd rt over 1f out: no prog: wknd fnl f* **10/1**

5444 **13** *11* **Midnight Man (FR)**[26] 6791 2-9-7 **65** (t) JoeyHaynes 10 21+
(K R Burke) *short of room and bmpd leaving stalls: in tch in midfield: rdn over 2f out: lost pl qckly over 1f out: bhd and eased ins fnl f* **7/1**

2m 11.15s (2.55) **Going Correction** -0.05s/f (Stan) **13** Ran SP% **124.0**
Speed ratings (Par 93): **87,86,84,84,84 83,82,81,81,80 79,73,64**
CSF £74.21 CT £950.82 TOTE £4.70: £1.70, £4.30, £4.70; EX 79.30 Trifecta £957.70.

Owner J David Abell **Bred** Peter Grimes & The Late Jackie Grimes **Trained** Middleham Moor, N Yorks

FOCUS
A modest nursery handicap on standard Polytrack. They went a modest gallop and there were some hard-luck stories in behind. Improved form from the front two, with 3rd-5th suggesting this level won't be far out.

7483 TOTEEXACTA MAIDEN STKS (PLUS 10 RACE) 1m (P)
6:15 (6:17) (Class 4) 2-Y-O **£3,946** (£1,174; £586; £293) **Stalls** Low

Form RPR

1 **Omeros** 2-9-5 0 JimCrowley 1 77+
(Hugo Palmer) *dwlt: hld up in tch in midfield: pushed along and clsd to join ldrs over 1f out: led ins fnl f: sn asserted and r.o wl: pushed out* **12/1**

4 **2** *3/4* **Sufi**[27] 6751 2-9-5 0 RyanMoore 3 75
(Richard Hannon) *chsd ldr: pushed along ent fnl 2f: rdn and sltly outpcd over 1f out: rallied to chse wnr wl ins fnl f: kpt on wl towards fin* **9/4**[1]

2403 **3** *1 1/4* **Fortune Of War**[7] 7306 2-9-0 77 CharlieBennett[(5)] 5 72
(Jane Chapple-Hyam) *chsd ldrs: effrt to chal wl over 1f out: rdn to ld 1f out: sn hdd and unable qck: kpt on same pce and lost 2nd wl ins fnl f* **8/1**[3]

352 **4** *3/4* **X Rated (IRE)**[9] 7239 2-9-5 0 AndrewMullen 6 70
(Mark Johnston) *led: drifted rt and rdn wl over 1f out: drvn and hrd pressed over 1f out: hdd 1f out: no ex and outpcd fnl 100yds* **10/1**

3 **5** *2 1/2* **Great Court (IRE)**[16] 7049 2-9-0 0 PatCosgrave 8 59
(Luca Cumani) *chsd ldng trio: rdn over 2f out: unable qck u.p and btn 5th 1f out: plugged on same pce ins fnl f* **9/4**[1]

0 **6** *3/4* **Addicted To You (IRE)**[9] 7247 2-9-5 0 JoeFanning 7 62
(Mark Johnston) *in tch in midfield: pushed along 3f out: c wd and effrt over 1f out: no imp and wl hld whn hung lft ins fnl f* **66/1**

60 **7** *1 3/4* **Jive Factor (USA)**[10] 7226 2-9-5 0 MartinHarley 2 58
(Ed Dunlop) *stdd after s: hld up in tch in last pair: effrt and no imp over 1f out: wknd ins fnl f* **50/1**

3 **8** *5* **Kissoffire (IRE)**[57] 5764 2-9-5 0 AndreaAtzeni 4 46
(Marco Botti) *dwlt: hld up in tch in last pair: pushed along over 3f out: rdn and no hdwy over 1f out: sn wknd* **11/4**[2]

1m 40.48s (0.58) **Going Correction** -0.05s/f (Stan) **8** Ran SP% **119.6**
Speed ratings (Par 97): **95,94,93,92,89 89,87,82**
CSF £41.24 TOTE £10.60: £2.20, £1.30, £2.30; EX 42.70 Trifecta £273.20.

Owner Chris Humber **Bred** Rabbah Bloodstock Limited **Trained** Newmarket, Suffolk

FOCUS
A fair juvenile maiden which went to subsequent Goodwood Group 3 winner Thikriyaat on his debut last season. Another promising newcomer won this renewal from off a respectable gallop.

7484 TOTEQUADPOT MAIDEN FILLIES' STKS (PLUS 10 RACE) 7f (P)
6:45 (6:49) (Class 4) 2-Y-O **£4,204** (£1,251; £625; £312) **Stalls** Low

Form RPR

02 **1** **Parlance (IRE)**[22] 6866 2-9-0 0 RyanMoore 3 82+
(Sir Michael Stoute) *mde all: rdn over 1f out: drew clr and styd on strly ins fnl f: readily* **9/4**[1]

2 *3 3/4* **Indian Blessing** 2-9-0 0 JimCrowley 1 72+
(Ed Walker) *chsd ldrs: nt clr run over 2f out: gap opened and chsd wnr wl over 1f out: sn pushed along: outpcd by wnr fnl f: kpt on for clr 2nd* **14/1**

50 **3** *2 1/2* **Patching**[33] 6578 2-9-0 0 JackMitchell 4 65
(Giles Bravery) *s.i.s: hld up in last trio: swtchd rt wl over 1f out: pushed along and hdwy 1f out: no threat to wnr but kpt on steadily ins fnl f: wnt 3rd on post* **100/1**

6 **4** *nse* **Dream Of Joy (IRE)**[13] 7118 2-9-0 0 AndreaAtzeni 2 65
(Roger Varian) *chsd ldrs: effrt in 4th 2f out: wnt 3rd ent fnl f: kpt on same pce u.p fnl 150yds: lost 3rd on post* **7/2**[2]

2 **5** *2 1/2* **Sea Tea Dea**[28] 6696 2-9-0 0 WilliamCarson 6 58
(Anthony Carson) *in tch in midfield: effrt 2f out: unable qck and outpcd over 1f out: wl hld fnl f* **14/1**

6 *1 1/2* **Awfaa (IRE)** 2-9-0 0 PaulHanagan 10 54+
(Sir Michael Stoute) *s.i.s: in tch in last trio: pushed along and hdwy to pass btn horses 1f out: n.d but kpt on ins fnl f* **7/1**

5 **7** *1 1/4* **Crimson Rosette (IRE)**[26] 6782 2-9-0 0 StevieDonohoe 8 51+
(Charlie Fellowes) *s.i.s and pushed along early: in tch in last trio: effrt over 1f out: no imp: n.d* **4/1**[3]

00 **8** *1 3/4* **Prairie Light**[51] 5995 2-8-9 0 MitchGodwin[(5)] 7 46
(Sylvester Kirk) *hld up in tch in midfield: rdn 3f out: outpcd over 1f out and btn whn swtchd rt 1f out: wknd fnl f* **100/1**

2 **9** *3/4* **Quick Artist (IRE)**[90] 4586 2-9-0 0 RobertHavlin 5 44
(Simon Crisford) *in tch in midfield: rdn over 2f out: lost pl over 1f out: sn wknd* **7/1**

34 **10** *4 1/2* **Unzipped**[16] 7056 2-9-0 0 JFEgan 9 32
(Stuart Edmunds) *chsd wnr tl wl over 1f out: sn lost pl u.p: bhd and eased ins fnl f* **20/1**

1m 25.64s (-1.56) **Going Correction** -0.05s/f (Stan) **10** Ran SP% **118.1**
Speed ratings (Par 94): **106,101,98,98,95 94,92,90,89,84**
CSF £37.05 TOTE £2.60: £1.10, £2.80, £17.70; EX 32.00 Trifecta £3442.10.

Owner Cheveley Park Stud **Bred** Wansdyke Farms Ltd & J M Burke **Trained** Newmarket, Suffolk

FOCUS
A fair juvenile fillies' maiden. They went a decent gallop and a clearly useful filly dominated. The opening level is fluid.

7485 TOTESWINGER FILLIES' H'CAP 7f (P)
7:15 (7:18) (Class 5) (0-75,81) 3-Y-O+ **£4,528** (£1,347; £673; £336) **Stalls** Low

Form RPR

1650 **1** **Baby Ballerina**[35] 6501 3-8-10 **66** BenCurtis 6 73
(Brian Ellison) *chsd ldr for 2f: swtchd rt and hdwy to chse ldr over 1f out: rdn to ld 1f out: styd on wl: rdn out* **20/1**

2410 **2** *2 1/4* **Pyla (IRE)**[37] 6453 4-8-10 **69** (v[1]) CliffordLee[(5)] 9 71
(Amy Murphy) *chsd ldrs: wnt 2nd 5f out tl led and rdn over 1f out: hdd and drvn 1f out: styd on same pce after* **8/1**

5411 **3** *1* **Beatbybeatbybeat**[8] 7272 3-9-3 **76** 6ex (v) AlistairRawlinson[(3)] 1 75
(Ismail Mohammed) *in tch in midfield: effrt 2f out: swtchd rt and hdwy over 1f out: drvn 1f out: wnt 3rd 100yds: no threat to ldrs and kpt on same pce after* **9/2**[2]

3110 **4** *hd* **Curious Fox**[22] 6878 3-8-12 **68** WilliamCarson 3 66
(Anthony Carson) *hld up in tch: effrt and nt clr run over 1f out: swtchd rt ent fnl f: styd on u.p ins fnl f: wnt 4th towards fin: nvr trbld ldrs* **10/1**

1500 **5** *3/4* **World's Greatest (USA)**[68] 5412 3-8-13 **69** (t[1]) PatCosgrave 7 65
(Stuart Williams) *hld up in tch in midfield: effrt and sme hdwy u.p over 1f out: styd on same pce ins fnl f* **6/1**[3]

0405 **6** *shd* **Perfect Alchemy (IRE)**[38] 6426 5-8-13 **72** CharlieBennett[(5)] 2 69
(Patrick Chamings) *hld up in tch in last trio: effrt towards inner over 1f out: swtchd rt and hdwy u.p 1f out: styd on same pce and no imp fnl 100yds* **8/1**

4611 **7** *nk* **Shypen**[5] 7363 3-9-4 **81** 6ex JaneElliott[(7)] 11 76
(George Margarson) *chsd ldrs: effrt 2f out: wnt 1f out: no imp: lost 3rd 100yds out: wknd towards fin* **7/2**[1]

5505 **8** *3/4* **Pink Martini (IRE)**[7] 7303 3-9-2 **72** (t) OisinMurphy 5 65
(Joseph Tuite) *wl in tch in midfield: effrt 2f out: nt clr run over 1f out: nvr enough room after tl swtchd lft ins fnl f: pushed along and kpt on same pce after* **8/1**

-200 **9** *3/4* **Performer**[90] 4593 3-8-12 **68** SeanLevey 10 59
(Richard Hannon) *s.i.s: in tch in last trio: pushed along over 1f out: no imp: n.d* **14/1**

4001 **10** *5* **Arize (IRE)**[23] 6851 3-8-10 **66** .... JoeFanning 8 44
(David Brown) *led tl rdn and hdd over 1f out: lost pl and eased ins fnl f*
8/1

1m 25.59s (-1.61) **Going Correction** -0.05s/f (Stan)
WFA 3 from 4yo+ 2lb **10** Ran SP% **119.7**
Speed ratings (Par 100): **107,104,103,103,102 102,101,100,100,94**
CSF £175.38 CT £879.81 TOTE £27.10: £5.00, £2.70, £2.10; EX 283.70 Trifecta £4204.00.
Owner Julie & Keith Hanson **Bred** Howard Barton Stud **Trained** Norton, N Yorks
■ Stewards' Enquiry : Oisin Murphy £280 fine; vaccinations in the passport did not comply

FOCUS
A fairly decent fillies' handicap. They went a proper gallop and the form should prove reliable.

7486 TOTEPOOL LIVE INFO DOWNLOAD THE APP H'CAP 1m (P)
7:45 (7:47) (Class 4) (0-80,79) 3-Y-O+ **£4,851** (£1,443; £721; £360) **Stalls** Low

Form RPR
3321 **1** **Irish Optimism (IRE)**[35] 6521 3-9-4 **79** .... JasonHart 2 88+
(John Quinn) *hld up in tch in midfield: gng wl and nt clr run over 2f out: hdwy to chse ldr over 1f out: rdn to ld jst ins fnl f: r.o wl: eased nr fin: readily*
3/1[1]

0345 **2** *1 1/4* **Mezzotint (IRE)**[21] 6899 7-9-7 **79** .... StevieDonohoe 1 86
(Lee Carter) *hld up in tch in last quartet: rdn and hdwy over 1f out: chsd wnr 100yds: styd on u.p but no threat to wnr*
9/1

1255 **3** *1 3/4* **Slovak (IRE)**[167] 2001 4-9-4 **76** .... LukeMorris 12 79
(James Tate) *led and crossed towards inner: rdn over 1f out: drvn and hdd jst ins fnl f: kpt on same pce after: lost 2nd fnl 100yds*
14/1

0640 **4** *1/2* **Palpitation (IRE)**[10] 7203 3-8-3 **67** .... AaronJones(3) 10 68
(David Brown) *in tch in midfield: effrt u.p over 1f out: kpt on ins fnl f: no threat to wnr*
33/1

460 **5** *2 1/4* **Marbooh (IRE)**[49] 6055 3-9-3 **78** .... JimCrowley 7 74
(David O'Meara) *stdd s: hld up in rr: rdn and hdwy on inner over 1f out: kpt on ins fnl f: nvr trbld ldrs*
7/1

-156 **6** *1 1/4* **With Pleasure**[130] 3187 3-8-11 **77** .... JoshDoyle(5) 4 70
(David O'Meara) *t.k.h: chsd ldrs: wnt 2nd briefly over 1f out: sn drvn and unable qck: wknd ins fnl f*
14/1

5600 **7** *3 1/2* **Boots And Spurs**[13] 7126 7-9-7 **79** ....(v) BenCurtis 8 65
(Scott Dixon) *chsd ldrs: 3rd and rdn over 2f out: unable qck and lost pl over 1f out: wknd ins fnl f*
12/1

-020 **8** *2 3/4* **Le Roi Du Temps (USA)**[66] 5482 3-9-2 **77** ....(p) OisinMurphy 3 55
(Ivan Furtado) *t.k.h: hld up in midfield: shifted rt after 1f out: effrt over 1f out: no imp and wl hld 1f out: wknd ins fnl f*
5/1[2]

0-1P **9** *1 1/4* **Eltham**[13] 7119 3-8-12 **76** .... JosephineGordon(3) 5 52
(Robyn Brisland) *hld up in tch in midfield: bmpd after 1f out: rdn over 2f out: sn struggling and lost pl over 1f out: wknd fnl f*
6/1[3]

6500 **10** *1/2* **Show Me Again**[21] 6899 3-9-0 **75** ....[1] MartinLane 9 49
(David Dennis) *dwlt: sn pushed along and rcvrd to chse ldr: rdn 2f out: lost pl over 1f out: wknd fnl f*
16/1

6200 **11** *nse* **Prosecute (FR)**[12] 7153 3-9-1 **76** .... MartinHarley 6 50
(David Simcock) *hld up in tch in rr: effrt over 1f out: no imp: wknd fnl f* **9/1**

4263 **12** *9* **New Street (IRE)**[94] 4459 5-9-0 **72** .... JFEgan 13 27
(Jim Best) *s.i.s and pushed along in rr: hdwy on outer into midfield 4f out: rdn 3f out: lost pl and bhd 2f out*
33/1

1m 38.43s (-1.47) **Going Correction** -0.05s/f (Stan)
WFA 3 from 4yo+ 3lb **12** Ran SP% **121.2**
Speed ratings (Par 105): **105,103,102,101,99 98,94,91,90,90 89,80**
CSF £31.40 CT £337.43 TOTE £3.70: £2.30, £3.50, £3.00; EX 31.30 Trifecta £178.20.
Owner Harlen Ltd **Bred** Cathal Ennis **Trained** Settrington, N Yorks

FOCUS
A fair handicap. Once again they went a proper gallop and it is solid form.

7487 @TOTEPOOLRACING WIN TICKETS ON TWITTER MAIDEN STKS 1m 5f 66y(P)
8:15 (8:15) (Class 5) 3-Y-O+ **£4,528** (£1,347; £673; £336) **Stalls** Low

Form RPR
03 **1** **Lord Topper**[15] 7063 3-9-5 0 .... JimCrowley 1 80
(Charles Hills) *hld up in tch in midfield: effrt over 2f out: clsd to chse ldrs and nt clr run 1f out: gap opened and chal between horses ins fnl f: rdn to ld fnl 50yds out: r.o wl*
8/1[3]

20 **2** *1/2* **Potters Lady Jane**[99] 4265 4-9-5 0 .... JosephineGordon(3) 2 74
(Lucy Wadham) *chsd ldrs: rdn over 2f out: hdwy to chse ldr over 1f out: drvn to ld 1f out: hrd pressed ins fnl f: hdd and styd on same pce fnl 50yds*
10/1

62 **3** *nse* **Going Up (IRE)**[59] 5716 3-9-5 0 .... PaulHanagan 3 79
(Rae Guest) *in tch in midfield: 4th and rdn over 1f out: hdwy u.p 1f out: styd on and ev ch wl ins fnl f: kpt on*
2/1[1]

3222 **4** *1 3/4* **Satish**[28] 6711 3-9-5 76 ....(b) RobertHavlin 8 76
(John Gosden) *hld up in tch in midfield: swtchd rt and clsd over 1f out: drvn ins fnl f: fnd nil and styd on same pce after*
5/2[2]

24 **5** *2 1/4* **Rock'n Gold**[14] 7102 3-9-5 0 .... PatCosgrave 5 73
(Luca Cumani) *t.k.h: led: rdn over 1f out: hdd and no ex 1f out: wknd ins fnl f: eased towards fin*
5/2[2]

0 **6** *3 1/4* **Lord Of The Valley**[106] 4001 3-9-5 0 .... JoeFanning 6 68
(Mark Johnston) *chsd ldr: rdn and ev ch 2f out: drvn and lost pl over 1f out: wknd ins fnl f*
20/1

4600 **7** *24* **Boru's Brook (IRE)**[16] 7052 8-9-13 0 .... JFEgan 7 32
(Jim Best) *s.i.s: detached in last: wnt 7th but stl nt on terms 5f out: rdn and lost tch 3f out: eased ins fnl f: t.o*
200/1

8 *124* **Samara Belle** 3-9-0 0 .... AdamBeschizza 4
(Christine Dunnett) *hld up in tch in 7th: rdn over 5f out: sn dropped to last and lost tch 4f out: t.o and eased fnl 3f*
200/1

2m 53.94s (0.34) **Going Correction** -0.05s/f (Stan)
WFA 3 from 4yo+ 8lb **8** Ran SP% **116.4**
Speed ratings (Par 103): **96,95,95,94,93 91,76,**
CSF £82.27 TOTE £6.60: £1.90, £2.90, £1.20; EX 36.80 Trifecta £247.90.
Owner Hillwood Racing,Mick & Janice Mariscotti **Bred** Theakston Stud **Trained** Lambourn, Berks

FOCUS
A fair staying maiden but they went a modest gallop until the tempo increased on the home bend.

7488 BOOK YOUR CHRISTMAS PARTY AT CHELMSFORDCITYRACECOURSE.COM H'CAP (DIV I) 6f (P)
8:45 (8:50) (Class 6) (0-55,55) 3-Y-O+ **£3,234** (£962; £481; £240) **Stalls** Centre

Form RPR
350U **1** **Humour (IRE)**[2] 7445 5-9-7 **55** ....(b) RobertHavlin 11 61
(Christine Dunnett) *s.i.s and bmpd s: detached in last early: clsd and wl in tch 2f out: nt clr run over 1f out: swtchd rt 1f out: r.o strly ins fnl f to ld last stride*
6/1[3]

0-00 **2** *shd* **Lady Bacchus**[36] 6478 3-8-11 **46** oh1 ....(b) ConnorBeasley 6 51
(Richard Guest) *taken down early: hld up in midfield: clsd and in tch 1/2-way: swtchd rt over 1f out: rdn and chal ins fnl f: led wl ins fnl f: hdd last stride*
33/1

1033 **3** *nk* **Burauq**[7] 7302 4-9-3 **51** ....(b) RichardKingscote 7 55
(Milton Bradley) *midfield: pushed along and clsd 2f out: rdn to chse ldrs over 1f out: ev ch ins fnl f: unable qck towards fin*
4/1[2]

3423 **4** *1 1/4* **Cadland Lad (IRE)**[10] 7201 3-9-0 **49** ....(vt) JimCrowley 8 49
(John Ryan) *chsd ldr: rdn to chal over 1f out: drvn and led 1f out: hdd wl ins fnl f: wknd towards fin*
11/8[1]

-023 **5** *2 1/2* **Wimboldsley**[12] 7144 5-9-2 **50** .... MichaelJMMurphy 3 43
(Scott Dixon) *taken down early: led: rdn over 1f out: hdd 1f out: wknd ins fnl f*
4/1[2]

0030 **6** *nse* **Simply Black (IRE)**[7] 7302 5-8-7 **46** oh1 ....(p) AnnStokell(5) 10 38
(Ann Stokell) *taken down early: wnt rt s: chsd ldrs: rdn over 1f out: unable qck and wknd ins fnl f*
20/1

0640 **7** *2 1/4* **Cytringan**[21] 6902 3-8-9 **47** .... SimonPearce(3) 2 33
(Lydia Pearce) *t.k.h: chsd ldrs: rdn over 1f out: unable qck and wknd ins fnl f*
10/1

0004 **8** *4 1/2* **Cecile Royale**[78] 5020 3-8-11 **46** oh1 .... OisinMurphy 9 18
(Stuart Williams) *a outpcd in last trio: n.d*
16/1

0/00 **9** *7* **Alberto**[52] 5954 6-8-5 **46** oh1 ....(p) JordanUys(7) 4
(Lisa Williamson) *fly j. as stalls opened: slowly away: a outpcd in rr: nvr on terms*
66/1

1m 12.91s (-0.79) **Going Correction** -0.05s/f (Stan)
WFA 3 from 4yo+ 1lb **9** Ran SP% **120.6**
Speed ratings (Par 101): **103,102,102,100,97 97,94,88,79**
CSF £184.62 CT £903.56 TOTE £7.30: £2.20, £7.20, £1.60; EX 329.90 Trifecta £836.00.
Owner The Humourites **Bred** Jeddah Bloodstock **Trained** Hingham, Norfolk
■ Playful Dude was withdrawn. Price at time of withdrawal 12/1. Rule 4 applies to bets struck prior to withdrawal but not to SP bets - deduct 5p in the pound. New market formed.

FOCUS
The first division of a moderate sprint handicap and, off a decent gallop, the winning time was marginally quicker.

7489 BOOK YOUR CHRISTMAS PARTY AT CHELMSFORDCITYRACECOURSE.COM H'CAP (DIV II) 6f (P)
9:15 (9:16) (Class 6) (0-55,55) 3-Y-O+ **£3,234** (£962; £481; £240) **Stalls** Centre

Form RPR
0040 **1** **Captain Scooby**[2] 7445 10-9-0 **48** ....(b) ConnorBeasley 3 53
(Richard Guest) *s.i.s: hld up in tch in last pair: nt clr run 2f out: clsd and squeezed through ins fnl f: drvn to chal wl ins fnl f: styd on to ld on post*
8/1

5046 **2** *nse* **Ryan Style (IRE)**[10] 7200 10-8-6 **47** oh1 ow1 ....(b) JordanUys(7) 6 52
(Lisa Williamson) *hld up in last pair: rdn and hdwy on outer over 1f out: drvn to ld wl ins fnl f: edgd rt towards fin and hdd on post*
16/1

5353 **3** *1* **Dream Ally (IRE)**[12] 7145 6-9-5 **53** ....(be) LukeMorris 10 55
(John Weymes) *hld up in tch: effrt 2f out: hrd drvn to chse ldrs 1f out: kpt on same pce wl ins fnl f*
8/1

5000 **4** *1/2* **Bushwise (IRE)**[7] 7302 3-8-12 **47** oh1 ow1 ....(p) JimCrowley 1 48
(Milton Bradley) *chsd ldrs: effrt on inner over 1f out: drvn and ev ch 1f out: unable qck and btn fnl 75yds*
8/1

4302 **5** *hd* **Kenstone (FR)**[10] 7200 3-9-1 **50** ....(p) OisinMurphy 8 50
(David Dennis) *sn chsd ldr: rdn to ld over 1f out: drvn and hrd pressed 1f out: hdd wl ins fnl f: no ex and wknd towards fin*
2/1[1]

4202 **6** *2 1/4* **Decisive (IRE)**[10] 7201 4-9-7 **55** ....(tp) WilliamCarson 9 48
(Anthony Carson) *chsd ldrs: effrt to chse ldrs over 1f out: no ex u.p 1f out: wknd ins fnl f*
7/2[2]

6000 **7** *5* **Single Summit**[99] 4278 4-8-12 **46** oh1 .... KierenFox 4 24
(J R Jenkins) *dwlt: in tch towards rr : effrt over 1f out: no imp: wknd ins fnl f*
25/1

650 **8** *nk* **Bemusement**[35] 6511 3-9-3 **53** .... JoeFanning 2 30
(Mark Johnston) *taken down early: led: rdn and hdd over 1f out: wknd fnl f*
5/1[3]

5056 **9** *2 1/4* **Nelson's Pride**[114] 3735 5-8-5 **46** oh1 .... RhiainIngram(7) 7 17
(Roger Ingram) *t.k.h: chsd ldrs: rdn and lost pl 1/2-way: bhd fnl f* **25/1**

1m 13.3s (-0.40) **Going Correction** -0.05s/f (Stan)
WFA 3 from 4yo+ 1lb **9** Ran SP% **119.1**
Speed ratings (Par 101): **100,99,98,97,97 94,88,87,84**
CSF £128.85 CT £1059.01 TOTE £9.50: £2.70, £4.40, £1.70; EX 117.20 Trifecta £1474.70.
Owner The Captain Scooby Syndicate **Bred** Hellwood Stud Farm & Paul Davies (h'Gate) **Trained** Ingmanthorpe, W Yorks

FOCUS
The second division of a moderate sprint handicap, which was marginally slower than the first, but it still paid to come from well off the pace. The winner has been rated to the best of this year's AW form.
T/Jkpt: Not Won. T/Plt: £345.60 to a £1 stake. Pool of £105407.70 - 222.61 winning tickets.
T/Qpdt: £38.10 to a £1 stake. Pool of £11949.24 - 232.05 winning tickets. **Steve Payne**

7480 DEAUVILLE (R-H)
Thursday, October 20
OFFICIAL GOING: Turf: good; polytrack: standard

7490a PRIX D'ENGLESQUEVILLE (CLAIMER) (2YO) (TURF) 6f
11:40 (12:00) 2-Y-O **£8,455** (£3,382; £2,536; £1,691; £845)

RPR
1 **Ekatea (FR)**[8] 7294 2-8-3 0 .... JeremieCatineau(5) 3 70
(C Laffon-Parias, France)
68/10

2 *hd* **Chaplin (FR)**[16] 7033 2-9-5 0 ....(b[1]) MickaelBarzalona 10 80
(Richard Hughes) *hld up in midfield: clsd to chsd ldrs fr 1/2-way: drvn appr fnl f: styd on u.p: jst hld*
9/1

3 *3/4* **Notre Sage (FR)**[86] 4750 2-8-8 0 .... RonanThomas 9 67
(P Decouz, France)
14/1

4 *1/2* **Finalize (FR)** 2-8-11 0 .... AntoineWerle 11 68
(T Lemer, France)
25/1

5 *hd* **Sirma Traou Land (FR)**[8] 7294 2-8-13 0 .... Pierre-CharlesBoudot 2 70
(B De Montzey, France)
14/1

6 *3/4* **Touching The Sky (IRE)**[8] 7294 2-9-5 0 .... ChristopheSoumillon 8 73
(Alex Fracas, France)
8/5[1]

7 *1 1/4* **Fa Ul Cuncert**[9] 2-8-11 0 .... AlexisBadel 7 62
(C Boutin, France)
26/1

8 *1/2* **Karyfanny (FR)**[62] 5698 2-9-1 0 ....(p) UmbertoRispoli 6 64
(S Labate, France)
22/1

The Form Book, Raceform Ltd, Newbury, RG14 5SJ

9 snk **Decapulse (IRE)**[135] 3006 2-8-8 0 AurelienLemaitre 1 57
(J-V Toux, France) **50/1**

10 1/2 **Assassinate (IRE)**[25] 6800 2-9-4 0 (b) JamieSpencer 5 65
(Paul Cole) *trckd ldrs: cl 3rd and ev ch 1 1/2f out: rdn and nt qckn over 1f out: wknd fnl 150yds* **5/1**[2]

11 2 **La Fibrossi (FR)** 2-8-6 0 FlorentGavilan(5) 4 52
(H-A Pantall, France) **66/10**[3]

1m 10.6s (-0.40) **11** Ran SP% **118.3**
WIN (incl. 1 euro stake): 7.80. PLACES: 2.60, 3.70, 3.40. DF: 40.50. SF: 53.60.
Owner Ecurie Mathieu Offenstadt **Bred** Stilvi Compania Financiera Sa **Trained** Chantilly, France

7491a PRIX ISONOMY (LISTED RACE) (2YO) (ROUND) (TURF) 1m (R)

1:20 (12:00) 2-Y-O **£23,897** (£9,558; £7,169; £4,779; £2,389)

RPR

1 **Al Wukair (IRE)**[20] 2-9-0 0 GregoryBenoist 5 102
(A Fabre, France) **19/10**[1]

2 1 3/4 **Gold Luck (FR)**[24] 2-8-10 0 MaximeGuyon 4 94
(F Head, France) **51/10**[2]

3 3/4 **Hebah (IRE)**[58] 2-8-11 0 ow1 ChristopheSoumillon 6 93
(J-C Rouget, France) **26/5**[3]

4 1 3/4 **Emmaus (IRE)**[31] 6632 2-9-0 0 Pierre-CharlesBoudot 8 92
(Roger Varian) *hld up in midfield: angled out and scrubbed along over 1 1/2f out but no immediate imp: kpt on u.p fnl f: nt pce to get on terms* **67/10**

5 1 3/4 **Medieval (IRE)**[25] 6801 2-9-0 0 (b) JamieSpencer 2 88
(Paul Cole) *disp ld on inner: led after 1 1/2f: hdd after 1/2-way and chsd ldr: rdn 1 1/2f out: sn btn and wknd ins fnl f* **56/10**

6 1 1/2 **Silver Cape (FR)**[17] 7031 2-8-10 0 EddyHardouin 1 81
(T Clout, France) **17/1**

7 1 1/4 **City Light (FR)**[31] 6638 2-9-0 0 TheoBachelot 3 82
(S Wattel, France) **26/5**[3]

8 2 **Do It In Rio (FR)** 2-8-10 0 CristianDemuro 7 73
(E J O'Neill, France) **50/1**

1m 41.97s (1.17) **8** Ran SP% **118.8**
WIN (incl. 1 euro stake): 2.90. PLACES: 1.40, 1.80, 1.90. DF: 6.70. SF: 11.50.
Owner Al Shaqab Racing **Bred** Ballylinch Stud **Trained** Chantilly, France

7492a PRIX DE MONTEILLERIE (CLAIMER) (3YO) (POLYTRACK) 1m 1f 110y

2:20 (12:00) 3-Y-O **£9,926** (£3,970; £2,977; £1,985; £992)

RPR

1 **Lord Of The North (IRE)**[48] 6104 3-9-2 0 Pierre-CharlesBoudot 5 86
(Gay Kelleway) *trckd ldng gp: 6th and gng wl 2 1/2f out: c wd into st: styd on fr 1 1/2f out: rdn and r.o if out: led fnl 110yds: comf* **12/5**[1]

2 3 **Ipanemo (FR)**[42] 3-9-4 0 CristianDemuro 12 82
(P Sogorb, France) **81/10**[2]

3 1/2 **Happy Cause (USA)**[12] 3-8-11 0 AurelienLemaitre 8 74
(S Cerulis, France) **10/1**

4 snk **Saint Joseph (FR)**[31] 3-8-4 0 ClementLecoeuvre(7) 4 74
(E Lellouche, France) **22/1**

5 hd **Downeva (FR)**[224] 3-8-9 0 NicolasBarzalona(6) 2 77
(F Vermeulen, France) **23/1**

6 1 1/2 **Identity Run Fast (IRE)**[19] 3-8-11 0 ChristopheSoumillon 11 70
(A Marcialis, Italy) **10/1**

7 1 1/2 **Penjack (FR)**[42] 3-9-5 0 (b) UmbertoRispoli 7 75
(G Botti, France) **9/1**

8 1 1/2 **Back To Bresil (FR)**[31] 3-8-8 0 (p) TheoBachelot 15 61
(S Wattel, France) **33/1**

9 6 **Maroc**[10] 7214 3-8-11 0 JamieSpencer 3 52
(Paul Cole) *drvn early: sn led: rdn 2 1/2f out: hdd 2f out: sn wknd* **12/1**

10 3/4 **Avec Laura**[108] 3-9-1 0 AlexisBadel 6 54
(Mme M Bollack-Badel, France) **19/1**

11 snk **Dosnueveuno (IRE)** 3-9-1 0 MaximeGuyon 9 54
(Alex Fracas, France) **83/10**[3]

12 1 1/2 **Threebagsue (IRE)**[47] 6140 3-8-8 0 (b) IoritzMendizabal 13 44
(J S Moore) *chsd ldrs on outer: rdn and wknd ins fnl 2f* **11/1**

13 7 **Equinoxe (FR)**[88] 3-8-11 0 (b) AdrienFouassier 14 32
(P-J Fertillet, France) **31/1**

14 7 **Corroyer (IRE)**[15] 3-8-13 0 EmmanuelEtienne(3) 1 23
(F Alloncle, France) **130/1**

15 9 **Going Viral (IRE)**[197] 1286 3-9-1 0 (p) AntoineHamelin 10 4
(Matthieu Palussiere, France) **21/1**

Owner Miss Gay Kelleway **Bred** J Kenny **Trained** Exning, Suffolk
WIN (incl. 1 euro stake): 3.40. PLACES: 1.70, 2.20, 3.00. DF: 18.30. SF: 33.40.

6326 DONCASTER (L-H)

Friday, October 21

OFFICIAL GOING: Good (7.7)
Wind: moderate 1/2 against Weather: fine

7493 MOBILE BETTING AT 188BET NURSERY H'CAP 1m (S)

1:30 (1:30) (Class 3) (0-95,92) 2-Y-O

£9,337 (£2,796; £1,398; £699; £349; £175) **Stalls** High

Form RPR

1463 1 **Mutawatheb (IRE)**[44] 6229 2-9-7 **92** PaulHanagan 1 95
(Richard Hannon) *t.k.h: led: pushed along 2f out: rdn over 1f out: drvn and hdd narrowly wl ins fnl f: rallied and edgd lft: led again towards fin* **5/2**[1]

126 2 nk **Society Red**[20] 6950 2-8-7 **78** PatrickMathers 6 80
(Richard Fahey) *hld up in rr: hdwy 2f out: rdn to chal ent fnl f: drvn to ld narrowly wl ins fnl f: edgd sltly rt and hdd nr fin* **13/2**

1055 3 nk **Aardwolf (USA)**[23] 6869 2-9-2 **87** WilliamBuick 2 89
(Mark Johnston) *trckd ldrs: hdwy on inner over 2f out: cl up wl over 1f out: rdn to chal ent fnl f: sn drvn and ev ch: n.m.r and sltly hmpd fnl 40 yds: no ex* **10/1**

2132 4 1 **Soldier's Girl (IRE)**[29] 6713 2-9-0 **85** RyanMoore 3 84
(Richard Hannon) *t.k.h: trckd wnr: cl up 3f out: rdn along wl over 1f out: drvn and no ex ins fnl f* **9/2**[3]

2211 5 hd **Zymyran**[22] 6903 2-9-0 **85** HarryBentley 4 84
(David Simcock) *dwlt and hld up in rr: hdwy over 2f out: rdn over 1f out: sn drvn and wknd ent fnl f* **7/2**[2]

4124 6 8 **Clef**[27] 6787 2-8-11 **82** TonyHamilton 8 62
(Richard Fahey) *trckd ldrs: effrt over 2f out: sn rdn and wknd over 1f out* **5/1**

0130 7 19 **Riviere Argentee (FR)**[53] 5967 2-8-12 **83** BenCurtis 5 20
(K R Burke) *cl up: pushed along wl over 2f out: rdn and wknd wl over 1f out* **40/1**

1m 38.25s (-1.05) **Going Correction** -0.10s/f (Good) 2y crse rec **7** Ran SP% **110.5**
Speed ratings (Par 99): **101,100,100,99,99 91,72**
CSF £17.84 CT £127.61 TOTE £3.30: £2.10, £3.30; EX 17.10 Trifecta £120.40.
Owner Hamdan Al Maktoum **Bred** Rosetown Bloodstock **Trained** East Everleigh, Wilts

FOCUS
Clerk of the course Roderick Duncan reported that only 4mm of rain had fallen over the previous seven days, and the going was given as good (GoingStick: 7.7). After riding in the opener Paddy Mathers said: "It is good ground" but William Buick said: "It is just on the easy side" and Paul Hanagan said: "It is just on the slow side of good but they are getting through it okay." They didn't go a great pace early on in this nursery, and as a result it turned into a bit of a dash, and they finished in a heap. Straightforward form rated around the third and fourth.

7494 188BET.CO.UK BRITISH STALLION STUDS EBF MAIDEN FILLIES' STKS (PLUS10 RACE) 1m (S)

2:00 (2:01) (Class 5) 2-Y-O **£4,528** (£1,347; £673; £336) **Stalls** High

Form RPR

6 1 **Fleeting Motion**[120] 3556 2-9-0 0 TomMarquand 3 80
(Richard Hannon) *trckd ldrs: led over 2f out: drvn and styd on wl fnl f* **25/1**

22 2 1 1/2 **Interweave**[34] 6578 2-9-0 0 RyanMoore 1 77
(Sir Michael Stoute) *trckd ldrs: effrt over 2f out: kpt on same pce last 150yds* **3/1**[2]

0 3 2 1/4 **Fashion Theory**[14] 7118 2-9-0 0 WilliamBuick 8 71
(Charlie Appleby) *dwlt: hdwy over 4f out: chsng ldrs 3f out: wknd last 100yds* **11/2**[3]

4 1 1/4 **Harebell (IRE)** 2-9-0 0 RichardKingscote 14 69+
(Ralph Beckett) *dwlt: swtchd lft after s: hld in rr: hdwy over 1f out: styd on steadily: will improve* **25/1**

2 5 3 **Scarlet Thrush (IRE)**[17] 7056 2-9-0 0 HarryBentley 10 62
(Marco Botti) *trckd ldrs: t.k.h: one pce over 1f out* **12/1**

6 hd **Dellaguista (IRE)** 2-9-0 0 JimCrowley 11 61+
(William Haggas) *dwlt: heled up in rr: hdwy over 1f out: kpt on steadily: will do bttr* **14/1**

462 7 1/2 **Washington Blue**[43] 6250 2-9-0 73 MartinHarley 12 60
(Clive Cox) *chsd ldrs: effrt over 2f out: lost pl over 1f out* **14/1**

5 8 1 1/2 **Prize Diva**[49] 6088 2-9-0 0 FrederikTylicki 5 57
(David Elsworth) *mid-div: effrt over 2f out: sn chsng ldrs: fdd fnl f* **14/1**

33 9 hd **Nellie's Dancer**[14] 7107 2-9-0 0 BenCurtis 6 56
(Scott Dixon) *led: hdd over 2f out: wknd fnl f* **50/1**

10 1/2 **Ouja** 2-9-0 0 FrankieDettori 13 55+
(John Gosden) *hld up towards rr: hdwy to chse ldrs 3f out: outpcd whn nt clr run 2f out: no ch after* **13/8**[1]

11 1/2 **Starlight Circus (IRE)** 2-9-0 0 LiamJones 2 54
(Marco Botti) *mid-div: sn drvn: hdwy to chse ldrs 3f out: lost pl over 1f out* **50/1**

00 12 1 1/4 **Newt**[17] 7049 2-9-0 0 RyanPowell 7 51
(Sir Mark Prescott Bt) *hld up in rr: outpcd 2f out: nvr a factor* **100/1**

0 13 4 1/2 **Plage Depampelonne**[53] 5966 2-9-0 0 PJMcDonald 4 41
(James Bethell) *chsd ldrs: reminders 3f out: lost pl 2f out* **100/1**

55 14 2 1/4 **Devoran**[23] 6874 2-9-0 0 DougieCostello 9 35
(Alan King) *t.k.h: trckd ldrs: lost pl over 2f out* **150/1**

1m 39.41s (0.11) **Going Correction** -0.10s/f (Good) **14** Ran SP% **120.4**
Speed ratings (Par 92): **95,93,91,90,87 86,86,84,84,84 83,82,77,75**
CSF £97.62 TOTE £41.90: £7.20, £1.30, £2.20; EX 199.00 Trifecta £1493.80.
Owner Saeed Suhail **Bred** P T Tellwright **Trained** East Everleigh, Wilts

FOCUS
A maiden that's produced some Group-class fillies over the years. A handy ride and experience counted for plenty in this season's running.

7495 188BET BRITISH STALLION STUDS EBF MAIDEN STKS (DIV I) 7f

2:35 (2:36) (Class 5) 2-Y-O **£4,528** (£1,347; £673; £336) **Stalls** High

Form RPR

6236 1 **Hyde Park**[37] 6486 2-9-5 85 FrankieDettori 5 94+
(John Gosden) *racd centre: mde all: pushed along and qcknd clr wl over 2f out: rdn over 1f out: kpt on strly* **7/2**[3]

43 2 5 **Sersar**[20] 6952 2-9-5 0 JimCrowley 8 81
(Ismail Mohammed) *trckd ldrs towards centre: hdwy over 2f out: rdn wl over 1f out: chsd wnr ins fnl f: no imp* **7/1**

2 3 1 1/2 **Radjash**[16] 7065 2-9-5 0 WilliamBuick 11 77
(Charlie Appleby) *racd towards stands side early stages: edgd lft to centre and hdwy to trck ldrs 1/2-way: rdn to chse wnr over 2f out: drvn over 1f out: kpt on same pce* **11/4**[2]

2 4 1 1/4 **Swiftsure (IRE)**[23] 6880 2-9-5 0 RyanMoore 7 74
(Sir Michael Stoute) *racd centre: chsd wnr: pushed along wl over 2f out: rdn wl over 1f out: sn one pce* **11/8**[1]

5 shd **To Dibba** 2-9-5 0 HarryBentley 4 74
(Roger Varian) *racd centre: in tch: hdwy to chse ldrs over 2f out: sn rdn and edgd lft: kpt on same pce fnl f* **20/1**

6 6 **Petit Filous** 2-9-5 0 JackMitchell 12 59
(Giles Bravery) *racd towards stands side early stages: in tch: edgd lft towards centre and pushed along 3f out: rdn 2f out:* **100/1**

0 7 2 **Mac's Kyllachy**[30] 6671 2-9-5 0 FrederikTylicki 6 54
(James Fanshawe) *dwlt:racd towards centre: midfield and pushed along 3f out: sn rdn and n.d* **100/1**

8 1/2 **Second Page** 2-9-5 0 TomMarquand 10 53
(Richard Hannon) *racd towards stands side early stages: t.k.h and prom: pushed along 1/2-way: rdn wl over 2f out: sn wknd* **25/1**

9 2 1/2 **Kaeso** 2-9-5 0 TomEaves 9 46
(Nigel Tinkler) *dwlt: racd towards stands side early stages: a towards rr* **100/1**

00 10 2 1/2 **Turning Gold**[20] 6952 2-9-5 0 RyanPowell 13 40
(Sir Mark Prescott Bt) *dwlt: racd towards stands side in early stages: rdn along 3f out: a rr* **100/1**

0 11 1/2 **Cape Baba**[34] 6590 2-9-5 0 GrahamGibbons 1 39
(Chris Wall) *racd centre: chsd wnr: rdn along 1/2-way: sn wkd* **100/1**

1m 25.78s (-0.52) **Going Correction** -0.10s/f (Good) **11** Ran SP% **117.1**
Speed ratings (Par 95): **98,92,90,89,89 82,79,79,76,73 73**
CSF £26.86 TOTE £5.00: £1.30, £1.50, £1.30; EX 24.80 Trifecta £75.70.
Owner K Abdullah **Bred** Juddmonte Farms Ltd **Trained** Newmarket, Suffolk

FOCUS
The faster of the two divisions by 0.14sec, and a good performance from the winner, who drew right away from some fair sorts.

7496 188BET BRITISH STALLION STUDS EBF MAIDEN STKS (DIV II) 7f
3:10 (3:11) (Class 5) 2-Y-O **£4,528** (£1,347; £673; £336) **Stalls** High

Form RPR

1 **Mirage Dancer** 2-9-5 0 RyanMoore 5 87+
(Sir Michael Stoute) *hld up towards rr: hdwy over 2f out: sn drvn: chsng ldrs over 1f out: edgd lft: styd on to ld last 50yds* **7/4**[1]

2433 **2** ½ **Tafaakhor (IRE)**[23] 6869 2-9-5 82 PaulHanagan 11 86
(Richard Hannon) *trckd ldrs: led over 2f out: edgd lft fnl f: hdd and no ex last 50yds* **5/1**[2]

0 **3** 1½ **Victory Angel (IRE)**[113] 3818 2-9-5 0 HarryBentley 1 82
(Roger Varian) *trckd ldrs: upsides over 1f out: kpt on same pce last 100yds* **20/1**

4 5 **Everything For You (IRE)** 2-9-5 0 TomEaves 2 70
(Kevin Ryan) *in rr: drvn over 3f out: hdwy over 1f out: kpt on to take modest 4th last 75yds* **12/1**[3]

3220 **5** 1 **Wigan Warrior**[76] 5150 2-9-5 75 PaulMulrennan 6 67
(David Brown) *chsd ldrs: drvn over 2f out: n.m.r appr fnl f: sn wknd* **20/1**

6 2½ **Flying Onsite (FR)** 2-9-5 0 AndrewMullen 3 61
(Nigel Tinkler) *dwlt: t.k.h: sn trcking ldrs: outpcd over 2f out: kpt on clsng stages* **100/1**

46 **7** ½ **Peace And Plenty**[78] 5073 2-9-5 0 MartinDwyer 12 60
(William Muir) *mid-div: hdwy to chse ldrs over 2f out: wknd over 1f out* **33/1**

8 2¾ **Valcartier (IRE)** 2-9-5 0 WilliamBuick 10 53
(John Gosden) *rr-div: hdwy to chse ldrs over 2f out: hung lft and wknd over 1f out* **7/4**[1]

0 **9** nk **Lesanti**[30] 6679 2-9-2 0 RobHornby(3) 4 52
(Ed McMahon) *led: hdd over 2f out: lost pl over 1f out* **80/1**

0 **10** 3 **Regal Mirage (IRE)**[14] 7125 2-9-2 0 RachelRichardson(3) 9 45
(Tim Easterby) *chsd ldrs: lost pl 2f out* **100/1**

11 3¾ **Rey Loopy (IRE)** 2-9-5 0 GrahamLee 13 35
(Ben Haslam) *in rr: drvn 3f out: nvr on terms* **100/1**

04 **12** 6 **Break The Silence**[26] 6808 2-9-5 0 BenCurtis 8 20
(Scott Dixon) *w ldrs: wknd 2f out: bhd whn eased clsng stages* **100/1**

1m 25.92s (-0.38) **Going Correction** -0.10s/f (Good) **12** Ran SP% **114.7**
Speed ratings (Par 95): **98,97,95,90,88 86,85,82,81,78 74,67**
CSF £10.37 TOTE £2.70: £1.20, £1.10, £3.80; EX 8.50 Trifecta £72.20.
Owner K Abdullah **Bred** Juddmonte Farms Ltd **Trained** Newmarket, Suffolk

FOCUS
This went to a well-bred, well-backed newcomer, with a useful running probably his best race yet in second. The principals edged towards the far side in the closing stages and the first three came clear.

7497 RACING POST/SIS BETTING SHOP MANAGER H'CAP 6f
3:45 (3:47) (Class 2) (0-105,104) 3-Y-O+**£19,407** (£5,775; £2,886; £1,443) **Stalls** High

Form RPR

6400 **1** **Muntadab (IRE)**[15] 7095 4-8-10 90 PJMcDonald 11 99
(Roger Fell) *led: rdn and hdd over 1f out: drvn and rallied ins fnl f to ld last 75 yds: kpt on* **33/1**

3320 **2** nk **Get Knotted (IRE)**[13] 7156 4-9-4 98 (p) PaulMulrennan 2 106
(Michael Dods) *trckd ldrs on inner: hdwy 2f out: rdn to chal over 1f out: drvn ins fnl f and ev ch: no ex towards fin* **11/1**

120 **3** nk **Solar Flair**[48] 6112 4-9-4 98 JimCrowley 4 105
(William Knight) *prom: cl up 2f out: rdn and ev ch ent fnl f: sn drvn and kpt on* **14/1**

0014 **4** hd **Dougan**[10] 7242 4-8-10 93 JosephineGordon(3) 13 99
(David Evans) *trckd ldrs: hdwy 2f out: str run on outer to ld over 1f out: drvn ins fnl f: hdd and no ex last 75 yds* **10/1**[3]

0006 **5** nk **George Bowen (IRE)**[13] 7156 4-8-11 91 TonyHamilton 17 96
(Richard Fahey) *hld up towards rr: hdwy 2f out: nt much over 1f out: sn rdn and styd on wl fnl f* **10/1**[3]

0630 **6** ¾ **Ninjago**[13] 7156 6-8-10 90 CamHardie 19 93
(Paul Midgley) *hld up towards rr: hdwy 2f out: rdn over 1f out: styd on fnl f* **22/1**

0233 **7** hd **Fendale**[7] 7315 4-8-9 89 (p) AndrewMullen 22 91
(Michael Dods) *hld up in rr: hdwy 2f out: n.m.r and swtchd rt over 1f out: sn rdn and edgd lft: kpt on towards fin* **12/1**

0065 **8** ½ **Red Pike (IRE)**[13] 7156 5-9-0 94 PaulHanagan 6 95
(Bryan Smart) *cl up: rdn along 2f out: drvn over 1f out: kpt on same pce ins fnl f* **11/1**

1160 **9** nk **Lincoln (IRE)**[12] 7186 5-9-1 95 GrahamLee 3 95
(Mick Channon) *in tch on inner: hdwy 2f out: rdn over 1f out: drvn and kpt on same pce fnl f* **22/1**

0206 **10** ¾ **Shared Equity**[104] 4136 5-9-5 99 DavidNolan 9 96
(Jedd O'Keeffe) *chsd ldrs: hdwy and cl up 2f out: rdn over 1f out: drvn and wknd fnl f* **16/1**

0300 **11** ¾ **Burnt Sugar (IRE)**[20] 6942 4-8-11 96 (bt) HollieDoyle(5) 5 91
(Richard Hannon) *s.i.s and rr: hdwy 2f out: sn rdn and kpt on fnl f* **18/1**

3101 **12** ½ **Ocean Sheridan (IRE)**[6] 7358 4-8-13 93 6ex ConnorBeasley 10 86
(Michael Dods) *midfield: effrt 2f out: sn rdn and no imp fnl f* **11/1**

3005 **13** ½ **Poyle Vinnie**[10] 7242 6-9-0 97 (p) AlistairRawlinson(3) 18 89
(Michael Appleby) *chsd ldrs on outer: hdwy 2f out: rdn over 1f out: wknd fnl f* **33/1**

0002 **14** hd **Blaine**[7] 7315 6-8-12 92 (b) TomEaves 7 83
(David Nicholls) *chsd ldrs: rdn along wl over 1f out: grad wknd* **16/1**

4000 **15** 2¼ **Johnny Barnes (IRE)**[34] 6558 4-9-10 104 FrankieDettori 16 88+
(John Gosden) *dwlt: a towards rr* **8/1**[2]

0000 **16** 1½ **Toofi (FR)**[48] 6112 5-9-3 97 FrederikTylicki 14 76+
(Robert Cowell) *a towards rr* **33/1**

2001 **17** 1 **New Bidder**[40] 6382 5-9-4 98 (b) GrahamGibbons 15 74
(David Barron) *dwlt and swtchd markedly lft s: a towards rr* **25/1**

0431 **18** 1¾ **C Note (IRE)**[10] 7241 3-9-8 103 6ex (b) RyanMoore 8 73
(Martyn Meade) *a towards rr* **13/2**[1]

0000 **19** 1 **Louis The Pious**[34] 6556 8-8-10 90 HarryBentley 20 57
(David O'Meara) *a rr* **40/1**

0350 **20** ¾ **Iseemist (IRE)**[20] 6943 5-9-0 94 ShaneGray 12 59
(John Gallagher) *cl up: rdn along 2f out: sn wknd* **100/1**

00 **21** 1½ **Clear Spring (IRE)**[47] 6161 8-9-4 98 [1] TomQueally 21 58
(John Spearing) *cl up on wd outside: pushed along 1/2-way: sn rdn and wknd* **100/1**

1m 11.42s (-2.18) **Going Correction** -0.10s/f (Good)
WFA 3 from 4yo+ 1lb **21** Ran SP% **124.8**
Speed ratings (Par 109): **110,109,109,108,108 107,107,106,106,105 104,103,102,102,99 97,96,93,92,91 89**
CSF £338.52 CT £5368.36 TOTE £49.50: £8.30, £3.30, £4.00, £2.60; EX 557.50 Trifecta £5095.60.
Owner Fell & High Hopes Partnership **Bred** Mrs James Wigan **Trained** Nawton, N Yorks

FOCUS
With the previous races suggesting the stands' side was not the place to be, the whole field tacked over to race centre to far side. It proved quite difficult to get competitive from too far back.

7498 HAGUE PRINT SOLUTIONS H'CAP 1m 6f 132y
4:20 (4:23) (Class 3) (0-95,95) 3-Y-O+
£12,450 (£3,728; £1,864; £932; £466; £234) **Stalls** Low

Form RPR

3114 **1** **Cape Cova (IRE)**[14] 7123 3-8-13 89 TomQueally 12 102
(John Gosden) *s.s: rn in snatches in detached last: gd hdwy over 2f out: 2nd 1f out: edgd lft: styd on to ld clsng stages* **4/1**[2]

312 **2** nk **Higher Power**[12] 7188 4-9-6 87 FrederikTylicki 3 99
(James Fanshawe) *trckd ldrs: qcknd to ld over 2f out: drvn over 1f out: hdd clsng stages* **7/2**[1]

313 **3** 5 **Ruscombe**[98] 4351 3-9-0 90 RyanMoore 11 95
(Sir Michael Stoute) *hld up towards rr: hdwy over 3f out: 3rd 1f out: sn n.m.r: kpt on one pce* **9/2**[3]

2321 **4** 7 **Arthur Mc Bride (IRE)**[12] 7183 7-9-4 85 6ex (t) ThomasBrown 6 81
(Nigel Twiston-Davies) *mid-div: drvn over 3f out: upsides over 2f out: wknd fnl f* **20/1**

0-22 **5** 3 **Not Never**[11] 7215 4-9-12 93 JimCrowley 13 85
(Hugo Palmer) *mid-div: swtchd rt 4f out: chsng ldrs over 2f out: wknd over 1f out* **5/1**

1151 **6** 2¾ **Champagne Champ**[11] 7215 4-9-11 92 6ex RichardKingscote 10 80
(Rod Millman) *chsd ldrs: led briefly 3f out: wknd over 1f out* **11/1**

422 **7** hd **Peterhouse (USA)**[27] 6794 4-8-6 78 (p) CliffordLee(5) 5 66
(Jason Ward) *hld up in rr: hdwy over 3f out: chsng ldrs over 2f out: wknd over 1f out* **22/1**

3050 **8** 1¼ **Gabrial's Star**[13] 7150 7-9-5 86 (b) DavidNolan 9 72
(Richard Fahey) *in rr: reminders over 3f out: nvr on terms* **50/1**

2000 **9** 6 **Gabrial The Hero (USA)**[13] 7150 7-10-0 95 TonyHamilton 4 73
(Richard Fahey) *mid-div: effrt 3f out: lost pl over 1f out* **50/1**

0000 **10** 4½ **The Twisler**[13] 7150 4-10-0 95 DougieCostello 8 67
(Jane Chapple-Hyam) *in rr: drvn 7f out: nvr a factor* **40/1**

0-23 **11** ½ **Major Mac**[12] 7183 4-8-9 76 oh2 (p) PJMcDonald 2 47
(Hughie Morrison) *drvn early to chse ldrs: led after 3f: hdd 3f out: lost pl 2f out* **18/1**

2412 **12** 1¼ **Multellie**[27] 6781 4-9-4 85 CamHardie 1 54
(Tim Easterby) *led early: chsd ldrs: lost pl over 2f out: sn bhd* **25/1**

6552 **13** 3½ **Noble Silk**[21] 6919 7-9-5 89 (v) JosephineGordon(3) 7 54
(Lucy Wadham) *sn led: hdd after 3f: lost pl over 2f out: sn bhd* **16/1**

3m 4.55s (-2.85) **Going Correction** +0.025s/f (Good)
WFA 3 from 4yo+ 9lb **13** Ran SP% **115.9**
Speed ratings (Par 107): **108,107,105,101,99 98,98,97,94,92 91,91,89**
CSF £16.21 CT £64.19 TOTE £4.20: £1.70, £1.80, £2.00; EX 20.20 Trifecta £57.50.
Owner Mohamed Obaida **Bred** Basil Brindley **Trained** Newmarket, Suffolk

FOCUS
A decent staying handicap run at what looked a good early pace.

7499 FREE SPINS AT 188BET CASINO H'CAP 1m 2f 60y
4:55 (4:55) (Class 3) (0-95,94) 3-Y-O **£12,938** (£3,850; £1,924; £962) **Stalls** Low

Form RPR

0464 **1** **Speed Company (IRE)**[34] 6559 3-9-7 94 RyanMoore 7 104
(John Quinn) *hld up in rr: hdwy over 2f out: swtchd rt and rdn over 1f out: str run ent fnl f: led last 50 yds* **8/1**

5313 **2** 1½ **Burguillos**[16] 7077 3-8-9 82 JimCrowley 6 89
(Alan King) *hld up in rr: stdy hdwy 3f out: trckd ldrs 2f out: rdn to chal ent fnl f: sn led: drvn and hdd last 50 yds: no ex* **7/2**[2]

1530 **3** ½ **Absolute Zero (IRE)**[28] 6753 3-9-0 87 HarryBentley 9 93
(Roger Varian) *trckd ldr: cl up 1/2-way: slt ld 2f out: sn rdn: hdd narrowly over 1f out: drvn and kpt on u.p fnl f* **14/1**

1101 **4** ¾ **Al Neksh**[37] 6489 3-9-4 91 FrankieDettori 4 96
(William Haggas) *trckd ldng pair: hdwy over 3f out: cl up 2f out: rdn and slt ld over 1f out: drvn and hdd jst ins fnl f: kpt on same pce towards fin* **9/4**[1]

3-23 **5** ¾ **Paris Magic**[14] 7106 3-8-6 82 (p) JosephineGordon(3) 3 85
(Hugo Palmer) *trckd ldrs: hdwy 3f out: rdn along wl over 1f out: sn drvn and kpt on same pce* **16/1**

1122 **6** 1½ **Rainbow Rebel (IRE)**[9] 7287 3-9-2 89 PJMcDonald 8 89
(Mark Johnston) *led: pushed along 3f out: sn rdn and hdd 2f out: grad wknd* **7/1**

31-5 **7** 2 **G K Chesterton (IRE)**[34] 6581 3-9-2 89 WilliamBuick 5 86
(Charlie Appleby) *trckd ldrs: hdwy and cl up 2f out: rdn 2f out: drvn and wknd appr fnl f* **4/1**[3]

31 **8** ¾ **Archippos**[99] 4313 3-8-10 83 ow1 DougieCostello 1 78
(Philip Kirby) *trckd ldng pair on inner: pushed along over 3f out: rdn over 2f out: sn wknd* **40/1**

2113 **9** 10 **Rubensian**[39] 6417 3-8-5 81 EdwardGreatrex(3) 2 57
(David Simcock) *hld up: hdwy on inner to chse ldrs 3f out: rdn over 2f out: sn drvn and wknd* **16/1**

2m 9.57s (0.17) **Going Correction** +0.025s/f (Good) **9** Ran SP% **117.5**
Speed ratings (Par 105): **100,98,98,97,97 96,94,93,85**
CSF £36.83 CT £393.36 TOTE £11.40: £2.60, £1.70, £4.40; EX 42.60 Trifecta £305.30.
Owner Wilson Woo **Bred** Rathasker Stud **Trained** Settrington, N Yorks

FOCUS
A decent handicap, and a smart performance from the winner.

7500 AMATEUR JOCKEYS ASSOCIATION OF GREAT BRITAIN AMATEUR RIDERS' H'CAP 1m 2f 60y
5:30 (5:32) (Class 5) (0-75,75) 3-Y-O+ **£4,991** (£1,548; £773; £387) **Stalls** Low

Form RPR

4331 **1** **Hardington**[28] 6737 3-10-6 75 (v) MrHHunt(3) 13 90
(Alan King) *gave problems gng to s: awkward s: hld up in rr: swtchd rt and gd hdwy over 2f out: led appr fnl f: edgd lft: sn clr: v readily* **6/1**[3]

6303 **2** *6* **Bahamian C**[7] 7336 5-9-11 **63**............................(t) MissEmilyBullock(5) 10 66
(Richard Fahey) *chsd ldrs: led over 2f out: hdd appr fnl f: kpt on same pce* **12/1**

0403 **3** *¾* **Woodacre**[4] 7412 9-10-11 **72**.......................... MrsCBartley 11 74
(Richard Whitaker) *chsd ldrs: n.m.r and swtchd rt over 2f out: one pce over 1f out: tk 3rd last 75yds* **8/1**

505 **4** *¾* **Polar Forest**[10] 7246 6-10-13 **74**......................(e) MissJoannaMason 16 74
(Richard Guest) *prom: effrt over 2f out: kpt on one pce* **25/1**

-403 **5** *1½* **Match My Fire (IRE)**[11] 7214 3-10-1 **67**.................. MissSBrotherton 17 64
(Ralph Beckett) *hld up in rr: hdwy over 2f out: kpt on: nvr nr ldrs* **9/2**[2]

0033 **6** *hd* **East India**[10] 7246 4-11-0 **75**.. MrSWalker 2 72
(George Baker) *mid-div: effrt over 3f out: one pce fnl 2f* **4/1**[1]

0P50 **7** *1¼* **Manny Owens (IRE)**[16] 7077 4-10-5 **71**.......................(t) MrJJO'Neill(5) 6 66
(Jonjo O'Neill) *mid-div: drvn over 5f out: one pce fnl 2f* **33/1**

0355 **8** *½* **Sakhalin Star (IRE)**[18] 7007 5-9-13 **65**............(e) MissPBridgwater(5) 12 59
(Richard Guest) *mid-div on outer: kpt on fnl 2f: nvr a threat* **25/1**

0335 **9** *nk* **Stardrifter**[13] 7159 4-10-3 **71**............................ MissFMcSharry(7) 15 64
(Richard Fahey) *hld up towards rr: hdwy on ins over 3f out: one pce whn n.m.r over 1f out* **7/1**

0000 **10** *1* **Inspector Norse**[31] 6647 5-10-0 **61** oh4.........................[1] MrWEasterby 4 52
(Tim Easterby) *led: t.k.h: hdd over 2f out: hung lft and wknd over 1f out* **40/1**

0000 **11** *½* **Cadmium**[15] 7097 5-10-0 **61** oh4.................................... MissCWalton 9 51
(Micky Hammond) *in rr: sme hdwy over 2f out: nvr a factor* **66/1**

400 **12** *2¾* **Albert Boy (IRE)**[16] 7078 3-9-8 **65**............................ MissMollyKing(5) 3 50
(Scott Dixon) *chsd ldrs: wkng whn n.m.r on inner over 1f out* **50/1**

3-50 **13** *nk* **Cadeau Magnifique**[13] 7159 4-10-7 **73**.......................... MrMEnnis(5) 7 57
(Richard Fahey) *sn drvn along: sn chsng ldrs: n.m.r and lost pl over 1f out* **16/1**

1221 **14** *4½* **Duke Of Yorkshire**[57] 5805 6-10-6 **70**....................(p) MissEEasterby(3) 1 46
(Tim Easterby) *sn chsng ldrs: wknd 2f out* **14/1**

4542 **15** *2¼* **Cold Fusion (IRE)**[18] 7014 3-9-9 **68**............................ MrTBenjamin(7) 5 40
(David Flood) *chsd ldrs: swtchd rt 3f out: lost pl 2f out* **50/1**

34 **16** *1¾* **Rayaa**[40] 6380 3-10-7 **73**..(t) MrDLQueally 8 41
(John Butler) *in rr: effrt on outer 3f out: sn wknd* **14/1**

3110 **17** *3* **Silver Alliance**[28] 6753 8-10-12 **73**................................(b) MrRBirkett 14 36
(Julia Feilden) *hld up in rr: hdwy over 4f out: sn chsng ldrs: wkng whn hmpd over 2f out: sn bhd* **25/1**

2m 10.65s (1.25) **Going Correction** +0.025s/f (Good) **17** Ran SP% **125.3**
WFA 3 from 4yo+ 5lb
Speed ratings (Par 103): **96,91,90,90,88 88,87,87,87,86 85,83,83,79,77 76,74**
CSF £71.93 CT £596.73 TOTE £6.80: £2.10, £3.10, £2.50, £5.40; EX 78.20 Trifecta £1075.20.
Owner The Fastnet Partnership **Bred** Litex Commerce **Trained** Barbury Castle, Wilts
■ Stewards' Enquiry : Mr H Hunt two-day ban: careless riding

FOCUS
A modest amateur riders' handicap.
T/Plt: £128.60 to a £1 stake. Pool: £92619.41, 525.46 winning units. T/Qpdt: £16.30 to a £1 stake. Pool: £10459.07, 473.68 winning units. **Joe Rowntree & Walter Glynn**

6570 NEWBURY (L-H)
Friday, October 21

OFFICIAL GOING: Good to soft (good in places; 5.8)
Wind: Moderate, behind Weather: Sunny spells

7501 SIA MAIDEN STKS (PLUS 10 RACE) (DIV I) 1m (S)
1:20 (1:21) (Class 4) 2-Y-O **£5,175** (£1,540; £769; £384) **Stalls** High

Form RPR

5 **1** **Rosarno (IRE)**[21] 6924 2-9-5 0.. JamieSpencer 5 81
(Charles Hills) *hld up towards rr: hdwy 2f out: drvn to ld ins fnl f* **11/1**

5 **2** *½* **International Law**[34] 6570 2-9-5 0.............................. JimmyFortune 7 80
(Brian Meehan) *dwlt: sn chsng ldrs: rdn 3f out: led 1f out tl ins fnl f: r.o* **14/1**

0 **3** *1¾* **Beach Break**[29] 6704 2-9-5 0.. FMBerry 6 76
(Ralph Beckett) *led: hrd rdn and hdd 1f out: kpt on same pce* **12/1**

34 **4** *½* **See Of Rome**[30] 6663 2-9-5 0.. ShaneKelly 10 75
(Richard Hughes) *a.p: kpt on u.p fnl 2f* **13/2**[3]

5 *2¾* **Sea Skimmer** 2-9-5 0... MartinLane 8 69
(Saeed bin Suroor) *prom tl outpcd 2f out: 5th and btn whn short of room over 1f out* **9/2**[2]

6 *½* **Surrey Hope (USA)** 2-9-5 0.. JFEgan 3 68
(Joseph Tuite) *bhd: rdn over 3f out: styd on fnl 2f* **66/1**

7 *nk* **Uae King** 2-9-5 0.. AndreaAtzeni 15 67
(Roger Varian) *prom tl rdn and btn 2f out* **7/2**[1]

8 *1¼* **Simoon (IRE)** 2-9-5 0... LiamKeniry 12 64
(Andrew Balding) *trckd ldrs: shkn up over 2f out: sn outpcd* **25/1**

0 **9** *3½* **Log Off (IRE)**[102] 4203 2-8-7 0........................... KatherineGlenister(7) 9 52
(David Evans) *a in midfield: rdn and btn 2f out* **200/1**

10 *6* **Pete So High (GER)** 2-9-5 0.. SeanLevey 2 43
(Richard Hannon) *bhd: rdn over 2f out: n.d* **16/1**

11 *4½* **Light Gunner (IRE)** 2-9-2 0.. EoinWalsh(3) 14 34
(Henry Tett) *dwlt: bhd: rdn 3f out: nvr nr ldrs* **200/1**

0 **12** *2* **Any Questions**[18] 7013 2-9-5 0...................................... AdamKirby 4 29
(William Knight) *dwlt: hrd rdn over 3f out: a bhd* **150/1**

13 *1¼* **Uptown Funk (IRE)** 2-9-5 0...................................... RobertHavlin 11 26
(John Gosden) *dwlt: nvr beyond midfield: rdn 3f out: sn bhd* **7/2**[1]

14 *2¾* **Weloof (FR)** 2-9-5 0... JamesDoyle 13 20
(Ed Dunlop) *in tch tl wknd 2f out* **16/1**

1m 43.76s (4.06) **Going Correction** +0.525s/f (Yiel) **14** Ran SP% **117.4**
Speed ratings (Par 97): **100,99,97,97,94 94,93,92,88,82 78,76,75,72**
CSF £150.59 TOTE £12.40: £3.40, £3.60, £5.30; EX 176.10 Trifecta £1568.30.
Owner Abdulla Al Khalifa **Bred** Wilgerbosdrift (uk) Ltd **Trained** Lambourn, Berks
■ Stewards' Enquiry : James Doyle one-day ban: failing to take all reasonable and permissible measures to obtain the best possible placing (1st Nov)

FOCUS
The going remained good to soft, good in places. Rail from 1m to 5f marker on round course moved in since last meeting, increasing race distances on the round course by 6yds. The first division of an interesting maiden, won by Midterm last year. Previous experience proved key with four of the six to have run before filling the first four places, while it was also noticeable that those who raced furthest from the stands' rail were at a big advantage. The winning time was 8.16sec outside standard and while they didn't go quick, it still suggested the ground was holding.

7502 JOIN THE HOT TO TROT SYNDICATE EBF STALLIONS MAIDEN STKS (PLUS 10 RACE) 6f 110y
1:50 (1:56) (Class 4) 2-Y-O **£4,269** (£1,270; £634; £317) **Stalls** High

Form RPR

340 **1** **Parfait (IRE)**[23] 6880 2-9-5 87.................................... JamesDoyle 4 84
(John Gosden) *mde virtually all: drvn and in control ins fnl f* **9/2**[3]

323 **2** *1* **Firefright (IRE)**[43] 6260 2-9-5 92................................ JamieSpencer 13 81
(Jeremy Noseda) *t.k.h: prom: pressed wnr after 2f: rdn over 1f out: kpt on* **15/8**[1]

3 *¾* **Yalawin (IRE)** 2-9-5 0.. AndreaAtzeni 15 79
(Roger Varian) *hld up in tch: effrt 2f out: kpt on fnl f* **3/1**[2]

4 *1¼* **Me Too Nagasaki (IRE)** 2-9-5 0.. JFEgan 2 76+
(Jeremy Noseda) *dwlt: hld up and bhd: brought to stands' side of gp fr 1/2-way: shkn up over 1f out: gd late hdwy* **50/1**

5 *2* **Rising (IRE)** 2-9-5 0.. JimmyFortune 5 70
(Brian Meehan) *dwlt: hld up and bhd: shkn up over 1f out: styd on wl fnl f* **50/1**

00 **6** *1½* **Alemaratalyoum (IRE)**[34] 6577 2-9-5 0........................ PatCosgrave 10 66
(Ed Dunlop) *in tch: rdn 2f out: one pce appr fnl f* **66/1**

00 **7** *3¼* **Orithia (USA)**[11] 7216 2-9-0 0....................................[1] FergusSweeney 14 52
(Seamus Durack) *towards rr: effrt over 2f out: sme late hdwy* **150/1**

8 *2* **Black Bolt (IRE)** 2-9-5 0.. DaneO'Neill 8 52
(Richard Hannon) *chsd ldrs tl wknd wl over 1f out* **20/1**

43 **9** *¾* **Things Happen**[15] 7090 2-9-5 0.................................. DanielTudhope 3 50
(David Evans) *towards rr: rdn 3f out: nvr rchd ldrs* **33/1**

10 *1* **Bay Watch (IRE)** 2-9-5 0.. OisinMurphy 12 47
(Andrew Balding) *a in midfield: outpcd and btn 2f out* **20/1**

06 **11** *1¾* **Mr Scaff (IRE)**[35] 6542 2-9-0 0................................ GeorgeWood(5) 9 42
(Paul Henderson) *mid-div: drvn along 1/2-way: n.d* **100/1**

12 *3¼* **Mellow** 2-9-0 0... RobertHavlin 11 28
(Hughie Morrison) *dwlt: t.k.h and sn in midfield: wknd over 2f out* **20/1**

00 **13** *2* **Silver Mist**[34] 6570 2-9-0 0.. KieranO'Neill 6 23
(Richard Hannon) *w wnr for 2f: rdn 1/2-way: lost pl over 2f out* **100/1**

14 *nk* **Mostahel** 2-9-5 0... SeanLevey 16 27
(Richard Hannon) *dwlt: sn chsng ldrs: wknd over 2f out* **16/1**

15 *½* **Highland Boy** 2-9-5 0... AdamKirby 1 25
(Clive Cox) *wnt lft s: rn green: sn wl bhd* **33/1**

040 **16** *13* **Koeman**[23] 6881 2-9-5 76... GeorgeBaker 7
(Mick Channon) *mid-div tl wknd over 2f out: eased whn no ch* **14/1**

1m 21.45s (2.15) **Going Correction** +0.525s/f (Yiel) **16** Ran SP% **115.9**
Speed ratings (Par 97): **108,106,106,104,102 100,96,94,93,92 90,86,84,84,83 68**
CSF £11.39 TOTE £5.60: £1.60, £1.10, £2.20; EX 14.20 Trifecta £47.40.
Owner Godolphin **Bred** Mogeely Stud **Trained** Newmarket, Suffolk

FOCUS
After the first race it was no surprise that the entire field soon made for the centre of the track. Few got into this. The form is rated around the runner-up's maiden form.

7503 SIA MAIDEN STKS (PLUS 10 RACE) (DIV II) 1m (S)
2:25 (2:29) (Class 4) 2-Y-O **£5,175** (£1,540; £769; £384) **Stalls** High

Form RPR

02 **1** **Sound Bar**[32] 6632 2-9-5 0.. FMBerry 12 81
(Ralph Beckett) *mde all: rdn 2f out: hung lft and rt fr over 1f out: clr ins fnl f: comf* **4/1**[3]

0 **2** *2¾* **Mathix (FR)**[28] 6751 2-9-5 0...................................... PatCosgrave 11 75
(William Haggas) *t.k.h and covered up: trckd ldrs: sltly outpcd over 2f out: rallied and chsd wnr over 1f out: a hld* **12/1**

3 *nk* **Hawridge Flyer** 2-9-5 0.. DaneO'Neill 15 74
(Stuart Kittow) *chsd ldrs: rdn and styd on fnl 2f* **66/1**

4 *½* **Solar Cross** 2-9-5 0.. GeorgeBaker 5 73
(Roger Charlton) *mid-div: rdn to chse ldrs over 2f out: styd on fnl f* **13/2**

5 *2¾* **Eagle Creek (IRE)** 2-9-5 0.. AndreaAtzeni 4 67
(Simon Crisford) *prom tl rdn and one pce appr fnl f* **7/2**[2]

6 *½* **Wine List** 2-9-5 0... OisinMurphy 13 66
(Andrew Balding) *dwlt: sn in midfield: effrt over 2f out: styd on same pce* **8/1**

7 *nse* **Road To Dubai (IRE)** 2-9-5 0.. RobertHavlin 7 66
(George Scott) *plld hrd: prom tl outpcd fnl 2f* **33/1**

8 *1* **Commander** 2-9-5 0... JamesDoyle 3 64
(Roger Varian) *chsd ldrs tl wknd 2f out* **5/2**[1]

9 *4* **London Master** 2-9-5 0.. TedDurcan 1 55
(Chris Wall) *dwlt: nvr trbld ldrs* **66/1**

10 *½* **Russian Regard (IRE)** 2-9-5 0.. RyanTate 2 54
(Jonathan Portman) *mid-div: outpcd over 2f out: sn btn* **50/1**

0 **11** *shd* **Tomsamcharlie**[12] 7187 2-9-5 0.................................. TimmyMurphy 6 54
(Gary Moore) *a towards rr: n.d fnl 3f* **125/1**

12 *¾* **About Glory** 2-9-5 0.. SeanLevey 9 52
(Richard Hannon) *sn in midfield: wknd over 2f out* **25/1**

13 *4½* **Champagne Reign (IRE)** 2-9-0 0....................................... JohnFahy 14 37
(J S Moore) *a bhd* **100/1**

0 **14** *19* **Black Prince (FR)**[12] 7187 2-9-5 0...................................... JFEgan 8
(Anthony Honeyball) *t.k.h: prom tl wknd 3f out* **100/1**

1m 44.37s (4.67) **Going Correction** +0.525s/f (Yiel) **14** Ran SP% **117.4**
Speed ratings (Par 97): **97,94,93,93,90 90,90,89,85,84 84,83,79,60**
CSF £47.76 TOTE £4.40: £1.50, £3.60, £15.90; EX 49.40 Trifecta £3475.80.
Owner K Abdullah **Bred** Juddmonte Farms Ltd **Trained** Kimpton, Hants

FOCUS
Again they came up the centre and the winning time was 0.61sec slower than the first division. The winner took this with some authority. The field finished a little compressed.

7504 KARL KING TRANSPORT FILLIES' H'CAP 1m 2f 6y
3:00 (3:01) (Class 4) (0-85,85) 3-Y-O+ **£4,851** (£1,443; £721; £360) **Stalls** Centre

Form RPR

4321 **1** **Entsar (IRE)**[31] 6661 3-9-4 **84**...................................... PatCosgrave 6 98+
(William Haggas) *led for 2f: settled off ldng pair in 3rd: led over 2f out: rdn clr over 1f out: comf* **11/2**[1]

1143 **2** *2½* **Lorelina**[26] 6803 3-8-8 **74**.. OisinMurphy 1 82
(Andrew Balding) *chsd clr ldrs in 5th: wnt 2nd over 1f out: no imp* **6/1**[2]

4654 **3** 3 ¼ **Somethingthrilling**[21] 6914 4-8-10 **78**.......................... JoshuaBryan(7) 7 80
(David Elsworth) *mid-div: rdn and hdwy 2f out: styd on fnl f* **8/1**

21 **4** 1 **Kullu (IRE)**[18] 7009 3-8-9 **75**.. StevieDonohoe 5 75
(Charlie Fellowes) *prom: wnt 4 l clr w ldr after 2f: outpcd fnl 2f* **15/2**[3]

1341 **5** 3 ¼ **Jawaayiz**[61] 5671 3-8-10 **81**.. GeorgeWood(5) 2 75
(Simon Crisford) *hld up off the pce in 7th: drvn along over 3f out: styd on same pce* **16/1**

1253 **6** 1 ½ **Blind Faith (IRE)**[11] 7204 3-8-13 **79**.............................. JamesDoyle 15 69+
(Luca Cumani) *plld hrd: c across fr wd stall to ld after 2f and wnt 4 l clr w one rival: hdd over 2f out: sn wknd* **10/1**

2610 **7** 1 ¾ **Sunscape (IRE)**[29] 6702 3-8-9 **75**.................................... RobertHavlin 4 62
(Hughie Morrison) *plld hrd in midfield: rdn 3f out: nvr able to chal* **33/1**

1320 **8** 1 ¾ **Inke (IRE)**[87] 4737 4-9-6 **81**..(p) AdamKirby 9 64
(Jim Boyle) *hld up in rr: shkn up and styd on fnl 2f* **33/1**

3106 **9** 1 ½ **Alyday**[13] 7153 3-9-1 **81**.. AndreaAtzeni 8 61
(Sir Michael Stoute) *bhd: rdn 3f out: n.d* **10/1**

3210 **10** nk **Bocking End (IRE)**[28] 6747 3-9-5 **85**............................. JamieSpencer 3 64
(Michael Bell) *chsd clr ldrs in 6th tl wknd 2f out* **14/1**

2230 **11** 3 ¼ **Daisy Bere (FR)**[80] 5006 3-9-0 **80**.................................. JoeyHaynes 14 53
(K R Burke) *stdd s and dropped in: bhd: rdn 4f out: nvr nr ldrs* **25/1**

6221 **12** 2 ½ **Shufoog**[43] 6268 3-8-12 **78**.. DaneO'Neill 16 46
(William Haggas) *a bhd* **8/1**

2324 **13** ¾ **Perceived**[62] 5650 4-9-0 **75**... FergusSweeney 10 41
(Henry Candy) *chsd clr ldrs in 4th tl wknd over 2f out* **14/1**

1450 **14** 14 **Della Valle (GER)**[23] 6876 3-8-9 **75**................................. TedDurcan 11 13
(Mike Murphy) *a bhd* **66/1**

-163 **15** 9 **Qamarain (USA)**[20] 6947 3-8-11 **77**...................................... FMBerry 12
(Brian Meehan) *mid-div: hrd rdn 3f out: sn wknd* **11/1**

2m 9.67s (0.87) **Going Correction** +0.40s/f (Good)
WFA 3 from 4yo+ 5lb **15** Ran SP% **120.6**
Speed ratings (Par 102): **112,110,107,106,104 102,101,100,98,98 95,93,93,82,74**
CSF £35.96 CT £269.09 TOTE £6.10: £2.20, £2.70, £2.90; EX 37.80 Trifecta £341.10.
Owner Al Shaqab Racing **Bred** Manister House Stud **Trained** Newmarket, Suffolk

FOCUS

Race distance increased by 6yds. A fair fillies' handicap in which the 3yos had taken the last five runnings and that trend continues. Despite the leaders appearing to go off quick, the pace held up surprisingly well.

7505 TOM'S PIES H'CAP 1m 7y(R)

3:35 (3:36) (Class 4) (0-85,85) 3-Y-O **£4,851** (£1,443; £721; £360) **Stalls** Centre

Form RPR

-111 **1** **Cloudberry**[42] 6300 3-9-6 **84**... GeorgeBaker 8 97+
(Roger Charlton) *stdd s: dwlt: hld up in rr: gd hdwy 2f out: led ins fnl f: drvn clr* **7/4**[1]

3140 **2** 2 ¼ **Grapevine (IRE)**[49] 6081 3-9-7 **85**.......................... MichaelJMMurphy 5 92
(Charles Hills) *stdd s: dwlt: t.k.h towards rr: hdwy over 2f out: led over 1f out tl ins fnl f: one pce* **12/1**

3510 **3** 1 ½ **Red Tea**[21] 6914 3-9-5 **83**... FMBerry 12 87
(Peter Hiatt) *mid-div: hrd rdn and hdwy over 1f out: styd on* **12/1**

3002 **4** 2 ¼ **Zzoro (IRE)**[16] 7077 3-9-3 **84**................................... KieranShoemark(3) 2 82
(Amanda Perrett) *in tch: rdn to press ldrs 2f out: no ex fnl f* **8/1**

0345 **5** hd **Flyboy (IRE)**[20] 6957 3-9-2 **80**..[1] DanielTudhope 7 78+
(David O'Meara) *in tch: effrt and nt clr run 2f out: swtchd lft: no imp* **5/1**[2]

14-0 **6** 1 ½ **Hells Babe**[18] 7017 3-9-2 **80**.. TimmyMurphy 1 74
(Jonjo O'Neill) *prom tl wknd wl over 1f out* **33/1**

200 **7** ½ **Navajo War Dance**[9] 7287 3-9-7 **85**..........................(v[1]) JamesDoyle 11 78
(K R Burke) *chsd ldrs: hrd rdn and lost pl over 2f out: n.d after* **11/2**[3]

0300 **8** hd **Drifting Spirit (IRE)**[26] 6811 3-8-11 **80**........................ AdamMcNamara(5) 9 73
(Richard Fahey) *towards rr: rdn 3f out: nvr able to chal* **14/1**

0350 **9** 5 **Take The Helm**[21] 6918 3-9-7 **85**...................................... JimmyFortune 4 66
(Brian Meehan) *stdd s and missed break: plld hrd in rr: rdn and struggling 3f out* **25/1**

1000 **10** 7 **Medburn Dream**[11] 7213 3-9-7 **85**.. AdamKirby 10 50
(Paul Henderson) *prom: led 3f out tl wknd wl over 1f out* **20/1**

1550 **11** 2 ½ **Billy Roberts (IRE)**[37] 6490 3-9-2 **80**.............................. JamieSpencer 3 40
(Richard Guest) *led tl 3f out: wknd wl over 1f out: eased whn no ch fnl f* **25/1**

1m 40.52s (1.82) **Going Correction** +0.40s/f (Good) **11** Ran SP% **117.0**
Speed ratings (Par 103): **106,103,102,100,99 98,97,97,92,85 83**
CSF £23.29 CT £204.32 TOTE £2.20: £1.20, £3.50, £3.10; EX 26.20 Trifecta £146.90.
Owner Beckhampton Stables Ltd **Bred** Carwell Equities Ltd **Trained** Beckhampton, Wilts

FOCUS

Race distance increased by 6yds. A fair 3yo handicap and unlike in the previous event, the runners came up the middle of the track after turning for home. With a few in here who like to force it, a good pace was always a likely and that suited the first two, who both came from the rear. The winner remains very much on the up.

7506 ZENERGI H'CAP 7f (S)

4:10 (4:11) (Class 4) (0-80,80) 3-Y-O+ **£4,690** (£1,395; £697; £348) **Stalls** High

Form RPR

0434 **1** **My Dad Syd (USA)**[7] 7333 4-8-8 **67**...................................(b) TedDurcan 10 77+
(Ian Williams) *disp ld: led over 3f out: rdn clr over 1f out: readily* **17/2**[3]

1300 **2** 1 ¼ **Cricklewood Green (USA)**[2] 7461 5-9-1 **79**.............. MitchGodwin(5) 4 86
(Sylvester Kirk) *dwlt: bhd and sn pushed along: hdwy and squeezed through over 1f out: styd on wl to take 2nd ins fnl f* **8/1**[2]

4352 **3** 2 ¾ **Topology**[11] 7204 3-9-2 **77**.. OisinMurphy 14 76
(Joseph Tuite) *chsd ldrs: rdn over 2f out: one pce appr fnl f* **10/1**

615 **4** shd **Posh Bounty**[27] 6770 5-9-2 **75**.. JFEgan 15 75
(Joseph Tuite) *sn towards rr: rdn and styd on wl fnl 2f* **25/1**

1050 **5** hd **Another Boy**[43] 6266 3-8-10 **76**..........................(p) GeorgiaCox(5) 12 74
(Ralph Beckett) *mid-div: hdwy to chse wnr 2f out: no ex and lost 2nd ins fnl f* **33/1**

1360 **6** 1 **Jimenez (IRE)**[13] 7153 3-9-5 **80**....................................(p) JimmyFortune 5 75
(Brian Meehan) *prom tl hrd rdn and no ex appr fnl f* **10/1**

0240 **7** nse **English Hero**[6] 7360 3-8-13 **74**... PatCosgrave 3 69
(John Mackie) *t.k.h: chsd ldrs tl outpcd fnl 2f* **25/1**

3060 **8** shd **Baltic Brave (IRE)**[26] 6806 5-9-2 **80**..................(t) CharlieBennett(5) 16 76
(Hughie Morrison) *towards rr tl shkn up and styd on fnl 2f* **25/1**

4050 **9** 1 **Captain Bob (IRE)**[23] 6878 5-8-8 **67**................................. JimmyQuinn 7 60+
(Robert Cowell) *dwlt: towards rr tl styd on fr over 1f out* **10/1**

0621 **10** 2 **Evening Attire**[17] 7059 5-9-0 **73**... JamesDoyle 13 61+
(William Stone) *awkward leaving stalls and missed break: towards rr: effrt over 2f out: n.d in midfield whn squeezed for room over 1f out* **10/1**

1220 **11** ½ **Tripartite (IRE)**[39] 6416 3-8-12 **73**...................................... DaneO'Neill 9 59
(Jeremy Gask) *chsd ldrs tl wknd over 1f out* **11/1**

4022 **12** ½ **Ballyer Rallyer (IRE)**[66] 5525 3-8-10 **71**...................... StevieDonohoe 17 56
(Daniel Mark Loughnane) *in tch tl hrd rdn and wknd wl over 1f out* **33/1**

3452 **13** ¾ **Short Work**[26] 6806 3-9-5 **80**...(b) FMBerry 11 63
(Ralph Beckett) *plld hrd in rr: nvr trbld ldrs* **10/1**

2545 **14** 3 **Russian Radiance**[42] 6299 4-9-4 **77**................................ GeorgeBaker 8 53
(Jonathan Portman) *in tch tl wknd over 2f out* **14/1**

2005 **15** 1 **Black Caesar (IRE)**[8] 7301 5-8-10 **69**............................. JamieSpencer 1 42
(Philip Hide) *disp ld tl over 3f out: wknd 2f out* **12/1**

-550 **16** 4 **Russian Reward (IRE)**[212] 1041 4-8-13 **75**............ KieranShoemark(3) 2 38
(Amanda Perrett) *chsd ldrs tl wknd over 2f out* **14/1**

5034 **17** 1 **Red Artist**[17] 7054 3-9-5 **80**...[1] AndreaAtzeni 6 39
(Simon Crisford) *a towards rr: hrd rdn and n.d 2f out* **13/2**[1]

1m 28.38s (2.68) **Going Correction** +0.525s/f (Yiel)
WFA 3 from 4yo+ 2lb **17** Ran SP% **127.2**
Speed ratings (Par 105): **105,103,100,100,100 98,98,98,97,95 94,94,93,89,88 84,83**
CSF £73.05 CT £731.88 TOTE £11.80: £2.80, £2.20, £2.80, £4.70; EX 110.10 Trifecta £2242.80.

Owner S Rudolf **Bred** Dr Christoph Berglar **Trained** Portway, Worcs

FOCUS

A competitive handicap and a wide-open betting market. Again they came up the middle and main action unfolded towards the far side.

7507 SIA "HANDS AND HEELS" APPRENTICE H'CAP (PART OF THE RACING EXCELLENCE INITIATIVE) 2m

4:45 (4:46) (Class 5) (0-75,75) 4-Y-O+ **£2,911** (£866; £432; £216) **Stalls** Centre

Form RPR

3562 **1** **London Prize**[7] 7320 5-9-7 **72**.. AdamMcNamara 1 82+
(Ian Williams) *hld up off the pce towards rr: smooth hdwy 4f out: led over 2f out: rdn and styd on wl* **11/10**[1]

5330 **2** 3 **Medburn Cutler**[26] 6804 6-9-7 **75**..............................(p) SeanMooney(3) 9 81
(Paul Henderson) *prom in chsng gp: rdn to chse wnr over 2f out: one pce fnl f* **11/1**

-464 **3** 1 ¼ **Northern Meeting (IRE)**[22] 6090 6-9-7 **72**..............(p) PatrickVaughan 10 77
(Robert Stephens) *dwlt: wl bhd tl hdwy to chse ldrs 2f out: styd on same pce appr fnl f* **33/1**

2043 **4** shd **Snowy Dawn**[22] 6906 6-9-3 **68**... JoshQuinn 12 72
(Steph Hollinshead) *hld up off the pce in 6th: hdwy and prom 3f out: styd on same pce fnl 2f* **12/1**

0-50 **5** 3 **Barizan (IRE)**[12] 7183 10-9-9 **74**.............................(vt) CallumRodriguez 4 75
(Brendan Powell) *hld up off the pce towards rr: rdn and styd on fnl 3f: nvr rchd ldrs* **11/1**

5566 **6** 5 **Shalimah (IRE)**[9] 7274 4-9-1 **69**...(v) WilliamCox(3) 8 64
(Clive Cox) *hld up off the pce in midfield: rdn 3f out: no imp* **16/1**

0U66 **7** ½ **Kissy Suzuki**[57] 5805 4-8-1 **57**.. TheodoreLadd(5) 6 51
(Hughie Morrison) *s.s: wl bhd tl sme hdwy 2f out: n.d* **25/1**

2213 **8** 1 **Miss Tiger Lily**[23] 6885 6-9-0 **68**...................................... JoshuaBryan(3) 5 61
(Harry Dunlop) *disp ld at gd pce and sn clr w one rival: led 1/2-way tl over 2f out: sn wknd* **15/2**[2]

1136 **9** ¾ **The New Pharaoh (IRE)**[17] 7053 5-9-10 **75**................. SamuelClarke 2 67
(Chris Wall) *dwlt: wl bhd tl modest effrt on inner 2f out: nvr nr ldrs* **10/1**[3]

6405 **10** 10 **Delagoa Bay (IRE)**[6] 7367 8-8-5 **56** oh2.......................... MitchGodwin 3 36
(Sylvester Kirk) *hld up off the pce in midfield: lost pl and in rr fnl 4f* **33/1**

3000 **11** hd **Giant Redwood (IRE)**[18] 7006 4-9-5 **70**..........................(p) LuluStanford 13 50
(Michael Bell) *chsd clr ldrs tl lost pl 4f out* **33/1**

2524 **12** 4 **The Ducking Stool**[79] 5035 9-9-0 **68**................................ LiamDoran(3) 7 43
(Julia Feilden) *chsd clr ldrs: lost pl 5f out: sn bhd* **16/1**

5400 **13** 10 **Wordiness**[13] 7158 8-9-6 **74**...................................... KatherineGlenister(3) 11 37
(David Evans) *disp ld tl 1/2-way: cl 2nd and wnt clr w ldr tl wknd over 3f out* **25/1**

3m 39.36s (7.36) **Going Correction** +0.40s/f (Good) **13** Ran SP% **121.1**
Speed ratings (Par 103): **97,95,94,94,93 90,90,90,89,84 84,82,77**
CSF £13.21 CT £258.43 TOTE £1.90: £1.20, £3.80, £9.10; EX 17.70 Trifecta £459.90.
Owner Mrs Margaret Forsyth **Bred** P And Mrs A G Venner **Trained** Portway, Worcs

FOCUS

Race distance increased by 6yds. A modest staying apprentice handicap featuring the winner, third and fourth from last year. The leaders went off far too quick and predictably set it up for a closer.

7508 RAYNER BOSCH CAR SERVICE H'CAP (FOR LADY AMATEUR RIDERS) 1m 4f 5y

5:20 (5:20) (Class 5) (0-75,75) 4-Y-O+ **£2,807** (£870; £435; £217) **Stalls** Centre

Form RPR

0-60 **1** **Syncopate**[60] 5724 7-10-7 **75**.. MissGAndrews 10 85
(Pam Sly) *in tch: effrt on inner and led 2f out: drvn clr over 1f out: styd on wl* **3/1**[1]

51U2 **2** 3 ½ **Jersey Jewel (FR)**[57] 5805 4-9-12 **71**................... MissCAGreenway(5) 2 75
(Tom Dascombe) *prom: lost pl over 9f out: rallied and pressed wnr 2f out: one pce* **6/1**[3]

0244 **3** 5 **Sherman McCoy**[17] 7043 10-9-8 **65**......................(p) MissBeckySmith(3) 8 61
(Marjorie Fife) *chsd ldr: led 3f out tl 2f out: sn btn* **6/1**[3]

1020 **4** 2 ½ **Glens Wobbly**[26] 6804 8-10-6 **74**.. MissBFrost 3 66
(Jonathan Geake) *led tl 3f out: wknd 2f out* **7/1**

6421 **5** 3 ¾ **Gaelic Silver (FR)**[67] 5485 10-9-8 **69**..................(p) MissBeckyButler(7) 4 55
(Gary Moore) *in tch tl wknd 2f out* **10/1**

4312 **6** 11 **Gracesome (IRE)**[23] 6871 5-9-9 **63**................................ MissMMullineaux 7 31
(Michael Blanshard) *in tch: lost pl 6f out: n.d fnl 2f* **10/1**

4024 **7** 4 ½ **Artful Rogue (IRE)**[17] 7053 5-10-2 **75**.........................(b) MissJCooley(5) 6 36
(Amanda Perrett) *t.k.h in rr: rapid hdwy to join ldrs 6f out: rdn and wknd 3f out* **4/1**[2]

0210 **8** 2 ¼ **Knight Of The Air**[50] 6066 4-9-6 **67**................................. MrsCPownall(7) 5 24
(Joseph Tuite) *t.k.h: chsd ldrs tl wknd over 3f out* **14/1**

5240 **9** 4 ½ **Grams And Ounces**[25] 6825 9-9-0 **61** oh3...............(tp) MissCMBerry(7) 9 11
(Grace Harris) *a in rr: bhd and drvn along 5f out* **25/1**

2000 **10** 24 **Ruzeiz (USA)**[156] 1747 7-9-0 **61** oh4...........................(p) MissJSpinkova(7) 1
(Peter Hedger) *towards rr: n.m.r over 9f out: wl bhd fnl 5f* **66/1**

2m 43.24s (7.74) **Going Correction** +0.40s/f (Good) **10** Ran SP% **116.3**
Speed ratings (Par 103): **90,87,84,82,80 72,69,68,65,49**
CSF £21.10 CT £101.83 TOTE £4.20: £1.50, £2.20, £2.30; EX 24.00 Trifecta £51.50.
Owner Mrs P M Sly **Bred** Meon Valley Stud **Trained** Thorney, Cambs

FOCUS

Race distance increased by 6yds. A modest lady amateurs' handicap and they finished well spread out.

T/Jkpt: Not Won. T/Plt: £326.00 to a £1 stake. Pool: £66127.98, 148.07 winning units. T/Qpdt: £37.30 to a £1 stake. Pool: £7834.66, 155.3 winning units. **Lee McKenzie**

[7362]WOLVERHAMPTON (A.W) (L-H)

Friday, October 21

OFFICIAL GOING: Tapeta: standard
Wind: Almost nil Weather: Cloudy

7509 ALMATY EXPRESS CLASSIFIED STKS — 5f 216y (Tp)
5:50 (5:50) (Class 6) 3-Y-0+ **£2,749** (£818; £408; £204) **Stalls** Low

Form — RPR

0300 **1** **Mr Conundrum**[25] 6835 3-9-0 46 ... PaddyAspell 10 54
(Lynn Siddall) *hld up: hdwy over 1f out: r.o to ld wl ins fnl f* **7/1**

3003 **2** *nk* **Krazy Paving**[24] 6852 4-8-10 51 ...(b) CallumShepherd(5) 4 53
(Anabel K Murphy) *chsd ldrs: rdn over 1f out: ev ch ins fnl f: r.o* **9/4**[1]

0000 **3** *2 1/2* **Whispering Wolf**[24] 6852 3-9-0 45 ... BarryMcHugh 6 46
(Suzzanne France) *chsd ldr tl led over 1f out: rdn, hdd and no ex wl ins fnl f* **12/1**

0460 **4** *nk* **Ershaad (IRE)**[13] 7144 4-9-1 54 ...(b) BenCurtis 9 45
(Shaun Harris) *sn pushed along into mid-div: hdwy over 2f out: rdn over 1f out: edgd lft and styd on same pce ins fnl f* **7/2**[3]

5 *1 1/4* **Captain K (IRE)**[544] 1707 4-9-1 34 ...[1] LiamKeniry 3 41
(Gordon Elliott, Ire) *chsd ldrs: shkn up over 1f out: no ex ins fnl f* **10/1**

2000 **6** *nse* **Rojina (IRE)**[184] 1574 3-8-7 48 ... JordanUys(7) 1 41
(Lisa Williamson) *led: rdn and hdd over 1f out: no ex ins fnl f* **50/1**

4405 **7** *1* **Golden Rosanna**[34] 6587 3-8-9 40 ... AnnaHesketh(5) 8 38
(Steph Hollinshead) *hld up: plld hrd: effrt over 1f out: nt trble ldrs* **14/1**

0-00 **8** *12* **Rouge Noir**[46] 6187 3-9-0 52 ...[1] MartinHarley 2
(Jeremy Noseda) *s.i.s: hdwy over 1f out: wknd fnl f* **3/1**[2]

0/5- **9** *11* **Lady Vellyn**[638] 248 4-9-1 27 ...[1] KieranO'Neill 5
(Matthew Salaman) *chsd ldrs: rdn over 3f out: wknd over 2f out* **100/1**

1m 14.04s (-0.46) **Going Correction** -0.225s/f (Stan)
WFA 3 from 4yo 1lb **9** Ran SP% **116.9**
Speed ratings (Par 101): **94,93,90,89,88 88,86,70,56**
CSF £23.43 TOTE £9.70: £2.50, £1.30, £3.30; EX 34.00 Trifecta £224.40.
Owner Jimmy Kay **Bred** The Hon Mrs R Pease & Highclere Stud **Trained** Colton, N Yorks

FOCUS
A weak event in which they went a good pace and the first two drew clear. The winner is rated back to his best.

7510 PORSCHE CENTRE WOLVERHAMPTON (S) STKS — 5f 216y (Tp)
6:20 (6:21) (Class 5) 2-Y-0 **£3,234** (£962; £481; £240) **Stalls** Low

Form — RPR

0623 **1** **Pulsating (IRE)**[13] 7143 2-8-1 66 ... HollieDoyle(5) 2 62
(Ali Stronge) *prom: n.m.r and lost pl after 1f: hdwy over 1f out: sn rdn: edgd lft and r.o to ld wl ins fnl f: sn clr* **13/8**[1]

3200 **2** *2 1/2* **Makman (IRE)**[16] 7073 2-8-11 68 ... MartinHarley 5 60
(Ed Dunlop) *led early: chsd ldrs: rdn over 1f out: styd on to go 2nd nr fin* **7/1**[3]

0452 **3** *hd* **Pavela (IRE)**[7] 7330 2-8-3 58 ... NathanEvans(3) 12 54
(Mick Channon) *sn prom: chsd ldr over 3f out: rdn over 1f out: styd on* **13/2**[2]

0566 **4** *hd* **Dazacam**[7] 7330 2-8-3 60 ... AaronJones(3) 8 53
(Michael Herrington) *chsd ldrs: led over 4f out: rdn over 1f out: hdd and unable qck wl ins fnl f* **16/1**

5 **5** *nk* **Jessiboo (IRE)**[10] 7259 2-8-6 0 ... BenCurtis 6 52
(Tom Dascombe) *sn led: hdd over 4f out: remained handy: rdn over 2f out: kpt on* **10/1**

2650 **6** *2 1/2* **Chiconomic (IRE)**[20] 6950 2-8-3 53 ...(b) NoelGarbutt(3) 9 45
(Rae Guest) *sn pushed along in rr: styd on ins fnl f: nvr nrr* **20/1**

6630 **7** *1/2* **Performing (IRE)**[11] 7228 2-8-11 65 ...[1] JasonHart 7 48
(John Quinn) *prom: rdn 1/2-way: wknd fnl f* **10/1**

5400 **8** *1/2* **Surfina**[22] 6895 2-8-6 50 ...(t) JoeFanning 3 42
(Dean Ivory) *s.i.s: hld up: shkn up and swtchd lft over 1f out: n.d* **66/1**

65 **9** *2 1/4* **Holy Roma**[11] 7208 2-8-6 0 ... LiamJones 1 35
(William Haggas) *s.i.s: pushed along in rr: hdwy over 1f out: sn rdn: wknd fnl f* **15/2**

2423 **10** *3/4* **Luduamf (IRE)**[40] 6366 2-9-2 61 ... KieranO'Neill 10 43
(Richard Hannon) *sn pushed along in rr: rdn over 2f out: no rspnse* **15/2**

005 **11** *11* **Lucky Return**[118] 3640 2-8-6 54 ...(b[1]) MartinDwyer 4
(Des Donovan, Ire) *mid-div: rdn 1/2-way: wknd over 2f out* **66/1**

1m 13.65s (-0.85) **Going Correction** -0.225s/f (Stan) **11** Ran SP% **119.3**
Speed ratings (Par 95): **96,92,92,92,91 88,87,87,84,83 68**
CSF £13.28 TOTE £2.30: £1.10, £2.20, £2.30; EX 14.40 Trifecta £56.60.No bid for the winners. Makman was subject to a friendly claim of £7,000.
Owner Mrs Bernice Stronge & Kevin Elliott **Bred** Mrs Margaret Sinanan **Trained** Eastbury, Berks

FOCUS
Not a bad juvenile seller in which the favourite was delivered wide down the middle from off a steady pace.

7511 BRITISH STALLION STUDS EBF MAIDEN STKS — 1m 1f 103y (Tp)
6:50 (6:50) (Class 5) 2-Y-0 **£3,234** (£962; £481; £240) **Stalls** Low

Form — RPR

2322 **1** **Whip Nae Nae (IRE)**[29] 6705 2-9-5 81 ... KieranO'Neill 3 80
(Richard Hannon) *sn led: hdd after 1f: chsd ldrs: rdn to go 2nd over 1f out: sn edgd lft: styd on u.p to ld wl ins fnl f: all out* **2/1**[1]

33 **2** *nse* **Draw Swords**[32] 6623 2-9-5 0 ... JackMitchell 7 80
(John Gosden) *hld up: hdwy and nt clr run over 1f out: sn rdn: r.o* **4/1**[2]

4 **3** *1/2* **Another Eclipse (IRE)**[18] 7013 2-9-5 0 ... MartinHarley 5 79
(David Simcock) *sn prom: chsd ldr over 7f out tl over 5f out: remained handy: rdn and hung rt over 2f out: edgd lft over 1f out: r.o* **6/1**

4 *1/2* **Andrassy Avenue (USA)** 2-9-5 0 ... MartinLane 6 78
(Charlie Appleby) *s.i.s: sn prom: chsd ldr 5f out tl led over 2f out: rdn over 1f out: edgd lft and hdd wl ins fnl f* **8/1**

04 **5** *nk* **Beautiful Escape (USA)**[34] 6578 2-9-0 0 ...[1] WilliamCarson 1 72+
(Saeed bin Suroor) *hld up: rdn over 2f out: hdwy over 1f out: nt clr run and swtchd rt ins fnl f: r.o* **5/1**[3]

52 **6** *7* **Powerful Love (IRE)**[10] 7247 2-9-5 0 ... JoeFanning 4 64
(Mark Johnston) *led after 1f: rdn and hdd over 2f out: wknd fnl f* **10/1**

2522 **7** *12* **Akkadian Empire**[8] 7297 2-9-5 75 ... MartinDwyer 2 41
(Mick Channon) *hld up: plld hrd: hdwy 5f out: rdn over 2f out: wknd wl over 1f out* **10/1**

1m 59.35s (-1.45) **Going Correction** -0.225s/f (Stan) 2y crse rec **7** Ran SP% **113.6**
Speed ratings (Par 95): **97,96,96,96,95 89,78**
CSF £9.93 TOTE £3.00: £2.00, £1.50; EX 9.60 Trifecta £59.10.
Owner Potensis Bloodstock Limited **Bred** Paul Starr **Trained** East Everleigh, Wilts

FOCUS
An interesting maiden, but a slow gallop and a bunched finish. The winner just needed to repeat his latest nursery form.

7512 FCL GLOBAL FORWARDING MAKING LOGISTICS PERSONAL H'CAP — 1m 4f 50y (Tp)
7:20 (7:22) (Class 4) (0-85,84) 3-Y-0+ **£5,822** (£1,732; £865; £432) **Stalls** Low

Form — RPR

-163 **1** **Natural Scenery**[92] 4561 3-8-13 81 ... JosephineGordon(3) 5 91+
(Saeed bin Suroor) *led 1f: remained handy: nt clr run over 2f out: shkn up: nt clr run and swtchd rt over 1f out: r.o to ld wl ins fnl f: sn clr: comf* **11/4**[2]

4363 **2** *2* **Second Serve (IRE)**[41] 6345 3-8-13 78 ...(p) RichardKingscote 6 85
(Mark Johnston) *led after 1f: hdd over 10f out: chsd ldr tl over 7f out: remained handy: rdn to ld ins fnl f: sn hdd and unable qck* **8/1**

330 **3** *1 1/4* **Ardamir (FR)**[35] 6549 4-9-6 78 ... FergusSweeney 12 83+
(Alan King) *hld up: pushed along and hdwy on outer 3f out: rdn to ld over 1f out: hdd and styd on same pce ins fnl f* **25/1**

4 *1 1/4* **Saint Contest (FR)**[162] 3-8-7 77 ... HollieDoyle(5) 4 80+
(Alan King) *hld up: nt clr run over 2f out: hdwy over 1f out: styd on: nt rch ldrs* **33/1**

1030 **5** *1/2* **Gawdawpalin (IRE)**[14] 7117 3-9-5 84 ... KieranO'Neill 3 86+
(Sylvester Kirk) *prom: lost pl after 1f: nt clr run over 2f out: hdwy over 1f out: r.o* **13/2**[3]

00-2 **6** *1* **Mohatem (USA)**[23] 6870 4-9-11 83 ... PaulHanagan 8 84
(Owen Burrows) *prom: chsd ldr over 7f out tl led over 2f out: rdn and hdd over 1f out: wknd wl ins fnl f* **5/2**[1]

362 **7** *2 1/2* **Miss Minuty**[51] 6019 4-9-1 78 ...[1] CharlieBennett(5) 7 75
(Alexandra Dunn) *s.i.s: hld up: rdn over 1f out: n.d* **40/1**

002 **8** *nk* **Open The Red**[22] 6892 4-9-6 78 ... JimCrowley 1 74
(Amanda Perrett) *hld up: hdwy 2f out: sn rdn: wknd fnl f* **8/1**

5-53 **9** *hd* **Callendula**[17] 7053 4-9-5 77 ...(p) MartinDwyer 2 73
(Clive Cox) *hld up: rdn over 1f out: nvr on terms* **33/1**

2043 **10** *8* **Space Mountain**[34] 6591 3-8-12 77 ... JoeFanning 11 60
(Mark Johnston) *hld up in tch: rdn over 2f out: wknd fnl f* **20/1**

2314 **11** *6* **Mayasa (IRE)**[66] 5526 3-9-1 80 ...(b) MartinHarley 10 53
(James Tate) *pushed along to ld over 10f out: rdn and hdd over 2f out: wknd wl over 1f out* **14/1**

10 **12** *14* **Testimonio**[26] 6804 3-9-1 80 ... MartinLane 9 31
(Luca Cumani) *s.i.s: hdwy over 8f out: rdn over 3f out: wknd over 2f out* **20/1**

2m 33.92s (-6.88) **Going Correction** -0.225s/f (Stan) course record
WFA 3 from 4yo 7lb **12** Ran SP% **119.2**
Speed ratings (Par 105): **113,111,110,110,109 109,107,107,107,101 97,88**
CSF £22.53 CT £464.32 TOTE £3.30: £1.50, £2.70, £5.70; EX 31.20 Trifecta £535.20.
Owner Godolphin **Bred** Darley **Trained** Newmarket, Suffolk

FOCUS
The feature race was an average handicap in which there was some trouble on the home bend. The first two were both well backed during the day and there was a new course record.

7513 JEAN STOCKLEY'S 80TH BIRTHDAY H'CAP — 7f 32y (Tp)
7:50 (7:55) (Class 6) (0-60,60) 3-Y-0+ **£2,749** (£818; £408; £204) **Stalls** High

Form — RPR

5532 **1** **Simply Me**[60] 5721 3-9-4 59 ...(p) RichardKingscote 3 68
(Tom Dascombe) *chsd ldrs: shkn up to ld wl ins fnl f: rdn out* **5/2**[1]

3604 **2** *1 1/2* **Coquine**[7] 7323 3-9-2 57 ... DanielTudhope 7 62
(David O'Meara) *s.i.s: hld up: hdwy over 1f out: sn rdn: r.o* **17/2**

5503 **3** *1/2* **Fashionable Spirit (IRE)**[11] 7200 3-9-5 60 ...(b) JimCrowley 5 64
(Amanda Perrett) *hld up in tch: nt clr run fr over 1f out tl ins fnl f: sn rdn: styd on same pce towards fin* **9/1**

0634 **4** *3/4* **Mrs Biggs**[10] 7261 4-9-0 58 ... PhilDennis(5) 9 61
(Declan Carroll) *disp ld tl wnt on over 1f out: rdn and hdd wl ins fnl f* **14/1**

4062 **5** *hd* **Beverley Bullet**[10] 7260 3-9-2 57 ... MartinDwyer 6 58
(Les Eyre) *hld up in tch: rdn over 1f out: styd on same pce ins fnl f* **7/2**[2]

6222 **6** *nk* **Infiniti (IRE)**[10] 7240 3-8-12 58 ...(p) GeorgeWood(5) 10 59
(Rae Guest) *hld up: rdn over 1f out: r.o towards fin: nvr nrr* **15/2**

4500 **7** *1/2* **Camdora (IRE)**[57] 5807 4-9-7 60 ...[1] TimmyMurphy 1 60
(Jamie Osborne) *hld up: swtchd lft and hdwy over 1f out: sn rdn: no ex wl ins fnl f* **12/1**

401 **8** *1 1/4* **Silver Springs (IRE)**[11] 7201 3-8-10 58 ... RhiainIngram(7) 8 54
(David Evans) *plld hrd and prom: rdn over 2f out: no ex fnl f* **20/1**

022 **9** *hd* **For Shia And Lula (IRE)**[10] 7261 7-9-3 59 ... JosephineGordon(3) 2 56
(Daniel Mark Loughnane) *disp ld tl rdn over 1f out: no ex ins fnl f* **6/1**[3]

0000 **10** *5* **The King's Steed**[15] 7096 3-9-0 58 ... AaronJones(3) 11 42
(Micky Hammond) *s.i.s: hld up: rdn over 2f out: a in rr* **125/1**

1m 28.12s (-0.68) **Going Correction** -0.225s/f (Stan)
WFA 3 from 4yo+ 2lb **10** Ran SP% **117.3**
Speed ratings (Par 101): **94,92,91,90,90 90,89,88,88,82**
CSF £24.89 CT £167.57 TOTE £3.60: £1.50, £3.40, £2.20; EX 27.90 Trifecta £161.20.
Owner Laurence Bellman **Bred** Highclere Stud **Trained** Malpas, Cheshire

FOCUS
Competitive stuff, though a sedate pace meant it paid to race prominently. It was dominated by 3yos.

7514 SUSAN BOX MEMORIAL H'CAP — 1m 141y (Tp)
8:20 (8:21) (Class 6) (0-65,65) 3-Y-0+ **£2,749** (£818; £408; £204) **Stalls** Low

Form — RPR

-000 **1** **Drago (IRE)**[6] 7368 4-9-8 64 ...[1] DanielTudhope 5 72
(David O'Meara) *hld up in tch: chsd ldr over 1f out: rdn to ld wl ins fnl f: r.o* **9/2**[2]

302 **2** *2* **Anneani (IRE)**[6] 7368 4-9-2 58 ... JFEgan 7 62
(David Evans) *chsd ldrs: led wl over 1f out: rdn and hdd wl ins fnl f* **5/2**[1]

5-35 **3** *3 1/2* **Paradise Palm**[251] 565 3-8-9 62 ... RhiainIngram(7) 13 59
(Philip McBride) *hld up: rdn over 2f out: hdwy over 1f out: styd on same pce fnl f* **50/1**

6403 **4** *nse* **Wasseem (IRE)**[17] 7035 3-9-3 63 ...(tp) MartinHarley 2 60
(Simon Crisford) *chsd ldrs: nt clr run over 1f out: sn rdn: styd on same pce fnl f* **6/1**[3]

0600 **5** *1 1/4* **Yasood (IRE)**[8] 7310 3-8-13 62 ...(p) JosephineGordon(3) 4 56
(Phil McEntee) *hld up: rdn over 2f out: hdwy and nt clr run over 1f out: nt trble ldrs* **20/1**

0020 **6** *nse* **Spirit Of Gondree (IRE)**[6] 7368 8-9-5 61 ...(b) RichardKingscote 3 55
(Milton Bradley) *hld up: nt clr run over 1f out: r.o towards fin: nvr nrr* **10/1**

1400 **7** *1 1/4* **Miss Lillie**[25] 6826 5-9-6 62 ...(p) JackMitchell 6 53
(Roger Teal) *hld up: hdwy over 1f out: sn rdn: wknd ins fnl f* **15/2**

653- **8** *1 3/4* **Siouxperhero (IRE)**[479] 3745 7-9-7 63 ...(p) MartinDwyer 1 51
(William Muir) *prom: rdn over 2f out: wknd over 1f out* **25/1**

0360 **9** *1* **Bush Beauty (IRE)**[24] 6851 5-9-5 **61** JimCrowley 11 46
(Eric Alston) *hld up: rdn on outer over 2f out: wknd fnl f* **6/1**[3]

0-05 **10** *1* **Mayfield Boy**[71] 5323 5-9-3 **59** CamHardie 12 42
(Antony Brittain) *prom: chsd ldr over 7f out: rdn and ev ch over 2f out: wknd fnl f* **25/1**

034 **11** *½* **African Trader (USA)**[38] 6441 3-9-5 **65** (t) DaleSwift 9 47
(Daniel Mark Loughnane) *hld up: plld hrd: rdn over 2f out: sn wknd* **25/1**

-430 **12** *3* **Locommotion**[11] 7212 4-9-7 **63** TomMarquand 10 39
(Matthew Salaman) *led: rdn and hdd wl over 1f out: wknd fnl f* **50/1**

1m 47.05s (-3.05) **Going Correction** -0.225s/f (Stan)
WFA 3 from 4yo+ 4lb **12** Ran SP% **116.4**
Speed ratings (Par 101): **104,102,99,99,97 97,96,95,94,93 93,90**
CSF £14.43 CT £496.31 TOTE £5.60: £1.90, £1.60, £17.90; EX 18.40 Trifecta £553.10.
Owner Dr Marwan Koukash **Bred** Sheikh Sultan Bin Khalifa Al Nayhan **Trained** Upper Helmsley, N Yorks

FOCUS
A moderate handicap and another slow gallop that caused several runners to be blocked in the straight. A minor pb from the winner.

7515 FCLGF.COM H'CAP (DIV I) 1m 1f 103y (Tp)
8:50 (8:50) (Class 6) (0-60,61) 3-Y-O+ **£2,749** (£818; £408; £204) **Stalls** Low

Form RPR

5000 **1** **Strummer (IRE)**[38] 6432 3-9-3 **57** (p) KevinStott 6 65
(Kevin Ryan) *hld up in tch: shkn up over 2f out: rdn to ld 1f out: r.o* **9/2**[1]

0433 **2** *2* **Spinning Rose**[10] 7257 4-9-8 **58** RobertWinston 13 62
(Dean Ivory) *a.p: chsd ldr over 3f out: rdn over 1f out: styd on same pce ins fnl f* **9/2**[1]

3301 **3** *¾* **Maverik**[8] 7300 8-9-11 **61** 6ex (tp) TomMarquand 2 64
(Ali Stronge) *led 1f: chsd ldrs: rdn over 1f out: styd on same pce wl ins fnl f* **9/1**

0200 **4** *1 ¼* **Frozon**[70] 5369 3-9-6 **60** DanielTudhope 11 60
(Marjorie Fife) *hld up: edgd lft over 2f out: hdwy over 1f out: sn rdn: styd on: nt rch ldrs* **20/1**

55 **5** *¾* **Medicean Queen (IRE)**[22] 6901 5-9-6 **59** (t) JosephineGordon(3) 9 58
(Phil McEntee) *chsd ldr after 1f: led 4f out: rdn and hdd 1f out: no ex ins fnl f* **12/1**

6305 **6** *½* **Paddy's Rock (IRE)**[25] 6839 5-9-5 **55** PaddyAspell 7 53
(Lynn Siddall) *hld up: rdn over 1f out: styd on ins fnl f: nvr nrr* **8/1**

504 **7** *nk* **Thatsthewaytodoit (IRE)**[20] 6967 3-8-12 **52** DaleSwift 8 49
(Daniel Mark Loughnane) *hld up: hdwy u.p over 2f out: hung lft fr over 1f out: wknd ins fnl f* **16/1**

6000 **8** *½* **Myboydaniel**[10] 7240 4-9-4 **57** (p) RobHornby(3) 3 54
(Derek Shaw) *hld up: edgd lft over 2f out: hdwy over 1f out: sn rdn: no ex fnl f* **50/1**

1064 **9** *½* **Free To Roam (IRE)**[10] 7260 3-8-6 **53** RhiainIngram(7) 1 49
(Philip McBride) *prom: lost pl whn hmpd over 2f out: n.d after* **15/2**[3]

0050 **10** *3* **Ferryview Place**[6] 7369 7-8-7 **50** (v) LukeCatton(7) 10 40
(Ian Williams) *dwlt: swtchd lft sn after s: hld up: nvr on terms* **14/1**

3000 **11** *½* **Moojaned (IRE)**[4] 7418 5-9-1 **58** AledBeech(7) 5 47
(David Evans) *hld up: a in rr* **7/1**[2]

2236 **12** *28* **Weardiditallgorong**[102] 4201 4-9-6 **56** (b) LiamKeniry 4
(Des Donovan, Ire) *led after 1f: hdd 4f out: rdn whn hmpd and wknd over 2f out: eased* **9/1**

1m 58.75s (-2.05) **Going Correction** -0.225s/f (Stan)
WFA 3 from 4yo+ 4lb **12** Ran SP% **118.7**
Speed ratings (Par 101): **100,98,97,96,95 95,95,94,94,91 91,66**
CSF £23.04 CT £177.58 TOTE £4.90: £1.80, £2.00, £2.20; EX 23.80 Trifecta £125.50.
Owner J E Pallister & J G Pallister **Bred** Heather Raw **Trained** Hambleton, N Yorks
■ Stewards' Enquiry : Rob Hornby three-day ban: careless riding (4-7 Nov)

FOCUS
The first division of this handicap was run at a moderate pace and it proved difficult to come from behind. The runner-up helpd to pin the level of the form.

7516 FCLGF.COM H'CAP (DIV II) 1m 1f 103y (Tp)
9:20 (9:21) (Class 6) (0-60,60) 3-Y-O+ **£2,749** (£818; £408; £204) **Stalls** Low

Form RPR

023 **1** **Gold Return (IRE)**[36] 6514 3-9-6 **60** ShaneKelly 8 66
(David Lanigan) *hld up: hdwy over 1f out: rdn and r.o to ld nr fin* **8/1**

0424 **2** *½* **Wootton Vale (IRE)**[10] 7256 3-8-12 **52** BarryMcHugh 9 57
(Richard Fahey) *chsd ldr: rdn over 2f out: hung lft over 1f out: ev ch ins fnl f: r.o* **5/1**[2]

0530 **3** *nk* **Cahar Fad (IRE)**[6] 7369 4-9-0 **50** (bt) AdamBeschizza 10 54
(Steph Hollinshead) *chsd ldrs: hmpd over 1f out: rdn to ld wl ins fnl f: hdd nr fin* **14/1**

5204 **4** *¾* **Inflexiball**[10] 7257 4-9-3 **58** CliffordLee(5) 3 61
(John Mackie) *chsd ldrs: rdn to ld ins fnl f: sn hdd and unable qck* **8/1**

1205 **5** *hd* **File Of Facts (IRE)**[34] 6593 3-9-5 **59** (vt) RichardKingscote 2 62
(Tom Dascombe) *led: rdn and hdd ins fnl f: no ex towards fin* **13/2**

3004 **6** *nse* **Russian Ranger (IRE)**[25] 6826 3-8-12 **57** (p) GeorgeWood(5) 4 60
(Jonathan Portman) *prom: racd keenly: rdn over 1f out: nt clr run and hung lft ins fnl f: kpt on* **16/1**

5000 **7** *2 ¾* **Win Lose Draw (IRE)**[18] 7010 4-9-6 **59** AlistairRawlinson(3) 11 56
(Michael Appleby) *mid-div: hdwy over 4f out: rdn over 2f out: styd on same pce fnl f* **16/1**

4233 **8** *1 ½* **Cool Music (IRE)**[57] 5805 6-9-7 **57** (p) CamHardie 12 52
(Antony Brittain) *hld up: rdn over 2f out: nvr nrr* **25/1**

0540 **9** *1 ½* **Whaleweigh Station**[30] 6677 5-9-7 **57** TimmyMurphy 1 49
(J R Jenkins) *hld up: rdn over 3f out: n.d* **40/1**

-500 **10** *2 ¼* **Kylea (IRE)**[11] 7211 3-9-1 **55** KieranO'Neill 5 42
(Richard Hannon) *mid-div: hdwy over 2f out: rdn over 1f out: wknd fnl f* **28/1**

333 **11** *shd* **Lady Canford (IRE)**[10] 7256 3-8-8 **51** JosephineGordon(3) 13 38
(James Bethell) *s.i.s: in rr whn hmpd over 7f out: rdn over 2f out: nvr on terms* **6/1**[3]

0642 **12** *¾* **Shift On Sheila**[24] 6857 3-9-1 **58** RobHornby(3) 7 44
(Pam Sly) *hmpd s: hld up: nt clr run over 2f out: n.d* **14/1**

0314 **13** *1 ½* **Overlord**[23] 6871 4-9-9 **59** (v) JimCrowley 6 42
(Mark Rimell) *prom: lost pl and hmpd over 7f out: hdwy over 2f out: sn rdn: wknd over 1f out* **9/2**[1]

1m 59.23s (-1.57) **Going Correction** -0.225s/f (Stan)
WFA 3 from 4yo+ 4lb **13** Ran SP% **119.5**
Speed ratings (Par 101): **97,96,96,95,95 95,92,91,90,88 88,87,86**
CSF £46.86 CT £562.60 TOTE £8.80: £2.10, £2.20, £3.80; EX 50.10 Trifecta £1017.20.
Owner Miss K J Keir **Bred** Seserve Sagl **Trained** Newmarket, Suffolk
■ Stewards' Enquiry : Adam Beschizza two-day ban: used whip above shoulder height (Nov 7-8)

FOCUS
The second division was run in a 0.48s slower time than the first and there was a bunched finish featuring mainly prominent runners. The front pair were near their recent form.
T/Plt: £30.00 to a £1 stake. Pool: £91,729.17 - 2,225.58 winning tickets T/Qpdt: £14.30 to a £1 stake. Pool: £10,263.82 - 528.18 winning tickets **Colin Roberts**

7337 DUNDALK (A.W) (L-H)
Friday, October 21

OFFICIAL GOING: Polytrack: standard

7517a CHRISTMAS PARTY NIGHTS AT DUNDALK CLAIMING RACE 1m 2f 150y(P)
6:05 (6:06) 3-Y-O+ **£4,522** (£1,397; £661; £294; £110)

RPR

1 **Hes Our Music (IRE)**[7] 7340 7-10-2 83 PatSmullen 12 82
(Patrick J Flynn, Ire) *sn led and mde rest: stl gng wl 2 l clr into st: rdn ent fnl f and kpt on wl u.p clsng stages where reduced advantage* **9/4**[1]

2 *½* **Elusive In Paris (IRE)**[14] 7134 7-9-8 74 (e) GaryHalpin(3) 3 76
(John James Feane, Ire) *in tch: 6th 1/2-way: hdwy u.p fr 2f out into 2nd ins fnl f: kpt on wl clsng stages: a hld* **10/3**[2]

3 *hd* **Power Grid (IRE)**[68] 5445 3-9-3 72 ColinKeane 11 74+
(John James Feane, Ire) *hld up: pushed along in rr of mid-div into st and hdwy 2f out to chse ldrs in 6th over 1f out: kpt on wl in 4th clsng stages to snatch 3rd on line: nrst fin* **10/1**

4 *nse* **Mandarin Monarch (IRE)**[6] 7371 3-9-1 80 KevinManning 9 72
(J S Bolger, Ire) *mid-div: 7th 1/2-way: hdwy bhd ldrs 2f out: no imp on wnr u.p in 3rd wl ins fnl f: denied 3rd on line* **5/1**[3]

5 *2 ¾* **Alnahar (IRE)**[21] 6928 6-9-7 69 DanielRedmond(5) 5 71
(Miss Natalia Lupini, Ire) *chsd ldrs: 3rd 1/2-way: rdn 2f out and no imp on wnr far side ent fnl f: one pce ins fnl f* **12/1**

6 *2 ¼* **Eighteen Summers (USA)**[24] 6863 9-9-2 72 WayneLordan 2 57
(Edward Lynam, Ire) *chsd ldrs: 4th 1/2-way: rdn 2f out and no imp on wnr far side ent fnl f: one pce ins fnl f* **8/1**

7 *4 ½* **San Quentin (IRE)**[13] 7139 5-9-12 74 (b) BillyLee 10 58
(Roger Fell) *hld up towards rr: rdn 2f out and sme hdwy into mod 7th ins fnl f: kpt on same pce: nvr trbld ldrs* **14/1**

8 *1 ½* **Dissertation**[5] 5817 4-8-12 47 [1] SeamieHeffernan 14 41
(Denis Gerard Hogan, Ire) *hld up: pushed along in 12th over 3f out and no imp into st: kpt on ins fnl f into nvr nrr 8th* **66/1**

9 *1* **Aphoristic (IRE)**[24] 6863 3-8-7 0 [1] ConorMcNamara(10) 13 50
(E McNamara, Ire) *dwlt and towards rr: pushed along after 1/2-way and no imp into st: kpt on one pce fnl 2f* **100/1**

10 *1 ¾* **Sas (IRE)**[6] 7372 3-9-8 75 (b) NGMcCullagh 4 52
(Denis W Cullen, Ire) *prom tl sn settled bhd ldr: 2nd 1/2-way: rdn in 2nd into st and sn no imp on wnr: wknd under 2f out* **25/1**

11 *¾* **Ravens Hill (IRE)**[31] 4673 3-9-0 55 ChrisHayes 1 42
(P J Prendergast, Ire) *mid-div: rdn and wknd fr under 2f out* **40/1**

12 *nk* **Maskoon**[28] 6759 5-10-2 70 (t) ColmO'Donoghue 6 52
(David Marnane, Ire) *settled bhd ldrs: 5th 1/2-way: rdn over 2f out and sn wknd* **14/1**

13 *1 ¾* **Aladdins Cave**[42] 6308 12-9-1 56 (tp) ShaneFoley 8 33
(R K Watson, Ire) *dwlt and pushed along in rr early: rdn and no imp 2f out* **66/1**

14 *2* **Ultra Thef (IRE)**[33] 6607 3-9-1 69 (bt[1]) GaryCarroll 7 35
(Ms Sheila Lavery, Ire) *mid-div: rdn in 9th 3f out and sn no ex: wknd fnl 2f* **33/1**

2m 13.03s (133.03)
WFA 3 from 4yo+ 6lb **14** Ran SP% **124.9**
CSF £9.39 TOTE £2.90: £1.30, £1.40, £3.10; DF 10.80 Trifecta £42.60.
Owner Mrs Patrick J Flynn **Bred** Liam Brennan **Trained** Carrick-On-Suir, Co Waterford **FOCUS**
The winner was not drawn well but Pat Smullen bounced him out early and made most of the running. That was probably the winning of the race and Hes Our Music remains a lovely sort for Dundalk.

7518 - 7519a (Foreign Racing) - See Raceform Interactive

7520a MERCURY STKS (LISTED RACE) 5f (P)
7:35 (7:36) 2-Y-O+
£19,522 (£6,286; £2,977; £1,323; £661; £330)

RPR

1 **Caspian Prince (IRE)**[10] 7250 7-9-13 107 (t) DeclanMcDonogh 4 113
(Roger Fell) *mde all: rdn 1 l clr 1 1/2f out: all out wl ins fnl f where strly pressed: hld on* **6/1**[2]

2 *hd* **Moviesta (USA)**[21] 6931 6-9-13 110 (p) BillyLee 9 112+
(Edward Lynam, Ire) *sn chsd ldrs: tk clsr order bhd ldrs over 1f out where rdn: impr into 2nd wl ins fnl f and strly pressed wnr clsng stages: jst hld* **9/1**

3 *½* **Medicean Man**[20] 6943 10-9-13 104 (tp) RonanWhelan 6 110
(Jeremy Gask) *hld up: tk clsr order in mid-div bef 1/2-way: hdwy far side fr 1/2-way to chse ldrs: rdn into 2nd briefly ins fnl f and no imp on wnr in 3rd clsng stages* **12/1**

4 *1* **The Happy Prince (IRE)**[19] 6983 4-10-2 112 (t) SeamieHeffernan 11 110
(A P O'Brien, Ire) *hld up in mid-div: hdwy far side fr 1/2-way to chse ldrs: rdn into 2nd briefly over 1f out and sn no imp on wnr: kpt on same pce in 4th wl ins fnl f* **7/1**[3]

5 *¾* **Chiclet (IRE)**[101] 4246 5-9-8 100 PatSmullen 8 99
(Tracey Collins, Ire) *cl up bhd ldr: rdn in 2nd under 2f out and no imp on wnr ent fnl f: kpt on same pce in 5th wl ins fnl f* **10/1**

6 *½* **Goldream**[19] 6990 7-9-13 112 (p) ChrisHayes 3 102
(Robert Cowell) *chsd ldrs: rdn 2f out and no imp on wnr u.p in 4th ent fnl f: one pce fnl f* **5/1**[1]

7 *nk* **Callender (IRE)**[48] 6147 2-8-9 97 ShaneFoley 7 95
(M Halford, Ire) *towards rr: sme hdwy after 1/2-way: kpt on in 7th wl ins fnl fi nvr nrr* **14/1**

8 *½* **Double Up**[31] 6642 5-9-13 105 (t) KevinManning 5 100
(Roger Varian) *chsd ldrs: rdn after 1/2-way and no imp on ldrs u.p in 7th over 1f out: one pce after* **6/1**[2]

9 *shd* **Fine Blend (IRE)**[20] 6943 3-9-8 97 GaryCarroll 1 95
(William Muir) *in rr of mid-div: swtchd lft fr 1/2-way and tk clsr order briefly far side 1f out: no ex and one pce ins fnl f* **33/1**

10 *hd* **Master Speaker (IRE)**[12] 7191 6-9-13 101 (bt) ColmO'Donoghue 2 98
(Martin Hassett, Ire) *dwlt and pushed along towards rr early: rdn after 1/2-way and no imp u.p in 10th wl ins fnl f: kpt on one pce* **16/1**

11 1 1/4 **Ardhoomey (IRE)**[40] 6384 4-10-4 112 (t) ColinKeane 13 99
(G M Lyons, Ire) *v s.i.s and detached in rr early: rdn in rr 2f out and kpt on one pce ins fnl f: nvr a factor* **7/1**[3]

12 1 1/4 **Hay Chewed (IRE)**[10] 7242 5-9-8 97 WayneLordan 14 84
(Conrad Allen) *chsd ldrs: rdn and no ex fr 1/2-way: wknd u.p over 1f out* **66/1**

13 nk **Seychelloise**[32] 6627 4-9-8 95 (b) LukeMorris 10 83
(Sir Mark Prescott Bt) *chsd ldrs: pushed along bef 1/2-way and no ex u.p 2f out: sn wknd* **12/1**

14 3/4 **Sahreej (IRE)**[26] 6819 3-9-13 86 LeighRoche 12 87
(Adrian Paul Keatley, Ire) *in rr of mid-div: rdn fr 1/2-way and sn no ex: wknd over 1f out* **66/1**

57.1s (57.10) **14** Ran SP% **123.2** CSF £60.32 TOTE £6.70: £2.40, £3.40, £4.30; DF 73.40 Trifecta £624.80.
Owner Stephen Louch **Bred** Ballygallon Stud Ltd **Trained** Nawton, N Yorks

FOCUS
This was an impressive display from the winner to keep up a strong pace to victory. He set a new track record of 57.1 seconds in doing so, and he has been rated in line with his recent best.

7521 - 7522a (Foreign Racing) - See Raceform Interactive

7523a BOOK YOUR CHRISTMAS PARTY AT DUNDALK H'CAP 7f (P)
9:05 (9:05) (70-100,99) 3-Y-O+ **£11,305** (£3,492; £1,654; £735; £275)

RPR

1 **Sevenleft (IRE)**[41] 6355 3-9-7 **94** [1] GaryCarroll 1 98
(Ms Sheila Lavery, Ire) *chsd ldrs: disp 4th at 1/2-way: impr to dispute ld fr 2f out and led narrowly u.p wl ins fnl f: all out clsng stages: jst hld on* **13/2**[2]

2 shd **Big Time (IRE)**[14] 7121 5-9-13 **98** (v) PatSmullen 3 103
(Kevin Ryan) *chsd ldrs: rdn into 3rd ins fnl f and kpt on wl clsng stages: jst failed* **7/4**[1]

3 nse **Reckless Endeavour (IRE)**[41] 6355 3-9-11 **98** ColinKeane 13 102+
(G M Lyons, Ire) *in rr of mid-div: hdwy nr side fr over 1f out: clsd u.p wl ins fnl f: nrst fin* **7/1**[3]

4 nk **Vitello**[21] 6931 3-9-3 **90** (p) ShaneFoley 7 93
(M Halford, Ire) *broke wl to ld tl hdd after 1f: 2nd 1/2-way: impr to dispute ld fr 2f out: ev ch tl hdd wl ins fnl f and no ex in 4th cl home* **12/1**

5 3/4 **Split The Atom (IRE)**[40] 6382 4-9-0 **85** (v) ColmO'Donoghue 12 87
(David Marnane, Ire) *dwlt and settled in rr: last appr st: prog fr 2f out to chse ldrs ent fnl f: rdn and kpt on u.p into 5th wl ins fnl f: nvr nrr* **20/1**

6 3/4 **Russian Soul (IRE)**[21] 6931 8-9-8 **98** ConorMcGovern[(5)] 10 98
(M Halford, Ire) *dwlt and settled towards rr early: impr into mid-div bef 1/2-way: rdn 2f out and no imp over 1f out: kpt on u.p into nvr nrr 6th clsng stages* **14/1**

7 1/2 **Ishebayorgrey (IRE)**[47] 6169 4-8-10 **81** WayneLordan 2 80
(Patrick Martin, Ire) *mid-div: rdn 2f out and no imp on ldrs ins fnl f: kpt on same pce* **14/1**

8 3/4 **Mcguigan (IRE)**[7] 7340 4-8-10 **81** (t) KevinManning 6 78
(J S Bolger, Ire) *in rr of mid-div: sme hdwy far side 1 1/2f out: kpt on one pce ins fnl f* **14/1**

9 nk **Shepherd's Purse**[68] 5442 4-9-9 **94** (p) ConnorKing 8 90
(Joseph G Murphy, Ire) *sn chsd ldrs: racd keenly early: clsr in 3rd at 1/2-way: rdn bhd ldrs under 2f out and sn no ex: wknd ins fnl f* **12/1**

10 1/2 **Have A Nice Day**[11] 7233 6-9-8 **93** LeighRoche 14 87
(Sabrina J Harty, Ire) *chsd ldrs: disp 4th at 1/2-way: rdn 2f out and no imp nr side in mid-div 1 1/2f out: one pce after* **25/1**

11 3/4 **Togoville (IRE)**[101] 4246 6-9-10 **98** (b) RossCoakley[(3)] 4 90
(Georgios Pakidis, Ire) *cl up bhd ldr tl led narrowly after 1f: 1 l clr at 1/2-way: rdn and hdd fr 2f out and sn no ex: wknd ins fnl f* **28/1**

12 nk **Northern Surprise (IRE)**[203] 1189 5-9-2 **87** BillyLee 11 79
(Timothy Doyle, Ire) *hld up: 13th appr st: pushed along in rr under 2f out and no imp ent fnl f: kpt on one pce ins fnl f* **14/1**

13 nk **Seanie (IRE)**[19] 6984 7-9-1 **91** (t) DonaghO'Connor[(5)] 5 82
(David Marnane, Ire) *mid-div early: rdn towards rr under 2f out and no imp* **20/1**

14 1/2 **Dont Bother Me (IRE)**[21] 6931 6-10-0 **99** (t) SeamieHeffernan 9 88
(Niall Moran, Ire) *chsd ldrs: 6th 1/2-way: rdn under 2f out and sn no ex: eased in mid-div ins fnl f* **9/1**

1m 23.49s (83.49)
WFA 3 from 4yo+ 2lb **14** Ran SP% **131.1**
Tote Aggregate: 2016: 112,486 - 2015: 171,220. Pick Six: Not won. Pool of 1,165.42 carried forward. CSF £18.86 CT £94.06 TOTE £7.40: £2.40, £1.40, £2.00; DF 23.20 Trifecta £152.70.
Owner John Lavery **Bred** J Kenny **Trained** Summerhill, Co. Meath
■ Stewards' Enquiry : Seamie Heffernan caution: failed to ride to draw
Shane Foley Fine 100 euro: failed to ride to draw
Colin Keane caution: failed to ride to draw

FOCUS
A four way go to the line and a gutsy display from the winner, who may have been helped by the first time tongue-tie. The runner-up helps set the level to his British turf best.
T/Jkpt: Not Won. T/Plt: @177.90. Pool: @4,058.02 **Brian Fleming**

7490 DEAUVILLE (R-H)
Friday, October 21

OFFICIAL GOING: Polytrack: standard; turf: good

7524a PRIX DU VAL MARTIN (CONDITIONS) (4YO+) (POLYTRACK) 1m 1f 110y
2:20 (2:20) 4-Y-O+ **£12,132** (£4,852; £3,639; £2,426; £1,213)

RPR

1 **Szoff (GER)**[476] 3873 6-9-0 0 AntoineHamelin 9 101
(A Wohler, Germany) **212/10**

2 1 **Sainte Amarante (FR)**[70] 5384 4-8-11 0 ow1 Pierre-CharlesBoudot 2 96
(Yves de Nicolay, France) **53/10**[3]

3 hd **Motabaary (IRE)**[22] 6-8-6 0 GuillaumeTrolleyDePrevaux[(8)] 4 99
(Mme Pia Brandt, France) **12/1**

4 snk **Ventaron (FR)**[49] 5-9-0 0 UmbertoRispoli 8 98
(V Luka Jr, Czech Republic) **9/1**

5 1 **Vodkato (FR)**[40] 8-9-0 0 (b) TheoBachelot 7 96
(S Wattel, France) **9/1**

6 hd **Broadway Boogie (IRE)**[146] 2713 4-9-3 0 ChristopheSoumillon 3 99
(J-C Rouget, France) **11/5**[1]

7 hd **Solar Deity (IRE)**[40] 6399 7-9-0 0 (p) MickaelBarzalona 5 95
(Jane Chapple-Hyam) *towards rr: hdwy on outer under 2f out: styd on fnl f: nt pce to trble ldrs* **24/1**

8 nk **Metropol (IRE)**[170] 5-9-0 0 MaximeGuyon 6 95
(Mme Pia Brandt, France) **11/1**

9 2 1/2 **Allez Henri (IRE)**[20] 5-9-3 0 (p) AlexisBadel 1 93
(D Prod'Homme, France) **4/1**[2]

10 3 **Tempete Nocturne (FR)**[174] 1876 5-9-0 0 MickaelForest 10 83
(J-P Gauvin, France) **11/1**

\n\x\x WIN (incl. 1 euro stake): 22.20 PLACES: 7.40, 2.60, 4.40. DF: 86.50. SF:
Owner UNIA Racing **Bred** Gestut Schlenderhan **Trained** Germany

7525a PRIX DE LA FONTAINE MARIE (CONDITIONS) (4YO+) (POLYTRACK) 6f 110y
2:55 (2:55) 4-Y-O+ **£12,132** (£4,852; £3,639; £2,426; £1,213)

RPR

1 **Lucky Team (FR)**[110] 4-9-0 0 (p) ThierryJarnet 1 87
(J Boisnard, France) **34/1**

2 hd **Kenouska (FR)**[43] 6272 4-8-11 0 ow1 (p) Pierre-CharlesBoudot 12 83
(P Sogorb, France) **76/10**[3]

3 snk **Wikita (FR)**[39] 5-8-10 0 AntoineWerle 5 82
(T Lemer, France) **15/1**

4 3/4 **Valbchek (IRE)**[61] 5678 7-9-0 0 (p) MickaelBarzalona 3 84
(Jane Chapple-Hyam) *w.w towards rr on inner: drvn and n.m.r 1 1/2f out: styd on fnl f: nvr quite on terms* **20/1**

5 snk **Saon Secret (FR)**[18] 7030 6-9-0 0 (b) UmbertoRispoli 6 83
(T Castanheira, France) **5/1**[2]

6 1 1/2 **Phu Hai (FR)**[20] 7-9-0 0 TheoBachelot 8 79
(V Luka Jr, Czech Republic) **8/1**

7 1 **Gamgoom**[12] 5-9-0 0 (b) EddyHardouin 4 76
(Mario Hofer, Germany) **9/1**

8 3/4 **Royal Prize**[18] 7030 6-9-0 0 (b) AlexisBadel 7 74
(Mme M Bollack-Badel, France) **76/10**[3]

9 snk **Kool And The Gang (IRE)**[25] 6-9-0 0 CyrilleStefan 10 74
(J Albrecht, Czech Republic) **53/1**

10 1 **Le Rebel (FR)**[50] 4-9-0 0 ChristopheSoumillon 2 71
(K Borgel, France) **10/1**

11 1 1/4 **Absalon (USA)**[25] 5-9-0 0 MaximeGuyon 11 67
(F Head, France) **12/5**[1]

12 1/2 **Mc Queen (FR)**[18] 7027 4-9-1 0 ClementLecoeuvre[(5)] 9 72
(Yasmin Almenrader, Germany) **24/1**

\n\x\x WIN (incl. 1 euro stake): 34.50. PLACES: 9.00, 3.70, 5.00. DF: 133.50. SF:
Owner Mme S Boulin Redouly & Haras Du Hoguenet **Bred** Mme S Boulin Redouly & Haras Du Hoguenet **Trained** France

7526 - (Foreign Racing) - See Raceform Interactive

7482 CHELMSFORD (A.W) (L-H)
Saturday, October 22

OFFICIAL GOING: Polytrack: standard
Wind: light, against Weather: dry

7527 TOTEPLACEPOT RACING'S FAVOURITE BET EBF MAIDEN STKS 6f (P)
5:30 (5:31) (Class 5) 2-Y-O **£3,234** (£962; £481; £240) **Stalls** Centre

Form RPR

3 **1** **Dubai Elegance**[140] 2885 2-9-0 0 WilliamCarson 10 80
(Saeed bin Suroor) *dwlt: hdwy to ld after 1f out and mde rest: rdn over 1f out: clr and in command ins fnl f: styd on: comf* **11/4**[1]

02 **2** 2 **Kingofmerrows (IRE)**[15] 7122 2-9-5 0 JFEgan 8 79
(David Evans) *chsd ldrs: pushed along over 3f out: swtchd out rt and effrt to chse wnr over 1f out: kpt on same pce ins fnl f* **9/2**[3]

033 **3** 2 **Houndstooth (IRE)**[17] 7071 2-9-5 73 LukeMorris 2 73
(Luca Cumani) *in tch in midfield: effrt on ins over 1f out: 3rd and drvn 1f out: styd on same pce ins fnl f* **5/1**

544 **4** 1 3/4 **Al Mansor (IRE)**[17] 7064 2-9-5 71 TimmyMurphy 9 68
(Richard Hannon) *t.k.h: led for 1f: chsd wnr tl over 4f out: swtchd rt and effrt over 1f out: no imp and styd on same pce fnl f* **7/2**[2]

5620 **5** 3 **Apple Scruffs (IRE)**[18] 7047 2-9-5 59 KierenFox 7 59
(Michael Attwater) *midfield: hdwy to chse ldrs 4f out: hung rt 3f out: wnt 2nd over 2f out tl unable qck u.p over 1f out: wknd fnl f* **50/1**

04 **6** 1 1/2 **Pyjamarama**[23] 6897 2-9-0 0 [1] JackMitchell 3 49
(Roger Varian) *broke wl sn stdd and in last pair after 1f: swtchd rt and effrt over 1f out: no imp and wl hld fnl f* **8/1**

4 **7** 3/4 **Echoism (IRE)**[7] 7356 2-9-0 0 JoeFanning 4 47
(Mark Johnston) *s.i.s: hld up in last pair: nt clr run over 1f out: effrt and hung lft over 1f out: no imp: wl hld and stl hanging fnl f* **12/1**

63 **8** nk **Liberatum**[13] 7184 2-9-5 0 (t) MartinHarley 1 51
(Hugo Palmer) *midfield: rdn over 2f out: wknd over 1f out* **6/1**

5420 **9** nk **Bizet (IRE)**[9] 7305 2-9-5 73 (p) DannyBrock 5 50
(John Ryan) *midfield: effrt on outer over 2f out: wknd over 1f out* **16/1**

6 **10** 11 **Verdi (IRE)**[12] 7224 2-9-5 0 StevieDonohoe 6 17
(John Ryan) *s.i.s: hdwy to chse wnr over 4f out tl ent fnl 2f: wknd over 1f out* **100/1**

1m 12.65s (-1.05) **Going Correction** -0.225s/f (Stan) **10** Ran SP% **125.7**
Speed ratings (Par 95): **98,95,92,90,86 84,83,82,82,67**
CSF £16.83 TOTE £3.70: £1.60, £2.30, £1.60; EX 18.30 Trifecta £68.60.
Owner Godolphin **Bred** Glebe Stud & J F Dean **Trained** Newmarket, Suffolk

FOCUS
A wide-open maiden on paper but very few got into it in truth, and the winner was given a good front-running ride having overcome a wide draw. Fair form.

7528 TOTEEXACTA FORECAST THE 1ST AND 2ND NURSERY H'CAP 5f (P)
6:05 (6:06) (Class 6) (0-60,60) 2-Y-O **£2,587** (£770; £384; £192) **Stalls** Low

Form RPR

0062 **1** **Gabridan (IRE)**[23] 6896 2-9-0 **53** (v) JackGarritty 1 56
(Richard Fahey) *chsd ldrs: swtchd rt and effrt to chse ldr over 1f out: edgd lft but styd on u.p ins fnl f: led last stride* **15/8**[1]

0553 **2** shd **Heavenly Cry**[23] 6895 2-8-9 **48** (b) WilliamCarson 3 51
(Phil McEntee) *sn rdn up to ld: rdn over 1f out: drvn ins fnl f: kpt on u.p: hdd last stride* **8/1**

000 **3** 2 3/4 **Sweet Sienna**[24] 6873 2-9-0 **53** RobertWinston 2 46
(Dean Ivory) *wnt rt s: in tch in midfield: effrt to chse ldng pair 1f out: styd on same pce and no imp ins fnl f* **14/1**

3U00 **4** 3/4 **Luxford**[16] 7099 2-9-0 **53** (b[1]) KierenFox 9 43
(John Best) *s.i.s: in tch in rr: hdwy u.p ent fnl f: swtchd rt and wnt 4th ins fnl f: styd on: no threat to ldrs* **16/1**

4044 **5** 3 1/4 **Ginger Truffle**[23] 6887 2-9-0 **53** StevieDonohoe 7 32
(Brett Johnson) *hld up towards rr: hung rt bnd over 3f out: effrt wd over 2f out: no imp over 1f out: wknd ins fnl f* **25/1**

6040 **6** *hd* **Red Savina**[40] 6420 2-8-6 **45**....(b[1]) BarryMcHugh 4 23
(Kevin Ryan) *in tch in midfield: rdn over 2f out: no imp u.p over 1f out: btn whn hmpd jst ins fnl f: wknd* **7/1**[3]

4056 **7** *nk* **Zipedee**[23] 6887 2-8-13 **52**.... DannyBrock 6 29
(John Ryan) *chsd ldr tl over 1f out: sn outpcd: lost 3rd 1f out: wknd fnl f* **8/1**

0042 **8** *1 1/4* **Miss Mayson**[10] 7275 2-9-7 **60**.... LukeMorris 12 32
(Roger Teal) *swtchd lft after s: towards rr: effrt and sme hdwy on outer over 2f out: no imp u.p over 1f out: wknd ins fnl f* **4/1**[2]

0000 **9** *6* **Sadieroseclifford (IRE)**[10] 7275 2-9-2 **55**.... JFEgan 8 6
(Denis Quinn) *chsd ldrs: rdn ent fnl f: lost pl over 1f out: wl btn and eased ins fnl f* **16/1**

1500 **10** *4* **Queen Celeste (IRE)**[18] 7041 2-9-7 **60**....[1] JoeFanning 10
(Mark Johnston) *sn dropped towards rr and hung rt: n.d* **20/1**

0346 **P** **Eid Rose**[136] 3008 2-8-8 **47**.... BenCurtis 5
(Scott Dixon) *rrd as stalls opened and v.s.a: immediately p.u and dismntd* **20/1**

1m 0.07s (-0.13) **Going Correction** -0.225s/f (Stan) **11** Ran SP% **121.3**
Speed ratings (Par 93): **92,91,87,86,81 80,80,78,68,62**
CSF £17.64 CT £160.23 TOTE £2.80: £1.20, £2.90, £3.90; EX 17.00 Trifecta £239.30.
Owner T Proctor **Bred** Sycamore Syndicate **Trained** Musley Bank, N Yorks

FOCUS
A weak nursery and, like the opener, the pace held up with most of these not landing a blow. Low draws dominated.

7529 TOTEPOOL BETTING ON ALL UK RACING CLAIMING STKS 1m (P)
6:40 (6:40) (Class 6) 3-Y-0+ **£2,911** (£866; £432; £216) **Stalls** Low

Form RPR

4300 **1** **Fort Bastion (IRE)**[15] 7121 7-9-8 88.... DanielTudhope 2 95
(David O'Meara) *in tch and a travelling wl: wnt 3rd and clsng 3f out: shkn up to ld ent fnl f: sn clr: eased towards fin: easily* **6/5**[1]

055 **2** *3 3/4* **Zaeem**[15] 7126 7-9-12 90....(p) DavidNolan 8 87
(Ivan Furtado) *chsd ldrs: wnt 2nd 3f out: ev ch over 1f out: clr 2nd but no ch w wnr ins fnl f: kpt on* **6/1**[2]

0360 **3** *2 1/2* **Majestic Myles (IRE)**[27] 6806 8-8-8 69.... KierenFox 3 63
(Lee Carter) *led: rdn and hdd over 1f out: wl hld 3rd and plugged in same pce ins fnl f* **8/1**[3]

330 **4** *3 3/4* **Schottische**[37] 6512 6-7-12 52....(p) LiamLewis-Salter(7) 1 51
(Alan Bailey) *in tch in midfield: effrt over 2f out: 4th and no imp over 1f out: wknd ins ffnl f* **25/1**

606 **5** *1/2* **Molten Lava (IRE)**[32] 6656 4-9-12 66....(b) MartinHarley 4 71
(Paul Cole) *hld up in midfield: rdn and no imp 2f out: wl hld over 1f out: wknd ins fnl f* **12/1**

030 **6** *1/2* **Pushaq (IRE)**[58] 5810 3-9-7 76.... DanielMuscutt 10 67
(Marco Botti) *stdd s: t.k.h: hld up towards rr: hdwy over 3f out: rdn and no imp over 1f out:* **12/1**

5000 **7** *5* **R Bar Open (FR)**[12] 7230 3-8-9 58....(p) JFEgan 7 43
(Dean Ivory) *hld up towards rr: rdn 3f out: wl btn over 1f out* **50/1**

6223 **8** *6* **Not Touch**[47] 6186 3-9-9 71.... AdamKirby 12 42
(Richard Hannon) *chsd ldr tl 3f out: sn u.p and lost pl: wknd over 1f out* **6/1**[2]

5300 **9** *3/4* **Artful Mind**[12] 7227 3-9-0 70....[1] StevieDonohoe 6 31
(Charlie Fellowes) *midfield but nvr on terms: rdn 3f out: sn struggling: wl btn over 1f out* **12/1**

-040 **10** *4 1/2* **Icy Blue**[37] 6512 8-8-5 46....(b[1]) NoelGarbutt(3) 9 13
(Adam West) *s.i.s: a bhd* **100/1**

00 **11** *1/4* **Pixel (IRE)**[132] 3194 3-7-13 0.... SophieScardifield(7) 5 12
(Denis Quinn) *s.i.s: a bhd* **100/1**

4044 **12** *2* **See You When (IRE)**[17] 7076 3-9-9 70.... TimmyMurphy 11 24
(Richard Hannon) *hld up in midfield: rdn 3f out: sn outpcd: wl bhd fnl f* **10/1**

1m 37.43s (-2.47) **Going Correction** -0.225s/f (Stan)
WFA 3 from 4yo+ 3lb **12** Ran SP% **125.1**
Speed ratings (Par 101): **103,99,96,93,92 92,87,81,80,75 75,73**
CSF £9.11 TOTE £2.00: £1.20, £2.00, £2.70; EX 11.20 Trifecta £57.50.Fort Bastion was claimed by Tom Dascombe for £10,000
Owner Sprint Thoroughbred Racing **Bred** L White & D McGregor **Trained** Upper Helmsley, N Yorks

FOCUS
No depth to this claimer and the favourite had an outstanding chance on these terms if able to get even within 10lb of his mark. He's rated close to his recent best.

7530 TOTEPOOL LIKE US ON FACEBOOK H'CAP 7f (P)
7:10 (7:11) (Class 3) (0-95,94) 3-Y-0+ **£7,439** (£2,213; £1,106; £553) **Stalls** Low

Form

2055 **1** **George William**[50] 6082 3-8-12 **87**.... TimmyMurphy 13 95+
(Richard Hannon) *hld up in tch in midfield on outer: rdn and hdwy to chse ldrs 2f out: chsd wnr over 1f out: styd on ins fnl f: led last strides* **14/1**

4100 **2** *hd* **He's No Saint**[15] 7121 5-9-1 **88**....(v) DanielTudhope 11 96
(David O'Meara) *sn led: rdn over 1f out: kpt on wl u.p ins fnl f: hdd and no ex last strides* **16/1**

030P **3** *2 1/4* **Passing Star**[106] 4104 5-8-13 **86**.... RobertWinston 10 88+
(Charles Hills) *hld up towards rr: swtchd rt and effrt over 1f out: hdwy u.p and edgd lft ins fnl f: styd on to snatch 3rd on post: nt rch ldrs* **10/1**

0352 **4** *nse* **Plucky Dip**[3] 7462 5-8-9 **82**.... DannyBrock 5 84
(John Ryan) *chsd ldrs: effrt over 1f out: 3rd and no imp 1f out: styd on same pce ins fnl f: lost 3rd on post* **4/1**[1]

4416 **5** *nse* **Valley Of Fire**[37] 6529 4-9-2 **89**....(b[1]) PatCosgrave 8 91+
(William Haggas) *taken down early: hld up in tch in midfield: nt clr run 2f out: swtchd lft and hdwy on inner over 1f out: kpt on u.p ins fnl f: nvr threatened ldrs* **5/1**[2]

0003 **6** *1 1/2* **Baddilini**[9] 7308 6-8-7 **85**....(p) PaddyPilley(5) 9 83
(Alan Bailey) *hld up in tch in midfield: swtchd rt and effrt u.p over 1f out: carried lft and kpt on same pce ins fnl f: nvr threatened ldrs* **14/1**

1000 **7** *3/4* **Highland Acclaim (IRE)**[33] 6627 5-9-3 **90**.... HarryBentley 12 86
(David O'Meara) *t.k.h: hld up wl in tch in midfield: effrt over 1f out: unable qck 1f out: styng on same pce whn edgd lft ins fnl f* **20/1**

4030 **8** *1* **Exchequer (IRE)**[50] 6082 5-9-4 **94**.... KieranShoemark(3) 2 87
(David Brown) *chsd ldrs: rdn over 1f out: unable qck and btn 1f out: wknd ins fnl f* **7/1**[3]

0040 **9** *3* **Musical Comedy**[62] 5678 5-9-0 **87**.... TomQueally 4 72
(Mike Murphy) *hld up in rr: swtchd rt over 1f out: sn rdn and no imp: wl hld but passed btn horses ins fnl f* **33/1**

2146 **10** *nse* **Philba**[206] 1153 4-9-2 **92**....(tp) AlistairRawlinson(3) 3 83+
(Michael Appleby) *broke wl: stdd and hld up in tch: effrt over 1f out: no imp and one pce after: wl hld whn hmpd wl ins fnl f* **25/1**

1000 **11** *hd* **Brazos (IRE)**[42] 6355 5-9-5 **92**....(b) MartinHarley 1 76
(James Tate) *hld up in tch in midfield: nt clr run over 1f out: gap opened and rdn 1f out: no imp: nvr trbld ldrs* **5/1**[2]

0003 **12** *2 1/4* **Al Khan (IRE)**[8] 7316 7-8-13 **86**.... TomEaves 6 64
(Kevin Ryan) *hld up towards rr: swtchd rt and effrt over 1f out: no imp and wl hld whn hmpd ins fnl f* **7/1**[3]

0004 **13** *9* **Clement (IRE)**[156] 2402 6-8-9 **82**.... JoeFanning 7 36
(John O'Shea) *hld up in rr: swtchd rt and effrt in centre over 1f out: no hdwy and sn btn: wknd fnl f* **50/1**

1352 **14** *6* **Loyalty**[219] 965 9-9-0 **87**....(v) MartinLane 15 25
(Derek Shaw) *chsd ldr tl lost pl u.p over 1f out: wknd and towards rr whn bdly hmpd wl ins fnl f* **20/1**

0500 **S** **Ghalib (IRE)**[35] 6560 4-9-5 **92**.... LukeMorris 14 83
(Ed Walker) *hld up in tch in midfield: nt clr run over 1f out: effrt u.p 1f out: keeping on same pce and no threat to ldrs whn squeezed for room: clipped heels and fell heavily wl ins fnl f* **14/1**

1m 24.51s (-2.69) **Going Correction** -0.225s/f (Stan)
WFA 3 from 4yo+ 2lb **15** Ran SP% **131.6**
Speed ratings (Par 107): **106,105,103,103,103 101,100,99,95,95 95,93,82,75,**
CSF £224.71 CT £2377.43 TOTE £15.10: £3.90, £5.90, £5.10; EX 439.30 Trifecta £4972.00 Part won..
Owner Lady Coventry & Partners **Bred** Rachel Countess Of Coventry **Trained** East Everleigh, Wilts

FOCUS
A big field and the sort of handicap that would throw up a different result every time it was run, but credit to the winner, the only three-year-old in the field, who was always trapped wide from his double-figure draw but still emerged on top.

7531 @TOTEPOOLRACING WIN TICKETS ON TWITTER H'CAP 1m 2f (P)
7:40 (7:42) (Class 5) (0-70,70) 3-Y-0+ **£3,557** (£1,058; £529; £264) **Stalls** Low

Form RPR

53 **1** **New Record (IRE)**[30] 6701 4-9-4 **67**.... RyanTate 4 75
(James Eustace) *led for 2f: chsd ldr after tl rdn to ld again 2f out: clr and styd on wl ins fnl f: rdn out* **6/1**

-300 **2** *1 1/2* **Sennockian Song**[12] 7223 3-8-8 **62**.... JoeFanning 2 67
(Mark Johnston) *chsd ldrs: effrt over 1f out: cl 4th 1f out: styd on to chse wnr wl ins fnl f: nvr enough pce to chal* **12/1**

4024 **3** *nk* **Transmitting**[12] 7214 3-8-13 **67**.... TedDurcan 5 71
(Sir Michael Stoute) *sn chsng ldrs and t.k.h: wnt 2nd whn edgd lft and sltly hmpd over 1f out: cl 3rd 1f out: kpt on same pce ins fnl f* **9/4**[1]

4210 **4** *1/2* **Blushes (FR)**[23] 6901 3-8-9 **63**....(b) TomEaves 1 66
(Ed Dunlop) *in tch in midfield: effrt on inner to chse wnr jst over 1f out: styd on same pce and no imp ins fnl f: lost 2 pls towards fin* **14/1**

34 **5** *5* **Tenerezza (IRE)**[23] 6901 3-8-12 **66**.... TomQueally 6 59
(David Lanigan) *stdd s: t.k.h: hld up in last pair: pushed along 3f out: no imp u.p over 1f out: wknd ins fnl f* **5/1**[3]

5060 **6** *nk* **Ruby Wednesday**[33] 6629 3-8-10 **64**.... KierenFox 7 56
(John Best) *in tch in midfield: pushed along 4f out: rdn over 2f out: unable qck over 1f out: wknd ins fnl f* **20/1**

1361 **7** *1/2* **Mercy Me**[12] 7205 4-9-7 **70**.... AdamKirby 9 61
(John Ryan) *hld up in tch in last pair: hdwy on outer over 3f out: rdn and unable qck over 1f out: wknd ins fnl f* **3/1**[2]

0536 **8** *6* **Topamichi**[30] 6701 6-9-6 **69**.... StevieDonohoe 3 48
(Mark H Tompkins) *chsd ldr tl led after 2f: hdd 2f out: sn u.p and lost pl over 1f out: wknd fnl f* **8/1**

2m 5.49s (-3.11) **Going Correction** -0.225s/f (Stan)
WFA 3 from 4yo+ 5lb **8** Ran SP% **117.0**
Speed ratings (Par 103): **103,101,101,101,97 96,96,91**
CSF £75.06 CT £210.69 TOTE £8.10: £2.20, £4.20, £1.10; EX 92.40 Trifecta £517.50.
Owner Jaber Ali Alsabah **Bred** G B Partnership **Trained** Newmarket, Suffolk

FOCUS
Ordinary handicap form in which the front four came clear and the winner showed a good attitude once hitting the front.

7532 TOTEPOOL COLLECT YOUR WINNINGS AT BETFRED SHOPS H'CAP 1m 5f 66y(P)
8:10 (8:13) (Class 7) (0-50,51) 3-Y-0 **£2,911** (£866; £432; £216) **Stalls** Low

Form RPR

0631 **1** **Work (IRE)**[9] 7309 3-9-8 **51**.... HarryBentley 4 60+
(David Simcock) *dwlt and jostling leaving stalls: sn in tch in midfield: wnt 3rd and clr of field gng strly over 2f out: led on bit 1f out: cruised clr: eased towards fin* **5/4**[1]

5450 **2** *2 3/4* **Regal Galaxy**[30] 6698 3-9-2 **45**.... StevieDonohoe 14 45+
(Mark H Tompkins) *hld up in last trio: hdwy on inner over 2f out: swtchd rt and rdn over 1f out: wnt 4th ins fnl f: styd on to snatch 2nd last strides: no threat to wnr* **50/1**

-005 **3** *hd* **Incus**[32] 6654 3-9-2 **45**.... PatCosgrave 12 45
(Ed de Giles) *hld up in midfield: hdwy to ld after 4f: rdn and clr in ldng trio over 2f out: hdd 1f out: sn brushed aside by wnr and kpt on same pce: lost 2nd last strides* **14/1**

000 **4** *1 1/4* **Murraqib (USA)**[18] 7052 3-9-2 **50**....(v[1]) PaddyBradley(5) 11 48
(Brett Johnson) *hld up in last trio: hdwy 3f out: chsd clr ldng trio wl over 1f out: kpt on ins fnl f: no threat to wnr* **50/1**

6300 **5** *1 3/4* **Triassic (IRE)**[16] 7104 3-9-6 **49**.... JoeFanning 1 45
(Mark Johnston) *chsd ldrs: 3rd and clr in ldng trio whn rdn over 2f out: no imp over 1f out: wknd ins fnl f* **8/1**[3]

4540 **6** *1 3/4* **Broughtons Mystery**[12] 7231 3-9-5 **48**.... DanielTudhope 10 41
(Henry Spiller) *hld up in last trio: sme hdwy over 2f out: nt clrest of runs over 1f out: kpt on ins fnl f: nvr trbld ldrs* **16/1**

0-65 **7** *3/4* **Lord Aslan (IRE)**[98] 4384 3-9-1 **47**.... RobHornby(3) 7 39
(Andrew Balding) *hld up in midfield: nt clr run and swtchd rt over 1f out: no imp fnl f: nvr trbld ldrs* **7/1**[2]

0-00 **8** *2* **King Of Cornwall (IRE)**[16] 7103 3-9-7 **50**.... TomQueally 3 40
(David Lanigan) *jostling leaving stalls: hld up in midfield: rdn 4f out: outpcd over 2f out: wknd over 1f out* **10/1**

0004 **9** *nk* **Nutzma**[12] 7230 3-9-2 **45**.... JohnFahy 6 34
(Mike Murphy) *t.k.h: chsd ldrs: 4th and outpcd u.p over 2f out: wknd over 1f out* **16/1**

0405 **10** *1/2* **Rob's Legacy**[56] 5888 3-8-11 **45**....[1] CharlieBennett(5) 13 33
(Shaun Harris) *a rr: rdn over 2f out: nvr on terms* **66/1**

0454 **11** *1/2* **Gilt Edged (IRE)**[16] 7103 3-9-5 **48**.... ShaneGray 9 36
(Julie Camacho) *hld up in tch towards rr: hdwy 4f out: outpcd over 2f out: nt clr run and swtchd rt over 1f out: wknd fnl f* **8/1**[3]

4055 **12** *35* **The Greedy Boy**[21] 6967 3-9-2 **45**.... TomEaves 2
(Mick Channon) *led tl after 4f: chsd ldrs tl lost pl u.p over 3f out: bhd over 1f out: eased ins fnl f: t.o* **7/1**[2]

056 **P** **Rayanne**[19] 7014 3-9-2 **45**.......................(t[1]) KieranO'Neill 8
(Sarah Hollinshead) *chsd ldrs tl swtchd rt and eased 4f out: p.u* **66/1**
2m 52.42s (-1.18) **Going Correction** -0.225s/f (Stan) **13** Ran SP% **126.1**
Speed ratings (Par 95): **94,92,92,91,90 89,88,87,87,87 86,65,**
CSF £101.01 CT £693.19 TOTE £2.10: £1.20, £10.10, £3.80; EX 85.50 Trifecta £926.90.

Owner Andrew Whitlock Racing Ltd **Bred** T Jones **Trained** Newmarket, Suffolk

FOCUS
A desperately weak handicap in which the favourite bolted up and was value for plenty more than the winning margin. The third and fourth help pin the level.

7533 FOLLOW US @CHELMSFORDCRC ON TWITTER H'CAP (DIV I) 5f (P)
8:40 (8:42) (Class 6) (0-65,68) 3-Y-O+ **£2,911** (£866; £432; £216) **Stalls** Low

Form RPR
221 **1** **Waneen (IRE)**[7] 7362 3-9-10 **68**.......................JFEgan 6 80
(Joseph Tuite) *mde all: rdn and asserted jst over 1f out: in command and styd on strly ins fnl f: rdn out* **2/1**[1]

3214 **2** *2½* **Kiringa**[21] 6958 3-9-4 **62**.......................KieranO'Neill 7 65
(Robert Cowell) *sn chsng wnr: rdn over 1f out: unable qck and outpcd by wnr 1f out: styd on same pce ins fnl f* **6/1**[3]

520 **3** *¾* **Head Space (IRE)**[16] 7092 8-9-0 **65**.......................AledBeech[(7)] 4 64
(David Evans) *hld up in tch in last trio: rdn over 1f out: hdwy 1f out: styd on to go 3rd towards fin: no threat to wnr* **5/1**[2]

0451 **4** *1* **Bilash**[71] 5378 9-8-4 **51**.......................JackDuern[(3)] 1 47
(Sarah Hollinshead) *chsd ldrs: rdn and unable qck over 1f out: no threat to wnr and styd on same pce ins fnl f* **16/1**

3005 **5** *hd* **Searanger (USA)**[21] 6959 3-9-6 **64**.......................[1] DougieCostello 8 60
(Rebecca Menzies) *wnt rt s: t.k.h: hld up in tch in midfield: effrt u.p over 1f out: no imp and styd on same pce ins fnl f* **16/1**

1332 **6** *¾* **Willow Spring**[10] 7276 4-8-4 **51**.......................NoelGarbutt[(3)] 3 43
(Conrad Allen) *taken down early: t.k.h: chsd ldrs: rdn over 1f out: unable qck 1f out: wknd ins fnl f* **8/1**

40-0 **7** *2¼* **Arctic Lynx (IRE)**[44] 6248 9-8-13 **62**.......................(p) AnnStokell[(5)] 2 46
(Ann Stokell) *taken down early: midfield: effrt over 1f out: no imp and styd on same pce and wl hld fnl f* **20/1**

1600 **8** *nse* **Lady Joanna Vassa (IRE)**[16] 7093 3-8-13 **57**.......................ConnorBeasley 9 42
(Richard Guest) *pushed rt s: t.k.h in midfield: rdn over 1f out: no ex and btn 1f out: wknd ins fnl f* **6/1**[3]

6301 **9** *1½* **Frangarry (IRE)**[19] 7018 4-8-9 **58**.......................(b) MitchGodwin[(5)] 10 37
(Alan Bailey) *pushed rt s: in tch in midfield: effrt u.p over 1f out: no imp: wl hld and styd on same pce ins fnl f* **8/1**

5660 **10** *1¾* **Louis Vee (IRE)**[154] 2458 8-8-7 **56**.......................CiaranMckee[(5)] 5 28
(John O'Shea) *a rr: effrt over 1f out: no hdwy: wknd fnl f* **25/1**
59.64s (-0.56) **Going Correction** -0.225s/f (Stan) **10** Ran SP% **121.2**
Speed ratings (Par 101): **95,91,89,88,87 86,83,83,80,77**
CSF £14.76 CT £55.43 TOTE £2.80: £1.20, £2.10, £2.10; EX 15.80 Trifecta £76.70.

Owner Stewart Brown **Bred** Roundhill Stud **Trained** Lambourn, Berks

FOCUS
Three previous winners in a race that looked fairly competitive for the grade beforehand, but, as has been the case so often this evening, the pace held up and nothing could land a glove on Waneen. He recorded a clear pb.

7534 FOLLOW US @CHELMSFORDCRC ON TWITTER H'CAP (DIV II) 5f (P)
9:10 (9:13) (Class 6) (0-65,65) 3-Y-O+ **£2,911** (£866; £432; £216) **Stalls** Low

Form RPR
0103 **1** **Horsforth**[10] 7290 4-8-13 **57**.......................(b) ConnorBeasley 8 64
(Richard Guest) *in tch: effrt on outer over 1f out: styd on u.p and ev ch 100yds out: led towards fin* **5/1**[3]

4015 **2** *½* **Zipedeedodah (IRE)**[19] 7018 4-9-6 **64**.......................(t) DanielTudhope 5 69
(Joseph Tuite) *in tch in midfield: hdwy u.p over 1f out: chsd ldr jst ins fnl f: sn led: kpt on: hdd and no ex towards fin* **11/4**[1]

136 **3** *¾* **Equijade**[31] 6669 3-9-6 **64**.......................LiamKeniry 4 68
(Robert Stephens) *hld up in tch in midfield: swtchd lft after 1f out: hdwy u.p over 1f out: ev ch wl ins fnl f: unable qck towards fin* **8/1**

1020 **4** *1¾* **Red Flute**[10] 7276 4-8-5 **52**.......................(v) TimClark[(3)] 7 48
(Denis Quinn) *led: rdn and edgd rt over 1f out: hdd ins fnl f: no ex: wknd fnl 75yds* **12/1**

0603 **5** *½* **Chandresh**[24] 6865 3-8-7 **51** oh3.......................(v) KieranO'Neill 1 46
(Robert Cowell) *chsd ldrs on inner: effrt u.p over 1f out: unable qck 1f out: wknd wl ins fnl f* **16/1**

2004 **6** *nse* **Shine Likeadiamond**[7] 7362 3-8-13 **57**.......................TomEaves 3 52
(Mick Channon) *hld up in tch towards rr: sltly impeded after 1f: effrt on inner over 1f out: styd on same pce and no imp ins fnl f* **10/1**

0325 **7** *nk* **Socialites Red**[11] 7255 3-9-4 **62**.......................(p) BenCurtis 2 56
(Scott Dixon) *chsd ldr early: in tch in midfield: effrt whn squeezed for room and hmpd over 1f out: swtchd lft ins fnl f: styd on same pce fnl 100yds* **7/2**[2]

0003 **8** *nk* **Smart Dj**[178] 1794 5-8-7 **51**.......................JFEgan 9 43
(Sarah Hollinshead) *stdd s and dropped in bhd: swtchd rt and effrt over 1f out: no imp and styd on same pce ins fnl f* **25/1**

350 **9** *1½* **Swanton Blue (IRE)**[43] 6296 3-9-7 **65**.......................PatCosgrave 10 53
(Ed de Giles) *chsd ldrs on outer: wnt 2nd 2f out: edgd lft u.p and unable qck over 1f out: lost 2nd and wknd ins fnl f* **8/1**

0455 **10** *2½* **Culloden**[41] 6374 4-8-11 **60**.......................CharlieBennett[(5)] 6 38
(Shaun Harris) *dwlt: sn rcvrd to chse ldr: lost 2nd 2f out: lost pl under over 1f out: wknd ins fnl f* **16/1**
59.47s (-0.73) **Going Correction** -0.225s/f (Stan) **10** Ran SP% **120.2**
Speed ratings (Par 101): **96,95,94,91,90 90,89,89,86,82**
CSF £19.79 CT £111.48 TOTE £5.60: £1.30, £1.60, £2.70; EX 24.00 Trifecta £176.60.

Owner Morecool Racing **Bred** Laundry Cottage Stud Farm **Trained** Ingmanthorpe, W Yorks

FOCUS
A wide-open and well run finale win which most of the field still held some sort of chance in the straight. The last challenger was the winning challenger.

T/Plt: £83.50 to a £1 stake. Pool: £76,147.70 - 665.45 winning units. T/Qpdt: £32.80 to a £1 stake. Pool: £10,626.24 - 239.03 winning units. **Steve Payne**

7493 DONCASTER (L-H)
Saturday, October 22

OFFICIAL GOING: Good (7.7)
Wind: moderate 1/2 behind Weather: changeable, light showers

7535 SUNBETS.CO.UK DOWNLOAD THE APP H'CAP 1m 2f 60y
1:35 (1:36) (Class 3) (0-90,90) 3-Y-O+ **£12,938** (£3,850; £1,924; £962) **Stalls** Low

Form RPR
0-56 **1** *hd* **Banditry (IRE)**[27] 6802 4-9-1 **81**.......................WilliamBuick 4 89
(Ian Williams) *dwlt: t.k.h: hld up in rr: hdwy 3f out: chsd ldrs 2f out: swtchd rt and rdn jst over 1f out: styng on whn sltly hmpd and swtchd lft jst ins fnl f: sn drvn: edgd lft and styd on wl towards fin* **9/1**

4325 **2** **Laurence**[29] 6753 4-9-7 **87**.......................RyanMoore 19 96
(Luca Cumani) *hld up towards rr: hdwy over 3f out: effrt on outer to chse ldrs 2f out: rdn to ld ent fnl f and sn edgd rt: drvn and hld on wl towards fin* **13/2**[2]

5650 **3** *hd* **American Artist (IRE)**[28] 6786 4-9-9 **89**.......................AndreaAtzeni 16 96+
(Roger Varian) *hld up: hdwy 2f out: rdn to chse ldrs over 1f out: drvn and styd on wl towards fin* **8/1**[3]

4033 **4** *hd* **Sennockian Star**[12] 7222 6-9-1 **81**.......................(v) PJMcDonald 13 88
(Mark Johnston) *midfield: pushed along and hdwy on outer 3f out: rdn along wl over 1f out: chal and ev ch ins fnl f: sn drvn: n.m.r and no ex towards fin* **16/1**

2S30 **5** *¾* **Jacbequick**[15] 7121 5-9-9 **89**.......................DanielTudhope 1 94
(David O'Meara) *midfield: hdwy wl over 2f out: chsd ldrs over 1f out: sn swtchd lft and rdn: kpt on towards fin* **25/1**

0401 **6** *2¼* **Beardwood**[12] 7222 4-9-3 **83**.......................(p) JimCrowley 18 84
(Mark Johnston) *hld up in rr: hdwy on wd outside 3f out: rdn to chse ldrs over 1f out: sltly hmpd jst ins fnl f: kpt on* **10/1**

2134 **7** *nse* **Character Onesie (IRE)**[28] 6772 4-8-10 **76**.......................TonyHamilton 17 77
(Richard Fahey) *hld up towards rr: hdwy on inner wl over 2f out: rdn wl over 1f out: styd on fnl f: nrst fin* **50/1**

5506 **8** *shd* **Hit The Jackpot (IRE)**[10] 7287 7-9-6 **89**.......................ShelleyBirkett[(3)] 6 90
(David O'Meara) *trckd ldrs on inner: hdwy 3f out: rdn to chal wl over 1f out: ev ch tl drvn and wknd fnl f* **20/1**

4312 **9** *1¼* **Malmoosa (IRE)**[21] 6948 3-9-5 **90**.......................PaulHanagan 2 88
(Brian Meehan) *trckd ldrs: hdwy 4f out: pushed along 3f out: rdn over 2f out: sn drvn and grad wknd* **9/1**

5606 **10** *¾* **Dance King**[14] 7159 6-9-0 **83**.......................(t) RachelRichardson[(3)] 10 80+
(Tim Easterby) *towards rr: hdwy over 2f out: rdn wl over 1f out: no imp fnl f* **16/1**

3504 **11** *½* **Ready (IRE)**[155] 2444 6-9-3 **86**.......................(p) JosephineGordon[(3)] 12 82
(Ivan Furtado) *prom: hdwy and cl up over 3f out: led 2f out and sn rdn: drvn and hdd ent fnl f: wknd* **100/1**

1524 **12** *hd* **Play Nicely**[12] 7229 4-8-12 **78**.......................GrahamGibbons 5 74
(David Barron) *nvr bttr than midfield* **16/1**

5030 **13** *nk* **Freewheel (IRE)**[15] 7108 6-8-10 **76**.......................JasonHart 7 71
(Garry Moss) *in tch: rdn along wl over 2f out: sn wknd* **25/1**

3340 **14** *¾* **Emerald (ITY)**[10] 7287 4-9-5 **85**.......................DanielMuscutt 9 79
(Marco Botti) *in tch: hdwy 3f out: sn chsng ldrs: rdn along 2f out: sn drvn and wknd* **14/1**

4510 **15** *9* **Mysterial**[21] 6957 6-8-8 **79**.......................PhilDennis[(5)] 8 55
(Declan Carroll) *sn led: pushed along 4f out: rdn and hdd 3f out: sn wknd* **50/1**

0000 **16** *4½* **Juste Pour Nous**[18] 7060 3-8-7 **78**.......................(b[1]) JoeFanning 14 46
(Mark Johnston) *chsd ldng trio: pushed along 3f out: rdn over 2f out: sn wknd* **25/1**

5221 **17** *1½* **Makzeem**[96] 4458 3-8-13 **87**.......................KieranShoemark[(3)] 15 52
(Roger Charlton) *cl up: led 3f out: rdn along and hdd 2f out: sn drvn and wknd over 1f out* **7/2**[1]

-664 **18** *1¾* **Bag Of Diamonds**[50] 6084 3-7-12 **76** oh3.......................TinaSmith[(7)] 11 38
(Richard Hannon) *midfield: rdn along 3f out: sn wknd* **50/1**

13-4 **19** *17* **Petrucci (IRE)**[157] 2377 4-9-4 **84**.......................[1] MartinLane 3 13
(Derek Shaw) *a towards rr: rdn along over 3f out: sn outpcd and bhd* **33/1**

/60- **20** *45* **Saxo Jack (FR)**[611] 616 6-9-3 **90**.......................[1] SophieKilloran[(7)] 20
(Sophie Leech) *stdd and swtchd lft s: hld up and a rr: outpcd and bhd fnl 2f* **100/1**
2m 7.67s (-1.73) **Going Correction** -0.05s/f (Good)
WFA 3 from 4yo+ 5lb **20** Ran SP% **127.2**
Speed ratings (Par 107): **103,104,103,103,102 101,101,101,100,99 99,98,98,98,90 87,86,84,71,35**
CSF £59.39 CT £490.94 TOTE £7.60: £2.30, £3.00, £2.60, £3.70; EX 87.60 Trifecta £883.90.
Owner Buxted Partnership **Bred** Darley **Trained** Portway, Worcs

FOCUS
There was 1.2mm of rain on Thursday but it had been dry since and the ground was unchanged from Friday's card, officially good all over. After riding in the opener Josephine Gordon said: "It is good ground, they are going in slightly," Paul Hanagan said: "It is just on the slow side of good" and Jason Hart said: "It is dead." A decent enough, competitive handicap to start, although not many unexposed types, and the pace was fast enough.

7536 SCOTT DOBSON 30TH BIRTHDAY MEMORIAL DONCASTER STKS (LISTED RACE) 6f
2:05 (2:07) (Class 1) 2-Y-O
£17,013 (£6,450; £3,228; £1,608; £807; £405) **Stalls** Centre

Form RPR
41 **1** **Rosie Briar**[29] 6733 2-8-10 78.......................RobHornby 2 95
(Andrew Balding) *trckd ldng pair towards far side: 2nd over 2f out: sn upsides: styd on to ld last 150yds: drvn rt out* **20/1**

1043 **2** *½* **Tomily (IRE)**[15] 7120 2-9-1 91.......................JimCrowley 1 99
(Richard Hannon) *led towards far side: jnd 2f out: hdd and no ex last 150yds* **8/1**

0215 **3** *nk* **Nuclear Power**[15] 7113 2-9-1 97.......................MartinDwyer 7 98
(William Muir) *t.k.h: sn trcking ldrs towards far side: kpt on same pce last 100yds* **6/1**[3]

13 **4** *1¼* **Khafoo Shememi (IRE)**[38] 6481 2-9-1 0.......................RyanMoore 3 94
(Richard Hannon) *chsd ldrs towards far side: drvn over 2f out: kpt on same pce fnl f* **7/1**

01 **5** *½* **Hilario**[50] 6086 2-9-1 85.......................AndreaAtzeni 5 93
(Charles Hills) *trckd ldrs centre: t.k.h: effrt over 2f out: kpt on same pce appr fnl f* **8/1**

6340 **6** *¾* **Grizzel (IRE)**[43] 6282 2-8-10 94.......................TomMarquand 9 86
(Richard Hannon) *hld up towards rr towards stands' side: effrt over 2f out: styd on wl fnl f: nt rch ldrs* **16/1**

0102 **7** ½ **Simmie (IRE)**[21] 6950 2-8-10 84 JimmyQuinn 10 84
(Sylvester Kirk) *chsd ldrs towards stands' side: effrt over 2f out: one pce over 1f out* **22/1**

4362 **8** 2 **Whirl Me Round**[21] 6954 2-9-1 83 KevinStott 11 83
(Kevin Ryan) *hld up in rr towards stands' side: sme hdwy over 1f out: nvr a factor* **16/1**

211 **9** 1¼ **Timeless Flight**[24] 6869 2-9-1 89 (t) WilliamBuick 8 80
(Charlie Appleby) *hld up in mid-div centre: effrt over 2f out: wknd and eased last 100yds* **11/2**[2]

011 **10** 3 **Comedy School (USA)**[15] 7120 2-8-10 88 PJMcDonald 6 65
(Mark Johnston) *in rr and sn drvn along centre: nvr on terms* **2/1**[1]

1626 **11** 1¼ **Angel Meadow**[29] 6734 2-8-10 85 PaulHanagan 4 62
(Micky Hammond) *s.s: hdwy towards far side over 2f out: lost pl over 1f out* **40/1**

1m 11.53s (-2.07) **Going Correction** -0.175s/f (Firm) **11** Ran SP% **121.0**
Speed ratings (Par 103): **106,105,104,103,102 101,100,98,96,92 90**
CSF £173.27 TOTE £28.00: £5.30, £2.50, £2.30; EX 222.80 Trifecta £2532.50.
Owner Dr J A E Hobby **Bred** J A E Hobby **Trained** Kingsclere, Hants

FOCUS
A weak 2yo Listed race and nothing got involved from off the pace, with the first three in those positions throughout. The third just abour repeated her Cornwallis Stakes figure.

7537 SUNBETS.CO.UK TOP PRICE TEMPLEGATE TIPS H'CAP 5f
2:40 (2:43) (Class 2) 3-Y-O+
£31,125 (£9,320; £4,660; £2,330; £1,165; £585) **Stalls** Centre

Form RPR

5150 **1** **Soie D'Leau**[27] 6819 4-8-13 96 TonyHamilton 17 105
(Kristin Stubbs) *prom: cl up 1/2-way: led 11/2f out and sn rdn: drvn ins fnl f: jst hld on* **14/1**

-11 **2** shd **Tithonus (IRE)**[27] 6819 5-7-13 87 (tp) KillianLeonard(5) 18 95
(Denis Gerard Hogan, Ire) *trckd ldrs towards outer: hdwy 2f out: rdn over 1f out: drvn and styd on strly fnl f: jst hld* **10/1**[1]

0004 **3** ½ **Bogart**[15] 7124 7-7-11 83 oh1 (p) NathanEvans(3) 9 89
(Kevin Ryan) *a cl up: rdn over 1f out and ev ch tl drvn and kpt on same pce towards fin* **12/1**[3]

313 **4** hd **Hilary J**[10] 7288 3-7-7 83 oh1 DavidEgan(7) 3 89
(Ann Duffield) *trckd ldrs on inner: hdwy and cl up 2f out: rdn to chal over 1f out: ev ch ins fnl f: sn drvn and no ex towards fin* **14/1**

2002 **5** nk **Confessional**[7] 7358 9-8-9 92 (be) CamHardie 7 96
(Tim Easterby) *trckd ldrs: pushed along and sltly outpcd wl over 1f out: sn rdn: styd on wl fnl f: nrst fin* **16/1**

0602 **6** ¾ **Dutch Masterpiece**[21] 6944 6-8-9 95 (b) HectorCrouch(3) 19 97
(Gary Moore) *trckd ldrs towards outer: hdwy 2f out: rdn over 1f out: drvn ent fnl f: no imp towards fin* **14/1**

0054 **7** ½ **Udontdodou**[7] 7358 3-8-2 85 AndrewMullen 4 86+
(Richard Guest) *dwlt and bhd: hdwy wl over 1f out: rdn and styd on strly fnl f: nrst fin* **12/1**[3]

0046 **8** nse **My Name Is Rio (IRE)**[15] 7124 6-8-6 89 (p) ConnorBeasley 13 89
(Michael Dods) *trckd ldrs: effrt wl over 1f out: sn rdn: drvn and kpt on same pce fnl f* **14/1**

3043 **9** shd **Gamesome (FR)**[11] 7250 5-8-11 94 DougieCostello 11 93
(Paul Midgley) *midfield: hdwy 2f out: rdn over 1f out: kpt on fnl f* **14/1**

0401 **10** shd **Robot Boy (IRE)**[15] 7124 6-8-13 96 GrahamGibbons 15 95
(David Barron) *qckly away and led: hdd over 3f out: cl up: rdn to chal 2f out: ev ch tl drvn ent fnl f and grad wknd* **10/1**[1]

2203 **11** 1 **Humidor (IRE)**[11] 7242 9-9-1 98 FergusSweeney 6 93+
(George Baker) *rr: hdwy 2f out: sn rdn and kpt on fnl f: nrst fin* **14/1**

-660 **12** nk **Orvar (IRE)**[14] 7156 3-8-10 93 AndreaAtzeni 12 88
(Robert Cowell) *chsd ldrs: rdn along and sltly outpcd wl over 1f out: kpt on fnl f* **25/1**

6055 **13** nse **Shipyard (USA)**[15] 7124 7-8-3 86 BenCurtis 22 80
(Michael Appleby) *chsd ldrs on wd outside: rdn along wl over 1f out: sn drvn and no imp* **10/1**[1]

1000 **14** nk **Mont Kiara (FR)**[22] 6916 3-8-10 93 TomEaves 10 87
(Kevin Ryan) *in tch: hdwy wl over 1f out: n.m.r and swtchd lft ent fnl f: sn rdn and no imp* **25/1**

5631 **15** shd **Mirza**[11] 7242 9-9-10 107 (p) JimCrowley 16 100
(Rae Guest) *chsd ldrs: rdn along wl over 1f out: grad wknd* **12/1**[3]

3000 **16** 1¼ **Dungannon**[21] 6944 9-8-2 85 (v) JimmyQuinn 2 73
(Andrew Balding) *a towards rr* **14/1**

0000 **17** 2 **Desert Law (IRE)**[7] 7358 8-8-7 90 PaulHanagan 14 71
(Paul Midgley) *cl up: led over 3f out: rdn 2f out: hdd 11/2f out and sn wknd* **33/1**

1002 **18** ½ **Kibaar**[15] 7124 4-8-4 87 (p) TomMarquand 20 66
(Kevin Ryan) *nvr bttr than midfield* **20/1**

05U0 **19** 1 **Huntsmans Close**[17] 7068 6-8-9 95 EoinWalsh(3) 21 70
(Robert Cowell) *in tch towards outer: rdn along 2f out: sn wknd* **50/1**

1006 **20** ½ **A Momentofmadness**[21] 6944 3-8-2 88 JosephineGordon(3) 5 63
(Charles Hills) *a rr* **11/1**[2]

0100 **21** 8 **Meadway**[66] 5555 5-8-6 94 (p) PhilDennis(5) 1 39
(Bryan Smart) *racd nr inner rail: in tch: rdn along 1/2-way: sn outpcd and bhd* **66/1**

58.19s (-2.31) **Going Correction** -0.175s/f (Firm) **21** Ran SP% **130.1**
Speed ratings (Par 109): **111,110,110,109,109 108,107,107,107,106 105,104,104,104,104 102,98,98,96,95 82**
CSF £142.37 CT £1800.08 TOTE £19.10: £4.30, £2.90, £3.10, £3.40; EX 200.90 Trifecta £2697.50.
Owner F A T J Partnership **Bred** Mrs M Lingwood **Trained** Norton, N Yorks
■ Stewards' Enquiry : Killian Leonard 4-day ban (5th & 7-9th Nov): used whip above permitted level

FOCUS
It doesn't come much more open than this sprint handicap.

7538 BET THROUGH THE RACING POST APP H'CAP 1m 4f
3:15 (3:16) (Class 2) (0-100,99) 3-Y-O+ **£16,172** (£4,812; £2,405; £1,202) **Stalls** Low

Form RPR

5-1 **1** **To Be Wild (IRE)**[86] 4792 3-8-10 93 JosephineGordon(3) 12 106+
(Hugo Palmer) *trckd ldrs: pushed along to ld 2f out: sn wnt clr: eased clsng stages: v readily* **6/1**[3]

1605 **2** 4 **Percy Street**[35] 6559 3-8-12 97 JordanVaughan(5) 1 101
(K R Burke) *led tl over 7f out: upsides over 2f out: kpt on same pce* **20/1**

0/0 **3** ½ **Wrangler**[19] 7015 5-9-0 87 RyanMoore 5 91+
(William Haggas) *hld up in rr: hdwy over 2f out: styd on wl fnl f: tk 3rd nr fin* **20/1**

4161 **4** 1 **Trendsetter (IRE)**[7] 7357 5-8-13 89 (p) AaronJones(3) 7 91
(Micky Hammond) *mid-div: effrt over 2f out: hung lft and kpt on same pce fnl f* **50/1**

4112 **5** ½ **Huge Future**[35] 6581 3-9-5 99 WilliamBuick 2 100
(Saeed bin Suroor) *w ldr: led briefly overall over 2f out: kpt on one pce* **4/1**[2]

31 **6** shd **Uae Prince (IRE)**[33] 6634 3-8-13 93 AndreaAtzeni 9 94
(Roger Varian) *mid-div: stdy hdwy over 2f out: one pce whn struck over hd by rival rdrs' whip over 1f out* **1/1**[1]

1100 **7** 8 **Ruwasi**[51] 6057 5-9-3 90 JimCrowley 11 78
(James Tate) *hld up in rr: sme hdwy 3f out: wknd over 1f out* **14/1**

3341 **8** hd **Mukhayyam**[28] 6794 4-9-0 90 (p) RachelRichardson(3) 13 78
(Tim Easterby) *swtchd lft after s: sn trcking ldrs: led over 7f out: styd alone far side over 4f out: hdd over 2f out: edgd rt and lost pl over 1f out* **20/1**

0000 **9** 4½ **My Reward**[14] 7150 4-9-6 93 JasonHart 4 74
(Tim Easterby) *hood removed v late: s.s: in rr: drvn and sme hdwy over 2f out: wknd over 1f out* **33/1**

-635 **10** 1 **Argus (IRE)**[12] 7215 4-9-2 89 GrahamGibbons 6 68
(Ralph Beckett) *trckd ldrs: reminders over 3f out: lost pl over 2f out* **10/1**

010 **11** 17 **Zamperini (IRE)**[24] 6884 4-9-1 88 JimmyFortune 10 40
(Mike Murphy) *hld up in rr: lost pl over 2f out: wl bhd whn eased last 100yds* **66/1**

2200 **12** 15 **Forgotten Hero (IRE)**[28] 6781 7-9-6 93 (t) DougieCostello 8 21
(Kim Bailey) *rr-div: t.k.h: brief effrt 3f out: bhd whn heavily eased over 1f out* **33/1**

2m 31.39s (-3.51) **Going Correction** -0.05s/f (Good)
WFA 3 from 4yo+ 7lb **12** Ran SP% **123.7**
Speed ratings (Par 109): **109,106,106,105,105 104,99,99,96,95 84,74**
CSF £122.84 CT £2283.50 TOTE £7.40: £1.90, £4.90, £4.20; EX 138.80 Trifecta £2374.20.
Owner Carmichael Jennings **Bred** Miss Mary Davison **Trained** Newmarket, Suffolk

FOCUS
Better could have been expected from the 5th and 6th, so maybe not as hot a race as it looked beforehand, but the winner showed himself significantly better than his mark. All bar Mukhayyam came middle to stands' side entering the straight.

7539 RACING POST TROPHY (GROUP 1) (ENTIRE COLTS & FILLIES) 1m (S)
3:50 (3:51) (Class 1) 2-Y-O
£113,420 (£43,000; £21,520; £10,720; £5,380; £2,700) **Stalls** Centre

Form RPR

2115 **1** **Rivet (IRE)**[14] 7149 2-9-1 114 AndreaAtzeni 5 116
(William Haggas) *set stdy pce: qcknd over 2f out: rdn over 1f out: drvn and kpt on wl fnl f* **11/4**[2]

2 **2** 1¾ **Yucatan (IRE)**[27] 6817 2-9-1 0 RyanMoore 2 112
(A P O'Brien, Ire) *hld up in tch: hdwy 3f out and sn pushed along: effrt wl over 1f out and sn rdn to chse wnr: drvn and ev ch ent fnl f: kpt on same pce towards fin* **11/8**[1]

1212 **3** nk **Salouen (IRE)**[20] 6987 2-9-1 105 TomMarquand 8 111
(Sylvester Kirk) *trckd ldrs: pushed along over 2f out: rdn over 1f out: drvn and kpt on wl fnl f* **16/1**

221 **4** nk **Raheen House (IRE)**[15] 7125 2-9-1 88 JimmyFortune 9 111
(Brian Meehan) *prom: pushed along over 2f out: rdn wl over 1f out: drvn and kpt on same pce fnl f* **16/1**

5 1¼ **Brutal (IRE)**[72] 5342 2-9-1 0 [1] ColinKeane 6 108
(G M Lyons, Ire) *hld up: hdwy nr stands rails over 2f out: rdn to chse ldrs over 1f out: drvn and one pce fnl f* **40/1**

1131 **6** ¾ **Sir Dancealot (IRE)**[14] 7155 2-9-1 105 JimCrowley 3 106+
(David Elsworth) *dwlt and hld up in rr: smooth hdwy on outer over 2f out and sn chsng ldrs: rdn and cl up over 1f out: wknd fnl f* **6/1**[3]

0 **7** 2¼ **Finn McCool (IRE)**[17] 7083 2-9-1 0 DonnachaO'Brien 1 101
(A P O'Brien, Ire) *trckd ldrs on outer: pushed along over 2f out: rdn wl over 1f out: sn wknd* **20/1**

610 **8** nk **Bay Of Poets (IRE)**[28] 6783 2-9-1 96 WilliamBuick 4 101
(Charlie Appleby) *hld up: hdwy 2f out: rdn to chse ldrs over 1f out: edgd rt and wknd appr fnl f* **25/1**

521 **9** 4½ **Contrapposto (IRE)**[17] 7074 2-9-1 85 MartinDwyer 7 92
(David Menuisier) *cl up: rdn along 2f out: drvn and wkng whn n.m.r and hmpd appr fnl f* **25/1**

323 **10** 2¼ **The Anvil (IRE)**[14] 7148 2-9-1 0 SeamieHeffernan 10 86
(A P O'Brien, Ire) *cl up nr stands rail: rdn along over 2f out: sn wknd* **9/1**

1m 37.08s (-2.22) **Going Correction** -0.175s/f (Firm) 2y crse rec **10** Ran SP% **119.7**
Speed ratings (Par 109): **104,102,101,101,100 99,97,97,92,90**
CSF £6.75 CT £51.25 TOTE £3.70: £1.40, £1.30, £3.60; EX 9.00 Trifecta £92.10.
Owner The Starship Partnership **Bred** Des Scott **Trained** Newmarket, Suffolk
■ Andrea Atzeni has now won the last four runnings of this event.

FOCUS
This didn't look a strong Group 1 for 2yos and it was run at an ordinary pace, but the form makes plenty of sense. It was probably towards the lower end of the race spectrum, rated around the runner-up.

7540 CROWNHOTEL-BAWTRY.COM APPRENTICE JOCKEYS' TRAINING SERIES FINAL H'CAP 7f
4:25 (4:26) (Class 4) (0-85,85) 3-Y-O **£6,469** (£1,925; £962; £481) **Stalls** Centre

Form RPR

5400 **1** **King Of Naples**[27] 6806 3-9-3 78 GeorgeWood 7 88
(James Fanshawe) *chsd ldrs: effrt and upsides appr fnl f: kpt on to ld post* **9/1**

1540 **2** shd **Briyouni (FR)**[19] 7005 3-9-4 79 LewisEdmunds 5 88
(Kevin Ryan) *hld up in mid-div: t.k.h: hdwy over 2f out: led over 1f out: hdd post* **13/2**[1]

5100 **3** 3 **Young John (IRE)**[68] 5488 3-9-3 83 HayleyIrvine(5) 9 84
(Richard Fahey) *hld up in rr: effrt over 2f out: edgd lft: kpt on to take modest 3rd post* **20/1**

0253 **4** hd **He's My Cracker**[44] 6255 3-9-1 81 WilliamCox(5) 3 81
(Clive Cox) *led: hdd over 1f out: one pce* **8/1**[3]

1105 **5** nk **Imperial State**[15] 7108 3-9-3 83 (t) JoshuaBryan(5) 6 83
(George Scott) *hld up in rr: hdwy over 2f out: nt clr run and swtchd rt over 1f out: kpt on fnl 100yds* **8/1**[3]

0400 **6** shd **Yosemite**[8] 7325 3-8-11 72 NatalieHambling 2 71
(Richard Fahey) *trckd ldrs: t.k.h: effrt over 2f out: one pce over 1f out* **12/1**

0406 **7** 2¾ **Desert Ruler**[15] 7126 3-9-1 76 SophieKilloran 12 68
(Jedd O'Keeffe) *hld up detached in last: hdwy 3f out: one pce over 1f out* **12/1**

3154 **8** ½ **Prying Pandora (FR)**[27] 6810 3-9-5 80 AdamMcNamara 4 71
(Richard Fahey) *dwlt: sn trcking ldrs: effrt over 2f out: fdd fnl 150yds* **13/2**[1]

The Form Book, Raceform Ltd, Newbury, RG14 5SJ

2023 **9** 1/2 **King Of Swing**[39] 6437 3-9-4 **79** GeorgiaCox 1 68
(James Given) *trckd ldrs: drvn over 2f out: wknd fnl 75yds* **7/1**[2]

003 **10** 1 1/4 **Royal Shaheen (FR)**[24] 6877 3-9-10 **85** RowanScott 10 71
(Alistair Whillans) *in rr: drvn over 3f out: reminders over 2f out: lost pl over 1f out* **10/1**

6140 **11** 3/4 **Explosive Power (IRE)**[22] 6918 3-9-5 **85** RussellHarris(5) 11 69
(K R Burke) *chsd ldrs: drvn and outpcd over 1f out* **20/1**

5212 **12** 1 1/2 **Alpine Dream (IRE)**[24] 6878 3-8-9 **73** (b) DavidEgan(3) 8 53
(Tim Easterby) *dwlt: t.k.h: hdwy to trck ldrs over 3f out: lost pl over 1f out* **7/1**[2]

1m 24.86s (-1.44) **Going Correction** -0.175s/f (Firm) **12** Ran SP% **117.9**
Speed ratings (Par 103): **101,100,97,97,96 96,93,93,92,91 90,88**
CSF £66.09 CT £1134.14 TOTE £9.00: £2.90, £2.40, £5.60; EX 72.40 Trifecta £1576.10.
Owner P S Ryan **Bred** Meon Valley Stud **Trained** Newmarket, Suffolk
■ Stewards' Enquiry : Rowan Scott 7-day ban (Nov 5th & 7-12th): used whip

FOCUS
A fair enough race, with the first two having dropped to handy marks.

7541 SAINT GOBAIN NURSERY H'CAP 7f
5:00 (5:00) (Class 3) (0-95,88) 2-Y-O **£12,291** (£3,657; £1,827; £913) **Stalls** Centre

Form RPR

6442 **1** **Masham Star (IRE)**[18] 7042 2-9-6 **87** PJMcDonald 5 93
(Mark Johnston) *cl up: led 4f out: rdn clr over 1f out: kpt on strly* **14/1**

11 **2** 1 1/2 **Andok (IRE)**[45] 6229 2-9-4 **85** TonyHamilton 12 87
(Richard Fahey) *in tch: hdwy on outer 2f out: rdn over 1f out: drvn and kpt on fnl f* **11/4**[1]

2152 **3** nk **Novoman (IRE)**[19] 7004 2-9-7 **88** RyanMoore 7 89
(William Haggas) *hld up in rr: hdwy 2f out and sn rdn: drvn ent fnl f: kpt on wl towards fin* **11/4**[1]

303 **4** shd **Lualiwa**[33] 6632 2-8-9 **76** KevinStott 11 77
(Kevin Ryan) *prom: cl up 3f out: rdn along 2f out: drvn ent fnl f: kpt on* **14/1**

244 **5** 1/2 **Miss Sheridan (IRE)**[92] 4603 2-7-11 **67** NathanEvans(3) 8 67
(Michael Easterby) *led 3f: cl up: rdn along 2f out: drvn jst over 1f out: kpt on* **33/1**

4012 **6** 1/2 **Aventinus (IRE)**[24] 6869 2-9-1 **82** JimCrowley 1 80
(Hugo Palmer) *cl up on outer: effrt over 2f out: rdn and ev ch over 1f out: drvn and kpt on same pce fnl f* **15/2**[3]

365 **7** 1 **Portledge (IRE)**[49] 6129 2-8-10 **77** DougieCostello 2 73
(James Bethell) *trckd ldrs: hdwy over 2f out: rdn wl over 1f out: drvn appr fnl f: one pce* **25/1**

451 **8** nk **Himself**[75] 5237 2-8-9 **76** TomMarquand 6 72
(Richard Hannon) *hld up in tch: hdwy over 2f out: rdn to chse ldrs and carried hd awkwardly over 1f out: sn nt clr run and wknd* **16/1**

6343 **9** nk **Golden Apollo**[36] 6534 2-8-10 **77** AndrewMullen 4 71
(Tim Easterby) *chsd ldrs: rdn along over 2f out: drvn and wknd over 1f out* **14/1**

41 **10** 1 1/2 **Cotinga**[137] 2990 2-8-10 **77** AndreaAtzeni 3 67
(Ralph Beckett) *a towards rr* **7/1**[2]

6120 **11** 7 **Evergate**[15] 7120 2-9-2 **86** JosephineGordon(3) 10 58
(Hugo Palmer) *a towards rr* **11/1**

1m 24.91s (-1.39) **Going Correction** -0.175s/f (Firm) **11** Ran SP% **118.6**
Speed ratings (Par 99): **100,98,97,97,97 96,95,95,94,93 85**
CSF £52.90 CT £145.74 TOTE £14.20: £3.50, £1.40, £1.60; EX 65.00 Trifecta £123.90.
Owner 3 Batterhams and a Reay **Bred** Petra Bloodstock Agency Ltd **Trained** Middleham Moor, N Yorks
■ Stewards' Enquiry : Kevin Stott caution: careless riding

FOCUS
This looked a competitive nursery but the improved winner, cannily ridden by P J McDonald, was allowed to get away in front. The runner-up continues to progress.

7542 JOIN RACING POST MEMBERS' CLUB CONDITIONS STKS 7f
5:35 (5:36) (Class 3) 3-Y-O+
£12,450 (£3,728; £1,864; £932; £466; £234) **Stalls** Centre

Form RPR

2224 **1** **Sovereign Debt (IRE)**[21] 6955 7-8-11 112 AndrewMullen 8 109+
(David Nicholls) *hld up towards rr: hdwy 3f out: hung lft and led over 1f out: drvn out* **6/1**[3]

/0-2 **2** 2 1/2 **Fannaan (USA)**[36] 6547 4-8-11 101 PaulHanagan 5 104+
(John Gosden) *hld up towards rr: hdwy 3f out: hmpd over 1f out: styd on to take modesr 2nd nr fin* **3/1**[2]

116 **3** nk **Castle Harbour**[129] 3269 3-8-9 100 WilliamBuick 6 100
(John Gosden) *in rr: effrt over 3f out: outpcd over 2f out: hdwy over 1f out: styd on to take modest 3rd nr fin* **7/4**[1]

1122 **4** 3/4 **Silent Attack**[48] 6181 3-8-9 102 AndreaAtzeni 1 98
(Saeed bin Suroor) *trckd one other far side: effrt over 2f out: chsd wnr 150yds out: kpt on same pce* **6/1**[3]

5104 **5** 1 **Kimberella**[11] 7250 6-8-11 108 GrahamGibbons 9 97
(David Nicholls) *t.k.h: led: hung rt and hdd over 1f out: kpt on same pce* **18/1**

4120 **6** 1 **Right Touch**[21] 6942 6-8-11 102 TonyHamilton 4 94
(Richard Fahey) *trckd overall ldr: drvn over 2f out: one pce over 1f out* **10/1**

0040 **7** 1/2 **Majestic Moon (IRE)**[28] 6764 6-8-11 89 MartinDwyer 3 93
(John Gallagher) *w overall ldr racing far side: one pce over 1f out* **40/1**

1310 **8** 1 1/2 **Dutch Law**[21] 6942 4-8-11 99 JimCrowley 7 89
(Hughie Morrison) *dwlt: in rr: bhd and drvn over 3f out: kpt on fnl f: nvr a factor* **8/1**

1m 24.04s (-2.26) **Going Correction** -0.175s/f (Firm) **8** Ran SP% **117.8**
WFA 3 from 4yo+ 2lb
Speed ratings (Par 107): **105,102,101,100,99 98,98,96**
CSF £25.19 TOTE £5.80: £1.50, £1.60, £1.40; EX 22.40 Trifecta £64.00.
Owner Lady O'Reilly **Bred** Yeomanstown Stud **Trained** Sessay, N Yorks

FOCUS
A good-quality conditions event.
T/Jkpt: Not Won. T/Plt: £884.40 to a £1 stake. Pool: £163,919.81 - 135.30 winning units. T/Qpdt: £239.10 to a £1 stake. Pool: £9,448.40 - 29.24 winning units. **Joe Rowntree & Walter Glynn**

7501 NEWBURY (L-H)
Saturday, October 22

OFFICIAL GOING: Good to soft
Wind: Moderate, behind Weather: Overcast start, sunny spells developing

7543 CONUNDRUM HR CONSULTING EBF STALLIONS MAIDEN FILLIES' STKS (PLUS 10 RACE) (DIV I) 1m (S)
1:15 (1:15) (Class 4) 2-Y-O **£5,175** (£1,540; £769; £384) **Stalls** Centre

Form RPR

1 **Crimson Rock (USA)** 2-9-0 0 FMBerry 10 83+
(Ralph Beckett) *wnt rt s: hld up: shkn up and hdwy 2f out: led ins fnl f: rdn out* **7/2**[1]

364 **2** nk **Elas Ruby**[28] 6782 2-9-0 71 FrankieDettori 3 82
(John Gosden) *in tch: effrt 2f out: str chal fnl f: r.o* **7/2**[1]

3 1 1/4 **Serenada** 2-9-0 0 HarryBentley 4 80+
(Roger Varian) *dwlt: sn trcking ldrs: led over 1f out: rn green: edgd lft and hdd ins fnl f: no ex nr fin* **9/2**[3]

4 6 **Star Rock** 2-9-0 0 RobertHavlin 5 66
(Hughie Morrison) *mid-div: rdn along and dropped to rr 1/2-way: styd on fnl 2f* **16/1**

5 2 1/4 **Silent Approach** 2-9-0 0 PatCosgrave 1 61
(William Haggas) *hld up in rr: rdn and sme hdwy over 1f out: nvr rchd ldrs* **4/1**[2]

0002 **6** 2 1/2 **Royal Melody**[7] 7366 2-9-0 62 (p) ShaneGray 6 56
(Heather Main) *led tl over 1f out: wknd fnl f* **50/1**

7 nse **Katabatika** 2-9-0 0 OisinMurphy 2 56
(Hughie Morrison) *prom tl wknd over 1f out* **6/1**

8 3 **Munstead Star** 2-9-0 0 LiamKeniry 9 49
(Andrew Balding) *nvr beyond midfield: bhd fnl 2f* **25/1**

9 nk **Precious Angel (IRE)** 2-9-0 0 SeanLevey 7 49
(Richard Hannon) *dwlt: bhd: brief effrt over 2f out: n.d* **16/1**

0 **10** 16 **Bed Of Diamonds**[28] 6762 2-9-0 0 TomQueally 8 13
(Adam West) *prom tl hrd rdn and wknd 2f out* **200/1**

1m 41.78s (2.08) **Going Correction** +0.325s/f (Good) **10** Ran SP% **115.0**
Speed ratings (Par 94): **102,101,100,94,92 89,89,86,86,70**
CSF £15.40 TOTE £4.80: £1.50, £1.60, £1.60; EX 14.00 Trifecta £64.10.
Owner H H Sheikh Mohammed Bin Khalifa Al Thani **Bred** Barnett Enterprises **Trained** Kimpton, Hants

FOCUS
The going was given as good to soft (GoingStick: 5.8) and the wind was half against in the home straight. Jockeys returning after the first said the ground was sticky and holding. The rail was out from the 8f point to the 5f marker on the Round course. The pace picked up from a fair way out here and the first three came right away in the closing stages. This is usually a decent maiden and some of these will progress markedly.

7544 WORTHINGTON'S ALZHEIMERS SOCIETY STKS (REGISTERED AS THE HORRIS HILL) (GROUP 3) (C&G) 7f (S)
1:45 (1:46) (Class 1) 2-Y-O
£22,684 (£8,600; £4,304; £2,144; £1,076; £540) **Stalls** Centre

Form RPR

3140 **1** **Pleaseletmewin (IRE)**[14] 7148 2-9-0 103 FMBerry 14 106
(Ralph Beckett) *prom: led and hung lft over 1f out: drvn clr ins fnl f* **16/1**

2110 **2** 2 1/4 **Kings Gift (IRE)**[28] 6783 2-9-0 92 PaulMulrennan 10 100
(Michael Dods) *chsd ldrs: hrd rdn and lost pl over 1f out: rallied to take 2nd nr fin* **20/1**

3150 **3** hd **Law And Order (IRE)**[14] 7148 2-9-0 99 MartinHarley 13 100
(James Tate) *chsd ldrs: hrd rdn over 1f out: styd on* **16/1**

2436 **4** 1 **Sea Fox (IRE)**[14] 7148 2-9-0 106 (t) AdamKirby 9 97
(David Evans) *led tl over 1f out: one pce* **10/1**

3405 **5** nk **Silver Line (IRE)**[14] 7155 2-9-0 103 FrederikTylicki 12 97
(Saeed bin Suroor) *bmpd s: plld hrd in rr: rdn and hdwy over 1f out: nrest at fin* **8/1**[3]

1 **6** 1/2 **Sultan Baybars**[31] 6671 2-9-0 0 [1] HarryBentley 15 95
(Roger Varian) *stdd in rr s: drvn along over 2f out: hdwy over 1f out: styd on same pce fnl f* **25/1**

12 **7** 3/4 **Eaton Square**[38] 6481 2-9-0 0 (p) FrankieDettori 5 94
(John Gosden) *prom: hrd rdn over 1f out: no ex fnl f* **6/1**[2]

1 **8** 2 1/2 **The Grape Escape (IRE)**[43] 6297 2-9-0 0 SeanLevey 3 87
(Richard Hannon) *hld up in tch: effrt over 2f out: hrd rdn and wknd over 1f out* **12/1**

16 **9** 2 1/2 **Lost At Sea**[14] 7155 2-9-0 0 JoeyHaynes 11 81
(K R Burke) *bmpd s: sn in midfield: rdn and dropped to rr 1/2-way: passed btn horses ins fnl f* **12/1**

1 **10** 3/4 **Musawaat**[36] 6542 2-9-0 0 DaneO'Neill 7 79
(Charles Hills) *mid-div: pushed along after 3f: wknd wl over 1f out: eased whn wl btn ins fnl f* **14/1**

1 **11** 3 1/2 **Gold Award (IRE)**[13] 7184 2-9-0 75 GrahamLee 4 70
(Mick Channon) *sn drvn along in rr* **33/1**

12 **12** 3 **Executive Force**[15] 7130 2-9-0 0 PatCosgrave 6 63
(William Haggas) *prom: drvn to chal over 2f out: wknd wl over 1f out: eased whn wl btn ins fnl f* **11/4**[1]

521 **13** 2 3/4 **City Of Joy**[21] 6952 2-9-0 84 PatSmullen 1 56
(Sir Michael Stoute) *bhd: sme hdwy 3f out: wknd over 2f out* **10/1**

1m 27.48s (1.78) **Going Correction** +0.325s/f (Good) **13** Ran SP% **115.6**
Speed ratings (Par 105): **102,99,99,98,97 97,96,93,90,89 85,82,79**
CSF £298.55 TOTE £21.00: £5.20, £5.70, £4.90; EX 539.30 Trifecta £1861.70 Part won..
Owner R Roberts **Bred** Ballykilbride Stud **Trained** Kimpton, Hants

FOCUS
A competitive Group 3 won by the only gelding in the line-up. Three of the first four had finished down the field in the Autumn Stakes last time out so it's hard to get too enthusiastic about the form. The form is rated roughly to the race par of the last right seasons.

7545 WORTHINGTON'S OCSL STKS (REGISTERED AS THE ST SIMON) (GROUP 3) 1m 4f 5y
2:20 (2:21) (Class 1) 3-Y-O+
£34,026 (£12,900; £6,456; £3,216; £1,614; £810) **Stalls** Centre

Form RPR

0225 **1** **Duretto**[21] 6940 4-9-4 100 GrahamLee 6 111
(Andrew Balding) *hld up in midfield: hdwy 2f out: styd on to ld wl ins fnl f* **20/1**

-131 **2** 1/2 **Mountain Bell**[42] 6321 3-8-8 100 OisinMurphy 10 107
(Ralph Beckett) *hld up in rr: gd hdwy 2f out: str chal ins fnl f: r.o* **9/1**

3113 **3** ¾ **Kings Fete**[21] 6940 5-9-7 112 PatSmullen 2 112
(Sir Michael Stoute) *prom: led over 3f out: hrd rdn and hdd wl ins fnl f: kpt on* **6/1**[3]

2656 **4** 2¼ **Sumbal (IRE)**[21] 6940 4-9-4 110 HarryBentley 3 105
(David Simcock) *chsd ldrs: drvn to dispute 2nd over 1f out: one pce* **12/1**

3664 **5** 1 **Western Hymn**[21] 6940 5-9-4 113 RobertHavlin 8 104
(John Gosden) *towards rr tl rdn and styd on fnl 2f* **8/1**

3141 **6** 2¼ **Frontiersman**[30] 6709 3-8-11 101 JamesDoyle 15 100
(Charlie Appleby) *prom tl no ex ins fnl f* **7/2**[1]

10 **7** 3¼ **Frosty Berry**[126] 3387 7-9-1 103 ShaneGray 5 92
(Ed de Giles) *stdd in rr s: sme hdwy 3f out: no further prog* **50/1**

5522 **8** 3 **Lady Of Camelot (IRE)**[15] 7119 4-9-1 104 NickyMackay 4 87
(John Gosden) *in tch: chal 3f out: hrd rdn and btn 2f out* **14/1**

2301 **9** 4½ **Twitch (IRE)**[10] 7271 4-9-1 100 (p) PatCosgrave 14 80
(Hugo Palmer) *towards rr: rdn and sme hdwy 3f out: no imp over 1f out* **33/1**

-240 **10** 6 **Koora**[65] 5586 4-9-1 109 JamieSpencer 9 70
(Luca Cumani) *bhd: rdn 3f out: sme hdwy over 1f out: n.d* **11/1**

-043 **11** 3¾ **Tashaar (IRE)**[35] 6571 4-9-4 106 FrankieDettori 7 67
(Richard Hannon) *mid-div tl wknd 2f out* **12/1**

24-1 **12** ½ **Memorial Day (IRE)**[30] 6715 5-9-4 109 AdamKirby 12 67
(Saeed bin Suroor) *in tch tl wknd 2f out* **11/2**[2]

3101 **13** 3 **Quarterback (GER)**[41] 6390 4-9-7 110 (p) DaneO'Neill 11 65
(Rune Haugen) *w ldrs tl wknd qckly 3f out* **33/1**

4150 **14** 9 **Black Night (IRE)**[21] 6940 4-9-4 83 JoeyHaynes 1 47
(J Moon, Jersey) *mid-div tl hrd rdn and wknd over 2f out* **200/1**

065 **15** 2 **Bazooka (IRE)**[5] 7418 5-9-4 75 RobertWinston 13 44
(David Flood) *a bhd* **200/1**

-361 **16** 40 **Bellajeu**[24] 6885 4-9-1 79 FMBerry 16
(Ralph Beckett) *led: styd alone on far rail in st: hdd over 3f out: sn wknd: bhd and eased fnl 2f* **66/1**

2m 38.19s (2.69) **Going Correction** +0.55s/f (Yiel)
WFA 3 from 4yo+ 7lb **16** Ran SP% **118.5**
Speed ratings (Par 113): **113,112,112,110,110 108,106,104,101,97 94,94,92,86,85 58**
CSF £181.10 TOTE £25.20: £5.50, £3.00, £2.10; EX 236.40 Trifecta £4108.60 Part won..
Owner Lord Blyth **Bred** Lord Blyth **Trained** Kingsclere, Hants

FOCUS
A big field and an open-looking Group 3. It was run at a decent gallop and the field gradually drifted towards the stands' side in the straight. A surprise step forward from the winner, but no fluke.

7546 BATHWICK TYRES H'CAP 1m 2f 6y
2:50 (2:51) (Class 2) (0-105,102) 3-Y-O+ **£12,938** (£3,850; £1,924; £962) **Stalls** Centre

Form RPR

0034 **1** **What About Carlo (FR)**[35] 6573 5-9-5 **95** TomQueally 5 104
(Eve Johnson Houghton) *chsd ldrs: led 2f out: drvn out* **7/1**[3]

2021 **2** 1¾ **Blair House (IRE)**[19] 7005 3-9-1 **96** (b) JamesDoyle 10 102
(Charlie Appleby) *mid-div: hdwy 2f out: chalng whn hung lft over 1f out: kpt on same pce* **4/1**[2]

0465 **3** ½ **Not So Sleepy**[42] 6321 4-9-10 **100** (t[1]) AdamKirby 9 105
(Hughie Morrison) *stdd in rr s: rdn and hdwy 2f out: styd on wl fnl f* **22/1**

1053 **4** shd **Imperial Aviator**[35] 6573 3-9-4 **99** OisinMurphy 2 104
(Roger Charlton) *prom: chalng whn carried lft over 1f out: one pce fnl f* **9/4**[1]

001 **5** shd **Storm Rock**[24] 6884 4-9-2 **92** HarryBentley 11 96
(Harry Dunlop) *in tch: drvn to chse ldrs 2f out: styd on* **9/1**

4300 **6** ¾ **Awake My Soul (IRE)**[44] 6261 7-9-3 **93** JamesSullivan 4 96
(Tom Tate) *bhd: rdn over 3f out: gd late hdwy* **33/1**

-350 **7** 1½ **Special Season**[154] 2473 3-8-12 **93** JamieSpencer 3 93
(William Haggas) *mid-div: rdn over 2f out: styd on same pce* **7/1**[3]

0000 **8** shd **Green Light**[12] 7215 5-9-0 **90** (b) FMBerry 8 90
(Ralph Beckett) *towards rr: drvn along and sme hdwy 2f out: nvr able to chal* **25/1**

6-00 **9** 2¼ **Sixth Sense (IRE)**[28] 6778 3-8-9 **90** PaulMulrennan 13 86
(Mark Johnston) *trckd ldr: led 3f out tl 2f out: wknd over 1f out* **33/1**

011 **10** 1¾ **Lord Ben Stack (IRE)**[28] 6775 4-9-7 **102** CliffordLee[(5)] 6 94
(K R Burke) *led tl 3f out: hrd rdn and wknd over 1f out* **8/1**

0200 **11** 2 **Gratzie**[8] 7316 5-8-11 **87** GrahamLee 1 75
(Mick Channon) *mid-div: hrd rdn 2f out: wknd over 1f out* **25/1**

0210 **12** 5 **Examiner (IRE)**[28] 6786 5-9-4 **94** SeanLevey 12 73
(Stuart Williams) *mid-div: rdn 3f out: wknd wl over 1f out* **25/1**

00 **13** 9 **Slowfoot (GER)**[49] 6142 8-9-0 **90** TimmyMurphy 7 52
(Jim Best) *a bhd: no ch fnl 3f* **100/1**

0600 **14** 1¾ **Balmoral Castle**[15] 7121 7-8-8 **91** Pierre-LouisJamin[(7)] 14 50
(Jonathan Portman) *prom tl wknd qckly over 2f out* **50/1**

2m 12.04s (3.24) **Going Correction** +0.55s/f (Yiel)
WFA 3 from 4yo+ 5lb **14** Ran SP% **121.6**
Speed ratings (Par 109): **109,107,107,107,107 106,105,105,103,101 100,96,89,87**
CSF £32.42 CT £603.27 TOTE £9.00: £2.30, £1.70, £5.90; EX 39.40 Trifecta £779.50.
Owner Anthony Pye-Jeary **Bred** Earl Haras Du Logis & J Ince **Trained** Blewbury, Oxon

FOCUS
A good handicap and again it looked a bit of an advantage to challenge centre to near side in the straight. The winner is rated back to his best.

7547 JLT STKS (REGISTERED AS THE RADLEY STAKES) (LISTED RACE) (FILLIES) 7f (S)
3:20 (3:22) (Class 1) 2-Y-O
£17,013 (£6,450; £3,228; £1,608; £807; £405) **Stalls** Centre

Form RPR

1 **1** **Cristal Fizz (IRE)**[50] 6071 2-9-0 0 FrankieDettori 4 100+
(William Haggas) *hld up towards rr: hdwy over 1f out: pushed along to ld fnl 50yds: comf* **4/1**[2]

1142 **2** nk **Glitter Girl**[15] 7114 2-9-0 101 PatCosgrave 3 99
(William Haggas) *travelled wl in midfield: smooth hdwy 2f out: led over 1f out: hrd rdn and hdd fnl 50yds: kpt on* **6/4**[1]

4110 **3** 2¼ **Pichola Dance (IRE)**[15] 7114 2-9-0 84 HarryBentley 11 93
(Roger Varian) *prom: led 2f out tl over 1f out: no ex ins fnl f* **25/1**

1 **4** nk **Castleacre**[22] 6925 2-9-0 0 JamieSpencer 7 93
(Hugo Palmer) *stdd s: plld hrd towards rr: hdwy over 1f out: r.o* **12/1**

1021 **5** 2¼ **Soul Silver (IRE)**[50] 6088 2-9-0 87 OisinMurphy 1 87
(David Simcock) *bhd: rdn 3f out: nrest at fin* **11/1**

21 **6** 1¾ **Peak Princess (IRE)**[56] 5861 2-9-0 80 SeanLevey 6 83
(Richard Hannon) *a abt same pl: hrd rdn and outpcd fnl 2f* **10/1**

1153 **7** ¾ **Rajar**[53] 5998 2-9-0 90 KieranO'Neill 8 81
(Richard Hannon) *plld hrd: trckd ldrs: rdn to chal 2f out: wknd over 1f out* **10/1**

10 **8** 1¼ **Emmie (IRE)**[63] 5703 2-9-0 80 PatSmullen 2 78
(Harry Dunlop) *towards rr: rdn over 2f out: nvr nr ldrs* **20/1**

5102 **9** 3¾ **Poet's Princess**[36] 6536 2-9-0 84 AdamKirby 5 68
(Hughie Morrison) *led tl 2f out: wknd over 1f out* **9/1**[3]

30 **10** 1½ **Vigee Le Brun (IRE)**[15] 7118 2-9-0 0 TomQueally 10 65+
(Brian Meehan) *rrd at s and missed break: rdn 3f out: a bhd* **66/1**

1003 **11** hd **Nasimi**[50] 6088 2-9-0 86 [1] JamesDoyle 9 64
(Charlie Appleby) *prom tl wknd wl over 1f out* **16/1**

1m 27.42s (1.72) **Going Correction** +0.325s/f (Good) **11** Ran SP% **120.2**
Speed ratings (Par 100): **103,102,100,99,97 95,94,92,88,86 86**
CSF £10.37 TOTE £4.90: £1.90, £1.10, £7.20; EX 10.10 Trifecta £136.70.
Owner Sheikh Juma Dalmook Al Maktoum **Bred** Norelands Bloodstock **Trained** Newmarket, Suffolk

FOCUS
An ordinary Listed race, and a one-two for William Haggas, but not in the order the market predicted. The form is well up to scratch for the race.

7548 CONUNDRUM HR CONSULTING EBF STALLIONS MAIDEN FILLIES' STKS (PLUS 10 RACE) (DIV II) 1m (S)
3:55 (3:57) (Class 4) 2-Y-O **£5,175** (£1,540; £769; £384) **Stalls** Centre

Form RPR

1 **Di Alta (IRE)** 2-9-0 0 [1] ThomasBrown 3 76+
(Ed Walker) *hld up: hdwy to ld over 1f out: drvn out* **20/1**

6 **2** nk **Dal Riata (IRE)**[8] 7329 2-9-0 0 DaneO'Neill 5 75
(Mark Johnston) *t.k.h: led tl over 1f out: kpt on wl* **16/1**

3 hd **Dynamic** 2-9-0 0 PatCosgrave 2 75+
(William Haggas) *hld up in rr: rapid hdwy over 1f out: pressed ldrs ins fnl f: r.o* **9/4**[1]

4 ½ **African Beat (IRE)** 2-9-0 0 JamesDoyle 8 74+
(John Gosden) *dwlt: sn in tch: rdn to chse ldrs over 1f out: styd on* **9/4**[1]

5 1¾ **Pondering** 2-9-0 0 CharlesBishop 6 70
(Eve Johnson Houghton) *missed break and rdn at s: towards rr tl styd on fr over 1f out* **25/1**

6 ½ **Music Lesson** 2-9-0 0 RobertHavlin 7 69
(Hughie Morrison) *chsd ldrs: rdn to chal wl over 1f out: no ex ins fnl f* **20/1**

7 3 **Trilliant (IRE)** 2-9-0 0 ShaneKelly 4 62
(David Lanigan) *chsd ldrs: rdn along fr 1/2-way: wknd 2f out* **10/1**[3]

04 **8** nk **Haraka (IRE)**[12] 7210 2-9-0 0 FMBerry 10 62
(Ralph Beckett) *prom tl wknd 1f out* **7/2**[2]

0 **9** 17 **Haldaw**[15] 7107 2-9-0 0 GrahamLee 1 24
(Mick Channon) *towards rr: sme hdwy over 2f out: sn rdn and wknd* **33/1**

0 **10** 14 **Sallee**[19] 7012 2-8-9 0 CiaranMckee[(5)] 9
(Adrian Wintle) *prom tl wknd qckly over 2f out* **200/1**

1m 43.68s (3.98) **Going Correction** +0.325s/f (Good) **10** Ran SP% **115.5**
Speed ratings (Par 94): **93,92,92,92,90 89,86,86,69,55**
CSF £276.57 TOTE £25.80: £4.70, £3.20, £1.20; EX 241.80 Trifecta £902.30.
Owner Robert Ng **Bred** Robert Ng **Trained** Upper Lambourn, Berks

FOCUS
There was a bunched finish to this maiden. It was the slower of the two divisions by 1.9sec and the form is rated towards the bottom end of the race average.

7549 SIR GERALD WHENT MEMORIAL NURSERY H'CAP 6f 8y
4:30 (4:31) (Class 3) (0-95,87) 2-Y-O **£6,469** (£1,925; £962; £481) **Stalls** Centre

Form RPR

1324 **1** **Fields Of Song (IRE)**[13] 7185 2-8-10 **76** ShaneGray 2 80
(Kevin Ryan) *prom: led over 1f out: drvn out* **11/2**[3]

5040 **2** nk **Letmestopyouthere (IRE)**[15] 7120 2-8-9 **80** CliffordLee[(5)] 11 83
(David Evans) *in tch: rdn to chse ldrs over 1f out: drvn nrly level ins fnl f: r.o* **7/1**

6040 **3** nk **Jet Setter (IRE)**[4] 7440 2-8-2 **68** NickyMackay 9 70
(Brian Meehan) *in tch: drvn to cl on ldrs 1f out: chal fnl 75 yds: r.o* **33/1**

110 **4** 1¼ **Northern Thunder (IRE)**[36] 6538 2-8-13 **79** SeanLevey 16 77
(Richard Hannon) *bmpd s: chsd ldrs: rdn to chal 2f out: one pce ins fnl f* **11/1**

431 **5** ½ **Scorching Heat**[41] 6375 2-8-10 **76** OisinMurphy 3 73
(Andrew Balding) *wnt rt s: led tl over 1f out: one pce* **5/1**[2]

2400 **6** ½ **Admiralty Arch**[31] 6664 2-9-0 **85** HollieDoyle[(5)] 5 80
(Richard Hannon) *hmpd s: towards rr tl rdn and styd on fnl 2f* **16/1**

0160 **7** ¾ **Kings Heart (IRE)**[12] 7228 2-8-0 **66** RyanPowell 15 59
(Mark Usher) *bmpd s: bhd: sme hdwy in midfield whn nt clr run over 1f out: fin wl* **33/1**

3515 **8** 1½ **Procurator (IRE)**[13] 7185 2-9-2 **82** JamesDoyle 6 71
(Richard Hannon) *bdly hmpd s: in tch tl rdn and no hdwy fnl 2f* **7/2**[1]

300 **9** 1¾ **Limelite (IRE)**[87] 4756 2-8-8 **74** KieranO'Neill 7 57
(Richard Hannon) *hmpd s: nvr trbld ldrs* **50/1**

4160 **10** 1½ **Reign On**[106] 4076 2-8-6 **72** JohnFahy 1 51
(Ralph Beckett) *in tch tl hrd rdn and wknd over 1f out* **33/1**

0630 **11** nk **Mr Hobbs**[13] 7185 2-8-4 **75** (b[1]) MitchGodwin[(5)] 8 53
(Sylvester Kirk) *w ldr tl wknd over 2f out: btn in midfield whn hung lft over 1f out* **10/1**

310 **12** 6 **The Amber Fort (USA)**[30] 6697 2-9-0 **80** RobertHavlin 13 40
(John Gosden) *rdn 1/2-way: a towards rr* **9/1**

5100 **13** 5 **Sayesse**[15] 7113 2-9-7 **87** GeorgeBaker 4 32
(Mick Channon) *outpcd: a bhd* **16/1**

0250 **14** ½ **Fair Power (IRE)**[19] 7016 2-8-6 **75** EdwardGreatrex[(3)] 12 19
(Sylvester Kirk) *in tch tl wknd over 2f out* **14/1**

5000 **15** 11 **Stringybark Creek**[11] 7258 2-8-9 **75** GrahamLee 14
(Mick Channon) *a towards rr: wl bhd fr 1/2-way* **66/1**

1m 14.48s (1.48) **Going Correction** +0.325s/f (Good) **15** Ran SP% **124.9**
Speed ratings (Par 99): **103,102,102,100,99 99,98,96,93,91 91,83,76,76,61**
CSF £43.75 CT £1223.15 TOTE £6.00: £1.80, £3.00, £11.20; EX 61.30 Trifecta £1480.00 Part won..
Owner Sheikh Juma Dalmook Al Maktoum **Bred** Ballyreddin Stud **Trained** Hambleton, N Yorks
■ Stewards' Enquiry : Shane Gray 5-day ban (5th & 7-10th Nov): careless riding

FOCUS
A competitive late-season nursery, rated around those finishing close up.

7550 WORTHINGTON'S "THE RUSHTON AND BRIDGE FAMILY TOGETHER" EBF STALLIONS FILLIES' H'CAP 7f (S)
5:05 (5:05) (Class 3) (0-95,95) 3-Y-O+ **£8,733** (£2,598; £1,298; £649) **Stalls** Centre

Form RPR

3600 **1** **Dawaa**[28] 6764 3-9-2 **92** PaulMulrennan 3 99
(Mark Johnston) *w ldr: led 1/2-way: hrd rdn over 1f out: styd on wl* **12/1**

1000 **2** 2 **Links Drive Lady**[13] 7186 8-8-7 **84** JackDuern[(3)] 1 87
(Dean Ivory) *chsd ldrs: wnt 2nd over 1f out: no imp* **25/1**

0105 **3** 1 ¾ **Iconic (IRE)**[30] 6710 4-8-8 **82**.......... OisinMurphy 6 80
(Henry Candy) *led tl 1/2-way: no ex fnl f* **15/2**[3]
4543 **4** 3 **Rebel Surge (IRE)**[42] 6340 3-8-6 **85**..........[1] EdwardGreatrex[(3)] 8 74
(Richard Spencer) *stdd s: hld up in rr: rdn and hdwy over 1f out: nvr rchd ldrs* **10/1**
3111 **5** 1 ¾ **Aflame**[35] 6576 3-8-12 **88**.......... PatSmullen 7 73
(Sir Michael Stoute) *prom: hrd rdn 2f out: wknd over 1f out* **2/1**[1]
3006 **6** 6 **Alqubbah (IRE)**[33] 6627 3-9-1 **91**..........[1] DaneO'Neill 2 60
(Ed Dunlop) *dwlt: sn chsng ldrs: hrd rdn and wknd over 1f out* **8/1**
41 **7** 11 **Perfectly Spirited**[21] 6960 3-8-5 **81** oh3.......... NickyMackay 5 22
(John Gosden) *stdd s: hld up in tch: wknd 2f out* **20/1**
4162 **8** ¾ **Clear Water (IRE)**[21] 6962 3-9-3 **93**.......... JamesDoyle 10 32
(Saeed bin Suroor) *mid-div tl wknd 2f out* **10/3**[2]
2444 **9** 3 **Dutch Mist**[28] 6770 3-8-9 **85**..........(v) ShaneGray 9 16
(Kevin Ryan) *a towards rr: n.d fnl 2f* **16/1**
-621 **10** 7 **Sunset Dream (IRE)**[60] 5735 3-8-5 **81** oh3.......... KieranO'Neill 11
(Richard Hannon) *wnt rt s: outpcd: a bhd* **10/1**

1m 27.52s (1.82) **Going Correction** +0.325s/f (Good)
WFA 3 from 4yo+ 2lb **10** Ran SP% **119.7**
Speed ratings (Par 104): **102,99,97,94,92 85,72,72,68,60**
CSF £275.67 CT £2400.96 TOTE £16.20: £3.30, £7.00, £2.30; EX 295.80 Trifecta £1056.70.
Owner Hamdan Al Maktoum **Bred** Shadwell Estate Company Limited **Trained** Middleham Moor, N Yorks

FOCUS
Few got into this, the pace holding up well and the early leaders finishing first and third.
T/Plt: £1,034.30 to a £1 stake. Pool of £91247.97 - 64.40 winning tickets. T/Qpdt: £39.60 to a £1 stake. Pool of £6675.12 - 124.50 winning tickets **Lee McKenzie**

7551a (Foreign Racing) - See Raceform Interactive

7526 MOONEE VALLEY (L-H)
Saturday, October 22

OFFICIAL GOING: Turf: good to soft

7552a ANTLER LUGGAGE MOONEE VALLEY GOLD CUP (GROUP 2) (4YO+) (TURF) 1m 4f 110y
6:10 (12:00) 4-Y-O+
£94,554 (£26,732; £13,366; £6,683; £3,712; £2,970)

RPR
1 **Grand Marshal**[21] 6978 6-9-2 0..........(t) BenMelham 6 111+
(Chris Waller, Australia) **18/1**
2 ¾ **Who Shot Thebarman (NZ)**[21] 6978 8-9-0 0..........(t) HughBowman 9 108
(Chris Waller, Australia) **17/5**[2]
3 3 ½ **Pentathlon (NZ)**[20] 6994 5-8-9 0.......... LukeNolen 10 97
(John Wheeler, New Zealand) **60/1**
4 nk **Excess Knowledge**[20] 6994 6-8-11 0.......... VladDuric 2 99
(Gai Waterhouse & Adrian Bott, Australia) **11/2**
5 5 **White Dollar Sign (AUS)**[9] 5-8-9 0..........(b[1]) HollyMcKechnie 5 89
(John Thom, Australia) **150/1**
6 2 **The Bandit (JPN)**[9] 4-8-9 0..........(t) CraigNewitt 3 86
(John D Sadler, Australia) **17/1**
7 2 ¼ **Gallante (IRE)**[35] 5-9-2 0..........(t) KerrinMcEvoy 4 89
(Robert Hickmott, Australia) **14/5**[1]
8 6 **Master Zephyr**[9] 4-8-9 0..........(t) DwayneDunn 1 72
(Darren Weir, Australia) **8/1**
9 15 **Second Wave (IRE)**[88] 4731 4-8-10 0 ow1.......... JamesMcDonald 7 49
(Charlie Appleby) **18/5**[3]
10 6 **Authoritarian (AUS)**[9] 5-8-11 0..........(bt) DanielMoor 8 41
(Lee & Anthony Freedman, Australia) **30/1**

2m 41.42s (161.42) **10** Ran SP% **113.6**
Owner C C Lai **Bred** Carwell Equities Ltd **Trained** Australia

7553a WILLIAM HILL COX PLATE (GROUP 1) (3YO+) (TURF) 1m 2f 44y
7:00 (12:00) 3-Y-O+
£915,841 (£217,821; £108,910; £64,356; £54,455; £49,504)

RPR
1 **Winx (AUS)**[14] 7179 5-9-0 0.......... HughBowman 3 130
(Chris Waller, Australia) **4/5**[1]
2 8 **Hartnell**[20] 6996 5-9-4 0.......... JamesMcDonald 7 118
(J O'Shea, Australia) **4/1**[2]
3 ¾ **Yankee Rose (AUS)**[14] 7173 3-7-7 0.......... DeanYendall 1 108
(David Vandyke, Australia) **12/1**[3]
4 1 **Vadamos (FR)**[41] 6394 5-9-4 0.......... MarkZahra 2 115+
(A Fabre, France) **20/1**
5 ¾ **Awesome Rock (AUS)**[14] 7182 5-9-4 0..........(t) StephenBaster 5 113
(Leon & Troy Corstens, Australia) **100/1**
6 ½ **Happy Clapper (AUS)**[21] 6977 6-9-4 0..........(p) BrentonAvdulla 4 112
(Patrick Webster, Australia) **50/1**
7 1 ¼ **Lucia Valentina (NZ)**[28] 6796 6-9-0 0.......... KerrinMcEvoy 9 106
(Kris Lees, Australia) **15/1**
8 hd **Hauraki (AUS)**[21] 6977 5-9-4 0..........(t) DwayneDunn 8 109
(J O'Shea, Australia) **30/1**
9 ¾ **Black Heart Bart (AUS)**[14] 7179 6-9-4 0.......... BradRawiller 6 108
(Darren Weir, Australia) **14/1**
10 1 ¼ **Happy Trails (AUS)**[20] 6996 9-9-4 0..........(b) BenMelham 10 105
(Paul Beshara, Australia) **100/1**

2m 6.35s (126.35)
WFA 3 from 5yo+ 5lb **10** Ran SP% **108.1**
Owner Magic Bloodstock Racing, R G Treweeke & Mrs D N Ke **Bred** Fairway Thoroughbreds **Trained** Australia

FOCUS
This had the look of a really classy renewal, but the winner blew them away to show once more she is something really special. The pace set by the fourth was decent, so the form is reliable, but the 5th and 6th limit the level.

7554 - (Foreign Racing) - See Raceform Interactive

7400 SAN SIRO (R-H)
Saturday, October 22

OFFICIAL GOING: Turf: good

7555a ST LEGER ITALIANO (GROUP 3) (3YO+) (TURF) 1m 6f
4:25 (12:00) 3-Y-O+ **£21,691** (£9,544; £5,205; £2,602)

RPR
1 **Dschingis Secret (GER)**[48] 6175 3-8-5 0.......... MartinSeidl 3 106
(Markus Klug, Germany) *plld hrd: restrained in 2nd: shkn up to ld wl over 2f out: drvn clr appr fnl f: styd on wl: won easing down* **19/10**[2]
2 7 **Troublemaker (ITY)** 3-8-5 0..........(b) CristianDemuro 1 96
(Stefano Botti, Italy) *w.w in midfield on inner: tk clsr order 2 1/2f out: chsd ldr wl over 1f out: kpt on fnl f: no ch w wnr* **33/4**
3 1 ¼ **Berghain (IRE)**[30] 6729 3-8-5 0.......... AlexanderPietsch 6 94
(J Hirschberger, Germany) *hld up in rr: hdwy 3f out: sn rdn chsd ldrs fr 1 1/2f out: kpt on at same pce fnl f: nvr plcd to chal* **28/1**
4 snk **Rock Of Romance (IRE)**[34] 6610 6-8-13 0.......... JozefBojko 2 93
(A Wohler, Germany) *led: hdd after 2f: trckd ldr: drvn to chal 3f out: kpt on at same pce fnl 1 1/2f* **59/10**
5 1 ½ **Always On Sunday (FR)**[28] 6-8-13 0.......... CarloFiocchi 7 91
(Radek Holcak, Czech Republic) *cl up: led after 2f: hdd wl over 2f out: grad lft bhd* **35/4**
6 hd **Tellina (SAF)**[34] 6610 7-8-13 0.......... EduardoPedroza 4 91
(A Wohler, Germany) *w.w in midfield on outer: dropped towards rr 1/2-way: rdn and effrt more than 2 1/2f out: sn btn* **37/20**[1]
7 13 **Durlindana**[13] 7198 4-8-9 0.......... FabioBranca 5 69
(Il Cavallo In Testa, Italy) *towards rr on outer: clsd 1/2-way to chse ldrs: rdn to chal 2 1/2f out: sn no further imp: dropped away fnl 1 1/2f* **39/10**[3]
P **Duca Di Mantova**[6] 7-8-13 0.......... DarioVargiu 8
(Il Cavallo In Testa, Italy) *towards rr on inner: reminders passing stables gng towards bkst: sn lost tch and p.u wl bef 1/2-way* **39/10**[3]

3m 1.2s (181.20)
WFA 3 from 4yo+ 9lb **8** Ran SP% **149.4**
WIN (incl. 1 euro stake): 2.85. PLACES: 1.77, 2.72, 6.28. DF: 18.98.
Owner Horst Pudwill **Bred** Gestut Park Wiedingen **Trained** Germany

7556 - 7557a (Foreign Racing) - See Raceform Interactive

6348 LEOPARDSTOWN (L-H)
Sunday, October 23

OFFICIAL GOING: Yielding (good to yielding in places)

7558a TRIGO STKS (LISTED RACE) 1m 2f
2:35 (2:35) 3-Y-O+
£20,606 (£6,636; £3,143; £1,397; £698; £349)

RPR
1 **Flying Fairies (IRE)**[7] 7392 3-8-11 92.......... GaryCarroll 9 102
(Joseph G Murphy, Ire) *broke wl to ld briefly tl sn settled bhd ldrs: 3rd 1/2-way: impr gng wl on outer to ld 1 1/2f out: rdn clr ent fnl f and styd on wl: comf* **11/1**
2 3 ¼ **Zawraq (IRE)**[560] 1362 4-9-7 111.......... PatSmullen 10 101+
(D K Weld, Ire) *settled in mid-div: gng wl in 7th 3f out and hdwy on outer to chse ldrs in 5th 1 1/2f out where rdn: clsd u.p into 2nd wl ins fnl f where no imp on wnr: kpt on same pce* **8/11**[1]
3 shd **Round Two (IRE)**[15] 7165 3-9-2 98.......... KevinManning 2 101
(J S Bolger, Ire) *hld up in mid-div: 5th 1/2-way: impr bhd ldrs under 2f out where sn n.m.r between horses and edgd lft: impr into 2nd u.p over 1f out: no imp on wnr wl ins fnl f where dropped to 3rd* **14/1**
4 ¾ **Ibergman (IRE)**[7] 7392 4-9-2 91.......... RonanWhelan 5 94
(Ms Sheila Lavery, Ire) *dwlt sltly and pushed along in rr early: clsr in 4th at 1/2-way: rdn bhd ldrs 1 1/2f out and wnt 3rd briefly 1f out where no imp on wnr: kpt on same pce in 4th wl ins fnl f* **25/1**
5 1 ½ **Santa Monica**[42] 6383 3-8-11 100.......... DeclanMcDonogh 1 91
(Charles O'Brien, Ire) *w.w towards rr: prog in 9th 1 1/2f out and kpt on ins fnl f into nvr nrr 5th: nvr trbld ldrs* **9/1**[3]
6 ½ **Hibiscus (IRE)**[7] 7393 3-8-11 95.......... SeamieHeffernan 3 90
(A P O'Brien, Ire) *hld up: 8th 1/2-way: tk clsr order into st and sn sltly impeded between horses: dropped to 8th ins fnl f tl kpt on again clsng stages into nvr threatening 6th* **13/2**[2]
7 1 **Stronger Than Me (IRE)**[42] 6389 8-9-7 93.......... BillyLee 4 93
(W T Farrell, Ire) *chsd ldrs early: 5th 1/2-way: rdn in 6th over 1f out and sn no imp on ldrs u.p in 5th: wknd clsng stages* **11/1**
8 ¾ **Avenante**[7] 7393 4-9-2 94.......... GaryHalpin 7 87
(John M Oxx, Ire) *cl up and sn led briefly tl settled bhd ldr: cl 2nd at 1/2-way: led over 2f out: sn rdn and hdd 1 1/2f out: wknd* **28/1**
9 1 ½ **My Brother (IRE)**[38] 6505 3-9-2 85..........(p) ChrisHayes 8 89
(Lee Smyth, Ire) *trckd ldrs tl sn led: narrow advantage at 1/2-way: rdn and hdd over 2f out: no imp on ldrs whn sn hmpd on inner under 2f out: kpt on one pce towards rr ins fnl f* **100/1**
10 ½ **Maneen**[7] 7394 3-9-2 97..........(v[1]) LeighRoche 6 88
(D K Weld, Ire) *towards rr: rdn and no imp 2f out: one pce after* **12/1**

2m 15.11s (6.91) **Going Correction** +0.80s/f (Soft)
WFA 3 from 4yo+ 5lb **10** Ran SP% **120.5**
Speed ratings: **104,101,101,100,99 99,98,97,96,96**
CSF £19.88 TOTE £14.90: £3.50, £1.02, £2.70; DF 33.10 Trifecta £1099.00.
Owner Mrs D P Magnier **Bred** Brittas Stud & Grange Stud **Trained** Fethard, Co Tipperary

FOCUS
Only two of these boasted three-figure ratings. All eyes were on \bZawraq\p who was returning from a long absence but strong in the market. The pace seemed quite generous and the winner is progressive.

7559a KILLAVULLAN STKS (GROUP 3) 7f
3:05 (3:05) 2-Y-O
£26,029 (£8,382; £3,970; £1,764; £882; £441)

RPR
1 **Making Light (IRE)**[20] 7019 2-9-0 0.......... PatSmullen 3 102
(D K Weld, Ire) *sn led briefly tl settled bhd ldrs: 3rd 1/2-way: gng wl bhd ldrs 1 1/2f out and rdn to ld narrowly ins fnl f: kpt on wl u.p to assert clsng stages* **3/1**[1]

2 *1* **Spirit Of Valor (USA)**[7] 7387 2-9-3 0.......................(t) DonnachaO'Brien 5 102
(A P O'Brien, Ire) *hld up and settled in rr after 1f: last at 1/2-way: rdn into 5th under 2f out and clsd u.p between horses into 2nd clsng stages: a hld by wnr* **7/2**[2]

3 *nk* **Taj Mahal (IRE)**[16] 7129 2-9-3 92............................(v) SeamieHeffernan 1 101
(A P O'Brien, Ire) *w ldrs and sn settled in 2nd: impr to ld narrowly 1f out tl sn hdd: no imp on wnr clsng stages where dropped to 3rd: kpt on same pce* **7/1**

4 *1/2* **Spanish Tenor (IRE)**[8] 7370 2-9-3 98...................................... BillyLee 6 100
(Timothy Doyle, Ire) *chsd ldrs: disp 4th at 1/2-way: rdn in 4th over 1f out and no imp on wnr wl ins fnl f: kpt on same pce* **11/2**[3]

5 *1 1/2* **Pipes Of Peace (IRE)**[108] 4067 2-9-3 0...............................[1] PBBeggy 9 96
(A P O'Brien, Ire) *w ldrs and sn led on outer: over 1 l clr at 1/2-way: rdn 1 1/2f out and strly pressed: hdd 1f out and no ex ins fnl 100yds where wknd into 5th* **25/1**

6 *4 1/4* **Born To Be (IRE)**[26] 6860 2-9-3 96.......................... DeclanMcDonogh 4 86
(John M Oxx, Ire) *in rr early tl settled towards rr after 1f: tk clsr order and disp 4th fr 1/2-way: rdn into st and sn no imp on ldrs u.p in 6th 1 1/2f out: one pce after* **8/1**

7 *41* **Holistic Approach (IRE)**[14] 7190 2-9-3 0..................... KevinManning 7
(J S Bolger, Ire) *chsd ldrs: pushed along in 6th after 1/2-way and no imp on ldrs into st: eased 1 1/2f out: t.o: coughing* **3/1**[1]

1m 31.15s (2.45) **Going Correction** +0.475s/f (Yiel) **7** Ran SP% **115.1**
Speed ratings: **105,103,103,102,101 96,49**
CSF £13.95 TOTE £3.20: £1.80, £1.60; DF 10.70 Trifecta £40.70.
Owner Moyglare Stud Farm **Bred** Moyglare Stud Farm Ltd **Trained** Curragh, Co Kildare

FOCUS
Not perhaps one of the stronger editions of this race, but a very satisfactory winning display by the only filly in the field.

7560 - 7562a (Foreign Racing) - See Raceform Interactive

6174 BADEN-BADEN (L-H)
Sunday, October 23

OFFICIAL GOING: Turf: soft

7563a ITTLINGEN - PREIS DER WINTERKONIGIN (GROUP 3) (2YO FILLIES) (TURF) 1m
3:10 (12:00) 2-Y-O
£44,117 (£16,911; £8,088; £4,411; £2,205; £1,470)

RPR

1 **Well Spoken (GER)** 2-9-2 0... AdriedeVries 5 103
(Markus Klug, Germany) *led: hdd bef 1/2-way: remained cl up travelling wl: regained ld appr 1 1/2f out: r.o and edgd rt thrght fnl f: jst hld on* **37/10**[1]

2 *hd* **Pemina (GER)**[29] 6797 2-9-2 0.................................. AlexanderPietsch 1 103
(J Hirschberger, Germany) *towards rr early: tk clsr order 1/2-way: hdwy over 2f out and chsd ldr appr 1f out: r.o u.p: jst failed* **111/10**

3 *4* **Arazza (GER)**[29] 6797 2-9-2 0.. FilipMinarik 4 94
(J Hirschberger, Germany) *nvr far away: rdn to chse ldrs 1 1/2f out: kpt on at same pce fnl f: wl hld by front two* **61/10**

4 *2 1/2* **Tusked Wings (IRE)** 2-9-2 0... MarcLerner 9 88
(Jean-Pierre Carvalho, Germany) *towards rr: hdwy over 2f out: styd on to chse ldrs appr fnl f: one pce u.p* **14/1**

5 *1 1/4* **Alwina (GER)** 2-9-2 0.. AntoineHamelin 12 86
(Henk Grewe, Germany) *cl up: led bef 1/2-way: drvn whn pressed 2f out: hdd 1 1/2f out: plugged on at one pce* **58/10**

6 *3* **Scapina (GER)** 2-9-2 0.. FrederikTylicki 3 79
(Henk Grewe, Germany) *chsd ldrs: cl 2nd fr 1/2-way: rdn and wknd fnl 2f* **26/5**[2]

7 *shd* **Wind Cries Mary (GER)** 2-9-2 0.................................... IanFerguson 2 79
(M Rulec, Germany) *towards rr: tk clsr order 2 1/2f out: rdn and no further imp under 2f out: sn btn* **28/1**

8 *3 1/2* **Windjammer (GER)** 2-9-2 0.. JozefBojko 8 71
(A Wohler, Germany) *racd in midfield: rdn and no prog over 2f out: sn btn* **13/1**

9 *1 1/4* **Saloon Sold (GER)**[29] 6797 2-9-2 0................................. MartinSeidl 6 68
(Markus Klug, Germany) *racd in midfield: short-lived effrt 2 1/2f out: sn wknd* **44/5**

10 *6 1/2* **Wadia (GER)** 2-9-2 0... EduardoPedroza 10 54
(A Wohler, Germany) *a towards rr: bhd fnl 2f* **92/10**

11 *3 1/2* **Frangipani (GER)** 2-9-2 0.. AndreasSuborics 11 46
(Andreas Lowe, Germany) *chsd ldrs on outer drvn 3f out: wknd wl over 1 1/2f out* **57/10**[3]

12 *13* **Night Adventure (GER)** 2-9-2 0.............................. MichaelCadeddu 7 18
(Jean-Pierre Carvalho, Germany) *w.w towards rr: rdn and btn over 2f out* **40/1**

1m 47.26s (8.15) **12** Ran SP% **129.1**
WIN (incl. 10 euro stake): 47. PLACES: 21, 30, 21. SF: 698..
Owner Gestut Rottgen **Bred** Gestut Rottgen **Trained** Germany

7564a BADEN-WURTTEMBERG-TROPHY - DEFI DU GALOP (GROUP 3) (3YO+) (TURF) 1m 2f
4:20 (12:00) 3-Y-O+ **£23,529** (£8,823; £4,411; £2,205; £1,470)

RPR

1 **Palace Prince (GER)**[20] 7028 4-8-11 0...............(p) AndreasHelfenbein 2 109
(Andreas Lowe, Germany) *chsd ldrs: disp 3rd on inner 5f out: drvn to ld 3f out: led field stands' side into st over 2f out: styd on wl u.p* **129/10**

2 *3* **Devastar (GER)**[20] 7028 4-9-2 0.. AdriedeVries 4 108
(Markus Klug, Germany) *settled in midfield: 5th and drvn 4f out: clsd to chse ldr fr 1 1/2f out: styd on u.p: nt pce to trble wnr: pair clr* **48/10**[2]

3 *6* **Star Victory (FR)**[21] 7002 5-9-0 0.............................. AnthonyCrastus 3 94
(J-L Dubord, France) *cl up: disp 3rd on outer 1 1/2f out: drvn to chsd ldrs 2f out: kpt on at one pce u.p* **47/10**[1]

4 *1/2* **Shutterbug (FR)**[21] 7002 4-9-0 0.........................(b) AntoineHamelin 8 93
(M Figge, Germany) *cl up: shkn up and led 4f out: hdd 3f out: rdn and no imp 2f out: kpt on at same pce fnl f* **6/1**[3]

5 *2 1/2* **Palang (USA)**[20] 7028 4-9-0 0.................................(b) AndreasSuborics 5 88
(Andreas Lowe, Germany) *sltly outpcd towards rr: tk clsr order bef 1/2-way: 6th and rdn 3f out: plugged on at one pce u.p* **153/10**

6 *1 3/4* **Nordico (GER)**[21] 6992 5-8-11 0...............................(p) StephenHellyn 7 82
(Mario Hofer, Germany) *towards rr: hdwy u.p over 3f out: rdn and no further imp 1f out: fdd ins fnl f* **8/1**

7 *4 1/2* **Capitano (GER)**[20] 7028 3-8-9 0.............................. AlexanderPietsch 1 76
(J Hirschberger, Germany) *led: hdd 4f out: remained cl up tl wknd u.p ins last 2f* **48/10**[2]

8 *11* **Ever Strong (GER)**[49] 8-8-11 0.. FilipMinarik 10 51
(Dr A Bolte, Germany) *towards rr: rdn and btn fr 3f out* **30/1**

9 *11* **Abendwind (GER)**[71] 5-8-11 0.. MarcLerner 6 29
(Waldemar Hickst, Germany) *prom: 6th and drvn along 3 1/2f out: sn btn: eased fnl f* **36/1**

10 *3* **Vif Monsieur (GER)**[77] 5219 6-8-11 0.......................... StefanieHofer 12 23
(Mario Hofer, Germany) *chsd ldrs: lost pl 1/2-way: wl btn fnl 2f* **143/10**

11 *3/4* **Incantator (GER)**[36] 6598 4-8-11 0..................................... JozefBojko 9 21
(A Wohler, Germany) *w.w in midfield: lost pl bef 1/2-way: nvr in contention* **119/10**

12 *hd* **Fair Mountain (GER)**[35] 6612 4-9-0 0........................ EduardoPedroza 13 24
(A Wohler, Germany) *chsd ldrs: dropped away bef 1/2-way: wl bhd fr 3f out* **61/10**

13 *1* **La Zamtoff (FR)**[126] 3454 4-8-10 0 ow2..................... WilliamsSaraiva 11 18
(C Le Lay, France) *w.w in midfield: rdn and no hdwy over 2 1/2f out: sn wknd* **243/10**

2m 12.04s (7.05)
WFA 3 from 4yo+ 5lb **13** Ran SP% **129.0**
WIN (incl. 10 euro stake): 139. PLACES: 37, 28, 21. SF: 1,179..
Owner Gestut Hony-Hof **Bred** Gestut Hony-Hof **Trained** Germany

2516 CAPANNELLE (R-H)
Sunday, October 23

OFFICIAL GOING: Turf: soft

7565a PREMIO RIBOT - MEM. LORETO LUCIANI (GROUP 3) (3YO+) (TURF) 1m
2:50 (12:00) 3-Y-O+ **£26,838** (£11,808; £6,441; £3,220)

RPR

1 **Greg Pass (IRE)**[7] 7400 4-9-3 0... DarioVargiu 3 106
(Il Cavallo In Testa, Italy) *a cl up: drvn to chal 2 1/2f out: sn rdn and led 2f out: r.o gamely u.p: jst hld on* **127/10**

2 *shd* **Basileus (IRE)**[28] 6823 3-9-1 0...................................... UmbertoRispoli 2 106
(Stefano Botti, Italy) *hld up in midfield: rdn over 2f out: styd on to chse ldrs 1 1/2f out: cl 3rd and n.m.r whn swtchd outside appr fnl f: r.o u.p: jst failed* **4/1**[2]

3 *2* **Clockwinder (IRE)**[49] 4-9-3 0..(p) FabioBranca 1 101
(Stefano Botti, Italy) *broke wl and led: sn hdd but remained cl up: rdn to chal fr 2f out and ev ch ent fnl f: no ex fnl 100yds* **162/10**

4 *2* **Priore Philip (ITY)**[350] 7767 5-9-3 0.................................. SilvanoMulas 8 97
(Stefano Botti, Italy) *settled towards rr: tk clsr order fr 1/2-way: rdn to chse ldrs 1 1/2f out: styd on same pce fnl f* **119/10**

5 *2 1/4* **Pabouche (IRE)**[35] 6611 3-8-11 0................................. AurelienLemaitre 7 87
(H-A Pantall, France) *settled bhd ldng trio: angled out and bmpd rival w 3f to go: cl 4th but hrd rdn fr 2f out: kpt on at one pce* **17/4**[3]

6 *7* **Shamalgan (FR)**[1050] 8210 9-9-3 0..................................... JiriPalik 6 75
(Artut Resulov, Czech Republic) *w.w in rr: plenty to do 1/2-way: tk clsr order 3f out: sn rdn and btn* **115/10**

7 *2 1/2* **Kaspersky (IRE)**[28] 6823 5-9-5 0.............................. CristianDemuro 5 72
(Endo Botti, Italy) *sn led: chal fr 2 1/2f out: sn rdn and hdd over 2f out: sn btn and eased ins fnl f* **11/20**[1]

8 *10* **Saint Bernard**[147] 2729 7-9-3 0..................................... SalvatoreSulas 4 47
(Simone Langiano, Italy) *hld up in fnl pair: bhd fr 3f out* **66/1**

1m 39.0s (-0.80)
WFA 3 from 4yo+ 3lb **8** Ran SP% **133.9**
WIN (incl. 10 euro stake): 13.70. PLACES: 5.24, 2.89, 5.05. DF: 30.07.
Owner Incolinx **Bred** Valdirone Soc Ag Sas Di Lualdi Lucia & C **Trained** Italy

7566a PREMIO LYDIA TESIO (GROUP 1) (3YO+ FILLIES & MARES) (TURF) 1m 2f
4:05 (12:00) 3-Y-O+ **£91,911** (£40,441; £22,058; £11,029)

RPR

1 **Sound Of Freedom (IRE)**[21] 4-9-0 0...........................(p) FabioBranca 4 107
(Stefano Botti, Italy) *a cl up: rdn to chal 2f out: disp ld 1 1/2f out and wnt on appr fnl f: styd on wl u.p last 150yds: readily* **3/1**[2]

2 *1 1/4* **Zghorta Dance (FR)**[85] 4904 3-8-10 0....................... IoritzMendizabal 8 105
(J-C Rouget, France) *w.w in midfield: drvn along and lost pl over 3f out: 10th and hrd rdn 2f out: began to stay on 1 1/2f out: r.o wl fnl f: wnt 2nd 75yds out: nt rch wnr* **69/20**

3 *1 1/2* **Laganore (IRE)**[16] 7119 4-9-0 0.. JimCrowley 11 101
(A J Martin, Ire) *w.w in last: hdwy wl over 2f out: nt clr run and sltly impeded 1 1/2f out: styd on fnl f: nvr on terms* **31/10**[3]

4 *hd* **Plein Air (IRE)**[21] 3-8-10 0... UmbertoRispoli 2 102
(Stefano Botti, Italy) *led: drvn over 2f out: hdd 1 1/2f out: kpt on gamely u.p* **3/1**[2]

5 *nse* **Persona Grata**[32] 6693 5-9-0 0.................................... CristianDemuro 9 101
(Ed Walker) *w.w bhd ldng gp: 5th and pushed along over 2 1/2f out: drvn to chal 2f out and disp ld 1 1/2f out: ev ch appr fnl f: sn hdd: styd on same pce: lost three pls fnl 75yds* **109/10**

6 *3/4* **Powder Snow (USA)**[28] 3-8-10 0.............................. AurelienLemaitre 6 100
(H-A Pantall, France) *w.w in midfield: rdn and clsd fr 2f out: 4th and styng on whn gap clsd and swtchd outside 150yds out: nt rcvr* **167/20**

7 *1* **Valuta Pregiata**[14] 7198 3-8-10 0....................................... SilvanoMulas 3 98
(Stefano Botti, Italy) *w.w towards rr of midfield: rdn and nt qckn 3f out: styd on fr over 1f out: nrest at fin* **269/10**

8 *1 1/2* **Wordless (IRE)**[14] 7198 4-9-0 0.. CarloFiocchi 5 94
(Stefano Botti, Italy) *hld up in tch: rdn to chse ldrs 2f out: wknd ins fnl f* **3/1**[2]

9 *1* **Thank You Bye Bye (FR)**[32] 6693 4-9-0 0................. GabrieleCongiu 1 92
(J-P Gauvin, France) *w.w towards rr: clsd over 2f out: kpt on at same pce fnl f* **38/1**

10 *1 1/2* **Blond Me (IRE)**[49] 6181 4-9-0 0.................................... JimmyFortune 10 89
(Andrew Balding) *w.w in fnl pair: last and rdn over 1 1/2f out: nvr in contention* **59/10**

11 8 **Sarandia (GER)**[21] 6998 3-8-10 0.................................. AndraschStarke 7 74
(P Schiergen, Germany) *cl up: rdn and nt qckn over 2f out sn btn: eased fnl f* **12/5**[1]

2m 3.7s (0.40)
WFA 3 from 4yo+ 5lb **11** Ran SP% **191.0**
win (incl. 1 euro stake); 4.02 (coupled with Plein Air & Wordless). PLACES: 2.00, 1.70, 1.60. DF: 58.58.
Owner Scuderia Effevi SRL **Bred** Razza Del Velino Srl **Trained** Italy

7567 - (Foreign Racing) - See Raceform Interactive

7264 SAINT-CLOUD (L-H)
Sunday, October 23

OFFICIAL GOING: Turf: good to soft

7568a PRIX DE FLORE (GROUP 3) (3YO+ FILLIES & MARES) (TURF) 1m 2f 110y
2:45 (2:45) 3-Y-O+ **£29,411** (£11,764; £8,823; £5,882; £2,941)

RPR

1 **Loving Things**[66] 5586 4-9-0 0.............................. ChristopheSoumillon 1 105+
(Luca Cumani) *chsd ldrs on inner: lost pl 3f out: sn rdn and angled out between horses: hdwy 2f out: led under 1 1/2f out: styd on to go clr ins fnl f: kpt up to her work: wl on top at fin* **7/1**

2 1 1/4 **Switching (USA)**[20] 7029 3-8-9 0.............................. MickaelBarzalona 3 104
(A Fabre, France) *tk a str hold: hld up in fnl trio: rowed along and hdwy on outer 2f out: 5th and styng on fr over 1f out: wnt 2nd cl home: nt trble wnr* **5/1**

3 hd **Furia Cruzada (CHI)**[30] 6752 5-9-0 0.............................. FrankieDettori 8 103
(John Gosden) *a cl up: cl 4th and pushed along 2f out: styd on to chse ldr over 1f out: styd on at same pce fnl f: lost 2nd cl home* **3/1**[2]

4 1 3/4 **Armande (IRE)**[19] 3-8-10 0 ow1.......................... Pierre-CharlesBoudot 7 101
(A Fabre, France) *hld up in rr: rdn and no imp over 2f out: styd on u.p fnl 1 1/2f: nt rch ldrs* **5/2**[1]

5 hd **Not Only Florina (IRE)**[43] 6357 3-8-9 0.............................. JulienAuge 2 100
(C Ferland, France) *settled in midfield on inner: drvn to chse ldrs 2f out: angled ins to chal wl under 1 1/2f out: kpt on at one pce* **8/1**

6 1 1/4 **Sharja Queen**[22] 6948 3-8-9 0.. AndreaAtzeni 4 97
(Roger Varian) *w.w in midfield on outer: rdn and no prog appr 2f out: kpt on u.p but nvr really in contention* **4/1**[3]

7 3/4 **Restiana (FR)**[20] 7029 3-8-9 0..............................(b) StephanePasquier 9 96
(P Sogorb, France) *dwlt and reminder s: rushed up to trck ldr after 1f: qcknd to ld over 3f out: rdn and wnt 2l clr appr 2f out: hdd under 1 1/2f out: wknd u.p fnl f* **33/1**

8 15 **Testarossa (POL)**[19] 5-9-0 0...................................... YohannBourgois 5 66
(P Sobry, France) *w.w in fnl trio: outpcd and drvn in last 3f out: lost tch over 1 1/2f out* **80/1**

9 4 1/2 **Spice Trail**[34] 3-8-9 0...(b) VincentCheminaud 6 58
(A Fabre, France) *led: hdd over 3f out: rdn and wknd appr fnl 1 1/2f* **9/1**

2m 15.58s (-4.02)
WFA 3 from 4yo+ 5lb **9** Ran SP% **128.0**
WIN (incl. 1 euro stake): 9.90. PLACES: 2.60, 1.90, 2.00. DF: 26.80. SF: 71.10.
Owner Normandie Stud Ltd **Bred** Normandie Stud Ltd **Trained** Newmarket, Suffolk

7569a PRIX ROYAL-OAK (GROUP 1) (3YO+) (TURF) 1m 7f 110y
3:25 (3:25) 3-Y-O+ **£147,051** (£58,830; £29,415; £14,694; £7,360)

RPR

1 **Vazirabad (FR)**[22] 6974 4-9-4 0.......................... ChristopheSoumillon 15 114+
(A De Royer-Dupre, France) *w.w towards rr: pushed along to cl more than 2f out: drvn to chse ldrs 1 1/2f out: sn rdn and led appr fnl f: styd on wl to go clr: won easing down* **13/8**[1]

2 1 3/4 **Endless Time (IRE)**[42] 6393 4-9-1 0.............................. WilliamBuick 13 109
(Charlie Appleby) *w.w in tch: rdn to ld 1 1/2f out: hdd appr fnl f: styd on u.p but no match for wnr* **12/1**

3 1/2 **Siljan's Saga (FR)**[21] 6989 6-9-1 0...................... Pierre-CharlesBoudot 6 108+
(J-P Gauvin, France) *w.w in midfield: c wd into st over 2 1/2f out: sn rdn and tk clsr order 2f out: wnt 4th over 1f out: styd on u.p fnl f: nvr on terms* **10/3**[2]

4 nk **Mille Et Mille**[22] 6974 6-9-4 0....................................... ThierryThulliez 11 111
(C Lerner, France) *a cl up: led over 3f out: rdn and rallied whn chal in home st: hdd 1 1/2f out: styd on same pce* **33/1**

5 1/2 **Sky Hunter**[32] 6666 6-9-4 0.. OlivierPeslier 7 110
(Saeed bin Suroor) *a.p: drvn to chse ldrs over 2 1/2f out: sltly outpcd and rdn 2f out: kpt on again u.p fr wl over 1f out* **13/2**[3]

6 shd **Quick Jack (IRE)**[43] 6350 7-9-4 0.. FMBerry 12 110
(A J Martin, Ire) *hld up towards rr: shkn up 2 1/2f out: 11th and styng on 1 1/2f out: kpt on fnl f: nvr nrr* **22/1**

7 3/4 **Slatina (IRE)**[39] 4-9-1 0..(p) TheoBachelot 5 106
(S Wattel, France) *racd in midfield: rdn and no real imp over 1 1/2f out: styd on at same pce fnl f* **40/1**

8 snk **Pallasator**[65] 5612 7-9-4 0.. OisinMurphy 10 109
(Sir Mark Prescott Bt) *w.w in fnl pair: hdwy wl over 1 1/2f out: kpt on ins fnl f: nt pce to get on terms* **8/1**

9 1 3/4 **Litigant**[8] 7349 8-9-4 0.. GeorgeBaker 8 107
(Joseph Tuite) *settled towards rr: prog u.p 2f out: sn btn and wl hld fnl f* **20/1**

10 2 **Settler's Son (IRE)**[18] 7088 5-9-4 0........................... SebastienMaillot 3 104
(J Michal, France) *w.w in midfield: clsd to chal 2 1/2f out: sn rdn and no ex: wknd wl over 1f out* **66/1**

11 1 1/4 **Penglai Pavilion (USA)**[36] 6582 6-9-4 0......................... JamesDoyle 14 103
(Charlie Appleby) *cl up: 4th and drvn along over 3f out: rdn and btn 2f out: plugged on at one pce* **16/1**

12 3/4 **Montaly**[50] 6118 5-9-4 0.. MaximeGuyon 1 102
(Andrew Balding) *led: hdd after 2 1/2f: remained cl up: rdn and rallied 2 1/2f out: wknd fnl 1 1/2f* **33/1**

13 10 **Candarliya (FR)**[42] 6393 4-9-1 0... AlexisBadel 4 87
(A De Royer-Dupre, France) *cl up: sltly outpcd and lost pl 3f out: rdn and wknd ent last 2f* **16/1**

14 6 **Justice Belle (IRE)**[31] 6708 4-9-1 0............................... FrankieDettori 2 80
(Ed Walker) *led after 2 1/2f: hdd over 3f out: wknd ins fnl 2f* **33/1**

15 dist **Mambomiss (FR)**[45] 6273 5-9-1 0............................... FranckBlondel 9
(D De Watrigant, France) *w.w in rr: outpcd in last 3f out: t.o* **66/1**

3m 29.23s (-9.47) **15** Ran SP% **128.4**
WIN (incl. 1 euro stake): 2.80 (Vazirabad coupled with Candarliya). PLACES: 1.30, 2.90, 1.30. DF: 24.10. SF: 27.30.
Owner H H Aga Khan **Bred** S C E A Haras De Son Altesse L'Aga Khan **Trained** Chantilly, France

FOCUS
This was an incredibly competitive renewal of this long-established Group 1 for stayers. The pace was predictably good due to the big field.

7239 LEICESTER (R-H)
Monday, October 24

OFFICIAL GOING: Good (good to firm in places on straight course; good to soft in places on round course; str 8.7, rnd 7.9)
Wind: Light across Weather: Fine

7570 HAYMARKET NURSERY H'CAP (DIV I) 7f
1:40 (1:42) (Class 6) (0-65,65) 2-Y-O **£2,587** (£770; £384; £192) **Stalls** High

Form RPR

004 1 **Raj Balaraaj (GER)**[44] 6314 2-9-6 **64**.............................. SteveDrowne 10 66
(George Baker) *hld up: pushed along and hdwy 2f out: rdn to ld wl ins fnl f: styd on* **8/1**

563 2 3/4 **Imperial City (USA)**[54] 6016 2-9-7 **65**............................. GeorgeBaker 7 65
(Charles Hills) *s.i.s: hld up: swtchd lft over 2f out: hdwy u.p over 1f out: styd on to go 2nd nr fin* **3/1**[1]

0605 3 nk **Gala Celebration (IRE)**[28] 6829 2-9-4 **62**....................... MartinDwyer 9 61
(John Gallagher) *plld hrd: sn led: rdn over 1f out: hdd and unable qck wl ins fnl f* **14/1**

6540 4 1 1/2 **Fancy Day (IRE)**[25] 6898 2-9-7 **65**.................................... RobertHavlin 2 61
(Mark Johnston) *chsd ldrs: wnt 2nd over 4f out: rdn and ev ch over 1f out: styd on same pce ins fnl f* **16/1**

400 5 1 **Skilful Lord (IRE)**[41] 6439 2-8-10 **54**................................... MartinLane 4 47
(Stuart Kittow) *hld up: hdwy 1/2-way: rdn over 1f out: kpt on* **25/1**

000 6 nk **Ten In The Hat (IRE)**[16] 7142 2-8-1 **50**.......................... GeorgeWood[(5)] 8 42
(Shaun Harris) *mid-div: hdwy 4f out: rdn over 2f out: styd on same pce fnl f* **100/1**

3500 7 nk **Our Boy John (IRE)**[17] 7109 2-9-1 **59**.......................... TonyHamilton 5 51
(Richard Fahey) *prom: lost pl after 1f: styd on u.p fr over 1f out* **7/1**

0005 8 nk **Fleeting Francesca**[20] 7047 2-8-6 **53**................. JosephineGordon[(3)] 6 44
(Chris Gordon) *chsd ldrs: pushed along 1/2-way: rdn and nt clr run over 1f out: no ex wl ins fnl f* **8/1**

1100 9 3 1/2 **Madam Prancealot (IRE)**[12] 7286 2-9-3 **61**...................... AdamKirby 11 43
(David Evans) *chsd ldr over 2f: remained handy: rdn over 2f out: wknd fnl f* **4/1**[2]

5063 10 3 1/2 **Accladora**[17] 7110 2-9-5 **63**.. DaneO'Neill 1 36
(Mark Johnston) *chsd ldrs: rdn over 2f out: wknd fnl f* **13/2**[3]

0043 11 23 **Ultimat Power (IRE)**[42] 6412 2-8-1 **48**..............(b) EdwardGreatrex[(3)] 14
(Mark Hoad) *prom: racd keenly: rdn 1/2-way: hung lft and wknd over 2f out* **25/1**

1m 26.39s (0.19) **Going Correction** -0.10s/f (Good) **11** Ran SP% **114.3**
Speed ratings (Par 93): **94,93,92,91,89 89,89,88,84,80 54**
CSF £30.76 CT £333.07 TOTE £10.80: £2.80, £1.90, £4.00; EX 39.60 Trifecta £451.80.
Owner George Baker **Bred** Fair Salinia Ltd **Trained** Manton, Wilts

FOCUS
The ground had dried out slightly on both tracks with the going on the straight course good, good to firm in places, while on the round course it was good, good to soft in places. False rail from the top of the hill in the back straight all the way to the winning line, increasing race distance on the round course by about 17yds. The first division of a moderate nursery to start and they came up the middle.

7571 HAYMARKET NURSERY H'CAP (DIV II) 7f
2:10 (2:10) (Class 6) (0-65,65) 2-Y-O **£2,587** (£770; £384; £192) **Stalls** High

Form RPR

050 1 **Wily Rumpus (IRE)**[32] 6712 2-9-3 **61**............................. ThomasBrown 7 65
(Ed Walker) *hld up: hdwy 1/2-way: rdn to ld over 1f out: edgd lft ins fnl f: styd on* **10/1**

046 2 3/4 **Harry Beau**[21] 7012 2-9-3 **61**... SeanLevey 10 63
(Richard Hannon) *chsd ldrs: rdn and ev ch over 1f out: styd on* **8/1**[2]

605 3 1 **Moonstone Rock**[14] 7216 2-9-5 **63**................................... PatCosgrave 14 63
(Jim Boyle) *hld up: hdwy over 2f out: rdn over 1f out: styd on* **8/1**[2]

5335 4 1/2 **Tigerfish (IRE)**[12] 7286 2-8-4 **48**... KieranO'Neill 3 46
(William Stone) *mid-div: hdwy over 2f out: rdn over 1f out: kpt on* **17/2**[3]

0364 5 1/2 **Breaking Free**[20] 7041 2-8-10 **54**.. JackGarritty 1 51
(John Quinn) *s.i.s: hld up: hdwy u.p and nt clr run over 1f out: styd on* **10/1**

006 6 1 **Charlie Chaplin (GER)**[53] 6044 2-9-5 **63**............................. AdamKirby 5 58
(Robert Eddery) *s.i.s: hld up: rdn over 2f out: hung lft and styd on ins fnl f: nt rch ldrs* **5/1**[1]

5605 7 1 1/2 **Royal Cosmic**[17] 7110 2-9-0 **58**.. TonyHamilton 8 49
(Richard Fahey) *mid-div: lost pl over 4f out: styd on towards fin* **14/1**

0000 8 nk **Gaia Princess (IRE)**[28] 6829 2-9-7 **65**.............................. RyanMoore 4 55
(Gary Moore) *s.i.s: hld up: swtchd lft over 1f out: styd on towards fin* **10/1**

600 9 1/2 **Toy Theatre**[20] 7049 2-9-4 **62**.. DaneO'Neill 9 51
(Mark Johnston) *prom: led over 4f out: rdn and hdd over 1f out: wknd ins fnl f* **25/1**

500 10 nk **Joshlee (IRE)**[38] 6543 2-9-4 **62**... ShaneKelly 11 50
(Richard Hughes) *sn led: hdd over 4f out: remained handy: rdn over 1f out: sn edgd lft and wknd* **20/1**

044 11 hd **Misty Moo**[13] 7244 2-8-5 **54**.. HollieDoyle[(5)] 12 42
(Michael Appleby) *chsd ldrs: rdn and ev ch over 1f out: wknd ins fnl f* **10/1**

3300 12 2 3/4 **Hazell Berry (IRE)**[23] 6963 2-8-0 **47**.................... JosephineGordon[(3)] 6 28
(David Evans) *chsd ldrs: pushed along 1/2-way: wknd over 1f out* **14/1**

0545 13 2 1/2 **Incentive**[28] 6830 2-9-7 **65**... TomQueally 13 39
(Stuart Kittow) *prom: rdn over 2f out: wkng whn hmpd ins fnl f* **10/1**

0664 14 15 **Yorkshire Star (IRE)**[28] 6828 2-8-7 **51**........................(b) WilliamCarson 2
(Bill Turner) *racd alone towards far side: prom to 1/2-way: rdn: hung rt and wknd over 2f out* **33/1**

1m 25.91s (-0.29) **Going Correction** -0.10s/f (Good) **14** Ran SP% **119.8**
Speed ratings (Par 93): **97,96,95,94,93 92,91,90,90,89 89,86,83,66**
CSF £85.27 CT £698.58 TOTE £9.80: £3.40, £3.30, £3.50; EX 123.90 Trifecta £2172.30 Part won..
Owner Robert Ng **Bred** Lucky Racing Syndicate **Trained** Upper Lambourn, Berks

FOCUS
A larger number were making their nursery debut on their fourth outing than in the first division and the first three were amongst them. The action unfolded more towards the nearside and the winning time was almost half a second quicker than the first leg.

7572 GUMLEY CLAIMING STKS 7f
2:40 (2:40) (Class 6) 3-4-Y-O **£2,587** (£770; £384; £192) **Stalls** High

Form RPR
2226 **1** **Infiniti (IRE)**[3] 7513 3-7-9 60 (p) HollieDoyle(5) 1 59
(Rae Guest) *s.i.s: hld up: hdwy over 2f out: led over 1f out: sn rdn: styd on* **7/2**[2]
4600 **2** *1* **Dodgy Bob**[9] 7360 3-8-9 75 ShaneGray 4 65
(Kevin Ryan) *hld up: hdwy over 2f out: swtchd rt over 1f out: r.o* **15/2**
000 **3** *3/4* **Sir Jack**[13] 7240 3-8-8 50 ow1 AdamBeschizza 6 62
(Tony Carroll) *s.i.s: sn pushed along in rr: hdwy over 1f out: r.o* **80/1**
4304 **4** *3/4* **Lilbourne Prince (IRE)**[7] 7415 3-9-3 72 AdamKirby 7 69
(David Evans) *chsd ldrs: rdn to ld over 2f out: hung rt and hdd over 1f out: no ex wl ins fnl f* **9/2**[3]
0150 **5** *1 3/4* **Monsieur Valentine**[42] 6408 4-8-9 61 TomMarquand 12 56
(Tony Carroll) *sn pushed along in rr: r.o ins fnl f: nvr nrr* **22/1**
-440 **6** *2* **Cockney Island**[9] 7363 4-7-13 70 JosephineGordon(3) 9 43
(Philip McBride) *prom: lost pl 1/2-way: hdwy over 1f out: sn rdn: no ex ins fnl f* **8/1**
0036 **7** *nk* **Mustn't Grumble (IRE)**[19] 7069 3-8-5 61 (p) KieranO'Neill 2 47
(Ivan Furtado) *hld up: hdwy 1/2-way: rdn over 2f out: no ex ins fnl f* **16/1**
2560 **8** *5* **Spirit Of Zeb (IRE)**[18] 7094 4-9-1 78 TonyHamilton 3 43
(Richard Fahey) *prom: racd keenly: wnt 2nd over 4f out: rdn and ev ch wl over 1f out: wknd fnl f* **5/2**[1]
2104 **9** *18* **Mecca's Missus (IRE)**[35] 6631 3-8-0 61 (b) NickyMackay 5
(Michael Wigham) *led: rdn and hdd over 2f out: wknd over 1f out* **16/1**
00 **10** *7* **Sense Of Snow (IRE)**[44] 6317 3-8-4 0 (bt1) GeorgeWood(5) 11
(William Muir) *prom over 4f* **125/1**
3004 **11** *2 1/4* **Jacksonfire**[13] 7240 4-8-7 49 (p) MartinDwyer 10
(Michael Mullineaux) *chsd ldrs: rdn 1/2-way: wknd over 2f out* **33/1**
00-0 **12** *40* **Stimulator**[20] 7052 3-8-2 32 EdwardGreatrex(3) 8
(Chris Gordon) *plld hrd and prom: wknd over 2f out: eased* **125/1**

1m 25.22s (-0.98) **Going Correction** -0.10s/f (Good)
WFA 3 from 4yo 2lb **12** Ran SP% **113.7**
Speed ratings (Par 101): **101,99,99,98,96 93,93,87,67,59 56,10**
CSF £27.73 TOTE £4.20: £1.60, £2.90, £10.70; EX 30.50 Trifecta £2208.50.Infiniti was claimed by Barry Leavy for £6,000
Owner Derek J Willis **Bred** Allevamento Ficomontanino Srl **Trained** Newmarket, Suffolk

FOCUS
A moderate claimer. The runner-up helps guide the level, along with the winner.

7573 SIS H'CAP 1m 60y
3:15 (3:15) (Class 2) (0-105,100) 3-Y-O+ **£12,938** (£3,850; £1,924; £962) **Stalls** Low

Form RPR
-143 **1** **El Vip (IRE)**[32] 6715 3-8-12 89 PatCosgrave 6 98+
(Luca Cumani) *hld up: rdn: swtchd lft and hdwy over 1f out: r.o to ld wl ins fnl f* **7/2**[1]
0210 **2** *1 1/2* **God Willing**[17] 7121 5-9-4 92 DanielTudhope 3 98
(Declan Carroll) *hld up in tch: rdn over 1f out: r.o* **4/1**[2]
3214 **3** *1/2* **Father Bertie**[10] 7316 4-9-4 92 (tp) DavidAllan 8 97
(Tim Easterby) *chsd ldr tl led over 1f out: sn rdn: hdd and unable qck wl ins fnl f* **7/1**
1320 **4** *3/4* **Knight Owl**[30] 6786 6-9-1 94 GeorgeWood(5) 2 97
(James Fanshawe) *chsd ldrs: rdn over 2f out: ev ch over 1f out: no ex towards fin* **8/1**
5016 **5** *2 3/4* **Highland Colori (IRE)**[9] 7354 8-9-12 100 (b) LiamKeniry 9 97
(Andrew Balding) *hld up: rdn over 2f out: r.o ins fnl f: nvr nrr* **8/1**
5424 **6** *3/4* **Beach Bar (IRE)**[26] 6884 5-9-4 95 JosephineGordon(3) 4 90
(Brendan Powell) *led: qcknd over 3f out: rdn and hdd over 1f out: wknd ins fnl f* **11/2**[3]
/050 **7** *1 3/4* **Quixote (GER)**[45] 6298 6-9-7 95 AdamKirby 7 86
(Tony Carroll) *hld up: rdn over 2f out: nvr on terms* **20/1**
4056 **8** *1/2* **Fox Trotter (IRE)**[10] 7316 4-9-2 90 TomQueally 1 80
(Brian Meehan) *s.i.s: hld up: rdn over 3f out: n.d* **12/1**
0603 **9** *1/2* **Finn Class (IRE)**[39] 6500 5-8-12 86 (p) SeanLevey 5 75
(Michael Dods) *chsd ldrs: rdn over 2f out: wknd over 1f out* **14/1**
1000 **10** *38* **Pintura**[47] 6225 9-9-2 90 (b) FrederikTylicki 10
(Alistair Whillans) *prom: rdn over 2f out: sn wknd* **40/1**

1m 45.08s (-0.02) **Going Correction** +0.225s/f (Good)
WFA 3 from 4yo+ 3lb **10** Ran SP% **113.9**
Speed ratings (Par 109): **109,107,107,106,103 102,101,100,100,62**
CSF £16.87 CT £93.45 TOTE £4.50: £2.00, £1.60, £1.90; EX 19.80 Trifecta £120.20.
Owner Al Shaqab Racing **Bred** Gestut Wittekindshof **Trained** Newmarket, Suffolk

FOCUS
Rail movement increased race distance by about 17yds. A decent handicap run at a good pace and form to view positively. It's been rated around the third.

7574 BRITISH STALLION STUDS EBF MAIDEN STKS (PLUS 10 RACE) 6f
3:45 (3:46) (Class 4) 2-Y-O **£6,469** (£1,925; £962; £481) **Stalls** High

Form RPR
23 **1** **Cuttin' Edge (IRE)**[47] 6224 2-9-5 0 GeorgeBaker 1 79
(William Muir) *sn prom: shkn up to ld over 1f out: r.o* **5/1**[2]
3233 **2** *1 1/2* **Stanhope**[45] 6295 2-9-5 77 PatCosgrave 13 75
(Mick Quinn) *chsd ldrs: nt clr run and swtchd rt over 1f out: rdn and edgd lft ins fnl f: r.o* **7/1**
44 **3** *1* **Dimitre**[38] 6543 2-9-5 0 FergusSweeney 8 72
(Henry Candy) *prom: racd keenly: jnd ldr 1/2-way: led wl over 1f out: sn rdn and hdd: no ex wl ins fnl f* **13/2**[3]
4 *nk* **Crafty Madam (IRE)** 2-9-0 0 AdamKirby 5 66+
(Clive Cox) *s.i.s: hld up: shkn up and hdwy over 1f out: r.o* **20/1**
42 **5** *3/4* **Contentment**[53] 6061 2-9-0 0 RyanMoore 12 63
(William Haggas) *led: rdn and hdd wl over 1f out: no ex ins fnl f* **6/4**[1]
0 **6** *3/4* **Mulzim**[16] 7157 2-9-5 0 DaneO'Neill 4 66
(Ed Dunlop) *hld up: hdwy over 3f out: rdn over 2f out: styd on same pce fnl f* **11/1**
032 **7** *1/2* **Secret Agent**[14] 7224 2-9-5 73 MartinDwyer 11 65
(William Muir) *racd keenly: w ldr over 2f: remained handy: rdn and ev ch over 1f out: styng on same pce whn nt clr run ins fnl f* **14/1**
00 **8** *4* **Coachella (IRE)**[19] 7071 2-9-0 0 CallumShepherd(5) 3 53
(Ed de Giles) *hld up: shkn up over 2f out: nvr on terms* **200/1**
344 **9** *hd* **No Not Again (IRE)**[15] 7184 2-9-5 73 SeanLevey 7 52
(Richard Hannon) *prom: rdn over 2f out: wknd fnl f* **9/1**
00 **10** *1/2* **Still Waiting**[77] 5244 2-9-5 0 RobertHavlin 2 51
(William Jarvis) *prom: hung rt and lost pl over 3f out: n.d after* **80/1**
11 *2 1/4* **Harvest Ranger** 2-9-2 0 AlistairRawlinson(3) 9 44
(Michael Appleby) *sn pushed along in rr: wknd over 2f out* **100/1**
0 **12** *1 1/4* **Angelical Eve (IRE)**[12] 7269 2-9-0 0 LiamKeniry 10 35
(George Baker) *hld up: hdwy over 3f out: rdn over 2f out: sn wknd* **66/1**

1m 12.83s (-0.17) **Going Correction** -0.10s/f (Good) **12** Ran SP% **116.5**
Speed ratings (Par 97): **97,95,93,93,92 91,90,85,85,84 81,79**
CSF £38.36 TOTE £5.20: £1.50, £2.20, £2.00; EX 43.30 Trifecta £210.10.
Owner Purple & Lilac Racing **Bred** P Hyland & C & J McHale **Trained** Lambourn, Berks

FOCUS
Just an ordinary maiden, but the winner was well backed and quickened up to win like a nice type. It's been rated around the first three.

7575 SIR GORDON RICHARDS H'CAP 1m 3f 183y
4:20 (4:20) (Class 2) (0-110,102) 3-Y-O+ **£18,903** (£5,658; £2,829; £1,416; £705) **Stalls** Low

Form RPR
0003 **1** **Tawdeea**[20] 7058 4-9-12 102 [1] DanielTudhope 4 109
(David O'Meara) *chsd ldrs: rdn to ld ins fnl f: styd on* **2/1**[1]
3004 **2** *1/2* **John Reel (FR)**[44] 6321 7-8-11 94 KatherineGlenister(7) 7 100
(David Evans) *racd keenly: trckd ldr: hung rt and led over 1f out: hdd ins fnl f: kpt on* **18/1**
0026 **3** *2 1/4* **Fattsota**[16] 7154 8-9-5 95 AdamKirby 6 97
(David O'Meara) *led: rdn over 2f out: hdd over 1f out: styd on same pce ins fnl f* **10/1**
2135 **4** *3/4* **Buonarroti (IRE)**[30] 6781 5-9-0 90 RyanMoore 2 91
(Declan Carroll) *hld up: shkn up over 2f out: styd on ins fnl f: nt trble ldrs* **10/3**[2]
202- **5** *1/2* **Dashing Star**[471] 4163 6-9-12 102 FrederikTylicki 5 102
(David Elsworth) *hld up: hdwy over 2f out: sn outpcd: r.o towards fin* **4/1**[3]
2405 **6** *1/2* **Stockhill Diva**[37] 6584 6-8-13 89 MartinDwyer 1 88
(Brendan Powell) *s.s: hld up: hdwy over 2f out: rdn and edgd rt over 1f out: no ex fnl f* **10/1**
3-00 **7** *13* **Moderah**[46] 6259 4-9-10 100 TomQueally 8 78
(James Fanshawe) *chsd ldrs: rdn over 2f out: wknd over 1f out* **8/1**

2m 34.85s (0.95) **Going Correction** +0.225s/f (Good) **7** Ran SP% **111.0**
Speed ratings (Par 109): **105,104,103,102,102 102,93**
CSF £36.57 CT £277.99 TOTE £2.80: £2.10, £9.60; EX 39.40 Trifecta £231.90.
Owner Middleham Park Racing LXVI **Bred** Shadwell Estate Company Limited **Trained** Upper Helmsley, N Yorks

FOCUS
Rail movement increased race distance by about 17yds. A warm handicap despite the two top weights being 8lb below the race ceiling, but they went no pace and it was hard to make up ground. The favourite still won this fair and square, though. The level is a bit fluid.

7576 COSSINGTON MEDIAN AUCTION MAIDEN FILLIES' STKS (PLUS 10 RACE) 6f
4:50 (4:51) (Class 5) 2-Y-O **£3,234** (£962; £481; £240) **Stalls** High

Form RPR
44 **1** **Mississippi Miss**[18] 7099 2-9-0 0 RobertHavlin 13 75
(Dr Jon Scargill) *w ldr 1f: remained handy: rdn to chse ldr over 1f out: styd on to ld nr fin* **5/1**[3]
54 **2** *3/4* **Lava Light**[26] 6866 2-9-0 0 DaneO'Neill 4 73
(Henry Candy) *racd keenly: led 5f out: rdn over 1f out: hdd nr fin* **11/4**[2]
2 **3** *2 1/2* **Sitar**[19] 7071 2-9-0 0 FrederikTylicki 2 65
(James Fanshawe) *chsd ldrs: swtchd lft over 2f out: rdn over 1f out: no ex ins fnl f* **7/4**[1]
4 *1* **Annie Fior (IRE)** 2-9-0 0 [1] TomQueally 5 64+
(Denis Coakley) *prom: hmpd and lost pl over 2f out: r.o towards fin* **50/1**
5 *1/2* **Little Miss Daisy** 2-9-0 0 MartinDwyer 15 61
(William Muir) *s.i.s: hdwy over 2f out: rdn over 1f out: styd on same pce ins fnl f* **28/1**
6266 **6** *1* **Cool Echo**[19] 7071 2-9-0 74 TonyHamilton 8 58
(J R Jenkins) *hld up: hdwy over 1f out: sn rdn: no ex ins fnl f* **8/1**
7 *shd* **Defining Moment** 2-9-0 0 MartinLane 9 60+
(Rae Guest) *hld up: hdwy over 3f out: nt clr run and lost pl over 2f out: kpt on fnl f* **25/1**
8 *2 1/2* **Tahiti** 2-9-0 0 PatCosgrave 14 50
(David Brown) *mid-div: hdwy over 3f out: rdn over 1f out: wknd ins fnl f* **6/1**
9 *3/4* **African Girl** 2-8-11 0 SimonPearce(3) 1 48
(Lydia Pearce) *chsd ldrs: rdn over 1f out: wknd ins fnl f* **66/1**
0 **10** *3 1/4* **Katie's Surprise (IRE)**[19] 7072 2-9-0 0 LiamKeniry 10 38
(John Butler) *plld hrd and prom: stdd and lost pl after 1f: n.d after* **150/1**
60 **11** *1 3/4* **Diamond Princess**[12] 7285 2-8-11 0 AlistairRawlinson(3) 7 33
(Michael Appleby) *sn led: hdd after 1f: chsd ldr tl rdn over 2f out: wknd over 1f out* **200/1**
12 *4 1/2* **Garboesque (IRE)** 2-9-0 0 TomMarquand 11 19
(Shaun Harris) *s.i.s: a in rr* **100/1**
00 **13** *2 3/4* **Diptych (USA)**[12] 7278 2-9-0 0 RyanPowell 6 11
(Sir Mark Prescott Bt) *prom: lost pl after 1f: sn pushed along: wknd wl over 1f out* **50/1**
14 *13* **Arya Stark** 2-9-0 0 WilliamCarson 12
(Tony Carroll) *s.i.s: outpcd* **50/1**

1m 13.32s (0.32) **Going Correction** -0.10s/f (Good) **14** Ran SP% **121.9**
Speed ratings (Par 92): **93,92,88,87,86 85,85,81,80,76 74,68,64,47**
CSF £18.73 TOTE £5.70: £1.70, £1.50, £1.30; EX 23.00 Trifecta £64.10.
Owner Silent Partners **Bred** Strawberry Fields Stud **Trained** Newmarket, Suffolk

FOCUS
A modest fillies' maiden and uncompetitive despite the size of the field. Previous experience proved important with the front three all having raced before.

7577 FOSSE WAY H'CAP (FOR GENTLEMAN AMATEUR RIDERS) 7f
5:20 (5:22) (Class 5) (0-70,70) 3-Y-O+ **£3,119** (£967; £483; £242) **Stalls** High

Form RPR
0000 **1** **Teversham**[20] 7062 3-10-0 56 oh3 MrJJO'Neill(5) 15 62
(Martin Smith) *s.i.s: bhd: hdwy over 1f out: sn rdn: r.o to ld last strides* **50/1**
2356 **2** *3/4* **Baltic Prince (IRE)**[7] 7417 6-11-0 68 MrBJames(5) 6 73
(Tony Carroll) *led 2f: led again over 2f out: rdn over 1f out: edgd rt ins fnl f: hdd last strides* **9/1**[3]
0312 **3** *shd* **Poor Duke (IRE)**[35] 6637 6-10-2 56 MrLewisStones(5) 3 61
(Michael Mullineaux) *hld up: pushed along over 2f out: hdwy over 2f out: rdn over 1f out: edgd rt ins fnl f: r.o* **14/1**

6361 **4** 1/2 **Rebel Lightning (IRE)**[13] 7240 3-11-5 **70** (b) MrSWalker 7 72
(Richard Spencer) *prom: chsd ldr 2f out: shkn up over 1f out: n.m.r ins fnl f: no ex towards fin* **15/8**[1]

204 **5** 1 **Strictly Art (IRE)**[38] 6541 3-10-9 **60** (p) MrRBirkett 12 60
(Alan Bailey) *prom: rdn 3f out: styd on* **14/1**

2235 **6** nk **Art Echo**[44] 6337 3-11-0 **68** (t) MrJHarding(3) 9 67
(Jonathan Portman) *hld up: hdwy over 2f out: rdn over 1f out: no ex ins fnl f* **12/1**

2400 **7** nse **Kingthistle**[20] 7059 3-11-0 **65** MrZBaker 4 64
(Ian Williams) *hld up: rdn over 2f out: r.o ins fnl f: nt trble ldrs* **10/1**

6024 **8** 1 **Janaab (IRE)**[25] 6907 6-11-5 **68** (t) MrWEasterby 8 65
(Tim Easterby) *mid-div: hdwy over 4f out: rdn over 2f out: styd on same pce ins fnl f* **6/1**[2]

5000 **9** 1 **Celtic Sixpence (IRE)**[10] 7333 8-10-3 **59** MrTPBroughton(7) 5 53
(Nick Kent) *chsd ldrs: rdn over 2f out: styd on same pce fnl f* **25/1**

400 **10** 1/2 **Living Leader**[14] 7212 7-10-4 **56** oh6 (bt) MrHHunt(3) 13 49
(Grace Harris) *hld up: rdn over 3f out: nvr on terms* **50/1**

1065 **11** 3/4 **Hijran (IRE)**[14] 7227 3-10-11 **69** (p) MrJamesKendrick(7) 10 59
(Michael Appleby) *s.i.s: in rr: rdn over 2f out: n.d* **10/1**

60-0 **12** 8 **Ishikawa (IRE)**[47] 6241 8-10-8 **60** [1] MrJoshuaNewman(3) 1 29
(Ali Stronge) *w ldrs: led 4f out tl hdd over 2f out: wknd over 1f out* **16/1**

5054 **13** 3 **Pennine Warrior**[30] 6769 5-10-13 **62** (p) MrAlexEdwards 14 23
(Scott Dixon) *chsd ldrs: rdn over 3f out: wknd over 2f out* **25/1**

0353 **14** 2 **Doctor Bong**[13] 7240 4-11-2 **70** [1] MrRichardPatrick(5) 2 26
(Grace Harris) *mid-div: rdn 1/2-way: hung rt and wknd over 2f out* **25/1**

1m 26.45s (0.25) **Going Correction** -0.10s/f (Good)
WFA 3 from 4yo+ 2lb **14** Ran SP% **119.6**
Speed ratings (Par 103): **94,93,93,92,91 90,90,89,88,88 87,78,74,72**
CSF £437.89 CT £6753.29 TOTE £48.80: £12.60, £3.10, £3.10; EX 915.10 TRIFECTA Not won..
Owner Strawberry Fields Stud **Bred** G & J Equestrian Of Newmarket **Trained** Newmarket, Suffolk
■ Stewards' Enquiry : Mr Lewis Stones two-day ban: used whip above permitted level (Nov 22,30)

FOCUS
A modest amateurs' handicap and a shock result. It's been rated around the front-running runner-up and third.
T/Jkpt: Not won. T/Plt: £595.70 to a £1 stake. Pool: £80,099.68 - 98.15 winning units. T/Qpdt: £74.00 to a £1 stake. Pool: £8,640.62 - 86.30 winning units. **Colin Roberts**

7329 REDCAR (L-H)
Monday, October 24

OFFICIAL GOING: Soft (good to soft in places; 7.3)
Wind: light 1/2 behind Weather: fine

7578 BRITISH STALLION STUDS EBF MAIDEN STKS 6f
1:50 (1:52) (Class 5) 2-Y-O **£3,234** (£962; £481; £240) **Stalls** Centre

Form RPR

3 **1** **Chipping (IRE)**[16] 7142 2-9-5 0 ConnorBeasley 10 77+
(Michael Dods) *chsd ldrs: led over 1f out: drvn out* **7/2**[3]

6652 **2** 1 **Bithynia (IRE)**[10] 7331 2-9-0 67 AndreaAtzeni 6 69
(Hugo Palmer) *led: hdd over 1f out: kpt on same pce last 100yds* **3/1**[2]

3 **3** 1 **Harvest Moon**[19] 7072 2-9-0 0 DavidNolan 11 66
(Richard Fahey) *chsd ldrs: outpcd over 3f out: hdwy over 2f out: 3rd appr fnl f: kpt on wl towards fin* **6/1**

42 **4** 2 1/4 **Sheikspear**[19] 7064 2-9-5 0 OisinMurphy 12 64
(Joseph Tuite) *chsd ldrs: one pce over 1f out* **9/4**[1]

53 **5** 1 3/4 **Oh Geno**[7] 7414 2-9-2 0 LouisSteward(3) 13 59
(Richard Spencer) *mid-div: hdwy over 2f out: kpt on same pce over 1f out* **12/1**

6 nk **Black Salt** 2-9-5 0 PhillipMakin 4 58
(David Barron) *swtchd lft s: t.k.h: hdwy to trck ldrs over 4f out: fdd over 1f out* **28/1**

600 **7** 1 1/4 **Babouska**[8] 7380 2-9-0 0 JamesSullivan 3 49
(Michael Easterby) *prom: one pce fnl 2f* **125/1**

8 nk **Indian Vision (IRE)** 2-9-5 0 PJMcDonald 14 53
(Micky Hammond) *dwlt: bhd and drvn along: sme hdwy over 1f out: nvr a factor* **100/1**

0 **9** 3/4 **Chaucer's Tale**[17] 7122 2-9-5 0 CamHardie 1 51
(Michael Easterby) *chsd ldrs: wknd over 1f out* **150/1**

44 **10** 1 **Vivardia (IRE)**[18] 7090 2-9-0 0 GrahamLee 8 43
(Ben Haslam) *in rr: sme hdwy over 1f out: nvr a factor* **40/1**

11 1 1/4 **Size Matters** 2-9-5 0 DougieCostello 2 44+
(Mark Walford) *dwlt: hdwy to chse ldrs over 4f out: lost pl over 1f out* **50/1**

0 **12** shd **Fairy Lock (IRE)**[20] 7040 2-9-0 0 GrahamGibbons 7 39
(David Barron) *mid-div: drvn 3f out: nvr a factor* **50/1**

020 **13** 3/4 **Ideal Bounty (IRE)**[8] 7381 2-9-5 0 NeilFarley 15 42
(Andrew Crook) *a towards rr* **66/1**

0 **14** 3/4 **Devil's Guard (IRE)**[38] 6535 2-9-5 0 JasonHart 5 40
(Keith Dalgleish) *in rr and sn drvn along: nvr on terms* **20/1**

0 **15** 7 **Ching Ching Lor (IRE)**[10] 7331 2-9-5 0 PaulMulrennan 9 19
(Declan Carroll) *in rr: edgd lft over 2f out: bhd whn heavily eased clsng stages* **150/1**

1m 13.48s (1.68) **Going Correction** +0.175s/f (Good) **15** Ran SP% **119.1**
Speed ratings (Par 95): **95,93,92,89,87 86,84,84,83,82 80,80,79,78,69**
CSF £13.44 TOTE £4.40: £1.70, £1.40, £2.30; EX 15.00 Trifecta £82.70.
Owner David W Armstrong **Bred** Mrs Helen Keaveney **Trained** Denton, Co Durham

FOCUS
There was another 0.5mm of rain the previous day and the ground was given as soft, good to soft in places. An ordinary 2yo maiden to start, but a nice enough winner. Straightforward form.

7579 RACING UK HD ON SKY 432 NURSERY H'CAP 5f
2:20 (2:20) (Class 6) (0-65,65) 2-Y-O **£2,587** (£770; £384; £192) **Stalls** Centre

Form RPR

000 **1** **Dusty Bin**[32] 6712 2-8-8 **52** KevinStott 3 65+
(Kevin Ryan) *chsd ldrs: led over 1f out: styd on wl: eased clsng stages* **11/2**[3]

5460 **2** 2 1/4 **Angel Palanas**[30] 6763 2-9-2 **65** CliffordLee(5) 7 65
(K R Burke) *led: hdd over 1f out: kpt: on same pce* **4/1**[1]

405 **3** 1 1/4 **Jorvik Prince**[55] 6009 2-8-13 **57** SamJames 10 53
(Karen Tutty) *hld up in mid-div: hdwy over 2f out: hung bdly lft overr 1f out: kpt on same pce* **25/1**

0025 **4** 3/4 **Myllachy**[59] 5833 2-8-8 **55** RachelRichardson(3) 11 48
(Tim Easterby) *swtchd lft after s: towards rr: hdwy over 1f out: kpt on: tk 4th nr fin* **7/1**

0456 **5** nk **Not Now Nadia (IRE)**[29] 6807 2-9-0 **58** [1] PaulMulrennan 1 50
(Michael Dods) *chsd ldrs: one pce over 1f out* **7/1**

0065 **6** nk **Scotch Myst**[63] 5712 2-8-9 **58** AdamMcNamara(5) 2 49
(Richard Fahey) *chsd ldrs: outpcd over 2f out: edgd lft and one pce over 1f out* **11/2**[3]

400 **7** 3 **Tranquil Tracy**[146] 2771 2-8-7 **51** ConnorBeasley 5 31
(John Norton) *in rr: edgd rt 2f out: kpt on fnl f: nvr a factor* **28/1**

4400 **8** 3/4 **Climax**[23] 6950 2-9-4 **62** JoeFanning 4 39
(Mark Johnston) *chsd ldrs: wknd over 1f out* **5/1**[2]

405 **9** 1/2 **Cool Run Girl (IRE)**[13] 7248 2-8-12 **56** PJMcDonald 8 31
(Iain Jardine) *sn chsng ldrs: outpcd over 2f out: lost pl over 1f out* **11/1**

6505 **10** 7 **Zebedee Cat (IRE)**[29] 6807 2-9-2 **60** (v) DougieCostello 9 10
(Iain Jardine) *chsd ldrs: lost pl over 1f out: bhd whn eased clsng stages* **18/1**

59.71s (1.11) **Going Correction** +0.175s/f (Good) **10** Ran SP% **113.3**
Speed ratings (Par 93): **98,94,92,91,90 90,85,84,83,72**
CSF £26.92 CT £513.20 TOTE £6.80: £2.40, £2.00, £6.50; EX 28.20 Trifecta £558.30.
Owner Mrs Janis Macpherson **Bred** Aston House Stud **Trained** Hambleton, N Yorks
■ Stewards' Enquiry : Adam McNamara two-day ban: used whip above permitted level (Nov 7-8)

FOCUS
This form looks okay for the grade. The second and third pin a solid enough level.

7580 EUROPEAN BREEDERS' FUND - DOUBLE TRIGGER EBF MAIDEN STKS 1m 1f
2:50 (2:52) (Class 5) 2-Y-O **£3,234** (£962; £481; £240) **Stalls** Low

Form RPR

423 **1** **Sofia's Rock (FR)**[59] 5834 2-9-5 78 PaulMulrennan 2 84
(Mark Johnston) *wnt rt s: mde all: clr over 3f out: styd on strly: unchal* **7/2**[2]

43 **2** 7 **Alqamar**[32] 6704 2-9-5 0 AndreaAtzeni 3 70
(Charlie Appleby) *carried rt s: trckd ldrs: effrt over 3f out: rdn to chse wnr 3f out: no imp and hung lft over 1f out* **4/6**[1]

3 1 3/4 **Bolder Bob (IRE)** 2-9-5 0 GrahamGibbons 5 67+
(David Barron) *clipped heels s: hld up in rr: hdwy and swtchd rt over 2f out: kpt on steadily: tk modest 3rd last 75yds: will improve* **16/1**

4 1 1/2 **Tewafeedj** 2-9-5 0 KevinStott 6 64
(Kevin Ryan) *trckd ldrs: lost pl over 6f out: hdwy 5f out: modest 3rd over 2f out: one pce* **33/1**

20 **5** 13 **Taxmeifyoucan (IRE)**[10] 7329 2-9-5 0 PhillipMakin 7 38
(Keith Dalgleish) *in rr: reminders over 3f out: bhd whn eased fnl f* **14/1**

03 **6** shd **Jukebox Jive (FR)**[12] 7273 2-9-5 0 OisinMurphy 8 37
(Anthony Honeyball) *trckd ldrs: drvn 4f out: lost pl over 2f out: sn bhd* **8/1**[3]

60 **7** hd **True Romance (IRE)**[10] 7318 2-9-5 0 TomEaves 1 37
(James Given) *dwlt: hdwy to trck ldrs after 2f: drvn over 3f out: lost pl over 2f out* **66/1**

8 6 **Moon Sun Star (IRE)** 2-9-5 0 DavidNolan 4 25
(David O'Meara) *carried rt s: hld up in mid-div: drvn over 3f out: lost pl over 2f out: bhd whn eased clsng stages* **14/1**

1m 53.21s (0.21) **Going Correction** +0.175s/f (Good) **8** Ran SP% **117.0**
Speed ratings (Par 95): **106,99,98,96,85 85,85,79**
CSF £6.30 TOTE £4.20: £1.10, £1.10, £4.50; EX 7.40 Trifecta £63.10.
Owner Mezzone Family 1 **Bred** Jean-Francois Gribomont **Trained** Middleham Moor, N Yorks

FOCUS
An uncompetitive maiden in which the improved winner was allowed a clear lead and the favourite disappointed. The level is a bit fluid.

7581 RACINGUK.COM/DAYPASS (S) STKS 1m 2f
3:25 (3:26) (Class 6) 3-5-Y-O **£2,726** (£805; £402) **Stalls** Low

Form RPR

1565 **1** **Ronya (IRE)**[23] 6953 5-9-3 58 DaleSwift 8 65
(Tracy Waggott) *chsd ldr: led over 1f out: fnd ex last 50yds* **12/1**

0500 **2** 1 3/4 **Devious Spirit (IRE)**[28] 6838 4-8-12 60 AdamMcNamara(5) 4 62
(Richard Fahey) *mid-div: drvn and modest 3rd over 3f out: 2nd over 1f out: sn upsides: kpt on same pce last 75yds* **10/1**

1102 **3** 4 1/2 **Miningrocks (FR)**[23] 6953 4-9-6 69 (v[1]) GerO'Neill(7) 9 64
(Declan Carroll) *rn wout declared tongue strap: swtchd lft after s: led: t.k.h: wnt clr over 3f out: drvn over 2f out: edgd rt and hdd over 1f out: sn wknd* **3/1**[2]

140 **4** 5 **Italian Beauty (IRE)**[30] 6772 4-8-12 72 BenCurtis 2 40+
(Brian Ellison) *in rr and sn pushed along: sme hdwy over 2f out: poor 4th 1f out* **1/1**[1]

0523 **5** 3 3/4 **Little Pippin**[28] 6839 3-8-7 52 BarryMcHugh 1 33
(Tony Coyle) *mid-div: t.k.h: effrt over 3f out: wknd over 2f out* **8/1**[3]

360 **6** 1 **Jasper Jay**[129] 3362 3-8-12 65 [1] DuranFentiman 3 36
(Tony Coyle) *hld up in rr: effrt over 3f out: lost pl over 2f out* **40/1**

564 **7** 2 1/4 **Eastern Shore (IRE)**[35] 6618 3-8-12 60 JoeyHaynes 6 32
(K R Burke) *chsd ldng pair: pushed along over 5f out: reminders over 3f out: lost pl over 2f out* **16/1**

6020 **8** 2 1/2 **Bertha Burnett (IRE)**[23] 6953 5-8-12 49 JamesSullivan 5 23
(Brian Rothwell) *up in rr: drvn over 4f out: nevedr on terms: eased clsng stages* **25/1**

2m 8.07s (0.97) **Going Correction** +0.175s/f (Good)
WFA 3 from 4yo+ 5lb **8** Ran SP% **115.1**
Speed ratings (Par 101): **103,101,98,94,91 90,88,86**
CSF £123.57 TOTE £12.40: £2.60, £2.40, £1.30; EX 107.30 Trifecta £770.30.Devious Spirit was bought by Iain Jardine for £6,000
Owner David Tate **Bred** P F Headon **Trained** Spennymoor, Co Durham

FOCUS
A moderate seller in which the 3rd did too much and the favourite under performed. The winner dictates the opening level.

7582 MARKET CROSS JEWELLERS H'CAP 1m 6f 19y
3:55 (3:55) (Class 5) (0-70,68) 3-Y-O **£3,234** (£962; £481; £240) **Stalls** Low

Form RPR

4535 **1** **Torremar (FR)**[21] 7008 3-9-7 **68** (p) TomEaves 3 76
(Kevin Ryan) *trckd ldrs: nt clr run and swtchd rt over 3f out: sn 2nd: led over 2f out: styd on strly fnl f: eased nr fin* **9/2**[2]

460 **2** 3 1/2 **Lady Natasha (IRE)**[53] 6052 3-8-13 **60** DougieCostello 1 62
(K R Burke) *hld up towards rr: hdwy after 4f: chsng ldrs over 3f out: 2nd over 1f out: hung lft and kpt on: no imp* **16/1**

0636 **3** 2 1/4 **Heavensfield**[62] 5749 3-9-6 **67** [1] StevieDonohoe 8 66
(Mark H Tompkins) *hld up towards rr: t.k.h: hdwy to chse ldrs over 3f out: 3rd and one pce 1f out* **10/1**

6204 **4** nk **Mikro Polemistis (IRE)**[20] 7045 3-8-9 **56** BenCurtis 7 54
(Brian Ellison) *hld up in rr: hdwy 4f out: chsng ldrs over 2f out: 4th and one pce 1f out* **4/1**[1]

3043 **5** 4 ½ **Adherence**^{21} 7008 3-8-11 **58**........................(p) BarryMcHugh 4 50
(Tony Coyle) *in rr: hdwy to chse ldrs 8f out: drvn over 5f out: lost pl over 3f out: kpt on fnl f* **11/2**^{3}

2342 **6** hd **Rockliffe**^{4} 5957 3-9-0 **61**........................ PJMcDonald 9 53
(Micky Hammond) *in rr: hdwy over 3f out: wknd over 1f out* **12/1**

1655 **7** hd **Young Tom**^{28} 6840 3-9-1 **62**........................ AndrewMullen 2 54
(Michael Appleby) *trckd ldrs: t.k.h: effrt over 2f out: wknd fnl f* **9/2**^{2}

6450 **8** 1 ½ **Calarules**^{21} 7008 3-8-10 **57**........................(b^{1}) JasonHart 6 46
(Tim Easterby) *drvn to ld: hdd over 3f out: wkng whn hmpd 2f out* **9/1**

0340 **9** 2 ½ **Disquotational**^{44} 6334 3-9-3 **64**........................^{1} OisinMurphy 5 54
(David Simcock) *sn trcking ldrs: t.k.h: hung lft and led over 3f out: hdd 2f out: wkng whn hmpd over 1f out* **10/1**

3m 6.41s (1.71) **Going Correction** +0.175s/f (Good) **9** Ran SP% **113.5**
Speed ratings (Par 101): **102,100,98,98,95 95,95,94,93**
CSF £71.19 CT £678.77 TOTE £4.70: £1.70, £4.80, £2.90; EX 86.00 Trifecta £870.20.
Owner Mrs Margaret Forsyth **Bred** E A R L Ecurie Haras D'Elbe **Trained** Hambleton, N Yorks
■ Stewards' Enquiry : Dougie Costello caution: careless riding

FOCUS

Just two previous winners in this, the 6th and 7th-placed finishers. The winner has been rated to form.

7583 RACING UK IN GLORIOUS HD MAIDEN STKS 7f

4:30 (4:30) (Class 5) 3-Y-O+ **£3,234** (£962; £481; £240) **Stalls** Centre

Form RPR

60 **1** **Glorious Poet**^{8} 7384 3-9-5 0........................ DougieCostello 2 77
(Ed Walker) *trckd ldrs: upsides over 3f out: led over 2f out: kpt on wl fnl 150yds* **25/1**

2 1 ¼ **Zabeel Prince (IRE)** 3-9-5 0........................ AndreaAtzeni 3 74
(Roger Varian) *trckd ldrs: pushed along over 2f out: chsd wnr last 100yds: no real imp* **5/6**^{1}

-25 **3** 2 ½ **Shah Of Armaan (IRE)**^{21} 7009 3-9-5 0........................ KevinStott 6 68
(Kevin Ryan) *led: hdd over 2f out: kpt on same pce fnl f to take 3rd post* **5/2**^{2}

4 **4** hd **Blue Cliffs (IRE)**^{10} 7335 3-9-5 0........................ AndrewMullen 1 67
(Michael Appleby) *chsd ldrs: effrt over 2f out: upsides and hung lft over 1f out: fdd clsng stages* **4/1**^{3}

4 **5** 6 **Einstein**^{10} 7327 3-9-5 0........................(t) TomEaves 5 51
(Mrs Ilka Gansera-Leveque) *stdd s: hld up: swtchd lft 3f out: chsng ldrs over 1f: sn wknd* **12/1**

6 8 **Sandstream** 3-9-5 0........................ JoeFanning 8 31
(Tracy Waggott) *t.k.h: w ldrs: lost pl 2f out: sn bhd* **40/1**

0P4 **7** 2 ¾ **Melodya (IRE)**^{25} 6905 3-9-0 0........................ BenCurtis 7 18
(Brian Ellison) *w ldrs: lost pl over 2f out: sn bhd* **100/1**

50 **8** 7 **Blynx**^{23} 6960 3-9-0 0........................ OisinMurphy 4
(David Simcock) *racd in last: swtchd lft over 3f out: lost pl over 2f out: sn bhd* **40/1**

1m 26.41s (1.91) **Going Correction** +0.175s/f (Good) **8** Ran SP% **120.5**
Speed ratings (Par 103): **96,94,91,91,84 75,72,64**
CSF £49.03 TOTE £32.80: £7.30, £1.10, £1.20; EX 116.90 Trifecta £334.30.
Owner Kangyu International Racing (HK) Limited **Bred** Bolton Grange **Trained** Upper Lambourn, Berks

FOCUS

A modest maiden. The third has been rated close to his latest form.

7584 RACING UK DAY PASS JUST £10 APPRENTICE H'CAP (DIV I) 6f

5:00 (5:00) (Class 6) (0-65,65) 3-Y-O+ **£2,587** (£770; £384; £192) **Stalls** Centre

Form RPR

5005 **1** **Be Bold**^{10} 7334 4-9-5 **65**........................ RowanScott$^{(3)}$ 2 72
(Rebecca Bastiman) *mid-div: hdwy over 2f out: chsd ldr 1f out: kpt on to ld last 50yds* **15/2**^{2}

0063 **2** nk **Questo**^{25} 6910 4-8-13 **56**........................ CharlieBennett 3 62
(Tracy Waggott) *chsd ldrs: hmpd and led over 1f out: hdd and no ex last 50yds* **10/1**

0103 **3** 3 ½ **Bold Spirit**^{13} 7253 5-9-4 **61**........................(vt) PhilDennis 1 57
(Declan Carroll) *trckd ldrs: t.k.h: effrt over 1f out: kpt on same pce* **15/2**^{2}

0231 **4** 1 ¼ **Gaelic Wizard (IRE)**^{41} 6451 8-9-6 **63**........................(v) GemmaTutty 8 55
(Karen Tutty) *hmpd s: in rr: hdwy and swtchd lft over 2f out: swtchd rt and nt clr run 1f out: kpt on same pce* **11/1**

5005 **5** hd **Piazon**^{47} 6235 5-9-5 **65**........................ CliffordLee$^{(3)}$ 7 56
(John Butler) *wnt rt s: led: hung lft and hdd over 1f out: kpt: on same pce* **11/2**^{1}

045 **6** 1 ¼ **Spirit Of Zebedee (IRE)**^{18} 7092 3-8-13 **62**........................(v) JoshQuinn$^{(5)}$ 11 50
(John Quinn) *chsd ldrs: one pce over 1f out* **9/1**^{3}

2060 **7** 2 **Adiator**^{73} 5355 8-8-4 **54**........................^{1} ManuelFernandes$^{(7)}$ 5 36
(Neville Bycroft) *mid-div: drvn and outpcd over 2f out: one pce over 1f out* **12/1**

6000 **8** 1 **Lackaday**^{13} 7255 4-9-3 **60**........................(v^{1}) AdamMcNamara 4 39
(Mark Walford) *chsd ldr: drvn over 2f out: one pce whn hmpd over 1f out* **9/1**^{3}

4020 **9** hd **Teetotal (IRE)**^{20} 7059 6-9-2 **62**........................(v) LewisEdmunds$^{(3)}$ 12 40
(Nigel Tinkler) *in rr: swtchd lft over 2f out: nvr a factor* **10/1**

313 **10** 5 **Longroom**^{20} 7046 4-9-1 **58**........................ JordanVaughan 9 21
(Noel Wilson) *n.m.r s: mid-div: outpcd over 2f out: wknd over 1f out* **11/2**^{1}

-026 **11** 5 **Shesnotforturning (IRE)**^{28} 6834 6-8-5 **51**.........(p) MeganNicholls$^{(3)}$ 10
(Ben Haslam) *mid-div: lost pl over 2f out: sn bhd* **25/1**

4465 **12** ½ **Kingfisher Girl**^{20} 7046 3-8-0 **51** oh5........................ BenRobinson$^{(7)}$ 13
(Michael Appleby) *in rr: bhd fnl 2f* **28/1**

1m 12.53s (0.73) **Going Correction** +0.175s/f (Good)
WFA 3 from 4yo+ 1lb **12** Ran SP% **115.8**
Speed ratings (Par 101): **102,101,96,95,95 93,90,89,89,82 75,75**
CSF £78.48 CT £433.69 TOTE £7.20: £2.40, £2.70, £2.80; EX 80.40 Trifecta £1093.40.
Owner Mrs P Bastiman **Bred** Simon Balding **Trained** Cowthorpe, N Yorks

FOCUS

Leg one of a moderate sprint handicap, and low-drawn runners dominated the finish. The winner has been rated to the best of this year's form.

7585 RACING UK DAY PASS JUST £10 APPRENTICE H'CAP (DIV II) 6f

5:30 (5:30) (Class 6) (0-65,65) 3-Y-O+ **£2,587** (£770; £384; £192) **Stalls** Centre

Form RPR

2124 **1** **Tricky Dicky**^{41} 6451 3-9-3 **64**........................ CliffordLee$^{(3)}$ 9 69
(Olly Williams) *chsd ldrs: effrt over 1f out: styd on to ld last 50yds* **7/4**^{1}

4423 **2** ½ **Wahaab (IRE)**^{13} 7254 5-9-5 **65**........................(p) LewisEdmunds$^{(3)}$ 13 69
(Iain Jardine) *chsd ldrs: effrt 2f out: swtchd rt appr fnl f: styd on to take 2nd fnl strides* **6/1**^{3}

4460 **3** nk **The Armed Man**^{18} 7096 3-8-5 **56**........................ PaulaMuir$^{(7)}$ 4 59
(Chris Fairhurst) *w ldrs: led over 3f out: hdd and no ex last 50yds* **17/2**

50-0 **4** 1 **Macho Mac**^{178} 1829 3-9-4 **62**........................ CharlieBennett 8 62
(Hughie Morrison) *trckd ldrs: t.k.h: kpt on same pce fnl f* **20/1**

2343 **5** ¾ **Letbygonesbeicons**^{28} 6836 3-8-11 **58**........................ RowanScott$^{(3)}$ 5 55
(Ann Duffield) *mid-div: hdwy to chse ldrs over 1f out: kpt on one pce* **8/1**

0604 **6** nk **Indian Pursuit (IRE)**^{10} 7324 3-8-12 **61**........................ JoshQuinn$^{(5)}$ 6 57
(John Quinn) *chsd ldrs: kpt on one pce fnl f* **4/1**^{2}

-650 **7** nk **Swansway**^{146} 2784 3-8-13 **57**........................ AnnaHesketh 11 53
(Michael Easterby) *mid-div: sn drvn along: outpcd over 2f out: kpt on appr fnl f* **25/1**

0401 **8** 2 ¼ **Captain Scooby**^{4} 7489 10-9-0 **64** 6ex........................(b) LisaTodd$^{(7)}$ 1 53
(Richard Guest) *s.s: bhd: sme hdwy over 2f out: nvr on terms* **22/1**

5501 **9** 14 **Goninodaethat**^{18} 7092 8-9-1 **58**........................ AdamMcNamara 7 5
(Jim Goldie) *led: hdd over 3f out: lost pl over 2f out: bhd whn eased over 1f out* **16/1**

0560 **10** 8 **Ay Up Audrey**^{11} 7302 5-8-5 **51** oh6........................(b) RhiainIngram$^{(3)}$ 3
(Rebecca Bastiman) *wnt lft s: in rr: bhd whn eased over 1f out* **66/1**

1m 13.52s (1.72) **Going Correction** +0.175s/f (Good)
WFA 3 from 5yo+ 1lb **10** Ran SP% **112.6**
Speed ratings (Par 101): **95,94,93,92,91 91,90,87,69,58**
CSF £11.16 CT £69.81 TOTE £2.60: £1.20, £1.70, £2.70; EX 11.30 Trifecta £114.30.
Owner Eight Gents and a Lady **Bred** Onslow, Stratton & Parry **Trained** Market Rasen, Lincs

FOCUS

The second division of a moderate sprint handicap. It's been rated around the winner.
T/Plt: £51.40 to a £1 stake. Pool: £57,883.78 - 821.04 winning units. T/Qpdt: £7.10 to a £1 stake. Pool: £6,046.84 - 625.65 winning units. **Walter Glynn**

7586 - 7587a (Foreign Racing) - See Raceform Interactive

7396 CHANTILLY (R-H)

Monday, October 24

OFFICIAL GOING: Polytrack: standard

7588a PRIX DU BUISSON CREUX (MAIDEN) (2YO COLTS & GELDINGS) (POLYTRACK) 6f 110y

1:35 (1:35) 2-Y-O **£9,926** (£3,970; £2,977; £1,985; £992)

RPR

1 **Greyway (FR)**^{19} 7086 2-9-2 0........................ IoritzMendizabal 4 82
(J-M Lefebvre, France) **39/10**^{3}

2 3 **African Ride**^{28} 2-9-2 0........................ MaximeGuyon 9 73
(C Laffon-Parias, France) **48/10**

3 1 ¼ **Brise De Mer (FR)**^{35} 6638 2-9-2 0........................ UmbertoRispoli 6 70
(George Baker) *a cl up: drvn to chse ldr 1 1/2f out: kpt on at same pce fnl f* **11/1**

4 snk **Coco City (FR)**^{31} 2-9-2 0........................ VincentCheminaud 14 69
(M Delcher Sanchez, France) **46/1**

5 snk **Pirandello**^{31} 2-9-2 0........................ MickaelBarzalona 13 69
(A Fabre, France) *w.w in midfield: hdwy on outer 2f out: styd on ins fnl f: nvr on terms* **17/5**^{1}

6 1 **Rise Hit (FR)**^{52} 2-9-2 0........................ LukasDelozier 12 66
(H-A Pantall, France) **98/10**

7 ½ **Mujeeb**^{24} 2-9-2 0........................ AurelienLemaitre 8 65
(F Head, France) **19/5**^{2}

8 1 ¼ **Graffiti (FR)**^{21} 2-9-2 0........................ StephanePasquier 10 61
(N Clement, France) **114/10**

9 1 ¼ **Antoni (IRE)** 2-8-11 0........................ AlexisBadel 3 53
(J E Hammond, France) **229/10**

10 12 **Ken Party (FR)**^{21} 7258 2-9-2 0........................ TonyPiccone 1 24
(Matthieu Palussiere, France) **38/1**

11 hd **Piscar D'Olhos (FR)**^{21} 2-9-2 0........................ AnthonyCrastus 7 24
(N Caullery, France) **38/1**

1m 17.26s (77.26) **11** Ran SP% **118.3**
PARI-MUTUEL (all including 1 euro stake): WIN 4.90; PLACE 1.90, 2.10, 3.30; DF 12.70; SF 26.60.
Owner Ecurie Melanie **Bred** Ecurie Haras Du Cadran, A Gilibert & A Von Gunten **Trained** France

7355 CATTERICK (L-H)

Tuesday, October 25

OFFICIAL GOING: Soft (6.4)

Wind: Virtually nil Weather: Fine and dry

7589 CATTERICKBRIDGE.CO.UK NOVICE STKS 5f

1:20 (1:20) (Class 5) 2-Y-O **£3,234** (£962; £481; £240) **Stalls** Low

Form RPR

1 **1** **Brian The Snail (IRE)**^{40} 6515 2-9-6 0........................ TonyHamilton 1 95+
(Richard Fahey) *cl up: led over 2f out: pushed clr over 1f out: readily* **6/5**^{1}

2221 **2** 7 **Tschierschen (IRE)**^{13} 7269 2-9-4 **74**........................ PatCosgrave 2 67
(William Haggas) *slt ld 2f: pushed along 2f out: rdn wl over 1f out: sn drvn and kpt ion same pce* **3/1**^{3}

2352 **3** 6 **Kiribati**^{14} 7248 2-9-2 **75**........................ JoeFanning 5 44
(Mark Johnston) *wnt rt s: racd towards stands rail and cl up: slt after 2f: hdd over 2f out and sn rdn: drvn over 1f out: kpt on one pce* **9/4**^{2}

0100 **4** 4 **Secret Potion**^{14} 7258 2-9-6 **77**........................ ShaneKelly 3 33
(Ronald Harris) *chsd ldrs: rdn along 2f out: sn drvn and wknd* **16/1**

0006 **5** 2 ¼ **Red Shanghai (IRE)**^{26} 6896 2-8-8 **40**........................ NoelGarbutt$^{(3)}$ 4 16
(Charles Smith) *chsd ldrs: rdn along 1/2-way: sn outpcd* **100/1**

1m 2.33s (2.53) **Going Correction** +0.55s/f (Yiel) **5** Ran SP% **108.1**
Speed ratings (Par 95): **101,89,80,73,70**
CSF £4.94 TOTE £1.60: £1.10, £1.50; EX 4.00 Trifecta £5.40.
Owner R A Fahey **Bred** A Kirwan **Trained** Musley Bank, N Yorks

FOCUS
The ground had dried out a little and the going was now officially soft all over (from soft, heavy in places). Bend into home straight out by 2yds, increasing 6f, 7f and 1m4f races by 6yds and 2m race by 12yds. An uncompetitive novice event to start and the jockeys wasted little time in coming stands' side in the testing ground. The favourite bolted up and the winning time was 4.03sec outside standard. Winning rider Tony Hamilton said: "It's soft ground", but Joe Fanning said: "I'd call it heavy." The winner has been rated with feet on the ground given the time of year.

7590 RACINGUK.COM H'CAP (DIV I) 5f 212y
1:50 (1:50) (Class 4) (0-80,80) 3-Y-O+ **£5,175** (£1,540; £769; £384) **Stalls** Low

Form RPR

1041 **1** **Royal Connoisseur (IRE)**[31] 6769 5-8-11 **77**........ NatalieHambling[(7)] 4 86
(Richard Fahey) *trckd ldng pair on inner: hdwy over 2f out: led wl over 1f out: sn rdn: hld on wl towards fin* **8/1**

1606 **2** ½ **Money Team (IRE)**[7] 7434 5-9-6 **79**........................... GrahamGibbons 3 86
(David Barron) *in tch: hdwy on inner over 2f out: rdn over 1f out: chal ent fnl f: sn drvn and ev ch tl no ex towards fin* **13/2**[3]

1505 **3** 1 **Ancient Astronaut**[8] 7413 3-8-12 **72**..................................... JasonHart 8 76
(John Quinn) *chsd ldr: cl up 1/2-way: rdn along 2f out and sn ev ch: drvn and kpt on same pce fnl f* **13/2**[3]

045 **4** ½ **Dandyleekie (IRE)**[7] 7433 4-9-7 **80**.............................. DanielTudhope 5 82
(David O'Meara) *trckd ldrs: effrt over 2f out: rdn over 1f out: drvn and kpt on same pce fnl f* **4/1**[1]

0000 **5** hd **The Hooded Claw (IRE)**[104] 4259 5-8-13 **72**..................... DavidAllan 7 74
(Tim Easterby) *led: rdn along over 2f out: hdd wl over 1f out: sn drvn and wknd fnl f* **8/1**

1450 **6** 2 ¾ **Gin In The Inn (IRE)**[15] 7221 3-9-2 **76**........................... TonyHamilton 1 69
(Richard Fahey) *hld up in rr: hdwy over 2f out: sn chsng ldrs: rdn over 1f out: no imp* **8/1**

2130 **7** 3 **Emerald Loch**[24] 6946 3-9-4 **78**... FMBerry 10 61
(Ralph Beckett) *cl up on outer: pushed along over 2f out: sn rdn and wknd wl over 1f out* **6/1**[2]

-000 **8** 2 ½ **See The Storm**[35] 6644 8-8-7 **66**....................................... PJMcDonald 2 41
(Ann Duffield) *a towards rr* **50/1**

3656 **9** 1 ¾ **Fantasy Justifier (IRE)**[8] 7415 5-8-10 **69**.......................... ShaneKelly 6 39
(Ronald Harris) *in tch: rdn along over 2f out: sn wknd* **18/1**

0243 **10** 17 **Art Obsession (IRE)**[11] 7325 5-9-2 **75**......................... PaulMulrennan 9
(Paul Midgley) *a rr: rdn along over 2f out: sn outpcd and eased in rr* **6/1**[2]

1m 17.68s (4.08) **Going Correction** +0.85s/f (Soft)
WFA 3 from 4yo+ 1lb **10** Ran SP% **115.8**
Speed ratings (Par 105): **106,105,104,103,103 99,95,92,89,67**
CSF £58.75 CT £369.00 TOTE £8.30: £2.30, £2.50, £2.10; EX 55.50 Trifecta £561.50.
Owner S & G Clayton, A Blower **Bred** Mrs Sheila Morrissey **Trained** Musley Bank, N Yorks

FOCUS
Rail movement increased race distance by 6yds. The first division of a fair sprint handicap and again they came stands' side after turning in. A winning time 6.86sec outside standard suggested the ground was softer on the round course. It's been rated around the runner-up.

7591 RACINGUK.COM H'CAP (DIV II) 5f 212y
2:20 (2:20) (Class 4) (0-80,80) 3-Y-O+ **£5,175** (£1,540; £769; £384) **Stalls** Low

Form RPR

6033 **1** **Ballesteros**[8] 7413 7-9-1 **79**...................................... AdamMcNamara[(5)] 6 86
(Richard Fahey) *trckd ldrs: hdwy over 2f out: cl up over 1f out: sn rdn: styd on wl to ld last 50 yds* **5/2**[1]

0226 **2** nk **Apricot Sky**[13] 7288 6-9-7 **80**... BarryMcHugh 8 86
(David Nicholls) *trckd ldr: cl up 1/2-way: led over 2f out: rdn over 1f out: drvn ins fnl f: hdd and no ex last 50 yds* **11/2**[2]

0601 **3** 1 ¼ **Coiste Bodhar (IRE)**[13] 7290 5-8-5 **71**................. NatalieHambling[(7)] 4 73
(Scott Dixon) *led: pushed along over 2f out: sn hdd and cl up: rdn wl over 1f out: kpt on same pce ent fnl f* **10/1**

000- **4** nk **Mehdi (IRE)**[395] 6746 7-9-2 **75**..(t) DavidNolan 7 76
(Richard Fahey) *in tch: effrt over 2f out: rdn and hdwy over 1f out: kpt on fnl f* **7/1**

0000 **5** ½ **Silhuette (IRE)**[18] 7126 3-9-1 **75**................................... PaulMulrennan 3 74
(Colin Teague) *hld up: hdwy jst over 2f out: rdn wl over 1f out: kpt on fnl f* **40/1**

1055 **6** ½ **Vincentti (IRE)**[15] 7221 6-9-4 **77**... ShaneKelly 5 75
(Ronald Harris) *midfield: swtchd lft and hdwy 2f out: rdn over 1f out: kpt on fnl f* **6/1**[3]

3353 **7** 5 **Rose Eclair**[10] 7363 3-8-12 **72**..(b) JasonHart 9 54
(Tim Easterby) *chsd ldng pair: rdn and hung lft 2f out: sn wknd* **12/1**

402 **8** ¾ **Bella's Venture**[22] 7011 3-8-7 **67**... BenCurtis 1 46
(John Gallagher) *a towards rr* **13/2**

00-0 **9** ¾ **Jubilee Brig**[150] 2677 6-9-3 **76**... NeilFarley 2 53
(Alan Swinbank) *a towards rr* **14/1**

1m 19.44s (5.84) **Going Correction** +1.125s/f (Soft)
WFA 3 from 5yo+ 1lb **9** Ran SP% **114.8**
Speed ratings (Par 105): **106,105,103,103,102 102,95,94,93**
CSF £15.99 CT £116.82 TOTE £3.60: £1.90, £1.50, £3.00; EX 14.60 Trifecta £89.90.
Owner Dr Marwan Koukash **Bred** Exors Of The Late J R Good **Trained** Musley Bank, N Yorks

FOCUS
Rail movement increased race distance by 6yds. They went a scorching pace in the conditions and the field were soon well spread out, but this was still a race in which it was hard to make up ground with the 1-2-3 at the line racing 4-2-1 rounding the home bend. The leaders were treading water at the end, though, and the winning time was 1.76sec slower than the first division. The winner has been rated close to this year's form, with the runner-up and third also close to form for now, but there's little solid here.

7592 BOOK NOW FOR NEW YEAR'S DAY H'CAP 1m 7f 177y
2:55 (2:55) (Class 5) (0-70,68) 3-Y-O+ **£2,911** (£866; £432; £216) **Stalls** Low

Form RPR

050/ **1** **Italian Riviera**[23] 5427 7-9-2 **56**.................................... [1] JamesSullivan 8 64+
(Kenneth Slack) *hld up in rr: hdwy over 5f out: sn trcking ldrs: cl up on bit 3f out: wd to stands side and led 2f out: rdn over 1f out: drvn ins fnl f: kpt on wl towards fin* **7/2**[1]

5324 **2** 1 **Cape Hideaway**[12] 4194 4-9-5 **59**....................................(p) JasonHart 1 66
(Mark Walford) *prom: cl up 1/2-way: led over 3f out: rdn along and hdd 2f out: drvn over 1f out: kpt on wl fnl f* **6/1**

0503 **3** 1 ¾ **Adrakhan (FR)**[10] 7361 5-8-9 **49** oh4................................. CamHardie 5 54
(Wilf Storey) *hld up towards rr: hdwy over 6f out: chsd ldrs over 3f out: cl up and wd st to stands rail whn hmpd over 2f out: sn swtchd lft: rdn and ev ch over 1f out: drvn and kpt on same pce fnl f* **16/1**

5005 **4** 13 **Topalova**[15] 7231 3-7-12 **51**...(p) NoelGarbutt[(3)] 2 40
(Mark H Tompkins) *midfield: hdwy 1/2-way: chsd ldrs 6f out: rdn along over 3f out: drvn and plugged on same pce fnl 2f* **10/1**

4603 **5** 7 **Hurry Home Poppa (IRE)**[11] 7332 6-10-0 **68**................. GrahamLee 10 49
(John Mackie) *hld up in rr: sme hdwy 4f out and sn pushed along: rdn 3f out: n.d* **11/2**

5262 **6** 8 **Northside Prince (IRE)**[17] 7138 10-9-11 **65**......................... BenCurtis 3 36
(Alan Swinbank) *trckd ldrs: pushed along 5f out: rdn 4f out: sn wknd* **8/1**

1321 **7** 1 ¾ **La Fritillaire**[22] 7006 4-9-7 **61**... TomEaves 7 30
(James Given) *prom: led 1/2-way: rdn along over 4f out: hdd over 3f out: sn drvn and wknd* **5/1**[3]

3662 **8** 5 **Dream Serenade**[21] 7045 3-8-0 **50** oh1......................... AndrewMullen 9 13
(Michael Appleby) *chsd ldrs: rdn along on outer over 4f out: wknd over 3f out* **9/2**[2]

30 **9** 6 **Politbureau**[129] 3417 9-9-10 **64**.......................................(p) PJMcDonald 4 20
(Micky Hammond) *a towards rr: outpcd and bhd fnl 3f* **33/1**

2060 **10** 99 **Symbolist (IRE)**[17] 7138 4-9-4 **58**.................................(v) PaulMulrennan 6
(John Norton) *sn led: pushed along and hdd 1/2-way: sn lost pl and bhd* **66/1**

3m 50.71s (18.71) **Going Correction** +1.125s/f (Soft)
WFA 3 from 4yo+ 10lb **10** Ran SP% **117.3**
Speed ratings (Par 103): **98,97,96,90,86 82,81,79,76,26**
CSF £24.84 CT £298.55 TOTE £4.30: £1.60, £2.20, £6.40; EX 28.50 Trifecta £461.50.
Owner Mrs Michelle Gleeson **Bred** J L C Pearce **Trained** Hilton, Cumbria

FOCUS
Rail movement increased race distance by 12yds. A modest staying handicap and they went steady in the conditions, but the first three still pulled miles clear. It's been rated around the runner-up.

7593 DINE AND VIEW AT CATTERICK RACES H'CAP 7f
3:25 (3:26) (Class 4) (0-85,85) 3-Y-O+ **£6,469** (£1,925; £962; £481) **Stalls** Low

Form RPR

0011 **1** **Shouranour (IRE)**[10] 7360 6-8-13 **82**............................(b) JoshDoyle[(5)] 8 91
(Alan Brown) *trckd ldrs: hdwy over 2f out: rdn along on stands rail to ld wl over 1f out: edgd lft ent fnl f: sn drvn and hld on wl towards fin* **11/2**[1]

6000 **2** nk **Boots And Spurs**[5] 7486 7-9-1 **79**.......................................(v) DaleSwift 3 87
(Scott Dixon) *rr: hdwy on inner over 2f out: chsd ldrs over 1f out and sn rdn: drvn to chal ins fnl f: ev ch tl no ex nr fin* **12/1**

0414 **3** 1 **Fingal's Cave (IRE)**[103] 4306 4-9-6 **84**......................... PJMcDonald 4 89
(Iain Jardine) *trckd ldrs on inner: hdwy over 2f out: rdn over 1f out: drvn and ev ch ent fnl f: kpt on same pce* **6/1**[2]

5206 **4** ¾ **Tadaany (IRE)**[19] 7095 4-9-2 **80**.................................... DanielTudhope 13 83
(David O'Meara) *trckd ldrs: hdwy over 2f out: rdn and ev ch over 1f out: sn drvn and kpt on same pce* **7/1**[3]

0640 **5** ½ **Lexington Times (IRE)**[19] 7095 4-9-7 **85**..................... JamesSullivan 1 87
(Ruth Carr) *dwlt and towards rr: hdwy 2f out: sn rdn and kpt on fnl f: nrst fin* **16/1**

4410 **6** ½ **Foresight (FR)**[27] 6883 3-8-12 **78**.. ShaneKelly 12 78
(David Simcock) *hld up: hdwy 3f out: chsd ldrs 2f out: rdn and ev ch over 1f out: sn drvn and kpt on same pce* **12/1**

0530 **7** 1 ¼ **Khelman (IRE)**[18] 7126 6-9-0 **83**............................ AdamMcNamara[(5)] 7 81
(Richard Fahey) *midfield: effrt over 2f out: sn rdn and no imp fnl f* **7/1**[3]

4000 **8** 2 ¼ **Westwood Hoe**[19] 7095 5-9-7 **85**.. BenCurtis 2 77
(Tony Coyle) *trckd ldrs on inner: hdwy 3f out: rdn along 2f out: sn drvn and wknd over 1f out* **10/1**

0000 **9** shd **Holiday Magic (IRE)**[25] 6914 5-8-13 **77**............................ CamHardie 14 68
(Michael Easterby) *nvr bttr than midfield* **16/1**

4000 **10** nse **Kalk Bay (IRE)**[18] 7126 9-9-4 **82**..................................(t) PaulMulrennan 11 73
(Michael Easterby) *dwlt: a towards rr* **40/1**

0030 **11** ½ **Newstead Abbey**[19] 7095 6-9-7 **85**............................. GrahamGibbons 5 75
(David Barron) *chsd ldrs: rdn along over 2f out: wknd over 1f out* **9/1**

0000 **12** 1 ¼ **Best Trip (IRE)**[18] 7124 9-9-5 **83**.. SamJames 6 70
(Marjorie Fife) *led: wd home turn to stands rail: rdn over 2f out: hdd wl over 1f out: sn wknd* **14/1**

6600 **13** 5 **Escalating**[19] 7094 4-9-2 **80**..(tp) AndrewMullen 9 54
(Michael Appleby) *a towards rr* **22/1**

2000 **14** 6 **Lucky Beggar (IRE)**[13] 7289 6-9-0 **78**............................... DavidAllan 15 36
(David C Griffiths) *in tch on outer: rdn along wl over 2f out: sn wknd* **16/1**

4600 **15** 3 ¾ **Rusty Rocket (IRE)**[53] 6080 7-8-11 **75**............................ JoeFanning 10 23
(Paul Green) *prom: rdn along wl over 2f out: sn wknd* **25/1**

1m 33.78s (6.78) **Going Correction** +1.125s/f (Soft)
WFA 3 from 4yo+ 2lb **15** Ran SP% **124.1**
Speed ratings (Par 105): **106,105,104,103,103 102,101,98,98,98 97,96,90,83,79**
CSF £71.12 CT £421.04 TOTE £6.00: £2.20, £4.90, £1.70; EX 101.10 Trifecta £596.50.
Owner David Lumley **Bred** His Highness The Aga Khan's Studs S C **Trained** Yedingham, N Yorks

FOCUS
Rail movement increased race distance by 6yds. A competitive handicap run at a true pace. The winner has been rated close to his old best, and the runner-up close to this year's form.

7594 EAT DRINK SLEEP NAGS HEAD PICKHILL H'CAP 1m 3f 214y
4:00 (4:01) (Class 4) (0-85,87) 3-Y-O+ **£5,175** (£1,540; £769; £384) **Stalls** Low

Form RPR

2320 **1** **Michael's Mount**[36] 6626 3-8-9 **73**................................(p) GrahamLee 11 83
(Ed Dunlop) *hld up towards rr: smooth hdwy over 4f out: cl up over 2f out: led wl over 1f out: rdn ent fnl f: styd on wl* **13/2**[3]

3142 **2** 1 ¾ **Tamayuz Magic (IRE)**[10] 7359 5-9-9 **80**..................(b) JamesSullivan 13 87
(Michael Easterby) *hld up towards rr: hdwy over 4f out: chsd ldrs 3f out: wd st and cl up: cl up 2f: sn rdn and ev ch: drvn ins fnl f: kpt on* **9/1**

6650 **3** 2 ¾ **Ingleby Hollow**[11] 7320 4-9-0 **76**................................(p) JoshDoyle[(5)] 1 79
(David O'Meara) *trckd ldr: led 3f out: rdn over 2f out: hdd wl over 1f out and sn drvn: kpt on same pce* **16/1**

2020 **4** 2 ½ **Sunglider (IRE)**[17] 7159 3-8-11 **75**.................................... SamJames 9 74
(David O'Meara) *hld up towards rr: hdwy 4f out: chsd ldrs 2f out: sn rdn: drvn and kpt on fnl f: nrst fin* **25/1**

0614 **5** 1 **Card High (IRE)**[10] 7359 6-9-6 **77**...................................(t) ShaneGray 8 74
(Wilf Storey) *in tch: hdwy 4f out: chsd ldrs 3f out: rdn along 2f out: sn drvn and kpt on one pce* **12/1**

5221 **6** 6 **Eez Eh (IRE)**[48] 6221 3-8-10 **74**.............................(p) ConnorBeasley 6 61
(Keith Dalgleish) *led: rdn along and hdd 3f out: drvn over 2f out and grad wknd* **9/1**

3313 **7** ¾ **Henry Smith**[10] 7359 4-9-5 **83**...............................(be) LewisEdmunds[(7)] 7 69
(Garry Moss) *hld up towards rr: hdwy wl over 2f out: sn rdn along and n.d* **5/1**[2]

5000 **8** 1 ¼ **Tapis Libre**[17] 7159 8-9-2 **80**................................ DanielleMooney[(7)] 2 64
(Jacqueline Coward) *a towards rr* **66/1**

203 **9** 1 **Henpecked**[7] 7435 6-8-8 **70**.....................................(p) GarryWhillans[(5)] 3 53
(Alistair Whillans) *chsd ldrs: rdn along over 3f out: sn wknd* **16/1**

062 **10** 2 ¼ **Astra Hall**10 7357 7-9-1 **72**........ AndrewMullen 10 51
(Michael Appleby) *prom: pushed along over 3f out: rdn over 2f out: sn drvn and wknd* **16/1**

0531 **11** 3 ¼ **Bahama Moon (IRE)**8 7412 4-10-2 **87** 6ex........ GrahamGibbons 14 61
(David Barron) *midfield: hdwy to trck ldrs 4f out: effrt 3f out: rdn over 2f out: sn wknd* **9/4**1

6410 **12** 2 ¼ **Deep Resolve (IRE)**188 1560 5-8-13 **70**........ BenCurtis 4 40
(Alan Swinbank) *chsd ldrs on inner: rdn along 4f out: sn wknd* **25/1**

3400 **13** 19 **Dubai Mission (IRE)**26 6899 3-8-8 **72**........ PJMcDonald 12 12
(Steve Flook) *a towards rr: bhd fnl 3f* **100/1**

0004 **14** 53 **English Summer**10 7357 9-9-7 **78**........(t) DavidNolan 5
(Richard Fahey) *a towards rr: outpcd and wl bhd fnl 3f* **20/1**

2m 50.4s (11.50) **Going Correction** +1.125s/f (Soft)
WFA 3 from 4yo+ 7lb **14** Ran SP% **121.0**
Speed ratings (Par 105): **106,104,103,101,100 96,96,95,94,93 91,89,76,41**
CSF £61.04 CT £912.02 TOTE £6.50: £2.40, £2.60, £6.40; EX 64.10 Trifecta £1770.70.
Owner Miltil Consortium **Bred** Southill Stud **Trained** Newmarket, Suffolk

FOCUS
Rail movement increased race distance by 6yds. A fair middle-distance handicap and they went a sensible pace. It's been rated around the runner-up to his C&D latest.

7595 JUMP SEASON NEXT ON NOVEMBER 30TH H'CAP (DIV I) 5f
4:30 (4:32) (Class 6) (0-65,65) 3-Y-O+ **£2,264** (£673; £336; £168) **Stalls** Low

Form RPR

0324 **1** **Whipphound**7 7444 8-8-11 **55**........(p) JamesSullivan 5 61
(Ruth Carr) *rr: hdwy wl over 1f out: chsd ldrs and swtchd rt towards stands rail jst ins fnl f: sn rdn and str run to ld nr line* **6/1**3

0222 **2** hd **Jacob's Pillow**19 7093 5-9-2 **65**........ RowanScott(5) 7 70
(Rebecca Bastiman) *trckd ldrs: hdwy to ld over 1f out: rdn ent fnl f: sn drvn and keeping on: hdd and no ex nr line* **6/1**3

4000 **3** nk **A J Cook (IRE)**21 7046 6-8-7 **51** oh1........ DavidAllan 8 55
(Ron Barr) *dwlt: hdwy wl over 1f out: rdn to chal ins fnl f: sn drvn and ev ch: no ex towards fin* **16/1**

0300 **4** 1 ½ **Minty Jones**69 5535 7-8-2 **51** oh4........(v) PhilDennis(5) 10 50
(Michael Mullineaux) *cl up: rdn to take slt ld 2f out: hdd over 1f out: drvn and kpt on same pce fnl f* **20/1**

5124 **5** 2 ¼ **Taffetta**7 7437 4-9-5 **63**........ BarryMcHugh 6 54
(Tony Coyle) *trckd ldrs whn n.m.r: bmpd and lost pl after 1f: towards rr: hdwy on inner 2f out: rdn and ev ch jst over 1f out: drvn and wknd fnl f* **9/2**2

2416 **6** nse **Coolcalmcollected (IRE)**7 7426 4-8-13 **57**........(p) PJMcDonald 1 48
(David Loughnane) *chsd ldrs: rdn along wl over 1f out: grad wknd* **4/1**1

6215 **7** ¾ **Diminutive (IRE)**13 7276 4-8-10 **54**........(p) StevieDonohoe 11 42
(Grace Harris) *towards rr: rdn along 1/2-way: sme late hdwy* **20/1**

0060 **8** ¾ **Hit The Lights (IRE)**13 7290 6-9-1 **59**........ PaulQuinn 9 44
(David Nicholls) *clsd up: rdn along over 2f out: sn wknd* **13/2**

0053 **9** 1 ¼ **Windforpower (IRE)**26 6909 6-9-0 **58**........(p) DaleSwift 2 39
(Tracy Waggott) *chsd ldrs: rdn along over 2f out: sn drvn and wknd* **16/1**

0006 **10** ½ **Sir Geoffrey (IRE)**21 7046 10-8-3 **54** ow2........(b) NatalieHambling(7) 3 33
(Scott Dixon) *slt ld: rdn along and hdd 2f out: grad wknd* **14/1**

0000 **11** ¾ **Mercers Row**19 7093 9-8-9 **60**........(b1) LewisEdmunds(7) 4 36
(Michael Herrington) *chsd ldrs: rdn along 2f out: sn drvn and wknd* **9/1**

1m 3.93s (4.13) **Going Correction** +0.825s/f (Soft) **11** Ran SP% **118.0**
Speed ratings (Par 101): **99,98,98,95,92 92,90,89,87,86 85**
CSF £42.09 CT £543.18 TOTE £7.00: £2.30, £1.80, £5.00; EX 41.70 Trifecta £935.20.
Owner Mrs Ruth A Carr **Bred** Mrs B Skinner **Trained** Huby, N Yorks
■ Stewards' Enquiry : Paul Quinn caution; entered wrong stalls

FOCUS
The first division of a moderate sprint handicap. The leaders may have gone off a shade too quick with the winner coming from a detached last.

7596 JUMP SEASON NEXT ON NOVEMBER 30TH H'CAP (DIV II) 5f
5:05 (5:05) (Class 6) (0-65,65) 3-Y-O+ **£2,264** (£673; £336; £168) **Stalls** Low

Form RPR

0001 **1** **Robbian**7 7444 5-8-0 **51** 6ex........ RPWalsh(7) 9 57
(Charles Smith) *chsd ldrs: rdn along and hdwy over 1f out: nt clr run and swtchd lft ent fnl f: sn drvn and kpt on wl to ld nr line* **7/1**3

0604 **2** hd **Kodimoor (IRE)**21 7046 3-8-7 **51** oh1........(bt) KieranO'Neill 1 57
(Christopher Kellett) *trckd ldrs on outer: hdwy wl over 1f out: sn chal and rdn: drvn and edgd rt ins fnl f: sn slt ld: hdd nr line* **7/1**3

4550 **3** 1 **Culloden**3 7534 4-8-9 **60**........(b) BenSanderson(7) 2 62
(Shaun Harris) *prom: cl up 2f out: rdn jst over 1f: ev ch whn n.m.r and hmpd ins fnl f: kpt on* **12/1**

2640 **4** ½ **Lydiate Lady**64 5714 4-8-12 **56**........ TonyHamilton 10 56
(Paul Green) *in tch: rdn along wl over 1f out: drvn and styd on wl fnl f* **15/2**

1222 **5** 1 **Compton River**14 7252 4-9-2 **65**........ PhilDennis(5) 11 61
(Bryan Smart) *trckd ldrs: hdwy nr stands rail and cl up 2f out: rdn to ld over 1f out: drvn and edgd lft jst ins fnl f: sn hdd & wknd* **5/2**1

0000 **6** hd **Balliol**20 7069 4-9-0 **58**........(b1) ShaneKelly 8 54
(Ronald Harris) *dwlt and towards rr: rdn along and hdwy over 1f out: kpt on fnl f: nrst fin* **12/1**

0013 **7** 3 ¼ **Knockamany Bends (IRE)**31 6774 6-8-9 **53**........(tp) BarryMcHugh 4 41
(John Wainwright) *sn led: rdn along and narrowly hdd over 1f out: drive: cl up and ev ch whn n.m.r and hmpd ins fnl f* **10/1**

0500 **8** 1 ½ **Captain Devious**10 7362 5-8-4 **51** oh6........1 NoelGarbutt(3) 7 29
(Grace Harris) *a towards rr* **50/1**

4050 **9** 1 ½ **Bapak Bangsawan**9 7386 6-8-6 **55** ow1........(v) AnnStokell(5) 5 28
(Ann Stokell) *prom: rdn along 2f out: sn wknd* **12/1**

0062 **10** shd **Emerald Bay**58 5920 3-8-13 **57**........ ShaneGray 6 31
(Ronald Thompson) *a towards rr* **20/1**

2040 **11** 7 **Native Falls (IRE)**45 6341 5-9-2 **60**........ StevieDonohoe 3 8
(Alan Swinbank) *cl up: rdn along 2f out: sn drvn and wknd* **13/2**2

1m 3.62s (3.82) **Going Correction** +0.825s/f (Soft) **11** Ran SP% **117.6**
Speed ratings (Par 101): **102,101,100,99,97 97,92,89,87,87 76**
CSF £55.36 CT £591.67 TOTE £7.60: £2.60, £2.50, £4.60; EX 74.30 Trifecta £1029.60.
Owner Rob Lewin **Bred** John Starbuck **Trained** Temple Bruer, Lincs
■ Stewards' Enquiry : Shane Gray £140.00 fine; passport did not comply.

FOCUS
The winning time was 0.31sec quicker than the first division and this time the principals came up the centre. The second and third help set the level.
T/Plt: £154.50 to a £1 stake Pool: £57,529.28 - 271.75 winning units. T/Qpdt: £29.60 to a £1 stake. Pool: £6,130.49 - 152.87 winning units. **Joe Rowntree**

7431 NEWCASTLE (A.W) (L-H)
Tuesday, October 25

OFFICIAL GOING: Tapeta: standard
Wind: Almost nil Weather: Overcast races 1-2

7597 AT THE RACES ON SKY 415 MAIDEN STKS 1m 4f 98y (Tp)
5:00 (5:00) (Class 5) 3-Y-O+ **£2,911** (£866; £432; £216) **Stalls** Low

Form RPR

52 **1** **St Malo (USA)**13 7280 3-9-5 0........ AndreaAtzeni 1 89+
(Roger Varian) *t.k.h: trckd ldr: rdn to ld over 2f out: drew clr fnl f* **8/11**1

4 **2** 6 **Mutadaffeq (IRE)**9 7384 3-9-5 80........ DanielTudhope 3 79
(David O'Meara) *led: rdn and hdd over 2f out: rallied: outpcd fnl f* **4/1**3

3 10 **Cape Dignity (IRE)** 3-9-2 0........ JosephineGordon(3) 4 63+
(Hugo Palmer) *slowly away: rn green in tch: drvn and struggling over 4f out: rallied to chse (clr) ldng pair over 2f out: edgd lft: sn no imp* **2/1**2

0 **4** 25 **First Of Never (IRE)**18 7106 10-9-12 0........ PaddyAspell 2 23
(Lynn Siddall) *hld up in tch: stdy hdwy 1/2-way: rdn and wknd fr 3f out: t.o* **100/1**

05 **5** 12 **Foible**87 4857 3-9-5 0........ TomEaves 5 4
(Mike Sowersby) *chsd ldrs: lost grnd 1/2-way: lost tch fr over 4f out: t.o* **66/1**

2m 38.64s (-2.46) **Going Correction** -0.125s/f (Stan)
WFA 3 from 10yo 7lb **5** Ran SP% **113.7**
Speed ratings (Par 103): **103,99,92,75,67**
CSF £4.47 TOTE £1.60: £1.10, £2.30; EX 3.80 Trifecta £4.20.
Owner China Horse Club **Bred** Merry Fox Stud Limited **Trained** Newmarket, Suffolk

FOCUS
An uncompetitive maiden run at a dawdle until halfway. When the pace quickened, the runners were soon strung out. The runner-up is the key to the form.

7598 AT THE RACES ON VIRGIN 535 NURSERY H'CAP 1m 5y (Tp)
5:30 (5:31) (Class 4) (0-80,74) 2-Y-O **£4,010** (£1,193; £596; £298) **Stalls** Centre

Form RPR

0441 **1** **Rashford's Double (IRE)**17 7140 2-8-13 **71**........ AdamMcNamara(5) 4 79+
(Richard Fahey) *in tch: stdy hdwy over 2f out: shkn up and qcknd to ld over 1f out: pushed out: comf* **5/4**1

0203 **2** 3 **Upgrade**10 7366 2-9-7 **74**........1 DougieCostello 3 73
(K R Burke) *led at ordinary gallop: rdn and hdd over 1f out: kpt on same pce fnl f* **8/1**

055 **3** ½ **Chocolate Box (IRE)**21 7034 2-9-7 **74**........ DanielTudhope 2 72
(Luca Cumani) *cl up: rdn and outpcd over 2f out: ralied over 1f out: kpt on: nt pce to chal* **5/2**2

4142 **4** 2 ¼ **Nepeta (USA)**17 7140 2-9-3 **70**........ JoeFanning 5 63
(Mark Johnston) *trckd ldrs: outpcd and edgd lft over 2f out: btn fnl f* **4/1**3

0510 **5** ¾ **Anythingknappen (IRE)**38 6554 2-8-13 **69**........ RachelRichardson(3) 1 60
(Tim Easterby) *chsd ldr to over 2f out: rdn and wknd over 1f out* **14/1**

1m 38.11s (-0.49) **Going Correction** -0.20s/f (Stan) **5** Ran SP% **110.8**
Speed ratings (Par 97): **94,91,90,88,87**
CSF £11.74 TOTE £2.10: £1.20, £2.60; EX 11.30 Trifecta £28.60.
Owner Middleham Park Racing XC **Bred** Manister House Stud **Trained** Musley Bank, N Yorks

FOCUS
A routine AW nursery run at a solid pace, with the winner appearing to be well handicapped.

7599 ELECTRON SERVICES NE LTD MEDIAN AUCTION MAIDEN STKS 6f (Tp)
6:00 (6:00) (Class 6) 2-Y-O **£2,264** (£673; £336; £168) **Stalls** Centre

Form RPR

6223 **1** **Mazyoun**24 6954 2-9-2 92........(b) JosephineGordon(3) 1 85
(Hugo Palmer) *t.k.h: w ldr: led briefly over 2f out: drvn and carried lft over 1f out: drifted rt and bmpd runner-up three times ins fnl f: kpt on to regain ld cl home* **1/8**1

2 shd **Holmeswood** 2-9-5 0........ PaulMulrennan 4 85+
(Michael Dods) *trckd ldrs: plld out and qcknd to ld 2f out: sn drifted lft: corrected whn carried rt and bmpd three times ins fnl f: kpt on: hdd cl home* **6/1**2

3 12 **Lily Fontana (IRE)** 2-8-9 0........ AdamMcNamara(5) 5 37
(Richard Fahey) *s.i.s: rn green and sn outpcd: plugged on to chse (clr) ldng pair ins fnl f: no imp* **9/1**3

0 **4** ½ **Red Douglas**17 7142 2-9-5 0........ BenCurtis 3 40
(Scott Dixon) *led: jst hdd whn hmpd 2f out: sn wknd* **50/1**

05 **5** 3 ½ **Enlighten Me (IRE)**10 7356 2-9-0 0........ JoeyHaynes 2 22
(Philip Kirby) *chsd ldrs: drvn and outpcd over 2f out: btn over 1f out* **100/1**

1m 9.95s (-2.55) **Going Correction** -0.20s/f (Stan) **5** Ran SP% **116.1**
Speed ratings (Par 93): **109,108,92,92,87**
CSF £1.86 TOTE £1.10: £1.02, £2.10; EX 1.80 Trifecta £3.80.
Owner Al Shaqab Racing **Bred** Cheveley Park Stud Ltd **Trained** Newmarket, Suffolk

FOCUS
Two above-average colts pulled well clear in this small-field maiden. Both runners in turn interfered with one other, but the runner-up appeared to be just held at the finish, so the stewards allowed the placings to stand. The winner has been rated a bit below, but may have run to his mark against a nice newcomer in second.

7600 ATTHERACES NURSERY H'CAP 5f (Tp)
6:30 (6:30) (Class 2) 2-Y-O **£9,056** (£2,695; £1,346; £673) **Stalls** Centre

Form RPR

0006 **1** **Spin Doctor**20 7073 2-8-6 **74**........ PatrickMathers 10 79
(Richard Fahey) *s.i.s: hld up: rdn and hdwy over 1f out: edgd lft and kpt on wl fnl f: led nr fin* **12/1**

0214 **2** hd **Harome (IRE)**45 6322 2-8-10 **78**........ PJMcDonald 7 82
(Roger Fell) *trckd ldrs: rdn to ld over 1f out: kpt on ins fnl f: hdd nr fin* **11/1**

4341 **3** 2 **Poet's Society**33 6697 2-9-7 **89**........ AndrewMullen 9 86
(Mark Johnston) *in tch: effrt and drvn wl over 1f out: kpt on same pce ins fnl f* **3/1**1

11 **4** hd **Lomu (IRE)**165 2196 2-9-3 **85**........ JasonHart 3 81
(Keith Dalgleish) *t.k.h: led tl edgd lft and hdd over 1f out: kpt on same pce ins fnl f* **6/1**

41 **5** 1 ¼ **White Royale (USA)**143 2913 2-8-8 **76**........ KevinStott 4 68
(Kevin Ryan) *hld up in tch: drvn and outpcd over 2f out: rallied fnl f: nvr able to chal* **9/2**3

0260 **6** nse **Ventura Secret (IRE)**24 6954 2-8-7 **75**........ DavidAllan 6 67
(Tim Easterby) *towards rr: drvn and outpcd over 2f out: rallied ins fnl f: kpt on: no imp* **14/1**

2532 **7** *shd* **Coolfitch (IRE)**[14] 7258 2-9-3 **85**.................................... DanielTudhope 5 76
(David O'Meara) *dwlt: hld up in tch: effrt and rdn over 1f out: outpcd ins fnl f* **7/2**[2]

252 **8** *3/4* **Prince Of Cool**[40] 6507 2-8-13 **81**.................................... TomEaves 2 70
(James Given) *trckd ldrs: rdn over 2f out: wknd fnl f* **9/1**

10 **9** *8* **Bay Station**[45] 6343 2-8-6 **74**.................................... PaulQuinn 1 34
(David Nicholls) *dwlt: tk keen hold and sn cl up: rdn over 2f out: wknd over 1f out* **33/1**

58.05s (-1.45) **Going Correction** -0.20s/f (Stan) **9** Ran SP% **115.3**
Speed ratings (Par 101): **103,102,99,99,97 97,96,95,82**
CSF £134.69 CT £416.94 TOTE £13.10: £2.70, £2.50, £1.70; EX 176.50 Trifecta £761.60.
Owner Cheveley Park Stud **Bred** Cheveley Park Stud Ltd **Trained** Musley Bank, N Yorks

FOCUS
A good nursery, run at a proper sprint tempo, in which the form should stand up. The runner-up has been rated to his best.

7601 VISIT ATTHERACES.COM H'CAP 1m 5y (Tp)
7:00 (7:01) (Class 6) (0-65,65) 3-Y-O+ **£2,587** (£770; £384; £192) **Stalls** Centre

Form RPR

6552 **1** **Testa Rossa (IRE)**[25] 6921 6-9-1 **62**....................(b) LewisEdmunds(7) 8 70
(Jim Goldie) *in tch: outpcd and edgd lft over 2f out: rallied over 1f out: led ins fnl f: kpt on wl* **8/1**

0101 **2** *3/4* **Totally Magic (IRE)**[11] 7326 4-9-11 **65**.................... BarryMcHugh 13 71
(Richard Whitaker) *led: drvn along 2f out: hdd ins fnl f: kpt on: hld nr fin* **3/1**[1]

3405 **3** *3/4* **Charles De Mille**[53] 6095 8-9-3 **57**.................................... JackGarritty 11 62
(Jedd O'Keeffe) *t.k.h: in tch: rdn and hung lft over 1f out: kpt on fnl f: hld towards fin* **33/1**

0356 **4** *1 1/4* **Broctune Papa Gio**[34] 6683 9-9-5 **64**.......................... CliffordLee(5) 14 66
(Keith Reveley) *prom: drvn along 2f out: kpt on same pce ins fnl f* **14/1**

3510 **5** *hd* **Im Dapper Too**[22] 7007 5-9-7 **61**.................................... SamJames 9 62
(John Davies) *trckd ldrs: effrt and chsd ldr 2f out to ins fnl f: sn no ex* **13/2**[3]

6465 **6** *1/2* **La Havrese (FR)**[11] 7326 5-9-8 **62**.................................... PaddyAspell 4 62
(Lynn Siddall) *hld up: rdn and outpcd over 2f out: rallied on far side of gp over 1f out: kpt on: no imp* **20/1**

040 **7** *1 1/4* **You'll Do**[115] 3886 3-9-3 **65**.................................... PhilDennis(5) 7 61
(Maurice Barnes) *hld up: pushed along over 2f out: hdwy over 1f out: kpt on fnl f: no imp* **50/1**

0506 **8** *1 1/4* **She's Electric (IRE)**[25] 6921 3-9-3 **60**....................(p) ConnorBeasley 10 53
(Keith Dalgleish) *hld up in tch: drvn and outpcd over 2f out: no imp whn checked over 1f out* **14/1**

0006 **9** *2* **Haidees Reflection**[19] 7097 6-9-2 **56**....................(b) DanielTudhope 12 46
(Jim Goldie) *hld up: rdn along 2f out: sn no imp* **25/1**

4303 **10** *3/4* **Arcane Dancer (IRE)**[11] 7326 3-9-7 **64**....................(p) PaulMulrennan 2 51
(Lawrence Mullaney) *in tch: rdn over 2f out: wknd fnl f* **8/1**

6204 **11** *1/2* **Jonofark (IRE)**[40] 6520 3-9-6 **63**.................................... JamesSullivan 5 49
(Brian Rothwell) *dwlt: bhd: drvn over 3f out: nvr on terms* **25/1**

3264 **12** *hd* **Bryght Boy**[48] 6241 3-9-7 **64**.................................... RichardKingscote 1 49
(Ed Walker) *midfield on wd outside: effrt and rdn over 2f out: wknd over 1f out* **4/1**[2]

5400 **13** *1 1/2* **Marcle (IRE)**[15] 7203 3-9-4 **61**.................................... GrahamGibbons 6 43
(Ed de Giles) *chsd ldr to over 2f out: wkng whn checked over 1f out* **10/1**

1026 **14** *1/2* **Whitkirk**[53] 6095 3-9-8 **65**.................................... GrahamLee 3 46
(Jedd O'Keeffe) *hld up in tch: drvn and outpcd over 2f out: sn btn* **14/1**

1m 36.94s (-1.66) **Going Correction** -0.20s/f (Stan)
WFA 3 from 4yo+ 3lb **14** Ran SP% **127.0**
Speed ratings (Par 101): **100,99,98,97,97 96,95,94,92,91 90,90,89,88**
CSF £32.07 CT £796.54 TOTE £8.10: £2.20, £1.90, £8.00; EX 36.50 Trifecta £1448.50.
Owner Mr & Mrs Gordon Grant **Bred** Hugo Merry And Khalid Al-Mudhaf **Trained** Uplawmoor, E Renfrews

FOCUS
A tight handicap run at a solid medium early pace, with the race for home developing fully 3f out. The winner has been rated to the balance of his recent form, while the runner-up and third help set the opening level.

7602 AT THE RACES H'CAP (DIV I) 7f 14y (Tp)
7:30 (7:34) (Class 6) (0-60,60) 3-Y-O+ **£2,587** (£770; £384; £192) **Stalls** Centre

Form RPR

0650 **1** **Faintly (USA)**[10] 7368 5-9-6 **59**....................(b) JamesSullivan 12 68
(Ruth Carr) *hld up: stdy hdwy over 2f out: effrt and swtchd lft over 1f out: rdn to ld ins fnl f: kpt on wl* **4/1**[2]

5002 **2** *1 1/4* **Gold Beau (FR)**[17] 7144 6-9-0 **60**....................(p) GerO'Neill(7) 11 66
(Kristin Stubbs) *racd jst away fr main gp towards stands' rail: prom: hdwy to ld over 1f out: hdd ins fnl f: kpt on same pce* **10/3**[1]

6030 **3** *1* **Fire Diamond**[45] 6347 3-8-12 **53**..............................[1] RichardKingscote 3 55
(Tom Dascombe) *mde most to over 1f out: rallied: kpt on same pce last 100yds* **13/2**

6000 **4** *2* **Lord Rob**[38] 6568 5-8-2 **46** oh1.................................... PhilDennis(5) 5 44
(David Thompson) *taken early to post: t.k.h: cl up: drvn over 2f out: no ex ins fnl f* **8/1**

250 **5** *2 1/4* **Euro Mac**[11] 7323 4-9-1 **54**..[1] KevinStott 7 46
(Neville Bycroft) *in tch: drvn and outpcd over 2f out: rallied ins fnl f: no imp* **16/1**

4166 **6** *1/2* **Castlerea Tess**[14] 7240 3-8-8 **49**.................................... PatrickMathers 9 39
(Sarah Hollinshead) *hld up: pushed along 1/2-way: hdwy wl over 1f out: outpcd ins fnl f* **20/1**

4006 **7** *3/4* **George Bailey (IRE)**[53] 6100 4-8-8 **47** oh1 ow1............ BarryMcHugh 1 36
(Suzzanne France) *hld up: rdn along over 2f out: wknd over 1f out* **20/1**

0061 **8** *3/4* **Rioja Day (IRE)**[19] 7097 6-8-12 **56**....................(b) AdamMcNamara(5) 6 43
(Jim Goldie) *w ldr to 1/2-way: sn drvn and outpcd: no imp fr over 1f out* **8/1**

3632 **9** *1* **Cooperess**[15] 7212 3-9-3 **58**....................(bt) KieranO'Neill 8 41
(Ali Stronge) *trckd ldrs: rdn over 2f out: wknd over 1f out* **11/2**[3]

00-6 **10** *2 1/4* **Wotabond**[188] 1564 3-8-6 **47**.................................... PaulQuinn 2 24
(Richard Whitaker) *hld up in tch: drvn and outpcd over 2f out: sn btn* **25/1**

00-0 **11** *8* **Boboli Gardens**[11] 7323 6-8-11 **50**....................(t) JoeyHaynes 10 8
(Susan Corbett) *wore hood in paddock: s.i.s: sn prom: struggling over 2f out: sn btn* **8/1**

1m 24.54s (-1.66) **Going Correction** -0.20s/f (Stan)
WFA 3 from 4yo+ 2lb **11** Ran SP% **124.4**
Speed ratings (Par 101): **101,99,98,96,93 93,92,91,90,87 78**
CSF £18.38 CT £90.52 TOTE £5.20: £1.70, £1.90, £3.00; EX 24.30 Trifecta £189.20.
Owner The Bottom Liners & Mrs R Carr **Bred** Juddmonte Farms Inc **Trained** Huby, N Yorks
■ Stewards' Enquiry : Kieran O'Neill caution; entered wrong stall

FOCUS
A modest handicap, but the pace was good, and that played into the hands of the previously disappointing winner. The winner has been rated not far off the best of this year's form.

7603 ATR MAIDEN FILLIES' STKS 6f (Tp)
8:00 (8:04) (Class 5) 3-Y-O+ **£2,911** (£866; £432; £216) **Stalls** Centre

Form RPR

5304 **1** **Lovin' Spoonful**[14] 7253 3-9-0 60.................................... ConnorBeasley 6 65
(Bryan Smart) *mde all: rdn clr over 1f out: edgd lft ins fnl f: kpt on strly* **6/4**[1]

5405 **2** *8* **Nefetari**[74] 5370 3-9-0 44...(b) DaleSwift 2 39
(Alan Brown) *w ldr to over 2f out: kpt on same pce fr over 1f out* **14/1**[3]

0 **3** *3/4* **Polish Empress**[24] 6960 3-8-11 0.......................... JosephineGordon(3) 1 37
(William Muir) *dwlt: in tch: drvn and outpcd over 2f out: plugged on fnl f: no imp* **9/4**[2]

-600 **4** *1/2* **Rathvale**[14] 7253 3-9-0 42..[1] BarryMcHugh 8 35
(Linda Perratt) *dwlt: hld up in tch: effrt over 2f out: one pce fr over 1f out* **33/1**

0000 **5** *3 3/4* **Jessie Allan (IRE)**[19] 7092 5-8-8 34.......................... JamieGormley(7) 4 23
(Jim Goldie) *prom: drvn and outpcd over 2f out: sn btn* **50/1**

00-0 **6** *3/4* **Nofizzophobia**[12] 7311 3-9-0 0.................................... JasonHart 7 21
(Derek Shaw) *dwlt: sn chsng ldrs: rdn over 2f out: wknd wl over 1f out* **50/1**

0-02 **7** *34* **Equinette (IRE)**[15] 7207 3-9-0 66.................................... PaulMulrennan 3
(Amanda Perrett) *fractious at s: plld hrd: trckd ldrs tl lost pl over 2f out: sn struggling: eased fr over 1f out* **9/4**[2]

1m 11.34s (-1.16) **Going Correction** -0.20s/f (Stan)
WFA 3 from 5yo 1lb **7** Ran SP% **115.1**
Speed ratings (Par 100): **99,88,87,86,81 80,35**
CSF £23.77 TOTE £2.50: £1.90, £5.00; EX 23.40 Trifecta £49.10.
Owner Albert Welch & Partners **Bred** Advantage Chemicals Holdings Ltd **Trained** Hambleton, N Yorks
■ Any Joy was withdrawn. Price at time of withdrawal 7/1. Rule 4 does not apply. New market formed.

FOCUS
A ordinary maiden run at a modest tempo until halfway. The winner has been rated to form.

7604 AT THE RACES H'CAP (DIV II) 7f 14y (Tp)
8:30 (8:30) (Class 6) (0-60,60) 3-Y-O+ **£2,587** (£770; £384; £192) **Stalls** Centre

Form RPR

0000 **1** **Great Colaci**[24] 6953 3-8-5 **46** oh1.................................... KieranO'Neill 8 54
(Keith Reveley) *mde all: rdn and edgd lft over 1f out: hrd pressed wl ins fnl f: hld on gamely* **25/1**

3654 **2** *shd* **Cliff (IRE)**[11] 7334 6-9-0 **60**.................................... LewisEdmunds(7) 11 69
(Nigel Tinkler) *hld up in tch: effrt and pushed along over 2f out: hdwy over 1f out: disp ld wl ins fnl f: jst hld* **2/1**[1]

2060 **3** *2 1/4* **Melgate Melody**[11] 7336 3-8-10 **51**.......................... GrahamGibbons 10 53
(Michael Easterby) *trckd ldrs: wnt 2nd and rdn over 2f out: kpt on same pce ins fnl f* **7/1**[3]

3006 **4** *3 1/4* **The Knave (IRE)**[11] 7323 3-9-0 **55**....................................(p) BenCurtis 6 49
(Scott Dixon) *pressed wnr to over 2f out: rdn and no ex fr over 1f out* **10/1**

6500 **5** *1/2* **Amber Crystal**[14] 7254 4-8-7 **46** oh1.................................... ShaneGray 7 39
(Linda Perratt) *hld up: stdy hdwy over 2f out: rdn over 1f out: kpt on ins fnl f: nt pce to chal* **80/1**

5645 **6** *1* **Cool Strutter (IRE)**[11] 7323 4-9-6 **59**..............................(b) SamJames 4 50
(Karen Tutty) *in tch: effrt and pushed along over 2f out: one pce fr over 1f out* **5/1**[2]

2200 **7** *3/4* **Deben**[14] 7261 3-9-3 **58**..(p) KevinStott 9 46
(Kevin Ryan) *t.k.h: prom: rdn over 2f out: wknd ins fnl f* **10/1**

0R00 **8** *nk* **Rolen Sly**[21] 7045 7-8-7 **46** oh1.................................... AndrewMullen 5 34
(Neville Bycroft) *hld up: outpcd and hung lft 3f out: nvr on terms after* **66/1**

6505 **9** *1 1/4* **The Name's Bond**[26] 6900 4-8-7 **46** oh1....................(v) PatrickMathers 2 31
(Richard Fahey) *dwlt: sn pushed along in midfield on far side: struggling over 2f out: sn btn* **5/1**[2]

0230 **10** *nse* **Centre Haafhd**[14] 7254 5-8-6 **50**....................(b) PhilDennis(5) 12 35
(Jim Goldie) *hld up on nr side of gp: drvn along over 2f out: wknd over 1f out* **16/1**

5030 **11** *11* **Cheeco**[40] 6512 4-8-7 **46** oh1.................................... JamesSullivan 3
(Ruth Carr) *stdd in rr: struggling over 2f out: sn btn* **16/1**

6001 **12** *1/2* **Circuitous**[14] 7254 8-9-2 **55**....................(v) TomEaves 1 10
(Keith Dalgleish) *in tch: drvn and struggling over 2f out: sn btn* **11/1**

1m 24.85s (-1.35) **Going Correction** -0.20s/f (Stan)
WFA 3 from 4yo+ 2lb **12** Ran SP% **124.0**
Speed ratings (Par 101): **99,98,96,92,92 90,90,89,88,88 75,75**
CSF £77.95 CT £422.72 TOTE £28.50: £6.00, £1.40, £3.20; EX 112.20 Trifecta £1703.40.
Owner Rug, Grub & Pub Partnership **Bred** Reveley Farms **Trained** Lingdale, Redcar & Cleveland

FOCUS
A low-grade race with a finish fought out by two horses who hadn't won a race between them in 35 previous attempts, but the pace was decent. The winner showed that his selling figure did not flatter him.
T/Plt: £9.90 to a £1 stake. Pool: £65,184.02 - 4779.62 winning units. T/Qpdt: £6.90 to a £1 stake. Pool: £8,192.61 - 867.97 winning units **Richard Young**

7527 CHELMSFORD (A.W) (L-H)
Wednesday, October 26

OFFICIAL GOING: Polytrack: standard
Wind: light, half behind Weather: light cloud

7605 TOTEPLACEPOT SIX PLACES IN SIX RACES MAIDEN AUCTION STKS 1m (P)
1:30 (1:30) (Class 5) 2-Y-O **£4,528** (£1,347; £673; £336) **Stalls** Low

Form RPR

32 **1** **Mister Manduro (FR)**[8] 7431 2-9-3 0.................................... JoeFanning 3 77
(Mark Johnston) *t.k.h: chsd ldr: hung rt bnd 4f out: rdn to ld over 1f out: clr and wandered lft ins fnl f: eased towards fin: easily* **10/11**[1]

55 **2** *4* **Makkadangdang**[76] 5324 2-8-10 0.................................... WilliamCox(7) 1 67
(Andrew Balding) *hld up in tch in last pair: effrt on inner and nt clr run over 1f out: hdwy 1f out: styd on to go 2nd towards fin: no ch w wnr* **8/1**

0623 **3** *1/2* **Captain Sue (IRE)**[44] 6421 2-8-1 69.................................... NicolaCurrie(7) 2 57
(Richard Hughes) *chsd ldng pair: effrt 2f out: rdn over 1f out: no imp: chsd clr wnr 100yds out: kpt on same pce and lost 2nd towards fin* **5/1**[3]

022 **4** 1 ½ **Otomo**[22] 7032 2-8-12 67 JamieSpencer 6 58
(Philip Hide) *led: rdn and hdd over 1f out: sn outpcd: lost wl btn 2nd 100yds out: wknd towards fin* **4/1**[2]

5 **5** 5 **Arab Moon**[23] 7012 2-9-1 0 MartinHarley 5 49
(William Knight) *dwlt: sn rcvrd and in tch in midfield: rdn 3f out: unable qck and btn over 1f out: wknd fnl f* **8/1**

0 **6** 5 **Arabela Dawn (IRE)**[12] 7328 2-8-11 0 DougieCostello 4 33
(John Quinn) *taken down early: stdd after s: t.k.h: hld up in rr: rdn over 1f out: sn btn and wknd* **50/1**

1m 39.19s (-0.71) **Going Correction** -0.275s/f (Stan) **6** Ran SP% **113.2**
Speed ratings (Par 95): **92,88,87,86,81 76**
CSF £9.36 TOTE £1.90: £1.10, £4.20; EX 9.00 Trifecta £33.00.
Owner The Originals **Bred** Mme Catherine Niederhauser **Trained** Middleham Moor, N Yorks

FOCUS
A modest maiden auction to start. The favourite didn't travel like a winner, but still proved much too good.

7606 TOTEPOOL RACECOURSE CASH BACK AVAILABLE (S) STKS 7f (P)
2:00 (2:01) (Class 6) 3-Y-O+ **£3,234** (£962; £481; £240) **Stalls** Low

Form RPR

4000 **1** **Unforgiving Minute**[45] 6372 5-9-2 87 AdamKirby 4 79
(John Butler) *hld up in tch in midfield: trckd ldng pair and gng wl 2f out: swtchd rt over 1f out: qcknd to ld ins fnl f: sn clr: easily* **4/5**[1]

2300 **2** 3 ¼ **Brasted (IRE)**[36] 6657 4-8-11 73 (t) PaddyBradley(5) 8 70
(Lee Carter) *chsd ldrs: wnt 2nd over 5f out: rdn and ev ch 2f out: drvn to ld 1f out: sn hdd and outpcd: edgd lft and one pced after* **9/1**[3]

3460 **3** ¾ **Fullon Clarets**[11] 7360 4-9-2 76 (p) DavidNolan 3 68
(Richard Fahey) *led: rdn 2f out: drvn and hdd 1f out: styd on same pce ins fnl f* **2/1**[2]

2150 **4** 2 ½ **Our Boy Jack (IRE)**[8] 7436 7-9-10 75 (p) PatCosgrave 1 69
(Conor Dore) *hld up in tch in midfield: rdn and unable qck over 1f out: no ch w wnr and kpt on same pce ins fnl f* **16/1**

5506 **5** nk **Hereward The Wake**[22] 7036 3-8-9 59 MitchGodwin(5) 6 59
(Sylvester Kirk) *niggled along in rr: rdn over 2f out: outpcd and no ch w wnr over 1f out: kpt on same pce ins fnl f* **33/1**

5000 **6** ¾ **Show Me Again**[6] 7486 3-9-0 75 (vt1) MartinLane 7 57
(David Dennis) *dwlt: in tch in last pair: rdn over 2f out: outpcd and btn over 1f out: plugged on same pce ins fnl f* **10/1**

6314 **7** 2 ½ **Masqueraded (USA)**[63] 5775 3-9-4 68 (v) JamieSpencer 2 55
(Gay Kelleway) *chsd ldng pair tl over 2f out: lost pl u.p over 1f out: wknd fnl f* **16/1**

1m 24.98s (-2.22) **Going Correction** -0.275s/f (Stan)
WFA 3 from 4yo+ 2lb **7** Ran SP% **122.7**
Speed ratings (Par 101): **101,97,96,93,93 92,89**
CSF £10.94 TOTE £2.10: £1.50, £3.40; EX 14.80 Trifecta £31.60.Winner bought in for £11,000. Fullon Clarets was claimed by Mrs L. J. Mongan for £8,000.
Owner Power Geneva Ltd **Bred** Equine Breeding Limited **Trained** Newmarket, Suffolk

FOCUS
An uncompetitive seller and all very straightforward for the favourite.

7607 TOTEQUADPOT FOUR PLACES IN FOUR RACES MAIDEN FILLIES' STKS 1m 2f (P)
2:30 (2:32) (Class 4) 3-Y-O+ **£8,086** (£2,406; £1,202; £601) **Stalls** Low

Form RPR

64 **1** **Aqualis**[167] 2183 3-9-0 0 RobertHavlin 6 83
(John Gosden) *mde all: dictated stdy gallop tl qcknd and edgd rt over 1f out: asserted 1f out: styd on wl and drew clr fnl f: comf* **5/4**[1]

22 **2** 4 **Trishuli Rock (IRE)**[64] 5735 3-8-9 0 GeorgeWood(5) 7 75
(Marco Botti) *t.k.h: hld up wl in tch in midfield: effrt in 3rd and hung lft over 1f out: no ch w wnr ins fnl f: kpt on same pce to go 2nd towards fin* **3/1**[3]

2325 **3** ½ **Casablanca (IRE)**[14] 7280 3-9-0 74 JamieSpencer 8 74
(Andrew Balding) *pressed wnr: rdn and ev ch wl over 1f out: wnt rt over 1f out: no ex and outpcd 1f out: plugged on same pce after: lost 2nd towards fin* **2/1**[2]

6 **4** 6 **Kerrera**[22] 7052 3-9-0 0 WilliamCarson 4 62
(Paul Webber) *t.k.h: chsd ldng pair: rdn ent fnl 2f: sn outpcd: 4th and wknd over 1f out* **25/1**

00 **5** 4 ½ **Mon Petite Etoile (FR)**[44] 6415 3-9-0 0 TomMarquand 5 53
(David Elsworth) *in tch in last pair: rdn over 3f out: outpcd u.p over 2f out: wl btn over 1f out* **66/1**

6 2 ¼ **Broughtons Salsa** 3-9-0 0 StevieDonohoe 1 49
(Henry Spiller) *in tch in last pair: rdn over 3f out: outpcd over 2f out: wl btn over 1f out* **33/1**

0 **7** 15 **Mighty Minks**[9] 7410 4-9-2 0 AlistairRawlinson(3) 3 19
(Michael Appleby) *s.i.s: t.k.h and wl in tch in midfield: rdn over 2f out: sn lost pl: bhd 1f out* **100/1**

2m 6.97s (-1.63) **Going Correction** -0.275s/f (Stan)
WFA 3 from 4yo+ 5lb **7** Ran SP% **112.0**
Speed ratings (Par 102): **95,91,91,86,83 81,69**
CSF £5.12 TOTE £2.20: £1.20, £2.10; EX 5.80 Trifecta £8.40.
Owner Al Asayl Bloodstock Ltd **Bred** Al Asayl Bloodstock Ltd **Trained** Newmarket, Suffolk

FOCUS
An uncompetitive fillies' maiden and the three with form on the board pulled well clear. It's been rated around the third.

7608 TOTEPOOLLIVEINFO.COM FOR RACING RESULTS H'CAP 1m 2f (P)
3:00 (3:01) (Class 2) 3-Y-O+ **£29,110** (£8,662; £4,329; £2,164) **Stalls** Low

Form RPR

-562 **1** **Banditry (IRE)**[4] 7535 4-8-11 **81** RobertHavlin 2 89
(Ian Williams) *trckd ldrs: effrt to chse ldr 2f out: led and edgd rt over 1f out: in command and r.o wl ins fnl f* **7/2**[2]

0162 **2** 1 ¼ **Brigliadoro (IRE)**[26] 6915 5-9-3 **92** PaddyBradley(5) 10 97
(Philip McBride) *stdd s and dropped in bhd after s: hld up in last pair: clsd and travelling strly over 1f out: nt clr run 1f out: sn swtchd rt and rdn: r.o to go 2nd nr fin: nvr gng to rch wnr* **16/1**

1310 **3** ¾ **Mithqaal (USA)**[18] 7153 3-8-6 **81** AndrewMullen 9 85
(Michael Appleby) *t.k.h: hld up in tch in midfield: effrt on inner over 1f out: chsd clr wnr wl ins fnl f: kpt on but no imp: lost 2nd nr fin* **14/1**

0620 **4** nse **Abareeq**[53] 6126 3-9-0 **89** JoeFanning 6 92
(Mark Johnston) *in tch in midfield: swtchd lft and effrt over 1f out: hdwy u.p to chal for placings 1f out: kpt on but no imp on wnr* **33/1**

5544 **5** ½ **Pactolus (IRE)**[60] 5874 5-9-0 **87** (t) AaronJones(3) 4 89
(Stuart Williams) *chsd ldrs: clsd to press ldrs and rdn 2f out: chsd wnr but unable qck jst ins fnl f: edgd lft and one pced fnl 100yds* **16/1**

123 **6** 1 **Lusory**[48] 6261 3-9-3 **92** [1] AdamKirby 1 93+
(Charlie Appleby) *s.i.s and rdn along early: in tch in last quartet: effrt on inner over 1f out: keeping on but not looking like getting on terms whn nt clr run and swtchd rt ins fnl f: one pced after* **7/4**[1]

211 **7** nse **Raising Sand**[12] 7316 4-9-10 **94** GeorgeBaker 11 94
(Jamie Osborne) *hld up in tch in last quartet: swtchd rt and effrt u.p over 1f out: keeping on same pce whn nudged jst ins fnl f* **7/1**[3]

4413 **8** 1 ¼ **Haalan**[59] 5932 4-9-8 **92** MartinHarley 5 90
(James Tate) *led: rdn 2f out: hdd over 1f out: unable qck u.p 1f out: lost 2nd 150yds out: wknd wl ins fnl f* **8/1**

4016 **9** 2 **Beardwood**[4] 7535 4-8-13 **83** (p) JamieSpencer 8 77
(Mark Johnston) *hld up in tch in last pair: c centre and effrt over 1f out: no imp u.p: wknd ins fnl f* **9/1**

0050 **10** 8 **Montsarrat (IRE)**[34] 6715 3-9-1 **90** MartinLane 7 68
(Mark Johnston) *pressed ldr: rdn over 2f out: lost pl u.p and bhd 1f out: wknd fnl f* **14/1**

2m 3.14s (-5.46) **Going Correction** -0.275s/f (Stan)
WFA 3 from 4yo+ 5lb **10** Ran SP% **120.2**
Speed ratings (Par 109): **110,109,108,108,107 107,107,106,104,98**
CSF £60.13 CT £714.58 TOTE £5.30: £1.70, £3.30, £4.00; EX 66.50 Trifecta £903.70.
Owner Buxted Partnership **Bred** Darley **Trained** Portway, Worcs

FOCUS
A quality handicap despite the absence of the top weight and likely favourite Very Talented. They didn't seem to go a great pace, but the winner did this very nicely. The third and fourth have been rated to form.

7609 ATTOTEPOOLRACING FILLIES' H'CAP 1m 2f (P)
3:30 (3:32) (Class 5) (0-70,70) 3-Y-O+ **£5,175** (£1,540; £769; £384) **Stalls** Low

Form RPR

-411 **1** **Estrella Eria (FR)**[20] 7103 3-8-5 **59** AndrewMullen 1 68
(George Peckham) *t.k.h: trckd ldrs: effrt to chse ldr 2f out: sn rdn and clr w ldr: drvn and upsides ins fnl f: styd on to ld on post* **9/4**[1]

2362 **2** nse **Forecaster**[27] 6901 3-9-2 **70** (v) AdamKirby 6 79
(Michael Bell) *w ldr tl led 7f out: rdn and qcknd 2f out: drvn and clr w wnr over 1f out: kpt on u.p: hdd on post* **7/2**[2]

132 **3** 6 **Unsuspected Girl (IRE)**[16] 7205 3-8-7 **68** SophieKilloran(7) 2 65
(David Simcock) *s.i.s: t.k.h: hld up in rr: hdwy on inner 2f out: rdn over 1f out: chsd clr ldng pair 1f out: no imp* **9/4**[1]

0630 **4** ¾ **East Coast Lady (IRE)**[16] 7205 4-9-2 **65** MartinLane 3 61
(William Stone) *s.i.s: hld up in rr: clsd on inner over 2f out: effrt to chse clr ldng pair over 1f out: no imp: wl hld 4th and one pced ins fnl f* **8/1**[3]

6500 **5** 1 **Gloryette**[91] 4777 3-8-13 **67** TedDurcan 8 61
(Ed Dunlop) *chsd ldrs: rdn ent fnl 2f: outpcd and btn over 1f out: wknd ins fnl f* **20/1**

555 **6** nse **Medicean Queen (IRE)**[5] 7515 5-8-7 **59** (t) JosephineGordon(3) 4 52
(Phil McEntee) *hld up in tch: nt clr run and swtchd lft over 1f out: no imp after* **14/1**

6300 **7** 1 **Lady Lunchalot (USA)**[36] 6662 6-8-4 **58** (p) MeganNicholls(5) 7 49
(Laura Mongan) *s.i.s: hld up in tch: hdwy on outer 5f out: outpcd whn nt clr run and swtchd lft over 1f out: nt clr run again and swtchd lft again 1f out: no imp* **25/1**

2540 **8** 4 ½ **La Celebs Ville (IRE)**[33] 6742 3-9-1 **69** (p) PatCosgrave 9 51
(Tom Dascombe) *led tl 7f out: chsd ldr: rdn over 3f out: 3rd and outpcd 2f out: wknd fnl f* **16/1**

100 **9** 11 **Simply Clever**[80] 5201 3-8-0 **57** AaronJones(3) 5 17
(David Brown) *in tch in midfield: rdn and lost pl 4f out: lost tch over 1f out* **33/1**

2m 4.54s (-4.06) **Going Correction** -0.275s/f (Stan)
WFA 3 from 4yo+ 5lb **9** Ran SP% **119.0**
Speed ratings (Par 100): **105,104,100,99,98 98,97,94,85**
CSF £10.41 CT £19.54 TOTE £3.30: £1.30, £1.30, £1.30; EX 11.60 Trifecta £20.90.
Owner Fawzi Abdulla Nass **Bred** D Chassagneux & E A R L Ecurie Loire **Trained** Newmarket, Suffolk

■ Stewards' Enquiry : Andrew Mullen two-day ban: used whip above permitted level (Nov 9-10)

FOCUS
A modest fillies' handicap, but a thrilling finish between the first two who pulled miles clear of the others. Few ever got into it. The runner-up is the key to the form.

7610 COLLECT ANY TOTEPOOL WINNINGS AT BETFRED SHOPS H'CAP 6f (P)
4:00 (4:01) (Class 3) (0-95,95) 3-Y-O+ **£16,172** (£4,812; £2,405; £1,202) **Stalls** Centre

Form RPR

6565 **1** **Boomerang Bob (IRE)**[12] 7315 7-9-0 **88** WilliamCarson 10 97
(Jamie Osborne) *chsd ldrs: effrt 2f out: pressed ldng pair over 1f out: edgd lft u.p but str chal ins fnl f: r.o to ld on post* **9/1**

5010 **2** nse **Doctor Sardonicus**[53] 6112 5-9-5 **93** MartinHarley 3 101
(David Simcock) *chsd ldrs: effrt 2f out: rdn and str chal over 1f out: drvn to ld 100yds out: hdd on post* **4/1**[2]

0000 **3** ¾ **Highland Acclaim (IRE)**[4] 7530 5-9-2 **90** DavidNolan 9 96
(David O'Meara) *led: rdn wl over 1f out: drvn and hrd pressed jst over 1f out: hdd 100yds out: no ex and one pce towards fin* **16/1**

1000 **4** 4 ½ **Highly Sprung (IRE)**[17] 7186 3-8-13 **88** JoeFanning 14 80
(Mark Johnston) *chsd ldr: rdn to press wnr over 2f out tl unable qck over 1f out: 4th and btn 1f out: wknd ins fnl f* **25/1**

400 **5** nk **Quatrieme Ami**[12] 7315 3-9-0 **94** PaddyBradley(5) 11 85
(Philip McBride) *midfield but nt on terms: rdn over 2f out: drvn and styd on same pce fr over 1f out* **14/1**

2046 **6** nse **Golden Amber (IRE)**[52] 6161 5-9-7 **95** RobertWinston 2 85+
(Dean Ivory) *hld up towards rr: swtchd lft 4f out: effrt in centre over 1f out: kpt on ins fnl f: nvr trbld ldrs* **8/1**

3303 **7** nse **Rex Imperator**[32] 6792 7-9-5 **93** (p) DanielTudhope 6 83
(David O'Meara) *awkward as stalls opened and s.i.s: off the pce towards rr: effrt and swtchd rt over 1f out: kpt on ins fnl f: nvr trbld ldrs* **6/1**[3]

000 **8** 1 **Steelriver (IRE)**[45] 6371 6-8-12 **89** AaronJones(3) 7 76
(David Barron) *s.i.s: off the pce in rr: swtchd rt and effrt over 1f out: kpt on ins fnl f: nvr trbld ldrs* **25/1**

5200 **9** ¾ **Intense Style (IRE)**[12] 7315 4-9-2 **90** (b) DavidAllan 8 75
(Les Eyre) *midfield but nvr on terms: rdn over 3f out: drvn and no hdwy over 2f out: wknd ins fnl f* **16/1**

3136 **10** shd **Distant Past**[11] 7358 5-9-1 **89** (p) ShaneGray 13 73
(Kevin Ryan) *chsd ldng quartet: effrt over 2f out: no imp over 1f out: wknd ins fnl f* **16/1**

0316 **11** 1 ¾ **Hakam (USA)**[32] 6792 4-8-13 **87** AndrewMullen 4 66+
(Michael Appleby) *hld up off the pce in rr: hmpd and dropped to last 4f out: rdn and swtchd lft over 1f out: no imp* **7/2**[1]

0010 **12** 3 1/4 **Handsome Dude**[39] 6556 4-8-13 **87**........................(b) GrahamGibbons 1 55
(David Barron) *a off the pce towards rr: rdn over 3f out: bhd 2f out: sn wknd* **7/1**

1m 10.41s (-3.29) **Going Correction** -0.275s/f (Stan)
WFA 3 from 4yo+ 1lb **12** Ran SP% **122.1**
Speed ratings (Par 107): **110,109,108,102,102 102,102,101,100,99 97,93**
CSF £46.26 CT £585.98 TOTE £10.70: £3.10, £2.00, £4.60; EX 52.50 Trifecta £721.70.
Owner The Melbourne 10 **Bred** Dr Dean Harron & Ederidge Ltd **Trained** Upper Lambourn, Berks

FOCUS
A warm sprint handicap and another thrilling finish, but few ever got into it with the early 1-2-3-4 finishing 3-4-2-1. The front-running third has been rated to form.

7611 BOOK TICKETS AT CHELMSFORDCITYRACECOURSE.COM H'CAP (DIV I) 6f (P)
4:30 (4:30) (Class 6) (0-65,65) 3-Y-O+ **£3,234** (£962; £481; £240) **Stalls** Centre

Form RPR

4655 **1** **Arlecchino's Rock**[22] 7038 3-8-5 **57**........................(p) LuluStanford(7) 5 64
(Mark Usher) *chsd ldrs: effrt on inner over 1f out: rdn and ev ch 1f out: led wl ins fnl f: r.o wl: rdn out* **6/1**[3]

3443 **2** 1/2 **Only Ten Per Cent (IRE)**[21] 7069 8-9-2 **63**.......... AlistairRawlinson(3) 8 69
(J R Jenkins) *t.k.h: chsd ldrs: effrt to chal over 1f out: drvn and led 100yds out: sn hdd and unable qck towards fin* **12/1**

2100 **3** 1/2 **Fleeting Dream (IRE)**[11] 7363 3-9-6 **65**........................(b) PatCosgrave 7 69
(William Haggas) *t.k.h: chsd ldr: rdn and ev ch over 1f out: led ent fnl f: hdd 100yds: no ex and one pced after* **7/1**

0021 **4** nk **Rock Warbler (IRE)**[18] 7145 3-9-3 **62**................................(t) KevinStott 3 65
(Oliver Greenall) *v.s.a: in rr: clsd and in tch 1/2-way: swtchd rt and effrt over 1f out: styd on wl fnl 100yds: nt rch ldrs* **11/4**[1]

6406 **5** 1 3/4 **Nellie Deen (IRE)**[37] 6629 3-9-6 **65**.............................. TomMarquand 1 63
(David Elsworth) *in tch in last trio: effrt over 1f out: kpt on same pce u.p ins fnl f: nvr enough pce to chal* **6/1**[3]

46U0 **6** nk **Darrell Rivers**[62] 5793 4-9-2 **60**... JoeFanning 4 57
(Giles Bravery) *led: rdn over 1f out: hdd jst over 1f out: losing pl whn squeezed for room jst ins fnl f: wknd fnl 100yds* **10/1**

0603 **7** 2 **Firesnake (IRE)**[15] 7255 3-8-11 **63**.................................. JordanUys(7) 6 54
(Lisa Williamson) *awkward leaving stalls and rdr lost off side iron: midfield: swtchd rt and hdwy over 3f out: chsd ldrs 2f out: lost pl over 1f out: wknd ins fnl f* **12/1**

3520 **8** 4 1/2 **Guanabara Bay (IRE)**[8] 7442 3-9-6 **65**..........................(b1) AdamKirby 9 42
(Martyn Meade) *t.k.h: hld up in tch: swtchd rt after 1f out: carried wd bnd over 3f out: swtchd rt and effrt in centre over 1f out: sn btn and wknd fnl f* **9/2**[2]

0000 **9** 4 1/2 **Wink Oliver**[16] 7203 4-9-7 **65**...(v1) MartinLane 2 29
(David Dennis) *a towards rr: carried wd bnd over 3f out: struggling u.p over 2f out: bhd fnl f* **12/1**

1m 12.32s (-1.38) **Going Correction** -0.275s/f (Stan)
WFA 3 from 4yo+ 1lb **9** Ran SP% **118.1**
Speed ratings (Par 101): **98,97,96,96,93 93,90,84,78**
CSF £76.37 CT £519.70 TOTE £8.20: £2.50, £2.20, £2.20; EX 104.80 Trifecta £1580.20.
Owner K Senior **Bred** The Aston House Stud **Trained** Upper Lambourn, Berks
■ Stewards' Enquiry : Pat Cosgrave caution: careless riding

FOCUS
The first division of a moderate sprint handicap and something of an unsatisfactory result, but the winner was always in the ideal position and was given a good ride.

7612 BOOK TICKETS AT CHELMSFORDCITYRACECOURSE.COM H'CAP (DIV II) 6f (P)
5:00 (5:00) (Class 6) (0-65,64) 3-Y-O+ **£3,234** (£962; £481; £240) **Stalls** Centre

Form RPR

3006 **1** **Himalayan Queen**[15] 7255 3-8-12 **63**........................ SophieKilloran(7) 2 68
(William Jarvis) *hld up in tch: clsd and swtchd rt over 1f out: hdwy to chse ldrs and drvn ins fnl f: r.o wl to ld towards fin* **8/1**

2155 **2** 1/2 **Mossy's Lodge**[21] 7069 3-9-4 **62**.. AdamKirby 1 66
(Anthony Carson) *chsd ldrs: rdn and swtchd rt over 1f out: drvn 1f out: ev ch ins fnl f: styd on* **9/2**[2]

5050 **3** 3/4 **Mighty Zip (USA)**[15] 7255 4-8-13 **63**............................(p) JordanUys(7) 9 64
(Lisa Williamson) *led and crossed to inner: rdn over 1f out: hdd and no ex towards fin* **12/1**

4532 **4** 1 1/2 **Summersault (IRE)**[43] 6461 5-9-7 **64**.......................... JamieSpencer 4 61
(Jamie Osborne) *hld up in tch in midfield: swtchd rt and effrt over 1f out: styd on same pce ins fnl f* **15/8**[1]

44 **5** 3 **Maymyo (IRE)**[21] 7069 5-9-2 **64**................................(t) MitchGodwin(5) 6 52
(Sylvester Kirk) *chsd ldr: rdn over 2f out: no ex and lost 2nd 1f out: wknd ins fnl f* **7/1**[3]

3650 **6** 1 1/2 **Loumarin (IRE)**[15] 7255 4-9-5 **62**.................................. AndrewMullen 5 45
(Michael Appleby) *chsd ldrs: rdn and unable qck over 1f out: wknd ins fnl f* **12/1**

3303 **7** 2 1/4 **Andalusite**[22] 7038 3-8-13 **57**..(p) JoeFanning 8 34
(Ed McMahon) *midfield tl dropped to rr and hung rt 4f out: nvr on terms after* **9/2**[2]

-000 **8** 1 **Los Cerritos (SWI)**[13] 7301 4-9-7 **64**.............................. RobertHavlin 7 38
(Sophie Leech) *sn outpcd in rr: n.d* **25/1**

1m 12.1s (-1.60) **Going Correction** -0.275s/f (Stan)
WFA 3 from 4yo+ 1lb **8** Ran SP% **114.0**
Speed ratings (Par 101): **99,98,97,95,91 89,86,85**
CSF £43.46 CT £433.61 TOTE £7.50: £2.00, £1.90, £3.60; EX 49.60 Trifecta £1024.30.
Owner Miss Samantha Dare **Bred** Usk Valley Stud **Trained** Newmarket, Suffolk

FOCUS
The winning time was 0.22sec faster than the first division.
T/Plt: £40.60 to a £1 stake. Pool: £52,295.93 - 939.98 winning units. T/Qpdt: £13.10 to a £1 stake. Pool: £4,486.82 - 253.2 winning units. **Steve Payne**

7457 KEMPTON (A.W) (R-H)
Wednesday, October 26

OFFICIAL GOING: Polytrack: standard to slow
Wind: Almost nil Weather: Some cloud

7613 RACINGUK.COM/DAYPASS H'CAP 1m 2f (P)
5:45 (5:47) (Class 6) (0-65,69) 3-Y-O+ **£2,264** (£673; £336; £168) **Stalls** Low

Form RPR

2423 **1** **Fast And Hot (IRE)**[30] 6827 3-9-3 **64**...........................(b) KieranO'Neill 2 71
(Richard Hannon) *in tch: rdn to chse ldrs over 1f out: boxed in ent fnl f: fnd gap and qcknd to ld nr fin* **9/2**[1]

6454 **2** 3/4 **Estibdaad (IRE)**[36] 6662 6-9-7 **63**..........................(t) MichaelJMMurphy 8 69
(Paddy Butler) *led: taken on and increased tempo 1/2-way: kpt on u.p fnl f: hdd and unable qck nr fin* **12/1**

5154 **3** nk **Tyrsal (IRE)**[21] 7078 5-9-7 **63**.. ShaneKelly 6 68
(Clifford Lines) *mid-div: hdwy over 1f out: r.o wl fnl f: clsng at fin* **9/1**

2243 **4** shd **Power Up**[28] 6871 5-9-4 **60**.. GeorgeBaker 1 65
(Jane Chapple-Hyam) *a.p: kpt on u.p fnl 2f* **5/1**[2]

11 **5** 3/4 **Bollihope**[8] 7435 4-9-13 **69** 6ex.................................. FergusSweeney 11 72
(Richard Guest) *towards rr: drvn along and rn wd ent st: styd on wl fr over 1f out* **13/2**[3]

1024 **6** 1 1/4 **Pacific Salt (IRE)**[34] 6700 3-9-4 **65**...................................... LiamKeniry 9 66
(Pam Sly) *plld hrd in 6th: rapid hdwy to join ldr 1/2-way tl over 1f out: disputing 2nd and hld whn squeezed for room ins fnl f* **7/1**

4544 **7** 1/2 **Paper Faces (USA)**[12] 7326 3-9-3 **64**.............................. HarryBentley 4 64
(Roger Varian) *chsd ldrs: lost pl and rdn over 3f out: styd on again fr over 1f out* **8/1**

1120 **8** 1/2 **First Summer**[15] 7246 4-9-4 **65**.................................... GeorgeWood(5) 3 64
(Shaun Harris) *mid-div: rdn over 2f out: styd on same pce* **16/1**

5000 **9** 1 1/2 **Aid To Africa (IRE)**[16] 7227 3-8-13 **63**.................. EdwardGreatrex(3) 13 59
(Michael Bell) *stdd s and dropped in: hld up and bhd: drvn along 3f out: styd on fnl f* **40/1**

260 **10** 3/4 **Ost Wind**[36] 6657 4-9-9 **65**... AdamBeschizza 14 60
(Michael Attwater) *prom: outpcd 3f out: btn in midfield whn n.m.r over 1f out* **33/1**

1104 **11** 1/2 **African Showgirl**[22] 7035 3-9-3 **64**................................ SteveDrowne 10 58
(George Baker) *towards rr: sme hdwy on outer 4f out: wknd over 2f out* **33/1**

4400 **12** 1 **Tee It Up Tommo (IRE)**[22] 7035 7-9-2 **61**...........(tp) HectorCrouch(3) 12 53
(Daniel Steele) *bhd: sme hdwy on inner over 3f out: wknd over 2f out* **33/1**

3005 **13** 1/2 **McDelta**[12] 7336 6-9-2 **63**...................................(p) CallumShepherd(5) 7 54
(Ian Williams) *a bhd* **14/1**

5604 **14** 2 **Live Dangerously**[22] 7037 6-9-4 **60**............................ DougieCostello 5 47
(John Bridger) *a bhd* **25/1**

2m 9.84s (1.84) **Going Correction** +0.075s/f (Slow)
WFA 3 from 4yo+ 5lb **14** Ran SP% **117.1**
Speed ratings (Par 101): **95,94,94,94,93 92,92,91,90,89 89,88,88,86**
CSF £53.80 CT £469.71 TOTE £5.00: £1.70, £3.20, £3.00; EX 55.90 Trifecta £474.80.
Owner Derek And Jean Clee **Bred** D D & Mrs J P Clee **Trained** East Everleigh, Wilts
■ Stewards' Enquiry : Kieran O'Neill caution: careless riding

FOCUS
Something of a tactical affair, and a bunched finish.

7614 100% PROFIT BOOST AT 32REDSPORT.COM H'CAP 1m 4f (P)
6:15 (6:17) (Class 6) (0-65,65) 3-Y-O+ **£2,264** (£673; £336; £168) **Stalls** Low

Form RPR

12-0 **1** **Halling's Wish**[36] 6659 6-9-10 **63**.............................(b) GeorgeBaker 9 69
(Gary Moore) *mde virtually all: hrd rdn 2f out: hld on wl* **7/1**[2]

6406 **2** 1 1/2 **Earthwindorfire**[22] 7037 5-9-4 **60**.....................(p) JosephineGordon(3) 1 64
(Geoffrey Deacon) *a.p: kpt on u.p fnl 2f* **7/1**[2]

4226 **3** 1/2 **Mamoo**[23] 7008 3-8-13 **59**...(p) ShaneKelly 13 62
(Mike Murphy) *chsd ldrs: rdn and styd on fnl 2f* **8/1**[3]

3140 **4** nk **Overlord**[5] 7516 4-9-6 **59**...(v) FergusSweeney 7 61
(Mark Rimell) *s.s: wl bhd tl gd hdwy on inner 2f out: one pce fnl f* **8/1**[3]

5600 **5** nse **Hold Hands**[15] 7257 5-9-2 **55**... TedDurcan 14 57
(Brendan Powell) *stdd s and dropped in towards rr: gd hdwy 2f out: one pce fnl f* **11/1**

-000 **6** nk **Miss Dusky Diva (IRE)**[7] 7463 4-8-12 **51** oh3............... KieranO'Neill 12 53
(David W Drinkwater) *t.k.h towards rr: last and drvn along 3f out: styd on fnl 2f* **66/1**

5304 **7** 3/4 **Multigifted**[13] 7300 3-8-5 **56**.. GeorgeWood(5) 10 57
(Michael Madgwick) *t.k.h: sn in tch on outer: rdn and lost pl over 2f out: styd on fnl f* **13/2**[1]

3000 **8** 1/2 **Smoky Hill (IRE)**[14] 7274 7-9-7 **60**.. JoeyHaynes 3 60
(Tony Carroll) *in tch: drvn along over 2f out: styd on same pce* **20/1**

5400 **9** 3/4 **Sunshineandbubbles**[26] 6920 3-8-11 **57**................(p) DougieCostello 4 56
(Daniel Mark Loughnane) *mid-div: effrt and in tch over 1f out: no ex fnl f* **16/1**

1-00 **10** 3/4 **Jersey Bull (IRE)**[30] 6827 4-9-7 **60**...................................... LiamKeniry 8 57
(Michael Madgwick) *bhd: hdwy and in tch 2f out: no imp fnl f* **16/1**

1504 **11** 1/2 **Hydrant**[21] 7078 10-9-10 **63**... ConnorBeasley 2 60
(Richard Guest) *prom: hrd rdn 3f out: wknd over 1f out* **14/1**

0102 **12** 1/2 **Maria's Choice (IRE)**[22] 7037 7-9-12 **65**..................(v) TimmyMurphy 11 61
(Jim Best) *in tch: hung rt over 2f out: sn outpcd* **14/1**

020- **13** 3/4 **Canadian Diamond (IRE)**[161] 7351 9-9-7 **60**............ AdamBeschizza 5 55
(Richard Rowe) *a bhd* **16/1**

11 **14** 11 **Flutterbee**[45] 6403 4-9-12 **65**.......................................(p) SteveDrowne 6 42
(George Baker) *mid-div tl wknd over 2f out* **8/1**[3]

2m 34.29s (-0.21) **Going Correction** +0.075s/f (Slow)
WFA 3 from 4yo+ 7lb **14** Ran SP% **117.2**
Speed ratings (Par 101): **103,102,101,101,101 101,100,100,99,99 99,98,98,90**
CSF £53.82 CT £404.19 TOTE £7.10: £2.30, £2.40, £2.60; EX 53.80 Trifecta £696.70.
Owner M Albon **Bred** B R Marsden **Trained** Lower Beeding, W Sussex

FOCUS
This was dictated from the front by the winner.

7615 RACING UK HD NURSERY H'CAP 6f (P)
6:45 (6:51) (Class 6) (0-60,60) 2-Y-O **£2,264** (£673; £336; £168) **Stalls** Low

Form RPR

4005 **1** **Geraldine (GER)**[14] 7275 2-9-2 **56**.. MartinHarley 7 59
(Stuart Williams) *hld up in midfield: hdwy and waited for gap over 1f out: qcknd to ld fnl strides* **3/1**[1]

6240 **2** hd **Seprani**[18] 7143 2-9-1 **60**.. GeorgeWood(5) 4 62
(Marco Botti) *prom: drvn level ins fnl f: led briefly nr fin: jst ct* **6/1**[3]

0335 **3** 1/2 **The Big Short**[27] 6896 2-9-6 **60**.................................. MichaelJMMurphy 3 61
(Charles Hills) *led: jnd ins fnl f: kpt on u.p: hdd nr fin* **13/2**

045 **4** 1 3/4 **Skellig Michael**[22] 7040 2-9-6 **60**.. TedDurcan 2 56
(Ben Haslam) *dwlt and squeezed out s: towards rr: hdwy on inner and hrd rdn 2f out: no imp fnl f* **16/1**

2013 **5** 3/4 **Rebel Heart**[27] 6887 2-9-1 **58**..(v) HectorCrouch(3) 1 51
(Bill Turner) *hld up in 6th: rdn over 2f out: styd on same pce* **9/1**

5040 **6** nk **Everkyllachy (IRE)**[22] 7047 2-9-0 **57**...............(b1) JosephineGordon(3) 11 50
(J S Moore) *chsd ldrs tl one pce appr fnl f* **9/1**

3043 **7** 1/2 **Spin Top**[14] 7275 2-9-5 **59**..(v) GeorgeBaker 8 50
(Joseph Tuite) *chsd ldr tl over 1f out: wknd ins fnl f* **9/2**[2]

604 **8** shd **Tea El Tee (IRE)**[16] 7224 2-9-4 **58**............................. DougieCostello 12 49
(Gay Kelleway) *bhd: rdn over 2f out: styng on at fin* **12/1**

6000 **9** 3 **Felstead Queen**36 6652 2-9-3 **57**........ ShaneKelly 9 39
(Joseph Tuite) *outpcd: a bhd* **50/1**
1m 12.98s (-0.12) **Going Correction** +0.075s/f (Slow) **9** Ran SP% **106.3**
Speed ratings (Par 93): **103,102,102,99,98 98,97,97,93**
CSF £17.94 CT £87.24 TOTE £3.50: £1.20, £2.70, £2.40; EX 19.40 Trifecta £99.20.
Owner Graf Stauffenberg **Bred** Graf U Grafin V Stauffenberg **Trained** Newmarket, Suffolk
■ Dixie Peach was withdrawn. Price at time of withdrawal 14/1. Rule 4 applies to all bets - deduction 5p in the pound

FOCUS
A moderate nursery.

7616 32RED ON THE APP STORE MAIDEN STKS 7f (P)
7:15 (7:18) (Class 5) 3-Y-O+ **£2,911** (£866; £432; £216) **Stalls** Low

Form RPR
3 **1** **Red Trooper (FR)**173 2005 3-9-5 0........ SteveDrowne 11 79+
(George Baker) *prom: led 1f out: rdn out* **7/2**2
66 **2** 1 **Princess Nia (IRE)**16 7218 3-9-0 0........ ShaneKelly 5 72
(Brian Meehan) *in tch: effrt over 2f out: jnd ldrs over 1f out: kpt on* **25/1**
2-54 **3** 1 **Senses Of Dubai**162 2321 3-9-5 75........ MichaelJMMurphy 12 74
(Jamie Osborne) *led: hrd rdn and hdd 1f out: kpt on same pce* **12/1**
4 1 1/2 **Fleeting Glimpse** 3-8-7 0........1 JoshuaBryan(7) 10 65+
(Andrew Balding) *hld up in midfield: rdn and hdwy over 1f out: kpt on fnl f* **33/1**
43 **5** 1 **Loveatfirstsight**13 7311 3-9-0 0........ AdamBeschizza 9 62
(Michael Attwater) *mid-div: hdwy 2f out: hrd rdn over 1f out: one pce* **9/1**3
63 **6** 3 **Commodity (IRE)**16 7218 3-9-5 0........ TedDurcan 3 59
(Sir Michael Stoute) *trckd ldrs: rdn 2f out: no rspnse* **10/11**1
3 **7** 1 1/4 **Hurricane Rock**23 7011 3-9-5 0........ GeorgeBaker 7 56
(Simon Dow) *wnt lft s: towards rr: rdn 2f out: nvr rchd ldrs* **10/1**
40 **8** 3/4 **Ross Raith Rover**13 7311 3-9-5 0........ JackMitchell 13 54
(Robert Eddery) *dwlt: nvr trbld ldrs* **50/1**
0 **9** hd **Scribner Creek (IRE)**7 7459 3-9-5 0........ DaleSwift 8 53
(Daniel Mark Loughnane) *stdd and bmpd s: t.k.h in rr: rdn over 2f out: n.d* **66/1**
10 3 3/4 **Magic Moments** 3-9-0 0........ FergusSweeney 1 38
(Alan King) *in tch on inner tl wknd wl over 1f out* **20/1**
5 **11** 2 **Piccola Poppy**16 7219 3-8-11 0........ JosephineGordon(3) 2 33
(John Bridger) *mid-div tl hrd rdn and wknd over 2f out* **150/1**
0 **12** 36 **Little Lizzie**23 7011 3-8-9 0........ MeganNicholls(5) 14
(Paddy Butler) *plld hrd: sn chsng ldrs: wknd qckly over 2f out* **150/1**
1m 26.19s (0.19) **Going Correction** +0.075s/f (Slow) **12** Ran SP% **117.7**
Speed ratings (Par 103): **101,99,98,97,95 92,91,90,89,85 83,42**
CSF £90.73 TOTE £4.90: £1.80, £5.90, £2.40; EX 104.40 Trifecta £804.90.
Owner PJL Racing 1 **Bred** Famille Niarchos **Trained** Manton, Wilts

FOCUS
A fair maiden.

7617 32RED.COM H'CAP 7f (P)
7:45 (7:45) (Class 4) (0-80,80) 3-Y-O+ **£4,690** (£1,395; £697; £348) **Stalls** Low

Form RPR
6213 **1** **Volition (IRE)**25 6964 3-9-2 **77**........ TedDurcan 2 83
(Sir Michael Stoute) *trckd ldrs gng wl on inner: led ins fnl f: drvn out* **4/1**1
4350 **2** nk **Major Crispies**32 6780 5-9-7 **80**........(t) GeorgeBaker 5 86
(Jeremy Gask) *t.k.h towards rr: effrt and swtchd lft 1f out: fin wl: snatched 2nd on line* **4/1**1
0234 **3** shd **Panther Patrol (IRE)**14 7267 6-8-10 **74**........(p) HollieDoyle(5) 3 80
(Eve Johnson Houghton) *chsd ldrs: hrd rdn over 1f out: r.o wl nr fin* **4/1**1
245 **4** 1/2 **Owaseyf (USA)**14 7281 3-9-4 **79**........ HarryBentley 9 83
(Roger Varian) *a.p: kpt on wl u.p fnl 2f* **4/1**1
3423 **5** nk **Anonymous John (IRE)**16 7221 4-9-2 **78**........ JosephineGordon(3) 4 82
(Dominic Ffrench Davis) *chsd ldrs: effrt and hrd rdn 2f out: r.o* **15/2**2
0013 **6** 1/2 **Gulland Rock**37 6637 5-8-12 **71**........ WilliamCarson 10 73
(Anthony Carson) *led: hrd rdn 2f out: hdd and one pce ins fnl f* **20/1**
060- **7** nk **Cayuga**355 7731 7-9-4 **77**........ JackMitchell 1 79
(Brett Johnson) *bhd: rdn and hdwy over 1f out: kpt on fnl f: nvr able to chal* **25/1**
5566 **8** 2 **Major Valentine**41 6510 4-8-5 **67**........ EdwardGreatrex(3) 8 63
(John O'Shea) *plld hrd: trckd ldrs on outer: hrd rdn and btn over 1f out* **20/1**
-106 **9** 4 **Muthraab Aldaar (IRE)**16 7204 3-8-11 **72**........ FergusSweeney 11 56
(Jim Boyle) *a in rr* **14/1**3
1m 26.23s (0.23) **Going Correction** +0.075s/f (Slow)
WFA 3 from 4yo+ 2lb **9** Ran SP% **111.8**
Speed ratings (Par 105): **101,100,100,99,99 99,98,96,91**
CSF £18.17 CT £65.56 TOTE £4.30: £1.90, £1.90, £1.90; EX 18.80 Trifecta £88.10.
Owner Cheveley Park Stud **Bred** Doc Bloodstock **Trained** Newmarket, Suffolk
■ Stewards' Enquiry : Hollie Doyle two-day ban: used whip above permitted level (Nov 9-10)

FOCUS
A competitive handicap, and the open betting was justified given the way they finished in a heap.

7618 32RED H'CAP 1m 4f (P)
8:15 (8:16) (Class 3) (0-90,87) 3-Y-O
£7,158 (£2,143; £1,071; £535; £267; £134) **Stalls** Low

Form RPR
1130 **1** **Marmajuke Bay**16 7215 3-8-13 **79**........(p) SteveDrowne 2 87+
(Mark Usher) *prom: sltly outpcd and hrd rdn over 2f out: styd on to ld fnl 50yds* **9/1**
1563 **2** 1 1/4 **Fashion Parade**21 7067 3-9-3 **83**........ MartinHarley 4 89
(Charles Hills) *chsd ldr: hung rt over 1f out: drvn to ld ins fnl f: hdd and one pce fnl 50yds* **6/1**2
2036 **3** 1/2 **Isharah (USA)**39 6565 3-8-12 **78**........ RichardKingscote 8 83
(Mark Johnston) *hld up in 5th: rdn over 2f out: styd on wl fnl f* **13/2**3
4633 **4** nk **Red Rannagh (IRE)**35 6675 3-9-6 **86**........(t) JamieSpencer 5 91+
(David Simcock) *stdd s: t.k.h in rr: rdn and n.m.r whn hung rt 2f out: styd on wl fnl f* **6/5**1
3126 **5** 1/2 **Duck A L'Orange (IRE)**68 5596 3-8-6 **75**........(p) EdwardGreatrex(3) 1 79
(Michael Bell) *led at modest pce: qcknd 3f out: hrd rdn 2f out: hdd and no ex ins fnl f* **14/1**
5420 **6** 2 1/4 **Maestro Mac (IRE)**22 7060 3-8-12 **78**........ FMBerry 7 78
(Hughie Morrison) *chsd ldrs: rdn and hung rt over 2f out: btn over 1f out* **17/2**
216 **7** 2 1/4 **Loveable Helen (IRE)**59 5927 3-9-0 **80**........ TonyHamilton 6 77
(Richard Fahey) *plld hrd towards rr: rdn and n.d fnl 2f* **10/1**
2m 33.03s (-1.47) **Going Correction** +0.075s/f (Slow) **7** Ran SP% **109.4**
Speed ratings (Par 105): **107,106,105,105,105 103,102**
CSF £55.53 CT £344.98 TOTE £8.50: £2.80, £3.30; EX 40.10 Trifecta £198.90.
Owner The Ridgeway Alchemist's **Bred** The Welldiggers Partnership **Trained** Upper Lambourn, Berks
■ Stewards' Enquiry : Martin Harley two-day ban: used whip above permitted level (Nov 9-10)

FOCUS
This was steadily run and turned into a bit of a dash up the straight.

7619 32RED CASINO H'CAP (DIV I) 1m (P)
8:45 (8:46) (Class 5) (0-70,74) 3-Y-O+ **£2,911** (£866; £432; £216) **Stalls** Low

Form RPR
4614 **1** **Fast Sprite (IRE)**44 6416 4-9-6 **69**........(v1) GeorgeBaker 7 76+
(John Best) *hld up in rr: hdwy over 1f out: squeezed through ins fnl f: str run to ld nr fin* **3/1**2
2121 **2** 1/2 **Zlatan (IRE)**9 7417 3-9-8 **74** 6ex........(p) HarryBentley 1 79
(Ed de Giles) *travelled strly in 4th: chal on bit and led 1f out: hrd rdn fnl f: hdd and no ex nr fin* **5/2**1
2342 **3** 1 1/2 **Polymnia**14 7272 3-8-12 **69**........ HollieDoyle(5) 8 71
(Richard Hannon) *hld up in 6th: hdwy over 1f out: edgd rt: styd on* **7/1**
0300 **4** nse **So Much Fun (IRE)**29 6856 3-9-1 **67**........(v1) MartinHarley 3 68
(Ismail Mohammed) *led for 1f: prom: drvn to chal 1f out: one pce ins fnl f* **16/1**
153 **5** 1 3/4 **Stormbound (IRE)**68 5592 7-9-6 **69**........ JamieSpencer 5 67
(Paul Cole) *chsd ldrs: outpcd over 1f out: disputing 4th and hld whn hmpd ins fnl f* **10/1**
6430 **6** nk **Star Of The Stage**16 7203 4-9-7 **70**........(p) AdamBeschizza 6 68
(Julia Feilden) *led after 1f and set stdy pce: qcknd 2f out: hdd and no ex 1f out* **10/1**
0334 **7** 2 1/4 **Chandon Elysees**36 6649 3-9-1 **67**........ FergusSweeney 4 59
(Gary Moore) *dwlt: hld up in 7th: rdn and unable to chal fnl 2f* **25/1**
4022 **8** 1 **Capolavoro (FR)**28 6872 5-9-4 **67**........ PatCosgrave 9 57
(Robert Cowell) *prom: rdn 2f out: disputing 4th and fading whn hmpd ins fnl f* **5/1**3
1340 **9** nse **Imperial Link**15 7240 4-8-8 **60**........ EdwardGreatrex(3) 2 50
(John O'Shea) *dwlt: bhd: rdn 2f out: n.d* **40/1**
1m 40.27s (0.47) **Going Correction** +0.075s/f (Slow)
WFA 3 from 4yo+ 3lb **9** Ran SP% **113.1**
Speed ratings (Par 103): **100,99,98,97,96 95,93,92,92**
CSF £10.65 CT £46.09 TOTE £4.00: £1.50, £1.40, £2.20; EX 15.80 Trifecta £50.80.
Owner N Dyshaev & The Boys Partnership **Bred** John Costello **Trained** Oad Street, Kent

FOCUS
The complexion of this race changed dramatically in the closing stages.

7620 32RED CASINO H'CAP (DIV II) 1m (P)
9:15 (9:15) (Class 5) (0-70,70) 3-Y-O+ **£2,911** (£866; £432; £216) **Stalls** Low

Form RPR
0526 **1** **Dana's Present**71 5503 7-9-4 **67**........ LiamKeniry 8 76
(Tom Dascombe) *hld up towards rr: hdwy on bit and swtchd lft 2f out: led over 1f out: edgd lft: drvn out* **7/1**3
2000 **2** 1 **Red Cossack (CAN)**21 7076 5-9-5 **68**........(t) RobertWinston 3 75
(Paul Webber) *dwlt: bhd: rdn and hdwy to chal 1f out: carried lft: kpt on* **8/1**
5560 **3** 4 **Furiant**19 7111 3-9-2 **68**........ RichardKingscote 6 65
(Mark Johnston) *hld up in 5th: rdn over 2f out: styd on same pce: wnt 3rd ins fnl f* **5/1**2
6043 **4** 1 1/2 **Shifting Star (IRE)**9 7417 11-9-6 **69**........(vt) WilliamCarson 9 63
(John Bridger) *led tl over 1f out: no ex fnl f* **8/1**
6104 **5** 1 1/2 **Prim And Proper**28 6872 5-8-13 **62**........(b) DanielMuscutt 5 53
(John Flint) *prom tl wknd over 1f out* **5/1**2
4430 **6** 2 3/4 **Anastazia**29 6851 4-9-1 **69**........ CliffordLee(5) 7 54
(Paul D'Arcy) *dwlt: sn in tch in 4th on outer: wknd 2f out* **7/4**1
4130 **7** 8 **Bridge Builder**28 6872 6-9-1 **64**........(p) TomMarquand 4 30
(Peter Hedger) *prom: jnd ldr 1/2-way tl 2f out: wknd over 1f out* **8/1**
1m 39.07s (-0.73) **Going Correction** +0.075s/f (Slow)
WFA 3 from 4yo+ 3lb **7** Ran SP% **115.5**
Speed ratings (Par 103): **106,105,101,99,98 95,87**
CSF £60.91 CT £306.17 TOTE £7.60: £3.30, £4.40; EX 54.10 Trifecta £235.60.
Owner Russell Jones & Partner **Bred** Newsells Park Stud **Trained** Malpas, Cheshire

FOCUS
This was set up for those coming from behind. It was the quicker of the two divisions by 1.2sec.
T/Plt: £236.00 to a £1 stake. Pool: £81,214.66 - 251.19 winning units T/Qpdt: £29.10 to a £1 stake. Pool: £8,036.81 - 203.95 winning units **Lee McKenzie**

7283 NOTTINGHAM (L-H)
Wednesday, October 26

OFFICIAL GOING: Good (good to soft in places; 7.5)
Wind: Light against Weather: Cloudy with sunny periods

7621 EBF STALLIONS GOLDEN HORN MAIDEN STKS (PLUS 10 RACE) (DIV I) 1m 75y
1:50 (1:56) (Class 4) 2-Y-O **£5,175** (£1,540; £769; £384) **Stalls** Centre

Form RPR
1 **Tartini (USA)** 2-9-1 0 ow1........1 RobertTart 2 82
(John Gosden) *in tch on inner: hdwy 3f out: swtchd rt to outer 2f out: rdn over 1f out: styd on strly to ld towards fin* **25/1**
2 **2** 1/2 **Dhajeej (IRE)**16 7225 2-9-0 0........ DaneO'Neill 12 80
(Roger Varian) *trckd ldr: cl up over 3f out: led wl over 2f out: rdn and edgd lft wl over 1f out: drvn ins fnl f: hdd and no ex towards fin* **2/1**2
3 1 1/4 **Alaik** 2-9-0 0........ OisinMurphy 4 77
(Saeed bin Suroor) *trckd ldng pair: hdwy on inner over 2f out: cl up whn n.m.r and hmpd wl over 1f out: sn swtchd rt and rdn: kpt on fnl f* **6/1**3
4 **4** 6 **Azam**34 6704 2-9-0 0........ FrankieDettori 11 63
(John Gosden) *prom: led after 1f: pushed along 3f out: rdn and hdd 2f out: sn n.m.r and hmpd: grad wknd* **6/5**1
0 **5** 3/4 **Melting Dew**21 7065 2-9-0 0........ WilliamBuick 3 61
(Sir Michael Stoute) *in tch: hdwy to chse ldrs wl over 2f out: sn rdn along and no imp* **9/1**
6 3/4 **Garbanzo (IRE)** 2-9-0 0........ ThomasBrown 9 60
(Ed Walker) *dwlt and towards rr: hdwy wl over 2f out: sn rdn along and no imp* **66/1**
00 **7** nk **Leapt**23 7013 2-9-0 0........ PaulMulrennan 7 59
(Roger Charlton) *t.k.h: trckd ldrs: pushed along 3f out: rdn over 2f out: grad wknd* **50/1**
00 **8** nse **Brimham Rocks**28 6881 2-9-0 0........ FMBerry 10 59
(Ralph Beckett) *chsd ldrs on outer: rdn along 3f out: wknd over 2f out* **150/1**

0 **9** *1* **Dream Machine (IRE)**[32] 6777 2-9-0 0 .... RichardKingscote 5 57
(Michael Bell) *towards rr: rdn along 3f out: plugged on fr over 1f out* **100/1**

10 *16* **Arcadian Sea (IRE)** 2-9-0 0 .... LiamKeniry 1 20
(William Jarvis) *dwlt: a rr: outpcd and bhd fnl 3f* **150/1**

1m 45.2s (-3.80) **Going Correction** -0.45s/f (Firm) 2y crse rec **10** Ran SP% **112.7**
Speed ratings (Par 97): **101,100,99,93,92 91,91,91,90,74**
CSF £73.20 TOTE £31.10: £5.00, £1.10, £2.00; EX 115.30 Trifecta £638.90.
Owner George Strawbridge **Bred** George Strawbridge Jr **Trained** Newmarket, Suffolk
■ Special Relation was withdrawn. Price at time of withdrawal 20/1. Rule 4 does not apply.
■ Stewards' Enquiry : Dane O'Neill caution: careless riding

FOCUS
The inner track was in use for the first time since April and all distances were as advertised. This looked the stronger of the two divisions and the time was a good bit quicker. John Gosden won this in 2014 with Golden Horn and he took it again this year, although not with the one the market implied he would.

7622 EBF STALLIONS GOLDEN HORN MAIDEN STKS (PLUS 10 RACE) (DIV II) 1m 75y

2:20 (2:21) (Class 4) 2-Y-O **£5,175** (£1,540; £769; £384) **Stalls** Centre

Form RPR

1 **Youmkin (USA)** 2-9-0 0 .... WilliamBuick 12 78
(Saeed bin Suroor) *trckd ldrs: hdwy 3f out: led 11/2f out: rdn clr ent fnl f: kpt on* **3/1**[1]

2 *1 1/2* **Face The Facts (IRE)** 2-9-0 0 .... FrankieDettori 6 75
(John Gosden) *trckd ldr: cl up 1/2-way: effrt and ev ch 11/2f out: sn rdn and kpt on same pce* **6/1**

3 *nk* **Itsakindamagic** 2-9-0 0 ....[1] LiamKeniry 11 74
(Andrew Balding) *dwlt: hdwy and in tch after 3f: effrt on outer to chse ldrs over 2f out: rdn wl over 1f out: kpt on fnl f* **33/1**

4 *1* **Steaming (IRE)** 2-9-0 0 .... FMBerry 9 72
(Ralph Beckett) *hld up in rr: hdwy on outer wl over 2f out: rdn wl over 1f out: styd on fnl f: nrst fin* **14/1**

0 **5** *2* **Envoy**[16] 7226 2-9-0 0 .... RyanTate 2 67
(James Eustace) *led: pushed along 3f out: rdn over 2f out: hdd and drvn 11/2f out: grad wknd* **16/1**

6 *3/4* **Scales Of Justice (IRE)** 2-9-0 0 .... RichardKingscote 1 65
(Charles Hills) *trckd ldrs: pushed along 3f out: rdn 2f out: grad wknd* **11/2**[3]

06 **7** *1 3/4* **Solo Mission**[16] 7225 2-9-0 0 .... TomQueally 10 61
(William Haggas) *rr: sme hdwy over 2f out: sn rdn and n.d* **14/1**

0 **8** *1 1/4* **Just In Time**[14] 7283 2-8-9 0 .... HollieDoyle[(5)] 4 58
(Alan King) *in tch: hdwy to chse ldrs 3f out: rdn along over 2f out: grad wknd* **20/1**

6 **9** *1* **Pow Wow**[35] 6664 2-9-0 0 .... PaulMulrennan 7 56
(Roger Charlton) *dwlt: t.k.h and hdwy on inner into midfield after 3f: effrt to chse ldrs 3f out: rdn along over 2f out: sn drvn and wknd over 1f out* **7/2**[2]

00 **10** *1 3/4* **Master Billie (IRE)**[55] 6044 2-9-0 0 .... MartinDwyer 3 52
(William Muir) *midfield: rdn along 3f out: sn wknd* **100/1**

11 *3/4* **Outcrop (IRE)** 2-9-0 0 .... JimmyFortune 5 50
(Hughie Morrison) *trckd ldrs: pushed along wl over 3f out: rdn wl over 2f out: sn wknd* **8/1**

1m 48.73s (-0.27) **Going Correction** -0.45s/f (Firm) **11** Ran SP% **115.9**
Speed ratings (Par 97): **83,81,81,80,78 77,75,74,73,71 70**
CSF £20.51 TOTE £2.80: £1.50, £2.60, £6.30; EX 17.00 Trifecta £108.30.
Owner Godolphin **Bred** Darley **Trained** Newmarket, Suffolk

FOCUS
This didn't look as strong as the first division and the time was a good bit slower, but still there were one or two likeable performances.

7623 ROA/RACING POST OWNERS JACKPOT H'CAP 1m 75y

2:50 (2:50) (Class 4) (0-85,83) 3-Y-O+ **£4,690** (£1,395; £697; £348) **Stalls** Centre

Form RPR

3410 **1** **Carnageo (FR)**[18] 7159 3-8-12 **77** .... TonyHamilton 8 86
(Richard Fahey) *hld up: hdwy 3f out: chsd ldrs over 2f out: rdn to ld jst over 1f out: drvn out* **8/1**

6450 **2** *nk* **Torrid**[23] 7010 5-8-12 **74** .... CamHardie 14 83+
(Michael Easterby) *hld up: hdwy 3f out: trckd ldrs 2f out: rdn over 1f out: chsd wnr ins fnl f: sn drvn and kpt on* **16/1**

0006 **3** *1 3/4* **Wilde Inspiration (IRE)**[33] 6736 5-9-0 **81** .... AdamMcNamara[(5)] 7 86
(Julie Camacho) *midfield: hdwy to trck ldrs over 3f out: effrt wl over 1f out: rdn and whn nt clr run and swtchd lft ent fnl f: sn drvn and kpt on wl towards fin* **7/1**[3]

4462 **4** *2 1/4* **Fast Dancer (IRE)**[17] 7189 4-9-7 **83** .... OisinMurphy 11 83
(Joseph Tuite) *towards rr: hdwy on wd outside 2f out: sn rdn and styd on wl fnl f: nrst fin* **6/1**[1]

0351 **5** *shd* **Stanley (GER)**[21] 7076 5-9-0 **76** .... GrahamLee 3 76
(Jonjo O'Neill) *trckd ldrs: cl up over 3f out: led wl over 2f out: rdn and hdd over 1f out: sn drvn and edgd rt ent fnl f: wknd* **13/2**[2]

000 **6** *1 1/2* **Auspicion**[23] 7010 4-8-11 **73** .... JamesSullivan 2 69
(Tom Tate) *hld up in rr: hdwy wl over 2f out: rdn wl over 1f out: styd on fnl f: nrst fin* **33/1**

1523 **7** *1* **Toboggan's Fire**[11] 7360 3-9-0 **79** .... PJMcDonald 15 72
(Ann Duffield) *midfield: hdwy 4f out: chsd ldrs 3f out: rdn along over 2f out: drvn over 1f out: grad wknd* **11/1**

2203 **8** *hd* **Planetaria (IRE)**[25] 6956 3-9-1 **80** .... JasonHart 12 72
(Garry Moss) *prom: cl up over 3f out: rdn along and ev ch 2f out: drvn and wknd appr fnl f* **10/1**

4022 **9** *1/2* **Sands Chorus**[16] 7227 4-9-0 **76** .... TomEaves 6 68
(James Given) *led: rdn along over 3f out: hdd wl over 2f out: sn drvn and grad wknd* **7/1**[3]

4120 **10** *2* **Nonno Giulio (IRE)**[19] 7126 5-9-1 **77** .... ConnorBeasley 10 65
(Roger Fell) *trckd ldrs: hdwy over 3f out and sn cl up: rdn along over 2f out: drvn wl over 1f out and sn wknd* **25/1**

1556 **11** *1/2* **Sunnua (IRE)**[11] 7360 3-9-0 **79** .... JackGarritty 13 64
(Richard Fahey) *midfield: hdwy on inner 3f out: chsd ldrs 2f out: sn rdn: drvn and wknd appr fnl f* **16/1**

100 **12** *6* **Zealous (IRE)**[68] 5616 3-9-2 **81** .... BenCurtis 4 53
(Alan Swinbank) *t.k.h: chsd ldrs: rdn along wl over 2f out: sn wknd* **16/1**

30-0 **13** *10* **Starfield**[13] 7308 7-9-3 **82** ....(v) RobHornby[(3)] 9 32
(Mandy Rowland) *clsd up: disp ld over 3f out: rdn along wl over 2f out: sn wknd* **150/1**

0-35 **14** *27* **Foolaad**[259] 518 5-9-0 **76** ....(t) TomQueally 1
(Roy Bowring) *t.k.h: a rr* **50/1**

2604 **15** *1/2* **Trinity Star (IRE)**[55] 6055 5-9-1 **77** ....(p) PaulMulrennan 5
(Michael Dods) *dwlt: a rr* **17/2**

1m 44.15s (-4.85) **Going Correction** -0.45s/f (Firm)
WFA 3 from 4yo+ 3lb **15** Ran SP% **118.7**
Speed ratings (Par 105): **106,105,103,101,101 100,99,98,98,96 95,89,79,52,52**
CSF £124.05 CT £966.73 TOTE £11.40: £2.80, £6.80, £2.80; EX 211.20 Trifecta £3895.20.
Owner The Up For Anything Syndicate **Bred** Viktor Timoshenko **Trained** Musley Bank, N Yorks

FOCUS
A fair handicap that set up for the closers, with them going a good gallop. A pb from the winner, and the third has been rated in line with his recent form, but the level is a bit fluid.

7624 RACING UK PROFITS RETURNED TO RACING H'CAP (DIV I) 1m 6f 15y

3:20 (3:21) (Class 4) (0-85,83) 3-Y-O+ **£4,690** (£1,395; £697; £348) **Stalls** Low

Form RPR

5621 **1** **London Prize**[5] 7507 5-9-1 **75** .... AdamMcNamara[(5)] 7 85+
(Ian Williams) *hld up and bhd: hdwy on wd outside over 3f out: led wl over 1f out: sn rdn clr: kpt on strly* **5/4**[1]

5053 **2** *3 1/4* **Coeur De Lion**[14] 7270 3-8-3 **72** .... HollieDoyle[(5)] 2 78
(Alan King) *prom: rdn along wl over 2f out: drvn over 1f out: styd on fnl f* **11/2**[2]

0114 **3** *hd* **Fire Jet (IRE)**[22] 7060 3-8-13 **77** .... TomQueally 1 82+
(John Mackie) *hld up and bhd: hdwy 3f out: chsd ldrs wl over 1f out: sn rdn and kpt on fnl f* **12/1**

3321 **4** *1 3/4* **Pastoral Music**[21] 7063 3-8-6 **75** .... CharlieBennett[(5)] 5 78
(Hughie Morrison) *trckd ldrs: hdwy over 3f out: rdn along over 2f out and sltly outpcd: sn drvn and kpt on fnl f* **14/1**

1133 **5** *3/4* **Captain Peacock**[33] 6735 3-8-12 **76** ....(v) RichardKingscote 11 78
(William Knight) *trckd ldr: led over 4f out: rdn along and hung lft 2f out: sn hdd and drvn: wknd over 1f out* **10/1**[3]

/410 **6** *3/4* **Zamoyski**[75] 5350 6-9-9 **78** ....(p) PJMcDonald 9 79
(Steve Gollings) *trckd ldrs: pushed along over 4f out: rdn 3f out: drvn over 2f out and plugged on one pce* **50/1**

1124 **7** *2 1/2* **Duke Of Diamonds**[23] 7006 4-9-2 **74** .... ShelleyBirkett[(3)] 10 71
(Julia Feilden) *.hld up towards rr: hdwy on outer over 3f out: pushed along whn n.m.r wl over 2f out: sn rdn and no imp* **20/1**

3311 **8** *1/2* **Transpennine Star**[43] 6438 3-9-1 **79** .... PaulMulrennan 6 76
(Michael Dods) *led: hdd over 4f out and sn pushed along: rdn over 3f out: drvn wl over 2f out and sn wknd* **12/1**

0630 **9** *1* **Swaheen**[32] 6781 4-9-9 **83** .... JoshDoyle[(5)] 3 78
(Julie Camacho) *midfield: hdwy over 3f out: rdn along wl over 2f out and sn btn* **10/1**[3]

2650 **10** *6* **Bulas Belle**[12] 7320 6-9-8 **77** .... GrahamLee 8 64
(Grant Tuer) *hld up towards rr: hdwy to trck ldrs after 5f: pushed along over 4f out: rdn along whn n.m.r wl over 2f out: sn wknd* **28/1**

500P **11** *29* **Tangba**[16] 7205 3-8-7 **71** ....[1] AndreaAtzeni 4 17
(Roger Varian) *in tch: rdn along 6f out: sn lost pl and bhd fnl 3f* **20/1**

3m 6.97s (-0.03) **Going Correction** 0.0s/f (Good)
WFA 3 from 4yo+ 9lb **11** Ran SP% **115.0**
Speed ratings (Par 105): **100,98,98,97,96 96,94,94,93,90 73**
CSF £7.06 CT £55.95 TOTE £2.30: £1.40, £1.50, £3.80; EX 10.10 Trifecta £75.00.
Owner Mrs Margaret Forsyth **Bred** P And Mrs A G Venner **Trained** Portway, Worcs

FOCUS
An ordinary handicap and the favourite proved much too good.

7625 RACING UK PROFITS RETURNED TO RACING H'CAP (DIV II) 1m 6f 15y

3:50 (3:50) (Class 4) (0-85,85) 3-Y-O+ **£4,690** (£1,395; £697; £348) **Stalls** Low

Form RPR

1203 **1** **Pointel (FR)**[22] 7060 3-9-3 **83** .... FrederikTylicki 11 90+
(James Fanshawe) *trckd ldrs: hdwy 3f out: chsd ldr over 2f out: chal over 1f out: rdn to ld ent fnl f: drvn and hld on wl towards fin* **11/4**[1]

1165 **2** *nk* **Corpus Chorister (FR)**[22] 7060 3-8-11 **77** .... MartinDwyer 4 83
(David Menuisier) *led: rdn along over 2f out: jnd over 1f out: hdd ent fnl f: sn drvn: rallied gamely and ev ch last 100 yds: no ex nr fin* **15/2**[3]

10-0 **3** *1 1/2* **Song Light**[28] 6870 6-8-12 **72** .... RobHornby[(3)] 8 76
(Seamus Mullins) *hld up in rr: hdwy over 3f out: effrt on inner to chse ldrs 2f out: drvn and kpt on fnl f* **12/1**

-001 **4** *shd* **Velvet Revolution**[16] 7223 3-8-7 **73** .... AndreaAtzeni 10 77+
(Marco Botti) *hld up in rr: hdwy 3f out: swtchd rt to outer and rdn along 2f out: drvn over 1f out: styd on wl fnl f* **7/2**[2]

1545 **5** *shd* **Ivanhoe**[28] 6885 6-8-10 **67** ....(v) RichardKingscote 6 71
(Michael Blanshard) *trckd ldrs: hdwy over 4f out: rdn along wl over 2f out: drvn wl over 1f out: kpt on same pce* **12/1**

6015 **6** *1 1/4* **Zenafire**[14] 7274 7-8-7 **67** ....(p) JackDuern[(3)] 2 69
(Sarah Hollinshead) *trckd ldrs: hdwy 4f out: rdn along wl over 2f out: drvn wl over 1f out: sn wknd* **20/1**

2104 **7** *hd* **Forth Bridge**[33] 6735 3-9-5 **85** ....(p) FrankieDettori 1 87
(Michael Bell) *trckd ldrs: effrt over 3f out: rdn along over 2f out: wknd wl over 1f out* **11/1**

402 **8** *1/2* **Marshall Aid (IRE)**[29] 6854 3-8-2 **68** .... JimmyQuinn 7 69
(Mark Usher) *reminders s: sn trcking ldrs: hdwy over 3f out: rdn wl over 2f out: drvn wl over 1f out: wknd* **16/1**

3512 **9** *8* **Parnell's Dream**[130] 3409 4-9-6 **77** .... FMBerry 3 67
(Ralph Beckett) *hld up: hdwy over 4f out: chsd ldrs 3f out: sn rdn along and btn 2f out* **8/1**

40-5 **10** *14* **Crystalise (IRE)**[49] 6239 4-8-10 **67** oh3 ow1 .... OisinMurphy 9 37
(Robert Stephens) *hld up towards rr: sme hdwy over 4f out: rdn along over 3f out: sn outpcd* **50/1**

2000 **11** *92* **Rideonastar (IRE)**[16] 7215 5-9-9 **80** .... BenCurtis 5
(Brendan Powell) *chsd ldng pair: sddle slipped after 3f: sn lost pl and virtually p.u over 5f out* **11/1**

3m 4.76s (-2.24) **Going Correction** 0.0s/f (Good)
WFA 3 from 4yo+ 9lb **11** Ran SP% **116.4**
Speed ratings (Par 105): **106,105,104,104,104 104,104,103,99,91 38**
CSF £23.46 CT £213.84 TOTE £3.70: £1.60, £2.50, £3.70; EX 25.50 Trifecta £306.10.
Owner Swinburn, Godfrey & French **Bred** Franklin Finance S A **Trained** Newmarket, Suffolk

FOCUS
Slightly more open than the first division, although the horses who were backed came to the fore. The fifth helps set the standard in a bunched finish.

7626 RACING UK IN GLORIOUS HD H'CAP 5f 13y

4:20 (4:25) (Class 5) (0-75,75) 3-Y-O+ **£1,888** (£1,888; £432; £216) **Stalls** High

Form RPR

133 **1** **Pensax Lad (IRE)**[14] 7268 5-9-7 **75**................................ OisinMurphy 12 83
(Ronald Harris) *racd stands' side: in rr: hdwy 2f out: styd on wl to dead-heat post* **9/1**
1223 **1** *dht* **Mysterious Look**[177] 1935 3-9-2 **73**.............................. RobHornby[(3)] 17 82
(Ed McMahon) *racd stands' side: hld up in rr: hdwy over 1f out: ld last 35yds: jnd post* **12/1**
3363 **3** *3/4* **Flying Bear (IRE)**[9] 7420 5-9-1 **69**................................ FrederikTylicki 15 74
(Jeremy Gask) *racd stands' side: mid-div: hdwy to chse ldrs over 1f out: hung lft and kpt on to take cl 3rd fnl stride* **6/1**[1]
311 **4** *1/2* **Bahamian Sunrise**[13] 7303 4-8-13 **72**..................(p) JordanVaughan[(5)] 1 75
(John Gallagher) *led: hdd and no ex last 35yds* **7/1**[2]
0260 **5** *1/2* **Nocturn**[9] 7415 7-9-0 **73**...(p) CiaranMckee[(5)] 2 74
(Ronald Harris) *chsd ldrs: keeping on same pce whn n.m.r 75yds out* **25/1**
1123 **6** *nk* **John Joiner**[47] 6296 4-8-4 **63**...................................... CharlieBennett[(5)] 3 63+
(Peter Hedger) *towards rr: hdwy over 1f out: kpt on clsng stages* **12/1**
3500 **7** *nk* **Bonjour Steve**[14] 7290 5-8-2 **61** oh1.............................(p) PhilDennis[(5)] 14 62
(Richard Price) *in rr: hdwy and nt clr run over 1f out: kpt on* **33/1**
3431 **7** *dht* **Storm Melody**[45] 6363 3-9-7 **75**....................................... GrahamLee 8 75+
(Jonjo O'Neill) *rr-div: effrt and nt clr run over 1f out: kpt on last 100yds* **6/1**[1]
5100 **9** *shd* **Show Palace**[41] 6506 3-8-12 **66**... TomEaves 7 66
(Jennie Candlish) *trckd ldrs gng wl: nt clr run over 1f out: swtchd lft and kpt on same pce last 100yds* **10/1**
6013 **10** *1 1/4* **Coiste Bodhar (IRE)**[1] 7591 5-8-10 **71**................... NatalieHambling[(7)] 9 65
(Scott Dixon) *w ldrs: fdd last 150yds* **11/1**
1003 **11** *3/4* **Sarabi**[8] 7437 3-9-1 **69**...(tp) BenCurtis 6 62
(Scott Dixon) *chsd ldrs: n.m.r over 2f out: wknd fnl f* **16/1**
4543 **12** *3/4* **Billyoakes (IRE)**[28] 6879 4-9-2 **70**..........................(p) RichardKingscote 4 59
(Charlie Wallis) *chsd ldrs: wknd appr fnl f* **8/1**[3]
2020 **13** *shd* **Jaarih (IRE)**[16] 7202 4-9-7 **75**......................................(b) PaulMulrennan 10 64
(Conor Dore) *mid-div: drvn 2f out: nvr a threat* **20/1**
630 **14** *nk* **Young Tiger**[33] 6744 3-8-7 **61** oh1.................................. JamesSullivan 16 50
(Tom Tate) *stdd s: hld up stands' side: t.k.h: swtchd lft over 2f out: chsng ldrs far side over 1f out: wknd fnl 150yds* **20/1**
0000 **15** *1/2* **Air Of York (IRE)**[14] 7267 4-8-8 **69**..................................... AledBeech[(7)] 5 55
(David Evans) *rrd at s: bhd: sme hdwy whn nt clr run over 1f out: hung rt and swtchd rt last 150yds: nvr on terms* **33/1**
535 **16** *3* **Sir Theodore (IRE)**[79] 5230 3-9-4 **75**........................[1] LouisSteward[(3)] 11 51
(Richard Spencer) *in rr stands' side: lost pl over 1f out: bhd whn eased clsng stages* **20/1**

59.77s (-1.73) **Going Correction** -0.225s/f (Firm) **16** Ran SP% **124.9**
Speed ratings (Par 103): **104,104,102,102,101 100,100,100,100,98 96,95,95,95,94 89**
WIN: PL £5.10, ML £6.10.; PLACES: PL £2.20, ML £2.90, FB £2.30, BS £2.00 EXACTA: PL-ML £50.60, ML-PL £45.60 CSF: PL-ML £51.90, ML-PL £53.61. TRICAST: PL-ML-FB £254.21, ML-PL-FB £259.43. TRIFECTA: PL-ML-FB £498.20, ML-PL-FB £417.90.
Owner S L Edwards **Bred** S L Edwards **Trained** Lichfield, Staffs
■ Stewards' Enquiry : Jordan Vaughan caution: careless riding

FOCUS
Perhaps no surprise to see the high-drawn runners emerge on top, with the middle-to-stands' side the place to be all day. It's been rated around the third.

7627 RACINGUK.COM INTERACTIVE MAIDEN STKS 1m 2f 50y
4:50 (4:54) (Class 5) 3-Y-O+ **£2,911** (£866; £432; £216) **Stalls** Low

Form RPR
22 **1** **First Voyage (IRE)**[16] 7218 3-9-5 0................................[1] WilliamBuick 5 87
(Charlie Appleby) *mde all: rdn over 1f out: wandered lft and rt ins fnl f: kpt on wl towards fin* **3/1**[2]
33 **2** *3/4* **Bybrook**[37] 6617 3-9-0 0.. OisinMurphy 11 79
(David Simcock) *trckd wnr: cl up 3f out: rdn to chal wl over 1f out: ev ch whn swtchd lft wl ins fnl f: kpt on* **12/1**
2303 **3** *3/4* **Blaze Of Hearts (IRE)**[16] 7229 3-9-5 78......................... FrederikTylicki 4 82
(Dean Ivory) *chsd ldng pair: hdwy over 2f out: rdn and ev ch over 1f out: drvn and kpt on same pce fnl f* **10/1**
52 **4** *3* **Dharoos (IRE)**[10] 7384 3-9-5 0...................................... DaneO'Neill 14 76
(John Gosden) *trckd ldrs: hdwy 3f out: pushed along over 2f out: rdn wl over 1f out: no imp fnl f* **6/4**[1]
2 **5** *1* **Just For You**[84] 5023 3-9-0 0... FMBerry 7 69
(James Fanshawe) *in tch: hdwy on outer tio chse ldrs 3f out: effrt over 2f out: sn rdn: drvn and no imp fnl f* **9/2**[3]
303 **6** *shd* **Blue Jean Baby**[32] 6795 3-8-9 77.......................... AdamMcNamara[(5)] 8 69
(George Scott) *hld up in tch: hdwy 3f out: rdn along over 2f out: kpt on one pce* **20/1**
-004 **7** *3 1/2* **Royal Flag**[19] 7106 6-9-10 68...(b[1]) BenCurtis 12 67
(Brian Ellison) *towards rr: hdwy 4f out: in tch over 2f out: sn rdn and n.d* **25/1**
460 **8** *shd* **Poppy Time**[27] 6901 3-9-0 65.. RyanTate 1 62
(James Eustace) *chsd ldrs: rdn along wl over 2f out: sn wknd* **100/1**
0 **9** *6* **Ravenswood**[22] 7052 3-9-5 0.................................. RichardKingscote 3 55
(Jonathan Portman) *a towards rr* **66/1**
10 *2 1/4* **Unblinking**[185] 3-9-5 0.. ThomasBrown 6 50
(Nigel Twiston-Davies) *dwlt: a bhd* **25/1**
11 *3 1/2* **Shakshuka (IRE)** 4-9-5 0.. GrahamLee 2 38
(Seamus Mullins) *a towards rr* **66/1**
12 *1/2* **Palindrome (USA)** 3-9-5 0...[1] TomEaves 13 42
(Ronald Thompson) *chsd ldrs: pushed along over 4f out: sn rdn and wknd* **33/1**
66 **13** *5* **Alidara (IRE)**[70] 5550 4-9-5 0......................................[1] TomQueally 9 27
(Emma Owen) *a towards rr* **200/1**

2m 13.15s (-1.15) **Going Correction** 0.0s/f (Good)
WFA 3 from 4yo+ 5lb **13** Ran SP% **119.8**
Speed ratings (Par 103): **104,103,102,100,99 99,96,96,91,90 87,86,82**
CSF £35.74 TOTE £4.10: £1.40, £2.80, £2.30; EX 31.20 Trifecta £160.60.
Owner Godolphin **Bred** Darley **Trained** Newmarket, Suffolk

FOCUS
Not a terribly strong maiden and two of the market leaders disappointed. The form is set around the third to begin with.

7628 AJA AMATEUR RIDERS' H'CAP 1m 2f 50y
5:20 (5:21) (Class 6) (0-60,66) 3-Y-O+ **£2,183** (£677; £338; £169) **Stalls** Low

Form RPR
0006 **1** **Whitchurch**[11] 7369 4-10-7 **49**.................................... MrBLynn[(3)] 14 56
(Philip Kirby) *mid-div: hdwy to trck ldrs 4f out: led over 2f out: edgd lft fnl 100yds: drvn out* **14/1**
5512 **2** *1* **Monday Club**[22] 7057 3-10-11 **60**....................................... MrMEnnis[(5)] 6 65
(Dominic Ffrench Davis) *chsd ldrs: styd on same pce fnl 100yds* **8/1**[3]
0440 **3** *hd* **Bridey's Lettuce (IRE)**[72] 5481 4-11-7 **60**....................... MrJHarding 12 65
(Ivan Furtado) *hld up in mid-div: hdwy over 3f out: chsng ldrs over 1f out: swtchd lft and styd on to take handy 3rd nr fin* **8/1**[3]
6425 **4** *1/2* **Dark Amber**[14] 7272 6-11-1 **57**.....................................(tp) MrWillPettis[(3)] 7 61
(Brendan Powell) *rr-div: hdwy over 3f out: chsng ldrs over 1f out: kpt on same pce* **6/1**[2]
2551 **5** *2* **Fast Play (IRE)**[9] 7421 4-11-8 **66** 6ex...........................(b) MrJEPerrett[(5)] 3 66
(Richard Hughes) *hld up in rr: hdwy on ins over 3f out: chsng ldrs over 1f out: kpt on one pce* **5/1**[1]
1264 **6** *1 3/4* **Hint Of Grey (IRE)**[120] 3738 3-11-2 **60**.................................... MrHHunt 1 57
(Don Cantillon) *s.i.s: hdwy 8f out: chsng ldrs over 3f out: one pce appr fnl f* **5/1**[1]
4246 **7** *nk* **Highlife Dancer**[16] 7231 8-10-12 **54**......................(v) MissSMDoolan[(3)] 10 51
(Mick Channon) *led: hdd over 2f out: rallied 1f out: one pce* **25/1**
3404 **8** *1/2* **Funny Oyster (IRE)**[16] 7211 3-10-6 **55**........................(v) MrJJO'Neill[(5)] 9 51
(George Baker) *chsd ldrs: edgd lft over 1f out: one pce* **8/1**[3]
2400 **9** *6* **Grams And Ounces**[5] 7508 9-10-12 **58**.................(tp) MissCMBerry[(7)] 5 43
(Grace Harris) *in rr: hdwy 4f out: lost pl over 2f out* **33/1**
0436 **10** *1 3/4* **Scent Of Power**[30] 6827 4-10-10 **54**.................... MrRichardPatrick[(5)] 15 36
(Barry Leavy) *hld up towards rr: effrt over 3f out: wknd 2f out* **10/1**
220 **11** *1* **Flag Of Glory**[60] 5883 9-10-9 **51**.................................(b) MissMEdden[(3)] 4 31
(Peter Hiatt) *mid-div: lost pl over 3f out* **25/1**
0405 **12** *nk* **Occasional Dream (IRE)**[22] 7057 3-10-4 **55**........... MrsCPownall[(7)] 16 34
(Joseph Tuite) *hld up in rr: sn bhd* **100/1**
3400 **13** *3 1/2* **Merchant Of Medici**[12] 7336 9-10-11 **55**.................. MrJoeWright[(5)] 13 28
(Micky Hammond) *mid-div: drvn over 3f out: sn lost pl* **33/1**
0000 **14** *26* **Ruzeiz (USA)**[5] 7508 7-10-11 **57**.........................(b[1]) MissJSpinkova[(7)] 11
(Peter Hedger) *racd v wd: chsd ldrs: lost pl 3f out: sn bhd: t.o whn hung rt fnl f* **66/1**
0050 **U** **Shining Romeo**[71] 5529 4-11-2 **60**.................................... MrBJames[(5)] 2
(Denis Quinn) *mid-div: crowded: stmbld and uns rdr sn after s* **16/1**

2m 14.06s (-0.24) **Going Correction** 0.0s/f (Good)
WFA 3 from 4yo+ 5lb **15** Ran SP% **118.6**
Speed ratings (Par 101): **100,99,99,98,97 95,95,95,90,88 88,87,84,64,**
CSF £112.91 CT £970.66 TOTE £18.70: £5.00, £2.60, £3.10; EX 181.00 Trifecta £3754.10.
Owner The Turf N' Surf Racing Partnership **Bred** D R Tucker **Trained** East Appleton, N Yorks

FOCUS
Moderate handicap form.
T/Jkpt: Not Won. T/Plt: £91.00 to a £1 stake. Pool: £65,823.08 - 527.53 winning units. T/Qpdt: £30.00 to a £1 stake. Pool: £4,912.0 - 121.02 winning units. **Joe Rowntree & Walter Glynn**

7629 - 7636a (Foreign Racing) - See Raceform Interactive

BENDIGO
Wednesday, October 26
OFFICIAL GOING: Turf: good

7637a JAYCO BENDIGO CUP (GROUP 3 H'CAP) (3YO+) (TURF) 1m 4f
6:00 (12:00) 3-Y-O+
£89,108 (£26,732; £13,366; £6,683; £3,712; £2,970)

RPR
1 **Francis Of Assisi (IRE)**[92] 4734 6-8-9 **0**....................... KerrinMcEvoy 6 99+
(Charlie Appleby) *chsd ldr: pushed along and qcknd to ld under 3f out: kicked clr wl over 1f out: easily* **11/2**[3]
2 *3* **Second Bullet (AUS)**[24] 6996 6-8-9 **0**.............................. DamianLane 7 93
(Danny O'Brien, Australia) *chsd ldng trio: outpcd and rdn 2 1/2f out: styd on ins fnl 1 1/2f: no ch w wnr* **11/2**[3]
3 *1/2* **Our Century (IRE)**[14] 5-8-9 **0**... KatelynMallyon 4 92
(Robert Hickmott, Australia) *settled in fnl pair: hdwy on outer more than 3 1/2f out: rdn and no imp wl over 2f out: styd on fr over 1f out: nvr on terms w wnr* **13/10**[1]
4 *3 1/2* **Bring Something (AUS)**[11] 6-8-11 **0**................................... LukeNolen 9 89
(Ken Keys, Australia) *w.w in rr: rdn and nt qckn over 2f out: styd on ins fnl f: nvr in contention* **10/1**
5 *hd* **Howard Be Thy Name (AUS)**[18] 4-9-2 **0**........................(b) JohnAllen 3 95
(Darren Weir, Australia) *w.w towards rr: styd on fr over 1f out: nvr trbld ldrs* **9/2**[2]
6 *2* **Desert Samurai (AUS)**[11] 5-8-9 **0**.....................................(t) CoryParish 5 83
(Adam O'Neill, Australia) *led: hdd after 1f: remained cl up: rdn and nt qckn over 2f out: wknd ins fnl f* **60/1**
7 *shd* **Go Dreaming (AUS)**[11] 7378 7-8-9 **0**................................. JustinPotter 8 83
(Grant Kluske, Australia) *rushed up on outer to ld after 1f: hdd under 3f out: dropped away ins fnl 1 1/2f* **20/1**
8 *3 3/4* **Blizzard (NZ)**[13] 6-8-9 **0**.. CraigAWilliams 2 77
(Emma-Lee & David Browne, New Zealand) *sn settled in midfield: lost pl and rdn wl over 2f out: sn btn* **40/1**
9 *nk* **Ferro Nero (NZ)**[14] 5-8-9 **0**.......................................(bt) MichaelWalker 1 77
(Nigel Blackiston, Australia) *hld up towards rr: effrt into midfield 3f out: rdn and wknd ins fnl f* **16/1**

2m 30.49s (150.49) **9** Ran SP% **116.2**
.
Owner Godolphin **Bred** Queen Cleopatra Syndicate **Trained** Newmarket, Suffolk

7638 - (Foreign Racing) - See Raceform Interactive

7605 CHELMSFORD (A.W) (L-H)
Thursday, October 27
OFFICIAL GOING: Polytrack: standard
Wind: Light, half behind Weather: Dry

7639 BET TOTEPLACEPOT AT BETFRED.COM MAIDEN STKS 6f (P)
5:40 (5:40) (Class 5) 2-Y-O **£3,881** (£1,155; £577; £288) **Stalls** Centre

Form RPR
3 **1** **The Feathered Nest (IRE)**[20] 7122 2-9-0 0................... TonyHamilton 4 75+
(Richard Fahey) *travelled strly: trckd ldng pair: effrt to chal over 1f out: led ent fnl f: rn green in front but in command ins fnl f: pushed out* **15/8**[1]
4 **2** *3/4* **Ascot Day (IRE)**[19] 7142 2-9-5 0..................................... TomEaves 6 76
(David Simcock) *chsd ldr: rdn to chal and carried rt wl over 1f out: sn rdn to ld: hdd ent fnl f: kpt on wl but a hld ins fnl f* **2/1**[2]
4 **3** *5* **Habbad (FR)**[22] 7065 2-9-5 0..................................... TomMarquand 7 61
(Richard Hannon) *chsd ldng trio: effrt ent fnl 2f: drvn and outpcd ent fnl f: chsd clr ldng pair 75yds out: kpt on same pce* **6/1**

 The Form Book, Raceform Ltd, Newbury, RG14 5SJ

00 **4** *1* **Embleton**[21] 7099 2-9-0 0... AdamBeschizza 3 53
(Charlie Wallis) *led: drifted rt bnd wl over 1f out: sn rdn and hdd: 3rd and outpcd 1f out: wknd ins fnl f* **100/1**

5 *2* **Sunlit Forest (USA)** 2-9-0 0.. WilliamCarson 5 47
(Saeed bin Suroor) *s.i.s: sn rcvrd and in tch in midfield: rdn ent fnl 2f: unable qck over 1f out: wknd 1f out* **5/1**[3]

43 **6** *2* **Dream Reversion**[13] 7331 2-9-5 0.. BenCurtis 8 46
(Tom Dascombe) *stdd s: t.k.h: hld up in tch in last pair: effrt 2f out: sn u.p and struggling: wknd jst over 1f out* **12/1**

7 *½* **Mockery (IRE)** 2-9-0 0.. AndrewMullen 1 40
(Mark Johnston) *fly j. leaving stalls and slowly away: a rr: rdn over 2f out: sn struggling: wknd over 1f out* **25/1**

1m 12.69s (-1.01) **Going Correction** -0.225s/f (Stan) **7** Ran SP% **111.6**
Speed ratings (Par 95): **97,96,89,88,85 82,82**
CSF £5.60 TOTE £2.60: £1.40, £1.20; EX 5.70 Trifecta £19.10.
Owner R A Fahey **Bred** Airlie Stud **Trained** Musley Bank, N Yorks

FOCUS
They went fairly steady early on but the first two came clear in the closing stages. The third and fourth help set the opening level.

7640 BET TOTESWINGER AT BETFRED.COM NURSERY H'CAP 1m (P)
6:10 (6:11) (Class 5) (0-70,70) 2-Y-O **£3,881** (£1,155; £577; £288) **Stalls** Low

Form RPR

5550 **1** **King's Coinage (IRE)**[26] 6963 2-8-13 **62**..........................[1] LiamKeniry 1 65
(Ed Walker) *chsd ldrs after 1f: wnt 2nd wl over 1f out: sn rdn: chal u.p ins fnl f: styd on to ld towards fin* **6/1**

5352 **2** *½* **Tagur (IRE)**[20] 7109 2-9-3 **66**...(p) TomEaves 4 68
(Kevin Ryan) *led: rdn and edgd lft over 1f out: drvn and hrd pressed ins fnl f: hdd and one pce towards fin* **7/2**[1]

440 **3** *nk* **The Blues Master (IRE)**[24] 7003 2-9-7 **70**.................... AndrewMullen 3 71
(Mark Johnston) *in tch in rr: nt clr run over 2f out: swtchd rt and hdwy 1f out: styd on strly ins fnl f: nt quite rch ldrs* **7/1**

6536 **4** *¾* **Keepup Kevin**[28] 6898 2-9-3 **69**...................................... RobHornby(3) 7 68
(Pam Sly) *chsd ldr for 1f out: styd handy: effrt and nt clr run over 1f out: swtchd rt 1f out: kpt on same pce ins fnl f* **5/1**[3]

424 **5** *½* **Flood Defence (IRE)**[20] 7107 2-9-0 **66**....................... LouisSteward(3) 2 64
(Chris Wall) *dwlt: in tch in midfield: effrt on inner over 1f out: chsd ldrs 1f out: styd on same pce ins fnl f* **9/2**[2]

0206 **6** *3 ¾* **Too Many Shots**[17] 7228 2-9-2 **65**...................................... KierenFox 10 54
(John Best) *dwlt and bustled along leaving stalls: lost pl u.p over 1f out: wknd ins fnl f* **14/1**

000 **7** *4* **Oxford Blu**[84] 5081 2-8-5 **61**................................... ManuelFernandes(7) 8 40
(Sir Mark Prescott Bt) *pitched leaving stalls: in tch in rr: swtchd rt wl over 1f out: sn btn: wknd fnl f* **16/1**

0314 **8** *2* **Let's Be Happy (IRE)**[48] 6289 2-9-3 **66**............................ ShaneKelly 6 41
(Richard Hughes) *in tch in midfield: hdwy to chse ldrs over 2f out: rdn over 1f out: sn btn and wknd* **12/1**

6320 **9** *3 ½* **Money In My Pocket (IRE)**[49] 6257 2-9-6 **69**............. TomMarquand 5 35
(Richard Hannon) *in tch towards rr: rdn and struggling over 2f out: bhd fnl f* **6/1**

1m 39.45s (-0.45) **Going Correction** -0.225s/f (Stan) **9** Ran SP% **118.4**
Speed ratings (Par 95): **93,92,92,91,90 87,83,81,77**
CSF £28.06 CT £153.17 TOTE £7.60: £2.30, £1.40, £2.80; EX 35.10 Trifecta £380.20.
Owner Brook Stud Partnership **Bred** Calumet Farm Llc **Trained** Upper Lambourn, Berks

FOCUS
A modest nursery.

7641 BET TOTEQUADPOT AT BETFRED.COM (S) H'CAP 1m 2f (P)
6:40 (6:43) (Class 6) (0-55,55) 3-Y-O+ **£3,234** (£962; £481; £240) **Stalls** Low

Form RPR

266/ **1** **Fast On (IRE)**[12] 7375 7-8-12 **46**.......................................(p) ShaneKelly 7 53
(Seamus Fahey, Ire) *hld up in tch in midfield: swtchd rt and effrt over 1f out: str run u.p to ld ins fnl f: r.o wl* **9/2**[1]

0500 **2** *1 ½* **Ferryview Place**[6] 7515 7-9-0 **48**............................(p) StevieDonohoe 9 52
(Ian Williams) *hld up in midfield: hdwy on inner over 1f out: drvn to chse ldrs ins fnl f: styd on to go 2nd last strides* **8/1**

0430 **3** *nk* **Frivolous Prince (IRE)**[17] 7231 3-8-0 **46**...................(bt[1]) AledBeech(7) 8 50
(David Evans) *hld up in midfield: rdn and hdwy over 1f out: chsng ldrs and styng on whn nt clr run 100yds out: swtchd rt and styd on to snatch 3rd last strides* **6/1**[3]

0305 **4** *nk* **Santadelacruze**[15] 7282 7-9-2 **50**..............................(b) AdamBeschizza 10 53
(Mark Hoad) *chsd ldrs: effrt over 1f out: drvn and ev ch ins fnl f: hdd and one pce ins fnl f: lost 2 pls: last strides* **12/1**

0060 **5** *½* **Synodic (USA)**[16] 7260 4-9-7 **55**.......................................(t) TomEaves 16 57
(Seamus Durack) *chsd ldrs: wnt 2nd 7f out: upsides ldr and travelling strly 2f out: rdn to ld over 1f out: hdd ins fnl f: no ex and outpcd towards fin* **20/1**

0005 **6** *¾* **Let There Be Light**[17] 7230 3-9-2 **55**.............................. AndrewMullen 2 55
(Gay Kelleway) *t.k.h: chsd ldr tl 7f out: styd prom: effrt on inner over 1f out: drvn to press ldrs 1f out: unable qck and one pce fnl 100yds* **16/1**

2300 **7** *1 ½* **Mister Marcasite**[12] 7369 6-9-1 **49**....................................[1] CamHardie 5 47
(Antony Brittain) *t.k.h: hld up wl in tch in midfield: effrt over 1f out: unable qck and styd on same pce ins fnl f* **11/1**

4206 **8** *½* **My Mistress (IRE)**[24] 5753 4-9-0 **48**...........................(p) LiamKeniry 3 45
(Phil McEntee) *hld up wl in tch in midfield: effrt to chse ldrs whn nt clr run and hmpd over 1f out: swtchd rt 1f out: kpt on same pce after* **20/1**

0003 **9** *1 ¼* **Mr Potter**[37] 6646 3-8-13 **52**... ConnorBeasley 14 46
(Richard Guest) *t.k.h: hld up in tch in midfield: effrt over 1f out: no imp and one pce ins fnl f* **12/1**

0000 **10** *1 ½* **Myboydaniel**[6] 7515 4-9-2 **53**.......................................(p) RobHornby(3) 13 44
(Derek Shaw) *taken down early: stdd s: t.k.h: hld up in rr: effrt and sme hdwy u.p over 1f out: no imp fnl f: nvr trbld ldrs* **20/1**

2200 **11** *1* **Wild Flower (IRE)**[16] 7240 4-9-2 **50**................................ KieranO'Neill 1 40
(Jimmy Fox) *stdd after s: hld up in rr: pushed along over 3f out: effrt over 1f out: no real imp: nvr trbld ldrs* **5/1**[2]

3000 **12** *7* **Heathfield Park (IRE)**[9] 7442 3-8-11 **50**.............................. BenCurtis 11 26
(William Stone) *stdd and dropped in bhd after s: hld up in rr: rdn 3f out: wknd over 1f out* **50/1**

400 **13** *¾* **Buachaillnaheirean (IRE)**[39] 5255 3-8-10 **49**............[1] TomMarquand 6 24
(Neil King) *stdd s: hld up in rr: rdn 2f out: sn wknd* **33/1**

3505 **14** *hd* **Claude Greenwood**[155] 2588 6-9-1 **49**.......................(b) WilliamCarson 4 23
(Tony Carroll) *led: rdn over 2f out: hdd and wandered over 1f out: sn btn and wknd qckly fnl f* **7/1**

0603 **15** *½* **Majestic Girl (IRE)**[28] 6900 3-8-5 **49**..........................(p) GeorgiaCox(5) 12 23
(Steve Flook) *in tch in midfield: lost pl over 2f out: rdn and bhd over 1f out* **12/1**

2m 6.92s (-1.68) **Going Correction** -0.225s/f (Stan)
WFA 3 from 4yo+ 5lb **15** Ran SP% **129.2**
Speed ratings (Par 101): **97,95,95,95,94 94,93,92,91,90 89,84,83,83,82**
CSF £40.13 CT £230.03 TOTE £4.60: £1.90, £3.30, £2.50; EX 59.60 Trifecta £294.80.There was no bid for the winner.
Owner Mrs B Fahey **Bred** Jaykayeen Breeding **Trained** Monasterevln, Co. Kildare

FOCUS
Open betting for this low-grade contest. The third has been rated near his best AW form.

7642 BET TOTEEXACTA AT BETFRED.COM H'CAP 1m (P)
7:10 (7:16) (Class 6) (0-60,63) 3-Y-O+ **£3,234** (£962; £481; £240) **Stalls** Low

Form RPR

360 **1** **Little Choosey**[45] 6424 6-9-2 **55**................................(bt) ConnorBeasley 2 65
(Roy Bowring) *broke wl: sn stdd and wl in tch in midfield: hdwy to chse wnr over 1f out: rdn to ld 1f out: sn in command: r.o wl* **10/1**

6050 **2** *2* **Rattle On**[17] 7214 3-9-4 **60**.. LiamKeniry 6 64
(Jim Boyle) *in tch in midfield: effrt and hdwy over 1f out: chsd clr wnr jst ins fnl f: no imp on wnr but kpt on wl for clr 2nd* **5/1**[3]

6266 **3** *3 ¼* **Touch Of Color**[14] 7298 3-8-13 **55**............................ AdamBeschizza 10 51
(Jane Chapple-Hyam) *chsd ldrs: effrt 2f out: chsd ldrs and unable qck 1f out: outpcd ins fnl f: hld on for 3rd wl ins fnl f* **12/1**

4220 **4** *¾* **Hidden Gem**[28] 6908 3-9-4 **60**.. DougieCostello 9 54
(Ed Walker) *hld up in tch in midfield: effrt whn nt clr run and swtchd lft over 1f out: kpt on ins fnl f: no threat to ldrs* **4/1**[2]

3304 **5** *shd* **Schottische**[5] 7529 6-8-6 **52**..............................(p) LiamLewis-Salter(7) 7 47
(Alan Bailey) *in tch in midfield: effrt over 1f out: styd on same pce ins fnl f: nvr threatened ldrs* **12/1**

4053 **6** *¾* **Captain Marmalade (IRE)**[17] 7211 4-9-4 **57**................. KieranO'Neill 12 51
(Jimmy Fox) *s.i.s and swtchd lft after s: hld up in rr: effrt over 1f out: hdwy u.p 1f out: nt clr run and swtchd lft ins fnl f: kpt on but nvr trbld ldrs* **16/1**

5652 **7** *¾* **Hawk Moth (IRE)**[14] 7299 8-9-4 **57**....................................(b) TomEaves 1 50
(John Spearing) *t.k.h: hld up in tch in midfield: effrt on inner over 1f out: nt clr run and swtchd rt ins fnl f: kpt on but no threat to ldrs* **12/1**

3111 **8** *½* **Bazzat (IRE)**[9] 7427 3-9-7 **63** 6ex..............................(p) StevieDonohoe 14 52
(John Ryan) *s.i.s: bustled along and stuck wd in last pair: hdwy 2f out: no imp u.p 1f out: btn eased off wl ins fnl f* **2/1**[1]

0050 **9** *1 ¼* **Lendal Bridge**[21] 7096 5-8-9 **48**... BenCurtis 4 35
(Tony Coyle) *chsd ldr for 3f: rdn and unable qck over 1f out: wknd ins fnl f* **12/1**

5534 **10** *nk* **Master Of Song**[51] 6212 9-8-12 **54**....................(p) AlistairRawlinson(3) 3 43
(Roy Bowring) *hld up towards rr: rdn and effrt over 1f out: hdwy but no threat to ldrs whn nt clr run and swtchd rt ins fnl f: nvr trbld ldrs* **16/1**

2-31 **11** *hd* **Hold Firm**[245] 707 4-8-12 **58**.. GeorgiaDobie(7) 5 46
(Mark H Tompkins) *hld up in tch in midfield: nt clr run over 2f out: effrt u.p over 1f out: keeping on but no threat to ldrs whn hmpd ins fnl f: no imp after* **16/1**

60-0 **12** *1 ¼* **Miss Uppity**[166] 2255 3-8-12 **54**....................................... LemosdeSouza 16 36
(Ivan Furtado) *sn led: clr over 2f out: rdn and hdd 1f out: sn wknd* **66/1**

003 **13** *2 ¾* **Foylesideview (IRE)**[145] 2901 4-8-5 **47**....................... NoelGarbutt(3) 13 24
(Harry Chisman) *hld up towards rr: rdn and effrt over 1f out: no imp and wknd ins fnl f* **16/1**

-050 **14** *½* **Mayfield Boy**[6] 7514 5-9-6 **59**... CamHardie 11 35
(Antony Brittain) *hld up towards rr: effrt and n.m.r over 1f out: no imp: wl btn fnl f* **33/1**

0200 **15** *½* **Zeteah**[9] 7426 6-8-7 **46**.. TomMarquand 15 20
(Tony Carroll) *midfield: rdn and losing pl over 2f out: bhd over 1f out: wknd fnl f* **50/1**

0066 **16** *2 ¼* **Guilded Rock**[17] 7211 3-8-4 **46** oh1..............................(bt) AndrewMullen 8 14
(Stuart Kittow) *chsd ldrs: wnt 2nd 5f out tl lost pl ent fnl 2f out: bhd fnl f* **33/1**

1m 38.7s (-1.20) **Going Correction** -0.225s/f (Stan)
WFA 3 from 4yo+ 3lb **16** Ran SP% **142.7**
Speed ratings (Par 101): **97,95,91,91,90 90,89,88,87,87 87,85,83,82,82 79**
CSF £68.56 CT £679.27 TOTE £13.90: £2.80, £1.90, £3.50, £1.60; EX 95.40 Trifecta £1504.20.
Owner K Nicholls **Bred** Mrs Sandra Fox **Trained** Edwinstowe, Notts

FOCUS
The first two drew clear in this moderate handicap. The winner has been rated a bit better than for her previous winning form this season.

7643 BET TOTETRIFECTA AT BETFRED.COM H'CAP 5f (P)
7:40 (7:43) (Class 4) (0-85,85) 3-Y-O+
£4,980 (£1,491; £745; £372; £186; £93) **Stalls** Low

Form RPR

4000 **1** **Silvanus (IRE)**[10] 7413 11-9-4 **82**.................................. DougieCostello 11 90
(Paul Midgley) *taken down early: sn led and mde rest: rdn over 1f out: pressed and edgd sltly lft 100yds out: lft in command towards fin* **25/1**

0130 **2** *1* **Stanghow**[38] 6633 4-9-7 **85**... CamHardie 1 89
(Antony Brittain) *chsd ldrs: effrt over 1f out: chsd wnr 1f out: sn dropped to 3rd and kpt on same pce ins fnl f: lft 2nd again towards fin* **5/1**[2]

4010 **3** *½* **Oriental Relation (IRE)**[27] 6927 5-9-5 **83**....................(v) TomEaves 3 86
(James Given) *chsd ldr: rdn over 1f out: 4th and kpt on same pce ins fnl f: lft 3rd towards fin* **7/1**[3]

1100 **4** *nk* **Outrage**[29] 6878 4-9-0 **81**... RobHornby(3) 4 90+
(Daniel Kubler) *dwlt: hld up in tch towards rr: hdwy 2f out: clsd on inner over 1f out: pressing wnr and gng for narrow gap on inner ins fnl f: hmpd and btn wl ins fnl f: nt rcvr and lost 2 pls nr fin* **8/1**

1244 **5** *½* **Dynamo Walt (IRE)**[17] 7202 5-9-3 **81**............................(v) MartinLane 2 83+
(Derek Shaw) *chsd ldrs: effrt over 1f out: chsng ldrs whn squeezed for room and hmpd 1f out: styd on same pce after* **4/1**[1]

2021 **6** *nk* **Burning Thread (IRE)**[15] 7268 9-9-1 **79**........................(b) ShaneKelly 7 78
(David Elsworth) *midfield: effrt 2f out: no imp u.p over 1f out: styd on same pce ins fnl f* **10/1**

21-0 **7** *nk* **Alkhor**[156] 2554 3-9-2 **80**.. TomMarquand 6 79
(Richard Hannon) *s.i.s and swtchd lft after s: racd in last trio: effrt on inner over 1f out: hdwy 1f out: kpt on ins fnl f: nvr trbld ldrs* **20/1**

1026 **8** *nk* **Excellent George**[40] 6583 4-9-1 **82**.........................(t) AaronJones(3) 10 78
(Stuart Williams) *hld up in last quartet: effrt over 1f out: kpt on ins fnl f: nvr trbld ldrs* **4/1**[1]

3130 **9** *1 ¼* **Come On Dave (IRE)**[47] 6324 7-9-4 **82**..........................(v) LiamKeniry 9 74
(John Butler) *taken down early: squeezed for room leaving stalls: in rr: effrt over 1f out: rdn and swtchd rt 1f out: sme hdwy but nvr threatening ldrs: eased towards fin* **12/1**

2450 **10** *1 ½* **Razin' Hell**[36] 6680 5-9-6 **84**..........(v) BenCurtis 12 71
(John Balding) *chsd ldrs on outer: rdn and unable qck over 1f out: wknd ins fnl f* **25/1**

5100 **11** *7* **King Crimson**[17] 7206 4-9-3 **81**.......... MartinHarley 5 42
(John Butler) *stdd into midfield after s: rdn over 1f out: no hdwy: wknd fnl f* **8/1**

1-00 **12** *17* **Swiss Affair**[15] 7289 4-9-2 **80**.......... AdamBeschizza 8
(Robert Cowell) *midfield: rdn and dropped to rr over 2f out: lost tch over 1f out* **33/1**

58.36s (-1.84) **Going Correction** -0.225s/f (Stan) **12** Ran SP% **123.6**
Speed ratings (Par 105): **105,103,102,102,101 100,100,99,97,95 84,57**
CSF £146.51 CT £1014.69 TOTE £24.30: £7.90, £2.60, £3.00; EX 205.10 Trifecta £6067.40.
Owner Colin Alton **Bred** Barronstown Stud And Mrs T Stack **Trained** Westow, N Yorks
■ Stewards' Enquiry : Dougie Costello three-day ban: careless riding (Nov 10-12)

FOCUS
Bar the unlucky-in-running fourth, the principals were up with the pace throughout.

7644 TOTEPOOL BETTING AT BETFRED.COM H'CAP 6f (P)
8:10 (8:11) (Class 5) (0-75,75) 3-Y-O+ **£3,881** (£1,155; £577; £288) **Stalls** Centre

Form RPR

0066 **1** **Dutch Golden Age (IRE)**[17] 7206 4-9-3 **71**.......... GeorgeBaker 2 84+
(Gary Moore) *broke wl and led early: trckd ldrs after 1f out: wnt 2nd and travelling strly wl over 1f out: shkn up to chal 1f out: led ins fnl f: sn rdn clr: comf* **3/1**[1]

0456 **2** *2 ½* **Penny Dreadful**[12] 7363 4-9-0 **68**..........(p) DaleSwift 3 73
(Scott Dixon) *sn led: rdn over 1f out: hdd ins fnl f: sn outpcd by wnr: kpt on for clr 2nd* **14/1**

243 **3** *1 ¼* **Gung Ho Jack**[58] 6000 7-9-4 **72**.......... KierenFox 13 73+
(John Best) *midfield: effrt u.p over 1f out: swtchd rt and hdwy ins fnl f: styd on strly to go 3rd towards fin: no ch w wnr* **7/1**[2]

520 **4** *1 ¼* **Vimy Ridge**[9] 7443 4-9-6 **74**..........(v) GrahamGibbons 1 71
(Alan Bailey) *in tch in midfield: effrt over 1f out: drvn and unable qck 1f out: kpt on same pce ins fnl f* **3/1**[1]

1326 **5** *¾* **Dusty Blue**[15] 7268 4-8-13 **70**.......... EoinWalsh(3) 4 65
(Tony Carroll) *hld up in tch in midfield: rdn 2f out: styd on same pce and no threat to wnr ins fnl f* **10/1**[3]

1233 **6** *¾* **Soaring Spirits (IRE)**[45] 6409 6-9-7 **75**..........(b) RobertWinston 12 67
(Dean Ivory) *chsd ldrs after 1f out: rdn and unable qck over 1f out: wknd ins fnl f* **12/1**

1343 **7** *½* **Chetan**[17] 7206 4-9-7 **75**..........(tp) AdamBeschizza 10 66
(Charlie Wallis) *taken down early: nvr bttr than midfield: rdn over 2f out: kpt on to pass btn horses ins fnl f: nvr trbld ldrs* **7/1**[2]

43 **8** *nk* **One Big Surprise**[14] 7303 4-9-2 **70**..........(p) ShaneKelly 6 60
(Richard Hughes) *dwlt:hld up in tch in midfield: rdn over 1f out: no imp and btn 1f out: wknd ins fnl f* **10/1**[3]

6040 **9** *nk* **Classic Pursuit**[9] 7430 5-9-1 **69**..........(p) MartinHarley 14 58
(Ivan Furtado) *hld up in last pair: sme hdwy on inner over 1f out: swtchd rt 1f out: n.d whn nt clr run again ins fnl f* **20/1**

-000 **10** *3 ¼* **Vroom (IRE)**[11] 7386 3-9-5 **74**.......... AdamKirby 7 52
(Gay Kelleway) *sn chsng ldr tl wl over 1f out: sn u.p and lost pl: wknd fnl f* **20/1**

0/ **11** *nse* **Higher Court (USA)**[1112] 7171 8-9-7 **75**.......... DougieCostello 9 53
(Emma Owen) *t.k.h: hld up in midfield: pushed along over 1f out: sn btn: wknd 1f out* **50/1**

5000 **12** *1 ¾* **Just Be Lucky (IRE)**[16] 7240 4-9-6 **74**..........(b) TomEaves 8 47
(Conor Dore) *a towards rr: n.d* **33/1**

4000 **13** *5* **Desert Strike**[45] 6425 10-9-2 **70**..........(p) LiamKeniry 11 27
(Conor Dore) *taken down early: t.k.h: hld up in tch in midfield: lost pl and bhd 2f out: wknd over 1f out* **25/1**

1m 11.31s (-2.39) **Going Correction** -0.225s/f (Stan)
WFA 3 from 4yo+ 1lb **13** Ran SP% **125.8**
Speed ratings (Par 103): **106,102,101,99,98 97,96,96,95,91 91,89,82**
CSF £50.78 CT £294.56 TOTE £3.60: £2.00, £5.00, £2.00; EX 52.70 Trifecta £441.80.
Owner R A Green **Bred** Denis Bergin **Trained** Lower Beeding, W Sussex
■ Stewards' Enquiry : Dougie Costello jockey said gelding ran too freely
Shane Kelly jockey said filly was slowly away

FOCUS
Few got into this, the first two swapping places with a furlong to go.

7645 BOOK YOUR CHRISTMAS PARTY AT CHELMSFORDCITYRACECOURSE.COM H'CAP (DIV I) 7f (P)
8:40 (8:40) (Class 6) (0-55,55) 3-Y-O+ **£3,234** (£962; £481; £240) **Stalls** Low

Form RPR

0060 **1** **Hipz (IRE)**[14] 7302 5-9-3 **51**..........(p) GeorgeBaker 13 64
(Laura Mongan) *stdd and switching lft after s: hld up in tch in midfield: gng wl and clsd to chse ldrs whn swtchd lft over 1f out: sn qcknd to ld: clr ins fnl f: comf* **8/1**[3]

4234 **2** *4* **Cadland Lad (IRE)**[7] 7488 3-8-10 **49**..........(t) JosephineGordon(3) 9 50
(John Ryan) *chsd ldrs: effrt over 1f out: chsd wnr 1f out: edgd lft and kpt on same pce ins fnl f* **11/4**[1]

060 **3** *½* **Moving Robe (IRE)**[16] 7240 3-8-7 **46** oh1.......... NoelGarbutt(3) 4 46
(Conrad Allen) *pushed along early and sn dropped to rr: rdn and hdwy over 1f out: edgd lft u.p and styd on ins fnl f: no threat to wnr* **25/1**

0522 **4** *shd* **Concur (IRE)**[17] 7211 3-8-11 **47**..........(bt[1]) KieranO'Neill 10 47
(Rod Millman) *t.k.h: hld up in tch in midfield: effrt over 2f out: styd on same pce u.p ins fnl f* **5/1**[2]

3300 **5** *hd* **Ertidaad (IRE)**[113] 4009 4-9-4 **52**..........(b) DougieCostello 12 53
(Emma Owen) *squeezed out sn after leaving stalls: hld up in last pair: effrt over 1f out: hdwy 1f out: hung lft ins fnl f: keeping on but no threat to ldrs whn nt clr run and eased cl home* **16/1**

0006 **6** *¾* **Cadeaux Pearl**[19] 7145 8-8-13 **47**.......... BenCurtis 5 45
(Scott Dixon) *led: rdn and edgd rt over 1f out: sn hdd and unable qck: wknd ins fnl f* **14/1**

0060 **7** *¾* **Back To Love (CAN)**[14] 7302 3-8-3 **46** oh1.......... MillyNaseb(7) 3 42
(Mark Gillard) *s.i.s: bhd: rdn and hdwy on inner ent fnl f: keeping on but no ch w wnr whn nt clr run and hmpd wl ins fnl f: nvr trbld ldrs* **50/1**

0040 **8** *3* **Cecile Royale**[7] 7488 3-8-7 **46** oh1.......... AaronJones(3) 6 33
(Stuart Williams) *chsd ldrs: rdn and unable qck over 1f out: wknd ins fnl f* **33/1**

0-00 **9** *1 ¼* **Cara's Request (AUS)**[16] 7254 11-9-7 **55**.......... StevieDonohoe 8 40
(David C Griffiths) *chsd ldr: rdn 2f out: unable qck and lost pl over 1f out: wkng whn sltly hmpd 100yds out* **14/1**

0-00 **10** *½* **My Bubba**[267] 431 4-8-12 **46**.......... DanielMuscutt 11 29
(John Flint) *in tch in midfield on outer: rdn over 1f out: no hdwy: wknd fnl f* **8/1**[3]

0 **11** *2* **Fastnet Prince (IRE)**[108] 4202 3-9-4 **54**.......... AdamKirby 1 31
(David Evans) *chsd ldrs: rdn 2f out: unable qck and btn ent fnl f: sn wknd* **11/4**[1]

-500 **12** *2 ¾* **Let It Go**[218] 1035 4-8-12 **46** oh1.......... TomMarquand 2 16
(Tony Carroll) *hld up in tch in midfield: rdn and lost pl over 2f out: bhd fnl f* **33/1**

1m 25.86s (-1.34) **Going Correction** -0.225s/f (Stan)
WFA 3 from 4yo+ 2lb **12** Ran SP% **123.1**
Speed ratings (Par 101): **98,93,92,92,92 91,90,87,85,85 83,79**
CSF £30.59 CT £559.53 TOTE £10.00: £3.00, £1.30, £8.80; EX 38.10 Trifecta £884.10.
Owner Aberdour Racing Club **Bred** Mrs Noelle Walsh **Trained** Epsom, Surrey
■ Stewards' Enquiry : Noel Garbutt caution: careless riding

FOCUS
The winner proved well treated on her return to the AW and soon put this to bed in the straight. Straightforward form.

7646 BOOK YOUR CHRISTMAS PARTY AT CHELMSFORDCITYRACECOURSE.COM H'CAP (DIV II) 7f (P)
9:10 (9:10) (Class 6) (0-55,55) 3-Y-O+ **£3,234** (£962; £481; £240) **Stalls** Low

Form RPR

3025 **1** **Rosie Crowe (IRE)**[42] 6512 4-8-10 **47**..........(v) JosephineGordon(3) 8 53
(Shaun Harris) *mde all: rdn over 1f out: styd on wl and in command ins fnl f: rdn out* **7/2**[2]

6- **2** *1 ¼* **Randall's Alannah (IRE)**[12] 7375 6-8-12 **46** oh1.......... MartinHarley 6 49
(Seamus Fahey, Ire) *in tch in midfield: effrt in 4th 2f out: kpt on u.p ins fnl f: snatched 2nd last stride: nvr enough pce to threaten wnr* **7/2**[2]

0-03 **3** *shd* **Bedazzling Lady (IRE)**[9] 7445 3-8-11 **47**.......... JackMitchell 2 48
(Robert Eddery) *chsd wnr for 2f: chsd ldrs after tl rdn to chse wnr again over 1f out: styd on same pce ins fnl f: lost 2nd last stride* **7/1**

0000 **4** *1 ¾* **Makhfar (IRE)**[22] 7070 5-9-4 **52**..........(v) PatCosgrave 4 51
(Kevin Morgan) *s.i.s: hld up in last quartet: rdn and hdwy over 1f out: kpt on ins fnl f: nvr threatened ldrs: eased cl home* **3/1**[1]

6600 **5** *1 ¼* **Noneedtotellme (IRE)**[28] 6902 3-8-10 **46** oh1.......... RyanPowell 3 39
(James Unett) *hld up in tch in midfield: effrt over 1f out: no imp 1f out: kpt on same pce ins fnl f* **25/1**

4460 **6** *1* **Baz's Boy**[28] 6894 3-8-10 **46**.......... DanielMuscutt 12 37
(John Flint) *chsd ldrs: wnt 2nd after 2f out tl unable qck u.p over 1f out: wknd ins fnl f* **16/1**

000 **7** *3 ¾* **Touch The Clouds**[9] 7445 5-8-12 **46** oh1.......... MartinLane 1 27
(William Stone) *in tch in midfield: u.p and struggling over 2f out: wknd fnl f* **16/1**

0500 **8** *1 ¼* **Steel Stockholder**[55] 6105 10-9-4 **52**.......... CamHardie 9 30
(Antony Brittain) *hld up in tch in last pair: rdn 3f out: no imp u.p over 1f out: wl hld fnl f* **25/1**

566 **9** *3* **The Excel Queen (IRE)**[13] 7336 3-9-5 **55**.......... BarryMcHugh 7 24
(Tony Coyle) *in tch in midfield: rdn and dropped to rr 4f out: drvn 3f out: n.d fnl 2f* **5/1**[3]

0060 **10** *2 ½* **Fearless Poppy**[9] 7444 3-8-7 **46** oh1..........(v) TimClark(3) 11 8
(Christine Dunnett) *a towards rr: rdn over 2f out: sn struggling: bhd fnl f* **50/1**

0-50 **11** *5* **Beat The Blues**[245] 707 4-9-3 **51**.......... StevieDonohoe 10 1
(Miss Joey Ellis) *midfield: rdn over 2f out: drvn and btn over 1f out: bhd fnl f* **33/1**

0450 **R** **Loud**[183] 1781 6-8-9 **46** oh1..........(b) SimonPearce(3) 5
(Lydia Pearce) *ref to r* **20/1**

1m 25.8s (-1.40) **Going Correction** -0.225s/f (Stan)
WFA 3 from 4yo+ 2lb **12** Ran SP% **127.7**
Speed ratings (Par 101): **99,97,97,95,94 92,88,87,83,80 75,**
CSF £16.60 CT £88.66 TOTE £4.60: £1.30, £2.00, £2.40; EX 23.00 Trifecta £146.10.
Owner R L Crowe **Bred** Liam Phelan **Trained** Carburton, Notts
■ Stewards' Enquiry : Simon Pearce two-day ban: used whip in way considered unacceptable (Nov 10-11)

FOCUS
Marginally the quicker of the two divisions. Ordinary form.
T/Jkpt: Not won. T/Plt: £486.40 to a £1 stake. Pool: £95,831.64. 143.81 winning units. T/Qpdt: £122.10 to a £1 stake. Pool: £11,601.06. 70.28 winning units. **Steve Payne**

6655 LINGFIELD (L-H)
Thursday, October 27

OFFICIAL GOING: Polytrack: standard
Wind: Fresh, across towards stands Weather: Fine, clouding over from race 3

7647 32RED CASINO/BRITISH STALLION STUDS EBF MAIDEN FILLIES' STKS (PLUS 10 RACE) 7f 1y(P)
1:40 (1:42) (Class 5) 2-Y-O **£3,363** (£1,001; £500; £250) **Stalls** Low

Form RPR

0 **1** **Mittens**[20] 7118 2-9-0 0.......... PatSmullen 4 76
(Sir Michael Stoute) *hld up in 5th: effrt over 1f out: rdn to ld wl ins fnl f* **3/1**[2]

2 *½* **Getna (USA)** 2-9-0 0.......... FrankieDettori 3 75
(Richard Hannon) *led: hrd rdn and hdd ins fnl f: kpt on* **11/2**[3]

3 *½* **Angel's Quest (FR)** 2-9-0 0.......... ShaneKelly 9 73
(Richard Hughes) *t.k.h: sn in midfield: shkn up and hdwy over 1f out: nrest at fin* **33/1**

3 **4** *1 ¼* **Shaaqaaf (IRE)**[15] 7278 2-9-0 0.......... DaneO'Neill 12 70
(John Gosden) *hld up in tch: shkn up over 2f out: styd on fnl f* **1/1**[1]

03 **5** *1 ¼* **Island Cloud**[15] 7277 2-9-0 0.......... OisinMurphy 7 67
(Heather Main) *pressed ldr tl 1f out: no ex* **6/1**

60 **6** *4 ½* **La Vie En Rose**[15] 7284 2-9-0 0.......... JoeFanning 2 54
(Mark Johnston) *sn prom on inner: wknd 2f out* **50/1**

00 **7** *¾* **Delirium (IRE)**[23] 7056 2-9-0 0.......... FrederikTylicki 10 52
(Ed de Giles) *s.s: bhd: shkn up over 2f out: sme late hdwy* **100/1**

00 **8** *2 ¼* **Last Word**[23] 7055 2-9-0 0.......... TomQueally 5 46
(David Lanigan) *a bhd* **100/1**

60 **9** *2 ¼* **Kyllachys Tale (IRE)**[23] 7066 2-9-0 0..........[1] GeorgeWood(6) 6 40
(Roger Teal) *outpcd after 2f: sn bhd and rdn along* **25/1**

06 **10** *12* **Modhilah (IRE)**[45] 6413 2-9-0 0.......... MartinHarley 8 8
(Harry Dunlop) *chsd ldrs on outer tl wknd 3f out* **66/1**

1m 24.3s (-0.50) **Going Correction** 0.0s/f (Stan) **10** Ran SP% **116.9**
Speed ratings (Par 92): **102,101,100,99,98 92,92,89,86,73**
CSF £18.94 TOTE £4.30: £1.10, £1.70, £5.60; EX 18.10 Trifecta £234.30.
Owner K Abdullah **Bred** Juddmonte Farms Ltd **Trained** Newmarket, Suffolk
■ The Bear Can Fly was withdrawn. Price at time of withdrawal 20-1. Rule 4 does not apply.
■ Stewards' Enquiry : Shane Kelly caution: careless riding

FOCUS
The first meeting of the fourth AW Championships season featuring two Listed events, one of them a fast-track qualifier. An ordinary fillies' maiden to start, with more than half the field qualifying for handicaps after this. The field was reduced by one when The Bear Can Fly was withdrawn after getting upset in the stalls.

7648 32REDSPORT.COM / BRITISH STALLION STUDS EBF MAIDEN STKS (DIV I) 7f 1y(P)
2:10 (2:12) (Class 5) 2-Y-O **£3,363** (£1,001; £500; £250) **Stalls** Low

Form RPR
5 **1** **Tai Sing Yeh (IRE)**[19] 7157 2-9-5 0 [1] WilliamBuick 9 74
(Charles Hills) *mde all: c across fr wd stall after 1f: hrd rdn and hld on wl fnl f* **7/4**[1]
0 **2** *1/2* **Sureyoutoldme (IRE)**[14] 7306 2-9-5 0 SeanLevey 7 73
(Richard Hannon) *chsd wnr thrght: kpt on u.p fnl f* **14/1**
3 *1/2* **Carigrad (IRE)** 2-9-2 0 JosephineGordon(3) 2 71
(Hugo Palmer) *mid-div: hdwy over 1f out: r.o ins fnl f* **9/4**[2]
30 **4** *1/2* **Tobrave (IRE)**[44] 6439 2-9-5 0 [1] AndreaAtzeni 5 70
(Roger Varian) *plld hrd: prom: rdn and sltly outpcd over 2f out: rallied 1f out: kpt on fnl f* **7/2**[3]
05 **5** *3 3/4* **Legendoire (IRE)**[120] 3770 2-9-5 0 MichaelJMMurphy 4 60
(John Gallagher) *prom tl wknd over 1f out* **100/1**
56 **6** *hd* **Leonidas (IRE)**[16] 7243 2-9-5 0 SteveDrowne 8 59
(Marcus Tregoning) *sn outpcd towards rr: styd on fnl 2f* **20/1**
7 *1 1/4* **Native Soldier (IRE)** 2-9-5 0 TomQueally 6 56
(William Haggas) *a towards rr* **10/1**
8 *5* **Peking Flyer (IRE)** 2-9-5 0 GeorgeBaker 3 42
(Ed Walker) *a bhd* **25/1**
9 *4 1/2* **De Little Engine (IRE)** 2-9-5 0 WilliamCarson 1 30
(Jamie Osborne) *in tch tl wknd over 2f out* **33/1**

1m 26.05s (1.25) **Going Correction** 0.0s/f (Stan) **9** Ran SP% **117.7**
Speed ratings (Par 95): **92,91,90,90,86 85,84,78,73**
CSF £27.15 TOTE £2.70: £1.10, £3.50, £1.90; EX 25.50 Trifecta £94.80.
Owner Hon Kit Cheung **Bred** Rabbah Bloodstock Limited **Trained** Lambourn, Berks

FOCUS
Another ordinary maiden which normally goes to a 2yo with previous experience and that was again the case. The pace was modest and the first two held those positions throughout, while the time was 1.75sec slower than the fillies in the opener.

7649 32REDSPORT.COM / BRITISH STALLION STUDS EBF MAIDEN STKS (DIV II) 7f 1y(P)
2:40 (2:44) (Class 5) 2-Y-O **£3,363** (£1,001; £500; £250) **Stalls** Low

Form RPR
1 **Across Dubai** 2-9-5 0 PatCosgrave 9 84
(William Haggas) *hld up in tch: effrt 2f out: r.o to ld fnl 100yds* **6/1**[2]
2 **2** *1* **Dubai Horizon (IRE)**[19] 7157 2-9-5 0 OisinMurphy 1 81
(Saeed bin Suroor) *dwlt: t.k.h and sn led: hrd rdn and hdd fnl 100yds: kpt on* **2/9**[1]
4 **3** *3* **Hajjam**[29] 6881 2-9-5 0 FrederikTylicki 3 73
(William Knight) *a.p: one pce appr fnl f* **10/1**[3]
00 **4** *hd* **Desert Grey (IRE)**[8] 7470 2-9-5 0 AndreaAtzeni 2 73
(Roger Varian) *chsd ldrs on inner: one pce ent fnl f* **33/1**
5 *6* **Know Your Limit (IRE)** 2-9-5 0 GeorgeBaker 4 56
(Ed Walker) *dwlt: bhd: shkn up over 2f out: sme late hdwy* **20/1**
6 *1/2* **Golden Opportunity** 2-9-5 0 MartinHarley 7 55
(James Tate) *dwlt: hld up in 6th: rdn and wknd 2f out* **20/1**
00 **7** *1/2* **Magdalene Fox**[14] 7307 2-9-5 0 AdamKirby 5 54
(Ed Dunlop) *outpcd: a towards rr* **50/1**
33 **8** *5* **Endeavour (IRE)**[52] 6183 2-9-5 0 SeanLevey 8 40
(Richard Hannon) *prom tl wknd and rn wd into st* **10/1**[3]
5 **9** *18* **Think So (IRE)**[32] 6808 2-9-5 0 JoeFanning 6
(Mark Johnston) *a towards rr: rdn and no ch fnl 3f* **25/1**

1m 24.27s (-0.53) **Going Correction** 0.0s/f (Stan) **9** Ran SP% **132.6**
Speed ratings (Par 95): **103,101,98,98,91 90,90,84,63**
CSF £8.61 TOTE £9.50: £1.30, £1.10, £2.20; EX 15.60 Trifecta £66.80.
Owner Sheikh Juma Dalmook Al Maktoum **Bred** Rabbah Bloodstock Limited **Trained** Newmarket, Suffolk

FOCUS
Painful viewing for long-odds-on backers, but the winner looks a nice prospect. The winning time was 1.78sec quicker than the first division and fractionally faster than the fillies in the opener.

7650 32RED EBF STALLIONS FLEUR DE LYS FILLIES' STKS (LISTED RACE) (ALL-WEATHER CHAMPIONSHIP QUALIFIER) 1m 1y(P)
3:10 (3:15) (Class 1) 3-Y£22,684 (£8,600; £4,304; £2,144; £1,076; £54015) **Stalls** High

0311 **1** **Muffri'Ha (IRE)**[19] 7152 4-9-6 109 PatCosgrave 2 111+
(William Haggas) *prom: led after 1f: qcknd 4 l clr over 1f out: comf* **5/4**[1]
0042 **2** *1 3/4* **Aljuljalah (USA)**[47] 6338 3-8-12 93 AndreaAtzeni 7 99
(Roger Varian) *t.k.h: sn in midfield: rdn 3f out: styd on to take 2nd ins fnl f* **9/1**
3652 **3** *1* **Home Cummins (IRE)**[20] 7121 4-9-1 94 (p) TonyHamilton 1 98
(Richard Fahey) *dwlt: t.k.h: prom on inner after 2f: kpt on u.p fnl 2f* **20/1**
123 **4** *nse* **Battlement**[26] 6939 3-8-12 95 PatSmullen 11 96+
(Roger Charlton) *dwlt: hld up in rr: rdn over 1f out: gd hdwy fnl f* **13/2**[3]
0000 **5** *1/2* **Volunteer Point (IRE)**[26] 6939 4-9-1 95 GrahamGibbons 4 96
(Mick Channon) *t.k.h at rr of midfield: rdn 3f out: nrest at fin* **20/1**
2112 **6** *hd* **Crowning Glory (FR)**[26] 6947 3-8-12 90 RichardKingscote 5 95
(Ralph Beckett) *chsd ldrs: outpcd over 2f out: styd on fnl f* **10/1**
0142 **7** *1/2* **Gold Sands (IRE)**[39] 6611 4-9-1 93 MartinHarley 6 95
(James Tate) *led for 1f: chsd wnr tl wknd over 1f out* **22/1**
-023 **8** *nk* **Squash**[173] 2034 3-8-12 102 OisinMurphy 9 93
(Philip McBride) *hld up towards rr: shkn up 2f out: styng on steadily at fin* **33/1**
2023 **9** *1 1/4* **Mise En Rose (USA)**[19] 7146 3-8-12 106 (p) WilliamBuick 12 90+
(Charlie Appleby) *hld up in rr on outer: effrt and rn v wd into st: rdn 3f out* **4/1**[2]
2454 **10** *1/2* **Johara (IRE)**[14] 7312 5-9-1 97 ShaneKelly 8 90
(H-F Devin, France) *chsd ldrs on outer: wnt 3rd 3f out: wknd over 1f out* **20/1**

1m 36.53s (-1.67) **Going Correction** 0.0s/f (Stan)
WFA 3 from 4yo+ 3lb **10** Ran SP% **118.4**
Speed ratings (Par 108): **108,106,105,105,104 104,104,103,102,101**
CSF £12.28 TOTE £2.20: £1.80, £2.60, £4.40; EX 16.10 Trifecta £127.50.
Owner Sheikh Juma Dalmook Al Maktoum **Bred** Lodge Park Stud **Trained** Newmarket, Suffolk

FOCUS
A warm fillies' Listed event and a fast-track qualifier for the Fillies and Mares Championship back here next Easter, but it proved a one-horse race. The form is set by the second, third, fourth and sixth.

7651 SUNBETS.CO.UK H'CAP 7f 1y(P)
3:45 (3:47) (Class 2) (0-105,102) 3-Y£01,971 (£3,583; £1,791; £896; £446) **Stalls** Low

Form RPR
301 **1** **Lord Of The Land (IRE)**[22] 7068 5-9-10 **102** (v) DanielTudhope 11 113
(David O'Meara) *mde all: 2 l ahd and in control over 1f out: rdn out* **4/1**[2]
0400 **2** *2* **Alfred Hutchinson**[20] 7121 8-9-2 **94** (p) AdamKirby 9 100
(David O'Meara) *chsd wnr thrght: kpt on u.p fnl 2f* **16/1**
0100 **3** *nk* **Oh This Is Us (IRE)**[33] 6788 3-9-6 **100** SeanLevey 3 104+
(Richard Hannon) *dwlt: hld up in midfield: rdn and hdwy over 1f out: styd on wl fnl f* **10/1**
2460 **4** *1 1/2* **Race Day (IRE)**[112] 4059 3-9-1 **98** (p) JosephineGordon(3) 2 98
(Saeed bin Suroor) *in tch: wnt 3rd on inner 2f out: one pce fnl f* **7/2**[1]
5022 **5** *1 3/4* **Intransigent**[16] 7241 7-9-5 **97** OisinMurphy 1 93
(Andrew Balding) *mid-div: effrt on inner over 1f out: styd on same pce* **7/1**
2000 **6** *hd* **Bint Dandy (IRE)**[26] 6947 5-9-1 **93** (b) MartinHarley 5 88
(Chris Dwyer) *in tch: effrt and hrd rdn over 1f out: no imp* **50/1**
1/3- **7** *1/2* **Faydhan (USA)**[561] 1420 4-9-8 **100** DaneO'Neill 8 94+
(John Gosden) *dwlt: towards rr: rdn over 2f out: styd on fnl f* **6/1**[3]
6100 **8** *1 1/4* **Barracuda Boy (IRE)**[33] 6788 6-9-5 **97** RichardKingscote 10 88
(Tom Dascombe) *dwlt: towards rr: rdn 2f out: sme late hdwy* **25/1**
3656 **9** *shd* **Charles Molson**[18] 7186 5-9-0 **92** JoeFanning 12 86+
(Patrick Chamings) *hld up towards rr: effrt and bdly hmpd over 1f out: nvr rchd ldrs* **14/1**
0000 **10** *shd* **Shyron**[27] 6914 5-9-0 **92** TomQueally 4 82
(George Margarson) *dwlt: nvr trbld ldrs* **25/1**
0660 **11** *3 1/4* **Forceful Appeal (USA)**[91] 4788 8-8-10 **88** NickyMackay 13 69
(Simon Dow) *stdd s: bhd: rdn 2f out: nvr nr ldrs* **100/1**
0600 **12** *shd* **Sea Of Flames**[112] 4065 3-9-6 **100** FrederikTylicki 7 80
(David Elsworth) *chsd ldrs on outer tl outpcd over 2f out* **11/1**
0410 **13** *1/2* **Cool Bahamian (IRE)**[29] 6878 5-8-4 **85** (v) EdwardGreatrex(3) 6 65
(Eve Johnson Houghton) *plld hrd in rr: drvn along and n.d ent st* **25/1**
0-12 **14** *nk* **Peril**[163] 2331 5-9-6 **98** RobertHavlin 14 77
(Simon Crisford) *prom tl wknd 2f out* **14/1**

1m 23.5s (-1.30) **Going Correction** 0.0s/f (Stan)
WFA 3 from 4yo+ 2lb **14** Ran SP% **120.1**
Speed ratings (Par 109): **107,104,104,102,100 100,99,98,98,98 94,94,93,93**
CSF £62.86 CT £625.10 TOTE £4.70: £1.50, £5.80, £3.70; EX 83.00 Trifecta £790.20.
Owner George Turner **Bred** Ammerland Verwaltung Gmbh **Trained** Upper Helmsley, N Yorks
■ Stewards' Enquiry : Dane O'Neill caution: careless riding

FOCUS
A warm handicap, but not many got into it with the 1-2-4 at halfway still in those positions at the line. A fine effort from the top weight to make all, though, and a 1-2 for trainer David O'Meara. The form has been rated at face value.

7652 32RED EBF STALLIONS RIVER EDEN FILLIES' STKS (LISTED RACE) 1m 5f (P)
4:20 (4:23) (Class 1) 3-Y-O+
£22,684 (£8,600; £4,304; £2,144; £1,076; £540) **Stalls** Low

Form RPR
-041 **1** **Bess Of Hardwick**[47] 6332 4-9-4 92 AndreaAtzeni 5 100+
(Luca Cumani) *t.k.h in midfield: rdn over 2f out: hdwy over 1f out: r.o to ld nr fin* **9/2**[2]
2 *nk* **Dogma (FR)**[22] 4-9-4 94 [1] AdamKirby 3 99
(S Wattel, France) *in tch: dashed into ld and qcknd 5 l clr 3f out: hrd rdn fnl f: hdd nr fin* **25/1**
-163 **3** *2 1/2* **Anzhelika (IRE)**[15] 7271 4-9-4 94 GeorgeBaker 8 95+
(David Lanigan) *hld up in rr: rdn and hdwy over 1f out: nrest at fin* **11/2**[3]
3133 **4** *nk* **Ruscombe**[6] 7498 3-8-10 90 PatSmullen 10 95+
(Sir Michael Stoute) *dwlt: towards rr: sme hdwy on outer 4f out: rdn and styd on wl fnl 2f* **7/2**[1]
130 **5** *3/4* **Yorkidding**[19] 7150 4-9-4 98 RichardKingscote 6 94+
(Mark Johnston) *sn in midfield: dropped to rr and rdn over 3f out: styd on wl fnl f* **8/1**
1-02 **6** *hd* **Last Tango Inparis**[105] 4331 3-8-10 100 FrederikTylicki 12 93
(Hughie Morrison) *prom: outpcd by ldr 3f out: fdd fnl f* **11/1**
3210 **7** *nk* **Kiltara (IRE)**[15] 7271 4-9-4 93 JoeFanning 2 93
(Mark Johnston) *prom: outpcd by ldr 3f out: no ex fnl f* **20/1**
0442 **8** *1* **All About Time**[19] 7139 4-9-4 85 DanielTudhope 11 91
(David O'Meara) *t.k.h in rr: rdn over 2f out: styd on wl fnl f* **33/1**
5410 **9** *1/2* **Flambeuse**[61] 5872 5-9-4 77 OisinMurphy 4 91?
(Harry Dunlop) *led at modest pce tl 3f out: wknd over 1f out* **100/1**
0221 **10** *7* **Eyeshine**[50] 6239 3-8-10 85 (p) FrankieDettori 9 80
(John Gosden) *nvr trbld ldrs* **9/2**[2]
3133 **11** *3/4* **Hereawi**[47] 6325 3-8-10 83 WilliamBuick 1 79
(Ralph Beckett) *in tch tl wknd 3f out* **25/1**
1515 **12** *6* **Novalina (IRE)**[27] 6917 3-8-10 86 PatCosgrave 7 70
(William Haggas) *prom tl wknd 3f out* **16/1**

2m 45.03s (-0.97) **Going Correction** 0.0s/f (Stan)
WFA 3 from 4yo+ 8lb **12** Ran SP% **115.7**
Speed ratings (Par 108): **102,101,100,100,99 99,99,98,98,94 93,89**
CSF £117.90 TOTE £5.50: £1.80, £4.70, £1.90; EX 87.30 Trifecta £550.20.
Owner Duke Of Devonshire **Bred** The Duke Of Devonshire **Trained** Newmarket, Suffolk

FOCUS
A competitive staying Listed event, but they went no pace and the tempo didn't pick up until inside the last half-mile. Muddling form. The runner-up has been rated to form but there are grounds for thinking the third, fourth and fifth are better than the bare form suggests.

7653 BETWAY H'CAP 1m 2f (P)
4:50 (4:52) (Class 5) (0-75,73) 3-Y-O+ **£3,234** (£962; £481; £240) **Stalls** Low

Form RPR
5160 **1** **Petite Jack**[49] 6268 3-9-5 **73** JackMitchell 1 81+
(Neil King) *trckd ldrs on inner: effrt over 1f out: led jst ins fnl f: rdn out* **8/1**
33-0 **2** *1 1/4* **Take Two**[23] 7043 7-9-2 **70** CallumShepherd(5) 11 75
(Alex Hales) *prom: rdn to chal 1f out: kpt on* **33/1**
1520 **3** *nk* **Port Paradise**[52] 6194 3-9-0 **68** JoeFanning 13 72
(William Jarvis) *prom: jnd ldr over 1f out: kpt on* **18/1**
1351 **4** *nk* **Hard Toffee (IRE)**[58] 6001 5-9-9 **72** RobertHavlin 7 75
(Conrad Allen) *led at gd pce tl jst ins fnl f: kpt on* **11/2**[2]
04 **5** *4* **Hungerford**[37] 6645 4-9-10 **73** TomQueally 4 68
(Eve Johnson Houghton) *prom tl hrd rdn and wknd over 1f out* **6/1**[3]

536 **6** ½ **The Salmon Man**[24] 7007 4-9-6 **72**.......................... EdwardGreatrex(3) 9 66
(Brendan Powell) *mid-div: effrt on outer over 2f out: styd on same pce* **13/2**
5300 **7** 1¾ **Choral Festival**[9] 7429 10-9-5 **68**.......................... DannyBrock 5 59
(John Bridger) *a abt same pl* **40/1**
1620 **8** 2¾ **Barren Brook**[28] 6889 9-9-8 **71**.......................... GeorgeBaker 3 56
(Laura Mongan) *dwlt: bhd: rdn 3f out: sme late hdwy* **25/1**
2630 **9** 2½ **New Street (IRE)**[7] 7486 5-9-9 **72**.......................... TimmyMurphy 8 52
(Jim Best) *towards rr: rdn 3f out: nvr rchd ldrs* **66/1**
6-33 **10** 1 **Trespassed (IRE)**[36] 4673 3-9-2 **70**..........................(t) JamieSpencer 10 48
(Gordon Elliott, Ire) *dwlt: nvr trbld ldrs* **9/1**
0050 **11** ½ **Cat Royale (IRE)**[35] 6701 3-9-1 **69**.......................... FrederikTylicki 6 46
(Jane Chapple-Hyam) *chsd ldrs tl wknd 3f out* **8/1**
4-1 **12** 6 **Squiggley**[32] 6805 3-9-4 **72**.......................... DaneO'Neill 12 37
(Henry Candy) *a towards rr* **5/2**[1]
51-5 **13** 10 **Artistic Flight (IRE)**[273] 357 4-9-2 **65**..........................(p) PatCosgrave 2 10
(Jim Boyle) *nvr gng wl in midfield: hung lft thrght: wknd 3f out: bhd and eased over 1f out* **25/1**

2m 4.82s (-1.78) **Going Correction** 0.0s/f (Stan)
WFA 3 from 4yo+ 5lb **13** Ran SP% **123.6**
Speed ratings (Par 103): **107,106,105,105,102 101,100,98,96,95 95,90,82**
CSF £261.90 CT £4578.00 TOTE £11.00: £2.90, £10.40, £5.70; EX 432.40.
Owner W Burn **Bred** Mrs Liz Nelson Mbe **Trained** Barbury Castle, Wiltshire

FOCUS
A modest handicap and you had to be up there with the 1-2-3-4-5 racing 5-4-2-1-3 at halfway. Muddling form set around the third to his best.

7654 SUN BETS ON THE APP STORE APPRENTICE H'CAP 7f 1y(P)
5:20 (5:27) (Class 6) (0-65,65) 3-Y-O+ **£1,678** (£1,678; £384; £192) **Stalls** Low

Form RPR
3402 **1** **Swiss Cross**[16] 7255 9-9-11 **64**..........................(tp) CallumShepherd 11 70
(Phil McEntee) *in tch: clsd on ldrs ent fnl f: r.o to dead-heat on line* **12/1**
0-00 **1** dht **Showtime Blues**[226] 943 4-9-7 **60**..........................[1] CharlieBennett 7 66
(Jim Boyle) *chsd ldrs: effrt over 1f out: drvn to ld fnl 50yds: ct for dead-heat on line* **9/1**
5440 **3** hd **Seek The Fair Land**[29] 6872 10-9-7 **63**..........................(v) PaddyBradley(3) 2 68
(Lee Carter) *mid-div: hdwy over 1f out: weaved through to join ldrs nr fin: jst denied* **3/1**[2]
00-0 **4** 1 **Chester Deelyte (IRE)**[279] 297 8-8-12 **51** oh6..........(p) MitchGodwin 6 54
(Lisa Williamson) *pressed ldr: led wl over 1f out: kpt on u.p fnl f: hdd fnl 50yds: no ex nr fin* **66/1**
2265 **5** 1 **Encapsulated**[42] 6509 6-9-5 **61**.......................... RhiainIngram(3) 13 61
(Roger Ingram) *prom: hrd rdn over 1f out: one pce fnl 100yds* **16/1**
0023 **6** ½ **Ten Rocks**[30] 6855 3-9-1 **61**.......................... JordanUys(5) 9 59
(Lisa Williamson) *led tl wl over 1f out: hrd rdn: one pce ins fnl f* **20/1**
305 **7** ¾ **Jazz Cat (IRE)**[14] 7311 3-9-9 **64**..........................(t) AdamMcNamara 5 60
(Paul Cole) *hmpd and in rr after 1f: rdn over 2f out: nrest at fin* **9/1**
5545 **8** hd **Lucky Louie**[23] 7059 3-9-7 **62**..........................(p) GeorgeWood 12 57
(Roger Teal) *towards rr: last and struggling 2f out: styd on fnl f* **7/1**
5225 **9** shd **New Rich**[92] 4763 6-9-12 **65**..........................(v) HollieDoyle 4 61
(Eve Johnson Houghton) *towards rr: rdn 2f out: styng on at fin* **11/4**[1]
0632 **10** 1¼ **Cascading Stars (IRE)**[21] 7096 4-9-2 **62**.......................... TobyEley(7) 1 55
(Daniel Mark Loughnane) *dwlt: sn chsng ldrs on inner: wknd 1f out* **6/1**[3]
3524 **11** hd **Arcanista (IRE)**[17] 7200 3-8-11 **59**..........................(tp) NicolaCurrie(7) 8 50
(Richard Hughes) *n.m.r and in rr after 1f: nvr nr ldrs* **8/1**

1m 25.57s (0.77) **Going Correction** 0.0s/f (Stan)
WFA 3 from 4yo+ 2lb **11** Ran SP% **129.4**
Speed ratings (Par 101): **95,95,94,93,92 91,91,90,90,89 89**
WIN: SC £5.10, SB £6.90; PL: SC £3.50, SB £4.20, STFL £2.10; EX: SC-SB £76.00, SB-SC 80.80; CSF: SC-SB £63.50, SB-SC £61.59; TC: SC-SB-STFL £213.44, SB-SC-STFL £209.40; TF: SC-SB-STFL £521.30, SB-SC-STFL £638.90.
Owner M B Spence **Bred** R J & S A Carter **Trained** Epsom, Surrey
Owner Steve Jakes **Bred** Lordship Stud **Trained** Newmarket, Suffolk
■ Sexton Blake was withdrawn. Price at time of withdrawal 9-2. Rule 4 applies to board prices prior to withdrawal - deduct 15p in the pound. New market formed. Royal Rettie was withdrawn. Price at time of withdrawal 40-1. Rule 4 does not apply.
■ Stewards' Enquiry : Callum Shepherd two-day ban: used whip above permitted level (Nov 10-11)
Charlie Bennett two-day ban: used whip above permitted level (Nov 10-11)

FOCUS
A moderate apprentice handicap to end with and a bunch finish with the judge unable to split the first two. The close fourth was effectively 13lb wrong, which rather holds the form down.
T/Plt: £112.20 to a £1 stake. Pool: £71,870.98. 467.42 winning units. T/Qpdt: £11.40 to a £1 stake. Pool: £7,822.64. 507.34 winning units. **Lee McKenzie**

7345 MAISONS-LAFFITTE (R-H)
Thursday, October 27
OFFICIAL GOING: Turf: soft

7655a PRIX ZEDDAAN (LISTED RACE) (2YO) (TURF) 6f (S)
1:20 (12:00) 2-Y-O **£23,897** (£9,558; £7,169; £4,779; £2,389)

RPR
1 **Private Matter**[41] 6538 2-8-13 0.......................... OlivierPeslier 1 100
(Richard Fahey) *sn trcking ldr: shkn up to ld wl over 2f out: sn drvn and wnt clr appr fnl f: styd on and a holding runner-up* **51/10**
2 1½ **Precieuse (IRE)**[15] 7291 2-8-10 0 ow1.......................... ChristopheSoumillon 4 93
(F Chappet, France) **42/10**[2]
3 6 **Vona (IRE)**[19] 7170 2-8-13 0.......................... Pierre-CharlesBoudot 9 78
(Richard Fahey) *w.w in midfield: clsd to chse ldrs 1/2-way: cl 4th and rdn 2f out but nt qckn: kpt on same pce fnl f* **11/2**
4 ¾ **Megan Lily (IRE)**[19] 7170 2-8-9 0.......................... ThierryJarnet 6 71
(Richard Fahey) *led: hdd wl over 2f out: sn lft bhd by ldr: kpt on at once pce u.p fnl f* **39/10**[1]
5 2 **Connacht Girl (IRE)**[40] 6555 2-8-9 0.......................... TonyPiccone 5 65
(K R Burke) *w.w towards rr: drvn 1/2-way: kpt on u.p fr over 1f out: nvr in contention* **13/1**
6 3 **Erica Bing**[40] 6555 2-8-9 0.......................... UmbertoRispoli 3 56
(Jo Hughes) *cl up: outpcd and rdn 1/2-way: grad dropped away* **22/1**
7 2½ **Bocca De La Verita (FR)**[20] 7136 2-8-9 0.......................... ThierryThulliez 8 49
(C Lerner, France) **43/5**
8 2 **Bay Of Biscaine (FR)**[53] 6174 2-8-13 0.......................... IoritzMendizabal 2 47
(Mario Hofer, Germany) **48/10**[3]
9 3 **Nofoemaypass (FR)**[19] 7170 2-8-13 0..........................(b[1]) AlexisBadel 7 38
(H-F Devin, France) **12/1**

1m 13.91s (0.51) **9** Ran SP% **118.3**
WIN (incl. 1 euro stake): 6.10. Places: 2.10, 2.10, 2.10. DF: 21.10. SF: 40.70..
Owner Cheveley Park Stud **Bred** Cheveley Park Stud Ltd **Trained** Musley Bank, N Yorks

7597 NEWCASTLE (A.W) (L-H)
Friday, October 28
OFFICIAL GOING: Tapeta: standard
Wind: Light, half against Weather: Overcast races 1-2

7656 PINNACLE-SHARE PRIZE DRAW H'CAP (DIV I) 1m 4f 98y (Tp)
4:40 (4:40) (Class 6) (0-65,65) 3-Y-O+ **£2,264** (£673; £336; £168) **Stalls** High

Form RPR
0003 **1** **Glasgon**[10] 7438 6-8-13 **50**.......................... ConnorBeasley 12 56
(Ray Craggs) *in tch: hdwy to chse clr ldr over 2f out: rdn and led over 1f out: edgd lft ins fnl f: drvn out* **14/1**
-445 **2** ½ **Magnolia Ridge (IRE)**[15] 4499 6-8-9 **46**..........................(p) JasonHart 14 51
(Mark Walford) *in tch: rdn over 3f out: rallied 2f out: kpt on wl fnl f to take 2nd nr fin* **50/1**
0-50 **3** nk **Angel In The Snow**[275] 345 3-8-4 **48**.......................... BenCurtis 11 53
(Brian Ellison) *t.k.h: hld up midfield: hdwy and hung lft over 2f out: chsd wnr over 1f out: kpt on fnl f: lost 2nd nr fin* **20/1**
0001 **4** 1 **Strummer (IRE)**[7] 7515 3-9-5 **63** 6ex..........................(p) KevinStott 10 66
(Kevin Ryan) *s.i.s: hld up: stdy hdwy and pushed along over 2f out: disp 2nd pl over 1f out to ins fnl f: no ex nr fin* **10/3**[1]
2/41 **5** 1½ **Miss Tree**[13] 7361 5-9-3 **54**.......................... DougieCostello 7 55
(John Quinn) *hld up midfield: stdy hdwy over 3f out: rdn along over 2f out: kpt on fnl f: nvr able to chal* **6/1**
0644 **6** 1½ **Nonchalant**[12] 7385 5-10-0 **65**..........................(b) PhillipMakin 2 64
(David O'Meara) *led: drew clr fr 4f out: rdn and hdd over 1f out: wknd ins fnl f* **7/1**
4022 **7** 1¼ **Stoneboat Bill**[17] 7257 4-9-5 **63**.......................... GerO'Neill(7) 6 60
(Declan Carroll) *s.i.s: hld up: stdy hdwy over 3f out: rdn 2f out: kpt on fnl f: no imp* **11/2**[3]
1044 **8** 6 **Yasir (USA)**[14] 7321 8-10-0 **65**.......................... PaulMulrennan 8 53
(Conor Dore) *hld up: pushed along and effrt over 2f out: nvr able to chal* **12/1**
362 **9** nk **Diletta Tommasa (IRE)**[27] 6965 6-9-4 **62**..........................(v) TobyEley(7) 13 49
(Daniel Mark Loughnane) *s.s: sn rcvrd and hld up: rdn and effrt on outside over 3f out: struggling fnl 2f* **9/1**
0604 **10** 1¼ **Exclusive Waters (IRE)**[10] 7438 6-9-4 **55**.......................... RobertWinston 5 41
(George Charlton) *hld up midfield: drvn and outpcd over 3f out: struggling fnl 2f* **20/1**
0050 **11** 6 **Zingiber**[10] 7438 4-8-9 **46** oh1.......................... CamHardie 3 23
(Wilf Storey) *chsd ldr tl rdn and wknd over 2f out* **100/1**
4202 **12** 8 **Aurora Gray**[17] 7425 3-9-1 **64**..........................[1] CharlieBennett(5) 1 29
(Hughie Morrison) *chsd ldrs: drvn over 3f out: wknd over 2f out* **5/1**[2]
000 **13** 11 **My Brown Eyed Girl**[118] 3886 3-8-3 **47** oh1 ow1.......... JoeyHaynes 9
(Susan Corbett) *hld up: rdn along over 4f out: struggling fnl 3f* **100/1**
6300 **14** 16 **Toola Boola**[14] 7332 6-9-8 **59**.......................... JackGarritty 4
(Jedd O'Keeffe) *in tch: pushed along 5f out: wknd over 3f out: t.o* **22/1**

2m 37.88s (-3.22) **Going Correction** -0.125s/f (Stan)
WFA 3 from 4yo+ 7lb **14** Ran SP% **124.1**
Speed ratings (Par 101): **105,104,104,103,102 101,100,96,96,95 91,86,79,68**
CSF £609.77 CT £13113.57 TOTE £20.20: £5.20, £13.50, £7.90; EX 854.60 TRIFECTA Not won..

Owner Ray Craggs **Bred** J L C Pearce **Trained** Sedgefield, Co Durham

FOCUS
This first leg of this handicap was run at a fair pace. Straightforward form rated around the principals.

7657 PINNACLE-SHARE PRIZE DRAW H'CAP (DIV II) 1m 4f 98y (Tp)
5:10 (5:10) (Class 6) (0-65,65) 3-Y-O+ **£2,264** (£673; £336; £168) **Stalls** High

Form RPR
0513 **1** **Kirtling**[21] 7105 5-9-13 **64**..........................(t) MartinLane 1 71
(Andi Brown) *s.i.s: hld up: gd hdwy on outside to ld over 1f out: rdn: edgd lft and idled ins fnl f: hld on nr fin* **4/1**[2]
3203 **2** nk **Tectonic (IRE)**[12] 7385 7-9-12 **63**..........................(v) ConnorBeasley 11 70
(Keith Dalgleish) *t.k.h: hld up: stdy hdwy whn nt clr run over 2f out to over 1f out: effrt and chsd wnr ins fnl f: kpt on: hld cl home* **7/1**[3]
00 **3** 1¾ **Aislabie (FR)**[25] 7008 3-9-6 **64**.......................... JasonHart 4 68
(Mark Walford) *trckd ldrs: hdwy to ld over 2f out: rdn and hdd over 1f out: edgd lft: lost 2nd and no ex ins fnl f* **22/1**
3125 **4** ¾ **Taopix**[21] 7105 4-9-2 **58**.......................... AdamMcNamara(5) 13 61
(Karen McLintock) *s.i.s: hld up: effrt on outside over 2f out: rdn and hung lft over 1f out: kpt on ins fnl f* **3/1**[1]
6652 **5** 1½ **Another Lincolnday**[12] 7385 5-9-10 **61**.......................... TomEaves 4 62
(Michael Herrington) *hld up midfield: stdy hdwy whn nt clr run over 2f out to over 1f out: rdn and kpt on fnl f: no imp* **7/1**[3]
000/ **6** ½ **Haaffa Sovereign**[836] 4304 5-8-9 **46** oh1.......................... JoeFanning 6 46
(Kevin Morgan) *t.k.h: prom: outpcd whn n.m.r over 1f out: btn fnl f* **33/1**
6030 **7** hd **Come On Lulu**[13] 7361 5-8-9 **46**..........................(b[1]) JamesSullivan 12 46
(David Thompson) *hld up in tch: effrt and rdn over 2f out: no ex fr over 1f out* **66/1**
6504 **8** 1¼ **Haymarket**[17] 7249 7-9-1 **55**.......................... JosephineGordon(3) 9 53
(R Mike Smith) *led to over 2f out: outpcd whn n.m.r over 1f out: sn btn* **12/1**
3244 **9** ¾ **Star Ascending (IRE)**[15] 2445 4-10-0 **65**.......................... DavidNolan 10 62
(Jennie Candlish) *cl up: rdn and ev ch briefly over 2f out: wknd over 1f out* **9/1**
0464 **10** 2½ **Gabrial's Hope (FR)**[12] 7382 7-9-2 **53**.......................... DaleSwift 3 46
(Tracy Waggott) *in tch: rdn along over 2f out: no imp wl over 1f out: sn btn* **25/1**
-051 **11** 1¼ **Bassett Bleu**[10] 7438 3-7-9 **46** oh1..........................(b) JamieGormley(7) 5 37
(Iain Jardine) *dwlt: hld up: rdn along over 2f out: sn btn* **4/1**[2]
-106 **12** nk **Whisky Marmalade (IRE)**[211] 1169 4-9-5 **56**.......................... CamHardie 8 46
(Ben Haslam) *hld up: rdn and outpcd over 2f out: sn btn* **40/1**
-002 **13** 5 **Insight (IRE)**[160] 2462 5-8-11 **48**..........................(p) DougieCostello 2 31
(Lucinda Egerton) *chsd ldrs tl rdn and wknd over 2f out* **50/1**

2m 40.73s (-0.37) **Going Correction** -0.125s/f (Stan)
WFA 3 from 4yo+ 7lb **13** Ran SP% **124.7**
Speed ratings (Par 101): **96,95,94,94,93 92,92,91,91,89 88,88,85**
CSF £31.67 CT £569.75 TOTE £4.50: £1.70, £2.40, £8.00; EX 34.20 Trifecta £720.70.

 The Form Book, Raceform Ltd, Newbury, RG14 5SJ

Owner Faith Hope And Charity **Bred** L P R Partnership **Trained** Newmarket, Suffolk
FOCUS
The second division was run in a 02.85s slower time, but the sedate early gallop didn't prevent those ridden from behind getting into the race.

7658 PINNACLE RACING "LIKE" US ON FACEBOOK MEDIAN AUCTION MAIDEN STKS (PLUS 10 RACE) 1m 5y (Tp)
5:45 (5:47) (Class 4) 2-Y-O **£3,946** (£1,174; £586; £293) **Stalls** Centre

Form RPR
3 **1** **Mojito (IRE)**[20] 7157 2-9-5 0 BenCurtis 5 80+
(William Haggas) *hld up: shkn up and hdwy 2f out: pushed along and led ent fnl f: edgd rt: kpt on strly* **1/2**[1]
03 **2** *2 1/4* **Somnambulist**[10] 7431 2-9-5 0 JasonHart 8 75
(Keith Dalgleish) *led: rdn 2f out: hdd ent fnl f: kpt on same pce* **40/1**
5 **3** *3* **Wordsearch (USA)**[14] 7329 2-9-2 0 JosephineGordon(3) 7 68
(Hugo Palmer) *chsd ldrs: drvn and outpcd over 2f out: rallied fnl f: nt rch first two* **9/2**[2]
2320 **4** *1 1/2* **Honourable**[20] 7147 2-9-0 70 TonyHamilton 1 60
(Richard Fahey) *prom: effrt and drvn along 2f out: wknd ins fnl f* **15/2**[3]
55 **5** *nk* **Poseidon (IRE)**[36] 6704 2-9-5 0 DougieCostello 3 64
(Ed Walker) *hld up in tch: rdn and outpcd over 2f out: rallied ins fnl f: nvr able to chal* **10/1**
02 **6** *nk* **Casina Di Notte (IRE)**[18] 7226 2-9-5 0 (b) DanielMuscutt 2 64
(Marco Botti) *prom: rdn over 2f out: wknd over 1f out* **15/2**[3]
7 *8* **Medici Moon** 2-9-5 0 DaleSwift 6 46
(Scott Dixon) *dwlt: rn green in rr: struggling over 2f out: sn btn* **125/1**
0 **8** *2 3/4* **Sunset Sally (IRE)**[27] 6952 2-9-0 0 CamHardie 4 35
(John Quinn) *in tch: rdn over 2f out: sn wknd* **125/1**
03 **9** *8* **Beaconsfield**[14] 7318 2-9-5 0 RobertWinston 10 23
(Hughie Morrison) *chsd ldr tl rdn and wknd over 1f out: eased whn btn ins fnl f* **10/1**

1m 39.13s (0.53) **Going Correction** -0.025s/f (Stan) **9** Ran SP% **124.7**
Speed ratings (Par 97): **96,93,90,89,88 88,80,77,69**
CSF £36.64 TOTE £1.50: £1.02, £7.60, £1.60; EX 26.20 Trifecta £106.40.
Owner Carmichael Jennings **Bred** Earl Ecurie Du Grand Chene **Trained** Newmarket, Suffolk
FOCUS
An average maiden in which the fair pace increased at halfway.

7659 AFFORDABLE SHARES AVAILABLE MAIDEN AUCTION STKS (PLUS 10 RACE) 7f 14y (Tp)
6:15 (6:17) (Class 4) 2-Y-O **£3,946** (£1,174; £586; £293) **Stalls** Centre

Form RPR
4 **1** **Crushed (IRE)**[21] 7125 2-8-11 0 BenCurtis 3 68
(William Haggas) *t.k.h early: cl up: led over 2f out: rdn and r.o wl fr over 1f out* **8/13**[1]
05 **2** *1 1/2* **Royal Icon**[12] 7380 2-8-10 0 KevinStott 11 63
(Kevin Ryan) *hld up: rdn and hdwy 2f out: chsd wnr 1f out: kpt on: nt pce to chal* **8/1**[3]
0 **3** *1/2* **Solent Meads (IRE)**[37] 6672 2-9-0 0 JosephineGordon(3) 9 69
(Daniel Kubler) *prom: effrt and rdn 2f out: kpt on same pce ins fnl f* **16/1**
06 **4** *1* **Sliceoflife**[15] 7306 2-9-3 0 DanielMuscutt 7 66
(Marco Botti) *t.k.h early: cl up: chal briefly over 2f out: rdn and one pce fnl f* **6/1**[2]
5 *3/4* **Cray (IRE)** 2-9-1 0 JoeFanning 10 62
(James Bethell) *hld up: pushed along and effrt over 2f out: no imp appr fnl f* **9/1**
6 *nse* **Eponina (IRE)** 2-8-6 0 CamHardie 5 53
(Ben Haslam) *trckd ldrs: effrt and rdn 2f out: wknd ins fnl f* **66/1**
7 *1 1/4* **Lady Kitty** 2-8-10 0 SamJames 12 54
(John Davies) *s.i.s: hld up: pushed along over 2f out: no imp fr over 1f out* **25/1**
0 **8** *5* **Hediddodinthe (IRE)**[16] 7283 2-8-13 0 ConnorBeasley 1 44
(Richard Guest) *s.i.s: hld up: rdn and outpcd over 2f out: sn btn* **66/1**
620 **9** *3/4* **Stevie Brown**[18] 7208 2-8-11 67 TomEaves 8 41
(David Brown) *in tch: drvn along over 2f out: wknd wl over 1f out* **14/1**
10 *2* **Delightfulsurprise** 2-8-6 0 JamesSullivan 6 31
(Scott Dixon) *s.i.s: bhd: struggling over 2f out: sn btn* **33/1**
06 **11** *1/2* **Dirty Randy (IRE)**[10] 7431 2-8-13 0 JasonHart 2 36
(Keith Dalgleish) *hld up: drvn and struggling over 2f out: sn wknd* **50/1**
00 **12** *8* **Unonothinjonsnow**[11] 7407 2-8-12 0 JacobButterfield(3) 4 18
(Richard Guest) *plld hrd: led to over 2f out: sn wknd* **100/1**

1m 27.34s (1.14) **Going Correction** -0.025s/f (Stan) **12** Ran SP% **122.6**
Speed ratings (Par 97): **92,90,89,88,87 87,86,80,79,77 76,67**
CSF £6.31 TOTE £1.50: £1.10, £1.90, £4.50; EX 9.10 Trifecta £67.10.
Owner B Haggas **Bred** J Manogue **Trained** Newmarket, Suffolk
FOCUS
A moderate maiden and another straightforward task for the well backed favourite, who made it a double on the night for William Haggas. The winner could be a good few lengths better than rated.

7660 ARRANGE A PINNACLE STABLE VISIT AT WYNYARD H'CAP 5f (Tp)
6:45 (6:46) (Class 5) (0-75,80) 3-Y-O+ **£2,911** (£866; £432; £216) **Stalls** Centre

Form RPR
0431 **1** **Rural Celebration**[10] 7437 5-9-12 80 6ex (v) GrahamGibbons 6 91
(David O'Meara) *mde virtually all: rdn along wl over 1f out: kpt on fnl f* **5/2**[1]
0032 **2** *3/4* **Dark Side Dream**[14] 7325 4-8-9 70 MillyNaseb(7) 7 77
(Chris Dwyer) *in tch: effrt and pushed along 2f out: chsd wnr ins fnl f: kpt on: nt pce to chal* **8/1**[3]
5323 **3** *nse* **Royal Brave (IRE)**[33] 6809 5-8-10 69 RowanScott(5) 11 76
(Rebecca Bastiman) *bhd: rdn and hdwy nr side of gp over 1f out: kpt on fnl f: nrst fin* **10/1**
4214 **4** *nk* **Astrophysics**[12] 7386 4-9-5 73 PaddyAspell 10 79
(Lynn Siddall) *hld up in tch: rdn and effrt over 1f out: kpt on ins fnl f* **8/1**[3]
0000 **5** *hd* **Clubland (IRE)**[41] 6589 7-9-0 68 JasonHart 2 73+
(Garry Moss) *hld up: rdn and hdwy towards far side of gp over 1f out: kpt on fnl f: no imp* **20/1**
4234 **6** *nse* **Innocently (IRE)**[27] 6959 5-8-9 68 (b) JoshDoyle(5) 8 73
(David O'Meara) *pressed wnr: rdn and ev ch 1/2-way: no ex ins fnl f* **16/1**
4036 **7** *1/2* **Sir Domino (FR)**[12] 7386 4-9-5 73 (b) KevinStott 13 76
(Kevin Ryan) *in tch in centre: hdwy to press wnr over 1f out to ins fnl f: sn no ex* **8/1**[3]
0600 **8** *1* **Imperial Legend (IRE)**[17] 7252 7-9-4 72 PaulQuinn 5 71
(David Nicholls) *s.i.s: bhd: rdn and hdwy over 1f out: no imp fnl f* **50/1**
6202 **9** *1/2* **Eternitys Gate**[12] 7386 5-9-4 75 (v) JosephineGordon(3) 4 73
(Ivan Furtado) *in tch: rdn and edgd lft over 1f out: sn outpcd* **9/2**[2]
1000 **10** *hd* **Point North (IRE)**[14] 7324 9-9-5 73 (b) PaulMulrennan 9 70
(John Balding) *hld up: rdn along 1/2-way: no imp fr over 1f out* **50/1**
0200 **11** *3/4* **Emjayem**[21] 7112 6-9-7 75 DaleSwift 14 69
(Ed McMahon) *bhd: rdn and hdwy over 2f out: hung lft: wknd over 1f out* **25/1**
0560 **12** *2 3/4* **Ayresome Angel**[10] 7437 3-9-2 70 ConnorBeasley 3 55
(Bryan Smart) *plld hrd: cl up towards far side: struggling over 2f out: sn btn* **80/1**
3122 **13** *3/4* **Twentysvnthlancers**[27] 6958 3-8-10 69 AdamMcNamara(5) 12 52
(Paul Midgley) *bhd: drvn along 1/2-way: nvr on terms* **14/1**
1500 **14** *1/2* **Jack Luey**[17] 7252 9-9-4 72 (b) TomEaves 1 52
(Lawrence Mullaney) *racd on far side of gp: w wnr to 1/2-way: sn struggling* **20/1**

58.65s (-0.85) **Going Correction** -0.025s/f (Stan) **14** Ran SP% **120.3**
Speed ratings (Par 103): **105,103,103,103,102 102,102,100,99,99 98,93,92,91**
CSF £20.81 CT £176.89 TOTE £3.20: £1.40, £3.50, £2.80; EX 26.40 Trifecta £117.90.
Owner Hambleton Racing Ltd - Two Chances **Bred** J A And M A Knox **Trained** Upper Helmsley, N Yorks
FOCUS
An ordinary sprint handicap and they went a good clip. The winner has been rated back to her best, with the third and fourth to their latest marks.

7661 GARY MOSS MAIDEN STKS 1m 5y (Tp)
7:15 (7:16) (Class 5) 3-Y-O+ **£2,911** (£866; £432; £216) **Stalls** Centre

Form RPR
53 **1** **Westward Ho (IRE)**[56] 6104 3-9-5 0 JoeFanning 3 81+
(James Bethell) *in tch: smooth hdwy to ld over 1f out: shkn up to go clr fnl f: readily* **7/4**[1]
65 **2** *2 1/2* **Dubawi Fifty**[12] 7384 3-9-5 0 DavidNolan 1 74
(Karen McLintock) *led: rdn and hdd over 1f out: kpt on fnl f: nt pce of wnr* **6/1**
52- **3** *1 3/4* **Initially**[353] 7787 3-9-0 0 GrahamGibbons 2 65
(Charles Hills) *t.k.h: pressed ldr: ev ch over 2f out to over 1f out: sn rdn and outpcd* **11/4**[2]
33 **4** *3 1/2* **Aloysius Hansom**[45] 6452 3-9-5 0 TomEaves 5 61
(Kevin Ryan) *stdd in last pl: stdy hdwy 3f out: rdn 2f out: sn one pce* **7/2**[3]
026 **5** *hd* **Secret Dreamer**[37] 6674 4-9-2 66 AdamMcNamara(5) 4 62
(Kevin Morgan) *prom: rdn over 2f out: outpcd fr over 1f out* **8/1**

1m 40.84s (2.24) **Going Correction** -0.025s/f (Stan)
WFA 3 from 4yo 3lb **5** Ran SP% **110.6**
Speed ratings (Par 103): **87,84,82,79,79**
CSF £12.45 TOTE £2.70: £1.40, £3.00; EX 12.90 Trifecta £50.90.
Owner Geoffrey Van Cutsem **Bred** Mrs F H Hay **Trained** Middleham Moor, N Yorks
FOCUS
A moderate maiden in which they set just a slow tempo. The winner has been rated as building on his C&D latst, and could possibly be a bit better at face value rated around the third and fourth.

7662 PINNACLERACING.CO.UK H'CAP 7f 14y (Tp)
7:45 (7:46) (Class 5) (0-75,74) 3-Y-O+ **£2,911** (£866; £432; £216) **Stalls** Centre

Form RPR
3250 **1** **Amood (IRE)**[45] 6435 5-9-7 74 (p) JasonHart 9 82+
(Simon West) *hld up: stdy hdwy over 1f out: rdn to ld wl ins fnl f: kpt on wl* **16/1**
4341 **2** *nk* **My Dad Syd (USA)**[7] 7506 4-9-6 73 6ex (b) RobertWinston 14 79
(Ian Williams) *cl up gng wl: led over 2f out: rdn over 1f out: hdd wl ins fnl f: kpt on* **3/1**[1]
3462 **3** *shd* **Athollblair Boy (IRE)**[21] 7111 3-8-8 70 LewisEdmunds(7) 10 75
(Nigel Tinkler) *in tch: hdwy over 1f out: sn rdn: ev ch ins fnl f: nt go past runner-up* **9/2**[2]
6531 **4** *shd* **Gun Case**[14] 7333 4-9-3 70 (p) DougieCostello 6 75
(Alistair Whillans) *hld up in tch: effrt and edgd lft over 1f out: ev ch and rdn ins fnl f: kpt on: hld nr fin* **5/1**[3]
0060 **5** *1/2* **Tellovoi (IRE)**[9] 7457 8-9-5 72 (v) JoeFanning 7 76
(Richard Guest) *t.k.h: led to over 2f out: rallied: kpt on same pce ins fnl f* **16/1**
1404 **6** *1 1/4* **Gone With The Wind (GER)**[48] 6347 5-8-10 68 (p) RowanScott(5) 11 69
(Rebecca Bastiman) *hld up: rdn along over 2f out: kpt on fnl f: nvr able to chal* **40/1**
00 **7** *1 1/2* **Crazy Tornado (IRE)**[34] 6772 3-9-2 71 ConnorBeasley 5 67
(Keith Dalgleish) *cl up: rdn over 2f out: no ex ent fnl f* **16/1**
5430 **8** *hd* **Hernando Torres**[20] 7141 8-8-13 66 (tp) CamHardie 13 62
(Michael Easterby) *hld up: rdn and effrt over 2f out: no imp over 1f out* **22/1**
2525 **9** *3/4* **Bahamian Bird**[14] 7324 3-9-0 69 TonyHamilton 3 62
(Richard Fahey) *prom: rdn over 2f out: outpcd over 1f out* **12/1**
2200 **10** *1* **Gold Flash**[24] 7051 4-9-5 72 (p) PhillipMakin 1 63
(Keith Dalgleish) *hld up: rdn and outpcd over 2f out: sn btn* **16/1**
4031 **11** *1 1/4* **Alice Thornton**[14] 7323 4-9-3 70 DavidNolan 4 58
(Martin Todhunter) *in tch: rdn over 2f out: wknd over 1f out* **9/2**[2]
0050 **12** *1 1/2* **Musaaid (IRE)**[14] 7324 4-8-13 66 (b[1]) GrahamGibbons 12 50
(Michael Easterby) *missed break: bhd: struggling over 2f out: sn btn* **14/1**

1m 24.7s (-1.50) **Going Correction** -0.025s/f (Stan)
WFA 3 from 4yo+ 2lb **12** Ran SP% **122.7**
Speed ratings (Par 103): **107,106,106,106,105 104,102,102,101,100 99,97**
CSF £65.88 CT £269.94 TOTE £21.80: £5.80, £2.00, £1.70; EX 87.10 Trifecta £693.50.
Owner C R Hirst **Bred** Shadwell Estate Company Limited **Trained** Middleham Moor, N Yorks
FOCUS
There was a fair pace for this handicap, which produced a four-way finish. The form is sound around the placed horses.

7663 PINNACLE RACING 20TH ANNIVERSARY APPRENTICE H'CAP 6f (Tp)
8:15 (8:16) (Class 5) (0-70,70) 3-Y-O+ **£2,911** (£866; £432; £216) **Stalls** Centre

Form RPR
4003 **1** **Meandmyshadow**[14] 7324 8-9-7 70 (b) JoshDoyle 7 77
(Alan Brown) *led towards far side of gp: rdn and hdd over 2f out: rallied and regained ld ins fnl f: hld on wl nr fin* **8/1**[3]
1006 **2** *hd* **Bay Mirage (IRE)**[14] 7333 3-8-10 63 (p) LewisEdmunds(3) 14 69
(Kevin Ryan) *cl up nr side of gp: led over 2f out: rdn and edgd rt over 1f out: hdd ins fnl f: kpt on: jst hld* **20/1**
046 **3** *1/2* **Epeius (IRE)**[21] 7111 3-8-10 63 MeganNicholls(3) 6 68
(Ben Haslam) *hld up towards rr: bmpd and lost pl over 3f out: rallied far side and prom over 2f out: kpt on fnl f: hld nr fin* **20/1**
0213 **4** *hd* **Caeser The Gaeser (IRE)**[24] 7059 4-8-9 65 (p) PaulaMuir(7) 12 69+
(Nigel Tinkler) *s.i.s: hld up: hdwy nr side of gp over 1f out: kpt on ins fnl f* **8/1**[3]
0320 **5** *3/4* **Fujin**[52] 6216 5-9-7 70 CharlieBennett 13 72
(Shaun Harris) *chsd ldrs: rdn over 2f out: effrt and ch ent fnl f: kpt on: no ex towards fin* **16/1**

5222 **6** 2 1/4 **Mr Orange (IRE)**[24] 7059 3-8-12 **69**....................(p) ManuelFernandes(7) 4 64
(Paul Midgley) *cl up on far side of gp: rdn and ev ch over 2f out: outpcd wknd ins fnl f* **7/2**[2]

0530 **7** 1 1/2 **Windforpower (IRE)**[3] 7595 6-8-9 **58**..............................(p) PhilDennis 1 48
(Tracy Waggott) *in tch on far side of gp: rdn and outpcd over 2f out: rallied over 1f out: sn no imp* **18/1**

060 **8** 1/2 **Fyrecracker (IRE)**[37] 6680 5-9-1 **64**........................... CallumShepherd 9 52
(Grant Tuer) *in tch centre: drvn and outpcd over 2f out: n.d after* **9/1**

1600 **9** 1/2 **Gypsy Major**[14] 7324 4-9-0 **63**................................(v) AdamMcNamara 10 50
(Garry Moss) *hld up on nr side of gp: drvn and outpcd over 2f out: sme late hdwy: nvr on terms* **20/1**

0320 **10** nk **Encantar**[14] 7325 3-9-0 **67**..(v) RowanScott(3) 11 53
(Ann Duffield) *hld up nr side of gp: drvn along over 2f out: no imp fr over 1f out* **10/1**

3354 **11** 2 1/2 **More Beau (USA)**[24] 7059 5-9-5 **68**.................................... HollieDoyle 5 46+
(David Nicholls) *t.k.h: hld up in tch: bmpd over 4f out: bmpd and squeezed out over 3f out: sn drvn along: wknd wl over 1f out* **11/4**[1]

000 **12** 2 **Doeadeer (IRE)**[31] 6851 3-8-7 **62**............................ PatrickVaughan(5) 2 33
(Keith Dalgleish) *taken early to post: t.k.h: hld up in tch: edgd rt and bmpd over 3f out: rdn over 2f out: wknd over 1f out* **40/1**

0050 **13** 5 **Monsieur Jimmy**[126] 3610 4-8-12 **66**................................ GerO'Neill(5) 8 21
(Declan Carroll) *tkl t.k.h: in tch: bmpd and lost pl over 3f out: sn struggling: btn fnl 2f* **33/1**

1m 10.81s (-1.69) **Going Correction** -0.025s/f (Stan)
WFA 3 from 4yo+ 1lb **13** Ran SP% **121.0**
Speed ratings (Par 103): **110,109,109,108,107 104,102,102,101,101 97,95,88**
CSF £164.86 CT £3176.68 TOTE £8.60: £2.80, £5.70, £4.60; EX 201.30 TRIFECTA Not won..
Owner G Morrill **Bred** M J Dawson **Trained** Yedingham, N Yorks

FOCUS
A moderate sprint handicap in which it paid to race race prominently. The winner has been rated similar to her C&D latest.
T/Plt: £545.00 to a £1 stake. Pool: £73,549.21 - 98.51 winning tickets T/Qpdt: £3.80 to a £1 stake. Pool: £11,992.60 - 2,287.20 winning tickets **Richard Young**

7465 NEWMARKET (R-H)

Friday, October 28

OFFICIAL GOING: Good (good to firm in places; 7.7)
Wind: light, half behind Weather: overcast

7664 BRITISH STALLION STUDS EBF MAIDEN STKS (PLUS 10 RACE) (DIV I) 7f

1:20 (1:22) (Class 4) 2-Y-O **£4,528** (£1,347; £673; £336) **Stalls** Low

Form RPR

1 **Giovanni Battista (IRE)** 2-9-0 0.................................. JimmyFortune 5 85+
(Brian Meehan) *mde all: pushed along 3f out: drvn over 1f out: kpt on gamely to forge ahd ins fnl f: rdn out* **25/1**

2 3/4 **Leshlaa (USA)** 2-9-0 0.. WilliamBuick 6 83+
(Saeed bin Suroor) *hld up wl in tch in midfield: effrt to chse ldrs 2f out: chal and edgd rt over 1f out: no ex and jst outpcd fnl 100yds* **5/1**[3]

3 **3** 5 **Founding Father (FR)**[18] 7216 2-9-0 0............................ JimCrowley 8 69
(James Tate) *w wnr: rdn over 2f out: unable qck and outpcd whn sltly hmpd 1f out: wknd ins fnl f* **13/8**[1]

56 **4** 1 1/4 **Call Me Grumpy (IRE)**[10] 7432 2-9-0 0......................... AndreaAtzeni 2 66
(Roger Varian) *chsd ldng pair: 4th and outpcd whn edgd lft over 1f out: wl hld and plugged on same pce after* **9/1**

4 **5** 3 1/4 **Blue On Blue (USA)**[15] 7306 2-9-0 0............................. FrankieDettori 4 57
(John Gosden) *keen to post: t.k.h: hld up in tch in midfield: rdn 3f out: sn outpcd: 5th and wl btn over 1f out* **7/4**[2]

6 nk **Astute Boy (IRE)** 2-9-0 0... FrederikTylicki 7 57
(Ed Vaughan) *s.i.s: hld up in last pair: effrt over 2f out: wl hld 6th and no imp whn rn green on downhill run over 1f out* **33/1**

7 1 3/4 **Salt Whistle Bay (IRE)** 2-9-0 0..................................... PatCosgrave 3 52
(Rae Guest) *hld up in tch in midfield: lost pl and pushed along over 2f out: sn btn: bhd over 1f out* **25/1**

8 nk **Retribution** 2-9-0 0... LiamKeniry 1 51
(David Lanigan) *stdd s: hld up in tch in last pair: pushed along over 2f out: sn btn and bhd over 1f out* **33/1**

1m 24.47s (-0.93) **Going Correction** -0.05s/f (Good) **8** Ran SP% **114.7**
Speed ratings (Par 97): **103,102,96,95,91 90,88,88**
CSF £139.57 TOTE £29.90: £6.50, £1.60, £1.10; EX 215.00 Trifecta £403.40.
Owner S E Sangster **Bred** Rathasker Stud **Trained** Manton, Wilts

FOCUS
Stands' side course used. Stalls: far side, except 1m4f and 2m: centre. The watered ground (3mm on Wednesday) was given as good, good to firm in places (GoingStick: 7.7). The re-positioning of the bend into the home straight increased the distance of the 1m4f and 2m races by 12yds. The wind was behind them up the straight. Something of a turn-up here, but there was no fluke about the way the winner scored, and the time compared very favourably with the second division (2.39sec quicker).

7665 BRITISH STALLION STUDS EBF MAIDEN STKS (PLUS 10 RACE) (DIV II) 7f

1:50 (1:53) (Class 4) 2-Y-O **£4,528** (£1,347; £673; £336) **Stalls** Low

Form RPR

33 **1** **Makkaar (IRE)**[17] 7243 2-9-0 0.. WilliamBuick 7 81
(Mark Johnston) *mde all: rdn wl over 1f out: forged ahd u.p ins fnl f: styd on* **5/1**

2 1 3/4 **Top Mission** 2-9-0 0.. JamesDoyle 3 76
(Saeed bin Suroor) *chsd wnr: rdn and ev ch whn edgd lft over 1f out: no ex and btn whn hung lft wl ins fnl f* **4/1**[3]

3 1 3/4 **Loujain (IRE)** 2-9-0 0.. DaneO'Neill 2 72
(John Gosden) *dwlt: sn rcvrd to chse ldrs: effrt over 1f out: styd on same pce ins fnl f* **3/1**[2]

4 nk **Ejaaby** 2-9-0 0.. AndreaAtzeni 4 71
(Roger Varian) *chsd ldrs: effrt and ev ch wl over 1f out: jst getting outpcd whn sltly short of room ent fnl f: kpt on same pce after* **11/4**[1]

5 5 **Prost (GER)** 2-9-0 0... FrederikTylicki 1 57
(Ed Vaughan) *dwlt and dropped in bhd after s: t.k.h in last pair: effrt ent fnl 2f: sn outpcd and hung lft over 1f out: wl hld and kpt on same pce after* **40/1**

6 nk **Screaming Gemini (IRE)** 2-9-0 0................................... JackMitchell 8 56
(Roger Varian) *in tch in midfield: effrt ent fnl 2f: sn outpcd and wl hld over 1f out: wknd ins fnl f* **14/1**

7 2 1/4 **Kuiper Belt (USA)** 2-9-0 0... ShaneKelly 5 50
(David Lanigan) *dwlt: hld up in tch in midfield: pushed along over 2f out: outpcd and btn wl over 1f out: wknd fnl f* **25/1**

8 3/4 **Daimochi (IRE)** 2-9-0 0... AdamKirby 9 48
(Clive Cox) *dwlt: in tch in last pair: effrt and rn green over 2f out: sn struggling and wl hld whn hung rt over 1f out* **11/2**

9 1 1/2 **Take A Turn (IRE)** 2-9-0 0... StevieDonohoe 6 44
(David Lanigan) *in tch in midfield: pushed along over 2f out: sn struggling: bhd fnl f* **80/1**

1m 26.86s (1.46) **Going Correction** -0.05s/f (Good) **9** Ran SP% **117.9**
Speed ratings (Par 97): **89,87,85,84,78 78,76,75,73**
CSF £25.61 TOTE £6.10: £1.70, £1.60, £1.30; EX 27.90 Trifecta £60.50.
Owner Hamdan Al Maktoum **Bred** Roundhill Stud **Trained** Middleham Moor, N Yorks

FOCUS
Much the slower of the two divisions, the winner dominating from the front and clocking a time 2.39sec slower than the first leg.

7666 NGK SPARK PLUGS H'CAP 1m 2f

2:25 (2:25) (Class 4) (0-85,84) 3-Y-O+ **£5,175** (£1,540; £769; £384) **Stalls** Low

Form RPR

1 **1** **Wadigor**[46] 6423 3-9-2 **81**.. AndreaAtzeni 8 100+
(Roger Varian) *t.k.h: hld up in tch: clsd to trck ldrs 4f out: shkn to ld and edging rt ent fnl f: stl drifting rt but drew wl clr fnl f: easily* **11/4**[1]

3252 **2** 7 **Rotherwick (IRE)**[11] 7419 4-9-10 **84**................................(t) JimCrowley 4 89
(Paul Cole) *hld up in tch in midfield: effrt 3f out: 3rd and drvn over 1f out: no ch w wnr and kpt on same pce ins fnl f: snatched 2nd last strides* **9/2**[2]

1061 **3** hd **Van Huysen (IRE)**[17] 7245 4-9-3 **77**................................ OisinMurphy 10 82
(Dominic Ffrench Davis) *t.k.h: chsd ldr tl led 1/2-way: rdn ent fnl 2f: hdd ent fnl f: sn outpcd and no ch w wnr: plugged on same pce after: lost 2nd last strides* **9/1**

4202 **4** nk **Compton Mill**[30] 6876 4-9-6 **80**.......................................(t) GeorgeBaker 3 84
(Hughie Morrison) *hld up in tch in midfield: dropped to rr 1/2-way: swtchd rt and effrt 2f out: slt impeded over 1f out: 4th and swtchd lft ins fnl f: kpt on: no ch w wnr* **11/2**

1353 **5** 3 3/4 **Dolphin Village (IRE)**[37] 6676 6-9-2 **83**.......................... DavidEgan(7) 7 80
(Jane Chapple-Hyam) *s.i.s: t.k.h: sn rcvrd and in midfield: hdwy to join ldr 5f out tl unable qck 2f out: wknd fnl f* **16/1**

315 **6** 6 **Bridge Of Sighs**[18] 7229 4-9-2 **76**..................................... PatCosgrave 6 61
(Martin Smith) *hld up in tch in rr: effrt ent fnl 2f: edgd rt and no imp over 1f out: wknd fnl f* **14/1**

0100 **7** 2 **Star Blaze**[33] 6803 3-9-1 **80**.. GrahamLee 9 61
(Mick Channon) *led tl 1/2-way: rdn 3f out: sn struggling: wknd over 1f out* **16/1**

6-4 **8** 4 1/2 **Charismatic Man (IRE)**[36] 6703 3-8-7 **72**................................ JFEgan 2 44
(Ralph Beckett) *in tch in midfield: rdn over 2f out: no imp whn edgd rt over 1f out: sn eased and bhd ins fnl f* **5/1**[3]

0630 **9** 3 1/4 **Pasaka Boy**[24] 7053 6-9-0 **74**...................................... RichardKingscote 5 39
(Jonathan Portman) *in tch in midfield: pushed along 3f out: sn struggling: bhd over 1f out* **10/1**

2m 3.05s (-2.75) **Going Correction** -0.05s/f (Good)
WFA 3 from 4yo+ 5lb **9** Ran SP% **114.4**
Speed ratings (Par 105): **109,103,103,103,100 95,93,90,87**
CSF £14.73 CT £96.15 TOTE £3.40: £1.50, £1.60, £2.90; EX 13.90 Trifecta £72.10.
Owner Sheikh Ahmed Al Maktoum **Bred** Panda Bloodstock **Trained** Newmarket, Suffolk

FOCUS
This handicap was taken apart by the unexposed winner. The three who chased him home arrived in form and set a solid level.

7667 IRISH STALLION FARMS "BOSRA SHAM" EBF FILLIES' STKS (LISTED RACE) 6f

3:00 (3:00) (Class 1) 2-Y-O

£17,013 (£6,450; £3,228; £1,608; £807; £405) **Stalls** Low

Form RPR

151 **1** **Spiritual Lady**[87] 4974 2-9-0 **96**...................................... FrankieDettori 10 101
(Philip McBride) *stdd after s: racd keenly and hld up in tch: swtchd lft and clsd on bit 2f out: pushed along and qcknd to ld jst over 1f out:wl in command ins fnl f: eased cl home: easily* **3/1**[1]

06 **2** 1 1/2 **Spy Ring (IRE)**[12] 7389 2-9-0 0...................................... OisinMurphy 9 97
(M D O'Callaghan, Ire) *chsd ldng trio: effrt 2f out: rdn and ev ch over 1f out: nvr matching pce of wnr but kpt on for 2nd ins fnl f* **16/1**

126 **3** 1 **Mystic Dawn (IRE)**[21] 7114 2-9-0 **98**................................ DaneO'Neill 5 94
(David Simcock) *dwlt: hld up in tch in rr: hdwy u.p over 1f out: styd on ins fnl f: wnt 3rd last strides: no ch w wnr* **7/1**[3]

1523 **4** nk **Perfect Angel (IRE)**[20] 7155 2-9-0 **100**.......................... MartinDwyer 7 93
(Andrew Balding) *chsd ldr: rdn to ld 2f: drvn and hdd over 1f out: styd on same pce ins fnl f* **10/3**[2]

3 **5** 3/4 **Classical Times**[14] 7314 2-9-0 0...................................... JamesDoyle 2 90
(Peter Chapple-Hyam) *hld up in tch: effrt to press ldrs u.p 2f out: edgd lft and unable qck over 1f out: kpt on same pce ins fnl f* **12/1**

135 **6** 1/2 **Pellucid**[34] 6784 2-9-0 **98**.. AdamKirby 1 89
(David Simcock) *taken down early: dwlt: hld up in tch towards rr: effrt u.p 2f out: shifted rt and no imp over 1f out: kpt on same pce ins fnl f* **8/1**

0300 **7** 2 1/4 **Dainty Dandy (IRE)**[57] 6063 2-9-0 **94**..........................[1] JimmyFortune 8 82
(Paul Cole) *taken down early: led: rdn and hdd 2f out: sn struggling and lost pl: wknd ins fnl f* **50/1**

100 **8** 3 1/2 **Easy Victory**[21] 7116 2-9-0 **88**..[1] JimCrowley 6 72
(Saeed bin Suroor) *in tch in midfield: effrt ent fnl 2f: sn struggling and lost pl over 1f out: wknd ins fnl f* **10/1**

21 **9** 2 1/2 **Loving**[10] 7439 2-9-0 0.. PatCosgrave 4 64
(William Haggas) *t.k.h: chsd ldrs: rdn to press ldrs ent fnl 2f: sn struggling and lost pl whn nt clrest of runs over 1f out: wknd fnl f: eased towards fin* **8/1**

1050 **10** nk **Romantic View**[20] 7147 2-9-0 **86**.......................................[1] WilliamBuick 3 63
(Charlie Appleby) *in tch in midfield: n.m.r over 2f out: effrt jst over 2f out: unable qck and lost pl over 1f out: wknd fnl f: eased towards fin* **20/1**

1m 11.08s (-1.12) **Going Correction** -0.05s/f (Good) **10** Ran SP% **112.2**
Speed ratings (Par 100): **105,103,101,101,100 99,96,91,88,88**
CSF £49.81 TOTE £4.10: £2.10, £4.30, £2.00; EX 51.30 Trifecta £363.20.
Owner PMRacing **Bred** J W Mitchell **Trained** Newmarket, Suffolk

FOCUS
This looked like quite a competitive Listed race, but the winner proved much too good.

7668 NEWMARKETRACECOURSES.CO.UK CONDITIONS STKS 6f
3:35 (3:35) (Class 3) 2-3-Y-O
£7,470 (£2,236; £1,118; £559; £279; £140) **Stalls** Low

Form RPR
2203 **1** **Aleef (IRE)**[13] 7358 3-9-10 91 ..... JimCrowley 2 93
(David O'Meara) *racd keenly: mde all: rdn 2f out: hld on wl u.p fnl 100yds: rdn out* **3/1**[2]

2161 **2** *nk* **Roll On Rory**[33] 6810 3-9-13 89 ..... (b) GrahamLee 1 95
(Jason Ward) *taken down early: chsd wnr tl over 1f out: rallied u.p to chse wnr again 100yds out: ev ch and kpt on u.p wl ins fnl f: hld cl home* **8/1**[3]

620 **3** *1 1/2* **Gale Song**[28] 6918 3-9-5 81 ..... WilliamBuick 3 82
(Ed Walker) *s.i.s: hld up in rr: clsd and in tch after 2f: hdwy u.p 1f out: wnt 3rd wl ins fnl f: kpt on same pce after: eased cl home* **12/1**

0134 **4** *1 3/4* **Fire Palace**[20] 7147 2-7-7 78 ..... DavidEgan(7) 4 72
(Robert Eddery) *in tch: hdwy to chse ldrs and rdn 3f out: unable qck over 1f out: wknd ins fnl f* **3/1**[2]

212 **5** *1/2* **Dubai One (IRE)**[15] 7305 2-8-0 83 ..... JimmyQuinn 5 70+
(Saeed bin Suroor) *t.k.h: chsd ldrs: effrt and hung rt over 1f out: wnt 2nd 1f out: no imp lost 100yds out: wknd towards fin* **5/2**[1]

2253 **6** *2* **Lagenda**[54] 6164 3-9-10 87 ..... (p) ShaneGray 6 74
(Kevin Ryan) *in tch: effrt over 2f out unable qck and dropped to last over 1f out: wknd ins fnl f* **8/1**[3]

1m 11.11s (-1.09) **Going Correction** -0.05s/f (Good) **6** Ran SP% **108.5**
Speed ratings: **105,104,102,100,99 96**
CSF £24.04 TOTE £3.80: £1.80, £2.70; EX 22.70 Trifecta £99.70.
Owner Nick Bradley Racing 8 **Bred** Sarah Fortune **Trained** Upper Helmsley, N Yorks

FOCUS
This race had gone to 2yos in eight of the previous ten years, but the two juveniles in this line-up finished well held. It's been rated around the third.

7669 EBF STALLIONS FEDERATION OF BLOODSTOCK AGENTS FILLIES' H'CAP 1m 4f
4:10 (4:10) (Class 3) (0-90,86) 3-Y-O+ **£9,056** (£2,695; £1,346; £673) **Stalls** Centre

Form RPR
1662 **1** **Hestina (FR)**[24] 7060 3-8-9 81 ..... GeorgiaCox(5) 2 91+
(Peter Chapple-Hyam) *t.k.h: trckd ldng pair: clsd to ld 2f out: sn rdn: clr 1f out: styd on: pushed out ins fnl f* **5/2**[2]

0445 **2** *1 3/4* **Persun**[18] 7222 4-9-5 79 ..... GrahamLee 4 84
(Mick Channon) *stdd s: hld up wl in tch: effrt 2f out: drvn over 1f out: kpt on to go 2nd towards fin: nvr enough pce to threaten wnr* **8/1**

2322 **3** *1/2* **Graceland (FR)**[37] 6667 4-9-6 83 ..... LouisSteward(3) 5 87
(Michael Bell) *stdd s: hld up in tch in rr: effrt on stands' rail 2f out: drvn ent fnl f: kpt on u.p but no threat to wnr: wnt 2nd last stride* **5/1**[3]

5113 **4** *shd* **Dawn Horizons**[61] 5927 3-9-5 86 ..... PatCosgrave 6 90
(William Haggas) *chsd wnr: rdn 2f out: drvn and no imp 1f out: kpt on same pce after: lost 2 pls towards fin* **6/4**[1]

0260 **5** *10* **Dora's Field (IRE)**[23] 7076 3-8-5 72 oh1 ..... JimmyQuinn 1 60
(Ed Dunlop) *dwlt: hld up in tch in last pair: rdn over 2f out: sn struggling: wknd over 1f out* **25/1**

3306 **6** *1 1/2* **Lovely Story (IRE)**[16] 7280 5-9-6 80 ..... GeorgeBaker 3 66
(Seamus Durack) *led: rdn over 2f out: hdd 2f out: lost pl and btn over 1f out: wknd fnl f* **8/1**

2m 30.46s (-1.54) **Going Correction** -0.20s/f (Firm)
WFA 3 from 4yo+ 7lb **6** Ran SP% **111.3**
Speed ratings (Par 104): **97,95,95,95,88 87**
CSF £21.44 TOTE £4.00: £2.40, £3.40; EX 22.10 Trifecta £68.00.
Owner Paul Hancock **Bred** Mlle Camille Collet & Mlle Louise Collet **Trained** Newmarket, Suffolk

FOCUS
Race distance increased by 12yds. A good performance from the winner here, as showed a nice turn of foot to land the spoils. It's been rated around the runner-up to her recent form.

7670 RACING UK HD H'CAP 2m
4:45 (4:46) (Class 3) (0-90,90) 3-Y-O+ **£7,762** (£2,310; £1,154; £577) **Stalls** Centre

Form RPR
3100 **1** **Star Rider**[20] 7150 4-10-0 90 ..... (p) JimmyFortune 8 103
(Hughie Morrison) *chsd ldrs: effrt to press ldrs 3f out: ev ch and drew clr w ldr over 1f out: led ins fnl f: styd on strly and drew clr fnl 75yds* **7/2**[1]

5411 **2** *4* **Alfredo (IRE)**[13] 7367 4-8-10 72 ..... (tp) OisinMurphy 2 80
(Seamus Durack) *chsd ldr: rdn to ld over 2f out: drvn and clr w wnr over 1f out: hdd ins fnl f: no ex and btn 100yds out: wknd towards fin* **6/1**[3]

2504 **3** *4 1/2* **October Storm**[14] 7332 3-7-12 73 ..... NathanEvans(3) 10 76
(Mick Channon) *stdd s: hld up in tch in last pair: effrt over 3f out: 4th and no imp over 1f out: plugged on to go 3rd ins fnl f* **9/1**

5000 **4** *1 1/4* **Grumeti**[20] 7150 8-9-7 83 ..... AdamKirby 9 85
(Alan King) *hld up in tch: hdwy into midfield 12f out: rdn to chal 3f out: outpcd and edgd rt over 1f out: wknd ins fnl f* **7/2**[1]

45 **5** *1* **Percy Veer**[28] 6919 4-9-8 84 ..... TomMarquand 5 84
(Sylvester Kirk) *chsd ldrs: rdn 3f out: sn outpcd: wl hld and plugged on same pce fr over 1f out* **9/1**

0430 **6** *3/4* **King Calypso**[47] 6362 5-8-2 71 oh1 ..... DavidEgan(7) 6 70
(Denis Coakley) *hld up in tch in midfield: rdn over 3f out: sn outpcd and wl hld whn wnt lft 2f out: no ch but plugged on ins fnl f* **16/1**

4100 **7** *3/4* **Albahar (FR)**[93] 4752 5-9-12 88 ..... (p) DaneO'Neill 7 87
(Chris Gordon) *stdd s: hld up in tch in rr: effrt over 3f out: struggling and no imp over 2f out: wl btn fnl 2f* **25/1**

4411 **8** *4* **Trevisani (IRE)**[65] 5767 4-9-12 88 ..... (v) GeorgeBaker 4 82
(David Lanigan) *led: rdn and hrd pressed 3f out: hdd over 2f out: sn dropped out: wknd over 1f out* **4/1**[2]

5210 **9** *14* **Medina Sidonia (IRE)**[25] 7006 4-8-8 73 ..... (p) RobHornby(3) 3 50
(Tim Easterby) *hld up in tch towards rr: rdn 5f out: sn struggling: bhd fnl 2f* **12/1**

3m 24.45s (-6.05) **Going Correction** -0.20s/f (Firm)
WFA 3 from 4yo+ 10lb **9** Ran SP% **116.2**
Speed ratings (Par 107): **107,105,102,102,101 101,100,98,91**
CSF £24.96 CT £174.56 TOTE £4.50: £1.40, £2.00, £3.00; EX 25.10 Trifecta £209.30.
Owner Ben & Sir Martyn Arbib **Bred** Arbib Bloodstock Partnership **Trained** East Ilsley, Berks

FOCUS
Race distance increased by 12yds. A decent enough staying race. It's been rated at face value for now, with a clear pb from the winner, and the third and fourth rated close to the balance of this year's form.

7671 DISCOVERNEWMARKET.CO.UK H'CAP 1m
5:15 (5:19) (Class 4) (0-80,80) 3-Y-O+ **£5,175** (£1,540; £769; £384) **Stalls** Low

Form RPR
15 **1** **Timeless Art (IRE)**[30] 6877 3-8-11 78 ..... CliffordLee(5) 1 91+
(K R Burke) *hld up in tch in midfield: rdn to ld 2f out: clr 1f out: styd on wl: rdn out* **8/1**[2]

1112 **2** *2* **Titan Goddess**[15] 7298 4-8-11 70 ..... ShaneKelly 10 78
(Mike Murphy) *s.i.s: hld up in tch in rr: hdwy 1/2-way: rdn to chse ldrs 2f out: chsd wnr 1f out: kpt on but no imp* **25/1**

4226 **3** *1 1/2* **Mister Music**[19] 7189 7-9-7 80 ..... TomMarquand 12 85+
(Tony Carroll) *stdd after s: hld up in tch in rr: effrt 2f out: hdwy over 1f out: styd on u.p ins fnl f: wnt 3rd towards fin* **14/1**

3451 **4** *3/4* **Invermere**[18] 7220 3-8-10 79 ..... NatalieHambling(7) 4 81
(Richard Fahey) *chsd ldrs: effrt and swtchd rt 2f out: styd on same pce ins fnl f* **9/1**[3]

0660 **5** *hd* **Eurystheus (IRE)**[20] 7159 7-9-1 77 ..... (tp) AlistairRawlinson(3) 2 80
(Michael Appleby) *s.i.s: sn rcvrd and in tch in midfield: rdn 3f out: kpt on ins fnl f: nvr enough pce to threaten ldrs* **20/1**

1524 **6** *nk* **Stosur (IRE)**[29] 6899 5-8-12 78 ..... (b) DavidEgan(7) 3 80
(Gay Kelleway) *w ldrs: rdn and ev ch 3f out: rdn and edgd rt 2f out: unable qck over 1f out: kpt on same pce ins fnl f* **33/1**

0015 **7** *1 1/4* **Mr Cool Cash**[17] 7253 4-8-8 67 ..... JFEgan 6 66
(Richard Guest) *hld up in tch in midfield: effrt and short of room ent fnl 2f: tried to rally over 1f out: kpt on same pce ins fnl f* **33/1**

0000 **8** *nse* **Directorship**[25] 7017 10-9-6 79 ..... FergusSweeney 9 78
(Patrick Chamings) *hld up in tch towards rr: effrt over 1f out: kpt on ins fnl f: nvr trbld ldrs* **33/1**

2622 **9** *nk* **Wings Of Esteem (IRE)**[31] 6856 3-8-6 68 ..... JimmyQuinn 7 65
(Martin Smith) *taken down early: hld up in tch towards rr: effrt whn nt clrest of runs and swtchd rt 2f out: no imp and kpt on same pce fr over 1f out* **11/1**

4221 **10** *1 1/2* **Pendo**[18] 7227 5-9-1 74 ..... KierenFox 18 69
(John Best) *w ldr tl led 1/2-way: rdn and hdd 2f out: no ex u.p: wknd ins fnl f* **10/1**

3455 **11** *4 1/2* **Flyboy (IRE)**[7] 7505 3-9-4 80 ..... (v1) GrahamLee 17 64+
(David O'Meara) *hld up in tch in midfield: clsd to chse ldrs 3f out: rdn and unable qck wl over 1f out: wknd ins fnl f: burst blood vessel* **12/1**

3566 **12** *8* **Prendergast Hill (IRE)**[39] 6628 4-9-7 80 ..... (p) JimCrowley 15 46
(Ed de Giles) *chsd ldrs: effrt ent fnl 2f out: outpcd and btn over 1f out: wknd fnl f* **9/1**[3]

0210 **13** *1 3/4* **Big Chill (IRE)**[19] 7189 4-8-11 75 ..... MitchGodwin(5) 11 37
(Patrick Chamings) *led tl 1/2-way: edgd rt 2f out: lost pl over 1f out: wknd fnl f* **25/1**

520 **14** *1 3/4* **Thecornishbarron (IRE)**[9] 7457 4-9-2 75 ..... AdamKirby 14 33
(John Ryan) *hld up in tch in midfield: rdn and struggling 3f out: bhd 2f out* **20/1**

3255 **15** *nk* **Ghinia (IRE)**[25] 7017 5-9-2 78 ..... RobHornby(3) 13 36
(Pam Sly) *in tch in midfield: rdn 3f out: lost pl 2f out: wknd over 1f out* **10/1**

5205 **16** *2 1/4* **Cadeaux Boxer**[97] 4639 3-9-2 78 ..... PatCosgrave 19 29
(Martin Smith) *stdd s: t.k.h: hld up in tch in rr: rdn ent fnl 2f: sn btn and bhd over 1f out* **50/1**

655- **17** *nse* **Gossiping**[494] 3461 4-9-4 77 ..... GeorgeBaker 8 29
(Gary Moore) *w ldrs: losing pl whn hmpd 2f out: eased over 1f out* **20/1**

3221 **18** *8* **Tomahawk Kid**[30] 6877 3-9-3 79 ..... JamesDoyle 16 12+
(Ian Williams) *in tch in midfield: clsd to press ldrs 3f out: rdn and ev ch 2f out tl lost action over 1f out: heavily eased after* **4/1**[1]

1m 37.76s (-0.84) **Going Correction** -0.05s/f (Good)
WFA 3 from 4yo+ 3lb **18** Ran SP% **124.7**
Speed ratings (Par 105): **102,100,98,97,97 97,96,95,95,94 89,81,79,78,77 75,75,67**
CSF £202.99 CT £2843.64 TOTE £10.50: £3.00, £4.40, £4.40, £2.00; EX 266.60 TRIFECTA Not won..
Owner Owners For Owners: Timeless Art **Bred** Sarl Elevage Du Haras De Bourgeauville **Trained** Middleham Moor, N Yorks

FOCUS
An open handicap on paper but there was a decisive winner. A clear pb from the winner, with the third a bit below this year's form.
T/Plt: £108.40 to a £1 stake. Pool: £76,404.34 - 514.13 winning tickets T/Qpdt: £39.10 to a £1 stake. Pool: £6,392.24 - 120.70 winning tickets **Steve Payne**

7672 - 7675a (Foreign Racing) - See Raceform Interactive

7629 DUNDALK (A.W) (L-H)
Friday, October 28

OFFICIAL GOING: Polytrack: standard

7676a IRISH STALLION FARMS EUROPEAN BREEDERS FUND COOLEY FILLIES STKS (LISTED) 1m (P)
7:30 (7:31) 3-Y-O+
£23,860 (£7,683; £3,639; £1,617; £808; £404)

RPR
1 **Kadra (IRE)**[21] 7131 3-9-0 97 ..... PatSmullen 6 102+
(M Halford, Ire) *mid-div early tl impr to chse ldrs after 2f: 5th 1/2-way: prog to chal in 2nd under 2f out and led over 1f out: kpt on wl u.p ins fnl f* **4/1**[1]

2 *1* **Desert Haze**[35] 6746 3-9-0 98 ..... ColmO'Donoghue 7 100
(Ralph Beckett) *hld up: pushed along in rr into st and hdwy u.p over 1f out: r.o wl into 2nd clsng stages: nt trble wnr* **7/1**

3 *1 1/2* **How High The Moon (IRE)**[12] 7392 3-9-0 92 ..... (v) SeamieHeffernan 13 97
(A P O'Brien, Ire) *mid-div: 7th 1/2-way: hdwy over 1f out to chse ldrs wl ins fnl f: kpt on same pce in 3rd clsng stages: nt trble wnr* **16/1**

4 *3/4* **Red Box**[69] 5645 3-9-3 101 ..... DeclanMcDonogh 10 98
(Sir Mark Prescott Bt) *chsd ldrs: 4th 1/2-way: rdn to chal over 1f out: sn no imp on wnr u.p in 2nd and one pce wl ins fnl f where dropped to 4th clsng stages* **9/2**[2]

5 *nk* **Lina De Vega (IRE)**[64] 5814 3-9-0 92 ..... RonanWhelan 11 94
(P J Prendergast, Ire) *towards rr early: 8th 1/2-way: prog under 2f out to chse ldrs 1f out: kpt on same pce in 5th wl ins fnl f: nvr on terms* **25/1**

6 nk **Mukaabra**[27] 6964 3-9-0 88..............................(p) MartinHarley 4 94
(James Tate) *in tch: 9th 1/2-way: pushed along over 2f out and sme hdwy u.p far side over 1f out to chse ldrs: no imp on wnr in 3rd briefly ins fnl f: wknd into 6th clsng stages* **13/2**[3]

7 1 1/2 **Midnight Crossing (IRE)**[79] 5313 3-9-0 91..................(b) ColinKeane 1 90
(Edward Lynam, Ire) *settled in rr of mid-div: 11th 3f out: sme hdwy u.p over 1f out where sn short of room and checked sltly between horses: swtchd rt and kpt on clsng stages: nvr nrr* **25/1**

8 hd **Hibiscus (IRE)**[5] 7558 3-9-0 94.............................. DonnachaO'Brien 9 90
(A P O'Brien, Ire) *hld up towards rr: 13th into st: hdwy under 2f out where n.m.r bhd horses: rdn over 1f out and kpt on ins fnl f: nvr nrr* **16/1**

9 1 **Colour Blue (IRE)**[27] 6939 5-9-3 97.............................. BillyLee 3 88
(W McCreery, Ire) *prom tl sn settled bhd ldrs: 6th 1/2-way: hdwy far side 2f out where n.m.r on inner: no imp on ldrs u.p ent fnl f and sn wknd* **7/1**

10 3/4 **Indrahar (IRE)**[21] 7131 3-9-0 90.............................. ShaneFoley 14 86
(M Halford, Ire) *settled in rr: 12th 3f out: rdn nr side 2f out and no imp over 1f out: kpt on one pce ins fnl f* **10/1**

11 shd **Erysimum (IRE)**[26] 6983 3-9-3 93.............................. LeighRoche 8 88
(W McCreery, Ire) *sn led: rdn w narrow advantage under 2f out and hdd over 1f out: wknd* **25/1**

12 1/2 **Cirin Toinne (IRE)**[40] 6604 3-9-0 97.............................. KevinManning 5 84
(J S Bolger, Ire) *chsd ldrs: clsr in 2nd fr 1/2-way: rdn and no ex 2f out: sn wknd* **16/1**

13 2 **Flirt (IRE)**[12] 7392 3-9-0 88..............................(p) WayneLordan 12 80
(David Wachman, Ire) *hld up: pushed along in 10th 3f out and no imp u.p over 2f out: sn wknd* **50/1**

14 1 1/2 **Suvenna (IRE)**[21] 7131 3-9-0 88.............................. ConorHoban 2 76
(M Halford, Ire) *sn trckd ldr: 3rd fr 1/2-way: rdn 2f out where edgd sltly lft and sn no ex: wknd 1 1/2f out* **12/1**

1m 36.14s (96.14)
WFA 3 from 5yo 3lb **14** Ran SP% **124.4**
CSF £31.64 TOTE £5.20: £2.20, £3.00, £4.60; DF 45.00 Trifecta £170.60.
Owner H H Aga Khan **Bred** His Highness The Aga Khan's Studs S C **Trained** Doneany, Co Kildare
■ Stewards' Enquiry : Martin Harley caution: used whip above shoulder height

FOCUS
On ratings at least this was not a strong contest, and with the winner likely to go to stud we may not know how good she could be as all of the indicators is that she is nothing but progressive. It's been rated around the balance of the first three, sixth and seventh.

7677 - 7679a (Foreign Racing) - See Raceform Interactive

[6911] COMPIEGNE (L-H)
Friday, October 28

OFFICIAL GOING: Turf: heavy

7680a PRIX DE LA MICHELETTE (CLAIMER) (3YO) (TURF) 1m
3:15 (3:15) 3-Y-O **£9,926** (£3,970; £2,977; £1,985; £992)

RPR

1 **Bronze Swan (IRE)**[41] 3-9-1 0..............................(p) MickaelBarzalona 6 80
(H-A Pantall, France) **127/10**

2 hd **Shiver In The River (FR)**[20] 3-8-4 0 ow1..................(b) PierreBazire(5) 2 74
(G Botti, France) **13/1**

3 nse **Virginie (FR)**[12] 3-8-3 0.............................. ClementLecoeuvre(5) 1 73
(T Clout, France) **78/10**

4 3 **Blonville (FR)**[23] 3-9-3 0.............................. SebastienMaillot 4 75
(Robert Collet, France) **43/10**[2]

5 1 1/2 **Time Shanakill (IRE)**[49] 6310 3-9-1 0.............. ChristopheSoumillon 10 70
(G Botti, France) **63/10**[3]

6 1/2 **Donuts Reyor (FR)**[17] 3-9-1 0.............................. MaximeGuyon 8 68
(Y Barberot, France) **83/10**

7 2 **Zalvados (FR)**[55] 3-9-1 0.............................. LukasDelozier 11 64
(H-A Pantall, France) **10/1**

8 3 **Predetermined (IRE)**[10] 3-9-2 0.............................. AlexisBadel 5 58
(H-F Devin, France) **3/1**[1]

9 3 **Vaporetto Capri (IRE)**[41] 3-8-11 0.................... EmmanuelEtienne(4) 9 50
(F Doumen, France) **29/1**

10 9 **Fils Prodigue (FR)**[10] 3-9-1 0.............................. RonanThomas 3 29
(F-H Graffard, France) **44/5**

11 5 **Be Bop Tango (FR)**[32] 6836 3-8-11 0..........................(p) TonyPiccone 7 14
(K R Burke) *hld up and a in rr: rdn in last 2f out: sn wl btn: eased: t.o* **65/1**

PARI-MUTUEL (all including 1 euro stake): WIN 13.70; PLACE 4.20, 4.50, 3.00; DF 84.50; SF 191.10
Owner Berend Van Dalfsen **Bred** Berend Van Dalfsen **Trained** France

7681 - 7686a (Foreign Racing) - See Raceform Interactive

[7639] CHELMSFORD (A.W) (L-H)
Saturday, October 29

OFFICIAL GOING: Polytrack: standard
Wind: virtually nil Weather: Fine

7687 TOTEPLACEPOT SIX PLACES IN SIX RACES APPRENTICE H'CAP 7f (P)
5:40 (5:40) (Class 4) (0-78,78) 3-Y-O+ **£5,175** (£1,540; £769; £384) **Stalls** Low

Form RPR

6210 1 **Sunset Dream (IRE)**[7] 7550 3-9-4 78.............................. HollieDoyle(3) 2 87
(Richard Hannon) *led: hdd over 5f out: trckd ldr: led again over 1f out: sn rdn: kpt on wl to draw clr fnl f* **11/4**[2]

0310 2 2 1/2 **Ravenhoe (IRE)**[25] 7051 3-9-4 75.............................. JoeDoyle 6 78+
(Mark Johnston) *hld up in rr: rdn over 2f out: hdwy on outside over 1f out: kpt on wl: edgd lft ins fnl f: wnt 2nd 75yds out* **10/1**

0050 3 1 **Captain Lars (SAF)**[10] 7461 7-9-3 72..............................(p) NoelGarbutt 5 73
(Derek Shaw) *trckd ldr: rdn to chal over 1f out: one pce and sn no ch w wnr fnl f: lost 2nd 75yds out* **10/1**

2354 4 3/4 **Inaam (IRE)**[22] 7111 3-8-11 71.............................. AdamMcNamara(3) 8 69
(Richard Fahey) *hld up: rdn and hdwy on outer over 2f out: one pce fnl f* **6/1**[3]

0106 5 1/2 **Be Royale**[17] 7281 6-8-9 71..............................(t) BenSanderson(7) 4 69
(Michael Appleby) *hld up in midfield: rdn and hdwy over 1f out: one pce* **16/1**

2060 6 4 1/2 **Great Fun**[47] 6416 5-9-2 74.............................. MitchGodwin(3) 3 59
(Michael Blake) *hld up: rdn 2f out: nvr threatened* **8/1**

2213 7 1 **Excellent Sounds**[73] 5551 3-9-3 77.............................. CharlieBennett(3) 1 59
(Hughie Morrison) *in tch: rdn 2f out: sn wknd* **9/4**[1]

334 8 3 1/2 **Rivers Of Asia**[226] 968 3-9-0 76.............................. PaddyBradley(5) 7 48
(Philip McBride) *in tch towards outer: rdn over 2f out: wknd over 1f out* **10/1**

0000 9 1 1/4 **Black Dave (IRE)**[189] 1625 6-9-1 77.............................. AledBeech(7) 9 47
(David Evans) *prom: led over 5f out: rdn whn hdd wl over 1f out: wknd* **40/1**

1m 25.3s (-1.90) **Going Correction** -0.225s/f (Stan)
WFA 3 from 5yo+ 2lb **9** Ran SP% **118.4**
Speed ratings (Par 105): **101,98,97,96,95 90,89,85,83**
CSF £31.42 CT £246.34 TOTE £4.80: £1.60, £3.00, £6.30; EX 35.30 Trifecta £284.70.
Owner Ecurie Des Charmes **Bred** Gigginstown House Stud **Trained** East Everleigh, Wilts

FOCUS
A fair handicap for apprentice riders.

7688 TOTEPOOL CHIP AND PIN BETTING NURSERY H'CAP 7f (P)
6:10 (6:11) (Class 5) (0-75,72) 2-Y-O **£4,528** (£1,347; £673; £336) **Stalls** Low

Form RPR

063 1 **Sans Souci Bay**[110] 4203 2-9-1 71.............................. MeganNicholls(5) 5 75+
(Richard Hannon) *hld up in midfield: rdn and hdwy over 1f out: led ins fnl f: kpt on* **12/1**

600 2 1/2 **Shadow Warrior**[59] 6034 2-9-1 66.............................. TomQueally 7 70+
(Paul D'Arcy) *hld up: pushed along whn short of room on a couple of occasions over 1f out: swtchd lft ent fnl f: r.o wl: wnt 2nd fnl 50yds: gaining at fin* **20/1**

330 3 1 1/2 **Buccaneers Cove (IRE)**[21] 7157 2-9-0 65.................... TonyHamilton 3 64
(Richard Fahey) *midfield: rdn and hdwy over 1f out: ev ch ins fnl f: one pce fnl 110yds* **7/1**[3]

2445 4 nk **Miss Sheridan (IRE)**[7] 7541 2-8-13 67.................... NathanEvans(3) 9 65
(Michael Easterby) *prom: rdn 2f out: one pce ins fnl f* **7/1**[3]

3210 5 1/2 **Miss Icon**[40] 6630 2-9-7 72.............................. JimmyQuinn 4 68
(Patrick Chamings) *trckd ldrs: rdn over 1f out: ev ch ins fnl f: no ex fnl 110yds* **16/1**

4222 6 1 3/4 **Texas Katie**[10] 7467 2-9-5 70..............................(p) PatCosgrave 2 62
(Archie Watson) *led: rdn and edgd rt over 1f out: hdd ins fnl f: wknd* **3/1**[2]

1000 7 1 1/4 **Percy Toplis**[43] 6536 2-9-2 67.............................. KevinStott 1 55
(Kevin Ryan) *trckd ldrs: rdn 2f out: wknd ins fnl f* **10/1**

5011 8 3/4 **Iftitah (IRE)**[22] 7109 2-9-2 67..............................(t) StevieDonohoe 8 53
(George Peckham) *dwlt: hld up in rr: rdn 2f out: nvr threatened* **11/4**[1]

2400 9 1 **Mia Cara**[11] 7440 2-8-12 63..............................(v[1]) JFEgan 11 47
(David Evans) *prom towards outer: rdn over 2f out: wknd over 1f out* **25/1**

4035 10 1 1/2 **Joyful Dream (IRE)**[17] 7294 2-8-12 63.............................. LiamKeniry 10 43
(J S Moore) *midfield: rdn 2f out: wknd over 1f out* **33/1**

655 11 3 1/2 **Pennington**[15] 7318 2-9-7 72.............................. JoeFanning 6 42
(Mark Johnston) *hld up: rdn 2f out: sn btn* **10/1**

0430 12 5 **Infatuated**[58] 6053 2-9-2 67.............................. DavidAllan 12 24
(Tim Easterby) *dwlt: hld up towards outer: rdn over 2f out: hung rt off bnd wl over 1f out: wknd* **33/1**

1m 26.44s (-0.76) **Going Correction** -0.225s/f (Stan) **12** Ran SP% **122.9**
Speed ratings (Par 95): **95,94,92,92,91 89,88,87,86,84 80,74**
CSF £237.95 CT £1815.98 TOTE £17.00: £4.50, £8.10, £3.00; EX 413.40 Trifecta £4373.50.
Owner J R Shannon **Bred** J R Shannon **Trained** East Everleigh, Wilts

FOCUS
Five of these were making their handicap debuts and they included the first three home.

7689 TOTEQUADPOT FOUR PLACES IN FOUR RACES STALLIONS EBF MAIDEN FILLIES' STKS (PLUS 10 RACE) 6f (P)
6:40 (6:41) (Class 5) 2-Y-O **£4,528** (£1,347; £673; £336) **Stalls** Centre

Form RPR

1 **First Priority** 2-9-0 0.............................. FrederikTylicki 5 79+
(Saeed bin Suroor) *dwlt: midfield on inner: pushed along over 1f out: hdwy appr fnl f: rdn ins fnl f: led 110yds out: edgd rt: kpt on* **5/2**[2]

35 2 1 **Millie's Kiss**[68] 5722 2-8-11 0.............................. LouisSteward(3) 1 76
(Philip McBride) *dwlt: hld up: sltly hmpd wl over 1f out: sn hdwy: rdn and kpt on fnl f* **6/1**[3]

2 3 1/2 **Dealer's Choice (IRE)**[13] 7380 2-9-0 0.............................. JackMitchell 8 75
(Roger Varian) *racd keenly: trckd ldrs: pushed along to ld over 1f out: rdn ins fnl f: hdd 110yds out: no ex* **4/5**[1]

2303 4 1 1/2 **Spinnaker Bay (IRE)**[19] 7217 2-9-0 72.............................. JoeFanning 3 70
(William Jarvis) *trckd ldrs: rdn over 1f out: no ex ins fnl f* **7/1**

5 4 **Flying Foxy** 2-9-0 0.............................. WilliamCarson 7 58
(Michael Wigham) *hld up: pushed along over 2f out: kpt on ins fnl f: nvr threatened* **50/1**

0 6 hd **Nuzha**[15] 7314 2-9-0 0.............................. JFEgan 6 57
(David Evans) *midfield: rdn 2f out: no imp* **100/1**

7 3 1/2 **Wotadoll** 2-9-0 0.............................. RobertWinston 9 50+
(Dean Ivory) *s.i.s: hld up: nvr threatened* **40/1**

66 8 1 1/2 **Aqdameya (IRE)**[11] 7424 2-9-0 0.............................. DaneO'Neill 2 42
(Mark Johnston) *led narrowly: rdn whn hdd over 1f out: wknd* **22/1**

4600 9 8 **The Lady Hysteria (IRE)**[47] 6419 2-9-0 37.................... DannyBrock 4 18
(Phil McEntee) *pressed ldr: rdn over 2f out: sn wknd* **100/1**

1m 12.91s (-0.79) **Going Correction** -0.225s/f (Stan) **9** Ran SP% **121.6**
Speed ratings (Par 92): **96,94,94,92,86 86,81,79,69**
CSF £18.23 TOTE £4.50: £1.20, £1.60, £1.10; EX 20.20 Trifecta £39.60.
Owner Godolphin **Bred** Darley **Trained** Newmarket, Suffolk

FOCUS
A fair maiden.

7690 TOTEPOOLLIVEINFO.COM FOR RACING RESULTS NURSERY H'CAP 6f (P)
7:10 (7:11) (Class 6) (0-65,65) 2-Y-O **£2,911** (£866; £432; £216) **Stalls** Centre

Form RPR

2461 1 **Acertwo**[30] 6896 2-9-7 65.............................. JFEgan 4 71
(Joseph Tuite) *mde all: pressed fr an early stage: rdn 2f out: kpt on* **7/2**[2]

2220 2 1/2 **Wentwell Yesterday (IRE)**[28] 6963 2-9-3 61.............. WilliamCarson 11 66
(Jamie Osborne) *midfield: rdn and hdwy over 1f out: kpt on wl fnl f* **8/1**

0001 3 1 1/2 **Dusty Bin**[5] 7579 2-9-0 58 6ex.............................. KevinStott 12 58+
(Kevin Ryan) *midfield: rdn along and outpcd 3f out: rallied and hdwy over 1f out: kpt on* **5/2**[1]

5532 4 1 3/4 **Heavenly Cry**[7] 7528 2-8-3 50..............................[1] JosephineGordon(3) 3 45
(Phil McEntee) *pressed ldr: rdn over 2f out: wknd fnl 110yds* **5/1**[3]

3130 5 1 1/4 **Harlequin Rose (IRE)**[11] 7423 2-8-5 52..................(v) NathanEvans(3) 6 43
(Mick Channon) *hld up: rdn 3f out: kpt on ins fnl f: nvr threatened ldrs* **11/1**

6454 6 1/2 **Tullinahoo (IRE)**[47] 6420 2-9-5 63.............................. OisinMurphy 5 53
(Denis Coakley) *slowly away: sn pushed along in rr: kpt on ins fnl f: nvr threatened* **8/1**

The Form Book, Raceform Ltd, Newbury, RG14 5SJ

066 **7** 3/4 **Like Minds**[17] 7269 2-8-2 **49** AaronJones(3) 9 36
(David Brown) *dwlt: hld up: rdn over 2f out: nvr threatened* **25/1**
340 **8** nk **Gracious Tom (IRE)**[63] 5890 2-9-7 **65** AdamKirby 7 51
(David Evans) *midfield: rdn 3f out: no imp* **6/1**
0646 **9** 6 **Radar Love (IRE)**[11] 7455 2-9-5 **63** LiamKeniry 8 31
(J S Moore) *chsd ldrs: rdn over 2f out: wknd appr fnl f* **33/1**
600 **10** 3 3/4 **Mr Enthusiastic**[53] 6214 2-8-12 **56** TonyHamilton 1 13
(Noel Wilson) *chsd ldrs: rdn over 2f out: wknd over 1f out* **66/1**
1m 12.67s (-1.03) **Going Correction** -0.225s/f (Stan) **10** Ran SP% **120.6**
Speed ratings (Par 93): **97,96,94,92,90 89,88,88,80,75**
CSF £32.43 CT £85.39 TOTE £4.20: £1.60, £2.60, £1.30; EX 30.10 Trifecta £77.90.
Owner B R Tregurtha **Bred** Mickley Stud & J Kent **Trained** Lambourn, Berks
FOCUS
A modest nursery.

7691 TOTEPOOL LIVE INFO DOWNLOAD THE APP H'CAP 1m (P)
7:40 (7:43) (Class 5) (0-75,75) 3-Y-O+ **£5,175** (£1,540; £769; £384) **Stalls** Low

Form RPR
0601 **1** **Qaffaal (USA)**[30] 6907 5-9-5 **73** GrahamGibbons 6 84+
(Michael Easterby) *dwlt: hld up: angled towards outer 2f out: rdn and gd hdwy wl over 1f out: led ins fnl f: edgd lft: kpt on* **7/4**[1]
1220 **2** 1 1/4 **Dark Wonder (IRE)**[11] 7436 4-9-4 **72** (p) RobertWinston 2 79
(Ivan Furtado) *midfield: rdn and hdwy over 1f out: kpt on* **6/1**[2]
-000 **3** 1 1/2 **Graceful James (IRE)**[50] 6300 3-9-1 **72** KieranO'Neill 3 75
(Jimmy Fox) *midfield: rdn and hdwy over 1f out: kpt on* **9/1**
6501 **4** 1/2 **Baby Ballerina**[9] 7485 3-9-1 **72** BenCurtis 11 73
(Brian Ellison) *led: rdn over 2f out: hdd ins fnl f: no ex* **7/1**[3]
010 **5** 1 1/2 **Tan Arabiq**[92] 4844 3-8-6 **66** TimClark(3) 13 64
(Michael Appleby) *dwlt: sn pressed ldr: rdn over 2f out: hung lft over 1f out: wknd fnl 110yds* **33/1**
2510 **6** nse **Pick A Little**[16] 7301 8-8-12 **71** MitchGodwin(5) 10 70
(Michael Blake) *trckd ldrs: rdn over 2f out: wknd ins fnl f* **33/1**
4306 **7** 1/2 **Skidby Mill (IRE)**[135] 3314 6-9-0 **68** PatCosgrave 14 66
(Laura Mongan) *midfield: rdn over 2f out: one pce and nvr threatened* **33/1**
4260 **8** nse **Billy Bond**[24] 7076 4-9-2 **73** (v) AdamMcNamara(3) 1 71
(Richard Fahey) *dwlt: hld up: rdn over 2f out: kpt on fnl f: nvr threatened* **8/1**
5300 **9** 2 1/2 **Fantasy Gladiator**[19] 7229 10-9-7 **75** (p) AndrewMullen 9 67
(Michael Appleby) *hld up: pushed along over 2f out: sme hdwy over 1f out: nvr threatened* **20/1**
6404 **10** 1 3/4 **Palpitation (IRE)**[9] 7486 3-8-5 **65** AaronJones(3) 12 63+
(David Brown) *trckd ldrs: rdn over 2f out: swtchd rt over 1f out: hmpd ins fnl f: eased* **12/1**
2452 **11** 13 **Heartstone (IRE)**[15] 7326 3-8-13 **70** RichardKingscote 7 27
(Charles Hills) *hld up: rdn 3f out: sn wknd* **6/1**[2]
4655 **12** 9 **Bushel (USA)**[107] 4303 6-9-1 **72** EoinWalsh(3) 4 9
(Tony Newcombe) *a rr* **33/1**
00/0 **13** 3 1/2 **Two No Bids (IRE)**[69] 5677 6-8-12 **69** JosephineGordon(3) 8
(Phil McEntee) *trckd ldrs: rdn over 3f out: wknd 2f out: eased* **50/1**
1m 38.08s (-1.82) **Going Correction** -0.225s/f (Stan)
WFA 3 from 4yo+ 3lb **13** Ran SP% **124.7**
Speed ratings (Par 103): **100,98,97,96,95 95,94,94,92,90 77,68,64**
CSF £11.77 CT £80.98 TOTE £2.70: £1.60, £1.90, £3.60; EX 13.90 Trifecta £157.00.
Owner Michael Burrows, Calam & Holdsworth **Bred** Shadwell Farm LLC **Trained** Sheriff Hutton, N Yorks
■ Stewards' Enquiry : Adam McNamara caution: careless riding
FOCUS
They went fairly steady early but the pace picked up a fair way out and the first three came from behind.

7692 BARKING BRICKWORK H'CAP 1m 5f 66y(P)
8:10 (8:11) (Class 6) (0-65,63) 3-Y-O **£3,234** (£962; £481; £240) **Stalls** Low

Form RPR
0-65 **1** **Regal Gait (IRE)**[124] 3727 3-9-2 **58** MartinHarley 5 65+
(Harry Whittington) *hld up in tch: rdn and hdwy over 1f out: styd on: led towards fin* **6/1**[3]
0211 **2** 1/2 **Iballisticvin**[25] 7039 3-9-4 **63** HectorCrouch(3) 1 69
(Gary Moore) *in tch: pushed along to chse ldr 2f out: rdn to ld narrowly ent fnl f: edgd lft fnl 75yds: hdd towards fin* **6/5**[1]
520 **3** 1 **Stonecoldsoba**[56] 6143 3-9-2 **58** AdamKirby 7 63
(David Evans) *trckd ldr: led wl over 2f out: sn rdn: hdd ent fnl f: edgd lft ins fnl f: one pce and hld in 3rd whn bit short of room nr fin* **8/1**
6154 **4** 2 **Dltripleseven (IRE)**[17] 7270 3-9-3 **59** ShaneKelly 2 61
(Richard Hughes) *slowly away: hld up in rr: rdn over 1f out: kpt on ins fnl f* **3/1**[2]
6222 **5** 1 3/4 **Rubis**[39] 6647 3-8-13 **58** AdamMcNamara(3) 8 57
(Richard Fahey) *hld up in tch towards outer: rdn 2f out: one pce and nvr threatened* **7/1**
5440 **6** 3 3/4 **Permera**[16] 7309 3-8-4 **49** (p) NoelGarbutt(3) 6 43
(Mark H Tompkins) *in tch: rdn 2f out: wknd fnl f* **25/1**
650 **7** 24 **Hodgkins Trust (IRE)**[11] 7427 3-7-12 **45** HollieDoyle(5) 4 6
(Julia Feilden) *led: rdn whn hdd wl over 2f out: sn wknd: eased* **50/1**
2m 51.67s (-1.93) **Going Correction** -0.225s/f (Stan) **7** Ran SP% **114.2**
Speed ratings (Par 99): **96,95,95,93,92 90,75**
CSF £13.63 CT £57.79 TOTE £5.90: £3.50, £1.70; EX 17.40 Trifecta £166.40.
Owner Paul G Jacobs **Bred** Peter Molony **Trained** Sparsholt, Oxfordshire
FOCUS
An ordinary handicap.

7693 COLLECT ANY TOTEPOOL WINNINGS AT BETFRED SHOPS H'CAP (DIV I) 6f (P)
8:40 (8:41) (Class 6) (0-60,60) 3-Y-O+ **£3,234** (£962; £481; £240) **Stalls** Centre

Form RPR
0414 **1** **Mambo Spirit (IRE)**[49] 6312 12-9-4 **60** EoinWalsh(3) 7 68
(Tony Newcombe) *hld up: rdn and hdwy over 1f out: led narrowly ent fnl f: hld on wl* **12/1**
5000 **2** nk **Camdora (IRE)**[8] 7513 4-9-4 **57** (t) TimmyMurphy 1 64
(Jamie Osborne) *dwlt: hld up: pushed along and hdwy wl over 1f out: rdn to chal strly ent fnl f: kpt on but a jst hld* **5/4**[1]
0333 **3** 2 **Burauq**[9] 7488 4-8-12 **51** (b) RichardKingscote 4 52
(Milton Bradley) *chsd ldrs: rdn over 2f out: ev ch over 1f out: one pce ins fnl f* **9/2**[2]
-002 **4** shd **Lady Bacchus**[9] 7488 3-8-6 **46** (b) ConnorBeasley 8 47
(Richard Guest) *chsd ldrs towards outer: rdn 2f out: forced to wd outside wl over 1f out: kpt on fnl f* **7/1**

0526 **5** 3/4 **Edith Weston**[31] 6865 3-8-8 **48** (p) JimmyQuinn 6 47
(Robert Cowell) *s.i.s: hld up: rdn 2f out: kpt on fnl f* **25/1**
0046 **6** 2 1/4 **Shine Likeadiamond**[7] 7534 3-9-2 **56** TonyHamilton 2 48
(Mick Channon) *chsd ldrs: rdn over 2f out: wknd fnl f* **8/1**
00-0 **7** nse **Named Asset**[117] 3953 4-8-12 **56** (p) GeorgeWood(5) 3 48
(Martin Bosley) *led narrowly: rdn over 2f out: hdd ent fnl f: wknd* **25/1**
0000 **8** 7 **Cloak And Degas (IRE)**[24] 7069 4-9-3 **59** (v) JosephineGordon(3) 9 30
(Tim McCarthy) *prom on outer: rdn over 2f out: wknd over 1f out* **14/1**
4010 **9** 11 **Silver Springs (IRE)**[8] 7513 3-9-5 **59** AdamKirby 5
(David Evans) *pressed ldr: rdn over 2f out: wknd over 1f out* **5/1**[3]
1m 12.34s (-1.36) **Going Correction** -0.225s/f (Stan)
WFA 3 from 4yo+ 1lb **9** Ran SP% **125.0**
Speed ratings (Par 101): **100,99,96,96,95 92,92,83,68**
CSF £29.80 CT £86.17 TOTE £12.70: £2.50, £1.20, £2.10; EX 34.30 Trifecta £154.10.
Owner Nigel Hardy **Bred** R Warren **Trained** Yarnscombe, Devon
FOCUS
This was run at a good gallop and the first two came from off the pace.

7694 COLLECT ANY TOTEPOOL WINNINGS AT BETFRED SHOPS H'CAP (DIV II) 6f (P)
9:10 (9:15) (Class 6) (0-60,60) 3-Y-O+ **£3,234** (£962; £481; £240) **Stalls** Centre

Form RPR
0451 **1** **Commanche**[30] 6902 7-8-12 **51** (b) MartinHarley 5 57
(Chris Dwyer) *mde all: rdn 2f out: strly pressed over 1f out: hld on wl* **6/4**[1]
0002 **2** 3/4 **Multi Quest**[11] 7445 4-8-11 **50** (b) RobertHavlin 4 54
(John E Long) *racd keenly: trckd ldrs: rdn 2f out: kpt on* **8/1**[3]
1600 **3** 1 1/2 **Le Manege Enchante (IRE)**[51] 6249 3-9-2 **59** (p) NoelGarbutt(3) 2 58
(Derek Shaw) *racd keenly in midfield: rdn 2f out: kpt on fnl f* **8/1**[3]
4402 **4** shd **Divine Call**[17] 7267 9-9-7 **60** (b) JoeFanning 3 59
(Milton Bradley) *hld up in rr: pushed along 2f out: rdn and kpt on ins fnl f: nrst fin* **5/1**[2]
0462 **5** 3/4 **Ryan Style (IRE)**[9] 7489 10-8-1 **47** (b) JordanUys(7) 1 44
(Lisa Williamson) *dwlt: hld up: rdn 2f out: kpt on fnl f* **8/1**[3]
6000 **6** 1/2 **Wilsons Ruby (IRE)**[15] 7324 3-9-4 **58** SamJames 6 53
(Marjorie Fife) *trckd ldrs: rdn over 2f out: wknd ins fnl f* **10/1**
5030 **7** 1 1/4 **Great Expectations**[11] 7442 8-9-4 **57** (vt) AdamKirby 8 48
(J R Jenkins) *stdd s: hld up: rdn 2f out: nvr threatened* **8/1**[3]
3-5 **8** 3/4 **Zeb's Fantasy (IRE)**[22] 7128 3-9-2 **56** [1] LemosdeSouza 9 45
(Amy Murphy) *prom: rdn over 2f out: wknd ins fnl f* **16/1**
5450 **9** 3 1/2 **Tally's Song**[14] 7362 3-8-3 **46** oh1 (p) JosephineGordon(3) 7 25
(Grace Harris) *hld up: rdn and sme hdwy on outer over 2f out: wknd over 1f out* **40/1**
1m 12.45s (-1.25) **Going Correction** -0.225s/f (Stan)
WFA 3 from 4yo+ 1lb **9** Ran SP% **118.5**
Speed ratings (Par 101): **99,98,96,95,94 94,92,91,86**
CSF £14.87 CT £76.29 TOTE £2.40: £1.20, £2.10, £2.50; EX 11.60 Trifecta £131.30.
Owner M M Foulger **Bred** Paramount Bloodstock **Trained** Newmarket, Suffolk
FOCUS
Marginally the slower of the two divisions.
T/Plt: £75.40 to a £1 stake. Pool of £91902.72 - 889.68 winning tickets. T/Qpdt: £3.60 to a £1 stake. Pool of £13067.23 - 2627.90 winning tickets. **Andrew Sheret**

7664 NEWMARKET (R-H)
Saturday, October 29
OFFICIAL GOING: Good to firm (good in places; 7.9)
Wind: virtually nil Weather: overcast

7695 EBF STALLIONS PRESTIGE VEHICLES MAIDEN FILLIES' STKS (PLUS 10 RACE) (DIV I) 7f
1:20 (1:21) (Class 4) 2-Y-O **£4,528** (£1,347; £673; £336) **Stalls** High

Form RPR
2 **1** **Cashla Bay**[15] 7314 2-9-0 0 RobertHavlin 13 82
(John Gosden) *hld up wl in tch: clsd to trck ldr 3f out: effrt to chal 2f out: rdn to ld over 1f out: forged ahd u.p ins fnl f: kpt on* **8/11**[1]
66 **2** 1 **Queen Of Time**[15] 7314 2-9-0 0 AdamKirby 8 79
(Henry Candy) *hld up in tch in midfield: hdwy 3f out: rdn to chse ldng pair over 1f out: styd on wl ins fnl f: wnt 2nd fnl 50yds: nvr getting to wnr* **11/1**
3 1 1/2 **Ashwaq** 2-9-0 0 FrankieDettori 3 75
(Richard Hannon) *led: jnd 2f out: sn rdn and hdd: no ex and btn ins fnl f: wknd and lost 2nd 50yds out* **8/1**[3]
4 2 1/4 **Multicultural (IRE)** 2-9-0 0 MartinHarley 7 69
(James Tate) *hld up in tch towards rr: hdwy 1/2-way: 4th and no imp over 1f out: kpt on same pce ins fnl f* **33/1**
5 2 1/4 **Isabel's On It** 2-9-0 0 PatCosgrave 12 63+
(William Haggas) *hld up in tch in last pair: swtchd lft and hdwy ent fnl 2f: drifting rt and no imp over 1f out: kpt on same pce ins fnl f* **6/1**[2]
5 **6** 3 1/2 **Lady Freyja**[22] 7107 2-9-0 0 DannyBrock 1 54
(John Ryan) *in tch in midfield: pushed along and hdwy 3f out: rdn to chse ldrs 2f out: rn green and unable qck over 1f out: wknd fnl f* **100/1**
7 1/2 **Zafaranah (USA)** 2-9-0 0 DaneO'Neill 4 52
(Roger Varian) *chsd ldrs: rdn over 2f out: sn struggling and lost pl 2f out: wknd over 1f out* **9/1**
40 **8** 1 **Echoism (IRE)**[7] 7527 2-9-0 0 WilliamBuick 9 50
(Mark Johnston) *chsd ldr tl 3f out: sn rdn and struggling: wknd over 1f out* **25/1**
00 **9** 3 1/4 **Oh It's Saucepot**[40] 6625 2-9-0 0 TedDurcan 5 41
(Chris Wall) *in tch in midfield: rdn 3f out: sn outpcd: wknd wl over 1f out* **80/1**
10 1/2 **Love And Be Loved** 2-8-11 0 JosephineGordon(3) 2 39
(Peter Chapple-Hyam) *chsd ldrs: rdn 3f out: sn struggling and lost pl: bhd over 1f out* **33/1**
11 1 1/2 **Meccabah (FR)** 2-9-0 0 OisinMurphy 10 35
(Andrew Balding) *s.i.s: in tch in midfield: rdn 3f out: sn outpcd: wknd over 1f out* **25/1**
12 1 **Miss Osier** 2-9-0 0 MartinDwyer 11 33
(Rae Guest) *stdd s: hld up in tch in rr: rdn over 2f out: sn btn and wknd 2f out* **100/1**
13 1/2 **Devon Cove** 2-8-9 0 CharlieBennett(5) 6 31
(Jane Chapple-Hyam) *s.i.s: in tch in rr: rdn over 2f out: sn outpcd and bhd 2f out* **200/1**
1m 25.23s (-0.17) **Going Correction** +0.025s/f (Good) **13** Ran SP% **118.9**
Speed ratings (Par 94): **101,99,98,95,93 89,88,87,83,83 81,80,79**
CSF £9.28 TOTE £1.70: £1.10, £2.80, £2.60; EX 11.70 Trifecta £69.40.
Owner Mrs C R Philipson & Mrs H Lascelles **Bred** Lofts Hall Stud & B Sangster **Trained** Newmarket, Suffolk

FOCUS

Stands' side course used. Stalls: stands' side for all races. The ground had dried out a little and was now good to firm, good in places (GoingStick 7.9), Stands-side course used. An interesting fillies' maiden to start and it can go to a nice type - The Fugue won a division of it in 2011. They came up the middle of the track and there were two groups initially, though they soon merged. Experience proved key, but there were some eye-catching performances from a couple of the newcomers. The time was 2.73 sec outside standard. The race average and the winner's debut shape the opening level.

7696 EBF STALLIONS PRESTIGE VEHICLES MAIDEN FILLIES' STKS (PLUS 10 RACE) (DIV II) 7f

1:50 (1:50) (Class 4) 2-Y-O **£4,528** (£1,347; £673; £336) **Stalls** High

Form RPR

4 **1** **Yellowhammer**[25] 7055 2-8-11 0 KieranShoemark(3) 8 78
(Roger Charlton) *hld up in tch: clsd to press ldrs and travelling strly over 2f out: shkn up to ld over 1f out: r.o wl pushed out* **8/1**

0 **2** 1 1/4 **Ettu**[25] 7055 2-9-0 0 JamesDoyle 9 75
(Jeremy Noseda) *t.k.h: chsd ldrs: rdn and ev ch whn wandered 2f out: 3rd and drvn 1f out: chsd wnr fnl 100yds: kpt on* **10/1**

3 1 **Luqyaa** 2-9-0 0 DaneO'Neill 7 72
(John Gosden) *in tch in midfield: hdwy 1/2-way: led 2f out: sn rdn: hdd over 1f out: no ex and styd on same pce ins fnl f* **8/1**

0 **4** 1 1/2 **Chicago Star**[15] 7314 2-9-0 0 TonyHamilton 13 68+
(Mick Channon) *hld up in rr: pushed along 2f out: rdn and hdwy 1f out: styd on strly ins fnl f: nvr trbld ldrs* **33/1**

6 **5** 3/4 **Ambrosia**[17] 7278 2-9-0 0 AndreaAtzeni 2 66
(Roger Varian) *hmpd leaving stalls: in tch in midfield: hdwy 1/2-way: rdn and pressing ldrs 2f out: unable qck over 1f out: wknd ins fnl f* **4/1**[2]

6 3/4 **Polly Glide (IRE)** 2-9-0 0 PatCosgrave 12 64
(Luca Cumani) *hld up in tch in rr: pushed along and hdwy wl over 1f out: kpt on steadily ins fnl f: nvr trbld ldrs* **25/1**

2 **7** 1/2 **Curlew River**[10] 7465 2-9-0 0 WilliamBuick 5 62
(Mark Johnston) *hmpd leaving stall: chsd ldrs: rdn 3f out: drvn and unable qck wl over 1f out: wknd ins fnl f* **2/1**[1]

8 2 1/4 **Miss Patience** 2-9-0 0 JimCrowley 6 56
(Peter Chapple-Hyam) *wnt rt leaving stalls: led tl 2f out: stl pressing ldrs but unable qck whn pushed along over 1f out: wknd ins fnl f* **20/1**

9 1 **Vice Versa** 2-9-0 0 TedDurcan 4 54
(Sir Michael Stoute) *hmpd leaving stalls and sn swtchd lft: in tch in midfield: pushed along 2f out: outpcd whn rn green and hung rt over 1f out: n.d and kpt on same pce after* **5/1**[3]

0 **10** 6 **Mordoree (IRE)**[25] 7056 2-9-0 0 [1] AdamKirby 11 38
(Clive Cox) *in tch in midfield: effrt 2f out: sn rn green and hung rt: wknd over 1f out* **66/1**

00 **11** 2 **How's Lucy**[35] 6782 2-9-0 0 DannyBrock 1 32
(Jane Chapple-Hyam) *chsd ldrs: rdn 3f out: sn lost pl: bhd over 1f out* **150/1**

0 **12** 7 **Our Cilla**[10] 7470 2-8-11 0 ShelleyBirkett(3) 3 13
(Julia Feilden) *hmpd leaving stalls: a towards but in tch: rdn over 2f out: sn wl btn* **150/1**

0 **13** 8 **Raspberry Princess**[10] 7466 2-9-0 0 OisinMurphy 10
(Stuart Williams) *in tch in midfield: rdn and lost pl qckly over 2f out: bhd over 1f out* **100/1**

1m 25.18s (-0.22) **Going Correction** +0.025s/f (Good) **13** Ran SP% **116.7**
Speed ratings (Par 94): **102,100,99,97,96 96,95,92,91,84 82,74,65**
CSF £79.48 TOTE £8.40: £2.00, £3.10, £2.90; EX 89.20 Trifecta £871.70.

Owner Lady Rothschild **Bred** Kincorth Investments Inc **Trained** Beckhampton, Wilts

FOCUS

They raced centre-to-nearside and, as in the first division, the first two in this contest had met before, finishing fourth and seventh respectively on their debuts in the same Leicester maiden. The winning time was fractionally faster than the first leg. A nice step forward from the winner, but the level is fluid.

7697 RACING UK HD NURSERY H'CAP 1m 1f

2:20 (2:23) (Class 4) (0-85,82) 2-Y-O **£5,175** (£1,540; £769; £384) **Stalls** High

Form RPR

3511 **1** **Count Calabash (IRE)**[48] 6366 2-9-7 **82** JimCrowley 2 89
(Paul Cole) *racd keenly: sn led and mde rest: rdn 2f out. clr and in command 1f out: styd on strly: readily* **11/4**[1]

264 **2** 3 1/2 **Challow (IRE)**[15] 7319 2-8-9 **70** LiamKeniry 3 70
(Sylvester Kirk) *hld up in tch in midfield: effrt ent fnl 2f: chsd clr wnr over 1f out: no ch w wnr but kpt on for clr 2nd* **6/1**

044 **3** 3 **Broughtons Knight**[19] 7209 2-8-10 **71** StevieDonohoe 6 65
(Henry Spiller) *t.k.h: hld up in tch in rr: bmpd after 1f: swtchd rt and effrt 2f out: unbalanced and no hdwy over 1f out: hdwy 1f out: wnt 3rd ins fnl f: kpt on but no threat to ldrs* **6/1**

5654 **4** 1/2 **Ocean Temptress**[52] 6240 2-8-0 **64** JosephineGordon(3) 1 57
(John Ryan) *t.k.h: sn chsng wnr: rdn over 2f out: unable qck and lost 2nd over 1f out: wknd ins fnl f* **14/1**

4411 **5** 3 **Katebird (IRE)**[9] 7482 2-8-10 **71** AndrewMullen 4 58
(Mark Johnston) *chsd ldrs: rdn 3f out: drvn and outpcd ent fnl 2f: swtchd rt over 1f out: no imp and wl hld after* **7/2**[2]

5213 **6** 1 **Quothquan (FR)**[26] 7016 2-8-3 **69** GeorgeWood(5) 5 54
(Michael Madgwick) *hld up in tch in last pair: effrt ent fnl 2f: no imp u.p and btn over 1f out: sn wknd* **5/1**[3]

232 **7** 8 **Peloton**[19] 7209 2-8-6 **67** KieranO'Neill 7 36
(Pat Phelan) *t.k.h: pressed wnr early: sn stdd into midfield: rdn and effrt to press ldrs 3f out: struggling 2f out: sn wknd* **8/1**

1m 51.4s (-0.30) **Going Correction** +0.025s/f (Good) **7** Ran SP% **111.9**
Speed ratings (Par 97): **102,98,96,95,93 92,85**
CSF £18.65 TOTE £3.20: £1.80, £3.40; EX 20.20 Trifecta £119.00.

Owner Trish Hall & Colin Fletcher **Bred** Miss S Von Schilcher **Trained** Whatcombe, Oxon

FOCUS

A fair staying nursery, but they went no pace early and that would have counted against a few, though the winner very much enjoyed the run of the race. The runner-up helps the opening level.

7698 BRITISH STALLION STUDS EBF MONTROSE FILLIES' STKS (LISTED RACE) 1m

2:55 (2:56) (Class 1) 2-Y-O

£17,013 (£6,450; £2,418; £2,418; £807; £405) **Stalls** High

Form RPR

1 **1** **Really Special**[23] 7099 2-9-0 0 JimCrowley 8 100+
(Saeed bin Suroor) *mde all: rdn wl over 1f out: asserting and edgd lft u.p 1f out: styd on strly and drew clr ins fnl f: pushed out towards fin* **2/1**[1]

14 **2** 2 3/4 **Kazimiera**[20] 7193 2-9-0 0 WilliamBuick 10 93
(Charlie Appleby) *in tch in midfield: clsd to trck ldng pair 3f out: effrt to chse wnr 2f out: unable qck and swtchd rt 1f out: styd on same pce ins fnl f* **9/2**[2]

1341 **3** 1/2 **Island Vision (IRE)**[21] 7147 2-9-0 87 MartinHarley 6 92
(David Simcock) *hld up in tch towards rr: effrt 2f out: hdwy u.p over 1f out: wnt 3rd ins fnl f: styd on but no threat to wnr* **6/1**[3]

1 **3** dht **Tansholpan**[17] 7284 2-9-0 0 AndreaAtzeni 4 92
(Roger Varian) *hld up in tch in last trio: effrt and nt clr run 2f out: rdn and hdwy over 1f out: wnt 4th and kpt on ins fnl f: no threat to wnr* **8/1**

1313 **5** nk **Teofonic (IRE)**[93] 4802 2-9-0 90 JoeFanning 9 91
(Mark Johnston) *hld up in tch in rr: effrt but hanging rt over 2f out: swtchd lft and hdwy 1f out: styd on ins fnl f: no ch w wnr* **8/1**

41 **6** 1 **Choumicha**[25] 7055 2-9-0 79 JamesDoyle 5 89
(Hugo Palmer) *chsd ldrs: rdn jst over 2f out: unable qck and lost pl over 1f out: plugged on same pce ins fnl f* **8/1**

1 **7** 1 **Billesdon Bess**[19] 7209 2-9-0 74 TomMarquand 11 86
(Richard Hannon) *dwlt: t.k.h: sn chsng wnr: rdn and lost 2nd 2f out: unable qck over 1f out: wknd ins fnl f* **22/1**

216 **8** 2 **Peak Princess (IRE)**[7] 7547 2-9-0 84 SeanLevey 2 82
(Richard Hannon) *chsd ldrs: rdn and struggling to qckn whn sltly impeded 2f out: lost pl and btn over 1f out: wknd ins fnl f* **14/1**

01 **9** 10 **Illaunmore (USA)**[25] 7049 2-9-0 80 RichardKingscote 7 59
(John Gosden) *restless in stalls: s.i.s: t.k.h: hdwy into midfield after 2f: rdn over 2f out: sn struggling: wknd over 1f out* **20/1**

2 **10** 6 **Bataka**[19] 7208 2-9-0 0 JosephineGordon 1 45
(Harry Dunlop) *wnt rt s: sn rcvrd and wl in touh in midfield: rdn 3f out: sn struggling: wknd wl over 1f out* **100/1**

1m 37.39s (-1.21) **Going Correction** +0.025s/f (Good) **10** Ran SP% **115.9**
Speed ratings (Par 100): **107,104,103,103,103 102,101,99,89,83**
Place 1.70 Kazimiera, 1.40 Tansholpan;TF: 13.20, 38.20; CSF £10.35 TOTE £2.90: £0.80, £1.90; EX 10.30.

Owner Godolphin **Bred** Darley **Trained** Newmarket, Suffolk

FOCUS

A warm Listed event, won by the likes of Timepiece and Blue Bunting within the last ten years. This year's winner could hardly have done it any easier. It's been rated as one of the better renewals.

7699 NEWMARKETRACECOURSES.CO.UK H'CAP 1m

3:30 (3:30) (Class 3) (0-95,92) 3-Y-O+ **£9,056** (£2,695; £1,346; £673) **Stalls** High

Form RPR

10-4 **1** **Greenside**[206] 1274 5-9-2 **87** DaneO'Neill 1 97
(Henry Candy) *racd in centre: hld up in tch in midfield overall: effrt 2f out: chsd ldrs u.p 1f out: r.o to ld 100yds out: r.o wl* **6/1**[3]

2210 **2** 1 **Makzeem**[7] 7535 3-8-13 **87** AndreaAtzeni 6 94
(Roger Charlton) *swtchd to centre after 2f: in tch in midfield: effrt over 2f out: drvn and ev ch over 1f out: led ins fnl f: sn hdd and styd on same pce after* **7/2**[1]

2143 **3** nk **Father Bertie**[5] 7573 4-9-7 **92** (tp) DavidAllan 10 99
(Tim Easterby) *racd nr stands' rail thrght: led: rdn 2f out: drvn and hrd pressed over 1f out: hdd ins fnl f: styd on same pce after* **4/1**[2]

1620 **4** 2 **Shady McCoy (USA)**[22] 7121 6-9-6 **91** JamesDoyle 7 93
(Ian Williams) *stdd s: hld up in tch in rr: racd nr stands' rail tl swtchd to centre 1/2-way: hdwy 2f out: rdn and ev ch over 1f out: wknd ins fnl f* **4/1**[2]

103 **5** 2 1/2 **Illustrissime (USA)**[26] 7005 3-9-0 **88** AdamKirby 8 84
(Roger Fell) *racd nr stands' side thrght: in tch in midfield: overall: effrt over 2f out: drvn and no imp over 1f out: kpt on same pce after* **8/1**

0010 **6** 1 1/2 **Jack's Revenge (IRE)**[15] 7316 8-9-3 **88** (vt) SteveDrowne 5 81
(George Baker) *swtchd to centre after 2f: hld up in tch in rr: effrt wl over 1f out: kpt on to pass btn horses ins fnl f: nvr trbld ldrs* **22/1**

264 **7** nk **In The Red (IRE)**[26] 7005 3-8-12 **86** TomMarquand 2 78
(Richard Hannon) *led centre gp and chsd overall ldr for 3f: styd chsng ldrs: unable qck u.p over 1f out: wknd ins fnl f* **11/1**

3050 **8** 2 3/4 **Two For Two (IRE)**[15] 7316 8-9-5 **90** (p) ConnorBeasley 3 76
(Roger Fell) *swtchd to centre after 2f: t.k.h: hld up in tch: effrt over 2f out: no imp: wknd over 1f out* **12/1**

250 **9** 1 3/4 **Mikmak**[56] 6132 3-8-13 **87** (b[1]) MartinDwyer 4 68
(William Muir) *awkward leaving stalls and hmpd sn after s: racd in centre: t.k.h: hdwy to ld gp and chsd overall ldr 5f out tl 2f out: sn lost pl: wknd fnl f* **25/1**

1m 37.56s (-1.04) **Going Correction** +0.025s/f (Good)
WFA 3 from 4yo+ 3lb **9** Ran SP% **111.8**
Speed ratings (Par 107): **106,105,104,102,100 98,98,95,93**
CSF £26.09 CT £92.59 TOTE £5.90: £2.10, £1.70, £1.50; EX 29.20 Trifecta £92.00.

Owner Clayton, Frost, Kebell & Turner **Bred** Lordship Stud **Trained** Kingston Warren, Oxon

FOCUS

A decent handicap, but a messy race. They soon split into two groups, but some of the riders didn't seem to know where they wanted to be and there was plenty of switching from one group to the other.

7700 JAMES SEYMOUR STKS (LISTED RACE) 1m 2f

4:05 (4:06) (Class 1) 3-Y-O+

£20,982 (£7,955; £3,981; £1,983; £995; £499) **Stalls** High

Form RPR

024- **1** **Energia Davos (BRZ)**[315] 8310 8-9-4 111 GeorgeBaker 6 113
(Jane Chapple-Hyam) *stdd s: hld up in tch in rr: rdn and hdwy 2f out: ev ch 1f out: bmpd and 100yds out: kpt on wl: rdn out* **11/1**

5150 **2** nk **Educate**[35] 6786 7-9-4 112 JamesDoyle 9 112
(Ismail Mohammed) *led: rdn: hdd and hung lft over 1f out: racing against stands' rails and ev ch ins fnl f: kpt on same pce fnl 100yds* **5/1**[3]

2000 **3** 3/4 **Master The World (IRE)**[14] 7354 5-9-4 107 (p) ShaneKelly 3 111
(David Elsworth) *hld up in tch in last pair: effrt over 2f out: hdwy u.p over 1f out: ev ch whn bmpd ins fnl f: kpt on same pce fnl 100yds* **11/1**

0522 **4** 1 3/4 **Basem**[23] 7101 5-9-4 108 (v[1]) WilliamCarson 4 107
(Saeed bin Suroor) *hld up wl in tch in midfield: clsd to join ldr jst over 2f out: led and rdn over 1f out: wnt sharply rt: bmpd rivals and hdd ins fnl f: nt rcvr and btn after* **9/2**[2]

0211 **5** 1 1/4 **Great Hall**[17] 7287 6-9-4 103 PatCosgrave 8 105
(Mick Quinn) *stdd s: hld up in tch in midfield: effrt over 2f out: drvn and unable qck 2f out: styd on same pce and no imp fr over 1f out* **12/1**

1254 **6** 3 1/4 **Ayrad (IRE)**[42] 6571 5-9-7 109 AndreaAtzeni 5 101
(Roger Charlton) *chsd ldr tl over 2f out: lost pl u.p and btn over 1f out: wknd ins fnl f* **11/2**

1111 **7** 3 **Baydar**[42] 6573 3-8-13 105 JosephineGordon 7 92
(Hugo Palmer) *chsd ldrs: rdn 4f out: drvn and struggling 3f out: lost pl and bhd 2f out: sn wknd* **13/8**[1]

2m 4.72s (-1.08) **Going Correction** +0.025s/f (Good)
WFA 3 from 4yo+ 5lb **7** Ran SP% **112.7**
Speed ratings (Par 111): **105,104,104,102,101 99,96**
CSF £62.26 TOTE £11.90: £4.70, £3.00; EX 77.10 Trifecta £1048.90.
Owner Bryan Hirst Ltd & Jane Chapple-Hyam **Bred** Haras Estrela Energia **Trained** Dalham, Suffolk
■ Stewards' Enquiry : William Carson caution: careless riding

FOCUS
An interesting Listed event, but an unsatisfactory race as although the field basically came up the centre, there were some strange antics late on with a couple of the principals hanging all over the place.

7701 "HATS OFF" TO STEVE BROWN BEN MARSHALL STKS (LISTED RACE) 1m
4:40 (4:42) (Class 1) 3-Y-O+
£20,982 (£7,955; £3,981; £1,983; £995; £499) **Stalls** High

Form RPR

00-2 **1** **Estidhkaar (IRE)**[19] 7213 4-9-2 109 DaneO'Neill 5 111
(Richard Hannon) *trckd ldr: effrt 2f out: rdn to chal over 1f out: sustained duel w ldr fnl f: styd on u.p to ld cl home* **7/2**[2]

42-4 **2** nk **Kool Kompany (IRE)**[19] 7213 4-9-2 103 SeanLevey 4 110
(Richard Hannon) *led: rdn 2f out: jnd over 1f out: sustained duel w wnr after: kpt on wl tl hdd and no ex cl home* **16/1**

23-1 **3** 3 1/4 **Latharnach (USA)**[28] 6955 4-9-5 113 WilliamBuick 6 106
(Charlie Appleby) *stdd s: hld up in tch in last trio: hdwy over 2f out: chsd ldng pair and drvn over 1f out: no imp* **7/4**[1]

2300 **4** shd **Donncha (IRE)**[14] 7354 5-9-2 100 AndreaAtzeni 2 102
(Robert Eddery) *hld up in tch in last trio: hdwy over 2f out: rdn and chsd clr ldng pair over 1f out: no imp and styd on same pce after* **8/1**

1 **5** 4 **Team Talk**[25] 7061 3-8-13 0 OisinMurphy 8 92
(Saeed bin Suroor) *hld up in tch in last trio: effrt over 2f out: 5th and no imp u.p over 1f out: wknd fnl f* **11/2**

4310 **6** 3/4 **C Note (IRE)**[8] 7497 3-8-13 101 (b) PaulMulrennan 3 90
(Martyn Meade) *stdd s: t.k.h: hld up in tch in midfield: wnt 3rd 3f out: rdn and unable qck 2f out: sn lost pl and wknd* **20/1**

1144 **7** 6 **Kylla Instinct**[51] 6246 3-8-8 82 TomMarquand 1 72
(Philip McBride) *in tch in midfield: rdn 3f out: sn struggling: bhd over 1f out* **100/1**

-111 **8** 19 **Murad Khan (FR)**[56] 6132 3-8-13 99 JimCrowley 7 33
(Hugo Palmer) *chsd ldrs: rdn and losing pl 3f out: bhd 2f out: eased fnl f* **5/1**[3]

1m 36.3s (-2.30) **Going Correction** +0.025s/f (Good)
WFA 3 from 4yo+ 3lb **8** Ran SP% **113.4**
Speed ratings (Par 111): **112,111,108,108,104 103,97,78**
CSF £55.01 TOTE £4.10: £1.60, £3.20, £1.20; EX 45.90 Trifecta £182.50.
Owner Hamdan Al Maktoum **Bred** BEC Bloodstock **Trained** East Everleigh, Wilts

FOCUS
Another interesting Listed event in which the first two in the betting were having their second starts back following long absences. Few ever got into this, despite a solid pace, and it provided a 1-2 for trainer Richard Hannon.

7702 TRACY HAWKES H'CAP 7f
5:15 (5:17) (Class 4) (0-85,89) 3-Y-O+ **£5,175** (£1,540; £769; £384) **Stalls** High

Form RPR

50/3 **1** **Via Via (IRE)**[42] 6579 4-9-2 **80** MartinHarley 3 89+
(James Tate) *stdd s: hld up in tch in last quartet: hdwy 2f out: rdn to chal 1f out: edgd lft and led ins fnl f: r.o wl* **6/1**[3]

5434 **2** 1 1/4 **Rebel Surge (IRE)**[7] 7550 3-9-4 **84** (p) JimCrowley 7 89
(Richard Spencer) *in tch in midfield: effrt 2f out: rdn and ev ch over 1f out: drvn to ld 1f out: hdd and styd on same pce ins fnl f* **8/1**

005 **3** hd **Free Code (IRE)**[29] 6914 5-9-3 **81** GrahamGibbons 1 86
(David Barron) *pressed ldr tl led 2f out: sn rdn: hdd 1f out and sn edgd rt: styd on same pce fnl 150yds* **8/1**

0221 **4** 3/4 **Harwoods Volante (IRE)**[11] 7443 5-9-11 **89** PhillipMakin 15 92
(David O'Meara) *stdd s: t.k.h: hld up in tch in midfield: effrt to chal over 1f out: drvn and styd on same pce ins fnl f* **8/1**

5013 **5** 1/2 **Chiswick Bey (IRE)**[26] 7010 8-8-8 **72** GeorgeChaloner 12 74
(Richard Fahey) *chsd ldrs: ecery ch 2f out: sn rdn: unable qck 1f out and kpt on same pce ins fnl f* **20/1**

1645 **5** dht **Shamaheart (IRE)**[28] 6956 6-9-6 **84** (p) PaulMulrennan 11 86+
(Geoffrey Harker) *t.k.h: hld up in tch in midfield: nt clr run and shuffled bk 2f out: hdwy 1f out: swtchd lft ins fnl f: styd on wl fnl 100yds: nt rch ldrs* **20/1**

3030 **7** shd **Regal Dan (IRE)**[22] 7126 6-9-2 **83** ShelleyBirkett(3) 5 87+
(David O'Meara) *t.k.h: chsd ldrs: effrt 2f out: ev ch over 1f out: squeezed for room and hmpd jst ins fnl f: nt rcvr and one pced after* **8/1**

3310 **8** 3/4 **My Target (IRE)**[29] 6914 5-9-5 **83** AdamKirby 4 83
(Michael Wigham) *hld up in tch in midfield: stuck bhd and wall of horses 2f out: swtchd lft over 1f out: kpt on ins fnl f: no threat to ldrs* **4/1**[1]

5653 **9** 1 1/4 **Realize**[29] 6914 6-9-4 **82** (t) OisinMurphy 8 85+
(Stuart Williams) *hld up in tch in midfield: nt clr run and swtchd rt over 1f out: hdwy and pressing ldrs whn squeezed for room and hmpd jst ins fnl f: nt rcvr and one pced after* **9/2**[2]

0000 **10** hd **Johnny Cavagin**[28] 6962 7-9-7 **85** (t) TomEaves 13 81
(Ronald Thompson) *hld up in tch in rr: effrt wl over 1f out: kpt on u.p ins fnl f: nvr threatened ldrs* **40/1**

4510 **11** 1/2 **Calvados Spirit**[44] 6529 3-9-2 **82** MartinDwyer 6 76
(William Muir) *stdd s: t.k.h: hld up in tch in last quartet: hdwy over 2f out: rdn and no imp over 1f out: nvr threatened ldrs* **16/1**

5500 **12** nk **Billy Roberts (IRE)**[8] 7505 3-8-12 **78** ConnorBeasley 9 71
(Richard Guest) *chsd ldrs: shifted lft and chal 2f out: unable qck u.p over 1f out: wknd ins fnl f* **33/1**

4-20 **13** 3 **Best Example (USA)**[11] 7428 4-9-6 **84** AdamBeschizza 2 70
(Julia Feilden) *s.i.s: hld up in tch in rr: effrt and swtchd lft over 1f out: no imp and wknd ins fnl f* **66/1**

0000 **14** 9 **Zacynthus (IRE)**[51] 6266 8-8-7 **74** JosephineGordon(3) 10 35
(Ivan Furtado) *led tl 2f out: sn lost pl and bhd 1f out: wknd* **33/1**

1m 26.23s (0.83) **Going Correction** +0.025s/f (Good)
WFA 3 from 4yo+ 2lb **14** Ran SP% **122.1**
Speed ratings (Par 105): **96,94,94,93,92 92,92,91,90,90 89,89,85,75**
CSF £50.07 CT £406.12 TOTE £6.70: £2.40, £3.20, £2.70; EX 61.60 Trifecta £363.70.
Owner Saeed Manana **Bred** Kenilworth House Stud **Trained** Newmarket, Suffolk

FOCUS
A competitive handicap, but a rough race with plenty of trouble as the winner hung left and the third hung right entering the last furlong. Several of these got very warm beforehand.
T/Plt: £143.00 to a £1 stake. Pool: £85,872.44 - 438.10 winning tickets T/Qpdt: £18.90 to a £1 stake. Pool: £7,141.63 - 278.76 winning tickets **Steve Payne**

7703 - 7705a (Foreign Racing) - See Raceform Interactive

7556 LEOPARDSTOWN (L-H)
Saturday, October 29

OFFICIAL GOING: Yielding (yielding to soft in places)

7706a THETOTE.COM KNOCKAIRE STKS (LISTED RACE) 7f
3:05 (3:07) 3-Y-O+
£20,389 (£6,566; £3,110; £1,382; £691; £345)

RPR

1 **Sovereign Debt (IRE)**[7] 7542 7-9-7 112 DeclanMcDonogh 2 112+
(David Nicholls) *disp early and settled bhd ldr after 1f: racd keenly early: dropped to 3rd after 2f: impr on outer into 2nd 1 1/2f out and rdn to ld ins fnl f: kpt on wl to assert clsng stages* **15/8**[1]

2 2 **Blue De Vega (GER)**[135] 3296 3-9-5 105 ColinKeane 1 106
(M D O'Callaghan, Ire) *disp early and settled bhd ldrs after 1f: wnt 2nd after 2f: impr to ld 1 1/2f out: sn rdn and hdd ins fnl f: kpt on wl wout matching wnr clsng stages* **9/2**[3]

3 1 1/2 **Downforce (IRE)**[27] 6984 4-9-7 98 BillyLee 4 103
(W McCreery, Ire) *chsd ldrs: 4th 1/2-way: rdn into 3rd cnt fnl f and no imp on ldrs: kpt on same pce: nt trble wnr* **9/1**

4 1 1/4 **Bebhinn (USA)**[20] 7191 3-9-0 99 ChrisHayes 6 93
(Kevin Prendergast, Ire) *hld up in tch: disp 6th at 1/2-way: rdn in 6th under 2f out and kpt on same pce into nvr threatening 4th wl ins fnl f: nvr trbld ldrs* **12/1**

5 1/2 **Rose De Pierre (IRE)**[13] 7392 3-9-3 103 PatSmullen 7 95
(D K Weld, Ire) *chsd ldrs: 5th 1/2-way: rdn into 4th ins fnl f and no imp on ldrs: one pce in 5th wl ins fnl f* **3/1**[2]

6 3/4 **Penny Pepper (IRE)**[13] 7392 4-9-2 87 GaryHalpin 8 91
(Kevin Prendergast, Ire) *dwlt and in rr: gng wl in 9th 3f out: rdn in 9th over 1f out and kpt on ins fnl f into nvr nrr 6th: nrst fin* **33/1**

7 1 1/2 **Master Speaker (IRE)**[8] 7520 6-9-7 101 (bt) ColmO'Donoghue 9 92
(Martin Hassett, Ire) *towards rr and pushed along briefly early: 12th appr st: rdn 2f out and sme modest hdwy on inner ins fnl f where n.m.r into nvr nrr 7th* **20/1**

8 3/4 **Final Frontier (IRE)**[104] 4433 3-9-5 101 ShaneFoley 3 89
(Mrs John Harrington, Ire) *towards rr early: clsr and disp 6th at 1/2-way: rdn under 2f out and no imp u.p in 6th 1 1/2f out: one pce fnl f* **33/1**

9 nk **Truffles (IRE)**[19] 7233 3-9-0 84 GaryCarroll 10 83
(Ms Sheila Lavery, Ire) *w ldrs and led after 1f: rdn and hdd 1 1/2f out: wknd* **66/1**

10 shd **Flight Risk (IRE)**[20] 7191 5-9-7 108 (t) KevinManning 12 89
(J S Bolger, Ire) *hld up in tch: disp 6th at 1/2-way: rdn under 2f out where hung sltly and sn no imp on ldrs: wknd* **14/1**

11 nk **Molly Dolly (IRE)**[36] 6746 4-9-2 96 [1] WayneLordan 13 83
(W T Farrell, Ire) *towards rr: last appr st: rdn and no imp 2f out: kpt on one pce ins fnl f* **20/1**

12 1 1/4 **Byzantium**[20] 7191 4-9-2 94 (v) RobbieDowney 11 79
(Edward Lynam, Ire) *w.w: 11th 3f out: rdn and no imp 2f out* **33/1**

13 7 1/2 **Collision Course (IRE)**[14] 7377 3-9-5 89 SeamieHeffernan 5 63
(A Oliver, Ire) *hld up: 10th 3f out: rdn and wknd 2f out* **100/1**

1m 28.57s (-0.13) **Going Correction** +0.30s/f (Good)
WFA 3 from 4yo+ 2lb **13** Ran SP% **123.2**
Speed ratings: **112,109,108,106,106 105,103,102,102,102 101,100,91**
CSF £9.96 TOTE £2.40: £1.80, £1.60, £2.60; DF 10.90 Trifecta £63.80.
Owner Lady O'Reilly **Bred** Yeomanstown Stud **Trained** Sessay, N Yorks

FOCUS
This was a really good Listed race. Five of the field were rated 101 or higher. The right horses fought out the finish. The form looks strong. The first two home were ridden positively. The third, sixth and ninth limit the form.

7707a THETOTE.COM EYREFIELD STKS (LISTED RACE) 1m 1f
3:40 (3:40) 2-Y-O
£20,389 (£6,566; £3,110; £1,382; £691; £345)

RPR

1 **Dubai Sand (IRE)**[19] 7235 2-9-3 0 KevinManning 2 101
(J S Bolger, Ire) *gd hdwy to trck ldr in 2nd after 1f: led narrowly 4f out: rdn clr over 1f out: styd on wl fnl f: ld reduced cl home* **7/1**

2 1/2 **Diodorus (IRE)**[19] 7235 2-9-3 85 (b[1]) MichaelHussey 7 100
(A P O'Brien, Ire) *racd in mid-div on inner: rdn and prog to chse ldrs in 4th 2f out: styd on wl into 2nd ins fnl f: nt rch wnr* **20/1**

3 1 1/2 **Youarewonder (IRE)**[13] 7390 2-9-3 85 DavidNolan 6 97
(John James Feane, Ire) *hld up: prog under 2f out in mid-div: wnt 5th ent fnl f: styd on wl into 3rd on line: nrst fin* **25/1**

4 nk **Percy (IRE)**[49] 6349 2-9-3 99 ColinKeane 5 96
(G M Lyons, Ire) *chsd ldrs in 4th: rdn in 3rd under 3f out: chsd ldr in 2nd under 2f out tl no imp ins fnl f: wknd cl home* **11/1**

5 nse **Butterflies (IRE)**[20] 7193 2-8-12 99 SeamieHeffernan 10 91
(A P O'Brien, Ire) *racd towards rr: last 4f out: swtchd rt 2f out to outer: styd on wl into 8th 1f out: kpt on strly into 5th cl home: nvr nrr* **10/1**

6 1/2 **Saltonstall**[21] 7161 2-9-3 0 ShaneFoley 11 95
(M Halford, Ire) *racd towards rr: prog whn short of room 2f out: kpt on wl on inner ins fnl f into 6th: nvr nrr* **11/2**[3]

7 2 **Bound (IRE)**[20] 7193 2-8-12 100 ColmO'Donoghue 9 86
(A P O'Brien, Ire) *racd in mid-div: pushed along 2f out: no imp appr fnl f: kpt on one pce* **7/1**

8 1 1/4 **Galilean (IRE)**[14] 7373 2-9-3 95 (p) DonnachaO'Brien 3 89
(A P O'Brien, Ire) *trckd ldrs in 3rd: rdn in 2nd 3f out: nt qckn under 2f out: wknd appr fnl f* **5/1**[2]

9 1 3/4 **Queen Anne's Lace (USA)**[20] 7193 2-8-12 99 PatSmullen 4 80
(D K Weld, Ire) *bit slowly away but sn chsd ldrs: rdn to cl in 3rd under 2f out: wknd ent fnl f: eased clsng stages* **10/3**[1]

10 7 1/2 **Three Jacks (IRE)**[27] 6982 2-9-3 0 WayneLordan 8 70
(Martin Hassett, Ire) *led v early on: sn settled in mid-div: pushed along over 3f out: no imp whn short of room under 2f out: sn no ex* **14/1**

11 4 1/2 **Vocal Activity (IRE)**[11] 7447 2-9-3 0........................... DanielRedmond 1 61
(J S Bolger, Ire) *sn led on inner: pressed and narrowly hdd 4f out: wknd qckly over 2f out* **66/1**

1m 56.81s (2.71) **Going Correction** +0.40s/f (Good) **11** Ran SP% **114.3**
Speed ratings: **103,102,101,100,100 100,98,97,96,89 85**
CSF £136.05 TOTE £6.20: £2.40, £5.00, £5.60; DF 170.90 Trifecta £1265.60.
Owner Godolphin **Bred** J S Bolger & Ennistown Stud **Trained** Coolcullen, Co Carlow

FOCUS

Jim Bolger won this Listed contest with Parish Boy in 2014 and Moonlight Magic in 2015. The hat-trick was completed by a maiden who was making it third time lucky. It might not have been the strongest renewal but there were five of the field rated 95 or higher. The pace was honest. The first two home were maidens. A nice step forward from the winner, but it's been rated as an ordinary renewal.

7708a TOTE NOVEMBER H'CAP (PREMIER HANDICAP) 1m 7f
4:15 (4:17) 3-Y-O+

£43,382 (£13,970; £6,617; £2,941; £1,470; £735)

RPR

1 **Golden Spear**[21] 7150 5-8-8 **87**..(t) ConorHoban 1 94+
(A J Martin, Ire) *sn settled off ldrs on inner: tk clsr order 3f out: wnt 3rd 2f out: rdn to press ldr in 2nd appr fnl f: on terms fnl 100yds: styd on wl to ld cl home* **7/1**[2]

2 1/2 **Nakeeta**[21] 7150 5-9-6 **99**... SeamieHeffernan 6 105
(Iain Jardine) *keen early on to trck ldrs: chsd ldrs tl gd prog in 2nd under 3f out: led under 2f out: strly pressed ins fnl f: kpt on wl: hdd cl home* **12/1**

3 2 **Magic Circle (IRE)**[56] 6118 4-9-4 **97**................................ PatSmullen 22 101+
(Ralph Beckett) *racd in mid-div: rdn 2f out in 11th: styd on wl into 5th ent fnl f: wnt 3rd ins fnl 100yds: nt rch principals* **8/1**[3]

4 1/2 **Guard of Honour (IRE)**[370] 7493 5-8-5 **84**.....................(b) ChrisHayes 2 87
(George Baker) *hld up: gd prog under 3f out: chsd ldrs in 4th under 2f out: wnt 3rd 1f out: nt qckn in 4th ins fnl 100yds: kpt on same pce* **16/1**

5 1 **Snow Falcon (IRE)**[32] 6864 6-8-11 **90**............................... ShaneFoley 7 92+
(Noel Meade, Ire) *racd in mid-div: prog whn sltly bmpd off home turn: styd on wl ins fnl f: nrst fin* **11/2**[1]

6 hd **Theophilus (IRE)**[6] 7562 5-8-4 **83**..................................(p) RoryCleary 16 85
(J S Bolger, Ire) *hld up: pushed along towards rr 4f out: gd hdwy on inner fr under 2f out: kpt on strly ins fnl f: nvr nrr* **33/1**

7 hd **Moonmeister (IRE)**[21] 7150 5-8-5 **89**..............................(t) OisinOrr(5) 21 90
(A J Martin, Ire) *bit slowly away and racd towards rr tl clsr on inner under 3f out: rdn in 4th appr fnl f: no ex ins fnl f: wknd clsng stages* **17/2**

8 2 **Artful Artist (IRE)**[20] 7195 7-8-0 **84**.........................(t) KillianLeonard(5) 3 83
(A J Martin, Ire) *racd towards rr: last at 1/2-way: prog whn short of room over 2f out: styd on wl ins fnl f: nvr on terms* **14/1**

9 1 1/2 **Rashaan (IRE)**[17] 7195 4-8-5 **84**.................................... NGMcCullagh 10 81
(Colin Kidd, Ire) *sn chsd ldrs: rdn and nt qckn over 2f out: no imp appr fnl f* **14/1**

10 1/2 **Renneti (FR)**[13] 7394 7-9-5 **108**................................. DannySheehy(10) 12 105
(W P Mullins, Ire) *racd in mid-div: clsr on outer to chse ldrs over 4f out: rdn in 5th 2f out: no imp appr fnl f: wknd* **10/1**

11 1/2 **Swamp Fox (IRE)**[20] 7195 4-8-9 **88**...........................(b) WayneLordan 15 84
(Joseph G Murphy, Ire) *racd in mid-div: pushed along on outer under 3f out: no imp appr fnl f* **10/1**

12 2 **Roconga (IRE)**[32] 6864 6-9-0 **93**.. BillyLee 18 87
(E J O'Grady, Ire) *hld up: bit short of room 2f out where swtchd lft and hmpd rival: sme prog appr fnl f: sn no imp and nt hrd rdn clsng stages* **11/1**

13 3/4 **Benkei (IRE)**[20] 7195 6-9-3 **96**..(t) ConnorKing 17 89
(H Rogers, Ire) *slowly away and sn rdn: rapid hdwy to press ldr in 2nd after 2f: rdn to ld under 3f out: hdd under 2f out and sn wknd* **33/1**

14 3/4 **Jennies Jewel (IRE)**[20] 7195 9-8-12 **98**........................ DenisLinehan(7) 5 90
(Jarlath P Fahey, Ire) *bit slowly away and hld up: rdn towards rr 3f out: prog whn short of room and swtchd lft under 2f out: kpt on one pce: nvr on terms* **14/1**

15 3/4 **Cradle Mountain (IRE)**[20] 7195 4-8-11 **93** ow2(tp) DonnachaO'Brien(3) 14 84
(Joseph Patrick O'Brien, Ire) *sn settled in mid-div: rdn along over 4f out on outer: chsd ldrs under 2f out in 5th: no imp appr fnl f: wknd* **16/1**

16 2 3/4 **Sir Ector (USA)**[31] 4436 9-8-10 **94**..................(b) DonaghO'Connor(5) 11 82
(Miss Nicole McKenna, Ire) *led: clly pressed after 2f tl hdd after 1/2-way: wknd fr 2f out* **50/1**

17 1 **Alton Bay (IRE)**[20] 7195 8-8-6 **85**....................................(t) LeighRoche 4 71
(Peter Fahey, Ire) *racd towards rr: sme prog on outer home turn: no imp over 1f out* **16/1**

18 shd **Chapter Seven**[13] 7394 7-8-8 **87**................................. EmilyFinnegan 23 73
(G M Lyons, Ire) *racd in mid-div: clsr to chse ldrs in 3rd at 1/2-way: pushed along and lost position 4f out: sn no ex* **50/1**

19 4 1/4 **Mandatario**[15] 7342 5-9-2 **95**..(t) KevinManning 13 76
(J S Bolger, Ire) *racd in mid-div: rdn over 3f out: no imp whn bdly hmpd under 2f out: no ex* **25/1**

20 1 3/4 **Tara Dylan (IRE)**[13] 7393 4-7-12 **84**..............................[1] SeanDavis(7) 19 63
(Thomas Mullins, Ire) *slowly away and racd towards rr tl sddle slipped and rapid hdwy to ld after 1/2-way: hdd under 3f out: wknd over 1f out and eased* **40/1**

21 7 **Queen Alphabet (IRE)**[49] 6350 7-8-9 **88**..............(t) DeclanMcDonogh 8 59
(Peter Fahey, Ire) *chsd ldr in 2nd: sn 3rd: 4th at 1/2-way: nt qckn whn short of room 2f out: eased over 1f out* **25/1**

22 7 **Wakea (USA)**[51] 2942 5-9-1 **94**.......................................(t) ColinKeane 9 56
(Karl Thornton, Ire) *racd in mid-div: quite keen: clsr on outer over 4f out: wknd home turn: eased fnl f* **14/1**

23 16 **Travertine (IRE)**[49] 6350 6-9-5 **103**............................ TomMadden(5) 20 46
(Niall Madden, Ire) *hld up: rdn along towards rr 4f out: no imp in rr 2f out and sn eased* **33/1**

3m 17.83s (1.83) **Going Correction** +0.40s/f (Good) **23** Ran SP% **150.9**
Speed ratings: **111,110,100,100,100 100,100,107,100,100 100,105,104,104,103 102,101,101,99,98 95,91,82**
CSF £99.11 CT £738.00 TOTE £9.50: £2.20, £3.00, £2.10, £3.40; DF 117.30 Trifecta £1930.70.
Owner Newtown Anner Stud Farm Ltd **Bred** D P And Mrs J A Martin **Trained** Summerhill, Co. Meath

■ Stewards' Enquiry : Billy Lee four-day ban: careless riding (tbn)

FOCUS

A top-notch November Handicap. Plenty of high-class stayers in the big field. A solid pace. A deserving winner. A courageous runner-up. A pb from the progressive winner.

7709 - 7711a (Foreign Racing) - See Raceform Interactive

6993 FLEMINGTON (L-H)
Saturday, October 29

OFFICIAL GOING: Good

7712a LEXUS STKS (GROUP 3 H'CAP) (3YO+) (TURF) 1m 4f 110y
3:40 (12:00) 3-Y-O+

£89,851 (£26,732; £13,366; £6,683; £3,712; £2,970)

RPR

1 **Oceanographer**[10] 7481 4-8-7 **0**....................................... KerrinMcEvoy 8 106+
(Charlie Appleby) *hld up to r 2nd last: last 3f out: plld wd for a run turning in: gd hdwy fr 2f out: stl 3 l bhd long time ldr ent fnl f: continued to cl: led fnl strides* **17/10**[1]

2 1/2 **Tom Melbourne (IRE)**[14] 5-8-8 **0**.......................................(t) GlenBoss 2 105
(Lee & Anthony Freedman, Australia) *led: clr after 2f: c bk to field 4f out: rdn clr 1 1/2f out: wknd last 50yds: hdd cl home* **17/5**[2]

3 3 **Tally (AUS)**[14] 7378 4-9-2 **0**.......................................(p) JamesMcDonald 9 111
(J O'Shea, Australia) *in rr of midfield early: sme hdwy bk st: rdn along 2f out: 2nd 1f out but unable to cl on ldr: kpt on fnl f* **10/1**

4 nk **De Little Engine (AUS)**[14] 7378 6-8-7 **0**........................ ChadSchofield 4 99
(Danny O'Brien, Australia) *hld up towards rr: rdn and kpt on fr 2f out: nrst fin* **17/2**

5 3 3/4 **Black Tomahawk (AUS)**[35] 7-8-7 **0**..........................(b[1]) CraigAWilliams 10 93
(Darren Weir, Australia) *chsd clr ldr: rdn 2f out: wknd fnl f* **14/1**

6 1/2 **Real Love (AUS)**[14] 7378 6-9-3 **0**.......................................(t) BradRawiller 5 102
(Darren Weir, Australia) *midfield: rdn and kpt on same pce fr over 2f out* **5/1**[3]

7 3 1/2 **Pentathlon (NZ)**[7] 7552 5-8-9 **0**.................................... MarkDuPlessis 6 89
(John Wheeler, New Zealand) *in tch: hdwy to trck ldrs 4f out: rdn 2f out: wknd over 1f out* **40/1**

8 3/4 **Transfer Allowance (AUS)**[16] 7-8-7 **0**.......................... ChrisSymons 12 85
(Peter Roche, Australia) *hld up in rr: rdn and no hdwy fr 2 1/2f out: passed btn rivals ins fnl f: nvr a factor* **200/1**

9 2 1/4 **Junoob**[14] 8-9-4 **0**..(bt) HughBowman 11 93
(Chris Waller, Australia) *trckd ldrs: wnt 2nd 4 1/2f out: rdn 3 1/2f out: lost pl over 2f out: wknd last 1 1/2f* **25/1**

10 shd **The Bandit (JPN)**[7] 7552 4-8-7 **0**.......................................(t) CraigNewitt 7 82
(John D Sadler, Australia) *hld up towards rr: effrt 2 1/2f out: sn btn: eased fnl f* **80/1**

11 3/4 **Rose Of Virginia (NZ)**[14] 7-8-7 **0**..........................(b[1]) BenEThompson 3 80
(Lee & Shannon Hope, Australia) *dwlt: t.k.h in midfield: rdn 2f out: wknd 1 1/2f out* **70/1**

12 3/4 **Hippopus (NZ)**[8] 7-8-7 **0**...(b) TimothyClark 1 79
(Gai Waterhouse & Adrian Bott, Australia) *trckd ldrs: grad lost pl fr 5f out: rdn under 3f out: btn 2f out* **150/1**

2m 35.68s (155.68) **12** Ran SP% **112.8**

Owner Godolphin **Bred** Earle I Mack **Trained** Newmarket, Suffolk

FOCUS

The standard is set around the second down to the fifth.

7713 - 7718a (Foreign Racing) - See Raceform Interactive

7555 SAN SIRO (R-H)
Saturday, October 29

OFFICIAL GOING: Turf: heavy

7719a PREMIO CHIUSURA (GROUP 3) (2YO+) (TURF) 7f
4:20 (12:00) 2-Y-O+ **£23,529** (£10,352; £5,647; £2,823)

RPR

1 **Princess Asta (FR)**[26] 7027 3-9-1 0.................................... CarloFiocchi 6 97
(Mario Hofer, Germany) *s.i.s: t.k.h towards rr of midfield: hdwy to ld 1f out: drvn out* **30/1**

2 1 1/4 **Dream Mover (IRE)**[52] 6232 3-9-4 0.................................. DarioVargiu 1 97
(Marco Botti) *sn led: rdn along 2f out: hdd 1f out: kpt on for 2nd: no ch w wnr* **47/10**[3]

3 1 1/2 **Sadalmelik (ITY)**[49] 3-9-1 0.. MarioSanna 7 90
(R Biondi, Italy) *racd in fnl pair: gd hdwy fnl f but unable to rch ldrs* **115/10**

4 1/2 **Antalya (GER)**[26] 7027 5-9-1 0... AdriedeVries 5 87
(Markus Klug, Germany) *prom: kpt on fnl f but nt the pce to chal* **67/10**

5 snk **Schang (GER)**[26] 7027 3-9-6 0... FedericoBossa 8 93
(P Vovcenko, Germany) *racd cl 2nd: rdn along and lost position fnl f* **19/4**

6 1/2 **Zapel**[146] 3-9-4 0.. SilvanoMulas 2 89
(Stefano Botti, Italy) *midfield: kpt on but nt the pce to chal* **89/20**[2]

7 nse **Justice Well**[42] 4-9-4 0.. FabioBranca 4 88
(Luciano Vitabile, Italy) *midfield: rdn along 1 1/2f out: unable qck: kpt on* **59/10**

8 nk **Shining Emerald**[26] 7027 5-9-6 0................................ EduardoPedroza 10 90
(A Wohler, Germany) *midfield on outer: rdn along 1 1/2f out: sn outpcd: rdn out* **2/1**[1]

9 2 **Double Dream (FR)**[38] 6693 3-9-1 0.................................... JozefBojko 3 80
(A Wohler, Germany) *t.k.h early: trckd ldrs: rdn along and lost pl 1f out: eased* **145/10**

10 10 **Harlem Shake (IRE)**[13] 5-9-4 0.. LucaManiezzi 9 55
(Marco Gasparini, Italy) *racd in fnl pair: btn and eased rt down 1f out* **102/10**

1m 24.9s (-3.30)
WFA 3 from 4yo+ 2lb **10** Ran SP% **140.7**
WIN (incl. 1 euro stake): 31.49. PLACES: 6.16, 2.66, 4.14. DF: 150.83.
Owner Stall Antanando **Bred** Mme G Forien & J-F Gribomont **Trained** Germany

6611 HANOVER (L-H)

Sunday, October 30

OFFICIAL GOING: Turf: good

7720a GROSSER PREIS DER BESITZERVEREINIGUNG FUR VOLLBLUTZUCHT (GROUP 3) (3YO+ FILLIES & MARES) (TURF) 1m 3f

1:25 (12:00) 3-Y-O+ **£23,529** (£8,823; £4,411; £2,205; £1,470)

RPR

1 **Son Macia (GER)**[57] 6152 3-8-13 0 IanFerguson 12 100
(Andreas Lowe, Germany) *prom on outer: chsd ldr wl over 2f out: rdn and sustained chal on stands' rail fnl f: led cl home* **124/10**

2 *nk* **Nazbanou (IRE)**[76] 3-8-13 0 MrVinzenzSchiergen 4 99
(P Schiergen, Germany) *chsd ldrs on inner: drvn to ld under 1 1/2f out: rallied gamely u.p whn chal ins fnl f: hdd cl home* **96/10**

3 *3/4* **Gambissara (FR)**[29] 6972 3-8-13 0 JozefBojko 1 98
(Lennart Hammer-Hansen, Germany) *w.w on inner in midfield: clsd to chsd ldrs 2f out: sn drvn and nt qckn: styd on fr 1 1/2f to chal ldr: no ex fnl 75yds* **112/10**

4 *1/2* **Kasalla (GER)**[35] 6822 3-8-13 0 AdriedeVries 10 97
(Markus Klug, Germany) *chsd ldr: drvn and nt qckn 2 1/2f out: sn rdn and styd on fnl f: unable to muster pce to chal* **13/10**[1]

5 *3* **Vallante (GER)** 3-8-13 0 AlexanderPietsch 8 91
(J Hirschberger, Germany) *led: tk field towards stands' side st: sn rdn whn chal: hdd under 1 1/2f out: dropped away grad ins fnl f* **91/10**

6 *nse* **Techno Queen (IRE)**[42] 6610 5-9-4 0 FilipMinarik 7 90
(T Potters, Germany) *w.w in rr: clsd fr 2 1/2f out: nvr got on terms w ldng gp: kpt on at same pce fnl 1 1/2f* **4/1**[2]

7 *4 1/2* **Rose Rized (GER)**[28] 6998 4-9-4 0 AndreasHelfenbein 9 82
(P Schiergen, Germany) *hld up in fnl pair: rdn and sme prog over 2f out: btn fr 1 1/2f out* **35/1**

8 *3/4* **She's Gina (GER)**[42] 6610 3-8-13 0 MaximPecheur 5 82
(Markus Klug, Germany) *plld: cl up under restraint: drvn to hold pl over 4f out: wl hld fr over 1 1/2f out* **29/1**

9 *7 1/2* **Eagle Eyes (GER)**[47] 3-8-13 0 MichaelCadeddu 3 68
(Jean-Pierre Carvalho, Germany) *settled in midfield: sltly outpcd and rdn 2f out: wknd ins fnl f* **17/2**[3]

10 *1 1/2* **Forever Gold (GER)** 3-8-13 0 AndreasSuborics 6 66
(Andreas Lowe, Germany) *w.w towards rr: rdn and btn ins fnl 2f* **91/10**

11 *1 1/4* **Myth**[46] 6497 3-8-13 0 MarcLerner 2 63
(Waldemar Hickst, Germany) *w.w towards rr: no hdwy u.p wl over 2f out: sn btn* **27/1**

12 *1/2* **La Dynamite (IRE)**[35] 3-8-13 0 MartinSeidl 11 62
(Markus Klug, Germany) *hld up in midfield: no imp whn rdn over 2f out: bhd ins fnl 1 1/2f* **182/10**

2m 28.86s (148.86)
WFA 3 from 4yo+ 6lb **12** Ran SP% **133.8**
WIN (incl. 10 euro stake): 134. PLACES: 36, 37, 40. SF: 1,658..
Owner Stall Elektrowelt24 De **Bred** Stall Sternstunde **Trained** Germany

7638 SAINT-CLOUD (L-H)

Sunday, October 30

OFFICIAL GOING: Turf: soft

7721a CRITERIUM INTERNATIONAL (GROUP 1) (2YO COLTS & FILLIES) (TURF) 7f

1:35 (12:00) 2-Y-O **£105,036** (£42,022; £21,011; £10,496; £5,257)

RPR

1 **Thunder Snow (IRE)**[22] 7149 2-9-0 0 ChristopheSoumillon 3 119
(Saeed bin Suroor) *ld early: hdd after 1f and chsd new ldr: led ent st over 2 1/2f out and tk field to stands' side: rdn 1 1/2f out: drvn clr ins fnl f: won easing down* **3/1**[3]

2 *5* **South Seas (IRE)**[22] 7149 2-9-0 0 OisinMurphy 1 107
(Andrew Balding) *a cl up on inner: drvn to chal 2f out: no match for wnr fr 1f out: kpt on at one pce* **11/4**[2]

3 *1 3/4* **Promise To Be True (IRE)**[28] 6986 2-8-10 0 SeamieHeffernan 6 98
(A P O'Brien, Ire) *cl up on outer: rdn and chsd ldng pair 2f out: kpt on at same pce u.p* **15/8**[1]

4 *2 1/2* **Tresorier**[27] 2-9-0 0 ThierryJarnet 9 96
(Mme C Head-Maarek, France) *w.w in rr: clsd 2 1/2f out: chsd ldrs 2f out: sn rdn and no further imp: plugged on ins fnl f* **22/1**

5 *3* **Boos (FR)**[16] 7347 2-8-10 0 CristianDemuro 7 84
(P Sogorb, France) *settled in fnl trio in inner: rdn and effrt 2f out: sn unable to cl: grad lft bhd* **16/1**

6 *1 1/4* **Mate Story (IRE)**[25] 7086 2-9-0 0 GregoryBenoist 8 85
(D Smaga, France) *w.w in fnl trio on outer: rdn and no real hdwy over 2f out: wl hld fnl 1 1/2f* **11/2**

7 *3* **King Of Spades (FR)**[16] 7347 2-9-0 0 (b) AntoineHamelin 5 78
(F Vermeulen, France) *hld up in midfield: dropped to last over 2f out: sn btn* **40/1**

8 *15* **Bay Of Poets (IRE)**[8] 7539 2-9-0 0 (b[1]) WilliamBuick 4 40
(Charlie Appleby) *led after 1f: pushed along and hdd over 2 1/2f out: sn wknd* **20/1**

U **Capchop (FR)**[18] 2-9-0 0 Pierre-CharlesBoudot 2
(P Sogorb, France) *uns rdr sn after leaving stalls* **33/1**

1m 28.2s (-4.00) **Going Correction** -0.20s/f (Firm) **9** Ran SP% **122.2**
Speed ratings: **114,108,106,103,100 98,95,78,**
WIN (incl. 1 euro stake): 3.10 (Thunder Snow coupled with Bay Of Poets). PLACES: 1.40, 1.70, 1.40. DF: 9.00. SF: 14.60.
Owner Godolphin **Bred** Darley **Trained** Newmarket, Suffolk

FOCUS
The second running of this Group 1 over 7f (formerly run over 1m) with Roderic O'Connor and Ectot probably the best winners of the race in recent seasons, though Almanzor finished only seventh in this last year. They went a decent gallop thanks to Bay Of Poets, but the winner was in a different league. A big boost for the Dewhurst form, with the first two here finishing fourth and sixth behind Churchill at Newmarket.

7722a CRITERIUM DE SAINT-CLOUD (GROUP 1) (2YO COLTS & FILLIES) (TURF) 1m 2f

2:45 (12:00) 2-Y-O **£105,036** (£42,022; £21,011; £10,496; £5,257)

RPR

1 **Waldgeist**[22] 7169 2-9-0 0 Pierre-CharlesBoudot 8 113
(A Fabre, France) *w.w in midfield: drvn and c stands' side st: rdn 2f out: styd on u.p fr 1 1/2f out: led 125yds out and asserted* **10/1**[3]

2 *1* **Best Solution (IRE)**[22] 7148 2-9-0 0 ChristopheSoumillon 11 111
(Saeed bin Suroor) *settled in rr of midfield: clsd and towards c stands' side fr 2 1/2f out: drvn to ld 2f out: sn rdn and edgd rt wl over 1f out: styd on u.p: hdd fnl 125yds: no ex* **17/2**[2]

3 *1/2* **Capri (IRE)**[35] 6817 2-9-0 0 SeamieHeffernan 4 110+
(A P O'Brien, Ire) *settled in midfield: dropped towards rr 4f out: clsd ins fnl 3f and pushed along to chse ldrs fr 2 1/2f out towards centre of trck: styd on u.p fr over 1f out: nt pce to get on terms w ldrs* **10/11**[1]

4 *nk* **Douglas Macarthur (IRE)**[36] 6783 2-9-0 0 DonnachaO'Brien 6 110
(A P O'Brien, Ire) *a cl up outside two rivals: led after 4f: rdn and hdd turning for home more than 2 1/2f out: rallied u.p to chse ldrs: styd on at same pce fnl f* **18/1**

5 *1 1/4* **Taj Mahal (IRE)**[7] 7559 2-9-0 0 (b[1]) PBBeggy 3 108
(A P O'Brien, Ire) *led: hdd after 4f: remained cl up between horses: drvn to ld turning for home more than 2 1/2f out: hdd 2f out: responded gamely u.p to stay w ldrs: gave best fnl 100yds* **28/1**

6 *1 3/4* **Prinz Hlodowig (FR)**[22] 7169 2-9-0 0 VincentCheminaud 2 104
(M Delzangles, France) *a cl up ins two rivals: kpt on u.p fr 2f out: fdd ins last half f* **16/1**

7 *1/2* **Cunco (IRE)**[22] 7151 2-9-0 0 RobertHavlin 5 103
(John Gosden) *chsd ldrs: rdn to hold pl 2 1/2f out: nt qckn u.p fr 2f out: plugged on at one pce* **18/1**

8 *1 1/2* **Frankuus (IRE)**[22] 7169 2-9-0 0 IoritzMendizabal 1 101
(Mark Johnston) *settled in midfield on inner: drvn 3f out but no real imp: kpt on at one pce u.p fnl 2f: nvr really in contention* **11/1**

9 *nk* **Wings Of Eagles (FR)**[22] 7151 2-9-0 0 ColmO'Donoghue 7 100
(A P O'Brien, Ire) *w.w towards rr: last over 2 1/2f out: rdn and effrt over 2f out: clsd a little but nvr trbld ldrs: one pce u.p fnl f* **33/1**

10 *5* **Warring States (JPN)**[27] 2-9-0 0 MickaelBarzalona 13 91
(A Wohler, Germany) *racd in fnl trio: sltly hmpd and dropped to last 1/2-way: n.d* **22/1**

11 *shd* **D'bai (IRE)**[13] 7409 2-9-0 0 (p) WilliamBuick 9 91
(Charlie Appleby) *w.w in fnl trio: pushed along and no imp wl after 1/2-way: btn fnl 2f* **16/1**

12 *nk* **Rich Legacy (IRE)**[23] 7116 2-8-10 0 OisinMurphy 12 87
(Ralph Beckett) *racd in fnl trio: clsd 2 1/2f out towards centre of trck: sn rdn and nt qckn: dropped away ins fnl 1 1/2f* **18/1**

13 *1 1/4* **Rekindling**[42] 6603 2-9-0 0 WayneLordan 10 88
(David Wachman, Ire) *chsd ldrs: drvn and no imp over 3f out: sn btn and wl hld last 1 1/2f* **22/1**

2m 12.73s (-3.27) **Going Correction** -0.20s/f (Firm) **13** Ran SP% **123.0**
Speed ratings: **105,104,103,103,102 101,100,99,99,95 95,95,94**
WIN (incl. 1 euro stake): 4.70. PLACES: 1.60, 2.10, 1.30. DF: 19.90. SF: 35.80.
Owner Gestut Ammerland, Newsells Park Stud & Mrs John Ma **Bred** The Waldlerche Partnership **Trained** Chantilly, France

FOCUS
A truly international contest with five raiders from Britain, five from Ireland (four of them representing Aidan O'Brien) and one from Germany. There were just two from the home side, but one of them took this convincingly. Despite a three-way share of the early lead, the pace was ordinary and a few took a grip. It paid to be handy and again the nearside was the place to be after turning in, with the first two racing closest to the hedge.

7723a PRIX PERTH (GROUP 3) (3YO+) (TURF) 1m

3:15 (12:00) 3-Y-O+ **£29,411** (£11,764; £8,823; £5,882; £2,941)

RPR

1 **Siyoushake (IRE)**[29] 6949 4-9-0 0 StephanePasquier 13 115+
(F Head, France) *w.w in rr: last and drvn 2f out: hdwy to chse ldrs under 2f out: sltly hmpd under 1 1/2f out: styd on to ld 1f out: sn clr: comf* **5/1**[2]

2 *1 3/4* **Crazy Horse**[20] 7213 3-8-11 0 RobertHavlin 4 110
(John Gosden) *keen early: a cl up on outer: drvn to chal between horses 1 1/2f out: led briefly over 1f out: hdd 1f out: styd on but no match for wnr* **7/4**[1]

3 *hd* **Kourkan (FR)**[23] 7137 3-8-11 0 ChristopheSoumillon 7 110
(J-M Beguigne, France) *settled in midfield: rdn bhd front rnk towards stands' rail over 1 1/2f out: angled towards centre of trck and sltly impeded eventual wnr 1 1/2f out: styd on the chse ldrs 1f out: nt pce to match wnr* **5/1**[2]

4 *1 1/2* **Steip Amach (IRE)**[43] 4-9-0 0 GregoryBenoist 9 108+
(D Smaga, France) *settled towards rr: shkn up and hdwy 2f out: styd on u.p fr over 1f out: nvr on terms* **15/2**[3]

5 *3/4* **Maximum Aurelius (FR)**[35] 6823 3-8-11 0 Pierre-CharlesBoudot 3 105
(F-H Graffard, France) *led: brought field to stands' side in st: rdn and hdd 1 1/2f out: kpt on at one pce* **11/1**

6 *1 3/4* **Show Day (IRE)**[35] 6824 3-8-8 0 MickaelBarzalona 5 98
(H-A Pantall, France) *w.w in midfield on inner: clsd to chse ldrs appr 2f out: hrd rdn to ld 1 1/2f out: hdd over 1f out: cl 4th whn squezzed out and snatched up ins fnl f: nt rcvr* **12/1**

7 *1 1/4* **Sussudio (FR)**[28] 6992 6-9-0 0 UmbertoRispoli 10 99
(Frau Hella Sauer, Germany) *hld up towards rr: sme late hdwy u.p: nvr trbld ldrs* **18/1**

8 *1* **Royal Julius (IRE)**[17] 3-8-11 0 AntoineHamelin 6 96
(A De Watrigant, France) *cl up on outer: rdn and no imp 2f out: sn btn* **16/1**

9 *1 1/4* **Rosebay (GER)**[35] 6824 5-8-10 0 IoritzMendizabal 1 90
(Markus Klug, Germany) *bhd ldrs on inner: rdn and dropped away 1 1/2f out: wl hld fnl f* **50/1**

10 *3* **Pas De Soucis (IRE)**[16] 7348 3-8-8 0 RonanThomas 11 83
(Robert Collet, France) *keen: hld up towards rr: rdn and btn fr 2f out* **17/2**

11 *5* **Wanderina (IRE)**[38] 6728 3-8-8 0.............................. AurelienLemaitre 2 71
(F Head, France) *chsd ldr on inner: rdn and nt qckn 2f out: sn btn* **14/1**
1m 43.24s (-4.26) **Going Correction** -0.20s/f (Firm)
WFA 3 from 4yo+ 3lb **11** Ran SP% **127.8**
Speed ratings: **113,111,111,109,108 107,105,104,103,100 95**
WIN (incl. 1 euro stake): 5.50. PLACES: 1.70, 1.40, 1.70. DF: 9.50. SF: 16.80.
Owner Roy Racing Ltd & A Morley **Bred** Aleyrion Bloodstock Ltd **Trained** France

7266 SANTA ANITA (L-H)
Saturday, October 29

OFFICIAL GOING: Turf: firm

7724a AUTUMN MISS STKS (GRADE 3) (3YO FILLIES) (TURF) 1m (T)
11:59 (12:00) 3-Y-O

£40,816 (£13,605; £8,163; £4,081; £1,360; £234)

RPR
1 **Cover Song (USA)**[132] 3-8-8 0............................... KentJDesormeaux 4 97
(Carla Gaines, U.S.A) **31/1**
2 *nse* **Danilovna (IRE)**[106] 4356 3-8-8 0.. FlavienPrat 1 97
(H Graham Motion, U.S.A) **6/4**[1]
3 *½* **Barleysugar (IRE)**[69] 5693 3-8-10 0................................ GaryStevens 5 98
(Edward Freeman, U.S.A) **69/10**
4 *nk* **Lady Valeur (IRE)**[69] 5693 3-8-8 0............................(b) RafaelBejarano 3 95
(Patrick Gallagher, U.S.A) **57/10**[3]
5 *½* **Belvoir Bay**[27] 3-8-12 0... NorbertoArroyoJr 10 98
(Peter Miller, U.S.A) **33/10**[2]
6 *½* **Dreamarcher (USA)**[303] 3-8-10 0..............................(b) MarioGutierrez 9 95
(Jerry Hollendorfer, U.S.A) **18/1**
7 *½* **Nodiac (IRE)**[27] 3-8-8 0... SantiagoGonzalez 6 92
(Philip D'Amato, U.S.A) **31/5**
8 *3 ½* **Lookout Sister (USA)**[210] 3-8-10 0........................... MartinAPedroza 7 86
(Jerry Hollendorfer, U.S.A) **64/1**
9 *2 ¾* **Sweet Dragon Fly**[21] 7146 3-8-8 0............................... JosephTalamo 8 77
(Paul Cole) **32/1**
10 *1* **Great Page (IRE)**[136] 3274 3-8-10 0...................(b[1]) TiagoJosuePereira 2 77
(Jerry Hollendorfer, U.S.A) **50/1**
1m 33.73s (-0.14) **10** Ran SP% **119.6**

Owner Spendthrift Farm LLC **Bred** Misty For Me Syndicate **Trained** USA

7613 KEMPTON (A.W) (R-H)
Monday, October 31

OFFICIAL GOING: Polytrack: standard to slow (the racing was abandoned after race 3 (3.20) due to injured jockeys)
Wind: Nil Weather: Fine, very mild

7725 100% PROFIT BOOST AT 32REDSPORT.COM H'CAP 7f (P)
2:20 (2:22) (Class 5) (0-70,70) 3-Y-O **£2,911** (£866; £432; £216) **Stalls** Low

Form RPR
2331 1 **Encore Moi**[21] 7203 3-9-2 **65**..(b) AndreaAtzeni 7 73
(Marco Botti) *hld up in midfield: stdy prog on inner fr over 2f out: chal fnl f: drvn ahd last 50yds* **3/1**[2]
5321 2 *nk* **Simply Me**[10] 7513 3-9-0 **63**....................................(p) RichardKingscote 3 70
(Tom Dascombe) *trckd ldr after 2f: gng wl over 2f out: shkn up to ld over 1f out: styd on fnl f but hdd last 50yds* **5/2**[1]
3 *½* **Plus Night (FR)**[162] 3-9-4 **67**... PatCosgrave 10 73
(Stuart Williams) *stdd s: hld up in last trio: pushed along and gd prog on outer jst over 2f out: pressed ldrs jst over 1f out: sn rdn and nt qckn: styd on nr fin but nvr really chal* **14/1**
6003 4 *2 ¾* **Caledonia Duchess**[30] 6960 3-9-7 **70**.................................... JoeyHaynes 5 68
(Jo Hughes) *awkward s: hld up in rr: rdn over 2f out: sme prog whn short of room briefly over 1f out: kpt on to take 4th last strides: n.d* **33/1**
6452 5 *¾* **Many Dreams (IRE)**[41] 6649 3-9-0 **66**.................. JosephineGordon(3) 8 62
(Mark Usher) *trckd ldrs: prog to ld 2f out: hdd over 1f out: fdd fnl f* **7/1**
066 6 *2 ¾* **Sexton Blake (IRE)**[44] 6592 3-8-11 **63**....................... HectorCrouch(3) 4 52
(Gary Moore) *trckd ldrs: shifted lft 2f out: rdn and no imp over 1f out: wknd fnl f* **5/1**[3]
-140 7 *5* **Sakhee's Jem**[16] 7364 3-9-4 **67**...................................... DougieCostello 9 42
(Gay Kelleway) *in tch in midfield: shkn up whn hmpd wl over 1f out: nt rcvr and wknd* **50/1**
10 8 *1* **Harmony Bay (IRE)**[44] 6592 3-9-2 **70**....................... MitchGodwin(5) 12 43
(Sylvester Kirk) *towards rr: rdn on outer 3f out: no prog* **33/1**
2220 9 *1 ½* **Sonnet (IRE)**[84] 5247 3-9-3 **66**.. AdamKirby 11 35
(David Evans) *v s.i.s: pushed along and detached in last: nvr a factor* **25/1**
0020 10 *1* **Flying Sakhee**[21] 7212 3-8-7 **56** oh4...............................[1] DannyBrock 6 22
(John Bridger) *chsd ldr 2f: rdn 1/2-way: wknd over 2f out* **66/1**
0353 11 *4* **Mockinbird (IRE)**[18] 7301 3-9-4 **67**..............................(b[1]) RyanPowell 2 22
(Sir Mark Prescott Bt) *led at str pce to 2f out: wknd rapidly* **8/1**
1m 25.16s (-0.84) **Going Correction** +0.025s/f (Slow) **11** Ran SP% **113.7**
Speed ratings (Par 101): **105,104,104,100,100 96,91,90,88,87 82**
CSF £9.99 CT £88.33 TOTE £3.80: £1.50, £1.10, £2.80; EX 11.00 Trifecta £48.30.
Owner Scuderia Vittadini Srl **Bred** Scuderia Vittadini Srl **Trained** Newmarket, Suffolk

FOCUS
The going was standard to slow. A modest 3yo handicap with a field consisting mainly of fillies and they filled the first two positions.

7726 BREEDERS SUPPORTING RACING EBF MAIDEN STKS (PLUS 10 RACE) (SIRE-RESTRICTED RACE) 7f (P)
2:50 (2:50) (Class 4) 2-Y-O **£6,469** (£1,925; £962; £481) **Stalls** Low

Form RPR
234 1 **Dick Tracy (IRE)**[19] 7283 2-9-5 81...................................... SeanLevey 1 81
(Richard Hannon) *led at mod pce: rdn and hdd wl over 1f out: styd pressing ldr and narrow advantage again ins fnl f: hld on wl* **7/2**[2]
3 2 *hd* **Yalawin (IRE)**[10] 7502 2-9-5 0....................................... AndreaAtzeni 2 80
(Roger Varian) *trckd ldrs: pushed into ld wl over 1f out: move nt decisive and narrowly hdd ins fnl f: nt qckn last 75yds* **5/6**[1]
3 *½* **Next Challenge (GER)** 2-9-5 0.. JimCrowley 4 79+
(Saeed bin Suroor) *hld up in rr: shkn up and prog over 2f out: chsd ldng pair over 1f out: rdn and styd on to to press them nr fin but nvr really got there* **5/1**[3]
0 4 *3 ¼* **Mafaaheem (IRE)**[44] 6577 2-9-5 0..................................... DaneO'Neill 3 70
(Owen Burrows) *t.k.h: trckd ldrs: cl enough jst over 2f out: racd awkwardly and fdd tamely over 1f out* **10/1**
06 5 *6* **Perla Blanca (USA)**[44] 6570 2-9-0 0.............................. SteveDrowne 5 49
(Marcus Tregoning) *in tch in rr tl outpcd over 2f out: no ch after* **66/1**
4 6 *2 ¾* **Jake's Hill**[26] 7074 2-9-5 0... TomQueally 6 46
(Eve Johnson Houghton) *mostly chsd wnr to over 2f out: hanging and wknd qckly* **14/1**
00 7 *1 ¾* **Imphal**[73] 5600 2-9-5 0.. MartinDwyer 8 42
(Marcus Tregoning) *racd on outer: in tch: wknd over 2f out* **66/1**
1m 26.74s (0.74) **Going Correction** +0.025s/f (Slow) **7** Ran SP% **112.2**
Speed ratings (Par 97): **96,95,95,91,84 81,79**
CSF £6.49 TOTE £3.90: £1.50, £1.30; EX 7.70 Trifecta £19.60.
Owner John Manley **Bred** Ballylinch Stud **Trained** East Everleigh, Wilts

FOCUS
An interesting juvenile maiden run 1.58 secs slower than the opening handicap due to an ordinary early gallop and the market leaders had it between them. The winner has been rated near his pre-race best.

7727 BREEDERS BACKING RACING EBF MAIDEN FILLIES' STKS 1m (P)
3:20 (3:26) (Class 5) 3-Y-O+ **£4,204** (£1,251; £625; £312) **Stalls** Low

Form RPR
2-22 1 **Madame Butterfly (IRE)**[175] 2094 4-9-3 75.............. GrahamGibbons 2 82
(David O'Meara) *taken down early: mde all: rdn wl clr fr 2f out: unchal* **9/4**[2]
506 2 *8* **Cutty Sark**[19] 7272 3-9-0 62... PatCosgrave 5 63
(Luca Cumani) *trckd wnr 3f: lft in 2nd again 1/2-way: rdn and easily outpcd fr 2f out* **9/1**
3 3 *2* **Tanzania Road (USA)**[69] 5735 3-9-0 0........................... MartinHarley 7 58+
(James Tate) *s.i.s: in rr: hmpd in melee 1/2-way: effrt to take 3rd wl over 1f out: no imp after* **8/1**
3 4 *2 ¾* **Issue**[40] 6674 3-9-0 0.. DanielMuscutt 6 52+
(James Fanshawe) *hld up in midfield: bdly hmpd in melee 1/2-way: no ch after* **2/1**[1]
5 *1 ¼* **Imasumaq (IRE)** 3-8-9 0..[1] GeorgeWood(5) 11 49+
(Marco Botti) *wl in rr: forced wd in melee 1/2-way: nvr on terms* **33/1**
0 6 *1 ¼* **Annabella**[18] 7311 3-9-0 0.. RyanTate 3 46
(Tim McCarthy) *reluctant to enter stall: dwlt: towards rr: lft in 3rd in melee 1/2-way: wknd 2f out* **66/1**
55 7 *1 ¾* **Rianna Star**[41] 6661 3-8-11 0.................................... HectorCrouch(3) 12 42
(Gary Moore) *racd on outer: hmpd in melee 1/2-way: bhd after* **66/1**
00 8 *18* **Miss Geronimo**[40] 6674 4-9-3 0................................. FergusSweeney 9
(Ken Cunningham-Brown) *in rr whn forced wd in melee 1/2-way: t.o* **66/1**
4065 F **Nellie Deen (IRE)**[5] 7611 3-9-0 65...............................[1] FrederikTylicki 1
(David Elsworth) *prom: trckd wnr after 3f: cl up on inner and sing to take t.k.h whn stmbld and fell 1/2-way* **14/1**
54 U **Sovrano Dolce (IRE)**[21] 7219 3-9-0 0............................... TedDurcan 8
(Mike Murphy) *in rr tl bdly hmpd and uns rdr in melee 1/2-way* **33/1**
40 B **Skara Mae (IRE)**[152] 2790 3-9-0 0............................... SteveDrowne 10
(Charles Hills) *in rr tl b.d in melee 1/2-way* **50/1**
543 B **Electrify (IRE)**[21] 7219 3-9-0 66.. JimCrowley 4
(Jeremy Noseda) *trckd ldrs: cl 4th whn b.d in melee 1/2-way* **5/1**[3]
1m 39.3s (-0.50) **Going Correction** +0.025s/f (Slow)
WFA 3 from 4yo 3lb **12** Ran SP% **120.9**
Speed ratings (Par 100): **103,95,93,90,89 87,86,68, ,**
CSF £22.59 TOTE £3.00: £1.10, £2.60, £2.30; EX 22.30 Trifecta £137.00.
Owner Sir Robert Ogden **Bred** Sir Robert Ogden **Trained** Upper Helmsley, N Yorks

FOCUS
A modest looking older horse fillies' maiden, but the complexion of the race changed following a melee on the home turn. Racing was subsequently abandoned just before 5pm. The level is a bit fluid. The winner has been rated back to the level of her debut form.

7728 32RED ON THE APP STORE H'CAP 1m (P)
(3:50) (Class 4) (0-85,) 3-Y-O £

7729 32RED.COM H'CAP 1m (P)
(4:20) (Class 3) (0-95,) 4-Y-O+

£

7730 32RED LONDON MIDDLE DISTANCE FINAL H'CAP 1m 3f (P)
(4:50) (Class 2) 3-Y-O+

£

7731 32RED CASINO H'CAP 7f (P)
(5:20) (Class 4) (0-85,) 4-Y-O+ £

T/Jkpt: £169.10. Pool of £26381.87 - 156.00 winning units. T/Plt: £3.70 to a £1 stake. Pool of £77622.88 - 15090.43 winning units. T/Qpdt: £1.80 to a £1 stake. Pool of £6819.30 - 2729.29 winning units. **Jonathan Neesom**

7725 KEMPTON (A.W) (R-H)
Tuesday, November 1

OFFICIAL GOING: Polytrack: standard to slow
Wind: Moderate, across towards stands Weather: Cloudy, becoming cold

7732 32RED AMATEUR RIDERS' H'CAP 1m 4f (P)
4:40 (4:41) (Class 4) (0-80,80) 3-Y-O+ **£4,523** (£1,402; £701; £350) **Stalls** Low

Form RPR
2550 1 **Safira Menina**[33] 6892 4-9-11 **68**.. MrBJames(5) 1 77
(Martin Smith) *t.k.h towards rr: rdn over 2f out: rapid hdwy over 1f out: str run to ld 50yds out: won gng away* **33/1**
5531 2 *1 ¾* **Ride The Lightning**[14] 7429 3-10-2 **74**.............................. MrSWalker 5 80
(Archie Watson) *prom: wnt 2nd 4f out: led over 1f out tl 50yds out: one pce* **11/8**[1]
0050 3 *nk* **Street Artist (IRE)**[61] 6050 6-10-9 **80**........................ MrJJO'Neill(5) 11 85
(David Nicholls) *prom: disp ld after 2f: led 5f out tl over 1f out: ev ch ins fnl f: one pce fnl 50yds* **12/1**
1U22 4 *1* **Jersey Jewel (FR)**[11] 7508 4-10-0 **71**................. MissCAGreenway(5) 2 74
(Tom Dascombe) *chsd ldrs: wnt 3rd 2f out: pressed ldrs ins fnl f: one pce* **12/1**

421 **5** *5* **Flower Of Love**[38] 6765 3-10-4 **76**..........................(t) MissSBrotherton 10 71
(Simon Crisford) *prom: rdn and struggling to hold pl 4f out: styd on same pce fnl 3f* **5/1**[2]
0515 **6** *nk* **Fern Owl**[18] 7320 4-10-2 **73**..(b) MrRPooles(5) 9 68
(Hughie Morrison) *mid-div: hdwy on outer 4f out: outpcd fnl 2f* **6/1**[3]
3002 **7** *nk* **Sennockian Song**[10] 7531 3-8-13 **62**................. MissEmmaBedford(5) 7 56
(Mark Johnston) *led for 2f then disp ld tl 5f out: outpcd and btn 3f out* **10/1**
2100 **8** *3/4* **Knight Of The Air**[11] 7508 4-9-8 **67**............................. MrsCPownall(7) 3 60
(Joseph Tuite) *t.k.h in 6th: outpcd 3f out: sn btn* **100/1**
4443 **9** *4* **Dakota City**[92] 4940 5-10-11 **77**..................................(v) MrRBirkett 4 63
(Julia Feilden) *bhd: modest hdwy and hrd rdn 2f out: no further prog* **18/1**
15-0 **10** *8* **Night Generation (GER)**[23] 7183 4-10-1 **74**.........(p) MissGLDouble(7) 6 48
(Chris Gordon) *sn towards rr: no ch fnl 3f* **50/1**
6463 **11** *22* **Spice Fair**[96] 4795 9-10-9 **78**.. MrHHunt(3) 8 16
(Mark Usher) *stdd s: a bhd: no ch fnl 3f* **12/1**
0460 **12** *7* **Star Anise (FR)**[52] 6335 5-9-2 **61** oh16..................(t) MissJMOlliver(7) 12
(Paddy Butler) *a bhd: no ch fnl 3f* **100/1**

2m 34.77s (0.27) **Going Correction** +0.025s/f (Slow)
WFA 3 from 4yo+ 6lb **12** Ran SP% **117.4**
Speed ratings (Par 105): **100,98,98,97,94 94,94,93,91,85 71,66**
CSF £77.97 CT £625.92 TOTE £88.60: £10.00, £1.20, £3.30; EX 235.80 Trifecta £2933.30.
Owner Four Winds Racing Partnership **Bred** Hascombe And Valiant Studs **Trained** Newmarket, Suffolk

FOCUS
A fairly decent amateur riders' middle-distance handicap. They went an initially modest gallop on standard to slow Polytrack. A confirmed hold-up horse managed to come home with a rare rattle, though, to reel in the more prominently-ridden front two, who got into a real scrap from over 2f out. The fourth helps with the opening level.

7733 32RED CASINO MAIDEN AUCTION STKS 7f (P)
5:10 (5:12) (Class 5) 2-Y-O **£2,911** (£866; £432; £216) **Stalls** Low

Form RPR
0 **1** **Black Bolt (IRE)**[11] 7502 2-9-2 0..................................... TimmyMurphy 4 84+
(Richard Hannon) *prom: led jst over 1f out: pushed clr* **1/1**[1]
2 *3 1/4* **Evening Hill** 2-9-1 0.. ShaneKelly 12 72+
(Richard Hughes) *chsd ldrs: effrt 2f out: styd on to take 2nd fnl 50yds* **20/1**
0 **3** *3/4* **Bahamian Paradise**[23] 7184 2-8-10 0............................ DavidProbert 13 65
(Hughie Morrison) *t.k.h: led tl jst over 1f out: no ex ins fnl f* **20/1**
45 **4** *2 1/4* **Power Home (IRE)**[50] 6421 2-8-4 0.......................... MeganNicholls(5) 2 58
(Denis Coakley) *mid-div: hdwy 2f out: styd on same pce* **7/1**[3]
5 *1* **Elusive Olivia (USA)** 2-8-10 0...[1] JFEgan 8 56+
(Joseph Tuite) *wnt lft and bmpd s: towards rr: rdn 3f out: styd on fnl 2f* **16/1**
0 **6** *1 1/4* **Forest Steps (IRE)**[34] 6867 2-8-3 0................................ HollieDoyle(5) 3 51
(J S Moore) *t.k.h: chsd ldrs tl outpcd fnl 2f* **25/1**
7 *1 1/4* **Ede's E Rider** 2-8-13 0.. KieranO'Neill 5 53
(Pat Phelan) *wnt lft s and missed break: nvr rchd ldrs* **50/1**
0 **8** *shd* **Highland Clearance (FR)**[14] 7439 2-8-10 0........................ JackMitchell 1 50
(Giles Bravery) *t.k.h towards rr: hdwy on inner 2f out: no ex over 1f out* **25/1**
9 *1/2* **Chough** 2-8-9 0.. LiamKeniry 6 47
(Hughie Morrison) *dwlt: nvr trbld ldrs* **20/1**
10 *1/2* **Settle Petal** 2-8-1 0.. SophieRalston(7) 14 45
(Pat Phelan) *s.s: hld up in rr: shkn up 2f out: n.d* **100/1**
11 *1 1/4* **Royal Sentiment (IRE)** 2-9-1 0.................................. WilliamCarson 11 49
(Jamie Osborne) *chsd ldrs tl wknd over 2f out* **16/1**
12 *1/2* **Prosecution** 2-9-1 0.. JimmyFortune 7 47
(Hughie Morrison) *dwlt and sltly hmpd s: bmpd after 1f: a bhd* **14/1**
13 *2* **Pleasure Requested (IRE)** 2-9-1 0.................................. JohnFahy 10 42
(Eve Johnson Houghton) *sn rdn up to chse ldr: wknd 2f out* **6/1**[2]
14 *11* **Sajah (IRE)** 2-8-6 0.. HectorCrouch(3) 9 8
(Harry Dunlop) *bmpd s: plld hrd: in tch tl rn wd and wknd ent st* **25/1**

1m 27.12s (1.12) **Going Correction** +0.025s/f (Slow) **14** Ran SP% **124.0**
Speed ratings (Par 96): **94,90,89,86,85 84,82,82,82,81 80,79,77,64**
CSF £30.74 TOTE £1.80: £1.10, £4.80, £6.20; EX 22.10 Trifecta £427.30.
Owner J Palmer-Brown/Potensis B'Stock & Ptnr **Bred** Tommy Burns **Trained** East Everleigh, Wilts

FOCUS
An ordinary juvenile maiden in terms of prior form, but the winner was entitled to come on considerably from his Newbury debut on good to soft the previous month, and ran out a taking winner.

7734 RACETECH 70TH ANNIVERSARY NURSERY H'CAP 1m (P)
5:40 (5:40) (Class 6) (0-60,60) 2-Y-O **£2,264** (£673; £336; £168) **Stalls** Low

Form RPR
656 **1** **Rake's Progress**[29] 7012 2-9-6 **59**.................................. JackMitchell 10 63
(Heather Main) *mde all: rdn over 2f out: hld on wl fnl f* **9/2**[2]
4406 **2** *1 1/2* **Dominating (GER)**[32] 6923 2-9-7 **60**.............................. DaneO'Neill 13 61+
(Mark Johnston) *dwlt: t.k.h: hdwy to chse wnr after 2f: n.m.r and swtchd rt over 1f out: kpt on same pce* **5/1**[3]
0006 **3** *nse* **Topmeup**[12] 7482 2-8-13 **52**.. JFEgan 5 53
(Stuart Edmunds) *mid-div: hdwy to dispute 2nd over 1f out: kpt on same pce* **6/1**
6004 **4** *3/4* **Masquerade Bling (IRE)**[14] 7423 2-9-7 **60**................... KieranO'Neill 14 59
(Simon Hodgson) *t.k.h towards rr: rdn over 2f out: nrest at fin* **8/1**
400 **5** *1 1/2* **Beepeecee**[33] 6888 2-9-3 **56**... ShaneKelly 12 52
(Richard Hughes) *chsd ldrs: effrt over 2f out: no ex fnl f* **9/1**
0430 **6** *1/2* **Ultimat Power (IRE)**[8] 7570 2-8-9 **48**...................(b) AdamBeschizza 9 42
(Mark Hoad) *prom tl hrd rdn and btn over 1f out* **20/1**
066 **7** *nk* **Gog Elles (IRE)**[26] 7098 2-8-7 **46**..................................... RyanPowell 1 40
(J S Moore) *towards rr: rdn over 2f out: styd on fnl f* **33/1**
0005 **8** *1 1/4* **Maysonri**[21] 7244 2-9-0 **53**... LiamKeniry 3 44
(Mark Hoad) *s.s: bhd: rdn 3f out: nvr rchd ldrs* **14/1**
4406 **9** *1 1/4* **Primrose Place**[28] 7047 2-9-5 **58**..............................(t) SeanLevey 4 46
(Richard Hannon) *mid-div: effrt and in tch 2f out: hrd rdn and wknd 1f out* **7/2**[1]
0000 **10** *3 3/4* **Hollow Crown**[31] 6963 2-8-10 **49**...............................(v[1]) JohnFahy 2 28
(Denis Coakley) *dwlt: a bhd* **33/1**
0065 **11** *15* **Pemberley House (IRE)**[50] 6420 2-9-2 **55**...................... JimmyFortune 8
(Paul D'Arcy) *prom tl wknd qckly wl over 1f out: eased whn no ch fnl f* **12/1**

1m 40.89s (1.09) **Going Correction** +0.025s/f (Slow) **11** Ran SP% **117.5**
Speed ratings (Par 94): **95,93,93,92,91 90,90,89,87,84 69**
CSF £26.66 CT £137.31 TOTE £6.30: £2.10, £2.80, £2.10; EX 34.20 Trifecta £218.10.
Owner Coxwell Partnership **Bred** Mr & Mrs A E Pakenham **Trained** Kingston Lisle, Oxon

FOCUS
A modest nursery handicap. The winner was likely to appreciate the return to the AW here and toughed it out from the front out of a wide draw. Those close up behind the winner suggest this is ordinary form.

7735 RACETECH CELEBRATES 70YRS SERVING HORSE RACING H'CAP (DIV I) 1m (P)
6:10 (6:10) (Class 6) (0-65,65) 3-Y-O+ **£2,264** (£673; £336; £168) **Stalls** Low

Form RPR
3145 **1** **Music Major**[28] 7035 3-9-2 **62**....................................... AdamBeschizza 1 67
(Michael Attwater) *prom: led 1f out: rdn out* **2/1**[2]
0325 **2** *1* **Rebel State (IRE)**[21] 7257 3-9-3 **63**.................................. DaneO'Neill 5 66
(Richard Spencer) *chsd ldrs: rdn over 2f out: styd on take 2nd ins fnl f* **15/8**[1]
213 **3** *1/2* **Bloodsweatandtears**[28] 7036 8-9-5 **63**............................. AmirQuinn 2 65
(William Knight) *t.k.h in 5th: effrt over 1f out: styd on fnl f* **6/1**[3]
4300 **4** *1 3/4* **Jessica Jo (IRE)**[16] 7385 3-9-0 **60**..................................(b[1]) JFEgan 10 58
(Mark Johnston) *chsd ldrs: rdn 1/2-way: led 2f out tl 1f out: no ex fnl f* **25/1**
0206 **5** *1/2* **Spirit Of Gondree (IRE)**[11] 7514 8-9-2 **60**..................(b) PatCosgrave 9 56
(Milton Bradley) *hld up in rr: rdn 3f out: nvr rchd ldrs* **9/1**
1045 **6** *6* **Prim And Proper**[6] 7620 5-9-4 **62**...........................(b) DanielMuscutt 4 45
(John Flint) *led tl 2f out: wknd over 1f out* **8/1**
3000 **7** *1* **Ron's Ballad**[19] 7298 3-8-5 **51** oh6.. KieranO'Neill 6 31
(Michael Madgwick) *dwlt: bhd: drvn along and sme hdwy on inner over 2f out: sn wknd* **80/1**

1m 40.8s (1.00) **Going Correction** +0.025s/f (Slow)
WFA 3 from 4yo+ 2lb **7** Ran SP% **108.6**
Speed ratings (Par 101): **96,95,94,92,92 86,85**
CSF £5.45 CT £14.22 TOTE £2.70: £2.30, £1.40; EX 6.20 Trifecta £18.70.
Owner The Attwater Partnership & J Daniels **Bred** Kevin Daniel Crabb **Trained** Epsom, Surrey

FOCUS
The first division of a modest handicap and the winning time was notably slower.

7736 RACETECH CELEBRATES 70YRS SERVING HORSE RACING H'CAP (DIV II) 1m (P)
6:40 (6:41) (Class 6) (0-65,64) 3-Y-O+ **£2,264** (£673; £336; £168) **Stalls** Low

Form RPR
1050 **1** **Ebbisham (IRE)**[101] 4641 3-9-3 **62**...................................... PatCosgrave 7 69
(Jim Boyle) *trckd ldr: led 2f out: rdn clr fnl f: comf* **13/2**
006 **2** *2 1/2* **Captain Courageous (IRE)**[19] 7311 3-9-4 **63**.................. GeorgeBaker 2 64+
(Ed Walker) *hld up towards rr: shkn up and hdwy over 1f out: r.o to take 2nd nr fin* **6/4**[1]
5-00 **3** *1/2* **Suitsus**[113] 4202 5-9-1 **58**.. TimmyMurphy 5 58
(Geoffrey Deacon) *hld up in 5th: hdwy to chse wnr over 1f out: one pce: lost 2nd nr fin* **33/1**
605 **4** *1 1/4* **Saleh (IRE)**[22] 7218 3-9-0 **64**......................................(e) PaddyBradley(5) 4 61
(Lee Carter) *chsd ldrs: rdn over 2f out: one pce* **7/1**
5005 **5** *2 1/2* **Gavarnie Encore**[14] 7427 4-8-7 **50**...................................(p) KieranO'Neill 8 41
(Michael Blanshard) *nvr gng wl in rr: nvr rchd ldrs* **5/1**[3]
0101 **6** *3* **Candesta (USA)**[14] 7426 6-9-3 **60**.................................. AdamBeschizza 9 45
(Julia Feilden) *led tl 2f out: wknd over 1f out* **4/1**[2]
04 **7** *1* **Welsh Inlet (IRE)**[14] 7426 8-8-7 **50** oh3......................... WilliamCarson 3 32
(John Bridger) *chsd ldrs tl wknd 2f out* **16/1**

1m 39.1s (-0.70) **Going Correction** +0.025s/f (Slow)
WFA 3 from 4yo+ 2lb **7** Ran SP% **111.3**
Speed ratings (Par 101): **104,101,101,99,97 94,93**
CSF £15.83 CT £286.82 TOTE £6.90: £2.70, £1.60; EX 19.60 Trifecta £188.30.
Owner The 'In Recovery' Partnership **Bred** John Quigley **Trained** Epsom, Surrey

FOCUS
The second division of a modest handicap. They went a decent gallop and the winning time was notably quicker. The winner has been rated back to this year's Bath form.

7737 32RED.COM H'CAP 6f (P)
7:10 (7:13) (Class 4) (0-85,85) 3-Y-O+ **£4,690** (£1,395; £697; £348) **Stalls** Low

Form RPR
2143 **1** **Mazzini**[32] 6916 3-9-6 **84**... GeorgeBaker 4 97+
(James Fanshawe) *hld up towards rr: hdwy over 1f out: led ins fnl f: rdn out* **15/8**[1]
5604 **2** *2* **Brilliant Vanguard (IRE)**[13] 7461 3-9-1 **79**........................ ShaneGray 3 86
(Kevin Ryan) *prom: wnt 2nd 2f out: unable qck fnl f* **11/2**[3]
1106 **3** *2* **Fang**[48] 6492 3-9-3 **81**.. DavidProbert 2 82
(William Jarvis) *led tl ins fnl f: no ex* **8/1**
21-0 **4** *3/4* **Tailwind**[14] 7443 3-9-2 **80**.. AndreaAtzeni 6 78
(Roger Varian) *sn chsng clr ldrs: effrt 2f out: one pce fnl f* **9/2**[2]
0000 **5** *3/4* **Rio Ronaldo (IRE)**[14] 7443 4-9-6 **84**............................ RobertWinston 11 80
(Mike Murphy) *sltly hmpd s and missed break: t.k.h towards rr: rdn and hdwy over 1f out: nvr rchd ldrs* **14/1**
4331 **6** *1 1/4* **Interlink (USA)**[22] 7207 3-9-0 **78**..................................... PatCosgrave 9 70
(Tony Coyle) *chsd ldr tl wknd 2f out* **10/1**
0140 **7** *nk* **Pandar**[22] 7221 7-9-1 **79**.. KierenFox 7 70
(Michael Attwater) *mid-div: rdn and lost pl over 3f out: sn struggling* **33/1**
363R **8** *2* **Bahamian Heights**[28] 7054 5-8-10 **77**............................... EoinWalsh(3) 1 61
(Robert Cowell) *dwlt: nvr trbld ldrs* **33/1**
0-00 **9** *1/2* **Picture Dealer**[43] 6627 7-9-3 **84**.................................. SimonPearce(3) 8 67
(Lydia Pearce) *dwlt and rdn s: mid-div on rail after 2f: effrt 2f out: btn over 1f out* **25/1**
000 **10** *13* **Townsville**[85] 5224 4-9-4 **82**.......................................(v[1]) PhillipMakin 10 23
(Keith Dalgleish) *chsd clr ldrs tl wknd over 2f out* **20/1**
0050 **11** *4 1/2* **Field Of Vision (IRE)**[31] 6944 3-9-0 **85**......................... SeanMooney(7) 5 12
(Joseph Tuite) *mid-div tl wknd 3f out* **25/1**

1m 11.64s (-1.46) **Going Correction** +0.025s/f (Slow) **11** Ran SP% **113.6**
Speed ratings (Par 105): **110,107,104,103,102 101,100,97,97,79 73**
CSF £10.41 CT £64.01 TOTE £2.40: £1.20, £2.30, £3.00; EX 11.90 Trifecta £69.90.
Owner Mr & Mrs P Hopper, Mr & Mrs M Morris **Bred** Jan & Peter Hopper **Trained** Newmarket, Suffolk

FOCUS
The feature contest was a decent sprint handicap. They went a proper gallop and the form should work out well. The runner-up has been rated to his best.

7738 32RED ON THE APP STORE H'CAP 7f (P)
7:40 (7:41) (Class 5) (0-75,75) 3-Y-O+ **£2,911** (£866; £432; £216) **Stalls** Low

Form RPR
5023 **1** **Veeraya**[34] 6872 6-8-7 **61**..(t) AdamBeschizza 12 68
(Julia Feilden) *chsd ldrs: drvn to ld ins fnl f: rdn out* **16/1**

5500 **2** ½ **Russian Reward (IRE)**[11] 7506 4-9-3 **71**.......................... JackMitchell 9 77
(Amanda Perrett) *in tch on inner: hmpd on 1st bnd: effrt and hrd rdn over 1f out: styd on fnl f* **16/1**

0200 **3** nk **Qortaaj**[80] 5386 3-8-11 **66**.......................................[1] JohnFahy 13 70
(David Loughnane) *led: hrd rdn and hdd ins fnl f: kpt on* **40/1**

1203 **4** ½ **Consulting**[27] 7066 3-9-6 **75**.. GeorgeBaker 5 78+
(Martyn Meade) *mid-div on inner: hmpd on 1st bnd: styd on wl fr over 1f out* **11/10**[1]

5204 **5** hd **Severus (GER)**[16] 7391 6-9-7 **75**................................ DavidProbert 7 78
(Des Donovan, Ire) *mid-div on outer: hdwy 2f out: styd on fnl f* **7/1**[3]

2125 **6** 3¾ **Let's Twist**[24] 7141 4-9-6 **74**...(b) ShaneGray 6 67
(Kristin Stubbs) *prom tl wknd over 1f out* **9/4**[2]

020 **7** 2½ **Picket Line**[91] 4990 4-9-7 **75**..................................... LiamKeniry 3 61
(Geoffrey Deacon) *t.k.h in midfield: outpcd over 2f out: n.d after* **12/1**

2060 **8** ¾ **Good Luck Charm**[19] 7301 7-9-3 **74**......................(b) HectorCrouch[(3)] 11 58
(Gary Moore) *dwlt: hld up in rr: hrd rdn 2f out: nvr rchd ldrs* **20/1**

0460 **9** nse **Take A Note**[19] 7301 7-9-5 **73**.......................(v) DanielMuscutt 1 57
(Patrick Chamings) *towards rr on inner: hmpd on 1st bnd: n.d* **14/1**

4605 **10** ¾ **Engaging Smile**[41] 6668 4-8-10 **64**................................ JoeyHaynes 10 46
(J Moon, Jersey) *prom tl wknd wl over 1f out* **50/1**

5066 **11** 2¾ **Lucky Di**[17] 7364 6-9-0 **68**.. TomMarquand 8 43
(Peter Hedger) *a bhd* **33/1**

6154 **12** 1¾ **Posh Bounty**[11] 7506 5-9-6 **74**... JFEgan 4 44
(Joseph Tuite) *dwlt: in tch in 5th after 2f: wknd over 2f out* **12/1**

0000 **13** 8 **Quintus Cerialis (IRE)**[59] 6138 4-9-0 **68**...................(p) TimmyMurphy 2 16
(Karen George) *bhd: sme hdwy on inner 2f out: wknd over 1f out* **33/1**

1m 25.37s (-0.63) **Going Correction** +0.025s/f (Slow)
WFA 3 from 4yo+ 1lb **13** Ran SP% **139.7**
Speed ratings (Par 103): **104,103,103,102,102 98,95,94,94,93 90,88,79**
CSF £273.07 CT £5467.96 TOTE £17.30: £4.20, £5.40, £10.00; EX 578.80 Trifecta £4012.10 Part won..
Owner Ahamed Farook **Bred** Roan Rocket Partners **Trained** Exning, Suffolk

FOCUS
A fair handicap. They went a decent gallop. It's been rated as ordinary form.

7739 100% PROFIT BOOST AT 32REDSPORT.COM H'CAP 2m (P)
8:10 (8:11) (Class 6) (0-65,69) 3-Y-0+ **£2,264** (£673; £336; £168) **Stalls** Low

Form RPR

4050 **1** **Delagoa Bay (IRE)**[11] 7507 8-9-1 **53**......................... EdwardGreatrex[(3)] 1 61
(Sylvester Kirk) *mid-div: hdwy on inner 3f out: clsd on clr ldr and led over 1f out: styd on wl* **16/1**

000 **2** 2 **Buckle Street**[50] 6415 3-9-3 **61**..(t) TomMarquand 14 67
(Martin Keighley) *wl bhd tl gd hdwy fnl 2f: tk 2nd ins fnl f* **16/1**

0502 **3** 4 **Endive**[20] 7270 4-10-0 **63**..(t) PatCosgrave 13 64
(Robert Stephens) *hld up in 5th: outpcd over 3f out: styd on to take 3rd ins fnl f* **15/2**[3]

2-01 **4** ¾ **Halling's Wish**[6] 7614 6-9-13 **69** 6ex...........................(b) JoshuaBryan[(7)] 4 69
(Gary Moore) *hld up in 6th: effrt and hrd rdn over 2f out: styd on same pce* **7/2**[1]

6213 **5** hd **Hiorne Tower (FR)**[54] 6245 5-9-11 **60**................................... KierenFox 5 60
(John Best) *led: wnt 10 l clr 4f out: sn rdn along: hdd & wknd over 1f out* **11/2**[2]

4350 **6** 6 **Dellbuoy**[28] 7039 7-8-7 **49**... SophieRalston[(7)] 3 41
(Pat Phelan) *prom: chsd ldr after 5f until wknd 2f out* **16/1**

40-2 **7** 1¼ **Londonia**[52] 6335 4-9-8 **60**..(t) RobHornby[(3)] 2 51
(Graeme McPherson) *towards rr: drvn along 3f out: nvr nr ldrs* **7/2**[1]

5000 **8** 2¼ **Last Summer**[64] 5958 5-9-0 **54**................................... CiaranMckee[(5)] 10 42
(Grace Harris) *mid-div: rdn 3f out: sn wknd* **66/1**

-650 **9** 4½ **Maison Brillet (IRE)**[230] 950 9-9-13 **62**......................(p) JackMitchell 8 45
(Clive Drew) *dwlt: towards rr: rdn 3f out: n.d* **40/1**

64-4 **10** 4½ **Newtown Cross (IRE)**[251] 695 6-8-12 **52**..................... HollieDoyle[(5)] 6 29
(Jimmy Fox) *a bhd* **12/1**

6130 **11** 7 **Ballyfarsoon (IRE)**[52] 6315 5-9-11 **60**......................(p) StevieDonohoe 7 29
(Ian Williams) *chsd ldrs tl wknd and rn wd on bnd 3f out* **8/1**

151- **12** 17 **Giant Sequoia (USA)**[566] 1411 12-9-0 **49**........................ DavidProbert 12
(Des Donovan, Ire) *a wl bhd* **16/1**

0/5- **13** 6 **Topolski (IRE)**[515] 2610 10-9-6 **55**... LiamKeniry 9
(David Arbuthnot) *prom tl wknd 4f out* **33/1**

3m 30.35s (0.25) **Going Correction** +0.025s/f (Slow)
WFA 3 from 4yo+ 9lb **13** Ran SP% **120.8**
Speed ratings (Par 101): **100,99,97,96,96 93,92,91,89,87 83,75,72**
CSF £249.72 CT £2087.87 TOTE £18.80: £4.40, £4.90, £2.80; EX 123.70 Trifecta £3579.20 Part won..
Owner Homebred Racing **Bred** J Ryan **Trained** Upper Lambourn, Berks

FOCUS
A modest staying handicap. They went a muddling gallop but the front-runner didn't quite get away from his field. The winner has been rated back to this year's best.
T/Jkpt: Not Won. T/Plt: £35.70 to a £1 stake. Pool: £75,026.29 - 1,529.88 winning tickets T/Qpdt: £8.80 to a £1 stake. Pool: £11,039.32 - 926.25 winning tickets **Lee McKenzie**

7578 REDCAR (L-H)
Tuesday, November 1

OFFICIAL GOING: Good to soft (7.8)
Wind: moderate 1/2 against Weather: fine, turning chilly

7740 IRISH STALLION FARMS EBF MAIDEN STKS (DIV I) 7f
12:40 (12:47) (Class 5) 2-Y-0 **£3,234** (£962; £481; £240) **Stalls** Centre

Form RPR

04 **1** **Original Choice (IRE)**[46] 6542 2-9-5 0.............................. BenCurtis 2 81
(William Haggas) *w ldrs: led 3f out: drvn and styd on wl fnl f* **5/2**[1]

2 1½ **Game Starter (IRE)** 2-9-5 0.. KevinStott 8 77+
(Saeed bin Suroor) *dwlt: in rr: hung lft over 3f out: hdwy over 2f out: chsd wnr fnl 150yds: no imp* **10/3**[2]

0 **3** 1 **Titi Makfi**[14] 7432 2-9-0 0.. JoeFanning 4 70
(Mark Johnston) *chsd ldrs: 2nd over 2f out: kpt on same pce fnl f* **14/1**

4 3¾ **Isabella (IRE)** 2-9-0 0.. SamJames 7 60
(David O'Meara) *mid-div: hdwy to chse ldrs over 2f out: one pce over 1f out* **9/1**

50 **5** shd **Pincheck (IRE)**[20] 7283 2-9-5 0.. MartinLane 16 64
(Luca Cumani) *t.k.h in rr: hdwy over 2f out: kpt on: nvr a threat* **16/1**

6 1¾ **Peaceful Passage (USA)** 2-9-0 0................................ RobertHavlin 12 55
(John Gosden) *towards rr: kpt on fnl 2f: nvr a factor* **11/2**[3]

06 **7** 2½ **Pindaric**[18] 7331 2-9-5 0.. AndrewMullen 1 53
(Alan Lockwood) *led: hdd 3f out: wknd over 1f out* **40/1**

8 hd **Power Power (IRE)** 2-9-5 0.. DanielMuscutt 10 53
(Marco Botti) *dwlt: wnt rt after s: in rr: kpt on fnl 2f: nvr a factor* **22/1**

460 **9** 3 **Mere Brow**[56] 6214 2-9-0 **64**.. ConnorBeasley 13 40
(Bryan Smart) *chsd ldrs: wknd appr fnl f* **22/1**

00 **10** ¾ **Urban Spirit (IRE)**[97] 4765 2-9-5 0................................ KeaganLatham 6 43
(David O'Meara) *prom: drvn over 2f out: grad wknd* **100/1**

0 **11** 1¼ **Cornerstone Lad**[25] 7125 2-9-5 0................................... JackGarritty 11 40
(Micky Hammond) *dwlt: hld up in rr: sme hdwy 3f out: nvr nr ldrs* **100/1**

12 2¼ **Bing Bang Bank (IRE)** 2-9-5 0...................................... GrahamGibbons 15 34
(David Barron) *in rr: sme hdwy over 2f out: wknd over 1f out* **16/1**

13 1½ **Crucial Response** 2-9-5 0.. GrahamLee 14 30
(Ben Haslam) *s.s: a towards rr* **66/1**

14 nk **Chionodoxa** 2-9-0 0.. DuranFentiman 5 24
(Tim Easterby) *prom: lost pl over 2f out* **200/1**

6 **15** ¾ **Four Kingdoms (IRE)**[21] 7247 2-9-5 0.......................... DougieCostello 9 27
(K R Burke) *a towards rr* **66/1**

430 **16** 2¾ **Luv U Always**[41] 6678 2-9-0 **52**.. DavidAllan 3 15
(Iain Jardine) *t.k.h: w ldrs: lost pl over 2f out: bhd whn eased clsng stages* **28/1**

1m 25.39s (0.89) **Going Correction** +0.225s/f (Good) **16** Ran SP% **115.5**
Speed ratings (Par 96): **103,101,100,95,95 93,90,90,87,86 84,82,80,80,79 76**
CSF £8.86 TOTE £3.30: £1.50, £1.30, £4.10; EX 13.30 Trifecta £166.10.
Owner A A Goodman **Bred** Ballybrennan Stud **Trained** Newmarket, Suffolk

FOCUS
A bright and sunny day helped bring down the curtain on Redcar for 2016. There was 1.5mm of overnight rain. This was largely made up of backward 2yos but still it wasn't a bad maiden.

7741 IRISH STALLION FARMS EBF MAIDEN STKS (DIV II) 7f
1:10 (1:15) (Class 5) 2-Y-0 **£3,234** (£962; £481; £240) **Stalls** Centre

Form RPR

1 **Pirate Look (IRE)** 2-9-5 0... DanielMuscutt 2 76+
(Marco Botti) *trckd ldrs: cl up 1/2-way: led 1½f out: rdn: green and edgd lft ins fnl f: kpt on* **9/1**[3]

66 **2** ¾ **Nastenka**[34] 6874 2-9-0 0......................................[1] ThomasBrown 9 69
(Ed Walker) *in tch: hdwy to trck ldrs over 2f out: rdn to chse wnr jst over 1f out: drvn and kpt on fnl f* **12/1**

3 1½ **Style And Grace (IRE)** 2-9-0 0...................................... RobertHavlin 4 65
(John Gosden) *dwlt: sn trcking ldrs: effrt over 2f out: sn swtchd lft and rdn wl over 1f out: styd on fnl f* **7/2**[1]

40 **4** 3¼ **Fleetfoot Jack (IRE)**[24] 7157 2-9-5 0........................ GrahamGibbons 10 62+
(David O'Meara) *towards rr: hdwy over 2f out: rdn over 1f out: kpt on wl fnl f: nrst fin* **9/1**[3]

6 **5** 1¼ **Golconda King (IRE)**[26] 7090 2-9-5 0............................. JackGarritty 3 58
(Richard Fahey) *led: rdn along 2f out: hdd 1½f out and grad wknd* **11/1**

44 **6** 1¾ **Iron Islands**[46] 6535 2-9-5 0.. DougieCostello 7 54
(K R Burke) *cl up: pushed along over 2f out: rdn and edgd lft wl over 1f out: sn wknd* **4/1**[2]

5 **7** nk **Alfred Richardson**[14] 7432 2-9-5 0.................................. SamJames 12 53
(John Davies) *prom: rdn along over 2f out: sn drvn and wknd* **16/1**

56 **8** 1¾ **Stubytuesday**[24] 7142 2-9-5 0...................................... JamesSullivan 6 49
(Michael Easterby) *towards rr: hdwy over 2f out: sn rdn and kpt on fnl f* **50/1**

00 **9** nk **Shackles**[14] 7432 2-9-5 0.. AndrewMullen 13 48
(Alistair Whillans) *chsd ldrs on outer: rdn along 3f out: sn wknd* **200/1**

10 nk **Pipe Dreamer** 2-9-5 0.. KevinStott 14 47
(Kevin Ryan) *dwlt: a towards rr* **12/1**

00 **11** 2¾ **Devil's Guard (IRE)**[8] 7578 2-9-0 0........................[1] ShirleyTeasdale[(5)] 15 40
(Keith Dalgleish) *in tch: rdn along 1/2-way: sn outpcd* **80/1**

6 **12** 7 **Breanski**[18] 7317 2-9-2 0... ShelleyBirkett[(3)] 5 22
(David O'Meara) *towards rr: pushed along 1/2-way: sn rdn: outpcd and bhd* **4/1**[2]

13 ¾ **Queen Starbond** 2-9-0 0.. GrahamLee 8 15
(Ben Haslam) *chsd ldrs: rdn along over 3f out: sn lost pl and bhd* **80/1**

00 **14** 31 **Ching Ching Lor (IRE)**[8] 7578 2-9-5 0.......................... PaulMulrennan 11
(Declan Carroll) *dwlt: a rr: outpcd and bhd fr 1/2-way* **250/1**

1m 27.15s (2.65) **Going Correction** +0.225s/f (Good) **14** Ran SP% **117.1**
Speed ratings (Par 96): **93,92,90,86,85 83,82,80,80,80 77,69,68,32**
CSF £109.41 TOTE £13.30: £3.50, £4.00, £1.40; EX 123.00 Trifecta £602.20.
Owner La Tesa Spa **Bred** Soc Agr La Tesa Srl **Trained** Newmarket, Suffolk

FOCUS
The weaker of the two divisions and the time was 1.76secs slower. Again the main action was on the far side. The starting point is fluid.

7742 HOLD YOUR CHRISTMAS PARTY HERE (S) STKS 1m
1:40 (1:40) (Class 6) 3-5-Y-0 **£2,726** (£805; £402) **Stalls** Centre

Form RPR

1200 **1** **Nonno Giulio (IRE)**[6] 7623 5-9-1 **77**.............................. JoshDoyle[(5)] 8 71
(Roger Fell) *trckd ldrs: led 3f out: drvn rt out: fnd ex towards fin* **5/4**[1]

0504 **2** nk **Bunker Hill Lass**[19] 7299 4-8-4 **51**..........................(p[1]) AnnaHesketh[(5)] 2 59
(Michael Appleby) *chsd ldrs: effrt over 2f out: upsides fnl f: no ex towards fin* **11/1**

1460 **3** 3 **Clayton Hall (IRE)**[14] 7436 3-9-4 **72**................................ PaddyAspell 6 63
(John Wainwright) *hld up in rr: hdwy over 2f out: hung lft over 1f out: kpt on one pce to take 3rd clsng stages* **22/1**

0540 **4** 1¼ **Percy's Gal**[56] 6216 5-8-9 **58**... SamJames 4 50
(Karen Tutty) *hld up in rr: t.k.h: hdwy over 2f out: w ldrs 1f out: fdd last 75yds* **9/2**[3]

5402 **5** 3 **Assisted**[43] 6618 3-8-12 **63**...(v[1]) JoeFanning 3 48
(Keith Dalgleish) *hld upo towards rr: hdwy over 3f out: sn trcking ldrs: effrt over 2f out: upsides over 1f out: hung lft: nt run on: wknd last 75yds: eased nr fin* **4/1**[2]

0056 **6** 4 **Let There Be Light**[5] 7641 3-9-4 **55**...........................[1] AndrewMullen 5 44
(Gay Kelleway) *in rr: drvn to chse ldrs over 2f out: lost pl over 1f out* **20/1**

0000 **7** 11 **Bahrikate**[48] 6478 3-8-7 **41**.. JoeDoyle 1 8
(Michael Herrington) *led: hdd 3f out: lost pl over 1f out* **50/1**

6004 **R** **Free One (IRE)**[61] 6047 4-9-0 **53**.......................................(p) DavidAllan 7
(Ivan Furtado) *ref to r: tk no part* **8/1**

1m 40.47s (3.87) **Going Correction** +0.225s/f (Good)
WFA 3 from 4yo+ 2lb **8** Ran SP% **113.1**
Speed ratings (Par 101): **89,88,85,84,81 77,66,**
CSF £16.03 TOTE £2.30: £1.10, £2.20, £4.10; EX 16.90 Trifecta £226.30.There was no bid for the winner.
Owner Stephen Louch **Bred** Ballygallon Stud Limited **Trained** Nawton, N Yorks

FOCUS
A very weak affair, run at an ordinary pace. The runner-up, rated to last year's best, limits the form.

7743 RACINGUK.COM/HD H'CAP 7f
2:10 (2:12) (Class 5) (0-75,75) 3-Y-O £2,911 (£866; £432; £216) **Stalls** Centre

Form RPR
1351 **1** **Enjoy Life (IRE)**[18] 7334 3-8-13 **67**....................(p) KevinStott 4 82+
(Kevin Ryan) *mde all: shkn up and wnt easily clr over 1f out: heavily eased clsng stages* **4/1**[1]
0403 **2** 4 **Kirkham**[18] 7333 3-8-11 **65**.................... JoeDoyle 7 68
(Julie Camacho) *hld up in mid-div: hdwy over 2f out: chsng ldrs over 1f out: styd on to take 2nd last 75yds: no ch w wnr* **6/1**[2]
1500 **3** 1 ¾ **Specialv (IRE)**[38] 6770 3-9-5 **73**....................(p) BenCurtis 2 71
(Brian Ellison) *mid-div: hdwy and edgd lft over 2f out: chsng wnr over 1f out: kpt on same pce* **13/2**[3]
1 **4** ¾ **Visitant**[67] 5843 3-9-0 **68**.................... JamesSullivan 10 64
(David Thompson) *in rr: hdwy 2f out: edgd lft and kpt on to take 4th nr fin* **16/1**
2400 **5** 1 **English Hero**[11] 7506 3-9-4 **72**.................... AndrewMullen 11 66
(John Mackie) *chsd ldrs: one pce over 1f out* **28/1**
4060 **6** ¾ **Desert Ruler**[10] 7540 3-9-5 **73**.................... GrahamLee 9 65
(Jedd O'Keeffe) *hld up in mid-div: effrt over 2f out: keeping on same pce whn n.m.r 100yds out* **8/1**
2215 **7** 3 ½ **Minminwin (IRE)**[31] 6946 3-8-10 **67**....................(vt) ShelleyBirkett(3) 15 49
(Gay Kelleway) *in rr: hdwy over 2f out: one pce over 1f out* **12/1**
360 **8** ½ **Anna Barkova (IRE)**[141] 3209 3-8-8 **62**.................... ConnorBeasley 8 43
(K R Burke) *trckd ldrs: effrt over 2f out: wknd over 1f out* **40/1**
2066 **9** ½ **Mustique (IRE)**[18] 7326 3-9-6 **74**.................... JackGarritty 3 53
(Richard Fahey) *chsd ldrs: drvn over 2f out: wknd over 1f out* **10/1**
501 **10** 1 **Sister Dude**[47] 6501 3-8-9 **68**.................... CliffordLee(5) 12 45
(K R Burke) *mid-div: drvn over 3f out: lost pl over 1f out* **14/1**
165 **11** 1 ½ **Donnelly's Rainbow (IRE)**[47] 6501 3-9-4 **72**.................... BarryMcHugh 6 45
(Rebecca Bastiman) *wnt rt s: sn chsng ldrs: drvn over 3f out: lost pl over 1f out* **20/1**
3665 **12** 1 ½ **Essenaitch (IRE)**[23] 7189 3-9-2 **70**.................... DavidAllan 14 39
(David Evans) *chsd ldrs: drvn over 2f out: lost pl over 1f out* **15/2**
6050 **13** 3 ½ **Forever A Lady (IRE)**[37] 6811 3-9-1 **74**.................... ShirleyTeasdale(5) 13 33
(Keith Dalgleish) *in rr: drvn over 3f out: nvr on terms* **33/1**
3330 **14** nk **Crystallographer (IRE)**[40] 6701 3-9-0 **68**..............[1] GrahamGibbons 16 26
(Daniel Mark Loughnane) *chsd ldrs: wkng whn hung lft over 1f out* **50/1**
0005 **15** 5 **Silhuette (IRE)**[7] 7591 3-9-7 **75**.................... PaulMulrennan 1 20
(Colin Teague) *w ldrs: edgd rt over 1f out: sn wknd: heavily eased clsng stages* **20/1**
2020 **P** **Flinty Fell (IRE)**[39] 6742 3-9-2 **70**.................... JoeFanning 5
(Keith Dalgleish) *prom: edgd lft over 2f out: sn lost pl and heavily eased: t.o whn p.u nr fin: b.b.v* **16/1**

1m 25.52s (1.02) **Going Correction** +0.225s/f (Good) **16** Ran SP% **126.0**
Speed ratings (Par 102): **103,98,96,95,94 93,89,89,88,87 85,83,79,79,73**
CSF £25.17 CT £160.66 TOTE £5.30: £1.80, £1.80, £2.30, £4.20; EX 30.00 Trifecta £316.50.
Owner CN Farm Limited **Bred** E Puerari & Mme D Ades-Hazan **Trained** Hambleton, N Yorks

FOCUS
This modest 3yo handicap looked wide open, but it fell apart from 2f out. Low numbers were again favoured. It's been rated around the runner-up.

7744 MURIEL NODDINGS BIRTHDAY CELEBRATION H'CAP 1m 2f
2:40 (2:40) (Class 3) (0-95,93) 3-Y-O+ £7,439 (£2,213; £1,106; £553) **Stalls** Low

Form RPR
0160 **1** **Beardwood**[6] 7608 4-9-0 **83**....................(p) JoeFanning 12 91
(Mark Johnston) *trckd ldrs: hdwy 3f out: led 2f out: sn rdn and edgd lft over 1f out: edgd rt ins fnl f: kpt on* **9/1**
3006 **2** ½ **Awake My Soul (IRE)**[10] 7546 7-9-10 **93**.................... JamesSullivan 13 100
(Tom Tate) *hld up towards rr: hdwy over 3f out: trckd ldrs over 2f out: swtchd rt and rdn over 1f out: styd on wl fnl f* **12/1**
345 **3** 1 **Michele Strogoff**[16] 7383 3-9-4 **91**.................... ConnorBeasley 9 96
(Roger Fell) *trckd ldrs: hdwy on inner over 3f out: rdn along 2f out: drvn over 1f out: kpt on* **10/1**
0053 **4** ¾ **Imshivalla (IRE)**[45] 6559 5-9-7 **90**.................... JackGarritty 7 94
(Richard Fahey) *sn led: pushed along 3f out: hdd and rdn 2f out: sn n.m.r and swtchd rt over 1f out: drvn and kpt on same pce fnl f* **11/1**
0002 **5** 2 ½ **Little Lady Katie (IRE)**[13] 7472 4-8-13 **87**.................... CliffordLee(5) 14 86
(K R Burke) *trckd ldrs: pushed along over 3f out: rdn wl over 2f out: sn one pce* **16/1**
0055 **6** nse **Indy (IRE)**[15] 7408 5-8-10 **79** oh2.................... GrahamGibbons 8 77
(David Barron) *cl up: pushed along 4f out: rdn 3f out: sn drvn and wknd* **17/2**[3]
2212 **7** 2 ¼ **Al Destoor**[15] 7412 6-8-12 **84**.................... AdamMcNamara(3) 6 78
(Jennie Candlish) *midfield: hdwy over 3f out: rdn along over 2f out: sn drvn and btn* **2/1**[1]
0006 **8** ½ **Tres Coronas (IRE)**[15] 7408 9-8-10 **79**.................... SamJames 2 72
(David Barron) *a towards rr* **9/1**
310 **9** nk **Archippos**[11] 7499 3-8-7 **80**.................... AndrewMullen 4 72
(Philip Kirby) *in tch on inner: pushed along over 3f out: sn rdn and wknd* **18/1**
S305 **10** 3 ½ **Jacbequick**[10] 7535 5-9-1 **89**....................(b) JoshDoyle(5) 5 74
(David O'Meara) *dwlt: hld up towards rr: sme hdwy on outer over 3f out: rdn along wl over 2f out: sn btn* **15/2**[2]
030 **11** 1 ¼ **Royal Shaheen (FR)**[10] 7540 3-8-10 **83**.................... PaulMulrennan 11 66
(Alistair Whillans) *a towards rr* **28/1**

2m 5.02s (-2.08) **Going Correction** +0.175s/f (Good)
WFA 3 from 4yo+ 4lb **11** Ran SP% **115.3**
Speed ratings (Par 107): **115,114,113,113,111 111,109,108,108,105 104**
CSF £109.75 CT £1100.28 TOTE £10.80: £3.00, £3.60, £3.10; EX 131.80 Trifecta £1277.00.
Owner A D Spence & M B Spence **Bred** Kirtlington Stud Ltd **Trained** Middleham Moor, N Yorks

FOCUS
It paid to be handy in this feature handicap. A length pb from the winner, with the runner-up rated close to this year's best.

7745 RACINGUK.COM/DAYPASS CLAIMING STKS 1m 2f
3:10 (3:11) (Class 6) 3-4-Y-O £2,726 (£805; £402) **Stalls** Low

Form RPR
0000 **1** **Hard To Handel**[25] 7108 4-9-5 78....................(p) JoshDoyle(5) 4 66+
(David O'Meara) *trckd ldr: effrt over 2f out: led over 1f out: edgd lft: drvn rt out* **8/11**[1]
6240 **2** ¾ **Highwayman**[67] 5845 3-9-6 62.................... JamesSullivan 1 65
(David Thompson) *trckd ldng pair: drvn 3f out: stmbld over 1f out: kpt on to take 2nd nr fin* **22/1**
-004 **3** ½ **Daleelak (IRE)**[22] 7227 3-8-13 69.................... JoeFanning 2 57
(Mark Johnston) *led: qcknd pce over 3f out: hdd over 1f out: swtchd rt 150yds out: kpt on one pce* **15/8**[2]
4303 **4** 1 ½ **Frivolous Prince (IRE)**[5] 7641 3-8-9 46....................(bt) BenCurtis 3 50
(David Evans) *racd in last thrght but wl in tch: effrt over 3f out: one pce fnl 2f* **9/1**[3]

2m 8.36s (1.26) **Going Correction** +0.175s/f (Good)
WFA 3 from 4yo 4lb **4** Ran SP% **107.0**
Speed ratings (Par 101): **101,100,100,98**
CSF £13.64 TOTE £1.60; EX 14.00 Trifecta £16.40.There was no bid for the winner.
Owner Middleham Park Racing XXV **Bred** Melody Bloodstock **Trained** Upper Helmsley, N Yorks

FOCUS
Dubious form.

7746 PAY FOR RACING UK VIA MOBILE H'CAP 1m 6f 19y
3:40 (3:40) (Class 6) (0-65,65) 3-Y-O+ £2,726 (£805; £402) **Stalls** Low

Form RPR
05 **1** **Buzz Boy (ITY)**[17] 7375 3-7-8 **46** oh1....................(v) DannySheehy(7) 5 55+
(Adrian Paul Keatley, Ire) *trckd ldr: cl up over 3f out: led wl over 2f out: rdn clr ent fnl f: kpt on strly* **6/1**[3]
0305 **2** 3 ¼ **Triple Eight (IRE)**[28] 7044 8-9-7 **58**.................... DougieCostello 6 61
(Philip Kirby) *trckd ldrs: hdwy 3f out: rdn and n.m.r wl over 1f out: drvn and kpt on fnl f* **28/1**
6560 **3** ½ **Perennial**[24] 7138 7-8-5 **47**....................(p) PhilDennis(5) 2 49
(Philip Kirby) *trckd ldrs: hdwy on outer over 3f out: rdn 2f out: drvn and kpt on fnl f* **14/1**
6522 **4** ¾ **Jan De Heem**[17] 7361 6-9-11 **62**.................... JamesSullivan 12 64
(Tina Jackson) *hld up in tch: hdwy on inner 3f out: effrt 2f out: sn rdn and n.m.r over 1f out: kpt on same pce fnl f* **17/2**
0440 **5** nse **Yasir (USA)**[4] 7656 8-10-0 **65**.................... PaulMulrennan 7 66
(Conor Dore) *hld up in rr: hdwy 3f out: rdn wl over 1f out: kpt on wl fnl f: nrst fin* **12/1**
0005 **6** ½ **Social Media**[50] 6424 3-8-9 **54**.................... GrahamLee 11 55
(Ed Dunlop) *hld up towards rr: effrt and sme hdwy 3f out: rdn over 2f out: n.d* **8/1**
2646 **7** 1 **Hint Of Grey (IRE)**[6] 7628 3-9-1 **60**.................... RobertHavlin 1 59
(Don Cantillon) *trckd ldng pair: hdwy and cl up over 2f our: rdn to chal wl over 1f out: drvn ent fnl f: sn wknd* **11/4**[1]
6050 **8** 1 ½ **Cavalieri (IRE)**[24] 7138 6-8-6 **50**....................(t) PaulaMuir(7) 8 47
(Philip Kirby) *a towards rr* **20/1**
5033 **9** 3 ½ **Adrakhan (FR)**[7] 7592 5-8-9 **46** oh1....................[1] KevinStott 10 39
(Wilf Storey) *trckd ldrs on inner: hdwy 4f out: rdn along 3f out: drvn over 2f out and sn wknd* **9/2**[2]
2020 **10** 7 **Ryan The Giant**[21] 7262 3-8-5 **50**....................(p) JoeFanning 3 34
(Keith Dalgleish) *led: pushed along 4f out: rdn and hdd wl over 2f out: sn drvn and btn* **7/1**
056- **F** **Sr Swing**[514] 2951 5-8-9 **46** oh1.................... AndrewMullen 4
(Peter Niven) *slipped and fell s* **40/1**

3m 11.03s (6.33) **Going Correction** +0.175s/f (Good)
WFA 3 from 4yo+ 8lb **11** Ran SP% **118.3**
Speed ratings (Par 101): **88,86,85,85,85 85,84,83,81,77**
CSF £165.45 CT £2251.77 TOTE £8.10: £2.70, £5.40, £4.20; EX 202.30 Trifecta £3354.60.
Owner Patrick J McCartan **Bred** Manuela Martinelli **Trained** Friarstown, Co. Kildare

FOCUS
A weak staying handicap, run at a routine pace. Another step up from the winner.

7747 THANKS & SEE YOU NEXT SEASON H'CAP 6f
4:10 (4:12) (Class 6) (0-60,60) 3-Y-O+ £2,726 (£805; £402) **Stalls** Centre

Form RPR
0632 **1** **Questo**[8] 7584 4-9-3 **56**.................... BenCurtis 5 67
(Tracy Waggott) *chsd ldrs: led wl over 1f out: drvn out* **5/2**[1]
2032 **2** ½ **Someone Exciting**[18] 7334 3-9-4 **60**.................... AdamMcNamara(3) 1 70
(David Thompson) *hld up towards rr: stdy hdwy over 1f out: chsd wnr last 150yds: no ex clsng stages* **4/1**[2]
5003 **3** 2 ¼ **Ki Ki**[49] 6451 4-9-7 **60**.................... ConnorBeasley 15 63
(Bryan Smart) *chsd ldrs: kpt on same pce fnl f: tk 3rd nr fin* **8/1**[3]
-063 **4** nk **Caribbean Spring (IRE)**[14] 7444 3-8-11 **57**.................... JaneElliott(7) 4 59
(George Margarson) *mid-div: hdwy over 2f out: kpt on same pce fnl f: tk 4th nr fin* **12/1**
540 **5** nk **Skadi**[39] 6744 4-9-2 **55**.................... NeilFarley 8 56
(Garry Moss) *chsd ldrs: kpt on same pce appr fnl f* **20/1**
4010 **6** 1 **Captain Scooby**[8] 7585 10-8-12 **58**....................(b) LisaTodd(7) 3 56
(Richard Guest) *s.i.s: in rr: hdwy over 2f out: chsng ldrs over 1f out: one pce* **33/1**
5004 **7** ½ **Tilsworth Micky**[14] 7445 4-9-0 **53**.................... DougieCostello 2 49
(J R Jenkins) *s.s: bhd: jhdwy over 2f out: kpt on fnl f* **25/1**
6000 **8** 1 ¼ **Goadby**[33] 6894 5-9-1 **54**....................[1] RobertHavlin 9 49
(John Holt) *chsd ldrs: one pce whn nt clr run over 1f out* **25/1**
4600 **9** ¾ **Secret Millionaire (IRE)**[83] 5295 9-9-5 **58**..............(p) PaulMulrennan 10 48
(Shaun Harris) *mid-div: effrt over 2f out: one pce* **50/1**
0003 **10** 1 ½ **A J Cook (IRE)**[7] 7595 6-8-11 **50**.................... DavidAllan 16 36
(Ron Barr) *chsd ldrs: fdd over 1f out* **20/1**
45-5 **11** ½ **Sea Of Hope (IRE)**[171] 2234 3-9-0 **60**.................... DannySheehy(7) 7 44
(Adrian Paul Keatley, Ire) *chsd ldrs: hung lft over 2f out: wknd fnl f* **4/1**[2]
-013 **12** 1 ½ **Novabridge**[241] 837 8-8-4 **46** oh1.................... RachelRichardson(3) 17 26
(Karen Tutty) *in rr: effrt over 2f out:sn chsng ldrs: lost pl over 1f out* **50/1**
0600 **13** ½ **Adiator**[8] 7584 8-9-1 **54**.................... KevinStott 12 32
(Neville Bycroft) *rr-div: sn drvn along: nvr a factor* **25/1**
6000 **14** ½ **Armelle (FR)**[123] 3843 5-8-8 **54**....................(p) NatalieHambling(7) 20 31
(Scott Dixon) *led: edgd lft over 4f out: hdd over 1f out: sn wknd* **33/1**
5000 **15** 2 ¾ **Lothair (IRE)**[49] 6435 7-9-4 **57**.................... JoeFanning 11 26
(Alan Swinbank) *hld up in rr: effrt over 2f out: hung lft: nvr on terms* **28/1**
5323 **16** ½ **Slim Chance (IRE)**[26] 7093 7-8-12 **58**....................(b) PaulaMuir(7) 14 25
(Simon West) *mid-div: effrt over 2f out: lost pl over 1f out* **25/1**
0000 **17** hd **Ivors Involvement (IRE)**[18] 7333 4-9-4 **57**..............(e) JamesSullivan 18 24
(Tina Jackson) *in rr: effrt over 2f out: sn wknd* **40/1**
010 **18** 5 **Dutch Dream**[18] 7323 3-9-2 **55**.................... GrahamLee 13 7
(Linda Perratt) *in rr: edgd rt over 2f out: sn bhd* **50/1**

1m 12.61s (0.81) **Going Correction** +0.225s/f (Good) **18** Ran SP% **129.9**
Speed ratings (Par 101): **103,102,99,98,98 97,96,94,93,91 91,89,88,87,84 83,83,76**
CSF £10.41 CT £76.51 TOTE £3.50: £1.50, £1.30, £2.30, £3.00; EX 12.80 Trifecta £48.70.
Owner John J Maguire **Bred** G Reed **Trained** Spennymoor, Co Durham
■ Ryedale Rio was withdrawn. Price at time of withdrawal 40/1. Rule 4 does not apply.

FOCUS
Not a bad sprint handicap for the class. In keeping with the bias, it paid to be drawn low.
T/Plt: £109.40 to a £1 stake. Pool: £55360.36, 369.07 winning units. T/Qpdt: £40.90 to a £1 stake. Pool: £4367.19, 79.0 winning units. **Walter Glynn & Joe Rowntree**

[7509]WOLVERHAMPTON (A.W) (L-H)

Tuesday, November 1

OFFICIAL GOING: Tapeta: standard

Wind: light, against Weather: overcast

7748 32RED.COM MAIDEN STKS 5f 20y (Tp)

1:30 (1:30) (Class 5) 2-Y-O **£3,557** (£1,058; £529; £264) **Stalls** Low

Form RPR

3002 **1** **Monte Cinq (IRE)**[16] 7381 2-9-0 70 TomEaves 1 76
(Jason Ward) *mde all: rdn and command 1f out: r.o wl: comf* **10/1**

05 **2** 2 **Dan Troop**[39] 6731 2-9-0 0 TonyHamilton 3 69
(Richard Fahey) *dwlt and niggled along early: t.k.h after 1f and hld up in tch in last trio: rdn and hdwy over 1f out: styd on wl ins fnl f: wnt 2nd towards fin: no threat to wnr* **12/1**

5 **3** ¾ **Kings Academy**[20] 7291 2-9-0 0 SeanLevey 5 66
(Paul Cole) *in tch in midfield: effrt to chse ldrs 2f out: wnt 2nd ins fnl f: kpt on but no imp on wnr: lost 2nd towards fin* **7/1**[3]

32 **4** ¾ **Rapid Ranger**[43] 6622 2-9-0 0 LiamKeniry 2 63
(Gary Moore) *t.k.h: chsd ldng pair: wnt 2nd 2f out: rdn over 1f out: fnd little and no imp 1f out: lost 2nd ins fnl f: wknd towards fin* **15/8**[1]

04 **5** ½ **Magique Touch**[22] 7216 2-8-6 0 (b[1]) JosephineGordon(3) 4 57
(Roger Charlton) *s.i.s and niggled along early: in tch in last pair: hdwy u.p on inner over 1f out: kpt on ins fnl f: nvr trbld ldrs* **10/1**

2225 **6** nk **Mr Pocket (IRE)**[66] 5876 2-9-0 75 PJMcDonald 8 61
(Paul Cole) *chsd ldrs: effrt in 4th 2f out: no imp over 1f out: styd on same pce ins fnl f* **11/4**[2]

66 **7** shd **Supreme Power (IRE)**[43] 6622 2-8-11 0 LouisSteward(3) 10 60
(Philip McBride) *midfield: rdn 2f out: swtchd lft 1f out: kpt on ins fnl f: nvr trbld ldrs* **20/1**

333 **8** 6 **Lady Molly (IRE)**[28] 7040 2-8-9 66 JasonHart 9 34
(Keith Dalgleish) *chsd wnr tl 2f out: sn struggling u.p: wl hld whn lost action and eased ins fnl f* **10/1**

0 **9** 1½ **Vicky Park**[15] 7414 2-8-6 0 JackDuern(3) 7 28
(Dean Ivory) *a towards rr: rdn and wd over 2f out wknd over 1f out: lost action and eased ins fnl f: fin lame* **50/1**

060 **10** 3½ **Lady Gwhinnyvere (IRE)**[34] 6873 2-8-9 30 TomMarquand 6 16
(John Spearing) *midfield: rdn 3f out: lost pl and bhd over 1f out* **100/1**

1m 0.68s (-1.22) **Going Correction** -0.10s/f (Stan) 2y crse rec **10** Ran SP% **116.6**

Speed ratings (Par 96): **105,101,100,99,98 98,97,88,85,80**

CSF £120.55 TOTE £13.40: £2.50, £3.30, £2.20; EX 98.20 Trifecta £618.30.

Owner John Sutton, Colin Cooley, Ian Cope **Bred** P O'Rourke **Trained** Middleham, N Yorks

FOCUS

A very ordinary maiden. The winner made all in a time only 0.68sec above standard, suggesting that the track was riding quite quick. Straightforward form.

7749 32RED CASINO NURSERY H'CAP (DIV I) 7f 32y (Tp)

2:00 (2:00) (Class 6) (0-65,65) 2-Y-O **£2,749** (£818; £408; £204) **Stalls** High

Form RPR

501 **1** **Alice's Dream**[31] 6961 2-8-13 62 (b[1]) GeorgeWood(5) 1 69+
(Marco Botti) *trckd ldrs: effrt 2f out: hdwy to chal 1f out: sn led and drew clr fnl 100yds: eased towards fin: readily* **13/2**[3]

050 **2** 3¼ **Impassioned**[21] 7259 2-9-3 61 [1] RyanPowell 7 60
(Sir Mark Prescott Bt) *chsd ldrs: wnt 2nd over 3f out: rdn to ld wl over 1f out: edgd lft 1f out: sn hdd and outpcd by wnr: hld on for 2nd cl home* **13/2**[3]

0000 **3** nse **Magic Journey (IRE)**[41] 6678 2-8-12 56 (b[1]) JasonHart 10 55
(John Quinn) *swtchd lft after s: t.k.h: hld up in tch in midfield: hdwy u.p 1f out: kpt on wl and pressing for 2nd cl home: no threat to wnr* **12/1**

5062 **4** 1 **Western Presence**[24] 7143 2-9-7 65 TonyHamilton 5 61
(Richard Fahey) *chsd ldrs: effrt on inner 2f out: chsd ldrs and drvn 1f out: no imp and kpt on same pce ins fnl f* **3/1**[1]

005 **5** ¾ **Arthurthedelegator**[115] 4133 2-9-4 65 NathanEvans(3) 8 60+
(Oliver Greenall) *hld up in last pair: nt clr run over 2f out: effrt and nt clr run again over 1f out: rdn and hdwy 1f out: kpt on ins fnl f: nvr trbld ldrs* **28/1**

5564 **6** hd **Life On Mars**[22] 7228 2-9-2 65 GeorgiaCox(5) 4 59
(William Haggas) *chsd ldr after 1f out tl over 3f out: sn rdn: lost pl over 1f out: kpt on same pce ins fnl f* **3/1**[1]

6046 **7** 1 **Silk Mill Blue**[25] 7109 2-9-5 63 GeorgeChaloner 9 55
(Richard Whitaker) *in tch in midfield on outer: rdn over 1f out: no imp over 1f out: plugged on same pce after* **6/1**[2]

6360 **8** 1¾ **Permanent**[43] 6632 2-9-5 63 RichardKingscote 3 50
(Daniel Kubler) *led: rdn and hdd wl over 1f out: unable qck over 1f out: wknd ins fnl f* **17/2**

560 **9** 4 **The Night Is Ours (IRE)**[14] 7455 2-8-13 60 JosephineGordon(3) 2 40
(J S Moore) *chsd ldr tl hmpd after 1f: steadily lost pl: rdn 3f out: wknd 2f out: bhd and eased wl ins fnl f* **22/1**

0060 **10** ½ **I Dare To Dream**[20] 7275 2-8-3 54 JordanUys(7) 6 30
(Lisa Williamson) *s.i.s: t.k.h: hld up in last pair: rdn ent fnl 2f: no hedaway: bhd and eased wl ins fnl f* **100/1**

1m 28.71s (-0.09) **Going Correction** -0.10s/f (Stan) **10** Ran SP% **118.0**

Speed ratings (Par 94): **96,92,92,91,90 90,88,86,82,81**

CSF £48.10 CT £512.42 TOTE £7.60: £4.10, £2.50, £3.50; EX 44.70 Trifecta £601.50.

Owner HH Shaikh Nader Mohamed Al Khalifa **Bred** Giles Wates **Trained** Newmarket, Suffolk

FOCUS

Low-ranking nursery form, but the quicker division by 0.53sec. A step forward from the winner.

7750 32RED CASINO NURSERY H'CAP (DIV II) 7f 32y (Tp)

2:30 (2:32) (Class 6) (0-65,65) 2-Y-O **£2,749** (£818; £408; £204) **Stalls** High

Form RPR

5401 **1** **A Sure Welcome**[14] 7423 2-8-9 53 (p) TomMarquand 6 56
(John Spearing) *in tch in midfield: effrt on outer 2f out: ev ch ins fnl f: styd on wl u.p to ld last strides* **8/1**

1000 **2** hd **Princess Way (IRE)**[22] 7228 2-9-1 59 RobertWinston 10 62
(David Evans) *chsd ldr for 1f: styd chsng ldrs: effrt over 1f out: led 1f out: kpt on wl: hdd and no ex last strides* **20/1**

330 **3** ½ **Golden Eye**[22] 7209 2-9-7 65 AdamKirby 5 66
(Sylvester Kirk) *stdd after s: in tch in midfield: shkn up 4f out: swtchd lft and hdwy u.p 1f out: ev ch ins fnl f: unable qck towards fin* **4/1**[1]

2642 **4** shd **Sheila's Return**[25] 7110 2-8-11 55 TomEaves 8 56
(Bryan Smart) *t.k.h: hld up wl in tch in midfield: effrt over 1f out: wnt between rivals and ev ch ins fnl f: unable qck towards fin: fin lame* **10/1**

0406 **5** nk **Everkyllachy (IRE)**[6] 7615 2-8-10 57 (b) JosephineGordon(3) 3 57
(J S Moore) *chsd ldrs: swtchd rt and effrt over 1f out: ev ch ins fnl f: unable qck towards fin* **14/1**

2336 **6** ½ **Galahad**[63] 6007 2-9-6 64 TonyHamilton 7 63
(Richard Fahey) *s.i.s: rcvrd and hdwy to join ldr after 1f out: led 5f out: rdn over 1f out: hdd 1f out: hung rt ins fnl f: wknd towards fin* **9/2**[2]

1424 **7** ¾ **Areyoutheway (IRE)**[56] 6208 2-9-4 65 AlistairRawlinson(3) 1 62
(Michael Appleby) *in tch in midfield: effrt on inner 2f out: hdwy u.p and pressing ldrs ins fnl f: styd on same pce wl ins fnl f* **11/1**

3650 **8** shd **Plato's Kode (IRE)**[13] 7467 2-9-7 65 [1] TomQueally 2 62
(Seamus Durack) *sn dropped to last pair: effrt and switching rt wl over 1f out: hdwy ins fnl f: styd on fnl 100yds: nvr trbld ldrs* **5/1**[3]

0543 **9** 1½ **Fair Selene**[28] 7047 2-9-3 61 (p) RyanTate 9 54
(Heather Main) *sn pushed into ld: hdd 5f out: styd w ldr: rdn over 1f out: no ex ins fnl f: wknd wl ins fnl f* **7/1**

436 **10** 2¾ **Affair**[62] 6035 2-9-0 63 CharlieBennett(5) 4 50
(Hughie Morrison) *sn in last pair: effrt 2f out: no imp and kpt on same pce fnl f: n.d* **9/1**

1m 29.24s (0.44) **Going Correction** -0.10s/f (Stan) **10** Ran SP% **117.3**

Speed ratings (Par 94): **93,92,92,92,91 91,90,90,88,85**

CSF £154.35 CT £755.89 TOTE £10.70: £2.70, £4.30, £1.70; EX 209.70 Trifecta £1374.80.

Owner Kinnersley Partnership 3 **Bred** Richard Evans Bloodstock **Trained** Kinnersley, Worcs

■ Stewards' Enquiry : Adam Kirby two-day ban: use of whip (15-16 Nov)

FOCUS

The slower division by 0.53sec. There was a very busy finish with any number holding a chance up the straight, and the first two home finished widest of all. Not form to get excited about given they finished so compressed.

7751 SUNBETS.CO.UK H'CAP 7f 32y (Tp)

3:00 (3:02) (Class 6) (0-60,60) 3-Y-O+ **£2,749** (£818; £408; £204) **Stalls** High

Form RPR

0001 **1** **Dark Confidant (IRE)**[13] 7463 3-9-3 58 DavidNolan 1 65
(Richard Fahey) *hld up in tch in midfield: swtchd rt over 1f out: rdn and hdwy between horses 1f out: led ins fnl f: styd on wl: rdn out* **5/1**[1]

220 **2** ½ **For Shia And Lula (IRE)**[11] 7513 7-9-6 60 AdamKirby 7 67
(Daniel Mark Loughnane) *hld up in tch in midfield: hdwy on outer over 1f out: drvn and chal ins fnl f: kpt on wl u.p but hld towards fin* **10/1**

-001 **3** 1¼ **Showtime Blues**[5] 7654 4-9-1 60 (p) CharlieBennett(5) 8 64
(Jim Boyle) *chsd ldrs: rdn and ev ch over 1f out: drvn to ld jst ins fnl f: sn hdd and styd on same pce fnl 100yds* **7/1**[3]

0055 **4** ½ **Misu Pete**[21] 7260 4-9-4 58 SteveDrowne 10 60
(Mark Usher) *hld up in tch in midfield: effrt u.p 2f out: hdwy and ev ch ins fnl f: styd on same pce fnl 100yds* **12/1**

3600 **5** ½ **Bush Beauty (IRE)**[11] 7514 5-9-0 59 SophieKilloran(5) 5 60
(Eric Alston) *hld up in tch in midfield: nt clr run on inner over 2f out: swtchd rt over 1f out: hdwy 1f out: swtchd rt again ins fnl f: styd on towards fin: no threat to ldrs* **8/1**

6500 **6** nk **Swansway**[8] 7585 3-8-13 57 NathanEvans(3) 3 57
(Michael Easterby) *in tch in midfield: rdn over 2f out: clsd and nt clr run ent fnl f: swtchd lft and squeezed between horses 1f out: kpt on same pce fnl 100yds* **6/1**[2]

4300 **7** 1¾ **Locommotion**[11] 7514 4-9-4 58 (be[1]) TomMarquand 9 54
(Matthew Salaman) *hld up in tch towards rr: effrt and hung lft over 1f out: kpt on ins fnl f: nvr trbld ldrs* **50/1**

0041 **8** 1 **No Refund (IRE)**[22] 7212 5-9-4 58 (p) PJMcDonald 12 52
(David Loughnane) *hdwy to join ldr after 1f tl led 5f out: rdn wl over 1f out: hdd jst ins fnl f: no ex and wknd fnl 100yds* **11/1**

0046 **9** 1½ **Moi Aussie**[21] 7261 3-9-3 58 MartinDwyer 6 47
(Ed McMahon) *t.k.h: led tl 5f out: styd upsides ldr: rdn wl over 1f out: unable qck 1f out: wknd ins fnl f* **12/1**

6540 **10** ¾ **Dr Red Eye**[45] 6568 8-9-2 59 (p) JosephineGordon(3) 2 47
(Scott Dixon) *t.k.h: chsd ldrs: unable qck u.p over 1f out: losing pl whn squeezed for room and hmpd 1f out: wknd ins fnl f* **14/1**

6042 **11** ¾ **Coquine**[11] 7513 3-9-2 57 PhillipMakin 11 42
(David O'Meara) *dwlt: sn pushed along and a towards rr: no hdwy u.p over 2f out: wknd fnl f* **7/1**[3]

0002 **12** 1¾ **National Service (USA)**[19] 7302 5-8-13 60 (tp) CallumRodriguez(7) 4 42
(Richard Ford) *fly j. as stalls opened and slowly away: hld up in tch towards rr: n.m.r over 2f out: rdn and no hdwy over 1f out: wknd ins fnl f* **8/1**

1m 28.15s (-0.65) **Going Correction** -0.10s/f (Stan)

WFA 3 from 4yo+ 1lb **12** Ran SP% **119.6**

Speed ratings (Par 101): **99,98,97,96,95 95,93,92,90,89 88,86**

CSF £55.53 CT £360.88 TOTE £4.70: £1.70, £2.90, £3.20; EX 38.30 Trifecta £388.90.

Owner D I Perry **Bred** Rabbah Bloodstock Limited **Trained** Musley Bank, N Yorks

FOCUS

Plenty had their chances in this workaday handicap.

7752 BETWAY SPRINT H'CAP 5f 20y (Tp)

3:30 (3:32) (Class 3) (0-95,94) 3-Y-O **£7,561** (£2,263; £1,131; £566; £282) **Stalls** Low

Form RPR

4211 **1** **Upstaging**[28] 7054 4-9-3 90 AdamKirby 1 100+
(Paul Cole) *hld up in tch towards rr: clsd and swtchd lft over 1f out: hrd drvn and hdwy ent fnl f: led wl ins fnl f: hung rt towards fin* **7/2**[1]

0303 **2** nk **Seeking Magic**[31] 6962 8-8-12 92 (t) WilliamCox(7) 2 101
(Clive Cox) *taken down early: broke fast: t.k.h: chsd ldr: rdn and ev ch over 1f out: led jst ins fnl f: hdd wl ins fnl f: kpt on same pce towards fin* **17/2**[3]

0003 **3** 1 **Highland Acclaim (IRE)**[6] 7610 5-9-0 87 DavidNolan 6 92
(David O'Meara) *chsd ldrs: effrt to chal ent fnl f: no ex and outpcd fnl 75yds* **7/2**[1]

0106 **4** 1¼ **Mappin Time (IRE)**[52] 6324 8-8-13 86 (be) JasonHart 5 87
(Tim Easterby) *s.i.s: pushed along and detached in last tl clsd 1/2-way: rdn and hdwy on inner over 1f out: drifted rt and kpt on ins fnl f* **14/1**

0000 **5** 1 **Zac Brown (IRE)**[20] 7288 5-9-4 94 (t) RobHornby(3) 8 91
(Charlie Wallis) *hld up in tch in midfield: effrt u.p over 1f out: kpt on same pce ins fnl f* **33/1**

1026 **6** hd **Just That Lord**[43] 6633 3-8-13 86 RobertWinston 10 83
(Bill Turner) *sn led and crossed to inner: rdn over 1f out: hdd jst ins fnl f: no ex and wknd fnl 100yds* **14/1**

4060 **7** ¾ **Seve**[38] 6793 4-8-9 82 RichardKingscote 11 76
(Tom Dascombe) *taken down early: t.k.h: chsd ldrs: rdn and unable qck over 1f out: wknd ins fnl f* **15/2**[2]

5302 **8** ½ **Top Boy**[22] 7202 6-8-11 **87**............................(v) NoelGarbutt(3) 3 79+
(Derek Shaw) *hld up in tch towards rr: hmpd and swtchd rt 4f out: swtchd rt over 2f out: effrt over 1f out: nt clr run ins fnl f: swtchd lft towards fin: nvr trbld ldrs* **16/1**

0103 **9** nse **Oriental Relation (IRE)**[5] 7643 5-8-10 **83**........................(v) TomEaves 7 75
(James Given) *taken down early: t.k.h: hld up in tch towards rr: effrt over 1f out: no imp u.p 1f out: plugged on same pce fnl f* **10/1**

2303 **10** ¾ **Memories Galore (IRE)**[28] 7054 4-8-11 **84**.................... TomQueally 9 73+
(Harry Dunlop) *s.i.s: sn rcvrd and in midfield: effrt 2f out: unable qck and btn 1f out: wknd ins fnl f* **17/2**[3]

1360 **11** 1 **Distant Past**[6] 7610 5-9-2 **89**..(v[1]) ShaneGray 4 75+
(Kevin Ryan) *towards rr: pushed wd over 2f out and sn dropped to last: no hdwy whn rdn over 1f out: bhd fnl f* **11/1**

1m 0.25s (-1.65) **Going Correction** -0.10s/f (Stan) **11** Ran SP% **116.8**
Speed ratings (Par 107): **109,108,106,104,103 103,101,101,100,99 98**
CSF £33.57 CT £114.19 TOTE £3.90: £1.80, £2.80, £1.40; EX 28.50 Trifecta £114.20.
Owner H R H Sultan Ahmad Shah **Bred** Glebe Stud **Trained** Whatcombe, Oxon

FOCUS
A decent sprint handicap which was run at a frenetic gallop. Upstaging was the fourth winner in five races on the card to come from stall 1. The runner-up helps set the standard.

7753 BETWAY MAIDEN STKS 1m 1f 103y (Tp)
4:00 (4:00) (Class 5) 3-Y-O+ **£3,557** (£1,058; £529; £264) **Stalls** Low

Form RPR

20 **1** **Alf Guineas (IRE)**[15] 7410 3-9-0 0.................................... TomQueally 5 76+
(John Gosden) *stdd after s: hld up in tch and travelled strly: clsd 2f out and sn pushed into ld: r.o wl: comf* **6/4**[2]

403 **2** 1½ **Stanley**[16] 7384 3-9-5 78.. AdamKirby 3 75+
(Luca Cumani) *chsd ldrs: effrt and hung lft over 1f out: chsd wnr 100yds out: kpt on for clr 2nd but no threat to wnr* **4/5**[1]

06 **3** 3½ **Spinart**[29] 7009 3-9-2 0.. RobHornby(3) 7 68
(Pam Sly) *chsd ldrs: effrt to chse ldr 2f out: unable qck over 1f out: lost 2nd 100yds out: wknd* **12/1**

0 **4** 1 **Dinsdale**[20] 7280 3-9-5 0... TomMarquand 6 66
(Michael Scudamore) *led: rdn and hdd over 1f out: wknd ins fnl f* **50/1**

55 **5** 2½ **Macksville (IRE)**[78] 5486 3-9-5 0.......................... RichardKingscote 2 61
(Jeremy Gask) *in tch in midfield: effrt 2f out: sn outpcd: wl hld and kpt on same pce ins fnl f* **33/1**

0 **6** ½ **Jackblack**[28] 7052 4-9-8 0.. JimmyQuinn 9 59
(Patrick Chamings) *hld up in tch in midfield: pushed along and outpcd over 1f out: wl hld and kpt on same pce ins fnl f* **100/1**

7 2 **Deeley's Double (FR)** 3-9-2 0.. EoinWalsh(3) 1 56
(Tony Carroll) *stdd s: t.k.h: hld up in rr: hdwy and hung rt bnd over 3f out: rdn over 1f out: no imp* **100/1**

0032 **8** 1 **Angelical (IRE)**[49] 6444 3-9-0 61.................................. TonyHamilton 10 48
(Daniel Mark Loughnane) *chsd ldr tl 2f out: swtchd rt and lost pl over 1f out: wknd fnl f* **10/1**[3]

0 **9** 17 **Look Who's There**[59] 6140 5-9-5 0................................ JackDuern(3) 8 17
(Sarah Hollinshead) *s.i.s: a towards rr: rdn 4f out: lost tch 3f out* **150/1**

10 7 **Sehail (USA)** 3-9-5 0... StevieDonohoe 4 3
(George Peckham) *s.i.s: rn green and a towards rr: lost tch 3f out: t.o* **14/1**

1m 59.94s (-0.86) **Going Correction** -0.10s/f (Stan)
WFA 3 from 4yo+ 3lb **10** Ran SP% **126.5**
Speed ratings (Par 103): **99,97,94,93,91 91,89,88,73,67**
CSF £3.34 TOTE £2.60: £1.10, £1.10, £3.70; EX 3.40 Trifecta £18.00.
Owner Mohamed Obaida **Bred** Rabbah Bloodstock Limited **Trained** Newmarket, Suffolk

FOCUS
Little depth to this maiden, which was run at a modest gallop. Muddling form rated around the third and fourth.

7754 BETWAY H'CAP 1m 1f 103y (Tp)
4:30 (4:30) (Class 6) (0-60,60) 3-Y-O+ **£2,749** (£818; £408; £204) **Stalls** Low

Form RPR

11 **1** **Protest (IRE)**[21] 7256 3-8-9 **56**.................................... MitchGodwin(5) 7 64
(Sylvester Kirk) *mde all: travelling strly and clr jst over 2f out: rdn over 1f out: tiring ins fnl f: drvn towards fin: a jst holding on* **11/4**[1]

0464 **2** nk **Two In The Pink (IRE)**[80] 5393 6-9-6 **59**.......................... AdamKirby 1 65+
(Ralph J Smith) *shuffled bk towards rr after 1f: in tch in last quartet: hdwy 3f out: swtchd rt and effrt over 1f out: hdwy u.p 1f out: chsd wnr wl ins fnl f: styd on: nvr quite getting to wnr* **17/2**

5002 **3** 1¾ **Enchanted Moment**[21] 7256 4-8-12 **54**..................(p) LouisSteward(3) 6 57
(Chris Wall) *chsd ldrs: rdn over 3f out: chsd wnr 2f out: kpt on but no real imp: lost 2nd wl ins fnl f* **9/2**[2]

3013 **4** 1 **Maverik**[11] 7515 8-9-7 **60**...(tp) TomMarquand 3 61
(Ali Stronge) *hld up in tch in midfield: swtchd rt and effrt u.p 2f out: kpt on same pce fr over 1f out* **10/1**

3500 **5** 1 **Percy Verence**[18] 7336 3-9-2 **58**....................................(t) JoeyHaynes 2 58
(K R Burke) *hld up in tch in last quartet: hdwy 2f out: kpt on same pce and no imp ins fnl f* **33/1**

4360 **6** hd **Scent Of Power**[6] 7628 4-8-10 **54**................................ GeorgeWood(5) 9 53
(Barry Leavy) *stdd and dropped in bhd after s: hld up in tch in rr: hdwy on inner 2f out: kpt on same pce ins fnl f* **16/1**

0001 **7** 1¼ **Thane Of Cawdor (IRE)**[21] 7257 7-9-4 **60**.......... JosephineGordon(3) 8 57
(Joseph Tuite) *hld up in tch in midfield: effrt u.p over 1f out: no imp 1f out: kpt on same pce ins fnl f* **7/1**[3]

0000 **8** ½ **Cadmium**[11] 7500 5-9-3 **56**... PJMcDonald 5 52
(Micky Hammond) *squeezed for room leaving stalls: hld up in tch in last quartet: switching rt and effrt wl over 1f out: sn no imp and kpt on same pce after* **25/1**

-000 **9** 6 **Thermal Column (IRE)**[14] 7435 4-9-4 **60**........... AlistairRawlinson(3) 11 44
(Michael Appleby) *in tch in midfield but stuck on outer: rdn over 2f out: wknd over 1f out* **8/1**

30P0 **10** 2 **Toffee Apple (IRE)**[16] 7385 3-8-13 **55**.............................. JasonHart 12 36
(Keith Dalgleish) *chsd ldr tl 2f out: sn lost pl u.p: wknd over 1f out: eased wl ins fnl f* **18/1**

0000 **11** 2½ **Gift From God**[22] 7212 3-8-13 **55**.................................(t) SteveDrowne 10 32
(Hugo Froud) *hld up in tch in rr: rdn and no rspnse over 2f out: sn wknd* **33/1**

3520 **12** nk **Golden Isles (IRE)**[36] 6827 3-9-3 **59**.............................. TomQueally 13 35
(J S Moore) *chsd ldrs tl over 2f out: sn lost pl: bhd and eased ins fnl f* **25/1**

5050 **13** 9 **Red Ruffian (IRE)**[28] 7048 3-8-11 **56**.............................. JackDuern(3) 4 15
(Dean Ivory) *squeezed for room leaving stalls: sn wl in tch in midfield: pushed along 3f out: sn lost pl: bhd and eased over 1f out* **16/1**

1m 59.82s (-0.98) **Going Correction** -0.10s/f (Stan)
WFA 3 from 4yo+ 3lb **13** Ran SP% **118.7**
Speed ratings (Par 101): **100,99,98,97,96 96,95,94,89,87 85,85,77**
CSF £24.96 CT £102.30 TOTE £2.60: £1.40, £3.10, £2.10; EX 23.80 Trifecta £98.80.
Owner Sylvester Kirk **Bred** Paget Bloodstock & Eadling Farm **Trained** Upper Lambourn, Berks

FOCUS
Just a moderate handicap, controlled in front by the winner.

7755 SUN BETS ON THE APP STORE APPRENTICE H'CAP 1m 141y (Tp)
5:00 (5:01) (Class 6) (0-65,65) 3-Y-O+ **£2,749** (£818; £408; £204) **Stalls** Low

Form RPR

3253 **1** **Roman De Brut (IRE)**[32] 6921 4-9-1 **63**.......................... TobyEley(7) 10 71
(Daniel Mark Loughnane) *chsd ldng pair tl wnt 2nd 2f out: sn rdn to ld: clr and edgd lft 1f out: styd on: rdn out* **11/2**[3]

1064 **2** 1¼ **Mary Le Bow**[134] 3476 5-9-5 **63**............................(t) CallumShepherd(3) 2 68
(Victor Dartnall) *hld up in tch towards rr: hdwy over 3f out: rdn to chse clr wnr 1f out: kpt on but nvr enough pce to chal* **14/1**

6350 **3** hd **Quoteline Direct**[29] 7010 3-9-1 **62**.................................. GeorgeWood(3) 1 69
(Micky Hammond) *hld up in tch in midfield: nt clr run ent fnl 2f: swtchd rt over 1f out: styd on wl u.p ins fnl f* **22/1**

3055 **4** 2¼ **Caledonia Laird**[17] 7368 5-9-4 **62**................................ GeorgiaCox(3) 5 62
(Jo Hughes) *t.k.h: hld up in tch in midfield: swtchd rt to outer 5f out: effrt and rdn to chse ldrs 2f out: unable qck over 1f out: styd on same pce after* **9/2**[2]

6210 **5** hd **Rock Icon**[19] 7310 3-8-13 **60**.. MitchGodwin(3) 3 61
(Patrick Chamings) *chsd ldrs: effrt on inner 2f out: unable qck over 1f out: kpt on same pce ins fnl f* **14/1**

4000 **6** ½ **Chelabella**[97] 4764 3-9-2 **65**.......................................(p) LuluStanford(5) 12 65
(Michael Bell) *dwlt and dropped in bhd after s: hld up in last trio: hdwy over 2f out: swtchd rt over 1f out: kpt on same pce ins fnl f* **25/1**

6266 **7** 2¼ **Our Little Sister (IRE)**[244] 789 3-8-13 **64**.............. TheodoreLadd(7) 6 59
(Hughie Morrison) *in tch in midfield: rdn and lost pl over 2f out: no threat to ldrs and kpt on same pce fnl 2f* **25/1**

0204 **8** ½ **Catastrophe**[17] 7368 3-9-5 **63**................................... JosephineGordon 7 57
(John Quinn) *t.k.h: led for 1f: styd pressing ldr: rdn 2f out: sn outpcd: wknd fnl f* **3/1**[1]

-353 **9** ¾ **Paradise Palm**[11] 7514 3-8-12 **61**.............................. RhiainIngram(5) 9 53
(Philip McBride) *t.k.h: led after 1f: rdn ent fnl 2f: sn hdd and unable qck: lost 2nd 1f out: wknd ins fnl f* **16/1**

50-6 **10** hd **Gambol (FR)**[31] 6965 6-9-3 **65**...................................(t[1]) LukeCatton(7) 13 56
(Ian Williams) *taken down early: stdd and dropped in bhd after s: hld up in rr: effrt wl over 1f out: no hdwy* **25/1**

0646 **11** nk **Rocket Ronnie (IRE)**[22] 7227 6-9-10 **65**.......................(b) RobHornby 8 55
(Ed McMahon) *t.k.h: hld up in tch in midfield: lost pl and rdn over 2f out: wl hld over 1f out* **9/2**[2]

6500 **12** 1¾ **Breakheart (IRE)**[237] 875 9-9-1 **63**............................ MichaelColes(7) 11 50
(Andrew Balding) *in tch but a towards rr: rdn over 2f out: n.d fnl 2f* **40/1**

1m 50.8s (0.70) **Going Correction** -0.10s/f (Stan)
WFA 3 from 4yo+ 3lb **12** Ran SP% **114.3**
Speed ratings (Par 101): **92,90,90,88,88 88,86,85,84,84 84,82**
CSF £69.97 CT £1581.25 TOTE £6.00: £1.90, £3.20, £6.20; EX 33.40 Trifecta £528.50.
Owner Phil Slater **Bred** Tinnakill Bloodstock **Trained** Baldwin's Gate, Staffs

FOCUS
This very modest apprentice handicap was run at a steady pace, and a number pulled too hard as a consequence. The front three and the winner's career to date are a good guide to the level in a straightforward handicap.
T/Plt: £330.60 to a £1 stake. Pool: £76321.38, 168.5 winning units. T/Qpdt: £8.80 to a £1 stake. Pool: £9903.18, 831.66 winning units. **Steve Payne**

7712 FLEMINGTON (L-H)
Tuesday, November 1

OFFICIAL GOING: Turf: good

7756a EMIRATES MELBOURNE CUP (GROUP 1) (3YO+) (TURF) 2m
4:00 (12:00) 3-Y-O+
£1,883,663 (£445,544; £222,772; £123,762; £86,633; £61,881)

RPR

1 **Almandin (GER)**[30] 6994 6-8-3 0.................................. KerrinMcEvoy 17 114
(Robert Hickmott, Australia) *towards rr of midfield: gd hdwy fr 3f out: rdn to chal 1 1/2f out: qcknd clr w 2nd 1f out: r.o wl: led narrowly clsng stages: rdn out* **10/1**

2 hd **Heartbreak City (FR)**[73] 5655 6-8-7 0...........................(t) JoaoMoreira 23 118
(A J Martin, Ire) *towards rr of midfield: hdwy fr 3f out: short of room 2 1/2f out: rdn 2f out: led narrowly 1 1/2f out: qcknd clr w wnr 1f out: r.o wl: hdd narrowly clsng stages* **18/1**

3 4¼ **Hartnell**[10] 7553 5-8-11 0... JamesMcDonald 12 117+
(J O'Shea, Australia) *midfield: gd hdwy fr 3 1/2f out: rdn and led briefly under 2f out: hdd 1 1/2f out: outpcd by front pair fnl f: kpt on* **9/2**[1]

4 2¼ **Qewy (IRE)**[13] 7481 6-8-2 0... CraigAWilliams 15 106
(Charlie Appleby) *in tch in midfield: rdn 2f out: kpt on fnl f: snatched 4th cl home* **20/1**

5 shd **Who Shot Thebarman (NZ)**[10] 7552 8-8-11 0.........(t) HughBowman 20 115
(Chris Waller, Australia) *hld up in rr: stdy hdwy fr 3f out: rdn over 2f out: styd on: nrst fin* **25/1**

6 shd **Almoonqith (USA)**[17] 7378 6-8-8 0...........................(b) MichaelWalker 19 112
(David A & B Hayes & Tom Dabernig, Australia) *towards rr: hdwy fr 3 1/2f out: wnt 4th 1 1/2f out: no imp on front three fnl f: no ex clsng stages* **30/1**

7 1 **Beautiful Romance**[39] 6747 4-8-4 0................................ DamianLane 1 107
(Saeed bin Suroor) *s.s: towards rr: rdn and kpt on steadily fr 2 1/2f out: n.d* **70/1**

8 ¾ **Exosphéric**[17] 7378 4-8-11 0... DamienOliver 13 113
(Lee & Anthony Freedman, Australia) *towards rr of midfield: sme hdwy fr over 3f out: rdn and kpt on same pce fr 1 1/2f out: n.d* **20/1**

9 ¾ **Pentathlon (NZ)**[3] 7712 5-8-2 0.................................... MarkDuPlessis 4 103
(John Wheeler, New Zealand) *towards rr: rdn and kpt on steadily on outer fr 3f out: nvr a factor* **80/1**

10 shd **Big Orange**[96] 4799 5-9-0 0...(p) JamieSpencer 7 115
(Michael Bell) *in tch: rdn and unable qck under 3f out: drvn 2f out: wknd last 75yds* **13/1**

11 *nk* **Grand Marshal**[10] 7552 6-8-8 0.......................................(t) BenMelham 9 108
(Chris Waller, Australia) *towards rr: rdn 3f out: kpt on steadily fr 1 1/2f out: nvr a factor* **30/1**

12 *hd* **Oceanographer**[3] 7712 4-8-3 0.................................. ChadSchofield 11 103
(Charlie Appleby) *towards rr of midfield: rdn and kpt on steadily fr 2f out: nvr a factor* **8/1**[3]

13 *3/4* **Bondi Beach (IRE)**[52] 6351 4-8-11 0................................ RyanMoore 5 110
(A P O'Brien, Ire) *hld up towards rr: rdn 3 1/2f out: kpt on steadily fnl 2f: nvr a factor* **12/1**

14 *3* **Grey Lion (IRE)**[13] 7481 4-8-3 0.. GlenBoss 16 99
(Matt Cumani, Australia) *in tch in midfield: rdn and effrt 2f out: wknd under 1f out* **40/1**

15 *hd* **Jameka (AUS)**[17] 7378 4-8-8 0.. NicholasHall 3 104
(Ciaron Maher, Australia) *midfield: sme hdwy 3 1/2f out: rdn over 2f out: wknd over 1f out* **15/2**[2]

16 *1 3/4* **Excess Knowledge**[10] 7552 6-8-6 0.................................. VladDuric 21 100
(Gai Waterhouse & Adrian Bott, Australia) *prom tl led after 4f: hdd 1/2-way: led 3f out: rdn and hdd under 2f out: sn wknd* **60/1**

17 *shd* **Our Ivanhoe (GER)**[17] 7378 6-9-0 0........................(bt) DwayneDunn 6 108
(Lee & Anthony Freedman, Australia) *midfield: pushed along 3f out: short of room and lost pl 2f out: sn rdn and btn* **50/1**

18 *5* **Sir John Hawkwood (IRE)**[17] 7378 7-8-7 0..............(t) BlakeSpriggs 14 95
(John P Thompson, Australia) *a towards rr* **80/1**

19 *shd* **Assign (IRE)**[24] 5-8-3 0.. KatelynMallyon 22 91
(Robert Hickmott, Australia) *trckd ldrs: rdn 4f out: wkng whn short of room over 2f out: sn btn* **50/1**

20 *1 1/4* **Gallante (IRE)**[10] 7552 5-8-8 0..(t) BlakeShinn 2 95
(Robert Hickmott, Australia) *towards rr of midfield: rdn and no significant hdwy fr 3f out: wknd 1 1/2f out* **50/1**

21 *hd* **Secret Number**[47] 6505 6-8-3 0.................................. StephenBaster 10 90
(Saeed bin Suroor) *in tch: hdwy to ld 1/2-way: rdn and hdd 3f out: wknd under 2f out* **30/1**

22 *2* **Wicklow Brave**[51] 6387 7-8-11 0.................................. FrankieDettori 24 95
(W P Mullins, Ire) *racd alone on outer first 3f: trckd ldrs after: rdn 3f out: wknd under 2f out* **15/1**

23 *3* **Curren Mirotic (JPN)**[37] 8-8-13 0..............................(t) TommyBerry 18 94
(Osamu Hirata, Japan) *led: hdd after 4f: trckd ldrs after: rdn over 4f out: lost pl 3f out: sn btn* **50/1**

24 *72* **Rose Of Virginia (NZ)**[3] 7712 7-8-0 0....................(b) BenEThompson 8 81
(Lee & Shannon Hope, Australia) *midfield: rdn and dropped towards rr 5f: sn struggling: t.o* **60/1**

3m 20.58s (0.94) **24** Ran SP% **117.0**

Owner N C Williams & Mr & Mrs L J Williams **Bred** Gestut Schlenderhan **Trained** Australia

FOCUS

This looked a wide-open renewal of the race that stops a nation and it was run at a good gallop, which wasn't the case last year. The field mostly headed down the middle of the track in the home straight for the final time and two came away to provide the public with a thrilling finish. The fifth, sixth and ninth help set the standard.

7655 MAISONS-LAFFITTE (R-H)

Tuesday, November 1

OFFICIAL GOING: Turf: soft

7757a PRIX MIESQUE (GROUP 3) (2YO FILLIES) (TURF) (STRAIGHT) 7f (S)

1:20 (12:00) 2-Y-O **£29,411** (£11,764; £8,823; £5,882; £2,941)

RPR

1 **Dame Du Roi (IRE)**[27] 7086 2-8-11 0......................... AurelienLemaitre 3 105
(F Head, France) *hld up: rdn in last over 1f out: r.o and chal fnl f: up to ld nring fin: shade cosily* **6/4**[1]

2 *1* **Kambura (FR)**[33] 6913 2-8-11 0........................... Jean-BernardEyquem 8 102
(K Borgel, France) *hld up: angled out and rdn to cl 2f out: chal and led fnl f: kpt on but worn down and hdd towards fin: no ex: jst on for hld 2nd* **11/1**

3 *hd* **Thais (FR)**[30] 6987 2-8-11 0................................ Pierre-CharlesBoudot 1 101
(P Bary, France) *midfield: rdn over 1f out: kpt on fnl f but nt quite pce of wnr: jst missed 2nd* **3/1**[3]

4 *1 1/4* **Elegante Bere (FR)**[30] 6986 2-8-11 0............................. ThierryJarnet 4 98
(D Guillemin, France) *midfield in tch: swtchd rt and rdn to chal over 1f out: ev ch ent fnl f: kpt on same pce and hld towards fin: jst prevailed for 4th* **15/2**

5 *hd* **Thrust Home (IRE)**[36] 2-8-11 0..............................(b) MaximeGuyon 2 97
(Y Durepaire, France) *trckd ldr: rdn to chal over 1f out: kpt on same pce and hld towards fin: jst denied 4th* **14/1**

6 *1 3/4* **Moonlit Show**[35] 6860 2-8-11 0..(p) BillyLee 6 93
(Charlie Fellowes) *led: rdn and strly pressed fr 2f out: hdd fnl f: no ex and fdd towards fin* **11/4**[2]

7 *3/4* **Upendi (FR)**[24] 7169 2-8-11 0....................................... GregoryBenoist 7 91
(Robert Collet, France) *trckd ldr: rdn to chal 2f out: ev ch ent fnl f: no ex and fdd towards fin* **33/1**

8 *4 1/2* **Sailana (GER)**[24] 2-8-11 0.. NicolasGuilbert 5 80
(Christina Bucher, Switzerland) *midfield: rdn 2f out: fnd little and sn btn: wknd into last* **28/1**

1m 27.9s (-0.10) **8** Ran SP% **124.8**

WIN (incl. 1 euro stake): 2.80. PLACES: 1.20, 1.70, 1.40. DF: 11.10. SF: 15.90.

Owner Mme P Ades-Hazan & E Puerari **Bred** E Puerari & Mme P Ades-Hazan **Trained** France

7758a PRIX DE SEINE-ET-OISE (GROUP 3) (3YO+) (TURF) 6f (S)

1:50 (12:00) 3-Y-O+ **£29,411** (£11,764; £8,823; £5,882; £2,941)

RPR

1 **The Right Man**[29] 7030 4-9-0 0......................... Francois-XavierBertras 12 110+
(D Guillemin, France) *hld up: smooth hdwy on outer over 1f out: rdn to chal ent fnl f and sn led: r.o and asserted: readily* **15/8**[1]

2 *2* **Porthilly (FR)**[30] 6990 6-8-10 0.. AlexisBadel 1 100
(J E Hammond, France) *led: rdn 2f out: kpt on but hdd fnl f: no ex w wnr after* **20/1**

3 *2* **La Rioja**[37] 6816 3-8-9 0.. OisinMurphy 8 92
(Henry Candy) *midfield: clsd and prom 1/2-way: rdn and effrt 2f out: kpt on same pce for 3rd fnl f* **4/1**[3]

4 *nk* **Finsbury Square (IRE)**[30] 6990 4-9-2 0...............(b) OlivierPeslier 13 98
(F Chappet, France) *hld up: rdn and hdwy over 1f out: kpt on but nt pce to chal front pair fnl f* **7/2**[2]

5 *1/2* **Aces (IRE)**[10] 4-9-0 0.. ThierryJarnet 9 95
(J E Hammond, France) *midfield: rdn 2f out: kpt on same pce and nt able to chal* **20/1**

6 *1* **Dhahmaan (IRE)**[27] 7068 3-8-13 0..............................(b) MaximeGuyon 3 90
(Marco Botti) *hld up in midfield: rdn over 2f out: kpt on u.p fnl f but nt able to chal: up for 6th post* **18/1**

7 *shd* **Love Spirit**[86] 5217 6-9-0 0.................................. Pierre-CharlesBoudot 4 91
(Louis Baudron, France) *in tch: rdn 2f out: kpt on same pce fnl f and nt able to chal: jst lost out for 6th* **5/1**

8 *nk* **Daring Match (GER)**[23] 5-9-0 0.................................. AntoineHamelin 6 90
(J Hirschberger, Germany) *trckd ldr: rdn for effrt 2f out: no ex fnl f: fdd* **16/1**

9 *5* **Damila (FR)**[51] 6391 3-8-11 0...................................... CristianDemuro 11 71
(H-A Pantall, France) *hld up: rdn 2f out: sn outpcd: eased whn btn fnl f* **14/1**

10 *4 1/2* **Marsh Hawk**[58] 6161 4-8-10 0.................................. StephanePasquier 2 56
(Richard Hannon) *trckd ldr: rdn and lost pl 2f out: sn btn: eased* **25/1**

11 *7* **Pupa Di Saronno (FR)**[29] 7030 5-8-10 0......................... FabriceVeron 7 33
(H-A Pantall, France) *in tch: rdn and lost pl 1/2-way: sn btn: eased* **25/1**

12 *nk* **Ross Castle (IRE)**[51] 6391 3-9-1 0...............................(p) TonyPiccone 5 37
(Matthieu Palussiere, France) *a in rr: eased whn btn: no factor* **33/1**

1m 11.8s (-1.60) **12** Ran SP% **131.6**

WIN (incl. 1 euro stake): 3.70. PLACES: 1.70, 3.00, 2.40. DF: 24.70. SF: 45.40.

Owner Pegase Bloodstock **Bred** Mme D Wigan **Trained** France

4928 MUNICH (L-H)

Tuesday, November 1

OFFICIAL GOING: Turf: soft

7759a PASTORIUS GROSSER PREIS VON BAYERN (GROUP 1) (3YO+) (TURF) 1m 4f

2:00 (12:00) 3-Y-O+ **£73,529** (£22,058; £11,029; £5,147; £2,205)

RPR

1 **Guignol (GER)**[16] 7402 4-9-6 0.................................. MichaelCadeddu 2 114
(Jean-Pierre Carvalho, Germany) *mde all: clr 1/2-way: rdn 2f out: styd on wl: reduced advantage fnl f but a doing more than enough* **33/1**

2 *1 3/4* **Racing History (IRE)**[17] 7353 4-9-6 0.................. IoritzMendizabal 6 111+
(Saeed bin Suroor) *prom in main body of field: rdn into st: styd on fnl f and clsng on wnr but nvr getting there: jst up for 2nd post:* **61/10**

3 *nse* **Hawkbill (USA)**[52] 6354 3-9-1 0....................................(p) WilliamBuick 5 112+
(Charlie Appleby) *sn prom in main body of field: rdn over 2f out: styd on fnl f and clsng on wnr but nvr getting there: jst lost out for 2nd post* **18/5**[2]

4 *2 1/2* **Iquitos (GER)**[37] 6822 4-9-6 0.. IanFerguson 7 107+
(H-J Groschel, Germany) *hld up in rr: rdn early in st: styd on steadily and wnt 4th ins fnl f: n.d* **54/10**

5 *1* **Savoir Vivre (IRE)**[30] 6989 3-9-1 0...................... ChristopheSoumillon 4 106+
(Jean-Pierre Carvalho, Germany) *trckd clr ldr: rdn early in st: no ex and fdd into 5th fnl f* **6/4**[1]

6 *5 1/2* **Algometer**[45] 6571 3-9-1 0.. FergusSweeney 1 98+
(David Simcock) *midfield: rdn into st: outpcd fnl 2f* **43/10**[3]

7 *nk* **Royal Solitaire (IRE)**[30] 6988 4-9-3 0................................ FilipMinarik 8 93+
(P Schiergen, Germany) *hld up: rdn over 2f out: outpcd fnl 2f* **122/10**

8 *16* **Sirius (GER)**[37] 6822 5-9-6 0...................................(b) AndreasSuborics 9 71+
(Andreas Lowe, Germany) *midfield: rdn into st: sn no imp: eased: t.o* **168/10**

9 *3 1/2* **Girolamo (GER)**[37] 7-9-6 0...................................(b) DennisSchiergen 10 65+
(P Schiergen, Germany) *hld up: rdn into st: no imp: eased: t.o* **29/1**

2m 37.42s (157.42)

WFA 3 from 4yo+ 6lb **9** Ran SP% **129.8**

WIN (incl. 10 euro stake): 335. PLACES: 49, 27, 17. SF: 14,812..

Owner Stall Ullmann **Bred** Stall Ullmann **Trained** Germany

FOCUS

This looked one of the most competitive German Group 1s of the year, but a few of these had question marks hanging over them. It produced a bit of a shock, and the ground seemed as described. The winner was given way too much rope in front.

7732 KEMPTON (A.W) (R-H)

Wednesday, November 2

OFFICIAL GOING: Polytrack: standard to slow

Wind: nil Weather: Clear, cold

7760 32RED ON THE APP STORE H'CAP 2m (P)

4:55 (4:55) (Class 6) (0-65,65) 3-Y-O **£2,264** (£673; £336; £168) **Stalls** Low

Form RPR

3040 **1** **Multigifted**[7] 7614 3-8-12 **56**.. LiamKeniry 6 62
(Michael Madgwick) *t.k.h in 5th on inner: swtchd off rail bef 1/2-way and hdwy on outer to sit handy: led over 5f out: stole a ld ent st: shkn up 3f out: 5 l clr over 1f out: pushed out fnl f: comf* **8/1**

00 **2** *1 1/4* **Southern States**[15] 7425 3-9-5 **63**.................................. RobertHavlin 2 67
(Lydia Richards) *hld up in 7th: rdn along in 6th 3f out: prog between horses ent fnl f: tk 2nd fnl 110yds: n.d to wnr* **10/1**

0052 **3** *3/4* **Balancing Time**[43] 6659 3-9-7 **65**................................... TomQueally 9 68
(Amanda Perrett) *settled in 5th: prog on inner over 4f out to sit in 3rd: rdn along over 2f out: kpt one one pce tl lost 2nd fnl 110yds* **10/11**[1]

6200 **4** *shd* **Moon Over Mobay**[58] 6194 3-8-13 **57**........................... DavidProbert 3 60
(Michael Blanshard) *hld up in 8th: rdn along over 4f out: kpt on one pce after* **20/1**

3344 **5** *6* **Le Tissier**[20] 7309 3-9-2 **60**..(p) KierenFox 10 56
(Michael Attwater) *handy in 4th on outer: shkn up 4f out: stl there in 5th over 2f out: wknd over 1f out* **6/1**[2]

5341 **6** *6* **Templier (IRE)**[70] 5783 3-9-4 **65**..............................(p) HectorCrouch(3) 5 54
(Gary Moore) *led: hdd over 5f out: rdn in 2nd over 2f out: wknd qckly fr over 1f out* **7/1**[3]

000 **7** *3 1/4* **Pixel (IRE)**[11] 7529 3-8-13 **60**..................................... TimClark(3) 7 45
(Denis Quinn) *in rr: bhd over 6f out: rdn over 3f out: sn hld* **100/1**

060 **8** *21* **Theocratic**[29] 7052 3-8-13 **57**.....................................(vt) StevieDonohoe 1 16
(Charlie Fellowes) *racd in 3rd: lost pl by 1/2-way: rdn along to hold tch over 4f out: no ex: t.o* **20/1**

0004 **9** *30* **Murraqib (USA)**[11] 7532 3-8-6 **50**..................................(v) MartinDwyer 8
(Brett Johnson) *chsd ldr: pushed along over 5f out: eased fr over 3f out: t.o* **20/1**

3m 30.4s (0.30) **Going Correction** 0.0s/f (Stan) **9** Ran SP% **114.6**
Speed ratings (Par 98): **99,98,98,97,94 91,90,79,64**
CSF £77.21 CT £140.56 TOTE £12.80: £2.10, £2.20, £1.70; EX 120.60 Trifecta £483.40.
Owner Mrs L N Harmes **Bred** Mrs L N Harmes **Trained** Denmead, Hants
■ Stewards' Enquiry : David Probert two-day ban: used whip above permitted level (Nov 16-17)

FOCUS
Most of these unexposed sorts were trying the marathon trip for the first time and there was a stop/start gallop. It looks unreliable form.

7761 100% PROFIT BOOST AT 32REDSPORT.COM MAIDEN FILLIES' STKS (PLUS 10 RACE) (DIV I) 1m (P)
5:25 (5:27) (Class 5) 2-Y-O **£2,911** (£866; £432; £216) **Stalls** Low

Form RPR

1 **Prosper** 2-9-0 0.. AndreaAtzeni 10 74
(Roger Varian) *restrained in 4th on inner: shkn up 2f out to chse clr ldr: gaining ent fnl f: led fnl 100yds* **20/1**

6 **2** *1/2* **Music Lesson**[11] 7548 2-9-0 0...................................... JimmyFortune 14 73
(Hughie Morrison) *led: shkn up 2f out: 3 l ld over 1f out: kpt on by wore down by wnr and hdd 100yds out* **25/1**

2 **3** *3/4* **Kitty Boo**[51] 6414 2-9-0 0.. AdamKirby 8 71+
(Luca Cumani) *sluggish s: sn pushed up to sit in mid-div: rdn on outside over 2f out: kpt on wl* **10/11**[1]

4 *1/2* **Ocean Of Love** 2-9-0 0.. MartinLane 11 70
(Saeed bin Suroor) *chsd ldr: rdn over 2f out: kpt on* **7/1**[2]

5 *1/2* **Cercle D'Or (IRE)** 2-9-0 0.. RobertHavlin 9 69
(John Gosden) *settled between horses chsng ldng pair: rdn over 2f out: kpt on* **14/1**

0 **6** *1/2* **Star Of Doha**[22] 7239 2-9-0 0.. SeanLevey 5 67
(Ralph Beckett) *settled in mid-divison on inner: rdn 2f out: kpt on one pce* **25/1**

7 *1/2* **Bois D'Ebene (IRE)** 2-8-11 0.................................. KieranShoemark[(3)] 2 66+
(Roger Charlton) *missed break and hld up in rr: n.m.r on heels ent st: rdn over 2f out: no immediate imp tl kpt on wl on outer fr over 1f out: nrst fin* **66/1**

8 *nk* **Mohallela (USA)** 2-9-0 0... DaneO'Neill 4 65
(Owen Burrows) *s.s: in rr-div: tk clsr order bnd: rdn over 2f out: kpt on* **10/1**[3]

5 **9** *1* **Penny Red**[29] 7050 2-9-0 0... RichardKingscote 3 63
(William Knight) *t.k.h in mid-dvision on inner: rdn over 2f out: kpt on* **16/1**

10 *1 1/2* **Fleur Forsyte** 2-9-0 0.. TomQueally 13 59
(James Fanshawe) *s.s: t.k.h on outer in rr: rdn along in rr w plenty to do over 2f out: styd on past btn horse fnl f* **25/1**

11 *shd* **Velvet Voice** 2-9-0 0... StevieDonohoe 7 59
(Mark H Tompkins) *covered up in mid-div: niggled along over 4f out: rdn over 2f out: kpt on on pce* **100/1**

5 **12** *1* **Lenoire**[21] 7285 2-9-0 0.. RobertTart 6 57
(John Gosden) *t.k.h in rr: rdn over 2f out: nvr involved* **16/1**

6 **13** *1 1/2* **Duke's Girl**[39] 6776 2-8-11 0...................................... LouisSteward[(3)] 12 53
(Michael Bell) *settled in 3rd on outside under restraint: rdn over 2f out: wknd over 1f out* **66/1**

14 *8* **Ghand (IRE)** 2-9-0 0.. JoeFanning 1 34
(Sir Michael Stoute) *rn green in rr: shkn up over 2f out: no rspnse and hands and heels after* **10/1**[3]

1m 40.67s (0.87) **Going Correction** 0.0s/f (Stan) **14** Ran SP% **121.8**
Speed ratings (Par 93): **95,94,93,93,92 92,91,91,90,88 88,87,86,78**
CSF £427.81 TOTE £12.00: £4.00, £6.10, £1.10; EX 377.70 Trifecta £1935.40.
Owner China Horse Club **Bred** Newsells Park Stud **Trained** Newmarket, Suffolk

FOCUS
The first division of a maiden that can throw up a fair sort, but they seemed to go a slow gallop which meant it paid to be prominent. The third has been rated below her debut form.

7762 100% PROFIT BOOST AT 32REDSPORT.COM MAIDEN FILLIES' STKS (PLUS 10 RACE) (DIV II) 1m (P)
5:55 (6:01) (Class 5) 2-Y-O **£2,911** (£866; £432; £216) **Stalls** Low

Form RPR

2 **1** **Golden Nectar**[21] 7278 2-9-0 0..................................... PatCosgrave 10 74
(Laura Mongan) *nt settled early chsng ldr: rdn 2f out: led 1f out: kpt on gamely whn pressed: jst hld on* **14/1**

3 **2** *nse* **Sea Tide**[21] 7284 2-9-0 0...[1] TomMarquand 2 74
(Hugo Palmer) *t.k.h chsng ldrs: travelling strly over 2f out: shkn up over 1f out: kpt on nring fin: jst hld* **6/5**[1]

4 **3** *1 3/4* **So Sleek**[21] 7285 2-9-0 0.. AdamKirby 12 70
(Luca Cumani) *sn led: shkn up over 2f out: hdd 1f out: wknd ins fnl f* **16/1**

4 *1 1/4* **Shenanigans (IRE)** 2-9-0 0.. AndreaAtzeni 1 67
(Roger Varian) *chsd ldrs: rdn over 2f out: kpt on tl wknd fnl f* **20/1**

4 **5** *1/2* **Star Rock**[11] 7543 2-9-0 0... JimmyFortune 8 66
(Hughie Morrison) *settled in mid-div on inner: rdn over 2f out: kpt on one pce* **10/1**

6 *hd* **Lady Bergamot (FR)** 2-9-0 0.. TomQueally 5 66+
(James Fanshawe) *in rr-div: rdn over 2f out: nt picked up tl ent fnl f: styd on wl* **40/1**

0 **7** *1* **Pobbles**[44] 6625 2-8-11 0....................................... KieranShoemark[(3)] 9 63
(Roger Charlton) *led early: settled in 3rd on inner: shkn up over 2f out on inner: stl there over 1f out: nvr involved fnl f* **33/1**

0 **8** *1 1/4* **Nargiza (USA)**[21] 7278 2-8-11 0.................................. LouisSteward[(3)] 13 60
(Chris Wall) *chsd ldrs on outer: rdn over 2f out: nt picked up* **66/1**

9 *nk* **Classified (IRE)** 2-8-9 0.. CallumShepherd[(5)] 6 60
(Ed de Giles) *s.s: in rr: rdn oevr 2f out: kpt on one pce* **100/1**

10 *1* **Bizzarria** 2-9-0 0.. RobertHavlin 4 57+
(John Gosden) *settled in mid-div: shkn up over 2f out: kpt on tl n.m.r ent fnl f: hands and heels after* **4/1**[2]

0 **11** *1/2* **Champagne Reign (IRE)**[12] 7503 2-9-0 0........................ JohnFahy 14 56
(J S Moore) *in rr-div: green and pushed along early: rdn over 2f out: wknd fnl f* **125/1**

12 *hd* **Everdina** 2-9-0 0.. ThomasBrown 11 56
(Ed Walker) *s.s: a in rr: rdn over 2f out: no imp* **50/1**

13 *3/4* **Ramya (IRE)** 2-9-0 0.. DaneO'Neill 7 54
(Sir Michael Stoute) *in rr-div: rdn along over 2f out: sn lft bhd* **10/1**

14 *3* **My Rosie (IRE)** 2-9-0 0.. NickyMackay 3 47
(John Gosden) *a in rr* **15/2**[3]

1m 41.88s (2.08) **Going Correction** 0.0s/f (Stan) **14** Ran SP% **123.3**
Speed ratings (Par 93): **89,88,87,85,85 85,84,83,82,81 81,81,80,77**
CSF £30.99 TOTE £12.00: £3.30, £1.40, £3.20; EX 43.20 Trifecta £315.90.
Owner Mrs P J Sheen **Bred** Beech Park Bloodstock Ltd **Trained** Epsom, Surrey

FOCUS
Slower than the first division and once again it paid to be on the pace. Two with experience fought out the close finish. The level is a bit fluid.

7763 IRISH STALLION FARMS EBF MAIDEN FILLIES' STKS (PLUS 10 RACE) 7f (P)
6:25 (6:31) (Class 5) 2-Y-O **£3,234** (£962; £481; £240) **Stalls** Low

Form RPR

1 **Daban (IRE)** 2-9-0 0.. RobertHavlin 4 78+
(John Gosden) *in rr-div on inner: tk clsr order over 2f out: gng wl bhd wall of horses waiting for gap over 1f: qcknd up smartly fr 1f out to ld fnl 100yds: cosily* **9/2**[2]

2 *1/2* **Thafeera (USA)** 2-9-0 0...[1] DaneO'Neill 11 74
(Charles Hills) *s.s: settled in 6th and t.k.h: rdn 2f out: kpt on wl on outer to snatch 2nd post* **25/1**

30 **3** *nk* **Ghadaayer (IRE)**[29] 7056 2-9-0 0.................................. JimmyFortune 8 73
(Sir Michael Stoute) *led after 1f: rdn 2f out: kpt on wl tl hdd 100yds out: lost 2nd post* **8/1**[3]

4 *1* **Tomyris** 2-9-0 0.. AndreaAtzeni 9 70
(Roger Varian) *in rr and rn green: shkn up 2f out and swtchd to inner: kpt on and styd on wl ins fnl f: nrst fin* **25/1**

5 *1/2* **My Lady Marie** 2-8-11 0..................................... KieranShoemark[(3)] 2 69
(Amanda Perrett) *settled in mid-divsion on inner: rdn 2f out: kpt on and ev ch ent fnl f: wknd fnl 110yds* **66/1**

0 **6** *nk* **Meshaykh (IRE)**[39] 6782 2-9-0 0.............................. RichardKingscote 13 68
(Sir Michael Stoute) *in rr: shkn up and prog up inner fr 2f out: rdn jst over 1f out: kpt on* **8/1**[3]

7 *1 1/4* **Royal Peace (IRE)** 2-9-0 0... SeanLevey 3 65
(Richard Hannon) *racd in 4th on inner: rdn 2f out: 3rd ent fnl f: wknd sn after* **33/1**

4 **8** *3* **Alouja (IRE)**[26] 7118 2-9-0 0... TomMarquand 7 57
(Hugo Palmer) *t.k.h on outer in rr-div: wdst of all 2f out: sme prog tl wknd fr 1f out* **11/8**[1]

0 **9** *1 1/4* **Mellow**[12] 7502 2-9-0 0..[1] LiamKeniry 5 53
(Hughie Morrison) *in rr: rdn 2f out: lft bhd after* **100/1**

4 **10** *hd* **Tazmania (IRE)**[62] 6062 2-9-0 0... AdamKirby 14 53
(Clive Cox) *chsd ldrw: rdn over 2f out: wknd fr over 1f out* **20/1**

11 *2 3/4* **Love Me Again** 2-9-0 0... StevieDonohoe 1 45
(Charlie Fellowes) *a in rr: no imp fr over 1f out* **100/1**

12 *1/2* **Alniyat** 2-9-0 0.. PatCosgrave 10 44
(Ed Dunlop) *settled in 5th: shkn up and drifted to centre over crse: sn no ex and wknd* **66/1**

13 *1 3/4* **Dream Waltz** 2-9-0 0.. NickyMackay 6 39
(John Gosden) *in rr: no imp fr over 2f out* **12/1**

62 **14** *3* **Dal Riata (IRE)**[11] 7548 2-9-0 0...................................... JoeFanning 12 31
(Mark Johnston) *t.k.h chsng ldrs on outer: rdn over 2f out: wknd qckly fr 2f out* **12/1**

1m 26.3s (0.30) **Going Correction** 0.0s/f (Stan) **14** Ran SP% **118.3**
Speed ratings (Par 93): **98,97,97,95,95 95,93,90,88,88 85,84,82,79**
CSF £117.65 TOTE £6.00: £2.30, £5.30, £2.20; EX 120.20 Trifecta £820.60.
Owner Abdullah Saeed Al Naboodah **Bred** Kildaragh Stud **Trained** Newmarket, Suffolk

FOCUS
Some well-bred and some expensive sorts from top stables were on show here and it appeared to have the hallmarks of a decent fillies' maiden. However, once again it appeared you needed to be on the front end of the pace.

7764 32RED.COM NURSERY H'CAP 7f (P)
6:55 (6:58) (Class 3) (0-90,90) 2-Y-O **£6,469** (£1,925; £962; £481) **Stalls** Low

Form RPR

110 **1** **Kananee (USA)**[141] 3247 2-9-7 **90**...................................[1] AndreaAtzeni 5 95
(Saeed bin Suroor) *settled in 3rd: gng wl over 2f out: rdn over 1f out: kpt on wl on outer to ld wl ins fnl f: cosily* **15/8**[1]

0111 **2** *3/4* **Mutahaady (IRE)**[38] 6800 2-9-0 **88**............................... CliffordLee[(5)] 7 91
(K R Burke) *sn led: rdn 2f out: hdd 1f out: kpt on wl ins fnl f to take 2nd nring fin* **11/2**[3]

4510 **3** *1/2* **Himself**[11] 7541 2-8-5 **74**... TomMarquand 2 76
(Richard Hannon) *settled in 4th: prog and upsides on inner over 2f out: rdn 2f out: led 1f out: wknd and lost two pls wl ins fnl f* **13/2**

215 **4** *2 3/4* **Zamjar**[20] 7305 2-8-11 **80**... PatCosgrave 6 74
(Ed Dunlop) *in rr: rdn 2f out: no imp after* **12/1**

2614 **5** *1 3/4* **Kodiac Khan (IRE)**[38] 6800 2-8-11 **80**............................ JoeFanning 3 70
(Mark Johnston) *settled in 5th: rdn 2f out: wknd after* **10/1**

2101 **6** *1 3/4* **Colonel Frank**[24] 7185 2-9-2 **85**.. AdamKirby 4 70
(Ed Walker) *t.k.h in ld early: settled bhd ldr after: rdn 2f out: no imp over 1f out: wknd* **11/4**[2]

1204 **7** *3 1/4* **Fastnet Spin (IRE)**[16] 7416 2-8-6 **78**...............(v) JosephineGordon[(3)] 1 54
(David Evans) *settled in 7th on inner: niggled along at 1/2-way: rdn 2f out: sn hld* **33/1**

1m 25.62s (-0.38) **Going Correction** 0.0s/f (Stan) **7** Ran SP% **109.9**
Speed ratings (Par 100): **102,101,100,97,95 93,89**
CSF £11.57 TOTE £2.90: £1.80, £2.20; EX 11.70 Trifecta £52.80.
Owner Godolphin **Bred** Darley **Trained** Newmarket, Suffolk

FOCUS
A small field, but all seven had won races and an above average nursery. It's been rated around the third to his previous form.

7765 32RED CASINO H'CAP 1m 4f (P)
7:25 (7:27) (Class 3) (0-95,95) 3-Y-O+
£7,158 (£2,143; £1,071; £535; £267; £134) **Stalls** Low

Form RPR

600 **1** **Prince Of Arran**[132] 3574 3-8-6 **83**................................ StevieDonohoe 3 96+
(Charlie Fellowes) *settled in 6th: rdn over 2f out: kpt on wl on inner to ld jst over 1f out: wnt clr* **5/2**[2]

0340 **2** *4* **Sunblazer (IRE)**[33] 6919 6-9-3 **95**.......................(t) JoshuaBryan[(7)] 10 100
(Kim Bailey) *in rr: rdn over 2f out w plenty to do: kpt on wl on outer fr over 1f out: tk 2nd 100yds out: nvr nrr* **14/1**

056 **3** *1 3/4* **Noble Gift**[29] 7058 6-9-5 **95**.................................. CallumShepherd[(5)] 6 97
(William Knight) *led: rdn over 2f out: kpt on wl tl hdd jst over 1f out: lost 2nd nring fin* **4/1**[3]

4540 **4** *3/4* **Energia Fox (BRZ)**[18] 7359 6-9-1 **86**.................................. JoeFanning 5 87
(Richard Fahey) *in last trio: rdn over 2f out: kpt on fr over 1f out on outer: kpt on* **12/1**

2112 **5** *1 1/4* **Cliff Face (IRE)**[82] 5350 3-8-5 **82**..................................... RyanPowell 4 81
(Sir Mark Prescott Bt) *settled in 4th bhd ldrs: squeezed up over 2f out: rdn 2f out: kpt on one pce after* **10/1**

1500 **6** *1* **Black Night (IRE)**[11] 7545 4-8-12 **83**.................................. JoeyHaynes 2 80
(J Moon, Jersey) *trckd ldrs: rdn over 2f out: kpt on and stl 3rd ent fnl f: wknd qckly after* **16/1**

1444 **7** *1/2* **Power Game**[38] 6802 4-9-4 **92**.................................. JosephineGordon(3) 8 89
(Saeed bin Suroor) *settled in 5th on outer: rdn over 2f out: kpt on tl wknd fr over 1f out* **9/4**[1]

5665 **8** *12* **Luv U Whatever**[207] 1336 6-9-8 **93**.................................. AdamKirby 9 70
(Michael Attwater) *settled in 2nd: pushed along ent st: sn struggling and wknd fr wl over 1f out* **33/1**

000 **9** *nk* **Slowfoot (GER)**[11] 7546 8-9-2 **87**.................................. TimmyMurphy 1 64
(Jim Best) *a in rr: lost pl fr over 3f out: nvr involved* **66/1**

2m 31.7s (-2.80) **Going Correction** 0.0s/f (Stan)
WFA 3 from 4yo+ 6lb **9** Ran SP% **113.1**
Speed ratings (Par 107): **109,106,105,104,103 103,102,94,94**
CSF £36.36 CT £135.02 TOTE £4.10: £1.50, £4.10, £1.50; EX 44.00 Trifecta £164.90.
Owner Saeed bel Obaida **Bred** Rabbah Bloodstock Limited **Trained** Newmarket, Suffolk
■ Stewards' Enquiry : Joshua Bryan caution: careless riding

FOCUS
A good handicap which was taken apart by the winner. The runner-up has been rated close to his best.

7766 32RED FLOODLIT STKS (LISTED RACE) 1m 4f (P)
7:55 (7:57) (Class 1) 3-Y-O+

£22,684 (£8,600; £4,304; £2,144; £1,076; £540) **Stalls** Low

Form RPR

6645 **1** **Western Hymn**[11] 7545 5-9-4 110.................................(v[1]) RobertHavlin 5 112
(John Gosden) *hld up in 6th: prog on outer ent st: rdn over 2f out: side by side w runner-up over 1f out whn began to drift lft and bmpd rival: continued to hang lft fnl f: on top cl home* **5/4**[1]

5030 **2** *1/2* **Star Storm (IRE)**[32] 6940 4-9-4 98.................................. TomQueally 7 111
(James Fanshawe) *in rr: angled wd ent st: pushed lft by wnr fr over 1f out: kpt on wl tl wknd last strides* **9/2**[2]

-434 **3** *4* **Restorer**[186] 1863 4-9-4 106.................................. MartinDwyer 1 105
(William Muir) *settled in 3rd: t.k.h: rdn in centre over 2f out: led 2f out: drifted rt fr over 1f out: hdd 1f out: kpt on one pce* **7/1**

305 **4** *5* **Yorkidding**[6] 7652 4-8-13 98.................................. RichardKingscote 8 92
(Mark Johnston) *settled in 4th on outer: shkn up ent st: rdn over 2f out: no imp on ldng trio fr over 1f out* **11/2**[3]

2515 **5** *1 1/4* **Berkshire (IRE)**[17] 7396 5-9-9 106.................................. TomMarquand 6 100
(Paul Cole) *t.k.h in last trio: rdn over 2f out: lft bhd fr over 1f out* **10/1**

-630 **6** *8* **Hamelin (IRE)**[138] 3340 6-9-4 102.................................(v) AdamKirby 4 82
(George Scott) *led after 1f: increased pce ent st: sn rdn hdd 2f out: wknd after* **10/1**

2100 **7** *5* **Kiltara (IRE)**[6] 7652 4-8-13 93.................................. JoeFanning 2 69
(Mark Johnston) *led 1f: pressed ldr on outer after: rdn 3f out where losing pl: lft bhd fr 2f out* **12/1**

2m 29.28s (-5.22) **Going Correction** 0.0s/f (Stan) **7** Ran SP% **116.4**
Speed ratings (Par 111): **117,116,114,110,109 104,101**
CSF £7.41 TOTE £2.20: £1.50, £2.80; EX 10.30 Trifecta £40.60.
Owner RJH Geffen and Rachel Hood **Bred** Newsells Park Stud **Trained** Newmarket, Suffolk
■ Stewards' Enquiry : Robert Havlin two-day ban: careless riding (Nov 16-17)

FOCUS
Subsequent Group 1 winners have taken this end of season Listed race in the past, but this didn't look to be a vintage renewal. The winner kept the race after a stewards' enquiry. The runner-up has been rated to his best for now.

7767 RACING UK HD H'CAP 1m 4f (P)
8:25 (8:28) (Class 6) (0-55,54) 3-Y-O **£2,264** (£673; £336; £168) **Stalls** Low

Form RPR

0035 **1** **Mr Marchwood**[14] 7463 3-8-11 **49**.................................. CallumShepherd(5) 7 57
(Sylvester Kirk) *hld up in rr on outer: prog wd ent st: rdn over 2f out: led over 1f out: sn clr and in n.d: hands and heels cl home* **6/1**[2]

063 **2** *4* **The Juggler**[23] 7231 3-9-6 **53**.................................. JimmyQuinn 11 55
(William Knight) *settled in 7th: rdn over 2f out: prog fr over 1f out: kpt on wl between horses fnl strides to snatch 2nd post: nrst fin* **7/1**[3]

4502 **3** *shd* **Regal Galaxy**[11] 7532 3-8-12 **45**.................................. StevieDonohoe 5 46
(Mark H Tompkins) *settled in 5th: rdn over 2f out: kpt on fr over 1f out: tk 3rd fnl strides* **7/1**[3]

0060 **4** *nk* **Master Of Heaven**[14] 7464 3-9-2 **49**.................................(tp) PatCosgrave 12 50
(Jim Boyle) *styd wd for 2f tl c across to ld bef bnd: rdn over 2f out: kpt on tl hdd over 1f out: styd on same pce fnl f tl lost two pls fnl strides* **17/2**

-400 **5** *1* **Trust The Man (IRE)**[14] 7464 3-9-5 **52**.................................. NickyMackay 1 51
(Simon Dow) *restrained and in last: rdn out wd over 2f out: kpt on fr over 1f out: styd on same pce fnl f* **16/1**

-006 **6** *3/4* **Dusty Raven**[27] 7103 3-9-5 **52**.................................(p) LiamKeniry 9 50
(Neil Mulholland) *difficult to settle for 3f in rr-div: gng wl in rr over 2f out whn tried to angle out: kpt on one pce after: eased fnl strides* **12/1**

604 **7** *1 1/4* **Pension Madness (IRE)**[23] 7231 3-9-0 **54**.................. LuluStanford(7) 4 50
(Mark Usher) *settled in 2nd: rdn over 2f out: stl there over 1f out: one pce fnl f* **7/1**[3]

0400 **8** *nk* **Wassail**[74] 5625 3-8-7 **45**.................................. MitchGodwin(5) 2 41
(Ed de Giles) *narrow ld on inner tl hdd and settled in 4th after 2f: rdn over 2f out: one pce after* **33/1**

5332 **9** *1 1/4* **Little Orchid**[29] 7039 3-9-2 **52**.................................. ShelleyBirkett(3) 3 46
(Julia Feilden) *t.k.h in rr: rdn over 2f out: nvr involved* **6/1**[2]

-456 **10** *5* **Moon Arrow (IRE)**[35] 6871 3-9-7 **54**.................................[1] AdamKirby 10 40
(Michael Blake) *racd in 3rd: rdn over 2f out: stl there over 1f out: wknd fnl f* **4/1**[1]

000 **11** *5* **Staplehurst (IRE)**[118] 4056 3-9-4 **54**.................................. JosephineGordon(3) 8 32
(Geoffrey Deacon) *settled in 8th: rdn over 2f out: sn squeezed up: pushed out after* **16/1**

2m 35.48s (0.98) **Going Correction** 0.0s/f (Stan) **11** Ran SP% **119.0**
Speed ratings (Par 98): **96,93,93,93,92 91,91,90,90,86 83**
CSF £48.32 CT £305.11 TOTE £7.90: £2.80, £4.80, £2.30; EX 56.10 Trifecta £368.90.
Owner Marchwood Aggregates **Bred** Mrs B E Moore **Trained** Upper Lambourn, Berks

FOCUS
A maiden handicap in all but name and these won't get many better opportunities to get off the mark. Weak form but an easy winner. The winner has been rated back to the best of this year's form.

T/Plt: £60.90 to a £1 stake. Pool: £95,932.86 - 1148.86 winning units. T/Qpdt: £32.10 to a £1 stake. Pool: £10,266.49 - 236.20 winning units. **Cathal Gahan**

7621 NOTTINGHAM (L-H)
Wednesday, November 2

OFFICIAL GOING: Good (good to soft in places; 7.8)
Wind: Virtually nil Weather: Fine & dry

7768 RACINGUK.COM NURSERY H'CAP 1m 75y
12:20 (12:20) (Class 5) (0-75,77) 2-Y-O **£2,911** (£866; £432; £216) **Stalls** Centre

Form RPR

4411 **1** **Rashford's Double (IRE)**[8] 7598 2-9-6 **77** 6ex... AdamMcNamara(3) 10 82+
(Richard Fahey) *rr early: smooth hdwy on inner over 4f out: sn trcking ldrs: cl up over 2f out: led wl over 1f out and sn rdn: drvn and kpt on wl towards fin* **13/8**[1]

2501 **2** *hd* **Phoenix Dawn**[16] 7416 2-8-13 **67**.................................(p) MartinDwyer 13 71
(Brendan Powell) *trckd ldrs: cl up 3f out: rdn along wl over 1f out: chsd wnr ins fnl f: kpt on wl towards fin* **33/1**

450 **3** *nk* **Ettihadi (IRE)**[42] 6663 2-9-2 **73**.................................[1] JosephineGordon(3) 1 76
(Hugo Palmer) *dwlt and sn pushed along into midfield on inner: trckd ldrs 1/2-way: effrt over 2f out: rdn wl over 1f out: styd on fnl f* **12/1**

3240 **4** *1* **Darkroom Angel**[24] 7185 2-8-13 **67**.................................. JohnFahy 7 68
(Clive Cox) *midfield: hdwy 3f out: chsd ldrs over 2f out: rdn wl over 1f out: kpt on u.p fnl f* **16/1**

205 **5** *3/4* **Wigan Warrior**[12] 7496 2-9-5 **73**.................................. PatCosgrave 14 72
(David Brown) *hld up: hdwy on wd outside 3f out: chsd ldrs 2f out: sn rdn: kpt on fnl f* **16/1**

0063 **6** *nk* **Sassoferrato (IRE)**[23] 7228 2-8-12 **66**.................................. GrahamGibbons 4 64
(Alan Bailey) *led: rdn along over 2f out: hdd wl over 1f out: sn drvn and grad wknd* **12/1**

0403 **7** *3/4* **Star Maker**[14] 7467 2-8-11 **70**.................................. MitchGodwin(5) 8 66
(Sylvester Kirk) *t.k.h in midfield: hdwy to chse ldrs 4f out: rdn along over 2f out: drvn wl over 1f out: kpt on same pce* **8/1**[3]

0066 **8** *nk* **Charlie Chaplin (GER)**[9] 7571 2-8-9 **63**.................................(b[1]) AndreaAtzeni 11 59
(Robert Eddery) *towards rr: hdwy on inner 3f out: chsd ldrs over 2f out: sn rdn and wknd over 1f out* **12/1**

410 **9** *hd* **Cotinga**[11] 7541 2-9-7 **75**.................................. OisinMurphy 12 70
(Ralph Beckett) *towards rr: effrt and sme hdwy over 3f out: rdn along wl over 2f out: sn no imp* **10/1**

6600 **10** *2 1/4* **Crucial Moment**[13] 7482 2-8-1 **58** ow1.................................. NathanEvans(3) 6 48
(Bill Turner) *prom: rdn along wl over 2f out: sn drvn and wknd* **50/1**

0066 **11** *1/2* **Come On Percy**[59] 6159 2-8-13 **67**.................................. GeorgeChaloner 3 56
(Richard Fahey) *chsd ldrs: rdn along wl over 2f out: sn wknd* **20/1**

U000 **12** *3 1/2* **She's Rosanna**[46] 6588 2-7-9 **54** oh8.................................. HollieDoyle(5) 5 35
(Steph Hollinshead) *in tch: rdn along 3f out: sn wknd* **100/1**

1541 **13** *3/4* **Tap Tap Boom**[14] 7467 2-9-7 **75**.................................. SteveDrowne 2 54
(George Baker) *prom: cl up 1/2-way: rdn along over 3f out: wknd over 2f out* **5/1**[2]

1m 45.14s (-3.86) **Going Correction** -0.425s/f (Firm) 2y crse rec **13** Ran SP% **120.5**
Speed ratings (Par 96): **102,101,101,100,99 99,98,98,98,95 95,91,91**
CSF £78.20 CT £537.20 TOTE £2.20: £1.10, £5.80, £4.00; EX 41.90 Trifecta £203.20.
Owner Middleham Park Racing XC **Bred** Manister House Stud **Trained** Musley Bank, N Yorks

FOCUS
Inner Track. Rail is set out 2yds on the home bend adding approximately 6yds to races 1, 2, 3 and 8. This modest nursery proved a sound test and the form looks fair. Winning rider Adam McNamara afterwards said the ground felt a "bit tacky." A minor pb from the runner-up.

7769 B&M INSTALLATIONS MAIDEN STKS (DIV I) 1m 75y
12:50 (12:54) (Class 5) 2-Y-O **£2,911** (£866; £432; £216) **Stalls** Centre

Form RPR

33 **1** **Crowned Eagle**[21] 7283 2-9-5 0.................................. RobertHavlin 14 84+
(John Gosden) *led after 1f: hung lft and styd on wl fnl 2f: v readily* **7/2**[2]

3 **2** *3 1/4* **Zumurudee (USA)**[27] 7100 2-9-5 0.................................. MartinHarley 1 76
(Marco Botti) *led 1f: chsd ldrs: kpt on same pce fnl f* **3/1**[1]

6 **3** *3/4* **Daira Prince (IRE)**[23] 7226 2-9-5 0.................................. AndreaAtzeni 2 75
(Roger Varian) *chsd ldrs: 3rd 1f out: styd on same pce* **5/1**

4 *3/4* **Master Singer (USA)** 2-9-5 0.................................. RobertTart 8 73+
(John Gosden) *mid-div: hdwy to trck ldrs over 3f out: kpt on same pce over 1f out* **20/1**

0 **5** *1 1/2* **Alshibaa (IRE)**[46] 6570 2-9-5 0.................................. DaneO'Neill 6 70
(William Haggas) *chsd ldrs: kpt on one pce over 1f out* **10/1**

4 **6** *4* **Solar Cross**[12] 7503 2-9-5 0.................................. GeorgeBaker 17 60
(Roger Charlton) *trckd ldrs: 2nd over 3f out: wknd over 1f out* **4/1**[3]

7 *1/2* **Incandescent** 2-8-9 0.................................. GeorgeWood(5) 9 54+
(James Fanshawe) *rr-div: drvn over 4f out: kpt on wl fnl 2f: will improve* **28/1**

0 **8** *nk* **Meyandi**[26] 7125 2-9-5 0.................................. LiamKeniry 3 59
(Andrew Balding) *prom: one pce fnl 2f* **50/1**

9 *1/2* **Lunar Jet** 2-9-5 0.................................. GrahamLee 5 57+
(John Mackie) *rr-div: hdwy 3f out: nvr nr ldrs* **100/1**

10 *1/2* **Gracious Diana** 2-9-0 0.................................. NickyMackay 7 51+
(John Gosden) *s.s: in rr: kpt on fnl 2f: nvr a factor* **25/1**

11 *1/2* **Tuff Rock (USA)** 2-9-5 0.................................. OisinMurphy 13 55+
(Ed Walker) *mid-div: kpt on fnl 2f: nvr a factor* **20/1**

12 *2* **Moans Cross (USA)** 2-9-5 0.................................. FergusSweeney 12 50
(Alan King) *hld up in rr: sme hdwy over 2f out: nvr on terms* **100/1**

5 **13** *2 1/2* **Medicean Dream (IRE)**[23] 7225 2-9-5 0.................................. PatCosgrave 4 45
(Luca Cumani) *mid-div: effrt over 3f out: wknd 2f out* **33/1**

14 *2 1/2* **Lorikeet (USA)** 2-9-5 0.................................. PJMcDonald 15 39
(Mark Johnston) *mid-div: lost pl 4f out: bhd fnl 2f* **50/1**

0 **15** *1* **Legalized**[21] 7285 2-9-0 0.................................. TomEaves 16 32
(James Given) *prom: lost pl over 2f out* **100/1**

16 *10* **Two Dollars (IRE)** 2-9-5 0.................................. SteveDrowne 10 14
(William Jarvis) *s.i.s: in rr: bhd fnl 3f: eased clsng stages* **100/1**

17 *7* **Twiston Shout (IRE)** 2-9-5 0.................................. TonyHamilton 11
(Richard Spencer) *s.i.s: in rr: bhd fnl 3f: eased* **100/1**

1m 45.41s (-3.59) **Going Correction** -0.425s/f (Firm) **17** Ran SP% **121.6**
Speed ratings (Par 96): **100,96,96,95,93 89,89,88,88,87 87,85,82,80,79 69,62**
CSF £12.70 TOTE £4.20: £1.50, £1.30, £1.80; EX 16.40 Trifecta £70.60.
Owner Lady Bamford **Bred** Lady Bamford **Trained** Newmarket, Suffolk

FOCUS
There was no hanging around in this interesting 2yo maiden. Straightforward form. The runner-up has been rated to his debut form.

7770 B&M INSTALLATIONS MAIDEN STKS (DIV II) 1m 75y
1:20 (1:21) (Class 5) 2-Y-O **£2,911** (£866; £432; £216) **Stalls** Centre

Form RPR
1 **Big Challenge (IRE)** 2-9-2 0 JosephineGordon(3) 11 84+
(Saeed bin Suroor) *trckd ldng pair: smooth hdwy and cl up 3f out: effrt 2f out and sn led: pushed clr appr fnl f: kpt on strly* **4/1**[2]

62 2 2 1/4 **Melodic Motion (IRE)**[21] 7284 2-9-0 0 OisinMurphy 4 70
(Ralph Beckett) *cl up: chal 3f out: led briefly over 2f out: sn rdn and hdd: drvn over 1f out: kpt on same pce* **11/8**[1]

3 shd **Wasatch Range** 2-9-5 0 RobertHavlin 15 75
(John Gosden) *trckd ldrs: hdwy on outer over 3f out: cl up over 2f out: rdn wl over 1f out: green and sn edgd lft: kpt on same pce fnl f* **7/1**

4 2 1/4 **Stone The Crows** 2-9-5 0 GeorgeBaker 2 70+
(Roger Charlton) *trckd ldrs: pushed along wl over 2f out: rdn wl over 1f out: n.m.r and sltly hmpd appr fnl f: sn one pce* **14/1**

5 shd **Buzz (FR)** 2-9-5 0 LiamKeniry 6 69+
(Hughie Morrison) *dwlt: sn in midfield: hdwy on outer wl over 2f out: rdn over 1f out: kpt on fnl f: nrst fin* **50/1**

6 1 3/4 **Royal Sunday (FR)** 2-9-5 0 FergusSweeney 5 65
(Alan King) *t.k.h: chsd ldrs: pushed along wl over 2f out: rdn wl over 1f out: sn no imp* **33/1**

45 7 2 **Mach One**[24] 7187 2-9-5 0 PaulMulrennan 3 61
(Clive Cox) *slt ld: rdn along 3f out: hdd over 2f out and grad wknd* **10/1**

00 8 1/2 **Dream Machine (IRE)**[7] 7621 2-9-5 0 WilliamCarson 12 59
(Michael Bell) *towards rr: sme hdwy over 3f out: sn rdn along and nvr nr ldrs* **100/1**

9 shd **Zeelander** 2-9-5 0 AndreaAtzeni 10 59
(Roger Varian) *in tch: pushed along 3f out: rdn along over 2f out: n.d* **5/1**[3]

10 nk **Belisa (IRE)** 2-9-0 0 TomEaves 9 53
(Ivan Furtado) *towards rr: sme hdwy over 3f out: rdn along wl over 2f out: n.d* **100/1**

11 11 **Eighth Circle (IRE)** 2-9-2 0 GaryHalpin(3) 16 33
(Henry Spiller) *a towards rr* **100/1**

12 9 **Shymkent** 2-9-5 0 JackMitchell 13 12
(Roger Varian) *s.i.s and sn pushed along: a rr* **25/1**

13 1 1/4 **Niseko** 2-9-5 0 MartinDwyer 14 10
(William Muir) *midfield: rdn along 3f out: woon wknd* **50/1**

1m 47.64s (-1.36) **Going Correction** -0.425s/f (Firm) **13** Ran SP% **120.7**
Speed ratings (Par 96): **89,86,86,84,84 82,80,80,79,79 68,59,58**
CSF £9.67 TOTE £4.50: £1.70, £1.20, £1.80; EX 10.30 Trifecta £45.50.
Owner Godolphin **Bred** Brucetown Farms Ltd **Trained** Newmarket, Suffolk

FOCUS
This second division of the 2yo maiden was another interesting heat. It was 2.23secs slower, though. The runner-up's previous effort would back the race being rated a lot higher, but she's been rated below that form here.

7771 LADY CECIL MORPHEUS H'CAP 5f 13y
1:55 (1:57) (Class 2) (0-110,109) 3-Y-O+ **£16,172** (£4,812; £2,405; £1,202) **Stalls** High

Form RPR
0360 1 **Gracious John (IRE)**[52] 6384 3-8-10 **105** KatherineGlenister(7) 4 112
(David Evans) *trckd ldr: shkn up and edgd rt to stands rail over 2f out: rdn wl over 1f out: slt ld ent fnl f: kpt on wl towards fin* **12/1**

100 2 1/2 **Perfect Pasture**[46] 6558 6-9-2 **107** (v) NathanEvans(3) 7 112
(Michael Easterby) *trckd wnr: swtchd lft and hdwy 2f out: rdn over 1f out: ch and drvn ins fnl f: kpt on* **7/1**

6000 3 nse **Justice Good (IRE)**[185] 1887 4-8-2 **95** oh3 HollieDoyle(5) 3 100
(David Elsworth) *led: rdn along wl over 1f out: hdd narrowly ent fnl f: sn drvn and kpt on* **14/1**

0430 4 1 1/2 **Double Up**[12] 7520 5-9-2 **104** (t) AndreaAtzeni 8 103
(Roger Varian) *trckd ldrs: hdwy 2f out: shkn up wl over 1f out: sn rdn and ch: drvn and kpt on same pce fnl f* **2/1**[1]

2030 5 1 3/4 **Humidor (IRE)**[11] 7537 9-8-9 **97** FergusSweeney 2 90
(George Baker) *chsd ldrs: rdn along 2f out: drvn over 1f out: kpt on one pce* **7/1**

016 6 1 3/4 **Mobsta (IRE)**[32] 6941 4-9-7 **109** GrahamLee 6 96
(Mick Channon) *towards rr: rdn along and outpcd 1/2-way: plugged on appr fnl f* **6/1**[3]

0040 7 nk **Maarek**[31] 6990 9-8-13 **104** GaryHalpin(3) 5 90
(Miss Evanna McCutcheon, Ire) *blind removed late and stmbld s: sn wl adrift and rdn along: hdwy over 1f out: kpt on fnl f* **8/1**

0140 8 2 1/2 **Demora**[18] 7358 7-8-11 **99** OisinMurphy 1 76
(Michael Appleby) *cl up on outer: rdn along over 2f out: sn wknd* **11/2**[2]

57.52s (-3.98) **Going Correction** -0.425s/f (Firm) course record **8** Ran SP% **113.5**
Speed ratings (Par 109): **114,113,113,110,107 105,104,100**
CSF £90.72 CT £1195.82 TOTE £18.50: £4.10, £2.20, £5.20; EX 116.40 Trifecta £2376.50.
Owner Terry Reffell **Bred** Skeaghmore Hill **Trained** Pandy, Monmouths

FOCUS
The feature handicap was a muddling affair, but it resulted in a new course record. The stands' rail was the place to be.

7772 RACING UK PROFITS RETURNED TO RACING H'CAP (DIV I) 5f 13y
2:30 (2:31) (Class 4) (0-85,85) 3-Y-O+ **£4,690** (£1,395; £697; £348) **Stalls** High

Form RPR
00-0 1 **Wentworth Falls**[19] 7315 4-9-7 **85** PhillipMakin 2 93
(Geoffrey Harker) *trckd ldrs: hdwy wl over 1f out: rdn ins fnl f: led last 75 yds* **16/1**

0234 2 nk **Straightothepoint**[44] 6633 4-9-3 **81** [1] ConnorBeasley 7 88
(Bryan Smart) *cl up: led 1/2-way: rdn over 1f out: drvn ins fnl f: hdd and no ex last 75 yds* **5/1**[1]

352 3 1/2 **Rosina**[33] 6927 3-9-3 **81** PJMcDonald 10 86+
(Ann Duffield) *hld up: hdwy 2f out: n.m.r and swtchd rt jst over 1f out: sn rdn and kpt on strly towards fin* **6/1**[2]

4310 4 3/4 **Storm Melody**[7] 7626 3-8-11 **75** GrahamLee 5 78+
(Jonjo O'Neill) *dwlt and towards rr: hdwy wl over 1f out: sn rdn and styd on wl fnl f: nrst fin* **7/1**[3]

0510 5 1/2 **Oeil De Tigre (FR)**[37] 6831 5-8-7 **71** WilliamCarson 3 72
(Tony Carroll) *hld up: hdwy on outer over 1f out: sn rdn and styd on fnl f* **20/1**

2550 6 hd **Elusivity (IRE)**[23] 7202 8-9-0 **78** (p) PaulMulrennan 6 78
(Conor Dore) *cl up: disp ld 2f out: sn rdn and hung lft ent fnl f: wknd* **25/1**

6422 7 1/2 **Silken Skies (IRE)**[21] 7289 3-9-0 **85** WilliamCox(7) 9 83
(Clive Cox) *chsd ldrs: rdn wl over 1f out: sn swtchd lft: drvn and kpt on same pce fnl f* **7/1**[3]

0621 8 1/2 **New Road Side**[21] 7288 3-9-0 **78** (v) JFEgan 11 74
(Richard Guest) *slt ld to 1/2-way: cl up and rdn wl over 1f out: drvn appr fnl f: grad wknd* **8/1**

0000 9 2 1/2 **Grandad's World (IRE)**[24] 7186 4-9-4 **82** TonyHamilton 8 82+
(Richard Fahey) *trckd ldrs: hdwy 1/2-way: rdn 2f out: sn wknd* **7/1**[3]

601 10 2 1/4 **Appleberry (IRE)**[21] 7289 4-8-13 **80** JosephineGordon(3) 1 59
(Michael Appleby) *chsd ldrs: rdn along 1/2-way: sn wknd* **12/1**

1331 11 1 3/4 **Pensax Lad (IRE)**[7] 7626 5-9-3 **81** 6ex OisinMurphy 4 54
(Ronald Harris) *a towards rr* **8/1**

58.6s (-2.90) **Going Correction** -0.425s/f (Firm) **11** Ran SP% **112.9**
Speed ratings (Par 105): **106,105,104,103,102 102,101,100,96,93 90**
CSF £90.42 CT £550.50 TOTE £18.30: £4.40, £1.50, £2.40; EX 135.50 Trifecta £980.10.
Owner Stockhill Racing Partnership **Bred** Newsells Park Stud **Trained** Thirkleby, N Yorks

FOCUS
A modest sprint handicap that saw a bunched finish down the middle.

7773 RACING UK PROFITS RETURNED TO RACING H'CAP (DIV II) 5f 13y
3:00 (3:00) (Class 4) (0-85,85) 3-Y-O+ **£4,690** (£1,395; £697; £348) **Stalls** High

Form RPR
0331 1 **Ballesteros**[8] 7591 7-9-5 **85** 6ex AdamMcNamara(3) 10 90
(Richard Fahey) *trckd ldrs: hdwy wl over 1f out: rdn to chal ent fnl f: led last 100 yds: drvn out* **7/1**

0130 2 nk **Coiste Bodhar (IRE)**[7] 7626 5-8-3 **73** ow2 NatalieHambling(7) 8 77
(Scott Dixon) *wnt lft s: led: rdn along 2f out: drvn and hdd ins fnl f: kpt on* **8/1**

6035 3 1/2 **Bondi Beach Boy**[33] 6926 7-9-1 **81** NathanEvans(3) 5 83
(James Turner) *dwlt and swtchd rt to stands rail s: sn cl up: chal 2f out: sn rdn and ev ch: drvn ins fnl f: no ex towards fin* **6/1**[3]

06-0 4 nk **Athas An Bhean**[38] 6819 3-8-12 **82** (t) DannySheehy(7) 3 83
(Adrian Paul Keatley, Ire) *chsd ldrs: hdwy and cl up 2f out: rdn over 1f out: drvn and ev ch whn hung lft ent fnl f: kpt on same pce* **16/1**

5106 5 1/2 **Swirral Edge**[43] 6653 3-8-13 **76** TomEaves 4 75
(David Brown) *dwlt and rr: swtchd rt to stands rail over 3f out: hdwy 2f out: sn chsng ldrs: rdn and kpt on same pce fnl f* **33/1**

55 6 1/2 **Diamond Lady**[21] 7288 5-8-12 **80** HollieDoyle(5) 9 78
(William Stone) *chsd ldr: rdn along 2f out: grad wknd fnl f* **8/1**

-400 7 nse **Merdon Castle (IRE)**[15] 7443 4-9-4 **81** (e) JamesSullivan 1 78
(Ruth Carr) *in tch: effrt 2f out: sn rdn and no imp fnl f* **10/1**

6062 8 1 1/4 **Money Team (IRE)**[8] 7590 5-9-1 **78** GrahamGibbons 2 71+
(David Barron) *in tch: rdn along 2f out: sn wknd* **7/2**[2]

1102 9 4 1/2 **Orient Class**[21] 7288 5-9-2 **84** CliffordLee(5) 7 61
(Paul Midgley) *chsd ldrs: rdn along 2f out: sn drvn and wknd* **11/4**[1]

59.45s (-2.05) **Going Correction** -0.425s/f (Firm) **9** Ran SP% **115.8**
Speed ratings (Par 105): **99,98,97,97,96 95,95,93,86**
CSF £61.70 CT £359.77 TOTE £5.70: £2.30, £2.90, £1.60; EX 66.40 Trifecta £628.00.
Owner Dr Marwan Koukash **Bred** Exors Of The Late J R Good **Trained** Musley Bank, N Yorks

FOCUS
The slower of the two divisions.

7774 B&M INSTALLATIONS H'CAP 5f 13y
3:30 (3:31) (Class 6) (0-65,68) 3-Y-O+ **£2,264** (£673; £336; £168) **Stalls** High

Form RPR
1031 1 **Horsforth**[11] 7534 4-9-3 **61** (b) ConnorBeasley 12 71
(Richard Guest) *trckd ldrs: hdwy nr stands rail 2f out: rdn to ld appr fnl f: drvn out* **8/1**[3]

1236 2 1 1/4 **John Joiner**[7] 7626 4-9-0 **63** CharlieBennett(5) 3 68
(Peter Hedger) *dwlt and bhd: hdwy on wd outside wl over 1f out: sn rdn: styd on wl fnl f* **7/1**[2]

2222 3 nk **Jacob's Pillow**[8] 7595 5-9-7 **65** PJMcDonald 1 69
(Rebecca Bastiman) *racd wd: prom: hdwy and cl up 2f out: sn rdn and ev ch: drvn ent fnl f: kpt on same pce* **6/1**[1]

3530 4 1/2 **Beau Mistral (IRE)**[21] 7290 7-8-13 **57** (p) WilliamCarson 15 60
(Tony Carroll) *trckd ldrs stands rail: effrt and nt clr run wl over 1f out: swtchd lft and rdn ent fnl f: sn drvn and kpt on same pce* **20/1**

3056 5 1/2 **Ambitious Icarus**[16] 7420 7-9-7 **65** (e) JFEgan 4 65
(Richard Guest) *awkward s and rr: hdwy wl over 1f out: swtchd lft and rdn ent fnl f: sn drvn to chse ldrs: no ex towards fin* **8/1**[3]

4403 6 nse **Mo Henry**[7] 7633 4-9-3 **68** 6ex (v) DannySheehy(7) 8 68
(Adrian Paul Keatley, Ire) *trckd ldrs: hdwy and cl up 1/2-way: led 2f out: sn rdn and hdd appr fnl f: drvn and kpt on same pce* **6/1**[1]

5000 7 nk **Bonjour Steve**[7] 7626 5-8-11 **60** (p) PhilDennis(5) 5 59
(Richard Price) *in tch: hdwy wl over 1f out: sn rdn and kpt on fnl f* **16/1**

1155 8 hd **Langley Vale**[21] 7267 7-9-7 **65** (v) JackMitchell 7 63
(Roger Teal) *chsd ldrs: cl up 1/2-way: rdn along wl over 1f out: grad wknd* **14/1**

50U1 9 nk **Humour (IRE)**[13] 7488 5-8-9 **58** ow1 (b) DavidParkes(5) 17 55
(Christine Dunnett) *dwlt and rr nr stands rail: hdwy 2f out: swtchd markedly lft and rdn over 1f out: kpt on* **25/1**

3416 10 3/4 **Toni's A Star**[37] 6831 4-9-1 **64** GeorgiaCox(5) 16 63
(Tony Carroll) *in tch nr stands rail: effrt and nt clr run wl over 1f out: swtchd lft and rdn ent fnl f: kpt on* **8/1**[3]

6U06 11 nk **Darrell Rivers**[7] 7611 4-8-13 **60** JosephineGordon(3) 13 54
(Giles Bravery) *chsd ldrs: rdn along wl over 1f out: grad wknd* **10/1**

200 12 1 1/4 **Oscars Journey**[30] 7018 6-9-5 **63** (v) TonyHamilton 9 52
(J R Jenkins) *sn led and cross towards stands rail: rdn along and hdd 2f out: sn wknd* **20/1**

060 13 1 3/4 **Gold Bud**[18] 7362 4-9-6 **64** SteveDrowne 11 47
(George Baker) *in tch: hdwy and nt clr run wl over 1f out: sn rdn and chsd ldrs ent fnl f: sn drvn and wknd* **33/1**

3010 14 nk **Frangarry (IRE)**[11] 7533 4-9-0 **58** (p[1]) GrahamGibbons 14 40
(Alan Bailey) *in tch: hdwy 2f: sn rdn and nt clr run: hld whn hmpd over 1f out* **16/1**

59.11s (-2.39) **Going Correction** -0.425s/f (Firm) **14** Ran SP% **118.2**
Speed ratings (Par 101): **102,100,99,98,97 97,97,97,96,95 94,92,90,89**
CSF £58.55 CT £374.25 TOTE £10.40: £3.10, £2.30, £2.50; EX 57.30 Trifecta £292.00.
Owner Morecool Racing **Bred** Laundry Cottage Stud Farm **Trained** Ingmanthorpe, W Yorks

FOCUS
A fair sprint handicap for the grade and another winner on the stands' rail. Straightforward form rated around the second and third.

7775 AJA GENTLEMAN AMATEUR RIDERS' H'CAP 1m 2f 50y
4:00 (4:00) (Class 5) (0-75,75) 3-Y-O+ **£2,807** (£870; £435; £217) **Stalls** Low

Form RPR
4423 **1** **Favorite Girl (GER)**[168] 2369 8-10-2 **63**.............. MrJamesKendrick(7) 7 72
(Michael Appleby) *sn led: hdd after 1f: led over 5f out: fnd ex clsng stages* **14/1**
115 **2** 1 **Bollihope**[7] 7613 4-10-12 **66**.............. MrSWalker 12 73
(Richard Guest) *hld up in mid-div: hdwy over 2f out: chal over 1f out: no ex clsng stages* **5/2**[1]
3032 **3** 1 ½ **Bahamian C**[12] 7500 5-10-4 **63**..............(t) MrMEnnis(5) 8 67
(Richard Fahey) *mid-div: drvn over 3f out: kpt on same pce last 150yds* **9/2**[2]
6106 **4** ¾ **Southern Strife**[18] 7359 5-11-0 **68**..............(b) MrWEasterby 2 71
(Tim Easterby) *dwlt: sn chsng ldrs: kpt on same pce fnl f* **6/1**[3]
3550 **5** 1 ¼ **Sakhalin Star (IRE)**[12] 7500 5-10-6 **63**..............(e) MrShaneQuinlan(3) 16 63
(Richard Guest) *led early: chsd ldrs: kpt on one pce appr fnl f* **10/1**
P500 **6** nse **Manny Owens (IRE)**[12] 7500 4-10-9 **68**..............(bt) MrJJO'Neill(5) 15 68
(Jonjo O'Neill) *hld up in rr: hdwy over 2f out: one pce appr fnl f* **10/1**
0000 **7** 1 ½ **Indian Chief (IRE)**[16] 7408 6-11-7 **75**.............. MrPMillman 9 72
(Rebecca Bastiman) *hld up in rr:t.k.h: hdwy over 3f out: chsng ldrs over 1f out: one pce* **10/1**
5054 **8** 2 ¾ **Polar Forest**[12] 7500 6-11-1 **72**..............(e) MrAlexFerguson(3) 6 64
(Richard Guest) *in rr: hdwy over 2f out: chsng ldrs over 1f out: sn wknd* **7/1**
1100 **9** 6 **Silver Alliance**[12] 7500 8-11-3 **71**..............(b) MrRBirkett 10 52
(Julia Feilden) *trckd ldrs: t.k.h: wknd over 1f out* **25/1**
60/6 **10** 1 ¼ **Star Of Namibia (IRE)**[16] 7410 6-10-2 **61** oh9........ MrLewisStones(5) 1 39
(Michael Mullineaux) *led after 1f: hdd over 5f out: lost pl 2f out* **33/1**
-000 **11** 1 ½ **Party Royal**[152] 2872 6-11-1 **69**..............(p) MrDHDunsdon 4 44
(Nick Gifford) *mid-div: effrt over 2f out: lost pl over 1f out* **50/1**
360 **12** 5 **Swiftee (IRE)**[142] 3236 3-10-6 **67**.............. MrJHarding(3) 13 33
(Ivan Furtado) *sn chsng ldrs: lost pl over 1f out: sn bhd* **25/1**
0-04 **13** 16 **Norse Castle**[278] 377 3-10-11 **69**.............. MrZBaker 3 5
(Martin Bosley) *s.i.s: hld up in rr: hdwy to chse ldrs far side ovedr 3f out: lost pl over 2f out: sn bhd* **40/1**

2m 13.75s (-0.55) **Going Correction** -0.425s/f (Firm)
WFA 3 from 4yo+ 4lb **13** Ran SP% **122.5**
Speed ratings (Par 103): **85,84,83,82,81 81,80,77,73,72 70,66,54**
CSF £48.18 CT £194.37 TOTE £17.30: £3.90, £1.30, £1.80; EX 56.00 Trifecta £189.20.
Owner Terry Pryke **Bred** Gestut Gorlsdorf **Trained** Oakham, Rutland

FOCUS
They came stands' side off the home bend in this moderate handicap for amateur riders.
T/Jkpt: Not Won. T/Plt: £913.60 to a £1 stake. Pool: £53,067.14 - 42.40 winning units. T/Qpdt: £182.10 to a 31 stake. Pool: £4,604.18 - 18.70 winning units. **Joe Rowntree & Walter Glynn**

7687 CHELMSFORD (A.W) (L-H)
Thursday, November 3

OFFICIAL GOING: Polytrack: standard
Wind: light, half behind Weather: dry, chilly

7776 TOTEPLACEPOT RACING'S FAVOURITE BET MAIDEN AUCTION STKS 6f (P)
4:40 (4:41) (Class 6) 2-Y-O **£2,264** (£673; £336; £168) **Stalls** Centre

Form RPR
064 **1** **Odelouca (IRE)**[22] 7278 2-8-7 70.............. DavidProbert 3 61
(Brendan Powell) *mde all: rdn over 1f out: asserted 1f out: edgd rt ins fnl f: kpt on and a doing enough ins fnl f* **11/4**[1]
0056 **2** nk **Lord Cooper**[22] 7275 2-9-1 55..............(tp) RenatoSouza 8 68
(Jose Santos) *sn chsng ldng pair: effrt 2f out: no imp tl styd on ins fnl f: wnt 2nd fnl 75yds: nvr quite getting to wnr* **12/1**
04 **3** 1 **Paquita Bailarina**[17] 7407 2-8-3 0.............. JosephineGordon(3) 5 56
(James Given) *w wnr: rdn over 1f out: unable qck 1f out: kpt on same pce ins fnl f: lost 2nd fnl 75yds* **6/1**
00 **4** ½ **Banta Bay**[30] 7032 2-8-13 0.............. KierenFox 1 62
(John Best) *chsd ldrs tl dropped to midfield after 2f: effrt 2f out: hdwy to chse ldrs 1f out: styd on same pce ins fnl f* **25/1**
5 ½ **Sattar (IRE)** 2-8-13 0.............. JimmyQuinn 4 60
(Martin Smith) *s.i.s: bhd: pushed along and swtchd rt over 1f out: hdwy 1f out: kpt on wl ins fnl f: no threat to ldrs* **20/1**
3440 **6** shd **No Not Again (IRE)**[10] 7574 2-8-11 73.............. HollieDoyle(5) 7 63
(Richard Hannon) *pressed ldrs for over 1f out: chsd ldrs after: effrt ent fnl 2f: unable qck over 1f out: kpt on same pce ins fnl f* **3/1**[2]
6 **7** 1 **Four Candles (IRE)**[23] 7259 2-8-13 0.............. PatCosgrave 2 57
(Philip McBride) *nvr bttr than midfield: lost pl and rdn over 2f out: drvn 1f out: kpt on same pce ins fnl f* **4/1**[3]
50 **8** ½ **Red Sniper (IRE)**[24] 7209 2-8-7 0..............[1] PaulHanagan 6 49
(Peter Chapple-Hyam) *s.i.s and pushed along in rr early: clsd and travelling bttr 1/2-way: edgd lft and no imp over 1f out: wl hld and one pced fnl f* **10/1**
00 **9** 6 **Not Now Mum**[49] 6524 2-8-13 0.............. RobertWinston 9 37
(Dean Ivory) *spooked and wnt sharply rt leaving stalls: sn rcvrd and in tch in midfield on outer: hung rt bnd over 3f out: lost pl and bhd over 1f out: eased ins fnl f* **16/1**

1m 12.48s (-1.22) **Going Correction** -0.275s/f (Stan) **9** Ran SP% **117.2**
Speed ratings (Par 94): **97,96,95,94,93 93,92,91,83**
CSF £37.28 TOTE £2.80: £1.20, £3.90, £1.80; EX 33.40 Trifecta £161.60.
Owner Tom Ford & Robert Peters **Bred** Piercetown Stud **Trained** Upper Lambourn, Berks

FOCUS
Just a modest maiden. It's been rated negatively.

7777 TOTEPOOL RACECOURSE CASH BACK AVAILABLE NURSERY H'CAP 6f (P)
5:15 (5:15) (Class 6) (0-65,71) 2-Y-O **£2,264** (£673; £336; £168) **Stalls** Centre

Form RPR
0350 **1** **Ninety Years Young**[20] 7313 2-9-2 **60**..............(b[1]) SeanLevey 1 68+
(David Elsworth) *mde all: rdn over 1f out: drvn ins fnl f: kpt on u.p and a doing enough ins fnl f* **11/4**[2]
2202 **2** ¾ **Wentwell Yesterday (IRE)**[5] 7690 2-8-12 **61**.............. LucyKBarry(5) 8 67
(Jamie Osborne) *chsd wnr and clr of field: rdn ent fnl 2f: unable qck over 1f out: kpt on same pce ins fnl f* **11/8**[1]
6060 **3** 3 ¼ **Lawfilly**[25] 7185 2-9-5 **63**.............. ShaneKelly 4 59
(Richard Hughes) *racd off the pce in 5th: effrt and hdwy over 1f out: chsd clr ldng pair jst over 1f out: flashed tail u.p but kpt on ins fnl f: nvr threatened ldng pair* **8/1**
500 **4** 5 **Dangerous Ends**[17] 7414 2-8-13 **57**.............. StevieDonohoe 5 38
(Brett Johnson) *sn pushed along and outpcd in last pair: rdn over 2f out: no imp but passed btn horses ins fnl f: n.d* **14/1**
065 **5** 1 ¾ **Aqshion Stations**[24] 7224 2-9-5 **63**.............. DavidProbert 2 39
(William Jarvis) *chsd clr ldng pair: rdn over 2f out: no imp and lost 3rd jst over 1f out: wknd fnl f* **6/1**[3]
600 **6** 2 ¾ **I Don't Believe It**[43] 6682 2-9-0 **58**.............. PJMcDonald 6 26
(Micky Hammond) *sn pushed along and outpcd in last pair: n.d* **16/1**
6000 **7** 3 **Newz Watch**[64] 6033 2-9-0 **58**.............. PatCosgrave 3 17
(Mick Quinn) *midfield: nvr on terms w ldng pair: rdn over 2f out: sn struggling and no imp: wknd fnl f* **16/1**

1m 12.63s (-1.07) **Going Correction** -0.275s/f (Stan) **7** Ran SP% **112.6**
Speed ratings (Par 94): **96,95,90,84,81 78,74**
CSF £6.69 CT £23.81 TOTE £4.30: £2.30, £1.30; EX 6.60 Trifecta £31.40.
Owner The Hot To Trot Syndicate **Bred** D And J Raeburn **Trained** Newmarket, Suffolk
■ Stewards' Enquiry : Lucy K Barry caution: careless riding

FOCUS
The two market leaders had this between them from some way out. The runner-up has been rated to his recent improvement.

7778 TOTEQUADPOT FOUR PLACES IN FOUR RACES CLAIMING STKS 7f (P)
5:50 (5:50) (Class 6) 3-Y-O+ **£2,911** (£866; £432; £216) **Stalls** Low

Form RPR
3001 **1** **Fort Bastion (IRE)**[12] 7529 7-9-10 90.............. RichardKingscote 1 97
(Tom Dascombe) *trckd ldrs: swtchd rt and pushed into ld over 1f out: readily wnt clr 1f out: easily* **4/7**[1]
0300 **2** 3 **Regal Dan (IRE)**[5] 7702 6-9-7 83.............. ShelleyBirkett(3) 7 86
(David O'Meara) *hld up in tch: cl 4th and effrt over 1f out: sn rdn: chsd clr wnr 150yds out: no imp but kpt on for clr 2nd* **4/1**[2]
0360 **3** 3 ¾ **Free Zone**[24] 7206 7-8-9 83..............(v) LucyKBarry(5) 2 66
(Jamie Osborne) *chsd ldrs: swtchd rt after 1f: chsd ldr over 4f out: rdn over 1f out: unable qck and lost 2nd 150yds out: wknd* **5/1**[3]
3002 **4** ½ **Brasted (IRE)**[8] 7606 4-8-11 73..............(t) PaddyBradley(5) 4 67
(Lee Carter) *led: rdn and hdd over 1f out: sn outpcd u.p: wknd ins fnl f* **12/1**
0400 **5** 3 **Spryt (IRE)**[16] 7436 4-9-4 70..............[1] PaulMulrennan 5 60
(Conor Dore) *hld up in midfield: effrt over 1f out: no imp: n.d* **50/1**
2-40 **6** 30 **Hearmenow (IRE)**[61] 6140 3-8-6 70..............(p) JosephineGordon(3) 6
(J S Moore) *chsd ldr tl over 4f out: lost pl and drifted wd bnd 2f out: sn bhd and eased ins fnl f: t.o* **33/1**
000 **7** 44 **Sense Of Snow (IRE)**[10] 7572 3-8-4 0..............(bt) GeorgeWood(5) 3
(William Muir) *last and no rspnse to press 4f out: sn lost tch: eased fnl 2f: t.o* **100/1**

1m 25.22s (-1.98) **Going Correction** -0.275s/f (Stan)
WFA 3 from 4yo+ 1lb **7** Ran SP% **113.9**
Speed ratings (Par 101): **100,96,92,91,88 54,3**
CSF £3.19 TOTE £1.50: £1.20, £2.10; EX 3.50 Trifecta £6.70.Fort Bastion was claimed by Brian Ellison for £12,000
Owner Owen Promotions Limited **Bred** L White & D McGregor **Trained** Malpas, Cheshire

FOCUS
A decent claimer. It's been rated around the first two.

7779 @TOTEPOOLRACING WIN TICKETS ON TWITTER H'CAP 1m 2f (P)
6:25 (6:28) (Class 2) (0-105,102) 3-Y-O+ **£11,971** (£3,583; £1,791; £896; £446) **Stalls** Low

Form RPR
10- **1** **Ijmaaly (IRE)**[525] 2646 4-9-5 **95**..............[1] PaulHanagan 2 104
(Saeed bin Suroor) *trckd ldrs: rdn to ld over 1f out: hrd pressed but keeping on wl whn bmpd wl ins fnl f: hld on wl cl home: gamely* **11/4**[1]
4004 **2** nk **Manson**[55] 6298 3-8-13 **93**.............. TimmyMurphy 5 101
(Dominic Ffrench Davis) *hld up in tch: nt clr run and swtchd rt over 1f out: hdwy u.p and edging lft ins fnl f: chal and bmpd rival 75yds: kpt on wl but hld cl home* **10/1**
14 **3** ½ **Erhaaf (USA)**[97] 4838 4-8-8 **84**.............. StevieDonohoe 6 91
(Charlie Fellowes) *s.i.s and pushed along in rr: clsd and in tch whn nt clr run over 1f out: hdwy ent fnl f: ev ch whn bmpd 75yds out: kpt on same pce towards fin* **7/1**[3]
1622 **4** 2 ½ **Brigliadoro (IRE)**[8] 7608 5-8-11 **92**.............. PaddyBradley(5) 3 94
(Philip McBride) *stdd s: hld up in tch: nt clr run over 2f out: hdwy on inner over 1f out: chsd ldrs and drvn 1f out: unable qck and wknd fnl 100yds* **11/4**[1]
5 6 **London (FR)**[13] 7521 3-8-1 **84**..............(t) JosephineGordon(3) 4 74
(Phil McEntee) *t.k.h: trckd ldrs: nt clrest of runs wl over 1f out: swtchd rt and unable qck over 1f out: wknd ins fnl f* **20/1**
110 **6** ½ **Lord Ben Stack (IRE)**[12] 7546 4-9-7 **102**.............. CliffordLee(5) 1 91
(K R Burke) *led: rdn over 2f out: drvn and hdd over 1f out: unable qck and btn 1f out: wknd ins fnl f* **6/1**[2]
3103 **7** 6 **Mithqaal (USA)**[8] 7608 3-8-3 **83** oh2.............. DannyBrock 8 60
(Michael Appleby) *t.k.h: chsd ldrs on outer: rdn over 3f out: lost pl u.p over 2f out: wknd over 1f out and bhd fnl f* **7/1**[3]
650 **8** 2 ¼ **Niceofyoutotellme**[56] 6261 7-9-0 **90**.............. RichardKingscote 7 63
(Ralph Beckett) *chsd ldr: rdn over 2f out: losing pl and n.m.r over 1f out: sn wknd and bhd fnl f* **14/1**

2m 2.5s (-6.10) **Going Correction** -0.275s/f (Stan)
WFA 3 from 4yo+ 4lb **8** Ran SP% **113.1**
Speed ratings (Par 109): **113,112,112,110,105 105,100,98**
CSF £31.46 CT £172.41 TOTE £3.20: £1.40, £2.60, £2.70; EX 29.60 Trifecta £231.30.
Owner Godolphin **Bred** Kildaragh Stud **Trained** Newmarket, Suffolk

FOCUS
A decent handicap run at a good gallop. The third has been rated as building on his C&D maiden win, but the fourth has been rated a bit off.

7780 TOTEPOOLLIVEINFO.COM FOR RACING RESULTS MAIDEN STKS 1m (P)
7:00 (7:04) (Class 5) 3-Y-O+ **£3,881** (£1,155; £577; £288) **Stalls** Low

Form RPR
2424 **1** **Cape Banjo (USA)**[39] 6805 3-9-5 79.............. RichardKingscote 5 79
(Ralph Beckett) *chsd ldr tl rdn to ld over 1f out: in command ins fnl f: styd on: rdn out* **Evs**[1]
22 **2** 2 ¾ **Wealth Tax**[21] 7311 3-9-5 0.............. MartinHarley 1 73
(Ed Dunlop) *trckd ldng pair: effrt to chse wnr over 1f out: edgd rt and one pced ins fnl f* **Evs**[1]

40B **3** *2* **Skara Mae (IRE)**[3] 7727 3-9-0 0.. SteveDrowne 3 64
(Charles Hills) *in tch in rr: wnt 4th 3f out: effrt over 1f out: 3rd and kpt on same pce ins fnl f: eased cl home* **33/1**[3]

0000 **4** *8* **Win Lose Draw (IRE)**[13] 7516 4-9-4 56................. AlistairRawlinson(3) 6 50
(Michael Appleby) *sn bustled up to ld: rdn and hdd over 1f out: sn btn and wknd fnl f* **33/1**[3]

0064 **5** *15* **Frankster (FR)**[31] 7009 3-9-5 70.......................................(t) PJMcDonald 2 15
(Micky Hammond) *in tch in 4th: rdn 4f out: dropped to last and struggling u.p 3f out: sn lost tch* **14/1**[2]

1m 38.45s (-1.45) **Going Correction** -0.275s/f (Stan)
WFA 3 from 4yo 2lb **5** Ran SP% **112.5**
Speed ratings (Par 103): **96,93,91,83,68**
CSF £2.25 TOTE £1.90: £1.40, £1.10; EX 2.60 Trifecta £10.60.
Owner A B Partnership **Bred** Reiley McDonald **Trained** Kimpton, Hants

FOCUS
An ordinary maiden in which only two mattered. The runner-up has been rated close to form for now.

7781 TOTEPOOL BETTING ON ALL UK RACING H'CAP 7f (P)
7:30 (7:32) (Class 4) (0-85,85) 3-Y-O+ **£5,175** (£1,540; £769; £384) **Stalls** Low

Form RPR

5001 **1** **Firmdecisions (IRE)**[21] 7308 6-9-6 **84**........................... PatCosgrave 12 93+
(Dean Ivory) *chsd ldrs: effrt 2f out: hdwy u.p to chse ldr ent fnl f: styd on wl u.p to ld cl home* **7/2**[2]

15-0 **2** *hd* **Haaf A Sixpence**[34] 6915 7-9-4 **85**.............................. HectorCrouch(3) 6 93
(Ralph Beckett) *led: rdn ent fnl 2f: drvn over 1f out: kpt on wl u.p: hdd cl home* **5/1**

5450 **3** *shd* **Russian Radiance**[13] 7506 4-9-3 **81**................................. MartinHarley 9 89+
(Jonathan Portman) *hld up in tch in midfield: effrt u.p over 1f out: wnt 3rd 1f out: styd on wl fnl 100yds: nt quite rch ldrs* **20/1**

1000 **4** *3 ¾* **Yourartisonfire**[15] 7461 6-9-2 **80**.......................................(p) LiamKeniry 1 78
(Lisa Williamson) *stdd after s: hld up in tch in last quartet: effrt and hdwy over 1f out: styd on ins fnl f: no threat to ldng trio: snatched 4th last stride* **50/1**

4024 **5** *shd* **Alejandro (IRE)**[15] 7462 7-9-7 **85**.................................. DavidNolan 3 83
(David O'Meara) *chsd ldr: effrt ent fnl 2f: 4th and no ex u.p 1f out: wknd ins fnl f: lost 4th last stride* **4/1**[3]

6560 **6** *hd* **Lyfka**[22] 7281 4-9-3 **81**...(t) PJMcDonald 10 78
(Paul Cole) *stdd and dropped in bhd after s: hld up in tch in last quartet: effrt and hdwy over 1f out: styd on ins fnl f: nvr trbld ldrs* **14/1**

2115 **7** *2* **Nouvelli Dancer (IRE)**[33] 6964 3-9-4 **83**..................... RobertWinston 4 74
(David C Griffiths) *chsd ldrs: effrt jst over 2f out: unable qck over 1f out: wknd ins fnl f* **11/1**

-006 **8** *1 ¾* **War Whisper (IRE)**[34] 6916 3-9-6 **85**................................. SeanLevey 2 71
(Richard Hannon) *in tch in midfield: effrt on inner over 1f out: no imp and wl hld 1f out: wknd ins fnl f* **11/4**[1]

1650 **9** *¾* **Showing Off (IRE)**[29] 7066 3-9-0 **79**................................. TomEaves 8 63
(Michael Wigham) *stdd after s: hld up in tch in last quartet: effrt over 1f out: no imp: nvr trbld ldrs* **18/1**

3610 **10** *3 ½* **Pearl Spectre (USA)**[190] 1775 5-9-0 **81**............. JosephineGordon(3) 11 56
(Phil McEntee) *in tch in midfield: rdn 3f out: lost pl and bhd over 1f out* **20/1**

6000 **11** *¾* **Captain Revelation**[29] 7066 4-9-2 **80**........................ RichardKingscote 7 53
(Tom Dascombe) *chsd ldrs early: steadily lost pl: bhd over 1f out* **20/1**

1m 24.62s (-2.58) **Going Correction** -0.275s/f (Stan)
WFA 3 from 4yo+ 1lb **11** Ran SP% **122.1**
Speed ratings (Par 105): **103,102,102,98,98 98,95,93,92,88 88**
CSF £21.16 CT £320.36 TOTE £4.40: £1.50, £2.10, £5.90; EX 33.80 Trifecta £716.70.
Owner White Bear Racing **Bred** Thomas O'Meara **Trained** Radlett, Herts

FOCUS
The first three finished clear here, the winner confirming the good impression he made on his last visit three weeks ago. It's been rated around the downgraded runner-up.

7782 DAVE (BARNEY) 70TH BIRTHDAY MAIDEN STKS 7f (P)
8:00 (8:02) (Class 5) 3-Y-O+ **£3,881** (£1,155; £577; £288) **Stalls** Low

Form RPR

00 **1** **Out Of The Ashes**[112] 4319 3-9-2 0..............................[1] EoinWalsh(3) 6 74
(John Butler) *hld up in tch: effrt and edgd rt over 1f out: chsd ldr ins fnl f: styd on to ld towards fin* **80/1**

222 **2** *nk* **Port Isaac (IRE)**[15] 7459 3-9-5 78.............................. GeorgeBaker 3 73
(Marcus Tregoning) *led: shkn up ent fnl f: pressed and rdn ins fnl f: hdd towards fin* **4/9**[1]

3 *3 ¾* **Dance Rebel** 3-9-0 0... GeorgeWood(5) 2 63
(Dr Jon Scargill) *chsd ldng trio: effrt over 1f out: unable qck 1f out: kpt on same pce after: wnt 3rd last strides* **12/1**[3]

3-06 **4** *nk* **Muatadel**[176] 2156 3-9-5 73... PaulHanagan 5 62
(Ed Dunlop) *chsd ldr: rdn over 1f out unable qck and lost 3rd ins fnl f: plugged on same pce: lost 3rd last strides* **11/4**[2]

0 **5** *13* **Pleadings (USA)**[21] 7311 3-9-5 0... KierenFox 7 27
(Charlie Wallis) *dwlt: hld up in tch: effrt over 1f out: sn edgd lft and wknd* **25/1**

6 *73* **Piccolilly** 3-9-0 0.. MartinLane 4
(Derek Shaw) *s.i.s: outpcd in rr: lost tch and eased 2f out: t.o* **33/1**

1m 25.95s (-1.25) **Going Correction** -0.275s/f (Stan) **6** Ran SP% **111.6**
Speed ratings (Par 103): **96,95,91,91,76**
CSF £118.85 TOTE £21.40: £15.60, £1.10; EX 79.50 Trifecta £443.70.
Owner David Fremel **Bred** D Fremel **Trained** Newmarket, Suffolk

FOCUS
There was quite a turn-up in this maiden. It's been rated on the negative side.
T/Jkpt: £1,666.60. Pool: £10,000 - 6 winning units. T/Plt: £15.50 to a £1 stake. Pool: £96,066.59 - 4510.53 winning units. T/Qpdt: £7.10 to a £1 stake. Pool: £10,310.41 - 1073.91 winning units.
Steve Payne

7711 CHANTILLY (R-H)
Thursday, November 3

OFFICIAL GOING: Polytrack: standard; turf: soft

7783a PRIX DU VIVIER MADAME (MAIDEN) (UNRACED 2YO) (POLYTRACK) 6f 110y
1:20 (1:20) 2-Y-O **£9,926** (£3,970; £2,977; £1,985; £992)

RPR

1 **Le Brivido (FR)** 2-9-2 0..................................... Pierre-CharlesBoudot 5 78
(A Fabre, France) **6/5**[1]

2 *2* **Uni** 2-8-13 0.. TonyPiccone 2 70
(F Chappet, France) **6/1**

3 *1 ¼* **Capitain Ken (FR)** 2-9-2 0.. CristianDemuro 6 69
(Gianluca Bietolini, Italy) **9/1**

4 *snk* **Andalouse Eria (FR)** 2-8-13 0.................................. IoritzMendizabal 1 66
(F Chappet, France) **59/10**[3]

5 *3 ½* **Indiscrete (FR)** 2-8-13 0... MaximeGuyon 3 56
(C Laffon-Parias, France) **12/5**[2]

6 *8* **Kendy Bay (FR)** 2-8-13 0.. TheoBachelot 4 34
(Gay Kelleway) *midfield: pushed along 2f out: no ex over 1f out: wknd into last: wl btn fnl f* **18/1**

WIN (incl. 1 euro stake): 2.20. PLACES: 1.40, 2.50. SF: 9.00
Owner HRH Prince Faisal Bin Khaled **Bred** J Bugada & Mme B Bugada **Trained** Chantilly, France

7784 - 7790a (Foreign Racing) - See Raceform Interactive

7656 NEWCASTLE (A.W) (L-H)
Friday, November 4

OFFICIAL GOING: Tapeta: standard
Wind: Almost nil Weather: Overcast races 1-2

7791 BREWIN DOLPHIN "CONFINED" H'CAP 1m 2f 42y (Tp)
3:50 (3:51) (Class 4) (0-85,84) 3-Y-O+ **£5,175** (£1,540; £769; £384) **Stalls** High

Form RPR

5040 **1** **Ready (IRE)**[13] 7535 6-9-0 **84**...................................(p) LewisEdmunds(7) 4 93
(Ivan Furtado) *trckd ldrs: plld out and rdn to ld over 1f out: edgd lft ins fnl f: kpt on wl* **3/1**[1]

5000 **2** *2* **L'Inganno Felice (FR)**[21] 7321 6-8-7 **70** oh3.................... CamHardie 8 75
(Iain Jardine) *blindfold slow to remove and s.i.s: hld up: hdwy on outside and ev ch over 1f out: sn rdn: sn chsng wnr: edgd lft ins fnl f: kpt on* **7/1**

0204 **3** *nk* **Sunglider (IRE)**[10] 7594 3-8-8 **75**..............................[1] GrahamGibbons 6 79
(David O'Meara) *prom: hdwy and cl up over 1f out: kpt on u.p ins fnl f* **4/1**[2]

450 **4** *1 ¾* **Storm King**[22] 7308 7-9-1 **78**.......................................[1] DavidAllan 9 79
(David C Griffiths) *hld up: rdn and effrt on outside over 2f out: kpt on fnl f: nt pce to chal* **6/1**[3]

4033 **5** *shd* **Woodacre**[14] 7500 9-8-8 **71**.. GeorgeChaloner 2 72
(Richard Whitaker) *t.k.h: trckd ldrs: effrt and ev ch over 1f out: wknd ins fnl f* **4/1**[2]

2600 **6** *2 ¾* **Argaki (IRE)**[28] 7108 6-8-9 **77**................................ ShirleyTeasdale(5) 7 72
(Keith Dalgleish) *pressed ldr: led over 2f out to over 1f out: rdn and wknd ins fnl f* **14/1**

0000 **7** *3 ¼* **Juste Pour Nous**[13] 7535 3-8-9 **76**...................................(b) JoeFanning 3 65
(Mark Johnston) *t.k.h: led to over 2f out: rdn and wknd over 1f out* **17/2**

0550 **8** *7* **Fray**[17] 7435 5-8-4 **70** oh3.. NathanEvans(3) 5 45
(Jim Goldie) *s.i.s: hld up: struggling over 2f out: sn btn* **33/1**

2m 9.72s (-0.68) **Going Correction** +0.075s/f (Slow)
WFA 3 from 5yo+ 4lb **8** Ran SP% **111.9**
Speed ratings (Par 105): **105,103,103,101,101 99,96,91**
CSF £23.36 CT £82.43 TOTE £6.00: £2.80, £3.50, £1.10; EX 27.40 Trifecta £143.20.
Owner Ron Hull **Bred** Kilshannig Stud **Trained** Wiseton, Nottinghamshire

FOCUS
A race confined to horses who had not won for a year. The runner-up and third have been rated close to form.

7792 HAY & KILNER MAIDEN AUCTION STKS 7f 14y (Tp)
4:20 (4:21) (Class 6) 2-Y-O **£2,587** (£770; £384; £192) **Stalls** Centre

Form RPR

4650 **1** **Peny Arcade**[44] 6678 2-9-0 55.................................. PaulMulrennan 5 57
(Alistair Whillans) *prom: effrt and drvn along over 1f out: led wl ins fnl f: kpt on u.p* **6/1**[3]

00 **2** *hd* **Chaucer's Tale**[11] 7578 2-9-3 0.............................. NathanEvans(3) 7 63
(Michael Easterby) *w ldr: led over 2f out: sn hrd pressed: hdd wl ins fnl f: kpt on: hld nr fin* **15/2**

43 **3** *¾* **Bourbonisto**[70] 5833 2-9-7 67.. GrahamLee 2 62
(Ben Haslam) *t.k.h: cl up on outside: drvn and ev ch over 1f out: one pce ins fnl f* **6/4**[1]

00 **4** *2* **Breathoffreshair**[30] 7071 2-9-9 0................................... ConnorBeasley 8 59
(Richard Guest) *hld up: rdn and outpcd over 2f out: rallied over 1f out: kpt on: nvr able to chal* **66/1**

00 **5** *hd* **Hediddodinthe (IRE)**[7] 7659 2-9-7 0.................................. JoeFanning 3 56
(Richard Guest) *s.i.s: hld up in tch: pushed along over 2f out: edgd lft and outpcd over 1f out: kpt on ins fnl f: no imp* **14/1**

6 *½* **Huddersfilly Town** 2-9-0 0.. TomEaves 1 48
(Ivan Furtado) *s.i.s: hld up: stdy hdwy over 2f out: rdn over 1f out: sn no ex* **16/1**

6 **7** *hd* **Musico (IRE)**[21] 7328 2-9-9 0... JoeyHaynes 4 56
(Patrick Holmes) *.prom: rdn over 2f out: sn outpcd: no imp fr over 1f out* **20/1**

8 *1 ½* **Oberyn (IRE)** 2-8-12 0.. MitchGodwin(5) 6 47
(Sylvester Kirk) *led to over 2f out: rallied: wknd ins fnl f* **5/2**[2]

1m 28.05s (1.85) **Going Correction** +0.075s/f (Slow) **8** Ran SP% **113.4**
Speed ratings (Par 94): **92,91,90,88,88 87,87,85**
CSF £48.96 TOTE £8.00: £2.30, £1.60, £1.10; EX 59.20 Trifecta £117.50.
Owner Mrs Helen Greggan **Bred** Bond Thoroughbred Corporation **Trained** Newmill-On-Slitrig, Borders

FOCUS
A moderate maiden.

7793 LYCETTS MAIDEN STKS 5f (Tp)
4:50 (4:50) (Class 5) 3-Y-O+ **£3,234** (£962; £481; £240) **Stalls** Centre

Form RPR

0022 **1** **Heiba (IRE)**[20] 7362 4-9-5 68.......................................[1] GrahamGibbons 3 68
(Robert Cowell) *mde virtually all: rdn along over 1f out: kpt on gamely fnl f* **8/11**[1]

533 **2** *½* **Eternalist**[20] 7362 3-8-7 59.. LewisEdmunds(7) 7 61
(Jim Goldie) *t.k.h: disp ld thrght: rdn over 1f out: kpt on fnl f: hld towards fin* **15/8**[2]

2350 **3** *1 ½* **Hot Stuff**[121] 3994 3-9-2 60...................................... GeorgeDowning(3) 2 61
(Tony Carroll) *t.k.h: prom: effrt and ev ch briefly over 1f out: no ex last 100yds* **10/1**[3]

-040 **4** *½* **Lilvanita (IRE)**[27] 7145 3-9-0 55.......................................(b[1]) BenCurtis 6 54
(Brian Ellison) *t.k.h: prom: outpcd and hd high 2f out: edgd lft and kpt on u.p ins fnl f* **22/1**

4052 **5** *7* **Nefetari**[10] 7603 3-8-9 44..(b) JoshDoyle(5) 5 29
(Alan Brown) *t.k.h early: cl up tl rdn and wknd over 1f out* **28/1**

6-60 **6** 1 1/4 **Valtashyra (IRE)**[55] 6317 3-8-9 39 ....(p) AnnStokell(5) 1 24
(Ann Stokell) *taken early to post: in tch on outside: struggling 1/2-way: sn btn* **150/1**

1m 0.28s (0.78) **Going Correction** +0.075s/f (Slow) **6** Ran SP% **110.2**
Speed ratings (Par 103): **96,95,92,92,80 78**
CSF £2.16 TOTE £1.50: £1.10, £1.30; EX 2.40 Trifecta £5.90.
Owner Saleh Al Homaizi & Imad Al Sagar **Bred** Fergus Cousins **Trained** Six Mile Bottom, Cambs

FOCUS
Pretty weak maiden form.

7794 LEATHERS LLP H'CAP (DIV I) 1m 5y (Tp)
5:20 (5:20) (Class 6) (0-60,60) 3-Y-O+ **£2,587** (£770; £384; £192) **Stalls** Centre

Form RPR
0650 **1** **Table Manners**[42] 6739 4-8-4 **48** .... HollieDoyle(5) 11 58
(Wilf Storey) *hld up midfield on nr side of gp: smooth hdwy to ld over 2f out: rdn and 3 l clr over 1f out: kpt on wl fnl f* **25/1**
2405 **2** 1 1/4 **Lozah**[29] 7097 3-8-12 **53** .... TonyHamilton 12 60
(Roger Fell) *hld up on nr side of gp: hdwy to chse (clr) wnr over 1f out: kpt on ins fnl f: no further imp towards fin* **16/1**
2431 **3** 1/2 **Galilee Chapel (IRE)**[21] 7336 7-9-5 **58** ....(b) DougieCostello 4 64
(Alistair Whillans) *hld up: rdn and outpcd over 3f out: gd hdwy over 1f out: kpt on fnl f: nrst fin* **14/1**
1401 **4** 1 1/2 **Thello**[34] 6953 4-8-13 **59** .... LewisEdmunds(7) 5 62
(Garry Moss) *t.k.h: cl up: carried lft over 2f out: rallied and swtchd rt over 1f out: kpt on same pce ins fnl f* **11/4**[1]
0004 **5** 5 **Lord Rob**[10] 7602 5-8-4 **46** oh1 .... NathanEvans(3) 10 38
(David Thompson) *taken early to post: prom: effrt and drvn over 2f out: wknd over 1f out* **10/1**
0356 **6** 1 **Grey Destiny**[71] 5808 6-9-4 **57** .... CamHardie 13 46
(Antony Brittain) *s.i.s: t.k.h in rr: hdwy and edgd lft 2f out: no imp fnl f* **16/1**
0001 **7** hd **Great Colaci**[10] 7604 3-8-10 **51** 6ex .... TomEaves 9 40
(Keith Reveley) *overall ldr on nr side of gp: drifted (lft) to far rail and hdd over 2f out: rdn and wknd fnl f* **6/1**[3]
0-03 **8** 1/2 **Rosy Ryan (IRE)**[42] 6742 6-9-1 **54** .... JamesSullivan 3 42
(Tina Jackson) *hld up on far side of gp: rdn over 2f out: sme hdwy over 1f out: nvr able to chal* **9/2**[2]
0003 **9** hd **Sir Jack**[11] 7572 3-8-9 **50** .... JoeyHaynes 2 37
(Tony Carroll) *s.i.s: hld up on far side of gp: drvn along 1/2-way: rallied: wknd fr 2f out* **15/2**
645 **10** 4 **Aneedh**[92] 5057 6-9-7 **60** ....(p) PaulMulrennan 6 39
(Clive Mulhall) *hld up towards rr: rdn along 1/2-way: no imp fr over 2f out* **25/1**
10 **11** 2 1/4 **Outlaw Torn (IRE)**[20] 7369 7-8-12 **51** ....(e) ConnorBeasley 14 25
(Richard Guest) *prom: drvn and outpcd over 2f out: sn btn* **14/1**
3620 **12** 5 **Call Me Crockett (IRE)**[27] 7145 4-8-11 **50** ....(p) PatrickMathers 1 13
(Noel Wilson) *in tch on far side of gp: drvn and struggling wl over 2f out: sn btn* **50/1**
050- **13** 11 **Stormont Bridge**[346] 4479 8-8-3 **47** ....(t) PhilDennis(5) 7
(Maurice Barnes) *midfield: drvn and struggling over 3f out: sn wknd* **100/1**
0005 **14** 3/4 **Afkar (IRE)**[31] 7048 8-9-3 **56** ....(p) DavidNolan 8
(Ivan Furtado) *prom: lost pl 1/2-way: sn struggling* **28/1**

1m 38.29s (-0.31) **Going Correction** +0.075s/f (Slow)
WFA 3 from 4yo+ 2lb **14** Ran SP% **119.2**
Speed ratings (Par 101): **99,97,97,95,90 89,89,89,88,84 82,77,66,65**
CSF £364.65 CT £5850.82 TOTE £35.00: £8.40, £5.50, £3.80; EX 566.70 Trifecta £4374.20.
Owner Geegeez.co.uk 1 **Bred** Raymond Clive Tooth **Trained** Muggleswick, Co Durham

FOCUS
A moderate handicap but not a bad performance from the winner.

7795 LEATHERS LLP H'CAP (DIV II) 1m 5y (Tp)
5:50 (5:52) (Class 6) (0-60,60) 3-Y-O+ **£2,587** (£770; £384; £192) **Stalls** Centre

Form RPR
0603 **1** **Melgate Melody**[10] 7604 3-8-10 **51** .... GrahamGibbons 1 57
(Michael Easterby) *mde all centre: rdn along 2f out: kpt on wl fnl f* **9/2**[3]
0030 **2** 2 **Mr Potter**[8] 7641 3-8-11 **52** .... ConnorBeasley 14 54
(Richard Guest) *hld up: hdwy in centre to chse wnr over 1f out: kpt on ins fnl f: nt pce to chal* **11/1**
0353 **3** 1/2 **Who's Shirl**[21] 7323 10-9-1 **54** .... PaulMulrennan 7 55
(Chris Fairhurst) *hld up: pushed along and hdwy stands' side 2f out: edgd lft and kpt on ins fnl f: nrst fin* **10/1**
5452 **4** 1 1/2 **Leonard Thomas**[17] 7442 6-9-4 **60** .... GeorgeDowning(3) 5 57
(Tony Carroll) *s.i.s: hld up in centre: hdwy to chse wnr over 2f out to over 1f out: kpt on same pce ins fnl f* **7/2**[1]
2060 **5** 1 1/4 **Stanlow**[24] 7262 6-8-9 **48** ow2 ....(v) TomEaves 10 42
(Michael Mullineaux) *s.i.s: hld up: rdn over 2f out: hdwy in centre over 1f out: kpt on same pce ins fnl f* **33/1**
1260 **6** 1/2 **I'm Super Too (IRE)**[45] 6647 9-8-12 **56** .... GemmaTutty(5) 12 51
(Karen Tutty) *rrd in stalls: hld up stands' side: rdn whn checked 3f out: kpt on fnl f: nvr able to chal* **20/1**
6150 **7** 1 1/2 **Highway Robber**[21] 7336 3-8-7 **53** .... HollieDoyle(5) 2 43
(Wilf Storey) *taken steadily to post: hld up on far side of centre gp: hdwy over 2f out: rdn and wknd over 1f out* **20/1**
500- **8** 3/4 **Southview Lady**[396] 6982 4-8-6 **48** .... RachelRichardson(3) 4 36
(Sean Regan) *prom centre: drvn along and outpcd over 2f out: sn n.d: btn fnl f* **100/1**
4440 **9** 1/2 **Border Bandit (USA)**[67] 5972 8-8-11 **50** ....(p) BenCurtis 3 37
(Tracy Waggott) *t.k.h: cl up on far side of centre gp: rdn over 2f out: wknd over 1f out* **12/1**
600 **10** shd **Bigbadboy (IRE)**[63] 6106 3-8-6 **47** .... JamesSullivan 8 34
(Clive Mulhall) *prom: rdn in centre over 2f out: edgd lft and sn wknd* **28/1**
4053 **11** 2 3/4 **Charles De Mille**[10] 7601 8-9-4 **57** .... JackGarritty 11 38
(Jedd O'Keeffe) *in tch: stdy hdwy in centre over 2f out: rdn: edgd lft and wknd over 1f out* **4/1**[2]
0210 **12** nk **Quadriga (IRE)**[140] 3342 6-9-3 **56** .... DougieCostello 9 36
(Chris Grant) *cl up towards stands' side: rdn over 2f out: wknd wl over 1f out* **20/1**
5060 **13** 2 **She's Electric (IRE)**[10] 7601 3-9-0 **60** ....[1] ShirleyTeasdale(5) 6 36
(Keith Dalgleish) *hld up in tch in centre: struggling over 2f out: wkng whn hung lft over 1f out* **16/1**

3360 **14** 17 **Breton Blues**[35] 6920 6-8-5 **47** ....(b) NathanEvans(3) 13
(Fred Watson) *s.i.s: in tch stands' side tl rdn and wknd wl over 2f out: sn lost tch: t.o* **12/1**

1m 39.22s (0.62) **Going Correction** +0.075s/f (Slow)
WFA 3 from 4yo+ 2lb **14** Ran SP% **120.8**
Speed ratings (Par 101): **99,97,96,95,93 93,91,91,90,90 87,87,85,68**
CSF £48.25 CT £491.26 TOTE £5.60: £2.00, £3.00, £3.00; EX 57.40 Trifecta £399.70.
Owner B Hoggarth & S Hull **Bred** Biddestone Stud Ltd **Trained** Sheriff Hutton, N Yorks

FOCUS
This was run in a similar time (0.07sec quicker) to the first division. Ordinary form.

7796 BREWIN DOLPHIN H'CAP 1m 5y (Tp)
6:20 (6:21) (Class 4) (0-85,85) 3-Y-O+ **£5,175** (£1,540; £769; £384) **Stalls** Centre

Form RPR
2066 **1** **Alexandrakollontai (IRE)**[16] 7472 6-8-13 **77** ....(b) JamesSullivan 4 89
(Alistair Whillans) *hld up in last pl: hdwy and swtchd to stands' rail over 2f out: qcknd to ld over 1f out: edgd lft and sn pushed clr: eased towards fin: readily* **22/1**
2030 **2** 3 1/2 **Planetaria (IRE)**[9] 7623 3-8-11 **80** .... AdamMcNamara(3) 9 84+
(Garry Moss) *led in centre: rdn along over 2f out: edgd rt and hdd over 1f out: kpt on fnl f: no ch w ready wnr* **6/1**[2]
0010 **3** shd **Lawyer (IRE)**[34] 6956 5-9-2 **80** .... GrahamGibbons 3 84
(David Barron) *hld up: shkn up and hdwy in centre over 1f out: rdn and r.o towards fin: nrst fin* **12/1**
P000 **4** nk **Edgar Balthazar**[29] 7095 4-9-7 **85** ....(p) PhillipMakin 8 88
(Keith Dalgleish) *s.i.s: hld up: reminders 1/2-way: rdn over 2f out: hdwy in centre over 1f out: kpt on fnl f: no imp* **16/1**
4061 **5** nk **Eastern Dragon (IRE)**[27] 7141 6-8-8 **77** ....(p) ShirleyTeasdale(5) 13 79
(Iain Jardine) *s.i.s: hld up: hdwy stands' side to chse ldrs over 1f out: kpt on same pce ins fnl f* **8/1**
0523 **6** 1 3/4 **Bell Heather (IRE)**[66] 6005 3-8-11 **77** .... GeorgeChaloner 2 75
(Richard Fahey) *prom in centre: drvn along over 2f out: no ex fnl f* **20/1**
6455 **7** 3 1/2 **Shamaheart (IRE)**[6] 7702 6-9-6 **84** ....(p) DavidAllan 6 74
(Geoffrey Harker) *hld up: hdwy on far side of gp over 2f out: no imp over 1f out* **9/1**
0004 **8** 6 **Miss Van Gogh**[50] 6500 4-9-7 **85** .... TonyHamilton 5 61
(Richard Fahey) *hld up in tch: drvn in centre over 2f out: wknd over 1f out* **11/1**
0003 **9** 3/4 **Mont Ras (IRE)**[28] 7108 9-9-5 **83** .... ConnorBeasley 10 58
(Roger Fell) *w ldr in centre: drvn along 3f out: wknd wl over 1f out* **9/2**[1]
2314 **10** 4 **Pumaflor (IRE)**[34] 6956 4-8-13 **82** ....(p) PhilDennis(5) 12 48
(Richard Whitaker) *hld up in tch on nr side of gp: rdn over 2f out: wknd over 1f out* **15/2**[3]
3040 **11** 2 **Woody Bay**[61] 6160 6-9-1 **79** .... DougieCostello 14 40
(Mark Walford) *midfield on nr side of gp: struggling over 2f out: sn btn* **20/1**
3125 **12** shd **Kiwi Bay**[44] 6683 11-8-13 **77** .... PaulMulrennan 11 38
(Michael Dods) *in tch in centre: lost pl over 2f out: sn wknd* **14/1**
1200 **13** 32 **Palmerston**[42] 6753 3-8-12 **78** .... BenCurtis 1
(Michael Appleby) *in tch on far side of gp: hung (lft) to far rail fr 1/2-way: struggling wl over 2f out: eased whn no ch over 1f out* **8/1**

1m 37.27s (-1.33) **Going Correction** +0.075s/f (Slow)
WFA 3 from 4yo+ 2lb **13** Ran SP% **118.9**
Speed ratings (Par 105): **109,105,105,105,104 103,99,93,92,88 86,86,54**
CSF £144.83 CT £1687.18 TOTE £30.10: £6.60, £3.50, £3.70; EX 170.50 Trifecta £1585.80.
Owner Chris Spark & William Orr **Bred** Sean O'Sullivan **Trained** Newmill-On-Slitrig, Borders

FOCUS
This was run at a good gallop and it suited the hold-up horses. The winner, third and fourth have been rated back to their best.

7797 GEORGE F WHITE H'CAP 7f 14y (Tp)
6:50 (6:50) (Class 6) (0-65,65) 3-Y-O+ **£2,587** (£770; £384; £192) **Stalls** Centre

Form RPR
0214 **1** **Rock Warbler (IRE)**[9] 7611 3-9-2 **62** ....(t) KevinStott 7 69+
(Oliver Greenall) *stdd s: hld up: stdy hdwy gng wl over 1f out: shkn up to ld ins fnl f: rdn and kpt on wl fnl f* **4/1**[2]
3300 **2** 3/4 **Space War**[21] 7334 9-9-2 **64** ....(t) NathanEvans(3) 8 70
(Michael Easterby) *prom on nr side of centre gp: led gng wl over 2f out: rdn and hdd ins fnl f: rallied: kpt on fin* **5/1**[3]
0006 **3** 3/4 **Thorntoun Lady (USA)**[17] 7437 6-8-10 **62** .... LewisEdmunds(7) 5 66
(Jim Goldie) *hld up in tch centre: rdn and hdwy over 1f out: kpt on ins fnl f* **28/1**
4045 **4** 1 1/4 **Custard The Dragon**[116] 4215 3-9-5 **65** .... JoeFanning 3 65
(John Mackie) *cl up centre: rdn and ev ch over 1f out: kpt on same pce ins fnl f* **20/1**
3564 **5** 1 3/4 **Broctune Papa Gio**[10] 7601 9-9-0 **64** .... CliffordLee(5) 13 61
(Keith Reveley) *cl up in stands' side gp: rdn over 2f out: edgd lft: kpt on same pce over 1f out* **9/1**
0 **6** 2 **Bromance**[17] 7435 3-9-5 **65** .... TomEaves 6 56
(Peter Niven) *hld up: hdwy on far side of centre gp over 2f out: no imp fr over 1f out* **40/1**
0000 **7** hd **French**[52] 6451 3-9-2 **62** .... CamHardie 14 52
(Antony Brittain) *t.k.h early: hld up in tch bhd stands' side ldrs: rdn and edgd lft over 2f out: no imp over 1f out* **100/1**
-660 **8** 1 1/4 **Destination Aim**[52] 6453 9-9-3 **62** .... GrahamLee 12 50
(Fred Watson) *cl up stands' side: rdn over 2f out: wknd over 1f out* **16/1**
0051 **9** nk **Be Bold**[11] 7584 4-9-1 **65** .... RowanScott(5) 10 52
(Rebecca Bastiman) *t.k.h: hld up on outside of stands' side quintet: pushed along over 2f out: no imp fr over 1f out* **11/2**
0400 **10** 2 1/4 **You'll Do**[10] 7601 3-9-0 **65** .... PhilDennis(5) 1 46
(Maurice Barnes) *hld up in tch in centre gp: struggling over 2f out: btn over 1f out* **25/1**
4232 **11** 1 **Wahaab (IRE)**[11] 7585 5-8-13 **65** ....(p) JamieGormley(7) 2 44
(Iain Jardine) *t.k.h: led centre to over 2f out: rdn and wknd over 1f out* **12/1**
5532 **12** shd **Napoleon Solo**[24] 7253 4-9-4 **63** .... GrahamGibbons 9 42
(David Barron) *t.k.h: hld up: swtchd to centre gp after 2f: rdn over 2f out: btn over 1f out* **10/3**[1]
2314 **13** 1 1/2 **Gaelic Wizard (IRE)**[11] 7584 8-8-13 **63** .... GemmaTutty(5) 4 38
(Karen Tutty) *t.k.h: cl up on far side of centre gp: rdn over 2f out: wknd wl over 1f out* **33/1**
0000 **14** 37 **Royal Normandy**[17] 7435 4-9-6 **65** ....(p[1]) BenCurtis 11
(Roger Fell) *s.i.s: bhd stands' side: lost tch 1/2-way: t.o* **33/1**

1m 26.56s (0.36) **Going Correction** +0.075s/f (Slow)
WFA 3 from 4yo+ 1lb **14** Ran SP% **120.1**
Speed ratings (Par 101): **100,99,98,96,94 92,92,90,90,88 86,86,85,42**
CSF £22.43 CT £502.65 TOTE £4.60: £1.90, £2.20, £9.10; EX 31.90 Trifecta £786.10.

Owner R A Royle & S Evason **Bred** Sir E J Loder **Trained** Oldcastle Heath, Cheshire

FOCUS

They went fairly steady early, but the winner still came from off the pace. The runner-up has been rated near his best from last year.

7798 CHUF H'CAP 6f (Tp)

7:20 (7:20) (Class 5) (0-75,77) 3-Y-O+ **£3,234** (£962; £481; £240) **Stalls** Centre

Form RPR

6423 **1** **Manatee Bay**[17] 7433 6-9-7 **75**...(v) TomEaves 4 85
(David Nicholls) *t.k.h: hld up: smooth hdwy over 1f out: rdn and led last 50yds: kpt on* **15/2**

3511 **2** *hd* **Enjoy Life (IRE)**[3] 7743 3-8-12 **73** 6ex...(p) LewisEdmunds[(7)] 1 82+
(Kevin Ryan) *pressed ldr: led gng wl over 2f out: pushed along over 1f out: rdn and veered rt ins fnl f: hdd last 50yds: kpt on: jst hld* **13/8**[1]

1440 **3** *2¼* **Magical Daze**[53] 6426 4-9-1 **69**... GrahamGibbons 8 71
(John Mackie) *t.k.h: prom: effrt and chsd wnr over 1f out to ins fnl f: kpt on same pce* **16/1**

0031 **4** *shd* **Meandmyshadow**[7] 7663 8-8-11 **70**...(b) JoshDoyle[(5)] 6 72
(Alan Brown) *led: rdn and hdd over 2f out: rallied: kpt on same pce ins fnl f* **7/1**[3]

3004 **5** *1¼* **Tavener**[87] 5269 4-8-8 **62** ow1...(p) DavidAllan 2 60
(David C Griffiths) *in tch: drvn and effrt on far side of gp over 1f out: no ex ins fnl f* **40/1**

00-4 **6** *nk* **Mehdi (IRE)**[10] 7591 7-9-7 **75**...(t) DavidNolan 12 72
(Richard Fahey) *hld up: rdn over 2f out: hdwy on nr side of gp over 1f out: no imp whn blkd fnl f* **9/1**

0411 **7** *nse* **Royal Connoisseur (IRE)**[10] 7590 5-9-2 **77** 6ex. NatalieHambling[(7)] 11 75
(Richard Fahey) *in tch on nr side of gp: rdn over 2f out: effrt over 1f out: one pce whn checked ins fnl f* **10/1**

2040 **8** *1½* **Lucky Lodge**[21] 7325 6-8-12 **66**...(p) CamHardie 5 58
(Antony Brittain) *rrd in stalls: s.i.s: bhd: rdn and outpcd over 2f out: sme late hdwy: nvr on terms* **33/1**

0000 **9** *nk* **Stocking**[28] 7112 4-9-7 **75**... ConnorBeasley 7 66
(Bryan Smart) *s.i.s: t.k.h: hld up: hdwy and prom over 1f out: no ex whn no room briefly ins fnl f: sn btn* **50/1**

041 **10** *5* **Slingsby**[21] 7325 5-9-0 **71**...(b) NathanEvans[(3)] 9 46
(Michael Easterby) *missed break: bhd on stands' rail (away fr main gp): rdn and hdwy 1/2-way: wknd wl over 1f out* **4/1**[2]

6600 **11** *¾* **Harmonic Wave (IRE)**[17] 7437 3-8-13 **67**... DougieCostello 3 40
(Rebecca Menzies) *in tch: rdn along over 2f out: wknd over 1f out* **100/1**

1500 **12** *2½* **Kestrel Call (IRE)**[53] 6425 3-9-6 **74**...(t) BenCurtis 10 39
(Michael Appleby) *cl up: rdn over 2f out: wknd over 1f out* **66/1**

1m 11.37s (-1.13) **Going Correction** +0.075s/f (Slow) **12** Ran SP% **117.2**

Speed ratings (Par 103): **110,109,106,106,104 104,104,102,102,95 94,91**

CSF £19.42 CT £198.06 TOTE £9.30: £2.20, £1.20, £4.70; EX 23.10 Trifecta £401.00.

Owner Alex Nicholls & Partner **Bred** Miss A J Rawding & P M Crane **Trained** Sessay, N Yorks

FOCUS

A fair sprint. The runner-up has been rated to her 7f Redcar win.

T/Plt: £307.10 to a £1 stake. Pool: £66,232.00 - 215.60 winning units. T/Qpdt: £205.70 to a £1 stake. Pool: £6,740.00 - 32.75 winning units. **Richard Young**

7799 - (Foreign Racing) - See Raceform Interactive

7672 DUNDALK (A.W) (L-H)

Friday, November 4

OFFICIAL GOING: Polytrack: standard

7800a CROWNE PLAZA HOTEL RACE & STAY H'CAP 5f (P)

6:35 (6:36) (45-65,65) 3-Y-O+ **£4,522** (£1,397; £661; £294; £110)

RPR

1 **Red All Star (IRE)**[9] 7633 6-8-3 **45**...(t) KillianLeonard[(5)] 13 56
(Gerard Keane, Ire) *mde all: rdn 2f out: strly pressed ins fnl f: kpt on gamely clsng stages* **12/1**

2 *½* **Strategic Force (IRE)**[9] 7633 5-9-7 **58**...(bt) NGMcCullagh 5 67+
(Gerard O'Leary, Ire) *chsd ldrs in 4th: clsr in 3rd over 1f out: kpt on wl towards outer into 2nd cl home: nt rch wnr* **6/4**[1]

3 *nse* **Dandysteps (IRE)**[129] 3758 5-8-8 **45**...[1] LeighRoche 1 54+
(Tracey Collins, Ire) *hld up on inner in mid-div: prog and swtchd rt under 2f out: swtchd to outer ins fnl f in 6th and styd on strly into 3rd cl home: nrst fin* **10/1**

4 *1¼* **Times In Anatefka (IRE)**[203] 1466 6-8-8 **45**...(tp) ShaneFoley 14 49
(Adrian Brendan Joyce, Ire) *trckd ldr in 2nd: travelled wl to press ldr under 2f out: kpt on wl tl no ex clsng stages and dropped to 4th* **8/1**[3]

5 *1½* **Roryslittlesister (IRE)**[16] 7474 6-8-1 **45**...(t) SeanDavis[(7)] 10 44
(S M Duffy, Ire) *bit slowly away and sn mid-div on outer: rdn 2f out: wnt 5th ent fnl f: no imp fnl 100yds: kpt on same pce* **20/1**

6 *nk* **Head Space (IRE)**[13] 7533 8-10-0 **65**... PatSmullen 12 63
(David Evans) *hld up towards outer: rdn over 2f out: kpt on wl on outer ins fnl f: nvr on terms* **7/1**[2]

7 *½* **Gower Princess**[9] 7629 5-8-3 **45**...[1] TomMadden[(5)] 4 41
(Miss Clare Louise Cannon, Ire) *chsd ldrs in 3rd on inner: rdn and nt qckn in 4th appr fnl f: no ex fnl 100yds* **33/1**

8 *¾* **Missile Command (IRE)**[94] 4998 8-8-8 **45**...(p) WayneLordan 2 38
(Jane M Foley, Ire) *rrd on leaving stalls: keen early on and sn mid-div: rdn and no imp ent fnl f: sn one pce* **12/1**

9 *1¼* **Sweetie Jar (IRE)**[94] 4997 3-9-3 **54**...(tp) ColinKeane 8 43
(John Joseph Murphy, Ire) *chsd early ldrs: 5th at 1/2-way: rdn and nt qckn over 1f out: sn no ex* **8/1**[3]

10 *nk* **Eye Glass (IRE)**[9] 7633 4-8-8 **45**...(v) RoryCleary 3 33
(T G McCourt, Ire) *sn rdn to chse early ldrs: strly rdn in mid-div at 1/2-way: no imp ent fnl f* **33/1**

11 *1* **Imprimatur (IRE)**[7] 7678 4-8-1 **45**...(b[1]) DannySheehy[(7)] 9 29
(John C McConnell, Ire) *hld up: rdn over 2f out: no imp and wandered u.p appr fnl f: no ex* **50/1**

12 *1* **Molans Mare (IRE)**[256] 673 6-8-1 **45**... AndrewBreslin[(7)] 7 26
(Jason Cairns, Ire) *racd in mid-div: rdn 1/2-way and dropped towards rr: swtchd lft to inner under 2f out: sn no ex* **50/1**

13 *½* **Warrior Chant (USA)**[2216] 6822 10-8-1 **45**...(t[1]) KeithMoriarty[(7)] 6 24
(Norman Cassidy, Ire) *slowly away: a towards rr: nvr a factor* **33/1**

14 *5½* **Prince Connoisseur (IRE)**[42] 6754 5-9-2 **56**...[1] GaryHalpin[(3)] 11 15
(John James Feane, Ire) *a in rr: nvr a factor* **8/1**[3]

58.93s (58.93) **14** Ran SP% **127.8**

CSF £30.54 CT £212.49 TOTE £15.60: £3.40, £1.10, £3.70; DF 41.10 Trifecta £600.80.

Owner Gaeltacht Partnership **Bred** Pat Reynolds **Trained** Trim, Co Meath

FOCUS

A low-grade handicap run at a good clip with a pillar-to-post winner. The second, third and fourth have been rated close to their best, with the fifth helping to set the standard.

7801a DUNDALK STADIUM CLAIMING RACE 1m (P)

7:05 (7:06) 3-Y-O+ **£4,522** (£1,397; £661; £294; £110)

RPR

1 **Hes Our Music (IRE)**[14] 7517 7-9-11 **80**... PatSmullen 8 81+
(Patrick J Flynn, Ire) *sn led: stl travelled wl 2f out and rdn to extend advantage over 1f out: styd on wl clsng stages* **6/4**[1]

2 *1* **Toccata Blue (IRE)**[21] 7340 6-9-9 **71**... ColinKeane 4 77
(G M Lyons, Ire) *chsd early ldrs on inner: sn settled in mid-div: prog under 2f out: wnt 4th ent fnl f: kpt on wl into 2nd cl home: nt rch wnr* **8/1**[3]

3 *hd* **Reckless Lad (IRE)**[61] 6169 6-9-9 **80**...(tp) OisinOrr[(5)] 9 81
(Patrick Martin, Ire) *hld up: gd prog over 1f out to chse ldrs in 3rd ent fnl f: wnt 2nd fnl 150yds: kpt on wl: ct for 2nd cl home* **12/1**

4 *1* **Specific Gravity (FR)**[14] 7522 8-9-1 **68**...(b) RonanWhelan 1 66+
(Adrian McGuinness, Ire) *chsd early ldrs on inner: sn dropped towards rr and rdn: prog over 1f out: kpt on wl ent fnl f: wnt 5th ins fnl 100yds: nvr nrr* **10/1**

5 *1¾* **Elusive In Paris (IRE)**[14] 7517 7-9-3 **72**...(e) GaryHalpin[(3)] 7 67
(John James Feane, Ire) *trckd ldr in 2nd: sn 3rd on inner: rdn in 2nd over 2f out: no imp on ldr ent fnl f: wknd fnl 100yds* **9/2**[2]

6 *hd* **Palavicini Run (IRE)**[9] 7629 3-8-11 **68**... DonaghO'Connor[(5)] 3 64
(J F Levins, Ire) *bit slowly away: sn mid-div: rdn 2f out: no imp ent fnl f in 6th: kpt on same pce* **20/1**

7 *1½* **Lilbourne Prince (IRE)**[11] 7572 3-9-1 **71**... DeclanMcDonogh 11 60
(David Evans) *racd in mid-div towards outer: pushed along over 2f out: kpt on same pce ins fnl f: nvr on terms* **14/1**

8 *nk* **Emperor Bob (IRE)**[14] 7518 4-8-13 **65**... AndrewBreslin[(7)] 10 62
(Patrick J McKenna, Ire) *sn chsd ldr in 2nd: rdn in 3rd 2f out: no ex appr fnl f: wknd* **50/1**

9 *½* **Manorov**[28] 7132 6-9-1 **64**...(vt) KillianLeonard[(5)] 2 61
(T G McCourt, Ire) *racd in mid-div: dropped towards rr after 2f: sme prog over 1f out: kpt on same pce: nvr on terms* **16/1**

10 *1¾* **Fire And Passion**[7] 7679 4-9-2 **70**...(v) DannySheehy[(7)] 13 60
(Adrian Paul Keatley, Ire) *racd in rr: sme prog 1/2-way: rdn and no imp under 2f out: wandered u.p ins fnl f* **20/1**

11 *nk* **Coilogshakeysirgin (IRE)**[20] 7376 9-8-11 **41**... RoryCleary 5 47
(Denis W Cullen, Ire) *chsd ldrs: rdn in 4th over 2f out: nt qckn over 1f out: sn wknd* **50/1**

12 *3½* **Vocal Experience (IRE)**[30] 7084 3-9-4 **72**... KevinManning 14 48
(J S Bolger, Ire) *chsd ldrs towards outer in 4th: rdn in 5th 3f out: nt qckn under 2f out: sn no ex: eased clsng stages* **16/1**

13 *2½* **Rocco's Delight**[109] 4443 4-8-6 **76**...[1] TomMadden[(5)] 6 34
(Shane Kieran Ryder, Ire) *racd in mid-div: pushed along and dropped to rr 3f out: sn no ex* **16/1**

14 *1* **Fiesole**[139] 5089 4-10-2 **79**... ConnorKing 12 50
(Eoin Doyle, Ire) *a towards rr: no imp under 2f out: nvr a factor* **50/1**

1m 36.73s (96.73)

WFA 3 from 4yo+ 2lb **14** Ran SP% **125.8**

CSF £13.69 TOTE £2.40: £1.20, £2.60, £4.00; DF 16.90 Trifecta £225.60.

Owner Mrs Patrick J Flynn **Bred** Liam Brennan **Trained** Carrick-On-Suir, Co Waterford

FOCUS

A fiercely competitive event for the grade with a number of established Polytrack performers doing battle.

7802a (Foreign Racing) - See Raceform Interactive

7803a DUNDALK STADIUM - LIGHT UP YOUR NIGHT H'CAP 6f (P)

8:05 (8:05) 3-Y-O+ **£10,852** (£3,352; £1,588; £705; £264)

RPR

1 **Dougan**[14] 7497 4-9-10 **98**... PatSmullen 1 105
(David Evans) *settled off ldrs on inner in 4th: rdn in 3rd over 1f out: styd on wl between horses to ld ins fnl 100yds: kpt on wl* **13/8**[1]

2 *nk* **Togoville (IRE)**[14] 7523 6-9-1 **92**...(b) RossCoakley[(3)] 6 98
(Georgios Pakidis, Ire) *led: rdn and kpt on wl appr fnl f: hdd ins fnl 100yds* **12/1**

3 *½* **Russian Soul (IRE)**[14] 7523 8-9-5 **93**...(p) ConorHoban 7 97
(M Halford, Ire) *slowly away and racd in rr: rdn under 2f out: wnt 4th ent fnl f: styd on strly into 3rd clsng stages: nrst fin* **7/1**

4 *¾* **Shepherd's Purse**[14] 7523 4-9-1 **89**...(p) GaryCarroll 2 91
(Joseph G Murphy, Ire) *trckd ldr in 2nd: rdn over 1f out: dropped to 3rd ins fnl 100yds: no ex in 4th clsng stages* **6/1**

5 *1¾* **Vitello**[14] 7523 3-8-13 **87**...(p) ShaneFoley 5 83
(M Halford, Ire) *chsd ldrs in 3rd tl rdn and nt qckn ent fnl f: sn one pce* **5/1**[2]

6 *½* **Complicit (IRE)**[40] 6821 5-8-6 **80**... WayneLordan 4 75
(J F Levins, Ire) *hld up: rdn in rr 2f out: kpt on one pce fnl f: nvr on terms* **11/2**[3]

7 *1* **Go Kart (IRE)**[26] 7192 3-8-0 **79**... TomMadden[(5)] 3 71
(P J Prendergast, Ire) *hld up in 5th: rdn and nt qckn appr fnl f: dropped to rr fnl 100yds* **10/1**

1m 11.09s (71.09) **7** Ran SP% **113.7**

CSF £22.60 TOTE £2.00: £1.30, £7.30; DF 27.60 Trifecta £84.20.

Owner Shropshire Wolves **Bred** Glebe Stud, J F Dean & Lady Trenchard **Trained** Pandy, Monmouths

FOCUS

A very competitive sprint handicap despite the small field, with four horses battling it out inside the last half furlong. A pb from the winner.

7804 - 7805a (Foreign Racing) - See Raceform Interactive

7312 LYON PARILLY (R-H)

Friday, November 4

OFFICIAL GOING: Turf: soft

7806a PRIX LA FLECHE (CONDITIONS) (4YO+) (TURF) 5f

12:35 (12:35) 4-Y-O+ **£6,985** (£2,794; £2,095; £1,397; £698)

RPR

1 **Winshine (FR)**[44] 5-9-5 0... TheoBachelot 6 82
(V Luka Jr, Czech Republic) **27/10**[2]

2 *1¼* **Kool And The Gang (IRE)**[14] 7525 6-9-4 0... CyrilleStefan 7 76
(J Albrecht, Czech Republic) **79/10**

3 *½* **Intibaah**[48] 6556 6-9-0 0... MaximeGuyon 5 70
(George Baker) *chsd ldng pair: rdn 1 1/2f out and nt qckn: styd on fnl f: nt pce to chal* **37/10**[3]

4 *nk* **Sunset Sail (IRE)**[19] 7398 4-9-0 0.................................... TonyPiccone 8 69
(Gerald Geisler, Germany) **13/1**

5 *1 ¼* **Robert Le Diable (FR)**[39] 7-9-6 0.................................. LouisBeuzelin 4 71
(J E Hammond, France) **19/10**[1]

6 *1 ½* **Lloydminster (FR)**[8] 6-9-6 0.. FabriceVeron 1 65
(Mlle C Cardenne, France) **24/1**

7 *1* **Pierre Precieuse (FR)**[8] 4-9-7 0................................ SebastienMaillot 2 63
(E Caroux, France) **29/1**

8 *2 ½* **Heave Ho (FR)**[13] 4-9-2 0......................................(b) StephanePasquier 3 49
(N Caullery, France) **9/1**

Owner www.trdelnik.com-Luka **Bred** S Hillou-Lespes & F Bragato **Trained** Czech Republic
WIN (incl. 1 euro stake): 3.70. PLACES: 1.40, 2.20, 1.80. DF: 14.00. SF: 24.20

7724 SANTA ANITA (L-H)
Friday, November 4

OFFICIAL GOING: Dirt: fast; turf: firm

7807a BREEDERS' CUP JUVENILE TURF (GRADE 1) (2YO COLTS & GELDINGS) (TURF) 1m (T)

9:25 (12:00) 2-Y-O

£374,149 (£115,646; £61,224; £34,013; £20,408; £6,802)

RPR

1 **Oscar Performance (USA)**[34] 2-8-10 0............................ JoseLOrtiz 13 114
(Brian A Lynch, Canada) *chsd ldr: rdn to ld under 2f out: drvn clr over 1f out: kpt on wl fnl f* **7/1**

2 *1 ¼* **Lancaster Bomber (USA)**[27] 7149 2-8-10 0............ SeamieHeffernan 1 111+
(A P O'Brien, Ire) *midfield: rdn 2f out: styd on wl fr 1 1/2f out: wnt 2nd ins fnl f: nt rch wnr* **9/1**

3 *nk* **Good Samaritan (USA)**[47] 2-8-10 0................................ JoelRosario 11 110+
(William Mott, U.S.A) *hld up towards rr: stdy hdwy on outer fr 3f out: rdn 2f out: drvn 1 1/2f out: styd on wl fnl f: nrst fin* **5/2**[1]

4 *3 ¼* **Ticonderoga (USA)**[26] 2-8-10 0................................(b) RafaelBejarano 14 103+
(Chad C Brown, U.S.A) *dwlt: in rr: rdn 2f out: wd into st: styd on fnl f: nrst fin* **20/1**

5 *½* **Big Score (USA)**[24] 7266 2-8-10 0.. FlavienPrat 6 102
(Tim Yakteen, U.S.A) *hld up towards rr of midfield: rdn and kpt on steadily fr under 2f out: nvr a factor* **6/1**[3]

6 *nk* **Made You Look (USA)**[65] 2-8-10 0............................ JavierCastellano 5 101
(Todd Pletcher, U.S.A) *in tch: rdn over 2f out: outpcd 1 1/2f out: kpt on steadily* **12/1**

7 *nk* **Channel Maker (CAN)**[47] 2-8-10 0.........................(b) JohnRVelazquez 3 100
(Daniel J Vella, Canada) *trckd ldrs: rdn 2f out: wknd 1f out* **28/1**

8 *1 ¼* **Keep Quiet (FR)**[26] 2-8-10 0.. FlorentGeroux 2 98
(Mark Casse, Canada) *trckd ldrs: rdn and unable qck 2f out: wknd 1f out* **22/1**

9 *hd* **Intelligence Cross (USA)**[41] 6785 2-8-10 0..................... RyanMoore 8 97
(A P O'Brien, Ire) *hld up towards rr: rdn 1 1/2f out: sme late hdwy: nvr a factor* **11/2**[2]

10 *nk* **Wellabled (USA)**[28] 2-8-10 0..(b) ETBaird 9 96
(Larry Rivelli, U.S.A) *led: rdn and hdd under 2f out: short of room 1 1/2f out: sn wknd* **33/1**

11 *1 ½* **Bowies Hero (USA)**[24] 7266 2-8-10 0..................(b) JulienRLeparoux 10 93
(Philip D'Amato, U.S.A) *midfield on outer: rdn and unable qck over 2f out: eased whn btn 1 1/2f out* **40/1**

12 *½* **Favorable Outcome (USA)**[27] 7177 2-8-10 0.................... IradOrtizJr 4 92
(Chad C Brown, U.S.A) *in tch: losing pl whn hmpd under 2f out: no ch after* **18/1**

13 *13 ¼* **J. S. Choice (USA)**[34] 2-8-10 0.............................. KentJDesormeaux 7 61
(Todd Pletcher, U.S.A) *a towards rr* **50/1**

14 *10 ½* **Rodaini (USA)**[27] 7148 2-8-10 0.................................... FrankieDettori 12 37
(Simon Crisford) *a in rr* **16/1**

1m 33.28s (-0.59) **14** Ran SP% **119.5**
PARI-MUTUEL (all including 2 usd stake): WIN 15.20; PLACE (1-2) 8.00, 11.20; SHOW (1-2-3) 5.60, 6.40, 3.40; SF 138.80.
Owner Amerman Racing Stables LLC **Bred** Mrs Jerry Amerman **Trained** Canada

FOCUS
The splits were 22.30, 23.58, 23.56, 23.84, and the final time was 0.73sec faster than the later fillies' edition. The form makes sense rated around the third, sixth and race averages.

7808a LAS VEGAS BREEDERS' CUP DIRT MILE (GRADE 1) (3YO+) (DIRT) 1m

10:05 (12:00) 3-Y-O+

£374,149 (£115,646; £61,224; £34,013; £20,408; £6,802)

RPR

1 **Tamarkuz (USA)**[27] 6-9-0 0.. MikeESmith 8 121
(Kiaran McLaughlin, U.S.A) *hld up towards rr: hdwy on outer fr under 4f out: rdn 2f out: led 1f out: drew clr fnl f: comf* **14/1**

2 *3 ½* **Gun Runner (USA)**[41] 3-8-11 0...................................... FlorentGeroux 9 112
(Steven Asmussen, U.S.A) *trckd ldrs: rdn to ld over 2f out: drvn 1 1/2f out: hdd 1f out: no ex clsng stages: jst hld 2nd* **5/1**[2]

3 *nk* **Accelerate (USA)**[40] 3-8-11 0.. TylerBaze 5 111
(John W Sadler, U.S.A) *midfield: rdn and in tch 3f out: kpt on gamely ins fnl f: nrly snatched 2nd: no ch w wnr* **40/1**

4 *½* **Dortmund (USA)**[34] 6980 4-9-0 0..................................(b) MartinGarcia 3 111+
(Bob Baffert, U.S.A) *chsd ldr: led 3f out: sn rdn: drvn and hdd over 2f out: wknd under 1f out* **8/13**[1]

5 *3 ¾* **Tom's Ready (USA)**[34] 3-8-11 0.. JoelRosario 2 101
(Dallas Stewart, U.S.A) *towards rr of midfield: rdn and kpt on steadily fr over 3f out: nvr a factor* **33/1**

6 *3 ¾* **Point Piper (USA)**[27] 6-9-0 0......................................(b) MarioGutierrez 4 94
(Jerry Hollendorfer, U.S.A) *hld up in rr: rdn and sme hdwy fr 3f out: nvr a factor* **33/1**

7 *4* **Vyjack (USA)**[27] 6-9-0 0.. FlavienPrat 1 85
(Philip D'Amato, U.S.A) *a towards rr* **16/1**

8 *hd* **Runhappy (USA)**[34] 4-9-0 0.. GaryStevens 7 84+
(Laura Wohlers, U.S.A) *led: rdn and hdd 3f out: wknd 2 1/2f out: eased* **7/1**[3]

9 *nk* **Texas Chrome (USA)**[39] 3-8-11 0.................................... CJMcMahon 6 83
(J R Caldwell, U.S.A) *midfield: rdn and lost pl 3f out: sn btn* **40/1**

1m 35.72s (95.72)
WFA 3 from 4yo+ 2lb **9** Ran SP% **114.4**
PARI-MUTUEL (all including 2 usd stake): WIN 25.80; PLACE (1-2) 9.40, 5.20; SHOW (1-2-3) 8.00, 4.60, 16.00; SF 100.40.
Owner Shadwell Stable **Bred** John D Gunther **Trained** USA

FOCUS
They went fast early and finished slowly - the splits were 22.45, 22.92, 24.63, 25.72 - and those who raced handily didn't get home. The winner's Dubai form could be rated this high.

7809a BREEDERS' CUP JUVENILE FILLIES TURF (GRADE 1) (2YO FILLIES) (TURF) 1m (T)

10:50 (12:00) 2-Y-O

£374,149 (£115,646; £61,224; £34,013; £20,408; £6,802)

RPR

1 **New Money Honey (USA)**[33] 6985 2-8-10 0............ JavierCastellano 3 110
(Chad C Brown, U.S.A) *t.k.h early: prom: effrt and rdn ent st: qckend to ld ins fnl f: kpt on strly* **9/1**

2 *½* **Coasted (USA)**[33] 6985 2-8-10 0.. MikeESmith 5 109+
(Leah Gyarmati, U.S.A) *hld up and bhd: stdy hdwy over 2f out: effrt and squeezed through over 1f out: angled off ins rail and chsd wnr wl ins fnl f: kpt on* **33/1**

3 *1* **Cavale Doree (FR)**[33] 6986 2-8-10 0.................................. FlavienPrat 8 107
(C Ferland, France) *s.i.s: hld up: stdy hdwy over 2f out: effrt and rdn over 1f out: kpt on fnl f to take 3rd nr fin: nt rch first two* **12/1**

4 *¾* **Lull (USA)**[23] 2-8-10 0.. JoelRosario 2 105
(Christophe Clement, U.S.A) *led at decent gallop: rdn ent st: hdd ins fnl f: no ex and lost two pls fnl 50yds* **40/1**

5 *1* **Rymska (FR)**[33] 6985 2-8-10 0.. IradOrtizJr 10 103+
(Chad C Brown, U.S.A) *hld up on outside: rdn along and angled to wd outside bnd ent st: kpt on wl fnl f: nvr able to chal* **20/1**

6 *nse* **La Coronel (USA)**[23] 2-8-10 0...................................... FlorentGeroux 13 102+
(Mark Casse, Canada) *hld up on outside: hdwy on outside into midfield over 2f out: sn rdn along: kpt on fnl f: no imp* **5/1**[3]

7 *½* **La Force (GER)**[25] 2-8-10 0.. RafaelBejarano 11 101
(Patrick Gallagher, U.S.A) *s.i.s: hld up: rdn and hdwy over 1f out: kpt on fnl f: nrst fin* **80/1**

8 *½* **Sweeping Paddy (USA)**[23] 2-8-10 0.............................. GaryStevens 14 100
(Dale Romans, U.S.A) *chsd ldr: drvn along over 2f out: wknd ent fnl f* **50/1**

9 *½* **Roly Poly (USA)**[41] 6784 2-8-10 0...................................... RyanMoore 12 99
(A P O'Brien, Ire) *trckd ldrs on ins: drvn along over 2f out: outpcd over 1f out: btn fnl f* **4/1**[1]

10 *2 ½* **Spain Burg (FR)**[42] 6748 2-8-10 0.................................. FrankieDettori 4 93
(Kathy Ritvo, U.S.A) *hld up in tch: stdy hdwy over 2f out: drvn along wl over 1f out: sn outpcd: btn fnl f* **9/2**[2]

11 *1* **Intricately (IRE)**[54] 6385 2-8-10 0.............................. DonnachaO'Brien 6 91
(Joseph Patrick O'Brien, Ire) *sn pushed along in midfield: drvn and outpcd over 2f out: sn wknd* **7/1**

12 *¾* **Happy Mesa (USA)**[25] 2-8-10 0.. JoseLOrtiz 9 89
(H Graham Motion, U.S.A) *hld up on outside: drvn along and struggling over 2f out: sn btn* **50/1**

13 *7 ¼* **Madam Dancealot (IRE)**[64] 6063 2-8-10 0.............. JohnRVelazquez 7 73
(Richard Baltas, U.S.A) *s.i.s: bhd: struggling over 3f out: sn lost tch* **40/1**

14 *2 ¼* **Hydrangea (IRE)**[28] 7116 2-8-10 0.......................... SeamieHeffernan 1 67
(A P O'Brien, Ire) *in tch on ins: drvn along over 2f out: sn wknd: eased whn btn appr fnl f* **6/1**

1m 34.01s (0.14) **14** Ran SP% **117.1**
PARI-MUTUEL (all including 2 usd stake): WIN 15.00; PLACE (1-2) 7.60, 17.40; SHOW (1-2-3) 5.20, 10.20, 10.60; SF 254.80.
Owner E Five Racing Thoroughbreds **Bred** WinStar Farm LLC **Trained** USA

FOCUS
The opening pace was similar to the earlier Juvenile Turf but the final time of this fillies' event was 0.73sec slower. The fourth has been rated to the better view of her form.

7810a LONGINES BREEDERS' CUP DISTAFF (GRADE 1) (3YO+ FILLIES & MARES) (DIRT) 1m 1f (D)

11:35 (12:00) 3-Y-O+

£748,299 (£231,292; £122,448; £68,027; £40,816; £13,605)

RPR

1 **Beholder (USA)**[33] 7000 6-8-12 0.................................... GaryStevens 8 124+
(Richard E Mandella, U.S.A) *trckd ldrs: rdn to dispute ld over 1f out: nosed ahd wl ins fnl f: hld on gamely* **4/1**[3]

2 *nse* **Songbird (USA)**[41] 6799 3-8-9 0.. MikeESmith 1 124+
(Jerry Hollendorfer, U.S.A) *led: rdn along whn jnd and protracted duel w wnr fr over 1f out: hdd wl ins fnl f: rallied gamely: jst hld* **11/10**[1]

3 *1 ¼* **Forever Unbridled (USA)**[34] 6970 4-8-12 0.................... JoelRosario 6 120
(Dallas Stewart, U.S.A) *hld up: hdwy over 2f out: chsng ldrs whn rdn and hung lft over 1f out: kpt on ins fnl f* **25/1**

4 *2 ½* **Stellar Wind (USA)**[33] 7000 4-8-12 0............................ VictorEspinoza 5 115
(John W Sadler, U.S.A) *dwlt: sn pushed along to chse ldng gp: swtchd to wd outside 1/2-way: drvn and outpcd over 2f out: edgd lft and kpt on ins fnl f: no imp* **5/2**[2]

5 *2 ¾* **I'm A Chatterbox (USA)**[26] 7197 4-8-12 0..................... FlorentGeroux 7 109
(J Larry Jones, U.S.A) *sn chsng ldr: drvn and lost 2nd over 2f out: wknd fnl f* **25/1**

6 *5 ½* **Curalina (USA)**[69] 5908 4-8-12 0................................ JohnRVelazquez 3 98
(Todd Pletcher, U.S.A) *in tch on ins: drvn and struggling over 2f out: sn wknd* **16/1**

7 *8 ½* **Land Over Sea (USA)**[41] 6799 3-8-9 0............................ MarioGutierrez 2 81
(Doug O'Neill, U.S.A) *hld up in tch on ins: struggling over 3f out: lost tch over 2f out: t.o* **100/1**

P **Corona Del Inca (ARG)**[187] 5-8-12 0................................ PabloGFalero 4
(Guillermo J Frenkel Santillan, Argentina) *hld up: drvn and struggling 4f out: sn lost tch: last and no ch whn broke down appr st: fatally injured* **100/1**

1m 49.2s (0.30)
WFA 3 from 4yo+ 3lb **8** Ran SP% **111.7**
PARI-MUTUEL (all including 2 usd stake): WIN 8.60; PLACE (1-2) 3.60, 3.20; SHOW (1-2-3) 3.00, 2.80, 4.40; SF 25.20.
Owner Spendthrift Farm LLC **Bred** Clarkland Farm **Trained** USA

FOCUS
One of the great Breeders' Cup races - the first six were multiple Grade 1 winners and two previous champions of this event ran 1-2, separated by only a nose after a memorable stretch duel. The splits were a gradually slowing 23.32, 23.84, 23.98, 25.01 and 13.05. A pb from the third.

7776 CHELMSFORD (A.W) (L-H)

Saturday, November 5

OFFICIAL GOING: Polytrack: standard
Wind: Light; half against Weather: Dry; chilly

7811 BREEDERS' CUP EXCLUSIVELY TONIGHT ON AT THE RACES APPRENTICE H'CAP 5f (P)

4:35 (4:36) (Class 5) (0-70,70) 3-Y-O+ **£2,911** (£866; £432; £216) **Stalls** Low

Form				RPR
6364	**1**		**Doctor Parkes**[18] 7430 10-8-13 **69**.................................. MillyNaseb(7) 6 (Stuart Williams) *bhd: clsd but nt clrest of runs fron wl over 1f out: swtchd rt and str run ins fnl f to ld 50yds: sn in command an d r.o wl* **7/2**[2]	78
0600	**2**	1 ¾	**Red Stripes (USA)**[26] 7202 4-9-0 **70**............................(b) JordanUys(7) 4 (Lisa Williamson) *trckd ldng pair: effrt and rdn to ld over 1f out: drvn ins fnl f: hdd 50yds: sn btn* **9/2**[3]	73
2020	**3**	½	**Racing Angel (IRE)**[35] 6946 4-9-2 **70**.......................... LuluStanford(5) 1 (Mick Quinn) *in tch in midfield: effrt over 1f out: hdwy to chse wnr 150yds: no imp: lost 2nd 100yds out and kpt on same pce after* **15/8**[1]	71
5430	**4**	½	**Billyoakes (IRE)**[10] 7626 4-9-6 **69**..........................(p) KieranShoemark 8 (Charlie Wallis) *in tch in last pair: effrt in centre over 1f out: styd on wl ins fnl f: nvr trbld ldrs* **8/1**	68
160	**5**	2	**Jumeirah Star (USA)**[52] 6479 3-9-3 **66**..........................(v) EoinWalsh 5 (Robert Cowell) *in tch in midfield: rdn over 2f out: no imp 1f out: wknd ins fnl f* **20/1**	58
6536	**6**	nk	**Noble Asset**[23] 7303 5-9-5 **68**....................................... EdwardGreatrex 7 (Milton Bradley) *chsd ldr: unable qck u.p over 1f out: wknd ins fnl f* **10/1**	59
0204	**7**	¾	**Red Flute**[14] 7534 4-8-7 **56** oh5..(v) TimClark 3 (Denis Quinn) *led tl over 1f out: no ex u.p 1f out: sn wknd* **14/1**	44
0006	**8**	2 ½	**Keep It Dark**[24] 7290 7-8-4 **60**...................................(v) AbbieWibrew(7) 2 (William Knight) *in tch in midfield: rdn over 1f out: no imp: wknd ins fnl f* **10/1**	39

59.82s (-0.38) **Going Correction** -0.05s/f (Stan) **8** Ran SP% **115.9**
Speed ratings (Par 103): **101,98,97,96,93 92,91,87**
CSF £19.98 CT £37.68 TOTE £4.20: £2.10, £1.20, £1.70; EX 18.40 Trifecta £55.90.
Owner Essex Racing Club 1 **Bred** Joseph Heler **Trained** Newmarket, Suffolk

FOCUS
A modest apprentice riders' sprint handicap. They went a decent gallop on standard Polytrack and the form makes sense. The downgraded runner-up and well-backed third could back this race being rated a bit better than at face value.

7812 ATTHERACES.COM/BREEDERSCUP MAIDEN STKS 7f (P)

5:10 (5:10) (Class 5) 2-Y-O **£3,150** (£943; £471; £236; £117) **Stalls** Low

Form				RPR
54	**1**		**Mamdood (IRE)**[23] 7297 2-9-5 0.................................... TomMarquand 1 (Richard Hannon) *broke wl sn restrained and trckd ldng pair: swtchd rt and effrt over 1f out: hdwy u.p and ev ch ins fnl f: led 75yds out: r.o wl* **10/1**	77
2	**2**	1	**El Cap (USA)**[39] 6850 2-9-5 0... DavidProbert 4 (Sir Michael Stoute) *broke wl: sn retrained and chsd ldng quartet: effrt to chse ldng trio over 1f out: drvn 1f out: ev ch ins fnl f: kpt on to 2nd cl home* **11/8**[1]	74
0	**3**	½	**Second Page**[15] 7495 2-9-5 0... KieranO'Neill 12 (Richard Hannon) *chsd ldr: effrt to chal and carried rt over 1f out: led and wnt lft u.p 100yds out: sn hdd and one pced: lost 2nd cl home* **33/1**	73
224	**4**	1 ¾	**Shabeeh (IRE)**[49] 6562 2-9-5 79....................................... MartinLane 10 (Mark Johnston) *sn led: rdn and hung rt over 1f out: hdd 100yds out: sn wknd* **20/1**	68
56	**5**	1	**Bedouin (IRE)**[17] 7470 2-9-5 0...................................(b) TimmyMurphy 6 (Luca Cumani) *stdd after s: hld up in tch in midfield: effrt towards inner over 1f out: chsd clr ldng quartet 1f out: styd on but nvr threatened ldrs* **14/1**	65+
0	**6**	2 ½	**Paradise Lake (IRE)**[17] 7468 2-9-5 0.............................. JackMitchell 5 (Sir Michael Stoute) *dwlt: rcvring into midfield whn squeezed for room and dropped to rr of main gp after 1f: c wd and effrt 2f out: styd on to pass btn horses fnl f: nvr trbld ldrs* **5/1**[3]	61+
065	**7**	1	**Veiled Secret (IRE)**[23] 7306 2-9-5 0................................. RyanPowell 7 (Sir Mark Prescott Bt) *t.k.h: effrt 2f out: sn edgd rt and outpcd: wl hld and kpt on same pce fnl f* **33/1**	56
	8	hd	**Fast Landing** 2-9-2 0... EdwardGreatrex(3) 11 (Saeed bin Suroor) *s.i.s: t.k.h: hld up in tch towards rr of main gp: wd and effrt 2f out: no imp and one pced fr over 1f out: nvr trbld ldrs* **7/2**[2]	55
	9	¾	**Flashy Snapper** 2-9-5 0... SteveDrowne 2 (Simon Crisford) *in tch in midfield: swtchd rt and effrt over 1f out: no imp and styd on same pce ins fnl f* **25/1**	53
0	**10**	¾	**Treagus**[17] 7468 2-9-5 0... StevieDonohoe 8 (Charlie Fellowes) *chsd ldrs: rdn 2f out: sn outpcd and btn: wknd ins fnl f* **66/1**	51
	11	nse	**Discovered (IRE)** 2-9-2 0....................................... KieranShoemark(3) 9 (Roger Charlton) *hld up in tch towards rr of main gp: swtchd rt and effrt wl over 1f out: sn pushed along and no imp: wknd ins fnl f* **16/1**	51
	12	1 ½	**King Otto** 2-9-5 0.. AdamBeschizza 3 (Phil McEntee) *in tch towards rr of main gp: rdn over 1f out: sn btn: wknd fnl f* **66/1**	47
	13	4	**Bradfield Magic (IRE)** 2-9-0 0............................ MichaelJMMurphy 13 (Charles Hills) *s.i.s: rn green and a rr* **33/1**	31+

1m 26.49s (-0.71) **Going Correction** -0.05s/f (Stan) **13** Ran SP% **123.1**
Speed ratings (Par 96): **102,100,100,98,97 94,93,92,92,91 91,89,84**
CSF £23.49 TOTE £12.40: £3.20, £1.10, £11.20; EX 35.60 Trifecta £1585.50.
Owner Hamdan Al Maktoum **Bred** Whitethorn Bloodstock **Trained** East Everleigh, Wilts

FOCUS
Not the strongest juvenile maiden form. A step forward from the winner.

7813 BREEDERS' CUP LIVE TONIGHT ON AT THE RACES H'CAP 1m (P)

5:40 (5:46) (Class 4) (0-80,85) 3-Y-O+ **£5,175** (£1,540; £769; £384) **Stalls** Low

Form				RPR
3653	**1**		**Chester Street**[84] 5412 3-8-13 **77**..........................[1] KieranShoemark(3) 1 (Roger Charlton) *hld up in tch in midfield: swtchd lft and effrt over 1f out: rdn and gd hdwy to ld ins fnl f: sn in command: eased towards fin: comf* **5/2**[1]	88
605	**2**	2 ¾	**Marbooh (IRE)**[16] 7486 3-9-2 **77**.. DavidProbert 2 (David O'Meara) *t.k.h: chsd ldr for 2f: trckd ldng pair after tl rdn to ld over 1f out: hdd ins fnl f: sn outpcd by wnr but hld on for 2nd fnl 75yds* **6/1**	82
2101	**3**	hd	**Sunset Dream (IRE)**[7] 7687 3-9-10 **85**......................... TimmyMurphy 7 (Richard Hannon) *stall malfunctioned and gate opened early: sn restrained and reloaded: t.k.h: trckd ldrs: effrt over 1f out: styd on same pce u.p ins fnl f* **5/1**[3]	89
5403	**4**	hd	**Squire**[17] 7457 5-9-0 **73**...(t) AdamBeschizza 9 (Michael Attwater) *s.i.s: pushed along and rcvrd to chse ldr after 2f tl over 1f out: styd on same pce ins fnl f* **10/1**	77
3102	**5**	1 ½	**Ravenhoe (IRE)**[7] 7687 3-9-0 **75**... MartinLane 4 (Mark Johnston) *in tch in last trio: u.p 3f out: drvn over 1f out: kpt on ins fnl f: nvr trbld ldrs* **9/2**[2]	76
3452	**6**	½	**Mezzotint (IRE)**[16] 7486 7-9-7 **80**................................. StevieDonohoe 3 (Lee Carter) *hld up in tch in last trio: effrt on inner over 1f out: nt clr run and swtchd rt 1f out: styd on same pce ins fnl f* **9/1**	79
0445	**7**	1	**Starboard**[64] 6084 7-9-0 **78**..............................(p) SophieKilloran(5) 5 (David Simcock) *taken down early: bustled along leaving stalls: sn dropped into last trio: in tch: effrt over 1f out: edgd lft u.p 1f out: no imp* **8/1**	75
1621	**8**	2 ½	**British Embassy (IRE)**[56] 6316 4-9-0 **80**.................... JoshuaBryan(7) 6 (Brian Barr) *v free to post: t.k.h: led: rdn and hdd over 1f out: wknd ins fnl f* **20/1**	71
3523	**9**	16	**Topology**[15] 7506 3-9-2 **77**.. DougieCostello 8 (Joseph Tuite) *trckd ldrs: pushed along and lost pl over 1f out: sn bhd: eased ins fnl f* **14/1**	32

1m 38.32s (-1.58) **Going Correction** -0.05s/f (Stan)
WFA 3 from 4yo+ 2lb **9** Ran SP% **119.3**
Speed ratings (Par 105): **105,102,102,101,100 99,98,96,80**
CSF £18.49 CT £71.97 TOTE £3.20: £1.60, £1.90, £1.90; EX 19.10 Trifecta £138.90.
Owner H R H Sultan Ahmad Shah **Bred** Cheveley Park Stud Ltd **Trained** Beckhampton, Wilts

FOCUS
A decent handicap. They went a proper gallop. The runner-up helps set the standard.

7814 YOUR BREEDERS' CUP GUIDE AT ATTHERACES.COM/BREEDERSCUP H'CAP 1m 6f (P)

6:10 (6:11) (Class 2) (0-105,105) 3-Y£01,971 (£3,583; £1,791; £896; £446) **Stalls** Low

Form				RPR
006	**1**		**Curbyourenthusiasm (IRE)**[57] 6284 5-10-0 **105**........ JamieSpencer 5 (David Simcock) *hld up in rr: swtchd rt and shkn up 3f out: clsd ton chse ldr over 1f out: led ins fnl f: pushed along and a doing enough after* **9/4**[1]	113+
0010	**2**	½	**Watersmeet**[49] 6573 5-9-8 **99**.. JoeFanning 6 (Mark Johnston) *trckd ldr tl pushed into ld jst over 2f out: drvn over 1f out: hdd ins fnl f: kpt on but a hld after* **5/1**[3]	106
2115	**3**	3 ¾	**Great Hall**[7] 7700 6-9-12 **103**....................................... PatCosgrave 3 (Mick Quinn) *trckd ldng pair: effrt jst over 2f out: stl cl enough and swtchd lft 1f out: sn drvn and fnd little: outpcd fnl 100yds* **8/1**	105
5260	**4**	3 ¾	**Haines**[49] 6582 5-9-0 **91**.. DavidProbert 4 (Andrew Balding) *hld up in tch in 4th: pushed along 2f out: swtchd rt over 1f out: sn outpcd and btn 1f out: wnt modest 4th ins fnl f* **9/2**[2]	88
0000	**5**	4 ½	**Rideonastar (IRE)**[10] 7625 5-8-9 **86** oh6......................... MartinDwyer 2 (Brendan Powell) *led and set stdy gallop: rdn and hdd over 2f out: unable qck over 1f out: wknd fnl f* **33/1**	76
15	**U**		**Winning Story**[182] 2036 3-8-10 **95**....................................... MartinLane 7 (Saeed bin Suroor) *stmbld and uns rdr sn after leaving stalls* **9/4**[1]	

3m 0.65s (-2.55) **Going Correction** -0.05s/f (Stan)
WFA 3 from 4yo+ 8lb **6** Ran SP% **110.4**
Speed ratings (Par 109): **105,104,102,100,97**
CSF £13.48 TOTE £3.30: £1.60, £2.40; EX 9.80 Trifecta £45.70.
Owner M Caine & J Barnett **Bred** Kevin J Molloy **Trained** Newmarket, Suffolk

FOCUS
The feature contest was a good quality handicap but one of the joint-favourites lost his jockey leaving the stalls. A muddling tempo then played into the hands of the classier winner who had twice been successful over shorter trips in the past. Muddling form. The runner-up has been rated close to his 4yo form.

7815 BREEDERS' CUP TURF LIVE ON ATTHERACES MAIDEN STKS 6f (P)

6:45 (6:45) (Class 5) 3-Y-O+ **£2,911** (£866; £432; £216) **Stalls** Centre

Form				RPR
6030	**1**		**Firesnake (IRE)**[10] 7611 3-8-12 63.............................. JordanUys(7) 6 (Lisa Williamson) *dwlt: t.k.h: hld up in tch in last pair: effrt over 1f out: hdwy u.p over 1f out: wnt 2nd 10yds out: styd on wl to ld last strides* **6/1**	64
3345	**2**	hd	**Cee Jay**[22] 7335 3-9-5 68...[1] AdamKirby 2 (Robert Cowell) *sn bustled along to ld: hung rt bnd wl over 1f out: drvn over 1f out: kpt on u.p: hdd last strides* **7/2**[3]	63
2342	**3**	2 ¼	**Cadland Lad (IRE)**[9] 7645 3-8-12 49........................... LuluStanford(7) 3 (John Ryan) *in tch in last pair: effrt and swtchd lft over 1f out: kpt on same pce ins fnl f: wnt 3rd towards fin* **10/3**[2]	56
	4	½	**Silently** 3-9-0 0... TimmyMurphy 8 (Daniel Kubler) *chsd ldrs: rdn over 1f out: styd on same pce u.p ins fnl f* **25/1**	49
4406	**5**	shd	**Cockney Island**[12] 7572 4-9-0 68..................................(p) PatCosgrave 5 (Philip McBride) *chsd ldr: ev ch and carried rt wl over 1f out: unable qck u.p 1f out: kpt on same pce ins fnl f* **2/1**[1]	49
05	**6**	3	**Pleadings (USA)**[2] 7782 3-9-5 0... KierenFox 1 (Charlie Wallis) *in tch: hdwy on inner to chse ldrs over 3f out: rdn over 2f out: unable qck u.p over 1f out: wknd fnl f* **20/1**	44
0236	**7**	2 ¾	**Ten Rocks**[9] 7654 3-9-5 59.. MartinDwyer 7 (Lisa Williamson) *taken down early: rdr struggling to remove hood and slowly away: styd wd: rcvrd and in tch after 2f: rdn over 2f out: lost pl and bhd over 1f out: wknd fnl f* **8/1**	36

1m 12.97s (-0.73) **Going Correction** -0.05s/f (Stan) **7** Ran SP% **112.6**
Speed ratings (Par 103): **102,101,98,98,97 93,90**
CSF £26.34 TOTE £8.00: £3.80, £1.80; EX 27.30 Trifecta £80.80.
Owner Pritchard & Woodward **Bred** Confey Stud **Trained** Saighton, Cheshire

FOCUS
A modest maiden. They went a respectable gallop and a horse with peak form over an extra furlong finished off the race much the strongest centrally. It's been rated around the exposed third.

7816 BREEDERS' CUP CLASSIC LIVE ON ATTHERACES H'CAP 1m 2f (P)

7:20 (7:20) (Class 4) (0-85,85) 3-Y-O+ **£4,851** (£1,443; £721; £360) **Stalls** Low

Form				RPR
122	**1**		**Burcan (FR)**[142] 3304 4-9-4 **82**....................................... DanielMuscutt 2 (Marco Botti) *led early: sn hdd and trckd leqading pair: shkn up and qcknd to ld over 1f out: in command 1f out: r.o strly: eased towards fin: comf* **2/1**[1]	94+
3304	**2**	3	**Craftsmanship (FR)**[19] 7418 5-9-2 **80**............................ JackMitchell 1 (Robert Eddery) *hld up in tch in last trio: effrt on inner over 1f out: hdwy u.p to chse clr wnr 150yds out: kpt on but no imp* **11/4**[2]	85

1112 **3** *nse* **Mia Tesoro (IRE)**[35] 6964 3-8-11 **79**.............................. StevieDonohoe 5 84+
(Charlie Fellowes) *taken down early: hld up in tch in midfield: effrt in centre over 1f out: styd on u.p and almost snatched 2nd: no threat to wnr* **7/1**

1055 **4** *2 ¾* **Cornelious (IRE)**[38] 6876 4-8-7 **71** oh3........................ AdamBeschizza 8 71
(Clifford Lines) *sn led and set stdy gallop: rdn and qcknd 2f out: hdd and unable qck over 1f out: lost 2nd 150yds: wknd* **12/1**

065 **5** *2* **Coillte Cailin (IRE)**[66] 6019 6-9-7 **85**.................................. AdamKirby 6 81
(Daniel Mark Loughnane) *dwlt: hld up in tch in last trio: effrt and wnt rt u.p over 1f out: no imp fnl f* **12/1**

511 **6** *½* **Ocean Eleven**[26] 7229 3-8-12 **80**....................................... DavidProbert 9 75
(John Ryan) *chsd ldr: rdn and pressing ldr jst over 2f out: sn outpcd and btn over 1f out: wknd ins fnl f* **9/2**[3]

1205 **7** *1 ½* **Ritasun (FR)**[19] 7419 3-8-7 **75**..(p) KieranO'Neill 7 67
(Richard Hannon) *in tch in midfield: rdn to cl and chsd ldrs jst over 2f out: outpcd and struggling whn wnt rt over 1f out: wknd fnl f* **9/1**

50P- **8** *6* **Kafeel (USA)**[492] 3804 5-9-0 **78**....................................(p) SteveDrowne 4 58
(Linda Jewell) *t.k.h: hld up in tch in midfield: rdn wl over 1f out: sn struggling and outpcd: wknd fnl f* **50/1**

1560 **9** *7* **Yul Finegold (IRE)**[34] 6048 6-8-13 **77**................................ MartinLane 3 43
(Conor Dore) *hld up in tch in midfield: rdn wl over 2f out: sn struggling: outpcd and btn over 1f out:. bhd fnl f* **33/1**

2m 6.46s (-2.14) **Going Correction** -0.05s/f (Stan)
WFA 3 from 4yo+ 4lb **9** Ran SP% **121.0**
Speed ratings (Par 105): **106,103,103,101,99 99,98,93,87**
CSF £8.02 CT £32.86 TOTE £3.10: £1.20, £1.80, £2.00; EX 9.70 Trifecta £52.00.
Owner Raed El Youssef **Bred** S F Bloodstock LLC **Trained** Newmarket, Suffolk

FOCUS
A decent handicap. They went a modest gallop but the form should stand up to close scrutiny. The front-running fourth helps set the standard.

7817 FOLLOW AT THE RACES ON TWITTER H'CAP 7f (P)
7:55 (7:57) (Class 6) (0-65,65) 3-Y-O+ **£2,264** (£673; £336; £168) **Stalls** Low

Form RPR
202 **1** **For Shia And Lula (IRE)**[4] 7751 7-9-2 **60**........................ AdamKirby 10 67
(Daniel Mark Loughnane) *mde all: rdn and wnt rt over 1f out: sustained duel w runner up fnl f: hld on wl ins fnl f: rdn out* **3/1**[1]

1552 **2** *nk* **Mossy's Lodge**[10] 7612 3-9-1 **63**................................ LouisSteward[(3)] 1 68
(Anthony Carson) *chsd wnr for 3f: styd chsng ldrs: rdn to chal and shifted rt over 1f out: sustained duel w wnr fnl f: kpt on wl but hld towards fin* **4/1**[2]

405 **3** *1 ¼* **Honcho (IRE)**[34] 6418 4-9-1 **59**.......................................(p) DannyBrock 8 62
(John Ryan) *t.k.h: chsd ldrs: wnt 2nd 5f out tl over 1f out: kpt on same pce u.p ins fnl f* **10/1**

0510 **4** *¾* **Garter (IRE)**[24] 7282 3-9-3 **62**................................... MichaelJMMurphy 9 62+
(Charles Hills) *hld up in tch in last quartet: effrt and switching lft over 1f out: wnt 4th ins fnl f: kpt on but nvr gng to rch ldrs* **6/1**[3]

4000 **5** *¾* **Mowhoob**[51] 6512 6-8-7 **51** oh3.......................................(t) JimmyQuinn 6 50+
(Brian Barr) *dwlt: hld up in tch in last quartet: effrt over 1f out: rdn and hdwy 1f out: styd on wl fnl 100yds: nt rch ldrs* **20/1**

4000 **6** *1* **Tee It Up Tommo (IRE)**[10] 7613 7-8-7 **58**............(p) KieranSchofield[(7)] 3 54
(Daniel Steele) *t.k.h: hld up in tch towards rr: effrt over 1f out: hdwy and swtchd lft ins fnl f: styd on: no threat to ldrs* **16/1**

6501 **7** *½* **Faintly (USA)**[11] 7602 5-9-4 **62**...................................(b) JamesSullivan 5 57
(Ruth Carr) *chsd ldrs: effrt whn nt clrest of runs and swtchd lft over 1f out: unable qck and kpt on same pce ins fnl f* **3/1**[1]

4024 **8** *½* **Divine Call**[7] 7694 9-9-2 **60**...(b) DougieCostello 11 53+
(Milton Bradley) *hld up in tch in midfield: nt clrest of runs over 1f out: swtchd rt and effrt ent fnl f: no imp and one pced after* **16/1**

500 **9** *2* **Ruby's Day**[45] 6680 7-9-3 **61**...[1] PatCosgrave 2 49
(David Brown) *taken down early: t.k.h: hld up in tch in midfield: rdn 2f out: unable qck u.p over 1f out: wknd ins fnl f* **20/1**

0000 **10** *1 ¾* **Wink Oliver**[10] 7611 4-9-4 **62**..(p) MartinLane 7 45+
(David Dennis) *hld up in tch: clsd to chse ldrs and rdn over 2f out: little rspnse and btn over 1f out: wknd fnl f* **25/1**

-500 **11** *1* **Caius College Girl (IRE)**[18] 7430 4-9-4 **65**.................. EoinWalsh[(3)] 4 46+
(Natalie Lloyd-Beavis) *s.i.s: t.k.h: hld up in rr: shkn up and no hdwy over 1f out: bhd ins fnl f* **33/1**

1m 26.21s (-0.99) **Going Correction** -0.05s/f (Stan)
WFA 3 from 4yo+ 1lb **11** Ran SP% **121.5**
Speed ratings (Par 101): **103,102,101,100,99 98,97,97,94,92 91**
CSF £14.62 CT £111.78 TOTE £3.90: £1.50, £1.90, £3.00; EX 15.70 Trifecta £107.00.
Owner Over The Moon Racing IV **Bred** A M F Persse **Trained** Baldwin's Gate, Staffs

FOCUS
A modest handicap but the form appears sound enough.
T/Plt: £21.00 to a £1 stake. Pool: £88,584.29 - 3,068.93 winning units T/Qpdt: £8.10 to a £1 stake. Pool: £10,133.51 - 923.76 winning units **Steve Payne**

7535 DONCASTER (L-H)
Saturday, November 5

OFFICIAL GOING: Good to firm (8.1)
Wind: Fresh; half against Weather: Fine but breezy

7818 BETFRED MOBILE COCK O'THE NORTH EBF MAIDEN STKS (PLUS 10 RACE) (DIV I) 6f
12:10 (12:11) (Class 4) 2-Y-O **£6,931** (£2,074; £1,037; £519; £258) **Stalls** High

Form RPR
0 **1** **Rely On Me (IRE)**[22] 7314 2-9-0 0................................. OisinMurphy 10 77+
(Andrew Balding) *mde all: rdn over 1f out: styd on strly* **6/1**[3]

2 *1 ¼* **Gloriux** 2-9-5 0.. GeorgeBaker 8 78
(Charles Hills) *t.k.h: trckd ldrs: hdwy 2f out: rdn over 1f out: styd on fnl f* **6/1**[3]

0 **3** *hd* **Harvest Wind (IRE)**[31] 7071 2-9-5 0................................ AdamKirby 12 78
(Clive Cox) *trckd ldrs on inner: hdwy over 2f out: swtchd lft and rdn to chse wnr over 1f out: kpt on same pce fnl f* **9/2**[2]

4 *2 ½* **Red Gunner** 2-9-5 0.. PatCosgrave 1 70+
(William Haggas) *midfield: hdwy over 2f out: rdn over 1f out: kpt on fnl f: nrst fin* **11/4**[1]

0 **5** *nk* **Widnes**[17] 7468 2-9-5 0... DavidProbert 2 69
(Alan Bailey) *trckd ldrs on outer: hdwy 2f out: sn rdn along and kpt on one pce* **66/1**

4 **6** *4 ½* **Must Be Amazing**[25] 7259 2-9-0 0..................................... MartinLane 7 51
(Jeremy Gask) *cl up: rdn along 2f out: grad wknd* **16/1**

554 **7** *2* **Captain Hawk**[155] 2847 2-9-2 78.............................. GeorgeDowning[(3)] 9 52
(Ian Williams) *t.k.h: hld up: a towards rr* **10/1**

8 *1 ¾* **Fantasy Keeper** 2-9-5 0... RobertWinston 3 45
(Michael Appleby) *cl up on outer: rdn along over 2f out: sn wknd* **18/1**

0 **9** *2 ¾* **Kaeso**[15] 7495 2-9-5 0.. TomEaves 4 36
(Nigel Tinkler) *a towards rr* **66/1**

10 *1 ½* **Sentinel** 2-9-5 0.. StevieDonohoe 5 32
(Charlie Fellowes) *a towards rr* **7/1**

11 *1 ½* **Coral Caye** 2-9-0 0... AdamBeschizza 6 22
(Steph Hollinshead) *dwlt: a rr* **66/1**

12 *12* **Ninedarter** 2-9-5 0.. GrahamLee 11
(Antony Brittain) *chsd ldrs: pushed along over 3f out: rdn over 2f out and sn wknd* **25/1**

1m 14.52s (0.92) **Going Correction** -0.075s/f (Good) **12** Ran SP% **114.5**
Speed ratings (Par 98): **90,88,88,84,84 78,75,73,69,67 65,49**
CSF £39.61 TOTE £6.40: £1.90, £2.40, £1.70; EX 44.00 Trifecta £383.40.
Owner Sheikh Juma Dalmook Al Maktoum **Bred** Old Carhue Stud **Trained** Kingsclere, Hants

FOCUS
Minimal rainfall (1.2mm Thursday, 1mm Friday, 0.2mm Saturday morning) and the going was given as good to firm (GoingStick: 8.1). The rail on the Round course was out 3yds from the 11.5f point to the 6f marker, adding about 9yds to the distances of the 1m2f and 1m4f races. This was steadily run (time was 2.14sec slower than the second division) and the winner dominated from the front. A step forward from the third, but the opening level is fluid.

7819 BETFRED MOBILE COCK O'THE NORTH EBF MAIDEN STKS (PLUS 10 RACE) (DIV II) 6f
12:40 (12:45) (Class 4) 2-Y-O **£6,931** (£2,074; £1,037; £519; £258) **Stalls** High

Form RPR
03 **1** **Victory Angel (IRE)**[15] 7496 2-9-5 0............................... AndreaAtzeni 10 82+
(Roger Varian) *gave problems and reluctant to go to s: trckd ldr: led over 1f out: drvn out* **2/1**[1]

2 *¾* **Omran** 2-9-5 0... DanielMuscutt 9 80+
(Marco Botti) *s.i.s: hld up: hdwy over 2f out: styd on fnl f: tk 2nd last 75yds* **8/1**[3]

64 **3** *2* **Somewhere Secret**[22] 7331 2-9-5 0.............................. PaulMulrennan 8 74
(Robert Cowell) *led: hung lft fr over 2f out: hdd over 1f out: kpt on same pce* **10/1**

3040 **4** *2 ¼* **Just An Idea (IRE)**[50] 6538 2-9-5 85.................................. MartinHarley 6 67
(Harry Dunlop) *chsd ldrs: one pce over 1f out* **6/1**[2]

3 **5** *½* **Wurood**[18] 7439 2-9-0 0... PaulHanagan 2 61
(William Haggas) *w ldrs: effrt over 2f out: one pce over 1f out* **2/1**[1]

6 *4 ½* **Jersey Heartbeat** 2-9-0 0.. SeanLevey 7 47
(Richard Hannon) *hld up in mid-div: effrt over 2f out: sn wknd* **14/1**

6 **7** *1 ¾* **Flying Onsite (FR)**[15] 7496 2-9-5 0...................................... TomEaves 11 47
(Nigel Tinkler) *swtchd lft after s: a towards rr* **66/1**

4 **8** *1* **Queens Royale**[31] 7071 2-9-0 0...................................... RobertWinston 3 39
(Michael Appleby) *trckd ldrs: t.k.h: hung rt and lost pl over 1f out: sn eased* **20/1**

0 **9** *3* **Indian Vision (IRE)**[12] 7578 2-9-5 0................................ PJMcDonald 4 35
(Micky Hammond) *mid-div: drvn over 2f out: sn lost pl* **66/1**

04 **10** *4 ½* **Red Douglas**[11] 7599 2-9-5 0... BenCurtis 5 21
(Scott Dixon) *in rr: hdwy to chse ldrs over 3f out: lost pl over 2f out* **100/1**

11 *76* **Flame And Fortune (IRE)** 2-9-5 0.............................. JamesSullivan 1
(Clive Mulhall) *uns rdr at s: s.s: reluctant and sn wl bhd: t.o fnl 4f: eased over 2f out: eventually completed* **100/1**

1m 12.38s (-1.22) **Going Correction** -0.075s/f (Good) **11** Ran SP% **117.5**
Speed ratings (Par 98): **105,104,101,98,97 91,89,88,84,78**
CSF £19.73 TOTE £3.20: £1.20, £2.80, £2.60; EX 21.30 Trifecta £179.20.
Owner Ziad A Galadari **Bred** Max Morris **Trained** Newmarket, Suffolk

FOCUS
This looked the stronger of the divisions on paper, and it was much the quicker (2.14sec) of the two legs. Solid form.

7820 BETFRED "RACING'S BIGGEST SUPPORTER" NURSERY H'CAP 6f
1:15 (1:19) (Class 4) (0-85,82) 2-Y-O **£7,115** (£2,117; £1,058; £529) **Stalls** High

Form RPR
3430 **1** **Golden Apollo**[14] 7541 2-9-0 **75**.. DavidAllan 7 81
(Tim Easterby) *hld up: hdwy over 2f out: rdn to chse ldrs over 1f out: chal ins fnl f: drvn and styd on wl to ld nr fin* **9/1**

21 **2** *nk* **Gheedaa (USA)**[24] 7279 2-9-6 **81**.................................... PaulHanagan 2 86
(William Haggas) *trckd ldr: hdwy 2f out: rdn to ld ent fnl f: drvn last 100 yds: hdd and no ex towards fin* **3/1**[1]

316 **3** *¾* **Anfaass (IRE)**[17] 7460 2-9-1 **76**... TomQueally 4 79
(George Margarson) *towards rr: hdwy on far rial over 1f out: sn rdn and styd on strly fnl f* **14/1**

3101 **4** *1 ½* **Savannah Slew**[18] 7440 2-9-4 **79**................................ PaulMulrennan 12 77
(James Given) *dwlt and rr: hdwy centre wl over 1rf out: sn rdn and styd on wl fnl f* **14/1**

5150 **5** *2 ¼* **Procurator (IRE)**[14] 7549 2-9-7 **82**.................................... SeanLevey 15 74
(Richard Hannon) *hld up in tch: hdwy over 2f out: rdn to chse ldrs over 1f out: kpt on same pce fnl f* **8/1**[3]

2142 **6** *hd* **Harome (IRE)**[11] 7600 2-9-6 **81**.. PJMcDonald 5 72
(Roger Fell) *racd towards far side: led: rdn along wl over 1f out: hdd and drvn ent fnl f: grad wknd* **16/1**

5424 **7** *1 ½* **Yarmouk (FR)**[33] 7004 2-8-8 **69**..............................(v[1]) GeorgeChaloner 20 56
(Richard Fahey) *racd towards stands side: hld up towards rr: hdwy wl over 2f out: rdn over 1f out: kpt on fnl f* **12/1**

1302 **8** *hd* **Naples Bay**[49] 6562 2-9-5 **80**... GrahamLee 9 66
(John Quinn) *towards rr centre: rdn along wl over 1f out: styd on fnl f* **20/1**

1052 **9** *½* **Turanga Leela**[31] 7073 2-9-2 **80**......................... JosephineGordon[(3)] 16 64
(Ian Williams) *racd centre: chsd ldrs: rdn along wl over 1f out: grad wknd* **11/1**

2300 **10** *hd* **La Casa Tarifa (IRE)**[42] 6787 2-9-2 **77**.................... RichardKingscote 1 61
(Mark Johnston) *dwlt: sn in tch towards far side: rdn along 2f out: grad wknd over 1f out* **14/1**

4212 **11** *nse* **Party Tiger**[18] 7440 2-8-13 **74**.. TonyHamilton 11 58
(Richard Fahey) *chsd ldrs towards centre: rdn along over 2f out: sn drvn and wknd* **15/2**[2]

6434 **12** *1 ¾* **Indie Rock**[42] 6768 2-8-6 **67**.. JoeFanning 19 45
(Mark Johnston) *racd towards stands rail: midfield: hdwy and in tch 22f out: sn rdn and wknd over 1f out* **20/1**

2606 **13** *2 ½* **Ventura Secret (IRE)**[11] 7600 2-8-8 **72**.............. RachelRichardson[(3)] 3 43
(Tim Easterby) *chsd ldrs towards far side: rdn along over 2f out: sn wknd* **25/1**

1511 **14** *nk* **Drop Kick Murphi (IRE)**[40] 6830 2-9-3 **78**...................... SteveDrowne 8 48
(George Baker) *towards rr: swtchd lft towards far rail and rdn along 2f out: n.d* **10/1**

630 **15** *¾* **Liberatum**[14] 7527 2-8-7 **68**... JamesSullivan 18 36
(Ruth Carr) *racd towards stands side: a towards rr* **40/1**

5336 **16** *½* **Wind In Her Sails (IRE)**[27] 7184 2-8-4 **70**.............(b[1]) GeorgeWood(5) 14 36
(Giles Bravery) *racd centre: chsd ldrs: rdn along over 2f out: wknd wl over 1f out* **33/1**

6414 **17** *20* **Zig Zag Girl**[170] 2404 2-8-6 **74**.....................................(b[1]) DavidEgan(7) 17
(Scott Dixon) *racd towards stands side: prom: rdn along wl over 2f out: sn outpcd and bhd* **50/1**

1m 12.05s (-1.55) **Going Correction** -0.075s/f (Good) **17** Ran SP% **129.6**
Speed ratings (Par 98): **107,106,105,103,100 100,98,98,97,97 97,94,91,91,90 89,62**
CSF £35.09 CT £326.51 TOTE £11.90: £2.80, £1.60, £3.00, £4.70; EX 58.70 Trifecta £1090.30.
Owner David Scott **Bred** Cheveley Park Stud Ltd **Trained** Great Habton, N Yorks

FOCUS
A huge field lined up for the first of the handicaps on the card, which predictably saw the leader set a good gallop. All the action happened middle to far side, so those drawn high that finished fairly close up need their performance upgrading a little. The winner has been rated in line with his earlier form over this trip.

7821 BETFRED "SUPPORTS JACK BERRY HOUSE" H'CAP 7f

1:50 (1:54) (Class 2) (0-105,105) 3-Y-O+

£18,675 (£5,592; £2,796; £1,398; £699; £351) **Stalls** High

Form RPR

1003 **1** **Oh This Is Us (IRE)**[9] 7651 3-9-5 **101**................................. SeanLevey 5 109
(Richard Hannon) *trckd ldrs: effrt over 1f out: styd on to ld last 75yds* **10/1**[3]

3361 **2** *nk* **Bertiewhittle**[29] 7126 8-8-6 **90**..................................... HectorCrouch(3) 6 98
(David Barron) *hld up in rr: hdwy over 1f out: kpt on wl last 100yds: tk 2nd clsng stages* **16/1**

0030 **3** *¾* **Al Khan (IRE)**[14] 7530 7-8-5 **86**... JoeDoyle 2 92
(Kevin Ryan) *trckd ldrs: upsides 100yds out: kpt on same pce* **25/1**

0125 **4** *nk* **Mount Tahan (IRE)**[30] 7095 4-8-10 **91**................................. KevinStott 8 96
(Kevin Ryan) *chsd ldrs: carried rt 1f out: kpt on same pce last 100yds* **12/1**

0065 **5** *¾* **George Bowen (IRE)**[15] 7497 4-8-10 **91**...................... TonyHamilton 11 94
(Richard Fahey) *mid-div: hdwy 2f out: carried rt 1f out: styd on same pce last 150yds* **7/1**[1]

1124 **6** *shd* **Boy In The Bar**[27] 7186 5-8-3 **87**.......................(b) JosephineGordon(3) 9 90
(Ian Williams) *trckd ldrs: hmpd 1f out: kpt on same pce* **9/1**[2]

1206 **7** *½* **Right Touch**[14] 7542 6-9-5 **100**...................................... PatrickMathers 3 102
(Richard Fahey) *w ldrs: led over 1f out: hdd last 75yds: fdd* **14/1**

0002 **8** *hd* **Withernsea (IRE)**[56] 6355 5-8-13 **97**........................ AdamMcNamara(3) 7 98
(Richard Fahey) *mid-div: swtchd rt and hdwy over 1f out: styng on at fin* **9/1**[2]

0106 **9** *¾* **Jack's Revenge (IRE)**[7] 7699 8-8-6 **87**.........................(vt) PJMcDonald 4 86
(George Baker) *hld up towards rr: hdwy over 1f out: kpt on: nvr a threat* **25/1**

0033 **10** *shd* **Dinkum Diamond (IRE)**[29] 7121 8-9-3 **98**..................... OisinMurphy 17 97
(Henry Candy) *led 3 others stands' side: edgd lft over 1f out: kpt on same pce: 1st of 4 that gp* **9/1**[2]

6204 **11** *1 ¼* **Shady McCoy (USA)**[7] 7699 6-8-10 **91**.......................... RobertHavlin 18 86
(Ian Williams) *dwlt: hld up last of 4 stands' side: effrt and swtchd rt over 1f out: kpt on same pce: 2nd of 4 that gp* **10/1**[3]

-200 **12** *1 ¼* **Flaming Spear (IRE)**[49] 6558 4-9-0 **95**........................ RobertWinston 1 90
(Kevin Ryan) *led: hdd over 1f out: wkng whn hung rt: n.m.r and eased 150yds out* **16/1**

0004 **13** *1 ½* **Highly Sprung (IRE)**[10] 7610 3-8-4 **86**............................ JoeFanning 19 73
(Mark Johnston) *chsd ldr stands' side: upsides over 2f out: wknd last 150yds* **33/1**

3002 **14** *1 ½* **Cricklewood Green (USA)**[15] 7506 5-8-1 **87** oh4 ow1 MitchGodwin(5) 16 71
(Sylvester Kirk) *hld up in 3rd stands' side: effrt over 2f out: sn chsng ldrs: wknd fnl f* **25/1**

0202 **15** *shd* **Albernathy**[36] 6918 3-8-8 **90**...[1] MartinLane 12 73
(Charlie Appleby) *hld up towards rr: effrt over 2f out: edgd rt over 1f out: nvr a threat* **9/1**[2]

6353 **16** *2* **London Protocol (FR)**[49] 6560 3-8-13 **95**..................(p) JoeyHaynes 10 72
(K R Burke) *trckd ldrs: wknd over 1f out* **16/1**

2102 **17** *1* **God Willing**[12] 7573 5-8-11 **92**.. JamieSpencer 15 67
(Declan Carroll) *in rr drvn over 2f out: nvr a factor* **10/1**[3]

1m 24.63s (-1.67) **Going Correction** -0.075s/f (Good)
WFA 3 from 4yo+ 1lb **17** Ran SP% **126.3**
Speed ratings (Par 109): **106,105,104,104,103 103,102,102,101,101 100,98,97,95,95 93,91**
CSF £158.50 CT £2226.09 TOTE £12.40: £3.70, £3.50, £5.90, £4.40; EX 169.10 Trifecta £3405.20 Part won..
Owner Team Wallop **Bred** Herbertstown House Stud **Trained** East Everleigh, Wilts

FOCUS
A competitive handicap and quite a bunched finish, the bigger group on the far side coming out well on top of the four who raced stands' side. The runner-up helps set the standard.

7822 BETFRED MOBILE WENTWORTH STKS (LISTED RACE) 6f

2:25 (2:25) (Class 1) 3-Y-O+

£28,355 (£10,750; £5,380; £2,680; £1,345; £675) **Stalls** High

Form RPR

4262 **1** **Growl**[21] 7350 4-9-3 114...(p) GrahamLee 7 113
(Richard Fahey) *hld up: hdwy 2f out: rdn to chal ins fnl f: sn drvn and carried sltly lft last 100 yds: led nr line* **2/1**[1]

040 **2** *nse* **Aeolus**[49] 6558 5-9-3 105.. GeorgeBaker 6 112
(Ed Walker) *trckd ldrs: hdwy on outer over 2f out: led over 1f out and sn rdn: jnd and drvn ins fnl f: edgd lft last 100 yds: hdd and no ex nr fin* **9/2**[3]

1045 **3** *2 ¾* **Kimberella**[14] 7542 6-9-3 105.. AndreaAtzeni 11 103
(David Nicholls) *t.k.h: trckd ldng pair: effrt and n.m.r wl over 1f out: sn nt clr run and swtchd lft jst over 1f out: rdn and kpt on fnl f* **8/1**

6001 **4** *2* **Dawaa**[14] 7550 3-8-12 98... PaulHanagan 1 92
(Mark Johnston) *trckd ldr: cl up 1/2-way: effrt 2f out: sn rdn and ev ch: drvn appr fnl f and kpt on same pce* **11/1**

5463 **5** *1* **Absolutely So (IRE)**[26] 7213 6-9-3 108............................. OisinMurphy 10 94
(Andrew Balding) *in tch: pushed along over 2f out: sn rdn and btn* **5/2**[2]

3000 **6** *¾* **Burnt Sugar (IRE)**[15] 7497 4-9-3 93...............................(bt) SeanLevey 4 91
(Richard Hannon) *dwlt: a rr* **20/1**

1051 **7** *hd* **Lady Macapa**[27] 7186 3-8-12 97.. MartinHarley 2 86
(William Knight) *led: pushed along over 2f out: rdn wl over 1f out: sn drvn: hdd & wknd* **8/1**

1m 11.61s (-1.99) **Going Correction** -0.075s/f (Good) **7** Ran SP% **115.4**
Speed ratings (Par 111): **110,109,106,103,102 101,101**
CSF £11.70 TOTE £2.30: £1.50, £3.10; EX 13.70 Trifecta £49.70.
Owner Dr Marwan Koukash **Bred** Kincorth Investments Inc **Trained** Musley Bank, N Yorks

FOCUS
Four of the original 11 came out, three of which were priced up at 12-1 or longer, so it was slightly weaker than it had looked at the overnight stage. Due to the small field, all of these remained stands' side and the early gallop wasn't overly strong. The runner-up sets the standard.

7823 BETFRED TV EBF STALLIONS BREEDING WINNERS GILLIES FILLIES' STKS (LISTED RACE) 1m 2f 60y

3:00 (3:01) (Class 1) 3-Y-O+ **£29,600** (£11,195; £5,595; £2,795) **Stalls** Low

Form RPR

3600 **1** **Carnachy (IRE)**[58] 6259 4-9-5 102................................ JamieSpencer 9 109
(David Simcock) *dwlt: in rr: piushed along early: hdwy over 2f out: led over 1f out: fnd ex clsng stages* **14/1**

5312 **2** *1* **Dubai Fashion (IRE)**[20] 7383 3-8-12 96......................... PaulHanagan 4 104
(Saeed bin Suroor) *hld up in mid-div: swtchd rt and hdwy over 2f out: upsides wnr over 1f out: kpt on same pce last 50yds* **4/1**[2]

5220 **3** *nk* **Lady Of Camelot (IRE)**[14] 7545 4-9-2 104...................... RobertHavlin 3 103+
(John Gosden) *hld up towards rr: hdwy over 2f out: swtchd rt over 1f out: styd on to take 3rd last 100yds: gng on at fin* **13/2**[3]

6-15 **4** *3 ½* **Dawn Of Hope (IRE)**[29] 7119 3-8-12 97.......................... AndreaAtzeni 5 96
(Roger Varian) *trckd ldrs: led narrowly 2f out: sn hdd: wknd fnl f* **9/1**

-140 **5** *3 ¾* **Materialistic**[29] 7119 3-8-12 98.. ShaneKelly 12 89
(Luca Cumani) *hld up towards rr: hdwy to chse ldrs over 2f out: wknd over 1f out* **22/1**

3211 **6** *nk* **Entsar (IRE)**[15] 7504 3-8-12 95.. PatCosgrave 16 88
(William Haggas) *trckd ldrs: led brifely over 2f out: wknd fnl f* **7/2**[1]

1050 **7** *1 ½* **Belle Travers**[64] 6107 4-9-2 80...................................... TonyHamilton 10 85
(Richard Fahey) *hld up towards rr: hdwy on ins over 3f out: kpt on fnl f* **66/1**

1040 **8** *nk* **Maleficent Queen**[21] 7351 4-9-5 105................................ PhillipMakin 2 87
(Keith Dalgleish) *hld up in mid-div: hdwy over 3f out: wknd over 1f out* **12/1**

4014 **9** *4* **Aljazzi**[48] 6604 3-9-1 101... AdamKirby 14 79
(Marco Botti) *mid-div: hdwy over 3f out: chsng ldrs over 2f out: wknd over 1f out* **8/1**

2046 **10** *¾* **Beauly**[87] 5307 3-8-12 98.. MartinHarley 15 75
(Charles Hills) *hld up in rr: effrt over 2f out: wknd over 1f out* **25/1**

0534 **11** *1* **Imshivalla (IRE)**[4] 7744 5-9-2 90.................................... PatrickMathers 7 73
(Richard Fahey) *mid-div: effrt over 3f out: wknd 2f out* **25/1**

-261 **12** *3* **Rahyah**[22] 7341 3-8-12 79...(p) JoeFanning 13 67
(Adrian Paul Keatley, Ire) *rr-div: sme hdwy over 2f out: lost pl over 1f out* **40/1**

4132 **13** *7* **Marsh Pride**[28] 7159 4-9-2 88... PJMcDonald 6 53
(K R Burke) *w ldr: lost pl over 2f out: bhd whn eased fnl 150yds* **28/1**

641 **14** *6* **Aqualis**[10] 7607 3-8-12 83.. NickyMackay 1 41
(John Gosden) *led: hdd over 2f out: sn lost pl: bhd whn eased fnl f* **16/1**

15 *17* **Ceol Na Nog (IRE)**[17] 7478 3-8-12 95.......................... KevinManning 17 7
(J S Bolger, Ire) *s.s: rapid hdwy on wd outside to join ldrs after 2f: drvn 4f out: lost pl over 2f out: bhd whn heavily eased over 1f out* **12/1**

2m 7.62s (-1.78) **Going Correction** 0.0s/f (Good)
WFA 3 from 4yo+ 4lb **15** Ran SP% **124.0**
Speed ratings (Par 108): **107,106,105,103,100 99,98,98,95,94 93,91,85,81,67**
CSF £66.11 TOTE £17.20: £4.40, £1.90, £2.50; EX 118.10 Trifecta £857.80.
Owner St Albans Bloodstock Limited **Bred** Summerhill & J Osborne **Trained** Newmarket, Suffolk

FOCUS
Race distance increased by about 9yds. Not a bad Listed race, and it was run at a solid gallop. A length pb from the winner, with the runner-up confirming her recent improvement.

7824 BETFRED NOVEMBER H'CAP 1m 4f

3:35 (3:35) (Class 2) 3-Y-O+

£49,800 (£14,912; £7,456; £3,728; £1,864; £936) **Stalls** Low

Form RPR

2205 **1** **Prize Money**[101] 4753 3-8-10 **107**...............................[1] GeorgeWood(5) 12 116
(Saeed bin Suroor) *hld up in midfield: hdwy 4f out: slt ld 3f out: rdn along and edgd rt over 1f out: drvn ent fnl f: kpt on gamely* **4/1**[2]

4030 **2** *¾* **Erik The Red (FR)**[42] 6786 4-8-9 **95**................................ KevinStott 19 103
(Kevin Ryan) *hld up: hdwy over 3f out: trckd ldrs over 2f out: effrt whn nt clr run over 1f out: sn swtchd lft and rdn: ev ch ins fnl f: sn drvn and kpt on same pce towards fin* **8/1**

1141 **3** *½* **Cape Cova (IRE)**[15] 7498 3-8-6 **98**..............................(b[1]) NickyMackay 8 105
(John Gosden) *hld up: hdwy on outer 4f out: chsd ldrs 2f out and sn rdn: drvn to chal ent fnl f: ev ch tl no ex towards fin* **3/1**[1]

3116 **4** *3 ½* **William Hunter**[44] 6709 4-7-10 **87**............................... HollieDoyle(5) 11 89+
(Alan King) *hld up in rr: hdwy on inner wl over 2f out: n.m.r wl over 1f out and sn rdn: styd on fnl f: nrst fin* **12/1**

0031 **5** *¾* **Tawdeea**[12] 7575 4-9-6 **106**......................................(p) GrahamGibbons 7 106
(David O'Meara) *hld up in rr: hdwy 3f out: rdn wl over 1f out: kpt on fnl f: nrst fin* **16/1**

1100 **6** *½* **Mistiroc**[28] 7150 5-8-10 **96**...(v) MartinHarley 20 96
(John Quinn) *prom: cl up after 3f: pushed along over 3f out: rdn over 2f out: drvn and kpt on same pce appr fnl f* **25/1**

3410 **7** *nk* **Mukhayyam**[14] 7538 4-8-2 **88**......................................(p) JamesSullivan 13 87
(Tim Easterby) *prom: rdn along wl over 2f out: drvn wl over 1f out: grad wknd appr fnl f* **40/1**

8 *½* **Qassem (IRE)**[63] 3-8-0 **95**...................................... JosephineGordon(3) 2 93
(Hugo Palmer) *prom: effrt 3f out and sn rdn along: drvn wl over 1f out: kpt on one pce* **14/1**

1614 **9** *1* **Trendsetter (IRE)**[14] 7538 5-7-10 **89**..........................(p) DavidEgan(7) 5 86
(Micky Hammond) *in tch: hdwy to chse ldrs 3f out: rdn along over 2f out: drvn and wknd appr fnl f* **40/1**

0263 **10** *½* **Fattsota**[12] 7575 8-8-6 **95**.. ShelleyBirkett(3) 4 91
(David O'Meara) *trckd ldrs: pushed along and sltly outpcd 3f out: sn rdn and n.m.r: kpt on u.p fnl 2f* **25/1**

0101 **11** *½* **Soldier In Action (FR)**[27] 7188 3-8-13 **105**...................... JoeFanning 15 100
(Mark Johnston) *led: rdn along 4f out: hdd 3f out: sn drvn and grad wknd* **15/2**[3]

3460 **12** *5* **Sir Chauvelin**[77] 5655 4-8-9 **95**...................................... PaulMulrennan 9 82
(Jim Goldie) *hld up: a towards rr* **20/1**

02-5 **13** 3/4 **Dashing Star**[12] 7575 6-9-0 **100** ShaneKelly 17 86
(David Elsworth) *in tch: hdwy to trck ldr 7f out: rdn along over 3f out: sn wknd* **14/1**

1354 **14** 1 1/4 **Buonarroti (IRE)**[12] 7575 5-8-2 **88** JimmyQuinn 23 72
(Declan Carroll) *hld up in rr: sme hdwy on wd outside over 3f out: sn rdn along and nvr a factor* **25/1**

320 **15** 7 **Montaly**[13] 7569 5-8-13 **99** OisinMurphy 10 72
(Andrew Balding) *hld up towards rr: effrt and sme hdwy over 3f out: sn rdn along and nvr a factor* **12/1**

2m 31.42s (-3.48) **Going Correction** 0.0s/f (Good)
WFA 3 from 4yo+ 6lb **15** Ran SP% **123.7**
Speed ratings (Par 109): **111,110,110,107,107 107,106,106,105,105 105,101,101,100,95**
CSF £33.55 CT £111.68 TOTE £4.60: £2.40, £2.80, £2.00; EX 36.40 Trifecta £118.90.
Owner Godolphin **Bred** Darley **Trained** Newmarket, Suffolk

FOCUS
Race distance increased by about 9yds. Eight of the 23 runners came out but only three after midday, which did include the potential market leader in Wrangler and last year's winner Litigant. Therefore, frustratingly for each-way punters, it left 15 runners, depriving them of a fourth-place payout in many places. The early gallop wasn't overly strong and plenty had some sort of chance in the home straight. The runner-up helps set the standard.

7825 BETFRED LOTTO "£100K CASH GIVEAWAY" APPRENTICE H'CAP (FUTURE STARS APPRENTICE SERIES) 7f

4:05 (4:12) (Class 3) (0-90,90) 3-Y-O+

£15,562 (£4,660; £2,330; £1,165; £582; £292) **Stalls** High

Form RPR

5302 **1** **Steel Train (FR)**[36] 6914 5-9-6 **88** ShelleyBirkett 12 99+
(David O'Meara) *chsd ldrs: led over 1f out: styd on wl* **14/1**

5402 **2** 2 **Briyouni (FR)**[14] 7540 3-9-2 **85** KevinStott 8 89
(Kevin Ryan) *hld up in rr: hdwy over 1f out: styd on to take 2nd last 75yds: no real imp* **8/1**[2]

0002 **3** 3/4 **Twin Appeal (IRE)**[29] 7126 5-9-5 **87** (b) HectorCrouch 1 93+
(David Barron) *dwlt: swtchd rt s: hld up in rr: swtchd rt over 1f out: styd on wl to take 3rd last 50yds* **11/4**[1]

2054 **4** 1 1/4 **Ballymore Castle (IRE)**[30] 7095 4-9-2 **84** AdamMcNamara 7 84
(Richard Fahey) *hld up in mid-div: hdwy over 1f out: kpt on wl to take 4th nr fin* **8/1**[2]

6032 **5** 1 1/2 **Sir Billy Wright (IRE)**[30] 7095 5-9-2 **87** CliffordLee(3) 17 83
(David Evans) *led: hdd over 1f out: wknd last 100yds* **12/1**

0050 **6** hd **Pastoral Player**[36] 6915 9-9-2 **87** CharlieBennett(3) 22 82
(Hughie Morrison) *hld up towards rr: effrt and nt clr run 2f out: kpt on fnl f* **25/1**

0111 **7** 1 3/4 **Shouranour (IRE)**[11] 7593 6-9-0 **85** (b) JoshDoyle(3) 9 75
(Alan Brown) *chsd ldrs: kpt on same pce over 1f out* **14/1**

0000 **8** hd **Winklemann (IRE)**[55] 6372 4-9-1 **90** JacobMitchell(7) 18 80
(Marco Botti) *chsd ldrs: hung rt over 1f out: one pce* **50/1**

4143 **9** 1 **Fingal's Cave (IRE)**[11] 7593 4-9-2 **84** GeorgeDowning 20 71
(Iain Jardine) *mid-div: effrt over 2f out: one pce* **14/1**

4165 **10** nk **Valley Of Fire**[14] 7530 4-8-13 **88** BenSanderson(7) 14 74
(Les Eyre) *chsd ldrs: one pce fnl 2f* **20/1**

0120 **11** nk **Hidden Rebel**[17] 7472 4-9-5 **87** JoeDoyle 6 72
(Alistair Whillans) *chsd ldrs: wknd over 1f out* **25/1**

02-0 **12** 1 1/2 **Jamaican Bolt (IRE)**[42] 6780 8-8-10 **85** PatrickVaughan(7) 3 66
(David O'Meara) *mid-div: effrt over 2f out: nvr a threat* **25/1**

3130 **13** hd **Fuwairt (IRE)**[35] 6956 4-9-2 **87** GeorgiaCox(3) 4 68
(Roger Fell) *rr-div: effrt 3f out: nvr a factor* **12/1**

3524 **14** 1 **Plucky Dip**[14] 7530 5-8-9 **84** JonathanFisher(7) 5 62
(John Ryan) *chsd ldrs: lost pl over 1f out* **22/1**

6405 **15** 2 3/4 **Lexington Times (IRE)**[11] 7593 4-9-2 **84** NathanEvans 11 55
(Ruth Carr) *w ldrs: wknd over 1f out* **16/1**

0400 **16** 2 1/4 **Musical Comedy**[14] 7530 5-9-0 **85** GeorgeWood(3) 21 50
(Mike Murphy) *chsd ldrs: edgd rt 2f out: sn wknd* **50/1**

2100 **17** 3/4 **Cincuenta Pasos (IRE)**[22] 7315 5-9-3 **88** HollieDoyle(3) 2 51
(Joseph Tuite) *mid-div: effrt over 2f out: sn wknd* **28/1**

1561 **18** 1 3/4 **Moonlightnavigator (USA)**[30] 7095 4-9-6 **88** JosephineGordon 13 46
(John Quinn) *chsd ldrs: drvn over 3f out: lost pl over 2f out: eased fnl f* **9/1**[3]

6655 **19** 5 **Maggie Pink**[25] 7241 7-9-8 **90** AlistairRawlinson 19 34
(Michael Appleby) *chsd ldrs: lost pl over 2f out: sn bhd: eased clsng stages* **33/1**

1m 24.47s (-1.83) **Going Correction** -0.075s/f (Good)
WFA 3 from 4yo+ 1lb **19** Ran SP% **131.1**
Speed ratings (Par 107): **107,104,103,102,100 100,98,98,97,96 96,94,94,93,90 87,86,84,79**
CSF £114.28 CT £422.90 TOTE £14.00: £3.80, £2.40, £1.60, £2.30; EX 175.80 Trifecta £543.60.

Owner Rasio Cymru I & Dutch Rose Partnerhsip **Bred** Erich Schmid **Trained** Upper Helmsley, N Yorks
■ Fourth Way was withdrawn. Price at time of withdrawal 16-1. Rule 4 does not apply.

FOCUS
The final British turf Flat race of the season was a wide-open affair and they headed down the centre of the track early on. The pace was sound but one runner pulled right away in the final stages. It's been rated a bit cautiously, the runner-up being rated to his C&D latest.
T/Jkpt: Not won. T/Plt: £305.20 to a £1 stake. Pool: £147,239.10 - 352.12 winning units T/Qpdt: £75.10 to a £1 stake. Pool: £13,576.81 - 133.76 winning units **Joe Rowntree & Walter Glynn**

7756 FLEMINGTON (L-H)

Saturday, November 5

OFFICIAL GOING: Turf: good

7826a QUEEN ELIZABETH STKS (GROUP 3 H'CAP) (3YO+) (TURF) 1m 5f

2:30 (12:00) 3-Y-O+

£89,851 (£26,732; £13,366; £6,683; £3,712; £2,970)

RPR

1 **Francis Of Assisi (IRE)**[10] 7637 6-9-2 **0** WilliamBuick 4 109+
(Charlie Appleby) *nudged along early to trck ldr: moved up to chal 2f out: led 1 1/2f out: burst clr: rdn out to win comf* **9/2**[2]

2 10 **Vengeur Masque (IRE)**[21] 7378 4-8-10 **0** PatrickMoloney 9 88
(Michael Moroney, Australia) **8/1**

3 3/4 **Tom Melbourne (IRE)**[7] 7712 5-9-1 **0** (t) DwayneDunn 8 92
(Lee & Anthony Freedman, Australia) **7/5**[1]

4 1 **De Little Engine (AUS)**[7] 7712 6-8-10 **0** ChadSchofield 6 85
(Danny O'Brien, Australia) **5/1**[3]

5 shd **Second Bullet (AUS)**[10] 7637 6-8-10 **0** DamianLane 7 85
(Danny O'Brien, Australia) **16/1**

6 shd **Howard Be Thy Name (AUS)**[10] 7637 4-9-2 **0** (b) BradRawiller 2 91
(Darren Weir, Australia) **16/1**

7 4 1/2 **Jim's Journey (AUS)**[236] 5-8-10 **0** (bt) BenClaridge 3 78
(Peter F Blanch, Australia) **25/1**

8 1/2 **Angel's Touch (AUS)**[8] 4-8-10 **0** DeanYendall 1 78
(Darren Weir, Australia) **12/1**

9 8 **Aagas (AUS)**[16] 5-8-10 **0** BenEThompson 5 66
(Todd Balfour, Australia) **150/1**

2m 41.13s (161.13) **9** Ran SP% **111.6**

Owner Godolphin **Bred** Queen Cleopatra Syndicate **Trained** Newmarket, Suffolk

7827 - 7828a (Foreign Racing) - See Raceform Interactive

7807 SANTA ANITA (L-H)

Saturday, November 5

OFFICIAL GOING: Dirt: fast; turf: firm

7829a SENATOR KEN MADDY STKS (GRADE 3) (3YO+ FILLIES & MARES) (TURF) 6f 110y

6:25 (12:00) 3-Y-O+

£40,816 (£13,605; £8,163; £4,081; £1,360; £234)

RPR

1 **Fair Point (USA)**[22] 4-8-9 0 (b) JoseLOrtiz 10 104
(Claude McGaughey III, U.S.A) **9/2**[3]

2 1 1/4 **Miss Double D'Oro (USA)**[413] 4-8-9 0 SantiagoGonzalez 7 101
(Neil Drysdale, U.S.A) **30/1**

3 1 1/4 **Most Beautiful**[57] 3-8-7 0 GaryStevens 4 95
(Thomas F Proctor, U.S.A) **149/10**

4 hd **Lady Shipman (USA)**[36] 4-8-13 0 IradOrtizJr 11 100
(Kiaran McLaughlin, U.S.A) **16/5**[1]

5 1 1/4 **Miss Katie Mae (IRE)**[34] 3-8-7 0 FlavienPrat 12 91
(H Graham Motion, U.S.A) **11/1**

6 3/4 **Acapulco (USA)**[175] 2263 3-8-7 0 RyanMoore 2 89
(Wesley A Ward, U.S.A) **17/5**[2]

7 hd **Off The Road (BRZ)**[34] 7000 5-8-9 0 TiagoJosuePereira 6 90
(Richard E Mandella, U.S.A) **66/1**

8 hd **Wild At Heart (USA)**[27] 4-8-9 0 MikeESmith 1 89
(Richard E Mandella, U.S.A) **117/10**

9 1/2 **Mehronissa**[35] 6941 4-8-9 0 FrankieDettori 8 88
(Ed Vaughan) *a towards rr: nvr a factor* **61/10**

10 hd **Entrechat (USA)**[552] 4-8-9 0 FlorentGeroux 9 87
(Neil Drysdale, U.S.A) **123/10**

11 nk **Juno (BRZ)**[27] 4-8-9 0 VictorEspinoza 5 87
(Richard E Mandella, U.S.A) **214/10**

12 1 1/4 **Snow Cloud (IRE)**[350] 7942 4-8-9 0 JamieTheriot 3 83
(James Cassidy, U.S.A) **91/1**

Owner Stuart S Janney III **Bred** WinStar Farm, Llc, M R Capital, Llc & Sam-Son Farm **Trained** USA

7830a 14 HANDS WINERY BREEDERS' CUP JUVENILE FILLIES (GRADE 1) (2YO FILLIES) (DIRT) 1m 110y(D)

7:05 (12:00) 2-Y-O

£748,299 (£231,292; £122,448; £68,027; £40,816; £13,605)

RPR

1 **Champagne Room (USA)**[34] 7001 2-8-10 0 MarioGutierrez 6 112+
(Peter Eurton, U.S.A) *chsd ldr: rdn over 2f out: led under 2f out: sn clr: pressed clsng stages but a holding on: comf* **28/1**

2 3/4 **Valadorna (USA)**[29] 2-8-10 0 JulienRLeparoux 3 110+
(Mark Casse, Canada) *hld up in rr: stdy hdwy fr over 2f out: rdn under 2f out: kpt on wl: nrst fin* **15/2**

3 3 1/4 **American Gal (USA)**[13] 2-8-10 0 (b) MikeESmith 12 103
(Bob Baffert, U.S.A) *midfield on outer: hdwy to trck ldrs 3f out: rdn and unable qck under 2f out: kpt on same pce* **5/1**[1]

4 1 **Daddys Lil Darling (USA)**[29] 7135 2-8-10 0 CoreyJLanerie 11 101
(Kenneth McPeek, U.S.A) *hld up towards rr: rdn 2 1/2f out: pushed wd into st: kpt on steadily: n.d* **11/1**

5 1 **Jamyson 'n Ginger (USA)**[27] 2-8-10 0 IradOrtizJr 7 99
(Rudy Rodriguez, U.S.A) *hld up in rr: drvn and kpt on steadily fr 2f out: nvr a factor* **12/1**

6 3 1/2 **Union Strike (USA)**[62] 2-8-10 0 MartinGarcia 9 91
(Craig Dollase, U.S.A) *dwlt: hld up towards rr: rdn 2f out: sme late hdwy: nvr a factor* **15/2**

7 1/2 **Noted And Quoted (USA)**[34] 7001 2-8-10 0 RafaelBejarano 10 90
(Bob Baffert, U.S.A) *led: rdn 2f out: hdd under 2f out: wknd over 1f out* **7/1**[3]

8 hd **Dancing Rags (USA)**[29] 7135 2-8-10 0 AngelCruz 8 90
(H Graham Motion, U.S.A) *midfield: hdwy to trck ldrs 4f out: rdn 3f out: drvn 2f out: wknd 1 1/2f out* **14/1**

9 1 1/4 **With Honors (USA)**[34] 7001 2-8-10 0 FlavienPrat 2 87
(J Keith Desormeaux, U.S.A) *in tch in midfield: rdn and unable qck 3f out: wknd 2f out* **16/1**

10 1/2 **Yellow Agate (USA)**[28] 7175 2-8-10 0 ManuelFranco 4 86
(Christophe Clement, U.S.A) *in tch: short of room and hmpd after 1f: in midfield after: rdn and unable qck 3f out: wknd steadily fr over 2f out* **11/2**[2]

11 hd **Sweet Loretta (USA)**[63] 6155 2-8-10 0 JavierCastellano 5 85
(Todd Pletcher, U.S.A) *trckd ldrs: stmbld after 1f: rdn and grad lost pl fr under 3f out: wknd over 1f out* **7/1**[3]

12 21 **Colorful Charades (USA)**[28] 7175 2-8-10 0 LuisSaez 1 39
(Rudy Rodriguez, U.S.A) *in tch: lost pl 4f out: t.o* **100/1**

1m 45.12s (2.70) **12** Ran SP% **113.6**
PARI-MUTUEL (all including 2 usd stake): WIN 69.20; PLACE (1-2) 26.60, 9.80; SHOW (1-2-3) 13.00, 6.60, 4.80; SF 723.60.
Owner Ciaglia, Exline-Border Et Al **Bred** Respite Farm **Trained** USA

FOCUS
They didn't look a great bunch beforehand and this was a slow race, splits of 23.77, 24.42, 24.82, 25.53 and 6.58 (last 0.5f), for a final time 2.52sec off the later Juvenile.

7831a BREEDERS' CUP FILLY & MARE TURF (GRADE 1) (3YO+ FILLIES & MARES) (TURF) 1m 2f (T)

7:43 (12:00) 3-Y-O+

£748,299 (£231,292; £122,448; £68,027; £40,816; £13,605)

RPR

1 **Queen's Trust**[21] 7351 3-8-8 0.. FrankieDettori 11 114+
(Sir Michael Stoute) *dwlt: hld up towards rr: rdn and hdwy fr 2f out: drvn 1 1/2f out: styd on wl to ld cl home* **5/1**[3]

2 *nse* **Lady Eli (USA)**[28] 7176 4-8-12 0.. IradOrtizJr 8 114+
(Chad C Brown, U.S.A) *hld up towards rr: stdy hdwy fr 3 1/2f out: drvn 1 1/2f out: styd on wl to ld 75yds out: hdd cl home* **5/2**[1]

3 *1* **Avenge (USA)**[35] 6981 4-8-12 0.. FlavienPrat 4 112
(Richard E Mandella, U.S.A) *chsd ldr: led after 2f: drvn 1 1/2f out: hdd 75yds out: no ex cl home* **20/1**

4 *¾* **Seventh Heaven (IRE)**[21] 7351 3-8-8 0.. RyanMoore 3 110+
(A P O'Brien, Ire) *midfield: rdn under 3f out: drvn 1 1/2f out: kpt on wl fnl f: nrst fin* **10/3**[2]

5 *1½* **Zipessa (USA)**[35] 6981 4-8-12 0.. JoeBravo 6 107
(Michael Stidham, U.S.A) *hld up in rr: drvn over 2f out: kpt on fnl f: nrst fin* **40/1**

6 *1¼* **Ryans Charm (USA)**[132] 6-8-12 0..(p) RafaelBejarano 9 105
(Patrick Gallagher, U.S.A) *hld up towards rr: nt clr run over 1f out: rdn and kpt on ins fnl f: n.d* **66/1**

7 *nse* **Sea Calisi (FR)**[28] 7176 4-8-12 0.. FlorentGeroux 1 105
(Chad C Brown, U.S.A) *in tch in midfield: hdwy on outer fr 3f out: rdn 2f out: drvn to chse ldr 1 1/2f out: wknd 1f out* **8/1**

8 *1¼* **Catch A Glimpse (USA)**[21] 7379 3-8-8 0.. JavierCastellano 2 102
(Mark Casse, Canada) *led: hdd after 2f: rdn 2f out: wknd under 1f out* **20/1**

9 *½* **Al's Gal (USA)**[20] 7404 5-8-12 0.. JoseLOrtiz 5 101
(Michael J Maker, U.S.A) *hld up towards rr: rdn 2f out: forced to switch 1f out: sme late hdwy: nvr a factor* **20/1**

10 *¾* **Sentiero Italia (USA)**[28] 7176 4-8-12 0.. JoelRosario 7 100
(Kiaran McLaughlin, U.S.A) *a towards rr* **16/1**

11 *½* **Nuovo Record (JPN)**[76] 5-8-12 0.. YutakaTake 13 99
(Makoto Saito, Japan) *midfield on outer: rdn and lost pl 2f out: sn btn* **12/1**

12 *1¼* **Kitcat (CHI)**[28] 4-8-12 0.. GonzaloUlloa 10 96
(Juan C Silva, Chile) *t.k.h: trckd ldrs: rdn 2f out: lost pl 1 1/2f out: sn btn* **100/1**

13 *1¾* **Pretty Perfect (IRE)**[21] 7351 3-8-8 0.. SeamieHeffernan 12 93
(A P O'Brien, Ire) *trckd ldrs: rdn under 3f out: lost pl 2 1/2f out: sn btn* **20/1**

1m 57.75s (-1.53)
WFA 3 from 4yo+ 4lb **13** Ran SP% **117.0**
PARI-MUTUEL (all including 2 usd stake): WIN 18.00; PLACE (1-2) 8.40, 3.20; SHOW (1-2-3) 5.80, 2.80, 7.40; SF 65.80.
Owner Cheveley Park Stud **Bred** Cheveley Park Stud Ltd **Trained** Newmarket, Suffolk

FOCUS
They went a good gallop, Avenge taking them along in 23.10, 46.16, 1:10.11, 1:34.12 and the winner crossed the line in 1:57.75. It's been rated around the balance of the winner, second, third, fifth and sixth.

7832a TWINSPIRES BREEDERS' CUP SPRINT (GRADE 1) (3YO+) (DIRT) 6f (D)

8:21 (12:00) 3-Y-O+

£561,224 (£173,469; £91,836; £51,020; £30,612; £10,204)

RPR

1 **Drefong (USA)**[70] 5910 3-8-12 0..(b) MartinGarcia 2 123+
(Bob Baffert, U.S.A) *cl up on ins: led and maintained decent gallop over 2f out: rdn along ent st: kpt on wl fnl f* **7/2**[2]

2 *nse* **Mind Your Biscuits (USA)**[42] 3-8-12 0..(b) JoelRosario 1 118
(Robert N Falcone Jr, U.S.A) *s.i.s: outpcd and detached on ins: rdn 1/2-way: hdwy and swtchd rt ent st: chsd clr ldng pair ins fnl f: clsng wl at fin* **25/1**

3 *3¼* **A. P. Indian (USA)**[29] 6-9-0 0.. JoeBravo 4 109
(Arnaud Delacour, U.S.A) *prom: effrt and chsd clr ldng pair 1/2-way: sn drvn along: edgd rt and no imp ent st: hld and lost 3rd pl ins fnl f* **9/4**[1]

4 *3¾* **Limousine Liberal (USA)**[29] 4-9-0 0..(b) JoseLOrtiz 7 97
(Ben Colebrook, U.S.A) *sn pushed along bhd ldng gp on wd outside: rdn and struggling wl over 2f out: sn btn* **8/1**[3]

5 *1½* **Delta Bluesman (USA)**[49] 6-9-0 0..(b) EmisaelJaramillo 3 93
(Jorge Navarro, U.S.A) *pressed ldng pair to 1/2-way: sn drvn along and outpcd: btn over 1f out* **20/1**

6 *24* **Noholdingback Bear (USA)**[42] 3-8-12 0.. EuricoRosaDaSilva 6 14
(Michael P De Paulo, Canada) *s.i.s: sn pushed along bhd ldng gp: struggling wl over 2f out: sn btn: eased whn no ch ent st* **16/1**

D *1¼* **Masochistic (USA)**[70] 6-9-0 0.. MikeESmith 5 121+
(Ronald W Ellis, U.S.A) *led at str tempo: hdd over 2f out: rallied and ev ch over 1f out: drvn and kpt on same pce ins fnl f: jst hld on for 2nd* **9/4**[1]

1m 8.79s (0.53) **7** Ran SP% **109.4**
PARI-MUTUEL (all including 2 usd stake): WIN 9.80; PLACE (1-2) 4.80, 4.00; SHOW (1-2-3) 3.80, 2.80, 4.60; SF 30.00.
Owner Baoma Corporation **Bred** Frederick M Allor, Michael T Barnett & Anthony M W **Trained** USA

FOCUS
The front two were duelling for most of the way, and finished slowly, but the closers weren't good enough to get to them. The splits were 21.49, 22.54, 24.76.

7833a BREEDERS' CUP TURF SPRINT (GRADE 1) (3YO+) (TURF) 6f 110y

9:05 (12:00) 3-Y-O+

£374,149 (£115,646; £61,224; £34,013; £20,408; £6,802)

RPR

1 **Obviously (IRE)**[28] 8-9-0 0.. FlavienPrat 2 115
(Philip D'Amato, U.S.A) *sn pushed along and led after 1f: mde rest: rdn and qcknd over 1f out: kpt on wl fnl f: jst lasted* **11/2**[2]

2 *nse* **Om (USA)**[28] 4-9-0 0.. GaryStevens 11 115+
(Dan L Hendricks, U.S.A) *s.i.s: bhd and outpcd: last and plenty to do 1/2-way: effrt and pushed along over 1f out: rapid hdwy fnl f: jst failed* **12/1**

3 *1* **Pure Sensation (USA)**[28] 5-9-0 0.. KendrickCarmouche 1 112
(Christophe Clement, U.S.A) *led 1f: chsd wnr: rdn along 2f out: kpt on same pce ins fnl f: no ex and lost 2nd pl towards fin* **14/1**

4 *1¼* **Calgary Cat (CAN)**[20] 7403 6-9-0 0.. LuisContreras 6 108+
(Kevin Attard, Canada) *bhd: rdn in last pl and plenty to do ent st: kpt on strly fnl f: nrst fin* **40/1**

5 *½* **Green Mask (USA)**[28] 5-9-0 0.. JulienRLeparoux 14 107+
(Brad H Cox, U.S.A) *t.k.h: hld up: n.m.r briefly ent st: gd hdwy fnl f: kpt on: nvr able to chal* **25/1**

6 *¾* **Holy Lute (USA)**[35] 6-9-0 0.. JamieTheriot 12 105
(James Cassidy, U.S.A) *sn pushed along towards rr: hdwy into midfield after 2f: hdwy to chse ldng pair over 2f out to last 100yds: sn outpcd* **20/1**

7 *¾* **Washington DC (IRE)**[34] 6990 3-8-12 0.. RyanMoore 7 101
(A P O'Brien, Ire) *sn towards rr: hdwy on ins into midfield 1/2-way: effrt and drvn ent st: sn no imp* **4/1**[1]

8 *1¼* **Undrafted (USA)**[28] 6-9-0 0.. JohnRVelazquez 10 99
(Wesley A Ward, U.S.A) *sn pushed along in midfield: effrt whn nt clr run over 2f out to over 1f out: kpt on fnl f: nvr able to chal* **11/1**

9 *½* **Mongolian Saturday (USA)**[28] 6-9-0 0.. CarlosMontalvo 3 98
(Enebish Ganbat, U.S.A) *chsd ldng pair: drvn along over 2f out: wknd over 1f out* **16/1**

10 *½* **A Lot (USA)**[77] 4-9-0 0.. JavierCastellano 8 96
(Chad C Brown, U.S.A) *s.i.s: towards rr: drvn along over 2f out: no imp over 1f out* **8/1**

11 *1¼* **Home Of The Brave (IRE)**[84] 5404 4-9-0 0.. JamesDoyle 4 93
(Hugo Palmer) *in tch: rdn along over 2f out: wknd over 1f out* **14/1**

12 *hd* **Celestine (USA)**[28] 7171 4-8-11 0.. JoelRosario 13 89
(William Mott, U.S.A) *broke wl fr wd draw but sn towards rr: rdn on outside over 2f out: sn btn* **7/1**[3]

13 *nk* **Ambitious Brew (USA)**[36] 6-9-0 0.. MikeESmith 9 91
(Martin F Jones, U.S.A) *midfield on outside: rdn and hung rt bnd over 2f out: wknd over 1f out* **12/1**

14 *7¾* **Karar**[34] 6991 4-9-0 0.. GregoryBenoist 5 69
(F-H Graffard, France) *rrd and lost grnd s: hdwy and in tch after 2f: rdn over 2f out: wknd wl over 1f out* **14/1**

1m 11.33s (71.33) **14** Ran SP% **119.6**
PARI-MUTUEL (all including 2 usd stake): WIN 9.60; PLACE (1-2) 5.20, 6.00; SHOW (1-2-3) 3.60, 4.40, 6.60; SF 58.20.
Owner Anthony Fanticola & Joseph Scardino **Bred** Miss Deirdre Cogan **Trained** North America

FOCUS
The looked pretty open, but the winner was able to set his own pace out in front (21.41, 43.08, 1:05.21 and 1:11.33) and just clung on at the line. It's been rated around the balance of the winner, second, fourth and fifth.

7834a SENTIENT JET BREEDERS' CUP JUVENILE (GRADE 1) (2YO COLTS & GELDINGS) (DIRT) 1m 110y(D)

9:43 (12:00) 2-Y-O

£748,299 (£231,292; £122,448; £68,027; £40,816; £13,605)

RPR

1 **Classic Empire (USA)**[28] 2-8-10 0..(b) JulienRLeparoux 5 123+
(Mark Casse, Canada) *chsd ldrs: led 3f out: rdn clr under 2f out: drvn fnl f: pressed cl home: hld on gamely* **11/2**[2]

2 *nk* **Not This Time (USA)**[49] 2-8-10 0.. RobbyAlbarado 10 122+
(Dale Romans, U.S.A) *bmpd s: midfield: stdy hdwy fr over 3f out: rdn 2 1/2f out: styd on wl to press wnr clsng stages* **7/2**[1]

3 *7½* **Practical Joke (USA)**[28] 7177 2-8-10 0.. JoelRosario 9 106
(Chad C Brown, U.S.A) *midfield: rdn and hdwy fr 2f out: drvn 1 1/2f out: sn outpcd by front pair: kpt on* **8/1**

4 *4¼* **Lookin At Lee (USA)**[28] 2-8-10 0..(b[1]) RicardoSantanaJr 11 96
(Steven Asmussen, U.S.A) *hld up in rr: drvn and kpt on steadily fr 2f out: n.d* **33/1**

5 *1½* **Syndergaard (USA)**[28] 7177 2-8-10 0.. JohnRVelazquez 2 93
(Todd Pletcher, U.S.A) *led: hdd 3f out: rdn 2f out: wknd 1 1/2f out* **11/2**[2]

6 *1¼* **Three Rules (USA)**[35] 2-8-10 0.. CornelioHVelasquez 6 90
(Jose Pinchin, U.S.A) *trckd ldrs: rdn 3f out: lost pl 2 1/2f out: sn btn* **10/1**

7 *1½* **Gormley (USA)**[35] 6979 2-8-10 0.. VictorEspinoza 7 87
(John Shirreffs, U.S.A) *in tch on outer: rdn over 3f out: drvn and lost pl 2 1/2f out: sn btn* **11/2**[2]

8 *½* **Klimt (USA)**[35] 6979 2-8-10 0..(b) RafaelBejarano 1 86
(Bob Baffert, U.S.A) *hld up towards rr: pushed along 4f out: rdn 3f out: nvr a factor* **7/1**[3]

9 *2½* **Term Of Art (USA)**[28] 2-8-10 0..(b) JosephTalamo 3 80
(Doug O'Neill, U.S.A) *a in rr* **100/1**

10 *1¾* **Theory (USA)**[21] 2-8-10 0.. JavierCastellano 4 76
(Todd Pletcher, U.S.A) *trckd ldrs: rdn along 4f out: lost pl 3f out: sn btn* **12/1**

11 *dist* **Star Empire**[21] 2-8-10 0..(b) TylerGaffalione 8
(Wesley A Ward, U.S.A) *dwlt: a towards rr: t.o* **66/1**

1m 42.6s (0.18) **11** Ran SP% **114.2**
PARI-MUTUEL (all including 2 usd stake): WIN 11.00; PLACE (1-2) 5.00, 4.60; SHOW (1-2-3) 3.80, 3.40, 4.60; SF 39.40.
Owner John C Oxley **Bred** Steven Nicholson & Brandi Nicholson **Trained** North America

FOCUS
This looked a potentially decent running of the Juvenile and, as it turned out, two of the 'right' types pulled a long way clear of a dual Grade 1 winner in third, with another fair gap back to the fourth, and the time was 2.52sec quicker than the earlier Juvenile Fillies. Probably a race to be positive about then. The splits were 23.05, 23.55, 23.88, 25.48, 6.64. Personal bests form the first two.

7835a LONGINES BREEDERS' CUP TURF (GRADE 1) (3YO+) (TURF) 1m 4f (T)

10:22 (12:00) 3-Y-O+

£1,496,598 (£462,585; £244,897; £136,054; £81,632; £27,210)

RPR

1 **Highland Reel (IRE)**[34] 6989 4-9-0 0.. SeamieHeffernan 12 121+
(A P O'Brien, Ire) *mde all: set modest tempo tl qcknd arnd 7 l clr passing 1/2-way: rdn over 2f out: kpt on wl: unchal: fine ride* **7/2**[3]

2 *1¾* **Flintshire**[35] 6968 6-9-0 0.. JavierCastellano 4 118+
(Chad C Brown, U.S.A) *t.k.h: prom on ins: rdn and hdwy to chse (clr) wnr ent st: kpt on fnl f but no ch of rching enterprisingly rdn wnr* **2/1**[1]

3 *2¼* **Found (IRE)**[21] 7353 4-8-11 0.. RyanMoore 10 112+
(A P O'Brien, Ire) *stmbld leaving stalls: t.k.h: hld up: pushed along and effrt over 2f out: hdwy to chse clr ldng pair ins fnl f: kpt on: nrst fin* **11/4**[2]

4 *2¼* **Ulysses (IRE)**[70] 5893 3-8-10 0.. FrankieDettori 7 113
(Sir Michael Stoute) *dwlt: t.k.h and sn in midfield: effrt and drvn along over 2f out: edgd lft over 1f out: kpt on same pce fnl f* **10/1**

5 *hd* **Ashleyluvssugar (USA)**34 5-9-0 0.............................(b) GaryStevens 5 111
(Peter Eurton, U.S.A) *trckd ldrs on outside: drvn along over 2f out: kpt on same pce fr over 1f out* **40/1**

6 *1/2* **Texas Ryano (USA)**34 5-9-0 0.....................................(b) FlavienPrat 11 110
(Carla Gaines, U.S.A) *hld up: last and plenty to do bnd appr st: rdn and kpt on fnl f: nvr able to chal* **100/1**

6 *dht* **Money Multiplier (USA)**35 6968 4-9-0 0................. JohnRVelazquez 9 110
(Chad C Brown, U.S.A) *t.k.h early: in tch on outside: rdn over 2f out: edgd lft and outpcd over 1f out* **25/1**

8 *hd* **Ectot**35 6968 5-9-0 0.. JoseLOrtiz 3 110
(Todd Pletcher, U.S.A) *chsd wnr: arnd 7 l down fr 1/2-way: drvn over 2f out: lost 2nd pl ent st: outpcd fnl f* **12/1**

9 *nse* **Ralis (USA)**34 3-8-10 0... MarioGutierrez 1 111
(Doug O'Neill, U.S.A) *hld up: effrt and rdn over 2f out: no imp fr over 1f out: btn fnl f* **100/1**

10 *1 1/4* **Twilight Eclipse (USA)**35 6968 7-9-0 0.......................... JoelRosario 8 107
(Thomas Albertrani, U.S.A) *midfield: effrt whn nt clr run and lost pl bnd over 2f out: sn drvn and n.d after* **100/1**

11 *1 3/4* **Da Big Hoss (USA)**56 5-9-0 0...................................... FlorentGeroux 2 105
(Michael J Maker, U.S.A) *t.k.h: hld up on outside: drvn along over 3f out: sn no imp: btn fnl 2f* **33/1**

12 *5 1/4* **Mondialiste (IRE)**28 7172 6-9-0 0................................ DanielTudhope 6 96
(David O'Meara) *t.k.h early: hld up on ins: drvn and struggling over 2f out: sn wknd* **20/1**

2m 23.0s (-3.65)
WFA 3 from 4yo+ 6lb **12** Ran SP% **116.0**
PARI-MUTUEL (all including 2 usd stake): WIN 9.60; PLACE (1-2) 5.20, 3.20; SHOW (1-2-3) 3.40, 2.40, 3.00; SF 28.80.
Owner Derrick Smith & Mrs John Magnier & Michael Tabor **Bred** Hveger Syndicate **Trained** Cashel, Co Tipperary

FOCUS
A sixth win in the Breeders' Cup Turf for Aidan O'Brien in the last 15 years, and a fine front-running ride by Seamie Heffernan on the winner, which took them along in 24.83, 48.00, 1:12.70, 1:36.16 and 1:59.34 before crossing the line in 2:23.00. The likes of the sixth and ninth limit the form.

7836a BREEDERS' CUP FILLY & MARE SPRINT (GRADE 1) (3YO+ FILLIES & MARES) (DIRT) 7f
11:01 (12:00) 3-Y-O+

£374,149 (£115,646; £61,224; £34,013; £20,408; £6,802)

RPR

1 **Finest City (USA)**61 4-8-12 0... MikeESmith 12 117
(Ian Kruljac, U.S.A) *prom: led under 2f out: rdn 1 1/2f out: drvn whn pressed wl ins fnl f: kpt on wl* **7/1**3

2 *3/4* **Wavell Avenue (CAN)**35 5-8-12 0................................. JoelRosario 10 115
(Chad C Brown, U.S.A) *hld up towards rr of midfield: stdy hdwy on outside fr 4f out: trckd ldrs 2f out: rdn 1 1/2f out: styd on wl to press wnr wl ins fnl f: no ex clsng stages* **10/1**

3 *1 1/4* **Paulassilverlining (USA)**35 4-8-12 0......................... JosephTalamo 9 112
(Michelle Nevin, U.S.A) *w ldr: led narrowly 2f out: rdn and hdd under 2f out: no ex ins fnl f* **12/1**

4 *3/4* **Tara's Tango (USA)**34 7000 4-8-12 0.......................(b) RafaelBejarano 3 110
(Jerry Hollendorfer, U.S.A) *in tch: rdn 3f out: short of room under 2f out: outpcd 1 1/2f out: kpt on* **6/1**2

5 *nk* **By The Moon (USA)**70 5909 4-8-12 0................................ JoseLOrtiz 6 109
(Michelle Nevin, U.S.A) *trckd ldrs: rdn 1 1/2f out: no ex fnl 100yds* **8/1**

6 *1 1/2* **Spelling Again (USA)**28 5-8-12 0....................................... LuisSaez 13 105
(Brad H Cox, U.S.A) *in tch in midfield: rdn under 3f out: lost pl 2f out: kpt on steadily fnl f* **66/1**

7 *hd* **Haveyougoneaway (USA)**70 5909 5-8-12 0........... JohnRVelazquez 2 105
(Thomas Morley, U.S.A) *midfield: rdn and kpt on same pce fr under 2f out* **4/1**1

8 *1 1/2* **Irish Jasper (USA)**28 4-8-12 0.. IradOrtizJr 11 101
(Chad C Brown, U.S.A) *hld up towards rr: rdn on outer 2 1/2f out: nvr able to chal and sme hdwy 1 1/2f out: fdd ins fnl f* **10/1**

9 *1/2* **Carina Mia (USA)**42 6799 3-8-10 0............................ JulienRLeparoux 8 97
(William Mott, U.S.A) *a towards rr* **4/1**1

10 *hd* **Wonder Gal (USA)**35 4-8-12 0............................ KendrickCarmouche 5 99
(Leah Gyarmati, U.S.A) *a towards rr* **33/1**

11 *3* **Gloryzapper (USA)**27 4-8-12 0...................................(b) StewartElliott 7 91
(Philip D'Amato, U.S.A) *led: rdn 2 1/2f out: hdd 2f out: wknd 1 1/2f out* **25/1**

12 *6 3/4* **Paola Queen (USA)**35 6970 3-8-10 0....................(b) JavierCastellano 1 70
(Gustavo Delgado, U.S.A) *a towards rr* **40/1**

13 *30* **Gomo (USA)**34 3-8-10 0.. MarioGutierrez 4
(Doug O'Neill, U.S.A) *a in rr: t.o* **40/1**

1m 22.37s (82.37)
WFA 3 from 4yo+ 1lb **13** Ran SP% **116.9**
PARI-MUTUEL (all including 2 usd stake): WIN 19.40; PLACE (1-2) 10.00, 13.80; SHOW (1-2-3) 6.60, 8.80, 9.20; SF 216.40.
Owner Seltzer Thoroughbreds **Bred** HnR Nothhaft Horseracing LLC **Trained** USA

FOCUS
A competitive race in which they went fast and finished slowly, 21.98, 22.84, 24.60, 12.95. The winner has been rated in line with her last dirt run, with the third, fourth and fifth helping to set the standard.

7837a BREEDERS' CUP MILE (GRADE 1) (3YO+) (TURF) 1m (T)
11:40 (12:00) 3-Y-O+

£748,299 (£231,292; £122,448; £68,027; £40,816; £13,605)

RPR

1 **Tourist (USA)**28 7172 5-9-0 0...(b) JoelRosario 5 120
(William Mott, U.S.A) *hld up in midfield on ins: effrt whn short of room bnd over 2f out: rdn and hdwy over 1f out: qcknd to ld against far rail ins fnl f: drvn out* **33/1**

2 *1/2* **Tepin (USA)**28 7171 5-8-11 0.................................... JulienRLeparoux 8 116+
(Mark Casse, Canada) *hld up in midfield on outside: rdn and edgd lft wl over 1f out: gd hdwy to chse wnr last 35yds: kpt on but a hld* **7/2**2

3 *1 1/4* **Midnight Storm (USA)**76 5-9-0 0............................ RafaelBejarano 13 116
(Philip D'Amato, U.S.A) *chsd clr ldr: rdn and hdwy to ld ent st: drvn: edgd lft and hdd ins fnl f: kpt on same pce and lost 2nd last 35yds* **25/1**

4 *nk* **Ironicus (USA)**28 7172 5-9-0 0... JoseLOrtiz 9 115+
(Claude McGaughey III, U.S.A) *hld up in midfield: effrt whn short of room briefly over 2f out: sn drvn along: gd hdwy fnl f: kpt on wl: nt pce to chal* **9/2**

5 *nk* **Miss Temple City (USA)**28 7172 4-8-11 0.................... EdgarSPrado 4 112
(H Graham Motion, U.S.A) *trckd ldrs on outside: effrt and drvn along 2f out: kpt on same pce ins fnl f* **25/1**

6 *1 1/4* **Limato (IRE)**34 6991 4-9-0 0.. HarryBentley 10 112
(Henry Candy) *hld up in tch: effrt and pushed along bnd over 2f out: edgd lft over 1f out: kpt on same pce ins fnl f* **11/4**1

7 *nse* **Ring Weekend (USA)**28 7172 5-9-0 0................(b) JohnRVelazquez 11 112
(H Graham Motion, U.S.A) *s.i.s: hld up on ins: effrt and rdn ent st: kpt on fnl f: no imp* **100/1**

8 *3/4* **Cougar Mountain (IRE)**29 7115 5-9-0 0............(p) DonnachaO'Brien 14 110
(A P O'Brien, Ire) *hld up: drvn along over 3f out: rallied on outside over 1f out: kpt on fnl f: nvr able to chal* **40/1**

9 *hd* **Hit It A Bomb (USA)**21 7352 3-8-11 0.................... SeamieHeffernan 12 108
(A P O'Brien, Ire) *hld up: drvn along over 2f out: sme hdwy fnl f: nvr rchd ldrs* **25/1**

10 *1/2* **Alice Springs (IRE)**35 6949 3-8-8 0.................................. RyanMoore 2 104
(A P O'Brien, Ire) *hld up: effrt and pushed along over 2f out: no imp fr over 1f out* **4/1**3

11 *2 3/4* **Spectre (FR)**55 6394 3-8-8 0....................................... JavierCastellano 3 98
(M Munch, Germany) *s.v.s: bhd: rdn and struggling 3f out: nvr on terms* **25/1**

12 *nse* **Dutch Connection**55 6394 4-9-0 0.................................. JamesDoyle 7 102
(Charles Hills) *hld up: rdn along and outpcd over 2f out: btn over 1f out* **25/1**

13 *nk* **Photo Call (IRE)**28 7171 5-8-11 0........................... KentJDesormeaux 6 98
(Todd Pletcher, U.S.A) *prom: rdn over 2f out: wknd qckly appr fnl f: eased whn btn* **16/1**

14 *2 1/4* **What A View (USA)**28 7172 5-9-0 0.................................(b) TylerBaze 1 96
(Kenneth D Black, U.S.A) *led at decent gallop and clr to wl over 3f out: rdn and hdd ent st: sn lost pl and struggling* **50/1**

1m 31.71s (-2.16)
WFA 3 from 4yo+ 2lb **14** Ran SP% **120.5**
PARI-MUTUEL (all including 2 usd stake): WIN 26.80; PLACE (1-2) 9.40, 4.60; SHOW (1-2-3) 6.20, 3.80, 6.60; SF 105.20.
Owner WinStar Farm LLC, Wachtel Stable & Gary Barber **Bred** WinStar Farm LLC **Trained** USA

FOCUS
They went a fast gallop, going 21.81, 44.61, 1:08.59, 1:20.37 and the winning time of 1:31.71 was just 0.02sec outside the track record. The winner got a dream run around the inside, while the European challengers disappointed, failing to make the first five. A pb from the wnner, with the third, fourth, fifth and seventh rated to their marks.

7829 SANTA ANITA (L-H)
Sunday, November 6
OFFICIAL GOING: Dirt: fast; turf: firm

7838a BREEDERS' CUP CLASSIC (GRADE 1) (3YO+) (DIRT) 1m 2f (D)
12:35 (12:00) 3-Y-O+

£2,244,897 (£693,877; £367,346; £204,081; £122,448; £40,816)

RPR

1 **Arrogate (USA)**71 5913 3-8-10 0....................................... MikeESmith 9 136
(Bob Baffert, U.S.A) *prom on outside: niggled along 1/2-way: hdwy to chse ldr over 2f out and sn clr of remainder: effrt and drvn over 1f out: sustained run fnl f to ld nr fin* **7/4**2

2 *1/2* **California Chrome (USA)**36 6980 5-9-0 0..............(b) VictorEspinoza 4 135+
(Art Sherman, U.S.A) *led: 2 l in front and gng wl appr st: rdn and edgd lft over 1f out: kpt on wl fnl f but worn down nr fin* **5/6**1

3 *10 3/4* **Keen Ice (USA)**30 4-9-0 0.. JavierCastellano 3 114
(Todd Pletcher, U.S.A) *broke wl but sn dropped to rr: rdn and hdwy over 3f out: chsd (clr) ldng pair over 1f out: kpt on fnl f: nvr able to chal* **50/1**

4 *nk* **Hoppertunity (USA)**29 7178 5-9-0 0.......................(b) JohnRVelazquez 8 113
(Bob Baffert, U.S.A) *bhd: rdn over 4f out: hdwy and angled to outside over 1f out: kpt on fnl f: nvr rchd ldrs* **20/1**

5 *4 1/4* **Melatonin (USA)**133 3703 5-9-0 0............................(b) JosephTalamo 6 104
(David Hofmans, U.S.A) *chsd ldr to over 2f out: drvn and wknd over 1f out* **20/1**

6 *3 1/2* **Frosted (USA)**64 6156 4-9-0 0..(b) JoelRosario 2 97
(Kiaran McLaughlin, U.S.A) *prom on ins: effrt and rdn 3f out: wknd ent st* **10/1**3

7 *4 3/4* **Effinex (USA)**29 7178 5-9-0 0..(b) FlavienPrat 1 88
(James Jerkens, U.S.A) *prom: rdn and outpcd over 3f out: wknd over 2f out* **50/1**

8 *1 1/4* **War Story (USA)**43 4-9-0 0..(b) ScottSpieth 7 85
(Mario Serey Jr, U.S.A) *fly-jmpd s: t.k.h early in rr: struggling over 4f out: nvr on terms* **150/1**

9 *dist* **Win The Space (USA)**36 6980 4-9-0 0........................(b) GaryStevens 5
(George Papaprodromou, U.S.A) *sn towards rr: rdn and struggling 4f out: sn btn: eased whn no ch early in st* **100/1**

2m 0.11s (0.23)
WFA 3 from 4yo+ 4lb **9** Ran SP% **115.1**
PARI-MUTUEL (all including 2 usd stake): WIN 5.40; PLACE (1-2) 2.80, 2.60; SHOW (1-2-3) 2.60, 2.40, 5.80; SF 10.00.
Owner Juddmonte Farms Inc **Bred** Clearsky Farms **Trained** USA

FOCUS
Just a day after the Distaff produced one of the great Breeders' Cup battles, this race was every bit as thrilling - it was an unforgettable meeting - and the level of form produced by the front two is brilliant. The fractions were 23.28, 23.87, 23.81, 24.76, 24.39, and the first two had the race to themselves up the stretch. The fourth, rated to his track form, helps set the standard.

7565 CAPANNELLE (R-H)
Sunday, November 6
OFFICIAL GOING: Turf: heavy

7839a PREMIO GUIDO BERARDELLI (GROUP 3) (2YO) (TURF) 1m 1f
1:15 (12:00) 2-Y-O **£25,735** (£11,323; £6,176; £3,088)

RPR

1 **Aethos (IRE)**21 7401 2-8-11 0...................................... SilvanoMulas 2 109
(Stefano Botti, Italy) *chsd ldr on out: sustained run to ld 1 1/2f out: drvn clr fnl f* **159/10**

2 9 **Holy Water (FR)**[126] 2-8-11 0 FabioBranca 7 92
(Stefano Botti, Italy) *led: sn 3l clr: rdn over 2 1/2f out: hdd 1 1/2f out: kpt on wl enough to hold 2nd wout being chal for it* **21/20**[1]

3 1 1/2 **Lunastorta (USA)** 2-8-8 0 CarloFiocchi 1 86
(Agostino Affe', Italy) *chsd ldr on inner: outpcd and rdn 2 1/2f out: kpt on at same pce fnl f: nvr trbld ldrs* **33/1**

4 hd **Dulciboy**[126] 2-8-11 0 Pierre-CharlesBoudot 6 89
(Stefano Botti, Italy) *w.w towards rr: 5th and rowed along 2 1/2f out: plugged on at same pce* **183/20**

5 1/2 **Devil's Bridge (IRE)**[32] 7075 2-8-11 0 CristianDemuro 5 88
(Richard Hannon) *racd bhd ldng trio on outer: stoked up and hdwy to chse ldr over 2 1/2f out: sn rdn and no more prog: one pce fnl f* **7/5**[2]

6 11 **Bridge Casadate (IRE)** 2-8-11 0 GermanoMarcelli 4 67
(Pierpaolo Sbariggia, Italy) *outpcd and drvn along leaving stalls: racd in fnl pair: scrubbed along and no imp 3f out: wknd fnl 2f* **116/1**

7 nk **Amore Hass (IRE)** 2-8-11 0 DarioVargiu 3 66
(Stefano Botti, Italy) *racd bhd ldng trio on inner: no hdwy u.p fr 3f out: wknd fnl 2f* **39/10**[3]

1m 53.0s (-1.70) **7 Ran SP% 130.4**
WIN (incl. 1 euro stake): 16.85. PLACES: 3.11, 1.34. DF: 11.92.
Owner We Bloodstock Srl **Bred** Sig Massimo Parri **Trained** Italy

7840a PREMIO CARLO E FRANCESCO ALOISI (GROUP 3) (2YO+) (TURF) 6f
2:20 (12:00) 2-Y-0+ **£23,529** (£10,352; £5,647; £2,823)

RPR

1 **Kathy Dream (IRE)**[113] 4-9-1 0 SalvatoreBasile 3 108
(Luigi Biagetti, Italy) *w.w in tch on inner: led 1/2-way: drvn clr appr fnl f: won easing down* **27/20**[1]

2 3 1/2 **Zapel**[8] 7719 3-9-4 0 CristianDemuro 11 100
(Stefano Botti, Italy) *led: hdd 1/2-way: sn outpcd and hrd rdn: styd on again wl over 1f out: no ch w wnr* **558/100**[3]

3 1 **Evil Spell**[168] 2518 4-9-1 0 CarloFiocchi 5 94
(Endo Botti, Italy) *a cl up: rdn and nt qckn appr 1f out: one pce fnl f* **66/10**

4 1 1/2 **Intense Life (IRE)**[21] 4-9-4 0 FabioBranca 2 92
(Endo Botti, Italy) *hld up towards rr: styd on fnl 1 1/2f out: nvr plcd to chal* **43/10**[2]

5 1/2 **Harlem Shake (IRE)**[8] 7719 5-9-4 0 LucaManiezzi 1 91
(Marco Gasparini, Italy) *w.w in rr: styd on late: nvr in contention* **558/100**[3]

6 1 3/4 **Trust You**[21] 4-9-4 0 Pierre-CharlesBoudot 10 85
(Endo Botti, Italy) *towards rr: sme hdwy over 2f out: rdn and one pce fnl f* **66/10**

7 5 **Pivotal Rio (IRE)**[611] 4-9-4 0 GermanoMarcelli 6 69
(F Boccardelli, Italy) *in rr on outer: no hdwy u.p fnl 2f* **198/10**

8 1/2 **Captain Chic (IRE)** 5-9-4 0 ChristianDiNapoli 4 67
(Giuseppe Ligas, Italy) *chsd ldng gp: rdn and no imp fr 2f out: sn wknd* **101/10**

9 nk **Facia De Tola**[21] 3-9-1 0 SilvanoMulas 9 63
(Stefano Botti, Italy) *a towards rr: rdn and btn fnl 2f* **168/10**

10 3/4 **Another Full Power (ITY)**[168] 2518 7-9-4 0 DarioVargiu 12 64
(M Grassi, Italy) *prom on outer: rdn and nt qckn over 1 1/2f out: sn wknd* **13/2**

11 dist **Axa Reim (IRE)**[841] 7-9-4 0 GiuseppeErcegovic 8
(F Boccardelli, Italy) *chsd ldrs: lost pl 1/2-way: bhd whn eased fnl f* **32/1**

1m 9.5s (-0.80) **11 Ran SP% 153.9**
WIN (incl. 1 euro stake); 2.34. PLACES: 1.51, 2.04, 2.75. DF: 17.45.
Owner Maicol Petretti **Bred** Allevamento Pian Di Neve Srl **Trained** Italy

7841a PREMIO ROMA GBI RACING (GROUP 1) (3YO+) (TURF) 1m 2f
3:30 (12:00) 3-Y-0+ **£91,911** (£40,441; £22,058; £11,029)

RPR

1 **Potemkin (GER)**[36] 6973 5-9-2 0 EduardoPedroza 2 113
(A Wohler, Germany) *in tch on inner: clsd steadily fr over 2 1/2f out: led appr fnl f and sn 2l clr: styd on wl fnl f* **11/4**[3]

2 1 1/2 **Robin Of Navan (FR)**[30] 7137 3-9-0 0 CristianDemuro 5 112
(Harry Dunlop) *a cl up: trckd ldr over 3f out and qcknd to ld 2 1/2f out: sn rdn and styd on: hdd appr fnl f: kpt on wl* **5/2**[2]

3 5 1/2 **Elliptique (IRE)**[56] 6395 5-9-2 0 Pierre-CharlesBoudot 4 99
(A Fabre, France) *w.w in rr: rdn and laboured rspnse 2 1/2f out: kpt on fnl f to go 3rd cl home: nvr trbld front two* **2/1**[1]

4 nse **Wireless (FR)**[36] 6975 5-9-2 0 TheoBachelot 7 99
(V Luka Jr, Czech Republic) *towards rr: sme hdwy 2f out: sn hrd rdn: kpt on fnl f: nvr on terms* **92/10**

5 3 **Circus Couture (IRE)**[21] 7400 4-9-2 0 DarioVargiu 3 93
(Stefano Botti, Italy) *w.w in midfield: rdn and clsd over 2f out: sn btn: one pce fnl f* **13/4**

6 9 1/2 **Bharuch (IRE)** 4-9-2 0 GermanoMarcelli 1 74
(Luigi Riccardi, Italy) *chsd ldr: rdn and nt qcknd 2 1/2f out: wknd ins fnl 2f* **233/10**

7 3 1/2 **Voice Of Love (IRE)**[21] 7400 3-9-0 0 FabioBranca 8 69
(Stefano Botti, Italy) *led: hdd 2 1/2f out: rdn and rallied: wknd wl over 1 1/2f out* **13/4**

8 3 1/2 **Diplomat (GER)**[21] 7400 5-9-2 0 CarloFiocchi 6 60
(Mario Hofer, Germany) *towards rr thrght: rdn and btn fnl 2f* **102/10**

9 7 **Basileus (IRE)**[14] 7565 3-9-0 0 SilvanoMulas 9 48
(Stefano Botti, Italy) *cl up on outer: lost pl sn after 1/2-way: wl bhd last 1 1/2f* **147/10**

2m 6.8s (3.50)
WFA 3 from 4yo+ 4lb **9 Ran SP% 164.8**
WIN (incl. 1 euro stake): 3.75. PLACES: 1.54, 1.58, 1.44. DF: 17.15.
Owner Klaus Allofs & Stiftung Gestut Fahrhof **Bred** Siftung Gestut Fahrhof **Trained** Germany

FOCUS
The first two have been rated to their marks.

[1689]KREFELD (R-H)
Sunday, November 6

OFFICIAL GOING: Turf: soft

7842a GROSSER PREIS VON LINK IN KREFELD DER TOLKE + FISCHER GRUPPE (GROUP 3) (2YO) (TURF) 1m 110y
12:30 (12:00) 2-Y-0 **£23,529** (£8,823; £4,411; £2,205; £1,470)

RPR

1 **Colomano**[21] 7399 2-9-2 0 MartinSeidl 7 103
(Markus Klug, Germany) *dwlt: w.w in fnl pair: last and drvn 2 1/2f out: clsd u.p fr 2f out: led ins fnl f: drvn out* **23/5**

2 1 3/4 **Kastano (GER)** 2-8-13 0 AndreasHelfenbein 1 96
(Markus Klug, Germany) *led: sn clr: scrubbed along over 1 12f out and styd on: hdd ins fnl f: one pce u.p: jst hld on for 2nd* **2/1**[1]

3 hd **Enjoy Vijay (GER)**[21] 7399 2-8-13 0 FilipMinarik 5 96
(P Schiergen, Germany) *w.w towards rr: prog on inner 2f out: styd on to go 3rd ins fnl f: jst failed to get up for 2nd: nvr cl enough to chal* **139/10**

4 3 **Savile Row (FR)**[32] 7086 2-8-13 0 EddyHardouin 3 89
(Frau Erika Mader, Germany) *keen: hld up in rr: hdwy on outer fr 2 1/2f out: chsd ldrs u.p 1 1/2f out: kpt on at one pce fnl f* **227/10**

5 2 1/2 **Amigo (GER)**[34] 2-8-13 0 BauyrzhanMurzabayev 6 84
(Eva Fabianova, Germany) *chsd ldr: rdn and no imp 2f out: one pce u.p fnl f* **127/10**

6 3/4 **Windstoss (GER)** 2-8-13 0 MaximPecheur 2 82
(Markus Klug, Germany) *chsd ldrs: sltly outpcd and rdn 2 1/2f out: kpt on at same pce fnl 1 1/2f* **43/5**

7 1 1/4 **Rolando (IRE)** 2-8-13 0 JozefBojko 9 79
(A Wohler, Germany) *keen: hld up in midfield: rdn and btn ins fnl 2f* **29/10**[2]

8 6 **Real Value (FR)**[21] 7399 2-9-2 0 StephenHellyn 8 69
(Mario Hofer, Germany) *hld up towards rr: rdn and edgd lft over 1 1/2f out: sn wknd* **19/5**[3]

9 6 **Ardashir (USA)**[21] 7399 2-8-13 0 (b) MichaelCadeddu 4 53
(Andreas Lowe, Germany) *chsd ldrs: rdn and no imp 2f out: bhd whn eased ins fnl f* **177/10**

1m 44.42s (-2.18) **9 Ran SP% 131.7**
WIN (incl. 10 euro stake): 56. PLACES: 18, 17, 33. SF: 164.
Owner Stall Reckendorf **Bred** Gestut Fahrhof **Trained** Germany

7843a GROSSER PREIS VON RONDO FOOD - NIEDERRHEIN-POKAL (GROUP 3) (3YO+) (TURF) 1m 2f 55y
1:45 (12:00) 3-Y-0+ **£23,529** (£8,823; £4,411; £2,205; £1,470)

RPR

1 **Amazona (GER)**[42] 4-8-11 0 AndreasHelfenbein 8 108
(Jean-Pierre Carvalho, Germany) *mde all: drvn 3l clr fr 2f out: styd on gamely u.p fnl f: nvr chal* **68/10**

2 1 3/4 **Palace Prince (GER)**[14] 7564 4-9-3 0 (p) EddyHardouin 5 110
(Andreas Lowe, Germany) *w.w in tch: rdn in pursuit of clr ldr fr wl over 1 1/2f out: styd on u.p: nvr able to get on terms* **21/10**[1]

3 2 1/4 **Devastar (GER)**[14] 7564 4-9-3 0 MartinSeidl 1 106
(Markus Klug, Germany) *settled in midfield: rdn and clsd fr 2f out: styd on at same pce fnl f: nvr able to chal* **14/5**[2]

4 4 1/2 **Matchwinner (GER)**[49] 6612 5-9-1 0 IanFerguson 6 95
(A Kleinkorres, Germany) *in rr and nt travelling too wl: rdn and styed on fr 2f out: nvr nrr* **132/10**

5 hd **Fair Mountain (GER)**[14] 7564 4-9-1 0 JozefBojko 9 95
(A Wohler, Germany) *nvr far off pce: rdn and nt qckn appr 2f out: grad lerft bhd* **172/10**

6 1 3/4 **Palang (USA)**[14] 7564 4-9-1 0 (b) FilipMinarik 4 91
(Andreas Lowe, Germany) *towards rr: rdn and effrt over 2f out: sn btn and nvr in contention* **113/10**

7 1 1/4 **Nordico (GER)**[14] 7564 5-8-13 0 (p) StephenHellyn 7 87
(Mario Hofer, Germany) *a towards rr: wl hld fnl 1 1/2f* **151/10**

8 22 **Felician (GER)**[21] 7400 8-8-13 0 MichaelCadeddu 11 43
(Ferdinand J Leve, Germany) *midfield on outer: lost pl and in rr 4f out: t.o* **26/1**

9 14 **Vif Monsieur (GER)**[14] 7564 6-8-13 0 KoenClijmans 3 15
(Mario Hofer, Germany) *prom on outer: drvn along after 1/2-way: hrd rdn and wknd fr 2f out: t.o* **127/10**

10 7 1/2 **Capitano (GER)**[14] 7564 3-8-10 0 AlexanderPietsch 10 1
(J Hirschberger, Germany) *chsd ldr on outer: rdn and no imp bef 2f out: wknd wl over 1 1/2f out: t.o* **114/10**

11 shd **Fast Lightning (GER)**[41] 3-8-8 0 MarcLerner 2
(Waldemar Hickst, Germany) *w.w in midfield: wknd u.p home st: t.o* **6/1**[3]

2m 3.79s (123.79)
WFA 3 from 4yo+ 4lb **11 Ran SP% 131.6**
WIN (incl. 10 euro stake): 78. PLACES: 20, 18, 17. SF: 244.
Owner Stall Ullmann **Bred** Stall Ullmann **Trained** Germany

7844 - (Foreign Racing) - See Raceform Interactive

[7791]NEWCASTLE (A.W) (L-H)
Monday, November 7

OFFICIAL GOING: Tapeta: standard
Wind: Moderate half against Weather: Sunny with showers

7845 PROTECTING YOUR WEALTH/EBF MAIDEN STKS 5f (Tp)
2:10 (2:11) (Class 5) 2-Y-0 **£3,234** (£962; £481; £240) **Stalls** Centre

Form RPR

0352 1 **Desert Sport (USA)**[30] 7142 2-9-5 71 JoeFanning 2 73
(Robert Cowell) *mde all: rdn appr fnl f: kpt on wl* **11/8**[1]

0 2 1 **Marseille (IRE)**[38] 6925 2-9-0 0 JoeDoyle 8 64
(Julie Camacho) *hld up in tch: hdwy to trck ldrs over 2f out: rdn to chse wnr jst over 1f out: drvn and edgd lft ins fnl f: kpt on* **6/1**

50 3 1 1/2 **Bombay Dream**[24] 7314 2-9-0 0 PatCosgrave 1 60
(William Haggas) *trckd ldrs on inner: hdwy to chse wnr over 2f out: sn rdn along: drvn ent fnl f: kpt on same pce* **7/4**[2]

4 4 7 **Flame Of Hope (IRE)**[34] 7040 2-9-0 0 GrahamGibbons 3 34
(David Barron) *prom: pushed along 1/2-way: rdn wl over 1f out: grad wknd* **4/1**[3]

0 **5** *5* **Paco Lady**[26] 7269 2-8-7 0 RPWalsh(7) 4 16
(Ivan Furtado) *towards rr: pushed along bef 1/2-way: sn outpcd* **100/1**

5056 **6** *1 3/4* **Shadow Wing (IRE)**[25] 7296 2-8-9 50 AnnStokell(5) 7 10
(Ann Stokell) *chsd ldrs: rdn along 1/2-way: sn drvn and wknd* **100/1**

00 **7** *1 1/2* **Mr Hill**[24] 7331 2-9-5 0 [1] PJMcDonald 6 9
(Rebecca Bastiman) *prom: rdn along 1/2-way: sn drvn and wknd* **100/1**

0 **8** *2 3/4* **Size Matters**[14] 7578 2-9-5 0 DougieCostello 5
(Mark Walford) *chsd ldrs: rdn along over 2f out: sn wknd* **33/1**

1m 0.01s (0.51) **Going Correction** +0.075s/f (Slow) **8** Ran SP% **118.7**
Speed ratings (Par 96): **98,96,94,82,74 72,69,65**
CSF £10.99 TOTE £2.30: £1.10, £1.60, £1.10; EX 11.30 Trifecta £21.10.
Owner Mohammed Al Shafar **Bred** Greenwood Lodge Farm Inc **Trained** Six Mile Bottom, Cambs

FOCUS
Fair efforts from the principals in this sprint maiden, the runner-up shaping well. The first three finished clear and the form is rated around the winner to his pre-race mark.

7846 @VERTEMAM FOLLOW US ON TWITTER H'CAP 2m 56y (Tp)
2:40 (2:40) (Class 5) (0-75,75) 3-Y-O+ **£3,557** (£1,058; £529; £264) **Stalls** Low

Form RPR

0521 **1** **Stamford Raffles**[46] 6698 3-8-12 **73** CharlieBennett(5) 4 80+
(Jane Chapple-Hyam) *trckd ldrs: hdwy over 4f out: cl up over 2f out: rdn to ld wl over 1f out: drvn ins fnl f: kpt on gamely towards fin* **7/2**[1]

5652 **2** *hd* **Aldreth**[30] 7158 5-9-8 **72** (b) NathanEvans(3) 2 78
(Michael Easterby) *trckd ldrs: hdwy 3f out: effrt wl over 1f out: rdn to chal ins fnl f: sn drvn and ev ch tl no ex nr fin* **8/1**

0500 **3** *1 1/4* **Cavalieri (IRE)**[6] 7746 6-8-13 **60** (tp) DougieCostello 3 65
(Philip Kirby) *hld up in tch: hdwy over 3f out: rdn over 1f out: styng on whn n.m.r ins fnl f: sn drvn and kpt on same pce towards fin* **40/1**

6525 **4** *2 1/4* **Another Lincolnday**[10] 7657 5-9-0 **61** GrahamLee 8 63
(Michael Herrington) *hld up: hdwy to trck ldrs 6f out: cl up 3f out: rdn and ev ch over 1f out: drvn and kpt on same pce fnl f* **12/1**

0434 **5** *1* **Snowy Dawn**[17] 7507 6-9-7 **68** GrahamGibbons 7 69
(Steph Hollinshead) *prom: hdwy to ld over 4f out: rdn along 3f out: hdd and drvn wl over 1f out: grad wknd* **4/1**[2]

4433 **6** *3/4* **Jan Smuts (IRE)**[22] 7382 8-8-6 **58** (tp) HollieDoyle(5) 10 58
(Wilf Storey) *hld up in rr: hdwy on outer over 3f out: chsd ldrs 2f out and sn rdn: drvn and no imp fnl f* **14/1**

5351 **7** *4 1/2* **Torremar (FR)**[14] 7582 3-9-4 **74** (p) TomEaves 9 68
(Kevin Ryan) *hld up in rr: stdy hdwy over 5f out: effrt to chse ldrs 3f out: rdn along 2f out: sn drvn and wknd fnl f* **9/2**[3]

0043 **8** *12* **Pray For Paris**[41] 6856 3-9-1 **71** PaulMulrennan 6 51
(Martyn Meade) *cl up: disp ld over 3f out: rdn along over 2f out: sn drvn. n.m.r and wknd* **13/2**

6503 **9** *12* **Ingleby Hollow**[13] 7594 4-9-9 **75** (p) JoshDoyle(5) 1 41
(David O'Meara) *sn led at stdy pce: pushed along over 5f out: hdd over 4f out and sn wknd* **16/1**

00-0 **P** **Precision Strike**[22] 7385 6-9-6 **67** (p) BarryMcHugh 5
(Richard Whitaker) *hld up: a towards rr: lost action over 1f out and sn p.u* **16/1**

3m 33.89s (-1.31) **Going Correction** 0.0s/f (Stan)
WFA 3 from 4yo+ 9lb **10** Ran SP% **113.4**
Speed ratings (Par 103): **103,102,102,101,100 100,98,92,86,**
CSF £30.90 CT £939.28 TOTE £4.20: £1.30, £1.90, £12.30; EX 24.90 Trifecta £2056.90.
Owner Mrs Jane Chapple-Hyam **Bred** C A Cyzer **Trained** Dalham, Suffolk

FOCUS
This was steadily run but the winner is progressive and is one to keep on side, the runner-up also shaping as if his turn is near. The form is rated a bit cautiously.

7847 BETWAY H'CAP 1m 4f 98y (Tp)
3:15 (3:15) (Class 4) (0-80,80) 3-Y-O+ **£5,175** (£1,540; £769; £384) **Stalls** High

Form RPR

5521 **1** **Ajman Prince (IRE)**[24] 7321 3-8-10 **72** JoeDoyle 13 83+
(Alistair Whillans) *hld up: hdwy on outer 5f out: trckd ldrs over 3f out: chal over 1f out: rdn ent fnl f: led last 100 yds: kpt on strly* **3/1**[1]

652 **2** *1 3/4* **Dubawi Fifty**[10] 7661 3-8-9 **71** GrahamLee 3 79
(Karen McLintock) *in tch: hdwy over 4f out: chsd ldrs over 2f out: pushed along wl over 1f out: rdn to chse ldng pair ent fnl f: sn drvn and kpt on same pce* **7/1**

1211 **3** *3/4* **The Resdev Way**[22] 7385 3-9-0 **76** BarryMcHugh 7 83+
(Richard Whitaker) *hld up in tch: hdwy to trck ldrs over 4f out: led wl over 2f out: rdn over 1f out: drvn ins fnl f: hdd and kpt on same pce last 100 yds* **9/2**[2]

1125 **4** *1* **Age Of Elegance (IRE)**[23] 7359 4-9-7 **77** (p) PJMcDonald 11 82
(Roger Fell) *trckd ldrs: hdwy over 3f out: effrt and nt clr run on inner wl over 1f out: swtchd rt to outer and rdn ent fnl f: kpt on* **20/1**

4666 **5** *nse* **Skiddaw Valleys**[24] 7332 4-8-12 **68** TonyHamilton 8 73
(Alan Swinbank) *prom: hdwy 5f out and sn cl up: led briefly jst over 3f out: sn rdn and hdd wl over 2f out: drvn over 1f out: kpt on same pce* **50/1**

6145 **6** *1 1/2* **Card High (IRE)**[13] 7594 6-9-1 **76** (t) HollieDoyle(5) 2 79
(Wilf Storey) *hld up in rr: hdwy on outer over 3f out: rdn to chse ldrs 2f out: drvn and no imp fnl f* **16/1**

364 **7** *1 1/2* **Azzir (IRE)**[21] 7412 4-9-0 **75** CliffordLee(5) 4 75
(K R Burke) *sltly hmpd after 11/2f: in tch on inner: pushed along over 4f out: sn rdn and grad wknd* **25/1**

42 **8** *nk* **Mutadaffeq (IRE)**[13] 7597 3-8-13 **75** GrahamGibbons 9 75
(David O'Meara) *led 2f: trckd ldr tl lft in ld over 4f out: sn rdn along: hdd jst over 3f out and grad wknd* **8/1**

0040 **9** *2 1/4* **Royal Flag**[12] 7627 6-8-11 **67** (b) BenCurtis 10 63
(Brian Ellison) *hld up: a towards rr* **25/1**

2032 **10** *hd* **Tectonic (IRE)**[10] 7657 7-8-11 **67** (v) ConnorBeasley 1 63
(Keith Dalgleish) *in tch on inner whn hmpd after 11/2f: t.k.h after: trckd ldrs: sltly hmpd over 4f out: sn rdn along and n.d* **20/1**

0000 **11** *7* **Weald Of Kent (USA)**[111] 4476 4-8-13 **72** AlistairRawlinson(3) 6 57
(Michael Appleby) *hld up: a rr* **100/1**

3400 **12** *7* **Hardstone (USA)**[23] 7365 5-9-10 **80** (t) PaulMulrennan 5 53
(Michael Dods) *trckd ldrs: hmpd over 4f out: sn rdn and wknd* **16/1**

0503 **P** **Street Artist (IRE)**[6] 7732 6-9-10 **80** PatCosgrave 12
(David Nicholls) *cl up: led after 2f tl lost action over 4f out and sn p.u* **5/1**[3]

2m 40.77s (-0.33) **Going Correction** 0.0s/f (Stan)
WFA 3 from 4yo+ 6lb **13** Ran SP% **115.4**
Speed ratings (Par 105): **101,99,99,98,98 97,96,96,94,94 90,85,**
CSF £20.86 CT £93.04 TOTE £3.70: £1.60, £2.70, £1.80; EX 26.10 Trifecta £184.50.
Owner J D Wright **Bred** Darley **Trained** Newmill-On-Slitrig, Borders

FOCUS
Progressive 3yos dominated in a race which appeals as strong form for the level. The form is rated slightly positively around the fourth.

7848 VERTEM MANAGEMENT MEDIAN AUCTION MAIDEN STKS 1m 4f 98y (Tp)
3:50 (3:51) (Class 6) 3-4-Y-O **£3,234** (£962; £481; £240) **Stalls** High

Form RPR

3 **1** **Vuela**[53] 6520 3-9-0 0 PatCosgrave 4 76+
(Luca Cumani) *sn trcking ldr: green and niggled along briefly 4f out: cl up 3f out: chal over 2f out: rdn to ld wl over 1f out: kpt on strly and clr fnl f* **6/5**[2]

2522 **2** *5* **Admiral's Sunset**[21] 7410 3-9-0 75 RobertHavlin 1 65
(Hughie Morrison) *led: pushed along and jnd 3f out: rdn over 2f out: hdd wl over 1f out: sn drvn and kpt on one pce* **10/11**[1]

3 *3 1/2* **Vision Of Beauty (FR)** 3-9-0 0 ConnorBeasley 3 59+
(Keith Dalgleish) *hld up in rr: hdwy 4f out: rdn: green and hung lft 3f out: sn chsng ldng pair and no imp* **25/1**

056/ **4** *9* **Ship Canal**[815] 5372 4-9-8 50 NathanEvans(3) 5 50
(Jacqueline Coward) *trckd ldrs: hdwy to chse ldng pair 4f out: rdn along 3f out: sn wknd* **100/1**

06 **5** *4 1/2* **Lord Of The Valley**[18] 7487 3-9-5 0 JoeFanning 2 43
(Mark Johnston) *trckd ldng pair on inner: pushed along 4f out: sn rdn and wknd 3f out* **14/1**[3]

2m 40.33s (-0.77) **Going Correction** 0.0s/f (Stan)
WFA 3 from 4yo 6lb **5** Ran SP% **109.3**
Speed ratings (Par 101): **102,98,96,90,87**
CSF £2.54 TOTE £2.10: £1.10, £1.10; EX 2.60 Trifecta £10.40.
Owner S Stuckey **Bred** Stuart Stuckey **Trained** Newmarket, Suffolk

FOCUS
A weakly contested late-season miaden, but a taking performance from the well-bred winner to readily see off a BHA 75-rated runner-up. The winner can do a lot better than the bare form.

7849 VERTEM.CO.UK EBF MAIDEN STKS 1m 5y (Tp)
4:20 (4:21) (Class 5) 2-Y-O **£3,234** (£962; £481; £240) **Stalls** Centre

Form RPR

54 **1** **Stradivarius (IRE)**[19] 7470 2-9-5 0 RobertHavlin 5 77
(John Gosden) *led at stdy pce: pushed along and qcknd over 2f out: rdn and hdd over 1f out: drvn ins fnl f: rallied wl to ld nr fin* **1/1**[1]

2 *hd* **Bowerman** 2-9-5 0 JackMitchell 2 77
(Roger Varian) *trckd ldrs: effrt and green wl over 1f out: rdn and styd on to chal ins fnl f: ev ch tl no ex nr fin* **7/1**[3]

3 *shd* **Mutarabby (IRE)** 2-9-5 0 PatCosgrave 6 76
(Saeed bin Suroor) *trckd ldng pair: hdwy and cl up wl over 2f out: rdn to take narrow ld over 1f out: drvn ins fnl f: hdd and no ex towards fin* **17/2**

4 *1/2* **Lethal Impact (JPN)** 2-9-5 0 OisinMurphy 7 75
(David Simcock) *hld up in tch: trckd ldrs over 2f out: effrt over 1f out: rdn and ch ins fnl f: kpt on* **11/2**[2]

5 **5** *3 1/2* **Teodoro (IRE)**[54] 6480 2-9-5 0 PaulMulrennan 1 67
(Tom Dascombe) *t.k.h: trckd wnr: pushed along over 2f out: rdn wl over 1f out: grad wknd* **10/1**

6 *1 1/2* **Bombay Marine (USA)** 2-9-5 0 RobertTart 3 64
(John Gosden) *trckd ldrs: rdn along and green over 2f out: sn outpcd* **7/1**[3]

1m 40.34s (1.74) **Going Correction** +0.075s/f (Slow) **6** Ran SP% **110.0**
Speed ratings (Par 96): **94,93,93,93,89 88**
CSF £8.14 TOTE £2.00: £1.20, £2.90; EX 8.90 Trifecta £63.80.
Owner B E Nielsen **Bred** Bjorn Nielsen **Trained** Newmarket, Suffolk

FOCUS
A muddling tempo and a blanket finish but it contained well-bred types from leading stables and it would be no surprise if it turns out to be quite a good maiden, the winner bringing some fairly useful form to the table courtesy of his Newmarket fourth. The bare form will probably prove little guide.

7850 FRESH APPROACH H'CAP 7f 14y (Tp)
4:50 (4:51) (Class 6) (0-55,55) 3-Y-O+ **£3,234** (£962; £481; £240) **Stalls** Centre

Form RPR

0303 **1** **Fire Diamond**[13] 7602 3-9-3 **52** (p) PaulMulrennan 5 59
(Tom Dascombe) *hld up towards rr: gd hdwy over 2f out: chsd ldrs over 1f out: sn rdn: drvn and stdy on to ld last 100 yds* **9/2**[2]

0302 **2** *1 1/4* **Mr Potter**[3] 7795 3-9-1 **50** ConnorBeasley 10 54
(Richard Guest) *hld up towards rr: hdwy over 2f out: rdn to chse ldrs over 1f out: drvn to chal and ev ch ins fnl f: kpt on* **11/4**[1]

5606 **3** *1/2* **Little Indian**[20] 7427 6-9-4 **52** DannyBrock 2 56
(J R Jenkins) *trckd ldrs: hdwy 3f out and sn cl up: rdn over 1f out: ev ch ins fnl f: sn drvn and kpt on* **14/1**

6005 **4** *hd* **Justice Pleasing**[39] 6905 3-9-2 **51** [1] PJMcDonald 12 53
(Roger Fell) *cl up: led 1/2-way: rdn and hdd 2f over 2f out: drvn to ld again appr fnl f: hdd and no ex last 100 yds* **33/1**

4655 **5** *2 1/4* **Yair Hill (IRE)**[27] 7254 8-8-11 **48** (p) RachelRichardson(3) 1 46
(Thomas Cuthbert) *prom: led over 2f out: rdn wl over 1f out: hdd appr fnl f: kpt on same pce* **9/1**

045 **6** *1 1/2* **Kopassus (IRE)**[95] 5065 4-9-1 **49** TomEaves 6 43
(Lawrence Mullaney) *midfield: hdwy over 3f out: rdn to chse ldrs wl over 1f out: sn no imp* **14/1**

0235 **7** *3/4* **Wimboldsley**[18] 7488 5-9-2 **50** BenCurtis 7 42
(Scott Dixon) *hld up in rr: hdwy 3f out: chsd ldrs and swtchd lft wl over 1f out: sn rdn and kpt on same pce* **12/1**

0606 **8** *2 3/4* **Diamond Avalanche (IRE)**[27] 7253 3-9-6 **55** GrahamLee 8 39
(Patrick Holmes) *chsd ldrs: rdn along over 3f out: sn wknd* **25/1**

0035 **9** *nk* **Mops Angel**[76] 5753 5-9-0 **51** (p) AlistairRawlinson(3) 11 35
(Michael Appleby) *dwlt: a towards rr* **17/2**[3]

0060 **10** *1/2* **Haidees Reflection**[13] 7601 6-9-6 **54** (p) OisinMurphy 14 37
(Jim Goldie) *dwlt: a towards rr* **20/1**

0600 **11** *1 1/2* **Jebel Tara**[24] 7323 11-9-3 **51** (bt) DaleSwift 3 30
(Alistair Whillans) *t.k.h: led: hdd 1/2-way: rdn along over 3f out: sn wknd* **25/1**

-000 **12** *9* **Solar Spirit (IRE)**[131] 3777 11-9-7 **55** JoeFanning 4 12
(Tracy Waggott) *trckd ldrs on inner: effrt 3f out: sn rdn along and wknd wl over 1f out* **16/1**

004R **R** **Free One (IRE)**[6] 7742 4-9-5 **53** TonyHamilton 13
(Ivan Furtado) *ref to r* **14/1**

1m 27.07s (0.87) **Going Correction** +0.075s/f (Slow)
WFA 3 from 4yo+ 1lb **13** Ran SP% **114.3**
Speed ratings (Par 101): **98,96,96,95,93 91,90,87,87,86 84,74,**
CSF £15.43 CT £162.88 TOTE £4.70: £1.50, £1.40, £5.40; EX 14.10 Trifecta £224.30.
Owner John Brown **Bred** John Brown **Trained** Malpas, Cheshire

FOCUS
Real low-grade fare and a couple of 3yos came to the fore after the early tempo had been very steady. The winner is rated a minor improver.

7851 INVESTING FOR THE FUTURE H'CAP (DIV I) 6f (Tp)
5:20 (5:21) (Class 5) (0-70,70) 3-Y-O+ **£2,308** (£2,308; £529; £264) **Stalls** Centre

Form RPR
3540 **1** **More Beau (USA)**[10] 7663 5-9-5 **68**...............................[1] BarryMcHugh 5 74
(David Nicholls) *hld up: hdwy over 2f out: chsd ldrs over 1f out: rdn to chal ent fnl f: sn drvn: led towards fin: jnd on line* **9/2**[1]

2320 **1** *dht* **Wahaab (IRE)**[3] 7797 5-8-12 **66**..........................(p) ShirleyTeasdale[(5)] 11 72
(Iain Jardine) *hld up: hdwy over 2f out: rdn to chse ldrs over 1f out: drvn ins fnl f: styd on wl to join ldr on line* **12/1**

1065 **3** *nse* **Be Royale**[9] 7687 6-9-7 **70**..(t) OisinMurphy 2 76
(Michael Appleby) *prom: chsd ldr 1/2-way: rdn to ld wl over 1f out: jnd and drvn ent fnl f: hdd towards fin: kpt on* **8/1**

0565 **4** *1 ¼* **Ambitious Icarus**[5] 7774 7-9-2 **65**..............................(e) ConnorBeasley 3 67+
(Richard Guest) *in tch: whn bmpd and lost pl over 3f out: hdwy over 2f out: rdn wl over 1f out: kpt on wl fnl f* **5/1**[2]

0503 **5** *nse* **Captain Lars (SAF)**[9] 7687 7-9-4 **70**..........................(p) NoelGarbutt[(3)] 10 72
(Derek Shaw) *trckd ldrs: hdwy over 2f out: rdn and cl up over 1f out: drvn and ev ch ent fnl f: kpt on same pce towards fin* **6/1**

16-0 **6** *1 ¼* **Ad Vitam (IRE)**[24] 7325 8-8-11 **60**....................................(bt) TomEaves 7 58
(Suzzanne France) *hld up in rr: hdwy over 2f out: sn rdn and kpt on fnl f* **25/1**

350 **7** *6* **Whozthecat (IRE)**[47] 6684 9-9-3 **66**.........................(vt) GrahamGibbons 1 45
(Declan Carroll) *led and sn clr: pushed along over 2f out: sn rdn: hdd wl over 1f out and sn wknd* **13/2**

4602 **8** *4* **Never In Doubt**[24] 7335 3-9-4 **67**................................. GeorgeChaloner 8 33
(Richard Whitaker) *chsd ldrs: rdn along over 2f out: sn wknd* **11/1**

43 **9** *2 ½* **Rock Canyon (IRE)**[32] 7092 7-8-7 **61**.............................. JoshDoyle[(5)] 9 19
(Linda Perratt) *chsd ldr: rdn along 1/2-way: wknd over 2f out* **25/1**

4562 **10** *3* **Penny Dreadful**[11] 7644 4-9-6 **69**..(p) DaleSwift 4 17
(Scott Dixon) *t.k.h: trckd ldrs: jinked lft over 3f out: rdn along 2f out: sn drvn and btn* **11/2**[3]

1m 11.72s (-0.78) **Going Correction** +0.075s/f (Slow) **10** Ran SP% **112.7**
Speed ratings (Par 103): **108,108,107,106,106 104,96,91,87,83**
WIN: 2.70 More Beau, 7.20 Wahaab; PL: 1.80 More Beau, 2.10 Be Royale, 4.80 Wahaab; EX: 31.30, 41.90; CSF: 28.25, 31.55; TC: 211.78, 235.41; TF: 186.10, 230.50;.
Owner Alex Nicholls & J Gee **Bred** Nursery Place **Trained** Sessay, N Yorks
Owner George Brian Davidson **Bred** Shadwell Estate Company Limited **Trained** Carrutherstown, D'fries & G'way

FOCUS
Run-of-the-mill fare but it provided a thrilling finish. The time was good compared to the second division.

7852 INVESTING FOR THE FUTURE H'CAP (DIV II) 6f (Tp)
5:50 (5:50) (Class 5) (0-70,70) 3-Y-O+ **£3,557** (£1,058; £529; £264) **Stalls** Centre

Form RPR
2134 **1** **Caeser The Gaeser (IRE)**[10] 7663 4-9-3 **66**...................(p) TomEaves 2 73
(Nigel Tinkler) *trckd ldrs: hdwy 2f out: rdn to take narrow ld 1f out: sn drvn and hld on gamely towards fin* **6/1**

0005 **2** *nk* **Clubland (IRE)**[10] 7660 7-9-5 **68**... NeilFarley 7 74
(Garry Moss) *hld up towards rr: hdwy 1/2-way: chsd ldrs over 1f out: rdn to chal ent fnl f: sn drvn and ev ch: no ex towards fin* **7/2**[1]

2004 **3** *shd* **Malaysian Boleh**[24] 7325 6-9-5 **68**....................................... BenCurtis 10 74+
(Brian Ellison) *hld up towards rr: hdwy over 2f out: rdn to chse ldrs over 1f out: styd on wl fnl f* **5/1**[2]

2164 **4** *shd* **Poppy In The Wind**[88] 5320 4-8-9 **63**..........................(v) JoshDoyle[(5)] 11 68
(Alan Brown) *in tch: hdwy on outer to join ldrs over 1f out: sn rdn to chal and ev ch: drvn wl ins fnl f: no ex towards fin* **14/1**

0456 **5** *1* **Spirit Of Zebedee (IRE)**[14] 7584 3-8-12 **61**.............(p) DougieCostello 1 63
(John Quinn) *hld up: hdwy wl over 1f out: rdn: n.m.r and swtchd lft ins fnl f: drvn and kpt on wl towards fin* **22/1**

0022 **6** *shd* **Gold Beau (FR)**[13] 7602 6-8-11 **60**...............................(p) TonyHamilton 4 62
(Kristin Stubbs) *led: rdn along and hdd over 2f out: drvn wl over 1f out: grad wknd* **11/2**[3]

5/10 **7** *½* **Lotara**[53] 6506 4-9-2 **65**.. OisinMurphy 5 65
(Jim Goldie) *trckd ldrs: effrt 2f out: rdn over 1f out: grad wknd* **14/1**

1135 **8** *1 ¼* **Portland Street (IRE)**[44] 6769 3-9-6 **69**....................(p) PaulMulrennan 9 65
(Bryan Smart) *chsd ldng pair: rdn along wl over 2f out: sn wknd* **13/2**

3205 **9** *1* **Fujin**[10] 7663 5-9-2 **70**.. CharlieBennett[(5)] 3 63
(Shaun Harris) *sn trcking ldr: cl up 1/2-way: rdn to ld over 2f out: drvn over 1f out: hdd appr fnl f: wknd* **8/1**

2606 **10** *nk* **Kodiac Lady (IRE)**[195] 1762 4-8-4 **58**............................. HollieDoyle[(5)] 8 50
(Simon West) *chsd ldrs: rdn along over 2f out: sn wknd* **40/1**

5120 **11** *1 ¼* **Charava (IRE)**[77] 5717 4-9-3 **66**....................................(v) JackGarritty 6 54
(Patrick Holmes) *hld up: a towards rr* **66/1**

1m 12.66s (0.16) **Going Correction** +0.075s/f (Slow) **11** Ran SP% **114.6**
Speed ratings (Par 103): **101,100,100,100,99 98,98,96,95,94 93**
CSF £26.12 CT £114.69 TOTE £5.30: £2.30, £1.50, £1.50; EX 28.50 Trifecta £163.80.
Owner Flying High Racing Club **Bred** Tom Foley **Trained** Langton, N Yorks

FOCUS
Another tight finish and it appears as solid form for the grade, the winner thriving and the runner-up on a good mark at present. It was the slower division.
T/Jkpt: £2,857.10. Pool: £10,000.00 - 3.20 winning units. T/Plt: £6.50 to a £1 stake. Pool: £92232.93, 10311.51 winning units. T/Qpdt: £2.50 to a £1 stake. Pool: £8396.11, 2390.46 winning units. **Joe Rowntree**

7845 NEWCASTLE (A.W) (L-H)
Tuesday, November 8

OFFICIAL GOING: Tapeta: standard
Wind: Virtually nil Weather: Cloudy

7853 BOWBURN HOTEL FILLIES' H'CAP 1m 4f 98y (Tp)
3:40 (3:40) (Class 5) (0-75,75) 3-Y-O+ **£3,234** (£962; £481; £240) **Stalls** High

Form RPR
1 **1** **Musaanada**[57] 6415 3-9-4 **75**... PaulHanagan 4 84+
(William Haggas) *sluggish s: green and sn pushed along: in tch after 1f: niggled along on outer over 4f out: rdn over 3f out: hdwy 2f out: led over 1f out: drvn and kpt on fnl f* **4/6**[1]

5664 **2** *¾* **Maulesden May (IRE)**[21] 7435 3-8-10 **67**..................... ConnorBeasley 5 74
(Keith Dalgleish) *hld up towards rr: hdwy on outer over 2f out: rdn to chse wnr ent fnl f: sn cl up and ev ch: drvn and kpt on same pce last 75yds* **12/1**

4264 **3** *3 ¼* **La Contessa (IRE)**[36] 7008 3-9-1 **72**............................... TonyHamilton 9 74
(Richard Fahey) *cl up: chal 3f out: sn ev ch: rdn wl over 1f out: kpt on same pce fnl f* **7/1**[2]

5206 **4** *shd* **Siren's Cove**[31] 7139 4-9-9 **74**..................................(b[1]) PaulMulrennan 7 76
(Kenneth Slack) *trckd ldng pair on outer: smooth hdwy and cl up 3f out: rdn along 2f out: drvn and kpt on same pce fnl f* **11/1**

2434 **5** *½* **Livella Fella (IRE)**[42] 6856 3-9-4 **75**.............................. PJMcDonald 8 76
(Keith Dalgleish) *t.k.h early: trckd ldrs: pushed along over 3f out: rdn along 2f out: kpt on one pce* **16/1**

2030 **6** *¾* **Henpecked**[14] 7594 6-9-0 **70**..............................(p) GarryWhillans[(5)] 1 70
(Alistair Whillans) *trckd ldrs: pushed along over 3f out: rdn over 2f out: sn drvn and grad wknd* **14/1**

1516 **6** *dht* **Raven Banner (IRE)**[58] 6378 3-9-0 **71**................................. DaleSwift 2 71
(Daniel Mark Loughnane) *hld up in tch: pushed along on inner over 3f out: rdn wl over 2f out: sn drvn and grad wknd* **40/1**

3252 **8** *5* **Shadow Spirit**[21] 7435 3-8-9 **71**.................................... JoshDoyle[(5)] 3 63
(Iain Jardine) *v.s.a and lost many l at s: detached tl tk clsr order 1/2-way: hdwy on wd outside and in tch over 2f out: sn rdn and wknd* **10/1**[3]

0436 **9** *6* **Notion Of Beauty (USA)**[23] 7385 3-8-6 **63**......................... BenCurtis 6 45
(K R Burke) *set stdy pce: pushed along and qcknd over 4f out: rdn along and jnd over 3f out: sn hdd & wknd* **20/1**

2m 40.1s (-1.00) **Going Correction** 0.0s/f (Stan)
WFA 3 from 4yo+ 6lb **9** Ran SP% **117.4**
Speed ratings (Par 100): **103,102,100,100,99 99,99,96,92**
CSF £10.52 CT £35.86 TOTE £1.50: £1.10, £2.60, £1.70; EX 10.60 Trifecta £50.60.
Owner Hamdan Al Maktoum **Bred** Windmill Farm Partnership **Trained** Newmarket, Suffolk

FOCUS
A fair fillies' handicap. There looks to be plenty more to come fom the winner and the form could be rated a shaade higher at face value.

7854 NEW SPA AT RAMSIDE HALL HOTEL NURSERY H'CAP 1m 5y (Tp)
4:15 (4:15) (Class 6) (0-65,63) 2-Y-O **£2,328** (£693; £346; £173) **Stalls** Centre

Form RPR
0001 **1** **Ronnie The Rooster**[32] 7110 2-9-5 **61**......................... GrahamGibbons 4 66+
(David Barron) *hld up towards rr: hdwy 3f out: sn trcking ldrs: cl up 2f out: rdn to take slt ld jst over 1f out: drvn ins fnl f: kpt on wl towards fin* **11/8**[1]

5404 **2** *1 ½* **Fancy Day (IRE)**[15] 7570 2-9-7 **63**............................ PaulMulrennan 7 64
(Mark Johnston) *led: rdn along 2f out: hdd narrowly jst over 1f out: sn drvn: kpt on same pce last 100 yds* **8/1**[3]

0400 **3** *nk* **Tael O' Gold**[32] 7110 2-9-1 **57**.. PatCosgrave 3 57
(Iain Jardine) *t.k.h: trckd ldrs: hdwy wl over 2f out: rdn over 1f out: drvn and kpt on fnl f* **8/1**[3]

0241 **4** *¾* **Volta Do Mar (IRE)**[25] 7330 2-9-5 **61**............................. TonyHamilton 1 60
(Richard Fahey) *trckd ldng pair: cl up over 3f out: rdn along wl over 1f out: drvn and kpt on same pce fnl f* **15/8**[2]

000 **5** *1* **Bodacious Name (IRE)**[48] 6679 2-8-13 **55**........................ TomEaves 6 51
(John Quinn) *hld up towards rr: hdwy 2f out: rdn over 1f out: kpt on fnl f: nrst fin* **20/1**

5060 **6** *nse* **Mystic Maeve (IRE)**[21] 7431 2-8-13 **55**.........................(p) JackGarritty 5 51
(Roger Fell) *trckd ldr: pushed along over 2f out: sn rdn and grad wknd* **12/1**

055 **7** *½* **Enlighten Me (IRE)**[14] 7599 2-8-5 **47**............................... JoeyHaynes 2 42
(Philip Kirby) *trckd ldrs: hdwy over 2f out: rdn along wl over 1f out: grad wknd* **40/1**

1m 42.78s (4.18) **Going Correction** -0.075s/f (Stan) **7** Ran SP% **114.0**
Speed ratings (Par 94): **76,74,74,73,72 72,71**
CSF £13.32 TOTE £2.30: £1.30, £2.50; EX 12.50 Trifecta £44.40.
Owner Ron Hull **Bred** Richard Kent & Robert Percival **Trained** Maunby, N Yorks

FOCUS
A modest nursery and very ordinary, straightforward form.

7855 RAMSIDE EVENT CATERING MAIDEN FILLIES' STKS (PLUS 10 RACE) 7f 14y (Tp)
4:45 (4:50) (Class 5) 2-Y-O **£2,911** (£866; £432; £216) **Stalls** Centre

Form RPR
2 **1** **Indian Blessing**[19] 7484 2-9-0 0................................ GrahamGibbons 8 75
(Ed Walker) *trckd ldrs: pushed along over 1f out: rdn ins fnl f: styd on strly to ld nr fin* **2/1**[1]

5 **2** *nk* **Isabel's On It**[10] 7695 2-9-0 0... PatCosgrave 9 74
(William Haggas) *in tch: hdwy over 2f out: led wl over 1f out: rdn ent fnl f: edgd lft last 100 yds: hdd and no ex nr fin* **3/1**[2]

3 *1* **Al Mayda (USA)** 2-8-11 0....................................[1] JosephineGordon[(3)] 2 72+
(Hugo Palmer) *trckd ldrs: hdwy over 2f out: cl up and rdn over 1f out: drvn and kpt on same pce fnl f* **10/1**

4 *¾* **Moonshine Dancer** 2-9-0 0... TomEaves 1 70+
(David Simcock) *dwlt and rr: gd hdwy over 2f out: rdn wl over 1f out: chsd ldrs ins fnl f: kpt on* **25/1**

5 *¾* **Crystal River** 2-9-0 0.. MartinLane 5 68
(Saeed bin Suroor) *dwlt: sn trcking ldrs: pushed along over 2f out: rdn wl over 1f out: kpt on same pce* **9/2**[3]

0 **6** *5* **Spirit Of Rome (IRE)**[31] 7157 2-9-0 0.............................. PJMcDonald 12 56
(James Bethell) *hld up towards rr: hdwy over 2f out: rdn along and kpt on fr over 1f out: nvr nr ldrs* **100/1**

65 **7** *3* **Seyadah**[35] 7049 2-9-0 0... TomMarquand 11 48
(Marco Botti) *cl up: pushed along over 3f out: rdn wl over 2f out and sn wknd* **12/1**

02 **8** *1* **Sulafah (IRE)**[20] 7466 2-9-0 0.. PaulHanagan 4 46
(Roger Varian) *prom: led 3f out: rdn along 2f out: sn hdd & wknd over 1f out* **5/1**

05 **9** *shd* **Judy Woods (IRE)**[31] 7142 2-9-0 0............................. PaulMulrennan 10 47+
(Bryan Smart) *t.k.h: a towards rr* **50/1**

00 **10** *1 ½* **Tilly Devine**[39] 6925 2-9-0 0.. BenCurtis 6 42
(Scott Dixon) *slt ld: pushed along 1/2-way: sn rdn and hdd 3f out: sn wknd* **200/1**

0 **11** *10* **You Look Different**[21] 7432 2-9-0 0................................. TonyHamilton 7 17
(Antony Brittain) *a towards rr* **200/1**

1m 26.6s (0.40) **Going Correction** -0.075s/f (Stan) **11** Ran SP% **117.8**
Speed ratings (Par 93): **94,93,92,91,90 85,81,80,80,78 67**
CSF £7.72 TOTE £3.20: £1.20, £1.50, £3.10; EX 10.00 Trifecta £77.50.
Owner P K Siu **Bred** Jocelyn Targett **Trained** Upper Lambourn, Berks
■ Nancy Hart was withdrawn. Price at time of withdrawal 11-1. Rule 4 applies to all bets. Deduction - 5p in the pound.

FOCUS
A maiden that should throw up a winner or two. The first five finished clear.

7856 RAMSIDE HALL HOTEL MEDIAN AUCTION MAIDEN FILLIES' STKS 7f 14y (Tp)
5:15 (5:17) (Class 6) 3-5-Y-O **£2,328** (£693; £346; £173) **Stalls** Centre

Form RPR

3300 **1** **Crystallographer (IRE)**[7] 7743 3-9-0 68 ....[1] GrahamGibbons 1 60+
(Daniel Mark Loughnane) *.trckd ldrs: hdwy wl over 1f out: rdn to ld appr fnl f: sn clr: kpt on* **10/11**[1]

60 **2** *4* **Poetic Queen (IRE)**[22] 7410 3-9-0 0 .... NeilFarley 5 50
(Eric Alston) *led: rdn along 2f out: drvn and hdd appr fnl f: kpt on same pce* **12/1**

5000 **3** *1¼* **Cosmic Dust**[31] 7145 3-9-0 43 ....[1] GeorgeChaloner 3 47
(Richard Whitaker) *trckd ldrs: pushed along over 2f out: rdn wl over 1f out: kpt on u.p fnl f* **12/1**

03 **4** *hd* **Polish Empress**[14] 7603 3-8-11 0 .... JosephineGordon(3) 6 46
(William Muir) *cl up: rdn along over 2f out: drvn over 1f out: sn wknd* **2/1**[2]

6 **5** *17* **Piccolilly**[5] 7782 3-8-11 0 .... NoelGarbutt(3) 4 4
(Derek Shaw) *dwlt: green and pushed along in rr whn jinked bdly ;lft after 1f: rdn along 3f out: outpcd and bhd fnl 2f* **100/1**

5 **6** *31* **Candy Express**[147] 3249 3-9-0 0 .... PaulMulrennan 2
(Clive Mulhall) *dwlt: in tch: pushed along to chse ldrs 4f out: rdn along over 3f out: sn outpcd and wl bhd fnl 2f* **7/1**[3]

1m 26.34s (0.14) **Going Correction** -0.075s/f (Stan) **6** Ran SP% **114.6**
Speed ratings (Par 98): **96,91,90,89,70 34**
CSF £14.00 TOTE £1.80: £1.10, £5.80; EX 11.70 Trifecta £58.70.
Owner B Dunn **Bred** W Maxwell Ervine **Trained** Baldwin's Gate, Staffs

FOCUS
This was a very weak maiden with no depth. The winner won as she was fully entitled to do.

7857 BAR BEYOND IN THE GATE H'CAP 1m 5y (Tp)
5:45 (5:46) (Class 5) (0-75,81) 3-Y-O+ **£2,911** (£866; £432; £216) **Stalls** Centre

Form RPR

5521 **1** **Testa Rossa (IRE)**[14] 7601 6-8-12 66 ....(b) TomMarquand 3 75
(Jim Goldie) *trckd ldrs: hdwy 3f out: rdn to ld over 1f out: drvn ins fnl f: kpt on wl towards fin* **7/1**[3]

-500 **2** *nk* **Cadeau Magnifique**[18] 7500 4-9-1 69 .... TonyHamilton 14 77+
(Richard Fahey) *trckd ldrs: hdwy wl over 2f out: rdn to chse ldrs over 1f out: drvn ins fnl f: kpt on wl towards fin* **14/1**

1324 **3** *nk* **Dark Intention (IRE)**[44] 6811 3-9-3 73 .... PaulHanagan 7 80
(Lawrence Mullaney) *prom: hdwy to ld over 2f out: rdn and hdd over 1f out: sn drvn and kpt wl fnl f* **5/1**[2]

0004 **4** *1* **Magic City (IRE)**[21] 7436 7-9-2 73 .... NathanEvans(3) 11 78
(Michael Easterby) *hld up towards rr: hdwy over 3f out: chsd ldrs 2f out: rdn over 1f out: drvn ins fnl f: keeping on same pce whn n.m.r and sltly hmpd towards fin* **4/1**[1]

0006 **5** *3½* **Auspicion**[13] 7623 4-9-4 72 .... TomEaves 6 69+
(Tom Tate) *hld up in rr: hdwy 2f out: rdn over 1f out: styd on strly fnl f: nrst fin* **8/1**

4202 **6** *2¼* **Green Howard**[21] 7436 8-9-7 75 .... PaulMulrennan 2 66
(Rebecca Bastiman) *trckd ldrs: hdwy on inner over 2f out: rdn and ev ch over 1f out: sn drvn and wknd fnl f* **7/1**[3]

2530 **7** *3* **Weather Front (USA)**[21] 7436 3-9-3 73 ....[1] GrahamLee 10 58
(Karen McLintock) *hld up in rr: hdwy over 2f out: rdn wl over 1f out: sn no imp* **4/1**[1]

2001 **8** *nse* **Nonno Giulio (IRE)**[7] 7742 5-9-8 81 6ex .... JoshDoyle(5) 8 65
(Roger Fell) *chsd ldrs: rdn along wl over 2f out: sn wknd* **20/1**

0000 **9** *½* **Balducci**[74] 5858 9-9-2 70 ....(b) PJMcDonald 5 53
(Roger Fell) *led: rdn along over 3f out: hdd over 2f out and sn wknd* **40/1**

1566 **10** *3* **With Pleasure**[19] 7486 3-9-5 75 .... GrahamGibbons 1 51
(David O'Meara) *chsd ldrs: rdn along 3f out: drvn and wknd 2f out* **9/1**

14-0 **11** *1¼* **Tafteesh (IRE)**[32] 7126 3-8-12 75 .... DanielleMooney(7) 4 49
(Michael Easterby) *in tch: hdwy to chse ldrs over 2f out: sn rdn and no imp* **40/1**

4113 **12** *5* **Beatbybeatbybeat**[19] 7485 3-9-5 75 ....(v) PatCosgrave 12 37
(Antony Brittain) *cl up: disp ld 3f out: rdn along over 2f out: sn drvn and wknd* **20/1**

4320 **13** *4* **Melabi (IRE)**[29] 7222 3-8-12 75 .... CallumRodriguez(7) 9 28
(Richard Ford) *prom: rdn along wl over 2f out: sn wknd* **20/1**

2200 **14** *10* **Rain In The Face**[136] 3653 3-9-2 72 .... BarryMcHugh 13 2
(Karen Tutty) *dwlt: a towards rr: rdn along 3f out: sn outpcd and bhd* **66/1**

1m 37.4s (-1.20) **Going Correction** -0.075s/f (Stan)
WFA 3 from 4yo+ 2lb **14** Ran SP% **130.1**
Speed ratings (Par 103): **103,102,102,101,97 95,92,92,92,89 87,82,78,68**
CSF £100.31 CT £566.71 TOTE £8.80: £2.60, £4.50, £2.10; EX 86.40 Trifecta £1205.00.
Owner Mr & Mrs Gordon Grant **Bred** Hugo Merry And Khalid Al-Mudhaf **Trained** Uplawmoor, E Renfrews

FOCUS
A competitive handicap but pretty ordinary form. The winner looks better than ever.

7858 HARDWICK HALL HOTEL H'CAP 6f (Tp)
6:15 (6:19) (Class 3) (0-95,93) 3-Y-O+ **£7,762** (£2,310; £1,154; £577) **Stalls** Centre

Form RPR

1132 **1** **Kenny The Captain (IRE)**[21] 7443 5-8-10 85 ..... RachelRichardson(3) 1 94
(Tim Easterby) *prom: cl up over 2f out: chal over 1f out: rdn to take narrow ld 1f out: sn drvn and kpt on wl* **8/1**

3000 **2** *nk* **Dragon King (IRE)**[53] 6537 4-8-11 83 ....[1] PaulMulrennan 13 91
(Michael Dods) *in tch: hdwy over 2f out: rdn to chse ldrs over 1f out: drvn to chal ent fnl f: ev ch: kpt on* **25/1**

3201 **3** *nse* **Jaywalker (IRE)**[21] 7433 5-8-10 82 .... PJMcDonald 4 90
(Rebecca Bastiman) *led: pushed along 2f out: rdn over 1f out: hdd narrowly 1f out: sn drvn and kpt on wl* **6/1**[3]

0540 **4** *2* **Udontdodou**[17] 7537 3-8-13 85 .... PaulHanagan 11 86
(Richard Guest) *hld up towards rr: hdwy over 2f out: swtchd rt and rdn over 1f out: drvn and kpt on fnl f: nrst fin* **3/1**[1]

44-0 **5** *nk* **King Robert**[208] 1442 3-9-7 93 .... ConnorBeasley 2 91
(Bryan Smart) *trckd ldrs: rdn along 2f out: drvn over 1f out: kpt on same pce fnl f* **14/1**

0100 **6** *1¾* **Handsome Dude**[13] 7610 4-9-0 86 ....(b) GrahamGibbons 6 81
(David Barron) *prom: rdn along over 2f out: drvn over 1f out: grad wknd* **14/1**

4004 **7** *1* **Another Wise Kid (IRE)**[25] 7315 8-9-4 90 .... GrahamLee 14 82
(Paul Midgley) *chsd ldrs on outer: rdn along 2f out: grad wknd* **18/1**

0000 **8** *¾* **Steelriver (IRE)**[13] 7610 6-9-1 87 .... TomEaves 5 76
(David Barron) *dwlt and rr: hdwy wl over 1f out: kpt on fnl f* **20/1**

0261 **9** *nk* **Cosmic Chatter**[22] 7413 6-9-0 86 ....(p) KevinStott 7 74
(Ruth Carr) *towards rr: hdwy on inner over 2f out: chsd ldrs over 1f out: sn rdn and wknd* **16/1**

0004 **10** *¾* **Showboating (IRE)**[24] 7360 8-9-1 87 .... BenCurtis 10 73
(John Balding) *in tch: rdn along wl over 2f out: sn drvn and wknd* **50/1**

2214 **11** *nk* **Harwoods Volante (IRE)**[10] 7702 5-8-12 89 .... JoshDoyle(5) 12 74
(David O'Meara) *a towards rr* **4/1**[2]

0003 **12** *nse* **Hawkeyethenoo (IRE)**[32] 7126 10-8-8 83 .... JosephineGordon(3) 9 68
(Jim Goldie) *towards rr: hdwy over 2f out: rdn to chse ldrs wl over 1f out: sn drvn and wknd* **12/1**

0000 **13** *2¼* **Zanetto**[56] 6449 6-8-8 87 .... JoshQuinn(7) 3 65
(John Quinn) *dwlt: a rr* **33/1**

0201 **14** *3¼* **Bossipop**[45] 6766 3-8-11 86 ....(b) RobHornby(3) 8 53
(Tim Easterby) *chsd ldrs: rdn along over 2f oyut: sn wknd* **8/1**

1m 9.9s (-2.60) **Going Correction** -0.075s/f (Stan) course record **14** Ran SP% **127.2**
Speed ratings (Par 107): **114,113,113,110,110 108,106,105,105,104 104,103,100,96**
CSF £207.59 CT £1341.05 TOTE £7.90: £2.20, £7.20, £1.90; EX 239.30 Trifecta £1247.00.
Owner Reality Partnerships V **Bred** Joe Foley & John Grimes **Trained** Great Habton, N Yorks

FOCUS
A decent sprint handicap and a good battle between the first three inside the last. Another pb from the winner.

7859 CANTEEN & COCKTAILS H'CAP (DIV I) 5f (Tp)
6:45 (6:47) (Class 6) (0-60,60) 3-Y-O+ **£2,393** (£712; £355; £177) **Stalls** Centre

Form RPR

3025 **1** **Groundworker (IRE)**[27] 7290 5-9-5 58 ....(t) PaulMulrennan 11 68
(Paul Midgley) *hld up: gd hdwy over 2f out: rdn and str run to ld over 1f out: kpt on strly* **7/4**[1]

0060 **2** *2* **Sir Geoffrey (IRE)**[14] 7595 10-8-12 58 ....(b) NatalieHambling(7) 9 61
(Scott Dixon) *led: rdn along 2f out: hdd over 1f out: drvn and edgd rt ent fnl f: kpt on* **33/1**

6046 **3** *shd* **Indian Pursuit (IRE)**[15] 7585 3-9-7 60 .... JackGarritty 3 62
(John Quinn) *trckd ldrs: hdwy wl over 1f out: rdn and styng on whn n.m.r ent fnl f: sn drvn and kpt on wl towards fin* **5/2**[2]

5300 **4** *1* **Windforpower (IRE)**[11] 7663 6-9-4 57 ....(p) DaleSwift 13 56
(Tracy Waggott) *in tch on outer: rdn along 2f out: drvn and kpt on fnl f* **8/1**[3]

6000 **5** *1* **Lady Joanna Vassa (IRE)**[17] 7533 3-9-2 55 .... ConnorBeasley 6 50
(Richard Guest) *t.k.h: chsd ldr: rdn along over 1f out: drvn and kpt on same pce fnl f* **12/1**

0030 **6** *nk* **A J Cook (IRE)**[7] 7747 6-8-13 52 .... KevinStott 12 46
(Ron Barr) *dwlt and rr: hdwy 2f out: sn rdn and kpt on fnl f* **12/1**

4501 **7** *1¼* **Very First Blade**[35] 7046 7-8-12 51 ....(be) TomEaves 10 41
(Michael Mullineaux) *chsd ldrs: rdn along wl over 1f out: grad wknd* **14/1**

0-06 **8** *½* **Nofizzophobia**[14] 7603 3-8-4 46 oh1 .... NoelGarbutt(3) 4 34
(Derek Shaw) *a towards rr* **100/1**

2300 **9** *hd* **Centre Haafhd**[14] 7604 5-8-9 48 ....[1] TomMarquand 7 35
(Jim Goldie) *a towards rr* **25/1**

4010 **10** *nk* **Pancake Day**[185] 2052 4-9-0 56 ....(v) JosephineGordon(3) 1 42
(David C Griffiths) *chsd ldr: cl up 2f out: sn rdn and wknd over 1f out* **20/1**

1200 **11** *shd* **Fortinbrass (IRE)**[31] 7144 6-9-5 58 .... JoeDoyle 5 44
(John Balding) *chsd ldrs: rdn along over 2f out: sn wknd* **12/1**

0306 **12** *1¼* **Simply Black (IRE)**[19] 7488 5-8-5 49 oh1 ow3 ....(p) AnnStokell(5) 8 30
(Ann Stokell) *dwlt: sn chsng ldrs: rdn along over 2f out: sn wknd* **66/1**

1000 **13** *2¼* **Under Approval**[35] 7046 5-8-11 50 ....(v) BarryMcHugh 2 23
(Karen Tutty) *towards rr: hdwy on inner to chse ldrs 2f out: sn rdn and wknd* **50/1**

58.15s (-1.35) **Going Correction** -0.075s/f (Stan) **13** Ran SP% **121.8**
Speed ratings (Par 101): **107,103,103,102,100 99,97,97,96,96 96,94,90**
CSF £80.44 CT £159.56 TOTE £2.60: £1.10, £7.70, £1.50; EX 54.00 Trifecta £186.20.
Owner Blackburn Family **Bred** Knockainey Stud **Trained** Westow, N Yorks

FOCUS
A moderate affair but it was won by a well-handicapped horse capable of winning again. He's rated to his September C&D form.

7860 CANTEEN & COCKTAILS H'CAP (DIV II) 5f (Tp)
7:15 (7:16) (Class 6) (0-60,59) 3-Y-O+ **£2,393** (£712; £355; £177) **Stalls** Centre

Form RPR

0024 **1** **Lady Bacchus**[10] 7693 3-8-8 46 ....(b) ConnorBeasley 12 54
(Richard Guest) *chsd ldrs on outer: hdwy 2f out: rdn to ld ent fnl f: drvn out* **11/2**[3]

0130 **2** *1¼* **Novabridge**[7] 7747 8-9-0 52 ....(b) JoeDoyle 3 55
(Karen Tutty) *chsd ldr: hdwy to ld 2f out: rdn over 1f out: hdd and drvn ent fnl f: kpt on same pce* **25/1**

6300 **3** *nk* **Young Tiger**[13] 7626 3-9-6 58 .... GrahamLee 11 60
(Tom Tate) *towards rr: hdwy 2f out: rdn over 1f out: styd on fnl f: nrst fin* **6/1**

0000 **4** *2½* **Mercers Row**[14] 7595 9-9-3 55 .... TomEaves 10 48
(Michael Herrington) *hld up in rr: hdwy wl over 1f out: sn rdn and kpt on fnl f: nrst fin* **20/1**

3454 **5** *½* **Men United (FR)**[91] 5270 3-9-6 58 ....(be[1]) TomMarquand 4 49
(Garry Moss) *led: rdn along and hdd 2f out: drvn over 1f out: wknd fnl f* **5/1**[2]

3241 **6** *2* **Whipphound**[14] 7595 8-9-2 57 ....(p) RachelRichardson(3) 5 41
(Ruth Carr) *towards rr: hdwy wl over 1f out: rdn and styd ion strly fnl f: nrst fin* **5/1**[2]

0202 **7** *nk* **Tinsill**[45] 6774 5-8-8 51 .... SophieKilloran(5) 6 34
(Nigel Tinkler) *towards rr:. hdwy on inner wl over 1f out: rdn and kpt on fnl f* **9/1**

4063 **8** *½* **Caymus**[44] 6813 3-8-5 48 ....(t) PhilDennis(5) 1 29
(Tracy Waggott) *in tch: hdwy to chse ldrs 2f out: sn rdn and wknd ent fnl f* **25/1**

3004 **9** *nk* **Minty Jones**[14] 7595 7-8-4 45 ....(v) NathanEvans(3) 9 25
(Michael Mullineaux) *chsd ldrs: pushed along 2f out: rdn wl over 1f out: sn drvn and wknd* **20/1**

0130 **10** *shd* **Knockamany Bends (IRE)**[14] 7596 6-9-0 52 ....(tp) BarryMcHugh 8 32
(John Wainwright) *in tch: rdn along 2f out: sn wknd* **33/1**

5252 **11** *nk* **Frank The Barber (IRE)**[10] 6909 4-9-7 59 ....(t) GrahamGibbons 13 38
(Steph Hollinshead) *prom: rdn along 2f out: sn drvn and wknd* **9/2**[1]

-464 **12** *½* **Life Of Fame**[40] 6909 3-8-12 57 .... PatrickVaughan(7) 7 34
(David O'Meara) *chsd ldrs: rdn along over 2f out: sn wknd* **7/1**

0005 **13** *6* **Jessie Allan (IRE)**[14] 7603 5-8-0 45 .... JamieGormley(7) 2
(Jim Goldie) *a towards rr* **100/1**

58.76s (-0.74) **Going Correction** -0.075s/f (Stan) **13** Ran SP% **124.8**
Speed ratings (Par 101): **102,100,99,95,94 91,91,90,89,89 89,88,78**
CSF £147.29 CT £899.76 TOTE £7.40: £2.70, £5.10, £2.80; EX 149.50 Trifecta £1675.50.
Owner Mrs Alison Guest **Bred** G Tomkins & J Luck **Trained** Ingmanthorpe, W Yorks

The Form Book, Raceform Ltd, Newbury, RG14 5SJ

FOCUS
The slower of the two divisions by 0.61sec. The third looks the best guide.
T/Jkpt: £1,333.30 to a £1 stake. Pool: £10,000 - 7.5 winning units T/Plt: £60.00 to a £1 stake. Pool: £83,846.74 - 1018.62 winning units T/Qpdt: £26.70 to a £1 stake. Pool: £10,708.12 - 296.15 winning units **Joe Rowntree**

7721 SAINT-CLOUD (L-H)
Tuesday, November 8

OFFICIAL GOING: Turf: very soft

7861a PRIX ISOLA BELLA - FONDS EUROPEEN DE L'ELEVAGE (LISTED RACE) (3YO+ FILLIES & MARES) (TURF) 1m
1:20 (1:20) 3-Y-0+ **£19,117** (£7,647; £5,735; £3,823; £1,911)

RPR
1 **Blossomtime**[25] 7348 3-8-11 0 ThierryJarnet 4 102+
(H-A Pantall, France) *midfield: smooth hdwy early in st and rdn to chal over 1f out: led fnl f: kpt on wl: shade cosily* **58/10**
2 ½ **Game Theory (IRE)**[34] 7087 4-9-3 0 StephanePasquier 1 105+
(N Clement, France) **21/10**[1]
3 3 **Saimaa (IRE)**[23] 7397 3-8-11 0 AlexisBadel 2 94
(H-F Devin, France) **71/10**
4 ½ **Incahoots**[48] 6693 4-9-3 0 AurelienLemaitre 8 97
(F Head, France) **10/1**
5 ½ **Coisa Boa (IRE)**[23] 7397 4-9-0 0 AntoineHamelin 7 93
(J E Hammond, France) **18/1**
6 snk **Golden Stunner (IRE)**[23] 7397 3-8-11 0 ChristopheSoumillon 6 91
(Ralph Beckett) *midfield: rdn early in st: styd on same pce and sn n.d* **23/5**[2]
7 2½ **Sant'Amanza (FR)**[38] 5-9-0 0 CristianDemuro 5 87
(R Le Dren Doleuze, France) **26/5**[3]
8 nk **Bandanetta (FR)**[16] 4-9-0 0 RaphaelMarchelli 3 86
(A Bonin, France) **23/1**
9 3 **Delve (IRE)**[38] 6939 3-8-11 0 OlivierPeslier 9 78
(Sir Michael Stoute) *trckd ldr: rdn and brief effrt into st: sn no ex and btn: wknd* **13/1**

1m 47.81s (0.31) **9 Ran SP% 119.0**
WFA 3 from 4yo+ 2lb
WIN (incl. 1 euro stake): 6.80. PLACES: 1.80, 1.60, 2.00. DF: 9.40. SF: 27.10.
Owner Godolphin SNC **Bred** Berend Van Dalfsen **Trained** France

7862a PRIX SOLITUDE (LISTED RACE) (3YO FILLIES) (TURF) 1m 2f
1:50 (1:50) 3-Y-0 **£20,220** (£8,088; £6,066; £4,044; £2,022)

RPR
1 **The Black Princess (FR)**[145] 3297 3-8-13 0 ChristopheSoumillon 8 103+
(John Gosden) *midfield in tch: rdn 2f out: styd on steadily and up to ld cl home* **19/10**[1]
2 ¾ **Maquette (USA)**[101] 4904 3-8-13 0 VincentCheminaud 1 101
(A Fabre, France) **10/1**
3 2 **Happy Approach (FR)**[21] 7456 3-8-13 0 AntoineHamelin 9 97+
(M Nigge, France) **11/1**
4 ½ **Divine Bere (FR)**[13] 3-8-13 0 AurelienLemaitre 3 96
(E Leenders, France) **14/1**
5 ½ **Switching (USA)**[16] 7568 3-9-3 0 Pierre-CharlesBoudot 6 99
(A Fabre, France) *hld up in midfield: rdn over 2f out: hung lft u.p and outpcd by ldrs fnl f* **12/5**[2]
6 1¾ **Dozule (FR)**[28] 3-8-13 0 CristianDemuro 5 92
(E Lellouche, France) **10/1**
7 1½ **Very Dashing**[36] 7029 3-8-13 0 StephanePasquier 2 89
(Luca Cumani) *trckd ldr on inner: rdn and effrt into st: no ex ent fnl f: wknd* **25/1**
8 2 **Salve Sicilia (FR)**[19] 3-8-13 0 MarcLerner 7 85
(Waldemar Hickst, Germany) **41/1**
9 15 **Edya**[36] 7029 3-8-13 0 AlexisBadel 10 55
(G Botti, France) **30/1**
10 nk **Deitee (FR)**[28] 7264 3-8-13 0 OlivierPeslier 4 54
(Louis Baudron, France) **66/10**[3]

2m 17.38s (1.38) **10 Ran SP% 119.7**
WIN (incl. 1 euro stake): 2.90. PLACES: 1.60, 2.80, 3.00. DF: 19.20. SF: 31.80.
Owner R J H Geffen **Bred** Petra Bloodstock Agency Ltd **Trained** Newmarket, Suffolk

7760 KEMPTON (A.W) (R-H)
Wednesday, November 9

OFFICIAL GOING: Polytrack: standard to slow
Wind: Across, moderate becoming light Weather: Cloudy, cold

7863 RACINGUK.COM H'CAP 5f (P)
4:25 (4:27) (Class 7) (0-50,50) 3-Y-0+ **£1,940** (£577; £288; £144) **Stalls** Low

Form RPR
0106 1 **Captain Scooby**[8] 7747 10-9-4 **49** (b) ConnorBeasley 5 55
(Richard Guest) *slowly away: detached in last and urged along: clsd over 1f out: styd on wl fnl f to ld last 75yds* **3/1**[1]
4054 2 ½ **Redalani (IRE)**[53] 6586 6-9-3 **48** (b) ShaneKelly 8 52
(Alan Brown) *pressed ldr: rdn over 1f out: narrow ld 150yds out: hdd and outpcd last 75yds* **10/1**
6035 3 ¾ **Chandresh**[18] 7534 3-9-3 **48** (v) KieranO'Neill 3 49
(Robert Cowell) *chsd ldrs: rdn 2f out: nt qckn over 1f out: kpt on fnl f to take 3rd last strides* **6/1**
2600 4 ½ **Give Us A Belle (IRE)**[42] 6865 7-9-3 **48** (v) RobertHavlin 2 48
(Christine Dunnett) *urged along to ld: hdd and one pce last 150yds* **8/1**
0052 5 ¾ **Presto Boy**[60] 6312 4-8-12 **50** (e) FinleyMarsh[(7)] 7 47
(Richard Hughes) *in tch: pushed along over 1f out: kpt on but nvr able to threaten* **5/1**[3]
1600 6 ½ **Topsoil**[43] 6852 3-9-3 **48** RenatoSouza 1 46
(Ronald Harris) *taken down early: reluctant to enter stall: t.k.h and racd awkwardly bhd ldng pair: trapped on inner fr over 1f out: lost pls fnl f* **7/2**[2]
2150 7 hd **Diminutive (IRE)**[15] 7595 4-9-3 **48** (p) StevieDonohoe 6 42
(Grace Harris) *a in last pair: detached in last 1f out: styd on last 100yds* **10/1**
0445 8 1½ **Hurricane Alert**[42] 6865 4-9-2 **47** (v) AdamBeschizza 9 36
(Mark Hoad) *taken down early: a towards rr: wknd fnl f* **12/1**

1m 0.73s (0.23) **Going Correction** -0.05s/f (Stan) **8 Ran SP% 115.2**
Speed ratings (Par 97): **96,95,94,93,92 91,90,88**
CSF £33.73 CT £171.08 TOTE £3.00: £1.10, £2.90, £2.50; EX 38.70 Trifecta £155.00.
Owner The Captain Scooby Syndicate **Bred** Hellwood Stud Farm & Paul Davies (h'Gate) **Trained** Ingmanthorpe, W Yorks

FOCUS
A very moderate sprint handicap. They went a decent gallop on standard to slow Polytrack which suited the winner.

7864 32RED H'CAP 5f (P)
4:55 (4:57) (Class 3) (0-95,92) 3-Y-0+
£7,158 (£2,143; £1,071; £535; £267; £134) **Stalls** Low

Form RPR
2445 1 **Dynamo Walt (IRE)**[13] 7643 5-8-7 **81** (v) NoelGarbutt[(3)] 3 88
(Derek Shaw) *t.k.h: chsd ldng pair: chal on inner fnl f: styd on best to ld last 50yds* **8/1**
000 2 hd **Calypso Choir**[39] 6946 3-8-3 **79** ow1 MitchGodwin[(5)] 6 85
(Sylvester Kirk) *chsd ldr: chal over 1f out: upsides 50yds out: jst outpcd* **12/1**
0266 3 nk **Just That Lord**[8] 7752 3-9-1 **86** WilliamCarson 4 91
(Bill Turner) *led at gd pce: rdn over 1f out: worn down last 50yds* **7/1**
1205 4 ¾ **Princess Tansy**[24] 7398 4-8-7 **78** oh1 (b[1]) TomMarquand 10 80+
(Gay Kelleway) *forced to r wd: disp 5th: rdn and styd on fr over 1f out to take 4th fnl f: nrst fin* **25/1**
1004 5 1¼ **Outrage**[13] 7643 4-8-10 **84** JosephineGordon[(3)] 2 82
(Daniel Kubler) *in tch disputing 5th: nt qckn over 1f out: kpt on fnl f: nvr able to threaten* **7/2**[1]
0216 6 1 **Burning Thread (IRE)**[13] 7643 9-8-1 **79** (b) DavidEgan[(7)] 1 73
(David Elsworth) *in tch disputing 5th: rdn and no prog over 1f out: n.d fnl f* **9/2**[2]
600 7 1¾ **Brother Tiger**[106] 4735 7-9-7 **92** AdamKirby 9 80
(David C Griffiths) *taken down early: chsd ldng trio: rdn 2f out: no imp and wknd fnl f* **6/1**[3]
406 8 1¾ **Krystallite**[48] 6699 3-8-7 **78** oh1 KieranO'Neill 8 60
(Scott Dixon) *slowly away: off the pce in 8th: nvr on terms* **12/1**
6000 9 ½ **El Viento (FR)**[54] 6539 8-8-11 **82** (v) PaulHanagan 7 62+
(Richard Fahey) *bdly outpcd in last: nvr a factor* **9/2**[2]

59.19s (-1.31) **Going Correction** -0.05s/f (Stan) **9 Ran SP% 115.7**
Speed ratings (Par 107): **108,107,107,106,104 102,99,96,96**
CSF £98.47 CT £706.51 TOTE £7.50: £2.20, £4.60, £2.60; EX 76.90 Trifecta £1798.80.
Owner Brian Johnson (Northamptonshire) **Bred** Dan Major **Trained** Sproxton, Leics
■ Stewards' Enquiry : Mitch Godwin two-day ban: used whip above permitted level (Nov 23-24)

FOCUS
A good sprint handicap. They went a decent pace and it was an exciting three-way go by the line. It proved difficult to make up ground from off the pace but the form is sound, taken at face value around the third and fourth.

7865 32RED CASINO MEDIAN AUCTION MAIDEN STKS 1m (P)
5:25 (5:29) (Class 6) 2-Y-0 **£2,264** (£673; £336; £168) **Stalls** Low

Form RPR
0 1 **Simoon (IRE)**[19] 7501 2-9-5 0 DavidProbert 8 74+
(Andrew Balding) *w.w in midfield: pushed along and no immediate prog over 2f out: shkn up over 1f out and stl only in 7th: r.o wl fnl f to ld last strides* **11/4**[1]
53 2 nk **Wordsearch (USA)**[12] 7658 2-9-2 0 JosephineGordon[(3)] 11 73
(Hugo Palmer) *trckd ldrs: shkn up and prog to ld wl over 1f out: drvn and more than a l ahd fnl f: styd on but hdd last strides* **7/2**[2]
3 1½ **Golden Wolf (IRE)** 2-9-5 0 ShaneKelly 6 70
(Richard Hughes) *wl in tch: shkn up and prog 2f out: chsd ldr 1f out: styd on but lost 2nd last 100yds* **50/1**
5 4 3 **Modern Life (IRE)**[22] 7424 2-9-5 0 SeanLevey 12 63
(David Elsworth) *plld way through to press ldr after 2f to 2f out: drvn over 1f out: outpcd after* **7/1**
0 5 ½ **Cape Cruiser (USA)**[37] 7012 2-9-5 0 JohnFahy 7 62
(Ralph Beckett) *wl in rr: drvn over 2f out: styd on fr over 1f out: nrst fin* **20/1**
0 6 ¾ **Take A Turn (IRE)**[12] 7665 2-9-5 0 GeorgeBaker 13 60
(David Lanigan) *settled in midfield: pushed along over 2f out: kpt on steadily fr over 1f out: nt disgracd* **50/1**
7 ½ **Speedo Boy (FR)** 2-9-5 0 RobertHavlin 4 59
(Ian Williams) *in tch: rdn over 2f out: one pce and nvr threatened* **50/1**
0 8 hd **Maori Bob (IRE)**[27] 7297 2-9-2 0 LouisSteward[(3)] 10 59
(Michael Bell) *pressed ldr 2f: styd cl up: rdn over 2f out: fdd over 1f out* **25/1**
6 9 1¼ **Nobleman (GER)**[31] 7187 2-9-5 0 JimmyFortune 3 56
(Hughie Morrison) *led to wl over 1f out: wknd qckly fnl f* **12/1**
32 10 1 **Salieri (FR)**[112] 4524 2-9-5 0 FergusSweeney 5 53
(Alan King) *t.k.h: chsd ldrs: effrt on inner 2f out: wknd jst over 1f out* **4/1**[3]
0 11 ¾ **Russian Regard (IRE)**[19] 7503 2-9-5 0 RyanTate 1 52
(Jonathan Portman) *dwlt: rcvrd into midfield: no prog 2f out: fdd* **50/1**
4 12 ½ **Babamunchkin**[21] 7466 2-9-0 0 PatCosgrave 9 45
(Michael Bell) *dwlt: a in rr: sltly impeded whn shkn up over 2f out: no prog* **9/2**
13 3¾ **Damsah (QA)** 2-8-11 0 NoelGarbutt[(3)] 14 37
(Conrad Allen) *mostly in last pair: brief effrt on outer 1/2-way: sn btn* **66/1**
14 4½ **Hot Lick** 2-9-2 0[1] RobHornby[(3)] 2 31
(Andrew Balding) *s.s: rn green and mostly in last: a bhd* **33/1**

1m 41.0s (1.20) **Going Correction** -0.05s/f (Stan) **14 Ran SP% 128.1**
Speed ratings (Par 94): **92,91,90,87,86 85,85,85,84,83 82,81,78,73**
CSF £12.38 TOTE £4.00: £1.50, £1.90, £8.80; EX 17.30 Trifecta £1223.80.
Owner Lord Blyth **Bred** Lemington Grange Stud **Trained** Kingsclere, Hants

FOCUS
An ordinary juvenile maiden. They went a modest gallop, but those on the lead didn't really settle, and the winner came with a rare late rattle. He took a nuce step forward from his debut.

7866 32RED ON THE APP STORE NURSERY H'CAP 1m (P)
5:55 (5:57) (Class 6) (0-60,60) 2-Y-0 **£2,264** (£673; £336; £168) **Stalls** Low

Form RPR
4062 1 **Dominating (GER)**[8] 7734 2-9-7 **60** PJMcDonald 11 67+
(Mark Johnston) *in tch bhd ldrs: shkn up over 2f out: clsd over 1f out: led ins fnl f: styd on wl* **9/2**[1]
000 2 1¼ **Still Waiting**[16] 7574 2-9-4 **57** RobertHavlin 10 61
(William Jarvis) *sn chsd ldrs: wnt 2nd wl over 1f out: clsd to chal jst ins fnl f: wnr sn wnt past and outpcd after* **14/1**

5333 **3** *3 ¼* **Moneyoryourlife**[29] 7244 2-9-4 **57** SeanLevey 4 54
(Richard Hannon) *led: had many in trble over 2f out: drvn over 1f out: hdd & wknd ins fnl f* **5/1**[2]

5000 **4** *½* **Our Boy John (IRE)**[16] 7570 2-9-4 **57** JackGarritty 8 53
(Richard Fahey) *off the pce in midfield: u.p over 2f out: kpt on fr over 1f out: nvr nrr* **10/1**

0050 **5** *nk* **Aventus (IRE)**[36] 7047 2-9-1 **54** PatCosgrave 2 49
(Jane Chapple-Hyam) *prom: chsd ldr wl over 2f out to wl over 1f out: fdd* **11/2**[3]

3600 **6** *1 ¾* **Quick Thought (IRE)**[32] 7147 2-9-2 **60** CallumShepherd(5) 7 51
(Dr Jon Scargill) *stdd s: hld up in last and wl off the pce: shkn up over 2f out: passed rivals fnl 2f: nvr involved* **9/2**[1]

3354 **7** *1* **Tigerfish (IRE)**[16] 7571 2-8-9 **48** KieranO'Neill 3 36
(William Stone) *chsd ldrs: pushed along 3f out: steadily wknd u.p fr 2f out* **8/1**

000 **8** *5* **Kingston Tasmania**[27] 7297 2-8-10 **52** (b[1]) RobHornby(3) 13 29
(Andrew Balding) *wl in rr: nvr a factor but modest late prog* **16/1**

2030 **9** *1* **Alligator**[20] 7482 2-9-7 **60** [1] AdamKirby 9 35
(Ed Dunlop) *wl away but sn lost pl: snatched up after 1f and dropped to rr: rdn over 2f out: no great prog* **10/1**

4005 **10** *1 ¾* **Beepeecee**[8] 7734 2-9-3 **56** [1] ShaneKelly 14 27
(Richard Hughes) *chsd ldrs on outer: lost grnd bnd 3f out: sn drvn: wknd 2f out* **16/1**

6000 **11** *2* **Hi There Silver (IRE)**[22] 7423 2-8-7 **46** ow1 TomMarquand 1 12
(Michael Madgwick) *lost pl on inner after 1f: brief effrt u.p over 2f out: sn no prog* **50/1**

0300 **12** *14* **Secret Ballerina**[41] 6896 2-8-9 **48** AdamBeschizza 6
(Julia Feilden) *dwlt: a wl in rr: t.o* **50/1**

000 **13** *3 ¾* **Venetian Proposal (IRE)**[28] 7277 2-8-8 **47** [1] WilliamCarson 5
(Zoe Davison) *chsd ldr to wl over 2f out: hanging bdly and wknd rapidly: t.o* **100/1**

1m 39.63s (-0.17) **Going Correction** -0.05s/f (Stan) 13 Ran SP% **121.1**
Speed ratings (Par 94): **98,96,93,93,92 90,89,84,83,82 80,66,62**
CSF £69.45 CT £344.47 TOTE £5.80: £1.80, £4.90, £1.70; EX 71.60 Trifecta £120.90.
Owner A D Spence **Bred** Gestut Etzean **Trained** Middleham Moor, N Yorks

FOCUS
A modest nursery handicap. The pace collapsed to a degree as the long-time leader got tired in the final furlong but the overall time was respectable for the grade. The form could rate a bit better.

7867 32RED/IRISH STALLION FARMS EBF MAIDEN STKS 6f (P)
6:25 (6:25) (Class 5) 2-Y-O **£3,234** (£962; £481; £240) **Stalls** Low

Form RPR

22 **1** **Hathiq (IRE)**[116] 4390 2-9-5 0 PaulHanagan 7 79+
(Owen Burrows) *trckd ldrs: smooth prog 2f out and poised to chal: shkn up to ld jst ins fnl f: drvn after and jst hld on* **10/11**[1]

2 *hd* **Cartographer** 2-9-0 0 DavidProbert 12 74+
(Martyn Meade) *settled in last pair: pushed along over 2f out: brought v wd and rdn over 1f out: gd prog after: tk 2nd ins fnl f: gaining on wnr at fin* **20/1**

3 *1 ½* **Saluti (IRE)** 2-9-5 0 RobertHavlin 11 74+
(Amanda Perrett) *trckd ldrs: gng strly 2f out: rdn to chal on inner 1f out: outpcd last 100yds* **50/1**

3 **4** *¾* **Ripp Orf (IRE)**[22] 7424 2-9-5 0 SeanLevey 6 72
(David Elsworth) *wl in rr: rdn over 2f out: styd on u.p fr over 1f out: nrst fin* **6/1**[3]

5 *½* **Big Tour (IRE)** 2-9-5 0 KevinStott 4 71
(Saeed bin Suroor) *prom: trckd ldr 1/2-way: rdn to chal and upsides 1f out: sn fdd* **5/2**[2]

0 **6** *1 ¼* **Delfie Lane**[121] 4205 2-9-5 0 ShaneKelly 1 67
(Richard Hughes) *led: rdn 2f out: hdd & wknd jst ins fnl f* **50/1**

0 **7** *¾* **Revel**[21] 7468 2-9-5 0 [1] AdamBeschizza 9 65
(Stuart Williams) *wl in rr: gd prog on inner 2f out: pushed along to trck ldrs jst over 1f out: nt clr run briefly ins fnl f: lost pls after: nt wout promise* **20/1**

0 **8** *1 ¼* **Nuncio**[53] 6570 2-9-5 0 GeorgeBaker 8 61
(Roger Charlton) *stdd s: hld up in last and sn so detached as to be nrly t.o: shuffled along over 2f out: kpt on fr over 1f out: likely improver* **33/1**

9 *nk* **Amenta (IRE)** 2-8-11 0 KieranShoemark(3) 2 55
(Roger Charlton) *in tch on inner: effrt 2f out: no prog over 1f out: wknd fnl f* **100/1**

10 *1 ¼* **Munro** 2-9-5 0 GrahamGibbons 10 56
(Ralph Beckett) *chsd ldrs but rn green: wknd over 1f out* **14/1**

53 **11** *7* **Peace Dreamer (IRE)**[27] 7296 2-9-0 0 PatCosgrave 3 30
(Robert Cowell) *chsd ldr: hung bdly lft bnd 3f out and sn dropped to rr* **25/1**

1m 12.53s (-0.57) **Going Correction** -0.05s/f (Stan) 11 Ran SP% **123.1**
Speed ratings (Par 96): **101,100,98,97,97 95,94,92,92,90 81**
CSF £28.75 TOTE £1.80: £1.10, £7.60, £7.10; EX 44.90 Trifecta £1456.70.
Owner Hamdan Al Maktoum **Bred** Shadwell Estate Company Limited **Trained** Lambourn, Berks

FOCUS
A fair juvenile maiden. The winner is talented, with an abundance of speed, and plenty displayed promise in behind. The form helps with the starting level.

7868 32RED.COM CONDITIONS STKS 7f (P)
6:55 (6:56) (Class 2) 3-Y-O+
£11,827 (£3,541; £1,770; £885; £442; £222) **Stalls** Low

Form RPR

0400 **1** **Chookie Royale**[35] 7068 8-9-3 104 (p) TomEaves 2 107
(Keith Dalgleish) *taken down early: difficult to load: mde all: decisive advantage fr 2f out: drvn over 1f out: styd on wl* **16/1**

0466 **2** *1 ¼* **Golden Amber (IRE)**[14] 7610 5-8-12 93 PJMcDonald 4 98
(Dean Ivory) *trckd ldng pair: shkn up over 2f out: sn chsd wnr: styd on but no imp fnl f* **33/1**

0200 **3** *1* **Donjuan Triumphant (IRE)**[25] 7350 3-9-2 113 [1] JackGarritty 1 99
(Richard Fahey) *t.k.h early: hld up in tch: rdn and prog to chse ldng pair over 1f out: kpt on but nvr able to threaten* **5/2**[2]

-054 **4** *¾* **Valbchek (IRE)**[19] 7525 7-9-3 90 (p) AdamKirby 8 98
(Jane Chapple-Hyam) *hld up in last trio: shkn up and prog 2f out: tk 4th fnl f: styd on but unable to threaten* **16/1**

3220 **5** *½* **Mitchum Swagger**[25] 7352 4-9-3 112 GeorgeBaker 3 97
(David Lanigan) *trckd ldrs: shkn up and nt qckn 2f out: n.d after: kpt on fnl f* **11/8**[1]

620- **6** *3* **Gabriel's Lad (IRE)**[389] 7282 7-9-3 105 TomQueally 6 89
(Denis Coakley) *stdd s: hld up in last: rdn 2f out: no great prog* **33/1**

4350 **7** *hd* **Emell**[25] 7354 6-9-3 95 (b) KieranO'Neill 7 88
(Richard Hannon) *mostly chsd wnr to 2f out: wknd over 1f out* **14/1**

0500 **8** *2* **Quixote (GER)**[16] 7573 6-9-3 95 GeorgeDowning 9 83
(Tony Carroll) *racd wd: a towards rr: last and struggling 2f out* **66/1**

/3-0 **9** *6* **Faydhan (USA)**[13] 7651 4-9-3 98 PaulHanagan 5 81
(John Gosden) *trckd ldrs: shkn up and no rspnse over 2f out: wknd over 1f out: eased* **4/1**[3]

1m 24.5s (-1.50) **Going Correction** -0.05s/f (Stan)
WFA 3 from 4yo+ 1lb 9 Ran SP% **116.5**
Speed ratings (Par 109): **106,104,103,102,102 98,98,96,89**
CSF £418.66 TOTE £16.70: £2.10, £6.40, £1.80; EX 206.30 Trifecta £1946.20.
Owner Raeburn Brick Limited **Bred** D And J Raeburn **Trained** Carluke, S Lanarks

FOCUS
A good quality conditions contest. The winner made all from a good draw in dominant fashion, and in a remarkably similar time to last year. He didn't need to be at his best.

7869 32RED LONDON MIDDLE DISTANCE FINAL H'CAP 1m 3f (P)
7:25 (7:29) (Class 2) 3-Y-O+
£34,237 (£10,252; £5,126; £2,563; £1,281; £643) **Stalls** Low

Form RPR

3124 **1** **Sixties Groove (IRE)**[33] 7117 3-9-4 **91** (p) AdamKirby 11 102+
(Jeremy Noseda) *hld up in last trio: rapid prog on inner over 2f out: rdn to ld jst over 1f out: hung lft fnl f but styd on wl* **5/2**[1]

222 **2** *½* **Rock Steady (IRE)**[35] 7067 3-8-11 **87** KieranShoemark(3) 5 97
(Roger Charlton) *hld up in midfield: clsd on ldrs gng strly fr 2f out: rdn to take 2nd wl ins fnl f: styd on but rather limited chal* **8/1**

6124 **3** *nk* **I Am Not Here (IRE)**[42] 6876 5-8-0 **75** DavidEgan(7) 6 84
(Brian Ellison) *hld up in midfield: gd prog 2f out to chal jst over 1f out: chsd wnr tl wl ins fnl f: hld whn short of room nr fin* **12/1**

2412 **4** *1 ¾* **Sam Missile (IRE)**[49] 6675 3-9-4 **91** GeorgeBaker 8 98
(James Fanshawe) *hld up in rr: rdn and prog fr 2f out: tk 4th fnl f: no imp ldng trio after* **11/4**[2]

0334 **5** *nk* **Sennockian Star**[18] 7535 6-9-0 **82** (v) PJMcDonald 1 88
(Mark Johnston) *trckd ldrs: clsd to chal wl over 1f out: fdd ins fnl f* **12/1**

6423 **6** *2 ½* **Charlies Mate**[42] 6870 5-9-0 **82** KierenFox 12 84
(John Best) *pushed up fr wd draw to ld after 1f: hdd & wknd jst over 1f out* **16/1**

6410 **7** *1 ¾* **Banish (USA)**[33] 7117 3-9-2 **92** (bt) JosephineGordon(3) 3 91
(Hugo Palmer) *t.k.h: trckd ldrs: rdn and nt qckn over 2f out: sn lost pl and btn* **8/1**

1060 **8** *hd* **Dutch Uncle**[116] 4399 4-9-2 **84** PatCosgrave 2 82
(Ed Dunlop) *led 1f: styd prom: tk 2nd over 2f out: upsides sn after: wknd over 1f out* **25/1**

325 **9** *1* **Plymouth Sound**[49] 6676 4-8-10 **78** (b) JohnFahy 7 75
(Eve Johnson Houghton) *in tch on outer in midfield: rdn and fnd nil 2f out: sn btn* **33/1**

100 **10** *nk* **Zamperini (IRE)**[18] 7538 4-9-5 **87** (b[1]) JimmyFortune 9 83
(Mike Murphy) *s.s: racd in last pair: effrt on inner over 2f out: sn no prog* **50/1**

15 **11** *¾* **Storm Rock**[18] 7546 4-9-10 **92** DavidProbert 10 90
(Harry Dunlop) *hld up towards rr: effrt whn hmpd 2f out: lost momentum and no ch after* **25/1**

6334 **12** *1* **Red Rannagh (IRE)**[14] 7618 3-8-13 **86** (t[1]) TomEaves 4 79
(David Simcock) *s.s: mostly in last: brought wd in st and no prog* **15/2**[3]

3-40 **13** *18* **Petrucci (IRE)**[18] 7535 4-8-13 **81** MartinLane 13 44
(Derek Shaw) *pushed up to press ldr after 2f: lost 2nd over 2f out and wknd rapidly: t.o* **50/1**

2m 19.87s (-2.03) **Going Correction** -0.05s/f (Stan)
WFA 3 from 4yo+ 5lb 13 Ran SP% **125.0**
Speed ratings (Par 109): **105,104,104,103,102 101,99,99,98,98 98,97,84**
CSF £23.32 CT £212.90 TOTE £3.50: £1.70, £2.70, £3.60; EX 26.80 Trifecta £334.70.
Owner Mrs Susan Roy **Bred** Minch Bloodstock **Trained** Newmarket, Suffolk
■ This event was rearranged from the meeting that was curtailed nine days earlier.

FOCUS
The feature contest was a good middle-distance handicap. The pace slowed down the back straight and the winning time suffered but it shouldn't be used as a stick to beat a convincing winner.

7870 100% PROFIT BOOST AT 32REDSPORT.COM H'CAP 1m 3f (P)
7:55 (8:00) (Class 6) (0-65,65) 3-Y-O+ **£2,264** (£673; £336; £168) **Stalls** Low

Form RPR

304 **1** **Art Of Swing (IRE)**[36] 7052 4-9-7 **62** GeorgeBaker 8 76+
(Gary Moore) *pressed ldr after 2f tl led over 2f out: shkn up and qckly clr: in n.d after* **6/1**[2]

356 **2** *5* **The Ginger Berry**[22] 7429 6-9-5 **65** CallumShepherd(5) 3 70+
(Dr Jon Scargill) *t.k.h: hld up towards rr: prog over 2f out: rdn to take 2nd jst over 1f out: kpt on but no ch w wnr* **7/1**[3]

5440 **3** *½* **Paper Faces (USA)**[14] 7613 3-9-2 **62** [1] JackMitchell 6 64
(Roger Varian) *led 2f: styd prom: rdn over 2f out: styd on to press for 2nd fnl f: no ch w wnr* **10/1**

0606 **4** *hd* **Ruby Wednesday**[18] 7531 3-9-1 **61** KierenFox 10 63
(John Best) *hld up in last trio: rdn and prog on inner fr 2f out: styd on fnl f: nrst fin* **16/1**

231 **5** *nk* **Gold Return (IRE)**[19] 7516 3-9-3 **63** ShaneKelly 12 64
(David Lanigan) *trckd ldrs: rdn and nt qckn over 2f out and sn outpcd: kpt on again fr over 1f out* **7/2**[1]

4542 **6** *½* **Estibdaad (IRE)**[14] 7613 6-9-9 **64** (t) MartinLane 4 64
(Paddy Butler) *cl up: rdn over 2f out: kpt on same pce fr over 1f out* **10/1**

1543 **7** *½* **Tyrsal (IRE)**[14] 7613 5-9-8 **63** AdamBeschizza 2 63
(Clifford Lines) *trckd ldrs: rdn 2f out: outpcd sn after: one pce fr over 1f out* **8/1**

3200 **8** *½* **Tommys Geal**[28] 7272 4-9-7 **62** TomQueally 13 61
(Michael Madgwick) *hld up in last trio: prog towards inner 2f out: trying to press for a pl whn nt clr run 1f out: no ch after* **33/1**

4062 **9** *hd* **Earthwindorfire**[14] 7614 5-9-3 **61** (p) JosephineGordon(3) 9 59
(Geoffrey Deacon) *led after 2f to over 2f out: sn no ch w wnr: lost 2nd jst over 1f out and wknd* **8/1**

0320 **10** *shd* **Angelical (IRE)**[8] 7753 3-9-1 **61** GrahamGibbons 1 59
(Daniel Mark Loughnane) *nvr bttr than midfield: rdn and no imp ldrs 2f out: one pce* **16/1**

6446 **11** *½* **Nonchalant**[12] 7656 5-9-8 **63** KieranO'Neill 7 61
(Hugo Froud) *hld up wl in rr: gng wl enough over 2f out: hanging whn impeded sn after: kpt on but no ch* **20/1**

4226 **12** *4* **Fair Comment**[44] 6825 6-9-5 **60** DavidProbert 5 51
(Michael Blanshard) *t.k.h: hld up towards rr: hanging and fnd nil whn rdn over 2f out* **10/1**

603/ **13** *3 ¾* **New Reaction**[398] 5282 5-9-2 **60** LouisSteward(3) 14 45
(Alexandra Dunn) *hld up in last: rdn and no prog 3f out* **100/1**

16-3 **14** 10 **Nebula Storm (IRE)**[72] 5958 9-9-4 **59**.......................(vt) SteveDrowne 11 28
(Michael Blake) *prog on wd outside to press ldng pair 1/2-way to 3f out: wknd rapidly: t.o* **20/1**

2m 22.28s (0.38) **Going Correction** -0.05s/f (Stan)
WFA 3 from 4yo+ 5lb **14** Ran SP% **123.7**
Speed ratings (Par 101): **96,92,92,91,91 91,90,90,90,90 89,87,84,77**
CSF £47.22 CT £426.11 TOTE £8.00: £2.70, £3.00, £4.50; EX 64.50 Trifecta £1095.00.
Owner T Jacobs & J E Harley **Bred** James Doyle **Trained** Lower Beeding, W Sussex

FOCUS
A modest middle-distance handicap. The winner took a decisive grip on proceedings from the top of the straight, even if he was well placed to do so off ordinary fractions.
T/Jkpt: Not won. T/Plt: £327.70 to a £1 stake. Pool: £81,534.23. 181.60 winning units. T/Qpdt: £33.10 to a £1 stake. Pool: £19,124.09. 427.32 winning units. **Jonathan Neesom**

7871 - 7878a (Foreign Racing) - See Raceform Interactive

7783 CHANTILLY (R-H)

Wednesday, November 9

OFFICIAL GOING: Polytrack: standard

7879a PRIX DE L'ALLEE MASSINE (CLAIMER) (2YO) (POLYTRACK) 6f 110y
1:05 (12:00) 2-Y-O **£9,926** (£3,970; £2,977; £1,985; £992)

RPR

1 **Admiralty Arch**[18] 7549 2-9-1 0.. AlexisBadel 5 81
(Richard Hughes) *w.w in tch: drvn to chal appr 1 1/2f out: led 1f out: r.o gamely* **16/5**[2]

2 1/2 **Bocca De La Verita (FR)**[13] 7655 2-8-13 0................. ThierryThulliez 4 78
(C Lerner, France) **89/10**

3 hd **La Fibrossi (FR)**[20] 7490 2-8-8 0...................................... FabriceVeron 7 72
(H-A Pantall, France) **14/1**

4 snk **Douceur D'Antan (FR)**[33] 7136 2-8-13 0.................... MaximeGuyon 11 77
(P Adda, France) **63/10**

5 1 **Holy Makfi**[8] 2-9-3 0..(b[1]) TheoBachelot 8 78
(J-Y Artu, France) **27/1**

6 1 **Neelanjali (FR)**[19] 2-9-1 0.................................... ChristopheSoumillon 9 73
(N Caullery, France) **47/10**[3]

7 hd **Notre Sage (FR)**[20] 7490 2-8-8 0...................................... RonanThomas 1 65
(P Decouz, France) **22/1**

8 2 **Sunday Winner (FR)**[8] 2-8-11 0..........................(b) StephanePasquier 6 63
(Y Gourraud, France) **17/1**

9 shd **Aothea (GER)** 2-8-8 0... AntoineHamelin 10 60
(J Hirschberger, Germany) **62/1**

10 3 **Frozen Queen (IRE)**[6] 2-8-8 0.................................. IoritzMendizabal 3 51
(D Windrif, France) **32/1**

11 5 **Chaplin (FR)**[8] 2-9-5 0...(p) Pierre-CharlesBoudot 2 48
(J Phelippon, France) **5/2**[1]

WIN (incl. 1 euro stake): 4.20. PLACES: 1.90, 2.80, 3.80. DF: 22.90. SF: 37.30
Owner The Queens & Partner **Bred** G B Partnership **Trained** Lambourn, Berkshire

7880 - (Foreign Racing) - See Raceform Interactive

7811 CHELMSFORD (A.W) (L-H)

Thursday, November 10

OFFICIAL GOING: Polytrack: standard
Wind: moderate, half against Weather: patchy cloud with showers

7881 BET TOTEPLACEPOT AT TOTESPORT.COM NURSERY H'CAP 7f (P)
4:25 (4:25) (Class 6) (0-60,60) 2-Y-O **£2,911** (£866; £432; £216) **Stalls** Low

Form RPR

0000 **1** **Fire Brigade**[31] 7228 2-9-3 **56**.. JamieSpencer 1 67+
(Michael Bell) *trckd ldrs: led travelling strly over 1f out: pushed out: comf* **3/1**[1]

000 **2** 1 1/4 **Orithia (USA)**[20] 7502 2-9-3 **56**.................................(t) FergusSweeney 7 61
(Seamus Durack) *mid-div: hdwy fr 2f out: rdn to chse wnr ins fnl f: kpt on but a being hld* **6/1**[3]

064 **3** 2 3/4 **Poppy May (IRE)**[48] 6732 2-8-11 **55**............................... PhilDennis[(5)] 2 53
(James Given) *led: rdn and hdd over 1f out: kpt on but no ex fnl f* **8/1**

4306 **4** 3/4 **Ultimat Power (IRE)**[9] 7734 2-8-8 **47**.....................(b) AdamBeschizza 11 43
(Mark Hoad) *in tch: rdn over 2f out: kpt on same pce fnl f* **33/1**

3000 **5** nk **Hazell Berry (IRE)**[17] 7571 2-7-13 **45**..........................(v) AledBeech[(7)] 4 40
(David Evans) *trckd ldrs: rdn over 2f out: kpt on same pce* **25/1**

000 **6** nk **Magdalene Fox**[14] 7649 2-9-7 **60**.................................(b[1]) AdamKirby 10 54
(Ed Dunlop) *bhd: rdn and hdwy over 1f out: kpt on ins fnl f but nt pce to get involved* **8/1**

0430 **7** hd **Whitby Bay**[34] 7109 2-8-7 **49**... NathanEvans[(3)] 8 42
(Michael Easterby) *hld up towards rr: hdwy whn swtchd lft ent fnl f: r.o: nvr trbld ldrs* **10/1**

04P0 **8** nk **Viola Park**[70] 6060 2-8-6 **45**... RyanTate 9 38
(Ronald Harris) *hld up towards rr: c wd ent st: kpt on fnl f: nvr trbld ldrs* **100/1**

6506 **9** 3/4 **Chiconomic (IRE)**[20] 7510 2-8-10 **52**...................(b) HectorCrouch[(3)] 12 43
(Rae Guest) *mid-div: rdn over 2f out: nvr any imp* **16/1**

0062 **10** 1 **Auric Goldfinger (IRE)**[37] 7047 2-9-5 **58**.......................... SeanLevey 6 46
(Richard Hannon) *prom: rdn and ev ch 2f out tl wknd ent fnl f* **4/1**[2]

0000 **11** 1 1/2 **Cheers All Round**[25] 7380 2-9-7 **60**.............................. TomQueally 5 44
(Henry Spiller) *nvr bttr than mid-div* **66/1**

4004 **12** 11 **Snoozy Sioux (IRE)**[29] 7275 2-9-7 **60**............................. PatCosgrave 3 14
(Martin Smith) *s.i.s: sn chsng ldrs: rdn over 2f out: wknd ent fnl f* **7/1**

1m 27.09s (-0.11) **Going Correction** -0.175s/f (Stan) **12** Ran SP% **118.3**
Speed ratings (Par 94): **93,91,88,87,87 86,86,86,85,84 82,70**
CSF £20.51 CT £134.57 TOTE £3.30: £1.20, £2.90, £3.30; EX 27.00 Trifecta £239.10.
Owner The Fitzrovians **Bred** Stowell Hill Ltd **Trained** Newmarket, Suffolk

FOCUS
They went a good pace in this modest nursery. A pb from the winner.

7882 BET TOTEEXACTA AT TOTESPORT.COM MEDIAN AUCTION MAIDEN STKS (DIV I) 7f (P)
4:55 (4:57) (Class 6) 2-Y-O **£2,911** (£866; £432; £216) **Stalls** Low

Form RPR

6 **1** **Volatile**[22] 7468 2-9-5 0.. MartinHarley 5 87+
(James Tate) *mde all: nudged clr ent fnl f: v easily* **7/4**[1]

43 **2** 1 3/4 **Nostalgie**[22] 7465 2-9-0 0.. PatCosgrave 4 73
(Rae Guest) *trckd ldrs: chal for 2nd over 1f out: kpt on to chse wnr ins fnl f but nvr any ch* **7/2**[2]

533 **3** 1 **Vanderbilt (IRE)**[37] 7034 2-9-5 83.................................. JamieSpencer 3 75
(Martyn Meade) *trckd ldrs: chsd wnr over 1f out where edging lft: kpt on but no ex fnl 120yds* **6/1**[3]

43 **4** 3 **Habbad (FR)**[14] 7639 2-9-5 0... SeanLevey 11 67
(Richard Hannon) *mid-div: rdn and hdwy on outer over 1f out: kpt on to go 4th ins fnl f* **14/1**

55 **5** 1/2 **Warm Words**[31] 7210 2-9-0 0.. JohnFahy 10 61
(Ralph Beckett) *trckd ldrs: rdn 2f out: sn one pce* **20/1**

53 **6** nk **Love Power (IRE)**[26] 7355 2-9-5 0....................................... GeorgeBaker 7 65
(Mark Johnston) *trckd ldr: rdn over 2f out: sn one pce* **10/1**

6 **7** 1 3/4 **Rosemay (FR)**[42] 6897 2-9-0 0... SteveDrowne 1 55
(Simon Crisford) *mid-div: rdn over 1f out: kpt on same pce* **12/1**

8 2 **Wonder Of Dubai (IRE)** 2-9-5 0.. TimmyMurphy 2 55+
(Jamie Osborne) *s.i.s: towards rr: sme late prog: nvr any threat* **50/1**

9 shd **Al Yarmouk** 2-9-5 0... RobertHavlin 6 54+
(John Gosden) *s.i.s: sn mid-div: rdn over 2f out: nvr threatened: fdd fnl f* **6/1**[3]

00 **10** 3 1/4 **Broughtons Admiral**[36] 7065 2-9-5 0................................. TomQueally 8 46
(Henry Spiller) *a towards rr* **100/1**

11 1/2 **Sunovarebel** 2-9-5 0.. GrahamGibbons 9 44
(Alan Bailey) *s.i.s: mid-div: rdn 3f out: wknd ent fnl f* **100/1**

50 **12** 6 **Medicean Dream (IRE)**[8] 7769 2-9-5 0.................................. AdamKirby 12 28
(Luca Cumani) *a towards rr* **25/1**

13 6 **Shillbourne Lad (IRE)** 2-8-12 0.................................. VictoriaWood[(7)] 13 12
(Bill Turner) *racd keenly on outer: in tch: rdn 3f out: wknd 2f out* **66/1**

1m 26.59s (-0.61) **Going Correction** -0.175s/f (Stan) **13** Ran SP% **124.6**
Speed ratings (Par 94): **96,94,92,89,88 88,86,84,84,80 79,72,66**
CSF £7.60 TOTE £2.90: £1.40, £1.20, £2.10; EX 8.50 Trifecta £40.70.
Owner Saeed Manana **Bred** Rabbah Bloodstock Limited **Trained** Newmarket, Suffolk

FOCUS
A fair maiden and the winner created a good impression. The form makes plenty of sense.

7883 BET TOTEEXACTA AT TOTESPORT.COM MEDIAN AUCTION MAIDEN STKS (DIV II) 7f (P)
5:25 (5:28) (Class 6) 2-Y-O **£2,911** (£866; £432; £216) **Stalls** Low

Form RPR

1 **High Waves (IRE)** 2-9-5 0... PatCosgrave 4 75+
(Saeed bin Suroor) *trckd ldrs: led ent fnl f: drifted lft: r.o wl: readily* **9/4**[2]

4 **2** 3/4 **Ejaaby**[13] 7665 2-9-5 0... PaulHanagan 6 73+
(Roger Varian) *trckd ldrs: led briefly jst over 1f out: carried lft fnl f: kpt on but a being hld* **11/10**[1]

0 **3** 2 1/2 **De Little Engine (IRE)**[14] 7648 2-9-0 0......................... LucyKBarry[(5)] 7 65
(Jamie Osborne) *led for 1f: trckd ldr: rdn t ld over 1f out: sn hdd: edgd lft: kpt on but no ex* **100/1**

5 **4** 1 3/4 **Know Your Limit (IRE)**[14] 7649 2-9-5 0............................. GeorgeBaker 2 61
(Ed Walker) *hld up towards rr: hdwy over 1f out: kpt on wl fnl f: snatched 4th cl home* **5/1**[3]

5 nk **Traveller (FR)** 2-9-5 0...[1] MichaelJMMurphy 9 60
(Charles Hills) *mid-div: rdn over 2f out: wnt 4th ent fnl f: drifted lft: kpt on: lost 4th cl home* **20/1**

66 **6** nse **Noble Ballad**[31] 7209 2-9-5 0.. JohnFahy 8 60
(Ralph Beckett) *mid-div: rdn 2f out: kpt on fnl f but nt pce to get involved* **33/1**

7 2 1/2 **Do You Know (IRE)** 2-9-0 0.. MartinHarley 10 48
(Marco Botti) *chsd ldrs: rdn over 2f out: fdd fnl f* **16/1**

00 **8** 1 **Chakra**[28] 7297 2-9-0 0.. TomMarquand 1 45
(Michael Bell) *mid-div: rdn over 2f out: wknd fnl f* **100/1**

00 **9** shd **Treagus**[5] 7812 2-9-5 0.. StevieDonohoe 5 50
(Charlie Fellowes) *nvr bttr than mid-div* **50/1**

60 **10** 1/2 **Pow Wow**[15] 7622 2-9-2 0.. KieranShoemark[(3)] 12 49
(Roger Charlton) *s.i.s: hung lft over 1f out: a towards rr* **16/1**

0 **11** 5 **Lady Of York**[22] 7466 2-9-0 0.. GrahamGibbons 11 30
(Alan Bailey) *led after 1f: rdn and hdd over 1f out: sn wknd* **66/1**

12 3 1/4 **Delagate This Lord** 2-9-5 0.. AdamKirby 3 26
(Bill Turner) *dwlt: a bhd* **33/1**

1m 27.09s (-0.11) **Going Correction** -0.175s/f (Stan) **12** Ran SP% **122.9**
Speed ratings (Par 94): **93,92,89,87,86 86,84,82,82,82 76,72**
CSF £5.04 TOTE £3.00: £1.10, £1.40, £16.10; EX 6.40 Trifecta £425.20.
Owner Godolphin **Bred** Richard Ahern **Trained** Newmarket, Suffolk

FOCUS
The second division of a fair maiden and the time was 0.5secs slower than the first leg. A few down the field limit the bare form.

7884 BET TOTEQUADPOT AT TOTESPORT.COM NURSERY H'CAP 5f (P)
5:55 (5:57) (Class 6) (0-65,66) 2-Y-O **£3,234** (£962; £481; £240) **Stalls** Low

Form RPR

4053 **1** **Jorvik Prince**[17] 7579 2-8-10 **53**.. SamJames 7 61
(Karen Tutty) *mde all: drifted lft fnl f: r.o: rdn out* **10/1**[3]

3501 **2** 2 **Ninety Years Young**[7] 7777 2-9-9 **66** 6ex.......................(b) SeanLevey 4 67
(David Elsworth) *bmpd leaving stalls: towards rr: hdwy over 1f out: r.o wl fnl f: snatched 2nd cl home* **6/4**[1]

5324 **3** nk **Heavenly Cry**[12] 7690 2-8-4 **50**...........................(b) JosephineGordon[(3)] 2 50
(Phil McEntee) *hmpd leaving stalls: in tch: trckd ldrs over 2f out: sn rdn: chsd wnr ins fnl f: lost 2nd cl home* **4/1**[2]

6060 **4** 1/2 **Little Nosegay (IRE)**[27] 7313 2-8-8 **58**.............................. AledBeech[(7)] 3 56
(David Evans) *s.i.s: towards rr: hdwy fr 2f out: chsd ldrs ent fnl f: kpt on tl no ex fnl 75yds* **16/1**

0656 **5** 3/4 **Scotch Myst**[17] 7579 2-8-13 **56**.. TonyHamilton 11 52
(Richard Fahey) *prom: rdn 2f out: sn one pce* **12/1**

0003 **6** nk **Sweet Sienna**[19] 7528 2-8-9 **52**....................................... KieranO'Neill 6 46
(Dean Ivory) *prom: rdn 2f out: one pce fnl f* **14/1**

0560 **7** 1 1/2 **Zipedee**[19] 7528 2-8-0 **50**.. LuluStanford[(7)] 1 39
(John Ryan) *wnt lft leaving stalls: in tch: effrt 2f out: wknd ins fnl f* **12/1**

0004 **8** nk **Glam'Selle**[24] 7414 2-8-11 **54**.. TomMarquand 8 42
(Ronald Harris) *racd keenly: trckd ldrs: rdn 2f out: wknd fnl f* **10/1**[3]

004 **9** 3 1/4 **Embleton**[14] 7639 2-9-3 **60**... AdamBeschizza 10 36
(Charlie Wallis) *s.i.s: a bhd* **33/1**

5400 **10** 3/4 **Halinka (IRE)**[36] 7073 2-9-0 **64**...............................(b[1]) DavidEgan[(7)] 5 38
(Roger Varian) *s.i.s: towards rr: hdwy on outer over 2f out: carried wd ent st: sn btn* **12/1**

U004 **11** 1 1/4 **Luxford**[19] 7528 2-8-9 **52**...(b) KierenFox 9 21
(John Best) *in tch on outer: rdn over 2f out: c wd ent st: sn wknd* **20/1**

59.77s (-0.43) **Going Correction** -0.175s/f (Stan) **11** Ran SP% **121.5**
Speed ratings (Par 94): **96,92,92,91,90 89,87,86,81,80 78**
CSF £26.14 CT £76.97 TOTE £14.00: £4.30, £1.30, £1.60; EX 45.80 Trifecta £199.00.
Owner Thoroughbred Homes Ltd **Bred** Hellwood Stud Farm & Mrs Jill Willows **Trained** Osmotherley, N Yorks

FOCUS
Just a modest nursery. The winner took a step forward.

7885 IRISH EBF MAIDEN FILLIES' STKS (PLUS 10 RACE) 1m (P)
6:25 (6:28) (Class 4) 2-Y-O **£5,175** (£1,540; £769; £384) **Stalls** Low

Form RPR

3642 **1** **Elas Ruby**[19] 7543 2-9-0 78 RobertHavlin 11 78
(John Gosden) *mid-div: hdwy 3f out: rdn over 1f out: str run ins fnl f: led fnl 70yds* **11/8**[1]

20 **2** 1/2 **Dubai Dunes**[37] 7050 2-8-11 0 JosephineGordon(3) 13 77
(Saeed bin Suroor) *pressed ldr: led over 2f out: rdn ins fnl f: no ex whn hdd fnl 70yds* **4/1**[3]

35 **3** 1 **Great Court (IRE)**[21] 7483 2-9-0 0 AdamKirby 5 75
(Luca Cumani) *trckd ldrs: rdn to chal 2f out: kpt on tl no ex fnl 75yds* **7/2**[2]

4 2 **Inconceivable (IRE)** 2-9-0 0 JohnFahy 8 70+
(Ralph Beckett) *racd keenly towards rr: hdwy fr 2f out: rdn over 1f out: styd on ins fnl f: wnt 4th towards fin* **12/1**

0 **5** 1 1/2 **Starlight Circus (IRE)**[20] 7494 2-9-0 0 TomMarquand 2 66
(Marco Botti) *mid-div: hdwy over 3f out: effrt over 2f out: wnt 4th over 1f out: no ex ins fnl f* **20/1**

04 **6** 1 3/4 **Duchess Of Fife**[22] 7458 2-9-0 0 MartinHarley 12 62
(William Knight) *trckd ldrs: rdn over 2f out: kpt on same pce* **33/1**

6 **7** nk **Lucrezia**[144] 3433 2-9-0 0 GrahamGibbons 9 61
(Sir Michael Stoute) *mid-div: swtchd rt over 5f out: rdn 3f out: nvr threatened* **6/1**

503 **8** 1 3/4 **Patching**[21] 7484 2-9-0 70 TonyHamilton 10 57
(Giles Bravery) *led tl over 2f out: sn rdn: wknd fnl f* **20/1**

00 **9** 6 **Log Off (IRE)**[20] 7501 2-8-7 0 AledBeech(7) 14 43
(David Evans) *a towards rr* **66/1**

0 **10** nk **Fortia**[23] 7441 2-9-0 0 PatCosgrave 1 42
(William Haggas) *mid-div: rdn over 3f out: wknd ent fnl f* **33/1**

11 1/2 **Life Happens** 2-9-0 0 RyanTate 3 41
(Jonathan Portman) *dwlt: a towards rr* **66/1**

12 1/2 **Secret Poet (IRE)** 2-9-0 0 TimmyMurphy 4 40
(Jamie Osborne) *a towards rr* **66/1**

13 1/2 **Afternoon (IRE)** 2-9-0 0 FergusSweeney 7 38
(Martyn Meade) *a towards rr* **33/1**

0 **14** 2 **Devon Cove**[12] 7695 2-9-0 0 DannyBrock 6 34
(Jane Chapple-Hyam) *mid-div: pushed along over 5f out: wknd 2f out* **100/1**

1m 39.2s (-0.70) **Going Correction** -0.175s/f (Stan) **14** Ran SP% **130.1**
Speed ratings (Par 95): **96,95,94,92,91 89,88,87,81,80 80,79,79,77**
CSF £7.03 TOTE £2.20: £1.10, £2.40, £1.50; EX 11.40 Trifecta £27.20.
Owner Newsells Park Stud **Bred** Newsells Park Stud **Trained** Newmarket, Suffolk
■ Stewards' Enquiry : Danny Brock three-day ban: careless riding (Nov 24-26)

FOCUS
An interesting maiden with the future in mind and the three market leaders were dominant. The winner confirmed that he#s improved, with the form straightforward in behind.

7886 @TOTEPOOLRACING WIN TICKETS ON TWITTER H'CAP 1m (P)
6:55 (7:00) (Class 5) (0-75,75) 3-Y-O+ **£4,528** (£1,347; £673; £336) **Stalls** Low

Form RPR

5002 **1** **Russian Reward (IRE)**[9] 7738 4-9-3 71 JackMitchell 12 80
(Amanda Perrett) *mde all: kpt on strly: rdn out* **7/1**

1210 **2** 1 **Footlight**[196] 1819 3-8-12 68 TonyHamilton 5 75
(Richard Fahey) *racd keenly: trckd ldrs: rdn to chse wnr over 1f out: kpt on but a being readily hld* **25/1**

0003 **3** 1 3/4 **Graceful James (IRE)**[12] 7691 3-9-2 72 KieranO'Neill 3 75
(Jimmy Fox) *racd keenly: trckd ldrs: rdn over 2f out: kpt on ins fnl f* **7/1**

3232 **4** nse **Exceeding Power**[90] 5357 5-9-4 75 JosephineGordon(3) 9 78
(Martin Bosley) *mid-div: rdn 2f out: swtchd rt over 1f out: r.o wl ins fnl f: chalng for 3rd towards fin* **6/1**[3]

643 **5** 1 **Willsy**[91] 5336 3-9-2 72 SamJames 1 73
(Karen Tutty) *mid-div: rdn 2f out: kpt on same pce fnl f* **25/1**

0552 **6** hd **Spiritual Star (IRE)**[22] 7457 7-8-13 72 PaddyBradley(5) 11 72
(Lee Carter) *mid-div: rdn over 2f out: kpt on same pce fnl f* **11/1**

0041 **7** 1 1/2 **Pivotman**[36] 7078 8-9-1 72 (bt) NathanEvans(3) 10 69
(Michael Easterby) *towards rr on outer: hdwy into midfield turning in: sn rdn: no further imp fnl f* **10/1**

5420 **8** 1/2 **Aqua Ardens (GER)**[38] 7017 8-9-5 73 (t) SteveDrowne 4 69
(George Baker) *hld up towards rr: rdn over 2f out: sme late prog: nvr any threat* **12/1**

/0-0 **9** 1/2 **Maskoon**[20] 7517 5-8-13 67 PaddyAspell 2 61
(Philip Kirby) *hld up towards rr: rdn 2f out: little imp* **20/1**

1504 **10** 1 **Our Boy Jack (IRE)**[15] 7606 7-9-2 70 (p) TomEaves 15 62
(Conor Dore) *trckd ldr: rdn over 2f out: wknd ent fnl f* **50/1**

0006 **11** 1/2 **Ruban (IRE)**[22] 7457 7-9-2 70 (t) PatCosgrave 6 61
(Stuart Williams) *mid-div: rdn 2f out: wknd fnl f* **7/2**[1]

3000 **12** hd **Fantasy Gladiator**[12] 7691 10-9-1 72 (p) AlistairRawlinson(3) 8 62
(Michael Appleby) *stdd s: last: drvn over 2f out: nvr any imp* **20/1**

2034 **13** 1 **Consulting**[9] 7738 3-9-5 75 JamieSpencer 7 63
(Martyn Meade) *trckd ldrs: rdn over 1f out: sn hld: wknd ins fnl f* **4/1**[2]

1m 38.78s (-1.12) **Going Correction** -0.175s/f (Stan)
WFA 3 from 4yo+ 2lb **13** Ran SP% **125.8**
Speed ratings (Par 103): **98,97,95,95,94 94,92,92,91,90 90,89,88**
CSF £182.76 CT £1341.88 TOTE £8.90: £2.70, £6.40, £2.70; EX 164.10 Trifecta £1742.60.
Owner A D Spence **Bred** Times Of Wigan Ltd **Trained** Pulborough, W Sussex

FOCUS
A fair, open-looking handicap, in which it paid to race prominently. Ordinary form, the winner having an unconvincing profile.

7887 BET TOTETRIFECTA AT TOTESPORT.COM H'CAP 7f (P)
7:25 (7:29) (Class 5) (0-70,69) 3-Y-O+ **£4,204** (£1,251; £625; £312) **Stalls** Low

Form RPR

4401 **1** **Vincenzo Coccotti (USA)**[30] 7255 4-9-1 66 HectorCrouch(3) 6 76
(Ken Cunningham-Brown) *mid-div: rdn over 2f out: hdwy wl over 1f out: r.o wl fnl f: led towards fin* **10/1**[3]

3466 **2** 3/4 **Curzon Line**[56] 6501 7-9-4 66 GrahamGibbons 4 74
(Michael Easterby) *trckd ldrs: rdn to ld over 1f out: sn edgd lft: kpt on: no ex whn hdd towards fin* **5/1**[2]

3002 **3** 3/4 **Space War**[6] 7797 9-8-13 64 (b) NathanEvans(3) 5 70
(Michael Easterby) *hld up towards rr: hdwy over 3f out: rdn in 7th ent fnl f: str run fnl 150yds: wnt 3rd cl home* **3/1**[1]

3060 **4** 3/4 **Skidby Mill (IRE)**[12] 7691 6-9-4 66 GeorgeBaker 14 70
(Laura Mongan) *hld up towards rr: hdwy fr 2f out: kpt on wl fnl f: wnt 4th cl home* **16/1**

4306 **5** 1/2 **Anastazia**[15] 7620 4-9-6 68 TomQueally 2 71
(Paul D'Arcy) *s.i.s: mid-div after 2f: hdwy on inner fnl bnd: rdn to chse ldng pair sn after: kpt on tl no ex fnl 75yds* **10/1**[3]

5005 **6** hd **World's Greatest (USA)**[21] 7485 3-9-4 67 (t) SeanLevey 7 68
(Stuart Williams) *mid-div: hdwy 3f out: rdn 2f out: kpt on same pce ins fnl f* **12/1**

3004 **7** 1 **So Much Fun (IRE)**[15] 7619 3-9-4 67 (v) MartinHarley 1 65
(Ismail Mohammed) *mid-div: hdwy over 3f out: led over 2f out: rdn and hdd whn hmpd ent fnl f: wknd* **12/1**

3213 **8** 5 **Desire**[27] 7334 4-9-4 66 TonyHamilton 12 52
(Richard Fahey) *towards rr: rdn 2f out: little imp whn swtchd rt over 1f out: nvr any threat* **10/1**[3]

0130 **9** 2 1/4 **Big Storm Coming**[27] 7333 6-9-7 69 TomEaves 13 49
(David Brown) *mid-div on outer: effrt over 2f out: wknd over 1f out* **10/1**[3]

0000 **10** 1 1/4 **Desert Strike**[14] 7644 10-9-4 66 (p) PaulMulrennan 3 42
(Conor Dore) *led tl over 2f out: wknd ent fnl f* **33/1**

0040 **11** 1 1/2 **Tagula Night (IRE)**[69] 6091 10-9-7 69 (tp) AdamKirby 9 41
(Dean Ivory) *trckd ldrs tl over 2f out: sn wknd* **14/1**

3603 **12** 3 3/4 **Majestic Myles (IRE)**[19] 7529 8-9-6 68 KierenFox 10 30
(Lee Carter) *pressed ldr tl rdn over 2f out: wknd over 1f out* **14/1**

1060 **13** 14 **Muthraab Aldaar (IRE)**[15] 7617 3-9-6 69 PatCosgrave 8
(Jim Boyle) *s.i.s: sn outpcd: a bhd* **25/1**

0061 **14** 9 **Himalayan Queen**[15] 7612 3-8-12 66 SophieKilloran(5) 11
(William Jarvis) *mid-div: rdn over 2f out: wknd over 1f out* **12/1**

1m 24.96s (-2.24) **Going Correction** -0.175s/f (Stan)
WFA 3 from 4yo+ 1lb **14** Ran SP% **127.1**
Speed ratings (Par 103): **105,104,103,102,101 101,100,94,92,90 89,84,68,58**
CSF £62.69 CT £195.30 TOTE £13.60: £3.80, £2.20, £1.80; EX 78.60 Trifecta £537.40.
Owner David Henery **Bred** Gainesway Thoroughbreds Ltd Et Al **Trained** Danebury, Hants
■ Stewards' Enquiry : Sophie Killoran jockey said filly never travelled and lost its action

FOCUS
A fair handicap and it was competitive for the grade. The form is rated around the third.

7888 TOTEPOOL BETTING AT TOTESPORT.COM H'CAP 1m 2f (P)
7:55 (7:56) (Class 6) (0-55,55) 3-Y-O+ **£2,911** (£866; £432; £216) **Stalls** Low

Form RPR

0000 **1** **Glorious Dancer**[29] 7282 4-9-4 52 AdamKirby 9 57
(Lee Carter) *trckd ldrs: rdn over 1f out: led jst ins fnl f: hld on: all out* **6/1**[2]

0061 **2** hd **Whitchurch**[15] 7628 4-9-5 53 TimmyMurphy 15 58
(Philip Kirby) *hld up last trio: hdwy over 1f out: rdn and r.o wl fnl 150yds: jst failed* **10/1**

0262 **3** 1/2 **Victoriously**[26] 7369 4-9-2 53 (p) NoelGarbutt(3) 10 57
(Andi Brown) *trckd ldr tl rdn over 1f out: kpt on fnl f* **3/1**[1]

3034 **4** 1 **Frivolous Prince (IRE)**[9] 7745 3-8-1 46 (bt) AledBeech(7) 12 48
(David Evans) *s.i.s: last pair: nt clr run briefly over 1f out: styd on fnl f: wnt 4th cl home* **7/1**[3]

5400 **5** nse **Whaleweigh Station**[20] 7516 5-9-5 53 RenatoSouza 1 55
(J R Jenkins) *in tch: hdwy on inner 2f out: rdn and ev ch ent fnl f: no ex cl home* **10/1**

403- **6** 1/2 **Spirit Of The Vale (IRE)**[362] 7862 3-8-6 47 [1] NathanEvans(3) 3 48
(Oliver Greenall) *led: rdn over 1f out: hdd jst ins fnl f: no ex* **20/1**

0064 **7** nk **Rainford Glory (IRE)**[26] 7369 6-9-0 48 (v[1]) BarryMcHugh 7 49
(Tim Fitzgerald) *trckd ldrs: rdn and ev ch over 1f out tl jst ins fnl f: no ex whn squeezed up towards fin* **10/1**

5340 **8** 5 **Master Of Song**[14] 7642 9-9-2 53 (p) AlistairRawlinson(3) 8 44
(Roy Bowring) *s.i.s: keen early: midfield: hdwy over 3f out: effrt over 2f out: fdd ins fnl f* **10/1**

6123 **9** nk **Moss Street**[11] 7421 6-9-7 55 (b) PaulMulrennan 2 45
(Conor Dore) *hld up bhd: rdn 3f out: nvr any imp* **3/1**[1]

2m 8.63s (0.03) **Going Correction** -0.175s/f (Stan)
WFA 3 from 4yo+ 4lb **9** Ran SP% **117.9**
Speed ratings (Par 101): **92,91,91,90,90 90,89,85,85**
CSF £65.37 CT £216.86 TOTE £6.60: £1.50, £2.90, £1.70; EX 65.00 Trifecta £272.90.
Owner Mrs I Marshall **Bred** D J And Mrs Deer **Trained** Epsom, Surrey

FOCUS
A low-grade handicap and they finished in a bit of a heap. Straightforward form.
T/Jkpt: Not won. T/Plt: £21.30 to a £1 stake. Pool: £99105.65, 3392.84 winning units. T/Qpdt: £7.30 to a £1 stake. Pool: £12576.46, 1266.0 winning units. **Tim Mitchell**

1706 SOUTHWELL (L-H)
Thursday, November 10

OFFICIAL GOING: Fibresand: standard
Wind: moderate 1/2 behind Weather: fine and sunny, overcast and showers after race 2 (12.55)

7889 SUNBETS.CO.UK H'CAP (DIV I) 1m (F)
12:25 (12:26) (Class 6) (0-65,65) 3-Y-O+ **£3,234** (£962; £481; £240) **Stalls** Low

Form RPR

5142 **1** **Barista (IRE)**[23] 7426 8-8-7 56 HollieDoyle(5) 9 67
(Brian Forsey) *mid-divission: chsng ldrs over 3f out: led over 1f out: forged clr* **7/1**[3]

3600 **2** 2 1/2 **Limerick Lord (IRE)**[31] 7200 4-8-6 53 (p) ShelleyBirkett(3) 6 58
(Julia Feilden) *trckd ldrs: led over 2f out: hdd over 1f out: kpt on same pce* **8/1**

0000 **3** 2 1/2 **General Tufto**[63] 6243 11-8-7 51 oh6 (b) JoeyHaynes 5 50
(Charles Smith) *in rr: bhd and drvn over 4f out: hdwy 3f out: kpt on to take 3rd clsng stages* **66/1**

2260 **4** 1 1/2 **Princess Peaches**[54] 6568 4-9-2 60 (p) PJMcDonald 3 55
(James Bethell) *chsd ldrs: kpt on same pce fnl f* **9/1**

6320 **5** 2 **Cascading Stars (IRE)**[14] 7654 4-9-4 62 GrahamGibbons 10 53
(Daniel Mark Loughnane) *chsd ldrs on outer: hung lft over 1f out: one pce* **8/1**

2324 **6** 3/4 **Niqnaaqpaadiwaaq**[38] 7010 4-9-7 65 NeilFarley 7 54
(Eric Alston) *led after 1f: hdd over 2f out: wknd fnl 150yds* **3/1**[1]

000 **7** 3 1/2 **Albert Boy (IRE)**[20] 7500 3-8-5 58 [1] NatalieHambling(7) 2 38
(Scott Dixon) *led 1f: chsd ldrs: swtchd rt over 1f out: sn wknd* **22/1**

5042 **8** 2 3/4 **Bunker Hill Lass**[9] 7742 4-8-4 51 oh4 (p) JosephineGordon(3) 8 25
(Michael Appleby) *s.i.s: racd wd: sme hdwy over 4f out: lost pl over 1f out in rr* **17/2**

6000 **9** 6 **Davey Boy**[36] 7078 3-9-0 63 LouisSteward(3) 4 22
(Michael Bell) *in rr: drvn to chse ldrs over 3f out: lost pl over 1f out* **11/1**

6304 **10** nk **East Coast Lady (IRE)**[15] 7609 4-9-6 64 BenCurtis 11 23
(William Stone) *s.s: hdwy on outside to chse ldrs over 4f out: sn drvn: lost pl 2f out* **9/2**[2]

The Form Book, Raceform Ltd, Newbury, RG14 5SJ

U- **11** ½ **Or So (USA)**[379] 7552 4-8-13 **60**....................(v) NoelGarbutt(3) 1 17
(Derek Shaw) *s.i.s: t.k.h: trcking ldrs after 2f: wknd 2f out* **33/1**

1m 42.01s (-1.69) **Going Correction** -0.15s/f (Stan)
WFA 3 from 4yo+ 2lb **11** Ran SP% **115.5**
Speed ratings (Par 101): **102,99,97,95,93 92,89,86,80,80 79**
CSF £59.75 CT £3370.83 TOTE £7.50: £1.40, £2.80, £12.70; EX 50.40 Trifecta £988.20.
Owner Three Oaks Racing & Mrs P Bosley **Bred** Rathasker Stud **Trained** Ash Priors, Somerset

FOCUS
The first meeting to take place on the Southwell Fibresand since the end of April with some cosmetic work having been done to parts of the track in the meantime. The first division of a moderate handicap to start. The winner was nesr his recent best.

7890 SUNBETS.CO.UK H'CAP (DIV II) 1m (F)
12:55 (12:55) (Class 6) (0-65,65) 3-Y-O+ **£3,234** (£962; £481; £240) **Stalls** Low

Form RPR
0106 **1** **Stun Gun**[28] 7310 6-9-6 **64**....................(p) TonyHamilton 7 72
(Derek Shaw) *trckd ldrs: rdn to ld appr fnl f: styd on wl: eased clsng stages* **9/2**[2]

5006 **2** 2 **Swansway**[9] 7751 3-8-10 **56**....................(b[1]) GrahamGibbons 10 59
(Michael Easterby) *chsd ldrs: edgd lft over 1f out: kpt on to take 2nd last 100yds* **2/1**[1]

2426 **3** 2½ **Unnoticed**[37] 7059 4-9-7 **65**.................... ShaneKelly 8 63
(Ollie Pears) *trckd ldrs: t.k.h: effrt over 2f out: one pce fnl f* **9/1**

0004 **4** 1¼ **Win Lose Draw (IRE)**[7] 7780 4-8-12 **56**.................... BenCurtis 4 51
(Michael Appleby) *led: hdd appr fnl f: one pce* **5/1**[3]

551P **5** 6 **Heads You Win**[157] 2968 3-9-4 **64**.................... WilliamCarson 9 45
(Jamie Osborne) *in rr: drvn and outpcd over 3f out: sn bhd* **11/1**

2-0 **6** ½ **Cahala Dancer (IRE)**[24] 7417 8-9-2 **60**....................(t) HarryPoulton 3 40
(Adam West) *chsd ldrs: outpcd and lost pl over 3f out* **50/1**

3601 **7** 6 **Little Choosey**[14] 7642 6-8-10 **61**....................(bt) KevinLundie(7) 6 27
(Roy Bowring) *in rr: outpcd and lost pl over 3f out* **11/2**

660 **8** ½ **The Excel Queen (IRE)**[14] 7646 3-8-7 **53**....................(b[1]) BarryMcHugh 1 18
(Tony Coyle) *trckd ldrs: lost pl over 1f out* **20/1**

1300 **9** 4 **Sober Up**[30] 7260 4-8-13 **57**....................(p) KierenFox 5 13
(Ivan Furtado) *s.i.s: sn detached in last* **16/1**

1m 42.57s (-1.13) **Going Correction** -0.15s/f (Stan)
WFA 3 from 4yo+ 2lb **9** Ran SP% **114.5**
Speed ratings (Par 101): **99,97,94,93,87 86,80,80,76**
CSF £13.76 CT £76.34 TOTE £6.20: £1.80, £1.40, £3.20; EX 18.00 Trifecta £127.50.
Owner John R Saville **Bred** Rothmere Bloodstock **Trained** Sproxton, Leics

FOCUS
The feature of this division was that half the field were beaten by halfway. The winning time was just over half a second slower than the first leg.A minor pb from the winner.

7891 32RED CASINO MAIDEN AUCTION STKS (PLUS 10 RACE) 7f (F)
1:25 (1:27) (Class 4) 2-Y-O **£4,204** (£1,251; £625; £312) **Stalls** Low

Form RPR
03 **1** **Red Guana (IRE)**[24] 7407 2-8-10 0.................... DavidProbert 8 69
(William Jarvis) *trckd ldrs: t.k.h: styd on to ld last 150yds* **25/1**

0224 **2** 1½ **Otomo**[15] 7605 2-8-13 66.................... GrahamLee 10 68
(Philip Hide) *w ldrs: led appr fnl f: hdd last 150yds: kpt on same pce* **4/1**[2]

6 **3** 2¾ **Golden Opportunity**[14] 7649 2-9-1 0.................... MartinHarley 13 63
(James Tate) *w ldrs: kpt on one pce fnl f* **4/1**[2]

052 **4** shd **Royal Icon**[13] 7659 2-8-12 68.................... KevinStott 6 59
(Kevin Ryan) *w ldrs: led over 4f out: hung lft over 1f out:sn hdd: wknd last 150yds* **6/1**[3]

4620 **5** ¾ **Washington Blue**[20] 7494 2-8-9 72.................... JosephineGordon(3) 4 57+
(Clive Cox) *led early: lost pl over 4f out: hdwy over 2f out: kpt on one pce* **11/4**[1]

00 **6** ½ **Lulu The Rocket**[23] 7441 2-8-6 0.................... KieranO'Neill 7 50
(Peter Chapple-Hyam) *s.i.s: hdwy over 2f out: kpt on one pce* **40/1**

7 ¾ **Royal Opera House (IRE)** 2-9-3 0.................... WilliamCarson 11 59
(Jamie Osborne) *sn chsng ldrs: one pce fnl 2f* **20/1**

330 **8** 9 **Nellie's Dancer**[20] 7494 2-8-3 63.................... NatalieHambling(7) 5 28
(Scott Dixon) *mid-div: hung lft and wknd over 1f out* **17/2**

5 **9** 1 **Sattar (IRE)**[7] 7776 2-9-3 0.................... TomMarquand 9 32
(Martin Smith) *sn led: hdd over 4f out: lost pl 2f out* **12/1**

0 **10** 2¼ **Harvest Ranger**[17] 7574 2-8-11 0.................... DannyBrock 3 20
(Michael Appleby) *t.k.h towards rr: sme hdwy on inner over 2f out: sn wknd* **100/1**

0 **11** hd **Chough**[9] 7733 2-8-12 0.................... PJMcDonald 1 20
(Hughie Morrison) *s.i.s: in rr: sme hdwy over 2f out: sn wknd* **25/1**

0 **12** 3¾ **Dragonite (IRE)**[26] 7366 2-9-1 0.................... OscarPereira 12 13
(Daniel Mark Loughnane) *mid-div: lost pl over 2f out* **100/1**

0 **13** 21 **Delightfulsurprise**[13] 7659 2-8-6 0.................... BenCurtis 2
(Scott Dixon) *in rr: wd bnd over 3f out: sn bhd: eased over 1f out: t.o* **100/1**

1m 28.77s (-1.53) **Going Correction** -0.15s/f (Stan) **13** Ran SP% **117.0**
Speed ratings (Par 98): **102,100,97,97,96 95,94,84,83,80 80,76,52**
CSF £116.63 TOTE £29.60: £6.00, £1.50, £2.10; EX 149.30 Trifecta £1004.70.
Owner G B Turnbull Ltd **Bred** Patrick Gleeson **Trained** Newmarket, Suffolk

FOCUS
A modest maiden for cheaply bought horses. The form is rated around the runner-up.

7892 BETWAY SPRINT H'CAP 5f (F)
1:55 (1:56) (Class 4) (0-85,84) 3-Y-O+ **£5,822** (£1,732; £865; £432) **Stalls** Centre

Form RPR
6112 **1** **Showdaisy**[23] 7437 3-9-4 **81**....................(p) GrahamGibbons 5 92
(Keith Dalgleish) *mde all: edgd lft over 1f out: styd on wl: eased nr fin* **13/2**[2]

0560 **2** 1¼ **Noble Storm (USA)**[29] 7288 10-8-11 **77**....................(p) RobHornby(3) 14 84
(Ed McMahon) *in rr: hdwy over 1f out: styd on wl to take 2nd nr fin* **20/1**

4500 **3** ½ **Razin' Hell**[14] 7643 5-9-6 **83**....................(v) BenCurtis 12 88
(John Balding) *trckd ldrs: 2nd over 1f out: kpt on same pce* **12/1**

5210 **4** nse **September Issue**[105] 4803 3-9-1 **78**.................... TonyHamilton 2 83
(Gay Kelleway) *mid-div: drvn over 2f out: chsng ldrs over 1f out: kpt on same pce* **9/2**[1]

6000 **5** nse **Escalating**[16] 7593 4-8-12 **78**....................(tp) AlistairRawlinson(3) 6 83+
(Michael Appleby) *mid-div: hdwy over 2f out: chsng ldrs over 1f out: kpt on same pce* **20/1**

6210 **6** hd **New Road Side**[8] 7772 3-9-1 **78**.................... ConnorBeasley 8 82
(Richard Guest) *chsd ldrs: one pce over 1f out* **7/1**[3]

4311 **7** 2 **Rural Celebration**[13] 7660 5-9-2 **84**....................(v) JoshDoyle(5) 9 81+
(David O'Meara) *sn outpcd: reminders over 2f out: hdwy over 1f out: nvr a threat* **15/2**

1030 **8** ½ **Oriental Relation (IRE)**[9] 7752 5-9-6 **83**....................(b) TomEaves 11 78
(James Given) *s.i.s: in rr: hdwy over 1f out: nvr a factor* **14/1**

5506 **9** nk **Elusivity (IRE)**[8] 7772 8-9-1 **78**....................(p) PaulMulrennan 7 72
(Conor Dore) *chsd ldrs: wknd over 1f out* **25/1**

1052 **10** 1½ **I'll Be Good**[24] 7413 7-8-13 **83**.................... BenRobinson(7) 10 72
(Brian Ellison) *chsd ldrs: drvn over 2f out: one pce* **8/1**

060 **11** ½ **Krystallite**[1] 7864 3-9-0 **77**.................... KieranO'Neill 13 64
(Scott Dixon) *chsd ldrs: wknd over 1f out* **80/1**

0353 **12** ½ **Bondi Beach Boy**[8] 7773 7-9-4 **81**.................... TomMarquand 3 66
(James Turner) *s.i.s: in rr: edgd rt over 1f out: nvr a factor* **9/1**

1000 **13** 8 **King Crimson**[14] 7643 4-9-3 **80**.................... TimmyMurphy 1 36
(John Butler) *hld up in rr: swtchd lft after s: nvr on terms* **20/1**

2610 **14** 9 **Van Gerwen**[24] 7413 3-9-4 **81**.................... PJMcDonald 4 5
(Les Eyre) *s.i.s: a detached in last* **16/1**

57.31s (-2.39) **Going Correction** -0.325s/f (Stan) **14** Ran SP% **116.5**
Speed ratings (Par 105): **106,104,103,103,103 102,99,98,98,95 95,94,81,67**
CSF £134.77 CT £1560.39 TOTE £5.50: £2.10, £6.00, £4.50; EX 147.00 Trifecta £3271.30.
Owner Ronnie Docherty & Partner **Bred** Patricia Ann Scott-Dunn **Trained** Carluke, S Lanarks

FOCUS
A competitive sprint handicap in which few got into it and those who raced centre to far side were favoured. A clear pb from the winner and the second's best run this year.

7893 32RED.COM NURSERY H'CAP 6f (F)
2:25 (2:29) (Class 2) 2-Y-O
£12,450 (£3,728; £1,864; £932; £466; £234) **Stalls** Low

Form RPR
0061 **1** **Spin Doctor**[16] 7600 2-8-9 **78**.................... GeorgeChaloner 6 84
(Richard Fahey) *chsd ldrs: drvn over 2f out: 2nd appr fnl f: led last 150yds: kpt on* **12/1**

1104 **2** nk **Parnassian (IRE)**[22] 7469 2-8-11 **85**.................... CliffordLee(5) 1 90
(K R Burke) *trckd ldrs: effrt over 2f out: led over 1f out: hdd last 150yds: no ex clsng stages* **4/1**[2]

4153 **3** 1½ **Erissimus Maximus (FR)**[23] 7440 2-8-2 **74**....... JosephineGordon(3) 10 75
(Chris Dwyer) *chsd ldrs on outer: hung rt and kpt on same pce fnl f* **7/1**

415 **4** ¾ **White Royale (USA)**[16] 7600 2-8-7 **76**.................... JoeDoyle 7 74
(Kevin Ryan) *led: hdd over 1f out: kpt on same pce* **6/1**[3]

6231 **5** nk **Pulsating (IRE)**[20] 7510 2-7-9 **69** oh2.................... HollieDoyle(5) 5 66
(Ali Stronge) *chsd ldrs: one pce fnl 2f* **12/1**

31 **6** hd **The Feathered Nest (IRE)**[14] 7639 2-8-13 **82**........... TonyHamilton 11 79+
(Richard Fahey) *s.i.s: sn chsng ldrs on outer: one pce fnl 2f* **3/1**[1]

2410 **7** 1¼ **Shamsaya (IRE)**[54] 6555 2-9-7 **90**.................... GrahamLee 4 83
(Simon Crisford) *in rr: outpcd over 3f out: sme hdwy over 2f out: nvr a factor* **11/1**

6336 **8** 6 **Tailor's Row (USA)**[54] 6563 2-8-10 **79**.................... PJMcDonald 8 54
(Mark Johnston) *stmbld s: in rr: sme hdwy on ins over 2f out: hung lft and lost pl over 1f out* **4/1**[2]

4523 **9** 6 **Pavela (IRE)**[20] 7510 2-7-9 **69** oh9....................[1] SophieKilloran(5) 3 26
(Scott Dixon) *chsd ldrs: lost pl over 1f out* **100/1**

4515 **10** 5 **Amathyst**[23] 7440 2-8-4 **73** ow2.................... DannyBrock 9 15
(Michael Appleby) *s.i.s: in rr: bhd whn eased over 1f out* **28/1**

1m 14.14s (-2.36) **Going Correction** -0.15s/f (Stan) **10** Ran SP% **119.9**
Speed ratings (Par 102): **109,108,106,105,105 104,103,95,87,80**
CSF £61.36 CT £381.56 TOTE £13.60: £3.40, £1.70, £2.30; EX 77.90 Trifecta £518.00.
Owner Cheveley Park Stud **Bred** Cheveley Park Stud Ltd **Trained** Musley Bank, N Yorks

FOCUS
A decent and valuable nursery, but none of these had any previous experience of racing on Fibresand. The winner is rated back to her best.

7894 SUNBETS.CO.UK DOWNLOAD THE APP MAIDEN STKS 7f (F)
2:55 (2:56) (Class 5) 3-Y-O+ **£3,881** (£1,155; £577; £288) **Stalls** Low

Form RPR
44 **1** **Blue Cliffs (IRE)**[17] 7583 3-9-2 0.................... AlistairRawlinson(3) 2 77+
(Michael Appleby) *dwlt and wnt rt s: sn chsng ldrs on outer: drvn over 3f out: led over 1f out: kpt on* **4/1**[3]

-543 **2** 1 **Senses Of Dubai**[15] 7616 3-9-5 74.................... WilliamCarson 4 72
(Jamie Osborne) *led: edgd rt over 2f out: hdd over 1f out: kpt on same pce* **11/4**[2]

3600 **3** 2 **Anna Barkova (IRE)**[9] 7743 3-9-0 62.................... BenCurtis 6 62
(K R Burke) *w ldrs: n.m.r and swtchd lft over 1f out: kpt on same pce* **10/1**

4 **4** 2½ **Fleeting Glimpse**[15] 7616 3-9-0 0.................... DavidProbert 5 55
(Andrew Balding) *trckd ldrs: t.k.h: rdn over 2f out: one pce* **5/2**[1]

5 **5** ¾ **Samphire Coast**[37] 7061 3-9-2 0.................... NoelGarbutt(3) 1 58
(Derek Shaw) *in rr and sn drvn along: hdwy over 2f out: one pce* **80/1**

3 **6** nk **Andanotherone (IRE)**[159] 2904 3-9-0 0.................... GrahamLee 3 52
(Simon Crisford) *trckd ldrs: rdn 3f out: one pce fnl 2f* **11/4**[2]

0500 **7** 23 **Vocalise**[23] 7445 3-9-0 29.................... JoeyHaynes 7
(Charles Smith) *w ldrs: drvn 4f out: wknd over 2f out: bhd whn eased clsng stages: t.o* **250/1**

1m 28.83s (-1.47) **Going Correction** -0.15s/f (Stan)
WFA 3 from 5yo 1lb **7** Ran SP% **112.6**
Speed ratings (Par 103): **102,100,98,95,94 94,68**
CSF £14.94 TOTE £5.70: £3.00, £1.90; EX 18.20 Trifecta £85.10.
Owner Mrs M A Pinney **Bred** Gce Farm Ltd **Trained** Oakham, Rutland

FOCUS
A moderate maiden, especially with a couple of the market leaders running moderately, but the winner is value for further than the winning margin. The form is rated around the second and third.

7895 BETWAY H'CAP 1m 4f (F)
3:25 (3:25) (Class 5) (0-70,74) 3-Y-O+ **£3,881** (£1,155; £577; £288) **Stalls** Low

Form RPR
6003 **1** **High Command (IRE)**[27] 7321 3-9-3 **69**.................... JackMitchell 12 80+
(Roger Varian) *w ldrs: led 7f out: styd on wl fnl 2f: readily* **5/4**[1]

5501 **2** 2½ **Safira Menina**[9] 7732 4-10-0 **74** 6ex.................... RyanPowell 1 78+
(Martin Smith) *sn detached in last: hdwy over 4f out: n.m.r over 2f out: sn chsng ldrs: kpt on to take 2nd last 75yds: no imp* **14/1**

5400 **3** 1¼ **Captain Swift (IRE)**[48] 6730 5-9-2 **62**.................... GrahamLee 4 64+
(John Mackie) *in rr: hdwy on outer 6f out: lost pl over 4f out: hdwy 2f out: kpt on to take 3rd post* **14/1**

300 **4** shd **Best Tamayuz**[30] 7257 5-8-7 **60**.................... NatalieHambling(7) 10 62
(Scott Dixon) *dwlt: t.k.h: sn trcking ldrs: 2nd over 3f out: one pce fnl f* **11/1**

4100 **5** ¾ **Deep Resolve (IRE)**[16] 7594 5-9-9 **69**.................... NeilFarley 5 70
(Alan Swinbank) *mid-div: hdwy over 4f out: 3rd over 2f out: one pce* **12/1**

6420 **6** 2 1/2 **Come Back King (IRE)**58 6445 3-9-4 **70** BenCurtis 2 67
(Michael Appleby) *hld up in mid-div: hdwy to chse ldrs over 3f out: one pce fnl 2f* **9/1**3

4004 **7** *hd* **Monzino (USA)**15 2853 8-8-7 **56** oh11 NoelGarbutt(3) 8 53
(Michael Chapman) *rr-div: hdwy over 4f out: kpt on fnl 2f: nvr a factor* **100/1**

463 **8** *9* **Rahmah (IRE)**23 7429 4-9-10 **70** PaulMulrennan 7 52
(Geoffrey Deacon) *chsd ldrs: drvn 5f out: wknd 2f out* **8/1**2

-P04 **9** *7* **Duc De Seville (IRE)**15 4024 4-8-10 **56** oh6 JoeyHaynes 3 27
(Michael Chapman) *chsd ldrs: lost pl after 3f: sn bhd* **100/1**

2440 **10** *nk* **Star Ascending (IRE)**13 7657 4-9-3 **63** (p) LiamKeniry 11 34
(Jennie Candlish) *dwlt: t.k.h: sn trcking ldrs: wknd over 2f out* **11/1**

4535 **11** 1/2 **Best Boy**58 6450 4-8-13 **59** (vt) DavidProbert 13 29
(David C Griffiths) *chsd ldrs: hung lft and lost pl over 2f out: sn heavily eased* **16/1**

0500 **12** *30* **Premier Currency (IRE)**92 5302 3-8-10 **62** PJMcDonald 6
(Mike Murphy) *led: hdd 7f out: lost pl over 2f out: sn bhd and eased: virtually p.u: t.o* **20/1**

2m 38.47s (-2.53) **Going Correction** -0.15s/f (Stan)
WFA 3 from 4yo+ 6lb **12** Ran SP% **115.9**
Speed ratings (Par 103): **102,100,99,99,98 97,97,91,86,86 85,65**
CSF £19.94 CT £172.22 TOTE £1.90: £1.10, £3.80, £4.80; EX 13.60 Trifecta £125.80.
Owner H R H Sultan Ahmad Shah **Bred** Greenwood Lodge Farm Inc **Trained** Newmarket, Suffolk

FOCUS
An ordinary middle-distance handicap and a slow-motion finish, but the favourite was much too good. The winner has clear potential to do better still.

7896 SUNBETS.CO.UK TOP PRICE ON ALL FAVOURITES ALL-WEATHER "HANDS AND HEELS" APPRENTICE H'CAP 7f (F)
3:55 (3:55) (Class 6) (0-60,60) 3-Y-O+ **£3,234** (£962; £481; £240) **Stalls** Low

Form RPR

6000 **1** **Alpha Tauri (USA)**119 4321 10-9-7 **60** BenRobinson(3) 3 67
(Charles Smith) *chsd ldrs: n.m.r 2f out: sn led: drvn out* **16/1**

4020 **2** 1/2 **Lmntrix**35 7103 4-9-6 **56** JaneElliott 6 62
(George Margarson) *chsd ldrs: 2nd over 1f out: no ex clsng stages* **13/2**3

0503 **3** 2 1/4 **Prisom (IRE)**30 7261 3-9-3 **59** WilliamCox(5) 8 58+
(Gay Kelleway) *hld up in mid-div: stdy hdwy over 3f out: kpt on to take 3rd last 75yds* **3/1**1

2350 **4** 2 3/4 **Wimboldsley**3 7850 5-8-11 **50** ManuelFernandes(3) 1 42
(Scott Dixon) *trckd ldrs: t.k.h: 2nd over 4f out: hung lft and led briefly 2f out: wknd last 100yds* **8/1**

5400 **5** 2 3/4 **Dr Red Eye**9 7751 8-9-4 **59** (b) LiamDoran(5) 2 44
(Scott Dixon) *led: hdd 2f out: wknd appr fnl f* **14/1**

4604 **6** 3/4 **Ershaad (IRE)**20 7509 4-8-11 **52** (b) BenSanderson(5) 13 35
(Shaun Harris) *in rr: sme hdwy over 2f out: nvr trbld ldrs* **14/1**

4166 **7** 2 1/4 **Coolcalmcollected (IRE)**16 7595 4-8-13 **56** (p) RossaRyan(7) 11 33
(David Loughnane) *dwlt: hdwy to trck ldrs after 2f: wknd over 1f out* **5/1**2

-000 **8** *shd* **Quina Brook (IRE)**56 6514 3-9-0 **56** TobyEley(5) 12 31
(Daniel Mark Loughnane) *mid-div: drvn 3f out: nvr a factor* **20/1**

0006 **9** 2 1/2 **Mr Chuckles (IRE)**35 7096 3-8-10 **52** (p) JamieGormley(5) 9 21
(Philip Kirby) *in rr and sn drvn along: outpcd 3f out* **9/1**

0540 **10** *13* **Pennine Warrior**17 7577 5-9-9 **59** (b) SamuelClarke 7
(Scott Dixon) *mid-div: effrt on ins over 2f out: lost pl over 1f out* **15/2**

0 **11** *4* **Captain Kendall (IRE)**225 1147 7-9-1 **51** (p) KieranSchofield 10
(Harry Chisman) *mid-div: effrt on ins over 2f out: edgd rt and lost pl over 1f out: sn bhd* **40/1**

1m 29.0s (-1.30) **Going Correction** -0.15s/f (Stan)
WFA 3 from 4yo+ 1lb **11** Ran SP% **114.3**
Speed ratings (Par 101): **101,100,97,94,91 90,88,88,85,70 65**
CSF £113.28 CT £401.85 TOTE £15.00: £3.50, £2.10, £1.60; EX 170.70 Trifecta £1342.10.
Owner J R Theaker **Bred** Flaxman Holdings Ltd **Trained** Temple Bruer, Lincs

FOCUS
A moderate "hands and heels" apprentice handicap and, despite a solid gallop the pace held up quite well. It went to a course specialist who was entitled to win off this mark/in this grade.
T/Plt: £1,035.30 to a £1 stake. Pool: £60093.22, 42.37 winning units. T/Qpdt: £105.50 to a £1 stake. Pool: £8270.75, 58.0 winning units. **Walter Glynn**

3733 LE CROISE-LAROCHE
Thursday, November 10
OFFICIAL GOING: Turf: heavy

7897a GRAND PRIX DU NORD (LISTED RACE) (3YO) (TURF) 1m 2f 110y
5:25 (12:00) 3-Y-O **£20,220** (£8,088; £6,066; £4,044; £2,022)

RPR

1 **Lily Passion**38 7029 3-8-13 0 ChristopheSoumillon 6 102
(P Bary, France) **5/1**3

2 1 3/4 **Saunter (FR)**34 7117 3-9-2 0 AurelienLemaitre 5 102
(David Menuisier) *sn midfield: rdn appr st: styd on u.p fnl f and jst up for 2nd post: no threat to wnr* **15/2**

3 *nse* **Le Juge (IRE)**17 7587 3-9-2 0 VincentCheminaud 7 102
(A Fabre, France) **31/5**

4 1 1/4 **Law Girl (FR)**136 3-8-13 0 StephanePasquier 4 96
(N Clement, France) **84/10**

5 3/4 **Sagaroi (FR)**23 7456 3-9-2 0 Francois-XavierBertras 9 98
(D Guillemin, France) **42/10**2

6 2 1/2 **Roche Rose (IRE)**100 5006 3-8-13 0 TonyPiccone 2 90
(E Lellouche, France) **14/1**

7 1 3/4 **Opulent D'Oroux (FR)**15 3-9-2 0 MaximeGuyon 8 90
(S Smrczek, Germany) **11/5**1

8 *15* **Accurate**10 3-9-2 0 RaphaelMarchelli 1 60
(A Fabre, France) **15/1**

9 *dist* **Boca Raton (IRE)**68 3-8-13 0 EddyHardouin 3
(E J O'Neill, France) **42/1**

WIN (incl. 1 euro stake): 4.30 (Lily Passion coupled with Roche Rose). PLACES: 2.20, 2.60, 2.10. DF: 23.20. SF: 44.80
Owner Ecurie Des Charmes **Bred** Aleyrion Bloodstock Ltd **Trained** Chantilly, France

7647 LINGFIELD (L-H)
Friday, November 11
OFFICIAL GOING: Polytrack: standard
Wind: virtually nil Weather: dry and bright

7898 £10 FREE AT 32RED.COM NURSERY H'CAP 7f 1y(P)
11:45 (11:46) (Class 5) (0-75,75) 2-Y-O **£3,234** (£962; £481; £240) **Stalls** Low

Form RPR

6214 **1** **Hersigh**23 7471 2-9-4 **75** 1 JosephineGordon(3) 4 79
(Saeed bin Suroor) *sn led and mde rest: shkn up over 1f out: kpt on under hands and heels riding and a doing enough ins fnl f* **9/4**1

0631 **2** 1/2 **Sans Souci Bay**13 7688 2-9-0 **75** TinaSmith(7) 14 78
(Richard Hannon) *hld up in tch in midfield: effrt on inner over 1f out: chsd ldrs u.p ins fnl f: styd on to snatch 2nd last strides* **9/1**

505 **3** *shd* **Sparkle**28 7314 2-9-2 **70** 1 AdamKirby 9 72
(Ed Dunlop) *hld up in tch in midfield: swtchd lft and effrt u.p over 1f out: styd on to chse wnr wl ins fnl f: kpt on: lost 2nd last strides* **7/1**3

0403 **4** *2* **Jet Setter (IRE)**20 7549 2-9-2 **70** JimmyFortune 3 67
(Brian Meehan) *chsd ldrs: effrt and rdn to chse wnr ent fnl f: no imp and one pced after: lost 2 pls wl ins fnl f* **8/1**

3522 **5** 3/4 **Tagur (IRE)**15 7640 2-9-0 **68** (p) TomEaves 8 63
(Kevin Ryan) *in tch in midfield: effrt over 1f out: drvn and no imp 1f out tl styd on fnl 100yds: nvr enough pce to threaten ldrs* **7/1**3

2226 **6** 1 1/4 **Texas Katie**13 7688 2-9-2 **70** (p) DavidProbert 12 62
(Archie Watson) *chsd ldrs: clsd to press wnr bnd 2f out: unable qck u.p over 1f out and lost 2nd ent fnl f: wknd fnl 100yds* **14/1**

055 **7** 1/2 **Legendoire (IRE)**15 7648 2-8-13 **67** MichaelJMMurphy 10 57
(John Gallagher) *in tch in midfield: effrt over 1f out: styd on same pce ins fnl f: nvr threatened ldrs* **50/1**

6340 **8** *nk* **Presence Process**23 7467 2-8-12 **71** PaddyBradley(5) 11 60
(Pat Phelan) *s.i.s: bhd: rdn over 1f out: styd on ins fnl f: nvr trbld ldrs* **50/1**

3256 **9** *nk* **Bellevarde (IRE)**57 6525 2-8-13 **72** 1 GeorgeWood(5) 13 61
(James Fanshawe) *hld up in tch towards rr: effrt over 1f out: sme hdwy ins fnl f: nvr trbld ldrs* **6/1**2

3643 **10** *nk* **Twiggy**48 6762 2-8-8 **67** CharlieBennett(5) 2 55
(Jane Chapple-Hyam) *squeezed for room s: sn bustled along in last quartet: rdn over 1f out: kpt on but nvr a threat to ldrs* **12/1**

F340 **11** *2* **Paddy A (IRE)**29 7306 2-8-13 **70** LouisSteward(3) 1 52
(Philip McBride) *bhd: pushed along over 4f out: nvr trbld ldrs* **16/1**

504 **12** 1 1/2 **Mr Maximum (USA)**24 7424 2-8-12 **66** LukeMorris 7 44
(Harry Dunlop) *a towards rr: drvn over 1f out: no prog and wknd ins fnl f* **12/1**

340 **13** *7* **Unzipped**22 7484 2-8-13 **67** StevieDonohoe 5 26
(Stuart Edmunds) *led for almost 1f: chsd wnr tl 2f out: sn u.p and lost pl: wknd over 1f out* **50/1**

1m 23.79s (-1.01) **Going Correction** -0.125s/f (Stan) **13** Ran SP% **125.0**
Speed ratings (Par 96): **100,99,99,97,96 94,94,93,93,93 90,89,81**
CSF £24.34 CT £132.63 TOTE £3.10: £1.70, £3.40, £1.90; EX 26.80 Trifecta £119.10.
Owner Godolphin **Bred** Darley **Trained** Newmarket, Suffolk
■ Stewards' Enquiry : Adam Kirby careless riding: caution
Stevie Donohoe jockey said filly lost action

FOCUS
An ordinary if competitive nursery to start and a straightforward all-the-way success for the favourite. The runner-up has been rated as building on his Chelmsford win, with the third also afforded minor improvement.

7899 BETWAY H'CAP 6f 1y(P)
12:15 (12:17) (Class 5) (0-75,74) 3-Y-O+ **£3,234** (£962; £360; £360) **Stalls** Low

Form RPR

1022 **1** **Kindly**27 7363 3-9-1 **73** GeorgeWood(5) 2 87
(Simon Crisford) *t.k.h: led for 1f: chsd ldr after: clsd and upsides over 1f out: pushed into ld ins fnl f: sn qcknd clr and r.o wl: comf* **3/1**2

2433 **2** 3 1/4 **Gung Ho Jack**15 7644 7-9-5 **72** KierenFox 1 75
(John Best) *in tch in midfield: nt clr run on inner over 2f out: rdn and hdwy over 1f out: chsd ldrs ins fnl f: styd on u.p to go 2nd towards fin: no threat to wnr: burst blood vessel* **5/2**1

3512 **3** *1* **Stormflower**25 7420 3-9-2 **69** DannyBrock 4 69
(John Bridger) *racd keenly: chsd wnr tl led after 1f out: jnd and rdn over 1f out: hdd jst ins fnl f: sn outpcd: wknd fnl 75yds* **12/1**

3240 **3** *dht* **Valmina**38 7038 9-9-1 **68** (t) LukeMorris 10 68
(Philip Hide) *stdd after s: hld up in last trio: hdwy on inner over 1f out: drvn and clsd ins fnl f: swtchd rt and kpt on fnl 100yds: no threat to wnr* **50/1**

0600 **5** *1* **The Big Lad**113 4563 4-9-5 **72** ShaneKelly 6 72+
(Richard Hughes) *hld up in midfield: effrt over 1f out: nt clr run and hmpd ent fnl f: pushed along and kpt on ins fnl f* **5/1**

4050 **6** 3/4 **Ebony N Ivory**46 6831 3-9-6 **73** DavidProbert 11 67
(Archie Watson) *chsd ldrs: unable qck u.p over 1f out: wknd ins fnl f* **14/1**

3641 **7** *nk* **Doctor Parkes**6 7811 10-9-2 **69** PatCosgrave 9 62
(Stuart Williams) *hld up in tch in midfield: rdn and unable qck over 1f out: sn btn and wknd ins fnl f* **7/2**3

0101 **8** 3/4 **Flowing Clarets**25 7415 3-9-4 **71** WilliamCarson 8 62
(John Bridger) *chsd ldrs: unable qck u.p over 1f out: wknd ins fnl f* **25/1**

6200 **9** *1* **Etaad (USA)**147 3354 5-8-13 **69** (b) HectorCrouch(3) 5 57
(Gary Moore) *s.i.s: sn pushed along in last trio: n.d* **14/1**

2236 **10** 3 1/4 **Colourbearer (IRE)**24 7444 9-9-1 **68** (t) BenCurtis 7 45
(Charlie Wallis) *taken down early: a last trio: no hdwy u.p over 1f out: wknd fnl f* **20/1**

1m 10.6s (-1.30) **Going Correction** -0.125s/f (Stan) **10** Ran SP% **124.1**
Speed ratings (Par 103): **103,98,97,97,96 95,94,93,92,87**
WIN: 4.00 Kindly; PL: 1.70 Kindly, 1.80 Stormflower, 1.50 Gung Ho Jack, 2.50 Valmina; EX: 12.80; CSF: 11.55; TC: 41.27, 164.94; TF: 41.20, 136.40;.
Owner The Johnstone Catridge Partnership **Bred** D Curran **Trained** Newmarket, Suffolk
■ Stewards' Enquiry : Kieren Fox vet reported gelding bled from the nose

FOCUS
An ordinary sprint handicap, but won in style by an unexposed and progressive filly. The field was reduced by one when Cinders was withdrawn after bolting before the start. It's been rated at face value, with the runner-up close to his best.

7900 32RED CASINO/EBF MAIDEN STKS 5f 6y(P)
12:45 (12:47) (Class 5) 2-Y-O **£3,363** (£1,001; £500; £250) **Stalls** High

Form RPR

1 **Team Meeting (USA)** 2-9-5 0 PatCosgrave 3 66+
(Saeed bin Suroor) *short of room and hmpd leaving stalls: sn in tch in midfield: hdwy on inner over 1f out: rdn to ld 1f out: r.o wl: rdn out* **8/11**[1]

3600 **2** 1 **Roundabout Magic (IRE)**[32] 7217 2-9-5 62 NickyMackay 7 62
(Simon Dow) *taken down early: stdd after s: hld up in tch in rr: hdwy on inner over 1f out: rdn to chse wnr ins fnl f: styd on same pce fnl 100yds* **20/1**

040 **3** 1¾ **Abundant Courage (IRE)**[35] 7122 2-9-5 69 JimmyFortune 9 56
(Brian Meehan) *chsd ldr: rdn over 1f out: unable qck u.p 1f out: styd on same pce ins fnl f* **11/1**

6 **4** hd **Gnaad (IRE)**[49] 6731 2-9-5 0 AdamKirby 1 55
(Robert Cowell) *led: drifted rt bnd wl over 1f out: hdd and no ex 1f out: kpt on same pce ins fnl f* **11/2**[3]

0366 **5** ½ **Lady Cleo (IRE)**[32] 7217 2-9-0 67 (t) DavidProbert 4 48
(Stuart Williams) *in tch in midfield: effrt over 1f out: unable qck* **4/1**[2]

345 **6** ¾ **Dontforgettocall**[67] 6189 2-9-5 68 TomMarquand 2 50
(Joseph Tuite) *wnt rt s: in tch in last trio: rdn jst over 2f out: sme hdwy u.p ins fnl f: nvr trbld ldrs* **16/1**

0 **7** 3¼ **Ballysampson**[63] 6295 2-9-5 0 FergusSweeney 6 39
(Roger Teal) *stdd after s: hld up in rr: rdn jst over 1f out: no imp: n.d* **66/1**

5 **8** ½ **Little Miss Daisy**[18] 7576 2-9-0 0 MartinDwyer 8 32
(William Muir) *dwlt: racd keenly: hdwy on outer after 1f: chsd ldrs 3f out tl hung rt: wd and lost pl bnd 2f out: bhd after* **16/1**

58.93s (0.13) **Going Correction** -0.125s/f (Stan) 8 Ran SP% **119.6**
Speed ratings (Par 96): **93,91,88,88,87 86,81,80**
CSF £21.16 TOTE £1.70: £1.10, £4.30, £2.30; EX 18.80 Trifecta £123.70.
Owner Godolphin **Bred** Darley **Trained** Newmarket, Suffolk

FOCUS
A moderate sprint maiden and although the hot favourite did enough to make a winning debut, the form doesn't look that strong with the placed horses rated 62 and 69. The fourth helps set the level.

7901 32RED.COM/BRITISH STALLION STUDS EBF FILLIES' H'CAP 1m 2f (P)
1:20 (1:20) (Class 3) (0-90,89) 3-Y-O **£9,136** (£2,734; £1,367; £684; £340) **Stalls** Low

Form RPR

2664 **1** **Indulged**[44] 6870 3-8-8 **81** GeorgeWood(5) 1 88
(James Fanshawe) *stdd s: hld up in tch in last pair: stl travelling wl and nt clr run ent fnl 2f: swtchd rt and bmpd rival wl over 1f out: hdwy to chal and wnt lft u.p ins fnl f: led 75yds out: r.o* **6/4**[1]

3415 **2** ¾ **Jawaayiz**[21] 7504 3-8-9 **80** HectorCrouch(3) 2 85
(Simon Crisford) *led: sn hdd and settled in 3rd: effrt to chse ldr whn nt clr run and swtchd rt ent fnl f: drvn and ev ch ins fnl f: styd on same pce towards fin* **5/1**[3]

2610 **3** ¾ **Rahyah**[6] 7823 3-8-11 **79** (p) DavidProbert 5 82
(Adrian Paul Keatley, Ire) *sn pushed up to ld: rdn and qcknd ent fnl 2f: drvn 1f out: hdd and one pced ins fnl f* **11/2**

3401 **4** 1 **Island Flame (IRE)**[42] 6922 3-8-7 **75** PatrickMathers 4 76
(Richard Fahey) *hld up in tch in last pair: effrt on outer wl over 1f out: chsng ldrs but keeping on same pce whn carried rt wl ins fnl f* **17/2**

110- **5** hd **Alinstante**[430] 6197 3-9-7 **89** LukeMorris 6 91
(Sir Mark Prescott Bt) *t.k.h: wl in tch in midfield: rdn and bmpd wl over 1f out: drvn over 1f out: keeping on same pce whn hmpd wl ins fnl f* **7/1**

1-30 **6** 5 **Farandine**[41] 6947 3-9-2 **84** AdamKirby 7 74
(Luca Cumani) *sn chsng ldr: rdn over 2f out: struggling to qckn whn short of room and lost pl jst over 1f out: wknd fnl f* **9/2**[2]

2m 4.99s (-1.61) **Going Correction** -0.125s/f (Stan) 6 Ran SP% **113.3**
Speed ratings (Par 103): **101,100,99,99,98 94**
CSF £9.53 TOTE £2.30: £1.60, £2.70; EX 9.40 Trifecta £40.70.
Owner Cheveley Park Stud **Bred** Cheveley Park Stud Ltd **Trained** Newmarket, Suffolk
■ Stewards' Enquiry : George Wood 2-day ban: careless riding (25-26 Nov)

FOCUS
A decent 3yo fillies' handicap, but they didn't go a great pace and a few pulled hard as a result, including the winner. The form is a bit fluid and muddling.

7902 SUNBETS.CO.UK H'CAP (DIV I) 1m 1y(P)
1:55 (1:56) (Class 4) (0-85,85) 3-Y-O+ **£5,175** (£1,540; £769; £384) **Stalls** High

Form RPR

5-02 **1** **Haaf A Sixpence**[8] 7781 7-9-4 **85** HectorCrouch(3) 7 94
(Ralph Beckett) *chsd ldr: shkn up to ld jst over 1f out: kpt on under mainly hands and heels riding and a doing enough ins fnl f* **9/2**[1]

1340 **2** 1¼ **Twin Point**[29] 7308 5-8-13 **77** (t) StevieDonohoe 6 83
(Charlie Fellowes) *taken down early: led: rdn and hdd over 1f out: kpt on same pce u.p ins fnl f* **8/1**

410 **3** 1 **Ripoll (IRE)**[23] 7462 3-8-7 **78** (t) MitchGodwin(5) 12 82+
(Sylvester Kirk) *hld up in rr: clsd and nt clrest of runs over 1f out: squeezed through and hdwy to chse ldng pair ins fnl f: r.o: nt rchd ldrs* **14/1**

210 **4** nk **Run To The Hills (USA)**[36] 7095 3-9-5 **85** LukeMorris 11 88+
(George Peckham) *stdd s: hld up in tch in last quartet on outer: rdn wl over 1f out: styd on wl ins fnl f: nt rchd ldrs* **5/1**[2]

3406 **5** hd **Presumido (IRE)**[23] 7461 6-9-4 **82** NickyMackay 10 85
(Simon Dow) *t.k.h: trckd ldrs: lost pl bnd 2f out: rdn jst over 1f out: hdwy ins fnl f: r.o wl fnl 100yds: nt rchd ldrs* **16/1**

3200 **6** nk **Inke (IRE)**[21] 7504 4-9-1 **79** (p) PatCosgrave 3 81
(Jim Boyle) *chsd ldrs: effrt in 4th 2f out: unable qck over 1f out: kpt on same pce ins fnl f* **12/1**

2640 **7** ½ **In The Red (IRE)**[13] 7699 3-9-4 **84** (b[1]) TomMarquand 4 85
(Richard Hannon) *t.k.h: chsd ldrs: rdn jst over 2f out: unable qck u.p over 1f out: lost 3rd and wknd ins fnl f* **7/1**[3]

3500 **8** nk **Take The Helm**[21] 7505 3-9-3 **83** JimmyFortune 8 85+
(Brian Meehan) *hld up in last trio: effrt and trying to switch rt over 1f out: hdwy ins fnl f: kpt on: nvr trbld ldrs* **7/1**[3]

2506 **9** nse **Franco's Secret**[24] 7428 5-9-2 **80** (p) SteveDrowne 2 80
(Peter Hedger) *stdd after s: hld up in last pair: effrt and wd bnd wl over 1f out: styd on ins fnl f: nvr trbld ldrs* **16/1**

1340 **10** ¾ **Character Onesie (IRE)**[20] 7535 4-8-12 **76** PatrickMathers 1 75+
(Richard Fahey) *in tch in midfield: nt clr run 2f out: effrt 1f out: nt clr run again and unable to cl ins fnl f: allowed to coast home after* **8/1**

3502 **11** 1¾ **Major Crispies**[16] 7617 5-9-3 **81** (t) AdamKirby 9 75
(Jeremy Gask) *in tch in midfield: effrt whn nt clr run and shuffled bk jst over 1f out: nvr enough room and bhd ins fnl f* **8/1**

0446 **12** nk **Danecase**[29] 7301 3-8-11 **77** FergusSweeney 5 70
(David Dennis) *in tch in midfield on outer: rdn and unable qck jst over 2f out: wknd fnl f* **20/1**

1m 36.34s (-1.86) **Going Correction** -0.125s/f (Stan)
WFA 3 from 4yo+ 2lb 12 Ran SP% **124.1**
Speed ratings (Par 105): **104,102,101,101,101 100,100,100,100,99 97,97**
CSF £42.48 CT £489.73 TOTE £4.70: £2.00, £3.40, £4.40; EX 53.60 Trifecta £756.00.
Owner Melody Racing **Bred** Melody Bloodstock **Trained** Kimpton, Hants

FOCUS
The first division of a fair handicap, but the front pair dominated throughout while there was trouble in behind. It's been rated around the first two.

7903 SUNBETS.CO.UK H'CAP (DIV II) 1m 1y(P)
2:30 (2:31) (Class 4) (0-85,85) 3-Y-O+ **£5,175** (£1,540; £769; £384) **Stalls** High

Form RPR

620 **1** **Carolinae**[41] 6939 4-8-12 **76** StevieDonohoe 11 85
(Charlie Fellowes) *stdd after s: hld up in last pair: clsd gng wl and swtchd lft over 1f out: qcknd to ld ins fnl f: r.o strly: comf* **7/1**[3]

500 **2** 1½ **Mikmak**[13] 7699 3-9-4 **84** [1] MartinDwyer 6 89
(William Muir) *hld up in tch in midfield: effrt to chse ldr over 1f out: drvn and ev ch 1f out: chsd wnr and r.o same pce fnl 100yds* **20/1**

5103 **3** ¾ **Red Tea**[21] 7505 3-9-3 **83** PatCosgrave 1 86
(Peter Hiatt) *wl in tch in midfield: effrt over 1f out: kpt on u.p ins fnl f* **7/1**[3]

5 **4** ½ **London (FR)**[8] 7779 3-9-4 **84** (t) AdamKirby 5 86
(Phil McEntee) *led: rdn and qcknd jst over 2f out: hrd drvn over 1f out: hdd ins fnl f: npo ex and wknd towards fin* **9/1**

4132 **5** ½ **Golden Wedding (IRE)**[23] 7461 4-8-13 **80** GeorgeDowning(3) 7 81
(Eve Johnson Houghton) *chsd ldng trio: effrt over 1f out: kpt on same pce ins fnl f* **5/1**[2]

-000 **6** 3 **Marcret (ITY)**[62] 6331 9-9-4 **82** DavidProbert 4 76
(James Unett) *hld up in tch in midfield: effrt and unable qck over 1f out: sn outpcd and wl hld fnl f* **33/1**

5241 **7** ½ **Dream Of Summer (IRE)**[23] 7457 3-8-12 **81** RobHornby(3) 12 74
(Andrew Balding) *chsd ldr and grad moved towards inner: rdn and lost 2nd over 1f out: wknd ins fnl f* **5/2**[1]

360- **8** ¾ **Torment**[432] 6130 3-8-12 **78** TomMarquand 3 69
(Richard Hannon) *hld up in tch in last trio: nt clr run over 1f out: no imp fnl f* **25/1**

55-0 **9** nk **Gossiping**[14] 7671 4-8-7 **74** HectorCrouch(3) 10 65
(Gary Moore) *stdd after s: hld up in tch in last pair: effrt on inner over 1f out: no imp and wl hld fnl f* **33/1**

30P3 **10** 1½ **Passing Star**[20] 7530 5-9-7 **85** LukeMorris 9 72
(Charles Hills) *hld up in tch in midfield: lost pl and drvn bnd wl over 1f out: no hdwy and bhd fnl f* **5/2**[1]

2620 **11** 3 **Like No Other**[29] 7308 3-9-1 **81** JimmyFortune 2 61
(Les Eyre) *chsd ldrs: rdn wl over 1f out: sn btn and wknd fnl f* **20/1**

1m 36.01s (-2.19) **Going Correction** -0.125s/f (Stan)
WFA 3 from 4yo+ 2lb 11 Ran SP% **128.1**
Speed ratings (Par 105): **105,103,102,102,101 98,98,97,97,95 92**
CSF £146.71 CT £1053.70 TOTE £8.80: £2.50, £6.00, £2.40; EX 206.10 Trifecta £1122.60.
Owner The Dalmunzie Devils Partnership **Bred** Meon Valley Stud **Trained** Newmarket, Suffolk

FOCUS
The winning time was 0.33sec quicker than the first division and, in a race run at a solid gallop, the winner showed an impressive turn of foot. The form is set around the runner-up and fourth.

7904 BETWAY MAIDEN STKS 1m 4f (P)
3:05 (3:06) (Class 5) 3-Y-O+ **£3,234** (£962; £481; £240) **Stalls** Low

Form RPR

34 **1** **Brodie**[30] 7280 3-9-0 0 JimmyFortune 6 78+
(Luca Cumani) *chsd ldr after 1f: rdn to press ldr 3f out: kpt on u.p: led ins fnl f: styd on: rdn out* **5/4**[1]

044 **2** ¾ **Adalene**[100] 5025 3-9-0 77 PatCosgrave 2 77
(David Simcock) *chsd ldr for 1f: chsd ldng pair: rdn and clr in ldng trio over 2f out: swtchd lft and drvn to chal ent fnl f: kpt on u.p: hld towards fin* **5/1**[3]

-243 **3** 1¼ **Statuesque**[36] 7102 3-9-0 76 AdamKirby 7 75
(Sir Michael Stoute) *led: rdn 3f out: drvn and hrd pressed over 1f out: hdd ins fnl f: no ex and outpcd fnl 75yds* **11/8**[2]

3 **4** 6 **Cape Dignity (IRE)**[17] 7597 3-9-5 0 [1] BenCurtis 3 70
(Hugo Palmer) *in tch in midfield: 4th and outpcd u.p 3f out: no imp and kpt on same pce after* **7/1**

0 **5** 10 **Divine Prince (GR)**[121] 4265 3-9-2 0 HectorCrouch(3) 4 54
(Amanda Perrett) *hld up in tch in midfield: shkn up 3f out: sn outpcd: wl btn fnl 2f* **25/1**

00 **6** ¾ **Ravenswood**[16] 7627 3-9-5 0 FergusSweeney 1 53
(Jonathan Portman) *s.i.s: in tch in rr: rdn over 3f out: sn struggling: wl btn 2f out* **66/1**

0 **7** 2¼ **Shakshuka (IRE)**[16] 7627 4-9-6 0 SteveDrowne 8 45
(Seamus Mullins) *hld up in tch in last pair: shkn up 3f out: sn outpcd and wl btn 2f out* **100/1**

00 **8** ¾ **Tractive Effort**[142] 3535 3-9-5 0 KierenFox 5 48
(Michael Attwater) *t.k.h: chsd ldng trio: rdn 4f out: outpcd and btn 3f out: bhd 2f out* **100/1**

2m 31.08s (-1.92) **Going Correction** -0.125s/f (Stan)
WFA 3 from 4yo 6lb 8 Ran SP% **123.0**
Speed ratings (Par 103): **101,100,99,95,89 88,87,86**
CSF £9.03 TOTE £2.30: £1.10, £1.60, £1.10; EX 11.60 Trifecta £19.50.
Owner Normandie Stud Ltd **Bred** Aston House Stud **Trained** Newmarket, Suffolk

FOCUS
A modest older-horse maiden and they only went an ordinary pace. The three market leaders, all fillies, dominated throughout. It's been rated around the runner-up.

7905 BETWAY APPRENTICE H'CAP 1m 4f (P)
3:40 (3:41) (Class 6) (0-65,65) 3-Y-O+ **£3,234** (£962; £481; £240) **Stalls** Low

Form RPR

3063 **1** **Courtsider**[48] 6765 4-9-9 **64** (v) RobHornby 9 73+
(Lucy Wadham) *s.i.s: hld up in rr: clsd and travelling strly over 2f out: chsng ldrs whn swtchd rt and squeezed through to chse ldr 1f out: pushed into ld ins fnl f: r.o wl: readily* **8/1**

1020 **2** 2¼ **Maria's Choice (IRE)**[16] 7614 7-9-8 **63** MichaelJMMurphy 7 65
(Jim Best) *led: rdn over 1f out: hdd and one pce ins fnl f* **16/1**

556 **3** *nk* **Medicean Queen (IRE)**[16] 7609 5-8-12 **56**.........(t) CallumShepherd(3) 4 58
(Phil McEntee) *chsd ldrs: effrt to chse ldrs over 1f out: kpt on same pce ins fnl f* **16/1**

6350 **4** *1 ¼* **Perfect Rhythm**[24] 7429 5-9-8 **63**.................................. HectorCrouch 5 63
(Patrick Chamings) *in tch in midfield: effrt and n.m.r over 1f out: kpt on same pce ins fnl f* **10/1**

5005 **5** *nk* **Gloryette**[16] 7609 3-9-1 **65**......................................(b¹) GeorgeWood(3) 12 64
(Ed Dunlop) *chsd ldrs: effrt over 1f out: kpt on same pce u.p ins fnl f* **6/1**²

2020 **6** *1* **Aurora Gray**[14] 7656 3-9-1 **65**.................................. CharlieBennett(3) 10 63
(Hughie Morrison) *chsd ldr tl 6f out: styd chsng ldrs: rdn over 1f out: sltly short of room 1f out: wknd ins fnl f* **7/1**

5300 **7** *1 ¼* **Trending (IRE)**[24] 7429 7-9-7 **65**..............................(t) DavidParkes(3) 11 61
(Jeremy Gask) *trckd ldrs: wnt 2nd 6f out: rdn and ev ch over 1f out: no ex 1f out: wknd ins fnl f* **10/1**

500 **8** *3* **Threediamondrings**[47] 6805 3-8-8 **58**......................¹ MitchGodwin(3) 13 49
(Brendan Powell) *hld up in rr: effrt over 2f out: keeping on but no threat to ldrs whn hmpd ent fnl f: no imp after* **20/1**

4340 **9** *2 ¾* **Peeps**[62] 6335 4-8-3 **51**..(p) GeorgiaDobie(7) 8 38
(Mark H Tompkins) *v.s.a: in rr but steadily rcvrd: effrt ent fnl 2f: no imp and wl hld whn hmpd ent fnl f* **12/1**

620 **B** **Diletta Tommasa (IRE)**[14] 7656 6-9-0 **62**.......................(v) TobyEley(7) 6 49+
(Daniel Mark Loughnane) *v.s.a: steadily rcvrd and in midfield 5f out: rdn 2f out: sn struggling and btn whn b.d ent fnl f* **13/2**³

5000 **U** **Salient**[23] 7464 12-8-11 **52**.. EdwardGreatrex 14 30+
(Michael Attwater) *in tch in midfield: rdn and lost pl over 2f out: bhd whn hmpd and uns rdr ent fnl f* **33/1**

3060 **F** **Bamako Du Chatelet (FR)**[24] 7429 5-9-8 **63**.........(p) GeorgeDowning 2 65+
(Ian Williams) *hld up in midfield: nt clr run over 2f out: clsd to chse ldrs over 1f out: effrt whn squeezed for room: clipped heels and fell heavily ent fnl f* **7/2**¹

1-50 **P** **Artistic Flight (IRE)**[15] 7653 4-9-5 **65**.....................(p) PaddyBradley(5) 3
(Jim Boyle) *hld up in last quartet: lost tch and eased 4f out: p.u 2f out: sddle slipped* **20/1**

2m 30.19s (-2.81) **Going Correction** -0.125s/f (Stan)
WFA 3 from 4yo+ 6lb **13** Ran SP% **123.6**
Speed ratings (Par 101): **104,102,102,101,101 100,99,97,95, , ,**
CSF £130.14 CT £2020.77 TOTE £9.60: £3.30, £5.50, £5.60; EX 170.80 Trifecta £4457.30.
Owner The Calculated Speculators **Bred** Mohammad Al Qatami **Trained** Newmarket, Suffolk

FOCUS
A moderate apprentice handicap and drama late on with the favourite Bamako Du Chatelet, who was trying for the same gap as the winner, running out of room and coming down over a furlong from home, bringing down Diletta Tommasa who in turn caused Salient to unseat his rider. The stewards were satisfied that the incident was accidental. The second and third help with the opening level.
T/Plt: £119.00 to a £1 stake. Pool: £52470.78, 321.81 winning units. T/Qpdt: £71.40 to a £1 stake. Pool: £4593.34, 47.6 winning units. **Steve Payne**

7748 WOLVERHAMPTON (A.W) (L-H)
Friday, November 11

OFFICIAL GOING: Tapeta: standard
Wind: Light behind Weather: Overcast

7906 £10 FREE AT 32RED.COM MAIDEN STKS 7f 32y (Tp)
4:15 (4:17) (Class 5) 2-Y-O **£3,234** (£962; £481; £240) **Stalls** High

Form RPR

2 **1** **Cliffs Of Capri**[29] 7307 2-9-5 0.. RobertHavlin 11 80
(Simon Crisford) *pushed along to go prom after 1f: chsd ldr over 4f out: shkn up over 2f out: rdn to ld over 1f out: styd on* **11/4**²

22 **2** *1 ¼* **Archer's Arrow (USA)**[23] 7458 2-9-2 0................ JosephineGordon(3) 3 77
(Saeed bin Suroor) *hld up: hdwy over 1f out: r.o to go 2nd wl ins fnl f: nt rch wnr* **7/2**³

6 **3** *1 ¾* **Never A Word (USA)**[155] 3054 2-9-5 0...........................¹ JamesDoyle 6 73
(Charlie Appleby) *sn pushed along in mid-div: hdwy 1/2-way: rdn and hung lft ins fnl f: styd on same pce* **5/1**

24 **4** *1 ¼* **Zefferino**[58] 6481 2-9-5 0... GeorgeBaker 8 69
(Roger Charlton) *led 6f out: rdn and hdd over 1f out: hung lft and no ex ins fnl f* **2/1**¹

0 **5** *½* **Enhancement (IRE)**[23] 7468 2-9-5 0.................................. SeanLevey 5 68+
(Richard Hannon) *trckd ldrs: shkn up over 1f out: hung lft and nt clr run ins fnl f: styd on same pce* **16/1**

6 *1 ¼* **Althib** 2-9-5 0...¹ PaulHanagan 7 65
(Charles Hills) *s.i.s: hld up: rdn over 1f out: r.o ins fnl f: nvr nrr* **9/1**

0 **7** *½* **Mutineer**[168] 2649 2-9-5 0.. MartinHarley 4 64
(Daniel Kubler) *led 1f: chsd ldr tl over 4f out: remained handy: rdn over 1f out: nt clr run and wknd ins fnl f* **100/1**

8 *2 ¾* **Cartavio (IRE)** 2-9-5 0.. ShaneKelly 12 57
(David Lanigan) *s.i.s: rdn 1/2-way: sme hdwy on outer over 2f out: wknd over 1f out* **66/1**

9 *hd* **My Aussie Rules** 2-9-5 0... JohnFahy 10 56
(Clive Cox) *chsd ldrs: pushed along 1/2-way: wknd wl over 1f out* **66/1**

00 **10** *3 ¾* **Sallee**[20] 7548 2-9-0 0.. ConnorBeasley 2 42
(Adrian Wintle) *hld up: pushed along over 2f out: sn wknd* **100/1**

0 **11** *2 ¼* **Retribution**[14] 7664 2-9-5 0.. TomQueally 1 41
(David Lanigan) *s.i.s: a in rr: pushed along 1/2-way: lost tch over 2f out* **80/1**

1m 28.25s (-0.55) **Going Correction** -0.15s/f (Stan) **11** Ran SP% **121.0**
Speed ratings (Par 96): **97,95,93,92,91 90,89,86,86,81 79**
CSF £13.36 TOTE £3.50: £1.20, £2.30, £1.30; EX 15.50 Trifecta £50.10.
Owner Rathordan Partnership **Bred** Glebe Farm Stud **Trained** Newmarket, Suffolk

FOCUS
A useful maiden run at a decent pace. The fourth has been rated below form.

7907 32RED CASINO MAIDEN STKS (DIV I) 1m 141y (Tp)
4:45 (4:46) (Class 5) 2-Y-O **£3,234** (£962; £481; £240) **Stalls** Low

Form RPR

6 **1** **First Nation**[31] 7239 2-9-5 0... JamesDoyle 9 79+
(Charlie Appleby) *chsd ldr over 7f out: led over 2f out: rdn over 1f out: r.o wl* **4/1**²

64 **2** *2 ¾* **Wild Shot**[36] 7100 2-9-5 0... RyanTate 2 71
(James Eustace) *chsd ldrs: rdn to chse wnr over 1f out: styd on same pce ins fnl f* **20/1**

0 **3** *½* **Lorikeet (USA)**[9] 7769 2-9-5 0....................................... PaulMulrennan 5 70
(Mark Johnston) *led: rdn and hdd over 2f out: edgd lft over 1f out: no ex ins fnl f* **100/1**

55 **4** *hd* **Quloob**[31] 7239 2-9-5 0.. PaulHanagan 1 70
(Owen Burrows) *prom: nt clr run 7f out: rdn over 1f out: r.o* **16/1**

35 **5** *nk* **Suspect Package (USA)**[43] 6904 2-9-5 0.......................... TimmyMurphy 3 69+
(James Fanshawe) *hld up: swtchd rt and hdwy over 1f out: r.o: nt rch ldrs* **14/1**

3 **6** *nk* **American History (USA)**[32] 7225 2-9-5 0...................... RobertHavlin 7 68
(John Gosden) *sn pushed along to chse ldrs: rdn over 2f out: no ex ins fnl f* **1/1**¹

7 *1 ¼* **Bahar (USA)** 2-9-5 0... SeanLevey 6 66
(Richard Hannon) *hld up: hdwy over 1f out: nt trble ldrs* **8/1**

0 **8** *4* **London Master**[21] 7503 2-9-5 0....................................... GeorgeBaker 10 57
(Chris Wall) *s.i.s: hld up: nvr on terms* **28/1**

9 *½* **Serenade The Stars (IRE)** 2-9-5 0.............................¹ MartinHarley 8 56
(James Tate) *prom: stdd and lost pl 7f out: n.d after* **25/1**

6 **10** *nk* **Nathan Mayer**[28] 7318 2-9-5 0...................................... GrahamGibbons 11 56
(Sir Michael Stoute) *sn prom on outer: rdn over 2f out: wknd over 1f out* **7/1**³

0 **11** *14* **Twiston Shout (IRE)**[9] 7769 2-9-5 0................................. LiamKeniry 4 26
(Richard Spencer) *s.i.s: sn pushed along in rr: wknd over 2f out* **100/1**

1m 49.11s (-0.99) **Going Correction** -0.15s/f (Stan) **11** Ran SP% **120.2**
Speed ratings (Par 96): **98,95,95,94,94 94,93,89,89,89 76**
CSF £86.30 TOTE £6.60: £1.90, £4.40, £9.80; EX 101.90 Trifecta £5698.20 Part Won..
Owner Godolphin **Bred** Darley **Trained** Newmarket, Suffolk

FOCUS
This pace was steady for this fair maiden. The runner-up has been rated to his mark.

7908 32RED CASINO MAIDEN STKS (DIV II) 1m 141y (Tp)
5:15 (5:16) (Class 5) 2-Y-O **£3,234** (£962; £481; £240) **Stalls** Low

Form RPR

4 **1** **African Beat (IRE)**[20] 7548 2-9-0 0.................................... JamesDoyle 5 74
(John Gosden) *prom: chsd ldr over 6f out: led over 1f out: sn rdn: r.o* **6/4**¹

2 *¾* **Flaming Marvel (IRE)** 2-9-5 0.. TomQueally 7 77+
(James Fanshawe) *hld up: rdn over 1f out: r.o wl ins fnl f: nt rch wnr* **40/1**

3 *1 ½* **Capital City (IRE)** 2-9-5 0... KevinStott 4 74+
(Saeed bin Suroor) *hld up: hdwy over 1f out: sn rdn: r.o* **5/1**³

0 **4** *nk* **Pete So High (GER)**[21] 7501 2-9-5 0................................. SeanLevey 2 74
(Richard Hannon) *hld up in tch: rdn over 1f out: r.o* **20/1**

03 **5** *shd* **Beach Break**[21] 7501 2-9-5 0.. GeorgeBaker 11 73
(Ralph Beckett) *sn led: rdn and hdd over 1f out: edgd lft and styd on same pce ins fnl f* **10/3**²

6 **6** *1 ½* **Sable Island (IRE)**[44] 6881 2-9-5 0............................. GrahamGibbons 8 70
(Sir Michael Stoute) *sn chsng ldrs: pushed along over 6f out: rdn over 1f out: no ex ins fnl f* **7/1**

6 **7** *½* **Screaming Gemini (IRE)**[14] 7665 2-9-5 0........................ JackMitchell 6 69
(Roger Varian) *mid-div: rdn and hung lft fr over 1f out: nt trble ldrs* **14/1**

8 *1 ¼* **War At Sea (IRE)** 2-9-5 0... JamieSpencer 10 67+
(David Simcock) *s.i.s and hmpd s: hld up: shkn up and styd on fnl f: nvr nrr* **20/1**

9 *2 ½* **My Brother Mike (IRE)** 2-9-5 0.. DaleSwift 3 61
(Daniel Mark Loughnane) *s.i.s: hld up: rdn over 1f out: hmpd ins fnl f: n.d* **100/1**

0 **10** *1 ¾* **Kuiper Belt (USA)**[14] 7665 2-9-5 0...................................... ShaneKelly 1 58
(David Lanigan) *plld hrd and prom: rdn over 2f out: wkng whn hung lft ins fnl f: eased* **40/1**

11 *5* **Hochfeld (IRE)** 2-9-5 0... PaulMulrennan 9 47
(Mark Johnston) *s.i.s and edgd rt s: hdwy over 6f out: rdn over 3f out: wknd wl over 1f out* **50/1**

1m 49.09s (-1.01) **Going Correction** -0.15s/f (Stan) **11** Ran SP% **116.3**
Speed ratings (Par 96): **98,97,96,95,95 94,93,92,90,88 84**
CSF £87.43 TOTE £2.40: £1.10, £8.00, £1.80; EX 89.30 Trifecta £207.10.
Owner Godolphin **Bred** Darley **Trained** Newmarket, Suffolk

FOCUS
An interesting maiden run at a steady pace. The field was compressed at the finish, though, and the time was quite ordinary.

7909 32RED.COM NURSERY H'CAP 1m 141y (Tp)
5:45 (5:45) (Class 2) 2-Y-O **£8,821** (£2,640; £1,320; £660; £329) **Stalls** Low

Form RPR

261 **1** **Commander Cole**[24] 7432 2-9-2 **94**.............................. JoshDoyle(5) 6 101+
(Saeed bin Suroor) *hld up: hdwy over 1f out: rdn to ld and hung lft wl ins fnl f: qcknd clr* **2/1**¹

4421 **2** *2 ¼* **Masham Star (IRE)**[20] 7541 2-9-6 **93**.......................... PaulMulrennan 4 95
(Mark Johnston) *w ldr: led wl over 1f out: edgd rt: rdn: edgd lft and hdd wl ins fnl f: sn outpcd* **7/1**

332 **3** *2* **Draw Swords**[21] 7511 2-8-7 **80**.. RobertHavlin 5 78
(John Gosden) *trckd ldrs: plld hrd: rdn and nt clr run over 1f out: edgd lft and styd on same pce ins fnl f* **3/1**²

2032 **4** *1 ¼* **Upgrade**[17] 7598 2-8-2 **75**...(p) JoeyHaynes 2 70
(K R Burke) *led at stdy pce: qcknd 3f out: sn rdn: hdd wl over 1f out: no ex ins fnl f* **20/1**

0101 **5** *shd* **Plant Pot Power (IRE)**[23] 7460 2-8-8 **86**...................... HollieDoyle(5) 3 81
(Richard Hannon) *trckd ldrs: racd keenly: rdn over 1f out: no ex ins fnl f* **11/2**

2115 **6** *hd* **Zymyran**[21] 7493 2-8-12 **85**.. JamieSpencer 1 80
(David Simcock) *hld up: shkn up and hung lft fr over 2f out: nvr on terms* **7/2**³

1m 48.91s (-1.19) **Going Correction** -0.15s/f (Stan) **6** Ran SP% **113.2**
Speed ratings (Par 102): **99,97,95,94,94 93**
CSF £16.75 TOTE £3.60: £1.90, £2.30; EX 13.60 Trifecta £65.30.
Owner Godolphin **Bred** Usk Valley Stud **Trained** Newmarket, Suffolk

FOCUS
They went a steady pace for this competitive handicap. The winner looks up to Listed class and the runner-up has been rated as backing up his latest effort.

7910 BETWAY CLASSIFIED STKS 1m 1f 103y (Tp)
6:20 (6:20) (Class 6) 3-Y-O+ **£2,587** (£770; £384; £192) **Stalls** Low

Form RPR

5416 **1** **Pensax Lady (IRE)**[31] 7256 3-8-13 53............................. GrahamGibbons 3 57
(Daniel Mark Loughnane) *hld up in tch: rdn to chse ldr over 1f out: r.o to ld wl ins fnl f* **4/1**²

040 **2** *¾* **Thatsthewaytodoit (IRE)**[21] 7515 3-8-10 50..... JosephineGordon(3) 12 56
(Daniel Mark Loughnane) *sn led: rdn clr over 1f out: hdd and unable qck wl ins fnl f* **8/1**

5023 **3** *shd* **Deftera Lad (IRE)**[23] 7463 4-9-2 50............................. TimmyMurphy 10 54
(Natalie Lloyd-Beavis) *hld up: hdwy over 1f out: r.o: nt quite rch ldrs* **7/1**³

0566 **4** *1 1/4* **Let There Be Light**[10] 7742 3-8-13 53 RobertHavlin 13 53
(Gay Kelleway) *mid-div: nt clr run over 2f out: hdwy over 1f out: r.o* **12/1**

0053 **5** *3/4* **Kay Sera**[60] 6424 8-8-13 55 EoinWalsh(3) 1 51
(Tony Newcombe) *hld up: nt clr run fr over 2f out tl swtchd lft over 1f out: swtchd rt ins fnl f: rdn: edgd lft and r.o towards fin: nvr nr to chal* **11/4**[1]

1020 **6** *2 1/4* **Desert Tango**[31] 7256 3-8-13 52 [1] TomEaves 4 47
(Michael Mullineaux) *mid-div: hdwy over 2f out: rdn over 1f out: no ex fnl f* **12/1**

-000 **7** *nk* **My Bubba**[15] 7645 4-9-2 44 LiamKeniry 7 46
(John Flint) *trckd ldrs: racd keenly: wnt 2nd 3f out tl rdn over 1f out: edgd lft and wknd ins fnl f* **16/1**

46-6 **8** *2 1/4* **McCarthy Mor (IRE)**[31] 7260 5-9-2 47 (v) KieranO'Neill 8 41
(Mandy Rowland) *s.i.s: hld up: plld hrd: nt clr run over 2f out: n.d* **18/1**

0-00 **9** *3/4* **Wild Bloom**[29] 7311 3-8-13 55 JamieSpencer 9 41
(Ed Vaughan) *chsd ldr after 1f tl over 6f out: remained handy: rdn over 2f out: wknd fnl f* **9/1**

0/0- **10** *3 1/4* **Xclusive**[14] 2697 6-9-2 48 ShaneKelly 6 34
(Ronald Harris) *plld hrd and prom: rdn over 2f out: wknd over 1f out* **16/1**

050 **11** *16* **Sonnentanz (IRE)**[29] 7311 3-8-13 55 MartinHarley 5 4
(Daniel Kubler) *hld up: swtchd rt over 7f out: pushed along and hdwy to chse ldr over 6f out: rdn and lost 2nd 3f out: wknd 2f out* **22/1**

00-0 **12** *12* **Custom (IRE)**[61] 6373 3-8-6 47 (b[1]) KieranSchofield(7) 11
(Daniel O'Brien) *plld hrd and prom: rdn over 3f out: wknd over 2f out* **100/1**

2m 0.64s (-0.16) **Going Correction** -0.15s/f (Stan)
WFA 3 from 4yo+ 3lb **12** Ran SP% **118.0**
Speed ratings (Par 101): **94,93,93,92,91 89,89,87,86,83 69,58**
CSF £36.04 TOTE £5.50: £2.30, £3.60, £1.20; EX 35.10 Trifecta £317.70.
Owner S & A Mares **Bred** Select Bloodstock & Melchior Bloodstock **Trained** Baldwin's Gate, Staffs

FOCUS
A modest contest run at an honest pace. It's been rated around the first four.

7911 BETWAY H'CAP 1m 1f 103y (Tp)
6:50 (6:50) (Class 5) (0-75,75) 3-Y-O+ **£3,234** (£962; £481; £240) **Stalls** Low

Form RPR

0001 **1** **Drago (IRE)**[21] 7514 4-9-2 70 GrahamGibbons 2 77+
(David O'Meara) *a.p: led over 1f out: rdn and hung lft ins fnl f: styd on* **9/2**[2]

3434 **2** *1/2* **Nonios (IRE)**[51] 6676 4-9-6 74 JamieSpencer 12 81+
(David Simcock) *s.i.s: hld up: hdwy: nt clr run and swtchd rt over 1f out: shkn up and edgd lft ins fnl f: r.o to go 2nd towards fin: nt rch wnr* **5/2**[1]

105 **3** *3/4* **Tan Arabiq**[13] 7691 3-8-6 66 JosephineGordon(3) 5 71
(Michael Appleby) *chsd ldr 2f: remained handy: rdn over 1f out: edgd lft and chsd wnr ins fnl f tl towards fin* **22/1**

5450 **4** *1 1/4* **Zabeel Star (IRE)**[34] 7141 4-9-2 70 JoeDoyle 3 71
(Graeme McPherson) *hld up in tch: rdn over 2f out: nt clr run wl ins fnl f: kpt on* **8/1**

6240 **5** *shd* **Enmeshing**[34] 7141 3-9-3 74 TomQueally 6 76+
(James Fanshawe) *hmpd sn after s: hld up: hdwy over 1f out: rdn and nt clr run ins fnl f: styd on* **15/2**[3]

0220 **6** *3/4* **Sands Chorus**[16] 7623 4-9-7 75 TomEaves 1 75
(James Given) *led: rdn and hdd over 2f out: no ex wl ins fnl f* **15/2**[3]

3000 **7** *shd* **Dunquin (IRE)**[116] 4455 4-8-13 67 LukeMorris 7 66
(John Mackie) *prom: chsd ldr after 2f tl led over 2f out: rdn and hdd over 1f out: edgd lft and no ex wl ins fnl f* **16/1**

600 **8** *3* **Loving Your Work**[24] 7429 5-8-13 67 ShaneKelly 4 60
(Ken Cunningham-Brown) *hld up in tch: rdn and hung lft fr over 1f out: nt run on* **40/1**

5261 **9** *hd* **Dana's Present**[16] 7620 7-9-4 72 LiamKeniry 13 65
(Tom Dascombe) *s.i.s: hld up: plld hrd: rdn over 2f out: n.d* **14/1**

10 *3/4* **Dance On The Hill (IRE)**[172] 4-9-3 71 GeorgeBaker 8 62
(Roger Charlton) *hld up: hdwy over 2f out: edgd lft: wknd and eased fnl f* **18/1**

0-00 **11** *2 1/4* **Seagull Star**[27] 7359 5-9-6 74 ConnorBeasley 10 60
(Keith Dalgleish) *hld up: rdn over 2f out: wknd over 1f out* **11/1**

6050 **12** *2 1/2* **Idol Deputy (FR)**[69] 6138 10-9-0 73 RachealKneller(5) 9 54
(James Bennett) *hld up: rdn over 2f out: wknd over 1f out* **25/1**

1m 57.07s (-3.73) **Going Correction** -0.15s/f (Stan) course record
WFA 3 from 4yo+ 3lb **12** Ran SP% **118.2**
Speed ratings (Par 103): **110,109,108,107,107 107,106,104,104,103 101,99**
CSF £15.65 CT £226.24 TOTE £3.60: £1.90, £1.10, £5.60; EX 17.40 Trifecta £300.60.
Owner Dr Marwan Koukash **Bred** Sheikh Sultan Bin Khalifa Al Nayhan **Trained** Upper Helmsley, N Yorks

FOCUS
The pace was steady for this open handicap. It's been rated around the third and fifth.

7912 BETWAY APP H'CAP 5f 216y (Tp)
7:20 (7:23) (Class 6) (0-60,60) 3-Y-O+ **£2,587** (£770; £384; £192) **Stalls** Low

Form RPR

0240 **1** **Divine Call**[6] 7817 9-9-7 60 (b) GeorgeBaker 9 66
(Milton Bradley) *hld up: hdwy over 1f out: qcknd to ld nr fin* **9/1**

5524 **2** *1/2* **Canford Belle**[23] 7463 3-9-1 54 PaddyAspell 1 59
(Grant Tuer) *sn pushed along to join ldr: led over 2f out: rdn over 1f out: hdd nr fin* **16/1**

0000 **3** *nk* **Bonjour Steve**[9] 7774 5-9-2 60 (p) PhilDennis(5) 2 64
(Richard Price) *chsd ldrs: rdn to go 2nd 1f out: r.o* **18/1**

4511 **4** *1/2* **Commanche**[13] 7694 7-9-1 54 (b) MartinHarley 7 56
(Chris Dwyer) *chsd ldrs: rdn over 2f out: styd on* **2/1**[1]

650 **5** *1 1/2* **Indigo Princess**[263] 679 3-9-4 60 AlistairRawlinson(3) 6 58
(Michael Appleby) *prom: outpcd over 2f out: rallied over 1f out: r.o* **33/1**

0000 **6** *hd* **Secret Bird (IRE)**[60] 6408 4-8-12 54 JackDuern(3) 10 51
(Dean Ivory) *led over 3f out: sn rdn: no ex ins fnl f* **25/1**

0U10 **7** *3/4* **Humour (IRE)**[9] 7774 5-9-4 57 (b) RobertHavlin 3 52
(Christine Dunnett) *mid-div: hdwy 2f out: rdn over 1f out: styd on same pce ins fnl f* **4/1**[2]

3023 **8** *nse* **Secret Witness**[62] 6311 10-9-5 58 (b) ShaneKelly 4 53
(Ronald Harris) *s.i.s: hld up: r.o towards fin: nvr nrr* **16/1**

0445 **9** *1/2* **Shahaama**[27] 7364 3-9-6 59 LukeMorris 8 52
(Jane Chapple-Hyam) *prom: lost pl over 4f out: rallied over 1f out: no ex fnl f* **6/1**[3]

2051 **10** *1* **Essaka (IRE)**[38] 7038 4-9-2 60 GeorgiaCox(5) 5 50
(Tony Carroll) *hld up in tch: plld hrd: rdn over 1f out: no ex fnl f* **8/1**

6030 **11** *1/2* **Ambitious Boy**[103] 4908 7-9-5 58 TimmyMurphy 13 47
(John O'Shea) *hld up: nvr on terms* **25/1**

0410 **12** *12* **No Refund (IRE)**[10] 7751 5-9-4 57 [1] JohnFahy 12 10
(David Loughnane) *hdwy over 4f out: rdn and wknd over 1f out* **11/1**

1m 13.62s (-0.88) **Going Correction** -0.15s/f (Stan) **12** Ran SP% **124.7**
Speed ratings (Par 101): **99,98,97,97,95 95,94,93,93,91 91,75**
CSF £148.03 CT £2599.98 TOTE £9.80: £3.00, £5.00, £5.70; EX 167.50 Trifecta £2421.20 Part Won..
Owner E A Hayward **Bred** Cheveley Park Stud Ltd **Trained** Sedbury, Gloucs

FOCUS
A modest handicap run at a sound pace. The likes of the runner-up highlight the limitations of the form.

7913 BETWAY SPRINT DISTANCE H'CAP 5f 20y (Tp)
7:50 (7:51) (Class 6) (0-58,58) 3-Y-O+ **£2,587** (£770; £384; £192) **Stalls** Low

Form RPR

4040 **1** **Captain Ryan**[38] 7038 5-9-1 56 JosephineGordon(3) 11 64
(Geoffrey Deacon) *hld up: hdwy over 1f out: rdn to ld ins fnl f: r.o* **17/2**

0100 **2** *1 1/4* **Harpers Ruby**[30] 7276 6-9-2 54 PaddyAspell 4 58
(Lynn Siddall) *led: rdn and edgd rt over 1f out: hdd ins fnl f: styd on same pce* **9/1**

6660 **3** *1 1/2* **Swendab (IRE)**[30] 7267 8-8-12 55 (b) CiaranMckee(5) 6 53
(John O'Shea) *chsd ldrs: rdn over 1f out: styd on* **12/1**

0000 **4** *3/4* **Goadby**[10] 7747 5-9-2 54 (p) RobertHavlin 1 49
(John Holt) *chsd ldr to 1/2-way: rdn over 1f out: styd on same pce ins fnl f* **12/1**

6404 **5** *1 1/4* **Lydiate Lady**[17] 7596 4-9-3 55 LukeMorris 2 46
(Paul Green) *chsd ldrs: rdn over 1f out: no ex ins fnl f* **8/1**

6000 **6** *1 1/2* **Secret Millionaire (IRE)**[10] 7747 9-9-6 58 (p) PaulMulrennan 9 44
(Shaun Harris) *hld up: racd wd 3f: swtchd lft ins fnl f: nvr on terms* **6/1**[3]

3566 **7** *hd* **Quality Art (USA)**[39] 7018 8-9-6 58 GrahamGibbons 7 43
(Simon Hodgson) *s.i.s: hdwy 2f out: rdn over 1f out: eased whn btn ins fnl f* **7/2**[1]

0-00 **8** *1/2* **Arctic Lynx (IRE)**[20] 7533 9-9-1 58 (p) AnnStokell(5) 3 41
(Ann Stokell) *chsd ldrs: rdn over 1f out: no ex fnl f* **25/1**

0-00 **9** *3/4* **Named Asset**[13] 7693 4-9-2 54 (p) MartinHarley 5 34
(Martin Bosley) *hld up: rdn over 1f out: nvr on terms* **10/1**

3030 **10** *1/2* **Andalusite**[16] 7612 3-9-5 57 (p) KevinStott 8 35
(Ed McMahon) *chsd ldrs: hung rt 1/2-way: sn rdn and wknd* **9/2**[2]

-640 **11** *24* **Palmina**[24] 7444 3-9-3 55 KieranO'Neill 10
(Dean Ivory) *mid-div: wknd 1/2-way* **40/1**

1m 1.25s (-0.65) **Going Correction** -0.15s/f (Stan) **11** Ran SP% **117.1**
Speed ratings (Par 101): **99,97,94,93,91 89,88,87,86,85 47**
CSF £82.37 CT £940.67 TOTE £9.90: £2.60, £3.20, £3.70; EX 94.90 Trifecta £828.80.
Owner A Lomax, B Mortimer, W H & J Simpson **Bred** Mrs C Lloyd **Trained** Compton, Berks

FOCUS
The pace was fair for this open handicap. The winner has been rated near the best of this year's form.
T/Plt: £248.40 to a £1 stake. Pool: £92,180.80 - 270.85 winning units T/Qpdt: £9.70 to a £1 stake. Pool: £12,903.24 - 977.10 winning units **Colin Roberts**

7914 - 7916a (Foreign Racing) - See Raceform Interactive

7871 DUNDALK (A.W) (L-H)
Friday, November 11

OFFICIAL GOING: Polytrack: standard

7917a IRISH STALLION FARMS EUROPEAN BREEDERS FUND MAIDEN (PLUS 10 RACE) 1m (P)
7:05 (7:07) 2-Y-O **£6,330** (£1,955; £926; £411; £154)

RPR

1 **Drake Passage (IRE)**[86] 5561 2-9-5 0 DeclanMcDonogh 2 84+
(John M Oxx, Ire) *mde all: narrow advantage gng wl into st: drvn clr ent fnl f and styd on wl: comf* **5/4**[1]

2 *2 1/4* **Shahroze (IRE)**[13] 7704 2-9-5 0 PatSmullen 3 78
(M Halford, Ire) *cl up: cl 2nd into st: sn rdn and no imp on wnr u.p over 1f out: kpt on same pce in 2nd wl ins fnl f* **5/2**[2]

3 *1* **X Rated (IRE)**[22] 7483 2-9-5 0 ShaneFoley 7 76
(Mark Johnston) *chsd ldrs: 5th 1/2-way: rdn bhd ldrs 2f out and tk clsr order ent fnl f where no imp on wnr: kpt on same pce in 3rd wl ins fnl f* **9/2**[3]

4 *nk* **Noble Intention (IRE)**[14] 7674 2-9-5 76 ColinKeane 6 75
(G M Lyons, Ire) *chsd ldrs: rdn 2f out and clsd u.p to dispute 2nd ent fnl f where no imp on wnr: sn dropped to 4th and kpt on same pce ins fnl f* **7/1**

5 *1/2* **Apparition (IRE)**[19] 7557 2-9-4 0 ow2 DonnachaO'Brien(3) 12 76
(Joseph Patrick O'Brien, Ire) *dwlt: sn settled in mid-div: impr bhd ldrs over 3f out: rdn 2f out and no imp on wnr in 6th over 1f out: kpt on ins fnl f* **12/1**

6 *3/4* **Ely Place (IRE)**[23] 7476 2-9-0 0 TomMadden(5) 8 72
(Mrs John Harrington, Ire) *settled in mid-div: 7th 1/2-way: rdn into 5th 1 1/2f out and no imp on wnr: kpt on same pce ins fnl f* **25/1**

7 *9* **Thunder Speed** 2-9-5 0 WayneLordan 9 50
(T Stack, Ire) *mid-div: 8th 1/2-way: rdn and no imp 2f out: one pce after* **25/1**

8 *2* **All The Mollies (IRE)**[28] 7338 2-9-0 0 RonanWhelan 10 41
(Adrian McGuinness, Ire) *loaded wout rdr: in rr of mid-div: pushed along in 9th 3f out and no imp into st: one pce fnl 2f* **80/1**

9 *1* **For Three (IRE)** 2-9-5 0 ConnorKing 13 43
(John Joseph Murphy, Ire) *towards rr: 10th 1/2-way: one pce fnl 2f: nvr involved* **66/1**

10 *7 1/2* **Schindlers Ark (USA)** 2-9-5 0 BillyLee 11 25+
(Charles O'Brien, Ire) *s.i.s and detached towards rr early: tk clsr order after 3f: pushed along under 4f out and no imp over 2f out* **40/1**

11 *2 1/4* **Michaels Boots**[26] 7387 2-9-0 0 KillianLeonard(5) 4 20
(Des Donovan, Ire) *chsd ldrs: 6th 1/2-way: rdn and wknd fr over 3f out* **100/1**

12 *4 3/4* **Run For The Roses (IRE)** 2-9-0 0 GaryCarroll 1 3+
(Augustine Leahy, Ire) *v s.i.s and detached in rr: tk clsr order at 1/2-way: rdn and no imp appr st: nvr a factor* **80/1**

13 *nk* **Safepac Lad** 2-9-5 0 EmmetMcNamara 14 8
(Des Donovan, Ire) *dwlt and towards rr: pushed along 4f out and no imp u.p appr st: nvr a factor* **80/1**

1m 38.22s (98.22) **13** Ran SP% **127.7**
CSF £4.60 TOTE £2.30: £1.02, £1.30, £1.50; DF 6.60 Trifecta £17.20.
Owner Mrs Barbara M Keller **Bred** Mr Albert Conneally **Trained** Currabeg, Co Kildare

FOCUS
A professional performance from the winner who should develop into an even better 3yo.

7918 - 7926a (Foreign Racing) - See Raceform Interactive

7002 STRASBOURG

Friday, November 11

OFFICIAL GOING: Turf: heavy

7927a PRIX DU CANAL DE LA MARNE-AU-RHIN (CLAIMER) (2YO) (TURF) 7f

11:00 (12:00) 2-Y-O **£5,882** (£2,352; £1,764; £1,176; £588)

RPR

1 **Nareia (GER)** 2-8-8 0 (p) MarcLerner 12 75
(Mario Hofer, Germany) **42/10**[2]

2 5 **Go Milady (FR)**[8] 2-9-1 0 (p) AntoineHamelin 13 70
(Matthieu Palussiere, France) **17/10**[1]

3 2 **Mashhad (FR)** 2-8-8 0 (b) RaphaelMarchelli 14 58
(Mlle Y Vollmer, France) **16/1**

4 11 **Mystery Sky (FR)**[13] 2-8-13 0 FranckForesi 8 35
(J Parize, France) **21/1**

5 2 **Countess Allegro (FR)**[102] 4965 2-8-11 0 TheoBachelot 10 28
(M Boutin, France) **44/5**

6 2 1/2 **Shaqoos (FR)**[66] 6208 2-8-8 0 ThomasHenderson 9 19
(Jo Hughes) *sltly outpcd early: towrads rr: bhd and drvn over 2f out: sme late hdwy: nvr anywhere nr ldrs* **41/1**

7 2 **Pole Celeste (FR)**[10] 2-9-1 0 (p) DelphineSantiago 6 21
(Robert Collet, France) **39/1**

8 7 1/2 **Batura Sar (FR)**[128] 2-8-9 0 MlleJohannaHeitz(6) 11 2
(M Boutin, France) **22/1**

9 1/4 **Defi Chope (FR)**[140] 2-8-13 0 SebastienMaillot 7
(C Boutin, France) **18/1**

10 3 1/2 **Blue Jasmine (FR)**[10] 2-8-8 0 MickaelBerto 2
(D De Waele, France) **23/1**

11 3 **Ken Party (FR)**[10] 2-9-4 0 (b) YohannBourgois 4
(Matthieu Palussiere, France) **30/1**

12 hd **Eblouis Moi (FR)**[10] 2-8-8 0 TonyPiccone 5
(A Giorgi, Italy) **17/1**

13 15 **Camaypaucha (FR)**[13] 2-9-2 0 RonanThomas 1
(M Boutin, France) **32/5**[3]

14 6 **Daisy Du Moulin (FR)** 2-8-11 0 AntonioPolli 3
(F Meckes, France) **85/1**

WIN (incl. 1 euro stake): 5.20. PLACES: 1.80, 1.40, 3.40. DF: 6.50. SF: 13.30
Owner Stall Helena **Bred** Harald Gritscher **Trained** Germany

7928 - (Foreign Racing) - See Raceform Interactive

7089 TOULOUSE

Friday, November 11

OFFICIAL GOING: Turf: heavy

7929a PRIX FILLE DE L'AIR (GROUP 3) (3YO+ FILLIES & MARES) (TURF) 1m 2f 110y

1:50 (12:00) 3-Y-O+ **£29,411** (£11,764; £8,823; £5,882; £2,941)

RPR

1 **Powder Snow (USA)**[19] 7566 3-8-9 0 AurelienLemaitre 5 105+
(H-A Pantall, France) *a.p: chsd ldr over 3f out: sn drvn and led ent fnl f: sn clr: won easing down* **92/10**

2 3 **Restiana (FR)**[19] 7568 3-8-9 0 (b) Roberto-CarlosMontenegro 13 99
(P Sogorb, France) *pressed ldr on outer: eased into ld sn after 1/2-way: rdn 1 1/2f out: hdd ent fnl f: no ex* **40/1**

3 2 1/2 **Rosental**[37] 7087 4-8-13 0 Pierre-CharlesBoudot 2 93
(Luca Cumani) *settled in midfield on inner: shuffled bk towards rr wl bef 1/2-way: hdwy on inner 2f out: rdn and styd on fnl f: nt pce to rch first two* **48/10**[3]

4 1/2 **Rostova (USA)**[26] 7397 3-8-9 0 VincentCheminaud 3 93
(Sir Michael Stoute) *nvr far off pce: 5th and drvn whn n.m.r under 2f out: sn rdn and styd on fnl f: unable to get on terms* **63/10**

5 2 1/2 **Five Fifteen (FR)**[37] 7089 4-8-13 0 (p) EddyHardouin 11 87
(X Thomas-Demeaulte, France) *w.w in rr: clsd into midfield after 1/2-way: rdn to dispute pls under 1 1/2f out: plugged on at one pce fnl f* **13/5**[1]

6 nk **Persona Grata**[19] 7566 5-8-13 0 ChristopheSoumillon 4 87
(Ed Walker) *w.w towards rr: 11th and drvn along over 2f out: styd on u.p wl ins fnl 1 1/2f: nvr rchd ldrs* **39/10**[2]

7 1/4 **Salve Venezia (GER)**[13] 4-8-13 0 AndreasHelfenbein 6 86
(Andreas Lowe, Germany) *towards rr: drvn and clsd a little wl over 1 1/2f out: one pce fnl f: nvr in contention* **46/1**

8 2 **Avenue Dargent (FR)**[47] 3-8-9 0 IoritzMendizabal 10 83
(J-M Osorio, Spain) *sn led: hdd after 2f and chsd ldr: rdn and nt qckn 2f out: grad lft bhd fr 1 1/2f out* **18/1**

9 4 1/2 **Gambissara (FR)**[12] 7720 3-8-9 0 JozefBojko 12 75
(Lennart Hammer-Hansen, Germany) *keen: hld up towards rr on outer: moved into midfield bef 1/2-way: rdn and btn 1 1/2f out* **12/1**

10 1 1/4 **Classe Vendome (FR)**[26] 7397 3-8-9 0 Francois-XavierBertras 1 72
(P Sogorb, France) *cl up on inner: lost pl wl over 3f out: bhd fnl 2f* **32/1**

11 dist **All About Time**[15] 7652 4-8-13 0 CristianDemuro 7
(David O'Meara) *racd in midfield on outer: drvn to chse ldr pair 3f out: sn rdn and wknd over 1 1/2f out* **50/1**

12 3/4 **Poti (SPA)**[12] 5-8-13 0 GregoryBenoist 9
(R Avial Lopez, Spain) *towards rr on outer: outpcd and scrubbed along in last after 4f: wl bhd and eased fnl 2f* **19/1**

13 18 **Cumbfree (IRE)**[85] 3-8-9 0 (p) EmilienRevolte 8
(X Thomas-Demeaulte, France) *midfield early: rapid hdwy on outer to ld after 2f: scrubbed along and hdd sn after 1/2-way: wknd fr 3f out: t.o* **59/1**

2m 15.25s (135.25)
WFA 3 from 4yo+ 4lb **13** Ran SP% **118.1**
WIN (incl. 1 euro stake): 10.20. PLACES: 3.40, 8.30, 2.50. DF: 148.90. SF: 216.20.
Owner Godolphin SNC **Bred** Darley **Trained** France

7898 LINGFIELD (L-H)

Saturday, November 12

OFFICIAL GOING: Polytrack: standard
Wind: light, behind Weather: rain

7930 32RED.COM / EBF NOVICE STKS 1m 1y(P)

11:45 (11:48) (Class 5) 2-Y-O **£3,363** (£1,001; £500; £250) **Stalls** High

Form RPR

2214 1 **Good Omen**[26] 7409 2-9-9 91 PatCosgrave 2 94+
(William Haggas) *mde all: set stdy gallop: pushed along and qcknd hugging inner on bnd 2f out: clr and in n.d 1f out: r.o wl: readily* **5/2**[3]

1 2 3 1/2 **Time To Study (FR)**[66] 6224 2-9-9 0 GeorgeBaker 4 85
(Mark Johnston) *chsd wnr: rdn to press wnr over 2f out: outpcd bnd 2f out: wl hld and kpt on same pce fr over 1f out* **7/4**[2]

16 3 1 3/4 **Sultan Baybars**[21] 7544 2-9-9 0 JackMitchell 3 81+
(Roger Varian) *awkward leaving stalls and dwlt: t.k.h hld up in tch in midfield: effrt but outpcd by ldng pair over 2f out: wl hld 3rd and one pced fr over 1f out* **11/8**[1]

00 4 1 1/2 **Ronni Layne**[24] 7465 2-8-11 0 RobertHavlin 5 65
(Conrad Allen) *stdd s: hld up in tch in rr: pushed along and outpcd over 2f out: no ch w wnr and kpt on same pce fr over 1f out* **100/1**

5 shd **Leopard (IRE)** 2-9-2 0 LukeMorris 1 70
(Paul Cole) *t.k.h: chsd ldng pair: rdn and outpcd by ldng pair over 2f out: wl hld and kpt on same pce fr over 1f out* **33/1**

1m 41.62s (3.42) **Going Correction** 0.0s/f (Stan) **5** Ran SP% **111.0**
Speed ratings (Par 96): **82,78,76,75,75**
CSF £7.38 TOTE £2.70: £1.20, £1.10; EX 6.90 Trifecta £9.90.
Owner A E Oppenheimer **Bred** Hascombe And Valiant Studs **Trained** Newmarket, Suffolk

FOCUS
An interesting little novice event despite the small field, but they went no pace and the winner was given a freebie up front. Muddling form.

7931 SUNBETS.CO.UK DOWNLOAD THE APP CLAIMING STKS 1m 1y(P)

12:15 (12:17) (Class 6) 3-Y-O **£2,587** (£770; £384; £192) **Stalls** High

Form RPR

4120 1 **Threebagsue (IRE)**[23] 7492 3-8-6 76 (b) JosephineGordon(3) 5 68
(J S Moore) *chsd ldr tl led 5f out: rdn wl over 1f out: kpt on wl u.p and a holding chalr ins fnl f* **9/4**[2]

0530 2 nk **Evidence (FR)**[47] 6827 3-8-8 62 DavidProbert 8 66
(Harry Dunlop) *chsd ldrs and styd wd early: wnt 2nd over 3f out: rdn and ev ch wl over 1f out: sustained chal but a hld ins fnl f* **12/1**

2050 3 1 1/4 **Ritasun (FR)**[7] 7816 3-9-0 73 (p) HollieDoyle(5) 6 74
(Richard Hannon) *niggled along in last pair: effrt on outer bnd 2f out: hdwy to chse ldng pair jst ins fnl f: kpt on but nvr enough pce to chal* **15/8**[1]

0440 4 1 1/4 **Lilbourne Prince (IRE)**[8] 7801 3-8-13 70 JFEgan 7 65
(David Evans) *in tch in midfield: effrt to chse ldrs over 1f out: unable qck u.p 1f out: kpt on same pce ins fnl f* **11/4**[3]

3060 5 2 3/4 **Tasteofexcellence (IRE)**[39] 7037 3-7-12 57 (b1) RhiainIngram(7) 4 51
(Roger Ingram) *hld up in tch in rr: effrt over 1f out: no imp and one pced fr over 1f out* **14/1**

3140 6 3/4 **Masqueraded (USA)**[17] 7606 3-8-9 68 (b1) LukeMorris 3 53
(Gay Kelleway) *chsd ldrs: rdn: unable qck and hung lft over 1f out: wknd fnl f* **14/1**

0000 7 4 1/2 **Musical Taste**[25] 7430 3-8-9 65 KieranO'Neill 1 42
(Pat Phelan) *sn pushed up to ld: hdd 5f out: lost 2nd over 3f out: wknd u.p over 1f out* **33/1**

0603 8 6 **Moving Robe (IRE)**[16] 7645 3-8-5 45 NoelGarbutt(3) 2 27
(Conrad Allen) *hld up in tch: rdn over 2f out: sn struggling: bhd fnl f* **50/1**

1m 37.56s (-0.64) **Going Correction** 0.0s/f (Stan) **8** Ran SP% **118.1**
Speed ratings (Par 98): **103,102,101,100,97 96,92,86**
CSF £30.40 TOTE £2.50: £1.10, £3.80, £1.30; EX 33.60 Trifecta £62.20.
Owner The Well Fleeced Partnership **Bred** S Couldrige **Trained** Upper Lambourn, Berks

FOCUS
A modest 3yo claimer with nothing officially rated above 76. Resolution appeared to win the day. It's been rated as routine form.

7932 BETWAY GOLDEN ROSE STKS (LISTED RACE) 6f 1y(P)

12:50 (12:51) (Class 1) 3-Y-O+

£22,684 (£8,600; £4,304; £2,144; £1,076; £540) **Stalls** Low

Form RPR

011 1 **Lord Of The Land (IRE)**[16] 7651 5-9-3 108 (v) JamesDoyle 8 114
(David O'Meara) *wl in tch in midfield: effrt to chse ldrs over 1f out: drvn to chal ins fnl f: led fnl 50yds: r.o wl: dismntd after fin: lame* **2/1**[1]

0010 2 3/4 **Mythmaker**[35] 7156 4-9-3 97 ConnorBeasley 4 111
(Bryan Smart) *led: rdn and fnd ex over 1f out: drvn and hrd pressed ins fnl f: hdd and one pce fnl 50yds* **16/1**

0453 3 1 1/2 **Kimberella**[7] 7822 6-9-3 105 PatCosgrave 3 106
(David Nicholls) *chsd ldrs: lft chsng ldr bnd wl over 1f out: sn rdn: lost 2nd and kpt on same pce ins fnl f* **10/1**

3601 4 1 1/4 **Gracious John (IRE)**[10] 7771 3-9-3 107 JFEgan 5 102
(David Evans) *t.k.h and hung rt: chsd ldr tl hung rt and lost pl bnd wl over 1f out: kpt on same pce fnl f* **7/1**[3]

5623 5 1/2 **Medicean Man**[22] 7520 10-9-3 107 (tp) NickyMackay 11 100
(Jeremy Gask) *off the pce in last pair: hdwy on inner over 1f out: wnt 5th ins fnl f: kpt on: nvr trbld ldrs* **20/1**

402 6 nk **Aeolus**[7] 7822 5-9-3 107 GeorgeBaker 7 99+
(Ed Walker) *hld up in tch in rr of main gp: effrt over 1f out: kpt on ins fnl f: nvr trbld ldrs* **4/1**[2]

6530 7 3/4 **Realize**[14] 7702 6-9-3 103 (t) SeanLevey 12 97
(Stuart Williams) *in tch in midfield but stuck wd: effrt 2f out: kpt on same pce u.p fr over 1f out* **20/1**

360 8 1 **Jane's Memory (IRE)**[48] 6816 4-9-0 104 MartinDwyer 10 91
(Rae Guest) *chsd ldrs: rdn ent fnl 2f: unable qck over 1f out: wknd ins fnl f* **33/1**

5026 9 hd **Dhahmaan (IRE)**[11] 7758 3-9-3 98 (b) LukeMorris 1 93
(Marco Botti) *bustled along leaving stalls: in tch in midfield: effrt and unable qck over 1f out: no imp u.p ins fnl f* **12/1**

6006 10 hd **Rivellino**[38] 7068 6-9-3 97 JoeyHaynes 2 93
(K R Burke) *bustled along leaving stalls: a towards rr: rdn over 1f out: no imp* **14/1**

U310 11 2 1/4 **Captain Colby (USA)**[35] 7156 4-9-3 101 (b) AdamKirby 6 85
(Ed Walker) *s.i.s and sn pushed along in rr: n.d* **9/1**

0105 **12** ½ **Outback Traveller (IRE)**[42] 6941 5-9-3 107.................... MartinHarley 9 84
(Robert Cowell) *in tch in midfield: rdn over 1f out: sn btn and wknd fnl f*
12/1

1m 10.03s (-1.87) **Going Correction** 0.0s/f (Stan) **12** Ran SP% **125.3**
Speed ratings (Par 111): **112,111,109,107,106 106,105,103,103,103 100,99**
CSF £39.97 TOTE £3.10: £1.20, £5.40, £3.20; EX 38.80 Trifecta £427.00.
Owner George Turner **Bred** Ammerland Verwaltung Gmbh **Trained** Upper Helmsley, N Yorks

FOCUS
A hot Listed sprint and there was no hanging about, but it was still important to be up there. This was a triumph for northern-based stables. The runner-up is the key to the form.

7933 SUNBETS.CO.UK H'CAP 1m 1y(P)
1:25 (1:26) (Class 2) (0-105,105) 3-Y-O+ **£11,971** (£3,583; £1,791; £896; £446) **Stalls** High

Form RPR

3100 **1** **My Target (IRE)**[14] 7702 5-8-5 **86**.............................. ConnorBeasley 3 95
(Michael Wigham) *hld up in tch: effrt and hdwy to chse ldrs 1f out: r.o wl to ld wl ins fnl f: pushed out*
8/1[3]

4002 **2** 1 **Alfred Hutchinson**[16] 7651 8-9-1 **96**..............................(p) AdamKirby 6 103
(David O'Meara) *chsd ldrs: effrt to chal 2f out: rdn to ld wl over 1f out: drvn 1f out: hdd and one pced wl ins fnl f*
6/1[2]

5600 **3** nse **Grey Mirage**[206] 1576 7-8-12 **93**.............................. LukeMorris 2 100
(Marco Botti) *broke wl stdd bk and hld up in tch: effrt over 1f out: drvn to chse ldrs 1f out: kpt on same pce u.p ins fnl f*
16/1

000 **4** ¾ **Keystroke**[36] 7121 4-8-11 **92**.............................. MartinHarley 11 97
(Jeremy Noseda) *in tch in midfield: effrt to chse ldrs wl over 1f out: chsd wnr jst over 1f out tl ins fnl f: outpcd wl ins fnl f*
6/1[2]

0620 **5** 2¼ **Georgian Bay (IRE)**[49] 6788 6-9-1 **96**..............................(v) JoeyHaynes 4 96
(K R Burke) *hld up in tch in midfield: hdwy 2f out: chsd ldrs and swtchd lft ent fnl f: no imp u.p ins fnl f*
12/1

6000 **6** ½ **Sea Of Flames**[16] 7651 3-9-1 **98**.............................. ShaneKelly 12 97
(David Elsworth) *taken down early: stdd s: hld up in rr: effrt and swtchd rt over 1f out: kpt on ins fnl f: nvr trbld ldrs*
14/1

3656 **7** 3 **Scottish Glen**[49] 6788 10-8-10 **94**.............................. HectorCrouch(3) 7 94+
(Patrick Chamings) *hld up in tch: effrt on inner whn nt clr run and hmpd over 1f out: swtchd rt 1f out: no imp fnl f*
10/1

1163 **8** nk **Castle Harbour**[21] 7542 3-9-8 **105**.............................. RobertHavlin 5 96
(John Gosden) *nt that wl away: pushed along and rcvrd to chse ldrs over 6f out: wnt 2nd 5f out tl 2f out: rdn and little rspnse over 1f out: wknd ins fnl f*
9/4[1]

4020 **9** 2¼ **Lunar Deity**[30] 7301 7-9-4 **99**.............................. PatCosgrave 8 85
(Stuart Williams) *hld up in tch towards rr: effrt over 1f out: no imp: nvr trbld ldrs*
16/1

0-00 **10** 3½ **Mutarakez (IRE)**[28] 7354 4-9-2 **97**..............................(b[1]) JimmyFortune 10 75
(Brian Meehan) *s.i.s: bhd and nvr travelling wl: n.d*
10/1

6-00 **11** nk **Jacob Black**[142] 3565 5-8-9 **90**.............................. DavidProbert 9 67
(Keith Dalgleish) *led tl rdn and hdd wl over 1f out: no ex u.p: wknd 1f out: bhd and eased wl ins fnl f*
25/1

6020 **12** ¾ **Captain Cat (IRE)**[45] 6884 7-9-8 **103**..............................(b) GeorgeBaker 1 79
(Tony Carroll) *led: sn hdd and chsd ldrs: effrt over 1f out: fnd nil and sn btn: wknd 1f out: bhd and eased wl ins fnl f*
14/1

1m 35.18s (-3.02) **Going Correction** 0.0s/f (Stan)
WFA 3 from 4yo+ 2lb **12** Ran SP% **125.3**
Speed ratings (Par 109): **115,114,113,113,110 110,107,107,104,101 101,100**
CSF £58.75 CT £775.30 TOTE £12.80: £3.40, £2.10, £4.70; EX 77.30 Trifecta £972.80.
Owner G Linder, M Wigham & J Williams **Bred** Darley **Trained** Newmarket, Suffolk

FOCUS
A warm handicap and a thrilling finish. Again you didn't want to be too far back. The runner-up helps set the standard.

7934 BETWAY CHURCHILL STKS (LISTED RACE) 1m 2f (P)
2:00 (2:04) (Class 1) 3-Y-O+
£25,519 (£9,675; £4,842; £2,412; £1,210; £607) **Stalls** Low

Form RPR

15 **1** **Team Talk**[14] 7701 3-8-12 93.............................. SeanLevey 10 111+
(Saeed bin Suroor) *hld up in last pair: effrt 2f out: clsd and swtchd rt over 1f out: str run u.p ins fnl f to ld cl home*
6/1[2]

1502 **2** ½ **Educate**[14] 7700 7-9-2 111.............................. JamesDoyle 7 110
(Ismail Mohammed) *chsd ldrs: effrt to chal 2f out: drvn to ld over 1f out: kpt on u.p ins fnl f: hdd and no ex cl home*
9/1

0003 **3** ½ **Master The World (IRE)**[14] 7700 5-9-2 108..............................(p) ShaneKelly 4 109
(David Elsworth) *dwlt: sn rcvrd and in tch in midfield: effrt over 1f out: hdwy to chse ldrs jst ins fnl f: styd on wl u.p fnl 100yds*
14/1

-111 **4** 1 **Grendisar (IRE)**[232] 1069 6-9-2 112..............................(p) AdamKirby 8 108+
(Marco Botti) *stdd after s: hld up in tch in last quartet: shkn up and hdwy over 1f out: chsd ldrs and rdn jst ins fnl f: kpt on but nvr gng to rch ldrs*
1/1[1]

5-30 **5** hd **Metropol (IRE)**[22] 7524 5-9-2 103.............................. TheoBachelot 5 107
(Mme Pia Brandt, France) *sn chsng ldr: clsd and upsides over 2f out: rdn to ld 2f out: hdd over 1f out: styd chalng tl no ex u.p 100yds out: wknd towards fin*
16/1

4343 **6** 2¾ **Restorer**[10] 7766 4-9-2 105.............................. MartinDwyer 11 101
(William Muir) *stdd and dropped in bhd after s: hld up rr: hdwy on inner over 1f out: swtchd rt 1f out: kpt on same pce and no imp ins fnl f* **16/1**

4100 **7** 1¼ **Flambeuse**[16] 7652 5-8-11 77.............................. DavidProbert 3 94?
(Harry Dunlop) *chsd ldrs: rdn 2f out: unable qck and lost pl over 1f out: wknd ins fnl f*
100/1

24-1 **8** hd **Energia Davos (BRZ)**[14] 7700 8-9-4 111.............................. GeorgeBaker 2 100
(Jane Chapple-Hyam) *in tch in midfield: effrt but unable qck over 1f out: wknd ins fnl f*
8/1[3]

5155 **9** 1 **Berkshire (IRE)**[10] 7766 5-9-4 105..............................(b) JimmyFortune 1 98
(Paul Cole) *racd keenly: led: jnd and rdn over 2f out: hdd 2f out: lost pl and btn over 1f out: wknd ins fnl f*
20/1

5020 **10** 16 **Maverick Wave (USA)**[28] 7353 5-9-2 107.............................. WilliamBuick 9 64
(John Gosden) *hld up in tch in last quartet: rdn 3f out: bhd over 1f out: eased ins fnl f*
6/1[2]

2m 2.56s (-4.04) **Going Correction** 0.0s/f (Stan)
WFA 3 from 4yo+ 4lb **10** Ran SP% **123.9**
Speed ratings (Par 111): **116,115,115,114,114 112,111,110,110,97**
CSF £62.83 TOTE £8.40: £2.30, £2.80, £3.80; EX 76.80 Trifecta £1114.70.
Owner Godolphin **Bred** Darley **Trained** Newmarket, Suffolk

FOCUS
A fascinating renewal of the Churchill Stakes with Grendisar, who has become a legend around here, holding centre stage, but in a race run at a generous pace a new kid appeared on the block. It's been rated around the principals.

7935 BETWAY MEDIAN AUCTION MAIDEN STKS 6f 1y(P)
2:35 (2:38) (Class 6) 3-5-Y-O **£2,587** (£770; £384; £192) **Stalls** Low

Form RPR

6 **1** **Beauden Barrett**[24] 7459 3-9-5 0..............................(t) GeorgeBaker 9 67+
(Jeremy Gask) *dwlt: hdwy to ld after 1f and mde rest: shkn up and drifted rt over 1f out: rdn ins fnl f: r.o wl*
11/10[1]

3 **2** 2¼ **La Fortuna**[33] 7207 3-9-0 0.............................. AdamBeschizza 8 55
(Charlie Wallis) *led for 1f: chsd ldrs after: effrt to chse wnr over 1f out: r.o same pce u.p ins fnl f*
9/2[3]

020 **3** 2 **Equinette (IRE)**[18] 7603 3-8-11 62..............................[1] KieranShoemark(3) 3 49
(Amanda Perrett) *w ldr for 1f: stdd bk into midfield after 1f: effrt to chse ldng pair over 1f out: no imp 1f out: one pced after*
5/2[2]

0 **4** 1 **Rigsby**[24] 7459 3-9-5 0..............................[1] KieranO'Neill 4 51
(Zoe Davison) *s.i.s: t.k.h: hld up in rr: effrt over 1f out: kpt on ins fnl f: wnt 4th towards fin: no threat to ldrs*
33/1

36 **5** ½ **Hangman Jury**[79] 5811 3-9-5 0.............................. ShaneKelly 5 50+
(Richard Hughes) *dwlt: t.k.h: hdwy on outer to chse ldrs 4f out: pushed along and awkward hd carriage 2f out: outpcd over 1f out: rdn and kpt on same pce ins fnl f*
7/1

0 **6** 1¾ **Secret Striker**[40] 7011 4-8-11 0.............................. HectorCrouch(3) 1 39
(Ken Cunningham-Brown) *in tch: hmpd and dropped towards rr 5f out: effrt ent fnl 2f: no imp over 1f out*
12/1

0- **7** 1 **Mistry**[402] 7033 3-9-0 0.............................. LiamKeniry 6 36
(Mark Usher) *chsd ldrs: wnt 2nd 4f tl over 1f out: wknd ins fnl f*
20/1

00 **8** 5 **Little Lizzie**[17] 7616 3-8-11 0.............................. NoelGarbutt(3) 7 21
(Paddy Butler) *in tch in midfield: rdn and lost pl over 1f out: wknd fnl f*
66/1

1m 12.72s (0.82) **Going Correction** 0.0s/f (Stan) **8** Ran SP% **123.8**
Speed ratings (Par 101): **94,91,88,87,86 84,82,76**
CSF £7.32 TOTE £2.40: £1.30, £1.50, £1.10; EX 7.20 Trifecta £15.30.
Owner Sarah O'Connell & Horses First Racing **Bred** Kirtlington Stud Ltd **Trained** Stockbridge, Hants

■ Wattaboutsteve was withdrawn not under orders. Price at time of withdrawal 4-1. Rule 4 applies to best struck prices prior to withdrawal but not to SP bets - deduction 20p in the pound. New market formed.

FOCUS
A modest older-horse maiden and straightforward for the favourite.

7936 BETWAY H'CAP (DIV I) 1m 2f (P)
3:10 (3:10) (Class 6) (0-60,62) 3-Y-O+ **£2,587** (£770; £384; £192) **Stalls** Low

Form RPR

526- **1** **Hallings Comet**[395] 6699 7-9-7 **60**.............................. KieranShoemark(3) 9 66
(Shaun Lycett) *chsd ldr: rdn to chal over 1f out: sustained chal u.p to ld 50yds out: jst hld on*
12/1

4642 **2** nse **Two In The Pink (IRE)**[11] 7754 6-9-12 **62**.............................. DavidProbert 6 68
(Ralph J Smith) *in tch in midfield: effrt to chse ldrs 2f out: drvn and clsd to chal jst ins fnl f: kpt on wl towards fin: jst hld*
7/2[2]

5040 **3** nk **Celtic Ava (IRE)**[45] 6871 4-9-2 **57**.............................. PaddyBradley(5) 10 62
(Pat Phelan) *hld up in tch in midfield: effrt to chse ldrs over 1f out: styd on wl u.p fnl 100yds: nt quite rch ldrs*
6/1[3]

-055 **4** hd **General Brook (IRE)**[37] 7103 6-9-2 **52**.............................. FergusSweeney 8 57
(John O'Shea) *led: rdn over 1f out: battled on wl u.p: hdd 50yds out: no ex and lost 2 pls cl home*
8/1

2060 **5** 2½ **My Mistress (IRE)**[16] 7641 4-8-6 **47**..............................(p) CallumShepherd(5) 3 47
(Phil McEntee) *hld up in tch in midfield: effrt to chse ldrs over 1f out: drvn and no imp ins fnl f*
16/1

3000 **6** nk **Lady Lunchalot (USA)**[17] 7609 6-9-6 **56**..............................(p) GeorgeBaker 1 56+
(Laura Mongan) *s.i.s: in rr: effrt but stl plenty to do wl over 1f out: sme hdwy and rdn 1f out: no imp ins fnl f*
7/4[1]

200 **7** 8 **Flag Of Glory**[17] 7628 9-9-0 **50**..............................(b) LiamKeniry 5 35
(Peter Hiatt) *t.k.h: hld up in last pair: effrt over 2f out: no rspnse and wknd over 1f out*
10/1

003 **8** 1½ **Outback Princess**[163] 2828 3-8-5 **48**.............................. NoelGarbutt(3) 4 30
(Gary Moore) *chsd ldrs: rdn over 3f out: lost pl 2f out: bhd fnl f*
10/1

020- **R** **Light Of Love**[90] 4-9-5 **55**.............................. MartinDwyer 7
(Brendan Powell) *walked out of stalls and ref to r*
33/1

2m 6.29s (-0.31) **Going Correction** 0.0s/f (Stan)
WFA 3 from 4yo+ 4lb **9** Ran SP% **118.7**
Speed ratings (Par 101): **101,100,100,100,98 98,91,90,**
CSF £55.37 CT £286.12 TOTE £15.50: £3.20, £1.40, £2.30; EX 57.70 Trifecta £401.10.
Owner Lord Blyth **Bred** Lord Blyth **Trained** Clapton-on-the-Hill, Gloucs

FOCUS
The first division of a moderate handicap and it paid to be handy. The first four finished in a heap.

7937 BETWAY H'CAP (DIV II) 1m 2f (P)
3:45 (3:45) (Class 6) (0-60,60) 3-Y-O+ **£2,587** (£770; £384; £192) **Stalls** Low

Form RPR

2225 **1** **Rubis**[14] 7692 3-9-2 **56**.............................. JackGarritty 10 62
(Richard Fahey) *t.k.h: midfield tl hdwy to join ldr after 2f: rdn over 1f out: led 1f out: hld on wl towards fin: all out*
3/1[1]

050U **2** nse **Shining Romeo**[17] 7628 4-9-5 **60**.............................. CliffordLee(5) 4 66
(Denis Quinn) *hld up in midfield: hdwy on inner over 1f out: str chal 100yds out: r.o: jst hld*
6/1[3]

4000 **3** ½ **Sunshineandbubbles**[17] 7614 3-9-0 **54**..............................(p) DavidProbert 8 59
(Daniel Mark Loughnane) *chsd ldrs: effrt over 1f out: kpt on wl u.p fnl 100yds*
5/1[2]

5005 **4** shd **Percy Verence**[11] 7754 3-9-2 **56**..............................[1] JoeyHaynes 6 61
(K R Burke) *hld up in tch in midfield: effrt 2f out: n.m.r jst over 1f out: hdwy 1f out: styd on wl u.p fnl 100yds*
5/1[2]

-000 **5** nk **Jersey Bull (IRE)**[17] 7614 4-9-8 **58**.............................. LiamKeniry 5 62
(Michael Madgwick) *hld up in tch in midfield: effrt 2f out: hdwy u.p 1f out: kpt on ins fnl f*
8/1

0320 **6** ½ **Understory (USA)**[37] 7103 9-9-0 **50**.............................. RyanTate 3 53
(Tim McCarthy) *led: jnd after 2f: rdn over 1f out: hdd 1f out: stl ev ch tl no ex and outpcd towards fin*
8/1

030 **7** 1 **Foylesideview (IRE)**[16] 7642 4-8-7 **46**.............................. NoelGarbutt(3) 7 47
(Harry Chisman) *stdd s: t.k.h: hld up in last pair: rdn and hdwy over 1f out: kpt on same pce ins fnl f*
16/1

-310 **8** ½ **Hold Firm**[16] 7642 4-9-0 **57**.............................. GeorgiaDobie(7) 1 57
(Mark H Tompkins) *t.k.h: chsd ldrs: effrt over 1f out: rdn 1f out: kpt on same pce ins fnl f*
9/1

-566 **9** *hd* **Josh Perry**[42] 6967 3-8-6 **46** oh1 ConnorBeasley 9 46
(Rod Millman) *hld up towards rr: rdn and hdwy on outer over 2f out: chsd ldrs but unable qck over 1f out: kpt on same pce ins fnl f* **16/1**

400 **10** *10* **Zorlu (IRE)**[33] 7219 3-9-5 **59** FergusSweeney 2 40
(John O'Shea) *awkward leaving stalls: hld up in rr: rdn over 2f out: no rspnse and sn btn: bhd fnl f* **33/1**

2m 8.05s (1.45) **Going Correction** 0.0s/f (Stan)
WFA 3 from 4yo+ 4lb **10** Ran SP% **119.5**
Speed ratings (Par 101): **94,93,93,93,93 92,92,91,91,83**
CSF £21.63 CT £89.18 TOTE £3.50: £1.50, £2.20, £2.20; EX 20.00 Trifecta £67.10.
Owner Mr & Mrs P Ashton **Bred** Mr & Mrs P Ashton **Trained** Musley Bank, N Yorks

FOCUS
Again the principals finished in a heap and the winning time was 1.76sec slower than the first division.
T/Plt: £99.90 to a £1 stake. Pool: £62,616.36 - 457.34 winning units. T/Qpdt: £44.60 to a £1 stake. Pool: £5,529.22 - 91.70 winning units. **Steve Payne**

7906 WOLVERHAMPTON (A.W) (L-H)

Saturday, November 12

OFFICIAL GOING: Tapeta: standard
Wind: Light across Weather: Overcast

7938 £10 FREE AT 32RED.COM NURSERY H'CAP 5f 216y (Tp)
5:45 (5:45) (Class 5) (0-75,75) 2-Y-O **£3,881** (£1,155; £577; £288) **Stalls** Low

Form RPR

2256 **1** **Mr Pocket (IRE)**[11] 7748 2-9-5 **73** (b[1]) TomQueally 5 77
(Paul Cole) *hld up in tch: swtchd rt over 2f out: rdn over 1f out: r.o to ld wl ins fnl f* **10/1**

2510 **2** *nk* **Marquee Club**[33] 7217 2-9-7 **75** WilliamCarson 8 78
(Jamie Osborne) *racd keenly: prom: wnt 2nd 4f out: rdn and ev ch ins fnl f: r.o* **10/1**

2135 **3** *¾* **Big Lachie**[36] 7120 2-9-7 **75** PatCosgrave 9 76
(Jamie Osborne) *s.i.s: hld up: rdn over 1f out: r.o ins fnl f: nt rch ldrs* **3/1**[1]

5023 **4** *nse* **Elegantly Bound (IRE)**[50] 6743 2-8-11 **68** JosephineGordon(3) 10 69
(James Given) *sn pushed along in rr: rdn over 1f out: r.o ins fnl f: nt rch ldrs* **4/1**[3]

2212 **5** *½* **Tschierschen (IRE)**[18] 7589 2-9-1 **74** GeorgiaCox(5) 2 73
(William Haggas) *trckd ldrs: plld hrd: rdn over 1f out: styd on* **7/2**[2]

1600 **6** *½* **Kings Heart (IRE)**[21] 7549 2-8-11 **65** SteveDrowne 3 63
(Mark Usher) *s.s: hld up: r.o ins fnl f: nt rch ldrs* **9/1**

233 **7** *¾* **Hamidans Girl (IRE)**[27] 7381 2-9-4 **72** TomMarquand 11 68
(Keith Dalgleish) *sn led: rdn over 2f out: hdd and no ex wl ins fnl f* **14/1**

4542 **8** *hd* **Black Bubba (IRE)**[34] 7184 2-9-4 **72** JFEgan 7 67
(David Evans) *prom: rdn over 2f out: styd on same pce fnl f* **9/1**

1544 **9** *4½* **Chevalier Du Lac (IRE)**[29] 7330 2-8-12 **66** KevinStott 6 48
(Conor Dore) *hld up: rdn over 2f out: hung lft fnl f: nvr on terms* **33/1**

0512 **10** *1¾* **Reckless Serenade (IRE)**[37] 7091 2-8-13 **72** ShirleyTeasdale(5) 1 48
(Keith Dalgleish) *chsd ldr 2f: remained handy: rdn over 2f out: wknd over 1f out* **12/1**

1m 13.12s (-1.38) **Going Correction** -0.275s/f (Stan) **10** Ran SP% **122.7**
Speed ratings (Par 96): **98,97,96,96,95 95,94,93,87,85**
CSF £110.96 CT £381.16 TOTE £11.90: £2.60, £2.90, £1.80; EX 136.40 Trifecta £667.10.
Owner Gatley & Baines **Bred** Kabansk Ltd & Rathbarry Stud **Trained** Whatcombe, Oxon

FOCUS
Heavy outbreaks of rain augmented the 9mm which the course had taken overnight. The higher banded of two nurseries held on the night, and still competitive fare despite the three absentees.

7939 32RED CASINO EBF MAIDEN FILLIES' STKS (PLUS 10 RACE) 5f 216y (Tp)
6:15 (6:17) (Class 5) 2-Y-O **£3,881** (£1,155; £577; £288) **Stalls** Low

Form RPR

3 **1** **Gorgeous Noora (IRE)**[37] 7099 2-9-0 0 AdamKirby 6 85+
(Luca Cumani) *mde all: 2 l ahd and rdn whn lft clr over 1f out: eased wl ins fnl f* **1/1**[1]

06 **2** *6* **Nuzha**[14] 7689 2-9-0 0 JFEgan 5 67
(David Evans) *plld hrd in 2nd pl 1f: settled 3rd and remained handy: rdn over 2f out: lft 2nd over 1f out: styd on same pce fnl f* **66/1**

23 **3** *1¾* **Sitar**[19] 7576 2-9-0 0 TomQueally 1 63
(James Fanshawe) *hld up in tch: plld hrd: rdn whn hmpd and lft 3rd over 1f out: edgd lft and styd on same pce fnl f* **8/1**[3]

5 **4** *¾* **Cheerfilly (IRE)**[31] 7277 2-9-0 0 RichardKingscote 13 60
(Tom Dascombe) *chsd ldrs: rdn over 2f out: styd on same pce fr over 1f out* **20/1**

0 **5** *¾* **Dream Waltz**[10] 7763 2-9-0 0 RobertHavlin 2 57
(John Gosden) *hld up: hdwy over 1f out: nt trble ldrs* **20/1**

6 *¾* **Sadhbh (IRE)** 2-9-0 0 KieranO'Neill 4 56+
(Richard Hannon) *s.i.s: hld up: hmpd over 1f out: nvr on terms* **40/1**

6 **7** *2¾* **Denver Spirit (IRE)**[25] 7439 2-9-0 0 TimmyMurphy 3 48
(Luca Cumani) *hld up: nt clr run wl over 2f out: n.d* **25/1**

00 **8** *½* **Dutch Cat**[31] 7277 2-9-0 0 JohnFahy 8 46
(Clive Cox) *hld up in tch: rdn over 2f out: hmpd and wknd over 1f out* **80/1**

0 **9** *1¾* **Wotadoll**[14] 7689 2-8-11 0 JackDuern(3) 10 42
(Dean Ivory) *hld up: rdn over 2f out: in rr whn hmpd over 1f out* **80/1**

10 *2¼* **Tai Hang Dragon (IRE)** 2-9-0 0 SeanLevey 9 34
(Richard Hannon) *s.i.s: in rr: pushed along and no ch whn hmpd over 1f out* **16/1**

11 *3¾* **Quintessential** 2-9-0 0 PatrickMathers 11 23
(Richard Fahey) *s.s: a in rr: bhd whn hmpd over 1f out* **40/1**

F **Exceedingly Sweet** 2-9-0 0 GeorgeChaloner 12
(Richard Fahey) *chsd wnr 5f out: 2 l down and rdn whn broke down and fell over 1f out: fatally injured* **33/1**

0 **U** **Harba (IRE)**[71] 6078 2-9-0 0 PatCosgrave 7 63+
(William Haggas) *hld up: sme hdwy whn hmpd and uns rdr over 1f out* **9/4**[2]

1m 13.5s (-1.00) **Going Correction** -0.275s/f (Stan) **13** Ran SP% **122.9**
Speed ratings (Par 93): **95,87,84,83,82 81,78,77,75,72 67,,**
CSF £120.12 TOTE £2.00: £1.30, £9.20, £2.00; EX 72.00.
Owner Saleh Al Homaizi & Imad Al Sagar **Bred** Kabansk Ltd & Rathbarry Stud **Trained** Newmarket, Suffolk

FOCUS
A ninth successive win in this race for a stable from Newmarket, and a very clear-cut one at that, but regrettably also a serious incident in behind.

7940 32RED.COM EBF STALLIONS MAIDEN STKS 1m 1f 103y (Tp)
6:45 (6:50) (Class 5) 2-Y-O **£3,881** (£1,155; £577; £288) **Stalls** Low

Form RPR

4 **1** **Andrassy Avenue (USA)**[22] 7511 2-9-5 0 AdamKirby 6 79+
(Charlie Appleby) *prom: reminder over 4f out: jnd ldr gng wl whn hung bdly rt wl over 1f out: rcvrd jst over 1f out: rdn to ld wl ins fnl f: edgd lft: r.o* **7/4**[1]

5 **2** *¾* **Eagle's Stare (IRE)**[40] 7003 2-9-5 0 WilliamCarson 8 75
(Saeed bin Suroor) *chsd ldr: led over 2f out: rdn over 1f out: edgd lft and hdd wl ins fnl f* **13/2**[2]

05 **3** *2* **Alshibaa (IRE)**[10] 7769 2-9-5 0 PatCosgrave 3 71
(William Haggas) *chsd ldrs: rdn over 2f out: styd on same pce ins fnl f* **7/1**[3]

0 **4** *1¼* **Medalla De Oro**[24] 7468 2-9-5 0 LukeMorris 7 68
(Peter Chapple-Hyam) *chsd ldrs: hung rt fr 1/2-way: rdn over 2f out: no ex fnl f* **20/1**

52 **5** *nk* **Avantgardist (GER)**[40] 7003 2-9-5 0 RichardKingscote 5 68
(Mark Johnston) *sn pushed along towards rr: hdwy over 1f out: nt trble ldrs* **11/1**

6 *1½* **Mr Davies** 2-9-5 0 TomQueally 4 65+
(David Brown) *s.v.s: hld up: sme hdwy over 2f out: sn outpcd: styd on ins fnl f* **66/1**

22 **7** *nk* **Vantage Point (IRE)**[31] 7273 2-9-5 0 RobertHavlin 2 65
(John Gosden) *led: rdn and hdd over 2f out: wknd fnl f* **7/4**[1]

8 *17* **Nothing Compares** 2-9-0 0 TomMarquand 1 27
(Mark Johnston) *sn outpcd* **33/1**

1m 58.96s (-1.84) **Going Correction** -0.275s/f (Stan) 2y crse rec **8** Ran SP% **116.1**
Speed ratings (Par 96): **97,96,94,93,93 91,91,76**
CSF £14.45 TOTE £2.80: £1.20, £1.90, £1.60; EX 13.60 Trifecta £58.10.
Owner Godolphin **Bred** Darley **Trained** Newmarket, Suffolk

FOCUS
Potentially a fair juvenile maiden for the time of year, and a winning effort well worth marking up.

7941 32REDSPORT.COM NURSERY H'CAP 1m 141y (Tp)
7:15 (7:17) (Class 6) (0-65,66) 2-Y-O **£2,911** (£866; £432; £216) **Stalls** Low

Form RPR

0666 **1** **Poetic Force (IRE)**[26] 7406 2-9-6 **64** (t) RichardKingscote 1 72
(Jonathan Portman) *led: hdd 7f out: chsd ldrs: wnt 2nd over 2f out: rdn to ld ins fnl f: edgd lft: styd on* **9/2**[1]

6000 **2** *1¾* **Armagnac (IRE)**[31] 7286 2-9-6 **64** AdamKirby 2 68
(Michael Bell) *pushed along to chse ldr: led 7f out: hdd 6f out: chsd ldr tl led again over 3f out: rdn over 2f out: hdd ins fnl f: styd on same pce* **8/1**

460 **3** *5* **Peace And Plenty**[22] 7496 2-9-4 **62** MartinDwyer 3 57
(William Muir) *prom: n.m.r and lost pl after 1f: hdwy u.p 2f out: styd on same pce fnl f* **6/1**

065 **4** *1¾* **Hold Me Tight (IRE)**[31] 7273 2-8-13 **60** JosephineGordon(3) 6 50
(J S Moore) *prom: rdn over 2f out: wknd ins fnl f* **25/1**

3303 **5** *shd* **Golden Eye**[11] 7750 2-9-3 **66** MitchGodwin(5) 8 56
(Sylvester Kirk) *chsd ldrs: rdn over 1f out: styd on same pce* **11/2**[3]

0633 **6** *¾* **All About The Pace**[39] 7032 2-9-2 **60** LiamKeniry 4 48
(Mark Usher) *hld up: rdn and flashed tail over 1f out: n.d* **28/1**

400 **7** *¾* **Echoism (IRE)**[14] 7695 2-9-4 **62** TomMarquand 7 49
(Mark Johnston) *mid-div: rdn over 2f out: hung lft fnl f: nvr trbld ldrs* **14/1**

0044 **8** *nk* **Masquerade Bling (IRE)**[11] 7734 2-9-2 **60** KieranO'Neill 11 46
(Simon Hodgson) *hld up: rdn over 1f out: nvr on terms* **14/1**

5040 **9** *3½* **Metronomic (IRE)**[31] 7286 2-9-4 **62** SeanLevey 9 41
(Richard Hannon) *prom: led over 6f out: hdd over 3f out: wknd and eased fnl f* **5/1**[2]

6050 **10** *hd* **Royal Cosmic**[19] 7571 2-8-13 **57** PatrickMathers 5 35
(Richard Fahey) *sn pushed along and prom: nt clr run and lost pl after 1f: pushed along over 5f out: bhd whn hrd rdn over 2f out* **8/1**

0113 **11** *4½* **Dragon Dream (IRE)**[25] 7423 2-9-3 **61** KierenFox 12 30
(Roger Ingram) *hld up: pushed along over 5f out: rdn and wknd over 2f out* **8/1**

060 **12** *2¾* **Bara Brith**[155] 3093 2-8-11 **55** JFEgan 10 18
(David Evans) *hld up: hdwy over 3f out: rdn and wknd over 2f out* **100/1**

1m 47.61s (-2.49) **Going Correction** -0.275s/f (Stan) 2y crse rec **12** Ran SP% **119.5**
Speed ratings (Par 94): **100,98,94,92,92 91,91,90,87,87 83,81**
CSF £40.30 CT £187.35 TOTE £5.90: £2.10, £3.10, £2.30; EX 46.60 Trifecta £360.80.
Owner The Sawgrass Survivors **Bred** S J Macdonald **Trained** Upper Lambourn, Berks

FOCUS
Few got into this extended mile nursery run at a searching pace.

7942 BETWAY MAIDEN STKS 1m 1f 103y (Tp)
7:45 (7:46) (Class 5) 3-Y-O+ **£3,881** (£1,155; £577; £288) **Stalls** Low

Form RPR

3 **1** **Hermann**[224] 1200 3-9-5 0 SeanLevey 4 81+
(Richard Hannon) *hld up in tch: racd keenly: shkn up over 1f out: rdn to ld ins fnl f: r.o* **2/1**[1]

25 **2** *½* **Just For You**[17] 7627 3-9-0 0 TomQueally 11 75+
(James Fanshawe) *s.i.s: hld up: hdwy over 2f out: hung lft over 1f out: r.o* **3/1**[2]

3 *1¼* **Condamine (IRE)** 3-9-5 0 RichardKingscote 8 77
(Jeremy Gask) *sn chsng ldr: ev ch fr over 2f out: rdn over 1f out: no ex wl ins fnl f* **14/1**

-253 **4** *1* **Shah Of Armaan (IRE)**[19] 7583 3-9-5 71 KevinStott 10 75
(Kevin Ryan) *chsd ldrs: rdn over 3f out: styd on same pce ins fnl f* **7/1**[3]

3622 **5** *1¼* **Forecaster**[17] 7609 3-9-0 75 (v) AdamKirby 6 67
(Michael Bell) *led: rdn over 2f out: hdd and no ex ins fnl f* **2/1**[1]

40 **6** *3½* **Phileas Fogg (IRE)**[37] 7102 3-9-2 0 JosephineGordon(3) 3 65
(Martyn Meade) *hld up in tch: rdn over 2f out: wknd fnl f* **25/1**

656- **7** *4½* **Ominotago**[445] 5722 4-9-0 69 AlistairRawlinson(3) 7 50
(Michael Appleby) *sn pushed along in mid-div: rdn over 3f out: wknd over 2f out* **40/1**

0 **8** *nk* **Bassino (USA)**[53] 6650 3-9-0 0 RachealKneller(5) 2 55
(James Bennett) *awkward leaving stalls: plld hrd and prom: rdn over 2f out: wknd over 1f out* **100/1**

06 **9** *¾* **Jackblack**[11] 7753 4-9-8 0 KierenFox 5 52
(Patrick Chamings) *hld up: a in rr: bhd fr 1/2-way* **80/1**

50 **10** *6* **Cougar Kid (IRE)**[33] 7218 5-9-3 0 CiaranMckee(5) 9 40
(John O'Shea) *s.i.s: a in rr: bhd fr 1/2-way* **100/1**

11 3 **Mamnoon (IRE)**41 3-9-5 0 TomMarquand 1 34
(Roy Brotherton) *hld up: a in rr: bhd fr 1/2-way* **80/1**

1m 58.07s (-2.73) **Going Correction** -0.275s/f (Stan)
WFA 3 from 4yo+ 3lb **11** Ran SP% **121.6**
Speed ratings (Par 103): **101,100,99,98,97 94,90,90,89,84 81**
CSF £8.50 TOTE £2.90: £1.50, £1.40, £4.10; EX 9.80 Trifecta £120.80.
Owner Michael Kerr-Dineen & Martin Hughes **Bred** Compagnia Generale Srl **Trained** East Everleigh, Wilts

FOCUS
The first event of the evening not limited to juveniles, and a winning time about 0.9 seconds quicker than that recorded by the errant Andrassy Avenue an hour earlier. Muddling form rated around the fourth and sixth.

7943 SUNBETS.CO.UK H'CAP (DIV I) 1m 141y (Tp)
8:15 (8:15) (Class 6) (0-60,60) 3-Y-O+ **£2,911** (£866; £432; £216) **Stalls** Low

Form RPR
53-0 **1** **Siouxperhero (IRE)**22 7514 7-9-7 **60** (p) MartinDwyer 6 66
(William Muir) *hld up: hdwy over 1f out: rdn and edgd lft ins fnl f: r.o to ld nr fin* **8/1**

2 ½ **Try Again (IRE)**103 4963 3-8-4 **46** oh1 (b) LukeMorris 2 52
(Paul W Flynn, Ire) *plld hrd and prom: rdn to chse ldr and hung lft over 1f out: led wl ins fnl f: hdd nr fin* **11/2**3

5 **3** ½ **Captain K (IRE)**22 7509 4-8-7 **46** oh1 (p) ConnorBeasley 5 50
(Gordon Elliott, Ire) *hld up: hdwy and nt clr run 1f out: sn rdn: r.o* **14/1**

0335 **4** ¾ **Dukes Meadow**30 7310 5-8-11 **57** RhiainIngram(7) 3 59
(Roger Ingram) *hld up: pushed along over 3f out: hdwy over 1f out: nt clr run ins fnl f: styd on* **5/1**2

5622 **5** 1 **Just Isla**38 7070 6-9-3 **56** (b) LiamKeniry 9 56
(John Flint) *prom: chsd ldr over 6f out tl led over 2f out: rdn and hung lft over 1f out: hdd and no ex wl ins fnl f* **11/1**

5641 **6** 1¾ **Secret Lightning (FR)**32 7261 4-8-11 **53** AlistairRawlinson(3) 8 50
(Michael Appleby) *prom: rdn over 2f out: styd on same pce fnl f* **9/4**1

6344 **7** ½ **Mrs Biggs**22 7513 4-8-12 **56** PhilDennis(5) 7 55
(Declan Carroll) *led: hdd after 1f: chsd ldrs: cl up whn hmpd over 1f out: styd on same pce ins fnl f* **13/2**

2004 **8** 3½ **Frozon**22 7515 3-9-3 **59** 1 AdamKirby 4 48
(Marjorie Fife) *led over 7f out: rdn and hdd over 2f out: nt clr run over 1f out: wknd fnl f* **13/2**

3400 **9** ½ **Imperial Link**17 7619 4-9-2 **58** EdwardGreatrex(3) 1 45
(John O'Shea) *s.i.s: hld up: a in rr* **33/1**

446 **10** ½ **Outrath (IRE)**65 6247 6-9-0 **53** TimmyMurphy 10 39
(Jim Best) *s.i.s: pushed along over 3f out: a in rr* **25/1**

1m 48.94s (-1.16) **Going Correction** -0.275s/f (Stan)
WFA 3 from 4yo+ 3lb **10** Ran SP% **122.4**
Speed ratings (Par 101): **94,93,93,92,91 90,89,86,86,85**
CSF £54.29 CT £623.37 TOTE £8.70: £2.40, £2.40, £3.20; EX 62.50 Trifecta £995.60.
Owner Muir Racing Partnership - Bath **Bred** J & J Waldron **Trained** Lambourn, Berks

FOCUS
The initially decent tempo to this moderate handicap slackened after 2f, but three of the first four places still went to closers.

7944 SUNBETS.CO.UK H'CAP (DIV II) 1m 141y (Tp)
8:45 (8:45) (Class 6) (0-60,60) 3-Y-O+ **£2,911** (£866; £432; £216) **Stalls** Low

Form RPR
0046 **1** **Russian Ranger (IRE)**22 7516 3-9-0 **56** (p) RichardKingscote 6 66+
(Jonathan Portman) *led 1f: chsd ldrs: wnt 2nd 3f out: led over 1f out: rdn clr fnl f* **7/4**1

40- **2** 4½ **Kubeba (IRE)**366 7821 5-9-7 **60** (b1) LukeMorris 1 60
(Paul Cole) *hld up in tch: racd keenly: rdn to chse ldr over 1f out: styd on same pce fnl f* **7/2**2

3004 **3** 1 **Jessica Jo (IRE)**11 7735 3-9-1 **57** (b) TomMarquand 3 55
(Mark Johnston) *sn pushed along in rr: hdwy 2f out: rdn over 1f out: styd on same pce fnl f* **9/1**

1006 **4** ½ **Mount Cheiron (USA)**30 7300 5-8-10 **56** (p) CallumRodriguez(7) 8 52
(Richard Ford) *s.s: hld up: hdwy over 1f out: no ex ins fnl f* **15/2**

2065 **5** 2¼ **Spirit Of Gondree (IRE)**11 7735 8-9-2 **58** (b) JosephineGordon(3) 5 50
(Milton Bradley) *chsd ldrs: rdn over 2f out: wknd fnl f* **6/1**3

6650 **6** 1½ **Zed Candy Girl**145 3474 6-9-3 **56** (p) AdamKirby 2 45
(Daniel Mark Loughnane) *hld up: hdwy u.p 2f out: wknd fnl f* **8/1**

000- **7** 7 **Club House (IRE)**414 6714 6-9-1 **57** EdwardGreatrex(3) 4 31
(Kevin Frost) *hld up: racd keenly: rdn: edgd lft and wknd over 1f out* **16/1**

0500 **8** nk **Jackpot**25 7426 6-8-7 **46** oh1 (p) MartinDwyer 7 19
(Brendan Powell) *led after 1f: rdn and hdd wl over 1f out: wknd fnl f* **33/1**

/000 **9** 45 **Alberto**23 7488 6-8-6 **48** oh1 ow2 (p) RobHornby(3) 9
(Lisa Williamson) *prom: chsd ldr over 6f out tl drvn along 3f out: wknd and eased over 2f out* **80/1**

1m 47.67s (-2.43) **Going Correction** -0.275s/f (Stan)
WFA 3 from 5yo+ 3lb **9** Ran SP% **115.8**
Speed ratings (Par 101): **99,95,94,93,91 90,84,83,43**
CSF £7.79 CT £42.29 TOTE £2.80: £1.10, £1.60, £2.80; EX 9.40 Trifecta £67.50.
Owner The Traditionalists **Bred** C J Foy **Trained** Upper Lambourn, Berks

FOCUS
A good pace on from the outset, and unsurprisingly the faster of the two divisions by 1.27 seconds.

7945 BETWAY H'CAP 5f 20y (Tp)
9:15 (9:16) (Class 5) (0-70,70) 3-Y-O+ **£3,881** (£1,155; £577; £288) **Stalls** Low

Form RPR
0152 **1** **Zipedeedodah (IRE)**21 7534 4-9-0 **66** (t) JosephineGordon(3) 2 75
(Joseph Tuite) *chsd ldrs: rdn to ld over 1f out: r.o* **9/2**1

3300 **2** 1 **Cruise Tothelimit (IRE)**47 6834 8-8-9 **63** CliffordLee(5) 1 68
(Patrick Morris) *mid-div: hdwy over 1f out: r.o u.p to go 2nd post* **20/1**

6002 **3** hd **Red Stripes (USA)**7 7811 4-9-7 **70** (b) KevinStott 3 74
(Lisa Williamson) *led: rdn and hdd over 1f out: styd on same pce ins fnl f: lost 2nd post* **5/1**2

5366 **4** nk **Noble Asset**7 7811 5-9-2 **65** LukeMorris 10 68
(Milton Bradley) *hld up in tch: rdn over 1f out: r.o* **9/1**

6024 **5** ½ **Powerful Dream (IRE)**73 6018 3-9-2 **70** CiaranMckee(5) 4 71+
(Ronald Harris) *s.i.s: in rr: hdwy over 1f out: r.o* **16/1**

5660 **6** ¾ **Quality Art (USA)**1 7913 8-8-6 **58** RobHornby(3) 5 57
(Simon Hodgson) *hld up: hdwy over 1f out: sn rdn: styd on same pce wl ins fnl f* **9/1**

0000 **7** 1¾ **Air Of York (IRE)**17 7626 4-9-4 **67** JFEgan 8 59
(David Evans) *s.i.s: outpcd* **7/1**3

0503 **8** 1¼ **Mighty Zip (USA)**17 7612 4-8-8 **62** (v) CharlieBennett(5) 11 50
(Lisa Williamson) *mid-div: rdn and hung lft fnl f: nvr trbld ldrs* **11/1**

3265 **9** 3 **Dusty Blue**16 7644 4-9-3 **69** EoinWalsh(3) 9 46
(Tony Carroll) *s.i.s: outpcd* **12/1**

2346 **10** ½ **Innocently (IRE)**15 7660 5-9-0 **68** (b) JoshDoyle(5) 6 43
(David O'Meara) *w ldr tl rdn 1/2-way: wkng whn hmpd ins fnl f* **9/2**1

-110 **11** 7 **China Excels**27 7386 9-9-6 **69** AdamKirby 7 19
(Mandy Rowland) *w ldr tl rdn 1/2-way: wknd over 1f out* **9/1**

1m 0.4s (-1.50) **Going Correction** -0.275s/f (Stan) **11** Ran SP% **122.2**
Speed ratings (Par 103): **101,99,99,98,97 96,93,91,87,86 75**
CSF £99.07 CT £388.49 TOTE £5.60: £2.00, £7.30, £2.20; EX 111.60 Trifecta £1675.10.
Owner D M Synergy & Mark Wellbelove **Bred** Tally-Ho Stud **Trained** Lambourn, Berks
■ Stewards' Enquiry : J F Egan caution: careless riding

FOCUS
A competitive sprint where it paid to sit just off the worst excesses of the pace. The winner has been rated back to his best and the third to his recent level.
T/Plt: £106.00 to a £1 stake. Pool: £120,803.30 - 831.77 winning tickets T/Qpdt: £28.10 to a £1 stake. Pool: £11,939.34 - 314.20 winning tickets **Colin Roberts**

7861 SAINT-CLOUD (L-H)
Saturday, November 12

OFFICIAL GOING: Turf: heavy

7946a PRIX DENISY (LISTED RACE) (3YO+) (TURF) 1m 7f 110y
2:45 (12:00) 3-Y-O+ **£19,117** (£7,647; £5,735; £3,823; £1,911)

RPR
1 **Nahual (FR)**42 6974 5-9-2 0 (p) MaximeGuyon 4 106
(J Bertran De Balanda, France) **29/10**2

2 ½ **Forgotten Rules (IRE)**28 7349 6-9-2 0 PatSmullen 3 105
(D K Weld, Ire) *w.w towards rr: drvn to cl under 2 1/2f out: kpt on to chse ldrs 1f out: styd on fnl f: nvr quite on terms w wnr* **13/5**1

3 2½ **Kloud Gate (FR)**27 7402 4-9-2 0 CristianDemuro 7 102
(Gianluca Bietolini, Italy) **102/10**

4 1½ **Eos Quercus (IRE)**14 7718 4-9-2 0 AlexandreRoussel 1 101
(N Leenders, France) **31/1**

5 hd **Return Ace**140 3665 4-8-13 0 GregoryBenoist 2 97
(James Fanshawe) *hld up in tch on inner: 6th and drvn 2 1/2f out: kpt on at same pce u.p fr over 1f out* **167/10**

6 ¾ **Golden Guepard (IRE)**19 5-9-2 0 Pierre-CharlesBoudot 9 99
(A Fabre, France) **54/10**3

7 2 **Pearl Dragon (FR)**19 5-9-2 0 VincentCheminaud 11 97
(M Delzangles, France) **87/10**

8 1¼ **Shalakar (FR)**25 7456 3-8-8 0 AlexisBadel 5 97
(M Delzangles, France) **41/1**

9 10 **Rock Of Romance (IRE)**21 7555 6-9-5 0 ChristopheSoumillon 8 87
(A Wohler, Germany) **87/10**

10 ¾ **Sandro Botticelli (IRE)**28 7349 4-9-5 0 (p) OlivierPeslier 6 86
(John Ryan) *hld up towards rr: rdn 2 1/2f out but no imp: bhd fnl 1 1/2f* **145/10**

11 4 **Valaynna (FR)**182 5-8-13 0 RonanThomas 10 75
(G Derat, France) **50/1**

3m 45.37s (6.67)
WFA 3 from 4yo+ 8lb **11** Ran SP% **118.2**
WIN (incl. 1 euro stake): 3.90. PLACES: 1.60, 1.50, 2.40. DF: 6.10. SF: 13.00.
Owner Emile Eyvaso **Bred** E Eyvaso **Trained** France

SANDOWN (AUS) (L-H)
Saturday, November 12

OFFICIAL GOING: Turf: good

7947a LADBROKES SANDOWN CUP (LISTED H'CAP) (3YO+) (TURF) 2m
2:35 (12:00) 3-Y-O+
£44,801 (£13,366; £6,683; £3,341; £1,856; £1,485)

RPR
1 **Qewy (IRE)**11 7756 6-9-3 **0** KerrinMcEvoy 1 108
(Charlie Appleby) **9/10**1

2 hd **Swacadelic (GER)**11 5-8-7 **0** (b) GlynSchofield 2 98
(Aaron Purcell, Australia) **11/2**3

3 3¾ **All I Survey (AUS)**11 5-8-7 **0** (v) PatrickMoloney 4 94
(Pat Carey, Australia) **30/1**

4 1 **Four Carat (GER)**11 5-8-8 **0** ow1 (bt) BenMelham 3 94
(Chris Waller, Australia) **16/1**

5 1¼ **De Little Engine (AUS)**7 7826 6-8-7 **0** DamianLane 5 91
(Danny O'Brien, Australia) **4/1**2

6 3¼ **Murphy's Delight (IRE)**11 6-8-7 **0** (t) CraigNewitt 6 88
(Chris Waller, Australia) **10/1**

7 4½ **Bring Something (AUS)**17 7637 6-8-7 **0** CraigAWilliams 8 83
(Ken Keys, Australia) **17/1**

8 2¾ **Tunes (AUS)**44 8-8-7 **0** (bt) MichellePayne 7 80
(Grant Young, Australia) **40/1**

3m 25.87s (205.87) **8** Ran SP% **114.2**

Owner Godolphin **Bred** Darley **Trained** Newmarket, Suffolk

7948a QUAYCLEAN ZIPPING CLASSIC (GROUP 2) (3YO+) (TURF) 1m 4f
5:00 (12:00) 3-Y-O+
£89,603 (£26,732; £13,366; £6,683; £3,712; £2,970)

RPR
1 **Beautiful Romance**11 7756 4-9-0 0 GlynSchofield 5 108+
(Saeed bin Suroor) **4/1**2

2 shd **Almoonqith (USA)**11 7756 6-9-4 0 (b) DamienOliver 4 112
(David A & B Hayes & Tom Dabernig, Australia) **9/2**3

3 hd **Big Orange**11 7756 5-9-4 0 (p) DamianLane 2 112
(Michael Bell) **9/2**3

4 4 **So Si Bon (AUS)**14 7715 3-7-13 0 CraigAWilliams 8 106
(Robbie Laing, Australia) **5/1**

5 hd **Who Shot Thebarman (NZ)**11 7756 8-9-4 0 (t) HughBowman 1 105
(Chris Waller, Australia) **27/10**1

6 3 **Transfer Allowance (AUS)**[14] 7712 7-9-4 0................ ChrisSymons 3 100
(Peter Roche, Australia) **150/1**
7 20 **Secret Number**[11] 7756 6-9-4 0.................................. StephenBaster 6 68
(Saeed bin Suroor) **7/1**
8 dist **Tristram's Sun (NZ)**[10] 8-9-4 0................................(b) KerrinMcEvoy 7
(Robbie Laing, Australia) **100/1**
2m 29.05s (149.05)
WFA 3 from 4yo+ 6lb **8** Ran SP% **114.2**

Owner Godolphin **Bred** Rabbah Bloodstock Limited **Trained** Newmarket, Suffolk

7949 - 7953a (Foreign Racing) - See Raceform Interactive

[7853] NEWCASTLE (A.W) (L-H)

Monday, November 14

OFFICIAL GOING: Tapeta: standard

Wind: Light across Weather: Overcast

7954 32RED.COM NURSERY H'CAP 1m 2f 42y (Tp)
2:00 (2:00) (Class 6) (0-65,67) 2-Y-O **£2,716** (£808; £404; £202) **Stalls** High

Form RPR
0000 1 **Oxford Blu**[18] 7640 2-9-3 **58**..(v[1]) LukeMorris 2 63+
(Sir Mark Prescott Bt) *prom: shkn up over 2f out: rdn to ld over 1f out: styd on wl* **5/1**[3]
606 2 3 **La Vie En Rose**[18] 7647 2-9-5 **60**.............................. PJMcDonald 6 59
(Mark Johnston) *hld up: pushed along over 3f out: hdwy to chse wnr over 1f out: no imp ins fnl f* **3/1**[1]
0005 3 3/4 **Bodacious Name (IRE)**[6] 7854 2-9-0 **55**.......................... TomEaves 3 53
(John Quinn) *hld up: hdwy over 2f out: rdn over 1f out: styd on same pce ins fnl f* **9/1**
6042 4 shd **Booshbash (IRE)**[84] 5719 2-9-4 **59**.......................... GrahamGibbons 1 57
(Ed Dunlop) *prom: nt clr run and swtchd lft over 1f out: sn rdn: no ex wl ins fnl f* **4/1**[2]
2066 5 2 **Too Many Shots**[18] 7640 2-9-7 **62**...................................... KierenFox 8 56
(John Best) *chsd ldr over 3f: remained handy: rdn and ev ch over 1f out: no ex ins fnl f* **3/1**[1]
005 6 2 1/2 **Siyahamba (IRE)**[27] 7431 2-9-5 **60**.............................. ConnorBeasley 4 50
(Bryan Smart) *hld up: racd keenly: hdwy to chse ldr over 6f out: pushed along 4f out: led over 2f out: rdn and hdd over 1f out: wknd ins fnl f* **5/1**[3]
0000 7 5 **Shadow Of Hercules (IRE)**[54] 6681 2-8-1 **45**.....(be[1]) NathanEvans(3) 5 26
(Michael Mullineaux) *led: rdn and hdd over 2f out: wknd over 1f out* **50/1**
2m 10.97s (0.57) **Going Correction** -0.025s/f (Stan) **7** Ran SP% **115.3**
Speed ratings (Par 94): **96,93,93,92,91 89,85**
CSF £20.72 CT £131.05 TOTE £6.30: £3.60, £1.60; EX 19.60 Trifecta £192.40.
Owner Mrs Olivia Hoare & J M Castle **Bred** Mrs Olivia Hoare **Trained** Newmarket, Suffolk

FOCUS
A modest nursery, in which all the runners were maidens and trying the longer trip for the first time. It proved quite a test and a small step forward from the winner.

7955 BETWAY STAYERS APPRENTICE H'CAP 2m 56y (Tp)
2:30 (2:30) (Class 5) (0-70,70) 3-Y-O+ **£3,234** (£962; £481; £240) **Stalls** Low

Form RPR
5003 1 **Cavalieri (IRE)**[7] 7846 6-9-2 **58**.......................................(tp) KevinStott 7 69
(Philip Kirby) *chsd ldrs: wnt 2nd 4f out: led on bit 2f out: shkn up and c readily clr fnl f: eased towards fin* **4/1**[2]
3212 2 4 1/2 **Alsacienne**[29] 7382 3-9-0 **70**................................[1] ManuelFernandes(5) 6 75
(Sir Mark Prescott Bt) *hld up: hdwy 12f out: chsd ldr 10f out: led 5f out: hdd 2f out: styd on same pce fnl f* **4/5**[1]
5023 3 4 **Endive**[13] 7739 4-9-7 **63**..(t) LouisSteward 2 63
(Robert Stephens) *chsd ldr 6f: remained handy: rdn over 3f out: styd on same pce fnl 2f* **9/2**[3]
5224 4 6 **Jan De Heem**[13] 7746 6-9-6 **62**................................ JosephineGordon 3 55
(Tina Jackson) *hld up: hdwy 4f out: rdn over 2f out: wknd over 1f out* **10/1**
- 5 nk **Rosarios (FR)**[116] 3-9-3 **68**... NathanEvans 5 60
(Rebecca Menzies) *hld up: hdwy 4f out: sn outpcd: kpt on to go mod 5th nr fin* **33/1**
5603 6 2 **Perennial**[13] 7746 7-8-9 **51** oh4..(p) JoeDoyle 4 41
(Philip Kirby) *hld up in tch: shkn up over 2f out: wknd over 1f out* **16/1**
032- 7 99 **Roughlyn**[478] 4632 7-8-9 **51** oh6...............................(b) ShirleyTeasdale 1
(Lisa Williamson) *led: clr after 2f tl 10f out: hdd 5f out: sn wknd* **50/1**
3m 34.06s (-1.14) **Going Correction** -0.025s/f (Stan)
WFA 3 from 4yo+ 9lb **7** Ran SP% **113.6**
Speed ratings (Par 103): **101,98,96,93,93 92,43**
CSF £7.47 TOTE £4.90: £2.10, £1.10; EX 8.60 Trifecta £32.30.
Owner The Cavalieri Partnership **Bred** Grange & Manister House Studs **Trained** East Appleton, N Yorks

FOCUS
A fair staying handicap, if not the strongest for the grade. The winner has been rated back to last winter's form.

7956 32RED CASINO NURSERY H'CAP 7f 14y (Tp)
3:00 (3:00) (Class 4) (0-85,82) 2-Y-O **£4,398** (£1,309; £654; £327) **Stalls** Centre

Form RPR
0200 1 **Textured (IRE)**[37] 7147 2-9-1 **76**.............................. GrahamGibbons 3 81
(Sir Michael Stoute) *pushed along in rr early: hdwy over 1f out: styd on u.p to ld towards fin* **20/1**
130 2 shd **Morning Suit (USA)**[66] 6275 2-9-1 **76**............................ PJMcDonald 9 81
(Mark Johnston) *hld up: hdwy 1/2-way: led wl over 1f out: sn rdn and hung lft: hdd towards fin* **20/1**
1020 3 3 **Norwegian Highness (FR)**[38] 7120 2-9-0 **75**.................. ShaneGray 8 72
(Kevin Ryan) *s.i.s: hld up: hdwy over 1f out: edgd lft and styd on same pce ins fnl f* **11/2**[3]
4454 4 1/2 **Miss Sheridan (IRE)**[16] 7688 2-8-2 **66**........................ NathanEvans(3) 6 62
(Michael Easterby) *w ldr tl wnt on 1/2-way: rdn and hdd wl over 1f out: styd on same pce ins fnl f* **7/1**
31 5 1 1/4 **Dubai Elegance**[23] 7527 2-9-6 **81**................................ WilliamCarson 2 74
(Saeed bin Suroor) *chsd ldrs: rdn and ev ch 2f out: no ex fnl f* **6/5**[1]
0252 6 4 1/2 **Bolt Phantom (USA)**[32] 7306 2-9-0 **78**................. AlistairRawlinson(3) 1 60
(Ismail Mohammed) *w ldrs: rdn over 2f out: wknd fnl f* **6/1**
055 7 4 **Wigan Warrior**[12] 7768 2-8-10 **71**.. TomEaves 4 43
(David Brown) *led to 1/2-way: sn rdn: wknd over 1f out* **20/1**
41 8 nk **Tor**[34] 7247 2-9-7 **82**.. JasonHart 7 53
(Keith Dalgleish) *s.i.s: wnt prom over 5f out: rdn and wknd over 2f out* **5/1**[2]
1m 27.01s (0.81) **Going Correction** +0.20s/f (Slow) **8** Ran SP% **118.6**
Speed ratings (Par 98): **103,102,99,98,97 92,87,87**
CSF £343.02 CT £2501.30 TOTE £14.10: £4.70, £4.20, £2.30; EX 108.80 Trifecta £759.00.
Owner Cheveley Park Stud **Bred** Timbre Partnership **Trained** Newmarket, Suffolk

FOCUS
A decent nursery and the first two pulled clear of the rest.

7957 SUNBETS.CO.UK H'CAP (DIV I) 7f 14y (Tp)
3:30 (3:30) (Class 4) (0-85,85) 3-Y-O+ **£5,175** (£1,540; £769; £384) **Stalls** Centre

Form RPR
1003 1 **Young John (IRE)**[23] 7540 3-9-3 **82**................................ JackGarritty 4 90
(Richard Fahey) *chsd ldrs: edgd lft over 2f out: rdn to ld and edgd rt ins fnl f: styd on* **10/1**
0000 2 1/2 **Holiday Magic (IRE)**[20] 7593 5-8-7 **74**...................... NathanEvans(3) 1 81
(Michael Easterby) *led: rdn and hdd ins fnl f: kpt on* **11/4**[1]
0661 3 3/4 **Alexandrakollontai (IRE)**[10] 7796 6-9-6 **84**.............(b) JamesSullivan 8 89
(Alistair Whillans) *sn pushed along in rr: rdn over 2f out: r.o ins fnl f: nt rch ldrs* **6/1**[3]
0002 4 1 1/4 **Boots And Spurs**[20] 7593 7-9-1 **79**................................(v) LukeMorris 2 81
(Scott Dixon) *chsd ldrs: rdn over 2f out: styd on* **14/1**
2131 5 3/4 **Volition (IRE)**[19] 7617 3-9-0 **79**.............................. RichardKingscote 3 78
(Sir Michael Stoute) *prom: chsd ldr 5f out: rdn and carried hd high ins fnl f: one pce* **7/2**[2]
1300 6 shd **War Department (IRE)**[27] 7433 3-9-0 **79**.......................(v) GrahamLee 7 77
(Keith Dalgleish) *hld up: hdwy over 1f out: sn rdn: nt rch ldrs* **14/1**
053 7 1 1/2 **Free Code (IRE)**[16] 7702 5-9-4 **82**............................ GrahamGibbons 5 77
(David Barron) *chsd ldrs: rdn 1/2-way: sn outpcd: n.d after* **8/1**
0030 8 1 **Mont Ras (IRE)**[10] 7796 9-9-5 **83**................................ ConnorBeasley 10 76
(Roger Fell) *prom: outpcd 1/2-way: nvr on terms after* **14/1**
242 9 1 **Tiger Jim**[39] 7094 6-9-4 **85**...................................... JosephineGordon(3) 6 75
(Jim Goldie) *hood removed late: dwlt: hdwy u.p over 2f out: wknd ins fnl f* **8/1**
052 10 3 1/2 **Marbooh (IRE)**[9] 7813 3-8-7 **77**................................... JoshDoyle(5) 9 56
(David O'Meara) *hld up: a in rr: rdn and wknd over 1f out* **6/1**[3]
1m 26.76s (0.56) **Going Correction** +0.20s/f (Slow)
WFA 3 from 5yo+ 1lb **10** Ran SP% **128.8**
Speed ratings (Par 105): **104,103,102,101,100 100,98,97,96,92**
CSF £41.81 CT £197.19 TOTE £16.80: £4.20, £1.30, £2.60; EX 86.70 Trifecta £439.30.
Owner Mrs A M Riney **Bred** Carpet Lady Partnership **Trained** Musley Bank, N Yorks

FOCUS
A decent, open-looking handicap and solid form with the winner on a fair mark on his best efforts.

7958 SUNBETS.CO.UK H'CAP (DIV II) 7f 14y (Tp)
4:00 (4:00) (Class 4) (0-85,85) 3-Y-O+ **£5,175** (£1,540; £769; £384) **Stalls** Centre

Form RPR
0000 1 **Kalk Bay (IRE)**[20] 7593 9-8-13 **80**..............................(t) NathanEvans(3) 6 87
(Michael Easterby) *hld up: hdwy over 2f out: nt clr run over 1f out: rdn and r.o to ld nr fin* **16/1**
6042 2 1/2 **Brilliant Vanguard (IRE)**[13] 7737 3-9-1 **80**........................ KevinStott 2 84
(Kevin Ryan) *trckd ldrs: plld hrd: rdn to ld wl ins fnl f: hdd nr fin* **7/2**[2]
4342 3 shd **Rebel Surge (IRE)**[16] 7702 3-9-6 **85**.............................. TomQueally 10 89
(Richard Spencer) *a.p: rdn to ld and edgd lft ins fnl f: sn hdd: r.o* **10/1**
1256 4 nk **Let's Twist**[13] 7738 4-8-10 **74**...(b) ShaneGray 9 78
(Kristin Stubbs) *led: rdn and hdd over 1f out: ev ch ins fnl f: styd on* **11/2**
5000 5 shd **Lil Sophella (IRE)**[26] 7472 7-9-5 **83**.............................. JackGarritty 3 87
(Patrick Holmes) *hld up: swtchd lft and r.o ins fnl f: nt rch ldrs* **33/1**
1300 6 1 **Jordan Sport**[26] 7462 3-9-3 **82**...................................... TonyHamilton 5 82
(David Simcock) *plld hrd and prom: rdn over 1f out: edgd lft and no ex wl ins fnl f* **4/1**[3]
1210 7 1/2 **Mon Beau Visage (IRE)**[30] 7360 3-9-0 **79**.............(p) GrahamGibbons 8 79
(David O'Meara) *hld up in tch: plld hrd: jnd ldr over 4f out: led over 1f out: rdn and hdd ins fnl f: no ex* **3/1**[1]
100- 8 1 **Jacquotte Delahaye**[412] 6831 5-8-13 **77**............................ TomEaves 4 74
(David Brown) *hld up: effrt and hung lft over 1f out: nt trble ldrs* **50/1**
0004 9 9 **Edgar Balthazar**[10] 7796 4-9-7 **85**.................................(p) GrahamLee 1 58
(Keith Dalgleish) *hld up: rdn and wknd over 2f out* **7/1**
0634 10 8 **Funding Deficit (IRE)**[27] 7433 6-8-7 **74**.............. JosephineGordon(3) 7 25
(Jim Goldie) *plld hrd and prom: rdn over 2f out: wknd over 1f out* **14/1**
1m 27.15s (0.95) **Going Correction** +0.20s/f (Slow)
WFA 3 from 4yo+ 1lb **10** Ran SP% **121.6**
Speed ratings (Par 105): **102,101,101,100,100 99,99,98,87,78**
CSF £74.61 CT £627.52 TOTE £20.10: £4.60, £1.60, £2.90; EX 104.20 Trifecta £1092.20.
Owner Linda Folwell, Steve Hull & David Swales **Bred** Wentworth Racing **Trained** Sheriff Hutton, N Yorks

FOCUS
The second division of a fair handicap and they finished in a bit of a heap, with the winner back to form off a good mark.

7959 BETWAY SPRINT H'CAP 6f (Tp)
4:30 (4:31) (Class 5) (0-75,75) 3-Y-O+ **£3,234** (£962; £481; £240) **Stalls** Centre

Form RPR
0065 1 **Savannah Beau**[50] 6809 4-8-13 **67**.................................... GrahamLee 9 74+
(Iain Jardine) *hld up: swtchd rt and hdwy over 1f out: r.o to ld nr fin* **8/1**
0322 2 nk **Dark Side Dream**[7] 7660 4-9-0 **71**.......................... JosephineGordon(3) 12 77
(Chris Dwyer) *hld up in tch: pushed along over 2f out: led over 1f out: rdn ins fnl f: hdd nr fin* **5/1**[3]
2351 3 nk **Compas Scoobie**[26] 7459 3-8-13 **74**............................ DavidEgan(7) 13 80+
(Roger Varian) *hld up: hdwy over 2f out: nt clr run over 1f out: r.o* **4/1**[1]
0005 4 nse **The Hooded Claw (IRE)**[20] 7590 5-9-3 **71**................(p) JamesSullivan 4 76
(Tim Easterby) *chsd ldrs: rdn and ev ch fr over 1f out: r.o* **12/1**
0605 5 shd **Tellovoi (IRE)**[17] 7662 8-9-3 **71**.......................................(v) KevinStott 10 76
(Richard Guest) *chsd ldr tl led over 2f out: rdn and hdd wl over 1f out: r.o* **16/1**
0052 6 1 3/4 **Clubland (IRE)**[7] 7852 7-9-0 **68**.. JasonHart 8 70+
(Garry Moss) *hld up in tch: nt clr run over 1f out: swtchd lft: styd on* **9/2**[2]
4005 7 nse **English Hero**[13] 7743 3-9-2 **70**.. TomQueally 14 69
(John Mackie) *hld up: hdwy over 1f out: sn rdn: no imp ins fnl f* **20/1**
3005 8 2 1/2 **Something Lucky (IRE)**[38] 7112 4-9-7 **75**....................(p) ShaneGray 1 66
(Kristin Stubbs) *hld up: hdwy over 1f out: sn rdn and flashed tail: no ex wl ins fnl f* **12/1**
3201 9 3/4 **Wahaab (IRE)**[7] 7851 5-8-13 **72** 6ex.......................(p) ShirleyTeasdale(5) 3 60
(Iain Jardine) *hld up: rdn 1/2-way: nt trble ldrs* **12/1**

The Form Book, Raceform Ltd, Newbury, RG14 5SJ

410 **10** *nk* **Slingsby**[10] 7798 5-9-3 **71**...............(v[1]) GrahamGibbons 7 58
(Michael Easterby) *dwlt: outpcd* **7/1**
3130 **11** *1* **Brockholes**[107] 4873 3-9-7 **75**............... ConnorBeasley 11 59
(Bryan Smart) *chsd ldrs: led wl over 1f out: sn rdn and hdd: wknd ins fnl f* **20/1**
0314 **12** *1 1/4* **Meandmyshadow**[10] 7798 8-9-5 **73**...............(b) DaleSwift 2 53
(Alan Brown) *chsd ldrs: rdn 1/2-way: wknd fnl f* **16/1**
0360 **13** *4* **Sir Domino (FR)**[17] 7660 4-9-4 **72**............... JackGarritty 5 39
(Patrick Holmes) *hld up: rdn and wknd over 1f out* **25/1**
1520 **14** *3 1/4* **Storm Trooper (IRE)**[34] 7252 5-8-13 **67**............... PaulQuinn 6 24
(David Nicholls) *led: rdn and hdd over 2f out: wknd over 1f out* **25/1**

1m 12.46s (-0.04) **Going Correction** +0.20s/f (Slow) **14** Ran SP% **130.5**
Speed ratings (Par 103): **108,107,107,107,107 104,104,101,100,99 98,96,91,87**
CSF £49.34 CT £192.16 TOTE £11.10: £3.40, £2.50, £2.10; EX 69.20 Trifecta £442.40.
Owner Market Avenue Racing Club Ltd **Bred** P Scholes **Trained** Carrutherstown, D'fries & G'way

FOCUS
A wide-open handicap and a thrilling finish, with the complexion of the race changing several times in the last half-furlong. The form has been rated around the second and fifth.

7960 SUN BETS ON THE APP STORE MAIDEN STKS 7f 14y (Tp)
5:00 (5:00) (Class 5) 3-Y-O+ **£3,234** (£962; £481; £240) **Stalls** Centre

Form RPR
4 **1** **Noble Star (IRE)**[216] 1397 3-9-5 0............... TomQueally 7 79
(James Fanshawe) *hld up: hdwy to chse ldr 1/2-way: rdn to ld over 1f out: styd on wl* **30/100**[1]
5320 **2** *4* **Napoleon Solo**[10] 7797 4-9-6 63............... GrahamGibbons 3 68
(David Barron) *led: rdn and hdd over 1f out: styd on same pce* **3/1**[2]
00 **3** *14* **Scribner Creek (IRE)**[19] 7616 3-9-5 0............... DaleSwift 6 29
(Daniel Mark Loughnane) *chsd ldrs: drvn along over 4f out: wknd wl over 1f out* **25/1**[3]
6 **4** *1 1/2* **Sandstream**[21] 7583 3-9-5 0............... BenCurtis 8 25
(Tracy Waggott) *prom: rdn over 2f out: wknd over 1f out* **50/1**
56/4 **5** *1 3/4* **Ship Canal**[7] 7848 4-9-3 50............... NathanEvans(3) 4 21
(Jacqueline Coward) *chsd ldrs: rdn 1/2-way: wknd 2f out* **25/1**[3]
/00- **6** *5* **Blythe Prince**[395] 7257 4-9-3 45............... AlistairRawlinson(3) 2 8
(Christopher Kellett) *s.i.s: a in rr: rdn and wknd over 2f out* **100/1**
0040 **7** *1/2* **Jacksonfire**[21] 7572 4-9-6 49...............(be[1]) TomEaves 1 7
(Michael Mullineaux) *chsd ldrs: rdn and hung lft over 2f out: sn wknd* **50/1**

1m 27.16s (0.96) **Going Correction** +0.20s/f (Slow)
WFA 3 from 4yo 1lb **7** Ran SP% **114.5**
Speed ratings (Par 103): **102,97,81,79,77 72,71**
CSF £1.43 TOTE £1.30: £1.10, £1.40; EX 1.70 Trifecta £7.00.
Owner Tang Wai Bun Tony **Bred** J Hanly, A Stroud & Castlemartin Sky **Trained** Newmarket, Suffolk

FOCUS
Little depth to this maiden and the short-priced favourite made no mistake. The form is taken at face value through the runner-up.

7961 BETWAY H'CAP 5f (Tp)
5:30 (5:36) (Class 6) (0-60,60) 3-Y-O+ **£2,458** (£731; £365; £182) **Stalls** Centre

Form RPR
0005 **1** **Lady Joanna Vassa (IRE)**[6] 7859 3-9-2 **55**............... ConnorBeasley 5 63
(Richard Guest) *hld up: hdwy and nt clr run over 1f out: rdn to ins fnl f: r.o* **7/1**
030 **2** *1/2* **Prigsnov Dancer (IRE)**[33] 7290 11-8-7 **46**............... JoeDoyle 8 50
(John Balding) *prom: rdn over 1f out: r.o* **12/1**
0045 **3** *nse* **Tavener**[10] 7798 4-9-4 **60**...............(p) JosephineGordon(3) 9 64
(David C Griffiths) *chsd ldrs: rdn to ld over 1f out: hdd ins fnl f: styd on* **7/2**[2]
230 **4** *nk* **Slim Chance (IRE)**[13] 7747 7-9-0 **56**...............(v) LouisSteward(3) 3 59
(Simon West) *hld up: hdwy over 1f out: sn rdn: r.o* **10/1**
6400 **5** *3/4* **Tribesman**[31] 7323 3-9-3 **56**...............[1] SamJames 2 56
(Marjorie Fife) *led 1f: remained w ldr: rdn and ev ch over 1f out: styd on* **7/1**
0463 **6** *1/2* **Indian Pursuit (IRE)**[6] 7859 3-9-7 **60**............... JackGarritty 4 59
(John Quinn) *prom: rdn over 1f out: styd on same pce ins fnl f* **2/1**[1]
0602 **7** *1 1/2* **Sir Geoffrey (IRE)**[6] 7859 10-9-5 **58**...............(b) BenCurtis 10 51
(Scott Dixon) *led after 1f: rdn and hdd over 1f out: wknd ins fnl f* **5/1**[3]
000 **8** *1/2* **Ruby's Day**[9] 7817 7-8-13 **59**............... TomDonoghue(7) 1 50
(David Brown) *s.i.s: hung lft thrght: n.d* **20/1**
0600 **9** *nk* **Misu Mac**[27] 7437 6-9-3 **59**............... NathanEvans(3) 6 49
(Neville Bycroft) *sn outpcd* **33/1**

1m 0.66s (1.16) **Going Correction** +0.20s/f (Slow) **9** Ran SP% **121.7**
Speed ratings (Par 101): **98,97,97,96,95 94,92,91,90**
CSF £91.20 CT £349.78 TOTE £8.20: £2.20, £3.40, £1.70; EX 105.40 Trifecta £990.00.
Owner www.primelawns.co.uk **Bred** Tom Radley **Trained** Ingmanthorpe, W Yorks

FOCUS
Just a modest sprint handicap with the winner well in on the best of her 2016 turf form.
T/Jkpt: Not won. T/Plt: £687.30 to a £1 stake. Pool: £93,784.06 - 99.60 winning units. T/Qpdt: £152.60 to a £1 stake. Pool: £9,400.91 - 45.57 winning units. **Colin Roberts**

7930 LINGFIELD (L-H)
Tuesday, November 15

OFFICIAL GOING: Polytrack: standard
Wind: Light, across Weather: Overcast, mild

7962 32RED.COM EBF MAIDEN STKS (DIV I) 1m 1y(P)
12:25 (12:29) (Class 5) 2-Y-O **£3,363** (£1,001; £500; £250) **Stalls** High

Form RPR
1 **Manangatang (IRE)** 2-8-12 0............... GabrieleMalune(7) 11 68+
(Luca Cumani) *slowly away: hld up in last: stl there 2f out but gng wl: gd prog on inner over 1f out: shkn up and r.o between rivals to ld last stride* **20/1**
2 *nse* **Cosmic Boy (IRE)** 2-9-5 0............... LukeMorris 2 68
(Marco Botti) *led 1f: styd cl up: rdn to chal 2f out: narrow ld 1f out: styd on but hdd last stride* **8/1**
0 **3** *hd* **Daimochi (IRE)**[18] 7665 2-9-5 0............... JohnFahy 7 67
(Clive Cox) *chsd ldr after 2f: rdn to ld over 1f out to 1f out: kpt on and stl upsides last strides: jst hld* **15/2**[3]
06 **4** *hd* **Addicted To You (IRE)**[26] 7483 2-9-5 0............... PaulMulrennan 4 67+
(Mark Johnston) *towards rr: shkn up and dropped to rr over 2f out: 9th whn swtchd to outer 1f: r.o wl fnl f and fin best of all* **9/1**
5 *hd* **Intermodal** 2-9-5 0............... RichardKingscote 3 67+
(Amanda Perrett) *t.k.h: trckd ldrs: shkn up 2f out: green and nt qckn over 1f out: styd on ins fnl f but nt as qckly as others* **15/8**[1]
06 **6** *3/4* **Beauchamp Opal**[34] 7284 2-9-0 0............... StevieDonohoe 6 60
(Charlie Fellowes) *pushed up to ld after 1f: hdd over 1f out but stl upsides tl fdd last 75yds* **12/1**
7 *nk* **Marettimo (IRE)** 2-9-5 0............... DavidProbert 8 64
(Charles Hills) *t.k.h: trckd ldrs: shkn up over 2f out: no imp over 1f out: kpt on fnl f but nt pce to threaten* **6/1**[2]
0 **8** *1/2* **Outcrop (IRE)**[20] 7622 2-9-5 0............... RobertWinston 1 63
(Hughie Morrison) *chsd ldrs: shkn up over 2f out: tried to cl over 1f out: kpt on but lost pls last 100yds* **10/1**
00 **9** *nk* **License To Thrill (USA)**[56] 6655 2-9-5 0............... NickyMackay 9 62
(Simon Dow) *hld up towards rr: pushed along fr 2f out: nvr landed a blow but kpt on steadily* **25/1**
55 **10** *4 1/2* **Arab Moon**[20] 7605 2-9-5 0............... GeorgeBaker 10 51
(William Knight) *mostly in last pair: brought wdst of all bnd 2f out: no prog* **9/1**
11 *1/2* **Sheila's Fancy (IRE)** 2-9-5 0............... DannyBrock 5 50
(J S Moore) *v difficult to load into stall: rn green in midfield on outer: pushed along sn after 1/2-way: wknd 2f out* **50/1**

1m 38.09s (-0.11) **Going Correction** -0.10s/f (Stan) **11** Ran SP% **119.3**
Speed ratings (Par 96): **96,95,95,95,95 94,94,93,93,89 88**
CSF £171.33 TOTE £34.00: £5.80, £2.10, £2.30; EX 215.40 Trifecta £1798.80.
Owner O T I Racing & Partner **Bred** Storm Bloodstock **Trained** Newmarket, Suffolk

FOCUS
They finished in a heap in this maiden.

7963 32RED.COM EBF MAIDEN STKS (DIV II) 1m 1y(P)
12:55 (12:58) (Class 5) 2-Y-O **£3,363** (£1,001; £500; £250) **Stalls** High

Form RPR
05 **1** **Melting Dew**[20] 7621 2-9-5 0............... GrahamGibbons 6 70
(Sir Michael Stoute) *led after 2f: mde rest: kicked on 3f out: rdn and jnd 2f out: gained narrow upper hand fr1f: hld on* **7/1**
5 **2** *nk* **Muqaatil (USA)**[32] 7317 2-9-5 0............... SeanLevey 8 69
(Richard Hannon) *led 2f: pressed wnr after: rdn to chal and upsides 2f out: nt qckn and jst hld ins fnl f: styd on nr fin* **5/2**[2]
6 **3** *hd* **Garbanzo (IRE)**[20] 7621 2-9-5 0............... GeorgeBaker 3 69
(Ed Walker) *reluctant to go to post and had to be dismntd and led: chsd ldrs: rdn in 5th over 2f out: clsd on inner over 1f out: chal 100yds out: nt qckn and hld after* **3/1**[3]
4 *nk* **High Mark (IRE)** 2-9-5 0............... DavidProbert 9 68+
(Saeed bin Suroor) *trckd ldng pair: rdn to chal 2f out: rn green and hanging persistently after: styd on but ch thrown away* **13/8**[1]
5 *5* **Angel Of Rome (IRE)** 2-9-0 0............... ShaneKelly 2 51+
(Richard Hughes) *chsd ldng pair: rdn and in tch over 2f out: wknd over 1f out* **33/1**
00 **6** *1* **Magic Beans**[27] 7458 2-9-5 0............... JimmyFortune 10 53
(Hughie Morrison) *in tch in midfield tl lft bhd fr 3f out: no ch after* **66/1**
7 *2 3/4* **Aware (IRE)** 2-9-5 0............... JamieSpencer 7 47
(Charles Hills) *s.i.s: hld up in last: no ch after ldrs skipped away 3f out: pushed along and kpt on steadily to pass rivals fnl f* **20/1**
8 *1 1/2* **Beyond Beyond** 2-9-5 0............... RobertWinston 4 43
(Hughie Morrison) *s.i.s: a towards rr: lft bhd fr 3f out* **40/1**
9 *4 1/2* **Look My Way** 2-9-5 0............... LiamKeniry 1 32
(Andrew Balding) *dwlt: sn wl in tch but rn green: wknd over 2f out* **33/1**
00 **10** *4* **Paco Dawn**[34] 7277 2-9-0 0............... TomEaves 5 18
(Philip Hide) *a in rr: wknd 3f out* **100/1**

1m 39.94s (1.74) **Going Correction** -0.10s/f (Stan) **10** Ran SP% **119.7**
Speed ratings (Par 96): **87,86,86,86,81 80,77,75,71,67**
CSF £24.50 TOTE £6.10: £1.70, £1.60, £1.10; EX 30.10 Trifecta £120.00.
Owner K Abdullah **Bred** Juddmonte Farms Ltd **Trained** Newmarket, Suffolk

FOCUS
The first four finished clear here, but it was the slower of the two divisions by 1.85sec.

7964 BETWAY H'CAP 6f 1y(P)
1:25 (1:26) (Class 6) (0-65,65) 3-Y-O+ **£2,911** (£866; £432; £216) **Stalls** Low

Form RPR
4021 **1** **Swiss Cross**[19] 7654 9-9-0 **65**...............(tp) CallumShepherd(5) 1 77
(Phil McEntee) *w.w in last trio: gap appeared on inner over 1f out and prog along it to ld jst ins fnl f: sn rdn clr* **10/3**[2]
2050 **2** *2 1/2* **Rigolleto (IRE)**[28] 7430 8-9-5 **65**...............(p) GeorgeBaker 6 70
(Anabel K Murphy) *led: drvn and edgd rt over 1f out: hdd and outpcd jst ins fnl f* **3/1**[1]
500 **3** *nk* **Swanton Blue (IRE)**[24] 7534 3-9-2 **62**............... JamieSpencer 5 66
(Ed de Giles) *plld hrd: prog on outer to chse ldr over 3f out to 2f out: encouraged along and kpt on to press for 2nd again nr fin* **11/2**
550 **4** *1/2* **Pharoh Jake**[43] 7018 8-9-2 **62**............... WilliamCarson 2 64
(John Bridger) *sn t.k.h: trckd ldr to over 3f out: rdn to go 2nd again 2f out to over 1f out: nt qckn* **14/1**
4403 **5** *2* **Seek The Fair Land**[19] 7654 10-8-12 **63**...............(v) PaddyBradley(5) 7 59
(Lee Carter) *trckd ldrs: effrt whn swtchd towards inner then out wd bnd 2f out: lost grnd and no ch after* **11/2**
2600 **6** *3/4* **Picansort**[33] 7302 9-9-5 **65**...............(v) ShaneKelly 4 59
(Peter Crate) *hld up in last trio: pushed along and no prog 2f out: fdd ins fnl f* **10/1**
4465 **7** *3 1/4* **Rosie Royce**[29] 7420 3-9-5 **65**............... JimmyFortune 10 49
(Henry Candy) *a in rr: rdn and no prog 2f out* **4/1**[3]

1m 11.55s (-0.35) **Going Correction** -0.10s/f (Stan) **7** Ran SP% **114.6**
Speed ratings (Par 101): **98,94,94,93,90 89,85**
CSF £13.85 CT £52.23 TOTE £3.90: £1.90, £1.70; EX 14.30 Trifecta £109.20.
Owner Steve Jakes **Bred** Lordship Stud **Trained** Newmarket, Suffolk

FOCUS
A modest if competitive sprint on paper, but the winner drew right away in the closing stages.

7965 BETWAY SPRINT H'CAP 6f 1y(P)
1:55 (1:55) (Class 4) (0-85,84) 3-Y-O+ **£5,175** (£1,540; £769; £384) **Stalls** Low

Form RPR
1-00 **1** **Alkhor**[19] 7643 3-9-2 **79**............... SeanLevey 1 88+
(Richard Hannon) *trckd ldng pair: produced to ld ins fnl f: drvn out and jst hld on* **8/1**
1100 **2** *shd* **Salvatore Fury (IRE)**[42] 7054 6-9-3 **80**...............(p) GrahamGibbons 3 88+
(Keith Dalgleish) *dwlt: hld up in midfield: waiting for a gap over 1f out: prog fnl f: clsd on wnr nr fin: jst failed* **16/1**
0036 **3** *3/4* **Baddilini**[24] 7530 6-9-4 **84**...............(p) EoinWalsh(3) 6 90
(Alan Bailey) *disp ld: drvn 2f out: hdd ins fnl f: kpt on same pce after* **5/1**[2]
4003 **4** *1/2* **Duke Cosimo**[28] 7434 6-9-2 **79**............... PJMcDonald 10 83
(Michael Herrington) *hld up in last quartet: prog on inner 2f out: rdn and styd on ins fnl f: nvr quite able to chal* **8/1**

1-56 **5** 3/4 **Parkour (IRE)**[120] 4460 3-9-3 **80**......(b) LukeMorris 5 82
(Marco Botti) *chsd ldrs: drvn 2f out: cl up 1f out: one pce u.p* **8/1**
6100 **6** 3/4 **Pearl Spectre (USA)**[12] 7781 5-9-2 **79**...... JosephineGordon 2 79
(Phil McEntee) *disp ld: drvn 2f out: hdd & wknd ins fnl f* **25/1**
0600 **7** 3/4 **Fleckerl (IRE)**[36] 7221 6-9-6 **83**......(p) PaulMulrennan 4 80
(Conor Dore) *s.s: hld up in last: stl there 2f out: sme prog on inner over 1f out and pushed along: nvr involved* **14/1**
2534 **8** nk **He's My Cracker**[24] 7540 3-9-3 **80**...... JohnFahy 9 76
(Clive Cox) *nvr bttr than midfield: drvn over 2f out: no prog but kpt on ins fnl f* **7/1**[3]
2024 **9** 1/2 **Gorokai (IRE)**[55] 6668 3-9-1 **78**...... JamieSpencer 7 73
(David Simcock) *hld up in last quartet: shkn up over 2f out: nvr on terms but kpt on fnl f* **7/1**[1]
6110 **10** nk **Shypen**[26] 7485 3-9-3 **80**...... TonyHamilton 8 74
(Richard Fahey) *chsd ldrs on outer: drvn 2f out: fdd over 1f out* **4/1**[1]
0510 **11** 5 **Lady Clair (IRE)**[72] 6164 3-9-7 **84**...... JoeyHaynes 11 62
(K R Burke) *racd on outer: a in rr: wknd over 1f out* **40/1**

1m 10.77s (-1.13) **Going Correction** -0.10s/f (Stan) **11** Ran SP% **121.3**
Speed ratings (Par 105): **103,102,101,101,100 99,98,97,97,96 90**
CSF £132.27 CT £729.22 TOTE £6.80: £2.60, £3.60, £3.00; EX 150.50 Trifecta £1554.00.
Owner Al Shaqab Racing **Bred** Whatton Manor Stud **Trained** East Everleigh, Wilts
■ Stewards' Enquiry : Graham Gibbons two-day ban: used whip without giving gelding time to respond (Nov 29-30)

FOCUS
An open affair won by an unexposed and improving type.

7966 32RED CASINO NURSERY H'CAP 5f 6y(P)
2:25 (2:25) (Class 5) (0-75,74) 2-Y-O **£3,234** (£962; £481; £240) **Stalls** High

Form RPR
2260 **1** **Assassinate (IRE)**[26] 7490 2-9-3 **70**......(bt) LukeMorris 6 74
(Paul Cole) *chsd ldrs: urged along 2f out: str run over 1f out to ld last 100yds then hung lft: styd on* **7/1**
1004 **2** 1/2 **Dandy Flame (IRE)**[35] 7258 2-9-2 **74**...... GeorgiaCox(5) 7 76+
(William Haggas) *outpcd in last and struggling: prog over 1f out: str run to take 2nd nr fin: nt rch wnr* **10/3**[1]
2343 **3** 1/2 **Street Jazz**[32] 7313 2-9-1 **68**......(b[1]) TomEaves 1 68
(James Given) *wl away fr gd draw: led: drvn over 1f out: hdd and outpcd last 100yds: bmpd nr fin* **5/1**[2]
3665 **4** nk **Lady Cleo (IRE)**[4] 7900 2-9-0 **67**......(t) SeanLevey 4 66
(Stuart Williams) *trckd ldrs: tk 2nd 1f out: clsng to chal whn wnr wnt past and then impeded: one pce last 75yds* **13/2**
0256 **5** 1/2 **Gerrard's Fur Coat**[35] 7258 2-9-5 **72**...... RichardKingscote 9 70
(Tom Dascombe) *spd fr wd draw to press ldng pair to 2f out: outpcd over 1f out: kpt on* **12/1**
5320 **6** nk **Miss Rosina (IRE)**[77] 6010 2-8-8 **68**...... JaneElliott(7) 2 64
(George Margarson) *hld up in midfield: pushed along and kpt on fr over 1f out: nvr able to threaten properly* **8/1**
542 **7** 1/2 **Lava Light**[22] 7576 2-9-7 **74**...... JimmyFortune 5 69
(Henry Candy) *dwlt: racd in last trio: rdn and no prog over 1f out: kpt on last 100yds but no ch* **6/1**[3]
3523 **8** 1 1/4 **Fethiye Boy**[34] 7269 2-9-3 **70**...... ShaneKelly 3 60
(Ronald Harris) *pressed ldr: drvn 2f out: lost 2nd and wknd 1f out* **10/1**
3034 **9** 1 **Spinnaker Bay (IRE)**[17] 7689 2-9-5 **72**...... JosephineGordon 10 59
(William Jarvis) *a in last pair: nvr a factor* **8/1**

58.38s (-0.42) **Going Correction** -0.10s/f (Stan) **9** Ran SP% **118.9**
Speed ratings (Par 96): **99,98,97,96,96 95,94,92,91**
CSF £31.56 CT £131.09 TOTE £6.70: £2.40, £2.00, £2.10; EX 25.50 Trifecta £194.50.
Owner PFI Cole Ltd, Mrs J Green & P Raphael **Bred** Ms Marie Higgins **Trained** Whatcombe, Oxon
■ Stewards' Enquiry : Luke Morris caution: careless riding

FOCUS
There was a good pace on in this sprint nursery with the winner back to his pre-raced level..

7967 BETWAY H'CAP 1m 2f (P)
2:55 (2:55) (Class 3) (0-95,91) 3-Y-O+ **£7,246** (£2,168; £1,084; £542; £270) **Stalls** Low

Form RPR
1601 **1** **Beardwood**[14] 7744 4-9-5 **86**......(p) GeorgeBaker 7 94
(Mark Johnston) *chsd ldr: clsd over 2f out: rdn to ld over 1f out: edgd rt ins fnl f and jnd: styd on wl nr fin* **9/2**[2]
0401 **2** nk **Ready (IRE)**[11] 7791 6-9-7 **88**......(p) JosephineGordon 3 95
(Ivan Furtado) *trckd ldng trio: shkn up over 2f out: prog on inner to chal jst over 1f out: w wnr 100yds out: nt qckn after* **12/1**
3050 **3** 3 **Jacbequick**[14] 7744 5-9-7 **88**...... GrahamGibbons 4 89
(David O'Meara) *in tch disputing 5th: rdn over 2f out: tried to cl on outer over 1f out: kpt on same pce fnl f to take 3rd last stride* **16/1**
500 **4** shd **Niceofyoutotellme**[12] 7779 7-9-4 **85**...... RichardKingscote 6 86
(Ralph Beckett) *led at str pce: 4 l clr 1/2-way: c bk to rivals over 2f out: hdd and no ex over 1f out: lost 3rd last stride* **11/1**
3500 **5** 1 1/2 **Special Season**[24] 7546 3-9-6 **91**...... WilliamCarson 2 89
(Jamie Osborne) *in tch disputing 5th: pushed along over 2f out: kpt on steadily fr over 1f out but nvr really involved* **13/2**
21 **6** nk **Strong Force**[40] 7102 3-8-10 **86**...... JoshDoyle(5) 8 83
(Saeed bin Suroor) *trckd ldng pair: shkn up over 2f out: wanting to hang and fnd little over 1f out: fdd* **6/5**[1]
4245 **7** 8 **Masterpaver**[54] 6715 5-9-7 **88**...... JamieSpencer 5 69
(Richard Fahey) *racd wd in 7th: nvr on terms: struggling fr 1/2-way: bhd 3f out* **11/2**[3]
000 **8** 26 **Slowfoot (GER)**[13] 7765 8-9-3 **84**...... TimmyMurphy 9 13
(Jim Best) *s.v.s: a wl detached in last: t.o* **100/1**

2m 2.23s (-4.37) **Going Correction** -0.10s/f (Stan)
WFA 3 from 4yo+ 4lb **8** Ran SP% **115.3**
Speed ratings (Par 107): **113,112,110,110,109 108,102,81**
CSF £56.29 CT £791.29 TOTE £6.70: £1.90, £2.30, £2.70; EX 50.30 Trifecta £349.40.
Owner A D Spence & M B Spence **Bred** Kirtlington Stud Ltd **Trained** Middleham Moor, N Yorks

FOCUS
A good handicap run at a decent clip, but probably not much depth to the form.

7968 SUNBETS.CO.UK CLAIMING STKS 7f 1y(P)
3:25 (3:25) (Class 6) 3-Y-O+ **£2,587** (£770; £384; £192) **Stalls** Low

Form RPR
0303 **1** **Al Khan (IRE)**[10] 7821 7-9-6 85...... LewisEdmunds(7) 5 88+
(Kevin Ryan) *hld up in last trio: stl there and brought wd bnd 2f out: urged along hands and heels fr over 1f out: str run fnl f to ld last strides* **9/4**[1]
0300 **2** hd **Exchequer (IRE)**[24] 7530 5-10-0 92...... SeanLevey 8 89
(David Brown) *led: drew clr 2f out: 4 l ahd 1f out: drvn and kpt on but hdd last strides* **11/4**[2]
1464 **3** 2 **Corporal Maddox**[63] 6442 9-9-8 76......(p) LukeMorris 2 77
(Ronald Harris) *in tch: rdn over 2f out: prog to dispute 2nd briefly jst ins fnl f: kpt on but nvr able to threaten* **14/1**
34-0 **4** 1/2 **Manolito**[47] 6899 4-9-3 72......(t) CharlieBennett(5) 11 76
(Hughie Morrison) *hld up in rr: pushed along 2f out: styd on ins fnl f to take 4th nr fin: nvr involved* **20/1**
2100 **5** 1/2 **Yeeoow (IRE)**[54] 6714 7-9-8 80...... JoeyHaynes 7 74
(K R Burke) *in tch: rdn over 2f out: one pce and nvr able to threaten* **12/1**
0552 **6** 1 1/2 **Zaeem**[24] 7529 7-9-0 88......(p) RPWalsh(7) 3 69
(Ivan Furtado) *t.k.h: chsd ldr: outpcd 2f out: lost 2nd and wknd 1f out* **6/1**
6043 **7** 2 **Port Lairge**[28] 7442 6-9-4 60......(v) MichaelJMMurphy 6 61
(John Gallagher) *chsd ldrs tl wknd 2f out* **66/1**
24-2 **8** 10 **Jan Van Hoof (IRE)**[226] 1215 5-9-6 87...... TonyHamilton 1 36
(Richard Fahey) *struggling to hold pl by 1/2-way: sn dropped away: t.o* **3/1**[3]

1m 23.37s (-1.43) **Going Correction** -0.10s/f (Stan) **8** Ran SP% **117.3**
Speed ratings (Par 101): **104,103,101,100,100 98,96,84**
CSF £8.94 TOTE £3.70: £1.50, £1.50, £3.00; EX 9.80 Trifecta £72.20.Exchequer was claimed by Mr A. Barnes for £16,000
Owner J C G Chua **Bred** Galadari Sons Stud Company Limited **Trained** Hambleton, N Yorks

FOCUS
A good claimer, but few got into it.

7969 BETWAY APPRENTICE H'CAP 1m 4f (P)
3:55 (3:56) (Class 6) (0-65,65) 3-Y-O **£2,264** (£673; £336; £168) **Stalls** Low

Form RPR
5000 **1** **Threediamondrings**[4] 7905 3-9-5 **58**......(t) EdwardGreatrex 2 64
(Brendan Powell) *mde all: set mod pce tl stretched on over 2f out and sn at least 2 l ahd: drvn over 1f out: hld on* **20/1**
0066 **2** 1/2 **Dusty Raven**[13] 7767 3-8-4 **50**......(p) DavidEgan(7) 3 55
(Neil Mulholland) *t.k.h early: trckd ldng pair: rdn to chse wnr 2f out: grad clsd fnl f but nvr quite able to chal* **8/1**
2112 **3** shd **Iballisticvin**[17] 7692 3-9-12 **65**...... HectorCrouch 7 70
(Gary Moore) *hld up disputing 7th: prog on outer over 2f out and wd bnd sn after: clsd over 1f out: kpt on but nvr quite able to chal* **5/2**[1]
2263 **4** 1/2 **Mamoo**[20] 7614 3-9-3 **59**......(p) CallumShepherd(3) 4 63
(Mike Murphy) *trckd ldrs in 5th: nt qckn whn pce lifted over 2f out: styd on ins fnl f and clsng at fin* **6/1**
0002 **5** 3/4 **Dancing Rainbow (GR)**[76] 6030 3-8-4 **46** oh1......(b) HollieDoyle(3) 8 49
(Amanda Perrett) *plld hrd early: hld up in 4th: rdn to dispute 2nd 2f out: kpt on same pce fr over 1f out and a hld* **20/1**
351 **6** 3 1/4 **Mr Marchwood**[13] 7767 3-9-0 **56**...... MitchGodwin(3) 5 54+
(Sylvester Kirk) *hld up in last pair: ldrs already gone whn nt clr run over 1f out and swtchd rt: styd on after but no ch* **3/1**[2]
3445 **7** 1/2 **Le Tissier**[13] 7760 3-9-1 **59**......(p) PaddyBradley(5) 1 56
(Michael Attwater) *settled disputing 7th: outpcd over 2f out: one pce and nvr on terms after* **10/1**
2660 **8** 1 3/4 **Our Little Sister (IRE)**[14] 7755 3-9-1 **61**...... TheodoreLadd(7) 11 55
(Hughie Morrison) *chsd ldrs on outer: outpcd over 2f out: nt clr run wl over 1f out and no ch after* **20/1**
5063 **9** 1/2 **Alcanar (USA)**[28] 7425 3-9-10 **63**...... GeorgeDowning 9 56+
(Tony Carroll) *hld up in last trio: shkn up over 3f out: no ntable prog* **5/1**[3]
005 **10** shd **Yasood (IRE)**[25] 7514 3-9-7 **60**......(p) JosephineGordon 10 53+
(Phil McEntee) *stdd s: hld up in last: no prog over 2f out* **25/1**
00 **11** 17 **Fastnet Prince (IRE)**[19] 7645 3-8-8 **50**......(t) LucyKBarry(3) 6 16
(Phil York) *chsd wnr to 2f out: wknd rapidly and eased: t.o* **50/1**

2m 33.35s (0.35) **Going Correction** -0.10s/f (Stan) **11** Ran SP% **124.8**
Speed ratings (Par 98): **94,93,93,93,92 90,90,89,88,88 77**
CSF £170.05 CT £554.11 TOTE £21.40: £5.40, £2.50, £2.10; EX 211.10 Trifecta £1264.20.
Owner Miss Louise Harbord **Bred** Richard Painter **Trained** Upper Lambourn, Berks

FOCUS
A moderate handicap stolen from the front.
T/Jkpt: Not won. T/Plt: £339.90 to a £1 stake. Pool: £70,227.32 - 150.81 winning units. T/Qpdt: £40.80 to a £1 stake. Pool: £8,512.51 - 154.35 winning units. **Jonathan Neesom**

7879 CHANTILLY (R-H)
Tuesday, November 15
OFFICIAL GOING: Polytrack: standard; turf: heavy

7970a PRIX DE LA CROIX SAINT-RIEUL (MAIDEN) (2YO FILLIES) (POLYTRACK) 7f
11:25 (12:00) 2-Y-O **£9,926** (£3,970; £2,977; £1,985; £992)

RPR
1 **Tikitiki (FR)**[22] 2-9-2 0...... StephanePasquier 8 77
(N Clement, France) **17/2**
2 snk **Creme De Cremes (FR)**[17] 2-9-2 0...... AntoineHamelin 12 77
(Matthieu Palussiere, France) **58/10**[3]
3 1 3/4 **Cool Esprit (IRE)** 2-8-11 0...... Pierre-CharlesBoudot 10 67
(A Fabre, France) **23/10**[1]
4 nse **Zouk (FR)**[32] 7346 2-9-2 0...... LouisBeuzelin 4 72
(P Bary, France) **23/1**
5 3/4 **La Breviere**[46] 6937 2-9-2 0...... ChristopheSoumillon 9 70
(F Chappet, France) **15/2**
6 1 1/2 **Sissi Doloise (FR)**[50] 2-8-8 0...... ClementLecoeuvre(8) 6 66
(A Bonin, France) **24/1**
7 3 **Nacida (GER)** 2-9-2 0...... StephenHellyn 5 58
(Yasmin Almenrader, Germany) **63/10**
8 5 **L'Invincible (FR)** 2-8-11 0...... VincentCheminaud 3 39
(A Fabre, France) **9/2**[2]
9 5 **Parinacota (FR)** 2-8-11 0...... DavidBreux 7 26
(Mlle V Dissaux, France) **77/1**
10 nk **Pelanca (FR)**[19] 2-9-2 0...... GregoryBenoist 2 30
(Yannick Fouin, France) **33/1**
11 3 **Kendy Bay (FR)**[12] 7783 2-9-2 0...... TheoBachelot 11 22
(Gay Kelleway) *trckd wnr: rdn and v brief effrt early in st: sn no ex and btn: wknd: eased* **45/1**
12 3 1/2 **Holy Romane (FR)** 2-8-11 0...... LukasDelozier 1 8
(H-A Pantall, France) **27/1**

WIN (incl. 1 euro stake): 9.50. PLACES: 2.20, 2.00, 1.60. DF: 17.10. SF: 39.10
Owner B J Lindsay **Bred** Haras Du Mont Dit Mont **Trained** Chantilly, France

7971a PRIX DES DIX CORS (CONDITIONS) (2YO) (POLYTRACK) 1m

11:55 (12:00) 2-Y-O

£15,205 (£6,147; £4,529; £2,911; £1,779; £1,132)

RPR

1 **Xo (FR)**[25] 2-8-13 0 MaximeGuyon 2 89
(Mme Pia Brandt, France) **11/5**[1]

2 1 ¼ **Touching The Sky (IRE)**[26] 7490 2-8-9 0 StephanePasquier 4 82
(Alex Fracas, France) **18/1**

3 snk **Admiralty Arch**[6] 7879 2-8-13 0 AlexisBadel 3 86
(Richard Hughes) *trckd ldr: rdn to chal 2f out: upsides and ev ch ent fnl f: hdd sn after: kpt on but no ex w wnr and lost 2nd fnl strides* **15/2**

4 1 **Mask Of Time (IRE)**[120] 2-8-9 0 VincentCheminaud 1 79
(A Fabre, France) **5/1**[3]

5 1 **La Fibre (FR)**[84] 5755 2-8-13 0 FranckBlondel 8 81
(M Pimbonnet, France) **8/1**

6 shd **Eldelbar (SPA)** 2-8-9 0 IoritzMendizabal 9 77
(M Delcher Sanchez, France) **23/1**

7 1 ¼ **Bebe D'Amour (FR)**[20] 2-8-6 0 EddyHardouin 6 71
(J-Y Artu, France) **30/1**

8 snk **Barbarigo (IRE)**[12] 2-8-13 0 TonyPiccone 5 77
(F Chappet, France) **16/1**

9 1 ¼ **Parauari (FR)**[129] 2-8-13 0 ChristopheSoumillon 7 74
(A De Royer-Dupre, France) **5/2**[2]

WIN (incl. 1 euro stake): 3.20. PLACES: 1.50, 3.90, 2.40. DF: 22.00. SF: 27.60

Owner Buck Racing **Bred** Buck Racing Ab **Trained** France

7972a PRIX YACOWLEF (LISTED RACE) (2YO) (TURF) 5f 110y

12:25 (12:00) 2-Y-O £23,897 (£9,558; £7,169; £4,779; £2,389)

RPR

1 **Simmie (IRE)**[24] 7536 2-8-10 0 GregoryBenoist 12 97
(Sylvester Kirk) *trckd ldrs: rdn to chal and led ent fnl f: r.o: asserted: readily* **11/1**

2 2 **Precieuse (IRE)**[19] 7655 2-8-11 0 ow1 ChristopheSoumillon 8 91
(F Chappet, France) **6/4**[1]

3 2 **Rajar**[24] 7547 2-8-10 0 TonyPiccone 5 84
(Richard Fahey) *trckd ldrs: rdn and effrt 2f out: kpt on and wnt 3rd cl home: nt pce of front pair* **21/1**

4 snk **Antonella** 2-8-10 0 RicardoSousaFerreira 10 83
(T J Martins Novais, Spain) **8/1**

5 ¾ **Megan Lily (IRE)**[19] 7655 2-8-10 0 ThierryJarnet 6 81
(Richard Fahey) *midfield in tch: rdn 2f out: kpt on same pce for wl hld 5th* **83/10**

6 1 ¼ **Becquamis (FR)**[38] 7170 2-9-3 0 AntoineWerle 11 84
(T Lemer, France) **53/10**[2]

7 4 **Cheries Amours (FR)**[38] 7170 2-8-10 0 MaximeGuyon 1 64
(T Castanheira, France) **16/1**

8 1 **Kocollada (IRE)**[39] 7120 2-8-10 0 FranckBlondel 4 60
(Richard Fahey) *hld up in tch: rdn over 1f out: sn outpcd and wknd: eased towards fin* **27/1**

9 ¾ **Tahoo (IRE)**[66] 6322 2-8-10 0 IoritzMendizabal 13 58
(K R Burke) *pushed along to be prom: rdn and outpcd fnl 2f: wknd: eased towards fin* **50/1**

10 20 **Reedanjas (IRE)**[56] 6641 2-8-11 0 ow1 (p) Pierre-CharlesBoudot 2
(Gay Kelleway) *hld up in tch: rdn and outpcd over 2f out: sn wl btn: eased: t.o* **58/10**[3]

11 8 **Highland Clearance (FR)**[14] 7733 2-8-10 0 VincentCheminaud 7
(Giles Bravery) *a towards rr: rdn bef 1/2-way: sn dropped to last and lost tch: eased and tailed rt off* **95/1**

1m 6.88s (2.38) **11 Ran SP% 117.8**

WIN (incl. 1 euro stake): 12.50. PLACES: 3.20, 1.40, 3.60. DF: 13.50. SF: 40.30.

Owner Neil Simpson **Bred** D Ryan, D S Ryan & R A Williams **Trained** Upper Lambourn, Berks

7863 KEMPTON (A.W) (R-H)

Wednesday, November 16

OFFICIAL GOING: Polytrack: standard

Wind: Light, behind Weather: Raining

7973 32RED ON THE APP STORE H'CAP 1m 2f (P)

4:10 (4:14) (Class 5) (0-70,70) 3-Y-O+ £2,911 (£866; £432; £216) Stalls Low

Form RPR

5316 1 **Solveig's Song**[48] 6889 4-9-3 67 (p) AdamKirby 13 77
(Steve Woodman) *hld up in rr: gng wl over 2f out: shkn up and prog fr rr on outer under 2f out: rdn over 1f out: stl plenty to do 1f out: qcknd wl and str run ins fnl f: jst got up post* **33/1**

366 2 shd **The Salmon Man**[20] 7653 4-9-3 70 EdwardGreatrex(3) 4 79
(Brendan Powell) *settled in 6th: shkn up over 2f out: rdn 2f out: prog to chse clr ldr over 1f out: led cl home: hdd post* **6/1**[3]

2444 3 1 ¼ **Choral Clan (IRE)**[28] 7457 5-9-6 70 JackMitchell 5 76
(Philip Mitchell) *settled bhd ldrs: rdn over 2f out: sn led wl over 1f out: 3 l ldr ent fnl f: wkng and hdd cl home* **5/1**[2]

5150 4 5 **Pink Ribbon (IRE)**[30] 7418 4-9-1 70 (p) MitchGodwin(5) 7 66
(Sylvester Kirk) *settled bhd ldrs: rdn over 2f out: kpt on one pce* **12/1**

0434 5 ¾ **Shifting Star (IRE)**[21] 7620 11-9-3 67 (vt) WilliamCarson 9 62
(John Bridger) *hld up in mid-div: rdn over 2f out: one pce st* **33/1**

050 6 hd **Camakasi (IRE)**[28] 7457 5-9-6 70 (t) TomMarquand 8 64
(Ali Stronge) *missed break: in rr: rdn over 2f out: kpt on wl* **50/1**

1152 7 1 ½ **Bollihope**[14] 7775 4-9-4 68 ConnorBeasley 11 59
(Richard Guest) *settled in mid-div: rdn over 2f out: lft bhd fr over 1f out* **9/2**[1]

6300 8 ¾ **New Street (IRE)**[20] 7653 5-9-6 70 TimmyMurphy 6 60
(Jim Best) *in rr on inner: rdn over 2f out: no imp after* **50/1**

0- 9 1 ¼ **Zoravan (USA)**[355] 8023 3-9-2 70 (v) JoeFanning 10 57
(Keith Dalgleish) *racd in 2nd: pushed up to ld over 2f out: hdd over 1f out: wknd after* **7/1**

6200 10 shd **Barren Brook**[20] 7653 9-9-6 70 GeorgeBaker 3 57
(Laura Mongan) *in rr: rdn over 2f out: kpt on one pce* **25/1**

5055 11 nk **Top Diktat**[29] 7429 8-9-1 68 HectorCrouch(3) 1 54
(Gary Moore) *in rr: rdn over 2f out: nvr involved* **6/1**[3]

0554 12 9 **Cornelious (IRE)**[11] 7816 4-9-4 68 (v) AdamBeschizza 12 36
(Clifford Lines) *racd in 4th: rdn over 2f out: wknd fr over 1f out* **8/1**

1023 13 10 **Miningrocks (FR)**[23] 7581 4-9-0 69 (t) PhilDennis(5) 2 17
(Declan Carroll) *sn led and set str gallop: hdd over 2f out: wknd st* **20/1**

0650 14 ¾ **Berkeley Vale**[30] 7417 5-9-4 68 [1] RobertWinston 14 15
(Roger Teal) *in rr-div on inner: rdn over 2f out: sn no ex and wknd* **16/1**

2m 5.7s (-2.30) **Going Correction** -0.05s/f (Stan)

WFA 3 from 4yo+ 4lb **14 Ran SP% 119.0**

Speed ratings (Par 103): **107,106,105,101,101 101,99,99,98,98 98,90,82,82**

CSF £209.15 CT £1181.41 TOTE £21.20: £5.60, £3.10, £1.50; EX 263.30 Trifecta £1722.60.

Owner Sally Woodman D Mortimer **Bred** Mrs Sally Woodman & Mr D Mortimer **Trained** East Lavant, W Sussex

■ Stewards' Enquiry : Edward Greatrex seven-day ban: used whip above permitted level (Nov 30-Dec 3,5-7)

FOCUS

They went a good gallop in this modest handicap. The first three finished clear and the form is rated around the third.

7974 RACING UK NURSERY H'CAP 7f (P)

4:40 (4:42) (Class 6) (0-65,65) 2-Y-O £2,264 (£673; £336; £168) Stalls Low

Form RPR

503 1 **King Of Nepal**[37] 7224 2-9-5 64 AdamKirby 4 78+
(Henry Candy) *settled bhd ldrs: shkn up and led over 1f out: 1 l up ent fnl f: hdd for a stride cl home: edgd lft and got bk up post* **11/2**[3]

0001 2 nk **Fire Brigade**[6] 7881 2-9-3 62 6ex JamieSpencer 7 75+
(Michael Bell) *hld up in rr: t.k.h: n.m.r tl prog between horses travelling strly over 1f out: rdn 1f out: led for a stride cl home: hdd post* **2/1**[1]

0636 3 6 **Sassoferrato (IRE)**[14] 7768 2-9-3 65 EoinWalsh(3) 1 64
(Alan Bailey) *racd in 3rd: upsides and rdn over 2f out: shkn up over 1f out: rdn and lft bhd by front two fnl f* **11/2**[3]

3100 4 1 **Sixties Habana**[28] 7460 2-9-0 64 PaddyBradley(5) 9 57
(Pat Phelan) *hld up in rr: rdn over 2f out: kpt on wl fr over 1f out* **66/1**

0600 5 2 ¾ **Latest Quest (IRE)**[37] 7217 2-8-12 62 MitchGodwin(5) 5 48
(Sylvester Kirk) *in rr: rdn 3f out: gd prog fr over 1f out: nvr nrr* **20/1**

5632 6 1 ½ **Imperial City (USA)**[23] 7570 2-9-6 65 LukeMorris 3 47
(Charles Hills) *hld up in mid-div: rdn over 2f out: kpt on one pce on outer fr over 1f out* **5/1**[2]

0002 7 1 **Princess Way (IRE)**[15] 7750 2-9-2 61 JFEgan 2 40
(David Evans) *settled in mid-div: rdn over 3f out: one pce st* **14/1**

000 8 2 **Penny Green**[29] 7441 2-9-6 65 [1] RyanTate 14 39
(James Eustace) *missed break and hld up: rdn over 2f out: no ex over 1f out* **66/1**

653 9 ¾ **Rita's Girl**[77] 6025 2-9-2 61 BenCurtis 11 33
(K R Burke) *in rr: rdn over 2f out: no imp over 1f out* **25/1**

5646 10 nk **Life On Mars**[15] 7749 2-9-5 64 (b[1]) MartinHarley 8 35
(William Haggas) *bhd ldrs: rdn over 2f out: one pce after* **14/1**

6053 11 nse **Moonstone Rock**[23] 7571 2-9-5 64 LiamKeniry 10 35
(Jim Boyle) *hld up in rr on outer: bmpd along ent st: no picked up after* **16/1**

560 12 5 **I Wouldn't Bother**[29] 7424 2-9-5 64 TimmyMurphy 6 21
(Daniel Kubler) *hld up in mid-div: c wd st: no imp and wknd fr over 1f out* **25/1**

0026 13 9 **Royal Melody**[25] 7543 2-9-3 62 (p) JackMitchell 13
(Heather Main) *led: hdd over 1f out: wknd qckly after* **25/1**

1m 25.67s (-0.33) **Going Correction** -0.05s/f (Stan) **13 Ran SP% 119.3**

Speed ratings (Par 94): **99,98,91,90,87 85,84,82,81,81 81,75,65**

CSF £15.52 CT £66.97 TOTE £7.80: £2.30, £1.10, £3.20; EX 23.20 Trifecta £133.90.

Owner First Of Many **Bred** Sir Eric Parker **Trained** Kingston Warren, Oxon

FOCUS

The first two drew nicely clear in this nursery. The winner was clearly well in and the second is progressive.

7975 32RED CASINO/EBFSTALLIONS.COM MAIDEN STKS (DIV I) 7f (P)

5:10 (5:12) (Class 5) 2-Y-O £3,234 (£962; £481; £240) Stalls Low

Form RPR

2 1 **Leshlaa (USA)**[19] 7664 2-9-5 0 AdamKirby 9 88+
(Saeed bin Suroor) *chsd ldrs: shkn up and led jst over 1f out: rdn and sn drew clr: easily* **4/11**[1]

03 2 5 **Titi Makfi**[15] 7740 2-9-0 0 JoeFanning 7 69
(Mark Johnston) *led: rdn over 1f out: hdd jst over 1f out: kpt on one pce: no ch w easy wnr* **12/1**[3]

3 2 **Daschas** 2-9-2 0 [1] KieranShoemark(3) 5 69
(Amanda Perrett) *settled in mid-div: rdn over 2f out: kpt on fr over 1f out* **16/1**

30 4 hd **Coastal Cyclone**[76] 6053 2-9-5 0 MartinHarley 14 68+
(Harry Dunlop) *in rr-div: rn green and hld together over 2f out: pushed along on outer and kpt on wl fr over 1f out: nvr nrr* **33/1**

3 5 1 ¼ **Wefait (IRE)**[159] 3108 2-9-5 0 SeanLevey 6 65
(Richard Hannon) *settled in 3rd: rdn over 2f out: kpt on one pce fr over 1f out* **7/1**[2]

0 6 ½ **Socrates**[74] 6108 2-9-5 0 TimmyMurphy 10 63
(Daniel Kubler) *in rr-div: n.m.r bhd horses over 2f out: shuffled along bhd horses fr 2f out: nvr involved* **100/1**

00 7 2 **Mac's Kyllachy**[26] 7495 2-9-5 0 TomQueally 11 58
(James Fanshawe) *racd in mid-div: rdn over 2f out: no ex* **50/1**

00 8 ½ **Mukallaf (IRE)**[37] 7226 2-9-5 0 JackMitchell 4 57
(Roger Varian) *hung rt s: in rr-div: rdn over 2f out: kpt on* **25/1**

9 1 ¾ **Falbon** 2-9-5 0 LukeMorris 2 52
(Marco Botti) *squeezed up s: in rr and green: rdn ent st no imp* **12/1**[3]

10 hd **Canadian Royal** 2-9-5 0 AdamBeschizza 12 51
(Stuart Williams) *settled in mid-div: pushed along over 2f out: no ex* **66/1**

60 11 2 ¼ **It's How We Roll (IRE)**[44] 7013 2-9-5 0 MichaelJMMurphy 3 45
(Charles Hills) *in rr: rdn over 2f out: no ex* **33/1**

00 12 2 ½ **Amherst Rock**[95] 5410 2-9-5 0 JFEgan 1 38
(John Butler) *in rr: pushed along over 2f out: no ex* **50/1**

000 13 5 **Not Now Mum**[13] 7776 2-9-5 55 LiamKeniry 13 25
(Dean Ivory) *t.k.h in mid-div: rdn over 2f out: wknd qckly fr over 1f out* **100/1**

1m 26.97s (0.97) **Going Correction** -0.05s/f (Stan) **13 Ran SP% 124.2**

Speed ratings (Par 96): **92,86,84,83,82 81,79,78,76,76 74,71,65**

CSF £6.11 TOTE £1.40: £1.10, £2.60, £4.90; EX 7.10 Trifecta £53.40.

Owner Godolphin **Bred** Darley **Trained** Newmarket, Suffolk

FOCUS
The short-priced favourite took this in comfortable fashion, but in a time 1.3sec slower than the preceding 0-65 nursery. There's better to come from the winner.

7976 32RED CASINO/EBFSTALLIONS.COM MAIDEN STKS (DIV II) 7f (P)
5:40 (5:41) (Class 5) 2-Y-O **£3,234** (£962; £481; £240) **Stalls** Low

Form RPR

1 **Chessman (IRE)** 2-9-5 0 RobertTart 2 83+
(John Gosden) *s.s: hld up in rr: gng wl in rr over 2f out: shkn up and prog through pack 2f out: qcknd up wl to ld wl ins fnl f: sn clr* **9/4[2]**

6 2 2 ¼ **Esprit De Corps**[42] 7065 2-9-5 0 GeorgeBaker 9 73
(Roger Charlton) *pushed up to press ldr after 2f: shkn up and led 2f out: hdd wl ins fnl f: no ex nr fin* **7/4[1]**

05 3 nk **Widnes**[11] 7818 2-9-2 0 EoinWalsh(3) 3 72
(Alan Bailey) *settled bhd ldrs: rdn over 2f out: kpt on one pce* **16/1**

4 ½ **Hadeeqa (IRE)** 2-9-0 0 GrahamLee 8 66
(Simon Crisford) *covered up in mid-div: rdn over 2f out: stdy prog fr over 1f out under hands and heels* **5/1[3]**

5 2 ¼ **Captain Pugwash (IRE)** 2-9-5 0 LiamKeniry 13 65
(Henry Spiller) *s.s: swtchd to inner and rdn over 2f out: kpt on fr over 1f out* **66/1**

0 6 3 ¼ **Prosecution**[15] 7733 2-9-5 0 JimmyFortune 4 56
(Hughie Morrison) *led: rdn over 2f out: hdd 2f out: wknd fnl f* **50/1**

00 7 ½ **Just In Time**[21] 7622 2-9-0 0 HollieDoyle(5) 1 55
(Alan King) *t.k.h in mid-div: rdn 2f out: no ex* **33/1**

000 8 ½ **Dream Machine (IRE)**[14] 7770 2-9-5 0 JamieSpencer 14 53
(Michael Bell) *hld up in rr on outer: prog on bnd ent st: rdn over 2f out: sn hld* **50/1**

9 1 ¼ **Master Archer (IRE)** 2-9-5 0 TomQueally 6 50
(James Fanshawe) *in rr: rdn over 2f out: kpt on one pce* **14/1**

10 ½ **Mazaaji (FR)** 2-9-5 0 StevieDonohoe 10 48
(George Peckham) *racd in mid-divsion: rdn over 2f out: nt qckn and wknd fr over 1f out* **66/1**

6 11 hd **Jersey Heartbeat**[11] 7819 2-9-0 0 SeanLevey 11 43
(Richard Hannon) *covered up in mid-divison: lost pl st: no ex fr 2f out* **20/1**

0 12 2 **Peking Flyer (IRE)**[20] 7648 2-9-5 0 AdamKirby 12 43
(Ed Walker) *mid-divsion on outer: rdn over 2f out: no ex* **12/1**

00 13 5 **Bed Of Diamonds**[25] 7543 2-9-0 0 TomMarquand 7 24
(Adam West) *settled bhd ldrs on outer: rdn over 2f out on outer: wknd qckly fr over 1f out* **100/1**

1m 26.91s (0.91) **Going Correction** -0.05s/f (Stan) **13** Ran SP% **119.6**
Speed ratings (Par 96): **92,89,89,88,85 82,81,81,79,79 78,76,70**
CSF £6.25 TOTE £3.20: £1.20, £1.60, £4.00; EX 8.00 Trifecta £63.10.
Owner Treasure Trove Partnership **Bred** Corduff Stud **Trained** Newmarket, Suffolk

FOCUS
Marginally the quicker of the two divisions. The winner impressed and the level of the form is fluid.

7977 100% PROFIT BOOST AT 32REDSPORT.COM MEDIAN AUCTION MAIDEN STKS 1m (P)
6:10 (6:11) (Class 6) 2-Y-O **£2,264** (£673; £336; £168) **Stalls** Low

Form RPR

22 1 **Qatar Man (IRE)**[66] 6368 2-9-5 0 LukeMorris 12 81
(Marco Botti) *plld hrd and sn led: rdn over 2f out: pressed by runner-up ins fnl f: plld out more nr fin* **10/11[1]**

4 2 ½ **Shenanigans (IRE)**[14] 7762 2-9-0 0 JackMitchell 11 75
(Roger Varian) *settled bhd ldrs on outer: rdn 2f out: almost upsides wnr ins fnl f: no ex nring fin* **15/2**

3 1 ¼ **Mustarrid (IRE)** 2-9-5 0 SeanLevey 6 77+
(Richard Hannon) *s.s: hld up in rr: prog over 2f out: kpt on w plenty to do fr 2f out: nrst fin* **6/1[3]**

0 4 1 ¾ **Sussex Ranger (USA)**[56] 6663 2-9-2 0 HectorCrouch(3) 8 73
(Gary Moore) *settled in mid-div: rdn 2f out: kpt on one pce fr over 1f out* **33/1**

0 5 2 ¼ **Bois D'Ebene (IRE)**[14] 7761 2-8-11 0 KieranShoemark(3) 10 63
(Roger Charlton) *settled bhd ldrs on outer: rdn and ev ch 2f out: wknd fnl f* **9/2[2]**

05 6 1 ¾ **Shambra (IRE)**[34] 7297 2-9-0 0 MartinHarley 13 59+
(James Tate) *mid-div on outer: shkn up over 2f out: one pce fr over 1f out* **14/1**

7 ½ **The Last Debutante** 2-9-0 0 JoeFanning 4 58
(Mark Johnston) *s.s: shkn up 2f out: kpt on fr over 1f out* **20/1**

0 8 2 ½ **Kissinger**[108] 4907 2-8-12 0 SophieScardifield(7) 2 57
(Michael Bell) *t.k.h in mid-div: n.m.r and shuffled along 2f out: wknd after* **66/1**

60 9 ½ **Nobleman (GER)**[7] 7865 2-9-5 0 JimmyFortune 9 56
(Hughie Morrison) *mid-div: rdn out wd over 2f out: no ex fr 1f out* **33/1**

0 10 1 ¼ **Hot Lick**[7] 7865 2-9-5 0 LiamKeniry 5 53
(Andrew Balding) *missed break and in rr: rdn over 2f out: no ex st* **66/1**

00 11 1 ¼ **Black Prince (FR)**[26] 7503 2-9-5 0 JFEgan 7 50
(Anthony Honeyball) *s.s: a in rr* **100/1**

0 12 1 ¾ **Precious Equity (FR)**[125] 4287 2-9-0 0 WilliamCarson 1 41
(David Menuisier) *led early: settled bhd ldr after: wknd qckly fr 2f out* **66/1**

13 2 ½ **Secret Willow** 2-9-5 0 RyanPowell 3 40
(John E Long) *hld up in rr: ct on heels on inner ent st and snatched up: nt picked up after and eased over 1f out* **66/1**

1m 41.41s (1.61) **Going Correction** -0.05s/f (Stan) **13** Ran SP% **120.9**
Speed ratings (Par 94): **89,88,87,85,83 81,81,78,78,76 75,73,71**
CSF £8.09 TOTE £1.70: £1.10, £1.80, £2.00; EX 8.80 Trifecta £28.60.
Owner Mubarak Al Naemi **Bred** Mubarak Al Naemi **Trained** Newmarket, Suffolk

FOCUS
Just a fair maiden, best rated through the winner.

7978 BRITISH STALLION STUDS EBF HYDE STKS (ALL WEATHER CHAMPIONSHIP FAST-TRACK QUALIFIER) (LISTED RACE) 1m (P)
6:40 (6:40) (Class 1) 3-Y-O+
£22,684 (£8,600; £4,304; £2,144; £1,076; £540) **Stalls** Low

1-11 1 **Ennaadd**[228] 1208 3-9-0 106 JackMitchell 3 117+
(Roger Varian) *settled bhd ldrs on inner: cruised into ld 2f out: rdn over 1f out: in n.d fnl f: easily* **5/2[2]**

0000 2 2 ¾ **You're Fired (IRE)**[90] 5585 5-9-2 103 JoeyHaynes 5 111
(K R Burke) *in rr: rdn over 2f out: kpt on: no ch w wnr* **16/1**

2411 3 1 **Sovereign Debt (IRE)**[18] 7706 7-9-4 112 DeclanMcDonogh 1 111
(David Nicholls) *settled bhd ldr: rdn over 2f out: nt qckn: kpt on one pce* **11/10[1]**

510 4 3 ¼ **Here Comes When (IRE)**[32] 7354 6-9-2 104 GrahamLee 2 101
(Andrew Balding) *hld up in rr: rdn over 2f out: one pce after* **8/1[3]**

1064 5 3 **Havre De Paix (FR)**[31] 7397 4-8-11 97 JoeFanning 7 89
(David Menuisier) *led: rdn wl over 2f out: hdd & wknd fr 2f out* **16/1**

0014 6 6 **Dawaa**[11] 7822 3-8-9 98 RichardKingscote 6 75
(Mark Johnston) *settled bhd ldrs: rdn 2f out: sn wknd* **14/1**

0020 7 14 **Calling Out (FR)**[217] 1425 5-9-2 105 JamieSpencer 8 48
(David Simcock) *settled bhd ldr on outer: lost pl bnd: no ex and wknd st* **14/1**

1m 36.45s (-3.35) **Going Correction** -0.05s/f (Stan)
WFA 3 from 4yo+ 2lb **7** Ran SP% **112.4**
Speed ratings (Par 111): **114,111,110,107,104 98,84**
CSF £38.18 TOTE £3.30: £1.50, £8.30; EX 48.50 Trifecta £96.80.
Owner Sheikh Ahmed Al Maktoum **Bred** Darley **Trained** Newmarket, Suffolk

FOCUS
A decent race and the winner impressed in putting his rivals away with the minimum of fuss. There wasn't much depth to this but the winner still put up a smart performance.

7979 32RED H'CAP 2m (P)
7:10 (7:10) (Class 2) (0-105,103) 3-Y-O+
£11,827 (£3,541; £1,770; £885; £442; £222) **Stalls** Low

Form RPR

3122 1 **Higher Power**[26] 7498 4-9-4 **93** TomQueally 2 106+
(James Fanshawe) *covered up in mid-div on inner: t.k.h: rdn 2f out: led jst under 1f out: styd on strly fnl f* **11/10[1]**

0025 2 2 **Steve Rogers (IRE)**[103] 5116 5-9-6 **95** JackMitchell 5 105
(Roger Varian) *led for 1f: settled bhd ldrs: rdn in centre over 2f out and sn led: hdd jst under 1f out: no imp on wnr ins fnl f* **14/1**

15U 3 2 ½ **Winning Story**[11] 7814 3-8-11 **95** SeanLevey 9 102
(Saeed bin Suroor) *racd in 3rd: rdn over 2f out: kpt on one pce* **6/1[2]**

0/03 4 2 ¼ **Wrangler**[25] 7538 5-8-12 **87** MartinHarley 7 91
(William Haggas) *hld up in rr-div: rdn on inner over 2f out: prog tl wknd fnl f* **7/1[3]**

455 5 nk **Percy Veer**[19] 7670 4-8-4 **84** oh2 MitchGodwin(5) 4 88
(Sylvester Kirk) *mostly mid-div: rdn over 2f out: kpt on fr over 1f out* **12/1**

4432 6 1 ¼ **First Mohican**[39] 7150 8-9-8 **102** HollieDoyle(5) 3 104
(Alan King) *missed break: racd in rr: rdn over 2f out: kpt on fr over 1f out* **10/1**

6604 7 4 ½ **Barye**[74] 6125 5-9-13 **102** ShaneKelly 1 99
(Richard Hughes) *racd in 4th: rdn over 2f out: kpt on one pce* **33/1**

1000 8 2 ¼ **Albahar (FR)**[19] 7670 5-8-10 **85** (p) LiamKeniry 11 79
(Chris Gordon) *missed break and lost several l: in rr: rdn and no imp fr over 2f out* **25/1**

2001 9 3 ½ **Oriental Fox (GER)**[30] 7411 8-10-0 **103** JoeFanning 10 93
(Mark Johnston) *led after 1f: rdn over 2f out: hdd 2f out: wknd fr over 1f out* **20/1**

3540 10 1 **Buonarroti (IRE)**[11] 7824 5-8-7 **87** PhilDennis(5) 6 76
(Declan Carroll) *in rr: no imp fr over 2f out* **66/1**

2540 11 7 **Gavlar**[144] 3658 5-9-3 **92** LukeMorris 12 72
(William Knight) *pressed ldr on outer: rdn over 3f out: sn wknd* **25/1**

0000 12 5 **The Twisler**[26] 7498 4-8-8 **90** RhiainIngram(7) 8 64
(Roger Ingram) *a in rr-div: pushed along over 4f out: no ex st* **40/1**

3m 28.56s (-1.54) **Going Correction** -0.05s/f (Stan)
WFA 3 from 4yo+ 9lb **12** Ran SP% **117.2**
Speed ratings (Par 109): **101,100,98,97,97 96,94,93,91,91 87,85**
CSF £16.33 CT £70.24 TOTE £2.10: £1.30, £3.20, £2.50; EX 17.50 Trifecta £98.30.
Owner Mrs Martin Armstrong **Bred** Mrs Martin Armstrong **Trained** Newmarket, Suffolk

FOCUS
A good-quality staying handicap and while it wasn't strong run, there are reasons to be positive about the first four.

7980 32RED.COM H'CAP 1m 4f (P)
7:40 (7:42) (Class 4) (0-85,85) 3-Y-O+ **£4,690** (£1,395; £697; £348) **Stalls** Low

Form RPR

1125 1 **Cliff Face (IRE)**[14] 7765 3-9-0 **81** LukeMorris 11 92
(Sir Mark Prescott Bt) *settled in mid-divsion: swtchd to outer over 2f out: sn rdn: kpt on wl to ld wl ins fnl f* **12/1**

0305 2 1 ¼ **Gawdawpalin (IRE)**[26] 7512 3-8-12 **84** MitchGodwin(5) 7 93
(Sylvester Kirk) *racd in mid-div: rdn over 2f out: led 2f out: kpt on wl in centre fr 1f out: hdd wl ins fnl f: no ex* **3/1[2]**

4604 3 1 ¼ **Plutocracy (IRE)**[50] 6854 6-9-7 **85** HectorCrouch(3) 3 92
(Gary Moore) *hld up in rr on inner: rdn on inner 2f out: kpt on wl and fr over 1f out: no ex nr fin* **9/1[3]**

21 4 1 ¼ **Timekeeping (IRE)**[30] 7410 3-9-4 **85** AdamKirby 1 90
(Saeed bin Suroor) *mid-divsion on outer: rdn over 2f out: kpt on one pce tl wknd wl ins fnl f* **1/1[1]**

-530 5 1 ½ **Callendula**[26] 7512 4-9-0 **75** (p) MartinHarley 6 78
(Clive Cox) *settled in mid-div: rdn over 2f out: kpt on one pce fnl f* **33/1**

3603 6 3 ¼ **Giantstepsahead (IRE)**[30] 7408 7-9-9 **84** TomQueally 5 81
(Alan Bailey) *led: rdn over 2f out: hdd 2f out: no ex and wknd fnl f* **14/1**

2024 7 hd **Compton Mill**[19] 7666 4-9-5 **80** (t) GeorgeBaker 13 77
(Hughie Morrison) *chsd ldrs: rdn over 2f out: upsides and ev ch 2f out: lft bhd by ldrs: one pce after* **14/1**

-601 8 1 ½ **Syncopate**[26] 7508 7-9-5 **80** LiamKeniry 14 75
(Pam Sly) *mid-div: rdn over 2f out out wd: no ex sn after* **33/1**

003/ 9 8 **Red Orator**[16] 4159 7-9-5 **80** TimmyMurphy 12 62
(Jim Best) *in rr: rdn and no imp fr over 3f out* **66/1**

5100 10 4 **Mysterial**[25] 7535 6-8-12 **78** PhilDennis(5) 4 53
(Declan Carroll) *chsd ldr on inner: rdn to hold pl over 3f out: rdn over 2f out: wknd sn after* **50/1**

5-10 11 33 **Southern Stars**[186] 2245 3-9-3 **84** NickyMackay 10 7
(John Gosden) *chsd ldrs: rdn along over 3f out: eased fr 2f out: t.o* **16/1**

000/ 12 16 **Man Of Plenty**[129] 3240 7-9-0 **75** (t) ShaneKelly 9
(Sophie Leech) *missed break: detached in rr and scrubbed along to try make up grnd: no imression and eased st: t.o* **66/1**

2m 30.99s (-3.51) **Going Correction** -0.05s/f (Stan)
WFA 3 from 4yo+ 6lb **12** Ran SP% **122.7**
Speed ratings (Par 105): **109,108,107,106,105 103,103,102,96,94 72,61**
CSF £48.80 CT £355.19 TOTE £14.00: £2.90, £1.60, £2.60; EX 63.60 Trifecta £343.10.
Owner Bluehills Racing Limited **Bred** Glashare House Stud **Trained** Newmarket, Suffolk

FOCUS
Not a bad handicap, and the right horses came to the fore, although not in the order the market predicted. A positive view has been taken of the form, with the winner resuming his progress.
T/Jkpt: £11,805.20 to a £1 stake. Pool: £29,513.15. 2.5 winning units. T/Plt: £16.10 to a £1 stake. Pool: £94,377.86. 4,263.70 winning units. T/Qpdt: £4.00 to a £1 stake. Pool: £13,248.36. 2,407.02 winning units. **Cathal Gahan**

The Form Book, Raceform Ltd, Newbury, RG14 5SJ

7881 CHELMSFORD (A.W) (L-H)

Thursday, November 17

OFFICIAL GOING: Polytrack: standard

Wind: light, medium Weather: dry, chilly

7981 TOTEPLACEPOT NURSERY H'CAP — 6f (P)

4:40 (4:40) (Class 6) (0-65,65) 2-Y-O **£2,911** (£866; £432; £216) **Stalls** Centre

Form RPR

2022 **1** **Wentwell Yesterday (IRE)**[14] 7777 2-9-7 **65**................ WilliamCarson 7 71
(Jamie Osborne) *broke wl: led for 1f: chsd ldr after: rdn to chal over 1f out: drvn to ld jst ins fnl f: styd on: rdn out* **5/1**[2]

045 **2** ½ **Magique Touch**[16] 7748 2-9-0 **61**..........................(b) KieranShoemark(3) 1 66
(Roger Charlton) *chsd ldrs: effrt wl over 1f out: ev ch ins fnl f: wnt 2nd 100yds out: kpt on but hld towards fin* **8/1**

0051 **3** ½ **Geraldine (GER)**[22] 7615 2-9-1 **59**.................................... MartinHarley 4 62
(Stuart Williams) *wl in tch in midfield: effrt over 1f out: swtchd rt jst ins fnl f: styd on wl fnl 100yds: wnt 3rd towards fin* **5/1**[2]

5664 **4** 1 **Dazacam**[27] 7510 2-8-13 **57**.. RobertWinston 2 57
(Michael Herrington) *taken down early: t.k.h: led after 1f: rdn over 1f out: drvn and hdd jst ins fnl f: no ex and lost 2 pls fnl 100yds* **14/1**

660 **5** shd **Supreme Power (IRE)**[16] 7748 2-9-3 **64**.................... LouisSteward(3) 3 64+
(Philip McBride) *in tch in midfield: effrt on inner over 1f out: swtchd rt jst ins fnl f: kpt on wl fnl 100yds: nvr enough pce to rch ldrs* **4/1**[1]

6002 **6** 1½ **Roundabout Magic (IRE)**[6] 7900 2-9-4 **62**.................... NickyMackay 8 57+
(Simon Dow) *taken down early: stdd s: hld up in rr: hdwy into midfield 1/2-way: effrt over 1f out: no imp and one pced fnl f* **10/1**

0624 **7** 4 **Western Presence**[16] 7749 2-9-7 **65**................................... JoeFanning 5 48+
(Richard Fahey) *hld up in last quartet: effrt 2f out: swtchd rt and sme hdwy over 1f out: no imp ins fnl f* **8/1**

0502 **8** 1¼ **Impassioned**[16] 7749 2-9-3 **61**...(p) LukeMorris 10 40
(Sir Mark Prescott Bt) *chsd ldrs: rdn over 1f out: fnd nil and sn btn: wknd fnl f* **6/1**[3]

0660 **9** 3 **Come On Percy**[15] 7768 2-9-5 **63**................................ PatrickMathers 11 33+
(Richard Fahey) *taken down early: a towards rr: rdn 2f out: no hdwy and bhd 1f out* **14/1**

650 **10** 2 **Dandy Roll (IRE)**[32] 7381 2-9-2 **63**............................. HectorCrouch(3) 6 27+
(Ralph Beckett) *hld up in last quartet: effrt 2f out: no hdwy: bhd 1f out* **12/1**

0000 **11** 2 **Chamasay**[38] 7208 2-8-11 **55**... LiamKeniry 12 13+
(J S Moore) *stdd s: t.k.h: no hdwy u.p over 1f out: bhd 1f out* **66/1**

1m 12.29s (-1.41) **Going Correction** -0.225s/f (Stan) **11** Ran SP% **121.5**

Speed ratings (Par 94): **100,99,98,97,97 95,89,88,84,81 78**

CSF £46.45 CT £219.12 TOTE £5.90: £1.30, £3.50, £1.90; EX 53.50 Trifecta £321.40.

Owner Ian Barratt, Stephen Short & Adam Signy **Bred** Tally-Ho Stud **Trained** Upper Lambourn, Berks

FOCUS

An interesting nursery, and it paid to race up with the lead considering few of those held up made much impression. Solid enough form.

7982 TOTEEXACTA FORECAST THE 1ST AND 2ND CONDITIONS STKS (PLUS 10 RACE) — 1m 2f (P)

5:15 (5:17) (Class 3) 2-Y-O **£9,703** (£2,887; £1,443; £721) **Stalls** Low

Form RPR

12 **1** **Time To Study (FR)**[5] 7930 2-9-7 0.................................... JoeFanning 2 85+
(Mark Johnston) *mde all: rdn and qcknd clr 2f out: in command and edgd rt 1f out: kpt on wl: comf* **11/10**[1]

6 **2** 2¼ **Peaceful Passage (USA)**[16] 7740 2-8-11 0.................. NickyMackay 3 71
(John Gosden) *chsd wnr: rdn ent fnl 2f: unable qck w wnr over 1f out: edgd lft and kpt on same pce ins fnl f* **8/1**

4216 **3** 4½ **Spring Jig (USA)**[29] 7471 2-9-7 81.................................[1] LukeMorris 4 73
(Hugo Palmer) *t.k.h: hld up in tch in 4th: effrt over 2f out: sn outpcd: no ch w wnr and battling for 3rd fr over 1f out: snatched 3rd last stride* **9/2**[3]

6 **4** shd **Mr Davies**[5] 7940 2-9-2 0.. SeanLevey 1 68
(David Brown) *chsd ldng pair: rdn over 2f out: sn drvn and outpcd: no ch w wnr and battling for 3rd fr over 1f out: lost 3rd last stride* **16/1**

5 ½ **Cross Step (USA)** 2-9-2 0... WilliamBuick 5 67+
(Charlie Appleby) *rn green in tch in rr: rdn over 3f out: effrt on outer over 2f out: wd and no imp bnd 2f out: wl hld and battling for 3rd fr over 1f out: kpt on same pce* **9/4**[2]

2m 5.17s (-3.43) **Going Correction** -0.225s/f (Stan) **5** Ran SP% **113.6**

Speed ratings (Par 100): **104,102,98,98,98**

CSF £10.94 TOTE £2.30: £1.40, £3.00; EX 11.90 Trifecta £32.30.

Owner Abdulla Al Mansoori **Bred** E A R L Haras Du Quesnay **Trained** Middleham Moor, N Yorks

FOCUS

The early gallop appeared to be far from quick and one got the impression that the winner was allowed to dominate his rivals. It's questionable if the bare form is worth any more.

7983 TOTEQUADPOT FOUR PLACES IN FOUR RACES CLAIMING STKS — 6f (P)

5:50 (5:50) (Class 6) 3-Y-O+ **£2,587** (£770; £384; £192) **Stalls** Centre

Form RPR

3603 **1** **Free Zone**[14] 7778 7-9-4 80...(v) MartinHarley 8 85
(Lee Carter) *lost nr front shoe on way to post: mde all: rdn over 1f out: kpt on wl ins fnl f: rdn out* **12/1**

6410 **2** ½ **Doctor Parkes**[6] 7899 10-8-5 74.. MillyNaseb(7) 3 78
(Stuart Williams) *chsd ldrs: effrt to press wnr over 1f out: ev ch ins fnl f: kpt on but hld towards fin* **5/1**

0146 **3** 1¾ **Sophisticated Heir (IRE)**[30] 7433 6-9-8 76..............(b) RobertWinston 4 82
(Michael Herrington) *trckd ldng trio: effrt over 1f out: 3rd and kpt on same pce ins fnl f* **9/2**

3002 **4** 2¾ **Regal Dan (IRE)**[14] 7778 6-9-9 83................................ ShelleyBirkett(3) 7 78
(David O'Meara) *chsd wnr tl over 1f out: 4th and outpcd whn wandered 1f out: wknd ins fnl f* **7/2**[3]

0005 **5** ¾ **Zac Brown (IRE)**[16] 7752 5-9-9 92.........................(t) KieranShoemark(3) 2 76
(Charlie Wallis) *s.i.s: t.k.h: hld up in tch in last trio: effrt over 1f out: kpt on same pce and no imp ins fnl f* **3/1**[2]

0002 **6** 6 **Links Drive Lady**[26] 7550 8-9-0 86.................................... JackDuern(3) 1 49
(Dean Ivory) *s.i.s: hld up in tch: effrt 2f out: swtchd rt over 1f out: wknd fnl f* **5/2**[1]

3-50 **7** ¾ **Zeb's Fantasy (IRE)**[19] 7694 3-8-9 53.....................(v[1]) LemosdeSouza 6 39
(Amy Murphy) *hld up in last trio: rdn 2f out: no hdwy and btn over 1f out: wknd fnl f* **100/1**

1m 11.46s (-2.24) **Going Correction** -0.225s/f (Stan) **7** Ran SP% **119.3**

Speed ratings (Par 101): **105,104,102,98,97 89,88**

CSF £73.68 TOTE £10.00: £3.80, £2.20; EX 45.90 Trifecta £329.80.

Owner Mrs S A Pearson **Bred** Richard Levin **Trained** Epsom, Surrey

FOCUS

A decent race of its type but being prominent was beneficial and the winner made all in a good time compared to Racing Post standard. Straightforward form rated around the first two.

7984 TOTEPOOLLIVEINFO.COM H'CAP — 7f (P)

6:25 (6:28) (Class 2) (0-105,110) 3-Y-O+

£12,450 (£3,728; £1,864; £932; £466; £234) **Stalls** Low

Form RPR

6560 **1** **Charles Molson**[21] 7651 5-8-12 **92**.................................... JoeFanning 5 103
(Patrick Chamings) *hld up in tch in last quartet and travelled strly: hdwy over 1f out: swtchd rt and chsd clr ldr 1f out: str run to ld wl ins fnl f: sn in command: comf* **11/2**[2]

1002 **2** 1½ **He's No Saint**[26] 7530 5-8-11 **91**.....................................(v) MartinHarley 8 98
(David O'Meara) *led: rdn and qcknd clr over 1f out: drvn ins fnl f: hdd and no ex wl ins fnl f* **6/1**[3]

0005 **3** 1 **Volunteer Point (IRE)**[21] 7650 4-9-0 **94**.......................... ShaneKelly 10 98
(Mick Channon) *hld up in tch in last quartet: effrt and swtchd lft over 1f out: hdwy u.p ins fnl f: styd on wl to go 3rd wl ins fnl f: no threat to wnr* **5/1**[1]

0103 **4** ¾ **Supersta**[161] 3055 5-9-2 **96**..(p) LukeMorris 3 98
(Michael Appleby) *taken down early: hld up in tch in midfield: swtchd rt and effrt over 1f out: hdwy u.p ins fnl f: styd on u.p: no threat to wnr* **5/1**[1]

3520 **5** ½ **Loyalty**[26] 7530 9-8-4 **87**..(v) NoelGarbutt(3) 2 88
(Derek Shaw) *chsd ldrs: 3rd and rdn over 2f out: chsd clr ldr over 1f out tl 1f out: kpt on same pce ins fnl f* **16/1**

0225 **6** hd **Intransigent**[21] 7651 7-8-8 **95**.. WilliamCox(7) 6 95
(Andrew Balding) *hld up in tch in midfield: rdn over 1f out: swtchd rt 1f out: styd on wl ins fnl f: no threat to wnr* **7/1**

6600 **7** nk **Forceful Appeal (USA)**[21] 7651 8-8-6 **86**...................... NickyMackay 7 88+
(Simon Dow) *stdd s: hld up in rr: effrt over 1f out: hdwy 1f out: keeping on but no threat to wnr whn nt clr run wl ins fnl f* **50/1**

6000 **8** 1½ **Mohab**[61] 6557 3-8-9 **90**.. ShaneGray 4 84
(Kevin Ryan) *chsd ldr tl over 5f out: rdn and unable qck over 1f out: wknd ins fnl f* **8/1**

016 **9** ¾ **That Is The Spirit**[37] 7241 5-9-2 **96**.............................. WilliamBuick 11 89
(David O'Meara) *dwlt: grad rcvrd to chse ldr over 5f out: rdn and unable qck over 1f out: btn and eased ins fnl f* **12/1**

2060 **10** 3½ **Right Touch**[12] 7821 6-9-5 **99**...................................... PatrickMathers 13 83
(Richard Fahey) *in tch in last quartet: effrt and wd bnd wl over 1f out: no imp u.p over 1f out: wl btn and hung lft ins fnl f* **8/1**

0363 **11** 3¼ **Baddilini**[2] 7965 6-8-5 **85** oh1...(p) KieranO'Neill 9 60
(Alan Bailey) *t.k.h: chsd ldrs: rdn over 2f out: sn struggling: lost pl over 1f out: bhd ins fnl f* **10/1**

1m 24.11s (-3.09) **Going Correction** -0.225s/f (Stan)

WFA 3 from 4yo+ 1lb **11** Ran SP% **122.4**

Speed ratings (Par 109): **108,106,105,104,103 103,103,101,100,96 92**

CSF £40.25 CT £183.45 TOTE £6.30: £2.10, £2.20, £2.20; EX 41.70 Trifecta £376.80.

Owner Trolley Action **Bred** Mrs Sheila Oakes **Trained** Baughurst, Hants

FOCUS

Undoubtedly the best race on the card and really open when considering the betting, but once again one horse was allowed to dominate and nearly stole it. The winner is rated close to his best.

7985 @TOTEPOOLRACING WIN TICKETS ON TWITTER H'CAP — 7f (P)

7:00 (7:01) (Class 5) (0-70,70) 3-Y-O+ **£4,204** (£1,251; £625; £312) **Stalls** Low

Form RPR

4662 **1** **Curzon Line**[7] 7887 7-9-3 **66**.. JoeFanning 13 81
(Michael Easterby) *chsd ldrs tl led over 5f out: mde rest: shkn up and readily qcknd clr over 1f out: in n.d 1f out: eased towards fin: eased towards fin: easily* **7/2**[1]

2000 **2** 3¼ **Gold Flash**[20] 7662 4-9-7 **70**......................................(b) RobertWinston 7 76
(Keith Dalgleish) *hld up in tch towards rr: swtchd rt and hdwy over 1f out: wnt 4th 1f out: styd on u.p to go 2nd towards fin: no ch w wnr* **14/1**

3311 **3** nk **Encore Moi**[17] 7725 3-9-5 **69**...(b) LukeMorris 11 73
(Marco Botti) *in tch in midfield: effrt in 4th 2f out: no ch w wnr but kpt on u.p to chse clr wnr 75yds out: no imp: lost 2nd towards fin* **7/2**[1]

0650 **4** 1¼ **Hijran (IRE)**[24] 7577 3-9-0 **67**.............................(p) AlistairRawlinson(3) 10 68
(Michael Appleby) *dwlt and pushed along leaving stalls: sn rcvrd and chsd ldrs after 1f: wnt 2nd over 3f out: rdn and unable qck 2f out: wl hld in 2nd 1f out: lost 2 pls fnl 75yds* **33/1**

3614 **5** 1¼ **Rebel Lightning (IRE)**[24] 7577 3-9-6 **70**........................(b) MartinHarley 3 67+
(Richard Spencer) *dwlt: in tch in last pair: clsd and nt clr run jst over 1f out: swtchd rt 1f out: styd on u.p ins fnl f: nvr trbld ldrs* **4/1**[2]

4242 **6** 1¼ **Oak Bluffs (IRE)**[37] 7254 5-8-13 **62**............................... PatrickMathers 8 57
(Richard Fahey) *wl in tch in midfield: clsd to chse ldrs 3f out: rdn and unable qck 2f out: wl hld over 1f out: wknd ins fnl f* **16/1**

1302 **7** ¾ **Remember Me**[38] 7203 3-9-1 **70**................................ CharlieBennett(5) 2 62
(Hughie Morrison) *stdd s: hld up in tch towards rr: effrt and swtchd lft jst over 1f out: kpt on same pce ins fnl f: nvr trbld ldrs* **6/1**[3]

2616 **8** nk **With Approval (IRE)**[73] 6184 4-8-12 **66**..............(p) CallumShepherd(5) 4 58
(Laura Mongan) *chsd ldr early: stdd bk into midfield after 3f: effrt over 1f out: no imp and wl hld fnl f* **33/1**

-240 **9** 1½ **Daring Day**[133] 4058 3-9-3 **67**.. StevieDonohoe 6 54
(George Peckham) *hld up in tch in midfield: swtchd rt and effrt u.p over 1f out: no imp and wl hld fnl f* **20/1**

5522 **10** ½ **Mossy's Lodge**[12] 7817 3-9-1 **65**...................................[1] WilliamCarson 5 51
(Anthony Carson) *led tl over 5f out: chsd ldr tl over 3f out: rdn over 2f out: unable qck and btn over 1f out: wknd ins fnl f* **14/1**

0604 **11** ¾ **Skidby Mill (IRE)**[7] 7887 6-9-3 **66**...................................... LiamKeniry 9 51
(Laura Mongan) *hld up in tch towards rr: pushed along over 3f out: no hdwy u.p over 1f out: wl hld fnl f* **16/1**

202 **12** ½ **Invade (IRE)**[51] 6851 4-9-2 **68**..(t) AaronJones(3) 1 51
(Stuart Williams) *hld up in rr: effrt on inner over 1f out: no imp: nvr trbld ldrs* **8/1**

4000 **13** 22 **Hammer Gun (USA)**[18] 7246 3-8-10 **63**.....................(v) NoelGarbutt(3) 12
(Derek Shaw) *s.i.s and pushed along: grad rcvrd and chsd ldrs after 2f: rdn over 2f out: sn struggling and lost pl qckly: bhd and eased ins fnl f: t.o* **80/1**

1m 25.05s (-2.15) **Going Correction** -0.225s/f (Stan)

WFA 3 from 4yo+ 1lb **13** Ran SP% **126.8**

Speed ratings (Par 103): **103,99,98,97,96 94,93,93,91,91 90,89,64**

CSF £56.53 CT £198.45 TOTE £4.70: £1.90, £4.70, £1.80; EX 72.50 Trifecta £592.20.

Owner The Golden Ratio Partnership **Bred** Darley **Trained** Sheriff Hutton, N Yorks

FOCUS
Given earlier evidence, it was surprising that a horse drawn widest was allowed to get to the front by all those inside it. He set fractions to suit and pulled well clear late on. The runner-up was close to his best and helps set the standard.

7986 TOTEPOOL RACECOURSE CASHBACK AVAILABLE H'CAP 1m (P)
7:30 (7:33) (Class 6) (0-60,60) 3-Y-O+ **£2,911** (£866; £432; £216) **Stalls** Low

Form RPR

0004 **1** **Makhfar (IRE)**[21] 7646 5-8-7 **51**............................(v) CallumShepherd[(5)] 4 58
(Kevin Morgan) *t.k.h: hld up towards rr: hdwy 4f out: effrt to chal over 1f out: rdn to ld ins fnl f: edgd lft: kpt on* **7/1**[3]

6505 **2** *hd* **Indigo Princess**[6] 7912 3-9-2 **60**........................... AlistairRawlinson[(3)] 3 66
(Michael Appleby) *in tch in midfield: swtchd lft: effrt and rdn to chal over 1f out: drvn to ld 1f out: hdd ins fnl f: kpt on u.p* **8/1**

3005 **3** *2 ¼* **Ertidaad (IRE)**[21] 7645 4-8-13 **52**................................(b) RobertWinston 5 53
(Emma Owen) *chsd ldrs: effrt and ev ch over 1f out: 3rd and kpt on same pce u.p ins fnl f* **12/1**

460 **4** *1 ¾* **Whispered Kiss**[38] 7218 3-8-11 **52**...................................... ShaneKelly 6 48
(Mike Murphy) *t.k.h: led for 2f: chsd ldrs: effrt and ev ch over 1f out: no ex 1f out: wknd ins fnl f* **11/1**

0014 **5** *2 ¼* **World Record (IRE)**[35] 7298 6-9-6 **59**........................ WilliamCarson 13 51
(Mick Quinn) *chsd ldrs: rdn and ev ch wl over 1f out: led and edgd lft over 1f out: sn hdd: wknd ins fnl f* **12/1**

045 **6** *nse* **Strictly Art (IRE)**[24] 7577 3-9-0 **58**................................(p) EoinWalsh[(3)] 2 48
(Alan Bailey) *dwlt: hld up in rr: effrt and c wd bnd 2f out: hung rt u.p over 1f out: styd on ins fnl f: nvr trbld ldrs* **9/2**[2]

2204 **7** *1 ½* **Hidden Gem**[21] 7642 3-9-4 **59**... LukeMorris 9 46
(Ed Walker) *dwlt: sn rcvrd and in tch in midfield: effrt 2f out: unable qck over 1f out: wl hld and hung lft ins fnl f* **7/2**[1]

5000 **8** *2* **Breakheart (IRE)**[16] 7755 9-9-0 **60**................................ MichaelColes[(7)] 1 43
(Andrew Balding) *hld up in tch in last quartet: effrt over 1f out: sme hdwy ins fnl f: nvr trbld ldrs* **16/1**

3530 **9** *1 ¼* **Paradise Palm**[16] 7755 3-8-12 **58**............................ PaddyBradley[(5)] 10 37
(Philip McBride) *in toouch in midfield: nt clr run and swtchd rt over 1f out: no imp: wknd ins fnl f* **16/1**

-556 **10** *1* **Mulled Wine**[220] 1389 3-9-5 **60**.. SteveDrowne 12 37
(John Best) *stdd s: hld up in tch in rr: effrt 2f out: no imp u.p over 1f out: wl hld fnl f* **25/1**

0605 **11** *¾* **Synodic (USA)**[21] 7641 4-9-1 **54**..................................(t) JackMitchell 11 30
(Seamus Durack) *midfield: hdwy to chse ldr after 2f out: rdn and no rspnse whn sltly short of room over 1f out: sn wknd* **9/2**[2]

3000 **12** *4 ½* **Officer In Command (USA)**[49] 6900 10-8-7 **46** oh1..(tp) KieranO'Neill 7 11
(Alan Bailey) *dwlt: niggled along in rr: n.d* **20/1**

00 **13** *2 ¼* **Uncle Dermot (IRE)**[31] 7417 8-9-5 **58**.............................. LiamKeniry 8 18
(Brendan Powell) *taken down early: hld up in tch in midfield: rdn and lost pl 2f out: bhd and eased ins fnl f* **16/1**

0600 **14** *¾* **Fearless Poppy**[21] 7646 3-7-12 **46** oh1........................(p) RPWalsh[(7)] 15 3
(Christine Dunnett) *chsd ldrs: led after 2f: rdn and hdd wl over 1f out: sn wknd* **66/1**

1m 39.47s (-0.43) **Going Correction** -0.225s/f (Stan)
WFA 3 from 4yo+ 2lb **14** Ran SP% **133.7**
Speed ratings (Par 101): **93,92,90,88,86 86,85,83,81,80 80,75,73,72**
CSF £68.21 CT £500.34 TOTE £7.80: £2.80, £3.80, £5.40; EX 91.80 Trifecta £1419.70.
Owner Roemex Ltd **Bred** Centaur Bloodstock Agency **Trained** Gazeley, Suffolk

FOCUS
A moderate handicap, in which the first three in the betting all ran below market expectations for one reason or another. The winner perhaps didn't even need to replicate this year's low 60s form.

7987 CHRISTMAS PARTIES AT CHELMSFORD CITY RACECOURSE H'CAP 1m 5f 66y(P)
8:00 (8:01) (Class 5) (0-70,68) 3-Y-O+
£4,046 (£1,211; £605; £302; £151; £76) **Stalls** Low

Form RPR

1113 **1** **Bracken Brae**[217] 1434 4-9-13 **67**................................ StevieDonohoe 3 73
(Mark H Tompkins) *led for 1f: settled in 3rd after 2f: effrt ent fnl 2f: swtchd rt and rdn to chal over 1f out: led ent fnl f: kpt on and a doing enough ins fnl f: eased nr fin* **5/1**

020 **2** *1* **Marshall Aid (IRE)**[22] 7625 3-9-7 **68**.................................. LiamKeniry 2 72
(Mark Usher) *led after 1f: rdn ent fnl 2f: drvn and hdd ent fnl f: kpt on same pce u.p fnl 150yds* **15/8**[1]

0030 **3** *shd* **Oyster Card**[29] 7464 3-8-2 **49**... LukeMorris 4 53
(Michael Appleby) *chsd ldrs: wnt 2nd after 2f: rdn over 3f out: drvn and ev ch over 1f out: kpt on same pce u.p ins fnl f* **4/1**[3]

5666 **4** *1 ¾* **Shalimah (IRE)**[27] 7507 4-9-6 **67**..................................(v) WilliamCox[(7)] 6 68
(Clive Cox) *in tch in midfield: rdn 3f out: edgd lft and unable qck over 1f out: hung lft and one pced ins fnl f* **7/2**[2]

4405 **5** *1 ½* **Yasir (USA)**[16] 7746 8-9-10 **64**... MartinLane 9 63
(Conor Dore) *sn in rr: clsd over 2f out: rdn over 1f out: unable qck and kpt on same pce ins fnl f* **10/1**

0245 **6** *1 ¾* **Whitstable Pearl (IRE)**[22] 6871 3-8-3 **53**.............. EdwardGreatrex[(3)] 1 49
(Sophie Leech) *hld up in tch in midfield: effrt wl over 1f out: edgd lft over 1f out: kpt on same pce and no imp ins fnl f* **8/1**

0000 **7** *3 ¼* **Pixel (IRE)**[15] 7760 3-8-1 **55**............................. SophieScardifield[(7)] 8 46
(Denis Quinn) *in tch in last pair: pushed along and unable qck 3f out: bhd and kpt on same pce fr over 1f out* **33/1**

2m 53.98s (0.38) **Going Correction** -0.225s/f (Stan)
WFA 3 from 4yo+ 7lb **7** Ran SP% **116.8**
Speed ratings (Par 103): **89,88,88,87,86 85,83**
CSF £15.40 CT £41.37 TOTE £5.00: £2.80, £2.40; EX 12.30 Trifecta £43.50.
Owner David P Noblett **Bred** Dullingham Park Stud & Mr D Noblett **Trained** Newmarket, Suffolk

FOCUS
The meeting concluded with a modest staying event, and it didn't look a stiff test. The time was 9.98 seconds slower than Racing Post standard. The form is rated around the second.

T/Plt: £261.50 to a £1 stake. Pool: £97,469.03 - 272.06 winning units. T/Qpdt: £64.60 to a £1 stake. Pool: £12,662.22 - 144.98 winning units. **Steve Payne**

7954 NEWCASTLE (A.W) (L-H)
Thursday, November 17

OFFICIAL GOING: Tapeta: standard
Wind: Moderate half against Weather: Cloudy

7988 32RED.COM EBF MAIDEN STKS 6f (Tp)
12:20 (12:22) (Class 5) 2-Y-O **£3,234** (£962; £481; £240) **Stalls** Centre

Form RPR

2 **1** **Holmeswood**[23] 7599 2-9-5 0.. PaulMulrennan 2 81+
(Michael Dods) *trckd ldrs: smooth hdwy on inner 2f out: rdn to ld jst ins fnl f: kpt on strly* **4/5**[1]

2 *1 ½* **Creek Walk (USA)** 2-9-0 0... JoshDoyle[(5)] 10 74+
(Saeed bin Suroor) *dwlt and rr: hdwy and in tch 1/2-way: chsd ldrs on outer wl over 1f out: cl up and rdn ent fnl f: sn chsng wnr: kpt on* **4/1**[2]

5 **3** *1 ¼* **Atteq**[145] 3633 2-9-5 0.. TonyHamilton 12 70
(Richard Fahey) *led: pushed along wl over 1f out: sn rdn: hdd jst ins fnl f: sn drvn and kpt on same pce* **4/1**[2]

4 *1 ½* **Suited** 2-9-0 0... DuranFentiman 7 61+
(Tim Easterby) *t.k.h: trckd ldrs: hdwy 2f out: sn rdn: kpt on u.p fnl f* **50/1**

5 *1 ¼* **La Guapita** 2-9-0 0.. BenCurtis 6 57
(Hugo Palmer) *prom: cl up 2f out: rdn over 1f out: grad wknd fnl f* **12/1**[3]

6 *½* **Brother McGonagall** 2-9-5 0... JasonHart 3 60
(Tim Easterby) *dwlt and towards rr: pushed along and hdwy over 2f out: rdn wl over 1f out: kpt on fnl f: nrst fin* **50/1**

00 **7** *nse* **Out Of Order (IRE)**[74] 6162 2-9-5 0........................... JamesSullivan 5 60
(Tim Easterby) *cl up: rdn along 2f out: drvn over 1f out: grad wknd* **100/1**

04 **8** *shd* **Doria Road (USA)**[71] 6223 2-9-0 0...................................... KevinStott 4 55
(Kevin Ryan) *towards rr: hdwy 2f out: rdn over 1f out: swtchd rt ent fnl f: kpt on wl towards fin* **20/1**

00 **9** *¾* **Fairy Lock (IRE)**[24] 7578 2-9-0 0.............................. GrahamGibbons 11 53
(David Barron) *trckd ldrs: pushed along 1/2-way: rdn over 2f out and sn wknd* **100/1**

10 *1 ½* **Mimic's Memory** 2-8-9 0.. RowanScott[(5)] 13 48
(Ann Duffield) *a towards rr* **66/1**

65 **11** *3 ¾* **Golconda King (IRE)**[16] 7741 2-9-5 0............................ DavidNolan 14 42
(Richard Fahey) *a towards rr* **20/1**

0 **12** *2 ½* **Garboesque (IRE)**[24] 7576 2-9-0 0.................................. GrahamLee 8 29
(Shaun Harris) *trckd ldrs: rdn along over 2f out: sn wknd* **100/1**

0 **13** *nk* **Pipe Dreamer**[16] 7741 2-9-5 0.. TomEaves 9 33
(Kevin Ryan) *a towards rr* **20/1**

1m 12.82s (0.32) **Going Correction** +0.05s/f (Slow) **13** Ran SP% **125.9**
Speed ratings (Par 96): **99,97,95,93,91 91,90,90,89,87 82,79,79**
CSF £4.11 TOTE £1.70: £1.10, £1.90, £1.50; EX 5.20 Trifecta £13.50.
Owner David W Armstrong **Bred** Highfield Farm Llp **Trained** Denton, Co Durham

FOCUS
An uncompetitive maiden despite the size of the field. The market principals duly dominated the finish and the winner looks a nice prospect.

7989 32RED CASINO CONDITIONS STKS (PLUS 10 RACE) (ALL-WEATHER CHAMPIONSHIP FAST-TRACK QUALIFIER) 6f (Tp)
12:50 (12:50) (Class 2) 2-Y-O **£12,938** (£3,850; £1,924; £962) **Stalls** Centre

Form RPR

1101 **1** **Kananee (USA)**[15] 7764 2-9-5 **96**.. KevinStott 3 101+
(Saeed bin Suroor) *cl up pulling hrd: effrt 2f out: rdn to ld ent fnl f: sn edgd rt: kpt on wl towards fin* **7/4**[1]

1140 **2** *nk* **Sutter County**[61] 6572 2-9-8 **96**.. PJMcDonald 5 103+
(Mark Johnston) *cl up: effrt 2f out: slt ld over 1f out: rdn and hdd ent fnl f: drvn and ev ch tl no ex towards fin* **6/1**

1042 **3** *2 ¼* **Parnassian (IRE)**[7] 7893 2-9-0 **85**.................................... JoeyHaynes 1 88
(K R Burke) *dwlt and hld up in rr: hdwy 2f out: rdn to chal over 1f out: ev ch: drvn and kpt on same pce ins fnl f* **7/2**[3]

1112 **4** *1* **Mutahaady (IRE)**[15] 7764 2-9-0 **90**...................................... BenCurtis 2 85
(K R Burke) *trckd ldrs: cl up 2f out and sn rdn: drvn over 1f out: kpt on same pce* **8/1**

2153 **5** *shd* **Nuclear Power**[26] 7536 2-9-0 **98**... GrahamLee 4 85
(William Muir) *slt ld: pushed along 2f out: sn rdn and hdd over 1f out: grad wknd* **11/4**[2]

1m 10.89s (-1.61) **Going Correction** +0.05s/f (Slow) **5** Ran SP% **110.6**
Speed ratings (Par 102): **112,111,108,107,107**
CSF £12.45 TOTE £2.00: £1.30, £3.10; EX 12.20 Trifecta £24.90.
Owner Godolphin **Bred** Darley **Trained** Newmarket, Suffolk

FOCUS
A fascinating conditions event and a qualifier for the 3yo Championship next Easter. All five runners were in a line across the track just after halfway. The time was good and the form is taken at face value.

7990 BETWAY SPRINT H'CAP 6f (Tp)
1:25 (1:27) (Class 3) (0-95,95) 3-Y-O+ **£7,561** (£2,263; £1,131; £566; £282) **Stalls** Centre

Form RPR

1000 **1** **Cornwallville (IRE)**[47] 6942 4-9-7 **95**............................... GrahamLee 12 104
(Roger Fell) *in tch: hdwy over 2f out: chsd ldrs over 1f out: rdn to ld ins fnl f: kpt on* **20/1**

3600 **2** *nk* **Distant Past**[16] 7752 5-8-11 **85**..................................(v) KevinStott 1 93
(Kevin Ryan) *in tch: hdwy on inner wl over 1f out: rdn to chal ins fnl f: ev ch: drvn and kpt on wl towards fin* **25/1**

6214 **3** *shd* **Spring Fling**[40] 7146 5-9-5 **93**... BenCurtis 10 101
(Henry Candy) *trckd ldrs: hdwy over 1f out: rdn and ev ch ins fnl f: drvn and kpt on wl towards fin* **7/1**

0650 **4** *½* **Red Pike (IRE)**[27] 7497 5-9-5 **93**................................. PaulMulrennan 13 99
(Bryan Smart) *prom towards stands side: hdwy and cl up 2f out: rdn to chal over 1f out: ev ch tl drvn ins fnl f and no ex last 50 yds* **7/1**

0000 **5** *nk* **Tatlisu (IRE)**[34] 7315 6-8-11 **85**.................................... TonyHamilton 2 90
(Richard Fahey) *trckd ldrs: hdwy to ld jst over 1f out and sn rdn: drvn and hdd wl ins fnl f: kpt on same pce towards fin* **25/1**

-141 **6** *½* **Spanish City**[30] 7434 3-8-10 **84**.. JackMitchell 7 88+
(Roger Varian) *towards rr: hdwy 2f out: rdn and n.m.r 1f out: sn drvn and kpt on* **7/4**[1]

2013 **7** *nk* **Jaywalker (IRE)**[9] 7858 5-8-8 **82**...................................... PJMcDonald 4 85
(Rebecca Bastiman) *led: rdn along 2f out: hdd jst over 1f out: grad wknd* **6/1**[3]

1064 **8** *¾* **Mappin Time (IRE)**[16] 7752 8-8-11 **85**............................(be) JasonHart 3 85
(Tim Easterby) *.hld up towards rr: hdwy wl over 1f out: rdn and kpt on fnl f: nrst fin* **33/1**

The Form Book, Raceform Ltd, Newbury, RG14 5SJ

0325 **9** ½ **Sir Billy Wright (IRE)**[12] 7825 5-8-6 **87**.............. KatherineGlenister(7) 8 86
(David Evans) *trckd ldr: effrt wl over 1f out: sn rdn and grad wknd fnl f* **16/1**
4050 **10** 1¾ **Lexington Times (IRE)**[12] 7825 4-9-1 **89**...................... JamesSullivan 5 82+
(Ruth Carr) *dwlt: a towards rr* **50/1**
1-00 **11** 2 **Mullionheir**[117] 4625 4-9-4 **92**.. KierenFox 6 79
(John Best) *in tch: effrt 2f out: sn rdn and no imp* **20/1**
0033 **12** 1¾ **Highland Acclaim (IRE)**[16] 7752 5-9-3 **91**...................... DavidNolan 11 72
(David O'Meara) *chsd ldrs towards stands side: rdn along wl over 1f out: sn wknd* **12/1**
0002 **13** 4½ **Dragon King (IRE)**[9] 7858 4-8-9 **83**........................(p) ConnorBeasley 14 50
(Michael Dods) *racd towards stands side:in tch: pushed along 1/2-way: sn rdn and wknd* **5/1**[2]

1m 12.16s (-0.34) **Going Correction** +0.05s/f (Slow) **13** Ran SP% **128.0**
Speed ratings (Par 107): **104,103,103,102,102 101,101,100,99,97 94,92,86**
CSF £444.35 CT £3976.51 TOTE £26.70: £6.40, £7.40, £2.60; EX 743.20 Trifecta £3715.10.
Owner Stephen Louch **Bred** Corrin Stud & Blackwater Bloodstock Ltd **Trained** Nawton, N Yorks

FOCUS
A decent sprint handicap in which they split into two early, though the two groups had converged by halfway and it produced a bunch finish. The form is rated around the winner, third and fourth.

7991 BETWAY MAIDEN STKS 1m 2f 42y (Tp)
1:55 (1:59) (Class 5) 3-Y-O+ **£3,234** (£962; £481; £240) **Stalls** High

Form RPR
0236 **1** **Kicking The Can (IRE)**[32] 7382 5-9-9 58........................... DavidNolan 6 67
(David Thompson) *hld up in tch: hdwy over 3f out: effrt on inner to chse ldrs 2f out: swtchd rt and rdn to chal 1f out: styd on to ld last 150 yds: drvn out* **10/1**
34 **2** 1¼ **Issue**[17] 7727 3-9-0 0.. TomQueally 7 60
(James Fanshawe) *towards rr: hdwy over 3f out: sn chsng ldrs: rdn over 1f out: drvn to chal ent fnl f: kpt on same pce towards fin* **7/4**[1]
2043 **3** 1¾ **Sunglider (IRE)**[13] 7791 3-9-5 75...........................(vt) GrahamGibbons 1 61
(David O'Meara) *slt ld: pushed along 3f out: rdn wl over 1f out: drvn ent fnl f: hdd last 150 yds: one pce* **15/8**[2]
4 5 **Maifalki (FR)**[46] 3-9-5 0.. JasonHart 10 51
(Mark Walford) *cl up: pushed along over 3f out: rdn along over 2f out: drvn wl over 1f out: sn one pce* **7/1**[3]
04 **5** 3½ **First Of Never (IRE)**[23] 7597 10-9-9 0.............................. PaddyAspell 5 44
(Lynn Siddall) *rr: sme hdwy 3f out: rdn along over 2f out: plugged on one pce* **100/1**
0 **6** 2¾ **Palindrome (USA)**[22] 7627 3-9-5 0..................................(p) TomEaves 9 39
(Ronald Thompson) *midfield: pushed along 4f out: rdn 3f out: n.d* **50/1**
60 **7** 1 **Miss Macchiato (IRE)**[171] 2741 3-9-0 0........................... PJMcDonald 3 32
(Keith Dalgleish) *chsd ldng pair: pushed along 1/2-way: rdn wl over 3f out: sn wknd* **33/1**
8 1¾ **Black Is Black (IRE)**[18] 3-9-5 0...................................... JamesSullivan 4 33
(Michael Easterby) *dwlt and towards rr: effrt and sme hdwy over 4f out: sn rdn along and wknd* **50/1**

2m 9.43s (-0.97) **Going Correction** -0.125s/f (Stan)
WFA 3 from 5yo+ 4lb **8** Ran SP% **100.6**
Speed ratings (Par 103): **98,97,95,91,88 86,85,84**
CSF £20.14 TOTE £10.30: £2.00, £1.10, £1.10; EX 25.30 Trifecta £34.90.
Owner D Mawer **Bred** William J M Morrissey **Trained** Bolam, Co Durham
■ Skara Mae was withdrawn. Price at time of withdrawal 4/1. Rule 4 applies to all bets - deduction 20p in the pound.

FOCUS
A modest older-horse maiden, weakened further when Skara Mae refused to enter the stalls, in which the third and fourth were soon in a clear lead. The winner didn't have to improve on this year's best.

7992 BETWAY H'CAP 1m 4f 98y (Tp)
2:25 (2:28) (Class 6) (0-60,60) 3-Y-O+ **£2,911** (£866; £432; £216) **Stalls** High

Form RPR
1254 **1** **Taopix**[20] 7657 4-9-8 **58**.. DavidNolan 12 65
(Karen McLintock) *trckd ldrs: cl up 4f out: led 2f out: rdn over 1f out: drvn ins fnl f: kpt on gamely towards fin* **11/2**[3]
0000 **2** ¾ **Canford Thompson**[20] 5365 3-9-2 **58**...................... GrahamGibbons 11 64
(Mark Walford) *hld up in rr: hdwy 3f out: in tch and rdn over 1f out: styd on strly fnl f* **25/1**
4313 **3** hd **Galilee Chapel (IRE)**[13] 7794 7-9-4 **59**................(b) GarryWhillans(5) 13 65
(Alistair Whillans) *hld up in midfield: hdwy on outer wl over 2f out: rdn to chse ldrs over 1f out: drvn and ev ch ins fnl f: kpt on* **11/1**
-503 **4** ¾ **Angel In The Snow**[20] 7656 3-8-7 **49**.............................. BenCurtis 5 55+
(Brian Ellison) *trckd ldrs: hdwy 3f out: chsd ldrs whn nt clr run over 2f out: sn swtchd lft to inner and rdn: styng on whn n.m.r ins fnl f: kpt on* **3/1**[1]
/415 **5** ½ **Miss Tree**[20] 7656 5-8-11 **54**.................................... JoshQuinn(7) 2 58+
(John Quinn) *hld up towards rr: hdwy wl over 2f out: rdn wl over 1f out: styd on wl fnl f* **6/1**
-460 **6** 1 **Merriment**[65] 6450 3-9-1 **57**..[1] TomEaves 7 59
(Peter Niven) *bhd: pushed along 1/2-way: rdn over 3f out: hdwy 2f out: styd on wl fnl f* **40/1**
5002 **7** ¾ **Devious Spirit (IRE)**[24] 7581 4-9-5 **60**........................... JoshDoyle(5) 14 61
(Iain Jardine) *hld up towards rr: hdwy on wd outside 3f out: rdn to chse ldrs wl over 1f out: sn drvn and wknd fnl f* **8/1**
5634 **8** 1¼ **Page Of Wands**[68] 6344 3-9-1 **57**....................................(v[1]) GrahamLee 8 56
(Karen McLintock) *in tch: hdwy to chse ldrs 3f out: cl up and rdn 2f out: drvn and wknd ent fnl f* **12/1**
0000 **9** 7 **Moojaned (IRE)**[27] 7515 5-8-12 **55**........................ KatherineGlenister(7) 4 44
(David Evans) *prom: cl up 4f out: rdn along 2f out: sn drvn and wknd over 1f out* **10/1**
4602 **10** 8 **Sebastian's Wish (IRE)**[30] 7438 3-8-11 **53**..............(b) BarryMcHugh 10 30
(Richard Whitaker) *led: rdn along and hdd 2f out: sn wknd* **9/1**
4500 **11** 6 **Calarules**[24] 7582 3-8-11 **53**...(b) DuranFentiman 1 21
(Tim Easterby) *midfield: pushed along over 4f out: rdn 3f out: nvr a factor* **40/1**
4000 **12** 7 **Merchant Of Medici**[22] 7628 9-9-2 **52**................................. PJMcDonald 6 9
(Micky Hammond) *midfield: pushed along over 5f out: rdn 4f out: sn wknd* **50/1**
600 **13** 2 **Whacking Bullock (IRE)**[192] 2109 3-8-11 **53**.............. JamesSullivan 9 7
(Daniel Mark Loughnane) *a towards rr* **100/1**
0031 **14** 4 **Glasgon**[20] 7656 6-9-3 **53**...(p) ConnorBeasley 3 1
(Ray Craggs) *trckd ldrs on inner: pushed along over 3f out: rdn wl over 2f out: sn wknd* **5/1**[2]

2m 39.13s (-1.97) **Going Correction** -0.125s/f (Stan)
WFA 3 from 4yo+ 6lb **14** Ran SP% **129.2**
Speed ratings (Par 101): **101,100,100,99,99 98,98,97,92,87 83,78,77,74**
CSF £150.47 CT £1509.08 TOTE £7.10: £2.20, £8.20, £3.70; EX 160.40 Trifecta £1896.80.
Owner Roger Stockdale **Bred** Lady Jennifer Green **Trained** Ingoe, Northumberland

FOCUS
A moderate handicap which saw a minor pb from the winner.

7993 ROA/RACING POST OWNERS' JACKPOT H'CAP 1m 4f 98y (Tp)
3:00 (3:00) (Class 5) (0-75,74) 3-Y-O+ **£3,234** (£962; £481; £240) **Stalls** High

Form RPR
0044 **1** **Heart Locket**[38] 7205 4-9-5 **69**.. PaulMulrennan 7 75
(Michael Easterby) *hld up towards rr: stdy hdwy over 3f out: trckd ldrs 2f out: effrt and n.m.r over 1f out: rdn ins fnl f: styd on wl to ld nr fin* **10/1**
0306 **2** nk **Henpecked**[9] 7853 6-9-6 **70**..(p) PJMcDonald 3 75
(Alistair Whillans) *trckd ldrs: hdwy over 3f out: cl up 2f out: rdn to ld over 1f out: drvn ins fnl f: hdd and no ex towards fin* **10/1**
003 **3** hd **Aislabie (FR)**[20] 7657 3-8-9 **65**... JasonHart 13 69
(Mark Walford) *hld up towards rr: stdy hdwy 3f out effrt on outer to chse ldrs over 1f out: rdn to chal ent fnl f: sn drvn and ev ch tl no ex towards fin* **12/1**
4316 **4** hd **Spinners Ball (IRE)**[75] 6121 3-9-4 **74**........................... TomMarquand 2 78
(Sylvester Kirk) *trckd ldrs on inner: hdwy over 2f out: rdn to chal over 1f out: drvn and ev ch ins fnl f: no ex towards fin* **7/1**[3]
3401 **5** 1¼ **Santiburi Spring**[30] 7425 3-8-12 **68**................................... KierenFox 12 70
(John Best) *hld up in rr: hdwy 3f out: chsd ldrs and n.m.r wl over 1f out: sn swtchd lft and rdn: kpt on fnl f* **7/1**[3]
0335 **6** ½ **Woodacre**[13] 7791 9-9-7 **71**... BarryMcHugh 4 72
(Richard Whitaker) *rrd s and blind removed late: lost many l and detached: jnd field 1/2-way: hdwy 3f out: rdn to chse ldrs over 1f out: n.m.r and swtchd rt ins fnl f: kpt on* **16/1**
2643 **7** nk **La Contessa (IRE)**[9] 7853 3-9-2 **72**.................................[1] TonyHamilton 5 73
(Richard Fahey) *trckd ldrs.: hdwy 3f out: rdn along 2f out: drvn appr fnl f: kpt on same pce* **8/1**
3514 **8** 10 **Hard Toffee (IRE)**[21] 7653 5-9-8 **72**................................. GrahamLee 9 57
(Conrad Allen) *prom and plld hrd early: cl up over 4f out: led over 2f out: sn rdn: hdd over 1f out and sn wknd* **6/1**[2]
2354 **9** 2¾ **Patent**[99] 5308 3-8-7 **63**... JamesSullivan 8 43
(Peter Niven) *a towards rr* **20/1**
6642 **10** 1 **Maulesden May (IRE)**[9] 7853 3-8-11 **67**.................. GrahamGibbons 10 46
(Keith Dalgleish) *trckd ldrs: effrt over 3f out: rdn along wl over 2f out: sn wknd* **3/1**[1]
4212 **11** 11 **Rocktherunway (IRE)**[37] 7251 7-9-8 **72**..................(b) ConnorBeasley 6 33
(Michael Dods) *cl up: led over 5f out: rdn along 3f out: sn hdd & wknd* **12/1**
4200 **12** 12 **San Quentin (IRE)**[27] 7517 5-9-4 **73**............................... JoshDoyle(5) 11 15
(Roger Fell) *hld up: hdwy on wd outside and tch over 2f out: sn rdn and wknd* **25/1**
4000 **13** 10 **Wordiness**[27] 7507 8-9-1 **72**...................................... KatherineGlenister(7) 1
(David Evans) *led: hdd over 5f out: rdn along 4f out: sn lost pl and bhd fnl 2f* **25/1**

2m 38.15s (-2.95) **Going Correction** -0.125s/f (Stan)
WFA 3 from 4yo+ 6lb **13** Ran SP% **127.3**
Speed ratings (Par 103): **104,103,103,103,102 102,102,95,93,93 85,77,71**
CSF £110.59 CT £1235.07 TOTE £17.20: £3.70, £4.50, £6.10; EX 154.70 Trifecta £4347.60.
Owner A Chandler & L Westwood 1 **Bred** Juddmonte Farms Ltd **Trained** Sheriff Hutton, N Yorks

FOCUS
A slightly better race than the previous 1m4f handicap, but a messy race with racing room at a premium up the straight. Ordinary form.

7994 SUNBETS.CO.UK H'CAP (DIV I) 7f 14y (Tp)
3:35 (3:37) (Class 6) (0-65,65) 3-Y-O+ **£2,264** (£673; £336; £168) **Stalls** Centre

Form RPR
6000 **1** **Gypsy Major**[20] 7663 4-9-3 **61**......................................(v) TomMarquand 6 68
(Garry Moss) *trckd ldrs: hdwy to ld 11/2f out: sn rdn: drvn ins fnl f: hld on wl towards fin* **20/1**
4032 **2** nk **Kirkham**[16] 7743 3-9-6 **65**.. JoeDoyle 12 70
(Julie Camacho) *trckd ldrs: hdwy to chal jst over 1f out: rdn and ev ch ins fnl f: drvn and no ex towards fin* **4/1**[2]
0063 **3** 1¾ **Thorntoun Lady (USA)**[13] 7797 6-9-1 **62**.............. GeorgeDowning(3) 9 64
(Jim Goldie) *hld up towards rr: hdwy 2f out: swtchd rt and rdn over 1f out: drvn and ch ins fnl f: kpt on same pce towards fin* **11/1**
3060 **4** 2 **Hold On Magnolia**[217] 1448 3-9-4 **63**................................. DavidNolan 3 59
(Richard Fahey) *trckd ldrs: hdwy over 2f out: rdn over 1f out: drvn ins fnl f: no imp* **16/1**
0023 **5** nk **Space War**[7] 7887 9-9-7 **65**..(b) PaulMulrennan 2 61
(Michael Easterby) *t.k.h: prom: effrt and ev ch 2f out: sn rdn: drvn and grad wknd fnl f* **2/1**[1]
-204 **6** nse **Dose**[30] 7442 3-9-1 **60**... TonyHamilton 1 55
(Richard Fahey) *trckd ldrs: rdn along over 2f out: drvn over 1f out and kpt on same pce* **7/1**
0000 **7** ¾ **Ivors Involvement (IRE)**[16] 7747 4-8-8 **52**.................. JamesSullivan 4 46
(Tina Jackson) *towards rr: hdwy wl over 1f out: sn rdn and kpt on fnl f* **50/1**
06 **8** ½ **Bromance**[13] 7797 3-9-1 **60**..(p) PJMcDonald 10 52
(Peter Niven) *towards rr: hdwy 2f out: sn rdn and kpt on fnl f* **10/1**
0000 **9** 1¾ **Royal Normandy**[13] 7797 4-9-4 **62**....................................(b) BenCurtis 8 51
(Roger Fell) *cl up: led over 3f out: rdn along 2f out: hdd over 1f out: sn drvn and wknd* **28/1**
0020 **10** 13 **National Service (USA)**[16] 7751 5-8-7 **58**........(tp) CallumRodriguez(7) 5 14
(Richard Ford) *dwlt: sn swtchd lft and hdwy to trck ldrs: cl up 1/2-way: rdn along 2f out: wknd over 1f out* **20/1**
0062 **11** 7 **Bay Mirage (IRE)**[20] 7663 3-9-6 **65**.................................(p) KevinStott 7 3
(Kevin Ryan) *t.k.h: slt ld: hdd over 3f out: rdn along over 2f out: sn wknd* **9/2**[3]

1m 26.44s (0.24) **Going Correction** +0.05s/f (Slow)
WFA 3 from 4yo+ 1lb **11** Ran SP% **122.3**
Speed ratings (Par 101): **100,99,97,95,95 94,94,93,91,76 68**
CSF £98.85 CT £976.11 TOTE £26.10: £5.60, £1.90, £3.60; EX 135.40 Trifecta £852.10.
Owner Pinnacle Duo Partnership **Bred** Bearstone Stud Ltd **Trained** Wynyard, Stockton-On-Tees

FOCUS
The first division of a moderate handicap. A slight pb from the winner, the next two offering some guidance.

7995 SUNBETS.CO.UK H'CAP (DIV II) 7f 14y (Tp)
4:10 (4:11) (Class 6) (0-65,65) 3-Y-O+ **£2,264** (£673; £336; £168) **Stalls** Centre

Form RPR
5010 **1** **Faintly (USA)**[12] 7817 5-9-4 **62**......................................(b) JamesSullivan 2 68
(Ruth Carr) *hld up in rr: hdwy wl over 1f out: effrt and nt clr run ent fnl f: sn rdn and styd on strly to ld last 50 yds* **9/2**[2]

200 **2** ½ **Sonnet (IRE)**[17] 7725 3-9-5 **64**.................................(v[1]) ConnorBeasley 12 68
(David Evans) *hld up: hdwy to chse ldrs on outer wl over 1f out: rdn to chal ent fnl f: ev ch tl drvn and no ex towards fin* **16/1**
6542 **3** nk **Cliff (IRE)**[23] 7604 6-9-3 **61**.................................... TomEaves 6 65
(Nigel Tinkler) *in tch: hdwy over 2f out and sn chsng ldrs: rdn over 1f out: led ins fnl f: sn drvn: hdd and no ex last 50 yds* **3/1**[1]
6456 **4** 1 **Cool Strutter (IRE)**[23] 7604 4-9-0 **58**..............................(b) SamJames 4 60
(Karen Tutty) *hld up towards rr: hdwy 2f out: rdn over 1f out: styd on wl fnl f: nrst fin* **11/1**
2604 **5** nk **Princess Peaches**[7] 7889 4-9-2 **60**............................(p) PJMcDonald 11 61
(James Bethell) *trckd ldrs: hdwy over 2f out: rdn over 1f out: ev ch ent fnl f: sn drvn and kpt on same pce* **10/1**
6060 **6** hd **Kodiac Lady (IRE)**[10] 7852 4-8-9 **58**...........................(e) HollieDoyle[(5)] 7 58
(Simon West) *chsd ldrs: rdn along 2f out: drvn over 1f out: kpt on same pce* **16/1**
4400 **7** hd **Border Bandit (USA)**[13] 7795 8-8-7 **51** oh4...................(p) BenCurtis 10 51
(Tracy Waggott) *cl up: led 2f out: rdn over 1f out: drvn and hdd ins fnl f: sn wknd* **20/1**
0600 **8** nk **Star Of Spring (IRE)**[101] 5223 4-9-5 **63**........................ BarryMcHugh 9 62
(Iain Jardine) *trckd ldrs: pushed along oevr 2f out: swtchd lft and rdn over 1f out: drvn and wknd fnl f* **6/1**
4-35 **9** nse **Miss Goldsmith (IRE)**[303] 249 3-9-6 **65**...................... TonyHamilton 8 63
(Richard Fahey) *t.k.h: hld up in rr: hdwy 2f out: rdn over 1f out: kpt on fnl f* **20/1**
/100 **10** 6 **Lotara**[10] 7852 4-9-7 **65**.. TomMarquand 5 49
(Jim Goldie) *trckd ldrs: pushed along wl over 2f out: rdn wl over 1f out: sn wknd* **16/1**
4000 **11** 1¼ **You'll Do**[13] 7797 3-9-1 **60**.. GrahamGibbons 1 40
(Maurice Barnes) *prom: rdn along 3f out: sn wknd* **16/1**
6606 **12** 2½ **Dark Forest**[50] 6872 3-9-4 **63**.. KevinStott 3 37
(Marjorie Fife) *wnt rt s: led. rdn along 3f out: hdd 2f out and sn wknd* **5/1**[3]

1m 26.73s (0.53) **Going Correction** +0.05s/f (Slow)
WFA 3 from 4yo+ 1lb **12** Ran SP% **124.6**
Speed ratings (Par 101): **98,97,97,95,95 95,95,94,94,87 86,83**
CSF £78.82 CT £256.60 TOTE £5.60: £1.80, £5.40, £1.50; EX 125.40 Trifecta £433.20.
Owner The Bottom Liners & Mrs R Carr **Bred** Juddmonte Farms Inc **Trained** Huby, N Yorks

FOCUS
The winning time was 0.29sec slower than the first division. The first two came from off the speed.
T/Jkpt: Not Won. T/Plt: £400.50 to a £1 stake. Pool: £64547.44, 117.63 winning units. T/Qpdt: £168.50 to a £1 stake. Pool: £6787.74, 29.8 winning units. **Joe Rowntree**

6107 FONTAINEBLEAU
Thursday, November 17

OFFICIAL GOING: Turf: very soft

7996a PRIX DE LA PINEDE (MAIDEN) (2YO FILLIES) (TURF) 6f
11:40 (12:00) 2-Y-O **£9,926** (£3,970; £2,977; £1,985; £992)

RPR
1 **Quindiana (FR)**[45] 2-9-2 0.. MaximeGuyon 4 88
(H-A Pantall, France) **17/10**[1]
2 5 **Coral Sea**[30] 7439 2-9-2 0..................................... ChristopheSoumillon 3 73
(Charles Hills) *a cl up: outpcd and rdn 2f out: styd on again to go 2nd ins fnl f: no ch w wnr and eased late on* **29/10**[2]
3 1 **Etoile Bere (FR)**[36] 7291 2-9-2 0............................ StephanePasquier 1 70
(N Clement, France) **18/5**[3]
4 1½ **Incantu (IRE)**[19] 2-9-2 0...(b) IoritzMendizabal 5 66
(F Chappet, France) **94/10**
5 1¼ **Astrella (GER)** 2-8-10 0...................................... ClementLecoeuvre[(6)] 8 62
(Waldemar Hickst, Germany) **138/10**
6 nk **Veldargent (FR)**[141] 2-9-2 0.. ThierryJarnet 6 61
(H-A Pantall, France) **111/10**
7 3 **Novela (IRE)**[41] 2-9-2 0.....................................(p) Pierre-CharlesBoudot 7 52
(Rod Collet, France) **116/10**
8 3 **Chiquit Indian (FR)**[91] 2-9-2 0................................... SebastienMaillot 2 43
(E Caroux, France) **54/1**

WIN (incl. 1 euro stake): 2.70. PLACES: 1.10, 1.20, 1.30. DF: 4.10. SF: 8.00
Owner Peter Rechsteiner **Bred** Peter Rechsteiner **Trained** France

7997a PRIX CONTESSINA (CONDITIONS) (3YO+) (TURF) 6f
12:10 (12:00) 3-Y-O+ **£14,705** (£5,882; £4,411; £2,941; £1,470)

RPR
1 **Spirit Quartz (IRE)**[45] 7030 8-9-6 0............................ JulianResimont 6 108
(N Caullery, France) **67/10**[3]
2 hd **Blue Soave (FR)**[45] 7030 8-9-0 0.. TonyPiccone 1 101
(F Chappet, France) **33/10**[2]
3 ½ **Hillbilly Boy (IRE)**[61] 6558 6-9-6 0........................ RichardKingscote 3 105
(Tom Dascombe) *broke wl: w ldrs early: sn chsng clr ldr: drvn after 1/2-way: styd on fnl f: nvr quite on terms* **12/1**
4 ½ **Rangali**[410] 6971 5-9-0 0..(b) ThierryJarnet 9 98
(D Guillemin, France) **11/5**[1]
5 2½ **Henrytheaeroplane (USA)**[768] 7097 4-9-1 0 ow1.......(p) RadekKoplik 5 91
(Z Koplik, Czech Republic) **31/1**
6 1½ **Saon Secret (FR)**[27] 7525 6-9-0 0...............................(b) MaximeGuyon 4 85
(T Castanheira, France) **36/5**
7 1 **Royal Prize**[27] 7525 6-9-0 0...(b) AlexisBadel 8 82
(Mme M Bollack-Badel, France) **14/1**
8 ½ **White Witch (USA)**[39] 3-9-0 0..................................... LukasDelozier 7 80
(H-A Pantall, France) *w.w in fnl trio: unable to cl u.p fr 2f out: nvr in contention* **9/1**
9 ¾ **Perfect Pasture**[15] 7771 6-9-0 0....................................(b) NathanEvans 2 78
(Michael Easterby) *chsd front rnk: rdn and no imp 2 1/2f out: fdd fnl f* **73/10**

1m 10.6s (70.60) **9** Ran SP% **119.2**
WIN (incl. 1 euro stake): 7.70. PLACES: 2.30, 1.30, 4.00. DF: 18.90. SF: 34.90.
Owner Mlle Charley Lauffer **Bred** Ballygallon Stud Ltd **Trained** France

7998a PRIX CERES (LISTED RACE) (3YO FILLIES) (TURF) 7f
1:20 (12:00) 3-Y-O **£20,220** (£8,088; £6,066; £4,044; £2,022)

RPR
1 **Narnia Dawn (IRE)**[49] 3-9-2 0.................................. StephanePasquier 5 96
(F-H Graffard, France) **61/10**[3]
2 ½ **Roshanara (FR)**[17] 3-9-2 0.................................. ChristopheSoumillon 4 95
(A De Royer-Dupre, France) **12/1**
3 snk **Blonville (FR)**[9] 3-9-2 0.. SebastienMaillot 2 94
(Robert Collet, France) **34/1**
4 snk **Blessed Silence (FR)**[19] 3-9-2 0.................................... OlivierPeslier 9 94
(J-M Beguigne, France) **13/1**
5 4 **Pietrafiore (IRE)**[34] 7348 3-9-2 0.. ThierryJarnet 6 83
(H-A Pantall, France) *settled towards rr: tk clsr order 1 1/2f out: styd on fnl f: no rch ldrs* **78/10**
6 ½ **Livinginafantasy (FR)**[56] 6728 3-9-2 0......................... ThierryThulliez 7 82
(S Wattel, France) **13/1**
7 nse **Squash**[21] 7650 3-9-2 0.. IoritzMendizabal 1 82
(Philip McBride) *keen: chsd ldr under a tight hold early: drvn 1/2-way and remained in tch: grad lft bhd by ldrs fr over 1f out* **49/10**[2]
8 1 **Grand Jete**[32] 3-9-2 0... VincentCheminaud 12 79
(D Smaga, France) **13/2**
9 1½ **Rien Que Pour Toi (FR)**[32] 3-9-2 0.......................... MaximeGuyon 10 75
(T Castanheira, France) **39/10**[1]
10 shd **Chanche The Life (IRE)**[19] 3-9-2 0.............................. EddyHardouin 3 75
(K Borgel, France) **22/1**
11 hd **Maisons (FR)**[32] 7397 3-9-2 0................................... ClementLecoeuvre 8 74
(E Lellouche, France) **41/1**
12 7 **Syrita (FR)**[34] 7348 3-9-2 0..(p) AlexisBadel 11 55
(M Nigge, France) **16/1**
13 20 **Basilia**[88] 3-9-2 0..(b) Pierre-CharlesBoudot 13
(Mme A Fabre, France) **18/1**

1m 30.9s (90.90) **13** Ran SP% **118.8**
WIN (incl. 1 euro stake): 7.10. PLACES: 2.40, 4.40, 7.80. DF: 44.10. 98.30.
Owner Mrs Robert G Ehrnrooth **Bred** Nordkappe Partnership **Trained** France

7999a PRIX DU COMITE DEPARTEMENTAL DU TOURISME DE SEINE-ET-MARNE (CLAIMER) (3YO) (TURF) 1m 1f
1:50 (12:00) 3-Y-O **£8,455** (£3,382; £2,536; £1,691; £845)

RPR
1 **Donuts Reyor (FR)**[20] 7680 3-8-11 0..................... LudovicBoisseau[(4)] 4 72
(Y Barberot, France) **8/1**
2 ½ **Gagner Sa Vie (ITY)**[207] 1686 3-8-13 0.............. NicolasBarzalona[(5)] 16 74
(G Botti, France) **12/1**
3 1¾ **Flying Fleur (FR)**[34] 3-8-0 0.. ThomasTrullier[(8)] 3 60
(N Clement, France) **42/1**
4 ¾ **Super Mac (FR)**[14] 3-8-13 0..................................... JeromeMoutard[(5)] 2 68
(Gianluca Bietolini, Italy) **61/10**[3]
5 nse **Alfieri (FR)**[39] 3-8-11 0.. ThibaultSpeicher[(4)] 14 65
(G Arizkorreta Elosegui, Spain) **11/2**[2]
6 ¾ **First Wheat**[43] 7076 3-9-2 0.. NathanEvans 13 65
(Michael Easterby) *towards rr of midfield: drvn 3 1/2f out: clsd fnl 2f and sn rdn: kpt on at same pce u.p fnl f: nt pce to get on terms* **28/1**
7 nse **Yooroppa (FR)**[9] 3-8-8 0.. MlleZoePfeil[(3)] 5 60
(Y Gourraud, France) **78/10**
8 ½ **Mon Bisou (IRE)**[18] 3-8-9 0...................................... MlleIsisMagnin[(6)] 12 63
(G Botti, France) **12/1**
9 2 **Valley Kid (FR)**[18] 3-8-8 0.. KyllanBarbaud[(8)] 7 59
(N Caullery, France) **39/1**
10 ¾ **Zanzi Way (FR)**[46] 3-8-6 0.. JeremyMoisan[(5)] 8 53
(Mlle T Puitg, France) **143/1**
11 1¼ **Carbutt's Ridge (IRE)**[17] 3-8-11 0.............. David-AndreSurveillant[(8)] 1 58
(N Caullery, France) **84/1**
12 snk **Dosnueveuno (IRE)**[28] 7492 3-8-11 0................... EmmanuelEtienne[(4)] 9 54
(Alex Fracas, France) **16/1**
13 snk **Going Viral (IRE)**[28] 7492 3-8-6 0........................(b) JeremieMonteiro[(5)] 18 50
(Matthieu Palussiere, France) **33/1**
14 snk **Motorbike (IRE)**[61] 3-8-8 0................................... AlexandreChesneau[(8)] 6 54
(G Botti, France) **43/1**
15 8 **Napadac (GER)** 3-8-6 0..................(b) GuillaumeTrolleyDePrevaux[(5)] 11 32
(P Schiergen, Germany) **11/1**
16 20 **Princesse Ava (FR)**[31] 3-8-5 0.................................(p) AdrienMoreau[(3)] 10
(Mlle S Delaroche, France) **110/1**
17 2 **Wikileaks (GER)** 3-9-3 0.. NicolasLarenaudie[(3)] 15
(Waldemar Hickst, Germany) **19/5**[1]

WIN (incl. 1 euro stake): 9.00. PLACES: 3.40, 5.60, 11.10. DF: 52.40. SF: 141.80
Owner Ecurie Des Monnaies **Bred** Mme J Royer **Trained** France

8000 - 8006a (Foreign Racing) - See Raceform Interactive

7988 NEWCASTLE (A.W) (L-H)
Friday, November 18

OFFICIAL GOING: Tapeta: standard
Wind: Light, half against

8007 HOP HOUSE 13 H'CAP 1m 2f 42y (Tp)
3:40 (3:42) (Class 4) (0-85,85) 3-Y-O+ **£4,851** (£1,443; £721; £360) **Stalls** High

Form RPR
3160 **1** **Purple Rock (IRE)**[41] 7159 4-8-11 **78**........................(t) NathanEvans[(3)] 8 86
(Michael Easterby) *hld up: stdy hdwy on outside over 2f out: rdn to ld ins fnl f: kpt on wl* **6/1**[2]
1254 **2** 1 **Age Of Elegance (IRE)**[11] 7847 4-8-13 **77**.................(p) PJMcDonald 14 83+
(Roger Fell) *pressed ldr: led 4f out: rdn 2f out: hdd ins fnl f: kpt on: hld nr fin* **7/1**[3]
2030 **3** ¾ **Rockwood**[32] 7408 5-8-9 **73**..(v) GrahamLee 3 78
(Karen McLintock) *t.k.h: hld up: smooth hdwy and prom over 2f out: rdn and kpt on fnl f* **9/1**
2300 **4** ½ **Daisy Bere (FR)**[28] 7504 3-8-10 **78**...................................... JoeyHaynes 11 82
(K R Burke) *hld up in midfield: hdwy over 2f out: prom whn nt clr run briefly over 1f out: kpt on ins fnl f: no imp* **10/1**
504 **5** hd **Storm King**[14] 7791 7-8-12 **76**... LukeMorris 5 79
(David C Griffiths) *in tch: hdwy over 2f out: drvn over 1f out: kpt on same pce ins fnl f* **16/1**
060 **6** 2¼ **Spes Nostra**[106] 5082 8-9-4 **82**...(b) DavidNolan 2 81+
(Iain Jardine) *hld up in midfield on ins: effrt whn nt clr run briefly 2f out: kpt on fnl f: nt pce to chal* **20/1**
0560 **7** ¾ **Theos Lolly (IRE)**[34] 7359 3-8-9 **77**.............................. TonyHamilton 12 74
(Richard Fahey) *t.k.h: in tch: rdn and effrt over 2f out: edgd rt and wknd ins fnl f* **8/1**

2160 **8** ½ **Loveable Helen (IRE)**[23] 7618 3-8-12 **80**......................[1] BarryMcHugh 9 76
(Richard Fahey) *t.k.h: trckd ldrs: effrt over 2f out: chsd wnr briefly over 1f out: wknd ins fnl f* **9/1**

1666 **9** 3 **Salmon Sushi**[34] 7365 5-9-7 **85**.. JasonHart 4 75
(Tim Easterby) *s.i.s: t.k.h in rr: rdn over 2f out: sme hdwy over 1f out: nvr able to chal* **6/1**[2]

004 **10** 1 ¼ **Corton Lad**[41] 7139 6-9-6 **84**..(tp) TomEaves 6 72
(Keith Dalgleish) *trckd ldrs: ev ch over 2f out: sn rdn: wknd appr fnl f* **12/1**

02-0 **11** 4 ½ **Final Countdown**[209] 1620 5-9-7 **85**................................ TomQueally 10 64
(Rebecca Menzies) *hld up: pushed along and edgd lft over 2f out: sn outpcd: btn over 1f out* **100/1**

5600 **12** 4 ½ **Yul Finegold (IRE)**[13] 7816 6-8-10 **74**.......................... JamesSullivan 13 44
(Conor Dore) *midfield: drvn along over 4f out: wknd over 2f out* **100/1**

2-31 **13** 3 ½ **Vizier**[60] 6617 3-8-9 **77**.. GrahamGibbons 1 40
(David O'Meara) *hld up: on ins: effrt and pushed along over 2f out: drvn and wknd over 1f out: b.b.v* **5/1**[1]

3150 **14** 2 ¾ **Royal Regent**[102] 5226 4-8-12 **76**.. JoeDoyle 7 33
(Lucy Normile) *led at ordinary gallop: hdd 4f out: rdn and wknd 2f out* **25/1**

2m 7.37s (-3.03) **Going Correction** -0.175s/f (Stan)
WFA 3 from 4yo+ 4lb **14** Ran SP% **122.1**
Speed ratings (Par 105): **105,104,103,103,103 101,100,100,97,96 93,89,86,84**
CSF £47.16 CT £384.08 TOTE £7.60: £2.90, £2.50, £3.30; EX 64.70 Trifecta £642.30.
Owner S Hull, M Blades, S Hollings & D Swales **Bred** Barronstown Stud **Trained** Sheriff Hutton, N Yorks

FOCUS
An open handicap run at an sound pace, and the form is sound too.

8008 FOR THE THIRSTY NURSERY H'CAP 1m 5y (Tp)
4:15 (4:16) (Class 5) (0-75,75) 2-Y-O **£2,911** (£866; £432; £216) **Stalls** Centre

Form RPR

3366 **1** **Galahad**[17] 7750 2-8-9 **63**.. TonyHamilton 7 67
(Richard Fahey) *hld up in tch: plld out and hdwy to ld appr fnl f: pushed out* **9/1**

4210 **2** 1 ¾ **Tonahutu (IRE)**[55] 6787 2-9-3 **71**...................................... LukeMorris 6 71
(Ed Vaughan) *trckd ldrs: smooth hdwy to ld briefly over 1f out: sn drvn: kpt on fnl f: nt pce of wnr* **8/1**

400 **3** 2 **Ourmullion**[44] 7064 2-8-9 **63**.. KierenFox 1 59
(John Best) *cl up: rdn and edgd lft over 2f out: kpt on same pce fnl f* **25/1**

4403 **4** 1 **The Blues Master (IRE)**[22] 7640 2-9-3 **71**......................... JoeFanning 3 64
(Mark Johnston) *trckd ldrs: rdn and hdwy to ld over 2f out to over 1f out: outpcd fnl f* **11/2**[3]

0250 **5** 3 ¾ **Hotfill**[35] 7319 2-9-0 **68**..[1] GrahamGibbons 5 53
(David Barron) *dwlt: plld hrd in tch: rdn and outpcd over 2f out: no imp fr over 1f out* **11/4**[2]

0324 **6** 3 ½ **Upgrade**[7] 7909 2-9-7 **75**..(p) JoeyHaynes 4 52
(K R Burke) *led: rdn and hdd over 2f out: rdn and wknd over 1f out* **6/1**

045 **7** 1 ¾ **Beautiful Escape (USA)**[28] 7511 2-9-0 **73**...................(p) JoshDoyle(5) 2 47
(Saeed bin Suroor) *rrd s: t.k.h in rr: drvn and outpcd wl over 2f out: sn btn* **9/4**[1]

1m 39.32s (0.72) **Going Correction** -0.025s/f (Stan) **7** Ran SP% **112.1**
Speed ratings (Par 96): **95,93,91,90,86 83,81**
CSF £73.06 CT £1716.77 TOTE £11.80: £4.20, £3.40; EX 47.80 Trifecta £740.30.
Owner Merchants and Missionaries **Bred** W A Tinkler **Trained** Musley Bank, N Yorks

FOCUS
Plenty of unexposed types in this nursery which was run at a steady pace. A minor pb from the winner.

8009 DOOM BAR MAIDEN AUCTION STKS 7f 14y (Tp)
4:45 (4:45) (Class 6) 2-Y-O **£2,264** (£673; £336; £168) **Stalls** Centre

Form RPR

6 **1** **Killermont Street (IRE)**[43] 7099 2-9-0 0.......................... JoeFanning 2 71
(Mark Johnston) *cl up on far side of gp: led over 2f out: drifted lft over 1f out: drifted rt ins fnl f: veered lft again nr fin: jst hld on* **2/1**[1]

526 **2** nse **Espresso Freddo (IRE)**[157] 3254 2-9-5 76........................ LukeMorris 7 76
(Sir Mark Prescott Bt) *in tch nr side of gp: hdwy to press wnr over 2f out: kpt on wl u.p fnl f: jst failed* **5/2**[2]

6 **3** 2 ½ **Eponina (IRE)**[21] 7659 2-9-0 0... GrahamLee 8 65
(Ben Haslam) *hld up on nr side of gp: hdwy to chse clr ldng pair over 1f out: kpt on ins fnl f: nt pce to chal* **16/1**

6350 **4** 2 **Pepys**[37] 7286 2-9-5 64... ConnorBeasley 5 65
(Bryan Smart) *hld up in tch: rdn centre over 2f out: hdwy over 1f out: sn no imp* **4/1**[3]

003 **5** 2 ¼ **Blue Rocks**[38] 7259 2-9-5 58... KevinStott 3 59
(Lisa Williamson) *t.k.h: prom in centre: outpcd and hung lft 2f out: no imp over 1f out* **28/1**

4200 **6** 3 ½ **Bizet (IRE)**[27] 7527 2-9-5 70...(p) TomQueally 4 50
(John Ryan) *led centre to over 2f out: rdn and wknd over 1f out* **7/1**

7 3 ¼ **Satis House** 2-9-0 0.. JoeyHaynes 1 37
(Susan Corbett) *s.i.s: t.k.h: hld up on far side of gp: outpcd and hung lft over 2f out: sn btn* **100/1**

8 4 ½ **Magical Molly Joe** 2-9-0 0.. GrahamGibbons 6 26
(David Barron) *cl up centre: rdn over 2f out: wknd wl over 1f out* **10/1**

1m 26.73s (0.53) **Going Correction** -0.025s/f (Stan) **8** Ran SP% **113.8**
Speed ratings (Par 94): **95,94,92,89,87 83,79,74**
CSF £7.08 TOTE £2.80: £1.10, £1.90, £3.70; EX 8.10 Trifecta £74.60.
Owner Douglas Livingston **Bred** Ballylinch Stud **Trained** Middleham Moor, N Yorks

FOCUS
Not a strong maiden but it saw an exciting finish between two racing wide apart. The form is rated around the second, fourth and fifth.

8010 CRABBIE'S ALCOHOLIC GINGER BEER H'CAP 5f (Tp)
5:15 (5:16) (Class 5) (0-75,75) 3-Y-O+ **£3,234** (£962; £481; £240) **Stalls** Centre

Form RPR

3233 **1** **Royal Brave (IRE)**[21] 7660 5-9-2 **70**................................ PJMcDonald 3 78
(Rebecca Bastiman) *cl up centre: effrt and rdn over 1f out: led ins fnl f: hld on wl cl home* **5/1**[3]

5020 **2** hd **Pearl Acclaim (IRE)**[31] 7434 6-9-7 **75**.........................(p) BarryMcHugh 9 82
(David Nicholls) *t.k.h: cl up stands' side: rdn and overall ldr over 1f out: hdd ins fnl f: rallied: jst hld* **11/2**

2144 **3** 1 **Astrophysics**[21] 7660 4-9-5 **73**.. PaddyAspell 14 77
(Lynn Siddall) *trckd stands' side ldrs: rdn to ld briefly over 1f out: kpt on ins fnl f* **9/2**[2]

0311 **4** nk **Horsforth**[16] 7774 4-8-11 **65**...(b) ConnorBeasley 7 68
(Richard Guest) *trckd centre ldr: rdn and ev ch over 1f out: kpt on same pce ins fnl f* **4/1**[1]

1302 **5** 1 ¼ **Coiste Bodhar (IRE)**[16] 7773 5-8-13 **74**.................. NatalieHambling(7) 2 72
(Scott Dixon) *overall ldr in centre: edgd rt and hdd over 1f out: no ex ins fnl f* **22/1**

6000 **6** ½ **Imperial Legend (IRE)**[21] 7660 7-9-2 **70**.......................... PaulQuinn 13 66
(David Nicholls) *s.i.s: sn pushed along at bk of stands' side gp: hdwy over 1f out: rdn and no imp fnl f* **10/1**

3200 **7** nse **Encantar**[21] 7663 3-8-5 **66**..(b) DavidEgan(7) 5 62
(Ann Duffield) *bmpd rival repeatedly sn after s: sn bhd ldng gp centre: drvn over 2f out: kpt on fnl f: no imp* **11/1**

000 **8** 1 ¼ **Top Of The Bank**[65] 6476 3-9-5 **73**................................(p) ShaneGray 10 65
(Kristin Stubbs) *hld up on outside of stands' side gp: rdn and edgd lft wl over 1f out: sn no imp* **40/1**

0433 **9** 1 **Archimedes (IRE)**[115] 4744 3-8-13 **67**.............................(t) LukeMorris 11 55
(David C Griffiths) *hld up stands' side gp: drvn and outpcd over 2f out: n.d after* **16/1**

2000 **10** 1 **Mossgo (IRE)**[32] 7420 6-9-3 **71**..(t) KierenFox 1 55
(John Best) *cl up on outside of centre gp: outpcd and edgd lft over 2f out: btn over 1f out* **25/1**

1410 **11** nse **Noble Act**[48] 6946 3-9-3 **71**.. GrahamLee 4 55
(Rae Guest) *bmpd repeatedly sn after s: bhd and outpcd centre: nvr on terms* **12/1**

0000 **12** 1 ¾ **Captain Dunne (IRE)**[54] 6809 11-8-9 **63**..................... JamesSullivan 12 41
(Tim Easterby) *led stands' side gp to over 1f out: sn rdn and wknd* **12/1**

59.05s (-0.45) **Going Correction** -0.025s/f (Stan) **12** Ran SP% **119.6**
Speed ratings (Par 103): **102,101,100,99,97 96,96,94,93,91 91,88**
CSF £32.26 CT £137.01 TOTE £6.00: £2.30, £2.40, £1.80; EX 38.80 Trifecta £143.10.
Owner James Edgar & William Donaldson **Bred** M Fahy **Trained** Cowthorpe, N Yorks

FOCUS
A competitive contest for the grade, run at a sound pace. Ordinary handiacp form.

8011 STELLA ARTOIS H'CAP 1m 5y (Tp)
5:45 (5:45) (Class 5) (0-75,75) 3-Y-O+ **£3,234** (£962; £481; £240) **Stalls** Centre

Form RPR

1605 **1** **Pike Corner Cross (IRE)**[30] 7457 4-8-13 **72**......... CallumShepherd(5) 1 89+
(Ed de Giles) *hld up on far side of gp: smooth hdwy to ld over 1f out: rdn and qcknd clr fnl f: readily* **10/1**

5002 **2** 3 ¼ **Cadeau Magnifique**[10] 7857 4-9-1 **69**............................ TonyHamilton 3 79
(Richard Fahey) *hld up: hdwy over 2f out: effrt and chsd wnr appr fnl f: kpt on: nt pce to chal* **2/1**[1]

2600 **3** 5 **Billy Bond**[20] 7691 4-9-2 **70**..(v) DavidNolan 12 69
(Richard Fahey) *hld up: hdwy nr side of gp and ev ch over 1f out: drvn and outpcd ins fnl f* **20/1**

14 **4** hd **Visitant**[17] 7743 3-8-11 **67**.. PatrickMathers 4 64
(David Thompson) *dwlt: sn pushed along in rr: hdwy and edgd lft over 1f out: kpt on fnl f: no imp* **6/1**[2]

2210 **5** 2 ½ **Pendo**[21] 7671 5-9-6 **74**.. KierenFox 11 66
(John Best) *dwlt: sn prom: led over 2f out to over 1f out: wknd fnl f* **9/1**[3]

6006 **6** 1 ½ **Argaki (IRE)**[14] 7791 6-9-6 **74**...................................... ConnorBeasley 14 63
(Keith Dalgleish) *hld up nr side of gp: drvn and outpcd over 3f out: rallied over 2f out: wknd fnl f* **12/1**

1064 **7** nk **Southern Strife**[16] 7775 5-8-13 **67**...............................(b) DuranFentiman 7 55
(Tim Easterby) *dwlt: hung lft and outpcd in rr: hdwy over 1f out: kpt on fnl f: nvr able to chal* **18/1**

0300 **8** ¾ **Muqarred (USA)**[58] 6684 4-9-2 **70**..................................(b[1]) PJMcDonald 5 56
(Roger Fell) *prom on far side of gp: drvn over 2f out: wknd wl over 1f out* **20/1**

000 **9** nk **Crazy Tornado (IRE)**[21] 7662 3-8-8 **69**..................... ShirleyTeasdale(5) 9 54
(Keith Dalgleish) *in tch: drvn and outpcd wl over 2f out: n.d after* **25/1**

4046 **10** ½ **Gone With The Wind (GER)**[21] 7662 5-8-13 **67**...........(p) LukeMorris 2 52
(Rebecca Bastiman) *hld up midfield: drvn and outpcd 3f out: btn fnl 2f* **20/1**

1250 **11** 11 **Kiwi Bay**[14] 7796 11-9-7 **75**... TomEaves 13 34
(Michael Dods) *chsd ldrs on nr side of gp: struggling wl over 2f out: sn btn* **66/1**

4225 **12** 14 **So It's War (FR)**[31] 7436 5-9-4 **72**...........................(p) GrahamGibbons 10
(Keith Dalgleish) *led at decent gallop: hdd over 2f out: sn wknd* **6/1**[2]

1025 **13** ½ **Ravenhoe (IRE)**[13] 7813 3-9-5 **75**.. JoeFanning 6
(Mark Johnston) *cl up: ev ch over 2f out: wknd and eased wl over 1f out* **12/1**

1m 37.71s (-0.89) **Going Correction** -0.025s/f (Stan)
WFA 3 from 4yo+ 2lb **13** Ran SP% **121.3**
Speed ratings (Par 103): **103,99,94,94,92 90,90,89,89,88 77,63,63**
CSF £28.54 CT £427.83 TOTE £13.00: £3.90, £1.40, £5.50; EX 41.10 Trifecta £536.40.
Owner Mrs Yvonne Fleet **Bred** Rockfield Farm **Trained** Ledbury, H'fords

FOCUS
The pace was sound for this fair handicap. The winner impressed, but this was out of line with his profile.

8012 OLD J SPICED RUM MAIDEN STKS 6f (Tp)
6:15 (6:17) (Class 5) 3-Y-O+ **£3,234** (£962; £481; £240) **Stalls** Centre

Form RPR

24- **1** **Tadaawol**[405] 7123 3-9-5 0.. PJMcDonald 2 71+
(Roger Fell) *hld up in tch: effrt and hdwy over 1f out: led ins fnl f: pushed out: comf* **11/8**[1]

0463 **2** ¾ **Epeius (IRE)**[21] 7663 3-9-5 64.. GrahamLee 7 68
(Ben Haslam) *prom: rdn to ld over 1f out: hdd ins fnl f: kpt on: nt pce of wnr* **9/4**[2]

0600 **3** 7 **The Cheese Gang**[60] 6616 4-9-5 43................................(t) JoeyHaynes 6 46
(Susan Corbett) *upset in stalls: t.k.h: pressed ldr: led over 2f out to over 1f out: rdn and outpcd fnl f* **66/1**

4 **4** 1 ¾ **Arctic Angel (IRE)**[39] 7207 3-9-5 0................................... TomQueally 5 40
(James Fanshawe) *t.k.h: prom: effrt and rdn over 1f out: outpcd fnl f* **11/4**[3]

2360 **5** 5 **Ten Rocks**[13] 7815 3-9-5 59.. KevinStott 8 24
(Lisa Williamson) *led to over 2f out: rdn and wknd over 1f out* **14/1**

500 **6** 6 **Blynx**[25] 7583 3-9-0 38.. KierenFox 3
(David Simcock) *s.i.s: bhd and sn drvn along: struggling 1/2-way: sn btn* **40/1**

7 shd **Royboy** 3-9-5 0.. TomEaves 1 4
(Ollie Pears) *dwlt: t.k.h in rr: struggling over 3f out: sn btn* **20/1**

1m 11.42s (-1.08) **Going Correction** -0.025s/f (Stan) **7** Ran SP% **114.9**
Speed ratings (Par 103): **106,105,95,93,86 78,78**
CSF £4.76 TOTE £2.20: £1.90, £1.20; EX 5.80 Trifecta £76.40.
Owner Fell, Hamilton & Smeaton **Bred** Christopher & Annabelle Mason **Trained** Nawton, N Yorks

FOCUS
Not a strong maiden. It was run at a fair pace and the front two pulled clear. The form is rated around the runer-up's C&D latest.

8013 STRONGARM-THE NORTHERN LEGEND APPRENTICE H'CAP 6f (Tp)
6:45 (6:50) (Class 6) (0-55,55) 3-Y-0+ **£2,264** (£673; £336; £168) **Stalls** Centre

Form RPR
3423 **1** **Cadland Lad (IRE)**[13] 7815 3-8-11 **49**....................(t) JonathanFisher[(7)] 8 56
(John Ryan) *towards rr: rdn over 1f out: gd hdwy to ld ins fnl f: edgd lft: kpt on wl* **8/1**[3]

0054 **2** *1/2* **Justice Pleasing**[11] 7850 3-9-1 **51**......................(tp) BenSanderson[(5)] 12 57
(Roger Fell) *in tch: pushed along over 2f out: hdwy over 1f out: pressed wnr ins fnl f: kpt on fin* **5/1**[2]

5265 **3** *1 1/2* **Edith Weston**[20] 7693 3-9-2 **47**..(p) JordanUys 6 48
(Robert Cowell) *missed break: bhd: edgd to far rail over 2f out: hdwy over 1f out: kpt on wl fnl f: nrst fin* **12/1**

6000 **4** *nk* **Jebel Tara**[11] 7850 11-9-6 **51**..(bt) BenRobinson 7 51
(Alistair Whillans) *led 1f: cl up: drvn and edgd lft over 2f out: kpt on ins fnl f* **16/1**

3533 **5** *shd* **Dream Ally (IRE)**[29] 7489 6-9-7 **52**..........................(be) PatrickVaughan 2 52
(John Weymes) *prom: rdn along over 2f out: rallied over 1f out: kpt on ins fnl f* **10/1**

1061 **6** *nse* **Captain Scooby**[9] 7863 10-9-3 **55** 6ex.........................(b) LisaTodd[(7)] 11 55
(Richard Guest) *missed break: bhd tl hdwy over 1f out: kpt on fnl f: no imp* **12/1**

0241 **7** *3/4* **Lady Bacchus**[10] 7860 3-9-7 **52** 6ex.................................(b) DavidEgan 9 49+
(Richard Guest) *t.k.h: led after 1f: clr over 2f out: pushed along and drifted (rt) to stands' rail over 1f out: hdd ins fnl f: sn btn* **9/4**[1]

4625 **8** *2 1/4* **Ryan Style (IRE)**[20] 7694 10-9-2 **47**................................(p) MillyNaseb 5 38
(Lisa Williamson) *s.i.s: bhd: hdwy 1/2-way: effrt over 1f out: wknd ins fnl f* **10/1**

3000 **9** *3/4* **Centre Haafhd**[10] 7859 5-8-12 **48**.......................(p) StephenCummins[(5)] 3 36
(Jim Goldie) *sn towards rr: rdn and outpcd over 2f out: n.d after* **16/1**

0060 **10** *shd* **George Bailey (IRE)**[24] 7602 4-9-0 **45**...................... KieranSchofield 10 33
(Suzzanne France) *t.k.h: prom: rdn over 2f out: wknd over 1f out* **20/1**

2040 **11** *1 3/4* **Carlovian**[38] 7261 3-9-0 **48**.. PaulaMuir[(3)] 13 31
(Christopher Kellett) *towards rr on nr side of gp: drvn along over 2f out: sn btn* **12/1**

0003 **12** *5* **Whispering Wolf**[28] 7509 3-8-11 **45**..................... RobertDodsworth[(3)] 1 13
(Suzzanne France) *in tch on far side of gp: struggling over 2f out: wknd over 1f out* **33/1**

0-04 **13** *7* **Chester Deelyte (IRE)**[22] 7654 8-9-1 **49**.........(p) ManuelFernandes[(3)] 14 14
(Lisa Williamson) *bhd and outpcd on nr side of gp: struggling 1/2-way: sn btn* **25/1**

1m 12.73s (0.23) **Going Correction** -0.025s/f (Stan) **13** Ran SP% **123.1**
Speed ratings (Par 101): **97,96,94,93,93 93,92,89,88,88 86,79,78**
CSF £48.13 CT £511.56 TOTE £10.10: £2.80, £2.50, £4.20; EX 57.40 Trifecta £881.10.
Owner J Ryan **Bred** G Bassi **Trained** Newmarket, Suffolk

FOCUS
A weak handicap run at a strong pace. A small pb from the winner.
T/Jkpt: Not won. T/Plt: £140.80 to a £1 stake. Pool: £88,767.71 - 460.02 winning tickets T/Qpdt: £5.00 to a £1 stake. Pool: £12,697.18 - 1,848.39 winning tickets **Richard Young**

8014 - 8023a (Foreign Racing) - See Raceform Interactive

7946 SAINT-CLOUD (L-H)
Friday, November 18

OFFICIAL GOING: Turf: heavy

8024a PRIX BELLE DE NUIT - FONDS EUROPEEN DE L'ELEVAGE (LISTED RACE) (3YO+ FILLIES & MARES) (TURF) 1m 4f 110y
1:05 (1:05) 3-Y-0+ **£19,117** (£7,647; £5,735; £3,823; £1,911)

RPR
1 **Diamonds Pour Moi**[168] 2869 3-8-13 0........................... AlexisBadel 13 103
(Ralph Beckett) *a.p: rdn into st: chal 2f out: led fnl f: styd on wl* **225/10**

2 *2* **Jollify (IRE)**[19] 3-8-13 0....................................... StephanePasquier 4 100
(A Fabre, France) *trckd ldr: led gng wl into st: rdn and strly pressed 2f out: styd on but hdd fnl f and hld towards fin* **13/2**[2]

3 *1 1/4* **Armande (IRE)**[26] 7568 3-8-13 0....................... Pierre-CharlesBoudot 16 98
(A Fabre, France)

4 *3 1/2* **Stone Roses (FR)**[44] 7087 4-9-4 0................................. ThierryJarnet 8 90
(F Head, France) **11/1**

5 *1 1/2* **Happy Approach (FR)**[10] 7862 3-8-13 0................. AntoineHamelin 15 90
(M Nigge, France) **16/1**

6 *3/4* **Pecking Order (IRE)**[71] 6273 4-9-4 0.......................... GregoryBenoist 2 87
(James Fanshawe) *in tch: rdn and effrt in st: outpcd by ldrs fnl 2f* **14/1**

7 *1 1/2* **Contribution**[97] 5461 4-9-4 0................................ VincentCheminaud 11 84
(A Fabre, France) **13/2**[2]

8 *3* **Notte D'Oro (IRE)**[53] 4-9-4 0... CristianDemuro 7 80
(Mme Pia Brandt, France) **30/1**

9 *1* **Last Tango Inparis**[22] 7652 3-8-13 0.......................... IoritzMendizabal 3 80
(Hughie Morrison) *led: rdn and hdd into st: no ex and wknd fnl 2f: eased towards fin* **11/1**

10 *9* **Slatina (IRE)**[26] 7569 4-9-4 0......................................(p) TheoBachelot 5 64
(S Wattel, France) **78/10**[3]

11 *3/4* **Matauri Jewel (IRE)**[23] 7638 3-8-13 0............................ ThierryThulliez 6 64
(M Delzangles, France) **33/1**

12 *3 1/2* **Event Mum (GER)**[27] 3-8-13 0.............................. ClementLecoeuvre 14 59
(Waldemar Hickst, Germany) **60/1**

13 *15* **Forever Gold (GER)**[19] 7720 3-8-13 0............................ FabriceVeron 9 35
(Andreas Lowe, Germany) **92/1**

14 *4* **Rosy Blush**[44] 7087 4-9-4 0... EddyHardouin 12 26
(Mme Pia Brandt, France) **24/1**

15 *20* **Petunia (IRE)**[58] 3-8-13 0... MaximeGuyon 1
(C Laffon-Parias, France) **30/1**

16 *nk* **Tiptree (IRE)**[37] 7271 3-8-13 0.............................. ChristopheSoumillon 10
(Luca Cumani) *midfield: rdn and lost pl qckly into st: sn btn: eased and t.o* **26/1**

2m 58.55s (178.55)
WFA 3 from 4yo 6lb **16** Ran SP% **119.9**
PARI-MUTUEL (all including 1 euro stake): WIN 23.50; PLACE 6.70, 2.40, 1.80; DF111.50; SF 324.50.
Owner Pearl Bloodstock Ltd **Bred** Hall Of Fame Stud Ltd **Trained** Kimpton, Hants

7962 LINGFIELD (L-H)
Saturday, November 19

OFFICIAL GOING: Polytrack: standard
Wind: virtually nil Weather: Bright, some cloud, rain after Race 5

8025 £10 FREE AT 32RED.COM (S) STKS 1m 1y(P)
11:50 (11:50) (Class 6) 2-Y-O **£2,587** (£770; £384; £192) **Stalls** High

Form RPR
2646 **1** **Bazwind (IRE)**[36] 7319 2-8-11 66.. JFEgan 1 52
(David Evans) *settled in mid-div on inner: rdn along 4f out: styd on wl fr over 1f out to ld cl home: jst hld on* **5/4**[1]

0050 **2** *hd* **Beepeecee**[10] 7866 2-8-11 52..(p) ShaneKelly 3 52
(Richard Hughes) *hld up in last: rdn over 3f out: c to centre ent st: no imp tl qcknd up wl fnl 150yds: jst failed* **8/1**

0350 **3** *1/2* **Joyful Dream (IRE)**[21] 7688 2-8-1 60............................ HollieDoyle[(5)] 4 46
(J S Moore) *sn led: rdn along over 2f out: hdd cl home and lost 2nd post* **4/1**[2]

0000 **4** *nk* **Hollow Crown**[18] 7734 2-8-6 45.................................... ConnorBeasley 8 45
(Denis Coakley) *pressed ldrs: rdn along over 2f out: stl 2nd 1f out: wknd fnl 100yds* **33/1**

0 **5** *2* **Royal Sentiment (IRE)**[18] 7733 2-8-11 0..................... WilliamCarson 6 45
(Jamie Osborne) *pushed along leaving stalls: sn settled bhd ldrs: rdn along 4f out: rdn and one pce fr over 1f out* **8/1**

5060 **6** *shd* **Chiconomic (IRE)**[9] 7881 2-8-3 49............................(b) NoelGarbutt[(3)] 5 40
(Rae Guest) *in last trio: rdn along out wd 4f out: one pce fr over 1f out* **12/1**

0300 **7** *6* **Alligator**[10] 7866 2-8-11 59...(b) TomQueally 7 31
(Ed Dunlop) *s.s: settled on outer in rr: rdn along 4f out: no ch over 1f out: pushed out* **6/1**[3]

5460 **8** *3 3/4* **Born To Please**[68] 6412 2-8-6 53.................................[1] KieranO'Neill 2 17
(Mark Usher) *settled rr-div on inner: rdn along to hold tch 4f out: lft bhd ent st: sn hld* **20/1**

1m 37.82s (-0.38) **Going Correction** -0.05s/f (Stan) **8** Ran SP% **116.3**
Speed ratings (Par 94): **99,98,98,98,96 95,89,86**
CSF £12.60 TOTE £2.20: £1.10, £2.80, £1.60; EX 11.90 Trifecta £61.50.There was no bid for the winner. Beepeecee was bought by Mr Richard Hughes (friendly) for £6,000. Royal Sentiment was bought by Mr M D I Usher for £6,000.
Owner B McCabe, L Cullimore, A Cooke **Bred** Paul McCarthy & Julie Carlton **Trained** Pandy, Monmouths

FOCUS
A moderate juvenile seller contested by eight maidens with none coming into the race in much form. It was a messy race too and few got into it, so isn't form to be positive about.

8026 SUNBETS.CO.UK DOWNLOAD THE APP H'CAP 7f 1y(P)
12:20 (12:21) (Class 6) (0-60,60) 3-Y-O+ **£2,587** (£770; £384; £192) **Stalls** Low

Form RPR
5104 **1** **Garter (IRE)**[14] 7817 3-9-6 **60**... LukeMorris 7 68
(Charles Hills) *sn settled bhd ldrs: rdn on inner over 1f out: led 1f out: drifted to centre fnl f: pushed out cl home* **11/4**[1]

5240 **2** *1/2* **Arcanista (IRE)**[23] 7654 3-9-4 **58**................................(bt) ShaneKelly 2 65
(Richard Hughes) *settled bhd ldrs on inner: rdn over 1f out: kpt on wl to press wnr fnl f* **9/1**

0601 **3** *1 1/2* **Hipz (IRE)**[23] 7645 5-9-6 **59**..(p) LiamKeniry 6 63
(Laura Mongan) *pressed ldr and t.k.h: rdn over 1f out: kpt on fnl f* **8/1**

0450 **4** *1 1/4* **Bingo George (IRE)**[68] 6408 3-8-13 **60**......................[1] JoshuaBryan[(7)] 9 59
(Andrew Balding) *covered up in mid-div in tch: rdn 2f out: kpt on one pce* **9/2**[2]

3000 **5** *1 1/4* **Aye Aye Skipper (IRE)**[40] 7211 6-8-6 **48**...............(t) HectorCrouch[(3)] 14 45+
(Ken Cunningham-Brown) *settled in rr fr wd draw: pushed along over 2f out: rdn over 1f out: kpt on wl fnl f: nrst fin* **16/1**

6063 **6** *3/4* **Little Indian**[12] 7850 6-9-0 **53**.. ConnorBeasley 4 48
(J R Jenkins) *hld up in rr: rdn over 1f out: kpt on wl fnl f* **7/1**[3]

4600 **7** *1/2* **Pearly Queen**[32] 7442 3-9-5 **59**.. RobertWinston 10 51
(Dean Ivory) *sn led: rdn over 1f out: hdd 1f out: wknd fnl f* **33/1**

1600 **8** *nk* **Arctic Flower (IRE)**[40] 7211 3-8-13 **53**............................ DannyBrock 13 45
(John Bridger) *settled bhd ldrs on outer: t.k.h early: lost pl 1/2-way into rr-div: squeezed up ent st: sn rdn and kpt on one pce fnl f* **33/1**

2655 **9** *1/2* **Encapsulated**[23] 7654 6-9-0 **60**...................................... RhiainIngram[(7)] 12 51
(Roger Ingram) *hld up in rr-div: rdn over 2f out: no ex fnl f* **14/1**

0040 **10** *1/2* **Tilsworth Micky**[18] 7747 4-8-13 **52**................................... TonyHamilton 1 42
(J R Jenkins) *mid-div on inner: rdn over 2f out: sn hld* **10/1**

6520 **11** *1* **Hawk Moth (IRE)**[23] 7642 8-9-3 **56**...........................(b) TomMarquand 5 43
(John Spearing) *in rr-div: got lit up for a f after 1f: settled in rr after: no ex fr over 1f out* **14/1**

3220 **12** *3/4* **Cool Crescendo**[189] 2255 3-9-6 **60**............................[1] RichardKingscote 11 44
(Jonathan Portman) *settled bhd ldrs on outer: upsides over 1f out: wknd qckly fnl f* **8/1**

1m 25.45s (0.65) **Going Correction** -0.05s/f (Stan)
WFA 3 from 4yo+ 1lb **12** Ran SP% **123.8**
Speed ratings (Par 101): **94,93,91,90,88 88,87,87,86,85 84,83**
CSF £29.72 CT £183.07 TOTE £3.60: £1.80, £3.10, £2.50; EX 31.50 Trifecta £235.30.
Owner Highclere Thoroughbred Racing (Walpole) **Bred** Herbertstown House Stud **Trained** Lambourn, Berks

FOCUS
A moderate handicap, dominated by the girls, and you just had to be handy. The third is the best guide.

8027 32RED CASINO/EBF STALLIONS MAIDEN STKS 5f 6y(P)
12:50 (12:51) (Class 5) 2-Y-O **£3,363** (£1,001; £500; £250) **Stalls** High

Form RPR
0026 **1** **Roundabout Magic (IRE)**[2] 7981 2-9-5 65.................... NickyMackay 4 62+
(Simon Dow) *settled bhd ldr and t.k.h: rdn over 1f out: kpt on wl to ld fnl 110yds* **4/1**[2]

3400 **2** *1 3/4* **Gracious Tom (IRE)**[21] 7690 2-9-5 62...................................... JFEgan 6 56
(David Evans) *pressed ldr on outer: shkn up over 2f out: rdn over 1f out: kpt on fnl f* **14/1**

3243 **3** *hd* **Heavenly Cry**[9] 7884 2-9-0 50..............................(b) CallumShepherd[(5)] 5 55
(Phil McEntee) *relucant to go to post: sn led: rdn over 1f out: hdd fnl 110yds and lost 2nd post* **20/1**

3653 **4** *shd* **Sheila's Palace**[39] 7258 2-8-9 62................................... HollieDoyle[(5)] 1 50
(J S Moore) *mid-div on rail: rdn over 1f out: kpt on wl fnl f* **8/1**

2006 **5** *3/4* **Cappananty Con**[107] 5072 2-9-5 72.............................[1] RobertWinston 7 52
(Dean Ivory) *settled bhd ldrs: rdn over 1f out: kpt on fnl f* **15/2**

6 *nk* **Termsnconditions (IRE)** 2-9-5 0 .... KieranO'Neill 3 51
(Tim Vaughan) *in rr: rdn 2f out: no imp tl styd on wl fnl f: nrst fin* **22/1**

2 7 *½* **Gloriux**[14] 7818 2-9-5 0 .... MichaelJMMurphy 8 49
(Charles Hills) *chsd ldrs out wd: c wd st: rdn over 1f out: kpt on wl ins fnl f* **1/1**[1]

06 8 *3 ¼* **Delfie Lane**[10] 7867 2-9-5 0 .... ShaneKelly 2 38
(Richard Hughes) *hld up in last: rdn over 1f out: sn no imp* **7/1**[3]

58.9s (0.10) **Going Correction** -0.05s/f (Stan) **8** Ran SP% **121.2**
Speed ratings (Par 96): **97,94,93,93,92 92,91,86**
CSF £60.39 TOTE £5.20: £1.50, £3.40, £4.60; EX 69.10 Trifecta £644.50.
Owner Six Mile Hill Racing **Bred** T F Lacy **Trained** Ashtead, Surrey

FOCUS
A weak and uncompetitive maiden in which those up with the pace again dominated. With the favourite disappointing the form is very limited, but the winner was well supported.

8028 32RED.COM EBF FILLIES' H'CAP 1m 1y(P)
1:25 (1:25) (Class 4) (0-85,85) 3-Y-O+ **£6,931** (£2,074; £1,037; £519; £258) **Stalls** High

Form RPR

6543 1 **Somethingthrilling**[29] 7504 4-8-8 **79** ow1 .... JoshuaBryan(7) 1 88+
(David Elsworth) *missed break and settled in rr on inner: swtchd to outside 2f out: c wdst into st: rdn in last over 1f out: sn qcknd up and gd prog fr 1f out: led 150yds out: comf* **2/1**[1]

4503 2 *1* **Russian Radiance**[16] 7781 4-9-5 **83** .... RichardKingscote 4 89
(Jonathan Portman) *covered up in mid-div: t.k.h: rdn over 1f out: kpt on wl and ev ch ent fnl f: kpt on ins fnl f* **5/1**[2]

0144 3 *1* **Normandie Lady**[33] 7419 3-8-11 **77** .... PatrickMathers 2 80
(Richard Fahey) *in rr: rdn 2f out: kpt on wl fr over 1f out: nrst fin* **11/1**

454 4 *1* **Owaseyf (USA)**[24] 7617 3-8-13 **79** ....[1] JackMitchell 9 79
(Roger Varian) *settled bhd ldr: rdn over 2f out and led wl over 1f out: kpt on tl hdd fnl 150yds and wknd nr fin* **11/2**[3]

5246 5 *nk* **Stosur (IRE)**[22] 7671 5-8-6 **77** ....(b) DavidEgan(7) 7 78
(Gay Kelleway) *chsd ldrs on outer: shkn up over 2f out: sn rdn and kpt on one pce fnl f* **10/1**

2143 6 *nse* **Catchment**[38] 7281 3-8-11 **80** .... KieranShoemark(3) 5 80
(Amanda Perrett) *led for 3f tl settled bhd ldrs: rdn over 1f out and ev ch ent fnl f: wknd last 110yds* **5/1**[2]

6050 7 *1 ¼* **Three Gracez**[177] 2621 4-9-1 **84** .... CallumShepherd(5) 3 82
(George Scott) *in rr-div on inner: rdn 2f out: kpt on tl wknd fnl f* **20/1**

460 8 *½* **Malmostosa**[40] 7220 3-8-8 **74** ....(b) TomMarquand 8 70
(Marco Botti) *in rr on outer: rdn 2f out: one pce st* **12/1**

5560 9 *6* **Sunnua (IRE)**[24] 7623 3-8-11 **77** .... TonyHamilton 10 59
(Richard Fahey) *pressed ldr tl led after 3f: rdn over 2f out: hdd wl over 1f out: wknd qckly fnl f* **14/1**

1m 36.61s (-1.59) **Going Correction** -0.05s/f (Stan)
WFA 3 from 4yo+ 2lb **9** Ran SP% **118.6**
Speed ratings (Par 102): **105,104,103,102,101 101,100,99,93**
CSF £12.31 CT £89.80 TOTE £3.40: £2.10, £1.70, £3.70; EX 13.70 Trifecta £141.70.
Owner Trebles Holford Thoroughbreds **Bred** Trebles Holford Farm Thoroughbreds **Trained** Newmarket, Suffolk

FOCUS
A fair fillies' handicap, but they didn't go a strong pace early. The main action unfolded down the centre of the track late on and the winner was impressive.

8029 SUNBETS.CO.UK CONDITIONS STKS 7f 1y(P)
2:00 (2:00) (Class 3) 3-Y-O+ **£7,246** (£2,168; £1,084; £542) **Stalls** Low

Form RPR

0022 1 **Alfred Hutchinson**[7] 7933 8-9-0 99 ....(p) MartinHarley 4 103
(David O'Meara) *pressed ldr in 2nd: rdn 2f out: upsides ent fnl f: kpt on best and led 150yds out: rdn out* **11/4**[2]

0210 2 *½* **Seychelloise**[29] 7520 4-8-9 94 ....(b) LukeMorris 5 97
(Sir Mark Prescott Bt) *sn led: rdn over 2f out: kpt on wl whn pressed by wnr fr over 1f out: hdd 150yds out: kpt on* **7/2**[3]

2003 3 *1* **Donjuan Triumphant (IRE)**[10] 7868 3-8-13 110 .... TonyHamilton 3 98
(Richard Fahey) *hld up in rr on outer: rdn over 2f out to cl: wanting to hang lft fr over 1f out: no imp on front pair fnl f* **11/10**[1]

4414 4 *1 ½* **Basil Berry**[45] 7068 5-9-2 97 ....(b) HectorCrouch(3) 2 100
(Chris Dwyer) *hld up in 3rd on inner: shkn up to hold pce w ldrs over 2f out: rdn over 1f out on inner: ev ch ent fnl f: sn wknd* **13/2**

1m 23.05s (-1.75) **Going Correction** -0.05s/f (Stan)
WFA 3 from 4yo+ 1lb **4** Ran SP% **109.8**
Speed ratings (Par 107): **108,107,106,104**
CSF £11.98 TOTE £3.30; EX 9.20 Trifecta £14.40.
Owner R C Bond **Bred** R C Bond **Trained** Upper Helmsley, N Yorks

FOCUS
An interesting little conditions event.

8030 BETWAY H'CAP (DIV I) 6f 1y(P)
2:35 (2:36) (Class 6) (0-65,71) 3-Y-O+ **£2,587** (£770; £384; £192) **Stalls** Low

Form RPR

0211 1 **Swiss Cross**[4] 7964 9-9-8 **71** 6ex ....(tp) CallumShepherd(5) 8 81
(Phil McEntee) *hld up in rr-div: prog gng wl over 2f out: rdn over 1f out: qcknd up and led wl ins fnl f: gng on at fin* **5/2**[1]

0060 2 *2 ¼* **Keep It Dark**[14] 7811 7-8-13 **57** .... MartinHarley 7 60+
(William Knight) *sn led: rdn 2f out: kpt on wl fr over 1f out: kpt on but hdd wl ins fnl f* **12/1**

0055 3 *1* **Piazon**[26] 7584 5-8-11 **62** .... JoshuaBryan(7) 6 62
(John Butler) *hld up in 3rd on inner: t.k.h: rdn 2f out: kpt on one pce fr over 1f out* **7/1**

1300 4 *1* **Bridge Builder**[24] 7620 6-9-4 **62** ....(p) TomMarquand 10 59
(Peter Hedger) *racd in 2nd on outer: rdn along wl over 2f out: kpt on one pce fr over 1f out* **12/1**

0032 5 *1* **Krazy Paving**[29] 7509 4-8-7 **51** ....(b) KieranO'Neill 5 45
(Anabel K Murphy) *mid-div on inner: pushed along over 2f out: kpt on one pce fnl f* **7/1**

5165 6 *shd* **Compton Prince**[88] 5736 7-9-3 **61** ....(b) LukeMorris 9 55
(Milton Bradley) *chsd ldrs: rdn over 2f out: one pce fr over 1f out tl wknd ins fnl f* **12/1**

3452 7 *hd* **Cee Jay**[14] 7815 3-9-5 **63** ....(p) TomQueally 1 56
(Robert Cowell) *in rr: rdn over 2f out: no imp fr over 1f out* **6/1**[3]

0124 8 *½* **Virile (IRE)**[39] 7255 5-9-4 **65** ....(bt) EdwardGreatrex(3) 2 57
(Sylvester Kirk) *sluggish s and push along to settled in rr: rdn along over 4f out for a few strides: no imp fr over 1f out* **11/4**[2]

0200 9 *76* **Flying Sakhee**[19] 7725 3-8-7 **51** oh1 ....(p) DannyBrock 4
(John Bridger) *cocked hd lft into next stall as gates opened and completely missed break: no ch after: t.o* **33/1**

1m 11.01s (-0.89) **Going Correction** -0.05s/f (Stan) **9** Ran SP% **120.5**
Speed ratings (Par 101): **103,100,98,97,96 95,95,94,**
CSF £35.31 CT £194.04 TOTE £3.40: £1.30, £4.50, £2.60; EX 36.30 Trifecta £344.00.
Owner Steve Jakes **Bred** Lordship Stud **Trained** Newmarket, Suffolk

FOCUS
The first division of a moderate sprint handicap won by an in-form horse who confirmed his form from earlier in the week.

8031 BETWAY H'CAP (DIV II) 6f 1y(P)
3:10 (3:10) (Class 6) (0-65,65) 3-Y-O+ **£2,587** (£770; £384; £192) **Stalls** Low

Form RPR

2036 1 **Head Space (IRE)**[15] 7800 8-9-5 **63** .... RobertWinston 1 69
(David Evans) *covered up in mid-div: clsd over 2f out: rdn jst over 1f out: kpt on wl and led 110yds out: rdn out* **5/1**[3]

3333 2 *½* **Burauq**[21] 7693 4-8-7 **51** ....(b) AdamBeschizza 7 56
(Milton Bradley) *t.k.h to post: restrained in rr: rdn over 1f out: kpt on wl but nt gng pce of wnr* **10/1**

5240 3 *1 ½* **Costa Filey**[52] 6878 5-9-5 **63** .... MartinHarley 6 63
(Ed Vaughan) *t.k.h bhd ldr: rdn over 1f out: kpt on wl tl wknd nring fin* **9/2**[2]

5654 4 *nk* **Ambitious Icarus**[12] 7851 7-9-4 **62** ....(e) ConnorBeasley 5 61+
(Richard Guest) *half-rrd s and missed break: t.k.h in rr: rdn over 1f out w plenty to do: kpt on wl ins fnl f: nrst fin* **11/4**[1]

0100 5 *¾* **Pancake Day**[11] 7859 4-8-11 **55** ....(v) StevieDonohoe 2 52
(David C Griffiths) *qckly into stride and sn led: rdn wl over 1f out: kpt on wl tl hdd 110yds: wknd after* **10/1**

2060 6 *hd* **Catalinas Diamond (IRE)**[38] 7276 8-8-4 **51** oh1.(t) EdwardGreatrex(3) 3 47
(Pat Murphy) *hld up in rr on inner: prog on rail turning in: rdn over 1f out: one pce fnl f* **16/1**

2355 7 *1 ¾* **Ghost Train (IRE)**[185] 2380 7-9-1 **59** ....(p) RyanTate 4 50
(Tim McCarthy) *stood stl in stalls and missed break by 10 l: in rr: ct up after 4f: mid-div out wd 3f out: rdn over 1f out: sn no ex* **8/1**

0314 8 *nk* **Full Of Promise**[35] 7363 3-9-4 **62** .... TonyHamilton 9 52
(Richard Fahey) *racd wd in mid-div: rdn wl over 1f out: wknd fr 1f out* **8/1**

0 9 *1 ½* **Harmony Bay (IRE)**[19] 7725 3-9-7 **65** .... TomMarquand 8 51
(Sylvester Kirk) *chsd ldrs: lost pl bef st: rdn over 1f out: no imp* **7/1**

1m 12.33s (0.43) **Going Correction** -0.05s/f (Stan) **9** Ran SP% **120.3**
Speed ratings (Par 101): **95,94,92,91,90 90,88,87,85**
CSF £56.12 CT £247.38 TOTE £7.00: £2.40, £3.80, £2.00; EX 65.50 Trifecta £487.70.
Owner Caerau-Ely Racing & E Evans **Bred** Castlemartin Stud And Skymarc Farm **Trained** Pandy, Monmouths

FOCUS
The winning time was 1.32sec slower than the first division. The winner is rated near his best form of the year.

8032 BETWAY SPRINT H'CAP 5f 6y(P)
3:45 (3:46) (Class 4) (0-85,86) 3-Y-O+ **£5,175** (£1,540; £769; £384) **Stalls** High

Form RPR

0600 1 **Seve**[18] 7752 4-9-2 **80** .... MartinHarley 1 91
(Tom Dascombe) *sn led and set gd gallop: shkn up and stole a ld ent st: rdn 1f out and fnd plenty for press ins fnl f* **5/2**[1]

3633 2 *1 ¼* **Flying Bear (IRE)**[24] 7626 5-8-8 **77** .... DavidParkes(5) 3 83
(Jeremy Gask) *chsd ldrs: rdn over 1f out: kpt on ins fnl f but nt get to wnr* **8/1**

1063 3 *½* **Fang**[18] 7737 3-9-2 **80** .... ShaneKelly 10 84+
(William Jarvis) *hld up in rr: shkn up and prog on inner fr over 1f out: kpt on fnl f* **6/1**[3]

4000 4 *½* **Shackled N Drawn (USA)**[90] 5669 4-8-13 **77** .... TomMarquand 8 79
(Peter Hedger) *racd freely in rr and stl racd keenly 3f out: rdn wl over 1f out and gd prog: upsides runner-up 1f out: wknd nring fin* **25/1**

2663 5 *nse* **Just That Lord**[10] 7864 3-9-8 **86** .... RobertWinston 4 88
(Bill Turner) *chsd ldr: rdn over 2f out: kpt on one pce fr over 1f out* **9/2**[2]

2054 6 *½* **Princess Tansy**[10] 7864 4-8-6 **77** ....(b) DavidEgan(7) 6 77
(Gay Kelleway) *racd in mid-div: shkn up 2f out: rdn over 1f out: one pce fnl f* **6/1**[3]

002 7 *½* **Calypso Choir**[10] 7864 3-8-13 **80** .... EdwardGreatrex(3) 5 79+
(Sylvester Kirk) *racd wd bhd ldrs: sltly hmpd 3f out: shkn up and c wd st: hung lft fr over 1f out: no imp fnl f* **6/1**[3]

1300 8 *1* **Come On Dave (IRE)**[23] 7643 7-9-3 **81** ....(v) LiamKeniry 7 76
(John Butler) *hld up on outer in rr: t.k.h: shkn up wl over 1f out to cl: sn rdn: no imp fr 1f out* **12/1**

2166 9 *¾* **Burning Thread (IRE)**[10] 7864 9-8-8 **79** ow1 ....(b) JoshuaBryan(7) 2 71
(David Elsworth) *mid-div on inner: rdn wl over 1f out: kpt on tl wknd fr 1f out* **14/1**

260 10 *5* **Bertie Blu Boy**[178] 2584 8-8-12 **83** ....(p) JordanUys(7) 9 57
(Lisa Williamson) *hld up in rr: rdn along on inner 2f out: no prog and wknd fr over 1f out* **33/1**

57.76s (-1.04) **Going Correction** -0.05s/f (Stan) **10** Ran SP% **121.9**
Speed ratings (Par 105): **106,104,103,102,102 101,100,99,97,89**
CSF £24.73 CT £116.36 TOTE £3.60: £1.40, £2.60, £2.70; EX 25.40 Trifecta £211.40.
Owner The Blue Nuns **Bred** Mrs P Good **Trained** Malpas, Cheshire

FOCUS
A fair sprint handicap and a gamble landed.
T/Plt: £288.60 to a £1 stake. Pool: £59314.89 - 149.99 winning units. T/Qpdt: £89.70 to a £1 stake. Pool: £3484.3 - 28.74 winning units. **Cathal Gahan**

7938 WOLVERHAMPTON (A.W) (L-H)
Saturday, November 19

OFFICIAL GOING: Tapeta: standard
Wind: Light behind Weather: Overcast

8033 32RED.COM NURSERY H'CAP 5f 216y (Tp)
5:45 (5:45) (Class 5) (0-75,77) 2-Y-O **£3,557** (£1,058; £529; £264) **Stalls** Low

Form RPR

1353 1 **Big Lachie**[7] 7938 2-9-7 **75** .... GrahamGibbons 6 79+
(Jamie Osborne) *hld up: racd keenly: hdwy 2f out: rdn to ld and edgd lft ins fnl f: r.o* **3/1**[1]

0234 2 *1 ½* **Elegantly Bound (IRE)**[7] 7938 2-9-0 **68** ....(b[1]) TomEaves 5 68
(James Given) *plld hrd and prom: rdn and ev ch 1f out: styd on same pce* **7/1**

430 **3** *shd* **Things Happen**[29] 7502 2-8-13 **67**.......... JFEgan 8 66
(David Evans) *w ldr tl wnt on 2f out: rdn and hdd ins fnl f: styd on same pce* **14/1**

1600 **4** *nk* **Reign On**[28] 7549 2-8-12 **69**.......... HectorCrouch(3) 2 67+
(Ralph Beckett) *s.i.s: hld up: hdwy and nt clr run over 1f out: r.o* **11/1**

052 **5** *3/4* **Dan Troop**[18] 7748 2-9-3 **71**.......... PaulMulrennan 1 67
(Richard Fahey) *chsd ldrs: rdn over 1f out: styd on same pce ins fnl f* **4/1**[2]

0506 **6** *hd* **Heaven's Rock (IRE)**[74] 6213 2-9-1 **69**..........(v[1]) RichardKingscote 7 64
(Tom Dascombe) *s.i.s: in rr: rdn over 1f out: r.o ins fnl f: nt rch ldrs* **14/1**

064 **7** *2* **Sliceoflife**[22] 7659 2-9-3 **71**.......... LukeMorris 3 60
(Marco Botti) *prom: racd keenly: rdn over 1f out: styd on same pce fnl f* **12/1**

0620 **8** *1 3/4* **Coping Stone**[49] 6950 2-8-12 **66**.......... SeanLevey 11 50
(David Brown) *stdd sn after s: hld up: nvr on terms* **25/1**

5102 **9** *nk* **Marquee Club**[7] 7938 2-9-9 **77**.......... WilliamCarson 10 60
(Jamie Osborne) *chsd ldrs: hung rt 1/2-way: rdn over 1f out: wknd ins fnl f* **6/1**[3]

0320 **10** *1 3/4* **Secret Agent**[26] 7574 2-9-4 **72**.......... JoeFanning 4 50
(William Muir) *led: rdn and hdd 2f out: wknd ins fnl f* **9/1**

1m 13.04s (-1.46) **Going Correction** -0.25s/f (Stan) **10** Ran SP% **115.0**
Speed ratings (Par 96): **99,97,96,96,95 95,92,90,89,87**
CSF £23.84 CT £252.91 TOTE £5.10: £2.60, £2.50, £5.30; EX 24.30 Trifecta £272.20.
Owner A F Tait **Bred** Mrs C Lloyd **Trained** Upper Lambourn, Berks

FOCUS
A fair nursery. They went a decent gallop on standard Tapeta and the form is straightforward.

8034 32RED CASINO EBF STALLIONS MAIDEN STKS 1m 141y (Tp)
6:15 (6:16) (Class 5) 2-Y-O **£3,881** (£1,155; £577; £288) **Stalls** Low

Form RPR

34 **1** **Anythingtoday (IRE)**[32] 7432 2-9-5 0.......... LukeMorris 12 79
(Hugo Palmer) *prom: chsd ldr 6f out tl led over 1f out: rdn out* **7/2**[2]

0 **2** *2 1/2* **Hochfeld (IRE)**[8] 7908 2-9-5 0.......... JoeFanning 10 74
(Mark Johnston) *led: rdn and hdd over 1f out: styd on same pce ins fnl f* **25/1**

3 *1* **Emirates Flight** 2-9-0 0.......... SeanLevey 8 67
(Saeed bin Suroor) *s.i.s: hdwy to chse ldrs after 1f: rdn over 1f out: styd on same pce ins fnl f* **9/4**[1]

4 **4** *1 1/4* **Harebell (IRE)**[29] 7494 2-9-0 0.......... RichardKingscote 9 64
(Ralph Beckett) *racd keenly: w ldr early: lost 2nd 6f out: remained handy: pushed along over 3f out: no ex ins fnl f* **9/4**[1]

5 *1/2* **Ebtkaar (IRE)** 2-9-5 0.......... JackMitchell 7 68+
(Roger Varian) *pushed along in rr early: hdwy over 3f out: styd on: nt rch ldrs* **11/2**[3]

6 *2 3/4* **Naupaka** 2-9-0 0.......... TomEaves 3 57+
(Brian Ellison) *hld up: r.o ins fnl f: nvr nrr* **25/1**

06 **7** *1/2* **Poet's Charm (IRE)**[75] 6183 2-9-5 0.......... SteveDrowne 4 61+
(Simon Crisford) *hld up: plld hrd: rdn over 2f out: nvr trbld ldrs* **22/1**

6 **8** *6* **Daily Trader**[44] 7100 2-9-2 0.......... EoinWalsh(3) 5 49
(David Evans) *lost pl after 1f: pushed along over 3f out: nvr trbld ldrs* **100/1**

40 **9** *1 3/4* **American Patrol (IRE)**[58] 6704 2-9-5 0.......... JFEgan 11 45
(Neil Mulholland) *mid-div: hdwy over 5f out: rdn over 3f out: wknd over 2f out* **66/1**

00 **10** *2 1/2* **Harvest Ranger**[9] 7891 2-9-2 0.......... AlistairRawlinson(3) 6 40
(Michael Appleby) *mid-div: rdn over 3f out: sn wknd* **200/1**

60 **11** *8* **Breanski**[18] 7741 2-9-2 0.......... ShelleyBirkett(3) 1 23
(David O'Meara) *a in rr: bhd fnl 4f* **50/1**

1m 48.16s (-1.94) **Going Correction** -0.25s/f (Stan) **11** Ran SP% **116.1**
Speed ratings (Par 96): **98,95,94,93,93 90,90,85,83,81 74**
CSF £86.43 TOTE £4.60: £1.40, £5.20, £1.30; EX 57.10 Trifecta £197.40.
Owner MPH Racing - II **Bred** T Whitehead **Trained** Newmarket, Suffolk

FOCUS
A fair juvenile maiden. They went a muddling gallop and it didn't help these inexperienced horses settle down to race. The winner is rated near his debut form.

8035 SUNBETS.CO.UK CLAIMING STKS 1m 141y (Tp)
6:45 (6:45) (Class 5) 3-Y-O+ **£3,557** (£1,058; £529; £264) **Stalls** Low

Form RPR

632- **1** **Mythical Madness**[348] 8132 5-9-2 92..........(p) DaleSwift 11 85+
(Brian Ellison) *hld up: hdwy over 1f out: shkn up to ld ins fnl f: rdn out* **4/1**[2]

4012 **2** *2* **Ready (IRE)**[4] 7967 6-9-0 88..........(p) GrahamGibbons 8 78
(Ivan Furtado) *chsd ldrs: rdn and ev ch ins fnl f: styd on same pce* **5/6**[1]

1404 **3** *nse* **Italian Beauty (IRE)**[26] 7581 4-8-8 69..........[1] WilliamCarson 6 72
(John Wainwright) *chsd ldr tl led over 1f out: rdn: edgd lft and hdd ins fnl f: styd on same pce* **50/1**

2610 **4** *1 1/4* **Dana's Present**[8] 7911 7-9-0 72.......... LiamKeniry 4 75
(Tom Dascombe) *hld up: plld hrd: hdwy over 1f out: rdn and hung lft ins fnl f: r.o* **12/1**

6200 **5** *1/2* **Chelwood Gate (IRE)**[197] 2006 6-8-9 74..........(v) HectorCrouch(3) 10 72
(Patrick Chamings) *pushed along in rr early: hdwy over 5f out: rdn over 1f out: no ex wl ins fnl f* **33/1**

4404 **6** *3/4* **Lilbourne Prince (IRE)**[7] 7931 3-8-4 68.......... KatherineGlenister(7) 7 72
(David Evans) *hld up: racd keenly: hdwy and nt clr run over 1f out: swtchd rt ins fnl f: r.o* **16/1**

6460 **7** *1 1/2* **Rocket Ronnie (IRE)**[18] 7755 6-8-10 62..........(b) KevinStott 1 65
(Ed McMahon) *led: clr over 6f out tl over 3f out: rdn and hdd over 1f out: wknd ins fnl f* **25/1**

0001 **8** *3/4* **Hard To Handel**[18] 7745 4-9-2 78..........(p) JoshDoyle(5) 5 74
(David O'Meara) *plld hrd and prom: shkn up over 1f out: wknd ins fnl f* **7/1**[3]

0420 **9** *7* **Bunker Hill Lass**[9] 7889 4-8-4 49..........(p) LukeMorris 9 41
(Michael Appleby) *sn prom: rdn over 3f out: wknd 2f out* **80/1**

-006 **10** *2* **Seven Clans (IRE)**[19] 5207 4-9-0 63.......... JoeFanning 3 46
(Neil Mulholland) *hld up: shkn up over 2f out: wknd over 1f out* **22/1**

60-0 **11** *30* **Saxo Jack (FR)**[28] 7535 6-9-2 85..........[1] TimmyMurphy 2
(Sophie Leech) *hld up: shkn up and wknd over 2f out* **28/1**

1m 47.03s (-3.07) **Going Correction** -0.25s/f (Stan)
WFA 3 from 4yo+ 3lb **11** Ran SP% **118.4**
Speed ratings (Par 103): **103,101,101,100,99 98,97,96,90,88 62**
CSF £7.24 TOTE £5.40: £1.60, £1.20, £5.80; EX 10.20 Trifecta £170.50.The winner was claimed by Mr D. O'Meara for £10,000. Ready was claimed by Miss Trish Marks for £8,000.
Owner Mrs Claire Ellison **Bred** Highbank Stud Llp **Trained** Norton, N Yorks

FOCUS
A big ratings spread in this decent claimer. The two horses who stood out on form, and in the betting, filled the first two placings off a respectable gallop.

8036 SUNBETS.CO.UK DOWNLOAD THE APP H'CAP (DIV I) 7f 32y (Tp)
7:15 (7:15) (Class 5) (0-75,75) 3-Y-O+ **£3,881** (£1,155; £577; £288) **Stalls** High

Form RPR

6210 **1** **Evening Attire**[29] 7506 5-9-0 **73**.......... HollieDoyle(5) 6 86
(William Stone) *mde virtually all: rdn over 1f out: styd on* **3/1**[1]

0220 **2** *3/4* **Capolavoro (FR)**[24] 7619 5-8-10 **67**.......... EoinWalsh(3) 10 78
(Robert Cowell) *chsd ldrs: rdn over 2f out: chsd wnr fnl f: styd on* **7/1**

5332 **3** *2 1/2* **Rio's Cliffs**[37] 7301 3-9-6 **75**.......... JackMitchell 4 78
(Martyn Meade) *chsd ldrs: rdn over 1f out: no ex ins fnl f* **10/3**[2]

3355 **4** *2 1/4* **Binky Blue (IRE)**[156] 3314 4-8-12 **66**.......... LukeMorris 3 64
(Daniel Mark Loughnane) *hld up: pushed along over 2f out: hdwy over 1f out: nt rch ldrs* **14/1**

0261 **5** *shd* **The Tichborne (IRE)**[145] 3729 8-8-10 **69**..........(v) JoshDoyle(5) 2 67
(Patrick Morris) *mid-div: hdwy over 2f out: rdn over 1f out: no ex ins fnl f* **22/1**

2336 **6** *2 1/2* **Soaring Spirits (IRE)**[23] 7644 6-9-7 **75**..........(b) RobertWinston 12 66
(Dean Ivory) *chsd wnr after 1f: rdn over 2f out: lost 2nd over 1f out: wknd ins fnl f* **14/1**

0000 **7** *nk* **Harry Holland**[46] 7051 4-9-0 **68**.......... RichardKingscote 11 58
(Tom Dascombe) *s.i.s: hld up: rdn over 2f out: nvr on terms* **9/1**

4100 **8** *1/2* **Mallymkun**[39] 7253 4-8-12 **71**.......... CliffordLee(5) 1 60
(K R Burke) *s.i.s: bhd and rdn over 2f out: nvr nrr* **11/1**

5003 **9** *shd* **Specialv (IRE)**[18] 7743 3-9-3 **72**..........(p) DaleSwift 5 60
(Brian Ellison) *hld up: rdn over 1f out: n.d* **6/1**[3]

0000 **10** *1* **Harwoods Star (IRE)**[32] 7444 6-9-4 **72**.......... JFEgan 8 58
(John Butler) *s.i.s: hld up: a in rr* **66/1**

5040 **11** *2 1/4* **Our Boy Jack (IRE)**[9] 7886 7-8-13 **67**..........(p) PaulMulrennan 7 47
(Conor Dore) *hld up in tch: shkn up on outer over 2f out: wknd over 1f out* **33/1**

1m 27.02s (-1.78) **Going Correction** -0.25s/f (Stan)
WFA 3 from 4yo+ 1lb **11** Ran SP% **115.3**
Speed ratings (Par 103): **100,99,96,93,93 90,90,89,89,88 86**
CSF £23.39 CT £74.75 TOTE £4.40: £1.40, £2.60, £1.60; EX 29.10 Trifecta £133.70.
Owner Miss Caroline Scott **Bred** Howard Barton Stud **Trained** West Wickham, Cambs

FOCUS
The first division of a fair handicap. They went a decent gallop and the form is sound.

8037 SUNBETS.CO.UK DOWNLOAD THE APP H'CAP (DIV II) 7f 32y (Tp)
7:45 (7:46) (Class 5) (0-75,75) 3-Y-O+ **£3,881** (£1,155; £577; £288) **Stalls** High

Form RPR

0000 **1** **Mr Christopher (IRE)**[31] 7457 4-9-4 **72**..........(p) RichardKingscote 11 82
(Tom Dascombe) *chsd ldr tl led over 1f out: rdn and edgd lft ins fnl f: styd on* **10/1**

3544 **2** *3/4* **Inaam (IRE)**[21] 7687 3-9-1 **70**.......... TonyHamilton 4 77
(Richard Fahey) *plld hrd and prom: rdn over 1f out: chsd wnr ins fnl f: r.o* **4/1**[1]

0043 **3** *3/4* **Malaysian Boleh**[12] 7852 6-9-0 **68**.......... TomEaves 5 74
(Brian Ellison) *hld up: hdwy over 1f out: rdn and hung lft ins fnl f: r.o* **4/1**[1]

0010 **4** *2 1/4* **Arize (IRE)**[30] 7485 3-8-11 **66**.......... SeanLevey 7 65
(David Brown) *sn led: rdn and hdd over 1f out: no ex ins fnl f* **16/1**

5505 **5** *1* **Personal Touch**[32] 7434 7-9-4 **75**.......... AlistairRawlinson(3) 2 72
(Michael Appleby) *hld up: rdn over 1f out: r.o ins fnl f: nt rch ldrs* **11/2**[2]

2003 **6** *hd* **Qortaaj**[18] 7738 3-8-13 **68**..........(t) JohnFahy 9 64+
(David Loughnane) *rrd s and lost many l: stl last wl over 1f out: r.o u.p ins fnl f: nrst fin* **4/1**[1]

5106 **7** *nse* **Pick A Little**[21] 7691 8-9-2 **70**.......... TimmyMurphy 6 67
(Michael Blake) *chsd ldrs: rdn over 1f out: wknd ins fnl f* **22/1**

6046 **8** *1/2* **Light From Mars**[45] 7066 11-9-3 **71**..........(p) LukeMorris 1 66
(Ronald Harris) *hld up: pushed along and sme hdwy over 1f out: no ex ins fnl f* **9/1**[3]

3530 **9** *3/4* **Doctor Bong**[26] 7577 4-8-13 **67**..........(b) StevieDonohoe 8 60
(Grace Harris) *s.i.s: hld up: rdn over 1f out: nvr on terms* **66/1**

4056 **10** *shd* **Perfect Alchemy (IRE)**[30] 7485 5-9-3 **71**.......... JoeFanning 10 64
(Patrick Chamings) *chsd ldrs: rdn over 1f out: wknd ins fnl f* **10/1**

4005 **11** *10* **Spryt (IRE)**[16] 7778 4-8-13 **67**..........(p) PaulMulrennan 12 33
(Conor Dore) *hld up: plld hrd: rdn over 2f out: wknd over 1f out* **33/1**

1m 26.98s (-1.82) **Going Correction** -0.25s/f (Stan)
WFA 3 from 4yo+ 1lb **11** Ran SP% **118.2**
Speed ratings (Par 103): **100,99,98,95,94 94,94,93,92,92 81**
CSF £49.38 CT £193.64 TOTE £12.40: £3.40, £2.00, £1.90; EX 63.90 Trifecta £272.90.
Owner Mrs M C Antrobus **Bred** Denis McDonnell **Trained** Malpas, Cheshire

FOCUS
The second division of a fair handicap. They went a decent gallop once again and the winning time was remarkably similar.

8038 BETWAY MIDDLE DISTANCE H'CAP 1m 4f 50y (Tp)
8:15 (8:16) (Class 6) (0-60,61) 3-Y-O+ **£2,911** (£866; £432; £216) **Stalls** Low

Form RPR

203 **1** **Stonecoldsoba**[21] 7692 3-9-2 **58**.......... RobertWinston 3 66
(David Evans) *prom: racd keenly: shkn up over 1f out: rdn to ld and hung lft wl ins fnl f: styd on* **11/4**[1]

50U2 **2** *1* **Shining Romeo**[7] 7937 4-9-11 **61**.......... LukeMorris 2 67
(Denis Quinn) *chsd ldrs: rdn to ld over 1f out: hdd and unable qck wl ins fnl f* **4/1**[2]

6005 **3** *nk* **Hold Hands**[24] 7614 5-9-5 **55**.......... RichardKingscote 5 61
(Brendan Powell) *s.i.s: hld up: hdwy 2f out: sn rdn: styd on* **4/1**[2]

3056 **4** *1* **Paddy's Rock (IRE)**[29] 7515 5-9-4 **54**.......... PaddyAspell 7 58
(Lynn Siddall) *hld up: hdwy and nt clr run over 1f out: nt rchd ldrs* **20/1**

0040 **5** *shd* **Frozon**[7] 7943 3-9-1 **57**.......... SamJames 8 61
(Marjorie Fife) *plld hrd and prom: stdd and lost pl over 10f out: hdwy over 1f out: r.o* **33/1**

5405 **6** *1 1/4* **Filament Of Gold (USA)**[77] 6143 5-9-7 **57**..........(p) TomEaves 11 59
(Roy Brotherton) *hld up: drvn along over 4f out: nt clr run and swtchd lft ins fnl f: r.o: nt rchd ldrs* **18/1**

0601 **7** *1 1/2* **Ali Bin Nayef**[24] 7262 4-9-4 **54**.......... ConnorBeasley 12 54
(Michael Wigham) *hld up: rdn over 1f out: nt clr run ins fnl f: nt trbld ldrs* **11/2**[3]

0035 **8** *nk* **King Olav (UAE)**[109] 4979 11-9-7 **60**.......... GeorgeDowning(3) 1 59
(Tony Carroll) *led 4f: chsd ldr: rdn to ld wl over 1f out: sn hdd: wknd ins fnl f* **25/1**

605 **9** *2* **Senor George (IRE)**[31] 7464 9-9-4 **54**.......... GrahamGibbons 9 50
(Simon Hodgson) *sn prom: rdn over 1f out: hmpd and wknd ins fnl f* **10/1**

-540 **10** 1 ¾ **Black Hole Sun**[39] 7256 4-9-2 **52**.................................. WilliamCarson 6 48
(Tony Carroll) *w ldr 4f: remained handy: rdn over 3f out: wknd ins fnl f* **40/1**

0000 **11** 3 **Flying Power**[35] 7367 8-9-2 **52**.................................(p) PaulMulrennan 10 46
(John Norton) *prom: racd keenly: led 8f out: rdn and hdd wl over 1f out: wknd fnl f* **10/1**

2m 39.17s (-1.63) **Going Correction** -0.25s/f (Stan)
WFA 3 from 4yo+ 6lb **11** Ran SP% **119.5**
Speed ratings (Par 101): **95,94,94,93,93 92,91,91,90,88 86**
CSF £13.16 CT £44.38 TOTE £3.10: £1.70, £1.90, £2.30; EX 15.10 Trifecta £105.40.

Owner Spiers & Hartwell Ltd **Bred** Mrs S A Hunt **Trained** Pandy, Monmouths

FOCUS
A moderate middle-distance handicap. They went a muddling gallop, but the right horses still came to the fore. The winner posted a minor pb.

8039 BETWAY MARATHON DISTANCE H'CAP 2m 119y (Tp)
8:45 (8:46) (Class 6) (0-60,60) 3-Y-O+ **£2,911** (£866; £432; £216) **Stalls** Low

Form RPR

0056 **1** **Social Media**[18] 7746 3-8-10 **53**... LukeMorris 7 58
(Ed Dunlop) *hld up in tch: rdn over 2f out: chsd ldr over 1f out: hung lft and styd on u.p to ld post* **4/1**[1]

200 **2** *hd* **Hier Encore (FR)**[78] 6090 4-9-4 **55**.......................... HectorCrouch(3) 10 60
(David Menuisier) *chsd ldr 14f out tl led over 3f out: rdn over 1f out: hdd post* **7/1**

0501 **3** ¾ **Delagoa Bay (IRE)**[18] 7739 8-9-8 **59**...................... EdwardGreatrex(3) 13 63
(Sylvester Kirk) *hld up: hdwy over 1f out: r.o: nt rch ldrs* **9/2**[2]

4563 **4** 2 ¼ **Sakhra**[35] 7367 5-8-12 **46**.. GrahamGibbons 9 47
(Mark Brisbourne) *prom: rdn over 2f out: styd on same pce ins fnl f* **9/1**

6620 **5** *nk* **Dream Serenade**[25] 7592 3-8-6 **52** ow3............................ TimClark(3) 1 51
(Michael Appleby) *chsd ldrs: nt clr run over 2f out: rdn over 1f out: no ex ins fnl f* **11/1**

642P **6** 1 **Graceful Lady**[37] 7309 3-8-12 **55**...................................... JackMitchell 8 55
(Robert Eddery) *hld up: hdwy 1/2-way: chsd ldr over 2f out tl rdn over 1f out: no ex ins fnl f* **11/2**[3]

5036 **7** 1 ½ **Lineman**[102] 5267 6-9-10 **58**...(b) SeanLevey 6 56
(Sarah Hollinshead) *hld up: hdwy u.p over 1f out: nt trble ldrs* **12/1**

0-50 **8** *nk* **Crystalise (IRE)**[24] 7625 4-9-12 **60**.................................. LiamKeniry 4 57
(Robert Stephens) *hld up in tch: nt clr run over 2f out: rdn over 1f out: wknd ins fnl f* **33/1**

1204 **9** 2 ¼ **Lorelei**[131] 4197 4-9-12 **60**.. TomMarquand 3 55
(William Muir) *hld up: hdwy and nt clr run over 1f out: rdn and no ex ins fnl f* **8/1**

0000 **10** 1 ¾ **Smoky Hill (IRE)**[24] 7614 7-9-10 **58**................................ JoeyHaynes 12 51
(Tony Carroll) *hld up: pushed along over 3f out: nt clr run over 2f out: nvr on terms* **20/1**

-600 **11** 2 **Lacey**[35] 7367 7-9-8 **56**...(b) KieranO'Neill 2 46
(Sarah Hollinshead) *s.i.s: hld up: nt clr run over 2f out: n.d* **33/1**

000 **12** 12 **Nightswift**[38] 7280 4-9-5 **53**.. TimmyMurphy 5 29
(James Evans) *led 1f: chsd ldrs: rdn over 2f out: sn wknd* **28/1**

3100 **13** 33 **Tarakkom (FR)**[150] 3528 4-9-10 **58**............................ WilliamCarson 11
(Peter Hiatt) *led at stdy pce after 1f: qcknd over 5f out: rdn and hdd over 3f out: wknd over 2f out* **28/1**

3m 38.37s (-5.33) **Going Correction** -0.25s/f (Stan)
WFA 3 from 4yo+ 9lb **13** Ran SP% **120.7**
Speed ratings (Par 101): **102,101,101,100,100 99,99,99,97,97 96,90,75**
CSF £30.14 CT £132.20 TOTE £4.60: £1.90, £3.00, £2.00; EX 39.40 Trifecta £207.30.

Owner Cliveden Stud **Bred** Cliveden Stud **Trained** Newmarket, Suffolk

FOCUS
A moderate staying handicap. They went a muddling tempo once again and plenty got trapped for room in a packing field, but three horses with sound enough claims beforehand came clear of their field. The bare form can't be rated much higher tha this.

8040 BETWAY H'CAP 5f 20y (Tp)
9:15 (9:15) (Class 5) (0-70,70) 3-Y-O+ **£3,881** (£1,155; £577; £288) **Stalls** Low

Form RPR

1521 **1** **Zipedeedodah (IRE)**[7] 7945 4-9-2 **70**.............................(t) JoshDoyle(5) 6 79+
(Joseph Tuite) *led 1f: chsd ldr tl led again 2f out: pushed out* **11/4**[1]

5035 **2** 1 ¼ **Captain Lars (SAF)**[12] 7851 7-9-4 **70**.........................(p) NoelGarbutt(3) 9 75+
(Derek Shaw) *hld up: hdwy over 1f out: rdn and hung lft ins fnl f: r.o* **15/2**

0245 **3** ¾ **Powerful Dream (IRE)**[7] 7945 3-9-6 **69**........................ RobertWinston 4 71
(Ronald Harris) *chsd ldrs: rdn over 1f out: styd on* **7/1**[3]

1363 **4** 1 **Equijade**[28] 7534 3-9-2 **65**.. LiamKeniry 8 63
(Robert Stephens) *trckd ldrs: plld hrd: rdn and edgd lft over 1f out: styd on same pce ins fnl f* **10/1**

4304 **5** *hd* **Billyoakes (IRE)**[14] 7811 4-9-5 **68**....................................(p) LukeMorris 7 66
(Charlie Wallis) *hld up in tch: rdn and swtchd lft over 1f out: styd on same pce ins fnl f* **7/1**[3]

0001 **6** 2 ¼ **Dreams Of Glory**[33] 7420 8-9-0 **66**........................... EdwardGreatrex(3) 5 56
(Ron Hodges) *w ldr tl led 4f out: rdn and hdd 2f out: wknd ins fnl f* **12/1**

0006 **7** ½ **Big Amigo (IRE)**[36] 7325 3-8-13 **62**............................ GrahamGibbons 2 50+
(Daniel Mark Loughnane) *pushed along in rr early: r.o ins fnl f: nvr nrr* **5/1**[2]

6606 **8** *shd* **Quality Art (USA)**[7] 7945 8-8-7 **56**.................................... JoeyHaynes 10 43
(Simon Hodgson) *chsd ldrs: rdn over 1f out: wknd ins fnl f* **20/1**

0030 **9** ¾ **Sarabi**[24] 7626 3-8-11 **67**...(tp) NatalieHambling(7) 3 52
(Scott Dixon) *hld up: plld hrd: rdn and swtchd rt over 1f out: nvr on terms* **7/1**[3]

0000 **10** 3 ½ **Los Cerritos (SWI)**[24] 7612 4-8-12 **61**.......................... SteveDrowne 1 33
(Sophie Leech) *a in rr* **50/1**

1m 0.91s (-0.99) **Going Correction** -0.25s/f (Stan) **10** Ran SP% **116.1**
Speed ratings (Par 103): **97,95,93,92,91 88,87,87,86,80**
CSF £23.64 CT £134.82 TOTE £3.70: £1.40, £2.90, £2.50; EX 29.90 Trifecta £136.00.

Owner D M Synergy & Mark Wellbelove **Bred** Tally-Ho Stud **Trained** Lambourn, Berks

FOCUS
A modest sprint handicap. The favourite proved utterly dominant.

T/Plt: £9.30 to a £1 stake. Pool: £127213.61 - 9939.77 winning units. T/Qpdt: £2.80 to a £1 stake. Pool: £12360.91 - 3240.3 winning units. **Colin Roberts**

8041 - (Foreign Racing) - See Raceform Interactive

7806 LYON PARILLY (R-H)
Saturday, November 19

OFFICIAL GOING: Turf: heavy

8042a PRIX DU GRAND CAMP (LISTED RACE) (3YO+) (TURF) 1m 4f
1:50 (12:00) 3-Y-O+ **£19,117** (£7,647; £5,735; £3,823; £1,911)

RPR

1 **Do Re Mi Fa Sol (FR)**[66] 6497 3-8-8 0........................ FranckBlondel 15 102
(P Decouz, France) **19/2**

2 5 ½ **Prince Nomad (FR)**[48] 7002 5-9-3 0........................... ThierryThulliez 14 96
(Eric Saint-Martin, France) **49/1**

3 *nse* **Cafe Royal (GER)**[21] 7718 5-9-3 0................................ MickaelForest 1 96
(Carina Fey, France) **13/1**

4 1 **Against Rules (FR)**[7] 4-9-0 0.. MaximeGuyon 10 91
(S Wattel, France) **31/5**[2]

5 1 ¾ **Baz (FR)**[37] 7312 6-9-3 0...(p) FabriceVeron 12 92
(F-H Graffard, France) **27/1**

6 *nse* **Madernia (IRE)**[45] 7087 4-9-0 0.................................... FrankPanicucci 7 88
(C Laffon-Parias, France) **54/1**

7 5 ½ **Al Haram (FR)**[32] 7456 3-8-11 0.................................. GregoryBenoist 8 83
(E Lellouche, France) **8/1**[3]

8 5 ½ **Coisa Boa (IRE)**[11] 7861 4-9-0 0................................. AntoineHamelin 3 71
(J E Hammond, France) **55/1**

9 1 ½ **Up Todate Du Casse (FR)**[224] 8-9-3 0.................. IoritzMendizabal 11 71
(F Plouganou, France) **32/1**

10 ¾ **Norse King (FR)**[147] 3683 7-9-6 0..................................... AlexisBadel 6 73
(Mme M Bollack-Badel, France) **11/1**

11 4 ½ **Spirit's Revench (FR)**[21] 7718 6-9-3 0........................ CristianDemuro 13 63
(P Demercastel, France) **17/1**

12 ¾ **Be Famous (GER)**[192] 4-9-3 0.. TonyPiccone 5 62
(Frau S Steinberg, Germany) **11/1**

13 4 ½ **Litigant**[27] 7569 8-9-3 0....................................... Pierre-CharlesBoudot 4 55
(Joseph Tuite) **11/5**[1]

14 11 **Laseen (IRE)**[45] 7089 5-9-0 0.. TheoBachelot 2 34
(J-P Gauvin, France) **9/1**

15 3 **Sylvanes (IRE)**[26] 4-9-0 0... MickaelBerto 9 29
(A De Royer-Dupre, France) **46/1**

2m 51.47s (17.96)
WFA 3 from 4yo+ 6lb **15** Ran SP% **119.5**
PARI-MUTUEL (all including 1 euro stake): WIN 10.50; PLACES: 3.50, 10.10, 4.60; DF: 221.10; SF: 366.00.
Owner Ecurie Seyssel **Bred** Haras De Saint-Voir **Trained** France

8043 - 8045a (Foreign Racing) - See Raceform Interactive

7981 CHELMSFORD (A.W) (L-H)
Monday, November 21

OFFICIAL GOING: Polytrack: standard
Wind: medium, half behind Weather: cloudy and dull, brightening up after race 3

8046 TOTEPLACEPOT RACING'S FAVOURITE BET NURSERY H'CAP 1m (P)
1:50 (1:53) (Class 6) (0-60,60) 2-Y-O **£3,234** (£962; £481; £240) **Stalls** Low

Form RPR

0424 **1** **Booshbash (IRE)**[7] 7954 2-9-6 **59**.................................... MartinHarley 7 62
(Ed Dunlop) *hld up in rr: rdn and hdwy to chse clr ldr over 1f out: r.o wl to ld 50yds: sn in command* **4/1**[2]

000 **2** 1 **How's Lucy**[23] 7696 2-8-11 **50**.. DannyBrock 6 51
(Jane Chapple-Hyam) *pressed ldr tl pushed into ld ent fnl 2f: rdn clr over 1f out: wandered and drvn ins fnl f: hdd and no ex 50yds out* **16/1**

060 **3** ¾ **Reynardo De Silver**[43] 7187 2-9-2 **58**....................(v[1]) HectorCrouch(3) 5 57
(Gary Moore) *midfield: effrt u.p over 1f out: wnt 3rd 100yds out and styd on wl towards fin: nt rchd ldrs* **14/1**

6000 **4** 1 **Babouska**[28] 7578 2-8-7 **49**.. NathanEvans(3) 13 46+
(Michael Easterby) *dwlt: in tch towards rr: swtchd lft and effrt wd over 2f out: hdwy over 1f out: wnt 3rd ent fnl f: kpt on but lost 3rd 100yds out: nvr gng to rch ldrs* **33/1**

0620 **5** 2 ¾ **Auric Goldfinger (IRE)**[11] 7881 2-9-4 **57**..................... TomMarquand 11 47
(Richard Hannon) *dwlt: t.k.h in rr: swtchd rt and effrt on outer 2f out: hdwy 1f out: styd on ins fnl f: nvr trbld ldrs* **16/1**

5004 **6** 6 **Dangerous Ends**[18] 7777 2-9-0 **53**............................... StevieDonohoe 4 30
(Brett Johnson) *in tch in midfield: effrt 2f out: sn struggling and outpcd: wknd fnl f* **20/1**

0004 **7** 1 ½ **Our Boy John (IRE)**[12] 7866 2-9-2 **55**........................ TonyHamilton 10 28
(Richard Fahey) *chsd ldrs: rdn ent fnl 2f: lost pl and btn over 1f out: wknd fnl f* **8/1**

4000 **8** 3 ½ **Echoism (IRE)**[9] 7941 2-9-5 **58**...................................... JoeFanning 1 23
(Mark Johnston) *broke wl: led tl ent fnl 2f: lost pl and btn over 1f out: wknd fnl f* **5/1**[3]

0660 **9** 2 ¾ **Charlie Chaplin (GER)**[19] 7768 2-9-7 **60**.........................[1] JackMitchell 3 19
(Robert Eddery) *s.i.s: sn pushed along in rr: rdn over 2f out: no hdwy and wl btn over 1f out* **7/2**[1]

0660 **10** 6 **Like Minds**[23] 7690 2-8-3 **45**... AaronJones(3) 8
(David Brown) *midfield: rdn and lost pl over 2f out: bhd over 1f out* **25/1**

4003 **11** 2 ½ **Tael O' Gold**[13] 7854 2-9-3 **56**.................................... ConnorBeasley 2
(Iain Jardine) *chsd ldrs: u.p and struggling ent fnl f: lost pl qckly over 1f out: sn bhd* **6/1**

3064 **P** **Ultimat Power (IRE)**[11] 7881 2-8-7 **46**......................(b) AdamBeschizza 9
(Mark Hoad) *sn dropped to rr and bustled along: eased after 2f and p.u 4f out* **20/1**

1m 41.1s (1.20) **Going Correction** -0.05s/f (Stan) **12** Ran SP% **120.8**
Speed ratings (Par 94): **92,91,90,89,86 80,79,75,72,66 64,**
CSF £63.00 CT £833.04 TOTE £5.90: £1.90, £5.20, £4.70; EX 93.30 Trifecta £2163.40.
Owner Mohammed Jaber **Bred** David & George Mullins **Trained** Newmarket, Suffolk

FOCUS
The track was power harrowed to four inches and gallop master finished to two inches. All race distances as advertised. A very modest nursery where the winner did well to win from a poor track position. The runner-up has been rated in keeping with her debut effort.

8047 @TOTEPOOLRACING FOLLOW US ON TWITTER NURSERY H'CAP 7f (P)
2:25 (2:26) (Class 5) (0-75,75) 2-Y-O **£4,528** (£1,347; £673; £336) **Stalls** Low

Form RPR
4611 **1** **Acertwo**[23] 7690 2-9-4 **72** JFEgan 4 82
(Joseph Tuite) *mde virtually all: rdn and fnd ex ent fnl f: in command and r.o wl fnl f: comf* **2/1**[1]

5011 **2** 3 ¾ **Alice's Dream**[20] 7749 2-8-12 **71** (b) CliffordLee(5) 3 71
(Marco Botti) *trckd ldng pair: effrt to chse wnr wl over 1f out: drvn and unable qck ent fnl f: wl hld but kpt on for clr 2nd fnl f* **11/4**[2]

352 **3** 5 **Millie's Kiss**[23] 7689 2-9-4 **75** LouisSteward(3) 1 64
(Philip McBride) *dwlt: in tch in rr: effrt over 2f out: rdn to chse ldng pair over 1f out: no imp and btn 1f out: wl hld and eased wl ins fnl f* **2/1**[1]

2006 **4** 8 **Bizet (IRE)**[3] 8009 2-9-2 **70** (v[1]) MartinHarley 2 35
(John Ryan) *sn w wnr and swtchd rt over 6f out: drvn and no rspnse over 2f out: dropped to last and wl btn over 1f out: eased ins fnl f* **6/1**[3]

1m 27.53s (0.33) **Going Correction** -0.05s/f (Stan) **4** Ran SP% **107.6**
Speed ratings (Par 96): **96,91,86,76**
CSF £7.55 TOTE £2.30; EX 5.60 Trifecta £5.10.
Owner B R Tregurtha **Bred** Mickley Stud & J Kent **Trained** Lambourn, Berks

FOCUS
Small on numbers but a competitive enough nursery, with the taking winner completing a hat-trick. Another step forward from the winner.

8048 TOTEQUADPOT FOUR PLACES IN FOUR RACES MAIDEN STKS 1m 2f (P)
3:00 (3:02) (Class 5) 3-Y-O+ **£5,175** (£1,540; £769; £384) **Stalls** Low

Form RPR
3-30 **1** **Hairdryer**[42] 7214 3-9-5 69 LiamKeniry 5 77
(Andrew Balding) *t.k.h: chsd ldr for 2f: trckd ldrs after but nvr settled: nt clr run over 2f out: effrt to ld and edge rt over 1f out: rdn and asserted ins fnl f: r.o wl: comf* **9/4**[1]

3423 **2** 1 ½ **Polymnia**[26] 7619 3-8-9 69 HollieDoyle(5) 1 69
(Richard Hannon) *hld up in tch in midfield: clsd on outer over 2f out: rdn to chal over 1f out: outpcd u.p ins fnl f: styd on same pce fnl 100yds* **5/2**[2]

3 2 ½ **Vogueatti (USA)** 3-8-9 0 CliffordLee(5) 4 64
(Marco Botti) *in tch in midfield: swtchd lft and effrt over 2f out: chsd ldng pair 1f out: styd on same pce and no imp after* **9/2**

050- **4** 6 **Twilight Angel**[663] 310 8-9-4 41 (v[1]) JFEgan 3 52?
(Emma Owen) *led: drifted rt and rdn wl over 1f out: sn hdd: 4th and wknd ins fnl f* **66/1**

3063 **5** 5 **Hepplewhite**[50] 6528 3-9-5 75 JackMitchell 8 47
(Robert Eddery) *chsd ldr after 2f: rdn ent fnl 2f: outpcd whn n.m.r over 1f out: sn btn and wknd fnl f* **3/1**[3]

5 **6** 2 **Imasumaq (IRE)**[21] 7727 3-9-0 0 LukeMorris 7 38
(Marco Botti) *in tch in last pair but niggled along at times: rdn 4f out: outpcd u.p and btn wl over 1f out: eased ins fnl f* **8/1**

6000 **7** 48 **Royal Mighty**[53] 6900 3-9-0 39 DannyBrock 6
(Jane Chapple-Hyam) *in tch in midfield: rdn over 3f out: dropped to rr and wl btn 2f out: lost tch and eased ins fnl f* **66/1**

0 **8** 10 **Zam I Am**[138] 4027 3-9-2 0 EoinWalsh(3) 2
(Christine Dunnett) *stdd s: hld up in rr: rdn over 2f out: sn btn: t.o and eased fnl f* **100/1**

2m 7.56s (-1.04) **Going Correction** -0.05s/f (Stan)
WFA 3 from 8yo 4lb **8** Ran SP% **117.6**
Speed ratings (Par 103): **102,100,98,94,90 88,50,42**
CSF £8.52 TOTE £3.20: £1.60, £1.10, £1.30; EX 8.60 Trifecta £32.70.
Owner Sir A Ferguson, P Done, G Mason **Bred** D D & Mrs J P Clee **Trained** Kingsclere, Hants

FOCUS
A modest maiden dominated by those at the head of the market. The fourth finished close enough for the value of the form to be doubted.

8049 TOTETRIFECTA PICK THE 1,2,3 H'CAP 1m (P)
3:30 (3:33) (Class 2) (0-105,102) 3-Y-O+**£22,641** (£6,737; £3,367; £1,683) **Stalls** Low

Form RPR
5445 **1** **Pactolus (IRE)**[26] 7608 5-8-5 **86** [1] AaronJones(3) 1 96
(Stuart Williams) *mde all and dictated gallop: rdn and kicked clr over 1f out: in command and r.o wl fnl f* **6/1**[3]

0033 **2** 2 ¼ **Chevallier**[60] 6710 4-8-8 **86** LukeMorris 13 91
(Archie Watson) *chsd ldrs: effrt to chse wnr wl over 1f out: kpt on u.p but no imp ins fnl f* **25/1**

3021 **3** hd **Steel Train (FR)**[16] 7825 5-9-3 **95** DanielTudhope 6 99+
(David O'Meara) *restless in stalls: hld up in rr: clsd and nt clr run jst over 1f out: swtchd rt and forced way out 1f out: r.o wl u.p ins fnl f* **5/1**[2]

6205 **4** ½ **Georgian Bay (IRE)**[9] 7933 6-9-3 **95** (vt) JoeyHaynes 5 98
(K R Burke) *hld up in tch towards rr: rdn and hdwy over 1f out: kpt on wl ins fnl f: no threat to wnr* **10/1**

0545 **5** 1 **Third Time Lucky (IRE)**[37] 7354 4-9-9 **101** TonyHamilton 14 102+
(Richard Fahey) *stdd and dropped in bhd after s: hld up in last: pushed along: clsng and switching rt over 1f out: hdwy and swtchd rt and then lft ins fnl f: kpt on wl: nvr threatened ldrs* **7/1**

0000 **6** shd **Solar Deity (IRE)**[31] 7524 7-9-5 **102** (p) CharlieBennett(5) 3 103
(Jane Chapple-Hyam) *hld up in tch in midfield: effrt 2f out: squeezed for room over 1f out: hdwy ins fnl f: styd on: nvr threatened wnr* **25/1**

1460 **7** 1 ¼ **Philba**[30] 7530 4-8-11 **92** (tp) AlistairRawlinson(3) 8 90
(Michael Appleby) *t.k.h: wl in tch in midfield: effrt u.p over 1f out: unable qck and styd on same pce fnl f* **100/1**

1001 **8** 1 ¼ **My Target (IRE)**[9] 7933 5-8-12 **90** ConnorBeasley 7 85
(Michael Wigham) *t.k.h: chsd ldrs tl restrained bk into midfield after 2f: effrt over 1f out: no imp and kpt on same pce fnl f* **9/2**[1]

5452 **9** ½ **Rousayan (IRE)**[38] 7316 5-8-7 **88** ShelleyBirkett(3) 4 82+
(David O'Meara) *in tch in midfield: effrt whn squeezed for room and hmpd over 1f out: rdn and kpt on ins fnl f: no threat to wnr* **10/1**

0011 **10** hd **Fort Bastion (IRE)**[18] 7778 7-8-12 **90** RobertWinston 10 83
(Brian Ellison) *in tch towards rr: effrt over 1f out: no imp and nudged rt 1f out: kpt on same pce after* **7/1**

0200 **11** 1 **Lunar Deity**[9] 7933 7-9-5 **97** AdamBeschizza 11 88
(Stuart Williams) *hld up towards rr: effrt and no imp over 1f out: nvr trbld ldrs* **25/1**

-220 **12** ¾ **Claim The Roses (USA)**[45] 7121 5-9-3 **95** MartinHarley 2 84
(Ed Vaughan) *chsd ldrs: rdn and unable qck over 1f out: btn 1f out: wknd ins fnl f* **7/1**

1433 **13** shd **Father Bertie**[23] 7699 4-9-0 **92** (tp) JasonHart 12 81
(Tim Easterby) *chsd ldr tl over 1f out: lost pl u.p and wknd ins fnl f* **20/1**

6204 **14** 9 **Abareeq**[26] 7608 3-8-9 **89** JoeFanning 9 56
(Mark Johnston) *midfield but stuck wd: rdn and dropped to rr over 1f out: bhd and hung lft ins fnl f* **14/1**

1m 37.66s (-2.24) **Going Correction** -0.05s/f (Stan)
WFA 3 from 4yo+ 2lb **14** Ran SP% **128.8**
Speed ratings (Par 109): **109,106,106,106,105 104,103,102,101,101 100,100,99,90**
CSF £162.42 CT £851.95 TOTE £7.30: £2.40, £5.50, £2.40; EX 181.60 Trifecta £1674.70.
Owner T W Morley & Mrs J Morley **Bred** Tom McDonald **Trained** Newmarket, Suffolk

FOCUS
A fiercely competitive handicap on paper where, as so often round here, a pace-setter took the spoils. The winner has been rated to the better view of his form.

8050 TOTESWINGER THREE WAYS TO WIN H'CAP 5f (P)
4:00 (4:01) (Class 2) (0-105,109) 3-Y-O+**£22,641** (£6,737; £3,367; £1,683) **Stalls** Low

Form RPR
1030 **1** **Encore D'Or**[150] 3606 4-8-12 **96** ShaneGray 10 108+
(Robert Cowell) *hld up in tch towards rr: clsd and nt clr run 1f out: gap opened and qcknd through to ld wl ins fnl f: r.o wl* **20/1**

2031 **2** 1 **Aleef (IRE)**[24] 7668 3-8-4 **91** ShelleyBirkett(3) 8 99
(David O'Meara) *led: rdn and fnd ex over 1f out: clr 1f out: hdd and no ex wl ins fnl f* **7/2**[1]

5U00 **3** 1 ¼ **Huntsmans Close**[30] 7537 6-8-9 **93** LukeMorris 6 97
(Robert Cowell) *taken down early: in tch in midfield: effrt over 1f out: kpt on u.p ins fnl f* **25/1**

3030 **4** shd **Bowson Fred**[72] 6327 4-9-0 **101** NathanEvans(3) 7 105
(Michael Easterby) *taken down early: chsd ldrs: wnt 2nd 2f out: rdn over 1f out: drvn and kpt on same pce ins fnl f: lost 2 pls fnl 75yds* **5/1**[2]

0102 **5** ½ **Doctor Sardonicus**[26] 7610 5-8-11 **95** MartinHarley 12 97
(David Simcock) *chsd ldrs: rdn and unable qck over 1f out: wknd ins fnl f* **5/1**[2]

4533 **6** hd **Kimberella**[9] 7932 6-9-6 **104** ConnorBeasley 9 105
(David Nicholls) *in tch in midfield: effrt over 1f out: kpt on u.p ins fnl f: nvr enough pce to chal* **6/1**[3]

1355 **6** dht **Guishan**[54] 6878 6-8-5 **92** ow2 TimClark(3) 1 93
(Michael Appleby) *taken down early: in tch in midfield: effrt on inner over 1f out: kpt on same pce ins fnl f* **20/1**

005 **8** nk **Quatrieme Ami**[26] 7610 3-8-8 **92** [1] TomMarquand 5 92
(Philip McBride) *hld up in tch in midfield: effrt and n.m.r over 1f out: swtchd lft and hdwy ins fnl f: kpt on: no threat to ldrs* **9/1**

0110 **9** ¾ **Upavon**[42] 7221 6-7-11 **88** (t) MillyNaseb(7) 3 85
(Stuart Williams) *rrd as stalls opened nd slowly away: detached in last: hdwy on inner over 1f out: kpt on ins fnl f: swtchd rt and nt clr run towards fin* **12/1**

1600 **10** 3 ¼ **Sir Maximilian (IRE)**[160] 3244 7-9-8 **109** GeorgeDowning(3) 2 95
(Ian Williams) *a towards rr: effrt over 1f out: no imp: nvr trbld ldrs* **7/1**

000 **11** ½ **Brother Tiger**[12] 7864 7-8-6 **90** JamesSullivan 11 74
(David C Griffiths) *taken down early: sn outpcd and stuck wd in midfield: bhd 1f out* **33/1**

0010 **12** ½ **Bosham**[80] 6080 6-9-0 **98** (b) JoeFanning 4 80
(Michael Easterby) *taken down early: chsd ldr tl 2f out: unable qck u.p over 1f out: wknd ins fnl f* **8/1**

58.44s (-1.76) **Going Correction** -0.05s/f (Stan) **12** Ran SP% **127.5**
Speed ratings (Par 109): **112,110,108,108,107 107,107,106,105,100 99,98**
CSF £91.85 CT £1847.81 TOTE £31.10: £6.70, £1.60, £6.40; EX 168.00 Trifecta £5455.30.
Owner J Morley, G Johnson & Newsells Park Stud **Bred** Newsells Park Stud **Trained** Six Mile Bottom, Cambs

FOCUS
A fiercely run sprint, with an impressive come-from-behind performance by the winner. It's been rated on the positive side.

8051 TOTEEXACTA FORECAST THE 1ST AND 2ND H'CAP 2m (P)
4:30 (4:35) (Class 4) (0-85,82) 3-Y-O+ **£8,086** (£2,406; £1,202; £601) **Stalls** Low

Form RPR
0014 **1** **Velvet Revolution**[26] 7625 3-8-10 **73** MartinHarley 2 88+
(Marco Botti) *hld up in midfield: wnt 3rd and travelling strly over 3f out: led over 1f out: sn nudged clr: eased wl ins fnl f: v easily* **9/4**[1]

6522 **2** 5 **Aldreth**[14] 7846 5-9-3 **74** NathanEvans(3) 1 80+
(Michael Easterby) *hld up in last pair: nt clr run over 3f out: rdn and hdwy jst over 2f out: styd on u.p to chse clr wnr 100yds out: nvr a threat* **3/1**[2]

000- **3** 3 **Yes Daddy (IRE)**[19] 5526 8-9-7 **75** (v[1]) LukeMorris 10 76
(Robert Stephens) *in tch in midfield: hdwy to chse ldr over 4f out: rdn to ld over 1f out: sn hdd and outpcd by wnr: lost 2nd and wknd fnl 100yds* **33/1**

5211 **4** 1 ¾ **Stamford Raffles**[14] 7846 3-8-8 **76** CharlieBennett(5) 5 75
(Jane Chapple-Hyam) *hld up in midfield: effrt over 2f out: hdwy under presure over 1f out: no ch w wnr but plugged on ins fnl f* **9/4**[1]

062 **5** 1 ½ **Lord Napier (IRE)**[143] 3845 3-9-5 **82** DannyBrock 3 80
(John Ryan) *hld up in midfield: effrt over 1f out: drvn over 1f out: no ch and plugged on same pce ins fnl f* **20/1**

000 **6** 1 **Teak (IRE)**[18] 7150 9-9-6 **74** (vt) StevieDonohoe 6 70
(Ian Williams) *bustled up to ld: hdd after 2f: chsd ldr tl led again 5f out: rdn over 2f out: hdd over 1f out: wknd fnl f* **12/1**[3]

6310 **7** 5 **Gleese The Devil (IRE)**[38] 7320 5-10-0 **82** TonyHamilton 4 72
(Richard Fahey) *hld up in rr: short lived effrt 2f out: no imp and wl btn 1f out* **14/1**

/002 **8** 1 ½ **Chartbreaker (FR)**[33] 4535 5-10-0 **82** (p) LiamKeniry 9 71
(Chris Gordon) *dwlt: sn bustled along and rcvrd to chse ldrs after 1f: rdn and lost pl whn n.m.r over 3f out: bhd over 1f out* **33/1**

1304 **9** 13 **Stormin Tom (IRE)**[44] 7158 4-9-7 **78** RachelRichardson(3) 8 51
(Tim Easterby) *chsd ldr tl led after 2f: hdd 5f out: rdn over 2f out: bhd over 1f out: wknd fnl f* **20/1**

3m 27.75s (-2.25) **Going Correction** -0.05s/f (Stan)
WFA 3 from 4yo+ 9lb **9** Ran SP% **116.3**
Speed ratings (Par 105): **103,100,99,98,97 96,94,93,87**
CSF £8.77 CT £163.53 TOTE £3.00: £1.10, £1.40, £6.10; EX 9.70 Trifecta £179.70.
Owner Heart of the South Racing & Partner **Bred** Newsells Park Stud **Trained** Newmarket, Suffolk
■ Plymouth Sound was withdrawn. Price at time of withdrawal 20/1. Rule 4 does not apply.

FOCUS
A competitive-looking staying contest that was run at a decent pace and turned into a procession by the progressive winner. The runner-up has been rated better than ever.

8052 CHRISTMAS PARTIES AT CCR H'CAP 7f (P)
5:00 (5:07) (Class 4) (0-80,86) 3-Y-O+ **£8,086** (£2,406; £1,202; £601) **Stalls** Low

Form RPR
1006 **1** **Pearl Spectre (USA)**[6] 7965 5-9-1 **79**.................. CallumShepherd(5) 12 90
(Phil McEntee) *chsd ldrs: effrt to ld and rdr dropped whip ent fnl f: r.o wl and a in command after* **33/1**
3-21 **2** *1 3/4* **Rockley Point**[39] 7311 3-8-10 **75**.................................... CliffordLee(5) 6 81
(Paul D'Arcy) *in tch in midfield: effrt in 6th 2f out: swtchd lft and chsd ldrs over 1f out: kpt on but no imp ins fnl f: wnt 2nd last strides* **7/1**[3]
3412 **3** *hd* **My Dad Syd (USA)**[24] 7662 4-9-1 **74**......................(v) RobertWinston 7 80
(Ian Williams) *sn led: rdn over 1f out: edgd rt and hdd ent fnl f: kpt on same pce ins fnl f: lost 2nd last strides* **5/1**[1]
1122 **4** *hd* **Titan Goddess**[24] 7671 4-9-0 **73**.. ShaneKelly 4 78
(Mike Murphy) *hld up towards rr: n.m.r 2f out: hdwy u.p 1f out: styd on wl fnl 100yds: nt rch ldrs* **12/1**
2141 **5** *nk* **Rock Warbler (IRE)**[17] 7797 3-8-7 **67**.........................(t) JamesSullivan 3 71
(Oliver Greenall) *hld up in midfield: swtchd rt and effrt over 1f out: kpt on but hung lft u.p ins fnl f* **8/1**
4526 **6** *1/2* **Mezzotint (IRE)**[16] 7813 7-9-7 **80**................................ MartinHarley 13 83
(Lee Carter) *hld up in last pair: nt clr run 2f out: swtchd lft and hdwy over 1f out: kpt on ins fnl f: nvr threatened ldrs* **16/1**
2343 **7** *1 1/4* **Panther Patrol (IRE)**[26] 7617 6-8-11 **75**......................(v) HollieDoyle(5) 8 75
(Eve Johnson Houghton) *wl in tch in midfield: hdwy to chse ldrs and rdn over 2f out: struggling to qckn and shifted rt jst 1f out: kpt on same pce after* **16/1**
2100 **8** *1/2* **Mon Beau Visage (IRE)**[7] 7958 3-9-5 **79**.................. DanielTudhope 11 77
(David O'Meara) *wl in tch in midfield: clsd to chse ldrs over 2f out: effrt over 1f out: struggling to qckn whn squeezed for room amd snatched up 1f out: kpt on but no threat to wnr ins fnl f* **9/1**
0021 **9** *1/2* **Russian Reward (IRE)**[11] 7886 4-9-3 **76**...................... JackMitchell 16 73
(Amanda Perrett) *chsd ldr: drvn and ev ch over 1f out: no ex and edgd rt 1f out: wknd ins fnl f* **8/1**
0001 **10** *1/2* **Kalk Bay (IRE)**[7] 7958 9-9-10 **86** 6ex........................(t) NathanEvans(3) 10 82
(Michael Easterby) *hld up towards rr: effrt u.p over 1f out: kpt on and edgd lft ins fnl f: nvr trbld ldrs* **10/1**
5236 **11** *1 1/2* **Bell Heather (IRE)**[17] 7796 3-9-3 **77**............................ TonyHamilton 14 68
(Richard Fahey) *hld up towards rr: effrt over 1f out: kpt on ins fnl f but nvr threatening ldrs* **33/1**
5566 **12** *nk* **Welliesinthewater (IRE)**[39] 7308 6-9-3 **79**..................(v) NoelGarbutt(3) 5 70
(Derek Shaw) *t.k.h: hld up in tch in midfield: effrt and no rspnse over 1f out: wl hld and plugged on same pce ins fnl f* **6/1**[2]
6500 **13** *3* **Showing Off (IRE)**[18] 7781 3-9-3 **77**............................ ConnorBeasley 2 59
(Michael Wigham) *hld up in rr: effrt over 1f out: no imp: n.d* **25/1**
3065 **14** *3/4* **Heartsong (IRE)**[34] 7430 7-8-7 **66**.................................... LukeMorris 9 47
(John Gallagher) *in tch in midfield: rdn over 1f out: sn lost pl: bhd fnl f* **66/1**
2564 **15** *3/4* **Let's Twist**[7] 7958 4-9-1 **74**..(b) ShaneGray 1 53
(Kristin Stubbs) *chsd ldrs: nt clr run on inner and shuffled bk over 2f out: rdn over 1f out: sn btn: bhd and eased ins fnl f* **5/1**[1]

1m 25.51s (-1.69) **Going Correction** -0.05s/f (Stan)
WFA 3 from 4yo+ 1lb **15** Ran SP% **132.1**
Speed ratings (Par 105): **107,105,104,104,104 103,102,101,101,100 98,98,95,94,93**
CSF £266.75 CT £1426.93 TOTE £41.50: £11.30, £3.10, £2.20; EX 545.60 Trifecta £7961.00.
Owner Steve Jakes **Bred** Estate Of Edward P Evans **Trained** Newmarket, Suffolk

FOCUS
A competitive finale that was won comprehensively by an outsider. A small pb from the winner.
T/Jkpt: Not Won. T/Plt: £512.40 to a £1 stake. Pool: £89145.58 - 126.98 winning units. T/Qpdt: £58.90 to a £1 stake. Pool: £10904.77 - 136.88 winning units. **Steve Payne**

7889 SOUTHWELL (L-H)
Tuesday, November 22
8053 Meeting Abandoned - Waterlogged track

8061 - (Foreign Racing) - See Raceform Interactive

7970 CHANTILLY (R-H)
Tuesday, November 22
OFFICIAL GOING: Polytrack: standard; turf: heavy

8062a PRIX HEROD (LISTED RACE) (2YO) (TURF) 7f
1:50 (12:00) 2-Y-O **£23,897** (£9,558; £7,169; £4,779; £2,389)

RPR
1 **Red Onion**[80] 6154 2-8-13 0...(p) ThierryThulliez 6 96
(C Lerner, France) **43/5**
2 *hd* **Charly Nova (FR)**[166] 2-8-10 0 ow1.............................. OlivierPeslier 10 93
(F Rossi, France) **63/10**[3]
3 *nse* **Charm Appeal (FR)**[21] 2-8-9 0.. AlexisBadel 7 91
(H-F Devin, France) **11/2**[2]
4 *3/4* **City Light (FR)**[33] 7491 2-8-13 0.................................... TheoBachelot 3 94
(S Wattel, France) **13/2**
5 *1 1/4* **Thrust Home (IRE)**[21] 7757 2-8-9 0..........................(b) IoritzMendizabal 5 86
(Y Durepaire, France) **14/1**
6 *1/2* **Mums The Word**[74] 6289 2-8-9 0...................................... ThierryJarnet 1 85
(Richard Fahey) *trckd ldr on inner: rdn 2f out: kpt on despite nt clrest of runs but probably nt pce to chal anyway* **15/1**
7 *3/4* **Sanjita (IRE)**[30] 2-8-9 0.. MaximeGuyon 8 83
(C Laffon-Parias, France) **10/1**
8 *nk* **Lucky Mistake (IRE)**[36] 7407 2-8-13 0........................ CristianDemuro 4 87
(J Reynier, France) **32/1**
9 *1/2* **Capchop (FR)**[23] 7721 2-8-13 0........................... Pierre-CharlesBoudot 2 85
(P Sogorb, France) **12/5**[1]
10 *10* **Re Run (IRE)**[35] 7432 2-8-13 0.........................(b1) ChristopheSoumillon 9 60
(Richard Fahey) *a in rr: no imp u.p st: eased appr fnl f* **8/1**

1m 30.1s (4.00) **10** Ran SP% **118.4**
WIN (incl. 1 euro stake): 9.60; PLACES: 2.60, 2.00, 2.10; DF: 40.90; SF: 95.20.
Owner Ecurie Salabi **Bred** T De La Heronniere & Mme M-J Goetschy **Trained** France

7973 KEMPTON (A.W) (R-H)
Wednesday, November 23
OFFICIAL GOING: Polytrack: standard to slow
Wind: Moderate, across (towards stands) Weather: Overcast

8063 LEWIS HUMPHRIS PALACE MAIDEN STKS 1m 2f (P)
4:25 (4:27) (Class 5) 2-Y-O **£2,911** (£866; £432; £216) **Stalls** Low

Form RPR
44 **1** **Azam**[28] 7621 2-9-5 0...[1] NickyMackay 9 80
(John Gosden) *trckd ldr: led wl over 2f out: shkn up and sn clr: unchal* **9/4**[1]
4 **2** *6* **Stone The Crows**[21] 7770 2-9-2 0........................ KieranShoemark(3) 11 69+
(Roger Charlton) *trckd ldrs: outpcd in 5th wl over 2f out: prog on outer after: kpt on to win battle for 2nd last strides: no ch w wnr* **6/1**
3 *shd* **Quality Moment (IRE)** 2-9-0 0.. KevinStott 8 64+
(Saeed bin Suroor) *hld up in midfield: outpcd over 2f out: prog on inner after: drvn to chse wnr over 1f out: no imp: kpt on but lost 2nd last strides* **5/1**[3]
6 **4** *4* **Hertford Dancer**[36] 7441 2-9-0 0................................ DavidProbert 12 57
(John Gosden) *prom: rdn to chse clr ldng pair wl over 2f out: tried to chal for 2nd over 1f out: one pce after* **10/1**
00 **5** *1* **Tomsamcharlie**[33] 7503 2-9-2 0.................................. HectorCrouch(3) 1 60
(Gary Moore) *s.i.s: hld up in rr: last over 3f out: gd prog over 2f out: styd on fnl f: no ch but shaped w promise* **100/1**
00 **6** *2 3/4* **Casado (IRE)**[47] 7125 2-9-5 0... KierenFox 2 55
(John Best) *led: clr w wnr whn hdd wl over 2f out: lost 2nd and wknd over 1f out* **100/1**
7 *3* **Soghan (IRE)** 2-9-5 0... SeanLevey 4 49
(John Gosden) *settled in midfield: outpcd wl over 2f out: pushed along and kpt on at same pce after: sme promise* **7/2**[2]
8 *5* **King Of Scotland (FR)** 2-9-5 0................................... RobertWinston 7 40
(Hughie Morrison) *s.s: hld up in last: brief effrt 4f out: no ch whn wd bnd 2f out* **50/1**
00 **9** *1* **Twiston Shout (IRE)**[12] 7907 2-9-5 0............................. TomMarquand 5 39
(Richard Spencer) *dwlt: a in rr: rdn and struggling 3f out* **250/1**
10 *2* **Inspector (IRE)** 2-9-5 0...[1] JimmyFortune 3 35
(Hugo Palmer) *chsd ldrs but rn in snatches: wknd qckly over 2f out* **25/1**
0 **11** *1 1/2* **Katabatika**[32] 7543 2-9-0 0.. RichardKingscote 6 27
(Hughie Morrison) *chsd ldng pair to wl over 2f out: wknd rapidly* **16/1**
3 **12** *hd* **Style And Grace (IRE)**[22] 7741 2-9-0 0............................ RobertTart 10 27
(John Gosden) *trapped out wd: dropped to rr 1/2-way: no ch over 2f out* **10/1**

2m 6.85s (-1.15) **Going Correction** -0.025s/f (Stan) **12** Ran SP% **116.2**
Speed ratings (Par 96): **103,98,98,94,94 91,89,85,84,83 81,81**
CSF £15.54 TOTE £3.10: £1.20, £2.00, £1.90; EX 14.70 Trifecta £69.60.
Owner Al Mirqab Racing **Bred** Newsells Park Stud **Trained** Newmarket, Suffolk

FOCUS
The pace picked up from a fair way out and they finished well strung out. The runner-up has been rated similar to his debut.

8064 100% PROFIT BOOST AT 32REDSPORT.COM H'CAP 7f (P)
4:55 (4:58) (Class 6) (0-65,65) 3-Y-O+ **£2,264** (£673; £336; £168) **Stalls** Low

Form RPR
5324 **1** **Summersault (IRE)**[28] 7612 5-9-5 **64**......................... WilliamCarson 11 71
(Jamie Osborne) *mde all: drvn 2f out: hld on u.p fnl f* **17/2**
0500 **2** *1* **Freddy With A Y (IRE)**[77] 6237 6-8-12 **62**................ DavidParkes(5) 1 66
(Paul Burgoyne) *awkward s: chsd ldrs on inner: pushed along fr over 2f out: kpt on fr over 1f out: snatched 2nd last stride despite jockey nt appearing to have a whip* **16/1**
1400 **3** *nse* **Sakhee's Jem**[23] 7725 3-9-5 **65**................................(p) TomMarquand 3 68
(Gay Kelleway) *prom: chsd wnr wl over 2f out: drvn and a jst hld fr over 1f out: lost 2nd last stride* **20/1**
666 **4** *1/2* **Sexton Blake (IRE)**[23] 7725 3-9-2 **62**...............................[1] ShaneKelly 6 64
(Gary Moore) *wl plcd bhd ldrs: rdn 2f out: nt qckn over 1f out: one pce after* **6/1**[3]
4000 **5** *1 1/4* **Kingthistle**[30] 7577 3-9-4 **64**.. StevieDonohoe 5 62
(Ian Williams) *s.i.s and rousted early: towards rr on inner: drvn and prog over 2f out: kpt on same pce u.p fr over 1f out* **5/1**[2]
1240 **6** *1 1/4* **Virile (IRE)**[4] 8030 5-9-3 **65**..................................(bt) CallumShepherd(3) 2 61
(Sylvester Kirk) *t.k.h early: hld up in midfield: rdn and no imp ldrs fr 2f out* **7/1**
0013 **7** *1/2* **Showtime Blues**[22] 7751 4-8-11 **61**........................(p) CharlieBennett(5) 8 56
(Jim Boyle) *mostly chsd wnr to wl over 2f out: steadily fdd* **8/1**
2250 **8** *1* **New Rich**[27] 7654 6-9-5 **64**...(v) JohnFahy 9 56
(Eve Johnson Houghton) *t.k.h: sn prog on wd outside to chse ldrs: nt qckn 2f out: wknd fnl f* **16/1**
0000 **9** *1/2* **Quintus Cerialis (IRE)**[22] 7738 4-9-6 **65**...................[1] TimmyMurphy 14 56
(Karen George) *t.k.h: hld up in rr: shkn up and limited prog fr over 2f out* **66/1**
1200 **10** *nse* **Charava (IRE)**[16] 7852 4-8-9 **61**.................................(v) PaulaMuir(7) 10 52
(Patrick Holmes) *hld up wl in rr: nudged along over 2f out: kpt on one pce* **50/1**
560 **11** *nk* **Popeswood (IRE)**[64] 6656 4-9-6 **65**............................ RobertWinston 12 55
(Lee Carter) *hld up wl in rr: shuffled along in last pl over 2f out: no great prog* **14/1**
4432 **12** *1 3/4* **Only Ten Per Cent (IRE)**[28] 7611 8-9-4 **63**.................. PaddyAspell 13 48
(J R Jenkins) *nvr bttr than midfield: rdn over 2f out: wknd over 1f out* **12/1**
4525 **13** *4* **Many Dreams (IRE)**[23] 7725 3-9-1 **64**........................ HectorCrouch(3) 7 37
(Mark Usher) *nvr gng wl and a towards rr: rdn and no prog 3f out: eased fnl f* **4/1**[1]

1m 26.19s (0.19) **Going Correction** -0.025s/f (Stan)
WFA 3 from 4yo+ 1lb **13** Ran SP% **119.4**
Speed ratings (Par 101): **97,95,95,95,93 92,91,90,90,90 89,87,83**
CSF £134.79 CT £2724.14 TOTE £7.20: £2.10, £5.40, £7.60; EX 141.60 Trifecta £6957.60.
Owner Mrs F Walwyn & Melbourne 10 Racing **Bred** Dr Dean Harron & Kemal Kurt **Trained** Upper Lambourn, Berks

FOCUS
A modest handicap dominated by the front-running winner. Straightforward form to rate.

8065 32RED.COM / BRITISH STALLION STUDS EBF MAIDEN STKS (DIV I) 6f (P)
5:25 (5:26) (Class 5) 2-Y-O **£3,234** (£962; £481; £240) **Stalls** Low

Form RPR
0 **1** **Munro**[14] 7867 2-9-5 0 RichardKingscote 1 75+
(Ralph Beckett) *mde all: drifted lft fr 2f out whn rdn: kpt on wl and a in command* **7/2**[2]
53 **2** *1* **Kings Academy**[22] 7748 2-9-5 0 JimmyFortune 4 72
(Paul Cole) *chsd wnr: brought wd in st and ended against nr side rail: rdn 2f out: kpt on but a hld* **9/4**[1]
3 *¾* **Fivetwoeight** 2-9-5 0 DanielMuscutt 11 70+
(Peter Chapple-Hyam) *dwlt: wl in rr: gd prog over 2f out: rdn to dispute 2nd over 1f out: kpt on same pce fnl f* **9/1**
00 **4** *2 ¼* **Nuncio**[14] 7867 2-9-2 0 KieranShoemark(3) 12 62
(Roger Charlton) *settled in rr: pushed along 3f out: kpt on fr 2f out and rdn to take ins fnl f: n.d* **14/1**
04 **5** *hd* **Five Star Frank**[95] 5631 2-9-5 0 JohnFahy 9 62
(Eve Johnson Houghton) *t.k.h early: sn hld up in midfield: lost pl over 2f out: stl looked green but kpt on fr over 1f out* **13/2**
40 **6** *nk* **Queens Royale**[18] 7819 2-9-0 0 RobertWinston 10 56
(Michael Appleby) *chsd ldrs: rdn over 2f out: no imp ldrs and one pce after* **20/1**
7 *1* **Ocean Promise (USA)** 2-9-0 0 ShaneKelly 3 53
(Richard Hughes) *prom: rdn over 2f out: one pce after and n.d fnl f* **33/1**
8 *5* **Roman Navigator (IRE)** 2-9-5 0 LukeMorris 2 42
(Marco Botti) *chsd ldrs: rdn over 2f out: wknd fnl f* **11/2**[3]
00 **9** *3 ¾* **Lily Cliff**[36] 7441 2-9-0 0 TomQueally 8 25
(Paul D'Arcy) *hld up in rr: sme prog over 2f out and w chsng gp over 1f out: sn wknd* **100/1**
60 **10** *2* **Four Candles (IRE)**[20] 7776 2-9-0 0 PaddyBradley(5) 6 23
(Philip McBride) *nvr bttr than midfield: no imp ldrs 2f out: wknd over 1f out* **33/1**
0 **11** *½* **Arya Stark**[30] 7576 2-8-11 0 GeorgeDowning(3) 5 17
(Tony Carroll) *a in rr: struggling over 2f out* **100/1**
12 *½* **Beach Dancer (IRE)** 2-9-5 0 (b[1]) WilliamCarson 7 20
(William Knight) *n.m.r s: tk fierece hold and hld up in last pair: nvr a factor* **16/1**

1m 13.11s (0.01) **Going Correction** -0.025s/f (Stan) **12** Ran SP% **116.9**
Speed ratings (Par 96): **98,96,95,92,92 92,90,84,79,76 75,75**
CSF £11.09 TOTE £4.40: £1.60, £1.20, £2.70; EX 14.50 Trifecta £118.90.
Owner Emma Capon & Mrs Simon Marsh **Bred** K Snell **Trained** Kimpton, Hants

FOCUS
A fairly modest maiden.

8066 32RED.COM / BRITISH STALLION STUDS EBF MAIDEN STKS (DIV II) 6f (P)
5:55 (5:55) (Class 5) 2-Y-O **£3,234** (£962; £481; £240) **Stalls** Low

Form RPR
343 **1** **Al Reeh (IRE)**[49] 7064 2-9-5 80 LukeMorris 1 81
(Marco Botti) *mde all: urged along 2f out: pressed and drvn fnl f and sn edgd lft: jst hld on* **8/11**[1]
3 **2** *hd* **Saluti (IRE)**[14] 7867 2-9-5 0 JackMitchell 10 80
(Amanda Perrett) *chsd wnr: rdn 2f out: trying to chal whn impeded 150yds out: styd on after and clsng at fin* **3/1**[2]
4 **3** *7* **Enfolding (IRE)**[118] 4805 2-9-5 0 TomQueally 12 59+
(James Fanshawe) *slowly away: t.k.h: hld up in rr: pushed along over 2f out and hanging: styd on pleasingly fnl f to take 3rd last strides* **10/1**[3]
0 **4** *½* **Zambezi Queen (IRE)**[180] 2637 2-8-11 0 CallumShepherd(3) 7 53
(Paul Cole) *t.k.h: chsd ldng trio: outpcd over 2f out: kpt on same pce to chal for 3rd last strides* **25/1**
00 **5** *hd* **Mellow**[21] 7763 2-9-0 0 RobertWinston 2 52
(Hughie Morrison) *chsd ldng pair: outpcd fr over 2f out: n.d after: lost 3rd last strides* **33/1**
0 **6** *shd* **Sentinel**[18] 7818 2-9-5 0 StevieDonohoe 4 57+
(Charlie Fellowes) *hld up in midfield: pushed along and outpcd over 2f out: shkn up over 1f out: styd on to press for a pl nr fin* **10/1**[3]
0 **7** *1 ½* **Canadian Royal**[7] 7975 2-9-5 0 [1] SeanLevey 9 53
(Stuart Williams) *t.k.h: hld up in midfield: outpcd over 2f out: pushed along and one pce after: possible improver* **50/1**
06 **8** *2 ¼* **Socrates**[7] 7975 2-9-5 0 TimmyMurphy 3 46
(Daniel Kubler) *appeared awkward s: t.k.h: hld up in rr: nudged along and no prog fnl 2f: possible improver* **33/1**
9 *1 ½* **Jannia** 2-9-0 0 ShaneKelly 11 36
(Eve Johnson Houghton) *v.s.a: a wl in rr: no ch fnl 2f* **50/1**
10 *3 ½* **Mister Freeze (IRE)** 2-9-5 0 [1] JohnFahy 5 31
(Clive Cox) *t.k.h: hld up in midfield: wknd over 2f out* **33/1**
11 *1 ¼* **Seeing Things (IRE)** 2-9-0 0 PaddyBradley(5) 6 27
(Philip McBride) *a in rr: bhd fnl 2f* **50/1**

1m 13.0s (-0.10) **Going Correction** -0.025s/f (Stan) **11** Ran SP% **119.6**
Speed ratings (Par 96): **99,98,89,88,88 88,86,83,81,76 75**
CSF £2.77 TOTE £1.60: £1.10, £1.30, £2.40; EX 3.30 Trifecta £9.20.
Owner Raed El Youssef **Bred** Oghill House Stud **Trained** Newmarket, Suffolk

FOCUS
The first two had this between them from passing the intersection and they finished well clear. It was the quicker of the two divisions, but only by 0.11sec.

8067 32RED ON THE APP STORE H'CAP 6f (P)
6:25 (6:25) (Class 5) (0-70,70) 3-Y-O+ **£2,911** (£866; £432; £216) **Stalls** Low

Form RPR
0006 **1** **Bold**[105] 5301 4-9-5 **70** (vt[1]) AdamBeschizza 9 78
(Stuart Williams) *mde all: stretched on over 2f out: drvn over 1f out: kpt on wl and a holding on* **3/1**[1]
0653 **2** *¾* **Be Royale**[16] 7851 6-9-5 **70** (t) RobertWinston 2 75
(Michael Appleby) *trckd ldrs: prog to chse wnr wl over 1f out: kpt on wl u.p but a hld* **5/1**[3]
2602 **3** *nk* **For Ayman**[36] 7430 5-8-12 **68** (t) JoshDoyle(5) 6 72
(Joseph Tuite) *hld up in rr: prog over 1f out: chsd ldng pair fnl f: styd on and grad clsd but unable to chal* **9/1**
5401 **4** *nk* **More Beau (USA)**[16] 7851 5-9-4 **69** (p) BarryMcHugh 4 72+
(David Nicholls) *impeded s: hld up in last: effrt over 2f out: nt clrest of runs over 1f out: hdwy to take 4th ins fnl f: styd on and nrst fin but unable to chal* **13/2**
6005 **5** *4 ½* **The Big Lad**[12] 7899 4-9-5 **70** ShaneKelly 12 59
(Richard Hughes) *hld up in rr: pushed along over 2f out: appeared briefly short of room over 1f out: shkn up and kpt on to take modest 5th ins fnl f: nvr involved* **6/1**
0400 **6** *nk* **Tagula Night (IRE)**[13] 7887 10-9-3 **68** (vt) SteveDrowne 1 56
(Dean Ivory) *prom: rdn over 2f out: wknd over 1f out* **16/1**
0000 **7** *½* **Vroom (IRE)**[27] 7644 3-8-12 **70** RhiainIngram(7) 5 56
(Gay Kelleway) *impeded s: hld up in last: brought wd in st: pushed along over 2f out: kpt on fnl f but no ch* **50/1**
2360 **8** *1 ¼* **Colourbearer (IRE)**[12] 7899 9-9-2 **67** (t) LukeMorris 10 49
(Charlie Wallis) *chsd wnr to wl over 1f out: wknd* **50/1**
0036 **9** *½* **Qortaaj**[4] 8037 3-9-3 **68** JohnFahy 8 48
(David Loughnane) *dwlt: tried to make prog fr rr but forced wd bnd over 3f out: struggling over 2f out: fdd* **9/2**[2]
1200 **10** *2 ½* **City Of Angkor Wat (IRE)**[92] 5736 6-9-2 **67** (p) TimmyMurphy 3 39
(Conor Dore) *wnt lft s: hld up towards rr: shkn up over 2f out: wknd over 1f out* **50/1**
2403 **11** *nk* **Cinders (IRE)**[35] 7459 3-9-3 **68** [1] JimmyFortune 11 40
(Hughie Morrison) *chsd ldrs: rdn over 2f out: sn lost pl and wknd over 1f out* **16/1**

1m 12.63s (-0.47) **Going Correction** -0.025s/f (Stan) **11** Ran SP% **115.1**
Speed ratings (Par 103): **102,101,100,100,94 93,93,91,90,87 87**
CSF £17.18 CT £119.07 TOTE £3.90: £1.60, £1.90, £2.50; EX 21.30 Trifecta £180.10.
Owner T W Morley & Mrs J Morley **Bred** Juddmonte Farms Ltd **Trained** Newmarket, Suffolk

FOCUS
A punt was landed in this modest sprint handicap. The form is rated around the second, third and fourth.

8068 32RED WILD FLOWER STKS (LISTED RACE) 1m 4f (P)
6:55 (6:56) (Class 1) 3-Y-O+
£22,684 (£8,600; £4,304; £2,144; £1,076; £540) **Stalls** Low

Form RPR
1 **1** **Crimean Tatar (TUR)**[124] 4597 3-9-0 94 JackMitchell 3 110+
(Hugo Palmer) *hld up in last pair: hanging and looked green whn asked for effrt over 2f out: rapid prog on outer over 1f out to chal fnl f: led last 100yds: r.o wl* **5/1**[2]
1/22 **2** *½* **Chemical Charge (IRE)**[142] 3964 4-9-6 107 SeanLevey 12 109
(Ralph Beckett) *t.k.h: trckd ldr 3f: styd cl up: prog to ld over 1f out: r.o but hdd and hld last 100yds* **8/1**
0061 **3** *2 ¼* **Curbyourenthusiasm (IRE)**[18] 7814 5-9-6 108 JamieSpencer 5 105
(David Simcock) *s.i.s: hld up in rr: prog on outer over 2f out to chal over 1f out: outpcd by ldng pair fnl f* **7/1**
6001 **4** *½* **Prince Of Arran**[21] 7765 3-9-0 92 StevieDonohoe 9 104+
(Charlie Fellowes) *snatched up after 1f in midfield: waiting for a gap over 2f out then impeded: prog to chse ldrs 1f out: styd on but nt pce to threaten* **13/2**[3]
1251 **5** *1* **Cliff Face (IRE)**[7] 7980 3-8-9 81 LukeMorris 10 98
(Sir Mark Prescott Bt) *hld up in midfield: cl up bhd ldrs and waiting for room 2f out: rdn and kpt on same pce fr over 1f out* **20/1**
0411 **6** *1 ¾* **Bess Of Hardwick**[27] 7652 4-9-3 98 JimmyFortune 8 97
(Luca Cumani) *hld up in rr: prog on outer 5f out to go prom: rdn to ld briefly wl over 1f out: wknd fnl f* **10/1**
0302 **7** *¾* **Star Storm (IRE)**[21] 7766 4-9-6 107 TomQueally 2 99+
(James Fanshawe) *hld up in midfield: nt clr run on inner over 2f out and swtchd out wd: tried to make prog over 1f out but nvr pce to threaten* **9/4**[1]
4653 **8** *1* **Not So Sleepy**[32] 7546 4-9-6 100 (t) LiamKeniry 11 97
(Hughie Morrison) *s.s: plld hrd and hld up in last: nvr a factor but passed a few late on* **50/1**
2 **9** *nk* **Dogma (FR)**[27] 7652 4-9-1 97 (tp) TheoBachelot 4 92
(S Wattel, France) *trckd ldrs towards outer: lost pl over 2f out: no hdwy over 1f out* **16/1**
5410 **10** *2* **Elysian Fields (GR)**[42] 7271 5-9-1 96 KieranShoemark 1 88
(Amanda Perrett) *prom on inner: rdn over 2f out: outpcd over 1f out: wknd* **33/1**
2203 **11** *¾* **Lady Of Camelot (IRE)**[18] 7823 4-9-1 104 NickyMackay 13 87
(John Gosden) *trckd ldr after 3f: led wl over 2f out to wl over 1f out: sn wknd* **12/1**
1026 **12** *13* **Eager Beaver**[53] 6951 4-9-1 81 TomMarquand 6 66
(William Muir) *led to wl over 2f out: wknd rapidly: t.o* **200/1**

2m 32.57s (-1.93) **Going Correction** -0.025s/f (Stan)
WFA 3 from 4yo+ 6lb **12** Ran SP% **117.2**
Speed ratings (Par 111): **105,104,103,102,102 101,100,99,99,98 97,89**
CSF £42.99 TOTE £5.60: £1.80, £2.50, £2.30; EX 40.70 Trifecta £417.80.
Owner V I Araci **Bred** Vefa Ibrahim Araci **Trained** Newmarket, Suffolk
■ Stewards' Enquiry : Sean Levey caution: careless riding

FOCUS
A good Listed race, but rather a messy affair from a pace perspective. The form is a bit fluid, but the runner-up has been rated to form for now, with the third closer to his earleir 1m4f form.

8069 32RED CASINO H'CAP 6f (P)
7:25 (7:26) (Class 2) (0-105,98) 3-Y-O+
£11,827 (£3,541; £1,770; £885; £442; £222) **Stalls** Low

Form RPR
0003 **1** **Justice Good (IRE)**[21] 7771 4-9-4 **95** SeanLevey 9 106
(David Elsworth) *trckd ldr: led 2f out and asserted over 1f out: drvn fnl f and styd on wl* **12/1**
0060 **2** *1 ¼* **Spring Loaded (IRE)**[81] 6112 4-9-7 **98** ShaneKelly 12 105
(Paul D'Arcy) *chsd ldng trio: rdn over 2f out: prog to take 2nd jst ins fnl f: styd on but no imp wnr last 100yds* **7/1**[3]
4040 **3** *nk* **Gentlemen**[73] 6371 5-9-0 **94** CallumShepherd(3) 10 100
(Phil McEntee) *chsd ldrs in 6th: rdn over 2f out: prog over 1f out: styd on to take 3rd nr fin: no threat* **20/1**
1003 **4** *¾* **Amazour (IRE)**[49] 7068 4-9-5 **96** MartinHarley 8 101+
(Ismail Mohammed) *s.i.s: hld up in rr: pushed along 2f out: prog over 1f out: styd on wl fnl f but a too much to do: eased last strides* **10/3**[1]
5651 **5** *nse* **Boomerang Bob (IRE)**[28] 7610 7-9-0 **91** WilliamCarson 5 94
(Jamie Osborne) *chsd ldng pair: rdn over 2f out: kpt on and stl in 3rd ins fnl f: one pce last 100yds* **6/1**[2]
3160 **6** *1 ½* **Hakam (USA)**[28] 7610 4-8-10 **87** TomMarquand 3 86
(Michael Appleby) *towards rr: rdn sn after 1/2-way: prog over 1f out: kpt on but nvr pce to threaten* **15/2**
0203 **7** *½* **Related**[65] 6627 6-9-4 **95** (b) LukeMorris 4 92
(Paul Midgley) *led: rdn and hdd 2f out: chsd wnr to jst ins fnl f: wknd* **7/1**[3]

00 **8** 2 **Kasbah (IRE)**[43] 7242 4-9-1 **95**................................. KieranShoemark(3) 7 86
(Amanda Perrett) *hld up towards rr and racd on outer: shkn up and no rspnse 2f out: wl btn after* **14/1**

325- **9** 1 1/4 **Lawmaking**[38] 3-9-2 **93**... LiamKeniry 2 80
(Henry Spiller) *s.i.s: hld up in last pair: shkn up over 2f out: no great prog* **33/1**

0006 **10** nk **Burnt Sugar (IRE)**[18] 7822 4-8-11 **93**........................(bt) HollieDoyle(5) 11 79
(Richard Hannon) *s.v.s: tried to make prog on wd outside bnd over 3f out: no hdwy 2f out* **7/1**[3]

-000 **11** 1/2 **Mullionheir**[6] 7990 4-9-1 **92**.. KierenFox 6 76
(John Best) *chsd ldrs: rdn and no prog 2f out: fdd over 1f out* **50/1**

-260 **12** 9 **Dutiful Son (IRE)**[264] 816 6-8-9 **86**................................... NickyMackay 1 41
(Simon Dow) *nvr bttr than midfield: wknd 2f out: t.o* **20/1**

1m 11.08s (-2.02) **Going Correction** -0.025s/f (Stan) **12** Ran SP% **115.4**
Speed ratings (Par 109): **112,110,109,108,108 106,106,103,101,101 100,88**
CSF £87.02 CT £1119.25 TOTE £14.70: £3.40, £2.40, £5.20; EX 104.40 Trifecta £2381.60.
Owner Robert Ng **Bred** Mrs C Regalado-Gonzalez **Trained** Newmarket, Suffolk

FOCUS
A good sprint handicap, even if the top weight weighed in 7lb below the race ceiling. As had been the case earlier on the card when pace had generally held up, it proved hard to get competitive from behind. The winner has been rated back to his best, with the runner-up and third to form.

8070 ALL WEATHER "HANDS AND HEELS" APPRENTICE SERIES H'CAP (PART OF THE RACING EXCELLENCE INITIATIVE) 1m (P)
7:55 (7:56) (Class 7) (0-50,50) 3-Y-O+ **£1,940** (£577; £288; £144) **Stalls** Low

Form RPR

0000 **1** **My Bubba**[12] 7910 4-8-11 **45**...[1] WilliamCox(5) 3 52
(John Flint) *hld up wl in rr: prog fr 1/2-way: weaved through fr 2f out to chal fnl f: led last 100yds: hld on wl* **10/1**

0662 **2** 1/2 **Henry Grace (IRE)**[36] 7427 5-9-1 **49**..........................(b) AledBeech(5) 14 55
(Jimmy Fox) *chsd ldrs on outer: clsd fr 2f out: led jst ins fnl f: hdd and one pce last 100yds* **9/2**[1]

054 **3** 2 1/2 **Santadelacruze**[27] 7641 7-9-7 **50**......................................(b) JordanUys 5 50
(Mark Hoad) *settled wl in rr: prog on wd outside fr 2f out: styd on wl to take 3rd last 50yds* **6/1**[2]

5050 **4** 1 1/4 **Claude Greenwood**[27] 7641 6-9-0 **48**....................(b) SophieRalston(5) 7 45+
(Tony Carroll) *pressed ldr and clr of rest: led over 2f out: hdd & wknd jst ins fnl f* **16/1**

2500 **5** 2 1/4 **Whip Up A Frenzy (IRE)**[41] 7310 4-9-1 **49**............. GabrieleMalune(5) 2 40
(Richard Rowe) *chsd ldrs: effrt on inner over 2f out: nt pce to threaten fr over 1f out* **11/1**

000 **6** 1 **Ravens Heart (IRE)**[156] 3464 4-9-4 **50**................. ManuelFernandes(3) 6 39
(Dean Ivory) *lost midfield pl after 3f: struggling in last trio over 2f out: kpt on fr over 1f out* **6/1**[2]

3000 **7** 3/4 **Secret Interlude (IRE)**[57] 6853 3-8-12 **50**.................. GeorgiaDobie(7) 1 36
(Jamie Osborne) *towards rr on inner: tried to make prog over 2f out: no hdwy over 1f out* **14/1**

00 **8** nse **Outlaw Torn (IRE)**[19] 7794 7-9-0 **50**.............................(e) LisaTodd(7) 13 37+
(Richard Guest) *led at str pce and clr w one rival: hdd over 2f out: wknd over 1f out* **16/1**

5000 **9** hd **Play The Blues (IRE)**[36] 7427 9-9-2 **45**..........................(t) MillyNaseb 11 32
(Henry Tett) *trckd ldrs: cl enough 2f out: wknd tamely over 1f out* **40/1**

5400 **10** 3 3/4 **Dalness Express**[35] 7463 3-8-13 **49**.............................. LiamDoran(5) 4 26
(John O'Shea) *s.v.s: detached in last pair: effrt over 2f out: nvr able to make much prog* **14/1**

00/0 **11** 3 1/2 **Frankie**[36] 7426 5-8-11 **47**.. SophieScardifield(7) 8 16
(Jimmy Fox) *chsd clr ldng pair to over 2f out: sn wknd* **33/1**

0005 **12** hd **Mowhoob**[18] 7817 6-9-5 **48**.......................................(t) JoshuaBryan 9 17
(Brian Barr) *s.v.s: nvr able to rcvr and bhd in last most of way* **8/1**[3]

0054 **13** 1/2 **Lutine Charlie (IRE)**[36] 7427 9-9-5 **48**....................(p) KieranSchofield 12 16
(Emma Owen) *racd on wd outside: chsd ldrs to 1/2-way: sn toiling in rr* **12/1**

0024 **14** 1 1/2 **Nidnod**[56] 6865 3-9-4 **49**.. JaneElliott 10 12
(John Bridger) *chsd clr ldng pair to over 2f out: wknd rapidly* **16/1**

1m 40.85s (1.05) **Going Correction** -0.025s/f (Stan)
WFA 3 from 4yo+ 2lb **14** Ran SP% **119.3**
Speed ratings (Par 97): **93,92,90,88,86 85,84,84,84,80 77,77,76,75**
CSF £53.94 CT £309.19 TOTE £11.80: £3.50, £2.00, £2.00; EX 61.90 Trifecta £687.20.
Owner Mrs N L Young **Bred** Mrs N L Young **Trained** Kenfig Hill, Bridgend

FOCUS
A low-grade handicap run at a good gallop. The winner has been rated back to last year's best effort.
T/Jkpt: Not Won. T/Plt: £92.00 to a £1 stake. Pool: £98,984.87 - 784.76 winning units T/Qpdt: £8.70 to a £1 stake. Pool: £12,499.02 - 1057.71 winning units **Jonathan Neesom**

8033 WOLVERHAMPTON (A.W) (L-H)
Wednesday, November 23

OFFICIAL GOING: Tapeta: standard
Wind: Light against Weather: Light rain

8071 32REDSPORT.COM NURSERY H'CAP 5f 216y (Tp)
12:30 (12:30) (Class 6) (0-65,71) 2-Y-O **£2,587** (£770; £384; £192) **Stalls** Low

Form RPR

0513 **1** **Geraldine (GER)**[6] 7981 2-9-1 **59**...................................... MartinHarley 3 65
(Stuart Williams) *trckd ldrs: shkn up to ld and edgd lft over 1f out: rdn and hung lft ins fnl f: r.o* **9/4**[1]

6006 **2** 1 1/2 **Kings Heart (IRE)**[11] 7938 2-9-6 **64**.................................. SteveDrowne 6 65
(Mark Usher) *hld up: hdwy over 1f out: r.o* **7/2**[3]

0221 **3** shd **Wentwell Yesterday (IRE)**[6] 7981 2-9-8 **71** 6ex........... LucyKBarry(5) 2 72
(Jamie Osborne) *chsd ldr tl over 4f out: remained handy: nt clr run wl over 1f out: sn rdn: styd on* **3/1**[2]

640 **4** 3 1/4 **Tranquil Daze (IRE)**[84] 6034 2-9-4 **62**................................. SeanLevey 7 53
(David Brown) *hld up in tch: shkn up over 1f out: styd on: nt trbld ldrs* **18/1**

050 **5** 3/4 **Judy Woods (IRE)**[15] 7855 2-9-4 **62**............................ ConnorBeasley 5 51
(Bryan Smart) *s.i.s: hld up: rdn: hung lft and nt clr run over 1f out: r.o ins fnl f: nvr nrr* **11/1**

0040 **6** 1 **Glam'Selle**[13] 7884 2-8-8 **52**.. KieranO'Neill 8 38
(Ronald Harris) *led: hung rt over 2f out: rdn and hdd over 1f out: wknd ins fnl f* **40/1**

5350 **7** hd **Affordability**[106] 5257 2-9-6 **64**... LukeMorris 1 49
(Daniel Mark Loughnane) *hld up in tch: rdn over 2f out: wknd ins fnl f* **18/1**

5500 **8** nk **Hugging The Rails (IRE)**[60] 6791 2-9-1 **59**......................... JasonHart 4 44
(Tim Easterby) *hld up: rdn over 2f out: nvr on terms* **12/1**

0603 **9** 2 1/4 **Lawfilly**[20] 7777 2-9-2 **60**.. RyanTate 9 38
(Richard Hughes) *sn pushed along and prom: chsd ldr over 4f out tl rdn over 1f out: n.m.r sn after: wknd fnl f* **10/1**

000 **10** 5 **Chillililli**[38] 7381 2-8-6 **50**... JoeFanning 10 13
(Bryan Smart) *in rr: shkn up and wknd over 1f out* **50/1**

1m 14.19s (-0.31) **Going Correction** -0.15s/f (Stan) **10** Ran SP% **118.0**
Speed ratings (Par 94): **96,94,93,89,88 87,86,86,83,76**
CSF £10.31 CT £23.83 TOTE £2.60: £1.10, £1.90, £1.50; EX 10.70 Trifecta £34.20.
Owner Graf Stauffenberg **Bred** Graf U Grafin V Stauffenberg **Trained** Newmarket, Suffolk

FOCUS
A moderate nursery dominated by the three market leaders. The race might be worth a shade more than rated.

8072 32RED ON THE APP STORE NURSERY H'CAP 7f 32y (Tp)
1:00 (1:01) (Class 6) (0-65,65) 2-Y-O **£2,587** (£770; £384; £192) **Stalls** High

Form RPR

4P00 **1** **Viola Park**[13] 7881 2-8-1 **45**.. RyanPowell 6 49
(Ronald Harris) *led 6f out: rdn and edgd lft over 1f out: styd on* **33/1**

4000 **2** 1/2 **Halinka (IRE)**[13] 7884 2-9-2 **60**... JackMitchell 9 64
(Roger Varian) *hld up: nt clr run over 1f out: r.o wl ins fnl f: wnt 2nd towards fin: nt rch wnr* **12/1**

0002 **3** 1 1/4 **Orithia (USA)**[13] 7881 2-9-2 **60**....................................(t) MartinHarley 1 60
(Seamus Durack) *prom: rdn to chse wnr and nt clr run over 1f out: styd on same pce wl ins fnl f* **2/1**[1]

0020 **4** 1 1/2 **Princess Way (IRE)**[7] 7974 2-9-3 **61**............................ RobertWinston 2 57
(David Evans) *led 1f: chsd wnr: rdn and lost 2nd over 1f out: styd on same pce ins fnl f* **4/1**[2]

3540 **5** nse **Tigerfish (IRE)**[14] 7866 2-8-3 **47**...................................... KieranO'Neill 5 43
(William Stone) *chsd ldrs: rdn over 1f out: styd on same pce ins fnl f* **7/1**

0500 **6** 1 1/4 **Ripper Street (IRE)**[90] 5796 2-9-7 **65**.................................. LukeMorris 3 58
(Ed Dunlop) *hld up: hdwy u.p 2f out: styd on same pce ins fnl f* **6/1**[3]

000 **7** 1 1/2 **Stag Party (IRE)**[115] 4907 2-9-3 **61**...................................... LiamKeniry 4 50
(Andrew Balding) *hld up: rdn over 1f out: nt trble ldrs* **7/1**

4050 **8** 3/4 **Gentleman Giles (IRE)**[100] 5484 2-9-1 **59**................. TimmyMurphy 10 46
(Jamie Osborne) *chsd ldrs: rdn over 2f out: wknd fnl f* **20/1**

0254 **9** 1 1/4 **Myllachy**[30] 7579 2-8-9 **53**.. DuranFentiman 8 37
(Tim Easterby) *hld up: rdn 1/2-way: nvr on terms* **10/1**

1m 29.72s (0.92) **Going Correction** -0.15s/f (Stan) **9** Ran SP% **117.1**
Speed ratings (Par 94): **88,87,86,84,84 82,81,80,78**
CSF £382.08 CT £1176.38 TOTE £43.40: £9.50, £3.40, £1.10; EX 1139.80 Trifecta £3918.90.
Owner John & Margaret Hatherell & RHS Ltd **Bred** Limestone Stud **Trained** Earlswood, Monmouths

FOCUS
Another moderate nursery and a boil-over, though the winner was backed at fancy odds before the off. The second has been rated near her pre-race form.

8073 32RED CASINO MAIDEN STKS (DIV I) 1m 141y (Tp)
1:30 (1:34) (Class 5) 2-Y-O **£3,234** (£962; £481; £240) **Stalls** Low

Form RPR

32 **1** **Zumurudee (USA)**[21] 7769 2-9-5 0................................... MartinHarley 7 87+
(Marco Botti) *w ldr tl led over 6f out: pushed clr fnl 2f: easily* **4/11**[1]

36 **2** 10 **American History (USA)**[12] 7907 2-9-5 0........................[1] RobertTart 11 66
(John Gosden) *s.i.s: hdwy over 6f out: rdn over 3f out: chsd wnr over 2f out: sn outpcd* **7/2**[2]

3 1/2 **Shee's Lucky** 2-9-0 0... JoeFanning 1 60
(Mark Johnston) *led: hdd over 6f out: chsd ldrs: rdn over 2f out: sn outpcd* **20/1**

0 **4** 1/2 **Lunar Jet**[21] 7769 2-9-5 0... PJMcDonald 3 64
(John Mackie) *hld up in tch: racd keenly: outpcd over 3f out: wnt 4th and edgd lft over 1f out: no further imp* **50/1**

5 1 **Ascot Week (USA)** 2-9-5 0... GrahamLee 8 62
(Owen Burrows) *sn given reminders in rr: bhd whn rdn and hung lft over 1f out: nvr nrr* **22/1**

0 **6** 1 3/4 **Look My Way**[8] 7963 2-9-5 0.. LiamKeniry 9 58
(Andrew Balding) *s.i.s: in rr: rdn over 1f out: nvr on terms* **80/1**

5 **7** nk **Leopard (IRE)**[11] 7930 2-9-5 0... TomQueally 10 57
(Paul Cole) *prom: chsd wnr over 6f out tl hung rt over 2f out: sn rdn and wknd* **20/1**

0 **8** 1/2 **Ghand (IRE)**[21] 7761 2-9-0 0.. GrahamGibbons 6 51
(Sir Michael Stoute) *sn pushed along and prom: rdn over 3f out: wknd 2f out* **14/1**[3]

00 **9** 1 **London Master**[12] 7907 2-9-2 0.................................. LouisSteward(3) 2 54
(Chris Wall) *hld up: shkn up over 1f out: nvr nr to chal* **40/1**

0 **10** 1 **Serenade The Stars (IRE)**[12] 7907 2-9-5 0..................(p) LukeMorris 4 52
(James Tate) *hld up: hdwy u.p over 2f out: sn wknd* **20/1**

1m 48.29s (-1.81) **Going Correction** -0.15s/f (Stan) **10** Ran SP% **126.5**
Speed ratings (Par 96): **102,93,92,92,91 89,89,89,88,87**
CSF £1.94 TOTE £1.30: £1.10, £1.20, £3.20; EX 2.60 Trifecta £19.50.
Owner Sheikh Mohammed Bin Khalifa Al Maktoum **Bred** Double K Llc, Brookdale & Jack Swain III **Trained** Newmarket, Suffolk

FOCUS
An uncompetitive maiden and a one-horse race. It's hard to pin down the level.

8074 32RED CASINO MAIDEN STKS (DIV II) 1m 141y (Tp)
2:05 (2:06) (Class 5) 2-Y-O **£3,234** (£962; £481; £240) **Stalls** Low

Form RPR

5243 **1** **X Rated (IRE)**[12] 7917 2-9-5 77... JoeFanning 7 76
(Mark Johnston) *mde all: rdn over 1f out: styd on* **11/8**[1]

352 **2** 3/4 **Jive Talking (IRE)**[58] 6828 2-8-11 73.......................... LouisSteward(3) 2 69
(Michael Bell) *chsd wnr 2f: remained handy: rdn to go 2nd again over 2f out: edgd lft ins fnl f: styd on* **3/1**[3]

0 **3** 1/2 **Speedo Boy (FR)**[14] 7865 2-9-2 0.......................... GeorgeDowning(3) 10 73
(Ian Williams) *hld up: hdwy over 2f out: rdn and hung lft over 1f out: r.o* **14/1**

4 3 3/4 **Oxford Thinking (IRE)** 2-9-5 0... GrahamLee 8 65+
(John Gosden) *s.i.s: hld up: plld hrd in rr early: styd on fr over 1f out: nvr nrr* **6/4**[2]

00 **5** 1 **Nargiza (USA)**[21] 7762 2-9-0 0.. MartinHarley 5 58
(Chris Wall) *prom: chsd wnr over 6f out tl rdn over 2f out: wknd ins fnl f* **20/1**

00 **6** 1 1/2 **Russian Regard (IRE)**[14] 7865 2-9-5 0.................................... RyanTate 3 60
(Jonathan Portman) *plld hrd and prom: rdn over 2f out: wknd over 1f out* **33/1**

0 **7** 2 1/2 **Delagate This Lord**[13] 7883 2-9-5 0...................................... LukeMorris 4 55
(Bill Turner) *hld up: rdn over 3f out: n.d* **66/1**

00 **8** 1 1/4 **Retribution**[12] 7906 2-9-5 0 .... TomQueally 9 52
(David Lanigan) *hld up: pushed along over 2f out: nvr on terms* **33/1**
00 **9** 2 1/2 **Dragonite (IRE)**[13] 7891 2-9-5 0 .... RyanPowell 1 47
(Daniel Mark Loughnane) *hld up in tch: plld hrd: nt clr run over 3f out: wknd over 2f out* **80/1**
1m 49.43s (-0.67) **Going Correction** -0.15s/f (Stan) **9** Ran SP% **127.1**
Speed ratings (Par 96): **96,95,94,91,90 89,87,86,83**
CSF £6.60 TOTE £2.70: £1.20, £1.30, £3.30; EX 7.00 Trifecta £39.90.
Owner Mark Johnston Racing Ltd **Bred** Mark Johnston Racing Ltd **Trained** Middleham Moor, N Yorks

FOCUS
Three pulled clear in this division and not many got into it. The winning time was 1.14sec slower than the first leg. It's been rated around the first two.

8075 £10 FREE AT 32RED.COM MAIDEN FILLIES' STKS 1m 141y (Tp)
2:35 (2:38) (Class 5) 3-Y-O+ **£3,234** (£962; £481; £240) **Stalls** Low

Form RPR
662 **1** **Princess Nia (IRE)**[28] 7616 3-9-2 70 .... JoeFanning 2 77+
(Brian Meehan) *mde all: rdn over 1f out: edgd rt: styd on* **11/2**
2 1 1/4 **Shahabad** 3-9-2 0 .... JackMitchell 10 73+
(Roger Varian) *trckd ldrs: shkn up over 2f out: edgd rt over 1f out: edgd lft and styd on to go 2nd wl ins fnl f: nt rch wnr* **7/4**[1]
222 **3** 1 1/4 **Trishuli Rock (IRE)**[28] 7607 3-9-2 75 .... LukeMorris 1 70
(Marco Botti) *chsd ldrs: pushed along over 3f out: rdn to chse wnr and hung rt over 1f out: styd on same pce and lost 2nd wl ins fnl f* **5/2**[2]
4035 **4** 1 1/4 **Ttainted Love**[44] 7220 4-9-2 75 .... (p) LouisSteward(3) 9 67
(Chris Wall) *hld up: hdwy 3f out: rdn over 1f out: styd on same pce fnl f* **11/4**[3]
5 **5** 3 **Dream Voice (IRE)**[165] 3145 3-9-2 0 .... PatrickMathers 8 60
(John Holt) *hld up: hdwy and edgd lft over 1f out: nt trble ldrs* **80/1**
6 1/2 **May Mist**[202] 4-9-2 0 .... EoinWalsh(3) 5 59
(Trevor Wall) *s.s: hld up: rdn over 1f out: r.o ins fnl f: nvr nrr* **100/1**
64 **7** 3/4 **Kerrera**[28] 7607 3-9-2 0 .... DougieCostello 6 57
(Paul Webber) *s.i.s: hld up: rdn over 1f out: nvr on terms* **28/1**
0 **8** 1/2 **Magic Moments**[28] 7616 3-9-2 0 .... MartinHarley 7 56
(Alan King) *chsd wnr tl rdn over 1f out: wknd fnl f* **40/1**
000 **9** 9 **Millady Percy**[44] 7218 3-8-13 31 .... AlistairRawlinson(3) 3 36
(Roy Brotherton) *hld up: plld hrd early: rdn over 2f out: sn wknd* **100/1**
54U **10** 1 3/4 **Sovrano Dolce (IRE)**[23] 7727 3-9-2 0 .... GrahamLee 4 31
(Mike Murphy) *hld up in tch: rdn over 3f out: wknd over 2f out* **28/1**
1m 48.49s (-1.61) **Going Correction** -0.15s/f (Stan)
WFA 3 from 4yo 3lb **10** Ran SP% **119.5**
Speed ratings (Par 100): **101,99,98,97,95 94,93,93,85,83**
CSF £15.69 TOTE £6.00: £1.30, £1.70, £1.10; EX 23.00 Trifecta £64.00.
Owner The Pony Club **Bred** Andrew Rosen **Trained** Manton, Wilts

FOCUS
An ordinary older-fillies' maiden and another race where the winner made all. Muddling form.

8076 32RED.COM FILLIES' H'CAP 1m 4f 50y (Tp)
3:10 (3:10) (Class 4) (0-80,79) 3-Y-O+ **£4,851** (£1,443; £721; £360) **Stalls** Low

Form RPR
4215 **1** **Flower Of Love**[22] 7732 3-9-0 **75** .... (t) MartinHarley 6 85+
(Simon Crisford) *chsd ldr tl led over 3f out: rdn clr and hung lft over 1f out: styd on: comf* **7/4**[1]
56-0 **2** 3 3/4 **Ominotago**[11] 7942 4-8-11 **66** .... BenCurtis 7 69
(Michael Appleby) *chsd ldrs: hung rt over 7f out: rdn over 3f out: chsd wnr over 2f out: rdr dropped reins wl over 1f out: styd on same pce fnl f* **25/1**
2200 **3** 1 **Zeehan**[156] 3468 3-8-11 **72** .... JoeFanning 3 73
(Clive Cox) *chsd ldrs: rdn over 4f out: hmpd and outpcd 2f out: styd on ins fnl f* **11/4**[2]
620 **4** 10 **Miss Minuty**[33] 7512 4-9-1 **77** .... JoshuaBryan(7) 2 62
(Alexandra Dunn) *s.i.s: hld up: hdwy and nt clr run over 2f out: wknd over 1f out* **4/1**[3]
5 9 **Chandos Belle (GER)**[32] 3-9-4 **79** .... JFEgan 1 50
(Stuart Edmunds) *led: rdn and hdd over 3f out: wkng whn nt clr run 2f out* **4/1**[3]
1306 **6** 1/2 **Topaling**[163] 3221 5-8-8 **66** .... TimClark(3) 4 36
(Mark H Tompkins) *hdwy 10f out: rdn over 3f out: wknd over 2f out* **14/1**
2m 37.83s (-2.97) **Going Correction** -0.15s/f (Stan)
WFA 3 from 4yo+ 6lb **6** Ran SP% **113.5**
Speed ratings (Par 102): **103,100,99,93,87 86**
CSF £42.50 TOTE £2.10: £1.20, £6.90; EX 34.30 Trifecta £74.60.
Owner Mohammed Al Nabouda **Bred** Rabbah Bloodstock Limited **Trained** Newmarket, Suffolk

FOCUS
A fair fillies' handicap though they went no great pace. The favourite hosed up. It's been rated cautiously.

8077 BETWAY H'CAP 1m 1f 103y (Tp)
3:40 (3:40) (Class 4) (0-80,80) 3-Y-O+ **£4,851** (£1,443; £721; £360) **Stalls** Low

Form RPR
4342 **1** **Nonios (IRE)**[12] 7911 4-9-4 **77** .... MartinHarley 12 89+
(David Simcock) *hld up in tch: tk clsr over 2f out: led over 1f out: rdn out* **2/1**[1]
6605 **2** 3 1/4 **Eurystheus (IRE)**[26] 7671 7-9-1 **77** .... (tp) AlistairRawlinson(3) 3 82
(Michael Appleby) *chsd ldrs: rdn and edgd lft over 1f out: styd on same pce ins fnl f* **9/1**
3064 **3** nse **Starlit Cantata**[44] 7222 5-8-13 **75** .... EdwardGreatrex(3) 9 80
(Eve Johnson Houghton) *prom: rdn and n.m.r over 1f out: styd on same pce ins fnl f* **12/1**
010 **4** shd **Bunbury**[117] 4839 4-8-13 **79** .... StephenCummins(7) 13 84
(Richard Hughes) *hld up: racd keenly: hdwy on outer over 2f out: styd on same pce ins fnl f* **22/1**
6300 **5** nk **Berlusca (IRE)**[46] 7159 7-9-7 **80** .... DanielTudhope 4 84+
(David O'Meara) *hld up: plld hrd: hdwy over 1f out: sn edgd lft: styd on same pce ins fnl f* **5/1**[3]
4431 **6** 2 **Iberica Road (USA)**[62] 6703 3-9-2 **78** .... (t) LiamKeniry 1 78
(Andrew Balding) *led: rdn and hdd over 1f out: no ex ins fnl f* **4/1**[2]
0006 **7** 1/2 **Marcret (ITY)**[12] 7903 9-9-6 **79** .... GrahamLee 6 78
(James Unett) *hld up: plld hrd: r.o ins fnl f: nt trble ldrs* **28/1**
4500 **8** 1 1/2 **Outback Blue**[44] 7204 3-8-11 **73** .... (t) JFEgan 2 69
(David Evans) *mid-div: sn pushed along: rdn 1/2-way: no imp fr over 1f out* **18/1**
6040 **9** 1 **Edge Of Heaven**[167] 3061 4-9-6 **79** .... RyanTate 11 73
(Jonathan Portman) *chsd ldrs: rdn over 2f out: wknd fnl f* **50/1**
5060 **10** nk **Franco's Secret**[12] 7902 5-8-12 **78** .... (v) JoshuaBryan(7) 7 71
(Peter Hedger) *s.i.s: hld up: rdn over 3f out: nvr on terms* **9/1**
-400 **11** 1 3/4 **Petrucci (IRE)**[14] 7869 4-9-1 **77** .... NoelGarbutt(3) 5 67
(Derek Shaw) *hld up: rdn over 3f out: n.d* **66/1**
25-5 **12** 4 1/2 **Pool House**[301] 349 5-8-5 **71** .... KevinLundie(7) 10 51
(Mike Murphy) *hld up: a in rr: wknd over 2f out* **66/1**
0-00 **13** 2 1/2 **Starfield**[28] 7623 7-9-4 **77** .... (v) KieranO'Neill 8 52
(Mandy Rowland) *chsd ldr: rdn and ev ch 2f out: wknd over 1f out* **150/1**
1m 59.17s (-1.63) **Going Correction** -0.15s/f (Stan)
WFA 3 from 4yo+ 3lb **13** Ran SP% **116.4**
Speed ratings (Par 105): **101,98,98,97,97 95,95,94,93,93 91,87,85**
CSF £19.55 CT £174.54 TOTE £3.30: £1.60, £3.50, £3.40; EX 24.70 Trifecta £220.10.
Owner Millingbrook Racing **Bred** Sheikh Sultan Bin Khalifa Al Nayhan **Trained** Newmarket, Suffolk
■ Stewards' Enquiry : Stephen Cummins ten-day ban: failed to take all reasonable and permissable measures to obtain best possible placing (Dec 7-10, 12-17)

FOCUS
A fair handicap, but the favourite took it apart. The runner-up has been rated close to form, and the fourth to a small pb.

8078 BETWAY SPRINT DISTANCE H'CAP 5f 20y (Tp)
4:10 (4:11) (Class 6) (0-65,65) 3-Y-O+ **£2,587** (£770; £384; £192) **Stalls** Low

Form RPR
2225 **1** **Compton River**[29] 7596 4-9-7 **65** .... ConnorBeasley 9 73
(Bryan Smart) *chsd ldrs: pushed along 1/2-way: rdn and hung lft fr over 1f out: r.o to ld wl ins fnl f* **9/2**[1]
0430 **2** 2 **Lady Nayef**[37] 7420 3-9-7 **65** .... (t) JFEgan 6 66+
(John Butler) *sn pushed along to dispute ld: wnt on 1/2-way: rdn over 1f out: hdd and unable qck wl ins fnl f* **9/1**
0000 **3** 1/2 **Desert Strike**[13] 7887 10-9-3 **64** .... (p) LouisSteward(3) 3 63
(Conor Dore) *chsd ldr: rdn 1/2-way: r.o* **8/1**
0453 **4** nk **Tavener**[9] 7961 4-8-13 **60** .... (p) NoelGarbutt(3) 4 58
(David C Griffiths) *hld up: rdn 1/2-way: r.o ins fnl f* **6/1**[3]
6000 **5** hd **Harmonic Wave (IRE)**[19] 7798 3-9-5 **63** .... (b[1]) PJMcDonald 10 60
(Rebecca Menzies) *hld up: r.o ins fnl f: nt rch ldrs* **22/1**
3002 **6** shd **Cruise Tothelimit (IRE)**[11] 7945 8-9-6 **64** .... GrahamLee 5 61
(Patrick Morris) *hld up in tch: rdn over 1f out: styd on* **7/1**
3664 **7** nse **Noble Asset**[11] 7945 5-9-4 **65** .... EdwardGreatrex(3) 1 62
(Milton Bradley) *mid-div: plld hrd: hdwy 1/2-way: rdn over 1f out: styd on same pce ins fnl f* **5/1**[2]
2653 **8** 3/4 **Roaring Rory**[89] 5855 3-9-7 **65** .... (p) DanielTudhope 8 59
(Ollie Pears) *hld up: rdn over 1f out: nt rch ldrs* **8/1**
5323 **9** 3/4 **Regal Miss**[73] 6374 4-9-3 **61** .... JoeFanning 2 52
(Patrick Chamings) *hld up: rdn over 1f out: nvr trbld ldrs* **7/1**
0516 **10** 1/2 **Pearl Noir**[173] 2863 6-9-0 **65** .... (b) NatalieHambling(7) 7 54+
(Scott Dixon) *pushed along to dispute ld to 1/2-way: rdn over 1f out: wknd ins fnl f* **22/1**
1m 0.86s (-1.04) **Going Correction** -0.15s/f (Stan) **10** Ran SP% **115.1**
Speed ratings (Par 101): **102,98,98,97,97 97,96,95,94,93**
CSF £44.41 CT £317.02 TOTE £5.20: £2.00, £3.70, £3.70; EX 51.80 Trifecta £372.20.
Owner The Smart Inagh River Partnership **Bred** Glebe Farm Stud **Trained** Hambleton, N Yorks

FOCUS
A moderate sprint handicap, but a complete burn up out in front with two duelling for the lead from the off. The runner-up helps with the opening level.
T/Plt: £6.00 to a £1 stake. Pool: £65094.75 - 7885.35 winning units. T/Qpdt: £3.20 to a £1 stake. Pool: £5469.53 - 1232.26 winning units. **Colin Roberts**

8046 CHELMSFORD (A.W) (L-H)
Thursday, November 24

OFFICIAL GOING: Polytrack: standard
Wind: medium,against Weather: dry

8079 BET TOTEPLACEPOT APPRENTICE H'CAP 6f (P)
4:25 (4:26) (Class 7) (0-50,55) 3-Y-O+ **£2,587** (£770; £384; £192) **Stalls** Centre

Form RPR
0006 **1** **Secret Bird (IRE)**[13] 7912 4-9-7 **50** .... LuluStanford 14 55
(Dean Ivory) *taken down early: chsd ldrs tl jnd ldr 4f out: rdn to ld over 1f out: hld on gamely ins fnl f: all out* **6/1**[2]
0525 **2** 1/2 **Presto Boy**[15] 7863 4-8-13 **49** .... (e) FinleyMarsh(7) 2 53
(Richard Hughes) *led early: sn hdd and chsd ldrs: effrt to press wnr ent fnl f: ev ch thrght fnl f: kpt on but a jst hld* **8/1**[3]
-000 **3** 1/2 **Named Asset**[13] 7913 4-9-4 **50** .... (p) JoshuaBryan(3) 7 52
(Martin Bosley) *chsd ldrs: effrt and edgd lft over 1f out: 3rd and kpt on u.p ins fnl f* **20/1**
6250 **4** 1/2 **Ryan Style (IRE)**[6] 8013 10-9-1 **47** .... (b) JordanUys(3) 4 48
(Lisa Williamson) *s.i.s: towards rr: hdwy into midfield 1/2-way: hdwy over 1f out: kpt on wl ins fnl f: nt rch ldrs* **8/1**[3]
0606 **5** hd **Catalinas Diamond (IRE)**[5] 8031 8-9-7 **50** .... (t) RhiainIngram 10 50
(Pat Murphy) *stdd after s: bhd: swtchd rt and effrt in centre over 1f out: hdwy 1f out: styd on wl ins fnl f: nt rch ldrs* **16/1**
3504 **6** 3/4 **Wimboldsley**[14] 7896 5-9-5 **48** .... NatalieHambling 11 46
(Scott Dixon) *midfield: effrt over 1f out: kpt on ins fnl f: nt rch ldrs* **10/1**
4231 **7** 1/2 **Cadland Lad (IRE)**[6] 8013 3-9-7 **55** 6ex .... (t) JonathanFisher(5) 8 51
(John Ryan) *bhd: effrt u.p over 1f out: hdwy and swtchd rt ins fnl f: styd on: nt rch ldrs* **4/1**[1]
-040 **8** 1 **Chester Deelyte (IRE)**[6] 8013 8-9-1 **49** .... (p) ManuelFernandes(5) 13 42
(Lisa Williamson) *dwlt: midfield but stuck wd thrght: rdn ent fnl 2f out: kpt on ins fnl f: nvr threatened ldrs* **50/1**
0505 **9** nk **Cuban Queen (USA)**[111] 5126 3-9-2 **50** .... GabrieleMalune(5) 5 42
(Jeremy Gask) *t.k.h: hld up in midfield: effrt u.p over 1f out: kpt on same pce ins fnl f* **10/1**
4500 **10** 1/2 **Wensara Dream**[36] 7463 3-9-0 **48** .... WilliamCox(5) 12 39
(Andrew Balding) *hld up in rr: hung rt over 4f out: effrt and hung lft over 1f out: swtchd rt ins fnl f: kpt on: nvr trbld ldrs* **22/1**
3060 **11** hd **Simply Black (IRE)**[16] 7859 5-9-2 **45** .... (p) KevinLundie 3 35
(Ann Stokell) *taken down early: chsd ldng quartet: rdn over 1f out: unable qck and wknd ins fnl f* **20/1**
0542 **12** 2 1/4 **Redalani (IRE)**[15] 7863 6-9-6 **49** .... (b) PaddyBradley 9 32
(Alan Brown) *chsd ldrs tl led over 4f out: rdn and hdd over 1f out: sn struggling: wknd ins fnl f* **14/1**
-033 **13** nk **Bedazzling Lady (IRE)**[28] 7646 3-8-12 **48** .... DarraghKeenan(7) 1 31
(Robert Eddery) *towards rr: effrt on inner over 1f out: keeping on but stl plenty to do whn nt clr run and hmpd 100yds out: nt rcvr and eased after* **4/1**[1]

 The Form Book, Raceform Ltd, Newbury, RG14 5SJ

-600 **14** *8* **Fred's Filly**[51] 7046 3-8-9 **45**...........................[1] VictoriaWood[(7)] 6 4
(Bill Turner) *midfield: rdn and lost pl over 2f out: bhd 1f out: wknd* **66/1**

1m 13.73s (0.03) **Going Correction** -0.125s/f (Stan) **14** Ran SP% **124.6**
Speed ratings (Par 97): **94,93,92,92,91 90,90,88,88,87 87,84,84,73**
CSF £52.04 CT £950.78 TOTE £7.10: £3.00, £2.80, £6.90; EX 59.60 Trifecta £1927.90.
Owner Radlett Racing **Bred** Hadi Al Tajir **Trained** Radlett, Herts

FOCUS
Ordinary form, with the 2nd/3rd helping to set a straightforward level.

8080 BET TOTEQUADPOT NURSERY H'CAP 1m 2f (P)
4:55 (4:56) (Class 6) (0-65,64) 2-Y-O **£2,587** (£770; £384; £192) **Stalls** Low

Form RPR

4603 **1** **Peace And Plenty**[12] 7941 2-9-5 **61**........................ MartinDwyer 1 69
(William Muir) *mde all: shkn up: edgd rt but readily wnt clr over 1f out: edging bk lft and r.o wl fnl f: comf* **9/2**[3]

4240 **2** *4 ½* **Areyoutheway (IRE)**[23] 7750 2-9-4 **63**.................. AlistairRawlinson[(3)] 7 63
(Michael Appleby) *racd in last pair: rdn and hdwy on inner over 1f out: wnt 2nd 75yds out: styd on: no ch w wnr* **20/1**

0660 **3** *½* **Gog Elles (IRE)**[23] 7734 2-7-12 **45**........................ HollieDoyle[(5)] 2 44
(J S Moore) *hld up in midfield: hdwy on inner over 1f out: styd on to chse clr wnr 100yds out: kpt on same pce and lost 2nd 75yds out* **25/1**

0001 **4** *1 ¼* **Oxford Blu**[10] 7954 2-9-8 **64** 6ex..........................(v) LukeMorris 8 61
(Sir Mark Prescott Bt) *t.k.h: hld up in midfield: swtchd rt and drvn over 1f out: no ch w wnr but kpt on u.p: snatched 4th last strides* **13/8**[1]

0505 **5** *hd* **Aventus (IRE)**[15] 7866 2-8-5 **52**...........................[1] CharlieBennett[(5)] 10 48
(Jane Chapple-Hyam) *chsd ldrs: effrt to chse wnr u.p 2f out: sn outpcd: lost 2nd and wknd fnl 100yds* **20/1**

4042 **6** *1 ¾* **Fancy Day (IRE)**[16] 7854 2-9-7 **63**........................ JoeFanning 6 57
(Mark Johnston) *wl in tch in midfield: nt clr run and shuffled bk jst over 2f out: gap opened and tried to rally jst over 1f out: no imp fnl f* **20/1**

0603 **7** *½* **Reynardo De Silver**[3] 8046 2-8-13 **58**......................(v) HectorCrouch[(3)] 5 51
(Gary Moore) *wnt lft s: a rr: effrt whn hung lft and hmpd over 1f out: wl hld and kpt on same pce after* **3/1**[2]

006 **8** *8* **Don't You Think**[119] 4786 2-8-6 **48**........................ RyanTate 4 26
(Richard Hughes) *squeezed for room and hmpd leaving stalls: rdn and rcvrd to chse ldrs after 2f and t.k.h: rdn and outpcd over 1f out: wknd fnl f* **25/1**

6544 **9** *4 ½* **Ocean Temptress**[26] 7697 2-9-6 **62**........................ JosephineGordon 3 32
(John Ryan) *wnt rt s: chsd ldr tl 2f out: drvn and lost pl over 1f out: sn wknd* **8/1**

0000 **10** *8* **Kingston Tasmania**[15] 7866 2-8-6 **48**........................ BenCurtis 9 4
(Andrew Balding) *in tch in midfield: lost pl u.p 2f out: bhd fnl f* **20/1**

2m 8.27s (-0.33) **Going Correction** -0.125s/f (Stan) **10** Ran SP% **119.1**
Speed ratings (Par 94): **96,92,92,91,90 89,89,82,79,72**
CSF £92.23 CT £2007.98 TOTE £7.00: £1.80, £3.50, £6.60; EX 88.20 Trifecta £2036.20.
Owner Muir Racing Partnership - Doncaster **Bred** Newsells Park Stud **Trained** Lambourn, Berks

FOCUS
The winner pulled well clear in this modest nursery.

8081 TOTEPOOLLIVEINFO.COM FOR RACING RESULTS MAIDEN FILLIES' STKS (PLUS 10 RACE) 7f (P)
5:25 (5:28) (Class 4) 2-Y-O **£4,528** (£1,347; £673; £336) **Stalls** Low

Form RPR

4 **1** **Annie Fior (IRE)**[31] 7576 2-9-0 0........................ TomQueally 8 74
(Denis Coakley) *t.k.h: chsd ldrs: effrt and drvn to chse ldrs 1f out: chal ins fnl f: styd on wl to ld towards fin* **16/1**

5 **2** *½* **Cercle D'Or (IRE)**[22] 7761 2-9-0 0........................ NickyMackay 13 73
(John Gosden) *styd wd early: chsd ldrs tl wnt 2nd 4f out: pushed into ld over 1f out: rdn ent fnl f: hdd and one pced towards fin* **6/1**[3]

3 **3** *2* **Al Mayda (USA)**[16] 7855 2-9-0 0........................(t) JosephineGordon 1 68
(Hugo Palmer) *chsd ldr: effrt whn nt clrest of runs and swtchd rt over 1f out: kpt on same pce ins fnl f* **5/2**[1]

4 *¾* **Pure Shores** 2-9-0 0........................ MartinLane 4 66
(Charlie Appleby) *wl in tch in midfield: effrt ent fnl 2f: unable qck and swtchd rt over 1f out: kpt on same pce ins fnl f* **3/1**[2]

00 **5** *½* **Pobbles**[22] 7762 2-8-11 0........................ KieranShoemark[(3)] 9 65+
(Roger Charlton) *hld up in last quartet: reminder over 1f out: hdwy and edging lft ins fnl f: kpt on wl fnl 100yds: nvr trbld ldrs* **33/1**

03 **6** *1* **Angel Of Darkness**[66] 6624 2-9-0 0........................ LukeMorris 6 62
(Charles Hills) *led: rdn and hdd over 1f out: no ex and btn 1f out: wknd ins fnl f* **6/1**[3]

7 *1* **Ebqaa (IRE)** 2-9-0 0........................ SteveDrowne 10 59
(Marcus Tregoning) *dwlt: racd in last trio: effrt and swtchd rt over 1f out: kpt on ins fnl f: wout threatening ldrs* **25/1**

0 **8** *¾* **Bradfield Magic (IRE)**[19] 7812 2-9-0 0........................ MichaelJMMurphy 7 57
(Charles Hills) *s.i.s: in rr of main gp: effrt over 1f out: kpt on same pce and no real imp fnl f* **66/1**

0 **9** *1* **Freediver**[51] 7055 2-9-0 0........................ GrahamGibbons 12 55
(Sir Michael Stoute) *dwlt: racd in rr of main gp: rdn over 1f out: no imp tl kpt on ins fnl f: nvr trbld ldrs* **17/2**

5 **10** *½* **My Lady Marie**[22] 7763 2-9-0 0........................ JackMitchell 5 54
(Amanda Perrett) *chsd ldrs early: stdd and in tch in midfield after 2f out: rdn and outpcd over 1f out: wknd ins fnl f* **8/1**

0 **11** *4 ½* **My Rosie (IRE)**[22] 7762 2-9-0 0........................(b[1]) RobertTart 2 42
(John Gosden) *sn bustled along in midfield and nvr gng wl: wknd over 1f out: bhd ins fnl f* **20/1**

00 **12** *31* **Proud Kate**[37] 7439 2-9-0 0...........................[1] AdamBeschizza 11
(Christine Dunnett) *restless in stalls: s.i.s: a detached in last: t.o fnl f* **150/1**

1m 26.04s (-1.16) **Going Correction** -0.125s/f (Stan) **12** Ran SP% **123.4**
Speed ratings (Par 95): **101,100,98,97,96 95,94,93,92,91 86,51**
CSF £109.19 TOTE £27.40: £5.80, £2.20, £1.40; EX 131.00 Trifecta £638.90.
Owner M D Ryan **Bred** M Ryan **Trained** West Ilsley, Berks

FOCUS
Just a fair maiden. The level is fluid, but the winner found some improvement from her debut.

8082 BET TOTEEXACTA MAIDEN AUCTION STKS 1m (P)
5:55 (5:58) (Class 5) 2-Y-O **£3,881** (£1,155; £577; £288) **Stalls** Low

Form RPR

6 **1** **Sadhbh (IRE)**[12] 7939 2-8-10 0........................ KieranO'Neill 9 68
(Richard Hannon) *chsd ldrs: swtchd rt over 1f out: drvn and str burst wl ins fnl f to ld on post* **16/1**

0 **2** *nse* **Do You Know (IRE)**[14] 7883 2-8-9 0........................ DanielMuscutt 4 67
(Marco Botti) *led and set steady gallop: rdn and qcknd over 1f out: drvn ins fnl f: kpt on u.p: hdd on post* **8/1**

0 **3** *¾* **Miss Osier**[26] 7695 2-8-7 0........................ MartinDwyer 8 63
(Rae Guest) *chsd ldr: rdn over 1f out: kpt on: unable qck and styd on same pce wl ins fnl f* **33/1**

03 **4** *¾* **Solent Meads (IRE)**[27] 7659 2-9-2 0........................ RichardKingscote 2 70
(Daniel Kubler) *hld up in tch in last trio: effrt on inner over 1f out: kpt on ins fnl f: wnt 4th last strides: nvr threatened ldrs* **5/1**[3]

0 **5** *shd* **The Last Debutante**[8] 7977 2-8-12 0........................ JoeFanning 7 67
(Mark Johnston) *t.k.h: hld up in tch in midfield: hdwy and edgd lft 1f out: wnt 4th ins fnl f: keeping on same pce and hld whn eased towards fin* **10/1**

6 **6** *¾* **Astute Boy (IRE)**[27] 7664 2-9-2 0........................ SteveDrowne 6 68
(Ed Vaughan) *dwlt: niggled along in last trio: hdwy and swtchd rt ins fnl f: styd on wout threatening ldrs* **7/1**

5 **7** *½* **Ferocity (IRE)**[46] 7184 2-8-13 0........................ LiamKeniry 10 64
(Robyn Brisland) *t.k.h: hld up in midfield: effrt and racd awkwardly over 1f out: hung lft and no imp ins fnl f* **11/4**[1]

454 **8** *1 ½* **Power Home (IRE)**[23] 7733 2-8-8 64........................ JosephineGordon 3 56
(Denis Coakley) *in tch in midfield: rdn and unable to 2f out: kpt on same pce and no imp over 1f out* **8/1**

0 **9** *¾* **Angel In Disguise (IRE)**[36] 7465 2-7-13 0........................ RhiainIngram[(7)] 11 52
(Philip McBride) *dwlt and pushed along early: hdwy to chse ldrs after 3f: rdn 3f out: carried lft and outpcd 1f out: wknd ins fnl f* **22/1**

10 *2 ¼* **Eugenie Feather (USA)** 2-8-7 0........................ LukeMorris 1 48
(Marco Botti) *chsd ldrs: rdn over 3f out: struggling and lost pl over 2f out: wknd over 1f out* **9/2**[2]

0 **11** *4 ½* **Pleasure Requested (IRE)**[23] 7733 2-9-1 0........................ JohnFahy 5 46
(Eve Johnson Houghton) *sn in rr and pushed along: no hdwy u.p over 1f out: bhd fnl f* **16/1**

1m 39.79s (-0.11) **Going Correction** -0.125s/f (Stan) **11** Ran SP% **124.4**
Speed ratings (Par 96): **95,94,94,93,93 92,92,90,89,87 83**
CSF £146.10 TOTE £21.20: £4.00, £3.30, £7.40; EX 229.70 Trifecta £7403.70.
Owner Mrs Anna Doyle **Bred** Mrs Eleanor Kent **Trained** East Everleigh, Wilts

FOCUS
An ordinary maiden, but an improved winner.

8083 BET TOTETRIFECTA H'CAP 6f (P)
6:25 (6:27) (Class 4) (0-85,85) 3-Y-O+ **£6,469** (£1,925; £962; £481) **Stalls** Centre

Form RPR

0061 **1** **Pearl Spectre (USA)**[3] 8052 5-9-4 **85** 6ex........................ CallumShepherd[(3)] 2 93
(Phil McEntee) *chsd ldrs: effrt to chal and drvn 1f out: kpt on gamely u.p to ld last strides* **7/2**[2]

0661 **2** *hd* **Dutch Golden Age (IRE)**[28] 7644 4-9-0 **78**........................ TomQueally 9 85
(Gary Moore) *led: rdn over 1f out: drvn and hrd pressed 1f out: kpt on gamely u.p tl hdd and no ex last strides* **14/1**

5240 **3** *hd* **Plucky Dip**[19] 7825 5-9-4 **82**........................ JosephineGordon 4 88
(John Ryan) *in tch in midfield: hdwy u.p over 1f out: chsd ldrs 1f out: ev ch 100yds out: kpt on wl* **6/1**

-204 **4** *nk* **Gold Club**[182] 2613 5-8-13 **77**........................ SeanLevey 11 82
(Ed McMahon) *chsd ldrs: effrt u.p over 1f out: drvn and ev ch 1f out: unable qck and styd on same pce wl ins fnl f* **16/1**

1-25 **5** *1* **King Cole (USA)**[124] 4662 3-9-3 **81**........................ JoeFanning 5 83+
(Robert Cowell) *hld up in tch in rr of main gp: hdwy on inner over 1f out: chsd ldrs ins fnl f: keeping on whn nt clr run and no imp wl ins fnl f* **5/2**[1]

-3 **6** *shd* **Zapper Cass (FR)**[88] 5946 3-9-5 **83**........................ DanielTudhope 7 85+
(Roger Fell) *hld up in tch in midfield: swtchd rt and effrt over 1f out: hdwy u.p over 1f out: kpt on wl fnl 100yds: nt rch ldrs* **22/1**

0040 **7** *nse* **Primrose Valley**[61] 6780 4-9-4 **85**........................(p) HectorCrouch[(3)] 1 87
(Ed Vaughan) *hld up in tch in midfield: swtchd rt and chsd ldrs over 1f out: rdn and nvr clrest of runs ins fnl f: kpt in same pce ins fnl f* **5/1**[3]

0045 **8** *½* **Outrage**[15] 7864 4-9-5 **83**........................ RichardKingscote 8 84+
(Daniel Kubler) *in tch in midfield: nt clr run and swtchd rt over 1f out: nt clr run again jst ins fnl f: kpt on same pce fnl 100yds* **14/1**

4231 **9** *hd* **Manatee Bay**[20] 7798 6-9-2 **80**........................(v) BarryMcHugh 14 79
(David Nicholls) *dwlt: sn rcvrd and in tch in midfield on outer: effrt u.p and bmpd over 1f out: kpt on same pce ins fnl f* **16/1**

0260 **10** *1* **Excellent George**[28] 7643 4-9-4 **82**........................(t) AdamBeschizza 12 78
(Stuart Williams) *chsd ldr tl unable qck and lost pl u.p over 1f out: wknd ins fnl f* **16/1**

0620 **11** *1 ¼* **Money Team (IRE)**[22] 7773 5-9-2 **80**........................ GrahamGibbons 3 72
(David Barron) *in tch in midfield: stuck bhd a wall of horses and swtchd rt over 1f out: no imp ins fnl f* **11/1**

12 *6* **Falcao (IRE)**[105] 5341 4-8-13 **77**........................ TimmyMurphy 10 50
(John Butler) *stdd and dropped in bhd after s: a detached in last: swtchd rt and wd bnd 2f out: nudged along and edgd lft over 1f out: no prog: eased wl ins fnl f* **25/1**

1m 11.92s (-1.78) **Going Correction** -0.125s/f (Stan) **12** Ran SP% **129.3**
Speed ratings (Par 105): **106,105,105,105,103 103,103,102,102,101 99,91**
CSF £57.71 CT £307.34 TOTE £5.70: £2.20, £3.10, £2.40; EX 67.10 Trifecta £442.00.
Owner Steve Jakes **Bred** Estate Of Edward P Evans **Trained** Newmarket, Suffolk

FOCUS
A competitive handicap and a bunched finish. The third helps set the standard, with the fourth close to form as well.

8084 COLLECT TOTEPOOL WINNINGS AT BETFRED SHOPS H'CAP 2m (P)
6:55 (6:57) (Class 5) (0-70,70) 3-Y-O+ **£4,204** (£1,251; £625; £312) **Stalls** Low

Form RPR

0031 **1** **Cavalieri (IRE)**[10] 7955 6-9-5 **61**........................(tp) KevinStott 11 72+
(Philip Kirby) *stdd s: hld up in last pair: clsd on bit 3f out: ev ch 2f out: sn led and rdn clr ent fnl f: easily* **5/1**[2]

4456 **2** *4 ½* **Voice Control (IRE)**[25] 7183 4-9-13 **69**...........................[1] LiamKeniry 8 73
(Laura Mongan) *s.i.s: hld up in tch in midfield: hdwy and nt clr run 3f out: swtchd rt and hdwy over 2f out: chsd ldng pair over 1f out: kpt on to go 2nd ins fnl f: no ch w wnr* **9/1**

5524 **3** *hd* **Lady Of Yue**[77] 6267 6-8-12 **61**...........................[1] LuluStanford[(7)] 5 65
(Eugene Stanford) *racd in last pair: nt clr run jst over 2f out: rdn and hdwy to chse ldng trio over 1f out: kpt on to go 3rd fnl 75yds: no ch w nr* **12/1**

0523 **4** *3 ½* **Balancing Time**[22] 7760 3-9-0 **65**...........................[1] JackMitchell 3 65
(Amanda Perrett) *t.k.h: hld up wl in tch in midfield: hdwy to ld 2f out: rdn and hdd over 1f out: sn outpcd by wnr: wknd and lost 2 pls ins fnl f* **7/4**[1]

5 *7* **Elusive Cowboy (USA)**[100] 5534 3-9-5 **70**........................ StevieDonohoe 4 61
(Stuart Edmunds) *hld up in tch in midfield: clsd to chse ldrs over 2f out: rdn and unable qck wl over 1f out: 5th and wl btn 1f out: wknd fnl f* **16/1**

0056 **6** *1 ¼* **Par Three (IRE)**[73] 6422 5-8-12 **54**........................(p) LukeMorris 7 44
(Tony Carroll) *reminders s: midfield: rdn 4f out: drvn and outpcd over 2f out: sn bhd : no ch but plugged on to pass btn horse fnl f* **33/1**

05-4 **7** 1 1/4 **Burning Desire (IRE)**17 488 5-9-3 **66**....................(tp) NicolaCurrie(7) 6 54
(Richard Hughes) *hld up in last trio: effrt on inner over 1f out: sn swtchd rt and no imp: wl hld and plugged on same pce ins fnl f* **33/1**

5-00 **8** 17 **Night Generation (GER)**23 7732 4-9-13 **69**.................(p) SeanLevey 10 37
(Chris Gordon) *chsd ldrs: shuffled bk into midfield and wd 6f out: rdn and no hdwy over 2f out: wknd over 1f out: sn bhd* **50/1**

6122 **9** nk **Free Bounty**49 7104 3-9-1 **66**...(t) JoeFanning 9 34
(Philip McBride) *chsd ldr: rdn and ev ch 4f out tl no ex 2f out: sn outpcd and wknd over 1f out: no ch and eased ins fnl f* **6/1**3

-014 **10** 23 **Halling's Wish**23 7739 6-9-8 **67**................................(b) HectorCrouch(3) 1 7
(Gary Moore) *trckd ldrs tl rdn to ld over 3f out: hdd over 2f out: sn btn and wknd over 1f out: wl btn and eased ins fnl f: t.o* **8/1**

2135 **11** 2 **Hiorne Tower (FR)**23 7739 5-9-3 **59**................................(v1) KierenFox 2
(John Best) *led: rdn 4f out: sn hdd: lost pl and bhd 2f out: t.o and eased ins fnl f* **8/1**

3m 29.05s (-0.95) **Going Correction** -0.125s/f (Stan)
WFA 3 from 4yo+ 9lb **11** Ran SP% **121.0**
Speed ratings (Par 103): **97,94,94,92,89 88,88,79,79,68 67**
CSF £50.35 CT £523.07 TOTE £5.70: £1.70, £2.70, £3.90; EX 53.30 Trifecta £392.60.
Owner The Cavalieri Partnership **Bred** Grange & Manister House Studs **Trained** East Appleton, N Yorks

FOCUS
A modest staying contest. The first three raced in the last four places early on. The runner-up has been rated to the balance of his form, with the third matching her old AW best.

8085 FOLLOW US ON TWITTER @CHELMSFORDCRC H'CAP (DIV I) 1m (P)
7:25 (7:28) (Class 6) (0-65,65) 3-Y-O+ **£3,234** (£962; £481; £240) **Stalls** Low

Form RPR

3040 **1** **East Coast Lady (IRE)**14 7889 4-9-0 **63**........................ HollieDoyle(5) 1 73
(William Stone) *broke wl and racd keenly in the ld: rdn and clr w rival over 1f out: forged ahd ins fnl f: styd on: rdn out* **9/2**2

1016 **2** 2 **Candesta (USA)**23 7736 6-8-9 **60**.................................. LiamDoran(7) 5 65
(Julia Feilden) *midfield: swtchd rt and hdwy over 1f out: rdn and styd on to chse wnr ins fnl f: kpt on wl but nvr getting to wnr* **12/1**

5-50 **3** 1 3/4 **Muzaahim (IRE)**281 607 5-8-11 **58**................................ EoinWalsh(3) 2 59
(Kevin Morgan) *s.i.s: hld up off the pce in rr: clsd and nt clr run over 1f out:* **10/1**

5430 **4** shd **Tyrsal (IRE)**15 7870 5-9-5 **63**....................................... AdamBeschizza 4 64
(Clifford Lines) *racd off the pce towards rr: effrt 2f out: hdwy u.p over 1f out: styd on ins fnl f: no threat to wnr* **8/1**

0502 **5** 1 **Rattle On**28 7642 3-9-2 **62**...1 TomQueally 9 60
(Jim Boyle) *chsd ldng trio: effrt in 3rd 2f out: hung lft u.p and no imp over 1f out: kpt on same pce ins fnl f* **2/1**1

1110 **6** nse **Bazzat (IRE)**28 7642 3-9-3 **63**......................................(p) MartinHarley 10 61
(John Ryan) *bustled along leaving stalls: chsd wnr: upsides 2f out: sn rdn and drew clr w wnr: no ex and btn ins fnl f: wknd fnl 100yds* **6/1**3

406 **7** 3 **Phileas Fogg (IRE)**12 7942 3-9-5 **65**....................... JosephineGordon 6 56
(Martyn Meade) *midfield: rdn 3f out: no imp u.p on inner over 1f out: wknd ins fnl f* **8/1**

060 **8** hd **Jackblack**12 7942 4-9-4 **62**.. KierenFox 3 53
(Patrick Chamings) *sn bustled along and off the pce towards rr: no imp u.p over 1f out: wknd ins fnl f* **12/1**

031- **9** 13 **Sir Lancelott**338 8354 4-9-7 **65**...................................... DanielTudhope 8 26
(David O'Meara) *broke wl: restrained to chse ldrs: 4th and wkng 2f out: bhd and eased wl ins fnl f* **10/1**

0-00 **10** 25 **Divasesque (IRE)**96 5636 3-8-2 **51** oh6........................ NoelGarbutt(3) 7
(Derek Shaw) *sn bhd: detached in last and struggling u.p 1/2-way: lost tch 2f out: t.o* **100/1**

1m 38.47s (-1.43) **Going Correction** -0.125s/f (Stan)
WFA 3 from 4yo+ 2lb **10** Ran SP% **122.6**
Speed ratings (Par 101): **102,100,98,98,97 97,94,93,80,55**
CSF £60.53 CT £527.23 TOTE £5.90: £2.40, £3.90, £2.80; EX 61.70 Trifecta £827.80.
Owner Miss Caroline Scott **Bred** Mountarmstrong Stud **Trained** West Wickham, Cambs

FOCUS
Few got into this. Straightforward form, with the runner-up to his recent C&D level.

8086 FOLLOW US ON TWITTER @CHELMSFORDCRC H'CAP (DIV II) 1m (P)
7:55 (7:55) (Class 6) (0-65,65) 3-Y-O+ **£3,234** (£962; £481; £240) **Stalls** Low

Form RPR

0246 **1** **Pacific Salt (IRE)**29 7613 3-9-2 **65**......................... CallumShepherd(3) 5 72
(Pam Sly) *trckd ldr and travelled strly: rdn to ld over 1f out: drvn and a doing enough ins fnl f: styd on* **9/2**3

2040 **2** 1 1/4 **Catastrophe**23 7755 3-9-1 **61**... JasonHart 2 65
(John Quinn) *hld up in tch in midfield: effrt 2f out: hdwy u.p 1f out: chsd wnr ins fnl f: kpt on but a hld* **7/1**

66-0 **3** 3/4 **Amor Invicto (IRE)**269 765 3-9-3 **63**..................(b1) RichardKingscote 3 65
(Daniel Kubler) *led: rdn ent fnl 2f: hdd over 1f out: kpt on same pce u.p ins fnl f* **25/1**

1421 **4** 3/4 **Barista (IRE)**14 7889 8-8-13 **62**....................................... HollieDoyle(5) 7 64
(Brian Forsey) *in tch in midfield: effrt over 1f out: sn rdn and styd on same pce ins fnl f* **7/1**

5052 **5** 1/2 **Tommy's Secret**42 7310 6-9-2 **65**.............................. CharlieBennett(5) 4 66
(Jane Chapple-Hyam) *chsd ldrs: rdn ent fnl 2f: drvn over 1f out: styd on same pce ins fnl f* **11/4**2

3252 **6** 3 1/4 **Rebel State (IRE)**23 7735 3-9-4 **64**..............................(vt1) LiamKeniry 1 56
(Richard Spencer) *stmbld leaving stalls: hld up in tch in last pair: effrt u.p and hung lft over 1f out: swtchd rt and no imp ins fnl f* **15/8**1

0600 **7** 9 **Muthraab Aldaar (IRE)**14 7887 3-9-5 **65**........................... JackMitchell 6 36
(Jim Boyle) *s.i.s: a rr: rdn 1/2-way: wknd and bhd over 1f out* **14/1**

516 **8** 1 3/4 **Anjuna Beach (USA)**218 1578 6-8-5 **54**............................ AnnStokell(5) 8 22
(Ann Stokell) *taken down early: t.k.h: hld up in tch in midfield: rdn and struggling jst over 2f out: bhd and hung lft over 1f out* **33/1**

1m 39.11s (-0.79) **Going Correction** -0.125s/f (Stan)
WFA 3 from 6yo+ 2lb **8** Ran SP% **118.1**
Speed ratings (Par 101): **98,96,96,95,94 91,82,80**
CSF £36.99 CT £714.24 TOTE £5.40: £1.50, £2.30, £6.90; EX 44.00 Trifecta £647.80.
Owner D L Bayliss & G A Libson **Bred** Tally-Ho Stud **Trained** Thorney, Cambs

FOCUS
The slower of the two divisions by 0.64sec. A minor pb from the winner, rated around the 2nd/3rd.
T/Plt: £22,683.70 to a £1 stake. Pool: £108,757.61 - 3.50 winning units. T/Qpdt: £554.20 to a £1 stake. Pool: £14,455.21 - 19.30 winning units. **Steve Payne**

8007 NEWCASTLE (A.W) (L-H)
Friday, November 25

OFFICIAL GOING: Tapeta: standard
Wind: Almost nil Weather: Sunny

8087 32RED.COM NURSERY H'CAP 1m 5y (Tp)
12:40 (12:43) (Class 6) (0-65,65) 2-Y-O **£2,587** (£770; £384; £192) **Stalls** Centre

Form RPR

4504 **1** **Dream Team**49 7110 2-9-0 **58**......................................(p) PaulMulrennan 4 63
(Michael Dods) *plld hrd in rr: stdy hdwy over 2f out: rdn to ld over 1f out: kpt on wl fnl f* **4/1**1

402 **2** 1 1/4 **Miss Danby (IRE)**115 4966 2-9-7 **65**.................................. JoeFanning 8 67
(Mark Johnston) *pressed ldr: led over 2f out: rdn: edgd lft and hdd over 1f out: kpt on same pce ins fnl f* **9/2**2

5305 **3** 1 1/4 **Lil's Affair (IRE)**49 7109 2-8-5 **49**....................................(p) LukeMorris 6 49
(Bryan Smart) *prom: rdn over 2f out: hdwy over 1f out: kpt on ins fnl f: nt enough pce to chal* **9/2**2

1000 **4** 1 **Madam Prancealot (IRE)**32 7570 2-9-2 **60**................ ConnorBeasley 2 57
(David Evans) *cl up: ev ch over 2f out to over 1f out: outpcd fnl f* **5/1**3

0540 **5** 1 1/4 **Belle's Angel (IRE)**56 6923 2-8-3 **47**..........................1 PatrickMathers 9 42
(Ann Duffield) *t.k.h early: cl up: rdn over 2f out: edgd lft and outpcd appr fnl f* **14/1**

440 **6** 3 3/4 **Vivardia (IRE)**32 7578 2-9-4 **62**... GrahamLee 1 48
(Ben Haslam) *hld up: rdn and outpcd wl over 2f out: rallied over 1f out: no imp fnl f* **16/1**

0606 **7** 1 **Mystic Maeve (IRE)**17 7854 2-8-7 **51**........................(p) TomMarquand 5 35
(Roger Fell) *led: rdn and hdd over 2f out: wknd over 1f out* **14/1**

0056 **8** 3 3/4 **Silver Gleam (IRE)**52 7041 2-9-2 **60** ow3......................... DougieCostello 10 36
(Chris Fairhurst) *s.i.s: hld up: rdn and outpcd over 2f out: sn btn* **40/1**

1m 41.29s (2.69) **Going Correction** +0.10s/f (Slow) **8** Ran SP% **94.7**
Speed ratings (Par 94): **90,88,87,86,85 81,80,76**
CSF £14.81 CT £42.20 TOTE £4.40: £1.60, £1.40, £1.60; EX 17.30 Trifecta £33.90.
Owner Denton Hall Racing Ltd **Bred** R G Percival **Trained** Denton, Co Durham
■ Magic Journey was withdrawn. Price at time of withdrawal 7/2f. Rule 4 applies to all bets - deduction 20p in the pound.
■ Stewards' Enquiry : Luke Morris four-day ban; used whip arm above shoulder height (9th-13th Dec)

FOCUS
The course was worked deeper earlier in the week as part of routine maintenance. The early pace wasn't particularly strong in this modest nursery. A pb from the winner and the 3rd fits.

8088 32RED.COM MAIDEN STKS (PLUS 10 RACE) 1m 5y (Tp)
1:15 (1:18) (Class 4) 2-Y-O **£4,204** (£1,251; £625; £312) **Stalls** Centre

Form RPR

1 **Middle Kingdom (USA)** 2-9-5 0.................................... NickyMackay 5 86+
(John Gosden) *missed break: hld up: shkn up and hdwy over 2f out: wnt 2nd over 1f out: led ins fnl f: pushed clr fnl f: readily* **5/1**3

2 3 1/2 **Mukalal** 2-9-5 0.. BenCurtis 6 76
(Marcus Tregoning) *plld hrd in midfield: gd hdwy to ld over 2f out: rdn and 3 l clr over 1f out: rdn: hung lft and hdd ins fnl f: no ch w ready wnr* **50/1**

3 1/2 **The Statesman**41 7370 2-9-5 0...................................... WilliamCarson 2 75
(Jamie Osborne) *trckd ldrs: rdn over 2f out: sn outpcd: rallied fnl f: kpt on: nrst fin* **15/8**1

03 **4** 1 **Lorikeet (USA)**14 7907 2-9-5 0... JoeFanning 3 73
(Mark Johnston) *led to over 2f out: rdn and kpt on same pce fr over 1f out* **8/1**

0 **5** 1 3/4 **Incandescent**23 7769 2-9-0 0.. TomQueally 4 64
(James Fanshawe) *trckd ldrs: rdn over 2f out: outpcd fr over 1f out* **6/1**

6 2 1/2 **Battle Ensign (USA)** 2-9-5 0.................................. JosephineGordon 9 64
(Saeed bin Suroor) *midfield: rdn and outpcd over 2f out: no imp fr over 1f out* **11/4**2

0 **7** 4 **Power Power (IRE)**24 7740 2-9-5 0..................................... LukeMorris 1 55
(Marco Botti) *hld up: stdy hdwy over 2f out: sn rdn: edgd lft and wknd over 1f out* **14/1**

5 **8** 1 3/4 **Cray (IRE)**28 7659 2-9-5 0... TomMarquand 7 51
(James Bethell) *bhd and pushed along: drvn and outpcd over 2f out: sme late hdwy: nvr on terms* **22/1**

9 2 3/4 **Noble Behest** 2-8-12 0... TylerSaunders(7) 12 45
(Marcus Tregoning) *hld up: pushed along over 4f out: hdwy over 2f out: wknd wl over 1f out* **100/1**

0 **10** nk **Belisa (IRE)**23 7770 2-9-0 0... GrahamLee 8 39
(Ivan Furtado) *trckd ldrs: rdn over 2f out: wknd wl over 1f out* **100/1**

0 **11** 3 1/4 **Light Gunner (IRE)**35 7501 2-9-2 0.................................. EoinWalsh(3) 10 37
(Henry Tett) *hld up: rdn and struggling over 2f out: sn btn* **100/1**

12 1/2 **Make Memories (USA)** 2-9-5 0......................................1 RobertTart 11 36
(John Gosden) *hld up: sn pushed along: struggling over 3f out: sn btn* **25/1**

1m 38.95s (0.35) **Going Correction** +0.10s/f (Slow) **12** Ran SP% **123.3**
Speed ratings (Par 98): **102,98,98,97,95 92,88,87,84,83 80,80**
CSF £246.94 TOTE £6.30: £2.00, £5.90, £1.50; EX 113.40 Trifecta £1285.30.
Owner China Horse Club **Bred** Lofts Hall Stud **Trained** Newmarket, Suffolk

FOCUS
A fair maiden, two newcomers coming out on top, with the third and fourth, rated up a tad, probably sound guides to the level.

8089 £10 FREE AT 32RED.COM MAIDEN STKS 7f 14y (Tp)
1:45 (1:48) (Class 5) 2-Y-O **£2,911** (£866; £432; £216) **Stalls** Centre

Form RPR

0 **1** **Native Soldier (IRE)**29 7648 2-9-5 0................................ TomQueally 6 72
(William Haggas) *s.s: hld up: gd hdwy over 1f out: led ins fnl f: pushed along and kpt on wl* **6/1**3

0 **2** nk **Al Yarmouk**15 7882 2-9-5 0... NickyMackay 8 71
(John Gosden) *in tch: pushed along: hdwy and ev ch over 1f out: pressed wnr wl ins fnl f: kpt on* **15/2**

43 **3** 1/2 **Envisaging (IRE)**91 5828 2-9-5 0.................................... DanielMuscutt 14 70
(James Fanshawe) *hld up: smooth hdwy to ld over 1f out: sn rdn: hdd ins fnl f: kpt on: hld cl home* **3/1**2

4 3 1/2 **Mesophere** 2-9-5 0.. RobertTart 4 61+
(John Gosden) *hld up midfield: pushed along and outpcd over 2f out: rallied over 1f out: kpt on fnl f: no imp* **7/1**

0 **5** 1 1/4 **Eighth Circle (IRE)**23 7770 2-9-5 0................................ TomMarquand 3 58
(Henry Spiller) *t.k.h: w ldr: rdn over 2f out: wknd over 1f out* **100/1**

	6	½	**Dreamofdiscovery (IRE)** 2-9-5 0 .... JoeDoyle 2	57+
			(Julie Camacho) *prom tl rdn and wknd over 1f out* **40/1**	
	7	½	**Life Won't Wait** 2-9-5 0 .... JasonHart 7	56+
			(John Quinn) *cl up: rdn over 2f of: wknd fnl f* **40/1**	
	8	hd	**Barwell (IRE)** 2-9-5 0 .... ConnorBeasley 10	55
			(Michael Dods) *t.k.h: hld up: stdy hdwy and shkn up over 1f out: kpt on fnl f: nvr nr ldrs* **12/1**	
00	9	1 ½	**Little Kingdom (IRE)**[42] 7330 2-9-1 0 ow1 .... DaleSwift 5	47
			(Tracy Waggott) *mde most to over 1f out: rdn and wknd fnl f* **200/1**	
022	10	1 ½	**Kingofmerrows (IRE)**[34] 7527 2-9-5 78 .... WilliamCarson 12	48
			(Jamie Osborne) *hld up midfield: drvn along over 2f out: wknd over 1f out* **2/1**[1]	
5	11	½	**Rainbow Chimes (IRE)**[159] 3433 2-8-9 0 .... RowanScott(5) 11	41
			(Ann Duffield) *in tch: lost pl over 2f out: sn wknd* **20/1**	
	12	½	**Lady Rowena** 2-9-0 0 .... JoeFanning 9	40
			(Mark Johnston) *hld up midfield: hdwy wl over 2f out: wknd over 1f out* **20/1**	
0	13	hd	**Rey Loopy (IRE)**[35] 7496 2-9-5 0 .... PaulMulrennan 1	45
			(Ben Haslam) *hld up: rdn and outpcd over 2f out: sn btn* **100/1**	
0	14	1	**Crucial Response**[24] 7740 2-9-5 0 .... GrahamLee 13	42
			(Ben Haslam) *hld up: drvn over 2f out: sn btn* **200/1**	

1m 29.16s (2.96) **Going Correction** +0.10s/f (Slow) **14** Ran SP% **122.0**
Speed ratings (Par 96): **87,86,86,82,80 80,79,79,77,75 75,74,74,73**
CSF £48.73 TOTE £6.80: £2.00, £2.80, £1.60; EX 53.40 Trifecta £245.10.
Owner Mohamed Obaida **Bred** Rabbah Bloodstock Limited **Trained** Newmarket, Suffolk

FOCUS
The pace gradually wound up here and the first three, two of whom came from the back of the field, finished clear, with all of them showing improved form.

8090 32RED.COM FILLIES' H'CAP — 1m 2f 42y (Tp)
2:20 (2:21) (Class 5) (0-75,75) 3-Y-O+ **£2,911** (£866; £432; £216) **Stalls** High

Form				RPR
252	1		**Just For You**[13] 7942 3-9-5 **74** .... TomQueally 8	81+
			(James Fanshawe) *prom: smooth hdwy 2f out: shkn up to ld 1f out: rdn and kpt on wl* **10/11**[1]	
2433	2	nk	**Statuesque**[14] 7904 3-9-6 **75** .... (v[1]) GrahamLee 2	81
			(Sir Michael Stoute) *pressed ldr: rdn to ld over 2f out: hdd 1f out: rallied: hld nr fin* **9/2**[3]	
2520	3	1 ½	**Shadow Spirit**[17] 7853 3-8-9 **71** .... JamieGormley(7) 7	74
			(Iain Jardine) *s.i.s: hld up: hdwy over 1f out: rdn and kpt on same pce ins fnl f* **10/1**	
5166	4	1 ¼	**Raven Banner (IRE)**[17] 7853 3-9-1 **70** .... DaleSwift 10	71
			(Daniel Mark Loughnane) *t.k.h: hld up in last pl: rdn over 2f out: kpt on fnl f: nvr able to chal* **20/1**	
4345	5	1	**Livella Fella (IRE)**[17] 7853 3-9-5 **74** .... ConnorBeasley 6	73
			(Keith Dalgleish) *prom: drvn and outpcd over 1f out: btn ins fnl f* **9/1**	
5441	6	1	**Princess Raihana**[57] 6901 3-9-2 **71** .... LukeMorris 1	68
			(Marco Botti) *led at stdy pce: rdn and hdd over 2f out: wknd fnl f* **4/1**[2]	

2m 15.79s (5.39) **Going Correction** +0.025s/f (Slow)
WFA 3 from 4yo+ 4lb **6** Ran SP% **114.4**
Speed ratings (Par 100): **79,78,77,76,75 74**
CSF £5.61 CT £24.00 TOTE £1.90: £1.20, £3.00; EX 6.10 Trifecta £27.90.
Owner John P McManus **Bred** Floors Farming, S Roy & Admington Hall **Trained** Newmarket, Suffolk

FOCUS
This weak fillies' handicap was steadily run and developed into a bit of a sprint.

8091 BETWAY H'CAP — 2m 56y (Tp)
2:55 (2:55) (Class 6) (0-60,57) 3-Y-O+ **£2,587** (£770; £384; £192) **Stalls** Low

Form				RPR
4606	1		**Merriment**[8] 7992 3-9-3 **57** .... (p) GrahamLee 3	66+
			(Peter Niven) *dwlt: hld up in tch: pushed along and outpcd over 4f out: rallied over 2f out: led over 1f out: rdn clr ins fnl f* **15/8**[1]	
4336	2	4 ½	**Jan Smuts (IRE)**[18] 7846 8-9-7 **57** .... (tp) HollieDoyle(5) 2	61
			(Wilf Storey) *t.k.h: cl up: wnt 2nd after 6f: led over 2f out to over 1f out: kpt on same pce ins fnl f* **11/4**[3]	
0006	3	1 ¾	**Waltz Darling (IRE)**[125] 4645 8-9-2 **47** .... JoeFanning 5	49
			(Keith Reveley) *s.i.s: sn chsng ldr: led after 4f: rdn and hdd over 2f out: outpcd over 1f out: no imp fnl f* **7/1**	
4452	4	1 ¼	**Magnolia Ridge (IRE)**[28] 7656 6-9-2 **47** .... (p) JasonHart 4	47
			(Mark Walford) *led 4f: cl up: drvn and outpcd 2f out: no imp after* **2/1**[2]	
0300	5	16	**Come On Lulu**[28] 7657 5-9-0 **45** .... (b) PatrickMathers 1	26
			(David Thompson) *prom: drvn and struggling over 4f out: lost tch over 2f out: t.o* **20/1**	

3m 34.89s (-0.31) **Going Correction** +0.025s/f (Slow)
WFA 3 from 5yo+ 9lb **5** Ran SP% **112.0**
Speed ratings (Par 101): **101,98,97,97,89**
CSF £7.56 TOTE £2.90: £1.60, £1.70; EX 7.90 Trifecta £24.10.
Owner G C Wragg **Bred** The Queen **Trained** Barton-le-Street, N Yorks

FOCUS
Not much of a race.

8092 SUNBETS.CO.UK H'CAP — 1m 5y (Tp)
3:30 (3:31) (Class 4) (0-80,80) 3-Y-O+ **£5,175** (£1,540; £769; £384) **Stalls** Centre

Form				RPR
2103	1		**Amazement (GER)**[161] 3364 3-9-5 **80** .... LukeMorris 11	93+
			(James Tate) *hld up: hdwy to ld over 1f out: drvn and kpt on wl fnl f* **5/1**[2]	
3006	2	1 ¼	**War Department (IRE)**[11] 7957 3-9-4 **79** .... (v) ConnorBeasley 8	88
			(Keith Dalgleish) *hld up: hdwy over 2f out: effrt and chsd wnr over 1f out: rdn and kpt on same pce ins fnl f* **12/1**	
5211	3	2 ¼	**Testa Rossa (IRE)**[17] 7857 6-8-10 **69** .... (b) TomMarquand 1	74
			(Jim Goldie) *prom: effrt and rdn over 2f out: kpt on same pce fnl f* **13/2**[3]	
0000	4	nk	**Balducci**[17] 7857 9-8-7 **66** .... BenCurtis 9	70
			(Roger Fell) *led: rdn over 2f out: hdd over 1f out: outpcd fnl f* **50/1**	
0065	5	1 ¾	**Auspicion**[17] 7857 4-8-13 **72** .... JamesSullivan 2	72
			(Tom Tate) *s.i.s: hld up: rdn over 3f out: hdwy over 1f out: kpt on fnl f: no imp* **7/1**	
0615	6	½	**Eastern Dragon (IRE)**[21] 7796 6-8-13 **77** .... (p) ShirleyTeasdale(5) 10	76
			(Iain Jardine) *hld up: rdn over 2f out: hdwy over 1f out: kpt on: nvr able to chal* **10/1**	
1035	7	hd	**The Lynch Man**[38] 7435 3-8-5 **66** .... (v) PatrickMathers 12	64
			(John Quinn) *prom: rdn over 2f out: outpcd fr over 1f out* **14/1**	
3400	8	nk	**Character Onesie (IRE)**[14] 7902 4-9-3 **76** .... DavidNolan 7	74
			(Richard Fahey) *hld up: rdn and effrt over 2f out: no imp over 1f out* **10/1**	
2064	9	¾	**Tadaany (IRE)**[31] 7593 4-9-0 **80** .... PatrickVaughan(7) 6	76
			(David O'Meara) *pressed ldrs: rdn and ev ch over 2f out: wknd oer 1f out* **20/1**	
531	10	4 ½	**Westward Ho (IRE)**[28] 7661 3-9-4 **79** .... JoeFanning 3	64
			(James Bethell) *in tch: effrt and rdn over 2f out: wknd over 1f out* **4/1**[1]	
006	11	3 ¼	**Pickett's Charge**[38] 7435 3-8-0 **66** .... HollieDoyle(5) 4	43
			(Richard Guest) *pressed ldr to over 2f out: sn rdn and wknd* **10/1**	
5300	12	½	**Weather Front (USA)**[17] 7857 3-8-11 **72** .... (v[1]) GrahamLee 5	48
			(Karen McLintock) *s.i.s: hld up: rdn and outpcd wl over 2f out: sn btn* **8/1**	

1m 38.21s (-0.39) **Going Correction** +0.10s/f (Slow)
WFA 3 from 4yo+ 2lb **12** Ran SP% **122.0**
Speed ratings (Par 105): **105,103,101,101,99 98,98,98,97,93 89,89**
CSF £65.94 CT £408.29 TOTE £5.40: £2.30, £4.90, £2.50; EX 81.00 Trifecta £235.30.
Owner Sheikh Juma Dalmook Al Maktoum **Bred** Gestut Ammerland **Trained** Newmarket, Suffolk

FOCUS
A fair handicap and the first two, who looked potentially well treated, came home well from off the pace.

8093 32RED CASINO MAIDEN FILLIES' STKS — 6f (Tp)
4:00 (4:02) (Class 5) 3-Y-O+ **£2,911** (£866; £432; £216) **Stalls** Centre

Form				RPR
	1		**Hackney Road** 3-9-0 0 .... TomQueally 1	72+
			(Henry Spiller) *t.k.h: hld up in tch: smooth hdwy to ld over 1f out: pushed out fnl f: comf* **8/1**[3]	
030	2	2 ¼	**Andys Girl (IRE)**[55] 6960 3-9-0 60 .... BenCurtis 7	63
			(Brian Ellison) *s.i.s: hld up: hdwy to chse wnr over 1f out: rdn and kpt on same pce ins fnl f* **10/1**	
002	3	1 ¼	**Sonnet (IRE)**[8] 7995 3-9-0 64 .... (v) ConnorBeasley 4	59
			(David Evans) *t.k.h: prom: effrt and ev ch briefly over 1f out: kpt on same pce fnl f* **13/8**[2]	
	4	hd	**Tibibit** 3-8-11 0 .... EoinWalsh(3) 6	58
			(Henry Tett) *s.i.s: hld up: rdn over 2f out: hdwy over 1f out: kpt on fnl f: no imp* **40/1**	
52-3	5	3 ½	**Initially**[28] 7661 3-9-0 68 .... LukeMorris 5	47
			(Charles Hills) *pressed ldr to over 2f out: drvn and wknd fr over 1f out* **11/10**[1]	
602	6	2 ¾	**Poetic Queen (IRE)**[17] 7856 3-9-0 55 .... NeilFarley 3	38
			(Eric Alston) *led tl rdn and hdd over 1f out: sn wknd* **20/1**	
65	7	1 ¼	**Any Joy (IRE)**[93] 5757 3-9-0 57 .... PaulMulrennan 2	34
			(Ben Haslam) *trckd ldrs: outpcd and hung lft over 2f out: sn wknd* **16/1**	

1m 12.13s (-0.37) **Going Correction** +0.10s/f (Slow) **7** Ran SP% **119.0**
Speed ratings (Par 100): **106,103,101,101,96 92,91**
CSF £85.13 TOTE £9.10: £3.80, £4.00; EX 79.60 Trifecta £240.00.
Owner Dethrone Racing **Bred** Whatton Manor Stud **Trained** Newmarket, Suffolk

FOCUS
They went a really good pace in this modest maiden and that suited those held up. Nevertheless, the winner, for whom there was some support, won comfortably. This has been rated around the runner-up.
T/Plt: £33.00 to a £1 stake. Pool: £66139.33 - 1462.75 winning units. T/Qpdt: £15.20 to a £1 stake. Pool: £5346.18 - 259.3 winning units. **Richard Young**

8071 WOLVERHAMPTON (A.W) (L-H)
Friday, November 25

OFFICIAL GOING: Tapeta: standard
Wind: Light against Weather: Fine

8094 BETWAY SPRINT DISTANCE H'CAP (DIV I) — 5f 216y (Tp)
4:15 (4:17) (Class 6) (0-65,69) 3-Y-O+ **£2,587** (£770; £384; £192) **Stalls** Low

Form				RPR
0420	1		**Coquine**[24] 7751 3-8-13 **57** ....[1] GrahamGibbons 13	63
			(David O'Meara) *pushed along in rr early: hdwy over 4f out: rdn over 1f out: led and hung lft ins fnl f: styd on* **10/1**	
6506	2	1	**Loumarin (IRE)**[30] 7612 4-9-2 **60** .... AndrewMullen 3	63
			(Michael Appleby) *s.i.s: hdwy to go prom 5f out: rdn to ld 1f out: hdd ins fnl f: styd on same pce* **12/1**	
2401	3	1 ¼	**Divine Call**[14] 7912 9-9-4 **62** .... (b) MartinHarley 8	61
			(Milton Bradley) *hld up: hdwy over 1f out: shkn up ins fnl f: styd on same pce* **5/1**[2]	
0361	4	½	**Head Space (IRE)**[6] 8031 8-9-11 **69** 6ex .... RobertWinston 11	67
			(David Evans) *broke wl: sn stdd and lost pl: rdn over 1f out: r.o ins fnl f: nt rch ldrs* **13/2**	
0401	5	½	**Captain Ryan**[14] 7913 5-9-3 **61** .... SteveDrowne 12	57
			(Geoffrey Deacon) *hld up: hdwy over 1f out: no ex wl ins fnl f* **11/2**[3]	
0002	6	hd	**Camdora (IRE)**[27] 7693 4-9-3 **61** .... (t) TimmyMurphy 10	57
			(Jamie Osborne) *hld up: shkn up over 1f out: r.o towards fin: nt trble ldrs* **9/2**[1]	
0301	7	¾	**Firesnake (IRE)**[20] 7815 3-8-12 **63** .... JordanUys(7) 9	56
			(Lisa Williamson) *hld up in tch: rdn over 1f out: no ex ins fnl f* **8/1**	
4005	8	½	**Dr Red Eye**[15] 7896 8-8-5 **56** .... (b) RPWalsh(7) 5	48
			(Scott Dixon) *w ldrs: led 4f out: rdn and hdd 1f out: no ex wl ins fnl f* **25/1**	
0500	9	nk	**Monsieur Jimmy**[28] 7663 4-9-1 **64** .... PhilDennis(5) 2	55
			(Declan Carroll) *hld up: hdwy over 1f out: no ex ins fnl f* **50/1**	
5010	10	1 ¼	**Anieres Boy**[44] 7290 4-9-0 **58** .... (t[1]) KevinStott 4	45
			(Oliver Greenall) *s.i.s: hld up: rdn over 1f out: nvr on terms* **9/1**	
0200	11	1	**Llewellyn**[119] 4848 8-9-7 **65** .... DanielTudhope 6	49
			(Declan Carroll) *sn led: hdd 4f out: rdn and ev ch over 1f out: wknd ins fnl f* **12/1**	
6020	12	2	**Sir Geoffrey (IRE)**[11] 7961 10-8-7 **58** .... (p) NatalieHambling(7) 7	36
			(Scott Dixon) *led early: chsd ldrs: rdn over 1f out: wknd ins fnl f* **33/1**	

1m 13.58s (-0.92) **Going Correction** -0.175s/f (Stan) **12** Ran SP% **117.9**
Speed ratings (Par 101): **99,97,96,95,94 94,93,92,92,90 89,86**
CSF £121.40 CT £686.33 TOTE £12.60: £3.20, £4.40, £2.10; EX 155.80 Trifecta £3386.30.
Owner R S Cockerill (Farms) Ltd **Bred** R S Cockerill (farms) Ltd **Trained** Upper Helmsley, N Yorks
■ Stewards' Enquiry : Martin Harley jockey said that the gelding lost its action in the home straight.

FOCUS
An ordinary handicap, with the winner finding a fraction on recent form.

8095 BETWAY SPRINT DISTANCE H'CAP (DIV II) — 5f 216y (Tp)
4:45 (4:47) (Class 6) (0-65,65) 3-Y-O+ **£2,587** (£770; £384; £192) **Stalls** Low

Form				RPR
003	1		**Swanton Blue (IRE)**[10] 7964 3-9-1 **62** .... CallumShepherd(3) 7	69
			(Ed de Giles) *hld up: hdwy and nt clr run fr over 1f out tl swtchd lft wl ins fnl f: r.o to ld nr fin* **7/1**[3]	

0-50 **2** *shd* **Baileys Pursuit**[72] 6487 4-9-2 **60** TonyHamilton 6 67
(Gay Kelleway) *chsd ldrs: sn pushed along: lost pl after 1f: hdwy over 1f out: rdn to ld and edgd rt ins fnl f: hdd nr fin* **9/1**

4640 **3** *hd* **Life Of Fame**[17] 7860 3-8-12 **56** GrahamGibbons 13 62
(David O'Meara) *mid-div: hdwy over 1f out: sn rdn: r.o wl* **16/1**

5660 **4** *1 ½* **Major Valentine**[30] 7617 4-9-7 **65** TimmyMurphy 3 70
(John O'Shea) *trckd ldrs: cl up whn hmpd and lost pl over 1f out: nt rcvr* **10/1**

1656 **5** *shd* **Compton Prince**[6] 8030 7-9-3 **61** (b) RobertWinston 4 62
(Milton Bradley) *chsd ldrs: rdn and ev ch ins fnl f: no ex towards fin* **12/1**

6-06 **6** *nk* **Ad Vitam (IRE)**[18] 7851 8-9-0 **58** (bt) BarryMcHugh 11 58
(Suzzanne France) *sn pushed along in rr: r.o ins fnl f: nvr nrr* **10/1**

0554 **7** *½* **Misu Pete**[24] 7751 4-8-13 **57** SteveDrowne 8 56
(Mark Usher) *in rr: rdn and r.o ins fnl f: nrst fin* **15/2**

1150 **8** *2 ½* **Intense Starlet (IRE)**[45] 7255 5-9-6 **64** (p) ShaneGray 12 55
(Marjorie Fife) *hld up: rdn over 1f out: nvr on terms* **16/1**

0-04 **9** *½* **Macho Mac**[32] 7585 3-8-12 **61** CharlieBennett(5) 5 51+
(Hughie Morrison) *plld hrd: sn w ldr: rdn to ld and hung lft over 1f out: hdd and no ex ins fnl f* **4/1**[1]

3500 **10** *1 ¾* **Whozthecat (IRE)**[18] 7851 9-9-7 **65** (vt) DanielTudhope 2 50+
(Declan Carroll) *sn led: rdn over 2f out: hdd over 1f out: nt clr run and wknd ins fnl f* **13/2**[2]

6003 **11** *1 ½* **Le Manege Enchante (IRE)**[27] 7694 3-8-11 **58** (p) NoelGarbutt(3) 1 41
(Derek Shaw) *s.i.s: in rr: running on whn rn out of room ins fnl f: n.d* **16/1**

0403 **12** *1* **Spowarticus**[139] 4142 7-8-12 **63** (b) RPWalsh(7) 10 40+
(Scott Dixon) *led early: chsd ldrs: hung rt over 2f out: sn rdn: wknd over 1f out* **33/1**

1m 13.66s (-0.84) **Going Correction** -0.175s/f (Stan) **12 Ran SP% 114.1**
Speed ratings (Par 101): **98,97,97,95,95 95,94,91,90,88 86,84**
CSF £65.93 CT £984.33 TOTE £5.80: £2.00, £3.70, £4.70; EX 63.30 Trifecta £765.80.
Owner Ian Gibson **Bred** Tally-Ho Stud **Trained** Ledbury, H'fords
■ Stewards' Enquiry : Callum Shepherd two-day ban; used his whip without giving his mount time to respond (9th-10th Dec)

FOCUS
The second division was run in a time similar to the first leg, again at a good pace. The winner was on a fair mark on this year's form.

8096 BETWAY MAIDEN STKS 1m 5f 194y (Tp)
5:15 (5:17) (Class 5) 3-Y-O+ **£2,911** (£866; £432; £216) **Stalls** Low

Form RPR

623 **1** **Going Up (IRE)**[36] 7487 3-9-5 83 MartinHarley 2 88+
(Rae Guest) *chsd ldr tl led over 8f out: rdn clr fr over 1f out* **8/13**[1]

0442 **2** *6* **Adalene**[14] 7904 3-9-0 77 ShaneKelly 6 73
(David Simcock) *chsd ldrs: wnt 2nd 3f out: rdn: hung lft and outpcd fr over 1f out* **15/8**[2]

0- **3** *2 ½* **Bossa Nova**[413] 7077 3-9-0 0 JosephineGordon 7 69
(Robyn Brisland) *prom: rn in snatches: rdn over 3f out: outpcd fr over 2f out* **33/1**

6 **4** *6* **Tayaar (IRE)**[62] 6765 3-9-5 0 RobertWinston 1 65
(John Ryan) *hld up: wknd over 2f out* **12/1**[3]

05 **5** *13* **Mackiri (IRE)**[39] 7410 3-9-5 0 AndrewMullen 3 47
(Michael Appleby) *led: hdd over 8f out: rdn and lost 2nd 3f out: wknd over 2f out* **100/1**

6 *8* **The Grey Hobbit** 3-8-11 0 CallumShepherd(3) 4 31
(Ed de Giles) *s.s: plld hrd in rr after 2f: wknd 3f out* **33/1**

3605 **7** *nk* **Ten Rocks**[7] 8012 3-8-12 59 JordanUys(7) 5 35
(Lisa Williamson) *hld up: plld hrd: rdn and wknd 3f out* **100/1**

3m 0.43s (-4.37) **Going Correction** -0.175s/f (Stan) **7 Ran SP% 112.3**
Speed ratings (Par 103): **105,101,100,96,89 84,84**
CSF £1.87 TOTE £1.90: £1.50, £1.10; EX 2.00 Trifecta £12.10.
Owner The Hornets **Bred** The Hornets **Trained** Newmarket, Suffolk

FOCUS
An uncompetitive maiden, with the favourite taking care of his main market rival with little fuss. This has been rated around the runner-up to a lesser view of her latest run.

8097 32RED CASINO NURSERY H'CAP 5f 20y (Tp)
5:45 (5:45) (Class 6) (0-65,65) 2-Y-O **£2,587** (£770; £384; £192) **Stalls** Low

Form RPR

6644 **1** **Dazacam**[8] 7981 2-8-13 **57** RobertWinston 8 63+
(Michael Herrington) *hld up: plld hrd: hmpd 3f out: hdwy and nt clr run over 1f out: shkn up to ld ins fnl f: r.o* **5/1**[3]

630 **2** *½* **Debonaire David**[98] 5593 2-9-2 **60** [1] ShaneKelly 3 64
(Richard Hughes) *s.i.s: hld up: hdwy and nt clr run over 1f out: rdn and r.o to go 2nd nr fin* **22/1**

6565 **3** *1 ¼* **Scotch Myst**[15] 7884 2-8-11 **55** TonyHamilton 2 55
(Richard Fahey) *led early: chsd ldrs: nt clr run and lost pl wl over 2f out: hdwy over 1f out: rdn and ev ch ins fnl f: no ex towards fin* **8/1**

0040 **4** *¾* **Oh So Dandy (IRE)**[51] 7073 2-9-0 **61** [1] NoelGarbutt(3) 1 58
(Derek Shaw) *s.i.s: sn pushed along in rr: nt clr run over 1f out: r.o towards fin: nt rch ldrs* **33/1**

0410 **5** *hd* **Snuggy (IRE)**[76] 6343 2-9-7 **65** GrahamGibbons 9 61
(David Barron) *chsd ldrs: rdn over 1f out: styd on same pce ins fnl f* **7/1**

0531 **6** *hd* **Jorvik Prince**[15] 7884 2-9-2 **60** ShaneGray 10 56
(Karen Tutty) *chsd ldrs: rdn over 1f out: ev ch ins fnl f: styd on same pce* **4/1**[1]

0420 **7** *nk* **Miss Mayson**[34] 7528 2-9-2 **60** DanielTudhope 5 54
(Roger Teal) *hld up: plld hrd: hdwy over 1f out: sn rdn: no ex ins fnl f* **9/2**[2]

042 **8** *½* **Flashing Light**[66] 6641 2-9-6 **64** AndrewMullen 7 57
(Tim Easterby) *sn w ldr: rdn to ld over 1f out: hdd and no ex ins fnl f* **20/1**

0403 **9** *2* **Abundant Courage (IRE)**[14] 7900 2-9-7 **65** JimmyFortune 6 50
(Brian Meehan) *sn led: rdn and hdd over 1f out: wknd ins fnl f* **5/1**[3]

0604 **10** *2 ¾* **Little Nosegay (IRE)**[15] 7884 2-8-13 **57** JohnFahy 11 33+
(David Evans) *hld up: plld hrd: pushed along on outer 1/2-way: styd on same pce fr over 1f out* **12/1**

1m 1.49s (-0.41) **Going Correction** -0.175s/f (Stan) **10 Ran SP% 114.9**
Speed ratings (Par 94): **96,95,93,92,91 91,90,90,86,82**
CSF £109.25 CT £883.86 TOTE £6.00: £1.90, £6.20, £2.50; EX 137.70 Trifecta £1262.40.
Owner Darren & Annaley Yates **Bred** Mr & Mrs D Yates **Trained** Cold Kirby, N Yorks

FOCUS
An okay low-grade nursery and a minor pb from the winner.

8098 32RED.COM FILLIES' CONDITIONS STKS (FAST-TRACK QUALIFIER) 7f 32y (Tp)
6:15 (6:16) (Class 2) 3-Y-O+
£11,827 (£3,541; £1,770; £885; £442; £222) **Stalls** High

Form RPR

0053 **1** **Volunteer Point (IRE)**[8] 7984 4-9-1 94 GrahamGibbons 6 97+
(Mick Channon) *hld up: racd keenly: hdwy over 1f out: shkn up to ld ins fnl f: r.o: comf* **15/8**[1]

103 **2** *1* **Dutch Destiny**[62] 6770 3-9-0 90 ShaneKelly 5 93
(William Haggas) *chsd ldrs: rdn and ev ch 1f out: styd on same pce ins fnl f* **5/1**[3]

4662 **3** *shd* **Golden Amber (IRE)**[16] 7868 5-9-1 98 PJMcDonald 2 94
(Dean Ivory) *led: hdd over 5f out: chsd ldr tl led again wl over 1f out: rdn and hdd ins fnl f: styd on same pce* **11/2**

2140 **4** *1* **Yeah Baby Yeah (IRE)**[42] 7348 3-9-0 93 (p) TonyHamilton 3 90
(Gay Kelleway) *hld up: rdn: nt clr run and edgd lft over 1f out: styd on towards fin* **7/1**

0006 **5** *¾* **Bint Dandy (IRE)**[29] 7651 5-9-1 91 (b) JosephineGordon 7 89
(Chris Dwyer) *chsd ldr: led over 5f out: rdn and hdd wl over 1f out: sn edgd lft: no ex wl ins fnl f* **10/1**

5606 **6** *½* **Lyfka**[22] 7781 4-9-1 78 (bt[1]) JimmyFortune 4 88?
(Paul Cole) *s.i.s: hld up: shkn up over 1f out: r.o: nt trble ldrs* **25/1**

2300 **P** **Squash**[8] 7998 3-9-0 98 MartinHarley 1
(Philip McBride) *rrd s and lost many l: sn p.u* **9/2**[2]

1m 26.97s (-1.83) **Going Correction** -0.175s/f (Stan)
WFA 3 from 4yo+ 1lb **7 Ran SP% 110.5**
Speed ratings (Par 96): **103,101,101,100,99 99,**
CSF £10.59 TOTE £2.30: £1.10, £2.90; EX 13.10 Trifecta £32.10.
Owner Box 41 **Bred** G Strawbridge & London Thoroughbred Services Ltd **Trained** West Ilsley, Berks

FOCUS
A decent Fast-Track Qualifier, in which they went an ordinary gallop, and the favourite won with a bit in hand. The 6th was a bit close for comfort and this has been rated cautiously.

8099 BETWAY H'CAP 5f 20y (Tp)
6:45 (6:45) (Class 5) (0-75,75) 3-Y-O+ **£3,234** (£962; £481; £240) **Stalls** Low

Form RPR

061 **1** **Royal Mezyan (IRE)**[40] 7386 5-9-2 **75** LouisSteward(3) 11 86
(Henry Spiller) *hld up: hdwy over 1f out: nt clr run and swtchd rt 1f out: rdn: edgd lft and r.o to ld wl ins fnl f* **8/1**

2400 **2** *1 ½* **Bush Warrior (IRE)**[73] 6461 5-9-2 **72** (v) JosephineGordon 4 78
(Anabel K Murphy) *prom: rdn to ld ins fnl f: sn hdd and unable qck* **12/1**

5060 **3** *½* **Elusivity (IRE)**[15] 7892 8-9-5 **75** (p) MartinHarley 2 79
(Conor Dore) *chsd ldr: rdn to ld 1f out: sn hdd: styd on same pce* **10/1**

0003 **4** *shd* **Landing Night (IRE)**[45] 7252 4-9-5 **75** (tp) PJMcDonald 8 79
(Rebecca Menzies) *s.i.s: hld up: nt clr run and swtchd rt over 1f out: rdn and r.o wl ins fnl f: nt rch ldrs* **10/1**

2231 **5** *hd* **Mysterious Look**[30] 7626 3-9-5 **75** KevinStott 3 78
(Ed McMahon) *chsd ldrs: rdn ins fnl f: styd on same pce* **5/1**[2]

2211 **6** *1* **Waneen (IRE)**[34] 7533 3-9-0 **75** JoshDoyle(5) 1 75
(Joseph Tuite) *chsd ldrs: rdn and edgd lft over 1f out: no ex ins fnl f* **7/2**[1]

5052 **7** *shd* **Taajub (IRE)**[43] 7303 9-9-3 **73** ShaneKelly 7 77+
(Peter Crate) *hld up: effrt and nt clr run ins fnl f: r.o towards fin* **11/2**[3]

0 **8** *nk* **Bahango (IRE)**[115] 4968 4-9-0 **73** (p) CallumShepherd(3) 5 71
(Patrick Morris) *s.i.s: hld up: rdn over 1f out: n.d* **33/1**

3025 **9** *nk* **Coiste Bodhar (IRE)**[7] 8010 5-8-11 **74** NatalieHambling(7) 6 71
(Scott Dixon) *led: rdn and hdd 1f out: no ex ins fnl f* **12/1**

-000 **10** *2 ¼* **Ticks The Boxes (IRE)**[212] 1787 4-9-5 **75** RobertWinston 9 64
(Michael Herrington) *hld up: racd keenly: nvr on terms* **7/1**

1m 0.63s (-1.27) **Going Correction** -0.175s/f (Stan) **10 Ran SP% 114.4**
Speed ratings (Par 103): **103,100,99,99,99 97,97,97,96,93**
CSF £97.43 CT £985.28 TOTE £9.80: £3.40, £4.20, £3.90; EX 105.80 Trifecta £1752.10.
Owner Peter-Robert Spiller **Bred** Mark Salmon **Trained** Newmarket, Suffolk

FOCUS
A competitive handicap for the grade and the form should work out. It's been rated around the runner-up.

8100 BETWAY MIDDLE DISTANCE H'CAP 1m 1f 103y (Tp)
7:15 (7:15) (Class 5) (0-75,75) 3-Y-O+ **£2,911** (£866; £432; £216) **Stalls** Low

Form RPR

0433 **1** **Sunglider (IRE)**[8] 7991 3-9-4 **75** (v) DanielTudhope 5 82
(David O'Meara) *hld up: hdwy over 1f out: rdn and edgd lft ins fnl f: r.o to ld nr fin* **5/1**[2]

0410 **2** *nk* **Pivotman**[15] 7886 8-9-4 **72** (bt) GrahamGibbons 3 78
(Michael Easterby) *chsd ldrs: rdn to ld wl ins fnl f: hdd nr fin* **5/1**[2]

00-2 **3** *¾* **Oregon Gift**[41] 7368 4-8-9 **63** JoeyHaynes 10 67
(Brian Ellison) *sn led: hdd after 1f: chsd ldrs: rdn to ld over 1f out: hdd wl ins fnl f* **15/2**[3]

0520 **4** *½* **The Third Man**[83] 6138 5-8-13 **70** (v[1]) LouisSteward(3) 1 76+
(Henry Spiller) *hld up in tch: nt clr run over 2f out: running on whn nowhere to go wl ins fnl f* **9/1**

053 **5** *2* **Tan Arabiq**[14] 7911 3-8-9 **66** AndrewMullen 8 65
(Michael Appleby) *chsd ldrs: led over 5f out: rdn and hdd over 1f out: no ex ins fnl f* **9/2**[1]

6456 **6** *2 ¾* **Beautiful Stranger (IRE)**[83] 6138 5-9-1 **69** (p) TonyHamilton 7 62
(Keith Dalgleish) *hld up: rdn over 1f out: nvr on terms* **25/1**

4-04 **7** *2 ¼* **Manolito**[10] 7968 4-8-13 **72** (t) CharlieBennett(5) 4 60
(Hughie Morrison) *hld up: rdn over 1f out: nvr trbld ldrs* **5/1**[2]

2040 **8** *2 ¾* **Sark (IRE)**[65] 6665 3-9-2 **73** (t) RobertWinston 6 56
(David Evans) *prom: rdn over 2f out: wknd over 1f out* **8/1**

45 **9** *9* **Hungerford**[29] 7653 4-9-3 **71** (b[1]) JohnFahy 9 35
(Eve Johnson Houghton) *racd wd and sn pushed along: led after 1f: hdd over 5f out: remained handy: rdn over 2f out: wknd over 1f out: eased* **10/1**

0406 **10** *19* **Chilworth Bells**[118] 4880 4-8-13 **67** (p) JosephineGordon 2
(Conor Dore) *broke wl: lost pl after 1f: drvn along over 4f out: wknd over 3f out* **66/1**

1m 58.48s (-2.32) **Going Correction** -0.175s/f (Stan)
WFA 3 from 4yo+ 3lb **10 Ran SP% 115.5**
Speed ratings (Par 103): **103,102,102,101,99 97,95,92,84,68**
CSF £29.93 CT £186.14 TOTE £6.80: £2.50, £1.70, £1.20; EX 33.20 Trifecta £117.90.
Owner G Brogan **Bred** Moyglare Stud Farm Ltd **Trained** Upper Helmsley, N Yorks
■ Stewards' Enquiry : Graham Gibbons caution: careless riding

FOCUS
A tight handicap and the winner has been rated back to his best.

8101 SUNBETS.CO.UK H'CAP 1m 141y (Tp)
7:45 (7:47) (Class 5) (0-75,78) 3-Y-O+ £2,911 (£866; £432; £216) Stalls Low

Form RPR
6051 1 **Pike Corner Cross (IRE)**[7] 8011 4-9-7 **78** 6ex.... CallumShepherd[(3)] 10 87+
(Ed de Giles) *hld up in tch: racd keenly: shkn up over 3f out: rdn to ld ins fnl f: r.o* **9/4**[2]
2206 2 ¾ **Sands Chorus**[14] 7911 4-9-6 **74**.... AndrewMullen 9 81
(James Given) *led: rdn over 1f out: hdd ins fnl f: kpt on* **6/1**[3]
24 3 ¾ **New Agenda**[18] 2577 4-9-7 **75**.... WilliamCarson 7 80
(Paul Webber) *chsd ldrs: rdn over 2f out: hung lft ins fnl f: styd on* **6/1**[3]
0500 4 nse **Idol Deputy (FR)**[14] 7911 10-8-11 **70**....(p) RachealKneller[(5)] 13 75
(James Bennett) *chsd ldrs: ct out wd: lost pl over 6f out: hdwy over 1f out: r.o* **50/1**
0011 5 ¾ **Drago (IRE)**[14] 7911 4-9-5 **73**.... DanielTudhope 5 76
(David O'Meara) *chsd ldrs: rdn over 1f out: styd on same pce ins fnl f* **2/1**[1]
5501 6 ¾ **Foie Gras**[43] 7310 6-8-12 **66**....(p) TonyHamilton 11 68
(Chris Dwyer) *hld up: nt clr run over 1f out: r.o ins fnl f: nvr nrr* **33/1**
-1P0 7 nk **Eltham**[36] 7486 3-9-4 **75**.... JosephineGordon 8 76
(Robyn Brisland) *prom: chsd ldr over 6f out tl rdn over 1f out: edgd lft and no ex ins fnl f* **22/1**
5-00 8 shd **Gossiping**[14] 7903 4-9-0 **71**.... HectorCrouch[(3)] 2 72
(Gary Moore) *hld up: rdn over 1f out: r.o ins fnl f: nrst fin* **25/1**
3414 9 ¾ **Lord Of The Storm**[39] 7417 8-8-13 **67**.... KierenFox 4 66
(Michael Attwater) *hld up: rdn over 2f out: hdwy over 1f out: styd on same pce ins fnl f* **22/1**
435 10 1 **Willsy**[15] 7886 3-8-13 **70**.... ShaneGray 12 67
(Karen Tutty) *s.i.s: hld up: rdn over 1f out: nvr on terms* **33/1**
5000 11 ¾ **St Patrick's Day (IRE)**[37] 7457 4-9-2 **70**.... PaddyAspell 1 68
(J R Jenkins) *hld up: shkn up over 1f out: nt clr run ins fnl f: n.d* **50/1**
660 12 1¾ **With Pleasure**[17] 7857 3-8-10 **72**.... JoshDoyle[(5)] 6 63
(David O'Meara) *hld up: plld hrd: rdn over 1f out: nvr on terms* **20/1**

1m 48.05s (-2.05) **Going Correction** -0.175s/f (Stan)
WFA 3 from 4yo+ 3lb **12** Ran SP% **119.8**
Speed ratings (Par 103): **102,101,100,100,99 99,99,98,98,97 96,95**
CSF £14.37 CT £72.65 TOTE £3.10: £1.50, £2.90, £1.70; EX 19.20 Trifecta £90.20.
Owner Mrs Yvonne Fleet **Bred** Rockfield Farm **Trained** Ledbury, H'fords

FOCUS
A fair handicap and the winner was completing a quick double under a penalty. The second helps set the level.
T/Plt: £1,290.40 to a £1 stake. Pool: £89,008.44 - 50.35 winning tickets T/Qpdt: £53.40 to a £1 stake. Pool: £10,564.47 - 146.17 winning tickets **Colin Roberts**

8102 - 8116a (Foreign Racing) - See Raceform Interactive

8023 SAINT-CLOUD (L-H)
Friday, November 25

OFFICIAL GOING: Turf: heavy

8117a PRIX TANTIEME (LISTED RACE) (3YO+) (TURF) 1m
12:50 (12:50) 3-Y-O+ £19,117 (£7,647; £5,735; £3,823; £1,911)

RPR
1 **Djiguite (FR)**[33] 4-9-1 0.... GregoryBenoist 6 111
(D Smaga, France) **39/10**[2]
2 2½ **Crazy Horse**[26] 7723 3-9-3 0.... ChristopheSoumillon 9 108
(John Gosden) *settled in midfield: 4th and rowed along over 2f out: styd on to chse ldr appr 1f out: kpt on fnl f: no ch w wnr* **1/1**[1]
3 hd **Maximum Aurelius (FR)**[26] 7723 3-9-3 0.... Pierre-CharlesBoudot 8 108
(F-H Graffard, France) **6/1**[3]
4 3 **Blossomtime**[17] 7861 3-9-0 0.... ThierryJarnet 7 98
(H-A Pantall, France) *w.w in fnl pair: hdwy 2f out: styd on fnl f: nvr on terms* **13/2**
5 snk **Whippa D'Or (FR)**[67] 4-8-11 0.... TheoBachelot 4 94
(S Wattel, France) **20/1**
6 snk **Wacaria (GER)**[26] 3-8-9 0.... AntoineHamelin 3 92
(A Wohler, Germany) **19/1**
7 1¾ **Sussudio (FR)**[26] 7723 6-9-7 0.... FilipMinarik 5 99
(Frau Hella Sauer, Germany) **15/1**
8 6 **Arcadia (FR)**[22] 4-8-11 0.... StephanePasquier 2 76
(F-H Graffard, France) **33/1**
9 5 **Nordico (GER)**[19] 7843 5-9-1 0....(p) StephenHellyn 1 68
(Mario Hofer, Germany) **47/1**

1m 51.82s (4.32)
WFA 3 from 4yo+ 2lb **9** Ran SP% **119.1**
WIN (incl. 1 euro stake): 4.90. PLACES: 1.30, 1.10, 1.40. DF: 5.30. SF: 13.30.
Owner Alain Louis-Dreyfus **Bred** R Nahas & A Louis-Dreyfus **Trained** Lamorlaye, France

8094 WOLVERHAMPTON (A.W) (L-H)
Saturday, November 26

OFFICIAL GOING: Tapeta: standard
Wind: Almost nil Weather: Fine, but misty at times

8118 32RED CASINO MAIDEN STKS 5f 20y (Tp)
5:15 (5:15) (Class 5) 2-Y-O £3,557 (£1,058; £529; £264) Stalls Low

Form RPR
1 **Rozy Boys** 2-9-5 0.... GrahamGibbons 9 77+
(David Barron) *s.s: sn swtchd lft: hdwy over 1f out: rdn: hung lft and r.o to ld nr fin* **33/1**
3 2 ¾ **The Daley Express (IRE)**[180] 2732 2-9-5 0.... DaleSwift 5 74
(Ed McMahon) *plld hrd and prom: rdn to ld ins fnl f: hdd nr fin* **9/1**
52 3 1¾ **Desert Mark (IRE)**[44] 7296 2-9-5 0.... AdamKirby 6 68
(John Butler) *led 1f: remained w ldr: rdn to ld over 1f out: hdd ins fnl f: styd on same pce* **7/2**[2]
05 4 1¼ **Enhancement (IRE)**[15] 7906 2-9-5 0.... SeanLevey 3 63
(Richard Hannon) *chsd ldrs: rdn and ev ch 1f out: styd on same pce* **5/2**[1]
3433 5 nk **Street Jazz**[11] 7966 2-9-0 68....(b) AndrewMullen 4 57
(James Given) *prom: hmpd 4f out: rdn and hung lft fr over 1f out: styd on same pce fnl f* **15/2**
63 6 2 **Atlanta Belle (IRE)**[59] 6866 2-9-0 0.... MartinHarley 7 50
(Chris Wall) *chsd ldrs: pushed along and hung rt 1/2-way: wknd ins fnl f* **6/1**
00 7 2 **Lesanti**[36] 7496 2-9-5 0.... PaulMulrennan 11 48
(Ed McMahon) *hld up: shkn up and hung lft fr over 1f out: nt trble ldrs* **100/1**
3 8 1½ **Lily Fontana (IRE)**[32] 7599 2-9-0 0.... TonyHamilton 10 37
(Richard Fahey) *s.s: outpcd* **33/1**
4 9 hd **Panther In Pink (IRE)**[88] 6009 2-8-9 0.... RowanScott[(5)] 1 37
(Ann Duffield) *n.m.r after s: sn pushed along towards rr: n.d* **50/1**
2330 10 1½ **Hamidans Girl (IRE)**[14] 7938 2-9-0 70.... JoeFanning 2 31
(Keith Dalgleish) *plld hrd: led 4f out: shkn up and hdd over 1f out: wknd ins fnl f* **9/2**[3]

1m 0.97s (-0.93) **Going Correction** -0.125s/f (Stan) **10** Ran SP% **113.9**
Speed ratings (Par 96): **102,100,98,96,95 92,89,86,86,84**
CSF £292.58 TOTE £32.40: £7.80, £2.80, £2.00; EX 242.30 Trifecta £2136.80.
Owner M Rozenbroek **Bred** Bumble Bloodstock And Catridge Farm Stud **Trained** Maunby, N Yorks

FOCUS
A fair maiden, and although the winner was a big price he might be useful.

8119 32RED.COM MAIDEN STKS (PLUS 10 RACE) 7f 32y (Tp)
5:45 (5:46) (Class 4) 2-Y-O £5,175 (£1,540; £769; £384) Stalls High

Form RPR
4 1 **Red Gunner**[21] 7818 2-9-5 0.... AdamKirby 5 78+
(William Haggas) *trckd ldrs: rdn and hung lft fr over 1f out: styd on u.p to ld wl ins fnl f* **2/1**[2]
2 2 ¾ **Doctor Bartolo (IRE)**[64] 6750 2-9-5 0.... LukeMorris 7 74
(Charles Hills) *s.i.s: pushed along to go prom 6f out: chsd ldr over 3f out: rdn to ld and hung lft fr over 1f out: hdd wl ins fnl f* **11/8**[1]
3 1¾ **Arnarson** 2-9-5 0.... GrahamGibbons 6 69
(Ed Dunlop) *prom: chsd ldr 6f out tl led 5f out: rdn and hdd over 1f out: styng on same pce whn nt clr run towards fin* **14/1**
0 4 ½ **Mazaaji (FR)**[10] 7976 2-9-5 0.... StevieDonohoe 2 68
(George Peckham) *trckd ldrs: pushed along and outpcd over 2f out: r.o ins fnl f* **66/1**
0 5 shd **Road To Dubai (IRE)**[36] 7503 2-9-5 0.... MartinHarley 9 68
(George Scott) *s.s: shkn up over 1f out: r.o ins fnl f: nt rch ldrs* **5/1**[3]
6 9 **Golden Harbour (FR)** 2-8-12 0....[1] JoshuaBryan[(7)] 1 46
(Brian Barr) *sn led: hdd 5f out: remained handy: rdn over 1f out: wkng whn hung lft ins fnl f* **66/1**
7 shd **Hermeneutics (USA)** 2-9-5 0.... ThomasBrown 3 46
(Ed Walker) *prom: lost pl 6f out: shkn up over 1f out: no ch whn nt clr run ins fnl f* **8/1**
8 1½ **Ventura Jazz** 2-9-0 0.... TonyHamilton 10 37
(Richard Fahey) *s.s: hld up: sme hdwy over 3f out: wknd over 2f out* **25/1**

1m 29.42s (0.62) **Going Correction** -0.125s/f (Stan) **8** Ran SP% **116.7**
Speed ratings (Par 98): **91,90,88,87,87 77,77,75**
CSF £5.20 TOTE £3.00: £1.10, £1.10, £3.40; EX 5.90 Trifecta £30.00.
Owner Simon Munir & Isaac Souede **Bred** Scea Haras De Saint Pair **Trained** Newmarket, Suffolk

FOCUS
This was run at a fairly ordinary early gallop. The opening level is fluid.

8120 SUN BETS ON THE APP STORE H'CAP (DIV I) 7f 32y (Tp)
6:15 (6:15) (Class 6) (0-55,55) 3-Y-O+ £2,911 (£866; £432; £216) Stalls High

Form RPR
3025 1 **Kenstone (FR)**[37] 7489 3-8-12 **52**....(p) HollieDoyle[(5)] 8 57
(Adrian Wintle) *prom: chsd ldr over 5f out: rdn to ld over 1f out: jst hld on* **12/1**
5300 2 shd **Sakhee's Rose**[60] 6853 6-9-5 **53**....(b) DaleSwift 5 59
(Ed McMahon) *broke wl: plld hrd: stdd and lost pl after 1f: nt clr run over 2f out: swtchd rt and hdwy over 1f out: sn rdn: r.o wl* **12/1**
6046 3 1½ **Ershaad (IRE)**[16] 7896 4-9-2 **50**....(b) LukeMorris 2 52
(Shaun Harris) *prom: rdn over 1f out: ev ch ins fnl f: no ex towards fin* **11/1**
5114 4 1¼ **Commanche**[15] 7912 7-9-6 **54**....(b) JosephineGordon 9 53
(Chris Dwyer) *pushed along to chse ldrs: led over 5f out: rdn and hdd over 1f out: styd on same pce ins fnl f* **7/2**[1]
0636 5 ¾ **Little Indian**[7] 8026 6-9-4 **52**.... ConnorBeasley 1 49
(J R Jenkins) *hld up: nt clr run over 2f out: hdwy over 1f out: rdn and hung rt ins fnl f: styd on u.p* **7/1**[3]
036 6 1¾ **Capital Gearing**[45] 7282 3-9-6 **55**....(b) TomMarquand 10 47
(Henry Spiller) *hld up: rdn over 1f out: hung lft ins fnl f: nt trble ldrs* **17/2**
53 7 ½ **Captain K (IRE)**[14] 7943 4-9-0 **48**....(p) LiamKeniry 6 40
(Gordon Elliott, Ire) *hld up: plld hrd: effrt and nt clr run over 1f out: styd on same pce fnl f* **4/1**[2]
6506 8 2¼ **Zed Candy Girl**[14] 7944 6-9-7 **55**....(v[1]) AdamKirby 7 41
(Daniel Mark Loughnane) *s.i.s: pushed along in rr early: rdn over 2f out: n.d* **7/1**[3]
0330 9 ½ **Bedazzling Lady (IRE)**[2] 8079 3-8-13 **48**.... JackMitchell 4 32
(Robert Eddery) *led: hdd over 5f out: chsd ldrs: rdn over 1f out: wknd fnl f* **14/1**
10 4½ **Fineasa Bee's Wing (IRE)**[15] 7921 3-9-4 **53**.... StevieDonohoe 3 26
(Adrian Brendan Joyce, Ire) *chsd ldrs: rdn over 2f out: wknd over 1f out* **14/1**

1m 28.3s (-0.50) **Going Correction** -0.125s/f (Stan)
WFA 3 from 4yo+ 1lb **10** Ran SP% **114.8**
Speed ratings (Par 101): **97,96,95,93,92 90,90,87,87,82**
CSF £144.40 CT £1666.42 TOTE £15.50: £3.30, £3.70, £3.40; EX 171.10 Trifecta £3275.00.
Owner Adrian Wintle **Bred** Guy Pariente Holding Sprl **Trained** Westbury-On-Severn, Gloucs

FOCUS
A moderate contest.

8121 SUN BETS ON THE APP STORE H'CAP (DIV II) 7f 32y (Tp)
6:45 (6:45) (Class 6) (0-55,55) 3-Y-O+ £2,911 (£866; £432; £216) Stalls High

Form RPR
0044 1 **Win Lose Draw (IRE)**[16] 7890 4-9-2 **53**....[1] AlistairRawlinson[(3)] 2 67+
(Michael Appleby) *chsd ldr: led over 2f out: rdn clr fr over 1f out* **9/2**[2]
1505 2 6 **Monsieur Valentine**[33] 7572 4-9-4 **55**.... GeorgeDowning[(3)] 6 55
(Tony Carroll) *hld up: hdwy: nt clr run and swtchd rt over 1f out: styd on to go 2nd nr fin: no ch w wnr* **5/1**[3]
50-6 3 nk **Tanzina**[96] 5710 4-9-5 **53**.... LukeMorris 1 52
(Laura Mongan) *prom: drvn along 1/2-way: chsd wnr over 1f out: styd on same pce fnl f* **14/1**
5252 4 ¾ **Presto Boy**[2] 8079 4-8-8 **49**....(e) FinleyMarsh[(7)] 9 46
(Richard Hughes) *hld up: hdwy 2f out: styd on same pce fnl f* **12/1**

0053 **5** *2 1/4* **Ertidaad (IRE)**[9] 7986 4-9-4 **52**.......................(b) ShaneKelly 8 43
(Emma Owen) *s.i.s: hld up: rdn and nt clr run over 1f out: nvr nrr* **15/2**

1666 **6** *nk* **Castlerea Tess**[32] 7602 3-8-10 **48**....................... JackDuern(3) 11 37
(Sarah Hollinshead) *hld up: pushed along 1/2-way: nvr on terms* **33/1**

6-2 **7** *1/2* **Randall's Alannah (IRE)**[30] 7646 6-8-13 **47**....................... MartinHarley 4 36
(Seamus Fahey, Ire) *led: rdn and hdd over 2f out: wknd fnl f* **3/1**[1]

0-66 **8** *1 1/2* **Shipshape Myfoot**[233] 1292 3-8-13 **51**....................... LouisSteward(3) 5 36
(Andrew Reid) *mid-div: hdwy 1/2-way: rdn over 2f out: wknd over 1f out* **80/1**

1660 **9** *2* **Coolcalmcollected (IRE)**[16] 7896 4-9-6 **54**.......................(p) PJMcDonald 3 35
(David Loughnane) *chsd ldrs: rdn over 2f out: wknd over 1f out* **13/2**

006 **10** *1 1/4* **Home Again**[38] 7463 3-9-3 **52**....................... RobertWinston 7 29
(Lee Carter) *hung rt thrght: prom tl wknd wl over 1f out* **11/1**

3000 **11** *1 1/4* **Locommotion**[25] 7751 4-9-5 **53**....................... TomMarquand 12 28
(Matthew Salaman) *hld up: racd keenly: a in rr* **18/1**

1m 27.6s (-1.20) **Going Correction** -0.125s/f (Stan)
WFA 3 from 4yo+ 1lb **11** Ran SP% **117.1**
Speed ratings (Par 101): **101,94,93,92,90 90,89,87,85,84 82**
CSF £27.18 CT £298.05 TOTE £5.20: £1.90, £2.10, £4.00; EX 29.10 Trifecta £309.60.
Owner Midest 1 **Bred** Nicholas Hartery **Trained** Oakham, Rutland

FOCUS
The quicker of the two divisions by 0.70sec, and a runaway winner who has been rated a fraction above his previous best.

8122 SUNBETS.CO.UK H'CAP 1m 141y (Tp)

7:15 (7:15) (Class 3) (0-95,95) 3-Y-O- **£7,561** (£2,263; £1,131; £566; £282) **Stalls** Low

Form RPR

004 **1** **Keystroke**[14] 7933 4-9-4 **92**....................... AdamKirby 10 101+
(Jeremy Noseda) *hld up: pushed along and hdwy over 1f out: edgd lft ins fnl f: r.o to ld nr fin* **11/8**[1]

32-1 **2** *hd* **Mythical Madness**[7] 8035 5-9-4 **92**.......................(p) GrahamGibbons 13 100
(David O'Meara) *a.p: rdn over 2f out: led wl ins fnl f: hdd nr fin* **7/1**[3]

0001 **3** *1 1/4* **Unforgiving Minute**[31] 7606 5-8-10 **87**....................... HectorCrouch(3) 5 92
(John Butler) *edgd lft s: hld up in tch: racd keenly: led over 1f out: rdn and hdd wl ins fnl f* **9/1**

5450 **4** *1/2* **Faithful Creek (IRE)**[64] 6753 4-8-11 **85**....................... LukeMorris 8 89
(Michael Appleby) *s.i.s: hld up: hdwy and hung lft over 1f out: styd on u.p* **8/1**

453 **5** *1 1/2* **Michele Strogoff**[25] 7744 3-9-0 **91**.......................(b[1]) ConnorBeasley 9 92
(Roger Fell) *plld hrd: w ldr tl led 3f out: rdn and hdd over 1f out: no ex ins fnl f* **6/1**[2]

1020 **6** *hd* **God Willing**[21] 7821 5-8-13 **92**....................... PhilDennis(5) 11 92
(Declan Carroll) *chsd ldrs: rdn over 2f out: no ex ins fnl f* **25/1**

4520 **7** *1* **Rousayan (IRE)**[5] 8049 5-9-0 **88**....................... MartinHarley 2 86
(David O'Meara) *hld up: shkn up over 1f out: r.o ins fnl f: nvr nrr* **8/1**

1430 **8** *nse* **Fingal's Cave (IRE)**[21] 7825 4-8-10 **84**....................... PJMcDonald 6 82
(Iain Jardine) *chsd ldrs: wnt 2nd over 2f out tl rdn over 1f out: no ex ins fnl f* **14/1**

0500 **9** *2* **Lexington Times (IRE)**[9] 7990 4-8-11 **85**....................... JamesSullivan 3 78
(Ruth Carr) *hmpd s: hld up: nvr nrr* **40/1**

0040 **10** *4* **Miss Van Gogh**[22] 7796 4-8-10 **84**....................... TonyHamilton 1 68
(Richard Fahey) *hld up: rdn over 1f out: n.d* **50/1**

0030 **11** *3/4* **Jack Of Diamonds (IRE)**[64] 6736 7-9-0 **88**....................... RobertWinston 4 70
(Roger Teal) *hmpd s: hld up: nvr on terms* **22/1**

-000 **12** *30* **Jacob Black**[14] 7933 5-8-12 **86**....................... JoeFanning 7
(Keith Dalgleish) *led over 5f: wknd 2f out* **28/1**

1m 45.43s (-4.67) **Going Correction** -0.125s/f (Stan) course record
WFA 3 from 4yo+ 3lb **12** Ran SP% **123.8**
Speed ratings (Par 107): **115,114,113,113,111 111,110,110,109,105 104,78**
CSF £11.19 CT £70.91 TOTE £2.20: £1.70, £1.90, £2.50; EX 11.00 Trifecta £89.40.
Owner Front Runner Racing III **Bred** Cheveley Park Stud Ltd **Trained** Newmarket, Suffolk

FOCUS
A decent handicap and a good performance from the winner, who quickened well. The level is a bit fluid, with a small pb from the runner-up.

8123 BETWAY H'CAP 1m 4f 50y (Tp)

7:45 (7:45) (Class 2) (0-105,100) 3-Y-O+
£11,827 (£3,541; £1,770; £885; £442; £222) **Stalls** Low

Form RPR

222 **1** **Rock Steady (IRE)**[17] 7869 3-8-8 **91**....................... KieranShoemark(3) 8 101
(Roger Charlton) *chsd ldr over 2f: remained handy: shkn up over 2f out: rdn to ld ins fnl f: styd on* **11/4**[2]

4120 **2** *1/2* **Cosmeapolitan**[50] 7117 3-8-12 **92**....................... FergusSweeney 5 101
(Alan King) *prom: rdn to ld over 1f out: edgd lft and hdd ins fnl f: styd on* **3/1**[3]

0503 **3** *3 1/4* **Jacbequick**[11] 7967 5-8-8 **87**....................... JoshDoyle(5) 1 91
(David O'Meara) *led 4f: chsd ldr tl led again over 2f out: rdn and hdd over 1f out: edgd lft and no ex ins fnl f* **18/1**

1221 **4** *shd* **Burcan (FR)**[21] 7816 4-9-2 **90**....................... LukeMorris 4 94
(Marco Botti) *chsd ldrs: nt clr run over 2f out: rdn over 1f out: edgd lft ins fnl f: styd on same pce* **2/1**[1]

06- **5** *3/4* **Hot Beat (IRE)**[433] 6573 4-9-3 **91**....................... MartinHarley 2 94
(David Simcock) *hld up: plld hrd: hdwy over 1f out: edgd lft and styd on same pce fnl f* **14/1**

5404 **6** *3/4* **Energia Fox (BRZ)**[24] 7765 6-8-10 **84**....................... TonyHamilton 6 85
(Richard Fahey) *hld up: hdwy and nt clr run over 1f out: edgd lft and no ex ins fnl f* **25/1**

050- **7** *12* **Buthelezi (USA)**[518] 3649 8-9-2 **90**....................... BenCurtis 7 72
(Brian Ellison) *s.i.s: hld up: wknd over 2f out* **25/1**

6306 **8** *2* **Hamelin (IRE)**[24] 7766 6-9-12 **100**.......................(bt[1]) StevieDonohoe 3 79
(George Scott) *hld up: plld hrd: wnt prom 10f out: led 8f out: rdn and hdd 2f out: wknd over 1f out* **14/1**

2m 38.3s (-2.50) **Going Correction** -0.125s/f (Stan)
WFA 3 from 4yo+ 6lb **8** Ran SP% **111.3**
Speed ratings (Par 109): **103,102,100,100,99 99,91,90**
CSF £10.79 CT £113.87 TOTE £3.20: £1.60, £1.40, £3.10; EX 11.10 Trifecta £90.90.
Owner Owners Group 011 **Bred** Martin Walsh **Trained** Beckhampton, Wilts

FOCUS
Muddling form. This was steadily run and developed into a bit of a sprint for the line.

8124 BETWAY MIDDLE DISTANCE H'CAP 1m 4f 50y (Tp)

8:15 (8:15) (Class 5) (0-70,70) 3-Y-O+ **£3,881** (£1,155; £577; £288) **Stalls** Low

Form RPR

6-40 **1** **Charismatic Man (IRE)**[29] 7666 3-9-4 **70**....................... RichardKingscote 6 80+
(Ralph Beckett) *chsd ldr: wnt 2nd over 2f out: led over 1f out: sn rdn: styd on wl: comf* **6/4**[1]

5515 **2** *3 1/4* **Fast Play (IRE)**[31] 7628 4-9-7 **67**.......................(b) ShaneKelly 5 71
(Richard Hughes) *plld hrd: hdwy 8f out: rdn to chse wnr fnl f: sn hung lft: styd on same pce* **15/2**[3]

0642 **3** *2* **Mary Le Bow**[25] 7755 5-9-1 **64**.......................(t) CallumShepherd(3) 10 65
(Victor Dartnall) *hld up: hdwy over 2f out: rdn over 1f out: no ex ins fnl f* **9/1**

4460 **4** *1 1/4* **Nonchalant**[17] 7870 5-9-2 **62**....................... FergusSweeney 4 61
(Hugo Froud) *hld up: hdwy over 1f out: styd on: nt trble ldrs* **20/1**

4055 **5** *nk* **Yasir (USA)**[9] 7987 8-9-3 **63**....................... PaulMulrennan 11 61
(Conor Dore) *s.i.s: hld up: racd wd fr over 3f out tl over 1f out: styd on: nt rch ldrs* **16/1**

4-50 **6** *1/2* **Commissar**[65] 6701 7-9-7 **67**.......................(tp) KieranO'Neill 8 65
(Mandy Rowland) *chsd ldrs: led over 3f out: rdn and hdd over 1f out: wknd ins fnl f* **66/1**

0040 **7** *6* **Marshal Dan Troop (IRE)**[28] 7709 3-8-12 **69**....................... GeorgiaCox(5) 7 57
(Robyn Brisland) *mid-div: lost pl 4f out: sn pushed along: wknd over 1f out* **10/1**

2000 **7** *dht* **Barren Brook**[10] 7973 9-9-7 **67**....................... LukeMorris 3 55
(Laura Mongan) *prom: rdn over 2f out: wknd fnl f* **33/1**

4603 **9** *1* **Clayton Hall (IRE)**[25] 7742 3-9-3 **69**....................... PaddyAspell 1 55
(John Wainwright) *hld up: pushed along and hdwy over 3f out: wknd over 1f out* **40/1**

0B3 **10** *4 1/2* **Skara Mae (IRE)**[23] 7780 3-9-0 **66**....................... MichaelJMMurphy 9 45
(Charles Hills) *led 2f: chsd ldr tl led again over 4f out: hdd over 3f out: sn rdn: wknd over 1f out* **12/1**

3322 **11** *99* **Speculator**[88] 6001 4-9-9 **69**.......................(p) AdamKirby 12
(John Butler) *chsd ldr tl led 10f out: pushed along and hdd over 4f out: wknd qckly* **4/1**[2]

2m 36.99s (-3.81) **Going Correction** -0.125s/f (Stan)
WFA 3 from 4yo+ 6lb **11** Ran SP% **116.1**
Speed ratings (Par 103): **107,104,103,102,102 102,98,98,97,94 28**
CSF £12.49 CT £77.14 TOTE £3.00: £1.20, £2.80, £2.40; EX 15.20 Trifecta £80.10.
Owner S Hanson **Bred** Salinity Service Ab **Trained** Kimpton, Hants

FOCUS
A weak race but a winner with potential.

8125 BETWAY APP H'CAP 1m 1f 103y (Tp)

8:45 (8:45) (Class 6) (0-55,55) 3-Y-O+ **£2,911** (£866; £432; £216) **Stalls** Low

Form RPR

2623 **1** **Victoriously**[16] 7888 4-9-5 **53**.......................(p) AdamKirby 6 60
(Andi Brown) *hld up: hdwy over 1f out: rdn and edgd lft ins fnl f: r.o to ld towards fin* **5/2**[1]

4161 **2** *1/2* **Pensax Lady (IRE)**[15] 7910 3-9-2 **53**....................... GrahamGibbons 8 59
(Daniel Mark Loughnane) *chsd ldrs: rdn over 1f out: ev ch ins fnl f: r.o* **7/1**[3]

000 **3** *nk* **Outlaw Torn (IRE)**[3] 8070 7-9-2 **50**.......................(e) ConnorBeasley 11 55
(Richard Guest) *plld hrd and prom: wnt 2nd over 6f out: rdn to ld over 1f out: hdd towards fin* **16/1**

0233 **4** *1 1/2* **Deftera Lad (IRE)**[15] 7910 4-8-13 **52**....................... CharlieBennett(5) 10 55
(Natalie Lloyd-Beavis) *hld up: hdwy over 1f out: nt clr run 1f out: styd on* **8/1**

5303 **5** *1 1/4* **Cahar Fad (IRE)**[36] 7516 4-9-2 **50**.......................(bt) AdamBeschizza 9 50
(Steph Hollinshead) *hld up: hdwy and hmpd over 5f out: rdn over 1f out: no ex ins fnl f* **8/1**

66/1 **6** *2 3/4* **Fast On (IRE)**[30] 7641 7-9-4 **52**.......................(p) MartinHarley 4 47
(Seamus Fahey, Ire) *broke wl and racd keenly: nt clr run and lost pl after 1f: hdwy over 1f out: sn rdn: no ex ins fnl f* **8/1**

0003 **7** *hd* **Sunshineandbubbles**[14] 7937 3-9-3 **54**.......................(p) LukeMorris 3 48
(Daniel Mark Loughnane) *sn pushed along to ld: hdd after 1f: chsd ldrs: rdn over 2f out: styd on same pce fr over 1f out* **14/1**

0023 **8** *2* **Enchanted Moment**[25] 7754 4-9-3 **54**.......................(p) LouisSteward(3) 13 44
(Chris Wall) *led after 1f: rdn and hdd over 1f out: wknd ins fnl f* **13/2**[2]

005- **9** *6* **New Tarabela**[350] 8198 5-9-4 **55**....................... GeorgeDowning(3) 1 34
(Tony Carroll) *hld up: drvn along over 4f out: n.d* **50/1**

0612 **10** *1 1/2* **Whitchurch**[16] 7888 4-9-6 **54**....................... TimmyMurphy 7 30
(Philip Kirby) *hld up: nvr on terms* **9/1**

4005 **11** *17* **Whaleweigh Station**[16] 7888 5-9-4 **52**....................... RenatoSouza 12
(J R Jenkins) *hld up in tch: plld hrd: hmpd over 5f out: rdn and wknd over 2f out* **25/1**

1m 59.77s (-1.03) **Going Correction** -0.125s/f (Stan)
WFA 3 from 4yo+ 3lb **11** Ran SP% **116.1**
Speed ratings (Par 101): **99,98,98,96,95 93,93,91,86,84 69**
CSF £19.35 CT £231.71 TOTE £3.00: £1.20, £2.40, £5.00; EX 20.10 Trifecta £443.60.
Owner Miss Linsey Knocker **Bred** E I Mack **Trained** Newmarket, Suffolk

FOCUS
A moderate heat in which the 2nd/3rd/4th help set the level.
T/Plt: £125.40 to a £1 stake. Pool: £121,660.64 - 707.67 winning units. T/Qpdt: £50.20 to a £1 stake. Pool: £14,469.56 - 213.21 winning units. **Colin Roberts**

8126 - (Foreign Racing) - See Raceform Interactive

6204 DEL MAR (L-H)

Saturday, November 26

OFFICIAL GOING: Turf: firm

8127a JIMMY DURANTE STKS (GRADE 3) (2YO FILLIES) (TURF) 1m

11:00 (12:00) 2-Y-O
£40,816 (£13,605; £8,163; £4,081; £1,360; £234)

RPR

1 **Journey Home (USA)** 2-8-8 0....................... DraydenVanDyke 4 96
(H Graham Motion, U.S.A) **79/10**[3]

2 *1 1/4* **Defiant Honor (USA)** 2-8-8 0....................... MikeESmith 1 93
(James J Toner, U.S.A) **13/5**[2]

3 *nk* **With Honors (USA)**[21] 7830 2-8-12 0....................... FlavienPrat 8 96
(J Keith Desormeaux, U.S.A) **21/10**[1]

4 *1 1/2* **Miss Sugars**[88] 6008 2-8-8 0....................... TylerBaze 11 89
(Jeff Mullins, U.S.A) **206/10**

5 *1 1/4* **Simmy's Temple**[238] 1199 2-8-8 0....................... NorbertoArroyoJr 10 86
(Doug O'Neill, U.S.A) **69/1**

6 *1/2* **Bella Luma (USA)** 2-8-8 0.......................(b) GaryStevens 2 85
(Ed Moger Jr, U.S.A) **43/1**

7 *1 1/4* **Happy Mesa (USA)**[22] 7809 2-8-8 0....................... JosephTalamo 12 82
(H Graham Motion, U.S.A) **19/1**

8 *3 1/4* **Tiburtina (IRE)**[63] 6797 2-8-8 0....................... VictorEspinoza 5 75
(Sylvester Kirk) *hld up: outpcd st: n.d* **269/10**

The Form Book, Raceform Ltd, Newbury, RG14 5SJ

9 1 ¾ **Mo'Vette (USA)** 2-8-8 0........ SantiagoGonzalez 3 71
(Richard Baltas, U.S.A) **93/10**

10 4 ¼ **How About Zero (USA)** 2-8-10 0........(b) MarioGutierrez 7 63
(Doug O'Neill, U.S.A) **269/10**

11 5 ¾ **Noble Dancer (IRE)**[127] 4613 2-8-8 0........ FernandoHernandezPerez 9 48
(Doug O'Neill, U.S.A) **101/1**

12 17 **La Force (GER)**[22] 7809 2-8-8 0........ BriceBlanc 13 8
(Patrick Gallagher, U.S.A) **9/1**

13 1 ¾ **Partyinthepaddock (USA)**[48] 2-8-8 0........ KentJDesormeaux 6 4
(Carla Gaines, U.S.A) **127/10**

Owner Sam-Son Farm **Bred** W S Farish & Kilroy Thoroughbred Partnership **Trained** USA

8128a (Foreign Racing) - See Raceform Interactive

2731 TOKYO (L-H)

Sunday, November 27

OFFICIAL GOING: Turf: firm

8129a JAPAN CUP (GRADE 1) (3YO+) (TURF) 1m 4f

6:40 (12:00) 3-Y-O£1,714,290 (£683,305; £426,312; £253,979; £169,379)

RPR

1 **Kitasan Black (JPN)**[48] 4-9-0 0........ YutakaTake 1 122+
(Hisashi Shimizu, Japan) **14/5**[1]

2 2 ½ **Sounds Of Earth (JPN)**[48] 5-9-0 0........ MircoDemuro 12 118
(Kenichi Fujioka, Japan) **112/10**

3 nk **Cheval Grand (JPN)**[21] 4-9-0 0........ YuichiFukunaga 17 118+
(Yasuo Tomomichi, Japan) **129/10**

4 ½ **Gold Actor (JPN)**[63] 5-9-0 0........ HayatoYoshida 3 117
(Tadashige Nakagawa, Japan) **7/2**[3]

5 nk **Real Steel (JPN)**[28] 4-9-0 0........ RyanMoore 16 117
(Yoshito Yahagi, Japan) **16/5**[2]

6 nk **Rainbow Line (JPN)**[35] 7567 3-8-9 0........ Christophe-PatriceLemaire 14 117
(Hidekazu Asami, Japan) **177/10**

7 nse **Iquitos (GER)**[26] 7759 4-9-0 0........ IanFerguson 5 116
(H-J Groschel, Germany) **135/1**

8 1 **One And Only (JPN)**[21] 5-9-0 0........ HironobuTanabe 7 115
(Shinsuke Hashiguchi, Japan) **107/1**

9 1 **Rouge Buck (JPN)**[28] 4-8-9 0........ KeitaTosaki 4 108
(Masahiro Otake, Japan) **141/10**

10 ¾ **Last Impact (JPN)**[48] 6-9-0 0........ YugaKawada 6 112
(Katsuhiko Sumii, Japan) **84/1**

11 nk **Tosen Basil (JPN)**[48] 4-9-0 0........ HiroyukiUchida 10 111
(Hideaki Fujiwara, Japan) **62/1**

12 hd **Nightflower (IRE)**[63] 6822 4-8-9 0........ AndraschStarke 15 106
(P Schiergen, Germany) **36/1**

13 ¾ **Dee Majesty (JPN)**[35] 7567 3-8-9 0........ MasayoshiEbina 9 111
(Yoshitaka Ninomiya, Japan) **13/2**

14 nk **Erupt (IRE)**[42] 7405 4-9-0 0........ Pierre-CharlesBoudot 8 109
(F-H Graffard, France) **39/1**

15 ½ **Hit The Target (JPN)**[48] 8-9-0 0........ FutoshiKomaki 13 108
(Keiji Kato, Japan) **239/1**

16 hd **Biche (JPN)**[42] 3-8-5 0........ HideakiMiyuki 2 105
(Yuichi Shikato, Japan) **59/1**

17 nk **Fame Game (JPN)**[21] 6-9-0 0........ HiroshiKitamura 11 108
(Yoshitada Munakata, Japan) **120/1**

2m 25.8s (0.30)
WFA 3 from 4yo+ 6lb **17** Ran SP% **125.6**
PARI-MUTUEL (all including 100 jpy stake): WIN 380; SHOW 150, 290, 330; DF 2570; SF 3990.
Owner Ono Shoji **Bred** Yanagawa Bokujo **Trained** Japan

FOCUS
Plenty of good horses in this year's Japan Cup, but only one front-runner.

8087 NEWCASTLE (A.W) (L-H)

Monday, November 28

OFFICIAL GOING: Tapeta: standard
Wind: Virtually nil Weather: Grey cloud

8130 32RED.COM MAIDEN FILLIES' STKS (PLUS 10 RACE) (DIV I) 1m 5y (Tp)

1:20 (1:20) (Class 5) 2-Y-O **£2,911** (£866; £432; £216) **Stalls** Centre

Form RPR

1 **Enable** 2-9-0 0........ RobertHavlin 4 83+
(John Gosden) *hld up towards rr: smooth hdwy 3f out: trckd ldrs 2f out: effrt to chal over 1f out: rdn to ld ent fnl f: kpt on strly* **7/2**[2]

2 3 ¾ **Gallifrey** 2-9-0 0........ RichardKingscote 2 75+
(Lucy Wadham) *dwlt and rr: hdwy over 3f out: rdn to chse ldrs over 1f out: kpt on wl fnl f* **8/1**

43 3 1 ¾ **Crimson Lake**[49] 7210 2-9-0 0........ LukeMorris 6 71
(David Simcock) *trckd ldng pair: pushed along over 2f out: rdn wl over 1f out: kpt on u.p fnl f* **4/1**[3]

6 4 shd **Dellaguista (IRE)**[38] 7494 2-9-0 0........ PatCosgrave 3 71
(William Haggas) *cl up: led wl over 1f out: sn jnd and rdn: hdd ent fnl f: sn edgd lft and one pce* **15/8**[1]

5 ¾ **Glamour Time** 2-9-0 0........ JackMitchell 7 69+
(Roger Varian) *dwlt and rr: hdwy over 2f out: rdn along wl over 1f out: kpt on fnl f* **6/1**

50 6 8 **Lenoire**[26] 7761 2-9-0 0........ NickyMackay 8 52+
(John Gosden) *slt ld: pushed along 3f out: rdn 2f out: sn hdd & wknd* **16/1**

06 7 6 **Spirit Of Rome (IRE)**[20] 7855 2-9-0 0........ TomQueally 9 39
(James Bethell) *chsd ldrs on outer: pushed along 3f out: sn rdn and wknd fnl 2f* **50/1**

8 2 ¼ **Touch Me (IRE)** 2-9-2 0 ow2........ DougieCostello 5 36
(K R Burke) *trckd ldrs: pushed along 3f out: rdn over 2f out: sn wknd* **33/1**

00 9 2 **Legalized**[26] 7769 2-9-0 0........ AndrewMullen 1 29
(James Given) *chsd ldrs: rdn along 3f out: sn wknd* **100/1**

1m 38.52s (-0.08) **Going Correction** -0.075s/f (Stan) 9 Ran SP% **114.2**
Speed ratings (Par 93): **97,93,91,91,90 82,76,74,72**
CSF £30.74 TOTE £4.10: £1.10, £3.00, £1.30; EX 28.60 Trifecta £113.10.
Owner K Abdullah **Bred** Juddmonte Farms Ltd **Trained** Newmarket, Suffolk

FOCUS
The surface had been worked deeper than normal before the meeting, but the time of this first race was reasonable. Some major yards were represented in the first division of this juvenile fillies' maiden and it fell to one of the newcomers, who scored readily.

8131 32RED.COM MAIDEN FILLIES' STKS (PLUS 10 RACE) (DIV II) 1m 5y (Tp)

1:50 (1:52) (Class 5) 2-Y-O **£2,911** (£866; £432; £216) **Stalls** Centre

Form RPR

1 **Vintage Folly** 2-9-0 0........ JosephineGordon 7 75+
(Hugo Palmer) *cl up: slt ld 2f out: rdn over 1f out: strly pressed ins fnl f: kpt on wl towards fin* **7/1**[3]

2 hd **Gymnaste (IRE)** 2-9-0 0........ RobertHavlin 6 74+
(John Gosden) *dwlt and hld up towards rr: smooth hdwy wl over 2f out: chsd ldrs over 1f out: rdn to chal ent fnl f: ev ch tl no ex nr fin* **4/6**[1]

002 3 1 ¾ **Plead**[47] 7285 2-9-0 70........ BenCurtis 1 70
(Archie Watson) *slt ld: pushed along 3f out: rdn and hdd 2f out: drvn over 1f out: kpt on wl fnl f* **25/1**

202 4 1 ¼ **Dubai Dunes**[18] 7885 2-9-0 77........ KevinStott 5 67
(Saeed bin Suroor) *t.k.h early: trckd ldrs: swtchd lft and hdwy over 1f out: rdn and ev ch ent fnl f: sn drvn and grad wknd* **11/4**[2]

0 5 ½ **Inchikhan**[47] 7285 2-9-0 0........ TomQueally 9 66
(James Fanshawe) *trckd ldrs on outer: hdwy 3f out: rdn along 2f out: kpt on same pce* **28/1**

662 6 2 ¼ **Nastenka**[27] 7741 2-9-0 72........ LukeMorris 2 61
(Ed Walker) *in tch on inner: pushed along 1/2-way: rdn and outpcd 3f out: drvn wl over 1f out: kpt on fnl f* **10/1**

0 7 1 ¼ **Velvet Voice**[26] 7761 2-9-0 0........ StevieDonohoe 4 58
(Mark H Tompkins) *trckd ldrs: pushed along over 3f out: sn rdn and wknd* **66/1**

8 1 **Champagne Pink (FR)** 2-9-2 0 ow2........ DougieCostello 8 58
(K R Burke) *chsd ldrs: pushed along over 3f out: sn rdn and wknd* **66/1**

9 ¾ **Zenovia (IRE)** 2-9-0 0........[1] PatCosgrave 3 54
(David Simcock) *a rr: rdn along wl over 2f out: sn outpcd* **33/1**

1m 39.35s (0.75) **Going Correction** -0.075s/f (Stan) 9 Ran SP% **121.5**
Speed ratings (Par 93): **93,92,91,89,89 87,85,84,84**
CSF £12.56 TOTE £13.00: £2.10, £1.30, £5.00; EX 27.60 Trifecta £313.20.
Owner R W Hill-Smith **Bred** London Thoroughbred Services Ltd **Trained** Newmarket, Suffolk

FOCUS
This second leg of the fillies' maiden was run 0.83sec slower than the first, with the pace holding up well. It looked a match according to the market, but that was not how it turned out.

8132 £10 FREE AT 32RED.COM NURSERY H'CAP 1m 5y (Tp)

2:20 (2:21) (Class 3) (0-95,95) 2-Y-O **£6,469** (£1,925; £962; £481) **Stalls** Centre

Form RPR

4212 1 **Masham Star (IRE)**[17] 7909 2-9-7 **95**........ PJMcDonald 4 100
(Mark Johnston) *mde all: rdn clr appr fnl f: kpt on strly* **2/1**[1]

1302 2 2 ¼ **Morning Suit (USA)**[14] 7956 2-8-6 **80**........ AndrewMullen 1 80
(Mark Johnston) *trckd ldng pair: effrt over 2f out: rdn and edgd lft over 1f out: drvn and kpt on fnl f* **9/2**[3]

1 3 ½ **Pirate Look (IRE)**[27] 7741 2-8-5 **79**........ LukeMorris 3 78
(Marco Botti) *hld up: hdwy 3f out: rdn to chse wnr and edgd lft over 1f out: drvn and kpt on same pce fnl f* **5/2**[2]

0126 4 1 ¼ **Aventinus (IRE)**[37] 7541 2-8-7 **81**........ JosephineGordon 2 77
(Hugo Palmer) *trckd wnr: niggled along wl over 2f out: rdn wl over 1f out: sn drvn and kpt on one pce* **5/2**[2]

1m 38.49s (-0.11) **Going Correction** -0.075s/f (Stan) 4 Ran SP% **108.7**
Speed ratings (Par 100): **97,94,94,93**
CSF £10.51 TOTE £2.60; EX 8.20 Trifecta £19.60.
Owner 3 Batterhams and a Reay **Bred** Petra Bloodstock Agency Ltd **Trained** Middleham Moor, N Yorks

FOCUS
A decent and competitive nursery despite the small field and the time was 0.03sec faster than the best of the two earlier maidens over the trip. The winner enjoyed the run of things and continues to progress.

8133 BETWAY MARATHON H'CAP 2m 56y (Tp)

2:50 (2:52) (Class 3) (0-95,91) 3-Y-O+ **£7,762** (£2,310; £1,154; £577) **Stalls** Low

Form RPR

11-0 1 **Good Run (FR)**[198] 2244 3-9-0 **91**........ AlistairRawlinson[(3)] 1 101+
(Saeed bin Suroor) *trckd ldrs: n.m.r on inner and lost pl 4f out: rr: swtchd rt to outer and hdwy 3f out: chsd ldrs 2f out: rdn to ld ent fnl f: kpt on wl* **2/1**[2]

5211 2 1 ½ **Ajman Prince (IRE)**[21] 7847 3-8-4 **78**........ JamesSullivan 5 86+
(Alistair Whillans) *hld up in rr: hdwy to trck ldrs and n.m.r 4f out: chsd ldng pair on inner: chal 2f out and n.m.r: rdn and hmpd over 1f out: squeezed through and drvn ent fnl f: chsd wnr: no imp* **5/4**[1]

0063 3 2 ½ **Royal Marskell**[131] 4520 7-9-11 **90**........ LukeMorris 2 95
(Gay Kelleway) *trckd ldrs: hdwy on outer over 5f out: chsd ldr over 3f out: rdn 2f out and sn edgd lft: drvn and ev ch appr fnl f: kpt on same pce* **9/1**

0003 4 1 ½ **Aramist (IRE)**[6] 7320 6-9-1 **80**........ RobertWinston 3 83
(Alan Swinbank) *hld up in rr: hdwy 5f out: chsd ldrs over 3f out: rdn along 2f out: sn drvn and one pce* **6/1**[3]

1362 5 hd **Lexi's Boy (IRE)**[66] 6740 8-9-5 **84**........(tp) DavidNolan 6 87
(Donald McCain) *cl up: led over 5f out: rdn along 2f out: drvn over 1f out: hdd ent fnl f and grad wknd* **22/1**

-425 6 12 **Grand Meister**[176] 1135 5-8-9 **81**........ JoshQuinn[(7)] 4 70
(John Quinn) *led: hdd over 5f out: cl up tl rdn along wl over 2f out and sn wknd* **20/1**

3m 35.01s (-0.19) **Going Correction** +0.175s/f (Slow)
WFA 3 from 5yo+ 9lb 6 Ran SP% **111.2**
Speed ratings (Par 107): **107,106,105,104,104 98**
CSF £4.76 TOTE £2.60: £1.40, £1.20; EX 5.50 Trifecta £19.20.
Owner Godolphin **Bred** Eric Puerari **Trained** Newmarket, Suffolk

FOCUS
The feature race and a good staying handicap with a couple of unexposed 3yos taking on older rivals, and they filled the first two places. The form looks sound enough.

8134 BETWAY APPRENTICE H'CAP 1m 4f 98y (Tp)

3:20 (3:24) (Class 6) (0-65,64) 3-Y-O+ **£2,587** (£770; £384; £192) **Stalls** High

Form RPR

004 1 **Go George Go (IRE)**[98] 5716 3-8-6 **48**........ CallumShepherd 4 54
(Alan Swinbank) *hld up towards rr: hdwy over 3f out: pushed along over 2f out: rdn to chse ldrs over 1f out: drvn ins fnl f: styd on wl to ld last 50 yds* **9/1**

3133 **2** *hd* **Galilee Chapel (IRE)**[11] 7992 7-9-5 **60**......................(b) RowanScott(5) 6 66
(Alistair Whillans) *hld up in rr: hdwy 3f out: rdn to chse ldrs wl over 1f out: swtchd rt and drvn ins fnl f: kpt on wl towards fin* **3/1**[1]
6/45 **3** *1 1/4* **Ship Canal**[14] 7960 4-8-10 **46**.. NathanEvans 10 50
(Jacqueline Coward) *cl up: chal over 2f out: rdn to ld over 1f out: drvn ins fnl f: hdd and no ex last 50 yds* **33/1**
0054 **4** *shd* **Percy Verence**[16] 7937 3-8-11 **56**................................(tp) CliffordLee(3) 9 60
(K R Burke) *cl up: led over 2f out: sn rdn: hdd over 1f out: sn drvn and ev ch: no ex last 50 yds* **7/2**[2]
0020 **5** *1* **Sennockian Song**[27] 7732 3-9-5 **61**................................ RossCoakley 8 63
(Mark Johnston) *cl up: led after 2f: hdd over 5f out: cl up: rdn along over 2f out: sn drvn and sltly outpcd: styng on whn n.m.r and swtchd rt ins fnl f: kpt on wl towards fin* **5/1**[3]
4403 **6** *hd* **Bridey's Lettuce (IRE)**[33] 7628 4-9-4 **61**............ ManuelFernandes(7) 3 63
(Ivan Furtado) *trckd ldrs: hdwy over 3f out: rdn along 2f out: drvn over 1f out: kpt on same pce fnl f* **5/1**[3]
6040 **7** *3/4* **Exclusive Waters (IRE)**[31] 7656 6-8-11 **52**........... NatalieHambling(5) 5 53
(George Charlton) *trckd ldrs: led over 5f out: rdn along and hdd over 2f out: drvn wl over 1f out: grad wknd fnl f* **20/1**
0300 **8** *2* **Rockabilly Riot (IRE)**[45] 7321 6-9-7 **57**............................... KevinStott 2 55
(Martin Todhunter) *midfield: effrt and sme hdwy 3f out: rdn along over 2f out: n.d* **20/1**
2443 **9** *3 1/2* **Sherman McCoy**[38] 7508 10-9-11 **64**..........................(p) HollieDoyle(3) 7 57
(Marjorie Fife) *slt ld 2f: trckd ldrs on outer: hdwy over 3f out: rdn along over 2f out: sn drvn and wknd* **9/1**
0P40 **10** *1/2* **Melodya (IRE)**[35] 7583 3-8-3 **45**.................................... ShelleyBirkett 12 37
(Brian Ellison) *a rr* **66/1**
0300 **11** *3/4* **Voice From Above (IRE)**[44] 7361 7-8-4 **47**..................(p) PaulaMuir(7) 1 38
(Patrick Holmes) *trckd ldrs on inner: hdwy over 4f out: rdn along over 3f out: sn wknd* **33/1**

2m 45.59s (4.49) **Going Correction** +0.175s/f (Slow)
WFA 3 from 4yo+ 6lb **11** Ran SP% **117.5**
Speed ratings (Par 101): **92,91,91,90,90 90,89,88,86,85 85**
CSF £34.13 CT £870.43 TOTE £10.40: £3.10, £1.50, £8.70; EX 41.90 Trifecta £2075.20.
Owner Lee Bond **Bred** Pat Grogan **Trained** Melsonby, N Yorks

FOCUS
A low grade but fairly competitive middle-distance apprentice handicap. They went very steadily early and it proved a race of changing fortunes in the straight.

8135 32RED CASINO FILLIES' H'CAP 7f 14y (Tp)
3:50 (3:50) (Class 5) (0-75,74) 3-Y-O+ **£2,911** (£866; £432; £216) **Stalls** Centre

Form RPR
5345 **1** **Colourfilly**[44] 7363 4-9-0 **67**......................................(p) RichardKingscote 6 74
(Tom Dascombe) *trckd ldrs: hdwy and cl up over 2f out: rdn to chal over 1f out: led last 150 yds: kpt on wl* **6/1**[3]
00-0 **2** *1 1/4* **Jacquotte Delahaye**[14] 7958 5-9-7 **74**......................... PaulMulrennan 5 78
(David Brown) *cl up: rdn to ld 11/2f out: drvn ent fnl f: hdd last 150 yds* **9/1**
3-41 **3** *2 1/2* **Tegara**[96] 5766 3-9-6 **74**.. TomQueally 1 70
(James Fanshawe) *hld up: hdwy wl over 1f out: rdn to chse ldng pair ent fnl f: sn drvn and no imp* **11/10**[1]
2130 **4** *1 1/4* **Desire**[18] 7887 4-8-13 **66**.. TonyHamilton 3 60
(Richard Fahey) *slt ld: hdd 1/2-way: cl up: rdn along over 2f out: sn drvn and kpt on one pce fnl f* **14/1**
6003 **5** *nse* **Anna Barkova (IRE)**[18] 7894 3-8-8 **62**.................................. BenCurtis 4 54
(K R Burke) *cl up: slt ld 1/2-way: rdn along 2f out: sn hdd: drvn and wknd over 1f out* **16/1**
0651 **6** *4* **Savannah Beau**[14] 7959 4-9-3 **70**.. GrahamLee 2 53
(Iain Jardine) *trckd ldrs. pushed along over 2f out:. rdn wl over 1f out: sn wknd* **3/1**[2]

1m 26.55s (0.35) **Going Correction** -0.075s/f (Stan)
WFA 3 from 4yo+ 1lb **6** Ran SP% **109.5**
Speed ratings (Par 100): **95,93,90,89,89 84**
CSF £51.66 TOTE £7.30: £3.20, £6.50; EX 48.50 Trifecta £151.50.
Owner Laurence Bellman **Bred** Michael E Broughton **Trained** Malpas, Cheshire
■ Stewards' Enquiry : Tom Queally two-day ban: used whip above shoulder height (Dec 12-13)

FOCUS
This ordinary but tightly-knit fillies' handicap was run at a sound enough gallop and two of the more experienced runners dominated.

8136 32REDSPORT.COM NURSERY H'CAP 5f (Tp)
4:20 (4:20) (Class 4) (0-85,83) 2-Y-O **£4,204** (£1,251; £625; £312) **Stalls** Centre

Form RPR
2125 **1** **Dubai One (IRE)**[31] 7668 2-9-7 **83**...................................[1] PatCosgrave 2 88+
(Saeed bin Suroor) *cl up: led wl over 1f out: rdn clr ent fnl f: kpt on wl* **6/4**[1]
1204 **2** *3/4* **Blue Suede (IRE)**[54] 7073 2-9-1 **77**................................. TonyHamilton 1 79
(Richard Fahey) *t.k.h early: hld up in rr: pushed along and hdwy 2f out: rdn over 1f out: styd on ins fnl f: sn drvn and edgd rt: kpt on* **12/1**
1533 **3** *1/2* **Erissimus Maximus (FR)**[18] 7893 2-8-12 **74**.......... JosephineGordon 4 75
(Chris Dwyer) *slt ld: rdn along and hdd wl over 1f out: sn drvn: kpt on fnl f* **11/2**[3]
3650 **4** *2 1/4* **Cajmere**[53] 7091 2-8-8 **70**.. RichardKingscote 6 62
(Tom Dascombe) *chsd ldrs on outer: rdn along wl over 1f out: drvn appr fnl f: wknd* **10/1**
4334 **5** *3 1/2* **Boater (IRE)**[140] 4195 2-9-4 **80**.. PJMcDonald 3 60
(Mark Johnston) *cl up: rdn along over 2f out: sn drvn and wknd* **11/2**[3]
0042 **6** *1 1/4* **Dandy Flame (IRE)**[13] 7966 2-8-8 **75**.............................. GeorgiaCox(5) 5 50
(William Haggas) *chsd ldrs: rdn along 2f out: wknd over 1f out* **7/2**[2]

58.79s (-0.71) **Going Correction** -0.075s/f (Stan) **6** Ran SP% **109.8**
Speed ratings (Par 98): **102,100,100,96,90 88**
CSF £19.38 TOTE £2.10: £1.50, £5.00; EX 18.80 Trifecta £88.70.
Owner Godolphin **Bred** Darley **Trained** Newmarket, Suffolk

FOCUS
A fair sprint nursery and a decisive success for the top weight and favourite.

8137 BETWAY SPRINT H'CAP 5f (Tp)
4:50 (4:51) (Class 6) (0-65,65) 3-Y-O+ **£2,264** (£673; £336; £168) **Stalls** Centre

Form RPR
1644 **1** **Poppy In The Wind**[21] 7852 4-9-1 **64**..........................(v) JoshDoyle(5) 13 72
(Alan Brown) *dwlt and in rr: hdwy after 2f: chsd ldrs 2f out: rdn to chal jst over 1f out: led ins fnl f: kpt on strly* **11/2**
026 **2** *1 3/4* **Cruise Tothelimit (IRE)**[5] 8078 8-9-6 **64**.......................... GrahamLee 11 66
(Patrick Morris) *prom: cl up 1/2-way: rdn to ld over 1f out: drvn and hdd ins fnl f: kpt on* **18/1**
3114 **3** *1/2* **Horsforth**[10] 8010 4-9-7 **65**..(b) ConnorBeasley 7 65+
(Richard Guest) *chsd ldrs: hdwy wl over 1f out: rdn ent fnl f: kpt on* **4/1**[2]
3003 **4** *1/2* **Young Tiger**[20] 7860 3-9-0 **58**.. JamesSullivan 12 56
(Tom Tate) *hld up in rr: hdwy wl over 1f out: swtchd rt and rdn jst ins fnl f: styd on: nrst fin* **9/2**[3]
0055 **5** *1* **Searanger (USA)**[37] 7533 3-9-5 **63**..............................(p) PJMcDonald 10 58
(Rebecca Menzies) *cl up: led 1/2-way: rdn and hdd over 1f out: sn drvn and kpt on same pce* **20/1**
4534 **6** *2* **Tavener**[5] 8078 4-9-2 **60**...(p) JosephineGordon 9 47
(David C Griffiths) *cl up: effrt 2f out: sn rdn and ev ch tl drvn and wknd fnl f* **8/1**
1260 **7** *shd* **Fuel Injection**[132] 4492 5-8-13 **57**...................................... JackGarritty 6 44
(Paul Midgley) *towards rr: hdwy wl over 1f out: rdn and kpt on fnl f* **40/1**
4545 **8** *1 1/2* **Men United (FR)**[20] 7860 3-8-13 **57**............................... TomMarquand 4 39
(Garry Moss) *a midfield* **12/1**
0600 **9** *3/4* **Hit The Lights (IRE)**[34] 7595 6-8-13 **57**.............................. PaulQuinn 8 36
(David Nicholls) *chsd ldrs: rdn along 2f out: sn drvn and wknd* **40/1**
0251 **10** *1 1/4* **Groundworker (IRE)**[20] 7859 5-9-6 **64**.......................(t) PaulMulrennan 2 38
(Paul Midgley) *in tch: rdn along wl over 1f out: sn btn* **9/4**[1]
5200 **11** *3/4* **Storm Trooper (IRE)**[14] 7959 5-9-7 **65**........................... BarryMcHugh 5 37
(David Nicholls) *led: hdd 1/2-way and sn rdn along: wknd wl over 1f out* **18/1**
0620 **12** *7* **Emerald Bay**[34] 7596 3-8-13 **57**..................................(v) RobertWinston 3
(Ronald Thompson) *prom: rdn along 2f out: sn wknd* **125/1**

58.68s (-0.82) **Going Correction** -0.075s/f (Stan) **12** Ran SP% **124.1**
Speed ratings (Par 101): **103,100,99,98,97 93,93,91,90,88 86,75**
CSF £100.88 CT £455.53 TOTE £7.30: £2.20, £4.30, £2.60; EX 77.60 Trifecta £498.60.
Owner Mrs M Doherty & Mrs W A D Craven **Bred** P Balding **Trained** Yedingham, N Yorks

FOCUS
A competitive field for this modest sprint handicap, but the time was 0.11sec faster than the preceding nursery. Those drawn high dominated the finish.
T/Jkpt: Not won. T/Plt: £363.50 to a £1 stake. Pool: £84,715.32 - 170.10 winning units. T/Qpdt: £98.80 to a £1 stake. Pool: £6,985.98 - 52.32 winning units. **Joe Rowntree**

8138 - (Foreign Racing) - See Raceform Interactive

[8130]NEWCASTLE (A.W) (L-H)
Tuesday, November 29

OFFICIAL GOING: Tapeta: standard
Wind: Light half against Weather: Fine and dry

8139 32RED CASINO MEDIAN AUCTION MAIDEN FILLIES' STKS (PLUS 10 RACE) 7f 14y (Tp)
1:20 (1:22) (Class 5) 2-Y-O **£3,234** (£962; £481; £240) **Stalls** Centre

Form RPR
42 **1** **Shenanigans (IRE)**[13] 7977 2-9-0 0................................... JackMitchell 7 80+
(Roger Varian) *trckd ldrs: cl up over 2f out: led 11/2f out: rdn clr ent fnl f: kpt on* **15/8**[2]
5 **2** *3 3/4* **La Guapita**[12] 7988 2-9-0 0................................... JosephineGordon 5 68
(Hugo Palmer) *trckd ldrs: swtchd rt and effrt wl over 1f out: rdn to chse wnr ins fnl f: kpt on* **10/1**
4 **3** *1 1/4* **Pattie**[66] 6776 2-9-0 0.. GrahamLee 1 65
(Mick Channon) *cl up: pushed along over 2f out: rdn wl over 1f out: kpt on same pce* **6/1**[3]
4 *4 1/2* **Thunderbell** 2-9-0 0.. BenCurtis 2 52
(Scott Dixon) *dwlt and rr: hdwy wl over 1f out: kpt on fnl f: nrst fin* **80/1**
432 **5** *3/4* **Nostalgie**[19] 7882 2-9-0 74.. PatCosgrave 6 50
(Rae Guest) *cl up: led over 2f out and sn rdn: hdd 11/2f out: sn drvn and wknd* **7/4**[1]
33 **6** *3/4* **Harvest Moon**[36] 7578 2-9-0 0... TonyHamilton 4 48
(Richard Fahey) *slt ld: pushed along 3f out: rdn and hdd over 2f out: sn wknd* **6/1**[3]
7 *2 1/4* **Thornton Mary** 2-9-0 0.. JamesSullivan 3 42
(Brian Rothwell) *dwlt: a rr* **150/1**

1m 27.76s (1.56) **Going Correction** +0.125s/f (Slow) **7** Ran SP% **110.7**
Speed ratings (Par 93): **96,91,90,85,84 83,80**
CSF £19.27 TOTE £2.80: £1.60, £4.00; EX 19.50 Trifecta £94.40.
Owner Ann Black,M Al Qatami & K M Al Mudhaf **Bred** Ringfort Stud **Trained** Newmarket, Suffolk

FOCUS
They went quite steady early on in this ordinary maiden. The winner almost certainly stepped up on previous form.

8140 BETWAY MAIDEN STKS (PLUS 10 RACE) 6f (Tp)
1:50 (1:52) (Class 4) 2-Y-O **£4,528** (£1,347; £673; £336) **Stalls** Centre

Form RPR
20 **1** **Six Strings**[136] 4394 2-9-5 0.. TonyHamilton 7 83+
(Richard Fahey) *hld up in rr: gd hdwy on outer over 2f out: slt ld jst over 1f out: rdn ins fnl f: kpt on* **13/8**[1]
6 **2** *shd* **Glorious Politics**[53] 7122 2-9-5 0.................................. GrahamGibbons 9 83+
(David Barron) *in tch: hdwy over 2f out: sn cl up: rdn to chal over 1f out: drvn ins fnl f and ev ch: no ex cl home* **11/4**[3]
332 **3** *3 3/4* **Rapid Rise (IRE)**[178] 2913 2-9-5 77.................................... PatCosgrave 1 71+
(David Brown) *cl up: led 1/2-way: rdn along wl over 1f out: hdd appr fnl f: sn drvn and kpt on same pce* **12/1**
23 **4** *1 1/2* **Dealer's Choice (IRE)**[31] 7689 2-9-0 0............................... JackMitchell 8 62
(Roger Varian) *trckd ldrs: effrt and cl up 2f out: sn rdn and grad wknd* **2/1**[2]
6 **5** *1 1/2* **Miss Montes**[91] 6009 2-9-0 0... ConnorBeasley 2 57
(Bryan Smart) *dwlt and towards rr: hdwy on inner 1/2-way: chsd ldrs over 2f out: sn rdn and grad wknd* **50/1**
6 **6** *2 1/4* **Brother McGonagall**[12] 7988 2-9-5 0.............................. DuranFentiman 3 56
(Tim Easterby) *t.k.h: trckd ldrs: pushed along over 2f out: sn rdn and wknd* **33/1**
0 **7** *nk* **Slave To Freedom**[45] 7355 2-8-9 0............................... RowanScott(5) 6 50
(Ann Duffield) *dwlt: t.k.h: a towards rr* **100/1**
64 **8** *1 1/4* **Red Mohican**[236] 1293 2-9-0 0.................................. JosephineGordon 5 46
(Phil McEntee) *led: hdd 1/2-way: sn rdn along and wknd fnl 2f* **25/1**
2 **9** *hd* **Wild Acclaim (IRE)**[138] 4308 2-9-5 0................................... GrahamLee 4 50
(Ann Duffield) *trckd ldrs: rdn along over 2f out: sn wknd* **20/1**

1m 12.53s (0.03) **Going Correction** +0.125s/f (Slow) **9** Ran SP% **120.3**
Speed ratings (Par 98): **104,103,98,96,94 91,91,89,89**
CSF £6.49 TOTE £2.40: £1.10, £1.40, £2.70; EX 7.40 Trifecta £53.40.
Owner Merchants and Missionaries **Bred** Andrew W Robson **Trained** Musley Bank, N Yorks

FOCUS
The first two finished nicely clear in this maiden and look useful types in the making. The winner has been rated to his debut C&D form.

8141 BETWAY H'CAP (DIV I) 1m 2f 42y (Tp)
2:20 (2:20) (Class 5) (0-70,70) 4-Y-0+ **£3,234** (£962; £481; £240) **Stalls** High

Form RPR

1520 **1** **Bollihope**[13] 7973 4-9-5 **68** ConnorBeasley 2 76
(Richard Guest) *hld up and bhd: hdwy 2f out: chsd ldrs jst over 1f out: sn rdn: drvn to chse ldr ins fnl f: styd on wl to ld on line* **9/2**

2541 **2** *nse* **Taopix**[12] 7992 4-8-12 **61** GrahamLee 4 69
(Karen McLintock) *sn trcking ldr: hdwy over 3f out: led over 2f out: rdn clr ent fnl f: kpt on: hdd on line* **3/1**[2]

0002 **3** *2 1/2* **L'Inganno Felice (FR)**[25] 7791 6-9-7 **70** PJMcDonald 7 73
(Iain Jardine) *trckd ldrs: hdwy 3f out and sn cl up: rdn and ev ch over 1f out: drvn and kpt on same pce fnl f* **4/1**[3]

2531 **4** *shd* **Roman De Brut (IRE)**[28] 7755 4-9-4 **67** DaleSwift 5 70
(Daniel Mark Loughnane) *hld up in tch: hdwy over 3f out: chsd ldrs over 2f out: sn rdn: drvn over 1f out: kpt on same pce* **13/2**

0-6 **5** *4 1/2* **Dancin Alpha**[204] 2092 5-8-9 **58** NeilFarley 9 52
(Alan Swinbank) *hld up in rr: hdwy on outer 3f out: chsd ldrs over 2f out: sn rdn and wknd over 1f out* **40/1**

4504 **6** *1/2* **Zabeel Star (IRE)**[18] 7911 4-9-3 **69** CallumShepherd[(3)] 8 62
(Graeme McPherson) *trckd ldrs: hdwy on outer over 3f out: cl up wl over 2f out: sn rdn and grad wknd* **11/4**[1]

5000 **7** *1/2* **Symbolic Star (IRE)**[60] 6921 4-8-6 **60** PhilDennis[(5)] 6 52
(Barry Murtagh) *a towards rr* **50/1**

0-00 **8** *2* **Maskoon**[19] 7886 5-9-3 **66** PaddyAspell 1 54
(Philip Kirby) *prom: rdn along on inner over 3f out: sn drvn and wknd* **20/1**

003 **9** *1 1/2* **Outlaw Torn (IRE)**[3] 8125 7-8-7 **56** oh6 (e) TomMarquand 3 41
(Richard Guest) *set gd pce and sn clr: pushed along 3f out: rdn and hdd over 2f out: sn wknd* **25/1**

2m 8.42s (-1.98) **Going Correction** +0.025s/f (Slow) **9** Ran SP% **116.2**
Speed ratings (Par 103): **108,107,105,105,102 101,101,99,98**
CSF £17.84 CT £58.29 TOTE £6.20: £2.10, £1.60, £1.80; EX 23.50 Trifecta £96.50.
Owner Mrs Alison Guest **Bred** Minster Stud And Mrs H Dalgety **Trained** Ingmanthorpe, W Yorks

FOCUS
This was run at a good pace, thanks to Outlaw Torn, and it was his patiently ridden stablemate who came out on top.

8142 BETWAY H'CAP (DIV II) 1m 2f 42y (Tp)
2:50 (2:51) (Class 5) (0-70,70) 4-Y-0+ **£3,234** (£962; £481; £240) **Stalls** High

Form RPR

0540 **1** **Polar Forest**[27] 7775 6-9-7 **70** (e) DanielTudhope 7 78
(Richard Guest) *trckd ldrs: hdwy 3f out: cl up 2f out: led over 1f out: sn rdn and kpt on strly* **7/2**[1]

0006 **2** *1 3/4* **Optima Petamus**[57] 7010 4-9-5 **68** (p) JackGarritty 8 72
(Patrick Holmes) *hld up in tch: hdwy 3f out: chsd ldrs 2f out: rdn to chal jst over 1f out: sn drvn and ev ch: kpt on same pce* **7/2**[1]

0320 **3** *3/4* **Tectonic (IRE)**[22] 7847 7-9-4 **67** (v) ConnorBeasley 6 70
(Keith Dalgleish) *plld hrd early and hld up in rr: hdwy 3f out: rdn and chsd ldrs over 1f out: drvn and kpt on same pce fnl f* **4/1**[2]

0506 **4** *1 1/4* **Camakasi (IRE)**[13] 7973 5-9-5 **68** (tp) TomMarquand 1 68
(Ali Stronge) *s.i.s and bhd: hdwy 4f out: chsd ldrs on outer over 2f out and sn rdn: drvn over 1f out: kpt on one pce* **8/1**

450 **5** *1 1/4* **Aneedh**[25] 7794 6-8-10 **59** (b) JamesSullivan 5 57
(Clive Mulhall) *chsd clr ldr: tk clsr order 4f out: rdn to ld over 2f out: hdd and drvn over 1f out: grad wknd* **25/1**

2500 **6** *2* **Nelson's Bay**[60] 6921 7-8-2 **56** oh2 HollieDoyle[(5)] 3 50
(Wilf Storey) *in tch on inner: hdwy 4f out: pushed along 3f out: rdn over 2f out and sn no imp* **12/1**

6603 **7** *1* **Highfield Lass**[59] 6953 5-8-7 **56** oh10 [1] AndrewMullen 4 48
(Michael Dods) *trckd ldng pair: hdwy over 4f out: cl up 3f out: rdn along 2f out: sn drvn and wknd over 1f out* **10/1**

5505 **8** *1 3/4* **Sakhalin Star (IRE)**[27] 7775 5-8-12 **61** (e) BenCurtis 2 49
(Richard Guest) *dwlt: a rr* **11/2**[3]

5040 **9** *6* **Hydrant**[14] 7614 10-8-5 **61** LisaTodd[(7)] 9 37
(Richard Guest) *led and sn clr: pushed along over 3f out: rdn and hdd over 2f out: sn wknd* **28/1**

2m 9.74s (-0.66) **Going Correction** +0.025s/f (Slow) **9** Ran SP% **115.0**
Speed ratings (Par 103): **103,101,101,100,99 97,96,95,90**
CSF £15.67 CT £50.12 TOTE £3.90: £1.50, £2.20, £1.60; EX 18.10 Trifecta £99.50.
Owner Alfa Site Services Ltd **Bred** Worksop Manor Stud **Trained** Ingmanthorpe, W Yorks

FOCUS
Something of a reproduction of the first division, in that the Richard Guest-trained Hydrant set a good gallop, and it was one of his stablemates who benefited. The time was 1.32sec slower than the first leg. The winner has been rated to his autumn turf form.

8143 BETWAY MARATHON H'CAP 2m 56y (Tp)
3:20 (3:21) (Class 5) (0-75,73) 3-Y-0 **£3,557** (£1,058; £529; £264) **Stalls** Low

Form RPR

6522 **1** **Dubawi Fifty**[22] 7847 3-9-7 **73** GrahamLee 2 85+
(Karen McLintock) *trckd clr ldr: tk clsr order over 3f out: led 2f out: sn rdn: drvn ins fnl f: kpt on strly* **6/4**[1]

6061 **2** *3 1/4* **Merriment**[4] 8091 3-8-9 **61** 6ex (p) GrahamGibbons 4 68
(Peter Niven) *trckd ldng pair: hdwy over 3f out: cl up over 2f out: chal wl over 1f out: sn rdn and ev ch tl drvn ins fnl f and kpt on same pce towards fin* **7/4**[2]

2122 **3** *nk* **Alsacienne**[15] 7955 3-9-4 **70** (p) LukeMorris 3 76
(Sir Mark Prescott Bt) *hld up towards rr: hdwy over 4f out: chsd ldrs over 2f out: rdn to chse ldng pair over 1f out: sn drvn and kpt on same pce* **11/4**[3]

1500 **4** *8* **Highway Robber**[25] 7795 3-7-11 **54** oh3 HollieDoyle[(5)] 1 50
(Wilf Storey) *in tch: hdwy over 4f out: rdn along wl over 2f out: plugged on one pce* **40/1**

5235 **5** *2 3/4* **Little Pippin**[36] 7581 3-7-9 **54** oh2 RPWalsh[(7)] 5 47
(Tony Coyle) *hld up: a bhd* **66/1**

6363 **6** *1 1/4* **Heavensfield**[36] 7582 3-8-13 **65** StevieDonohoe 6 56
(Mark H Tompkins) *t.k.h: set v stdy pce and sn clr: pushed along 3f out: rdn over 2f out: sn hdd & wknd* **16/1**

3m 43.38s (8.18) **Going Correction** +0.025s/f (Slow) **6** Ran SP% **112.8**
Speed ratings (Par 102): **80,78,78,74,72 72**
CSF £4.49 TOTE £3.00: £1.40, £1.20; EX 5.50 Trifecta £11.40.
Owner Paul & Clare Rooney **Bred** Hesmonds Stud Ltd **Trained** Ingoe, Northumberland

FOCUS
An ordinary staying contest run at a steady pace, but the winner can probably go on and rate higher.

8144 32RED.COM FILLIES' H'CAP 1m 5y (Tp)
3:50 (3:51) (Class 5) (0-70,70) 4-Y-0+ **£3,557** (£1,058; £529; £264) **Stalls** Centre

Form RPR

0310 **1** **Alice Thornton**[32] 7662 4-9-7 **70** DavidNolan 2 76
(Martin Todhunter) *trckd ldng pair: trckd ldng pair: hdwy 3f out: sn cl up: rdn to ld 11/2f out: drive and edgd lft ins fnl f: kpt on wl* **2/1**[2]

3533 **2** *1 3/4* **Who's Shirl**[25] 7795 10-8-0 **56** oh2 PaulaMuir[(7)] 5 57
(Chris Fairhurst) *hld up in tch: hdwy on wd outside 2f out: rdn over 1f out: chsd wnr ins fnl f: kpt on* **6/1**[3]

6501 **3** *1 1/4* **Table Manners**[25] 7794 4-8-2 **56** oh3 HollieDoyle[(5)] 4 54
(Wilf Storey) *led: pushed along over 2f out: sn rdn and hdd 11/2f out: kpt on same pce fnl f* **11/10**[1]

060 **4** *1* **Saint Helena (IRE)**[48] 7272 8-8-12 **61** (b) TimmyMurphy 6 57
(Mark Gillard) *dwlt: sn trcking ldrs: hdwy and cl up on inner over 2f out: rdn wl over 1f out: sn drvn and kpt on one pce* **10/1**

0040 **5** *3 3/4* **Swiss Lait**[46] 7336 5-8-7 **56** (p) JamesSullivan 3 43
(Patrick Holmes) *cl up: rdn along wl over 2f out: sn outpcd* **28/1**

1m 40.91s (2.31) **Going Correction** +0.125s/f (Slow) **5** Ran SP% **107.8**
Speed ratings (Par 100): **93,91,90,89,85**
CSF £13.03 TOTE £3.00: £1.50, £2.60; EX 10.30 Trifecta £16.70.
Owner Javas Charvers **Bred** Dunchurch Lodge Stud Co **Trained** Orton, Cumbria

FOCUS
A modest fillies' handicap run at an ordinary early gallop.

8145 SUNBETS.CO.UK H'CAP 1m 5y (Tp)
4:20 (4:22) (Class 6) (0-60,60) 3-Y-0 **£2,587** (£770; £384; £192) **Stalls** Centre

Form RPR

4052 **1** **Lozah**[25] 7794 3-9-3 **56** JackGarritty 12 64+
(Roger Fell) *hld up in rr: gd hdwy over 2f out: chsd ldrs over 1f out: rdn to ld ins fnl f: kpt on strly* **5/1**[1]

0605 **2** *2 1/2* **Hightime Girl**[123] 4833 3-9-6 **59** (tp) ConnorBeasley 4 61
(Roger Fell) *dwlt and rr: hdwy over 2f out: rdn to chse ldrs over 1f out: drvn and kpt on wl fnl f* **50/1**

0062 **3** *1/2* **Swansway**[19] 7890 3-9-0 **56** NathanEvans[(3)] 14 57
(Michael Easterby) *trckd ldrs: hdwy 3f out and sn cl up: rdn to ld 11/2f out: hdd ins fnl f: kpt on* **5/1**[1]

060 **4** *3/4* **Bromance**[12] 7994 3-9-4 **57** (p) GrahamLee 9 56
(Peter Niven) *in tch: hdwy to chse ldrs 2f out: rdn over 1f out: kpt on same pce fnl f* **9/1**

2046 **5** *1* **Dose**[12] 7994 3-9-5 **58** DavidNolan 10 55
(Richard Fahey) *trckd ldrs: hdwy 3f out and sn cl up: rdn 2f out and ev ch: drvn and wknd appr fnl f* **7/1**[3]

0010 **6** *1 1/2* **Great Colaci**[25] 7794 3-8-6 **48** CallumShepherd[(3)] 8 42
(Keith Reveley) *slt ld: hdd 1/2-way: led again 3f out: rdn over 2f out: hdd 11/2f out: sn drvn and grad wknd* **7/1**[3]

5033 **7** *8* **Prisom (IRE)**[19] 7896 3-9-5 **58** LukeMorris 2 34
(Gay Kelleway) *midfield: hdwy to chse ldrs over 2f out: rdn wl over 1f out: sn btn* **6/1**[2]

334 **8** *1/2* **Aloysius Hansom**[32] 7661 3-9-7 **60** KevinStott 6 35
(Kevin Ryan) *trckd ldng pair: cl up over 3f out: rdn along wl over 2f out: sn wknd* **7/1**[3]

0600 **9** *nk* **Back To Love (CAN)**[33] 7645 3-8-7 **46** oh1 BenCurtis 13 20
(Mark Gillard) *in tch on outer: rdn along 3f out: sn drvn and wknd* **22/1**

2040 **10** *2 3/4* **Jonofark (IRE)**[35] 7601 3-9-7 **60** [1] JamesSullivan 11 28
(Brian Rothwell) *cl up: slt ld 1/2-way: rdn and hdd 3f out: sn wknd* **80/1**

0060 **11** *1/2* **Mr Chuckles (IRE)**[19] 7896 3-8-9 **48** PJMcDonald 7 15
(Philip Kirby) *chsd ldrs: rdn along over 2f out: sn wknd* **20/1**

0625 **12** *20* **Beverley Bullet**[39] 7513 3-9-6 **59** RobertWinston 5
(Les Eyre) *plld hrd: chsd ldrs: rdn along 3f out: sn wknd* **7/1**[3]

0000 **13** *2 1/2* **Captain Gerald**[42] 7426 3-8-9 **48** (p) JosephineGordon 1
(John Ryan) *racd wd: chsd ldrs: rdn along 3f out: sn wknd* **33/1**

1m 39.4s (0.80) **Going Correction** +0.125s/f (Slow) **13** Ran SP% **122.9**
Speed ratings (Par 98): **101,98,98,97,96 94,86,86,85,83 82,62,60**
CSF £281.16 CT £1379.53 TOTE £6.30: £1.60, £11.50, £2.20; EX 324.70 Trifecta £2004.80.
Owner Trendy Ladies **Bred** Shutford Stud And O F Waller **Trained** Nawton, N Yorks

FOCUS
A moderate handicap in which the pace gradually increased and the closers came to the fore. A one-two for Roger Fell.

8146 SUN BETS ON THE APP STORE CLASSIFIED STKS 7f 14y (Tp)
4:50 (4:51) (Class 6) 3-Y-0+ **£2,587** (£770; £384; £192) **Stalls** Centre

Form RPR

3022 **1** **Mr Potter**[22] 7850 3-9-5 52 (e) ConnorBeasley 13 60
(Richard Guest) *hld up towards rr: smooth hdwy 2f out: rdn to ld ins fnl f: drvn out* **4/1**[1]

-030 **2** *3/4* **Rosy Ryan (IRE)**[25] 7794 6-9-6 53 JamesSullivan 6 59
(Tina Jackson) *hld up and bhd: hdwy 2f out: nt clr run and swtchd rt over 1f out: sn rdn and styd on wl fnl f* **7/1**[3]

2310 **3** *1 3/4* **Cadland Lad (IRE)**[5] 8079 3-8-12 52 (t) JonathanFisher[(7)] 2 54
(John Ryan) *trckd ldrs: hdwy 2f out: rdn over 1f out: drvn and kpt on fnl f* **8/1**

0463 **4** *shd* **Ershaad (IRE)**[3] 8120 4-9-6 50 (b) LukeMorris 8 54
(Shaun Harris) *cl up: rdn along 2f out: drvn and ev ch ent fnl f: kpt on same pce* **10/1**

0600 **5** *1/2* **George Bailey (IRE)**[11] 8013 4-9-3 42 NathanEvans[(3)] 4 53
(Suzzanne France) *cl up: rdn wl over 1f out and ev ch: drvn ins fnl f: no ex last 75 yds* **80/1**

0542 **6** *nk* **Justice Pleasing**[11] 8013 3-9-5 52 (p) PJMcDonald 3 51
(Roger Fell) *slt ld: rdn along wl over 1f out: drvn ent fnl f: sn hdd and no ex last 75 yds* **6/1**[2]

6600 **7** *shd* **The Excel Queen (IRE)**[19] 7890 3-9-5 50 (v[1]) BarryMcHugh 12 51
(Tony Coyle) *hld up towards rr: swtchd lft towards far side and hdwy over 2f out: rdn to chse ldrs over 1f out: kpt on fnl f* **50/1**

0606 **8** *hd* **Kodiac Lady (IRE)**[12] 7995 4-9-1 55 (e) HollieDoyle[(5)] 9 52
(Simon West) *chsd ldrs: rdn along 2f out: sn drvn and no imp* **10/1**

05-0 **9** *1* **Desert Chief**[135] 4425 4-9-3 44 (p[1]) AlistairRawlinson[(3)] 10 49
(Michael Appleby) *in tch: hdwy 3f out: rdn along over 2f out: sn drvn and btn* **12/1**

5362 **10** *1 1/4* **Just Fab (IRE)**[41] 7463 3-9-5 53 [1] TomMarquand 14 45
(Ali Stronge) *towards rr: rdn along bef 1/2-way: nvr a factor* **8/1**

5242 **11** ½ **Canford Belle**[18] 7912 3-9-5 54 PaddyAspell 1 44
(Grant Tuer) *trckd ldrs: hdwy and cl up over 2f out: rdn to chal over 1f out: ev ch tl drvn ent fnl f and sn wknd* **11/1**

456 **12** 11 **Kopassus (IRE)**[22] 7850 4-9-6 47 PaulMulrennan 7 17
(Lawrence Mullaney) *cl up: rdn along 2f out: sn wknd* **12/1**

6-60 **13** 7 **McCarthy Mor (IRE)**[18] 7910 5-9-3 45 CallumShepherd(3) 5
(Mandy Rowland) *chsd ldrs: rdn along over 2f out: sn wknd* **20/1**

040- **14** 50 **Badalona Breeze (IRE)**[349] 8245 3-9-5 45 AndrewMullen 11
(Michael Appleby) *midfield: rdn along 1/2-way: sn lost pl and bhd* **80/1**

1m 27.12s (0.92) **Going Correction** +0.125s/f (Slow)
WFA 3 from 4yo+ 1lb **14** Ran SP% **120.1**
Speed ratings (Par 101): **99,98,96,96,95 95,95,94,93,92 91,79,71,13**
CSF £30.31 TOTE £5.10: £1.90, £3.10, £2.40; EX 38.70 Trifecta £293.60.
Owner A Turton, J Blackburn & Partner **Bred** P Balding **Trained** Ingmanthorpe, W Yorks

FOCUS
They went a good gallop and two of those at the back of the field early came through to take the first two places.
T/Plt: £21.20 to a £1 stake. Pool: £82452.71 - 2837.3 winning units. T/Qpdt: £4.80 to a £1 stake. Pool: £8383.22 - 1287.18 winning units. **Joe Rowntree**

8147a (Foreign Racing) - See Raceform Interactive

7524 DEAUVILLE (R-H)
Tuesday, November 29

OFFICIAL GOING: Polytrack: standard

8148a PRIX PETITE ETOILE (LISTED RACE) (3YO FILLIES) (POLYTRACK) 1m 1f 110y
1:50 (1:50) 3-Y-O **£20,220** (£8,088; £6,066; £4,044; £2,022)

RPR

1 **Dawn Of Hope (IRE)**[24] 7823 3-9-2 0 MaximeGuyon 9 96
(Roger Varian) *midfield: rdn and hdwy on outer early in st: chal and led over 1f out: styd on* **23/5**[3]

2 1 **Endless Summer (ITY)**[80] 6357 3-9-2 0 CristianDemuro 5 94
(M Guarnieri, Italy) **67/10**

3 hd **Magnolea (IRE)**[44] 7397 3-9-2 0 ChristopheSoumillon 10 94
(J-C Rouget, France) **29/10**[1]

4 nk **Battlement**[33] 7650 3-9-2 0 VincentCheminaud 6 93
(Roger Charlton) *trckd ldr: rdn to chal over 1f out: kpt on wout matching wnr fnl f: dropped to 4th towards fin* **7/2**[2]

5 ½ **I Am Charlie (FR)**[26] 3-9-2 0 TheoBachelot 13 92
(J-P Gauvin, France) **15/1**

6 hd **Divine Bere (FR)**[21] 7862 3-9-2 0 AurelienLemaitre 7 92
(E Leenders, France) **15/1**

7 shd **Boreale (USA)**[20] 7880 3-9-2 0 StephanePasquier 8 91
(N Clement, France) **69/10**

8 ½ **Blink (FR)**[95] 3-9-2 0 RonanThomas 1 90
(F-H Graffard, France) **33/1**

9 6 **Kalinda (SPA)**[30] 3-9-2 0 EmilienRevolte 12 78
(A Carrasco Sanchez, Spain) **71/1**

10 shd **Ibazz**[31] 7711 3-9-2 0 PierreBazire 2 78
(G Botti, France) **46/1**

11 1¼ **Aktoria (FR)**[31] 7711 3-9-2 0 (b) OlivierPeslier 3 75
(C Laffon-Parias, France) **26/1**

12 1 **Newrock (IRE)**[127] 4723 3-9-2 0 GregoryBenoist 4 73
(X Thomas-Demeaulte, France) **19/1**

WIN (incl. 1 euro stake): 5.60. Places: 2.00, 2.10, 1.70. DF: 23.90. SF: 63.50.
Owner Imad Al Sagar **Bred** Gerrardstown House Stud **Trained** Newmarket, Suffolk

8063 KEMPTON (A.W) (R-H)
Wednesday, November 30

OFFICIAL GOING: Polytrack: standard to slow
Wind: Almost nil Weather: Clear, cold

8149 100% PROFIT BOOST AT 32REDSPORT.COM H'CAP 5f (P)
4:25 (4:25) (Class 6) (0-60,60) 3-Y-O+ **£2,264** (£673; £336; £168) **Stalls** Low

Form RPR

4000 **1** **Fly True**[47] 7334 3-9-2 60 [1] DavidParkes(5) 1 69
(Jeremy Gask) *in tch on inner: prog wl over 1f out: clsd qckly to ld last 150yds: shkn up and sn clr* **8/1**

0001 **2** 2¾ **Ask The Guru**[49] 7276 6-9-5 58 (p) KierenFox 3 57
(Michael Attwater) *led: rdn over 1f out: hdd and outpcd last 150yds* **3/1**[1]

5304 **3** ½ **Beau Mistral (IRE)**[28] 7774 7-9-0 56 (p) GeorgeDowning(3) 5 53
(Tony Carroll) *t.k.h: hld up in rr: rdn and prog over 1f out: styd on to take 3rd nr fin and clsd on runner-up* **9/2**[3]

0060 **4** 1¼ **Excellent Aim**[58] 7018 9-9-0 60 JaneElliott(7) 7 53
(George Margarson) *nt on terms in midfield: rdn over 1f out: kpt on fnl f: n.d* **14/1**

3-66 **5** nk **Leith Bridge**[311] 320 4-9-2 55 LiamKeniry 4 47
(Mark Usher) *chsd ldng trio: appeared short of room on inner over 1f out: wknd last 100yds* **40/1**

4343 **6** 1½ **Tasaaboq**[134] 4472 5-8-10 56 (t) JonathanFisher(7) 10 42
(Phil McEntee) *stdd s fr wdst draw: hld up in last: brought v wd bnd 2f out: pushed along and kpt on fnl f: nvr involved* **16/1**

1000 **7** shd **Charlie Lad**[219] 1721 4-9-3 56 JosephineGordon 9 42
(Daniel Mark Loughnane) *chsd ldr after 1f to jst over 1f out: wknd qckly* **14/1**

8 nk **Pick Of Any (IRE)**[69] 6725 3-9-2 58 EoinWalsh(3) 2 43
(Tony Carroll) *pushed along in last: a outpcd* **7/1**

0432 **9** 1¾ **Deer Song**[105] 5554 3-9-4 57 DannyBrock 8 36
(John Bridger) *chsd ldr 1f: styd prom tl wknd qckly over 1f out* **15/2**

0051 **10** 1¼ **Lady Joanna Vassa (IRE)**[16] 7961 3-9-5 58 ConnorBeasley 6 32
(Richard Guest) *blindfold off as stalls opened and nt the best away: a in rr: pushed along and no prog over 1f out: wknd last 150yds* **4/1**[2]

59.63s (-0.87) **Going Correction** -0.075s/f (Stan) **10** Ran SP% **120.2**
Speed ratings (Par 101): **103,98,97,95,95 92,92,92,89,87**
CSF £33.30 CT £125.67 TOTE £12.20: £3.30, £1.90, £1.60; EX 43.60 Trifecta £233.40.
Owner G Carstairs **Bred** The Kathryn Stud **Trained** Stockbridge, Hants

FOCUS
A moderate sprint handicap.

8150 32RED H'CAP 5f (P)
4:55 (4:56) (Class 4) (0-85,83) 3-Y-O+ **£4,690** (£1,395; £697; £348) **Stalls** Low

Form RPR

3030 **1** **Memories Galore (IRE)**[29] 7752 4-9-6 82 LukeMorris 3 95+
(Harry Dunlop) *trckd ldrs: pushed into ld jst ins fnl f: sn clr: v comf* **15/8**[1]

6031 **2** 2½ **Free Zone**[13] 7983 7-9-6 82 (v) ConnorBeasley 6 85
(Lee Carter) *trckd ldr: rdn to ld over 1f out: hdd jst ins fnl f: no ch w wnr but clung on for 2nd* **11/2**[3]

0-46 **3** nk **Mehdi (IRE)**[26] 7798 7-8-12 74 PatrickMathers 4 76
(Richard Fahey) *s.i.s and then short of room: in rr: prog on inner over 1f out: kpt on to press runner-up nr fin* **8/1**

4451 **4** hd **Dynamo Walt (IRE)**[21] 7864 5-9-3 82 (v) NoelGarbutt(3) 5 83
(Derek Shaw) *chsd ldrs: rdn over 1f out: kpt on to press for a pl ins fnl f: no ch w wnr* **4/1**[2]

033 **5** 1½ **Just Us Two (IRE)**[51] 7202 4-9-7 83 (p) PatCosgrave 10 79+
(Robert Cowell) *hld up in last fr wdst draw: stl there jst over 1f out: pushed along and fin quite wl: nrst fin* **13/2**

0/0 **6** 1 **Higher Court (USA)**[34] 7644 8-8-10 72 StevieDonohoe 8 64
(Emma Owen) *racd on outer: hld up in rr: 8th jst over 1f out: shkn up and kpt on but no ch* **40/1**

2025 **7** ½ **Archie Stevens**[49] 7268 6-8-2 71 KatherineGlenister(7) 7 61
(David Evans) *racd on outer: chsd ldrs: awkward bnd 2f out: wknd fnl f* **16/1**

1660 **8** ¾ **Burning Thread (IRE)**[11] 8032 9-8-13 75 (b) ShaneKelly 9 66+
(David Elsworth) *t.k.h: hld up in rr: trying to make prog whn ct bhd wkng rival jst ins fnl f: no ch after* **12/1**

0000 **9** 3¼ **King Crimson**[20] 7892 4-9-1 77 TimmyMurphy 2 53
(John Butler) *racd freely: led to over 1f out: wknd rapidly* **20/1**

59.01s (-1.49) **Going Correction** -0.075s/f (Stan) **9** Ran SP% **115.4**
Speed ratings (Par 105): **108,104,103,103,100 99,98,97,92**
CSF £12.37 CT £66.40 TOTE £2.50: £1.60, £2.00, £2.70; EX 13.10 Trifecta £85.90.
Owner Windflower Overseas Holdings Inc **Bred** Windflower Overseas Holdings Inc **Trained** Lambourn, Berks

FOCUS
A fair sprint and a good performance from the class-dropping winner, who looks a possible improver on the AW.

8151 32RED.COM/ IRISH STALLION FARMS EBF MAIDEN FILLIES' STKS (PLUS 10 RACE) (DIV I) 6f (P)
5:25 (5:27) (Class 5) 2-Y-O **£3,234** (£962; £481; £240) **Stalls** Low

Form RPR

1 **Endless Charm** 2-9-0 0 AdamKirby 7 75+
(Charlie Appleby) *mde all: pushed along and drew clr fr 2f out: in n.d after: eased nr fin* **11/10**[1]

6 **2** 3¼ **Tisbutadream (IRE)**[159] 3613 2-9-0 0 TimmyMurphy 3 65+
(David Elsworth) *hld up in midfield: pushed along on outer over 2f out: prog over 1f out: styd on to take 2nd last 50yds: no ch w wnr* **5/1**[3]

3 ½ **Monteamiata (IRE)** 2-9-0 0 ThomasBrown 1 64+
(Ed Walker) *prom: shkn up to chse wnr 2f out but sn outpcd: one pce after and lost 2nd last 50yds* **25/1**

0 **4** 1¼ **Ocean Promise (USA)**[7] 8065 2-9-0 0 ShaneKelly 10 60
(Richard Hughes) *chsd ldrs on outer: urged along wl over 2f out: outpcd wl over 1f out: kpt on nr fin* **14/1**

0 **5** shd **Warba (IRE)**[160] 3555 2-9-0 0 JFEgan 8 59
(Ms N M Hugo) *chsd wnr to 2f out: one pce after u.p* **14/1**

00 **6** hd **Dandy Walk**[69] 6696 2-9-0 0 LukeMorris 2 59
(Chris Wall) *chsd ldrs: rdn sn after 1/2-way: no great prog but kpt on to press for 4th ins fnl f* **16/1**

0 **7** ¾ **Love And Be Loved**[32] 7695 2-8-9 0 GeorgiaCox(5) 11 57
(Peter Chapple-Hyam) *dwlt: nvr bttr than midfield: pushed along and no imp ldrs fnl 2f* **40/1**

8 1 **Bird To Love** 2-9-0 0 RichardKingscote 9 54
(Ralph Beckett) *slowly away: hld up in last pair: pushed along and kpt on steadily fnl 2f but nvr able to get involved* **4/1**[2]

9 ¾ **Celerity (IRE)**[82] 6302 2-8-11 0 EoinWalsh(3) 5 51
(David Evans) *dwlt: rchd midfield after 2f: shkn up and no imp ldrs over 2f out: fdd fnl f* **50/1**

10 2¼ **Sparkling Cossack** 2-9-0 0 SteveDrowne 6 45
(Jeremy Gask) *slowly away: detached in last mostly: nvr a factor* **50/1**

60 **11** ½ **Jersey Heartbeat**[14] 7976 2-9-0 0 TomMarquand 4 43
(Richard Hannon) *a in rr: struggling by 1/2-way* **25/1**

1m 13.36s (0.26) **Going Correction** -0.075s/f (Stan) **11** Ran SP% **117.6**
Speed ratings (Par 93): **95,90,90,88,88 87,86,85,84,81 80**
CSF £6.28 TOTE £1.90: £1.10, £1.70, £6.10; EX 7.80 Trifecta £123.20.
Owner Godolphin **Bred** New England, Mount Coote & P Barrett **Trained** Newmarket, Suffolk

FOCUS
This was dominated by the favourite, who had an easy time of it in front, but promise from the placed horses too.

8152 32RED.COM/ IRISH STALLION FARMS EBF MAIDEN FILLIES' STKS (PLUS 10 RACE) (DIV II) 6f (P)
5:55 (5:57) (Class 5) 2-Y-O **£3,234** (£962; £481; £120; £120) **Stalls** Low

Form RPR

1 **Pavillon** 2-9-0 0 AdamKirby 6 73+
(Clive Cox) *slowly away: rn green in last: taken to wd outside and rapid prog 2f out: swept into the ld 150yds out: hung rt and stl green but a holding on* **7/1**[3]

3 **2** ½ **Ashwaq**[32] 7695 2-9-0 0 TomMarquand 5 71+
(Richard Hannon) *trckd ldrs: impeded on inner and dropped to 6th 1/2-way: effrt over 2f out: rdn and clsd on ldr fnl f: tk 2nd last 75yds but hld by wnr* **10/11**[1]

3 ¾ **Porto Ferro (IRE)**[42] 7473 2-9-0 0 RichardKingscote 8 69
(Dr Jon Scargill) *trckd ldrs gng wl: prog and pushed into ld over 1f out: rdn and hdd fnl 150yds: kpt on but hld in 3rd last 75yds* **11/2**[2]

5205 **4** 1¼ **Sun Angel (IRE)**[68] 6733 2-9-0 73 LukeMorris 11 65
(Henry Candy) *prom: drvn to chal over 1f out: one pce ins fnl f* **11/1**

4 dht **Mitigate** 2-9-0 0 ShaneKelly 4 65
(David Elsworth) *slowly away: hld up in 11th: pushed along and stdy prog on inner fr 2f out: kpt on fnl f: fair debut* **16/1**

6 1 **Sayem** 2-9-0 0 ThomasBrown 2 62
(Ed Walker) *towards rr: pushed along fr 2f out: nvr threatened ldrs but kpt on steadily: nt disgrcd* **33/1**

00 **7** ½ **Chough**[20] 7891 2-9-0 0 LiamKeniry 3 60
(Hughie Morrison) *hld up towards rr: nudged along over 2f out: in tch over 1f out: reminders and no prog ins fnl f: likely improver* **66/1**

8 ½ **Ghaseedah** 2-9-0 0 RobertHavlin 10 59
(Simon Crisford) *dwlt: wl in rr: shkn up 2f out: kpt on same pce after: nt disgracd* **7/1**[3]

9 *nse* **Cherry Leyf** 2-9-0 0 PatCosgrave 1 58
(Stuart Williams) *towards rr: pushed along over 2f out: nvr on terms but kpt on steadily: nt disgracd* **33/1**

0445 **10** 2 **Ginger Truffle**[39] 7528 2-9-0 51 StevieDonohoe 7 52
(Brett Johnson) *racd freely: led 1f and again over 3f out: hdd & wknd over 1f out* **100/1**

00 **11** 1¾ **Wotadoll**[18] 7939 2-9-0 0 RobertWinston 9 46
(Dean Ivory) *prog on outer fr midfield to chse ldrs 1/2-way: rdn 2f out: fdd fnl f* **50/1**

12 2½ **Sugar Plum (IRE)** 2-9-0 0 WilliamCarson 12 38
(Bill Turner) *quick prog fr wdst draw to ld after 1f: hdd over 3f out and rn green: wknd rapidly over 1f out* **100/1**

1m 13.43s (0.33) **Going Correction** -0.075s/f (Stan) **12** Ran SP% **118.3**
Speed ratings (Par 93): **94,93,92,90,90 89,88,88,87,85 82,79**
CSF £13.44 TOTE £8.60: £2.30, £1.10, £2.00; EX 18.90 Trifecta £73.90.
Owner Mondial Racing & Robert Haim **Bred** J Bernstein & R Haim **Trained** Lambourn, Berks

FOCUS
Marginally the slower of the two divisions. The field were compressed at the line and hard to think this is great form.

8153 32RED ON THE APP STORE NURSERY H'CAP 1m (P)
6:25 (6:25) (Class 5) (0-75,75) 2-Y-O £3,234 (£962; £481; £240) **Stalls** Low

Form RPR

434 **1** **Habbad (FR)**[20] 7882 2-9-2 70 TomMarquand 7 74
(Richard Hannon) *towards rr: rdn over 2f out: prog over 1f out: led last 150yds: hld on u.p* **16/1**

524 **2** ½ **Emenem**[83] 6264 2-8-12 66 JFEgan 9 69
(Simon Dow) *settled in last trio: rdn over 2f out: rapid prog on wd outside over 1f out: tk 2nd last 75yds and pressed wnr: nt qckn last strides* **16/1**

2136 **3** 1 **Quothquan (FR)**[32] 7697 2-9-1 69 LiamKeniry 10 70
(Michael Madgwick) *stmbld s: hld up in last: gd prog on inner over 2f out: drvn and styd on fnl f: nvr quite able to chal* **20/1**

41 **4** ¾ **African Beat (IRE)**[19] 7908 2-9-7 75 RobertHavlin 13 74
(John Gosden) *s.i.s: rapid prog to chse ldng trio after 2f: drvn over 2f out: grad clsd to chal 1f out but then outpcd by those coming fr bhd* **3/1**[1]

6661 **5** *shd* **Poetic Force (IRE)**[18] 7941 2-9-5 73 (t) RichardKingscote 14 72+
(Jonathan Portman) *sn trckd ldr: rdn 2f out: led jst over 1f out: hdd and fdd last 150yds* **4/1**[2]

532 **6** 1 **Wordsearch (USA)**[21] 7865 2-9-7 75 JosephineGordon 12 71
(Hugo Palmer) *racd on outer: 6th 1/2-way: sn pushed along: nvr pce to chal but kpt on u.p fnl 2f* **5/1**[3]

3661 **7** 1¼ **Galahad**[12] 8008 2-9-1 69 PatrickMathers 4 62
(Richard Fahey) *dwlt: rapid prog on inner to chse ldrs after s: urged along 1/2-way: nvr pce to threaten but plugged on tl fdd last 100yds* **8/1**

5630 **8** *nk* **Mullarkey**[42] 7467 2-9-4 72 KierenFox 2 64
(John Best) *chsd ldng pair: awkward passage on inner over 2f out then racd awkwardly: wknd jst over 1f out* **20/1**

0550 **9** 2¾ **Legendoire (IRE)**[19] 7898 2-8-9 63 MichaelJMMurphy 3 49
(John Gallagher) *chsd ldrs to 1/2-way: lost pl and struggling over 2f out* **50/1**

2404 **10** ½ **Darkroom Angel**[28] 7768 2-8-13 67 JohnFahy 6 52
(Clive Cox) *nvr bttr than midfield on outer: rdn and no prog over 2f out* **12/1**

113 **11** ¾ **Lord Clenaghcastle (IRE)**[57] 7033 2-9-1 72 HectorCrouch[(3)] 1 55+
(Gary Moore) *led at str pce: rdn and hdd jst over 1f out: wknd rapidly* **7/1**

6030 **12** *nk* **Lawfilly**[7] 8071 2-8-6 60 [1] RyanTate 5 42
(Richard Hughes) *a in rr: struggling over 2f out* **50/1**

6320 **13** *nk* **Oceanus (IRE)**[47] 7319 2-9-5 73 [1] LukeMorris 8 54
(Ed Dunlop) *a in rr: rdn and no prog wl over 2f out* **25/1**

1m 38.56s (-1.24) **Going Correction** -0.075s/f (Stan) **13** Ran SP% **122.0**
Speed ratings (Par 96): **103,102,101,100,100 99,98,98,95,94 94,93,93**
CSF £237.23 CT £5069.49 TOTE £19.10: £4.80, £4.20, £5.60; EX 295.50 Trifecta £4781.80.
Owner Salem Fahad S A Ghorab **Bred** Stilvi Compania Financiera **Trained** East Everleigh, Wilts

FOCUS
This was run at a good gallop and it was set up for the closers. The winner is improving.

8154 32RED CASINO H'CAP 1m (P)
6:55 (6:58) (Class 5) (0-70,70) 3-Y-O+ £2,911 (£866; £432; £216) **Stalls** Low

Form RPR

3562 **1** **Baltic Prince (IRE)**[37] 7577 6-9-3 69 GeorgeDowning[(3)] 1 77
(Tony Carroll) *pushed up to ld fr ins draw: kicked clr 2f out: stl clr ins fnl f: drvn and jst hld on* **16/1**

1451 **2** *nk* **Music Major**[29] 7735 3-9-0 65 AdamBeschizza 10 71
(Michael Attwater) *settled in last quartet: gd prog on outer jst over 2f out: tk 2nd fnl f: clsd on wnr after: need a few more strides* **7/1**[2]

0002 **3** 1 **Red Cossack (CAN)**[35] 7620 5-9-7 70 (t) RobertWinston 9 75
(Paul Webber) *hld up in last: gd prog on outer fr 2f out: wavering sltly but drvn to take 3rd ins fnl f: kpt on but nvr able to chal* **10/1**

0501 **4** 1¾ **Ebbisham (IRE)**[29] 7736 3-9-2 67 PatCosgrave 5 67
(Jim Boyle) *trckd ldrs: rdn and nt qckn over 2f out: kpt on same pce fr over 1f out: nvr able to chal* **3/1**[1]

535 **5** ¾ **Stormbound (IRE)**[35] 7619 7-9-4 67 (b) LukeMorris 4 66
(Paul Cole) *in tch in midfield: rdn over 2f out: kpt on fr over 1f out: nt pce to threaten* **8/1**

1010 **6** 3¼ **Flowing Clarets**[19] 7899 3-9-2 67 JosephineGordon 3 58
(John Bridger) *chsd ldrs: rdn and prog to take 2nd 2f out to 1f out: wknd fnl f* **33/1**

5410 **7** 1¾ **Check 'Em Tuesday (IRE)**[46] 7368 3-9-1 66 TomMarquand 12 53
(Daniel Mark Loughnane) *racd in last quartet: no prog over 2f out: kpt on fnl f: no ch* **20/1**

6323 **8** 1 **Believe It (IRE)**[51] 7203 4-9-3 66 [1] ShaneKelly 11 51
(Richard Hughes) *nvr bttr than midfield: shkn up and no prog over 2f out* **15/2**[3]

0000 **9** *nk* **Harry Holland**[11] 8036 4-9-3 66 RichardKingscote 14 51
(Tom Dascombe) *wl away fr wdst draw: prom: chsd wnr 1/2-way to 3f out: wknd qckly jst over 1f out* **10/1**

3-01 **10** 1½ **Siouxperhero (IRE)**[18] 7943 7-9-0 63 (p) MartinDwyer 8 44
(William Muir) *sn pushed along in midfield: no prog 2f out* **14/1**

1 **11** 8 **Rightway (IRE)**[126] 4773 5-9-5 68 AdamKirby 2 31
(Tony Carroll) *chsd wnr to 1/2-way and again 3f out to 2f out: wknd rapidly: t.o* **8/1**

520 **12** 1 **Haabis (USA)**[237] 1287 3-9-2 67 StevieDonohoe 7 27
(George Peckham) *a towards rr and nvr gng wl: t.o* **16/1**

4345 **13** 3¾ **Shifting Star (IRE)**[14] 7973 11-9-3 66 (vt) WilliamCarson 6 18
(John Bridger) *chsd ldrs 5f: wknd qckly: t.o* **25/1**

1m 38.61s (-1.19) **Going Correction** -0.075s/f (Stan)
WFA 3 from 4yo+ 2lb **13** Ran SP% **119.6**
Speed ratings (Par 103): **102,101,100,98,98 94,93,92,91,90 82,81,77**
CSF £121.44 CT £1231.31 TOTE £18.20: £4.60, £2.10, £3.80; EX 143.70 Trifecta £1276.60.
Owner A Mills **Bred** William Pilkington **Trained** Cropthorne, Worcs

FOCUS
A good performance from the winner, who is something of a course specialist and recorded a personal best.

8155 RACINGUK.COM H'CAP 1m 4f (P)
7:25 (7:28) (Class 6) (0-60,60) 3-Y-O+ £2,264 (£673; £336; £168) **Stalls** Low

Form RPR

0005 **1** **Jersey Bull (IRE)**[18] 7937 4-9-8 58 LiamKeniry 2 66
(Michael Madgwick) *hld up in midfield: smooth prog 3f out: shkn up to ld over 1f out: rdn clr fnl f* **8/1**

6010 **2** 2¾ **Ali Bin Nayef**[11] 8038 4-9-4 54 AdamKirby 5 58
(Michael Wigham) *chsd ldng trio: rdn wl over 2f out: kpt on fr over 1f out to take 2nd last 75yds* **15/2**[3]

0053 **3** ¾ **Hold Hands**[11] 8038 5-9-5 55 RichardKingscote 1 57
(Brendan Powell) *trckd ldng pair: clsd to ld 2f out: rdn and hdd over 1f out: one pce and lost 2nd last 75yds* **4/1**[2]

4254 **4** 1 **Dark Amber**[35] 7628 6-9-7 57 JosephineGordon 12 58
(Brendan Powell) *dwlt: hld up in last pair: pushed along over 3f out: rdn and kpt on fr 2f out: nt pce to rch ldrs* **10/1**

4450 **5** *nk* **Le Tissier**[15] 7969 3-8-10 57 (p) PaddyBradley[(5)] 7 57
(Michael Attwater) *chsd ldrs: lost pl and drvn 3f out: kpt on again fr over 1f out: n.d* **10/1**

516 **6** 1½ **Mr Marchwood**[15] 7969 3-8-11 56 CallumShepherd[(3)] 10 54
(Sylvester Kirk) *hld up in last pair: rdn over 2f out: one pce and no ch to threaten* **9/4**[1]

5060 **7** ¾ **Lions Charge (USA)**[79] 6411 9-9-6 56 SteveDrowne 8 53
(Seamus Mullins) *nvr beyond midfield: rdn 3f out: no imp ldrs* **16/1**

2260 **8** 2 **Fair Comment**[21] 7870 6-9-9 59 DavidProbert 14 53
(Michael Blanshard) *trckd ldr after 2f: poised to chal 3f out: rdn and fnd nil over 2f out: sn wknd* **20/1**

1302 **9** ¾ **Sexy Secret**[51] 7231 5-9-4 57 (p) SimonPearce[(3)] 3 49
(Lydia Pearce) *led: urged along over 3f out: hdd & wknd 2f out* **16/1**

365 **10** 2 **Hangman Jury**[18] 7935 3-9-2 58 ShaneKelly 11 47
(Richard Hughes) *t.k.h: hld up in last trio: pushed along over 2f out: no prog and sn btn* **25/1**

3200 **11** 3½ **Angelical (IRE)**[21] 7870 3-9-4 60 [1] LukeMorris 13 44
(Daniel Mark Loughnane) *chsd ldr 2f: styd prom tl wknd over 2f out* **20/1**

3400 **P** **Peeps**[19] 7905 4-9-1 51 (b) StevieDonohoe 9
(Mark H Tompkins) *ref to r tl rest of field had gone 1f: pottered arnd tl p.u 1/2-way* **25/1**

2m 34.92s (0.42) **Going Correction** -0.075s/f (Stan)
WFA 3 from 4yo+ 6lb **12** Ran SP% **120.8**
Speed ratings (Par 101): **95,93,92,92,91 90,90,88,88,87 84,**
CSF £64.30 CT £278.17 TOTE £10.30: £2.50, £2.30, £2.00; EX 80.40 Trifecta £463.60.
Owner Mrs Susan Bunney **Bred** Rathasker Stud **Trained** Denmead, Hants

FOCUS
A moderate affair, rated around the front pair, and routine form.

8156 BIG DAVE H'CAP 7f (P)
7:55 (7:59) (Class 6) (0-60,60) 3-Y-O+ £2,264 (£673; £336; £168) **Stalls** Low

Form RPR

000 **1** **Medicean El Diablo**[95] 5896 3-9-4 59 TomMarquand 7 66
(Jimmy Fox) *hld up in rr: hmpd after 2f and dropped to last pair: drvn and gd prog on inner over 2f out: clsd on ldrs fnl f: styd on to ld nr fin* **10/1**

3205 **2** ¾ **Cascading Stars (IRE)**[20] 7889 4-9-6 60 LukeMorris 1 66
(Daniel Mark Loughnane) *trckd ldrs on inner: rdn to ld wl over 1f out: kpt on u.p fnl f: hdd nr fin* **7/1**

400 **3** ½ **Ross Raith Rover**[35] 7616 3-9-3 58 JackMitchell 5 62
(Robert Eddery) *tried to trck ldrs but nt pce to hold pl: urged along and dropped to rr 3f out: gd prog u.p on outer 2f out: styd on to take 3rd nr fin* **7/1**

2402 **4** *nk* **Arcanista (IRE)**[11] 8026 3-9-5 60 (bt) ShaneKelly 2 63
(Richard Hughes) *t.k.h: trckd ldrs: chal and w ldr wl over 1f out tl ins fnl f: nt qckn* **5/1**[2]

2426 **5** 1 **Oak Bluffs (IRE)**[13] 7985 5-9-6 60 PatrickMathers 12 61
(Richard Fahey) *trapped out wd in midfield: rdn and no prog over 2f out: styd on fr over 1f out: nrst fin* **9/1**

0000 **6** ½ **Wink Oliver**[25] 7817 4-9-5 59 (p) PatCosgrave 10 59
(Jo Hughes) *awkward s: wl in rr: rdn and prog on outer over 1f out: kpt on fnl f: nvr quite pce to threaten* **16/1**

0456 **7** *nk* **Prim And Proper**[29] 7735 5-9-5 59 (b) DanielMuscutt 14 58
(John Flint) *hld up towards rr: prog whn nt clr run over 1f out: kpt on same pce after and unable to rch ldrs* **25/1**

0000 **8** 3¾ **Nasri**[128] 4715 10-9-3 57 StevieDonohoe 13 47
(Emma Owen) *pressed ldrs on outer: lost pl over 2f out: steadily wknd* **20/1**

100 **9** *hd* **Blackthorn Stick (IRE)**[203] 2155 7-9-1 60 DavidParkes[(5)] 11 49
(Paul Burgoyne) *taken down early: hld up in midfield: rdn to cl on ldrs over 1f out: nt qckn jst ins fnl f: heavily eased last 100yds* **16/1**

5000 **10** 1 **Caius College Girl (IRE)**[25] 7817 4-9-1 60 [1] CharlieBennett[(5)] 9 46
(Natalie Lloyd-Beavis) *taken down early: hld up in midfield: swtchd rt 5f out: effrt 2f out: no prog over 1f out: wknd* **25/1**

0634 **11** 1 **Caribbean Spring (IRE)**[29] 7747 3-8-9 57 JaneElliott[(7)] 4 40
(George Margarson) *mostly in last and nvr a factor* **6/1**[3]

053 **12** *hd* **Honcho (IRE)**[15] 7817 4-9-5 59 (p) AdamKirby 3 42
(John Ryan) *led but pressed: hdd & wknd qckly wl over 1f out* **5/2**[1]

U-0 **13** 2¼ **Or So (USA)**[20] 7889 4-9-0 57 (v) NoelGarbutt[(3)] 8 34
(Derek Shaw) *taken down early: reluctant to enter stall: w ldr to over 2f out: wknd rapidly* **50/1**

1m 26.26s (0.26) **Going Correction** -0.075s/f (Stan)
WFA 3 from 4yo+ 1lb **13** Ran SP% **129.8**
Speed ratings (Par 101): **95,94,93,93,92 91,91,86,86,85 84,84,81**
CSF £82.09 CT £544.36 TOTE £12.60: £3.50, £2.50, £3.20; EX 85.20 Trifecta £676.10.
Owner Sugar Syndicate **Bred** Pantile Stud **Trained** Collingbourne Ducis, Wilts
■ Stewards' Enquiry : Charlie Bennett three-day ban: careless riding (Dec 14-16)

Jack Mitchell seven-day ban: used whip above permitted level (Dec 14-20)

FOCUS

A bit of a messy race, but the winner and third could have more to offer this winter.

T/Jkpt: Not won. T/Plt: £345.00 to a £1 stake. Pool: £101,187.14 - 214.06 winning units. T/Qpdt: £126.90 to a £1 stake. Pool: £11,370.97 - 66.30 winning units. **Jonathan Neesom**

8025 LINGFIELD (L-H)

Wednesday, November 30

OFFICIAL GOING: Polytrack: standard

Wind: virtually nil Weather: sunny, chilly

8157 SUNBETS.CO.UK EBF MAIDEN STKS — 1m 1y(P)

12:10 (12:10) (Class 5) 3-Y-O+ **£3,363** (£1,001; £500; £250) **Stalls** High

Form RPR

1 **Blue Revelation**[485] 4952 3-9-5 0 .... GeorgeBaker 2 75+
(Paul Webber) *trckd ldng pair: shkn up and clsd to press ldrs over 1f out: rdn to ld ins fnl f: idling in front and eased towards fin* **5/4**[1]

0- 2 ½ **Mornington**[487] 4859 3-8-12 0 .... TylerSaunders(7) 6 71
(Marcus Tregoning) *s.i.s: hld up in tch: effrt to chse ldrs over 1f out: cl 3rd 1f out: rdn ins fnl f: wnt 2nd fnl 50yds: kpt on* **8/1**[3]

4 3 ½ **Tarseekh**[175] 3023 3-9-5 0 .... JackMitchell 9 70
(Roger Varian) *trckd ldr tl shkn up to ld 2f out: rdn over 1f out: hdd and styd on same pce ins fnl f* **11/8**[2]

0505 4 8 **Farrah's Choice**[82] 6278 4-9-2 45 .... TomMarquand 4 47?
(James Grassick) *led tl 2f out: drvn and unable qck over 1f out: wknd ins fnl f* **66/1**

5 *shd* **Summer Falls (IRE)** 3-8-7 0 .... LuluStanford(7) 7 46
(Rae Guest) *s.i.s: sn rcvrd and wl in tch in midfield: pushed along 2f out: sn outpcd and wl hld over 1f out* **25/1**

00 6 6 **Race Time (USA)**[60] 6960 3-9-0 0 .... TimmyMurphy 1 31
(Seamus Durack) *hld up in rr of main gp: pushed along and outpcd 2f out: sn wl btn* **33/1**

7 *155* **Portland Belle (IRE)** 3-9-0 0 .... (bt1) RichardKingscote 3
(Jeremy Gask) *v.s.a: flashing tail and ref to r properly: sn t.o* **12/1**

1m 38.5s (0.30) **Going Correction** 0.0s/f (Stan)
WFA 3 from 4yo 2lb **7** Ran SP% **113.6**
Speed ratings (Par 103): **98,97,97,89,88 82,**
CSF £11.73 TOTE £1.90: £1.60, £3.90; EX 12.70 Trifecta £19.70.
Owner Saleh Al Homaizi & Imad Al Sagar **Bred** Saleh Al Homaizi & Imad Al Sagar **Trained** Mollington, Oxon

FOCUS

A moderate older-horse maiden, dominated by the three market leaders all of whom had been gelded since last seen.

8158 32RED.COM FILLIES' H'CAP — 7f 1y(P)

12:40 (12:41) (Class 3) (0-90,87) 3-Y-O+ **£7,561** (£2,263; £1,131; £566; £282) **Stalls** Low

Form RPR

1214 1 **Bargain Buy**[175] 3039 3-9-4 82 .... PatCosgrave 8 91
(William Haggas) *stdd and awkward leaving stalls: dropped in and hld up in last trio: gap opened and gd hdwy wl over 1f out: rdn to ld 1f out: r.o wl: rdn out* **4/1**[1]

1100 2 1¼ **Shypen**[15] 7965 3-9-1 79 .... JackGarritty 2 85
(Richard Fahey) *t.k.h: hld up in tch in midfield: effrt whn carried rt and impeded bnd wl over 1f out: rallied 1f out: styd on wl to go 2nd fnl 50yds: nvr getting to wnr* **6/1**[2]

2410 3 ¾ **Summer Icon**[193] 2466 3-9-9 87 .... GeorgeBaker 5 91
(Mick Channon) *chsd ldrs: effrt and pressed ldng pair over 1f out: wnt 2nd ins fnl f: kpt on same pce after: lost 2nd 50yds out* **20/1**

6066 4 1 **Lyfka**[5] 8098 4-9-1 78 .... (tp) LukeMorris 4 80
(Paul Cole) *hld up in tch in last trio: carried rt and nt clr run bnd wl over 1f out: rallied 1f out: styd on wl u.p fnl 100yds: no threat to ldrs* **7/1**[3]

3423 5 *nk* **Rebel Surge (IRE)**[16] 7958 3-9-7 85 .... (p) TomQueally 1 85
(Richard Spencer) *led: jnd 3f out: rdn 2f out: hdd 1f out: no ex u.p and outpcd ins fnl f* **7/1**[3]

0450 6 *hd* **Lady Lydia (IRE)**[207] 2034 5-9-2 82 .... NoelGarbutt(3) 7 83
(Gay Kelleway) *stdd s: t.k.h: hld up in tch in last pair: rdn 2f out: hdwy on inner over 1f out: kpt on same pce and no imp ins fnl f* **50/1**

3113 7 ¾ **Encore Moi**[13] 7985 3-8-1 72 ow3 .... (b) LuluStanford(7) 6 70
(Marco Botti) *in tch in midfield: effrt and drifted wd bnd: styd on same pce u.p fnl f* **4/1**[1]

1201 8 1¼ **Threebagsue (IRE)**[18] 7931 3-8-12 76 .... (b) JosephineGordon 11 71
(J S Moore) *chsd ldrs: ev ch 3f out: carried rt and lost pl bnd wl over 1f out: drifted bk lft and no imp over 1f out: kpt on same pce after* **25/1**

5032 9 *shd* **Russian Radiance**[11] 8028 4-9-7 84 .... RichardKingscote 9 79
(Jonathan Portman) *hld up in tch in midfield: carried rt and nt clr run wl over 1f out: swtchd lft and tried to rally over 1f out: no imp ins fnl f* **7/1**[3]

5112 10 3¼ **Enjoy Life (IRE)**[26] 7798 3-8-13 77 .... (p) KevinStott 10 62
(Kevin Ryan) *chsd ldrs: ev ch 3f out: hung rt bnd wl over 1f out: lost pl and drifted bk lft over 1f out: wknd ins fnl f* **6/1**[2]

1240 11 2½ **Pretty Bubbles**[57] 7054 7-9-5 82 .... (v) AdamKirby 3 62
(J R Jenkins) *in tch in midfield: rdn and carried lft over 1f out: wknd ins fnl f* **25/1**

1m 22.77s (-2.03) **Going Correction** 0.0s/f (Stan)
WFA 3 from 4yo+ 1lb **11** Ran SP% **120.5**
Speed ratings (Par 104): **111,109,108,107,107 107,106,104,104,100 98**
CSF £27.46 CT £444.50 TOTE £3.20: £1.40, £2.90, £5.70; EX 31.70 Trifecta £357.00.
Owner Sheikh Rashid Dalmook Al Maktoum **Bred** Shane & Nicola O'Neill & R Kent **Trained** Newmarket, Suffolk
■ Stewards' Enquiry : Richard Kingscote caution: careless riding

FOCUS

A decent fillies' handicap, but a slightly messy race. The unexposed winner did it nicely, though.

8159 32REDPOKER.COM NURSERY H'CAP — 7f 1y(P)

1.10 (1.17) (Class 5) (0-70,70) 2-Y-O **£2,911** (£800; £432; £216) **Stalls** Low

Form RPR

6004 1 **Reign On**[11] 8033 2-9-3 69 .... HectorCrouch(3) 10 76+
(Ralph Beckett) *in tch in last trio: swtchd rt and hdwy over 1f out: rdn and wnt between rivals to ld 1f out: fnd ex whn chal ins fnl f: r.o wl* **8/1**

6363 2 ¾ **Sassoferrato (IRE)**[14] 7974 2-9-1 64 .... PatCosgrave 13 69
(Jo Hughes) *restrained and dropped in towards rr after 1f: hmpd over 2f out: hdwy and swtchd rt over 1f out: str chal ins fnl f: unable qck w wnr and btn fnl 50yds* **7/1**[3]

032 3 2½ **Titi Makfi**[14] 7975 2-9-7 70 .... AndrewMullen 2 68
(Mark Johnston) *wl in tch in midfield: swtchd rt over 1f out: hdwy and swtchd rt again ins fnl f: kpt on u.p to go 3rd wl ins fnl f: no threat to ldng pair* **7/1**[3]

6205 4 ½ **Washington Blue**[20] 7891 2-9-7 70 .... AdamKirby 4 67
(Clive Cox) *in tch in midfield: n.m.r over 2f out: shuffled bk and edgd lft over 1f out: hdwy 1f out: styd on u.p ins fnl f: no threat to ldng pair* **8/1**

2266 5 2 **Texas Katie**[19] 7898 2-9-5 68 .... (p) LukeMorris 5 59
(Archie Watson) *w ldr: rdn to ld 2f out: drvn over 1f out: hdd 1f out: sn outpcd and wknd fnl 100yds* **7/1**[3]

5012 6 1¼ **Ninety Years Young**[20] 7884 2-9-4 67 .... (b) ShaneKelly 9 55
(David Elsworth) *in tch in midfield: shuffled bk to rr and nt clrest of runs over 1f out: swtchd rt and hdwy 1f out: rdn and kpt on to pass btn horses ins fnl f: nvr trbld ldrs* **7/1**[3]

4034 7 *nk* **Jet Setter (IRE)**[19] 7898 2-8-13 69 .... (b1) JordanUys(7) 1 56
(Brian Meehan) *bustled along leaving stalls: chsd ldrs: effrt on inner and pressed ldrs over 1f out: unable qck 1f out: wknd ins fnl f* **6/1**[2]

466 8 1½ **Ejabah (IRE)**[79] 6414 2-9-0 66 .... LouisSteward(3) 8 49
(Chris Wall) *dropped to rr and swtchd lft sn after s: pushed along at times in rr: rdn and hdwy on inner over 1f out: no imp ins fnl f: nvr trbld ldrs* **20/1**

330 9 1¼ **Endeavour (IRE)**[34] 7649 2-9-5 68 .... TomMarquand 3 48
(Richard Hannon) *taken down early: led but awkward hd carriage: rdn and hdd 2f out: stl ev ch tl no ex u.p 1f out: wknd ins fnl f* **20/1**

030 10 8 **Beaconsfield**[33] 7658 2-9-7 70 .... KierenFox 14 28
(Hughie Morrison) *pushed up to press ldrs but stuck v wd thrght: lost pl bnd wl over 1f out: sn wl btn and bhd fnl f* **20/1**

6340 11 *shd* **Elementary**[42] 7467 2-9-6 69 .... GeorgeBaker 6 27
(Michael Bell) *pressed ldrs: rdn wl over 1f out: fnd nil and wkng whn hmpd over 1f out: bhd fnl f* **5/1**[1]

0640 12 ¾ **Sliceoflife**[11] 8033 2-8-13 69 .... LuluStanford(7) 7 25
(Marco Botti) *pressed ldrs but wd thrght: lost pl 2f out: bhd fnl f* **14/1**

1m 24.46s (-0.34) **Going Correction** 0.0s/f (Stan) **12** Ran SP% **124.1**
Speed ratings (Par 96): **101,100,97,96,94 93,92,90,89,80 80,79**
CSF £64.15 CT £417.61 TOTE £10.90: £3.00, £2.20, £2.60; EX 95.30 Trifecta £1341.80.
Owner What Asham Partnership **Bred** J A And M A Knox **Trained** Kimpton, Hants

FOCUS

An ordinary nursery and a five-way battle for the early lead set it up for the closers. The winner has been rated back to his early season figure.

8160 BETWAY CONDITIONS STKS — 1m 2f (P)

1:40 (1:43) (Class 2) 3-Y-O+ **£11,827** (£3,541; £1,770; £885; £442; £222) **Stalls** Low

Form RPR

6052 1 **Battalion (IRE)**[61] 6932 6-9-4 104 .... WilliamCarson 7 109
(Jamie Osborne) *s.i.s: hld up in tch in last pair: gap opened and qcknd on inner to ld over 1f out: sn in command: r.o wl: comf* **7/2**[2]

0033 2 4 **Master The World (IRE)**[18] 7934 5-9-4 108 .... (p) ShaneKelly 2 101
(David Elsworth) *s.i.s: hld up in last pair: nt clr run bnd 2f out: swtchd lft and hdwy over 1f out: rdn and styd on ins fnl f: wnt 2nd last strides: no ch w wnr* **5/4**[1]

5431 3 *nk* **Somethingthrilling**[11] 8028 4-8-13 84 .... TomMarquand 3 95
(David Elsworth) *trckd ldng pair: rdn 2f out: swtchd rt jst over 1f out: drvn and chsd clr wnr jst ins fnl f: kpt on but no ch w wnr: lost 2nd last strides* **12/1**

0042 4 1¼ **Manson**[27] 7779 3-9-0 95 .... TimmyMurphy 5 98+
(Dominic Ffrench Davis) *stdd after s: t.k.h: hld up in tch in midfield: effrt whn short of room and hmpd jst over 1f out: nt clr run again 1f out: rdn and kpt on same pce ins fnl f* **5/1**[3]

0533 5 2 **Pinzolo**[52] 7188 5-9-4 98 .... TomQueally 6 94
(Ismail Mohammed) *sn chsng ldr tl unable qck and lost pl over 1f out: wknd ins fnl f* **6/1**

0122 6 1½ **Ready (IRE)**[11] 8035 6-9-4 91 .... (p) SteveDrowne 4 91
(Clare Ellam) *led: rdn and hdd over 1f out: sn edgd rt and outpcd: wknd ins fnl f* **66/1**

0400 7 2 **Bancnuanaheireann (IRE)**[67] 6786 9-9-4 104 .... AlistairRawlinson 1 87
(Michael Appleby) *wl in tch in midfield: rdn and outpcd bnd 2f out: bhd ins fnl f* **14/1**

2m 2.74s (-3.86) **Going Correction** 0.0s/f (Stan)
WFA 3 from 4yo+ 4lb **7** Ran SP% **113.5**
Speed ratings (Par 109): **115,111,111,110,108 107,106**
CSF £8.14 TOTE £4.70: £2.10, £1.70; EX 10.60 Trifecta £65.10.
Owner Melbourne 10 Racing **Bred** Kildaragh Stud **Trained** Upper Lambourn, Berks

FOCUS

An interesting conditions event, but they didn't go much of a pace. The winner was still impressive, though.

8161 BETWAY H'CAP (DIV I) — 1m 4f (P)

2:10 (2:11) (Class 4) (0-80,79) 3-Y-O+ **£5,175** (£1,540; £769; £384) **Stalls** Low

Form RPR

5402 1 **Priors Brook**[51] 7222 5-9-4 73 .... LiamKeniry 5 81
(Andrew Balding) *hld up in tch in midfield: effrt over 1f out: led jst ins fnl f: edgd rt briefly wl ins fnl f: styd on* **11/4**[2]

0240 2 ½ **Artful Rogue (IRE)**[40] 7508 5-9-2 74 .... KieranShoemark(3) 9 81
(Amanda Perrett) *t.k.h: hld up in tch in last quartet: effrt over 1f out: styd on to chse wnr ins fnl f: kpt on but a hld* **7/1**

3-02 3 1 **Take Two**[34] 7653 7-8-13 71 .... CallumShepherd(3) 6 76
(Alex Hales) *t.k.h: chsd ldr tl rdn to ld over 1f out: hdd jst ins fnl f: no ex and styd on same pce fnl 100yds* **9/1**

3164 4 ¾ **Spinners Ball (IRE)**[13] 7993 3-8-13 74 .... TomMarquand 4 80+
(Sylvester Kirk) *hld up wl in tch in midfield: clsd to chse ldrs but nt clr run over 1f out: trying to switch rt 1f out: stl nt clrest of runs and swtchd rt again wl ins fnl f: kpt on: unable to chal* **5/2**[1]

3214 5 ½ **Pastoral Music**[35] 7624 3-8-9 75 .... CharlieBennett(5) 2 78
(Hughie Morrison) *chsd ldrs: effrt over 1f out: kpt on same pce u.p ins fnl f: hld whn nudged rt wl ins fnl f* **6/1**[3]

4420 6 1 **Excellent Puck (IRE)**[200] 1999 6-9-9 78 .... FergusSweeney 3 79
(Shaun Lycett) *led and set stdy gallop: rdn and qcknd wl over 1f out: hdd over 1f out: unable qck: outpcd wl ins fnl f* **12/1**

4643 7 *nk* **Northern Meeting (IRE)**[40] 7507 6-9-3 72 .... (p) AdamBeschizza 1 73+
(Robert Stephens) *s.i.s: hld up in tch in rr: effrt and nt clr run over 1f out: swtchd lft and hdwy ent fnl f: kpt on but no threat to ldrs* **12/1**

0-00 8 2 **El Campeon**[161] 3525 4-9-4 73 .... NickyMackay 8 71
(Simon Dow) *stdd after s: t.k.h: hld up in tch towards rr: effrt and nt clrest of runs over 1f out: no imp ins fnl f: sddle slipped* **25/1**

0000 **9** *hd* **Juste Pour Nous**[26] 7791 3-8-11 **72**.............................. AndrewMullen 10 69
(Mark Johnston) *chsd ldrs: rdn and lost pl over 1f out: wknd ins fnl f* **20/1**

4215 **10** *12* **Gaelic Silver (FR)**[40] 7508 10-9-7 **79**........................(p) HectorCrouch(3) 7 57
(Gary Moore) *stdd s: t.k.h: hld up in tch in last trio: effrt 2f out: outpcd u.p over 1f out: sn wknd* **20/1**

2m 33.77s (0.77) **Going Correction** 0.0s/f (Stan)
WFA 3 from 4yo+ 6lb **10** Ran SP% **120.8**
Speed ratings (Par 105): **97,96,96,95,95 94,94,92,92,84**
CSF £22.72 CT £157.87 TOTE £3.00: £1.30, £2.60, £2.70; EX 24.20 Trifecta £169.40.
Owner Mrs L Alexander **Bred** Mrs L M Alexander **Trained** Kingsclere, Hants

FOCUS
The first division of a fair middle-distance handicap, but they went no pace and it became a 3f sprint.

8162 BETWAY H'CAP (DIV II) 1m 4f (P)
2:40 (2:41) (Class 4) (0-80,79) 3-Y-O+ **£5,175** (£1,540; £769; £384) **Stalls** Low

Form RPR

1601 **1** **Petite Jack**[34] 7653 3-9-2 **77**.. JackMitchell 8 90+
(Neil King) *stdd s: hld up in rr: swtchd rt and v wd bnd 2f out: hdwy to chse clr ldng pair jst ins fnl f: qckned and str run to ld 50yds out: sn in command: readily* **5/2**[1]

0363 **2** *1 1/4* **Isharah (USA)**[35] 7618 3-9-3 **78**...................................... AndrewMullen 1 86
(Mark Johnston) *dwlt: sn rcvrd to chse ldrs: wnt 2nd jst over 2f out: drvn and chalng over 1f out: led ins fnl f: hdd and outpcd by wnr fnl 50yds* **5/1**

1265 **3** *2 1/4* **Duck A L'Orange (IRE)**[35] 7618 3-8-13 **74**...........(p) RichardKingscote 2 78
(Michael Bell) *led: rdn wl over 1f out: clr w chalr 1f out: hdd and no ex ins fnl f: wknd towards fin* **9/2**[3]

303 **4** *1/2* **Ardamir (FR)**[40] 7512 4-9-9 **78**....................................... FergusSweeney 9 82+
(Alan King) *hld up in tch in last trio: clsd whn bmpd bnd wl over 1f out: trying to switch rt whn nt clr run and swtchd bk sharply lft over 1f out: rdn and kpt on ins fnl f* **3/1**[2]

3066 **5** *1 3/4* **Topaling**[7] 8076 5-8-11 **66**.. StevieDonohoe 4 67
(Mark H Tompkins) *in tch in midfield: effrt wl over 1f out: chsd clr ldng pair 1f out: no imp and one pce after* **66/1**

5012 **6** *nk* **Safira Menina**[20] 7895 4-9-5 **74**.. RyanPowell 7 74
(Martin Smith) *hmpd leaving stalls: hld up in tch in rr: nt clr run 2f out: shkn up and effrt on inner over 1f out: kpt on same pce ins fnl f: swtchd rt towards fin* **16/1**

0360 **7** *3* **Clovelly Bay (IRE)**[121] 4940 5-8-10 **72**....................... TylerSaunders(7) 6 68
(Marcus Tregoning) *wnt rt leaving stalls: t.k.h: chsd ldrs: shkn up: edgd lft and unable qck over 1f out: wknd ins fnl f* **16/1**

5305 **8** *1 1/2* **Callendula**[14] 7980 4-9-4 **73**...(p) AdamKirby 5 66
(Clive Cox) *wl in tch in midfield: effrt and edgd lft wl over 1f out: hmpd: swtchd rt and unable qck over 1f out: wknd ins fnl f* **7/1**

4550 **9** *25* **Genuine Approval (IRE)**[63] 6870 3-9-4 **79**................. RobertWinston 3 32
(John Butler) *chsd ldr tl jst over 2f out: lost pl qckly and hung rt bnd 2f out: wl bhd and eased ins fnl f: t.o* **16/1**

2m 31.54s (-1.46) **Going Correction** 0.0s/f (Stan)
WFA 3 from 4yo+ 6lb **9** Ran SP% **120.1**
Speed ratings (Par 105): **104,103,101,101,100 99,97,96,80**
CSF £16.20 CT £54.84 TOTE £3.50: £1.10, £2.30, £1.50; EX 19.70 Trifecta £66.70.
Owner W Burn **Bred** Mrs Liz Nelson Mbe **Trained** Barbury Castle, Wiltshire
■ Stewards' Enquiry : Tyler Saunders two-day ban: careless riding (Dec 14-15)

FOCUS
This didn't look strongly run either, but the winning time was still 2.23sec quicker than the first division.

8163 SUNBETS.CO.UK TOP PRICE ON ALL FAVOURITES H'CAP 7f 1y(P)
3:10 (3:14) (Class 5) (0-70,70) 3-Y-O+ **£3,234** (£962; £481; £120; £120) **Stalls** Low

Form RPR

6054 **1** **Saleh (IRE)**[29] 7736 3-8-12 **62**... RobertWinston 3 70
(Lee Carter) *hld up in tch in midfield: hdwy on inner over 1f out: str chal ins fnl f: r.o wl to ld last strides* **7/1**[3]

6145 **2** *hd* **Rebel Lightning (IRE)**[13] 7985 3-9-6 **70**.......................(b) AdamKirby 14 77
(Richard Spencer) *chsd ldr: rdn and ev ch 2f out: drvn fnl f: kpt on* **4/1**[2]

3 **3** *nse* **Plus Night (FR)**[30] 7725 3-9-5 **69**.................................. PatCosgrave 13 76
(Stuart Williams) *led: rdn over 1f out: drvn ins fnl f: hdd and no ex last strides* **13/8**[1]

1024 **4** *1 3/4* **Polar Kite (IRE)**[48] 7310 8-8-11 **65**............................. PaddyBradley(5) 8 68
(Michael Attwater) *hld up in tch in midfield: clsd on inner over 1f out: rdn ins fnl f: kpt on: nvr trbld ldrs* **20/1**

510- **4** *dht* **Miss Blondell**[446] 6278 3-9-4 **68**...................................... SteveDrowne 7 70
(Marcus Tregoning) *chsd ldrs: rdn over 1f out: stl cl enough 1f out: no ex and wknd wl ins fnl f* **33/1**

135 **6** *hd* **Chiswick Bey (IRE)**[32] 7702 8-8-11 **67**.................. NatalieHambling(7) 9 70
(Richard Fahey) *t.k.h: chsd ldrs: rdn over 1f out: kpt on same pce ins fnl f* **15/2**

2403 **7** *1 1/2* **Valmina**[19] 7899 9-9-3 **66**..(t) LukeMorris 5 65
(Philip Hide) *hld up in tch in midfield: effrt over 1f out: drvn 1f out: kpt on same pce ins fnl f* **12/1**

6040 **8** *2* **Skidby Mill (IRE)**[13] 7985 6-8-10 **66**.................................. OllieJago(7) 6 59
(Laura Mongan) *t.k.h early: chsd ldrs tl lost pl 2f out: shkn up and btn over 1f out: wknd and hung lft ins fnl f* **16/1**

0660 **9** *1 1/4* **Lucky Di**[29] 7738 6-9-2 **65**... TomMarquand 4 55
(Peter Hedger) *awkward leaving stalls and s.i.s: hld up in tch in last pair: effrt over 1f out: kpt on same pce ins fnl f: nvr trbld ldrs* **20/1**

2000 **10** *hd* **Etaad (USA)**[19] 7899 5-9-0 **66**....................................... HectorCrouch(3) 10 55
(Gary Moore) *in tch in midfield: rdn and unable qck over 1f out: wknd ins fnl f* **20/1**

4300 **11** *1/2* **Sehayli (IRE)**[72] 6629 3-9-0 **67**..................................... LouisSteward(3) 2 54
(Lee Carter) *hld up in tch in last pair: effrt over 1f out: no imp: nvr trbld ldrs* **20/1**

0000 **12** *1 3/4* **Musical Taste**[18] 7931 3-8-12 **62**... JFEgan 12 44
(Pat Phelan) *hld up in tch in last trio: effrt on inner over 1f out: no imp and wl hld whn eased wl ins fnl f* **66/1**

1m 25.6s (0.80) **Going Correction** 0.0s/f (Stan)
WFA 3 from 5yo+ 1lb **12** Ran SP% **119.4**
Speed ratings (Par 103): **95,94,94,92,92 92,90,88,87,86 86,84**
CSF £31.86 CT £69.18 TOTE £8.60: £2.20, £1.50, £1.20; EX 45.10 Trifecta £205.70.
Owner Only One Bid Partnership **Bred** Stowell Park Stud **Trained** Epsom, Surrey

FOCUS
An ordinary handicap and not many got into it, but a thrilling finish between the first three.

8164 BETWAY AMATEUR RIDERS' H'CAP 1m 7f 169y(P)
3:40 (3:40) (Class 6) (0-60,57) 3-Y-O+ **£2,495** (£774; £386; £193) **Stalls** Low

Form RPR

1544 **1** **Dltripleseven (IRE)**[32] 7692 3-9-12 **57**........................... MrJJO'Neill(7) 9 66+
(Richard Hughes) *stdd s: hld up in last pair: hdwy to trck ldrs over 4f out: shkn up to join ldrs over 1f out: pushed into ld ins fnl f: sn qcknd clr: easily* **6/5**[1]

3321 **2** *3 1/4* **Master Burbidge**[227] 695 5-10-10 **56**.....................(p) MrJamesKing(3) 1 60
(Neil Mulholland) *led tl over 12f out: chsd ldr tl 9f out: wnt 2nd again 4f out: rdn and ev ch over 1f out: edgd lft and outpcd by wnr ins fnl f* **2/1**[2]

6300 **3** *1 1/2* **Sund City (FR)**[42] 7464 3-9-9 **52**............................. MrShaneQuinlan(5) 3 54
(Harry Dunlop) *chsd ldrs: hdwy to ld over 12f out: rdn over 1f out: hdd ins fnl f: sn outpcd and hld in 3rd whn nt clrest of runs towards fin* **7/1**[3]

1000 **4** *nse* **Tarakkom (FR)**[11] 8039 4-10-7 **57**............................... MissMollyKing(7) 2 59
(Peter Hiatt) *chsd ldrs: 4th and stl travelling wl over 2f out: pushed along over 1f out: kpt on same pce and swtchd rt ins fnl f* **25/1**

1-60 **5** *3/4* **Grand Facile**[285] 634 4-10-2 **52**..........................(v) MissBeckyButler(7) 5 54
(Gary Moore) *in tch: pushed along 6f out: 5th and rdn over 2f out: keeping on but no ch w wnr whn nt clr run and swtchd rt towards fin* **25/1**

/5-0 **6** *6* **Topolski (IRE)**[29] 7739 10-10-7 **50**........................... MissSBrotherton 4 44
(David Arbuthnot) *in tch in midfield: rdn and outpcd over 4f out: 6th and wl hld over 2f out: no imp after* **12/1**

5044 **7** *13* **Leyland (IRE)**[20] 7421 7-9-10 **46**...................................(b) MrWillPettis(7) 6 25
(Natalie Lloyd-Beavis) *in tch in midfield: swtchd rt and hdwy to chse ldr 10f out: rdn 5f out: lost pl u.p over 3f out: bhd and eased ins fnl f* **16/1**

0- **8** *4 1/2* **Moveable Asset (IRE)**[65] 8257 8-10-5 **55**..................(t) MrCAJones(7) 8 28
(Henry Tett) *nvr gng wl in rr: lost tch 3f out* **50/1**

-500 **9** *3 1/4* **Crystalise (IRE)**[11] 8039 4-10-7 **57**......................... MrSeanHoulihan(7) 7 26
(Robert Stephens) *stuck wd: hld up in tch: drvn 4f out: sn btn: bhd over 2f out* **12/1**

3m 24.81s (-0.89) **Going Correction** 0.0s/f (Stan)
WFA 3 from 4yo+ 9lb **9** Ran SP% **122.2**
Speed ratings (Par 101): **102,100,99,99,99 96,89,87,85**
CSF £3.92 CT £11.78 TOTE £2.10: £1.10, £1.10, £1.80; EX 4.50 Trifecta £20.80.
Owner Advantage Chemicals Holdings Ltd **Bred** Advantage Chemicals Holdings Ltd **Trained** Upper Lambourn, Berkshire

FOCUS
A moderate amateur riders' handicap, but a fine ride from the winning jockey.
T/Plt: £79.80 to a £1 stake. Pool: £62,741.55 - 573.84 winning units. T/Qpdt: £12.40 to a £1 stake. Pool: £7,648.07 - 453.75 winning units. **Steve Payne**

8147 DEAUVILLE (R-H)
Wednesday, November 30
OFFICIAL GOING: Polytrack: standard

8165a PRIX LYPHARD (LISTED RACE) (3YO+) (POLYTRACK) 1m 1f 110y
1:35 (12:00) 3-Y-O+ **£19,117** (£7,647; £5,735; £3,823; £1,911)

RPR

1 **Mr Owen (USA)**[74] 6601 4-9-0 0.................................... OlivierPeslier 7 109
(F Rohaut, France) **33/10**[1]

2 *3* **Al Debel (FR)**[91] 3-8-11 0.. GregoryBenoist 12 104
(J Reynier, France) **53/10**[3]

3 *1 1/2* **Ecureuil (USA)**[60] 4-9-0 0... MaximeGuyon 8 100
(C Ferland, France) **11/2**

4 *shd* **Sea Front (FR)**[59] 6988 5-8-11 0 ow1.................. ChristopheSoumillon 5 97
(E Libaud, France) **9/1**

5 *snk* **Nice To See You (FR)**[22] 3-8-11 0.........................(p) SebastienMaillot 1 100
(Robert Collet, France) **20/1**

6 *1 1/2* **Sainte Amarante (FR)**[40] 7524 4-8-10 0.................... CristianDemuro 11 92
(Yves de Nicolay, France) **18/1**

7 *3/4* **Ame Bleue**[53] 7176 4-9-0 0.................................. Pierre-CharlesBoudot 9 95
(A Fabre, France) **4/1**[2]

8 *1 3/4* **Funny Kid (USA)**[247] 3-8-11 0... JulienAuge 10 92
(C Ferland, France) **31/1**

9 *3/4* **Taratchi (FR)**[44] 4-9-0 0.. FabriceVeron 14 90
(J Parize, France) **36/1**

10 *snk* **Vodkato (FR)**[40] 7524 8-9-0 0...(b) TheoBachelot 4 89
(S Wattel, France) **13/1**

11 *1 1/2* **Energia Davos (BRZ)**[18] 7934 8-9-3 0................................ MartinDwyer 2 89
(Jane Chapple-Hyam) **21/1**

12 *shd* **Game Theory (IRE)**[22] 7861 4-9-0 0........................ StephanePasquier 13 86
(N Clement, France) **15/1**

WIN (incl. 1 euro stake): 4.30. PLACES: 1.70, 1.90, 2.00. DF: 11.60. SF: 25.00.
Owner Qatar Racing Ltd **Bred** Derry Meeting Farm **Trained** Sauvagnon, France

8166 - 8173a (Foreign Racing) - See Raceform Interactive

8079 CHELMSFORD (A.W) (L-H)
Thursday, December 1
OFFICIAL GOING: Polytrack: standard
Wind: virtually nil Weather: dry and chilly

8174 TOTEPLACEPOT NURSERY H'CAP 6f (P)
4:10 (4:10) (Class 5) (0-70,69) 2-Y-O **£2,911** (£866; £432; £216) **Stalls** Centre

Form RPR

0452 **1** **Magique Touch**[14] 7981 2-8-12 **63**......................(b) KieranShoemark(3) 4 73
(Roger Charlton) *trckd ldng pair: swtchd rt and chsd ldr wl over 1f out: rdn to ld 1f out: styd on strly: rdn out* **3/1**[1]

5100 **2** *2 1/2* **Manners Please**[59] 7016 2-9-7 **69**.............................. RichardKingscote 5 72
(Ralph Beckett) *hld up in midfield: swtchd rt and effrt over 1f out: wnt 4th 1f out: styd on wl to go 2nd 50yds out: no threat to wnr* **9/1**

062 **3** *3/4* **Nuzha**[19] 7939 2-9-4 **66**... JFEgan 8 66
(David Evans) *led: rdn over 1f out: hdd and no ex 1f out: styd on same pce ins fnl f: lost 2nd 50yds out* **20/1**

2213 **4** *1 1/4* **Wentwell Yesterday (IRE)**[8] 8071 2-9-7 **69**.............. WilliamCarson 10 66
(Jamie Osborne) *chsd ldrs: effrt to chse ldng pair over 1f out: no imp and kpt on same pce ins fnl f* **4/1**[2]

2402 **5** *2* **Seprani**[36] 7615 2-8-7 **62**...[1] LuluStanford(7) 1 53
(Marco Botti) *dwlt: sn in tch in midfield: pushed along 2f out: rdn and kpt on same pce fr over 1f out* **5/1**[3]

010 **6** ½ **Uncle Charlie (IRE)**[43] 7467 2-9-0 **67**............................ RowanScott(5) 2 56
(Ann Duffield) *dwlt: hld up in last pair: rdn and hdwy on inner over 1f out: kpt on ins fnl f: nvr trbld ldrs* **5/1**3

4406 **7** ¾ **No Not Again (IRE)**[28] 7776 2-9-0 **67**............................ HollieDoyle(5) 7 54
(Richard Hannon) *pushed along in last quartet: rdn wl over 1f out: hdwy 1f out: kpt on ins fnl f: nvr trbld ldrs* **10/1**

0345 **8** 2 **Oudwood**[52] 7228 2-9-4 **66**............................ DanielTudhope 9 47
(David O'Meara) *chsd ldrs: rdn and unable qck over 1f out: lost pl and wknd fnl f* **10/1**

060 **9** 1 **Delfie Lane**[12] 8027 2-9-4 **66**............................ ShaneKelly 13 44
(Richard Hughes) *dwlt: a bhd: n.d* **50/1**

3206 **10** 5 **Miss Rosina (IRE)**[16] 7966 2-9-4 **66**............................ AdamKirby 12 29
(George Margarson) *chsd ldr tl wl over 1f out: lost pl over 1f out: bhd ins fnl f* **16/1**

000 **11** 4½ **Dutch Cat**[19] 7939 2-8-4 **52**............................ LukeMorris 6
(Clive Cox) *a towards rr: shkn up over 1f out: no rspnse: bhd ins fnl f* **33/1**

1m 11.98s (-1.72) **Going Correction** -0.175s/f (Stan) **11** Ran SP% **122.1**
Speed ratings (Par 96): **104,100,99,98,95 94,93,91,89,83 77**
CSF £31.87 CT £475.49 TOTE £3.60: £1.10, £4.20, £5.20; EX 37.60 Trifecta £574.60.
Owner Mrs M D Stewart **Bred** Wellsummers Stud **Trained** Beckhampton, Wilts

FOCUS
A modest nursery with the form taken at face value.

8175 @TOTEPOOL TWEET US YOUR #TOTEELFIE MAIDEN STKS (PLUS 10 RACE) 6f (P)
4:45 (4:45) (Class 4) 2-Y-O **£5,822** (£1,732; £865; £432) **Stalls** Centre

Form RPR

304 **1** **Coastal Cyclone**[15] 7975 2-9-5 71............................ DavidProbert 8 73
(Harry Dunlop) *t.k.h: chsd ldrs: effrt to chal and edgd lft over 1f out: drvn to ld ins fnl f: kpt on* **7/2**3

424 **2** nk **Arzaak (IRE)**[97] 5820 2-9-5 74............................ JosephineGordon 4 73
(Chris Dwyer) *wl in tch in midfield: rdn 2f out: chsng ldrs whn squeezed out and hmpd over 1f out: swtchd rt and rallied ins fnl f: styd on wl u.p: wnt 2nd towards fin: nt quite rch wnr* **8/1**

532 **3** ¾ **Kings Academy**[8] 8065 2-9-5 0............................ LukeMorris 5 70
(Paul Cole) *chsd ldr: drvn 2f out: led u.p 1f out: sn hdd and styd on same pce ins fnl f* **13/8**1

254 **4** nk **Her Terms**[55] 7122 2-9-0 74............................ PatCosgrave 2 65
(William Haggas) *trckd ldrs: nt clr run and trying to switch rt over 1f out: stl nt clr run tl wl ins fnl f: rdn and styd on towards fin* **11/4**2

045 **5** ½ **Five Star Frank**[8] 8065 2-9-5 0............................ RobertWinston 1 67
(Eve Johnson Houghton) *racd keenly: led: rdn over 1f out: hdd 1f out: no ex and one pce ins fnl f* **8/1**

2244 **6** hd **Shabeeh (IRE)**[26] 7812 2-9-5 77............................ AndrewMullen 7 67
(Mark Johnston) *in tch in midfield: effrt 2f out: drvn over 1f out: kpt on ins fnl f: nvr enough pce to rch ldrs* **10/1**

400 **7** ¾ **Vibes (IRE)**[44] 7424 2-9-5 0............................ WilliamCarson 3 65
(Jamie Osborne) *stdd s: hld up in tch in last trio: effrt over 1f out: hdwy and hung lft ins fnl f: kpt on: nt clr run towards fin* **25/1**

8 nk **Canberra Cliffs (IRE)**[92] 6039 2-9-0 0............................ LiamKeniry 9 59
(Don Cantillon) *stdd s: hld up in tch in last trio: effrt over 1f out: kpt on ins fnl f: nvr enough pce to rch ldrs* **25/1**

9 2½ **Alfonso Manana (IRE)** 2-9-5 0............................ TomEaves 6 56
(James Given) *s.i.s: hld up in rr: pushed along 2f out: drvn over 1f out: kpt on same pce and no imp ins fnl f* **50/1**

1m 13.12s (-0.58) **Going Correction** -0.175s/f (Stan) **9** Ran SP% **128.0**
Speed ratings (Par 98): **96,95,94,94,93 93,92,91,88**
CSF £34.68 TOTE £5.20: £1.70, £2.50, £1.20; EX 34.00 Trifecta £112.80.
Owner Malcolm Aldis & Susan Abbott Racing **Bred** Kempsons Stud **Trained** Lambourn, Berks

FOCUS
A bit of a messy race and they finished in a heap.

8176 #TOTEELFIE WIN A £50 FREE BET H'CAP 6f (P)
5:15 (5:15) (Class 4) (0-80,89) 3-Y-O+ **£6,469** (£1,925; £962; £481) **Stalls** Centre

Form RPR

6210 **1** **Captain Dion**[47] 7360 3-9-6 **79**............................ KevinStott 4 91
(Kevin Ryan) *mde all: rdn ent fnl f: fnd ex and wnt clr ins fnl f: r.o wl: eased towards fin* **6/1**3

-565 **2** 2 **Parkour (IRE)**[16] 7965 3-9-6 **79**............................ LukeMorris 3 85
(Marco Botti) *chsd ldrs: wnt 2nd and drvn ent fnl f: styd on same pce u.p ins fnl f* **8/1**

1463 **3** 1¼ **Sophisticated Heir (IRE)**[14] 7983 6-9-6 **79**..............(b) RobertWinston 5 81
(Michael Herrington) *hld up in tch in midfield: swtchd lft and effrt over 1f out: chsd ldng pair and drvn ins fnl f: styd on same pce fnl 100yds* **12/1**

6612 **4** ½ **Dutch Golden Age (IRE)**[7] 8083 4-9-5 **78**............................ GeorgeBaker 8 78
(Gary Moore) *chsd ldrs: effrt over 1f out: sn rdn and unable qck: kpt on same pce ins fnl f* **3/1**1

2044 **5** ¾ **Gold Club**[7] 8083 5-9-4 **77**............................ DaleSwift 9 75
(Ed McMahon) *wl in tch in midfield: rdn jst over 2f out: styd on same pce u.p and no imp fr over 1f out* **7/1**

4235 **6** ¾ **Anonymous John (IRE)**[36] 7617 4-9-5 **78**............................ JFEgan 1 74
(Dominic Ffrench Davis) *hld up in tch in midfield: effrt over 1f out: swtchd lft and kpt on wl ins fnl f: no threat to wnr* **8/1**

0000 **7** ½ **El Viento (FR)**[22] 7864 8-9-6 **79**............................(v) JackGarritty 2 73
(Richard Fahey) *hld up in tch in midfield: effrt over 1f out: nt clr run and swtchd lft ins fnl f: kpt on fnl 100yds: no threat to wnr* **16/1**

0005 **8** 1¼ **Varsovian**[125] 4839 6-9-3 **79**............................ JackDuern(3) 7 69
(Dean Ivory) *stuck wd: hld up in tch: effrt ent fnl 2f: sme hdwy u.p 1f out: kpt on: nvr trbld ldrs* **16/1**

0611 **9** shd **Pearl Spectre (USA)**[7] 8083 5-9-13 **89** 12ex.......... CallumShepherd(3) 6 79
(Phil McEntee) *hld up in midfield: effrt ent fnl 2f: edgd lft u.p 1f out: styd on same pce ins fnl f* **7/2**2

-000 **10** hd **Picture Dealer**[30] 7737 7-9-4 **80**............................1 SimonPearce(3) 11 69
(Lydia Pearce) *squeezed out leaving stalls and sn swtchd lft: bhd: effrt over 1f out: swtchd lft ins fnl f: nvr trbld ldrs* **33/1**

3316 **11** nk **Interlink (USA)**[30] 7737 3-9-2 **75**............................ BenCurtis 10 63
(Tony Coyle) *taken down early: pressed wnr tl unable qck over 1f out: wknd and edgd rt ins fnl f* **14/1**

104 **12** 1½ **September Issue**[21] 7892 3-9-5 **78**............................ DougieCostello 14 61
(Gay Kelleway) *stdd s and hld up in rr: effrt over 1f out: no imp: nvr trbld ldrs* **25/1**

3430 **13** 1 **Panther Patrol (IRE)**[10] 8052 6-8-11 **75**..................(v) HollieDoyle(5) 13 55
(Eve Johnson Houghton) *in tch in midfield: effrt ent fnl 2f: edgd lft and no imp over 1f out: wknd ins fnl f* **16/1**

0034 **14** 3¼ **Welease Bwian (IRE)**[49] 7303 7-8-10 **76**............................ MillyNaseb(7) 12 46
(Stuart Williams) *dwlt: a towards rr: rdn over 1f out: no prog: bhd ins fnl f* **33/1**

1m 11.28s (-2.42) **Going Correction** -0.175s/f (Stan) **14** Ran SP% **138.0**
Speed ratings (Par 105): **109,106,104,104,103 102,101,99,99,99 98,96,95,91**
CSF £61.00 CT £436.47 TOTE £6.50: £2.30, £3.10, £4.20; EX 65.40 Trifecta £807.00.
Owner T A Rahman **Bred** Miss R J Dobson **Trained** Hambleton, N Yorks

FOCUS
A competitive handicap on paper, but few got involved. The winner has been rated to the better view of his Pontefract win, and the runner-up as close to his best.

8177 TOTETRIFECTA PICK THE 1,2,3 H'CAP 1m (P)
5:45 (5:47) (Class 3) (0-90,90) 3-Y-O+ **£9,703** (£2,887; £1,443; £721) **Stalls** Low

Form RPR

6011 **1** **Qaffaal (USA)**[33] 7691 5-8-9 **78**............................ GrahamGibbons 10 89
(Michael Easterby) *hld up in tch in midfield: clsd and travelling strly over 1f out: rdn to chse ldr jst over 1f out: led ins fnl f: r.o strly: readily* **8/1**3

5205 **2** 2¾ **Loyalty**[14] 7984 9-8-13 **85**............................(v) NoelGarbutt(3) 1 90
(Derek Shaw) *pushed along leaving stalls: chsd ldr tl 4f out: styd prom: rdn to ld over 1f out: hdd ins fnl f: kpt on same pce after* **20/1**

0332 **3** hd **Chevallier**[10] 8049 4-9-3 **86**............................ LukeMorris 3 93+
(Archie Watson) *hld up in tch in midfield: nt clr run over 1f out: sn swtchd rt and bmpd rival: edging lft u.p but r.o wl ins fnl f: no threat to wnr* **9/2**1

1300 **4** 1 **Fuwairt (IRE)**[26] 7825 4-9-4 **87**............................ ShaneKelly 6 89
(Roger Fell) *stdd after s: hld up in last quartet: swtchd rt and effrt over 1f out: hdwy 1f out: edgd lft and r.o wl ins fnl f: no threat to wnr* **10/1**

5005 **5** ¾ **Special Season**[16] 7967 3-9-6 **90**............................ WilliamCarson 2 91
(Jamie Osborne) *hld up in tch in midfield and travelled strly: nt clr run 2f out: swtchd rt and effrt over 1f out: styd on same pce ins fnl f* **8/1**3

6000 **6** 1¼ **Forceful Appeal (USA)**[14] 7984 8-9-1 **84**............................ NickyMackay 9 85+
(Simon Dow) *stdd after s: hld up in last pair: swtchd rt and effrt over 1f out: nt clr run and hmpd 1f out: pushed along and kpt on ins fnl f: no threat to wnr* **16/1**

3031 **7** ½ **Al Khan (IRE)**[16] 7968 7-9-4 **87**............................ TomEaves 12 83
(Kevin Ryan) *chsd ldrs: drvn and effrt but unable qck over 1f out: wknd ins fnl f* **25/1**

1060 **8** shd **Jack's Revenge (IRE)**[26] 7821 8-9-3 **86**..................(vt) SteveDrowne 11 82
(George Baker) *hld up in tch in midfield: effrt jst over 2f out: struggling to qckn whn bmpd and pushed rt over 1f out: no imp fnl f* **33/1**

0005 **9** nk **Lil Sophella (IRE)**[17] 7958 7-8-13 **82**............................ JackGarritty 7 78
(Patrick Holmes) *hld up in rr: effrt over 1f out: hdwy and swtchd rt 1f out: kpt on ins fnl f: no threat to ldrs* **50/1**

-021 **10** 4½ **Haaf A Sixpence**[20] 7902 7-9-2 **88**............................ HectorCrouch(3) 8 73
(Ralph Beckett) *t.k.h: chsd ldrs: effrt over 1f out: sn hrd drvn and unable qck: wknd ins fnl f* **5/1**2

0500 **11** 1½ **Two For Two (IRE)**[33] 7699 8-9-5 **88**............................(p) PJMcDonald 16 70
(Roger Fell) *towards rr: rdn 3f out: drvn over 2f out and no hdwy: lost pl over 1f out: wknd fnl f* **33/1**

5002 **12** 1 **Mikmak**[20] 7903 3-9-2 **86**............................(p) MartinDwyer 14 65
(William Muir) *dwlt: hdwy to chse ldrs after 2f: jnd ldr 4f out tl led wl over 1f out: sn rdn and hdd: wknd fnl f* **25/1**

0011 **13** 1 **Firmdecisions (IRE)**[28] 7781 6-9-4 **87**............................ PatCosgrave 4 64
(Dean Ivory) *hld up in tch towards rr: rdn jst over 2f out: swtchd rt and sme hdwy u.p jst over 1f out: edgd bk lft and no hdwy 1f out: wknd ins fnl f* **9/2**1

0010 **14** 8 **My Target (IRE)**[10] 8049 5-9-7 **90**............................ AdamKirby 13 49
(Michael Wigham) *led: hdd wl over 1f out: sn btn and lost pl: bhd ins fnl f* **12/1**

4316 **15** 6 **Iberica Road (USA)**[8] 8077 3-8-8 **78**............................(t) DavidProbert 5 23
(Andrew Balding) *wl in tch in midfield: rdn and lost pl jst over 2f out: bhd whn hung lft 1f out: eased ins fnl f* **9/1**

1m 36.89s (-3.01) **Going Correction** -0.175s/f (Stan)
WFA 3 from 4yo+ 1lb **15** Ran SP% **128.2**
Speed ratings (Par 107): **108,105,105,104,103 102,101,101,101,96 95,94,93,85,79**
CSF £171.29 CT £845.42 TOTE £8.70: £2.80, £6.70, £1.80; EX 143.30 Trifecta £1073.70.
Owner Michael Burrows, Calam & Holdsworth **Bred** Shadwell Farm LLC **Trained** Sheriff Hutton, N Yorks

■ Stewards' Enquiry : Luke Morris caution: careless riding

FOCUS
The winner put up a good performance to take this. It's been rated around the runner-up.

8178 TOTEEXACTA FORECAST THE 1ST AND 2ND H'CAP 1m (P)
6:15 (6:18) (Class 5) (0-75,75) 3-Y-O+ **£5,175** (£1,540; £769; £384) **Stalls** Low

Form RPR

4034 **1** **Squire**[26] 7813 5-9-5 **73**............................(t) AdamBeschizza 10 81
(Michael Attwater) *led early: chsd ldrs: effrt to chal 1f out: rdn and r.o wl to ld wl ins fnl f* **7/1**2

600 **2** ½ **With Pleasure**[6] 8101 3-9-3 **72**............................ DanielTudhope 13 79
(David O'Meara) *chsd ldrs: wnt 2nd 5f out: rdn to chal over 1f out: drvn to ld 1f out: hdd and one pce wl ins fnl f* **33/1**

0401 **3** 1½ **East Coast Lady (IRE)**[7] 8085 4-8-12 **69** 6ex...... CallumShepherd(3) 15 72
(William Stone) *sn led: rdn 2f out: drvn and hdd 1f out: no ex and styd on same pce ins fnl f* **12/1**

1110 **4** hd **Multitask**[43] 7457 6-9-7 **75**............................ AdamKirby 4 78
(Gary Moore) *hld up in tch in midfield: swtchd rt and clsd over 1f out: chsd ldrs and hrd drvn ent fnl f: kpt on same pce fnl 150yds* **11/4**1

340 **5** ¾ **Rivers Of Asia**[33] 7687 3-9-4 **73**............................(t) PatCosgrave 2 74
(Philip McBride) *hld up in midfield: rdn and hdwy over 1f out: kpt on u.p ins fnl f: nvr gng to rch ldrs* **25/1**

2324 **6** ¾ **Exceeding Power**[21] 7886 5-9-0 **75**............................ JoshuaBryan(7) 6 74+
(Martin Bosley) *hld up in tch in midfield: effrt and nt clr run over 1f out: swtchd rt and bmpd rival 1f out: kpt on ins fnl f: nvr gng to rch ldrs* **7/1**2

0043 **7** 1½ **Daleelak (IRE)**[30] 7745 3-8-12 **67**............................ AndrewMullen 1 63
(Mark Johnston) *chsd ldrs: rdn ent fnl 2f: unable qck u.p over 1f out: wknd ins fnl f* **12/1**

6003 **8** ½ **Billy Bond**[13] 8011 4-9-1 **69**............................ JackGarritty 11 64
(Richard Fahey) *s.i.s: hld up in rr: hdwy on inner u.p over 1f out: shifting rt and kpt on same pce ins fnl f* **20/1**

0000 **9** nse **Fantasy Gladiator**[21] 7886 10-9-1 **69**............................(p) RobertWinston 12 64
(Michael Appleby) *hld up in tch but stuck wd: effrt over 1f out: no imp whn bmpd and pushed rt 1f out: kpt on same pce after* **33/1**

2116 **10** ¾ **Gracious George (IRE)**[259] 965 6-9-3 **71**............................ TimmyMurphy 7 64
(Jimmy Fox) *hld up in tch in midfield: c wd bnd 2f out: sn pushed along: rdn and kpt on same pce ins fnl f* **25/1**

1224 **11** 3/4 **Titan Goddess**[10] 8052 4-9-5 **73**.......................... ShaneKelly 9 64
(Mike Murphy) *t.k.h: hld up in tch towards rr: effrt and switching lft over 1f out: nt clr run and sltly hmpd jst over 1f out: kpt on same pce ins fnl f* **7/1**[2]

5526 **12** 3/4 **Spiritual Star (IRE)**[21] 7886 7-8-12 **71**.......................... PaddyBradley(5) 3 61
(Lee Carter) *hld up in tch in midfield: nt clr run and switching rt over 1f out: effrt whn squeezed out and bdly hmpd 1f out: nt rcvr and one pce after* **10/1**[3]

6546 **13** 1 **Boycie**[58] 7051 3-8-12 **72**..........................(b) HollieDoyle(5) 5 59
(Richard Hannon) *hld up in tch in last quartet: effrt u.p over 1f out: no prog and wl hld fnl f* **7/1**[2]

2000 **14** nk **Cottesloe (IRE)**[42] 6876 7-9-4 **72**.......................... LiamKeniry 14 59
(Neil Mulholland) *s.i.s: hld up in rr: shkn up over 1f out: rdn and no imp fnl f* **20/1**

5016 **15** 1 3/4 **Foie Gras**[6] 8101 6-8-12 **66**..........................(p) JosephineGordon 8 49
(Chris Dwyer) *wl in tch in midfield: rdn and lost pl over 1f out: bhd ins fnl f* **20/1**

1m 38.52s (-1.38) **Going Correction** -0.175s/f (Stan)
WFA 3 from 4yo+ 1lb **15** Ran SP% **129.0**
Speed ratings (Par 103): **99,98,97,96,96 95,93,93,93,92 91,91,90,89,87**
CSF £234.42 CT £2755.56 TOTE £9.20: £2.90, £10.90, £3.50; EX 370.30 Trifecta £6201.90 Part won..
Owner The Attwater Partnership **Bred** Darley **Trained** Epsom, Surrey
■ Stewards' Enquiry : Joshua Bryan two-day ban: careless riding (Dec 15-16)

FOCUS
The pace held up quite well and it proved hard to get into it from behind. The winner has been rated close to his best.

8179 TOTEPOOL RACECOURSE CASH BACK AVAILABLE H'CAP 1m 2f (P)
6:45 (6:47) (Class 6) (0-60,60) 3-Y-O+ **£3,234** (£962; £481; £240) **Stalls** Low

Form RPR

6050 **1** **Synodic (USA)**[14] 7986 4-9-0 **53**..........................(t) JackMitchell 9 62+
(Seamus Durack) *hld up in midfield: clsd to trck ldrs and nt clr run over 1f out: swtchd rt ins fnl f: qcknd to ld wl ins fnl f: sn in command* **10/1**

2106 **2** 1 1/2 **Monna Valley**[51] 7257 4-9-4 **60**.......................... AaronJones(3) 8 64
(Stuart Williams) *t.k.h: chsd ldrs: rdn to chal over 1f out: sn drvn: kpt on to ld 100yds out: sn hdd and one pce after* **6/1**[2]

6232 **3** nk **Ahraam (IRE)**[27] 6243 3-9-2 **58**.......................... LukeMorris 2 61
(Harry Whittington) *chsd ldrs: effrt over 1f out: sn drvn: kpt on u.p ins fnl f* **2/1**[1]

550 **4** 1 1/4 **Rianna Star**[31] 7727 3-8-13 **58**.......................... HectorCrouch(3) 13 59
(Gary Moore) *led: rdn over 2f out: drvn and hdd 100yds out: no ex and wknd towards fin* **25/1**

-064 **5** 1/2 **Purple Belle**[50] 7282 3-7-13 **46** oh1.......................... HollieDoyle(5) 4 46
(Jimmy Fox) *sn dropped towards rr and pushed along: hdwy u.p and edgd rt 1f out: kpt on ins fnl f* **16/1**

5050 **6** 1/2 **The Name's Bond**[37] 7604 4-8-7 **46** oh1.......................... PatrickMathers 7 45
(Richard Fahey) *hld up in tch in midfield: nt clr run over 1f out: rdn ent fnl f: kpt on u.p fnl 100yds* **14/1**

0000 **7** 1/2 **Aid To Africa (IRE)**[36] 7613 3-9-1 **60**..........................[1] LouisSteward(3) 5 59
(Michael Bell) *hld up in tch in midfield: effrt over 1f out: nt clrest of runs and switching rt 1f out: kpt on same pce ins fnl f* **8/1**

3354 **8** 3/4 **Dukes Meadow**[19] 7943 5-8-11 **57**.......................... RhiainIngram(7) 6 54
(Roger Ingram) *hld up in tch in midfield: shuffled bk towards rr and rdn wl over 1f out: hdwy 1f out: kpt on ins fnl f: no threat to ldrs* **8/1**

0554 **9** 1/2 **General Brook (IRE)**[19] 7936 6-8-13 **52**.......................... FergusSweeney 15 48
(John O'Shea) *chsd ldr after 2f: upsides ldr 3f out: rdn ent fnl 2f: no ex u.p and btn 1f out: wknd ins fnl f* **14/1**

0041 **10** nk **Makhfar (IRE)**[14] 7986 5-9-0 **56**..........................(v) CallumShepherd(3) 10 52
(Kevin Morgan) *stdd s: t.k.h: hld up in rr: effrt and c wd over 1f out: edgd rt 1f out: rdn and kpt on ins fnl f: nvr trbld ldrs* **7/1**[3]

0010 **11** 6 **Thane Of Cawdor (IRE)**[30] 7754 7-9-7 **60**.......................... JosephineGordon 14 45
(Joseph Tuite) *t.k.h: hld up in midfield but stuck wd: clsd to chse ldrs 3f out: rdn and fnd little over 1f out: sn wknd* **25/1**

4406 **12** 3/4 **Permera**[33] 7692 3-8-0 **49** ow2.......................... GeorgiaDobie(7) 1 33
(Mark H Tompkins) *stdd after s: hld up in rr: c wd and effrt over 1f out: sn sltly impeded and no prog after: wknd fnl f: b.b.v* **20/1**

6416 **13** 1/2 **Secret Lightning (FR)**[19] 7943 4-8-11 **53**.......................... AlistairRawlinson(3) 12 36
(Michael Appleby) *t.k.h: chsd ldrs: rdn and unable qck over 1f out: sn lost pl and wknd 1f out* **20/1**

-060 **P** **Supa Seeker (USA)**[281] 690 10-8-7 **46** oh1.......................... JFEgan 11
(Emma Owen) *a towards rr: rdn 5f out: lost tch over 3f out: t.o and p.u 1f out: b.b.v* **50/1**

2m 6.99s (-1.61) **Going Correction** -0.175s/f (Stan)
WFA 3 from 4yo+ 3lb **14** Ran SP% **129.8**
Speed ratings (Par 101): **99,97,97,96,96 95,95,94,94,94 89,88,88,**
CSF £69.80 CT £176.03 TOTE £12.50: £3.70, £2.70, £1.40; EX 94.00 Trifecta £361.40.
Owner A M Gibbons **Bred** Flaxman Holdings Limited **Trained** Upper Lambourn, Berkshire
■ Stewards' Enquiry : Georgia Dobie five-day ban: used whip when out of contention (Dec 15-19)

FOCUS
A moderate handicap, but an easy winner who has been rated back to his better form.

8180 BOOK TICKETS @CHELMSFORDCITYRACECOURSE.COM H'CAP 1m 5f 66y(P)
7:15 (7:16) (Class 7) (0-50,50) 3-Y-O+ **£2,911** (£866; £432; £216) **Stalls** Low

Form RPR

0/ **1** **Shan Dun na nGall (IRE)**[47] 6935 5-9-5 **48**..........................(vt[1]) LemosdeSouza 2 55
(Amy Murphy) *hld up in tch in midfield: effrt over 1f out: nt clr run and swtchd rt 1f out: rdn and r.o wl to ld fnl 50yds: sn in command* **16/1**

6433 **2** 1 1/4 **Top Set (IRE)**[51] 7262 6-9-2 **45**..........................(p) TimmyMurphy 3 49
(Richard Phillips) *hld up in rr: swtchd rt and steadily clsd fr 5f out: urged along to chse ldr jst over 1f out: upsides ins fnl f: rdn to ld 75yds out: sn hdd and outpcd* **14/1**

0650 **3** 1 1/4 **Solid Justice (IRE)**[69] 6739 5-9-2 **45**.......................... DavidProbert 4 47
(Tim Vaughan) *led: rdn over 2f out: drvn ent fnl f: hdd 75yds out: sn outpcd* **9/2**[2]

500 **4** nk **Cougar Kid (IRE)**[19] 7942 5-9-3 **46**..........................(p) AdamKirby 10 48
(John O'Shea) *hld up in tch in midfield: effrt over 1f out: hdwy and edgd lft u.p 1f out: kpt on same pce ins fnl f* **9/4**[1]

0662 **5** 2 1/4 **Dusty Raven**[16] 7969 3-9-1 **50**..........................(p) LiamKeniry 14 49
(Neil Mulholland) *t.k.h: chsd ldr for 3f: styd chsng ldrs: rdn over 2f out: unable qck and edgd lft 1f out: wknd ins fnl f* **9/2**[2]

4005 **6** nk **Trust The Man (IRE)**[29] 7767 3-9-1 **50**.......................... NickyMackay 1 48
(Simon Dow) *t.k.h: hld up in tch in midfield: effrt 2f out: chsng ldrs u.p whn squeezed for room and hmpd jst ins fnl f: nt rcvr and one pced after* **5/1**[3]

0040 **7** hd **Monzino (USA)**[16] 7895 8-9-2 **48**.......................... LouisSteward(3) 5 46
(Michael Chapman) *hld up in last pair: nt clr run 3f out: swtchd rt and effrt over 1f out: hdwy u.p 1f out: styd on ins fnl f: nvr trbld ldrs* **50/1**

0046 **8** 1/2 **Hooks Lane**[51] 7262 4-9-7 **50**.......................... StevieDonohoe 9 47
(Shaun Harris) *hld up in last pair: swtchd rt and effrt over 1f out: kpt on ins fnl f: nvr trbld ldrs* **20/1**

5664 **9** 3 **Let There Be Light**[20] 7910 3-9-1 **50**.......................... RobertHavlin 8 43
(Gay Kelleway) *stdd s: t.k.h: hld up in tch in midfield: nt clr run and swtchd rt over 1f out: no imp and wl hld fnl f* **12/1**

0640 **10** 2 1/4 **Rainford Glory (IRE)**[21] 7888 6-9-4 **47**.......................... BarryMcHugh 6 37
(Tim Fitzgerald) *hld up in tch in midfield: unable qck u.p over 1f out: wknd ins fnl f* **16/1**

5001 **11** 10 **Fleetwood Poppy**[114] 5261 4-9-1 **47**.......................... CallumShepherd(3) 13 22
(Michael Attwater) *t.k.h early: hld up in tch in midfield: rdn jst over 2f out: n.m.r and swtchd lft over 1f out: no hdwy: wknd fnl f* **25/1**

4000 **12** 7 **Street Art (IRE)**[51] 7262 4-9-4 **47**.......................... ShaneKelly 12 12
(Mike Murphy) *t.k.h: chsd ldr after 3f: rdn over 2f out: unable qck over 1f out: btn whn short of room 1f out: sn wknd and eased* **50/1**

32-0 **13** 4 1/2 **Roughlyn**[17] 7955 7-9-2 **45**..........................(b) LukeMorris 11 3
(Lisa Williamson) *t.k.h: chsd ldrs: rdn over 2f out: sn lost pl: bhd and eased over 1f out* **33/1**

4500 **14** 11 **Hall Of Beauty**[162] 3528 4-8-9 **45**.......................... JaneElliott(7) 7
(Shaun Harris) *hld up in last pair: rdn 4f out: sn struggling: bhd 2f out: t.o* **50/1**

2m 53.15s (-0.45) **Going Correction** -0.175s/f (Stan)
WFA 3 from 4yo+ 6lb **14** Ran SP% **127.4**
Speed ratings (Par 97): **94,93,92,92,90 90,90,90,88,87 80,76,73,67**
CSF £220.29 CT £1193.23 TOTE £24.30: £6.30, £2.90, £2.30; EX 207.50 Trifecta £1338.20.
Owner J Melo **Bred** Donal Mac A Bhaird **Trained** Newmarket, Suffolk

FOCUS
A weak handicap and ordinary form as befits the grade.

8181 2017 CCR MEMBERSHIP NOW AVAILABLE H'CAP 6f (P)
7:45 (7:45) (Class 5) (0-67,67) 3-Y-O+ **£3,396** (£1,010; £505; £252) **Stalls** Centre

Form RPR

3045 **1** **Billyoakes (IRE)**[12] 8040 4-9-6 **66**..........................(p) BenCurtis 3 75
(Charlie Wallis) *chsd ldrs: rdn to chal over 1f out: sn led and edgd rt: clr ins fnl f: styd on* **5/1**[3]

4000 **2** 1 3/4 **Spice Mill (IRE)**[99] 5760 3-9-6 **66**..........................(tp) AndrewMullen 5 69
(Michael Appleby) *s.i.s: hld up in last pair: hdwy on inner to chse ldrs over 1f out: chsd clr wnr 1f out: kpt on* **25/1**

5615 **3** 1/2 **Quite A Story**[52] 7203 4-9-1 **66**.......................... CharlieBennett(5) 6 68
(Patrick Chamings) *taken down early: hld up in tch in midfield: effrt u.p over 1f out: kpt on ins fnl f: no threat to wnr* **4/1**[2]

4520 **4** 1/2 **Cee Jay**[12] 8030 3-8-11 **60**..........................(p) EoinWalsh(3) 14 60
(Robert Cowell) *s.i.s: sn pushed along to rcvr: wnt 2nd 4f out: rdn to ld over 1f out: hdd ent fnl f: no ex u.p: wknd towards fin* **10/3**[1]

3344 **5** nse **Indian Affair**[50] 7268 6-9-7 **67**..........................(bt) AdamKirby 9 67
(Milton Bradley) *hld up towards rr: effrt over 1f out: edgd lft and hdwy ins fnl f: kpt on: nvr trbld ldrs* **10/3**[1]

6550 **6** 3/4 **Encapsulated**[12] 8026 6-8-5 **58**.......................... RhiainIngram(7) 1 56
(Roger Ingram) *taken down early and led to post: hld up in tch: hdwy and swtchd rt 2f out: swtchd bk lft and rdn over 1f out: kpt on same pce ins fnl f* **8/1**

2500 **7** nk **New Rich**[8] 8064 6-9-4 **64**..........................(b) RobertWinston 11 61+
(Eve Johnson Houghton) *hld up in rr: rdn over 1f out: hdwy u.p ins fnl f: nt clr run and eased towards fin* **8/1**

U100 **8** 1/2 **Humour (IRE)**[20] 7912 5-8-11 **57**..........................(b) RobertHavlin 13 52
(Christine Dunnett) *hld up towards rr: swtchd rt and effrt over 1f out: sme hdwy but no threat to wnr 1f out: short of room and no hdwy wl ins fnl f* **14/1**

0054 **9** 1/2 **Triple Dream**[63] 6894 11-9-6 **66**.......................... JosephineGordon 10 59
(Milton Bradley) *chsd ldrs: rdn wl over 1f out: unable qck 1f out: wknd fnl 75yds* **25/1**

2403 **10** 2 3/4 **Costa Filey**[12] 8031 5-9-2 **62**.......................... LukeMorris 7 47
(Ed Vaughan) *in tch in midfield: drvn and carried lft over 1f out: wknd ins fnl f: eased towards fin* **5/1**[3]

0050 **11** 4 **Spryt (IRE)**[12] 8037 4-9-3 **63**..........................(p) PaulMulrennan 2 35
(Conor Dore) *led: edgd rt 4f out: rdn and hdd over 1f out: hung lft and wknd ins fnl f: eased fnl 100yds* **14/1**

0000 **12** 1/2 **Roy's Legacy**[50] 7290 7-8-12 **58**.......................... TomMarquand 4 28
(Shaun Harris) *chsd ldr tl squeezed for room and lost pl 4f out: dropped to rr and no rspnse to press over 1f out: wknd fnl f* **50/1**

1m 12.39s (-1.31) **Going Correction** -0.175s/f (Stan) **12** Ran SP% **127.5**
Speed ratings (Par 103): **101,98,98,97,97 96,95,95,94,90 85,84**
CSF £134.25 CT £567.55 TOTE £6.30: £1.90, £7.40, £1.90; EX 126.60 Trifecta £915.40.
Owner Roalco Limited **Bred** Mrs M Cusack **Trained** Ardleigh, Essex
■ Stewards' Enquiry : Eoin Walsh two-day ban: careless riding (Dec 15-16)

FOCUS
An ordinary sprint handicap. The winner has been rated close to this year's best.
T/Jkpt: Not won. T/Plt: £594.20 to a £1 stake. Pool of £124,672.53 - 153.14 winning tickets. T/Qpdt: £111.70 to a £1 stake. Pool of £13,968.55 - 92.52 winning tickets. **Steve Payne**

8182 - 8187a (Foreign Racing) - See Raceform Interactive

[8118]WOLVERHAMPTON (A.W) (L-H)
Friday, December 2

OFFICIAL GOING: Tapeta: standard
Wind: Nil Weather: Overcast

8188 SUNBETS.CO.UK APPRENTICE H'CAP 7f 32y (Tp)
4:10 (4:11) (Class 6) (0-65,65) 3-Y-O+ **£2,587** (£770; £384; £192) **Stalls** High

Form RPR

5423 **1** **Cliff (IRE)**[15] 7995 6-9-3 **61**.......................... JosephineGordon 9 69
(Nigel Tinkler) *sn pushed along to go prom: shkn up and nt clr run over 4f out: rdn to ld and edgd lft wl ins fnl f* **7/2**[2]

5052 **2** 1/2 **Indigo Princess**[15] 7986 3-9-5 **63**.......................... AlistairRawlinson 4 70
(Michael Appleby) *chsd ldr: led over 1f out: rdn and hdd wl ins fnl f* **7/2**[2]

-350 **3** 1 1/2 **Miss Goldsmith (IRE)**[15] 7995 3-9-2 **63**.......................... NatalieHambling(3) 2 66
(Richard Fahey) *chsd ldrs: rdn over 1f out: styd on same pce wl ins fnl f* **16/1**

0000 **4** 1/2 **Air Of York (IRE)**[20] 7945 4-9-7 **65**.......................... KieranShoemark 7 67
(David Evans) *hld up: shkn up over 2f out: hdwy over 1f out: r.o: nt rch ldrs* **5/2**[1]

4263 **5** 3/4 **Unnoticed**[22] 7890 4-9-6 **64**.......[1] TimClark 3 65
(Ollie Pears) *plld hrd and prom: hmpd over 4f out: nt clr run and lost pl wl over 3f out: hung rt over 2f out: hdwy over 1f out: styd on u.p* **11/1**
3246 **6** 1 **Niqnaaqpaadiwaaq**[22] 7889 4-9-6 **64**....... LouisSteward 5 62
(Eric Alston) *led: rdn and hdd over 1f out: no ex ins fnl f* **7/1**[3]
2406 **7** 1/2 **Virile (IRE)**[9] 8064 5-9-6 **64**.......(b) MitchGodwin 8 60+
(Sylvester Kirk) *s.i.s: hld up: rdn over 1f out: sn edgd lft: nvr nrr* **9/1**
0 **8** 2 1/2 **Coillte Mach**[48] 7368 3-9-5 **63**.......[1] JoshDoyle 6 53+
(David O'Meara) *s.i.s: hld up: rdn over 1f out: n.d* **50/1**
0000 **9** 2 1/2 **Royal Normandy**[15] 7994 4-9-0 **58**.......(b) NoelGarbutt 12 42
(Roger Fell) *sn pushed along into mid-div: rdn and lost pl 1/2-way: wknd over 2f out* **33/1**
0100 **10** hd **Anieres Boy**[7] 8094 4-9-0 **58**.......(t) KevinStott 10 42
(Oliver Greenall) *prom: edgd lft over 4f out: rdn over 2f out: sn hung lft: wknd over 1f out* **28/1**

1m 28.62s (-0.18) **Going Correction** -0.15s/f (Stan) **10** Ran SP% **118.1**
Speed ratings (Par 101): **95,94,92,92,91 90,89,86,83,83**
CSF £16.21 CT £178.43 TOTE £4.30: £1.30, £1.80, £4.90; EX 18.80 Trifecta £148.80.
Owner W F Burton **Bred** John O'Connor **Trained** Langton, N Yorks

FOCUS
A modest apprentice handicap and a deserved breakthrough success for the winner. Straightforward form. The third has been rated to her best yet.

8189 32RED.COM MEDIAN AUCTION MAIDEN STKS 7f 32y (Tp)
4:40 (4:42) (Class 6) 2-Y-O **£2,587** (£770; £384; £192) **Stalls** High

Form RPR
3 **1** **Mustarrid (IRE)**[16] 7977 2-9-5 0....... TimmyMurphy 4 85+
(Richard Hannon) *chsd ldrs: wnt 2nd 2f out: shkn up to ld 1f out: r.o wl* **5/6**[1]
5262 **2** 5 **Espresso Freddo (IRE)**[14] 8009 2-9-5 76....... LukeMorris 3 70
(Sir Mark Prescott Bt) *racd keenly: led at stdy pce: qcknd over 2f out: rdn and hdd 1f out: sn outpcd* **15/2**
3 1 1/2 **Joys Delight** 2-9-0 0....... GrahamGibbons 7 61
(Daniel Mark Loughnane) *s.i.s: hld up: nt clr run over 2f out: hdwy over 1f out: styd on to go 3rd nr fin* **100/1**
5333 **4** shd **Vanderbilt (IRE)**[22] 7882 2-9-5 79.......(b[1]) DavidProbert 9 66
(Martyn Meade) *trckd ldrs: rdn and hung lft over 1f out: styd on same pce* **3/1**[2]
2 **5** shd **Cosmic Boy (IRE)**[17] 7962 2-9-5 0....... DanielMuscutt 6 66
(Marco Botti) *chsd ldr: rdn and lost 2nd 2f out: hung lft over 1f out: no ex fnl f* **5/1**[3]
6 1/2 **Critical Thinking (IRE)** 2-9-5 0....... AdamBeschizza 5 65
(Julia Feilden) *sn pushed along in rr: nt trble ldrs* **100/1**
00 **7** 1 1/2 **Delagate This Lord**[9] 8074 2-9-5 0....... AdamKirby 1 61
(Bill Turner) *hld up: rdn over 2f out: wknd over 1f out* **100/1**

1m 27.71s (-1.09) **Going Correction** -0.15s/f (Stan) **7** Ran SP% **111.0**
Speed ratings (Par 94): **100,94,92,92,92 91,90**
CSF £7.62 TOTE £1.70: £1.30, £2.00; EX 6.60 Trifecta £109.70.
Owner Hamdan Al Maktoum **Bred** John Malone **Trained** East Everleigh, Wilts

FOCUS
A fair maiden and a wide-margin winner.

8190 SUN BETS ON THE APP STORE CLASSIFIED CLAIMING STKS (DIV I) 1m 141y (Tp)
5:10 (5:12) (Class 5) 3-Y-O+ **£3,234** (£962; £481; £240) **Stalls** Low

Form RPR
1140 **1** **Jumbo Prado (USA)**[163] 3514 7-8-10 66.......(b) GrahamGibbons 4 74
(Daniel Mark Loughnane) *chsd ldrs: shkn up to ld over 1f out: rdn clr ins fnl f* **4/1**[2]
0060 **2** 2 1/2 **Seven Clans (IRE)**[13] 8035 4-8-6 60.......(b[1]) JFEgan 10 63
(Neil Mulholland) *sn prom: rdn over 3f out: chsd wnr and hung lft fnl f: styd on same pce* **6/1**
3/2- **3** hd **Glorious Asset**[367] 8066 4-8-7 67....... HectorCrouch[(3)] 9 67
(Ivan Furtado) *sn led: hdd over 6f out: chsd ldr: rdn over 1f out: edgd lft and styd on same pce fnl f* **12/1**
1406 **4** 3/4 **Masqueraded (USA)**[20] 7931 3-8-2 65.......(b) LukeMorris 1 59
(Gay Kelleway) *mid-div: rdn over 2f out: hdwy over 1f out: no imp ins fnl f* **9/1**
5 3/4 **Sarakova (IRE)**[60] 7022 3-8-2 45....... RyanPowell 2 57
(Kevin Frost) *hld up: hdwy u.p over 1f out: nt trble ldrs* **50/1**
6650 **6** 1/2 **Essenaitch (IRE)**[31] 7743 3-8-5 66....... KatherineGlenister[(7)] 5 66
(David Evans) *sn chsng ldr: led over 6f out: rdn and hdd over 1f out: no ex ins fnl f* **7/2**[1]
6021 **7** 1 1/2 **Attain**[135] 4531 7-8-5 67....... ShelleyBirkett[(3)] 8 56
(Julia Feilden) *in rr: hdwy u.p over 1f out: styng on same pce whn nt clr run wl ins fnl f* **4/1**[2]
5300 **8** 2 3/4 **Doctor Bong**[13] 8037 4-8-10 64.......(b) StevieDonohoe 3 52
(Grace Harris) *chsd ldrs: rdn over 2f out: wknd over 1f out* **33/1**
4043 **9** 14 **Italian Beauty (IRE)**[13] 8035 4-8-12 69.......(p) WilliamCarson 7 22
(John Wainwright) *sn pushed along in rr: rdn over 3f out: wknd over 2f out* **5/1**[3]
0000 **10** 31 **Officer In Command (USA)**[15] 7986 10-8-3 43 ow1(tp) NickyMackay 6
(Alan Bailey) *s.i.s: outpcd* **40/1**

1m 48.28s (-1.82) **Going Correction** -0.15s/f (Stan)
WFA 3 from 4yo+ 2lb **10** Ran SP% **118.2**
Speed ratings (Par 103): **102,99,99,98,98 97,96,94,81,54**
CSF £28.39 TOTE £4.50: £1.40, £1.70, £3.20; EX 31.80 Trifecta £266.40.
Owner J T Stimpson **Bred** Mr & Mrs Foreman Hardy **Trained** Baldwin's Gate, Staffs

FOCUS
A modest claimer, in which a course specialist came to the fore. The runner-up has been rated to form for now.

8191 SUN BETS ON THE APP STORE CLASSIFIED CLAIMING STKS (DIV II) 1m 141y (Tp)
5:45 (5:45) (Class 5) 3-Y-O+ **£3,234** (£962; £481; £240) **Stalls** Low

Form RPR
4566 **1** **Beautiful Stranger (IRE)**[7] 8100 5-8-10 69.......(p) ConnorBeasley 7 73
(Keith Dalgleish) *s.i.s: pushed along in rr early: hdwy over 1f out: r.o u.p to ld wl ins fnl f* **7/4**[1]
2615 **2** 1 1/4 **The Tichborne (IRE)**[13] 8036 8-8-3 67.......(v) NathanEvans[(3)] 2 66
(Patrick Morris) *chsd ldrs: led over 1f out: sn rdn: hdd wl ins fnl f* **7/2**[2]
4600 **3** 5 **Rocket Ronnie (IRE)**[13] 8035 6-8-2 62.......(b) AndrewMullen 4 51
(Ed McMahon) *led: plld hrd: rdn and hdd over 1f out: wknd ins fnl f* **4/1**[3]
4100 **4** 3/4 **Ubla (IRE)**[74] 6629 3-8-12 70.......(t) LukeMorris 6 61
(Gay Kelleway) *chsd ldr: hung rt over 2f out: sn rdn and ev ch: no ex fnl f* **7/2**[2]

6-60 **5** 1/2 **Q Ten Girl (IRE)**[52] 7240 3-8-6 63.......(v) JosephineGordon 8 54
(James Unett) *hld up: hdwy over 1f out: wknd ins fnl f* **33/1**
6 1/2 **Ocotillo (IRE)**[71] 6725 3-8-0 35....... RyanPowell 5 46
(Kevin Frost) *prom: lost pl over 6f out: hdwy u.p over 1f out: wknd fnl f* **80/1**
4200 **7** 1 **Bunker Hill Lass**[13] 8035 4-7-9 49.......(p) JaneElliott[(7)] 9 44
(Michael Appleby) *chsd ldrs: rdn over 3f out: wknd fnl f* **20/1**

1m 47.9s (-2.20) **Going Correction** -0.15s/f (Stan)
WFA 3 from 4yo+ 2lb **7** Ran SP% **109.7**
Speed ratings (Par 103): **103,101,97,96,96 95,95**
CSF £7.36 TOTE £2.60: £1.90, £1.70; EX 7.80 Trifecta £25.10.
Owner Weldspec Glasgow Limited **Bred** D Veitch & B Douglas **Trained** Carluke, S Lanarks

FOCUS
The front two pulled clear in the second division of this modest claimer. The winner has been rated close to his spring AW form.

8192 BETWAY H'CAP 5f 216y (Tp)
6:15 (6:16) (Class 3) (0-95,94) 3-Y-O+ **£7,403** (£2,216; £1,108; £554; £276) **Stalls** Low

Form RPR
5-25 **1** **Nimr**[161] 3600 3-9-1 **88**....... BarryMcHugh 8 99
(Richard Fahey) *s.i.s: hdwy over 3f out: rdn to ld and edgd lft wl ins fnl f: r.o* **6/1**[3]
1100 **2** nk **Upavon**[11] 8050 6-9-1 **88**.......(t) PatCosgrave 3 101+
(Stuart Williams) *s.i.s: hld up: hdwy and nt clr run over 1f out: swtchd rt ins fnl f: r.o wl* **9/2**[1]
3004 **3** 1 1/4 **Aguerooo (IRE)**[62] 6962 3-9-6 **93**.......(p) AdamKirby 11 99
(Richard Hannon) *s.i.s: hld up: hdwy and nt clr run over 1f out: swtchd rt: rdn and ev ch wl ins fnl f: unable qck towards fin* **15/2**
4-05 **4** shd **King Robert**[24] 7858 3-9-5 **92**....... ConnorBeasley 1 101+
(Bryan Smart) *hld up: hdwy and nt clr run fr over 1f out tl ins fnl f: r.o* **9/2**[1]
0330 **5** 1 1/2 **Highland Acclaim (IRE)**[15] 7990 5-9-3 **90**....... DavidNolan 10 91
(David O'Meara) *sn chsng ldr: rdn and ev ch ins fnl f: styd on same pce* **9/1**
3311 **6** 1 3/4 **Ballesteros**[30] 7773 7-9-0 **87**....... JackGarritty 5 82
(Richard Fahey) *chsd ldrs: rdn over 1f out: hmpd sn after: no ex ins fnl f* **20/1**
0055 **7** nk **Zac Brown (IRE)**[15] 7983 5-9-3 **90**.......(t) WilliamCarson 9 84
(Charlie Wallis) *sn led: rdn over 1f out: hdd & wknd wl ins fnl f* **33/1**
3250 **8** 2 3/4 **Sir Billy Wright (IRE)**[15] 7990 5-8-9 **85**....... EoinWalsh[(3)] 13 71
(David Evans) *pushed along in rr on outer early: shkn up and hung rt over 3f out: nvr on terms* **14/1**
4000 **9** 1/2 **Merdon Castle (IRE)**[30] 7773 4-9-0 **87**.......(e) JamesSullivan 6 71
(Ruth Carr) *prom: hmpd and lost pl over 5f out: n.d after* **25/1**
3556 **10** 1/2 **Guishan**[11] 8050 6-9-0 **90**....... TimClark[(3)] 2 72
(Michael Appleby) *sn pushed along to chse ldrs: rdn over 1f out: wknd ins fnl f* **22/1**
0040 **11** nk **Another Wise Kid (IRE)**[24] 7858 8-9-1 **88**....... DougieCostello 7 69
(Paul Midgley) *plld hrd and prom: wknd over 1f out* **22/1**
U003 **12** 2 1/2 **Huntsmans Close**[11] 8050 6-9-6 **93**....... LukeMorris 4 66
(Robert Cowell) *hld up: plld hrd: rdn and hung rt over 2f out: nt clr run over 1f out: sn wknd* **11/2**[2]

1m 12.15s (-2.35) **Going Correction** -0.15s/f (Stan) course record **12** Ran SP% **114.7**
Speed ratings (Par 107): **109,108,106,106,104 102,102,98,97,97 96,93**
CSF £29.24 CT £207.76 TOTE £6.80: £2.30, £1.90, £2.40; EX 36.00 Trifecta £220.90.
Owner Al Shaqab Racing **Bred** Mr & Mrs G Middlebrook **Trained** Musley Bank, N Yorks

FOCUS
A good-quality sprint, in which there were a couple of hard luck stories, but the winner had a bit in reserve despite the narrow winning margin. The third has been rated to the better view of his form.

8193 BETWAY MIDDLE DISTANCE H'CAP 1m 4f 50y (Tp)
6:45 (6:46) (Class 6) (0-65,65) 3-Y-O **£2,749** (£818; £408; £204) **Stalls** Low

Form RPR
006 **1** **Major Ben**[109] 5486 3-9-5 **63**....... AdamKirby 3 68
(David Evans) *hld up: hdwy over 1f out: rdn and edgd lft ins fnl f: r.o u.p to ld post* **6/1**
4403 **2** shd **Paper Faces (USA)**[23] 7870 3-9-4 **62**.......(p) JackMitchell 10 67
(Roger Varian) *led: hdd over 10f out: chsd ldrs: shkn up to ld over 1f out: rdn ins fnl f: hdd post* **11/2**[3]
04 **3** shd **Burnside (FR)**[33] 7057 3-9-2 **60**.......(v) RobertHavlin 11 65
(Ian Williams) *led over 10f out: rdn and hdd over 1f out: rallied ins fnl f: r.o* **40/1**
166 **4** 1/2 **Mr Marchwood**[2] 8155 3-8-12 **56**....... LiamKeniry 4 60
(Sylvester Kirk) *prom: rdn over 1f out: r.o* **11/2**[3]
064 **5** nk **Limonata (IRE)**[79] 6485 3-9-5 **63**....... LukeMorris 9 67
(Harry Whittington) *prom: chsd ldr over 9f out tl 8f out: remained handy: rdn over 3f out: edgd lft ins fnl f: r.o* **3/1**[1]
050 **6** 1/2 **Lost The Moon**[57] 7102 3-9-3 **61**....... StevieDonohoe 12 66
(Mark H Tompkins) *hld up: hdwy and nt clr run over 1f out: swtchd lft ins fnl f: r.o: nt rch ldrs* **11/1**
555 **7** nk **Macksville (IRE)**[31] 7753 3-9-2 **65**....... DavidParkes[(5)] 5 67
(Jeremy Gask) *hld up: racd on outer rnd the home turn: rdn over 1f out: r.o ins fnl f: nt rch ldrs* **9/2**[2]
1053 **8** 1 **Rainbow Lad (IRE)**[126] 4847 3-8-11 **55**....... BenCurtis 2 56
(Michael Appleby) *chsd ldrs: rdn over 1f out: styd on same pce ins fnl f* **11/2**[3]
3320 **9** 3 **Little Orchid**[30] 7767 3-8-5 **52**....... ShelleyBirkett[(3)] 1 48
(Julia Feilden) *hld up: hdwy over 1f out: wknd wl ins fnl f* **28/1**
4360 **10** nk **Notion Of Beauty (USA)**[24] 7853 3-9-2 **60**.......(v[1]) DougieCostello 6 56
(K R Burke) *mid-div: hdwy to chse ldr 8f out: rdn and ev ch wl over 1f out: wknd ins fnl f* **22/1**

2m 38.97s (-1.83) **Going Correction** -0.15s/f (Stan) **10** Ran SP% **122.2**
Speed ratings (Par 98): **100,99,99,99,99 99,98,98,96,95**
CSF £40.20 CT £1240.40 TOTE £7.30: £2.30, £2.30, £8.30; EX 44.90 Trifecta £387.00.
Owner Usk Valley Stud **Bred** Usk Valley Stud **Trained** Pandy, Monmouths
■ Stewards' Enquiry : Robert Havlin two-day ban: use of whip (16-17 Dec)

FOCUS
A modest, open-looking handicap, in which the pace was steady and it developed into a sprint up the straight. It's hard to rate the race any higher than this starting point when taking into account the likes of the fourth.

8194 BETWAY APP H'CAP 1m 1f 103y (Tp)
7:15 (7:16) (Class 6) (0-60,60) 3-Y-O **£2,587** (£770; £384; £192) **Stalls** Low

Form RPR
3005 **1** **General Hazard (IRE)**[176] 3080 3-9-6 **59**....... AdamKirby 5 71+
(Michael Bell) *hld up: rdn and hung lft over 2f out: hdwy wl over 1f out: sn hung bdly lft: drvn to ld 1f out: sn clr* **15/8**[1]

4560 **2** 3 3/4 **Moon Arrow (IRE)**[30] 7767 3-8-13 **52**......................(v[1]) StevieDonohoe 7 57
(Michael Blake) *s.i.s: hld up: rdn over 2f out: hdwy over 1f out: hung lft and styd on: no ch w wnr* **16/1**

2251 **3** 3/4 **Rubis**[20] 7937 3-8-12 **58**.......................... NatalieHambling(7) 2 63
(Richard Fahey) *hld up: hdwy and nt clr run over 1f out: swtchd rt and r.o ins fnl f* **13/2**[2]

0043 **4** 1 1/2 **Jessica Jo (IRE)**[20] 7944 3-9-2 **55**..........................(b) AndrewMullen 4 58
(Mark Johnston) *mid-div: hdwy over 5f out: rdn whn bdly hmpd over 1f out: styd on towards fin* **10/1**

0402 **5** 2 1/2 **Thatsthewaytodoit (IRE)**[21] 7910 3-8-13 **52**......... JosephineGordon 13 48+
(Daniel Mark Loughnane) *sn led: hdd 7f out: chsd ldr tl led again over 2f out: rdn and hdd 1f out: wknd wl ins fnl f* **12/1**

5304 **6** 1 **Pivotal Dream (IRE)**[62] 6966 3-8-2 **46** oh1................ CharlieBennett(5) 8 40
(Mark Brisbourne) *sn prom: rdn whn hmpd over 1f out: wknd wl ins fnl f* **14/1**

2202 **7** 4 1/2 **Go On Gal (IRE)**[53] 7230 3-9-1 **57**.............................. ShelleyBirkett(3) 12 42
(Julia Feilden) *mid-div: lost pl over 4f out: hmpd over 2f out: n.d after* **10/1**

0405 **8** 1 3/4 **Frozon**[13] 8038 3-9-3 **56**.. DaleSwift 6 38
(Marjorie Fife) *plld hrd and prom: rdn whn bdly hmpd over 1f out: wknd ins fnl f* **14/1**

6 **9** 1 1/2 **Trump Card (IRE)**[35] 7677 3-8-7 **46** oh1.............................(t) BenCurtis 3 37
(Conor O'Dwyer, Ire) *plld hrd and prom: rdn over 2f out: bdly hmpd and wknd over 1f out* **7/1**[3]

6645 **10** 2 1/4 **Kilim**[107] 5548 3-9-7 **60**..[1] JFEgan 10 35
(John Berry) *pushed along early in rr: stl in rr whn hmpd over 2f out: n.d* **16/1**

0060 **11** 2 3/4 **Somepink (IRE)**[62] 6966 3-8-7 **46** oh1.............................. LukeMorris 1 16
(Daniel Mark Loughnane) *sn pushed along and a in rr: bhd fnl 3f* **100/1**

03-6 **12** 2 1/4 **Spirit Of The Vale (IRE)**[22] 7888 3-8-4 **46**...........(bt[1]) NathanEvans(3) 9 23
(Oliver Greenall) *chsd ldr: led 7f out: rdn and hdd over 2f out: bdly hmpd and eased over 1f out* **25/1**

1m 59.32s (-1.48) **Going Correction** -0.15s/f (Stan) **12** Ran SP% **116.4**
Speed ratings (Par 98): **100,96,96,94,92 91,87,86,84,82 80,78**
CSF £34.97 CT £167.18 TOTE £2.80: £1.40, £5.20, £2.10; EX 38.30 Trifecta £267.00.
Owner R P B Michaelson **Bred** London Thoroughbred Services Ltd **Trained** Newmarket, Suffolk
■ Stewards' Enquiry : Adam Kirby nine-day ban: careless riding (16 - 22 Dec, 26-27 Dec)

FOCUS
A moderate handicap, but run at a strong pace.

8195 BETWAY MAIDEN STKS — 1m 1f 103y (Tp)
7:45 (7:48) (Class 5) 3-4-Y-O — **£3,234** (£962; £481; £240) **Stalls** Low

Form RPR

4 **1** **Maifalki (FR)**[15] 7991 3-9-5 0.. DougieCostello 5 77
(Mark Walford) *hld up: plld hrd early: hdwy over 2f out: rdn to ld wl ins fnl f: r.o* **14/1**

2 1 1/4 **Sea Dweller** 3-9-0 0.. WilliamCarson 6 69
(Anthony Carson) *chsd ldr tl over 3f out: shkn up over 2f out: led ins fnl f: sn edgd lft and hdd: styd on same pce* **5/1**[3]

55 **3** 1 1/4 **Dream Voice (IRE)**[9] 8075 3-9-0 0.................................. PatrickMathers 3 67
(John Holt) *chsd ldrs: rdn over 2f out: styd on* **20/1**

2223 **4** 1 **Trishuli Rock (IRE)**[9] 8075 3-9-0 75............................. DanielMuscutt 2 65
(Marco Botti) *led: qckn over 2f out: rdn and hdd ins fnl f: styd on same pce* **9/4**[2]

6 **5** 1 1/4 **May Mist**[9] 8075 4-8-13 0.. EoinWalsh(3) 7 62
(Trevor Wall) *s.i.s: hld up: rdn over 3f out: r.o ins fnl f: nvr nrr* **33/1**

3 **6** 1/2 **Condamine (IRE)**[20] 7942 3-9-5 0.......................... RichardKingscote 8 66
(Jeremy Gask) *prom: jnd ldr over 3f out tl rdn over 1f out: wknd ins fnl f* **8/13**[1]

7 2 3/4 **Raashdy (IRE)** 3-9-5 0.. LukeMorris 1 60
(Peter Hiatt) *s.i.s: rdn over 3f out: n.d* **25/1**

-000 **8** 18 **North Bay Lady (IRE)**[289] 602 4-9-2 34......................(b) PaddyAspell 4 17
(John Wainwright) *sn pushed along in rr: rdn and wknd fnl 3f* **66/1**

2m 2.32s (1.52) **Going Correction** -0.15s/f (Stan)
WFA 3 from 4yo 2lb **8** Ran SP% **129.1**
Speed ratings (Par 103): **87,85,84,83,82 82,79,63**
CSF £87.03 TOTE £21.80: £3.70, £1.60, £5.50; EX 117.40 Trifecta £1017.20.
Owner Lamont Racing **Bred** M Daguzan-Garros & C Sainte Marie **Trained** Sherriff Hutton, N Yorks

FOCUS
An ordinary maiden that looked a match on paper, but there was a bit of an upset as the two form principals failed to live up to market expectations. Muddling form rated around the third and fifth.
T/Plt: £103.20 to a £1 stake. Pool: £110,061.44 - 778.41 winning tickets T/Qpdt: £26.70 to a £1 stake. Pool: £11,346.85 - 314.09 winning tickets **Colin Roberts**

8196 - (Foreign Racing) - See Raceform Interactive

8102 DUNDALK (A.W) (L-H)
Friday, December 2

OFFICIAL GOING: Polytrack: standard

8197a CHRISTMAS PARTY NIGHTS AT DUNDALK STADIUM H'CAP — 5f (P)
6:00 (6:00) 3-Y-O+ — **£7,235** (£2,235; £1,058; £470; £176)

RPR

1 **Oneoveryou (IRE)**[14] 8014 5-8-6 **72**.................................(t) ConorHoban 1 80
(S J Mahon, Ire) *pressed ldr in 2nd tl led 2f out: strly pressed clsng stages: kpt on wl* **28/1**

2 shd **Russian Soul (IRE)**[28] 7803 8-9-13 **93**..........................(p) ShaneFoley 8 101+
(M Halford, Ire) *hld up: rdn under 2f out: clsr in 6th 1f out: styd on strly into 3rd clsng stages where short of room: fin 3rd: plcd 2nd* **5/1**[3]

3 nk **Aggression (IRE)**[14] 8014 4-8-11 **80**.............................. ShaneBKelly(3) 7 88+
(M D O'Callaghan, Ire) *settled off ldrs tl clsr 2f out in 5th: rdn on outer into 3rd ent fnl f: styd on strly u.p into 2nd clsng stages where edgd lft: nt quite rch wnr: fin 2nd: disqualified and plcd 3rd - caused interference* **6/4**[1]

4 hd **Go Kart (IRE)**[14] 8014 3-8-4 **75**...............................(v[1]) KillianLeonard(5) 13 81
(P J Prendergast, Ire) *chsd ldrs in 3rd: wnt 2nd appr fnl f: kpt on same pce fnl 100yds: dropped to 4th cl home* **25/1**

5 1 1/4 **Split The Atom (IRE)**[14] 8015 4-8-10 **81**.......................(b[1]) OisinOrr(5) 12 83
(David Marnane, Ire) *bit slowly away and racd in rr: prog over 1f out: wnt 8th ent fnl f: kpt on strly into 5th cl home: nrst fin* **9/1**

6 1/2 **Swiss Cross**[13] 8030 9-8-13 **82**...........................(tp) CallumShepherd(3) 5 82
(Phil McEntee) *racd in mid-div on inner: rdn under 2f out: no imp in 7th ent fnl f: kpt on wl again clsng stages* **7/1**

7 shd **Dance Alone**[21] 7914 3-8-6 **72**...................................(vt[1]) RoryCleary 10 72
(Damian Joseph English, Ire) *chsd ldrs in 4th: rdn and nt qckn ins fnl f: wknd clsng stages* **14/1**

8 1 1/2 **Eleuthera**[7] 8107 4-8-5 **76**... AnaO'Brien(5) 14 70
(J F Levins, Ire) *hld up on outer: sme prog ent fnl f: kpt on wl: nvr nrr* **50/1**

9 1 3/4 **Bainne (IRE)**[14] 8014 6-8-8 **79**................................. DonaghO'Connor(5) 4 67
(J F Levins, Ire) *bit slowly away and sn towards rr: prog whn swtchd to inner under 2f out: kpt on same pce fnl f: nvr on terms* **33/1**

10 nk **Complicit (IRE)**[14] 8014 5-8-11 **77**................................ MichaelHussey 9 64
(J F Levins, Ire) *racd towards rr: rdn 1/2-way: kpt on ins fnl f: nvr on terms* **33/1**

11 nk **Sahreej (IRE)**[14] 8014 3-8-9 **82**...............................(v[1]) DannySheehy(7) 2 68
(Adrian Paul Keatley, Ire) *led tl hdd 2f out: 5th ent fnl f: sn wknd* **9/2**[2]

12 1 1/2 **Master Bond**[14] 8014 7-8-6 **77**................................ ConorMcGovern(5) 11 57
(John C McConnell, Ire) *racd in mid-div: rdn and no imp under 2f out: sn no ex* **25/1**

13 1 1/2 **Your Pal Tal**[14] 8014 6-8-4 **70** oh1.................................... WayneLordan 3 45
(J F Levins, Ire) *in rr early: sn mid-div: rdn and nt qckn appr fnl f: wknd* **20/1**

14 1 3/4 **Mulzamm (IRE)**[340] 8380 4-10-4 **98**.........................(t) SeamieHeffernan 6 67
(James McAuley, Ire) *racd in mid-div: pushed along 2f out: no imp and dropped to rr ent fnl f* **20/1**

59.45s (59.45) **14** Ran SP% **132.5**
CSF £165.63 CT £369.45 TOTE £39.50: £7.50, £1.70, £1.02; DF 321.50 Trifecta £2509.80.
Owner Michael O'Dea **Bred** Michael O'Dea **Trained** Kilcolgan, Co Galway

FOCUS
A dramatic finish, and one would have to expect that Russian Soul would have won this had he got a clear run. A stewards' inquiry was called and they took the view that Russian Soul and Aggression's placings should be switched. Michael Halford's servant is was unlucky not to notch his 11th career win. The winner has been rated to her mark.

8198 - 8204a (Foreign Racing) - See Raceform Interactive

8188 WOLVERHAMPTON (A.W) (L-H)
Saturday, December 3

OFFICIAL GOING: Tapeta: standard
Wind: Light against Weather: Overcast

8205 SUNBETS.CO.UK H'CAP (DIV I) — 7f 32y (Tp)
5:15 (5:15) (Class 5) (0-75,75) 3-Y-O+ — **£3,881** (£1,155; £577; £288) **Stalls** High

Form RPR

2202 **1** **Capolavoro (FR)**[14] 8036 5-8-12 **69**................................. EoinWalsh(3) 7 79
(Robert Cowell) *hld up: pushed along and hdwy over 1f out: led ins fnl f: r.o wl* **3/1**[2]

61 **2** 2 1/4 **Beauden Barrett**[21] 7935 3-9-7 **75**..................................(t) GeorgeBaker 9 79
(Jeremy Gask) *sn chsng ldr: rdn to ld 1f out: hdd ins fnl f: styd on same pce* **7/1**[3]

0044 **3** 1 **Magic City (IRE)**[25] 7857 7-9-2 **73**............................... NathanEvans(3) 3 74+
(Michael Easterby) *dwlt: hld up: pushed along and nt clr run over 1f out: r.o ins fnl f: wnt 3rd nr fin* **11/8**[1]

0250 **4** 1/2 **Ravenhoe (IRE)**[15] 8011 3-9-6 **74**.................................... PJMcDonald 5 74
(Mark Johnston) *led: rdn and hdd 1f out: no ex ins fnl f* **9/1**

0034 **5** 3/4 **Caledonia Duchess**[33] 7725 3-8-12 **66**..........................[1] JoeyHaynes 6 64
(Jo Hughes) *s.i.s: hld up: rdn 1/2-way: hung lft and styd on fr over 1f out: nt trble ldrs* **16/1**

5055 **6** 2 3/4 **Personal Touch**[14] 8037 7-9-5 **73**...................................... LukeMorris 1 63
(Michael Appleby) *trckd ldrs: plld hrd: rdn over 1f out: sn hung lft: wknd ins fnl f* **10/1**

2410 **7** 3/4 **Satchville Flyer**[52] 7288 5-9-0 **71**......................... KieranShoemark(3) 8 59
(David Evans) *plld hrd and prom: rdn over 2f out: wknd over 1f out* **33/1**

3366 **8** hd **Soaring Spirits (IRE)**[14] 8036 6-9-3 **71**..................(b) RobertWinston 2 59
(Dean Ivory) *chsd ldrs: rdn over 1f out: wknd ins fnl f* **14/1**

0000 **9** 2 **Top Of The Bank**[15] 8010 3-9-2 **70**................................(p) ShaneGray 4 52
(Kristin Stubbs) *hld up: rdn over 1f out: wknd fnl f* **66/1**

1m 26.91s (-1.89) **Going Correction** -0.20s/f (Stan) **9** Ran SP% **115.7**
Speed ratings (Par 103): **102,99,98,97,96 93,92,92,90**
CSF £24.47 CT £40.38 TOTE £3.10: £1.20, £2.60, £1.10; EX 25.00 Trifecta £62.60.
Owner Cyril Humphris & Partner **Bred** Cyril Humphris **Trained** Six Mile Bottom, Cambs

FOCUS
A fair contest for the grade.

8206 SUNBETS.CO.UK H'CAP (DIV II) — 7f 32y (Tp)
5:45 (5:45) (Class 5) (0-75,75) 3-Y-O+ — **£3,881** (£1,155; £577; £288) **Stalls** High

Form RPR

2045 **1** **Severus (GER)**[32] 7738 6-9-2 **75**................................. MitchGodwin(5) 9 83
(Des Donovan, Ire) *chsd ldrs: stdd and lost pl after 1f: hdwy 2f out: rdn and r.o to ld towards fin* **13/2**[3]

0454 **2** shd **Custard The Dragon**[29] 7797 3-8-10 **64** ow1........... GrahamGibbons 10 71
(John Mackie) *chsd ldrs: rdn to ld ins fnl f: hdd towards fin* **11/1**

403 **3** 1 **Energia Flavio (BRZ)**[74] 6644 6-9-6 **74**........................ StevieDonohoe 5 78+
(Ian Williams) *hld up: hdwy over 1f out: shkn up and swtchd rt ins fnl f: r.o to go 3rd post: nt rch ldrs* **11/2**[2]

0340 **4** shd **Consulting**[23] 7886 3-9-7 **75**... DavidProbert 2 79+
(Martyn Meade) *chsd ldr: nt clr run over 2f out: led sn after: rdn and hdd ins fnl f: styd on same pce* **11/2**[2]

4011 **5** 2 1/4 **Vincenzo Coccotti (USA)**[23] 7887 4-9-0 **71**............. HectorCrouch(3) 1 69
(Ken Cunningham-Brown) *mid-div: pushed along and hdwy over 1f out: carried rt ins fnl f: styd on same pce* **7/2**[1]

0 **6** 1 **Dominium (USA)**[54] 7206 9-9-0 **73**.........................(b) DavidParkes(5) 7 68
(Jeremy Gask) *hld up: rdn over 1f out: r.o ins fnl f: nvr nrr* **14/1**

6002 **7** 1 3/4 **Dodgy Bob**[40] 7572 3-9-4 **72**.. ShaneGray 4 63
(Kevin Ryan) *sn chsng ldrs: rdn over 1f out: wknd ins fnl f* **8/1**

0015 **8** 4 1/2 **Evanescent (IRE)**[47] 7415 7-9-0 **68**................................. RobertWinston 3 46
(Tony Carroll) *led: hung rt and hdd over 2f out: sn rdn: wknd fnl f* **9/1**

-000 **9** 1 1/2 **Gossiping**[8] 8101 4-9-1 **69**...[1] ShaneKelly 6 43
(Gary Moore) *hld up: rdn over 1f out: a in rr* **12/1**

1000 **10** 2 1/2 **Mallymkun**[14] 8036 4-8-11 **70**................................. JordanVaughan(5) 8 38
(K R Burke) *s.s: hdwy over 4f out: rdn over 2f out: sn wknd* **25/1**

1m 26.98s (-1.82) **Going Correction** -0.20s/f (Stan) **10** Ran SP% **114.0**
Speed ratings (Par 103): **102,101,100,100,98 96,94,89,88,85**
CSF £73.76 CT £427.43 TOTE £8.90: £3.10, £4.00, £2.30; EX 83.00 Trifecta £917.70.
Owner W P Flynn **Bred** Capricorn Stud **Trained** Dualla, Co Tipperary

FOCUS
The pace was sound for this open handicap. The runner-up has been rated back to his early 3yo form.

8207 SUN BETS ON THE APP STORE H'CAP — 1m 141y (Tp)
6:15 (6:15) (Class 6) (0-60,66) 3-Y-O+ £2,911 (£866; £324; £324) Stalls Low

Form RPR
003 1 **Scribner Creek (IRE)**[19] 7960 3-9-2 57 DaleSwift 13 65
(Daniel Mark Loughnane) *s.i.s: swtchd lft sn after: hld up: pushed along: hdwy and swtchd lft 1f out: r.o to ld wl ins fnl f:* **50/1**
4656 2 1 1/4 **La Havrese (FR)**[39] 7601 5-9-7 60 PaddyAspell 9 65
(Lynn Siddall) *hld up: hdwy to ld over 1f out: rdn: edgd lft and hdd wl ins fnl f* **9/1**
4260 3 1 1/4 **Dovil's Duel (IRE)**[59] 7078 5-9-4 60 HectorCrouch(3) 8 64
(Tony Newcombe) *swtchd lft sn after s: hld up: hdwy and nt clr run over 1f out: sn rdn: styd on same pce wl ins fnl f* **10/1**
0554 3 dht **Caledonia Laird**[32] 7755 5-9-7 60 JoeyHaynes 1 64+
(Jo Hughes) *chsd ldrs: pushed along over 3f out: nt clr run over 1f out: styd on same pce wl ins fnl f* **8/1**
3100 5 7 **Hold Firm**[21] 7937 4-9-3 56 StevieDonohoe 7 44
(Mark H Tompkins) *mid-div: hdwy and nt clr run over 1f out: wknd ins fnl f* **12/1**
00-0 6 nk **Club House (IRE)**[21] 7944 6-9-1 54 (p) RyanPowell 4 41
(Kevin Frost) *prom: nt clr run wl over 1f out: sn rdn: hmpd and wknd ins fnl f* **20/1**
0-2 7 3/4 **Kubeba (IRE)**[21] 7944 5-9-7 60 (b) LukeMorris 11 46
(Paul Cole) *mid-div: rdn over 3f out: nt clr run over 1f out: wknd fnl f* **13/2**[2]
2105 8 2 1/2 **Rock Icon**[32] 7755 3-9-3 58 KierenFox 5 39
(Patrick Chamings) *led: rdn and hdd wl over 1f out: wknd ins fnl f* **7/1**[3]
0441 9 2 1/4 **Win Lose Draw (IRE)**[7] 8121 4-9-10 66 (p) AlistairRawlinson(3) 2 42
(Michael Appleby) *w ldr tl led wl over 1f out: sn rdn: edgd lft and hdd: wknd fnl f* **9/4**[1]
0202 10 1 3/4 **Lmntrix**[23] 7896 4-9-6 59 AdamKirby 10 31
(George Margarson) *chsd ldrs: rdn over 2f out: wknd and eased fnl f* **7/1**[3]
5060 11 5 **Zed Candy Girl**[7] 8120 6-9-2 55 GrahamGibbons 3 27
(Daniel Mark Loughnane) *hld up: hdwy and hmpd over 1f out: eased* **22/1**

1m 47.53s (-2.57) **Going Correction** -0.20s/f (Stan)
WFA 3 from 4yo+ 2lb 11 Ran SP% **118.1**
Speed ratings (Par 101): **103,101,100,100,94 94,93,91,89,87 83**
PL: Scribner Creek £12.50, La Havrese £3.40, Dovil's Duel £1.70, Caledonia Laird £0.90; EX: £792.50; CSF: £446.40; TC: SC/LH/DD £2420.76, SC/LH/CL £2022.78; TF: £2599.70 TOTE £32.60.
Owner David Slater **Bred** Holborn Trust Co **Trained** Baldwin's Gate, Staffs

FOCUS
This was competitive enough for the grade. It was strongly run and suited the closers.

8208 32RED.COM EBF MAIDEN STKS — 1m 141y (Tp)
6:45 (6:45) (Class 5) 2-Y-O £3,881 (£1,155; £577; £288) Stalls Low

Form RPR
02 1 **Hochfeld (IRE)**[14] 8034 2-9-5 0 PJMcDonald 5 78
(Mark Johnston) *chsd ldr: rdn to ld and hung lft ins fnl f: styd on* **10/1**
2 1/2 **Bois de Boulogne (USA)** 2-9-5 0 [1] RobertHavlin 3 77
(John Gosden) *mid-div: nt clr run over 2f out: hdwy over 1f out: chse wnr ins fnl f: r.o* **5/1**[3]
2 3 1 3/4 **Flaming Marvel (IRE)**[22] 7908 2-9-5 0 TomQueally 11 73
(James Fanshawe) *s.i.s: hld up: hdwy over 1f out: sn edgd lft: styd on: nt rch ldrs* **11/8**[1]
2 4 nse **Getna (USA)**[37] 7647 2-9-0 0 AdamKirby 10 68
(Richard Hannon) *led: rdn over 1f out: hdd ins fnl f: styd on same pce* **7/2**[2]
60 5 1/2 **Lucrezia**[23] 7885 2-9-0 0 (v[1]) GrahamGibbons 7 67
(Sir Michael Stoute) *prom: rdn over 1f out: kpt on* **18/1**
0 6 1 3/4 **Big Sigh (IRE)**[71] 6750 2-9-5 0 GeorgeBaker 4 68
(Chris Wall) *prom: rdn over 1f out: no ex wl ins fnl f* **12/1**
7 1 3/4 **Whatelseaboutyou (IRE)**[101] 5784 2-9-0 0 BarryMcHugh 8 60
(Richard Fahey) *mid-div: hdwy over 2f out: sn rdn: styd on same pce fr over 1f out* **33/1**
56 8 nk **Khattar**[60] 7034 2-9-5 0 (bt[1]) JosephineGordon 1 64
(Hugo Palmer) *hld up in tch: rdn over 3f out: no ex fnl f* **33/1**
642 9 1 1/2 **Wild Shot**[22] 7907 2-9-5 72 RyanTate 12 63
(James Eustace) *chsd ldrs: rdn over 2f out: wknd fnl f* **12/1**
10 2 **William Booth (IRE)** 2-9-5 0 RyanPowell 6 57
(Daniel Mark Loughnane) *s.i.s: hld up: rdn over 2f out: n.d* **100/1**
00 11 nk **Champagne Reign (IRE)**[31] 7762 2-9-0 0 JohnFahy 9 51
(J S Moore) *sn outpcd* **100/1**
12 3/4 **Dream Magic (IRE)** 2-9-5 0 OscarPereira 2 54
(Daniel Mark Loughnane) *s.i.s: shkn up over 2f out: a in rr* **100/1**
60 13 1 **Daily Trader**[14] 8034 2-9-2 0 EoinWalsh(3) 13 52
(David Evans) *hld up: rdn over 2f out: a towards rr* **100/1**

1m 47.83s (-2.27) **Going Correction** -0.20s/f (Stan) 13 Ran SP% **120.6**
Speed ratings (Par 96): **102,101,100,99,99 97,96,96,94,93 92,92,91**
CSF £59.18 TOTE £12.70: £3.10, £1.70, £1.70; EX 78.40 Trifecta £267.40.
Owner Sheikh Hamdan bin Mohammed Al Maktoum **Bred** Kenilworth House Stud **Trained** Middleham Moor, N Yorks

FOCUS
Some powerful yards were represented in this maiden which was run at a strong pace.

8209 32RED.COM CONDITIONS STKS (PLUS 10 RACE) (FAST-TRACK QUALIFIER) — 5f 20y (Tp)
7:15 (7:16) (Class 2) 2-Y-O £9,451 (£2,829; £1,414; £708; £352) Stalls Low

Form RPR
1251 1 **Dubai One (IRE)**[5] 8136 2-8-9 83 PatCosgrave 6 87+
(Saeed bin Suroor) *chsd ldr tl led over 1f out: shkn up and edgd lft ins fnl f: r.o* **11/4**[2]
212 2 1/2 **Gheedaa (USA)**[28] 7820 2-8-9 86 BenCurtis 2 86
(William Haggas) *trckd ldrs: plld hrd: rdn over 1f out: chsd wnr wl ins fnl f: r.o* **7/2**[3]
1402 3 1/2 **Sutter County**[16] 7989 2-9-0 103 PJMcDonald 5 89
(Mark Johnston) *edgd rt s: hld up: rdn over 1f out: r.o wl towards fin: nt rch ldrs* **1/1**[1]
0021 4 1/2 **Monte Cinq (IRE)**[32] 7748 2-9-0 78 TomEaves 1 87
(Jason Ward) *led: rdn and hdd over 1f out: styng on same pce whn nt clr run wl ins fnl f* **40/1**
13 5 1 **Visionary (IRE)**[210] 2023 2-9-0 0 AdamKirby 7 83
(Robert Cowell) *s.i.s: hld up: r.o ins fnl f: nvr nrr* **18/1**
1 6 nk **Rozy Boys**[7] 8118 2-9-0 80 GrahamGibbons 3 85
(David Barron) *hld up: plld hrd and hung lft thrght: hdwy over 1f out: sn rdn: eased whn nt clr run wl ins fnl f* **7/1**

1m 0.36s (-1.54) **Going Correction** -0.20s/f (Stan) 2y crse rec 6 Ran SP% **119.1**
Speed ratings (Par 102): **104,103,102,101,100 99**
CSF £13.77 TOTE £3.50: £1.30, £2.80; EX 13.90 Trifecta £30.30.
Owner Godolphin **Bred** Darley **Trained** Newmarket, Suffolk

FOCUS
An interesting contest. They went a sound pace and the winner looks useful. Another step up from the fourth, and he might be the key to the level.

8210 BETWAY H'CAP — 1m 5f 194y (Tp)
7:45 (7:46) (Class 2) (0-105,102) 3-Y-O+
£12,450 (£3,728; £1,864; £932; £466; £234) Stalls Low

Form RPR
0102 1 **Watersmeet**[28] 7814 5-9-12 100 PJMcDonald 1 107
(Mark Johnston) *led: stdd pce 10f out: qcknd over 3f out: rdn and hdd ins fnl f: rallied to ld post* **14/1**
2221 2 nse **Rock Steady (IRE)**[7] 8123 3-8-12 96 KieranShoemark(3) 2 103
(Roger Charlton) *chsd ldrs: rdn to ld ins fnl f: hdd post* **7/2**[2]
034 3 1 1/4 **Wrangler**[17] 7979 5-8-13 87 PatCosgrave 3 92+
(William Haggas) *prom: rdn over 1f out: styd on* **4/1**[3]
2450 4 nk **Masterpaver**[18] 7967 5-8-5 86 NatalieHambling(7) 11 91
(Richard Fahey) *chsd wnr: pushed along over 2f out: rdn and ev ch ins fnl f: no ex towards fin* **33/1**
6040 5 hd **Barye**[17] 7979 5-9-13 101 ShaneKelly 8 105+
(Richard Hughes) *hld up: hdwy over 1f out: r.o: nt rch ldrs* **66/1**
15U3 6 1 1/2 **Winning Story**[17] 7979 3-9-0 95 KevinStott 7 97
(Saeed bin Suroor) *chsd ldrs: rdn over 2f out: no ex fnl f* **4/1**[3]
143 7 2 1/4 **Erhaaf (USA)**[30] 7779 4-8-12 86 StevieDonohoe 5 85
(Charlie Fellowes) *hld up: swtchd rt and nt clr run over 1f out: nvr trbld ldrs* **2/1**[1]
4326 8 shd **First Mohican**[17] 7979 8-10-0 102 JosephineGordon 6 101
(Alan King) *s.i.s: hld up: rdn over 1f out: nvr on terms* **14/1**
4- 9 1/2 **Novis Adventus (IRE)**[255] 4-9-10 98 AdamKirby 4 96
(Jeremy Noseda) *hld up in tch: rdn over 1f out: no ex fnl f* **33/1**
3402 10 3/4 **Sunblazer (IRE)**[31] 7765 6-9-0 95 (t) JoshuaBryan(7) 9 92
(Kim Bailey) *hld up: racd keenly: hdwy over 2f out: rdn over 1f out: no ex fnl f* **20/1**
0633 11 hd **Royal Marskell**[5] 8133 7-9-2 90 LukeMorris 10 87
(Gay Kelleway) *s.s: rdn over 2f out: n.d* **40/1**

3m 2.26s (-2.54) **Going Correction** -0.20s/f (Stan)
WFA 3 from 4yo+ 7lb 11 Ran SP% **123.5**
Speed ratings (Par 109): **99,98,98,98,97 97,95,95,95,95 94**
CSF £63.32 CT £244.35 TOTE £9.30: £3.50, £1.60, £1.60; EX 66.60 Trifecta £194.70.
Owner J Barson **Bred** Stetchworth & Middle Park Studs **Trained** Middleham Moor, N Yorks

FOCUS
They went a steady pace for this decent handicap which suited those prominent.

8211 BETWAY MARATHON DISTANCE H'CAP — 2m 119y (Tp)
8:15 (8:15) (Class 6) (0-65,65) 3-Y-O+ £2,911 (£866; £432; £216) Stalls Low

Form RPR
/01- 1 **Medicine Hat**[322] 6980 5-9-13 64 SamJames 4 74+
(Marjorie Fife) *plld hrd and prom: stdd and lost pl after 2f: hdwy over 2f out: led over 1f out: hung lft and pushed clr fnl f* **13/2**
2060 2 7 **Hallstatt (IRE)**[36] 5183 10-9-12 63 (t) LukeMorris 1 65
(John Mackie) *mid-div: hdwy to chse ldrs 13f out: rdn over 3f out: chsd wnr fnl f: no imp* **33/1**
0555 3 1 3/4 **Yasir (USA)**[7] 8124 8-9-10 61 PaulMulrennan 11 61
(Conor Dore) *s.i.s: hld up: hdwy over 2f out: rdn over 1f out: styd on same pce fnl f* **9/1**
5634 4 hd **Sakhra**[14] 8039 5-8-6 46 RyanPowell(3) 3 45
(Mark Brisbourne) *hld up: hdwy over 1f out: sn rdn: styd on same pce* **20/1**
5013 5 1 1/2 **Delagoa Bay (IRE)**[14] 8039 8-9-4 60 MitchGodwin(5) 10 57
(Sylvester Kirk) *hld up: hdwy over 3f out: sn rdn: hung lft over 1f out: styd on same pce* **7/1**
0055 6 1/2 **Gloryette**[22] 7905 3-9-4 63 [1] AdamKirby 2 60
(Ed Dunlop) *chsd ldrs: rdn and ev ch over 2f out: wknd fnl f* **9/2**[2]
2040 7 2 3/4 **Lorelei**[14] 8039 4-9-7 58 JosephineGordon 7 52
(William Muir) *hld up: hdwy over 4f out: led over 2f out: rdn and hdd over 1f out: wknd fnl f* **14/1**
6000 8 21 **Lacey**[14] 8039 7-8-12 52 (b) JackDuern(3) 12 20
(Sarah Hollinshead) *hld up: hdwy over 5f out: sn rdn: wknd 3f out* **40/1**
5420 9 1 1/2 **Cold Fusion (IRE)**[29] 7500 3-9-6 65 TomQueally 9 32
(David Flood) *chsd ldr after 1f: ldr wnt clr 13f out: tk clsr order over 4f out: led wl over 2f out: sn rdn and hdd: wknd over 1f out* **16/1**
3000 10 26 **Trending (IRE)**[22] 7905 7-9-12 63 (t) GeorgeBaker 5
(Jeremy Gask) *led: wnt clr 13f out: c bk to the field over 4f out: hdd wl over 2f out: hmpd and wknd sn after* **5/1**[3]
11 4 1/2 **Tortueuse (IRE)**[15] 8021 9-8-9 46 oh1 [1] BenCurtis 8
(David Peter Dunne, Ire) *chsd ldrs: rdn over 4f out: sn wknd* **33/1**
002 12 3 1/2 **Hier Encore (FR)**[14] 8039 4-9-3 57 HectorCrouch(3) 6
(David Menuisier) *mid-div: drvn along over 4f out: wknd over 3f out* **7/2**[1]

3m 34.97s (-8.73) **Going Correction** -0.20s/f (Stan) course record
WFA 3 from 4yo+ 8lb 12 Ran SP% **118.5**
Speed ratings (Par 101): **112,108,107,107,107 106,105,95,94,82 80,78**
CSF £211.33 CT £1935.02 TOTE £7.40: £2.70, £7.60, £2.90; EX 170.90 Trifecta £1569.00.
Owner Mrs Sarah Pearson **Bred** Mrs S M Pearson **Trained** Stillington, N Yorks

FOCUS
An open handicap run at a sound pace. The fourth helps pin the level.

8212 BETWAY MAIDEN STKS — 1m 4f 50y (Tp)
8:45 (8:45) (Class 5) 3-Y-O+ £3,557 (£1,058; £529; £264) Stalls Low

Form RPR
3 1 **Snobbery (IRE)**[103] 5723 3-9-5 0 GeorgeBaker 4 68+
(Roger Charlton) *chsd ldrs: wnt 2nd over 2f out: led on bit over 1f out: easily* **4/9**[1]
3353 2 2 1/4 **Lobster Cocktail (IRE)**[45] 7464 3-9-5 55 (t) LukeMorris 8 59
(Ed Walker) *hld up: hdwy u.p over 2f out: styd on to go 2nd nr fin: no ch w wnr* **7/1**
3 3 nk **Vision Of Beauty (FR)**[26] 7848 3-9-0 0 ConnorBeasley 1 54
(Keith Dalgleish) *led at stdy pce: qcknd over 3f out: rdn and hdd over 1f out: no ex ins fnl f* **5/1**[3]

00/6 **4** *3 ¾* **Haaffa Sovereign**[36] 7657 5-9-3 43.............................. JoshuaBryan(7) 7 53?
(Kevin Morgan) *chsd ldrs: rdn over 2f out: styd on same pce fr over 1f out* **33/1**

062- **5** *1 ¼* **Star Of Lombardy (IRE)**[373] 7997 3-9-0 68..................... PJMcDonald 5 46
(Mark Johnston) *chsd ldr tl rdn over 2f out: hung lft over 1f out: wknd fnl f* **11/4**[2]

6 *10* **House Of Frauds (IRE)** 8-9-7 0.................................... EoinWalsh(3) 2 35
(Tony Newcombe) *s.s: hld up: plld hrd in rr: effrt over 2f out: sn wknd* **33/1**

00 **7** *3 ¾* **Look Who's There**[32] 7753 5-9-7 0.................................. JackDuern(3) 6 29
(Sarah Hollinshead) *hld up: rdn over 3f out: sn wknd* **80/1**

0-0 **8** *9* **Dream Journey (IRE)**[157] 3769 3-9-0 0............................... BenCurtis 3 10
(Daniel O'Brien) *hld up: rdn and wknd over 3f out* **50/1**

2m 40.68s (-0.12) **Going Correction** -0.20s/f (Stan)
WFA 3 from 5yo+ 5lb **8 Ran SP% 134.2**
Speed ratings (Par 103): **92,90,90,87,86 80,77,71**
CSF £6.43 TOTE £1.40: £1.10, £1.80, £2.00; EX 5.70 Trifecta £18.80.
Owner Lady Rothschild **Bred** N Cable & M Smith **Trained** Beckhampton, Wilts
■ Stewards' Enquiry : Connor Beasley 2-day ban (17-18 Dec): used whip in incorrect place

FOCUS
An uncompetitive maiden. The winner did not need to match his debut effort, while the runner-up has been rated to his latest for now.
T/Plt: £236.20 to a £1 stake. Pool: £119,588.96 - 369.57 winning units. T/Qpdt: £50.60 to a £1 stake. Pool: £11,453.23 - 167.43 winning units. **Colin Roberts**

8213 - 8226a (Foreign Racing) - See Raceform Interactive

8157 LINGFIELD (L-H)
Monday, December 5

OFFICIAL GOING: Polytrack: standard
Wind: Light, across Weather: Fine, crisp

8227 32REDBINGO.COM MAIDEN STKS 1m 2f (P)
11:50 (11:56) (Class 5) 2-Y-O **£3,234** (£962; £481; £240) **Stalls** Low

Form RPR

0023 **1** **Plead**[7] 8131 2-9-0 70... JackMitchell 2 72
(Archie Watson) *led 1f: trckd ldng pair after: gng strly whn taking 2nd over 2f out: rdn to ld last 100yds: styd on wl* **8/1**

4034 **2** *2* **The Blues Master (IRE)**[17] 8008 2-9-5 70..................... AndrewMullen 4 73
(Mark Johnston) *in tch in midfield: pushed along 5f out: effrt on inner over 2f out: rdn and styd on wl fnl f to take 2nd last strides* **12/1**

3 *nk* **Naseem (IRE)** 2-9-5 0.. NickyMackay 7 72
(John Gosden) *led after 1f: rdn 2 l clr 2f out: hdd 100yds out: fdd and lost 2nd last strides* **13/2**[3]

3 **4** *nse* **The Statesman**[10] 8088 2-9-5 0...................................... WilliamCarson 5 72
(Jamie Osborne) *hld up in midfield: pushed along over 2f out: rdn and styd on fr over 1f out: nrly snatched 3rd but nvr able to threaten* **13/8**[1]

064 **5** *1 ¼* **Addicted To You (IRE)**[20] 7962 2-9-5 71........................ GeorgeBaker 8 70
(Mark Johnston) *s.i.s: hld up in rr: taken to wd outside and prog over 3f out: wd bnd 2f out: kpt on fr over 1f out but nvr able to threaten* **8/1**

62 **6** *¾* **Peaceful Passage (USA)**[18] 7982 2-9-0 0................... RobertHavlin 10 64
(John Gosden) *trckd ldrs: rdn to dispute 2nd briefly over 2f out: outpcd over 1f out: one pce after* **7/2**[2]

00 **7** *16* **Serenade The Stars (IRE)**[12] 8073 2-9-5 0.................(b[1]) LukeMorris 9 42
(James Tate) *chsd ldr after 1f: rdn over 3f out: lost 2nd over 2f out and stmbld bdly sn after: wknd and eased* **33/1**

0 **8** *½* **Make Memories (USA)**[10] 8088 2-9-5 0.........................(v[1]) RobertTart 6 37
(John Gosden) *trckd ldrs: rdn 3f out: wknd rapidly over 2f out* **40/1**

9 *shd* **Dervish** 2-8-12 0... GabrieleMalune(7) 3 37
(Luca Cumani) *a in rr: lost tch over 4f out: wl bhd fnl 3f* **25/1**

0 **10** *1 ½* **Nothing Compares**[23] 7940 2-9-0 0.............................. PJMcDonald 12 29
(Mark Johnston) *urged along towards rr bef 1/2-way: wknd over 3f out: sn bhd* **66/1**

11 *26* **Franny Nisbet** 2-9-0 0.. MartinDwyer 1
(William Muir) *s.v.s: rn green and a detached in last: t.o* **50/1**

2m 3.3s (-3.30) **Going Correction** -0.025s/f (Stan) **11 Ran SP% 116.2**
Speed ratings (Par 96): **112,110,110,110,109 108,95,95,95,94 73**
CSF £92.47 TOTE £7.70: £2.10, £2.90, £2.70; EX 87.50 Trifecta £672.90.
Owner C R Hirst **Bred** Cheveley Park Stud Ltd **Trained** Upper Lambourn, West Berks

FOCUS
John Gosden and Mark Johnston were well represented in this juvenile maiden, but neither had the winner and this form looks just fair at best. Straightforward form to rate.

8228 DOWNLOAD THE BETWAY APP H'CAP 5f 6y(P)
12:20 (12:26) (Class 5) (0-70,70) 3-Y-O+ **£3,234** (£962; £481; £240) **Stalls** High

Form RPR

0221 **1** **Heiba (IRE)**[31] 7793 4-9-4 **68**......................................(p) GrahamGibbons 6 76
(Robert Cowell) *trckd ldr: shkn up to ld over 1f out: in command after: rdn out* **3/1**[1]

5123 **2** *¾* **Stormflower**[24] 7899 3-9-5 **69**.. DannyBrock 7 73
(John Bridger) *chsd ldrs on outer: rdn fr 1/2-way: kpt on to take 2nd ins fnl f: a hld* **5/1**[3]

1600 **3** *½* **Aragon Knight**[146] 4224 3-9-3 **70**...............................(b) HectorCrouch(3) 1 75+
(Heather Main) *sn prom on inner: trckd ldng pair over 1f out: tried to squeeze through sn after but no room and snatched up: styd on but nt rcvr* **4/1**[2]

4100 **4** *½* **Noble Act**[17] 8010 3-9-4 **68**... NickyMackay 2 68
(Rae Guest) *chsd ldrs: rdn and nt qckn over 1f out: styd on again ins fnl f* **12/1**

2650 **5** *nk* **Dusty Blue**[23] 7945 4-9-0 **67**...................................... GeorgeDowning(3) 5 66
(Tony Carroll) *mostly in last pair: rdn 2f out: styd on fnl f: nrst fin but too late to threaten* **11/1**

00 **6** *nk* **Bahango (IRE)**[10] 8099 4-9-3 **70**...............................(p) CallumShepherd(3) 3 68
(Patrick Morris) *n.m.r after s and towards rr: in tch whn hmpd jst over 2f out: no ch after but kpt on fr over 1f out* **20/1**

0000 **7** *½* **Mossgo (IRE)**[17] 8010 6-9-4 **68**...(t) KierenFox 4 64
(John Best) *wl away and won battle for ld: hdd over 1f out: wknd fnl f* **8/1**

5456 **8** *2 ¼* **Diamond Charlie (IRE)**[120] 5189 8-9-6 **70**............................(p) JFEgan 8 58
(Simon Dow) *trapped out wd and a towards rr: wd bnd 2f out: fdd* **8/1**

6225 **9** *2* **Jack The Laird (IRE)**[88] 6248 3-9-2 **66**.....................(p) RobertWinston 9 47
(Dean Ivory) *trapped out wd and sn in last pair: nvr a factor* **7/1**

59.0s (0.20) **Going Correction** -0.025s/f (Stan) **9 Ran SP% 117.2**
Speed ratings (Par 103): **97,95,95,94,93 93,92,88,85**
CSF £18.36 CT £61.21 TOTE £4.20: £1.40, £1.90, £2.00; EX 14.90 Trifecta £125.80.
Owner Saleh Al Homaizi & Imad Al Sagar **Bred** Fergus Cousins **Trained** Six Mile Bottom, Cambs
■ Stewards' Enquiry : Graham Gibbons 3-day ban (19-21 Dec): careless riding

FOCUS
A modest sprint handicap. A length pb from the winner, with the runner-up rated to form.

8229 32RED.COM / EBF MAIDEN STKS (PLUS 10 RACE) 5f 6y(P)
12:50 (12:55) (Class 4) 2-Y-O **£4,269** (£1,270; £634; £317) **Stalls** High

Form RPR

50 **1** **Little Miss Daisy**[24] 7900 2-9-0 0.................................... MartinDwyer 7 62
(William Muir) *hld up after modest s: stl in last pair over 1f out: str run on outer after: led last 50yds* **33/1**

0 **2** *nk* **Fantasy Keeper**[30] 7818 2-9-5 0.................................... AndrewMullen 5 66
(Michael Appleby) *towards rr but in tch: rdn and clsd on ldrs over 1f out: chal and upsides 75yds out: jst outpcd by wnr nr fin* **20/1**

5420 **3** *½* **Black Bubba (IRE)**[23] 7938 2-9-5 69.. JFEgan 1 64
(David Evans) *chsd ldrs on inner: rdn over 1f out: led ins fnl f: hdd and outpcd last 50yds* **4/1**[3]

2433 **4** *½* **Heavenly Cry**[16] 8027 2-9-5 55.............................(v[1]) JosephineGordon 4 62
(Phil McEntee) *taken down early: t.k.h: trckd ldrs: rdn and nt qckn over 1f out: kpt on again ins fnl f: nvr able to chal* **20/1**

4335 **5** *shd* **Street Jazz**[9] 8118 2-9-0 68.. TomEaves 6 57
(James Given) *led: hrd pressed over 1f out: hdd and no ex ins fnl f* **11/2**

436 **6** *hd* **Dream Reversion**[39] 7639 2-9-5 66......................... RichardKingscote 2 61
(Tom Dascombe) *t.k.h: hld up in last pair: stl there whn swtchd off rail 1f out: pushed along and styd on wl last 150yds: nrst fin* **7/2**[2]

0065 **7** *½* **Cappananty Con**[16] 8027 2-9-5 68.............................. RobertWinston 9 59
(Dean Ivory) *spd fr wd draw to press ldng pair: rdn over 1f out: chal and upsides ins fnl f: wilted bdly last 100yds* **11/1**

04 **8** *½* **Zambezi Queen (IRE)**[12] 8066 2-8-11 0............... CallumShepherd(3) 3 53
(Paul Cole) *towards rr: rdn on inner over 1f out: one pce and no great prog* **16/1**

3523 **9** *1 ¼* **Kiribati**[41] 7589 2-9-5 72.. GeorgeBaker 10 53
(Mark Johnston) *trapped out wd in midfield: rdn 1/2-way: already struggling whn hanging and wd bnd 2f out: no ch after* **11/4**[1]

0 **10** *½* **Defining Moment**[42] 7576 2-9-0 0.................................... MartinLane 8 46
(Rae Guest) *pressed ldr to over 1f out: wknd* **14/1**

59.47s (0.67) **Going Correction** -0.025s/f (Stan) **10 Ran SP% 117.6**
Speed ratings (Par 98): **93,92,91,90,90 90,89,88,86,86**
CSF £560.68 TOTE £45.60: £8.50, £5.10, £1.50; EX 535.30 Trifecta £6536.60 Part won..
Owner Mrs J M Muir **Bred** Hungerford Park Stud **Trained** Lambourn, Berks

FOCUS
A modest juvenile sprint maiden. The level is fluid, but the winner has been rated to her pre-race form, and the fourth to a minor pb.

8230 32REDSPORT.COM (S) STKS 6f 1y(P)
1:25 (1:30) (Class 6) 2-Y-O **£2,911** (£866; £432; £216) **Stalls** Low

Form RPR

4002 **1** **Gracious Tom (IRE)**[16] 8027 2-9-0 60.................................... JFEgan 9 66
(David Evans) *pressed ldr: led wl over 1f out: sn jnd: battled on wl fnl f* **4/1**[3]

2315 **2** *nk* **Pulsating (IRE)**[25] 7893 2-8-10 67.......................... CallumShepherd(3) 5 64
(Ali Stronge) *trckd ldrs: chal on outer 2f out: jnd wnr over 1f out: upsides after but nt qckn last 100yds and jst hld* **9/4**[1]

0430 **3** *1 ½* **Spin Top**[40] 7615 2-9-0 58...(v) LiamKeniry 6 61
(Joseph Tuite) *hld up in rr: prog over 1f out: shkn up and kpt on to take 3rd ins fnl f: unable to chal* **12/1**

3503 **4** *½* **Joyful Dream (IRE)**[16] 8025 2-8-9 58.......................[1] JosephineGordon 1 54
(J S Moore) *trckd ldng pair: cl up on inner over 1f out: sn rdn and nt qckn: one pce after* **7/1**

6600 **5** *2* **Come On Percy**[18] 7981 2-9-0 60.. JackGarritty 2 53
(Richard Fahey) *a abt same pl: one pce whn rdn over 1f out and no imp on ldrs* **15/2**

50 **6** *1 ¼* **Hollywood Style**[47] 7465 2-8-9 0.. LukeMorris 3 44
(William Knight) *pushed along in last: effrt 2f out: hanging and one pce after* **20/1**

6120 **7** *1* **Baby Gal**[59] 7120 2-8-13 74... JackMitchell 8 45
(Giles Bravery) *a in rr: wd bnd 2f out and no prog after* **7/2**[2]

0 **8** *6* **Shillbourne Lad (IRE)**[25] 7882 2-9-0 0........................ WilliamCarson 4 28
(Bill Turner) *led to wl over 1f out: wknd rapidly* **50/1**

1m 12.45s (0.55) **Going Correction** -0.025s/f (Stan) **8 Ran SP% 111.7**
Speed ratings (Par 94): **95,94,92,91,89 87,86,78**
CSF £12.75 TOTE £5.50: £1.70, £1.20, £3.00; EX 16.30 Trifecta £90.70.There was no bid for the winner.
Owner Terry Reffell **Bred** Golden Vale Stud **Trained** Pandy, Monmouths

FOCUS
A moderate juvenile seller. The winner has been rated back to his pre-race best.

8231 BETWAY H'CAP 1m 2f (P)
1:55 (2:00) (Class 3) (0-90,90) 3-Y-O **£7,561** (£2,263; £1,131; £566; £282) **Stalls** Low

Form RPR

0613 **1** **Van Huysen (IRE)**[38] 7666 4-8-8 **77**.. JFEgan 2 85
(Dominic Ffrench Davis) *trckd ldng pair: wnt 2nd 2f out: rdn to ld jst over 1f out: edgd rt but hld on wl* **12/1**

1631 **2** *nk* **Natural Scenery**[45] 7512 3-9-0 **89**.........................[1] AlistairRawlinson(3) 6 96
(Saeed bin Suroor) *trckd ldng quartet: rdn over 2f out: clsd on inner over 1f out: styd on to take 2nd ins fnl f: hanging rt and hld nr fin* **7/4**[1]

6011 **3** *nk* **Beardwood**[20] 7967 4-9-7 **90**...(p) GeorgeBaker 3 96
(Mark Johnston) *led: kicked on over 2f out: hdd jst over 1f out: edgd rt and styd on same pce: lost 2nd ins fnl f* **3/1**[2]

12-0 **4** *¾* **High Baroque (USA)**[198] 2484 4-9-2 **85**...................... BarryMcHugh 13 90
(Richard Fahey) *trckd ldng trio: rdn over 2f out: threatened to cl 1f out: one pce ins fnl f* **25/1**

5033 **5** *¾* **Jacbequick**[9] 8123 5-8-13 **87**... JoshDoyle(5) 7 90
(David O'Meara) *trckd ldr to 2f out: nt qckn over 1f out: one pce after* **14/1**

10-5 **6** *¾* **Alinstante**[24] 7901 3-9-3 **89**.. LukeMorris 8 91
(Sir Mark Prescott Bt) *t.k.h: hld up towards rr: rdn over 2f out: kpt on same pce and n.d* **14/1**

1601 **7** *¾* **Purple Rock (IRE)**[17] 8007 4-8-9 **81**......................(t) NathanEvans(3) 1 81
(Michael Easterby) *hld up towards rr: gng wl enough in 7th over 2f out but plenty to do: effrt on inner over 1f out: one pce and nvr able to threaten* **9/2**[3]

2001 **8** *1 ½* **Bluegrass Blues (IRE)**[48] 7428 6-9-3 **89**.............. HectorCrouch(3) 5 86
(Heather Main) *hld up in last pair: rdn and no prog 2f out* **14/1**

1311 **9** *½* **Marshgate Lane (USA)**[199] 2444 7-9-7 **90**...................(p) LiamKeniry 11 86
(Neil Mulholland) *t.k.h: hld up in last pair: plenty to do over 2f out: shkn up and hanging wl over 1f out: no prog* **14/1**

0000 **10** *25* **Ocean Tempest**^{135} 4644 7-9-5 **88** .... AdamKirby 9 34
(John Ryan) *racd on outer in midfield: wknd 3f out: sn t.o* **50/1**

2m 2.83s (-3.77) **Going Correction** -0.025s/f (Stan)
WFA 3 from 4yo+ 3lb **10** Ran SP% **119.7**
Speed ratings (Par 107): **114,113,113,112,112 111,111,109,109,89**
CSF £34.25 CT £84.55 TOTE £15.70: £3.70, £1.10, £1.60; EX 47.30 Trifecta £234.70.
Owner Prof C D Green **Bred** Prof C Green **Trained** Lambourn, Berks

FOCUS
A useful handicap, but it proved hard to make up significant ground. It's been rated around the winner and third.

8232 BETWAY SPRINT H'CAP 5f 6y(P)
2:30 (2:35) (Class 2) (0-105,107) 3-Y-O+ **£11,971** (£3,583; £1,791; £896; £446) **Stalls** Low

Form RPR
6014 **1** **Gracious John (IRE)**^{23} 7932 3-9-9 **107** .... JFEgan 2 115
(David Evans) *t.k.h: trckd ldrs: wnt 2nd over 1f out and sn chalng: led last 100yds: styd on wl* **10/3**^{2}

0100 **2** *1* **Bosham**^{14} 8050 6-8-8 **95** ....(bt) NathanEvans$^{(3)}$ 5 99
(Michael Easterby) *led: rdn and pressed over 1f out: hdd and outpcd last 100yds* **14/1**

00 **3** *hd* **Kasbah (IRE)**^{12} 8069 4-8-8 **92** .... JackMitchell 1 96
(Amanda Perrett) *hld up in midfield: prog on inner over 1f out: tk 3rd ins fnl f: clsng on runner-up at fin* **6/1**^{3}

0301 **4** *1 ¼* **Encore D'Or**^{14} 8050 4-9-4 **102** .... ShaneGray 3 101+
(Robert Cowell) *hld up in midfield: dropped towards rr and plenty to do wl over 1f out: shkn up and styd on to take 4th wl ins fnl f: no ch* **2/1**^{1}

3020 **5** *¾* **Top Boy**^{34} 7752 6-8-0 **87** ....(v) NoelGarbutt$^{(3)}$ 4 83
(Derek Shaw) *dwlt: hld up in last: pushed along and styd on fr over 1f out on inner: nrst fin but nvr involved* **25/1**

0050 **6** *shd* **Poyle Vinnie**^{45} 7497 6-8-10 **94** .... LukeMorris 7 90
(Michael Appleby) *t.k.h: hld up in last pair: stl there over 1f out: styd on ins fnl f: nrst fin but no ch* **14/1**

0000 **7** *¾* **Sign Of The Kodiac (IRE)**^{107} 5657 3-9-2 **100** .... TomEaves 6 93
(James Given) *chsd ldng pair 2f: styd cl up: nt qckn over 1f out: lost pl fnl f* **16/1**

6001 **8** *¾* **Seve**^{16} 8032 4-8-2 **86** oh1 .... JosephineGordon 9 77
(Tom Dascombe) *chsd ldr to over 2f out: wknd over 1f out* **10/1**

6000 **9** *1 ¾* **Sir Maximilian (IRE)**^{14} 8050 7-9-9 **107** .... AdamKirby 8 91
(Ian Williams) *hld up in rr fr wd draw: sme prog into midfield over 1f out: wknd fnl f* **12/1**

0104 **10** *2 ¼* **Sandfrankskipsgo**^{93} 6114 7-8-4 **88** .... NickyMackay 10 64
(Peter Crate) *spd fr wd draw: prom: chsd ldr over 2f out to over 1f out: wknd qckly* **33/1**

57.85s (-0.95) **Going Correction** -0.025s/f (Stan) **10** Ran SP% **113.5**
Speed ratings (Par 109): **106,104,104,102,100 100,99,98,95,91**
CSF £47.81 CT £267.22 TOTE £4.30: £1.50, £3.20, £2.10; EX 46.40 Trifecta £237.10.
Owner Terry Reffell **Bred** Skeaghmore Hill **Trained** Pandy, Monmouths

FOCUS
A decent sprint handicap and a smart winner. A clear pb from the winner, with the runner-up back to some form from the front.

8233 32RED ON THE APP STORE FILLIES' H'CAP 6f 1y(P)
3:00 (3:05) (Class 4) (0-85,84) 3-Y-O+ **£5,175** (£1,540; £769; £384) **Stalls** Low

Form RPR
2400 **1** **Pretty Bubbles**^{5} 8158 7-9-5 **82** ....(v) GeorgeBaker 2 89
(J R Jenkins) *hld up in last pair: prog over 1f out: coaxed along and clsd between rivals to ld last 100yds: cosily* **6/1**^{3}

6130 **2** *¾* **Evening Starlight**^{49} 7420 3-8-3 **66** .... RyanTate 7 70
(Ron Hodges) *fast away fr wd draw: led: rdn over 1f out: hdd last 100yds: kpt on* **33/1**

0400 **3** *shd* **Primrose Valley**^{11} 8083 4-9-4 **84** ....(p) HectorCrouch$^{(3)}$ 1 88
(Ed Vaughan) *hld up off the pce in midfield: prog on inner 2f out w gap available: rdn to chal fnl f: outpcd last 100yds* **6/4**^{1}

4321 **4** *3* **Hyland Heather (IRE)**^{90} 6218 3-9-1 **78** .... JackGarritty 6 72
(Richard Fahey) *cl up bhd ldr: rdn and fnd little over 1f out: one pce after* **7/1**

435 **5** *nk* **Loveatfirstsight**^{40} 7616 3-8-4 **67** .... LukeMorris 8 60
(Michael Attwater) *s.i.s: mostly in last pair: rdn wl over 1f out: styd on late but no ch* **7/1**

0610 **6** *nk* **Himalayan Queen**^{25} 7887 3-7-13 **67** .... SophieKilloran$^{(5)}$ 4 59
(William Jarvis) *hld up off the pce: nudged along and no prog over 1f out* **17/2**

56 **7** *½* **Diamond Lady**^{33} 7773 5-9-1 **78** .... MartinLane 3 69
(William Stone) *chsd ldr 2f: styd prom: drvn 2f out: wknd fnl f and eased* **11/2**^{2}

5620 **8** *2 ½* **Penny Dreadful**^{28} 7851 4-7-13 **69** ....(p) RPWalsh$^{(7)}$ 5 52
(Scott Dixon) *pushed up on wd outside to chse ldr after 2f: on terms whn wd bnd 2f out: sn lost pl and no ch* **20/1**

1m 11.23s (-0.67) **Going Correction** -0.025s/f (Stan) **8** Ran SP% **112.9**
Speed ratings (Par 102): **103,102,101,97,97 97,96,93**
CSF £159.86 TOTE £7.20: £2.00, £5.50, £1.30; EX 125.10 Trifecta £767.10.
Owner Mark Goldstein **Bred** Southill Stud **Trained** Royston, Herts

FOCUS
A fair fillies' handicap. The winner has been rated to her turf win in July.

8234 100% DEPOSIT BONUS AT BETWAY H'CAP 6f 1y(P)
3:30 (3:39) (Class 6) (0-65,63) 3-Y-O+ **£2,911** (£866; £432; £216) **Stalls** Low

Form RPR
0003 **1** **Desert Strike**^{12} 8078 10-9-7 **63** ....(p) PaulMulrennan 3 70
(Conor Dore) *taken down early: mde all: rdn over 1f out: styd on wl and nvr in any real danger* **9/2**^{2}

3332 **2** *1 ¼* **Burauq**^{16} 8031 4-8-11 **53** ....(b) JosephineGordon 2 56
(Milton Bradley) *prom: chsd wnr jst over 2f out: rdn and no imp over 1f out: kpt on* **4/1**^{1}

6065 **3** *¾* **Catalinas Diamond (IRE)**^{11} 8079 8-8-7 **49** ....(t) JFEgan 7 50
(Pat Murphy) *hld up in rr: prog on outer jst over 1f out: styd on ins fnl f to take 3rd nr fin* **7/1**

0300 **4** *nse* **Great Expectations**^{37} 7694 8-9-0 **56** ....(vt) FergusSweeney 5 57
(J R Jenkins) *t.k.h: hld up towards rr: urged along and prog over 1f out: styd on ins fnl f: nrly snatched 3rd* **14/1**

0262 **5** *shd* **Cruise Tothelimit (IRE)**^{7} 8137 8-9-7 **63** .... LiamKeniry 1 64
(Patrick Morris) *cl up: disp 2nd on inner over 2f out to over 1f out: one pce and lost pls nr fin* **6/1**

2000 **6** *½* **Flying Sakhee**^{16} 8030 3-8-8 **50** ....(p) WilliamCarson 10 49
(John Bridger) *s.i.s: sn in midfield: rdn and nt qckn over 1f out: one pce after* **66/1**

650 **7** *¾* **Indiana Dawn**^{51} 7362 3-9-4 **60** .... AdamBeschizza 6 57
(Robert Stephens) *hld up in rr: effrt 2f out: rdn and kpt on fr over 1f out: nt pce to threaten* **25/1**

0600 **8** *nk* **Dishy Guru**^{75} 6669 7-9-3 **59** ....(v) TomEaves 9 55
(Michael Blanshard) *slowly away: mostly in last of main field: rdn and kpt on fr over 1f out: no ch* **12/1**

0602 **9** *½* **Keep It Dark**^{16} 8030 7-9-2 **58** .... LukeMorris 8 52
(William Knight) *chsd ldrs: rdn and nt qckn wl over 1f out: lost pl and wl hld after* **5/1**^{3}

4030 **10** *2* **Spowarticus**^{10} 8095 7-8-11 **60** ....(v) NatalieHambling$^{(7)}$ 12 48
(Scott Dixon) *chsd wnr and racd on outer: hung rt over 2f out: wd bnd sn after and dropped to rr: no ch over 1f out* **33/1**

3550 **11** *92* **Ghost Train (IRE)**^{16} 8031 7-9-3 **59** ....(p) MartinLane 4
(Tim McCarthy) *ref to r tl rest had gone 1f: pottered rnd in own time* **6/1**

1m 11.76s (-0.14) **Going Correction** -0.025s/f (Stan) **11** Ran SP% **118.6**
Speed ratings (Par 101): **99,97,96,96,96 95,94,94,93,90**
CSF £22.74 CT £128.11 TOTE £5.80: £1.90, £1.40, £2.80; EX 23.70 Trifecta £138.70.
Owner Andrew Page **Bred** Mrs Mary Rowlands **Trained** Hubbert's Bridge, Lincs

FOCUS
A moderate sprint handicap. Straightforward form to rate.
T/Jkpt: Not won. T/Plt: £197.40 to a £1 stake. Pool: £74,882.83 - 276.82 winning tickets T/Qpdt: £14.20 to a £1 stake. Pool: £12,664.32 - 657.58 winning tickets **Jonathan Neesom**

7889 SOUTHWELL (L-H)
Tuesday, December 6

OFFICIAL GOING: Fibresand: standard
Wind: Virtually Nil Weather: Foggy & Poor visibility

8235 32RED CASINO NURSERY H'CAP 1m (F)
11:50 (11:51) (Class 6) (0-65,65) 2-Y-O **£3,234** (£962; £481; £240) **Stalls** Low

Form RPR
5041 **1** **Dream Team**^{11} 8087 2-9-6 **64** ....(p) PaulMulrennan 3 70
(Michael Dods) *trckd ldrs: hdwy over 2f out: rdn to ld jst over 1f out: kpt on wl fnl f* **6/1**

555 **2** *½* **Warm Words**^{26} 7882 2-9-7 **65** .... RichardKingscote 2 70
(Ralph Beckett) *cl up: slt ld over 2f out: rdn and hdd jst over 1f out: drvn and rallied ins fnl f: kpt on* **4/1**^{2}

0055 **3** *4 ½* **Arthurthedelegator**^{35} 7749 2-9-5 **63** .... KevinStott 11 57
(Oliver Greenall) *hld up in rr: swtchd lft to inner after 2f: hdwy over 3f out: pushed along over 2f out: sn rdn to chse ldrs. kpt on fnl f* **10/1**

0002 **4** *nk* **Still Waiting**^{27} 7866 2-9-3 **61** .... RobertHavlin 5 54
(William Jarvis) *chsd ldng pair: effrt over 2f out and sn rdn along: drvn wl over 1f out: kpt on same pce* **7/2**^{1}

6336 **5** *4* **All About The Pace**^{24} 7941 2-8-13 **57** .... LiamKeniry 8 41
(Mark Usher) *awkward s and sn pushed along: in tch: rdn along wl over 2f out: drvn over 1f out and kpt on one pce* **20/1**

6461 **6** *2 ¾* **Bazwind (IRE)**^{17} 8025 2-9-7 **65** ....(v^{1}) JFEgan 12 42
(David Evans) *chsd ldrs: rdn along over 2f out: sn drvn and kpt on one pce* **5/1**^{3}

6200 **7** *¾* **Valley Lodge**^{84} 6440 2-9-4 **62** .... AdamBeschizza 13 37
(Julia Feilden) *midfield: hdwy and in tch over 3f out: rdn along wl over 2f out: sn btn* **50/1**

0000 **8** *1 ¼* **Stag Party (IRE)**^{13} 8072 2-8-13 **57** .... DavidProbert 1 29
(Andrew Balding) *sn led on inner: pushed along over 3f out: rdn and hdd over 2f out: sn wknd* **16/1**

066 **9** *shd* **Beauchamp Opal**^{21} 7962 2-9-5 **63** .... StevieDonohoe 6 35
(Charlie Fellowes) *midfield: rdn along on outer over 2f out: n.d* **9/1**

6530 **10** *2 ½* **Rita's Girl**^{20} 7974 2-9-0 **58** .... BenCurtis 14 24
(K R Burke) *midfield: hdwy on outer over 3f out: rdn along over 2f out: sn wknd* **16/1**

0502 **11** *24* **Deleyll**^{49} 7423 2-8-13 **57** ow1 ....^{1} TimmyMurphy 7
(John Butler) *a rr: outpcd and bhd fr over 3f out* **22/1**

1m 43.21s (-0.49) **Going Correction** -0.075s/f (Stan) **11** Ran SP% **115.1**
Speed ratings (Par 94): **99,98,94,93,89 86,86,84,84,82 58**
CSF £28.82 CT £240.08 TOTE £5.10: £1.80, £1.70, £3.50; EX 32.30 Trifecta £418.90.
Owner Denton Hall Racing Ltd **Bred** R G Percival **Trained** Denton, Co Durham

FOCUS
The last Flat meeting here was called off due to waterlogging and since then the surface had been opened up down to the membrane and then rolled back. Clerk of the course Roderick Duncan said that "it walks quite quick." A foggy day and the visibility was poor. This was a modest nursery but the first two came nicely clear.

8236 BETWAY CLASSIFIED CLAIMING STKS 6f (F)
12:20 (12:21) (Class 6) 3-Y-O+ **£3,234** (£962; £481; £240) **Stalls** Low

Form RPR
0000 **1** **Vroom (IRE)**^{13} 8067 3-8-0 67 ....(p) GabrieleMalune$^{(7)}$ 10 78
(Gay Kelleway) *prom: led wl over 2f out: clr appr fnl f: kpt on strly* **16/1**

0000 **2** *3 ¼* **Ticks The Boxes (IRE)**^{11} 8099 4-7-13 70 ....^{1} NathanEvans$^{(3)}$ 7 63
(Michael Herrington) *t.k.h: in tch: hdwy to chse ldrs over 2f out: sn rdn: styd on to chse wnr ins fnl f: sn no imp* **7/1**^{3}

2000 **3** *¾* **Fortinbrass (IRE)**^{28} 7859 6-8-7 56 .... JoeDoyle 1 66
(John Balding) *trckd ldrs: hdwy wl over 2f out: chsd wnr over 1f out: sn rdn and kpt on same pce* **14/1**

0001 **4** *2 ½* **Alpha Tauri (USA)**^{26} 7896 10-8-2 65 .... NoelGarbutt$^{(3)}$ 3 57
(Charles Smith) *hld up in rr: hdwy on inner 2f out: rdn over 1f out: styd on fnl f: nrst fin* **8/1**

2000 **5** *shd* **Llewellyn**^{11} 8094 8-7-10 62 .... RhiainIngram$^{(7)}$ 6 54
(Declan Carroll) *led: rdn along over 2f out: sn rdn along and grad wknd* **20/1**

6050 **6** *1* **Ten Rocks**^{11} 8096 3-8-4 55 ow1 .... BenCurtis 5 52
(Lisa Williamson) *dwlt: rdn along and sme hdwy over 2f out: nvr a factor* **50/1**

0050 **7** *1 ½* **Dr Red Eye**^{11} 8094 8-7-12 53 ....(v) RPWalsh$^{(7)}$ 8 49
(Scott Dixon) *cl up: rdn along wl over 2f out: sn drvn and wknd* **40/1**

3000 **8** *1 ½* **Sober Up**^{26} 7890 4-8-3 55 ....(p) JoeyHaynes 4 42
(Ivan Furtado) *a rr* **25/1**

105 **9** *shd* **Oeil De Tigre (FR)**^{34} 7772 5-8-4 70 .... LukeMorris 2 43
(Tony Carroll) *towards rr: hdwy 1/2-way: in tch and rdn along over 2f out: sn btn* **13/8**^{1}

2050 **10** *1 ¼* **Fujin**^{29} 7852 5-8-3 69 .... JosephineGordon 12 38
(Shaun Harris) *chsd ldrs: rdn along wl over 2f out: sn wknd* **3/1**^{2}

5160 **11** *shd* **Pearl Noir**^{13} 8078 6-8-3 62 ow1 ....(p) NatalieHambling$^{(7)}$ 9 45
(Scott Dixon) *chsd ldrs: rdn along 1/2-way: sn wknd* **33/1**

0000 **12** *18* **Armelle (FR)**[35] 7747 5-8-5 49......................................(p) KieranO'Neill 13
(Scott Dixon) *a rr* **80/1**
1m 15.68s (-0.82) **Going Correction** -0.075s/f (Stan) **12** Ran SP% **116.4**
Speed ratings (Par 101): **102,97,96,93,93 91,89,87,87,86 85,61**
CSF £113.57 TOTE £24.40: £5.60, £1.90, £2.90; EX 135.50 Trifecta £1774.80.There was no bid for the winner.
Owner Buy,Clarke,Whatley & Panther Racing **Bred** Paul & T J Monaghan **Trained** Exning, Suffolk

FOCUS
A moderate heat, but a good performance from the winner nonetheless. A minor pb from the winner, with the third helping to set the opening level.

8237 32RED.COM BRITISH STALLION STUDS EBF MAIDEN STKS 7f (F)
12:50 (12:51) (Class 5) 2-Y-O **£3,881** (£1,155; £577; £288) **Stalls** Low

Form RPR
224 **1** **Syndicate**[63] 7049 2-9-0 78.. RichardKingscote 4 81
(Ralph Beckett) *cl up on inner: led 3f out: rdn along 2f out: drvn clr ins fnl f: kpt on* **11/8**[1]
53 **2** *3* **Atteq**[19] 7988 2-9-5 0.. DavidNolan 7 78
(Richard Fahey) *slt ld: hdd 3f out and sn pushed along: rdn 2f out: drvn and ev ch over 1f out: kpt on same pce fnl f* **11/4**[2]
3 *10* **Lady Volante (IRE)**[76] 6686 2-9-0 0.................................... JFEgan 10 47
(David Evans) *trckd ldrs: hdwy to chse ldng pair wl over 2f out: sn rdn along and kpt on one pce* **14/1**
620 **4** *2* **Dal Riata (IRE)**[34] 7763 2-9-0 75..................................... PJMcDonald 8 42
(Mark Johnston) *chsd ldrs: rdn along on inner over 2f out: sn drvn and one pce* **17/2**
0 **5** *hd* **Medici Moon**[39] 7658 2-8-12 0.. RPWalsh(7) 12 46
(Scott Dixon) *stdd s and hld up in rr: hdwy wl over 2f out: styd on appr fnl f: nrst fin* **50/1**
006 **6** *¾* **Shaqoos (FR)**[25] 7927 2-9-0 0.. JoeyHaynes 9 40
(Jo Hughes) *midfield: hdwy wl over 2f out: sn rdn along and plugged on one pce* **100/1**
3 **7** *6* **Shee's Lucky**[13] 8073 2-9-0 0.. AndrewMullen 5 24
(Mark Johnston) *a towards rr* **8/1**[3]
0 **8** *½* **My Aussie Rules**[25] 7906 2-9-5 0..................................... AdamKirby 2 28
(Clive Cox) *a towards rr* **8/1**[3]
9 *¾* **Knightsbridge Liam (IRE)** 2-9-2 0.............................. NathanEvans(3) 3 26
(Michael Easterby) *a towards rr* **40/1**
00 **10** *3¾* **Pleasure Requested (IRE)**[12] 8082 2-9-5 0............. RobertWinston 11 16
(Eve Johnson Houghton) *a towards rr* **50/1**
00 **11** *15* **Delightfulsurprise**[26] 7891 2-9-0 0................................. KieranO'Neill 13
(Scott Dixon) *in tch: rdn along 1/2-way: sn outpcd* **250/1**
600 **12** *7* **Copa Beech**[55] 7283 2-9-5 26..(b[1]) DuranFentiman 1
(Olly Williams) *chsd ldng pair on inner: rdn along wl over 2f out: sn wknd* **150/1**
0 **13** *26* **Thornton Frank**[124] 5067 2-9-5 0.................................... JamesSullivan 6
(Brian Rothwell) *dwlt: a bhd* **150/1**
1m 29.86s (-0.44) **Going Correction** -0.075s/f (Stan) **13** Ran SP% **117.3**
Speed ratings (Par 96): **99,95,84,81,81 80,73,73,72,68 51,43,13**
CSF £4.80 TOTE £2.50: £1.50, £1.20, £3.10; EX 5.90 Trifecta £33.60.
Owner K Abdullah **Bred** Juddmonte Farms Ltd **Trained** Kimpton, Hants

FOCUS
Only two mattered in this from some way out.

8238 DOWNLOAD THE BETWAY APP H'CAP 1m 6f (F)
1:20 (1:20) (Class 5) (0-75,75) 3-Y-O+ **£3,881** (£1,155; £577; £288) **Stalls** Low

Form RPR
0031 **1** **High Command (IRE)**[26] 7895 3-9-7 75.............................. JackMitchell 6 94+
(Roger Varian) *trckd ldrs: hdwy and cl up over 3f out: led over 2f out: sn rdn: clr ins fnl f: kpt on* **1/2**[1]
4206 **2** *4½* **Come Back King (IRE)**[26] 7895 3-9-0 68.........................(b[1]) BenCurtis 2 78
(Michael Appleby) *trckd ldr: led over 4f out: jnd and rdn along 3f out: hdd over 2f out and sn drvn: kpt on same pce fnl f* **8/1**[2]
202 **3** *15* **Marshall Aid (IRE)**[19] 7987 3-9-0 68.................................. LiamKeniry 4 57
(Mark Usher) *chsd ldrs: rdn along 4f out: drvn wl over 2f out: sn outpcd* **9/1**[3]
1005 **4** *2½* **Deep Resolve (IRE)**[26] 7895 5-9-3 67.................... CallumShepherd(3) 5 53
(Alan Swinbank) *hld up: hdwy to chse ldrs over 4f out: rdn along over 3f out: sn drvn and one pce* **11/1**
0000 **5** *5* **Albert Boy (IRE)**[26] 7889 3-7-9 56 oh1.................................. RPWalsh(7) 7 35
(Scott Dixon) *in tch: rdn along over 5f out: sn outpcd and bhd* **80/1**
4003 **6** *2½* **Captain Swift (IRE)**[26] 7895 5-9-1 62................................ GrahamLee 3 37
(John Mackie) *hld up: effrt and sme hdwy 1/2-way: rdn along over 4f out: sn wknd* **12/1**
6000 **7** *32* **Yul Finegold (IRE)**[18] 8007 6-9-9 70..............................[1] PaulMulrennan 1
(Conor Dore) *led: rdn along and hdd over 4f out: sn wknd and bhd* **33/1**
3m 6.88s (-1.42) **Going Correction** -0.075s/f (Stan)
WFA 3 from 5yo+ 7lb **7** Ran SP% **108.0**
Speed ratings (Par 103): **101,98,89,88,85 84,65**
CSF £4.35 TOTE £1.40: £1.10, £2.60; EX 5.40 Trifecta £24.90.
Owner H R H Sultan Ahmad Shah **Bred** Greenwood Lodge Farm Inc **Trained** Newmarket, Suffolk

FOCUS
This was a proper test and the first two finished well clear. An improved showing from the runner-up in the first-time blinkers, but with little solid in behind.

8239 SUNBETS.CO.UK H'CAP 7f (F)
1:50 (1:52) (Class 4) (0-80,80) 3-Y-O+ **£5,822** (£1,732; £865; £432) **Stalls** Low

Form RPR
0000 **1** **Captain Revelation**[33] 7781 4-9-5 78........................ RichardKingscote 9 89
(Tom Dascombe) *in tch: hdwy to trck ldrs wl over 2f out: chsd ldng pair over 1f out: rdn to chal ent fnl f: kpt on wl to ld nr fin* **9/2**[2]
0024 **2** *½* **Boots And Spurs**[22] 7957 7-8-11 77....................(v) NatalieHambling(7) 6 87
(Scott Dixon) *trckd ldng pair: hdwy over 2f out: rdn to ld jst over 1f out: drvn ins fnl f: hdd and no ex towards fin* **13/2**
5340 **3** *2¼* **He's My Cracker**[21] 7965 3-9-4 77.. AdamKirby 8 81
(Clive Cox) *rdn along s and sn slt ld: rdn along 2f out: hdd jst over 1f out: sn drvn and kpt on same pce* **4/1**[1]
0556 **4** *1¼* **Personal Touch**[3] 8205 7-9-0 73.. LukeMorris 10 74
(Michael Appleby) *trckd ldrs: hdwy 3f out: rdn wl over 1f out: drvn and kpt on same pce fnl f* **9/1**
-000 **5** *¾* **Starfield**[13] 8077 7-9-2 75..(b[1]) JosephineGordon 7 74
(Mandy Rowland) *sn cl up: rdn along wl over 2f out: drvn wl over 1f out: grad wknd* **25/1**
1060 **6** *2½* **Dusky Dawn**[178] 3152 4-9-3 76... BenCurtis 14 68
(Alan Swinbank) *midfield: hdwy wl over 2f out: sn rdn and no imp* **16/1**
530 **7** *hd* **Free Code (IRE)**[22] 7957 5-9-7 80................................ GrahamGibbons 3 72
(David Barron) *dwlt and rr tl sme late hdwy* **6/1**[3]
6055 **8** *3½* **Tellovoi (IRE)**[22] 7959 8-8-12 71.................................(v) ConnorBeasley 1 54
(Richard Guest) *chsd ldrs on inner: rdn along 3f out: sn drvn and wknd* **10/1**
5660 **9** *1½* **Welliesinthewater (IRE)**[15] 8052 6-9-2 78..................(v) NoelGarbutt(3) 2 57
(Derek Shaw) *in tch: rdn along 1/2-way: sn lost pl and towards rr* **8/1**
00-0 **10** *3½* **War Singer (USA)**[114] 1620 9-9-5 78.........................(bt) StevieDonohoe 13 48
(Johnny Farrelly) *s.i.s: a bhd* **25/1**
0 **11** *1½* **Falcao (IRE)**[12] 8083 4-9-2 75.. TimmyMurphy 4 41
(John Butler) *a rr* **40/1**
0000 **12** *2¾* **Another Go (IRE)**[50] 7412 3-9-6 79...................................... NeilFarley 12 38
(Alan Swinbank) *a rr* **40/1**
1m 28.75s (-1.55) **Going Correction** -0.075s/f (Stan) **12** Ran SP% **114.5**
Speed ratings (Par 105): **105,104,101,100,99 96,96,92,90,86 85,81**
CSF £31.25 CT £124.12 TOTE £5.30: £2.20, £2.50, £1.70; EX 29.50 Trifecta £136.30.
Owner Cheshire Racing **Bred** Downfield Cottage Stud **Trained** Malpas, Cheshire

FOCUS
There was a good pace on here and that suited the winner. A length pb from the winner, with the runner-up helping to set the standard. A length pb from the winner, with the runner-up helping to set the standard.

8240 SUN BETS ON THE APP STORE H'CAP (DIV I) 1m (F)
2:20 (2:20) (Class 5) (0-70,70) 3-Y-O+ **£3,881** (£1,155; £577; £288) **Stalls** Low

Form RPR
3560 **1** **Anton Chigurh**[94] 6138 7-9-5 68............................... RichardKingscote 8 79+
(Tom Dascombe) *trckd ldrs: smooth hdwy over 2f out: rdn to ld over 1f out: rdn and kpt on strly fnl f* **4/1**[1]
-040 **2** *2½* **Gatillo**[145] 4319 3-9-6 70.. AdamKirby 7 74
(Philip McBride) *sn cl up: led wl over 2f out: rdn and hdd over 1f out: drvn and kpt on same pce fnl f* **9/1**
1040 **3** *1* **African Showgirl**[41] 7613 3-8-13 63.......................... JosephineGordon 2 65
(Ivan Furtado) *in tch: hdwy over 2f out: rdn wl over 1f out: styd on fnl f: nrst fin* **28/1**
3004 **4** *nk* **Best Tamayuz**[26] 7895 5-8-3 59......................................(p) RPWalsh(7) 11 60
(Scott Dixon) *cl up: led after 11/2f: rdn along 3f out: sn hdd: drvn and grad wknd fnl 2f* **13/2**
1060 **5** *2* **Pick A Little**[17] 8037 8-9-3 66.. LukeMorris 1 63
(Michael Blake) *slt ld 11/2f: cl up: rdn along 3f out: grad wknd fnl 2f* **20/1**
0003 **6** *nk* **General Tufto**[26] 7889 11-8-4 56 oh9............................(b) NoelGarbutt(3) 6 52
(Charles Smith) *rr and sn pushed along: rdn along 1/2-way: styd on fnl 2f: nrst fin* **50/1**
6636 **7** *2½* **First Wheat**[19] 7999 3-9-3 70..(e[1]) NathanEvans(3) 5 60
(Michael Easterby) *hmpd and lost pl s: sn bhd: hdwy over 3f out: in tch and rdn along over 2f out: n.d* **9/2**[2]
1061 **8** *¾* **Stun Gun**[26] 7890 6-9-5 68...(p) MartinLane 12 57
(Derek Shaw) *prom: rdn along over 3f out: sn wknd* **5/1**[3]
0350 **9** *1* **The Lynch Man**[11] 8101 3-9-1 65.................................(e[1]) DougieCostello 4 51
(John Quinn) *in tch: rdn along over 3f out: n.d* **14/1**
0202 **10** *nk* **Maria's Choice (IRE)**[25] 7905 7-9-0 63......................... TimmyMurphy 3 49
(Jim Best) *a towards rr* **33/1**
0002 **11** *4* **Gold Flash**[19] 7985 4-9-7 70...(b) RobertWinston 10 46
(Keith Dalgleish) *trckd ldrs: cl up on outer 1/2-way: effrt 3f out: sn rdn along and wknd fnl 2f* **9/2**[2]
0400 **12** *14* **Our Boy Jack (IRE)**[17] 8036 7-9-1 64.............................(p) PaulMulrennan 9 8
(Conor Dore) *a towards rr* **40/1**
1m 43.12s (-0.58) **Going Correction** -0.075s/f (Stan)
WFA 3 from 4yo+ 1lb **12** Ran SP% **118.6**
Speed ratings (Par 103): **99,96,95,95,93 92,90,89,88,88 84,70**
CSF £38.19 CT £910.83 TOTE £5.30: £1.80, £3.40, £7.50; EX 50.80 Trifecta £1904.30.
Owner Panarea Racing & Partner **Bred** Mr & Mrs G Middlebrook **Trained** Malpas, Cheshire

FOCUS
A modest but competitive handicap. It's been rated around the winner to his C&D win in April.

8241 SUN BETS ON THE APP STORE H'CAP (DIV II) 1m (F)
2:50 (2:50) (Class 5) (0-70,70) 3-Y-O+ **£3,881** (£1,155; £577; £288) **Stalls** Low

Form RPR
1300 **1** **Big Storm Coming**[26] 7887 6-9-5 68.................................... AdamKirby 9 81
(David Brown) *trckd ldrs: hdwy over 3f out: rdn to ld over 2f out: drvn clr ent fnl f: kpt on* **8/1**
0004 **2** *3½* **Balducci**[11] 8092 9-9-1 64.. BenCurtis 3 69
(Roger Fell) *trckd ldrs: hdwy over 2f out: rdn to chse wnr ent fnl f: sn drvn and no imp* **11/2**[3]
0000 **3** *3* **St Patrick's Day (IRE)**[11] 8101 4-9-5 68.........................(v) PaddyAspell 5 66
(J R Jenkins) *pushed along s and towards rr: hdwy 1/2-way: swtchd wd and rdn 2f out: drvn and kpt on fnl f: tk 3rd nr line* **5/1**[2]
2062 **4** *hd* **Royal Holiday (IRE)**[71] 6838 9-9-7 70........................(p) RobertWinston 7 68
(Marjorie Fife) *cl up: led 3f out: sn rdn and hdd over 2f out: chsd wnr: drvn over 1f out and kpt on same pce: lost 3rd nr line* **4/1**[1]
3030 **5** *1¼* **Arcane Dancer (IRE)**[42] 7601 3-8-10 63....................(p) NathanEvans(3) 8 58
(Lawrence Mullaney) *cl up: rdn along over 2f out: drvn over 1f out: grad wknd* **10/1**
6002 **6** *7* **Limerick Lord (IRE)**[26] 7889 4-8-4 56 oh2..............(p) ShelleyBirkett(3) 1 35
(Julia Feilden) *in tch: hdwy 3f out: rdn along over 2f out: sn drvn and no imp* **16/1**
5000 **7** *3½* **Whozthecat (IRE)**[11] 8095 9-8-8 62..............................(vt) PhilDennis(5) 2 33
(Declan Carroll) *slt ld on inner: rdn along over 3f out: sn hdd and grad wknd* **33/1**
6434 **8** *1* **Call Out Loud**[141] 4443 4-9-4 67...[1] LukeMorris 6 35
(Michael Appleby) *chsd ldrs: effrt over 2f out and sn rdn: drvn wl over 1f out: sn wknd* **8/1**
3533 **9** *3¼* **Summer Collection (IRE)**[164] 3673 3-9-6 70..................... JoeyHaynes 4 31
(K R Burke) *a rr* **12/1**
0000 **10** *18* **Genres**[87] 6346 4-9-2 65... NeilFarley 10
(Alan Swinbank) *a rr* **10/1**
0400 **11** *6* **Marshal Dan Troop (IRE)**[10] 8124 3-9-1 65............. PaulMulrennan 11
(Robyn Brisland) *midfield: rdn along wl over 3f out: sn outpcd and bhd* **12/1**
1m 42.93s (-0.77) **Going Correction** -0.075s/f (Stan)
WFA 3 from 4yo+ 1lb **11** Ran SP% **116.7**
Speed ratings (Par 103): **100,96,93,93,92 85,81,80,77,59 53**
CSF £51.18 CT £250.41 TOTE £8.20: £3.10, £1.90, £2.10; EX 56.00 Trifecta £376.50.
Owner Fishlake Commercial Motors Ltd **Bred** Bearstone Stud Ltd **Trained** Averham Park, Notts

FOCUS
The pace slackened and a few got held up in traffic on the turn in, which allowed the winner, who was taken wide by Adam Kirby, the momentum to kick clear of his rivals early in the straight. It was the quicker of the two divisions by 0.19sec. The winner has been rated close to his old best.

8242 BETWAY H'CAP 5f (F)
3:20 (3:22) (Class 6) (0-60,60) 3-Y-O+ £3,234 (£962; £481; £240) Stalls Centre

Form RPR
0553 **1** **Piazon**[17] 8030 5-9-0 **60**........(be[1]) DarraghKeenan(7) 12 70
(John Butler) *trckd ldrs: hdwy wl over 1f out: led ent fnl f: sn rdn and kpt on strly* **10/1**
0604 **2** 1 3/4 **Excellent Aim**[6] 8149 9-9-0 **60**........ JaneElliott(7) 4 64
(George Margarson) *trckd ldrs towards far side: hdwy wl over 1f out: rdn and ev ch ins fnl f: sn drvn and kpt on* **5/1**[1]
4005 **3** 3/4 **Tribesman**[22] 7961 3-9-2 **55**........(t) SamJames 14 56
(Marjorie Fife) *in tch: pushed along and hdwy 2f out: rdn to chse ldrs over 1f out: styd on wl fnl f* **20/1**
0510 **4** 1 1/4 **Lady Joanna Vassa (IRE)**[6] 8149 3-9-5 **58**........ ConnorBeasley 9 55
(Richard Guest) *slt ld: hdd 1/2-way: cl up and rdn wl over 1f out: drvn and kpt on fnl f* **12/1**
0060 **5** 3/4 **Big Amigo (IRE)**[17] 8040 3-9-4 **60**........ EoinWalsh(3) 10 54
(Daniel Mark Loughnane) *rr: hdwy 2f out: rdn over 1f out: styd on wl fnl f: nrst fin* **16/1**
1005 **6** 1 1/2 **Pancake Day**[17] 8031 4-9-1 **54**........(v) JFEgan 6 42
(David C Griffiths) *cl up: led 1/2-way: rdn wl over 1f out: drvn and hdd ent fnl f: wknd* **6/1**[2]
000 **7** nk **Oscars Journey**[34] 7774 6-9-7 **60**........(v) PaddyAspell 1 47
(J R Jenkins) *prom far side: cl up 1/2-way: rdn and ev ch over 1f out: sn drvn and kpt on same pce fnl f* **6/1**[2]
0500 **8** 3/4 **Bapak Bangsawan**[42] 7596 6-9-2 **60**........(v) AnnStokell(5) 3 45
(Ann Stokell) *prom: hdwy and cl up 1/2-way: rdn and ev ch wl over 1f out: wknd ent fnl f* **8/1**[3]
0430 **9** 1/2 **Port Lairge**[21] 7968 6-9-4 **60**........ NoelGarbutt(3) 11 43
(Michael Chapman) *dwlt and sn rdn along in rr: styd on u.p fnl 2f* **28/1**
5503 **10** 3/4 **Culloden**[42] 7596 4-9-2 **60**........(b) CharlieBennett(5) 7 40
(Shaun Harris) *trckd ldrs: smooth hdwy and cl up over 2f out: sn ev ch: rdn over 1f out: wknd* **12/1**
0200 **11** 1/2 **Sir Geoffrey (IRE)**[11] 8094 10-8-9 **55**........(b) NatalieHambling(7) 8 33
(Scott Dixon) *a towards rr* **10/1**
2600 **12** hd **Fuel Injection**[8] 8137 5-9-4 **57**........(p) JackGarritty 13 35
(Paul Midgley) *cl up: disp ld 1/2-way: rdn over 2f out: sn drvn and grad wknd* **16/1**
6000 **13** 1/2 **Hit The Lights (IRE)**[8] 8137 6-9-4 **57**........(v) PaulQuinn 2 33
(David Nicholls) *dwlt: sn pushed along and hdwy to chse ldrs 1/2-way: rdn 2f out and sn wknd* **11/1**
0200 **14** 6 **Lady Elizabeth (IRE)**[73] 6774 3-8-8 **54**........(p) RPWalsh(7) 5 8
(Scott Dixon) *prom: rdn along bef 1/2-way: sn lost pl and bhd fnl 2f* **80/1**

1m 0.25s (0.55) **Going Correction** +0.15s/f (Slow) **14** Ran SP% **119.5**
Speed ratings (Par 101): **101,98,97,95,93 91,90,89,88,87 86,86,85,76**
CSF £57.82 CT £1026.52 TOTE £10.60: £3.10, £2.30, £5.80; EX 59.30 Trifecta £720.30.
Owner Royale Racing Syndicate **Bred** Peter Baldwin **Trained** Newmarket, Suffolk

FOCUS
They went a good pace in this ordinary sprint handicap. The second and third help set the standard.
T/Jkpt: £36,131.80 to a £1 stake. Pool: £54,197.74 - 1.5 winning units. T/Plt: £86.60 to a £1 stake. Pool: £68055.53 - 573.04 winning units. T/Qpdt: £8.20 to a £1 stake. Pool: £7510.31 - 669.79 winning units. **Joe Rowntree**

8149 KEMPTON (A.W) (R-H)
Wednesday, December 7

OFFICIAL GOING: Polytrack: standard to slow
Weather: cloudy

8243 32RED ON THE APP STORE MAIDEN STKS 6f (P)
3:45 (3:45) (Class 5) 2-Y-O £3,234 (£962; £481; £240) Stalls Low

Form RPR
1 **Medahim (IRE)** 2-9-5 0........ SeanLevey 5 87+
(Richard Hannon) *hld up in mid-div on inner: pushed along and tk clsr order over 1f out: sn rdn and qcknd up wl to ld ins fnl f: easily* **12/1**
32 **2** 3 1/4 **Saluti (IRE)**[14] 8066 2-9-5 0........ RobertHavlin 6 77
(Amanda Perrett) *broke wl: sn settled in 4th: rdn jst over 2f out: picked up ins fnl f to grab 2nd post: no ch w wnr* **6/5**[1]
0220 **3** nse **Kingofmerrows (IRE)**[12] 8089 2-9-5 77........ WilliamCarson 4 77
(Jamie Osborne) *sn led at stdy pce: rdn over 2f out: hdd ins fnl f: kpt on one pce and lost 2nd fnl stride* **12/1**
3002 **4** 1 1/2 **Juan Horsepower**[54] 7319 2-9-5 76........ KieranO'Neill 8 72
(Richard Hannon) *settled in 2nd: rdn along 2f out and sn disp ld: wandered sltly under rt hand drive ins fnl f: rdr changed whip and styd on one pce* **8/1**[3]
0 **5** 3 1/4 **Bay Watch (IRE)**[47] 7502 2-9-5 0........ DavidProbert 9 62
(Andrew Balding) *covered up in mid-div: rdn along in centre 2f out: kpt on one pce fr over 1f out* **10/1**
6 1 1/2 **Private Mission** 2-9-5 0........ RobertWinston 10 58
(Hughie Morrison) *hld up in rr: rdn over 2f out: no imp on ldrs and pushed out hands and heels fr over 1f out* **33/1**
7 nk **Milburn Jack** 2-9-5 0........ AdamKirby 7 57
(Clive Cox) *hld up in rr: rdn over 2f out: sn hld* **9/4**[2]
00 **8** 2 1/2 **Young Officer (IRE)**[104] 5792 2-9-5 0........ TomQueally 2 49
(Brian Meehan) *in rr and rn green: rdn on inner over 2f out: no imp fr over 1f out* **66/1**
06 **9** shd **Sentinel**[14] 8066 2-9-5 0........ StevieDonohoe 11 49
(Charlie Fellowes) *c across fr wd draw to sit in rr-div on outer: niggled along over 2f out: no ex fr over 1f out: hands and heels after* **33/1**
000 **10** 1 1/2 **Highland Clearance (FR)**[22] 7972 2-9-0 0........ JackMitchell 3 40
(Giles Bravery) *settled bhd ldr on rail: rdn over 2f out: wknd qckly fr over 1f out* **100/1**

1m 13.72s (0.62) **Going Correction** +0.075s/f (Slow) **10** Ran SP% **120.2**
Speed ratings (Par 96): **98,93,93,91,87 85,84,81,81,79**
CSF £27.53 TOTE £9.90: £2.70, £1.20, £2.50; EX 30.00 Trifecta £143.80.
Owner Al Shaqab Racing **Bred** Paul McEnery **Trained** East Everleigh, Wilts

FOCUS
The going was standard to slow. A fair maiden run at a steady pace. The third, fourth and a few down the field offer perspective to the level.

8244 CURTIS ENGINEERING SOLUTIONS NURSERY H'CAP 7f (P)
4:15 (4:15) (Class 5) (0-75,74) 2-Y-O £3,234 (£962; £481; £240) Stalls Low

Form RPR
5242 **1** **Emenem**[7] 8153 2-8-13 **66**........ JFEgan 2 72
(Simon Dow) *racd bhd ldr in tch: niggled along to hold pl at 1/2-way: rdn over 2f out: led 2f out: kpt on wl fr over 1f out: sn in control and pushed out wl ins fnl f* **11/4**[1]
4303 **2** 1 3/4 **Things Happen**[18] 8033 2-9-1 **68**........ RobertWinston 9 69
(David Evans) *racd in 2nd on outer: rdn over 2f out: ev ch 2f out: outpcd ent fnl f: kpt on again nr fin* **10/1**
066 **3** 1/2 **Heaven's Rock (IRE)**[18] 8033 2-9-1 **68**........(v) RichardKingscote 5 68
(Tom Dascombe) *sn led: rdn over 2f out: hdd 2f out: picked up again ins fnl f* **9/1**
2120 **4** nk **Party Tiger**[32] 7820 2-9-7 **74**........ DavidNolan 3 73
(Richard Fahey) *settled bhd ldrs: rdn 2f out where swtchd to inner: ev ch over 1f out: no ex wl ins fnl f and wknd cl home* **7/1**[3]
5053 **5** 1 **Sparkle**[26] 7898 2-9-6 **73**........ AdamKirby 6 70+
(Ed Dunlop) *hld up in mid-div: rdn over 2f out: kpt on wl fr over 1f out tl wknd last strides* **11/2**[2]
005 **6** shd **Pobbles**[13] 8081 2-9-1 **71**........ KieranShoemark(3) 4 68+
(Roger Charlton) *sltly hmpd s: hld up in rr on inner: niggled along over 2f out: rdn 2f out: pushed out fnl f: nvr involved* **16/1**
1004 **7** 1/2 **Sixties Habana**[21] 7974 2-8-9 **62**........ KieranO'Neill 8 57+
(Pat Phelan) *in rr: lots to do ent st: drifted to ins rail 2f out: one pce ins fnl f* **33/1**
61 **8** nk **Sadhbh (IRE)**[13] 8082 2-9-1 **68**........ SeanLevey 1 62+
(Richard Hannon) *hld up in mid-div on inner: rdn along over 2f out: kpt on one pce fnl f* **7/1**[3]
04U0 **9** 2 3/4 **Broughtons Story**[51] 7407 2-8-12 **65**........ StevieDonohoe 11 52+
(Henry Spiller) *in last: plenty to do ent st: rdn over 2f out: sme hdwy fr over 1f out* **66/1**
053 **10** 3/4 **Widnes**[21] 7976 2-9-1 **71**........ EoinWalsh(3) 12 56+
(Alan Bailey) *squeezed up s: sn in rr: rdn over 2f out: no ex fr over 1f out* **20/1**
2342 **11** 1 1/2 **Elegantly Bound (IRE)**[18] 8033 2-9-1 **68**........ TomEaves 13 49+
(James Given) *hld up in rr on outer: pushed along on bnd: rdn over 2f out: sn lft bhd and pushed out after* **11/1**
040 **12** 2 3/4 **Haraka (IRE)**[46] 7548 2-8-11 **67**........ HectorCrouch(3) 7 41+
(Ralph Beckett) *in rr: struggling wl over 3f out: no imp st* **8/1**

1m 27.19s (1.19) **Going Correction** +0.075s/f (Slow) **12** Ran SP% **120.7**
Speed ratings (Par 96): **96,94,93,93,91 91,91,90,87,86 85,82**
CSF £31.60 CT £228.91 TOTE £3.30: £1.40, £3.90, £3.60; EX 34.60 Trifecta £447.60.
Owner Robert Moss and Christopher Brennan **Bred** D R Tucker **Trained** Ashtead, Surrey

FOCUS
The pace was sound for this open handicap. A tiny step forward from the winner.

8245 100% PROFIT BOOST AT 32REDSPORT.COM MAIDEN STKS (DIV I) 1m (P)
4:45 (4:46) (Class 5) 2-Y-O £3,234 (£962; £481; £240) Stalls Low

Form RPR
1 **Son Of The Stars** 2-9-5 0........ SeanLevey 9 80+
(Richard Hannon) *t.k.h bhd ldrs: rdn and led wl over 1f out: qcknd up and in command ent fnl f: pushed out wl ins fnl f: easily* **8/1**
2 3 1/4 **Opinionate** 2-9-5 0........ RobertHavlin 2 72
(Amanda Perrett) *s.s and pushed up to sit in rr-div on inner: gng wl over 2f out: rdn on inner 2f out: styd on wl fnl f: improver* **8/1**
00 **3** 1 3/4 **Outcrop (IRE)**[22] 7962 2-9-5 0........ LiamKeniry 1 68
(Hughie Morrison) *sn led: rdn over 2f out: hdd over 1f out: kpt on again ins fnl f* **14/1**
0 **4** shd **Master Archer (IRE)**[21] 7976 2-9-5 0........ TomQueally 10 68
(James Fanshawe) *settled in mid-div: rdn over 2f out: kpt on wl fr over 1f out on outer: styng on at fin: nvr nrr* **6/1**
034 **5** 1 **Lorikeet (USA)**[12] 8088 2-9-5 72........ PJMcDonald 12 65
(Mark Johnston) *settled bhd ldrs: rdn over 2f out: kpt on one pce* **7/2**[1]
0 **6** 1 1/2 **Sunovarebel**[27] 7882 2-9-5 0........ JoeyHaynes 6 62
(Alan Bailey) *racd in mid-div: rdn over 2f out: kpt on one pce fnl f* **66/1**
7 1 1/4 **Mikey Ready (USA)** 2-9-5 0........[1] LukeMorris 4 59
(Ed Walker) *racd in mid-div: effrt over 2f out: sn no imp and kpt on one pce* **4/1**[2]
8 2 **Beyond Recall** 2-9-0 0........ PatCosgrave 11 49
(Luca Cumani) *settled in 2nd: rdn jst over 2f out: wknd fr over 1f out* **12/1**
0 **9** 1 1/4 **Beyond Beyond**[22] 7963 2-9-5 0........ RobertWinston 3 51
(Hughie Morrison) *mid-div on inner: rdn over 2f out: kpt on wl fr over 1f out: nvr nrr* **50/1**
10 nk **Footman (GER)** 2-9-5 0........ AdamKirby 5 50+
(Richard Hughes) *awkward s and lost pl early: hld up in rr: n.m.r on heels ent st: nvr involved fr over 1f out* **11/2**[3]
06 **11** 2 1/2 **Look My Way**[14] 8073 2-9-5 0........ DavidProbert 8 44
(Andrew Balding) *in rr: rdn over 2f out: nvr a factor* **25/1**
0 **12** nk **Secret Poet (IRE)**[27] 7885 2-9-0 0........ WilliamCarson 7 39
(Jamie Osborne) *hld up in rr: rdn over 2f out: sn hld* **100/1**
13 hd **Glassalt** 2-9-0 0........ MartinHarley 13 38
(Michael Bell) *in rr on outer: niggled over 3f out on outer to take clsr order: rdn st: sn hld* **33/1**

1m 41.59s (1.79) **Going Correction** +0.075s/f (Slow) **13** Ran SP% **119.7**
Speed ratings (Par 96): **94,90,89,88,87 86,85,83,81,81 79,78,78**
CSF £68.62 TOTE £9.50: £2.90, £3.00, £4.80; EX 83.50 Trifecta £1477.80.
Owner Ahmad Abdulla Al Shaikh **Bred** Southill Stud **Trained** East Everleigh, Wilts

FOCUS
An interesting maiden. The level is fluid.

8246 100% PROFIT BOOST AT 32REDSPORT.COM MAIDEN STKS (DIV II) 1m (P)
5:15 (5:19) (Class 5) 2-Y-O £3,234 (£962; £481; £240) Stalls Low

Form RPR
5 **1** **Intermodal**[22] 7962 2-9-5 0........ RobertHavlin 1 76
(Amanda Perrett) *broke wl and reluctantly led for 4f: settled bhd ldr after: rdn over 2f out: picked up wl ent fnl f: sn battling w runner-up gng hd-to-hd: jst got up post* **11/4**[1]
04 **2** nse **Pete So High (GER)**[26] 7908 2-9-5 0........ SeanLevey 10 76
(Richard Hannon) *racd bhd ldrs tl led after 4f: rdn over 2f out: kpt on wl: chal and wnt hd-to-hd w wnr ins fnl f: jst lost out* **11/4**[1]

04 3 ¾ **Sussex Ranger (USA)**[21] 7977 2-9-2 0 HectorCrouch(3) 7 74
(Gary Moore) *settled bhd ldrs: rdn over 2f out: kpt on one pce tl styd on ins fnl f: gng on at fin* **8/1**[3]

5 4 2 **Alkashaaf (USA)**[77] 6671 2-9-5 0 DavidProbert 6 69
(Archie Watson) *settled bhd ldr and t.k.h: prom and rdn over 2f out: kpt on wl: hld by ldrs wl ins fnl f: eased fnl 50yds* **7/1**[2]

5 1 ¼ **Makaarim** 2-9-5 0 LukeMorris 13 66+
(Marco Botti) *in rr on outer: impr on bnd ent st: rdn over 2f out: kpt on wl fr over 1f out: nvr nrr* **8/1**[3]

6 shd **Button Up (IRE)** 2-9-0 0 GrahamGibbons 8 61+
(Sir Michael Stoute) *hld up in mid-div: rdn over 2f out: pushed out fnl f: kpt on* **11/1**

06 7 1 ¼ **Prosecution**[21] 7976 2-9-5 0 LiamKeniry 2 63
(Hughie Morrison) *settled bhd ldrs on inner: gng wl over 2f out: sn pushed along: no ex and shuffled along ins fnl f* **40/1**

8 2 ¾ **Bessemer Lady** 2-9-0 0 RichardKingscote 12 52
(Ralph Beckett) *settled in rr-div: rdn 2f out: sn no ch and pushed out fr over 1f out* **16/1**

9 ½ **Seaborn (IRE)** 2-9-5 0 RobertWinston 5 55
(Simon Hodgson) *t.k.h in rr: shuffled along fr over 2f out: kpt on past btn horses fr over 1f out* **100/1**

0 10 3 ½ **Noble Behest**[12] 8088 2-8-12 0 TylerSaunders(7) 3 47
(Marcus Tregoning) *mid-div: rdn 2f out: no ex fr over 1f out* **100/1**

11 2 **Mambo Dancer** 2-9-5 0 PJMcDonald 4 42
(Mark Johnston) *in rr: rdn along bef 1/2-way: lft bhd fr 2f out* **16/1**

12 3 ¼ **Innstigator** 2-9-5 0 KierenFox 11 34
(Ralph J Smith) *s.s: sn pushed up into mid-div: pushed along over 2f out: wknd fr over 1f out* **66/1**

00 13 2 ¼ **Lady Of York**[27] 7883 2-9-0 0 JoeyHaynes 9 24
(Alan Bailey) *a in rr* **150/1**

1m 41.16s (1.36) **Going Correction** +0.075s/f (Slow) **13** Ran SP% **114.7**
Speed ratings (Par 96): **96,95,95,93,91 91,90,87,87,83 81,78,76**
CSF £8.50 TOTE £3.20: £1.40, £2.00, £2.40; EX 10.90 Trifecta £55.60.
Owner K Abdullah **Bred** Juddmonte Farms Ltd **Trained** Pulborough, W Sussex

FOCUS
Not a bad maiden. They went an honest pace and it paid to race handy.

8247 32RED CASINO MAIDEN STKS 1m (P)
5:45 (5:47) (Class 5) 3-Y-O+ **£3,234** (£962; £481; £240) **Stalls** Low

Form RPR

5432 1 **Senses Of Dubai**[27] 7894 3-9-5 71 WilliamCarson 1 66
(Jamie Osborne) *marginally led: rdn over 2f out: 2 l up ent fnl f: kpt up to work fnl 110yds: hld on* **1/1**[1]

2 nk **Tifl** 3-9-5 0 LiamKeniry 6 65
(Heather Main) *missed break and t.k.h in rr: shkn up 2f out: prog being rdn along ent fnl f: gaining fnl 150yds: nt get to wnr* **16/1**[3]

5660 3 7 **Josh Perry**[25] 7937 3-9-5 45 (v[1]) RyanTate 5 48
(Rod Millman) *disp ld: rdn over 2f out: no ex fr over 1f out* **40/1**

4 4 2 **Gamrah (IRE)**[113] 5527 3-9-0 0 MartinHarley 8 38
(James Tate) *settled in 3rd: rdn on outer over 2f out: one pce after* **11/10**[2]

000/ 5 2 **Birdie Must Fly**[792] 7014 4-9-1 39 TimmyMurphy 3 33
(Jimmy Fox) *racd in 4th: rdn over 2f out: no ex fnl f* **66/1**

00 6 2 ¼ **Shakshuka (IRE)**[26] 7904 4-9-1 0 SteveDrowne 4 28
(Seamus Mullins) *racd in 5th: shkn up over 3f out: btn fr over 1f out* **50/1**

1m 41.4s (1.60) **Going Correction** +0.075s/f (Slow)
WFA 3 from 4yo 1lb **6** Ran SP% **109.4**
Speed ratings (Par 103): **95,94,87,85,83 81**
CSF £15.23 TOTE £2.20: £1.30, £4.30; EX 13.70 Trifecta £55.90.
Owner Nas Bashir **Bred** Shadwell Estate Company Limited **Trained** Upper Lambourn, Berks

FOCUS
The pace was honest for this uncompetitive maiden. The winner didn't need to match his previous maiden form to win.

8248 RACING UK HD H'CAP 7f (P)
6:15 (6:16) (Class 6) (0-65,65) 3-Y-O **£2,587** (£770; £384; £192) **Stalls** Low

Form RPR

3031 1 **Fire Diamond**[30] 7850 3-8-13 57 (p) RichardKingscote 5 66
(Tom Dascombe) *hld up in mid-div on inner: trckd runner-up over 1f out: sn rdn on inner and wnt hd-to-hd w runner-up ent fnl f: kpt on wl tl led nr fin* **7/2**[2]

1041 2 nk **Garter (IRE)**[18] 8026 3-9-5 63 LukeMorris 2 71
(Charles Hills) *settled bhd ldrs on inner: travelling strly over 2f out: rdn between horses over 1f out and sn led: kpt on wl gng hd-to-hd w wnr ins fnl f: kpt on tl hld fnl strides* **4/1**[3]

4512 3 2 ½ **Music Major**[7] 8154 3-9-7 65 AdamBeschizza 7 66+
(Michael Attwater) *hld up in rr: plenty to do over 2f out: sn rdn and stl in last of pack over 1f out: gd prog ent fnl f: tk 3rd wl ins fnl f: gng on nr fin* **5/2**[1]

20-5 4 1 **Lightsome**[75] 6754 3-8-13 57 MartinHarley 4 56
(Harry Dunlop) *settled in rr-div: shkn up and rdn over 1f out: ev ch ent fnl f: no ex ins fnl f and lost 3rd nr fin* **10/1**

6664 5 1 ¾ **Sexton Blake (IRE)**[14] 8064 3-9-0 61 (p) HectorCrouch(3) 6 55
(Gary Moore) *settled in mid-div: rdn over 2f out: kpt on one pce* **7/1**

4320 6 4 **Deer Song**[7] 8149 3-8-13 57 DannyBrock 3 40
(John Bridger) *racd in 3rd on outer: rdn over 2f out: struggling over 1f out: wknd after* **50/1**

2446 7 ½ **Tahiti One**[56] 7276 3-8-9 53 WilliamCarson 9 35
(Tony Carroll) *racd wl in rr: wl bhd ent st: sn rdn: no ex fr over 1f out* **40/1**

2526 8 ½ **Rebel State (IRE)**[13] 8086 3-9-6 64 (v) AdamKirby 8 44
(Richard Spencer) *sn led at stdy pce: qcknd tempo ent st: shkn up and rdn over 2f out: hdd over 1f out: wknd fnl f* **9/1**

6000 9 2 **Arctic Flower (IRE)**[18] 8026 3-8-7 51 JosephineGordon 1 26
(John Bridger) *settled bhd ldr on rail: rdn over 2f out: rdn and pushed aside over 1f out: wknd qckly after* **40/1**

1m 26.32s (0.32) **Going Correction** +0.075s/f (Slow) **9** Ran SP% **109.2**
Speed ratings (Par 98): **101,100,97,96,94 90,89,88,86**
CSF £16.14 CT £35.95 TOTE £5.00: £1.20, £1.60, £1.20; EX 19.70 Trifecta £42.40.
Owner John Brown **Bred** John Brown **Trained** Malpas, Cheshire

FOCUS
They went a good pace for this open handicap which was dominated by the two last-time-out winners.

8249 32RED H'CAP 1m 3f (P)
6:45 (6:46) (Class 4) (0-85,83) 3-Y-O+ **£4,690** (£1,395; £697; £348) **Stalls** Low

Form RPR

041- 1 **Towerlands Park (IRE)**[364] 8153 3-9-6 83 GeorgeBaker 3 97+
(Michael Bell) *settled bhd ldrs: travelling strly ent st: cruised into ld 2f out: rdn over 1f out: in command ins fnl f: chal cl home but plld out more* **6/4**[1]

655 2 1 **Coillte Cailin (IRE)**[32] 7816 6-9-10 83 DanielTudhope 12 92+
(David O'Meara) *hld up in rr-dividon: c wdst st: rdn over 2f out: kpt on wl fr over 1f out to take 2nd nr fin* **11/1**[3]

3535 3 nk **Dolphin Village (IRE)**[40] 7666 6-9-4 82 CharlieBennett(5) 7 90
(Jane Chapple-Hyam) *hld up in mid-div: rdn over 2f out: kpt on wl fr over 1f out tl lost 2nd cl home* **8/1**[2]

0600 4 3 ½ **Dutch Uncle**[28] 7869 4-9-10 83 MartinHarley 13 85
(Ed Dunlop) *hld up in mid-div: gd hdwy over 2f out: rdn over 1f out: nt qckn but kpt on ins fnl f* **8/1**[2]

4633 5 ½ **Alcatraz (IRE)**[37] 6316 4-9-5 78 (tp) PatCosgrave 14 79
(George Baker) *hld up in rr: rdn 2f out on inner: kpt on wl fr over 1f out: nvr nrr* **25/1**

6052 6 nse **Eurystheus (IRE)**[14] 8077 7-9-1 77 (tp) AlistairRawlinson(3) 5 78
(Michael Appleby) *chsd ldrs: rdn over 2f out: kpt on one pce* **11/1**[3]

115 7 2 ¼ **Tangramm**[203] 2377 4-9-10 83 RobertWinston 2 80
(Dean Ivory) *hld up in rr-div: rdn and prog fr over 1f out: no ex fnl f* **14/1**

3661 8 3 ½ **Inniscastle Lad**[51] 7419 4-9-8 81 (b) AdamKirby 11 72
(Stuart Williams) *led: rdn over 2f out: sn hdd: kpt on one pce after* **8/1**[2]

9 shd **Foresee (GER)**[85] 3-9-6 83 DavidProbert 1 74
(Tony Carroll) *chsd ldrs on inner: rdn over 2f out: sn no ex and wknd fr over 1f out* **14/1**

4046 10 ½ **Energia Fox (BRZ)**[11] 8123 6-9-9 82 DavidNolan 9 72
(Richard Fahey) *hld up in rr: rdn 2f out: no imp after* **16/1**

0P-0 11 6 **Kafeel (USA)**[32] 7816 5-8-13 72 (p) SteveDrowne 10 52
(Linda Jewell) *settled bhd ldrs on inner: rdn 2f out: wknd nt long after* **100/1**

0-24 12 1 ¼ **Golden Jubilee (USA)**[307] 447 7-9-6 79 (p) ThomasBrown 6 57
(Nigel Twiston-Davies) *settled bhd ldrs on outer: rdn over 2f out: sn hld* **25/1**

0000 13 15 **Slowfoot (GER)**[22] 7967 8-9-9 82 TimmyMurphy 4 34
(Jim Best) *hld up in rr: nvr involved: t.o* **66/1**

2m 20.87s (-1.03) **Going Correction** +0.075s/f (Slow)
WFA 3 from 4yo+ 4lb **13** Ran SP% **119.4**
Speed ratings (Par 105): **106,105,105,102,102 102,100,97,97,97 93,92,81**
CSF £18.49 CT £106.82 TOTE £2.30: £1.20, £4.10, £2.30; EX 22.50 Trifecta £143.10.
Owner W J and T C O Gredley **Bred** Lynch Bages Ltd **Trained** Newmarket, Suffolk

FOCUS
A competitive handicap run at a sound pace. It's been rated around the third.

8250 32REDSPORT.COM H'CAP 2m (P)
7:15 (7:16) (Class 4) (0-85,85) 3-Y-O+ **£4,690** (£1,395; £697; £348) **Stalls** Low

Form RPR

613/ 1 **Beltor**[29] 7043 5-9-4 75 PatCosgrave 5 86
(Robert Stephens) *hld up in rr-div on inner: shkn up over 3f out and tk clsr order in centre fr 2f out: rdn to chse clr ldr wl over 1f out: had ldr in sights ent fnl f: kpt on wl to ld under 1f out: pushed out nr fin* **5/1**

3-13 2 1 ¼ **Wolf Of Windlesham (IRE)**[24] 2392 4-8-13 70 JFEgan 1 79
(Stuart Edmunds) *settled bhd ldrs: rdn over 2f out and ev ch on inner 1f out: tk 2nd jst under 1f out: kpt on wl* **7/2**[2]

214 3 3 ¼ **Timekeeping (IRE)**[21] 7980 3-9-6 85 AdamKirby 4 90
(Saeed bin Suroor) *racd in 3rd: pressed ldr at 1/2-way: kicked and committed for home off bnd: kpt on wl and clr advantage 2f out: hrd rdn over 1f out w ld diminishing: hdd under 1f out: wknd nr fin* **7/4**[1]

4555 4 2 **Percy Veer**[21] 7979 4-9-11 82 [1] GeorgeBaker 6 85
(Sylvester Kirk) *hld up in rr: rdn 3f out: kpt on one pce fr over 1f out: nvr nrr* **4/1**[3]

5156 5 1 ½ **Fern Owl**[36] 7732 4-9-1 72 (b) LiamKeniry 7 73
(Hughie Morrison) *settled bhd ldrs: rdn over 2f out: kpt on one pce after* **14/1**

1131 6 nk **Bracken Brae**[20] 7987 4-8-13 70 StevieDonohoe 11 71
(Mark H Tompkins) *settled in rr-div: rdn over 2f out: no ch w ldr ent fnl f: pushed out* **20/1**

3100 7 4 ½ **Gleese The Devil (IRE)**[16] 8051 5-9-8 79 DavidNolan 12 74
(Richard Fahey) *hld up in rr: rdn over 2f out on inner: no ex sn after* **33/1**

0000 8 6 **Wordiness**[20] 7993 8-8-6 70 KatherineGlenister(7) 13 58
(David Evans) *in rr: no imp fr over 3f out: nvr involved* **50/1**

10-0 9 8 **Katie Gale**[22] 2194 6-9-7 78 AndrewMullen 3 57
(Michael Appleby) *led: hdd over 3f out: sn rdn and wknd fr 2f out: t.o* **66/1**

0044 10 1 ¼ **Knight's Parade (IRE)**[21] 5334 6-9-6 77 (tp) DougieCostello 9 54
(Sarah Humphrey) *a in rr: rdn and no ex fr over 2f out: t.o* **66/1**

0/42 11 6 **Harry Hunt**[12] 7183 9-9-8 82 CallumShepherd(3) 10 52
(Graeme McPherson) *settled bhd ldrs on outer: disp over 6f out: rdn wl over 2f out: eased fr over 1f out: t.o* **33/1**

4331 12 54 **Alberta (IRE)**[30] 6267 7-9-12 83 TimmyMurphy 8
(Jim Best) *a in rr: struggling wl over 4f out: sn eased: t.o* **25/1**

3m 30.44s (0.34) **Going Correction** +0.075s/f (Slow)
WFA 3 from 4yo+ 8lb **12** Ran SP% **121.4**
Speed ratings (Par 105): **102,101,99,98,98 97,95,92,88,87 84,57**
CSF £22.12 CT £43.18 TOTE £4.90: £2.40, £1.90, £1.10; EX 27.20 Trifecta £74.80.
Owner Alison Mossop **Bred** Stewart Aitken **Trained** Penhow, Newport

FOCUS
The pace was steady for this fair handicap. It's possibly better than rated.

T/Jkpt: Not Won. T/Plt: £117.20 to a £1 stake. Pool: £73,280.66 - 456.23 winning units. T/Qpdt: £19.40 to a £1 stake. Pool: £8,598.59 - 326.36 winning units. **Cathal Gahan**

8227 LINGFIELD (L-H)

Wednesday, December 7

OFFICIAL GOING: Polytrack: standard

Wind: Fresh, half behind Weather: Cloudy, mild

8251 SUN BETS BET £10 GET £20 FREE H'CAP — 1m 1y(P)

12:05 (12:06) (Class 4) (0-85,85) 3-Y-O+ **£5,175** (£1,540; £769; £384) **Stalls** High

Form RPR

0006 **1** **Forceful Appeal (USA)**[6] 8177 8-9-6 **84** .... LukeMorris 11 93
(Simon Dow) *stdd fr wd draw and hld up: prog 1/2-way to trck ldrs over 2f out: shkn up over 1f out: r.o to ld last 150yds: readily* **6/1**[3]

-043 **2** ¾ **Constantino (IRE)**[178] 3187 3-9-1 **80** .... JackGarritty 3 90+
(Richard Fahey) *cl up on inner: trying to make an effrt whn nowhere to go and hmpd jst over 1f out: swtchd rt and r.o to take 2nd last 75yds: no ch to chal* **5/1**[2]

6201 **3** 1 **Carolinae**[26] 7903 4-9-6 **84** .... StevieDonohoe 9 89
(Charlie Fellowes) *hld up in rr fr wd draw: prog over 1f out: shkn up and r.o fnl f to take 3rd last strides* **9/2**[1]

0001 **4** ½ **Mr Christopher (IRE)**[18] 8037 4-8-12 **76** ....(p) RichardKingscote 7 80
(Tom Dascombe) *led after 2f: hrd pressed over 1f out: hdd and one pce last 150yds* **12/1**

31 **5** nk **Red Trooper (FR)**[42] 7616 3-8-13 **78** .... SteveDrowne 1 81
(George Baker) *led 2f: styd cl up: drvn to chal on inner 1f out and sn upsides: one pce last 150yds* **5/1**[2]

5000 **6** shd **Take The Helm**[26] 7902 3-9-4 **83** .... TomQueally 5 89+
(Brian Meehan) *trckd ldrs: lost pl 3f out and in rr: making prog whn nt clr run 1f out: styd on nr fin but nt rcvr* **5/1**[2]

5526 **7** ½ **Zaeem**[22] 7968 7-9-4 **85** ....(p) HectorCrouch(3) 4 87
(Ivan Furtado) *pressed ldr after 3f: rdn to chal over 1f out: wknd ins fnl f* **20/1**

8 2 ¾ **My Fantasea (IRE)**[61] 7134 3-9-1 **80** .... AdamKirby 8 75
(David Evans) *pressed ldrs on outer: rdn 3f out: on terms wl over 1f out: sn wknd* **10/1**

0-46 **9** 1 ¾ **Intensical (IRE)**[152] 4094 5-8-13 **77** .... TomEaves 6 68
(Ivan Furtado) *hld up and sn wl in rr: detached in 10th over 2f out and pushed along: no ch after and nvr involved* **33/1**

3156 **10** 1 ½ **Bridge Of Sighs**[40] 7666 4-8-11 **75** .... PatCosgrave 10 63
(Martin Smith) *dwlt: a in rr: wknd over 1f out* **10/1**

306 **11** 17 **Torch**[51] 7418 3-9-0 **79** .... TimmyMurphy 2 28
(John Butler) *struggling in last after 3f: t.o* **33/1**

1m 36.84s (-1.36) **Going Correction** -0.05s/f (Stan)
WFA 3 from 4yo+ 1lb **11** Ran SP% **119.0**
Speed ratings (Par 105): **104,103,102,101,101 101,100,98,96,94 77**
CSF £35.77 CT £150.81 TOTE £8.80: £2.60, £2.40, £1.20; EX 41.20 Trifecta £158.60.
Owner Mark McAllister **Bred** Juddmonte Farms Inc **Trained** Ashtead, Surrey

FOCUS
Probably a fair race for the grade, run at a solid pace. The third and fourth help set the standard.

8252 SUNBETS.CO.UK (S) STKS — 7f 1y(P)

12:35 (12:35) (Class 6) 3-Y-O+ **£2,911** (£866; £432; £216) **Stalls** Low

Form RPR

2005 **1** **Chelwood Gate (IRE)**[18] 8035 6-8-9 73 ....(v) HectorCrouch(3) 8 74
(Patrick Chamings) *s.s: racd in last trio and stl there jst over 2f out: gd prog over 1f out and swtchd to inner: sustained effrt to ld last 75yds* **5/1**[3]

2012 **2** nk **Ballylare**[106] 5743 3-9-4 80 .... KierenFox 10 79
(John Best) *pressed ldr: led 3f out: drvn for home over 1f out: kpt on but hdd last 75yds* **3/1**[1]

6104 **3** 1 ¾ **Dana's Present**[18] 8035 7-9-4 72 .... LiamKeniry 6 74
(Tom Dascombe) *hld up in rr: prog to trck ldrs 2f out: shkn up and styd on to take 3rd last 100yds: nt pce to chal* **6/1**

0024 **4** ¾ **Brasted (IRE)**[34] 7778 4-8-12 71 ....(t) MartinHarley 7 66
(Lee Carter) *racd on outer: sn chsd ldng pair: pressed wnr wl over 2f out: rdn and nt qckn wl over 1f out: one pce after* **4/1**[2]

6013 **5** 1 ¼ **Hipz (IRE)**[18] 8026 5-8-13 59 ....(p) PatCosgrave 2 64
(Laura Mongan) *t.k.h: cl up: chsd ldng pair over 2f out tl jst ins fnl f: wknd* **11/1**

4560 **6** ½ **Prim And Proper**[7] 8156 5-8-13 59 ....(b) DanielMuscutt 4 63
(John Flint) *hld up in midfield: shkn up to cl on ldrs on inner over 1f out: fdd ins fnl f* **20/1**

6600 **7** ¾ **Lucky Di**[7] 8163 6-8-7 65 ....[1] LukeMorris 11 55
(Peter Hedger) *hld up in rr: shkn up over 2f out and detached fr ldng gp: nvr any ch but plugged on fnl f* **14/1**

5002 **8** 7 **Greyfriarschorista**[163] 3726 9-9-4 77 .... AdamKirby 5 47
(David Evans) *in tch tl wknd 2f out: bhd fnl f* **5/1**[3]

5000 **9** 6 **Jackpot**[25] 7944 6-8-0 41 ....(p) LuluStanford(7) 1 20
(Brendan Powell) *led to 3f out: sn wknd qckly: bhd over 1f out* **66/1**

0210 **10** 14 **Layla's Hero (IRE)**[78] 6644 9-9-9 72 ....(v) CallumShepherd(3) 3 1
(Roger Teal) *sn pushed along in last: brief effrt on outer over 3f out: wknd rapidly over 2f out: t.o* **16/1**

1m 24.05s (-0.75) **Going Correction** -0.05s/f (Stan) **10** Ran SP% **119.8**
Speed ratings (Par 101): **102,101,99,98,97 96,95,87,81,65**
CSF £21.00 TOTE £5.80: £2.00, £1.50, £2.00; EX 25.30 Trifecta £154.50.No bid for the winner. Ballylare was claimed by Mr L A Carter for £6,000.
Owner P R Chamings **Bred** Jusoor Syndicate **Trained** Baughurst, Hants

FOCUS
This seller was well run. The fifth and sixth are the key to the level.

8253 BETWAY H'CAP (DIV I) — 1m 4f (P)

1:05 (1:06) (Class 5) (0-75,75) 3-Y-O+ **£3,234** (£962; £481; £240) **Stalls** Low

Form RPR

5312 **1** **Ride The Lightning**[36] 7732 3-9-5 **75** .... LukeMorris 2 84+
(Archie Watson) *trckd ldng pair: clsd to ld 2f out: drvn 2 l clr over 1f out: kpt on* **7/4**[1]

4015 **2** 1 ½ **Santiburi Spring**[20] 7993 3-8-11 **67** .... KierenFox 1 72
(John Best) *trckd ldrs: rdn over 2f out: no imp tl styd on fnl f to take 2nd last 100yds: unable to chal* **6/1**[2]

3610 **3** 1 ¼ **Mercy Me**[46] 7531 4-9-5 **70** .... AdamKirby 5 73
(John Ryan) *hld up in 6th: prog on outer over 3f out: rdn to chal 2f out: outpcd by wnr over 1f out: one pce and lost 2nd last 100yds* **6/1**[2]

4430 **4** ½ **Dakota City**[36] 7732 5-9-10 **75** ....(v) AdamBeschizza 3 77
(Julia Feilden) *dwlt: hld up in 7th: effrt over 2f out: rdn and kpt on same pce fr over 1f out* **12/1**

0126 **5** 1 ¼ **Safira Menina**[7] 8162 4-9-9 **74** .... RyanPowell 8 76+
(Martin Smith) *awkward to load: slowly away: hld up in last: prog 2f out: trying to cl but pl prospects at best whn hmpd 1f out: nt rcvr* **12/1**

1544 **6** ½ **Mystikana**[50] 7429 3-8-13 **69** ....[1] SteveDrowne 9 68
(Marcus Tregoning) *pressed ldr: led 3f out to 2f out: wknd fnl f* **6/1**[2]

5360 **7** 5 **Goldslinger (FR)**[144] 4381 4-9-7 **72** .... RobertWinston 6 63
(Dean Ivory) *chsd ldrs: rdn over 3f out: wknd over 2f out* **20/1**

5131 **8** 1 **Kirtling**[40] 7657 5-9-4 **69** ....(t) MartinLane 7 59
(Andi Brown) *dwlt: hld up in last pair: prog on wd outside 3f out: drvn and wd bnd 2f out: wknd qckly over 1f out: eased* **7/1**[3]

5540 **9** 9 **Cornelious (IRE)**[21] 7973 4-9-2 **67** ....(p) RobertTart 4 42
(Clifford Lines) *led: rdn 4f out: hdd 3f out: wknd rapidly over 2f out* **8/1**

2m 30.6s (-2.40) **Going Correction** -0.05s/f (Stan)
WFA 3 from 4yo+ 5lb **9** Ran SP% **123.0**
Speed ratings (Par 103): **106,105,104,103,103 102,99,98,92**
CSF £13.62 CT £55.81 TOTE £2.50: £1.10, £1.80, £2.40; EX 12.50 Trifecta £46.40.
Owner The Ride The Lightning Partnership **Bred** Usk Valley Stud **Trained** Upper Lambourn, West Berks

FOCUS
This ordinary handicap was run at a fairly leisurely pace until around halfway, and it was the slower division by 0.41sec. It's been rated around the second and third.

8254 BETWAY H'CAP (DIV II) — 1m 4f (P)

1:35 (1:35) (Class 5) (0-75,75) 3-Y-O+ **£3,234** (£962; £481; £240) **Stalls** Low

Form RPR

2402 **1** **Artful Rogue (IRE)**[7] 8161 5-9-6 **74** .... KieranShoemark(3) 3 85
(Amanda Perrett) *hld up in tch: wnt 3rd over 2f out but 4 l bhd ldng pair: clsd qckly over 1f out: rdn to ld 150yds out: wanting to hang but sn drew away* **13/8**[1]

0556 **2** 1 ¾ **River Dart (IRE)**[63] 7067 4-9-10 **75** .... GeorgeBaker 1 83
(Tony Carroll) *trckd ldrs: wnt 2nd over 3f out: led 2f out gng strly: shkn up over 1f out: hdd and outpcd last 150yds but wl clr of rest* **9/2**[3]

0665 **3** 9 **Topaling**[7] 8162 5-8-12 **63** .... StevieDonohoe 2 57
(Mark H Tompkins) *in tch: rdn and no prog over 3f out: sn outpcd: kpt on u.p fr 2f out to take modest 3rd last 100yds* **20/1**

450 **4** 4 **Hungerford**[12] 8100 4-9-3 **68** ....[1] TomQueally 8 55
(Eve Johnson Houghton) *led: drvn and hdd 2f out: wknd qckly over 1f out: lost 3rd last 100yds* **12/1**

2145 **5** hd **Pastoral Music**[7] 8161 3-9-0 **75** .... CharlieBennett(5) 7 62
(Hughie Morrison) *slowly away: rapid prog to press ldng pair after 2f on outer: lost pl and wknd wl over 2f out* **4/1**[2]

6320 **6** ¾ **Maroc**[48] 7492 3-8-13 **69** ....[1] LukeMorris 9 55
(Paul Cole) *t.k.h: hld up in last pair: rdn over 3f out: lft wl bhd over 2f out* **5/1**

0500 **7** 2 ½ **Comedy House**[127] 4995 8-8-10 **61** oh9 ....(v) KieranO'Neill 5 43
(Michael Madgwick) *slowly away: hld up in last: rdn and no prog 3f out: sn no ch* **33/1**

241 **8** 3 ½ **Officer Drivel (IRE)**[102] 5895 5-9-5 **70** .... TimmyMurphy 6 46
(Jim Best) *pressed ldr to over 3f out: wknd qckly over 2f out* **14/1**

2m 30.19s (-2.81) **Going Correction** -0.05s/f (Stan)
WFA 3 from 4yo+ 5lb **8** Ran SP% **115.0**
Speed ratings (Par 103): **107,105,99,97,97 96,94,92**
CSF £9.19 CT £103.51 TOTE £2.70: £1.30, £2.30, £4.00; EX 9.50 Trifecta £116.40.
Owner Mr & Mrs F Cotton, Mr & Mrs P Conway **Bred** Michael Morrissey **Trained** Pulborough, W Sussex

FOCUS
The quicker division by 0.41sec, the first two finishing well clear. The first two are both on good marks compared to their back form and there's a chance both could prove a bit better than rated.

8255 BETWAY MEDIAN AUCTION MAIDEN STKS — 1m 2f (P)

2:05 (2:05) (Class 6) 3-5-Y-O **£2,587** (£770; £384; £192) **Stalls** Low

Form RPR

0030 **1** **Sunshineandbubbles**[11] 8125 3-8-11 54 ....(p) GeorgeDowning(3) 5 63
(Daniel Mark Loughnane) *led: pressed 3f out: narrowly hdd over 2f out: fought on and led again over 1f out: jst hld on* **16/1**

662 **2** shd **The Salmon Man**[21] 7973 4-9-8 73 .... AdamKirby 6 68
(Brendan Powell) *hld up in 3rd: trckd ldr 1/2-way: shkn up to chal 3f out: rdn to take narrow ld over 2f out: hdd over 1f out: jst hld after tl clsd nr fin: jst failed* **1/2**[1]

0-2 **3** ½ **Mornington**[7] 8157 3-8-12 0 .... TylerSaunders(7) 1 67
(Marcus Tregoning) *dwlt and sltly impeded s: hld up in last: brought to chal on outer 3f out: hanging and nt qckn 2f out: hld after but clsd on ldng pair nr fin* **9/4**[2]

0006 **4** 4 **Chelabella**[36] 7755 3-8-7 63 ....(p) LuluStanford(7) 3 60+
(Michael Bell) *trckd ldr to 1/2-way: dropped to last 3f out: pushed along over 2f out: in tch but hld whn sddle slipped and nrly uns rdr 1f out: wknd* **14/1**[3]

2m 8.06s (1.46) **Going Correction** -0.05s/f (Stan)
WFA 3 from 4yo 3lb **4** Ran SP% **110.0**
Speed ratings (Par 101): **92,91,91,88**
CSF £26.14 TOTE £17.00; EX 31.80 Trifecta £52.70.
Owner Amazing Racing **Bred** Mickley Stud **Trained** Baldwin's Gate, Staffs

FOCUS
A tight finish to this weak event. It's not easy to find the positives in this race.

8256 SUNBETS.CO.UK H'CAP — 7f 1y(P)

2:35 (2:35) (Class 3) (0-95,95) 3-Y-O+ **£7,246** (£2,168; £1,084; £542; £270) **Stalls** Low

Form RPR

0022 **1** **He's No Saint**[20] 7984 5-9-4 **92** ....(v) DanielTudhope 8 99
(David O'Meara) *mde all: rdn over 1f out: hrd pressed last 100yds: hld on wl* **5/2**[1]

0000 **2** shd **Shyron**[41] 7651 5-9-2 **90** .... RyanPowell 6 96
(George Margarson) *s.i.s: hld up in last pair: prog on inner over 1f out: tk 2nd last 100yds and str chal after: jst hld last strides* **12/1**

0510 **3** ½ **Mr Bossy Boots (IRE)**[133] 4758 5-9-3 **94** ....(t) KieranShoemark(3) 7 98
(Amanda Perrett) *hld up in last trio: shkn up over 2f out: prog on outer over 1f out: rdn and r.o fnl f to take 3rd last strides* **6/1**[3]

0505 **4** hd **Joey's Destiny (IRE)**[59] 7186 6-8-13 **87** .... SteveDrowne 2 91
(George Baker) *hld up in midfield: shkn up over 2f out: hanging and nt qckn over 1f out: styd on ins fnl f to press for 3rd nr fin* **10/1**

6110 **5** nse **Pearl Spectre (USA)**[6] 8176 5-8-9 **86** .... CallumShepherd(3) 5 90
(Phil McEntee) *chsd wnr: rdn 2f out: no imp and hld 1f out: lost 2nd and one pce last 100yds* **6/1**

0520 **6** nk **Gallipoli (IRE)**[165] 3635 3-8-13 **87** .... JackGarritty 4 90
(Richard Fahey) *disp 3rd pl to 1/2-way: rdn and struggling over 2f out: rallied 1f out: kpt on nr fin* **12/1**

4065 **7** 1 **Presumido (IRE)**[26] 7902 6-8-7 **81** .... LukeMorris 1 81
(Simon Dow) *t.k.h: trckd ldng pair: rdn 2f out: no imp jst over 1f out: sn lost pl and fdd* **8/1**

6003 **8** 1 **Grey Mirage**[25] 7933 7-9-7 **95** ....(p) MartinHarley 9 92
(Marco Botti) *t.k.h: hld up in last: stl there whn shkn up over 1f out: no prog* **7/2**[2]

1m 23.04s (-1.76) **Going Correction** -0.05s/f (Stan) **8** Ran SP% **117.3**
Speed ratings (Par 107): **108,107,107,107,107 106,105,104**
CSF £34.83 CT £142.63 TOTE £3.10: £1.20, £4.70, £1.90; EX 42.40 Trifecta £312.60.
Owner Peter R Ball & All About York Partners **Bred** Follow The Flag Partnership **Trained** Upper Helmsley, N Yorks
■ Stewards' Enquiry : Callum Shepherd two-day ban: use of whip (21-22 Dec)

FOCUS
A tight finish to this good handicap, which was only 0.84sec outside the standard. It's been rated as ordinary form for the grade.

8257 DOWNLOAD THE BETWAY APP H'CAP 1m 2f (P)
3:05 (3:05) (Class 6) (0-65,65) 3-Y-O+ **£2,587** (£770; £384; £192) **Stalls** Low

Form RPR

0051 **1** **General Hazard (IRE)**[5] 8194 3-9-3 **65** 6ex..................... PatCosgrave 1 75+
(Michael Bell) *hld up in midfield: prog over 2f out: rdn over 1f out: clsd to ld last 100yds: drvn clr* **4/6**[1]

42P- **2** 1 1/4 **Goodby Inheritence**[384] 7901 4-9-4 **63** ....(t) GeorgeBaker 8 70
(Seamus Durack) *hld up in midfield alongside wnr: prog over 2f out: rdn over 1f out: styd on wl to take 2nd last 50yds but no threat* **7/1**[2]

4660 **3** 1 1/4 **Combe Hay (FR)**[58] 7214 3-9-0 **65** ....[1] LouisSteward(3) 9 69
(Henry Spiller) *trckd ldng pair: wnt 2nd wl over 2f out: rdn to ld wl over 1f out: fnd little in front: hdd and outpcd last 100yds* **12/1**

5426 **4** 3/4 **Estibdaad (IRE)**[28] 7870 6-9-2 **64** ....(t) CallumShepherd(3) 6 67
(Paddy Butler) *led 1f: trckd ldr: led wl over 2f out: hdd wl over 1f out: one pce ins fnl f* **12/1**

2000 **5** hd **Tommys Geal**[28] 7870 4-9-2 **61** .... DanielMuscutt 2 63
(Michael Madgwick) *hld up in rr: prog 2f out: 7th 1f out: rdn and styd on: nrst fin* **20/1**

3340 **6** 1/2 **Chandon Elysees**[42] 7619 3-9-2 **64** .... FergusSweeney 4 65
(Gary Moore) *trckd ldrs: cl up and rdn 2f out: one pce fr over 1f out* **20/1**

0U22 **7** 1/2 **Shining Romeo**[18] 8038 4-9-2 **61** .... LukeMorris 3 62
(Denis Quinn) *t.k.h: trckd ldrs: chsd ldng pair over 2f out: nt clr run bhd them over 1f out: sn lost 3rd and fdd* **8/1**[3]

20B **8** 2 3/4 **Diletta Tommasa (IRE)**[26] 7905 6-9-2 **61** .... JosephineGordon 11 56
(Daniel Mark Loughnane) *slowly away and early reminders in detached last: effrt on wd outside over 3f out: lft bhd by ldng gp over 2f out* **20/1**

-040 **9** 1 1/4 **Norse Castle**[35] 7775 3-9-3 **65** .... JackGarritty 7 58
(Martin Bosley) *t.k.h: hld up towards rr: rdn and no prog over 2f out: no ch after* **100/1**

4304 **10** 1/2 **Tyrsal (IRE)**[13] 8085 5-9-2 **61** ....(p) AdamBeschizza 13 53
(Clifford Lines) *slowly away: hld up wl in rr: no prog whn short of room briefly 2f out* **14/1**

51P5 **11** 1 **Heads You Win**[27] 7890 3-9-2 **64** .... TimmyMurphy 5 54
(Jamie Osborne) *trckd ldrs: trapped bhd wkng rival fr wl over 2f out and dropped to rr sn after: no ch over 1f out* **40/1**

502- **12** 1 1/2 **Idle Talker (IRE)**[415] 7350 4-9-6 **65** .... LiamJones 10 52
(Nick Gifford) *nvr bttr than midfield: lft bhd over 2f out* **33/1**

0000 **13** 4 **Barren Brook**[11] 8124 9-8-13 **65** .... OllieJago(7) 12 45
(Laura Mongan) *dwlt: pushed up on outer to chse ldrs: wknd qckly over 2f out* **50/1**

4060 **14** 8 **Chilworth Bells**[12] 8100 4-9-5 **64** ....(b[1]) MartinLane 14 28
(Conor Dore) *furiously drvn to ld after 1f fr wd draw: hdd & wknd rapidly wl over 2f out: t.o* **66/1**

2m 5.48s (-1.12) **Going Correction** -0.05s/f (Stan)
WFA 3 from 4yo+ 3lb **14** Ran SP% **129.8**
Speed ratings (Par 101): **102,101,100,99,99 98,98,96,95,94 94,92,89,83**
CSF £5.65 CT £41.12 TOTE £1.40: £1.10, £2.70, £4.40; EX 7.40 Trifecta £100.30.
Owner R P B Michaelson **Bred** London Thoroughbred Services Ltd **Trained** Newmarket, Suffolk
■ Stewards' Enquiry : Josephine Gordon jockey said that the filly was slowly away
Luke Morris jockey said the gelding was denied a clear run
Timmy Murphy jockey said that the filly was denied a clear run

FOCUS
This looks fair form for the grade. The fourth is among those that helps set the level.

8258 SUNBETS.CO.UK ALL-WEATHER "HANDS AND HEELS" APPRENTICE SERIES H'CAP (PART OF RACING EXCELLENCE) 1m 1y(P)
3:35 (3:36) (Class 6) (0-65,65) 3-Y-O+ **£2,587** (£770; £384; £192) **Stalls** High

Form RPR

4035 **1** **Seek The Fair Land**[22] 7964 10-9-6 **63** ....(v) JaneElliott 1 70
(Lee Carter) *hld up: stl in last trio and rest fought it out 2f out: prog on inner over 1f out: led last 100yds: sn in command* **12/1**

0030 **2** 1 1/4 **Swot**[91] 6241 4-9-3 **60** ....(p) KieranSchofield 2 64
(Roger Teal) *trckd ldrs: effrt on outer to ld wl over 1f out: hrd pressed fnl f: hdd last 100yds: kpt on* **4/1**[1]

3 hd **Sheer Intensity (IRE)**[60] 7163 3-8-10 **59** .... KatherineGlenister(5) 4 63
(David Evans) *settled off the pce: prog 2f out: clsd to chal 1f out: nt qckn last 150yds* **16/1**

1005 **4** 1 3/4 **Hold Firm**[4] 8207 4-8-6 **56** .... GeorgiaDobie(7) 7 56
(Mark H Tompkins) *led at str pce 2f: chsd ldng pair: lost pl 2f out then short of room and dropped towards rr: styd on again fnl f* **8/1**

133 **5** 1 1/2 **Bloodsweatandtears**[36] 7735 8-8-13 **63** .... AbbieWibrew(7) 8 59
(William Knight) *racd v wd towards rr: prog 3f out: nudged along to take 4th 1f out and looked a threat: wknd last 100yds* **8/1**

1106 **6** 2 1/2 **Bazzat (IRE)**[13] 8085 3-8-13 **62** ....(v[1]) JonathanFisher(5) 6 52
(John Ryan) *slowly away: mostly in last trio: tried to make prog wl over 1f out: sn no great hdwy* **5/1**[2]

0130 **7** 1 **Showtime Blues**[14] 8064 4-8-11 **61** ....(p) DarraghKeenan(7) 5 49
(Jim Boyle) *racd wd: tried to cl on ldrs 2f out: no hdwy over 1f out: fdd* **4/1**[1]

0000 **8** 1 **Breakheart (IRE)**[20] 7986 9-8-7 **57** .... MichaelColes(7) 3 43
(Andrew Balding) *hld up in last trio: pushed along and no prog 2f out* **16/1**

2021 **9** 1 1/4 **For Shia And Lula (IRE)**[32] 7817 7-9-1 **63** .... TobyEley(5) 10 46
(Daniel Mark Loughnane) *pressed ldr after 2f: led 3f out: hdd & wknd qckly wl over 1f out* **11/2**[3]

6030 **10** 2 1/4 **Majestic Myles (IRE)**[27] 7887 8-9-3 **65** .... WilliamCox(5) 9 43
(Lee Carter) *led after 2f and maintained str pce: hdd 3f out: wknd qckly 2f out* **7/1**

1m 38.5s (0.30) **Going Correction** -0.05s/f (Stan)
WFA 3 from 4yo+ 1lb **10** Ran SP% **126.2**
Speed ratings (Par 101): **96,94,94,92,91 88,87,86,85,83**
CSF £64.64 CT £615.07 TOTE £15.30: £4.20, £2.50, £6.20; EX 97.40 Trifecta £1359.60.
Owner John Joseph Smith **Bred** Raimon Bloodstock **Trained** Epsom, Surrey
■ Stewards' Enquiry : Toby Eley vet said the gelding had finished lame on its right-fore and had lost a left-fore shoe
Jonathan Fisher jockey said the gelding was slowly away

FOCUS
A contested lead to this weak event. The winner has been rated a little higher than his recent best, while the runner-up fits the opening level.
T/Plt: £171.80 to a £1 stake. Pool: £63,810.90 - 271.05 winning units. T/Qpdt: £75.20 to a £1 stake. Pool: £4,166.91 - 41.0 winning units. **Jonathan Neesom**

8259 - 8275a (Foreign Racing) - See Raceform Interactive

8174 CHELMSFORD (A.W) (L-H)
Thursday, December 8

OFFICIAL GOING: Polytrack: standard
Wind: light, half behind Weather: dry

8276 TOTEPLACEPOT RACING'S FAVOURITE BET NURSERY H'CAP 7f (P)
4:20 (4:21) (Class 6) (0-60,59) 2-Y-O **£2,587** (£770; £384; £192) **Stalls** Low

Form RPR

0006 **1** **Bruny Island (IRE)**[51] 7423 2-8-9 **47** .... StevieDonohoe 12 51
(Charlie Fellowes) *hld up towards rr: clsd over 2f out: trckd ldrs over 1f out: squeezed through to chal 1f out: led 100yds out: r.o strly and sn in command* **9/1**

P001 **2** 1 3/4 **Viola Park**[15] 8072 2-8-12 **50** .... RyanPowell 2 49
(Ronald Harris) *chsd ldr tl led over 2f out: rdn and hrd pressed wl over 1f out: edgd lft u.p 1f out: hdd and one pce fnl 100yds* **10/1**

6205 **3** shd **Auric Goldfinger (IRE)**[17] 8046 2-9-4 **56** ....(b[1]) SeanLevey 3 55
(Richard Hannon) *chsd ldrs: rdn and chal wl over 1f out: ev ch tl unable to match pce of wnr and one pce fnl 100yds* **5/1**[2]

0400 **4** nk **Metronomic (IRE)**[26] 7941 2-9-6 **58** .... KieranO'Neill 7 56
(Richard Hannon) *t.k.h: hld up in tch in midfield: hdwy over 2f out: rdn and ev ch ent fnl f* **7/1**[3]

0500 **5** 3 1/4 **Gentleman Giles (IRE)**[15] 8072 2-9-5 **57** .... WilliamCarson 4 46
(Jamie Osborne) *wl in tch in midfield: effrt to chse ldrs over 1f out: pressing ldrs whn squeezed for room and hmpd 1f out: nt rcvr and one pce after* **16/1**

6005 **6** 2 1/4 **Latest Quest (IRE)**[22] 7974 2-9-7 **59** .... AdamKirby 9 42
(Sylvester Kirk) *hld up in tch in midfield: effrt ent fnl 2f: outpcd u.p over 1f out: wl hld and plugged on same pce fnl f* **5/1**[2]

400 **7** hd **American Patrol (IRE)**[19] 8034 2-9-5 **57** .... JFEgan 1 40
(Neil Mulholland) *hld up in rr: sme hdwy into midfield but nt on terms w ldrs whn swtchd rt bnd 2f out: swtchd bk lft and hdwy jst ins fnl f: kpt on: nvr trbld ldrs* **16/1**

0002 **8** 3/4 **How's Lucy**[17] 8046 2-9-1 **53** .... DannyBrock 8 34
(Jane Chapple-Hyam) *chsd ldrs: effrt 2f out: unable qck u.p over 1f out: wknd fnl f* **3/1**[1]

5405 **9** 1/2 **Tigerfish (IRE)**[15] 8072 2-8-8 **46** ....[1] BenCurtis 14 25
(William Stone) *hld up in rr: rdn and wd bnd 2f out: plugged on but nvr threatened ldrs* **16/1**

5600 **10** 3 3/4 **Zipedee**[28] 7884 2-8-9 **47** ....[1] JosephineGordon 5 16
(John Ryan) *racd keenly: led tl over 2f out: lost pl u.p over 1f out: wknd fnl f* **33/1**

600 **11** 2 3/4 **Dolly Dimples**[57] 7278 2-9-7 **59** .... DavidProbert 15 21
(William Jarvis) *dwlt: sn in midfield but stuck wd: rdn over 2f out: sn struggling and wknd over 1f out* **25/1**

0006 **12** 1/2 **Magdalene Fox**[28] 7881 2-9-3 **58** ....(b) CallumShepherd(3) 10 19
(Ed Dunlop) *hld up in midfield: swtchd rt and effrt over 1f out: sn outpcd and btn: wknd fnl f* **10/1**

0500 **13** 1 3/4 **Cambridge Favorite**[78] 6681 2-8-10 **55** ....(bt[1]) LuluStanford(7) 13 11
(Mrs Ilka Gansera-Leveque) *a towards rr: rdn outpcd over 2f out: wl btn over 1f out* **50/1**

600 **14** 2 3/4 **Four Candles (IRE)**[15] 8065 2-9-1 **53** ....[1] LiamKeniry 11 1
(Philip McBride) *s.i.s: a in rr: outpcd over 2f out: wl btn over 1f out* **20/1**

050 **15** 14 **Take This Waltz**[70] 6888 2-8-12 **50** .... LukeMorris 6
(Bill Turner) *midfield: rdn over 2f out: sn struggling and lost pl wl over 1f out: bhd 1f out: eased fnl f* **50/1**

1m 26.53s (-0.67) **Going Correction** -0.225s/f (Stan) **15** Ran SP% **132.1**
Speed ratings (Par 94): **94,92,91,91,87 85,85,84,83,79 76,75,73,70,54**
CSF £100.15 CT £530.67 TOTE £13.40: £4.10, £3.20, £3.00; EX 154.20 Trifecta £1377.70.
Owner Saffron House Stables Partnership **Bred** Forenaghts Stud **Trained** Newmarket, Suffolk
■ Stewards' Enquiry : Ryan Powell caution: careless riding

FOCUS
A moderate nursery.

8277 @TOTEPOOL TWEET US YOUR #TOTEELFIE MAIDEN AUCTION STKS 7f (P)
4:55 (4:55) (Class 6) 2-Y-O **£2,587** (£770; £384; £192) **Stalls** Low

Form RPR

0 **1** **Royal Opera House (IRE)**[28] 7891 2-9-1 0 .... WilliamCarson 7 84+
(Jamie Osborne) *mde all: stl travelling strly over 2f out: shkn up and readily wnt clr over 1f out: styd on strly: easily* **5/1**[3]

2 7 **Shadow Beauty** 2-8-13 0 .... DanielMuscutt 3 63
(Marco Botti) *pushed along and rn green early: in tch in midfield: nt clr run over 2f out: hdwy over 1f out: wnt 2nd 100yds out: kpt on: no ch w wnr* **11/4**[1]

6 **3** nk **Petit Filous**[48] 7495 2-8-13 0 .... JackMitchell 5 62
(Giles Bravery) *t.k.h: hld up wl in tch in midfield: effrt and hung lft over 1f out: chalng for 2nd u.p 1f out: no ch w wnr and kpt on same pce ins fnl f* **6/1**

25 **4** 2 **Sea Tea Dea**[49] 7484 2-8-6 0 .... LukeMorris 8 50
(Anthony Carson) *chsd wnr: rdn 2f out: sn drvn and outpcd: wl hld 2nd 1f out: lost 2 pls fnl 100yds* **3/1**[2]

5 1 3/4 **Circuit** 2-8-6 0 .... ConnorBeasley 2 45
(Mick Quinn) *s.i.s: in rr: sme hdwy u.p over 1f out: kpt on but nvr nr ldrs* **50/1**

5 **6** 1/2 **Camaradorie (IRE)**[50] 7466 2-8-7 0 .... SimonPearce(3) 4 49
(Lydia Pearce) *hld up in tch: clsd and nt clr run over 2f out: swtchd rt and rdn over 1f out: no prog and wl hld fnl f* **25/1**

20 **7** 3/4 **Bataka**[40] 7698 2-8-8 0 JosephineGordon 1 44
(Harry Dunlop) *chsd ldrs: rdn and unable qck over 2f out: lost pl over 1f out: wknd fnl f* **7/1**

66 **8** 2 1/4 **Astute Boy (IRE)**[14] 8082 2-9-3 0 AdamKirby 10 46
(Ed Vaughan) *dwlt: a towards rr and styd wd: sltly hmpd 4f out: effrt 2f out: sn outpcd* **7/1**

0 **9** 4 **Lady Rowena**[13] 8089 2-8-6 0 PJMcDonald 6 25
(Mark Johnston) *chsd ldrs: rdn 3f out: sn struggling and lost pl wl over 1f out: bhd fnl f* **20/1**

P **Crystal Stanza (IRE)** 2-8-13 0 StevieDonohoe 9
(Charlie Fellowes) *edgd rt and dropped to last 4f out: lost tch and eased over 2f out: p.u and dismntd ins fnl f* **20/1**

1m 25.6s (-1.60) **Going Correction** -0.225s/f (Stan) **10** Ran SP% **122.9**
Speed ratings (Par 94): **100,92,91,89,87 86,85,83,78,**
CSF £19.42 TOTE £5.70: £2.20, £1.70, £2.90; EX 25.50 Trifecta £232.50.
Owner Melbourne 10 Racing **Bred** Shortgrove Manor Stud **Trained** Upper Lambourn, Berks

FOCUS
This proved very straightforward for the winner, who drew right away in the straight.

8278 #TOTEELFIE WIN A £50 FREE BET H'CAP 7f (P)
5:25 (5:29) (Class 7) (0-50,50) 3-Y-O+ **£2,264** (£673; £336; £168) **Stalls** Low

Form RPR

0000 **1** **Turaathy (IRE)**[79] 6651 3-9-4 **50** EoinWalsh(3) 5 56
(Tony Newcombe) *dwlt: hld up towards rr: hdwy 3f out: sn pushed along: swtchd rt and rdn over 1f out: chsd wnr ins fnl f: r.o wl u.p to ld last strides* **10/1**

0-66 **2** hd **Menelik (IRE)**[327] 216 7-9-7 **50** (vt) AdamKirby 14 56
(Des Donovan, Ire) *chsd ldrs: drvn to ld over 1f out: kpt on u.p: hdd last strides* **6/1**[3]

5035 **3** 1 3/4 **Fossa**[58] 7261 6-8-12 **46** CharlieBennett(5) 13 47
(Mark Brisbourne) *stdd and dropped in bhd after s: hld up in rr: hdwy over 1f out: swtchd rt 1f out: kpt on u.p ins fnl f: wnt 3rd towards fin* **10/1**

0251 **4** 1/2 **Rosie Crowe (IRE)**[42] 7646 4-9-7 **50** (v) JosephineGordon 6 50
(Shaun Harris) *chsd ldrs: drvn over 1f out: no ex 1f out and kpt on same pce u.p ins fnl f* **9/4**[1]

6006 **5** 2 **Topsoil**[29] 7863 3-9-5 **48** [1] RenatoSouza 11 42
(Ronald Harris) *racd keenly: sn led: rdn and hdd over 1f out: no ex 1f out: wknd ins fnl f* **16/1**

0540 **6** 1/2 **Lutine Charlie (IRE)**[15] 8070 9-9-4 **47** (p) TomQueally 10 40
(Emma Owen) *hld up towards rr: sme hdwy over 1f out: swtchd lft jst ins fnl f: kpt on: nvr trbld ldrs* **14/1**

5000 **7** hd **Arizona Snow**[56] 7302 4-9-6 **49** LukeMorris 4 41
(Ronald Harris) *in tch in midfield: effrt over 1f out: unable qck ent fnl f: wknd ins fnl f* **12/1**

6400 **8** shd **Cytringan**[49] 7488 3-8-13 **45** SimonPearce(3) 1 37
(Lydia Pearce) *hld up in tch in midfield: nt clr run over 2f out: clsd on inner over 1f out: rdn and cl enough 1f out: fnd little and wknd wl ins fnl f* **20/1**

03 **9** 1 **Bold Max**[196] 2610 5-9-4 **47** (p) KieranO'Neill 9 36
(Zoe Davison) *hld up in midfield: n.m.r briefly over 1f out: sn rdn: edgd lft and kpt on same pce ins fnl f: nvr trbld ldrs* **12/1**

6365 **10** 1 1/4 **Little Indian**[12] 8120 6-9-7 **50** DannyBrock 7 36
(J R Jenkins) *bustled along early: hld up towards rr: swtchd rt and effrt bnd 2f out: no hdwy over 1f out: kpt on same pce ins fnl f: nvr trbld ldrs* **5/1**[2]

1000 **11** 3 **Chandrayaan**[180] 3146 9-9-4 **47** (v) RobertHavlin 3 25
(John E Long) *hld up in last quartet: nt clr run over 1f out: no imp 1f out: n.d* **33/1**

0400 **12** 1 1/2 **Chester Deelyte (IRE)**[14] 8079 8-8-11 **45** (p) MitchGodwin(5) 12 19
(Lisa Williamson) *in tch in midfield: rdn over 3f out: lost pl u.p over 1f out: wknd fnl f* **16/1**

0050 **13** 15 **Mowhoob**[15] 8070 6-8-12 **48** (t) JoshuaBryan(7) 16
(Brian Barr) *chsd ldr tl wl over 1f out: sn lost pl: bhd and eased ins fnl f: burst blood vessel* **12/1**

450R **R** **Loud**[42] 7646 6-8-13 **45** (v) TimClark(3) 8
(Denis Quinn) *ref to r* **33/1**

1m 26.56s (-0.64) **Going Correction** -0.225s/f (Stan) **14** Ran SP% **132.1**
Speed ratings (Par 97): **94,93,91,91,88 88,88,88,86,85 82,80,63,**
CSF £74.43 CT £657.40 TOTE £17.50: £4.30, £2.40, £4.60; EX 126.60 Trifecta £3954.60.
Owner David Freeman **Bred** Forenaghts Stud **Trained** Yarnscombe, Devon
■ Home Again was withdrawn at the start. Rule 4 applies to board prices prior to withdrawal - deduction 10p in the pound. New market formed

FOCUS
A low-grade handicap.

8279 TOTEPOOLLIVEINFO.COM FOR RACING RESULTS H'CAP 1m (P)
5:55 (5:58) (Class 2) (0-105,103) 3-Y-O+ **£12,938** (£3,850; £1,924; £962) **Stalls** Low

Form RPR

6531 **1** **Chester Street**[33] 7813 3-8-4 **84** JosephineGordon 2 92
(Roger Charlton) *chsd ldrs: wnt 2nd and swtchd rt over 1f out: drvn and ev ch ins fnl f: r.o to ld on post* **9/2**[2]

0111 **2** nse **Qaffaal (USA)**[7] 8177 5-8-2 **84** 6ex NathanEvans(3) 7 92+
(Michael Easterby) *hld up in tch towards rr: clsd on outer over 2f out: shkn up to chse ldrs 1f out: sn rdn and chalng: r.o to ld wl ins fnl f: hdd on post* **10/3**[1]

3323 **3** 3/4 **Chevallier**[7] 8177 4-8-8 **87** LukeMorris 9 93
(Archie Watson) *racd keenly: led: rdn and fnd ex over 1f out: hrd drvn 1f out: hdd and one pced fnl 50yds* **6/1**

4451 **4** 1/2 **Pactolus (IRE)**[17] 8049 5-8-10 **92** (tp) AaronJones(3) 3 97+
(Stuart Williams) *hld up in tch: swtchd rt and hdwy 1f out: r.o u.p ins fnl f* **5/1**[3]

535 **5** 1/2 **Michele Strogoff**[12] 8122 3-8-10 **90** [1] ConnorBeasley 1 94
(Roger Fell) *hld up in tch in midfield: nt clr run over 2f out: hdwy to chse ldrs and hrd drvn 1f out: kpt on same pce fnl 100yds* **5/1**[3]

2052 **6** 2 1/2 **Loyalty**[7] 8177 9-8-3 **85** (v) NoelGarbutt(3) 6 83
(Derek Shaw) *awkward leaving stalls: in tch in midfield: nt clr run over 2f out: hdwy u.p over 1f out: kpt on same pce ins fnl f* **25/1**

2000 **7** nk **Lunar Deity**[17] 8049 7-9-2 **95** SeanLevey 11 92
(Stuart Williams) *stdd s: hld up in tch in rr: effrt over 1f out: kpt on ins fnl f: nvr trbld ldrs* **50/1**

0400 **8** 1 3/4 **Majestic Moon (IRE)**[47] 7542 6-9-7 **100** AdamBeschizza 4 93
(Julia Feilden) *chsd ldrs: shuffled bk and n.m.r over 1f out: wl hld and one pced fnl f* **100/1**

1034 **9** hd **Supersta**[21] 7984 5-9-1 **94** (p) AdamKirby 8 87
(Michael Appleby) *in tch in midfield: shkn up over 1f out: rdn and btn 1f out: wknd ins fnl f* **8/1**

0110 **10** 1 1/4 **Fort Bastion (IRE)**[17] 8049 7-8-11 **90** BenCurtis 10 80
(Brian Ellison) *chsd ldr tl unable qck and lost pl over 1f out: wknd fnl f* **20/1**

0013 **11** 2 **Unforgiving Minute**[12] 8122 5-8-5 **87** HectorCrouch(3) 5 72
(John Butler) *in tch towards rr: shkn up and n.m.r over 1f out: no imp: bhd ins fnl f* **9/1**

20-6 **P** **Gabriel's Lad (IRE)**[29] 7868 7-9-10 **103** TomQueally 12
(Denis Coakley) *s.i.s: t.k.h: in rr: lost action and p.u over 4f out (fatally injured)* **50/1**

1m 36.68s (-3.22) **Going Correction** -0.225s/f (Stan)
WFA 3 from 4yo+ 1lb **12** Ran SP% **123.5**
Speed ratings (Par 109): **107,106,106,105,105 102,102,100,100,99 97,**
CSF £20.00 CT £96.06 TOTE £5.70: £2.00, £1.50, £1.90; EX 22.50 Trifecta £81.20.
Owner H R H Sultan Ahmad Shah **Bred** Cheveley Park Stud Ltd **Trained** Beckhampton, Wilts

FOCUS
There was a tight finish to this decent handicap. It's been rated around the third.

8280 TOTEPOOL RACECOURSE CASH BACK AVAILABLE H'CAP 5f (P)
6:25 (6:26) (Class 4) (0-80,79) 3-Y-O+ **£5,175** (£1,540; £769; £384) **Stalls** Low

Form RPR

5622 **1** **Monumental Man**[77] 6699 7-9-2 **74** (p) KierenFox 7 82
(Michael Attwater) *bhd: stl last and shkn up over 1f out: swtchd lft and hdwy 1f out: str run ins fnl f to ld last strides* **6/1**[2]

5204 **2** nk **Vimy Ridge**[42] 7644 4-9-1 **73** RobertWinston 3 80
(Alan Bailey) *hld up in midfield: clsd over 1f out: rdn to chse ldr jst ins fnl f: drvn and ev ch fnl 50yds: r.o: wnt 2nd last strides* **6/1**[2]

020 **3** nk **Calypso Choir**[19] 8032 3-9-7 **79** AdamKirby 10 85+
(Sylvester Kirk) *broke wl to ld and crossed to inner: rdn over 1f out: drvn ins fnl f: kpt on u.p: hdd and no ex last strides* **8/1**[3]

0352 **4** 1 1/4 **Captain Lars (SAF)**[19] 8040 7-8-9 **70** (p) NoelGarbutt(3) 6 74+
(Derek Shaw) *off the pce in last: rdn and hdwy over 1f out: gng for gap whn hmpd jst ins fnl f: hdwy 100yds out: chsng ldrs but hld whn nt clr run and eased towards fin* **8/1**[3]

0/06 **5** 1/2 **Higher Court (USA)**[8] 8150 8-8-11 **72** HectorCrouch(3) 11 72
(Emma Owen) *off the pce towards rr: effrt over 1f out: styd on wl ins fnl f: nvr trbld ldrs* **33/1**

2116 **6** 1 1/4 **Waneen (IRE)**[13] 8099 3-9-3 **75** JFEgan 5 70
(Joseph Tuite) *chsd ldrs: rdn over 1f out: unable qck u.p and wknd ins fnl f* **8/1**[3]

5211 **7** 1 1/2 **Zipedeedodah (IRE)**[19] 8040 4-9-0 **75** (t) NathanEvans(3) 1 65
(Joseph Tuite) *chsd ldr tl over 2f out: chsd ldr u.p again over 1f out: edgd lft: lost 2nd and btn jst ins fnl f: wknd fnl 100yds* **4/1**[1]

0202 **8** nk **Pearl Acclaim (IRE)**[20] 8010 6-9-5 **77** (p) BarryMcHugh 12 66
(David Nicholls) *midfield: hung rt bnd 4f out tl 2f out: effrt over 1f out: no imp and one pce fnl f* **10/1**

600 **9** 3/4 **Krystallite**[28] 7892 3-9-2 **74** [1] BenCurtis 2 60
(Scott Dixon) *midfield: effrt over 1f out: clsng whn swtchd rt and hmpd jst ins fnl f: nt rcvr and no imp after* **16/1**

2605 **10** 1 3/4 **Nocturn**[43] 7626 7-8-13 **71** (p) LukeMorris 4 51
(Ronald Harris) *off the pce towards rr: effrt and no imp over 1f out: wl hld and one pce fnl f* **12/1**

3000 **11** 3 **Come On Dave (IRE)**[19] 8032 7-9-7 **79** (b) LiamKeniry 9 48
(John Butler) *chsd ldrs: rdn to chse ldr over 2f out tl lost pl over 1f out: wknd ins fnl f* **8/1**[3]

0004 **12** 16 **Shackled N Drawn (USA)**[19] 8032 4-9-4 **76** JosephineGordon 8
(Peter Hedger) *chsd ldrs tl lost pl u.p over 1f out: bhd and eased ins fnl f* **16/1**

59.01s (-1.19) **Going Correction** -0.225s/f (Stan) **12** Ran SP% **124.5**
Speed ratings (Par 105): **100,99,99,97,96 94,91,91,90,87 82,56**
CSF £44.21 CT £304.36 TOTE £6.30: £2.30, £3.00, £3.30; EX 47.30 Trifecta £309.90.
Owner Richard and Nicola Hunt **Bred** Christopher Chell **Trained** Epsom, Surrey

FOCUS
This was run at a strong gallop and was set up for a closer. Straightforward form rated around the first four.

8281 COLLECT TOTEPOOL WINNINGS AT BETFRED SHOPS MEDIAN AUCTION MAIDEN STKS 1m 5f 66y(P)
6:55 (6:56) (Class 6) 3-5-Y-O **£2,587** (£770; £384; £192) **Stalls** Low

Form RPR

2003 **1** **Zeehan**[15] 8076 3-9-0 72 [1] AdamKirby 3 69
(Clive Cox) *chsd ldrs: rdn 4f out: hdwy to ld wl over 1f out: asserted u.p jst ins fnl f: eased towards fin* **8/11**[1]

2 1 **Burning Heat (IRE)**[29] 3-9-5 70 RyanTate 5 73
(James Eustace) *hld up in midfield: trckd ldrs and nt clr run over 2f out: rdn to chse wnr over 1f out: kpt on same pce ins fnl f* **7/2**[2]

5550 **3** 6 **Versant**[51] 7429 4-9-11 67 (t) RobertWinston 2 65
(Lee Carter) *t.k.h: hld up in rr: swtchd rt and hdwy 3f out: rdn to chse ldng pair and hung lft over 1f out: wknd ins fnl f* **7/1**[3]

05 **4** 11 **Time To Tango (IRE)**[226] 1767 5-9-11 0 LiamKeniry 7 47
(Joseph Tuite) *racd keenly: led: stdd gallop 8f out: hdd wl over 1f out: sn rdn and unable qck: 4th and btn whn hung rt 1f out: wknd ins fnl f* **16/1**

0604 **5** 1 3/4 **Master Of Heaven**[36] 7767 3-9-0 48 (tp) CharlieBennett(5) 4 44
(Jim Boyle) *chsd ldr: rdn and ev ch over 2f out: unable qck and lost pl over 1f out: 5th and wkng whn carried rt and hmpd 1f out* **20/1**

6 1 3/4 **Moorstone**[26] 4-9-6 0 JackMitchell 6 37
(Giles Bravery) *s.i.s: hld up in last pair: rdn over 3f out: outpcd and btn over 1f out: wknd over 1f out* **9/1**

00/0 **7** 2 1/2 **Amadiva (IRE)**[52] 7421 5-9-6 37 (b[1]) TimmyMurphy 1 33
(Martin Bosley) *midfield: lost pl and rdn over 3f out: bhd over 1f out* **66/1**

2m 50.87s (-2.73) **Going Correction** -0.225s/f (Stan)
WFA 3 from 4yo+ 6lb **7** Ran SP% **114.8**
Speed ratings (Par 101): **99,98,94,87,86 85,84**
CSF £3.55 TOTE £1.60: £1.10, £2.00; EX 3.90 Trifecta £14.20.
Owner Mondial Racing **Bred** Ruby Bloodstock Limited **Trained** Lambourn, Berks

FOCUS
A modest maiden.

8282 BOOK TICKETS AT CHELMSFORDCITYRACECOURSE.COM H'CAP 1m 2f (P)
7:25 (7:28) (Class 5) (0-75,76) 3-Y-O+ **£3,881** (£1,155; £577; £288) **Stalls** Low

Form RPR

0033 **1** **Graceful James (IRE)**[28] 7886 3-9-1 **72** KieranO'Neill 7 80
(Jimmy Fox) *chsd ldr tl 6f out: rdn to chse ldr again 2f out: edgd rt and rdn to ld 1f out: hld on cl home* **9/2**[2]

2000 **2** shd **San Quentin (IRE)**[21] 7993 5-9-3 **71** (b) AdamKirby 6 78
(Roger Fell) *hld up in rr: swtchd rt and effrt over 1f out: hdwy u.p 1f out: str run and chal wl ins fnl f: jst hld* **9/1**

-330 **3** *1* **Thahab Ifraj (IRE)**[77] 6702 3-8-10 **67**..............................[1] LukeMorris 11 72
(Ismail Mohammed) *in tch in midfield: effrt over 2f out: hdwy and swtchd rt over 1f out: pressed ldrs wl ins fnl f: hld whn squeezed out and snatched up last strides* **10/1**

6030 **4** *1 1/2* **Glenalmond (IRE)**[50] 7457 4-9-1 **72**........................... HectorCrouch(3) 9 74
(Daniel Steele) *stdd and dropped in after s: hld up in last trio: swtchd rt and hdwy over 1f out: chsd ldrs and swtchd lft wl ins fnl f: kpt on* **14/1**

045 **5** *3/4* **Storm King**[20] 8007 7-9-7 **75**.................................(p[1]) JosephineGordon 3 76
(David C Griffiths) *t.k.h: chsd ldrs: swtchd rt and hdwy to ld 6f out: hdd 3f out: rdn over 1f out: no ex ins fnl f: wknd towards fin* **3/1[1]**

6002 **6** *hd* **With Pleasure**[7] 8178 3-8-12 **69**.. BenCurtis 8 69
(David O'Meara) *led tl 6f out: chsd ldr tl led again 3f out: rdn and edgd rt over 1f out: hdd 1f out: wknd ins fnl f* **3/1[1]**

4140 **7** *2 1/2* **Lord Of The Storm**[13] 8101 8-8-12 **66**.................................. KierenFox 1 61
(Michael Attwater) *in tch in midfield: effrt over 2f out: hdwy u.p over 1f out: wknd ins fnl f* **8/1[3]**

3000 **8** *13* **New Street (IRE)**[22] 7973 5-9-0 **68**.. JFEgan 10 37
(Jim Best) *chsd ldrs: rdn and ev ch over 3f out tl over 2f out: wknd over 1f out: bhd and eased ins fnl f* **25/1**

6550 **9** *10* **Bushel (USA)**[40] 7691 6-8-13 **70**....................................... EoinWalsh(3) 5 19
(Tony Newcombe) *in tch in midfield: effrt over 2f out: sn struggling: wknd over 1f out: bhd ins fnl f* **33/1**

3220 **10** *11* **Speculator**[12] 8124 4-9-1 **69**...(p) TimmyMurphy 2
(John Butler) *hld up in last trio: outpcd whn swtchd rt 4f out: t.o fnl 2f* **10/1**

2m 5.51s (-3.09) **Going Correction** -0.225s/f (Stan)
WFA 3 from 4yo+ 3lb **10** Ran SP% **120.9**
Speed ratings (Par 103): **103,102,102,100,100 100,98,87,79,70**
CSF £46.55 CT £393.59 TOTE £5.20: £1.50, £2.60, £3.10; EX 43.90 Trifecta £535.20.
Owner Abacus Employment Services Ltd **Bred** D Fuller **Trained** Collingbourne Ducis, Wilts

FOCUS
There was another tight finish to this handicap. The runner-up has been rated close to his best.
T/Plt: £176.80 to a £1 stake. Pool: £106,782.53 - 440.71 winning units T/Qpdt: £23.10 to a £1 stake. Pool: £13,764.37 - 440.72 winning units **Steve Payne**

8139 NEWCASTLE (A.W) (L-H)
Friday, December 9

OFFICIAL GOING: Tapeta: standard
Wind: Light, across

8283 CONCEPT PERSONNEL H'CAP 1m 4f 98y (Tp)
3:10 (3:10) (Class 4) (0-85,83) 3-Y-O+ **£4,690** (£1,395; £697; £348) **Stalls** High

Form RPR

1243 **1** **I Am Not Here (IRE)**[30] 7869 5-9-5 **78**.................................. BenCurtis 8 89
(Brian Ellison) *hld up: smooth hdwy on outside to ld over 2f out: rdn over 1f out: kpt on strly to draw clr fnl f* **5/2[1]**

3632 **2** *3 1/4* **Isharah (USA)**[9] 8162 3-9-0 **78**.. PJMcDonald 5 84
(Mark Johnston) *prom: effrt and ev ch briefly over 2f out: sn chsng wnr: kpt on fnl f: nt pce to chal* **4/1[2]**

2064 **3** *1/2* **Siren's Cove**[31] 7853 4-9-0 **73**...................................(b) PaulMulrennan 10 78
(Kenneth Slack) *hld up: rdn and hdwy on outside over 2f out: disp 2nd pl over 1f out to ins fnl f: kpt on same pce towards fin* **20/1**

0441 **4** *1 3/4* **Heart Locket**[22] 7993 4-8-9 **71**.................................... NathanEvans(3) 12 73
(Michael Easterby) *stdd s: hld up: pushed along and hdwy 2f out: drifted lft and kpt on wl fnl f: nrst fin* **7/1[3]**

4331 **5** *shd* **Sunglider (IRE)**[14] 8100 3-9-0 **78** ow1.......................(v) DanielTudhope 11 80
(David O'Meara) *hld up: rdn and hdwy over 2f out: kpt on same pce ins fnl f* **8/1**

3062 **6** *1* **Henpecked**[22] 7993 6-8-12 **71**...(p) JoeDoyle 3 72
(Alistair Whillans) *hld up midfield: stdy hdwy over 2f out: rdn over 1f out: outpcd ins fnl f* **10/1**

040 **7** *8* **Corton Lad**[21] 8007 6-9-5 **83**.................................(tp) ShirleyTeasdale(5) 2 71
(Keith Dalgleish) *trckd ldrs: rdn over 2f out: wknd over 1f out* **40/1**

2542 **8** *1 1/2* **Age Of Elegance (IRE)**[21] 8007 4-9-5 **78**.................(p) ConnorBeasley 7 63
(Roger Fell) *pressed ldr: led over 3f out to over 2f out: rdn and wknd over 1f out* **8/1**

6660 **9** *13* **Salmon Sushi**[21] 8007 5-9-10 **83**.. JasonHart 9 48
(Tim Easterby) *prom: rdn and outpcd over 2f out: wknd wl over 1f out* **12/1**

0606 **10** *20* **Spes Nostra**[21] 8007 8-9-8 **81**...(b) TomEaves 4 14
(Iain Jardine) *led to over 3f out: rdn and wknd fr 2f out: t.o* **16/1**

1456 **11** *41* **Card High (IRE)**[32] 7847 6-9-2 **75**.................................(t) ShaneGray 1
(Wilf Storey) *hld up: struggling over 3f out: sn btn: t.o* **33/1**

510 **12** *12* **Flower Power**[12] 7158 5-9-6 **79**....................................... BarryMcHugh 6
(Tony Coyle) *dwlt: bhd and nvr gng wl: lost tch fr over 3f out: t.o* **50/1**

2m 38.38s (-2.72) **Going Correction** -0.10s/f (Stan)
WFA 3 from 4yo+ 5lb **12** Ran SP% **118.1**
Speed ratings (Par 105): **105,102,102,101,101 100,95,94,85,72 44,36**
CSF £11.37 CT £163.87 TOTE £3.30: £1.50, £1.70, £5.20; EX 12.80 Trifecta £240.80.
Owner Koo's Racing Club **Bred** John Reilly **Trained** Norton, N Yorks

FOCUS
Deep decompaction work had been carried out on the surface and it was expected to rise slightly slower than of late. A fair handicap, won fairly comfortably by the class-dropping favourite. The runner-up and third have been rated close to form.

8284 NORTHERN INSIGHT NURSERY H'CAP 1m 5y (Tp)
3:40 (3:42) (Class 6) (0-60,59) 2-Y-O **£2,587** (£770; £384; £192) **Stalls** Centre

Form RPR

0004 **1** **Babouska**[18] 8046 2-8-7 **48**... NathanEvans(3) 7 52
(Michael Easterby) *mde all: rdn along 2f out: kpt on strly fnl f* **11/4[1]**

006 **2** *1 1/2* **Lulu The Rocket**[29] 7891 2-8-13 **56**.............................. GeorgiaCox(5) 10 57
(Peter Chapple-Hyam) *hld up in tch: hdwy over 2f out: effrt and chsd wnr over 1f out: plugged on same pce ins fnl f* **7/2[2]**

0040 **3** *nk* **Our Boy John (IRE)**[18] 8046 2-9-1 **53**.............................. JackGarritty 2 53
(Richard Fahey) *stdd s: hld up: rdn and hdwy over 2f out: disp 2nd pl over 1f out to ins fnl f: kpt on same pce* **7/1**

0654 **4** *2 1/2* **Hold Me Tight (IRE)**[27] 7941 2-9-5 **57**............................ LiamKeniry 11 52
(J S Moore) *prom: hdwy to chse wnr over 2f out to over 1f out: rdn and outpcd ins fnl f* **7/1**

440 **5** *shd* **Misty Moo**[46] 7571 2-8-11 **52**.................................. AlistairRawlinson(3) 3 46
(Michael Appleby) *dwlt: hld up: rdn and outpcd over 2f out: rallied over 1f out: no imp fnl f* **18/1**

050 **6** *1 1/4* **Masterfilly (IRE)**[128] 5036 2-9-7 **59**................................. ThomasBrown 9 51
(Ed Walker) *dwlt: sn in tch: rdn over 2f out: sn outpcd: no imp fr over 1f out* **12/1**

0030 **7** *1* **Tael O' Gold**[18] 8046 2-9-3 **55**...................................... PatCosgrave 8 44
(Iain Jardine) *prom: rdn over 2f out: wknd appr fnl f* **14/1**

4065 **8** *11* **Everkyllachy (IRE)**[38] 7750 2-9-5 **57**...................................(b) JohnFahy 4 22
(J S Moore) *cl up: rdn over 2f out: wknd over 1f out* **16/1**

3053 **9** *10* **Lil's Affair (IRE)**[14] 8087 2-8-11 **49**............................(p) ConnorBeasley 6
(Bryan Smart) *pressed wnr to over 2f out: sn lost pl and struggling: t.o* **4/1[3]**

1m 42.4s (3.80) **Going Correction** +0.20s/f (Slow) **9** Ran SP% **119.4**
Speed ratings (Par 94): **89,87,87,84,84 83,82,71,61**
CSF £12.88 CT £62.36 TOTE £3.70: £1.60, £1.60, £2.00; EX 18.50 Trifecta £103.50.
Owner A G Black & M Burrows **Bred** Alan Black And M W Easterby **Trained** Sheriff Hutton, N Yorks

FOCUS
A moderate nursery dominated from the front by the winner.

8285 AVANT HOMES NURSERY H'CAP 5f (Tp)
4:15 (4:15) (Class 6) (0-65,64) 2-Y-O **£2,587** (£770; £384; £192) **Stalls** Centre

Form RPR

6441 **1** **Dazacam**[14] 8097 2-9-5 **62**.. RobertWinston 10 72+
(Michael Herrington) *hld up: smooth hdwy to ld over 1f out: shkn up and qcknd clr ins fnl f: pushed out: comf* **6/4[1]**

300 **2** *2* **Luv U Always**[38] 7740 2-8-7 **50**....................................... PJMcDonald 11 51
(Iain Jardine) *hld up: rdn and hdwy over 1f out: chsd wnr ins fnl f: kpt on: nt pce to chal* **11/1**

055 **3** *nk* **Royal Celebration**[76] 6789 2-8-10 **53**.......................... ConnorBeasley 9 53
(Bryan Smart) *in tch: hdwy to chse ldr over 2f out: rdn and ev ch over 1f out: lost 2nd and one pce ins fnl f* **7/1[3]**

4105 **4** *1 1/4* **Snuggy (IRE)**[14] 8097 2-9-7 **64**.. SamJames 6 59
(David Barron) *hld up: rdn and hdwy wl over 1f out: kpt on ins fnl f: nt pce to chal* **7/1[3]**

6200 **5** *1 3/4* **Coping Stone**[20] 8033 2-9-7 **64**... PatCosgrave 5 53
(David Brown) *hld up bhd ldng gp: effrt and hdwy over 1f out: kpt on same pce ins fnl f* **7/2[2]**

0636 **6** *3/4* **Champagne Queen**[122] 5257 2-8-13 **56**....................... PaulMulrennan 2 42
(Rae Guest) *dwlt: bhd and sn pushed along: hdwy on far side of gp over 1f out: nvr able to chal* **16/1**

5044 **7** *1/2* **Khelly's Edge**[75] 6807 2-8-10 **53**...(p) BenCurtis 3 38
(Scott Dixon) *t.k.h: led to over 1f out: rdn and wknd ins fnl f* **20/1**

0404 **8** *3/4* **Oh So Dandy (IRE)**[14] 8097 2-9-3 **60**..............................(p) MartinLane 7 42
(Derek Shaw) *dwlt: sn pushed along in rr: hdwy on far side of gp 1/2-way: rdn and no imp over 1f out* **12/1**

2060 **9** *7* **King Of Castilla**[83] 6588 2-8-11 **57**.............................. NathanEvans(3) 1 14
(John Murray) *prom: rdn over 2f out: wknd wl over 1f out* **28/1**

346P **10** *1* **Eid Rose**[48] 7528 2-8-4 **47**... KieranO'Neill 8
(Scott Dixon) *chsd ldr to 1/2-way: drvn and wknd wl over 1f out* **100/1**

0420 **11** *4* **Flashing Light**[14] 8097 2-9-5 **62**.. DuranFentiman 4 1
(Tim Easterby) *chsd ldrs: rdn over 2f out: sn struggling* **33/1**

1m 0.46s (0.96) **Going Correction** +0.20s/f (Slow) **11** Ran SP% **121.3**
Speed ratings (Par 94): **100,96,96,94,91 90,89,88,77,75 69**
CSF £20.18 CT £96.71 TOTE £2.30: £1.10, £3.60, £2.70; EX 20.40 Trifecta £163.60.
Owner Darren & Annaley Yates **Bred** Mr & Mrs D Yates **Trained** Cold Kirby, N Yorks

FOCUS
The well-backed winner landed this ordinary nursery in the manner of a filly who can cope with a rise in class.

8286 NOT ON THE MARKET H'CAP 1m 5y (Tp)
4:50 (4:51) (Class 5) (0-75,74) 3-Y-O+ **£2,911** (£866; £432; £216) **Stalls** Centre

Form RPR

2113 **1** **Testa Rossa (IRE)**[14] 8092 6-8-13 **69**..................(b) GeorgeDowning(3) 8 82
(Jim Goldie) *hld up: pushed along and hdwy over 2f out: led and clr w runner-up ins fnl f: kpt on gamely* **11/2[2]**

0- **2** *hd* **Absolute Blast (IRE)**[544] 3211 4-9-5 **72**......................... PJMcDonald 11 84
(Iain Jardine) *hld up in tch: smooth hdwy to ld wl over 1f out: rdn and hdd but clr of rest ins fnl f: rallied: hld cl home* **13/2[3]**

144 **3** *6* **Visitant**[21] 8011 3-8-12 **66**... AndrewMullen 12 64
(David Thompson) *t.k.h: in tch: effrt and pushed along over 2f out: plugged on fnl f: nt rch first two* **7/1**

3000 **4** *hd* **Muqarred (USA)**[21] 8011 4-9-0 **67**................................. ConnorBeasley 10 65
(Roger Fell) *hld up: rdn over 2f out: hdwy over 1f out: kpt on ins fnl f: nt pce to chal* **14/1**

5645 **5** *3 3/4* **Broctune Papa Gio**[35] 7797 9-8-9 **62**.............................. KieranO'Neill 13 51
(Keith Reveley) *cl up: led over 2f out to wl over 1f out: sn drvn and outpcd* **22/1**

2534 **6** *2 3/4* **Shah Of Armaan (IRE)**[27] 7942 3-9-5 **73**............................ TomEaves 6 56
(Kevin Ryan) *dwlt: hld up: stdy hdwy over 2f out: rdn and no imp fr over 1f out* **10/1**

2500 **7** *1 3/4* **Kiwi Bay**[21] 8011 11-9-5 **72**... PaulMulrennan 7 51
(Michael Dods) *prom: drvn and outpcd wl over 2f out: n.d after* **50/1**

2102 **8** *3/4* **Footlight**[29] 7886 3-9-3 **71**.. DavidNolan 5 48
(Richard Fahey) *hld up in tch: stdy hdwy over 2f out: rdn and wknd over 1f out* **14/1**

0042 **9** *hd* **Balducci**[3] 8241 9-8-11 **64**.. BenCurtis 3 41
(Roger Fell) *prom: drvn along over 2f out: wknd wl over 1f out* **11/2[2]**

4000 **10** *3/4* **Petrucci (IRE)**[16] 8077 4-9-6 **73**..[1] MartinLane 9 48
(Derek Shaw) *dwlt: hld up: rdn over 2f out: nvr on terms* **50/1**

0300 **11** *1/2* **Freewheel (IRE)**[48] 7535 6-9-7 **74**.................................... PatCosgrave 2 48
(Garry Moss) *in tch: drvn and outpcd over 2f out: sn btn* **11/2[2]**

0066 **12** *2 3/4* **Argaki (IRE)**[21] 8011 6-8-13 **71**...............................(p) ShirleyTeasdale(5) 1 38
(Keith Dalgleish) *led to over 2f out: sn rdn and wknd* **28/1**

6500 **13** *2 3/4* **Hellavashock**[65] 6268 3-8-13 **67**.................................... RobertWinston 14 28
(Alistair Whillans) *hld up: shortlived effrt over 2f out: wknd over 1f out* **125/1**

441 **14** *10* **Blue Cliffs (IRE)**[29] 7894 3-9-3 **74**........................ AlistairRawlinson(3) 4 12
(Michael Appleby) *hld up in tch: rdn over 2f out: wknd wl over 1f out* **5/1[1]**

1m 39.33s (0.73) **Going Correction** +0.20s/f (Slow)
WFA 3 from 4yo+ 1lb **14** Ran SP% **123.6**
Speed ratings (Par 103): **104,103,97,97,93 91,89,88,88,87 87,84,81,71**
CSF £40.88 CT £261.83 TOTE £7.40: £2.60, £2.50, £2.50; EX 46.90 Trifecta £667.70.
Owner Mr & Mrs Gordon Grant **Bred** Hugo Merry And Khalid Al-Mudhaf **Trained** Uplawmoor, E Renfrews

FOCUS
The first two came well clear here. Another clear pb from the winner.

8287 NEIGH ONE WILL GIVE YOU A BETTER DEAL H'CAP 7f 14y (Tp)
5:20 (5:23) (Class 5) (0-75,74) 3-Y-O+ **£3,234** (£962; £481; £240) **Stalls** Centre

Form RPR
5442 **1** **Inaam (IRE)**[20] 8037 3-9-5 **72** DavidNolan 2 81
(Richard Fahey) *prom on far side of gp: wnt 2nd over 2f out: led and rdn over 1f out: hld on wl fnl f* **8/1**
5640 **2** *1* **Let's Twist**[18] 8052 4-9-6 **73** (b) ShaneGray 3 79
(Kristin Stubbs) *reluctant to enter stalls: led on far side of gp: rdn and hdd over 1f out: rallied: kpt on same pce ins fnl f* **8/1**
0020 **3** *1 1/2* **Dodgy Bob**[6] 8206 3-9-5 **72** JoeDoyle 1 74
(Kevin Ryan) *hld up on far side of gp: stdy hdwy over 2f out: effrt and rdn over 1f out: kpt on same pce ins fnl f* **11/1**
2010 **4** *1 1/2* **Wahaab (IRE)**[25] 7959 5-8-9 **67** (p) ShirleyTeasdale(5) 10 65
(Iain Jardine) *hld up: hdwy on nr side of gp over 2f out: rdn and no imp fr over 1f out* **16/1**
0-02 **5** *3* **Jacquotte Delahaye**[11] 8135 5-9-7 **74** PaulMulrennan 6 64
(David Brown) *bmpd s: hld up: rdn and outpcd over 2f out: kpt on fnl f: nvr able to chal* **7/1**[3]
0-00 **6** *1* **Jubilee Brig**[45] 7591 6-9-7 **74** NeilFarley 7 61
(Alan Swinbank) *prom: drvn along over 2f out: wknd over 1f out* **33/1**
0460 **7** *nk* **Sunnyside Bob (IRE)**[79] 6680 3-9-4 **71** BarryMcHugh 5 57
(Neville Bycroft) *blkd s: hld up: rdn over 2f out: sn no imp: btn over 1f out* **80/1**
0360 **8** *nk* **Qortaaj**[16] 8067 3-9-0 **67** (b) SamJames 11 52
(David Loughnane) *hld up in tch on nr side of gp: rdn and effrt over 2f out: wknd over 1f out* **10/1**
24-1 **9** *1 3/4* **Tadaawol**[21] 8012 3-9-5 **72** PJMcDonald 4 53
(Roger Fell) *wnt rt s: in tch: drvn along over 2f out: wknd over 1f out* **7/4**[1]
0001 **10** *3* **Gypsy Major**[22] 7994 4-8-11 **64** (v) PatCosgrave 9 37
(Garry Moss) *in tch: drvn and outpcd over 2f out: sn btn* **5/1**[2]
0000 **11** *5* **Murdanova (IRE)**[102] 5969 3-8-12 **65** TomEaves 8 24
(Karen McLintock) *racd on nr side of gp: chsd ldr to over 2f out: sn rdn and wknd* **25/1**

1m 27.1s (0.90) **Going Correction** +0.20s/f (Slow) **11** Ran SP% **119.1**
Speed ratings (Par 103): **102,100,99,97,94 92,92,92,90,86 81**
CSF £70.43 CT £521.00 TOTE £8.80: £2.10, £2.90, £3.10; EX 71.70 Trifecta £614.40.
Owner Yorkshire Connections Ltd **Bred** John Doyle **Trained** Musley Bank, N Yorks

FOCUS
The three who raced more towards the far side dominated here. The runner-up has been rated to his penultimate C&D form.

8288 ASCENT HOMES H'CAP (DIV I) 6f (Tp)
5:50 (5:57) (Class 6) (0-55,58) 3-Y-O+ **£2,587** (£770; £384; £192) **Stalls** Centre

Form RPR
1144 **1** **Commanche**[13] 8120 7-9-2 **54** (b) GeorgiaCox(5) 5 68
(Chris Dwyer) *cl up: led 1/2-way: rdn clr over 1f out: kpt on strly fnl f* **5/1**[2]
0-00 **2** *4* **Gettin' Lucky**[77] 6744 3-8-12 **45** AndrewMullen 1 47
(John Balding) *in tch: hdwy to chse (clr) wnr wl over 1f out: kpt on fnl f: no imp* **14/1**
3001 **3** *1 3/4* **Mr Conundrum**[49] 7509 3-9-5 **52** PaddyAspell 12 49
(Lynn Siddall) *stdd s: hld up on nr side of gp: hdwy over 1f out: edgd lft ins fnl f: kpt on: nt pce to chal* **8/1**[3]
0221 **4** *1 1/4* **Mr Potter**[10] 8146 3-9-11 **58** 6ex (e) ConnorBeasley 6 51
(Richard Guest) *dwlt: hld up: rdn along 1/2-way: hdwy over 1f out: kpt on fnl f: nrst fin* **5/2**[1]
03 **5** *1 3/4* **Hadley**[16] 2425 3-9-5 **52** JasonHart 4 40
(Tracy Waggott) *t.k.h and sn cl up: effrt and ev ch briefly over 2f out: outpcd fr over 1f out* **33/1**
0004 **6** *1/2* **Jebel Tara**[21] 8013 11-9-1 **48** (bt) PaulMulrennan 13 34
(Alistair Whillans) *hld up: rdn over 2f out: nt clr run briefly over 1f out: no imp fnl f* **12/1**
0600 **7** *1 1/4* **Simply Black (IRE)**[15] 8079 5-8-8 **46** ow1 (p) AnnStokell(5) 14 29
(Ann Stokell) *hld up midfield on nr side of gp: pushed along and effrt over 2f out: wknd over 1f out* **50/1**
05 6 **8** *shd* **Oddsocks (IRE)**[57] 7302 4 8 9 **45** GcorgcDowning(3) 11 27
(Tony Carroll) *bhd: pushed along 1/2-way: no imp fr 2f out* **28/1**
2653 **9** *1/2* **Edith Weston**[21] 8013 3-8-12 **45** (p) KieranO'Neill 2 26
(Robert Cowell) *dwlt: hld up on far side of gp: rdn over 2f out: wknd over 1f out* **10/1**
4100 **10** *2* **No Refund (IRE)**[28] 7912 5-9-6 **53** (p) PJMcDonald 8 28
(David Loughnane) *cl up: drvn along and outpcd over 2f out: sn wknd* **14/1**
0050 **11** *nk* **Jessie Allan (IRE)**[31] 7860 5-8-12 **45** JoeDoyle 9 19
(Jim Goldie) *prom on nr side of gp: struggling over 2f out: sn wknd* **150/1**
0-06 **12** *1* **Upper Lambourn (IRE)**[297] 596 8-8-5 **45** MeganEllingworth(7) 3 16
(John Holt) *led on far side of gp to 1/2-way: rdn and wknd fr 2f out* **66/1**
5046 **13** *3 3/4* **Wimboldsley**[15] 8079 5-9-0 **47** BenCurtis 10 7
(Scott Dixon) *in tch: drvn and struggling over 2f out: sn wknd* **11/1**

1m 13.7s (1.20) **Going Correction** +0.20s/f (Slow) **13** Ran SP% **105.3**
Speed ratings (Par 101): **100,94,92,90,88 87,86,85,85,82 82,80,75**
CSF £52.55 CT £357.91 TOTE £6.60: £2.00, £4.60, £2.40; EX 53.60 Trifecta £489.70.
Owner M M Foulger **Bred** Paramount Bloodstock **Trained** Newmarket, Suffolk
■ Skadi was withdrawn. Price at time of withdrawal 9/2. Rule 4 applies to all bets - deduction 15p in the pound.

FOCUS
A moderate sprint handicap.

8289 ASCENT HOMES H'CAP (DIV II) 6f (Tp)
6:20 (6:25) (Class 6) (0-55,55) 3-Y-O+ **£2,587** (£770; £384; £192) **Stalls** Centre

Form RPR
5301 **1** **Suni Dancer**[57] 7302 5-8-9 **46** oh1 GeorgeDowning(3) 10 56+
(Tony Carroll) *missed break: hld up: gd hdwy over 1f out: rdn to ld ent fnl f: sn clr* **7/1**
525 **2** *2 1/4* **Nefetari**[35] 7793 3-8-12 **46** oh1 (b) BenCurtis 11 49
(Alan Brown) *led: rdn and hdd ent fnl f: kpt on: nt pce of wnr* **28/1**
2420 **3** *3/4* **Canford Belle**[10] 8146 3-9-6 **54** PaddyAspell 9 55
(Grant Tuer) *hld up in tch: rdn over 2f out: hdwy over 1f out: kpt on ins fnl f* **6/1**[3]
0000 **4** *1/2* **Centre Haafhd**[21] 8013 5-8-12 **46** oh1 (b) AndrewMullen 6 46
(Kenneth Slack) *t.k.h early: prom: rdn over 2f out: kpt on same pce ins fnl f* **6/1**[3]
5005 **5** *1/2* **Amber Crystal**[45] 7604 4-8-12 **46** oh1 TomEaves 13 44
(Linda Perratt) *hld up: rdn and hdwy over 1f out: no imp ins fnl f* **25/1**
0353 **6** *3 1/2* **Chandresh**[30] 7863 3-9-0 **48** (v) KieranO'Neill 2 36
(Robert Cowell) *cl up tl rdn and wknd over 1f out* **9/1**
4240 **7** *3/4* **Sea Of Green**[90] 6341 4-8-10 **47** NathanEvans(3) 4 32
(Jim Goldie) *hld up in tch: drvn and outpcd over 2f out: no imp fr over 1f out* **8/1**
4050 **8** *nk* **Golden Rosanna**[49] 7509 3-8-9 **46** oh1 JackDuern(3) 12 30
(Steph Hollinshead) *prom: rdn over 2f out: wknd over 1f out* **40/1**
5050 **9** *shd* **Autumn Tonic (IRE)**[293] 658 4-9-6 **54** SamJames 7 38
(David Barron) *prom: effrt and pushed along over 2f out: wknd over 1f out* **5/1**[2]
2546 **10** *9* **Isntshesomething**[62] 7144 4-9-3 **51** (p) ConnorBeasley 5 8
(Richard Guest) *t.k.h early: trckd ldrs tl rdn and wknd over 1f out* **4/1**[1]
5160 **11** *shd* **Anjuna Beach (USA)**[15] 8086 6-9-0 **53** AnnStokell(5) 1 10
(Ann Stokell) *s.i.s: bhd and outpcd: struggling and detached 1/2-way: nvr on terms* **25/1**

1m 13.0s (0.50) **Going Correction** +0.20s/f (Slow) **11** Ran SP% **112.4**
Speed ratings (Par 101): **104,101,100,99,98 94,93,92,92,80 80**
CSF £174.56 CT £1073.69 TOTE £6.40: £2.10, £5.20, £2.30; EX 94.10 Trifecta £355.90.
Owner Ian Furlong **Bred** Mickley Stud And Mr G A Greaves **Trained** Cropthorne, Worcs
■ Major Muscari was withdrawn. Price at time of withdrawal 14/1. Rule 4 applies to all bets - deduction 5p in the pound

FOCUS
This was the quicker of the two divisions by 0.70sec.

8290 AVANT HOMES MEDIAN AUCTION MAIDEN STKS 5f (Tp)
6:50 (6:56) (Class 5) 3-5-Y-O **£2,911** (£866; £432; £216) **Stalls** Centre

Form RPR
0 **1** **Monsieur Paddy**[67] 7011 3-9-5 0 JoeyHaynes 5 68
(Tony Carroll) *dwlt: hld up in tch: hdwy to ld over 1f out: rdn out fnl f* **18/1**
6026 **2** *3/4* **Poetic Queen (IRE)**[14] 8093 3-9-0 55 PatCosgrave 7 59
(Eric Alston) *prom: rdn along 1/2-way: chsd wnr ins fnl f: kpt on: hld nr fin* **14/1**
4 **3** *3/4* **Dandilion (IRE)**[90] 6317 3-9-0 0 (t) KieranO'Neill 6 56
(Alex Hales) *pressed ldr: rdn and ev ch over 1f out: kpt on same pce ins fnl f* **2/1**[1]
4 *1 3/4* **Diamond Indulgence** 3-8-11 0 [1] NoelGarbutt(3) 8 50
(Derek Shaw) *dwlt: t.k.h: hld up: stdy hdwy 1/2-way: sn rdn: kpt on ins fnl f: nt pce to chal* **66/1**
5332 **5** *shd* **Eternalist**[35] 7793 3-9-0 60 JoeDoyle 4 50
(Jim Goldie) *t.k.h: led: rdn and hdd over 1f out: no ex fnl f* **2/1**[1]
2000 **6** *2 1/4* **Lady Elizabeth (IRE)**[3] 8242 3-8-7 54 RPWalsh(7) 9 42
(Scott Dixon) *hld up: drvn and outpcd 1/2-way: kpt on fnl f: nvr able to chal* **80/1**
3503 **7** *nse* **Hot Stuff**[35] 7793 3-9-2 60 GeorgeDowning(3) 3 46
(Tony Carroll) *t.k.h: cl up: rdn over 2f out: wknd appr fnl f* **11/2**[3]
0 **8** *1/2* **Royboy**[21] 8012 3-9-5 0 TomEaves 10 45
(Ollie Pears) *dwlt: bhd: drvn and struggling 1/2-way: nvr on terms* **28/1**
3- **9** *2 1/4* **Private Donald**[357] 8287 3-9-2 0 EoinWalsh(3) 2 36
(Robert Cowell) *dwlt: t.k.h and in tch: rdn over 2f out: wknd over 1f out* **9/2**[2]
10 *23* **Diamond Eagle (IRE)** 4-9-0 0 CharlieBennett(5) 1
(Shaun Harris) *s.s: a struggling in rr* **100/1**

1m 0.68s (1.18) **Going Correction** +0.20s/f (Slow) **10** Ran SP% **119.3**
Speed ratings (Par 103): **98,96,95,92,92 89,88,88,84,47**
CSF £240.31 TOTE £21.80: £5.10, £2.80, £1.20; EX 321.40 Trifecta £1864.20.
Owner Mayden Stud **Bred** Mayden Stud, J A And D S Dewhurst **Trained** Cropthorne, Worcs

FOCUS
This was a weak maiden. The third has been rated similar to her debut.
T/Plt: £177.40 to a £1 stake. Pool: £77,296.35 - 318.05 winning tickets T/Qpdt: £55.90 to a £1 stake. Pool: £9,261.81 - 122.42 winning tickets **Richard Young**

8291 - 8304a (Foreign Racing) - See Raceform Interactive

8283 NEWCASTLE (A.W) (L-H)
Saturday, December 10

OFFICIAL GOING: Tapeta: standard
Wind: Light, across Weather: Overcast

8305 PINNACLE-SHARE PRIZE DRAW MAIDEN STKS 1m 5y (Tp)
12:15 (12:16) (Class 5) 2-Y-O **£2,911** (£866; £432; £216) **Stalls** Centre

Form RPR
1 **Poetique (IRE)** 2-9-5 0 RobertHavlin 6 86+
(John Gosden) *reluctant to enter stalls: s.i.s: sn prom: shkn up to ld over 1f out: drew clr ins fnl f: eased towards fin: promising* **4/5**[1]
4 **2** *8* **Oxford Thinking (IRE)**[17] 8074 2-9-5 0 NickyMackay 10 66+
(John Gosden) *t.k.h: led: rdn over 2f out: hdd over 1f out: kpt on same pce* **9/2**[3]
0 **3** *2* **Nick Vedder**[57] 7318 2-9-0 0 JordanVaughan(5) 9 62
(K R Burke) *chsd ldrs: rdn and outpcd over 2f out: rallied over 1f out: kpt on fnl f: nvr able to chal* **16/1**
525 **4** *2 3/4* **Avantgardist (GER)**[28] 7940 2-9-5 73 PJMcDonald 5 56
(Mark Johnston) *cl up: rdn along 3f out: edgd lft and outpcd over 1f out: sn no imp* **9/1**
5 *nse* **Royal Flute** 2-9-0 0 JasonHart 4 50
(Mark Walford) *s.i.s: rn green in rr: hdwy over 1f out: kpt on fnl f: nvr able to chal* **100/1**
0 **6** *2 1/2* **My Brother Mike (IRE)**[29] 7908 2-9-5 0 AndrewMullen 8 50
(Daniel Mark Loughnane) *t.k.h: chsd ldrs: drvn over 2f out: edgd lft and wknd over 1f out* **33/1**
00 **7** *3/4* **Size Matters**[33] 7845 2-9-5 0 DougieCostello 3 48
(Mark Walford) *s.i.s: hld up: pushed along and struggling over 2f out: sn wknd* **100/1**
8 *2 3/4* **Ignacio Zuloaga (IRE)** 2-9-5 0 JoeyHaynes 7 42
(Jo Hughes) *chsd ldng gp: drvn over 3f out: wknd over 2f out* **33/1**
0 **9** *8* **Satis House**[22] 8009 2-8-9 0 GarryWhillans(5) 2 20
(Susan Corbett) *hld up: drvn and struggling over 2f out: sn wknd* **100/1**
10 *19* **Oden** 2-9-5 0 JackMitchell 1
(Roger Varian) *s.i.s: sn prom: rdn over 3f out: wknd over 2f out: lost tch and eased over 1f out* **7/2**[2]

1m 40.35s (1.75) **Going Correction** +0.175s/f (Slow) **10** Ran SP% **120.7**
Speed ratings (Par 96): **98,90,88,85,85 82,81,79,71,52**
CSF £5.02 TOTE £1.70: £1.10, £1.50, £3.60; EX 6.30 Trifecta £45.60.
Owner Godolphin **Bred** Darley **Trained** Newmarket, Suffolk

 The Form Book, Raceform Ltd, Newbury, RG14 5SJ

FOCUS
Not much depth to this but a useful winner.

8306 PINNACLE RACING "LIKE" US ON FACEBOOK H'CAP (DIV I) 1m 5y (Tp)
12:50 (12:50) (Class 6) (0-60,60) 3-Y-O+ **£2,587** (£770; £384; £192) **Stalls** Centre

Form RPR

6000 **1** **Star Of Spring (IRE)**[23] 7995 4-9-7 **60**.......................... MartinDwyer 12 70+
(Iain Jardine) *t.k.h: hld up: gd hdwy nr side of gp over 1f out: led ins fnl f: pushed clr* **9/2**[1]

5013 **2** 3 ¼ **Table Manners**[11] 8144 4-8-11 **53**................................ NathanEvans(3) 2 55
(Wilf Storey) *trckd ldrs: drvn along over 2f out: rallied to ld over 1f out: edgd lft and hdd ins fnl f: kpt on same pce* **9/2**[1]

4564 **3** 1 ¼ **Cool Strutter (IRE)**[23] 7995 4-9-5 **58**............................(b) SamJames 13 59
(Karen Tutty) *hld up: hdwy whn nt clr run over 2f out to over 1f out: rdn and kpt on ins fnl f: nt rch first two* **8/1**[3]

3440 **4** ½ **Mrs Biggs**[28] 7943 4-8-12 **56**..................................(b) PhilDennis(5) 9 54
(Declan Carroll) *led to over 2f out: sn rdn: rallied and ev ch over 1f out: no ex ins fnl f* **15/2**[2]

65 **5** nk **Dancin Alpha**[11] 8141 5-9-3 **56**... NeilFarley 1 53
(Alan Swinbank) *in tch: hdwy to ld over 2f out: rdn and hdd over 1f out: no ex ins fnl f* **10/1**

0302 **6** ¾ **Rosy Ryan (IRE)**[11] 8146 6-9-1 **54**................................ JamesSullivan 7 50
(Tina Jackson) *t.k.h: hld up: rdn over 2f out: hdwy and edgd lft over 1f out: no imp fnl f* **9/2**[1]

00-0 **7** 2 **Percy's Lass**[57] 7326 4-9-2 **55**.. BenCurtis 14 46
(Brian Ellison) *hld up: drvn and outpcd over 2f out: rallied over 1f out: kpt on fnl f: no imp* **20/1**

1300 **8** ½ **Basingstoke (IRE)**[238] 1498 7-9-7 **60**...................(p) JosephineGordon 5 50
(Daniel Mark Loughnane) *prom: rdn 3f out: rallied: outpcd fr over 1f out* **14/1**

000F **9** 1 ¾ **Disclosure**[60] 7261 5-9-7 **60**.. JasonHart 3 46
(Les Eyre) *taken early to post: s.i.s: sn in tch: rdn and ev ch briefly over 1f out: wknd ins fnl f* **18/1**

0003 **10** ½ **Cosmic Dust**[32] 7856 3-8-10 **50**.................................. ConnorBeasley 10 35
(Richard Whitaker) *hld up in tch: drvn and outpcd over 2f out: n.d after* **25/1**

4U00 **11** ¾ **Patron Of Explores (USA)**[235] 1556 5-8-7 **46** oh1....(t) AndrewMullen 8 30
(Patrick Holmes) *s.i.s: bhd: rdn and hdwy over 2f out: no further imp fr over 1f out* **50/1**

0250 **12** 1 **Cyflymder (IRE)**[152] 4200 10-8-5 **51**..................... NatalieHambling(7) 11 32
(David C Griffiths) *t.k.h: cl up tl rdn and wknd fr 2f out* **80/1**

3400 **13** 1 ½ **Master Of Song**[30] 7888 9-8-5 **51**..................................(v[1]) KevinLundie(7) 6 29
(Roy Bowring) *t.k.h: prom tl rdn and wknd over 2f out* **22/1**

0600 **14** 12 **Haidees Reflection**[33] 7850 6-8-10 **49**.................................. JoeDoyle 4
(Jim Goldie) *s.i.s: bhd: struggling 1/2-way: sn lost tch* **25/1**

1m 40.27s (1.67) **Going Correction** +0.175s/f (Slow)
WFA 3 from 4yo+ 1lb **14** Ran SP% **118.4**
Speed ratings (Par 101): **98,94,93,93,92 91,89,89,87,87 86,85,83,71**
CSF £20.70 CT £163.80 TOTE £4.50: £1.50, £2.00, £3.50; EX 26.30 Trifecta £118.60.
Owner I J Jardine **Bred** Mrs Mary Gallagher **Trained** Carrutherstown, D'fries & G'way

FOCUS
A moderate handicap but the winner was formerly rated much higher.

8307 PINNACLE RACING "LIKE" US ON FACEBOOK H'CAP (DIV II) 1m 5y (Tp)
1:25 (1:26) (Class 6) (0-60,61) 3-Y-O+ **£2,587** (£770; £384; £192) **Stalls** Centre

Form RPR

4524 **1** **Leonard Thomas**[36] 7795 6-9-3 **59**.......................(p) GeorgeDowning(3) 4 67
(Tony Carroll) *s.i.s: hld up: hdwy over 1f out: rdn to ld wl ins fnl f: hld on wl cl home* **15/2**[3]

0521 **2** nk **Lozah**[11] 8145 3-9-7 **61**.. JackGarritty 12 68
(Roger Fell) *hld up: hdwy over 2f out: effrt and disp ld fr over 1f out: kpt on fnl f: hld nr fin* **6/5**[1]

4005 **3** nk **Mr Sundowner (USA)**[110] 5729 4-8-11 **50**.....................(t) ShaneGray 10 56
(Wilf Storey) *hld up: smooth hdwy on nr side of gp to ld over 1f out: sn rdn: edgd lft and hdd wl ins fnl f: no ex cl home* **25/1**

0604 **4** 3 **Bromance**[11] 8145 3-9-2 **56**..(p) AndrewMullen 7 56
(Peter Niven) *midfield: rdn along 3f out: rallied and ev ch briefly over 1f out: no ex last 100yds* **9/2**[2]

0434 **5** 1 ¾ **Jessica Jo (IRE)**[8] 8194 3-9-0 **54**...............................(b) PJMcDonald 9 50
(Mark Johnston) *prom: rdn along over 2f out: hdwy and ev ch briefly over 1f out: wknd ins fnl f* **8/1**

0000 **6** 1 ¾ **Breathless**[72] 6907 4-9-7 **60**...(t) PaulMulrennan 6 52
(Clive Mulhall) *hld up: hdwy on far side of gp over 2f out: rdn over 1f out: wknd fnl f* **80/1**

0030 **7** ½ **Outlaw Torn (IRE)**[11] 8141 7-8-12 **51**........................(e) ConnorBeasley 5 42
(Richard Guest) *prom: drvn along over 2f out: rallied: wknd fnl f* **11/1**

0000 **8** 2 ½ **Ivors Involvement (IRE)**[23] 7994 4-8-10 **49**............... JamesSullivan 14 34
(Tina Jackson) *t.k.h: hld up: hdwy whn n.m.r briefly wl over 1f out: effrt whn hmpd over 1f out: sn no ex* **20/1**

6026 **9** nk **Ada Misobel (IRE)**[130] 4972 3-8-11 **54**...................(p) NathanEvans(3) 11 39
(Garry Moss) *t.k.h: w ldr: clr of rest over 5f out: led over 3f out to over 1f out: sn wknd* **14/1**

2000 **10** 2 ¾ **Charava (IRE)**[17] 8064 4-8-12 **58**.................................[1] PaulaMuir(7) 13 37
(Patrick Holmes) *hld up midfield: rdn and edgd lft over 2f out: wknd wl over 1f out* **66/1**

03 **11** 2 **Let Right Be Done**[127] 5114 4-9-3 **56**...................................... TomEaves 1 30
(Linda Perratt) *hld up: rdn along over 2f out: wknd over 1f out* **25/1**

6000 **12** 1 ¾ **Tom's Anna (IRE)**[87] 6478 6-8-0 **46** oh1........................... RPWalsh(7) 8 16
(Sean Regan) *led: clr w one other over 5f out: hdd over 3f out: rdn and wknd wl over 1f out* **100/1**

6060 **13** ½ **Kodiac Lady (IRE)**[11] 8146 4-8-10 **54**.....................(e) SophieKilloran(5) 2 23
(Simon West) *hld up on far side of gp: struggling over 2f out: sn btn* **33/1**

2000 **14** 6 **Bunker Hill Lass**[8] 8191 4-8-1 **47**..................................(p) JaneElliott(7) 3 3
(Michael Appleby) *in tch: rdn along over 3f out: wknd over 2f out* **50/1**

1m 40.18s (1.58) **Going Correction** +0.175s/f (Slow)
WFA 3 from 4yo+ 1lb **14** Ran SP% **122.6**
Speed ratings (Par 101): **99,98,98,95,93 91,91,88,88,85 83,82,81,75**
CSF £16.10 CT £239.89 TOTE £9.20: £2.30, £1.20, £8.00; EX 24.20 Trifecta £465.20.
Owner Mrs E Arundel **Bred** Wedgewood Estates **Trained** Cropthorne, Worcs

FOCUS
A slightly quicker time than the first division.

8308 AFFORDABLE SHARES AVAILABLE H'CAP 5f (Tp)
2:00 (2:00) (Class 3) (0-95,95) 3-Y-O+ **£7,762** (£2,310; £1,154; £577) **Stalls** Centre

Form RPR

4514 **1** **Dynamo Walt (IRE)**[10] 8150 5-8-5 **82**.......................(v) NoelGarbutt(3) 10 89
(Derek Shaw) *hld up: rdn and hdwy over 1f out: kpt on wl fnl f: led last stride* **14/1**

1121 **2** shd **Showdaisy**[30] 7892 3-8-8 **87**...................................(p) ShirleyTeasdale(5) 3 94+
(Keith Dalgleish) *taken early to post: t.k.h: disp ld: led and rdn over 1f out: drifted lft ins fnl f: kpt on wl: hdd last stride* **8/1**

0301 **3** nk **Memories Galore (IRE)**[10] 8150 4-9-1 **89**.................... PaulMulrennan 7 95+
(Harry Dunlop) *trckd ldrs: smooth hdwy and ev ch over 1f out to ins fnl f: sn rdn: kpt on: no ex nr fin* **7/4**[1]

5003 **4** hd **Razin' Hell**[30] 7892 5-8-9 **83**..(v) BenCurtis 11 88
(John Balding) *hld up: rdn and hdwy over 1f out: chsd ldrs ins fnl f: kpt on: hld nr fin* **18/1**

0640 **5** shd **Mappin Time (IRE)**[23] 7990 8-8-9 **83**.............................(be) JasonHart 1 88
(Tim Easterby) *bhd: drvn and outpcd after 2f: rallied over 1f out: kpt on wl fnl f: nrst fin* **18/1**

0506 **6** ½ **Poyle Vinnie**[5] 8232 6-9-3 **94**.................................. AlistairRawlinson(3) 8 98
(Michael Appleby) *taken early to post: hld up: smooth hdwy to chse ldrs wl over 1f out: sn rdn: edgd lft and kpt on same pce ins fnl f* **6/1**[3]

-36 **7** shd **Zapper Cass (FR)**[16] 8083 3-8-9 **83**.. TomEaves 9 85
(Roger Fell) *hld up: rdn over 2f out: hdwy fnl f: kpt on wl: nrst fin* **10/1**

0450 **8** 1 ½ **Outrage**[16] 8083 4-8-8 **82**... JosephineGordon 6 80
(Daniel Kubler) *chsd ldrs: rdn along 1/2-way: one pce whn edgd lft ins fnl f: hld whn n.m.r briefly last 50yds* **10/1**

1000 **9** ¾ **Meadway**[49] 7537 5-9-4 **92**...(p) ConnorBeasley 5 86
(Bryan Smart) *in tch: outpcd whn hung lft over 2f out: btn over 1f out* **25/1**

0400 **10** 1 ¼ **Another Wise Kid (IRE)**[8] 8192 8-8-11 **85**.....................[1] PJMcDonald 4 75
(Paul Midgley) *bhd and sn drvn along: nvr on terms* **25/1**

1002 **11** ¾ **Bosham**[5] 8232 6-9-4 **95**..(bt) NathanEvans(3) 2 82
(Michael Easterby) *mounted on crse and taken early to post: disp ld to over 1f out: sn rdn and wknd* **11/2**[2]

58.65s (-0.85) **Going Correction** +0.175s/f (Slow) **11** Ran SP% **120.2**
Speed ratings (Par 107): **113,112,112,112,111 111,110,108,107,105 104**
CSF £124.19 CT £302.36 TOTE £19.00: £4.20, £2.40, £1.20; EX 147.20 Trifecta £1205.50.
Owner Brian Johnson (Northamptonshire) **Bred** Dan Major **Trained** Sproxton, Leics
■ Stewards' Enquiry : Shirley Teasdale two-day ban; careless riding (26th-27th Dec)

FOCUS
This was run at a fast, contested pace and the runner-up and third probably want their efforts upgrading. It's hard to rate the race positively given the bunched finish.

8309 ARRANGE A PINNACLE STABLE VISIT AT WYNYARD H'CAP 2m 56y (Tp)
2:35 (2:35) (Class 6) (0-60,59) 3-Y-O+ **£2,587** (£770; £384; £192) **Stalls** Low

Form RPR

0/1 **1** **Shan Dun na nGall (IRE)**[9] 8180 5-9-5 **52**.............(vt) LemosdeSouza 6 59
(Amy Murphy) *hld up: gd hdwy on outside to ld over 2f out: rdn and edgd lft ins fnl f: kpt on strly* **11/2**[2]

3320 **2** 1 ½ **Maple Stirrup (IRE)**[126] 5155 4-9-2 **56**............................ PaulaMuir(7) 7 61
(Patrick Holmes) *hld up: hdwy far rail over 3f out: chsd wnr over 1f out: kpt on fnl f: nt pce to chal* **16/1**

0200 **3** 1 ¼ **Ryan The Giant**[39] 7746 3-8-8 **49**...........................(p) ConnorBeasley 11 53
(Keith Dalgleish) *hld up: hdwy far side and disp 2nd pl over 1f out: kpt on same pce ins fnl f* **13/2**[3]

2361 **4** 1 **Chestnut Storm (IRE)**[61] 7231 3-9-4 **59**....................... RobertHavlin 10 62
(Brian Barr) *hld up: rdn along 3f out: hdwy on outside over 1f out: kpt on fnl f: nt pce to chal* **14/1**

3362 **5** 1 ½ **Jan Smuts (IRE)**[15] 8091 8-9-7 **57**..........................(tp) NathanEvans(3) 4 58
(Wilf Storey) *prom: effrt and ev ch over 2f out: sn rdn: kpt on same pce over 1f out* **9/1**

0063 **6** shd **Waltz Darling (IRE)**[15] 8091 8-9-0 **47**...........................(b) KieranO'Neill 9 48
(Keith Reveley) *hld up: gd hdwy to chse ldrs 6f out: led briefly over 2f out: edgd lft: outpcd fr over 1f out* **16/1**

0566 **7** ½ **Par Three (IRE)**[16] 8084 5-9-2 **52**.........................(p) GeorgeDowning(3) 1 52
(Tony Carroll) *hld up midfield: hdwy and prom over 3f out: rdn and edgd lft 2f out: sn outpcd* **25/1**

-000 **8** 1 ¼ **Crakehall Lad (IRE)**[100] 4971 5-9-0 **47**..............................(p) NeilFarley 2 45
(Andrew Crook) *hld up: rdn over 3f out: hdwy over 1f out: kpt on: no imp* **28/1**

4155 **9** 8 **Miss Tree**[23] 7992 5-9-7 **54**.. DougieCostello 14 43
(John Quinn) *t.k.h: hld up midfield on outside: effrt and pushed along over 2f out: wknd over 1f out* **2/1**[1]

605- **10** 6 **The Special House (IRE)**[513] 4296 4-9-10 **57**.................. BenCurtis 12 39
(Brian Ellison) *led and clr w one other to 6f out: hdd over 2f out: wknd wl over 1f out* **20/1**

0330 **11** 2 **Adrakhan (FR)**[39] 7746 5-9-2 **49**.. ShaneGray 3 28
(Wilf Storey) *hld up: drvn and struggling over 4f out: n.d after* **12/1**

5040 **12** nse **Haymarket**[43] 7657 7-9-1 **53**... GarryWhillans(5) 13 32
(R Mike Smith) *t.k.h: chsd ldr and clr of rest to 6f out: rdn and ev ch over 2f out: wknd over 1f out* **25/1**

56-F **13** 7 **Sr Swing**[10] 7746 5-8-12 **45**... AndrewMullen 8 16
(Peter Niven) *hld up in tch: drvn and lost pl over 3f out: sn struggling* **66/1**

0510 **14** 36 **Bassett Bleu**[43] 7657 3-8-7 **48**...(b) MartinDwyer 5
(Iain Jardine) *t.k.h: chsd clr ldng pair: drvn over 3f out: rallied: wknd qckly wl over 1f out: t.o* **10/1**

3m 38.85s (3.65) **Going Correction** +0.25s/f (Slow)
WFA 3 from 4yo+ 8lb **14** Ran SP% **124.7**
Speed ratings (Par 101): **100,99,98,98,97 97,97,96,92,89 88,88,84,66**
CSF £87.52 CT £600.91 TOTE £6.90: £2.30, £4.10, £2.60; EX 78.10 Trifecta £744.00.
Owner J Melo **Bred** Donal Mac A Bhaird **Trained** Newmarket, Suffolk

FOCUS
A muddling sort of tempo to this moderate staying handicap.

8310 GARRY MOSS MAIDEN STKS 1m 4f 98y (Tp)
3:10 (3:10) (Class 5) 3-4-Y-O **£3,234** (£962; £481; £240) **Stalls** High

Form RPR

-235 **1** **Paris Magic**[50] 7499 3-9-5 81..................................(b[1]) JosephineGordon 5 82
(Hugo Palmer) *hld up in last pl: hdwy over 2f out: rdn to ld over 1f out: sn clr* **11/8**[2]

6622 **2** 4 ½ **Henry Croft**[109] 5742 3-9-2 82.................................... GeorgeDowning(3) 3 75
(Tony Carroll) *in tch: rdn over 4f out: rallied and chsd clr ldr over 2f out to over 1f out: sn chsng wnr: no imp fnl f* **7/2**[3]

06 **3** *4* **Palindrome (USA)**^{23} 7991 3-9-5 0 ShaneGray 4 68?
(Ronald Thompson) *chsd ldr to 1/2-way: prom: effrt and rdn 3f out: outpcd fnl 2f* **100/1**

4332 **4** *¾* **Statuesque**^{15} 8090 3-9-0 77 (b^{1}) RobertHavlin 1 62
(Sir Michael Stoute) *led at ordinary gallop: qcknd clr bnd over 3f out: drvn and hdd over 1f out: folded tamely* **5/4**^{1}

5 *49* **Psychology**^{14} 3-9-5 0 ConnorBeasley 2
(Kenny Johnson) *missed break: sn rcvrd and chsd ldrs: wnt 2nd 1/2-way: drvn and wknd fr 3f out: eased whn no ch fnl f* **100/1**

2m 43.07s (1.97) **Going Correction** +0.25s/f (Slow) **5** Ran SP% **110.8**
Speed ratings (Par 103): **103,100,97,96,64**
CSF £6.64 TOTE £2.30: £1.40, £2.40; EX 6.40 Trifecta £53.40.
Owner Abdulla Al Mansoori **Bred** Bolton Grange **Trained** Newmarket, Suffolk

FOCUS
An uncompetitive maiden. It's doubtful the winner had to improve to get off the mark.

8311 PINNACLERACING.CO.UK H'CAP — 7f 14y (Tp)
3:45 (3:48) (Class 2) (0-105,98) 3-Y-**£12,602** (£3,772; £1,886; £944; £470) **Stalls** Centre

Form RPR

0213 **1** **Steel Train (FR)**^{19} 8049 5-8-11 **95** PatrickVaughan$^{(7)}$ 5 104
(David O'Meara) *hld up: hdwy 2f out: rdn to ld 1f out: drifted lft and hrd pressed ins fnl f: kpt on wl cl home* **3/1**^{1}

3004 **2** *nk* **Fuwairt (IRE)**^{9} 8177 4-8-10 **87** ConnorBeasley 4 95
(Roger Fell) *hld up: gd hdwy over 1f out: rdn and ev ch ins fnl f: edgd lft: kpt on: hld cl home* **9/2**^{2}

0600 **3** *¾* **Right Touch**^{23} 7984 6-9-7 **98** JackGarritty 7 104
(Richard Fahey) *hld up in tch: hdwy and ev ch briefly appr fnl f: kpt on: hld towards fin* **14/1**

2403 **4** *2* **Plucky Dip**^{16} 8083 5-8-5 **82** DannyBrock 11 83
(John Ryan) *hld up in tch: rdn over 2f out: kpt on fnl f: nvr able to chal* **8/1**^{3}

4115 **5** *shd* **Lefortovo (FR)**^{72} 6911 3-8-11 **88** RobertHavlin 9 88
(Jo Hughes) *chsd ldr to over 1f out: rdn and outpcd fnl f* **18/1**

0001 **6** *3* **Cornwallville (IRE)**^{23} 7990 4-9-7 **98** JosephineGordon 2 90
(Roger Fell) *hld up: rdn and outpcd over 2f out: kpt on ins fnl f: no imp* **3/1**^{1}

0544 **7** *¾* **Valbchek (IRE)**^{31} 7868 7-9-4 **95** (p) MartinDwyer 10 85
(Jane Chapple-Hyam) *led: rdn over 2f out: hdd 1f out: sn btn: eased cl home* **10/1**

420 **8** *2 ½* **Tiger Jim**^{26} 7957 6-8-1 **81** NathanEvans$^{(3)}$ 1 64
(Jim Goldie) *prom: drvn and outpcd over 2f out: n.d after* **18/1**

6003 **9** *nk* **Kingsley Klarion (IRE)**^{143} 4519 3-8-11 **88** PJMcDonald 3 71
(Mark Johnston) *chsd ldrs: drvn along over 2f out: wknd wl over 1f out* **25/1**

4144 **10** *5* **Basil Berry**^{21} 8029 5-9-6 **97** (b) AndrewMullen 8 66
(Chris Dwyer) *chsd ldrs: drvn along fr 3f: wknd wl over 1f out* **10/1**

1m 25.98s (-0.22) **Going Correction** +0.175s/f (Slow) **10** Ran SP% **118.5**
Speed ratings (Par 109): **108,107,106,104,104 100,100,97,96,91**
CSF £16.63 CT £165.42 TOTE £3.90: £1.60, £1.60, £4.30; EX 17.10 Trifecta £145.80.
Owner Rasio Cymru I & Dutch Rose Partnerhsip **Bred** Erich Schmid **Trained** Upper Helmsley, N Yorks

■ Stewards' Enquiry : Patrick Vaughan two-day ban; used whip above the permitted level (26th-27th Dec)

FOCUS
The pace was steady to begin with but picked up plenty early enough, with the principals coming from the back. A small pb from the winner, with the third rated close to his turf best.

8312 FORWARD ASSIST VETERANS CHARITY H'CAP — 5f (Tp)
4:15 (4:17) (Class 6) (0-55,55) 3-Y-O+ **£2,587** (£770; £384; £192) **Stalls** Centre

Form RPR

1302 **1** **Novabridge**^{32} 7860 8-8-13 **52** (b) GemmaTutty$^{(5)}$ 9 58
(Karen Tutty) *cl up: led 2f out: sn hrd pressed: hld on wl towards fin* **17/2**

2410 **2** *½* **Lady Bacchus**^{22} 8013 3-9-2 **50** (b) ConnorBeasley 4 54
(Richard Guest) *prom: hdwy to press wnr over 1f out: drvn along and kpt on fnl f: hld nr fin* **5/2**^{1}

0006 **3** *2* **Secret Millionaire (IRE)**^{29} 7913 9-9-2 **55** (p) CharlieBennett$^{(5)}$ 6 52
(Shaun Harris) *s.i.s: hld up: hdwy on far side of gp over 1f out: kpt on ins fnl f: nt pce to chal* **7/1**^{3}

0306 **4** *½* **A J Cook (IRE)**^{32} 7859 6-9-2 **50** AndrewMullen 13 45
(Ron Barr) *hld up: drvn along 1/2-way: rallied over 1f out: kpt on fnl f: nrst fin* **18/1**

0616 **5** *½* **Captain Scooby**^{22} 8013 10-9-4 **52** (b) DougieCostello 2 45+
(Richard Guest) *missed break: bhd and detached: gd hdwy on far side of gp fnl f: fin strly* **14/1**

5320 **6** *¾* **Zebelini (IRE)**^{67} 7046 4-8-8 **49** ^{1} KevinLundie$^{(7)}$ 8 40
(Roy Bowring) *led to 2f out: drvn and no ex fnl f* **14/1**

-000 **7** *hd* **Arctic Lynx (IRE)**^{29} 7913 9-9-1 **54** (p) AnnStokell$^{(5)}$ 10 44
(Ann Stokell) *taken early to post: bhd: pushed along and hdwy over 1f out: kpt on fnl f: no imp* **66/1**

0302 **8** *hd* **Prigsnov Dancer (IRE)**^{26} 7961 11-8-13 **47** JoeDoyle 11 36
(John Balding) *sn towards rr: outpcd 1/2-way: kpt on ins fnl f: no imp* **10/1**

0053 **9** *nk* **Tribesman**^{4} 8242 3-9-7 **55** ^{1} SamJames 14 43
(Marjorie Fife) *towards rr: drvn and outpcd 1/2-way: n.d after* **3/1**^{2}

3030 **10** *1 ¾* **Birrafun (IRE)**^{112} 5636 3-9-4 **52** RobertHavlin 1 34
(Ann Duffield) *in tch: gng wl over 2f out: rdn over 1f out: sn wknd* **33/1**

-500 **11** *1 ½* **Zeb's Fantasy (IRE)**^{23} 7983 3-9-2 **50** (v) LemosdeSouza 3 26
(Amy Murphy) *chsd ldrs: rdn over 2f out: wknd over 1f out* **33/1**

0056 **12** *1 ¼* **Pancake Day**^{4} 8242 4-9-6 **54** (v) JosephineGordon 12 26
(David C Griffiths) *cl up tl rdn and wknd over 1f out* **12/1**

1m 0.31s (0.81) **Going Correction** +0.175s/f (Slow) **12** Ran SP% **119.4**
Speed ratings (Par 101): **100,99,96,95,94 93,92,92,92,89 86,84**
CSF £29.83 CT £163.00 TOTE £7.50: £2.40, £2.10, £2.90; EX 20.80 Trifecta £159.20.
Owner Thoroughbred Homes Ltd **Bred** Bishopswood Bloodstock & Trickledown Stud **Trained** Osmotherley, N Yorks

FOCUS
A moderate sprint handicap.
T/Plt: £25.60 to a £1 stake. Pool: £57,424.74 - 1,636.94 winning units. T/Qpdt: £12.30 to a £1 stake. Pool: £3,684.46 - 221.22 winning units. **Richard Young**

8205 WOLVERHAMPTON (A.W) (L-H)
Saturday, December 10

OFFICIAL GOING: Tapeta: standard
Wind: Light across Weather: Raining

8313 32RED.COM MAIDEN STKS — 5f 20y (Tp)
5:15 (5:15) (Class 5) 2-Y-O **£3,881** (£1,155; £577; £288) **Stalls** Low

Form RPR

6504 **1** **Cajmere**^{12} 8136 2-9-5 68 RichardKingscote 6 77
(Tom Dascombe) *mde all: rdn and hung rt over 1f out: styd on u.p* **11/2**

2544 **2** *1 ½* **Her Terms**^{9} 8175 2-9-0 70 ^{1} PatCosgrave 9 67
(William Haggas) *hmpd s: sn chsng wnr: rdn and edgd rt over 1f out: styd on same pce ins fnl f* **7/2**^{2}

32 **3** *¾* **The Daley Express (IRE)**^{14} 8118 2-9-5 0 GeorgeBaker 11 69+
(Ed McMahon) *hmpd s: hld up: nt clr run wl over 1f out: hdwy sn after: rdn and hung lft ins fnl f: r.o* **11/8**^{1}

2 **4** *2* **Speed Freak**^{133} 4879 2-9-0 70 (v) SeanLevey 10 57
(Ralph Beckett) *s.i.s and hmpd s: hld up: hdwy over 1f out: nt rch ldrs* **10/1**

4640 **5** *½* **Hathfa (FR)**^{77} 6762 2-9-0 72 AdamKirby 3 55
(Richard Hughes) *chsd ldrs: rdn over 1f out: no ex ins fnl f* **9/2**^{3}

66 **6** *½* **Brother McGonagall**^{11} 8140 2-9-5 0 DuranFentiman 2 59
(Tim Easterby) *hld up in tch: rdn over 1f out: no ex fnl f* **25/1**

0 **7** *7* **Sugar Plum (IRE)**^{10} 8152 2-9-0 0 WilliamCarson 4 28
(Bill Turner) *edgd rt s: sn prom: rdn 1/2-way: wknd over 1f out* **100/1**

0 **8** *nse* **Oberyn (IRE)**^{36} 7792 2-8-11 0 EdwardGreatrex$^{(3)}$ 5 28
(Sylvester Kirk) *s.i.s: sn pushed along and a in rr* **33/1**

0 **9** *3* **Quintessential**^{28} 7939 2-9-0 0 BarryMcHugh 7 17
(Richard Fahey) *sn outpcd* **66/1**

050 **10** *1 ¼* **Elmley Queen**^{115} 5542 2-8-9 50 MitchGodwin$^{(5)}$ 8 13
(Roy Brotherton) *edgd rt s: chsd ldrs: hung rt fr over 3f out: rdn and wknd over 1f out* **100/1**

1m 1.83s (-0.07) **Going Correction** +0.025s/f (Slow) **10** Ran SP% **117.2**
Speed ratings (Par 96): **101,98,97,94,93 92,81,81,76,74**
CSF £24.68 TOTE £8.90: £2.30, £1.30, £1.30; EX 27.00 Trifecta £76.60.
Owner John Dance **Bred** A H And C E Robinson Partnership **Trained** Malpas, Cheshire

FOCUS
The track was harrowed to full depth on Monday and re-instated with a gallop master prior to this meeting. The early pace wasn't that strong and the front two dominated throughout.

8314 BETWAY SPRINT H'CAP — 5f 216y (Tp)
5:45 (5:47) (Class 3) (0-90,90) 3-Y-O-**£7,561** (£2,263; £1,131; £566; £282) **Stalls** Low

Form RPR

0300 **1** **Oriental Relation (IRE)**^{30} 7892 5-8-12 **81** (v) TomEaves 10 88
(James Given) *led: rdn and hdd over 1f out: rallied gamely to ld nr fin* **25/1**

6515 **2** *nk* **Boomerang Bob (IRE)**^{17} 8069 7-9-7 **90** WilliamCarson 8 96
(Jamie Osborne) *chsd ldrs: shkn up to ld over 1f out: rdn ins fnl f: hdd nr fin* **11/4**^{1}

4633 **3** *nk* **Sophisticated Heir (IRE)**^{9} 8176 6-8-10 **79** ow1...(b) RobertWinston 12 84
(Michael Herrington) *trckd ldrs: edgd lft over 5f out: rdn and ev ch ins fnl f: unable qck towards fin* **13/2**

0000 **4** *2* **Steelriver (IRE)**^{32} 7858 6-9-1 **84** AdamKirby 9 83+
(David Barron) *hld up: plld hrd: nt clr run over 1f out: swtchd rt sn after: r.o wl towards fin* **5/1**^{2}

1005 **5** *½* **Yeeoow (IRE)**^{25} 7968 7-8-10 **79** JoeyHaynes 13 76
(K R Burke) *chsd ldr: rdn over 2f out: no ex ins fnl f* **28/1**

0031 **6** *¾* **Young John (IRE)**^{26} 7957 3-9-3 **86** DavidNolan 5 81
(Richard Fahey) *plld hrd and prom: hmpd over 5f out: rdn over 1f out: styd on same pce ins fnl f* **11/2**^{3}

3305 **7** *hd* **Highland Acclaim (IRE)**^{8} 8192 5-9-6 **89** DavidProbert 2 83
(David O'Meara) *plld hrd and prom: hmpd over 5f out: rdn over 1f out: no ex fnl f* **7/1**

1002 **8** *1 ¾* **Salvatore Fury (IRE)**^{25} 7965 6-8-13 **82** (p) PatCosgrave 7 70
(Keith Dalgleish) *s.i.s: hld up: rdn over 1f out: nt trble ldrs* **14/1**

6000 **9** *nk* **Fleckerl (IRE)**^{25} 7965 6-8-12 **81** (p) PaulMulrennan 6 68
(Conor Dore) *dwlt: nvr nrr* **20/1**

4100 **10** *¾* **Cool Bahamian (IRE)**^{44} 7651 5-8-13 **85** (v) EdwardGreatrex$^{(3)}$ 3 70
(Eve Johnson Houghton) *chsd ldrs: hmpd and lost pl over 5f out: n.d after* **20/1**

530 **11** *½* **Equally Fast**^{99} 6080 4-8-11 **80** ^{1} LiamKeniry 4 63
(Peter Hiatt) *hld up: plld hrd: swtchd rt over 4f out: hdwy over 3f out: wknd over 1f out* **40/1**

5540 **12** *4 ½* **Illegally Blonde (IRE)**^{260} 1070 3-8-13 **87** LucyKBarry$^{(5)}$ 1 56
(Jamie Osborne) *prom: nt clr run and lost pl over 5f out: rdn over 1f out: wknd fnl f* **20/1**

1m 13.39s (-1.11) **Going Correction** +0.025s/f (Slow) **12** Ran SP% **115.2**
Speed ratings (Par 107): **108,107,107,104,103 102,102,100,99,98 98,92**
CSF £84.19 CT £518.72 TOTE £28.70: £6.80, £1.50, £2.30; EX 117.80 Trifecta £1567.90.
Owner The Cool Silk Partnership **Bred** Brendan Laffan & Michael McCormick **Trained** Willoughton, Lincs

■ Stewards' Enquiry : Robert Winston four-day ban; careless riding (26th-29th Dec)

FOCUS
A competitive sprint handicap on paper, but the pace held up well. It's been rated around the first two.

8315 DOWNLOAD THE BETWAY APP H'CAP (DIV I) — 5f 216y (Tp)
6:15 (6:17) (Class 6) (0-65,65) 3-Y-O+ **£2,911** (£866; £432; £216) **Stalls** Low

Form RPR

4201 **1** **Coquine**^{15} 8094 3-9-4 **62** (p) DanielTudhope 9 69
(David O'Meara) *chsd ldrs: rdn to ld 1f out: all out* **5/1**^{2}

0235 **2** *shd* **Space War**^{23} 7994 9-9-2 **65** (t) MeganNicholls$^{(5)}$ 10 72
(Michael Easterby) *hld up in tch: rdn over 1f out: chsd wnr and edgd lft wl ins fnl f: r.o* **6/1**^{3}

6603 **3** *1 ½* **Swendab (IRE)**^{29} 7913 8-8-5 **54** (b) MitchGodwin$^{(5)}$ 7 56
(John O'Shea) *led: rdn and hdd 1f out: no ex nr fin* **22/1**

-502 **4** *1 ¾* **Baileys Pursuit**^{15} 8095 4-9-3 **61** AdamKirby 5 58
(Gay Kelleway) *sn pushed along and prom: rdn over 2f out: styd on same pce fnl f* **9/4**^{1}

4013 **5** *shd* **Divine Call**^{15} 8094 9-9-4 **62** (b) GeorgeBaker 2 59
(Milton Bradley) *hld up: r.o ins fnl f: nt rch ldrs* **8/1**

0003 **6** *½* **Bonjour Steve**^{29} 7912 5-8-10 **59** (p) PhilDennis$^{(5)}$ 13 54
(Richard Price) *chsd ldrs: rdn over 1f out: wknd wl ins fnl f* **16/1**

0360 **7** 3/4 **Mustn't Grumble (IRE)**[47] 7572 3-9-2 **60**.............. RichardKingscote 12 53
(David Loughnane) *chsd ldr: rdn over 2f out: lost 2nd over 1f out: wknd ins fnl f* **14/1**

2000 **8** *nse* **City Of Angkor Wat (IRE)**[17] 8067 6-9-6 **64**............(p) PaulMulrennan 3 57
(Conor Dore) *hld up: hdwy u.p over 1f out: styd on same pce fnl f* **16/1**

0300 **9** 2 **Ambitious Boy**[29] 7912 7-8-10 **54**.................................. FergusSweeney 1 41
(John O'Shea) *s.i.s: hld up: rdn over 2f out: n.d* **25/1**

2416 **10** *nk* **Whipphound**[32] 7860 8-8-12 **56**...................................(p) JamesSullivan 6 42
(Ruth Carr) *hld up: rdn over 2f out: n.d* **25/1**

4141 **11** 1 **Mambo Spirit (IRE)**[42] 7693 12-9-4 **65**........................... EoinWalsh(3) 4 48
(Tony Newcombe) *s.i.s: hld up: shkn up over 2f out: nvr on terms* **20/1**

0325 **12** 3 **Krazy Paving**[21] 8030 4-8-7 **51**...(b) JohnFahy 11 25
(Anabel K Murphy) *hld up: rdn over 2f out: a in rr* **25/1**

0030 **13** 22 **Smart Dj**[49] 7534 5-8-7 **51** oh2... JFEgan 8
(Sarah Hollinshead) *hld up: racd keenly: pushed along and sme hdwy over 2f out: wknd wl over 1f out: eased* **25/1**

1m 14.19s (-0.31) **Going Correction** +0.025s/f (Slow) **13** Ran SP% **115.8**
Speed ratings (Par 101): **103,102,100,98,98 97,96,96,94,93 92,88,58**
CSF £29.78 CT £593.66 TOTE £5.50: £2.30, £2.40, £6.90; EX 33.00 Trifecta £1244.60.
Owner R S Cockerill (Farms) Ltd **Bred** R S Cockerill (farms) Ltd **Trained** Upper Helmsley, N Yorks

FOCUS
An ordinary sprint handicap.

8316 DOWNLOAD THE BETWAY APP H'CAP (DIV II) 5f 216y (Tp)

6:45 (6:47) (Class 6) (0-65,65) 3-Y-O+ **£2,911** (£866; £432; £216) **Stalls** Low

Form RPR

6604 **1** **Major Valentine**[15] 8095 4-9-7 **65**................................... TimmyMurphy 4 72
(John O'Shea) *mde virtually all: rdn over 1f out: jst hld on* **7/1**[3]

6565 **2** *hd* **Compton Prince**[15] 8095 7-9-2 **60**.......................(b) RichardKingscote 12 66
(Milton Bradley) *led early: chsd ldrs: rdn and edgd lft ins fnl f: r.o* **20/1**

0004 **3** *nk* **Air Of York (IRE)**[8] 8188 4-9-6 **64**.. JFEgan 1 70
(David Evans) *chsd ldrs: pushed along over 3f out: rdn over 1f out: r.o* **4/1**[2]

3436 **4** 1 **Tasaaboq**[10] 8149 5-8-6 **55**..(t) PhilDennis(5) 9 58
(Phil McEntee) *hld up: hdwy and nt clr run over 1f out: r.o: nt rch ldrs* **22/1**

2450 **5** 1 **Generalyse**[107] 5797 7-8-7 **58**......................................(b) JoshuaBryan(7) 2 58
(Anabel K Murphy) *sn pushed along to chse ldrs: rdn over 1f out: no ex wl ins fnl f* **33/1**

0031 **6** 1 1/4 **Swanton Blue (IRE)**[15] 8095 3-9-3 **64**.................... CallumShepherd(3) 7 60
(Ed de Giles) *mid-div: hmpd wl over 3f out: sn rdn: styd on u.p fr over 1f out: nt trble ldrs* **4/1**[2]

62-2 **7** 1/2 **Declamation (IRE)**[159] 3940 6-8-13 **57**........................ RobertWinston 5 51
(Alistair Whillans) *chsd ldrs: wnt 2nd over 2f out: sn ev ch: rdn over 1f out: no ex ins fnl f* **13/8**[1]

400 **8** 1 **Angelito**[58] 7303 7-8-13 **60**... EoinWalsh(3) 6 51
(Tony Newcombe) *s.i.s: in rr tl styd on ins fnl f* **33/1**

1441 **9** 1 1/4 **Kaaber (USA)**[74] 6853 5-8-4 **53**...............................(b) MitchGodwin(5) 11 41
(Roy Brotherton) *hld up: nvr on terms* **18/1**

5062 **10** 1 3/4 **Loumarin (IRE)**[15] 8094 4-9-4 **62**...................................... TomQueally 13 44
(Michael Appleby) *prom: chsd ldr over 4f out tl rdn over 2f out: wknd fnl f* **16/1**

6600 **11** 2 3/4 **Louis Vee (IRE)**[49] 7533 8-8-10 **54**............................... FergusSweeney 3 28
(John O'Shea) *s.i.s: a in rr* **50/1**

4514 **12** 8 **Bilash**[49] 7533 9-8-4 **51** oh1.. JackDuern(3) 8 1
(Sarah Hollinshead) *prom: lost pl after 1f: rdn over 2f out: wknd over 1f out* **50/1**

1m 14.57s (0.07) **Going Correction** +0.025s/f (Slow) **12** Ran SP% **120.7**
Speed ratings (Par 101): **100,99,99,98,96 95,94,93,91,89 85,74**
CSF £143.71 CT £651.57 TOTE £8.30: £2.40, £4.50, £1.80; EX 98.80 Trifecta £429.70.
Owner Pete Smith & Ally Hunter **Bred** J R Salter **Trained** Elton, Gloucs

FOCUS
Once again the pace held up. This was run in a time 0.38sec slower than the first division.

8317 BETWAY H'CAP 1m 1f 103y (Tp)

7:15 (7:16) (Class 2) (0-105,101) 3-Y-O+
£15,562 (£4,660; £2,330; £1,165; £582; £292) **Stalls** Low

Form RPR

2-12 **1** **Mythical Madness**[14] 8122 5-9-3 **94**..........................(p) DanielTudhope 4 103+
(David O'Meara) *hld up in tch: shkn up over 1f out: led ins fnl f: sn rdn: r.o* **3/1**[1]

3345 **2** *nk* **Sennockian Star**[31] 7869 6-8-5 **82**.......................................(v) JFEgan 11 89
(Mark Johnston) *sn pushed along and prom: chsd ldr over 7f out: rdn over 3f out: led ins fnl f: sn hdd: r.o* **14/1**

2100 **3** 1 1/4 **Examiner (IRE)**[49] 7546 5-9-2 **93**... SeanLevey 13 97+
(Stuart Williams) *hld up: r.o wl ins fnl f: nt rch ldrs* **20/1**

0006 **4** *hd* **Solar Deity (IRE)**[19] 8049 7-9-9 **100**...............................(p) AdamKirby 6 104
(Jane Chapple-Hyam) *hld up: rdn over 1f out: edgd lft and r.o ins fnl f: nt trble ldrs* **12/1**

1340 **5** 3/4 **Perfect Cracker**[177] 3304 8-8-13 **90**.. RyanTate 2 92
(Clive Cox) *plld hrd: led at stdy pce 2f: remained handy: shkn up over 1f out: styd on same pce ins fnl f* **33/1**

4504 **6** *nk* **Faithful Creek (IRE)**[14] 8122 4-8-7 **84**.................................. BenCurtis 7 86
(Michael Appleby) *chsd ldrs: rdn over 2f out: edgd lft and styd on same pce ins fnl f* **11/2**

4065 **7** *nk* **Winterlude (IRE)**[105] 3435 6-9-7 **98**.................................... TomQueally 3 99
(Jennie Candlish) *hld up: rdn over 1f out: r.o ins fnl f: nvr nrr* **28/1**

2054 **8** 1/2 **Georgian Bay (IRE)**[19] 8049 6-8-12 **94**................(vt) JordanVaughan(5) 1 94
(K R Burke) *hld up in tch: rdn over 1f out: no ex ins fnl f* **22/1**

5455 **9** *hd* **Third Time Lucky (IRE)**[19] 8049 4-9-10 **101**.................... DavidNolan 9 101
(Richard Fahey) *chsd ldrs: led over 7f out: qcknd over 2f out: rdn and hdd ins fnl f: no ex* **7/2**[2]

6140 **10** *shd* **Trendsetter (IRE)**[35] 7824 5-8-8 **88**.........................(p) AaronJones(3) 10 88
(Micky Hammond) *hld up: rdn over 1f out: running on whn nt clr run wl ins fnl f: nt rch ldrs* **50/1**

1226 **11** 3 **Ready (IRE)**[10] 8160 6-8-13 **90**..............................(p) RichardKingscote 5 83
(Clare Ellam) *w ldr 2f: remained handy: rdn over 2f out: wknd ins fnl f* **66/1**

0000 **12** 2 1/2 **Afonso De Sousa (USA)**[64] 7121 6-8-10 **90**...... AlistairRawlinson(3) 12 78
(Michael Appleby) *hld up: nvr on terms* **40/1**

3421 **13** 1 1/4 **Nonios (IRE)**[17] 8077 4-8-7 **84**.. DavidProbert 8 69
(David Simcock) *plld hrd and prom: lost pl over 7f out: hdwy over 2f out: rdn over 1f out: wknd fnl f* **5/1**[3]

2m 0.09s (-0.71) **Going Correction** +0.025s/f (Slow) **13** Ran SP% **115.0**
Speed ratings (Par 109): **104,103,102,102,101 101,101,100,100,100 97,95,94**
CSF £40.82 CT £712.65 TOTE £3.20: £1.10, £4.00, £7.00; EX 40.20 Trifecta £1435.80.
Owner J C G Chua **Bred** Highbank Stud Llp **Trained** Upper Helmsley, N Yorks

FOCUS
A good handicap. Nothing really wanted to go on and so Third Time Lucky was allowed to stride on, and the pace picked up once he got rolling. It's been rated around the runner-up.

8318 BETWAY MIDDLE H'CAP 1m 4f 50y (Tp)

7:45 (7:46) (Class 6) (0-65,65) 3-Y-O+ **£2,911** (£866; £432; £216) **Stalls** Low

Form RPR

1332 **1** **Galilee Chapel (IRE)**[12] 8134 7-9-7 **62**........................(b) BarryMcHugh 6 68
(Alistair Whillans) *hld up: hdwy over 1f out: rdn and r.o to ld whn hmpd towards fin* **9/2**[2]

043 **2** *nk* **Burnside (FR)**[8] 8193 3-9-1 **61**.................................(v) StevieDonohoe 12 67
(Ian Williams) *chsd ldrs: rdn and edgd lft wl ins fnl f: ld towards fin: sn hdd: styd on* **14/1**

0001 **3** *nk* **Threediamondrings**[25] 7969 3-8-11 **60**................(t) EdwardGreatrex(3) 3 65
(Brendan Powell) *chsd ldr tl led over 2f out: rdn and edgd lft ins fnl f: hung rt and hdd nr fin* **15/2**

0205 **4** 1 3/4 **Sennockian Song**[12] 8134 3-9-0 **60**................................. PJMcDonald 2 62
(Mark Johnston) *led: rdn and hdd over 2f out: styng on same pce whn nt clr run wl ins fnl f* **6/1**[3]

5550 **5** 2 1/4 **Macksville (IRE)**[8] 8193 3-9-0 **65**.................................. DavidParkes(5) 1 64
(Jeremy Gask) *hld up: hdwy over 6f out: nt clr run over 2f out tl wl over 1f out: sn rdn: styd on same pce fnl f* **6/1**[3]

064- **6** 1 3/4 **Krafty One**[151] 8107 4-9-0 **55**.. PatCosgrave 4 51
(Michael Scudamore) *hld up: hdwy 7f out: rdn over 1f out: wknd ins fnl f* **33/1**

4256 **7** *nk* **Iona Island**[53] 7425 3-9-3 **63**.. LiamKeniry 8 58
(Peter Hiatt) *hld up: rdn over 1f out: edgd lft: nvr nrr* **28/1**

2031 **8** 3/4 **Stonecoldsoba**[21] 8038 3-9-1 **61**.................................... RobertWinston 10 55
(David Evans) *hld up in tch: plld hrd: pushed along over 3f out: wknd fnl f* **7/2**[1]

4400 **9** 1 1/4 **Star Ascending (IRE)**[30] 7895 4-9-5 **60**...........................[1] TomQueally 7 52
(Jennie Candlish) *s.i.s: hld up: rdn over 2f out: nt clr run over 1f out: a in rr* **16/1**

1254 **10** *hd* **Happy Jack (IRE)**[28] 2781 5-8-12 **53**......................(b) RichardKingscote 9 45
(Dai Burchell) *chsd ldrs: rdn over 2f out: wknd fnl f* **15/2**

-506 **11** 1 3/4 **Commissar**[14] 8124 7-9-9 **64**....................................(tp) AdamKirby 11 53
(Mandy Rowland) *s.i.s: hld up: drvn over 1f out: wknd fnl f* **16/1**

2m 40.09s (-0.71) **Going Correction** +0.025s/f (Slow)
WFA 3 from 4yo+ 5lb **11** Ran SP% **117.3**
Speed ratings (Par 101): **103,102,102,101,99 98,98,98,97,97 95**
CSF £65.81 CT £466.20 TOTE £5.10: £1.70, £3.80, £2.90; EX 49.40 Trifecta £524.80.
Owner A C Whillans **Bred** Tally-Ho Stud **Trained** Newmill-On-Slitrig, Borders
■ Stewards' Enquiry : Edward Greatrex caution; careless riding

FOCUS
Just a modest heat, but a thrilling finish.

8319 SUNBETS.CO.UK H'CAP 7f 32y (Tp)

8:15 (8:20) (Class 4) (0-80,80) 3-Y-O+ **£5,175** (£1,540; £769; £384) **Stalls** High

Form RPR

0002 **1** **Holiday Magic (IRE)**[26] 7957 5-9-3 **76**............................ JamesSullivan 7 85
(Michael Easterby) *plld hrd and prom: rdn and hung lft ins fnl f: r.o to ld post* **5/2**[1]

103 **2** *nk* **Ripoll (IRE)**[29] 7902 3-9-0 **78**..................................(t) MitchGodwin(5) 3 86
(Sylvester Kirk) *chsd ldr: shkn up to ld over 1f out: rdn and hung lft ins fnl f: hdd post* **11/2**[3]

5300 **3** 2 **Free Code (IRE)**[4] 8239 5-9-4 **80**........................... CallumShepherd(3) 2 83
(David Barron) *hld up in tch: rdn over 1f out: styd on* **10/1**

2101 **4** 1 **Evening Attire**[21] 8036 5-9-4 **77**.. MartinLane 1 77
(William Stone) *sn led: rdn and hdd over 1f out: no ex ins fnl f* **15/2**

612 **5** *nk* **Beauden Barrett**[7] 8205 3-9-2 **75**.......................(t) RichardKingscote 8 74
(Jeremy Gask) *s.i.s: hld up: hdwy over 1f out: kpt on* **10/1**

1154 **6** *hd* **Eljaddaaf (IRE)**[98] 6123 5-9-4 **77**............................... RobertWinston 12 76+
(Dean Ivory) *hld up: plld hrd: rdn over 1f out: styd on: nt trble ldrs* **9/1**

0040 **7** 1 **Clement (IRE)**[49] 7530 6-9-7 **80**..................................... FergusSweeney 6 76
(John O'Shea) *hld up: plld hrd: rdn over 1f out: nt trble ldrs* **66/1**

2-16 **8** 3 3/4 **Cambodia (IRE)**[197] 2654 3-9-3 **76**................................ GeorgeBaker 11 62+
(Chris Wall) *chsd ldrs: rdn over 2f out: wknd fnl f* **3/1**[2]

0-00 **9** 6 **Saxo Jack (FR)**[21] 8035 6-9-2 **80**..........................(t[1]) SophieKilloran(5) 9 50
(Sophie Leech) *hld up: pushed along 1/2-way: wknd over 2f out* **66/1**

5000 **10** 1 1/4 **Showing Off (IRE)**[19] 8052 3-9-2 **75**.................................. AdamKirby 4 41
(Michael Wigham) *in rr: drvn along 1/2-way: wknd over 2f out* **33/1**

1m 28.4s (-0.40) **Going Correction** +0.025s/f (Slow) **10** Ran SP% **114.8**
Speed ratings (Par 105): **103,102,100,99,98 98,97,93,86,84**
CSF £16.20 CT £114.53 TOTE £3.40: £1.50, £2.20, £3.30; EX 15.10 Trifecta £93.60.
Owner A Saha **Bred** Mrs Ann Fortune **Trained** Sheriff Hutton, N Yorks

FOCUS
A fair handicap. A small pb from the runner-up.

8320 SUN BETS ON THE APP STORE MAIDEN STKS 7f 32y (Tp)

8:45 (8:50) (Class 5) 3-Y-O+ **£3,557** (£1,058; £529; £264) **Stalls** High

Form RPR

33 **1** **New Signal**[72] 6905 3-9-5 0.. DanielTudhope 5 69+
(David O'Meara) *mde all: rdn over 1f out: styd on* **2/1**[1]

2040 **2** 1 **Hidden Gem**[23] 7986 3-8-11 57..................................(t[1]) AaronJones(3) 4 61
(Stuart Williams) *chsd wnr over 4f: wnt 2nd again over 1f out: styd on* **8/1**

4- **3** 1 **Raise The Game (IRE)**[611] 1290 3-9-0 0.................... JordanVaughan(5) 1 64
(Bill Turner) *mid-div: hdwy 2f out: nt clr run ins fnl f: styd on* **40/1**

3 **4** *shd* **Dance Rebel**[37] 7782 3-9-0 0.. MitchGodwin(5) 9 63
(Dr Jon Scargill) *chsd ldrs: chsd wnr over 2f out tl rdn and edgd lft over 1f out: styd on same pce fnl f* **18/1**

0 **5** 1 1/4 **Deeley's Double (FR)**[39] 7753 3-9-2 0................................ EoinWalsh(3) 11 60
(Tony Carroll) *hld up: hdwy over 1f out: r.o: nt trble ldrs* **20/1**

6 *shd* **Tell A Story** 3-9-0 0.. PatCosgrave 12 54
(David Simcock) *s.i.s: flashed tail at times: shkn up and r.o ins fnl f: nt trble ldrs* **14/1**

7 *hd* **Life Of Luxury** 3-9-5 0... PaulMulrennan 6 59
(Mark Brisbourne) *s.i.s: hld up: hdwy and nt clr run over 1f out: swtchd rt: styd on: nt trble ldrs* **9/2**[2]

44 **8** 3/4 **Fleeting Glimpse**[30] 7894 3-8-7 0.................................. JoshuaBryan(7) 10 52
(Andrew Balding) *plld hrd and prom: rdn over 1f out: no ex ins fnl f* **7/1**

24 **9** 5 **I Can't Stop**[262] 1036 3-9-0 0... RobertWinston 8 38
(Milton Bradley) *mid-div: rdn over 2f out: edgd lft and wknd over 1f out* **20/1**

60- **10** 1 **Irvine Lady (IRE)**[469] 5881 3-9-0 0... JFEgan 2 36
(Gay Kelleway) *chsd ldrs: rdn over 2f out: wknd fnl f* **18/1**

11 *1* **Waggle (IRE)** 3-9-5 0 AdamKirby 3 38
(Michael Wigham) *s.i.s: pushed along 3f out: n.d* **5/1**[3]
12 *35* **Ocean Kave**[138] 6-9-5 0 RyanPowell 7
(Tony Newcombe) *s.i.s: a in rr: bhd fr 1/2-way* **100/1**
1m 29.94s (1.14) **Going Correction** +0.025s/f (Slow) **12** Ran SP% **121.9**
Speed ratings (Par 103): **94,92,91,91,90 90,89,88,83,82 80,40**
CSF £18.67 TOTE £2.90: £1.40, £1.90, £10.00; EX 17.80 Trifecta £1113.00.
Owner Hamad Rashed Bin Ghedayer **Bred** Scuderia Blueberry SRL **Trained** Upper Helmsley, N Yorks
FOCUS
A modest maiden. Two of the newcomers were gambled on but neither troubled the judge.
T/Plt: £106.40 to a £1 stake. Pool: £115,615.49 - 792.83 winning units. T/Qpdt: £51.80 to a £1 stake. Pool: £9,235.50 - 131.88 winning units. **Colin Roberts**

8321 - 8328a (Foreign Racing) - See Raceform Interactive

[8217] SHA TIN (R-H)
Sunday, December 11
OFFICIAL GOING: Turf: good

8329a LONGINES HONG KONG VASE (GROUP 1) (3YO+) (TURF) 1m 4f
6:00 (12:00) 3-Y-O+ **£823,555** (£317,863; £166,155; £86,690; £50,569)

RPR
1 **Satono Crown (JPN)**[42] 4-9-0 0 (t) JoaoMoreira 9 122
(Noriyuki Hori, Japan) *hld up on ins: stdy hdwy whn nt clr run over 3f out: effrt and weaved through to chse clr ldr over 1f out: drvn and sustained run fnl f: led nr fin* **195/10**
2 *1/2* **Highland Reel (IRE)**[36] 7835 4-9-0 0 RyanMoore 10 121
(A P O'Brien, Ire) *led: hdd briefly after 5f: rdn and qcknd over 3 l clr over 1f out: kpt on fnl f: hdd nr fin* **1/2**[1]
3 *6 3/4* **One Foot In Heaven (IRE)**[56] 7396 4-9-0 0 ChristopheSoumillon 4 110
(A De Royer-Dupre, France) *hld up: effrt and hdwy over 2f out: chsd clr ldng pair 1f out: kpt on: nt pce to chal* **18/1**
4 *3/4* **Nuovo Record (JPN)**[17] 5-8-10 0 YasunariIwata 12 105
(Makoto Saito, Japan) *t.k.h: hld up: n.m.r after 2f: dropped to last pl 1/2-way: effrt and hdwy over 1f out: kpt on fnl f: no imp* **43/5**[2]
5 *nk* **Smart Layer (JPN)**[57] 6-8-10 0 (t) YutakaTake 13 105
(Ryuji Okubo, Japan) *hld up midfield on outside: hdwy and prom over 3f out: drvn along over 2f out: kpt on same pce fr over 1f out* **68/1**
6 *nk* **Benzini (AUS)**[15] 7-9-0 0 (p) RosieMyers 11 108
(Adrian & Harry Bull, New Zealand) *s.i.s: hld up: nt clr run over 3f out to over 2f out: rdn and hdwy over 1f out: no further imp ins fnl f* **136/1**
7 *1 1/4* **Garlingari (FR)**[105] 5947 5-9-0 0 (p) StephanePasquier 8 106
(Mme C Barande-Barbe, France) *hld up midfield: drvn and outpcd over 2f out: rallied on outside fnl f: kpt on: nt pce to chal* **85/1**
8 *1/2* **Quechua (ARG)**[21] 6-9-0 0 BVorster 14 105
(Patrick Shaw, Singapore) *sn niggled along in rr: last and outpcd over 2f out: plugged on fnl f: nvr able to chal* **216/1**
9 *shd* **Flame Hero (NZ)**[21] 7-9-0 0 (v) ZacPurton 5 105
(L Ho, Hong Kong) *hld up midfield: drvn along over 3f out: shortlived effrt on outside 2f out: sn outpcd: btn fnl f* **51/1**
10 *3* **Eastern Express (IRE)**[21] 4-9-0 0 (bt) SilvestreDeSousa 2 100
(J Size, Hong Kong) *trckd ldr 3f: cl up: effrt and regained 2nd pl over 2f out to over 1f out: wknd fnl f* **28/1**
11 *3* **Big Orange**[29] 7948 5-9-0 0 (v) DamianLane 7 95
(Michael Bell) *awkward s: t.k.h and sn in tch: hdwy to ld briefly after 5f: drvn and outpcd over 3f out: sn struggling: btn over 1f out: eased* **17/1**
12 *8* **Silverwave (FR)**[70] 6989 4-9-0 0 MaximeGuyon 1 83
(P Bary, France) *in tch: rdn along over 2f out: wknd wl over 1f out* **9/1**[3]
13 *shd* **Helene Happy Star (IRE)**[21] 5-9-0 0 (t) HughBowman 6 83
(John Moore, Hong Kong) *chsd ldrs: wnt 2nd briefly after 3f: effrt and regained 2nd pl over 3f out to over 2f out: sn wknd* **10/1**
14 *3 1/2* **Anticipation (IRE)**[21] 5-9-0 0 (bt) NeilCallan 3 77
(A S Cruz, Hong Kong) *t.k.h: in tch: drvn and outpcd wl over 2f out: sn wknd* **34/1**
2m 26.22s (-1.98) **14** Ran SP% **123.9**
PARI-MUTUEL (all including 10 hkd stake): WIN 204.50; PLACE 41.50, 10.50, 39.50; DF 142.50.
Owner Hajime Satomi **Bred** Northern Racing **Trained** Japan
FOCUS
Not the strongest Group 1 but it did have a proven performer at that level as favourite, and he only just lost out to one rival, the pair clear. The second and fourth have been rated in line with their recent form.

8330a LONGINES HONG KONG SPRINT (GROUP 1) (3YO+) (TURF) 6f
6:40 (12:00) 3-Y-O+ **£923,380** (£356,392; £186,295; £97,197; £56,698)

RPR
1 **Aerovelocity (NZ)**[21] 8-9-0 0 (vt) ZacPurton 2 120
(P O'Sullivan, Hong Kong) *trckd ldrs: effrt and drvn along over 1f out: led ins fnl f: hld on wl cl home* **66/10**
2 *shd* **Lucky Bubbles (AUS)**[21] 5-9-0 0 BrettPrebble 5 120+
(K W Lui, Hong Kong) *hld up: angled lft and hdwy wl over 1f out: rdn and kpt on strly fnl f: jst hld* **6/5**[1]
3 *3/4* **Peniaphobia (IRE)**[21] 5-9-0 0 (tp) SilvestreDeSousa 1 117
(A S Cruz, Hong Kong) *t.k.h: led: rdn over 1f out: hdd ins fnl f: kpt on same pce* **10/1**
4 *1/2* **Amazing Kids (NZ)**[21] 5-9-0 0 JoaoMoreira 7 116
(J Size, Hong Kong) *sn pushed along in last pair: rdn and hdwy on ins over 1f out: kpt on ins fnl f* **59/10**[2]
5 *1/2* **Signs Of Blessing (IRE)**[57] 7350 5-9-0 0 StephanePasquier 13 114+
(F Rohaut, France) *hld up on outside: drvn along over 2f out: hdwy fnl f: nrst fin* **123/1**
6 *shd* **Takedown (AUS)**[15] 4-9-0 0 (bt) TimothyClark 6 114
(G W Moore, Australia) *midfield: drvn along over over 2f out: kpt on u.p ins fnl f: nt pce to chal* **24/1**
7 *nk* **Not Listenin'tome (AUS)**[21] 6-9-0 0 (t) HughBowman 4 113
(John Moore, Hong Kong) *hld up midfield on ins: nt clr run over 2f out to wl over 1f out: sn drvn along: kpt on fnl f: no imp* **89/10**
8 *1 1/2* **Super Jockey (NZ)**[91] 6398 8-9-0 0 KarisTeetan 9 108
(A T Millard, Hong Kong) *pressed ldr: drvn along over 1f out: outpcd fnl f* **102/1**
9 *nk* **Strathmore (AUS)**[21] 5-9-0 0 (bt) NeilCallan 3 107
(A T Millard, Hong Kong) *prom on ins: drvn along over 2f out: outpcd over 1f out: btn ins fnl f* **55/1**
10 *1/2* **Big Arthur (JPN)**[70] 6999 5-9-0 0 RyanMoore 12 105
(Kenichi Fujioka, Japan) *midfield on outside: effrt and drvn along over 2f out: wknd appr fnl f* **6/1**[3]
11 *nk* **Rebel Dane (AUS)**[51] 7526 7-9-0 0 (b) BenMelham 8 104
(Gary Portelli, Australia) *trckd ldrs: drvn along over 2f out: wknd over 1f out* **80/1**
12 *1 3/4* **Red Falx (JPN)**[70] 6999 5-9-0 0 MircoDemuro 10 99
(Tomohito Ozeki, Japan) *s.i.s: bhd: drvn along whn blkd 2f out: sn no imp: btn over 1f out* **15/1**
13 *3* **Growl**[36] 7822 4-9-0 0 (p) GrahamLee 11 89
(Richard Fahey) *bhd on outside: drvn and shortlived effrt whn blkd 2f out: sn wknd* **260/1**
1m 8.8s (68.80) **13** Ran SP% **122.0**
PARI-MUTUEL (all including 10 hkd stake): WIN 75.50; PLACE 19.00, 12.00, 33.00; DF 83.00.
Owner Daniel Yeung Ngai **Bred** N E Schick & S J Till **Trained** Hong Kong
FOCUS
There weren't many hard-luck stories, apart perhaps from those forced to start from wide stalls. Those weren't necessarily unlucky in their runs, but had plenty of work on to get involved. The third, fourth and sixth have been rated to their marks.

8332a LONGINES HONG KONG MILE (GROUP 1) (3YO+) (TURF) 1m
7:50 (12:00) 3-Y-O **£1,147,985** (£443,082; £231,611; £120,840; £70,490)

RPR
1 **Beauty Only (IRE)**[21] 5-9-0 0 (t) ZacPurton 13 119
(A S Cruz, Hong Kong) *hld up towards rr of midfield: hdwy on outer fr under 3f out: rdn 2 1/2f out: led 1f out: kpt on wl* **5/1**[3]
2 *1/2* **Helene Paragon (FR)**[21] 4-9-0 0 HughBowman 5 118
(John Moore, Hong Kong) *hld up towards rr of midfield: rdn 1 1/2f out: styd on wl fnl f: nrst fin* **49/10**[2]
3 *1/2* **Joyful Trinity (IRE)**[21] 4-9-0 0 GeraldMosse 11 117
(John Moore, Hong Kong) *midfield: rdn over 2f out: gd hdwy fr 1 1/2f out: ev ch 150yds out: no ex clsng stages* **14/1**
4 *nk* **Contentment (AUS)**[21] 6-9-0 0 (e) BrettPrebble 6 116+
(J Size, Hong Kong) *trckd ldrs: rdn 2f out: kpt on gamely: nvr quite able to chal* **14/1**
5 *shd* **Logotype (JPN)**[42] 6-9-0 0 MircoDemuro 2 116+
(Tsuyoshi Tanaka, Japan) *trckd ldrs: rdn 1 1/2f out: kpt on wl fnl f: nt quite able to chal* **12/1**
6 *3/4* **Able Friend (AUS)**[21] 7-9-0 0 (p) JoaoMoreira 14 114
(John Moore, Hong Kong) *hld up in rr: rdn and gd hdwy on outer fr under 2f out: nt quite able to chal: no ex last 100yds* **11/5**[1]
7 *nk* **Satono Aladdin (JPN)**[21] 8045 5-9-0 0 (t) YugaKawada 8 114+
(Yasutoshi Ikee, Japan) *in rr: rdn 2f out: kpt on ins fnl f: nrst fin* **11/1**
8 *3/4* **Romantic Touch (AUS)**[21] 6-9-0 0 (t) MatthewChadwick 4 112
(A S Cruz, Hong Kong) *midfield: rdn over 2f out: outpcd 1 1/2f out: kpt on ins fnl f* **52/1**
9 *1/2* **Neorealism (JPN)**[21] 8045 5-9-0 0 (p) RyanMoore 9 111+
(Noriyuki Hori, Japan) *chsd ldr: rdn 2f out: led over 1f out: hdd 1f out: wknd last 150yds* **11/1**
10 *shd* **Cougar Mountain (IRE)**[36] 7837 5-9-0 0 (tp) DonnachaO'Brien 7 110
(A P O'Brien, Ire) *towards rr of midfield: rdn and kpt on steadily fr 2f out: n.d* **158/1**
11 *nk* **Giant Treasure (USA)**[21] 5-9-0 0 (b) ChristopheSoumillon 10 110
(Richard Gibson, Hong Kong) *hld up in rr: rdn and kpt on steadily fr 1 1/2f out: n.d* **26/1**
12 *3/4* **Sun Jewellery (AUS)**[21] 5-9-0 0 (t) SilvestreDeSousa 3 108
(J Size, Hong Kong) *in tch: rdn and outpcd under 2f out: no ex last 75yds* **9/1**
13 *2 1/2* **Beauty Flame (IRE)**[21] 6-9-0 0 (t) KCLeung 12 102+
(A S Cruz, Hong Kong) *broke wl and led: rdn 2f out: hdd over 1f out: wknd fnl f* **46/1**
14 *3* **Packing Pins (NZ)**[21] 6-9-0 0 MaximeGuyon 1 95
(P F Yiu, Hong Kong) *in tch in midfield: rdn 2 1/2f out: wknd steadily fr 2f out: eased whn btn* **50/1**
1m 33.48s (-1.22) **14** Ran SP% **122.9**
PARI-MUTUEL (all including 10 hkd stake): WIN 60.00; PLACE 18.00, 20.50, 45.00; DF 161.00.
Owner Eleanor Kwok Law Kwai Chun & Patrick Kwok Ho Chuen **Bred** Massimo Parri **Trained** Hong Kong
FOCUS
The favourite and local star Able Friend failed to fire, so it gave the result an open look. Not many lengths separated the majority of the field at the end. Being drawn wide didn't prove an issue. The winner has been rated to his best.

8333a LONGINES HONG KONG CUP (GROUP 1) (3YO+) (TURF) 1m 2f
8:30 (12:00) 3-Y-O **£1,247,810** (£481,611; £251,751; £131,348; £76,619)

RPR
1 **Maurice (JPN)**[42] 5-9-0 0 (t) RyanMoore 8 124+
(Noriyuki Hori, Japan) *dwlt: towards rr: rdn 2f out: styd on strly to ld 150yds out: sn in command: drvn out* **3/4**[1]
2 *3* **Secret Weapon**[21] 6-9-0 0 (t) ZacPurton 3 118
(C H Yip, Hong Kong) *midfield: rdn under 2f out: kpt on wl ins fnl f: tk 2nd cl home: no ch w wnr* **10/1**
3 *1/2* **Staphanos (JPN)**[42] 5-9-0 0 ChristopheSoumillon 7 117
(Hideaki Fujiwara, Japan) *racd in 3rd bhd clr ldr: rdn to go 2nd 2f out: dropped to 4th 1f out: kpt on same pce* **17/1**
4 *shd* **Lovely Day (JPN)**[42] 6-9-0 0 HughBowman 2 117
(Yasutoshi Ikee, Japan) *in tch in main gp: rdn and hdwy fr under 2f out: nt quite able to chal: no ex last 50yds* **22/1**
5 *nk* **Blazing Speed**[21] 7-9-0 0 (t) NeilCallan 4 116
(A S Cruz, Hong Kong) *midfield: rdn 2 1/2f out: hdwy fr 1 1/2f out: drvn 1f out: nt able to chal: no ex clsng stages* **11/1**
6 *3/4* **Horse Of Fortune (SAF)**[35] 6-9-0 0 SilvestreDeSousa 10 115
(A T Millard, Hong Kong) *midfield: rdn and kpt on same pce fr 2 1/2f out* **71/1**
7 *nk* **Elliptique (IRE)**[35] 7841 5-9-0 0 Pierre-CharlesBoudot 9 114
(A Fabre, France) *towards rr: rdn 2f out: kpt on ins fnl f: n.d* **69/1**
8 *3/4* **Designs On Rome (IRE)**[21] 6-9-0 0 JoaoMoreira 6 113
(John Moore, Hong Kong) *dwlt: towards rr: rdn 2 1/2f out: kpt on steadily fnl f: n.d* **69/10**[2]
9 *1 1/2* **Queens Ring (JPN)**[28] 7953 4-8-10 0 MircoDemuro 11 106
(Keiji Yoshimura, Japan) *towards rr of midfield: rdn and no significant hdwy fr 2 1/2f out* **10/1**
10 *3/4* **A Shin Hikari (JPN)**[42] 5-9-0 0 YutakaTake 1 108+
(Masanori Sakaguchi, Japan) *led: clr fr 7f out: rdn 2f out: wknd over 2f out: hdd 150yds: lost several positions clsng stages* **76/10**[3]

11 *1* **Gun Pit (AUS)**[21] 6-9-0 0........(bt) KarisTeetan 5 106
(C Fownes, Hong Kong) *towards rr of midfield: rdn and outpcd 2f out: wknd ins fnl f* **85/1**

12 *5* **Helene Super Star (USA)**[21] 6-9-0 0........(tp) GeraldMosse 12 96
(A S Cruz, Hong Kong) *chsd clr ldr: rdn 2 1/2f out: wknd 1 1/2f out: eased whn btn* **93/1**

2m 0.95s (-0.45) **12** Ran SP% **122.9**
PARI-MUTUEL (all including 10 hkd stake): WIN 17.50; PLACE 11.00, 27.50, 38.50; DF 118.50.
Owner Kazumi Yoshida **Bred** Togawa Bokujo **Trained** Japan

FOCUS
This had been billed as the last great clash between two retiring Japanese superstars, but only one of that pair proved up to his pre-race hype. The third and seventh help set the standard, with the first two rated to the better view of their previous form.

8331 - 8335a (Foreign Racing) - See Raceform Interactive

7928 TOULOUSE
Sunday, December 11

OFFICIAL GOING: Turf: soft

8336a PRIX MAX SICARD - 15TH ETAPE DU DEFI DU GALOP (LISTED RACE) (3YO+) (TURF) 1m 4f
2:15 (12:00) 3-Y-O+ **£22,058** (£8,823; £6,617; £4,411; £2,205)

RPR

1 **Satanicjim (IRE)**[115] 7-9-1 0........ AdrienFouassier 9 108
(Alain Couetil, France) **16/1**

2 *2* **Chemical Charge (IRE)**[18] 8068 4-9-5 0........ GregoryBenoist 12 109
(Ralph Beckett) *t.k.h: hld up bhd ldrs: 4th and drvn 2f out: styd on to ld narrowly briefly wl ins fnl f: hdd 100yds out: no ex* **5/2**[1]

3 *1 1/2* **Holdthasigreen (FR)**[43] 7718 4-9-10 0........(p) WilliamsSaraiva 15 112
(C Le Lay, France) **44/5**

4 *1 1/4* **Star Victory (FR)**[28] 7951 5-9-5 0........ IoritzMendizabal 7 105
(J-L Dubord, France) **7/1**[3]

5 *1/2* **Lily Passion**[31] 7897 3-8-11 0........ RonanThomas 2 101
(P Bary, France) **12/1**

6 *shd* **Master's Spirit (IRE)**[28] 7951 5-9-5 0........ FranckBlondel 13 104
(J Reynier, France) **44/5**

7 *1* **Prince Nomad (FR)**[22] 8042 5-9-1 0........ EddyHardouin 4 98
(Eric Saint-Martin, France) **16/1**

8 *3 1/2* **Shutterbug (FR)**[28] 7951 4-9-5 0........(b) AntoineHamelin 1 96
(M Figge, Germany) **11/1**

9 *5 1/2* **Saane (FR)**[43] 7718 5-9-1 0........ MickaelForest 5 84
(G Taupin, France) **63/1**

10 *1 1/2* **Spirit's Revench (FR)**[22] 8042 6-9-1 0........ HugoJourniac 3 81
(P Demercastel, France) **54/1**

11 *nse* **Quiliano (IRE)**[23] 3-8-10 0........ LukasDelozier 8 81
(C Aubert, France) **11/1**

12 *2 1/2* **Ziga**[92] 6356 5-8-11 0........ JulienGrosjean 6 73
(G Arizkorreta Elosegui, Spain) **85/1**

13 *11* **Eos Quercus (IRE)**[29] 7946 4-9-1 0........ AlexandreRoussel 16 60
(N Leenders, France) **44/1**

14 *5 1/2* **Flambeuse**[29] 7934 5-8-11 0........ Roberto-CarlosMontenegro 10 47
(E Leenders, France) **107/1**

15 *7 1/2* **Best Fouad (FR)**[28] 7951 5-9-10 0........ Francois-XavierBertras 11 48
(F Rohaut, France) **66/10**[2]

2m 29.28s (-3.02)
WFA 3 from 4yo+ 5lb **15** Ran SP% **118.5**
WIN (incl. 1 euro stake): 17.00. PLACE: 3.50, 1.90, 3.60. DF: 14.90. SF: 48.10.
Owner Mme Karine Perreau & Couetil Elevage **Bred** Moorpark Stud **Trained** France

8313 WOLVERHAMPTON (A.W) (L-H)
Monday, December 12

OFFICIAL GOING: Tapeta: standard
Wind: Nil Weather: Misty

8337 BETWAY AMATEUR RIDERS' H'CAP 1m 1f 103y (Tp)
2:10 (2:10) (Class 5) (0-75,75) 3-Y-O+ **£3,119** (£967; £483; £242) **Stalls** Low

Form RPR

243 **1** **New Agenda**[17] 8101 4-10-11 **75**........ MrMJPKendrick(3) 7 84
(Paul Webber) *a.p: rdn to ld over 1f out: r.o* **11/8**[1]

401 **2** *3 3/4* **Polar Forest**[13] 8142 6-10-13 **74**........(e) MrSWalker 8 75
(Richard Guest) *hld up: hdwy over 4f out: rdn over 1f out: styd on to go 2nd wl ins fnl f* **6/4**[2]

0000 **3** *1 3/4* **Black Dave (IRE)**[44] 7687 6-10-8 **74**........ MrJFlook(5) 4 71
(David Evans) *led over 8f out: rdn and hdd over 1f out: no ex ins fnl f* **25/1**

-060 **4** *1 1/2* **Munaawib**[254] 1202 8-9-7 **61** oh3........(bt) MissSPeacock(7) 5 55
(Ray Peacock) *prom: chsd ldr over 7f out: rdn over 2f out: styd same pce fnl f* **150/1**

3045 **5** *3/4* **Schottische**[46] 7642 6-10-0 **61** oh10........(p) MissJoannaMason 10 54
(Alan Bailey) *hld up: hdwy over 2f out: rdn over 1f out: styd on same pce* **33/1**

456 **6** *nk* **Strictly Art (IRE)**[25] 7986 3-9-7 **61** oh5........(p) MissJCooley(5) 2 53
(Alan Bailey) *prom: lost pl over 5f out: shkn up and edgd lft over 1f out: styd on* **11/1**

44-3 **7** *1* **Noguchi (IRE)**[318] 382 11-9-13 **67**........(p) MissEBushe(7) 6 57
(Chris Dwyer) *s.i.s: hld up: pushed along over 3f out: nt trble ldrs* **10/1**[3]

4050 **8** *10* **Sayedaati Saadati (IRE)**[63] 7223 3-9-9 **61** oh1.... MissAliceHaynes(3) 1 30
(John Butler) *plld hrd: led 1f: chsd ldrs: pushed along over 3f out: wknd wl over 1f out* **25/1**

0100 **9** *3 1/4* **Thane Of Cawdor (IRE)**[11] 8179 7-9-7 **61** oh2........ MrsCPownall(7) 9 23
(Joseph Tuite) *hld up: hdwy over 3f out: rdn over 2f out: wknd over 1f out* **16/1**

2m 0.89s (0.09) **Going Correction** 0.0s/f (Stan)
WFA 3 from 4yo+ 2lb **9** Ran SP% **116.7**
Speed ratings (Par 103): **99,95,94,92,92 91,90,82,79**
CSF £3.58 CT £29.26 TOTE £2.30: £1.30, £1.10, £3.70; EX 4.10 Trifecta £45.30.
Owner Bowden C Magee **Bred** Juddmonte Farms Ltd **Trained** Mollington, Oxon

FOCUS
Little depth to this, with five of these out the handicap, but the well-backed winner is a lightly raced improver and the second had won last time, so gives the form a solid look.

8338 BETWAY (S) STKS 1m 4f 50y (Tp)
2:40 (2:40) (Class 6) 3-Y-O+ **£2,749** (£818; £408; £204) **Stalls** Low

Form RPR

0010 **1** **Hard To Handel**[23] 8035 4-9-9 76........[1] DanielTudhope 1 62
(David O'Meara) *hld up: pushed along over 1f out: hdwy fnl f: rdn: hung lft and r.o to ld last strides* **9/4**[2]

614P **2** *nk* **Street Outlaw (IRE)**[121] 5398 3-9-4 64........(p) AndrewMullen 5 62
(Daniel Mark Loughnane) *chsd ldr after 1f: led wl over 1f out: sn rdn and hung lft: carried hd high ins fnl f: hdd last strides* **7/1**[3]

3 *3 3/4* **All Dolled Up (IRE)**[58] 7375 4-8-8 50........ AliceMills(5) 4 46
(Sarah-Jayne Davies) *prom: rdn over 1f out: styd on same pce fnl f* **125/1**

2540 **4** *shd* **Happy Jack (IRE)**[2] 8318 5-9-4 53........(b) HollieDoyle(5) 2 56
(Dai Burchell) *racd keenly and prom: rdn: hung lft and nt clr run over 1f out: kpt on towards fin* **22/1**

013- **5** *nk* **Rhombus (IRE)**[468] 5974 6-9-4 95........ AdamKirby 3 50
(John Butler) *led: shkn up over 2f out: hdd wl over 1f out: nt clr run sn after: rdn: hung lft and no ex ins fnl f* **1/2**[1]

2m 46.42s (5.62) **Going Correction** 0.0s/f (Stan)
WFA 3 from 4yo+ 5lb **5** Ran SP% **115.1**
Speed ratings (Par 101): **81,80,78,78,78**
CSF £17.86 TOTE £3.00: £1.10, £2.80; EX 11.10 Trifecta £120.20.
Owner Middleham Park Racing XXV **Bred** Melody Bloodstock **Trained** Upper Helmsley, N Yorks
■ Stewards' Enquiry : Andrew Mullen caution: careless riding

FOCUS
Not form to be positive about.

8339 BETWAY MARATHON DISTANCE H'CAP 1m 5f 194y (Tp)
3:10 (3:13) (Class 5) (0-75,81) 3-Y-O+ **£3,234** (£962; £481; £240) **Stalls** Low

Form RPR

-000 **1** **El Campeon**[12] 8161 4-9-11 **72**........ JFEgan 5 78
(Simon Dow) *hld up in tch: pushed along over 3f out: rdn to ld over 1f out: edgd lft ins fnl f: styd on* **6/1**[2]

0311 **2** *3/4* **High Command (IRE)**[6] 8238 3-9-13 **81** 6ex........ JackMitchell 3 86
(Roger Varian) *led 1f: chsd ldrs: wnt 2nd over 8f out: led over 2f out: rdn and hdd over 1f out: styd on same pce ins fnl f* **1/4**[1]

4345 **3** *1/2* **Snowy Dawn**[35] 7846 6-9-6 **67**........ AdamBeschizza 2 71
(Steph Hollinshead) *led after 1f: sn hdd: chsd ldr tl over 8f out: remained handy: nt clr run over 2f out: rdn over 1f out: styd on* **15/2**[3]

3600 **4** *17* **Notion Of Beauty (USA)**[10] 8193 3-8-3 **57**........(v) JoeyHaynes 4 37
(K R Burke) *led over 12f out: rdn and hdd over 2f out: wknd over 1f out* **33/1**

465/ **5** *9* **Skilled**[123] 5346 5-9-13 **74**........ GeorgeBaker 1 42
(Anabel K Murphy) *dwlt: hld up and a bhd: wknd over 2f out* **25/1**

3m 4.02s (-0.78) **Going Correction** 0.0s/f (Stan)
WFA 3 from 4yo+ 7lb **5** Ran SP% **112.8**
Speed ratings (Par 103): **102,101,101,91,86**
CSF £8.34 TOTE £8.30: £2.20, £1.10; EX 13.80 Trifecta £21.80.
Owner Robert Moss **Bred** L Norris **Trained** Ashtead, Surrey

FOCUS
Another beaten odds-on shot and muddling form.

8340 32RED CASINO MEDIAN AUCTION MAIDEN STKS 1m 1f 103y (Tp)
3:40 (3:43) (Class 6) 2-Y-O **£2,749** (£818; £408; £204) **Stalls** Low

Form RPR

64 **1** **Hertford Dancer**[19] 8063 2-9-0 0........ RobertHavlin 3 72
(John Gosden) *chsd ldrs: wnt 2nd over 2f out: rdn to ld over 1f out: hung lft ins fnl f: styd on* **11/4**[2]

43 **2** *1/2* **Pattie**[13] 8139 2-9-0 0........ MartinHarley 7 71
(Mick Channon) *hld up: hdwy over 2f out: rdn and ev ch ins fnl f: unable qck towards fin* **9/1**

22 **3** *1 1/4* **Doctor Bartolo (IRE)**[16] 8119 2-9-5 0........ AdamKirby 11 73+
(Charles Hills) *hld up: hdwy and hung lft fr over 1f out: sn hrd rdn: wnt 3rd nr fin* **7/4**[1]

034 **4** *hd* **Solent Meads (IRE)**[18] 8082 2-9-5 70........(b[1]) GeorgeBaker 5 73
(Daniel Kubler) *disp ld tl led over 3f out: rdn and hdd over 1f out: styd on same pce ins fnl f* **10/1**

5 *1/2* **Percy B Shelley** 2-9-5 0........ NickyMackay 6 72+
(John Gosden) *hld up: shkn up and hung lft ins fnl f: r.o: nt rch ldrs* **9/2**[3]

4325 **6** *1 1/2* **Nostalgie**[13] 8139 2-9-0 74........ PatCosgrave 2 64
(Rae Guest) *chsd ldrs: rdn over 1f out: nt clr run ins fnl f: styd on same pce* **8/1**

05 **7** *1 1/4* **The Last Debutante**[18] 8082 2-9-0 0........ JoeFanning 9 62
(Mark Johnston) *s.i.s: sn rcvrd into mid-div: hdwy over 2f out: rdn over 1f out: no ex ins fnl f* **10/1**

000 **8** *6* **Delagate This Lord**[10] 8189 2-9-5 59........ JFEgan 4 55
(Bill Turner) *mid-div: pushed along whn nt clr run 2f out: n.d after* **125/1**

0 **9** *2 3/4* **Dream Magic (IRE)**[9] 8208 2-8-12 0........ TobyEley(7) 10 50
(Daniel Mark Loughnane) *hld up: pushed along over 2f out: hit rails wl over 1f out: nvr on terms* **125/1**

00 **10** *14* **Hot Lick**[26] 7977 2-9-5 0........ DavidProbert 8 24
(Andrew Balding) *chsd ldrs: rdn and wkng whn hmpd over 2f out* **125/1**

00 **11** *1* **Kissinger**[26] 7977 2-9-5 0........ StevieDonohoe 1 22
(Michael Bell) *disp ld 6f: wknd 2f out* **50/1**

2m 0.79s (-0.01) **Going Correction** 0.0s/f (Stan) **11** Ran SP% **124.8**
Speed ratings (Par 94): **100,99,98,98,97 96,95,90,87,75 74**
CSF £30.08 TOTE £4.10: £1.70, £2.50, £1.30; EX 35.00 Trifecta £111.90.
Owner 5 Hertford Street Racing Club **Bred** Highclere Stud **Trained** Newmarket, Suffolk

FOCUS
Just a modest maiden and a slightly unsatisfactory race, but there were one or two for the notebook.

8341 32RED.COM CLAIMING STKS 1m 141y (Tp)
4:10 (4:11) (Class 5) 2-Y-O **£3,396** (£1,010; £505; £252) **Stalls** Low

Form RPR

6615 **1** **Poetic Force (IRE)**[12] 8153 2-9-10 73........(t) GeorgeBaker 6 72
(Jonathan Portman) *chsd ldrs: wnt 2nd over 5f out: led over 1f out: edgd lft: rdn out* **4/9**[1]

5055 **2** *3 1/4* **Aventus (IRE)**[18] 8080 2-8-5 50........(b) CharlieBennett(5) 4 50
(Jane Chapple-Hyam) *led: rdn and hdd over 1f out: no ex ins fnl f* **16/1**

4616 **3** *hd* **Bazwind (IRE)**[6] 8235 2-8-12 65........ JFEgan 3 52
(David Evans) *pushed along to chse ldr: lost 2nd over 5f out: remained handy: rdn over 2f out: sn outpcd: styd on ins fnl f* **13/2**[2]

0004 **4** 1 1/2 **Madam Prancealot (IRE)**[17] 8087 2-8-7 58.............. AdamBeschizza 7 43
(David Evans) *hld up: hdwy over 4f out: rdn and outpcd over 2f out: n.d after* **10/1**[3]
0606 **5** 1/2 **Chiconomic (IRE)**[23] 8025 2-7-12 47........................(e[1]) NoelGarbutt[(3)] 5 36
(Rae Guest) *hld up: rdn over 2f out: nvr trbld ldrs* **28/1**
0000 **6** 1 1/4 **Penny Green**[26] 7974 2-8-5 60...(b[1]) RyanTate 1 38
(James Eustace) *s.i.s: hld up: nt clr run wl over 1f out: nvr on terms* **22/1**
7 1 **Glenamoy (IRE)**[82] 6691 2-8-5 0..........................(v[1]) JosephineGordon 2 36
(Harry Dunlop) *prom: lost pl over 4f out: rdn over 2f out: wknd over 1f out* **12/1**

1m 49.88s (-0.22) **Going Correction** 0.0s/f (Stan) **7** Ran SP% **113.0**
Speed ratings (Par 96): **100,97,96,95,95 94,93**
CSF £9.39 TOTE £1.50: £1.10, £5.40; EX 8.60 Trifecta £34.40.Poetic Force was claimed by Mr A W Carroll for £12,000
Owner The Sawgrass Survivors **Bred** S J Macdonald **Trained** Upper Lambourn, Berks

FOCUS
A few disappointing sorts and the market was bang on. Weak form behind the standout winner.

8342 SUNBETS.CO.UK DOWNLOAD THE APP MAIDEN STKS 1m 141y (Tp)
4:40 (4:43) (Class 5) 3-Y-O+ **£3,234** (£962; £481; £240) **Stalls** Low

Form RPR
0 **1** **Raashdy (IRE)**[10] 8195 3-9-5 0.. AdamKirby 3 69
(Peter Hiatt) *chsd ldrs: rdn over 1f out: styd on u.p to ld wl ins fnl f* **12/1**
65 **2** hd **May Mist**[10] 8195 4-8-13 0... EoinWalsh[(3)] 4 64
(Trevor Wall) *chsd ldr tl led over 2f out: rdn and hdd wl ins fnl f: styd on* **8/1**[3]
3 1 1/4 **Belabour** 3-9-5 0.. JFEgan 8 66
(Mark Brisbourne) *s.i.s: hld up: pushed along and hdwy on outer over 2f out: rdn over 1f out: kpt on* **9/1**
4 2 1/2 **Champagne Freddie** 3-9-5 0.................................... FergusSweeney 7 60
(John O'Shea) *s.i.s: hld up: hdwy and hung lft fr over 1f out: nt rch ldrs* **16/1**
43 **5** nk **Tarseekh**[12] 8157 3-9-5 0.. JackMitchell 9 60
(Roger Varian) *chsd ldrs: rdn and edgd rt over 1f out: styd on same pce* **4/6**[1]
0-00 **6** 1 **Fire Empress**[159] 4017 3-9-0 43..[1] RyanPowell 2 52?
(James Unett) *hld up: effrt and nt clr run over 1f out: nvr trbld ldrs* **100/1**
6-03 **7** 2 1/4 **Amor Invicto (IRE)**[18] 8086 3-9-5 62....................(b) JosephineGordon 1 52
(Daniel Kubler) *led: hdd over 2f out: hmpd and wknd ins fnl f* **11/4**[2]
00 **7** dht **Bassino (USA)**[30] 7942 3-9-0 0................................ RachealKneller[(5)] 6 52
(James Bennett) *s.i.s: hld up: rdn over 2f out: n.d* **22/1**

1m 50.99s (0.89) **Going Correction** 0.0s/f (Stan)
WFA 3 from 4yo 2lb **8** Ran SP% **126.7**
Speed ratings (Par 103): **96,95,94,92,92 91,89,89**
CSF £113.18 TOTE £12.20: £2.40, £2.10, £2.50; EX 90.50 Trifecta £1525.60.
Owner P W Hiatt **Bred** Shadwell Estate Company Limited **Trained** Hook Norton, Oxon

FOCUS
The front two in the market ran poorly (this race saw a third odds-on loser on the card) and the form looks moderate.

8343 SUNBETS.CO.UK H'CAP 1m 141y (Tp)
5:10 (5:10) (Class 5) (0-75,76) 3-Y-O+ **£3,396** (£1,010; £505; £252) **Stalls** Low

Form RPR
2062 **1** **Sands Chorus**[17] 8101 4-9-8 76.. TomEaves 2 83
(James Given) *led: hdd 7f out: chsd ldr tl led again over 2f out: rdn over 1f out: styd on gamely* **11/2**[3]
0022 **2** nk **Cadeau Magnifique**[24] 8011 4-9-3 71................................ DavidNolan 1 77
(Richard Fahey) *prom: chsd wnr 2f out: rdn and ev ch ins fnl f: styd on* **1/1**[1]
1600 **3** 1 3/4 **House Of Commons (IRE)**[54] 7462 3-9-1 74...... AlistairRawlinson[(3)] 5 76
(Michael Appleby) *hld up: hdwy 2f out: rdn over 1f out: styd on* **9/2**[2]
1401 **4** 1/2 **Jumbo Prado (USA)**[10] 8190 7-9-2 70............................(b) AdamKirby 4 71
(Daniel Mark Loughnane) *hld up: rdn over 2f out: hdwy over 1f out: nt rch ldrs* **6/1**
0400 **5** 2 1/4 **Edge Of Heaven**[19] 8077 4-9-2 75.................................... MitchGodwin[(5)] 6 71
(Jonathan Portman) *hld up in tch: rdn and edgd lft over 1f out: no ex fnl f* **25/1**
5004 **6** 6 **Idol Deputy (FR)**[17] 8101 10-8-11 70....................(p) RachealKneller[(5)] 8 52
(James Bennett) *hld up: pushed along on outer over 2f out: nvr on terms* **14/1**
6506 **7** nk **Essenaitch (IRE)**[10] 8190 3-8-0 63...................... KatherineGlenister[(7)] 7 44
(David Evans) *chsd ldrs: rdn over 2f out: sn wknd* **18/1**
0005 **8** 2 3/4 **Starfield**[6] 8239 7-9-7 75..(b) JosephineGordon 3 50
(Mandy Rowland) *pushed along to chse ldr: led 7f out: rdn and hdd over 2f out: wknd over 1f out* **33/1**

1m 47.96s (-2.14) **Going Correction** 0.0s/f (Stan)
WFA 3 from 4yo+ 2lb **8** Ran SP% **116.6**
Speed ratings (Par 103): **109,108,107,106,104 99,99,96**
CSF £11.64 CT £27.51 TOTE £5.60: £2.00, £1.20, £1.40; EX 13.90 Trifecta £47.80.
Owner The Cool Silk Partnership **Bred** Worksop Manor Stud **Trained** Willoughton, Lincs

FOCUS
A fair handicap, but just an ordinary pace and the first two were always well placed.
T/Plt: £370.50 to a £1 stake. Pool: £72,522.66 - 142.88 winning units. T/Qpdt: £154.40 to a £1 stake. Pool: £6,054.55 - 29.00 winning units. **Colin Roberts**

8235 SOUTHWELL (L-H)
Tuesday, December 13

OFFICIAL GOING: Fibresand: standard
Wind: Light half against Weather: Grey cloud

8344 32RED CASINO NURSERY H'CAP 6f (F)
12:00 (12:00) (Class 6) (0-60,66) 2-Y-O **£3,234** (£962; £481; £240) **Stalls** Low

Form RPR
0021 **1** **Gracious Tom (IRE)**[8] 8230 2-9-13 66 6ex.............................. JFEgan 1 74
(David Evans) *slt ld on inner: rdn 2f out: drvn clr appr fnl f: kpt on* **5/1**[2]
5653 **2** 2 **Scotch Myst**[18] 8097 2-9-2 55.. JackGarritty 11 57
(Richard Fahey) *wnt bdly lft s: sn cl up: rdn along 2f out: drvn wl over 1f out: kpt on fnl f* **11/2**[3]
535 **3** nk **Oh Geno**[50] 7578 2-9-9 62.. AdamKirby 12 63
(Richard Spencer) *prom: effrt and cl up 2f out: sn rdn: drvn and kpt on fnl f* **3/1**[1]
000 **4** 4 1/2 **Fairy Lock (IRE)**[26] 7988 2-9-5 58................................ AndrewMullen 2 46
(David Barron) *chsd ldrs on inner: rdn along over 2f out: drvn wl over 1f out: kpt on u.p fnl f* **16/1**

5005 **5** 3/4 **Gentleman Giles (IRE)**[5] 8276 2-9-4 57..................... WilliamCarson 10 42
(Jamie Osborne) *towards rr: hdwy on outer wl over 2f out: rdn and edgd lft jst over 1f out: kpt on fnl f: nrst fin* **11/2**[3]
6040 **6** 1 1/4 **Tea El Tee (IRE)**[48] 7615 2-9-3 56......................................[1] JoeFanning 6 38
(Gay Kelleway) *sltly hmpd and swtchd rt after 150 yds: t.k.h: chsd ldrs: cl up 1/2-way: rdn along 2f out: drvn and edgd lft over 1f out: sn one pce* **7/1**
6000 **7** 5 **Bella Duchess (IRE)**[93] 6388 2-8-6 45...................... JosephineGordon 8 12
(David C Griffiths) *towards rr: hdwy on outer and in tch 1/2-way: rdn along over 2f out: grad wknd* **33/1**
0643 **8** 3/4 **Poppy May (IRE)**[33] 7881 2-9-1 54.......................................[1] TomEaves 9 18+
(James Given) *dwlt and rr: hdwy and in tch 1/2-way: rdn along 2f out: sn edgd lft and wknd* **7/1**
46P0 **9** 1 **Eid Rose**[4] 8285 2-8-1 47..(b[1]) RPWalsh[(7)] 7 8
(Scott Dixon) *a towards rr* **100/1**
4000 **10** 3/4 **Tranquil Tracy**[50] 7579 2-8-12 51.................................. ConnorBeasley 4 10
(John Norton) *a towards rr* **33/1**
0550 **11** 1/2 **Enlighten Me (IRE)**[35] 7854 2-8-6 45.............................. JoeyHaynes 13
(Philip Kirby) *racd wd: in tch: rdn along wl over 2f out: sn drvn and wknd* **50/1**
600 **12** 3 1/4 **Diamond Princess**[50] 7576 2-8-6 45.................................... BenCurtis 3
(Michael Appleby) *prom and hmpd after 150 yds: chsd ldrs: rdn along 1/2-way: sn wknd* **20/1**

1m 15.24s (-1.26) **Going Correction** -0.20s/f (Stan) **12** Ran SP% **116.9**
Speed ratings (Par 94): **100,97,96,90,89 88,81,80,79,78 77,73**
CSF £30.69 CT £98.24 TOTE £5.60: £1.90, £2.00, £1.60; EX 31.30 Trifecta £98.20.
Owner Terry Reffell **Bred** Golden Vale Stud **Trained** Pandy, Monmouths
■ Stewards' Enquiry : Connor Beasley trainer said that the filly was outpaced in the early stages and subsequently didn't face the kickback
Jack Garritty one-day ban: failed to keep straight after the stalls (27 Dec)

FOCUS
The principals dominated. Without the winner it was a maiden nursery in all but name.

8345 BETWAY H'CAP 6f (F)
12:30 (12:31) (Class 5) (0-75,77) 3-Y-O+ **£4,528** (£1,347; £673; £336) **Stalls** Low

Form RPR
5060 **1** **Bring On A Spinner**[102] 6072 3-8-13 68..................(be[1]) AaronJones[(3)] 3 81+
(Stuart Williams) *trckd ldng pair: hdwy and cl up 2f out: sn chal: rdn to ld ent fnl f: edgd lft and kpt on wl* **5/2**[1]
0000 **2** 2 **Harwoods Star (IRE)**[24] 8036 6-9-6 72................................(be) JFEgan 7 78
(John Butler) *awkward s and pushed along towards rr: rdn along over 2f out: hdwy over 1f out: drvn to chse ldrs and n.m.r ins fnl f: kpt on wl towards fin* **33/1**
0001 **3** hd **Vroom (IRE)**[7] 8236 3-9-0 73 6ex............................(p) GabrieleMalune[(7)] 1 78
(Gay Kelleway) *cl up: led 1/2-way: rdn wl over 1f out: drvn and hdd ent fnl f: sn edgd lft and kpt on* **9/1**
5564 **4** 2 1/4 **Personal Touch**[7] 8239 7-9-1 70............................ AlistairRawlinson[(3)] 5 68
(Michael Appleby) *chsd ldrs: hdwy over 2f out: rdn wl over 1f out: drvn and no imp fnl f* **15/2**
0242 **5** hd **Boots And Spurs**[7] 8239 7-9-4 77........................(v) NatalieHambling[(7)] 2 81+
(Scott Dixon) *trckd ldrs on inner: hdwy wl over 2f out: sn rdn: drvn over 1f out: n.m.r ent fnl f: kpt on same pce* **7/2**[2]
4330 **6** nk **Archimedes (IRE)**[25] 8010 3-8-13 65....................(t) JosephineGordon 4 61
(David C Griffiths) *slt ld: hdd 1/2-way: cl up: rdn along 2f out: drvn over 1f out: kpt on same pce* **33/1**
0526 **7** 1 3/4 **Clubland (IRE)**[29] 7959 7-9-2 68...................................... TomMarquand 11 59
(Garry Moss) *stdd s and swtchd lft: towards rr: hdwy over 2f out: sn rdn and n.d* **5/1**[3]
0451 **8** 1 1/4 **Billyoakes (IRE)**[12] 8181 4-9-6 72.......................................(p) BenCurtis 8 59
(Charlie Wallis) *chsd ldrs: rdn along 2f out: sn drvn and wknd* **12/1**
06 **8** dht **Dominium (USA)**[10] 8206 9-8-13 70..........................(b) DavidParkes[(5)] 6 57
(Jeremy Gask) *dwlt: a towards rr* **16/1**
-200 **10** 5 **Extortion**[98] 6215 3-9-7 73.. ConnorBeasley 9 44
(Bryan Smart) *racd wd and towards rr: rdn along over 2f out: sn outpcd* **16/1**
4100 **11** nse **Satchville Flyer**[10] 8205 5-9-2 68...................................... AdamKirby 10 38
(David Evans) *rr: wd st: a bhd* **33/1**

1m 14.89s (-1.61) **Going Correction** -0.20s/f (Stan) **11** Ran SP% **117.5**
Speed ratings (Par 103): **102,99,99,96,95 95,93,91,91,84 84**
CSF £97.72 CT £644.93 TOTE £3.80: £1.40, £7.40, £2.90; EX 112.60 Trifecta £1123.80.
Owner J W Parry **Bred** J W Parry **Trained** Newmarket, Suffolk

FOCUS
It again paid to be handy in this modest sprint handicap and the main action was on the far rail.

8346 BETWAY MEDIAN AUCTION MAIDEN STKS 6f (F)
1:00 (1:02) (Class 6) 3-5-Y-O **£3,234** (£962; £481; £240) **Stalls** Low

Form RPR
63- **1** **Mr Morse**[591] 1867 3-9-5 0.. BenCurtis 6 66
(Brian Ellison) *trckd ldng pair: hdwy 1/2-way and sn cl up: rdn to ld wl over 1f out: drvn ent fnl f: kpt on wl towards fin* **2/1**[2]
5030 **2** nk **Vivre La Reve**[124] 5335 4-9-0 48..[1] RyanPowell 8 60
(James Unett) *chsd ldrs: hdwy over 2f out: rdn to chal over 1f out: ev ch: drvn ins fnl f: kpt on* **20/1**
4632 **3** hd **Epeius (IRE)**[25] 8012 3-9-5 64.. GrahamLee 9 65
(Ben Haslam) *trckd ldrs: hdwy on outer 1/2-way: cl up over 2f out: rdn to chal over 1f out: ev ch: drvn ins fnl f: kpt on* **4/5**[1]
0/06 **4** 5 **Saxony**[132] 5009 5-8-9 30... LucyKBarry[(5)] 5 45
(Matthew Salaman) *cl up on inner: led after 2f: rdn along 1/2-way: sn hdd and drvn: one pce fr wl over 1f out* **100/1**
434 **5** 1 1/4 **Freeze A Crowd (IRE)**[146] 4511 3-8-9 42..............(t) MeganNicholls[(5)] 7 41
(Ben Haslam) *slt ld 2f: cl up: rdn to ld again wl over 2f out: hdd wl over 1f out: sn drvn and grad wknd* **16/1**
0400 **6** hd **Tilsworth Micky**[24] 8026 4-9-5 50...................................... JoeFanning 4 45
(J R Jenkins) *a towards rr* **7/1**[3]
/5-0 **7** 16 **Lady Vellyn**[53] 7509 4-8-11 27..................................(p) NoelGarbutt[(3)] 1
(Matthew Salaman) *in tch: rdn along over 3f out: sn outpcd and bhd* **100/1**
0506 **U** **Ten Rocks**[7] 8236 3-8-12 55.. JordanUys[(7)] 3
(Lisa Williamson) *rrd bdly and uns rdr s* **8/1**

1m 16.3s (-0.20) **Going Correction** -0.20s/f (Stan) **8** Ran SP% **125.1**
Speed ratings (Par 101): **93,92,92,85,84 83,62,**
CSF £42.06 TOTE £3.30: £1.10, £4.30, £1.10; EX 57.30 Trifecta £146.20.
Owner Mrs J A Martin **Bred** Bishopswood Bloodstock & Trickledown Stud **Trained** Norton, N Yorks

FOCUS
There was a tight three-way finish to this weak maiden. The third clouds the form.

8347 32RED.COM FILLIES' H'CAP 1m (F)
1:30 (1:31) (Class 4) (0-80,76) 3-Y-O+ **£6,469** (£1,925; £962; £481) **Stalls** Low

Form RPR

2465 **1** **Stosur (IRE)**[24] 8028 5-9-10 **76**..(b) AdamKirby 6 82
(Gay Kelleway) *mde all: rdn wl over 1f out: drvn ins fnl f: kpt on wl towards fin* **10/3**[2]

0606 **2** *nk* **Dusky Dawn**[7] 8239 4-9-10 **76**.. BenCurtis 4 81
(Alan Swinbank) *chsd wnr: pushed along and hdwy 2f out: rdn over 1f out: drvn to chal and ev ch ins fnl f: no ex towards fin* **9/2**[3]

0403 **3** *1* **African Showgirl**[7] 8240 3-8-10 **63**.......................... JosephineGordon 8 66
(Ivan Furtado) *trckd ldrs: hdwy 2f out: swtchd lft and rdn to chse ldng pair over 1f out: sn chal on inner and ev ch tl drvn and no ex last 100 yds* **3/1**[1]

0305 **4** *2 1/2* **Arcane Dancer (IRE)**[7] 8241 3-8-10 **63**..............................(p) TomEaves 1 60
(Lawrence Mullaney) *trckd ldng pair on inner: pushed along wl over 2f out: rdn wl over 1f out: kpt on same pce* **14/1**

4516 **5** *nse* **Sattelac**[89] 6504 3-9-1 **68**... ConnorBeasley 2 65
(Keith Dalgleish) *trckd ldrs: pushed along and sltly outpcd over 3f out: hdwy over 2f out: sn rdn and no imp fnl f* **8/1**

6200 **6** *7* **Penny Dreadful**[8] 8233 4-8-10 **69**....................................... RPWalsh(7) 5 50
(Scott Dixon) *dwlt: a rr* **33/1**

6504 **7** *10* **Hijran (IRE)**[26] 7985 3-8-12 **65**....................................(p) RobertWinston 7 51
(Michael Appleby) *chsd ldrs on outer: pushed along over 3f out: rdn wl over 1f out: wknd wl over 1f out: sn eased and bhd* **3/1**[1]

0500 **8** *5* **Miramonte Dancer (IRE)**[102] 6105 3-8-2 **58**................. NoelGarbutt(3) 3 4
(David C Griffiths) *dwlt and rr: rdn along 1/2-way: sn outpcd and bhd* **50/1**

1m 42.31s (-1.39) **Going Correction** -0.20s/f (Stan)
WFA 3 from 4yo+ 1lb **8** Ran SP% **113.9**
Speed ratings (Par 102): **98,97,96,94,94 87,77,72**
CSF £18.61 CT £48.91 TOTE £4.10: £1.10, £1.90, £1.30; EX 19.40 Trifecta £59.10.
Owner Brian C Oakley **Bred** Mervyn Stewkesbury **Trained** Exning, Suffolk

FOCUS
An ordinary fillies' handicap where once more those racing handily held sway.

8348 BETWAY CLAIMING STKS 1m 3f (F)
2:00 (2:00) (Class 6) 3-Y-O+ **£3,234** (£962; £481; £240) **Stalls** Low

Form RPR

1432 **1** **Tatting**[224] 1952 7-9-1 75.. PaulMulrennan 2 78
(Lawrence Mullaney) *trckd ldrs: hdwy 3f out: rdn along wl over 1f out: sn cl up: led ent fnl f: pushed out* **11/8**[1]

0001 **2** *1 1/4* **Brigadoon**[122] 4967 9-8-11 73.. RobertWinston 8 71
(Michael Appleby) *cl up: led 4f out: rdn along 2f out: drvn and hdd ent fnl f: kpt on u.p* **3/1**[3]

0641 **3** *2 1/2* **Vercingetorix (IRE)**[31] 5547 5-9-9 76..............................(p) GrahamLee 6 79
(Harriet Bethell) *trckd ldng pair: pushed along and hdwy 3f out: rdn wl over 1f out: drvn appr fnl f: kpt on same pce* **10/1**

4200 **4** *3/4* **Cold Fusion (IRE)**[10] 8211 3-8-2 62.......................... JosephineGordon 4 61
(David Flood) *slt ld: hdd 4f out and sn pushed along: rdn over 2f out: drvn over 1f out: kpt on same pce* **14/1**

13-5 **5** *14* **Rhombus (IRE)**[1] 8338 6-9-11 95... AdamKirby 1 57
(John Butler) *trckd ldrs: pushed along on inner 4f out: rdn 3f out: sn outpcd* **9/4**[2]

0550 **6** *30* **Striking Nigella**[113] 5729 6-8-1 1.. NoelGarbutt(3) 3
(Michael Chapman) *a rr: rdn along over 4f out: sn outpcd and bhd* **150/1**

2m 26.11s (-1.89) **Going Correction** -0.20s/f (Stan)
WFA 3 from 4yo+ 4lb **6** Ran SP% **114.3**
Speed ratings (Par 101): **98,97,95,94,84 62**
CSF £6.09 TOTE £2.70: £1.40, £2.00; EX 7.10 Trifecta £27.10.There was no bid for the winner.
Owner The Usual Suspects **Bred** Darley **Trained** Great Habton, N Yorks

FOCUS
Not a bad claimer on paper, but most arrived with something to prove.

8349 BETWAY SPRINT H'CAP 5f (F)
2:30 (2:30) (Class 5) (0-75,75) 3-Y-O+ **£4,528** (£1,347; £673; £336) **Stalls** Centre

Form RPR

0034 **1** **Landing Night (IRE)**[18] 8099 4-9-7 **75**..........................(tp) PJMcDonald 6 84
(Rebecca Menzies) *hld up: hdwy wl over 1f out: effrt and nt clr run ent over 1f out: sn rdn and squeezed through to ld last 110 yds: sn drvn and kpt on* **6/1**[2]

0250 **2** *nk* **Archie Stevens**[13] 8150 6-9-1 **69**.. JFEgan 11 77
(David Evans) *chsd ldrs: hdwy 2f out: rdn to chal over 1f out: drvn and slt ld ent fnl f: hdd and no ex last 110 yds* **28/1**

6-1 **3** *1/2* **Berlios (IRE)**[285] 798 3-9-5 **73**.................................. AndrewMullen 4 80+
(David Barron) *racd towards far rail: rr: hdwy over 1f out: sn rdn and styd on wl fnl f: nrst fin* **5/1**[1]

3160 **4** *1* **Interlink (USA)**[12] 8176 3-9-4 **72**.. BenCurtis 13 75
(Tony Coyle) *racd stands side: towards rr: rdn along 2f out: hdwy over 1f out: drvn and kpt on fnl f: nrst fin* **6/1**[2]

000 **5** *1/2* **Jack Luey**[46] 7660 9-9-2 **70**...(b) TomEaves 9 71
(Lawrence Mullaney) *in tch: rdn along and outpcd 1/2-way: drvn wl over 1f out: kpt on fnl f* **66/1**

5060 **6** *nk* **Powerful Wind (IRE)**[128] 5189 7-9-3 **71**.......................... AdamBeschizza 8 71
(Charlie Wallis) *slt ld: rdn wl over 1f out: drvn and edgd rt 1f out: sn hdd and grad wknd* **14/1**

2315 **7** *nk* **Mysterious Look**[18] 8099 3-9-7 **75**...................................... GrahamLee 2 74
(Ed McMahon) *racd nr far rail: chsd ldrs: rdn along wl over 1f out: drvn and kpt on same pce fnl f* **5/1**[1]

2420 **8** *1/2* **You're Cool**[98] 6215 4-9-1 **69**... RobertWinston 1 66
(John Balding) *cl up: rdn along wl over 1f out: drvn and wknd ent fnl f* **9/1**

0250 **9** *1/2* **Coiste Bodhar (IRE)**[18] 8099 5-8-9 **70**................. NatalieHambling(7) 10 65
(Scott Dixon) *chsd ldrs: rdn along 2f out: sn drvn and wknd appr fnl f* **33/1**

0603 **10** *nk* **Elusivity (IRE)**[18] 8099 8-9-6 **74**.................................(p) PaulMulrennan 3 68
(Conor Dore) *cl up: rdn 2f out: ev ch tl drvn and wknd appr fnl f* **10/1**

0000 **11** *1 1/2* **Crosse Fire**[64] 7202 4-9-0 **75**..(p) RPWalsh(7) 7 64+
(Scott Dixon) *slowly away and a bhd* **7/1**[3]

350 **12** *9* **Sir Theodore (IRE)**[48] 7626 3-9-6 **74**...................................... AdamKirby 5 31
(Richard Spencer) *racd towards far side: in tch: rdn 2f out: sn lost pl and bhd* **22/1**

0050 **13** *22* **Something Lucky (IRE)**[29] 7959 4-9-5 **73**.......................(p) ShaneGray 12
(Kristin Stubbs) *dwlt: stmbld and rdr lost iron s: a bhd* **14/1**

59.43s (-0.27) **Going Correction** +0.025s/f (Slow) **13** Ran SP% **119.1**
Speed ratings (Par 103): **103,102,101,100,99 98,98,97,96,96 93,79,44**
CSF £170.89 CT £939.24 TOTE £4.20: £2.30, £6.80, £1.70; EX 131.50 Trifecta £1283.10.
Owner John Dance **Bred** Mrs Claire Doyle **Trained** Mordon, Co. Durham

FOCUS
This very well-contested sprint handicap was run at a frantic pace. The main action was down the middle and the winner has been rated close to his best.

8350 SUNBETS.CO.UK H'CAP (DIV I) 7f (F)
3:00 (3:00) (Class 6) (0-65,65) 3-Y-O+ **£3,234** (£962; £481; £240) **Stalls** Low

Form RPR

-040 **1** **Macho Mac**[18] 8095 3-9-1 **59**.. RobertHavlin 4 79+
(Hughie Morrison) *trckd ldrs: smooth hdwy over 2f out: led on bit wl over 1f out: clr ent fnl f: readily* **6/1**[2]

0623 **2** *6* **Swansway**[14] 8145 3-8-9 **56**.. NathanEvans(3) 6 58
(Michael Easterby) *towards rr: hdwy over 2f out: rdn wl over 1f out: drvn and styd on fnl f: no ch w wnr* **5/4**[1]

0014 **3** *1/2* **Alpha Tauri (USA)**[7] 8236 10-9-7 **65**................................ MartinLane 11 66
(Charles Smith) *towards rr: hdwy 3f out: rdn to chse ldrs over 1f out: drvn and kpt ion fnl f* **9/1**

3500 **4** *1* **Paladin (IRE)**[76] 6872 7-8-12 **61**.................................. MitchGodwin(5) 2 59
(Michael Blake) *prom: cl up 1/2-way: rdn 2f out and ev ch: drvn over 1f out and grad wknd* **14/1**

0005 **5** *4* **Llewellyn**[7] 8236 8-8-13 **62**...(b) PhilDennis(5) 3 49
(Declan Carroll) *slt ld: rdn along wl over 2f out: drvn and hdd wl over 1f out: grad wknd* **10/1**

0000 **6** *1 1/4* **Secret Glance**[65] 7189 4-9-7 **65**.................................. AdamBeschizza 8 49
(Richard Rowe) *rr: hdwy 2f out: sn rdn and plugged on one pce* **13/2**[3]

4300 **7** *1* **Port Lairge**[7] 8242 6-8-13 **60**.. NoelGarbutt(3) 7 41
(Michael Chapman) *rr and sn rdn along: hdwy u.p over 2f out: drvn over 1f out: plugged on* **33/1**

100 **8** *1* **Quadriga (IRE)**[39] 7795 6-8-11 **55**.................................. DougieCostello 9 33
(Chris Grant) *chsd ldrs: rdn along wl over 2f out: sn wknd* **16/1**

0546 **9** *2 3/4* **Firgrove Bridge (IRE)**[85] 6636 4-8-7 **51** oh6.................. RyanPowell 10 22
(Kevin Frost) *s.i.s: a bhd* **33/1**

0000 **10** *1* **Locommotion**[17] 8121 4-8-7 **51** oh1..........................(e[1]) KieranO'Neill 1 19
(Matthew Salaman) *chsd ldrs on inner: rdn along over 3f out: sn outpcd* **66/1**

0500 **11** *2 1/4* **Dr Red Eye**[7] 8236 8-8-2 **53**...[1] RPWalsh(7) 5 15
(Scott Dixon) *cl up: rdn along 3f out: sn wknd* **25/1**

1m 27.54s (-2.76) **Going Correction** -0.20s/f (Stan) **11** Ran SP% **114.9**
Speed ratings (Par 101): **107,100,99,98,93 92,91,90,87,85 83**
CSF £13.09 CT £68.93 TOTE £5.90: £2.30, £1.30, £2.30; EX 19.60 Trifecta £114.20.
Owner A McAlpine H Scott-Barrett A Struthers **Bred** Longdon Stud **Trained** East Ilsley, Berks

FOCUS
This moderate handicap looks sound and has been rated around the runner-up..

8351 SUNBETS.CO.UK H'CAP (DIV II) 7f (F)
3:30 (3:30) (Class 6) (0-65,65) 3-Y-O+ **£3,234** (£962; £481; £240) **Stalls** Low

Form RPR

4542 **1** **Custard The Dragon**[10] 8206 3-9-7 **65**.................................. JoeFanning 6 73
(John Mackie) *cl up: chal 2f out: rdn to ld ins fnl f: sn drvn and jst hld on* **11/4**[1]

2635 **2** *nse* **Unnoticed**[11] 8188 4-9-4 **62**..(t) RobertWinston 8 70
(Ollie Pears) *cl up: led wl over 1f out and sn rdn: drvn and hdd ins fnl f: rallied last 50 yds: jst hld* **5/1**[3]

0044 **3** *3 1/4* **Best Tamayuz**[7] 8240 5-8-8 **59**..............................(p) NatalieHambling(7) 10 58
(Scott Dixon) *dwlt and rr: hdwy on outer over 2f out: rdn to chse ldng pair over 1f out: drvn and no imp fnl f* **7/2**[2]

2052 **4** *4* **Cascading Stars (IRE)**[13] 8156 4-9-3 **61**.............................. AdamKirby 7 49
(Daniel Mark Loughnane) *chsd ldrs: rdn along over 2f out: drvn wl over 1f out: one pce* **15/2**

5450 **5** *nk* **Men United (FR)**[15] 8137 3-8-10 **54**............................... TomMarquand 9 41
(Garry Moss) *qckly away and led: rdn along 3f out: hdd wl over 1f out: sn drvn and grad wknd* **14/1**

4404 **6** *2 3/4* **Mrs Biggs**[3] 8306 4-8-7 **56**...(b) PhilDennis(5) 5 36
(Declan Carroll) *in tch: rdn along 1/2-way: drvn over 2f out: sn wknd* **8/1**

0500 **7** *3/4* **Spryt (IRE)**[12] 8181 4-9-2 **60**...(b) PaulMulrennan 2 38
(Conor Dore) *chsd ldrs on inner: rdn along 3f out: sn drvn and wknd* **25/1**

4160 **8** *5* **Secret Lightning (FR)**[12] 8179 4-8-6 **53** ow1........................ TimClark(3) 1 18
(Michael Appleby) *in tch: rdn along 3f out: sn btn* **20/1**

0645 **9** *4* **Trust Me Boy**[56] 7442 8-9-5 **63**.. RobertHavlin 4 17
(John E Long) *in tch: rdn along and outpcd 1/2-way: sn swtchd rt to outer: wd st and bhd* **12/1**

6000 **10** *hd* **Fearless Poppy**[26] 7986 3-8-0 **51** oh6.................................(v) RPWalsh(7) 3 4
(Christine Dunnett) *n.m.r and snatched up shortly after s: a rr* **100/1**

1m 28.07s (-2.23) **Going Correction** -0.20s/f (Stan) **10** Ran SP% **112.4**
Speed ratings (Par 101): **104,103,100,95,95 92,91,85,81,80**
CSF £15.52 CT £47.45 TOTE £3.70: £1.50, £1.60, £1.60; EX 15.90 Trifecta £49.70.
Owner Derbyshire Racing **Bred** Mr & Mrs Kevan Watts **Trained** Church Broughton , Derbys

FOCUS
They went a sound pace in this second division of the 7f handicap and the first two were prominent throughout. It was 0.53sec slower than the first.
T/Jkpt: £10,000.00 to a £1 stake. Pool: £10,000.00 - 1.0 winning unit. T/Plt: £19.30 to a £1 stake. Pool: £72,248.46 - 2,721.62 winning units. T/Qpdt: £4.80 to a £1 stake. Pool: £6,951.59 - 1,070.30 winning units. **Joe Rowntree**

8243 KEMPTON (A.W) (R-H)
Wednesday, December 14

OFFICIAL GOING: Polytrack: standard to slow
Wind: light behind Weather: clear

8352 "BOY ABOUT TOWN BARBERS HORNCHURCH" MEDIAN AUCTION MAIDEN STKS 6f (P)
4:05 (4:07) (Class 6) 2-Y-O **£2,264** (£673; £336; £168) **Stalls** Low

Form RPR

3 **1** **Fivetwoeight**[21] 8065 2-9-5 0.. LukeMorris 1 75
(Peter Chapple-Hyam) *chsd ldr on inner: rdn on inner 2f out: kpt on wl fr over 1f out to ld fnl 110yds* **15/8**[1]

34 **2** *1* **Ripp Orf (IRE)**[35] 7867 2-9-5 0.. SeanLevey 5 72
(David Elsworth) *covered up in mid-div: rdn between horses 2f out: angling to outer fr over 1f out tl clr ent fnl f: kpt on wl ins fnl f to grabbed 2nd post: nvr nrr* **5/2**[2]

035 **3** *nse* **Island Cloud**[48] 7647 2-9-0 70................................. RichardKingscote 10 67
(Heather Main) *sn led: rdn 2f out: kpt on wl whn pressed ent fnl f: hdd 110yds out: lost 2nd post* **9/1**

63 **4** *1 1/2* **Golden Opportunity**[34] 7891 2-9-5 0 MartinHarley 11 68
(James Tate) *pressed ldr on outer: upside ldr whn rdn 2f out: kpt on pce ins fnl f* **10/1**

5 **5** *1 3/4* **Captain Pugwash (IRE)**[28] 7976 2-9-5 0 LiamKeniry 3 62
(Henry Spiller) *hld up in mid-div on inner: rdn 2f out: ev ch ent fnl f: one pce after* **5/1**[3]

0 **6** *1* **Innstigator**[7] 8246 2-9-2 0 HectorCrouch(3) 8 59
(Ralph J Smith) *hld up in rr: rdn over 2f out: prog ent fnl f: nvr nrr* **150/1**

3200 **7** *1/2* **Secret Agent**[25] 8033 2-9-5 69 MartinDwyer 2 58
(William Muir) *chsd ldrs: rdn 2f out: no imp ent fnl f and kpt on one pce* **16/1**

4000 **8** *3/4* **Vibes (IRE)**[13] 8175 2-9-5 73 WilliamCarson 6 56
(Jamie Osborne) *fly-leaped s and t.k.h: sltly hmpd 2f out: rdn sn after: no imp on ldrs ent fnl f: kpt on nicely under hands and heels* **14/1**

9 *2* **Jai Hanuman (IRE)** 2-9-5 0 [1] FergusSweeney 7 50
(Seamus Durack) *hld up in rr: rdn along over 2f out: lft bhd over 1f out* **20/1**

6 **10** *3/4* **Golden Harbour (FR)**[18] 8119 2-8-12 0 (t) JoshuaBryan(7) 4 47
(Brian Barr) *in rr: rdn on inner over 2f out: sn hld* **100/1**

0 **11** *hd* **African Girl**[51] 7576 2-8-11 0 SimonPearce(3) 12 42
(Lydia Pearce) *wnt lft s: racd in mid-div on outer: rdn over 2f out: sn struggling and wknd fnl f* **100/1**

12 *6* **Captain Sedgwick (IRE)** 2-9-0 0 TomMarquand 9 24
(John Spearing) *hld up in rr: pushed along to hold pl over 3f out: rdn over 2f out: no rspnse and pushed out hands and heels fr over 1f out* **100/1**

1m 13.02s (-0.08) **Going Correction** -0.025s/f (Stan) **12** Ran SP% **120.1**
Speed ratings (Par 94): **99,97,97,95,93 91,91,90,87,86 86,78**
CSF £6.52 TOTE £3.00: £1.60, £1.70, £2.40; EX 8.30 Trifecta £39.00.
Owner Raed El Youssef **Bred** Mrs Mary Taylor & Kirtlington Stud **Trained** Newmarket, Suffolk

FOCUS
The pace held up well in this maiden. The winner was always well placed.

8353 32RED/BRITISH STALLION STUDS EBF MAIDEN STKS (DIV I) 7f (P)

4:40 (4:42) (Class 5) 2-Y-O **£3,234** (£962; £481; £240) **Stalls** Low

Form RPR

4 **1** **Me Too Nagasaki (IRE)**[54] 7502 2-9-5 0 JFEgan 1 76
(Jeremy Noseda) *dwlt: settled bhd ldrs on inner: travelling wl over 2f out: sn rdn and led over 1f out: rdn out* **4/7**[1]

004 **2** *3/4* **Desert Grey (IRE)**[48] 7649 2-9-5 74 JimCrowley 4 74
(Roger Varian) *led: hdd after 1f: pressed ldr on inner after: rdn to ld over 2f out: hdd over 1f out: kpt on after* **6/1**[3]

3 *1 1/4* **Al Sail (FR)** 2-9-5 0 SeanLevey 5 71
(Richard Hannon) *covered up in mid-div: tk clsr order over 2f out: rdn 2f out: ev ch ent fnl f and rn green: wknd fnl strides* **9/2**[2]

00 **4** *1/2* **Mutineer**[33] 7906 2-9-5 0 RichardKingscote 7 69
(Daniel Kubler) *wnt rt s: t.k.h bhd ldrs: rdn over 2f out: kpt on* **33/1**

5 *1/2* **Rock N Roll Global (IRE)** 2-9-5 0 ShaneKelly 6 68
(Richard Hughes) *hld up in rr-div: rdn over 2f out: kpt on one pce fr over 1f out* **25/1**

6 *1 1/4* **Bo Selecta (IRE)** 2-9-5 0 LiamKeniry 3 65
(Richard Spencer) *settled bhd ldrs: rdn on inner 2f out: no ex wl ins fnl f* **33/1**

06 **7** *1 1/2* **Take A Turn (IRE)**[35] 7865 2-9-5 0 TomQueally 2 60
(David Lanigan) *in rr: rdn on inner over 2f out: kpt on one pce after* **40/1**

8 *2 1/2* **Shouldertoshoulder** 2-9-2 0 AaronJones(3) 9 54
(Stuart Williams) *reluctant to load: hld up in rr: rdn 2f out: kpt on one pce* **33/1**

2446 **9** *3/4* **Shabeeh (IRE)**[13] 8175 2-9-5 74 PJMcDonald 12 52
(Mark Johnston) *sn pushed up fr wd draw to ld after 1f: hdd over 2f out: rdn 2f out: wknd over 1f out* **12/1**

00 **10** *2 1/2* **My Aussie Rules**[8] 8237 2-9-5 0 AdamKirby 10 45
(Clive Cox) *outpcd in rr: scrubbed along at 1/2-way to hold tch: wl bhd ent st: gng on under hands and heels fr over 1f out* **33/1**

00 **11** *1/2* **Secret Poet (IRE)**[7] 8245 2-9-0 0 WilliamCarson 11 39
(Jamie Osborne) *restless in stalls: a in rr: rdn over 2f out: sn hld* **100/1**

0 **12** *15* **Seeing Things (IRE)**[21] 8066 2-9-5 0 JohnFahy 8 3
(Philip McBride) *t.k.h in mid-div on outer: settled bttr by 1/2-way: rdn over 2f out: sn no imp and cantered home* **100/1**

1m 26.88s (0.88) **Going Correction** -0.025s/f (Stan) **12** Ran SP% **123.8**
Speed ratings (Par 96): **93,92,90,90,89 88,86,83,82,79 79,62**
CSF £4.42 TOTE £1.60: £1.10, £1.60, £1.30; EX 5.30 Trifecta £14.90.
Owner C Fox, B Wilson & R Levitt **Bred** Kevin Walsh **Trained** Newmarket, Suffolk

FOCUS
A fair maiden and once again it didn't pay to be too far off the pace. The hot favourite wasn't overly impressive.

8354 32RED/BRITISH STALLION STUDS EBF MAIDEN STKS (DIV II) 7f (P)

5:10 (5:15) (Class 5) 2-Y-O **£3,234** (£962; £481; £240) **Stalls** Low

Form RPR

3 **1** **Daschas**[28] 7975 2-9-2 0 (t) KieranShoemark(3) 4 77+
(Amanda Perrett) *settled in mid-divsion on inner: tk clsr order 3f out: shkn up over 2f out: rdn 2f out and wl over 1f out: qcknd away fr gp ent fnl f: in command and rdn out fnl f* **11/4**[2]

0 **2** *3 3/4* **Footman (GER)**[7] 8245 2-9-5 0 ShaneKelly 7 67+
(Richard Hughes) *hld up in rr-div on inner: swtchd to centre 2f out: travelling powerfully whn nt clr run over 1f out: n.d to wnr whn gap opened ent fnl f: nudged out after: likely improver* **16/1**

54 **3** *1* **Know Your Limit (IRE)**[34] 7883 2-9-5 0 LukeMorris 12 63
(Ed Walker) *hld up in mid-div: in centre ent st: shkn up and drifted to inner rail fr 2f out: kpt on nicely ins fnl f* **8/1**[3]

60 **4** *nk* **Screaming Gemini (IRE)**[33] 7908 2-9-5 0 JimCrowley 6 62
(Roger Varian) *settled bhd ldrs: pushed along ntering st: no imp tl kpt on wl fr over 1f out: nvr nrr* **7/4**[1]

5 *2 1/4* **Greyjoy (IRE)** 2-9-0 0 MitchGodwin(5) 10 56
(Sylvester Kirk) *pressed ldr: upsides and rdn ent st: no ex fr over 1f out* **25/1**

0 **6** *1 1/4* **Mister Freeze (IRE)**[21] 8066 2-9-5 0 (t) AdamKirby 9 53
(Clive Cox) *led: rdn over 2f out: hdd wl over 1f out: sn wknd* **40/1**

7 *1/2* **Brother In Arms (IRE)** 2-9-5 0 WilliamCarson 2 52
(Jamie Osborne) *hld up in rr: rdn over 2f out: no imp and kpt on one pce* **8/1**[3]

06 **8** *nk* **Sunovarebel**[7] 8245 2-9-5 0 JoeyHaynes 8 51
(Alan Bailey) *reluctant to load: chsd ldrs on outer: rdn over 2f out: no ex and wknd ins fnl f* **25/1**

06 **9** *1/2* **Mr Mac**[56] 7458 2-9-5 0 TomMarquand 5 49
(Peter Hedger) *hld up in rr: pushed along over 1f out: nvr involved: likely improver* **100/1**

00 **10** *8* **Raspberry Princess**[46] 7696 2-9-0 0 [1] PatCosgrave 1 23
(Stuart Williams) *a in rr: rdn over 2f out and no rspnse* **50/1**

11 *2 1/4* **Caracas** 2-9-5 0 GeorgeBaker 11 22+
(Roger Charlton) *missed break: a in rr* **8/1**[3]

12 *6* **Millie May** 2-8-9 0 HollieDoyle(5) 3
(Jimmy Fox) *in rr: scrubbed along bef 1/2-way: no imp st* **66/1**

1m 26.89s (0.89) **Going Correction** -0.025s/f (Stan) **12** Ran SP% **116.8**
Speed ratings (Par 96): **93,88,87,87,84 83,82,82,81,72 70,63**
CSF £41.79 TOTE £3.70: £1.50, £3.50, £2.40; EX 39.00 Trifecta £258.00.
Owner K Abdullah **Bred** Juddmonte Farms Ltd **Trained** Pulborough, W Sussex

FOCUS
The winner came right away from them, but the time was almost identical to the first division.

8355 32RED ON THE APP STORE MAIDEN AUCTION STKS 1m (P)

5:40 (5:42) (Class 5) 2-Y-O **£2,911** (£866; £432; £216) **Stalls** Low

Form RPR

5 **1** **Buzz (FR)**[42] 7770 2-8-13 0 LiamKeniry 7 78+
(Hughie Morrison) *settled in mid-div on inner: rdn 2f out in centre: gd prog ent fnl f: led wl ins fnl f: gng on at fin* **3/1**[1]

2 *2 1/4* **Dubaitwentytwenty** 2-8-7 0 JosephineGordon 14 65
(Hugo Palmer) *mid-div on outer: rdn 2f out: kpt on wl fr over 1f out to grab 2nd cl home* **11/2**[2]

0 **3** *shd* **Settle Petal**[43] 7733 2-8-6 0 JFEgan 10 64
(Pat Phelan) *pressed ldr on inner tl led at 1/2-way: rdn jst over 2f out: kpt on bravely tl hdd wl ins fnl f: wknd nr fin and lost 2nd post* **50/1**

4 *1* **Let Rip (IRE)** 2-8-13 0 MartinHarley 11 68
(Henry Candy) *chsd ldrs: rdn over 2f out: kpt on fr over 1f out* **6/1**[3]

5 *hd* **Bermondsey Belle (IRE)** 2-8-10 0 DavidProbert 8 65+
(Lucy Wadham) *in rr: rdn over 2f out: gd prog fr over 1f out: nvr nrr* **16/1**

0 **6** *3/4* **Moonlight Silver**[93] 6413 2-8-10 0 MartinDwyer 9 63
(William Muir) *racd in rr: rdn 2f out: kpt on one pce* **16/1**

50 **7** *nk* **My Lady Marie**[20] 8081 2-8-4 0 HollieDoyle(5) 2 61
(Amanda Perrett) *in rr: rdn over 2f out: kpt on one pce* **11/2**[2]

05 **8** *2 3/4* **Cape Cruiser (USA)**[35] 7865 2-9-0 0 RichardKingscote 13 60
(Ralph Beckett) *sn led on outer: hdd at 1/2-way: remained pressing ldr: wknd fnl f* **11/2**[2]

0 **9** *1/2* **Eugenie Feather (USA)**[20] 8082 2-8-7 0 LukeMorris 5 52
(Marco Botti) *chsd ldrs: rdn 2f out: wknd sn after* **25/1**

0 **10** *1* **Ede's E Rider**[43] 7733 2-8-11 0 KieranO'Neill 4 54
(Pat Phelan) *t.k.h in rr-div on inner: rdn 2f out: no imp* **33/1**

05 **11** *3 1/4* **Royal Sentiment (IRE)**[25] 8025 2-9-0 0 SteveDrowne 6 49
(Mark Usher) *settled in mid-div: rdn 2f out: no imp and wknd* **40/1**

6 **12** *5* **Kenyan (FR)**[63] 7273 2-9-1 0 FergusSweeney 12 39
(Seamus Durack) *mid-div on outer: rdn wl over 2f out: wknd in st* **66/1**

13 *4* **Lyrica's Lion (IRE)** 2-8-12 0 AdamBeschizza 3 26
(Mark Hoad) *in rr: nvr gng enough pce* **100/1**

U **Asmahan** 2-8-8 0 RobertHavlin 1
(Simon Crisford) *stopped to a walk on leaving stalls and sed bucking: gave rdr no ch: uns rdr sn after* **17/2**

1m 40.03s (0.23) **Going Correction** -0.025s/f (Stan) **14** Ran SP% **121.4**
Speed ratings (Par 96): **97,94,94,93,93 92,92,89,89,88 84,79,75,**
CSF £18.34 TOTE £4.20: £1.90, £2.00, £15.10; EX 22.90 Trifecta £1143.10.
Owner Bevan, Pickford & Angliss **Bred** Christian Maillaut & Matthieu Maillaut **Trained** East Ilsley, Berks

FOCUS
This probably didn't take a lot of winning, but the winner is value for more.

8356 32RED H'CAP 1m (P)

6:10 (6:11) (Class 4) (0-85,85) 3-Y-O+ **£4,690** (£1,395; £697; £348) **Stalls** Low

Form RPR

0650 **1** **Presumido (IRE)**[7] 8256 6-9-3 **81** JFEgan 12 90
(Simon Dow) *broke wl and restrained leaving stalls to sit in last: gd prog on inner fr over 2f out: sn rdn and qcknd up wl to ld over 1f out: pressed by runner-up on inner fnl f: kpt on wl and asserted fnl strides* **10/1**

0600 **2** *1/2* **Franco's Secret**[21] 8077 5-8-13 **77** (v) TomMarquand 6 85
(Peter Hedger) *hld up in rr: rdn to chse wnr fr over 1f out: ev ch wl ins fnl f: no ex nr fin* **10/1**

0020 **3** *4 1/2* **Mikmak**[13] 8177 3-9-6 **85** (p) MartinDwyer 1 83
(William Muir) *settled in mid-div: rdn over 2f out: kpt on one pce: but no ch w ldng pair* **7/1**[3]

0020 **4** *2* **Cricklewood Green (USA)**[39] 7821 5-8-8 **77** MitchGodwin(5) 7 70
(Sylvester Kirk) *in rr: rdn over 2f out: kpt on fr off the pce fr over 1f out: nvr nrr* **12/1**

60-0 **5** *1* **Torment**[33] 7903 3-8-11 **76** SeanLevey 2 67
(Richard Hannon) *chsd ldrs: rdn and ev ch 2f out: no ex ent fnl f and wknd* **12/1**

5240 **6** *1 1/4* **Byres Road**[214] 2237 3-9-0 **79** PJMcDonald 5 67
(Mark Johnston) *chsd ldrs: rdn 2f out: no ex and one pce fnl f* **10/1**

2600 **7** *1/2* **Dutiful Son (IRE)**[21] 8069 6-9-5 **83** LukeMorris 10 70
(Simon Dow) *in rr: rdn over 2f out: kpt on one pce* **10/1**

5004 **8** *2* **Niceofyoutotellme**[29] 7967 7-9-6 **84** RichardKingscote 3 66
(Ralph Beckett) *sn led: rdn over 2f out: hdd over 1f out: no ex and wknd ent fnl f* **3/1**[1]

0210 **9** *nk* **Russian Reward (IRE)**[23] 8052 4-8-12 **76** JimCrowley 9 57
(Amanda Perrett) *racd in mid-div: rdn over 2f out: nt qckn and one pce after* **9/2**[2]

5020 **10** *5* **Major Crispies**[33] 7902 5-8-11 **80** (t) DavidParkes(5) 8 50
(Jeremy Gask) *settled in mid-div on inner: rdn over 2f out: no ex and wknd after* **14/1**

0004 **11** *21* **Yourartisonfire**[41] 7781 6-9-0 **78** (p) LiamKeniry 4
(Lisa Williamson) *pressed ldr: rdn over 2f out: wknd qckly sn after: t.o* **25/1**

030 **12** *40* **Freight Train (IRE)**[82] 6753 4-8-8 **77** (p) HollieDoyle(5) 11
(Adrian Wintle) *mid-div early: struggling at 1/2-way: eased st: t.o* **50/1**

1m 37.89s (-1.91) **Going Correction** -0.025s/f (Stan)
WFA 3 from 4yo+ 1lb **12** Ran SP% **119.9**
Speed ratings (Par 105): **108,107,103,101,100 98,98,96,95,90 69,29**
CSF £107.44 CT £765.61 TOTE £10.70: £3.00, £4.00, £2.60; EX 139.70 Trifecta £862.10.
Owner Robert Moss **Bred** Lynn Lodge Stud **Trained** Ashtead, Surrey

The Form Book, Raceform Ltd, Newbury, RG14 5SJ

FOCUS
The leaders went off too quick here and the principals came from off the pace. A small personal best from the winner.

8357 100% PROFIT BOOST AT 32REDSPORT.COM FILLIES' H'CAP 7f (P)
6:40 (6:40) (Class 5) (0-75,75) 3-Y-O+ **£2,911** (£866; £432; £216) **Stalls** Low

Form RPR
3323 **1** **Rio's Cliffs**[25] 8036 3-9-7 **75**....(b[1]) DavidProbert 1 84
(Martyn Meade) *settled in 4th on inner: swtchd to outer wl over 2f out: shkn up and stalked ldng pair over 1f: rdn ent fnl f: qcknd up and led under 1f out: kpt on wl* **7/2**[2]
-423 **2** *2* **Palenville (IRE)**[133] 5027 3-9-7 **75**.... RobertHavlin 5 79
(Simon Crisford) *led: rdn over 1f out: hdd under 1f out: kpt on one pce to hold 2nd* **2/1**[1]
1130 **3** *½* **Encore Moi**[14] 8158 3-9-1 **69**....(b) LukeMorris 6 72
(Marco Botti) *chsd ldr: rdn over 1f out: ev ch ent fnl f: kpt on one pce* **2/1**[1]
0106 **4** *4½* **Flowing Clarets**[14] 8154 3-8-12 **66**.... JosephineGordon 4 57
(John Bridger) *settled in 3rd: shkn up 2f out: lft bhd over 1f out: wknd after* **14/1**
-630 **5** *½* **Lucymai**[277] 924 3-9-6 **74**.... RobertWinston 8 63
(Dean Ivory) *settled in last: niggled along over 2f out: lost tch w ldrs 2f out: on pce after* **15/2**[3]

1m 25.34s (-0.66) **Going Correction** -0.025s/f (Stan) **5** Ran SP% **107.3**
Speed ratings (Par 100): **102,99,99,94,93**
CSF £10.33 TOTE £4.30: £1.80, £2.40; EX 11.70 Trifecta £18.70.
Owner Mrs Jane Newett **Bred** Ladyswood Stud **Trained** Newmarket, Suffolk

FOCUS
A small field, but a tight betting heat between the first three in the market. A clear personal best from the winner.

8358 32RED CASINO FILLIES' H'CAP 6f (P)
7:10 (7:12) (Class 5) (0-70,71) 3-Y-O+ **£2,911** (£866; £432; £216) **Stalls** Low

Form RPR
1 **1** **Hackney Road**[19] 8093 3-9-7 **70**.... TomQueally 3 76+
(Henry Spiller) *in rr on inner and t.k.h: shkn up and swtchd to outer over 1f out: allowed to gather stride and moved clsr on heels of ldrs ent fnl f: sn rdn and kpt on best to ld nr fin* **2/1**[1]
5020 **2** *½* **Lolita**[91] 6487 4-9-7 **70**.... FergusSweeney 9 74
(J R Jenkins) *fly-leaped s and rdr did wl to stay in sddle: gd pce out wd and pressed ldr after 2f: rdn over 2f out: led wl over 1f out: hrd pressed in line of five ent fnl f: sn hdd: kpt on wl to take 2nd post* **25/1**
0000 **3** *shd* **Musical Taste**[14] 8163 3-8-8 **57**.... JFEgan 1 61
(Pat Phelan) *hld up in rr-div: rdn over 2f out: ev ch in line of five ent fnl f: led 110yds out: kpt on wl tl hdd and lost two pls fin* **25/1**
0000 **4** *¾* **Englishwoman**[79] 6831 3-9-7 **70**.... AdamKirby 7 71
(David Evans) *chsd ldrs: rdn over 2f out: ev ch in line of five ent fnl f: kpt on* **8/1**
1605 **5** *½* **Jumeirah Star (USA)**[39] 7811 3-8-12 **64**....(v) EoinWalsh(3) 6 64
(Robert Cowell) *chsd ldr on inner: rdn over 2f out: ev ch in line of five ent fnl f: kpt on one pce nr fin* **25/1**
0026 **6** *1* **Camdora (IRE)**[19] 8094 4-8-12 **61**....(t) TimmyMurphy 4 57
(Jamie Osborne) *t.k.h in rr: rdn over 2f out: kpt on wl on wd outside fr over 1f out: nvr nrr* **6/1**[3]
1302 **7** *nse* **Evening Starlight**[9] 8233 3-9-3 **66**.... LukeMorris 11 62
(Ron Hodges) *sn led: rdn over 2f out and ev ch in line of five ent fnl f: wknd ins fnl f* **12/1**
6532 **8** *¾* **Be Royale**[21] 8067 6-9-7 **70**....(t) RobertWinston 2 64
(Michael Appleby) *racd in rr-div: rdn over 2f out: wknd ins fnl f* **9/4**[2]
0006 **9** *¾* **Flying Sakhee**[9] 8234 3-8-0 **56** oh6....(p) JaneElliott(7) 5 48
(John Bridger) *t.k.h early in mid-div: tk clsr order to pressed ldrs on outer ent 3f out: rdn over 2f out: wknd after* **66/1**
0203 **10** *8* **Equinette (IRE)**[32] 7935 3-8-8 **60**.... KieranShoemark(3) 8 26
(Amanda Perrett) *settled in mid-div: rdn over 2f out: wknd after* **25/1**

1m 13.11s (0.01) **Going Correction** -0.025s/f (Stan) **10** Ran SP% **114.1**
Speed ratings (Par 100): **98,97,97,96,95 94,94,93,92,81**
CSF £59.16 CT £983.66 TOTE £3.30: £1.80, £6.50, £5.70; EX 60.50 Trifecta £1284.10.
Owner Dethrone Racing **Bred** Whatton Manor Stud **Trained** Newmarket, Suffolk

FOCUS
Most of these looked pretty exposed, but the winner was the exception and once again she overcame racing keenly to score.

8359 RACING UK H'CAP 2m (P)
7:40 (7:41) (Class 6) (0-60,60) 3-Y-O+ **£2,264** (£673; £336; £168) **Stalls** Low

Form RPR
20-0 **1** **Canadian Diamond (IRE)**[49] 7614 9-9-10 **58**.... AdamBeschizza 11 67
(Richard Rowe) *hld up in mid-div on outer: gd prog ent st: shkn up over 2f out to chse down ldr: sn rdn and led over 1f out: in command and pushed out ins fnl f* **17/2**
3003 **2** *2¼* **Sund City (FR)**[14] 8164 3-8-9 **51**.... DavidProbert 14 55
(Harry Dunlop) *chsd ldrs: rdn over 3f out: kpt on wl tl wnr wnt by over 1f out: no ch after and kpt on one pce* **8/1**
5553 **3** *¾* **Yasir (USA)**[11] 8211 8-9-12 **60**.... PaulMulrennan 13 63
(Conor Dore) *s.s: in rr: rdn over 3f out: gd prog fr rr 2f out: kpt on wl under hands and heels fr over 1f out: nvr nrr* **12/1**
0000 **4** *nk* **Lily Edge**[85] 6659 7-9-0 **48**....(v) DannyBrock 9 51
(John Bridger) *hld up in mid-div: rdn between horses over 3f out: kpt on one pce fr over 1f out* **20/1**
0135 **5** *1½* **Delagoa Bay (IRE)**[11] 8211 8-9-7 **60**.... MitchGodwin(5) 4 61
(Sylvester Kirk) *in rr: rdn over 3f out: n.m.r between horses over 2f out: swtchd to centre and kpt on one pce* **7/1**[3]
0303 **6** *¾* **Oyster Card**[27] 7987 3-8-7 **49**.... LukeMorris 3 49
(Michael Appleby) *chsd ldrs: rdn over 3f out: kpt on one pce* **4/1**[2]
6500 **7** *1* **Maison Brillet (IRE)**[43] 7739 9-9-10 **58**....(p) RobertHavlin 7 57
(Clive Drew) *settled in mid-div: rdn over 3f out: no imp and kpt on one pce* **25/1**
0401 **8** *nse* **Multigifted**[42] 7760 3-9-3 **59**.... LiamKeniry 8 58
(Michael Madgwick) *t.k.h bhd ldr: plld way into ld over 10f out: rdn and kicked for home over 3f out: coming bk to chsng gp over 2f out: hdd & wknd fr over 1f out* **5/2**[1]
4-40 **9** *1¼* **Newtown Cross (IRE)**[43] 7739 6-9-2 **50**.... KieranO'Neill 5 48
(Jimmy Fox) *a in rr: rdn over 3f out: no imp* **20/1**
0000 **10** *5* **Pixel (IRE)**[27] 7987 3-8-7 **52**.... TimClark(3) 2 44
(Denis Quinn) *hld up in rr: rdn ent st: no imp* **66/1**
0000 **11** *3¼* **Ruzeiz (USA)**[49] 7628 7-9-12 **60**.... TomMarquand 10 48
(Peter Hedger) *a in rr: nvr involved* **40/1**
-605 **12** *11* **Grand Facile**[14] 8164 4-9-1 **52**....(v) HectorCrouch(3) 12 26
(Gary Moore) *t.k.h in mid-div on outer: hrd rdn 4f out: wknd fr 3f out* **16/1**
0004 **13** *94* **Tarakkom (FR)**[14] 8164 4-9-8 **56**.... WilliamCarson 1
(Peter Hiatt) *led tl hdd over 10f out: settled bhd ldr after: rdn wl over 3f out: sn struggling and eased fr over 2f out: t.o* **12/1**

3m 29.78s (-0.32) **Going Correction** -0.025s/f (Stan)
WFA 3 from 4yo+ 8lb **13** Ran SP% **118.5**
Speed ratings (Par 101): **99,97,97,97,96 96,95,95,95,92 90,85,38**
CSF £70.63 CT £824.74 TOTE £9.80: £2.60, £2.70, £3.30; EX 109.50 Trifecta £2925.60.
Owner Nicholls Family **Bred** J S Bolger **Trained** Sullington, W Sussex

FOCUS
An ordinary staying contest, but an emphatic winner.
T/Plt: £45.70 to a £1 stake. Pool: £56,625.98 - 903.37 winning units. T/Qpdt: £35.80 to a £1 stake. Pool: £8,471.97 - 175.10 winning units. **Cathal Gahan**

8251 LINGFIELD (L-H)
Wednesday, December 14

OFFICIAL GOING: Polytrack: standard
Wind: light, behind Weather: sunny

8360 32RED.COM NURSERY H'CAP 1m 1y(P)
11:40 (11:41) (Class 4) (0-85,78) 2-Y-O **£5,175** (£1,540; £769; £384) **Stalls** High

Form RPR
6145 **1** **Kodiac Khan (IRE)**[42] 7764 2-9-7 **78**.... JoeFanning 3 82
(Mark Johnston) *dwlt: sn rcvrd and w ldr: pushed along to ld 2f out: forged ahd u.p ent fnl f: styd on wl: rdn out* **6/1**
014 **2** *1* **Hajaj (IRE)**[56] 7460 2-9-5 **76**.... StevieDonohoe 5 78
(Charlie Fellowes) *stdd and dropped in bhd after s: effrt and swtchd lft over 1f out: hdwy and swtchd lft again ins fnl f: sn chsng wnr: kpt on but a hld* **5/2**[2]
21 **3** *nk* **Golden Nectar**[42] 7762 2-9-6 **77**.... PatCosgrave 2 78
(Laura Mongan) *trckd ldrs: hdwy on outer to join ldrs 3f out: hung rt bnd 2f out: rallied to chse wnr 1f out: 3rd and styd on pce fnl 100yds* **5/1**[3]
3400 **4** *1¾* **Presence Process**[33] 7898 2-8-12 **69**.... JFEgan 1 66
(Pat Phelan) *trckd ldrs: effrt ent fnl 2f: unable qck ent fnl f: kpt on same pce fnl 150yds* **10/1**
6312 **5** *3* **Sans Souci Bay**[33] 7898 2-9-0 **78**.... TinaSmith(7) 4 67
(Richard Hannon) *t.k.h: led: hdd 2f out: unable qck u.p ent fnl f: wknd ins fnl f* **11/8**[1]

1m 37.89s (-0.31) **Going Correction** -0.075s/f (Stan) **5** Ran SP% **110.7**
Speed ratings (Par 98): **98,97,96,94,91**
CSF £21.22 TOTE £6.50: £2.30, £1.70; EX 21.10 Trifecta £76.50.
Owner Hussain Alabbas Lootah **Bred** John P Mangan & John S Mangan **Trained** Middleham Moor, N Yorks

FOCUS
A modest nursery in which they only went a steady pace early.

8361 32RED CASINO EBF MAIDEN FILLIES' STKS (PLUS 10 RACE) (DIV I) 7f 1y(P)
12:10 (12:12) (Class 5) 2-Y-O **£3,363** (£1,001; £500; £250) **Stalls** Low

Form RPR
52 **1** **Cercle D'Or (IRE)**[20] 8081 2-9-0 0.... RobertHavlin 6 73
(John Gosden) *mde all: rdn over 1f out: forged ahd u.p ins fnl f: styd on wl: rdn out* **4/6**[1]
2 *¾* **Harbour Grey (IRE)** 2-9-0 0.... SeanLevey 9 71
(Richard Hannon) *chsd wnr: rdn and ev ch over 1f out: styd on same pce ins fnl f* **12/1**
5 **3** *3¼* **Parisian Chic (IRE)**[63] 7279 2-9-0 0.... RobertWinston 1 62
(Lee Carter) *chsd ldrs: rdn over 1f out: styd on same pce and no imp on ldng pair fnl f* **33/1**
0000 **4** *¾* **Venetian Proposal (IRE)**[35] 7866 2-9-0 44....(p) DanielMuscutt 5 60
(Zoe Davison) *chsd ldng trio: effrt u.p over 1f out: styd on same pce and no imp on ldng pair fnl f* **100/1**
5 *1½* **Flood Warning** 2-9-0 0.... AdamKirby 4 56+
(Clive Cox) *restless in stalls: fly j. leaving stalls and slowly away: keen and rn green in last trio: nt clr run over 2f out: shkn up over 1f out: pushed along and styd on wl ins fnl f: nvr trbld ldrs* **11/4**[2]
0 **6** *nk* **Lady Hester (USA)**[93] 6414 2-9-0 0.... NickyMackay 2 55
(John Gosden) *in tch in midfield: 5th and outpcd whn rdn over 2f out: kpt on same pce and no threat to ldrs after* **5/1**[3]
00 **7** *1* **Bradfield Magic (IRE)**[20] 8081 2-9-0 0.... MichaelJMMurphy 3 53
(Charles Hills) *hld up in tch in last quartet: pushed along and effrt on inner 2f out: one pced and no imp after* **25/1**
8 *hd* **Sandy Shores** 2-9-0 0.... JoeFanning 7 52
(Brian Meehan) *s.i.s: t.k.h: hld up in tch in last trio: pushed along and outpcd 2f out: n.d and kpt on same pce after* **50/1**
0 **9** *4½* **Shiloh**[71] 7056 2-9-0 0.... SteveDrowne 10 40
(Simon Crisford) *in tch in midfield but niggled along: rdn and outpcd over 2f out: wknd over 1f out* **33/1**
0 **10** *8* **Lady Parker (IRE)**[198] 2748 2-9-0 0.... JohnFahy 8 18
(J S Moore) *s.i.s: t.k.h: hedl up in tch in last trio: pushed along and outpcd over 2f out: wknd 2f out* **100/1**

1m 25.64s (0.84) **Going Correction** -0.075s/f (Stan) **10** Ran SP% **124.7**
Speed ratings (Par 93): **92,91,87,86,84 84,83,83,78,68**
CSF £11.80 TOTE £1.80: £1.10, £2.60, £7.70; EX 12.30 Trifecta £129.50.
Owner Sangster, Lascelles & McCalmont **Bred** Fleche D'Or Partnership **Trained** Newmarket, Suffolk

FOCUS
An uncompetitive fillies' maiden in which the first four held those positions throughout. The proximity of the 44-rated fourth doesn't do much for the form.

8362 32RED CASINO EBF MAIDEN FILLIES' STKS (PLUS 10 RACE) (DIV II) 7f 1y(P)
12:45 (12:46) (Class 5) 2-Y-O **£3,363** (£1,001; £500; £250) **Stalls** Low

Form RPR
6 **1** **Sayem**[14] 8152 2-9-0 0.... ThomasBrown 3 78
(Ed Walker) *chsd ldrs: wnt 2nd 2f out: rdn and ev ch ent fnl f: led ins fnl f: r.o wl* **14/1**
02 **2** *1¼* **Ettu**[46] 7696 2-9-0 0.... JimCrowley 4 75
(Jeremy Noseda) *led: rdn over 1f out: hdd ins fnl f: styd on same pce after* **4/7**[1]
4 **3** *1½* **Mitigate**[14] 8152 2-9-0 0.... ShaneKelly 7 71
(David Elsworth) *hld up in tch in last trio: hdwy on outer over 2f out: rdn to chse ldrs 2f out: hung lft and styd on same pce ins fnl f* **4/1**[2]

4 hd **Ifubelieveindreams (IRE)** 2-9-0 0[1] SeanLevey 2 66+
(Ismail Mohammed) *dwlt: hld up in tch in last pair: rdn and hdwy over 1f out: kpt on same pce ins fnl f: fin 5th: promoted to 4th* **12/1**

0 5 2 1/2 **Marwa**[160] 4064 2-9-0 0 PatCosgrave 8 61
(Ed Dunlop) *hld up in tch in midfield: swtchd rt and effrt 2f out: unable qck over 1f out: nt clrest of runs and wknd ins fnl f* **20/1**

6 1 3/4 **Defiance (IRE)** 2-9-0 0 LukeMorris 5 54
(James Tate) *chsd ldr tl 2f out: sn u.p and outpcd over 1f out: btn whn nt clr run and swtchd rt ins fnl f* **16/1**

0 7 1 1/4 **Jannia**[21] 8066 2-8-11 0 EdwardGreatrex(3) 1 51
(Eve Johnson Houghton) *in tch in midfield: effrt on inner wl over 1f out: sn outpcd and bhd whn nt clr run and swtchd rt ins fnl f* **66/1**

8 1 **Vivian Ward** 2-9-0 0 RobertHavlin 6 48
(John Gosden) *dwlt: sn rcvrd and in tch in midfield: swtchd lft and unable qck over 1f out: btn whn squeezed for room ins fnl f: wknd* **17/2[3]**

D 1 1/2 **Zilza (IRE)** 2-9-0 0 MartinDwyer 9 66
(Conrad Allen) *s.i.s and flashed tail leaving stalls: in tch in last pair: effrt on outer bnd 2f out: hdwy and hung lft 1f out: stl hanging but kpt on ins fnl f: nvr trbld ldrs* **50/1**

1m 25.53s (0.73) **Going Correction** -0.075s/f (Stan) **9** Ran SP% **122.6**
Speed ratings (Par 93): **92,90,88,86,84 82,80,79,87**
CSF £23.82 TOTE £20.50: £3.10, £1.10, £1.40; EX 33.90 Trifecta £113.70.
Owner B Greenwood & I Dodds-Smith **Bred** Saleh Al Homaizi & Imad Al Sagar **Trained** Upper Lambourn, Berks

FOCUS
This looked the stronger division, run at a solid pace, and the winning time was 0.11sec faster than the first leg.

8363 BETWAY STAYERS H'CAP 1m 7f 169y(P)
1:20 (1:21) (Class 5) (0-75,77) 3-Y-O+ **£3,234** (£962; £481; £240) **Stalls** Low

Form RPR

4112 1 **Alfredo (IRE)**[47] 7670 4-9-8 **73** (tp) GeorgeBaker 5 88+
(Seamus Durack) *in tch in midfield: clsd to join ldr over 2f out: led 2f out: rdn and asserting whn edgd lft over 1f out: in command fnl f: eased towards fin: easily* **4/6[1]**

2130 2 3 3/4 **Miss Tiger Lily**[54] 7507 6-9-3 **68** JimCrowley 2 73
(Harry Dunlop) *chsd ldr tl led over 2f out: rdn and hdd 2f out: outpcd whn swtchd rt over 1f out: wl hld but kpt on for clr 2nd fnl f* **9/2[2]**

00-3 3 3 **Yes Daddy (IRE)**[23] 8051 8-9-9 **74** (v) LukeMorris 4 75
(Robert Stephens) *chsd ldrs: effrt over 2f out: unable qck u.p 2f out: wnt 3rd 1f out: no threat to wnr and one pce after* **8/1[3]**

6-30 4 1 1/2 **Winter Spice (IRE)**[203] 2582 5-9-12 **77** AdamKirby 7 77
(Clive Cox) *taken down early: stdd and dropped in after s: hld up in last pair: swtchd rt and effrt over 2f out: no imp: wl hld and kpt on same pce fr over 1f out* **8/1[3]**

5152 5 nk **Fast Play (IRE)**[18] 8124 4-9-3 **68** (b) ShaneKelly 3 67
(Richard Hughes) *stdd s: hld up in last pair: swtchd rt and effrt over 2f out: no imp u.p 2f out: wl hld and kpt on same pce after* **12/1**

150 6 2 1/2 **Ravens Quest**[93] 6416 3-9-2 **75** DannyBrock 1 71
(John Ryan) *led: rdn and hdd over 2f out: 3rd and outpcd 2f out: wl hld whn lost 3rd 1f out: wknd fnl f* **16/1**

3m 20.0s (-5.70) **Going Correction** -0.075s/f (Stan)
WFA 3 from 4yo+ 8lb **6** Ran SP% **114.0**
Speed ratings (Par 103): **111,109,107,106,106 105**
CSF £4.17 TOTE £1.50: £1.10, £2.60; EX 4.80 Trifecta £13.60.
Owner Stephen Tucker & Keith McIntosh **Bred** Colin Kennedy **Trained** Upper Lambourn, Berkshire

FOCUS
A modest staying handicap, but the favourite could hardly have been more impressive. They went an even pace.

8364 BETWAY CLASSIFIED (S) STKS 1m 2f (P)
1:50 (1:50) (Class 6) 3-Y-O+ **£2,911** (£866; £432; £216) **Stalls** Low

Form RPR

0000 1 **Juste Pour Nous**[14] 8161 3-9-0 69[1] JoeFanning 5 66
(Mark Johnston) *in tch in last trio: effrt on outer bnd 2f out: hdwy u.p 1f out: led 100yds out: r.o: rdn out* **11/4[2]**

3206 2 3/4 **Maroc**[7] 8254 3-9-0 69 LukeMorris 8 65
(Paul Cole) *t.k.h: chsd ldrs: drvn over 2f out: edgd lft u.p over 1f out: hdwy to ld jst ins fnl f: hdd 100yds out: kpt on same pce after* **5/2[1]**

0210 3 nk **Attain**[12] 8190 7-9-0 66 AaronJones(3) 7 64
(Julia Feilden) *hld up in tch in rr: effrt and hdwy on inner over 1f out: ev ch 1f out: styd on same pce fnl 100yds* **4/1[3]**

3000 4 1 1/2 **Artful Mind**[53] 7529 3-9-0 68[1] DanielMuscutt 2 61
(John Flint) *t.k.h: hld up in tch in last pair: effrt and n.m.r over 1f out: kpt on u.p ins fnl f: no threat to ldrs* **12/1**

2260 5 1 1/4 **Dalavand (IRE)**[135] 4942 3-9-0 53 (t) PatCosgrave 1 59
(Laura Mongan) *in tch in midfield: effrt and jostled over 1f out: pressing ldrs and drvn 1f out: sn no ex: wknd ins fnl f and btn whn swtchd rt towards fin* **12/1**

5-50 6 1 1/4 **Pool House**[21] 8077 5-9-3 69 JimCrowley 4 56
(Mike Murphy) *led tl 6f out: chsd ldr tl led again 2f out: sn rdn: hdd jst ins fnl f: sn outpcd and btn whn pushed rt towards fin* **6/1**

0000 7 3/4 **Yul Finegold (IRE)**[8] 8238 6-8-12 70 (b[1]) SophieKilloran(5) 3 57
(Conor Dore) *stdd s: t.k.h in last pair: nt settle and hdwy on outer after 2f: led 6f out tl 2f out: sn rdn and no ex: btn whn nt clr run 1f out: wknd* **8/1**

2m 5.2s (-1.40) **Going Correction** -0.075s/f (Stan)
WFA 3 from 5yo+ 3lb **7** Ran SP% **116.0**
Speed ratings (Par 101): **102,101,101,99,98 97,97**
CSF £10.41 TOTE £3.20: £2.30, £1.70; EX 9.20 Trifecta £30.20.The winner was bought by David Pipe for 7,000gns. Maroc was claimed by Mrs Nikki Evans for £6,000. Attain was claimed by Mr A. M. B. Watson for £6,000.
Owner Robin Holleyhead **Bred** Burns Farm Stud **Trained** Middleham Moor, N Yorks

FOCUS
A modest seller, but quite a finish. The third and fifth set the level.

8365 BETWAY SPRINT H'CAP 6f 1y(P)
2:25 (2:28) (Class 6) (0-65,69) 3-Y-O+ **£3,234** (£962; £481; £240) **Stalls** Low

Form RPR

3004 1 **Bridge Builder**[25] 8030 6-9-4 **62** (p) TomMarquand 10 71
(Peter Hedger) *sn led and crossed to inner: rdn and kicked clr over 1f out: clr and styd on strly fnl f* **15/2**

3600 2 2 1/4 **Colourbearer (IRE)**[21] 8067 9-9-6 **64** (t) AdamBeschizza 8 66
(Charlie Wallis) *led early: chsd wnr tl 4f out: styd chsng ldrs: effrt to chse wnr again 2f out: styd on same pce u.p fr over 1f out* **14/1**

5000 3 shd **New Rich**[13] 8181 6-9-4 **62** (b) JohnFahy 7 64
(Eve Johnson Houghton) *sn dropped to rr: rdn and hdwy 1f out: r.o wl ins fnl f: no threat to wnr* **11/2[3]**

5504 4 3/4 **Pharoh Jake**[29] 7964 8-9-3 **61** WilliamCarson 6 61
(John Bridger) *midfield: effrt 2f out: chsd clr ldng pair 1f out: kpt on but no real imp: lost 3rd towards fin* **11/1**

3010 5 1 **Firesnake (IRE)**[19] 8094 3-8-10 **61** JordanUys(7) 4 58
(Lisa Williamson) *hld up in last trio: rdn and hdwy over 1f out: kpt on ins fnl f: nvr trbld ldrs* **7/1**

0540 6 1 1/4 **Triple Dream**[13] 8181 11-9-6 **64** JosephineGordon 1 57
(Milton Bradley) *shifted rt s: in tch in midfield: effrt and wd bnd 2f out: no imp over 1f out: wknd ins fnl f* **8/1**

3000 7 hd **Sehayli (IRE)**[14] 8163 3-9-1 **64**[1] PaddyBradley(5) 9 56
(Lee Carter) *s.i.s: bhd: effrt over 1f out: sme hdwy 1f out: kpt on ins fnl f: nvr trbld ldrs* **16/1**

0031 8 2 1/2 **Desert Strike**[9] 8234 10-9-11 **69** 6ex (p) PaulMulrennan 11 54
(Conor Dore) *nt that wl away: midfield tl hdwy to chse ldr after 2f tl 2f out: sn u.p and struggling: wknd fnl f* **5/1[2]**

5010 9 2 1/4 **Last Star Falling (IRE)**[64] 7255 3-8-13 **64** (b) LuluStanford(7) 5 42
(Henry Spiller) *t.k.h: hld up in tch in midfield: no rspnse and lost pl u.p over 1f out: wknd fnl f* **9/2[1]**

4030 10 20 **Valmina**[14] 8163 9-9-7 **65** (t) LukeMorris 2
(Philip Hide) *wl in tch in midfield: rdn 2f out: unable qck over 1f out: no imp and wl hld whn eased jst over 1f out: virtually p.u ins fnl f: dismntd after fin: lame* **5/1[2]**

1m 11.08s (-0.82) **Going Correction** -0.075s/f (Stan) **10** Ran SP% **123.2**
Speed ratings (Par 101): **102,99,98,97,96 94,94,91,88,61**
CSF £112.58 CT £635.59 TOTE £8.80: £2.90, £4.80, £1.80; EX 68.60 Trifecta £660.30.
Owner P C F Racing Ltd **Bred** D J And Mrs Deer **Trained** Hook, Hampshire
■ Royal Rettie was withdrawn. Price at time of withdrawal 40/1. Rule 4 does not apply.

FOCUS
A moderate sprint handicap, but they didn't hang about and the winner was decisive.

8366 BETWAY MAIDEN STKS 1m 4f (P)
3:00 (3:00) (Class 5) 3-Y-O+ **£3,363** (£1,001; £500; £250) **Stalls** Low

Form RPR

1 **Dream Love** 3-9-0 0 RobertHavlin 8 71
(Simon Dow) *hld up in tch towards rr: hdwy over 2f out: rdn to chse ldrs over 1f out: chsd clr ldr ins fnl f: styd on wl to ld last strides* **50/1**

4422 2 nk **Adalene**[19] 8096 3-9-0 76[1] JimCrowley 2 70
(David Simcock) *chsd ldr for 3f out: wnt 2nd again 6f out tl led jst over 2f out: rdn and kicked clr over 1f out: u.p and hung lft ins fnl f: hdd last strides* **1/1[1]**

00 3 nk **Pinkie Brown (FR)**[34] 5486 4-9-10 0 DougieCostello 3 74
(Neil Mulholland) *t.k.h: hld up in tch in midfield: effrt to chse ldr wl over 1f out: lost 2nd but kpt on u.p ins fnl f: pressing ldrs towards fin* **7/1**

0 4 1 1/4 **Diamond Kut**[86] 6634 3-9-5 0 DavidProbert 5 72
(Andrew Balding) *stdd s: t.k.h early: hld up in tch towards rr: hdwy 5f out: nt clr run and hmpd bnd 2f out: swtchd rt over 1f out: kpt on wl ins fnl f: nt rch ldrs* **15/2**

36 5 2 3/4 **Condamine (IRE)**[12] 8195 3-9-5 0 GeorgeBaker 6 68
(Jeremy Gask) *stdd after s and t.k.h early: hld up in last: swtchd rt 6f out: hdwy on outer over 2f out: kpt on same pce fr over 1f out* **5/1[3]**

00- 6 5 **Touched By Love (USA)**[407] 7673 3-9-5 0 AdamKirby 10 60
(Ismail Mohammed) *midfield: hdwy to chse ldr 9f out tl 6f out: shkn up ent fnl 2f: lost pl and btn over 1f out: wknd fnl f* **4/1[2]**

05 7 6 **Divine Prince (GR)**[33] 7904 3-9-2 0 KieranShoemark(3) 4 50
(Amanda Perrett) *led tl rdn and hdd jst over 2f out: lost pl over 1f out: fdd fnl f* **50/1**

64 8 1 1/4 **Tayaar (IRE)**[19] 8096 3-9-5 0 RobertWinston 9 48
(John Ryan) *t.k.h early: hld up in midfield: rdn and dropped to rr over 2f out: sn struggling: bhd over 1f out* **16/1**

00 9 156 **Thenobleprankster (IRE)**[148] 4477 7-9-10 0 StevieDonohoe 7
(Emma Owen) *chsd ldr for 3f out: sn niggled along: lost pl and bhd 6f out: lost tch qckly 4f out: sn eased and t.o* **100/1**

2m 33.04s (0.04) **Going Correction** -0.075s/f (Stan)
WFA 3 from 4yo+ 5lb **9** Ran SP% **121.7**
Speed ratings (Par 103): **96,95,95,94,92 89,85,84,**
CSF £106.90 TOTE £37.10: £6.40, £1.10, £2.10; EX 132.70 Trifecta £1098.40.
Owner T Staplehurst **Bred** T Staplehurst **Trained** Ashtead, Surrey

FOCUS
An uncompetitive older-horse maiden and a dramatic finish.

8367 BETWAY APPRENTICE H'CAP 1m 4f (P)
3:30 (3:31) (Class 5) (0-70,73) 3-Y-O+ **£3,234** (£962; £481; £240) **Stalls** Low

Form RPR

3600 1 **Clovelly Bay (IRE)**[14] 8162 5-9-5 **70** TylerSaunders(7) 5 80
(Marcus Tregoning) *broke wl: sn stdd and hld up in tch in midfield: effrt to chse ldr wl over 1f out: sn chalng: led ins fnl f: r.o wl* **10/1**

0511 2 1 1/4 **General Hazard (IRE)**[7] 8257 3-9-7 **73** 6ex LuluStanford(3) 7 81
(Michael Bell) *t.k.h: hld up in tch in midfield: hdwy to ld 2f out: rdn and edgd lft over 1f out: hdd and one pced ins fnl f* **6/4[1]**

0403 3 2 **Celtic Ava (IRE)**[32] 7936 4-8-6 **57** SophieRalston(7) 1 62
(Pat Phelan) *t.k.h: led for 2f: styd chsng ldrs: nt clr run over 2f out: rdn to chse ldng pair over 1f out: kpt on same pce ins fnl f* **9/1**

5064 4 6 **Camakasi (IRE)**[15] 8142 5-9-9 **67** MitchGodwin 4 62
(Ali Stronge) *hld up in tch in rr of main gp: effrt ent fnl 2f: sn outpcd: no threat to ldrs and kpt on same pce fnl f* **20/1**

0140 5 1 **Halling's Wish**[20] 8084 6-9-6 **67** (b) PaddyBradley(3) 6 61
(Gary Moore) *chsd ldrs tl led 10f out: rdn and hdd 2f out: struggling whn sltly hmpd over 1f out: sn wknd* **16/1**

1223 6 4 1/2 **Alsacienne**[15] 8143 3-9-0 **70** (b[1]) ManuelFernandes(7) 3 56
(Sir Mark Prescott Bt) *t.k.h: chsd ldrs: wnt 2nd after 3f: ev ch and wnt lft over 2f out: sn rdn: wd and lost pl bnd 2f out: wknd and hung lft fnl f* **5/1[3]**

6460 7 1 1/4 **Epsom Day (IRE)**[181] 3306 3-8-13 **69** OllieJago(7) 2 53
(Laura Mongan) *awkward leaving stalls and slowly away: in tch in rr of main gp: rdn ent fnl 2f out: sn outpcd and wknd over 1f out* **16/1**

0631 8 33 **Courtsider**[33] 7905 4-9-11 **69** (v) GeorgiaCox 8
(Lucy Wadham) *stood stl as stalls opened and lost many l s: grad rcvrd and 8 l last 4f out: rdn over 2f out: sn btn: eased wl over 1f out: t.o* **3/1[2]**

2m 30.45s (-2.55) **Going Correction** -0.075s/f (Stan)
WFA 3 from 4yo+ 5lb **8** Ran SP% **117.3**
Speed ratings (Par 103): **105,104,102,98,98 95,94,72**
CSF £26.21 CT £147.44 TOTE £14.90: £3.10, £1.20, £2.40; EX 36.20 Trifecta £223.80.
Owner M P N Tregoning **Bred** Elton Lodge Stud **Trained** Whitsbury, Hants

FOCUS
An ordinary apprentice handicap and another race where things changed late on.

T/Plt: £36.60 to a £1 stake. Pool: £46,222.92 - 921.50 winning units. T/Qpdt: £8.40 to a £1 stake. Pool: £5,469.51 - 481.80 winning units. **Steve Payne**

8165 DEAUVILLE (R-H)

Wednesday, December 14

OFFICIAL GOING: Polytrack: standard

8368a PRIX DE LA PIGEONNIERE (CONDITIONS) (3YO) (POLYTRACK) 6f 110y

10:15 (12:00) 3-Y-O **£10,661** (£4,264; £3,198; £2,132; £1,066)

RPR

1 **Cersei**[41] 3-8-10 0 ... StephanePasquier 6 88
(F Rohaut, France) **81/10**

2 1 1/2 **Lbretha (FR)**[44] 3-8-5 0 ... ClementLecoeuvre(5) 3 84
(F-H Graffard, France) **37/10**[2]

3 snk **Aguerooo (IRE)**[12] 8192 3-9-0 0 ... (p) CristianDemuro 7 87
(Richard Hannon) *racd in midfield on outer: 5l 4th and drvn 2 1/2f out: styd on ent fnl f to chse eventual wnr: lost 2nd cl home* **2/1**[1]

4 3 **Basilia**[27] 7998 3-8-11 0 ow1 ... (b) Pierre-CharlesBoudot 4 76
(Mme A Fabre, France) **68/10**

5 nk **Basse Reine (FR)**[150] 3-8-10 0 ... YohannBourgois 8 74
(M Figge, Germany) **133/10**

6 hd **Denga (IRE)**[44] 3-8-10 0 ... (p) TheoBachelot 5 73
(S Wattel, France) **41/10**[3]

7 1 1/4 **Nimo (FR)**[46] 3-9-0 0 ... SebastienMaillot 1 73
(E Caroux, France) **26/1**

8 10 **Predetermined (IRE)**[47] 7680 3-9-0 0 ... MaximeGuyon 2 44
(H-F Devin, France) **98/10**

Owner Hh Sheikh Khalifa Bin Zayed Al Nahyan **Bred** Al Asayl Bloodstock Ltd **Trained** Sauvagnon, France

WIN (incl. 1 euro stake): 9.10. PLACES: 1.80, 1.40, 1.20. DF: 22.50. SF: 43.00

8369 - 8376a (Foreign Racing) - See Raceform Interactive

8276 CHELMSFORD (A.W) (L-H)

Thursday, December 15

OFFICIAL GOING: Polytrack: standard

Wind: light, half behind Weather: dry

8377 TOTEPLACEPOT SIX PLACES IN SIX RACES MEDIAN AUCTION MAIDEN STKS 7f (P)

4:40 (4:40) (Class 5) 2-Y-O **£3,881** (£1,155; £577; £288) **Stalls** Low

Form RPR

2 1 **Omran**[40] 7819 2-9-5 0 ... DanielMuscutt 6 84+
(Marco Botti) *hld up in tch in midfield: clsd to trck ldrs and travelling strly 2f out: shkn up and qcknd to ld ent fnl f: sn rdn and in command: r.o strly: easily* **4/7**[1]

4 2 6 **Special Relation (IRE)**[65] 7239 2-9-5 0 ... LiamKeniry 5 66
(Hughie Morrison) *hld up in tch in midfield: clsd to trck ldrs 2f out: shkn up on inner over 1f out: rdn and outpcd by wnr 1f out: kpt on to go 2nd fnl 75yds: no ch w wnr* **8/1**

0 3 1 1/4 **Falbon**[29] 7975 2-9-5 0 ... TomMarquand 7 62
(Marco Botti) *sn bustled along to ld: hdd over 3f out: rdn and ev ch over 1f out: sn outpcd: plugged on same pce and lost 2nd fnl 75yds* **16/1**

03 4 2 3/4 **Second Page**[40] 7812 2-9-5 0 ... KieranO'Neill 9 55
(Richard Hannon) *bustled along leaving stalls: sn chsng ldrs: effrt over 1f out: unable qck and hung lft ent fnl f: wknd ins fnl f* **9/2**[2]

32 5 3/4 **Preobrajenska**[174] 3592 2-9-0 0 ... AdamKirby 8 48
(Michael Bell) *sn w ldr tl led over 3f out: rdn over 1f out: sn hdd and no ex: wknd ins fnl f* **5/1**[3]

00 6 2 1/2 **Maori Bob (IRE)**[36] 7865 2-9-5 0 ... StevieDonohoe 2 46
(Michael Bell) *sn off the pce in last pair: pushed along 3f out: no ch but sme hdwy to pass btn horses over 1f out: n.d* **25/1**

00 7 nk **Noble Attitude (FR)**[182] 3315 2-9-5 0 ... KierenFox 1 45
(John Best) *in tch in midfield: rdn and outpcd over 2f out: wknd u.p over 1f out* **50/1**

8 4 **La Isla Bonita** 2-9-0 0 ... TomQueally 3 30
(Richard Spencer) *awkward leaving stalls and s.i.s: a outpcd in rr* **25/1**

0 9 9 **Secret Willow**[29] 7977 2-9-5 0 ... RyanPowell 10 10
(John E Long) *dwlt: in tch in midfield: rdn and outpcd over 2f out: hung lft and wknd over 1f out* **150/1**

1m 25.2s (-2.00) **Going Correction** -0.175s/f (Stan) **9 Ran SP% 125.8**

Speed ratings (Par 96): **104,97,95,92,91 88,88,83,73**

CSF £7.16 TOTE £1.50: £1.10, £2.20, £5.50; EX 7.20 Trifecta £59.80.

Owner H E S Al-Kaabi **Bred** Bugley Stud & D B Clark **Trained** Newmarket, Suffolk

FOCUS

Probably not the deepest race and this proved very straightforward for the odds-on favourite.

8378 TOTEPOOLLIVEINFO.COM H'CAP 7f (P)

5:15 (5:15) (Class 5) (0-75,77) 3-Y-O+ **£4,204** (£1,251; £625; £312) **Stalls** Low

Form RPR

2105 1 **Pendo**[27] 8011 5-9-6 73 ... KierenFox 6 80
(John Best) *taken down early: hld up in tch in midfield: rdn over 2f out: drvn over 1f out: styd on strly fnl 100yds to ld on post* **7/1**[3]

1452 2 nse **Rebel Lightning (IRE)**[15] 8163 3-9-3 70 ... (b) AdamKirby 7 77
(Richard Spencer) *chsd ldrs: effrt u.p over 1f out: drvn to chal 1f out: sn led: kpt on: hdd on post* **9/2**[2]

33 3 1/2 **Plus Night (FR)**[15] 8163 3-9-2 69 ... PatCosgrave 4 76+
(Stuart Williams) *trckd ldng trio: effrt on inner whn bdly hmpd over 1f out: sn swtchd rt and rallied u.p ins fnl f: kpt on wl fnl 100yds* **2/1**[1]

4013 4 1 **East Coast Lady (IRE)**[14] 8178 4-8-12 70 ... HollieDoyle(5) 2 73
(William Stone) *sn bustled up to join ldr: rdn and ev ch whn edgd lft over 1f out: no ex 100yds out: wknd towards fin* **9/2**[2]

0050 5 1/2 **Varsovian**[14] 8176 6-9-7 77 ... JackDuern(3) 5 79
(Dean Ivory) *w ldr tl led over 5f out: rdn over 1f out: hdd jst ins fnl f: no ex 100yds out: wknd towards fin* **7/1**[3]

4643 6 5 **Corporal Maddox**[30] 7968 9-9-9 76 ... (p) LukeMorris 3 64
(Ronald Harris) *racd in last trio: rdn over 3f out: no imp u.p and btn over 1f out: no ch and edgd lft ins fnl f* **10/1**

0304 7 1/2 **Glenalmond (IRE)**[7] 8282 4-9-5 72 ... StevieDonohoe 8 59
(Daniel Steele) *bhd: pushed along over 2f out: c centre st but no imp u.p over 1f out: n.d* **14/1**

-461 8 10 **Bobby Benton (IRE)**[94] 6408 5-9-4 71 ... TimmyMurphy 1 31
(Jim Best) *off the pce in last pair: pushed along over 2f out: no imp and wl btn over 1f out: wknd* **16/1**

1m 25.53s (-1.67) **Going Correction** -0.175s/f (Stan) **8 Ran SP% 116.3**

Speed ratings (Par 103): **102,101,101,100,99 93,93,81**

CSF £39.13 CT £86.73 TOTE £9.30: £2.80, £1.60, £1.20; EX 55.80 Trifecta £186.00.

Owner Brett Hopson **Bred** Miss Sue Parkinson **Trained** Oad Street, Kent

■ Stewards' Enquiry : Hollie Doyle caution: careless riding

FOCUS

A tight finish to this fair handicap, but ordinary form.

8379 TOTEQUADPOT FOUR PLACES IN FOUR RACES CLAIMING STKS 1m (P)

5:50 (5:51) (Class 6) 3-Y-O **£2,911** (£866; £432; £216) **Stalls** Low

Form RPR

2010 1 **Threebagsue (IRE)**[15] 8158 3-8-2 74 ... (b) LuluStanford(7) 5 74
(J S Moore) *mde all: rdn over 1f out: kpt on u.p and a holding chalr ins fnl f* **7/2**

2504 2 1 **Ravenhoe (IRE)**[12] 8205 3-9-0 72 ... PJMcDonald 2 77
(Mark Johnston) *chsd ldrs: effrt to chse wnr ent fnl 2f: drvn to press wnr 1f out: kpt on same pce and a hld ins fnl f* **3/1**[3]

0503 3 2 **Ritasun (FR)**[33] 7931 3-8-12 73 ... (p) HollieDoyle(5) 1 75
(Richard Hannon) *hld up in rr: effrt 3f out: hdwy ent fnl 2f: no imp u.p over 1f out: wnt 3rd and kpt on fnl 50yds: nvr enough pce to chal* **5/2**[2]

0026 4 2 **With Pleasure**[7] 8282 3-9-2 75 ... AdamKirby 3 70
(David O'Meara) *t.k.h: in tch in 4th: effrt to cl ent fnl 2f: drvn and no imp over 1f out: lost 3rd 50yds out and eased towards fin* **13/8**[1]

6030 5 9 **Moving Robe (IRE)**[33] 7931 3-8-2 45 ... NoelGarbutt(3) 6 38
(Conrad Allen) *t.k.h: chsd ldr tl lost pl ent fnl 2f: wknd fnl f* **66/1**

1m 39.9s **Going Correction** -0.175s/f (Stan) **5 Ran SP% 115.4**

Speed ratings (Par 98): **93,92,90,88,79**

CSF £14.90 TOTE £4.50: £2.30, £1.30; EX 13.90 Trifecta £24.20.

Owner The Well Fleeced Partnership **Bred** S Couldrige **Trained** Upper Lambourn, Berks

■ Stewards' Enquiry : Lulu Stanford two-day ban: used whip above permitted level (Dec 29-30)

FOCUS

An ordinary claimer and straightforward form.

8380 @TOTEPOOL TWEET US YOUR #TOTEELFIE H'CAP 6f (P)

6:25 (6:25) (Class 4) (0-85,83) 3-Y-O+ **£6,469** (£1,925; £962; £481) **Stalls** Centre

Form RPR

0000 1 **El Viento (FR)**[14] 8176 8-9-1 77 ... (v) PatrickMathers 8 86
(Richard Fahey) *bustled along in rr: hdwy over 1f out: chsng ldrs and swtchd rt 1f out: str run u.p fnl 100yds to ld cl home* **25/1**

4034 2 3/4 **Plucky Dip**[5] 8311 5-9-6 82 ... (p) DannyBrock 1 89
(John Ryan) *in tch in midfield: swtchd rt and hdwy 2f out: rdn and ev ch 1f out: led 100yds out: hdd and no ex cl home* **4/1**[2]

3524 3 1 **Captain Lars (SAF)**[7] 8280 7-8-8 70 ... (p) JFEgan 5 74
(Derek Shaw) *chsd ldr: rdn over 2f out: drvn over 1f out: ev ch 1f out: unable qck and one pce fnl 100yds* **7/1**

1002 4 3/4 **Shypen**[15] 8158 3-9-5 81 ... DavidNolan 4 82
(Richard Fahey) *in tch in midfield: effrt over 1f out: swtchd rt 1f out: kpt on same pce u.p ins fnl f* **7/2**[1]

0312 5 1/2 **Free Zone**[15] 8150 7-9-6 82 ... (v) MartinHarley 9 83
(Lee Carter) *led: rdn over 1f out: drvn 1f out: hdd 100yds out: no ex and eased towards fin* **16/1**

2055 6 1 1/4 **Florencio**[57] 7461 3-9-7 83 ... [1] AdamKirby 7 79
(Marco Botti) *in rr: effrt ent fnl 2f: drvn over 1f out: kpt on ins fnl f: nvr threatened ldrs* **5/1**[3]

-001 7 1 3/4 **Alkhor**[30] 7965 3-9-6 82 ... SeanLevey 2 72
(Richard Hannon) *trckd ldrs: effrt over 1f out: ev ch 1f out: no ex and btn ins fnl f: wknd qckly fnl 100yds* **7/2**[1]

0000 8 5 **Picture Dealer**[14] 8176 7-8-12 77 ... (t) SimonPearce(3) 3 51
(Lydia Pearce) *v.s.a and lost many l at s: nvr on terms* **20/1**

600 9 3 **Bertie Blu Boy**[26] 8032 8-9-4 80 ... (v) LiamKeniry 10 45
(Lisa Williamson) *stuck wd: chsd ldrs tl 1/2-way: lost pl and bhd over 1f out: sn wknd* **50/1**

5652 10 1 1/2 **Parkour (IRE)**[14] 8176 3-9-4 80 ... LukeMorris 6 57
(Marco Botti) *chsd ldrs: rdn and lost pl over 1f out: wknd and hung lft over 1f out: eased ins fnl f* **8/1**

1m 11.56s (-2.14) **Going Correction** -0.175s/f (Stan) **10 Ran SP% 121.2**

Speed ratings (Par 105): **107,106,104,103,103 101,99,92,88,86**

CSF £125.35 CT £823.44 TOTE £21.60: £6.40, £1.70, £2.70; EX 185.60 Trifecta £1321.10.

Owner John Nicholls Ltd/David Kilburn **Bred** Ballykilbride Stud **Trained** Musley Bank, N Yorks

FOCUS

There was a good gallop on here and the first two came from well off the pace.

8381 #TOTEELFIE WIN A £50 FREE BET FILLIES' H'CAP 1m 2f (P)

7:00 (7:02) (Class 5) (0-75,77) 3-Y-O+ **£4,204** (£1,251; £625; £312) **Stalls** Low

Form RPR

2145 1 **Zain Arion (IRE)**[114] 5746 3-8-11 68 ... JFEgan 3 76
(John Butler) *chsd ldrs: rdn to ld over 1f out: sn hrd pressed and hdd jst ins fnl f: rallied gamely u.p to ld again last strides* **16/1**

0643 2 hd **Starlit Cantata**[22] 8077 5-9-7 75 ... (p) JohnFahy 6 82
(Eve Johnson Houghton) *hld up in tch: clsd to trck ldrs 2f out: rdn to chal over 1f out: led jst ins fnl f: kpt on u.p: hdd last strides* **7/1**[3]

6103 3 3/4 **Mercy Me**[8] 8253 4-9-2 70 ... AdamKirby 9 76
(John Ryan) *in tch in last trio: hdwy 5f out: effrt on inner to chse ldrs over 1f out: wnt 3rd ins fnl f: kpt on u.p* **5/1**[1]

4625 4 3 **Tabla**[141] 4773 4-9-0 68 ... MartinHarley 4 68
(Lee Carter) *wnt rt and bmpd s: t.k.h: hld up in tch in midfield: clsd to trck ldrs and pushed lft over 1f out: sn rdn: no ex ins fnl f: wknd fnl 100yds* **10/1**

4416 5 5 **Princess Raihana**[20] 8090 3-9-0 71 ... [1] DanielMuscutt 1 61
(Marco Botti) *led for 1f: chsd ldr after tl rdn to ld and edgd lft over 1f out: sn hdd and no ex: wknd ins fnl f* **6/1**[2]

0522 6 2 1/2 **Indigo Princess**[13] 8188 3-8-7 64 ... LukeMorris 2 49
(Michael Appleby) *chsd ldrs: shkn up ent fnl 2f: sn u.p and outpcd: wknd fnl f* **5/1**[1]

4232 7 1/2 **Polymnia**[24] 8048 3-8-7 69 ... (b[1]) HollieDoyle(5) 5 53
(Richard Hannon) *s.i.s: hld up in tch in rr: effrt over 1f out: sme hdwy and edgd rt 1f out: kpt on ins fnl f: nvr trbld ldrs* **6/1**[2]

5230 8 1 1/2 **Dame Judi (IRE)**[81] 6805 3-9-3 74 ... (p) RobertHavlin 12 55
(Simon Crisford) *hld up in tch in midfield: effrt ent fnl 2f: sn struggling and hung lft u.p over 1f out: wknd* **16/1**

1600 9 1 1/4 **Loveable Helen (IRE)**[27] 8007 3-9-6 77 ... DavidNolan 8 55
(Richard Fahey) *t.k.h: led after 1f tl rdn and hdd over 1f out: losing pl whn hmpd sn after: wknd fnl f* **9/1**

34 **10** *11* **Celestial Bay**[280] 884 7-9-7 **75**.................................... GeorgeBaker 11 31
(Sylvester Kirk) *hld up in rr: shkn up over 1f out: no imp whn sltly hmpd 1f out: wknd* **25/1**

064 **11** *11* **Maqam (IRE)**[117] 5623 3-8-9 **66**.. SeanLevey 7
(Richard Hannon) *in tch in midfield: rdn over 2f out: sn struggling: wknd over 1f out* **6/1**[2]

2434 **12** *7* **Power Up**[50] 7613 5-8-0 **61** oh1.................................. RhiainIngram[(7)] 10
(Roger Ingram) *in tch in midfield: rdn over 2f out: sn lost pl: bhd and eased over 1f out: t.o* **25/1**

2m 5.44s (-3.16) **Going Correction** -0.175s/f (Stan)
WFA 3 from 4yo+ 3lb **12** Ran SP% **127.2**
Speed ratings (Par 100): **105,104,104,101,97 95,95,94,93,84 75,70**
CSF £132.90 CT £659.41 TOTE £21.20: £5.00, £2.60, £2.20; EX 186.60 Trifecta £943.30.
Owner Asaad Al Banwan **Bred** Lynch Bages & Camas Park Stud **Trained** Newmarket, Suffolk

FOCUS
A competitive fillies' handicap rated around the third. It was run at a good gallop.

8382 TOTEPOOL RACECOURSE CASH BACK AVAILABLE H'CAP 1m (P)
7:30 (7:32) (Class 6) (0-65,65) 3-Y-O+ **£3,234** (£962; £481; £240) **Stalls** Low

Form RPR

0400 **1** **Skidby Mill (IRE)**[15] 8163 6-9-6 **64**................................. GeorgeBaker 5 71
(Laura Mongan) *mde all: shkn up and kicked clr over 1f out: kpt on under hands and heels riding ins fnl f: a jst lasting home* **6/1**[3]

5055 **2** *nse* **Almanack**[103] 6137 6-8-13 **60**...................................... NathanAlison[(3)] 1 67
(Mark Pattinson) *chsd ldrs: effrt ent fnl 2f: swtchd rt and rdn over 1f out: chsd clr wnr ent fnl f: styd on wl u.p ins fnl f: jst failed* **8/1**

5260 **3** *3* **Rebel State (IRE)**[8] 8248 3-9-5 **64**..................................[1] AdamKirby 6 65
(Richard Spencer) *hld up tch in midfield: effrt and clsd to chse ldrs whn r.oto heels: hmpd and wnt sharply rt jst over 1f out: rallied u.p ins fnl f: styd on* **8/1**

0365 **4** *¾* **Jazri**[145] 4656 5-8-9 **53**..(b) AdamBeschizza 4 51
(Milton Bradley) *hld up in tch in last quartet: rdn hdwy over 1f out: kpt on same pce ins fnl f* **16/1**

4566 **5** *1 ¼* **Strictly Art (IRE)**[3] 8337 3-8-11 **56**.............................(p) RobertHavlin 11 51
(Alan Bailey) *bustled along leaving stalls: sn chsng ldrs: rdn jst over 2f out: stl chsng ldrs but struggling to qckn whn pushed rt and hmpd jst over 1f out kpt on same pce ins fnl f* **12/1**

0465 **6** *nk* **Dose**[16] 8145 3-8-12 **57**.. PatrickMathers 9 52
(Richard Fahey) *in tch in midfield: effrt jsut over 2f out: drvn over 1f out: edgd lft 1f out: kpt on but no threat to ldrs ins fnl f* **7/1**

0430 **7** *3 ½* **Daleelak (IRE)**[14] 8178 3-9-6 **65**................................. PJMcDonald 13 52
(Mark Johnston) *chsd ldr: rdn ent fnl 2f: unable qck and edgd rt jst over 1f out: wknd ins fnl f* **7/1**

5560 **8** *nk* **Mulled Wine**[28] 7986 3-8-12 **57**.. KierenFox 3 43
(John Best) *hld up in tch in last quartet: pushed over 2f out: effrt on inner but no imp over 1f out: kpt on same pce ins fnl f* **14/1**

0402 **9** *1* **Catastrophe**[21] 8086 3-9-3 **62**..[1] LukeMorris 8 46
(John Quinn) *in tch in midfield: shkn up over 3f out: lost pl ent fnl 2f: no rspnse to press over 1f out: wknd fnl f* **9/2**[2]

4034 **10** *1* **Wasseem (IRE)**[55] 7514 3-9-3 **62**................................(tp) MartinHarley 2 45
(Simon Crisford) *in tch in midfield: effrt to chse ldrs whn pushed rt and hmpd jst over 1f out: hmpd again 1f out: nt rcvr and wl hld fnl f* **10/3**[1]

-500 **11** *4 ½* **Storming Ambition**[120] 5554 3-8-3 **51**......................(b[1]) NoelGarbutt[(3)] 7 22
(Conrad Allen) *hld up in tch in last quartet: rdn 3f out: sn struggling: wknd fnl f* **66/1**

0000 **12** *nk* **Quintus Cerialis (IRE)**[22] 8064 4-9-3 **61**...............(tp) TimmyMurphy 10 31
(Karen George) *dwlt: hld up in rr and stuck wd: shkn up over 1f out: sn btn: wknd fnl f* **33/1**

1m 38.93s (-0.97) **Going Correction** -0.175s/f (Stan)
WFA 3 from 4yo+ 1lb **12** Ran SP% **127.4**
Speed ratings (Par 101): **97,96,93,93,91 91,88,87,86,85 81,81**
CSF £57.82 CT £407.62 TOTE £5.40: £2.00, £2.80, £2.70; EX 54.80 Trifecta £728.40.
Owner Charlie's Starrs **Bred** Michael O'Mahony **Trained** Epsom, Surrey

FOCUS
Few got into this with the winner making most of the ease in grade.

8383 BUY TICKETS AT CHELMSFORDCITYRACECOURSE.COM H'CAP 6f (P)
8:00 (8:02) (Class 7) (0-50,50) 3-Y-O+ **£2,587** (£770; £384; £192) **Stalls** Centre

Form RPR

4006 **1** **Tilsworth Micky**[2] 8346 4-9-7 **50**.................................... GeorgeBaker 12 57+
(J R Jenkins) *hld up in midfield: clsd ent fnl 2f: swtchd rt and hdwy over 1f out: rdn and hung lft ent fnl f: upsides and stl hanging whn bmpd ldr ins fnl f: led and pushed clr wl ins fnl f* **4/1**[1]

0000 **2** *1* **Arizona Snow**[7] 8278 4-9-6 **49**.....................................(p) LukeMorris 6 53
(Ronald Harris) *chsd ldrs and travelled strly: clsd and upsides ldr over 1f out: drvn to ld 1f out: sn jnd and bmpd ins fnl f: hdd and outpcd wl ins fnl f* **7/1**

0004 **3** *1 ¾* **Bushwise (IRE)**[56] 7489 3-9-2 **45**..........................(b[1]) AdamBeschizza 4 44
(Milton Bradley) *chsd ldrs: effrt and swtchd lft and rt over 1f out: kpt on same pce ins fnl f* **6/1**[3]

0065 **4** *½* **Topsoil**[7] 8278 3-9-5 **48**..(p) RenatoSouza 3 45
(Ronald Harris) *restless in stalls: t.k.h: led after 1f: rdn over 1f out: hdd 1f out: no ex ins fnl f: wknd wl ins fnl f* **4/1**[1]

-060 **5** *½* **Upper Lambourn (IRE)**[6] 8288 8-8-9 **45**.................(t) KevinLundie[(7)] 13 41
(John Holt) *midfield: effrt and clsd on outer ent fnl 2f: drvn over 1f out: kpt on ins fnl f: nvr threatened ldrs:* **33/1**

4650 **6** *1 ½* **Kingfisher Girl**[52] 7584 3-9-0 **46**.........................[1] AlistairRawlinson[(3)] 10 37
(Michael Appleby) *off the pce in midfield: rdn 3f out: drvn over 1f out: kpt on ins fnl f: nvr enough pce to threaten ldrs* **14/1**

5456 **7** *3 ¾* **Justice Rock**[117] 5636 3-9-5 **48**....................................(p) AdamKirby 5 28
(Phil McEntee) *bustled along to ld for 1f: chsd ldr: wandered u.p over 1f out: outpcd and sltly hmpd 1f out: wknd ins fnl f* **6/1**[3]

0550 **8** *½* **Just Marion (IRE)**[202] 2647 4-9-2 **45**...........................(b[1]) JohnFahy 7 24
(Clare Ellam) *sn outpcd and wl off the pce in last pair: rdn over 2f out: styd on to pass btn horses ins fnl f: n.d* **33/1**

2460 **9** *1* **Imjin River (IRE)**[106] 3822 9-9-1 **49**...........................(t) HollieDoyle[(5)] 14 25
(William Stone) *stdd and dropped in bhd after s: hld up off the pce in last trio: rdn over 1f out: sme hdwy ins fnl f: nvr trbld ldrs* **20/1**

0-60 **10** *½* **Pacabag**[57] 7459 3-9-3 **46**.. KierenFox 8 20
(Peter Hedger) *rdn sn after s: sn off the pce in last trio and pushed along: no imp u.p over 1f out: nvr on terms* **14/1**

2504 **11** *1 ¾* **Ryan Style (IRE)**[21] 8079 10-8-11 **47**.........................(v) JordanUys[(7)] 2 16
(Lisa Williamson) *sn niggled along and a off the pce in last quartet: n.d* **5/1**[2]

5054 **12** *1 ¼* **Farrah's Choice**[15] 8157 4-9-6 **49**.................................. TomMarquand 11 14
(James Grassick) *bustled along leaving stalls and pressed ldrs early: sn struggling to go pce and midfield after 2f: lost pl u.p 2f out: bhd 1f out* **25/1**

1m 13.28s (-0.42) **Going Correction** -0.175s/f (Stan) **12** Ran SP% **125.6**
Speed ratings (Par 97): **95,93,91,90,90 88,83,82,81,80 78,76**
CSF £32.96 CT £173.94 TOTE £5.80: £2.10, £2.60, £2.50; EX 36.60 Trifecta £272.80.
Owner M Ng **Bred** Michael Ng **Trained** Royston, Herts

FOCUS
A weak handicap, but there was a good gallop on. The winner was thrown in on old form and the race has been rated around the placed horses.
T/Plt: £134.50 to a £1 stake. Pool: £97,360.91 - 528.21 winning units T/Qpdt: £77.60 to a £1 stake. Pool: £9,814.97 - 93.5 winning units **Steve Payne**

8305 NEWCASTLE (A.W) (L-H)
Thursday, December 15

OFFICIAL GOING: Tapeta: standard
Wind: Light half behind Weather: Overcast

8384 32RED.COM IRISH STALLION FARMS EBF MAIDEN STKS 7f 14y (Tp)
12:50 (12:50) (Class 5) 2-Y-O **£3,557** (£1,058; £529; £264) **Stalls** Centre

Form RPR

1 **Brittanic (IRE)** 2-9-5 0... TomEaves 3 74+
(David Simcock) *hld up in rr: swtchd rt and hdwy over 2f out: trckd ldrs over 1f out: chal on bit ent fnl f: shkn up and qcknd to ld towards fin* **7/1**

3 **2** *½* **Arnarson**[19] 8119 2-9-5 0.. DavidProbert 9 71
(Ed Dunlop) *trckd ldrs: hdwy over 2f out: led 11/2f out: rdn and jnd ent fnl f: sn drvn: hdd and no ex towards fin* **10/3**[2]

3 *2 ¼* **Dubai Art** 2-9-5 0.. BarryMcHugh 8 65
(Richard Fahey) *dwlt and t.k.h towards rr: hdwy on outer over 2f out: chsd ldrs over 1f out: sn rdn and kpt on fnl f* **16/1**

4 *1* **Mount Rock** 2-9-2 0.. NathanEvans[(3)] 5 63
(Michael Easterby) *prom: effrt and cl up 2f out: sn rdn: green and sltly outpcd over 1f out: kpt on same pce u.p fnl f* **50/1**

5 *¾* **Mountain Angel (IRE)** 2-9-5 0.. PaulMulrennan 4 61
(Roger Varian) *t.k.h early: cl up: effrt over 2f out and ev ch: rdn wl over 1f out: drvn and kpt on same pce appr fnl f* **9/1**

6 *nse* **Cloud Dragon (IRE)** 2-9-5 0................................ JosephineGordon 10 61
(Hugo Palmer) *trckd ldrs: cl up 1/2-way: led over 2f out: rdn and hdd 11/2f out: sn drvn and grad wknd* **5/1**[3]

7 *1 ¾* **Fear The Fury (USA)** 2-9-5 0...................................... DougieCostello 2 57
(K R Burke) *t.k.h: trckd ldrs: cl up 3f out: rdn along over 2f out: sn btn* **7/4**[1]

0 **8** *1* **Whatelseaboutyou (IRE)**[12] 8208 2-9-0 0........................ JackGarritty 6 49
(Richard Fahey) *in tch: effrt over 2f out: sn rdn along and wknd* **16/1**

00 **9** *1 ¼* **Rey Loopy (IRE)**[20] 8089 2-9-5 0.................................... GrahamLee 7 51
(Ben Haslam) *chsd ldrs: rdn along 3f out: sn wknd* **150/1**

6 **10** *shd* **Dreamofdiscovery (IRE)**[20] 8089 2-9-5 0............................ JoeDoyle 1 51
(Julie Camacho) *.a towards rr* **28/1**

00 **11** *8* **Crucial Response**[20] 8089 2-9-0 0.......................... MeganNicholls[(5)] 11 31
(Ben Haslam) *led: rdn along 3f out: hdd over 2f out and sn wknd* **200/1**

1m 29.25s (3.05) **Going Correction** +0.20s/f (Slow) **11** Ran SP% **116.9**
Speed ratings (Par 96): **90,89,86,85,84 84,82,81,80,80 70**
CSF £30.22 TOTE £8.60: £2.30, £1.40, £3.50; EX 40.90 Trifecta £476.90.
Owner Never Say Die Partnership **Bred** Fountain Syn & Flaxman Stables **Trained** Newmarket, Suffolk

FOCUS
A fair maiden in which the early gallop was just an ordinary one. The winner looks the sort to hold his own in stronger company.

8385 SUNBETS.CO.UK H'CAP 7f 14y (Tp)
1:20 (1:21) (Class 4) (0-85,85) 3-Y-O+ **£5,822** (£1,732; £865; £432) **Stalls** Centre

Form RPR

0310 **1** **Al Khan (IRE)**[14] 8177 7-9-0 **85**.................................... LewisEdmunds[(7)] 7 93
(Kevin Ryan) *t.k.h early: trckd ldrs: smooth hdwy over 2f out: led appr fnl f: sn rdn and kpt on wl* **10/3**[1]

6200 **2** *¾* **Like No Other**[34] 7903 3-9-0 **78**.. JasonHart 1 84
(Les Eyre) *t.k.h early: cl up: led wl over 2f out: rdn over 1f out: hdd appr fnl f: sn drvn and kpt on* **33/1**

0062 **3** *1* **War Department (IRE)**[20] 8092 3-9-4 **82**........................(v) JoeFanning 8 85
(Keith Dalgleish) *t.k.h early: trckd ldrs: hdwy 2f out: swtchd lft and rdn over 1f out: kpt on fnl f* **6/1**[3]

0550 **4** *hd* **Tellovoi (IRE)**[9] 8239 8-8-7 **71**..(v) ShaneGray 12 74
(Richard Guest) *slowly away and racd towards stands side: rapid hdwy to ld after 11/2f: pushed along 3f out: sn rdn and hdd: cl up tl drvn ent fnl f and kpt on same pce* **20/1**

5000 **5** *½* **Lexington Times (IRE)**[19] 8122 4-9-4 **82**..................... JamesSullivan 9 83
(Ruth Carr) *hld up: hdwy over 2f out: rdn over 1f out: sn chsng ldrs: drvn and no imp fnl f* **12/1**

1006 **6** *½* **Handsome Dude**[37] 7858 4-9-7 **85**.............................(b) AndrewMullen 13 85
(David Barron) *rr: hdwy wl over 1f out: sn rdn and styd on wl fnl f: nrst fin* **20/1**

0050 **7** *½* **Lil Sophella (IRE)**[14] 8177 7-8-10 **81**................................ PaulaMuir[(7)] 11 80
(Patrick Holmes) *dwlt and towards rr: hdwy and in tch 1/2-way: pushed along and sltly outpcd over 2f out: sn rdn and styd on fnl f* **16/1**

3101 **8** *½* **Alice Thornton**[16] 8144 4-8-10 **74**.. GrahamLee 6 71
(Martin Todhunter) *led 11/2f: cl up: rdn along over 2f out: drvn over 1f out and grad wknd* **12/1**

4300 **9** *1* **Fingal's Cave (IRE)**[19] 8122 4-8-10 **81**...................... JamieGormley[(7)] 3 76
(Iain Jardine) *dwlt: sn in tch: chsd ldrs over 3f out: rdn along over 2f out: wknd over 1f out* **8/1**

1-04 **10** *nse* **Tailwind**[44] 7737 3-9-0 **78**.. PaulMulrennan 10 73
(Roger Varian) *hld up towards rr: hdwy over 2f out: chsd ldrs over 1f out: sn rdn and wknd fnl f* **7/2**[2]

0600 **11** *2 ¾* **Althareeb (IRE)**[75] 6966 6-0-13 **77**................................ DougieCostello 2 64
(Sally Hall) *dwlt: a towards rr* **40/1**

2360 **12** *1* **Bell Heather (IRE)**[24] 8052 3-8-9 **73**............................. BarryMcHugh 5 57
(Richard Fahey) *hld up: a towards rr* **20/1**

0000 **13** *3 ¾* **Westwood Hoe**[51] 7593 5-9-6 **84**.. BenCurtis 4 58
(Tony Coyle) *prom: rdn along over 2f out: sn wknd* **14/1**

1m 27.18s (0.98) **Going Correction** +0.20s/f (Slow) **13** Ran SP% **118.3**
Speed ratings (Par 105): **102,101,100,99,99 98,98,97,96,96 93,92,87**
CSF £124.84 CT £669.99 TOTE £3.50: £1.40, £10.50, £2.10; EX 133.20 Trifecta £1051.40.
Owner J C G Chua **Bred** Galadari Sons Stud Company Limited **Trained** Hambleton, N Yorks

FOCUS
Not the strongest of races for the grade, but a useful effort from the winner who was well backed. The early gallop wasn't overly strong.

8386 BETWAY CLASSIFIED STKS 1m 4f 98y (Tp)
1:50 (1:51) (Class 6) 3-Y-O+ **£2,911** (£866; £432; £216) **Stalls** High

Form RPR

0041 **1** **Go George Go (IRE)**[17] 8134 3-8-13 51 JoeFanning 11 63+
(Alan Swinbank) *trckd ldrs: hdwy over 2f out: rdn to ld jst over 1f out: drvn and edgd lft ins fnl f: kpt on wl* **7/4**[1]

00-0 **2** 1 3/4 **My Renaissance**[30] 3031 6-9-4 49 AndrewMullen 6 57
(Sam England) *trckd ldr: cl up 3f out: led over 2f out: rdn over 1f out: sn hdd and drvn: kpt on same pce ins fnl f* **33/1**

4005 **3** shd **Tred Softly (IRE)**[198] 2772 3-8-13 55 (b) JasonHart 7 57
(John Quinn) *trckd ldrs: hdwy 3f out: chsd ldr wl over 1f out: sn rdn and ev ch: n.m.r ent fnl f: kpt on same pce* **7/1**[3]

600 **4** 6 **Miss Macchiato (IRE)**[28] 7991 3-8-13 42 TomEaves 8 48
(Keith Dalgleish) *led: pushed along over 3f out:. rdn and hdd over 2f out: sn drvn and kpt on one pce* **50/1**

1060 **5** 1 **Whisky Marmalade (IRE)**[48] 7657 4-9-4 54 PaulMulrennan 5 47
(Ben Haslam) *hld up towards rr: hdwy 3f out: rdn to chse ldrs over 1f out: drvn and no imp fnl f* **25/1**

0102 **6** nk **Ali Bin Nayef**[15] 8155 4-9-4 54 DougieCostello 3 46
(Michael Wigham) *trckd ldrs: hdwy wl over 2f out: rdn wl over 1f out: sn drvn and kpt on one pce* **8/1**

/453 **7** 1/2 **Ship Canal**[17] 8134 4-9-1 46 NathanEvans(3) 14 45
(Jacqueline Coward) *hld up and bhd: hdwy on wd outside wl over 2f out: rdn wl over 1f out: kpt on fnl f* **10/1**

5004 **8** 1/2 **Highway Robber**[16] 8143 3-8-13 51 ShaneGray 2 45
(Wilf Storey) *midfield: hdwy over 3f out: rdn along to chse ldrs over 2f out: sn drvn and wknd over 1f out* **25/1**

2355 **9** nk **Little Pippin**[16] 8143 3-8-6 52 RPWalsh(7) 13 44
(Tony Coyle) *hld up: a rr* **33/1**

6340 **10** 1 **Page Of Wands**[28] 7992 3-8-13 55 (v) GrahamLee 12 43
(Karen McLintock) *hld up towards rr: pushed along over 3f out: rdn over 2f out: no hdwy* **5/2**[2]

000- **11** 1/2 **Sabha (IRE)**[456] 6441 4-9-4 50 JoeyHaynes 9 42
(K R Burke) *a towards rr* **22/1**

3005 **12** 3 1/4 **Come On Lulu**[20] 8091 5-9-4 44 (b) JamesSullivan 1 37
(David Thompson) *prom: rdn along 3f out: sn wknd* **100/1**

2m 44.37s (3.27) **Going Correction** +0.20s/f (Slow)
WFA 3 from 4yo+ 5lb **12** Ran SP% **118.5**
Speed ratings (Par 101): **97,95,95,91,91 90,90,90,90,89 89,86**
CSF £74.86 TOTE £2.60: £1.20, £7.90, £2.90; EX 55.80 Trifecta £392.20.
Owner Lee Bond **Bred** Pat Grogan **Trained** Melsonby, N Yorks

FOCUS
A low-grade event, but a reasonable gallop and the first three pulled clear. The winner is the type to make further progress.

8387 DOWNLOAD THE BETWAY APP H'CAP 1m 4f 98y (Tp)
2:20 (2:20) (Class 5) (0-70,69) 3-Y-O+ **£2,308** (£2,308; £529; £264) **Stalls** High

Form RPR

2223 **1** **High On Light**[76] 6922 3-9-3 67 SamJames 3 76
(David Barron) *trckd ldng pair: hdwy 3f out and sn cl up: led 2f out: rdn over 1f out: drvn ins fnl f: kpt on: jnd on line* **13/2**[2]

3642 **1** dht **Airton**[62] 7321 3-9-5 69 JosephineGordon 9 78+
(James Bethell) *hld up and bhd: hdwy on wd outside 2f out: rdn over 1f out: drvn to chse ldr and edgd lft ins fnl f: styd on gamely to join ldr on line* **10/11**[1]

2361 **3** 5 **Kicking The Can (IRE)**[28] 7991 5-9-5 64 BarryMcHugh 2 65
(David Thompson) *trckd ldrs: hdwy over 2f out: rdn over 1f out: sn drvn and kpt on same pce fnl f* **15/2**

3203 **4** 4 **Tectonic (IRE)**[16] 8142 7-9-8 67 (v) JasonHart 4 62
(Keith Dalgleish) *in tch: hdwy over 2f out: rdn to chse ldrs over 1f out: sn ev ch: drvn ent fnl f: sn btn* **14/1**

0612 **5** 1 3/4 **Merriment**[16] 8143 3-8-12 62 (p) TomEaves 7 54
(Peter Niven) *hld up towards rr: hdwy 3f out: rdn to chse ldrs over 1f out: sn drvn and wknd* **7/1**[3]

-000 **6** 1/2 **Maskoon**[16] 8141 5-9-4 63 PaddyAspell 6 55
(Philip Kirby) *hld up towards rr: hdwy 3f out: rdn along 2f out: n.d* **28/1**

0544 **7** hd **Percy Verence**[17] 8134 3-8-6 56 (tp) JoeyHaynes 1 47
(K R Burke) *trckd ldng pair on inner: hdwy 3f out: rdn along over 2f out: sn drvn and wknd* **11/1**

0000 **8** 1 3/4 **You'll Do**[28] 7995 3-8-7 57 JoeFanning 8 46
(Maurice Barnes) *sn slt ld: pushed along over 3f out: rdn wl over 2f out: sn hdd & wknd* **22/1**

00-0 **9** 8 **Beaumont's Party (IRE)**[226] 1201 9-9-5 64 DougieCostello 5 41
(Chris Grant) *cl up: rdn along 3f out: sn wknd* **50/1**

2m 41.51s (0.41) **Going Correction** +0.20s/f (Slow)
WFA 3 from 5yo+ 5lb **9** Ran SP% **114.7**
Speed ratings (Par 103): **106,106,102,100,98 98,98,97,91**
WIN: A £0.90, HOL £3.40; PLACE: A £1.10, HOL £2.30, KTC £2.10; EXACTA: A-HOL £4.10, HOL-A £8.10 CSF: A-HOL £3.46, HOL-A £6.24; TRICAST: A-HOL-KTC £14.13, HOL-A-KTC £22.98; TRIFECTA: A-HOL-KTC £15.90, HOL-A-KTC £25.40;.
Owner Clarendon Thoroughbred Racing **Bred** Clive Dennett **Trained** Middleham Moor, N Yorks
Owner D G Pryde **Bred** Highclere Stud **Trained** Maunby, N Yorks

FOCUS
A modest handicap in which the gallop was no more than fair. The first two look capable of winning again this winter.

8388 32RED.COM MAIDEN FILLIES' STKS 1m 5y (Tp)
2:55 (2:58) (Class 5) 3-Y-O+ **£3,557** (£1,058; £529; £264) **Stalls** Centre

Form RPR

1 **Notte Illuminata (IRE)**[65] 3-8-9 0 JordanVaughan(5) 5 76
(K R Burke) *t.k.h: trckd ldrs: smooth hdwy 3f out: cl up 2f out: sn chal: rdn to take slt ld ent fnl f: drvn out* **6/4**[2]

243- **2** 1 3/4 **Amber Mystique**[448] 6687 3-9-0 74 ShaneGray 4 72
(Kristin Stubbs) *cl up: led over 3f out: jnd and rdn over 1f out: hdd narrowly ent fnl f: sn drvn and ev ch tl edgd lft and no ex last 100 yds* **14/1**

42- **3** 3 **Ribbing (USA)**[510] 4597 3-9-0 0 TomEaves 3 65
(David Simcock) *t.k.h early: hld up: hdwy 3f out: chsd ldrs 2f out: sn rdn and kpt on same pce* **11/8**[1]

0- **4** nse **Shadele (IRE)**[433] 7077 3-9-0 0 GrahamLee 1 65
(Jeremy Noseda) *cl up: pushed along 3f out: rdn 2f out: sn drvn and kpt on same pce* **7/2**[3]

0 **5** 13 **Madame Bond**[111] 5843 4-9-1 0 JoeFanning 2 35
(Sally Hall) *led: pushed along and hdd over 3f out: rdn along over 2f out: sn wknd* **66/1**

6 5 **Scannermandango** 3-8-11 0 GeorgeDowning(3) 6 24
(Jim Goldie) *dwlt: a towards rr: outpcd and bhd fr over 2f out* **40/1**

1m 42.18s (3.58) **Going Correction** +0.20s/f (Slow)
WFA 3 from 4yo 1lb **6** Ran SP% **114.9**
Speed ratings (Par 100): **90,88,85,85,72 67**
CSF £22.27 TOTE £2.40: £1.20, £3.80; EX 18.20 Trifecta £22.30.
Owner Mrs Elaine M Burke **Bred** Swordlestown Little **Trained** Middleham Moor, N Yorks

FOCUS
Fair form from the principals, but an uncompetitive maiden in which half of the six-strong field were returning from lengthy absences. A slow pace means this bare form isn't very reliable.

8389 BETWAY H'CAP 6f (Tp)
3:30 (3:30) (Class 5) (0-75,75) 3-Y-O+ **£3,557** (£1,058; £529; £264) **Stalls** Centre

Form RPR

3404 **1** **Consulting**[12] 8206 3-9-7 75 (b[1]) DavidProbert 2 86
(Martyn Meade) *t.k.h early: cl up: rdn to ld 11/2f out: drvn out* **9/2**[2]

4123 **2** 1 3/4 **My Dad Syd (USA)**[24] 8052 4-9-6 74 (v) RobertWinston 6 79
(Ian Williams) *prom: cl up 1/2-way: effrt wl over 1f out: sn rdn to chal: drvn ent fnl f: kpt on same pce* **9/4**[1]

100 **3** nk **Slingsby**[31] 7959 5-8-13 70 (p) NathanEvans(3) 5 74
(Michael Easterby) *in tch: hdwy 2f out: rdn over 1f out: drvn and kpt on wl fnl f* **9/1**

0104 **4** 1 **Wahaab (IRE)**[6] 8287 5-8-8 67 (p) ShirleyTeasdale(5) 1 68
(Iain Jardine) *chsd ldrs: rdn along wl over 1f out: drvn ent fnl f and kpt on same* **11/1**

3222 **5** 2 3/4 **Dark Side Dream**[31] 7959 4-8-13 72 GeorgiaCox(5) 3 64
(Chris Dwyer) *led: rdn along over 2f out: drvn and hdd 11/2f out: grad wknd* **9/2**[2]

0433 **6** 1/2 **Malaysian Boleh**[26] 8037 6-9-0 68 TomEaves 8 58
(Brian Ellison) *hld up: hdwy wl over 1f out: sn rdn and no imp fnl f* **9/1**

4014 **7** nk **More Beau (USA)**[22] 8067 5-9-1 69 (p) BarryMcHugh 9 58
(David Nicholls) *in tch on outer: hdwy 1/2-way: rdn to chse ldrs 2f out: wknd over 1f out* **5/1**[3]

0000 **8** 3/4 **Point North (IRE)**[48] 7660 9-9-4 72 (b) PaulMulrennan 10 59
(John Balding) *a rr* **33/1**

6340 **9** 3 3/4 **Funding Deficit (IRE)**[31] 7958 6-9-0 71 GeorgeDowning(3) 4 46
(Jim Goldie) *dwlt: a rr* **33/1**

0405 **10** 1/2 **Jess**[163] 3985 3-8-11 65 ShaneGray 7 38
(Kevin Ryan) *chsd ldrs: rdn along 1/2-way: sn wknd* **50/1**

1m 11.4s (-1.10) **Going Correction** +0.20s/f (Slow) **10** Ran SP% **120.0**
Speed ratings (Par 103): **115,112,112,110,107 106,106,105,100,99**
CSF £15.34 CT £89.76 TOTE £5.60: £1.90, £1.40, £3.00; EX 19.20 Trifecta £119.70.
Owner J Anderson & J Spence 1 **Bred** Ladyswood Stud **Trained** Newmarket, Suffolk

FOCUS
A fair handicap, but although the gallop was sound those held up were at a bit of a disadvantage. A personal best from the winner back sprinting.

8390 BETWAY SPRINT H'CAP 5f (Tp)
4:05 (4:06) (Class 6) (0-65,65) 3-Y-O+ **£2,911** (£866; £432; £216) **Stalls** Centre

Form RPR

4302 **1** **Lady Nayef**[22] 8078 3-9-7 65 (t) RobertWinston 12 73
(John Butler) *trckd ldrs: hdwy and cl up over 2f out: rdn to chal over 1f out: drvn to ld ins fnl f: kpt on wl u.p towards fin* **5/1**[2]

1143 **2** 1/2 **Horsforth**[17] 8137 4-9-7 65 (b) JoeFanning 13 71
(Richard Guest) *trckd ldrs: hdwy and cl up 2f out: rdn to take slt ld jst over 1f out: drvn and hdd ins fnl f: no ex last 100 yds* **15/8**[1]

0555 **3** 1 3/4 **Searanger (USA)**[17] 8137 3-9-4 62 DougieCostello 2 62
(Rebecca Menzies) *towards rr: hdwy 2f out: rdn to chse ldrs over 1f out: drvn and kpt on same pce ins fnl f* **16/1**

0005 **4** 3/4 **Harmonic Wave (IRE)**[22] 8078 3-9-4 62 [1] BenCurtis 11 59
(Rebecca Menzies) *hld up towards rr: hdwy wl over 1f out: sn rdn and kpt on wl fnl f* **17/2**

1000 **5** hd **Lotara**[28] 7995 4-8-12 59 GeorgeDowning(3) 1 55+
(Jim Goldie) *rr: hdwy over 1f out: sn swtchd rt and rdn: styd on wl fnl f: nrst fin* **14/1**

2000 **6** 1 **Storm Trooper (IRE)**[17] 8137 5-9-4 62 BarryMcHugh 10 55
(David Nicholls) *sn led: rdn along 2f out: drvn and hdd jst over 1f out: wknd fnl f* **20/1**

3412 **7** 1 1/2 **Noah Amor (IRE)**[138] 4855 3-9-7 65 PaulQuinn 9 52
(David Nicholls) *prom: rdn along 2f out: grad wknd* **11/2**[3]

6165 **8** hd **Captain Scooby**[5] 8312 10-8-8 52 (b) ShaneGray 7 39
(Richard Guest) *dwlt and rr tl sme late hdwy* **12/1**

6530 **9** 1/2 **Roaring Rory**[22] 8078 3-9-5 63 (p) TomEaves 6 48
(Ollie Pears) *cl up: rdn along wl over 1f out: grad wknd appr fnl f* **25/1**

1500 **10** 1 1/4 **Intense Starlet (IRE)**[20] 8095 5-9-4 62 (p) SamJames 3 42
(Marjorie Fife) *a towards rr* **9/1**

0000 **11** 1/2 **Long Awaited (IRE)**[89] 6589 8-9-6 64 (b) PaulMulrennan 8 43
(Conor Dore) *a towards rr* **33/1**

-240 **12** 2 3/4 **Busy Bimbo (IRE)**[119] 5582 7-9-3 61 (b) GrahamLee 5 30
(John Murray) *chsd ldrs: rdn along over 2f out: sn wknd* **50/1**

6003 **P** **The Cheese Gang**[27] 8012 4-8-7 51 oh5 (t) JoeyHaynes 4
(Susan Corbett) *chsd ldrs tl lost action and p.u 2f out* **33/1**

59.18s (-0.32) **Going Correction** +0.20s/f (Slow) **13** Ran SP% **124.1**
Speed ratings (Par 101): **110,109,106,105,104 103,100,100,99,97 96,92,**
CSF £14.46 CT £152.51 TOTE £7.00: £2.00, £1.40, £4.80; EX 18.20 Trifecta £303.50.
Owner Greenstead Hall Racing Ltd **Bred** Greenstead Hall Racing Ltd **Trained** Newmarket, Suffolk

FOCUS
A run-of-the-mill handicap in which the pace was good thoughout and sound form for the level.

T/Plt: £31.30 to a £1 stake. Pool: £66,401.75 - 1545.96 winning units T/Qpdt: £7.20 to a £1 stake. Pool: £4,866.37 - 497.2 winning units **Joe Rowntree**

8182 MEYDAN (L-H)
Thursday, December 15

OFFICIAL GOING: Dirt: fast

8391a THE LINCOLN MKT TROPHY (MAIDEN) (DIRT) 7f (D)
3:05 (3:05) 2-3-Y-O **£16,635** (£5,545; £3,049; £1,663; £831)

RPR

1 **Cosmo Charlie (USA)** 2-9-0 PatDobbs 1 87
(Doug Watson, UAE) *soon led, rdn clr 2 1/2f out, ran on wl, comfortably* **13/2**[3]

2 2 3/4 **Capezzano (USA)**[118] 5615 2-9-0 ColmO'Donoghue 5 80+
(Charlie Appleby) *mid-division, chsd leaders 3f out, ran on wl fnl 2f but no ch wth winner* **5/4**[1]

3 3 1/4 **Mazeed (USA)** 2-9-0 AdriedeVries 3 71
(M F De Kock, South Africa) *tracked leaders, ev ch 2f out, one pace fnl 1 1/2f* **7/4**[2]

4 6 3/4 **Dawwass (USA)** 2-9-0 TadhgO'Shea 6 53
(S Seemar, UAE) *never nr to chal but ran on fnl 2f* **14/1**

5 7 3/4 **Kahrab (IRE)**[28] 8000 2-9-0 72 BReis 7 32
(R Bouresly, Kuwait) *tracked leaders til wknd fnl 2f* **16/1**

6 10 1/2 **Sabegg (USA)** 2-9-0 (t) DaneO'Neill 2 4
(A bin Harmash, UAE) *never nr to challenge* **10/1**

7 4 1/2 **Al Zeem (USA)**[42] 7784 2-9-0 (t) AntonioFresu 4
(A bin Harmash, UAE) *bumped at strt, al in rear* **25/1**

1m 25.02s (-0.08) **Going Correction** +0.35s/f (Slow) **7** Ran SP% **119.6**
Speed ratings: **114,110,107,99,90 78,73**
CSF: 16.10.
Owner Kildare Stud - Frankie O'Connor **Bred** Roger S Braugh Jr **Trained** United Arab Emirates

8392- 8595a (Foreign Racing) - See Raceform Interactive

8396a THE DUBAI CREEK MILE SPONSORED BY LINCOLN MKZ (LISTED RACE) (DIRT) 1m (D)
6:00 (6:00) 3-Y-O+
£27,726 (£9,242; £4,621; £2,310; £1,386; £924)

RPR

1 **Fitzgerald (USA)**[28] 8005 4-9-0 95 (t) AntonioFresu 12 113+
(A bin Harmash, UAE) *at rear, smooth prog 2 1/2f out, led 1 1/2f out, ran on wl, easy* **33/1**

2 5 1/4 **Farrier (USA)**[264] 1106 8-9-0 104 RichardMullen 2 101+
(S Seemar, UAE) *slowly into strd, nvr nr to chal but ran on fnl 2f, nrst finish* **20/1**

3 3/4 **Cool Cowboy (USA)**[34] 7923 5-9-2 112 PatDobbs 7 101
(Doug Watson, UAE) *tracked ldr, led 2f out, hdd 1 1/2f out but ran on well* **15/8**[1]

4 2 1/4 **Le Bernardin (USA)**[285] 842 7-9-3 110 (t) TadhgO'Shea 6 97
(A R Al Rayhi, UAE) *tracked leaders, ev ch 3f out, ran on same pace fnl 2f* **9/4**[2]

5 1 1/2 **Footbridge (USA)**[301] 624 6-9-0 106 (b) ColmO'Donoghue 3 91
(Charlie Appleby) *soon led, hdd 3f out, wknd fnl 1f* **12/1**

6 hd **Long Water (USA)**[6] 8301 5-9-0 85 (b) GeorgeBuckell 4 90
(H Al Alawi, UAE) *slowly into strd, nvr better than mid-division* **50/1**

7 6 1/4 **Need To Know (SAF)**[28] 8004 8-9-0 103 (bt) SaeedAlMazrooei 11 76
(A R Al Rayhi, UAE) *never nr to challenge* **33/1**

8 1/2 **Earnshaw (USA)**[11] 8214 5-9-0 107 (bt) FernandoJara 5 75
(S bin Ghadayer, UAE) *never better than mid-division* **14/1**

9 2 3/4 **Maftool (USA)**[264] 1101 4-9-0 112 DaneO'Neill 1 68
(M Al Mheiri, UAE) *never better than mid-division* **3/1**[3]

10 1 1/4 **Frankyfourfingers (FR)**[343] 92 6-9-0 111 SamHitchcott 10 65
(S bin Ghadayer, UAE) *tracked ldr til wknd fnl 2f* **12/1**

11 9 **Fauvism (USA)**[320] 408 7-9-0 95 BReis 8 45
(R Bouresly, Kuwait) *always in rear* **100/1**

12 8 **Dormello (IRE)**[270] 1020 8-9-0 109 ChrisHayes 9 26
(D Selvaratnam, UAE) *always in rear* **25/1**

1m 37.52s (0.02) **Going Correction** +0.35s/f (Slow) **12** Ran SP% **130.0**
Speed ratings: **113,107,107,104,103 103,96,96,93,92 83,75**
CSF: 586.83.
Owner Buti Bintooq Almarri **Bred** Darley **Trained** United Arab Emirates

8384 NEWCASTLE (A.W) (L-H)
Friday, December 16

OFFICIAL GOING: Tapeta: standard
Wind: Virtually nil Weather: Cloudy

8397 32RED.COM MAIDEN FILLIES' STKS (PLUS 10 RACE) 1m 5y (Tp)
12:25 (12:26) (Class 5) 2-Y-O **£3,557** (£1,058; £529; £264) **Stalls** Centre

Form RPR

0 **1** **Bizzarria**[44] 7762 2-9-0 0 RobertHavlin 1 72+
(John Gosden) *trckd ldrs: hdwy over 2f out: rdn to ld appr fnl f: kpt on wl* **5/2**[2]

3026 **2** 1 **Mums The Word**[24] 8062 2-9-0 87 JackGarritty 4 70
(Richard Fahey) *trckd ldrs: effrt over 1f out: rdn to chal ent fnl f and ev ch: drvn and kpt on same pce last 100 yds* **6/4**[1]

6 **3** 3/4 **Naupaka**[27] 8034 2-9-0 0 TomEaves 3 68
(Brian Ellison) *hld up in rr: hdwy 2f out: rdn over 1f out: kpt on wl fnl f* **11/2**[3]

30 **4** nk **Shee's Lucky**[10] 8237 2-9-0 0 PJMcDonald 7 67
(Mark Johnston) *cl up on outer: effrt 2f out: sn rdn and ev ch: drvn ent fnl f: kpt on same pce* **9/1**

0 **5** 2 **Zenovia (IRE)**[18] 8131 2-9-0 0 PaulMulrennan 5 63
(David Simcock) *hld up in rr: hdwy wl over 1f out: rdn and kpt on fnl f: nrst fin* **10/1**

0 **6** 6 **Touch Me (IRE)**[18] 8130 2-9-0 0 DougieCostello 6 50
(K R Burke) *cl up: led 21/2f out: rdn wl over 1f out: drvn and hdd appr fnl f: sn wknd* **66/1**

0 **7** 5 **Thornton Mary**[17] 8139 2-9-0 0 JamesSullivan 8 39
(Brian Rothwell) *a rr* **150/1**

6204 **8** 19 **Dal Riata (IRE)**[10] 8237 2-9-0 75 JasonHart 2
(Mark Johnston) *slt ld: rdn along 3f out: sn hdd & wknd* **12/1**

1m 41.31s (2.71) **Going Correction** +0.10s/f (Slow) **8** Ran SP% **112.9**
Speed ratings (Par 93): **90,89,88,87,85 79,74,55**
CSF £6.42 TOTE £3.10: £1.10, £1.20, £1.80; EX 6.80 Trifecta £24.10.
Owner A E Oppenheimer **Bred** Hascombe And Valiant Studs **Trained** Newmarket, Suffolk

FOCUS
A modest fillies' maiden with the two market leaders dominating the finish. The runner-up's mark of 87 probably shouldn't be used as the benchmark.

8398 32RED.COM NURSERY H'CAP 7f 14y (Tp)
1:00 (1:00) (Class 6) (0-65,66) 2-Y-O **£2,911** (£866; £432; £216) **Stalls** Centre

Form RPR

0553 **1** **Arthurthedelegator**[10] 8235 2-9-2 63 NathanEvans(3) 3 67
(Oliver Greenall) *trckd ldrs: hdwy over 2f out: led 11/2f out and sn rdn: drvn ins fnl f: jst hld on* **9/2**[3]

0013 **2** shd **Dusty Bin**[48] 7690 2-9-6 64 PJMcDonald 6 68
(Garry Moss) *trckd ldrs: hdwy 2f out: rdn over 1f out: sn chsng wnr: drvn ins fnl f: styd on strly: jst failed* **3/1**[2]

2505 **3** shd **Hotfill**[28] 8008 2-9-8 66 SamJames 2 70
(David Barron) *dwlt and hld up in rr: swtchd rt and hdwy 2f out: rdn over 1f out: sn chsng ldng pair: drvn ins fnl f: styd on strly towards fin* **5/1**

0000 **4** 4 1/2 **Good Time Ahead (IRE)**[60] 7406 2-9-7 65 PaddyAspell 5 57
(Philip Kirby) *cl up: pushed along over 2f out: rdn wl over 1f out: grad wknd* **16/1**

000 **5** 1/2 **Mukallaf (IRE)**[30] 7975 2-9-8 66 [1] PaulMulrennan 7 57
(Roger Varian) *hld up towards rr: pushed along over 2f out: sn rdn: plugged on fnl f* **6/1**

0061 **6** nk **Bruny Island (IRE)**[8] 8276 2-8-9 53 6ex StevieDonohoe 4 43
(Charlie Fellowes) *t.k.h: in tch: effrt over 2f out: sn rdn and btn* **9/4**[1]

5405 **7** 2 3/4 **Belle's Angel (IRE)**[21] 8087 2-7-10 45 (p) HollieDoyle(5) 1 28
(Ann Duffield) *led: rdn along over 2f out: hdd wl over 1f out: sn wknd* **22/1**

1m 26.96s (0.76) **Going Correction** +0.10s/f (Slow) **7** Ran SP% **115.1**
Speed ratings (Par 94): **99,98,98,93,93 92,89**
CSF £18.66 TOTE £5.40: £2.60, £2.60; EX 18.50 Trifecta £74.40.
Owner E A Brook **Bred** Howard Barton Stud **Trained** Oldcastle Heath, Cheshire

FOCUS
A moderate if straightforward nursery formwise, with little separating the first three.

8399 BETWAY MARATHON H'CAP 2m 56y (Tp)
1:35 (1:35) (Class 4) (0-85,82) 3-Y-O+ **£5,175** (£1,540; £769; £384) **Stalls** Low

Form RPR

2114 **1** **Stamford Raffles**[25] 8051 3-9-0 76 StevieDonohoe 2 84+
(Jane Chapple-Hyam) *trckd ldr: cl up 1/2-way: led 2f out and sn rdn: drvn ent fnl f: kpt on strly* **11/2**[2]

4125 **2** 1 1/4 **Zakatal**[170] 3784 10-10-0 82 PJMcDonald 7 86
(Rebecca Menzies) *t.k.h: trckd ldrs: hdwy 3f out: rdn to chse wnr jst over 1f out: drvn and ev ch jst ins fnl f: kpt on same pce towards fin* **25/1**

5222 **3** nk **Aldreth**[25] 8051 5-9-4 75 (b) NathanEvans(3) 1 79
(Michael Easterby) *trckd ldng pair on inner: hdwy over 2f out: effrt and n.m.r over 1f out: sn swtchd rt and rdn: drvn and ch ent fnl f: kpt on* **7/1**

5221 **4** nk **Dubawi Fifty**[17] 8143 3-9-3 79 DavidNolan 6 82
(Karen McLintock) *set stdy pce: pushed along and qcknd over 3f out: rdn over 2f out: sn hdd: cl up and drvn over 1f out: kpt on same pce* **5/4**[1]

0643 **5** hd **Siren's Cove**[7] 8283 4-9-5 73 (b) PaulMulrennan 3 76
(Kenneth Slack) *trckd ldrs: hdwy over 3f out: rdn along over 2f out: drvn over 1f out: kpt on fnl f* **13/2**[3]

1161 **6** nk **Mister Bob (GER)**[84] 6740 7-9-8 76 (p) DougieCostello 5 79
(James Bethell) *t.k.h: hld up in rr: hdwy over 2f out: rdn over 1f out: styd on wl fnl f: nrst fin* **16/1**

0311 **7** 7 **Cavalieri (IRE)**[22] 8084 6-8-9 68 (tp) HollieDoyle(5) 8 62
(Philip Kirby) *hld up towards rr: sme hdwy on inner over 2f out: sn rdn along and n.d* **8/1**

0034 **8** 1/2 **Aramist (IRE)**[18] 8133 6-9-11 79 BenCurtis 4 73
(Alan Swinbank) *trckd ldrs on outer: pushed along 3f out: rdn over 2f out: sn outpcd* **12/1**

4256 **9** 4 **Grand Meister**[18] 8133 5-9-4 79 JoshQuinn(7) 9 68
(John Quinn) *t.k.h: trckd ldrs on outer: effrt 3f out: rdn along over 2f out: sn btn* **50/1**

3m 43.29s (8.09) **Going Correction** +0.45s/f (Slow)
WFA 3 from 4yo+ 8lb **9** Ran SP% **116.2**
Speed ratings (Par 105): **97,96,96,96,95 95,92,92,90**
CSF £127.88 CT £974.71 TOTE £6.30: £2.00, £4.90, £1.80; EX 131.50 Trifecta £743.50.
Owner Mrs Jane Chapple-Hyam **Bred** C A Cyzer **Trained** Dalham, Suffolk

FOCUS
A fair staying handicap with a few of these coming into the race in decent form, but they only went a moderate pace and it suited those ridden handily.

8400 BETWAY H'CAP 1m 2f 42y (Tp)
2:10 (2:13) (Class 6) (0-60,60) 3-Y-O+ **£2,911** (£866; £432; £216) **Stalls** High

Form RPR

4014 **1** **Thello**[42] 7794 4-9-3 59 LouisSteward(3) 8 67
(Garry Moss) *trckd ldrs: hdwy over 2f out: led wl over 1f out: rdn and kpt on strly fnl f* **2/1**[1]

036 **2** 1 **Bridey's Lettuce (IRE)**[18] 8134 4-9-7 60 DavidNolan 13 65
(Ivan Furtado) *set stdy pce: pushed along and qcknd 3f out: rdn 2f out: sn hdd and drvn: kpt on* **5/1**[3]

0405 **3** 1 1/4 **Swiss Lait**[17] 8144 5-9-0 53 JamesSullivan 10 56
(Patrick Holmes) *rr: pushed along over 3f out: rdn and hdwy 2f out: chsd ldrs over 1f out: kpt on wl fnl f* **100/1**

5050 **4** nk **Sakhalin Star (IRE)**[17] 8142 5-9-6 59 (e) DougieCostello 3 61
(Richard Guest) *plld hrd: trckd ldrs on inner: effrt 2f out: n.m.r and sltly hmpd jst over 1f out: kpt on wl fnl f* **14/1**

6052 **5** 1/2 **Hightime Girl**[17] 8145 3-8-10 59 (tp) BenSanderson(7) 7 61
(Roger Fell) *hld up and bhd: hdwy over 2f out: rdn along on inner over 1f out: kpt on fnl f: nrst fin* **8/1**

3400 **6** nk **Page Of Wands**[1] 8386 3-8-13 55 (v) TomEaves 6 56
(Karen McLintock) *t.k.h: trckd ldrs: hdwy on outer 3f out: rdn along over 1f out:. kpt on same pce fnl f* **11/1**

-560 **7** nk **Life Knowledge (IRE)**[184] 3287 4-9-1 54 JackGarritty 5 54
(Patrick Holmes) *.t.k.h: trckd ldng pair: effrt on inner over 1f out: sn n.m.r and swtchd rt: sn drvn and one pce* **12/1**

0020 **8** 1 **Devious Spirit (IRE)**[29] 7992 4-9-7 60 [1] PJMcDonald 9 59
(Iain Jardine) *dwlt: a towards rr* **7/2**[2]

The Form Book, Raceform Ltd, Newbury, RG14 5SJ

-000 **9** *nse* **Stamp Duty (IRE)**[80] 6857 8-8-7 **46** oh1........................... BarryMcHugh 4 45
(Suzzanne France) *hld up towards rr: hdwy over 2f out: in tch and rdn along whn hmpd over 1f out: sn one pce* **50/1**

505 **10** *1 3/4* **Aneedh**[17] 8142 6-9-4 **57**...............................(b) PaulMulrennan 11 52
(Clive Mulhall) *sn trcking ldr: cl up 4f out: rdn along wl over 2f out: grad wknd* **25/1**

6120 **11** *2 1/4* **Whitchurch**[20] 8125 4-8-10 **54**........................ HollieDoyle[(5)] 12 45
(Philip Kirby) *hld up: a towards rr* **12/1**

560- **12** *1 1/2* **Jordaura**[408] 7713 10-8-4 **46** oh1.............................. NathanEvans[(3)] 1 35
(John Murray) *a towards rr* **28/1**

0000 **13** *2 1/4* **Symbolic Star (IRE)**[17] 8141 4-8-13 **57**........................ PhilDennis[(5)] 14 42
(Barry Murtagh) *t.k.h: chsd ldrs on outer: pushed along 3f out: sn rdn and wknd* **25/1**

2m 12.8s (2.40) **Going Correction** +0.45s/f (Slow)
WFA 3 from 4yo+ 3lb **13** Ran SP% **127.8**
Speed ratings (Par 101): **108,107,106,105,105 105,105,104,104,102 101,99,98**
CSF £12.40 CT £815.57 TOTE £3.10: £1.40, £2.20, £10.60; EX 18.70 Trifecta £5223.10.
Owner James Gaffney **Bred** Mickley Stud & Mr W T Whittle **Trained** Wynyard, Stockton-On-Tees
■ Stewards' Enquiry : Jack Garritty three-day ban; careless riding (30th-31st Jan)

FOCUS
A moderate handicap in which they went an even pace and the market got it right.

8401 SUNBETS.CO.UK CLASSIFIED STKS 7f 14y (Tp)
2:45 (2:45) (Class 6) 3-Y-O+ **£2,911** (£866; £432; £216) **Stalls** Centre

Form RPR

5426 **1** **Justice Pleasing**[17] 8146 3-8-7 52............................(p) BenSanderson[(7)] 7 57
(Roger Fell) *trckd ldng pair: hdwy to ld 21/2f out and sn rdn clr: kpt on fnl f* **2/1**[1]

4203 **2** *1* **Canford Belle**[7] 8289 3-8-9 54.. PhilDennis[(5)] 2 55
(Grant Tuer) *hld up in rr: hdwy over 2f out: chsd wnr over 1f out: sn rdn: kpt on fnl f* **9/2**[3]

3026 **3** *4* **Rosy Ryan (IRE)**[6] 8306 6-9-0 54.................................... JamesSullivan 4 45
(Tina Jackson) *trckd ldrs: effrt over 2f out: sn rdn and edgd lft: drvn over 1f out: sn one pce* **9/4**[2]

6005 **4** *1 1/2* **George Bailey (IRE)**[17] 8146 4-8-11 48.......................... NathanEvans[(3)] 6 41
(Suzzanne France) *cl up: led 1/2-way: rdn and hdd 21/2f out: sn drvn and grad wknd* **8/1**

6000 **5** *3 1/4* **The Excel Queen (IRE)**[17] 8146 3-9-0 48...................... BarryMcHugh 3 33
(Tony Coyle) *chsd ldrs: rdn along over 2f out: drvn wl over 1f out: sn btn* **7/1**

5460 **6** *12* **Isntshesomething**[7] 8289 4-9-0 51..............................(e) PaulMulrennan 1 3
(Richard Guest) *in tch: rdn along wl over 2f out: sn outpcd and bhd* **14/1**

0/0- **7** *5* **Red Legacy**[503] 4888 8-8-11 12.. RachelRichardson[(3)] 5
(Sean Regan) *slt ld: hdd 1/2-way: sn rdn and wknd* **80/1**

1m 27.29s (1.09) **Going Correction** +0.10s/f (Slow) **7** Ran SP% **113.8**
Speed ratings (Par 101): **97,95,91,89,85 72,66**
CSF £11.38 TOTE £3.00: £1.70, £2.10; EX 10.60 Trifecta £22.10.
Owner R G Fell **Bred** D R Botterill **Trained** Nawton, N Yorks

FOCUS
A particularly moderate 0-55 classified event with the seven runners having a combined career record of 3-118. Five of these met in a similar event over C&D last month and the 2-5-6-7-11 from there finished 3-4-1-5-2 this time.

8402 BETWAY CLAIMING STKS 6f (Tp)
3:20 (3:20) (Class 6) 3-Y-O+ **£2,911** (£866; £432; £216) **Stalls** Centre

Form RPR

5 **1** **Doc Sportello (IRE)**[228] 1937 4-8-13 78........................[1] HarryPoulton 4 86
(Adam West) *t.k.h early: led 2f: cl up: led again over 2f out: rdn wl over 1f out: edgd lft ins fnl f: kpt on* **66/1**

2503 **2** *2 1/2* **Intibaah**[42] 7806 6-9-1 89..[1] PJMcDonald 6 81
(George Baker) *trckd ldrs: hdwy over 2f out: rdn over 1f out: drvn ent fnl f: sn one pce* **9/4**[1]

5200 **3** *3 1/4* **Among Angels**[205] 2579 4-8-8 78...............................(b[1]) NathanEvans[(3)] 5 67
(Daniel Mark Loughnane) *chsd ldrs: rdn along 2f out: sn drvn and kpt on one pce* **7/1**

0106 **4** *nk* **Fairway To Heaven (IRE)**[79] 6883 7-8-11 82.............. DougieCostello 1 66
(Michael Wigham) *slowly away and bhd: hdwy 2f out: sn swtchd rt and rdn: kpt on fnl f* **7/1**

0055 **5** *3/4* **Yeeoow (IRE)**[6] 8314 7-8-13 79.. JoeyHaynes 8 66
(K R Burke) *cl up: slt ld after 2f: rdn along and hdd over 2f out: drvn wl over 1f out: sn wknd* **5/2**[2]

2310 **6** *1 1/4* **Manatee Bay**[22] 8083 6-9-3 80..(v) TomEaves 2 66
(David Nicholls) *hld up in tch: effrt over 2f out: sn rdn and n.d* **11/4**[3]

64 **7** *33* **Sandstream**[32] 7960 3-9-3 0... JasonHart 3
(Tracy Waggott) *chsd ldrs: rdn along 1/2-way: sn outpcd and bhd* **200/1**

1m 11.94s (-0.56) **Going Correction** +0.10s/f (Slow) **7** Ran SP% **113.0**
Speed ratings (Par 101): **107,103,99,98,97 96,52**
CSF £206.25 TOTE £32.10: £16.10, £2.00; EX 177.70 Trifecta £676.80.Doc Sportello was claimed by Mr M. Herrington for £10,000.
Owner Mrs J West **Bred** J Hutchinson **Trained** Epsom, Surrey

FOCUS
Not a bad claimer, with those holding an official mark rated between 78 and 89, but this was a shock for most punters.

8403 BETWAY SPRINT H'CAP 5f (Tp)
3:50 (3:51) (Class 4) (0-80,82) 3-Y-O+ **£5,498** (£1,636; £817; £408) **Stalls** Centre

Form RPR

4500 **1** **Outrage**[6] 8308 4-9-6 **82**...(b[1]) GeorgeDowning[(3)] 11 93+
(Daniel Kubler) *hld up in rr: gd hdwy 2f out: chsd ldrs over 1f out: chal ent fnl f: sn rdn: kpt on wl to last 75 yds* **15/2**

0600 **2** *1/2* **Foxy Forever (IRE)**[67] 7202 6-9-5 **78**........................... DougieCostello 6 87
(Michael Wigham) *prom: cl up over 2f out: led wl over 1f out: rdn ent fnl f: drvn and hdd last 75 yds: no ex* **9/2**[1]

611 **3** *1 1/2* **Royal Mezyan (IRE)**[21] 8099 5-9-4 **80**........................ LouisSteward[(3)] 9 84
(Henry Spiller) *in tch: hdwy over 2f out: rdn and ev ch jst over 1f out: sn drvn and kpt on same pce* **9/2**[1]

0341 **4** *nk* **Landing Night (IRE)**[3] 8349 4-9-8 **81** 6ex..................(tp) PJMcDonald 10 84
(Rebecca Menzies) *trckd ldrs: cl up 1/2-way: effrt and ev ch over 1f out: sn rdn and kpt on same pce* **8/1**

6441 **5** *nse* **Poppy In The Wind**[18] 8137 4-8-10 **69**................................(v) BenCurtis 5 72
(Alan Brown) *chsd ldrs: rdn wl over 1f out: drvn and kpt on same pce fnl f* **5/1**[2]

1300 **6** *1/2* **Brockholes**[32] 7959 3-9-0 **73**... PaulMulrennan 7 74
(Bryan Smart) *led: rdn along over 2f out: hdd wl over 1f out: sn drvn and grad wknd* **22/1**

-000 **7** *1/2* **Richter Scale (IRE)**[59] 7437 3-8-9 **68**.................................... TomEaves 1 67+
(Iain Jardine) *in tch: hdwy to chse ldrs wl over 1f out: sn rdn and no imp fnl f* **33/1**

0500 **8** *3/4* **Something Lucky (IRE)**[3] 8349 4-9-0 **73**.....................(p) JamesSullivan 8 71
(Kristin Stubbs) *dwlt and rr: hdwy wl over 1f out: sn rdn and kpt on fnl f: nrst fin* **20/1**

5003 **9** *hd* **Fredricka**[70] 7112 5-9-3 **76**.. JasonHart 12 72
(David Barron) *dwlt and rr: hdwy wl over 1f out: sn rdn and kpt on fnl f: nrst fin* **7/1**[3]

1 **10** *1/2* **Nuala Tagula (IRE)**[84] 6744 3-8-6 **68**........................ NathanEvans[(3)] 13 62
(John Quinn) *in tch on outer: hdwy to chse ldrs 1/2-way: rdn along 2f out: sn drvn and wknd appr fnl f* **16/1**

1000 **11** *1/2* **Invincible Ridge (IRE)**[65] 7289 8-9-5 **81**............ RachelRichardson[(3)] 2 73
(Eric Alston) *prom towards far side: rdn along 2f out: drvn and wknd over 1f out* **18/1**

2020 **12** *nk* **Pearl Acclaim (IRE)**[8] 8280 6-9-4 **77**............................(p) BarryMcHugh 4 68
(David Nicholls) *t.k.h: in tch: pushed along 2f out: sn rdn and wknd* **10/1**

0006 **13** *2 1/2* **Imperial Legend (IRE)**[28] 8010 7-8-9 **68**.............................(p) PaulQuinn 3 50
(David Nicholls) *plld hrd: prom: rdn along over 2f out: sn wknd* **25/1**

59.42s (-0.08) **Going Correction** +0.10s/f (Slow) **13** Ran SP% **124.5**
Speed ratings (Par 105): **104,103,100,100,100 99,98,97,97,96 95,95,91**
CSF £40.99 CT £176.73 TOTE £9.80: £3.00, £2.60, £1.80; EX 69.30 Trifecta £667.60.
Owner D Blunt & G Middlebrook **Bred** Trickledown Stud Limited **Trained** Lambourn, Berks

FOCUS
A fair sprint handicap with those who raced centre to nearside favoured. The third, fourth and fifth help set the standard.
T/Plt: £76.30 to a £1 stake. Pool: £60,570.12 - 579.26 winning tickets T/Qpdt: £23.30 to a £1 stake. Pool: £5,097.85 - 161.90 winning tickets **Joe Rowntree**

8337 WOLVERHAMPTON (A.W) (L-H)
Friday, December 16

OFFICIAL GOING: Tapeta: standard
Wind: Light behind Weather: Overcast

8404 32RED CASINO MAIDEN AUCTION STKS 7f 32y (Tp)
3:45 (3:47) (Class 5) 2-Y-O **£3,557** (£1,058; £529; £264) **Stalls** High

Form RPR

1 **Mr Minerals** 2-9-3 0.. ShaneKelly 4 79+
(Richard Hughes) *hld up: hdwy over 2f out: shkn up to ld ins fnl f: r.o wl: comf* **8/11**[1]

63 **2** *4* **Petit Filous**[8] 8277 2-8-13 0.. PatCosgrave 3 62
(Giles Bravery) *led 1f: chsd ldr: rdn and ev ch ins fnl f: edgd lft and styd on same pce* **7/2**[2]

3 *3 1/4* **Deliberator** 2-8-13 0... WilliamCarson 8 54
(William Knight) *s.i.s: in rr: shkn up over 1f out: r.o to go 3rd post* **11/2**[3]

640 **4** *nk* **Red Mohican**[17] 8140 2-8-10 58..............................[1] JosephineGordon 6 50
(Phil McEntee) *led 6f out: rdn over 1f out: hdd & wknd ins fnl f* **20/1**

06 **5** *1/2* **Forest Steps (IRE)**[45] 7733 2-8-7 0................................... KieranO'Neill 2 46
(J S Moore) *prom: rdn and hung lft over 1f out: styd on same pce* **40/1**

6 *2* **Allegheny Bay (IRE)** 2-8-13 0.. LiamKeniry 1 47+
(J S Moore) *s.s: nt clr run over 1f out: nvr nrr* **25/1**

0 **7** *1/2* **Champagne Pink (FR)**[18] 8131 2-8-7 0.................. JordanVaughan[(5)] 9 45
(K R Burke) *prom: rdn over 2f out: hung lft and wknd over 1f out* **16/1**

000 **8** *6* **Champagne Reign (IRE)**[13] 8208 2-8-7 57............................ JohnFahy 7 25
(J S Moore) *chsd ldrs tl rdn and wknd over 1f out* **25/1**

9 *nse* **Trautmann (IRE)** 2-9-3 0... LukeMorris 5 35
(Daniel Mark Loughnane) *s.i.s: sn pushed along in rr: drvn 1/2-way: hung lft and wknd over 1f out* **20/1**

1m 28.83s (0.03) **Going Correction** -0.075s/f (Stan) **9** Ran SP% **121.0**
Speed ratings (Par 96): **96,91,87,87,86 84,83,77,77**
CSF £3.32 TOTE £1.70: £1.10, £1.10, £2.00; EX 4.60 Trifecta £12.70.
Owner R P Gallagher **Bred** Bearstone Stud Ltd **Trained** Upper Lambourn, Berkshire

FOCUS
An ordinary maiden, in which a newcomer proved much the best.

8405 32RED.COM NURSERY H'CAP 7f 32y (Tp)
4:15 (4:16) (Class 4) (0-85,85) 2-Y-O **£5,498** (£1,636; £817; £408) **Stalls** High

Form RPR

41 **1** **Dr Julius No**[207] 2536 2-9-7 **85**..................................... RichardKingscote 2 91+
(Ralph Beckett) *prom: stdd and lost pl after 1f: shkn up and hdwy 1f out: r.o to ld wl ins fnl f* **7/2**[2]

402 **2** *1/2* **Letmestopyouthere (IRE)**[55] 7549 2-9-5 **83**........................ JFEgan 7 87
(David Evans) *s.i.s: hld up: pushed along and hdwy on outer over 2f out: rdn to ld ins fnl f: sn hdd: kpt on* **6/1**[3]

3360 **3** *1 3/4* **Tailor's Row (USA)**[36] 7893 2-9-0 **78**................................ JoeFanning 6 77
(Mark Johnston) *chsd ldr 6f out: led over 4f out: rdn and edgd lft over 1f out: hdd ins fnl f: styd on same pce* **9/1**

663 **4** *1/2* **Heaven's Rock (IRE)**[9] 8244 2-8-4 **68**.............................[1] WilliamCarson 5 66
(Tom Dascombe) *sn led: hdd over 4f out: remained handy: nt clr run over 2f out: nt clr run again and swtchd rt over 1f out: styd on same pce ins fnl f* **6/1**[3]

650 **5** *3/4* **Portledge (IRE)**[55] 7541 2-8-10 **74**........................... JosephineGordon 4 70
(James Bethell) *hld up in tch: rdn over 1f out: styd on same pce fnl f* **8/1**

4544 **6** *1 1/4* **Miss Sheridan (IRE)**[32] 7956 2-8-1 **65**.............................. LukeMorris 3 58
(Michael Easterby) *chsd ldrs: rdn whn nt clr run over 1f out: no ex ins fnl f* **10/1**

41 **7** *1 1/2* **Red Gunner**[20] 8119 2-9-1 **79**... PatCosgrave 8 69
(William Haggas) *s.i.s: hdwy over 5f out: chsd ldr over 3f out tl rdn over 1f out: wknd ins fnl f* **15/8**[1]

1m 28.08s (-0.72) **Going Correction** -0.075s/f (Stan) **7** Ran SP% **115.8**
Speed ratings (Par 98): **101,100,98,97,97 95,93**
CSF £25.14 CT £174.17 TOTE £3.50: £2.20, £2.50; EX 18.60 Trifecta £147.60.
Owner Chelsea Thoroughbreds - Doctor No **Bred** Miss J Chaplin **Trained** Kimpton, Hants

FOCUS
A useful nursery won by a progressive type who could reach a rating in the low 90s.

8406 £10 FREE AT 32RED.COM MAIDEN STKS 5f 216y (Tp)
4:45 (4:46) (Class 5) 2-Y-O **£3,557** (£1,058; £529; £264) **Stalls** Low

Form RPR

2 **1** **Second Thought (IRE)**[202] 2696 2-9-5 0.............................. PatCosgrave 8 82+
(William Haggas) *hld up in tch: led on bit 1f out: easily* **4/11**[1]

6522 **2** *1 3/4* **Bithynia (IRE)**[53] 7578 2-9-0 69.. JFEgan 7 65
(David Evans) *led: pushed along 2f out: rdn and hdd 1f out: styd on same pce* **4/1**[2]

3 1/2 **School Run (IRE)** 2-9-0 0 .... JoeFanning 10 64
(David O'Meara) *racd keenly and prom: wnt 2nd over 4f out: shkn up and ev ch over 1f out: styd on same pce ins fnl f* **8/1**[3]
0 4 shd **Alfonso Manana (IRE)**[15] 8175 2-9-5 0 .... RichardKingscote 4 69
(James Given) *prom: pushed along 1/2-way: rdn and hung lft over 1f out: styd on* **11/1**
5 3 **Highly Focussed (IRE)** 2-9-5 0 .... LukeMorris 6 59
(Ann Duffield) *chsd ldrs: rdn over 2f out: wknd ins fnl f* **25/1**
40 6 1 1/2 **Panther In Pink (IRE)**[20] 8118 2-9-0 0 .... ShaneGray 12 50
(Ann Duffield) *hld up: rdn over 1f out: nvr on terms* **66/1**
0 7 1/2 **Ventura Jazz**[20] 8119 2-9-0 0 .... PatrickMathers 2 48
(Richard Fahey) *s.i.s: sn pushed along in rr: nvr nrr* **33/1**
00 8 nk **Slave To Freedom**[17] 8140 2-8-9 0 .... RowanScott(5) 13 47
(Ann Duffield) *hld up: pushed along 1/2-way: n.d* **66/1**
9 1 **Fiery Spice (IRE)** 2-9-2 0 .... EoinWalsh(3) 1 49
(Robert Cowell) *s.s: outpcd: hung lft fr over 2f out* **20/1**

1m 14.44s (-0.06) **Going Correction** -0.075s/f (Stan) 9 Ran SP% **127.3**
Speed ratings (Par 96): **97,94,94,93,89 87,87,86,85**
CSF £2.54 TOTE £1.30: £1.10, £1.30, £2.10; EX 2.80 Trifecta £8.40.
Owner Liam Sheridan **Bred** Tally-Ho Stud **Trained** Newmarket, Suffolk

FOCUS
An uncompetitive maiden and easy pickings for the short-priced favourite.

8407 BETWAY H'CAP 5f 216y (Tp)
5:15 (5:19) (Class 2) (0-105,100) 3-Y-O £12,349 (£3,696; £1,848; £925; £460) **Stalls** Low

Form RPR
3006 1 **Jordan Sport**[32] 7958 3-8-3 **82** .... WilliamCarson 10 91
(David Simcock) *led: hdd over 4f out: remained handy: chsd ldr over 2f out: shkn up to ld over 1f out: rdn out* **11/1**
0403 2 1/2 **Gentlemen**[23] 8069 5-9-1 **94** .... JosephineGordon 8 101
(Phil McEntee) *chsd ldrs: rdn over 2f out: r.o* **8/1**
1441 3 3/4 **Dougan**[42] 7803 4-9-7 **100** .... JFEgan 7 105+
(David Evans) *hld up in tch: racd keenly: rdn over 1f out: r.o* **3/1**[1]
6002 4 3/4 **Distant Past**[29] 7990 5-8-8 **87** ....(p) ShaneGray 2 89
(Kevin Ryan) *sn pushed along and prom: rdn and hung lft over 1f out: styd on* **22/1**
2030 5 1/2 **Related**[23] 8069 6-9-1 **94** ....(b) LukeMorris 9 95
(Paul Midgley) *chsd ldrs: wnt 2nd over 3f out tl rdn over 2f out: styd on same pce ins fnl f* **12/1**
0550 6 hd **Zac Brown (IRE)**[14] 8192 5-8-5 **87** ....(t) RobHornby(3) 11 87
(Charlie Wallis) *sn w ldr: led over 4f out: rdn and hdd over 1f out: no ex wl ins fnl f* **28/1**
1-00 7 nk **Angelic Lord (IRE)**[279] 921 4-9-7 **100** .... RichardKingscote 1 99
(Tom Dascombe) *hld up: styd on fr over 1f out: nt trble ldrs* **14/1**
1002 8 1 **Upavon**[14] 8192 6-8-12 **91** ....(t) PatCosgrave 4 89+
(Stuart Williams) *s.s: hld up: rdn and hung lft ins fnl f: nt clr run towards fin: nt trble ldrs* **7/2**[2]
2000 9 nk **Suzi's Connoisseur**[69] 7156 5-9-4 **97** ....(vt) AdamBeschizza 3 94+
(Stuart Williams) *s.s: hld up: styng on whn nt clr run wl ins fnl f* **10/1**
003 10 1 1/2 **Kasbah (IRE)**[11] 8232 4-8-10 **92** .... KieranShoemark(3) 6 82
(Amanda Perrett) *hld up: rdn over 1f out: nt trble ldrs* **13/2**[3]
3116 11 1/2 **Ballesteros**[14] 8192 7-8-6 **85** .... PatrickMathers 5 73
(Richard Fahey) *mid-div: sn pushed along: rdn over 2f out: wknd fnl f* **25/1**

1m 12.61s (-1.89) **Going Correction** -0.075s/f (Stan) course record 11 Ran SP% **115.1**
Speed ratings (Par 109): **109,108,107,106,105 105,105,103,103,101 100**
CSF £91.61 CT £332.63 TOTE £14.40: £3.40, £2.30, £1.40; EX 125.70 Trifecta £553.30.
Owner M Khan X2 Pip Walter Harry Wigan **Bred** Rabbah Bloodstock Limited **Trained** Newmarket, Suffolk

FOCUS
A competitive sprint, in which the pace held up, and strong AW form rated around the runner-up.

8408 BETWAY SPRINT DISTANCE H'CAP (DIV I) 5f 20y (Tp)
5:45 (5:47) (Class 6) (0-55,55) 3-Y-O+ **£2,749** (£818; £408; £204) **Stalls** Low

Form RPR
0061 1 **Secret Bird (IRE)**[22] 8079 4-8-12 **53** .... LuluStanford(7) 10 61
(Dean Ivory) *mde all: rdn over 1f out: edgd lft ins fnl f: r.o* **7/2**[1]
3536 2 2 **Chandresh**[7] 8289 3-9-0 **48** ....(b[1]) LukeMorris 1 49
(Robert Cowell) *chsd ldrs: chsd wnr over 1f out: sn rdn: styd on same pce ins fnl f* **9/1**
4364 3 1/2 **Tasaaboq**[6] 8316 5-9-7 **55** ....(t) JosephineGordon 9 54
(Phil McEntee) *pushed along in rr early: rdn over 1f out: hung lft and r.o ins fnl f* **7/2**[1]
6060 4 1 1/2 **Quality Art (USA)**[27] 8040 8-9-3 **54** .... RobHornby(3) 2 48
(Simon Hodgson) *prom: rdn over 1f out: styd on same pce ins fnl f* **8/1**
0353 5 1 **Fossa**[8] 8278 6-8-12 **46** .... WilliamCarson 3 37
(Mark Brisbourne) *prom: rdn and hung lft fr over 1f out: styd on* **13/2**[3]
-303 6 hd **Fanci That (IRE)**[65] 7276 3-9-5 **53** .... PatCosgrave 5 42
(Rae Guest) *hld up: hdwy over 1f out: no ex ins fnl f* **5/1**[2]
2524 7 1 1/2 **Presto Boy**[20] 8121 4-8-9 **50** ....(e) NicolaCurrie(7) 6 34
(Richard Hughes) *s.i.s: pushed along early in rr: rdn and hung lft ins fnl f: nt trble ldrs* **11/1**
3326 8 2 1/4 **Willow Spring**[55] 7533 4-9-0 **51** .... TimClark(3) 7 27
(Denis Quinn) *chsd ldrs: rdn over 1f out: wknd ins fnl f* **22/1**
0-06 9 1 1/4 **Zophilly (IRE)**[206] 2560 3-9-2 **55** ....(t[1]) DavidParkes(5) 4 26
(Jeremy Gask) *hld up: rdn over 1f out: n.d* **50/1**
U-00 10 hd **Or So (USA)**[16] 8156 4-9-1 **52** ....(v) NoelGarbutt(3) 8 23
(Derek Shaw) *s.i.s: outpcd* **40/1**
6200 11 hd **Emerald Bay**[18] 8137 3-9-7 **55** ....(b[1]) LiamKeniry 11 25
(Ronald Thompson) *chsd wnr tl rdn over 1f out: wknd fnl f* **66/1**

1m 1.28s (-0.62) **Going Correction** -0.075s/f (Stan) 11 Ran SP% **114.1**
Speed ratings (Par 101): **101,97,97,94,93 92,90,86,84,84 84**
CSF £33.90 CT £119.03 TOTE £4.50: £1.60, £2.70, £1.40; EX 39.30 Trifecta £138.30.
Owner Cynthia Smith & Radlett Racing **Bred** Hadi Al Tajir **Trained** Radlett, Herts
■ Stewards' Enquiry : Lulu Stanford one-day ban; did not keep straight from the stalls (30th Dec)
Liam Keniry one-day ban; did not keep straight from the stalls (30th Dec)

FOCUS
A low-grade handicap dominated by the winner. The second and third highlight the limitations of the form.

8409 BETWAY SPRINT DISTANCE H'CAP (DIV II) 5f 20y (Tp)
6:15 (6:15) (Class 6) (0-55,55) 3-Y-O+ **£2,749** (£818; £408; £204) **Stalls** Low

Form RPR
1650 1 **Captain Scooby**[1] 8390 10-9-4 **52** ....(b) JFEgan 7 61
(Richard Guest) *hld up: hdwy and edgd rt over 1f out: led ins fnl f: edgd lft: rdn out* **6/1**[3]
6042 2 1 1/4 **Kodimoor (IRE)**[52] 7596 3-9-5 **53** ....(bt) KieranO'Neill 4 57
(Christopher Kellett) *s.i.s: hld up: hdwy over 1f out: rdn and ev ch whn edgd rt ins fnl f: no ex towards fin* **10/3**[1]
5460 3 1 1/2 **Fabulous Flyer**[135] 5007 3-8-8 **47** .... DavidParkes(5) 10 46
(Jeremy Gask) *s.i.s: hld up: nt clr run over 1f out: rdn and r.o ins fnl f: nt rch ldrs* **25/1**
0000 4 nk **Eland Ally**[73] 7046 8-9-3 **51** ....(b) JosephineGordon 8 49
(Anabel K Murphy) *prom: racd keenly: rdn over 1f out: styd on* **16/1**
0000 5 shd **Roy's Legacy**[15] 8181 7-9-7 **55** .... TomMarquand 9 52
(Shaun Harris) *chsd ldr: led over 1f out: rdn and hdd ins fnl f: styd on same pce* **16/1**
0026 6 1 **Whispering Soul (IRE)**[80] 6852 3-9-6 **54** .... PatCosgrave 2 48
(Brian Baugh) *chsd ldrs: rdn and edgd lft over 1f out: no ex ins fnl f* **8/1**
0000 7 1/2 **Charlie Lad**[16] 8149 4-9-7 **55** .... LukeMorris 6 47
(Daniel Mark Loughnane) *mid-div: hdwy 1/2-way: rdn over 1f out: styd on same pce fnl f* **6/1**[3]
-665 8 shd **Leith Bridge**[16] 8149 4-9-5 **53** .... LiamKeniry 11 44
(Mark Usher) *hld up: hdwy whn hmpd over 1f out: n.d after* **9/1**
4450 9 3/4 **Hurricane Alert**[37] 7863 4-8-12 **46** oh1 .... AdamBeschizza 5 35
(Mark Hoad) *prom: plld hrd: rdn and nt clr run over 1f out: no ex fnl f* **20/1**
1002 10 6 **Harpers Ruby**[35] 7913 6-9-7 **55** .... PaddyAspell 3 22
(Lynn Siddall) *chsd ldrs: rdn over 1f out: sn wknd* **4/1**[2]
1300 11 nk **Knockamany Bends (IRE)**[38] 7860 6-9-1 **49** ....(tp) WilliamCarson 1 15
(John Wainwright) *led: rdn and hdd over 1f out: wknd fnl f* **18/1**

1m 1.54s (-0.36) **Going Correction** -0.075s/f (Stan) 11 Ran SP% **118.4**
Speed ratings (Par 101): **99,97,96,94,93 92,91,91,90,80 80**
CSF £26.46 CT £482.02 TOTE £6.40: £2.20, £2.00, £7.00; EX 32.40 Trifecta £1400.00.
Owner The Captain Scooby Syndicate **Bred** Hellwood Stud Farm & Paul Davies (h'Gate) **Trained** Ingmanthorpe, W Yorks

FOCUS
The second division was run 0.26sec slower than the first leg. The fast pace suited the winner. The runner-up helps with the opening level.

8410 BETWAY APP H'CAP 1m 4f 50y (Tp)
6:45 (6:46) (Class 6) (0-60,60) 3-Y-O+ **£2,749** (£818; £408; £204) **Stalls** Low

Form RPR
0535 1 **Kay Sera**[35] 7910 8-9-1 **54** .... EoinWalsh(3) 10 60
(Tony Newcombe) *hld up: hdwy over 2f out: hung lft fr over 1f out: r.o u.p to ld nr fin* **6/1**[3]
0400 2 1/2 **Hydrant**[17] 8142 10-9-10 **60** .... JFEgan 8 65
(Richard Guest) *led: rdn over 1f out: hdd nr fin* **33/1**
0002 3 shd **Canford Thompson**[29] 7992 3-9-5 **60** .... JoeFanning 2 65
(Mark Walford) *hld up: pushed along over 2f out: hdwy and nt clr run over 1f out: rdn and hung lft ins fnl f: r.o* **13/8**[1]
1062 4 1/2 **Monna Valley**[15] 8179 4-9-7 **60** .... AaronJones(3) 1 64
(Stuart Williams) *chsd ldrs: rdn and ev ch ins fnl f: unable qck towards fin* **9/2**[2]
0530 5 2 **Rainbow Lad (IRE)**[14] 8193 3-8-13 **54** .... LukeMorris 9 55
(Michael Appleby) *chsd ldr after 1f: rdn over 1f out: styd on same pce ins fnl f* **8/1**
6035 6 2 **Kerry Icon**[59] 7438 3-8-5 **46** oh1 .... WilliamCarson 12 44
(Iain Jardine) *plld hrd and prom: rdn over 2f out: nt clr run over 1f out: no ex ins fnl f* **25/1**
4056 7 nk **Filament Of Gold (USA)**[27] 8038 5-9-6 **56** ....(p) JosephineGordon 4 53
(Roy Brotherton) *hld up: rdn over 2f out: styd on: nt trble ldrs* **9/1**
220 8 3/4 **Tingo In The Tale (IRE)**[79] 6871 7-9-8 **58** .... TimmyMurphy 11 54
(Sophie Leech) *chsd ldrs: rdn whn nt clr run over 1f out: hung lft and no ex fnl f* **20/1**
300 9 1 **Foylesideview (IRE)**[34] 7937 4-8-10 **46** oh1 .... MartinDwyer 6 41
(Harry Chisman) *hld up: hdwy over 3f out: rdn over 1f out: wknd ins fnl f* **16/1**
336/ 10 2 3/4 **Sweeping Rock (IRE)**[57] 7182 6-9-3 **53** ....(t) TomMarquand 5 43
(John Spearing) *prom: rdn over 2f out: wknd ins fnl f* **66/1**
0564 11 15 **Paddy's Rock (IRE)**[27] 8038 5-9-3 **53** .... PaddyAspell 7 19
(Lynn Siddall) *hld up: rdn over 3f out: sn wknd* **10/1**
0000 12 5 **Briac (FR)**[65] 7280 5-8-10 **46** oh1 .... JohnFahy 3 4
(Jim Best) *s.i.s: hdwy into mid-div: 10f out: rdn and wknd over 3f out* **50/1**

2m 40.73s (-0.07) **Going Correction** -0.075s/f (Stan)
WFA 3 from 4yo+ 5lb 12 Ran SP% **121.6**
Speed ratings (Par 101): **97,96,96,96,94 93,93,92,92,90 80,77**
CSF £200.15 CT £472.56 TOTE £7.30: £2.20, £6.90, £1.10; EX 85.10.
Owner Nigel Hardy **Bred** Nigel Hardy **Trained** Yarnscombe, Devon

FOCUS
A modest handicap, but it was competitive for the grade and has been rated around the principals.

8411 BETWAY MIDDLE DISTANCE H'CAP 1m 1f 103y (Tp)
7:15 (7:16) (Class 6) (0-65,67) 3-Y-O **£2,749** (£818; £408; £204) **Stalls** Low

Form RPR
0005 1 **Kingthistle**[23] 8064 3-9-5 **63** .... StevieDonohoe 8 69
(Ian Williams) *plld hrd early in 2nd: rdn over 1f out: styd on u.p to ld post* **4/1**[2]
1P50 2 nse **Heads You Win**[9] 8257 3-9-6 **64** .... TimmyMurphy 11 70
(Jamie Osborne) *led: rdn over 1f out: hdd post* **33/1**
3600 3 1 1/4 **Qortaaj**[7] 8287 3-9-9 **67** .... ShaneKelly 6 71
(David Loughnane) *hld up in tch: rdn ins fnl f: styd on same pce* **8/1**
0031 4 2 1/2 **Scribner Creek (IRE)**[13] 8207 3-9-4 **62** .... DaleSwift 7 61
(Daniel Mark Loughnane) *plld hrd and prom: rdn over 1f out: no ex ins fnl f* **9/4**[1]
3046 5 1 **Pivotal Dream (IRE)**[14] 8194 3-8-7 **51** oh6 .... LukeMorris 4 48
(Mark Brisbourne) *hld up: hdwy u.p over 1f out: styd on same pce ins fnl f* **20/1**
050 6 3/4 **Yasood (IRE)**[31] 7969 3-8-13 **57** ....(v[1]) JosephineGordon 9 52
(Phil McEntee) *s.i.s: wnt prom over 6f out: rdn over 2f out: no ex fnl f* **12/1**
315 7 2 1/2 **Gold Return (IRE)**[37] 7870 3-9-5 **63** .... JFEgan 2 54
(John Ryan) *plld hrd and prom: rdn over 2f out: wknd ins fnl f* **5/1**[3]
40-0 8 4 1/2 **Mr Globetrotter (USA)**[236] 1671 3-9-7 **65** .... MartinDwyer 1 47
(Iain Jardine) *s.i.s: hld up: rdn over 3f out: nvr on terms* **7/1**
00 9 22 **Coillte Mach**[14] 8188 3-9-2 **60** .... PatCosgrave 10
(David O'Meara) *hld up: plld hrd and hung rt: hdwy over 4f out: wknd over 2f out* **18/1**
600 10 3 1/4 **Just For Show (IRE)**[122] 5504 3-9-1 **62** .... KieranShoemark(3) 3
(Shaun Lycett) *hld up: rdn and wknd over 3f out* **25/1**

2m 3.05s (2.25) **Going Correction** -0.075s/f (Stan) 10 Ran SP% **115.6**
Speed ratings (Par 98): **87,86,85,83,82 82,79,75,56,53**
CSF £130.86 CT £1009.83 TOTE £5.20: £2.20, £5.60, £2.70; EX 149.90 Trifecta £821.00.
Owner E A Brook **Bred** R C Bond **Trained** Portway, Worcs

The Form Book, Raceform Ltd, Newbury, RG14 5SJ

FOCUS
Just a modest handicap.
T/Plt: £50.60 to a £1 stake. Pool: £86,058.34 - 1,240.86 winning tickets T/Qpdt: £9.80 to a £1 stake. Pool: £11,259.01 - 846.54 winning tickets **Colin Roberts**

8412 - 8419a (Foreign Racing) - See Raceform Interactive

[8368]DEAUVILLE (R-H)
Friday, December 16

OFFICIAL GOING: Polytrack: standard

8420a PRIX DE GIBERVILLE (MAIDEN) (2YO) (POLYTRACK) 7f 110y
11:55 (12:00) 2-Y-O **£9,926** (£3,970; £2,977; £1,985; £992)

RPR
1 **Prost (GER)**[49] 7665 2-9-2 0 GregoryBenoist 8 78
(Ed Vaughan) *broke wl: chsd ldng pair: 3rd and drvn 1 1/2f out: styd on to ld ins fnl f: rdn out to hold off runner-up* **117/10**
2 *hd* **Desert Strom (IRE)**[70] 2-8-13 0 MaximeGuyon 5 75
(Mme Pia Brandt, France) **14/1**
3 *1 3/4* **Black Poweer (FR)** 2-9-2 0 Pierre-CharlesBoudot 2 73
(P Sogorb, France) **3/1**[1]
4 *1/2* **Aluqdah (FR)** 2-9-2 0 SebastienMartino 4 72
(H-A Pantall, France) **29/1**
5 *nk* **Sandara (FR)**[70] 2-8-13 0 TheoBachelot 11 69
(H-F Devin, France) **9/1**
6 *1 1/4* **Cicada (FR)** 2-8-13 0 ThierryThulliez 3 66
(Y Durepaire, France) **13/1**
7 *1* **Etoile Bere (FR)**[29] 7996 2-8-13 0 StephanePasquier 1 63
(N Clement, France) **42/10**[2]
8 *shd* **Couville (FR)**[109] 5986 2-8-13 0 CristianDemuro 12 63
(Mme Pia Brandt, France) **26/5**[3]
9 *1/2* **Merci Patron (FR)**[155] 4330 2-9-0 0 ow1 JulianResimont(3) 14 66
(N Caullery, France) **36/1**
10 *3/4* **Gasalto (FR)**[18] 2-8-10 0 ClementLecoeuvre(6) 15 63
(F-H Graffard, France) **55/1**
11 *1* **Malefique (FR)** 2-8-5 0 TristanBaron(8) 7 58
(H-A Pantall, France) **112/1**
12 *3/4* **Galpi (IRE)**[38] 2-8-13 0 LukasDelozier 16 56
(H-A Pantall, France) **44/1**
13 *7* **L'Astrolabe (FR)**[152] 2-8-13 0 IoritzMendizabal 9 40
(J Baudron, France) **74/10**
14 *3/4* **Parinacota (FR)**[16] 2-8-13 0 DavidBreux 13 38
(Mlle V Dissaux, France) **60/1**
15 *4* **Septimius (IRE)** 2-8-10 0 ow1 ThibaultSpeicher(4) 6 29
(E J O'Neill, France) **122/1**
16 *5* **Nouvelle Vision (FR)** 2-8-13 0 FabriceVeron 10 17
(E Libaud, France) **47/1**

WIN (incl. 1 euro stake): 12.70. PLACES: 4.50, 3.90, 2.30. DF: 97.50. SF: 209.00
Owner Hawkes Anzac Partnership **Bred** Lord W Huntingdon U L Norris **Trained** Newmarket, Suffolk

8421a PRIX DE LA TUILERIE (H'CAP) (4YO+) (POLYTRACK) 1m 1f 110y
2:05 (12:00) 4-Y-O+ **£5,514** (£2,205; £1,654; £1,102; £551)

RPR
1 **Taboule**[109] 6-9-5 0 FabriceVeron 8 61
(Carla O'Halloran, France) **22/1**
2 *1 3/4* **Golden Buck (FR)**[17] 6-9-3 0 JeromeCabre 6 55
(P Van De Poele, France) **51/10**[2]
3 *hd* **Bubble Brook (FR)**[21] 5-9-3 0 PierreBazire 2 55
(S Kobayashi, France) **42/10**[1]
4 *1/2* **Gentle Maine (IRE)**[70] 6-9-4 0 (b) MaximeGuyon 4 55
(J-M Beguigne, France) **63/10**[3]
5 *nk* **Uphold**[129] 5281 9-9-4 0 (b) IoritzMendizabal 10 54
(Gay Kelleway) *chsd ldrs on outer: drvn to ld 2f out: sn rdn and hdd appr fnl f: kpt on at one pce* **24/1**
6 *nk* **Orpello (IRE)**[21] 7-9-5 0 (p) MickaelForest 7 54
(Mme G Rarick, France) **9/1**
7 *hd* **Anouma Freedom (FR)**[58] 5-9-6 0 (p) TristanNormand 14 55
(H De Nicolay, France) **49/1**
8 *1/2* **Lady's Spring (FR)**[17] 5-9-3 0 StephaneLaurent 13 51
(Mlle G Gadbled, France) **38/1**
9 *1* **My Darling Memory (FR)**[17] 5-9-6 0 MarcNobili 9 52
(Rod Collet, France) **15/1**
10 *snk* **Ciaratza (FR)**[28] 4-9-4 0 (p) LudovicBoisseau 11 50
(Mme S Adet, France) **31/1**
11 *shd* **Vol Dolois (FR)**[21] 6-9-1 0 (b) ClementLecoeuvre(5) 1 51
(A Bonin, France) **63/10**[3]
12 *nk* **Live Miracle (USA)**[54] 4-9-5 0 (b) TheoBachelot 3 50
(P Monfort, France) **12/1**
13 *snk* **Chicago Bere (FR)**[31] 4-9-4 0 EddyHardouin 16 48
(Leo Braem, Belgium) **14/1**
14 *3* **Eba Chope (FR)**[21] 5-9-4 0 AntoineHamelin 12 42
(Mme M-C Naim, France) **52/1**
15 *4* **Albertochop (FR)**[31] 4-9-2 0 (b) SebastienMaillot 5 32
(T Van Den Troost, Belgium) **20/1**
16 *3/4* **Arluno (FR)**[58] 7-9-1 0 QuentinGervais(3) 15 33
(J-Y Artu, France) **37/1**

Owner Martial Prouheze **Bred** Biddestone Stud **Trained** France
WIN (incl. 1 euro stake): 23.60. Places: 5.50, 2.30, 2.00. DF: 78.90. SF: 175.50.

8422a PRIX DE LA BRIQUETERIE (H'CAP) (4YO+) (POLYTRACK) 1m 1f 110y
2:40 (12:00) 4-Y-O+ **£4,779** (£1,911; £1,433; £955; £477)

RPR
1 **Godric**[53] 4-9-4 0 MaximeGuyon 5 58
(J Carayon, France) **9/5**[1]
2 *2* **Freedom Tales (FR)**[107] 5-9-2 0 (b) LudovicBoisseau 12 52
(L Cendra, France) **37/1**
3 *2* **Levelyne (FR)**[117] 4-9-5 0 FabriceVeron 11 51
(J Bourgeais, France) **33/1**
4 *nk* **Fantastic Way (FR)**[212] 7-9-0 0 (b) JeremieMonteiro(5) 15 50
(Mme C Barande-Barbe, France) **63/1**
5 *nk* **Trois Points (FR)**[106] 4-9-6 0 IoritzMendizabal 9 51
(Gay Kelleway) *w.w in fnl 3rd on inner: in fnl quartet and pushed along over 3f out: hdwy on inner appr 1 1/2f out: kpt on at same pce u.p fnl f: nvr able to get on terms* **11/1**
6 *hd* **Jazz Et Salsa (FR)**[21] 5-9-4 0 (b) EddyHardouin 3 48
(J-L Mace, France) **13/1**
7 *hd* **Bridjnaia (FR)**[21] 7-9-6 0 (p) SylvainRuis 2 50
(C Bauer, France) **28/1**
8 *3/4* **Susukino (FR)**[497] 7-9-2 0 MlleAlisonMassin(3) 8 47
(S Kobayashi, France) **25/1**
9 *1/2* **Thats Notall Folks (IRE)**[441] 6-9-5 0 StephaneBreux 10 46
(J-P Sauvage, France) **52/1**
10 *nse* **L'Homme Du Lys (FR)**[106] 6-9-3 0 JeromeCabre 6 44
(J-L Guillochon, France) **44/5**
11 *nk* **Raffinee (FR)**[166] 5-9-4 0 GregoryBenoist 1 45
(D Smaga, France) **7/1**[2]
12 *1 3/4* **Layman Junior (FR)**[109] 8-9-5 0 (b) DelphineSantiago 7 42
(S Bossert, France) **22/1**
13 *shd* **American Way (FR)**[17] 4-9-3 0 (p) EmmanuelEtienne 4 40
(M Aubry, France) **25/1**
14 *3/4* **Dauphine De France (FR)**[423] 4-9-3 0 (b) AntoineHamelin 16 38
(J Parize, France) **37/1**
15 *4* **Stormy Star (FR)**[802] 7-9-4 0 TheoBachelot 14 31
(J-V Toux, France) **13/1**
16 *7* **Blue Bere (FR)**[109] 5-9-5 0 (p) GuillaumeFourrier 13 18
(Freddy Grizon, France) **81/10**[3]

WIN (incl. 1 euro stake): 2.80. Places: 1.50, 7.40, 6.30. DF: 66.20. SF: 121.40.
Owner Mlle Alicia Bretel **Bred** Chasemore Farm **Trained** France

[8360]LINGFIELD (L-H)
Saturday, December 17

OFFICIAL GOING: Polytrack: standard
Wind: light, across Weather: foggy

8423 32RED.COM NOVICE STKS 1m 1y(P)
11:45 (11:45) (Class 5) 2-Y-O **£3,881** (£1,155; £577; £288) **Stalls** High

Form RPR
3250 1 **Mr Scaramanga**[97] 6388 2-9-9 99 JimCrowley 4 78
(Simon Dow) *stdd s: hld up in tch in rr: swtchd rt and effrt wl over 1f out: in narrow ld wl ins fnl f: kpt on* **30/100**[1]
04 2 *hd* **Ocean Promise (USA)**[17] 8151 2-8-4 0 FinleyMarsh(7) 2 65
(Richard Hughes) *broke wl: led: rdn over 1f out: 2nd and ev ch wl ins fnl f: kpt on* **12/1**
04 3 *2 1/4* **Mazaaji (FR)**[21] 8119 2-9-2 0 [1] StevieDonohoe 3 65
(George Peckham) *chsd ldr: rdn ent fnl 2f: 3rd and one pced wl ins fnl f* **8/1**[3]
0 4 *1 1/4* **King Of Scotland (FR)**[24] 8063 2-9-2 0 RobertWinston 1 62
(Hughie Morrison) *trckd ldrs: effrt wl over 1f out: 4th and one pced wl ins fnl f* **7/1**[2]

1m 40.16s (1.96) **Going Correction** -0.05s/f (Stan) 4 Ran SP% **108.2**
Speed ratings (Par 96): **88,87,85,84**
CSF £4.71 TOTE £1.10; EX 4.40 Trifecta £11.00.
Owner Robert Moss and Christopher Brennan **Bred** Lordship Stud **Trained** Ashtead, Surrey

FOCUS
An uncompetitive novice event in which the visibility was poor due to the fog. The red-hot favourite got the job done, but only just. The level is fluid.

8424 DOWNLOAD THE BETWAY APP H'CAP 1m 4f (P)
12:15 (12:15) (Class 2) (0-100,101) 3-Y-O+ **£11,971** (£3,583; £1,791; £896; £446) **Stalls** Low

Form RPR
5335 1 **Pinzolo**[17] 8160 5-9-7 97 SeanLevey 4 108
(Ismail Mohammed) *mde all and set stdy: pushed along and clr 2f out: in command and styd on wl fr over 1f out* **5/2**[1]
0405 2 *2 1/4* **Barye**[14] 8210 5-9-11 101 ShaneKelly 1 108
(Richard Hughes) *stdd s: hld up in last pair: clsd and swtchd rt over 2f out: effrt in 4th 2f out: kpt on u.p to chse clr ldr ins fnl f: nvr getting on terms and eased towards fin* **3/1**[2]
3315 3 *1 3/4* **Rydan (IRE)**[84] 6775 5-9-0 90 (v) TomQueally 2 94
(Gary Moore) *in tch in midfield: effrt to chse ldrs 2f out: styd on same pce fr over 1f out* **6/1**
3060 4 *2* **Hamelin (IRE)**[21] 8123 6-9-7 97 StevieDonohoe 6 98
(George Scott) *stdd s: hld up in tch in last pair: effrt in 6th 2f out: kpt on ins fnl f: wnt 4th towards fin: no threat to wnr* **16/1**
4-0 5 *3/4* **Novis Adventus (IRE)**[14] 8210 4-9-6 96 MartinHarley 3 96
(Jeremy Noseda) *chsd wnr for 2f: styd chsng ldrs tl wnt 2nd again and rdn over 2f out: no imp: lost 2nd and wknd ins fnl f* **10/1**
4020 6 *6* **Sunblazer (IRE)**[14] 8210 6-8-12 95 (t) JoshuaBryan(7) 7 85
(Kim Bailey) *hld up in tch in midfield: effrt 2f out: no imp and sn outpcd: wknd fnl f* **10/1**
6650 7 *1 1/4* **Luv U Whatever**[45] 7765 6-9-1 91 LukeMorris 8 79
(Michael Attwater) *chsd wnr after 2f: shkn up over 4f out: drvn and lost pl over 2f out: wknd over 1f out* **25/1**
5400 8 *104* **Gavlar**[31] 7979 5-9-0 90 JimCrowley 5
(William Knight) *in tch in midfield: rdn and lost pl over 4f out: lost tch qckly: t.o and virtually p.u over 1f out* **4/1**[3]

2m 27.93s (-5.07) **Going Correction** -0.05s/f (Stan) 8 Ran SP% **115.8**
Speed ratings (Par 109): **114,112,111,110,109 105,104,**
CSF £10.31 CT £39.65 TOTE £3.70: £1.50, £1.40, £2.10; EX 10.20 Trifecta £43.70.
Owner Sultan Ali **Bred** Fittocks Stud **Trained** Newmarket, Suffolk

FOCUS
A warm middle-distance handicap, but it became a tactical event in the murk. The winner has been rated close to his old form, with the runner-up running as well as ever.

8425 32RED CASINO (S) STKS 5f 6y(P)
12:50 (12:51) (Class 6) 2-Y-O **£2,911** (£866; £432; £216) **Stalls** High

Form RPR
4303 1 **Spin Top**[12] 8230 2-9-0 58 (v) LiamKeniry 7 64
(Joseph Tuite) *mde all: pushed along and clr over 1f out: kpt on wl fnl f: unchal* **5/1**[3]
05 2 *2* **Warba (IRE)**[17] 8151 2-8-9 0 JFEgan 9 52
(Mohamed Moubarak) *chsd wnr after 1f: effrt over 1f out: sn drvn: clr 2nd but no imp on wnr fnl f: kpt on* **7/2**[2]

4203 **3** 2 1/2 **Black Bubba (IRE)**[12] 8229 2-9-0 67 PatCosgrave 4 48
(David Evans) *t.k.h: hld up in midfield: effrt 2f out: chsd ldng pair ent fnl f: one pced and no imp fnl f* **11/10**[1]

0300 **4** 3/4 **Lawfilly**[17] 8153 2-8-9 56 (e[1]) ShaneKelly 1 40
(Richard Hughes) *in tch in midfield: effrt 2f out: 4th and flashed tail u.p ins fnl f: one pced* **8/1**

0 **5** 1 3/4 **Port Master**[77] 6952 2-9-0 0 MartinHarley 2 39
(Ann Duffield) *stdd s: in tch in last trio: effrt wl over 1f out: no imp fnl f: nvr trbld ldrs* **12/1**

6 nse **Tanksalot (IRE)**[71] 7129 2-8-9 0 LukeMorris 5 34
(Harry Dunlop) *in tch in midfield: hdwy to chse ldrs 3f out: rdn 2f out: lost pl and btn over 1f out: wknd fnl f* **20/1**

7 3/4 **Brean Flyer** 2-8-6 0 EdwardGreatrex(3) 8 31
(Bill Turner) *dwlt: hld up in rr: effrt wl over 1f out: no imp: n.d* **25/1**

6000 **8** nk **Zipedee**[9] 8276 2-8-9 44 (t[1]) DannyBrock 6 30
(John Ryan) *hld up in tch in last trio: effrt and wd bnd 2f out: no hdwy: n.d* **33/1**

00 **9** 1 1/2 **Shillbourne Lad (IRE)**[12] 8230 2-9-0 0 WilliamCarson 3 29
(Bill Turner) *chsd wnr for 1f: styd chsng ldrs: unable qck over 1f out: wknd ins fnl f* **50/1**

59.01s (0.21) **Going Correction** -0.05s/f (Stan) **9** Ran SP% **118.8**
Speed ratings (Par 94): **96,92,88,87,84 84,83,83,80**
CSF £22.65 TOTE £5.90: £1.20, £2.50, £1.10; EX 26.80 Trifecta £44.20.There was no bid for the winner
Owner The Spin Top Partnership **Bred** Newsells Park Stud **Trained** Lambourn, Berks

FOCUS
Effectively a maiden seller and a moderate one at that. The front pair held those positions throughout.

8426 EBF STALLIONS BREEDING WINNERS FILLIES' CONDITIONS STKS 1m 1y(P)
1:25 (1:25) (Class 3) 3-Y-O+ **£10,396** (£3,111; £1,555; £778; £387) **Stalls** High

Form RPR

4313 **1** **Somethingthrilling**[17] 8160 4-9-1 90 JimCrowley 4 95+
(David Elsworth) *hld up in tch in midfield: rdn and hdwy over 1f out: led ins fnl f: sn in command and r.o strly: readily* **7/4**[2]

4103 **2** 2 1/4 **Summer Icon**[17] 8158 3-9-0 87 MartinHarley 2 89
(Mick Channon) *led: rdn and qcknd 2f out: drvn ent fnl f: hdd ins fnl f: sn outpcd by wnr and one pced after* **8/1**[3]

2141 **3** 1/2 **Bargain Buy**[17] 8158 3-9-0 87 PatCosgrave 5 88+
(William Haggas) *stdd and dropped in bhd after s: hld up in tch in rr: effrt on inner whn nt clr run over 1f out: hdwy ent fnl f: kpt on: no threat to wnr* **6/4**[1]

0065 **4** 1 **Bint Dandy (IRE)**[22] 8098 5-8-10 90 (p[1]) GeorgiaCox(5) 7 86
(Chris Dwyer) *chsd ldrs: effrt to chse ldr 2f out: drifted rt and lost pl over 1f out: kpt on same pce ins fnl f* **10/1**

3004 **5** 1/2 **Daisy Bere (FR)**[29] 8007 3-8-9 78 JordanVaughan(5) 6 84
(K R Burke) *hld up in tch in last pair: effrt 2f out: kpt on same pce ins fnl f: no threat to wnr* **16/1**

1404 **6** 3 **Yeah Baby Yeah (IRE)**[22] 8098 3-9-5 92 (p) AaronJones(3) 1 85
(Gay Kelleway) *chsd ldr tl 2f out: sn rdn and unable qck: wknd ins fnl f* **10/1**

1m 36.19s (-2.01) **Going Correction** -0.05s/f (Stan)
WFA 3 from 4yo+ 1lb **6** Ran SP% **111.5**
Speed ratings (Par 104): **108,105,105,104,103 100**
CSF £15.54 TOTE £2.70: £1.40, £3.10; EX 14.20 Trifecta £27.00.
Owner Trebles Holford Thoroughbreds **Bred** Trebles Holford Farm Thoroughbreds **Trained** Newmarket, Suffolk

FOCUS
A decent fillies' conditions event, but a race of contrasting fortunes for the two market leaders. The form is set around the runner-up, with the fifth also limiting the form.

8427 BETWAY QUEBEC STKS (LISTED RACE) 1m 2f (P)
2:00 (2:01) (Class 1) 3-Y-O+
£22,684 (£8,600; £4,304; £2,144; £1,076; £540) **Stalls** Low

Form RPR

0521 **1** **Battalion (IRE)**[17] 8160 6-9-3 106 WilliamCarson 5 103+
(Jamie Osborne) *dwlt: hld up in tch in midfield: clsd to chse ldrs on inner and nt clr run 2f out: wnt 2nd and swtchd rt and over 1f out: qcknd to ld jst ins fnl f: r.o strly* **9/2**

3122 **2** 1 1/2 **Dubai Fashion (IRE)**[42] 7823 3-8-9 100 PatCosgrave 3 95+
(Saeed bin Suroor) *chsd ldrs: effrt over 1f out: hdwy u.p 1f out: chsd wnr 100yds out: kpt on but no threat to wnr* **9/4**[2]

1114 **3** 1/2 **Grendisar (IRE)**[35] 7934 6-9-3 112 (p) GeorgeBaker 6 99+
(Marco Botti) *stdd s: hld up in tch in last pair: clsd and nt clrst of runs over 1f out: hdwy ent fnl f: edgd lft u.p ins fnl f: wnt 3rd and kpt on fnl 100yds: no threat to wnr* **15/8**[1]

0061 **4** 1 1/4 **Forceful Appeal (USA)**[10] 8251 8-9-3 88 JFEgan 7 96
(Simon Dow) *stdd s: hld up in rr: rdn over 1f out: hdwy 1f out: swtchd rt ins fnl f: kpt on to go 4th last strides: no threat to wnr* **50/1**

5404 **5** nk **Brandybend (IRE)**[62] 7395 4-8-12 96 LukeMorris 1 90
(Marco Botti) *led and set stdy gallop: rdn and qcknd 3f out: 3 l clr 2f: drvn over 1f out: hdd jst ins fnl f: lost 2nd 100yds out: wknd* **33/1**

5022 **6** 8 **Educate**[35] 7934 7-9-3 111 JimCrowley 2 87
(Ismail Mohammed) *chsd ldr tl unable qck u.p over 1f out: lost pl and btn whn lost action and heavily eased ins fnl f (fatally injured)* **7/2**[3]

1033 **7** 3/4 **Mercy Me**[2] 8381 4-8-12 70 DavidProbert 4 73
(John Ryan) *in tch in midfield: rdn jst over 2f out: lost pl over 1f out: wknd and bhd ins fnl f* **125/1**

2m 4.06s (-2.54) **Going Correction** -0.05s/f (Stan)
WFA 3 from 4yo+ 3lb **7** Ran SP% **111.7**
Speed ratings (Par 111): **108,106,106,105,105 98,98**
CSF £14.31 TOTE £5.70: £2.10, £1.80; EX 17.00 Trifecta £49.70.
Owner Melbourne 10 Racing **Bred** Kildaragh Stud **Trained** Upper Lambourn, Berks

FOCUS
A fascinating Listed contest run at a true pace. Muddling form, limited by the fourth and seventh.

8428 BETWAY H'CAP 1m 4f (P)
2:35 (2:35) (Class 6) (0-65,71) 3-Y-O **£3,234** (£962; £481; £240) **Stalls** Low

Form RPR

5234 **1** **Balancing Time**[23] 8084 3-9-6 64 (p) JimCrowley 1 72
(Amanda Perrett) *trckd ldr: effrt ent fnl 2f: rdn and styd on to ld ins fnl f: rdn out* **7/4**[1]

0013 **2** 1 3/4 **Threediamondrings**[7] 8318 3-9-0 61 (t) EdwardGreatrex(3) 8 66
(Brendan Powell) *led: rdn ent fnl 2f: hdd and styd on same pce ins fnl f* **5/1**

-312 **3** 4 1/2 **Reckless Wave (IRE)**[135] 5064 3-9-4 62 ThomasBrown 4 60
(Ed Walker) *stdd s: t.k.h: hld up in rr: clsd and nt clr run ent fnl 2f: rdn and hdwy jst over 1f out: kpt on ins fnl f to snatch 3rd last strides: no threat to ldng pair* **7/2**[2]

0061 **4** nk **Major Ben**[15] 8193 3-9-7 65 JFEgan 3 63
(David Evans) *hld up in midfield: effrt jst over 1f out: chsd clr ldng pair 1f out: no imp and kpt on same pce: lost 3rd last strides* **9/2**[3]

3650 **5** 4 1/2 **Hangman Jury**[17] 8155 3-8-12 56 ShaneKelly 9 46
(Richard Hughes) *stdd s: t.k.h: hld up in rr: clsd over 2f out: rdn: awkward hd carriage and no imp over 1f out* **33/1**

645 **6** shd **Limonata (IRE)**[15] 8193 3-9-5 63 [1] MartinHarley 2 53
(Harry Whittington) *t.k.h: chsd ldrs: wnt 3rd 4f out tl outpcd over 1f out: wknd fnl f* **7/1**

000 **7** 6 **Tractive Effort**[36] 7904 3-8-5 49 LukeMorris 5 30
(Michael Attwater) *stdd s: hld up in last trio: shkn up over 3f out: rdn over 2f out: no hdwy and hung lft over 1f out: wknd fnl f* **25/1**

0605 **8** 1 **Tasteofexcellence (IRE)**[35] 7931 3-8-4 55 RhiainIngram(7) 6 34
(Roger Ingram) *chsd ldrs: rdn 4f out: lost pl bnd 2f out: sn bhd* **40/1**

2m 31.79s (-1.21) **Going Correction** -0.05s/f (Stan) **8** Ran SP% **115.2**
Speed ratings (Par 98): **102,100,97,97,94 94,90,89**
CSF £10.84 CT £27.41 TOTE £2.70: £1.10, £1.70, £1.50; EX 12.40 Trifecta £35.70.
Owner John Connolly & Odile Griffith **Bred** W And R Barnett Ltd **Trained** Pulborough, W Sussex

FOCUS
A moderate 3yo handicap run at an ordinary gallop and another race where those ridden handily were favoured, the front two dominating throughout. Probably another step forward from the runner-up.

8429 BETWAY SPRINT H'CAP (DIV I) 5f 6y(P)
3:10 (3:15) (Class 5) (0-70,71) 3-Y-O+ **£3,234** (£962; £481; £240) **Stalls** High

Form RPR

6006 **1** **Picansort**[32] 7964 9-9-0 62 (b) ShaneKelly 1 71
(Peter Crate) *in tch towards rr: hdwy 1/2-way: trcking ldrs and swtchd lft ent fnl 2f: wnt between rivals and pushed into ld ins fnl f: reminder towards fin: kpt on* **14/1**

3653 **2** 1/2 **Dream Farr (IRE)**[184] 3307 3-9-6 68 (t) ThomasBrown 6 75
(Ed Walker) *s.i.s: sn outpcd and pushed along in rr: hdwy whn nt clr run and swtchd lft 1f out: r.o wl to go 2nd towards fin: nvr quite getting to wnr* **17/2**

1405 **3** 3/4 **Cherry Kool**[86] 6699 3-9-9 71 PatCosgrave 4 76
(Stuart Williams) *in tch in midfield: rdn to chal over 1f out: drvn to ld jst ins fnl f: sn hdd and one pced wl ins fnl f: lost 2nd towards fin* **11/4**[1]

0016 **4** 1 **Dreams Of Glory**[28] 8040 8-9-4 66 AdamBeschizza 8 67
(Ron Hodges) *in tch in midfield: effrt wl over 1f out: kpt on u.p ins fnl f: nvr enough pce to chal* **25/1**

2502 **5** 1/2 **Archie Stevens**[4] 8349 6-9-7 69 RobertWinston 3 68
(David Evans) *w ldr tl rdn to ld over 1f out: hdd jst ins fnl f: no ex and wknd wl ins fnl f* **7/2**[2]

1232 **6** 1/2 **Stormflower**[12] 8228 3-9-7 69 DannyBrock 10 66
(John Bridger) *chsd ldrs: rdn wl over 1f out: unable qck ent fnl f: styd on same pce ins fnl f* **10/1**

2453 **7** 2 **Powerful Dream (IRE)**[28] 8040 3-9-6 68 LukeMorris 2 58
(Ronald Harris) *in tch in midfield: effrt on inner 2f out: drvn and pressing ldrs ent fnl f: no ex and btn ins fnl f: wknd fnl 100yds* **7/1**

4560 **8** 1/2 **Diamond Charlie (IRE)**[12] 8228 8-9-5 67 (p) JFEgan 5 55
(Simon Dow) *dwlt: hld up in last pair: wd bnd 2f out: no imp and kpt on same pce fr over 1f out* **5/1**[3]

0012 **9** hd **Ask The Guru**[17] 8149 6-8-10 58 (p) KierenFox 7 46
(Michael Attwater) *in tch in last trio: rdn and no imp over 1f out: wl hld and one pced ins fnl f* **11/1**

1600 **10** 6 **Annie Salts**[87] 6680 3-8-10 63 GeorgiaCox(5) 9 29
(Chris Dwyer) *taken down early: led: rdn and hdd over 1f out: sn struggling and sltly impeded: wknd ins fnl f* **33/1**

58.08s (-0.72) **Going Correction** -0.05s/f (Stan) **10** Ran SP% **119.5**
Speed ratings (Par 103): **103,102,101,99,98 97,94,93,93,83**
CSF £130.45 CT £441.16 TOTE £16.70: £4.10, £2.80, £1.50; EX 203.40 Trifecta £1440.70.
Owner Peter Crate **Bred** Miss Brooke Sanders **Trained** Newdigate, Surrey

FOCUS
The first division of an ordinary sprint handicap and predictably there was no hanging about. A clear pb from the runner-up, while the third helps set the standard.

8430 BETWAY SPRINT H'CAP (DIV II) 5f 6y(P)
3:40 (3:42) (Class 5) (0-70,70) 3-Y-O+ **£3,234** (£962; £481; £240) **Stalls** High

Form RPR

0055 **1** **The Big Lad**[24] 8067 4-9-5 68 (e[1]) ShaneKelly 2 78
(Richard Hughes) *chsd ldrs: clsd over 2f out: effrt to chal 1f out: rdn to ld wl ins fnl f: rdn out* **11/4**[1]

0000 **2** 1/2 **Mossgo (IRE)**[12] 8228 6-9-2 65 (t) KierenFox 6 73
(John Best) *led and clr w rival tl 2f out: rdn over 1f out: hdd wl ins fnl f: kpt on same pce after* **9/1**

1004 **3** nk **Noble Act**[12] 8228 3-9-4 67 MartinHarley 9 74
(Rae Guest) *w ldr and clr of field tl 2f out: rdn over 1f out: styd on same pce ins fnl f* **12/1**

5044 **4** 1 1/4 **Pharoh Jake**[3] 8365 8-8-12 61 WilliamCarson 8 63
(John Bridger) *chsd ldrs: clsd over 2f out: swtchd rt jst over 1f out: kpt on same pce u.p ins fnl f* **12/1**

5004 **5** hd **Temple Road (IRE)**[150] 4529 8-8-13 62 (bt) AdamBeschizza 1 64+
(Milton Bradley) *dwlt and pushed along leaving stalls: midfield: clsd and swtchd lft jst over 1f out: drvn to press ldrs 1f out: no ex 100yds out: wknd towards fin* **16/1**

0001 **6** 3/4 **Fly True**[17] 8149 3-9-0 68 DavidParkes(5) 3 67+
(Jeremy Gask) *taken down early: short of room sn after s and dropped to rr: hdwy on inner over 1f out: kpt on ins fnl f: swtchd rt wl ins fnl f: nvr trbld ldr* **3/1**[2]

6003 **7** 1 1/4 **Aragon Knight**[12] 8228 3-9-4 70 (b) HectorCrouch(3) 7 65
(Heather Main) *stdd s: t.k.h: effrt 2f out: no imp over 1f out: kpt on same pce ins fnl f* **4/1**[3]

6050 **8** 2 1/4 **Nocturn**[9] 8280 7-9-6 69 (p) LukeMorris 4 55
(Ronald Harris) *a towards rr: n.d* **9/1**

5-25 **9** 2 1/2 **Nora Batt (IRE)**[108] 6018 3-9-6 69 JFEgan 5 46
(David Evans) *midfield and sn pushed along: rdn and no imp over 1f out: wknd ins fnl f* **16/1**

0000 **10** *5* **Rubheira**[147] 4658 4-8-0 **56** oh11....(b) RPWalsh(7) 10 15
(Paul Burgoyne) *stdd after s: sn dropped to rr and n.d* **100/1**
58.51s (-0.29) **Going Correction** -0.05s/f (Stan) **10** Ran SP% **119.8**
Speed ratings (Par 103): **100,99,98,96,96 95,93,89,85,77**
CSF £29.35 CT £267.76 TOTE £4.10: £1.80, £3.10, £3.40; EX 28.90 Trifecta £374.00.
Owner Don Churston & Ray Greatorex **Bred** Lookout Partnership **Trained** Upper Lambourn, Berkshire

FOCUS
The winning time was nearly half a second slower than the first division. It's rated around the second and third.
T/Plt: £10.50 to a £1 stake. Pool: £50,382.69 - 3,491.84 winning units. T/Qpdt: £6.00 to a £1 stake. Pool: £4,030.26 - 491.69 winning units. **Steve Payne**

8420 DEAUVILLE (R-H)
Saturday, December 17
OFFICIAL GOING: Polytrack: standard (last three races abandoned due to fog)

8431a PRIX LUTHIER (LISTED RACE) (3YO+) (POLYTRACK) 7f 110y
1:20 (12:00) 3-Y-O+ **£19,117** (£7,647; £5,735; £3,823; £1,911)

RPR
1 **Qurbaan (USA)**[66] 7292 3-8-13 0.... Francois-XavierBertras 6 106
(F Rohaut, France) **39/10**[3]
2 *snk* **Sovereign Debt (IRE)**[31] 7978 7-9-2 0.... AndrewMullen 10 109
(David Nicholls) *led: sn 3l clr: rdn whn chal fnl f: rallied u.p: hdd cl home (poor visibility: fog)* **29/10**[2]
3 *1* **King Malpic (FR)**[49] 7711 3-8-13 0.... OlivierPeslier 8 103
(T Lemer, France) **14/5**[1]
4 *hd* **Ross (IRE)**[34] 7952 4-8-13 0.... EddyHardouin 3 103
(P Schiergen, Germany) **118/10**
5 *1 1/4* **Tamil Nadu**[48] 4-8-13 0.... CristianDemuro 9 99
(Andrea Renzi, Italy) **20/1**
6 *2* **You're Back (USA)**[34] 7952 3-8-9 0.... MaximeGuyon 2 90
(H-A Pantall, France) *settled towards rr of midfield: one pce fnl f (poor visibility: fog)* **7/1**
7 *shd* **Orcia (IRE)**[61] 4-8-9 0.... FranckBlondel 1 90
(H-F Devin, France) **32/1**
8 *5* **Nice To See You (FR)**[17] 8165 3-8-13 0....(p) SebastienMaillot 7 82
(Robert Collet, France) **142/10**
9 *hd* **Keravnos (FR)**[34] 6-8-13 0.... DavidMorisson 5 81
(C Gourdain, France) **58/1**
10 *nk* **Harry's Son (AUS)**[76] 6991 5-8-13 0.... FrankPanicucci 4 80
(C Alonso Pena, Spain) **101/10**
1m 25.12s (85.12) **10** Ran SP% **117.8**
WIN (incl. 1 euro stake): 4.90. PLACES: 1.60, 1.40, 1.40. DF: 6.90. SF: 17.80.
Owner Hamdan Al Maktoum **Bred** Justin Carthy **Trained** Sauvagnon, France

8432 - 8442a (Foreign Racing) - See Raceform Interactive

8423 LINGFIELD (L-H)
Sunday, December 18
OFFICIAL GOING: Polytrack: standard
Wind: Nil Weather: Grey, slightly misty

8443 32RED.COM MAIDEN FILLIES' STKS (PLUS 10 RACE) 7f 1y(P)
12:25 (12:25) (Class 5) 2-Y-O **£3,234** (£962; £481; £240) **Stalls** Low

Form RPR
64 **1** **Dellaguista (IRE)**[20] 8130 2-9-0 0.... PatCosgrave 1 73+
(William Haggas) *trckd ldng pair: clsd on inner fr 2f out: shkn up to ld 1f out: styd on* **11/4**[2]
55 **2** *1 1/4* **Circulate**[67] 7278 2-9-0 0.... JoeFanning 2 70
(Tom Clover) *led: rdn and pressed 2f out: hdd 1f out: one pce but jst hld on for 2nd* **20/1**
3 *nse* **Dreaming Of Paris** 2-9-0 0.... RichardKingscote 8 70
(William Haggas) *s.i.s: sn in 5th: pushed along and prog over 1f out: styd on and nrly snatched 2nd* **10/1**
4 **4** *1/2* **Moonshine Dancer**[40] 7855 2-9-0 0.... MartinHarley 7 69
(David Simcock) *hld up in last: prog over 1f out: rdn and r.o fnl f to press plcd horses nr fin* **2/1**[1]
3 **5** *1* **Monteamiata (IRE)**[18] 8151 2-9-0 0.... ThomasBrown 5 66
(Ed Walker) *chsd ldr: tried to chal 2f out: nt qckn over 1f out: sn lost 2nd and one pce* **6/1**
6 *2 3/4* **Influent (IRE)** 2-9-0 0.... JimCrowley 6 58
(Hugo Palmer) *mostly in last pair: shkn up and no prog 2f out* **3/1**[3]
7 *2 1/2* **Girl Squad** 2-9-0 0....[1] JosephineGordon 4 52
(William Jarvis) *urged along in 4th: wknd wl over 1f out* **40/1**
1m 25.8s (1.00) **Going Correction** +0.025s/f (Slow) **7** Ran SP% **115.6**
Speed ratings (Par 93): **95,93,93,92,91 88,85**
CSF £52.67 TOTE £4.00: £1.50, £7.00; EX 42.00 Trifecta £160.80.
Owner David & Yvonne Blunt **Bred** M Gittins **Trained** Newmarket, Suffolk

FOCUS
The pace was not strong in this maiden and the hold-up performers couldn't land a major blow. The runner-up helps guide the level.

8444 32RED CASINO NURSERY H'CAP 6f 1y(P)
12:55 (12:56) (Class 4) (0-85,80) 2-Y-O **£4,528** (£1,347; £673; £336) **Stalls** Low

Form RPR
01 **1** **Munro**[25] 8065 2-9-6 **79**.... RichardKingscote 1 83+
(Ralph Beckett) *wl away: led to 1/2-way: sltly impeded over 2f out: rdn over 1f out: led on inner jst ins fnl f: kpt on wl* **7/4**[1]
154 **2** *1/2* **Zamjar**[46] 7764 2-9-5 **78**....(b[1]) LukeMorris 2 79
(Ed Dunlop) *t.k.h: trckd wnr 1f: styd cl up: rdn to chal on outer fnl f and upsides wnr: nt qckn last 75yds* **6/1**
0426 **3** *1 1/2* **Dandy Flame (IRE)**[20] 8136 2-9-2 **75**.... PatCosgrave 4 72
(William Haggas) *hld up in last: plenty to do whn prog 2f out: rdn and r.o to take 3rd last 100yds: no imp ldng pair after* **15/2**
154 **4** *2 1/2* **White Royale (USA)**[38] 7893 2-8-9 **75**.... LewisEdmunds(7) 6 64
(Kevin Ryan) *racd wd: in tch: outpcd over 2f out: wd bnd sn after: n.d over 1f out* **7/2**[2]
0261 **5** *1* **Roundabout Magic (IRE)**[29] 8027 2-8-7 **66** ow2.... JFEgan 5 52
(Simon Dow) *plld hrd and jnd wnr after 1f: led 1/2-way: hanging over 2f out: hdd & wknd jst ins fnl f* **4/1**[3]
2100 **6** *3/4* **Kamra (USA)**[87] 6697 2-9-7 **80**....(v) JimCrowley 3 64
(Jeremy Noseda) *sn hld up: outpcd over 2f out: pushed along and no prog after* **12/1**
1m 11.78s (-0.12) **Going Correction** +0.025s/f (Slow) **6** Ran SP% **112.3**
Speed ratings (Par 98): **101,100,98,95,93 92**
CSF £12.76 TOTE £2.30: £1.40, £3.10; EX 12.20 Trifecta £44.10.
Owner Emma Capon & Mrs Simon Marsh **Bred** K Snell **Trained** Kimpton, Hants

FOCUS
They went a steady pace but the unexposed favourite showed a good attitude to score in his first nursery. The runner-up has been rated close to his earlier form.

8445 BETWAY STAYERS H'CAP 1m 7f 169y(P)
1:30 (1:30) (Class 6) (0-65,68) 3-Y-O **£2,911** (£866; £432; £216) **Stalls** Low

Form RPR
0206 **1** **Aurora Gray**[37] 7905 3-9-7 **64**.... JimCrowley 4 72
(Hughie Morrison) *hld up in rr: gng best whn prog over 2f out: tk 2nd fnl f: rdn to ld last 100yds: styd on wl* **7/1**[3]
0432 **2** *1 1/2* **Burnside (FR)**[8] 8318 3-9-6 **63**....(p) StevieDonohoe 7 69
(Ian Williams) *cl up: gng bttr than most 3f out: chsd ldr 2f out: rdn to ld jst over 1f out: styd on but hdd and outpcd last 100yds* **5/1**[2]
002 **3** *2 1/4* **Southern States**[46] 7760 3-9-6 **63**.... RobertHavlin 1 66
(Lydia Richards) *mde most: rdn over 2f out: hdd and outpcd jst over 1f out* **5/1**[2]
0056 **4** *1 3/4* **Trust The Man (IRE)**[17] 8180 3-8-7 **50** ow1.... JFEgan 2 51
(Simon Dow) *t.k.h early: trckd ldrs: lost pl and pushed along over 2f out: kpt on same pce fr over 1f out: nvr chal* **7/1**[3]
0152 **5** *2 1/2* **Santiburi Spring**[11] 8253 3-9-11 **68**.... KierenFox 5 66
(John Best) *t.k.h: hld up tl prog and prom 1/2-way: rdn 3f out: wknd over 1f out* **7/2**[1]
2004 **6** *3/4* **Moon Over Mobay**[46] 7760 3-8-13 **56**....[1] DavidProbert 6 53
(Michael Blanshard) *hld up in last: rdn over 2f out: no great prog* **14/1**
2634 **7** *1 3/4* **Mamoo**[33] 7969 3-9-2 **59**.... ShaneKelly 8 54
(Mike Murphy) *mostly pressed ldr: rdn 3f out: lost 2nd and wknd 2f out* **5/1**[2]
0025 **8** *4* **Dancing Rainbow (GR)**[33] 7969 3-7-11 **45**....(b) HollieDoyle(5) 3 35
(Amanda Perrett) *hld up in last pair: rdn and no prog 3f out: wknd over 1f out* **8/1**
3m 21.92s (-3.78) **Going Correction** +0.025s/f (Slow) **8** Ran SP% **115.0**
Speed ratings (Par 98): **110,109,108,107,106 105,104,102**
CSF £41.98 CT £191.46 TOTE £7.20: £2.20, £2.20, £2.40; EX 37.40 Trifecta £180.40.
Owner Wardley Bloodstock **Bred** Lakin Bloodstock/Wardley Bloodstock **Trained** East Ilsley, Berks

FOCUS
A minor handicap but several of the runners were unexposed at this trip and the winner got off the mark in decent style. It's been rated as sound form for the level.

8446 BETWAY H'CAP 1m 2f (P)
2:05 (2:05) (Class 4) (0-85,83) 3-Y-O+ **£5,175** (£1,540; £769; £384) **Stalls** Low

Form RPR
6131 **1** **Van Huysen (IRE)**[13] 8231 4-9-4 **80**.... SeanLevey 1 86
(Dominic Ffrench Davis) *hld up in midfield: prog over 2f out: chsd ldr over 1f out: rdn and styd on wl on inner to ld last 50yds* **11/4**[1]
0104 **2** *nk* **Bunbury**[25] 8077 4-9-7 **83**.... ShaneKelly 5 88
(Richard Hughes) *t.k.h: hld up in 4th: prog to ld 2f out: drvn on outer fnl f: worn down last 50yds* **6/1**[3]
6004 **3** *1 1/4* **Dutch Uncle**[11] 8249 4-9-6 **82**.... MartinHarley 10 85+
(Ed Dunlop) *hld up in last pair fr wd draw: gng wl but only 9th over 2f out and wdst of all bnd sn after: rdn and r.o fr over 1f out to take 3rd nr fin: too much to do* **9/2**[2]
0020 **4** *1/2* **Saint Honore**[164] 4049 4-8-3 **72**.... SophieRalston(7) 6 74
(Pat Phelan) *t.k.h: hld up in midfield: pushed along over 2f out: limited prog tl styd on wl last 150yds to press for 3rd nr fin* **40/1**
0106 **5** *nk* **Zain Emperor (IRE)**[95] 6490 3-8-13 **78**.... JFEgan 3 79
(John Butler) *cl up bhd ldng pair: pushed along over 2f out: nt qckn over 1f out: kpt on same pce after* **12/1**
-200 **6** *1 3/4* **Best Example (USA)**[50] 7702 4-9-4 **80**....[1] AdamBeschizza 2 78
(Julia Feilden) *hld up in midfield: nowhere to go on inner over 2f out: drvn and effrt over 1f out: one pce* **25/1**
7 *2* **Spin Point (IRE)**[420] 7494 4-8-10 **75**.... GeorgeDowning(3) 9 69
(Ian Williams) *racd wd in midfield: rdn 3f out: no prog over 1f out: wknd* **7/1**
6636 **8** *2* **Ansaab**[50] 5932 8-9-6 **82**....[1] LukeMorris 7 72
(Marjorie Fife) *sn trckd ldr: chal 1/2-way: led 3f out to 2f out: wknd over 1f out* **16/1**
6400 **9** *3/4* **In The Red (IRE)**[37] 7902 3-9-3 **82**.... TomMarquand 4 70
(Richard Hannon) *sn led: pressed 1/2-way: hdd 3f out: wknd 2f out* **6/1**[3]
0436 **10** *nk* **Modernism**[85] 6794 7-9-5 **81**.... StevieDonohoe 8 69
(Ian Williams) *hld up in last: detached and pushed along over 3f out: no prog* **10/1**
2m 4.28s (-2.32) **Going Correction** +0.025s/f (Slow)
WFA 3 from 4yo+ 3lb **10** Ran SP% **114.9**
Speed ratings (Par 105): **110,109,108,108,108 106,105,103,102,102**
CSF £18.90 CT £71.32 TOTE £3.70: £1.20, £2.10, £2.00; EX 18.10 Trifecta £49.50.
Owner Prof C D Green **Bred** Prof C Green **Trained** Lambourn, Berks

FOCUS
The favourite battled well to complete a double in this decent handicap. A small pb from the winner.

8447 BETWAY MIDDLE DISTANCE H'CAP 1m 4f (P)
2:35 (2:35) (Class 4) (0-85,85) 3-Y-O+ **£5,175** (£1,540; £769; £384) **Stalls** Low

Form RPR
6043 **1** **Plutocracy (IRE)**[32] 7980 6-9-7 **85**....(p) TimmyMurphy 1 92
(Gary Moore) *hld up in midfield: prog fr 2f out gng wl: pushed along to take 2nd ins fnl f: shkn up to ld last 75yds: fnd enough to assert* **8/1**
3121 **2** *1/2* **Ride The Lightning**[11] 8253 3-8-11 **80**.... LukeMorris 3 86
(Archie Watson) *disp ld 1f: chsd ldng pair: rdn 2f out: led on inner wl over 1f out: kpt on u.p but hdd last 75yds* **11/4**[2]
11 **3** *1/2* **Cape Discovery**[216] 2313 4-9-6 **84**.... ShaneKelly 4 89
(Richard Hughes) *t.k.h: disp ld 1f then restrained into midfield: effrt 2f out: tried to cl w wnr fnl f: styd on but a jst outpcd* **11/2**
4021 **4** *nk* **Artful Rogue (IRE)**[11] 8254 5-8-13 **80**.... KieranShoemark(3) 8 85
(Amanda Perrett) *pressed ldr after 1f to wl over 1f out: styd on fnl f but a jst outpcd* **4/1**[3]
000 **5** *1/2* **Zamperini (IRE)**[39] 7869 4-9-7 **85**....(b) MartinDwyer 6 89
(Mike Murphy) *trckd ldrs: wd bnd 2f out and nt qckn wl over 1f out: styd on again ins fnl f* **20/1**

0000 **6** *1* **The Twisler**[32] 7979 4-9-0 **85** RhiainIngram(7) 7 87
(Roger Ingram) *led after 1f after nthing else wanted to: kicked on 3f out: hdd wl over 1f out: wknd ins fnl f* **40/1**

31 **7** *3/4* **Hermann**[36] 7942 3-8-13 **82** SeanLevey 5 83+
(Richard Hannon) *hld up in rr: rdn over 2f out and nt wl plcd as sprint began: one pce and no prog* **9/4**[1]

6534 **8** *3 1/4* **Gabrial The Terror (IRE)**[99] 6346 6-8-10 **74** StevieDonohoe 9 70
(Ian Williams) *dwlt: hld up in last pair: lft bhd fr 3f out: hanging on inner over 1f out* **40/1**

0000 **9** *4* **Slowfoot (GER)**[11] 8249 8-9-0 **78** LiamKeniry 2 68
(Jim Best) *c out of stall slowly: hld up in last pair: pushed along 4f out: wknd 2f out* **66/1**

2m 32.81s (-0.19) **Going Correction** +0.025s/f (Slow)
WFA 3 from 4yo+ 5lb **9** Ran SP% **115.1**
Speed ratings (Par 105): **101,100,100,100,99 99,98,96,93**
CSF £29.44 CT £133.07 TOTE £9.40: £2.40, £1.30, £2.00; EX 36.80 Trifecta £174.20.

Owner Power Geneva Ltd **Bred** Bjorn Nielsen **Trained** Lower Beeding, W Sussex

FOCUS
Four last-time-out winners lined up in this handicap. They went a stop-start gallop and there was a bunched finish. The runner-up has been rated as running as well as ever.

8448 DOWNLOAD THE BETWAY APP H'CAP 1m 4f (P)
3:05 (3:07) (Class 6) (0-65,65) 3-Y-O+ **£2,911** (£866; £432; £216) **Stalls** Low

Form RPR

060F **1** **Bamako Du Chatelet (FR)**[37] 7905 5-9-8 **63**.......(p) RichardKingscote 3 71
(Ian Williams) *wl in tch: rdn to cl on ldrs 2f out: chal 1f out: drvn ahd last 100yds* **9/4**[2]

2 *1/2* **My Matador (IRE)**[158] 4284 5-9-7 **65** [1] KieranShoemark(3) 6 72
(Victor Dartnall) *trckd ldr after 4f: rdn to ld 2f out: kpt on u.p: hdd last 100yds* **14/1**

2600 **3** *1 1/4* **Fair Comment**[18] 8155 6-9-2 **57** DavidProbert 4 62
(Michael Blanshard) *hld up in midfield: prog wl over 1f out: rdn and r.o fnl f to take 3rd nr fin: no ch to chal* **16/1**

2P-2 **4** *shd* **Goodby Inheritence**[11] 8257 4-9-10 **65**.......(t) GeorgeBaker 1 70
(Seamus Durack) *chsd ldr 4f: styd prom: rdn over 2f out: cl enough 1f out: one pce fnl f* **15/8**[1]

0051 **5** *1/2* **Jersey Bull (IRE)**[18] 8155 4-9-9 **64** LiamKeniry 8 68
(Michael Madgwick) *t.k.h: hld up: dropped to rr over 3f out: prog on inner wl over 1f out but ldrs already gone: styd on but no ch to threaten* **8/1**[3]

3504 **6** *3/4* **Perfect Rhythm**[37] 7905 5-9-3 **61** HectorCrouch(3) 7 64
(Patrick Chamings) *hld up in midfield: rdn and nt qckn 2f out: kpt on fr over 1f out* **8/1**[3]

0400 **7** *1 1/4* **Norse Castle**[11] 8257 3-9-1 **61** TimmyMurphy 11 62
(Martin Bosley) *led fr wdst draw but set mod pce: tried to kick on 3f out: hdd 2f out: wknd fnl f* **40/1**

2560 **8** *2 1/4* **Iona Island**[8] 8318 3-8-12 **61** EoinWalsh(3) 9 58
(Peter Hiatt) *hld up in last trio: poorly plcd whn pce lifted over 2f out: pushed along and no prog: nvr involved* **20/1**

0010 **9** *3 3/4* **Fleetwood Poppy**[17] 8180 4-8-7 **51** oh4 EdwardGreatrex(3) 2 43
(Michael Attwater) *hld up in midfield: lost pl on inner over 2f out: no ch whn sltly impeded wl over 1f out* **33/1**

/50- **10** *3/4* **Bridge That Gap**[552] 3234 8-8-9 **57**.......(p) RhiainIngram(7) 5 47
(Roger Ingram) *hld up in last pair: outpcd fr 3f out: nvr on terms after* **100/1**

6422 **11** *3* **Two In The Pink (IRE)**[36] 7936 6-9-8 **63** LukeMorris 10 48
(Ralph J Smith) *chsd ldrs: rdn on outer over 2f out: sn wknd* **14/1**

2m 34.24s (1.24) **Going Correction** +0.025s/f (Slow)
WFA 3 from 4yo+ 5lb **11** Ran SP% **118.1**
Speed ratings (Par 101): **96,95,94,94,94 93,93,91,89,88 86**
CSF £32.87 CT £417.98 TOTE £3.40: £1.40, £4.00, £3.70; EX 42.90 Trifecta £536.40.

Owner Macable Partnership **Bred** S N C Ecurie Jouenne Gerard **Trained** Portway, Worcs

FOCUS
The pace was steady in this ordinary handicap and not many got involved from off the pace. The winner has been rated to his better level of recent times.

8449 SUNBETS.CO.UK MAIDEN STKS 1m 1y(P)
3:35 (3:36) (Class 5) 3-Y-O+ **£3,234** (£962; £481; £240) **Stalls** High

Form RPR

0-5 **1** **Karisma (IRE)**[198] 2877 3-9-0 0 JoeFanning 6 80+
(Roger Varian) *stdd s: hld up in last pair: smooth prog on outer 2f out: led 1f out: sn clr: easily* **15/8**[1]

2 *3 3/4* **Galinthias** 4-9-3 0 HectorCrouch(3) 4 73
(Simon Dow) *trckd ldrs: rdn to try to cl over 1f out but wnr sn cruised by: kpt on to take 2nd last 100yds* **10/1**

030 **3** *1 1/2* **Wonderful Life (IRE)**[150] 4546 3-9-0 75 TomMarquand 5 63
(Richard Spencer) *trckd ldr: led jst over 2f out: hdd and one pce 1f out* **11/2**

6 **4** *2 1/2* **Tell A Story**[8] 8320 3-9-0 0 PatCosgrave 2 57
(David Simcock) *trckd ldrs: shkn up 2f out: flashed tail and outpcd after* **11/4**[2]

06 **5** *8* **Annabella**[48] 7727 3-9-0 0 RyanTate 1 38
(Tim McCarthy) *hld up in last pair: wknd 2f out: sn bhd* **50/1**

0402 **6** *13* **Hidden Gem**[8] 8320 3-8-11 60.......(t) AaronJones(3) 3
(Stuart Williams) *led to jst over 2f out: wknd qckly: t.o* **7/2**[3]

1m 38.67s (0.47) **Going Correction** +0.025s/f (Slow)
WFA 3 from 4yo 1lb **6** Ran SP% **110.1**
Speed ratings (Par 103): **98,94,92,90,82 69**
CSF £20.12 TOTE £2.50: £1.20, £4.50; EX 21.10 Trifecta £67.80.

Owner Miss Yvonne Jacques **Bred** Mrs Cherry Faeste **Trained** Newmarket, Suffolk

FOCUS
A modest maiden and the leading form contender powered clear on her return.

T/Jkpt: £15,200.10. Pool: £22,800.27 - 1.5 winning units T/Plt: £88.00 to a £1 stake. Pool: £75,674.15 - 627.53 winning units T/Qpdt: £17.00 to a £1 stake. Pool: £8,352.97 - 361.96 winning units **Jonathan Neesom**

8450 - 8452a (Foreign Racing) - See Raceform Interactive

8377 CHELMSFORD (A.W) (L-H)
Monday, December 19

OFFICIAL GOING: Polytrack: standard
Wind: virtually nil Weather: overcast

8453 TOTEPLACEPOT RACING'S FAVOURITE BET NURSERY H'CAP 5f (P)
1:45 (1:45) (Class 5) (0-75,77) 2-Y-O **£3,881** (£1,155; £577; £288) **Stalls** Low

Form RPR

4411 **1** **Dazacam**[10] 8285 2-9-6 **73** RobertWinston 7 81+
(Michael Herrington) *taken down early: hld up in midfield: clsd and nt clr run jst over 2f out: hdwy between horses over 1f out: rdn and qcknd to ld 150yds: r.o wl and gng away at fin* **6/1**[3]

0455 **2** *1* **Five Star Frank**[18] 8175 2-9-4 **71** JimCrowley 3 73
(Eve Johnson Houghton) *chsd ldrs: swtchd rt and effrt over 1f out: ev ch and drvn 150yds: styd on same pce fnl 100yds* **6/1**[3]

5333 **3** *1 1/2* **Erissimus Maximus (FR)**[21] 8136 2-9-7 **74** JosephineGordon 4 71
(Chris Dwyer) *chsd ldrs on outer: rdn 2f out: drvn over 1f out: kpt on same pce u.p ins fnl f* **9/2**[2]

1020 **4** *1* **Marquee Club**[30] 8033 2-9-10 **77** WilliamCarson 10 70
(Jamie Osborne) *off the pce in last pair: effrt and swtchd rt over 1f out: kpt on u.p ins fnl f: nt rch ldrs* **16/1**

5442 **5** *nk* **Her Terms**[9] 8313 2-8-10 **68**.......(p) GeorgiaCox(5) 1 60
(William Haggas) *led: rdn over 1f out: hdd 150yds out: wknd fnl 75yds* **11/4**[1]

501 **6** *1/2* **Little Miss Daisy**[14] 8229 2-8-10 **63** MartinDwyer 6 53
(William Muir) *s.i.s and swtchd lft after s: bhd: rdn and swtchd rt over 1f out: kpt on ins fnl f: nvr trbld ldrs* **11/1**

2565 **7** *3/4* **Gerrard's Fur Coat**[34] 7966 2-9-2 **69** RichardKingscote 8 56
(Tom Dascombe) *midfield: effrt u.p over 1f out: unable qck and styd on same pce fnl f* **7/1**

3355 **8** *2 3/4* **Street Jazz**[14] 8229 2-8-13 **66** TomEaves 5 44
(James Given) *midfield: rdn and dropped towards rr over 2f out: bhd over 1f out* **14/1**

623 **9** *3 3/4* **Nuzha**[18] 8174 2-8-13 **66** JFEgan 2 30
(David Evans) *chsd ldr tl lost pl qckly over 1f out: bhd and eased ins fnl f* **7/1**

59.62s (-0.58) **Going Correction** -0.175s/f (Stan) **9** Ran SP% **119.3**
Speed ratings (Par 96): **97,95,93,91,90 90,88,84,78**
CSF £43.26 CT £181.12 TOTE £4.10: £1.80, £2.40, £2.00; EX 27.00 Trifecta £79.00.
Owner Darren & Annaley Yates **Bred** Mr & Mrs D Yates **Trained** Cold Kirby, N Yorks
FOCUS
An ordinary nursery but an improving winner. The runner-up has been rated close to his previous C&D run.

8454 TOTEPOOLRACING LIKE US ON FACEBOOK MAIDEN STKS 6f (P)
2:15 (2:15) (Class 5) 2-Y-O **£3,881** (£1,155; £577; £288) **Stalls** Centre

Form RPR

54 **1** **Alkashaaf (USA)**[12] 8246 2-9-5 0 [1] DavidProbert 7 76
(Archie Watson) *dwlt and pushed along leaving stalls: sn chsng ldr: rdn and sltly outpcd whn drifted rt bnd wl over 1f out: styd on to ld 150yds out: edgd lft but hld on wl after* **7/1**[3]

4242 **2** *nk* **Arzaak (IRE)**[18] 8175 2-9-5 75 JosephineGordon 5 75
(Chris Dwyer) *chsd ldrs: carried rt bnd wl over 1f out: hdwy u.p over 1f out: ev ch 150yds out: kpt on but a jst hld* **11/10**[1]

6405 **3** *1 1/4* **Hathfa (FR)**[9] 8313 2-9-0 68.......(be[1]) ShaneKelly 6 66
(Richard Hughes) *led: pushed clr ent fnl 2f: drvn ent fnl f: sn hdd and one pced fnl 100yds* **12/1**

203 **4** *nk* **Kingofmerrows (IRE)**[12] 8243 2-9-5 78 WilliamCarson 4 71
(Jamie Osborne) *in tch in midfield: effrt ent fnl 2f: drvn to press ldrs 1f out: kpt on same pce fnl 100yds* **9/4**[2]

0 **5** *1 1/4* **Canberra Cliffs (IRE)**[18] 8175 2-9-0 0 LiamKeniry 1 62
(Don Cantillon) *hld up in tch in last pair: effrt over 1f out: no imp and kpt on same pce ins fnl f* **12/1**

6 **6** *6* **Termsnconditions (IRE)**[30] 8027 2-9-5 0 KieranO'Neill 3 49
(Tim Vaughan) *dwlt: in tch in last pair: rdn over 2f out: struggling and outpcd 2f out: bhd ins fnl f* **20/1**

1m 12.1s (-1.60) **Going Correction** -0.175s/f (Stan) **6** Ran SP% **111.0**
Speed ratings (Par 96): **103,102,100,100,98 90**
CSF £14.95 TOTE £9.40: £3.10, £1.10; EX 16.80 Trifecta £73.00.
Owner The Keg Partnership **Bred** Shadwell Farm LLC **Trained** Upper Lambourn, West Berks
FOCUS
An ordinary juvenile sprint maiden.

8455 TOTEQUADPOT FOUR PLACES IN FOUR RACES H'CAP 1m (P)
2:50 (2:51) (Class 4) (0-80,80) 3-Y-O+ **£5,175** (£1,540; £769; £384) **Stalls** Low

Form RPR

0021 **1** **Holiday Magic (IRE)**[9] 8319 5-9-7 **80** JamesSullivan 3 92+
(Michael Easterby) *t.k.h: trckd ldrs: pushed along and hdwy to ld over 1f out: in command fnl f: comf* **4/6**[1]

0204 **2** *1 1/2* **Cricklewood Green (USA)**[5] 8356 5-8-13 **77** MitchGodwin(5) 9 84
(Sylvester Kirk) *s.i.s: bhd: effrt in 5th over 2f out: hdwy u.p over 1f out: chsd wnr ins fnl f: kpt on but* **9/2**[3]

5266 **3** *1 1/4* **Mezzotint (IRE)**[28] 8052 7-9-6 **79** MartinHarley 8 83
(Lee Carter) *hld up in tch in midfield: effrt wl over 1f out: chsd wnr 1f out: 3rd and kpt on same pce fnl 150yds* **4/1**[2]

0020 **4** *6* **Greyfriarschorista**[12] 8252 9-8-8 **74** KatherineGlenister(7) 6 64
(David Evans) *led: rdn wl over 1f out: sn hdd and no ex: wknd ins fnl f* **33/1**

410 **5** *1 1/2* **Officer Drivel (IRE)**[12] 8254 5-8-11 **70** JFEgan 2 57
(Jim Best) *w ldr for 2f: styd chsng ldrs tl rdn and lost pl over 1f out: wknd fnl f* **12/1**

4610 **6** *2 1/4* **Bobby Benton (IRE)**[4] 8378 5-8-12 **71**.......(v) TimmyMurphy 5 53
(Jim Best) *chsd ldrs: hdwy to join ldr after 2f: shkn up over 1f out: sn lost pl and wknd fnl f* **33/1**

060 **7** *7* **Torch**[12] 8251 3-8-13 **76** HectorCrouch(3) 4 40
(John Butler) *stdd s: a off the pce in rr: n.d* **25/1**

124- **8** *4 1/2* **Austin Friars**[63] 1603 4-8-11 **70** JohnFahy 1 25
(Jim Best) *dwlt: rdn along and sn rcvrd to chse ldrs: lost pl 4f out: wl bhd over 1f out* **20/1**

1m 38.16s (-1.74) **Going Correction** -0.175s/f (Stan)
WFA 3 from 4yo+ 1lb **8** Ran SP% **120.4**
Speed ratings (Par 105): **101,99,98,92,90 88,81,77**
CSF £4.18 CT £7.52 TOTE £1.70: £1.10, £1.50, £1.10; EX 5.00 Trifecta £9.80.
Owner A Saha **Bred** Mrs Ann Fortune **Trained** Sheriff Hutton, N Yorks

The Form Book, Raceform Ltd, Newbury, RG14 5SJ

FOCUS
This was all about the favourite. A step up from the winner on this year's form, with the third rated to the balance of his recent form.

8456 @TOTEPOOL TWEET US WITH YOUR #TOTEELFIE H'CAP 7f (P)
3:20 (3:20) (Class 4) (0-80,81) 3-Y-O+ **£6,469** (£1,925; £962; £481) **Stalls** Low

Form RPR

0122 **1** **Ballylare**[12] 8252 3-9-5 **77**...................... MartinHarley 8 85
(Lee Carter) *hld up in tch in midfield: effrt jst over 2f out: hdwy u.p over 1f out: chal 1f out: sustained effrt u.p to ld 50yds out* **8/1**

0640 **2** ½ **Tadaany (IRE)**[24] 8092 4-9-0 **79**...................... PatrickVaughan(7) 7 85
(David O'Meara) *chsd ldrs: effrt and drvn to chal over 1f out: led 1f out: kpt on u.p: hdd and no ex 50yds out* **12/1**

001 **3** 1 ¼ **Out Of The Ashes**[46] 7782 3-9-4 **79**...................... (t) EoinWalsh(3) 2 82
(Mohamed Moubarak) *chsd ldng trio: effrt 2f out: hdwy u.p over 1f out: pressed ldrs 1f out: styd on same pce fnl 100yds* **14/1**

0400 **4** 1 ¼ **Clement (IRE)**[9] 8319 6-9-5 **77**...................... (v) FergusSweeney 5 77
(John O'Shea) *s.i.s: hld up in tch in midfield: nt clr run ent fnl 2f: rdn and hdwy over 1f out: nt clr run and swtchd rt ins fnl f: styd on wl fnl 100yds: nt rch ldrs* **14/1**

0115 **5** ½ **Vincenzo Coccotti (USA)**[16] 8206 4-8-10 **71**...................... HectorCrouch(3) 3 70
(Ken Cunningham-Brown) *broke wl: sn stdd and keen in midfield: effrt ent fnl 2f: swtchd lft and rdn to press ldrs over 1f out: struggling to qckn whn squeezed for room and hmpd jst ins fnl f: one pced after* **4/1**[2]

1032 **6** ½ **Ripoll (IRE)**[9] 8319 3-9-4 **81**...................... (t) MitchGodwin(5) 10 78+
(Sylvester Kirk) *t.k.h: hld up in last trio: effrt but stl plenty to do over 2f out: hdwy over 1f out: carried rt and sltly impeded jst ins fnl f: kpt on: nvr trbld ldrs* **9/2**[3]

-212 **7** ½ **Rockley Point**[28] 8052 3-9-5 **77**...................... TomQueally 4 73
(Paul D'Arcy) *chsd ldr: rdn to ld over 1f out: drvn and hdd 1f out: no ex and wknd ins fnl f* **3/1**[1]

-415 **8** 1 **Masarzain (IRE)**[75] 7066 3-9-7 **79**...................... TomEaves 1 72
(James Given) *sn led: rdn and hdd over 1f out: no ex u.p and wknd ins fnl f* **6/1**

0000 **9** 3 **Showing Off (IRE)**[9] 8319 3-9-0 **72**...................... ConnorBeasley 6 57
(Michael Wigham) *stdd s: hld up in last trio: effrt 2f out: no hdwy: n.d* **40/1**

1250 **10** 13 **Flying Fantasy**[149] 4627 4-9-3 **75**...................... PatCosgrave 9 25
(Stuart Williams) *stdd after s: hld up in rr: effrt wd wl over 1f out: no hdwy and sn wknd* **7/1**

1m 25.37s (-1.83) **Going Correction** -0.175s/f (Stan) **10** Ran SP% **124.5**
Speed ratings (Par 105): **103,102,101,99,99 98,97,96,93,78**
CSF £106.17 CT £1368.31 TOTE £10.00: £2.90, £4.50, £4.00; EX 120.10 Trifecta £2117.70.
Owner Mrs S A Pearson **Bred** J H Mayne **Trained** Epsom, Surrey

FOCUS
A fair handicap. A small pb from the winner, with the runner-up rated close to his turf best.

8457 #TOTEELFIE WIN A £50 FREE BET H'CAP 7f (P)
3:50 (3:51) (Class 6) (0-60,59) 3-Y-O+ **£2,587** (£770; £384; £192) **Stalls** Low

Form RPR

0251 **1** **Kenstone (FR)**[23] 8120 3-8-12 **55**...................... (p) HollieDoyle(5) 6 65
(Adrian Wintle) *chsd ldrs: rdn to chal over 1f out: led ent fnl f: styd on strly and drew clr ins fnl f: readily* **4/1**[1]

0050 **2** 3 ¼ **Zabdi**[61] 7463 3-9-2 **54**...................... RobertWinston 10 55
(Lee Carter) *t.k.h: chsd ldr: rdn to chal over 1f out: chsd wnr and kpt on same pce ins fnl f* **8/1**

4050 **3** 2 ¾ **Emily Goldfinch**[194] 3038 3-9-7 **59**...................... JosephineGordon 7 53
(Phil McEntee) *led: rdn wl over 1f out: hdd jst over 1f out: wknd ins fnl f* **25/1**

1000 **4** nk **Humour (IRE)**[18] 8181 5-9-4 **56**...................... (b) RobertHavlin 13 51
(Christine Dunnett) *hld up in midfield: nt clrest of run and swtchd lft over 1f out: shkn up ent fnl f: kpt on u.p fnl 100yds: no threat to wnr* **10/1**

3004 **5** shd **Great Expectations**[14] 8234 8-9-3 **55**...................... (vt) FergusSweeney 5 47
(J R Jenkins) *t.k.h: hld up in midfield: effrt over 1f out: sn drvn: styd on same pce and no imp fnl f* **8/1**

6500 **6** 2 ¼ **Indiana Dawn**[14] 8234 3-9-4 **56**...................... AdamBeschizza 1 42
(Robert Stephens) *hld up in tch in midfield: effrt on inner over 1f out: no imp: wl hld and one pced fnl f* **12/1**

34-4 **7** ¾ **Powered (IRE)**[72] 7166 3-8-12 **57**...................... KatherineGlenister(7) 11 41
(David Evans) *t.k.h early: hld up towards rr: effrt 2f out: no hdwy u.p: nvr trbld ldrs* **7/1**[3]

6000 **8** 3 ½ **Pearly Queen**[30] 8026 3-9-1 **56**...................... JackDuern(3) 3 31
(Dean Ivory) *towards rr: rdn over 2f out: no real hdwy: no ch but plugged on to pass btn horses fnl f* **20/1**

056 **9** 1 ¼ **Pleadings (USA)**[44] 7815 3-8-7 **45**...................... [1] KieranO'Neill 9 17
(Charlie Wallis) *s.i.s: sn bustled and rcvrd to r in midfield: effrt u.p to chse ldrs over 2f out: lost pl and btn over 1f out: wknd fnl f* **12/1**

4000 **10** hd **Imperial Link**[37] 7943 4-9-1 **56**...................... EdwardGreatrex(3) 8 27
(John O'Shea) *in tch in midfield: rdn 2f out: sn struggling: wknd fnl f* **28/1**

4450 **11** 2 ½ **Shahaama**[38] 7912 3-9-4 **56**...................... LukeMorris 2 20
(Jane Chapple-Hyam) *dwlt and bustled along leaving stalls: last pair: no hdwy u.p over 1f out: n.d* **6/1**[2]

560 **12** 1 ¼ **Frap**[90] 6646 3-9-6 **58**...................... StevieDonohoe 4 19
(Ian Williams) *a rr: rdn and no hdwy whn carried lft over 1f out: no ch whn swtchd rt 1f out* **6/1**[2]

0000 **13** 2 ¾ **Nasri**[19] 8156 10-9-2 **54**...................... TomQueally 12 7
(Emma Owen) *chsd ldrs but stuck wd: lost pl qckly ent fnl 2f: hung lft and eased over 1f out* **16/1**

1m 25.67s (-1.53) **Going Correction** -0.175s/f (Stan) **13** Ran SP% **125.7**
Speed ratings (Par 101): **101,97,94,93,93 91,90,86,84,84 81,80,77**
CSF £36.86 CT £737.88 TOTE £4.40: £1.80, £4.00, £7.40; EX 50.00 Trifecta £3096.50.
Owner Adrian Wintle **Bred** Guy Pariente Holding Sprl **Trained** Westbury-On-Severn, Gloucs

FOCUS
Few got into this moderate handicap. The balance of the placed horses' form suggests this is weak form, but it's equally feasible that the race could be rated as much as 6lb better.

8458 TOTEPOOL RACECOURSE CASH BACK AVAILABLE H'CAP 1m (P)
4:20 (4:22) (Class 6) (0-65,70) 3-Y-O+ **£2,587** (£770; £384; £192) **Stalls** Low

Form RPR

0162 **1** **Candesta (USA)**[25] 8085 6-9-1 **62**...................... ShelleyBirkett(3) 7 68
(Julia Feilden) *trckd ldrs: wnt 2nd 2f out: rdn to chal over 1f out: pushed along ins fnl f: kpt on to ld towards fin* **7/1**

4001 **2** ½ **Skidby Mill (IRE)**[4] 8382 6-9-12 **70** 6ex...................... GeorgeBaker 8 75
(Laura Mongan) *led: jnd and shkn up over 1f out: clr w wnr and rdn ins fnl f: hdd and no ex towards fin* **5/2**[1]

1066 **3** 3 ½ **Bazzat (IRE)**[12] 8258 3-9-2 **61**...................... (p) JimCrowley 10 57
(John Ryan) *in tch in midfield: effrt ent fnl 2f: drvn to chse clr ldng pair over 1f out: one pced and no imp ins fnl f* **4/1**[2]

0525 **4** 1 ¾ **Tommy's Secret**[25] 8086 6-9-2 **65**...................... PaddyBradley(5) 9 58
(Jane Chapple-Hyam) *chsd ldrs: unable qck u.p over 1f out: no imp and one pced ins fnl f* **9/2**[3]

0000 **5** 2 **Party Royal**[47] 7775 6-9-7 **65**...................... (e[1]) MartinDwyer 2 53+
(Nick Gifford) *t.k.h: hld up in last trio: effrt on inner over 1f out: sme hdwy 1f out: kpt on ins fnl f: nvr trbld ldrs* **7/1**

0244 **6** hd **Polar Kite (IRE)**[19] 8163 8-9-3 **64**...................... RobHornby(3) 14 52
(Michael Attwater) *stdd s: hld up towards rr: rdn and hdwy ent fnl 2f: edgd lft u.p over 1f out: no imp and kpt on same pce ins fnl f* **10/1**

5000 **7** 2 **Premier Currency (IRE)**[39] 7895 3-9-1 **60**...................... [1] ShaneKelly 3 42
(Mike Murphy) *racd keenly: chsd ldr: drvn and lost 2nd 2f out: lost pl and btn over 1f out: wknd fnl f* **12/1**

4460 **8** shd **Outrath (IRE)**[37] 7943 6-8-7 **51**...................... (t) JFEgan 1 34
(Jim Best) *hld up in midfield: pushed along over 2f out: no imp over 1f out: kpt on same pce ins fnl f: nvr trbld ldrs* **20/1**

600 **9** 1 **Swiftee (IRE)**[47] 7775 3-9-5 **64**...................... [1] TomEaves 5 44
(Ivan Furtado) *stdd s: t.k.h: hld up in rr: swtchd rt and effrt over 1f out: no imp: n.d* **20/1**

0-40 **10** 5 **Gabrial The Thug (FR)**[319] 437 6-9-0 **58**...................... StevieDonohoe 12 27
(Ian Williams) *hld up in midfield: lost pl ent fnl 2f: no rspnse to press over 1f out: bhd fnl f* **14/1**

0000 **11** ¾ **New Street (IRE)**[11] 8282 5-9-7 **65**...................... TimmyMurphy 13 33
(Jim Best) *midfield and stuck wd: hdwy to chse ldrs 1/2-way: lost pl over 1f out: bhd fnl f* **33/1**

600 **12** 1 ¼ **Popeswood (IRE)**[26] 8064 4-9-4 **62**...................... RobertWinston 6 27
(Lee Carter) *s.i.s: a bhd* **14/1**

1m 38.65s (-1.25) **Going Correction** -0.175s/f (Stan)
WFA 3 from 4yo+ 1lb **12** Ran SP% **134.3**
Speed ratings (Par 101): **99,98,95,93,91 91,89,88,87,82 82,80**
CSF £27.68 CT £88.12 TOTE £8.70: £2.30, £1.50, £2.10; EX 28.60 Trifecta £117.50.
Owner Mrs Jo Lambert **Bred** Juddmonte Farms Inc **Trained** Exning, Suffolk

FOCUS
Another race in which few were involved, and modest form. A minor career pb from the winner.

8459 2017 CCR MEMBERSHIP NOW AVAILABLE H'CAP 1m 6f (P)
4:50 (4:53) (Class 6) (0-65,66) 3-Y-O+ **£2,911** (£866; £432; £216) **Stalls** Low

Form RPR

0506 **1** **Lost The Moon**[17] 8193 3-9-3 **61**...................... StevieDonohoe 1 73+
(Mark H Tompkins) *trckd ldrs: rdn to ld over 1f out: in command and styd on strly fnl f: easily* **5/4**[1]

6064 **2** 6 **Ruby Wednesday**[40] 7870 3-9-3 **61**...................... KierenFox 8 64
(John Best) *hld up in midfield: nt clr run and shuffled bk over 2f out: rdn and hdwy over 1f out: chsd clr wnr ins fnl f: kpt on* **11/1**

0340 **3** 1 ¼ **Karam Albaari (IRE)**[79] 6965 8-10-1 **66**...................... (v) GeorgeBaker 4 67
(J R Jenkins) *s.i.s: hld up in rr: clsd 3f out: nt clr run wl over 1f out: swtchd rt over 1f out: rdn 1f out: kpt on to go 3rd last strides: no ch w wnr* **8/1**

0-35 **4** nk **Istimraar (IRE)**[22] 6618 5-10-0 **65**...................... (tp) JosephineGordon 6 66
(Alexandra Dunn) *chsd ldrs: effrt 2f out: chsd wnr jst over 1f out: no imp and sn outpcd: kpt on same pce and lost 2 pls ins fnl f* **16/1**

4505 **5** 7 **Le Tissier**[19] 8155 3-8-9 **56**...................... (p) RobHornby(3) 2 48
(Michael Attwater) *chsd ldr tl jst over 2f out: sn u.p and unable qck: 5th and wknd fnl f* **5/1**[3]

0-46 **6** 5 **Demand Respect**[98] 6423 3-8-2 **46** oh1...................... KieranO'Neill 5 31
(Henry Spiller) *rn wout declared tongue tie: midfield: rdn 3f out: drvn and no hdwy 2f out: wknd over 1f out* **20/1**

0400 **7** hd **Lorelei**[16] 8211 4-9-4 **55**...................... MartinDwyer 9 40
(William Muir) *hld up in last pair: rdn over 3f out: swtchd rt and no hdwy wl over 1f out: sn wknd* **12/1**

4032 **8** 2 ¼ **Paper Faces (USA)**[17] 8193 3-9-5 **63**...................... (p) JimCrowley 7 45
(Roger Varian) *led: rdn ent fnl 2f: hdd over 1f out and sn struggling: wknd fnl f* **3/1**[2]

0500 **9** 2 ¾ **Sayedaati Saadati (IRE)**[7] 8337 3-9-2 **60**...................... [1] JFEgan 3 39
(John Butler) *in tch in midfield: rdn 3f out: lost pl and bhd over 1f out: eased fnl f* **33/1**

3m 0.09s (-3.11) **Going Correction** -0.175s/f (Stan)
WFA 3 from 4yo+ 7lb **9** Ran SP% **126.8**
Speed ratings (Par 101): **101,97,96,96,92 89,89,88,86**
CSF £19.84 CT £92.14 TOTE £2.40: £1.20, £2.80, £2.40; EX 19.60 Trifecta £121.30.
Owner AEDOS & Tompkins **Bred** John Brenchley & Dullingham Park **Trained** Newmarket, Suffolk

FOCUS
A moderate contest but a winner to keep on side. The runner-up has been rated to form up in trip.
T/Jkpt: Not Won. T/Plt: £70.20 to a £1 stake. Pool: £83,242.97 - 865.48 winning units. T/Qpdt: £26.90 to a £1 stake. Pool: £8,723.98 - 239.29 winning units. **Steve Payne**

8460 - 8461a (Foreign Racing) - See Raceform Interactive

[8352]KEMPTON (A.W) (R-H)
Tuesday, December 20

OFFICIAL GOING: Polytrack: standard
Wind: Moderate, half behind Weather: Fine

8462 32REDSPORT.COM H'CAP 1m 2f (P)
2:10 (2:11) (Class 5) (0-70,71) 3-Y-O+ **£2,911** (£866; £432; £216) **Stalls** Low

Form RPR

5046 **1** **Zabeel Star (IRE)**[21] 8141 4-9-5 **68**...................... LiamKeniry 7 77
(Graeme McPherson) *s.i.s: racd in 9th: rdn and prog over 2f out: clsd to take 2nd fnl f: styd on wl to ld last 75yds* **8/1**

5535 **2** 1 ¼ **Fastnet Blast (IRE)**[67] 7321 3-9-0 **66**...................... (b) ThomasBrown 2 73
(Ed Walker) *trckd ldrs: gng wl whn prog over 2f out: shkn up to ld over 1f out: hdd and outpcd last 75yds* **5/1**[2]

5460 **3** 1 ½ **Boycie**[19] 8178 3-8-12 **69**...................... HollieDoyle(5) 10 73+
(Richard Hannon) *pushed along and dropped to last after 2f: stl there 3f out and long way off the pce: waiting for room 2f out: gd prog over 1f out: r.o wl to take 3rd last strides* **12/1**

0023 **4** ½ **Red Cossack (CAN)**[20] 8154 5-9-7 **70**...................... (t) PatCosgrave 11 73
(Paul Webber) *dwlt: settled in 10th: rdn and prog 2f out: styd on to chse ldng pair ins fnl f: no imp and lost 3rd last strides* **7/1**[3]

0500 **5** 1 ½ **Cat Royale (IRE)**[54] 7653 3-9-1 **67**...................... (p) DannyBrock 3 67
(Jane Chapple-Hyam) *trckd ldrs: prog to press ldr over 3f out: rdn to ld over 2f out to over 1f out: fdd* **14/1**

0005 **6** 2¾ **Tommys Geal**[13] 8257 4-9-11 **60**.................................. DanielMuscutt 13 54
(Michael Madgwick) *hld up in last quartet: pushed along and prog on inner over 2f out: unable to threaten ldrs over 1f out: wknd ins fnl f* **20/1**

0420 **7** ¾ **Runaiocht (IRE)**[167] 4009 6-8-7 **61**..........................(b) DavidParkes(5) 5 55
(Paul Burgoyne) *taken down early: awkward s: in tch in midfield: nt clr run on inner 2f out: hmpd over 1f out and dropped to rr: kpt on again last 150yds* **25/1**

3450 **8** ½ **Shifting Star (IRE)**[20] 8154 11-9-0 **63**.......................(vt) WilliamCarson 8 55
(John Bridger) *chsd ldrs: rdn wl over 2f out: wknd over 1f out* **50/1**

4264 **9** 1¼ **Estibdaad (IRE)**[13] 8257 6-8-9 **63**...........................(t) MitchGodwin(5) 4 52
(Paddy Butler) *racd in ldng trio: rdn 3f out: wknd over 1f out* **12/1**

3540 **10** 1 **Dukes Meadow**[19] 8179 5-8-0 **56**................................ RhiainIngram(7) 1 43
(Roger Ingram) *mde most to 1/2-way: rdn over 3f out: wknd over 1f out* **25/1**

3161 **11** 1½ **Solveig's Song**[34] 7973 4-9-5 **71**.........................(p) EdwardGreatrex(3) 12 55
(Steve Woodman) *mostly in last quartet: drvn 3f out: last and wl btn 2f out* **8/1**

000 **12** ¾ **Loving Your Work**[39] 7911 5-9-2 **65**................................ JimCrowley 14 48
(Ken Cunningham-Brown) *mostly in last quartet: struggling over 2f out* **16/1**

4504 **13** 2¾ **Hungerford**[13] 8254 4-9-3 **66**..(p) TomQueally 6 43
(Eve Johnson Houghton) *pressed ldrs: quick move to ld 1/2-way: pressed and rdn over 3f out: hdd over 2f out: wknd qckly over 1f out and eased* **12/1**

262 **14** 19 **Dream Ruler**[63] 7429 5-9-5 **68**......................................(tp) GeorgeBaker 9 7
(Jeremy Gask) *chsd ldrs: rdn 3f out: sn wknd: eased whn no ch: t.o* **4/1**[1]

2m 5.47s (-2.53) **Going Correction** -0.10s/f (Stan)
WFA 3 from 4yo+ 3lb **14** Ran SP% **121.4**
Speed ratings (Par 103): **106,105,103,103,102 100,99,99,98,97 96,95,93,78**
CSF £46.07 CT £490.84 TOTE £11.10: £3.30, £2.20, £4.30; EX 77.20 Trifecta £787.60.
Owner The Self Preservation Society & Partner **Bred** G Morrin **Trained** Upper Oddington, Gloucs

FOCUS
A modest handicap. There was a stop-start gallop but the pace picked up a fair way out. The winner has been rated back to form, with the fourth helping to set the level.

8463 32RED H'CAP 5f (P)
2:40 (2:41) (Class 4) (0-85,87) 3-Y-0+ **£4,690** (£1,395; £697; £348) **Stalls** Low

Form RPR

5001 **1** **Outrage**[4] 8403 4-9-9 **87** 6ex.................................(b) RichardKingscote 10 100+
(Daniel Kubler) *stdd s fr wdst draw: hld up wl off the pce in rr: stdy prog over 1f out: brought between rivals and r.o to ld last 50yds* **5/1**[1]

0000 **2** 1 **Come On Dave (IRE)**[12] 8280 7-8-13 **77**.......................(v) LiamKeniry 1 84
(John Butler) *fast away fr ins draw: led at str pce and had field strung out: 2 l clr 1f out: mown down last 50yds* **20/1**

0203 **3** nk **Calypso Choir**[12] 8280 3-8-10 **79**................................. MitchGodwin(5) 9 85
(Sylvester Kirk) *prom on outer: rdn to chse ldr briefly ins fnl f: styd on but a hld* **7/1**

0010 **4** hd **Seve**[15] 8232 4-9-2 **85**.. AnnaHesketh(5) 6 90
(Tom Dascombe) *chsd ldng quartet and in tch: urged along on inner over 1f out: kpt on and pressed for 3rd nr fin* **11/1**

0004 **5** nk **Steelriver (IRE)**[10] 8314 6-9-5 **83**... MartinHarley 8 87+
(David Barron) *stdd s fr wd draw: hld up wl off the pce in rr: effrt over 1f out: styd on fnl f but nt pce to chal* **5/1**[1]

5000 **6** 1½ **Normal Equilibrium**[166] 4066 6-9-4 **82**.............................. PatCosgrave 3 81
(Robert Cowell) *prom: rdn over 1f out: wknd ins fnl f* **6/1**[2]

1040 **7** 1¾ **Sandfrankskipsgo**[15] 8232 7-9-7 **85**.............................. GeorgeBaker 7 80
(Peter Crate) *chsd ldr: rdn and no imp over 1f out: lost 2nd and wkng whn bmpd ins fnl f* **9/1**

1240 **8** 2¾ **Miracle Garden**[106] 6195 4-9-1 **79**....................................(p) JimCrowley 4 62
(Roy Brotherton) *hld up off the pce: rdn and no prog over 1f out* **10/1**

6332 **9** 1¼ **Flying Bear (IRE)**[31] 8032 5-8-9 **78**.............................. DavidParkes(5) 5 56
(Jeremy Gask) *a struggling in last trio* **12/1**

2240 **10** 1 **Masamah (IRE)**[87] 6766 10-8-12 **76**............................ StevieDonohoe 2 50
(Ian Williams) *dwlt: detached in last and nt gng wl: a bhd* **13/2**[3]

58.87s (-1.63) **Going Correction** -0.10s/f (Stan) **10** Ran SP% **113.3**
Speed ratings (Par 105): **109,107,106,106,106 103,100,96,94,92**
CSF £102.02 CT £709.99 TOTE £6.20: £2.00, £4.90, £2.80; EX 90.50 Trifecta £1225.30.
Owner D Blunt & G Middlebrook **Bred** Trickledown Stud Limited **Trained** Lambourn, Berks

FOCUS
This was a well-run sprint. The runner-up has been rated to his handicap best since rejoining John Butler, while the third has been rated to his November C&D form.

8464 32RED/BRITISH STALLION STUDS EBF MAIDEN FILLIES' STKS (PLUS 10 RACE) (DIV I) 1m (P)
3:10 (3:10) (Class 4) 2-Y-O **£4,269** (£1,270; £634; £317) **Stalls** Low

Form RPR

2 **1** **Gallifrey**[22] 8130 2-9-0 0.. RichardKingscote 7 78
(Lucy Wadham) *trckd ldr after 2f: shkn up to ld wl over 1f out: sn pressed and rdn: asserted last 150yds* **5/4**[1]

4232 **2** 1¼ **Magical Forest (IRE)**[110] 6044 2-9-0 73......................... MartinHarley 3 75
(Marco Botti) *cl up: rdn to press wnr over 1f out and sn clr of rest: styd on but hld last 150yds* **4/1**[3]

0 **3** 4½ **Glassalt**[13] 8245 2-9-0 0... StevieDonohoe 1 64
(Michael Bell) *in tch: chsd clr ldng trio over 2f out: pushed along to take 3rd ins fnl f: no ch w ldng pair but styd on* **66/1**

0 **4** 1½ **Vrika Bay**[145] 4801 2-9-0 0.. WilliamCarson 10 61
(Robert Eddery) *wl in rr: sme prog 2f out but ldrs already wl clr: kpt on to win battle for 4th nr fin* **33/1**

0 **5** ½ **Beyond Recall**[13] 8245 2-9-0 0... PatCosgrave 6 59
(Luca Cumani) *towards rr: lost tch w ldrs wl over 2f out: no ch after: plugged on late* **20/1**

05 **6** nk **Starlight Circus (IRE)**[40] 7885 2-9-0 0........................ TomMarquand 11 59+
(Marco Botti) *broke on terms but sn shuffled bk to last: urged along 1/2-way: no prog tl styd on wl fnl f* **20/1**

7 shd **Mayflair** 2-8-9 0.. MitchGodwin(5) 4 58
(Jonathan Portman) *chsd ldr 2f: styd in tch to over 2f out: no ch after* **33/1**

0320 **8** shd **Snow Squaw**[120] 5722 2-9-0 75.. JimCrowley 2 58
(David Elsworth) *led: rdn and hdd wl over 1f out: sn outpcd: wknd and lost several pls nr fin* **7/2**[2]

9 19 **Piaffe (USA)** 2-9-0 0.. SeanLevey 8 13
(Ralph Beckett) *s.i.s: early reminder and sn chsd ldrs: wknd 3f out: t.o* **6/1**

1m 39.4s (-0.40) **Going Correction** -0.10s/f (Stan) **9** Ran SP% **117.9**
Speed ratings (Par 95): **98,96,92,90,90 89,89,89,70**
CSF £6.19 TOTE £2.30: £1.10, £1.40, £4.60; EX 6.40 Trifecta £149.80.
Owner Chasemore Farm **Bred** Mr & Mrs A E Pakenham **Trained** Newmarket, Suffolk

FOCUS
Just a fair maiden. It's been rated around the runner-up.

8465 32RED/BRITISH STALLION STUDS EBF MAIDEN FILLIES' STKS (PLUS 10 RACE) (DIV II) 1m (P)
3:40 (3:44) (Class 4) 2-Y-O **£4,269** (£1,270; £634; £317) **Stalls** Low

Form RPR

1 **Precious Ramotswe** 2-9-0 0.. RobertHavlin 2 76+
(John Gosden) *trckd ldng pair: led on inner wl over 1f out: pushed along firmly and in command fnl f: readily* **8/15**[1]

2 2¼ **Flight Of Fantasy** 2-9-0 0... RichardKingscote 10 70+
(Harry Dunlop) *trckd ldng trio: shkn up over 2f out: styd on u.p to take 2nd jst ins fnl f: no ch w wnr* **10/1**

3 hd **Nurse Nightingale** 2-9-0 0.. JimCrowley 11 70+
(Hugo Palmer) *sn towards rr: shkn up and prog 2f out: styd on fnl f to press for 2nd nr fin* **7/1**[3]

0323 **4** 2 **Titi Makfi**[20] 8159 2-9-0 70... PJMcDonald 8 65
(Mark Johnston) *chsd ldr: tried to chal 2f out but sn one pce u.p* **6/1**[2]

25 **5** 1¾ **Scarlet Thrush (IRE)**[60] 7494 2-9-0 0.................................. JFEgan 6 61
(Marco Botti) *led to wl over 1f out: wknd fnl f* **10/1**

6 2 **Tomorrow Mystery** 2-9-0 0.. WilliamCarson 4 56+
(Jamie Osborne) *s.i.s: sn in tch in rr: lft bhd over 2f out: fin quite wl last 150yds* **33/1**

7 2 **Awaayil (IRE)** 2-9-0 0.. MartinHarley 1 51
(James Tate) *nvr bttr than 5th: lft bhd fr over 2f out* **16/1**

0 **8** ½ **Life Happens**[40] 7885 2-9-0 0... RyanTate 3 50
(Jonathan Portman) *in tch: rdn over 2f out: sn btn* **50/1**

00 **9** 7 **Katie's Surprise (IRE)**[57] 7576 2-9-0 0............................. LiamKeniry 5 33
(John Butler) *broke on terms but sn restrained into last: pushed along bhd over 2f out: nvr involved* **66/1**

1m 40.6s (0.80) **Going Correction** -0.10s/f (Stan) **9** Ran SP% **122.5**
Speed ratings (Par 95): **92,89,89,87,85 83,81,81,74**
CSF £8.04 TOTE £1.40: £1.10, £2.30, £1.90; EX 9.10 Trifecta £40.80.
Owner A E Oppenheimer **Bred** Hascombe And Valiant Studs **Trained** Newmarket, Suffolk
■ Night Poetry was withdrawn. Price at time of withdrawal 2/1. Rule 4 applies to bets struck prior to withdrawal - deduction 30p in the pound. New market formed. Everdina was withdrawn. Price at time of withdrawal 50/1. Rule 4 does not apply.

FOCUS
This looked the more interesting of the two divisions, even in the absence of Night Poetry, who was withdrawn at the start, but it was the slower of the two legs by 1.2sec.

8466 32RED ON THE APP STORE NURSERY H'CAP 1m (P)
4:10 (4:11) (Class 5) (0-75,75) 2-Y-O **£3,234** (£962; £481; £240) **Stalls** Low

Form RPR

2054 **1** **Washington Blue**[20] 8159 2-9-1 **69**................................[1] MartinHarley 3 72
(Clive Cox) *trckd ldng pair: rdn and clsd to ld wl over 1f out: hrd pressed and drvn fnl f: hld on wl* **11/1**

1363 **2** hd **Quothquan (FR)**[20] 8153 2-9-3 **71**...................................... LiamKeniry 2 74+
(Michael Madgwick) *t.k.h: trckd ldrs disputing 5th: prog to go 2nd jst over 1f out: str chal ins fnl f: jst hld* **6/1**[3]

4060 **3** ¾ **No Not Again (IRE)**[19] 8174 2-8-5 **64**........................... HollieDoyle(5) 8 65
(Richard Hannon) *settled in 9th: rdn over 2f out: prog over 1f out: styd on wl to take 3rd wl ins fnl f* **33/1**

414 **4** ¾ **African Beat (IRE)**[20] 8153 2-9-7 **75**............................... RobertHavlin 5 76
(John Gosden) *hld up in 7th: nt clr run briefly 2f out: prog over 1f out: kpt on but nvr pce to threaten* **11/8**[1]

4U00 **5** ¾ **Broughtons Story**[13] 8244 2-8-8 **62**........................... StevieDonohoe 13 59
(Henry Spiller) *racd in 8th: shkn up and nt qckn over 2f out: styd on fnl f: nrst fin* **100/1**

355 **6** nk **Suspect Package (USA)**[39] 7907 2-9-5 **73**................. DanielMuscutt 11 69
(James Fanshawe) *s.i.s: towards rr fr wd draw: shkn up over 2f out: styd on quite wl fnl f: nrst fin* **8/1**

3306 **7** ½ **Suffragette City (IRE)**[62] 7467 2-9-0 **68**...................... TomMarquand 4 63
(Richard Hannon) *chsd ldrs disputing 5th: rdn and tried to cl fr 2f out: one pce over 1f out* **16/1**

3246 **8** nk **Upgrade**[32] 8008 2-9-5 **73**.. DougieCostello 9 67
(K R Burke) *sn pressed ldr: led over 2f out to wl over 1f out: wknd fnl f* **40/1**

0056 **9** nk **Pobbles**[13] 8244 2-8-13 **70**....................................... KieranShoemark(3) 10 64
(Roger Charlton) *hld up in rr: pushed along and sme prog 2f out: no hdwy fnl f: nvr involved* **25/1**

063 **10** ½ **Spirit Of Belle**[62] 7458 2-9-0 **73**.................................... PaddyBradley(5) 7 66
(Pat Phelan) *hld up in last pair and racd wd: no prog tl rdn and styd on fr over 1f out: nvr involved* **20/1**

2421 **11** hd **Emenem**[13] 8244 2-9-4 **72**.. JFEgan 14 64
(Simon Dow) *hld up in last trio fr wdst draw: pushed along and no prog 3f out: nt knocked abt whn no ch fnl 2f* **4/1**[2]

6300 **12** nse **Mullarkey**[20] 8153 2-9-3 **71**... KierenFox 12 63
(John Best) *hld up in last: pushed along and sme prog 2f out: no hdwy fnl f: nvr involved* **20/1**

0426 **13** 10 **Fancy Day (IRE)**[26] 8080 2-8-8 **62**....................................... MartinLane 6 30
(Mark Johnston) *led to over 2f out: wknd rapidly: t.o* **33/1**

2530 **14** 2¼ **Baileys Apprentice**[64] 7406 2-8-13 **67**............................ PJMcDonald 1 30
(Mark Johnston) *chsd ldng pair to over 2f out: wknd rapidly: t.o* **25/1**

1m 39.43s (-0.37) **Going Correction** -0.10s/f (Stan) **14** Ran SP% **128.2**
Speed ratings (Par 96): **97,96,96,95,94 94,93,93,93,92 92,92,82,80**
CSF £73.66 CT £2216.55 TOTE £13.20: £3.30, £1.90, £8.70; EX 84.10 Trifecta £1827.70.
Owner Cavendish Bloodstock Racing **Bred** Cavendish Bloodstock **Trained** Lambourn, Berks
■ Stewards' Enquiry : Martin Harley two-day ban: used whip above permitted level (Jan 3-4)

FOCUS
The early pace wasn't overly strong and they finished in a bit of a heap. It's been rated around the winner back to her pre-race best.

8467 100% PROFIT BOOST AT 32REDSPORT.COM NURSERY H'CAP 6f (P)
4:40 (4:41) (Class 6) (0-65,69) 2-Y-O **£2,264** (£673; £336; £168) **Stalls** Low

Form RPR

0562 **1** **Lord Cooper**[47] 7776 2-9-2 **60**.....................................(tp) RenatoSouza 2 68
(Jose Santos) *chsd ldrs in 5th: clsd on inner over 2f out: rdn to ld over 1f out: kpt on wl* **10/1**

302 **2** 1¾ **Debonaire David**[25] 8097 2-9-5 **63**...................................(t) ShaneKelly 8 66
(Richard Hughes) *sltly awkward s: chsd ldrs in 6th: shkn up over 2f out: clsd over 1f out: kpt on wl to take 2nd last strides: no ch to chal* **4/1**[2]

1054 **3** nk **Snuggy (IRE)**[11] 8285 2-9-4 **62**.. MartinHarley 1 64
(David Barron) *chsd ldng pair to 2f out: kpt on wl u.p to take 3rd again last stride* **9/1**

0211 **4** *shd* **Gracious Tom (IRE)**[7] 8344 2-9-11 **69** 6ex................................ JFEgan 6 71
(David Evans) *chsd ldr: rdn to ld 2f out: hdd over 1f out and sn wl hld by wnr: lost 2 pls nr fin* **5/2**[1]

430 **5** *½* **Fair Selene**[49] 7750 2-9-2 **60**..(p) LiamKeniry 3 60
(Heather Main) *chsd ldng trio: rdn over 2f out: kpt on to press for a pl ins fnl f: one pce nr fin* **16/1**

4366 **6** *4 ½* **Dream Reversion**[15] 8229 2-9-7 **65**........................ RichardKingscote 7 52
(Tom Dascombe) *mostly in 7th and nt on terms w ldrs: shkn up and no imp over 2f out: no ch after* **7/1**[3]

2665 **7** *hd* **Texas Katie**[20] 8159 2-9-8 **66**...................................(b[1]) DavidProbert 5 52+
(Archie Watson) *racd freely: led at str pce: hdd 2f out: wknd qckly fnl f* **4/1**[2]

000 **8** *¾* **Miriam Violet**[71] 7210 2-7-10 **45**..................................... HollieDoyle[(5)] 4 29
(Paul Henderson) *a abt 8th and sn pushed along: nvr on terms and nvr a factor* **66/1**

000 **9** *1 ¾* **Chough**[20] 8152 2-9-2 **60**... JimCrowley 10 38
(Hughie Morrison) *a in rr: rdn and no prog over 2f out* **14/1**

506 **10** *½* **Hollywood Style**[15] 8230 2-8-3 **50**.......................... EdwardGreatrex[(3)] 9 27
(William Knight) *dwlt: a in rr: rdn and no prog over 2f out* **50/1**

3463 **11** *3 ½* **Zaatar (IRE)**[144] 4815 2-9-2 **60**.. PJMcDonald 12 26
(Mick Channon) *dropped in fr wd draw: t.k.h and hld up in last pair: no prog over 2f out: no ch after* **25/1**

6400 **12** *¾* **Sliceoflife**[20] 8159 2-9-0 **65**.......................................[1] JacobMitchell[(7)] 11 29
(Marco Botti) *tk fierce hold and hld up in last: racd awkwardly and nvr any prog* **25/1**

1m 12.08s (-1.02) **Going Correction** -0.10s/f (Stan) **12** Ran SP% **123.9**
Speed ratings (Par 94): **102,99,99,99,98 92,92,91,88,88 83,82**
CSF £50.83 CT £396.95 TOTE £12.60: £3.40, £2.40, £3.00; EX 73.90 Trifecta £571.90.
Owner R Cooper Racing Ltd **Bred** Miss K Rausing **Trained** Upper Lambourn, Berks

FOCUS
This was run at a decent pace. The winner has been rated as replicating his latest form.

8468 "NOEL BHOYS" H'CAP 1m 4f (P)

5:10 (5:10) (Class 6) (0-55,55) 3-Y-O+ **£2,264** (£673; £336; £168) **Stalls** Centre

Form RPR

0000 **1** **Stand Guard**[237] 1796 12-9-6 **54**.. LiamKeniry 12 60
(John Butler) *hld up towards rr: prog over 2f out: clsd to ld jst over 1f out: sn wl in command: rdn out* **10/1**

42P6 **2** *¾* **Graceful Lady**[31] 8039 3-9-1 **54**.. PatCosgrave 3 58
(Robert Eddery) *t.k.h: hld up in tch: prog to go 3rd over 3f out: drvn over 2f out: kpt on to take 2nd ins fnl f but unable to chal* **11/2**[3]

0000 **3** *nk* **Staplehurst (IRE)**[48] 7767 3-8-12 **51**...............................[1] TimmyMurphy 8 54
(Geoffrey Deacon) *broke on terms but sn restrained and in last after 3f: stl there 3f out: gd prog and scythed through fr 2f out to take 3rd ins fnl f: too much to do* **33/1**

0004 **4** *1 ¾* **Lily Edge**[6] 8359 7-9-0 **48**...(v) DannyBrock 14 49
(John Bridger) *chsd ldrs: lost pl fr 1/2-way: rdn over 2f out towards rr: kpt on fr over 1f out: n.d* **14/1**

5000 **5** *nk* **Comedy House**[13] 8254 8-8-13 **52**........................ MeganNicholls[(5)] 7 52
(Michael Madgwick) *dwlt: wl in rr: wdst of all bnd 3f out: rdn and kpt on fnl 2f: nrst fin* **20/1**

0032 **6** *½* **Sund City (FR)**[6] 8359 3-8-12 **51**...................................... DavidProbert 2 50
(Harry Dunlop) *led: drew clr fr 4f out: drvn over 2f out: c bk to rivals and hdd jst over 1f out: wknd* **11/8**[1]

0000 **7** *hd* **Tractive Effort**[3] 8428 3-8-10 **49**.. KierenFox 5 48
(Michael Attwater) *t.k.h: prom: lost pl over 3f out: plugged on u.p fr over 1f out* **20/1**

0000 **8** *2* **Smoky Hill (IRE)**[31] 8039 7-9-7 **55**.................................... JoeyHaynes 11 51
(Tony Carroll) *hld up in midfield on outer: rdn over 2f out: no prog over 1f out and wl hld after* **9/2**[2]

0040 **9** *1* **Murraqib (USA)**[48] 7760 3-8-10 **49**..............................(v) StevieDonohoe 1 43
(Brett Johnson) *prom: chsd clr ldr 4f out to wl over 1f out: wknd* **33/1**

0600 **10** *1 ½* **Silver Lining (IRE)**[64] 7421 4-9-2 **50**.............................. RobertHavlin 13 42
(Mark Hoad) *hld up in tch: prog on inner to dispute 2nd briefly 2f out: sn wknd* **50/1**

3200 **11** *4 ½* **Little Orchid**[18] 8193 3-8-7 **51**.. HollieDoyle[(5)] 4 36
(Julia Feilden) *a towards rr: struggling over 2f out* **16/1**

0336 **12** *2 ¾* **Hermosa Vaquera (IRE)**[14] 6891 6-9-2 **50**..............(p) FergusSweeney 6 30
(Gary Moore) *hld up in rr: quick prog on outer to go prom 1/2-way: wknd 3f out* **16/1**

1600 **13** *27* **Catharina**[153] 4527 4-8-13 **52**..................................... LuluStanford[(5)] 10
(Dean Ivory) *t.k.h: pressed ldr: lost 2nd 4f out and wknd rapidly: t.o* **20/1**

2m 35.03s (0.53) **Going Correction** -0.10s/f (Stan)
WFA 3 from 4yo+ 5lb **13** Ran SP% **125.3**
Speed ratings (Par 101): **94,93,93,92,91 91,91,90,89,88 85,83,65**
CSF £61.73 CT £1798.35 TOTE £14.50: £3.40, £2.10, £12.40; EX 102.90 Trifecta £1577.20.
Owner Miss Alice Haynes **Bred** Juddmonte Farms Ltd **Trained** Newmarket, Suffolk

FOCUS
An ordinary handicap, but a welcome return to form for a veteran AW performer. Those in behind the winner set the level.

8469 RACING UK ALL WEATHER "HANDS AND HEELS" APPRENTICE H'CAP (RACING EXCELLENCE INITIATIVE) 1m (P)

5:40 (5:40) (Class 5) (0-70,72) 4-Y-O+ **£3,234** (£962; £481; £240) **Stalls** Low

Form RPR

3230 **1** **Believe It (IRE)**[20] 8154 4-8-9 **65**................................(b) NicolaCurrie[(7)] 5 73
(Richard Hughes) *pressed ldr for 1f then settled in 2nd: clsd to chal over 1f out: led jst ins fnl f: styd on wl* **5/1**[3]

5621 **2** *1 ½* **Baltic Prince (IRE)**[20] 8154 6-9-4 **72**............................ AledBeech[(5)] 6 77
(Tony Carroll) *led: def advantage after 2f: pushed along over 1f out: hdd jst ins fnl f: kpt on* **5/2**[1]

-503 **3** *4 ½* **Muzaahim (IRE)**[26] 8085 5-8-4 **58**.................................. TobyEley[(5)] 2 53
(Kevin Morgan) *in tch: chsd ldng pair over 3f out: no imp 2f out: lost grnd fnl f* **7/1**

1160 **4** *2 ¼* **Gracious George (IRE)**[19] 8178 6-9-0 **70**.................... FinleyMarsh[(7)] 1 59
(Jimmy Fox) *hld up: jst in tch in 5th over 2f out: sn outpcd by ldrs: tk modest 4th nr fin* **4/1**[2]

5355 **5** *¾* **Stormbound (IRE)**[20] 8154 7-8-12 **66**..........................(b) WilliamCox[(5)] 4 54
(Paul Cole) *hld up: wd bnd 1/2-way: in tch in 4th over 2f out: wknd over 1f out* **4/1**[2]

0351 **6** *1 ¼* **Seek The Fair Land**[13] 8258 10-9-3 **66**............................(v) JaneElliott 8 51
(Lee Carter) *hld up: v wd bnd 1/2-way and lost grnd: nvr on terms after* **8/1**

-000 **7** *4 ½* **Put The Boot In (IRE)**[200] 695 4-8-8 **57**............................ JordanUys 7 32
(Barry Brennan) *chsd ldng pair to over 3f out: sn dropped to rr and looked reluctant* **66/1**

0053 **8** *½* **Hannington**[174] 2977 5-8-11 **67**...................................(tp) JacobMitchell[(7)] 3 40
(Barry Brennan) *v awkward s and slowly away: mostly in last and nvr a factor* **25/1**

1m 38.78s (-1.02) **Going Correction** -0.10s/f (Stan) **8** Ran SP% **114.2**
Speed ratings (Par 103): **101,99,95,92,92 90,86,85**
CSF £17.87 CT £87.41 TOTE £5.10: £1.80, £1.30, £2.00; EX 20.10 Trifecta £95.70.
Owner Richard Hughes **Bred** The Kathryn Stud **Trained** Upper Lambourn, Berkshire

FOCUS
Only two ever really mattered in this apprentice handicap. It's been rated around the runner-up to his latest C&D career best.
T/Plt: £301.70 to a £1 stake. Pool: £84,366.87 - 204.10 winning units. T/Qpdt: £29.80 to a £1 stake. Pool: £9,623.73 - 238.28 winning units. **Jonathan Neesom**

8344 SOUTHWELL (L-H)

Tuesday, December 20

OFFICIAL GOING: Fibresand: standard
Wind: Moderate half against Weather: Fine 7 dry

8470 SUNBETS.CO.UK DOWNLOAD THE APP H'CAP (DIV I) 1m (F)

12:00 (12:01) (Class 6) (0-55,55) 3-Y-O+ **£3,234** (£962; £481; £240) **Stalls** Low

Form RPR

0036 **1** **General Tufto**[14] 8240 11-8-13 **47**....................................(b) JoeyHaynes 5 56
(Charles Smith) *sn pushed along towards rr: hdwy over 3f out: rdn to chse ldrs over 2f out: styd on to ld ent fnl f: sn drvn clr and edgd lft: kpt on strly* **7/1**

655 **2** *2 ½* **Dancin Alpha**[10] 8306 5-9-6 **54**... JoeFanning 9 55
(Alan Swinbank) *rr and pushed along: sn swtchd rt to outer: hdwy 3f out: rdn along 2f out: drvn to chse ldrs over 1f out: edgd lft ins fnl f: kpt on* **3/1**[1]

0366 **3** *nk* **Capital Gearing**[24] 8120 3-9-4 **53**...............................(b) PaulMulrennan 12 52
(Henry Spiller) *prom: cl up 1/2-way: rdn to ld 2f out: drvn and edgd rt over 1f out: hdd ent fnl f: kpt on same pce* **7/1**

4634 **4** *2* **Ershaad (IRE)**[21] 8146 4-9-1 **49**....................................(b) LukeMorris 10 45
(Shaun Harris) *dwlt: sn in tch: chsd ldrs 3f out: rdn 2f out: sn drvn and kpt on fnl f* **8/1**

0535 **5** *¾* **Ertidaad (IRE)**[24] 8121 4-9-3 **51**..............................(v) RobertWinston 8 45
(Emma Owen) *chsd ldrs: rdn over 2f out: drvn over 1f out: sn one pce* **6/1**[3]

0504 **6** *3 ¾* **Claude Greenwood**[27] 8070 6-8-11 **48**..............(b) GeorgeDowning[(3)] 11 33
(Tony Carroll) *prom: rdn along over 2f out: drvn wl over 1f out: grad wknd* **10/3**[2]

6 **7** *shd* **Ocotillo (IRE)**[18] 8191 3-8-11 **46** oh1.................................. RyanPowell 7 30
(Kevin Frost) *slt ld: rdn along 3f out: hdd 2f out: sn drvn and grad wknd* **33/1**

0000 **8** *11* **Sober Up**[14] 8236 4-9-4 **52**...(p) TomEaves 2 12
(Ivan Furtado) *a towards rr* **33/1**

0000 **9** *1* **Rupert Boy (IRE)**[62] 7463 3-9-3 **52**.. BenCurtis 4 9
(Scott Dixon) *chsd ldrs 3f: outpcd and bhd fr 1/2-way* **14/1**

4-06 **10** *7* **Chesham Rose (IRE)**[163] 3053 3-9-2 **51**................(v[1]) AdamBeschizza 3
(Dave Roberts) *cl up on inner: rdn along wl over 2f out: sn wknd* **66/1**

00-6 **11** *7* **Blythe Prince**[36] 7960 4-8-5 **46** oh1.................................(b[1]) RPWalsh[(7)] 1
(Christopher Kellett) *chsd ldrs on inner: pushed along and n.m.r 1/2-way: sn wknd* **100/1**

1m 42.97s (-0.73) **Going Correction** -0.175s/f (Stan)
WFA 3 from 4yo+ 1lb **11** Ran SP% **113.5**
Speed ratings (Par 101): **96,93,93,91,90 86,86,75,74,67 60**
CSF £26.80 CT £155.17 TOTE £7.70: £3.00, £1.30, £2.30; EX 32.80 Trifecta £269.40.
Owner J R Theaker **Bred** Hascombe And Valiant Studs **Trained** Temple Bruer, Lincs
■ Stewards' Enquiry : Joey Haynes two-day ban: used whip above permitted level (Jan 3-4)

FOCUS
A weak handicap, though made more interesting by the presence of a local legend who proved that fairytales do come true. The third has been rated 4lb off this year's form.

8471 SUNBETS.CO.UK DOWNLOAD THE APP H'CAP (DIV II) 1m (F)

12:30 (12:31) (Class 6) (0-55,55) 3-Y-O+ **£3,234** (£962; £481; £240) **Stalls** Low

Form RPR

0000 **1** **Shearian**[115] 5887 6-8-9 **48**.. PhilDennis[(5)] 4 62
(Declan Carroll) *trckd ldrs: hdwy on inner and n.m.r over 2f out: squeezed through to ld 11/2f out: sn rdn clr: readily* **6/1**[2]

0455 **2** *4 ½* **Schottische**[8] 8337 6-9-3 **51**..(b) LukeMorris 3 53
(Alan Bailey) *in tch: hdwy 3f out: chsd ldrs 2f out: rdn to chse wnr over 1f out: sn drvn and no imp* **17/2**

4345 **3** *3* **Jessica Jo (IRE)**[10] 8307 3-9-4 **53**..................................(b) JoeFanning 2 47
(Mark Johnston) *slt ld on inner: rdn along wl over 2f out: edgd rt and hdd 11/2f out: sn drvn and kpt on same pce* **5/1**[1]

000 **4** *4* **Quadriga (IRE)**[7] 8350 6-9-2 **55**................................ MeganNicholls[(5)] 7 41
(Chris Grant) *rr: hdwy over 2f out: sn rdn and kpt on appr fnl f: nrst fin* **16/1**

4000 **5** *½* **Master Of Song**[10] 8306 9-8-7 **48**................................(vt) KevinLundie[(7)] 12 32
(Roy Bowring) *sn cl up on outer: effrt over 2f out and sn rdn: drvn and edgd rt over 1f out: sn edgd lft and grad wknd* **13/2**[3]

5 **6** *1 ¼* **Sarakova (IRE)**[18] 8190 3-9-1 **50**.. RyanPowell 6 31
(Kevin Frost) *in tch: hdwy to chse ldrs over 3f out: rdn along 2f out: swtchd lft and drvn appr fnl f: kpt on one pce* **12/1**

0030 **7** *hd* **Sir Jack**[46] 7794 3-9-3 **55**...................................... GeorgeDowning[(3)] 10 35
(Tony Carroll) *rr and sn pushed along: rdn over 3f out: styd on fnl 2f: n.d* **5/1**[1]

4025 **8** *nk* **Thatsthewaytodoit (IRE)**[18] 8194 3-9-3 **52**........................ DaleSwift 9 31
(Daniel Mark Loughnane) *prom: pushed along over 3f out: rdn wl over 2f out: sn wknd* **6/1**[2]

0605 **9** *2 ½* **Stanlow**[46] 7795 6-8-12 **46**..(be) TomEaves 1 21
(Michael Mullineaux) *midfield: hdwy on inner and in tch over 3f out: rdn to chse ldrs over 2f out: sn drvn and wknd* **33/1**

0-00 **10** *6* **Miss Uppity**[54] 7642 3-9-3 **52**.. LemosdeSouza 5 12
(Ivan Furtado) *a rr* **33/1**

3464 **11** *2 ¼* **Luv U Lucky**[214] 2448 4-8-12 **46** oh1................................ JoeyHaynes 8 2
(Jo Hughes) *cl up: rdn along wl over 2f out: sn drvn and wknd* **8/1**

0-00 **12** *85* **Dream Journey (IRE)**[17] 8212 3-8-11 **46** oh1.................... BenCurtis 11
(Daniel O'Brien) *in tch: pushed along after 3f: rdn along 1/2-way: sn outpcd and bhd: eased fnl 2f* **66/1**

1m 42.17s (-1.53) **Going Correction** -0.175s/f (Stan)
WFA 3 from 4yo+ 1lb **12** Ran SP% **117.8**
Speed ratings (Par 101): **100,95,92,88,88 86,86,86,83,77 75,**
CSF £55.24 CT £228.36 TOTE £5.70: £2.30, £3.80, £1.90; EX 63.40 Trifecta £503.50.
Owner Mrs Sarah Bryan **Bred** Minehart Developments Ltd **Trained** Malton, N Yorks

FOCUS
The winning time was 0.8sec quicker than the first division and they finished well spread out. Straightforward form.

8472 BETWAY MEDIAN AUCTION MAIDEN STKS 5f (F)
1:00 (1:04) (Class 5) 3-5-Y-O **£4,528** (£1,347; £673; £336) **Stalls** Centre

Form RPR

0005 **1** **Gorgeous (FR)**[111] 6036 3-8-11 43 GeorgeDowning[(3)] 10 56
(Tony Carroll) *racd towards stands side: towards rr: hdwy 1/2-way/ edgd lft 2f out: sn rdn to chse ldrs: chal and hung lft 1f out: drvn to ld and edgd lft ins fnl f: kpt on wl towards fin* **33/1**

32 **2** *nk* **La Fortuna**[38] 7935 3-9-0 0 LukeMorris 8 55
(Charlie Wallis) *cl up: rdn 2f out and sn edgd lft. chal wl over 1f out: drvn and ev ch ent fnl f: hrd drvn and kpt on* **7/2**[1]

3-0 **3** *hd* **Private Donald**[11] 8290 3-9-2 0 [1] EoinWalsh[(3)] 11 59+
(Robert Cowell) *cl up: led over 3f out: rdn along 2f out: jnd and drvn over 1f out: edgd lft and hdd ins fnl f: kpt on* **12/1**

4 **4** *1 1/4* **Diamond Indulgence**[11] 8290 3-8-11 0 NoelGarbutt[(3)] 7 50
(Derek Shaw) *in tch: hdwy 1/2-way: rdn to chse ldrs over 1f out: drvn and kpt on same pce fnl f* **11/1**

35 **5** *1 3/4* **Hadley**[11] 8288 3-9-5 50 JasonHart 1 48+
(Tracy Waggott) *cl up: rdn along 2f out: drvn over 1f out: sn wknd* **10/1**[3]

04 **6** *1/2* **Rigsby**[38] 7935 3-9-5 0 KieranO'Neill 2 47+
(Zoe Davison) *racd towards far side: rdn along after 1f and towards rr: hdwy 2f out: sn drvn and n.d* **14/1**

-006 **7** *2 1/2* **Clever Divya**[179] 3625 3-9-0 52 JoeFanning 5 33
(J R Jenkins) *dwlt: a towards rr* **6/1**[2]

0000 **8** *1 3/4* **Single Summit**[61] 7489 4-9-5 37 (v) ConnorBeasley 9 31
(J R Jenkins) *slt ld: hdd over 3f out: cl up: rdn 2f out: sn drvn and grad wknd* **33/1**

0006 **9** *3/4* **Lady Elizabeth (IRE)**[11] 8290 3-9-0 50 BenCurtis 3 24
(Scott Dixon) *prom: rdn along 1/2-way: sn wknd* **20/1**

6-56 **10** *hd* **Don't Tell Jo Jo**[122] 5628 3-9-2 34 NathanEvans[(3)] 6 28
(Bill Turner) *racd towards far side: a towards rr* **50/1**

1m 0.34s (0.64) **Going Correction** +0.10s/f (Slow) **10** Ran SP% **80.9**
Speed ratings (Par 103): **98,97,97,95,92 91,87,84,83,83**
CSF £67.03 TOTE £23.90: £4.40, £1.20, £3.30; EX 71.80 Trifecta £666.40.
Owner Wedgewood Estates **Bred** Mme Liza Judd **Trained** Cropthorne, Worcs
■ Poetic Queen was withdrawn. Price at time of withdrawal 7/4F. Rule 4 applies to all bets - deduction 35p in the pound.

FOCUS
A moderate older-horse maiden with the winner rated 43, and weakened further by the withdrawal of the favourite Poetic Queen after she refused to enter the stalls. It's been rated around the runner-up and third.

8473 BETWAY H'CAP 6f (F)
1:30 (1:31) (Class 5) (0-75,75) 3-Y-O+ **£4,528** (£1,347; £673; £336) **Stalls** Low

Form RPR

0002 **1** **Ticks The Boxes (IRE)**[14] 8236 4-8-13 **67** (p) RobertWinston 8 84+
(Michael Herrington) *prom: effrt 2f out and sn edging lft: chsd ldr over 1f out: rdn to ld and carried hd awkwardly ent fnl f: sn clr: kpt on wl* **8/1**[3]

0002 **2** *3 1/4* **Harwoods Star (IRE)**[7] 8345 6-8-11 **72** (be) JoshuaBryan[(7)] 10 77
(John Butler) *in tch: rdn along and hdwy wl over 1f out: drvn and kpt on fnl f* **8/1**[3]

0013 **3** *1/2* **Vroom (IRE)**[7] 8345 3-8-10 **71** (p) GabrieleMalune[(7)] 2 74
(Gay Kelleway) *cl up: rdn along 2f out: drvn over 1f out: kpt on same pce fnl f* **4/1**[2]

005 **4** *3/4* **Jack Luey**[7] 8349 9-9-2 **70** (b) TomEaves 14 71
(Lawrence Mullaney) *qckly away and sn led: rdn wl over 1f out: drvn and hdd ent fnl f: grad wknd* **25/1**

1604 **5** *nse* **Interlink (USA)**[7] 8349 3-9-4 **72** BenCurtis 11 73+
(Tony Coyle) *midfield on outer: hdwy and wd st: rdn wl over 1f out: kpt on fnl f: nrst fin* **11/4**[1]

0500 **6** *nk* **Fujin**[14] 8236 5-8-8 **67** CharlieBennett[(5)] 13 67
(Shaun Harris) *prom: rdn along over 2f out: drvn wl over 1f out: grad wknd* **25/1**

0002 **7** *shd* **Spice Mill (IRE)**[19] 8181 3-8-13 **67** (tp) LukeMorris 9 67+
(Michael Appleby) *dwlt and towards rr: hdwy and wd st: rdn and in tch wl over 1f out: kpt on fnl f: nrst fin* **10/1**

6505 **8** *1/2* **Dusty Blue**[15] 8228 4-8-8 **65** GeorgeDowning[(3)] 12 63+
(Tony Carroll) *prom on outer: effrt over 2f out: rdn along wl over 1f out: sn drvn and one pce* **25/1**

0150 **9** *4 1/2* **Evanescent (IRE)**[17] 8206 7-8-8 **65** EoinWalsh[(3)] 6 49
(Tony Carroll) *nvr bttr than midfield* **14/1**

0000 **10** *1/2* **Crosse Fire**[7] 8349 4-9-7 **75** KieranO'Neill 4 57
(Scott Dixon) *v.s.a: a rr* **12/1**

-350 **11** *1 1/2* **Foolaad**[55] 7623 5-8-4 **65** (t) KevinLundie[(7)] 5 42
(Roy Bowring) *a rr* **10/1**

-614 **12** *9* **Secret Clause**[201] 2834 3-8-5 **66** RPWalsh[(7)] 1 14
(Michael Appleby) *in tch on inner: hdwy to chse ldrs 1/2-way: rdn along 2f out: sn wknd* **33/1**

2100 **13** *4 1/2* **Layla's Hero (IRE)**[13] 8252 9-9-1 **72** (b) RobHornby[(3)] 7 6
(Roger Teal) *a rr: bhd and outpcd fr 1/2-way* **28/1**

1m 15.6s (-0.90) **Going Correction** -0.175s/f (Stan) **13** Ran SP% **119.4**
Speed ratings (Par 103): **99,94,94,93,92 92,92,91,85,85 83,71,65**
CSF £65.77 CT £307.72 TOTE £10.20: £2.80, £3.00, £2.00; EX 79.70 Trifecta £301.20.
Owner Darren & Annaley Yates **Bred** John B Hughes **Trained** Cold Kirby, N Yorks

FOCUS
An ordinary sprint handicap and you had to be handy. The runner-up gives the form a bit of substance after his back-to-form C&D latest, and the third has been rated close to his recent C&D form.

8474 BETWAY SPRINT H'CAP 5f (F)
2:00 (2:02) (Class 6) (0-65,65) 3-Y-O+ **£3,234** (£962; £481; £240) **Stalls** Centre

Form RPR

5531 **1** **Piazon**[14] 8242 5-9-0 **65** (be) JoshuaBryan[(7)] 1 74
(John Butler) *racd nr far rail: trckd ldr: hdwy to ld 11/2f out: rdn clr ent fnl f: kpt on wl* **6/4**[1]

0300 **2** *1 1/2* **Sarabi**[31] 8040 3-9-7 **65** (p) BenCurtis 4 69
(Scott Dixon) *racd towards far side: in tch: rdn along and sltly outpcd 1/2-way: swtchd lft and hdwy wl over 1f out: drvn to chse wnr ins fnl f: kpt on* **14/1**

3306 **3** *1 1/4* **Archimedes (IRE)**[7] 8345 3-9-7 **65** (t) RobertWinston 5 65
(David C Griffiths) *trckd ldrs centre: effrt 2f out and sn rdn along: drvn and kpt on fnl f* **9/2**[2]

0036 **4** *nk* **Bonjour Steve**[10] 8315 5-8-10 **59** (p) PhilDennis[(5)] 14 57+
(Richard Price) *hld up and towards rr: pushed along bef 1/2-way: rdn 2f out: styd on wl fnl f: nrst fin* **12/1**

3600 **5** *nk* **Mustn't Grumble (IRE)**[10] 8315 3-8-13 **57** LukeMorris 2 54
(David Loughnane) *chsd ldrs: rdn along 2f out: drvn over 1f out: kpt on same pce* **13/2**[3]

2520 **6** *1* **Frank The Barber (IRE)**[42] 7860 4-9-0 **58** (t) AdamBeschizza 12 52+
(Steph Hollinshead) *in tch centre: hdwy to chse ldrs 2f out: sn rdn: drvn and kpt on same pce fnl f* **25/1**

5000 **7** *1/2* **Bapak Bangsawan**[14] 8242 6-8-8 **57** (be[1]) AnnStokell[(5)] 3 49
(Ann Stokell) *racd towards far side: slt ld: rdn along 2f out: sn edgd rt and hdd: grad wknd* **25/1**

0022 **8** *1 1/4* **Multi Quest**[52] 7694 4-8-8 **52** (b) RyanPowell 8 39
(John E Long) *towards rr centre: hdwy 2f out: sn rdn and kpt on fnl f: nrst fin* **20/1**

1600 **9** *nk* **Pearl Noir**[14] 8236 6-8-9 **60** (b) NatalieHambling[(7)] 10 46
(Scott Dixon) *cl up centre: rdn along 2f out: sn drvn and wknd over 1f out* **66/1**

0 **10** *1 3/4* **Pick Of Any (IRE)**[20] 8149 3-8-8 **55** EoinWalsh[(3)] 9 35
(Tony Carroll) *a towards rr* **20/1**

5030 **11** *1* **Culloden**[14] 8242 4-8-10 **59** CharlieBennett[(5)] 11 35
(Shaun Harris) *a towards rr* **33/1**

2000 **12** *2 1/4* **Sir Geoffrey (IRE)**[14] 8242 10-8-8 **52** (b) KieranO'Neill 7 20
(Scott Dixon) *racd towards far side: a rr* **20/1**

000 **13** *hd* **Oscars Journey**[14] 8242 6-9-0 **58** (vt) JoeFanning 13 26
(J R Jenkins) *in tch towards stands side: rdn along 2f out: sn wknd* **16/1**

59.53s (-0.17) **Going Correction** +0.10s/f (Slow) **13** Ran SP% **118.2**
Speed ratings (Par 101): **105,102,100,100,99 98,97,95,94,91 90,86,86**
CSF £21.77 CT £82.54 TOTE £2.10: £1.20, £3.70, £1.80; EX 26.00 Trifecta £93.00.
Owner Royale Racing Syndicate **Bred** Peter Baldwin **Trained** Newmarket, Suffolk

FOCUS
A moderate sprint handicap with the action unfolding towards the far side. The runner-up has been rated to the best of this year's AW form.

8475 SUNBETS.CO.UK H'CAP 7f (F)
2:30 (2:31) (Class 3) (0-90,90) 3-Y-O+
£9,960 (£2,982; £1,491; £745; £372; £187) **Stalls** Low

Form RPR

1030 **1** **Mithqaal (USA)**[47] 7779 3-8-12 **81** AndrewMullen 11 94
(Michael Appleby) *trckd ldrs: hdwy on outer 2f out: rdn to chal over 1f out: drvn to ld ins fnl f kpt on strly* **11/4**[1]

4600 **2** *2* **Philba**[29] 8049 4-9-4 **90** (tp) AlistairRawlinson[(3)] 14 98
(Michael Appleby) *trckd ldrs: hdwy and cl up over 2f out: rdn to ld over 1f out: hdd and drvn ins fnl f: kpt on* **8/1**

0001 **3** *shd* **Captain Revelation**[14] 8239 4-8-13 **82** LukeMorris 10 90
(Tom Dascombe) *chsd ldrs: rdn along over 2f out: drvn over 1f out: kpt on wl fnl f* **7/1**[3]

5260 **4** *2 1/2* **Zaeem**[13] 8251 7-8-7 **83** (p) RPWalsh[(7)] 7 85
(Ivan Furtado) *hld up towards rr: hdwy over 2f out: rdn wl over 1f out: kpt on fnl f: nrst fin* **20/1**

0210 **5** *1* **Haaf A Sixpence**[19] 8177 7-9-2 **88** HectorCrouch[(3)] 12 87
(Ralph Beckett) *slt ld: rdn 2f out: hdd and drvn over 1f out: grad wknd* **5/1**[2]

0600 **6** *nk* **Jack's Revenge (IRE)**[19] 8177 8-9-1 **84** (bt) RobertWinston 9 82
(George Baker) *hld up: hdwy 2f out: rdn to chse ldrs and n.m.r on inner over 1f out: sn drvn and kpt on same pce* **8/1**

0316 **7** *1 1/4* **Young John (IRE)**[10] 8314 3-9-3 **86** DavidNolan 6 81
(Richard Fahey) *in tch: effrt over 2f out: sn rdn along to chse ldrs: swtchd lft and drvn jst over 1f out: no imp* **16/1**

1105 **8** *nk* **Pearl Spectre (USA)**[13] 8256 5-9-3 **86** PaulMulrennan 8 82
(Phil McEntee) *cl up: rdn along over 2f out: drvn over 1f out and grad wknd* **7/1**[3]

0040 **9** *3/4* **Showboating (IRE)**[42] 7858 8-9-2 **85** ShaneGray 13 77
(John Balding) *dwlt: a towards rr* **25/1**

0300 **10** *1* **Jack Of Diamonds (IRE)**[24] 8122 7-9-0 **86** RobHornby[(3)] 1 76
(Roger Teal) *a rr* **66/1**

2425 **11** *6* **Boots And Spurs**[7] 8345 7-8-10 **79** (v) KieranO'Neill 2 53
(Scott Dixon) *in tch on inner: rdn along bef 1/2-way: sn outpcd and bhd* **16/1**

014 **12** *3/4* **Bouclier (IRE)**[116] 5825 6-8-10 **82** GeorgeDowning[(3)] 4 54
(Tony Carroll) *trckd ldrs on inner: rdn along 3f out: sn wknd* **25/1**

0000 **13** *nse* **Merdon Castle (IRE)**[18] 8192 4-9-1 **84** (e) JamesSullivan 5 56
(Ruth Carr) *a rr* **66/1**

1110 **14** *1 3/4* **Shouranour (IRE)**[45] 7825 6-9-2 **85** (b) TomEaves 3 52
(Alan Brown) *cl up on inner: rdn along 3f out: sn wknd* **25/1**

1m 26.84s (-3.46) **Going Correction** -0.175s/f (Stan) **14** Ran SP% **121.6**
Speed ratings (Par 107): **112,109,109,106,105 105,103,103,102,101 94,93,93,91**
CSF £23.15 CT £130.21 TOTE £3.70: £1.70, £3.30, £2.20; EX 36.00 Trifecta £245.00.
Owner The Horse Watchers **Bred** Extern Developments Ltd **Trained** Oakham, Rutland
■ Stewards' Enquiry : Hector Crouch two-day ban: careless riding (Jan 3-4)

FOCUS
A decent Fibresand handicap run at a strong pace with a three-way battle for the lead. It provided a 1-2 for trainer Michael Appleby. A clear pb from the winner, with the second and third helping to set a sound-looking standard.

8476 BETWAY STAYERS H'CAP 1m 6f (F)
3:00 (3:00) (Class 5) (0-75,75) 3-Y-O+ **£4,528** (£1,347; £673; £336) **Stalls** Low

Form RPR

0601 **1** **Western Prince**[86] 6812 3-9-2 **71** BenCurtis 2 81+
(Michael Appleby) *t.k.h: hld up in rr: smooth hdwy over 3f out: led on bit 2f out: pushed clr over 1f out: readily* **7/4**[1]

3600 **2** *3 3/4* **Goldslinger (FR)**[13] 8253 4-9-7 **69** RobertWinston 7 74
(Dean Ivory) *led: rdn along over 2f out: sn hdd and drvn: kpt on: no ch w wnr* **8/1**

0-00 **3** *4* **Katie Gale**[13] 8250 6-9-13 **75** AndrewMullen 4 74
(Michael Appleby) *trckd ldrs: pushed along over 3f out: rdn wl over 2f out: sn drvn and kpt on same pce* **8/1**

525- **4** *1 3/4* **Serenity Now (IRE)**[269] 8272 8-9-4 **73** BenRobinson[(7)] 5 70
(Brian Ellison) *hld up: stdy hdwy on outer 4f out: wd st and cl up over 2f out: rdn and hung lft over 1f out: sn drvn and one pce* **10/1**

0000 **5** *10* **Petrucci (IRE)**[11] 8286 4-9-4 **69** (p) NoelGarbutt[(3)] 1 52
(Derek Shaw) *trckd ldng pair on inner: hdwy over 3f out: rdn along wl over 2f out: sn drvn and wknd* **25/1**

1265 **6** *1 1/2* **Safira Menina**[13] 8253 4-9-9 **74** TimClark[(3)] 6 54
(Martin Smith) *hld up in rr: niggled along 5f out: sme hdwy 3f out: sn rdn and btn* **3/1**[2]

0400 **7** *3* **Spiritoftomintoul**[178] 3639 7-9-10 **75**....................(t) GeorgeDowning[(3)] 3 51
(Tony Carroll) *trckd ldr: rdn along over 3f out: drvn wl over 2f out: sn wknd* **11/2**[3]

3m 5.87s (-2.43) **Going Correction** -0.175s/f (Stan)
WFA 3 from 4yo+ 7lb **7** Ran SP% **111.9**
Speed ratings (Par 103): **99,96,94,93,87 87,85**
CSF £15.82 TOTE £2.40: £1.40, £4.20; EX 16.00 Trifecta £79.80.
Owner Craig Buckingham **Bred** Dayton Investments Ltd **Trained** Oakham, Rutland

FOCUS
An ordinary handicap and quite a test with the pace a fair one. The form might prove a bit better than rated.

8477 DOWNLOAD THE BETWAY APP H'CAP 1m 3f (F)
3:30 (3:30) (Class 5) (0-75,75) 3-Y-O+ **£4,528** (£1,347; £673; £336) **Stalls** Low

Form RPR

2062 **1** **Come Back King (IRE)**[14] 8238 3-9-1 **70**........................(b) BenCurtis 12 81+
(Michael Appleby) *trckd ldrs: hdwy 5f out and sn cl up: chal 2f out and sn rdn: drvn over 1f out: styd on to ld ins fnl f: kpt on strly* **9/4**[1]

-000 **2** *2 3/4* **Seagull Star**[39] 7911 5-9-5 **70**..................................(p) ConnorBeasley 14 77
(Keith Dalgleish) *trckd ldr: led 1/2-way: jnd and rdn 2f out: drvn over 1f out: hdd ins fnl f: no ex last 75 yds* **10/1**

3303 **3** *1* **Thahab Ifraj (IRE)**[12] 8282 3-8-13 **68**................................. LukeMorris 4 73
(Ismail Mohammed) *in tch: hdwy over 3f out: chsd ldrs 2f out: sn rdn and kpt on same pce* **9/2**[3]

0624 **4** *7* **Royal Holiday (IRE)**[14] 8241 9-9-5 **70**.....................(p) RobertWinston 10 63
(Marjorie Fife) *led: hdd 1/2-way: cl up: rdn along 3f out: drvn 2f out and kpt on one pce* **14/1**

650 **5** *4* **Bazooka (IRE)**[59] 7545 5-9-8 **73**..................................... PaulMulrennan 7 59
(David Flood) *hld up in rr: hdwy over 3f out: rdn over 2f out: plugged on: n.d* **20/1**

3000 **6** *1/2* **Port Lairge**[7] 8350 6-8-5 **61** oh2....................................... PhilDennis[(5)] 13 46
(Michael Chapman) *in tch: hdwy on outer to chse ldrs 4f out: rdn along wl over 2f out: sn drvn and plugged on one pce* **66/1**

U220 **7** *2* **Shining Romeo**[13] 8257 4-8-7 **61**.................................... TimClark[(3)] 8 43
(Denis Quinn) *hld up towards rr: gd hdwy on inner 4f out: in tch 3f out: sn rdn and no imp* **20/1**

3020 **8** *1/2* **Firestorm (GER)**[44] 4050 5-9-6 **71**.. TomEaves 6 52
(Michael Attwater) *trckd ldrs: pushed along over 3f out: rdn wl over 2f out: sn drvn and wknd* **28/1**

0000 **9** *2* **Ralphy Lad (IRE)**[98] 6438 5-8-11 **62**.................................. JoeFanning 9 40
(Alan Swinbank) *in tch: rdn along over 3f out: sn drvn and wknd* **4/1**[2]

0033 **10** *3* **Scrafton**[194] 3052 5-8-10 **64**.................................... GeorgeDowning[(3)] 11 37
(Tony Carroll) *a towards rr* **16/1**

5030 **11** *2 3/4* **The Lock Master (IRE)**[207] 2663 9-9-10 **75**...............(p) AndrewMullen 5 43
(Michael Appleby) *a towards rr* **14/1**

/06- **12** *3/4* **Sailors Warn (IRE)**[10] 5221 9-9-7 **72**.................................... DaleSwift 2 39
(Daniel Mark Loughnane) *a towards rr* **40/1**

4310 **13** *2 1/2* **Solarmaite**[214] 2445 7-8-8 **66**......................................(bt) KevinLundie[(7)] 1 29
(Roy Bowring) *chsd ldrs: rdn along 4f out: sn wknd* **40/1**

0040 **14** *1 3/4* **English Summer**[56] 7594 9-9-10 **75**.................................. RyanPowell 3 35
(Ian Williams) *a rr* **50/1**

2m 23.85s (-4.15) **Going Correction** -0.175s/f (Stan)
WFA 3 from 4yo+ 4lb **14** Ran SP% **118.6**
Speed ratings (Par 103): **108,106,105,100,97 96,95,95,93,91 89,88,87,85**
CSF £23.53 CT £96.62 TOTE £3.50: £1.60, £3.60, £1.70; EX 29.10 Trifecta £141.30.
Owner Craig Buckingham **Bred** Darley **Trained** Oakham, Rutland

FOCUS
A modest handicap and few got into it. It's been rated loosely around the third for now.
T/Plt: £22.30 to a £1 stake. Pool: £74,402.34 - 2,430.33 winning units. T/Qpdt: £4.60 to a £1 stake. Pool: £7,096.03 - 1,130.97 winning units. **Joe Rowntree**

8397 NEWCASTLE (A.W) (L-H)
Wednesday, December 21

OFFICIAL GOING: Tapeta: standard
Wind: Breezy, half against Weather: Cloudy, bright

8478 SUNBETS.CO.UK H'CAP 1m 5y (Tp)
1:30 (1:31) (Class 3) (0-95,95) 3-Y-O **£7,246** (£2,168; £1,084; £542; £270) **Stalls** Centre

Form RPR

2000 **1** **Flaming Spear (IRE)**[46] 7821 4-9-4 **92**......................... RobertWinston 1 103
(Kevin Ryan) *t.k.h: cl up: led after 2f: mde rest: hrd pressed and edgd rt over 1f out: rdn out fnl f* **20/1**

0432 **2** *1 1/4* **Constantino (IRE)**[14] 8251 3-8-9 **84**................................. JoeFanning 5 91
(Richard Fahey) *prom: rdn over 2f out: hdwy over 1f out: pressed wnr ins fnl f: kpt on: hld nr fin* **8/1**

0042 **3** *1/2* **Fuwairt (IRE)**[11] 8311 4-9-2 **90**.................................... ConnorBeasley 13 97
(Roger Fell) *stdd s: hld up: smooth hdwy and prom over 1f out: sn rdn: kpt on ins fnl f* **8/1**

041 **4** *1/2* **Keystroke**[25] 8122 4-9-7 **95**.. GrahamLee 12 101+
(Jeremy Noseda) *hld up midfield: stdy hdwy over 2f out: effrt and pressed wnr over 1f out to ins fnl f: one pce last 100yds* **15/8**[1]

1100 **5** *nk* **Fort Bastion (IRE)**[13] 8279 7-9-0 **88**................................... BenCurtis 10 93
(Brian Ellison) *missed break: hld up: rdn over 2f out: hdwy over 1f out: kpt on ins fnl f* **50/1**

1402 **6** *1 1/4* **Briardale (IRE)**[75] 7108 4-8-11 **85**.................................. PatCosgrave 8 87
(James Bethell) *hld up: rdn over 2f out: hdwy over 1f out: kpt on fnl f: no imp* **16/1**

0540 **7** *1/2* **Georgian Bay (IRE)**[11] 8317 6-9-0 **93**.................(vt) JordanVaughan[(5)] 2 94
(K R Burke) *led 2f: pressed wnr: rdn and ev ch over 1f out: outpcd ins fnl f* **33/1**

5000 **8** *nk* **Quixote (GER)**[42] 7868 6-9-2 **93**............................ GeorgeDowning[(3)] 3 93
(Tony Carroll) *dwlt: hld up: rdn over 2f out: hdwy over 1f out: kpt on fnl f: no imp* **4/1**[2]

5355 **9** *3/4* **Michele Strogoff**[13] 8279 3-9-0 **89**........................ JosephineGordon 11 87
(Roger Fell) *t.k.h: trckd ldrs: rdn over 2f out: wknd over 1f out* **18/1**

5000 **10** *1/2* **Two For Two (IRE)**[20] 8177 8-8-11 **85**.............................. PJMcDonald 7 83
(Roger Fell) *hld up midfield: drvn and outpcd over 2f out: n.d after* **50/1**

0300 **11** *7* **Mont Ras (IRE)**[37] 7957 9-8-1 **82**................................ BenSanderson[(7)] 4 63
(Roger Fell) *t.k.h: in tch tl rdn and wknd over 2f out* **100/1**

0511 **12** *3/4* **Pike Corner Cross (IRE)**[26] 8101 4-8-5 **82**.................. RobHornby[(3)] 9 62
(Ed de Giles) *t.k.h: in tch: rdn over 2f out: wknd wl over 1f out* **16/1**

1031 **13** *12* **Amazement (GER)**[26] 8092 3-8-11 **86**................................ LukeMorris 6 37
(James Tate) *hld up: drvn and struggling over 2f out: sn wknd* **7/1**[3]

1m 39.91s (1.31) **Going Correction** +0.225s/f (Slow)
WFA 3 from 4yo+ 1lb **13** Ran SP% **119.1**
Speed ratings (Par 107): **102,100,100,99,99 98,97,97,96,96 89,88,76**
CSF £167.33 CT £1448.11 TOTE £28.00: £5.70, £1.80, £2.60; EX 235.60 Trifecta £2475.60.
Owner Tony Bloom **Bred** Gerry Flannery Developments **Trained** Hambleton, N Yorks

FOCUS
The early gallop was pretty sedate and the winner dominated throughout. The form has been rated at face value around the third.

8479 BETWAY CONDITIONS STKS (ALL-WEATHER CHAMPIONSHIP FAST-TRACK QUALIFIER) 2m 56y (Tp)
2:00 (2:00) (Class 2) 3-Y-O+ **£12,602** (£3,772; £1,886; £944; £470) **Stalls** Low

Form RPR

5U36 **1** **Winning Story**[18] 8210 3-8-9 95.. PatCosgrave 5 109
(Saeed bin Suroor) *dwlt: sn pressing ldr: led gng wl over 3f out: rdn appr 2f out: kpt on wl fnl f* **7/2**[2]

3260 **2** *1 3/4* **First Mohican**[18] 8210 8-9-3 101... HollieDoyle 2 107
(Alan King) *prom: hdwy to chse wnr over 2f out: rdn and kpt on fnl f: nt pce to chal* **10/1**

0252 **3** *2 1/2* **Steve Rogers (IRE)**[35] 7979 5-9-3 98................................ JackMitchell 1 104
(Roger Varian) *t.k.h early: trckd ldrs: rdn along over 2f out: kpt on same pce ins fnl f* **5/1**[3]

3020 **4** *3/4* **Star Storm (IRE)**[28] 8068 4-9-3 107.................................. TomQueally 8 103
(James Fanshawe) *hld up: smooth hdwy on outside and prom over 1f out: sn rdn: kpt on same pce fnl f* **13/8**[1]

0010 **5** *2 3/4* **Oriental Fox (GER)**[35] 7979 8-9-3 103.............................. JoeFanning 7 100
(Mark Johnston) *hld up in tch: stdy hdwy over 2f out: rdn and wknd fr over 1f out* **14/1**

12-4 **6** *hd* **Guard of Honour (IRE)**[53] 7708 5-9-3 88.................(b) RobertWinston 6 100?
(George Baker) *t.k.h: hld up: drvn along over 2f out: btn over 1f out* **12/1**

0005 **7** *3 1/4* **Gang Warfare**[113] 5999 5-9-3 100.................................. PatrickMathers 3 96
(Jamie Osborne) *hld up in tch: drvn and outpcd over 2f out: sn n.d: btn over 1f out* **13/2**

50-0 **8** *20* **Buthelezi (USA)**[25] 8123 8-9-3 87... BenCurtis 4 72
(Brian Ellison) *led to over 3f out: rdn and wknd over 2f out: t.o* **66/1**

3m 31.65s (-3.55) **Going Correction** +0.225s/f (Slow)
WFA 3 from 4yo+ 8lb **8** Ran SP% **115.3**
Speed ratings (Par 109): **117,116,114,114,113 113,111,101**
CSF £38.13 TOTE £4.80: £1.80, £2.60, £1.20; EX 39.30 Trifecta £224.10.
Owner Godolphin **Bred** Darley **Trained** Newmarket, Suffolk

FOCUS
A decent contest and it went to the only 3yo in the line-up. The second and third set the standard.

8480 BETWAY H'CAP 1m 4f 98y (Tp)
2:30 (2:30) (Class 5) (0-70,71) 3-Y-O+ **£3,557** (£1,058; £529; £264) **Stalls** High

Form RPR

0411 **1** **Go George Go (IRE)**[6] 8386 3-8-7 **57** 6ex.......................... JoeFanning 3 70
(Alan Swinbank) *trckd ldr: led on bit over 2f out: shkn up and qcknd clr over 1f out: readily* **4/6**[1]

0626 **2** *6* **Henpecked**[12] 8283 6-9-12 **71**...(p) PJMcDonald 1 75
(Alistair Whillans) *trckd ldrs: rdn over 2f out: chsd (clr) wnr over 1f out: edgd lft u.p ins fnl f: no imp* **11/4**[2]

5330 **3** *2 1/2* **Summer Collection (IRE)**[15] 8241 3-9-0 **69**.......... JordanVaughan[(5)] 4 68
(K R Burke) *in tch: rdn over 2f out: hdwy and edgd lft over 1f out: plugged on fnl f: no imp* **16/1**

0000 **4** *nk* **Wordiness**[14] 8250 8-9-2 **68**................................... KatherineGlenister[(7)] 6 67+
(David Evans) *slowly away: hld up: shkn up 2f out: kpt on fnl f: nvr able to chal* **28/1**

6420 **5** *1 1/4* **Maulesden May (IRE)**[34] 7993 3-9-7 **71**...................... ConnorBeasley 2 68
(Keith Dalgleish) *t.k.h: led at stdy pce: rdn and hdd over 2f out: lost 2nd over 1f out: wknd ins fnl f* **8/1**[3]

1200 **6** *8* **First Summer**[56] 7613 4-9-4 **63**... LukeMorris 5 47
(Shaun Harris) *t.k.h: hld up in tch: drvn and struggling wl over 2f out: sn btn* **28/1**

2m 44.51s (3.41) **Going Correction** +0.225s/f (Slow)
WFA 3 from 4yo+ 5lb **6** Ran SP% **110.5**
Speed ratings (Par 103): **97,93,91,91,90 84**
CSF £2.58 TOTE £1.50: £1.10, £1.50; EX 3.00 Trifecta £13.00.
Owner Lee Bond **Bred** Pat Grogan **Trained** Melsonby, N Yorks

FOCUS
They didn't go much of a gallop early on, but it was still a straightforward success for the odds-on favourite. The runner-up has been rated to her penultimate C&D form.

8481 SUNBETS ON THE APP STORE MAIDEN STKS 1m 5y (Tp)
3:00 (3:01) (Class 5) 3-Y-O+ **£3,234** (£962; £481; £240) **Stalls** Centre

Form RPR

1 **Roller**[200] 3-9-2 0.. NathanEvans[(3)] 3 75+
(Michael Easterby) *t.k.h early: cl up: led gng wl over 2f out: rdn and qcknd over 1f out: pushed out fnl f* **11/4**[2]

34 **2** *2* **Singapore Sling**[13] 7218 3-9-5 0....................................... TomQueally 4 69
(James Fanshawe) *t.k.h early: hld up in tch: stdy hdwy to chse wnr over 1f out: sn rdn: kpt on same pce ins fnl f* **5/6**[1]

3 *4 1/2* **John Milton (IRE)** 3-9-5 0.. GrahamLee 7 58+
(Karen McLintock) *dwlt: rn green in rr: drvn and outpcd over 2f out: rallied over 1f out: kpt on fnl f: no ch w first two* **12/1**

5 **4** *2* **Psychology**[11] 8310 3-9-5 0.. DougieCostello 6 53
(Kenny Johnson) *dwlt: hld up: stdy hdwy over 2f out: rdn over 1f out: sn no imp* **200/1**

0556 **5** *5* **Gloryette**[18] 8211 3-9-0 61... LukeMorris 5 36
(Ed Dunlop) *led to over 2f out: rdn and wknd fr over 1f out* **13/2**[3]

55 **6** *1 3/4* **Samphire Coast**[41] 7894 3-9-2 0.............................. NoelGarbutt[(3)] 1 37
(Derek Shaw) *t.k.h: cl up: rdn over 2f out: wknd wl over 1f out* **25/1**

7 *hd* **Persian Steel (IRE)**[22] 4-9-6 0.. BenCurtis 2 38
(Brian Ellison) *dwlt: t.k.h and sn prom on outside: pushed along 2f out: sn wknd* **25/1**

1m 41.86s (3.26) **Going Correction** +0.225s/f (Slow)
WFA 3 from 4yo 1lb **7** Ran SP% **110.4**
Speed ratings (Par 103): **92,90,85,83,78 76,76**
CSF £4.98 TOTE £4.30: £2.20, £1.40; EX 6.70 Trifecta £28.70.
Owner Irkroy Racing & Andrew Pollock **Bred** Juddmonte Farms Ltd **Trained** Sheriff Hutton, N Yorks

FOCUS
A fair maiden and a good performance from the winner. The first two have been rated close to their previous maiden bests.

8482 DOWNLOAD THE BETWAY APP H'CAP (DIV I) 6f (Tp)
3:30 (3:30) (Class 6) (0-65,65) 3-Y-O+ **£2,911** (£866; £432; £216) **Stalls** Centre

Form RPR
-066 **1** **Ad Vitam (IRE)**[26] 8095 8-8-13 **57**....(bt) TomEaves 3 66
(Suzzanne France) *hld up: effrt and swtchd rt over 1f out: sn rdn: kpt on wl fnl f to ld nr fin* **14/1**
4231 **2** *nk* **Cliff (IRE)**[19] 8188 6-9-5 **63**.... JosephineGordon 5 71
(Nigel Tinkler) *cl up: pushed along briefly over 3f out: smooth hdwy to ld ins fnl f: sn rdn: kpt on: hdd nr fin* **11/4**[1]
0633 **3** *1 3/4* **Thorntoun Lady (USA)**[34] 7994 6-9-0 **61**.... GeorgeDowning[(3)] 2 64
(Jim Goldie) *dwlt: hld up: stdy hdwy 2f out: rdn and kpt on fnl f: nt rch first two* **8/1**
3435 **4** *hd* **Letbygonesbeicons**[58] 7585 3-8-13 **57**.... JoeDoyle 7 59
(John Balding) *t.k.h early: in tch: rdn and effrt 2f out: kpt on same pce ins fnl f* **7/1**[3]
0302 **5** *1/2* **Andys Girl (IRE)**[26] 8093 3-9-4 **62**.... BenCurtis 9 63
(Brian Ellison) *hld up in tch: rdn over 2f out: hdwy over 1f out: edgd lft and no ex ins fnl f* **8/1**
0000 **6** *2 1/2* **Top Of The Bank**[18] 8205 3-9-7 **65**.... ShaneGray 4 58
(Kristin Stubbs) *prom: rdn along 2f out: sn outpcd: btn fnl f* **20/1**
0000 **7** *shd* **Best Trip (IRE)**[57] 7593 9-9-6 **64**....(t) SamJames 1 57
(Marjorie Fife) *led: rdn over 1f out: hdd ins fnl f: sn wknd* **7/1**[3]
0040 **8** *hd* **Minty Jones**[43] 7860 7-8-2 **51** oh6....(v) PhilDennis[(5)] 6 43
(Michael Mullineaux) *t.k.h: cl up tl rdn and wknd over 1f out* **100/1**
6352 **9** *3/4* **Unnoticed**[8] 8351 4-9-4 **62**....(t) RobertWinston 8 52
(Ollie Pears) *t.k.h: in tch: hdwy over 2f out: sn rdn: wknd fnl f* **3/1**[2]

1m 13.34s (0.84) **Going Correction** +0.225s/f (Slow) **9** Ran SP% **111.3**
Speed ratings (Par 101): **103,102,100,100,99 96,95,95,94**
CSF £49.90 CT £326.90 TOTE £12.00: £3.20, £1.40, £2.30; EX 38.00 Trifecta £332.00.
Owner Newstart Partnership **Bred** Michelle Morgan **Trained** Norton, N Yorks

FOCUS
There was a good pace on here and that played into the hands of the winner. The winner has been rated as building on this year's form and getting close to last year's level.

8483 DOWNLOAD THE BETWAY APP H'CAP (DIV II) 6f (Tp)
4:00 (4:01) (Class 6) (0-65,64) 3-Y-O+ **£2,911** (£866; £432; £216) **Stalls** Centre

Form RPR
0604 **1** **Hold On Magnolia**[34] 7994 3-9-5 **62**.... DavidNolan 4 67
(Richard Fahey) *in tch: smooth hdwy to ld over 1f out: sn rdn: kpt on wl fnl f* **6/1**[3]
0030 **2** *3/4* **Le Manege Enchante (IRE)**[26] 8095 3-8-11 **57**....(p) NoelGarbutt[(3)] 7 60
(Derek Shaw) *hld up: pushed along over 2f out: hdwy over 1f out: chsd wnr ins fnl f: kpt on* **25/1**
-550 **3** *3/4* **Tango Sky (IRE)**[249] 1489 7-9-6 **63**.... PaulMulrennan 5 64
(Paul Midgley) *prom: hdwy to press wnr over 1f out to ins fnl f: rdn and edgd lft: kpt on same pce* **20/1**
2400 **4** *1/2* **Sea Of Green**[12] 8289 4-8-7 **50** oh5.... KieranO'Neill 6 51
(Jim Goldie) *in tch: pushed along whn nt clr run and swtchd rt over 1f out: kpt on ins fnl f: nvr able to chal* **40/1**
-011 **5** *hd* **Quiet Warrior (IRE)**[104] 6249 5-9-1 **61**.... GeorgeDowning[(3)] 9 59
(Tony Carroll) *taken steadily to post: stdd s: plld hrd in rr: effrt and hdwy nr side of gp over 1f out: rdn and one pce fnl f* **11/10**[1]
2625 **6** *1 1/4* **Cruise Tothelimit (IRE)**[16] 8234 8-9-7 **64**.... GrahamLee 1 59
(Patrick Morris) *t.k.h: cl up on outside of gp: drvn and ev ch briefly over 1f out: wknd ins fnl f* **16/1**
0226 **7** *nk* **Gold Beau (FR)**[44] 7852 6-9-3 **60**....(p) JosephineGordon 3 54
(Kristin Stubbs) *cl up: rdn over 2f out: rallied and ch over 1f out: wknd ins fnl f* **9/2**[2]
6403 **8** *1 1/2* **Life Of Fame**[26] 8095 3-9-0 **57**....(b[1]) DougieCostello 2 46
(Mark Walford) *dwlt: hld up: effrt and pushed along over 2f out: wknd over 1f out* **14/1**
0620 **9** *4* **Bay Mirage (IRE)**[34] 7994 3-9-7 **64**....(p) TomEaves 8 41
(Kevin Ryan) *led tl rdn and hdd over 1f out: wknd fnl f* **12/1**

1m 14.1s (1.60) **Going Correction** +0.225s/f (Slow) **9** Ran SP% **111.4**
Speed ratings (Par 101): **98,97,96,95,95 93,93,91,85**
CSF £138.12 CT £2709.85 TOTE £6.60: £1.80, £5.50, £4.10; EX 114.70 Trifecta £1340.70.
Owner Dan Gilbert **Bred** Dan Gilbert **Trained** Musley Bank, N Yorks

FOCUS
A modest sprint handicap and the slower of the two divisions by 0.76sec. Ordinary form rated around the first four.

8484 BETWAY SPRINT H'CAP 5f (Tp)
4:30 (4:30) (Class 2) (0-105,110) 3-Y-O+ **£11,971** (£3,583; £1,791; £896; £446) **Stalls** Centre

Form RPR
0024 **1** **Distant Past**[5] 8407 5-8-3 **87**....(v) JoeDoyle 7 96
(Kevin Ryan) *mde all: rdn and edgd lft ent fnl f: kpt on wl: unchal* **7/2**[2]
0141 **2** *1 1/2* **Gracious John (IRE)**[16] 8232 3-9-5 **110**.... KatherineGlenister[(7)] 9 114
(David Evans) *pressed wnr: pushed along and effrt over 1f out: kpt on same pce last 100yds* **4/1**[3]
6040 **3** *nk* **Line Of Reason (IRE)**[80] 6990 6-9-4 **102**.... PaulMulrennan 8 105
(Paul Midgley) *dwlt: sn pushed along in rr: rdn and hdwy on nr side of gp over 1f out: edgd lft and kpt on fnl f* **9/2**
5141 **4** *1 1/4* **Dynamo Walt (IRE)**[11] 8308 5-7-13 **86** oh2....(v) NoelGarbutt[(3)] 3 84
(Derek Shaw) *t.k.h: hld up: rdn and hdwy on far side of gp over 1f out: kpt on same pce ins fnl f* **14/1**
0205 **5** *1* **Top Boy**[16] 8232 6-8-2 **86**....(v) PatrickMathers 6 80
(Derek Shaw) *in tch: rdn along over 2f out: sn outpcd: kpt on fnl f: no imp* **12/1**
0111 **6** *hd* **Caspian Prince (IRE)**[61] 7520 7-9-12 **110**....(t) GrahamLee 10 104
(Roger Fell) *taken steadily to post: chsd ldrs: effrt and drvn along over 1f out: wknd ins fnl f* **5/2**[1]
0000 **7** *1* **Sign Of The Kodiac (IRE)**[16] 8232 3-9-0 **98**.... TomEaves 4 88
(James Given) *dwlt: t.k.h and sn cl up: rdn over 2f out: wknd over 1f out* **14/1**
0030 **8** *3 3/4* **Huntsmans Close**[19] 8192 6-8-8 **92**.... LukeMorris 1 69
(Robert Cowell) *prom: drvn and outpcd over 2f out: wknd over 1f out* **25/1**

58.46s (-1.04) **Going Correction** +0.225s/f (Slow) **8** Ran SP% **113.8**
Speed ratings (Par 109): **117,114,114,112,110 110,108,102**
CSF £17.76 CT £62.65 TOTE £4.60: £1.60, £1.60, £2.00; EX 21.60 Trifecta £61.50.
Owner J C G Chua **Bred** J E Rose **Trained** Hambleton, N Yorks

FOCUS
A good sprint handicap and a gamble was landed. The winner has been rated to this year's turf best, and the runner-up close to form.

8485 100% DEPOSIT BONUS AT BETWAY H'CAP 5f (Tp)
5:00 (5:01) (Class 6) (0-60,59) 3-Y-O+ **£2,587** (£770; £384; £192) **Stalls** Centre

Form RPR
3021 **1** **Novabridge**[11] 8312 8-8-12 **55**....(b) GemmaTutty[(5)] 4 62
(Karen Tutty) *t.k.h early: prom: hdwy to ld over 1f out: drvn and kpt on wl fnl f* **6/1**[3]
0030 **2** *1 1/4* **Whispering Wolf**[33] 8013 3-8-7 **45**.... BarryMcHugh 9 47
(Suzzanne France) *chsd ldrs: rdn and outpcd over 2f out: rallied over 1f out: kpt on wl to take 2nd nr fin: nt rch wnr* **80/1**
3004 **3** *nse* **Windforpower (IRE)**[43] 7859 6-9-4 **56**....(p) DaleSwift 13 58
(Tracy Waggott) *dwlt: hld up: pushed along 1/2-way: hdwy on nr side of gp fnl f: kpt on: nrst fin* **10/1**
0005 **4** *nse* **Lotara**[6] 8390 4-9-4 **59**.... GeorgeDowning[(3)] 2 61
(Jim Goldie) *mounted on crse: dwlt: bhd and sn pushed along: hdwy on far side of gp over 1f out: kpt on fnl f* **6/1**[3]
0005 **5** *nk* **Roy's Legacy**[5] 8409 7-8-12 **55**.... CharlieBennett[(5)] 1 56
(Shaun Harris) *pressed ldr: rdn and ev ch over 1f out: kpt on ins fnl f: no ex and lost three pls towards fin* **8/1**
6000 **6** *nk* **Fuel Injection**[15] 8242 5-9-2 **54**....(p) JackGarritty 10 53
(Paul Midgley) *led: rdn and hdd over 1f out: rallied: kpt on same pce last 100yds* **25/1**
3064 **7** *nse* **A J Cook (IRE)**[11] 8312 6-8-11 **49**.... AndrewMullen 8 48
(Ron Barr) *sn towards rr: rdn along 1/2-way: hdwy fnl f: kpt on: nrst fin* **16/1**
0422 **8** *hd* **Kodimoor (IRE)**[5] 8409 3-9-1 **53**....(bt) KieranO'Neill 11 52
(Christopher Kellett) *prom: rdn along 2f out: kpt on same pce ins fnl f* **9/2**[2]
04 **9** *nk* **Slim Chance (IRE)**[37] 7961 7-8-10 **55**....(v) PaulaMuir[(7)] 3 53
(Simon West) *taken early to post: in tch on far side of gp: pushed along 1/2-way: rallied: effrt over 1f out: kpt on same pce ins fnl f* **16/1**
0605 **10** *3/4* **Big Amigo (IRE)**[15] 8242 3-9-3 **58**.... EoinWalsh[(3)] 7 57+
(Daniel Mark Loughnane) *fly-jmpd s: bhd and sn pushed along: stdy hdwy over 1f out: keeping on but no imp whn nt clr run ins fnl f* **7/2**[1]
5010 **11** *1 1/4* **Very First Blade**[43] 7859 7-8-13 **51**....(p) TomEaves 14 41
(Michael Mullineaux) *hld up midfield on nr side of gp: pushed along over 2f out: sn no imp: wknd fnl f* **33/1**
5104 **12** *3/4* **Lady Joanna Vassa (IRE)**[15] 8242 3-9-5 **57**.... ConnorBeasley 6 45
(Richard Guest) *t.k.h in midfield: pushed along and effrt over 1f out: no imp whn nt clr run briefly ins fnl f: sn btn and eased* **10/1**
0000 **13** *1/2* **Arctic Lynx (IRE)**[11] 8312 9-8-9 **52**....(p) AnnStokell[(5)] 12 38
(Ann Stokell) *taken early to post: midfield: pushed along over 2f out: wkng whn checked ins fnl f* **66/1**

1m 0.07s (0.57) **Going Correction** +0.225s/f (Slow) **13** Ran SP% **119.5**
Speed ratings (Par 101): **104,102,101,101,101 100,100,100,100,98 96,95,94**
CSF £437.90 CT £4823.50 TOTE £5.70: £2.00, £13.00, £3.30; EX 359.60 Trifecta £7756.20.
Owner Thoroughbred Homes Ltd **Bred** Bishopswood Bloodstock & Trickledown Stud **Trained** Osmotherley, N Yorks

FOCUS
An ordinary but competitive sprint handicap. They finished in a heap behind the winner. The form makes sense rated around the second to the fifth.
T/Plt: £198.50 to a £1 stake. Pool: £84,724.93 - 311.52 winning units. T/Qpdt: £27.00 to a £1 stake. Pool: £9,052.13 - 247.78 winning units. **Richard Young**

8453 CHELMSFORD (A.W) (L-H)
Thursday, December 22

OFFICIAL GOING: Polytrack: standard
Wind: virtually nil Weather: sunny

8486 WEATHERBYS RACING DIARIES MAIDEN STKS (PLUS 10 RACE) 1m (P)
12:50 (12:52) (Class 3) 2-Y-O **£12,291** (£3,657; £1,827; £913) **Stalls** Low

Form RPR
3 **1** **Naseem (IRE)**[17] 8227 2-9-5 0.... JimCrowley 16 90+
(John Gosden) *broke wl fr wd draw to press ldr tl led ent fnl 2f: sn rdn and qcknd clr over 1f out: r.o strly: impressive* **5/1**[3]
5 **2** *5* **Auberge Du Lac (IRE)**[76] 7125 2-9-5 0.... JamieSpencer 3 78+
(David Simcock) *hld up in tch in 5th: effrt in 3rd whn sltly hmpd and swtchd rt over 1f out: styd on to go 2nd 100yds out: no ch w wnr* **3/1**[2]
63 **3** *1 1/2* **Garbanzo (IRE)**[37] 7963 2-9-5 0.... GeorgeBaker 1 74
(Ed Walker) *chsd ldng: effrt to chse clr wnr and hung lft over 1f out: kpt on same pce and no ch w wnr: lost 2nd 100yds out* **5/1**[3]
4 *3* **Arctic Sea** 2-9-5 0.... PJMcDonald 4 67
(Paul Cole) *chsd ldng trio: effrt and no imp over 1f out: no ch w wnr and kpt on same pce fnl f* **50/1**
2 **5** *1/2* **Bois de Boulogne (USA)**[19] 8208 2-9-5 0....(p) RobertHavlin 10 66
(John Gosden) *midfield: effrt and wd bnd 2f out: hdwy u.p over 1f out: styd on ins fnl f: no ch w wnr* **6/4**[1]
04 **6** *hd* **Medalla De Oro**[40] 7940 2-9-5 0.... LukeMorris 15 66+
(Peter Chapple-Hyam) *t.k.h: hld up towards rr: swtchd lft and dropped in bhd after 2f: swtchd rt and effrt but plenty to do over 1f out: hdwy u.p 1f out: styd on: nvr trbld ldrs* **50/1**
7 *1* **Shamrokh (IRE)** 2-9-5 0....[1] NickyMackay 8 63
(John Gosden) *in tch in midfield: rdn over 2f out: outpcd by wnr wl over 1f out: kpt on same pce u.p ins fnl f* **12/1**
00 **8** *1/2* **Velvet Voice**[24] 8131 2-9-0 0.... JoeyHaynes 2 57
(Mark H Tompkins) *midfield: rdn jst over 2f out: sn outpcd by wnr: wl hld and kpt on same pce fr over 1f out* **100/1**
9 *3 3/4* **Mirimar (IRE)** 2-9-5 0.... TomMarquand 9 53
(Ed Vaughan) *short of room leaving stalls and s.i.s: hld up in rr: swtchd rt over 1f out:sme hdwy 1f out: kpt on: nvr trbld ldrs* **100/1**
10 *3/4* **Moamar** 2-9-5 0.... DavidProbert 13 52
(Ed Dunlop) *midfield: effrt ent fnl 2f: rn green and hung lft over 1f out: sn lost pl and btn: eased fnl f* **33/1**
11 *1 1/2* **Olive Branch (IRE)** 2-9-0 0.... StevieDonohoe 12 43
(Sir Michael Stoute) *s.i.s: niggled along towards rr: rdn over 1f out: no imp: n.d* **33/1**
12 *4 1/2* **Malt Teaser (FR)** 2-9-5 0.... KierenFox 5 38
(John Best) *towards rr: rdn over 1f out: sn struggling and btn: wknd fnl f* **100/1**
0042 **13** *3/4* **Desert Grey (IRE)**[8] 8353 2-9-5 74.... JoeFanning 7 36
(Roger Varian) *led tl rdn and hdd ent fnl 2f: lost pl and btn over 1f out: wknd fnl f* **14/1**

The Form Book, Raceform Ltd, Newbury, RG14 5SJ

0 **14** 3 1/2 **Dervish**17 8227 2-9-5 0 PatCosgrave 14 28
(Luca Cumani) *stuck wd in midfield: rdn over 3f out: lost pl and bhd 2f out: sn wknd* **100/1**
15 11 **Breakenridge** 2-9-5 0 MartinHarley 11 3
(William Knight) *a rr: lost tch 2f out* **100/1**
1m 38.11s (-1.79) **Going Correction** -0.05s/f (Stan) **15** Ran SP% **127.4**
Speed ratings (Par 100): **106,101,99,96,96 95,94,94,90,89 88,83,83,79,68**
CSF £21.11 TOTE £6.20: £1.70, £1.70, £1.80; EX 29.40 Trifecta £97.00.
Owner Hamdan Al Maktoum **Bred** Oghill House Stud **Trained** Newmarket, Suffolk

FOCUS
Not a bad maiden, certainly decent prize money for a race like this, and many of the top Newmarket yards were represented. It proved one-way traffic, though.

8487 WINNER.CO.UK BEATEN BY A LENGTH FREE BET H'CAP 1m (P)
1:20 (1:22) (Class 4) (0-80,80) 3-Y-O+ **£8,086** (£2,406; £1,202; £601) **Stalls** Low

Form RPR
5504 **1** **Tellovoi (IRE)**7 8385 8-8-12 **71** (v) DougieCostello 2 79
(Richard Guest) *t.k.h: hld up in tch: hdwy to chse ldrs 3f out: effrt jst over 2f out: hdwy and rdn to chse ldrs jst ins fnl f: styd on u.p to ld last stride* **16/1**
4520 **2** shd **Street Duel (USA)**151 4687 3-9-6 **80** SeanLevey 4 87
(Ismail Mohammed) *chsd ldr: rdn to ld over 1f out: drvn 1f out: kpt on u.p: hdd last stride* **9/2**2
4421 **3** 1 1/4 **Inaam (IRE)**13 8287 3-9-1 **75** TonyHamilton 8 79+
(Richard Fahey) *t.k.h: hld up in tch in rr: nt clr run over 2f out: swtchd rt and rdn 1f out: hdwy and swtchd rt again wl ins fnl f: styd on towards fin* **10/1**
4450 **4** shd **Starboard**47 7813 7-9-3 **76** (b) JamieSpencer 1 83+
(David Simcock) *taken down early: hld up in tch towards rr: swtchd rt and hdwy over 1f out: swtchd lft and pressed ldr jst ins fnl f: n.m.r and sltly impeded wl ins fnl f: wknd towards fin* **7/1**3
0341 **5** 1 3/4 **Squire**21 8178 5-9-4 **77** (t) AdamBeschizza 5 78
(Michael Attwater) *chsd ldrs: effrt wl over 1f out: unable qck and one pce ins fnl f* **9/2**2
3246 **6** 1 3/4 **Exceeding Power**21 8178 5-8-8 **74** JoshuaBryan(7) 9 71
(Martin Bosley) *in tch towards rr: effrt over 1f out: unable qck ent fnl f: wknd ins fnl f* **12/1**
6621 **7** 1 1/2 **Curzon Line**35 7985 7-8-13 **75** NathanEvans(3) 3 68
(Michael Easterby) *led: rdn and hdd over 1f out: lost 2nd jst ins fnl f: sn wknd* **6/4**1
4005 **8** 1 1/2 **Edge Of Heaven**10 8343 4-9-2 **75** LukeMorris 7 65
(Jonathan Portman) *in tch in midfield: hung lft u.p over 1f out: sn lost pl and wknd fnl f* **28/1**
1m 38.77s (-1.13) **Going Correction** -0.05s/f (Stan)
WFA 3 from 4yo+ 1lb **8** Ran SP% **115.0**
Speed ratings (Par 105): **103,102,101,101,99 98,96,95**
CSF £86.70 CT £776.05 TOTE £21.80: £5.00, £2.10, £2.00; EX 132.30 Trifecta £1188.40.
Owner G Smith **Bred** Whisperview Trading Ltd **Trained** Ingmanthorpe, W Yorks

FOCUS
A fair handicap run at a true pace, but quite a rough race and a bit of a turn up.

8488 WINNER.CO.UK BET & WATCH H'CAP 2m (P)
1:50 (1:54) (Class 6) (0-65,61) 3-Y-O+ **£3,234** (£962; £481; £240) **Stalls** Low

Form RPR
0350 **1** **King Olav (UAE)**33 8038 11-9-8 **58** GeorgeDowning(3) 1 65
(Tony Carroll) *led: sn hdd and chsd ldr tl led again over 2f out: rdn over 1f out: drvn 1f out: pressed wl ins fnl f: kpt on but hld towards fin* **7/1**
5533 **2** 3/4 **Yasir (USA)**8 8359 8-9-13 **60** MartinHarley 4 66
(Conor Dore) *hld up in rr: clsd over 2f out: effrt to chse wnr over 1f out: drvn 1f out: styd on to press wnr wl ins fnl f: hld towards fin* **9/4**2
2003 **3** 3 3/4 **Ryan The Giant**12 8309 3-8-8 **49** (p) JoeFanning 2 51
(Keith Dalgleish) *in tch in last pair: nt clr run over 2f out: swtchd rt and hdwy over 1f out: chsd ldng pair ins fnl f: kpt on but nvr enough pce to chal* **15/8**1
055 **4** 1 1/2 **Mackiri (IRE)**27 8096 3-8-7 **48** LukeMorris 3 48
(Michael Appleby) *chsd ldrs: drvn 3f out: edgd lft u.p and chsd wnr wl over 1f out tl over 1f out: sn outpcd: plugged on same pce ins fnl f* **6/1**
6653 **5** 7 **Topaling**15 8254 5-10-0 **61** StevieDonohoe 7 52
(Mark H Tompkins) *hld up in rr: effrt ent fnl 2f: drvn over 1f out: no imp: kpt on same pce ins fnl f* **5/1**3
0000 **6** 1/2 **Pixel (IRE)**8 8359 3-8-8 **52** (v1) TimClark(3) 6 43
(Denis Quinn) *racd keenly: sn led: hdd and rdn over 2f out: lost pl over 1f out: wknd fnl f* **20/1**
3m 32.58s (2.58) **Going Correction** -0.05s/f (Stan)
WFA 3 from 5yo+ 8lb **6** Ran SP% **113.8**
Speed ratings (Par 101): **91,90,88,88,84 84**
CSF £23.63 TOTE £8.20: £3.40, £1.70; EX 26.40 Trifecta £78.30.
Owner Cover Point Racing **Bred** Darley **Trained** Cropthorne, Worcs

FOCUS
A moderate staying handicap and the pace was ordinary. The finish was fought out between two comparative veterans. The third is limited and helps set the level.

8489 WEATHERBYS STALLION BOOK CONDITIONS STKS 7f (P)
2:20 (2:23) (Class 2) 3-Y-O+
£28,012 (£8,388; £4,194; £2,097; £1,048; £526) **Stalls** Low

Form RPR
5300 **1** **Realize**40 7932 6-9-3 102 (t) SeanLevey 3 109
(Stuart Williams) *hld up in tch: swtchd rt and effrt over 1f out: hdwy u.p to chal jst ins fnl f: r.o wl to ld towards fin* **11/4**1
0033 **2** 1/2 **Donjuan Triumphant (IRE)**33 8029 3-9-3 105 TonyHamilton 9 107
(Richard Fahey) *led: rdn over 1f out: drvn and hrd pressed ins fnl f: kpt on tl hdd and one pced towards fin* **6/1**3
2045 **3** hd **Dragon Mall (USA)**99 6482 3-9-3 105 JamieSpencer 4 106
(David Simcock) *t.k.h: hld up in tch in midfield: swtchd rt over 1f out: hdwy u.p 1f out: swtchd lft and hdwy ins fnl f: styd on wl fnl 100yds: nt quite rch ldrs* **10/3**2
0000 **4** 1/2 **Fanciful Angel (IRE)**126 5585 4-9-3 104 DanielMuscutt 10 105
(Marco Botti) *t.k.h: hld up in tch in midfield: effrt and edgd lft u.p over 1f out: hdwy ins fnl f: styd on wl towards fin: nt quite rch ldrs* **6/1**3
6623 **5** 3/4 **Golden Amber (IRE)**27 8098 5-8-12 95 PatCosgrave 5 98
(Dean Ivory) *chsd ldrs tl wnt 2nd 5f out: rdn and pressed ldr over 1f out tl no ex ins fnl f: kpt on same pce fnl 100yds* **14/1**
3106 **6** 1 3/4 **C Note (IRE)**54 7701 3-9-3 99 DavidProbert 7 98
(Martyn Meade) *chsd ldng trio: pushed along ent fnl 2f: unable qck u.p over 1f out: no imp ins fnl f: hld and eased towards fin* **8/1**
0260 **7** 1 3/4 **Dhahmaan (IRE)**40 7932 3-9-3 98 LukeMorris 6 93
(Marco Botti) *in tch in rr: rdn jst over 2f out: styd on same pce ins fnl f: nvr threatened ldrs* **14/1**
0221 **8** shd **He's No Saint**15 8256 5-9-3 94 (v) MartinHarley 1 93
(David O'Meara) *chsd ldr for 2f: styd prom: rdn and unable qck over 1f out: wknd ins fnl f* **7/1**
5440 **9** 1 1/2 **Valbchek (IRE)**12 8311 7-9-3 92 (p) StevieDonohoe 8 89
(Jane Chapple-Hyam) *s.i.s and swtchd lft after s: hld up in rr: no imp u.p over 1f out: n.d* **50/1**
1m 24.94s (-2.26) **Going Correction** -0.05s/f (Stan) **9** Ran SP% **117.2**
Speed ratings (Par 109): **110,109,109,108,107 105,103,103,101**
CSF £20.04 TOTE £4.30: £1.60, £2.20, £1.40; EX 19.90 Trifecta £94.80.
Owner JKB Racing **Bred** M J Watson **Trained** Newmarket, Suffolk

FOCUS
A warm conditions event and a decent pace. The right horses came to the fore.

8490 WINNER.CO.UK MOBILE LOYALTY FREE BETS H'CAP 7f (P)
2:50 (2:51) (Class 5) (0-70,72) 3-Y-O+ **£5,175** (£1,540; £769; £384) **Stalls** Low

Form RPR
0001 **1** **Medicean El Diablo**22 8156 3-8-13 **62** TomMarquand 2 71+
(Jimmy Fox) *hld up in tch in midfield on inner: rdn and hdwy over 1f out: led ins fnl f: r.o wl* **5/1**2
/065 **2** 1 1/4 **Higher Court (USA)**14 8280 8-9-7 **70** StevieDonohoe 3 75
(Emma Owen) *sn led: rdn over 1f out: hdd ins fnl f: no ex and one pced after* **14/1**
4510 **3** 3/4 **Billyoakes (IRE)**9 8345 4-9-9 **72** (p) ShaneKelly 5 75
(Charlie Wallis) *t.k.h: trckd ldrs: wnt 2nd and rdn over 1f out: 3rd and kpt on same pce ins fnl f* **20/1**
333 **4** 1/2 **Plus Night (FR)**7 8378 3-9-3 **69** AaronJones(3) 4 71
(Stuart Williams) *in tch in midfield: effrt over 1f out: edgd lft u.p 1f out: kpt on same pce ins fnl f* **1/1**1
5540 **5** 3 **Misu Pete**27 8095 4-8-7 **56** DavidProbert 7 50
(Mark Usher) *hld up in tch in midfield: effrt and unable qck over 1f out: no imp and one pced fnl f* **14/1**
2150 **6** shd **Minminwin (IRE)**51 7743 3-9-3 **66** (vt) LukeMorris 12 59
(Gay Kelleway) *s.i.s and swtchd lft after s: in tch in last pair: shkn up ent fnl 2f: styd on u.p ins fnl f: nvr trbld ldrs* **25/1**
3020 **7** 3/4 **Remember Me**35 7985 3-9-7 **70** RobertHavlin 9 61
(Hughie Morrison) *t.k.h: hld up in tch in midfield: effrt oer 1f out: unable qck u.p 1f out: no imp and one pced after* **10/1**
5665 **8** 1/2 **Strictly Art (IRE)**7 8382 3-8-7 **56** (p) JoeFanning 10 46
(Alan Bailey) *stdd after s: t.k.h: hld up in tch in rr on outer: no imp u.p over 1f out: kpt on same pce after* **16/1**
0136 **9** 1 1/2 **Gulland Rock**57 7617 5-9-7 **70** WilliamCarson 6 56
(Anthony Carson) *chsd ldr: rdn over 2f out: lost 2nd over 1f out and wknd ins fnl f* **20/1**
4600 **10** 1 1/4 **Sunnyside Bob (IRE)**13 8287 3-9-5 **68** PJMcDonald 11 50
(Neville Bycroft) *in tch: effrt 2f out: lost pl u.p over 1f out: wknd ins fnl f* **33/1**
4306 **11** 2 1/2 **Star Of The Stage**57 7619 4-9-5 **68** DanielMuscutt 8 44
(John Butler) *hld up in tch in rr: shkn up and n.m.r over 1f out: rdn and no hdwy ent fnl f: wknd ins fnl f* **8/1**3
1m 26.11s (-1.09) **Going Correction** -0.05s/f (Stan) **11** Ran SP% **122.4**
Speed ratings (Par 103): **104,102,101,101,97 97,96,96,94,93 90**
CSF £70.93 CT £927.75 TOTE £5.80: £1.70, £4.70, £4.80; EX 100.80 Trifecta £1171.60.
Owner Sugar Syndicate **Bred** Pantile Stud **Trained** Collingbourne Ducis, Wilts

FOCUS
An ordinary handicap and the first four pulled clear.

8491 WINNER.CO.UK ACCA CLUB MAIDEN STKS 1m 2f (P)
3:20 (3:22) (Class 4) 3-Y-O+ **£8,086** (£2,406; £1,202; £601) **Stalls** Low

Form RPR
3 **1** **Vogueatti (USA)**31 8048 3-9-0 0 DanielMuscutt 3 73
(Marco Botti) *wnt rt s: led for 1f: chsd ldr tl 7f out: clsd qckly over 3f out to press ldr over 2f out: rdn and wnt clr w rival over 1f out: led jst ins fnl f: kpt on: rdn out* **5/6**1
2 **2** 1/2 **Sea Dweller**20 8195 3-9-0 0 WilliamCarson 2 72
(Anthony Carson) *midfield: clsd on clr ldrs over 3f out: led on inner over 2f out: rdn and wnt clr w wnr over 1f out: hdd jst ins fnl f: kpt on same pce fnl 100yds: hld whn eased cl home* **11/4**2
054 **3** 8 **Avoidable**297 768 3-9-5 0 JamieSpencer 6 61
(David Simcock) *hld up in rr: clsd on clr ldrs over 3f out: trcking ldrs over 2f out: sn rdn and outpcd: wl hld and plugged on same pce fr over 1f out: wnt modest 3rd wl ins fnl f* **4/1**3
45 **4** 3/4 **Einstein**59 7583 3-9-5 0 (t) LukeMorris 4 60
(Mrs Ilka Gansera-Leveque) *hmpd s: t.k.h: hld up in tch in last pair: clsd on clr ldrs over 3f out: trckd ldrs over 2f out: sn rdn and outpcd: lost modest 3rd wl ins fnl f* **14/1**
50-4 **5** 8 **Twilight Angel**31 8048 8-9-3 49 (v) StevieDonohoe 5 39
(Emma Owen) *hmpd s: rcvrd to ld after 1f: hdd 1/2-way: lost pl u.p over 2f out: bhd over 1f out* **33/1**
5000 **6** 4 **Let It Go**56 7645 4-9-0 32 GeorgeDowning(3) 1 31
(Tony Carroll) *stdd s: plld v hrd and ref to settle: chsd ldr 7f out: led 1/2-way tl hdd over 2f out: sn dropped out and bhd over 1f out* **66/1**
2m 8.09s (-0.51) **Going Correction** -0.05s/f (Stan)
WFA 3 from 4yo+ 3lb **6** Ran SP% **112.3**
Speed ratings (Par 105): **100,99,93,92,86 83**
CSF £3.38 TOTE £1.80: £1.10, £1.60; EX 3.70 Trifecta £6.20.
Owner Khalid Bin Ali Al Khalifa **Bred** Haymarket Farm Llc **Trained** Newmarket, Suffolk

FOCUS
A poor maiden in which the two outsiders went tearing off in front while the others ignored them. The big two in the market eventually dominated and they had a protracted battle up the straight, getting close to each other in the final furlong.

8492 KEITH OSBORNE'S 60TH BIRTHDAY H'CAP 1m 2f (P)
3:50 (3:52) (Class 7) (0-50,50) 3-Y-O+ **£3,234** (£962; £481; £240) **Stalls** Low

Form RPR
6045 **1** **Master Of Heaven**14 8281 3-9-2 **48** (tp) PatCosgrave 1 54
(Jim Boyle) *rdn along early: chsd ldrs: swtchd lft and rdn to chal over 1f out: sustained chal u.p to ld towards fin* **7/2**1
0300 **2** 1/2 **Outlaw Torn (IRE)**12 8307 7-9-7 **50** (e) JoeFanning 12 55
(Richard Guest) *chsd ldr tl led 2f out: sn rdn: kpt on wl u.p tl hdd and no ex towards fin* **10/1**
5002 **3** hd **Ferryview Place**56 7641 7-9-6 **49** (vt) StevieDonohoe 13 54
(Ian Williams) *hld up towards rr: rdn and hdwy wd over 1f out: styd on strly u.p to go 3rd wl ins fnl f: nt quite rch ldrs* **5/1**2

3-60 **4** 1 **Spirit Of The Vale (IRE)**[20] 8194 3-9-0 **46**...............(t) JamesSullivan 11 49
(Oliver Greenall) *in tch in midfield: hmpd 2f out: rallied u.p ent fnl f: kpt on:wnt 4th cl home* **25/1**

3206 **5** ½ **Understory (USA)**[40] 7937 9-9-6 **49**................................ LukeMorris 15 51
(Tim McCarthy) *chsd ldrs: rdn to chal over 1f out tl no ex and btn 100yds out: wknd and lost 2 pls towards fin* **16/1**

5406 **6** 1¼ **Lutine Charlie (IRE)**[14] 8278 9-9-3 **46**............................(p) ShaneKelly 5 47
(Emma Owen) *t.k.h: hld up wl in tch: effrt ent fnl f: fnd little and btn whn short of room ins fnl f: eased towards fin* **25/1**

0305 **7** 1¾ **Moving Robe (IRE)**[7] 8379 3-8-13 **45**............................[1] RobertHavlin 7 42
(Conrad Allen) *hld up towards rr: effrt u.p over 1f out: kpt on u.p ins fnl f: nvr trbld ldrs* **25/1**

-032 **8** shd **White Dog (IRE)**[308] 622 4-9-0 **50**..............................[1] KevinLundie[(7)] 4 46
(Sarah Humphrey) *t.k.h: hld up in tch in midfield: effrt on inner and little rspnse over 1f out: kpt on same pce ins fnl f* **7/1**[3]

0050 **9** ½ **Whaleweigh Station**[26] 8125 5-9-7 **50**.........................(p) GeorgeBaker 3 45
(J R Jenkins) *stdd after s and t.k.h early: hld up in rr: shkn up and effrt over 1f out: sme hdwy and edgd lft u.p 1f out: kpt on same pce after* **5/1**[2]

6603 **10** ¾ **Josh Perry**[15] 8247 3-9-4 **50**...(v) RyanTate 10 44
(Rod Millman) *t.k.h: hld up wl in tch in midfield: hdwy u.p to chse ldrs over 2f out: lost pl over 1f out: btn whn sltly hmpd and wnt rt ins fnl f: wknd* **16/1**

0000 **11** 2¼ **Clock On Tom**[53] 7231 6-8-10 **46**........................... PatrickVaughan[(7)] 14 36
(Denis Quinn) *hld up in midfield: swtchd rt and effrt over 2f out: v wd and no hdwy over 1f out: wknd ins fnl f* **25/1**

0006 **12** 5 **Ravens Heart (IRE)**[29] 8070 4-9-2 **48**............................ JackDuern[(3)] 6 29
(Dean Ivory) *led tl 2f: sn lost pl and btn: wknd and bhd ins fnl f* **7/1**[3]

0645 **13** 2 **Purple Belle**[21] 8179 3-8-13 **45**...................................... TomMarquand 8 22
(Jimmy Fox) *a towards rr: rdn and wknd over 1f out* **10/1**

6506 **14** 1¼ **Magic Mirror**[82] 6966 3-9-0 **46**....................................... DougieCostello 2 21
(Mark Rimell) *hld up in rr: n.d* **33/1**

2m 7.37s (-1.23) **Going Correction** -0.05s/f (Stan)
WFA 3 from 4yo+ 3lb **14** Ran SP% **128.8**
Speed ratings (Par 97): **102,101,101,100,100 99,97,97,97,96 94,90,89,88**
CSF £39.98 CT £185.89 TOTE £4.20: £2.10, £4.20, £1.60; EX 51.60 Trifecta £413.10.
Owner Maid In Heaven Partnership **Bred** Qatar Bloodstock Ltd **Trained** Epsom, Surrey

FOCUS
Races don't come much worse than this, but it was competitive. A bit of a punt was landed, though. The second, third and fourth help set the level.
T/Plt: £163.40 to a £1 stake. Pool: £69,959.47 - 312.49 winning units. T/Qpdt: £18.80 to a £1 stake. Pool: £6,685.27 - 262.92 winning units. **Steve Payne**

8404 WOLVERHAMPTON (A.W) (L-H)
Thursday, December 22

OFFICIAL GOING: Tapeta: standard
Wind: Fresh behind Weather: Cloudy

8493 32RED.COM FILLIES' H'CAP 7f 32y (Tp)
1:30 (1:31) (Class 5) (0-75,76) 3-Y-O+ **£4,204** (£1,251; £625; £312) **Stalls** High

Form RPR

0104 **1** **Arize (IRE)**[33] 8037 3-8-13 **66**.. TomEaves 4 71
(David Brown) *mde all: shkn up over 2f out: rdn over 1f out: styd on u.p* **12/1**

-413 **2** ¾ **Tegara**[24] 8135 3-9-4 **71**.. TomQueally 2 74
(James Fanshawe) *chsd wnr: hung rt and rdn wl over 1f out: r.o* **5/6**[1]

510 **3** shd **First Experience**[88] 6806 5-9-6 **76**........................(v) LouisSteward[(3)] 5 79
(Lee Carter) *hld up: hdwy over 1f out: sn rdn: r.o* **13/2**[3]

3503 **4** hd **Miss Goldsmith (IRE)**[20] 8188 3-8-9 **62**......................... BarryMcHugh 6 64
(Richard Fahey) *chsd ldrs: carried rt wl over 1f out: sn rdn: r.o* **11/2**[2]

3554 **5** 1¾ **Binky Blue (IRE)**[33] 8036 4-8-13 **66**......................... JosephineGordon 1 63
(Daniel Mark Loughnane) *chsd ldrs: rdn over 1f out: styd on same pce ins fnl f* **8/1**

3261 **6** 2½ **Nag's Wag (IRE)**[122] 5725 3-9-7 **74**.................................... LiamKeniry 3 65
(George Baker) *s.i.s: hld up: shkn up over 2f out: styd on same pce* **8/1**

1m 28.61s (-0.19) **Going Correction** -0.075s/f (Stan) **6** Ran SP% **113.2**
Speed ratings (Par 100): **98,97,97,96,94 91**
CSF £23.21 TOTE £14.60: £5.30, £1.10; EX 33.30 Trifecta £168.90.
Owner Mrs Sandra Brown & Mrs Ann Harrison **Bred** Peter Onslow & T Whelan **Trained** Averham Park, Notts
■ Stewards' Enquiry : Barry McHugh two-day ban: use of whip (5-6 Jan)

FOCUS
A fair handicap and a tactical affair, in which the winner was never headed.

8494 32RED CASINO MEDIAN AUCTION MAIDEN STKS 5f 20y (Tp)
2:00 (2:00) (Class 5) 2-Y-O **£3,881** (£1,155; £577; £288) **Stalls** Low

Form RPR

0024 **1** **Juan Horsepower**[15] 8243 2-9-5 75...............................[1] KieranO'Neill 1 73
(Richard Hannon) *mde all: rdn over 1f out: styd on* **9/4**[2]

0650 **2** 1¾ **Cappananty Con**[17] 8229 2-9-5 65.................................. GrahamLee 5 67
(Dean Ivory) *hld up: hdwy 2f out: hung lft and r.o to go 2nd wl ins fnl f: no ch w wnr* **12/1**

2000 **3** 4 **Secret Agent**[8] 8352 2-9-5 69.. MartinDwyer 7 52+
(William Muir) *hld up: rdn over 1f out: r.o to go 3rd post: nt trble ldrs* **8/1**[3]

4334 **4** nk **Heavenly Cry**[17] 8229 2-9-5 64..............................(v) JosephineGordon 3 51
(Phil McEntee) *chsd wnr: rdn over 1f out: no ex ins fnl f* **16/1**

323 **5** nk **The Daley Express (IRE)**[12] 8313 2-9-5 78........................ DaleSwift 2 50
(Ed McMahon) *chsd ldrs: rdn and hung lft over 1f out: no ex fnl f* **4/5**[1]

6 6 **Tink** 2-9-0 0.. JFEgan 6 24
(Mark Brisbourne) *s.s: hld up: plld hrd early: rdn over 1f out: wknd fnl f* **100/1**

3205 **7** 9 **Irish Melody (IRE)**[146] 4842 2-9-5 64.........................(p) AndrewMullen 4
(Bill Turner) *chsd ldrs: pushed along 1/2-way: sn wknd* **50/1**

1m 1.42s (-0.48) **Going Correction** -0.075s/f (Stan) **7** Ran SP% **114.0**
Speed ratings (Par 96): **100,97,90,90,89 80,65**
CSF £28.27 TOTE £3.10: £1.70, £2.90; EX 38.50 Trifecta £146.90.
Owner Middleham Park Racing LXXXIII **Bred** Max Weston **Trained** East Everleigh, Wilts

FOCUS
An ordinary maiden. The winner only had to reproduce the balance of his recent form to score.

8495 BETWAY SPRINT H'CAP 5f 20y (Tp)
2:30 (2:30) (Class 5) (0-75,75) 3-Y-O+ **£3,881** (£1,155; £577; £288) **Stalls** Low

Form RPR

5243 **1** **Captain Lars (SAF)**[7] 8380 7-9-2 **70**..............................(v) JFEgan 7 82
(Derek Shaw) *hld up: hdwy over 1f out: r.o to ld wl ins fnl f* **9/4**[1]

2251 **2** 1½ **Compton River**[29] 8078 4-9-2 **70**.................................. ConnorBeasley 2 77
(Bryan Smart) *led 1f: chsd ldr tl rdn to ld over 1f out: hdd and unable qck wl ins fnl f* **7/2**[2]

2211 **3** ½ **Heiba (IRE)**[17] 8228 4-9-3 **71**......................................(p) LiamKeniry 4 76
(Robert Cowell) *chsd ldrs: rdn over 1f out: styd on same pce wl ins fnl f* **9/2**[3]

4102 **4** 1¼ **Doctor Parkes**[35] 7983 10-8-13 **74**................................ MillyNaseb[(7)] 5 75
(Stuart Williams) *hld up in tch: rdn and nt clr run ins fnl f: styd on same pce* **8/1**

6000 **5** 1¼ **Krystallite**[14] 8280 3-9-4 **72**... KieranO'Neill 6 68
(Scott Dixon) *s.i.s: hld up: n.m.r 4f out: hdwy 2f out: sn rdn: no ex ins fnl f* **20/1**

2000 **6** nk **Emjayem**[55] 7660 6-9-4 **72**.. DaleSwift 8 67
(Ed McMahon) *chsd ldrs: pushed along 1/2-way: rdn and edgd lft ins fnl f: styd on same pce* **20/1**

0023 **7** 1¼ **Red Stripes (USA)**[40] 7945 4-9-2 **70**..............................(b) TomEaves 1 61
(Lisa Williamson) *led 4f out: rdn and hdd over 1f out: no ex ins fnl f* **16/1**

4002 **8** nk **Bush Warrior (IRE)**[27] 8099 5-9-4 **72**.................(v) JosephineGordon 10 62
(Anabel K Murphy) *hld up: rdn 1/2-way: nvr trbld ldrs* **14/1**

2110 **9** ¾ **Zipedeedodah (IRE)**[14] 8280 4-9-2 **75**.......................(t) HollieDoyle[(5)] 9 62
(Joseph Tuite) *hld up: pushed along over 1f out: nvr on terms* **6/1**

1m 0.64s (-1.26) **Going Correction** -0.075s/f (Stan) **9** Ran SP% **118.6**
Speed ratings (Par 103): **107,104,103,101,99 99,97,96,95**
CSF £10.39 CT £31.59 TOTE £2.90: £1.50, £1.50, £1.50; EX 11.90 Trifecta £45.30.
Owner Chris Hamilton **Bred** Klawervlei Stud **Trained** Sproxton, Leics

FOCUS
A fair sprint handicap and they went a good pace throughout.

8496 BETWAY SPRINT MAIDEN STKS 5f 216y (Tp)
3:00 (3:01) (Class 5) 3-Y-O+ **£3,557** (£1,058; £529; £264) **Stalls** Low

Form RPR

02- **1** **Song Of Shadows**[548] 3489 3-9-5 0..........................[1] ConnorBeasley 2 76+
(Michael Wigham) *trckd ldrs: plld hrd: shkn up to ld over 1f out: r.o: comf* **13/8**[1]

44 **2** 1¾ **Arctic Angel (IRE)**[34] 8012 3-9-5 0.................................. TomQueally 10 67
(James Fanshawe) *hld up: r.o ins fnl f: wnt 2nd post: no ch w wnr* **9/1**

045 **3** hd **Q Cee**[68] 7362 3-9-0 65.. LuluStanford[(5)] 5 66
(Eugene Stanford) *chsd ldrs: rdn over 2f out: styd on to chse wnr wl ins fnl f tl lost 2nd post* **9/2**[3]

4 1¼ **Grainne's Dream (IRE)**[27] 8104 3-9-0 66...........................(v) JFEgan 4 57
(W McCreery, Ire) *w ldr: rdn and ev ch over 1f out: styd on same pce ins fnl f* **7/2**[2]

43 **5** 2 **Dandilion (IRE)**[13] 8290 3-9-0 0....................................(t) KieranO'Neill 1 51
(Alex Hales) *sn led: rdn and hdd over 1f out: edgd lft and wknd wl ins fnl f* **14/1**

0-0 **6** 1 **Mistry**[40] 7935 3-9-0 0.. LiamKeniry 6 47
(Mark Usher) *hld up: hdwy 2f out: sn rdn: no ex fnl f* **100/1**

5204 **7** ¾ **Cee Jay**[21] 8181 3-9-2 59...(v) EoinWalsh[(3)] 7 50
(Robert Cowell) *pushed along in rr early: rdn over 2f out: edgd lft over 1f out: n.d* **6/1**

8 ½ **London Rebel (IRE)** 3-9-0 0.. GrahamLee 8 43
(Richard Spencer) *s.i.s: rdn over 1f out: nvr on terms* **20/1**

00 **9** 12 **Royboy**[13] 8290 3-9-5 0.. TomEaves 3 10
(Ollie Pears) *chsd ldrs over 3f* **100/1**

1m 14.02s (-0.48) **Going Correction** -0.075s/f (Stan) **9** Ran SP% **116.2**
Speed ratings (Par 103): **100,97,97,95,93 91,90,90,74**
CSF £17.82 TOTE £2.40: £1.10, £3.00, £2.10; EX 24.00 Trifecta £86.70.
Owner G Linder & D Hassan **Bred** Darley **Trained** Newmarket, Suffolk

FOCUS
An uncompetitive maiden and the favourite made no mistake.

8497 BETWAY APP H'CAP 1m 4f 50y (Tp)
3:30 (3:30) (Class 7) (0-50,50) 3-Y-O+ **£2,264** (£673; £336; £168) **Stalls** Low

Form RPR

0-02 **1** **My Renaissance**[7] 8386 6-9-8 **49**................................ AndrewMullen 5 57+
(Sam England) *chsd ldrs: hmpd and lost pl over 3f out: hdwy and nt clr run over 1f out: led ins fnl f: r.o* **7/2**[1]

5660 **2** 1¾ **Par Three (IRE)**[12] 8309 5-9-9 **50**..............................(p) LiamKeniry 8 53
(Tony Carroll) *hld up: hdwy over 1f out: sn rdn: r.o* **12/1**

4332 **3** nse **Top Set (IRE)**[21] 8180 6-9-6 **47**.................................(p) MartinDwyer 3 50
(Richard Phillips) *hld up: nt clr run fr over 2f out tl rdn: swtchd lft and hdwy over 1f out: r.o: nt rch ldrs* **9/2**[2]

0006 **4** ½ **Miss Dusky Diva (IRE)**[57] 7614 4-9-8 **49**........................ GrahamLee 12 51
(David W Drinkwater) *prom: chsd ldr 5f out: rdn to ld over 1f out: hdd ins fnl f: styd on same pce* **10/1**[3]

0444 **5** ½ **Right Madam (IRE)**[15] 7262 4-9-6 **47**.......................(p) KieranO'Neill 2 49
(Sarah Hollinshead) *hld up: bhd 8f out: pushed along on outer over 2f out: hung lft and r.o ins fnl f: nt trbld ldrs* **20/1**

4530 **6** ¾ **Ship Canal**[7] 8386 4-9-5 **46**.. JackGarritty 1 46
(Jacqueline Coward) *chsd ldrs: rdn over 1f out: edgd lft and styd on same pce ins fnl f* **10/1**[3]

0/64 **7** nk **Haaffa Sovereign**[19] 8212 5-9-4 **48**............................ EoinWalsh[(3)] 9 49
(Kevin Morgan) *prom: chsd ldr over 9f out: hung lft over 7f out: lost 2nd 5f out: nt clr run over 3f out: sn rdn: styd on same pce fnl f* **12/1**

5005 **8** nk **Whip Up A Frenzy (IRE)**[29] 8070 4-9-5 **46**...................... RyanPowell 6 45
(Richard Rowe) *sn led: rdn and hdd over 1f out: no ex ins fnl f* **12/1**

0000 **9** 1½ **Moccasin (FR)**[21] 4425 7-9-5 **46**..................................(v) SamJames 11 43
(Geoffrey Harker) *hld up: hdwy 4f out: rdn over 1f out: no ex ins fnl f* **16/1**

6400 **10** 3¼ **Rainford Glory (IRE)**[21] 8180 6-9-5 **46**.....................(p) BarryMcHugh 7 38
(Tim Fitzgerald) *hld up: hdwy over 3f out: rdn over 2f out: wknd fnl f* **16/1**

0460 **11** nk **Hooks Lane**[21] 8180 4-9-2 **48**................................ CharlieBennett[(5)] 10 39
(Shaun Harris) *chsd ldrs: hmpd and lost pl over 3f out: rdn over 2f out: wknd fnl f* **12/1**

5004 **12** 2½ **Cougar Kid (IRE)**[21] 8180 5-9-5 **46**.............................(v[1]) TimmyMurphy 4 35
(John O'Shea) *hld up in tch: n.m.r over 3f out: nt clr run over 2f out: sn rdn: wknd fnl f* **7/2**[1]

2m 39.51s (-1.29) **Going Correction** -0.075s/f (Stan) **12** Ran SP% **128.1**
Speed ratings (Par 97): **101,99,99,99,99 98,98,98,97,95 94,93**
CSF £51.73 CT £203.67 TOTE £3.80: £1.50, £4.20, £2.00; EX 46.80 Trifecta £194.60.
Owner Panther Racing Ltd **Bred** Aston House Stud **Trained** Guiseley, West Yorkshire

The Form Book, Raceform Ltd, Newbury, RG14 5SJ

FOCUS
A low-grade handicap. The form is ordinary but could perhaps be rated a pound higher.

8498 BETWAY H'CAP 1m 1f 103y (Tp)
4:00 (4:00) (Class 5) (0-75,81) 3-Y-O+ £4,204 (£1,251; £625; £312) Stalls Low

Form RPR
41 1 **Maifalki (FR)**[20] 8195 3-9-5 **75** TomEaves 13 85
(Mark Walford) *racd keenly and sn trcking ldr: led wl over 1f out: rdn and hung lft ins fnl f: styd on* **16/1**
0222 2 1 1/2 **Cadeau Magnifique**[10] 8343 4-9-3 **71** [1] JackGarritty 5 76
(Richard Fahey) *chsd ldrs: rdn over 2f out: chsd wnr ins fnl f: styd on same pce* **9/4**[1]
1235 3 nk **Zephyros (GER)**[116] 5925 5-8-6 **63** RobHornby(3) 7 68+
(David Bridgwater) *hld up: hdwy over 1f out: rdn and swtchd rt ins fnl f: r.o* **33/1**
5112 4 shd **General Hazard (IRE)**[8] 8367 3-8-12 **71** LouisSteward(3) 6 76+
(Michael Bell) *hld up: hdwy over 1f out: styd on: eased last stride* **9/4**[1]
2431 5 3/4 **New Agenda**[10] 8337 4-9-13 **81** 6ex TomQueally 1 84
(Paul Webber) *trckd ldrs: racd keenly: rdn over 1f out: styd on same pce ins fnl f* **11/2**[2]
5661 6 1 **Beautiful Stranger (IRE)**[20] 8191 5-9-4 **72** (p) ConnorBeasley 3 73
(Keith Dalgleish) *hld up: hdwy u.p over 1f out: nt rch ldrs* **16/1**
012 7 nk **Polar Forest**[10] 8337 6-9-6 **74** (v[1]) JFEgan 4 74
(Richard Guest) *s.i.s: hld up: hdwy over 2f out: rdn over 1f out: styd on same pce fnl f* **14/1**
P-00 8 2 1/4 **Kafeel (USA)**[15] 8249 5-8-13 **67** (p) SteveDrowne 12 63
(Linda Jewell) *led: rdn and hdd wl over 1f out: wknd ins fnl f* **25/1**
5204 9 1 1/4 **The Third Man**[27] 8100 5-9-3 **71** (v) LiamKeniry 9 64
(Henry Spiller) *hld up: shkn up over 1f out: sn hung lft: nvr on terms* **7/1**[3]
3200 10 2 1/4 **Melabi (IRE)**[44] 7857 3-8-10 **73** CallumRodriguez(7) 10 61
(Richard Ford) *hld up: rdn over 2f out: n.d* **66/1**
34-0 11 hd **Steady Major (IRE)**[100] 6464 4-9-0 **73** CharlieBennett(5) 2 61
(Mark Brisbourne) *prom: rdn over 2f out: wknd fnl f* **100/1**
0060 12 3/4 **Marcret (ITY)**[29] 8077 9-9-7 **75** GrahamLee 11 61
(James Unett) *hld up: shkn up over 2f out: wknd over 1f out* **16/1**
5200 13 7 **Haabis (USA)**[22] 8154 3-8-8 **64** (vt[1]) AndrewMullen 8 36
(George Peckham) *hld up in tch: rdn over 2f out: sn wknd* **50/1**

1m 59.27s (-1.53) **Going Correction** -0.075s/f (Stan)
WFA 3 from 4yo+ 2lb **13** Ran SP% **125.0**
Speed ratings (Par 103): **103,101,101,101,100 99,99,97,96,94 94,93,87**
CSF £53.41 CT £1258.27 TOTE £16.50: £4.00, £1.50, £5.70; EX 79.10 Trifecta £3596.10.
Owner Lamont Racing **Bred** M Daguzan-Garros & C Sainte Marie **Trained** Sherriff Hutton, N Yorks
■ Stewards' Enquiry : Louis Steward 10-day ban: failed to ride out for third (5-7, 9-14, 16 Jan)

FOCUS
A fair handicap in which it paid to race handily.

8499 SUNBETS.CO.UK H'CAP (DIV I) 1m 141y (Tp)
4:30 (4:31) (Class 6) (0-55,55) 3-Y-O+ £2,846 (£847; £423; £211) Stalls Low

Form RPR
2334 1 **Deftera Lad (IRE)**[26] 8125 4-9-4 **52** TimmyMurphy 8 58+
(Natalie Lloyd-Beavis) *hld up: hmpd over 7f out: hdwy over 1f out: r.o to ld wl ins fnl f* **4/1**[2]
000 2 1 **Simply Clever**[57] 7609 3-9-5 **55** TomEaves 1 58
(David Brown) *led over 7f out: rdn over 1f out: hdd and unable qck wl ins fnl f* **20/1**
0-63 3 3/4 **Tanzina**[26] 8121 4-9-5 **53** LiamKeniry 6 54
(Laura Mongan) *led 1f: chsd ldr: rdn and ev ch fr over 1f out tl no ex towards fin* **8/1**
0044 4 1 1/2 **Orlando Rogue (IRE)**[121] 5734 4-9-7 **55** ConnorBeasley 10 53
(Keith Dalgleish) *chsd ldrs: rdn over 1f out: styd on same pce ins fnl f* **7/4**[1]
000 5 2 **Thrtypointstothree (IRE)**[85] 5383 5-8-9 **46** oh1(bt) EdwardGreatrex(3) 4 40
(Nikki Evans) *chsd ldrs: rdn over 2f out: nio ex ins fnl f* **33/1**
0600 6 3/4 **Zed Candy Girl**[19] 8207 6-9-0 **55** (p) TobyEley(7) 9 48
(Daniel Mark Loughnane) *hld up: hmpd over 7f out: hdwy over 3f out: rdn over 1f out: no ex ins fnl f* **14/1**
0600 7 hd **Kodiac Lady (IRE)**[12] 8307 4-8-12 **51** (e) HollieDoyle(5) 5 43
(Simon West) *hld up in tch: racd keenly: pushed along over 2f out: no ex fnl f* **7/1**[3]
6005 8 1 **Noneedtotellme (IRE)**[56] 7646 3-8-7 **46** oh1 RobHornby(3) 13 36
(James Unett) *hld up: rdn over 1f out: nvr trbld ldrs* **20/1**
0064 9 hd **Mount Cheiron (USA)**[40] 7944 5-9-0 **55** (p) CallumRodriguez(7) 2 45
(Richard Ford) *hld up: nt clr run wl over 1f out: nt trble ldrs* **7/1**[3]
6-66 10 nk **Seamoor Secret**[316] 513 4-8-12 **46** oh1 (t) KieranO'Neill 3 36
(Alex Hales) *hld up in tch: nt clr run over 2f out: rdn whn hmpd 1f out: wknd ins fnl f* **50/1**
5460 11 1 **Firgrove Bridge (IRE)**[9] 8350 4-8-12 **46** oh1 (p) RyanPowell 12 33
(Kevin Frost) *hld up: plld hrd: rdn over 1f out: n.d* **25/1**
5-06 12 11 **Moment To Dream**[220] 2292 4-9-1 **49** [1] JohnFahy 7 13
(Ken Wingrove) *hld up and a in rr* **66/1**
05-0 13 7 **New Tarabela**[26] 8125 5-8-12 **53** AledBeech(7) 11 2
(Tony Carroll) *hld up: a in rr* **20/1**

1m 49.71s (-0.39) **Going Correction** -0.075s/f (Stan)
WFA 3 from 4yo+ 2lb **13** Ran SP% **123.7**
Speed ratings (Par 101): **98,97,96,95,93 92,92,91,91,91 90,80,74**
CSF £87.65 CT £652.02 TOTE £5.00: £1.60, £5.50, £2.50; EX 68.00 Trifecta £430.40.
Owner Y Mustafa **Bred** S O'Sullivan **Trained** East Garston, Berks
■ Stewards' Enquiry : Rob Hornby three-day ban: careless riding (5-7 Jan)

FOCUS
Another low-grade handicap, in which the pace was ordinary. Those close up behind the winner help set the level.

8500 SUNBETS.CO.UK H'CAP (DIV II) 1m 141y (Tp)
5:00 (5:03) (Class 6) (0-55,55) 3-Y-O+ £2,846 (£847; £423; £211) Stalls Low

Form RPR
0000 1 **Pipers Piping (IRE)**[160] 4369 10-8-10 **47** RobHornby(3) 3 52
(Mandy Rowland) *prom: rdn over 2f out: nt clr run and swtchd rt ins fnl f: r.o to ld towards fin* **25/1**
0006 2 1/2 **Playful Dude (USA)**[79] 7057 3-9-5 **55** [1] JosephineGordon 5 59
(Phil McEntee) *led: racd keenly: hdd over 5f out: chsd ldr: rdn over 1f out: led wl ins fnl f: sn hdd: styd on* **14/1**
543 3 hd **Santadelacruze**[29] 8070 7-9-3 **51** (b) AdamBeschizza 4 55
(Mark Hoad) *chsd ldrs: rdn over 1f out: ev ch ins fnl f: styd on* **12/1**
0465 4 hd **Pivotal Dream (IRE)**[6] 8411 3-8-5 **46** oh1 CharlieBennett(5) 9 50
(Mark Brisbourne) *hld up: hdwy over 3f out: rdn over 1f out: r.o* **12/1**
0054 5 3/4 **Hold Firm**[15] 8258 4-9-7 **55** TomQueally 11 58
(Mark H Tompkins) *chsd ldr: rein broke and led over 5f out: rdn over 1f out: hdd wl ins fnl f* **7/1**[3]
3654 6 1 3/4 **Jazri**[7] 8382 5-9-5 **53** (b) JFEgan 10 51
(Milton Bradley) *hld up: hdwy on outer over 2f out: rdn over 1f out: styd on same pce ins fnl f* **8/1**
6044 7 hd **Bromance**[12] 8307 3-9-5 **55** (p) AndrewMullen 2 55
(Peter Niven) *hld up: plld hrd: nt clr run over 2f out: r.o ins fnl f: nvr nrr* **3/1**[1]
6505 8 1 1/4 **Star Links (USA)**[15] 8261 10-8-12 **46** oh1 (b) JohnFahy 1 41
(S Donohoe, Ire) *prom: stdd and losing pl whn hmpd after 1f: n.d after* **7/2**[2]
600 9 3/4 **Nouvelle Ere**[169] 3997 5-9-0 **55** AledBeech(7) 12 49
(Tony Carroll) *chsd ldrs: rdn over 2f out: no ex fnl f* **22/1**
6666 10 2 1/2 **Castlerea Tess**[26] 8121 3-8-10 **46** oh1 KieranO'Neill 6 34
(Sarah Hollinshead) *chsd ldrs: rdn over 2f out: wknd over 1f out* **28/1**
0001 11 shd **My Bubba**[29] 8070 4-8-9 **50** (t) WilliamCox(7) 8 38
(John Flint) *hld up in tch: plld hrd: rdn over 2f out: wknd over 1f out* **15/2**
0060 12 32 **Never To Be (USA)**[71] 7274 5-9-3 **54** (vt) CallumShepherd(3) 13
(Nikki Evans) *s.i.s: hld up: stmbld and stirrup leather broke over 2f out: eased* **11/1**
06- 13 1 1/2 **Ede's The Business**[151] 4899 5-8-12 **46** oh1 (b) RyanPowell 7
(Ken Wingrove) *s.i.s: outpcd* **66/1**

1m 49.57s (-0.53) **Going Correction** -0.075s/f (Stan)
WFA 3 from 4yo+ 2lb **13** Ran SP% **126.1**
Speed ratings (Par 101): **99,98,98,98,97 95,95,94,94,91 91,63,61**
CSF £346.67 CT £2633.81 TOTE £22.10: £6.50, £5.60, £3.90; EX 899.70 Trifecta £3334.20.
Owner Miss M E Rowland **Bred** Drumhass Stud **Trained** Lower Blidworth, Notts
■ Stewards' Enquiry : Adam Beschizza two-day ban: use of whip (5-6 Jan)

FOCUS
The second division was run 0.14sec quicker than the first leg. The third and fourth give perspective to the level.
T/Plt: £61.80 to a £1 stake. Pool: £58,956.53 - 695.54 winning units. T/Qpdt: £6.10 to a £1 stake. Pool: £9,211.87 - 1,104.78 winning units. **Colin Roberts**

8501 - 8523a (Foreign Racing) - See Raceform Interactive

[8493] WOLVERHAMPTON (A.W) (L-H)
Monday, December 26

OFFICIAL GOING: Tapeta: standard
Wind: Fresh, behind Weather: Fine

8524 BETWAY MIDDLE H'CAP 1m 4f 50y (Tp)
1:00 (1:02) (Class 5) (0-75,77) 3-Y-O+ £4,204 (£1,251; £625; £312) Stalls Low

Form RPR
5 1 **Elusive Cowboy (USA)**[18] 8084 3-8-13 **68** StevieDonohoe 6 76
(Stuart Edmunds) *chsd ldr tl rdn to ld over 2f out: styd on u.p* **16/1**
0132 2 1 1/4 **Threediamondrings**[9] 8428 3-8-5 **63** (t) EdwardGreatrex(3) 2 69
(Brendan Powell) *a.p: chsd wnr and edgd lft over 1f out: rdn: hung rt and lft ins fnl f: styd on* **4/1**[3]
4414 3 3 **Heart Locket**[17] 8283 4-9-3 **70** NathanEvans(3) 7 71
(Michael Easterby) *chsd ldrs: rdn over 2f out: sn outpcd: edgd lft over 1f out: styd on to go 3rd nr fin* **3/1**[2]
4304 4 nk **Dakota City**[19] 8253 5-9-10 **74** (v) AdamBeschizza 10 75
(Julia Feilden) *s.i.s: hld up: hdwy u.p over 1f out: hung lft ins fnl f: styd on same pce* **9/1**
5203 5 1 3/4 **Shadow Spirit**[31] 8090 3-9-2 **71** PJMcDonald 4 69
(Iain Jardine) *prom: rdn over 2f out: nt clr run over 1f out: no ex ins fnl f* **10/1**
0000 6 1 1/2 **Cottesloe (IRE)**[18] 8178 7-9-6 **70** DougieCostello 3 65
(Neil Mulholland) *hld up: rdn over 2f out: nvr on terms* **14/1**
3315 7 nk **Sunglider (IRE)**[17] 8283 3-9-8 **77** (v) PaulMulrennan 5 72
(David O'Meara) *hld up: racd keenly: rdn over 2f out: hung lft and wknd fr over 1f out* **11/4**[1]
0101 8 1 **Hard To Handel**[14] 8338 4-9-12 **76** SteveDrowne 1 69
(Clare Ellam) *hld up: sme hdwy u.p over 1f out: wknd fnl f* **25/1**
2343 9 shd **Oratorio's Joy (IRE)**[107] 6315 6-9-13 **77** TimmyMurphy 8 70
(Jamie Osborne) *hld up: hdwy 5f out: wknd wl over 2f out* **14/1**
0301 10 shd **Sunshineandbubbles**[19] 8255 3-8-5 **60** (p) JosephineGordon 9 53
(Daniel Mark Loughnane) *led: rdn and hdd over 2f out: wknd fnl f* **20/1**

2m 38.07s (-2.73) **Going Correction** -0.10s/f (Stan)
WFA 3 from 4yo+ 5lb **10** Ran SP% **118.6**
Speed ratings (Par 103): **105,104,102,101,100 99,99,98,98,98**
CSF £80.47 CT £252.39 TOTE £25.10: £5.00, £1.80, £1.70; EX 104.80 Trifecta £497.00.
Owner J Humberstone **Bred** Darley **Trained** Newport Pagnell, Bucks

FOCUS
Just an ordinary 61-75 handicap in which the early pace was strong but it slowed markedly after three furlongs and the hold-up horses struggled to get involved. A step up on his Irish form from the winner, with the third a bit off her recent levels.

8525 32RED.COM NURSERY H'CAP 1m 141y (Tp)
1:35 (1:38) (Class 3) (0-95,90) 2-Y-O £7,876 (£2,357; £1,178; £590; £293) Stalls Low

Form RPR
4210 1 **Emenem**[6] 8466 2-7-12 **72** HollieDoyle(5) 6 75
(Simon Dow) *hld up: hdwy over 2f out: rdn to ld and edgd lft ins fnl f: r.o* **11/4**[2]
55 2 1/2 **Mailshot (USA)**[113] 6180 2-9-7 **90** JasonHart 4 92
(Mark Johnston) *led at stdy pce: qcknd over 2f out: rdn over 1f out: hung rt and hdd ins fnl f: bmpd sn after: r.o* **5/1**
6151 3 nse **Poetic Force (IRE)**[14] 8341 2-8-4 **73** (t) JoeyHaynes 2 75
(Tony Carroll) *chsd ldrs: rdn over 1f out: hung rt and ev ch ins fnl f: r.o* **4/1**[3]
021 4 3 1/4 **Hochfeld (IRE)**[23] 8208 2-8-8 **77** PJMcDonald 5 72
(Mark Johnston) *chsd ldr: rdn and hung rt over 2f out: nt clr run and no ex ins fnl f* **5/2**[1]
022 5 shd **Letmestopyouthere (IRE)**[10] 8405 2-8-9 **85** KatherineGlenister(7) 3 80
(David Evans) *hld up in tch: rdn and nt clr run over 2f out: styd on same pce fnl f* **11/2**
014 6 shd **Woodukheleyfit**[159] 4523 2-8-0 **69** RyanPowell 1 64
(Sylvester Kirk) *s.i.s: hld up: rdn over 1f out: nt trble leaaders* **16/1**

1m 50.7s (0.60) **Going Correction** -0.10s/f (Stan) **6** Ran SP% **113.2**
Speed ratings (Par 100): **93,92,92,89,89 89**
CSF £16.88 TOTE £3.90: £1.70, £2.60; EX 19.60 Trifecta £70.50.
Owner Robert Moss and Christopher Brennan **Bred** D R Tucker **Trained** Ashtead, Surrey
■ Stewards' Enquiry : Joey Haynes jockey caution: future conduct in races.

FOCUS
There was a decent gallop to this nursery, but with just half a length separating the first three and the first two hanging right the form may not be strong.

8526 32RED CASINO EBF MAIDEN STKS — 5f 20y (Tp)
2:05 (2:05) (Class 5) 2-Y-O — **£4,204** (£1,251; £625; £312) **Stalls** Low

Form — RPR

3550 **1** **Street Jazz**[7] 8453 2-9-0 66 ....(b) TomEaves 2 — 70
(James Given) *mde all: rdn and edgd rt over 1f out: jst hld on* **11/2**[3]

3322 **2** *nk* **Coral Sea**[39] 7996 2-8-11 74 .... CallumShepherd(3) 4 — 69
(Charles Hills) *a.p: chsd wnr 1/2-way: rdn over 1f out: r.o* **5/2**[1]

24 **3** *shd* **Speed Freak**[16] 8313 2-8-11 68 ....(b[1]) HectorCrouch(3) 10 — 69
(Ralph Beckett) *a.p: pushed along 1/2-way: rdn and swtchd lft ins fnl f: r.o* **7/2**[2]

54 **4** *6* **Absolutely Awesome**[252] 1520 2-9-5 0 .... JosephineGordon 1 — 52
(Scott Dixon) *chsd ldrs: pushed along 1/2-way: wknd fnl f* **8/1**

5 *3* **De Vegas Kid (IRE)**[69] 7450 2-9-2 0 .... GeorgeDowning(3) 7 — 41
(Tony Carroll) *sn outpcd: nvr nrr* **8/1**

6 *2 1/4* **Wishing Time (IRE)** 2-9-0 0 .... PaulMulrennan 3 — 28+
(David O'Meara) *chsd wnr to 1/2-way: hung rt and wknd over 1f out* **7/2**[2]

00 **7** *4* **Quintessential**[16] 8313 2-9-0 0 .... BarryMcHugh 6 — 14
(Richard Fahey) *sn outpcd* **40/1**

8 *1* **Fast Tack (IRE)** 2-9-5 0 .... JasonHart 5 — 15
(John Quinn) *s.i.s: outpcd* **16/1**

30 **9** *shd* **Lily Fontana (IRE)**[30] 8118 2-9-0 0 .... TonyHamilton 8 — 10
(Richard Fahey) *s.i.s: outpcd* **28/1**

1m 1.03s (-0.87) **Going Correction** -0.10s/f (Stan) — **9** Ran SP% **122.4**
Speed ratings (Par 96): **102,101,101,91,86 83,76,75,75**
CSF £20.95 TOTE £6.80: £1.60, £1.40, £1.60; EX 23.80 Trifecta £69.60.
Owner The Cool Silk Partnership **Bred** Laundry Cottage Stud Farm **Trained** Willoughton, Lincs

FOCUS
The winner dominated this modest maiden throughout. It's been rated around the balance of the first three.

8527 BETWAY APP H'CAP (DIV I) — 1m 1f 103y (Tp)
2:35 (2:37) (Class 6) (0-60,62) 3-Y-O+ — **£2,911** (£866; £432; £216) **Stalls** Low

Form — RPR

0605 **1** **My Mistress (IRE)**[44] 7936 4-8-7 46 ....(p) JosephineGordon 4 — 54
(Phil McEntee) *hld up in tch: racd keenly: rdn to ld and hung lft ins fnl f: styd on* **20/1**

5351 **2** *1/2* **Kay Sera**[10] 8410 8-9-0 56 .... EoinWalsh(3) 6 — 63
(Tony Newcombe) *hld up: hdwy over 1f out: rdn and hung lft ins fnl f: styd on* **4/1**[1]

210 **3** *2 1/2* **Kristal Hart**[27] 2144 7-9-5 58 ....(p) DougieCostello 3 — 60
(Neil Mulholland) *led: hdd over 7f out: chsd ldr who wnt clr 5f out: tk clsr order over 2f out: rdn and ev ch whn carried lft ins fnl f: no ex towards fin* **12/1**

4000 **4** *1 1/2* **Star Ascending (IRE)**[16] 8318 4-9-4 57 ....(v[1]) TonyHamilton 8 — 56
(Jennie Candlish) *sn chsng ldr: led over 7f out: wnt clr 5f out tl c bk to the field over 2f out: rdn over 1f out: hdd: edgd lft and no ex ins fnl f* **12/1**

6562 **5** *1 1/2* **La Havrese (FR)**[23] 8207 5-9-9 62 .... PaddyAspell 2 — 59
(Lynn Siddall) *hld up: hdwy over 2f out: no ex fnl f* **6/1**[3]

0000 **6** *1/2* **Stamp Duty (IRE)**[10] 8400 8-8-7 46 oh1 .... BarryMcHugh 7 — 42
(Suzzanne France) *hld up: hdwy over 2f out: rdn over 1f out: wknd ins fnl f* **14/1**

3035 **7** *1 1/4* **Cahar Fad (IRE)**[30] 8125 4-8-10 49 ....(bt) AdamBeschizza 1 — 42
(Steph Hollinshead) *chsd ldrs: rdn over 1f out: wknd ins fnl f* **8/1**

1612 **8** *1/2* **Pensax Lady (IRE)**[30] 8125 3-8-13 54 .... StevieDonohoe 10 — 46
(Daniel Mark Loughnane) *s.i.s: hld up: rdn over 2f out: nvr on terms* **7/1**

3002 **9** *1/2* **Outlaw Torn (IRE)**[4] 8492 7-8-11 50 ....(e) ConnorBeasley 9 — 41
(Richard Guest) *chsd ldrs: rdn over 2f out: wknd and eased fnl f* **9/2**[2]

0000 **10** *1/2* **Los Cerritos (SWI)**[37] 8040 4-9-5 58 ....[1] SteveDrowne 5 — 48
(Oliver Greenall) *prom: lost pl over 7f out: rdn over 2f out: wknd over 1f out* **9/1**

4300 **11** *5* **Daleelak (IRE)**[11] 8382 3-9-7 62 .... PJMcDonald 11 — 43
(Mark Johnston) *s.i.s: sn prom: lost pl over 5f out: rdn and wknd over 2f out* **8/1**

1m 59.34s (-1.46) **Going Correction** -0.10s/f (Stan)
WFA 3 from 4yo+ 2lb — **11** Ran SP% **124.0**
Speed ratings (Par 101): **102,101,99,98,96 96,95,94,94,93 89**
CSF £103.84 CT £1045.45 TOTE £25.50: £6.30, £2.00, £3.30; EX 194.50 Trifecta £1395.30.
Owner Miss Robin Blaze McEntee **Bred** Helen Smith & Sally Mullen **Trained** Newmarket, Suffolk

FOCUS
An ordinary 45-60 handicap run at a modest pace.

8528 BETWAY APP H'CAP (DIV II) — 1m 1f 103y (Tp)
3:10 (3:10) (Class 6) (0-60,60) 3-Y-O+ — **£2,911** (£866; £432; £216) **Stalls** Low

Form — RPR

0023 **1** **Ferryview Place**[4] 8492 7-8-10 49 ....(vt) StevieDonohoe 7 — 56
(Ian Williams) *s.i.s: pushed along in rr early: hdwy over 1f out: rdn: edgd lft and r.o to ld nr fin* **9/4**[1]

4604 **2** *nk* **Nonchalant**[30] 8124 5-9-7 60 .... SteveDrowne 1 — 66
(Hugo Froud) *led: rdn over 2f out: hdd nr fin* **5/1**[2]

0344 **3** *1/2* **Frivolous Prince (IRE)**[46] 7888 3-8-0 46 ....(vt) HollieDoyle(5) 4 — 51
(David Evans) *mid-div: hdwy over 2f out: rdn over 1f out: r.o* **6/1**[3]

0504 **4** *1 1/4* **Sakhalin Star (IRE)**[10] 8400 5-9-5 58 ....(e) ConnorBeasley 10 — 61
(Richard Guest) *chsd ldrs: rdn over 1f out: swtchd lft ins fnl f: styd on same pce* **13/2**

0000 **5** *1* **Caius College Girl (IRE)**[26] 8156 4-9-4 57 .... TimmyMurphy 2 — 58
(Natalie Lloyd-Beavis) *chsd ldr: rdn over 1f out: no ex wl ins fnl f* **20/1**

000 **6** *1 3/4* **Foylesideview (IRE)**[10] 8410 4-8-7 46 oh1 .... JosephineGordon 3 — 44
(Harry Chisman) *chsd ldrs: rdn over 2f out: no ex ins fnl f* **10/1**

0410 **7** *shd* **Makhfar (IRE)**[25] 8179 5-9-0 56 ....[1] CallumShepherd(3) 11 — 54
(Kevin Morgan) *hld up: hdwy over 1f out: sn rdn: styd on same pce fnl f* **8/1**

2603 **8** *8* **Dovil's Duel (IRE)**[23] 8207 5-9-4 60 .... HectorCrouch(3) 8 — 42
(Tony Newcombe) *hld up: racd keenly: wknd over 1f out* **5/1**[2]

0-00 **9** *2* **Percy's Lass**[16] 8306 4-8-13 52 .... TomEaves 9 — 31
(Brian Ellison) *hld up in tch: pushed along and lost pl over 3f out: wknd over 2f out* **20/1**

-006 **10** *6* **Fire Empress**[14] 8342 3-8-11 52 .... RyanPowell 5 — 19
(James Unett) *hld up: plld hrd: rdn over 2f out: wknd and eased over 1f out* **25/1**

1m 59.95s (-0.85) **Going Correction** -0.10s/f (Stan)
WFA 3 from 4yo+ 2lb — **10** Ran SP% **125.3**
Speed ratings (Par 101): **99,98,98,97,96 94,94,87,85,80**
CSF £14.24 CT £63.98 TOTE £3.10: £1.50, £2.80, £2.30; EX 22.10 Trifecta £70.10.
Owner Ian Williams **Bred** Bishopswood Bloodstock & Trickledown Stud **Trained** Portway, Worcs

FOCUS
The second division of a 45-60 handicap, but the pace was fair and the time was marginally slower than the first division.

8529 BETWAY H'CAP — 1m 1f 103y (Tp)
3:45 (3:46) (Class 2) (0-105,103) 3-Y-O+
£12,450 (£3,728; £1,864; £932; £466; £234) **Stalls** Low

Form — RPR

0614 **1** **Forceful Appeal (USA)**[9] 8427 8-8-12 **91** .... TomMarquand 1 — 99
(Simon Dow) *chsd ldrs: nt clr run over 1f out: rdn and r.o to ld wl ins fnl f* **16/1**

3405 **2** *3/4* **Perfect Cracker**[16] 8317 8-8-11 **90** .... RyanTate 6 — 96
(Clive Cox) *hld up in tch: racd keenly: shkn up over 1f out: r.o* **10/1**

0042 **3** *nk* **John Reel (FR)**[63] 7575 7-8-11 **97** .... KatherineGlenister(7) 4 — 102
(David Evans) *chsd ldr over 7f out tl led over 5f out: rdn over 2f out: hdd over 1f out: r.o* **20/1**

1000 **4** *shd* **Our Channel (USA)**[153] 4731 5-9-10 **103** .... WilliamCarson 5 — 108
(Jamie Osborne) *plld hrd: led: hdd over 5f out: chsd ldr tl rdn to ld again over 1f out: hdd wl ins fnl f* **16/1**

1003 **5** *hd* **Examiner (IRE)**[16] 8317 5-9-0 **93** .... AdamBeschizza 9 — 98+
(Stuart Williams) *hld up: rdn and r.o ins fnl f: nt rch ldrs* **11/4**[2]

2-04 **6** *shd* **High Baroque (USA)**[21] 8231 4-8-6 **85** .... BarryMcHugh 7 — 90
(Richard Fahey) *chsd ldrs: rdn over 1f out: r.o* **5/1**[3]

0064 **7** *hd* **Solar Deity (IRE)**[16] 8317 7-9-7 **100** ....(p) StevieDonohoe 8 — 104+
(Jane Chapple-Hyam) *hld up: rdn over 1f out swtchd rt and r.o ins fnl f: nt rch ldrs* **10/1**

0650 **8** *1 1/2* **Winterlude (IRE)**[16] 8317 6-9-5 **98** .... TimmyMurphy 11 — 99
(Jennie Candlish) *hld up: hdwy 4f out: rdn over 2f out: hung lft and styd on same pce fnl f* **14/1**

2260 **9** *nk* **Ready (IRE)**[16] 8317 6-8-10 **89** ....(p) SteveDrowne 3 — 89
(Clare Ellam) *hld up in tch: rdn over 1f out: no ex wl ins fnl f* **33/1**

-121 **10** *1 1/2* **Mythical Madness**[16] 8317 5-9-4 **97** ....(p) PaulMulrennan 10 — 94
(David O'Meara) *hld up: hdwy over 1f out: sn rdn: no ex ins fnl f* **9/4**[1]

4340 **11** *3/4* **Castilo Del Diablo (IRE)**[222] 2377 7-8-11 **90** ....(p) TomEaves 2 — 86
(David Simcock) *hld up: rdn over 1f out: nvr on terms* **25/1**

1m 59.5s (-1.30) **Going Correction** -0.10s/f (Stan) — **11** Ran SP% **122.3**
Speed ratings (Par 109): **101,100,100,99,99 99,99,98,97,96 95**
CSF £168.78 CT £3226.03 TOTE £17.60: £4.30, £3.00, £6.20; EX 173.80 Trifecta £3578.90.
Owner Mark McAllister **Bred** Juddmonte Farms Inc **Trained** Ashtead, Surrey

FOCUS
A competitive handicap, but the pace wasn't strong, and as it developed into a sprint up the straight those who raced prominently were favoured. It's been rated around the runner-up.

8530 BETWAY SPRINT CONDITIONS STKS — 5f 216y (Tp)
4:15 (4:16) (Class 2) 3-Y-O+
£12,450 (£3,728; £1,864; £932; £466; £234) **Stalls** Low

Form — RPR

0602 **1** **Spring Loaded (IRE)**[33] 8069 4-9-4 99 .... ShaneKelly 2 — 113
(Paul D'Arcy) *hld up: hdwy over 1f out: led ins fnl f: r.o: comf* **11/8**[1]

0102 **2** *2 3/4* **Mythmaker**[44] 7932 4-9-4 105 .... ConnorBeasley 6 — 104
(Bryan Smart) *led: rdn over 1f out: hdd and unable qck ins fnl f* **7/2**[2]

4032 **3** *1 1/4* **Gentlemen**[10] 8407 5-9-4 96 .... JosephineGordon 3 — 100
(Phil McEntee) *prom: racd keenly: rdn over 1f out: styd on same pce* **8/1**

124 **4** *hd* **Final Venture**[121] 5863 4-9-4 104 .... PaulMulrennan 1 — 99
(Paul Midgley) *trckd ldrs: plld hrd: rdn over 1f out: no ex ins fnl f* **8/1**

4413 **5** *2 1/2* **Dougan**[10] 8407 4-9-4 100 .... EoinWalsh 5 — 91
(David Evans) *hld up: rdn over 1f out: nvr on terms* **9/2**[3]

52 **6** *3/4* **Lightscameraction (IRE)**[76] 7242 4-9-7 108 ....(b) TonyHamilton 4 — 92
(Gay Kelleway) *sn chsng ldr: rdn over 1f out: wknd ins fnl f* **10/1**

1m 11.88s (-2.62) **Going Correction** -0.10s/f (Stan) course record — **6** Ran SP% **113.8**
Speed ratings (Par 109): **113,109,107,107,104 103**
CSF £6.55 TOTE £2.30: £1.40, £2.10; EX 7.30 Trifecta £33.50.
Owner Rowley Racing **Bred** Swordlestown Little **Trained** Newmarket, Suffolk
■ Stewards' Enquiry : Connor Beasley one-day ban: failed to ride to draw (Jan 9)

FOCUS
A competitive sprint run at a sound gallop. The runner-up's latest effort might not be as good as it looked and he's been rated to the rest of his form, with the third close to his latest career-best C&D handicap run.

8531 SUNBETS.CO.UK H'CAP — 7f 32y (Tp)
4:45 (4:46) (Class 5) (0-75,77) 3-Y-O+ — **£4,204** (£1,251; £625; £312) **Stalls** High

Form — RPR

1014 **1** **Evening Attire**[16] 8319 5-9-4 **77** .... HollieDoyle(5) 10 — 86
(William Stone) *mde all: rdn over 1f out: edgd rt ins fnl f: r.o* **9/2**[2]

4336 **2** *1* **Malaysian Boleh**[11] 8389 6-8-13 **67** ....(b) TomEaves 2 — 73
(Brian Ellison) *hld up: hdwy over 1f out: r.o* **10/1**

0014 **3** *shd* **Mr Christopher (IRE)**[19] 8251 4-9-8 **76** ....(p) AdamBeschizza 11 — 82
(Tom Dascombe) *chsd wnr over 5f out: rdn over 1f out: styd on* **6/1**[3]

2021 **4** *3/4* **Capolavoro (FR)**[23] 8205 5-9-3 **74** .... EoinWalsh(3) 8 — 78
(Robert Cowell) *mid-div: rdn over 1f out: r.o ins fnl f: nt rch ldrs* **3/1**[1]

3300 **5** *nk* **Smokethatthunders (IRE)**[156] 4627 6-9-7 **75** .... StevieDonohoe 4 — 78
(James Unett) *chsd ldrs: rdn over 2f out: styd on* **12/1**

1415 **6** *nk* **Rock Warbler (IRE)**[35] 8052 3-8-13 **67** ....(t) JamesSullivan 6 — 69+
(Oliver Greenall) *hld up: hdwy over 1f out: r.o* **13/2**

5042 **7** *nk* **Ravenhoe (IRE)**[11] 8379 3-9-4 **72** .... PJMcDonald 3 — 74
(Mark Johnston) *chsd ldrs: rdn over 2f out: no ex wl ins fnl f* **7/1**

356 **8** *nk* **Chiswick Bey (IRE)**[26] 8163 8-8-12 **66** .... TonyHamilton 1 — 67
(Richard Fahey) *mid-div: rdn over 2f out: hdwy over 1f out: styd on* **16/1**

0000 **9** *1 1/2* **Harry Holland**[26] 8154 4-8-9 **63** .... JosephineGordon 5 — 60
(Tom Dascombe) *hld up: rdn over 1f out: nt trble ldrs* **12/1**

3614 **10** *2 3/4* **Head Space (IRE)**[31] 8094 8-8-6 **67** .... KatherineGlenister(7) 9 — 56
(David Evans) *chsd ldrs: rdn over 1f out: wknd fnl f* **20/1**

3600 **11** *2 3/4* **Bell Heather (IRE)**[11] 8385 3-9-2 **70** .... BarryMcHugh 7 — 52
(Richard Fahey) *hld up: shkn up over 2f out: nt trble ldrs* **16/1**

1m 27.76s (-1.04) **Going Correction** -0.10s/f (Stan) — **11** Ran SP% **124.3**
Speed ratings (Par 103): **101,99,99,98,98 98,97,97,95,92 89**
CSF £52.26 CT £285.99 TOTE £5.40: £1.80, £2.60, £2.70; EX 64.60 Trifecta £374.50.
Owner Miss Caroline Scott **Bred** Howard Barton Stud **Trained** West Wickham, Cambs

FOCUS
A fair handicap for the grade run at a sound pace from the outset. The third has been rated to his penultimate C&D win.
T/Plt: £810.40 to a £1 stake. Pool: £64,735.81. 58.31 winning tickets. T/Qpdt: £76.00 to a £1 stake. Pool: £3,910.52. 38.07 winning tickets. **Colin Roberts**

8532 - 8534a (Foreign Racing) - See Raceform Interactive

8524 WOLVERHAMPTON (A.W) (L-H)

Tuesday, December 27

OFFICIAL GOING: Tapeta: standard

Wind: Light behind Weather: Overcast

8535 BETWAY APP H'CAP — 5f 20y (Tp)

1:05 (1:06) (Class 6) (0-65,65) 3-Y-O+ **£2,425** (£721; £360; £180) **Stalls** Low

Form RPR

0000 **1** **Richter Scale (IRE)**[11] 8403 3-9-7 **65** MartinDwyer 2 73
(Iain Jardine) *a.p: rdn to ld over 1f out: edgd rt: styd on* **5/2**[1]

0164 **2** ½ **Dreams Of Glory**[10] 8429 8-9-7 **65** DavidProbert 1 71
(Ron Hodges) *w ldr tl wnt on 3f out: rdn: edgd rt and hdd over 1f out: styd on* **9/2**[2]

0045 **3** 1¼ **Temple Road (IRE)**[10] 8430 8-9-2 **60** (bt) RichardKingscote 7 62
(Milton Bradley) *hld up: racd keenly: hdwy 2f out: shkn up ins fnl f: styd on same pce towards fin* **7/1**[3]

10 **4** 1¼ **Nuala Tagula (IRE)**[11] 8403 3-9-7 **65** JasonHart 3 62
(John Quinn) *sn prom: rdn over 1f out: styd on same pce ins fnl f* **8/1**

6640 **5** 1½ **Noble Asset**[34] 8078 5-9-6 **64** DougieCostello 6 56
(Milton Bradley) *s.i.s: hld up: hdwy over 1f out: nt trble ldrs* **10/1**

0000 **6** 2½ **City Of Angkor Wat (IRE)**[17] 8315 6-9-4 **62** (p) TomEaves 9 45
(Conor Dore) *in rr: rdn over 1f out: nvr on terms* **16/1**

5600 **7** nk **Diamond Charlie (IRE)**[10] 8429 8-9-1 **64** HollieDoyle(5) 10 46
(Simon Dow) *hld up: racd keenly: rdn over 1f out: nvr nrr* **15/2**

2250 **8** nk **Jack The Laird (IRE)**[22] 8228 3-9-3 **64** (b) JackDuern(3) 11 45
(Dean Ivory) *hld up: rdn over 1f out: nvr on terms* **14/1**

5030 **9** ¾ **Mighty Zip (USA)**[45] 7945 4-8-12 **61** (p) CharlieBennett(5) 4 39
(Lisa Williamson) *led 2f: rdn and ev ch 2f out: wknd fnl f* **20/1**

0000 **10** 2½ **Long Awaited (IRE)**[12] 8390 8-9-2 **60** (b) MartinHarley 5 29
(Conor Dore) *hld up: hdwy over 1f out: wknd fnl f* **25/1**

3213 **11** 2¼ **David's Beauty (IRE)**[92] 6832 3-9-3 **61** PatCosgrave 8 22
(Brian Baugh) *chsd ldrs: sn pushed along: wknd over 1f out* **16/1**

1m 1.03s (-0.87) **Going Correction** -0.125s/f (Stan) **11** Ran SP% **118.3**

Speed ratings (Par 101): **101,100,98,96,93 89,89,88,87,83 80**

CSF £13.14 CT £71.71 TOTE £3.30: £1.40, £2.10, £2.20; EX 14.50 Trifecta £82.80.

Owner New Approach Racing Limited **Bred** Max Morris **Trained** Carrutherstown, D'fries & G'way

FOCUS

A moderate sprint handicap and few ever got into it.

8536 £10 FREE AT 32RED.COM MAIDEN AUCTION STKS — 5f 216y (Tp)

1:40 (1:43) (Class 6) 2-Y-O **£2,425** (£721; £360; £180) **Stalls** Low

Form RPR

50 **1** **Ferocity (IRE)**[33] 8082 2-9-0 0 PatCosgrave 4 72+
(Robyn Brisland) *a.p: racd keenly: wnt 2nd 2f out: shkn up to ld over 1f out: edgd lft ins fnl f: r.o wl* **11/8**[1]

6404 **2** 4½ **Red Mohican**[11] 8404 2-8-10 57 (t) JosephineGordon 2 54
(Phil McEntee) *s.i.s: hld up: racd keenly: hdwy over 2f out: rdn and hung lft over 1f out: styd on to go 2nd wl ins fnl f* **7/1**[3]

04 **3** ½ **Alfonso Manana (IRE)**[11] 8406 2-9-3 0 RichardKingscote 10 60
(James Given) *broke wl on outer: sn pushed along: lost pl after 1f: rdn and edgd lft over 1f out: styd on to go 3rd post* **5/2**[2]

3500 **4** nk **Affordability**[34] 8071 2-8-12 60 SteveDrowne 8 53
(Daniel Mark Loughnane) *led: rdn: edgd rt and hdd over 1f out: no ex ins fnl f* **10/1**

00 **5** ½ **Oberyn (IRE)**[17] 8313 2-8-6 0 MitchGodwin(5) 6 51
(Sylvester Kirk) *hld up: hdwy over 1f out: sn rdn: styd on same pce ins fnl f* **33/1**

00 **6** 1 **Love And Be Loved**[27] 8151 2-8-3 0 GeorgiaCox(5) 1 45
(Peter Chapple-Hyam) *chsd ldrs: rdn over 1f out: wknd ins fnl f* **10/1**

7 3¼ **Flying Fynn (IRE)** 2-8-13 0 ow2 RenatoSouza 3 40
(Jose Santos) *w ldr over 3f: sn rdn: wknd fnl f* **20/1**

8 3 **Rockalater** 2-8-7 0 MartinDwyer 7 25
(Sylvester Kirk) *s.i.s: rn green in rr: nvr on terms* **14/1**

00 **9** 1¾ **Lady Rowena**[19] 8277 2-8-7 0 AndrewMullen 5 20
(Mark Johnston) *sn pushed along towards rr: wknd over 2f out* **33/1**

00 **10** 7 **Sugar Plum (IRE)**[17] 8313 2-8-7 0 WilliamCarson 9
(Bill Turner) *chsd ldr tl rdn and wknd over 2f out* **66/1**

1m 14.3s (-0.20) **Going Correction** -0.125s/f (Stan) **10** Ran SP% **120.2**

Speed ratings (Par 94): **96,90,89,88,88 86,82,78,76,66**

CSF £11.94 TOTE £2.30: £1.10, £2.00, £1.50; EX 12.40 Trifecta £37.70.

Owner Franconson Partners **Bred** Anglia Bloodstock Ltd & Mr C Humber **Trained** Newmarket, Suffolk

FOCUS

A moderate maiden auction event and ultimately a one-horse race. The time, along with the runner-up and fifth point to caution over the bare form.

8537 32RED CASINO MAIDEN STKS — 1m 141y (Tp)

2:15 (2:17) (Class 5) 2-Y-O **£3,072** (£914; £456; £228) **Stalls** Low

Form RPR

5 **1** **Makaarim**[20] 8246 2-9-5 0 DanielMuscutt 7 75+
(Marco Botti) *mde virtually all: rdn over 1f out: edgd lft ins fnl f: styd on* **2/1**[2]

042 **2** 2 **Pete So High (GER)**[20] 8246 2-9-5 74 JosephineGordon 12 70
(Richard Hannon) *a.p: chsd wnr 2f out: rdn and hung lft over 1f out: styd on* **7/4**[1]

3 1¼ **Bowban** 2-9-5 0 TomEaves 5 68
(Brian Ellison) *chsd ldrs: rdn over 2f out: sn outpcd: styd on fnl f* **9/1**

0 **4** 1¼ **Caracas**[13] 8354 2-9-5 0 RichardKingscote 11 65
(Roger Charlton) *hld up: hdwy over 1f out: nt trble ldrs* **28/1**

0 **5** ½ **William Booth (IRE)**[24] 8208 2-9-5 0 RyanPowell 1 64
(Daniel Mark Loughnane) *prom: nt clr run over 2f out: rdn over 1f out: styd on same pce* **100/1**

304 **6** 1 **Shee's Lucky**[11] 8397 2-9-0 70 AndrewMullen 3 57
(Mark Johnston) *chsd ldrs: rdn over 2f out: no ex fnl f* **16/1**

0 **7** 3¼ **Mikey Ready (USA)**[20] 8245 2-9-5 0 (t) ThomasBrown 4 55+
(Ed Walker) *hld up: shkn up over 1f out: nvr on terms* **7/1**[3]

8 ½ **Costa Percy** 2-9-5 0 DougieCostello 2 54
(K R Burke) *mid-div: pushed along over 2f out: n.d* **50/1**

5 **9** 3½ **Bermondsey Belle (IRE)**[13] 8355 2-9-0 0 DavidProbert 9 42
(Lucy Wadham) *chsd wnr tl rdn 2f out: wknd fnl f* **10/1**

0 **10** 5 **Mambo Dancer**[20] 8246 2-9-5 0 JasonHart 10 36
(Mark Johnston) *sn pushed along in rr: nvr on terms* **50/1**

11 3 **Major Tom** 2-9-2 0 AlistairRawlinson(3) 6 30
(Michael Appleby) *in rr whn nt clr run after 1f: sn pushed along: nvr on terms* **80/1**

66 **12** 21 **Termsnconditions (IRE)**[8] 8454 2-9-5 0 PatCosgrave 13
(Tim Vaughan) *prom: rdn over 3f out: wknd over 2f out* **100/1**

13 10 **Born Legend (IRE)** 2-9-5 0 SteveDrowne 8
(Charles Hills) *s.s: a bhd* **20/1**

1m 48.72s (-1.38) **Going Correction** -0.125s/f (Stan) **13** Ran SP% **122.5**

Speed ratings (Par 96): **101,99,98,97,96 95,92,92,89,84 82,63,54**

CSF £5.79 TOTE £3.40: £1.40, £1.40, £2.00; EX 6.80 Trifecta £36.00.

Owner Sheikh Mohammed Bin Khalifa Al Maktoum **Bred** Essafinaat Ltd **Trained** Newmarket, Suffolk

FOCUS

This was a rather better maiden, forever associated with the winning debut of Jack Hobbs two years ago, and while this year's winner is unlikely to reach his heights, he still did this nicely. The runner-up's mark of 74 rates the benchmark.

8538 32RED.COM EBF FILLIES' H'CAP — 1m 141y (Tp)

2:50 (2:53) (Class 2) (0-105,98) 3-Y-O+

£16,807 (£5,032; £2,516; £1,258; £629; £315) **Stalls** Low

Form RPR

0045 **1** **Daisy Bere (FR)**[10] 8426 3-8-3 **79** oh1 (p) JoeyHaynes 5 83
(K R Burke) *s.i.s: sn prom: chsd ldr over 2f out: led over 1f out: sn rdn and hung rt: r.o* **6/1**[3]

2013 **2** ¾ **Carolinae**[20] 8251 4-8-10 **84** StevieDonohoe 2 87+
(Charlie Fellowes) *hld up: hdwy and nt clr run over 1f out: shkn up to chal whn hmpd 1f out: edgd rt: r.o* **6/5**[1]

531 **3** hd **Gleaming Girl**[120] 5973 4-8-5 **79** oh1 JosephineGordon 4 81
(David Simcock) *hld up: shkn up over 2f out: r.o ins fnl f* **4/1**[2]

300P **4** ¾ **Squash**[32] 8098 3-9-8 **98** DavidProbert 3 98
(Philip McBride) *hld up: rdn whn carried rt 1f out: r.o ins fnl f* **6/1**[3]

4651 **5** 2 **Stosur (IRE)**[14] 8347 5-8-2 **79** (b) AaronJones(3) 1 74
(Gay Kelleway) *led: clr over 6f out tl c bk to the field: 3f out: rdn and hdd over 1f out: no ex ins fnl f* **12/1**

4046 **6** 1 **Yeah Baby Yeah (IRE)**[10] 8426 3-9-0 **90** TonyHamilton 6 83
(Gay Kelleway) *prom: rdn over 2f out: hmpd 1f out: no ex* **8/1**

0430 **7** 1½ **Italian Beauty (IRE)**[25] 8190 4-8-2 **79** oh10 (p) NathanEvans(3) 7 69
(John Wainwright) *chsd ldr tl rdn over 2f out: wknd ins fnl f* **80/1**

1m 48.31s (-1.79) **Going Correction** -0.125s/f (Stan)

WFA 3 from 4yo+ 2lb **7** Ran SP% **114.1**

Speed ratings (Par 96): **102,101,101,100,98 97,96**

CSF £13.61 TOTE £8.70: £3.20, £1.50; EX 21.80 Trifecta £70.30.

Owner Mrs Elaine M Burke **Bred** S N C Regnier & San Gabriel Inv Inc **Trained** Middleham Moor, N Yorks

FOCUS

Probably not the best Class 2 handicap ever run, with the top weight 7lb below the race ceiling and three of the seven fillies out of the weights. Although the early pace was generous, it had slowed down by halfway and it became a rough race. It's been rated around the first three.

8539 BETWAY H'CAP — 1m 1f 103y (Tp)

3:25 (3:26) (Class 4) (0-85,85) 3-Y-O+ **£4,690** (£1,395; £697; £348) **Stalls** Low

Form RPR

552 **1** **Coillte Cailin (IRE)**[20] 8249 6-9-7 **85** MartinHarley 6 93
(David O'Meara) *hld up: hdwy over 1f out: led ins fnl f: sn rdn and edgd lft: styd on* **11/4**[1]

6144 **2** ½ **Toga Tiger (IRE)**[103] 6517 9-8-13 **77** RichardKingscote 10 84
(Kevin Frost) *hld up: hdwy over 1f out: rdn and ev ch ins fnl f: r.o* **20/1**

5305 **3** 2¼ **Mica Mika (IRE)**[93] 6802 8-8-13 **84** NatalieHambling(7) 5 87+
(Richard Fahey) *prom: lost pl over 3f out: hdwy and nt clr run over 1f out: swtchd rt ins fnl f: r.o* **33/1**

3005 **4** nk **Berlusca (IRE)**[34] 8077 7-9-2 **80** ShaneKelly 4 82
(David O'Meara) *hld up: hdwy over 1f out: rdn and ev ch ins fnl f: styd on same pce* **10/1**

3452 **5** 1¼ **Sennockian Star**[17] 8317 6-9-7 **85** (v) AndrewMullen 9 84
(Mark Johnston) *chsd ldrs: rdn to ld over 1f out: hdd and no ex ins fnl f* **7/2**[2]

1000 **6** 1½ **Gleese The Devil (IRE)**[20] 8250 5-8-12 **76** TonyHamilton 3 72
(Richard Fahey) *hld up: r.o ins fnl f: nvr nrr* **20/1**

5046 **7** hd **Faithful Creek (IRE)**[17] 8317 4-9-6 **84** (p) TomEaves 11 79
(Michael Appleby) *s.i.s: hld up: hdwy over 3f out: rdn and nt clr run over 1f out: sn hung lft: wknd wl ins fnl f* **5/1**[3]

0 **8** 2¼ **My Fantasea (IRE)**[20] 8251 3-8-12 **78** StevieDonohoe 2 69
(David Evans) *s.i.s: sn prom: rdn over 2f out: wknd fnl f* **14/1**

-415 **9** nk **Aldeburgh**[197] 3219 7-9-5 **83** ThomasBrown 13 73
(Nigel Twiston-Davies) *chsd ldrs: rdn over 2f out: wknd ins fnl f* **18/1**

2042 **10** ½ **Cricklewood Green (USA)**[8] 8455 5-8-7 **76** MitchGodwin(5) 8 65
(Sylvester Kirk) *s.i.s: hld up: hdwy 4f out: rdn over 2f out: wknd ins fnl f* **13/2**

0- **11** 1¼ **Restive (IRE)**[78] 7233 3-8-12 **78** MartinDwyer 7 64
(Iain Jardine) *plld hrd: trckd ldrs: led 5f out: rdn and hdd over 1f out: wknd ins fnl f* **16/1**

0000 **12** 2½ **Ocean Tempest**[22] 8231 7-9-6 **84** (p) JosephineGordon 1 65
(John Ryan) *sn pushed along to ld: hdd 5f out: rdn over 2f out: wknd over 1f out* **40/1**

1m 58.05s (-2.75) **Going Correction** -0.125s/f (Stan)

WFA 3 from 4yo+ 2lb **12** Ran SP% **120.7**

Speed ratings (Par 105): **107,106,104,104,103 101,101,99,99,98 97,95**

CSF £66.34 CT £1532.56 TOTE £3.80: £1.90, £3.70, £7.70; EX 25.20 Trifecta £943.80.

Owner Peter J Moran **Bred** Whisperview Trading Ltd **Trained** Upper Helmsley, N Yorks

FOCUS

A fair and competitive handicap with the first two coming with their efforts widest from off the pace. The third would have matched his AW career best with a clear run.

8540 BETWAY MARATHON H'CAP — 1m 5f 194y (Tp)

4:00 (4:01) (Class 6) (0-60,60) 3-Y-O+ **£2,425** (£721; £360; £180) **Stalls** Low

Form RPR

0036 **1** **Captain Swift (IRE)**[21] 8238 5-9-10 **60** [1] AndrewMullen 11 66
(John Mackie) *prom: rdn to ld over 1f out: styd on u.p* **9/1**

0360 **2** ½ **Lineman**[38] 8039 6-9-3 **56** (b) JackDuern(3) 1 61
(Sarah Hollinshead) *hld up: hdwy 4f out: led over 2f out: rdn and hdd over 1f out: styd on* **20/1**

0564 **3** 1½ **Trust The Man (IRE)**[9] 8445 3-8-8 **51** ow2 AdamBeschizza 4 54
(Simon Dow) *chsd ldrs: rdn over 2f out: styd on* **9/2**[3]

0/11 **4** ½ **Shan Dun na nGall (IRE)**[17] 8309 5-9-6 **56** (vt) LemosdeSouza 9 58
(Amy Murphy) *s.i.s: hld up: hdwy over 1f out: styd on: nt rch ldrs* **7/2**[1]

0033 **5** ½ **Ryan The Giant**^{5} 8488 3-8-3 **49** ....(v^{1}) NathanEvans$^{(3)}$ 6 51
(Keith Dalgleish) *chsd ldr over 8f: remained handy: nt clr run over 2f out: rdn over 1f out: styd on same pce fnl f* **4/1**^{2}

0003 **6** ¾ **Staplehurst (IRE)**^{7} 8468 3-8-8 **51** ....(t) JosephineGordon 10 52
(Geoffrey Deacon) *s.i.s: hld up: r.o ins fnl f: nvr nrr* **7/1**

1664 **7** 1½ **Mr Marchwood**^{25} 8193 3-8-13 **56** .... TomMarquand 5 54
(Sylvester Kirk) *hld up: nt clr run over 1f out: nvr on terms* **9/2**^{3}

0560 **8** 3½ **Filament Of Gold (USA)**^{11} 8410 5-9-5 **55** ....(p) TomEaves 12 48
(Roy Brotherton) *chsd ldrs: wnt 2nd over 5f out: ev ch over 2f out: sn rdn: edgd lft and wknd ins fnl f* **20/1**

0-06 **9** 2¼ **Major Franko**^{7} 1174 4-8-12 **48** .... StevieDonohoe 2 38
(Sarah-Jayne Davies) *mid-div: lost pl over 6f out: rdn over 2f out: sme hdwy over 1f out: eased whn btn ins fnl f* **66/1**

3665 **10** 1½ **Thou Swell (IRE)**^{286} 957 4-9-3 **60** .... BenSanderson$^{(7)}$ 3 48
(Shaun Harris) *s.i.s: hld up: rdn over 3f out: n.d* **33/1**

0320 **11** 3¾ **White Dog (IRE)**^{5} 8492 4-9-0 **50** ....(t) DougieCostello 7 32
(Sarah Humphrey) *led at stdy pce: rdn and hdd over 2f out: wknd over 1f out* **20/1**

0000 **12** 45 **Street Art (IRE)**^{26} 8180 4-8-10 **46** oh1 ....(t) MartinDwyer 13
(Mike Murphy) *hld up in tch: plld hrd: hung lft over 5f out: rdn and wknd over 2f out* **40/1**

3m 3.79s (-1.01) **Going Correction** -0.125s/f (Stan)
WFA 3 from 4yo+ 7lb **12** Ran SP% **122.2**
Speed ratings (Par 101): **97,96,95,95,95 94,94,92,90,89 87,62**
CSF £181.16 CT £928.59 TOTE £11.30: £3.20, £7.20, £1.80; EX 236.50 Trifecta £1839.90.
Owner Mrs Sue Adams **Bred** Mrs Michele Craig White **Trained** Church Broughton , Derbys

FOCUS
A moderate staying handicap and they didn't go a great pace. The runner-up has been rated to the best of this year's form.

8541 BETWAY SPRINT H'CAP (DIV I) 5f 216y (Tp)
4:30 (4:32) (Class 6) (0-55,55) 3-Y-O+ **£2,425** (£721; £360; £180) **Stalls** Low

Form RPR

60 **1** **Ocotillo (IRE)**^{7} 8470 3-8-12 **46** oh1 .... RyanPowell 2 53
(Kevin Frost) *sn pushed along and prom: rdn to ld over 1f out: edgd lft: styd on* **20/1**

4250 **2** 1 **Major Muscari (IRE)**^{107} 6373 8-9-7 **55** ....(p) TomMarquand 1 60
(Shaun Harris) *s.i.s: hld up: hdwy and n.m.r over 1f out: styd on same pce towards fin* **9/1**

3643 **3** ½ **Tasaaboq**^{11} 8408 5-9-6 **54** ....(tp) JosephineGordon 3 57
(Phil McEntee) *trckd ldrs: racd keenly: rdn and swtchd lft over 1f out: styd on same pce wl ins fnl f* **2/1**^{1}

6000 **4** 1¼ **Louis Vee (IRE)**^{17} 8316 8-8-12 **51** ....(p) GeorgiaCox$^{(5)}$ 4 50
(John O'Shea) *s.i.s: hld up: hdwy over 1f out: r.o* **9/1**

4410 **5** nk **Kaaber (USA)**^{17} 8316 5-9-5 **53** ....(b) TomEaves 5 51
(Roy Brotherton) *hld up: hdwy fnl f: nt rch ldrs* **8/1**

4460 **6** hd **Tahiti One**^{20} 8248 3-9-4 **52** ....(b^{1}) WilliamCarson 10 49
(Tony Carroll) *prom: led and edgd lft over 4f out: rdn and hdd over 1f out: no ex ins fnl f* **15/2**^{3}

0045 **7** ½ **Great Expectations**^{8} 8457 8-9-4 **55** ....(vt) AlistairRawlinson$^{(3)}$ 12 51
(J R Jenkins) *hld up: hdwy over 2f out: rdn over 1f out: kpt on* **9/2**^{2}

6600 **8** 5 **Barnsdale**^{182} 3734 3-8-5 **46** oh1 .... MeganEllingworth$^{(7)}$ 8 27
(John Holt) *led 5f out: sn hdd: chsd ldrs: rdn over 1f out: wknd ins fnl f* **66/1**

4045 **9** 3¼ **Lydiate Lady**^{46} 7913 4-9-5 **53** .... TonyHamilton 6 25
(Paul Green) *prom tl rdn and wknd over 1f out* **10/1**

3020 **10** 1¾ **Prigsnov Dancer (IRE)**^{17} 8312 11-8-9 **46** .... NathanEvans$^{(3)}$ 13 12
(John Balding) *led: hdd 5f out: chsd ldrs: hmpd over 4f out: rdn over 2f out: wknd over 1f out* **16/1**

6100 **11** ¾ **Ciaras Cookie (IRE)**^{174} 4005 4-9-1 **52** .... JackDuern$^{(3)}$ 9 16
(Mandy Rowland) *prom: lost pl over 4f out: rdn over 2f out: sn wknd* **50/1**

0000 **12** 3 **Alberto**^{45} 7944 6-8-8 **49** ow3 ....(p) JordanUys$^{(7)}$ 7 4
(Lisa Williamson) *s.i.s: a in rr: wknd over 2f out* **66/1**

1m 14.46s (-0.04) **Going Correction** -0.125s/f (Stan) **12** Ran SP% **119.1**
Speed ratings (Par 101): **95,93,93,91,90 90,90,83,79,76 75,71**
CSF £187.41 CT £468.58 TOTE £26.00: £6.00, £2.70, £1.50; EX 252.30 Trifecta £845.60.
Owner Kevin Frost **Bred** Barronstown Stud **Trained** Market Drayton, Shropshire

FOCUS
The first division of the 0-55 sprint handicap and not the easiest winner to find.

8542 BETWAY SPRINT H'CAP (DIV II) 5f 216y (Tp)
5:00 (5:02) (Class 6) (0-55,55) 3-Y-O+ **£2,425** (£721; £360; £180) **Stalls** Low

Form RPR

0 **1** **Athassel**^{81} 7133 7-8-12 **46** oh1 .... StevieDonohoe 13 53
(David Evans) *hld up: hdwy over 1f out: rdn and hung lft ins fnl f: r.o to ld nr fin* **8/1**^{3}

0600 **2** ½ **Mr Chuckles (IRE)**^{28} 8145 3-8-12 **46** ....(p) AndrewMullen 1 52
(Daniel Mark Loughnane) *chsd ldrs: rdn over 2f out: led wl ins fnl f: hdd nr fin* **14/1**

6033 **3** 2 **Swendab (IRE)**^{17} 8315 8-9-0 **53** ....(b) MitchGodwin$^{(5)}$ 9 53
(John O'Shea) *led: rdn over 2f out: hdd wl ins fnl f* **13/2**^{2}

040 **4** ½ **Slim Chance (IRE)**^{6} 8485 7-9-0 **55** ....(p) PaulaMuir$^{(7)}$ 2 53
(Simon West) *prom: racd keenly: rdn over 1f out: styd on* **18/1**

5335 **5** hd **Dream Ally (IRE)**^{39} 8013 6-9-3 **51** ....(be) MartinHarley 4 48
(John Weymes) *hld up in tch: rdn over 1f out: styd on same pce ins fnl f* **4/1**^{1}

0063 **6** nk **Secret Millionaire (IRE)**^{17} 8312 9-9-6 **54** ....(p) TomMarquand 3 51
(Shaun Harris) *hld up: hmpd over 3f out: hdwy over 1f out: sn rdn: styd on same pce wl ins fnl f* **10/1**

3535 **7** ¾ **Fossa**^{11} 8408 6-8-7 **46** .... CharlieBennett$^{(5)}$ 10 40
(Mark Brisbourne) *hld up: hdwy over 1f out: no clr run ins fnl f: nt trble ldrs* **16/1**

3011 **8** 3 **Suni Dancer**^{18} 8289 5-9-2 **53** .... GeorgeDowning$^{(3)}$ 7 38
(Tony Carroll) *s.i.s: hld up: nvr nrr* **4/1**^{1}

0200 **9** ¾ **National Service (USA)**^{40} 7994 5-9-0 **55** ....(tp) CallumRodriguez$^{(7)}$ 6 38
(Richard Ford) *s.i.s: hld up: nvr on terms* **9/1**

0013 **10** 1 **Mr Conundrum**^{18} 8288 3-9-4 **52** .... PaddyAspell 11 32
(Lynn Siddall) *hld up: rdn over 1f out: n.d* **10/1**

0653 **11** hd **Catalinas Diamond (IRE)**^{22} 8234 8-9-1 **49** ....(t) SteveDrowne 5 28
(Pat Murphy) *prom: rdn over 1f out: eased whn btn fnl f* **14/1**

0405 **12** 8 **Justice (IRE)**^{75} 7302 3-8-12 **46** oh1 ....(p) RenatoSouza 8
(Jose Santos) *chsd ldr tl rdn over 2f out: wknd over 1f out* **33/1**

0043 **13** 4 **Bushwise (IRE)**^{12} 8383 3-8-12 **46** oh1 ....(b) AdamBeschizza 12
(Milton Bradley) *prom: rdn over 2f out: sn wknd* **25/1**

1m 13.35s (-1.15) **Going Correction** -0.125s/f (Stan) **13** Ran SP% **123.9**
Speed ratings (Par 101): **102,101,98,98,97 97,96,92,91,90 89,79,73**
CSF £119.44 CT £811.76 TOTE £8.70: £2.50, £6.20, £2.30; EX 168.40 Trifecta £1721.20.
Owner Mrs E Evans **Bred** Moyns Park Estate And Stud Ltd **Trained** Pandy, Monmouths

FOCUS
The winning time was 1.11sec quicker than the first leg. The winner was even harder to find than the winner of the first leg on all known evidence, but someone knew. The winner has been rated back to his best.
T/Plt: £103.50 to a £1 stake. Pool: £76,069.65 - 536.32 winning units. T/Qpdt: £87.70 to a £1 stake. Pool: £4,964.97 - 41.86 winning units. **Colin Roberts**

8543 - 8553a (Foreign Racing) - See Raceform Interactive

^{8443}LINGFIELD (L-H)
Wednesday, December 28

OFFICIAL GOING: Polytrack: standard
Wind: nil Weather: Fog, clearing after Race 3

8554 BETWAY APPRENTICE (S) STKS 1m 4f (P)
11:40 (11:40) (Class 6) 3-Y-O+ **£2,264** (£673; £336; £168) **Stalls** Low

Form RPR

0635 **1** **Hepplewhite**^{37} 8048 3-8-7 72 ....^{1} JordanUys$^{(5)}$ 6 68
(Robert Eddery) *trckd ldrs: rdn to ld ins fnl f: hld on wl* **11/4**^{1}

2150 **2** hd **Gaelic Silver (FR)**^{28} 8161 10-9-4 75 ....(p) HectorCrouch$^{(3)}$ 3 71
(Gary Moore) *hld up in last pair: prog over 1f out to chal ins fnl f: r.o but jst hld* **7/2**^{2}

5-40 **3** 1¾ **Burning Desire (IRE)**^{15} 8084 5-8-7 63 ....(bt^{1}) FinleyMarsh$^{(10)}$ 4 64
(Richard Hughes) *in tch: prog on inner to ld wl over 1f out: hdd and one pce ins fnl f* **12/1**

5563 **4** 1½ **Medicean Queen (IRE)**^{47} 7905 5-8-12 55 ....(t) JosephineGordon 1 57
(Phil McEntee) *led 1f: trckd ldrs: rdn over 2f out: cl up 1f out: fdd* **7/2**^{2}

0000 **5** 3½ **Barren Brook**^{21} 8257 9-8-11 62 .... OllieJago$^{(10)}$ 5 60
(Laura Mongan) *t.k.h: hld up: dropped to last over 2f out: sn btn* **20/1**

0004 **6** 1 **Artful Mind**^{14} 8364 3-9-2 65 ....(tp) DanielMuscutt 7 59
(John Flint) *a in last pair: no prog 2f out* **8/1**

450 **7** 1 **Forced Family Fun**^{18} 3533 6-8-7 69 .... AmeliaGlass$^{(10)}$ 8 53
(George Baker) *led after 1f: hdd & wknd qckly wl over 1f out* **13/2**^{3}

2m 31.08s (-1.92) **Going Correction** -0.10s/f (Stan)
WFA 3 from 5yo+ 5lb **7** Ran SP% **108.0**
Speed ratings (Par 101): **102,101,100,99,97 96,96**
CSF £11.02 TOTE £3.70: £2.70, £1.70; EX 11.70 Trifecta £103.50.The winner was bought by Foursome Thoroughbreds for 7,200gns
Owner Robert Eddery **Bred** Meon Valley Stud **Trained** Newmarket, Suffolk

FOCUS
A moderate apprentice seller to start and they went a steady pace in the fog. The first two were best in at the weights. It's been rated as straightforward form around the principals.

8555 SUNBETS.CO.UK DOWNLOAD THE APP H'CAP 7f 1y(P)
12:10 (12:11) (Class 6) (0-65,65) 3-Y-O+ **£2,264** (£673; £336; £168) **Stalls** Low

Form RPR

0311 **1** **Fire Diamond**^{21} 8248 3-9-4 **62** ....(p) RichardKingscote 11 69
(Tom Dascombe) *dwlt: sn in midfield: drvn on outer 2f out: str run fnl f to ld last stride* **3/1**^{1}

0541 **2** nse **Saleh (IRE)**^{28} 8163 3-9-7 **65** .... AdamKirby 8 72
(Lee Carter) *chsd ldrs: drvn to dispute 3rd 2f out: r.o fnl f to ld last strides: hdd post* **3/1**^{1}

5506 **3** ½ **Encapsulated**^{27} 8181 6-8-6 **57** .... RhiainIngram$^{(7)}$ 7 63
(Roger Ingram) *led after 1f: clr 1/2-way: hdd and no ex last strides* **25/1**

0302 **4** ¾ **Swot**^{21} 8258 4-8-13 **60** ....(p) HectorCrouch$^{(3)}$ 3 64
(Roger Teal) *towards rr: rdn over 2f out: styd on wl fnl f: nrst fin* **5/1**^{2}

0135 **5** hd **Hipz (IRE)**^{21} 8252 5-8-12 **59** ....(p) CallumShepherd$^{(3)}$ 12 62
(Laura Mongan) *awkward s: rcvrd to chse ldr over 5f out: rdn to cl fnl f but lost 3 pls nr fin* **25/1**

2446 **6** hd **Polar Kite (IRE)**^{9} 8458 8-9-3 **64** .... RobHornby$^{(3)}$ 10 67
(Michael Attwater) *hld up wl in rr: stl there 2f out: gd prog fnl f: nrst fin* **16/1**

0231 **7** ¾ **Veeraya**^{57} 7738 6-9-7 **65** ....(t) AdamBeschizza 2 66
(Julia Feilden) *chsd ldrs: no imp over 1f out: kpt on same pce* **11/2**^{3}

4060 **8** 3 **Virile (IRE)**^{26} 8188 5-9-4 **62** ....(bt) GeorgeBaker 13 54
(Sylvester Kirk) *dwlt: mostly in last pair tl prog 2f out: one pce fnl f:* **16/1**

5606 **9** 1¼ **Prim And Proper**^{21} 8252 5-9-0 **58** ....(p) DanielMuscutt 9 47
(John Flint) *prom: disp 3rd 2f out: wknd* **25/1**

3610 **10** nse **Tulip Dress**^{102} 6592 3-9-4 **62** .... WilliamCarson 6 51
(Anthony Carson) *disp ld 1f: prom tl wknd over 1f out* **50/1**

0006 **11** nk **Top Of The Bank**^{7} 8482 3-9-7 **65** .... TonyHamilton 4 53
(Kristin Stubbs) *disp ld 1f: lost pl and btn 2f out* **33/1**

0000 **12** shd **Sehayli (IRE)**^{14} 8365 3-9-4 **62** .... KieranO'Neill 1 50
(Lee Carter) *s.s: a wl in rr* **25/1**

6450 **13** ½ **Trust Me Boy**^{15} 8351 8-9-4 **62** .... RobertHavlin 5 48
(John E Long) *chsd ldrs early: in rr 2f out* **66/1**

4000 **14** 2 **Bookmaker**^{189} 3522 6-9-0 **58** ....(b) DannyBrock 14 39
(John Bridger) *dwlt: a struggling in rr* **33/1**

1m 24.39s (-0.41) **Going Correction** -0.10s/f (Stan) **14** Ran SP% **118.5**
Speed ratings (Par 101): **98,97,97,96,96 96,95,91,90,90 89,89,89,86**
CSF £9.81 CT £189.68 TOTE £3.60: £1.50, £1.70, £7.20; EX 13.00 Trifecta £307.80.
Owner John Brown **Bred** John Brown **Trained** Malpas, Cheshire

FOCUS
A moderate if competitive handicap and another race where the visibility wasn't great, but it provided a thrilling finish. It's hard to rate the race any higher than this.

8556 32RED.COM EBF MAIDEN STKS (DIV I) 7f 1y(P)
12:45 (12:46) (Class 5) 2-Y-O **£3,363** (£1,001; £500; £250) **Stalls** Low

Form RPR

1 **Ay Ay (IRE)** 2-9-5 0 .... ShaneKelly 8 75+
(David Elsworth) *chsd ldrs: wnt 3rd over 2f out: rdn to cl fnl f: r.o to ld last strides: shade cleverly* **7/2**^{3}

4443 **2** hd **Sidewinder (IRE)**^{125} 5792 2-9-5 72 .... RichardKingscote 6 73
(Tom Dascombe) *chsd ldr: chal fr 2f out tl led ins fnl f: styd on but hdd last strides* **13/8**^{1}

3 1¼ **Blue Dahlia (IRE)**^{106} 6460 2-9-0 0 .... AndrewMullen 1 63
(Mark Johnston) *led: rdn 2f out: hdd and one pce ins fnl f* **7/1**

4 7 **Sublime** 2-9-0 0 .... RyanTate 2 44
(Rod Millman) *chsd ldrs: outpcd fr 2f out: nt disgracd* **25/1**

00 **5** 1¼ **Beyond Beyond**^{21} 8245 2-9-5 0 .... AdamKirby 7 46
(Hughie Morrison) *chsd ldng pair to over 2f out: wknd* **16/1**

00 **6** ½ **Ede's E Rider**^{14} 8355 2-9-5 0 .... KieranO'Neill 9 45
(Pat Phelan) *s.i.s: hld up in rr: nvr involved: possible improver* **40/1**

60 **7** ½ **Kenyan (FR)**^{14} 8355 2-9-5 0 ....^{1} FergusSweeney 10 43
(Seamus Durack) *dwlt: a wl in rr* **50/1**

8 2 3/4 **Street Jester** 2-9-5 0 AdamBeschizza 3 36
(Robert Stephens) *s.s: a wl in rr* **20/1**

9 4 1/2 **Duxbury** 2-9-5 0 TonyHamilton 4 24
(Richard Fahey) *rn green and sn pushed along towards rr: wknd 2f out* **11/4**[2]

1m 25.6s (0.80) **Going Correction** -0.10s/f (Stan) **9** Ran SP% **118.4**
Speed ratings (Par 96): **91,90,88,80,79 78,78,75,69**
CSF £9.53 TOTE £4.40: £1.30, £1.10, £1.80; EX 11.60 Trifecta £48.60.
Owner Mrs Doreen Tabor **Bred** Eyrefield Lodge Stud **Trained** Newmarket, Suffolk

FOCUS
An ordinary maiden and for a long time it looked as though the two form horses would dominate it, but a newcomer proved too good for them both. The runner-up, who is the key to the level, has been rated as running as well as ever.

8557 32RED.COM EBF MAIDEN STKS (DIV II) 7f 1y(P)
1:15 (1:18) (Class 5) 2-Y-O **£3,363** (£1,001; £500; £250) **Stalls** Low

Form RPR

6 **1** **Private Mission**[21] 8243 2-9-5 0 AdamKirby 6 71
(Hughie Morrison) *trckd ldr: rdn to ld 2f out: drvn and styd on fnl f* **7/1**

43 **2** 2 **Enfolding (IRE)**[35] 8066 2-9-5 0 DanielMuscutt 8 66+
(James Fanshawe) *s.i.s: hld up in last trio: wdst of all bnd 2f out and shkn up: r.o wl fnl f to take 2nd last strides* **5/1**[2]

0 **3** nk **Thetrioandme (IRE)**[138] 5371 2-9-5 0 KierenFox 2 65
(John Best) *t.k.h: chsd ldng pair: rdn 2f out: kpt on fnl f to press for 2nd nr fin* **16/1**

420 **4** hd **Re Run (IRE)**[36] 8062 2-9-5 0[1] TonyHamilton 3 65
(Richard Fahey) *t.k.h: trckd ldrs: rdn 2f out: kpt on same pce and chal for 2nd nr fin* **5/4**[1]

5 nk **Spinwheel** 2-9-0 0 AndrewMullen 1 59
(Mark Johnston) *led: rdn and hdd 2f out: hanging over 1f out: one pce and lost 3 pls nr fin* **16/1**

6 hd **Dragons Voice** 2-9-5 0 GeorgeBaker 9 63
(Philip Hide) *in tch in midfield: shkn up 2f out: kpt on to press for a pl ins fnl f: one pce nr fin* **50/1**

62 **7** 1 **Tisbutadream (IRE)**[28] 8151 2-9-0 0 TimmyMurphy 7 59
(David Elsworth) *trckd ldrs: lost pl and pushed along whn taken wd bnd 2f out: nt on terms after: kpt on* **6/1**[3]

55 **8** 1 1/4 **Captain Pugwash (IRE)**[14] 8352 2-9-5 0 RobertHavlin 10 57
(Henry Spiller) *dwlt: swtchd to inner and hld up in last trio: pushed along over 2f out: kpt on one pce after* **10/1**

5 **9** 3/4 **Greyjoy (IRE)**[14] 8354 2-9-0 0 MitchGodwin(5) 4 55
(Sylvester Kirk) *nvr bttr than midfield: no prog 2f out: fdd fnl f* **14/1**

0 **10** 6 **Seaborn (IRE)**[21] 8246 2-9-2 0 RobHornby(3) 5 39
(Simon Hodgson) *a in last trio: wknd over 2f out: sn bhd* **66/1**

1m 25.64s (0.84) **Going Correction** -0.10s/f (Stan) **10** Ran SP% **118.9**
Speed ratings (Par 96): **91,88,88,88,87 87,86,85,84,77**
CSF £42.82 TOTE £8.20: £2.20, £1.70, £6.30; EX 41.40 Trifecta £870.90.
Owner Kerr-Dineen, Eason, Rothwell & Malpas **Bred** New England Stud, Myriad & T Vestey **Trained** East Ilsley, Berks

FOCUS
The winning time was fractionally slower than the first division. The level is fluid.

8558 BETWAY APP H'CAP 1m 7f 169y(P)
1:45 (1:48) (Class 4) (0-85,83) 3-Y-O+ **£4,690** (£1,395; £697; £348) **Stalls** Low

Form RPR

1121 **1** **Alfredo (IRE)**[14] 8363 4-9-13 **82** (tp) GeorgeBaker 1 91+
(Seamus Durack) *dwlt: hld up in 7th: prog over 1f out: drvn to chal ins fnl f: r.o wl to ld last strides* **13/8**[2]

-401 **2** hd **Charismatic Man (IRE)**[32] 8124 3-9-1 **78** RichardKingscote 2 86+
(Ralph Beckett) *trckd ldrs in 5th: gap appeared and clsd qckly to ld 1f out: drvn and r.o wl fnl f but hdd last strides* **11/10**[1]

0001 **3** 3 1/2 **El Campeon**[16] 8339 4-9-3 **75** HectorCrouch(3) 6 79
(Simon Dow) *hld up in last: prog on inner over 1f out: rdn to take 3rd last 75yds but no ch w ldng pair* **8/1**[3]

4545 **4** 3/4 **Cotton Club (IRE)**[133] 5553 5-10-0 **83** RyanTate 7 86
(Rod Millman) *hld up in 6th: rdn on outer 2f out: sn outpcd: kpt on to take 4th last strides* **16/1**

1440 **5** 1/2 **Midtech Star (IRE)**[171] 2887 4-9-13 **82** (p) AdamKirby 8 84
(Ian Williams) *pushed up to ld after 1f: rdn over 3f out: hdd 1f out: immediately btn* **20/1**

2023 **6** 1/2 **Marshall Aid (IRE)**[22] 8238 3-8-4 **67** KieranO'Neill 3 69
(Mark Usher) *trckd ldng pair: rdn and tried to chal on inner over 1f out: wl outpcd fnl f* **16/1**

0-50 **7** 4 1/2 **Tindaro (FR)**[18] 6356 9-9-11 **80** (tp) WilliamCarson 4 76
(Paul Webber) *led 1f: styd prom: rdn over 2f out: wknd qckly over 1f out* **33/1**

0222 **8** 1/2 **Saborido (USA)**[126] 5767 10-9-10 **79** (b) RobertHavlin 5 75
(Amanda Perrett) *trckd ldr after 2f: rdn over 2f out: wknd qckly over 1f out* **14/1**

3m 21.06s (-4.64) **Going Correction** -0.10s/f (Stan)
WFA 3 from 4yo+ 8lb **8** Ran SP% **123.0**
Speed ratings (Par 105): **107,106,105,104,104 104,102,101**
CSF £4.13 CT £10.37 TOTE £2.50: £1.30, £1.10, £2.30; EX 4.40 Trifecta £16.00.
Owner Stephen Tucker & Keith McIntosh **Bred** Colin Kennedy **Trained** Upper Lambourn, Berkshire

FOCUS
A fair staying handicap and a fascinating game of cat and mouse between the big two in the betting, both of whom were held up for a late run. It's been rated around the third and fourth to their recent form.

8559 SUNBETS.CO.UK MAIDEN STKS 1m 1y(P)
2:20 (2:25) (Class 5) 3-Y-O+ **£2,911** (£866; £432; £216) **Stalls** High

Form RPR

43-2 **1** **Amber Mystique**[13] 8388 3-9-0 74 TonyHamilton 6 71
(Kristin Stubbs) *pressed ldr: rdn 2f out: styd on to ld ins fnl f: drvn out* **6/1**[3]

2 **2** 3/4 **Galinthias**[10] 8449 4-9-3 0 HectorCrouch(3) 4 75+
(Simon Dow) *s.i.s and racd in last trio: rdn and prog on inner 2f out: styd on fnl f to take 2nd last strides but nvr quite pce to chal* **5/2**[1]

3 nk **Wahiba (GER)**[388] 3-9-0 0 DanielMuscutt 3 68
(Marco Botti) *t.k.h: led: hanging rt bnd over 4f out: rdn 2f out: hdd and nt qckn ins fnl f: lost 2nd last strides* **10/3**[2]

2 **4** 3/4 **Tifl**[21] 8247 3-9-5 0 JackMitchell 1 71
(Heather Main) *reluctant to enter stall: trckd ldrs: rdn to chal on inner jst over 1f out: nt qckn ins fnl f and hld after* **5/2**[1]

5 **5** hd **Summer Falls (IRE)**[28] 8157 3-8-11 0 AaronJones(3) 10 66
(Rae Guest) *hld up in last trio: shkn up 2f out: prog on inner over 1f out: styd on fnl f and nrst fin* **33/1**

00 **6** 2 1/4 **Magic Moments**[35] 8075 3-9-0 0 FergusSweeney 9 61
(Alan King) *hld up in 7th: taken wd bnd 2f out and pushed along: sme prog fnl f but nvr on terms: one pce last 50yds* **33/1**

065F **7** 2 3/4 **Nellie Deen (IRE)**[58] 7727 3-9-0 63 ShaneKelly 5 54
(David Elsworth) *chsd ldrs: rdn and wknd over 1f out* **8/1**

4-3 **8** shd **Raise The Game (IRE)**[18] 8320 3-9-5 0 WilliamCarson 7 59
(Bill Turner) *chsd ldrs: rdn over 2f out: wknd over 1f ut* **20/1**

9 2 **Mount Vesuvius (IRE)**[22] 8-9-6 0 (t) MartinDwyer 2 55
(Paul Henderson) *slowly away: a last and nvr a factor* **66/1**

0052 **P** **Pacohontas**[144] 5167 3-9-0 51 RobertHavlin 8
(John E Long) *in tch tl lost action over 4f out and p.u: fatally injured* **50/1**

1m 37.01s (-1.19) **Going Correction** -0.10s/f (Stan)
WFA 3 from 4yo+ 1lb **10** Ran SP% **119.7**
Speed ratings (Par 103): **101,100,99,99,99 96,94,93,91,**
CSF £21.18 TOTE £5.90: £1.80, £1.40, £1.50; EX 24.10 Trifecta £99.40.
Owner The G-Guck Group **Bred** Avenue Farm Stud **Trained** Norton, N Yorks

FOCUS
A modest older horse maiden though four of the ten runners had finished second in their most recent starts. They finished in a bit of a heap, though. The winner has been rated close to form, but the level if a bit fluid in behind.

8560 32RED CASINO EBF NURSERY H'CAP 7f 1y(P)
2:55 (2:59) (Class 5) (0-70,70) 2-Y-O **£3,881** (£1,155; £577; £288) **Stalls** Low

Form RPR

0201 **1** **Vatican Hill (IRE)**[106] 6446 2-9-1 **70** LucyKBarry(5) 6 76
(Jamie Osborne) *hld up in 6th: prog wl over 1f out: rdn to ld last 150yds: r.o wl* **25/1**

004 **2** 1 **Nuncio**[35] 8065 2-9-4 **68** GeorgeBaker 1 71
(Roger Charlton) *hld up in 5th: prog over 1f out along w wnr: chal ins fnl f: r.o but a jst outpcd* **2/1**[1]

2054 **3** nse **Sun Angel (IRE)**[28] 8152 2-9-6 **70** AdamKirby 4 73
(Henry Candy) *chsd ldng trio: rdn to take 2nd briefly over 1f out: outpcd fnl f* **7/1**[3]

3400 **4** 2 1/4 **Elementary**[28] 8159 2-8-13 **66** LouisSteward(3) 8 63
(Michael Bell) *stdd s: hld up in last pair: stl last over 2f out: gd prog over 1f out: shkn up and r.o wl to take 3rd last stride: too late to threaten ldng pair* **20/1**

000 **5** 1 1/4 **License To Thrill (USA)**[43] 7962 2-9-3 **67** RobertHavlin 2 62
(Simon Dow) *s.i.s: racd in 7th and off the pce: kpt on fr over 1f out: n.d* **12/1**

010 **6** nse **Melissa Jane**[76] 7305 2-9-1 **68** CallumShepherd(3) 7 62
(Henry Spiller) *towards rr and off the pce: rdn 2f out: styd on fnl f: nrst fin but n.d* **22/1**

0126 **7** 1 **Ninety Years Young**[28] 8159 2-9-3 **67** (b) ShaneKelly 10 58
(David Elsworth) *led at str pce and stretched field: stl 3 l clr over 1f out: hdd & wknd last 150yds* **7/1**[3]

6610 **8** shd **Galahad**[28] 8153 2-9-4 **68** TonyHamilton 3 59
(Richard Fahey) *rdn in 8th pl by 1/2-way and a struggling w the pce: no prog* **5/1**[2]

666 **9** 1 **Noble Ballad**[48] 7883 2-9-2 **66** RichardKingscote 11 54
(Ralph Beckett) *mostly in last trio and nvr a factor* **8/1**

5055 **10** shd **Rita's Man (IRE)**[90] 6898 2-9-4 **68** TomMarquand 9 56
(Richard Hannon) *chsd ldr at str pce to over 1f out: wknd* **16/1**

0400 **11** 1 1/2 **Mungo Madness**[70] 7471 2-9-2 **66** AdamBeschizza 5 50
(Julia Feilden) *a struggling in rr* **33/1**

4004 **12** hd **Presence Process**[14] 8360 2-8-9 **66** SophieRalston(7) 13 49
(Pat Phelan) *plld hrd: hld up: wl in rr fr 1/2-way* **20/1**

3200 **13** 3/4 **Oceanus (IRE)**[28] 8153 2-9-6 **70** (b[1]) JosephineGordon 14 51
(Ed Dunlop) *chsd ldr at str pce to over 1f out: wknd rapidly* **25/1**

1m 23.23s (-1.57) **Going Correction** -0.10s/f (Stan) **13** Ran SP% **124.2**
Speed ratings (Par 96): **104,102,100,100,98 98,97,97,96,96 94,94,93**
CSF £72.23 CT £1136.03 TOTE £24.50: £5.30, £2.00, £6.10; EX 103.30 Trifecta £4153.30.
Owner J A Osborne **Bred** Mrs Gillian McCalmont **Trained** Upper Lambourn, Berks

FOCUS
An ordinary nursery, but no hanging about. The race might have been rated a bit high but it's worth taking a chance it'll work out.

8561 BETWAY H'CAP 6f 1y(P)
3:30 (3:31) (Class 4) (0-80,80) 3-Y-O+ **£4,690** (£1,395; £697; £348) **Stalls** Low

Form RPR

1116 **1** **Swiss Cross**[26] 8197 9-9-2 **78** (tp) CallumShepherd(3) 9 85
(Phil McEntee) *hld up towards rr: prog 2f out: rdn over 1f out: styd on wl fnl f to ld last 2 strides* **8/1**

4332 **2** nse **Gung Ho Jack**[47] 7899 7-9-0 **73** KierenFox 3 79
(John Best) *chsd ldrs: rdn into 3rd over 1f out: clsd on ldr fnl f: jnd him last strides but jst pipped by wnr* **9/2**[2]

6333 **3** shd **Sophisticated Heir (IRE)**[18] 8314 6-9-6 **79** (b) TomEaves 2 85+
(Michael Herrington) *pressed ldr: led wl over 1f out and sent for home: drvn fnl f: collared last 2 strides* **5/2**[1]

2042 **4** 1 **Vimy Ridge**[20] 8280 4-9-1 **74** RobertHavlin 6 76
(Alan Bailey) *hld up in last pair: prog wl over 1f out: drvn to take 4th last 75yds: no imp ldng trio after* **7/1**[3]

2356 **5** 1 1/4 **Anonymous John (IRE)**[27] 8176 4-9-4 **77** GeorgeBaker 7 78+
(Dominic Ffrench Davis) *hld up in last: making prog whn rn into trble and snatched up 150yds out: r.o nr fin but unable to rcvr* **9/2**[2]

0505 **6** 1/2 **Varsovian**[13] 8378 6-9-0 **76** JackDuern(3) 10 73
(Dean Ivory) *chsd ldrs on outer: pushed along whn wdst of all bnd 2f out and sn dropped to last pair: styd on again fnl 150yds* **15/2**

3214 **7** nk **Hyland Heather (IRE)**[23] 8233 3-9-4 **77** (p) TonyHamilton 4 73
(Richard Fahey) *sn towards rr: rdn and prog on inner over 1f out: no hdwy fnl f* **20/1**

000 **8** 3/4 **Bertie Blu Boy**[13] 8380 8-9-4 **77** (b) TomMarquand 5 71
(Lisa Williamson) *led at str pce: hdd wl over 1f out: lost 2nd and wknd fnl f* **20/1**

3020 **9** nse **Evening Starlight**[14] 8358 3-8-1 **67** FinleyMarsh(7) 1 60
(Ron Hodges) *chsd ldrs: rdn and wknd over 1f out* **18/1**

0520 **10** nk **I'll Be Good**[48] 7892 7-9-7 **80** DaleSwift 8 72
(Brian Ellison) *chsd ldng trio: rdn over 2f out: wknd over 1f out* **16/1**

0300 **11** 1 1/4 **Noble Deed**[124] 5827 6-8-13 **72** JosephineGordon 12 60
(Michael Attwater) *racd wd: nvr beyond midfield: rdn over 2f out: struggling in last pair over 1f out* **66/1**

1m 10.5s (-1.40) **Going Correction** -0.10s/f (Stan) **11** Ran SP% **122.5**
Speed ratings: **105,104,104,103,101 101,100,99,99,99 97**
CSF £44.89 CT £121.84 TOTE £5.50: £2.40, £2.00, £1.50; EX 39.70 Trifecta £73.90.

Owner Steve Jakes **Bred** Lordship Stud **Trained** Newmarket, Suffolk

FOCUS

A fair sprint handicap and a dramatic finish. It's been rated around the runner-up.
T/Jkpt: £6,666.60 to a £1 stake. Pool: £10,000.00 - 1.50 winning units T/Plt: £20.90 to a £1 stake. Pool: £74,274.16 - 2,588.53 winning units T/Qpdt: £6.40 to a £1 stake. Pool: £7,689.97 - 884.51 winning units **Jonathan Neesom**

8562 - (Foreign Racing) - See Raceform Interactive

8532 DEAUVILLE (R-H)

Wednesday, December 28

OFFICIAL GOING: Polytrack: standard

8563a PRIX MISS SATAMIXA (LISTED RACE) (FAST-TRACK QUALIFIER) (3YO+ FILLIES & MARES) (POLYTRACK) — 7f 110y

1:35 (12:00) 3-Y-O+ **£19,117** (£7,647; £5,735; £3,823; £1,911)

RPR

1 **Realtra (IRE)**[452] 6925 4-8-13 0 ow2 .... ChristopheSoumillon 2 107
(Roger Varian) *in tch: shkn up to chal over 1f out and led ent fnl f: r.o wl: readily* **7/2**[1]

2 1 1/2 **Caointiorn (FR)**[98] 6693 5-8-11 0 ....(p) MorganDelalande 3 101
(S Wattel, France) **26/5**[2]

3 3/4 **Via Firenze (IRE)**[30] 3-8-11 0 .... FabriceVeron 15 100
(Mme Pia Brandt, France) **10/1**

4 hd **I Am Charlie (FR)**[29] 8148 3-8-11 0 .... GabrieleCongiu 13 99
(J-P Gauvin, France) **18/1**

5 1 **Galantes Ivresses (FR)**[9] 3-8-11 0 .... JeromeCabre 1 97
(Yves de Nicolay, France) **54/10**[3]

6 3/4 **Villebaudon (FR)**[75] 7348 3-8-11 0 .... AlexandreRoussel 4 95
(C Ferland, France) **23/1**

7 3/4 **Seychelloise**[39] 8029 4-8-11 0 ....(b) TonyPiccone 12 93
(Sir Mark Prescott Bt) *led: rdn 2f out: hdd over 1f out: no ex: fdd* **18/1**

8 hd **Ella Diva (FR)**[75] 7348 3-8-11 0 .... RonanThomas 5 92
(N Caullery, France) **46/1**

9 shd **Volunteer Point (IRE)**[33] 8098 4-8-11 0 .... MartinHarley 9 92
(Mick Channon) *hld up in midfield: rdn over 1f out: outpcd: n.d* **10/1**

10 1 1/4 **Pietrafiore (IRE)**[41] 7998 3-8-11 0 .... MickaelBarzalona 14 89
(H-A Pantall, France) *in rr: rdn 2f out: kpt on but nvr threatened* **22/1**

11 3 **Havre De Paix (FR)**[42] 7978 4-8-11 0 .... AntoineHamelin 6 81
(David Menuisier) *trckd ldr: rdn to chal 2f out: no ex over 1f out: wknd* **33/1**

12 1 1/2 **Whippa D'Or (FR)**[33] 8117 4-8-11 0 .... StephanePasquier 8 78
(S Wattel, France) **14/1**

13 2 1/2 **Wacaria (GER)**[33] 8117 3-8-11 0 .... JozefBojko 7 71
(A Wohler, Germany) **34/1**

14 2 1/2 **Mukaabra**[61] 7676 3-8-11 0 .... ThierryThulliez 10 65
(F Chappet, France) **22/1**

15 1 1/2 **You're Back (USA)**[11] 8431 3-8-11 0 .... LukasDelozier 16 61
(H-A Pantall, France) *midfield on outer: rdn into st: no ex appr fnl f: wknd* **23/1**

16 3/4 **Sainte Amarante (FR)**[28] 8165 4-8-11 0 .... Francois-XavierBertras 11 60
(Yves de Nicolay, France) **18/1**

1m 25.42s (85.42) **16** Ran SP% **119.6**
WIN (incl. 1 euro stake): 4.30. Places: 1.80, 1.70, 3.30. DF: 10.50. SF: 27.50..
Owner Yasushi Kubota **Bred** Tom & Geraldine Molan **Trained** Newmarket, Suffolk

755 DOHA

Wednesday, December 28

OFFICIAL GOING: Turf: good

8564a AL RAYYAN STKS (CONDITIONS) (2YO) (TURF) — 7f

3:40 (12:00) 2-Y-O **£38,775** (£11,224; £11,224; £4,081; £2,721)

RPR

1 **Pazeer (FR)**[111] 6270 2-9-2 0 .... EduardoPedroza 9
(Ibrahim Al Malki, Qatar)

2 3/4 **Perfect Storm (IRE)**[66] 7560 2-9-2 0 .... SaleemGolam 2
(Ibrahim Al Malki, Qatar)

2 dht **Trouble Of Course (FR)**[87] 2-9-2 0 ....(t) Per-AndersGraberg 13
(Niels Petersen, Norway)

4 1 1/4 **Catch A Wave (IRE)**[66] 7560 2-9-2 0 .... AlanMunro 3
(Debbie Mountain, Qatar)

5 shd **Notalot (IRE)**[82] 7120 2-9-2 0 ....(v) StephaneLadjadj 7
(Hilal Kobeissi, Qatar)

6 nk **Moi Moi Moi (IRE)**[78] 7263 2-9-2 0 .... AlbertoSanna 11
(Ibrahim Al Malki, Qatar)

7 nk **What A Surprise (IRE)**[96] 6750 2-9-2 0 .... Jean-BaptisteHamel 5
(Ibrahim Al Malki, Qatar)

8 hd **Hyper Hyper**[36] 8061 2-9-2 0 .... AdriedeVries 12
(Mario Hofer, Germany)

9 1 1/2 **Hakeem (FR)**[155] 4732 2-9-2 0 .... RichardMullen 6
(J Smart, Qatar)

10 1 3/4 **Masham Star (IRE)**[30] 8132 2-9-2 0 .... PJMcDonald 4
(Mark Johnston) *sn disputing: rdn and hdd 2f out: no ex ent fnl f: wknd*

11 1 3/4 **Scudding (USA)**[195] 3301 2-8-11 0 .... HarryBentley 10
(Mohammed Jassim Ghazali, Qatar)

12 1 1/4 **Ras Al Qimmah (FR)**[186] 2-8-11 0 .... PierantonioConvertino 1
(Mohammed Jassim Ghazali, Qatar)

13 16 **Master Degree (IRE)**[74] 7366 2-9-2 0 ....(t) XavierZiani 8
(Debbie Mountain, Qatar)

Owner Abdulatif Hussain Al-Emadi **Bred** Haras De S.A. Aga Khan Scea **Trained** Qatar

8470 SOUTHWELL (L-H)

Thursday, December 29

OFFICIAL GOING: Fibresand: standard

Wind: Virtually nil Weather: Fine & dry

8565 BETWAY STAYER'S H'CAP — 2m (F)

11:45 (11:45) (Class 5) (0-75,75) 3-Y-O+ **£4,528** (£1,347; £673; £336) **Stalls** Low

Form RPR

1565 1 **Fern Owl**[22] 8250 4-9-10 **71** ....(b) LiamKeniry 3 85+
(Hughie Morrison) *trckd ldng pair: smooth hdwy 4f out and sn cl up: led wl over 2f out and sn pushed wl clr: heavily eased towards fin* **2/1**[2]

-003 2 8 **Katie Gale**[9] 8476 6-10-0 **75** .... AndrewMullen 5 75
(Michael Appleby) *cl up: led over 6f out: jnd 4f out and sn rdn along: hdd wl over 2f out: sn drvn and kpt on: no ch w wnr* **9/1**

0040 3 12 **Tarakkom (FR)**[15] 8359 4-8-9 **56** .... KieranO'Neill 6 42
(Peter Hiatt) *trckd ldrs on outer: effrt 4f out: rdn along over 3f out: sn drvn and plugged on one pce* **25/1**

01-1 4 6 **Medicine Hat**[26] 8211 5-9-11 **72** .... SamJames 1 50
(Marjorie Fife) *hld up: hdwy to trck ldrs 6f out: effrt over 3f out and sn rdn along: drvn wl over 2f out and sn one pce* **11/10**[1]

6002 5 4 1/2 **Goldslinger (FR)**[9] 8476 4-9-5 **69** .... JackDuern[(3)] 2 42
(Dean Ivory) *led: edgd rt and reminders paddock bnd 10f out: pushed along on inner 1/2-way: hdd over 6f out: sn rdn along and lost pl: outpcd fr wl over 3f out* **7/1**[3]

3636 6 60 **Heavensfield**[30] 8143 3-8-8 **63** .... StevieDonohoe 4
(Mark H Tompkins) *trckd ldrs: pushed along over 7f out: rdn along 6f out: sn lost tch and bhd fnl 4f* **25/1**

3m 52.49s (6.99) **Going Correction** +0.45s/f (Slow)
WFA 3 from 4yo+ 8lb **6** Ran SP% **111.1**
Speed ratings (Par 103): **100,96,90,87,84 54**
CSF £19.10 TOTE £3.10: £1.20, £3.00; EX 18.40 Trifecta £117.40.
Owner Sir Thomas Pilkington **Bred** Sir Thomas Pilkington **Trained** East Ilsley, Berks

FOCUS

An ordinary staying handicap and a proper stamina test. If this had been a boxing match the referee would have stopped it before the 2f pole. A fairly big pb from the winner, with the runner-up rated close to her latest effort.

8566 BETWAY H'CAP (DIV I) — 1m 3f (F)

12:15 (12:16) (Class 6) (0-60,61) 3-Y-O+ **£3,234** (£962; £481; £240) **Stalls** Low

Form RPR

5004 1 **Paladin (IRE)**[16] 8350 7-9-5 **60** .... MitchGodwin[(5)] 2 69
(Michael Blake) *hld up towards rr: hdwy to trck ldrs 4f out: chsd ldr wl over 2f out: rdn to chal wl over 1f out: drvn ent fnl f: styd on to ld last 75 yds* **12/1**

362 2 nk **Bridey's Lettuce (IRE)**[13] 8400 4-9-11 **61** .... DavidNolan 8 70
(Ivan Furtado) *awkward and reminders s: sn prom: cl up 1/2-way: led over 2f out: rdn and jnd wl over 1f out: drvn ent fnl f: hdd and no ex last 75 yds* **7/2**[3]

0300 3 15 **Sir Jack**[9] 8471 3-8-12 **55** .... GeorgeDowning[(3)] 3 40
(Tony Carroll) *hld up towards rr: pushed along and hdwy 4f out: rdn to chse ldrs 3f out: drvn 2f out and sn one pce* **16/1**

3532 4 3 1/4 **Lobster Cocktail (IRE)**[26] 8212 3-9-3 **57** ....(t) ThomasBrown 7 36
(Ed Walker) *trckd ldrs: smooth hdwy on outer 4f out: cl up over 3f out and sn pushed along: rdn wl over 2f out: sn drvn and one pce* **9/4**[1]

0005 5 1/2 **Albert Boy (IRE)**[23] 8238 3-8-13 **53** .... KieranO'Neill 9 32
(Scott Dixon) *cl up: slt ld after 3f: pushed along 4f out: rdn and hdd over 3f out: drvn over 2f out and sn wknd* **28/1**

0660 6 10 **Rail Dancer**[73] 7421 4-9-2 **52** ....(p) AdamBeschizza 5 15
(Richard Rowe) *chsd ldrs: rdn along over 3f out: drvn and wknd over 2f out* **10/3**[2]

5044 7 6 **Sakhalin Star (IRE)**[3] 8528 5-9-8 **58** ....(e) ConnorBeasley 1 11
(Richard Guest) *trckd ldrs on inner: pushed along 1/2-way and sn lost pl: rr and swtchd rt to outer wl over 3f out: sn drvn and n.d* **10/1**

0400 8 14 **Murraqib (USA)**[9] 8468 3-8-9 **49** ....(b[1]) MartinDwyer 6
(Brett Johnson) *racd wd: sn outpcd and a rr: bhd fr 1/2-way* **20/1**

0200 9 22 **Ramblow**[80] 7230 3-9-2 **59** .... AlistairRawlinson[(3)] 4
(Michael Appleby) *slt ld: hdd after 3f: rdn along 4f out: sn drvn and wknd* **10/1**

2m 32.47s (4.47) **Going Correction** +0.45s/f (Slow)
WFA 3 from 4yo+ 4lb **9** Ran SP% **116.0**
Speed ratings (Par 101): **101,100,89,87,87 79,75,65,49**
CSF £54.11 CT £687.28 TOTE £15.30: £3.00, £1.60, £5.50; EX 68.00 Trifecta £1317.90.
Owner The Moonlighters **Bred** Jim McCormack **Trained** Trowbridge, Wilts

FOCUS

The first division of a moderate handicap and a war of attrition, with the first two pulling clear. The runner-up has been rated back to his pre-race best.

8567 BETWAY H'CAP (DIV II) — 1m 3f (F)

12:45 (12:46) (Class 6) (0-60,60) 3-Y-O+ **£3,234** (£962; £481; £240) **Stalls** Low

Form RPR

0000 1 **Moojaned (IRE)**[42] 7992 5-9-2 **52** .... AndrewMullen 8 59
(David Evans) *trckd ldrs: pushed along on outer 1/2-way: hdwy 4f out: led over 3f out: rdn over 2f out: drvn and kpt on strly fnl f* **3/1**[2]

0006 2 1 3/4 **Port Lairge**[9] 8477 6-9-3 **58** .... PhilDennis[(5)] 5 62
(Michael Chapman) *midfield: hdwy 4f out: rdn to chse wnr 2f out: drvn over 1f out: kpt on same pce fnl f* **25/1**

0053 3 1/2 **Tred Softly (IRE)**[14] 8386 3-9-0 **54** ....(b) JasonHart 3 57
(John Quinn) *in tch: hdwy over 4f out: chsd ldrs over 3f out: rdn to chse ldng pair over 2f out: drvn wl over 1f out: kpt on u.p fnl f* **9/2**[3]

0001 4 4 **Stand Guard**[9] 8468 12-9-10 **60** 6ex .... LiamKeniry 7 57
(John Butler) *in tch: pushed along and lost pl 1/2-way: sn towards rr: hdwy 4f out: rdn to chse ldrs over 2f out: sn drvn and no imp* **5/2**[1]

0005 5 4 **Master Of Song**[9] 8471 9-8-6 **49** ow1 ....(p) KevinLundie[(7)] 9 40
(Roy Bowring) *t.k.h: cl up: led over 5f out: rdn along over 3f out: sn hdd and drvn: grad wknd* **15/2**

0040 6 2 3/4 **Nutzma**[68] 7532 3-8-6 **46** oh1 .... KieranO'Neill 6 32
(Mike Murphy) *prom: cl up 5f out: rdn along over 3f out: drvn and wknd over 2f out* **16/1**

4002 7 15 **Hydrant**[13] 8410 10-9-10 **60** .... ConnorBeasley 2 22
(Richard Guest) *v.s.a and bhd: hdwy 1/2-way: in tch 4f out: chsd ldrs over 3f out: sn rdn and wknd* **11/1**

6460 8 5 **Hint Of Grey (IRE)**[23] 7746 3-9-5 **59** .... JosephineGordon 1 13
(Don Cantillon) *a towards rr: bhd fnl 3f* **8/1**

 The Form Book, Raceform Ltd, Newbury, RG14 5SJ

6000 **9** *51* **Catharina**[9] 8468 4-8-13 **52**........ JackDuern(3) 4
(Dean Ivory) *slt ld: rdn along 1/2-way: sn hdd: wknd qckly over 4f out and sn bhd* **50/1**

2m 32.87s (4.87) **Going Correction** +0.45s/f (Slow)
WFA 3 from 4yo+ 4lb **9** Ran SP% **114.7**
Speed ratings (Par 101): **100,98,98,95,92 90,79,76,38**
CSF £72.08 CT £334.36 TOTE £3.90: £1.60, £6.60, £2.00; EX 79.30 Trifecta £434.00.
Owner Robert Emmanuel **Bred** Shadwell Estate Company Limited **Trained** Pandy, Monmouths

FOCUS
The winning time was 0.4sec slower than the first division. Straightforward form.

8568 32RED CASINO NURSERY H'CAP 1m (F)
1:15 (1:15) (Class 6) (0-65,65) 2-Y-O **£3,234** (£962; £481; £240) **Stalls** Low

Form RPR

0400 **1** **Haraka (IRE)**[22] 8244 2-9-6 **64**........ (b[1]) RichardKingscote 7 70
(Ralph Beckett) *towards rr: hdwy and swtchd rt over 2f out: rdn to chse ldng pair over 1f out: sn drvn: styd on strly to ld wl ins fnl f* **13/2**[3]

600 **2** *1 1/2* **Daily Trader**[26] 8208 2-8-11 **55**........ AndrewMullen 8 57
(David Evans) *cl up: led over 4f out: hdd over 2f out and sn rdn: drvn and kpt on ins fnl f* **10/1**

0552 **3** *1 3/4* **Aventus (IRE)**[17] 8341 2-8-2 **51**........ (b) CharlieBennett(5) 11 49
(Jane Chapple-Hyam) *prom: cl up 1/2-way: rdn to ld over 2f out: drvn over 1f out: hdd and no ex wl ins fnl f* **7/1**

0004 **4** *3 1/4* **Good Time Ahead (IRE)**[13] 8398 2-9-4 **62**........ PaddyAspell 3 52
(Philip Kirby) *towards rr: hdwy on inner over 3f out: rdn wl over 2f out: kpt on appr fnl f* **33/1**

044 **5** *1* **Charlie Rascal (FR)**[119] 6044 2-9-6 **64**........ JosephineGordon 6 52
(Peter Chapple-Hyam) *trckd ldrs: rdn along wl over 2f out: drvn wl over 1f out: grad wknd* **5/1**[2]

0403 **6** *1/2* **Our Boy John (IRE)**[20] 8284 2-8-10 **54**........ TonyHamilton 4 40
(Richard Fahey) *in tch: hdwy to chse ldrs over 2f out: rdn to chse ldng pair wl over 1f out: sn drvn and grad wknd* **11/1**

0132 **7** *5* **Dusty Bin**[13] 8398 2-9-7 **65**........ KieranO'Neill 2 39+
(Garry Moss) *chsd ldrs: rdn along over 2f out: drvn wl over 1f out: sn wknd* **4/1**[1]

2402 **8** *4* **Areyoutheway (IRE)**[35] 8080 2-9-3 **64**........ (p) AlistairRawlinson(3) 9 29
(Michael Appleby) *swtchd rt to outer after 1f: in tch: rdn along wl over 2f out: sn drvn and btn* **4/1**[1]

4360 **9** *1/2* **Affair**[58] 7750 2-8-10 **61**........ TheodoreLadd(7) 5 25
(Hughie Morrison) *in tch: rdn along 1/2-way: drvn over 2f out. sn wknd* **28/1**

2000 **10** *3/4* **Valley Lodge**[23] 8235 2-8-10 **57**........[1] ShelleyBirkett(3) 10 19
(Julia Feilden) *led: hdd over 4f out: cl up: rdn along 3f out: drvn and wknd over 2f out* **22/1**

0012 **11** *23* **Viola Park**[21] 8276 2-8-7 **51**........ RyanPowell 1
(Ronald Harris) *chsd ldrs on inner: rdn along 1/2-way: sn lost pl and bhd* **12/1**

1m 46.77s (3.07) **Going Correction** +0.45s/f (Slow) **11** Ran SP% **118.4**
Speed ratings (Par 94): **102,100,98,95,94 94,89,85,84,83 60**
CSF £68.61 CT £473.75 TOTE £7.80: £3.10, £4.50, £2.90; EX 128.20 Trifecta £766.20.
Owner Andy Smith and Friends **Bred** March Thoroughbreds **Trained** Kimpton, Hants

FOCUS
Quite a dramatic finish to this moderate nursery. There are obvious question marks about the class-dropping winner, who had blinkers on for the first time, repeating this form.

8569 32RED.COM MAIDEN AUCTION STKS 5f (F)
1:50 (1:50) (Class 5) 2-Y-O **£4,528** (£1,347; £673; £336) **Stalls** Centre

Form RPR

6230 **1** **Nuzha**[10] 8453 2-8-6 66........ AndrewMullen 1 72+
(David Evans) *cl up:. chal wl over 1f out: rdn to ld ent fnl f: styd on strly* **7/2**[2]

634 **2** *4 1/2* **Golden Opportunity**[15] 8352 2-8-13 71........ RobertHavlin 8 63
(James Tate) *cl up: chal over 2f out: led briefly 11/2f out: sn rdn and hdd ent fnl f: drvn and kpt on same pce* **10/11**[1]

3 *2 3/4* **Mia Tia** 2-8-13 0........ TomEaves 6 53
(James Given) *swtchd rt s and trckd ldrs: hdwy to ld 1/2-way: rdn along and hdd 11/2f out: sn drvn and kpt on same pce* **7/1**

4 *4* **Jungle George** 2-8-12 0........[1] KieranO'Neill 2 38
(Scott Dixon) *dwlt: sn in tch on outer: rdn along 1/2-way: kpt on same pce* **25/1**

64 **5** *5* **Oakley Pride (IRE)**[143] 5244 2-8-6 0........[1] RhiainIngram(7) 5 21
(Gay Kelleway) *slt ld: hdd 1/2-way: sn rdn along 2f out: sn drvn and wknd* **12/1**

0065 **6** *shd* **Red Shanghai (IRE)**[65] 7589 2-8-6 40........ NoelGarbutt(3) 7 16
(Charles Smith) *rr: outpcd and bhd fr 1/2-way* **66/1**

3360 **7** *1 1/4* **Wind In Her Sails (IRE)**[54] 7820 2-8-13 66........ JackMitchell 4 16
(Giles Bravery) *cl up: rdn along bef 1/2-way: sn lost pl and bhd* **6/1**[3]

2050 **8** *6* **Irish Melody (IRE)**[7] 8494 2-8-11 64........ (b[1]) NathanEvans(3) 3
(Bill Turner) *a rr: rdn along: outpcd and bhd fr 1/2-way* **33/1**

1m 1.51s (1.81) **Going Correction** +0.275s/f (Slow) **8** Ran SP% **117.4**
Speed ratings (Par 96): **96,88,84,78,70 69,67,58**
CSF £7.18 TOTE £5.30: £1.50, £1.10, £1.80; EX 9.20 Trifecta £34.30.
Owner Naser Buresli **Bred** Mascalls Stud **Trained** Pandy, Monmouths

FOCUS
A moderate sprint maiden and the front three had it to themselves from some way out. There's little depth to this form behind the winner.

8570 SUNBETS.CO.UK MAIDEN STKS 7f (F)
2:25 (2:27) (Class 5) 3-Y-O+ **£3,881** (£1,155; £577; £288) **Stalls** Low

Form RPR

3202 **1** **Napoleon Solo**[45] 7960 4-9-5 63........ AndrewMullen 3 69+
(David Barron) *mde all: rdn wl over 1f out: drvn and hung lft ins fnl f: kpt on* **7/4**[1]

0062 **2** *1 1/2* **Playful Dude (USA)**[7] 8500 3-9-5 55........ JosephineGordon 2 63
(Phil McEntee) *prom: effrt on inner 3f out and sn rdn: drvn along 2f out: kpt on fnl f* **9/2**[3]

355 **3** *5* **Loveatfirstsight**[24] 8233 3-9-0 65........ AdamBeschizza 7 45
(Michael Attwater) *prom: rdn along 3f out: drvn 2f out: kpt on one pce* **5/2**[2]

4 *1 1/2* **Treaty Of Rome (USA)**[501] 5428 4-9-5 60........ (v[1]) TonyHamilton 9 45
(Derek Shaw) *cl up on outer: rdn to chal over 2f out: sn drvn and ev ch tl wknd appr fnl f* **7/1**

0 **5** *1 3/4* **Waggle (IRE)**[19] 8320 3-9-5 0........ ConnorBeasley 6 41
(Michael Wigham) *towards rr: pushed along over 3f out: rdn over 2f out: kpt on u.p fnl f: n.d* **14/1**

000- **6** *4* **Frank Cool**[463] 6645 3-9-2 55........ GeorgeDowning(3) 5 30
(Tony Carroll) *in tch: hdwy wl over 2f out: rdn to chse ldrs and hung lft wl over 1f out: sn drvn and wknd* **25/1**

44 **7** *3/4* **Diamond Indulgence**[9] 8472 3-8-11 0........ NoelGarbutt(3) 4 23
(Derek Shaw) *in tch on inner: rdn along 1/2-way: drvn over 2f out: sn wknd* **14/1**

8 *12* **Barbary Prince** 4-9-0 0........ CharlieBennett(5) 8
(Shaun Harris) *dwlt: a rr* **66/1**

0 **9** *2 3/4* **Diamond Eagle (IRE)**[20] 8290 4-9-5 0........ TomMarquand 1
(Shaun Harris) *a rr* **80/1**

1m 32.79s (2.49) **Going Correction** +0.45s/f (Slow) **9** Ran SP% **115.5**
Speed ratings (Par 103): **103,101,95,93,91 87,86,72,69**
CSF £9.96 TOTE £3.10: £1.50, £1.20, £1.50; EX 9.60 Trifecta £19.10.
Owner Let's Be Lucky Racing 7 **Bred** Southill Stud **Trained** Maunby, N Yorks

FOCUS
A moderate older-horse maiden in which the order didn't change much. The winner has been rated to form.

8571 BETWAY SPRINT H'CAP 5f (F)
3:00 (3:00) (Class 4) (0-80,78) 3-Y-O-**£7,876** (£2,357; £1,178; £590; £293) **Stalls** Centre

Form RPR

2431 **1** **Captain Lars (SAF)**[7] 8495 7-9-5 **76** 6ex........ (v) TonyHamilton 7 88
(Derek Shaw) *prom: hdwy 2f out: rdn to chal ent fnl f: sn drvn and kpt on wl to ld last 50 yds* **4/1**[1]

5311 **2** *nk* **Piazon**[9] 8474 5-8-7 **71** 6ex........ (be) JoshuaBryan(7) 14 82
(John Butler) *racd centre: prom: smooth hdwy to ld wl over 1f out: jnd and drvn ent fnl f: hdd and no ex last 50 yds* **9/2**[2]

0000 **3** *2 1/2* **Crosse Fire**[9] 8473 4-9-1 **72**........ KieranO'Neill 6 74
(Scott Dixon) *dwlt: sn trcking ldrs towards far side: hdwy 2f out: rdn over 1f out: kpt on wl fnl f* **14/1**

0230 **4** *1/2* **Red Stripes (USA)**[7] 8495 4-8-6 **70**........ (b) JordanUys(7) 3 70
(Lisa Williamson) *racd towards far side: slt ld: rdn along over 2f out: hdd wl over 1f out: sn drvn and kpt on same pce fnl f* **12/1**

5260 **5** *2 1/4* **Clubland (IRE)**[16] 8345 7-8-10 **67**........ AndrewMullen 9 59
(Garry Moss) *midfield: hdwy 2f out: sn rdn and kpt on fnl f: nrst fin* **16/1**

0061 **6** *2 1/4* **Bold**[36] 8067 4-8-13 **73**........ (vt) AaronJones(3) 12 57
(Stuart Williams) *racd centre: chsd ldrs: rdn along 2f out: kpt on same pce* **4/1**[1]

0000 **7** *nk* **Invincible Ridge (IRE)**[13] 8403 8-9-2 **78**........ PhilDennis(5) 2 61
(Eric Alston) *racd towards far rail: cl up: disp ld 1/2-way: rdn along 2f out: drvn over 1f out and kpt on same pce* **22/1**

6221 **8** *1* **Monumental Man**[21] 8280 7-9-5 **76**........ (p) KierenFox 11 55
(Michael Attwater) *racd centre: chsd ldrs: rdn along over 2f out: kpt on same pce* **13/2**

2006 **9** *2 1/4* **Penny Dreadful**[16] 8347 4-8-10 **67**........ (b[1]) TomMarquand 10 38
(Scott Dixon) *dwlt: a towards rr* **40/1**

0021 **10** *nse* **Ticks The Boxes (IRE)**[9] 8473 4-8-13 **73** 6ex........ (p) NathanEvans(3) 13 44
(Michael Herrington) *racd towards stands side: a towards rr* **6/1**[3]

6140 **11** *hd* **Secret Clause**[9] 8473 3-8-4 **66**........ HollieDoyle(5) 1 36
(Michael Appleby) *a towards rr* **25/1**

0000 **12** *1 1/4* **King Crimson**[29] 8150 4-9-3 **74**........ TimmyMurphy 4 40
(John Butler) *dwlt: plld hrd: a towards rr* **33/1**

0-00 **13** *5* **Spiraea**[157] 4708 6-9-2 **73**........ TomEaves 8 21
(Ivan Furtado) *a rr* **25/1**

1m 0.57s (0.87) **Going Correction** +0.275s/f (Slow) **13** Ran SP% **123.5**
Speed ratings (Par 105): **104,103,99,98,95 91,91,89,85,85 85,83,75**
CSF £21.10 CT £246.00 TOTE £3.80: £1.90, £1.80, £6.60; EX 20.50 Trifecta £290.30.
Owner Chris Hamilton **Bred** Klawervlei Stud **Trained** Sproxton, Leics

FOCUS
A fair sprint handicap with the action unfolding centre-to-far side. A thrilling battle between the front pair. The winner has been rated as back close to his AW best.

8572 BETWAY CLASSIFIED STKS 6f (F)
3:30 (3:31) (Class 6) 3-Y-O+ **£3,234** (£962; £481; £240) **Stalls** Low

Form RPR

0060 **1** **Clever Divya**[9] 8472 3-9-0 52........ TonyHamilton 9 57
(J R Jenkins) *prom: rdn along and sltly outpcd 11/2f out: drvn and styd on wl fnl f to ld nr fin* **50/1**

0530 **2** *1/2* **Tribesman**[19] 8312 3-9-0 54........ (t) SamJames 14 56
(Marjorie Fife) *chsd ldrs hdwy on outer over 2f out: rdn wl over 1f out: drvn and ev ch ins fnl f: kpt on* **7/1**[3]

6433 **3** *nk* **Tasaaboq**[2] 8541 5-9-0 54........ (tp) JosephineGordon 13 55
(Phil McEntee) *chsd ldrs: hdwy on outer over 2f out: rdn wl over 1f out: drvn and ev ch ins fnl f: kpt on* **11/2**[2]

4505 **4** *nk* **Men United (FR)**[16] 8351 3-9-0 53........ KieranO'Neill 1 54
(Garry Moss) *led: rdn clr 2f out: drvn over 1f out: wknd ins fnl f: hdd and no ex towards fin* **10/1**

0500 **5** *nk* **Autumn Tonic (IRE)**[20] 8289 4-9-0 52........ (b) AndrewMullen 8 53
(David Barron) *t.k.h: hld up: n.m.r after 1f and sn swtchd rt: hdwy and wd st: rdn 2f out: styd on strly fnl f: nrst fin* **12/1**

0302 **6** *3/4* **Vivre La Reve**[16] 8346 4-9-0 55........ RyanPowell 7 51
(James Unett) *towards rr: hdwy 2f out: nt clr run and swtchd lft towards inner over 1f out: sn rdn and styd on: nrst fin* **12/1**

3206 **7** *hd* **Zebelini (IRE)**[19] 8312 4-8-7 48........ (tp) KevinLundie(7) 6 50
(Roy Bowring) *clsd up: rdn wl over 1f out: drvn ent fnl f: grad wknd last 100 yds* **25/1**

-002 **8** *1/2* **Gettin' Lucky**[20] 8288 3-8-11 46........ CallumShepherd(3) 4 49
(John Balding) *chsd ldrs: hdwy 2f out: rdn over 1f out: drvn and one pce fnl f* **11/2**[2]

5-00 **9** *1/2* **Desert Chief**[30] 8146 4-8-11 44........ (p) AlistairRawlinson(3) 12 47
(Michael Appleby) *dwlt and bhd: rdn and hdwy on inner over 1f out: styd on: nrst fin* **8/1**

050 **10** *3/4* **Cuban Queen (USA)**[35] 8079 3-9-0 48........[1] AdamBeschizza 5 45
(Julia Feilden) *in tch: effrt over 2f out: sn rdn and no imp* **14/1**

0560 **11** *4 1/2* **Pleadings (USA)**[10] 8457 3-9-0 40........ (vt[1]) RichardKingscote 2 32
(Charlie Wallis) *in tch on inner: hdwy over 2f out: rdn wl over 1f out: wknd appr fnl f* **14/1**

4102 **12** *8* **Lady Bacchus**[19] 8312 3-9-0 51........ (b) ConnorBeasley 11 8
(Richard Guest) *in tch: rdn along 2f out: sn drvn and wknd* **3/1**[1]

1m 19.26s (2.76) **Going Correction** +0.45s/f (Slow) **12** Ran SP% **123.0**
Speed ratings (Par 101): **99,98,97,97,97 96,95,95,94,93 87,76**
CSF £385.56 TOTE £50.10: £7.70, £2.50, £1.90; EX 353.20 Trifecta £3494.40.
Owner Ms Aurelija Juskaite **Bred** Mrs Wendy Jenkins **Trained** Royston, Herts

■ Stewards' Enquiry : Sam James jockey ban: four-day ban (12-16 Jan) - used whip above permitted level.

FOCUS
A moderate classified event and they finished in a heap, so not form to dwell on, especially with a 50-1 winner. It's been rated negatively.
T/Plt: £92.50 to a £1 stake. Pool: £70,701.93 - 557.58 winning units T/Qpdt: £22.20 to a £1 stake. Pool: £6,663.85 - 222.01 winning units **Joe Rowntree**

8564 DOHA
Thursday, December 29

OFFICIAL GOING: Turf: good

8573a QATAR DERBY (LOCAL GROUP 1) (3YO) (TURF) 1m 2f
4:45 (12:00) 3-Y-O **£193,877** (£74,829; £37,414; £20,408; £13,605)

RPR
1 **Noor Al Hawa (FR)**[88] 6992 3-9-2 0 AdriedeVries 9 105+
(A Wohler, Germany)
2 3 **Gerrard's Quest**[306] 756 3-9-2 0 PatCosgrave 16 99+
(Mohammed Hussain, Qatar)
3 3/4 **Al Mohalhal (IRE)**[109] 6382 3-9-2 0 DarrenWilliams 15 97
(Majed Seifeddine, Qatar)
4 1 3/4 **Opera Baron**[306] 756 3-9-2 0 (p) HarryBentley 8 94
(Mohammed Jassim Ghazali, Qatar)
5 nk **Open 'n Shut**[205] 2998 3-9-2 0 (t) EduardoPedroza 7 93
(Ibrahim Al Malki, Qatar)
6 nk **Barwod**[149] 5004 3-9-2 0 MarcoMonteriso 3 92
(J Smart, Qatar)
7 1/2 **Cameraman**[445] 7144 3-9-2 0 (b) StephaneLadjadj 2 91
(Zuhair Mohsen, Qatar)
8 1 **Top Face (USA)**[144] 3-9-2 0 TomLukasek 6 89
(M Al Ramzani, Qatar)
9 1 **Life Imitates Art (USA)**[362] 3-9-2 0 AlbertoSanna 4 87
(J Smart, Qatar)
10 1/2 **French Encore**[306] 756 3-9-2 0 AlanMunro 10 86
(Debbie Mountain, Qatar)
11 hd **Thewayyouwish (IRE)**[117] 6153 3-9-2 0 PierantonioConvertino 12 86
(Mohammed Jassim Ghazali, Qatar)
12 shd **Noble House (GER)**[130] 5696 3-9-2 0 KoenClijmans 14 86
(Mario Hofer, Germany)
13 2 **Fourioso (FR)**[96] 6798 3-9-2 0 GeraldAvranche 1 82
(M Al Yaqout, Qatar)
14 1 3/4 **Scarlet Dragon**[83] 7117 3-9-2 0 JimCrowley 5 78
(Eve Johnson Houghton) *sltly slow to stride: towards rr on inner: racd a little keenly: nudged along sn after 1/2-way: 10th and drvn 2 1/2f out but no imp: rdn over 1 1/2f out: wl hld fnl f*
15 1/2 **Ard San Aer (IRE)**[306] 756 3-9-2 0 (b) OlivierPeslier 13 77
(M Al Yaqout, Qatar)
16 dist **More Than A Dream (IRE)**[117] 3-9-2 0 Per-AndersGraberg 11
(H Al Jehani, Qatar)

2m 0.51s (120.51) **16** Ran

Owner Al Wasmiyah Farm **Bred** Rabbah Bloodstock Limited **Trained** Germany

8391 MEYDAN (L-H)
Thursday, December 29

OFFICIAL GOING: Dirt: fast

8574a EGA CASTHOUSE TROPHY (MAIDEN) (DIRT) 7f (D)
2:30 (2:30) 2-3-Y-O **£16,635** (£5,545; £3,049; £1,663; £831)

RPR
1 **Capezzano (USA)**[14] 8391 2-9-0 86 ColmO'Donoghue 3 86+
(Charlie Appleby) *slowly into strd, trkd leaders, rdn to ld 1f out, ran on well* **2/1**[2]
2 2 **Fawree (USA)** 2-9-0 BernardFayd'Herbe 10 81+
(M F De Kock, South Africa) *slowly into strd, mid-division, ran on fnl 2f but no ch wth winner* **9/1**[3]
3 1/2 **Bee Jersey (USA)** 2-9-0 PatDobbs 9 79
(Doug Watson, UAE) *soon led, hdd 1f out but ran on same pace* **7/4**[1]
4 7 1/2 **Cape Of Eagles (USA)**[76] 7337 2-9-0 80 MarcMonaghan 7 59
(Fawzi Abdulla Nass, Bahrain) *chased leaders, ran on same pace fnl 2f* **12/1**
5 hd **Dawwass (USA)**[14] 8391 2-9-0 RichardMullen 5 58
(S Seemar, UAE) *mid-division, ran on same pace fnl 2 1/2f* **20/1**
6 3 3/4 **Bourbon Gleam (USA)** 2-8-9 SamHitchcott 11 44
(Doug Watson, UAE) *chased leaders, ran on same pace fnl 2f* **20/1**
7 5 1/4 **Sharp Defence (USA)**[41] 8017 2-9-0 TadhgO'Shea 8 34
(S Seemar, UAE) *slowly into strd, nvr better than mid-division* **14/1**
8 1/2 **Hidden Journey (USA)**[180] 2-9-0 85 (t) ChrisHayes 2 33
(D Selvaratnam, UAE) *never nr to chal but ran on fnl 2f* **10/1**
9 1/2 **Voice Of The North (USA)**[42] 8000 2-9-0 FernandoJara 12 31
(S Seemar, UAE) *never better than mid-division* **25/1**
10 2 **Al Abyad (USA)**[12] 8442 2-9-0 (t) DaneO'Neill 4 26
(A bin Harmash, UAE) *tracked leaders til wknd fnl 3f* **33/1**
11 8 1/2 **Big Sigh (IRE)**[26] 8208 2-8-10 GeorgeBuckell(4) 1 3
(Ismail Mohammed) *never nr to challenge* **33/1**
12 1 3/4 **Modhilah (IRE)**[28] 8182 2-8-9 60 AntonioFresu 6
(S Seemar, UAE) *never better than mid-division* **66/1**

1m 24.41s (-0.69) **12** Ran SP% **123.9**
CSF: 19.60.
Owner Godolphin **Bred** Darley **Trained** Newmarket, Suffolk

8575a EGA AL TAWEELAH ALUMINA TROPHY (CONDITIONS) (DIRT) 7f (D)
3:05 (3:05) 2-3-Y-O **£19,963** (£6,654; £3,659; £1,996; £998)

RPR
1 **Van Der Decken**[131] 5646 2-9-2 103 DaneO'Neill 3 99+
(Charlie Appleby) *slowly into strd, nr rear, rdn 3f out, ran on wl fnl 2f to ld 1f out* **9/2**[3]
2 1 3/4 **Fly At Dawn (USA)**[82] 7151 2-9-5 98 ColmO'Donoghue 7 97
(Charlie Appleby) *tracked ldr, led briefly 2f out, hdd 1f out but ran on well* **5/4**[1]
3 1/2 **Complimenti (USA)** 2-8-7 SamHitchcott 1 84
(Doug Watson, UAE) *soon led, hdd 2f out but ran on well* **10/1**
4 5 1/2 **Nomorerichblondes (USA)**[28] 8182 2-8-11 84 (t) AntonioFresu 8 73
(A bin Harmash, UAE) *always mid-division* **10/1**
5 9 **Mufeed (USA)**[42] 8000 2-9-2 85 RichardMullen 4 54
(S Seemar, UAE) *tracked ldr til outpcd 3f out* **7/2**[2]
6 hd **Nalout (USA)**[20] 8304 2-8-3 60 ow3 CameronNoble(7) 6 47
(S Seemar, UAE) *never nr to challenge* **100/1**
7 hd **Arborist (IRE)**[28] 8186 2-9-2 78 (bt) TadhgO'Shea 2 52
(A R Al Rayhi, UAE) *always in rear* **66/1**
8 5 **Call To War (USA)**[195] 2-9-2 89 (t) ChrisHayes 5 39
(D Selvaratnam, UAE) *never better than mid-division* **8/1**

1m 25.56s (0.46) **8** Ran SP% **116.6**
CSF: 10.76.
Owner Godolphin **Bred** Cheveley Park Stud Ltd **Trained** Newmarket, Suffolk

8576a EGA BILLETS TROPHY (MAIDEN) (DIRT) 1m (D)
3:40 (3:40) 2-Y-O+ **£16,635** (£5,545; £3,049; £1,663; £831)

RPR
1 **Somerset House (USA)** 2-8-7 (b) ColmO'Donoghue 9 81+
(Charlie Appleby) *tracked leaders, led 1 1/2f out, ran on well* **7/2**[2]
2 3 **Mazeed (USA)**[14] 8391 2-8-7 AntonioFresu 3 74+
(M F De Kock, South Africa) *tracked ldr, ev ch 2f out, ran on well* **2/1**[1]
3 7 1/2 **Cachao**[20] 8304 3-8-13 73 (t) AdamMcLean(6) 13 52
(A bin Harmash, UAE) *near rear, ran on fnl 2 1/2f but nvr dangerous* **33/1**
4 3/4 **Shillong**[6] 8520 3-9-5 (t) FernandoJara 5 50
(H Al Alawi, UAE) *soon led, hdd 1 1/2f out, ran on same pace* **14/1**
5 1 3/4 **Just Pretend (USA)**[293] 912 3-9-5 TadhgO'Shea 8 46
(S Seemar, UAE) *slowly into strd, nvr nr to chal but ran on fnl 2 1/2f* **16/1**
6 shd **Dangerous Thought (USA)**[248] 1703 3-9-5 68 PatDobbs 4 46
(Doug Watson, UAE) *never better than mid-division* **66/1**
7 nk **Vivernus (USA)**[14] 8392 3-9-2 GeorgeBuckell(3) 7 45
(M Al Mheiri, UAE) *tracked leaders til outpcd fnl 3f* **9/2**[3]
8 3 1/2 **Sea Urchin (IRE)**[6] 8520 4-9-2 JacobButterfield 11 34
(R Bouresly, Kuwait) *never better than mid-division* **40/1**
9 nk **Pradesh (IRE)**[28] 8183 3-9-5 70 (t) SamHitchcott 10 36
(M Ibrahim, UAE) *never better than mid-division* **14/1**
10 2 1/4 **Al Madam (USA)**[28] 8182 2-8-7 ow2 (t) DaneO'Neill 2 36
(A bin Harmash, UAE) *slowly into strd, nvr better than mid-division* **16/1**
11 12 1/2 **Arcarius**[28] 8183 3-9-0 IKoyuncu(5) 12
(M Ibrahim, UAE) *never nr to challenge* **100/1**
12 3 **Eaglecraft (USA)**[14] 8392 3-9-5 SMazur 16
(I Al Hadhrami, UAE) *raced in rear but ran on fnl 2 1/2f* **100/1**
13 1 3/4 **Tribalism (USA)**[5] 8522 3-9-5 64 (t) ChrisHayes 14
(A Al Shamsi, UAE) *always in rear* **25/1**
14 7 1/4 **Henrytheghost (USA)**[392] 8100 4-9-6 57 (v) MarcMonaghan 6
(Fawzi Abdulla Nass, Bahrain) *tracked leaders, til outpcd fnl 2 1/2f* **66/1**
15 5 **Anbar**[20] 8304 4-9-6 55 (b) GokhanKocakaya 1
(R Bouresly, Kuwait) *never better than mid-division* **66/1**
16 5 3/4 **Dubai Post (IRE)**[14] 8392 5-9-6 55 PaoloSirigu 15
(Miss B Deutrom, UAE) *always in rear* **66/1**

1m 39.36s (1.86)
WFA 2 from 3yo 20lb 3 from 4yo+ 1lb **16** Ran SP% **116.0**
CSF: 11.25.
Owner Godolphin **Bred** Darley **Trained** Newmarket, Suffolk

8578a EGA EXCELLENCE TROPHY (H'CAP) (DIRT) 7f (D)
4:50 (4:50) (85-98,98) 3-Y-O+ **£21,072** (£7,024; £3,863; £2,107; £1,053)

RPR
1 **Desert Force**[28] 8184 4-9-4 **97** PatDobbs 4 114+
(Doug Watson, UAE) *soon led, clr 2 1/2f out, ran on wl, impressive* **10/11**[1]
2 7 3/4 **Heavy Metal**[14] 8395 6-9-5 **98** AntonioFresu 5 92
(S bin Ghadayer, UAE) *mid-division, ran on fnl 2 1/2f but no ch wth winner* **14/1**
3 2 **Comicas (USA)**[237] 1991 3-9-5 **98** (b) ColmO'Donoghue 7 87
(Charlie Appleby) *tracked ldr, ev ch 2 1/2f out, wknd fnl 1f* **5/2**[2]
4 1 1/2 **Riflescope (IRE)**[166] 4399 3-8-9 **89** RichardMullen 9 73
(S Seemar, UAE) *tracked leaders, ev ch 3f out, one pace fnl 2f* **50/1**
5 3/4 **Winslow (USA)**[383] 8208 4-8-11 **91** SamHitchcott 3 73
(Doug Watson, UAE) *slowly into strd, nvr nr to chal but ran on fnl 2 1/2f* **11/1**
6 1 1/4 **Philosopher (IRE)**[28] 8185 4-8-5 **90** ow1 (b) AdamMcLean(6) 6 69
(S bin Ghadayer, UAE) *tracked leaders, til wknd fnl 3f* **40/1**
7 2 **Alareef (SAF)**[293] 916 6-8-9 **89** (b) DaneO'Neill 8 62
(M F De Kock, South Africa) *never better than mid-division* **10/1**[3]
8 3/4 **Ajraam (USA)**[34] 8115 6-9-2 **95** FernandoJara 2 67
(M Al Mheiri, UAE) *never better than mid-division* **10/1**[3]
9 25 **Not A Given (USA)**[348] 229 7-8-11 **91** (t) TadhgO'Shea 1
(A R Al Rayhi, UAE) *slowly into strd, al in rear* **25/1**
10 9 1/2 **English Deer (IRE)**[664] 808 6-8-8 **88** (t) JacobButterfield 10
(A R Al Rayhi, UAE) *never nr to challenge* **66/1**

1m 23.97s (-1.13) **10** Ran SP% **123.9**
CSF: 18.08; TRICAST: 30.27.
Owner Mohd Khalifa Al Basti **Bred** Newsells Park Stud **Trained** United Arab Emirates

8579 - 8581a (Foreign Racing) - See Raceform Interactive

8478 NEWCASTLE (A.W) (L-H)
Friday, December 30

OFFICIAL GOING: Tapeta: standard
Wind: Breezy, half against Weather: Fine, dry

8582 32RED.COM NURSERY H'CAP 6f (Tp)
12:50 (12:50) (Class 4) (0-85,81) 2-Y-O **£6,469** (£1,925; £962; £481) **Stalls** Centre

Form RPR
542 1 **Zamjar**[12] 8444 2-9-7 **78** (b) JosephineGordon 2 83
(Ed Dunlop) *t.k.h: hld up in tch: shkn up and hdwy to ld over 1f out: rdn clr ins fnl f* **10/3**
0241 2 3 **Juan Horsepower**[8] 8494 2-9-5 **81** 6ex (p) HollieDoyle(5) 1 77
(Richard Hannon) *trckd ldrs: drvn and chsd wnr over 1f out: one pce whn edgd lft ins fnl f* **11/4**[1]

544 **3** *2* **White Royale (USA)**[12] 8444 2-8-11 **75** ... LewisEdmunds(7) 3 65
(Kevin Ryan) *led to over 1f out: rdn and wknd ins fnl f* **3/1**[2]

4004 **4** *1 ½* **Metronomic (IRE)**[22] 8276 2-8-1 **58** ... KieranO'Neill 5 44
(Richard Hannon) *trckd ldr tl rdn and outpcd over 2f out: no imp fr over 1f out* **6/1**

61 **5** *3* **Killermont Street (IRE)**[42] 8009 2-9-1 **72** ... JoeFanning 4 54
(Mark Johnston) *dwlt: sn prom: hdwy to chse wnr over 2f out to over 1f out: wknd and eased ins fnl f* **16/5**[3]

1m 13.15s (0.65) **Going Correction** +0.125s/f (Slow) **5** Ran SP% **112.8**
Speed ratings (Par 98): **100,96,93,91,87**
CSF £13.11 TOTE £3.20: £1.50, £2.00; EX 9.00 Trifecta £21.90.
Owner Abdullah Saeed Al Naboodah **Bred** Manor Farm Stud (rutland) **Trained** Newmarket, Suffolk

FOCUS
A trappy nursery to open this eight-race card but the pace looked sound and the winner cruised up from off the speed to open his all-weather account. There was little depth to the race, so it's questionable how literally the form should be rated.

8583 BETWAY SPRINT H'CAP 6f (Tp)
1:20 (1:22) (Class 3) (0-95,96) 3-Y-O+ **£9,451** (£2,829; £1,414; £708; £352) **Stalls** Centre

Form RPR

0034 **1** **Amazour (IRE)**[37] 8069 4-9-6 **96** ... LouisSteward(3) 4 106
(Ismail Mohammed) *hld up: stdy hdwy over 1f out: sn rdn: led ins fnl f: hld on wl* **5/2**[1]

5066 **2** *nk* **Poyle Vinnie**[20] 8308 6-9-7 **94** ... TomEaves 3 103
(Michael Appleby) *taken early to post: trckd ldrs: led gng wl over 1f out: rdn: edgd rt and hdd ins fnl f: kpt on: hld towards fin* **11/1**

0011 **3** *½* **Outrage**[10] 8463 4-9-3 **93** 6ex ... (b) GeorgeDowning(3) 5 100
(Daniel Kubler) *dwlt: t.k.h in rr: rdn and hdwy on nr side of gp over 1f out: ch ins fnl f: kpt on: hld nr fin* **14/1**

2101 **4** *¾* **Captain Dion**[29] 8176 3-8-12 **85** ... ShaneGray 7 90
(Kevin Ryan) *led: rdn over 2f out: hdd over 1f out: kpt on same pce ins fnl f* **6/1**[3]

0005 **5** *nk* **Tatlisu (IRE)**[43] 7990 6-8-12 **85** ... TonyHamilton 1 89
(Richard Fahey) *hld up: pushed along on far side of gp over 1f out: kpt on ins fnl f: nvr able to chal* **16/1**

0414 **6** *hd* **Rich Again (IRE)**[84] 7112 7-8-8 **81** ... (b) PJMcDonald 9 84
(James Bethell) *hld up in tch: effrt nr side of gp over 1f out: kpt on same pce ins fnl f* **20/1**

-054 **7** *1 ¾* **King Robert**[28] 8192 3-9-5 **92** ... ConnorBeasley 11 90
(Bryan Smart) *t.k.h: hld up in tch on nr side of gp: effrt and drvn over 1f out: no ex ins fnl f* **3/1**[2]

0001 **8** *shd* **El Viento (FR)**[15] 8380 8-8-8 **81** ... (v) PatrickMathers 8 78
(Richard Fahey) *in tch: drvn and outpcd over 2f out: rallied ins fnl f: kpt on: no imp* **16/1**

5032 **9** *1* **Intibaah**[14] 8402 6-9-0 **87** ... (p) SteveDrowne 6 81
(George Baker) *trckd ldrs: effrt and ev ch over 1f out: wknd ins fnl f* **40/1**

0066 **10** *1* **Handsome Dude**[15] 8385 4-8-10 **83** ... (b) AndrewMullen 2 74
(David Barron) *prom on far side of gp: rdn over 2f out: wknd over 1f out* **20/1**

0305 **11** *1 ¼* **Related**[14] 8407 6-9-5 **92** ... (b) MartinLane 10 79
(Paul Midgley) *w ldr tl rdn and wknd wl over 1f out* **12/1**

1m 12.1s (-0.40) **Going Correction** +0.125s/f (Slow) **11** Ran SP% **114.3**
Speed ratings (Par 107): **107,106,105,104,104 104,101,101,100,99 97**
CSF £29.15 CT £319.54 TOTE £3.60: £1.50, £3.10, £2.50; EX 29.00 Trifecta £111.00.
Owner Sheikh Juma Dalmook Al Maktoum **Bred** J F Tuthill **Trained** Newmarket, Suffolk

FOCUS
A competitive enough sprint handicap in which the first three home were the top three in the handicap. Straightforward form rated around the principals.

8584 BETWAY H'CAP 1m 4f 98y (Tp)
1:50 (1:50) (Class 4) (0-85,86) 3-Y-O+ **£6,469** (£1,925; £962; £481) **Stalls** High

Form RPR

6322 **1** **Isharah (USA)**[21] 8283 3-9-3 **80** ... JoeFanning 4 87
(Mark Johnston) *dwlt: sn cl up: wnt 2nd after 2f: led gng wl over 2f out: rdn and edgd lft wl ins fnl f: hld on wl* **2/1**[1]

4504 **2** *nk* **Masterpaver**[27] 8210 5-9-7 **86** ... NatalieHambling(7) 3 92
(Richard Fahey) *trckd ldr 2f: cl up: pushed along and outpcd over 2f out: rallied and ev ch whn blkd wl ins fnl f: kpt on* **4/1**[3]

014 **3** *½* **Island Flame (IRE)**[49] 7901 3-8-12 **75** ... PatrickMathers 5 80
(Richard Fahey) *trckd ldrs: effrt and pressed wnr over 1f out to ins fnl f: kpt on: hld nr fin* **8/1**

2351 **4** *3 ¾* **Paris Magic**[20] 8310 3-9-5 **82** ... (b) JosephineGordon 6 81
(Hugo Palmer) *t.k.h: hld up: stdy hdwy over 3f out: rdn over 2f out: no imp fr over 1f out* **9/4**[2]

120 **5** *1 ¼* **Polar Forest**[8] 8498 6-9-2 **74** ... (e) ConnorBeasley 8 71
(Richard Guest) *hld up: rdn over 2f out: no imp fr over 1f out* **10/1**

0/ **6** *5* **Lac Leman (GER)**[327] 5-9-5 **77** ... JamesSullivan 1 66
(Pauline Robson) *t.k.h: led to over 2f out: rdn and wknd over 1f out* **28/1**

1010 **7** *13* **Hard To Handel**[4] 8524 4-9-4 **76** ... SteveDrowne 2 44
(Clare Ellam) *hld up in tch: drvn and outpcd over 2f out: sn wknd* **40/1**

2m 39.37s (-1.73) **Going Correction** +0.10s/f (Slow)
WFA 3 from 4yo+ 5lb **7** Ran SP% **110.2**
Speed ratings (Par 105): **109,108,108,105,105 101,93**
CSF £9.59 CT £46.27 TOTE £2.70: £1.70, £2.30; EX 8.90 Trifecta £34.50.
Owner Abdulla Al Mansoori **Bred** M Buckley, M Buckley & K L Ramsey **Trained** Middleham Moor, N Yorks
■ Stewards' Enquiry : Steve Drowne jockey said gelding moved poorly throughout

FOCUS
A trappy little heat and the result may well have been different had the runner-up not been squeezed for room when making good progress up the rail in the closing stages, but the winning distance was always going to mean he had no chance of getting the race in the Stewards' room. The runner-up has been rated to his best since early 2015 and the third to form.

8585 BETWAY MAIDEN STKS 1m 2f 42y (Tp)
2:20 (2:21) (Class 5) 3-Y-O+ **£4,528** (£1,347; £673; £336) **Stalls** High

Form RPR

4222 **1** **Adalene**[16] 8366 3-9-0 74 ... (b1) TomEaves 8 72+
(David Simcock) *hld up in tch: smooth hdwy to ld over 2f out: sn qckned clr on bridle: drifted to far rail ins fnl f: v easily* **10/11**[1]

2 *6* **Codeshare**[38] 4-9-8 0 ... JoeFanning 7 60
(Alan Swinbank) *dwlt: t.k.h in rr: hdwy on outside to chse (clr) wnr 2f out: plugged on fnl f: no imp* **7/2**[2]

5-36 **3** *1 ½* **On Fire**[228] 2306 3-9-5 62 ... PJMcDonald 1 57
(James Bethell) *t.k.h early: hld up: rdn and outpcd over 3f out: rallied over 2f out: kpt on fnl f: no imp* **15/2**

0 **4** *nk* **Persian Steel (IRE)**[9] 8481 4-9-1 0 ... BenRobinson(7) 2 56
(Brian Ellison) *dwlt: t.k.h and sn trcking ldrs: drvn along over 2f out: one pce fr over 1f out* **80/1**

0543 **5** *nk* **Chorus of Lies**[26] 5517 4-9-8 53 ... DaleSwift 5 56
(Tracy Waggott) *t.k.h: cl up: rdn and outpcd over 2f out: no imp fr over 1f out* **25/1**

2402 **6** *5* **Highwayman**[59] 7745 3-9-5 62 ... JosephineGordon 3 46
(David Thompson) *t.k.h: led at stdy pce: rdn and hdd over 2f out: wknd over 1f out* **12/1**

3 **7** *3 ¼* **John Milton (IRE)**[9] 8481 3-9-5 0 ... DavidNolan 6 39
(Karen McLintock) *hld up: rdn and outpcd over 4f out: no imp fr over 2f out* **4/1**[3]

00 **8** *27* **Diamond Eagle (IRE)**[1] 8570 4-9-8 0 ... PaddyAspell 4
(Shaun Harris) *t.k.h: cl up tl rdn and wknd 3f out: t.o* **125/1**

2m 10.99s (0.59) **Going Correction** +0.10s/f (Slow)
WFA 3 from 4yo 3lb **8** Ran SP% **119.9**
Speed ratings (Par 103): **101,96,95,94,94 90,87,66**
CSF £4.69 TOTE £1.90: £1.10, £1.50, £2.00; EX 6.00 Trifecta £21.20.
Owner Qatar Racing Limited **Bred** Qatar Bloodstock Ltd **Trained** Newmarket, Suffolk

FOCUS
This looked weak on paper and most were keen and pulling for their heads as they went no gallop early, so although the winner bolted up. It's not hard to have reservations about this form. It's been rated around the third and fifth, but the level is fluid..

8586 DOWNLOAD THE BETWAY APP H'CAP 1m 2f 42y (Tp)
2:50 (2:51) (Class 6) (0-65,65) 3-Y-O+ **£3,234** (£962; £481; £240) **Stalls** High

Form RPR

3321 **1** **Galilee Chapel (IRE)**[20] 8318 7-9-7 **65** ... (b) BarryMcHugh 3 72
(Alistair Whillans) *t.k.h: hld up midfield: effrt and rdn 2f out: led ent fnl f: kpt on wl towards fin* **9/1**

060 **2** *¾* **Pickett's Charge**[35] 8092 3-9-4 **65** ... ConnorBeasley 10 71
(Richard Guest) *t.k.h: hld up: hdwy and prom over 1f out: chsd wnr ins fnl f: kpt on fin* **8/1**[3]

5412 **3** *nk* **Taopix**[31] 8141 4-9-6 **64** ... DavidNolan 12 69
(Karen McLintock) *t.k.h: in tch: hdwy against far rail and led over 1f out to ent fnl f: sn one pce* **3/1**[2]

0000 **4** *¾* **Genres**[24] 8241 4-9-4 **62** ... JoeFanning 13 66
(Alan Swinbank) *hld up: stdy hdwy on outside over 2f out: effrt and shkn up over 1f out: kpt on ins fnl f* **14/1**

0141 **5** *½* **Thello**[14] 8400 4-9-2 **63** ... LouisSteward(3) 4 66
(Garry Moss) *t.k.h: hld up midfield: effrt and rdn over 1f out: kpt on same pce ins fnl f* **5/2**[1]

2513 **6** *1 ¼* **Rubis**[28] 8194 3-8-4 **58** ... NatalieHambling(7) 1 59
(Richard Fahey) *t.k.h: cl up: rdn and ev ch briefly over 1f out: no ex ins fnl f* **9/1**

0000 **7** *2* **Los Cerritos (SWI)**[4] 8527 4-8-11 **58** ... NathanEvans(3) 14 55
(Oliver Greenall) *cl up: led over 2f out to over 1f out: rdn and wknd ins fnl f* **40/1**

/2-3 **8** *½* **Glorious Asset**[28] 8190 4-9-6 **64** ... TomEaves 8 60
(Ivan Furtado) *in tch: pushed along over 2f out: edgd lft and outpcd fr over 1f out* **25/1**

4053 **9** *nk* **Swiss Lait**[14] 8400 5-8-9 **53** ... JamesSullivan 5 49
(Patrick Holmes) *s.i.s: hld up: rdn and hdwy over 2f out: no further imp fr over 1f out* **50/1**

0020 **10** *nse* **Hydrant**[1] 8567 10-8-13 **60** ... GeorgeDowning(3) 6 55
(Richard Guest) *led at ordinary gallop: rdn and hdd over 2f out: wknd over 1f out: eased whn btn ins fnl f* **50/1**

0200 **11** *¾* **Devious Spirit (IRE)**[14] 8400 4-9-1 **59** ... AndrewMullen 7 53
(Iain Jardine) *s.s: hld up on ins: rdn and shortlived effrt 2f out: sn no imp: btn fnl f* **11/1**

0400 **12** *nk* **Royal Flag**[53] 7847 6-8-13 **64** ... BenRobinson(7) 11 58
(Brian Ellison) *s.i.s: hld up: rdn along on outside over 3f out: no imp fr 2f out* **12/1**

0420 **13** *2 ½* **Balducci**[21] 8286 9-9-6 **64** ... TonyHamilton 2 53
(Roger Fell) *t.k.h: hld up midfield: struggling over 2f out: sn wknd* **33/1**

0-00 **14** *¾* **Beaumont's Party (IRE)**[15] 8387 9-9-1 **59** ... DougieCostello 9 47
(Chris Grant) *hld up in tch: rdn over 2f out: wknd wl over 1f out* **100/1**

2m 11.09s (0.69) **Going Correction** +0.10s/f (Slow)
WFA 3 from 4yo+ 3lb **14** Ran SP% **121.5**
Speed ratings (Par 101): **101,100,100,99,99 98,96,96,95,95 95,95,93,92**
CSF £76.54 CT £272.70 TOTE £8.40: £2.20, £3.30, £1.70; EX 111.80 Trifecta £428.80.
Owner A C Whillans **Bred** Tally-Ho Stud **Trained** Newmill-On-Slitrig, Borders
■ Stewards' Enquiry : Connor Beasley caution; careless riding.

FOCUS
The sort of contest that would throw up a different result every time it was run but the first and third have been in good form of late so they give the for a reasonable feel in the circumstances. Another slight pb from the winner.

8587 SUNBETS.CO.UK H'CAP (DIV I) 1m 5y (Tp)
3:20 (3:20) (Class 6) (0-65,67) 3-Y-O+ **£3,234** (£962; £481; £240) **Stalls** Centre

Form RPR

6232 **1** **Swansway**[17] 8350 3-8-9 **57** ... NathanEvans(3) 4 66+
(Michael Easterby) *hld up in last pl: rdn and qcknd on nr side of gp to ld appr fnl f: sn clr: pricked ears: idled and edgd lft ins fnl f: kpt on* **2/1**[1]

0440 **2** *1 ½* **Bromance**[8] 8500 3-8-10 **55** ... (p) JamesSullivan 7 60
(Peter Niven) *hld up: effrt whn nt clr run over 2f out: nt clr run and swtchd rt over 1f out: hdwy to chse wnr towards fin: kpt on* **11/2**[2]

3500 **3** *¾* **Foolaad**[10] 8473 5-9-0 **65** ... (t) KevinLundie(7) 9 69
(Roy Bowring) *led: rdn and qcknd 2f out: hdd appr fnl f: sn one pce: lost 2nd towards fin* **20/1**

0-20 **4** *1 ¼* **What Usain**[158] 4715 4-9-3 **64** ... [1] AlistairRawlinson(3) 11 65
(Michael Appleby) *hld up on nr side of gp: rdn over 2f out: hdwy wl over 1f out: kpt on fnl f: nvr able to chal* **12/1**

0030 **5** *¾* **Billy Bond**[29] 8178 4-9-9 **67** ... TonyHamilton 5 67
(Richard Fahey) *hld up: pushed along on far side of gp over 2f out: kpt on fnl f: nt pce to chal* **6/1**[3]

4033 **6** *¾* **African Showgirl**[17] 8347 3-9-4 **63** ... JosephineGordon 1 60
(Ivan Furtado) *t.k.h: in tch: effrt on far side of gp over 2f out: edgd lft and no imp over 1f out* **14/1**

6455 **7** *1 ½* **Broctune Papa Gio**[21] 8286 9-9-2 **60** ... KieranO'Neill 8 55
(Keith Reveley) *hld up midfield: drvn and outpcd over 2f out: plugged on ins fnl f: nvr rchd ldrs* **12/1**

5000 **8** *2 ½* **Hellavashock**[21] 8286 3-9-0 **64** ... RowanScott(5) 10 52
(Alistair Whillans) *prom: rdn over 2f out: wknd over 1f out* **66/1**

3241 **9** *2 ¼* **Celtic Artisan (IRE)**[99] 6700 5-9-0 **58** ow2 ... (tp) DougieCostello 6 42
(Rebecca Menzies) *cl up: drvn along over 2f out: wknd over 1f out* **12/1**

6045 **10** ½ **Princess Peaches**[43] 7995 4-9-0 **58**..............................(p) PJMcDonald 3 41
(James Bethell) *in tch: drvn along over 2f out: wknd wl over 1f out* **12/1**

3334 **11** 1¼ **Dominannie (IRE)**[174] 4145 3-9-5 **64**..................................... JoeFanning 2 43
(Alan Swinbank) *t.k.h: cl up on far side of gp: rdn over 2f out: wknd over 1f out* **9/1**

1m 39.28s (0.68) **Going Correction** +0.125s/f (Slow)
WFA 3 from 4yo+ 1lb **11** Ran SP% **116.7**
Speed ratings (Par 101): **101,99,98,97,96 96,94,92,89,89 88**
CSF £12.26 CT £173.50 TOTE £2.90: £1.50, £2.20, £6.40; EX 15.20 Trifecta £247.40.
Owner W H & Mrs J A Tinning **Bred** Pontchartrain Stud **Trained** Sheriff Hutton, N Yorks

FOCUS
An open handicap full of horses that struggle to win but it was won fairly decisively by a horse who has been knocking at the door of late.

8588 SUNBETS.CO.UK H'CAP (DIV II) 1m 5y (Tp)
3:50 (3:50) (Class 6) (0-65,66) 3-Y-O+ **£3,234** (£962; £481; £240) **Stalls** Centre

Form RPR

6600 **1** **The Magic Pencil (IRE)**[99] 6701 3-9-3 **62**........................(p) TomEaves 9 68
(Kevin Ryan) *mde all: set ordinary gallop: rdn and qckn d wl over 1f out: drifted lft ins fnl f: hld on wl towards fin* **5/1**[3]

6345 **2** nk **Newmarket Warrior (IRE)**[168] 4335 5-9-1 **66**.....(p) JamieGormley(7) 11 72
(Iain Jardine) *hld up in last pl: stdy hdwy whn nt clr run over 1f out: swtchd rt and gd hdwy to chsd wnr ins fnl f: edgd lft: kpt on fin* **7/1**

4265 **3** ¾ **Oak Bluffs (IRE)**[30] 8156 5-9-1 **59**.................................... BarryMcHugh 6 64
(Richard Fahey) *prom: effrt and chsd wnr over 2f out: edgd lft and lost 2nd ins fnl f: kpt on same pce nr fin* **8/1**

0500 **4** 1½ **Jessie Allan (IRE)**[21] 8288 5-8-7 **51** oh6......................... JamesSullivan 3 52
(Jim Goldie) *hld up: hdwy nr side of gp over 1f out: edgd lft ins fnl f: kpt on same pce* **200/1**

5212 **5** ½ **Lozah**[20] 8307 3-9-5 **64**... TonyHamilton 2 63
(Roger Fell) *stdd s: hld up bhd ldng gp on outside: effrt and hdwy over 1f out: no imp fnl f* **2/1**[1]

5332 **6** 1¾ **Who's Shirl**[31] 8144 10-8-5 **56**.. PaulaMuir(7) 7 52
(Chris Fairhurst) *dwlt: t.k.h: hld up: rdn and outpcd over 2f out: rallied and edgd rt ins fnl f: kpt on: nvr able to chal* **18/1**

4300 **7** 2¼ **Hernando Torres**[63] 7662 8-9-4 **65**..........................(tp) NathanEvans(3) 1 56
(Michael Easterby) *prom: effrt and rdn 2f out: wknd ins fnl f* **9/2**[2]

030 **8** 3 **Let Right Be Done**[20] 8307 4-8-11 **55**................................ ShaneGray 5 40
(Linda Perratt) *hld up midfield: effrt and hdwy wl over 1f out: btn ins fnl f* **40/1**

31-0 **9** ½ **Sir Lancelott**[36] 8085 4-8-12 **63**.............................. PatrickVaughan(7) 10 47
(David O'Meara) *hld up: rdn and outpcd over 2f out: n.d after* **20/1**

3123 **10** 3 **Poor Duke (IRE)**[67] 7577 6-8-13 **57**...................................... JoeFanning 8 34
(Michael Mullineaux) *chsd ldrs on nr side of gp: rdn over 2f out: wknd wl over 1f out* **25/1**

3001 **11** 3½ **Crystallographer (IRE)**[52] 7856 3-9-5 **64**..................(p) AndrewMullen 4 32
(Daniel Mark Loughnane) *t.k.h: chsd wnr to over 2f out: sn rdn and wknd* **12/1**

1m 40.4s (1.80) **Going Correction** +0.125s/f (Slow)
WFA 3 from 4yo+ 1lb **11** Ran SP% **116.3**
Speed ratings (Par 101): **96,95,94,93,92 91,88,85,85,82 78**
CSF £38.04 CT £280.99 TOTE £5.60: £1.90, £2.80, £2.60; EX 46.50 Trifecta £361.30.
Owner Mrs J Ryan **Bred** J & L Young / Darlacher Ltd **Trained** Hambleton, N Yorks

FOCUS
There must be a good chance this was run at steady fractions early given the leader was able to kick from the front and hold on, but without instant access to sectionals, it's impossible to back that theory up.

8589 SUN BETS ON THE APP STORE H'CAP 7f 14y (Tp)
4:20 (4:21) (Class 6) (0-55,55) 3-Y-O+ **£3,234** (£962; £481; £240) **Stalls** Centre

Form RPR

0106 **1** **Great Colaci**[31] 8145 3-9-0 **48**.. KieranO'Neill 3 55
(Keith Reveley) *cl up in centre: rdn to ld over 2f out: edgd lft ins fnl f: kpt on wl* **5/1**[2]

0132 **2** 1¾ **Table Manners**[20] 8306 4-9-0 **53**.................................... HollieDoyle(5) 1 56
(Wilf Storey) *prom on far side of gp: effrt and chsd wnr over 1f out: edgd lft: kpt on same pce ins fnl f* **7/1**

552 **3** 1¼ **Dancin Alpha**[10] 8470 5-9-6 **54**.. JoeFanning 14 54
(Alan Swinbank) *hld up on nr side of gp: rdn and hdwy over 2f out: edgd lft and kpt on ins fnl f: nt rch first two* **6/1**[3]

2214 **4** 1¼ **Mr Potter**[21] 8288 3-9-7 **55**...(e) ConnorBeasley 2 51
(Richard Guest) *hld up: hdwy far side of gp over 2f out: rdn over 1f out: kpt on same pce fnl f* **6/1**[3]

6050 **5** nk **Stanlow**[10] 8471 6-9-1 **49** ow3......................................(v) DougieCostello 7 45
(Michael Mullineaux) *dwlt: bhd on nr side of gp: drvn and outpcd 3f out: rallied fnl f: kpt on: nt pce to chal* **50/1**

0053 **6** ½ **Mr Sundowner (USA)**[20] 8307 4-9-1 **52**..................(t) NathanEvans(3) 13 46
(Wilf Storey) *prom on nr side of gp: drvn and edgd lft over 2f out: kpt on same pce over 1f out* **10/3**[1]

0000 **7** 1 **Secret Interlude (IRE)**[37] 8070 3-8-8 **49**................ BenSanderson(7) 11 41
(Roger Fell) *dwlt: bhd on nr side of gp: outpcd over 2f out: sme late hdwy: nvr on terms* **40/1**

2514 **8** nk **Rosie Crowe (IRE)**[22] 8278 4-9-2 **50**..................... JosephineGordon 10 41
(Shaun Harris) *prom on nr side of gp: rdn along over 2f out: wknd over 1f out* **22/1**

2032 **9** 1 **Canford Belle**[14] 8401 3-9-1 **54**... PhilDennis(5) 9 43
(Grant Tuer) *midfield in centre: rdn and outpcd over 2f out: btn over 1f out* **12/1**

0000 **10** ½ **Symbolic Star (IRE)**[14] 8400 4-8-12 **53**................ CallumRodriguez(7) 5 40
(Barry Murtagh) *hld up on far side of gp: stdy hdwy and in tch bef 1/2-way: rdn and wknd fr 2f out* **22/1**

0046 **11** 1¼ **Jebel Tara**[21] 8288 11-8-13 **47**.......................................(bt) PJMcDonald 4 31
(Alistair Whillans) *midfield in centre: drvn and outpcd over 2f out: btn over 1f out* **40/1**

252 **12** 3 **Nefetari**[21] 8289 3-8-13 **47**...(b) TomEaves 6 24
(Alan Brown) *led in centre: edgd rt and hdd over 2f out: wknd wl over 1f out* **33/1**

4004 **13** nk **Sea Of Green**[9] 8483 4-8-9 **46** oh1............................ GeorgeDowning(3) 8 22
(Jim Goldie) *dwlt: t.k.h: hld up centre: drvn over 2f out: sn wknd* **18/1**

5665 **14** 8 **The Big Day (IRE)**[102] 6631 3-8-12 **53**.................... KieranSchofield(7) 12 9
(Nigel Tinkler) *in tch on nr side of gp: rdn and hung bdly lft fr wl over 2f out: sn struggling* **33/1**

1m 26.85s (0.65) **Going Correction** +0.125s/f (Slow) **14** Ran SP% **115.2**
Speed ratings (Par 101): **101,99,97,96,95 95,94,93,92,92 90,87,86,77**
CSF £35.00 CT £219.35 TOTE £6.10: £2.30, £2.50, £2.30; EX 44.40 Trifecta £315.70.
Owner Rug, Grub & Pub Partnership **Bred** Reveley Farms **Trained** Lingdale, Redcar & Cleveland

FOCUS
Only a few in-form contenders in an ordinary event and the winner landed a bit of a punt. The winner has been rated similar to his C&D win in October.
T/Plt: £30.50 to a £1 stake. Pool: £120,081.30 - 2,872.53 winning units T/Qpdt: £9.40 to a £1 stake. Pool: £8,626.70 - 676.90 winning units **Richard Young**

8554 LINGFIELD (L-H)
Saturday, December 31

OFFICIAL GOING: Polytrack: standard
Wind: almost nil Weather: mostly cloudy

8590 SUNBETS.CO.UK H'CAP 1m 1y(P)
12:25 (12:25) (Class 5) (0-75,77) 3-Y-O **£3,234** (£962; £481; £240) **Stalls** High

Form RPR

2406 **1** **Byres Road**[17] 8356 3-9-11 **77**.. JasonHart 4 85
(Mark Johnston) *trckd ldr: edgd lft over 1f out: led ent fnl f: r.o wl: rdn out* **6/1**

1020 **2** ½ **Footlight**[22] 8286 3-9-4 **70**.. TonyHamilton 2 77
(Richard Fahey) *trckd ldr: effrt on inner whn nt clr run and swtchd rt over 1f out: sn rdn: r.o wl fnl 120yds: wnt 2nd cl home* **14/1**

405 **3** 1¼ **Rivers Of Asia**[30] 8178 3-9-6 **72**...(t) AdamKirby 1 76
(Philip McBride) *led: rdn over 2f out: hdd ent fnl f: no ex* **7/1**

0-05 **4** 1¼ **Torment**[17] 8356 3-9-7 **73**.. SeanLevey 10 74
(Richard Hannon) *hld up: hdwy 2 out: sn rdn: kpt on same pce fnl f* **7/1**

5014 **5** ½ **Ebbisham (IRE)**[31] 8154 3-9-1 **67**.. JimCrowley 9 67
(Jim Boyle) *mid-div: rdn 2f out: nt pce to get involved* **4/1**[2]

5123 **6** 1 **Music Major**[24] 8248 3-9-1 **67**....................................... AdamBeschizza 7 65
(Michael Attwater) *hld up: rdn 2f out: little imp* **5/1**[3]

4530 **7** hd **Pc Dixon**[113] 6294 3-8-12 **67**.. GeorgeDowning(3) 8 64
(Mick Channon) *s.i.s: bhd: sme prog over 1f out: no further imp fnl f* **25/1**

2320 **8** 3¾ **Polymnia**[16] 8381 3-8-9 **68**.. TinaSmith(7) 6 57
(Richard Hannon) *mid-div: rdn over 2f out: nvr threatened: fdd fnl f* **16/1**

0P00 **9** 3½ **Kristoff (IRE)**[93] 6891 3-8-0 **59** oh14.............................. RhiainIngram(7) 5 40
(Jim Boyle) *trckd ldrs tl rdn over 2f out: hung lft and wknd over 1f out* **66/1**

3113 **10** 6 **German Whip**[103] 6629 3-9-2 **71**.................................. HectorCrouch(3) 3 38
(Gary Moore) *mid-div: rdn over 2f out: wknd over 1f out* **7/2**[1]

1m 35.84s (-2.36) **Going Correction** -0.225s/f (Stan) **10** Ran SP% **116.1**
Speed ratings (Par 102): **102,101,100,99,98 97,97,93,90,84**
CSF £85.71 CT £458.26 TOTE £7.10: £2.40, £4.30, £2.50; EX 91.30 Trifecta £424.80.
Owner Robin Holleyhead **Bred** Usk Valley Stud **Trained** Middleham Moor, N Yorks

FOCUS
The early pace was pretty steady and few got into it, the first three racing in the first three places virtually throughout.

8591 32RED CASINO MEDIAN AUCTION MAIDEN STKS 7f 1y(P)
12:55 (12:57) (Class 6) 2-Y-O **£2,911** (£866; £432; £216) **Stalls** Low

Form RPR

06 **1** **Touch Me (IRE)**[15] 8397 2-8-9 0..............................[1] JordanVaughan(5) 2 63
(K R Burke) *trckd ldrs: rdn to chal wl over 1f out: led fnl 100yds: kpt on wl* **16/1**

6440 **2** ½ **Peachey Carnehan**[85] 7109 2-9-5 63..............................(v[1]) AdamKirby 1 67
(Michael Attwater) *led: rdn 2f out: kpt on tl no ex and hdd fnl 100yds* **10/1**

03 **3** 1 **Settle Petal**[17] 8355 2-9-0 0... JFEgan 3 59
(Pat Phelan) *trckd ldrs: rdn 2f out: kpt on ins fnl f* **7/1**[3]

3060 **4** ¾ **Suffragette City (IRE)**[11] 8466 2-9-0 66................(b[1]) TomMarquand 11 57
(Richard Hannon) *hld up: shkn up over 2f out: hdwy over 1f out: r.o wl fnl f but n.d to ldrs* **9/4**[1]

6 **5** 2 **Critical Thinking (IRE)**[29] 8189 2-9-5 0.................... AdamBeschizza 10 57
(Julia Feilden) *mid-div: rdn over 2f out: kpt on ins fnl f but nt pce to get on terms* **10/1**

6 nk **Beatisa** 2-9-0 0... RichardKingscote 8 51+
(Ed Walker) *hld up: hung lft fnl 2f: kpt o but no threat fnl f* **15/2**

06 **7** 1 **Innstigator**[17] 8352 2-9-2 0.. HectorCrouch(3) 12 53
(Ralph J Smith) *hld up: hdwy on outer over 3f out: rdn over 2f out: no further imp (sddle slipped)* **14/1**

0 **8** ¾ **Malt Teaser (FR)**[9] 8486 2-9-5 0.. KierenFox 13 51
(John Best) *hld up towards rr: sme late prog: nvr any danger* **33/1**

4 **9** shd **Zilza (IRE)**[17] 8362 2-9-0 0.. MartinDwyer 4 46
(Conrad Allen) *prom tl rdn over 2f out: kpt on tl no ex fnl 120yds* **4/1**[2]

00 **10** ½ **Eugenie Feather (USA)**[17] 8355 2-9-0 0...................... DanielMuscutt 9 45
(Marco Botti) *mid-div: rdn over 2f out: nvr threatened: fdd fnl f* **22/1**

11 2¼ **Dawn Goddess** 2-9-0 0.. TimmyMurphy 7 39
(Gary Moore) *nvr bttr than mid-div* **33/1**

12 13 **Maarit (IRE)** 2-9-0 0.. ShaneKelly 5
(Denis Coakley) *mid-div: rdn over 2f out: wkng whn squeezed up jst over 1f out* **16/1**

1m 23.85s (-0.95) **Going Correction** -0.225s/f (Stan) **12** Ran SP% **121.9**
Speed ratings (Par 94): **96,95,94,93,91 90,89,88,88,88 85,70**
CSF £168.38 TOTE £23.30: £5.40, £2.80, £2.00; EX 243.80 Trifecta £2733.90.
Owner Hassan Al Abdulmalik **Bred** H A A M Al-Abdulmalik **Trained** Middleham Moor, N Yorks

FOCUS
Just a modest maiden, and in something of a carbon copy of the first race on the card, Adam Kirby controlled the pace in front most of the way but was denied late on. The race could be rated up to 5lb higher around those behind the first two, but this looks a sensible starting level.

8592 32RED.COM NURSERY H'CAP 7f 1y(P)
1:30 (1:31) (Class 4) (0-85,80) 2-Y-O **£4,528** (£1,347; £673; £336) **Stalls** Low

Form RPR

0041 **1** **Reign On**[31] 8159 2-9-0 **76**.. HectorCrouch(3) 1 80+
(Ralph Beckett) *trckd ldrs: rdn over 1f out: led ins fnl f: kpt on wl* **9/4**[1]

3603 **2** ¾ **Tailor's Row (USA)**[15] 8405 2-9-4 **77**.................................. JasonHart 5 79
(Mark Johnston) *led: rdn 2f out: hdd ins fnl f: kpt on* **9/1**

3000 **3** ½ **Mullarkey**[11] 8466 2-8-10 **69**... KierenFox 2 70
(John Best) *trckd ldr: rdn and ev ch 2f out tl ent fnl f: kpt on* **9/1**

3125 **4** ½ **Sans Souci Bay**[17] 8360 2-9-5 **78**...................................... SeanLevey 7 77
(Richard Hannon) *trckd ldrs: rdn over 1f out: r.o wl fnl 120yds* **6/1**

2631 **5** 3½ **Chica De La Noche**[80] 7277 2-9-3 **76**...................................... JFEgan 4 66
(Simon Dow) *hld up in tch: rdn over 2f out: nt pce to get involved* **9/2**[3]

410 **6** ¾ **Red Gunner**[15] 8405 2-9-4 **77**.......................................[1] AdamKirby 6 65
(William Haggas) *hld up in tch: rdn over 2f out: nt pce to get on terms* **4/1**[2]

2106 **7** *6* **Bee Case**[100] 6697 2-9-2 **80** HollieDoyle(5) 3 52+
(Simon Dow) *sitting down whn stalls opened: nvr rcvrd: a detached in last* **12/1**
1m 25.26s (0.46) **Going Correction** -0.225s/f (Stan) **7** Ran SP% **110.9**
Speed ratings (Par 98): **88,87,86,86,82 81,74**
CSF £21.78 TOTE £2.50: £1.40, £4.40; EX 22.60 Trifecta £177.60.
Owner What Asham Partnership **Bred** J A And M A Knox **Trained** Kimpton, Hants

FOCUS
A fair nursery and the winner looks progressive. The level is quite straightforward behind the winner.

8593 SUNBETS BET £10 GET £20 FREE H'CAP 1m 1y(P)
2:05 (2:05) (Class 2) (0-105,100) 3-Y-O+ **£11,971** (£3,583; £1,791; £896; £446) **Stalls** High

Form RPR
0100 **1** **My Target (IRE)**[30] 8177 5-8-13 **89** ConnorBeasley 2 97
(Michael Wigham) *mid-div: hdwy over 2f out: rdn over 1f out: r.o strly fnl f: led fnl 75yds* **5/1**[2]
1112 **2** *½* **Qaffaal (USA)**[23] 8279 5-8-8 **87** NathanEvans(3) 9 93
(Michael Easterby) *mid-div: swtchd rt and rdn over 1f out: r.o wl ins fnl f: snatched 2nd fnl stride* **9/2**[1]
5103 **3** *hd* **Mr Bossy Boots (IRE)**[24] 8256 5-9-4 **94** (t) JimCrowley 10 100
(Amanda Perrett) *trckd ldrs: rdn over 2f out: ev ch fnl 120yds: no ex cl home: lost 2nd fnl stride* **8/1**
3265 **4** *½* **Bold Prediction (IRE)**[140] 5419 6-8-13 **89** ThomasBrown 6 94
(Ed Walker) *broke wl: led: rdn 2f out: hdd fnl 75yds: no ex* **12/1**
4550 **5** *hd* **Third Time Lucky (IRE)**[21] 8317 4-9-9 **99** TonyHamilton 7 104+
(Richard Fahey) *mid-div: nt clr run briefly ent fnl f: r.o wl fnl 120yds* **9/2**[1]
5400 **6** *½* **Georgian Bay (IRE)**[10] 8478 6-8-10 **91** (v) JordanVaughan(5) 8 94
(K R Burke) *hld up: hung lft ent fnl f but kpt on wl wout ever looking dangerous* **10/1**
0221 **7** *½* **Alfred Hutchinson**[42] 8029 8-9-10 **100** (p) AdamKirby 11 102+
(David O'Meara) *s.i.s: bhd: nt clr run briefly 1f out: fin strly but nvr a threat* **15/2**[3]
0P30 **8** *1* **Passing Star**[50] 7903 5-8-4 **83** CallumShepherd(3) 1 83
(Charles Hills) *in tch: rdn to chse ldrs wl over 1f out: no ex fnl 120yds* **16/1**
6501 **9** *¾* **Presumido (IRE)**[17] 8356 6-8-11 **87** JFEgan 3 85
(Simon Dow) *hld up: r.o ins fnl f but nvr threatening to get on terms* **10/1**
0030 **10** *1 ½* **Grey Mirage**[24] 8256 7-9-5 **95** (p) JosephineGordon 5 90
(Marco Botti) *trckd ldrs: rdn 2f out: fdd fnl f* **16/1**
4000 **11** *3* **Majestic Moon (IRE)**[23] 8279 6-9-7 **97** AdamBeschizza 4 85
(Julia Feilden) *racd keenly: sn pressing ldr: rdn 2f out: wknd fnl f* **66/1**
0000 **12** *6* **Lunar Deity**[23] 8279 7-8-11 **94** MillyNaseb(7) 12 68
(Stuart Williams) *s.i.s: a towards rr* **33/1**
1m 34.34s (-3.86) **Going Correction** -0.225s/f (Stan) **12** Ran SP% **118.0**
Speed ratings (Par 109): **110,109,109,108,108 108,107,106,105,104 101,95**
CSF £27.60 CT £182.09 TOTE £6.00: £2.20, £2.30, £2.90; EX 32.80 Trifecta £260.50.
Owner G Linder, M Wigham & J Williams **Bred** Darley **Trained** Newmarket, Suffolk

FOCUS
A good handicap. They finished in a bit of a heap as the pace horses weakened and the closers came through. The course record was lowered by 0.17sec.

8594 BETWAY MIDDLE DISTANCE H'CAP 1m 4f (P)
2:40 (2:43) (Class 3) (0-95,95) 3-Y-O+ **£7,561** (£2,263; £1,131; £566; £282) **Stalls** Low

Form RPR
2214 **1** **Burcan (FR)**[35] 8123 4-9-2 **90** DanielMuscutt 1 98
(Marco Botti) *mid-div: hdwy over 2f out: rdn over 1f out: led ins fnl f: strly chal fnl 120yds: hld on* **7/1**[3]
0-56 **2** *nse* **Alinstante**[26] 8231 3-8-9 **88** RyanPowell 3 96+
(Sir Mark Prescott Bt) *hld up towards rr: hdwy on inner fnl bnd: nt clr run whn swtchd lft ent fnl f: rdn for str chal fnl 120yds: jst hld* **20/1**
6312 **3** *1* **Natural Scenery**[26] 8231 3-8-9 **91** AlistairRawlinson(3) 8 97+
(Saeed bin Suroor) *mid-div: hdwy to ld over 2f out: rdn over 1f out: hdd ins fnl f: no ex* **10/11**[1]
4525 **4** *¾* **Sennockian Star**[4] 8539 6-8-11 **85** JasonHart 7 90+
(Mark Johnston) *trckd ldrs: lost pl bhd wkng horse over 2f out: rdn wl over 1f out: styd on wl but hld fnl f* **16/1**
3153 **5** *nk* **Rydan (IRE)**[14] 8424 5-9-2 **90** (v) ShaneKelly 4 94
(Gary Moore) *mid-div: rdn 2f out: styd on fnl f* **20/1**
6330 **6** *2 ¼* **Royal Marskell**[28] 8210 7-9-2 **90** AdamKirby 5 91
(Gay Kelleway) *hld up towards rr: rdn and hdwy 3f out: ev ch wl over 1f out: wknd ent fnl f* **33/1**
540 **7** *nse* **Silver Quay (IRE)**[89] 7015 4-9-4 **92** GeorgeBaker 10 93
(Jamie Osborne) *hld up towards rr: rdn and hdwy jst over 1f out: styd on fnl f but no threat* **14/1**
1212 **8** *3* **Ride The Lightning**[13] 8447 3-8-2 **81** JosephineGordon 2 77
(Archie Watson) *disp ld tl rdn over 2f out: fdd fnl f* **8/1**
0020 **9** *5* **Havana Beat (IRE)**[84] 7150 6-9-2 **93** GeorgeDowning(3) 11 81
(Tony Carroll) *sn trcking ldrs: pushed along over 4f out: wknd 2f out* **40/1**
0343 **10** *1 ¾* **Wrangler**[28] 8210 5-8-8 **87** GeorgiaCox(5) 6 72
(William Haggas) *disp ld tl rdn over 2f out: sn wknd* **5/1**[2]
2m 27.09s (-5.91) **Going Correction** -0.225s/f (Stan) course record
WFA 3 from 4yo+ 5lb **10** Ran SP% **120.1**
Speed ratings (Par 107): **110,109,109,108,108 107,107,105,101,100**
CSF £140.04 CT £245.90 TOTE £6.90: £2.00, £6.90, £1.10; EX 158.90 Trifecta £575.60.
Owner Raed El Youssef **Bred** S F Bloodstock LLC **Trained** Newmarket, Suffolk

FOCUS
A good handicap and a tight finish. Another track record was broken here, the previous standard being beaten by 0.84sec.

8595 BETWAY APP H'CAP 6f 1y(P)
3:15 (3:15) (Class 6) (0-65,67) 3-Y-O+ **£3,234** (£962; £481; £240) **Stalls** Low

Form RPR
0000 **1** **Born To Finish (IRE)**[114] 6249 3-9-0 **58** (p) MartinLane 1 66
(Jeremy Gask) *hld up: hdwy over 1f out: str run ins fnl f: led fnl 60yds: readily* **3/1**[1]
6002 **2** *1 ½* **Colourbearer (IRE)**[17] 8365 9-9-7 **65** (t) AdamBeschizza 2 69
(Charlie Wallis) *led: rdn 2 l clr wl over 1f out: hdd fnl 60yds: no ex* **5/1**[2]
5406 **3** *1 ¼* **Triple Dream**[17] 8365 11-9-1 **62** HectorCrouch(3) 9 62
(Milton Bradley) *chsd ldrs: rdn to chse ldr jst over 1f out tl ins fnl f: kpt on same pce* **16/1**
3445 **4** *¾* **Indian Affair**[30] 8181 6-9-9 **67** (bt) DougieCostello 10 65
(Milton Bradley) *mid-div: rdn and hdwy over 1f out: kpt on ins fnl f* **8/1**
0003 **5** *hd* **Musical Taste**[17] 8358 3-9-1 **59** JFEgan 3 56
(Pat Phelan) *mid-diviion: drvn along over 3f out: kpt on ins fnl f: nvr gng pce to get involved* **8/1**
5652 **6** *½* **Compton Prince**[21] 8316 7-9-3 **61** (b) RichardKingscote 12 56
(Milton Bradley) *pressed ldr tl rdn wl over 1f out: no ex fnl 120yds* **7/1**
0000 **7** *1 ¼* **Cloak And Degas (IRE)**[63] 7693 4-8-13 **57** (b) RyanTate 4 49
(Tim McCarthy) *trckd ldrs: rdn over 2f out: one pce fnl f* **25/1**
0006 **8** *½* **City Of Angkor Wat (IRE)**[4] 8535 6-9-4 **62** (p) TimmyMurphy 6 52
(Conor Dore) *hmpd s: towards rr: sme late prog: nvr a threat* **8/1**
6000 **9** *½* **Indus Valley (IRE)**[88] 7048 9-8-11 **55** (b) KieranO'Neill 7 44
(Lee Carter) *towards rr: sme late prog: n.d* **18/1**
6055 **10** *7* **Jumeirah Star (USA)**[17] 8358 3-9-4 **62** (v) AdamKirby 5 30
(Robert Cowell) *wnt lft s: reminders: mid-div: drvn 3f out: wknd 2f out* **11/2**[3]
600 **11** *¾* **Frap**[12] 8457 3-8-12 **56** StevieDonohoe 8 21
(Ian Williams) *sn outpcd: a towards rr* **16/1**
1m 10.31s (-1.59) **Going Correction** -0.225s/f (Stan) **11** Ran SP% **123.8**
Speed ratings (Par 101): **101,99,97,96,96 95,93,93,92,83 82**
CSF £18.55 CT £219.19 TOTE £4.20: £1.80, £2.10, £5.00; EX 24.70 Trifecta £222.50.
Owner Crowd Racing Partnership **Bred** B Kennedy & Mrs Ann Marie Kennedy **Trained** Stockbridge, Hants

FOCUS
A punt was landed in this modest sprint. The level has a standard feel about it behind the winner.

8596 BETWAY H'CAP 5f 6y(P)
3:45 (3:46) (Class 6) (0-60,60) 3-Y-O+ **£3,234** (£962; £481; £240) **Stalls** High

Form RPR
0453 **1** **Temple Road (IRE)**[4] 8535 8-9-7 **60** (bt) GeorgeBaker 6 68
(Milton Bradley) *hld up: hdwy over 1f out: led fnl 120yds: r.o wl: readily* **11/10**[1]
0055 **2** *¾* **Roy's Legacy**[10] 8485 7-8-10 **54** CharlieBennett(5) 4 59
(Shaun Harris) *led: rdn wl over 1f out: hdd fnl 120yds: no ex* **8/1**
0444 **3** *¾* **Pharoh Jake**[14] 8430 8-9-7 **60** WilliamCarson 2 63
(John Bridger) *trckd ldrs: rdn over 1f out: kpt on same pce* **5/1**[2]
5206 **4** *¾* **Frank The Barber (IRE)**[11] 8474 4-9-4 **57** (bt) AdamBeschizza 5 57
(Steph Hollinshead) *racd keenly: trckd ldrs: rdn over 1f out: kpt on same pce fnl f* **12/1**
0120 **5** *1 ¼* **Ask The Guru**[14] 8429 6-9-4 **57** (p) KierenFox 1 52
(Michael Attwater) *in tch: rdn 2f out: kpt on but nt pce to get on terms* **6/1**[3]
0000 **6** *hd* **Charlie Lad**[15] 8409 4-9-0 **53** JosephineGordon 8 48
(Daniel Mark Loughnane) *in tch: rdn 2f out: sn one pce* **14/1**
3206 **7** *nk* **Deer Song**[24] 8248 3-9-3 **56** DannyBrock 7 50
(John Bridger) *trckd ldrs: rdn wl over 1f out: sn one pae* **20/1**
6501 **8** *4 ½* **Captain Scooby**[15] 8409 10-9-3 **56** (b) JFEgan 3 33
(Richard Guest) *slowly away: sn rousted along: a last* **8/1**
58.2s (-0.60) **Going Correction** -0.225s/f (Stan) **8** Ran SP% **119.9**
Speed ratings (Par 101): **95,93,92,91,89 89,88,81**
CSF £11.68 CT £35.02 TOTE £2.00: £1.10, £2.30, £1.80; EX 12.30 Trifecta £46.80.
Owner J M Bradley **Bred** Paul Monaghan **Trained** Sedbury, Gloucs

FOCUS
An ordinary sprint, but the well-backed favourite won in cosy fashion.
T/Plt: £279.10 to a £1 stake. Pool: £91,043.38 - 238.07 winning units. T/Qpdt: £13.80 to a £1 stake. Pool: £8,784.56 - 470.54 winning units. **Tim Mitchell**

8579a (Foreign Racing) - See Raceform Interactive

Index to meetings Flat 2016

† Abandoned
* All-Weather
(M) Mixed meeting

INDEX TO FLAT RACING

Horses are shown in alphabetical order; the trainer's name follows the name of the horse. The figures to the right are current master ratings for all-weather and turf; the all-weather rating is preceded by the letter 'a'.Underneath the horse's name is its age, colour and sex in abbreviated format e.g. 6 b g indicates the horse is six-years-old, bay in colour, and a gelding.The descriptive details are followed by the race numbers of the races in which it has taken part in chronological order; a superscript figure indicates its finishing position in that race (brackets indicate it was the winner of the race).

Aagas (AUS) *Todd Balfour* 66
4 b g Golden Snake(USA) Brindabella (AUS) (Bellotto (USA))
7826a^{9}

Aaman (IRE) *Bernard Llewellyn* a54 46
10 gr g Dubai Destination(USA) Amellnaa (IRE) (Sadler's Wells (USA))
1830^{5}

Aardwolf (USA) *Mark Johnston* a81 91
2 bb g Cape Cross(IRE) Desert Gazelle (USA) (Smart Strike (CAN))
(3058) 3356^{4} (4090) 4925a^{7} 5416^{5} 6869^{5} 7493^{3}

Aared (IRE) *Kevin Prendergast* a79 93
4 b g Shamardal(USA) Adaala (USA) (Sahm (USA))
5941a^{3}

Abaco Ridge *Ralph Beckett* 70
3 b f Bahamian Bounty Echo Ridge (IRE) (Oratorio (IRE))
1524^{11} 1892^{4} 2823^{6}

Abacus *Michael Bell*
2 b c Sixties Icon Friendlier (Zafonic (USA))
7470^{10}

Abareeq *Mark Johnston* a92 81
3 ch g Haatef(USA) Hafawa (IRE) (Intikhab (USA))
770^{2} ◆ (976) ◆ 1603^{8} 2029^{11} 3187^{9} (3783) 4453^{2} 4797^{13} 5292^{6} 5892^{2} 6126^{12} 7608^{4} 8049^{14}

Abatement *Roger Charlton* 63
2 b g Bated Breath Iwunder (IRE) (King's Best (USA))
4989^{6} 6108^{10}

Abba Forever (FR) *R Rohne*
2 gr f Soave(GER) Abbasanta (IRE) (Highest Honor (FR))
5698a^{15}

Abberley Dancer (IRE) *J S Moore* a69 57
3 b f Lilbourne Lad(IRE) Babberina (IRE) (Danehill Dancer (IRE))
152^{3} ◆ 459^{5} 638^{4} 2373^{7} 2824^{7} 3725^{3} 4085^{5} 5078^{5}

Abbey Angel (IRE) *Richard Fahey* a90 90
4 b m Arcano(IRE) Sanna Bay (IRE) (Refuse To Bend (IRE))
172^{2} (240) (422) 749^{7} 886^{4} 1016a^{8}

Abdon *Sir Michael Stoute* 113
3 b c Cacique(IRE) Kinnaird (IRE) (Dr Devious (IRE))
1866^{2} ◆ 3296^{8} (5160) 6505^{3} 7152^{4}

Abe Lincoln (USA) *Jeremy Noseda* a99 104
3 b c Discreet Cat(USA) Truly Blushed (USA) (Yes It's True (USA))
836^{10} 2161^{5} 3299^{2}

Abendwind (GER) *Waldemar Hickst* 95
5 b g Wiesenpfad(FR) Adela (GER) (Tannenkonig (IRE))
7564a^{9}

Aberdonian *Jeremy Gask* a52
2 b g Royal Applause Delaware Dancer (IRE) (Danehill Dancer (IRE))
3472^{6} 4209^{6} 4938^{10}

Aberlady (USA) *Sir Michael Stoute* a71 69
3 bb f Arch(USA) Visit (Oasis Dream)
2050^{5} 2770^{5} ◆ 3599^{3} 5302^{4} 5935^{3} 6851^{6}

Abertillery *Michael Blanshard* a57 47
4 b g Shamardal(USA) Nantyglo (Mark Of Esteem (IRE))
141^{7} 709^{5} 950^{6} 2210^{11} 3489^{7} 4531^{7} 4995^{9} 6651^{12} 6891^{7}

Abiding Star (USA) *Edward Allard* a104
3 b c Uncle Mo(USA) Abiding (USA) (Dynaformer (USA))
2499a^{11}

Abiento (IRE) *Richard Fahey* 78
2 b g Requinto(IRE) Nose One's Way (IRE) (Revoque (IRE))
3516^{3} 4343^{2} ◆ 4866^{5} 5615^{8} (6319) 6954^{13}

Abingdon (USA) *Sir Michael Stoute* a69 111
3 b f Street Cry(IRE) Justlookdontouch (IRE) (Galileo (IRE))
(1989) (3060) 4883^{2} (5587) ◆ 6259^{5}

Abi Scarlet (IRE) *Scott Dixon* a80 56
7 b m Baltic King Petarga (Petong)
135^{5} 276^{5} 581^{3} 893^{11} 1298^{2} 1401^{4}

A Bit Of Ginger *Ann Duffield* 48
2 b f Camacho Hel's Angel (IRE) (Pyrus (USA))
5756^{6} 6448^{6} 6641^{7} 7041^{9}

Ablaze *Laura Mongan* a53 44
2 ch f Arcano(IRE) Angry Bark (USA) (Woodman (USA))
2764^{6} 4457^{8} 5764^{9}

Able Dash *Michael Blake* a73 71
6 ch g Dutch Art Evasive Quality (FR) (Highest Honor (FR))
1002^{4} 1434^{4} 2605^{P}

Able Friend (AUS) *John Moore* 128
6 ch g Shamardal(USA) Ponte Piccolo (NZ) (Volksraad)
8332a^{6}

Able Jack *Andrew Balding* a77 85
3 b g Iffraaj Solva (Singspiel (IRE))
1270^{9} 4010^{10} (4563) 4789^{5} 6123^{7}

Abonos (IRE) *Simon West* a56 10
4 b m Approve(IRE) Topiary (IRE) (Selkirk (USA))
136^{7} 937^{7} 1495^{15} 1676^{15} 2778^{9}

Aboulie (IRE) *J-C Rouget* 101
3 b f Exceed And Excel(AUS) Anja (IRE) (Indian Ridge)
1374a^{14} 2232a^{9}

About Glory *Richard Hannon* 52
2 b c Nayef(USA) Lemon Rock (Green Desert (USA))
7503^{12}

Abouttimeyoutoldme *Ralph Beckett*
2 ch g Mastercraftsman(IRE) Mary Boleyn (IRE) (King's Best (USA))
6945^{8} 7458^{9}

Above N Beyond *Tom Dascombe* a93 108
3 ch c Exceed And Excel(AUS) Hill Welcome (Most Welcome)
836^{6} 1975^{2} 2473^{3} 3299^{23} 4887^{5} (6778)

Above The Rest (IRE) *David Barron* a84 106
5 b g Excellent Art Aspasias Tizzy (USA) (Tiznow (USA))
1627^{12} 3346^{5} 4665^{2} 5640^{3} ◆ 5871^{5} 6382a^{15} (6764)

A Boy Named Sue *Peter Niven* a38 51
3 b g Monsieur Bond(IRE) Elusive Sue (USA) (Elusive Quality (USA))
2784^{7} 3224^{6} 4006^{11} 4600^{3} 4973^{6} 5732^{10}

Abraham (IRE) *J R Barry* a85 92
4 b g Hernando(FR) Guana (FR) (Sillery (USA))
3680a^{4} 4850a^{2}

Abrahams Blessing (IRE) *R P Burns* a58 49
8 b g Fasliyev(USA) Ouija's Sister (Groom Dancer (USA))
(6422) (Dead)

Absalon (USA) *F Head* a87 93
5 ch g Giant's Causeway(USA) Wakigoer (USA) (Miswaki (USA))
7525a^{11}

Absolute Blast (IRE) *Iain Jardine* a84 97
4 b m Kodiac Perfect Fun (Marju (IRE))
8286^{2} ◆

Absolutely Awesome *Scott Dixon* a52 60
2 ch c Choisir(AUS) Milton Of Campsie (Medicean)
1199^{5} 1520^{4} 8526^{4}

Absolutely So (IRE) *Andrew Balding* a98 113
6 b g Acclamation Week End (Selkirk (USA))
2030^{5} 3386^{4} 6558^{6} 7213^{3} 7822^{5}

Absolute Zero (IRE) *Roger Varian* 94
3 b g Cape Cross(IRE) Emsiyah (USA) (Bernardini (USA))
2299^{5} 2891^{9} 3824^{3} (4459) (4945) 5240^{5} 6489^{3} 6753^{15} 7499^{3}

Abstraction (IRE) *Miss Natalia Lupini* a98 106
6 b h Majestic Missile(IRE) Bronze Queen (IRE) (Invincible Spirit (IRE))
745^{8} 1730a^{3} 3696a^{13} 4735^{9}

Abu Khadra (IRE) *Richard Fahey* 47
3 b c Oasis Dream Flashy Wings (Zafonic (USA))
2809^{6}

Abundant Courage (IRE) *Brian Meehan* a65 55
2 gr g Zebedee Dane Thyme (IRE) (Danetime (IRE))
5077^{9} 6673^{4} 7122^{8} 7900^{3} 8097^{9}

Abushamah (IRE) *Ruth Carr* 89
5 b g Nayef(USA) Adaala (USA) (Sahm (USA))
1122^{7} ◆ 1380^{2} 1924^{9} 2256^{2} 2527^{6} (3364) 4368^{4} 4894^{6} 5180^{11} 5419^{2} 5514^{4} 6217^{13} 6956^{7}

Acapulco (USA) *Wesley A Ward* a90 113
3 ch f Scat Daddy(USA) Global Finance (USA) (End Sweep (USA))
7829a^{6}

Accelerate (USA) *John W Sadler* a113
3 ch c Lookin At Lucky(USA) Issues (USA) (Awesome Again (CAN))
7808a^{3}

Accento *Hugo Palmer* a73 70
2 b g Elusive Quality(USA) Azameera (IRE) (Azamour (IRE))
4545^{4} 5676^{3}

Accession (IRE) *Charlie Fellowes* a96 104
7 b g Acclamation Pivotal's Princess (IRE) (Pivotal)
(1441) 2027^{14} 3386^{16} 4152^{8} 5174^{2} 6547^{3} 7241^{3}

Accidental Agent *Eve Johnson Houghton* 87
2 b c Delegator Roodle (Xaar)
4270^{6} (4907) 5829^{2} ◆ (6950)

Accino (GER) *R Rohne* 91
4 bb h Mamool(IRE) Appena La (IRE) (Tirol)
2516a^{8}

Accladora *Mark Johnston* a63 61
2 b f Acclamation Keladora (USA) (Crafty Prospector (USA))
1342^{4} 1583^{3} 2104^{5} 6440^{7} 6963^{6} 7110^{3} 7570^{10}

Acclaim The Nation (IRE) *Eric Alston* a80 68
3 b g Acclamation Dani Ridge (IRE) (Indian Ridge)
2333^{2} ◆ (3879) ◆ 5643^{6} 6133^{6} 6476^{9}

Acclamatio (IRE) *A J Martin* a54 54
2 b g Acclamation Incitatus Girl (IRE) (Galileo (IRE))
7387a^{6}

Acclio (IRE) *James Tate* a88 87
5 b m Acclamation Hovering (IRE) (In The Wings)
(2032) 3405^{4} 5677^{4} (6246)

Accord D'Argent (FR) *Y Barberot* a79 65
3 gr f Kendargent(FR) Accordia (USA) (Smart Strike (CAN))
(128a)

Accurate *A Fabre* a95 96
3 b c Zoffany(IRE) More Respect (IRE) (Spectrum (IRE))
2141a^{9} 7897a^{8}

Ace Master *Roy Bowring* a89 78
8 ch g Ballet Master(USA) Ace Maite (Komaite (USA))
2238^{6} 2540^{5} 3821^{5} 4496^{3} (5034)

Ace Of Arts (IRE) *P J F Murphy* a54 10
4 b m Art Connoisseur(IRE) Alleged Touch (USA) (Alleged (USA))
2610^{9}

Ace Rebel *Richard Spencer*
3 ch c Bahamian Bounty Quadrophenia (College Chapel)
2039^{9}

Acertwo *Joseph Tuite* a82 59
2 b f Approve(IRE) Annellis (UAE) (Diesis)
4756^{14} 5258^{2} 5511^{4} 6412^{6} (6896) (7690) (8047)

Aces (IRE) *J E Hammond* 97
4 b h Dark Angel(IRE) Cute Ass (IRE) (Fath (USA))
6391a^{8} 7758a^{5}

Achnaha (IRE) *George Weaver* 98
5 b m Haatef(USA) Sanna Bay (IRE) (Refuse To Bend (IRE))
3088a^{2}

Aclaim (IRE) *Martyn Meade* a79 115
3 b c Acclamation Aris (IRE) (Danroad (AUS))
(1442) ◆ 2719a^{3} 3165^{6} 4393^{7} ◆ 5409^{5} (6075) ◆ (6547) (7115)

A Coeur Ouvert (FR) *H-A Pantall* a14 42
10 b g Dano-Mast Lady Stapara (IRE) (Lead On Time (USA))
1846a^{8}

Acombboy *Marjorie Fife*
2 b g Paco Boy(IRE) Birdie (Alhaarth (IRE))
4765^{14}

Acroleina (IRE) *H Rogers* a67 60
5 b m Captain Gerrard(IRE) Ask Jenny (IRE) (Marju (IRE))
6462a^{3}

Across Dubai *William Haggas* a84
2 b c Cape Cross(IRE) Saadiah (IRE) (Dubai Destination (USA))
(7649) ◆

Across The Stars (IRE) *Sir Michael Stoute* a84 113
3 b c Sea The Stars(IRE) Victoria Cross (IRE) (Mark Of Esteem (IRE))
(1265) 2036^{3} 2896^{10} (3337) ◆ 5557^{3}

Acrux *David Lanigan* a84 50
3 b g Dansili Ikat (IRE) (Pivotal)
4857^{7} (5811) 6484^{8}

Action Pursuits *Adrian Paul Keatley* 55
3 br c Pastoral Pursuits Enthralled (Zafonic (USA))
2957^{5}

Activation *Hughie Morrison* a53 55
4 b g Stimulation(IRE) Patteresa Girl (Auction House (USA))
354^{5} 521^{2}

Active Spirit (IRE) *Doug Watson* a94 87
5 ch g Pivotal Local Spirit (USA) (Lion Cavern (USA))
12a^{10} (407a) 718a^{2}

Act Of Freedom (IRE) *Charlie Appleby* 70
2 gr g Dark Angel(IRE) Sodashy (IRE) (Noverre (USA))
3463^{4} 4040^{4} 5237^{3} 5989^{6}

Actonetaketwo *Ron Hodges* a56 52
6 b m Act One Temple Dancer (Magic Ring (IRE))
127^{5} 334^{8} 355^{3} 563^{8} 787^{6}

Actualisation *John Quinn* 75
2 b g Exceed And Excel(AUS) Eluding (Street Cry (IRE))
3705^{4} 4188^{3} 5107^{4} 6716^{4} 7003^{4} 7406^{3}

Adaay (IRE) *William Haggas* 116
4 b h Kodiac Lady Lucia (IRE) (Royal Applause)
1606^{6} 2691^{8} 3664^{2} 4433a^{4} 6328^{3} 7352^{7}

Adalene *David Simcock* a77 76
3 b f Makfi Marine Bleue (IRE) (Desert Prince (IRE))
1608^{8} 3194^{4} 5025^{4} 7904^{2} 8096^{2} 8366^{2} (8585)

Ada Lovelace *John Gallagher* a80 76
6 b m Byron Satin Braid (Diktat)
1950^{3} (3307) 4198^{10} 4585^{11} 5599^{9}

Adamant (GER) *Sir Michael Stoute* 76
2 gr c Dalakhani(IRE) Attima (Zafonic (USA))
6211^{4} (7013)

Ada Misobel (IRE) *Garry Moss* a55 57
3 b f Alfred Nobel(IRE) Startarette (USA) (Dixieland Band (USA))
248^{7} 896^{3} 1486^{4} (1710) 2784^{2} 3604^{6} 3896^{7} 4498^{2} 4972^{6} 8307^{9}

Adam's Ale *Mark Walford* 97
7 b g Ishiguru(USA) Aqua (Mister Baileys)
1218^{15} 1644^{6} 2188^{15} 2803^{8} 3265^{7} (4345) 4896^{6} 5274^{5} 5780^{6} 6012^{6} 6718^{6}

Addicted To Luck *Jo Hughes* a45 69
3 b f Myboycharlie(IRE) Fortunately (Forzando)
1745^{7} 2044^{11} (3494) 3898^{6} 5230^{4} 6506^{7} 7364^{9}

Addicted To You (IRE) *Mark Johnston* a70 36
2 ch c Medicean Adalawa (IRE) (Barathea (IRE))
7247^{8} 7483^{6} 7962^{4} 8227^{5}

Addictive Dream (IRE) *Garry Moss* a85 91
9 ch g Kheleyf(USA) Nottambula (IRE) (Thatching)
508^{2} 938^{3}

Adham (IRE) *James Tate* a82 92
3 b c Dream Ahead(USA) Leopard Creek (Weldnaas (USA))
45^{3} 322^{4} ◆ 2982^{6} 4014^{5}

Adherence *Tony Coyle* 64
3 b g Sir Percy Straight Laced (Refuse To Bend (IRE))
1587^{4} 2124^{2} 2348^{2} 2772^{6} 3715^{4} 4255^{3} 5481^{13} 6647^{4} 7008^{3} 7582^{5}

Adiator *Neville Bycroft* 70
8 b m Needwood Blade Retaliator (Rudimentary (USA))
1254^{2} 1676^{8} 3484^{9} 4006^{2} 4240^{8} 4454^{6} 5355^{11} 7584^{7} 7747^{13}

Admirable Art (IRE) *Tony Carroll* a59 65
6 b g Excellent Art Demi Voix (Halling (USA))
36^{11} 231^{8} 424^{5} 590^{7} 943^{9} 1295^{6} 1544^{4} (2285a) 3732^{4} ◆ (3973) 6407^{2} (7298)

Admirals Choice *Robert Eddery* a41
3 b g Mount Nelson Admirable Spirit (Invincible Spirit (IRE))
77^{8} 4992^{9}

Admiral's Sunset *Hughie Morrison* a68 80
3 b f Mount Nelson Early Evening (Daylami (IRE))
1962^{2} ◆ 2548^{5} 3063^{2} 7410^{2} 7848^{2}

Admiralty Arch *Richard Hughes* a86 90
2 b c Archipenko(USA) Aldeburgh Music (IRE) (In The Wings)
1579a^{4} (2193) ◆ 3382^{8} 4330a^{2} 5447a^{4} 6260^{15} 6664^{8} 7549^{6} (7879a) 7971a^{3}

Adool (IRE) *D K Weld* 100
3 ch f Teofilo(IRE) Khulood (USA) (Storm Cat (USA))
4326a^{3} (5313a) ◆ 5939a^{9}

Adrakhan (FR) *Wilf Storey* a28 54
5 b g Martaline Annee De La Femme (IRE) (Common Grounds)
2914^{9} 3886^{6} 4235^{11} 5064^{11} 6619^{5} 7044^{7} 7361^{3} 7592^{3} 7746^{9} 8309^{11}

Adventureman *Ruth Carr* a64 70
4 b g Kyllachy Constitute (USA) (Gone West (USA))
1047^{12} 1241^{8} 1841^{5} 2092^{4} (2661) 3220^{8}

Adventure Seeker (IRE) *Ed Vaughan* a97 84
5 gr g Dalakhani(IRE) Adventure (USA) (Unbridled's Song (USA))
2377^{11}

Adventure Zone (IRE) *Lee Carter* a70 55
3 b g Elnadim(USA) Eliza Doolittle (Royal Applause)
253^{7} (335) 443^{5} 613^{5} 4518^{8} (5775) 6268^{6} 7014^{5}

Adventurous (IRE) *Mark Johnston* a104 108
3 b c Invincible Spirit(IRE) Rosia (IRE) (Mr Prospector (USA))
836^{11} 1208^{2} 1424^{4} 1991^{7}

Ad Vitam (IRE) *Suzzanne France* a67 67
8 ch g Ad Valorem(USA) Love Sonnet (Singspiel (IRE))
7325^{10} 7851^{6} 8095^{6} (8482)

Aegean Boy *John Bridger* a54 45
3 b g Paco Boy(IRE) Anosti (Act One)
798^{4} ◆ 935^{7} 1151^{6} 2143^{7} 5088^{9} 7048^{10}

Aegean Secret *Kevin Ryan* 32
2 b c Equiano(FR) Aegean Mystery (Dr Fong (USA))
5476^{10} 5884^{18} 6448^{7}

Aelius *Michael Easterby* 65
2 ch g Sepoy(AUS) Syvilla (Nayef (USA))
6162^{5} 7157^{9}

Aeolus *Ed Walker* a99 112
5 b g Araafa(IRE) Bright Moll (Mind Games)
1439^{4} 1862^{6} 2475^{5} 3244^{10} 4393^{4} 6558^{9} 7822^{2} 7932^{6}

Aerovelocity (NZ) *P O'Sullivan* 125
7 b g Pins(AUS) Exodus (NZ) (Kaapstad (NZ))
1911a^{8} (8330a)

Aethos (IRE) *Stefano Botti* 109
2 ch c Dragon Pulse(IRE) Quela (GER) (Acatenango (GER))
7401a^{6} (7839a)

Afandem (IRE) *Hugo Palmer* 107
2 b c Vale Of York(IRE) Al Mahmeyah (Teofilo (IRE))
(1850) 2390^{3} (3254) 4076^{5} (4750a) 5656^{2} (6068a) 6282^{4} 7113^{4} ◆

A Few Dollars More (IRE) *Andrew Slattery* a75 82
4 b g Moss Vale(IRE) Lady Naomi (USA) (Distant View (USA))
3696a^{5}

Affair *Hughie Morrison* a50 65
2 b f Sakhee's Secret Supatov (USA) (Johannesburg (USA))
2997^{4} 3555^{3} 6035^{6} 7750^{10} 8568^{9}

Affaire Solitaire (IRE) *P Khozian* a101 112
6 b h Danehill Dancer(IRE) Arlesienne (IRE) (Alzao (USA))
1023a^{3} 1375a^{3}

Affectionate Lady (IRE) *Keith Reveley* a62 62
5 b m Dandy Man(IRE) Agouti (Pennekamp (USA))
431^{5} 609^{7} 876^{3} (1120) 1382^{2} 1926^{2} 2329^{2} 4144^{2} 4445^{5}

Affinia Fifty (IRE) *Thomas Gibney* a18 12
6 b m Refuse To Bend(IRE) Newgate Lodge (IRE) (Namid)
7474a^{12}

Affoburg (FR) *Simone Brogi* 64
2 b g Sageburg(IRE) Affolante (USA) (Whywhywhy (USA))
1118a^{5} 5186a^{8}

Affordability *Daniel Mark Loughnane* a65 59
2 b g Bushranger(IRE) Munaa's Dream (Oasis Dream)
2104^{2} 2822^{10} 3654^{5} 4221^{3} 4712^{5} 5257^{9} 8071^{7} 8536^{4}

A Fitting Finale *Kevin Ryan* a24 53
3 b f Indesatchel(IRE) Amused (Prince Sabo)
2740^{4} 3209^{8} 4258^{9} 5369^{8}

Afjaan (IRE) *William Haggas* a106 105
4 b g Henrythenavigator(USA) Elusive Galaxy (IRE) (Elusive City (USA))
4263^{2} ◆ 4758^{6} 5552^{2} (6126) 6942^{7} ◆ 7354^{4} ◆

Afkar (IRE) *Ivan Furtado* a75 49
8 b g Invincible Spirit(IRE) Indienne (IRE) (Indian Ridge)
(246) 449^{2} 581^{8} 2918^{12} 3729^{7} 4729^{10} 5273^{10} 5729^{10} 6373^{9} 7048^{5} 7794^{14}

Aflame *Sir Michael Stoute* a74 94
3 b f Shamardal(USA) Magical Romance (IRE) (Barathea (IRE))
1930^{2} 2904^{2} 3406^{3} (5038) (5752) (6576) 7550^{5}

Afnaan *Saeed bin Suroor* a54 62
3 ch c Raven's Pass(USA) Almansoora (USA) (Bahri (USA))
1897^4

Afonso De Sousa (USA) *Michael Appleby* a107 90
6 br g Henrythenavigator(USA) Mien (USA) (Nureyev (USA))
215^2 333^3 530^3 $757a^{14}$ 1089^7 1629^{14} 5651^{12} 6372^8 7121^7 8317^{12}

African Beat (IRE) *John Gosden* a76 74
2 b f Cape Cross(IRE) Rythmic (Dubai Destination (USA))
7548^4 (7908) 8153^4 8466^4

African Blessing *David Barron* a72 73
3 ch g Mount Nelson Bella Beguine (Komaite (USA))
(1151) ◆ 4835^4 5224^3 ◆ 5643^5

African Friend (IRE) *Henry Candy* 40
3 b g Equiano(FR) Fontanally Springs (IRE) (Namid)
1451^4

African Girl *Lydia Pearce* a42 48
2 b f Equiano(FR) Tychy (Suave Dancer (USA))
7576^9 8352^{11}

African Grey *David Barron* 54
2 gr g Kheleyf(USA) Elbow Beach (Choisir (AUS))
3222^6 3874^5 4405^8

African Ride *C Laffon-Parias* a73 75
2 b c Candy Ride(ARG) Paiota Falls (USA) (Kris S (USA))
$7588a^2$

African Showgirl *Ivan Furtado* a66 65
3 ch f Showcasing Georgie The Fourth (IRE) (Cadeaux Genereux)
1420^5 ◆ 1829^8 2372^5 3003^{11} 3973^2 4936^{10} (5055) (5823) 6444^9 7035^4 7613^{11} 8240^3 8347^3 8587^6

African Trader (USA) *Daniel Mark Loughnane* a47 60
3 bb c Lonhro(AUS) Nasaieb (IRE) (Fairy King (USA))
4041^9 5260^3 6441^4 7514^{11}

Afternoon (IRE) *Martyn Meade* a38
2 b f Rip Van Winkle(IRE) Necklace (Darshaan)
7885^{13}

Afzal (FR) *T J O'Mara* a52 59
3 ch g Iffraaj Adelfia (IRE) (Sinndar (IRE))
$4899a^5$

Again Charlie (FR) *C Delcher-Sanchez* 95
3 ch c Medecis Tiptonia (USA) (Kendor (FR))
(6356a)

Against Rules (FR) *S Wattel* a71 91
4 b m Aussie Rules(USA) Around Me (IRE) (Johannesburg (USA))
$8042a^4$

Against The Odds *Paul Cole* a89 90
3 b c Champs Elysees Generous Diana (Generous (IRE))
(1479) 2209^4 2638^4 (4207) 4920^2 5147^4 5761^3 6591^2 7123^{11}

Agama (GER) *F Kurz* 92
6 ch m Sholokhov(IRE) Ariana (GER) (Dashing Blade)
$6611a^{10}$

Agatas Legacy (IRE) *Michael Dods* 47
3 b f Fastnet Rock(AUS) Agata (FR) (Poliglote)
1449^4

Agathonia (USA) *Charlie Appleby* a78 73
2 b f Street Cry(IRE) Regency Romance (Diktat)
6206^4 6624^2 7050^2

Agenor (GER) *C Von Der Recke* 85
5 b g Medicean Acerba (GER) (Monsun (GER))
3387^{13}

Agent Gibbs *John O'Shea* a89 91
4 ch g Bertolini(USA) Armada Grove (Fleetwood (IRE))
1081^3 1568^8 1934^3 2176^5 3192^3 3533^7 4311^4 4920^6 5574^4 (6165) (6445)

Agent Murphy *Brian Meehan* 116
5 b h Cape Cross(IRE) Raskutani (Dansili)
$757a^4$

Age Of Elegance (IRE) *Roger Fell* a83 84
4 b m Makfi Elegant Pride (Beat Hollow)
1588^5 3983^9 4409^5 4476^4 4702^3 4977^2 (5292) (5918) 6957^2 7359^5 7847^4 8007^2 8283^8

Age Of Innocence *Derek Shaw* a74 67
5 b g Invincible Spirit(IRE) Elusive Legend (USA) (Elusive Quality (USA))
133^5

Agerzam *Ronald Harris* a74 66
6 b g Holy Roman Emperor(IRE) Epiphany (Zafonic (USA))
106^{10} 192^7 685^4 857^3 ◆ 919^6 1150^4 1264^2 1533^{12} 2765^{10} 3098^8 3317^3 3994^{12} 4484^2 5773^5

Aggression (IRE) *M D O'Callaghan* a88 84
4 br g Marju(IRE) Radha (Bishop Of Cashel)
$8197a^3$

Aghaany *Roger Varian* 83
3 gr f Dubawi(IRE) Hathrah (IRE) (Linamix (FR))
2470^7 (3059) 4130^6

Agha Des Mottes (FR) *Ian Williams* 45
6 b g Mister Sacha(FR) Java Des Mottes (FR) (Passing Sale (FR))
3856^6

Agnes Stewart (IRE) *Edward Lynam* 90
4 gr m Lawman(FR) Anice Stellato (IRE) (Dalakhani (IRE))
$3692a^5$ $5095a^6$

Agree (IRE) *Brian Ellison* 93
3 b g Zebedee Refuse To Give Up (IRE) (Refuse To Bend (IRE))
(1524) ◆ (2693) 3980^3

Agreement (IRE) *Nikki Evans* a43 66
6 b g Galileo(IRE) Cozzene's Angel (USA) (Cozzene (USA))
1450^9 1830^4 2131^4 3099^4 3767^4 4591^6 4816^6

Aguerooo (IRE) *Richard Hannon* a98 84
3 b g Monsieur Bond(IRE) Vision Of Peace (IRE) (Invincible Spirit (IRE))
(3) 131^2 262^3 (559) (881) 1070^8 1168^3 1865^8 6780^{12} 6962^4 8192^3 $8368a^3$

Ahead Of Time *David Simcock* a69
2 b c Dream Ahead(USA) Malladore (IRE) (Lawman (FR))
3032^3

Ahlan Bil Zain (FR) *David Simcock* a75 64
2 bb c Elusive City(USA) Fall View (Pivotal)
7012^4 ◆ (7431)

Ahlan Emarati (IRE) *S Seemar* a51 76
4 b g Holy Roman Emperor(IRE) Indaba (IRE) (Indian Ridge)
$91a^{12}$ $370a^{11}$

Ahraam (IRE) *Harry Whittington* a62 58
3 b g Roderic O'Connor(IRE) Simla Sunset (IRE) (One Cool Cat (USA))
376^8 4498^6 5019^2 5610^3 6243^2 8179^3

Aid To Africa (IRE) *Michael Bell* a71 61
3 b g Big Bad Bob(IRE) El Soprano (IRE) (Noverre (USA))
633^2 746^4 5681^5 6265^9 6629^{11} 7227^9 7613^9 8179^7

Aimez La Vie (IRE) *Richard Fahey* 74
2 br f Arcano(IRE) La Vita E Bella (IRE) (Definite Article)
4298^4 5771^2 ◆ 6762^2 ◆ 7147^3

Aiming For Rio (FR) *A Fabre* 88
2 ch f Rio De La Plata(USA) Tevara (Compton Place)
$1579a^5$ 3382^7 $4750a^6$

Aimless Lady (FR) *F Vermeulen* a57 90
4 bb m Peer Gynt(JPN) Poet's Studio (USA) (Bertrando (USA))
$3092a^5$

Aim To Please (FR) *F Doumen* a89 109
3 b f Excellent Art Midnight Flash (IRE) (Anabaa Blue)
$1309a^5$ $2282a^{10}$ $2945a^3$ $5498a^3$ (6693a) $7404a^{11}$

Ainippe (IRE) *G M Lyons* 106
4 b m Captain Rio Imitation (Darshaan)
$1939a^3$ $2497a^7$ $2923a^8$

Ainslie (IRE) *Gordon Elliott* a73 66
4 rg g Mastercraftsman(IRE) Capriole (Noverre (USA))
$6465a^6$

Air Force Blue (USA) *A P O'Brien* 125
3 b c War Front(USA) Chatham (USA) (Maria's Mon (USA))
1864^{12} $2496a^7$ 4151^{12} $5213a^7$

Airley (FR) *R Labit* a65 74
5 b m Slickly(FR) Airlight (IRE) (Trempolino (USA))
$512a^9$

Air Of Astana (IRE) *Hugo Palmer* a86 74
4 b g Equiano(FR) Fairnilee (Selkirk (USA))
603^4 968^3 1161^2 1651^6 2328^{11}

Air Of Glory (IRE) *John Spearing* a48
6 ch g Shamardal(USA) Balloura (USA) (Swain (IRE))
7368^{13}

Airoforce (USA) *Mark Casse* a114 114
3 rg c Colonel John(USA) Chocolate Pop (USA) (Cuvee (USA))
$4173a^{10}$

Air Of York (IRE) *David Evans* a92 83
4 b g Vale Of York(IRE) State Secret (Green Desert (USA))
213^{11} 503^7 694^7 923^{10} 1528^7 1634^{13} 2587^4 3124^6 3783^6 4211^9 4291^5 4481^2 4908^7 5403^{15} 5825^9 6589^8 7267^8 7626^{15} 7945^7 8188^4 8316^3

Air Pilot *Ralph Beckett* 117
7 b g Zamindar(USA) Countess Sybil (IRE) (Dr Devious (IRE))
1425^2 $1909a^7$ (3544a) 4666^4 5652^{10}

Air Squadron *Ralph Beckett* a82 85
6 b g Rail Link Countess Sybil (IRE) (Dr Devious (IRE))
2699^9 3784^3 4353^4 5321^5 6582^{13}

Airton *James Bethell* a78 71
3 b g Champs Elysees Fly In Style (Hernando (FR))
1410^4 3323^7 (4549) 5365^3 5975^6 6450^4 7321^2 (8387)

Air Vice Marshal (USA) *A P O'Brien* 111
3 b c War Front(USA) Gold Vault (USA) (Arch (USA))
1864^4 $2496a^6$

Aislabie (FR) *Mark Walford* a69 66
3 gr g Soldier Of Fortune(IRE) Someries (FR) (Kendor (FR))
2804^4 4313^4 4682^7 7008^8 7657^3 7993^3 ◆

Ajaya *William Haggas* 113
3 b c Invincible Spirit(IRE) Nessina (USA) (Hennessy (USA))
2692^6 4824^{16}

A J Cook (IRE) *Ron Barr* a48 58
6 b g Mujadil(USA) Undertone (IRE) (Noverre (USA))
2052^{RR} 2423^{10} 3925^4 4771^3 (4931) 5278^4 5483^{10} 6680^{18} 7046^8 7595^3 7747^{10} 7859^6 8312^4 8485^7

Ajeeb (NZ) *S Seemar* 106
6 b g Al Maher(AUS) Destiny (AUS) (Bureaucracy (NZ))
$91a^5$ $370a^{12}$

Ajig *Eve Johnson Houghton* a71 73
5 ch m Bahamian Bounty Atwirl (Pivotal)
14^8 191^4 607^2 777^8 977^6

Ajmal (IRE) *A Fabre* 90
2 b c Shamardal(USA) Adja (IRE) (Rock Of Gibraltar (IRE))
$7086a^5$

Ajman Bridge *Roger Varian* a71 111
6 ch g Dubawi(IRE) Rice Mother (IRE) (Indian Ridge)
2482^5 3340^{15} 6333^6

Ajman King (IRE) *Roger Varian* 85
2 ch c Lope De Vega(IRE) Third Dimension (FR) (Suave Dancer (USA))
6880^5 7283^2 ◆

Ajman Prince (IRE) *Alistair Whillans* a86 21
3 b g Manduro(GER) Jumaireyah (Fairy King (USA))
5366^4 5716^7 6104^5 6921^5 7105^2 (7321) (7847) 8133^2

Ajman Princess (IRE) *Roger Varian* 105
3 b f Teofilo(IRE) Reem Three (Mark Of Esteem (IRE))
1608^2 ◆ 1989^2 2735^2 3297^2 $4416a^{11}$

Ajraam (USA) *M Al Mheiri* a95 95
6 b g Daaher(CAN) Abby Road (IRE) (Danehill (USA))
$8578a^8$

Ajwad *R Bouresly* a67 86
3 b c Rock Of Gibraltar(IRE) Afrodita (IRE) (Montjeu (IRE))
$536a^3$ $807a^4$

Akavit (IRE) *Ed de Giles* a41 82
4 b g Vale Of York(IRE) Along Came Molly (Dr Fong (USA))
6445^8 6965^8 7274^P

Akbulat *A Savujev* 60
3 b g Invincible Spirit(IRE) Summer's Lease (Pivotal)
$3120a^8$

Akhlaaq *Owen Burrows* 87
2 b c New Approach(IRE) Misheer (Oasis Dream) (5304) 6228^4

Akihiro (JPN) *A Fabre* 113
2 b c Deep Impact(JPN) Baahama (IRE) (Anabaa (USA))
(6270a)

Akinspirit (IRE) *Nikki Evans* a61 49
12 b g Invincible Spirit(IRE) Akebia (USA) (Trempolino (USA))
233^4 674^8

Akkadian Empire *Mick Channon* a41 75
2 b g Arabian Gleam Floral Beauty (Shamardal (USA))
5952^4 6264^2 6664^5 6888^2 7297^2 7511^7

Akohol (IRE) *F Head* a55 72
3 b c Invincible Spirit(IRE) Never Green (IRE) (Halling (USA))
$1311a^7$ $2456a^6$

Aksum *Michael Bell* a56 50
3 b f Cacique(IRE) Quiet (Observatory (USA))
258^6 1148^4 1705^4 2608^5 2968^4 3975^7

Aktoria (FR) *C Laffon-Parias* a90 80
3 bl f Canford Cliffs(IRE) Granadilla (Zafonic (USA))
$1309a^{11}$ $8148a^{11}$

Al *Luca Cumani* a88 88
4 b g Halling(USA) Incarnation (IRE) (Samum (GER))
4153^3 4888^6 6209^4 6854^3

Alabaster (USA) *Saeed bin Suroor* a93
4 br h Medaglia d'Oro(USA) Lady Pegasus (USA) (Fusaichi Pegasus (USA))
$94a^7$

Al Abyad (USA) *A bin Harmash* a56
2 gr c Awesome Of Course(USA) Silver Shannon (USA) (Pentelicus (USA))
$8574a^{10}$

Aladdine *F Head* 89
2 b f Naaqoos Katerini (FR) (Cacique (IRE))
$5497a^3$

Aladdins Cave *R K Watson* a65 43
12 b g Rainbow Quest(USA) Flight Of Fancy (Sadler's Wells (USA))
$7517a^{13}$

Alaik *Saeed bin Suroor* 77
2 b c New Approach(IRE) Hawaafez (Nayef (USA))
7621^3 ◆

Alakhana (FR) *F Head* 100
3 b f Dalakhani(IRE) Dubai (IRE) (Galileo (IRE))
$4331a^4$ (6497a) $7312a^3$

Alamgiyr (IRE) *A De Royer-Dupre* a68 84
4 b g Desert Style(IRE) Alaiyma (IRE) (Refuse To Bend (IRE))
$3936a^{11}$

Alamode *Marcus Tregoning* 103
3 ch f Sir Percy Almamia (Hernando (FR))
3274^{19} 3911^6 4826^{11}

A L'Anglaise *A Fabre* a79 78
3 b f Invincible Spirit(IRE) Alabelle (Galileo (IRE))
$5907a^8$

Alans Pride (IRE) *Michael Dods* a58 50
4 ch g Footstepsinthesand True Crystal (IRE) (Sadler's Wells (USA))
1696^5 2303^7 3262^9 3732^3 4214^3 4486^5 4772^8 5068^{10} 5517^5 5729^3 6095^3

Alapinta *Ralph Beckett* 63
2 b f Medicean Altruiste (Montjeu (IRE))
5373^5 6578^7 7466^7

Alaraz (SPA) *G Arizkorreta Elosegui* 88
4 b h Le Havre(IRE) Tadea (FR) (Bering)
$5502a^7$

Alareef (SAF) *M F De Kock* a89
5 b g Stronghold Modraj (Machiavellian (USA))
$12a^8$ $183a^3$ (39a) $535a^4$ $8578a^7$

Alaskan Breeze (IRE) *Brian Meehan* 66
3 b f Fastnet Rock(AUS) Arabian Mirage (Oasis Dream)
2483^8 3059^6 4367^{13} 5013^7

Alatan Blaze (ITY) *Endo Botti* 99
5 b h Distant Way(USA) Shalimar (ITY) (College Chapel)
$2518a^{13}$

Alba Dawn (IRE) *Keith Dalgleish* 61
3 ch f Compton Place Pink Delight (IRE) (Rock Of Gibraltar (IRE))
1667^8 2359^9 3017^7 3549^{12}

Albahar (FR) *Chris Gordon* a88 95
5 gr g Dark Angel(IRE) Downland (USA) (El Prado (IRE))
1653^3 (619) 1417^5 1987^4 (2392) 3657^{13} 4752^{16} 7670^7 7979^8

Albecq *Mrs A Malzard* 38
4 b g Paco Boy(IRE) Helen Sharp (Pivotal)
$2080a^4$ $2285a^4$ $2955a^{10}$ $3381a^8$

Alben Star (IRE) *Richard Fahey* a114 100
8 b g Clodovil(IRE) Secret Circle (Magic Ring (IRE))
166^3 4831^0 7457^3 ◆ (1066) 1197^8 1644^8 4865^{10} 5418^{12}

Albernathy *Charlie Appleby* 95
3 ch c Dubawi(IRE) La Pelegrina (USA) (Redoute's Choice (AUS))
2161^{10} 3026^2 3908^9 6918^2 7821^{15}

Alberta (IRE) *Jim Best* 86
7 ch g Choisir(AUS) Akita (IRE) (Foxhound (USA))
3508^4 4384^3 5255^3 (6267) 8250^{12}

Albert Boy (IRE) *Scott Dixon* a62 73
3 ch g Falco(USA) Trumbaka (IRE) (In The Wings)
678^3 785^3 1200^4 (1379) 1816^2 2269^6 3355^7 3841^4 5471^8 7078^{14} 7500^{12} 7889^7 8238^5 8566^5

Albert Hall (USA) *A Chaille-Chaille* a61 69
11 b g Stravinsky(USA) Albertine (FR) (Irish River (FR))
$5452a^{10}$

Albert Herring *Jonathan Portman* a46 54
4 b g Tobougg(IRE) Balsamita (FR) (Midyan (USA))
5573^6

Alberto *Lisa Williamson* a4
6 b g Bertolini(USA) Al Awaalah (Mukaddamah (USA))
4716^9 5954^{15} 7488^9 7944^9 8541^{12}

Albertochop (FR) *T Van Den Troost* a53 50
4 ch h Deportivo Perle De Star (FR) (Indian Rocket)
$8421a^{15}$

Albizu Campos *Lawrence Mullaney* 57
2 b c Mastercraftsman(IRE) Lolita Lebron (IRE) (Royal Applause)
3633^9 4133^4 4914^5 5799^5 6446^{10}

Alcanar (USA) *Tony Carroll* a65 63
3 ch g Teofilo(USA) Badalona (Cape Cross (IRE))
968^7 2440^5 2790^8 4385^6 7425^3 7969^9

Alcatraz (IRE) *George Baker* a79 88
4 b g Camacho Spring Opera (IRE) (Sadler's Wells (USA))
1716^3 ◆ 2868^4 3557^4 4081^6 5234^3 6316^3 8249^5 ◆

Alcazar *David Simcock* a74 93
2 b c Rio De La Plata(USA) Zarkiyna (FR) (Sendawar (IRE))
3093^4 (3561) 4622^6

Aldair *Richard Hannon* a69 73
3 b c Pastoral Pursuits Tremelo Pointe (IRE) (Trempolino (USA))
1146^3 (1485) 2044^5 2545^8 4562^8 5375^6 6231^{13}

Al Debel (FR) *J Reynier* a104
3 b g Distorted Humor(USA) Negligee (USA) (Northern Afleet (USA))
$8165a^2$

Aldeburgh *Nigel Twiston-Davies* a89 86
7 b g Oasis Dream Orford Ness (Selkirk (USA))
605^4 (2043) 3219^5 8539^9

Al Destoor *Jennie Candlish* a84 89
6 ch g Teofilo(IRE) In A Silent Way (IRE) (Desert Prince (IRE))
4875^2 6160^2 ◆ (7077) 7412^2 7744^7

Aldreth *Michael Easterby* a83 76
5 b g Champs Elysees Rowan Flower (IRE) (Ashkalani (IRE))
1560^5 2018^3 2912^2 3149^2 4101^4 4935^5 5350^6 6503^5 7158^2 7846^2 8051^2 8399^3

Aldrin (FR) *Charlie Appleby* 74
3 b c New Approach(IRE) Trip To The Moon (Fasliyev (USA))
4546^4 6805^3

Aleator (USA) *Sir Mark Prescott Bt* a95 92
4 b g Blame(USA) Alma Mater (Sadler's Wells (USA))
(121) 353^6

Aleef (IRE) *David O'Meara* a99 97
3 b c Kodiac Okba (USA) (Diesis)
(2156) ◆ 2972^8 4889^2 6633^2 7124^{19} 7358^3 (7668) 8050^2

Al Egda *John Gosden* 58
3 b f Poet's Voice Perfect Spirit (IRE) (Invincible Spirit (IRE))
2395^7

Alejandro (IRE) *David O'Meara* a90 91
7 b g Dark Angel(IRE) Carallia (IRE) (Common Grounds)
2361^2 2910^3 3115^{11} 3518^2 4611^5 4917^5 5866^2 6082^8 6320^4 6764^7 7308^2 7462^4 7781^5

Aleko *Mark Johnston* a65 66
3 b c Cape Cross(IRE) Monnavanna (IRE) (Machiavellian (USA))
1238^4 1777^2 1992^3 3026^6 4317^5

Aleksandar *Jim Goldie* a68 72
7 ch g Medicean Alexander Celebre (IRE) (Peintre Celebre (USA))
1665^9

Alemaratalyoum (IRE) *Ed Dunlop* 66
2 ch c Lope De Vega(IRE) Heart Of Ice (IRE) (Montjeu (IRE))
6211^9 6577^9 7502^6

Alert *Andrew Slattery* a61 72
4 b m Zamindar(USA) Tereshkina (IRE) (Sadler's Wells (USA))
2370^5

Alexander M (IRE) *Mark Johnston* 26
2 ch g Mastercraftsman(IRE) Naomh Geileis (USA) (Grand Slam (USA))
4188^9

Alexandrakollontai (IRE) *Alistair Whillans* a89 88
6 b m Amadeus Wolf Story (Observatory (USA))
1215^{14} 1694^6 2016^{15} 2420^3 (2737) ◆ 3021^4 3518^3 4318^7 4700^7 5419^9 5836^8 6096^2 6811^{12} 7108^6 7472^6 (7796) 7957^3

Alexios Komnenos (IRE) *J Stack* 105
2 b c Choisir(AUS) Alexiade (IRE) (Montjeu (IRE))
$4574a^2$

Alex My Boy (IRE) *A Wohler* 115
5 b h Dalakhani(IRE) Alexandrova (IRE) (Sadler's Wells (USA))
$1688a^8$ $2286a^2$

Alfahad (IRE) *Ed Dunlop* a64 76
3 b c New Approach(IRE) Al Tamooh (IRE) (Dalakhani (IRE))
2008^6 6104^6

Alfajer *Marco Botti* a96 103
4 b m Mount Nelson Sakhee's Song (IRE) (Sakhee (USA))
1065[3] 3979[12] 4826[10]

Alfa Manifesto (FR) *Matthieu Palussiere* a66 72
2 b c Whipper(USA) Fairy Dress (USA) (Fasliyev (USA))
(4187a) 5141a[4] 5568a[5] *5755a[10]* 6015a[6]

Alfarris (FR) *William Haggas* 69
2 b c Shamardal(USA) Rose Et Noire (IRE) (Dansili)
6750[5] 7226[4]

Al Fatih (IRE) *Steve Flook* a49 70
5 b g Montjeu(IRE) Sky High Flyer (Anabaa (USA))
1640[2] ◆ 6254[6] 7245[3]

Alfawaris *Owen Burrows* 82
2 b c Frankel Kareemah (IRE) (Peintre Celebre (USA))
6570[3] 7470[3]

Alf Guineas (IRE) *John Gosden* a82
3 b f Sea The Stars(IRE) Sayyedati Storm (USA) (Storm Cat (USA))
7102[2] ◆ 7410[9] *(7753)*

Alfieri (FR) *G Arizkorreta Elosegui* a71 65
3 b g Naaqoos Jolie Et Belle (FR) (Oratorio (IRE))
7999a[5]

Alfie's Angel (IRE) *Bryan Smart* 72
2 b c Dark Angel(IRE) Penolva (IRE) (Galileo (IRE))
3208[3] ◆ 3749[3] 4699[3] 5318[5] 5884[8]

Alfie The Pug *Pat Phelan* a59
4 b g Pastoral Pursuits Kapsiliat (IRE) (Cape Cross (IRE))
168[5] 257[5]

Alfonso Manana (IRE) *James Given* a69
2 ch c Dutch Art Chance For Romance (Entrepreneur)
8175[9] 8406[4] 8536[3]

Alfred Hutchinson *David O'Meara* a103 104
8 ch g Monsieur Bond(IRE) Chez Cherie (Wolfhound (USA))
1629[5] ◆ 2191[17] 3163[3] *3565[9]* 4665[5] 5585[14] *6372[4]* 6778[8] 7121[15] *7651[2] 7933[2] (8029) 8593[7]*

Alfredo (IRE) *Seamus Durack* a91 80
4 ch g Arcano(IRE) Western Sky (Barathea (IRE))
2414[15] 5255[5] 6031[4] *(6659) (7367)* 7670[2] *(8363)* ◆ *(8558)*

Alfred Richardson *John Davies* a60 53
2 ch g Dapper Vera Richardson (IRE) (Dutch Art)
7432[5] 7741[7]

Al Furat (USA) *Ron Barr* a9 47
8 b g El Prado(IRE) No Frills (IRE) (Darshaan)
1675[10] 1952[4] 2409[11] 2573[7] 3921[12] 4260[9] 4767[6]

Algaith (USA) *Owen Burrows* a104 109
4 b g Dubawi(IRE) Atayeb (USA) (Rahy (USA))
3273[28] 4688[2]

Algometer *David Simcock* 114
3 gr c Archipenko(USA) Albanova (Alzao (USA))
1605[2] (2432) 2896[7] (6571) 7759a[6]

Al Haayelah *Roger Varian* a59 43
2 b f Showcasing Disposition (Selkirk (USA))
6673[10] 6925[5] 7439[5]

Al Haffanah (IRE) *Richard Hannon* a48 23
3 b f Acclamation Street Style (IRE) (Rock Of Gibraltar (IRE))
1798[11] 4056[12]

Alhamareer (IRE) *Paul Webber* a52 30
4 ch g Teofilo(IRE) Ribot's Guest (IRE) (Be My Guest (USA))
342[8]

Al Hamd (IRE) *Ed Dunlop* a80 77
3 b g Intikhab(USA) Bakoura (Green Desert (USA))
(1036) 1409[7] 2179[12] 3187[5] *3605[10]*

Al Hamdany (IRE) *Marco Botti* a87 100
2 b c Kodiac Easy Times (Nayef (USA))
2604[4] 4975[2] 5505[2] (6240) 7409[2]

Al Haram (FR) *E Lellouche* a74 102
3 b c Sea The Stars(IRE) En Public (FR) (Rainbow Quest (USA))
3450a[3] 7456a[7] 8042a[7]

Al Hawraa *Kevin Ryan* 67
3 b f Iffraaj Kashoof (Green Desert (USA))
3014[2] 3850[5] 4313[3] 5757[2] 6541[10]

Al Hayyah (IRE) *F Rohaut* 100
3 b f Lope De Vega(IRE) Black Dahlia (Dansili)
1685a[8] 6357a[3]

Alhella *Mick Quinn* a77 76
4 b m Kyllachy Maid In The Shade (Forzando)
67[4] 349[8] 969[7] 1237[7] 1700[5] 2537[10] 3078[11]

Ali Bin Nayef *Michael Wigham* a58 46
4 b g Nayef(USA) Maimoona (IRE) (Pivotal)
190[6] 356[5] 7691[2] 982[7] 1169[2] 1500[10] 5303[6] 5749[7] *(7262) 8038[7] 8155[2] 8386[6]*

Alicante Dawn *Bryan Smart* 100
2 ch c Equiano(FR) Sofonisba (Rock Of Gibraltar (IRE))
3148[3] (3515) (4602) (5977)

Alice's Dream *Marco Botti* a71 61
2 b f Showcasing Amandian (IRE) (Indian Ridge)
2793[5] 3433[4] 5930[5] *6670[11] (6961) (7749) 8047[2]*

Alice Springs (IRE) *A P O'Brien* 118
3 ch f Galileo(IRE) Aleagueoftheirown (IRE) (Danehill Dancer (IRE))
1369a[3] 1888[3] 2282a[7] 3339[3] (4107) 4926a[8] (6352a) (6949) 7837a[10]

Alice Thornton *Martin Todhunter* a76 66
4 b m Hurricane Run(IRE) Alice Alleyne (IRE) (Oasis Dream)
3550[6] 5178[2] 5757[4] 6226[9] 7096[3] *(7323) 7662[11] (8144) 8385[8]*

Alidara (IRE) *Emma Owen* a37 27
4 ch m Manduro(GER) Artisia (IRE) (Peintre Celebre (USA))
5025[6] 5550[6] 7627[13]

Alignement *C Laffon-Parias* 108
3 b c Pivotal Soldata (USA) (Maria's Mon (USA))
2283a[12] 4185a[6] (5699a) 6973a[4]

Alinstante *Sir Mark Prescott Bt* a96 88
3 b f Archipenko(USA) Algarade (Green Desert (USA))
7901[5] 8231[6] 8594[2]

Ali Spirit (IRE) *Matthieu Palussiere* a84 78
3 b c Invincible Spirit(IRE) Citron Presse (USA) (Lemon Drop Kid (USA))
(6310a) 6911a[7]

A Little Bit Dusty *Conor Dore* a65 60
8 ch g Needwood Blade Dusty Dazzler (IRE) (Titus Livius (FR))
251[3] 445[4] 577[3]

Alizoom (IRE) *Roger Varian* a77 88
3 gr g Invincible Spirit(IRE) Lady Springbank (IRE) (Choisir (AUS))
1607[7] 2650[4] (3138) 3689[6] 5253[2] 5743[3] 6255[6] 6883[3]

Al Jazi (IRE) *F Rohaut* 110
3 b f Canford Cliffs(IRE) Rainbow Crossing (Cape Cross (IRE))
(4826)

Aljazzi *Marco Botti* a94 103
3 b f Shamardal(USA) Nouriya (Danehill Dancer (IRE))
1476[4] ◆ 1888[10] (5158) 6604a[4] 7823[9]

Aljezeera *Luca Cumani* 83
2 b f Frankel Dynaforce (USA) (Dynaformer (USA))
(5387)

Al Johrah *H-F Devin* 109
2 b f Bated Breath Bea Remembered (Doyen (IRE))
3270[2] 4694a[2] 5690a[4] 6694a[5]

Aljuljalah (USA) *Roger Varian* a99 99
3 b f Exchange Rate(USA) Ruler's Charm (USA) (Cape Town (USA))
2220[2] ◆ 3274[18] 4105[8] 6113[4] 6338[2] *7650[2]*

Alkashaaf (USA) *Archie Watson* a78
2 b g More Than Ready(USA) Abby Road (IRE) (Danehill (USA))
6671[5] 8246[4] (8454)

Alketios (GR) *Chris Gordon* a72 69
5 b g Kavafi(IRE) Mazea (IRE) (Montjeu (IRE))
647 777[7] *2006[6]* 3064[12] *3522[11] 5509[8]*

Al Khafji *Jeremy Gask* a78 70
3 ch g New Approach(IRE) Wadaat (Diktat)
2580[4] 3103[5] *6138[5]*

Al Khan (IRE) *Kevin Ryan* a96 97
7 b g Elnadim(USA) Popolo (IRE) (Fasliyev (USA))
50[6] 290[10] 486[10] 1871[8] 1993[5] 2257[2] (2361) 2684[12] 4399[8] 4758[9] 5640[7] 6557[13] 7316[3] *7530[12]* 7821[3] *(7968) 8177[7] (8385)*

Al Khazaaliya (USA) *Todd Pletcher* 87
4 b m Blame(USA) Erhu (USA) (Tactical Cat (USA))
3088a[5]

Alkhor *Richard Hannon* a88 59
3 b g Exceed And Excel(AUS) Ruse (Diktat)
2554[8] *7643[7] (7965) 8380[7]*

Al Kirana (IRE) *Richard Hannon* a45 60
3 b f Exceed And Excel(AUS) Ripalong (IRE) (Revoque (IRE))
441[5]

All About The Pace *Mark Usher* a58 51
2 ch f Sixties Icon Phoebe Woodstock (IRE) (Grand Lodge (USA))
3555[8] *3986[6] 5809[3]* 7032[3] *7941[6] 8235[5]*

All About Time *David O'Meara* a91 90
4 b m Azamour(IRE) Up And About (Barathea (IRE))
2236[7] 3291[4] 6134[4] *7139[2] 7652[8]* 7929a[11]

All Dolled Up (IRE) *Sarah-Jayne Davies* a46 46
4 b m Aussie Rules(USA) All On Sugar (GER) (Red Ransom (USA))
8338[3]

Allegheny Bay (IRE) *J S Moore* a47
2 b g Power Allegheny Creek (IRE) (Teofilo (IRE))
8404[6]

Allen's Folly *Peter Hiatt* a42 50
3 b f Captain Gerrard(IRE) Rabarama (Xaar)
3148 1132[6] 1414[10] 1761[5] 2143[3] 2372[6]

Allez Henri (IRE) *D Prod'Homme* a97 91
5 b g Footstepsinthesand Macotte (FR) (Nicolotte)
7524a[9]

All For The Best (IRE) *Robert Stephens* a79 76
4 b g Rip Van Winkle(IRE) Alleluia (Caerleon (USA))
1760[5] 2392[5]

Allfredandnobell (IRE) *Micky Hammond* a44 57
3 b g Alfred Nobel(IRE) Its In The Air (IRE) (Whipper (USA))
1671[5] 2308[9] 2553[9] 2801[6] 3982[6] 4375[3] *5064[8]* 5921[2] 6840[6]

Alliance Secrete (FR) *T Castanheira* a86 87
2 bb c Sageburg(IRE) Gentle Tap (Beat Hollow)
4924a[3]

Alligator *Ed Dunlop* a60 55
2 ch g Sepoy(AUS) See You Later (Emarati (USA))
3524[8] 3819[7] 4053[9] *6045[2]* 6313[8] *6963[3] 7482[12] 7866[9] 8025[7]*

All I Survey (AUS) *Pat Carey* 97
4 b g Domesday(AUS) Duchess Drive (IRE) (Halling (USA))
7481a[6] 7947a[3]

All My Love (IRE) *Pam Sly* a79 83
4 b m Lord Shanakill(USA) Afilla (Dansili)
1221[3] ◆ 1717[3] ◆ 4462[5] *5526[2]* 6527[4]

Allnecessaryforce (FR) *Alex Hales* a76 79
6 gr g Verglas(IRE) Kosmic View (USA) (Distant View (USA))
1531[2]

All Or Nothin (IRE) *Paddy Butler* a44 74
7 b g Majestic Missile(IRE) Lady Peculiar (CAN) (Sunshine Forever (USA))
563[9] 1042[8] 1544[9] 2402[7]

All Talk N No Do (IRE) *Seamus Durack* a83 98
5 b g Kodiac Woodren (USA) (Woodman (USA))
3351[8] 4077[5] 4581[11] 6283[9] 6775[8]

All The Mollies (IRE) *Adrian McGuinness* a47
2 ch f Intense Focus(USA) Madam Gaffer (Tobougg (IRE))
7917a[8]

All The Rage *Sir Mark Prescott Bt* a79 60
3 b f Dubawi(IRE) Intrigued (Darshaan)
3071[5] *3318[2] 3652[4] 4018[4] (6137) 6241[6]* ◆ *6702[5] 6922[2] 7205[3]*

All The Winds (GER) *Shaun Lycett* a80 81
11 ch g Samum(GER) All Our Luck (GER) (Spectrum (IRE))
267[8] 330[3] 922[8] 1417[8] 6457[4]

Allux Boy (IRE) *Nigel Tinkler* 72
2 b g Iffraaj Ms Victoria (IRE) (Fasliyev (USA))
2014[5] 3167[8] (3416) 4167[6] (5265) 6213[4]

All You (IRE) *David O'Meara* a72 77
4 b g Siyouni(FR) Diamond Light (USA) (Fantastic Light (USA))
823[7] 1124[11] *1502[5] 1762[3]* (1925) 2347[5] 2672[2] 2811[7]

Al Madam (USA) *A bin Harmash* a61
2 b f To Honor And Serve(USA) Hug It Out (USA) (Medaglia d'Oro (USA))
8576a[10]

Almanack *Mark Pattinson* a71 56
6 b g Haatef(USA) Openness (Grand Lodge (USA))
683[6] 860[2] 1114[6] 1498[2] 4369[5] 4772[7] *5503[5] 6137[5] 8382[2]*

Almandin (GER) *Robert Hickmott* 114
6 b g Monsun(GER) Anatola (GER) (Tiger Hill (IRE))
(7756a)

Al Mansor (IRE) *Richard Hannon* a72 61
2 gr c Dark Angel(IRE) Atullia (GER) (Tertullian (USA))
6211[5] *6671[4] 7064[4] 7527[4]*

Almanzor (FR) *J-C Rouget* 129
3 b c Wootton Bassett Darkova (USA) (Maria's Mon (USA))
1580a[3] (2140a) (2946a) (5499a) ◆ (6354a) (7353)

Almargo (IRE) *S bin Ghadayer* a92 106
5 b g Invincible Spirit(IRE) Alexander Youth (IRE) (Exceed And Excel (AUS))
374a[8]

Al Markhiya (IRE) *Richard Hannon* 21
3 b f Arcano(IRE) Danetime Out (IRE) (Danetime (IRE))
4361[13]

Almashooqa (AUS) *Owen Burrows* a26 96
3 b f Bernardini(USA) Joy Of Flight (AUS) (Flying Spur (AUS))
184a[6] 451a[7] 723a[5] 807a[8] 6746[13]

Al Mayda (USA) *Hugo Palmer* a72
2 ch f Distorted Humor(USA) Ms. Margaret H (USA) (Point Given (USA))
7855[3] 8081[3]

Almeira (IRE) *N Caullery* 43
2 b f Henrythenavigator(USA) Aiboa (IRE) (King Charlemagne (USA))
1579a[6]

Almela (IRE) *D K Weld* 110
4 b m Sea The Stars(IRE) Aliya (IRE) (Darshaan)
5095a[2] (6200a) 6972a[2]

Almizhar (IRE) *Ed Dunlop* 38
2 b c Dark Angel(IRE) La Reine Mambo (USA) (High Yield (USA))
6480[9] 6704[11]

Almodovar (IRE) *David Lanigan* a113 115
4 b g Sea The Stars(IRE) Melodramatic (IRE) (Sadler's Wells (USA))
(2377) 3384[3] ◆ 5558[7] 6505[P]

Al Mohalhal (IRE) *Majed Seifeddine* a89 99
3 b g Acclamation Secret Question (USA) (Rahy (USA))
3332a[2] 5941a[24] 6382a[17] 8573a[3]

Almoonqith (USA) *David A & B Hayes & Tom Dabern* a88 112
6 bb h Dynaformer(USA) Bohemian Lady (USA) (Carson City (USA))
7378a[4] 7756a[6] 7948a[2]

Almoreb (IRE) *Richard Hannon* 63
2 b c Raven's Pass(USA) Macadamia (IRE) (Classic Cliche (IRE))
7470[7]

Almorox *C Ferland* a92 93
4 b g Rip Van Winkle(IRE) Totem (USA) (Mizzen Mast (USA))
660a[6]

Almost Gemini (IRE) *Kenneth Slack* a72 77
7 gr g Dylan Thomas(IRE) Streetcar (IRE) (In The Wings)
(1244) 3149[6]

Almost Spanish (IRE) *Scott Dixon* a24
3 b f Rock Of Gibraltar(IRE) Spanish Quest (Rainbow Quest (USA))
2608[8] 4648[12]

Almuhalab *Ruth Carr* 72
5 bb g Dansili Ghanaati (USA) (Giant's Causeway (USA))
1588[7] 2441[7] 2773[5] 3366[4] 3943[8] 4446[6] (5114) 6095[4] 6621[9]

Al Muheer (IRE) *Tom Dascombe* a78 74
11 b g Diktat Dominion Rose (USA) (Spinning World (USA))
37[7]

Almunther (IRE) *J E Hammond* 76
3 b g Invincible Spirit(IRE) Adaala (USA) (Sahm (USA))
5385a[12]

Almutamarred (USA) *Kevin Morgan* a72 56
4 ch g Street Cry(IRE) Sortita (GER) (Monsun (GER))
428[5] 582[7] 1049[2] 1675[9] *(3564)* 4277[6] 5392[7] *(5842)* 6730[9] *7385[9]*

Al Mutanabi (IRE) *G E Mikhalides* 78
3 b c Footstepsinthesand Boragh Jamal (IRE) (Namid)
1311a[3]

Al Nafoorah *Ed Dunlop* a68 70
2 b f Bated Breath Cat O' Nine Tails (Motivator)
2211[7] 6077[2] *7049[7]*

Alnahar (IRE) *Miss Natalia Lupini* a73 73
6 br g Bahri(USA) My Causeway Dream (IRE) (Giant's Causeway (USA))
7517a[5]

Alnajmah *Owen Burrows* 95
3 br f Dansili Joanna (IRE) (High Chaparral (IRE))
6746[7] 7119[6]

Alnashama *Charles Hills* a77 92
4 b g Dubawi(IRE) Ghanaati (USA) (Giant's Causeway (USA))
2010[3] (4157) (4839) (5514) 6082[9]

Alnasl (IRE) *Owen Burrows* 56
2 b f Tamayuz Arwaah (IRE) (Dalakhani (IRE))
5846[7]

Al Nasser Alwashik *Roger Fell* 84
3 b g Intikhab(USA) Crystal Moments (Haafhd)
3264[6] 3483[3] ◆ 3856[4] 4241[3] 4607[3] 6877[10] 7007[3] (7246)

Al Neksh *William Haggas* 99
3 b g Zoffany(IRE) Mount Crystal (IRE) (Montjeu (IRE))
2541[3] ◆ (3023) (4092) ◆ 4827[14] (6489) ◆ 7499[4]

Alniyat *Ed Dunlop* a44
2 ch f Sepoy(AUS) Agata Laguna (IRE) (Elnadim (USA))
7763[12]

Along The Shore (IRE) *Joseph Patrick O'Brien* a62 75
4 b m Dylan Thomas(IRE) Golden Dancer (IRE) (Sadler's Wells (USA))
2114a[10] 4813a[10]

A Lot (USA) *Chad C Brown* 108
4 b h Tapit(USA) Overly Tempting (USA) (In Excess I (IRE))
7833a[10]

Alouja (IRE) *Hugo Palmer* a57 71
2 ch f Raven's Pass(USA) Artisti (Cape Cross (IRE))
7118[4] *7763[8]*

A Lovable Rogue *R Mike Smith* 64
4 b g Dutch Art Dance Card (Cape Cross (IRE))
1878[6] 2201[4]

Aloysius Hansom *Kevin Ryan* a61 61
3 b g High Chaparral(IRE) Crystany (IRE) (Green Desert (USA))
5979[3] 6452[3] *7661[4] 8145[8]*

Alphabetical Order *David O'Meara* a67 84
8 b g Alflora(IRE) Lady Turk (FR) (Baby Turk)
567[4] 675[4] (1121) (1222) (1586) 2194[11]

Alpha Delphini *Bryan Smart* 114
5 b g Captain Gerrard(IRE) Easy To Imagine (USA) (Cozzene (USA))
(1666) 2259[5] 2665[3] (4112) (4584) (5863) ◆ 6574[2]

Alpha Tauri (USA) *Charles Smith* a76 60
10 b g Aldebaran(USA) Seven Moons (JPN) (Sunday Silence (USA))
24[6] 133[2] 176[5] 278[4] 367[6] 523[2] 598[10] 893[7] 1154[3] 1401[5] 1712[6] 3838[10] 4006[8] 4321[9] *(7896) 8236[4] 8350[3]*

Alphonsus *John M Oxx* a103 101
3 b c Invincible Spirit(IRE) Ela Athena (Ezzoud (IRE))
2067a[5] 3677a[8] 4433a[8]

Alpine Dream (IRE) *Tim Easterby* 78
3 b f Dream Ahead(USA) Infamous Angel (Exceed And Excel (AUS))
2674[10] 4043[6] 4861[5] 5537[2] (6436) 6878[2] 7540[12]

Al Qahwa (IRE) *M Halford* 101
3 b g Fast Company(IRE) Cappuccino (IRE) (Mujadil (USA))
2719a[7]

Alqamar *Charlie Appleby* 76
2 b c Dubawi(IRE) Moonsail (Monsun (GER))
6054[4] ◆ 6704[3] 7580[2]

Alqubbah (IRE) *Ed Dunlop* a92 96
3 b f Arcano(IRE) Musharakaat (IRE) (Iffraaj)
1599[2] 2042[3] ◆ 2466[8] 3116[10] *6627[6]* ◆ 7550[6]

Alquffaal *Roger Varian* 85
3 br g Dansili Cuis Ghaire (IRE) (Galileo (IRE))
1784[7] 3160[7] (3715) 6794[5]

Alrahma *F Head* 110
2 br f Shamardal(USA) Albaraah (IRE) (Oasis Dream)
(4925a) 5690a[2]

Al Rayyan (IRE) *Majed Seifeddine* a87 85
4 ch g Danehill Dancer(IRE) Inca Trail (USA) (Royal Academy (USA))
744a[15]

Al Razi (USA) *S Seemar* a90 51
9 b g Distorted Humor(USA) Sweet Serendipity (USA) (Salt Lake (USA))
369a[6]

Al Reeh (IRE) *Marco Botti* a81 83
2 br c Invincible Spirit(IRE) Dffra (IRE) (Refuse To Bend (IRE))
5876[3] ◆ 6524[4] *7064[3] (8066)*

Alsaaden *Richard Hannon* 88
3 b f Acclamation Bahia Breeze (Mister Baileys)
1977[5] 2683[2] 3130[9] 4105[11]

Alsacienne *Sir Mark Prescott Bt* a77 68
3 gr f Dalakhani(IRE) Alabastrine (Green Desert (USA))
5749[3] 5993[2] *(6593)* 7382[2] *7955[2] 8143[3] 8367[6]*

Al Saham *Saeed bin Suroor* a94 110
7 b g Authorized(IRE) Local Spirit (USA) (Lion Cavern (USA))
285a[2]

Al Sail (FR) *Richard Hannon* a71
2 b c Kendargent(FR) Golden Lily (FR) (Dolphin Street (FR))
8353[3]

Al Sailiyah (IRE) *Richard Hannon* a66 72
3 b f Acclamation Raja (IRE) (Pivotal)
1337[3] 1814[6] (2288) 2642[6] 2905[5]

Al's Gal (USA) *Michael J Maker* 110
5 b m English Channel(USA) Dans La Ville (CHI) (Winning (USA))
5430a[2] (7404a) 7831a[9]

Al Shahaniya (IRE) *John Quinn* a81 89
3 ch f Zoffany(IRE) Sweet Kristeen (USA) (Candy Stripes (USA))
2420[6] (3213) 4105[7] 4630[3] ◆ 5671[2] 6032[4] 6811[6]

Alshan Fajer *J R Jenkins* a82 55
6 ch g Lemon Drop Kid(USA) Illuminise (IRE) (Grand Lodge (USA))
256[6] (399) 556[5] 779[5] 983[5] 1717[9] *2582[10] 2995[3]*

Alshaqee *William Haggas* a79 70
3 b c Equiano(FR) Impressible (Oasis Dream)
16[5] 262[4] 322[3]
Alshibaa (IRE) *William Haggas* a71 70
2 br g New Approach(IRE) Amjaad (Dansili)
6570[7] 7769[5] 7940[3]
Al's Memory (IRE) *David Evans* a71 77
7 b g Red Clubs(IRE) Consensus (IRE) (Common Grounds)
1443[3] ◆ (191) 424[7] 616[6] 942[5] 1326[3] (2079a) 2324[9] 2769[5]
Alsvinder *David O'Meara* a85 66
3 b c Footstepsinthesand Notting Hill (BRZ) (Jules (USA))
1669[3] (2333) 2863[7]
Alsylal Dolois (FR) *A Bonin* a61 63
2 ch g Naaqoos Fancy Diamond (GER) (Ransom O'War (USA))
1118a[12] 7345a[7]
Altaira *Tony Carroll* a61 74
5 b h Dubawi(IRE) Peach Pearl (Invincible Spirit (IRE))
164[5] 435[10] 672[7] 1390[11] 2461[4] 3064[10] 3490[3] 4992[3] 5055[3] 5625[6] 6188[3]
Altarsheed (IRE) *Richard Hannon* a86 91
3 b g Lilbourne Lad(IRE) Lilakiya (IRE) (Dr Fong (USA))
1288[3] 1610[9] 2694[3] (3102) 3861[6]
Altesse *J S Bolger* 102
5 ch m Hernando(FR) Alvarita (Selkirk (USA))
(1279a)
Altharoos (IRE) *Sally Hall* a64 85
6 br g Sakhee(USA) Thamara (USA) (Street Cry (IRE))
3565[8] 4374[5] 4894[10] 5886[5] 6217[7] 6956[11] 8385[11]
Althib *Charles Hills* a65
2 b c Dansili Great Heavens (Galileo (IRE))
7906[6] ◆
Altiko Tommy (IRE) *George Baker* a64 64
2 b g Kodiac Altishaan (Darshaan)
2082[5] 3742[7] 5304[8] 5770[2] (6045) 6670[3]
Alton Bay (IRE) *Peter Fahey* a84 89
8 b g Pushkin(IRE) Miss Chapman (IRE) (Imperial Ballet (IRE))
6582[4] 7195a[9] 7708a[17]
Aluqdah (FR) *H-A Pantall* a72
2 b c Zoffany(IRE) Halo De Lune (Halling (USA))
8420a[4]
Alveena (IRE) *D K Weld* 99
4 ch m Medicean Aliyfa (IRE) (Spinning World (USA))
3697a[3] 4850a[10] (7196a)
Al Waab (IRE) *Majed Seifeddine* a99 109
6 ch g Danehill Dancer(IRE) Aunt Julia (In The Wings)
757a[12]
Alwafaa (IRE) *Owen Burrows* a77 68
2 b f Invincible Spirit(IRE) Ghandoorah (USA) (Forestry (USA))
5930[4] 6867[3]
Alwahsh (IRE) *William Haggas* 63
2 b c Dubawi(IRE) Gile Na Greine (IRE) (Galileo (IRE))
6577[8]
Alwalaa (IRE) *Mark Johnston* 66
2 b f Elzaam(AUS) Aljana (IRE) (Exceed And Excel (AUS))
1921[3] 2295[3] 3143[3]
Al Wathna *J-C Rouget* a91 102
3 b f Nayef(USA) Lemon Twist (IRE) (Marju (IRE))
2944a[2] (3935a) 5461a[7]
Always A Dream *Chris Wall* a67 51
3 b f Oasis Dream Always Remembered (IRE) (Galileo (IRE))
2108[9] 3731[5] (5248) 5515[8] 6238[5] 7062[12]
Alwaysandforever (IRE) *Luca Cumani* 80
2 b f Teofilo(IRE) Deep Winter (Pivotal)
6206[2]
Always Endeavour *Daniel Mark Loughnane* a33
3 b f Amadeus Wolf Anaya (Tobougg (IRE))
423[9] 679[9] 925[7]
Always Hope (GER) *Andreas Lowe* 75
3 b f Lord Of England(GER) All An Star (Galileo (IRE))
3207a[11]
Always On Sunday (FR) *Radek Holcak* 91
6 b h Sunday Break(JPN) Good Blend (FR) (Darshaan)
7555a[5]
Always Resolute *Brian Ellison* a64 86
5 b g Refuse To Bend(IRE) Mad Annie (USA) (Anabaa (USA))
(2233) (2406) 3409[3] (3639) 4491[2] ◆ 4721a[9] 6540[3] 7150[11]
Always Smile (IRE) *Saeed bin Suroor* a91 116
4 b m Cape Cross(IRE) Eastern Joy (Dubai Destination (USA))
(2191) ◆ 3271[3] 4107[3] 4826[4] 6949[2]
Always Summer *James Fanshawe* a80 65
3 b f Flatter(USA) Air Kiss (Red Ransom (USA))
2767[10] 3601[8] 4265[6] 4836[4] 5680[2] (6508) (7382) ◆
Always Thankful *Ismail Mohammed* a68 70
2 b f Showcasing Thankful (Diesis)
6454[4] 7099[5]
Always Welcome (USA) *John Gosden* a84 43
3 ch g Elusive Quality(USA) No Matter What (USA) (Nureyev (USA))
2239[12]
Alwina (GER) *Henk Grewe* 86
2 b f Areion(GER) Alte Dame (GER) (Dashing Blade)
7563a[5]
Al Wukair (IRE) *A Fabre* 102
2 b c Dream Ahead(USA) Macheera (IRE) (Machiavellian (USA))
(7491a)
Alyaa (IRE) *Conrad Allen* a73 76
3 b f Iffraaj Queenie Keen (IRE) (Refuse To Bend (IRE))
(679) 1061[7] 1867[4] 3039[6] 3519[7] (4787) 5588[10] 6299[6] 6806[7]
Al Yaboob (IRE) *Ali Jan* a63 33
3 b g Arcano(IRE) Red Blossom (USA) (Silver Hawk (USA))
536a[13]
Al Yarmouk *John Gosden* a71
2 b c Holy Roman Emperor(IRE) Disco Volante (Sadler's Wells (USA))
7882[9] 8089[2]
Alyday *Sir Michael Stoute* a74 84
3 ch f Kyllachy Dayrose (Daylami (IRE))
1723[3] (3350) ◆ 4391[8] 7153[6] 7504[9]
Alyssa *Ralph Beckett* a74 102
3 b f Sir Percy Almiranta (Galileo (IRE))
2815[3] (3727) (4303) (5331) 6259[10] (6917)
Alyssum (IRE) *J S Bolger* a64 76
3 ch f New Approach(IRE) Alasha (IRE) (Barathea (IRE))
7393a[14]
Al Zaman (IRE) *Simon Crisford* 81
2 bb c Cacique(IRE) Flowers Of Spring (IRE) (Celtic Swing)
7074[2] ◆
Alzammaar (USA) *Warren Greatrex* a60 66
5 b g Birdstone(USA) Alma Mater (Sadler's Wells (USA))
4661[7]
Alzebarh (IRE) *James Fanshawe* a53 55
3 ch f Poet's Voice Dubai Pearl (IRE) (Refuse To Bend (IRE))
2321[6] 2784[8] 3319[5] 4021[2]
Al Zeem (USA) *A bin Harmash*
2 gr c Old Fashioned(USA) Twilights Prayer (USA) (Allen's Prospect (USA))
8391a[7]
Amaany *Charles Hills* 78
3 br f Teofilo(IRE) Almass (IRE) (Elnadim (USA))
3769[3] 4361[11] (6650)
Amabilis *Ralph Beckett* 90
2 b f Champs Elysees Pure Joy (Zamindar (USA))
4147[2] ◆ 4801[2] 5401[3] (6472) 7147[5] ◆
Amadeus Rox (FR) *Alan King* a57 46
2 b g Falco(USA) Vittoria Vetra (Danehill Dancer (IRE))
5081[6] 5740[11] 7012[9]
Amadiva (IRE) *Martin Bosley* a33 32
5 b m Amadeus Wolf Divine Quest (Kris)
7421[7] 8281[7]
A Magic Man (IRE) *Henk Grewe*
2 gr c Lawman(FR) Ayun Tara (FR) (Martaline)
7401a[7]
Amakhala (USA) *Charlie Appleby* 57
2 br g Candy Ride(ARG) Androeah (USA) (Arch (USA))
7243[8]
Amalina (FR) *N Caullery* a70 44
3 gr f Martaline Annee De La Femme (IRE) (Common Grounds)
716a[5] 1357a[9]
Amantius *Johnny Farrelly* a68 60
7 b g Multiplex Ghana (GER) (Bigstone (IRE))
3403[8] 3991[9] 4979[2] 5745[3] 6422[2]
Amanto (GER) *Paul Nicholls* a72 66
6 b g Medicean Amore (GER) (Lando (GER))
698[3] 882[6]
Amathyst *Michael Appleby* a15 69
2 ch f Bahamian Bounty Wish You Luck (Dubai Destination (USA))
2963[6] 3613[3] 5756[4] 6275[5] (7091) 7440[5] 7893[10]
Amaze Me *Robyn Brisland* a85 98
4 ch m Aqlaam Princess Miletrian (IRE) (Danehill (USA))
72[6]
Amazement (GER) *James Tate* a93 83
3 ch g Lope De Vega(IRE) Aglow (Spinning World (USA))
245[2] 1662[2] (2271) 2654[7] 3364[3] (8092) 8478[13]
Amazing Blue Sky *Ruth Carr* a53 51
10 b g Barathea(IRE) Azure Lake (USA) (Lac Ouimet (USA))
251[8] 521[4] 684[8]
Amazing Charm *James Tate* a55 66
4 ch m King's Best(USA) Bint Doyen (Doyen (IRE))
3823[13] 4568[4] 5010[6] 5749[5] 6513[6]
Amazing Kids (NZ) *J Size* 116
4 b g Falkirk(NZ) Cadence (NZ) (Rhythm (USA))
1911a[5] 8330a[4]
Amazing Maria (IRE) *David O'Meara* 118
5 gr m Mastercraftsman(IRE) Messias Da Silva (USA) (Tale Of The Cat (USA))
1886[3] 3242[6] 4107[7] 4926a[6] 6749[4]
Amazing Moon *Richard Hughes* a45
3 b f Aqlaam Bint Doyen (Doyen (IRE))
814[10] 1000[8]
Amazing Red (IRE) *Ed Dunlop* 89
3 b c Teofilo(FR) Artisia (IRE) (Peintre Celebre (USA))
1426[6] (1784)
Amazona (GER) *Jean-Pierre Carvalho* 108
4 b m Dubawi(IRE) Amarette (GER) (Monsun (GER))
1822a[7] 2727a[10] (7843a)
Amazour (IRE) *Ismail Mohammed* a106 90
4 b g Azamour(IRE) Choose Me (IRE) (Choisir (AUS))
1394[7] (3656) 4338[11] 6056[7] 7068[3] 8069[4] (8583)
Ambassadorial (USA) *M Halford* a105
2 b c Elusive Quality(USA) Tactfully (IRE) (Discreet Cat (USA))
(7130a)
Amber Crystal *Linda Perratt* a44 46
4 b m Multiplex Glitz (IRE) (Hawk Wing (USA))
1692[11] 2359[8] 2572[9] 2812[7] 5225[8] 5582[5] 5804[4] 5838[6] 6347[9] 6616[7] 6813[6] 6835[5] 7092[7] 7254[10] 7604[5] 8289[5]
Amber Flush *Martin Smith* a13 77
7 b m Sir Harry Lewis(USA) Sari Rose (FR) (Vertical Speed (FR))
1273[7] 1772[9] 3913[13] 5176[7]
Amberine *Malcolm Saunders* 50
2 b f Equiano(FR) Crimson Fern (IRE) (Titus Livius (FR))
4261[12] 4790[6]
Amber Mystique *Kristin Stubbs* a72 76
3 ch f Sakhee(USA) Dame De Noche (Lion Cavern (USA))
8388[2] (8559)
Ambiance (IRE) *Katharina Stenefeldt* a66 100
5 b g Camacho Thawrah (IRE) (Green Desert (USA))
3992a[8]
Ambiguity (IRE) *Joseph Patrick O'Brien* 88
2 b c Fastnet Rock(AUS) Descant (USA) (Nureyev (USA))
2494a[3] 3247[18] 4171a[6] 4414a[6] 5212a[5]
Ambitious Boy *John O'Shea* a81 58
7 bl g Striking Ambition Cherished Love (IRE) (Tomba)
433[11] 1186[9] 1341[6] 1724[6] 2130[9] 3510[6] 4084[7] 4506[3] 4908[8] 7912[11] 8315[9]
Ambitious Brew (USA) *Martin F Jones* a105 106
6 bb g Tizbud(USA) Kathwen (USA) (Forest Wildcat (USA))
7833a[13]
Ambitious Icarus *Richard Guest* a67 71
7 b g Striking Ambition Nesting Box (Grand Lodge (USA))
1444[11] 1634[3] 1879[6] 2016[9] 2346[6] 2846[3] 2975[5] 3217[5] 3494[4] 3713[4] 3907[4] 6479[3] 6878[13] 7289[5] 7420[6] 7774[5] 7851[4] 8031[4]
Ambitious Rosie *Tony Carroll* a42 55
5 b m Striking Ambition Cerulean Rose (Bluegrass Prince (IRE))
35[7] 216[7] 412[4] 602[9]
Ambriel (IRE) *Michael Dods* 78
3 gr f Dark Angel(IRE) Skehana (IRE) (Mukaddamah (USA))
3213[9] 5858[9] 6501[3] 7220[10]
Ambrosia *Roger Varian* a64 66
2 b f Frankel Pearling (USA) (Storm Cat (USA))
7278[6] 7696[5]
Ambuscade *Hughie Morrison* a55
3 b f Dick Turpin(IRE) Tarqua (IRE) (King Charlemagne (USA))
3319[10]
Ame Bleue *A Fabre* a96 107
4 ch m Dubawi(IRE) Aquarelliste (FR) (Danehill (USA))
1232a[5] 1822a[6] 2727a[7] 5691a[2] 6598a[2] 8165a[7]
Amelia Dream *Mick Channon* 72
2 ch f Kyllachy Lady Scarlett (Woodman (USA))
5400[5] 5705[4] 6111[5]
Amenable (IRE) *Ann Stokell* a48 79
9 b g Bertolini(USA) Graceful Air (IRE) (Danzero (AUS))
25[8] 895[6] 1899[9] 4485[8]
Amenta (IRE) *Roger Charlton* a55
2 b f Roderic O'Connor(IRE) Pale Light (USA) (Lemon Drop Kid (USA))
7867[9]
American Artist (IRE) *Roger Varian* a76 96
4 ch g Danehill Dancer(IRE) American Adventure (USA) (Miswaki (USA))
1620[2] 1972[5] 2752[6] 6298[5] ◆ 6786[14] 7535[3]
American Craftsman (IRE) *Jedd O'Keeffe* a34 43
2 gr g Mastercraftsman(IRE) Quiet Mouse (USA) (Quiet American (USA))
5150[7] 7432[10]
American Freedom (USA) *Bob Baffert* a115
3 b c Pulpit(USA) Gottcha Last (USA) (Pleasant Tap (USA))
5913a[2]
American Gal (USA) *Bob Baffert* a103 89
2 b f Concord Point(USA) American Story (USA) (Ghostzapper (USA))
7830a[3]
American History (USA) *John Gosden* a68 75
2 bb c High Chaparral(IRE) Spinning Time (USA) (Giant's Causeway (USA))
7225[3] 7907[6] 8073[2]
American Hope (USA) *Saeed bin Suroor* a103 109
5 b g Lemon Drop Kid(USA) Cedrat (FR) (Enrique)
284a[2] 624a[4] (810a)
American Hustle (IRE) *Brian Ellison* a69 70
4 b m Jeremy(USA) Love In May (IRE) (City On A Hill (USA))
1565[3] 1631[7] 2332[3] 3610[9] 4490[5] 5757[3] 6502[9]
American Life (FR) *Sophie Leech* a53 63
9 bb g American Post Poplife (FR) (Zino)
1244[4] (1523) 2018[9]
American Patriot (USA) *Todd Pletcher* 106
3 bb c War Front(USA) Life Well Lived (USA) (Tiznow (USA))
5429a[3]
American Patrol (IRE) *Neil Mulholland* a45 58
2 ch c Rio De La Plata(USA) Gutter Press (IRE) (Raise A Grand (IRE))
5121[4] 6704[10] 8034[9] 8276[7]
American Song (FR) *C Plisson* 38
2 b g American Post Lilli Star (FR) (Fly To The Stars)
3871a[15]
American Way (FR) *M Aubry* a64 29
4 ch m American Post Green Way (FR) (Green Tune (USA))
8422a[13]
American Whipper (FR) *J-C Rouget* a77 56
3 b g Whipper(USA) Abondante (USA) (Thunder Gulch (USA))
5385a[8]
Amherst Rock *John Butler* a38 60
2 ch g Exceed And Excel(AUS) Frigid (Indian Ridge)
4545[9] 5410[7] 7975[12]
Amie Noire (GER) *Wido Neuroth* a86 97
5 bb m Soldier Of Fortune(IRE) Autriche (IRE) (Acatenango (GER))
3449a[2] 6390a[7] (7395a)
Amigo (GER) *Eva Fabianova* 84
2 ch c Lord Of England(GER) All Night Long (GER) (Ransom O'War (USA))
7842a[5]
Amirant (GER) *E Leenders* a87 103
8 b g Shirocco(GER) A Winning Dream (GER) (Law Society (USA))
7088a[4]
Amirli (IRE) *Alistair Whillans* a51 74
5 ch g Medicean Amenapinga (FR) (Spinning World (USA))
2618[9] 3706[3] 4099[2] (4828) 5118[3] 6346[5]
Amisha (FR) *J Parize* a43 79
3 b f Naaqoos Star Dancing (Danehill Dancer (IRE))
2172a[7]
Amis Reunis *Colin Teague* a30 42
7 b m Bahamian Bounty Spring Clean (FR) (Danehill (USA))
130[9] 418[9] 4513[6] 4771[7] 5278[6] 5483[6] ◆ 5839[6] 6616[6] 6835[8] 7046[9]
Amlad (IRE) *Ed Dunlop* 79
2 ch c Lope De Vega(IRE) Pietra Dura (Cadeaux Genereux)
4103[9] 4533[8] 5848[4]
Amlak *Richard Hannon* a76 72
2 b f Invincible Spirit(IRE) Forgotten Me (IRE) (Holy Roman Emperor (IRE))
1988[4] 2219[5] 3128[4] 6141[2] 6658[2]
A Momentofmadness *Charles Hills* a84 92
3 b g Elnadim(USA) Royal Blush (Royal Applause)
(954) 1271[3] (2751) (3193) 4062[19] 4803[16] 6944[6] 7537[20]
Amona (IRE) *Andreas Lowe* 104
4 rg m Aussie Rules(USA) Abbasharjah (GER) (Tiger Hill (IRE))
4696a[6] 5454a[6] 6152a[7]
Among Angels *Daniel Mark Loughnane* a85 80
4 b g Acclamation Love Action (IRE) (Motivator)
250[4] 508[5] 944[2] 1634[14] 2579[11] 8402[3]
Amood (IRE) *Simon West* a82 81
5 ch g Elnadim(USA) Amanah (USA) (Mr Prospector (USA))
2345[8] 3168[6] 3553[3] ◆ 4360[2] 4889[5] 6435[7] (7662)
Amore Hass (IRE) *Stefano Botti* 90
2 b c Azamour(IRE) Hassaya (IRE) (King's Best (USA))
7839a[7]
Amor Invicto (IRE) *Daniel Kubler* a65 67
3 b g Holy Roman Emperor(IRE) Love In The Mist (USA) (Silver Hawk (USA))
765[10] 8086[3] 8342[7]
Amour De Nuit (IRE) *Sir Mark Prescott Bt* a107 109
4 b g Azamour(IRE) Umthoulah (IRE) (Unfuwain (USA))
(1963) 3387[6] 4031a[4] 6526[4] 6974a[10]
Ampere (FR) *A Fabre* 116
4 b h Galileo(IRE) Amorama (FR) (Sri Pekan (USA))
1375a[12]
Amthal (IRE) *Lucy Wadham* a71 70
7 b m Dalakhani(IRE) Al Ihtithar (IRE) (Barathea (IRE))
3642[3] (5130)
Amy Blair *Keith Dalgleish* a28 57
3 b g Captain Gerrard(IRE) Shalad'Or (Golden Heights)
510[5] 3153[8] 4444[10] 4874[7] 5152[8] 5578[7] (5835) (6839) 7249[6]
Amy Gardner *James Given* a56 54
2 b f Bated Breath Cesseras (IRE) (Cape Cross (IRE))
3902[7] 4404[5] 4842[3] 5351[2] 5853[3] 6045[3]
Amyntas (ITY) *Stefano Botti* 103
2 b c Desert Prince(IRE) A Touch Wild (USA) (Touch Gold (USA))
7401a[3]
Anaerobio (ARG) *M F De Kock* a78 110
8 b h Catcher In The Rye(IRE) Potra Anala (ARG) (Potrillon (ARG))
95a[4] 282a[4] (373a) 744a[8]
Anagallis (IRE) *John Balding* a4 62
3 b f Elusive Pimpernel(USA) Adjtiya (IRE) (Green Desert (USA))
365[7]
Anamba *M Halford* 104
3 b f Shamardal(USA) Anamato (AUS) (Redoute's Choice (AUS))
(2716a) 3274[6]
Anantapur (FR) *S Cerulis* a81 81
4 b g Lawman(FR) Relais D'Aumale (Rainbow Quest (USA))
(4901a) 5501a[2]
Anastazia *Paul D'Arcy* a78 80
4 br m Kyllachy Meddle (Diktat)
2213[4] 2401[5] 3038[10] 3823[4] 4362[8] (5090) 5337[4] 5935[4] 6510[3] 6851[7] 7620[6] 7887[5]
Anaximandros (USA) *Mikhail Yanakov* a96
3 b c Hard Spun(USA) Dragon Fly (FR) (Sadler's Wells (USA))
5913a[13]
Anbar *R Bouresly* a53
4 br h Thewayyouare(USA) Elegant Times (IRE) (Dansili)
8576a[15]
An Cailin Orga (IRE) *J S Bolger* 92
3 ch f Galileo(IRE) Finsceal Beo (IRE) (Mr Greeley (USA))
3630a[6] 4416a[6] 7393a[13]
Ancient Astronaut *John Quinn* a64 81
3 b g Kodiac Tatora (Selkirk (USA))
1243[4] 1599[6] 2239[15] 3568[5] 4134[4] (5960) 6435[5] 6878[9] 7413[5] 7590[3]
Ancient Cross *Michael Easterby* a69 88
12 b g Machiavellian(USA) Magna Graecia (IRE) (Warning)
541[4] 799[7] 1341[3] 1496[6] 1648[3] 2416[5] 2856[2] (3016)
Ancient History (IRE) *A Fabre* 105
3 ch c Shamardal(USA) Antiquities (Kaldounevees (FR))
7152[6]
Ancient World (USA) *Charles Hills* a59 50
3 ch g Giant's Causeway(USA) Satulagi (USA) (Officer (USA))
1036[7] 2700[10]
Andalouse Eria (FR) *F Chappet* a66
2 bb f Rio De La Plata(USA) Berroscoberro (FR) (Octagonal (NZ))
7783a[4]

Andalucia (SPA) *G Arizkorreta Elosegui* 76
5 b m Pyrus(USA) Abril (FR) (Anabaa (USA))
5249a[4]
Andalusite *Ed McMahon* a59 63
3 br f Equiano(FR) Kammaan (Diktat)
3209[4] 3900[3] *4472[2] 5078[4]* 5570 [3] 6361[3] 6680[8] 7038[3] *7612[7] 7913[10]*
Andanotherone (IRE) *Simon Crisford* a52 67
3 b f Kodiac Itsanothergirl (Reprimand)
2904[3] ◆ *7894[6]*
Andar *Clive Cox* a76 83
3 rg c Hellvelyn Rioliina (IRE) (Captain Rio)
2693[2] ◆ 3127[2] 3643[5] 4344[3] 5408[6]
Andaz *Marjorie Fife* a70 57
3 b f Makfi Waafiah (Anabaa (USA))
742 679[6] 3153[9] 3838[5] 4424[10] 4600[6] *5130[6]*
Andok (IRE) *Richard Fahey* 87
2 b c Elzaam(AUS) My Causeway Dream (IRE) (Giant's Causeway (USA))
(4423) ◆ (6229) 7541[2]
Andrassy Avenue (USA) *Charlie Appleby* a79
2 b c Street Cry(IRE) Suez (Green Desert (USA))
7511[4] (7940) ◆
An Duine Uasal (IRE) *Adrian Paul Keatley* a78 76
3 b g Alfred Nobel(IRE) Dany Song (USA) (Yankee Victor (USA))
4288[6]
Andys Girl (IRE) *Brian Ellison* a63 61
3 gr f Clodovil(IRE) Fishy (Irish River (FR))
1669[9] 6218[3] *6960[7] 8093[2] 8482[5]*
Aneedh *Clive Mulhall* a57 54
6 b g Lucky Story(USA) Seed Al Maha (USA) (Seeking The Gold (USA))
1202[11] 2672[4] 3480[6] 4724[4] 5057[5] *7794[10] 8142[5] 8400[10]*
Anfaass (IRE) *George Margarson* a60 79
2 ro c Vale Of York(IRE) Webcast (IRE) (Verglas (IRE))
5410[3] (6448) *7460[6]* 7820[3]
An Fear Ciuin (IRE) *Richard Ford* a81 83
5 b g Galileo(IRE) Potion (Pivotal)
(1405) 2820[5] 3942[5] 4935[7] (5758) (6279) 7357[3]
Anfield *Mick Quinn* a46 42
5 b m Captain Gerrard(IRE) Billie Holiday (Fairy King (USA))
217[8] 258[5] 363[4]
Anfitrion Sale (ARG) *Y Al Blooshi* a104 22
4 ch h Not For Sale(ARG) Potrabrite (ARG) (Potrillon (ARG))
373a[12] *537a[8] 840a[6]*
Angel Baby (FR) *J-C Rouget* a74
2 b f Canford Cliffs(IRE) Shabanou (FR) (Shamardal (USA))
5460a[2]
Angel Down *Henry Candy* 80
2 b g Kyllachy Falling Angel (Kylian (USA))
2997[6] 3813[5] (5202) 5583[16]
Angel Flores (IRE) *Lee Carter* a78 32
5 b m Art Connoisseur(IRE) Emmas Princess (IRE) (Bahhare (USA))
1811[6] 2155[9] 3317[4] 6249[12] 6902[13]
Angel Gabrial (IRE) *Richard Fahey* a93 109
7 b g Hurricane Run(IRE) Causeway Song (USA) (Giant's Causeway (USA))
1081[12] 1967[8] 2486[3] *3658[16]* 6118[9] 6781[3] 7150[15]
Angel Grace (IRE) *David Menuisier* a60 77
3 gr f Dark Angel(IRE) Light Sea (IRE) (King's Best (USA))
(1270) 1759[4] 5975[10] 7412[6]
Angelical (IRE) *Daniel Mark Loughnane* a59 64
3 b f Dark Angel(IRE) Ladylishandra (IRE) (Mujadil (USA))
3609[11] 4546[8] 5486[3] 6444[2] *7753[8] 7870[10] 8155[11]*
Angelical Dancer (FR) *Marco Botti* a73 84
3 gr g Dark Angel(IRE) Sundancer (Hernando (FR))
603[2] 968[5] 1140[8]
Angelical Eve (IRE) *George Baker* 35
2 gr f Dark Angel(IRE) First Lady (IRE) (Indian Ridge)
7269[7] 7574[12]
Angelic Guest (IRE) *Mick Channon* 67
3 gr f Dark Angel(IRE) Kelsey Rose (Most Welcome)
1628[4] 1998[7] 2505[6] 2968[5] 3740[9]
Angelic Lord (IRE) *Tom Dascombe* a99 104
4 b g Dark Angel(IRE) Divine Design (IRE) (Barathea (IRE))
4831[2] 921[8] 8407[7]
Angel In Disguise (IRE) *Philip McBride* a52 43
2 b f Vale Of York(IRE) Meynell (Sakhee (USA))
7465[8] *8082[9]*
Angel In The Snow *Brian Ellison* a55
3 ch g Haafhd Chilly Filly (IRE) (Montjeu (IRE))
5[5] 345[8] 7656[3] 7992[4]
Angelito *Tony Newcombe* a75 65
7 ch g Primo Valentino(IRE) Supreme Angel (Beveled (USA))
3674[11] 3995[5] 6296[4] ◆ 6832[9] 7303[11] *8316[8]*
Angel Meadow *Micky Hammond* 86
2 b f Mayson Memo (Groom Dancer (USA))
(3112) 3663[6] 6538[2] 6734[6] 7536[11]
Angel Of Darkness *Charles Hills* a67 42
2 b f Dark Angel(IRE) Chelsea Morning (USA) (Giant's Causeway (USA))
3812[9] *6624[3] 8081[6]*
Angel Of Light (IRE) *Jo Hughes* a44 1
4 b m Dark Angel(IRE) Riymaisa (IRE) (Traditionally (USA))
1499[7] 1739[12] *7052[8]*
Angel Of Rome (IRE) *Richard Hughes* a51
2 gr f Mastercraftsman(IRE) Bright Sapphire (IRE) (Galileo (IRE))
7963[5] ◆
Angel Palanas *K R Burke* a60 65
2 b g Mayson Scottish Exile (IRE) (Ashkalani (IRE))
4981[5] 5476[4] *6099[6]* 6763[8] 7579[2]
Angels Above (IRE) *John Butler* a54 50
4 b g Dark Angel(IRE) Fag End (IRE) (Treasure Kay)
1295[9] 1548[6]

Angel's Acclaim (IRE) *Kevin Ryan* 62
2 gr f Dark Angel(IRE) Miss Otis (Danetime (IRE))
2535[7]
Angel's Quest (FR) *Richard Hughes* a73
2 b f Dark Angel(IRE) Lilac Charm (IRE) (Marju (IRE))
7647[3] ◆
Angel's Touch (AUS) *Darren Weir* 78
3 br f Dane Shadow(AUS) Zabere (AUS) (Dehere (USA))
7826a[8]
Angel Way (IRE) *John Gallagher* a68 79
7 b m Trans Island Zilayah (USA) (Zilzal (USA))
41[6] 162[6] 1269[7] 1898[7] 3530[3] 3811[6] 4744[5]
Angie Baby *J S Moore* 40
2 b f Compton Place Angie And Liz (IRE) (Spectrum (IRE))
2641[6] 2902[6]
Angie's Girl *Clive Cox* a63 72
3 b f Exceed And Excel(AUS) Expedience (USA) (With Approval (CAN))
1257[4] 2337[8] 2980[4] *3527[5]* 4262[3] 4878[5] 5330[10]
Anginola (IRE) *David Dennis* a47 42
7 b m Kodiac Lady Montekin (Montekin)
232[7] 378[9]
Anglo Paddy (IRE) *Neil Mulholland*
7 ch m Mountain High(IRE) Hazel Sylph (IRE) (Executive Perk)
630[6]
Anglophile *Charlie Appleby* a106 98
5 ch g Dubawi(IRE) Anna Palariva (IRE) (Caerleon (USA))
(317) 1067[2] (Dead)
Angrywhitepyjamas (IRE) *William Muir* a80 65
3 b g Manduro(GER) Ornellaia (IRE) (Mujadil (USA))
3400[3] *(4213) 5026[6]*
Anieres Boy *Oliver Greenall* a61 60
4 b g Kheleyf(USA) Place Morny (IRE) (Cadeaux Genereux)
2053[3] 2418[2] *2919[11]* 3268[9] 3484[15] 6506[5] 6959[8] *(7200)* 7290[13] *8094[10] 8188[10]*
Anjuna Beach (USA) *Ann Stokell* a60 60
6 b g Artie Schiller(USA) Hidden Temper (USA) (Miswaki (USA))
32[2] 79[2] 175[2] 326[2] 904[5] (1263) 1578[6] 8086[8] 8289[11]
Ankle (FR) *C Ferland* 102
3 ch c Shamardal(USA) Polygreen (FR) (Green Tune (USA))
2140a[4] 3183a[7]
Anna Barkova (IRE) *K R Burke* a62 59
3 b f Invincible Spirit(IRE) Skiphall (Halling (USA))
1814[3] 2304[6] 3209[9] 7743[8] *7894[3] 8135[5]*
Annabella *Tim McCarthy* a46
3 b f Approve(IRE) Ashlinn (IRE) (Ashkalani (IRE))
7311[12] 7727[6] 8449[5]
Annakrista (GER) *Zoe Davison* a58 54
8 b m Kallisto(GER) Annabelle (GER) (Esclavo (FR))
127[6] 289[2] 417[7] 461[5] 622[8] 941[3] 1049[6]
Anna Lou (FR) *B Drieux* a51 69
4 bb m Anabaa Blue Lilou Prospect (FR) (Loup Solitaire (USA))
3092a[7]
Anna Mia (GER) *Melanie Sauer* 93
4 ch m Monsun(GER) Queen's Hall (Singspiel (IRE))
1907a[8] 4253a[9]
Anneani (IRE) *David Evans* a62 60
4 b m Bushranger(IRE) Hazium (IRE) (In The Wings)
787[4] 986[7] 2436[7] 3020[11] *(4214)* 5513[2] *5610[2] 6137[3] 6593[3]* 6826[13] *7368[2] 7514[2]*
Annie Fior (IRE) *Denis Coakley* a74 64
2 ch f Finsceal Fior(IRE) Annamanamoux (USA) (Leroidesanimaux (BRZ))
7576[4] ◆ *(8081)*
Annie Salts *Chris Dwyer* a66 69
3 b f Zebedee Dazzling View (USA) (Distant View (USA))
2372[9] 3000[9] (5041) *5370[6] 6248[7]* 6680[16] *8429[10]*
Annie T *Paul Midgley* 42
3 b f Makfi Hanella (IRE) (Galileo (IRE))
1562[11] 2576[11]
Annigoni (IRE) *Ruth Carr* a49 57
4 b g Excellent Art Aspen Falls (IRE) (Elnadim (USA))
2507[9] *2915[9]* 3212[5] 3706[4] 4489[7] 5117[6] *6424[2]* 7045[7]
Anniversarie *John Norton* a57 39
4 ch m Major Cadeaux Razzle (IRE) (Green Desert (USA))
383[4] 568[10] 1768[10]
Announcement *Ronald Thompson* a56 54
5 ch m Proclamation(IRE) Anapola (GER) (Polish Precedent (USA))
569[10]
Annoushka *Mrs Ilka Gansera-Leveque* a43 57
3 b f Proclamation(IRE) Anapola (GER) (Polish Precedent (USA))
5380[5] *6855[4]*
Anonymous John (IRE) *Dominic Ffrench Davis* a97 80
4 gr g Baltic King Helibel (IRE) (Pivotal)
4[2] 288[7] 338[8] 749[8] 923[8] 2391[12] 3594[3] 4460[4] 5773[2] 7221[3] *7617[5] 8176[6] 8561[5]*
Anonymous Lady (IRE) *Adrian Paul Keatley* a81 88
4 b m Le Cadre Noir(IRE) Dany Song (USA) (Yankee Victor (USA))
(1693) (2364) 4540a[7] *5441a[5]* 6539[12]
Another Angel (IRE) *Michael Dods* a76 64
2 b c Dark Angel(IRE) Kermana (IRE) (Selkirk (USA))
1377[3] ◆ 1850[4] *2913[3]*
Another Boy *Ralph Beckett* a69 78
3 ch g Paco Boy(IRE) Kurtanella (Pastoral Pursuits)
1176[8] 1452[3] *2446[7]* 2981[9] (3111) 3908[7] 4306[5] 6266[7] 7506[5]

Another Day *Robert Cowell* a25
3 b f Monsieur Bond(IRE) Madam President (Royal Applause)
5509[10] 5721[11]
Another Desperado (IRE) *Rebecca Bastiman* 42
3 b g Approve(IRE) Kind Regards (IRE) (Unfuwain (USA))
1494[6] 1870[5] 2667[9] 3293[5] 5041[8] 5354[13] 5803[10]
Another Eclipse (IRE) *David Simcock* a79 67
2 b c Lope De Vega(IRE) Black Dahlia (Dansili)
7013[4] *7511[3]*
Another Full Power (ITY) *M Grassi* 90
7 b g Mujahid(USA) Miss Schivani (IRE) (Marju (IRE))
2518a[11] 7840a[10]
Another Go (IRE) *Alan Swinbank* a38 87
3 gr g Strategic Prince Golden Rose (GER) (Winged Love (IRE))
958[5] (1123) (1411) 4153[8] 5865[9] 6500[13] 7412[10] *8239[12]*
Another Lincolnday *Michael Herrington* a66 68
5 ch g Desideratum Another Paris (Paris House)
2051[5] 3052[5] 3480[7] 3942[7] *4645[4]* (5435) 6227[6] 6519[6] *6906[5] 7385[2] 7657[5] 7846[4]*
Another Squeeze *Peter Hiatt* a29 38
8 gr m Proclamation(IRE) Tight Squeeze (Petoski)
5208[5] 5958[9] 6891[9]
Another Touch *Richard Fahey* 101
3 b g Arcano(IRE) Alsalwa (IRE) (Nayef (USA))
1851[2] 2473[9] 4448[7] (5175) 5616[5] 6557[8] 7153[2]
Another Wise Kid (IRE) *Paul Midgley* a82 97
8 b g Whipper(USA) Romancing (Dr Devious (IRE))
923[12] 1197[6] 3250[4] 3891[4] 4667[14] 6944[12] 7315[4] *7858[7] 8192[11] 8308[10]*
Anouma Freedom (FR) *H De Nicolay* a58 65
5 b g Hannouma(IRE) Miss Freedom (FR) (Freedom Cry)
8421a[7]
Ansaab *Marjorie Fife* a98 87
8 b g Cape Cross(IRE) Dawn Raid (IRE) (Docksider (USA))
31[2] 353[3] 656[6] 4650[6] 5198[3] ◆ 5932[6] *8446[8]*
An Saighdiur (IRE) *Andrew Slattery* a84 103
9 b g Acclamation Brief Sentiment (IRE) (Brief Truce (USA))
1015a[4] 1127a[3] 5941a[13] 6556[8] 6984a[11]
Anshika (IRE) *Ollie Pears*
2 b f Elzaam(AUS) Model Looks (IRE) (Majestic Missile (IRE))
4404[9] 4842[6]
Antalya (GER) *Markus Klug* 97
5 b m Areion(GER) Annina (GER) (Diktat)
5695a[8] 6611a[8] 7027a[2] 7719a[4]
Anticipation (IRE) *A S Cruz* 106
5 b g Fastnet Rock(AUS) Small Sacrifice (IRE) (Sadler's Wells (USA))
8329a[14]
Antigua (SWE) *Tommy Gustafsson* 77
4 ch m Archipenko(USA) On Light (SWE) (Midyan (USA))
3448a[6]
Antinori (IRE) *S Seemar* a97 97
10 b g Fasliyev(USA) Albavilla (Spectrum (IRE))
93a[7] 285a[10] 538a[6] 811a[13]
Antioco (IRE) *Richard Fahey* 70
3 b g Motivator Haraplata (GER) (Platini (GER))
1971[P]
Antiquarium (IRE) *Charlie Appleby* a109 106
4 b g New Approach(IRE) Antillia (Red Ransom (USA))
2482[4] *(3658)* 5655[8]
Anton Chigurh *Tom Dascombe* a79 73
7 b g Oasis Dream Barathiki (Barathea (IRE))
437[3] 598[7] (1058) 1640[10] *(1707) 2444[3]* 3398[7] 3849[3] 4348[5] 4933[6] *6138[9] (8240)*
Antonella *T J Martins Novais* 83
2 b f Dream Ahead(USA) Al Janadeirya (Oasis Dream)
7972a[4]
Antoni (IRE) *J E Hammond* a53
2 b g Arcano(IRE) Art Work (Zafonic (USA))
7588a[9]
Antonio Joli (IRE) *Jo Hughes* a63 44
4 b g Arcano(IRE) Snowtime (IRE) (Galileo (IRE))
342[6] 567[8] 1140[7] 1561[11] 5232[7]
Antonoe (USA) *P Bary* 103
3 bb f First Defence(USA) Ixora (USA) (Dynaformer (USA))
1581a[3] 2282a[12] 5498a[11]
Anushka Noo Noo *Ollie Pears* 68
3 b f Makfi Triple Edition (USA) (Lear Fan (USA))
1448[14] 2306[10] 4454[12] 5278[10]
Any Guest (IRE) *George Margarson* 56
3 b g Zoffany(IRE) Princess Speedfit (FR) (Desert Prince (IRE))
2553[10] 3080[6] 3734[7] 5338[4]
Any Joy (IRE) *Ben Haslam* a34 57
3 b f Zoffany(IRE) For Joy (Singspiel (IRE))
1597[5] 1998[6] 5757[5] *8093[7]*
Any Questions *William Knight* 47
2 ch c Poet's Voice Funday (Daylami (IRE))
7013[10] 7501[12]
Anythingknappen (IRE) *Tim Easterby* a60 71
2 b f Arcano(IRE) Knapton Hill (Zamindar (USA))
4765[8] 5516[5] (5854) 6554[11] *7598[5]*
Anythingtoday (IRE) *Hugo Palmer* a79 82
2 b c Zoffany(IRE) Corking (IRE) (Montjeu (IRE))
6880[3] ◆ *7432[4] (8034)* ◆
Any Time *John Joseph Murphy* a47 51
3 b f Zamindar(USA) Penchee (Grand Lodge (USA))
5096a[16]
Anzhelika (IRE) *David Lanigan* a95 98
4 ch m Galileo(IRE) Ange Bleu (USA) (Alleged (USA))
(4940) 5587[6] 7271[3] *7652[3]*
Aothea (GER) *J Hirschberger* a60
2 b f Areion(GER) Aotearoa (FR) (Doyen (IRE))
7879a[9]

Apache Glory (USA) *Daniel Mark Loughnane* a76 63
8 bb m Cherokee Run(USA) Jumeirah Glory (USA) (Deputy Minister (CAN))
38[12] 316[4] (724) 832[6]
Apache Myth *James Eustace* a62 56
3 ch f Sakhee's Secret Indian Angel (Indian Ridge)
2009[13] *2578[8]* 3720[5]
Apache Song *Rod Millman* 72
3 ch f Mount Nelson Pantita (Polish Precedent (USA))
1386[3] 1739[8] 2415[4] 4956[3] 5822[3] 6441[2] 6650[4] 7272[3]
Apache Storm *Michael Appleby* a90 95
4 ch m Pivotal Best Side (IRE) (King's Best (USA))
4[5] 220[5] 359[3] 492[2] 580[5] 771[9] (1003) 1318[6] 2223[7]
Apamurra (USA) *Mark Johnston* a57 67
2 b f Lonhro(AUS) Alizes (NZ) (Rory's Jester (AUS))
2874[3] 3106[5] *5469[6]* 6564[10] *7143[7]*
Apex King (IRE) *Ed Dunlop* 97
2 b c Kodiac Rainbowskia (FR) (Rainbow Quest (USA))
2756[7] (3408) (4622) 5646[4]
Aphoristic (IRE) *E McNamara* a50 8
3 ch g Street Cry(IRE) Sutra (USA) (Meadowlake (USA))
7517a[9]
Apilobar (FR) *F Vermeulen* 108
3 b c Slickly(FR) Popee (FR) (Take Risks (FR))
2076a[4] 2946a[5]
A. P. Indian (USA) *Arnaud Delacour* a125
6 b g Indian Charlie(USA) Ender's Sister (USA) (A.P. Indy (USA))
7832a[3]
Apoleon (GER) *Frau Anna Schleusner-Fruhriep* 99
6 br g Ogatonango(GER) Abisou (GER) (Goofalik (USA))
7028a[9]
Apollo Eleven (IRE) *Michael Appleby* a74 50
7 b g Manduro(GER) Arlesienne (IRE) (Alzao (USA))
1092[6] 1598[P] *2105[3] 2916[9] 4478[7]*
Apollon (FR) *A Bonin* a46 51
8 ch g Green Tune(USA) Aegle (IRE) (Night Shift (USA))
5281a[12] 5700a[6]
Apparition (IRE) *Joseph Patrick O'Brien* a76 66
2 br g Dream Ahead(USA) Bluebell Park (USA) (Gulch (USA))
7917a[5]
Appeared *Roger Varian* a90 97
4 b g Dubawi(IRE) Appearance (Galileo (IRE))
(500) 1430[3] (2163) ◆ 2487[9] 6709[3]
Appease *E Sheehy* a53 54
7 b g Oasis Dream Penchee (Grand Lodge (USA))
822[7]
Appiano (FR) *W Menuet* a61 72
5 b g Orpen(USA) Appearance (GER) (Monsun (GER))
7295a[2]
Appleberry (IRE) *Michael Appleby* a63 85
4 b m Approve(IRE) Passage To India (IRE) (Indian Ridge)
2737[4] 3218[3] 3714[3] 4034[6] *6926[11]* (7289) 7772[10]
Apple Betty (IRE) *J-C Rouget* 107
3 b f Galileo(IRE) Absolutelyfabulous (IRE) (Mozart (IRE))
2726a[3] 4904a[3] 6152a[4]
Applejack Lad *Michael Smith* a53 63
5 ch g Three Valleys(USA) Fittonia (FR) (Ashkalani (IRE))
1560[2] *2329[10]* 4260[11] *5065[6] 6739[8] 6920[12]*
Apple Scruffs (IRE) *Michael Attwater* a60 64
2 gr g Fast Company(IRE) La Chita Bonita (IRE) (Verglas (IRE))
2429[5] 2874[5] *3404[7]* 4315[8] 4738[5] 5052[6] 6440[2] *7047[12] 7527[5]*
Appleton *David O'Meara* 87
3 ch g Showcasing Valentina Guest (IRE) (Be My Guest (USA))
3131[7] 5199[6]
Applicator (USA) *Mikhail Yanakov* 105
3 b c Henrythenavigator(USA) River Flower (USA) (Strodes Creek (USA))
4173a[7]
Appointed *Tim Easterby* 87
2 b f Delegator Celestial Harmony (Polish Precedent (USA))
(2404) 4296[3] 4884[6] ◆ 6229[2] ◆ (6433) ◆ 6954[11]
Appointment Only *John Joseph Murphy* a74 27
3 b g Aqlaam Guermantes (Distant Relative)
(7339a)
Approaching Star (FR) *Dai Burchell* a37 44
5 ch m New Approach(IRE) Madame Arcati (IRE) (Sinndar (IRE))
1049[7] 3748[2] 4088[6] 4592[4]
Approbare (IRE) *T M Walsh* a58 61
4 b g Approve(IRE) Tabrina (IRE) (Fasliyev (USA))
6463a[2]
Apres Midi (IRE) *K R Burke* 82
3 b f Galileo(IRE) Rose Bonheur (Danehill Dancer (IRE))
2835[3] 3343[2] 4682[2] (5581)
Apricot Sky *David Nicholls* a64 86
6 ch g Pastoral Pursuits Miss Apricot (Indian Ridge)
1672[11] 1869[12] 2261[8] 2531[3] (3326) 3552[8] 3875[5] 4608[13] 5479[2] 6012[2] 6080[8] 6324[2] 6793[2] 7288[6] 7591[2]
Aprovado (IRE) *Michael Dods* a85 86
4 b g Approve(IRE) Aldburgh (Bluebird (USA))
1879[8] 2677[11] 3326[7] 3713[9] 4544[11] 5224[2] 5714[5] *5969[7]* (6216) 6435[4] *(6927)*
Apterix (FR) *Brian Ellison* a75 93
6 b g Day Flight Ohe Les Aulmes (FR) (Lute Antique (FR))
3657[18]

Aqdameya (IRE) *Mark Johnston* a55 61
2 ch f Tamayuz Classic Falcon (IRE) (Dubawi (IRE))
7055[6] 7424[6] 7689[8]

Aqshion Stations *William Jarvis* a60 41
2 b g Aqlaam Shersha (IRE) (Priolo (USA))
5792[9] 6673[6] 7224[5] 7777[5]

Aqua Ardens (GER) *George Baker* a92 92
8 b g Nayef(USA) Arduinna (GER) (Winged Love (IRE))
1344[6] 2587[8] 2934[9] 3803[8] 4132[5] 4305[3] 4868[5] 5793[4] 6402a[2] 7017[9] 7886[8]

Aqua Libre *Philip McBride* a78 85
3 b f Aqlaam Be Free (Selkirk (USA))
4105[6] 4548[5] 5123[4]

Aqualis *John Gosden* a83 79
3 b f Sea The Stars(IRE) Rosamixa (FR) (Linamix (FR))
1392[6] 2183[4] (7607) 7823[14]

Aquaphobia (USA) *Arnaud Delacour* 101
3 b c Giant's Causeway(USA) Pussycat Doll (USA) (Real Quiet (USA))
4173a[11]

Aquila Solitaria (IRE) *Il Cavallo In Testa* 96
3 b f Raven's Pass(USA) Alta Fedelta (Oasis Dream)
1685a[6] 2518a[3]

Arabda *Patrick Wahl* 90
5 bb m Elnadim(USA) Ghizlaan (USA) (Seeking The Gold (USA))
3448a[4]

Arabela Dawn (IRE) *John Quinn* a43
2 b f Delegator Arabela (IRE) (Medicean)
7328[7] 7605[6]

Arabian Hope (USA) *Saeed bin Suroor* 74
2 b f Distorted Humor(USA) Achieving (USA) (Bernardini (USA))
2211[4]

Arabian Night *John Gosden* 37
3 b f Oasis Dream Solaia (USA) (Miswaki (USA))
2505[12]

Arabian Oasis *Philip Kirby* a72 79
4 b g Oasis Dream Love Divine (Diesis)
1853[4] 2328[12] 3118[12]

Arabian Queen (IRE) *David Elsworth* 116
4 b m Dubawi(IRE) Barshiba (IRE) (Barathea (IRE))
1886[2] 2894[7] 6488[3] 6949[6]

Arable *P Schaerer* a76 87
5 ch g Three Valleys(USA) Cut Corn (King's Theatre (IRE))
664a[9]

Arab Moon *William Knight* a51 54
2 b g Elnadim(USA) Albeed (Tiger Hill (IRE))
7012[5] 7605[5] 7962[10]

Arab Poet *Sir Michael Stoute* a84 90
3 ch g Poet's Voice Floral Beauty (Shamardal (USA))
1585[2] 2466[4] 3155[5] 4402[6] 5507[3]

Arab Spring (IRE) *Sir Michael Stoute* a116 118
6 b h Monsun(GER) Spring Symphony (IRE) (Darshaan)
5159[3] ◆ 5558[11] (6125) 6940[2] 7402a[4]

Aragon Knight *Heather Main* a78 69
3 b g Kheleyf(USA) Midnight Allure (Aragon)
(1753) 2314[6] 3407[7] 4224[7] 8228[3] ◆ 8430[7]

Aramadyh *Jim Best* a52 47
5 gr m Authorized(IRE) Swift Dispersal (Shareef Dancer (USA))
2292[7] 3402[10] 4019[9]

Aramist (IRE) *Alan Swinbank* a84 84
6 gr g Aussie Rules(USA) Mistic Sun (Dashing Blade)
1493[11] 1880[8] 3657[10] 4162[9] 7320[3] 8133[4] 8399[8]

Arantes *R Mike Smith* a42 66
5 b g Sixties Icon Black Opal (Machiavellian (USA))
2198[10] 3347[6] 3920[7] 4189[3] 4491[7] 4875[8] 5154[7] 5715[8] 6921[9]

A Raving Beauty (GER) *A Wohler* 88
3 rg f Mastercraftsman(IRE) Anabasis (GER) (High Chaparral (IRE))
2730a[4]

Arazza (GER) *J Hirschberger* 98
2 b f Areion(GER) Aloe (GER) (Lomitas)
(6797a) 7563a[3]

Arborist (IRE) *A R Al Rayhi* a52 77
2 gr c Dark Angel(IRE) Ride For Roses (IRE) (Barathea (IRE))
3859[10] 4533[5] (4988) 5595[9] 6330[5] 8575a[7]

Arbourfield (IRE) *Mrs Prunella Dobbs* a65 62
4 b g Moss Vale(IRE) Shoooz (IRE) (Soviet Star (USA))
7339a[6]

Arcada (IRE) *Joseph Patrick O'Brien* 107
2 b g Rip Van Winkle(IRE) Applause (IRE) (Danehill Dancer (IRE))
5683a[3] 6783[3]

Arcadia (FR) *F-H Graffard* a76 79
4 ch m Lope De Vega(IRE) Ramzia (IRE) (Soviet Star (USA))
8117a[8]

Arcadian Sea (IRE) *William Jarvis* 20
2 b g Born To Sea(IRE) Drombeg Dawn (IRE) (Orpen (USA))
7621[10]

Arcamante (ITY) *K R Burke* a54 76
5 b g High Chaparral(IRE) Caractere (IRE) (Indian Ridge)
78[8]

Arcamist *Charles Hills* a61 79
3 gr f Arcano(IRE) Good Enough (FR) (Mukaddamah (USA))
1392[13] (2405) 3071[2] 3949[4]

Arcanada (IRE) *Tom Dascombe* a91 109
3 ch g Arcano(IRE) Bond Deal (IRE) (Pivotal)
1115[3] (1623) 1975[8] 3299[4] (3635) (5616) 6482[6]

Arcane Dancer (IRE) *Lawrence Mullaney* a67 67
3 b f Arcano(IRE) La Reine Mambo (USA) (High Yield (USA))
1584[8] (1927) 2306[5] 2674[6] 3366[7] 3877[3] 4454[11] (4729) 5322[2] 5782[4] 5919[3] 7254[8] 7326[3] 7601[10] 8241[5] 8347[4]

Arcanista (IRE) *Richard Hughes* a65 63
3 ch f Arcano(IRE) Cattiva Generosa (Cadeaux Genereux)
2128[5] 3989[12] 4388[8] 4796[2] 5167[3] 6317[5] 6677[2] 7200[4] 7654[11] 8026[2] 8156[4]

Arcano Gold (IRE) *Richard Fahey* 90
4 ch g Arcano(IRE) Azia (IRE) (Desert Story (IRE))
1221[8] (1526)

Arcarius *M Ibrahim* a62
3 ch c Dubawi(IRE) Isobel Archer (Oasis Dream)
8576a[11]

Archangel Raphael (IRE) *Amanda Perrett* a100 101
4 b g Montjeu(IRE) La Sylvia (IRE) (Oasis Dream)
1336[6] 1569[6] 2979[5] 6074[7] 6919[11]

Archer's Arrow (USA) *Saeed bin Suroor* a77 79
2 b c Lonhro(AUS) Midnight Music (IRE) (Dubawi (IRE))
6952[2] 7458[2] 7906[2]

Archery Peak *Luca Cumani* 84
4 b g Arch(USA) Come Touch The Sun (IRE) (Fusaichi Pegasus (USA))
(7219) ◆

Archie (IRE) *Clive Cox* a92 93
4 b g Fast Company(IRE) Winnifred (Green Desert (USA))
1204[4] ◆ 1993[6] 3055[2] 4104[3] ◆ 5156[6] 6210[7]

Archie's Advice *Keith Dalgleish* a74 84
5 b g Archipenko(USA) Flylowflylong (IRE) (Danetime (IRE))
38[6] 179[2] 708[6] (1884) 2811[4] 3286[2] 3884[2] 4190[4] (4446) 4871[7] 6772[9]

Archie Stevens *David Evans* a81 73
6 b g Pastoral Pursuits Miss Wells (IRE) (Sadler's Wells (USA))
142[8] 484[3] ◆ 604[7] 685[2] 764[6] 5896[5] 6017[2] 6195[7] 6669[2] 7268[5] 8150[7] 8349[2] 8429[5]

Archimedes (IRE) *David C Griffiths* a68 71
3 b g Invincible Spirit(IRE) Waveband (Exceed And Excel (AUS))
2846[7] 3625[4] 4280[3] 4744[3] 8010[9] 8345[6] 8474[3]

Archimento *Ed Dunlop* a70 83
3 ch g Archipenko(USA) Caribana (Hernando (FR))
1397[3] 1755[3] 2307[2] 3281[2]

Archipeligo *Iain Jardine* a79 78
5 b g Archipenko(USA) Red Slew (Red Ransom (USA))
200[4] (332) 566[4] 2093[6] 2811[5]

Archipentura *J R Jenkins* a44 59
4 b m Archipenko(USA) Bookiesindex Girl (IRE) (Rakti)
1597[10] 2312[9] 3720[7] 4718[12] 5753[7]

Archippos *Philip Kirby* 79
3 b g Archipenko(USA) Sparkling Clear (Efisio)
2957[3] (4313) 7499[8] 7744[9]

Archi's Affaire *Michael Dods* 53
2 ch g Archipenko(USA) Affaire D'Amour (Hernando (FR))
5271[9] 5884[7]

Architecture (IRE) *Hugo Palmer* 115
3 b f Zoffany(IRE) Brigayev (ITY) (Fasliyev (USA))
2035[2] 2869[2] ◆ 3297[8] 4416a[2] 5220a[3] 7351[6]

Arch Villain (IRE) *Amanda Perrett* a103 107
7 b g Arch(USA) Barzah (IRE) (Darshaan)
(194) (614) ◆ 3658[18] 4734[14] (5144)

Arc Royal *Tom Dascombe* 88
2 ch g Arcano(IRE) Royal Blush (Royal Applause)
1635[5] 2682[3] 3054[2] 4802[11] 5637[2] (6275) 7120[6]

Arctic Angel (IRE) *James Fanshawe* a67
3 b g Dark Angel(IRE) Charlene Lacy (IRE) (Pips Pride)
7207[4] 8012[4] 8496[2]

Arctic Feeling (IRE) *Richard Fahey* a66 101
8 ch g Camacho Polar Lady (Polar Falcon (USA))
(1408) 2188[7] 2488[15] 2898[9] 3656[12] 4112[6] 4667[15] 5555[9] 5991[10] 6537[6] 6779[14] 7124[15] 7413[4]

Arctic Flower (IRE) *John Bridger* a51 60
3 gr f Roderic O'Connor(IRE) Just In Love (FR) (Highest Honor (FR))
2186[9] 2586[9] 4017[2] 4388[6] (4641) 5167[6] 5721[10] 7211[8] 8026[8] 8248[9]

Arctic Lynx (IRE) *Ann Stokell* a46 48
9 b g One Cool Cat(USA) Baldemara (FR) (Sanglamore (USA))
6248[9] 7533[7] 7913[8] 8312[7] 8485[13]

Arctic Sea *Paul Cole* a67
2 bb c Oasis Dream Rainbow Dancing (Rainbow Quest (USA))
8486[4] ◆

Ardad (IRE) *John Gosden* 108
2 b c Kodiac Good Clodora (IRE) (Red Clubs (IRE))
(3037) ◆ (3247) 4060[9] 5654[7] (6282) 6990a[9]

Ardamir (FR) *Alan King* a83 79
4 b g Deportivo Kiss And Cry (FR) (Nikos)
4265[3] 4948[3] 5742[3] 6549[7] 7512[3] 8162[4]

Ardashir (USA) *Andreas Lowe* 72
2 bb c Hat Trick(JPN) Diva Dyna (USA) (Grand Slam (USA))
7399a[8] 7842a[9]

Ardez (FR) *P Van De Poele* a80 63
3 b g Youmzain(IRE) Autumn Forest (FR) (Exit To Nowhere (USA))
2456a[3]

Ardhoomey (IRE) *G M Lyons* a103 116
4 b g Dark Angel(IRE) Moy Joy (IRE) (Orpen (USA))
3201a[2] 3696a[4] 4413a[5] (6384a) 7520a[11]

Ardmore (IRE) *J S Bolger* 73
5 b g Whipper(USA) Ard Fheis (IRE) (Lil's Boy (USA))
1014a[7]

Ard San Aer (IRE) *M Al Yaqout* 77
3 b c Acclamation Allannah Abu (Dubawi (IRE))
756a[9] 8573a[15]

Areen (IRE) *David O'Meara* 106
3 b c Kodiac Falcolnry (IRE) (Hawk Wing (USA))
2192[F] (Dead)

Areen Heart (FR) *Richard Fahey* 78
2 b c Exceed And Excel(AUS) Reine Zao (FR) (Alzao (USA))
6129[2] (6640)

Areyoutheway (IRE) *Michael Appleby* a63 66
2 ch g Thewayyouare(USA) Grenouillere (USA) (Alysheba (USA))
1741[5] 2266[3] (3361) 4509[4] 4982[2] 6208[4] 7750[7] 8080[2] 8568[8]

Argaki (IRE) *Keith Dalgleish* a76 85
6 ch g Strategic Prince Amathusia (Selkirk (USA))
1445[9] 3518[11] 5802[2] 6225[6] 6500[10] 7108[9] 7791[6] 8011[6] 8286[12]

Argante (FR) *Nicky Henderson* a81 62
7 bb g Singspiel(IRE) Abyaan (IRE) (Ela-Mana-Mou)
4941[5]

Argenterie *Marcus Tregoning* 91
2 ch f Archipenko(USA) Sterling Sound (USA) (Street Cry (IRE))
4801[3] ◆ (6062) 6748[7]

Argent Knight *Christopher Kellett* a77 86
6 gr g Sir Percy Tussah (Daylami (IRE))
(1550) 1665[2] (1987) 3639[5] 4664[7] 4912[7]

Argot *Charlie Longsdon* a51 63
5 b g Three Valleys(USA) Tarot Card (Fasliyev (USA))
583[5] 3767[3]

Argus (IRE) *Ralph Beckett* 91
4 b g Rip Van Winkle(IRE) Steel Princess (IRE) (Danehill (USA))
4115[6] 6333[3] 7215[5] 7538[10]

Argyle (IRE) *William Muir* a71 72
3 gr g Lawman(FR) All Hollows (IRE) (Dalakhani (IRE))
1532[2] 2411[7] 3778[2] 4636[3] 5398[3] 5830[5] 6730[12]

Ariena (IRE) *Clive Cox* 81
2 b f Arcano(IRE) Xena (IRE) (Mull Of Kintyre (USA))
2997[3] 4054[2] (4586) 5794[6]

Aristocles (IRE) *Stuart Edmunds* a55 74
3 b g High Chaparral(IRE) Amathusia (Selkirk (USA))
1386[6] 1784[6] ◆ 2300[7] (2798) 3615[4] 7320[6]

Aristocracy *Sally Randell* a55
5 b g Royal Applause Pure Speculation (Salse (USA))
957[6]

Aristocratic *Sir Michael Stoute* a85 84
3 b f Exceed And Excel(AUS) Peeress (Pivotal)
1701[3] 2431[2] 4105[9] (5300) 6299[3] 7281[2]

Arithmetic (IRE) *Charles Hills* 73
3 b g Invincible Spirit(IRE) Multiplication (Marju (IRE))
1270[7] 2306[2] 3189[3] 4986[3] 5362[3] 6956[14]

Arize (IRE) *David Brown* a71 69
3 b f Approve(IRE) Raise (USA) (Seattle Slew (USA))
1703[8] 2255[4] 2777[7] 4604[7] (6851) 7485[10] 8037[4] (8493)

Arizona (GER) *Waldemar Hickst* a56
4 b m Areion(GER) Aliette (FR) (Lando (GER))
5452a[8]

Arizona Snow *Ronald Harris* a59 40
4 b g Phoenix Reach(IRE) Calgary (Pivotal)
54[2] 143[6] 272[4] 596[2] 2458[3] 2537[5] 3734[10] 3953[8] 7302[13] 8278[7] 8383[2]

Arizona State (USA) *A P O'Brien* a57 57
2 b c Scat Daddy(USA) Barometer (USA) (Point Given (USA))
7387a[5]

Arizona Sunrise *Tina Jackson* a55 74
3 b g Sakhee's Secret Phoenix Rising (Dr Fong (USA))
783[5] (1667) 6347[10] 7007[10]

Arkaitz (SPA) *Ana Imaz Ceca* 108
5 b h Pyrus(USA) Lady Cree (IRE) (Medicean)
5502a[15]

Arlecchino's Leap *Mark Usher* a88 85
4 br g Kheleyf(USA) Donna Giovanna (Mozart (IRE))
1724[4] (2430) 2934[7] 3803[7] 4519[5] (5810) 6914[13]

Arlecchino's Rock *Mark Usher* a64 63
3 ch g Rock Of Gibraltar(IRE) Xtra Special (Xaar)
2506[12] 3062[7] 3786[10] 4262[5] 4820[4] 5605[4] 5807[6] 6592[5] 7038[5] (7611)

Arles (FR) *A Wohler* 103
4 b m Monsun(GER) Attachee De Presse (IRE) (Danehill (USA))
1907a[3]

Arluno (FR) *J-Y Artu* a55 48
7 gr g Chichicastenango(FR) Ambrosianella` (FR) (Take Risks (FR))
4927a[11] 8421a[16]

Armagnac (IRE) *Michael Bell* a68 68
2 br c Arcano(IRE) Folle Blanche (USA) (Elusive Quality (USA))
4856[6] 5371[8] 5848[10] 7286[11] 7941[2] ◆

Armande (IRE) *A Fabre* 101
3 b f Sea The Stars(IRE) Alpine Snow (IRE) (Verglas (IRE))
2944a[3] 3452a[U] 7568a[4] 8024a[3]

Armandihan (IRE) *Kevin Ryan* 77
2 b c Zoffany(IRE) Flying Flag (IRE) (Entrepreneur)
6499[3] ◆ 7329[3]

Armelle (FR) *Scott Dixon* a48 61
5 b m Milk It Mick Park Ave Princess (IRE) (Titus Livius (FR))
1254[6] 1600[8] 2053[11] 3843[13] 7747[14] 8236[12]

Arms Around Me (IRE) *James Given* a54 74
4 ch g Lope De Vega(IRE) Mexican Milly (IRE) (Noverre (USA))
1756[6] 2441[5] 2915[10] 3214[3] 3478[7]

Arnarson *Ed Dunlop* a71
2 b c Exceed And Excel(AUS) Islandia (USA) (Johar (USA))
8119[3] 8384[2] ◆

Arnold *Ann Duffield* 59
2 b g Equiano(FR) Azurinta (IRE) (Azamour (IRE))
6712[4] 7072[7] 7355[4]

Arnold Lane (IRE) *Mick Channon* a96 96
7 b h Footstepsinthesand Capriole (Noverre (USA))
290[3] 486[8] 727[4] 1068[10] 1335[8] 1563[4] 1993[3] 2391[3] (2934) 3358[12] 3895[9] 4305[2] 4758[11] 5419[14] 6082[6]

Arod (IRE) *Peter Chapple-Hyam* a69 121
5 b h Teofilo(IRE) My Personal Space (USA) (Rahy (USA))
1774[3] 4151[18] 5449a[10] 5873[3] 6601a[5]

Arousal *Tina Jackson* 37
4 b m Stimulation(IRE) Midnight Mover (IRE) (Bahamian Bounty)
5715[11]

Arquus (IRE) *Ed de Giles* a41
3 b g Lilbourne Lad(IRE) Charaig (Rainbow Quest (USA))
4939[11]

Arrest Warrant *Michael Easterby* a48 59
3 b g Acclamation Dream Day (Oasis Dream)
3609[8] 4041[10]

Arriella *John Davies* a38 42
4 b m Dapper Bedtime Blues (Cyrano De Bergerac)
3287[9] 3774[6] 4971[9]

Arrogate (USA) *Bob Baffert* a136
3 rg c Unbridled's Song(USA) Bubbler (USA) (Distorted Humor (USA))
(5913a) (7838a)

Arrowtown *Michael Easterby* a75 81
4 b m Rail Link Protectress (Hector Protector (USA))
1586[6] ◆ 2836[3] 3844[2] 4230[2] ◆ 6163[4]

Arrowzone *Ivan Furtado* a81 95
5 b g Iffraaj Donna Giovanna (Mozart (IRE))
(2216) 3435[4] 4650[7] 5933[6] 6559[2] 6802[3] 7287[5]

Arsenale (GER) *Michael Appleby* a67 56
5 b m Nicaron(GER) Alte Rose (GER) (Monsun (GER))
358[6] 425[8] 577[4] 601[5] 876[7] 1058[5] 1654[8] 2733[3]

Artbeat (IRE) *Julia Feilden* a52 57
4 b m Dutch Art Easy Beat (IRE) (Orpen (USA))
54[9] 525[10] 1676[2] 2013[7]

Art Charter (FR) *K R Burke* a52 65
4 b m Artiste Royal(IRE) Lady Sylvester (USA) (Elusive Quality (USA))
180[4]

Art Collection (FR) *Gary Moore* a82 78
3 b g Shakespearean(IRE) Renascent Rahy (Rahy (USA))
2818[8] 3689[8] 4051[8] 4268[2] 6409[6] 7066[8]

Art Echo *Jonathan Portman* a77 80
3 b g Art Connoisseur(IRE) Madhaaq (IRE) (Medicean)
1828[10] 2412[9] 3816[8] 4365[10] 5087[2] 5711[2] 6066[3] 6337[5] 7577[6]

Artful Artist (IRE) *A J Martin* a35 87
7 b g Excellent Art Silly Goose (IRE) (Sadler's Wells (USA))
7195a[4] 7708a[8]

Artful Mind *John Flint* a73 66
3 b g Cape Cross(IRE) Tiriana (Common Grounds)
(70) 495[5] 1185[5] 2413[6] 3053[5] 6337[3] ◆ 6646[9] 7227[10] 7529[9] 8364[4] 8554[6]

Artful Prince *James Given* a78 92
6 ch g Dutch Art Royal Nashkova (Mujahid (USA))
1633[7] 2043[8] 2347[8] 2743[7] (3212) 3517[15] 4026[9] 4568[5] 5122[12] 5540[4] 6221[12] 6876[15]

Artful Rogue (IRE) *Amanda Perrett* a85 79
5 b g Excellent Art Szabo (IRE) (Anabaa (USA))
4868[15] 5413[4] 6065[8] 6676[2] 7053[4] 7508[7] 8161[2] (8254) 8447[4]

Arthenus *James Fanshawe* a92 108
4 b g Dutch Art Lady Hen (Efisio)
1861[6] ◆ 2246[12] 3383[4] 4165[16] 5500a[2] (6178a) 6973a[7]

Art History (IRE) *Zoe Davison* a47 53
8 gr g Dalakhani(IRE) What A Picture (FR) (Peintre Celebre (USA))
2876[6] 5724[12]

Arthur Mc Bride (IRE) *Nigel Twiston-Davies* 88
7 bb g Royal Anthem(USA) Lucky Diverse (IRE) (Lucky Guest)
5623[2] 6052[3] 6634[2] (7183) 7498[4]

Arthur's Queen (FR) *Carroll Gray* a64 61
5 b m Soldier Of Fortune(IRE) Tintagel (Oasis Dream)
1831[6] 2131[7] 2634[12]

Arthurs Secret *John Quinn* a72 77
6 ch g Sakhee's Secret Angry Bark (USA) (Woodman (USA))
103[4] 425[7] 2678[4] 3418[3] (3903) 5758[2]

Arthurthedelegator *Oliver Greenall* a67 60
2 b c Delegator Markova's Dance (Mark Of Esteem (IRE))
3472[8] 3633[7] 4133[5] 7749[5] 8235[3] (8398)

Articus (FR) *A Wohler* a95 109
4 b h Areion(GER) Almerita (GER) (Medicean)
2723a[2] (4253a) 4928a[5] 7378a[13]

Artigiano (USA) *Charlie Appleby* a102 94
6 ch g Distorted Humor(USA) Angel Craft (USA) (A.P. Indy (USA))
94a[4] 627a[6] 812a[5]

Artisandra (FR) *William Knight* a16 49
3 ch f Mastercraftsman(IRE) Kezia (FR) (Spectrum (IRE))
1551[12] 2212[10] 2823[7]

Artistic Flight (IRE) *Jim Boyle* a70 44
4 b g Art Connoisseur(IRE) Robin (Slip Anchor)
357[5] 7653[13] 7905[P]

Artists Model (IRE) *Henry Candy* a64 82
3 b f Dutch Art Zarwala (IRE) (Polish Precedent (USA))
2848[5] 5515[3] 6066[2] (6635) 7246[2]

Art Obsession (IRE) *Paul Midgley* a79 88
5 b g Excellent Art Ghana (IRE) (Lahib (USA))
1444[7] 1844[5] 2238[7] 3168[4] (3646) 4608[12] 5182[9] 6136[2] 6718[4] 7325[3] 7590[10]

Art Of Swing (IRE) *Gary Moore* a76 42
4 b g Excellent Art Shahmina (IRE) (Danehill (USA))
5709[3] 5996[8] 7052[4] (7870)

Art Of Zapping (FR) *T Castanheira* a80 77
5 b g Desert Style(IRE) Any Colour (Anshan)
3184a[10]

Artplace (IRE) *Carina Fey* a103 99
6 b g Teofilo(IRE) Ginostra (Oasis Dream)
3090a[10]

Artscape *Dean Ivory* a71
4 b g Iffraaj Artisti (Cape Cross (IRE))
6247^{4}
Art Scholar (IRE) *Michael Appleby* a80 67
9 b g Pyrus(USA) Marigold (FR) (Marju (IRE))
267^{6} 446^{5} 940^{2} 1161^{6} 1588^{6}
Artsteelwork *Denis Quinn* 31
2 b f Fast Company(IRE) Etymology (Rail Link)
3073^{8}
Art Wave (IRE) *M Al Mheiri* a100 79
5 ch h Art Connoisseur(IRE) Musical Review (UAE) (Jade Robbery (USA))
$623a^{8}$
Art World (IRE) *James Coyle* a36 40
4 b g Art Connoisseur(IRE) Human Touch (Oasis Dream)
$2229a^{12}$ $7474a^{11}$
Arty Campbell (IRE) *Bernard Llewellyn* a87 88
6 b g Dylan Thomas(IRE) Kincob (USA) (Kingmambo (USA))
1987^{9} 2392^{10} 2782^{7} 4012^{2} (4912) (5553) 5999^{3} 6582^{12} 6919^{4}
Aru Cha Cha *Roger Ingram* a67 51
5 b g Myboycharlie(IRE) Royal Arruhan (Royal Applause)
20^{6} 690^{6} 1049^{9}
Arvios *C Laffon-Parias* a74 74
4 ch h Medicean Akrivi (IRE) (Tobougg (IRE))
$4074a^{8}$
Arwa (IRE) *Charles Hills* 82
2 b f Holy Roman Emperor(IRE) Another Storm (USA) (Gone West (USA))
4063^{8} (5516) 6257^{7} 6787^{6} 7151^{10}
Arya Stark *Tony Carroll* a51
2 b f Piccolo Night Affair (Bold Edge)
7576^{14} 8065^{11}
Arya Tara (IRE) *Joseph Patrick O'Brien* a48 94
3 b f Dylan Thomas(IRE) Anadiyla (IRE) (Barathea (IRE))
$5002a^{7}$ $5660a^{3}$
Aryeh (IRE) *Hugo Palmer* a61
2 ch f Exceed And Excel(AUS) Height Of Summer (IRE) (Alhaarth (IRE))
4011^{6}
Arzaak (IRE) *Chris Dwyer* a75 71
2 br g Casamento(IRE) Dixieland Kiss (USA) (Dixie Union (USA))
2756^{4} ◆ 5229^{2} 5820^{4} 8175^{2} 8454^{2}
Asaas (USA) *Roger Varian* a75 77
2 ch c Distorted Humor(USA) Affectionately (Galileo (IRE))
3058^{4} 4349^{4} 7307^{4}
As A Dream (IRE) *Nikki Evans* a62 56
4 b m Azamour(IRE) Wedding Dream (Oasis Dream)
237^{9} 547^{3} 876^{8} 985^{10}
Asafoetida (IRE) *Peter Chapple-Hyam* a65 55
3 b f Pivotal Embraced (Pursuit Of Love)
591^{4} 699^{4} 1297^{3} 2639^{5} 3493^{9}
Asama Blue (IRE) *William Haggas* 83
3 b f Fastnet Rock(AUS) Butterfly Blue (IRE) (Sadler's Wells (USA))
(2653)
Asbury Boss (IRE) *M Halford* 95
5 gr g Dalakhani(IRE) Nick's Nikita (IRE) (Pivotal)
$3680a^{8}$ $4721a^{5}$ $6350a^{16}$
Ascot Angel (FR) *J-C Rouget* 67
2 b c Dark Angel(IRE) Lady Ascot (IRE) (Excellent Art)
$5348a^{7}$
Ascot Day (IRE) *David Simcock* a76
2 b c Kheleyf(USA) My Lucky Liz (IRE) (Exceed And Excel (AUS))
7142^{4} 7639^{2}
Ascot Week (USA) *Owen Burrows* a62
2 bb c Lonhro(AUS) Millenia (Unfuwain (USA))
8073^{5}
Ascription (IRE) *Keith Dalgleish* 115
7 b g Dansili Lady Elgar (IRE) (Sadler's Wells (USA))
6558^{17} 6837^{5}
Asfaar (IRE) *Brian Meehan* 90
2 b g Sir Prancealot(IRE) Duchess Of Foxland (IRE) (Medecis)
1454^{8} 3093^{8} 4297^{3} 4786^{2}
Ashaadd (IRE) *D Selvaratnam* a59 97
6 b g Dansili Vital Statistics (Indian Ridge)
$370a^{2}$ $623a^{6}$
Ashadihan *Kevin Ryan* a102 105
3 b f Kyllachy Miss Delila (USA) (Malibu Moon (USA))
(2034) 3339^{6} ◆ 4107^{5} 6746^{10}
Ashazuri *Jonathan Portman* a70 47
2 b f Dick Turpin(IRE) Shesha Bear (Tobougg (IRE))
3812^{12} 5119^{9} 7049^{6}
Ashford Island *Adam West* a50 56
3 b g Munnings(USA) Falling Angel (Kylian (USA))
87^{8} 327^{4} 436^{3} 785^{5} 948^{5} (1162) 1792^{9} 2293^{2} 2969^{2} 3490^{6} 4316^{8} 5087^{7} 6373^{10} 7231^{13}
A Shin Erwin (IRE) *Hidemasa Nakao* 105
5 b h Shamardal(USA) La Ina (GER) (Monsun (GER))
3242^{10}
A Shin Hikari (JPN) *Masanori Sakaguchi* 126
5 gr h Deep Impact(JPN) Catalina (USA) (Storm Cat (USA))
(2568a) 3272^{6} $8333a^{10}$
Ashleyluvssugar (USA) *Peter Eurton* a87 113
5 b g Game Plan(USA) Ashley's Folly (USA) (Urgent Request (IRE))
$7835a^{5}$
Ashpan Sam *David W Drinkwater* a63 105
7 b g Firebreak Sweet Patoopie (Indian Ridge)
2898^{8} 3386^{25} 4136^{9} 4632^{5} 5390^{4} ◆ 5641^{9} 5991^{2} ◆ 6633^{9}
Ashraf (IRE) *D K Weld* 102
4 b g Cape Cross(IRE) Askeria (IRE) (Sadler's Wells (USA))
$1018a^{22}$ $4070a^{10}$ $4747a^{15}$
Ashurst Beacon *Brian Ellison* 71
2 b g Avonbridge Espagnolette (Oasis Dream)
5058^{5} 5433^{4} $6388a^{13}$ 7248^{4}
Ashwaq *Richard Hannon* a71 75
2 ch f Sepoy(AUS) Blaugrana (IRE) (Exceed And Excel (AUS))
7695^{3} 8152^{2}
Asian Wing (IRE) *John James Feane* a73 73
7 ch g Hawk Wing(USA) Blue Beacon (Fantastic Light (USA))
$208a^{8}$ 545^{8} $3680a^{9}$ 4920^{3}
Asidious Alexander (IRE) *Simon Crisford* 101
2 ch f Windsor Knot(IRE) Birthday Present (Cadeaux Genereux)
(3597) 4106^{7} (4902a) $5703a^{2}$ $6271a^{3}$ 7114^{11}
Askari *Roger Varian* a66 64
3 b g Sea The Stars(IRE) Loulwa (IRE) (Montjeu (IRE))
2175^{10} 2619^{5} 3160^{11}
Ask Dad *Damian Joseph English* a66 72
6 b g Intikhab(USA) Don't Tell Mum (IRE) (Dansili)
$2229a^{5}$
Asker (IRE) *Nick Lampard* 23
8 b g High Chaparral(IRE) Pay The Bank (High Top)
4995^{8}
Ask The Guru *Michael Attwater* a71 69
6 b g Ishiguru(USA) Tharwa (IRE) (Last Tycoon)
100^{5} 604^{4} 714^{3} 775^{2} 903^{6} 1150^{8} (1782) 2088^{3} 2931^{9} 3159^{6} 3316^{8} 4536^{7} 5105^{3} 5599^{3} 5928^{8} 6296^{8} 6660^{8} (7276) 8149^{2} 8429^{9} 8596^{5}
Asmahan *Simon Crisford*
2 b f Casamento(IRE) Finnmark (Halling (USA))
8355^{U}
A Soldier's Life (IRE) *Charlie Appleby* 103
5 b g Authorized(IRE) Aynthia (USA) (Zafonic (USA))
3340^{6} 4734^{11} 6526^{2}
Aspasius (GER) *Gary Moore* a55 62
4 b g Desert Prince(IRE) Aspasia Lunata (GER) (Tiger Hill (IRE))
3522^{13} 4993^{3} 6406^{10}
Aspen Again (IRE) *David Menuisier* 68
3 b f Intikhab(USA) Deira Dubai (Green Desert (USA))
1436^{8} 1989^{9}
Aspens Shadow *Grace Harris*
4 ch m Captain Gerrard(IRE) Aspen Ridge (IRE) (Namid)
9841^{1}
Aspirer *A Fabre* 54
2 b f Frankel Nebraska Tornado (USA) (Storm Cat (USA))
$6639a^{10}$
Assanilka (FR) *Harry Dunlop* a79 93
2 b f Diamond Green(FR) Regal Step (Royal Applause)
(7050) $7480a^{5}$
Assassinate (IRE) *Paul Cole* a74 74
2 b g Tagula(IRE) Ten Spot (IRE) (Intikhab (USA))
$1579a^{10}$ (1776) 1944^{2} $2280a^{2}$ 6800^{6} $7490a^{10}$ (7966)
Assault On Rome (IRE) *Mark Johnston* a83 89
4 b m Holy Roman Emperor(IRE) Naomh Geileis (USA) (Grand Slam (USA))
24^{3} 58^{8} 260^{6} 422^{5}
Assertive Agent *Tony Carroll* a66 63
6 b m Assertive Agent Kensington (Mujahid (USA))
143^{8} 872^{2} 1042^{3} 1794^{5} 2609^{3} (3734) 3993^{9} 5105^{2} (6677)
Assertor *Tony Carroll* 28
2 b f Assertive Blue Goddess (IRE) (Blues Traveller (IRE))
6733^{8}
Assign (IRE) *Robert Hickmott* 102
5 b g Montjeu(IRE) Belesta (Xaar)
$7756a^{19}$
Assisted *Keith Dalgleish* a42 61
3 ch g Motivator More Sirens (IRE) (Night Shift (USA))
219^{4} 4702^{5} 5517^{4} 6137^{10} 6618^{2} 7742^{5}
Assume (IRE) *David Wachman* 101
4 b m Fastnet Rock(AUS) Alsharq (IRE) (Machiavellian (USA))
$2716a^{12}$ $4218a^{2}$ $5313a^{3}$ $5564a^{5}$
Asterina *A De Royer-Dupre* a74 97
3 ch f Dalakhani(IRE) Altamira (Peintre Celebre (USA))
$2455a^{4}$
Astley Hall *Mohammed Jassim Ghazali* 89
3 ch g Dutch Art Haigh Hall (Kyllachy)
$756a^{10}$
Astra Hall *Michael Appleby* a65 79
7 ch m Halling(USA) Star Precision (Shavian)
53^{4} 251^{6} 386^{2} 498^{3} 637^{2} 684^{4} 801^{7} 1004^{10} (1248) (1560) ◆ 2399^{3} 6566^{7} 7043^{6} 7357^{2} 7594^{10}
Astrella (GER) *Waldemar Hickst* 62
2 b f Lawman(FR) Atalia (GER) (Sholokhov (IRE))
$7996a^{5}$
Astrolabe (IRE) *Tom Dascombe* 69
2 b f Born To Sea(IRE) Aquanaut (Dansili)
5387^{8} 6077^{3}
Astronereus (IRE) *Amanda Perrett* 114
5 ch h Sea The Stars(IRE) Marie Rheinberg (GER) (Surako (GER))
(2241) 3384^{9} 3913^{5}
Astronomy's Choice *John Gosden* 84
2 b f Redoute's Choice(AUS) Astronomy Domine (Galileo (IRE))
(7118)
Astrophysics *Lynn Siddall* a79 79
4 ch g Paco Boy(IRE) Jodrell Bank (IRE) (Observatory (USA))
4032^{7} 4608^{19} 5032^{7} 5582^{4} 6093^{2} (6476) ◆ 7386^{4} 7660^{4} 8010^{3}
Astrosecret *Mark H Tompkins* a66 66
3 b f Halling(USA) Optimistic (Reprimand)
1179^{6} 3359^{7} 3990^{8} 5763^{4} 6886^{8}
Astrowizard *Mark H Tompkins* a44
3 ch g Zamindar(USA) Mega (IRE) (Petardia)
3359^{11} 6703^{10} 7280^{12}
Astrum *Donald McCain* a17 15
6 gr g Haafhd Vax Star (Petong)
6058^{8}
Astute Boy (IRE) *Ed Vaughan* a68 57
2 b g Arcano(IRE) Spa (Sadler's Wells (USA))
7664^{6} 8082^{6} 8277^{8}
Asulaman (GER) *S Cerulis* a88 73
9 b g Sulamani(IRE) Andrelhina (Tirol)
(3376a)
A Sure Welcome *John Spearing* a56 53
2 b g Pastoral Pursuits Croeso Bach (Bertolini (USA))
2344^{4} 2822^{7} 4016^{8} 4907^{7} 5770^{5} 6313^{4} 6875^{7} (7423) (7750)
Atacama (SPA) *Ana Imaz Ceca*
3 ch c Gentlewave(IRE) Princess Skippie (USA) (Skip Away (USA))
$5502a^{14}$
Atalan *Hughie Morrison* a72 76
4 b g Azamour(IRE) Capriolla (In The Wings)
(2502) 3409^{6} 4535^{6} 5267^{5} 7183^{9}
Atalanta Bay (IRE) *Marcus Tregoning* a70 52
6 b m Strategic Prince Wood Sprite (Mister Baileys)
4381^{10} 4979^{3} 5737^{2} 6090^{5}
Atalante *Andrew Balding* a65 69
3 b f Cape Cross(IRE) Sabria (USA) (Miswaki (USA))
1577^{7} 3720^{4} 4565^{3} ◆ 5009^{4}
Ataman (IRE) *Chris Wall* a78 83
4 b g Sholokhov(IRE) Diora (IRE) (Dashing Blade)
2043^{6} 3061^{4} 4028^{6} 6416^{6} 7222^{8}
Ataman Ermak (IRE) *S Gouyette* a76 52
5 b g Galileo(IRE) Missvinski (USA) (Stravinsky (USA))
$1846a^{7}$ $5216a^{5}$ $5700a^{5}$
Athas An Bhean *Adrian Paul Keatley* 87
3 b f Royal Applause Dusty Moon (Dr Fong (USA))
$6819a^{15}$ 7773^{4}
Athassel *David Evans* a57 53
7 ch g Dalakhani(IRE) Hope Island (IRE) (Titus Livius (FR))
$6462a^{9}$ (8542)
Athenian Garden (USA) *Paddy Butler* a54 27
9 b m Royal Academy(USA) Webee (USA) (Kingmambo (USA))
232^{6} 382^{9} 674^{9} 870^{7} 1239^{5} 1547^{10}
Athenry Boy (IRE) *J T Gorman* 68
4 br g Excellent Art Dancing With Stars (IRE) (Where Or When (IRE))
$4813a^{9}$
Athletic *Andrew Reid* a78 79
7 b g Doyen(IRE) Gentle Irony (Mazilier (USA))
221^{8} ◆ 433^{12} 712^{5} ◆ 2247^{13} 2934^{10} 3571^{3} 4089^{10} 4402^{5} 4839^{7} 5892^{3} 6579^{7} 6872^{9}
Athlon (IRE) *David Lanigan* a95 94
3 b g Arakan(USA) Alexander Divine (Halling (USA))
2152^{4} ◆ 2639^{2} (3236) (3959) (5724) 6048^{2} 7015^{3}
Athollblair Boy (IRE) *Nigel Tinkler* a75 73
3 ch g Frozen Power(IRE) Ellxell (IRE) (Exceed And Excel (AUS))
1788^{9} 2337^{2} 2981^{8} 3439^{10} 4605^{4} 5179^{9} 5537^{3} 5978^{4} 6216^{6} 7111^{2} 7662^{3}
Athou Du Nord (FR) *Ali Stronge* a31
6 b g Voix Du Nord(FR) Orathou Du Plaid (FR) (Lute Antique (FR))
3651^{6}
Atkinson Grimshaw (FR) *Andrew Balding* 74
2 ch c Rio De La Plata(USA) Cosabawn (IRE) (Barathea (IRE))
6288^{6} 6828^{3}
Atlanta Belle (IRE) *Chris Wall* a74 33
2 ch f Zebedee Tara Too (IRE) (Danetime (IRE))
6515^{6} 6866^{3} 8118^{6}
Atlantic Splash *Nikki Evans*
6 ch g Dreams End Atlantic Lady (GER) (Dashing Blade)
5255^{9}
Atlantic Sun *Richard Hannon* a104 103
3 br c Roderic O'Connor(IRE) Robema (Cadeaux Genereux)
1991^{2} 2627^{2} 3672^{6} 4065^{5} 4665^{4} 5472^{3} (7168a)
Atlas (IRE) *M D O'Callaghan* a66 76
3 b g Acclamation Sheer Bliss (IRE) (Sadler's Wells (USA))
$7391a^{11}$
Atomic Rush (SAF) *M F De Kock* 93
5 b h Dynasty(SAF) Ice Tibbs (SAF) (Casey Tibbs (IRE))
$93a^{6}$
Atone *Sir Michael Stoute* 83
3 b f Oasis Dream Midsummer (Kingmambo (USA))
1608^{11} (2395)
Atrafan (IRE) *Alan Brown* a60 51
2 b g Atraf Up Front (IRE) (Up And At 'Em)
5477^{8} 5966^{7} 6274^{6} 7109^{4}
Atrayu (IRE) *Paul D'Arcy* a69 44
3 b g Jeremy(USA) Feis Ceoil (IRE) (Key Of Luck (USA))
1257^{10} 1710^{2} 1792^{3} 2107^{2} 3069^{12} 3499^{5} 3906^{9} 5248^{8}
Atreus *Michael Easterby* a62 64
4 b g Indesatchel(IRE) Devassa (Reel Buddy (USA))
1120^{16} 1323^{6} 1654^{2} 2096^{7} 2330^{11} 2660^{2} 2906^{3} 3153^{4} 3777^{3} 4005^{6}
Atta Alla *R Bouresly* a59
3 ch c Archipenko(USA) Rosa De Mi Corazon (USA) (Cozzene (USA))
$185a^{7}$
Attain *Julia Feilden* a72 64
7 b g Dansili Achieve (Rainbow Quest (USA))
55^{6} (222) 672^{3} (1340) 1751^{4} 2507^{8} 3072^{6} 3354^{9} 4234^{2} (4531) 8190^{7} 8364^{3}
Attendu (FR) *C Laffon-Parias* 113
3 b c Acclamation Gwenseb (FR) (Green Tune (USA))
$1308a^{2}$ $2283a^{9}$ (2927a) $5217a^{6}$ $6272a^{2}$ $6991a^{5}$
Attenzione (IRE) *S Donohoe* a58 8
5 b g Shamardal(USA) Fig Tree Drive (USA) (Miswaki (USA))
1500^{4}
Atteq *Richard Fahey* a78 68
2 b c Invincible Spirit(IRE) Wallis (King's Best (USA))
3633^{5} 7988^{3} 8237^{2}
Attest *Amanda Perrett* a65 74
3 b g Cacique(IRE) Change Course (Sadler's Wells (USA))
3535^{3} 4657^{5} 5723^{6}
At The Beach *Richard Hannon* a65 65
2 ch c Harbour Watch(IRE) Almatinka (IRE) (Indian Ridge)
2173^{10} 2748^{4} 3301^{3} 4386^{6} 4802^{14} 5707^{5} 6191^{6} (7275)
Attitude Rocks *Clive Cox* a60 45
3 b c Dansili Dorelia (IRE) (Efisio)
219^{9} 691^{8} 1036^{6} 3062^{13} 4269^{9} 5326^{10}
Attraction Ticket *Joanne Foster*
7 b g Selkirk(USA) Trick (IRE) (Shirley Heights)
3711^{10} 6719^{8}
Atty Persse (IRE) *Roger Charlton* 85
2 b c Frankel Dorcas Lane (Norse Dancer (IRE))
(6480)
Atwix *Lucy Wadham* a79 83
4 br m Sakhee(USA) Atwirl (Pivotal)
1144^{4} ◆ 1552^{4} 2415^{3} (4785) 5053^{9}
Aubenas (FR) *F Chappet* 95
3 ch c Siyouni(FR) Dexandra (GR) (Evippos (GR))
$5699a^{8}$
Auberge Du Lac (IRE) *David Simcock* a78 66
2 b c Lope De Vega(IRE) Red Kyte (Hawk Wing (USA))
7125^{5} 8486^{2}
Aufsteiger (FR) *P Schiergen* 94
2 b c Meshaheer(USA) Moon Romance (FR) (Nayef (USA))
$5348a^{5}$
Augusta Ada *Bryan Smart* 69
5 b m Byron Preference (Efisio)
4428^{10} 5379^{5}
Aumerle *Shaun Lycett* a78 44
4 b g Authorized(IRE) Succinct (Hector Protector (USA))
357^{4} 704^{6} 882^{5} 1391^{8} 2105^{5}
Auntie Barber (IRE) *Stuart Williams* a70 73
3 b f Elusive City(USA) Lady Stardust (Spinning World (USA))
1146^{DSQ} ◆ (1779) 2181^{5}
Auntie Joy (USA) *Brendan P Walsh* 102
3 b f Uncle Mo(USA) Rejoicing (USA) (Forestry (USA))
$4174a^{6}$
Auntinet *John Gosden* a78
3 b f Invincible Spirit(IRE) Cozy Maria (USA) (Cozzene (USA))
1960^{6}
Aureana *Ralph Beckett* 46
2 b f Kyllachy Going For Gold (Barathea (IRE))
4054^{8}
Auric Goldfinger (IRE) *Richard Hannon* a58 49
2 b c Kyllachy Ghenwah (FR) (Selkirk (USA))
4988^{8} 5505^{6} 5764^{7} 6253^{8} 6652^{6} 7047^{2} 7881^{10} 8046^{5} 8276^{3}
Aurora Gray *Hughie Morrison* a72 67
3 gr f Rip Van Winkle(IRE) Summer's Eve (Singspiel (IRE))
3059^{9} 4480^{5} ◆ 5011^{6} 5627^{4} 5823^{2} 6901^{9} 7425^{2} 7656^{12} 7905^{6} (8445)
Auspicion *Tom Tate* a72 84
4 b g Dansili Superstar Leo (IRE) (College Chapel)
788^{7} 1643^{7} 2121^{8} (2662) 3166^{3} 3717^{4} 4808^{7} 6160^{13} 7010^{14} 7623^{6} 7857^{5} 8092^{5}
Aussi Celebre (IRE) *Mlle I Essig* 40
7 gr g Aussie Rules(USA) Femme Celebre (IRE) (Peintre Celebre (USA))
$6938a^{11}$
Aussie Lyrics (FR) *Mrs C Gilbert* a67 77
6 gr g Aussie Rules(USA) Operam (Kris)
$2952a^{4}$ $3918a^{3}$ (4698a) $5459a^{2}$
Aussie Ruler (IRE) *Daniel Mark Loughnane* a50 66
4 br g Aussie Rules(USA) Experiment (IRE) (Whipper (USA))
2342^{7} 3610^{8} 3953^{4} 4771^{11}
Aussie Valentine (IRE) *P D Deegan* a95 98
5 b g Aussie Rules(USA) Love Valentine (IRE) (Fruits Of Love (USA))
$1018a^{2}$
Austerity (IRE) *Alan Swinbank* 58
3 br g Elnadim(USA) Royal Reprieve (FR) (Celtic Swing)
2048^{6} 2349^{8}
Austin Friars *Jim Best* a25 16
4 b g New Approach(IRE) My Luigia (IRE) (High Estate)
8455^{8}
Australian Queen *David Elsworth* a76 94
3 b f Fastnet Rock(AUS) Barshiba (IRE) (Barathea (IRE))
163^{2} (654) 1890^{8} 2160^{5} 2869^{8} 3534^{3} ◆ 3911^{7} 5307^{8} 5645^{10}
Authoritarian (AUS) *Lee & Anthony Freedman* 41
4 b g Authorized(IRE) Special Dream (AUS) (Stravinsky (USA))
$7552a^{10}$
Authorized Spirit *John Best* a59 59
4 b m Authorized(IRE) World Spirit (Agnes World (USA))
(348) 724^{4}
Author's Dream *William Knight* a55 59
3 gr g Authorized(IRE) Spring Dream (IRE) (Kalanisi (IRE))
1826^{10} 2700^{7}
Autocratic *Sir Michael Stoute* a82 108
3 b c Dubawi(IRE) Canda (USA) (Storm Cat (USA))
1639^{4} 2790^{2} (3160) 4108^{2} ◆ 6573^{11} (7154)
Automated *Gordon Elliott* a66 81
5 b g Authorized(IRE) Red Blooded Woman (USA) (Red Ransom (USA))
$7195a^{13}$

Automotive *Julia Feilden* a72 65
8 b g Beat Hollow Bina Ridge (Indian Ridge)
173[11] 563[10]
Autor (IRE) *Z Koplik* 108
6 b g Authorized(IRE) Kansas (Kahyasi)
6974a[12]
Autre Princess (IRE) *Eric Alston* a14
3 b f Strategic Prince Molly Marie (IRE) (Fasliyev (USA))
298[9] 544[5] 785[11]
Autumn Blossom (USA) *Mark Johnston* a68 57
3 b f Bernardini(USA) Late Romance (USA) (Storm Cat (USA))
63[8] 366[4] 1584[7] 2123[9]
Autumn Chorus *John Bridger* a5 17
3 ch f Piccolo Filemot (Largesse)
5300[10] 6674[11] 7011[12] 7459[11]
Autumn Glow *Miss Joey Ellis* 32
2 b f Sir Percy Steady Rain (Zafonic (USA))
7465[9]
Autumn Surprise (IRE) *Tim Easterby* 66
3 b f Yeats(IRE) Septembers Hawk (IRE) (Machiavellian (USA))
3886[2] 4633[P] 6052[8] 6795[4]
Autumn Tonic (IRE) *David Barron* a68 44
4 b g Approve(IRE) Trempjane (Lujain (USA))
124[5] 482[7] 615[5] 658[7] 8289[9] 8572[5]
Auxiliary *Patrick Holmes* a71 79
3 b g Fast Company(IRE) Lady Xara (IRE) (Xaar)
2532[6] 3775[5] 4241[6] 4871[6] 6028[3] 6344[8] 7076[8] 7435[7] ◆
Available (IRE) *John Mackie* a80 86
7 b m Moss Vale(IRE) Divert (IRE) (Averti (IRE))
1186[4] (1341) 2238[2] 2621[2] 3394[7] 4211[4] (4608)
Avalanche Express *William Muir* a75 77
4 ch h Pivotal Irresistible (Cadeaux Genereux)
1151[5] 3035[3] 3989[3] 4717[9] 6907[10]
Avantgardist (GER) *Mark Johnston* a68 70
2 ch c Campanologist(USA) Avocette (GER) (Kings Lake (USA))
6716[5] 7003[2] 7940[5] 8305[4]
Av A Word *Daniel Kubler* a59 39
2 b g Aussie Rules(USA) Real Me (Mark Of Esteem (IRE))
5237[7] 5676[7] 6319[9]
Avec Laura *Mme M Bollack-Badel* a71 22
3 ch g Manduro(GER) Sign Of Life (Haafhd)
7492a[10]
Avenante *John M Oxx* 97
4 b m Champs Elysees Averna (Heraldiste (USA))
1279a[6] 3202a[6] (3630a) 6200a[4] 6350a[14] 7393a[9] 7558a[8]
Avenge (USA) *Richard E Mandella* 112
4 bb m War Front(USA) Lerici (USA) (Woodman (USA))
7831a[3]
Aventinus (IRE) *Hugo Palmer* a82 80
2 b c Zoffany(IRE) Luminous Gold (Fantastic Light (USA))
2489[4] 3524[2] 4188[4] 4825[14] (6368) 6869[2] 7541[6] 8132[4]
Aventus (IRE) *Jane Chapple-Hyam* a50 54
2 b c Zebedee Irish Design (IRE) (Alhaarth (IRE))
4877[8] 5304[9] 5959[8] 6313[7] 6670[5] 7047[9] 7866[5] 8080[5] 8341[2] 8568[3]
Avenue Dargent (FR) *J-M Osorio* 83
3 ch f Kendargent(FR) Corfu (IRE) (Daylami (IRE))
5249a[5] 7929a[8]
Avenue Des Champs *Jane Chapple-Hyam* a70 71
4 b g Champs Elysees Penang Cry (Barathea (IRE))
(950) (1434) 1760[4] 2605[7]
Avenue Of Stars *Karen McLintock* a74 81
3 b g Makfi Clifton Dancer (Fraam)
(1111) (1788) 2650[14] 3646[4] 4193[5] 6027[10] 6714[11] 7111[12]
Aviator (FR) *T Poche* a56 56
7 b g Motivator Summer Wave (IRE) (King's Best (USA))
1618a[6]
Avocadeau (IRE) *Stuart Kittow* a38 77
5 b g Lawman(FR) Christmas Cracker (FR) (Alhaarth (IRE))
5308[7] 5776[5] 6825[11]
Avoidable *David Simcock* a69
3 b g Iffraaj Ever Rigg (Dubai Destination (USA))
40[9] 331[5] 768[4] 8491[3]
Avon Breeze *Richard Whitaker* a71 95
7 b m Avonbridge African Breeze (Atraf)
1522[4] (1644) 1968[3] 2267[5] 5417[17] 6012[5] 6556[18] 6780[11] 7126[8] 7413[7]
Avon Pearl *Rune Haugen* a93 99
7 ch g Avonbridge Warden Rose (Compton Place)
375a[9] 628a[7] 812a[3] 1957a[4] 3449a[6]
Avon Scent *Christopher Mason* 43
6 b m Avonbridge Ferrybridge (IRE) (Mister Baileys)
2849[5] 3514[7] 4290[8] 5252[6] 5953[10]
Awaayil (IRE) *James Tate* a51
2 b f Iffraaj Lady Pitrizza (IRE) (Night Shift (USA))
8465[7]
Await The Storm (IRE) *Hugo Palmer* a72 72
2 ch g Fast Company(IRE) Stormchaser (IRE) (Titus Livius (FR))
1889[5] 2757[5] 3321[3] 3858[6] 6789[6] 7098[2] 7330[10]
Awake My Soul (IRE) *Tom Tate* a64 102
7 ch g Teofilo(IRE) Field Of Hope (IRE) (Selkirk (USA))
1245[7] 2157[4] 3666[3] 5651[16] 6261[7] 7546[6] 7744[2]
Aware (IRE) *Charles Hills* a47
2 b c Lawman(FR) Viz (IRE) (Darshaan)
7963[7]
Away In May *John Spearing* a30 49
5 gr m Proclamation(IRE) Loch Shiol (IRE) (Selkirk (USA))
1132[9] 1529[7] 1715[9] 2645[9] 3624[11]
Awaywiththegreys (IRE) *Peter Bowen* 88
9 gr g Whipper(USA) Silver Sash (GER) (Mark Of Esteem (IRE))
4230[5]
Awesome Allan (IRE) *David Evans* 81
2 b g Acclamation Spring Approach (Tiger Hill (IRE))
(1384) 1713[3] 1965[5] 2371[6] 5510[7] (7073)
Awesome Quality (USA) *James Tate* a79 64
3 b g Elusive Quality(USA) Awesome Maneuver (USA) (Awesome Again (CAN))
2998[6] (3567) ◆ 3821[6] 5367[3] 6656[8]
Awesome Rock (AUS) *Leon & Troy Corstens* 115
4 b h Fastnet Rock(AUS) Awesome Planet (AUS) (Giant's Causeway (USA))
7553a[5]
Awesome Rock (IRE) *Roger Ingram* a53 42
7 ch g Rock Of Gibraltar(IRE) Dangerous Diva (IRE) (Royal Academy (USA))
233[2] 348[5] 653[3] 1239[8] 3031[7] 4197[2] 5021[3] 5261[5] 5777[9] 6411[8] 7104[5]
Awesome Speed (USA) *Alan E Goldberg* a100
3 bb c Awesome Again(CAN) Speedy Escape (USA) (Aptitude (USA))
2499a[9]
Awfaa (IRE) *Sir Michael Stoute* a54
2 b f Shamardal(USA) Elraabeya (CAN) (Seeking The Gold (USA))
7484[6]
Awtaad (IRE) *Kevin Prendergast* 122
3 br c Cape Cross(IRE) Asheerah (Shamardal (USA))
(1938a) (2496a) 3245[3] 4754[8] (6353a) 7352[4]
Axa Reim (IRE) *F Boccardelli*
7 b g Cape Cross(IRE) My Personal Space (USA) (Rahy (USA))
7840a[11]
Ayahuasca (USA) *Takashi Kodama* a73 90
6 ch h Johar(USA) Eulogize (Pivotal)
1802[6]
Ay Ay (IRE) *David Elsworth* a75
2 b c Pour Moi(IRE) Chatline (IRE) (One Cool Cat (USA))
(8556) ◆
Aydoun (IRE) *D K Weld* 92
3 ch g Mastercraftsman(IRE) Alaya (IRE) (Ela-Mana-Mou)
6917[7]
Aye Aye Skipper (IRE) *Ken Cunningham-Brown* a63 58
6 b g Captain Marvelous(IRE) Queenfisher (Scottish Reel)
2187[6] 2647[5] 3724[2] 5326[3] 5953[9] 6826[11] 7211[9] 8026[5]
Ayguemorte (FR) *P-L Guerin* a66 66
3 b g Vertigineux(FR) Aiguille Du Midi (FR) (Fly To The Stars)
511a[9]
Ayla's Emperor *John Flint* a52 64
7 b m Holy Roman Emperor(IRE) Ayla (IRE) (Daylami (IRE))
7274[13]
Ayrad (IRE) *Roger Charlton* 113
5 ch g Dalakhani(IRE) Sweet Firebird (IRE) (Sadler's Wells (USA))
1604[3] 2241[2] 2947a[6] (3860) 4821[2] 5893[5] 6571[4] 7700[6]
Ayresome Angel *Bryan Smart* a55 72
3 ch f Captain Gerrard(IRE) Almunia (IRE) (Mujadil (USA))
2218[13] 4032[8] 4514[8] 6133[5] 6809[6] 7437[10] 7660[12]
Ayr Of Elegance *Philip Hide* a71 77
4 b m Motivator Gaelic Swan (IRE) (Nashwan (USA))
1266[2] 1810[3] 2400[2] 2932[9] 4661[2] 5262[P]
Ay Up Audrey *Rebecca Bastiman* 56
5 b m Desideratum Smiddy Hill (Factual (USA))
1151[12] 2047[2] 2304[8] 3368[11] 3941[7] 4257[7] 6615[7] 6834[5] 7092[6] 7302[11] 7585[10]
Azaelia (FR) *Simone Brogi* a80 108
3 b f Turtle Bowl(IRE) Azalee (IRE) (Peintre Celebre (USA))
2455a[2] 3452a[4] ◆
Azagal (IRE) *Tim Easterby* 83
5 b m Azamour(IRE) Brave Madam (IRE) (Invincible Spirit (IRE))
1624[2] 2223[4] 2737[3] 2855[6] 3419[6]
Azaly (IRE) *Owen Burrows* a57
2 ch g Sepoy(AUS) Azzoom (IRE) (Cadeaux Genereux)
7064[7]
Azam *John Gosden* a80 73
2 b c Dansili Giants Play (USA) (Giant's Causeway (USA))
6704[4] ◆ 7621[4] (8063)
Azari *Il Cavallo In Testa* 93
4 b g Azamour(IRE) Atasari (IRE) (Whipper (USA))
2729a[6] 3455a[8]
Azerelle (IRE) *Tim Easterby* a52 52
4 ch m Arcano(IRE) Simply Topping (IRE) (Exceed And Excel (AUS))
136[4]
Azhar *Saeed bin Suroor* a79 64
3 b f Exceed And Excel(AUS) Nitya (FR) (Indian Ridge)
2237[9] 3714[7]
Azilian *Paul Cole* a83 63
4 b h Azamour(IRE) Zietory (Zieten (USA))
1934[6] (2445) 2605[2] 3184a[3]
Azizaan *Roger Varian* 81
3 b c Dubawi(IRE) Pearling (USA) (Storm Cat (USA))
1622[8] 2340[2] ◆ 2861[6]
Azraff (IRE) *Marco Botti* a100 104
4 b g Paco Boy(IRE) Gee Kel (IRE) (Danehill Dancer (IRE))
1195[17] 1478[2] (2246) 3273[4] 4165[7] 4823[9] 5585[9] 6786[11]
Azrur (IRE) *Keith Dalgleish* a78 73
6 b g Sir Percy Tiger Spice (Royal Applause)
893[2] (1044) 1252[12] 1664[3] 1841[7] 2660[6]
Azure Amour (IRE) *Rod Millman* a59 61
4 b m Azamour(IRE) Al Euro (FR) (Mujtahid (USA))
1413[9] 2144[3] 3064[11] 3997[6] 4507[4] 5010[5] 5625[2] 6022[9]
Azzeccagarbugli (IRE) *Stefano Botti* 103
3 b c Kodiac Consultant Stylist (IRE) (Desert Style (IRE))
2729a[4] 6823a[8]
Azzir (IRE) *K R Burke* a75 83
4 gr g Echo Of Light Lady Georgina (Linamix (FR))
3395[3] (3983) 4190[3] 6773[6] 7412[4] 7847[7]
Baadi *Charlie Fellowes* 93
4 b g Dansili Dashing (IRE) (Sadler's Wells (USA))
(1529) (2549) ◆ 3670[4] 5145[10] 6573[15]
Baashiq (IRE) *Roger Varian* 82
2 b c New Approach(IRE) Fatanah (IRE) (Green Desert (USA))
6952[4] (7329)
Babalugats (IRE) *Tim Easterby* 44
2 br f Elzaam(AUS) Ellanova (Kyllachy)
2404[7] 2970[5] 3477[6] 6026[4] 6681[13]
Babamunchkin *Michael Bell* a45 63
2 b f Henrythenavigator(USA) Babycakes (IRE) (Marju (IRE))
7466[4] ◆ 7865[12]
Babel Ouest (FR) *W Mongil* a74 58
8 b g Bachir(IRE) Belle De L'Ouest (FR) (Quai Voltaire (USA))
5452a[2] (7295a)
Babel's Book (FR) *F-H Graffard* 85
3 b c Iffraaj Ponentina (FR) (Lando (GER))
2948a[3]
Babouska *Michael Easterby* a52 49
2 b f Monsieur Bond(IRE) Prices Lane (Gentleman's Deal (IRE))
3321[6] 3772[10] 7380[10] 7578[7] 8046[4] (8284)
Baby Ballerina *Brian Ellison* a73 72
3 b f Kheleyf(USA) Markova's Dance (Mark Of Esteem (IRE))
1448[12] 1788[8] 2742[13] 4003[3] (4973) 5537[6] 5759[5] 6501[13] (7485) 7691[4]
Babyfact *Malcolm Saunders* a30 74
5 b m Piccolo Pennyspider (IRE) (Redback)
1533[7] 2146[4] 2697[6] 4155[5] 4264[2] (4506) 5009[2] ◆ 5330[2] (5599) (5928) 6363[9] 7267[11]
Baby Gal *Giles Bravery* a52 77
2 b f Royal Applause Our Gal (Kyllachy)
1799[6] (2535) 3254[2] 7120[16] 8230[7]
Baby Helmet *Robert Cowell* a58 40
2 ch g Helmet(AUS) Lady Gorgeous (Compton Place)
7355[6]
Baccarat (IRE) *Charlie Appleby* a72 114
7 ch g Dutch Art Zut Alors (IRE) (Pivotal)
(723a) 1439[6] 2031[2] 2546[8] 4865[15] 5418[3] 5880[3] 6458[2]
Bacchus *Brian Meehan* 93
2 ch g Kheleyf(USA) Rumbled (Halling (USA))
3058[5] (3808) ◆ 4148[2] 6285[6] 6705[8]
Bachelorhood *Charlie Appleby* 76
3 b g New Approach(IRE) Most Charming (FR) (Darshaan)
(3019) ◆ 4655[3]
Backinanger *Kevin Ryan* 54
2 b g Royal Applause Giusina Mia (USA) (Diesis)
4423[12] 5477[10] 6477[10]
Back Off Mate (IRE) *A L T Moore* a58 77
8 b g Old Vic Flyhalf (IRE) (Be My Native (USA))
208a[12]
Backontheroadagain (IRE) *Matthieu Palussiere* 74
2 gr c Zebedee Gladstone Street (IRE) (Waajib (IRE))
5141a[8]
Back To Bond *Richard Fahey* 76
3 ch g Monsieur Bond(IRE) Nicola's Dream (Alhaarth (IRE))
1622[7] (2349) 2907[11] 4116[8] 4607[7] 5181[2] 5729[14] 5860[5]
Back To Bresil (FR) *S Wattel* a75 69
3 b f Muhtathir Miss Recif (IRE) (Exit To Nowhere (USA))
7492a[8]
Back To Love (CAN) *Mark Gillard* a42 35
3 b f Street Cry(IRE) Song And Danz (USA) (Unbridled's Song (USA))
4660[8] 5238[6] 5766[7] 6290[11] 7038[6] 7302[14] 7645[7] 8145[9]
Badalona Breeze (IRE) *Michael Appleby* a34
3 br f Big Bad Bob(IRE) Rose Mandarin (IRE) (Tiger Hill (IRE))
8146[14]
Baddilini *Alan Bailey* a102 76
6 b g Bertolini(USA) Baddi Heights (FR) (Shirley Heights)
290[7] 503[8] 657[3] 771[5] 1545[6] 2361[6] 2754[4] 3115[13] 3185[7] 5552[11] 5678[11] 6627[8] 7308[3] 7530[6] 7965[3] 7984[11]
Bad Girl Caoimhe (IRE) *Brian Ellison* 73
3 br f Big Bad Bob(IRE) Sumostars (IRE) (Refuse To Bend (IRE))
1246[2] ◆ 1562[2] 3213[7] 3948[6] 4861[6]
Bad Penny (IRE) *John Quinn* a55 66
3 b f Kodiac Double Fantasy (GER) (Indian Ridge)
1562[4] 2011[4] 2574[3] ◆
Bag Of Diamonds *Richard Hannon* a81 73
3 b c Lilbourne Lad(IRE) Milnagavie (Tobougg (IRE))
4953[6] 5649[6] 6084[4] 7535[18]
Bahaarah (IRE) *Richard Hannon* 101
3 b f Iffraaj Love Intrigue (IRE) (Marju (IRE))
1867[7] 4391[2] 4651[2] ◆ 5175[6] 6557[10]
Bahamadam *Eve Johnson Houghton* a82 82
2 b f Bahamian Bounty Pelagia (IRE) (Lycius (USA))
(4951) 5632[5] 6063[6] 6882[3]
Bahama Moon (IRE) *David Barron* 93
4 b g Lope De Vega(IRE) Bahama Bay (GER) (Dansili)
(1122) ◆ 1613[4] 2010[11] 3806[10] 4001[9] 6217[5] 7287[3] (7412) 7594[11]
Bahamas (IRE) *Marco Botti* 103
2 b c Rip Van Winkle(IRE) Gwyllion (USA) (Red Ransom (USA))
(3598) 4622[5] 6116[5] 7401a[2]
Bahamian Bird *Richard Fahey* a71 68
3 b f Bahamian Bounty Ride The Wind (Cozzene (USA))
4007[5] 4604[4] (5151) 6027[2] 6502[5] 6908[2] 7324[5] 7662[9]
Bahamian Boy *Hughie Morrison* a64 59
3 ch g Paco Boy(IRE) Bahamian Babe (Bahamian Bounty)
2083[2] 3003[5] 4009[8] 4498[12] 5248[4] 5808[4] 6047[8]
Bahamian C *Richard Fahey* a72 67
5 b g Bahamian Bounty Amandian (IRE) (Indian Ridge)
1664[6] 2296[10] 3801[5] 4341[5] 5883[6] 6432[3] 6772[7] 7336[3] 7500[2] 7775[3]
Bahamian Dollar *James Tate* a83 84
3 b g Bahamian Bounty Penny Ha'penny (Bishop Of Cashel)
2349[4] (2740) 4360[4] 6123[3] 6583[10]
Bahamian Heights *Robert Cowell* a82 82
5 b g Bahamian Bounty Tahirah (Green Desert (USA))
2480[9] 3068[5] 4051[5] ◆ 4569[3] 5372[6] 5679[3] 7054[RR] 7737[8]
Bahamian Paradise *Hughie Morrison* a65 33
2 ch f Bahamian Bounty Amanjena (Beat Hollow)
7184[8] 7733[3]
Bahamian Sunrise *John Gallagher* a80 80
4 ch g Bahamian Bounty Tagula Sunrise (IRE) (Tagula (IRE))
1110[7] 1175[5] 2028[15] 2396[4] 2846[2] 3487[2] 3741[2] 4295[10] 4809[3] (6479) (7303) 7626[4]
Bahamian Sunshine *Richard Fahey* a68 71
3 ch g Bahamian Bounty Tagula Sunrise (IRE) (Tagula (IRE))
131[5] 419[2] 726[4] 783[2] 1126[2] (1313) 2255[5] 2571[4] 2864[2] 5195[6] 5732[8] 6140[6] 6522[8] 6836[4]
Bahango (IRE) *Patrick Morris* a79 50
4 b g Bahamian Bounty Last Tango (IRE) (Lion Cavern (USA))
764[2] 1255[9] 1843[5] 2523[4] 3268[6] 3851[4] 4968[12] 8099[8] 8228[6]
Bahar (USA) *Richard Hannon* a66
2 b g First Defence(USA) La Rignana (USA) (Galileo (IRE))
7907[7]
Bahia Del Duque (FR) *J-P Domalain* a60 61
8 b g Enrique Perspective (FR) (Funambule (USA))
5216a[15]
Bahkit (IRE) *Alan Swinbank* 55
2 b g Intikhab(USA) Pink Moon (IRE) (Namid)
3416[6] 3854[9] 5058[6]
Bahrikate *Michael Herrington* 38
3 b f Bahri(USA) Dispol Katie (Komaite (USA))
2835[11] 3710[3] 4972[10] 5537[10] 5972[9] 6478[7] 7742[7]
Baie D'Amour (FR) *K R Burke* a61 74
2 ch f Never On Sunday(FR) Baie Des Fleurs (FR) (Chelsea Manor)
1284a[U] 4140[2] 4678[6] 5698a[4] 5988a[7]
Bailarico (IRE) *Charlie Appleby* 52
3 b g Dubawi(IRE) Baila Me (GER) (Samum (GER))
6520[5] 7410[4]
Baileys Apprentice *Mark Johnston* a51 71
2 ch f Mastercraftsman(IRE) Jalissa (Mister Baileys)
4975[5] 5290[3] 5861[2] 6377[5] 6875[3] 7406[8] 8466[14]
Baileys Concerto (IRE) *Dianne Sayer* 67
10 b g Bach(IRE) None The Wiser (IRE) (Dr Massini (IRE))
4934[8]
Baileys En Premier (FR) *Chris Dwyer* a74 63
5 b g Exceed And Excel(AUS) Numberonedance (USA) (Trempolino (USA))
58[7] 491[8]
Baileys Galaxy (FR) *Mark Johnston* a62 33
3 b g Elusive City(USA) Kosmic View (USA) (Distant View (USA))
5478[8] 6094[5] 6920[U]
Baileys Mirage (FR) *Chris Dwyer* a90 82
5 bb m Desert Style(IRE) Baileys Dancer (Groom Dancer (USA))
(1139) (1334) (1754) (1811) 2032[2] (2621) 3279[3] 3714[8] 4475[7] 5882[6] 6927[9]
Baileys Perle (IRE) *Chris Dwyer* a59 63
3 ch f Dutch Art Sister Agnes (IRE) (Dr Fong (USA))
2177[13] 2483[7] 3038[11] 5808[11] 6514[7]
Baileys Pursuit *Gay Kelleway* a67 43
4 ch m Pastoral Pursuits Royal Mistress (Fasliyev (USA))
5038[5] 6487[7] 8095[2] 8315[4]
Baileys Showgirl (FR) *Mark Johnston* a26 98
2 b f Sepoy(AUS) Tanguista (FR) (War Chant (USA))
3301[7] (3749) ◆ (4620a) 5703a[3] 6177a[3] 6986a[10]
Baileys Temptress (FR) *F Doumen* 73
2 ch f Medicean Khelwa (FR) (Traditionally (USA))
5698a[5] 6639a[8]
Bailiwick *Karen George* a68
5 b g Oratorio(IRE) Imperial Bailiwick (IRE) (Imperial Frontier (USA))
231[4] 321[7] 590[4] 769[5] 1120[14] 2635[12]
Bainne (IRE) *J F Levins* a67 85
6 b m Strategic Prince Laemeen (IRE) (Danehill Dancer (IRE))
4748a[4] 6819a[10] 8197a[9]
Baitha Alga (IRE) *Jassim Al Ghazali* 102
4 b h Fast Company(IRE) Tawaafur (Fantastic Light (USA))
755a[13]
Bajan Rebel *Michael Easterby* a51 69
5 ch m Bahamian Bounty Silca Key (Inchinor)
(1565) (1845) 2045[3] (3020) 3521[2] 3708[3] 4043[5] 4684[2] 5018[3] 5523[5] 5887[4] 6347[5]
Bajan Spice (IRE) *Ann Duffield* 48
2 b f Pastoral Pursuits Centenerola (USA) (Century City (IRE))
3416[7] 4097[5]
Baker *Robyn Brisland* a68 56
4 b g Teofilo(IRE) Meydan Princess (IRE) (Choisir (AUS))
295[8] 4718[9] 5471[7] 6512[10]
Baker Street *Tom Dascombe* 60
2 ch g Bahamian Bounty Aliante (Sir Percy)
3108[7] 3854[8] 4981[6] 6319[8]

Bakht A Rawan (IRE) *Stuart Kittow* a34 82
4 b g Rip Van Winkle(IRE) Foolish Ambition (GER) (Danehill Dancer (IRE))
(1317) (1916) 2688^{2} 3219^{3} 4138^{6} 5965^{5}

Balance *Richard Fahey* a68 80
3 ch f Pivotal Danella (FR) (Highest Honor (FR))
4191^{3} ◆ 4985^{4} 5973^{3} (6502) ◆

Balance Sheet (IRE) *Jedd O'Keeffe* a30
2 ch g Casamento(IRE) Mystery Hill (USA) (Danehill (USA))
5966^{12} 7432^{11}

Balancing Time *Amanda Perrett* a72 62
3 b g Pivotal Time On (Sadler's Wells (USA))
2175^{11} 2414^{10} 2929^{5} 6659^{2} 7760^{3} 8084^{4} (8428)

Balashakh (USA) *David Simcock* a68
2 b c Blame(USA) She Has Aptitude (USA) (Aptitude (USA))
5764^{4} 6655^{3}

Balducci *Roger Fell* a70 77
9 b g Dansili Miss Meltemi (IRE) (Miswaki Tern (USA))
2297^{6} 3421^{2} 3849^{7} 4611^{13} 5179^{11} 5858^{10} 7857^{9} 8092^{4} ◆ 8241^{2} 8286^{9} 8586^{13}

Balgair *Jonathan Portman* 78
2 ch g Foxwedge(AUS) Glencal (Compton Place)
(4270) 6260^{14} 6705^{6}

Balios (IRE) *David Simcock* a83 115
4 ch h Shamardal(USA) Elle Galante (GER) (Galileo (IRE))
843a^{4}

Ballard Down (IRE) *William Knight* a84 88
3 b g Canford Cliffs(IRE) Mackenzie's Friend (Selkirk (USA))
1992^{4} 2565^{5} 3465^{4}

Ballesteros *Richard Fahey* a81 90
7 ch g Tomba Flamenco Dancer (Mark Of Esteem (IRE))
1408^{11} 1874^{7} 2238^{15} 3133^{2} 3638^{2} 4632^{7} 5153^{6} 6080^{12} 6766^{3} 7413^{3} (7591) (7773) 8192^{6} 8407^{11}

Ballet Concerto *Sir Michael Stoute* a91 102
3 b g Dansili Ballet Ballon (USA) (Rahy (USA))
1386^{5} 4235^{2} (5023) ◆ (5933) 6132^{2}

Balliol *Ronald Harris* a72 62
4 b g Exceed And Excel(AUS) Cinerama (IRE) (Machiavellian (USA))
4544^{9} 4952^{8} 5546^{7} 5797^{14} 7069^{9} 7596^{6} ◆

Ballista (IRE) *Tom Dascombe* a91 74
8 b g Majestic Missile(IRE) Ancient Secret (Warrshan (USA))
86^{4} 580^{4} 878^{2} 974^{2} 1084^{5} 1744^{5} 1969^{8}

Ballroom Angel *Philip Hide* a56 35
4 gr m Dark Angel(IRE) Ballroom Dancer (IRE) (Danehill Dancer (IRE))
(1005) 1138^{9} 1556^{7} 3314^{8}

Ballyanna *David Evans* a60
2 b f Royal Applause Glorious Dreams (USA) (Honour And Glory (USA))
4713^{5} (5606) 6139^{8} 6419^{5}

Ballybacka Queen (IRE) *P A Fahy* 102
5 b m Hurricane Run(IRE) Zankara (FR) (Linamix (FR))
1279a^{2} 2189^{6} 3630a^{10} 4850a^{11}

Ballycoyle Girl (IRE) *Tony Coyle* 26
3 b f Manduro(GER) Gwyllion (USA) (Red Ransom (USA))
1920^{3} 2774^{9}

Ballydoyle (IRE) *A P O'Brien* 115
3 b f Galileo(IRE) Butterfly Cove (USA) (Storm Cat (USA))
1888^{2} 3452a^{6} 4174a^{13} 5430a^{12}

Ballyer Rallyer (IRE) *Daniel Mark Loughnane* a73 66
3 ch g Dylan Thomas(IRE) Ridiforza (FR) (Starborough)
2109^{5} 3267^{4} 3982^{9} 4258^{2} 5525^{2} 7506^{12}

Ballyfarsoon (IRE) *Ian Williams* a65 62
5 ch g Medicean Amzara (IRE) (Montjeu (IRE))
150^{10} 1004^{7} 2634^{3} (2813) 3999^{2} 4226^{6} (5680) 6022^{3} 6315^{11} 7739^{11}

Ballyglasheen (IRE) *Evan Williams* a77 75
6 ch g Galileo(IRE) Luas Line (IRE) (Danehill (USA))
165^{2} 382^{5}

Ballylare *Lee Carter* a85 83
3 b g Mullionmileanhour(IRE) Retainage (USA) (Polish Numbers (USA))
3406^{2} 4134^{7} (5169) 5743^{2} 8252^{2} (8456)

Ballymore Castle (IRE) *Richard Fahey* 102
4 br g Invincible Spirit(IRE) Ballymore Lady (USA) (War Chant (USA))
1218^{8} 1522^{9} 1887^{12} 2476^{6} 3980^{5} 4569^{2} 4862^{20} 5512^{5} 6082^{2} 6539^{13} 6560^{5} 7095^{4} 7825^{4}

Ballynanty (IRE) *Andrew Balding* a104 74
4 gr g Yeats(IRE) Reina Blanca (Darshaan)
19^{6} 317^{2} 1067^{3} 3913^{14} 5655^{18}

Ballysampson *Roger Teal* a39
2 b c Equiano(FR) The Fugative (Nicholas (USA))
6295^{11} 7900^{7}

Balmont Belle (IRE) *Barry Leavy* a51 51
6 b m Balmont(USA) Social Set (IRE) (Key Of Luck (USA))
2127^{6}

Balmoral Castle *Jonathan Portman* a61 98
7 b g Royal Applause Mimiteh (USA) (Maria's Mon (USA))
(1775) 4731^{8} 6075^{6} 6786^{31} 7121^{12} 7546^{14}

Balmusette *Keith Reveley* 61
7 b m Halling(USA) Tcherina (IRE) (Danehill Dancer (IRE))
1123^{9} 1955^{5} 2338^{7} (3417) 4045^{9}

Baltic Beau *Richard Fahey* a57 57
2 b c Camacho Baltic Sea (IRE) (Baltic King)
(1813) 2265^{3} 3114^{7} 6222^{4} ◆ 7109^{3} 7330^{5}

Baltic Brave (IRE) *Hughie Morrison* a90 93
5 b g Baltic King Negria (IRE) (Al Hareb (USA))
2032^{3} 2430^{4} 3061^{8} 3849^{5} 4599^{2} 4839^{3} 5403^{10} 5934^{6} 6806^{10} 7506^{8}

Baltic Knight (IRE) *B Al Abed* a88 110
6 b g Baltic King Night Of Joy (IRE) (King's Best (USA))
(744a)

Baltic Prince (IRE) *Tony Carroll* a77 73
6 b g Baltic King Brunswick (Warning)
1631^{12} 2491^{10} 3013^{9} 4089^{2} 5104^{2} 5832^{3} 6280^{5} 7417^{6} 7577^{2} (8154) 8469^{2}

Baltic Raider (IRE) *Michael Dods* 80
3 b g Baltic King Frippet (IRE) (Ela-Mana-Mou)
1243^{9} 2695^{13} 3753^{9} 4844^{8}

Balty Boys (IRE) *Brian Ellison* a106 117
7 b g Cape Cross(IRE) Chatham Islands (USA) (Elusive Quality (USA))
1491^{3} 1774^{7} 2191^{16} 3273^{26} 4165^{17} 4625^{19} 5146^{8}

Bamako Du Chatelet (FR) *Ian Williams* a72 70
5 gr g Voix Du Nord(FR) Royale Du Chatelet (FR) (Sleeping Car (FR))
164^{6} 358^{4} 724^{3} (1748) (2326) ◆ (2397) 2876^{3} 3844^{7} 4551^{6} 7429^{11} 7905^{F} (8448)

Bamber Bridge (IRE) *Michael Dods* 94
2 gr c Dark Angel(IRE) Nashira (Prince Sabo)
(5577) 6260^{4} 6950^{13}

Banaadeer (AUS) *M F De Kock* 105
4 br g More Than Ready(USA) Provence (AUS) (Redoute's Choice (AUS))
91a^{10} 280a^{7} 373a^{2} 810a^{7}

Banaadeer (IRE) *Doug Watson* a99 101
5 ch h Tamayuz Loose Julie (IRE) (Cape Cross (IRE))
723a^{7}

Bancnuanaheireann (IRE) *Michael Appleby* a111 99
9 b g Chevalier(IRE) Alamanta (IRE) (Ali-Royal (IRE))
93a^{14} 283a^{10} 540a^{14} 5146^{4} 6075^{8} 6786^{29} 8160^{7}

Bandanetta (FR) *A Bonin* a94 94
4 b m Soldier Of Fortune(IRE) Bandaneira (GER) (Tertullian (USA))
5906a^{3} 7861a^{8}

Banditry (IRE) *Ian Williams* a89 89
4 b g Iffraaj Badalona (Cape Cross (IRE))
6301^{5} 6802^{6} (7535) (7608) ◆

Banham (USA) *Roger Charlton* a71 74
3 gr g Exchange Rate(USA) Palisade (USA) (Gone West (USA))
1287^{5} 1738^{5} 3110^{4} 3766^{6}

Banish (USA) *Hugo Palmer* a97 88
3 b g Smart Strike(CAN) Beyond Our Reach (IRE) (Danehill Dancer (IRE))
1339^{2} ◆ 1837^{2} (2320) 2892^{15} 3957^{2} 4710^{6} 6286^{4} (6870) ◆ 7117^{13} 7869^{7}

Bank Of Burden (USA) *Niels Petersen* a100 104
9 ch g Hawk Wing(USA) Wewantitall (Pivotal)
4329a^{9} 5187a^{3} 5950a^{3} 6390a^{10}

Bank Of Gibraltar *Martin Smith* a86 78
4 ch g Rock Of Gibraltar(IRE) Banksia (Marju (IRE))
(74) 1142^{5} 2324^{6} 3035^{5} 6416^{3} 7066^{12}

Banksea *Luca Cumani* 105
3 b g Lawman(FR) Stars In Your Eyes (Galileo (IRE))
1992^{2} 2538^{2} ◆ (3435) ◆ 4108^{5} 4797^{12} 5616^{2} ◆ 6331^{2} 6786^{19}

Bannock (IRE) *A bin Harmash* a86 86
7 b g Bertolini(USA) Laoub (USA) (Red Ransom (USA))
284a^{10}

Bannock Town *Linda Perratt* 10
5 b g Denounce Miss Pigalle (Good Times (ITY))
3022^{8} 4309^{7} 4705^{5} 5222^{10} 5838^{7} 6003^{4} 6506^{19} 6774^{9} 7093^{13} 7253^{11}

Ban Shoof *Ismail Mohammed* a77 75
3 b g Shirocco(GER) Pasithea (IRE) (Celtic Swing)
(1184) 1602^{7} 1994^{7} 4549^{4} 5333^{6} 6626^{4} 6870^{8}

Banta Bay *John Best* a62 24
2 b g Kheleyf(USA) Atnab (USA) (Riverman (USA))
6369^{7} 7032^{7} 7776^{4}

Banzari *H-F Devin* 110
4 b m Motivator Bantu (Cape Cross (IRE))
(5384a) (6598a) 7404a^{3}

Bapak Asmara (IRE) *Kevin Ryan* a63 87
4 ro g Zebedee Sheba Five (USA) (Five Star Day (USA))
1672^{3} 2364^{9} 3956^{3} 4896^{10} 6079^{3}

Bapak Bangsawan *Ann Stokell* a64 53
6 b g Pastoral Pursuits Nsx (Roi Danzig (USA))
133^{7} 250^{7} 364^{5} 868^{7} 5826^{8} 6381^{4} 6653^{7} 7093^{5} 7386^{13} 7596^{9} 8242^{8} 8474^{7}

Baraboy (IRE) *Barry Murtagh* 65
6 b g Barathea(IRE) Irina (IRE) (Polar Falcon (USA))
6221^{9}

Bara Brith *David Evans* a18 53
2 b f Hellvelyn Crazy Chris (Ishiguru (USA))
1086^{10} 2976^{6} 3093^{7} 7941^{12}

Baraweez (IRE) *Brian Ellison* a84 107
6 b g Cape Cross(IRE) Aquarelle Bleue (Sadler's Wells (USA))
2191^{7} 3164^{6} 3565^{6} 4163^{7} 4747a^{5} 4921a^{5} 5555^{13} 6558^{20}

Barbarigo (IRE) *F Chappet* a78
2 b g Canford Cliffs(IRE) Lally Mut (ITY) (Muhtathir)
(4183a) 5447a^{3} (5988a) 7293a^{4} 7971a^{8}

Barbary Prince *Shaun Harris*
4 ch g Dapper La Vie Est Belle (Makbul)
8570^{8}

Barbs Princess *Charles Hills* a81 78
6 ch m Bahamian Bounty Halland Park Girl (IRE) (Primo Dominie)
269^{2} 364^{7}

Barchan (USA) *Roger Varian* a81 68
4 b g War Front(USA) Malamado (USA) (Broken Vow (USA))
1606^{7} 2243^{12} 3242^{12} 7352^{13}

Bargain Buy *William Haggas* a91 84
3 ch f Tamayuz Peace Summit (Cape Cross (IRE))
(1146) ◆ 1572^{2} (2532) 3039^{4} (8158) ◆ 8426^{3}

Barhanpour (FR) *A De Royer-Dupre* a80 77
3 bb c Raven's Pass(USA) Balankiya (IRE) (Darshaan)
1240a^{3}

Barista (IRE) *Brian Forsey* a67 69
8 b g Titus Livius(FR) Cappuccino (IRE) (Mujadil (USA))
1456^{8} 5954^{7} 6254^{5} (6636) 7070^{4} 7426^{2} (7889) 8086^{4}

Barizan (IRE) *Brendan Powell* 75
10 b g Kalanisi(IRE) Behra (IRE) (Grand Lodge (USA))
6544^{5} 7183^{7} 7507^{5}

Barjeel (USA) *William Haggas* a84
3 b c Speightstown(USA) Listen To My Song (USA) (Unbridled's Song (USA))
6905^{2} 7311^{4}

Barkston Ash *Eric Alston* a38 95
8 b g Kyllachy Ae Kae Ae (USA) (King Of Kings (IRE))
1215^{16} 1444^{3} 1787^{2} 1879^{3} 2016^{3} 2259^{12} 3753^{5} 3892^{5} ◆ 4873^{4} 5161^{8} 6079^{16}

Barleysugar (IRE) *Edward Freeman* a97 99
3 b f Kyllachy Caster Sugar (USA) (Cozzene (USA))
1809^{3} 2479^{2} 2789^{2} 7724a^{3}

Barlongueta (IRE) *M Delcher Sanchez* 87
2 b f Fol Parade(ARG) Solita (USA) (Thunder Gulch (USA))
3006a^{7} 7480a^{7}

Barnaby Brook (CAN) *Robyn Brisland* a68 56
6 b g North Light(IRE) Mascara (USA) (Milwaukee Brew (USA))
527^{2} (702) (2566) 2899^{3} 6890^{4} 7310^{3}

Barnacle *Emma Owen* a46 46
7 b g Compton Place Bombalarina (IRE) (Barathea (IRE))
3031^{5} 4197^{5} 5303^{8}

Barnet Fair *David Nicholls* a90 97
8 br g Iceman Pavement Gates (Bishop Of Cashel)
2258^{5} 2488^{8} 3150^{7} 4079^{15} 4862^{18} 5390^{9} 6072^{12}

Barney McGrew (IRE) *Michael Dods* a58 79
13 b g Mark Of Esteem(IRE) Success Story (Sharrood (USA))
2238^{8} 3610^{6}

Barney Roy *Richard Hannon* 84
2 b c Excelebration(IRE) Alina (IRE) (Galileo (IRE))
(6777)

Barnmore *Peter Hedger* a81 73
8 b g Royal Applause Veronica Franco (Darshaan)
953^{3} 1418^{3} 1916^{6}

Barnsdale *John Holt* a37 48
3 b g Stimulation(IRE) Seren Teg (Timeless Times (USA))
730^{8} 883^{6} 970^{8} 1249^{6} 1554^{6} 3140^{7} 3734^{12} 8541^{8}

Baron Bolt *Paul Cole* a81 96
3 br g Kheleyf(USA) Scarlet Royal (Red Ransom (USA))
(1249) 1487^{2} 1935^{6} 3036^{2} 3614^{3} (4003) (5759) ◆ 7213^{5}

Baroncello (GER) *Andreas Lowe* 94
3 b c Medecis Balsamia (GER) (Speedmaster (GER))
2315a^{6}

Barracuda Boy (IRE) *Tom Dascombe* a105 104
6 b g Bahamian Bounty Madame Boulangere (Royal Applause)
288^{3} 657^{2} 923^{5} 1083^{5} 2031^{4} 2898^{14} 3250^{6} (4644) 5389^{7} 6788^{12} 7651^{8}

Barren Brook *Laura Mongan* a80 77
9 b g Beat Hollow Carinthia (IRE) (Tirol)
256^{11} 815^{4} 1933^{7} 2588^{2} 3802^{6} (4020) 4459^{6} 5994^{2} 6889^{9} 7653^{8} 7973^{10} 8124^{7} 8257^{13} 8554^{5}

Barrington (IRE) *Charles Hills* 98
2 b c Casamento(IRE) Mia Divina (Exceed And Excel (AUS))
2204^{4} (2543) ◆ 4060^{6}

Barroche (IRE) *Clive Cox* 98
2 b f Kodiac Dark Arts (USA) (Royal Anthem (USA))
2310^{2} (2637) ◆ 3270^{6} (4503) 5359^{4} 6068a^{3}

Barsanti (IRE) *Roger Varian* a100 114
4 b g Champs Elysees Silver Star (Zafonic (USA))
(708) (1089) ◆ (2222) 3436^{3} 4164^{2} (5611) 6752^{2}

Bartack (IRE) *Abdulla Kuwaiti* a83 99
6 b g Acclamation Bentley's Bush (IRE) (Barathea (IRE))
744a^{6}

Bartholomew J (IRE) *Lydia Pearce* 42
2 ch g Fast Company(IRE) Mana (IRE) (Motivator)
4738^{6} 5332^{11} 5876^{8}

Bartok (IRE) *John Gosden* a70
3 b c Iffraaj City Dancer (IRE) (Elusive City (USA))
65^{2} 298^{2} (Dead)

Barton Lodge (IRE) *David Simcock* a78
3 b c Fastnet Rock(AUS) Queen Cleopatra (IRE) (Kingmambo (USA))
(287) ◆

Barwah (USA) *Peter Niven* a69 62
5 b m Discreet Cat(USA) Enfiraaj (USA) (Kingmambo (USA))
2053^{10} (2329) (3013) 3952^{9} 4429^{5} 5068^{4} (5844) 5973^{2} 6742^{7} 6908^{8}

Barwell (IRE) *Michael Dods* a55
2 b g Rock Of Gibraltar(IRE) Agata (FR) (Poliglote)
8089^{8}

Barwick *George Baker* a91 94
8 b g Beat Hollow Tenpence (Bob Back (USA))
(1568) 2313^{3} 2897^{9} 3889^{16}

Barwod *J Smart* 108
3 b c Lope De Vega(IRE) Atlanda (FR) (Hernando (FR))
1024a^{2} 2281a^{5} 5004a^{6} 8573a^{6}

Barye *Richard Hughes* a108 98
5 b g Archipenko(USA) Oblige (Robellino (USA))
(99) ◆ 793^{6} 5173^{6} 5611^{8} 6125^{4} 7979^{7} 8210^{5} 8424^{2} ◆

Basateen (IRE) *Doug Watson* 107
4 ch g Teofilo(IRE) Tasha's Dream (USA) (Woodman (USA))
(721a) 1106a^{10}

Basem *Saeed bin Suroor* a107 113
5 b h Pivotal Gonbarda (GER) (Lando (GER))
3273^{25} 4165^{5} 6157a^{2} 7101^{2} 7700^{4}

Bashiba (IRE) *Nigel Tinkler* 94
5 ch g Iffraaj Nightswimmer (IRE) (Noverre (USA))
1601^{11} 2016^{11} 2305^{3} 2775^{3} 3056^{5} (3956) 4488^{4} (5390) 6114^{3} 6779^{P} 7124^{12}

Basil Bear *Deborah Sanderson*
4 b g Indesatchel(IRE) Summer Gift (Cadeaux Genereux)
1027^{7}

Basil Berry *Chris Dwyer* a103 101
5 b g Tobougg(IRE) Dolly Coughdrop (IRE) (Titus Livius (FR))
333^{2} 501^{4} 833^{7} 923^{7} 3573^{6} 4741^{4} ◆ 5934^{4} (6458) 7068^{4} 8029^{4} 8311^{10}

Basileus (IRE) *Stefano Botti* 106
3 ch c Dream Ahead(USA) Miss Mariduff (USA) (Hussonet (USA))
1686a^{7} 6823a^{6} 7565a^{2} 7841a^{9}

Basilia *Mme A Fabre* a87 83
3 b f Fastnet Rock(AUS) Bargouzine (USA) (Stravinsky (USA))
(2141a) 7998a^{13} 8368a^{4}

Basingstoke (IRE) *Daniel Mark Loughnane* a64 41
7 b g Elusive City(USA) Ryninch (IRE) (Dr Devious (IRE))
2^{2} 526^{2} 682^{2} 776^{2} (936) 1047^{3} 1120^{7} 1498^{7} 8306^{8}

Basma *Owen Burrows* a65 74
3 b f Exceed And Excel(AUS) Miss Chicane (Refuse To Bend (IRE))
791^{2} 1431^{7}

Basse Reine (FR) *M Figge* a74 69
3 b f Touch Down(GER) Bakufu (IRE) (King's Best (USA))
3764a^{3} 8368a^{5}

Bassett Bleu *Iain Jardine* a49 49
3 b c Wootton Bassett Lafontaine Bleu (Piccolo)
5228^{9} 6966^{5} (7438) 7657^{11} 8309^{14}

Bassino (USA) *James Bennett* a55 26
3 b g Street Cry(IRE) Show Me The Roses (USA) (Storm Cat (USA))
6650^{8} 7942^{8} 8342^{7}

Bassmah *Ismail Mohammed* 68
2 b f Harbour Watch(IRE) Secret Night (Dansili)
3818^{5} ◆ 4298^{5} 5119^{5}

Bastille (GER) *P Schiergen* 94
3 b f Saddex Boccassini (GER) (Artan (IRE))
1513a^{6} 6824a^{7}

Bastille Day *David Elsworth* a90 95
4 ch g Champs Elysees Vivianna (Indian Ridge)
1775^{3} ◆ 2214^{5} (2819) ◆ (3523) ◆ (4048) 4654^{5} 4776^{6} 6126^{8} 6786^{24}

Bataka *Harry Dunlop* a44 60
2 ch f Mount Nelson Dominica (Alhaarth (IRE))
7208^{2} 7698^{10} 8277^{7}

Bateel (IRE) *David Simcock* 107
4 b m Dubawi(IRE) Attractive Crown (USA) (Chief's Crown (USA))
1855^{2} 2465^{5} (3662) 5691a^{5} 7351^{13}

Bathos (IRE) *Mark Johnston* a81 92
3 b c Poet's Voice Santolina (USA) (Boundary (USA))
1080^{7} 2029^{6} (2393) 2892^{13} 4108^{7} 4399^{7} 4868^{12} 5865^{8} 6209^{6} 6753^{20}

Bathtub Stella (USA) *Tom Dascombe* 34
2 rg f Hat Trick(JPN) Tarika (USA) (Cozzene (USA))
3134^{5}

Battaash (IRE) *Charles Hills* 101
2 b g Dark Angel(IRE) Anna Law (IRE) (Lawman (FR))
(2371) 3247^{12} 6228^{3} 6734^{3} 7113^{3}

Battalion (IRE) *Jamie Osborne* a110 105
6 b g Authorized(IRE) Zigarra (Halling (USA))
1475^{4} 1973^{5} 2464^{6} 3383^{10} 5651^{5} 6932a^{2} (8160) (8427)

Battered *William Haggas* 84
2 b g Foxwedge(AUS) Swan Wings (Bahamian Bounty)
4161^{6} 4663^{3} (6524) 7120^{2}

Battersea *Roger Varian* 111
5 b g Galileo(IRE) Gino's Spirits (Perugino (USA))
(453a) 811a^{4} 4061^{4} 5402^{5} 5655^{4} 6283^{5}

Battle Ensign (USA) *Saeed bin Suroor* a64
2 b c Arch(USA) Rate Of Exchange (USA) (Exchange Rate (USA))
8088^{6}

Battlement *Roger Charlton* a96 97
3 gr f Dansili Scuffle (Daylami (IRE))
984^{2} ◆ (1235) 2178^{4} (3034) (4599) 5205^{2} 6939^{3} ◆ 7650^{4} 8148a^{4}

Battle Of Bosworth (IRE) *Paul Cole* a35 37
3 b g Duke Of Marmalade(IRE) Muskoka Dawn (USA) (Miswaki (USA))
7310^{11}

Battle Of Marathon (USA) *John Ryan* a84 114
4 b g War Front(USA) Sayedah (IRE) (Darshaan)
95a^{12} 189a^{8} 372a^{5} 540a^{7} 748^{8} 1196^{3} 1425^{5} 1774^{2} 3273^{5} 4127^{10}

Battle Of Wits (IRE) *J S Moore* a47 52
2 b g Fast Company(IRE) Mirandassister (IRE) (Titus Livius (FR))
2147^{5} 2747^{9} 2997^{7} 4015^{6} 4386^{4} 5141a^{7} 6253^{6} 6313^{5} 6961^{7}

Battleroftheboyne (IRE) *Eamonn O'Connell* a55 77
7 b g Majestic Missile(IRE) Khaytada (IRE) (Doyoun)
7474a^{10}

Batts Rock (IRE) *Michael Bell* a79 87
3 b g Fastnet Rock(AUS) Be My Queen (IRE) (Sadler's Wells (USA))
(1499) 2252^{3}

Batura Sar (FR) *M Boutin* a39 53
2 b f Sunday Break(JPN) Misery Hill (FR) (Nombre Premier)
1021a^{4} 7927a^{8}

Bayan Kasirga (IRE) *Richard Fahey* a79 80
6 b m Aussie Rules(USA) Gwyllion (USA) (Red Ransom (USA))
200^{5} 382^{8} 566^{6} (636) 890^{6} (1166) 1586^{7} (2093) 2564^{4} ◆ 3251^{6} 3636^{8} 4049^{8} 4646^{6}

Baybaskan (TUR) *Fehmi Demir* 86
4 b h Flier's Fantasy(TUR) Best Queen (TUR) (Kayabey (TUR))
6179a[6]

Baydar *Hugo Palmer* a83 111
3 b c Rock Of Gibraltar(IRE) Splashdown (Falbrav (IRE))
1992[8] (3355) (4650) (5647) (6573) 7700[7]

Bay Mirage (IRE) *Kevin Ryan* a69 66
3 b g Kheleyf(USA) Choosey Girl (IRE) (Choisir (AUS))
2307[8] 2957[6] (4310) 4830[8] 5537[9] 7333[6] 7663[2] 7994[11] 8483[9]

Bay Of Angels (IRE) *Stuart Williams* a44
2 br f Dark Angel(IRE) Shehira (FR) (Sendawar (IRE))
5202[10] 6696[13] 6866[10]

Bay Of Biscaine (FR) *Mario Hofer* 82
2 gr c Mastercraftsman(IRE) Britney (FR) (Kheleyf (USA))
6174a[7] 7655a[8]

Bay Of Poets (IRE) *Charlie Appleby* a82 101
2 b c Lope De Vega(IRE) Bristol Bay (IRE) (Montjeu (IRE))
4379[6] ◆ (6085) 6783[8] 7539[8] 7721a[8]

Bay Of St Malo (IRE) *Richard Hannon* a76 78
3 b f Canford Cliffs(IRE) Distant Skies (Tiger Hill (IRE))
1860[14] 2181[7] 2431[6] (2968) 3740[3] (4087) 4556[3] 4819[4] 6299[7] 6657[5] 6893[5]

Bayrir (FR) *N Al Mandeel* a81 89
7 b g Medicean Balankiya (IRE) (Darshaan)
93a[12] 455a[10]

Bay Station *David Nicholls* a34 74
2 b f Camacho Hazelhurst (IRE) (Night Shift (USA))
(5317) 6343[10] 7600[9]

Bayston Hill *Mark Usher* a71 71
2 br g Big Bad Bob(IRE) Jessica Ennis (USA) (English Channel (USA))
2535[2] ◆ 2963[2] 3404[2] 3986[2] 5251[2] 5594[8] (6404) 6950[14]

Bay Watch (IRE) *Andrew Balding* a62 47
2 b c Harbour Watch(IRE) Karuga (Kyllachy)
7502[10] 8243[5]

Baz (FR) *F-H Graffard* a79 104
6 b g Mount Nelson Zelah (IRE) (Alzao (USA))
6178a[5] 7312a[5] 8042a[5]

Bazaruto *Abduljabar Ali* 92
9 ch h Pivotal Isla Azul (IRE) (Machiavellian (USA))
755a[10]

Bazooka (IRE) *David Flood* a77 82
5 b g Camacho Janadam (IRE) (Mukaddamah (USA))
1144[9] (1390) 1885[9] 2114a[12] 2582[7] 3690[2] 4795[4] 5405[7] 6379[6] 7418[5] 7545[15] 8477[5]

Baz's Boy *John Flint* a37 50
3 b g Compton Place Spunger (Fraam)
1829[6] 2784[10] 3975[6] 4292[11] (4796) 5706[4] 5954[4] 6291[6] 6894[10] 7646[6]

Bazula (IRE) *Tim Easterby* a28 53
3 b g Tagula(IRE) Lilly Be (IRE) (Titus Livius (FR))
1524[8] 1870[6] 2333[8] 3014[4] 3710[8] 4410[9] 4600[9] 4973[5] 5278[5] 5920[10]

Bazwind (IRE) *David Evans* a52 72
2 b g Lilbourne Lad(IRE) Gay Heroine (Caerleon (USA))
3093[5] 3495[4] 3742[2] 4287[2] 4386[2] 5229[6] 7091[4] 7319[6] (8025) 8235[6] 8341[3]

Bazzat (IRE) *John Ryan* a67 55
3 ch g Roderic O'Connor(IRE) Compradore (Mujtahid (USA))
2348[7] 2608[4] 2829[4] 3033[9] 4204[4] 4567[7] 4936[2] 5263[4] 6047[7] 6187[3] 6407[3] (6900) (7282) (7427) 7642[8] 8085[6] 8258[6] 8458[3]

B B Queen (IRE) *Clive Cox* a47 48
2 br f Big Bad Bob(IRE) Gold Queen (Grand Lodge (USA))
5771[5] 6250[9] 6625[13] 7275[10]

Beach Bar (IRE) *Brendan Powell* a49 101
5 b g Azamour(IRE) Toasted Special (USA) (Johannesburg (USA))
94a[8] 189a[5] 375a[4] 628a[6] 812a[2] 1196[12] 5146[5] 5962[4] 6364[2] 6884[4] 7573[6]

Beach Break *Ralph Beckett* a73 76
2 b c Cacique(IRE) Wemyss Bay (Sadler's Wells (USA))
6704[8] 7501[3] 7908[5]

Beach Dancer (IRE) *William Knight* a20
2 b c Footstepsinthesand All Night Dancer (IRE) (Danehill Dancer (IRE))
8065[12]

Beach Patrol (USA) *Chad C Brown* 108
3 bb c Lemon Drop Kid(USA) Bashful Bertie (USA) (Quiet American (USA))
4173a[3] (5429a)

Beachy Head (IRE) *A R Al Rayhi* a106 74
5 b h Shamardal(USA) Chaquiras (USA) (Seeking The Gold (USA))
369a[4] 535a[7]

Beacon Rock (IRE) *A P O'Brien* 109
3 ch c Galileo(IRE) Remember When (IRE) (Danehill Dancer (IRE))
1370a[3] 2069a[4] (2510a) 3337[2] 4332a[8]

Beaconsfield *Hughie Morrison* a28 69
2 b c Foxwedge(AUS) Italian Connection (Cadeaux Genereux)
6881[12] 7318[3] 7658[9] 8159[10]

Beadlam (IRE) *Roger Fell* a11 67
3 ch f Frozen Power(IRE) Pivotal Role (Pivotal)
2122[7] 2835[12] 3249[4] 3750[8] 3877[U] (4972) 5277[9] 5355[4] 5803[2] (6646) 6908[11]

Bearag *David O'Meara* a62 53
2 b f Dutch Art Cats Eyes (Echo Of Light)
6477[8] 6925[4] 7380[3]

Beardwood *Mark Johnston* a96 91
4 ch g Dutch Art Valentina Guest (IRE) (Be My Guest (USA))
1522[6] 2259[3] 2679[4] 3419[3] 3645[6] ◆ 4894[5] 6217[10] 6753[4] ◆ 6956[10] (7222) 7535[6] 7608[9] (7744) (7967) 8231[3]

Bear Essentials (IRE) *David O'Meara* 68
2 b c Kodiac Jacquelin Jag (IRE) (Fayruz)
2956[4] 3321[7] 3939[3] 4602[8] 5833[9] 7091[5]

Bear Faced *Sir Mark Prescott Bt* a94 82
3 b g Intikhab(USA) Hulcote Rose (IRE) (Rock Of Gibraltar (IRE))
(402) ◆ 638[3] (828a) 972a[3] 1071[7] 2870[7]

Bear Valley (IRE) *Mark Johnston* 97
2 b c Manduro(GER) Shane (GER) (Kornado)
3248[2] 3808[2] (4304) (4802) 5556[6] 6707[8] 7151[12]

Beatbybeatbybeat *Antony Brittain* a75 74
3 ch f Poet's Voice Beat As One (Medicean)
1389[4] 1804[7] 5515[5] 6337[4] (7035) ◆ (7272) 7485[3] 7857[12]

Beatisa *Ed Walker* a51
2 b f Intikhab(USA) Bea Menace (USA) (Mizzen Mast (USA))
8591[6]

Beat The Ballot (IRE) *Tracey Collins* a74 81
7 br g Big Bad Bob(IRE) Cosmic Speed Queen (USA) (On To Glory (USA))
4748a[15]

Beat The Blues *Miss Joey Ellis* a61 59
4 b m Aqlaam Beat As One (Medicean)
158[5] 707[8] 7646[11]

Beauchamp Opal *Charlie Fellowes* a60 56
2 b f Pastoral Pursuits Orange Sunset (IRE) (Roanoke (USA))
6782[10] 7284[6] 7962[6] 8235[9]

Beauchamp Pasha *Harry Dunlop* a28
3 b g Pastoral Pursuits Ashford Castle (USA) (Bates Motel (USA))
2816[9] 4384[7]

Beauden Barrett *Jeremy Gask* a79
3 b g Dick Turpin(IRE) Riccoche (IRE) (Oasis Dream)
7459[6] (7935) 8205[2] 8319[5]

Beauly *Charles Hills* a75 100
3 ch f Sea The Stars(IRE) Pickle (Piccolo)
(591) 2245[7] 3060[2] 3297[13] 4610[4] 5307[6] 7823[10]

Beau Mistral (IRE) *Tony Carroll* a53 62
7 ch m Windsor Knot(IRE) Carpet Lover (IRE) (Fayruz)
1600[7] 2905[2] 3217[6] 3397[5] 3898[3] 4763[4] (5105) 5827[4] 6312[3] 6832[5] 7018[3] 7290[7] 7774[4] ◆ 8149[3]

Beaumont's Party (IRE) *Chris Grant* a47 77
9 b g High Chaparral(IRE) Miss Champagne (FR) (Bering)
1201[11] 8387[9] 8586[14]

Beausant *George Baker* a68 81
4 ch g Orientor Hanella (IRE) (Galileo (IRE))
1057[7] (1456) 2205[2] (2367)

Beau Satchel *Adrian McGuinness* a82 84
6 b g Indesatchel(IRE) Sweet Patoopie (Indian Ridge)
(4748a) 4899a[3] 5941a[14] 6984a[10]

Beau Strata (IRE) *Clive Mulhall* 45
2 b f Dandy Man(IRE) Stratospheric (Slip Anchor)
3433[7] 3947[8] 4451[9] 5861[6]

Beautiful Escape (USA) *Saeed bin Suroor* a72 68
2 b f Elusive Quality(USA) Aviacion (BRZ) (Know Heights (IRE))
4261[9] 6578[4] 7511[5] 8008[7]

Beautiful Heroine (IRE) *F-H Graffard* 106
5 b m High Chaparral(IRE) Blue Sail (USA) (Kingmambo (USA))
1375a[10] 1822a[4] 2727a[6] 4696a[8]

Beautiful Morning *Luca Cumani* 103
3 b f Galileo(IRE) Date With Destiny (IRE) (George Washington (IRE))
2245[2] ◆ 6747[5]

Beautiful Romance *Saeed bin Suroor* 114
4 b m New Approach(IRE) Mazuna (IRE) (Cape Cross (IRE))
(2189) ◆ 3384[5] 4864[5] 6747[3] 7756a[7] (7948a)

Beautiful Stranger (IRE) *Keith Dalgleish* a74 78
5 b g Iffraaj Monarchy (IRE) (Common Grounds)
788[3] ◆ 1152[4] 2362[7] 2959[6] 3517[11] (3922) 4189[5] 4435[6] 5291[4] 5779[5] 6138[6] 8100[6] (8191) 8498[6]

Beauty Flame (IRE) *A S Cruz* 117
6 br g Footstepsinthesand Lucy Diamonds (IRE) (Orpen (USA))
1912a[6] 8332a[13]

Beauty Night *Clive Cox* a76 75
3 b g Showcasing Night Symphonie (Cloudings (IRE))
(1238) 2044[2] 2545[11] 4288[9] 5287[5]

Beauty Of Love *Mme Pia Brandt* 81
2 b f Elusive City(USA) Breath Of Love (USA) (Mutakddim (USA))
(6937a)

Beauty Only (IRE) *A S Cruz* 119
5 b g Holy Roman Emperor(IRE) Goldendale (IRE) (Ali-Royal (IRE))
1912a[4] (8332a)

Beauty's Forte (IRE) *Declan Carroll* a63 53
5 b g Kyllachy Viking Fair (Zamindar (USA))
144[10] 201[11] 542[10] 682[8] 801[11]

Beauty Sleep (IRE) *William Haggas* a77 80
3 b f Rip Van Winkle(IRE) Rasana (Royal Academy (USA))
2009[5] 2505[8] 3350[2] 4384[2] 4792[3] (5681) 6527[3]

Beaverbrook *Mark Johnston* a102 99
3 b c Cape Cross(IRE) Bint Almatar (USA) (Kingmambo (USA))
1080[3] 1567[6] 1866[5] 2473[8] 3341[9] 4863[7] 5173[8] 6057[4] 6379[5]

Bebe Cherie (FR) *Markus Klug* 96
4 b m Youmzain(IRE) Shamaniya (IRE) (Doyoun)
2286a[3] 6151a[5] 6610a[8]

Bebe D'Amour (FR) *J-Y Artu* a71 66
2 ro f Montmartre(FR) Prudence Royale (FR) (Loup Solitaire (USA))
7971a[7]

Bebhinn (USA) *Kevin Prendergast* 102
3 b f Street Boss(USA) Passion Overflow (USA) (Hennessy (USA))
3681a[6] 6816a[5] 7191a[3] 7706a[4]

Be Bold *Rebecca Bastiman* a68 72
4 ch g Assertive Marysienka (Primo Dominie)
1447[10] 1879[7] 2857[6] 4259[7] 4700[5] 5224[8] 5858[8] 7334[5] (7584) 7797[9]

Be Bop Tango (FR) *K R Burke* 77
3 b g Soul City(IRE) Divine Poesie (FR) (Enrique)
1275[6] 1789[6] 2693[12] 3924[7] 5478[6] 6836[6] 7680a[11]

Becca Campbell (IRE) *Eve Johnson Houghton* a45 72
3 b f Roderic O'Connor(IRE) Scottendale (Zilzal (USA))
1734[3] 2590[5] 2967[4] 4021[5] (5101) 5513[3] 5923[6] (6405) 6646[8] (7037) 7245[6]

Beck And Call *Henry Candy* 74
2 b f Holy Roman Emperor(IRE) Gosbeck (Dubawi (IRE))
4350[3] ◆ 5304[3]

Becky The Thatcher *Micky Hammond* 74
3 b f Mastercraftsman(IRE) Fairmont (IRE) (Kingmambo (USA))
2269[5] 2831[4] 3323[4] 3778[4] 4255[2] 4847[2] 5420[6] 5888[3] 7045[11]

Become Aware *Tim Etherington* a37 45
4 b g Sakhee(USA) Sainte Gig (FR) (Saint Cyrien (FR))
37[6]

Becquamis (FR) *T Lemer* 98
2 bb g Vertigineux(FR) Becquamour (FR) (Septieme Ciel (USA))
4750a[4] 5497a[6] (7170a) 7972a[6]

Becquarius (FR) *Eric Saint-Martin* a63 70
6 b g Medecis Berangele (FR) (Medaaly)
4903a[10] 6938a[9]

Bective (IRE) *J F Levins* a66 90
2 b g Approve(IRE) Raindancing (IRE) (Tirol)
2717a[4]

Bedale *Ernst Oertel* a28 107
5 b g Cape Cross(IRE) Beta (Selkirk (USA))
453a[13] 627a[14]

Bedazzling Lady (IRE) *Robert Eddery* a48 48
3 rg f Zebedee Malta (USA) (Gone West (USA))
6902[12] 7445[3] 7646[3] 8079[13] 8120[9]

Bed Of Diamonds *Adam West* a24 43
2 ch f Bated Breath Bedara (Barathea (IRE))
6762[8] 7543[10] 7976[13]

Bedouin (IRE) *Luca Cumani* a65 71
2 b g High Chaparral(IRE) Jewel In The Sand (IRE) (Bluebird (USA))
6945[5] 7470[6] 7812[5]

Bedrock *William Haggas* 90
3 b g Fastnet Rock(AUS) Gemstone (IRE) (Galileo (IRE))
1623[3] 2099[3] 2393[10] (3399) 4554[2] 6484[2] 6876[3]

Bee Case *Simon Dow* a83 73
2 br f Showcasing Binabee (Galileo (IRE))
2817[4] 4951[2] (5469) 5998[9] 6697[6] 8592[7]

Beechmount Whisper (IRE) *P J Prendergast* a80 79
4 b g Kodiac Miss Me (Marju (IRE))
6465a[2]

Bee Jersey (USA) *Doug Watson* a79
2 ch c Jersey Town(USA) Bees (USA) (Rahy (USA))
8574a[3]

Beepeecee *Richard Hughes* a52 46
2 b g Henrythenavigator(USA) Roedean (IRE) (Oratorio (IRE))
6183[4] 6439[7] 6888[7] 7734[5] 7866[10] 8025[2]

Be Famous (GER) *Frau S Steinberg* 93
4 b g Kamsin(GER) Bandeira (GER) (Law Society (USA))
8042a[12]

Beggers Luck *Eric Wheeler* a68 43
6 b m Lucky Story(USA) Dropitlikeit's Hot (IRE) (Tagula (IRE))
60[7] 355[4] 2442[9]

Beholder (USA) *Richard E Mandella* a124
6 b m Henny Hughes(USA) Leslie's Lady (USA) (Tricky Creek (USA))
(7810a)

Beijing *A Fabre* a68 90
3 b c Dubawi(IRE) Board Meeting (IRE) (Anabaa (USA))
3543a[5]

Be Kool (IRE) *Brian Ellison* a71 75
3 b g Approve(IRE) Accounting (Sillery (USA))
(1345) ◆ 1804[6] 2674[7] 3130[7] 3567[3] 4643[3] 5845[8] (6265)

Belabour *Mark Brisbourne* a66
3 b g Bernardini(USA) Criticism (Machiavellian (USA))
8342[3]

Belango (GER) *Frau R Weissmeier* a66 102
10 ch g Tertullian(USA) Brighella (GER) (Lomitas)
715a[5]

Belardo (IRE) *Roger Varian* 122
4 b h Lope De Vega(IRE) Danaskaya (IRE) (Danehill (USA))
(1198) ◆ 1606[4] (2243) 3242[2]

Bel Canto (JPN) *Koichi Tsunoda* 115
5 ch m Sakura Bakushin O(JPN) Celebrar (JPN) (Boston Harbor (USA))
1104a[12]

Beleave *Luke Dace* a70 78
3 gr f Avonbridge Grezie (Mark Of Esteem (IRE))
(400) ◆ 678[RR] (817) 1071[8] 3111[5] 3816[2]

Belga Bere (FR) *E Leenders* a75 49
5 b m Peer Gynt(JPN) Arrondie (FR) (Inchinor)
5216a[6]

Belgian Bill *George Baker* a106 110
8 b h Exceed And Excel(AUS) Gay Romance (Singspiel (IRE))
189a[6] 540a[10] 625a[5] 4165[11] 4823[4] 5329[6] (6157a)

Believable *Sir Michael Stoute* a74 74
2 b f Acclamation Irresistible (Cadeaux Genereux)
4063[7] 5469[5] (6087) 6630[3]

Believe It (IRE) *Richard Hughes* a73 59
4 b h Rip Van Winkle(IRE) Have Faith (IRE) (Machiavellian (USA))
144[4] ◆ 201[7] (696) 2635[10] 2769[2] 3780[8] 4355[6] 4876[3] 5808[2] 7203[3] 8154[8] (8469)

Belisa (IRE) *Ivan Furtado* a39 53
2 ch f Lope De Vega(IRE) Fleche Brisee (USA) (Dynaformer (USA))
7770[10] 8088[10]

Bella Alissa *Peter Chapple-Hyam* 71
2 b f Dutch Art Crazy Too (IRE) (Invincible Spirit (IRE))
5869[3] ◆

Bella Blur *Eugene Stanford* a62
4 ch m Showcasing Ellablue (Bahamian Bounty)
1491[0] 6137[12]

Bella Donna Borget (FR) *J Bertran De Balanda* 97
4 b m Early March Jasmine Des Bordes (FR) (Epervier Bleu)
1232a[7]

Bella Duchess (IRE) *David C Griffiths* a38 41
2 b f Big Bad Bob(IRE) Spinning Gold (Spinning World (USA))
1443[6] 1799[8] 5884[9] 6388a[30] 8344[7]

Bellajeu *Ralph Beckett* a82 95
4 b m Montjeu(IRE) Arbella (Primo Dominie)
3665[3] 6050[6] (6885) 7545[16]

Bella Luma (USA) *Ed Moger Jr* 85
2 ch f Ministers Wild Cat(USA) Bold Roberta (USA) (Bold Badgett (USA))
8127a[6]

Bellamay *John Weymes* 44
2 b f Foxwedge(AUS) Steeple (Selkirk (USA))
1921[9] 2417[6] 2739[9]

Bella's Boy (IRE) *John Ryan* a37 52
3 b g Lovelace Cosa Deasa (IRE) (Barathea (IRE))
5474[6]

Bella's Venture *John Gallagher* 67
3 bg f Hellvelyn Fayre Bella (Zafeen (FR))
1597[4] 2234[8] 7011[2] 7591[8]

Bellcanto (GER) *S Smrczek* a72 76
4 b g Areion(GER) Bergwelt (GER) (Solarstern (FR))
7398a[8]

Belle De Belle (FR) *P Sogorb* a61 90
2 b f Big Bad Bob(IRE) Green Girl (FR) (Lord Of Men)
5186a[3]

Belledesert *Steph Hollinshead* 90
3 b f Pastoral Pursuits Ocean Blaze (Polar Prince (IRE))
1452[5] (2372) 2693[8] 4093[6] 4547[4] (5284) (5379) 6164[4] 6878[11] 7146[11]

Belle Diva (IRE) *Ralph Beckett* a77 57
2 b f Dark Angel(IRE) Red Intrigue (IRE) (Selkirk (USA))
5304[6] (6625)

Belleire (FR) *M Nigge* 61
2 ch f Soldier Of Fortune(IRE) Eire (Medicean)
6639a[6]

Belle Mare Plage *Stuart Williams* a68 53
3 b f Canford Cliffs(IRE) Flora Trevelyan (Cape Cross (IRE))
1933 (258) 2823[5] 4525[4] 5195[3] 6373[6]

Belle Meade (IRE) *Richard Fahey* 94
2 ch f Roderic O'Connor(IRE) Hazardous (Night Shift (USA))
(4371) 5172[7] 5870[6] 6555[3]

Belle Of Seville *Dominic Ffrench Davis* a34 48
3 b f Duke Of Marmalade(IRE) Kekova (Montjeu (IRE))
1265[3] 2183[12] 2548[9] 4210[11]

Belle Peinture (FR) *Alan Lockwood* a38 41
5 ch m Peintre Celebre(USA) Grosgrain (USA) (Diesis)
2746[10] 3072[10] 3774[10] 4234[11] 5319[8] 5726[3] 6438[13]

Belle's Angel (IRE) *Ann Duffield* a45 53
2 gr f Dark Angel(IRE) Belle Of The Blues (IRE) (Blues Traveller (IRE))
2344[7] 2739[5] 3222[7] 5112[5] 5719[4] 6923[9] 8087[5] 8398[7]

Belle Travers *Richard Fahey* 85
4 ch m Bahamian Bounty Forthefirstime (Dr Fong (USA))
1756[4] 2174[11] 2811[2] 3291[2] (3711) 4138[9] 4808[5] 6107a[7] 7823[7]

Bellevarde (IRE) *James Fanshawe* a73 74
2 b f Kodiac Pearl Mountain (IRE) (Pearl Of Love (IRE))
3526[3] ◆ 4363[2] 4951[5] 6525[6] 7898[9]

Bell Heather (IRE) *Richard Fahey* a75 79
3 b f Iffraaj Burren Rose (USA) (Storm Cat (USA))
2029[4] 2299[6] 3152[8] 3591[2] 4139[7] 4631[5] 5062[2] 6005[3] 7796[6] 8052[11] 8385[12] 8531[11]

Bell Of The Ball (IRE) *Liam Lennon* 60
6 b m Bachelor Duke(USA) Grangehill Dancer (IRE) (Danehill Dancer (IRE))
4194[2]

Bellotta *Jonathan Portman* a63
3 ch f Nayef(USA) Ela Paparouna (Vettori (IRE))
699[5] ◆

Bell Weir *Dianne Sayer* 72
8 gr g Tobougg(IRE) Belly Dancer (IRE) (Danehill Dancer (IRE))
(5155) 5541[3] 6227[4]

Beltor *Robert Stephens* a86 80
5 b g Authorized(IRE) Carahill (AUS) (Danehill (USA))
(8250)

Belvoir Bay *Peter Miller* a99 100
3 b f Equiano(FR) Path Of Peace (Rock Of Gibraltar (IRE))
7724a[5]

Bemusement *Mark Johnston* a50 47
3 b f Exceed And Excel(AUS) Sweet Folly (IRE) (Singspiel (IRE))
102[6] 5731[5] 6511[7] 7489[8]

Be My Sea (IRE) *Tony Carroll* a84 84
5 b g Sea The Stars(IRE) Bitooh (Diktat)
567[3] (864) 957[4] 1296[2] 1852[3] 2582[3] (2820) 3862[7] 4752[6] 5553[7] 6362[2] 7183[4]

Bengal Lancer *Ian Williams* 71
2 gr c Hellvelyn Bens Georgie (IRE) (Opening Verse (USA))
3196[3] 3805[5] 4371[3]

Benidiction (IRE) *K R Burke* a84 62
2 ch f Zebedee Elizabelle (IRE) (Westerner)
1443[7] 2196[7] 2675[5] 3008[2] (3820) 5931[7] 6343[6] 6768[2] 7313[5]

Benjamin Thomas (IRE) *John Quinn* 75
2 b g Mayson Strudel (IRE) (Spectrum (IRE))
6712[2] 7407[2]

Benkei (IRE) *H Rogers* 103
6 b g Galileo(IRE) Bywayofthestars (Danehill (USA))
4721a[3] 5660a[4] 6350a[6] 6820a[7] 7195a[8] 7708a[13]

Bennelong *Lee Carter* a60 51
10 b g Bahamian Bounty Bundle Up (USA) (Miner's Mark (USA))
62[5] 606[8] 950[4] 1262[9] 1547[8] 2006[7] 2326[3] 3522[12] 7427[13]

Benoordenhout (IRE) *T Le Brocq* a64 55
5 br g Footstepsinthesand Tara Too (IRE) (Danetime (IRE))
1518a[4] (2954a) 3380a[2] 4698a[4] 5458a[5] 6402a[3]

Ben Rumson (IRE) *Timothy Doyle* a53 53
4 b g Ask La Protagonista (IRE) (Night Shift (USA))
5900a[5]

Benzini (AUS) *Adrian & Harry Bull* 108
6 bb g Tale Of The Cat(USA) Paris Perfume (AUS) (Kurofune (USA))
8329a[6]

Beolmaui Kkum (USA) *Baik Kwang Yeol* a37
6 bb h Put It Back(USA) Wild Dixie Gal (USA) (Wild Event (USA))
6399a[11]

Be Perfect (USA) *Ruth Carr* a89 87
7 b g Street Cry(IRE) Binya (GER) (Royal Solo (IRE))
747[6] 1081[10] 1493[8] 1642[11] 2199[4] 2685[8] 3345[3] (3659) 4311[7] 4969[5] 5434[6] 6083[9] (6565) 6854[5] 7139[5]

Bequia (IRE) *Martyn Meade* 74
2 ch f Helmet(AUS) Bunditten (IRE) (Soviet Star (USA))
5119[2] 7439[8]

Beraymi (IRE) *A Fabre* 97
3 b f Manduro(GER) Tempete (Dubai Millennium)
2115a[4] 6497a[3]

Berengaria (IRE) *Mark Johnston* a83 80
2 b f Teofilo(IRE) Belle Josephine (Dubawi (IRE))
4801[4] ◆ (5196) ◆ 5632[4]

Beret (FR) *Harry Dunlop* a57 69
3 b g Sageburg(IRE) Moonavvara (IRE) (Sadler's Wells (USA))
128a[2]

Berghain (IRE) *J Hirschberger* 94
3 ch c Medicean Basilea Gold (GER) (Monsun (GER))
1908a[6] 3453a[4] 4186a[7] 7555a[3]

Bergholt (IRE) *Philip Hide* a71 75
3 b g Sir Percy Sularina (IRE) (Alhaarth (IRE))
1288[4] 1750[7] 2393[3] ◆ 2640[5] 3110[5] 5875[4] 6701[9] 7222[6]

Bering Empress (IRE) *Mme C Head-Maarek* a78 73
2 b f Holy Roman Emperor(IRE) Gagarina (IRE) (Galileo (IRE))
5698a[12]

Berkeley Vale *Roger Teal* a80 83
5 b g Three Valleys(USA) Intriguing Glimpse (Piccolo)
(1173) (1756) 2324[5] 3109[4] 4081[8] 4868[13] 5609[8] 6365[6] 7076[5] 7417[8] 7973[14]

Berkshire (IRE) *Paul Cole* a100 111
5 b h Mount Nelson Kinnaird (IRE) (Dr Devious (IRE))
2464[8] 3377a[7] 4392[2] 4821[5] (5894) 7396a[5] 7766[5] 7934[9]

Berkshire Beauty *Andrew Balding* a64 35
4 b m Aqlaam Salim Toto (Mtoto)
(336) 429[5]

Berkshire Boy (IRE) *Andrew Balding* 83
2 b g Elzaam(AUS) Circuit City (IRE) (Exit To Nowhere (USA))
(1915) ◆ 2240[U] 2682[7] 5821[2] 6260[19]

Berling (IRE) *Jessica Long* a88 103
9 gr g Montjeu(IRE) Danaskaya (IRE) (Danehill (USA))
3449a[4] 5187a[9] 5950a[8] 7400a[7]

Berlios (IRE) *David Barron* a80 72
3 b g Excellent Art Endless Peace (IRE) (Russian Revival (USA))
(798) 8349[3] ◆

Berlusca (IRE) *David O'Meara* a90 66
7 b g Holy Roman Emperor(IRE) Shemanikha (FR) (Sendawar (IRE))
160[3] 465[4] (2688) 4113[10] 4717[6] 5246[3] 6517[12] 7159[18] 8077[5] 8539[4]

Bermondsey *Luca Cumani* a99 97
4 b g Galileo(IRE) Barter (Daylami (IRE))
(3109) ◆ 4583[6] 5647[4] 6261[6] 6573[14] 7383[4]

Bermondsey Belle (IRE) *Lucy Wadham* a65
2 b f Sir Percy Bermondsey Girl (Bertolini (USA))
8355[5] 8537[9]

Bernie's Boy *Andrew Balding* a79 85
3 b g Lilbourne Lad(IRE) Stoney Cove (IRE) (Needwood Blade)
618[2] (874) 1071[6] 3908[4] 4532[3] 5649[3] 6576[7]

Bernisdale *John Flint* a48 66
8 ch m Bertolini(USA) Carradale (Pursuit Of Love)
199[8] 1450[8] (3747) (4226) 4507[3] 4913[3] 5232[3] 6315[5]

Be Royale *Michael Appleby* a79 76
6 b m Byron Sofia Royale (Royal Applause)
80[4] 260[5] 415[3] 523[4] 564[3] 780[4] 953[4] 1252[6] 4630[8] 5090[7] (6522) 6644[8] 7281[6] 7687[5] 7851[3] 8067[2] 8358[8]

Berrahri (IRE) *John Best* a80 82
5 b g Bahri(USA) Band Of Colour (IRE) (Spectrum (IRE))
313[6] 588a[3] 664a[3] 900[3] 1144[10] 2151[2] 2651[2] 4138[3]

Bertha Burnett (IRE) *Brian Rothwell* a8 55
5 gr m Verglas(IRE) Starsazi (Observatory (USA))
1412[7] 2525[4] 3479[4] 3642[6] 3952[11] 5729[2] 6953[9] 7581[8]

Bertie Bishop *Brian McMath* a42 10
4 b g Myboycharlie(IRE) Razor Sharp (Bering)
1184[9] 1765[6] 2980[7]

Bertie Blu Boy *Lisa Williamson* a89 63
8 b g Central Park(IRE) Shaymee's Girl (Wizard King)
879[2] 1175[2] 1836[2] 2003[6] 2584[13] 8032[10] 8380[9] 8561[8]

Bertie Buoy *Richard Guest* a61 41
3 b g Bertolini(USA) Tide Of Love (Pursuit Of Love)
763[4] (820) 947[6]

Bertie Moon *Lydia Pearce* a70 86
6 b g Bertolini(USA) Fleeting Moon (Fleetwood (IRE))
164[11] (1201) 1222[2] 3129[7] 4550[3] (5267) (5334) 7158[7]

Bertiewhittle *David Barron* a94 98
8 ch g Bahamian Bounty Minette (Bishop Of Cashel)
290[5] 486[12] 599[6] 833[5] 1153[7] 1394[2] 1627[4] 2247[4] 3358[10] 4299[7] 4893[4] 5389[2] 6210[3] 6276[3] 6560[6] (7126) 7821[2]

Beshara (FR) *A De Royer-Dupre* 83
3 b f Cape Cross(IRE) Behkara (IRE) (Kris)
6273a[10]

Besharah (IRE) *William Haggas* a98 112
3 b f Kodiac Dixieland Kiss (USA) (Dixie Union (USA))
1476[3] 2282a[4] 3339[10] 4114[2] 4826[5]

Beslon (FR) *C Ferland* a72 67
2 b g Rajsaman(FR) Influence (FR) (Dansili)
5348a[8] 5755a[6]

Besotted (IRE) *P Sogorb* a84 104
3 ch f Dutch Art Tender Is Thenight (IRE) (Barathea (IRE))
2945a[2] 4184a[8] 6693a[12]

Bessemer Lady *Ralph Beckett* a52
2 b f Cacique(IRE) Blast Furnace (IRE) (Sadler's Wells (USA))
8246[8]

Bess Of Hardwick *Luca Cumani* a100 97
4 b m Dansili Request (Rainbow Quest (USA))
4078[8] 5328[4] (6332) (7652) ◆ 8068[6]

Best Away (FR) *Ruth Carr* 60
2 b g Intikhab(USA) Blue Best (ITY) (Mujahid (USA))
2852[3] 5756[9] 6446[6]

Best Bid (IRE) *John Quinn* a56 60
2 ch f Mayson High Reserve (Dr Fong (USA))
1951[4] 2404[3] 6925[8] 7330[8]

Best Boy *David C Griffiths* a68 64
4 b g Myboycharlie(IRE) Best Dancer (King's Best (USA))
4455[9] 5057[4] 5481[5] 5918[3] 6450[5] 7895[11]

Best Example (USA) *Julia Feilden* a91 70
4 ch g King's Best(USA) Born Something (IRE) (Caerleon (USA))
240[2] 7428[9] 7702[13] 8446[6]

Best Fouad (FR) *F Rohaut* 107
5 bb g King's Best(USA) Raheefa (USA) (Riverman (USA))
8336a[15]

Best In The World (IRE) *A P O'Brien* 105
3 b f Galileo(IRE) Red Evie (IRE) (Intikhab (USA))
1507a[4] 2160[7] 3202a[3] 4435a[6] (5002a) 6383a[2] 7404a[12]

Best Laid Plans *James Tate* a71 71
3 br f Diktat Najraan (Cadeaux Genereux)
1798[9] 4027[2] 4806[3] 5608[2] 6855[2] 7327[2]

Best New Show (IRE) *David Evans* a67 67
3 gr f Clodovil(IRE) Serious Delight (Lomond (USA))
249[2] (423)

Best Not Argue (IRE) *John Joseph Murphy* a63 79
4 b m Acclamation Laurentina (Cadeaux Genereux)
6984a[9]

Best Of Days *Hugo Palmer* 110
2 b c Azamour(IRE) Baisse (High Chaparral (IRE))
(4533) ◆ 5556[2] (6783)

Best Of Oregon (USA) *Ed Walker* a66 71
3 ch g Cape Blanco(IRE) Wicked Sting (USA) (Devil His Due (USA))
976[4] 1738[11]

Best Of Times *Saeed bin Suroor* 111
4 b g Dubawi(IRE) Nabati (USA) (Rahy (USA))
2684[9] ◆ 3383[6] 3910[13] 4731[5]

Best Solution (IRE) *Saeed bin Suroor* 111
2 b c Kodiac Al Andalyya (USA) (Kingmambo (USA))
3954[3] (4736) 6180a[3] 6707[4] ◆ (7148) 7722a[2]

Best Tamayuz *Scott Dixon* a77 70
5 ch g Tamayuz Pink Ivory (Sakhee (USA))
1[4] 598[3] 802[2] 866[6] 956[6] 1202[8] (2507) 3219[2] 3617[6] 4377[4] 5102[3] 6921[8] 7257[9] 7895[4] 8240[4] 8351[3]

Best Trip (IRE) *Marjorie Fife* a58 91
9 b g Whipper(USA) Tereed Elhawa (Cadeaux Genereux)
658[6] 1563[5] 1869[2] (2238) 2857[2] 3115[5] 3646[7] (4259) 4514[9] 5417[10] 5641[7] 6539[23] 7124[17] 7593[12] 8482[7]

Bethellie Pride *Lynn Siddall* a9
6 b m Misu Bond(IRE) Sunset Lady (IRE) (Red Sunset)
102[10] 298[10] 679[11] 1167[6]

Bethnal Green *Robyn Brisland* a57 55
4 ch m Cockney Rebel(IRE) Exodia (Dr Fong (USA))
2443[7] 3145[7] 4740[5] 5630[6]

Betsalottie *John Bridger* a65 63
3 cg g Aqlaam Si Belle (IRE) (Dalakhani (IRE))
65[6] 219[7] 691[9] 874[3] 1259[2] 1388[6] 1860[4] (2325) 3236[3] 3816[3] 4635[7] 4936[11] 6194[2] 6662[11] 7425[9]

Bettercallphoenix *David C Griffiths* 41
3 b g Motivator Opening Ceremony (USA) (Quest For Fame)
3609[14] 4690[5] 5811[8]

Betty Boo (IRE) *Shaun Harris* a13 51
6 ch m Thousand Words Poker Dice (Primo Dominie)
1495[7] 2013[9] 2423[11] 3777[2] 6902[14] 7046[10]

Beverley Bullet *Les Eyre* a63 65
3 b g Makfi Don't Tell Mary (IRE) (Starcraft (NZ))
1584[2] 1927[8] 2674[8] 5322[4] 5732[7] 5860[6] 7260[2] 7513[5] 8145[12]

Bewdley *Ray Peacock*
11 b m Best Of The Bests(IRE) Garota De Ipanema (FR) (Al Nasr (FR))
35[10]

Beyond Argument (IRE) *David Simcock* a32 53
4 b g Galileo(IRE) Thought Is Free (Cadeaux Genereux)
2792[8]

Beyond Beyond *Hughie Morrison* a51
2 b g Shirocco(GER) Riverine (Risk Me (FR))
7963[8] 8245[9] 8556[5]

Beyond Recall *Luca Cumani* a59
2 b f Cacique(IRE) Forgotten Dreams (IRE) (Olden Times)
8245[8] 8464[5]

Beyond The Edge *Christopher Mason* 15
4 ch m Compton Place Edge Of Gold (Choisir (AUS))
2848[10] 3744[8]

B Fifty Two (IRE) *Charles Hills* a85 104
7 br g Dark Angel(IRE) Petite Maxine (Sharpo)
95a[5] 370a[8] 2206[4] 3386[26] 4152[14] 4846[4] 5678[7] 5880[8]

Bharuch (IRE) *Luigi Riccardi* 74
4 gr h Footstepsinthesand Bysshe (Linamix (FR))
7841a[6]

Bianca Minola (FR) *David Menuisier* 64
2 ch f Shakespearean(IRE) Transylvania (FR) (Motivator)
4397[9] 5740[9] 6376[2] 7209[5]

Biche (JPN) *Yuichi Shikato* 112
3 b f Deep Impact(JPN) Barancella (FR) (Acatenango (GER))
8129a[16]

Bickershaw *Roger Ingram* a45 48
4 b g Equiano(FR) Ring Of Love (Magic Ring (IRE))
630[5] 776[6]

Bidder *P Bary* a78 59
3 b c Oasis Dream Love The Rain (Rainbow Quest (USA))
5907a[9]

Bien Nommee (FR) *F Doumen* a61 61
3 b f Whipper(USA) Another Name (USA) (Giant's Causeway (USA))
716a[10]

Biff Johnson (IRE) *Keith Dalgleish* a86 85
4 b g Dansili Sagacious (IRE) (Dalakhani (IRE))
(438) (491) 693[2] (766) 2328[10] 2888[5] 3347[3] 3520[13] 3920[4] 4406[7] 5837[14] 6160[12] 7357[5]

Big Amigo (IRE) *Daniel Mark Loughnane* a73 70
3 b g Bahamian Bounty Goldamour (IRE) (Fasliyev (USA))
(544) 954[4] 1452[10] 1977[4] 2446[6] 3111[10] 3591[8] 4215[6] 5059[2] 5643[8] 6453[8] 6790[9] 7325[6] 8040[7] 8242[5] 8485[10]

Big Arthur (JPN) *Kenichi Fujioka* 120
5 b h Sakura Bakushin O(JPN) Siyabona (USA) (Kingmambo (USA))
8330a[10]

Bigbadboy (IRE) *Clive Mulhall* a51 49
3 b g Big Bad Bob(IRE) Elegantly (IRE) (Rock Of Gibraltar (IRE))
3014[6] 3483[6] 4972[9] 6106[7] 7795[10]

Big Baz (IRE) *William Muir* a114 111
6 b g Pivotal Gracefully (IRE) (Orpen (USA))
187a[2] 372a[14] 720a[6] 1068[4] 7152[8]

Big Blue *A Fabre* a87 109
4 ch h Galileo(IRE) Board Meeting (IRE) (Anabaa (USA))
5218a[3] 6178a[6]

Big Blue Kitten (USA) *Chad C Brown* a100 115
8 b h Kitten's Joy(USA) Spent Gold (USA) (Unaccounted For (USA))
6600a[8]

Big Challenge (IRE) *Saeed bin Suroor* 84
2 ch c Sea The Stars(IRE) Something Mon (USA) (Maria's Mon (USA))
(7770) ◆

Big Chill (IRE) *Patrick Chamings* a57 85
4 b g Acclamation Royal Consort (IRE) (Green Desert (USA))
2698[4] 3405[9] 4157[2] 5017[12] 5544[2] (6441) 7189[12] 7671[13]

Big City Boy (IRE) *Phil McEntee* a58 53
8 b g Tamarisk(IRE) Cuddles (IRE) (Taufan (USA))
46[7]

Big City Dreamin (USA) *Wesley A Ward* a89 49
2 ch f Iqbaal(USA) Teriffany (USA) (Fusaichi Pegasus (USA))
3247[16]

Bigger And Better *Richard Hannon* a57 76
3 b c Fastnet Rock(AUS) Interlace (Pivotal)
1930[7] 2366[2] (2639) 3033[7] 3905[2] 5256[3] 5875[7] 6737[4] (7214) ◆

Big Kenny *Peter Winks*
5 b g Multiplex Jezadil (IRE) (Mujadil (USA))
6647[12]

Big Lachie *Jamie Osborne* a79 76
2 b c Camacho Ryan's Quest (IRE) (Mukaddamah (USA))
2976[3] 3247[19] 3647[9] 4221[2] 4553[5] 5008[3] 5598[2] 6010[2] (6295) ◆ 6763[3] 7120[5] 7938[3] (8033)

Big Larry (IRE) *Nigel Tinkler* 52
3 b g Windsor Knot(IRE) Telltime (IRE) (Danetime (IRE))
3014[U] 4518[7] 4760[5]

Big McIntosh (IRE) *John Ryan* a63 63
4 b g Bushranger(IRE) Three Decades (IRE) (Invincible Spirit (IRE))
2582[11] 4099[10]

Bigmouth Strikes (IRE) *David Menuisier* 67
3 ch g Raven's Pass(USA) Chiosina (IRE) (Danehill Dancer (IRE))
4521[8] 5168[4] 5928[10]

Big Orange *Michael Bell* a82 119
5 b g Duke Of Marmalade(IRE) Miss Brown To You (IRE) (Fasliyev (USA))
1102a[2] 1863[3] (4061) (4799) 7756a[10] 7948a[3] 8329a[11]

Big Red *Rebecca Bastiman* 50
4 ch m Sakhee's Secret Hickleton Lady (IRE) (Kala Shikari)
1412[5] 2409[13] 2666[5] 3220[4] 3624[2] ◆ 3943[3] 4424[13] 6621[5] 6839[8] 7298[7]

Big Score (USA) *Tim Yakteen* 108
2 bk c Mr. Big(USA) Not Unusual (USA) (Unusual Heat (USA))
(7266a) 7807a[5]

Big Shoes (IRE) *Charles Hills* a54 49
3 br g Big Bad Bob(IRE) Caro Mio (IRE) (Danehill Dancer (IRE))
(688) 896[4] 1141[5] 1705[5] 2124[7]

Big Sigh (IRE) *Ismail Mohammed* a68 55
2 ch c Raven's Pass(USA) Sospira (Cape Cross (IRE))
6750[7] 8208[6] ◆ 8574a[11]

Big Storm Coming *David Brown* a81 73
6 b g Indesatchel(IRE) Amber Valley (Foxhound (USA))
332[8] (6453) 6700[3] 7333[10] 7887[9] (8241)

Big Time (IRE) *Kevin Ryan* a103 103
5 br g Kheleyf(USA) Beguine (USA) (Green Dancer (USA))
240[7] (360) 494[4] 599[3] 749[4] 1195[16] 2679[2] 2910[2] 3115[9] 3594[2] (4305) 5871[3] 7121[8] 7523a[2]

Big Time Baby (IRE) *Tom Dascombe* 105
2 b c Dandy Man(IRE) Royal Majestic (Tobougg (IRE))
(2847) 3295[7] (4091) 4755[5] (5656)

Big Time Dancer (IRE) *Brian Ellison* 72
3 b g Zoffany(IRE) Final Opinion (IRE) (King's Theatre (IRE))
1673[7] 2019[4] 2522[3] 3210[7] (5322) (5576)

Big Toms Girl *Simon Dow* a3
4 ch m Shirocco(GER) Plaisterer (Best Of The Bests (IRE))
400[10]

Big Tour (IRE) *Saeed bin Suroor* a71
2 b c Dubawi(IRE) Alsindi (IRE) (Acclamation)
7867[5]

Big Whiskey (IRE) *David Nicholls* a69 90
6 ch g Ad Valorem(USA) El Opera (IRE) (Sadler's Wells (USA))
2862[7] 6683[3]

Bijin (FR) *H-A Pantall* a65 68
2 b f Holy Roman Emperor(IRE) Hayaku (USA) (Arch (USA))
7291a[4]

Bilash *Sarah Hollinshead* a47 54
9 gr g Choisir(AUS) Goldeva (Makbul)
589[8] 1164[4] 5127[5] (5378) 7533[4] 8316[12]

Bilidn *Laura Young* a12 34
8 b m Tiger Hill(IRE) Brightest Star (Unfuwain (USA))
3746[10]

Bilko's Back (IRE) *Susan Corbett* a52 38
4 b g Big Bad Bob(IRE) Chica Roca (USA) (Woodman (USA))
4682[11] 5366[5] 6104[8] 6618[6] 7105[11]

Billabong (MOR) *P Bary* a102 107
7 rg h Gentlewave(IRE) Lunattori (Vettori (IRE))
757a[2] 5428a[5]

Billesdon Bess *Richard Hannon* 86
2 br f Dick Turpin(IRE) Coplow (Manduro (GER))
(7209) 7698[7]

Bills Delight *Bill Turner* a30 39
2 b f Compton Place Sing Alana Sing (Singspiel (IRE))
1086[7] 1543[7] 3511[8] 4195[7]

Billy Big (IRE) *Philip D'Amato* 95
2 b g Royal Applause Nutkin (Act One)
7266a[7]

Billy Bond *Richard Fahey* a76 77
4 b g Monsieur Bond(IRE) Princess Cocoa (IRE) (Desert Sun)
(179) 4232[5] 4986[6] 5779[4] 6221[2] 6645[6] 7076[7] 7691[8] 8011[3] 8178[8] 8587[5]

Billyoakes (IRE) *Charlie Wallis* a75 76
4 b g Kodiac Reality Check (IRE) (Sri Pekan (USA))
198[10] 508[7] 581[6] 4714[10] 5169[2] 5673[4] 6296[5] 6479[4] 6879[3] 7626[12] 7811[4] 8040[5] (8181) 8345[8] 8490[3]

Billy Roberts (IRE) *Richard Guest* a54 85
3 b g Multiplex Mi Amor (IRE) (Alzao (USA))
924[9] 1276[9] (1584) 2095[2] ◆ (2907) 3389[5] 5437[5] 6490[8] 7505[11] 7702[12]

Billy's Boots *Andrew Reid* a56 66
2 ch g Winker Watson Solmorin (Fraam)
1454[5] 1635[2] 1915[9] (2933) 3114[3] 3232[3] 3472[3]

Billy Slater *Richard Fahey* 82
4 br g Pastoral Pursuits Procession (Zafonic (USA))
2686[5] 3286[6]

Bin Battuta *Saeed bin Suroor* 85
2 ch c Dubawi(IRE) Land Of Dreams (Cadeaux Genereux)
(2976) 4150[7]

Bing Bang Bank (IRE) *David Barron* 34
2 br g Big Bad Bob(IRE) Causeway Charm (USA) (Giant's Causeway (USA))
7740[12]

Bingo George (IRE) *Andrew Balding* a68 66
3 b g Holy Roman Emperor(IRE) Kalleidoscope (Pivotal)
959[3] 1638[9] 2322[10] 5711[4] 6184[5] 6408[9] 8026[4]

Binky Blue (IRE) *Daniel Mark Loughnane* a74 65
4 b m Approve(IRE) Sabander Bay (USA) (Lear Fan (USA))
35[3] (87) (297) 355[2] 502[2] (859) 943[6] 1268[3] 1754[3] 2655[5] 3314[5] 8036[4] 8493[5]

Bint Aldar *Robert Cowell* 78
3 b f Zoffany(IRE) Maggie Lou (IRE) (Red Ransom (USA))
4708[6]

Bint Arcano (FR) *Julie Camacho* a75 77
3 ch f Arcano(IRE) Rosa Mundi (Alhaarth (IRE))
679[3] (824) 1137[8] 3213[5] (4043) ◆ 4605[5] 5973[4] 6426[3]

Bint Dandy (IRE) *Chris Dwyer* a102 93
5 b m Dandy Man(IRE) Ceol Loch Aoidh (IRE) (Medecis)
774[2] 1065[2] 1576[5] 2026[4] 2789[4] 3271[12] 3848[4] 5190[2] 5396[7] 6529[9] 6947[11] 7651[6] 8098[5] 8426[4]

Binzart (IRE) *Majed Seifeddine* a84 85
3 ch c Dandy Man(IRE) Silca Conegliano (IRE) (Alhaarth (IRE))
756a[15]

Biodynamic (IRE) *K R Burke* a68 95
3 b c New Approach(IRE) Doctrine (Barathea (IRE))
(1140) 1438[3] 1974[4] 2896[13] 4108[10]

Biologist (IRE) *William Haggas* a60 65
2 b f Sir Prancealot(IRE) Miss Rosie (Librettist (USA))
2902[8] 3902[5] 6369[6] 6696[5] 6961[6]

Bionic Indian *Michael Easterby* a55 54
4 b g Acclamation Strawberry Moon (IRE) (Alhaarth (IRE))
201[9] 525[2] 547[2] 707[3] 898[10] 986[U] 1320[3] (1556) 1795[4] 2013[11]

Biotic *Rod Millman* a88 83
5 b g Aqlaam Bramaputra (IRE) (Choisir (AUS))
1480[5] ◆ 1933[4] 2549[9] 2978[6] 4013[7] 5071[3] 5649[5] 6128[6] 6870[5]

Birchfield Lady *Robert Eddery* a14 36
2 b f Mullionmileanhour(IRE) Alectrona (FR) (Invincible Spirit (IRE))
3820[3] 3897[5] 4526[6]

Birchwood (IRE) *Richard Fahey* 113
3 b c Dark Angel(IRE) Layla Jamil (IRE) (Exceed And Excel (AUS))
2283a[13] 3664[7] (4135) 4733[7] 5613[5] 6991a[6]

Birdcage *Richard Fahey* a68 83
3 b f Showcasing Trinny (Rainbow Quest (USA))
5643[10] 6013[6] 6770[9]

Birdie Must Fly *Jimmy Fox* a33 24
4 ch m Major Cadeaux Musical Day (Singspiel (IRE))
8247[5]

Birdie Queen *Gary Moore* a82 75
6 b m Pastoral Pursuits Silver Miss (FR) (Numerous (USA))
80[5] 561[7] 713[5]

Birdman (IRE) *David O'Meara* a97 111
6 b g Danehill Dancer(IRE) Gilded Vanity (IRE) (Indian Ridge)
1196[4] ◆ 1629[13] 2191[13] 2744[6] 3688[4] 4165[19] 4846[3] 5585[15]

Bird To Love *Ralph Beckett* a54
2 b f Delegator Bird Over (Bold Edge)
8151[8]

Birikyno *Matthew Salaman* a42 42
5 b g Piccolo Alvarinho Lady (Royal Applause)
2969[7]

Birkdale (IRE) *David O'Meara* a47 74
3 b g Elnadim(USA) Duquesa (IRE) (Intikhab (USA))
(2809) 3753[8] 4714[12]

Birrafun (IRE) *Ann Duffield* a56 54
3 gr f Zebedee Flower Bowl (IRE) (Noverre (USA))
531[5] 659[4] 765[4] (1045) 4236[3] 4512[8] 4944[3] 5636[9] 8312[10]

Birthday Prince (GER) *Frau Erika Mader* a68 93
8 ch g Areion(GER) Birthday Spectrum (GER) (Spectrum (IRE))
3992a[6]

Birthplace (IRE) *Joseph Patrick O'Brien* a49 80
3 ch g Galileo(IRE) Ask For The Moon (FR) (Dr Fong (USA))
3341[16]

Bishnoi (FR) *G Doleuze* a57 63
3 gr f Cima De Triomphe(IRE) Mantissa (Oratorio (IRE))
128a[9]

Bishop Wulstan (IRE) *Peter Bowen* a40 54
5 b g Oratorio(IRE) Laurentine (USA) (Private Account (USA))
3999[7] 4483[7]

Bismarck The Flyer (IRE) *Ollie Pears* a58 63
2 b g Requinto(IRE) Livia's Wake (IRE) (Galileo (IRE))
4053[13] 4473[7] (4842) 5177[2] (5351) 6471[3] 7110[7]

Bithynia (IRE) *David Evans* a68 69
2 b f Kodiac Alexander Confranc (IRE) (Magical Wonder (USA))
2410[3] 4756[6] 5317[6] 6010[5] 7331[2] 7578[2] 8406[2]

Bit Of A Lad (IRE) *David Brown* a64 19
3 b g Lilbourne Lad(IRE) Sacred Love (IRE) (Barathea (IRE))
952[9] 2118[5]

Bit Of A Quirke *Mark Walford* 61
3 ch g Monsieur Bond(IRE) Silk (IRE) (Machiavellian (USA))
1216[6] 1524[5] 2039[5] 2777[6] 3579[2] 3982[2] 4681[2] 6432[6]

Bittern (IRE) *Emmet Mullins* a83 61
4 ch m New Approach(IRE) Oiseau Rare (FR) (King's Best (USA))
208a[3]

Bitty Kitty (USA) *Brendan P Walsh* a86 94
6 ch m Kitten's Joy(USA) Littlebitoflove (USA) (High Yield (USA))
5185a[8]

Bizet (IRE) *John Ryan* a74 68
2 b g Helmet(AUS) Morinda (Selkirk (USA))
4837[4] 5332[5] 6034[4] 6369[2] 7305[10] 7527[9] 8009[6] 8047[4]

Biz Heart (IRE) *Stefano Botti* 107
3 ch g Roderic O'Connor(IRE) Biz Bar (Tobougg (IRE))
2517a[4]

Biz Power (IRE) *Stefano Botti* 102
2 b c Power Biz Bar (Tobougg (IRE))
3701a[2] 4925a[4] 7401a[5]

Bizzarria *John Gosden* a72
2 ch f Lemon Drop Kid(USA) Lynnwood Chase (USA) (Horse Chestnut (SAF))
7762[10] (8397)

Blackadder *Mark Gillard* 52
4 b g Myboycharlie(IRE) Famcred (Inchinor)
346[10]

Black Agnes (IRE) *Lee Smyth* a69 59
3 b f Holy Roman Emperor(IRE) Nice To Know (FR) (Machiavellian (USA))
4313[5] 5223[7] 7339a[11]

Blackasyourhat (IRE) *Michael Attwater* a62 46
4 b g Le Cadre Noir(IRE) Mattrah (USA) (Machiavellian (USA))
442[9] 615[7] 837[7] 970[7] 1138[4] 5636[10] 7145[5]

Black Beach *Jassim Al Ghazali* 74
3 b c Footstepsinthesand Eraadaat (IRE) (Intikhab (USA))
756a[8]

Black Benny (IRE) *J P Broderick* a55 72
11 br g Close Conflict(USA) Treen (IRE) (Charnwood Forest (IRE))
2114a[8]

Black Bess *Jim Boyle* a69 88
3 br f Dick Turpin(IRE) Spring Clean (FR) (Danehill (USA))
1176[2] ◆ 2002[7] (2823) 3111[3] (3689) (4306) 5148[7] 5488[8] 6806[3]

Black Bolt (IRE) *Richard Hannon* a84 52
2 br c Cape Cross(IRE) Safiya Song (IRE) (Intikhab (USA))
7502[8] (7733) ◆

Black Bubba (IRE) *David Evans* a67 71
2 b g Arcano(IRE) Assumption (IRE) (Beckett (IRE))
3531[4] 3808[5] 4790[4] 7184[2] 7938[8] 8229[3] 8425[3]

Black Caesar (IRE) *Philip Hide* a77 75
5 b g Bushranger(IRE) Evictress (IRE) (Sharp Victor (USA))
(1544) 1780[2] 2401[2] 2934[8] 6806[14] 7301[5] 7506[15]

Black Cherry *Richard Hannon* 105
4 b m Mount Nelson Arctic Char (Polar Falcon (USA))
1858[3] 2464[3] 3271[7] 3979[2] 4582[6] 5645[11] 6939[14]

Black Dave (IRE) *David Evans* a71 70
6 b g Excellent Art Miss Latina (IRE) (Mozart (IRE))
(88) 169[7] (349) 546[4] 734[7] 866[7] 1318[8] 1625[14] 7687[9] 8337[3] ◆

Blackdown Warrior *Rod Millman* a41 49
3 b g Showcasing Showery (Rainbow Quest (USA))
1829[7] 2143[2] 2458[9] 3513[6] 4202[7] 4992[5] 5953[13]

Black Grass *Michael Easterby* a79 80
3 b g Monsieur Bond(IRE) Alustar (Emarati (USA))
1126[11] 1249[2] (1558) (2854) (3420) (3471) 3611[2] 4612[11]

Black Hambleton *Bryan Smart* 67
3 b g Dick Turpin(IRE) Duena (Grand Lodge (USA))
2306[11]

Black Hawk War (USA) *A P O'Brien* 100
3 b c War Front(USA) Lasting Code (USA) (Lost Code (USA))
7372a[2]

Black Heart Bart (AUS) *Darren Weir* 122
5 b g Blackfriars(AUS) Sister Theresa (AUS) (At Talaq (USA))
7553a[9]

Black Hole Sun *Tony Carroll* a54
4 ch m Black Sam Bellamy(IRE) Black Annie (IRE) (Anshan)
161[5] 318[4] 7256[9] 8038[10]

Black Iceman *Lydia Pearce* a52 41
8 gr g Iceman Slite (Mind Games)
354[11] 622[4] 796[6] 3067[7]

Black Is Black (IRE) *Michael Easterby* a33
3 b g Big Bad Bob(IRE) Dazzling Dancer (Nashwan (USA))
7991[8]

Black Isle Boy (IRE) *David O'Meara* a60
2 b g Elzaam(AUS) Shadow Mountain (Selkirk (USA))
2913[5]

Blacklister *Mick Channon* a79 83
3 br g Lawman(FR) Lebenstanz (Singspiel (IRE))
314[2] 361[2] (557) 887[6] 1389[2] 1584[6] 2044[8] 2341[2] 3558[6] 3906[4] (4382) (4681) (5201) 5616[15] 6084[8]

Black Magic (IRE) *Richard Fahey* 73
3 gr g Poet's Voice Centifolia (FR) (Kendor (FR))
1630[8] 2336[10]

Black Max (FR) *H-A Pantall* 101
3 b c Fuisse(FR) Okapina (FR) (Okawango (USA))
2551a[2] 5217a[9] 6272a[14]

Black Minstrel (IRE) *John O'Shea* a69 66
7 b g Dylan Thomas(IRE) Overlook (Generous (IRE))
222[3] (463) 568[6] 708[3] 862[10]

Black Night (IRE) *J Moon* a80 97
4 b h Excellent Art Starfish (IRE) (Galileo (IRE))
(2952a) 3918a[4] (6402a) 6666[5] 6940[7] 7545[14] 7765[6]

Blackout (FR) *Richard Hannon* 92
3 b c Dream Ahead(USA) Belle Masquee (IRE) (Oratorio (IRE))
1571[6] 2161[17] (3062) (3357)

Black Poweer (FR) *P Sogorb* a73
2 bb c Power Love And War (GER) (War Blade (GER))
8420a[3]

Black Prince (FR) *Anthony Honeyball* a50 31
2 b g Falco(USA) Thamara (USA) (Street Cry (IRE))
7187[9] 7503[14] 7977[11]

Black Redstart *Alan Bailey* a49 54
2 b f Big Bad Bob(IRE) Red Roxanne (Rock Of Gibraltar (IRE))
1437[8] 1799[2] 2007[11] 2933[7] 3592[5] 5128[3] 5528[7] 6044[8] 6808[2]

Black Salt *David Barron* 58
2 b g Equiano(FR) Marine Girl (Shamardal (USA))
7578[6]

Black Sea (FR) *A De Royer-Dupre* a92 104
3 b c Dubai Destination(USA) Goleta (IRE) (Royal Applause)
4783a[2] 6597a[4]

Black Sea (IRE) *A P O'Brien* 100
3 b c Galileo(IRE) Christmas Kid (USA) (Lemon Drop Kid (USA))
2190[9] 2946a[14]

Blackthorn Stick (IRE) *Paul Burgoyne* a65 40
7 b g Elusive City(USA) Hi Lyla (IRE) (Lahib (USA))
68[8] 257[2] 403[5] 608[4] 777[10] 951[8] 1147[2] (1415) 1735[12] 2155[7] 8156[9]

Black Tie Bob (IRE) *J S Moore* 6
2 br g Big Bad Bob(IRE) Marion Antoinette (IRE) (Antonius Pius (USA))
4815[8] 5549[12] 6208[9]

Black Tomahawk (AUS) *Darren Weir* 98
6 bk g Seul Amour(NZ) Willisa (AUS) (Vite Cheval (NZ))
7712a[5]

Black Trilby (IRE) *Clive Cox* 83
2 ch c Helmet(AUS) Reine De Romance (IRE) (Vettori (IRE))
2757[7] 4866[3] ◆ 5615[7]

Black Truffle (FR) *Mark Usher* a70 50
6 b g Kyllachy Some Diva (Dr Fong (USA))
144[5] 387[2] 608[7] 943[8] 1117[3] 1326[5] 1555[10]

Black Vale (IRE) *Phil McEntee* a66 24
5 b g Moss Vale(IRE) Limit (IRE) (Barathea (IRE))
174[9] 217[5] 270[7] 355[6] 837[4] 895[7] 1138[11] 1833[5]

Blades Lad *Peter Niven* a79 64
7 ch g Haafhd Blades Girl (Bertolini (USA))
(446) (940) 1028[3]

Blagger *Richard Guest* 37
3 ch g Major Cadeaux Brogue Lanterns (IRE) (Dr Devious (IRE))
1564[8] 1698[5] 2801[10]

Blaine *David Nicholls* a82 104
6 ch g Avonbridge Lauren Louise (Tagula (IRE))
2258[8] 2488[7] (2898) 3656[9] 4338[12] 4865[26] 5857[13] 6556[14] 7315[2] 7497[14]

Blair House (IRE) *Charlie Appleby* 102
3 ch g Pivotal Patroness (Dubawi (IRE))
(2340) 2907[2] 4104[10] 6803[2] ◆ (7005) 7546[2]

Blairmayne (IRE) *Miss Natalia Lupini* a58 79
3 b c Zebedee Amended (Beat Hollow)
6382a[13]

Blakeney Point *Roger Charlton* a85 94
3 b g Sir Percy Cartoon (Danehill Dancer (IRE))
1860[3] (2300) ◆ 2909[11] 3768[3] 4778[2] (6127) ◆ (6325) 7123[6]

Blanco (USA) *George Baker* a50
3 b g Cape Blanco(IRE) Nimue (USA) (Speightstown (USA))
65[10] 6805[10] 7459[7]

Blast Of Faith (IRE) *Richard Hughes* a28 53
2 b c Myboycharlie(IRE) Art Of Dance (Medicean)
3301[8] 3485[7] 4479[7] 4982[4] 5719[7] 6253[7]

Blastofmagic *David Dennis* a35 60
2 gr g Hellvelyn Elegant Pursuit (Pastoral Pursuits)
4638[7] 5668[3] 6214[6] 6678[16] 7275[7]

Blaze Of Hearts (IRE) *Dean Ivory* a70 82
3 b c Canford Cliffs(IRE) Shesthebiscuit (Diktat)
4458[2] 4955[3] 5765[9] 7229[3] 7627[3]

Blaze To Win (TUR) *Aydin Kucukaksoy* 103
5 b h Win River Win(USA) Lovely Blaze (TUR) (Sri Pekan (USA))
6179a[4]

Blazing Mighty *Robyn Brisland* a72 75
3 ch f Mighty Exodia (Dr Fong (USA))
4978[5] 5550[4] 6049[3] 6457[2]

Blazing Speed *A S Cruz* 119
7 b g Dylan Thomas(IRE) Leukippids (IRE) (Sadler's Wells (USA))
1690a[3] 8333a[5]

Blending *John Gosden* 87
2 b f Medicean Panzanella (Dansili)
4357[3] (4885) 6258[6]

Blenheim Warrior *Richard Hughes* a62 76
4 gr g Galileo(IRE) Crystal Swan (IRE) (Dalakhani (IRE))
1651[4] 1826[6] 2210[3] (3002) 4483[2] 5526[7] 6380[6]

Blessed Silence (FR) *J-M Beguigne* 94
3 ch f Siyouni(FR) Blanc Sur Blanc (IRE) (Hold That Tiger (USA))
6912a[5] 7998a[4]

Bletchley *Ralph Beckett* 103
2 b f Makfi An Ghalanta (IRE) (Holy Roman Emperor (IRE))
(2793) 3336[2] 4106[6] 6555[10]

Blind Faith (IRE) *Luca Cumani* a81 83
3 ch f Zoffany(IRE) Guajira (FR) (Mtoto)
(3305) 5603[2] 6378[5] 7204[3] 7504[6]

Bling King *Geoffrey Harker* a45 79
7 b g Haafhd Bling Bling (IRE) (Indian Ridge)
2618[7] 2915[12] 3367[1] (4498) 6226[8] 6683[7]

Blink (FR) *F-H Graffard* a90 81
3 b f Pour Moi(IRE) Blue Blue Sky (IRE) (Anabaa (USA))
8148a[8]

Blistering Dancer (IRE) *Tony Carroll* a49 55
6 b g Moss Vale(IRE) Datura (Darshaan)
168[2] 355[5] 431[3] ◆ 730[2] 1138[5] 1319[4] (1676) 2447[11] 3040[4] 3469[3] 3993[2] 4202[5] 5628[12]

Blithe Spirit *Eric Alston* a62 100
5 b m Byron Damalis (IRE) (Mukaddamah (USA))
1272[5] 1968[7] 2895[5] 3637[2] (4632) 4735[16] 5641[6] 6779[12] 7124[11]

Blizzard (NZ) *Emma-Lee & David Browne* 94
5 gr g Any Suggestion(AUS) Deune (AUS) (Green Line Express (USA))
7637a[8]

Blond Me (IRE) *Andrew Balding* 109
4 ch m Tamayuz Holda (IRE) (Docksider (USA))
(1858) 3271[11] 4127[9] 5645[2] (6181a) 7566a[10]

Blonville (FR) *Robert Collet* a72 94
3 bl f Le Havre(IRE) La Mouche (Dubawi (IRE))
(3007a) 5349a[8] (6912a) 7680a[4] 7998a[3]

Blood Moon *G M Lyons* a93 97
3 b g Equiano(FR) First Eclipse (IRE) (Fayruz)
2272a[6] 4246a[8]

Bloodsweatandtears *William Knight* a65 69
8 b g Barathea(IRE) Celestial Princess (Observatory (USA))
709[4] 877[8] 1546[4] 3739[2] (6407) 7036[3] 7735[3] 8258[5]

Bloomin Lovely (IRE) *John Quinn* a61 72
2 b f Helmet(AUS) Dorothy Dene (Red Ransom (USA))
4451[6] 4943[4] 5637[3] 6257[11] 7140[7]

Blossomtime *H-A Pantall* 102
3 b f Shamardal(USA) Bal De La Rose (IRE) (Cadeaux Genereux)
1898[2] 3039[3] 7348a[7] (7861a) 8117a[4]

Blue Amazon (IRE) *Lee Carter* a63 45
4 b m Acclamation Amazon Beauty (IRE) (Wolfhound (USA))
292[3] 460[3] 669[5]

Blue Bahia (IRE) *Mark Johnston* a72 76
2 b f Big Bad Bob(IRE) Brazilian Bride (IRE) (Pivotal)
8556[3]

Blue Bayou *Brian Meehan* 107
3 ch f Bahamian Bounty Oshiponga (Barathea (IRE))
1888[13] 3274[20]

Blue Bere (FR) *Freddy Grizon* a48 49
5 b m Hold That Tiger(USA) Miss Fine (FR) (Kaldoun (FR))
8422a[16]

Blue Bounty *Mark H Tompkins* a70 52
5 ch g Bahamian Bounty Laheen (IRE) (Bluebird (USA))
143[2] 230[2] 444[2] (659) 775[3] 937[4] 1133[4] 2584[6] 3040[7] 3316[7] 3822[7]

Blue Cliffs (IRE) *Michael Appleby* a77 67
3 b g Canford Cliffs(IRE) Lapistanera (IRE) (Cape Cross (IRE))
7335[4] 7583[4] (7894) ◆ 8286[14]

Blue Creek *Charlie Appleby* a94
3 b c Street Cry(IRE) Blue Bunting (USA) (Dynaformer (USA))
(8a) 407a[2] 839a[3]

Blue De Vega (GER) *M D O'Callaghan* a77 112
3 b c Lope De Vega(IRE) Burning Heights (GER) (Montjeu (IRE))
1938a[2] 2496a[3] 3296[7] 7706a[2]

Blue Geranium (IRE) *John Gosden* a67 77
3 b f Dansili Super Sleuth (IRE) (Selkirk (USA))
1436[3] 2004[6] 2606[5] 3038[6] 4318[6] (4743) 5374[6]

Bluegrass Blues (IRE) *Heather Main* a93 92
6 gr g Dark Angel(IRE) Dear Catch (IRE) (Bluebird (USA))
(4081) 4894[14] 5545[2] 6076[7] 6915[12] (7428) ◆ 8231[8]

Blue Hussar (IRE) *Micky Hammond* 97
5 b g Montjeu(IRE) Metaphor (USA) (Woodman (USA))
1493[3] 2222[7] 3162[8] 4407[4] 5031[4] 5611[13] 6794[4] 7359[8]

Blue Illusion *Charlie Appleby*
2 b f Dubawi(IRE) Blue Bunting (USA) (Dynaformer (USA))
6782[14]

Blue Jacket (USA) *Dianne Sayer* 69
5 ro m Mizzen Mast(USA) Complex (USA) (Unbridled's Song (USA))
1495[2] (2096) 2855[2] 3153[7]

Blue Jasmine (FR) *D De Waele* 54
2 gr f Rajsaman(FR) Sanja (FR) (Anabaa Blue)
7927a[10]

Blue Jay (FR) *Ronald Thompson* a24 46
3 b g Anabaa Blue Romantic Notion (IRE) (Mujadil (USA))
2307[7] 3982[12] 4275[6] 6967[9]

Blue Jean Baby *George Scott* a55 77
3 ch f Poet's Voice Ring Of Esteem (Mark Of Esteem (IRE))
4367[3] 4978[7] 6795[3] 7627[6]

Blue Melody Girl (IRE) *James Given* a57 46
4 b m Captain Rio Salingers Star (IRE) (Catcher In The Rye (IRE))
32[9] 150[12]

Blue Mischief *Miss Joey Ellis*
5 ch g Bahamian Bounty Question (USA) (Coronado's Quest (USA))
7011[16]

Blue Moon Rising (IRE) *Michael Bell* 72
3 ch f Dream Ahead(USA) Wedding Gown (Dubai Destination (USA))
2904[5] 3899[4] 4596[6]

Blue On Blue (USA) *John Gosden* a67 57
2 ch c More Than Ready(USA) Alina (USA) (Came Home (USA))
7306[4] 7664[5]

Blue Point (IRE) *Charlie Appleby* 116
2 b c Shamardal(USA) Scarlett Rose (Royal Applause)
(3065) ◆ (4297) 4798[2] (5654) ◆ 6785[2] 7149[3]

Blue Rambler *Ian Williams* 106
6 b g Monsun(GER) La Nuit Rose (FR) (Rainbow Quest (USA))
6118[3] ◆ 7150[6]

Blue Revelation *Paul Webber* a75 77
3 b g Exceed And Excel(AUS) Epiphany (Zafonic (USA))
(8157)

Blue Rocks *Lisa Williamson* a59 31
2 b g Indesatchel(IRE) Mabinia (IRE) (Cape Cross (IRE))
5637[8] 6274[7] 7259[3] 8009[5]

Bluesbreaker (IRE) *Damian Joseph English* a68 84
4 b g Fastnet Rock(AUS) Jalisco (IRE) (Machiavellian (USA))
6819a[18]

Blues Dancer *J H Culloty* a33 46
4 b g Norse Dancer(IRE) Indiana Blues (Indian Ridge)
5900a[16]

Blue Sea Of Ibrox (IRE) *Mrs A Corson* a74 78
8 gr m Subtle Power(IRE) Jerpoint Rose (IRE) (Roselier (FR))
30[4] 566[8] 884[5] 4698a[3] 5459a[7] 6403a[3]

Blue Silk *Roger Charlton*
3 b f Compton Place Silky Dawn (IRE) (Night Shift (USA))
2848[9]

Blue Skimmer (IRE) *P J Prendergast* a73 74
4 b g Arcano(IRE) Cattiva Generosa (Cadeaux Genereux)
4813a[13]

Blue Soave (FR) *F Chappet* a88 102
8 ch g Soave(GER) Rhapsody In Blue (FR) (Bering)
1618a[2] 6272a[7] 7030a[7] 7997a[2]

Blue Sonic *Linda Perratt* 71
6 gr m Proclamation(IRE) Big Mystery (IRE) (Grand Lodge (USA))
1693[4] 2364[7] 2524[3] 3924[5] 3944[8] 4488[9] 5152[4] 5225[3] ◆

Blue Suede (IRE) *Richard Fahey* a79 78
2 b f Requinto(IRE) Shoooz (IRE) (Soviet Star (USA))
3106[2] 3686[2] 4011[4] 4558[3] 5008[2] (5283) 5741[2] 6538[7] 7073[4] 8136[2]

Blue Surf *Amanda Perrett* a104 107
7 ch g Excellent Art Wavy Up (IRE) (Brustolon)
99[3] 317[4] 499[3] 1067[5] 1475[5] 2897[10] 3670[6] 5145[9] 5647[3] 6089[5]

Blue Top *Dai Burchell* a51 60
7 b g Millkom Pompey Blue (Abou Zouz (USA))
1450[11] 1831[8] (2850) (3999)

Blue Vision (FR) *Alan Swinbank* a56
3 ch g Loup Breton(IRE) Blueprint (USA) (Shadeed (USA))
202[5] 524[4] 892[3] 1163[7]

Bluff (USA) *D Selvaratnam* a101
4 ch g Tapit(USA) Ermine Slippers (USA) (El Prado (IRE))
183a[7]

Bluff Crag *Andrew Balding* 77
3 b g Canford Cliffs(IRE) Camp Riverside (USA) (Forest Camp (USA))
1276[7] 2212[3] (3558) 4241[8] 4909[5] 6231[4] 7076[11]

Blu Marshall (ITY) *Il Cavallo In Testa* 78
2 b c Blu Air Force(IRE) Raganella (IRE) (Fasliyev (USA))
3701a[5]

Blumenfee (GER) *J Hirschberger* a87 97
3 bb f Soldier Hollow Bella Flora (GER) (Slip Anchor)
3916a[5]

Blushes (FR) *Ed Dunlop* a67 62
3 b f Siyouni(FR) Pink And Red (USA) (Red Ransom (USA))
(948) 1725[7] 2576[5] 4370[4] 5241[2] (6513) 6901[8] 7531[4]

Blushing Red (FR) *Ed Dunlop* 62
2 ch c Le Havre(IRE) Boliche (Key Of Luck (USA))
7225[4]

Blushing Rose *Sir Michael Stoute* a82 81
2 ch f Dalakhani(IRE) Russelliana (Medicean)
4885[3] (5722) 6575[6] 6787[3] ◆

Blusterysky (FR) *M Narduzzi* a64 64
2 b c Myboycharlie(IRE) Eternal Beauty (USA) (Zafonic (USA))
7454a[9]

Blyde River (IRE) *F-X De Chevigny* a57 64
5 b g Shamardal(USA) Bunting (USA) (Private Account (USA))
512a[11]

Blynx *David Simcock* a27 33
3 b f Equiano(FR) Desert Lynx (IRE) (Green Desert (USA))
6459[5] 6960[10] 7583[8] 8012[6]

Blythe Prince *Christopher Kellett* a8 41
4 b g Dutch Art Arculinge (Paris House)
7960[6] 8470[11]

Blythe Star (IRE) *Christopher Kellett* a46 44
4 b g Thewayyouare(USA) Run To Jane (IRE) (Doyoun)
1649[7]

Boater (IRE) *Mark Johnston* a83 83
2 b f Helmet(AUS) Cercle D'Amour (USA) (Storm Cat (USA))
(1086) ◆ 2219[2] 2670[4] 2908[3] 3819[3] 4195[4] 8136[5]

Bobbio (FR) *N Caullery* a62 78
3 b g Diamond Green(FR) Carnet De Bal (Kingsalsa (USA))
5946a[14] 6310a[5]

Bobby Benton (IRE) *Jim Best* a53 73
5 b g Invincible Spirit(IRE) Remarkable Story (Mark Of Esteem (IRE))
3125[4] 4656[6] (6408) 8378[8] 8455[6]

Bobbys Helmet (IRE) *David C Griffiths*
2 b g Helmet(AUS) Ready When You Are (IRE) (Royal Applause)
3854[10] 6054[12]

Bobby's Kitten (USA) *D K Weld* a57 117
5 b h Kitten's Joy(USA) Celestial Woods (USA) (Forestry (USA))
(1127a)

Bobby Vee *Dean Ivory* a54 68
2 ch f Camacho Miss Lesley (Needwood Blade)
2822[4] ◆ 3404[8] 4261[2] (4759) 5707[3] 6440[9]

Bobby Wheeler (IRE) *Clive Cox* 98
3 b g Pivotal Regal Rose (Danehill (USA))
1603[9] (4080) 4867[2] 5616[14] 6109[18]

Boboli Gardens *Susan Corbett* a56 31
6 b g Medicean Park Crystal (IRE) (Danehill (USA))
7323[11] 7602[11]

Bob's Boy *Jose Santos* a53 61
3 b g Showcasing Tech Zinne (Zinaad)
2590[10] 3401[3] 3765[2] 4275[9] 5021[7] (5625) 6315[7] 6827[7] 7230[6] 7421[2]

Boca Raton (IRE) *E J O'Neill* 73
3 b f Approve(IRE) Kaaba (Darshaan)
7897a[9]

Bocca Baciata (IRE) *Mrs John Harrington* 113
4 bb m Big Bad Bob(IRE) Sovana (IRE) (Desert King (IRE))
1227a[4] 2167a[3] 2512a[4] 3695a[2] (4435a) 5691a[10] 7351[10]

Bocca De La Verita (FR) *C Lerner* a78 76
2 gr f Literato(FR) Burghelarab (IRE) (Dubai Destination (USA))
(7136a) 7655a[7] 7879a[2]

Bocelli *Simon Crisford* a43
2 b g Poet's Voice Indian Love Bird (Efisio)
6655[9]

Bocking End (IRE) *Michael Bell* a79 88
3 b f Paco Boy(IRE) Miss Wells (IRE) (Sadler's Wells (USA))
(706) 1758[4] (2108) 2783[2] 3107[3] 3667[3] 4761[2] (5415) 6747[7] 7504[10]

Bodacious Name (IRE) *John Quinn* a53 51
2 b g Famous Name Nice Wee Girl (IRE) (Clodovil (IRE))
5728[7] 6099[8] 6679[8] 7854[5] 7954[3]

Body Sculpt (FR) *S Kobayashi* 98
2 gr f Kendargent(FR) Vital Body (FR) (Gold Away (IRE))
5186a[2] 6177a[4] 6986a[11]

Boethius *Tim Vaughan* a67
3 b g Manduro(GER) Perfect Note (Shamardal (USA))
7280[10]

Bogardus (IRE) *Patrick Holmes* a72 73
5 b g Dalakhani(IRE) Sugar Mint (IRE) (High Chaparral (IRE))
38[8] 256[2] ◆ 2832[6] 3563[4] 4099[4] 4686[6] (5264) 5841[12] 6684[8]

Bogart *Kevin Ryan* a78 100
7 ch g Bahamian Bounty Lauren Louise (Tagula (IRE))
2158[14] 2488[2] 3188[11] 3606[7] 4112[14] 6537[11] 7124[4] 7537[3]

Bognor (USA) *Michael Attwater* a85 73
5 b g Hard Spun(USA) Ms Blue Blood (USA) (A.P. Indy (USA))
581[4] 788[2] 866[4] 967[7] 1702[7] 2187[5] 2849[4] 3220[7] 3497[6] 4020[3] 4305[5] 4635[3] 4880[5]

Bogsnog (IRE) *Kristin Stubbs* a68 72
6 b g Moss Vale(IRE) Lovers Kiss (Night Shift (USA))
36[3] 144[8] 271[6] 857[5] 1180[5] 1496[5] 2013[4] 2360[7] 3016[3] 3984[6] 4513[2] 5277[3] 6100[7]

Bohemian Flame (IRE) *Andrew Balding* 94
2 b g Zoffany(IRE) Red Japonica (Daylami (IRE))
(2180) 2624[3] 4060[7] 6260[11]

Bohemian Origin (IRE) *J S Moore* a49 52
3 ch g Zoffany(IRE) Rainbow Lyrics (IRE) (Rainbow Quest (USA))
87[7] 147[3]

Bohemian Rapsody (FR) *Enrique Leon Penate* a82 99
6 b g Jarn Marion La Coquine (FR) (Al Nasr (FR))
7292a[8]

Bohemian Rhapsody (IRE) *Brendan Powell* a66 80
7 b g Galileo(IRE) Quiet Mouse (USA) (Quiet American (USA))
1144[8] 1390[5] 1933[9] (2463) 2932[5] 3533[8] 4381[8] 5262[4] 5963[8]

Bohemian Rhapsody (SPA) *Enrique Leon Penate* 93
6 ch m Dyhim Diamond(IRE) Solina (GER) (Acatenango (GER))
6070a[8]

Boherbuoy (IRE) *David Wachman* 91
4 b g Galileo(IRE) Potion (Pivotal)
4811a[4] 6389a[10]

Bois D'Ebene (IRE) *Roger Charlton* a66
2 b f Big Bad Bob(IRE) Mpumalanga (Observatory (USA))
7761[7] 7977[5]

Bois de Boulogne (USA) *John Gosden* a77
2 b c Street Cry(IRE) Rosa Parks (Sadler's Wells (USA))
8208[2] ◆ 8486[5]

Boite (IRE) *Warren Greatrex* 100
6 b g Authorized(IRE) Albiatra (USA) (Dixieland Band (USA))
(3351) ◆ 4581[7]

Bokan (FR) *Wido Neuroth* a96 100
4 b g Soldier Of Fortune(IRE) Paree (IRE) (Desert Prince (IRE))
4329a[2] 5950a[5] 6390a[5]

Bold *Stuart Williams* a78 54
4 b g Oasis Dream Minority (Generous (IRE))
1887[15] 2587[10] 3571[10] 5301[6] (8067) 8571[6]

Boldbob (IRE) *Micky Hammond* 49
4 gr g Verglas(IRE) Special Park (USA) (Trempolino (USA))
1121[7] 1842[3] 2501[9]

Bolder Bob (IRE) *David Barron* 67
2 b g Big Bad Bob(IRE) Semiquaver (IRE) (Mark Of Esteem (IRE))
7580[3]

Bold Grove *Edward Bevan* a49 45
4 b g Proclamation(IRE) Trysting Grove (IRE) (Cape Cross (IRE))
2448[10] 2542[8] 3070[6] 3554[8] 3743[10] 4088[5] 4289[6] 6636[7]

Bold Henmie (IRE) *Philip Kirby* a60 57
5 b g Henrythenavigator(USA) Seminole Lass (USA) (Indian Charlie (USA))
2343[5] 5971[8]

Bold Max *Zoe Davison* a56 46
5 b g Assertive Jane's Payoff (IRE) (Danetime (IRE))
143[9] 297[8] 528[3] 617[3] 895[4] 1949[8] 2610[3] 8278[9]

Bold Prediction (IRE) *Ed Walker* a95 95
6 b g Kodiac Alexander Eliott (IRE) (Night Shift (USA))
(172) 620[2] (749) 920[4] 1993[11] 2868[12] 3303[3] 4026[2] 4868[6] 5419[5] 8593[4]

Bold Runner *Jose Santos* a74 79
5 ch g Mount Nelson Music In Exile (USA) (Diesis)
7183[15]

Bold Spirit *Declan Carroll* a55 70
5 b g Invincible Spirit(IRE) Far Shores (USA) (Distant View (USA))
1489[7] 1565[13] 2741[8] 2856[8] 2974[11] (3777) 4848[8] 4970[4] 5354[12] (5760) 6569[7] 7253[3] 7584[3]

Bold Thady Quill (IRE) *K J Condon* a83 106
9 ch g Tale Of The Cat(USA) Jazzie (FR) (Zilzal (USA))
1018a[15] 1127a[4]

Bollihope *Richard Guest* a76 73
4 ch g Medicean Hazy Dancer (Oasis Dream)
1169[4] 1413[3] 1500[9] 4730[6] (6921) (7435) 7613[5] ◆ 7775[2] 7973[7] (8141)

Bollin Ted *Tim Easterby* 54
2 b g Haafhd Bollin Greta (Mtoto)
4609[7] 5637[7]

Bollywood Dream *Peter Hedger* a53 27
4 b m Sleeping Indian Act Three (Beat Hollow)
2397[8] 3031[11]

Bolting (USA) *F-H Graffard* a91 104
3 b r War Front(USA) Beta Leo (USA) (A.P. Indy (USA))
3269[14] 4905a[8]

Bolt Phantom (USA) *Ismail Mohammed* a76 76
2 b c Exchange Rate(USA) Miss Liberty (FR) (Statue Of Liberty (USA))
2500[2] 3247[13] 3712[2] 6697[5] 7306[2] 7956[6]

Bomba (FR) *Charley Rossi* a64 91
2 b f Hannouma(IRE) Piquetera (Oratorio (IRE))
3182a[4]

Bombay Dream *William Haggas* a63 65
2 ch f Sepoy(AUS) Indiana Blues (Indian Ridge)
6867[5] 7314[7] 7845[3]

Bombay Marine (USA) *John Gosden* a64
2 b c War Front(USA) Bel Air Beauty (USA) (Smart Strike (CAN))
7849[6]

Bombay Night (FR) *H-A Pantall* a71 76
3 b c Wootton Bassett Blue Roses (IRE) (Oratorio (IRE))
(2172a)

Bomber Etches *Scott Dixon* a37
3 b g Hellvelyn Little Greenbird (Ardkinglass)
363[7] 507[4] 798[6] 2560[5] 5278[11]

Bombilate (USA) *Charlie Appleby* a73 80
3 b f Kitten's Joy(USA) Wild Chant (USA) (War Chant (USA))
(1798) 2339[2] 3001[7]

Bonchard *Emma Owen* 27
3 b f Champs Elysees Five Fields (USA) (Chester House (USA))
1609[11] 3094[10]

Bond Bombshell *David O'Meara* a53 78
3 ch f Monsieur Bond(IRE) Fashion Icon (USA) (Van Nistelrooy (USA))
1839[3] ◆ 2334[11] (3009) 3423[2] 4426[2] (4726) 5296[6] 5867[7] 6475[9] 6790[5] (6958) 7252[11]

Bondi Beach (IRE) *A P O'Brien* 119
4 b h Galileo(IRE) One Moment In Time (IRE) (Danehill (USA))
(2275a) 5095a[3] 6351a[3] 7756a[13]

Bondi Beach Babe *James Turner* a57 75
6 b m Misu Bond(IRE) Nice One (Almaty (IRE))
2334[12] (2856) 3880[2] 4295[4]

Bondi Beach Boy *James Turner* a78 89
7 b g Misu Bond(IRE) Nice One (Almaty (IRE))
(2261) 2488[9] 2665[4] (3638) 4112[11] 4373[8] 5479[6] 6012[11] 6793[3] 6926[5] 7773[3] 7892[12]

Bond Mystery *Natalie Lloyd-Beavis* a32 49
4 b g Monsieur Bond(IRE) Scooby Dooby Do (Atraf)
1548[5] 2285a[6] 2955a[5] 2899[8] 3492[7] 4504[6]

Bond Starprincess *Ben Haslam* 43
4 ch m Monsieur Bond(IRE) Presidium Star (Presidium)
3642[8] 4515[6]

Bond's Tricks *Ronald Thompson* a47 55
3 ch g Monsieur Bond(IRE) Triple Tricks (IRE) (Royal Academy (USA))
48[7] 565[6]

Bond Trader *Clive Cox* a71 69
3 b g Monsieur Bond(IRE) Bidding Time (Rock Of Gibraltar (IRE))
824[3] 2578[9] 2999[6] 3816[6] 7417[7]

Bonfire Bank (IRE) *John C McConnell* a36 61
3 br g Intense Focus(USA) Cuiseach (IRE) (Bachelor Duke (USA))
1014a[12]

Bongrace (IRE) *Kevin Ryan* a80 80
2 ch f Helmet(AUS) Wish List (IRE) (Mujadil (USA))
2756[9] 3548[4] 4037[5] (4487) (5066) 5407[6] (5967) 6258[8]

Bonhomie *Michael Bell* a72 68
3 b f Shamardal(USA) Bonnie Doon (IRE) (Grand Lodge (USA))
1562[3] 2585[3] 3558[3] (4718) 5302[9] 5860[4] 6893[6]

Bonjour Baby *K R Burke* a64 66
3 ch f Duke Of Marmalade(IRE) Briery (IRE) (Salse (USA))
582[4]

Bonjour Steve *Richard Price* a67 68
5 b g Bahamian Bounty Anthea (Tobougg (IRE))
1595[12] 2130[6] 2697[8] 3217[9] (5230) 5546[3] 5955[5] 6255[9] 7290[9] 7626[7] 7774[7] 7912[3] 8315[6] 8474[4] ◆

Bonnie Arlene (IRE) *Mark Johnston* a54 63
2 b f Excelebration(IRE) Pioneer Bride (USA) (Gone West (USA))
1443[4] 1641[4] 2082[4] 2612[4] 3186[4] 3852[5] 6026[3] 6743[8] 7244[2]

Bonnoption *R Le Gal* a63 62
5 b m Myboycharlie(IRE) Slyta (FR) (Slickly (FR))
2806a[6] 4927a[12]

Bonusdargent (FR) *Mme Pia Brandt* a95 99
4 b h Kendargent(FR) Quadded Bere (FR) (Epistolaire (IRE))
6178a[4] 7312a[6]

Booborowie (IRE) *Jeremy Gask* a53 72
3 b g Big Bad Bob(IRE) Rejuvenation (IRE) (Singspiel (IRE))
3744[3] 4347[4] 5380[3] 6268[7] 7063[5]

Bookmaker *John Bridger* a67 47
6 b g Byron Cankara (IRE) (Daggers Drawn (USA))
(97) 316[8] (608) 777[10] 1262[4] 2153[4] 2379[8] 2872[12] 3522[10] 8555[14]

Book Of Days (FR) *M Rulec* a64 61
5 bb m Definite Article Jetarsu (IRE) (King's Theatre (IRE))
(5700a)

Book Of Poetry (IRE) *Mark Johnston* a65 67
2 b c Poet's Voice Duniatty (Green Desert (USA))
2119[3] ◆ 2358[6] 4047[5] 5171[2] 6903[3]

Boolass (IRE) *Brian Ellison* a74 45
4 b m Bushranger(IRE) Silent Secret (IRE) (Dubai Destination (USA))
(133) 246[4]

Boomerang Bob (IRE) *Jamie Osborne* a104 93
7 b h Aussie Rules(USA) Cozzene's Pride (USA) (Cozzene (USA))
220[2] ◆ 288[2] 483[5] 663a[2] 816[4] 923[4] 2898[10] 3279[2] 3656[5] 5098a[6] 5678[6] 6112[5] 6962[6] 7315[5] (7610) 8069[5] 8314[2]

Booming Delight (IRE) *William Haggas* 96
3 b g Fastnet Rock(AUS) Starship (IRE) (Galileo (IRE))
(2695) 3299[6]

Boom Junior *Tony Carroll* a41 27
3 b c Compton Place Khyber Knight (IRE) (Night Shift (USA))
48[3] 345[9] 700[4] 896[5] 1141[7] 3740[11]

Boomshackerlacker (IRE) *George Baker* a100 106
6 gr g Dark Angel(IRE) Allegrina (IRE) (Barathea (IRE))
189a[4] ◆ 373a[10] 628a[5] 3273[19] (4395) 4823[5] 5941a[7]

Boom The Groom (IRE) *Tony Carroll* a106 111
5 b g Kodiac Ecco Mi (IRE) (Priolo (USA))
288[4] (677) 745[6] 1066[4] 2895[7] 3386[18] 4126[10] (4735) (5555) 6574[6] 7242[6]

Boonga Roogeta *Peter Charalambous* a89 88
7 b m Tobougg(IRE) Aberlady Bay (IRE) (Selkirk (USA))
33[2] 72[3] 212[7] 632[6] 900[5] 1171[5]

Boos (FR) *P Sogorb* 107
2 b f Dream Ahead(USA) La Belliere (IRE) (Kheleyf (USA))
4750a[2] 7347a[2] 7721a[5]

Booshbash (IRE) *Ed Dunlop* a62 56
2 gr f Dark Angel(IRE) Surrey Storm (Montjeu (IRE))
3261[10] 4261[6] 4762[7] 5297[4] 5719[2] 7954[4] (8046)

Boost *Sir Mark Prescott Bt* a74
2 b f Pivotal Hooray (Invincible Spirit (IRE))
2376[3] 2817[3]

Boots And Spurs *Scott Dixon* a87 88
7 b g Oasis Dream Arctic Char (Polar Falcon (USA))
58[3] (134) 866[5] 1215[8] 1478[6] (3645) 3895[2] 4163[5] 4644[6] 4894[7] 7126[7] 7486[7] 7593[2] 7957[4] 8239[2] 8345[5] 8475[11]

Bop It *David O'Meara* a61 78
7 b g Misu Bond(IRE) Forever Bond (Danetime (IRE))
2524[9] 3168[10] 3610[5] 4608[2] 5060[9]

Borak (IRE) *Bernard Llewellyn* a74 82
4 b g Kodiac Right After Moyne (IRE) (Imperial Ballet (IRE))
6279[6]

Bora Rock (IRE) *P Schiergen* 99
3 b c Rock Of Gibraltar(IRE) Bora Blues (Peintre Celebre (USA))
3453a[7] 4186a[5]

Border Bandit (USA) *Tracy Waggott* a61 50
8 b g Selkirk(USA) Coretta (IRE) (Caerleon (USA))
1924[10] 2121[12] 2917[8] 3367[11] 3605[12] 3717[10] 5030[4] 5521[4] 5729[4] 5972[7] 7795[9] 7995[7]

Boreale (USA) *N Clement* a91 59
3 bb f Makfi Aurore (USA) (Arch (USA))
8148a[7]

Born Innocent (IRE) *John Patrick Shanahan* a51 75
3 gr f Dark Angel(IRE) Navajo Princess (IRE) (Indian Ridge)
(2571) 3285[5] (3553) ◆ 3753[2] 4873[12] 6769[3] 7059[9] 7252[13]

Born Legend (IRE) *Charles Hills*
2 b c Born To Sea(IRE) Hallowed Park (IRE) (Barathea (IRE))
8537[13]

Born To Be (IRE) *John M Oxx* 98
2 b c Born To Sea(IRE) Duquesa (IRE) (Intikhab (USA))
6860a[2] 7559a[6]

Born To Boogie *Chris Grant* a44 59
2 b f Bahri(USA) Turtle Dove (Tobougg (IRE))
1443[3] 1921[10] 2424[7] 3561[6] 4404[6]

Born To Finish (IRE) *Jeremy Gask* a73 66
3 b g Dark Angel(IRE) Music Pearl (IRE) (Oratorio (IRE))
1431[2] 1745[3] 2186[6] 3098[7] 3725[5] 4009[10] 5059[7] 5769[7] 6249[7] (8595)

Born To Fly (IRE) *Christine Dunnett* a55 24
5 b m Kodiac Cayambe (IRE) (Selkirk (USA))
3146[11] 3624[10] 4388[10]

Born To Please *Mark Usher* a43 57
2 b f Stimulation(IRE) Heart Felt (Beat Hollow)
2747[8] 3232[2] 4270[5] 4937[4] 5719[6] 6412[12] 8025[8]

Borough Boy (IRE) *Derek Shaw* a84 83
6 b g Jeremy(USA) Ostrusa (AUT) (Rustan (HUN))
56[6] 250[6] 426[4] (520) 694[5] 901[6] 938[2] ◆ 1528[9] 1634[4] 1958[3] 7054[10] 7443[10]

Boru's Brook (IRE) *Jim Best* a35 36
8 b g Brian Boru Collybrook Lady (IRE) (Mandalus)
5709[4] 5850[6] 6415[13] 7052[11] 7487[7]

Boscaccio (GER) *Christian Sprengel* 105
3 b c Mount Nelson Bianca De Medici (Medicean)
(3453a) 4186a[8] 6175a[10]

Bo Selecta (IRE) *Richard Spencer* a65
2 b c Dream Ahead(USA) Chicane (Motivator)
8353[6]

Bosham *Michael Easterby* a104 81
6 b g Shamardal(USA) Awwal Malika (USA) (Kingmambo (USA))
28[4] (56) 323[3] (359) (439) (529) 677[6] 835[3] (966) 1066[11] 3606[10] 3875[10] 4112[19] 4514[10] (5295) 6080[14] 8050[12] 8232[2] 8308[11]

Bossa Nova *Robyn Brisland* a69 39
3 b f High Chaparral(IRE) Marcellinas Angel (Anabaa (USA))
8096[3]

Bossipop *Tim Easterby* a83 92
3 ch g Assertive Opopmil (IRE) (Pips Pride)
(1448) 2049[3] 2650[2] 2972[3] 3292[2] 4344[6] 4643[5] 5643[9] 5978[2] 6537[15] (6766) 7858[14]

Bossy Guest (IRE) *Mick Channon* 107
4 b g Medicean Ros The Boss (IRE) (Danehill (USA))
95a[10] 372a[11] 720a[9] 1425[7] 2464[7] 3273[6] ◆ 4152[11] 4625[24]

Boston Blue *Tony Carroll* a53 68
9 b g Halling(USA) City Of Gold (IRE) (Sadler's Wells (USA))
289^3 417^8 634^7 1174^5

Botanical Lady (IRE) *H Rogers* 63
5 b m Moss Vale(IRE) Diskretion (GER) (Acatenango (GER))
7474a^9

Botany Bay (IRE) *Charles O'Brien* a71 99
4 b g Galileo(IRE) Honour Bright (IRE) (Danehill (USA))
2881a^4 3680a^5 5559^5 6151a^4

Both Sides *Andrew Balding* a79 92
3 b g Lawman(FR) Pearl Dance (USA) (Nureyev (USA))
1160^2 (1961) 2244^5 ◆ 3110^2 ◆ 3861^3 ◆ 4808^2 6484^3

Bouclier (IRE) *Tony Carroll* a85 88
6 ch h Zamindar(USA) Bastet (IRE) (Giant's Causeway (USA))
416^5 (955) (1178) 1566^4 2754^{10} (3487) 5825^4 *8475^{12}*

Bounce *Henry Candy* a89 97
3 b f Bahamian Bounty Black Belt Shopper (IRE) (Desert Prince (IRE))
2736^3 ◆ 4062^3

Bound (IRE) *A P O'Brien* 96
2 ch f Galileo(IRE) Remember When (IRE) (Danehill Dancer (IRE))
5937a^7 7193a^2 7707a^7

Boundsy (IRE) *Richard Fahey* 77
2 ch g Dandy Man(IRE) Chiba (UAE) (Timber Country (USA))
1641^3 (2570) 3208^4 4394^{14} 4629^2 5917^3 6322^2 6950^{10}

Bounty Pursuit *Michael Appleby* a59 60
4 b g Pastoral Pursuits Poyle Dee Dee (Oasis Dream)
2964^2 3009^3

Bouquet De Flores (USA) *Charlie Appleby* a66 79
2 b f Street Cry(IRE) Floristry (Fasliyev (USA))
4064^7 4756^3 6454^3 6873^{12}

Bourbon Gleam (USA) *Doug Watson* a44
2 b f Not Bourbon(CAN) Halo's Gleam (USA) (Halo (USA))
8574a^6

Bourbonisto *Ben Haslam* a62 70
2 ch g Stimulation(IRE) Psychic's Dream (Oasis Dream)
2235^2 2570^8 2807^4 4167^4 5833^3 *7792^3*

Bourges (FR) *E Lellouche* 88
3 bl f Le Havre(IRE) Aglaia (IRE) (Invincible Spirit (IRE))
6069a^8

Bournemouth Belle *Richard Hannon* a74 85
3 b f Canford Cliffs(IRE) Ellbeedee (IRE) (Dalakhani (IRE))
1432^5 1898^5

Bourree (GER) *Andreas Lowe* 111
4 b m Siyouni(FR) Bearlita (GER) (Lomitas)
2727a^8

Boutan *Bernard Llewellyn* 73
3 gr f Tobougg(IRE) High Tan (High Chaparral (IRE))
1275^7 1860^{11} 2586^6 3740^8 (4316) 4518^2 (4760) 5197^3 (5957) 7014^4

Bow And Arrow *Charlie Appleby* a84 98
4 b g Iffraaj Isobel Archer (Oasis Dream)
2033^7

Bowban *Brian Ellison* a68
2 b c Makfi Serafina's Flight (Fantastic Light (USA))
8537^3 ◆

Bow Creek (IRE) *J O'Shea* a105 115
5 b h Shamardal(USA) Beneventa (Most Welcome)
1912a^{12}

Bowdler's Magic *David Thompson* a68 70
9 b g Hernando(FR) Slew The Moon (ARG) (Kitwood (USA))
2746^5 *2916^5* 4045^3 4935^4 4971^2 *5970^6*

Bowerman *Roger Varian* a77
2 b c Dutch Art Jamboretta (IRE) (Danehill (USA))
7849^2

Bowies Hero (USA) *Philip D'Amato* 104
2 b c Artie Schiller(USA) Remembered (USA) (Sky Mesa (USA))
7266a^8 7807a^{11}

Bowl Imperior *Mrs A Malzard* a47 51
4 ch g Raven's Pass(USA) Turtle Point (USA) (Giant's Causeway (USA))
2952a^7 3381a^7 3918a^6 4696a^2 5459a^6 6403a^2

Bowsers Bold *Roger Ingram* a64 58
5 gr g Firebreak Cristal Clear (IRE) (Clodovil (IRE))
7063^6

Bowson Fred *Michael Easterby* a106 107
4 b g Monsieur Bond(IRE) Bow Bridge (Bertolini (USA))
(1321) 1650^2 1964^4 (2658) *(2787) 3277^2 3606^2* 4126^6 4735^3 5555^{14} 6119^3 6327^{20} *8050^4*

Boxeur (IRE) *F Rossi* 97
3 b c Slickly(FR) Joha (FR) (Johann Quatz (FR))
7292a^6

Boxing Shadows *Les Eyre* a69 70
6 b g Camacho Prima Ballerina (Pivotal)
98^2 (196) (292) 733^7 1255^{10} 2808^4 2975^3 3268^7 5354^9

Boychick (IRE) *Ed Walker* a58 54
3 b g Holy Roman Emperor(IRE) Al Saqiya (USA) (Woodman (USA))
3141^7 3765^{11} 4275^{11} (4992) *5630^2 6243^3*

Boycie *Richard Hannon* a75 79
3 b c Paco Boy(IRE) Eve (Rainbow Quest (USA))
519^7 678^5 1176^9 2184^3 (2402) 3614^4 *4010^9* (4588) 5076^2 5412^6 6266^5 6579^4 *7051^6 8178^{13} 8462^3*

Boyfriend Brian (IRE) *G M Lyons* 98
2 b g Big Bad Bob(IRE) Danzelline (Danzero (AUS))
5136a^2

Boy In The Bar *Ian Williams* a72 96
5 ch g Dutch Art Lipsia (IRE) (Dubai Destination (USA))
1143^{10} 3580^6 (5744) (6072) 6792^2 7186^4 7821^6

Boynton (USA) *Charlie Appleby* 114
2 ch c More Than Ready(USA) Baffled (USA) (Distorted Humor (USA))
(2873) (4150) 4732^3

Brabbham (USA) *A bin Harmash* a90
6 b h Bernardini(USA) Easter Bunnette (USA) (Carson City (USA))
8a^3 (718a) ◆

Bracken Brae *Mark H Tompkins* a76 56
4 b m Champs Elysees Azure Mist (Bahamian Bounty)
170^2 (622) (731) (884) 1434^3 *(7987) 8250^6*

Bradfield Magic (IRE) *Charles Hills* a57
2 b f Holy Roman Emperor(IRE) Magic Eye (IRE) (Nayef (USA))
7812^{13} 8081^8 8361^7

Bradleysintown (IRE) *Michael Dods* 62
3 ch g Thousand Words Anazah (USA) (Diesis)
1123^4 1379^5 2428^6

Braes Of Lochalsh *Jim Goldie* 80
5 b g Tiger Hill(IRE) Gargoyle Girl (Be My Chief (USA))
(1852) 2487^{10} 3345^2 4101^7 4381^6 6561^7

Brahma *Hughie Morrison* 60
3 b g Mount Nelson Swan Queen (In The Wings)
4458^{11} 4955^6 5486^7

Brametot (IRE) *J-C Rouget* 97
2 b c Rajsaman(FR) Morning Light (GER) (Law Society (USA))
(7263a)

Bramshill Lass *Amanda Perrett* a63 48
7 ch m Notnowcato Disco Ball (Fantastic Light (USA))
435^4

Brancaio (FR) *K Borgel* a67
3 b c Denon(USA) Brictop (USA) (Mizzen Mast (USA))
5704a^3

Branch Line (IRE) *Andrew Slattery* 85
2 b g Rip Van Winkle(IRE) Disco Lights (Spectrum (IRE))
5136a^5

Brando *Kevin Ryan* 119
4 ch g Pivotal Argent Du Bois (USA) (Silver Hawk (USA))
(1427) 2188^2 3386^2 (3909) 4413a^2 5614^9 (6558) 7350^3

Brandon Castle *Simon West* a82 86
4 b g Dylan Thomas(IRE) Chelsey Jayne (IRE) (Galileo (IRE))
337^7 975^5 1166^4 1531^3 3798^2 4381^3 4888^4 5918^4 6323^4 6730^7

Brandybend (IRE) *Marco Botti* a90 98
4 b m Galileo(IRE) Elusive Wave (IRE) (Elusive City (USA))
1232a^2 2363^5 3088a^4 3979^{13} 7395a^4 *8427^5*

Brassbound (USA) *Michael Appleby* a92 57
8 b g Redoute's Choice(AUS) In A Bound (AUS) (Ashkalani (IRE))
6^4 440^8 619^7 (891) 1296^6 1760^{11}

Brasted (IRE) *Lee Carter* a79 57
4 ch g Footstepsinthesand Ellen (IRE) (Machiavellian (USA))
172^5 349^2 616^2 4204^3 *6128^{12} 6657^8 7606^2 7778^4 8252^4*

Bravadora (IRE) *Scott Dixon* a17 19
3 b f Roderic O'Connor(IRE) Viscoumtess Brave (IRE) (Law Society (USA))
984^{10} 2271^7 3850^8

Brave Anna (USA) *A P O'Brien* 112
2 b f War Front(USA) Liscanna (IRE) (Sadler's Wells (USA))
(3336) 5686a^6 6385a^6 (6784)

Brave Archibald (IRE) *Paul Cole* a79 75
3 b g Arch(USA) Muneefa (USA) (Storm Cat (USA))
2044^3 2291^2 ◆ *2900^9* 4046^8 (4522) *4880^2 (5704a)*

Brave Decision *Brett Johnson* a71 42
9 gr g With Approval(CAN) Brave Vanessa (USA) (Private Account (USA))
173^6

Brave Hero *Saeed bin Suroor* a86 99
3 ch g Poet's Voice Classical Dancer (Dr Fong (USA))
1438^5 1867^8 (6529) 6918^4

Brave Richard (IRE) *J R Jenkins* a70
5 b g Jeremy(USA) Certainly Brave (Indian Ridge)
51^2

Bravery (IRE) *A P O'Brien* a82 102
3 b c Galileo(IRE) Lady Icarus (Rainbow Quest (USA))
2496a^4 2946a^{10} 3912^7 6389a^{12} 7196a^4

Bravo Echo *Michael Attwater* a93 85
10 b g Oasis Dream Bold Empress (USA) (Diesis)
727^8

Bravo Girl (FR) *Waldemar Hickst* 97
4 ch m Lord Of England(GER) Arlekinada (Lycius (USA))
1907a^2 7028a^8

Bravo Zolo (IRE) *Jeremy Noseda* a105 109
4 b g Rip Van Winkle(IRE) Set Fire (IRE) (Bertolini (USA))
560^3 (767) 1196^2 ◆ 6786^{23} (7292a)

Brazen Spirit *Clive Cox* a76 78
4 gr g Zebedee Never Say Deya (Dansili)
67^6 416^4 782^7 3004^6 4291^9 5744^{11} *6235^2* 7268^8

Brazos (IRE) *James Tate* a76 98
5 gr h Clodovil(IRE) Shambodia (IRE) (Petardia)
2833^7 3358^6 3622^4 (4299) 4625^{10} 5389^{10} 6355a^7 *7530^{11}*

Braztime *Richard Hannon* a72 62
2 b f Canford Cliffs(IRE) Briery (IRE) (Salse (USA))
4762^5 *5242^3* 6534^6

Breakable *Tim Easterby* 100
5 ch m Firebreak Magic Myth (IRE) (Revoque (IRE))
1563^6 2223^3 2420^5 2890^4 (3884) 4630^2 (5419) (5640) 6331^5

Breakenridge *William Knight* a3
2 b c Lawman(FR) Western Pearl (High Chaparral (IRE))
8486^{15}

Breakheart (IRE) *Andrew Balding* a72 90
9 b g Sakhee(USA) Exorcet (FR) (Selkirk (USA))
165^6 263^5 491^9 875^9 7755^{12} 7986^8 8258^8

Breaking Free *John Quinn* 55
2 ch g Kyllachy Hill Welcome (Most Welcome)
1850^5 2301^{10} 3873^7 4364^3 4869^6 7041^4 ◆ 7571^5

Break The Silence *Scott Dixon* 44
2 b g Rip Van Winkle(IRE) In A Silent Way (IRE) (Desert Prince (IRE))
3598^8 6808^4 7496^{12}

Breakwater Bay (IRE) *Tim Easterby* 58
2 b g Lilbourne Lad(IRE) Aqualina (IRE) (King's Theatre (IRE))
3248^6 5414^8 5884^{14}

Brean Flyer *Bill Turner* a52
2 b f Phenomena Lois Lane (Striking Ambition)
8425^7

Brean Golf Birdie *Bill Turner* a48 31
4 br m Striking Ambition Straight As A Die (Pyramus (USA))
20^8 79^8

Breanski *David O'Meara* a23 69
2 b c Delegator Jubilee (Selkirk (USA))
7317^6 7741^{12} *8034^{11}*

Brean Splash Susie *Bill Turner* a20 57
5 b m Tobougg(IRE) Straight As A Die (Pyramus (USA))
528^9 2047^6

Breathe Easy (IRE) *Gavin Cromwell* a77 92
6 ch g Redback Inishmac (IRE) (Danehill Dancer (IRE))
5941a^{12} 6389a^2

Breathless *Clive Mulhall* a67 15
4 b g Royal Applause Ada River (Dansili)
(939) 1241^{10} 1631^{11} 6568^{12} *6907^{12} 8307^6*

Breathoffreshair *Richard Guest* a59 14
2 b g Bated Breath Stormy Weather (Nashwan (USA))
6712^{11} 7071^{10} *7792^4*

Brendan (IRE) *Jim Goldie* 48
3 b g Elnadim(USA) My (King's Best (USA))
1216^7 1849^7

Brendan Brackan (IRE) *G M Lyons* a102 107
7 b g Big Bad Bob(IRE) Abeyr (Unfuwain (USA))
1509a^2 2067a^4 3677a^7 4747a^8 (7372a)

Bretherton *Jassim Al Ghazali* a87 98
5 ch g Exceed And Excel(AUS) Cliche (IRE) (Diktat)
744a^4

Breton Blues *Fred Watson* a47 41
6 b g Street Cry(IRE) Many Colours (Green Desert (USA))
3014^{10} 4146^6 4683^7 *5366^3 5971^3 6738^6 6920^{10} 7795^{14}*

Bretoncelles (FR) *Harry Dunlop* a76 58
3 b f Le Havre(IRE) Carolles (FR) (Medicean)
2767^3 4272^7

Breton Rock (IRE) *David Simcock* 116
6 b g Bahamian Bounty Anna's Rock (IRE) (Rock Of Gibraltar (IRE))
1606^3 2691^4 (3664) 6117^5 (6328) 7352^{10}

Brex Drago (ITY) *Stefano Botti* 104
4 b h Mujahid(USA) Shibuni's Thea (IRE) (Barathea (IRE))
3455a^5 7400a^5

Brexit *Pat Phelan* a43 57
2 b f Bahamian Bounty Famcred (Inchinor)
2748^5 3555^6 *4524^4* 5165^5

Briac (FR) *Jim Best* a36 36
5 b g Kapgarde(FR) Jarwin Do (FR) (Grand Tresor (FR))
4657^7 4840^7 5544^9 *6511^9 7280^{13} 8410^{12}*

Brian The Snail (IRE) *Richard Fahey* 95
2 gr c Zebedee Sweet Irish (Shamardal (USA))
(6515) (7589) ◆

Briardale (IRE) *James Bethell* a91 88
4 b g Arcano(IRE) Marine City (JPN) (Carnegie (IRE))
1250^{10} 1588^4 1923^7 *(2618) 3563^2* (4611) 5376^4 6753^{12} *7108^2 8478^6*

Brick Lane *Robyn Brisland* a80 43
3 ch f Bahamian Bounty Medicea Sidera (Medicean)
2443^4 2767^9 3145^4 *4718^5 (5808) (6426)* ◆ *6510^2 7204^5*

Bridal March *Mark Johnston* a64 67
2 ch f Casamento(IRE) Exultate Jubilate (USA) (With Approval (CAN))
2437^4 3134^2 *3404^3* 3872^3 4487^2 5112^3 *6923^{10}* 7286^{14}

Bridey's Lettuce (IRE) *Ivan Furtado* a70 65
4 b g Iffraaj Its On The Air (IRE) (King's Theatre (IRE))
1390^6 2233^{11} 3191^4 5183^4 5481^8 7628^3 *8134^6 8400^2 8566^2*

Bridge Builder *Peter Hedger* a71 60
6 b g Avonbridge Amazing Dream (IRE) (Thatching)
143^3 (168) 237^2 257^3 1147^4 (1261) 2380^3 6872^{12} 7620^7 8030^4 (8365)

Bridge Casadate (IRE) *Pierpaolo Sbariggia* 67
2 br c Casamento(IRE) Coffee Date (USA) (Bob And John (USA))
7839a^6

Bridge Of Sighs *Martin Smith* a75 80
4 ch g Avonbridge Ashantiana (Ashkalani (IRE))
(621) (1751) 2174^7 2623^2 *3276^4* 4868^8 *6702^3* (6889) 7229^5 7666^6 *8251^{10}*

Bridge That Gap *Roger Ingram* a47 46
8 b h Avonbridge Figura (Rudimentary (USA))
8448^{10}

Bridjnaia (FR) *C Bauer* a50 50
7 b m Policy Maker(IRE) La Pelaude (FR) (Marignan (USA))
512a^8 8422a^7

Brief Angel (IRE) *Thomas Cooper* a29 40
3 gr f Dark Angel(IRE) Brief Sentiment (IRE) (Brief Truce (USA))
1014a^{17}

Brief Visit *Andrew Balding* 90
3 b f Fastnet Rock(AUS) Brevity (USA) (Street Cry (IRE))
2009^{12} 3194^5 3981^2 (4761) ◆

Brigadoon *Michael Appleby* a73 73
9 b g Compton Place Briggsmaid (Elegant Air)
2439^7 3118^{14} 4095^9 (4967) *8348^2*

Bright Applause *Tracy Waggott* a40 70
8 b g Royal Applause Sadaka (USA) (Kingmambo (USA))
2836^5 3774^7

Bright Flash *David Brown* 92
4 ch m Dutch Art Quadri (Polish Precedent (USA))
(1664) ◆ 2236^8 4556^2 5874^{10}

Brigliadoro (IRE) *Philip McBride* a97 95
5 ch g Excellent Art Milady's Pride (Machiavellian (USA))
401^3 886^2 1204^8 ◆ 3115^7 (4028) 6753^6 6915^2 *7608^2 7779^4*

Brilliant Vanguard (IRE) *Kevin Ryan* a86 86
3 b g Fast Company(IRE) Alyska (IRE) (Owington)
(1524) ◆ 2161^{16} (2802) 3292^6 3908^5 5759^6 6714^9 *7461^4 7737^2 7958^2*

Brimham Rocks *Ralph Beckett* 59
2 b g Fastnet Rock(AUS) Colima (IRE) (Authorized (IRE))
6439^8 6881^{13} 7621^8

Brindle *Richard Fahey* a54 63
4 b m Iffraaj Anglezarke (IRE) (Acclamation)
713^8

Bring On A Spinner *Stuart Williams* a81 72
3 b g Kheleyf(USA) Posy Fossil (USA) (Malibu Moon (USA))
(5) (181) 2314^5 3105^7 4744^6 6072^{11} *(8345)*

Bring Something (AUS) *Ken Keys* 98
5 b g Sebring(AUS) Metellus (AUS) (Naturalism (NZ))
7637a^4 7947a^7

Brisanto *M G Mintchev* 107
4 b h Dansili Briseida (Pivotal)
2074a^6 4928a^7 5500a^4 7028a^4

Brise De Mer (FR) *George Baker* a70 74
2 b c Miesque's Son(USA) Lisselan Firefly (IRE) (Monashee Mountain (USA))
2203^8 2873^7 3971^4 4802^7 ◆ 5348a^2 6638a^6 *7588a^3*

Briseide (IRE) *D Zarroli* a53 67
2 ch f Approve(IRE) Solaria (IRE) (Desert Prince (IRE))
6015a^8 *7294a^6*

Britannia Boy *Mark Usher* a46 38
3 b g Royal Applause Caledonia Princess (Kyllachy)
1734^{13} 2184^8 *2608^3 4210^6 4527^{10}* 5016^4

British Embassy (IRE) *Brian Barr* a75 85
4 b g Clodovil(IRE) Embassy Belle (IRE) (Marju (IRE))
1595^8 2347^{13} 2810^2 3220^5 3253^4 3363^2 3804^3 (3876) 3952^{12} (5030) *5609^6* 6021^2 ◆ (6316) *7813^8*

Brittanic (IRE) *David Simcock* a74
2 ch c Excelebration(IRE) Fountain Of Peace (USA) (Kris S (USA))
(8384) ◆

Brittleton *Harry Dunlop* a69 87
4 b g Aqlaam Fairy Dance (IRE) (Zafonic (USA))
2392^{11} 4057^3 (4550) 6163^{12} 7320^{12}

Briyouni (FR) *Kevin Ryan* 89
3 b g Siyouni(FR) Brianza (USA) (Thunder Gulch (USA))
(2506) ◆ 2801^5 3357^3 (4605) 5180^5 6132^4 7005^8 7540^2 7825^2

Broadhaven Honey (IRE) *Ed McMahon* 77
2 b f Harbour Watch(IRE) Honeymead (IRE) (Pivotal)
2295^2 2793^4 4451^2 5511^6 (6477) 6830^3 ◆ (7217)

Broadsword (IRE) *Kevin Frost* a48 44
4 ch m Dandy Man(IRE) Petticoat Hill (UAE) (Timber Country (USA))
1184^6 1653^{11} 2653^{10}

Broadway Boogie (IRE) *J-C Rouget* a99 99
4 b h Distorted Humor(USA) Grande Melody (IRE) (Grand Lodge (USA))
7524a^6

Broadway Icon *Jeremy Noseda* a80 58
3 b c Sixties Icon Funny Girl (IRE) (Darshaan)
219^5 352^3

Brockholes *Bryan Smart* a74 80
3 ch f Equiano(FR) Rivalry (Medicean)
1814^2 2303^2 3209^3 (3775) ◆ 4259^3 4873^{10} *7959^{11} 8403^6*

Brocklebank (IRE) *Simon Dow* a98 89
7 b g Diamond Green(FR) La Stellina (IRE) (Marju (IRE))
353^4 485^8

Broctune Papa Gio *Keith Reveley* a66 76
9 b g Tobougg(IRE) Fairlie (Halling (USA))
2773^{14} 3366^{12} (4772) *5367^7 5972^3* 6220^5 6683^6 *7601^4 7797^5 8286^5 8587^7*

Brodie *Luca Cumani* a78 70
3 gr f Sea The Stars(IRE) Dali's Grey (Linamix (FR))
5996^3 ◆ *7280^4 (7904)*

Brody's Cause (USA) *Dale Romans* a114
3 b c Giant's Causeway(USA) Sweet Breanna (CAN) (Sahm (USA))
2063a^7 3181a^6

Brogan *Tom Dascombe* a64 77
2 b f Pivotal Roger Sez (IRE) (Red Clubs (IRE))
5298^3 6223^3 6648^2 (7319)

Broken Stones (IRE) *Kevin Ryan* 107
2 br c Requinto(IRE) Positive Step (IRE) (Footstepsinthesand)
(2489) 4060^3 (4653) ◆

Broklyn Baby (FR) *Matthieu Palussiere* 75
2 bb c Elusive City(USA) Reine Violette (FR) (Fly To The Stars)
4924a^5

Bromance *Peter Niven* a60 65
3 b g Showcasing Romantic Destiny (Dubai Destination (USA))
7435[11] 7797[6] 7994[8] 8145[4] 8307[4] 8500[7] 8587[2] ◆

Bromley Cross (IRE) *Brian Ellison* a65 58
3 ch g Dandy Man(IRE) Marianne's Dancer (IRE) (Bold Fact (USA))
765[5] 1111[3] 1494[4] 2776[6] 3368[9] 3611[4]

Bromyard (IRE) *David Simcock* a89 68
4 b g Dark Angel(IRE) Zoudie (Ezzoud (IRE))
18[2] (313)

Bronte Flyer *Ann Duffield* 77
3 ch f Nayef(USA) Shohrah (IRE) (Giant's Causeway (USA))
2029[9] 4036[5] 4727[5]

Bronze Angel (IRE) *Marcus Tregoning* a95 114
7 b g Dark Angel(IRE) Rihana (IRE) (Priolo (USA))
1425[8] 6786[15] 7354[16]

Bronze Beau *Kristin Stubbs* a43 79
9 ch g Compton Place Bella Cantata (Singspiel (IRE))
1447[12] 1559[6] 1878[2] 2202[6] 2418[6] 3009[2] 3136[2] 3494[5] (3755) 3925[9] 4452[12] 4874[5] 5320[9] 5582[9] 6023[4] (6680) 6959[3] 7290[11]

Bronze Swan (IRE) *H-A Pantall* a71 85
3 b c Turtle Bowl(IRE) Rosey De Megeve (Efisio)
(7680a)

Brooke's Point *Neil Mulholland* 52
3 b g Cape Cross(IRE) Forest Pearl (USA) (Woodman (USA))
3769[13] 4156[10] 4660[6] 5572 [2] ◆

Brooklyn's Rose (IRE) *G M Lyons* 96
2 b f Holy Roman Emperor(IRE) Right Key (IRE) (Key Of Luck (USA))
4573a[5] 5686a[7] 6860a[4]

Brorocco *Andrew Balding* a76 90
3 b g Shirocco(GER) Lady Brora (Dashing Blade)
1242[6] 1575[7] 3156[4] 3483[2] 4213[3] (4838) (5333) 5932[4] 6277[3] 6581[3]

Brosnan (IRE) *J F Levins* a79 87
4 ch m Champs Elysees Clytha (Mark Of Esteem (IRE))
4218a[12]

Brother In Arms (IRE) *Jamie Osborne* a52
2 b c Kodiac Cool Cousin (IRE) (Distant Relative)
8354[7]

Brother Khee *Wilf Storey* a41 32
5 ch g Sakhee's Secret Cugina (Distant Relative)
2307[11] 2914[6]

Brother McGonagall *Tim Easterby* a60
2 b g Equiano(FR) Anatase (Danehill (USA))
7988[6] 8140[6] 8313[6]

Brother Tiger *David C Griffiths* a98 89
7 b g Singspiel(IRE) Three Secrets (IRE) (Danehill (USA))
4[3] 213[6] (492) 966[2] 3277[6] 4112[7] 4735[12] 7864[7] 8050[11]

Broughtons Admiral *Henry Spiller* a48
2 b g Born To Sea(IRE) Chanter (Lomitas)
6671[7] 7065[10] 7882[10]

Broughtons Berry (IRE) *Willie Musson* a53 51
5 b m Bushranger(IRE) Larrocha (IRE) (Sadler's Wells (USA))
354[6] 695[7] 1807[3] 2400[4] 2781[6]

Broughtons Fancy *Andrew Reid* a69 71
3 b f Pastoral Pursuits Lifetime Romance (IRE) (Mozart (IRE))
380[2] (565) 924[8] 1137[5] 1313[2] 1573[3] (1764) (2184) 2586[3] 2823[2] (3473) 4269[7] 4787[4] 5725[8] 6592[8]

Broughtons Harmony *Willie Musson* a69
4 ch m Nayef(USA) Park Melody (IRE) (Refuse To Bend (IRE))
3076[6]

Broughtons Knight *Henry Spiller* a68 68
2 b g Foxwedge(AUS) Disco Ball (Fantastic Light (USA))
3463[7] 6672[4] 7209[4] ◆ 7697[3]

Broughtons Mystery *Henry Spiller* a54 38
3 b f Sakhee's Secret Enchanted Princess (Royal Applause)
1792[7] ◆ 2325[4] 2967[10] 4596[9] 4936[4] 6047[5] 6514[4] 7231[10] 7532[6]

Broughtons Salsa *Henry Spiller* a49
3 b f Royal Applause Reeling N' Rocking (IRE) (Mr Greeley (USA))
7607[6]

Broughtons Story *Henry Spiller* a65 53
2 b g Royal Applause News Desk (Cape Cross (IRE))
2997[8] 5077[4] 5809[U] 7407[9] 8244[9] 8466[5]

Broughtons Vision *Willie Musson* a75 59
3 b g Kheleyf(USA) Read Federica (Fusaichi Pegasus (USA))
2544[7] 2998[7] 3614[6] 4718[3] (5720) 6629[2] 6899[6]

Brownie (FR) *Bent Olsen* a75 106
4 b h Sunday Break(JPN) Tropical Mark (Mark Of Esteem (IRE))
1957a[6] (5098a) (5950a)

Brown Velvet *K Kukk* a38 45
4 b m Kodiac Silkenveil (IRE) (Indian Ridge)
1517a[6] 2284a[4] 2954a[3] 3917a[5] 5457a[4] 6401a[3]

Bruntingthorpe (IRE) *Dean Ivory* a48 36
3 b g Thousand Words Cooke's Bar (IRE) (Invincible Spirit (IRE))
1577[8] 2107[5]

Bruny Island (IRE) *Charlie Fellowes* a51 58
2 ch c Bahamian Bounty Prianca (GER) (Diktat)
4140[5] 4678[10] 5029[7] 5675[9] 6252[7] 7109[12] 7423[6] (8276) 8398[6]

Brutal (IRE) *G M Lyons* 108
2 b c Pivotal Loreto (IRE) (Holy Roman Emperor (IRE))
7539[5]

Bryght Boy *Ed Walker* a67 68
3 b g Paco Boy(IRE) Bright Moll (Mind Games)
2234[6] 2864[6] 3648[3] 4269[2] 5525[6] 6241[4] 7601[12]

Buachaillnaheirean (IRE) *Neil King* a24 44
3 b g Desert Millennium(IRE) Run Sweetheart (Bold Run (FR))
2825[4] 3508[10] 5255[7] 7641[13]

Bubble Bath *Daniel Kubler* a73
2 br f Big Bad Bob(IRE) Plume (Pastoral Pursuits)
4938[3] 5549[7]

Bubble Brook (FR) *S Kobayashi* a55 53
5 b m Great Journey(JPN) Bubble Gum Girl (FR) (Green Tune (USA))
8421a[3]

Bubbly Bailey *J R Jenkins* a67 45
6 b g Byron Night Gypsy (Mind Games)
196[5] 872[11] 1150[9] 1833[8] 5509[9] 7070[11] 7276[10]

Bubbly Bellini (IRE) *Adrian McGuinness* a65 84
9 b g Mull Of Kintyre(USA) Gwapa (IRE) (Imperial Frontier (USA))
(1015a) 6382a[11] 6819a[14] 6984a[6] 7475a[9]

Buccaneers Cove (IRE) *Richard Fahey* a64 66
2 b g Footstepsinthesand Primissima (GER) (Second Set (IRE))
6009[3] 6679[3] 7157[11] 7688[3]

Buccaneers Vault (IRE) *Michael Dods* a87 81
4 gr g Aussie Rules(USA) Heaven's Vault (IRE) (Hernando (FR))
1625[8] 2345[4] 2917[7] 3517[16] 4684[9] (4830) 5179[7] 5859[5] 6926[7] 7434[2]

Buckland Beau *Charlie Fellowes* a86 82
5 b g Rock Of Gibraltar(IRE) Heavenly Whisper (IRE) (Halling (USA))
(33) (605) 779[6] 1093[5] 1716[6] 2791[2] 4129[7] 5333[5] 6048[8]

Buckleberry *Jonathan Portman* a73 72
4 ch g Sakhee's Secret Smart Hostess (Most Welcome)
875[6]

Buckle Street *Martin Keighley* a67 41
3 br g Cacique(IRE) Rose Row (Act One)
3769[8] 5486[9] 6415[8] 7739[2]

Buckstay (IRE) *Peter Chapple-Hyam* a110 114
6 b g Lawman(FR) Stella Del Mattino (USA) (Golden Gear (USA))
2027[3] 3386[5] 4152[9] 4733[4] (5472) 6328[4] 6942[5]

Buddhist Monk *Dagmar Geissmann* a42 91
11 b g Dr Fong(USA) Circle Of Light (Anshan)
587a[2]

Bueller (USA) *A Fabre* a81 87
3 b c Medaglia d'Oro(USA) Cheeky Charm (USA) (A.P. Indy (USA))
4439a[8]

Buena Luna *Sir Mark Prescott Bt* a27 34
2 ch f Bahamian Bounty Half Moon Hotel (With Approval (CAN))
6244[11] 7099[11] 7439[7]

Buffering (AUS) *Robert Heathcote* 120
8 b g Mossman(AUS) Action Annie (AUS) (Anabaa (USA))
(1104a) 1911a[14]

Bukle (IRE) *Rod Millman* a35 63
3 b g Approve(IRE) Rumline (Royal Applause)
1828[4] 2341[7] 4818[6] 7310[12]

Bulas Belle *Grant Tuer* 86
6 b m Rob Roy(USA) Bula Rose (IRE) (Alphabatim (USA))
2406[6] (2971) 3437[11] 4664[2] 5321[6] 6163[5] 7320[7] 7624[10]

Bulge Bracket *Tom Dascombe* a52 57
3 b g Great Journey(JPN) Baldovina (Tale Of The Cat (USA))
1740[12] 2553[11]

Bullington Bear (FR) *Jane Chapple-Hyam* a75
3 b c Youmzain(IRE) Maternelle (FR) (Machiavellian (USA))
1479[2]

Bun An Churraigh *Michael Mullineaux*
2 ch c Equiano(FR) Azlaa (Dubawi (IRE))
7331[11]

Bunbury *Richard Hughes* a88 82
4 b g Dansili Ithaca (USA) (Distant View (USA))
691[7] 1715[4] ◆ 1931[5] ◆ 3234[8] (4463) ◆ 4839[8] 8077[4] ◆ 8446[2]

Bunce (IRE) *Linda Perratt* a72 79
8 b g Good Reward(USA) Bold Desire (Cadeaux Genereux)
1666[6] 1843[4] 2523[3] 3150[14] 3709[5] 4100[5] 4488[10] 4834[4] (5225) 5780[8] 6093[6] 6341[3] 6506[4] 6813[5] 7093[4] 7252[5]

Bunker Hill Lass *Michael Appleby* a50 59
4 ch m Kheleyf(USA) Incony (Daggers Drawn (USA))
277[5] 5055[7] 5513[10] 5797[9] 6637[5] 7062[9] 7299[4] 7742[2] 7889[8] 8035[9] 8191[7] 8307[14]

Buonarroti (IRE) *Declan Carroll* a89 93
5 b g Galileo(IRE) Beauty Is Truth (IRE) (Pivotal)
1493[7] 2157[11] 2487[7] 2897[8] 3920[2] (4703) ◆ 6379[3] 6781[5] 7575[4] 7824[14] 7979[10]

Burano (IRE) *David O'Meara* a80 96
7 ch g Dalakhani(IRE) Kalimanta (IRE) (Lake Coniston (IRE))
1221[2] ◆ 1620[5] 1978[2] 2487[4] 3162[10] 3391[6] 4407[13] 4717[8] 4945[4]

Buratino (IRE) *Mark Johnston* a95 117
3 ch c Exceed And Excel(AUS) Bergamask (USA) (Kingmambo (USA))
1864[9] 2692[4] 3655[7] 4393[8] 4822[8]

Burauq *Milton Bradley* a63 54
4 b g Kyllachy Riccoche (IRE) (Oasis Dream)
167[9] 320[4] 442[4] 615[6] 873[4] 1042[6] 1138[8] 3486[7] 3734[9] 3993[7] 4292[9] 5126[6] 5509[4] (6312) 6853[12] 6894[3] 7302[3] 7488[3] 7693[3] 8031[2] 8234[2]

Burcan (FR) *Marco Botti* a98
4 ch g Astronomer Royal(USA) Sentimental Union (USA) (Dixie Union (USA))
(778) 1430[2] 3304[2] (7816) ◆ 8123[4] (8594)

Burger And Fries (FR) *C Ferland* 97
3 bb c Sageburg(IRE) Figarie (USA) (Bernardini (USA))
1582a[5]

Burguillos *Alan King* 89
3 ch c Lope De Vega(IRE) Hazy Dancer (Oasis Dream)
2208[3] 2861[2] 3769[5] 4480[3] (6294) 7077[3] 7499[2]

Burma Star *D K Weld* 78
3 ch f Shamardal(USA) Shamayel (Pivotal)
5313a[8]

Burmese *Marcus Tregoning* a94 111
4 b g Sir Percy Swan Queen (In The Wings)
1772[5] ◆ 2625[4] 3298[5] 6284[4] 6974a[7] 7411[2]

Burmese Whisper *Andrew Balding* a70 68
3 b c Approve(IRE) Annellis (UAE) (Diesis)
77[3] 268[4]

Burner (IRE) *Olly Williams* a43 72
4 b g High Chaparral(IRE) Breathe (FR) (Ocean Of Wisdom (USA))
1202[4] 1595[6] 1925[11] 2343[8]

Burneston *James Bethell* 68
4 br g Rock Of Gibraltar(IRE) Grain Of Gold (Mr Prospector (USA))
1136[8]

Burning Blaze *Brian Ellison* a82 80
6 b g Danroad(AUS) Demeter (USA) (Diesis)
278[3] 449[5] (953) 1143[3] 1625[2] 1958[5] 2491[6] 2910[8] 3421[3] 4627[17] 5037[6] 5845[12] 5968[7]

Burning Desire (IRE) *Richard Hughes* a73 67
5 b g Galileo(IRE) Flames (Blushing Flame (USA))
488[4] 8084[7] 8554[3]

Burningfivers (IRE) *Joseph Tuite* a64 71
3 b g Paco Boy(IRE) All Embracing (IRE) (Night Shift (USA))
3036[7] 3786[6] 4485[6]

Burning Heat (IRE) *James Eustace* a73 73
3 b g Rock Of Gibraltar(IRE) Burning Damask (USA) (Thunder Gulch (USA))
8281[2]

Burning Love (IRE) *Adam West* a58 47
3 b f Kodiac Think (FR) (Marchand De Sable (USA))
248[9] 565[4] 5572 [8] 5775[3] 6187[8] 6514[10] 7256[13]

Burning Thread (IRE) *David Elsworth* a89 84
9 b g Captain Rio Desert Rose (Green Desert (USA))
106[4] 484[2] 655[6] 1175[4] 3233[9] 3995[10] 4461[8] 5032[4] 5305[6] 5751[2] 5882[9] 6717[2] (7268) 7643[6] 7864[6] 8032[9] 8150[8]

Burnside (FR) *Ian Williams* a69 45
3 gr g Kendargent(FR) Tishkara (FR) (Xaar)
6219[9] 7057[4] 8193[3] 8318[2] 8445[2]

Burnt Cream *Martin Bosley* a56 56
9 b m Exceed And Excel(AUS) Basbousate Nadia (Wolfhound (USA))
98[5] 292[7] 2845[10] 5335[9]

Burn The Boats (IRE) *Mike Murphy* a90 81
7 br g Big Bad Bob(IRE) Forever Phoenix (Shareef Dancer (USA))
1204[7] 1959[5] 2862[9]

Burnt Pavlova (USA) *A bin Harmash* a69 61
3 b f Big Brown(USA) Pavlova (USA) (Stravinsky (USA))
184a[7] 536a[11]

Burnt Sugar (IRE) *Richard Hannon* a79 106
4 b h Lope De Vega(IRE) Lady Livius (IRE) (Titus Livius (FR))
3195[7] 3386[6] 4860[5] 5143[10] 6207[3] 6287[7] 6942[16] 7497[11] 7822[6] 8069[10]

Burren View Lady (IRE) *Denis Gerard Hogan* a80 72
6 br m Dansili Westerly Gale (USA) (Gone West (USA))
(6462a)

Burrishoole Abbey (IRE) *K R Burke* 89
2 b c Acclamation Xeralda (IRE) (Xaar)
2611[7] (3516) 4622[9] 5560[12] 6536[12]

Burtonwood *Julie Camacho* a69 72
4 b g Acclamation Green Poppy (Green Desert (USA))
1341[5] 1790[2] (3010) 3882[4] 4452[8] 4726[3] 5032[3] 5320[7] 5867[6] 6475[4]

Buscavidas (IRE) *A Carrasco Sanchez* 96
5 b h Acclamation Trill (Highest Honor (FR))
1231a[7]

Bush Beauty (IRE) *Eric Alston* a68 75
5 b m Bushranger(IRE) Scottendale (Zilzal (USA))
1631[6] 2409[6] 2529[3] (3132) 3594[5] 3810[3] 4348[2] 5062[7] 6055[3] ◆ 6426[6] 6851[9] 7514[9] 7751[5]

Bushel (USA) *Tony Newcombe* a76 75
6 b g Street Cry(IRE) Melhor Ainda (USA) (Pulpit (USA))
6[3] 266[3] 1737[5] 2367[4] 3002[6] 3560[5] 4303[5] 7691[12] 8282[9]

Bushephalus (IRE) *Ivan Furtado* a71 72
4 gr g Dark Angel(IRE) White Daffodil (IRE) (Footstepsinthesand)
3068[10] 3266[6] 3907[8] 4528[3]

Bushtiger (IRE) *Ruth Carr* a43 44
4 b g Bushranger(IRE) Emma's Surprise (Tobougg (IRE))
1845[8] 2528[3] 2810[5] 3020[9] 3921[7] 4314[10]

Bush Warrior (IRE) *Anabel K Murphy* a78 55
5 b g Bushranger(IRE) Lady Corduff (IRE) (Titus Livius (FR))
100[2] 319[8] (671) 784[2] 1178[4] 5259[8] 6461a[9] 8099[2] 8495[8]

Bushwise (IRE) *Milton Bradley* a50 61
3 b f Bushranger(IRE) Validate (Alhaarth (IRE))
820[6] 1497[3] (1829) (2143) 2559[9] 2824[3] 3513[5] 4085[10] 6852[8] 7302[10] 7489[4] 8383[3] 8542[13]

Buskin River (IRE) *Richard Hannon* 65
2 b c Kodiac Miss Smilla (Red Ransom (USA))
2649[8] 3529[9] 4075[11] 4825[16] 6191[2]

Bussa *S J Mahon* a56 54
8 b g Iceman Maid To Dance (Pyramus (USA))
6464a[10]

Busta Nellie *Simon Dow* a37 34
3 ch f Pastoral Pursuits Vezere (USA) (Point Given (USA))
87[11]

Busy Bimbo (IRE) *John Murray* a30 65
7 b m Red Clubs(IRE) Unfortunate (Komaite (USA))
4834[2] 5110[4] 5582[10] 8390[12]

Busy Earning (FR) *Niels Petersen* a24
3 b c Canford Cliffs(IRE) Diamond Star (IRE) (Daylami (IRE))
539a[7]

Busy Street *Alan Swinbank* a80 84
4 b g Champs Elysees Allegro Viva (USA) (Distant View (USA))
890[2] 1586[2] 2163[7] 2663[4] 5434[7] 7359[11]

Buteo Bai (IRE) *Lucy Wadham* a29 63
3 b f Big Bad Bob(IRE) Spring Will Come (IRE) (Desert Prince (IRE))
4740[3] 5086[5] 5672[4] (6185) 6406[9]

Buthelezi (USA) *Brian Ellison* a72 75
8 b g Dynaformer(USA) Ntombi (USA) (Quiet American (USA))
8123[7] 8479[8]

Butterflies (IRE) *A P O'Brien* 95
2 b f Galileo(IRE) Mariah's Storm (USA) (Rahy (USA))
5937a[3] 7193a[5] 7707a[5]

Button Down *Josie Carroll* a83 108
5 b m Oasis Dream Modesta (IRE) (Sadler's Wells (USA))
6600a[7]

Button Up (IRE) *Sir Michael Stoute* a61
2 b f So You Think(NZ) Star Ruby (IRE) (Rock Of Gibraltar (IRE))
8246[6] ◆

Buxted Dream (USA) *Luca Cumani* a61
2 gr c Dream Ahead(USA) America Nova (FR) (Verglas (IRE))
3315[7]

Buyer Beware (IRE) *Patrick Holmes* a43 88
4 br g Big Bad Bob(IRE) Adoring (IRE) (One Cool Cat (USA))
6794[8]

Buying Trouble (USA) *David Evans* a89 106
3 b f Hat Trick(JPN) Lotus Sutra (USA) (Kingmambo (USA))
(432) ◆ (612) ◆ 1115[2] 1623[10] 2242[3] 2736[6] 2875[2] 3392[3] 4540a[2] 5880[2]

Buzz (FR) *Hughie Morrison* a78 69
2 gr c Motivator Tiysha (IRE) (Araafa (IRE))
7770[5] (8355)

Buzz Boy (ITY) *Adrian Paul Keatley* a33 55
3 ch g Buzzword Echad (IRE) (Kris Kin (USA))
4290[7] 5222[5] (7746)

Buzz Lightyere *Michael Attwater* a61 63
3 b g Royal Applause Lady Gloria (Diktat)
1931[12] 2293[4] ◆ 2828[2] 3256[6] 4267[6] 5720[9] 6187[7] 7282[9] 7464[13]

Buzzy (GER) *Guido Forster* 76
3 b c Mamool(IRE) Best Tune (King's Best (USA))
4186a[9] 6610a[11]

Bybrook *David Simcock* 79
3 b f Dubawi(IRE) Diary (IRE) (Green Desert (USA))
6135[3] 6617[3] 7627[2]

Bygones For Coins (IRE) *Kenny Johnson* a15 26
8 ch m Danroad(AUS) Reservation (IRE) (Common Grounds)
2916[10]

Byrd In Hand (IRE) *John Bridger* a55 57
9 b g Fasliyev(USA) Military Tune (IRE) (Nashwan (USA))
1899[5] 2323[13] 2872[4]

Byres Road *Mark Johnston* a85 84
3 ch g Pivotal Croeso Cariad (Most Welcome)
40[2] 219[3] (361) 1220[5] 1446[2] 1571[4] 2237[7] 8356[6] (8590)

By Rights *Tony Carroll* a73 74
5 b m Byron Legend House (FR) (Grand Lodge (USA))
(146) 3397[8] 3892[2]

Byron Beauty (IRE) *H Rogers* a42 66
8 b m Byron Latin Beauty (IRE) (Sadler's Wells (USA))
4813a[15]

Byron Blue (IRE) *Brian Barr* a44 43
7 br g Dylan Thomas(IRE) High Society (IRE) (Key Of Luck (USA))
6022[7]

Byronegetonefree *Stuart Coltherd* a55 46
5 b g Byron Lefty's Dollbaby (USA) (Brocco (USA))
2089[4] 2813[8] (2916) 3704[7] 4645[10] 6102[5] (6738) 6920[6]

Byron Flyer *Ian Williams* a76 82
5 b g Byron Nursling (IRE) (Kahyasi)
(259) ◆ 6804[4]

By The Law *Tim Easterby* 67
3 b g New Approach(IRE) Walk On Bye (IRE) (Danehill Dancer (IRE))
4521[5] 4845[3] 5388[8]

By The Moon (USA) *Michelle Nevin* a110
4 bb m Indian Charlie(USA) By The Light (USA) (Malibu Moon (USA))
7836a[5]

Byzantium *Edward Lynam* a69 101
4 ch m Dutch Art Spring Green (Bahamian Bounty)
2042[10] 2923a[7] 4540a[6] 5816a[7] 7191a[5] 7706a[12]

Cabal *Geoffrey Harker* a72 77
9 br m Kyllachy Secret Flame (Machiavellian (USA))
1125[9] 1412[6] 1926[6] 2655[4] 2918[2] 3214[7] 3366[2] 3952[5] (4240) 4429[4] 4986[4] 5180[6] 5521[7] 5973[5] 6453[10]

Cabbies Lou *Richard Ford* a13 68
4 b m Sakhee's Secret Regal Run (USA) (Deputy Minister (CAN))
388[10]

Cabuchon (GER) *David Evans* a60 55
9 b g Fantastic Light(USA) Catella (GER) (Generous (IRE))
2326[8]

Caccini (FR) *Adam Wyrzyk* 104
3 b c American Post Courances (FR) (Simon Du Desert (FR))
5454a[5]

Cachao *A bin Harmash* a77
3 br c New Approach(IRE) Mambo Halo (USA) (Southern Halo (USA))
153[2] 377[2] 8576a[3]

Cacica *George Scott* a75 68
3 b f Cacique(IRE) Moonlight Mystery (Pivotal)
2968[3] 3810[4] 4301[4] 5529[2] 6334[3] (6965) 7205[5]

Cadeau Magnifique *Richard Fahey* a79 74
4 b g Dutch Art Cadeau Speciale (Cadeaux Genereux)
5579[5] 7159[17] 7500[13] 7857[2] ◆ 8011[2] ◆ 8343[2] 8498[2]

Cadeaux Boxer *Martin Smith* 77
3 ch g Major Cadeaux Ashantiana (Ashkalani (IRE))
2175^{9} 3104^{5} 3572^{2} ◆ 4149^{8} 4639^{5} 7671^{16}

Cadeaux Pearl *Scott Dixon* a59 57
8 b g Acclamation Anneliina (Cadeaux Genereux)
25^{5} 178^{5} 430^{4} 681^{5} 936^{4} 1047^{9} 2872^{10} 4516^{7} 7145^{6} 7645^{6}

Cadela Rica *Gay Kelleway* a27 30
2 b f Compton Place Millennium Heiress (Singspiel (IRE))
3073^{9} 4064^{10} 6421^{8}

Cadland Lad (IRE) *John Ryan* a56 52
3 b g Lilbourne Lad(IRE) Hari's Gift (IRE) (Ivan Denisovich (IRE))
1574^{3} 2609^{2} 3070^{5} 3489^{4} 4279^{8} 4518^{6} 5338^{5} 5636^{3} 5769^{3} 6249^{4} 6902^{2} 7201^{3} 7488^{4} 7645^{2} 7815^{3} (8013) 8079^{7} 8146^{3}

Cadmium *Micky Hammond* a52 71
5 b m Major Cadeaux Miss Mirasol (Sheikh Albadou)
1247^{3} 1884^{8} 3551^{5} 3952^{13} 4335^{7} 6569^{8} 7097^{10} 7500^{11} 7754^{8}

Caerleon Kate *Rod Millman* a43 45
4 ch m Medicean Towaahi (IRE) (Caerleon (USA))
1748^{10} 2634^{6} 3492^{4}

Caesaria (IRE) *N Branchu* a52 87
6 br g Hannouma(IRE) Sweet Shop (Grand Lodge (USA))
(512a)

Caeser The Gaeser (IRE) *Nigel Tinkler* a73 70
4 b g Captain Rio Alchimie (IRE) (Sri Pekan (USA))
2416^{8} 2974^{9} 3478^{12} 3599^{7} 4516^{3} 4771^{2} 5068^{8} (5535) 5887^{8} 6451^{2} (6685) 7059^{3} 7663^{4} (7852)

Cafe Nervosa (IRE) *James Unett* a5
3 b f Excellent Art Namoos (USA) (Sahm (USA))
384^{12}

Cafe Royal (GER) *Carina Fey* a83 96
5 ch g Nicaron(GER) Cariera (GER) (Macanal (USA))
8042a^{3}

Cafoo (IRE) *Ed Dunlop* a57
3 ch c Makfi Kournikova (SAF) (Sportsworld (USA))
1499^{5} 1961^{5}

Caged Lightning (IRE) *Steve Gollings* a82 81
6 b g Haatef(USA) Rainbow Melody (IRE) (Rainbows For Life (CAN))
1760^{7}

Cahala Dancer (IRE) *Adam West* a40 47
8 ch m Elnadim(USA) Ranma (In The Wings)
7417^{9} 7890^{6}

Cahar Fad (IRE) *Steph Hollinshead* a62 40
4 b g Bushranger(IRE) Tarbiyah (Singspiel (IRE))
39^{4} (107) 569^{2} 862^{6} 4052^{7} 4456^{15} 5130^{8} 5610^{5} 6857^{3} 7369^{7} 7516^{3} 8125^{5} 8527^{7}

Cahill (IRE) *Ronald Harris* a86 80
4 b g Lawman(FR) Malaspina (IRE) (Whipper (USA))
66^{4} 588a^{9}

Cailin Mor (IRE) *M Halford* a81 95
4 b m Lope De Vega(IRE) Capall An Ibre (IRE) (Traditionally (USA))
1018a^{17} 4747a^{9} 4921a^{4} 5564a^{3} 5941a^{23} 6983a^{10}

Cainhoe Star *Anthony Carson* a56
3 ch g Pivotal Celeste (Green Desert (USA))
952^{8} 1091^{9} 1337^{9}

Cairdiuil (IRE) *I Madden* a62 78
10 b g Bachelor Duke(USA) Lilabelle (IRE) (Lil's Boy (USA))
4899a^{2}

Cai Shen (IRE) *Grace Harris* a47 48
8 ch g Iffraaj Collada (IRE) (Desert Prince (IRE))
121^{6} 244^{9}

Caitie (IRE) *Paul Cole* a59 76
3 b f Canford Cliffs(IRE) The Shrew (Dansili)
1572^{9} 2373^{6} (2642) 3353^{2} 4085^{2} 4365^{2} 4835^{3} 6831^{3} 7415^{8}

Caius College Girl (IRE) *Natalie Lloyd-Beavis* a74 66
4 b m Royal Applause Galeaza (Galileo (IRE))
558^{5} 6442^{8} 7430^{8} 7817^{11} 8156^{10} 8528^{5}

Cajmere *Tom Dascombe* a77 70
2 b g Kyllachy Percolator (Kheleyf (USA))
2648^{3} 3167^{7} 3633^{3} 6139^{6} 6743^{5} 7091^{8} 8136^{4} (8313)

Cajoled (FR) *George Scott* a74 81
3 b f High Chaparral(IRE) Dolphina (USA) (Kingmambo (USA))
(2044) ◆ 2394^{9} 3824^{5}

Calantha (FR) *A Wohler* 93
3 gr f Literato(FR) Caucasienne (FR) (Galileo (IRE))
6824a^{5}

Calare (IRE) *Charlie Appleby* 98
2 ch f Dubawi(IRE) Calando (USA) (Storm Cat (USA))
(3186) 4560^{2} 4902a^{2} 5703a^{7} (7193a)

Calarules *Tim Easterby* a21 60
3 gr g Aussie Rules(USA) Ailincala (IRE) (Pursuit Of Love)
5716^{6} 6014^{4} 6452^{5} 7008^{7} 7582^{8} 7992^{11}

Calder Prince (IRE) *Tom Dascombe* a94 103
3 gr g Dark Angel(IRE) Flame Of Ireland (IRE) (Fasliyev (USA))
185a^{3} 536a^{6} 807a^{7} (2477) 2870^{8} 3269^{15} 4136^{4} 4665^{3} 4867^{11} 6547^{7} 7213^{6}

Caledonia Duchess *Jo Hughes* a70 41
3 b f Dutch Art Granuaile O'Malley (IRE) (Mark Of Esteem (IRE))
1723^{8} 2004^{5} 3989^{6} 4641^{7} 5330^{9} 6960^{3} 7725^{4} 8205^{5}

Caledonia Laird *Jo Hughes* a71 70
5 b g Firebreak Granuaile O'Malley (IRE) (Mark Of Esteem (IRE))
201^{8} (590) 681^{2} 900^{6} 1269^{3} 2006^{5} 3125^{5} 3514^{5} 4640^{3} ◆ 5386^{3} 5887^{15} 6872^{5} 7368^{5} 7755^{4} 8207^{3} ◆

Caledonian Gold *Paul D'Arcy* a48 44
3 b f Acclamation Moonlight Rhapsody (IRE) (Danehill Dancer (IRE))
7310^{9} 7442^{7}

Calgary Cat (CAN) *Kevin Attard* a108 109
6 ch g Cowtown Cat(USA) Big Sink Star (USA) (A.P. Indy (USA))
6400a^{4} (7403a) 7833a^{4}

Calibration (IRE) *Martyn Meade* 85
2 b c Excelebration(IRE) Dance Troupe (Rainbow Quest (USA))
4580^{3} 5600^{2} 6486^{2} 7016^{2} ◆

California (IRE) *John Gosden* a95 105
4 b m Azamour(IRE) Maskaya (IRE) (Machiavellian (USA))
1855^{7} 2797^{6} (4078) (4800) 6259^{3} 7351^{12}

California Chrome (USA) *Art Sherman* a135 116
5 ch h Lucky Pulpit(USA) Love The Chase (USA) (Not For Love (USA))
(722a) (1108a) 7838a^{2}

Californiadreaming (IRE) *A P O'Brien* a55 80
3 b f Fastnet Rock(AUS) Descant (USA) (Nureyev (USA))
2509a^{8} 3539a^{9} 4218a^{13} 4540a^{10}

California Lad *Harry Dunlop* a78 76
3 b g Aussie Rules(USA) Medaille D'Or (With Approval (CAN))
778^{2} 1000^{3} 2098^{3} 3145^{6} 4213^{2} (5163) 6032^{5} 7246^{6}

California Tee *Matthieu Palussiere* 80
2 ch f Kheleyf(USA) Quintrell (Royal Applause)
3507a^{3} 4750a^{5} 5497a^{5} 6068a^{7}

California Whip (USA) *Richard Hannon* 104
3 ch c Giant's Causeway(USA) Canterbury Lace (USA) (Danehill (USA))
1603^{3} 2161^{2} 2473^{2} ◆ 3299^{3}

Callaghan (GER) *Tom Gretton* a38 60
3 b g Cacique(IRE) Cent Cheveux Blanc (GER) (Pentire)
2652^{13}

Callender (IRE) *M Halford* a95 97
2 b c Exceed And Excel(AUS) Much Faster (IRE) (Fasliyev (USA))
3247^{5} 7520a^{7}

Callendula *Clive Cox* a88 81
4 ch m Halling(USA) Oatey (Master Willie)
6267^{5} 7053^{3} 7512^{9} 7980^{5} 8162^{8}

Calling Out (FR) *David Simcock* a103 107
5 bb g Martaline Exit The Straight (IRE) (Exit To Nowhere (USA))
372a^{7} 628a^{11} 1198^{2} 1425^{9} 7978^{7}

Calliope *Kenneth Slack* a60 70
3 b f Poet's Voice Costa Brava (IRE) (Sadler's Wells (USA))
2291^{8} 3033^{10} 4159^{8} (5481) 6006^{3}

Call Me Crockett (IRE) *Noel Wilson* a66 52
4 ch g Intense Focus(USA) Forest Storm (USA) (Woodman (USA))
1695^{7} 2092^{7} 2528^{6} 3153^{6} 3476^{7} 3943^{7} 4144^{3} 4456^{11} 5576^{3} 5835^{6} 6478^{2} 7145^{11} 7794^{12}

Call Me Grumpy (IRE) *Roger Varian* a59 66
2 b g Holy Roman Emperor(IRE) Miss Rochester (IRE) (Montjeu (IRE))
7064^{5} 7432^{6} 7664^{4}

Call Out Loud *Michael Appleby* a56 72
4 b g Aqlaam Winner's Call (Indian Ridge)
1317^{6} (1596) 1899^{6} 3214^{6} 3599^{4} 4089^{3} 4443^{4} 8241^{8}

Call Provision (USA) *Chad C Brown* 98
3 ch g Lemon Drop Kid(USA) Run In (USA) (Dynaformer (USA))
4173a^{13}

Call To War (USA) *D Selvaratnam* a39
2 ch c High Cotton(USA) All Saint's Day (USA) (Gold Case (USA))
8575a^{8}

Caltra Colleen *Gay Kelleway* a67 71
4 b m Sixties Icon Mistic Magic (IRE) (Orpen (USA))
14^{5} 158^{4}

Calvados Spirit *William Muir* a81 85
3 b g Invincible Spirit(IRE) Putois Peace (Pivotal)
2790^{3} 3412^{4} 4358^{5} (5743) 6529^{11} 7702^{11}

Calvinist *Brian Meehan* 95
3 b g Holy Roman Emperor(IRE) Sharp Relief (IRE) (Galileo (IRE))
6484^{6} (7123) ◆

Calypso Choir *Sylvester Kirk* a85 86
3 ch f Bahamian Bounty Heavenly Song (IRE) (Oratorio (IRE))
1453^{8} 1865^{6} 3105^{2} 4398^{12} 5744^{9} 6946^{10} 7864^{2} 8032^{7} 8280^{3} ◆ 8463^{3}

Calypso Delegator (IRE) *Micky Hammond* 53
3 b g Lilbourne Lad(IRE) Amber Nectar (IRE) (Barathea (IRE))
2271^{5} 2831^{6} 3215^{5} 3715^{8} 4301^{3} 4681^{4} 6004^{6} 7044^{12}

Camakasi (IRE) *Ali Stronge* a79 62
5 b g Camacho Innocence (Unfuwain (USA))
3957^{7} 4520^{5} 7457^{8} 7973^{6} 8142^{4} 8367^{4}

Camanche Grey (IRE) *Ben Haslam* a51 54
5 gr g Camacho Sense Of Greeting (IRE) (Key Of Luck (USA))
293^{8} 732^{4} 1164^{7} 1709^{8} 4236^{4} 6745^{8}

Camaradorie (IRE) *Lydia Pearce* a49 48
2 ch f Camacho Lady Duxyana (Most Welcome)
7466^{5} 8277^{6}

Camargue *Mark Johnston* a77 83
2 b f Invincible Spirit(IRE) Chaquiras (USA) (Seeking The Gold (USA))
1437^{3} ◆ 1719^{2} (1988) 3270^{14} 4091^{4} 4503^{2} 4884^{5} 5638^{7} 5998^{4} 6954^{10} 7258^{7}

Camaypaucha (FR) *M Boutin* a49 46
2 ch f Spirit One(FR) Vassileva (FR) (Lomitas)
7927a^{13}

Cambodia (IRE) *Chris Wall* a77 76
3 ch g Fast Company(IRE) Remarkable Story (Mark Of Esteem (IRE))
(2109) 2654^{6} 8319^{8}

Cambridge Favorite *Mrs Ilka Gansera-Leveque* a11 60
2 b f Aussie Rules(USA) Sanctum (Medicean)
3074^{9} 5196^{5} 5846^{10} 6681^{15} 8276^{13}

Camdora (IRE) *Jamie Osborne* a67 57
4 b m Arcano(IRE) Crimphill (IRE) (Sadler's Wells (USA))
174^{2} ◆ (270) ◆ (528) 617^{2} 859^{4} 969^{4} 3743^{5} 5270^{7} 5807^{8} 7513^{7} 7693^{2} 8094^{6} 8358^{6}

Camelot Kitten (USA) *Chad C Brown* 108
3 b c Kitten's Joy(USA) Celestial Woods (USA) (Forestry (USA))
4173a^{4}

Cameraman *Zuhair Mohsen* 91
3 b g Rail Link Photographic (Oasis Dream)
8573a^{7}

Camerone (IRE) *Ralph Beckett* 70
2 b f Galileo(IRE) Louvain (IRE) (Sinndar (IRE))
6480^{4} ◆ (7034) ◆

Caminel (IRE) *Keith Henry Clarke* a66 41
5 b m Kyllachy Jalissa (Mister Baileys)
2229a^{11}

Camino *Henry Spiller* a42 42
3 b f Equiano(FR) Juncea (Elnadim (USA))
5078^{7} 5725^{7} 6587^{6} 7427^{10}

Camlann (IRE) *John Joseph Hanlon* 68
5 b g Cape Cross(IRE) Elle Galante (GER) (Galileo (IRE))
4813a^{3}

Camp Creek (CAN) *Rachel Halden* 100
3 rg g Dunkirk(USA) Go Go Neigh (CAN) (Storm Boot (USA))
6600a^{6}

Campillo (FR) *J Phelippon* a91 98
7 b g Lando(GER) Milisa (FR) (Anabaa (USA))
7292a^{5}

Camprock (FR) *Mme Pia Brandt* a71 106
3 b f Myboycharlie(IRE) Camporese (IRE) (Sadler's Wells (USA))
(1541a) 2316a^{2} 3452a^{11}

Canadian Diamond (IRE) *Richard Rowe* a72 67
9 ch g Halling(USA) Six Nations (USA) (Danzig (USA))
7614^{13} (8359)

Canadian Royal *Stuart Williams* a53
2 b g Royal Applause Emily Carr (IRE) (Teofilo (IRE))
7975^{10} 8066^{7}

Canary Row (IRE) *P J Prendergast* 95
6 b g Holy Roman Emperor(IRE) Fresh Mint (IRE) (Sadler's Wells (USA))
4921a^{6} 5941a^{8} 6984a^{4}

Canberra Cliffs (IRE) *Don Cantillon* a62 70
3 b f Canford Cliffs(IRE) Gloved Hand (Royal Applause)
8175^{8} 8454^{5}

Can Can Dream *Olly Williams* 50
2 b f Stimulation(IRE) Can Can Dancer (Fantastic Light (USA))
3290^{12} 4040^{7} 5272^{10} 5377^{9} 5861^{7} 6678^{14}

Cancan Katy *Tom Dascombe* a23 81
3 b f Canford Cliffs(IRE) Katy Nowaitee (Komaite (USA))
1597^{8} 2303^{6} 3899^{5}

Cancellara *Michael Attwater* a36
4 b g Kheleyf(USA) Royal Ivy (Mujtahid (USA))
2005^{12}

Cancilla (FR) *P Sogorb* a75 63
2 b f Wootton Bassett Diva Aggressiva (Tobougg (IRE))
6015a^{4}

Candarliya (FR) *A De Royer-Dupre* 115
4 gr m Dalakhani(IRE) Candara (FR) (Barathea (IRE))
1688a^{2} 2727a^{3} (4333a) 5692a^{2} 6393a^{5} 7569a^{13}

Candelisa (IRE) *Jedd O'Keeffe* a94 100
3 br c Dream Ahead(USA) Vasilia (Dansili)
1243^{2} 1851^{7} 2871^{5} 3566^{5} 4644^{3} 5616^{3} 6225^{7}

Candelita *Clare Ellam* a23 23
9 b m Trade Fair Gramada (IRE) (Cape Cross (IRE))
5459a^{4} 6020^{9}

Candesta (USA) *Julia Feilden* a68 54
6 b g First Defence(USA) Wandesta (Nashwan (USA))
247^{6} 609^{9} 776^{3} 1578^{4} 2323^{4} 2899^{7} (6478) 6826^{12} (7426) 7736^{6} 8085^{2} (8458)

Candide (FR) *A Fabre* 104
3 b c Turtle Bowl(IRE) Circus Key (IRE) (Key Of Luck (USA))
1580a^{9} 5948a^{8}

Candy Banter (USA) *Kevin Ryan* a46 50
3 b f Distorted Humor(USA) Sweet Hope (USA) (Lemon Drop Kid (USA))
327^{5}

Candy Boy (USA) *Doug Watson* a112
5 b h Candy Ride(ARG) She's An Eleven (USA) (In Excess I (IRE))
1108a^{7}

Candyco *F-H Graffard* a66
2 b f Equiano(FR) Candycakes (IRE) (Cape Cross (IRE))
4187a^{3}

Candy Express *Clive Mulhall* 46
3 b f Fast Company(IRE) Sugar Mountain (IRE) (Lomitas)
3249^{5} 7856^{6}

Candy Real (USA) *Gianluca Bietolini* a88
3 ch c Candy Ride(ARG) Beauty O' Gwaun (IRE) (Rainbow Quest (USA))
1240a^{4}

Canessar (FR) *M Delzangles* 94
3 b c Kendargent(FR) Candara (FR) (Barathea (IRE))
3450a^{4}

Canford Bay (IRE) *Michael Dods* 49
2 b c Canford Cliffs(IRE) Maundays Bay (IRE) (Invincible Spirit (IRE))
4371^{5} ◆

Canford Belle *Grant Tuer* a64 58
3 b f Canford Cliffs(IRE) Ballyea (IRE) (Acclamation)
1420^{7} 1745^{5} 2143^{6} 2964^{3} 3734^{6} 3786^{4} 4647^{11} 5355^{5} 5803^{5} 6569^{2} 7463^{4} 7912^{2} 8146^{11} 8289^{3} 8401^{2} 8589^{9}

Canford Crossing (IRE) *David Nicholls* a73 65
3 b g Canford Cliffs(IRE) Smartest (IRE) (Exceed And Excel (AUS))
287^{8} 582^{5} 746^{5} 1584^{9} 2015^{7} 2425^{7}

Canford Kilbey (IRE) *Michael Easterby* a47 56
3 b f Canford Cliffs(IRE) Sweet Namibia (IRE) (Namid)
1126^{8} 1325^{7} 4425^{10} 4705^{4} 5355^{14} 5972^{10}

Canford Lilli (IRE) *Eve Johnson Houghton* a57 76
3 b f Canford Cliffs(IRE) Aine (IRE) (Danehill Dancer (IRE))
1246^{8} 3720^{8} 5168^{6} 5525^{7} 6251^{2} 6649^{6} 7011^{7}

Canford Thompson *Mark Walford* a71 52
3 b g Canford Cliffs(IRE) Sadie Thompson (IRE) (King's Best (USA))
275^{7} 2306^{9} 4973^{7} 5365^{7} 7992^{2} 8410^{3}

Canizay (IRE) *Ronald Harris*
2 ch g Tagula(IRE) Baltic Dip (IRE) (Benny The Dip (USA))
5952^{7}

Canndal (FR) *Ahmed Kobeissi* 105
4 b h Medicean Clodovina (IRE) (Rock Of Gibraltar (IRE))
757a^{8}

Cannock Chase (USA) *Sir Michael Stoute* a72 120
5 b h Lemon Drop Kid(USA) Lynnwood Chase (USA) (Horse Chestnut (SAF))
(1973)

Canny Kool *Brian Ellison* 103
4 b g Kheleyf(USA) Kool Acclaim (Royal Applause)
1969^{3} 2438^{6} 3250^{7}

Canny Style *Kevin Ryan* a61 75
3 b f Canford Cliffs(IRE) Stylish One (IRE) (Invincible Spirit (IRE))
1111^{7} 1448^{7} 1725^{4} 2428^{5} 2864^{8} 3289^{6} 4233^{4} 4872^{3} 5513^{7} (6029) (6620) (7249)

Canonbury (IRE) *Sir Michael Stoute* a78 78
3 bb f Oasis Dream Islington (IRE) (Sadler's Wells (USA))
4978^{3} 6019^{3} (6278)

Cantankerous *Daniel Mark Loughnane* a50 47
5 b g Myboycharlie(IRE) Akhira (Emperor Jones (USA))
731^{3} 1169^{8} 1182^{4} 1322^{7} 1649^{4}

Can't Change It (IRE) *David Simcock* a44 102
5 gr g Verglas(IRE) All Tied Up (IRE) (Desert Prince (IRE))
(2391) 3566^{12} 4823^{12} 5871^{13} (6331) 7241^{4}

Can't Do Spells *Tim Easterby* 66
2 b g Camacho Magic Myth (IRE) (Revoque (IRE))
4890^{5} 5536^{4} 7122^{9}

Canterbury Quad (FR) *Henry Spiller* 73
2 b f Motivator Coiffure (King's Best (USA))
6077^{4} 7346a^{3}

Canyari (IRE) *Richard Fahey* a73 95
5 b g Dandy Man(IRE) Morna's Fan (FR) (Lear Fan (USA))
1848^{8} 2158^{8} 2476^{11} 2679^{10} 3168^{19} 5161^{6} 6718^{9} 7415^{9} (Dead)

Caointiorn (FR) *S Wattel* a102 105
5 b m Stormy River(FR) Champagnepouryoyo (USA) (Bering)
3938a^{3} 5948a^{2} 6693a^{7} 8563a^{2}

Cap Canaille (USA) *Jeremy Noseda* a71 62
3 br c Giant's Causeway(USA) Cassis (USA) (Red Ransom (USA))
4458^{5} 5681^{4}

Capchop (FR) *P Sogorb* 101
2 b c Captain Chop(FR) Gooseley Lane (Pyramus (USA))
7721a^{U} 8062a^{9}

Cape Baba *Chris Wall* a44 39
2 b c Cape Cross(IRE) Eclaircie (IRE) (Thunder Gulch (USA))
6590^{11} 7495^{11}

Cape Banjo (USA) *Ralph Beckett* a80 85
3 ch g Cape Blanco(IRE) Magic Of Love (Magic Ring (IRE))
1091^{6} 1828^{9} 2321^{2} 3110^{7} 3996^{2} 4710^{2} 5198^{4} 6301^{2} 6805^{4} (7780)

Cape Byron *Roger Varian* 86
2 ch c Shamardal(USA) Reem Three (Mark Of Esteem (IRE))
7243^{2} (7468)

Cape Cova (IRE) *John Gosden* a83 105
3 b g Cape Cross(IRE) Sina Cova (IRE) (Barathea (IRE))
2929^{6} 3359^{2} 3845^{3} (4265) (4859) 7123^{4} ◆ (7498) 7824^{3}

Cape Cruiser (USA) *Ralph Beckett* a62 48
2 ch g Cape Blanco(IRE) Skip A Dare (USA) (Skip Away (USA))
7012^{8} 7865^{5} 8355^{8}

Cape Crusader (IRE) *Michael Dods* a20 44
3 br g Kheleyf(USA) Naddwah (Pivotal)
1673^{10} 3603^{4} 4445^{6} 5069^{11} 6106^{12}

Cape Crystal (IRE) *Sir Mark Prescott Bt* a83 59
3 b f Cape Cross(IRE) Lady Rockfield (IRE) (Rock Of Gibraltar (IRE))
2108^{7} 2784^{4} 3141^{10} (5529) (5610) 5841^{3} (6701)

Cape Dignity (IRE) *Hugo Palmer* a70
3 b c Teofilo(IRE) Eclaircie (IRE) (Thunder Gulch (USA))
7597^{3} 7904^{4}

Cape Discovery *Richard Hughes* a89 89
4 ch g Shamardal(USA) Kotsi (IRE) (Nayef (USA))
(1933) (2313) 8447^{3}

Cape Falcone *James Tate* a63 61
2 b f Camacho Asinara (GER) (Big Shuffle (USA))
4209^{4} 4564^{5} 5242^{8} 5809^{5}

Cape Hideaway *Mark Walford* 66
4 b g Mount Nelson Amiata (Pennekamp (USA))
1201^{8} 1675^{5} 2233^{5} 2745^{3} 3418^{2} 4194^{4} 7592^{2}

Cape Icon *Clive Cox* a93 72
5 b g Mount Nelson Cape Merino (Clantime)
(2378) 3303^{4} 4625^{14} 5156^{13} 6126^{9}

Capelena *Miss Joey Ellis* a59 58
5 br m Cape Cross(IRE) Roslea Lady (IRE) (Alhaarth (IRE))
55^{3} 348^{10} 3620^{5} 4200^{4} 5739^{P}

Capelita *Michael Appleby* a91 76
5 b m Cape Cross(IRE) Zamhrear (Singspiel (IRE))
503[6] 632[4] 774[3] 1041[3] 1418[4] 1898[8]

Cape Love (USA) *David O'Meara* 64
3 ch g Cape Blanco(IRE) Matroshka (IRE) (Red Ransom (USA))
1446[4] 2269[7] 5919[5]

Cape Of Eagles (USA) *Fawzi Abdulla Nass* a81 68
2 b c Cape Blanco(IRE) Aj's Gal (USA) (Monashee Mountain (USA))
8574a[4]

Cape Of Glory (IRE) *Keith Dalgleish* a91 91
3 br c Cape Cross(IRE) Stairway To Glory (IRE) (Kalanisi (IRE))
(29) (182) 1971[6] 4153[6] 5520[2] 5837[12] 6142[4]

Cape Peninsular *James Tate* a85 65
3 b f Cape Cross(IRE) Najam (Singspiel (IRE))
1063[3] ◆ 1989[10] 3990[3] 6423[2] 6661[2]

Cape Speed (FR) *Mark Johnston* a95 72
3 b g Cape Cross(IRE) At A Great Rate (USA) (Arch (USA))
(315) (434) 1071[9] 1438[9] 5437[4] 6126[11] 6372[6] 6803[10]

Cape Spirit (IRE) *Andrew Balding* a56 61
4 b m Cape Cross(IRE) Fearless Spirit (USA) (Spinning World (USA))
1735[13] 2436[4] 3031[3] 3498[14] 4082[2] 4499[2] 5106[3] 5777[7] 6022[4] 6315[10]

Capezzano (USA) *Charlie Appleby* a86 76
2 b c Bernardini(USA) Cableknit (USA) (Unbridled's Song (USA))
5615[9] 8391a[2] (8574a)

Capitain Ken (FR) *Gianluca Bietolini* a71
2 gr c Tin Horse(IRE) Landa Vision (FR) (Lando (GER))
7783a[3]

Capital City (IRE) *Saeed bin Suroor* a74
2 b c Acclamation Carioca (IRE) (Rakti)
7908[3]

Capital Gearing *Henry Spiller* a56 69
3 b g Makfi Dicara (GER) (Royal Applause)
1276[8] 1486[8] 2553[4] 3080[11] 6405[10] 7070[3] 7282[6] 8120[6] 8470[3]

Capitano (GER) *J Hirschberger* 106
3 b c Paolini(GER) Carabiola (FR) (Grape Tree Road)
1689a[4] 2711a[8] 5219a[5] 5696a[2] 7028a[2] 7564a[7] 7843a[10]

Capolavoro (FR) *Robert Cowell* a79 73
5 b g Sulamani(IRE) Farnesina (FR) (Anabaa (USA))
(2442) ◆ 3259[2] 3349[3] 4008[4] 5103[7] 6237[2] 6872[2] 7619[8] 8036[2] (8205) 8531[4]

Caponova (IRE) *Tom Dascombe* a66 79
3 b g Bushranger(IRE) Satin Cape (IRE) (Cape Cross (IRE))
1638[12] (2652) (3053) ◆ (3395) 4342[7] 5391[5] 6684[10] 6876[9] 7245[2]

Capo Rosso (IRE) *Tom Dascombe* a101 104
6 b g Red Clubs(IRE) Satin Cape (IRE) (Cape Cross (IRE))
125[4] 560[6] 1001[6] 1344[2] 1797[2] 2033[2] 2684[6] (3055) 3390[12] 4688[7] 5146[7] 5640[11] 6081[9] 6764[10] 7316[5]

Cappadocia (IRE) *John James Feane* a65 63
6 b g Mujadil(USA) Green Vision (IRE) (Green Desert (USA))
(2229a)

Cappananty Con *Dean Ivory* a73 72
2 gr g Zebedee Fairmont (IRE) (Kingmambo (USA))
2235[7] 3032[2] 3647[2] 4015[7] 4394[10] 5072[6] 8027[5] 8229[7] 8494[2]

Cappielow Park *Ali Stronge* a49 31
7 b g Exceed And Excel(AUS) Barakat (Bustino)
1547[11]

Cappy Brown *Alan Bailey* a49 54
3 b g Showcasing Corndavon (USA) (Sheikh Albadou)
105[8] 291[7] 327[8] 1162[12] 1548[10] 2825[6]

Capri (IRE) *A P O'Brien* 113
2 gr c Galileo(IRE) Dialafara (FR) (Anabaa (USA))
(5136a) (6817a) 7722a[3] ◆

Capricious Cantor (IRE) *Ed Dunlop* a79 95
3 b f Cape Cross(IRE) Alleluia (Caerleon (USA))
59[3] (1179) ◆ 2035[4] 3297[11]

Caprior Bere (FR) *K R Burke* a99 91
4 b g Peer Gynt(JPN) Hush Hush (USA) (Horse Chestnut (SAF))
1563[3]

Cap Sizun (FR) *Frau M Muller* 95
7 b g Gold Away(IRE) Texaloula (FR) (Kendor (FR))
664a[6]

Captain America (SWE) *Annike Bye Hansen* a91 96
6 b g Academy Award(IRE) Muja Maiy (IRE) (Mujadil (USA))
3449a[10]

Captain Bob (IRE) *Robert Cowell* 78
5 b g Dark Angel(IRE) Birthday Present (Cadeaux Genereux)
1318[5] ◆ 1530[7] 1887[14] 2253[8] 3159[5] 3414[5] 4079[14] 4726[4] 5039[4] 5744[7] 6453[5] 6878[8] 7506[9]

Captain Carleton (IRE) *Adrian Paul Keatley* a81 78
7 b g Artan(IRE) Mary Carleton (Halling (USA))
6561[16]

Captain Cat (IRE) *Tony Carroll* a112 111
7 bb g Dylan Thomas(IRE) Mother Of Pearl (IRE) (Sadler's Wells (USA))
125[2] 485[4] (692) 1068[5] 1774[6] 3273[20] 3672[2] 6884[9] 7933[12]

Captain Chic (IRE) *Giuseppe Ligas* 67
5 br h Captain Rio Minimal Chic (IRE) (King's Best (USA))
7840a[8]

Captain Colby (USA) *Ed Walker* a85 107
4 b g Bernstein(USA) Escape To Victory (Salse (USA))
3656[13] 4112[4] ◆ 4741[U] 5555[3] ◆ (6327) 7156[20] 7932[11]

Captain Courageous (IRE) *Ed Walker* a64 65
3 b g Canford Cliffs(IRE) Annacloy Pearl (IRE) (Mull Of Kintyre (USA))
6441[9] 7009[7] 7311[6] 7736[2]

Captain Cullen (IRE) *Joseph Anthony Murray* a96 84
7 b g Strategic Prince Missouri (Charnwood Forest (IRE))
4415a[16]

Captain Devious *Grace Harris* a1 50
5 b g Captain Gerrard(IRE) Aspen Ridge (IRE) (Namid)
1556[10] 4289[12] 5007[4] 5378[9] 5628[5] 6363[12] 7362[11] 7596[8]

Captain Dion *Kevin Ryan* a91 88
3 gr g Equiano(FR) Bandanna (Bandmaster (USA))
1789[2] 2695[10] 3775[6] 5412[2] (6718) 7360[11] (8176) 8583[4]

Captain Dunne (IRE) *Tim Easterby* a41 80
11 b g Captain Rio Queen Bodicea (IRE) (Revoque (IRE))
1672[10] 2261[7] 2775[4] 4100[10] 4514[11] 5274[4] 5762[7] 6324[9] 6680[7] 6809[8] 8010[12]

Captain Felix *George Scott* a74 76
4 b g Captain Gerrard(IRE) Sweet Applause (IRE) (Acclamation)
88[6] 215[7] 2672[6] 3030[7] 4020[2] (4427) 4767[2] 5750[4]

Captain George (IRE) *Michael Blake* a60 67
5 b g Bushranger(IRE) High Society Girl (IRE) (Key Of Luck (USA))
(1004) 1182[5] 2370[6] 2634[2] 3999[5] 4995[4] (6022) 6315[2] 7274[8]

Captain Gerald *John Ryan* a56 58
3 b g Captain Gerrard(IRE) My Heart's On Fire (IRE) (Beat Hollow)
1768[8] 2608[9] (2828) 2967[8] 3906[7] 4021[3] 4740[6] 5122[9] 5399[8] 6046[9] 7426[9] 8145[13]

Captain Hawk *Ian Williams* 73
2 b g Acclamation Vintage Gardenia (Selkirk (USA))
1770[5] 2358 [5] 2847[4] 7818[7]

Captain James (FR) *Mrs C Gilbert* a13 51
6 bb g Linngari(IRE) Chopassing (FR) (Indian Rocket)
1519a[2] 2285a[9] 2955a[6] 3381a[5] 5458a[2]

Captain Joey (IRE) *Charles Hills* 43
3 b g Kodiac Archetypal (IRE) (Cape Cross (IRE))
1892[9] 2359 [10] 3146[9]

Captain Joy (IRE) *Tracey Collins* a110 98
7 gr g Dark Angel(IRE) Ardea Brave (IRE) (Chester House (USA))
(1068) 1957a[8] 4326a[7] 5343a[5]

Captain K (IRE) *Gordon Elliott* a50
4 b g Captain Rio Zenana (IRE) (Lucky Guest)
7509[5] 7943[3] 8120[7]

Captain Kendall (IRE) *Harry Chisman* a55 25
7 b g Clodovil(IRE) Queen's Lace (IRE) (King's Best (USA))
607[6] 1147[9] 7896[11]

Captain Lars (SAF) *Derek Shaw* a92 82
6 b g Captain Al(SAF) Polar Charge (Polar Falcon (USA))
(23) 134[4] 360[7] 508[8] 694[9] 938[9] 1215[3] 1530[4] 1634[2] 1869[10] 5507[8] 7054[5] 7461[9] 7687[3] 7851[5] 8040[2] 8280[4] 8380[3] (8495) (8571)

Captain Marmalade (IRE) *Jimmy Fox* a59 60
4 gr g Duke Of Marmalade(IRE) Elisium (Proclamation (IRE))
2579[12] 3233[6] 4058[8] 5259[9] 6066[4] 6241[12] 6826[5] 7211[3] 7642[6]

Captain Morgan (DEN) *Marc Stott* 89
5 b g Diamond Green(FR) Bonny Scotland (IRE) (Redback)
5187a[10] 5950a[10]

Captain Morley *David Simcock* a81 104
5 b g Hernando(FR) Oval Office (Pursuit Of Love)
843a[6] 2486[8] 3436[5] 6884[3]

Captain Navarre *Lydia Pearce* a84 86
4 b g Excellent Art Quantum (IRE) (Alhaarth (IRE))
(1093)

Captain Oats (IRE) *Pam Ford* a42 59
13 b g Bahhare(USA) Adarika (Kings Lake (USA))
4225[4] 4995[6] 5575 [3] 6020[7]

Captain Of Comerce (DEN) *Jan Bjordal* 89
4 b g Captain Rio Zuccini Business (IRE) (Entrepreneur)
5950a[11]

Captain Peacock *William Knight* a79 80
3 b g Champs Elysees Blast Furnace (IRE) (Sadler's Wells (USA))
(1259) ◆ 1860[7] 2615[6] 3493[4] 4273[2] (5232) (5398) 6127[3] 6735[3] 7624[5]

Captain Peaky *Patrick Holmes* a64 65
3 b g Captain Gerrard(IRE) Multi-Sofft (Northern State (USA))
4258[3] ◆ 5731[3] 6567[5] 6907[6] 7327[3]

Captain Power (IRE) *Edward Lynam* a72 95
4 b g Captain Rio Invincible Power (IRE) (Invincible Spirit (IRE))
4415a[5] 6382a[7] 6819a[12] 7475a[5]

Captain Pugwash (IRE) *Henry Spiller* a65
2 b g Sir Prancealot(IRE) Liscoa (IRE) (Foxhound (USA))
7976[5] 8352[5] 8557[8]

Captain Revelation *Tom Dascombe* a90 60
4 ch g Captain Rio Agony Aunt (Formidable I (USA))
24[2] ◆ 581[2] 670[3] (802) (866) 1274[10] 1997[2] 2689[11] 3594[6] 4094[8] 6521[7] 7066[13] 7781[11] (8239) ◆ 8475[3]

Captain Ryan *Geoffrey Deacon* a64 62
5 b g Captain Gerrard(IRE) Ryan's Quest (IRE) (Mukaddamah (USA))
2396[6] (2845) 3994[3] 4506[4] 5007[6] 5928[4] 6363[14] 6832[4] 7038[7] (7913) 8094[5]

Captain Scooby *Richard Guest* a61 57
10 b g Captain Rio Scooby Dooby Do (Atraf)
733[4] 869[7] 963[6] 1138[3] ◆ 1255[2] 1481[4] (1525) 1878[7] (2524) 2919[7] 2974[10] 4931[10] 5069[5] 5717[9] 6522[5] 6615[9] 6909[9] 7092[9] 7145[4] 7445[8] (7489) 7585[8] 7747[6] (7863) 8013[6] 8312[5] 8390[8] (8409) 8596[8]

Captain Sedgwick (IRE) *John Spearing* a24
2 b f Approve(IRE) Alinda (IRE) (Revoque (IRE))
8352[12]

Captain Sue (IRE) *Richard Hughes* a68 67
2 ch f Tamayuz Correct (Oasis Dream)
4938[8] 5549[6] 6035[2] 6421[3] 7605[3]

Captain Swift (IRE) *John Mackie* a66 70
5 br g Captain Rio Grannys Reluctance (IRE) (Anita's Prince)
2296[9] 2836[10] 3641[5] 3844[4] 4934[10] 6730[8] 7895[3] 8238[6] (8540)

Capton *Henry Candy* a64 72
3 b g Cape Cross(IRE) Flavian (Catrail (USA))
5486[2] ◆ 6294[5] 7052[3]

Caracas *Roger Charlton* a65
2 b c Cacique(IRE) Bourbonella (Rainbow Quest (USA))
8354[11] 8537[4] ◆

Caracci Apache (IRE) *Eve Johnson Houghton* 50
6 b g High Chaparral(IRE) Campanella (GER) (Lomitas)
4792[11] 6052[12]

Caramuru (IRE) *Richard Hannon* a70
2 b c Casamento(IRE) Zaynaba (IRE) (Traditionally (USA))
6085[3] 6623[4]

Cara's Request (AUS) *David C Griffiths* a43 50
10 gr g Urgent Request(IRE) Carahill (AUS) (Danehill (USA))
6028[9] 7254[9] 7645[9]

Caravaggio (USA) *A P O'Brien* a94 118
2 gr c Scat Daddy(USA) Mekko Hokte (USA) (Holy Bull (USA))
(2494a) (3243) (5212a)

Carbon Dating (IRE) *John Patrick Shanahan* a76 102
4 b g The Carbon Unit(USA) Advertising Space (IRE) (Galileo (IRE))
3019[2] 4312[4] 4634[3] (4875) 5837[5] 6286[5]

Carbutt's Ridge (IRE) *N Caullery* a58 65
3 br g Alfred Nobel(IRE) Tallassee (Indian Ridge)
(48) 274[3] 597[4] 3285[3] (3579) 3816[5] 7999a[11]

Carcharias (IRE) *Ed de Giles* a56 64
3 b g Kodiac Princess Atoosa (USA) (Gone West (USA))
1768[11] 2610[5] 3319[8] (4289) 4506[7] 5235[2] (5572) 6047[6] 7048[3] (7299)

Card High (IRE) *Wilf Storey* a79 81
6 b g Red Clubs(IRE) Think (FR) (Marchand De Sable (USA))
1250[6] 3659[8] 6134[6] (6566) 7359[4] 7594[5] 7847[6] 8283[11]

Cardinal Palace (IRE) *J A Nash* a80 80
6 b g Papal Bull Heat (King's Best (USA))
4721a[6]

Cardinal Walter (IRE) *Nicky Henderson* a94 95
7 bb g Cape Cross(IRE) Sheer Spirit (IRE) (Caerleon (USA))
2194[4] 3657[7] 5381[10]

Carducci *Richard Hannon* 72
2 b f Poet's Voice Gee Kel (IRE) (Danehill Dancer (IRE))
4397[7] 4856[3] 5324[2] (5922)

Careless Rapture *Mark H Tompkins* a25 14
3 ch f Champs Elysees Cushat Law (IRE) (Montjeu (IRE))
4942[12] 5473[7] 6030[4]

Carenot (IRE) *William Haggas* 83
3 b f Iffraaj Sahara Sky (IRE) (Danehill (USA))
(1589) (5602)

Caribbean Blue (ITY) *G Botti* a91 104
3 b c Storm Mountain(IRE) Certosa Di Pavia (ITY) (Haafhd)
5699a[2]

Caribbean Spring (IRE) *George Margarson* a40 63
3 b g Dark Angel(IRE) Bogini (IRE) (Holy Roman Emperor (IRE))
3823[12] 4570[6] 7444[3] 7747[4] 8156[11]

Carigrad (IRE) *Hugo Palmer* a71
2 b c Excelebration(IRE) Blissful Beat (Beat Hollow)
7648[3] ◆

Carina Mia (USA) *William Mott* a113
3 bb f Malibu Moon(USA) Miss Simpatia (ARG) (Southern Halo (USA))
7836a[9]

Carlovian *Christopher Kellett* a56 51
3 b g Acclamation Mimisel (Selkirk (USA))
1257[5] 1792[4] 2506[10] 3731[11] 3988[9] 4848[4] 5270[3] 5578[2] 5889[11] 6436[4] 7261[7] 8013[11]

Carlton Choice (IRE) *Louis Baudron* a61
2 b g Bushranger(IRE) Choice House (USA) (Chester House (USA))
4124a[8]

Carlton Frankie *Michael Easterby* 76
2 b f Equiano(FR) Valiant Runner (Haafhd)
2219[9] (7122)

Carnachy (IRE) *David Simcock* 109
4 gr m Mastercraftsman(IRE) Market Day (Tobougg (IRE))
(1855) 2241[3] 3888[6] 5691a[9] 6259[9] (7823)

Carnageo (FR) *Richard Fahey* a55 86
3 b g Pivotal Sudarynya (IRE) (Sadler's Wells (USA))
1584[5] ◆ 2341[3] (2801) 3026[4] 3950[5] 4406[3] 5154[4] (5975) 7159[7] (7623)

Carnival King (IRE) *Brian Meehan* a61 93
4 b g Arcano(IRE) Validate (Alhaarth (IRE))
1195[19] 2247[10] 2934[11] 4839[2] 5403[12] (5934) 6529[7] 6915[13]

Carntop *Ralph Beckett* 106
3 b g Dansili Milford Sound (Barathea (IRE))
2036[2] 3337[5] 6752[6]

Carol (IRE) *Ed Dunlop* a60 74
2 b f Acclamation Miss Topsy Turvy (IRE) (Mr Greeley (USA))
4147[5] 4885[5] 6111[2] 6624[5]

Carolinae *Charlie Fellowes* a89 80
4 ch m Makfi You Too (Monsun (GER))
675[3] 2205[4] (3314) (5037) ◆ 5677[6] 6579[2] 6939[15] (7903) 8251[3] 8538[2] ◆

Carosamel (IRE) *D Prod'Homme* 76
3 b f Henrythenavigator(USA) Viking Splendor (USA) (Giant's Causeway (USA))
5385a[13]

Carpe Diem Lady (IRE) *Clive Cox* a57 81
3 b f Acclamation Greenisland (IRE) (Fasliyev (USA))
1572[7] 2178[2] 2431[3] 2968[2] ◆ 4206[7] 4596[2] 5891[3] 6893[2] 7220[3]

Carpet Elegance (IRE) *Thomas J Farrell* a33 46
11 b g Definite Article Tricky Dee (IRE) (Religiously (USA))
5900a[6]

Carpe Vita (IRE) *David O'Meara* a63 78
4 b m Montjeu(IRE) Dance Parade (USA) (Gone West (USA))
2427[3] 2805[4] 4550[7] 5262[5] 7332[8]

Carragold *Antony Brittain* a75 81
10 b g Diktat Shadow Roll (IRE) (Mark Of Esteem (IRE))
1501[8] 1952[6] 2618[14]

Carrera *Mrs A Malzard* a48 48
6 b g Sixties Icon Aileen's Gift (IRE) (Rainbow Quest (USA))
1519a[7] (2080a) 2285a[8] 2955a[4] 3381a[6]

Carrington (FR) *Charlie Appleby* a86 91
3 b g New Approach(IRE) Winning Family (IRE) (Fasliyev (USA))
(1851) 2237[6] 3299[14] 4339[4] 4797[7]

Carr Lane *Michael Easterby*
3 b f Piccolo Leominda (Lion Cavern (USA))
331[10]

Carry Me Home *Charles Hills* a85 90
3 b g Dark Angel(IRE) Toffee Vodka (IRE) (Danehill Dancer (IRE))
466[2] 633[3] (880) 1896[2] 2209[10] 4013[2] 4827[3] (5413) 6709[4]

Carry On Deryck *Saeed bin Suroor* a93 111
4 b g Halling(USA) Mullein (Oasis Dream)
(628a) 3273[9] 4165[12] 4823[6] 6786[2] 7152[2]

Carry On Sydney *Oliver Sherwood* a39 44
6 ch g Notnowcato River Fantasy (USA) (Irish River (FR))
7183[13]

Carson City *Richard Fahey* 74
2 ch c Excelebration(IRE) Humhum (Medicean)
2119[2] 3128[2] 3939[4] 4394[19] 4891[6] 5931[8]

Cartago *John Gosden* a70 99
3 b g Dansili Kilo Alpha (King's Best (USA))
2244[2] ◆ 2892[10] 4108[13]

Cartavio (IRE) *David Lanigan* a66
2 b c Cacique(IRE) Star Cluster (Observatory (USA))
7906[8]

Carthage (IRE) *Brian Ellison* a53 85
5 b g Mastercraftsman(IRE) Pitrizzia (Lando (GER))
2163[20] 3660[5] (4237) 5275[4] 6267[9]

Cartier (IRE) *David Simcock* a66 84
4 b m Montjeu(IRE) Rosamixa (FR) (Linamix (FR))
(2427) 2753[3] 4501[4]

Cartmell Cleave *Stuart Kittow* a90 97
4 br g Pastoral Pursuits There's Two (IRE) (Ashkalani (IRE))
1990[7] 2547[4] 3068[8] 4079[16] (4889) 5648[7] 6112[9] 6627[4] 7186[11]

Cartographer *Martyn Meade* a74
2 b f Henrythenavigator(USA) Right Answer (Lujain (USA))
7867[2] ◆

Cartographic (USA) *David Evans* a67 62
4 b g Henrythenavigator(USA) Good Student (ARG) (Louis Quatorze (USA))
(232) ◆ 348[4] 568[5] 724[2] 982[2] 1347[2] 1501[3] 2461[3] 2872[P] (Dead)

Cartwright *Sir Mark Prescott Bt* a79 91
3 b g High Chaparral(IRE) One So Marvellous (Nashwan (USA))
4882[5] ◆ (5263) (5718) ◆ 6370[3] (6719) (6906)

Carzoff (FR) *Alain Couetil* 97
3 b c Zoffany(IRE) Cartama (Mark Of Esteem (IRE))
6392a[5] 7456a[5]

Casablanca (IRE) *Andrew Balding* a77 77
3 b f Cape Blanco(IRE) Wonderful Town (USA) (Bernstein (USA))
4806[5] 5550[2] 6278[3] 6765[2] 7280[5] 7607[3]

Casaclare (IRE) *Jonjo O'Neill* 54
2 b g Casamento(IRE) Sarah Ann (IRE) (Orpen (USA))
4707[10] 5890[6] 6189[3]

Casado (IRE) *John Best* a55 49
2 b g Casamento(IRE) Sense Of Greeting (IRE) (Key Of Luck (USA))
6570[8] 7125[12] 8063[6]

Cascabel (SPA) *Barbara Valenti* a70 92
7 ch m Dyhim Diamond(IRE) Channel (SPA) (Sharp N' Early (IRE))
5249a[6]

Cascadia (IRE) *Ivan Furtado* a62 46
5 br m Mujadil(USA) Tucum (IRE) (Diktat)
157[7]

Cascading Stars (IRE) *Daniel Mark Loughnane* a77 66
4 b m Tagula(IRE) Subtle Affair (IRE) (Barathea (IRE))
223[4] 415[6] 456[6] 1595[9] 2379[10] 3096[4] 4006[4] ◆ 5068[12] 5393[6] 5953[3] 7096[2] 7654[10] 7889[5] 8156[2] 8351[4]

Case Key *Michael Appleby* a77 80
3 gr g Showcasing Fluttering Rose (Compton Place)
1112[3] 1452[9] 1935[10] 3407[6] (5195) 5408[3] 6492[7] 6810[6] 7308[11]

Cash Control (USA) *Brad H Cox* 103
5 b m Pioneerof The Nile(USA) Hidden Assets (USA) (Mt. Livermore (USA))
7171a[6]

Cash In Mind (FR) *E J O'Neill* a79 93
5 b g Creachadoir(IRE) Dynamic Dream (USA) (Dynaformer (USA))
6178a[7]

Cashla Bay *John Gosden* 82
2 b f Fastnet Rock(AUS) Rose Blossom (Pastoral Pursuits)
7314[2] ◆ (7695)

Cashman (FR) *A Wohler* a72 97
3 ch c Soldier Of Fortune(IRE) Crystals Sky (FR) (Hernando (FR))
3453a[9]

Casila (IRE) *Ann Duffield* a27 66
4 b m High Chaparral(IRE) Miletrian (IRE) (Marju (IRE))
3099[11]

Casina Di Notte (IRE) *Marco Botti* a64 72
2 ch g Casamento(IRE) Nightswimmer (IRE) (Noverre (USA))
5764[10] 7226[2] 7658[6]

Casino (FR) *P Khozian* 82
4 b h Montjeu(IRE) Legerete (USA) (Rahy (USA))
7396a[6]

Caspian Gold (IRE) *Richard Hughes* a37 62
2 ch g Born To Sea(IRE) Eminence Gift (Cadeaux Genereux)
6264[5] 6880[9] 7259[9]

Caspian Prince (IRE) *Roger Fell* a113 113
7 ch g Dylan Thomas(IRE) Crystal Gaze (IRE) (Rainbow Quest (USA))
280a[3] 450a[8] 626a[4] 723a[6] (2895) 4166[5] 4584[13] 5863[10] (6642) (7250) (7520a) 8484[6]

Cassandane (IRE) *Shaun Harris* a32 64
4 br m Jeremy(USA) Princess Atoosa (USA) (Gone West (USA))
1202[10] 2086[6] 4099[11]

Cassie *Ben Pauling* a66
6 b m Refuse To Bend(IRE) Strictly Cool (USA) (Bering)
1063[4] 1184[7]

Cassina De Pomm (ITY) *Stefano Botti* 101
3 b f Pounced(USA) Clever Annie (IRE) (Danehill Dancer (IRE))
2730a[11]

Cassis Sunset (IRE) *Miss Evanna McCutcheon* 36
3 b f Roderic O'Connor(IRE) Sonic Night (IRE) (Night Shift (USA))
1014a[9]

Castanea *Ronald Harris* a49 57
4 ch g Pivotal Invitee (Medicean)
150[6] 255[3] 549[3] 2462[11] 3488[6] 4482[5]

Castellated *Richard Hannon* a74 78
2 b f Teofilo(IRE) Portal (Hernando (FR))
6206[3] 6625[3] (7273)

Casterbridge *Eric Alston* a83 85
4 b g Pastoral Pursuits Damalis (IRE) (Mukaddamah (USA))
1046[4] ◆ 1321[8] 1447[6] 1869[3] 2346[9] 3892[10] 4345[3] 6324[3] 6766[9] 7094[5] 7413[6]

Castilo Del Diablo (IRE) *David Simcock* a100 85
7 br g Teofilo(IRE) Hundred Year Flood (USA) (Giant's Causeway (USA))
194[4] 499[4] 614[5] 861[4] 1089[3] 1209[4] 2377[10] 8529[11]

Castleacre *Hugo Palmer* a80 93
2 ch f Exceed And Excel(AUS) Cloud Castle (In The Wings)
(6925) 7547[4] ◆

Castle Guest (IRE) *M Halford* a65 97
7 b g Rock Of Gibraltar(IRE) Castelletto (Komaite (USA))
4070a[3] 6389a[5]

Castle Harbour *John Gosden* a96 102
3 b c Kyllachy Gypsy Carnival (Trade Fair)
(1397) (2161) 3269[6] 7542[3] ◆ 7933[8]

Castle Hill Cassie (IRE) *Ben Haslam* 60
2 ch f Casamento(IRE) Angel Bright (IRE) (Dark Angel (IRE))
6682[3]

Castlemorris King *Brian Barr* a41 38
8 br g And Beyond(IRE) Brookshield Baby (IRE) (Sadler's Wells (USA))
781[6] 1085[9]

Castlerea Tess *Sarah Hollinshead* a51 49
3 ch f Pastoral Pursuits Zartwyda (IRE) (Mozart (IRE))
104[8] 544[3] 820[8] 1497[8] 2425[4] (2741) 5338[6] 7240[6] 7602[6] 8121[6] 8500[10]

Castle Talbot (IRE) *Richard Hughes* a60 70
4 b g Rock Of Gibraltar(IRE) Louve Sacree (USA) (Seeking The Gold (USA))
717[2] 2144[5] 2566[4] 3031[6] (3258) 3739[3] 4388[2] 4777[3] 5252[5] 5610[6]

Catalan (IRE) *Hughie Morrison* a71 75
3 b f Duke Of Marmalade(IRE) Twice The Ease (Green Desert (USA))
1708[2] ◆ (2307) 3152[5] 4086[6]

Catalinas Diamond (IRE) *Pat Murphy* a61 59
8 b m One Cool Cat(USA) Diamondiferous (USA) (Danzig (USA))
872[5] 1261[6] 1533[10] 1913[5] 2845[5] 3510[9] 3994[14] 4224[8] 5007[5] 5282[2] 5628[2] 6363[16] 6832[6] 7276[8] 8031[6] 8079[5] 8234[3] 8542[11]

Catastrophe *John Quinn* a65 65
3 b g Intikhab(USA) Mrs Snaffles (IRE) (Indian Danehill (IRE))
4036[6] 4607[8] 5540[8] 6541[2] 7078[7] 7368[4] 7755[8] 8086[2] 8382[9]

Catcall (FR) *P Sogorb* 116
7 b g One Cool Cat(USA) Jurata (IRE) (Polish Precedent (USA))
1172a[3] 1618a[3] 2943a[2] 3796a[7] 6391a[9]

Catch A Glimpse (USA) *Mark Casse* 112
3 ch f City Zip(USA) Halo River (USA) (Irish River (FR))
(4174a) 7379a[7] 7831a[8]

Catch A Wave (IRE) *Debbie Mountain* 84
2 b g Approve(IRE) Casablanca Jewel (IRE) (Kalanisi (IRE))
8564a[4]

Catchment *Amanda Perrett* a83 79
3 b f Oasis Dream Mirror Lake (Dubai Destination (USA))
3147[2] 4660[2] 5168[2] (5551) 6483[4] 7281[3] 8028[6]

Catharina *Dean Ivory* a46 55
4 ch m Dutch Art Lambadora (Suave Dancer (USA))
1415[11] 1654[11] (2901) 3620[6] 3999[10] 4527[8] 8468[13] 8567[9]

Cat O'Mountain (USA) *Charlie Appleby* a111 48
6 br g Street Cry(IRE) Thunder Kitten (USA) (Storm Cat (USA))
188a[9] 627a[11]

Cat Royale (IRE) *Jane Chapple-Hyam* a75 78
3 b c Lilbourne Lad(IRE) Call This Cat (IRE) (One Cool Cat (USA))
287[2] (603) 1185[6] (1532) 2209[11] 3617[7] 5122[7] 6128[5] 6701[11] 7653[11] 8462[5] ◆

Cat Silver *Sir Michael Stoute* a74 75
3 b g Dansili Catopuma (USA) (Elusive Quality (USA))
6511[3] 7229[7]

Catskill Mountains (IRE) *Roger Varian* a64 59
3 b g Rip Van Winkle(IRE) Cawett (IRE) (Danehill Dancer (IRE))
1930[9] 2320[7] 2835[6] 3652[8]

Catwilldo (IRE) *Garvan Donnelly* a55 69
6 b m One Cool Cat(USA) Hypocrisy (Bertolini (USA))
2229a[8] 5225[2] 6506[13]

Cause And Effect (IRE) *Ralph Beckett* a67 59
3 b g Big Bad Bob(IRE) Special Cause (IRE) (Fasliyev (USA))
2998[9] 3744[5] 5302[11]

Causey Arch (IRE) *Michael Dods* a39 75
3 b g Jeremy(USA) Coill Cri (IRE) (Shinko Forest (IRE))
1622[9] 2048[10] 2652[9] 3287[2] (3710) (3943) 4241[4] 5975[7] 6838[9] 7111[8]

Cautionary Note *Nigel Tinkler* 65
3 bb f Roderic O'Connor(IRE) Precautionary (Green Desert (USA))
2776[10] 3604[9] 4410[7] 4426[5] 4944[5]

Cautious Choice (IRE) *J S Moore* a38 46
2 b f Elzaam(AUS) On Thin Ice (IRE) (Verglas (IRE))
3555[11] 4526[5] 5120[3] 5528[6] 6313[6] 6961[9]

Cautious Optimism *William Muir* a54 76
3 ch g Showcasing Queen Of Havana (USA) (King Of Kings (IRE))
1809[9] 2981[11] 4046[6] 4482[3] 5517[6] 6631[6]

Cavale Doree (FR) *C Ferland* 107
2 b f Sunday Break(JPN) Sweet Alabama (FR) (Enrique)
(4924a) (5703a) 6986a[5] 7809a[3]

Cavalieri (IRE) *Philip Kirby* a72 60
6 b g Oratorio(IRE) Always Attractive (IRE) (King's Best (USA))
4045[10] 4430[3] 5183[9] 5481[9] 5758[6] 6219[10] 7045[5] 7138[8] 7746[8] 7846[3] (7955) (8084) 8399[7]

Cavaprun (FR) *C Baillet* a79 88
2 b g Siyouni(FR) Atabaska (FR) (Ashkalani (IRE))
(1118a) 3182a[7]

Cayirli (FR) *Seamus Durack* a96 101
4 b g Medicean Clarinda (FR) (Montjeu (IRE))
1089[4] 2024[6] 2468[5] 3387[2] 3913[9] 6283[11] 6974a[8] 7411[4]

Cay Location (IRE) *Ed de Giles* a25
3 b g Bahamian Bounty Desert Location (Dubai Destination (USA))
863[9] 1113[11] 2128[6]

Caymus *Tracy Waggott* a29 50
3 b f Compton Place Midnight Sky (Desert Prince (IRE))
1029[6] 1922[12] 2834[11] 3268[13] 4096[4] 5920[8] 6341[6] 6813[3] 7860[8]

Cayuga *Brett Johnson* a86 83
7 b g Montjeu(IRE) Ithaca (USA) (Distant View (USA))
7617[7]

Cazalys (FR) *E J O'Neill* 75
2 b f Deportivo Thandiswa (FR) (Zamindar (USA))
5005a[6]

Ceaseless (IRE) *James Tate* 92
4 b m Iffraaj Sheer Bliss (IRE) (Sadler's Wells (USA))
2797[8] 5123[6] 5933[3] 6710[12]

Cecile Royale *Stuart Williams* a33 37
3 b f Royal Applause George's Gift (Haafhd)
1337[10] 1753[8] 3267[9] 4570[8] 5020[4] 7488[8] 7645[8]

Ceecubed (IRE) *Jeremy Noseda* a71 23
3 b f Canford Cliffs(IRE) Chincoteague (IRE) (Daylami (IRE))
2767[7]

Cee Jay *Robert Cowell* a71 65
3 ch g Kyllachy Intermission (IRE) (Royal Applause)
126[2] 765[3] 902[3] 1337[4] 7335[5] 7815[2] 8030[7] 8181[4] 8496[7]

Celanova (FR) *J-C Rouget* 100
2 b f Exceed And Excel(AUS) Clarinda (FR) (Montjeu (IRE))
(5005a)

Ce La Vie *Keith Dalgleish* 80
2 ch f Dutch Art Chase The Lady (USA) (Atticus (USA))
(7356)

Celebration *Richard Fahey* 92
3 b g Equiano(FR) Bold Bidder (Indesatchel (IRE))
1492[2] ◆ 1977[3] 2554[2] (3131) 4112[8] 4803[4] 5657[6] 6263[20] 6944[7]

Celebration Day (IRE) *Simon Crisford* a75 83
3 b g Raven's Pass(USA) Bunting (Shaadi (USA))
1610[7] 2471[5] 3102[6]

Celerity (IRE) *David Evans* a51 47
2 ch f Casamento(IRE) Shinko Dancer (IRE) (Shinko Forest (IRE))
8151[9]

Celestation *Mark Johnston* 75
2 b f Excelebration(IRE) Coventina (IRE) (Daylami (IRE))
5289[4] 5615[4] 6035[5] (6762)

Celestial Bay *Sylvester Kirk* a80 75
7 b m Septieme Ciel(USA) Snowy Mantle (Siberian Express (USA))
(420) 636[3] 884[4] 8381[10]

Celestial Dancer (FR) *Michael Appleby* a52 34
4 bb m Dr Fong(USA) Rabeera (Beat Hollow)
251[2] 368[10] 674[2] 1048[5] 1182[2] 2370[9]

Celestial Path (IRE) *Sir Mark Prescott Bt* a105 110
4 br g Footstepsinthesand Miss Kittyhawk (IRE) (Hawk Wing (USA))
2074a[4] 2867[5] 4163[2] 4823[10] 5652[7] 6786[6]

Celestial Spheres (IRE) *Charlie Appleby* 84
2 b c Redoute's Choice(AUS) Copernica (IRE) (Galileo (IRE))
3108[2] 4274[4] 5828[2] 6455[2] (6663)

Celestial Vision (USA) *Miss Joey Ellis* a38 50
4 b g Henrythenavigator(USA) Damini (USA) (Seeking The Gold (USA))
174[11]

Celestine (USA) *William Mott* 119
4 bb m Scat Daddy(USA) Mona Mia (USA) (Monarchos (USA))
(3178a) 7171a[3] 7833a[12]

Celestra *Alan King* a67
3 b f Doyen(IRE) Triple Cee (IRE) (Cape Cross (IRE))
699[2] 1179[4] 2368[P]

Celtic Artisan (IRE) *Rebecca Menzies* a60 58
5 ch g Dylan Thomas(IRE) Perfectly Clear (USA) (Woodman (USA))
107[4] 383[2] ◆ 463[3] ◆ (527) 702[4] 982[10] 4234[7] 4425[3] 4772[2] 5114[4] (6700) 8587[9]

Celtic Ava (IRE) *Pat Phelan* a66 56
4 b m Peintre Celebre(USA) Denices Desert (Green Desert (USA))
(237) (347) (672) 951[4] 2814[4] 3230[7] 4050[5] 4459[8] 5994[4] 6871[11] 7936[3] 8367[3]

Celtic Power *Jim Goldie* a46 70
4 b g Rail Link Biloxi (Caerleon (USA))
1881[5] 2575[4] 3149[13] 4430[6] 4634[7] 5183[5] 5842[6] 6619[6]

Celtic Sixpence (IRE) *Nick Kent* a47 79
8 b m Celtic Swing Penny Ha'penny (Bishop Of Cashel)
1600[5] 3132[2] 3807[5] 4807[5] 5386[7] 6635[8] 7333[8] 7577[9]

Celticus (IRE) *Stefano Botti* 100
6 b h Stroll(USA) Bois Joli (IRE) (Orpen (USA))
2073a[6]

Cemcem (TUR) *Metin Sacan* a101
5 b h Akindayim(IRE) Gloriana (TUR) (Marlin (USA))
6157a[3]

Central Square (IRE) *Roger Varian* 111
4 b g Azamour(IRE) Lucky Clio (IRE) (Key Of Luck (USA))
(2098) 2744[2] (3391) ◆ 4115[4] (6261) 7154[3]

Centre Haafhd *Kenneth Slack* a54 53
5 b g Haafhd Deira Dubai (Green Desert (USA))
3924[9] 4444[9] 4932[8] 5369[7] 5729[9] 6106[2] 6347[3] 7254[11] 7604[10] 7859[9] 8013[9] 8289[4]

Centuro (USA) *Jonjo O'Neill* a63 63
3 ch g Cape Blanco(IRE) Cats Copy (USA) (Cat's Career (USA))
2044[9] 2639[4] 4273[6]

Century Dream (IRE) *Simon Crisford* 87
2 b c Cape Cross(IRE) Salacia (IRE) (Echo Of Light)
6108[5] 6751[3] (7283)

Ceol An Ghra (IRE) *J S Bolger* 85
3 b f Teofilo(IRE) Key To Coolcullen (IRE) (Royal Academy (USA))
1369a[7]

Ceol Na Nog (IRE) *J S Bolger* 95
3 b f Teofilo(IRE) Ard Fheis (IRE) (Lil's Boy (USA))
7823[15]

Cercle D'Or (IRE) *John Gosden* a73
2 b f Acclamation Fleche D'Or (Dubai Destination (USA))
7761[5] 8081[2] (8361)

Cerise Firth *Steph Hollinshead* a31 50
4 b m Pastoral Pursuits Vermilion Creek (Makbul)
681[8]

Cersei *F Rohaut* a88 83
3 b f Invincible Spirit(IRE) Elle Galante (GER) (Galileo (IRE))
(1814) 3218[2] 3644[3] 5205[3] 6013[2] (8368a)

Certain Time *Peter Hiatt* 40
4 b g Cape Cross(IRE) Copperbeech (IRE) (Red Ransom (USA))
5255[8] 5723[8]

Certerach (IRE) *M Halford* a90 107
8 b g Halling(USA) Chartres (IRE) (Danehill (USA))
285a[12] 453a[11] 811a[2] 1102a[10]

Certificate *Roger Varian* a103 114
5 ch g Pivotal Graduation (Lomitas)
50[2] 486[2] 3566[6] (5389) (5871) 6955[2] 7115[4]

Certification (IRE) *Andrew Crook* a75 78
6 b g Authorized(IRE) Most Charming (FR) (Darshaan)
1722[6]

Certified (IRE) *James Tate* a84
3 ch f Raven's Pass(USA) Guarantia (Selkirk (USA))
(3989) 4474[7] 5551[7]

Cerulean Silk *Tony Carroll* a51 44
6 b m Striking Ambition Cerulean Rose (Bluegrass Prince (IRE))
46[6] 341[5] 513[3] 730[4] 1026[3] 3993[10] 5007[10] 5826[4] 6586[5]

Cetta's Hill *Stuart Edmunds* a51
3 gr f Al Namix(FR) Melancholy Hill (IRE) (Marju (IRE))
1346[7] 1962[7]

Cevedale (FR) *Mlle B Renk* 34
3 ch f Vespone(IRE) Continental Kid (IRE) (Exit To Nowhere (USA))
7265a[11]

Ceyhan *Joseph Tuite* 72
4 ch h Rock Of Gibraltar(IRE) Alla Prima (IRE) (In The Wings)
1529[3] ◆ 3845[10]

Chababa Rosetgri (FR) *H De Nicolay* a63 63
2 b f Recharge(IRE) Zambaba (FR) (Le Balafre (FR))
2724a[10] 3006a[10] 4965a[2] 5279a[7] 5988a[6]

Chadic *R P McNamara* a46 86
4 b g Echo Of Light Hawsa (USA) (Rahy (USA))
4721a[10]

Chain Of Daisies *Henry Candy* a102 111
4 b m Rail Link Puya (Kris)
2363[7] 3608[5] (5307) (5893)

Chakra *Michael Bell* a45 58
2 ch f Notnowcato Ming Meng (IRE) (Intikhab (USA))
6776[10] 7297[9] 7883[8]

Chalieb *Nigel Tinkler* a53 62
2 b f Exceed And Excel(AUS) Alkhana (IRE) (Dalakhani (IRE))
4040[8] 4856[8] 5272[5] 7110[8]

Challow (IRE) *Sylvester Kirk* a67 72
2 b g Acclamation Starlight Smile (USA) (Green Dancer (USA))
2203[7] 2873[5] 3524[5] 4076[3] 5239[2] 7033[6] 7319[4] 7697[2]

Chamasay *J S Moore* a13 45
2 ch c Sayif(IRE) Miss Chamanda (IRE) (Choisir (AUS))
2748[8] 5052[7] 6314[7] 7208[7] 7981[11]

Champagne Bob *Richard Price* a61 74
4 gr g Big Bad Bob(IRE) Exclusive Approval (USA) (With Approval (CAN))
2187[10] 2827[8] 3220[6] 3745[3] 4354[4] 5060[5] 5408[2] 5736[3] 6381[3] 6636[5]

Champagne Champ *Rod Millman* a82 96
4 b g Champs Elysees Maramba (Rainbow Quest (USA))
1598[4] 2582[2] 3533[2] 3862[5] (4795) (6083) 6582[5] (7215) 7498[6]

Champagne City *Mark Johnston* 100
3 ch g Tobougg(IRE) City Of Angels (Woodman (USA))
2481[4] 2892[12] 3887[3] 4797[14]

Champagne Freddie *John O'Shea* a60
3 b g Sleeping Indian Shes Minnie (Bertolini (USA))
8342[4]

Champagne Or Water (IRE) *W McCreery* a71 98
5 b m Captain Rio Former Drama (USA) (Dynaformer (USA))
(6495a)

Champagne Pink (FR) *K R Burke* a58
2 b f Teofilo(IRE) Carruba (IRE) (Marju (IRE))
8131[8] 8404[7]

Champagne Queen *Rae Guest* a42 55
2 ch f Showcasing Night Haven (Night Shift (USA))
2902[7] 4022[6] 4638[3] ◆ 5257[6] 8285[6]

Champagne Reign (IRE) *J S Moore* a56 37
2 b f Casamento(IRE) Reign Of Fire (IRE) (Perugino (USA))
7503[13] 7762[11] 8208[11] 8404[8]

Champagne Room (USA) *Peter Eurton* a112
2 b f Broken Vow(USA) Lucky To Be Me (USA) (Bernstein (USA))
(7830a)

Champagne Rules *Sharon Watt* a48 62
5 gr g Aussie Rules(USA) Garabelle (IRE) (Galileo (IRE))
1248[6] 1391[12] 2618[12] 2836[9] 3498[9] 4872[11] 6432[11] 6619[4] 6840[7]

Champion Harbour (IRE) *Richard Fahey* a63 62
2 b g Harbour Watch(IRE) Drastic Measure (Pivotal)
1482[3] 1850[7] 3654[4] 4167[5] 4595[4] 5265[3] 5806[2] 6222[5] 6743[12]

Championship (IRE) *A bin Harmash* a90 108
5 ch g Exceed And Excel(AUS) Aljafliyah (Halling (USA))
720a[10] 810a[2]

Chancery (USA) *David O'Meara* a62 102
8 bb g Street Cry(IRE) Follow That Dream (Darshaan)
1219[2] 1645[4] 2222[8] 3666[5] 4407[12] 5651[11] 6261[8] 7154[7] 7383[7]

Chanche The Life (IRE) *K Borgel* a68 87
3 b f Frozen Power(IRE) Pivot D'Amour (Pivotal)
7998a[10]

Chandon Elysees *Gary Moore* a67 62
3 b f Champs Elysees Upstream (Prince Sabo)
3059[12] 4991[3] 6247[3] 6649[4] 7619[7] 8257[6]

Chandos Belle (GER) *Stuart Edmunds* a64 72
3 b f Mamool(IRE) Chandos Rose (IRE) (Mull Of Kintyre (USA))
8076[5]

Chandrayaan *John E Long* a51 48
9 ch g Bertolini(USA) Muffled (USA) (Mizaaya)
87[5] 237[7] 412[8] 696[6] (876) 1035[8] 1834[8] 3146[10] 8278[11]

Chandresh *Robert Cowell* a49 59
3 b f Holy Roman Emperor(IRE) Cloud's End (Dubawi (IRE))
2435[7] 3976[2] 4517[10] 4855[7] 5626[6] 6408[11] 6865[3] 7534[5] 7863[3] 8289[6] 8408[2]

Chanducoq (FR) *J-P Gallorini* 94
3 b c Voix Du Nord(FR) Cardounika (FR) (Nikos)
1582a[6]

Channel Maker (CAN) *Daniel J Vella* 103
2 ch g English Channel(USA) In Return (USA) (Horse Chestnut (SAF))
7807a[7]

Chant (IRE) *Ann Duffield* a66 78
6 b g Oratorio(IRE) Akarita (IRE) (Akarad (FR))
3118[10] (4686) 4967[3] 6006[4] 6719[4]

Chantecler *Neil Mulholland* a73 75
5 b g Authorized(IRE) Snow Goose (Polar Falcon (USA))
2369[2] 3766[3] 4711[5] 5208[3] 5629[2] 6365[9]

Chantegrive (FR) *Adrien Desespringalle* a17 41
3 b f Youmzain(IRE) Queens Coach (American Post)
7265a[12]

Chantilly Fraise (FR) *P Sogorb* 67
2 b f Myboycharlie(IRE) Chantilly Creme (USA) (Johannesburg (USA))
4924a[4]

Chaotic Carnival *Julien Lemee* a42 59
5 b g Montjeu(IRE) Remote Romance (USA) (Irish River (FR))
2318a[7]

Chaparrachik (IRE) *Amanda Perrett* a69 72
2 b g High Chaparral(IRE) Chocolat Chaud (IRE) (Excellent Art)
4103[11] 6297[4] *6623[5]*

Chapeau Bleu (IRE) *Mrs C Gilbert* a69 53
4 b m Haatef(USA) La Petite Bleue (GER) (Fantastic Light (USA))
1517a[5] 2284a[8] 3380a[6] 3917a[3] 5456a[4]

Chapess *Philip McBride* a55
3 b f Pastoral Pursuits Inchcoonan (Emperor Jones (USA))
1063[10] 1179[5] 1961[6] 2784[12] 4214[12]

Chaplin (FR) *J Phelippon* a48 91
2 b c Myboycharlie(IRE) Lady Oriande (Makbul)
4594[6] (5229) 5821[3] 7033[7] 7490a[2] *7879a[11]*

Chaplin Bay (IRE) *Ruth Carr* a76 82
4 b g Fastnet Rock(AUS) Green Castle (IRE) (Indian Ridge)
1489[2] ◆ (2201) 2416[4] 2857[4] 3284[4] 3807[2] 3980[2] 4094[2] 4830[3] (5075) 5859[4] 6643[3] *7141[4]* 7360[5]

Chapter One (IRE) *D K Weld* 57
4 b g Pivotal Towards (USA) (Fusaichi Pegasus (USA))
4899a[15]

Chapter Seven *G M Lyons* a77 102
7 ch g Excellent Art My First Romance (Danehill (USA))
7708a[18]

Character Onesie (IRE) *Richard Fahey* a75 81
4 b g Dark Angel(IRE) Flame Keeper (IRE) (Pivotal)
1625[9] 2257[7] 2688[8] 3398[5] 4089[7] 4683[3] 5223[2] ◆ (5750) 6280[3] 6772[4] 7535[7] *7902[10] 8092[8]*

Charamba *James Given*
3 b f Sir Percy Rahcak (IRE) (Generous (IRE))
6795[7]

Charava (IRE) *Patrick Holmes* a54 68
4 br g Captain Marvelous(IRE) Sweet Compliance (Safawan)
2918[13] 3479[7] 4102[5] (4445) 4701[2] 5717[8] *7852[11] 8064[10] 8307[10]*

Charioteer *Ed Dunlop* 70
3 b g Champs Elysees Skyrider (IRE) (Dalakhani (IRE))
2098[10] *2815[10]* 3434[4]

Charismatic Man (IRE) *Ralph Beckett* a86 44
3 b g Dalakhani(IRE) On Fair Stage (IRE) (Sadler's Wells (USA))
6703[4] 7666[8] *(8124)* ◆ *8558[2]* ◆

Charles Camoin (IRE) *Sylvester Kirk* a102 98
8 b g Peintre Celebre(USA) Birthday (IRE) (Singspiel (IRE))
485[P]

Charles De Mille *Jedd O'Keeffe* a62 64
8 b g Tiger Hill(IRE) Apple Town (Warning)
(2046) 2555[3] 2661[3] 4425[4] 5114[7] 6095[5] *7601[3] 7795[11]*

Charles Molson *Patrick Chamings* a103 104
5 b g Monsieur Bond(IRE) Arculinge (Paris House)
2206[8] 2434[7] 2898[16] 3671[6] 4366[8] 4862[5] 5403[3] 6109[6] 6788[5] 7186[6] *7651[9] (7984)*

Charles The Great (IRE) *John Moore* 118
7 b g Holy Roman Emperor(IRE) Jojeema (Barathea (IRE))
1911a[11]

Charlie Bear *Jamie Osborne* a91 63
4 b g Myboycharlie(IRE) Millennium Heiress (Singspiel (IRE))
1752[6] 2628[12] *3303[7]* 4208[10] *4717[4] 5526[3] (6128) (6676)*

Charlie Beer Punt (IRE) *Tom Dascombe* a56 57
2 ch c Nathaniel(IRE) Quiet Protest (USA) (Kingmambo (USA))
1543[4] 3008[4] *3730[8]*

Charlie Chaplin (GER) *Robert Eddery* a61 59
2 b g Lope De Vega(IRE) Campina (Oasis Dream)
1889[8] 2193[8] *6044[6]* 7571[6] 7768[8] *8046[9]*

Charlie Lad *Daniel Mark Loughnane* a64 72
4 b g Myboycharlie(IRE) Night Owl (Night Shift (USA))
136[3] 241[6] 732[2] (837) 1059[7] 1133[7] 1721[7] 8149[7] 8409[7] 8596[6]

Charlie Parker (IRE) *Dominic Ffrench Davis* a45 40
3 b g Myboycharlie(IRE) Solaria (IRE) (Desert Prince (IRE))
1259[11] 1740[9] 2700[12] 3765[10]

Charlie Rascal (FR) *Peter Chapple-Hyam* a62 64
2 b c Myboycharlie(IRE) Rascafria (USA) (Johannesburg (USA))
4856[7] 5792[4] *6044[4] 8568[5]*

Charlie's Approval (IRE) *Ben Haslam* 53
4 b m Approve(IRE) Authenticate (Dansili)
1379[6] 2047[3] 2778[8] 4257[5]

Charlies Mate *John Best* a88 72
5 br g Myboycharlie(IRE) Retainage (USA) (Polish Numbers (USA))
(263) 518[4] 712[3] 779[4] 1093[3] 1430[5] 2324[7] 2827[6] *5724[4] 6128[2] 6870[3] 7869[6]*

Charlie's Star *Laura Mongan* a59 58
4 b m Hellvelyn Sweet Sorrow (IRE) (Lahib (USA))
155[5] 255[8] 514[12]

Charlie Victor *Clive Cox* 42
2 b g Myboycharlie(IRE) Audrey Brown (Mind Games)
2583[7] 4053[11]

Charlie Wells (IRE) *Eve Johnson Houghton* a83 61
5 b g High Chaparral(IRE) Numbers Game (Rainbow Quest (USA))
693[5] (5262) 5767[4] 6362[7]

Charly Green (FR) *P Leblanc* a62 51
4 b g Fuisse(FR) Tornad Des Bieffes (FR) (Le Fou (IRE))
4901a[9]

Charly Nova (FR) *F Rossi* 93
2 b f Myboycharlie(IRE) Terra Nova (FR) (American Post)
8062a[2]

Charm Appeal (FR) *H-F Devin* 91
2 b f Canford Cliffs(IRE) Tara's Force (IRE) (Acclamation)
(7291a) 8062a[3]

Charmed Company (IRE) *Keith Dalgleish* 7
3 b f Fast Company(IRE) Lucky Leigh (Piccolo)
1562[10]

Charming Kitten (USA) *D K Weld* a106 105
6 b h Kitten's Joy(USA) Iteration (USA) (Wild Again (USA))
5660a[5]

Charming Thought *Charlie Appleby* 108
4 b h Oasis Dream Annabelle's Charm (IRE) (Indian Ridge)
3195[4] 4393[6] 5613[9]

Charm Park *Geoffrey Harker* 9
6 b g Desideratum Queen's Lodge (IRE) (Grand Lodge (USA))
2804[7]

Charmy *Andrew Balding* a72 73
3 b f Yeats(IRE) Saturday Girl (Peintre Celebre (USA))
2109[4] 2749[3]

Chartbreaker (FR) *Chris Gordon* a71 85
5 b g Shirocco(GER) Caucasienne (FR) (Galileo (IRE))
3246[15] 4077[12] 4535[2] *8051[8]*

Chartreuse (IRE) *F Head* a79 109
3 b f Lawman(FR) Bufera (IRE) (King's Best (USA))
1581a[5] 4184a[2] 5498a[2] 6693a[5]

Chastushka (IRE) *John Gosden* 97
3 br f Poet's Voice Sesmen (Inchinor)
2245[6] 3667[5]

Chatterton (IRE) *Paul W Flynn* a64 45
6 b g Excellent Art Elba (IRE) (Ela-Mana-Mou)
5132[6]

Chaucer's Tale *Michael Easterby* a63 51
2 b g Poet's Voice Grand Slam Maria (FR) (Anabaa (USA))
7122[12] 7578[9] *7792[2]*

Chautauqua (AUS) *Michael, Wayne & John Hawkes* 124
5 gb g Encosta De Lago(AUS) Lovely Jubly (AUS) (Lion Hunter (AUS))
(1911a)

Chauvelin *Nigel Tinkler* a54 74
5 b g Sir Percy Enforce (USA) (Kalanisi (IRE))
601[6] 1004[6] 1170[5] 1343[5] 1500[8] 1748[4] 2110[7] 2781[3] 2962[2] (3288) 3325[2] 3844[6] 4099[9] 4260[2] 4489[6] (4724) 5117[4] 5726[4] 6219[2] 6438[8] 7044[9]

Chebsey Beau *John Quinn* a72 82
6 b g Multiplex Chebsey Belle (IRE) (Karinga Bay)
1493[14] 2051[11] 2888[4] 3942[3] 4634[4] 5061[3] *5970[3]* 6519[3]

Check 'Em Tuesday (IRE) *Daniel Mark Loughnane* a66 62
3 b f Kodiac Wait Watcher (IRE) (Fath (USA))
1723[4] 2780[5] 3634[4] 4102[6] 4587[5] *5132[4] (7048) 7368[10] 8154[7]*

Cheeco *Ruth Carr* a45
4 ch g Shami Mandarin Lady (Timeless Times (USA))
986[5] 1295[7] 6105[3] 6512[11] 7604[11]

Cheeky Angel (IRE) *Michael Dods* 70
3 gr f Dark Angel(IRE) Cheeky Weeky (Cadeaux Genereux)
2049[11] 3521[9] 4043[4] 4429[7] ◆

Cheeky Fox *Marcus Tregoning* 41
2 b f Foxwedge(AUS) Cheeky Girl (College Chapel)
3812[10] 4801[10]

Cheeni *Jim Goldie* 45
4 ch m Orientor Class Wan (Safawan)
4096[3] 4492[8] 6098[10] 6341[13] 6615[8] 6774[8] 7093[6]

Cheerfilly (IRE) *Tom Dascombe* a60
2 br f Excelebration(IRE) Classic Remark (IRE) (Dr Fong (USA))
7277[5] 7939[4]

Cheerful Character (IRE) *Richard Fahey* a62 31
2 b f Tagula(IRE) Eucharist (IRE) (Acclamation)
4601[10] *5244[2] 6141[3]* 6768[5] *7143[13]*

Cheers All Round *Henry Spiller* a44 52
2 b f Royal Applause Shadow Of The Sun (Red Ransom (USA))
2404[8] 6035[7] 6404[8] *7380[8] 7881[11]*

Cheers Buddy (IRE) *Lee Smyth* a62 57
8 b g Acclamation Victorian Dancer (IRE) (Groom Dancer (USA))
5222[3] ◆ 5576[4] 6838[11]

Chefchaouen (IRE) *J S Moore* a62 34
4 b m Dylan Thomas(IRE) Love Thirty (Mister Baileys)
127[3] 348[7]

Cheikeljack (FR) *H-A Pantall* 112
3 b c Myboycharlie(IRE) Senderlea (IRE) (Giant's Causeway (USA))
1024a[5] (1308a) 3338[6] 4433a[6]

Chelabella *Michael Bell* a69 56
3 b f Medicean Agrippina (Timeless Times (USA))
1798[4] 2574[8] 3878[7] 4764[9] *7755[6] 8255[4]*

Chella Thriller (SPA) *Ralph J Smith* a68 50
7 b m Chevalier(IRE) Arundhati (IRE) (Royal Academy (USA))
1278[6] 2153[11] 3402[4] 4200[6] 5399[4] 5708[9]

Chelsea Corsage (IRE) *A Oliver* a72 78
2 b f Teofilo(IRE) Galley (Zamindar (USA))
7193a[6]

Chelsea Lad (IRE) *Martyn Meade* 102
3 b c Clodovil(IRE) Yali (IRE) (Orpen (USA))
1623[2] (2479)

Chelsea's Boy (IRE) *Clive Cox* 80
3 gr g Rip Van Winkle(IRE) St Roch (IRE) (Danehill (USA))
1739[10] 2398[2] ◆ (3103) 4131[9] 4778[4] 5331[4] 6193[3] 7060[6]

Chelwood Gate (IRE) *Patrick Chamings* a74 77
6 gr g Aussie Rules(USA) Jusoor (USA) (El Prado (IRE))
263[2] 414[3] ◆ *629[3] 782[3] 953[6] 1173[2]* 1530[11] *2006[8] 8035[5] (8252)*

Chemical Charge (IRE) *Ralph Beckett* a109 109
4 ch h Sea The Stars(IRE) Jakonda (USA) (Kingmambo (USA))
2924a[2] 3692a[2] *8068[2]* 8336a[2]

Chempedak Bay (IRE) *Paul Cole* a60 63
3 ch g Exceed And Excel(AUS) Snowdrops (Gulch (USA))
1389[8] 2639[6]

Chene Boppe (FR) *J-M Baudrelle* a61 64
6 ch g Turtle Bowl(IRE) Beggars Belief (IRE) (Common Grounds)
3184a[12]

Cheongu (USA) *I Seo* a90
4 ch h Old Fashioned(USA) So Much Fun (USA) (Speightstown (USA))
90a[5] 719a[9]

Cheries Amours (FR) *T Castanheira* 87
2 b f Air Chief Marshal(IRE) Cherie Bibie (FR) (Statue Of Liberty (USA))
6068a[6] 7170a[8] 7972a[7]

Cherry Kool *Stuart Williams* a77 74
3 b f Kheleyf(USA) Pretty Kool (Inchinor)
1812[3] 2435[8] (4820) 5285[4] 6363[8] *6699[5] 8429[3]*

Cherry Leyf *Stuart Williams* a58
2 b f Kheleyf(USA) Pretty Kool (Inchinor)
8152[9]

Cherry Street *John Berry* a73 60
7 b g Alhaarth(IRE) Weqaar (USA) (Red Ransom (USA))
676[6] 898[6]

Cherry Wine (USA) *Dale Romans* a115 83
3 rg c Paddy O'Prado(USA) C. S. Royce (USA) (Unbridled's Song (USA))
2499a[2] 3181a[7] 5429a[8]

Chesham Rose (IRE) *Dave Roberts*
3 gr f Mastercraftsman(IRE) Rose's Destination (IRE) (Dubai Destination (USA))
384[8] 3053[6] *8470[10]*

Chessman (IRE) *John Gosden* a83
2 b c Acclamation Dulcian (IRE) (Shamardal (USA))
(7976) ◆

Chess Master (IRE) *Charlie Appleby* 75
3 br g Shamardal(USA) Cassandra Go (IRE) (Indian Ridge)
2207[7]

Chester Deelyte (IRE) *Lisa Williamson* a54 47
8 b m Desert Style(IRE) Bakewell Tart (IRE) (Tagula (IRE))
297[9] 7654[4] 8013[13] 8079[8] 8278[12]

Chester'slittlegem (IRE) *Mrs A Corson* a28 19
7 b m Atraf Ceylon Round (FR) (Royal Applause)
1517a[3] 2081a[2] 2284a[6] 2953a[4]

Chester Street *Roger Charlton* a92 83
3 b g Invincible Spirit(IRE) Expressive (Falbrav (IRE))
1891[4] 2299[3] 3156[6] 4709[5] 5412[3] *(7813) (8279)*

Chestnut Fire *M Halford* a100 86
4 ch g Showcasing Music In Exile (USA) (Diesis)
4748a[6]

Chestnut Storm (IRE) *Brian Barr* a67 63
3 ch f Rip Van Winkle(IRE) Always Attractive (IRE) (King's Best (USA))
925[6] 1179[8] 1740[7] ◆ 3015[3] *4210[2]* 4450[3] *5079[6]* (7231) *8309[4]*

Chetan *Charlie Wallis* a78 76
4 b g Alfred Nobel(IRE) Island Music (IRE) (Mujahid (USA))
(68) 167[2] (607) 955[6] 2584[11] *2821[6]* 3486[9] *3989[8]* 4278[2] (4570) (4878) *(5736)* 6269[3] 6580[4] *7206[3] 7644[7]*

Cheval Blanche (USA) *Michael Bell* 71
2 gr f Stay Thirsty(USA) Primrose Hill (USA) (Giant's Causeway (USA))
(2771) 3336[12]

Cheval Grand (JPN) *Yasuo Tomomichi* 118
4 ch h Heart's Cry(JPN) Halwa Sweet (JPN) (Machiavellian (USA))
8129a[3]

Chevalier Du Lac (IRE) *Conor Dore* a66 78
2 b g Sir Prancealot(IRE) Crimson Sunrise (IRE) (Holy Roman Emperor (IRE))
1921[2] (2344) ◆ 2908[6] 3282[4] 3707[4] 5974[3] (6208) 6446[5] *6961[4]* 7330[4] *7938[9]*

Chevallier *Archie Watson* a93 91
4 b g Invincible Spirit(IRE) Magical Romance (IRE) (Barathea (IRE))
1142[4] 1775[8] (2628) 3910[12] 5976[8] 6320[3] 6710[3] *8049[2] 8177[3] 8279[3]*

Chevise (IRE) *Steve Woodman* a71 70
8 b m Holy Roman Emperor(IRE) Lipica (IRE) (Night Shift (USA))
403[7]

Chez Vegas *Scott Dixon* a54 77
3 gr g Hellvelyn Lola Sapola (IRE) (Benny The Dip (USA))
935[4] ◆ *1151[8]* (2234) 3644[5]

Chica De La Noche *Simon Dow* a76 78
2 b f Teofilo(IRE) Welsh Cake (Fantastic Light (USA))
2467[5] 2990[6] 5400[U] *6244[2]* 6454[6] *6897[3] (7277) 8592[5]*

Chicadoro *Ralph Beckett* 98
3 b f Paco Boy(IRE) Going For Gold (Barathea (IRE))
1890[2] 3297[9]

Chicago Bere (FR) *Leo Braem* a60 52
4 b g Peer Gynt(JPN) Fitness Queen (USA) (Gilded Time (USA))
8421a[13]

Chicago School (IRE) *Mark Johnston* a72 52
3 ch g Approve(IRE) Ms Sasha Malia (IRE) (Verglas (IRE))
1132[3] 1809[7]

Chicago Star *Mick Channon* 68
2 b f Exceed And Excel(AUS) Librettista (AUS) (Elusive Quality (USA))
7314[8] 7696[4]

Chickenfortea (IRE) *Eric Alston* a49 60
2 gr g Clodovil(IRE) Kardyls Hope (IRE) (Fath (USA))
2196[6] 2648[5] 3128[8] 4308[4] *5364[6]* 6213[3] 6678[2]

Chiclet (IRE) *Tracey Collins* a103 100
5 b m Dandy Man(IRE) Springfort (IRE) (Captain Rio)
3696a[12] *(4246a) 7520a[5]*

Chiconomic (IRE) *Rae Guest* a43 56
2 b f Clodovil(IRE) Ashdali (IRE) (Grand Lodge (USA))
4738[8] 5202[9] 5668[2] 6252[6] *6895[5]* 6950[24] *7510[6] 7881[9] 8025[6] 8341[5]*

Chiefofchiefs *Charlie Fellowes* 79
3 b c Royal Applause Danvers (Cape Cross (IRE))
4840[3] 5850[2]

Chief Spirit *James Eustace* a68 82
4 b g Norse Dancer(IRE) Indian Angel (Indian Ridge)
2651[9]

Childesplay *Heather Main* a90 94
5 ch m Byron Parting Gift (Cadeaux Genereux)
1003[2] 1394[5] 1990[10] *2621[4]* 3061[9] *3405[5]* 4627[16]

Chillie Billie *J Larkin* a67 66
7 ch g Piccolo Chilly Cracker (Largesse)
4748a[7] 4899a[9] 7391a[10]

Chilli Jam *Ed de Giles* a61 57
3 b g Mastercraftsman(IRE) Wosaita (Generous (IRE))
2506[5] 3141[6] 3482[10]

Chillililli *Bryan Smart* a48
2 ch f Monsieur Bond(IRE) Stunning Icon (Dr Fong (USA))
6515[10] *6925[9] 7381[9] 8071[10]*

Chilli Spice (IRE) *J P Murtagh* a81 92
3 ch f Manduro(GER) Contrary (IRE) (Mark Of Esteem (IRE))
4331a[8] *7342a[6]*

Chil The Kite *Hughie Morrison* a89 117
7 b g Notnowcato Copy-Cat (Lion Cavern (USA))
3672[4] 4392[7] 5585[16] 6786[22] 7354[18]

Chilworth Bells *Conor Dore* a78 68
4 ch g Sixties Icon Five Bells (IRE) (Rock Of Gibraltar (IRE))
(1202) 1588[3] (1952) *2328[5]* 2663[7] 3135[3] *3403[5] 3659[10] 4201[4]* 4531[8] *4880[6] 8100[10] 8257[14]*

Chilworth Icon *Debbie Mountain* a92 97
6 b g Sixties Icon Tamara Moon (IRE) (Acclamation)
755a[11]

China Excels *Mandy Rowland* a68 74
9 b g Exceed And Excel(AUS) China Beauty (Slip Anchor)
(1059) (2120) *7386[7] 7945[11]*

China Girl (IND) *William Knight* a68 72
4 b m Dancing Forever(USA) Oriental Lady (IRE) (King's Best (USA))
1808[3] 1947[7] 2872[3] 3673[4]

Chinese Soldier (FR) *Stijn Derycke* a54 50
4 ch g Soldier Of Fortune(IRE) Mandarine (FR) (Desert Prince (IRE))
7295a[9]

Chinese Spirit (IRE) *R Mike Smith* 12
2 gr g Clodovil(IRE) In The Ribbons (In The Wings)
6833[7]

Ching Ching Lor (IRE) *Declan Carroll* 19
2 b g Elzaam(AUS) Art Critic (USA) (Fusaichi Pegasus (USA))
7331[9] 7578[15] 7741[14]

Chionodoxa *Tim Easterby* 24
2 ch f Haafhd Bollin Nellie (Rock Hopper)
7740[14]

Chip Or Pellet *Nigel Tinkler* a57 50
3 b g Hellvelyn Concentration (IRE) (Mind Games)
2302[3] 3423[3] 3948[10] 4426[7] 4855[4] 5041[2] 5920[5] *6744[4] (6909)*

Chipping (IRE) *Michael Dods* a70 77
2 b c Dark Angel(IRE) Bean Uasal (IRE) (Oasis Dream)
7142[3] (7578)

Chiquit Indian (FR) *E Caroux* 58
2 b f Indian Danehill(IRE) Chiquitita (IRE) (Oratorio (IRE))
3763a[7] 7996a[8]

Chiringuita (USA) *James Bethell* a64 93
3 rg f Hard Spun(USA) Silver Games (IRE) (Verglas (IRE))
2789[8] 3519[4] 4105[3]

Chiron (IRE) *Keith Dalgleish* 24
7 b g Celtic Swing Jane Digby (IRE) (Magical Strike (USA))
2094[3] 3886[9] 4682[12] 6438[15]

Chiswick Bey (IRE) *Richard Fahey* a72 74
8 b g Elusive City(USA) Victoria Lodge (IRE) (Grand Lodge (USA))
2121[4] 2421[6] 3166[12] 3517[8] 4081[3] 4627[5] 5033[2] 5540[6] 6028[5] 6231[10] (6683) 7010[3] 7702[5] *8163[6] 8531[8]*

Chloe's Image *Philip Kirby* a60 60
6 b m Lucky Story(USA) Iwunder (IRE) (King's Best (USA))
27[9]

Chocala (IRE) *Alan King* a80 96
6 b g Rock Of Gibraltar(IRE) Arbella (Primo Dominie)
(5642) 6279[2] 6781[6]

Chochenyo *Bryan Smart* 35
2 b g Kheleyf(USA) Unwrapit (USA) (Tapit (USA))
3283[8]

Chocolate Box (IRE) *Luca Cumani* a72 67
2 b c Zoffany(IRE) Chocolate Mauk (USA) (Cozzene (USA))
6054[10] 6523[5] 7034[5] *7598[3]*

Cholpon Ata (FR) *Mme P Butel* a21 57
2 gr f Rajsaman(FR) Karalka (IRE) (Brief Truce (USA))
3763a[5] 4471a[7] 4965a[5] *7455a[15]*

Chookie Royale *Keith Dalgleish* a114 88
8 ch g Monsieur Bond(IRE) Lady Of Windsor (IRE) (Woods Of Windsor (USA))
(166) 483[7] 921[7] 1066[10] 3655[4] 4299[16] *7068[8] (7868)* ◆

Chookie's Lass *Keith Dalgleish* a68 68
5 ch m Compton Place Lady Of Windsor (IRE) (Woods Of Windsor (USA))
1402[2] 1692[2] *2334[8]* 2808[6] 3553[5] 3755[2] 4488[6] *5078[6]* 5804[5]

Chookie Valentine *Keith Dalgleish* a49 42
3 b g Approve(IRE) Lady Of Windsor (IRE) (Woods Of Windsor (USA))
863[6] 958[4] 3020[10] 3710[7]

Chopsoave (FR) *N Caullery* a76 63
8 ch h Soave(GER) Moon Serenade (Key Of Luck (USA))
1034a[6]

Choral Clan (IRE) *Philip Mitchell* a76 76
5 b g Oratorio(IRE) Campbellite (Desert Prince (IRE))
(964) 1899[3] 2379[5] (2769) (3402) 4201[2] 4773[2] 5076[4] 6701[4] 7457[4] 7973[3]

Choral Festival *John Bridger* a70 74
10 b m Pivotal Choirgirl (Unfuwain (USA))
2205[3] 2623[3] 2930[5] 3721[3] (4784) 5207[5] 5994[3] 6876[7] 7429[10] 7653[7]

Choreographer (IRE) *Roger Varian* 96
3 ch c Sea The Stars(IRE) Evensong (GER) (Waky Nao)
(1715) ◆ 2190[7] 3337[9]

Chorlton House *Ian Williams* a67 65
4 ch g Compton Place Really Ransom (Red Ransom (USA))
(161) 676[10]

Chorus of Lies *Tracy Waggott* a62 61
4 b g Teofilo(IRE) Cherry Orchard (IRE) (King's Best (USA))
1028[4] 1923[10] 2618[8] 3418[5] 4099[7] 4427[5] 4767[4] 5517[3] 8585[5]

Chosen Character (IRE) *Tom Dascombe* a71 93
8 b g Choisir(AUS) Out Of Thanks (IRE) (Sadler's Wells (USA))
1247[7] (1631) 2441[2] 3124[7] (3398) 3855[4] 4917[9] 5156[12] 6055[6] 6280[8]

Chotto (IRE) *George Scott* a53 50
2 b f Royal Applause Alta Definizione (IRE) (Hawk Wing (USA))
1799[7] 2235[5] 3820[2] 4638[8]

Chough *Hughie Morrison* a60
2 b f Dutch Art Port Charlotte (Oasis Dream)
7733[9] 7891[11] 8152[7] 8467[9]

Choumicha *Hugo Palmer* a68 89
2 b f Paco Boy(IRE) Galicuix (Galileo (IRE))
6625[4] (7055) 7698[6]

Christmas Hamper (IRE) *Michael Appleby* a67 68
4 b g Dubawi(IRE) Gift Range (IRE) (Spectrum (IRE))
1399[P] 1675[6] (2089) 2501[6] 2887[4] 3437[4]

Christmas Light *Alan Lockwood* a37 62
9 b m Zafeen(FR) Arabian Dancer (Dansili)
3253[7] 4260[6] 4724[6]

Chrysolite (JPN) *Hidetaka Otonashi* a116
6 b h Gold Allure(JPN) Chrysoprase (JPN) (El Condor Pasa (USA))
(6399a)

Chupalla *Mark Johnston* a92 64
2 b f Helmet(AUS) Dubai Sunrise (USA) (Seeking The Gold (USA))
(1087) ◆ 2624[5]

Churchill (IRE) *A P O'Brien* 120
2 b c Galileo(IRE) Meow (IRE) (Storm Cat (USA))
(3382) ◆ (4574a) (5683a) (6386a) (7149)

Ciacona (IRE) *A De Royer-Dupre* 66
3 b f Oasis Dream Caesarine (FR) (Pivotal)
5385a[11]

Ciao Cielo (GER) *David Barron* a83 64
4 br g Lord Of England(GER) Celebration Night (IRE) (Hawk Wing (USA))
52[4]

Ciaras Cookie (IRE) *Mandy Rowland* a54 24
4 b m Approve(IRE) Preach (IRE) (Danehill Dancer (IRE))
54[6] 174[8] 270[4] 388[8] 525[5] 596[4] 790[6] (895) 3474[12] 4005[13] 8541[11]

Ciaratza (FR) *Mme S Adet* a50 58
4 gr g Confuchias(IRE) Premiraza (FR) (Nombre Premier)
8421a[10]

Cicada (FR) *Y Durepaire* a66
2 b f Holy Roman Emperor(IRE) Celestina Agostino (USA) (Street Cry (IRE))
8420a[6]

Ciel Rouge *Charlie Wallis* a47 54
2 b f Champs Elysees Artistic Blue (USA) (Diesis)
3275[5] 3613[5] 4016[7] 6670[13] 6896[4]

Cima Jelois (FR) *Robert Collet* 53
2 bb f Cima De Triomphe(IRE) Jenne Jelois (FR) (My Risk (FR))
4471a[8] 6015a[10]

Cincuenta Pasos (IRE) *Joseph Tuite* a76 93
5 ch g Footstepsinthesand Sweet Nicole (Okawango (USA))
1318[3] ◆ 1929[3] 2391[4] 2679[3] 2934[6] 3571[2] 3895[6] 6339[2] (6442) 6915[10] 7315[12] 7825[17]

Cinders (IRE) *Hughie Morrison* a73 51
3 b f Lilbourne Lad(IRE) The Fairies Did It (USA) (Elusive Quality (USA))
2004[2] 5766[2] 6251[4] 6657[9] 7459[3] 8067[11]

Cinque Port *Richard Hughes* a77
2 ch c Compton Place Jump Ship (Night Shift (USA))
6671[2] 7064[8]

Circuit *Mick Quinn* a45
2 b f Foxwedge(AUS) Lady Circe (USA) (Spinning World (USA))
8277[5]

Circuitous *Keith Dalgleish* a58 65
8 b g Fasliyev(USA) Seren Devious (Dr Devious (IRE))
2416[10] 2906[10] 3880[7] 4102[2] 4490[4] 4683[5] 4830[6] 5114[6] 5535[10] 7144[10] (7254) 7604[12]

Circulate *Tom Clover* a70
2 b f Dutch Art Royal Whisper (Royal Applause)
6866[5] 7278[5] 8443[2]

Circus Couture (IRE) *Stefano Botti* 114
4 ch h Intikhab(USA) Bois Joli (IRE) (Orpen (USA))
(1516a) 2073a[2] 2728a[2] 3455a[3] 6612a[3] 7400a[2] 7841a[5]

Cirencester *Ralph Beckett* 76
2 b f Sea The Stars(IRE) Columella (Kyllachy)
6111[3] (6716)

Cirin Toinne (IRE) *J S Bolger* a84 97
3 ch f Galileo(IRE) Sister Angelina (USA) (Saint Ballado (CAN))
6383a[4] 6604a[10] 7676a[12]

Citadel *John Wainwright* 49
3 ch g Haafhd Preference (Efisio)
1126[7] 1819[5] 2124[8] 3015[4] 3482[12] 4450[5] 5517[8]

Citisonsmith (IRE) *Tony Carroll* a51 36
4 b g Amadeus Wolf Ink Pot (USA) (Green Dancer (USA))
232[5] 653[9] 796[8] 1039[9] 1456[12] 1768[2]

City By The Bay *Richard Hannon* a68 64
3 b c Myboycharlie(IRE) October Winds (USA) (Irish River (FR))
1701[5] 2005[5] ◆ 2701[5]

City Chic (USA) *Charlie Appleby* a88 80
3 bb f Street Cry(IRE) Divine Dixie (USA) (Dixieland Band (USA))
5123[7] 6964[4]

City Dreamer (IRE) *Alan King* 66
2 ch g Casamento(IRE) Cadescia (IRE) (Cadeaux Genereux)
3859[8] 4989[4] 5740[8] 7016[7]

City Dreams (IRE) *Philip Kirby* a60
6 b m Rakti Attymon Lill (IRE) (Marju (IRE))
1004[2] 1136[2] 1322[8]

City Ground (USA) *Michael Appleby* a71 74
9 bb g Orientate(USA) Magnet (USA) (Seeking The Gold (USA))
(2899) 3064[2] 3917a[2] (5056) 5883[4] 6221[5] 6737[6] 7078[6]

City Light (FR) *S Wattel* 94
2 b c Siyouni(FR) Light Saber (FR) (Kendor (FR))
(6638a) 7491a[7] 8062a[4]

City Limits *Luca Cumani* a47 75
2 ch c Nathaniel(IRE) Wait It Out (USA) (Swain (IRE))
5505[7] 6297[5] 6663[5] ◆

City Of Angkor Wat (IRE) *Conor Dore* a83 53
6 b g Elusive City(USA) Kathleen Rafferty (IRE) (Marju (IRE))
703[10] (856) 942[2] 1341[4] 1648[6] 1803[5] 2309[7] 2856[10] (3726) 3985[2] 4714[13] 5736[8] 8067[10] 8315[8] 8535[6] 8595[8]

City Of Ideas *John Gosden* a74 77
3 b c Dansili Gertrude Bell (Sinndar (IRE))
1738[3] 2411[5] 3728[8]

City Of Joy *Sir Michael Stoute* 81
2 b g Elusive City(USA) Ammo (IRE) (Sadler's Wells (USA))
5600[5] ◆ 6570[2] ◆ (6952) 7544[13]

City Of Night (IRE) *Julie Camacho* a64 67
4 b g Elusive City(USA) Testama (FR) (Testa Rossa (AUS))
1117[9] 2329[3] 2773[2] 3366[6] (4454) 5030[8]

Cj Parker *Jim Boyle* a66 63
2 ch f Harbour Watch(IRE) Blonde (IRE) (Pivotal)
2747[4] 3275[4] 4270[13] 5251[5] 5989[8] 6236[10] 7098[5]

Claim The Roses (USA) *Ed Vaughan* a98 96
5 bb g Speightstown(USA) Reboot (USA) (Rubiano (USA))
1153[2] ◆ 6529[2] 7121[18] 8049[12]

Claire's Secret *Philip McBride* a66 62
2 ch f Sakhee's Secret Akathea (Barathea (IRE))
5119[7] 5792[2] (7304)

Clandon *Brett Johnson* a41
3 b g Sakhee's Secret Whassup (FR) (Midyan (USA))
5681[7] 6674[10]

Clarabel *Garry Moss* a23 56
3 b f Major Cadeaux Neardown Beauty (IRE) (Bahhare (USA))
6104[10] 6617[4]

Claret Cloak (IRE) *Emma Lavelle*
9 b g Vinnie Roe(IRE) Bewildered (IRE) (Prince Sabo)
630[P] (Dead)

Cla Rock (IRE) *William Haggas* a60 56
3 b f Iffraaj Blessed Biata (USA) (Mr Greeley (USA))
140[8]

Clary (IRE) *James Unett* a71 61
6 b m Clodovil(IRE) Kibarague (Barathea (IRE))
14[2] 324[3] 977[2] 1171[3] 6137[4] 6700[6] 7272[4]

Classe Vendome (FR) *P Sogorb* a43 100
3 gr f Kendargent(FR) Place Vendome (FR) (Dr Fong (USA))
2928a[5] 3274[14] 7397a[11] 7929a[10]

Classical Rose *Charlie Fellowes* a80 74
4 b m Amadeus Wolf Monaazalah (IRE) (Green Desert (USA))
1702[4] (2324) 3030[6] 6656[3]

Classical Times *Peter Chapple-Hyam* 90
2 b f Lawman(FR) Sunday Times (Holy Roman Emperor (IRE))
7314[3] ◆ 7667[5]

Classic Collection *Saeed bin Suroor* a89 101
4 b g Cape Cross(IRE) Local Spirit (USA) (Lion Cavern (USA))
1629[15] 7058[5]

Classic Colori (IRE) *Martin Keighley* a56 54
9 b g Le Vie Dei Colori Beryl (Bering)
5071[6] 5485[3]

Classic Empire (USA) *Mark Casse* a123
2 b c Pioneerof The Nile(USA) Sambuca Classica (USA) (Cat Thief (USA))
(7834a)

Classic Flyer *David O'Meara* a74 70
4 b g Stimulation(IRE) Tranquil Flight (Oasis Dream)
159[6] 2808[7] 3307[8] 4229[2] (4309) 4512[4] 4647[7] (5368) 5605[9] 5968[5] 7059[7] 7324[9]

Classic Mission *Jonathan Portman* a74 72
5 ch g Bahamian Bounty Triple Cee (IRE) (Cape Cross (IRE))
101[2] 382[6] 640[9] 2930[3] 3560[8] 4551[5] 5547[3] 6001[4] 6892[8]

Classic Pursuit *Ivan Furtado* a67 80
5 b g Pastoral Pursuits Snake's Head (Golden Snake (USA))
2040[2] ◆ 2342[4] 3610[11] (5060) 5269[3] 5512[6] 6072[14] 6680[4] 7430[7] 7644[9]

Classic Seniority *Marjorie Fife* a80 95
4 b g Kyllachy Dramatic Solo (Nayef (USA))
198[5] 655[10] 1444[4] 2016[8] 2491[3] 2961[3] (3115) (3344) 3645[8] 4193[7] 4627[4] 4862[9] ◆ 5403[9] (6280) (6539)

Classic Villager *Michael Appleby* a68 95
4 b g Authorized(IRE) Sablonne (USA) (Silver Hawk (USA))
2024[8] 6561[10] 7412[11]

Classified (IRE) *Ed de Giles* a60
2 b f Lope De Vega(IRE) Crossbreeze (USA) (Red Ransom (USA))
7762[9]

Classy Anne *Jim Goldie* 88
6 ch m Orientor Class Wan (Safawan)
1666[5] 2364[2] 2572[4] 3150[6] 3393[6] 3944[2] (4100) 4632[6] 4831[7] 5153[2] 5836[9] 6537[2]

Claude Greenwood *Tony Carroll* a45 44
6 b g Lucky Story(USA) Greenmeadow (Sure Blade (USA))
232[3] (505) 801[10] 1239[3] 1778[5] 2323[8] 2588[5] 7641[14] 8070[4] 8470[6]

Claudia Octavia *Werner Glanz* a64 78
5 br m Holy Roman Emperor(IRE) Chalosse (Doyoun)
5452a[5]

Claudio Monteverdi (IRE) *A P O'Brien* 99
3 b c Galileo(IRE) Dance For Fun (Anabaa (USA))
1567[4] 2883a[2] 3679a[8]

Claymore (IRE) *Bernard Llewellyn* a71 73
3 gr c Kodiac Krasotka (IRE) (Soviet Star (USA))
2044[7] 2322[5] 2864[14] 3740[4] 3985[4] 4480[4]

Clayton *Gary Moore* a81 104
7 b g Peintre Celebre(USA) Blossom (Warning)
1569[4]

Clayton Hall (IRE) *John Wainwright* a74 63
3 b g Lilbourne Lad(IRE) Hawk Dance (IRE) (Hawk Wing (USA))
768[2] 1113[7] 1406[4] 2012[5] (2694) 3596[4] 4607[6] 7436[13] 7742[3] 8124[9]

Clear As A Bell (IRE) *Tim Easterby* 60
2 ch f Choisir(AUS) Brilliant Crystal (Compton Place)
2007[12] 2424[3] 3839[3] 4451[7] 5712[8] 6222[10] 6564[9]

Clear Evidence *Michael Bell* a76 79
3 b g Cape Cross(IRE) Rainbow's Edge (Rainbow Quest (USA))
2122[4] 2652[11] 3615[2] 4033[4] (4655) 5331[3] (5830) ◆ 6325[4] 6906[2]

Clear Focus (IRE) *T G McCourt* a51 50
5 ch m Intense Focus(USA) Sofistication (IRE) (Dayjur (USA))
6466a[3]

Clear Leader (USA) *Micky Hammond* a31 50
3 b g Hard Spun(USA) Laureldean Gale (USA) (Grand Slam (USA))
6104[9] 6567[6]

Clear Spell (IRE) *Alistair Whillans* a69 75
5 b g Tamayuz Beat The Rain (Beat Hollow)
2575[5] 3395[4] 3751[RR] 5065[RR]

Clear Spring (IRE) *John Spearing* a69 106
8 b g Chineur(FR) Holly Springs (Efisio)
1887[10] (2206) 2434[4] 3195[5] 3671[4] 5488[13] 6161[7] 7497[21]

Clear Water (IRE) *Saeed bin Suroor* a97 86
3 b f Hard Spun(USA) Storm Lily (USA) (Storm Cat (USA))
1436[4] (2483) 4104[6] 6962[2] 7550[8]

Clef *Richard Fahey* 86
2 b f Dutch Art Humouresque (Pivotal)
3134[3] (3874) (4296) 4884[4] (5407) ◆ 5877[2] 6787[4] 7493[6]

Clement (IRE) *John O'Shea* a87 60
6 b g Clodovil(IRE) Winnifred (Green Desert (USA))
257[4] (355) (403) (482) 727[3] ◆ 816[7] 1041[7] 1335[9] 2402[4] 7530[13] 8319[7] 8456[4]

Clemento (IRE) *Richard Hughes* 53
2 b c Canford Cliffs(IRE) Street Style (IRE) (Rock Of Gibraltar (IRE))
6881[7]

Clem Fandango (FR) *Keith Dalgleish* 100
2 b f Elzaam(AUS) Question (USA) (Coronado's Quest (USA))
1583[2] ◆ (1951) 2670[2] 3270[3] 4394[3] 5584[6] (6538) ◆ 7113[2]

Clenymistra (IRE) *Marco Botti* a57 55
2 ch f Poet's Voice Expedience (USA) (With Approval (CAN))
3592[6] 4357[6] 5854[6] 6963[8] 7482[2]

Cleo Fan (ITY) *Stefano Botti* 111
5 b h Mujahid(USA) Cuprea (IRE) (Best Of The Bests (IRE))
1516a[6]

Cleonte (IRE) *A Fabre* 101
3 ch c Sir Percy Key Figure (Beat Hollow)
1582a[4] (5448a) 6176a[3]

Clergyman *Rebecca Bastiman* a44 77
4 b g Pastoral Pursuits Doctor's Note (Pursuit Of Love)
1874[4] ◆ 2305[9] 3150[15] 3924[8] 4608[15] 4970[7] 5887[17] 6910[5]

Clevedon Court *Gary Moore* a55 45
3 b f Royal Applause Bow River Arch (USA) (Arch (USA))
345[2] 436[8] 4992[6] 6187[9]

Clever Bob (IRE) *Joseph Tuite* a72 78
3 br g Big Bad Bob(IRE) Clever Millie (USA) (Cape Canaveral (USA))
2012[4] 2640[3] 3468[6] 4158[6] (4639) 5832[6] 6265[7] 6657[6] 7417[2]

Cleverconversation (IRE) *Jane Chapple-Hyam* a55 74
3 ro f Thewayyouare(USA) Monet's Lady (IRE) (Daylami (IRE))
2179[6] 2795[5] 3039[7] 4215[7] 4881[9] 5374[8] 5677[11]

Clever Cookie *Peter Niven* 116
8 b g Primo Valentino(IRE) Mystic Memory (Ela-Mana-Mou)
1273[2] 1772[2] (2221) 3298[7] 5612[5] 6284[7]

Clever Divya *J R Jenkins* a57 48
3 b f Archipenko(USA) Clever Omneya (USA) (Toccet (USA))
1597[7] 2234[11] 3625[6] 8472[7] (8572)

Cliff (IRE) *Nigel Tinkler* a73 69
6 b g Bachelor Duke(USA) Silesian (IRE) (Singspiel (IRE))
893[9] 1124[4] 1595[2] 1926[5] 2491[5] 2773[8] 3262[6] 3880[3] 4684[3] 5323[6] 6907[5] 7334[4] 7604[2] 7995[3] (8188) 8482[2] ◆

Cliff Bay (IRE) *Keith Dalgleish* a55 55
2 b g Elzaam(AUS) Lost Highway (IRE) (Danehill Dancer (IRE))
3548[7] 3939[7] 4188[7] 6923[5]

Cliff Edge (IRE) *Roger Varian* a66 65
3 b g Canford Cliffs(IRE) That's My Style (Dalakhani (IRE))
1931[8] 2340[6] 2835[5] 3738[6] 6662[3] 6921[4] 7214[9] 7425[4]

Cliff Face (IRE) *Sir Mark Prescott Bt* a98 84
3 b f Canford Cliffs(IRE) Kotdiji (Mtoto)
1392[7] 1798[12] 2009[9] 4018[2] (4880) (5100) 5350[2] 7765[5] (7980) 8068[5]

Cliffhanger *Paul Cole* a69 77
3 b f Canford Cliffs(IRE) Copy-Cat (Lion Cavern (USA))
1723[6] 2606[4] ◆ (2904) ◆ 3357[10] 3649[4] 4881[7]

Cliffmeena (IRE) *Alex Hales* a60 32
3 b f Canford Cliffs(IRE) Yasmeena (USA) (Mr Greeley (USA))
2980[6] 4215[8]

Cliffords Reprieve *John Gerard Fitzgerald* a45 33
8 b g Kheleyf(USA) Bijan (IRE) (Mukaddamah (USA))
6462a[10]

Cliffs Of Capri *Simon Crisford* a80
2 b g Canford Cliffs(IRE) Shannon Spree (Royal Applause)
7307[2] (7906)

Cliffs Of Dover *Charles Hills* a63 69
3 b g Canford Cliffs(IRE) Basanti (USA) (Galileo (IRE))
1804[5] 2639[3] 3063[5]

Climax *Mark Johnston* a44 65
2 b f Acclamation Blue Rocket (IRE) (Rock Of Gibraltar (IRE))
3290[2] 3873[3] 4405[4] 5352[4] 6419[10] 6950[12] 7579[8]

Clip Art *Jamie Osborne* 43
2 b f Acclamation Semaphore (Zamindar (USA))
3511[6]

Clive Clifton (IRE) *Phil York* a68 65
3 b g Wootton Bassett Dearest Daisy (Forzando)
140[2] ◆ 265[4] 524[3] (725) 1137[6] 1238[5] 2152[9] 3955[2] 4204[2] 5397[8] 5830[4]

Cloak And Degas (IRE) *Tim McCarthy* a71 48
4 b g Sakhee's Secret Coup De Torchon (FR) (Namid)
28[7] 1928[13] 2379[13] 7069[7] 7693[8] 8595[7]

Clockmaker (IRE) *Conor Dore* a77 92
10 b g Danetime(IRE) Lady Ingabelle (IRE) (Catrail (USA))
1[2] 49[2] 367[4] 446[3] 598[9] 792[2] 890[8] 3595[8] 4094[10] 4497[6]

Clock On Tom *Denis Quinn* a55 63
6 b g Trade Fair Night Owl (Night Shift (USA))
(155) (362) 505[9] 527[4] 702[2] 870[12] 1578[9] 3401[9] 6514[9] 7231[11] 8492[11]

Clockwinder (IRE) *Stefano Botti* 101
4 b h Intikhab(USA) Ars Nova (IRE) (Barathea (IRE))
7565a[3]

Clodianna (IRE) *Roger Charlton* a73 67
3 gr f Clodovil(IRE) Indiannie Moon (Fraam)
243[4]

Clonard Street *A J Martin* 103
4 b g Archipenko(USA) Moi Aussi (USA) (Mt. Livermore (USA))
6389a[21]

Clondaw Warrior (IRE) *W P Mullins* a49 112
9 br g Overbury(IRE) Thespian (IRE) (Tiraaz (USA))
3387[3] 5428a[2] 6284[8]

Clon Rocket (IRE) *John Holt* a60 51
3 b g Lilbourne Lad(IRE) Ryalahna (IRE) (High Chaparral (IRE))
1485[5] 1817[6] 2336[9] 2974[8] 3439[4] 4321[8] 4848[11] 5368[7] 5887[14] 6522[6] 6790[8] 7145[9]

Closer To Home (IRE) *David Pipe* a81 49
4 b g Soldier Of Fortune(IRE) Maid For Music (IRE) (Dubai Destination (USA))
779[8]

Cloth Of Stars (IRE) *A Fabre* 114
3 b c Sea The Stars(IRE) Strawberry Fledge (USA) (Kingmambo (USA))
(1230a) (2076a) 2896[8] 4332a[3]

Clotilde *William Knight* a85 103
4 br m Dubawi(IRE) Mary Boleyn (IRE) (King's Best (USA))
(1158) (1268) (1932) 2689[2] 3672[3] 3979[11] 5645[12]

Cloudberry *Roger Charlton* a88 97
3 b g Pivotal Clouded Leopard (USA) (Danehill (USA))
(3769) (6084) (6300) (7505) ◆

Cloud Dragon (IRE) *Hugo Palmer* a61
2 br c Dark Angel(IRE) Karliysha (IRE) (Kalanisi (IRE))
8384[6]

Clouded Gold *Michael Appleby* a55 44
4 ch g Resplendent Glory(IRE) Segretezza (IRE) (Perugino (USA))
3843[11] 4370[8] 6105[7]

Cloud Monkey (IRE) *Martin Todhunter* a68 83
6 bb g Marju(IRE) Sweet Clover (Rainbow Quest (USA))
2163[11] 3263[7] 4044[6] 7043[5]

Cloud Nine (FR) *Tony Carroll* a34 56
3 b f Sakhee(USA) Heaven (Reel Buddy (USA))
516[7] 2177[8]

Cloud Seven *Chris Wall* a88 77
4 br g New Approach(IRE) Regrette Rien (USA) (Unbridled's Song (USA))
1418[7] 2214[8] 3783[3]

Clovelly Bay (IRE) *Marcus Tregoning* a81 80
5 b g Bushranger(IRE) Crystalline Stream (FR) (Polish Precedent (USA))
2367[3] 2888[7] 3690[3] 4476[6] 4940[7] 8162[7] (8367)

Club House (IRE) *Kevin Frost* a41 37
6 b g Marju(IRE) Idesia (IRE) (Green Desert (USA))
7944[7] 8207[6]

Clubland (IRE) *Garry Moss* a89 52
7 b g Red Clubs(IRE) Racjilanemm (Kyllachy)
198[2] (508) 694[10] 938[6] 1444[15] 2857[8] 3580[8] 4496[9] 5034[8] 5797[10] 6131[7] 6589[7] 7660[5] 7852[2] 7959[6] ◆ 8345[7] 8571[5]

Club Wexford (IRE) *J S Bolger* 87
5 b g Lawman(FR) Masnada (IRE) (Erins Isle)
1015a[2]

Clumber Place *John Balding* 39
10 ch m Compton Place Inquirendo (USA) (Roberto (USA))
2655[10]

Clumber Street *Lee Carter* a64 53
5 ch g Compton Place Tinnarinka (Observatory (USA))
2562[3] (3317) 4536[5]

C Note (IRE) *Martyn Meade* a98 104
3 b g Iffraaj Alexander Queen (IRE) (King's Best (USA))
(1315) ◆ 1773[5] 3269[10] 4395[4] 6338[3] (7241) 7497[18] 7701[6] 8489[6]

Coachella (IRE) *Ed de Giles* 53
2 gr g Kyllachy Indian Belle (IRE) (Indian Ridge)
5890[15] 7071[9] 7574[8]

Coarse Cut (IRE) *Eve Johnson Houghton* a69 74
3 b g Duke Of Marmalade(IRE) Keladora (USA) (Crafty Prospector (USA))
1718[4] 2563[4] 3509[7] (4024) (4942) (5286) 5746[2] 6315[4]

Coastal Cyclone *Harry Dunlop* a73 67
2 b c Canford Cliffs(IRE) Seasonal Cross (Cape Cross (IRE))
4989[3] 6053[9] 7975[4] ◆ (8175)

Coasted (USA) *Leah Gyarmati* 109
2 b f Tizway(USA) Malibu Pier (USA) (Malibu Moon (USA))
7809a[2]

Cockle Town Boy *Brendan Powell* a57 47
4 ch g Cockney Rebel(IRE) Rare Cross (IRE) (Cape Cross (IRE))
241[3] 589[2]

Cockney Blue *Malgorzata Fabianska* 74
3 b f Cockney Rebel(IRE) However (IRE) (Hector Protector (USA))
3207a[9]

Cockney Boy *John Gallagher* 61
3 ch g Cockney Rebel(IRE) Menha (Dubawi (IRE))
2207[14] 3736[10] 4847[7] 5053[7]

Cockney Island *Philip McBride* a56 75
4 b m Cockney Rebel(IRE) Island Rhapsody (Bahamian Bounty)
6459[4] 6879[4] 7363[8] 7572[6] 7815[5]

Cocoa Beach (IRE) *Sir Mark Prescott Bt* a86 63
3 b f Acclamation Smart Coco (USA) (Smarty Jones (USA))
(102) ◆ 315[3] 4643[2] 5285[8] 5955[10] 6926[8]

Coco City (FR) *M Delcher Sanchez* a69 61
2 b c Elusive City(USA) Coco (USA) (Storm Bird (CAN))
7588a[4]

Coco John (FR) *Mlle B Renk* 21
2 gr g Rajsaman(FR) Continental Kid (IRE) (Exit To Nowhere (USA))
6638a[16]

Coco La Belle (IRE) *Tim Easterby* a34 59
2 b f Sir Prancealot(IRE) Dry Lightning (Shareef Dancer (USA))
2852[4] 3261[11] 3881[6] 4404[2] 4843[4] 5364[10] 5974[2] 6446[7] 6678[19]

Coconut Creme *William Haggas* 65
2 b f Cape Cross(IRE) Soft Centre (Zafonic (USA))
7441[5] ◆

Code Of Honor *Saeed bin Suroor* a77 103
6 b g Zafeen(FR) Verbal Intrigue (USA) (Dahar (USA))
93a[8] 538a[2]

Code Red *William Muir* 112
4 ch h Bahamian Bounty Just Devine (IRE) (Montjeu (IRE))
1637[10] 2546[7] 5926[6] 7115[11]

Codeshare *Alan Swinbank* a60
4 b g Dansili Clepsydra (Sadler's Wells (USA))
8585[2]

Coeur De Lion *Alan King* a66 78
3 b g Pour Moi(IRE) Hora (Hernando (FR))
3535[5] 4056[10] 5129[5] 7270[3] 7624[2]

Coeur Dolois (IRE) *A Bonin* a57 60
5 b g High Chaparral(IRE) Tallulah Bell (USA) (Gone West (USA))
5281a[4]

Coherent (IRE) *William Haggas* a73 77
3 b g Rip Van Winkle(IRE) Hold Off (IRE) (Bering)
1411[2] ◆ 4028[3]

Cohesion *D Smaga* 103
3 b g Champs Elysees Winter Bloom (USA) (Aptitude (USA))
5218a[6] 6597a[5]

Coif (IRE) *A Fabre* a91 76
3 b f Shamardal(USA) Hairpin (USA) (Bernardini (USA))
1541a[9] 5006a[4] 5987a[8]

Coillte Cailin (IRE) *David O'Meara* a93 78
6 b m Oratorio(IRE) Forest Walk (IRE) (Shinko Forest (IRE))
(160) (465) 734[2] ◆ 888[3] 4850a[13] 5489[6] 6019[5] 7816[5] 8249[2] (8539)

Coillte Mach *David O'Meara* a53 65
3 b g Royal Applause Bassinet (USA) (Stravinsky (USA))
7368[11] 8188[8] 8411[9]

Coilogshakeysirgin (IRE) *Denis W Cullen* a47 49
9 br g Expelled(USA) Coilog Supreme (IRE) (Supreme Leader)
7801a[11]

Coisa Boa (IRE) *J E Hammond* 93
4 b m Lawman(FR) Ragazza Mio (IRE) (Generous (IRE))
7397a[10] 7861a[5] 8042a[8]

Coiste Bodhar (IRE) *Scott Dixon* a72 77
5 b g Camacho Nortolixa (FR) (Linamix (FR))
133[6] 340[7] 937[6] 961[4] (1026) 1154[6] 1298[3] 1401[7] 1495[11] (1790) 2040[6] 2622[7] (3268) 4039[8] 4874[6] 7018[10] (7290) 7591[3] 7626[10] 7773[2] 8010[5] 8099[3] 8349[9]

Cold As Ice (SAF) *William Haggas* a108 100
4 b m Western Winter(USA) Viva (SAF) (National Assembly (CAN))
483[3] ◆ 1065[5]

Cold Fusion (IRE) *David Flood* a61 76
3 b f Frozen Power(IRE) Tuscania (USA) (Woodman (USA))
361[3] 633[4] 814[6] (4356) 4635[4] 5508[5] 6370[4] 7014[2] 7500[15] 8211[9] 8348[4]

Cold Snap (IRE) *William Jarvis* a71 83
3 b g Medicean Shivering (Royal Applause)
2156[3] ◆ (2544) ◆

Cole Porter (IRE) *A P O'Brien* 86
3 b c Galileo(IRE) A Z Warrior (USA) (Bernardini (USA))
3341[12]

Colibri (IRE) *Hugo Palmer* 99
2 b c Redoute's Choice(AUS) High Days (IRE) (Hennessy (USA))
4866[8] 5356[4] (6183)

Collect Art (IRE) *Mohammed Jassim Ghazali* a54 82
9 b g Footstepsinthesand Night Scent (IRE) (Scenic)
755a[12]

Collected (USA) *Bob Baffert* a106 96
3 ch c City Zip(USA) Helena Bay (Johannesburg (USA))
2499a[10]

Collision Course (IRE) *A Oliver* a70 92
3 gr g Fast Company(IRE) Anam Chara (IRE) (Soviet Star (USA))
1938a[5] 7706a[13]

Collodi (GER) *Neil Mulholland* a77 76
7 b g Konigstiger(GER) Codera (GER) (Zilzal (USA))
1640[6] 2872[5] 3064[4] 3905[5] (6444) (6662)

Colomano *Markus Klug* 103
2 b c Cacique(IRE) Codera (GER) (Zilzal (USA))
7399a[5] (7842a)

Colombe Bleu *Tony Coyle* 68
3 b f Manduro(GER) Blue Dream (IRE) (Cadeaux Genereux)
2674[9] 3367[12] 3604[7] 5181[4] 5483[12]

Colonel Bossington (IRE) *William Knight* a74 60
3 b g Azamour(IRE) Ros The Boss (IRE) (Danehill (USA))
1091[3] 1577[6] 2156[7] 2818[6] 6123[6] 6576[8]

Colonel Frank *Ed Walker* a79 84
2 b g Dutch Art Loquacity (Diktat)
3818[6] ◆ 5077[2] (6009) 6536[7] (7185) 7764[6]

Colonel Samsen (USA) *Eoin Harty* 85
2 b g Colonel John(USA) Blondz Away (USA) (Skip Away (USA))
7266a[10]

Colonial Classic (FR) *John Gosden* a90 96
3 b f Dansili Flame Of Hestia (IRE) (Giant's Causeway (USA))
(3990) 4668[3] 5382[2] (5927) 6497a[9] 6951[7]

Color Force (IRE) *Gay Kelleway* a49 54
3 gr f Dark Angel(IRE) Amistad (GER) (Winged Love (IRE))
2177[12] 2904[6] 5338[3] 7463[7]

Colorful Charades (USA) *Rudy Rodriguez* a83
2 rg f Discreet Cat(USA) Laila's Punch (USA) (Two Punch (USA))
7830a[12]

Colourbearer (IRE) *Charlie Wallis* a77 61
9 ch g Pivotal Centifolia (FR) (Kendor (FR))
28[6] 319[10] 426[11] 799[8] (1159) 1341[2] 1712[2] 2765[3] 7444[6] 7899[10] 8067[8] 8365[2] 8595[2]

Colour Blue (IRE) *W McCreery* a88 102
5 b m Holy Roman Emperor(IRE) Catch The Blues (IRE) (Bluebird (USA))
4218a[5] 5564a[4] (6355a) 6939[5] 7676a[9]

Colourfilly *Tom Dascombe* a74 72
4 ch m Compton Place Where's Broughton (Cadeaux Genereux)
127[4] 456[4] 564[2] 667[4] 1725[3] 2403[3] (2655) 3132[9] 4240[5] 5247[5] 5523[3] 6426[4] 7363[5] (8135)

Colour Guard *M Al Mheiri* a72 69
8 b g Shamardal(USA) Colorvista (Shirley Heights)
12a[6]

Colour My World *Ed McMahon* a57 55
6 gr g With Approval(CAN) Nadeszhda (Nashwan (USA))
429[7] 681[6] 1117[2] 1595[5] 2442[4]

Colour Play (USA) *Mark Johnston* 65
3 b f Medaglia d'Oro(USA) Blue Duster (USA) (Danzig (USA))
3769[9] 4235[5] ◆ 4761[6]

Columbanus (IRE) *Kenneth Slack*
5 b g Jeremy(USA) Shamah (Unfuwain (USA))
1253[13]

Column *James Fanshawe* a84 90
3 b g Mount Nelson Tottie (Fantastic Light (USA))
1623[5] 4104[9] 4776[3] 5933[4] 6736[5] 7428[4]

Comadoir (IRE) *Paul Burgoyne* a52 50
10 ch g Medecis Hymn Of The Dawn (USA) (Phone Trick (USA))
87[3] 1263[5] 1781[4] 2969[9]

Comanche Chieftain (CAN) *Michael Appleby* a74 71
4 b g Broken Vow(USA) Platinum Preferred (CAN) (Vindication (USA))
212[2] 438[2] ◆ 708[4] 890[4] ◆ 1028[2] 1347[3] 2445[6] 4237[3] 4785[7]

Combative *Amanda Perrett* a86 95
3 b c Sinndar(IRE) Intense (Dansili)
(1575) ◆ 2413[5] 3532[6] 4827[5] ◆ 5147[2] 6110[9] 6526[6]

Combe Hay (FR) *Henry Spiller* a69 64
3 b f Elusive City(USA) Coiffure (King's Best (USA))
1708[4] 2178[6] 3894[6] 7214[7] 8257[3]

Come Alive *A Fabre* 104
3 b f Dansili Portrayal (USA) (Saint Ballado (CAN))
2282a[8] 2928a[2] 5498a[6] 6272a[11]

Come Back King (IRE) *Michael Appleby* a81 69
3 ch g Pivotal Queen Consort (USA) (Kingmambo (USA))
4895[6] 5438[4] ◆ 5731[2] 6445[7] 7895[6] 8238[2] ◆ (8477)

Comedia Eria (FR) *P Monfort* a79 79
4 b m Lope De Vega(IRE) Vola Vola (IRE) (Danehill Dancer (IRE))
5906a[6]

Comedy House *Michael Madgwick* a68 58
8 b g Auction House(USA) Kyle Akin (Vettori (IRE))
156[6] 634[10] 950[5] 3767[8] 4995[7] 8254[7] 8468[5]

Comedy King (IRE) *Richard Fahey* 88
5 bb g Dansili Comic (IRE) (Be My Chief (USA))
4634[12] 4919[9]

Comedy School (USA) *Mark Johnston* 91
2 b f Distorted Humor(USA) Cheeky Charm (USA) (A.P. Indy (USA))
2162[8] (6732) (7120) ◆ 7536[10]

Come On Come On (IRE) *Clive Cox* 78
2 br c Lord Shanakill(USA) Maridiyna (IRE) (Sinndar (IRE))
(6888)

Come On Dave (IRE) *John Butler* a92 80
7 b g Red Clubs(IRE) Desert Sprite (IRE) (Tagula (IRE))
4[6] 323[5] 359[4] 655[3] 966[3] (2562) 3638[3] 6324[7] 7643[9] 8032[8] 8280[11] 8463[2]

Come On Lulu *David Thompson* a46 47
5 ch m Calcutta Flashing Floozie (Muhtarram (USA))
4260[12] 4648[9] 5726[6] 6738[10] 7044[3] 7361[8] 7657[7] 8091[5] 8386[12]

Come On Percy *Richard Fahey* a53 70
2 b c Sir Percy Collette's Choice (Royal Applause)
4161[8] 4663[7] 5476[6] 6159[6] 7768[11] 7981[9] 8230[5]

Comicas (USA) *Charlie Appleby* a87 73
3 ch g Distorted Humor(USA) Abby's Angel (USA) (Touch Gold (USA))
(536a) 807a[2] 1991[6] 8578a[3]

Comino (IRE) *Kevin Ryan* 89
5 b g Tagula(IRE) Malta (USA) (Gone West (USA))
1563[12] 2256[10] 2679[14] 3708[9] 4893[12] 5859[6] 6502[10]

Commanche *Chris Dwyer* a68 65
7 ch g Sleeping Indian Happy Memories (IRE) (Thatching)
1154[8] 1533[11] 1945[4] 2309[3] 2584[7] 2964[4] 3822[3] 4278[11] 5797[4] 6249[5] (6902) (7694) 7912[4] 8120[4] (8288)

Commander *Roger Varian* 64
2 b c Frankel Model Queen (USA) (Kingmambo (USA))
7503[8]

Commander Blue *Steph Hollinshead* 18
2 b g Royal Applause Dream In Waiting (Oasis Dream)
2119[8] 2500[U]

Commander Cole *Saeed bin Suroor* a101 71
2 b c Kyllachy Welsh Angel (Dubai Destination (USA))
6295[2] 6873[6] (7432) (7909) ◆

Commander Won (IRE) *Dermot Anthony McLoughlin* a64 69
4 bb g Zamindar(USA) Sheboygan (IRE) (Grand Lodge (USA))
2114a[11]

Commanding Role *Michael Blanshard* a26 52
3 ch f Major Cadeaux Cultural Role (Night Shift (USA))
1141[9] 2107[6]

Commissar *Mandy Rowland* a74 70
7 b g Soviet Star(USA) Sari (Faustus (USA))
88[5] 6701[12] 8124[6] 8318[11]

Commissioned (IRE) *Gordon Elliott* 103
6 b g Authorized(IRE) Zelda (IRE) (Caerleon (USA))
(3387) 4799[P]

Commodity (IRE) *Sir Michael Stoute* a59 75
3 ch g Dutch Art Royale Danehill (IRE) (Danehill (USA))
1397[6] 7218[3] 7616[6]

Commodore (IRE) *George Baker* a93 90
4 b g Kodiac Deportment (Barathea (IRE))
1418[2] ◆ 2246[13] 4299[4] 5075[6] (6123) 6736[9]

Common Touch (IRE) *Willie Musson* a75 75
8 ch g Compton Place Flying Finish (FR) (Priolo (USA))
546[8]

Communicator *Andrew Balding* a88 91
8 b g Motivator Goodie Twosues (Fraam)
244[3] 556[6] 983[4] 1642[6] 2782[6] 3639[3] 4752[15] 5642[6] 6362[5]

Company *Richard Hannon* 65
2 ch f Pivotal Invitee (Medicean)
3812[3] 4707[7] 5705[7] 6440[5]

Company Asset (IRE) *Kevin Ryan* a80 83
3 ch f Fast Company(IRE) Changari (USA) (Gulch (USA))
3213[4] ◆ 4116[5] 4548[2] 5179[3] 5514[7] 6113[5] 7108[7]

Comparative *Lydia Pearce* a62 61
4 b g Oasis Dream Indication (Sadler's Wells (USA))
2379[14] 3069[15]

Comparinka *Scott Dixon* a55 60
3 ch f Compton Place Tinnarinka (Observatory (USA))
510[6] 820[2] 1670[6] 3069[7] 4240[11]

Compas Scoobie *Roger Varian* a80 75
3 br g Kheleyf(USA) Fantastic Santanyi (Fantastic Light (USA))
1755[5] 2109[2] 2349[3] 3145[2] 3899[3] 6583[5] (7459) 7959[3]

Competent *Kristin Stubbs* a71 55
4 b g Compton Place Pantita (Polish Precedent (USA))
342[3] 789[2] 1085[3] 2093[13]

Complicit (IRE) *J F Levins* a101 81
5 b g Captain Rio Molomo (Barathea (IRE))
125[3] 485[6] 748[7] 1069[7] 1629[10] 2246[9] 2819[8] 7803a[6] 8197a[10]

Complimenti (USA) *Doug Watson* a84
2 ch f Congrats(USA) Goldilocks' Cat (USA) (Seeking The Gold (USA))
8575a[3]

Complimentor (IRE) *Hilal Kobeissi* a104 104
6 ch g Acclamation Lovely Blossom (FR) (Spinning World (USA))
755a[14]

Comprise *Michael Bell* 76
2 b g Pivotal Constitute (USA) (Gone West (USA))
6071[3] 6731[2]

Compromise *Conor Dore* a40
3 ch g Compton Place Palinisa (FR) (Night Shift (USA))
275[10] 557[8] 697[6] 824[8] 1162[6] 1292[4]

Compton Brave *J R Jenkins* 39
2 b g Compton Place Willmar (IRE) (Zafonic (USA))
6524[11] 7072[10] 7414[8]

Compton Lady (IRE) *Ismail Mohammed* a37 66
3 b f Compton Place Treble Seven (USA) (Fusaichi Pegasus (USA))
1703[6] 3236[10]

Compton Lane *Rod Millman* a53 75
2 b g Compton Place Dubai Affair (Dubawi (IRE))
1770[7] 2180[3] 3231[2] (6440) 6658[10] 7217[13]

Compton Mews *Les Eyre* 53
3 ch f Compton Place Dhuyoof (IRE) (Sinndar (IRE))
3879[6] 4492[9] 4845[5] 5920[11]

Compton Mill *Hughie Morrison* a77 84
4 b g Compton Place Classic Millennium (Midyan (USA))
2296[5] 2791[5] (3617) 4561[4] 5071[2] 6301[7] 6876[2] 7666[4] 7980[7]

Compton Park *Les Eyre* a73 84
9 ch h Compton Place Corps De Ballet (IRE) (Fasliyev (USA))
2857[10] 3265[8] 3646[2] 3980[11] 4428[4] 4608[10] 4896[9] 5859[7]

Compton Poppy *Tony Carroll* a66 83
2 b f Compton Place Miss Poppy (Averti (IRE))
3511[7] 4756[11] (5542) 6507[6]

Compton Prince *Milton Bradley* a66 44
7 ch g Compton Place Malelane (IRE) (Prince Sabo)
167[6] 320[2] (442) 658[4] 889[2] 3259[7] 3735[10] 3984[7] 4389[5] (5126) 5194[6] 5736[5] 8030[6] 8095[5] 8316[2] 8595[6]

Compton River *Bryan Smart* a77 67
4 b g Compton Place Inagh River (Fasliyev (USA))
1255[5] 1668[4] 2052[6] 2423[2] 2778[5] 3368[7] 3779[2] (4228) (4968) 5354[2] 6745[2] 7252[2] 7596[5] (8078) 8495[2]

Compton's Gee Wiz (IRE) *Brett Johnson*
2 b f Compton Place Private Means (Dansili)
2583[9] 3232[9]

Compton Sky (USA) *Jo Hughes* 62
3 b g Sky Mesa(USA) See How She Runs (USA) (Maria's Mon (USA))
1740[13] 2828[9]

Computable *Tim Easterby* 80
2 ch c Compton Place Kummel Excess (IRE) (Exceed And Excel (AUS))
2162[7] 2800[2] 3112[6] 5583[12] (7248)

Concord (IRE) *Marcus Tregoning* a69 64
4 b g Mawatheeq(USA) Amhooj (Green Desert (USA))
2876[5]

Concur (IRE) *Rod Millman* a47 50
3 ch g Approve(IRE) Tradmagic (IRE) (Traditionally (USA))
1146[6] 1734[9] 2148[3] 2590[9] 3198[6] 4290[4] 4796[4] 5570[7] 5954[5] 6361[2] 7211[2] 7645[4]

Condamine (IRE) *Jeremy Gask* a77
3 b g Duke Of Marmalade(IRE) Miracolia (IRE) (Montjeu (IRE))
7942[3] 8195[6] 8366[5]

Confessional *Tim Easterby* a85 97
9 b g Dubawi(IRE) Golden Nun (Bishop Of Cashel)
1968[6] 2259[8] 2613[9] (2931) 3151[9] 3637[4] (4032) 4373[5] 4735[6] 5390[2] 5641[5] 6119[2] 6327[12] 6779[7] 7358[2] 7537[5]

Confident Kid *Saeed bin Suroor* a73 81
3 b g Dubawi(IRE) Longing To Dance (Danehill Dancer (IRE))
3856[2] 4690[2] 6014[3] 6423[4]

Confrontation (USA) *Kiaran McLaughlin* a109
6 br g War Pass(USA) Successfully Sweet (USA) (Successful Appeal (USA))
(454a) 1105a[6]

Confrontational (IRE) *John Joseph Murphy* a89 86
2 b c Footstepsinthesand Chevanah (IRE) (Chevalier (IRE))
2494a[6] 4171a[4] 7130a[5]

Conistone *James Bethell* a56 68
2 ch f Poet's Voice Protectress (Hector Protector (USA))
2254[2] 2779[5] 4603[5] 5549[10] 6213[2] 6713[9]

Conkering Hero (IRE) *Joseph Tuite* a69 41
2 ch g Arakan(USA) Brioney (IRE) (Barathea (IRE))
5890[12] 6087[4] 6881[9]

Connacht Girl (IRE) *K R Burke* 87
2 b f Dark Angel(IRE) Fairy Flight (USA) (Fusaichi Pegasus (USA))
5072[3] 5727[2] 6555[6] 7655a[5]

Connect (USA) *Chad C Brown* a115
3 bb c Curlin(USA) Bullville Belle (USA) (Holy Bull (USA))
5913a[6]

Connemera Queen *Tracy Waggott* 65
3 ch f Major Cadeaux Cashleen (USA) (Lemon Drop Kid (USA))
1815[6] (2304) 3213[8] 5973[9] 6502[11]

Connie O'Meara (IRE) *Robert Eddery*
3 b f Roderic O'Connor(IRE) Korabushka (Selkirk (USA))
1313[4]

Conquerant *Ismail Mohammed* a72 79
5 ch g Dubawi(IRE) The World (Dubai Destination (USA))
12a[3] 407a[4]

Conqueress (IRE) *Tom Dascombe* 77
2 ch f Dandy Man(IRE) Sesmen (Inchinor)
3186[2] 3592[3] 4397[2] 5387[2] (5772)

Conquest Enforcer (CAN) *Mark Casse* 108
3 b c Into Mischief(USA) Keen Victory (USA) (Victory Gallop (CAN))
7403a[3]

Conry (IRE) *Ian Williams* a53 74
10 ch g Captain Rio Altizaf (Zafonic (USA))
3849[6] 6226[5] ◆

Conselice *Stefano Botti* 98
3 gr f Showcasing Dictatrix (Diktat)
(1685a) 2730a[13]

Considered Opinion *Ralph Beckett* 83
2 b f Redoute's Choice(AUS) Forest Crown (Royal Applause)
5400[2]

Consistant *Brian Baugh* a64 69
8 b g Reel Buddy(USA) Compact Disc (IRE) (Royal Academy (USA))
1676[5] 2130[3] (2974) 3743[2] 4321[7] 4932[6] 5797[11]

Consortium (IRE) *Neil King* a73 68
4 b g Teofilo(IRE) Wish List (IRE) (Mujadil (USA))
(637) 786[2]

Constable Clouds (USA) *Gary Moore* a59 56
3 b g Blame(USA) For Spacious Skies (USA) (Golden Missile (USA))
2293[6] 3003[3] 3319[4] 3988[8]

Constantino (IRE) *Richard Fahey* a94 83
3 b c Danehill Dancer(IRE) Messias Da Silva (USA) (Tale Of The Cat (USA))
2161[9] 2654[4] 3187[3] 8251[2] 8478[2]

Consulting *Martyn Meade* a86 78
3 ch c Kyllachy Doctor's Note (Pursuit Of Love)
3360[6] 3978[8] 4502[4] (5027) 5832[2] 6580[9] 7066[3] 7738[4] 7886[13] 8206[4] (8389)

Conte Colorate (FR) *Mlle M Henry* a65 64
7 b g Le Vie Dei Colori Contessina (IRE) (Medicean)
5281a[6]

Contendit *Michael Easterby* a47 31
3 b g Indesatchel(IRE) Hope Chest (Kris)
2553[12] 6646[14] 7260[9]

Contentment (AUS) *J Size* 117
5 ch g Hussonet(USA) Jemison (AUS) (Commands (AUS))
1912a[2] 8332a[4]

Contentment *William Haggas* 78
2 b f Cacique(IRE) Cartimandua (Medicean)
5400[4] 6061[2] 7574[5]

Contingency *Jane Chapple-Hyam* a75 77
3 b f Champs Elysees Cyclone Connie (Dr Devious (IRE))
3235[12] 3781[6] 4367[10] 5398[2] 6127[4] 6885[2]

Continuum *Peter Hedger* 95
7 bb g Dansili Clepsydra (Sadler's Wells (USA))
1893[9] 4077[7] 4581[8] 5358[2]

Contrapposto (IRE) *David Menuisier* 92
2 b c Cacique(IRE) Interim Payment (USA) (Red Ransom (USA))
4649[5] 5615[2] ◆ (7074) ◆ 7539[9]

Contrast (IRE) *Richard Hannon* 96
2 ch c Dutch Art Israar (Machiavellian (USA))
4387[4] (5108) 6116[4] 6546[4]

Contribution *A Fabre* 106
4 b m Champs Elysees Concentric (Sadler's Wells (USA))
1822a[3] 2727a[4] 4696a[4] 5461a[3] 8024a[7]

Control Centre (IRE) *Richard Hannon* a68 56
2 b c Dragon Pulse(IRE) Margaux Magique (IRE) (Xaar)
2082[6] 3032[4] 3813[14] 5806[9] 6208[5] (6588) 6961[2]

Convergence (IRE) *Debbie Mountain* a106 109
4 b h Cape Cross(IRE) Zahoo (IRE) (Nayef (USA))
744a[12]

Convey *Sir Michael Stoute* a92 117
4 b g Dansili Insinuate (USA) (Mr Prospector (USA))
1637[7] 2191[2] 2691[2] 3273[22] 4127[7] (4688) 5404[6] 5926[2] 6117[3] 6955[5]

Cookie Ring (IRE) *Patrick Holmes* a66 50
5 b g Moss Vale(IRE) Talah (Danehill (USA))
107[9] (257) 608[3] (617) 792[5] ◆ 904[2] 1131[6] 1262[7] 1700[4] 2096[8]

Cook Islands (IRE) *A P O'Brien* a101 100
3 b g Fastnet Rock(AUS) Tree Chopper (USA) (Woodman (USA))
1370a[4] 1994[5]

Cool Angel (IRE) *William Muir* a57 10
3 gr f Zebedee Malthouse Mistress (IRE) (Peintre Celebre (USA))
2375[13] 3720[9] 6101[3] 6677[10]

Cool Bahamian (IRE) *Eve Johnson Houghton* a87 90
5 b g Bahamian Bounty Keritana (FR) (One Cool Cat (USA))
2430[8] 2547[7] (2903) 3414[13] 4862[27] 5488[4] (5852) 6878[10] 7651[13] 8314[10]

Cool Baranca (GER) *Dianne Sayer* 39
10 b m Beat Hollow Cool Storm (IRE) (Rainbow Quest (USA))
5726[9]

Cool Beans *Roy Bowring* a58 54
4 b g Kyllachy Stellar Brilliant (USA) (Kris S (USA))
150[11] 251[5] 822[6] 1049[5] 1295[3] 4498[11]

Cool Breeze (IRE) *David Simcock* 37
2 b f Dream Ahead(USA) Dead Cool (Kyllachy)
6078[9] 6454[9]

Coolcalmcollected (IRE) *David Loughnane* a75 74
4 b m Acclamation Jalissa (Mister Baileys)
1125[4] 1252[10] 2416[9] 3078[12] 3750[11] 5355[3] 5734[3] 6568[2] 6853[4] (7211) 7426[6] 7595[6] 7896[7] 8121[9]

Cool Climate (IRE) *Richard Fahey* 73
2 br c Bated Breath Spanish Sun (USA) (El Prado (IRE))
5371[7] 5959[6] 6679[2] 7319[3]

Cool Cowboy (USA) *Doug Watson* a111
5 ch h Kodiak Kowboy(USA) Grand Breeze (USA) (Grand Slam (USA))
186a[2] (374a) 624a[2] (842a) 1101a[3] 8396a[3]

Cool Crescendo *Jonathan Portman* a44 42
3 b f Royal Applause Cool Catena (One Cool Cat (USA))
104[3] 1045[3] 1292[2] 1420[2] 2255[12] 8026[12]

Cool Echo *J R Jenkins* a52 73
2 b f Mount Nelson Ellcon (IRE) (Royal Applause)
2793[6] 3718[2] 6088[6] 7071[6] 7576[6]

Cool Esprit (IRE) *A Fabre* a67
2 gr f Invincible Spirit(IRE) Coolnagree (IRE) (Dark Angel (IRE))
7970a[3]

Coolfitch (IRE) *David O'Meara* a86 82
2 b f Roderic O'Connor(IRE) Farbenspiel (IRE) (Desert Prince (IRE))
(1443) 2219[7] 2670[5] 3143[4] (4679) 4869[5] 5741[3] 6343[2] 6538[5] 7073[3] 7258[2] 7600[7]

Cool Macavity (IRE) *Nicky Henderson* a75 91
8 b g One Cool Cat(USA) Cause Celebre (IRE) (Peintre Celebre (USA))
4077[3] 5358[7]

Coolmore (IRE) *A P O'Brien* 106
3 ch f Galileo(IRE) You'resothrilling (USA) (Storm Cat (USA))
1396[5] 2509a[10] 3452a[5] 4174a[3] 5430a[10]

Cool Music (IRE) *Antony Brittain* a62 61
6 b m One Cool Cat(USA) Musicology (USA) (Singspiel (IRE))
39[3] 1114[5] 2915[3] 3842[4] 4716[2] 5083[3] 5805[3] 7516[8]

Cool Run Girl (IRE) *Iain Jardine* a41 55
2 br f Lord Shanakill(USA) Fantastic Anna (IRE) (Fantastic Light (USA))
5577[4] 6925[12] 7248[5] 7579[9]

Cool Silk Boy (IRE) *James Given* a69 58
3 b g Big Bad Bob(IRE) Kheleyf's Silver (IRE) (Kheleyf (USA))
57[5] 322[7] 797[3] 2854[8] 5855[4]

Cool Silk Girl *James Given* 25
3 br f Motivator Captain's Paradise (IRE) (Rock Of Gibraltar (IRE))
1920[4] 4027[6]

Cool Star (FR) *A Bonin* a59 59
11 ch g Starborough Valverda (USA) (Irish River (FR))
512a[10]

Cool Strutter (IRE) *Karen Tutty* a60 65
4 b g Kodiac Cassava (IRE) (Vettori (IRE))
416[7] 561[9] 893[5] 1044[6] 1625[13] 2379[6] 2643[3] 3880[6] 4454[9] 4771[6] 5368[10] (6105) 6451[5] 6685[6] 7144[4] 7323[5] 7604[6] 7995[4] 8306[3]

Cool Team (IRE) *Hugo Palmer* a77
2 b g Tamayuz Coolminx (IRE) (One Cool Cat (USA))
6924[2]

Cool Thunder (IRE) *Kevin Prendergast* 99
3 b f Shamardal(USA) Asfurah's Dream (IRE) (Nayef (USA))
2509a[5] 7392a[12]

Cooperess *Ali Stronge* a61 61
3 b f Sixties Icon Vilnius (Imperial Dancer)
2415[7] 3198[7] 3734[3] 3970[4] (4269) 4562[3] 5076[6] 6291[3] 7212[2] 7602[9]

Coorg (IRE) *Chris Dwyer* a81 41
4 ch g Teofilo(IRE) Creese (Halling (USA))
(61) (157) (358)

Copa Beech *Olly Williams* 13
2 ch c Paco Boy(IRE) My Girl Jode (Haafhd)
3576[6] 4371[14] 7283[11] 8237[12]

Coping Stone *David Brown* a67 67
2 b f Bahamian Bounty Brick Tops (Danehill Dancer (IRE))
2771[3] 5272[8] 5771[6] 6419[2] 6950[18] 8033[8] 8285[5]

Copper Baked (FR) *K R Burke* 72
2 bb f Never On Sunday(FR) Shakila (Cadeaux Genereux)
4063[6] 4487[3] 5986a[6]

Copper Cavalier *Michael Blanshard* a59
5 ch g Haafhd Elle Crystal (Mozart (IRE))
615[2] ◆ 1042[7] 1533[15] 1833[4] 2155[4] 3648[8] 3984[9]

Copper Knight (IRE) *Hugo Palmer* 89
2 b g Sir Prancealot(IRE) Mystic Dream (Oasis Dream)
1422[4] 1713[2] (1965) 2624[6] 3247[21] 4394[21]

Coprah *Cathrine Erichsen* a87 102
8 b g Bertolini(USA) Oatcake (Selkirk (USA))
1957a[11] (3449a) 5950a[4] 6942[14]

Coquine *David O'Meara* a69 57
3 b f Monsieur Bond(IRE) Stolen Glance (Mujahid (USA))
2681[5] 3249[8] 4258[4] 4972[8] 5369[3] 5807[3] 6106[6] 6685[17] 7323[4] 7513[2] 7751[11] (8094) (8315)

Corail (IRE) *P D Deegan* 96
4 ch m Lope De Vega(IRE) Croisiere (USA) (Capote (USA))
1016a[11] 1127a[6] 3332a[6]

Coral Caye *Steph Hollinshead* 22
2 b f Pastoral Pursuits Vermilion Creek (Makbul)
7818[11]

Coral Cluster (IRE) *Thomas Cleary* a43 48
4 b m Intense Focus(USA) Balloura (USA) (Swain (IRE))
6463a[5]

Coral Island *David O'Meara* a50
3 ch f Equiano(FR) Windermere Island (Cadeaux Genereux)
105[7]

Coral Sea *Charles Hills* a69 73
2 gr f Excelebration(IRE) Tropical Paradise (IRE) (Verglas (IRE))
3812[2] 4503[3] 5542[3] 7439[2] 7996a[2] 8526[2]

Cordite (IRE) *Jim Boyle* a81 96
5 ch g Footstepsinthesand Marion Haste (IRE) (Ali-Royal (IRE))
134[6] 1545[4] 2032[5] 2868[5] 3534[12] 4048[4] 4532[5] 5357[9] 6806[8] 7418[2]

Cordon (USA) *Pavel Vashchenko* 95
3 bb c Archarcharch(USA) Golden Desert (USA) (Vindication (USA))
5429a[6]

Coreczka (IRE) *Miss Clare Louise Cannon* a72 58
5 b m Intense Focus(USA) Szewinska (Green Desert (USA))
36[4] 2363[8]

Corella (IRE) *Clive Cox* 53
3 b f Dream Ahead(USA) Nashira (Prince Sabo)
3059[13] 3850[4] 5168[5] 5953[7] 6407[9]

Coressos (FR) *Roberto Di Paolo* a62 63
5 b g Dalakhani(IRE) Nearthyka (IRE) (Sadler's Wells (USA))
5281a[8]

Corinthe (FR) *J-P Gauvin* 56
2 bb f Makfi Cornucopia (FR) (Kaldounevees (FR))
5986a[10]

Corinthian *Roger Varian* 93
3 b g Sea The Stars(IRE) Contradictive (USA) (Kingmambo (USA))
(2440) ◆ 3814[2] 6781[4] 7123[10]

Cork (FR) *F Monnier* a72 53
3 b g Redback Crosshaven (IRE) (Cape Cross (IRE))
5704a[2]

Corked (IRE) *Hugo Palmer* a72 72
3 b f Mastercraftsman(IRE) Dama'A (IRE) (Green Desert (USA))
1798[2] 2183[7] 3996[3] 4743[3]

Cornborough *Mark Walford* 78
5 ch g Sir Percy Emirates First (IRE) (In The Wings)
1241[6] 1631[2]

Cornelious (IRE) *Clifford Lines* a78 72
4 b g Cape Cross(IRE) Fantastic Spring (USA) (Fantastic Light (USA))
33[7] 2174[12] 2623[11] 3523[5] 4009[2] ◆ 4528[5] 5503[4] (5795) 6128[10] 6701[5] 6876[5] 7816[4] 7973[12] 8253[9]

Cornerstone Lad *Micky Hammond* 50
2 b g Delegator Chapel Corner (IRE) (Alhaarth (IRE))
7125[8] 7740[11]

Cornwallville (IRE) *Roger Fell* a104 103
4 ch h Makfi Morinqua (IRE) (Cadeaux Genereux)
2485[9] 3346[2] 3890[6] 4338[5] 4667[8] (5403) 6355a[8] 6788[10] 6942[17] (7990) 8311[6]

Corny (FR) *C Ferland* a61 77
3 gr f Makfi Orellana (USA) (With Approval (CAN))
2115a[6]

Coroberee (IRE) *John Gosden* 90
3 b c Dansili Cabaret (IRE) (Galileo (IRE))
(1483)

Corona Borealis *Martin Todhunter* 90
5 b g Galileo(IRE) Incheni (IRE) (Nashwan (USA))
2406[3] 4162[7] 4664[9]

Corona Del Inca (ARG) *Guillermo J Frenkel Santillan* a108
4 b m Luhuk(USA) Inca Brava (ARG) (Acceptable (USA))
7810a[P]

Coronation Cottage *Malcolm Saunders* 63
2 b f Pastoral Pursuits Avrilo (Piccolo)
4287[3] 5072[4] 5542[5] 6016[7]

Coronation Day *James Tate* a86 79
3 b f Bahamian Bounty Queensgate (Compton Place)
1723[2] 2177[6] 3422[3] (4258) 4742[4] 5247[2] (5478) (7281)

Coronet *John Gosden* 96
2 gr f Dubawi(IRE) Approach (Darshaan)
(6206) (7151) ◆

Corporal Maddox *Ronald Harris* a86 83
9 b g Royal Applause Noble View (USA) (Distant View (USA))
260[4] 546[4] (878) 944[6] 1142[6] 1634[5] 1997[9] 2643[6] 3405[6] 4132[3] 4608[6] (4908) 5357[4] 5793[6] 6442[4] 7968[3] 8378[6]

Corpus Chorister (FR) *David Menuisier* 83
3 b f Soldier Of Fortune(IRE) Bridge Of Peace (Anabaa (USA))
1755[4] 2505[4] 3355[3] 3906[5] 5326[9] (5746) (6334) 6527[6] 7060[5] 7625[2]

Correggio *Micky Hammond* 85
6 ch g Bertolini(USA) Arian Da (Superlative)
2556[11] 3166[15] 3711[7] 4237[2] 4892[7] 5293[3] 6058[5] 7043[9]

Corridor Kid (IRE) *Derek Shaw* a62 74
3 b g Kodiac All In Clover (IRE) (Bahri (USA))
1669[2] 5862[5] 6101[7] 6879[13]

Corroyer (IRE) *F Alloncle* a70 73
3 ch g Arcano(IRE) Hambye (Distant Relative)
1079[7] 1815[2] 2914[4] (3838) 5349a[6] 6310a[12] 7492a[14]

Corton Lad *Keith Dalgleish* a91 92
6 b g Refuse To Bend(IRE) Kelucia (IRE) (Grand Lodge (USA))
465[5] 888[6] 1999[4] 2199[3] 2688[5] (2832) 3391[3] 3950[3] 4407[10] 6559[7] 7139[4] 8007[10] 8283[7]

Corybas (FR) *Mlle A Voraz* a53 60
4 ch g Montmartre(FR) Rafale Pearl (FR) (Verbier (FR))
5216a[12]

Cosachope (FR) *P Sogorb* 101
2 b f Soave(GER) First Chope (FR) (Indian Rocket)
3182a[6] (3937a) 4694a[6] 6068a[5] 6694a[7]

Cosette (IRE) *Bernard Llewellyn* a69 82
5 b m Champs Elysees Luanas Pearl (IRE) (Bahri (USA))
420[8] 566[11] 693[7] 946[4] 1343[6] (1830) (2149) 3767[2] 4483[5]

Cosmeapolitan *Alan King* a101 97
3 b g Mawatheeq(USA) Cosmea (Compton Place)
3156[5] 3557[3] 4207[2] 4827[4] (5406) 6121[2] 7117[9] 8123[2]

Cosmica Sidera (IRE) *D Smaga* 95
3 b f Galileo(IRE) Bywayofthestars (Danehill (USA))
6497a[5]

Cosmic Beau (IRE) *Tom Dascombe* 66
2 ch c Dandy Man(IRE) High Inthe Sky (IRE) (High Chaparral (IRE))
1621[4] 1915[7] 2732[5] 3232[4] 3897[7]

Cosmic Boy (IRE) *Marco Botti* a68
2 b c Fast Company(IRE) Moon Shine (FR) (Groom Dancer (USA))
7962[2] 8189[5]

Cosmic Chatter *Ruth Carr* a74 90
6 b g Paris House Paradise Eve (Bahamian Bounty)
1046[6] 1321[9] 1869[6] 2346[8] 3021[2] 3553[2] 3753[3] 4569[4] (4896) 5182[3] 5372[2] 6079[11] 6714[2] 6927[6] (7413) 7858[9]

Cosmic Dust *Richard Whitaker* a47 47
3 b f Equiano(FR) Cosmic Song (Cosmonaut)
3776[5] 4005[9] 4410[8] 5277[5] 5920[7] 6909[8] 7145[7] 7856[3] 8306[10]

Cosmic Halo *Richard Fahey* a72 60
7 ch m Halling(USA) Cosmic Case (Casteddu)
88[3] 256[5] 420[5] 631[2] 672[2] 773[4] 1266[3] 1786[5] 2043[7] 2672[9]

Cosmic Ray *Daniel Mark Loughnane* a32 81
4 b g Phoenix Reach(IRE) Beat Seven (Beat Hollow)
2256[11] 2734[10] 5793[8] 6028[12]

Cosmic Sky *Tim Easterby* 52
2 b f Harbour Watch(IRE) Foolish Lady (IRE) (Exceed And Excel (AUS))
2254[8] 3902[8] 4405[7] 6026[6]

Cosmic Statesman *Richard Fahey* a64 71
4 ch g Halling(USA) Cosmic Case (Casteddu)
170[4] 354[4]

Cosmic Storm *Ralph Beckett* a70 78
3 br f Sea The Stars(IRE) Riotous Applause (Royal Applause)
2009[8] 2320[3] 3959[5] 4549[2] 5201[4] (5592) 6021[8]

Cosmic Tigress *John Quinn* a61 61
5 b m Tiger Hill(IRE) Cosmic Case (Casteddu)
789[5] ◆ 1346[5] 1873[5] 2233[6] 3018[7] (5781) 6438[3] 7045[6] 7367[2]

Cosmo Charlie (USA) *Doug Watson* a87
2 br c Stay Thirsty(USA) Lake Como (USA) (Salt Lake (USA))
(8391a)

Cosmopolitan Girl (IRE) *Robert Cowell* a74 82
3 b f Dream Ahead(USA) Absolute Music (USA) (Consolidator (USA))
(3127) 4585[2] ◆ 5040[3]

Costa Esmeralda (FR) *J A Remolina Diez* a66
2 b c Naaqoos Midnight Miracle (IRE) (Danehill Dancer (IRE))
7422a[4]

Costa Filey *Ed Vaughan* a71 72
5 b g Pastoral Pursuits Cosmic Destiny (IRE) (Soviet Star (USA))
3159[3] 3780[10] 4952[5] 5599[5] 6051[2] 6669[4] 6878[16] 8031[3] 8181[10]

Costa Percy *K R Burke* a54
2 b g Sir Percy Costa Brava (IRE) (Sadler's Wells (USA))
8537[8]

Cotai Glory *Charles Hills* 117
4 ch h Exceed And Excel(AUS) Continua (USA) (Elusive Quality (USA))
1862[12] 2438[2] 3244[2] 4151[13] 4824[8] 5614[4] 6384a[9] (6574) 6990a[10]

Cote D'Azur *Les Eyre* a85 101
3 ch c Champs Elysees Florentia (Medicean)
2322[2] ◆ 2674[5] 3824[2] (4476) ◆ (4607) (4818) ◆ (5520) 5865[4] ◆ 6277[2] 6753[2] 7154[4]

Cote Match (FR) *C Lerner* a46 41
2 b f Excelebration(IRE) Cotes D'Armor (FR) (Numerous (USA))
6639a[13]

Cotillion *Ian Williams* a74 74
10 b g Sadler's Wells(USA) Riberac (Efisio)
440[6] 2041[2] 5642[8] 6163[10] (6773)

Cotinga *Ralph Beckett* a60 73
2 ch f Paco Boy(IRE) Hobby (Robellino (USA))
2376[4] (2990) 7541[10] 7768[9]

Coto (IRE) *M J Tynan* a79 81
4 b m Fast Company(IRE) Let Me Shine (USA) (Dixie Union (USA))
(2334) (2622) 3392[8] 4585[3]

Cottesloe (IRE) *Neil Mulholland* a82 81
7 b g Teofilo(IRE) Vignelaure (IRE) (Royal Academy (USA))
160[6] 266[5] 488[5] 3617[2] 4138[2] 4634[9] 5574[7] 6876[8] 8178[14] 8524[6]

Cotton Club (IRE) *Rod Millman* a92 82
5 b g Amadeus Wolf Slow Jazz (USA) (Chief's Crown (USA))
1654 (440) 1209[5] 1893[6] 2392[7] 2932[2] 3784[4] 4535[5] 4912[4] 5553[5] 8558[4]

Cougar Kid (IRE) *John O'Shea* a48 43
5 b g Yeats(IRE) Western Skylark (IRE) (Westerner)
6765[5] 7218[9] 7942[10] 8180[4] ◆ 8497[12]

Cougar Mountain (IRE) *A P O'Brien* 118
5 b h Fastnet Rock(AUS) Descant (USA) (Nureyev (USA))
1226a[7] 2067a[2] 3242[8] 3677a[5] 5343a[2] 6328[6] (6749) 7115[5] 7837a[8] 8332a[10]

Could Should Would (IRE) *A Oliver* a81 81
4 b m Jeremy(USA) All Day (CHI) (Jaded Dancer (USA))
4748a[13]

Coulsty (IRE) *Richard Hannon* 114
5 b h Kodiac Hazium (IRE) (In The Wings)
1439[7] 1637[2] 2030[4] 3386[12] 3891[2] (4846) 6272a[4] 6991a[8]

Count Calabash (IRE) *Paul Cole* 89
2 b g Big Bad Bob(IRE) Tinaheely (IRE) (Intikhab (USA))
4270[3] ◆ 4907[5] (5052) (6366) ◆ (7697)

Countermand *Andrew Balding* a86 79
4 b g Authorized(IRE) Answered Prayer (Green Desert (USA))
7[4]

Countermeasure *Roger Charlton* a88 114
4 b g American Post Namaskar (Dansili)
2819[2] ◆ 3912[4] 4666[3] 5652[6] (6073)

Counterweight (IRE) *Sir Michael Stoute* 80
2 b f Azamour(IRE) Drama Class (IRE) (Caerleon (USA))
5524[9] 6874[2] 7441[9]

Countess Allegro (FR) *M Boutin* a53 64
2 b f Sageburg(IRE) Chansonette (GER) (Singspiel (IRE))
1118a[11] 3763a[4] 4965a[6] 7927a[5]

Count Montecristo (FR) *Kevin Ryan* a71 88
4 b g Siyouni(FR) Blackberry Pie (USA) (Gulch (USA))
2121[6] 2832[2] *3605[11]* 5886[14]

Count Octave *Andrew Balding* 74
2 b c Frankel Honorine (IRE) (Mark Of Esteem (IRE))
7187[3]

Count Of Carabass (IRE) *Miss Hilary McLoughlin* a57 65
5 b g Ad Valorem(USA) Three Pennies (Pennekamp (USA))
7474a[7]

Country Blue (FR) *Mrs A Malzard* 60
7 bl g Country Reel(USA) Exica (FR) (Exit To Nowhere (USA))
1517a[2] 2081a[3] 2284a[5] (2953a) 6401a[2]

County Wexford (IRE) *Miss Joey Ellis* a66 57
5 b g Teofilo(IRE) Tiffed (USA) (Seattle Slew (USA))
1805[6] 2174[13] *2605[4]* 4320[4] *4979[6]* 5710[8]

Coup De Grace (IRE) *Pat Phelan* a73 65
7 b g Elusive City(USA) No Way (IRE) (Rainbows For Life (CAN))
234[8] 2582[12]

Coup De Vent *John O'Shea* a58 59
5 b m Tobougg(IRE) Pigment (Zamindar (USA))
61[4] 569[8] 1548[11] 2127[2] 2461[5] *2607[3]* 3096[6] 3748[8]

Courage Under Fire (USA) *A P O'Brien* 105
2 b c War Front(USA) Charming (USA) (Seeking The Gold (USA))
5212a[2] 5556[5] 7113[7]

Courier *Marjorie Fife* a63 89
4 b m Equiano(FR) Pivotal Drive (IRE) (Pivotal)
2347[3] 2660[4] 3262[3] 4240[2] 4604[2] (4932) (5276) (5836) 6276[7] 6539[10] 6770[2] 7126[12]

Court Minstrel (IRE) *Evan Williams* a62
9 b g Court Cave(IRE) Theatral (Orchestra)
318[3]

Courtsider *Lucy Wadham* a73 68
4 b m Kyllachy Elhareer (IRE) (Selkirk (USA))
2321[9] 4361[3] 5037[7] 6337[6] 6765[3] *(7905)* ◆ *8367[8]*

Cousin Khee *Hughie Morrison* a95 91
9 b g Sakhee(USA) Cugina (Distant Relative)
3657[19]

Couville (FR) *Mme Pia Brandt* a63 72
2 bb f Hurricane Cat(USA) Realdad (ARG) (Victory Speech (USA))
5986a[3] *8420a[8]*

Coverham (IRE) *James Bethell* a59 59
2 b g Bated Breath Mark Too (IRE) (Mark Of Esteem (IRE))
1783[6] *2617[7]* 3416[3] 4090[2] 4510[3] *4937[3] 5675[4]* 6564[5] 6678[3]

Cover Song (USA) *Carla Gaines* 97
3 b f Fastnet Rock(AUS) Misty For Me (IRE) (Galileo (IRE))
(7724a)

Cracker'Star (FR) *C Plisson* a62 56
3 ch c Muhtathir Star Davis (FR) (Starborough)
1311a[11] 5907a[13]

Crack Shot (IRE) *James Tate* a75 81
4 ch h Lope De Vega(IRE) Slap Shot (IRE) (Lycius (USA))
82[4] 620[U] (Dead)

Cracksman *John Gosden* 91
2 b c Frankel Rhadegunda (Pivotal)
(7470) ◆

Cradle Mountain (IRE) *Joseph Patrick O'Brien* a60 96
4 b g Mastercraftsman(IRE) Sea Picture (IRE) (Royal Academy (USA))
7195a[2] 7708a[15]

Craftsmanship (FR) *Robert Eddery* a89 88
5 ch g Mastercraftsman(IRE) Jennie Jerome (IRE) (Pivotal)
(900) 1195[21] 1861[12] 2978[7] *3303[6] 4199[4]* 4868[3] *6048[3]* 6753[16] 7418[4] *7816[2]* ◆

Crafty Madam (IRE) *Clive Cox* 66
2 gr f Mastercraftsman(IRE) Dani Ridge (IRE) (Indian Ridge)
7574[4] ◆

Craggaknock *Mark Walford* 88
5 b g Authorized(IRE) Goodie Twosues (Fraam)
1493[4] 1853[2] 2163[5]

Crakehall Lad (IRE) *Andrew Crook* a45 42
5 ch g Manduro(GER) My Uptown Girl (Dubai Destination (USA))
731[9] 4194[7] 4971[7] *8309[8]*

Cranberry Park (IRE) *Brian Ellison* a47 45
3 b f Acclamation Queen Padme (IRE) (Halling (USA))
1710[4] 2360[6] 3838[7]

Cranwell *George Baker* a53 58
4 b m Nayef(USA) First Bloom (USA) (Fusaichi Pegasus (USA))
5308[6] 6020[3] 6406[3] ◆ 6890[6]

Crashing Thew Life *Sheena West* a63 61
6 b g Tobougg(IRE) Kalmina (USA) (Rahy (USA))
1174[3] 1807[9]

Craven's Legend (IRE) *A Fabre* 100
3 b c Invincible Spirit(IRE) Prudenzia (IRE) (Dansili)
4439a[5]

Cray (IRE) *James Bethell* a62
2 b c Rip Van Winkle(IRE) Amaya (USA) (Kingmambo (USA))
7659[5] 8088[8]

Crazy (GER) *David Dennis* a62 69
7 b m Nicaron(GER) Chato's Girl (GER) (Chato (USA))
30[3] ◆ *157[3]*

Crazy Chic (IRE) *Stuart Williams* a102 86
5 gr g Exceed And Excel(AUS) Martines (FR) (Linamix (FR))
503[2] (1204) 2027[16]

Crazy Horse *John Gosden* 115
3 b c Sleeping Indian Mainstay (Elmaamul (USA))
2283a[6] (7213) 7723a[2] 8117a[2]

Crazy Queen *Anthony Carson* a29
4 ch m Le Fou(IRE) Queen Of Norway (USA) (Woodman (USA))
26[8]

Crazy Tornado (IRE) *Keith Dalgleish* a77 74
3 b g Big Bad Bob(IRE) All Day (CHI) (Jaded Dancer (USA))
5151[5] 5537[5] ◆ 5717[3] (6028) 6344[7] 6772[8] *7662[7] 8011[9]*

Create A Dream (USA) *Wesley A Ward* 101
2 b f Oasis Dream Anabaa's Creation (IRE) (Anabaa (USA))
(1770) 3336[4]

Creator (USA) *Steven Asmussen* a119
3 rg c Tapit(USA) Morena (PER) (Privately Held (USA))
2063a[13] (3181a) 5913a[7]

Creek Walk (USA) *Saeed bin Suroor* a74
2 b g Street Cry(IRE) Badminton (Zieten (USA))
7988[2]

Creeping Ivy (IRE) *A J Martin* a70 49
4 br m Mustameet(USA) Just Like Ivy (CAN) (Street Cry (IRE))
5900a[3]

Creggs Pipes (IRE) *Andrew Slattery* a73 107
4 ch m Rip Van Winkle(IRE) Sophie Germain (IRE) (Indian Ridge)
(4218a) (4747a) 5814a[2] 6352a[7] 6983a[5]

Creme De Cremes (FR) *Matthieu Palussiere* a77 80
2 b f Rio De La Plata(USA) Creme De Cuvee (USA) (Cuvee (USA))
7170a[6] *7970a[2]*

Crescent (IRE) *Ahmed Kobeissi* 99
4 ch h Galileo(IRE) Coralita (IRE) (Night Shift (USA))
744a[11]

Cresendo (IRE) *J S Bolger* a67 62
3 b c Vocalised(USA) Rachida (IRE) (Hurricane Run (IRE))
7391a[14]

Crew Cut (IRE) *Stuart Williams* a81 89
8 gr g Acclamation Carabine (USA) (Dehere (USA))
1215[15] 1530[8] (1929) *3279[5]* 4360[7] 4889[10] 5408[5]

Cribbs Causeway (IRE) *Roger Charlton* 29
2 b f Rip Van Winkle(IRE) Bristol Fashion (Dansili)
7284[11]

Cricklewood Green (USA) *Sylvester Kirk* a84 86
5 ch g Bob And John(USA) B Berry Brandy (USA) (Event Of The Year (USA))
1775[16] *2324[4]* 3061[6] 3557[10] 4081[11] (5017) (5674) 6266[3] 6914[12] *7461[7]* 7506[2] 7821[14] *8356[4] 8455[2] 8539[10]*

Crimean Tatar (TUR) *Hugo Palmer* a110 96
3 b c Sea The Stars(IRE) Unity (IRE) (Sadler's Wells (USA))
(4597) ◆ *(8068)*

Crimson Lake *David Simcock* a71 71
2 b f Makfi Liberty Chery (Statue Of Liberty (USA))
6336[4] ◆ 7210[3] *8130[3]*

Crimson Rock (USA) *Ralph Beckett* 83
2 b f Fastnet Rock(AUS) Maryinsky (IRE) (Sadler's Wells (USA))
(7543)

Crimson Rosette (IRE) *Charlie Fellowes* a51 65
2 b f Teofilo(IRE) Crimson Ribbon (USA) (Lemon Drop Kid (USA))
6782[5] ◆ *7484[7]*

Cristal Fizz (IRE) *William Haggas* 100
2 ch f Power Effervesce (IRE) (Galileo (IRE))
(6071) (7547)

Critical Speed (IRE) *Sylvester Kirk* a68 70
4 ch m Pivotal Speed Cop (Cadeaux Genereux)
1324[4] 1765[4] 2320[6] 3497[2] 3817[4]

Critical Thinking (IRE) *Julia Feilden* a65
2 b c Art Connoisseur(IRE) Cookie Cutter (IRE) (Fasliyev (USA))
8189[6] 8591[5]

Croft Ranger (IRE) *Michael Dods* a23 64
3 b g Bushranger(IRE) Alexander Duchess (IRE) (Desert Prince (IRE))
(1383) 1927[7] 2576[9] *5841[13]* 7097[9]

Crombay (IRE) *Tim Easterby* a30 68
3 b f Approve(IRE) Ms Cromby (IRE) (Arakan (USA))
1647[6] (2050) 2534[6] 3397[7] 3847[5] 4256[5] 5730[4] 6506[6] 6958[9] *7437[11]*

Croquembouche (IRE) *Ed de Giles* a92 99
7 b g Acclamation Wedding Cake (IRE) (Groom Dancer (USA))
1620[4] 2222[4] 2752[2] 3109[12] 4115[9] 4561[5] 5405[2] 5964[6] 6709[2] *7365[10]*

Cross Cave *Emma Owen* a63
3 b f Rail Link Valentine Girl (Alzao (USA))
3305[5]

Crosse Fire *Scott Dixon* a93 66
4 b g Monsieur Bond(IRE) Watersilk (IRE) (Fasliyev (USA))
(21) 250[3] (338) 580[3] (894) 966[5] 1218[13] 1566[6] *1801[2] 1958[9]* 4514[5] *5678[12]* 6506[17] *6926[10] 7202[10] 8349[11] 8473[10] 8571[3]* ◆

Cross Examine (IRE) *David Simcock* a52 54
3 b g Roderic O'Connor(IRE) Red Vale (IRE) (Halling (USA))
47[4] 328[7] 419[3]

Cross Step (USA) *Charlie Appleby* a67
2 b g Kitten's Joy(USA) Maid Service (USA) (Arch (USA))
7982[5]

Crowned Eagle *John Gosden* 84
2 b c Oasis Dream Gull Wing (IRE) (In The Wings)
6777[3] ◆ 7283[3] (7769) ◆

Crowning Glory (FR) *Ralph Beckett* a95 95
3 b f Speightstown(USA) Forest Crown (Royal Applause)
2178[5] *2783[3]* (4206) 4788[2] (5965) (6483) 6947[2] *7650[6]*

Crowning Star (IRE) *Steve Woodman* a47 47
7 b g Royal Applause Dossier (Octagonal (NZ))
252[6] 347[9] 690[2] 876[10] 1035[6] 1742[11]

Crucial Moment *Bill Turner* a54 62
2 b g Pivotal Moonglow (Nayef (USA))
1199[8] 3529[6] 4274[6] *4937[7] 7482[9]* 7768[10]

Crucial Response *Ben Haslam* a42 30
2 b g Pivotal Respondez (Oasis Dream)
7740[13] *8089[14] 8384[11]*

Cruiseliner (BRZ) *Takashi Kodama* a51 105
4 b m Wild Event(USA) Quantia Exata (BRZ) (Trempolino (USA))
6932a[7]

Cruise Tothelimit (IRE) *Patrick Morris* a68 68
8 b g Le Vie Dei Colori Kiva (Indian Ridge)
5162[6] 5535[3] 5762[3] ◆ 6451[9] 6834[7] *7945[2] 8078[6] 8137[2] 8234[5] 8483[6]*

Crushed (IRE) *William Haggas* a68 66
2 b g Beat Hollow Sel (Salse (USA))
7125[4] *(7659)*

Cry Fury *Sophie Leech* a67 80
8 b g Beat Hollow Cantanta (Top Ville (IRE))
3651[2] 4716[5] 5131[3] 6424[6]

Cryogenics (IRE) *Rebecca Menzies* 35
2 b g Frozen Power(IRE) New Blossom (IRE) (Shirocco (GER))
5728[10]

Cryptic (IRE) *Luca Cumani* a84 71
3 br g Lord Shanakill(USA) Privet (IRE) (Cape Cross (IRE))
1703[2] ◆ *2322[8]* 3079[8] 4607[5] *5302[2]* 6254[3] *(6629) (7051) 7428[3]*

Cryptonite (IRE) *Michael Appleby* 55
2 br c Dark Angel(IRE) Bowness (Efisio)
6833[6] 7331[5]

Crystal Bleu *Miss V Haigh* a63 47
2 b f Equiano(FR) Crystal Plum (IRE) (Rock Of Gibraltar (IRE))
7291a[7]

Crystal Dome *Ed Dunlop* a74 70
2 b c Dansili Crystal Maze (Gone West (USA))
4775[7] 5332[7] *5676[6]* (6681) *7140[4]* 7406[7]

Crystalise (IRE) *Robert Stephens* a58 37
4 b m Nayef(USA) Crystal Power (USA) (Pleasant Colony (USA))
6239[5] 7625[10] *8039[8] 8164[9]*

Crystallographer (IRE) *Daniel Mark Loughnane* a67 66
3 br f Big Bad Bob(IRE) Desert Alchemy (IRE) (Green Desert (USA))
2375[3] 3475[3] 4027[3] *6701[10]* 7743[14] *(7856) 8588[11]*

Crystal Malt (IRE) *Richard Hannon* a76 75
4 b m Intikhab(USA) Elegantly (IRE) (Rock Of Gibraltar (IRE))
80[6]

Crystal Money (FR) *J-Y Artu* 62
2 ch f Fuisse(FR) Mont Doree (FR) (Mansonnien (FR))
5698a[13]

Crystal Ocean *Sir Michael Stoute* 80
2 b c Sea The Stars(IRE) Crystal Star (Mark Of Esteem (IRE))
6577[2] ◆

Crystal River *Saeed bin Suroor* a68
2 b f Dubawi(IRE) Inner Secret (USA) (Singspiel (IRE))
7855[5]

Crystal Secret *John Bridger* 56
2 b f Sayif(IRE) Laser Crystal (IRE) (King's Theatre (IRE))
1527[4] 2696[6] 3555[9] 4304[4] 4786[3] 5325[7] 5770[6] *7423[11]*

Crystal Stanza (IRE) *Charlie Fellowes* a27
2 b g Poet's Voice Clear Impression (IRE) (Danehill (USA))
8277[P]

Crystal Zvezda *Sir Michael Stoute* a77 109
4 ch m Dubawi(IRE) Crystal Star (Mark Of Esteem (IRE))
1886[9] 2189[7]

Cry Wolf *James Evans* a73
3 ch g Street Cry(IRE) Love Charm (Singspiel (IRE))
7052[2] 7280[7]

Cuban Isabela *Stuart Williams* 67
2 b f Harbour Watch(IRE) Madam Mojito (USA) (Smart Strike (CAN))
4951[9] 5772[4]

Cuban Queen (USA) *Julia Feilden* a47 34
3 ro f Elusive Quality(USA) One Smokin' Lady (USA) (Smoke Glacken (USA))
635[5] 1497[4] (1794) 2155[5] 2964[8] *3320[5]* 4202[9] *5126[5] 8079[9] 8572[10]*

Cubswin (IRE) *Roger Charlton* 58
2 b f Zamindar(USA) Moonlight Rhapsody (IRE) (Danehill Dancer (IRE))
6061[6]

Cuevo Especial (FR) *N Branchu* a37
7 bb g Marchand De Sable(USA) Swandor (USA) (Swain (IRE))
512a[7]

Cuff (IRE) *A P O'Brien* 102
2 ch f Galileo(IRE) Massarra (Danehill (USA))
(2718a) 3336[5]

Cullingworth (IRE) *Richard Fahey* a32 86
2 b c Kodiac Think (FR) (Marchand De Sable (USA))
1082[10] (1377) 2240[5] 2664[4] 3388[3] 4090[3] 6275[4]

Culloden *Shaun Harris* a63 62
4 b h Kyllachy Mamounia (IRE) (Green Desert (USA))
3843[7] (4096) *(4472) 4647[10]* 4980[4] 5762[5] *6374[5] 7534[10]* 7596[3] *8242[10] 8474[11]*

Cultured Knight *Richard Hughes* a75 79
3 ch g Compton Place Cultured Pride (IRE) (King's Best (USA))
432[2] (531) 797[2] 2185[2] 2314[4] 3144[3]

Culturehull *Les Eyre* 40
3 b f Dabbers Ridge(IRE) The Pen (Lake Coniston (IRE))
3643[11] 4235[10] 5757[6]

Cumbfree (IRE) *X Thomas-Demeaulte* a70
3 b f Footstepsinthesand Cumbrian Princess (Mtoto)
7929a[13]

Cunco (IRE) *John Gosden* 103
2 b c Frankel Chrysanthemum (IRE) (Danehill Dancer (IRE))
(2204) ◆ 3382[3] ◆ 4150[4] 5595[4] 6116[3] 7151[2] 7722a[7]

Cupid's Arrow (IRE) *Ruth Carr* 64
2 b g Majestic Missile(IRE) Kiss And Don'Tell (USA) (Rahy (USA))
3216[3] 5884[6] 6448[8] 7041[2]

Cuppacoffee (IRE) *Ann Duffield* 84
2 b c Intense Focus(USA) Breedj (IRE) (Acclamation)
(2265) 2682[4] 3282[2] (3881) 6734[10] 7073[8]

Cuppatee (IRE) *Ann Duffield* a59 66
3 b f Canford Cliffs(IRE) Fanditha (IRE) (Danehill Dancer (IRE))
2802[11] 3479[12] 3948[8] 4848[2] 4973[3] *5369[6] 5839[7]* 6216[10]

Curalina (USA) *Todd Pletcher* a118
4 ch m Curlin(USA) Whatdreamsrmadeof (USA) (Graeme Hall (USA))
7810a[6]

Curbyourenthusiasm (IRE) *David Simcock* a113 114
5 gr g Mastercraftsman(IRE) Mohican Princess (Shirley Heights)
2221[2] ◆ 4799[10] 5612[7] 6284[6] *(7814) 8068[3]*

Curious Fox *Anthony Carson* a72 64
3 b f Bertolini(USA) Doric Lady (Kyllachy)
1414[6] 1753[6] 3280[6] (3735) 4262[11] *5126[3] (5554) (6091)* 6878[15] *7485[4]*

Curlew River *Mark Johnston* 77
2 b f Casamento(IRE) Dubai Opera (USA) (Dubai Millennium)
7465[2] 7696[7]

Currency Converter (USA) *D K Weld* 100
2 gr c Exchange Rate(USA) Ruby's Realm (USA) (Empire Maker (USA))
4574a[3]

Curren Mirotic (JPN) *Osamu Hirata* 116
8 ch g Heart's Cry(JPN) Star Mie (USA) (A.P. Indy (USA))
7756a[23]

Current State (IRE) *T Stack* a73 90
4 b m High Chaparral(IRE) Thoughtful (IRE) (Acclamation)
3084a[6] 3677a[9]

Curriculum *William Haggas* a82 56
3 b g New Approach(IRE) Superstar Leo (IRE) (College Chapel)
5023[4] 5544[3] *(6511)*

Curry (IRE) *Richard Hannon* 58
2 b f Acclamation Marvada (IRE) (Elusive City (USA))
4756[13] 5869[9]

Curtain Call *Richard Fahey* a78 86
3 b f Acclamation Apace (IRE) (Oasis Dream)
1763[3] 2218[6] 3131[5] (3552) ◆

Curtsy (IRE) *Hughie Morrison* 56
2 ch f Galileo(IRE) Acts Of Grace (USA) (Bahri (USA))
5995[6] 6578[9] 7210[7]

Curve Ball (IRE) *Richard Hughes* 74
2 b c Requinto(IRE) Royal Esteem (Mark Of Esteem (IRE))
3813[12] 4837[2] 5237[5]

Curzon Line *Michael Easterby* a81 74
7 b g Dubawi(IRE) Polska (USA) (Danzig (USA))
24[9] 179[7] (2409) 2661[2] ◆ 3367[3] 4089[4] 5033[6] 6501[6] *7887[2] (7985) 8487[7]*

Custard The Dragon *John Mackie* a76 61
3 b g Kyllachy Autumn Pearl (Orpen (USA))
242[2] ◆ *(380) 1137[7]* 1485[4] 1638[7] 3399[4] *4215[5] 7797[4] 8206[2] (8351)*

Custom (IRE) *Daniel O'Brien* a36
3 b f Lilbourne Lad(IRE) Margaux Magique (IRE) (Xaar)
6373[11] 7910[12]

Custom Cut (IRE) *David O'Meara* a101 120
7 b g Notnowcato Polished Gem (IRE) (Danehill (USA))
1198[3] 1425[4] 2067a[8] 2867[3] 4127[4] 5343a[4] 5652[3] 6117[4] 6353a[2] 6749[5] 7152[7]

Cuttin' Edge (IRE) *William Muir* 79
2 b c Rip Van Winkle(IRE) How's She Cuttin' (IRE) (Shinko Forest (IRE))
5820[2] 6224[3] (7574) ◆

Cutty Sark *Luca Cumani* a63 61
3 b f Dylan Thomas(IRE) L'Affaire Monique (Machiavellian (USA))
5375[5] 6365[8] 7272[6] *7727[2]*

Cydalise (FR) *H-A Pantall* a54
2 ch f Siyouni(FR) Angel Of Harlem (FR) (Holy Roman Emperor (IRE))
7455a[7]

Cyflymder (IRE) *David C Griffiths* a46 57
10 b g Mujadil(USA) Nashwan Star (IRE) (Nashwan (USA))
97[9] 429[11] 2661[7] 3153[2] 3599[5] *4200[8] 8306[12]*

Cymraeg Bounty *Iain Jardine* 97
4 ch g Bahamian Bounty Croeso Cusan (Diktat)
1631[3] (2526) (2959) 3517[13] (3945) 4700[4] (5182) (5825)

Cymric (USA) *John Gosden* 112
3 b c Kitten's Joy(USA) Fastbridled (USA) (Unbridled's Song (USA))
1866^{8} 2627^{5} 3245^{4} 4065^{2} 4822^{9}

Cymro (IRE) *Tom Dascombe* 108
4 b g Dark Angel(IRE) Dictatrice (FR) (Anabaa (USA))
(1493) ◆ 1995^{4} 3340^{12} 3697a^{4} 5639^{10} (6057) 6545^{4}

Cyril *Gordon Elliott* a69 89
4 b g Rail Link Nurse Gladys (Dr Fong (USA))
1493^{15} 1923^{3} 2487^{11} 2688^{7} 3920^{9} *6465a^{10}*

Cytringan *Lydia Pearce* a37 48
3 b f Equiano(FR) Scisciabubu (IRE) (Danehill (USA))
3850^{9} 4565^{6} 5260^{4} *6902^{9} 7488^{7} 8278^{8}*

Czabo *Mick Channon* 104
3 b f Sixties Icon Fiumicino (Danehill Dancer (IRE))
(1603) 2220^{4} 2509a^{4} (2928a) 3339^{13}

Czech It Out (IRE) *Amanda Perrett* 99
6 b g Oratorio(IRE) Naval Affair (IRE) (Last Tycoon)
1856^{8} 2391^{5} 3534^{8} 4758^{15} 7189^{4}

Daafik *Simon Crisford* 76
3 b g Shamardal(USA) Princess Danah (IRE) (Danehill (USA))
2340^{3} 3104^{3}

Dabadiyan (IRE) *Gary Moore* a88 87
6 b g Zamindar(USA) Dabista (IRE) (Highest Honor (FR))
440^{9}

Daban (IRE) *John Gosden* a78
2 b f Acclamation Malaspina (IRE) (Whipper (USA))
(7763)

Da Big Hoss (USA) *Michael J Maker* 114
5 ch h Lemon Drop Kid(USA) Lady Struck Gold (USA) (Touch Gold (USA))
(5428a) 7835a^{11}

Dabyah (IRE) *John Gosden* 111
2 b f Sepoy(AUS) Samdaniya (Machiavellian (USA))
(4147) ◆ (6548) 6986a^{3}

Dacita (CHI) *Chad C Brown* 114
4 ch m Scat Daddy(USA) Daja (CHI) (Seeker's Reward (CAN))
(3119a)

Dacoity *Richard Fahey* 74
3 b g Dick Turpin(IRE) Todber (Cape Cross (IRE))
1524^{7} 2337^{4} 2886^{6} 3422^{6}

Daddys Lil Darling (USA) *Kenneth McPeek* a106
2 b f Scat Daddy(USA) Miss Hot Salsa (USA) (Houston (USA))
7830a^{4}

Daffodil Mulligan *J S Moore* a57 49
2 b f Showcasing Anapola (GER) (Polish Precedent (USA))
1895^{5} 2457^{4} 3507a^{7} 4879^{4} *(5297) 5755a^{13} 5988a^{10}*

Daghash *Stuart Kittow* a82 84
7 b g Tiger Hill(IRE) Zibet (Kris)
1987^{12} 2699^{8} 2971^{3} 4230^{6}

Dagobert Duke *C Boutin* a78 72
6 ch g Duke Of Marmalade(IRE) Victoria Page (FR) (Anabaa (USA))
3184a^{4}

Dagonet (IRE) *Roger Charlton* a83 68
2 b g Sir Prancealot(IRE) Dubai Diamond (Octagonal (NZ))
6295^{7} 6873^{3} *(7424)*

Dahl (IRE) *Mark Johnston* 66
2 b c Shamardal(USA) Illandrane (IRE) (Cape Cross (IRE))
4649^{7} 5250^{2} 5670^{5}

Dahlia Bere (FR) *J Phelippon* a41 60
3 ch f Sunday Break(JPN) Arrondie (FR) (Inchinor)
2172a^{10}

Daily Bulletin (USA) *John Gosden* a102 88
3 b c Medaglia d'Oro(USA) Life At Ten (USA) (Malibu Moon (USA))
5175^{4} 5601^{8} *(6372)* 6753^{17} *7101^{5}*

Daily News *Roger Varian* 68
3 b g Street Cry(IRE) Zeeba (IRE) (Barathea (IRE))
3028^{4} 4056^{6} 4597^{5} 6827^{5}

Daily Trader *David Evans* a57
2 ch g Medicean Danehill Destiny (Danehill Dancer (IRE))
7100^{6} 8034^{8} 8208^{13} 8568^{2}

Daimochi (IRE) *Clive Cox* a67 48
2 b c Excelebration(IRE) Quiritis (Galileo (IRE))
7665^{8} *7962^{3}*

Dainty Dandy (IRE) *Paul Cole* 96
2 b f Dandy Man(IRE) Pinewoods Lily (IRE) (Indian Ridge)
(2885) ◆ 3336^{7} 4623^{3} 5359^{10} 6063^{9} 7667^{7}

Daioni *Richard Hughes* a53
3 b f Green Horizon Calon Lan (Nayef (USA))
140^{11} 2083^{6}

Daira Prince (IRE) *Roger Varian* 75
2 b c Dubawi(IRE) Chiang Mai (IRE) (Sadler's Wells (USA))
7226^{6} 7769^{3}

Daisy Bere (FR) *K R Burke* a84 84
3 b f Peer Gynt(JPN) Jackette (USA) (Mr Greeley (USA))
40^{12} (275) 522^{2} ◆ *1155^{4}* (1759) 2694^{2} 2973^{2} 3596^{3} *5006a^{7}* 7504^{11} *8007^{4}* ◆ *8426^{5} (8538)*

Daisy Boy (IRE) *Stuart Williams* a89 82
5 b g Cape Cross(IRE) Muluk (IRE) (Rainbow Quest (USA))
(357) 619^{5} (1430) 1802^{5} 4561^{6} 5198^{5} 5964^{4} 6892^{4}

Daisy Du Moulin (FR) *F Meckes*
2 ch f Arc Royal(GER) Tequeromas (GER) (Platini (GER))
7927a^{14}

Dakota City *Julia Feilden* a82 72
5 b g Three Valleys(USA) West Dakota (USA) (Gone West (USA))
(164) 399^{4} (566) 922^{5} 3570^{4} 4277^{4} 4566^{4} *4940^{3} 7732^{9} 8253^{4} 8524^{4}*

Dakota Gold *Michael Dods* 81
2 b g Equiano(FR) Joyeaux (Mark Of Esteem (IRE))
5476^{3} (6002) 6536^{13} 6950^{5}

Dalaki (IRE) *Des Donovan* a73 71
5 b g Dalakhani(IRE) Lunda (IRE) (Soviet Star (USA))
566^{3} 1222^{5} 1561^{9} *2105^{4} 2814^{3}* 2887^{6} 4813a^{16}

Dalalah *Richard Guest* a57 58
3 b f Exceed And Excel(AUS) Bashasha (USA) (Kingmambo (USA))
105^{11} 1670^{8} 2359^{4} 3069^{11} 3603^{3} 4365^{6} 4770^{12} 4972^{7}

Dalavand (IRE) *Laura Mongan* a60 60
3 ch g Tamayuz Kirunavaara (IRE) (Galileo (IRE))
770^{5} 1079^{9} 1701^{9} 2325^{5} 2851^{4} 3256^{4} 4024^{2} *4212^{2} 4527^{6} 4942^{10} 8364^{5}*

Daleelak (IRE) *Mark Johnston* a63 72
3 b g Arcano(IRE) Alshamatry (USA) (Seeking The Gold (USA))
1750^{8} 6957^{10} 7227^{4} 7745^{3} *8178^{7} 8382^{7} 8527^{11}*

Daleside *Michael Bell*
3 b f Vale Of York(IRE) Al Cobra (IRE) (Sadler's Wells (USA))
2774^{8}

Dalgarno (FR) *N Clement* 98
3 b c Sea The Stars(IRE) Jakonda (USA) (Kingmambo (USA))
2281a^{4}

Dal Harraild *William Haggas* 114
3 ch g Champs Elysees Dalvina (Grand Lodge (USA))
1610^{11} (2909) 4131^{3} ◆ (4863) 6110^{3} (6752)

Daliance (IRE) *Noel Williams* a71 68
7 ch g Dalakhani(IRE) Everlasting Love (Pursuit Of Love)
2194^{10} 2805^{6} 6885^{9}

Dallas Affair *F Head* 43
2 b f Soldier Hollow Daytona (GER) (Lando (GER))
6937a^{11}

Dalmarella Dancer (IRE) *K R Burke* a72 71
5 gr m Mastercraftsman(IRE) Ting A Greeley (Mr Greeley (USA))
1202^{13} 2343^{4} 2860^{RR} 3230^{4} 3467^{RR}

Dalmatian Sea (GER) *A Wohler* 83
3 b f Lord Of England(GER) Dubavint (GER) (Monsun (GER))
3207a^{12}

Dalness Express *John O'Shea* a49 30
3 b g Firebreak Under My Spell (Wizard King)
1451^{5} 4310^{4} *6674^{8} 7463^{8} 8070^{10}*

Dal Riata (IRE) *Mark Johnston* a42 75
2 br f Raven's Pass(USA) Dinka Raja (USA) (Woodman (USA))
7329^{6} 7548^{2} *7763^{14} 8237^{4} 8397^{8}*

Dalshand (FR) *A De Royer-Dupre* 98
3 ch g New Approach(IRE) Daltaiyma (IRE) (Doyoun)
7088a^{5}

Dalton *David O'Meara* 66
2 b c Mayson Pious (Bishop Of Cashel)
2358^{3} 2830^{4}

Dame D'Id (FR) *A Lyon* a50 73
3 bl f Gold Away(IRE) Eretria (USA) (Dynaformer (USA))
716a^{11}

Dame Du Roi (IRE) *F Head* 105
2 b f Dark Angel(IRE) Uruguay (IRE) (Authorized (IRE))
5703a^{5} 7086a^{2} (7757a)

Dame Judi (IRE) *Simon Crisford* a75 79
3 b f Shamardal(USA) Miss Hepburn (USA) (Gone West (USA))
2312^{2} 3059^{5} 3684^{5} *5527^{2} 6415^{3}* 6805^{9} *8381^{8}*

Damila (FR) *H-A Pantall* a94 106
3 b f Milanais(FR) Dawaes (FR) (Marchand De Sable (USA))
1309a^{6} 2232a^{3} 2943a^{6} (3796a) 5217a^{7} 6391a^{11} 7758a^{9}

Damour (GER) *Markus Klug* 97
4 b m Azamour(IRE) Desabina (GER) (Big Shuffle (USA))
4031a^{3}

Damsah (QA) *Conrad Allen* a37
2 b f Gio Ponti(USA) Kitten Love (USA) (Kitten's Joy (USA))
7865^{13}

Dana's Present *Tom Dascombe* a76 71
7 ch g Osorio(GER) Euro Empire (USA) (Bartok I (IRE))
82^{8} 595^{6} 788^{8} 1093^{10} 1387^{7} 1916^{5} ◆ 4463^{2} ◆ *5503^{6} (7620) 7911^{9} 8035^{4} 8252^{3}*

Dance Alone *Damian Joseph English* a78 76
3 gr g Bahamian Bounty Palais Glide (Proclamation (IRE))
1524^{3} 2049^{15} 2667^{2} 2974^{14} 3948^{2} 4410^{5} 4870^{2} 5195^{2} (5862) 6475^{6} 6717^{7} *7324^{6} 8197a^{7}*

Dance Band (IRE) *Roger Varian* a69 58
3 b f Danehill Dancer(IRE) Maidin Maith (IRE) (Montjeu (IRE))
2177^{14} 2505^{9} 2904^{7} *(3527)* 6182^{5} *6851^{10}*

Dance King *Tim Easterby* a76 94
6 ch g Danehill Dancer(IRE) One So Wonderful (Nashwan (USA))
(2017) 2744^{8} 3435^{3} 3889^{6} 4407^{5} 5157^{6} 6559^{9} 7159^{6} 7535^{10} ◆

Dance Of Fire *Andrew Balding* a91 94
4 b g Norse Dancer(IRE) Strictly Dancing (IRE) (Danehill Dancer (IRE))
172^{3} ◆ *(530) 594^{5} 871^{5}* 1978^{3} 2484^{5} 3534^{5} 3855^{2}

Dance On The Hill (IRE) *Roger Charlton* a62 80
4 br m Danehill Dancer(IRE) Hitra (USA) (Langfuhr (CAN))
7911^{10}

Dance Rebel *Dr Jon Scargill* a63
3 b g Cockney Rebel(IRE) Slave To The Rythm (IRE) (Hamas (IRE))
7782^{3} 8320^{4}

Dance Teacher (IRE) *Ralph Beckett* 71
2 ch f Lope De Vega(IRE) Fairnilee (Selkirk (USA))
4988^{2} 5615^{12} 6880^{4}

Dance The Dream *Marcus Tregoning* 96
3 b f Sir Percy Shadow Dancing (Unfuwain (USA))
3535^{7} 4056^{3} (5255) 6110^{7} (7060) ◆

Dance With Kate *Polly Gundry* 27
5 b m Hamairi(IRE) Vercheny (Petoski)
3684^{8} 3996^{9} 4657^{9} 5256^{5}

Dancin Alpha *Alan Swinbank* a55 49
5 ch g Bahamian Bounty Phoebe Woodstock (IRE) (Grand Lodge (USA))
2092^{6} *8141^{5} 8306^{5} 8470^{2} 8589^{3}*

Dancing Alligator *Stuart Williams* 15
2 b c Delegator Perfect Act (Act One)
6751^{8}

Dancing Dragon (IRE) *George Baker* 50
2 b f Dragon Pulse(IRE) Abbeyleix Lady (IRE) (Montjeu (IRE))
6404^{4}

Dancing Elegance *Michael Bell* 66
2 ch f Nathaniel(IRE) Parisian Elegance (Zilzal (USA))
3556^{4} 4603^{8}

Dancing Noretta (IRE) *K J Condon* a64 77
4 b m Big Bad Bob(IRE) Shaimaa (IRE) (Fantastic Light (USA))
6466a^{2}

Dancing Rags (USA) *H Graham Motion* a108 67
2 b f Union Rags(USA) Home Court (USA) (Storm Cat (USA))
7830a^{8}

Dancing Rainbow (GR) *Amanda Perrett* a49 47
3 b f Tiantai(USA) Rainbow Way (High Chaparral (IRE))
2182^{10} 2929^{9} 3958^{10} 5101^{7} 5777^{10} 6030^{2} *7969^{5} 8445^{8}*

Dancing Star *Andrew Balding* 113
3 b f Aqlaam Strictly Dancing (IRE) (Danehill Dancer (IRE))
(2185) (2875) 3165^{2} ◆ (4062) (4865) 6120^{9}

Dancingwithangels (IRE) *Thomas Cleary* a63 75
7 gr m Dark Angel(IRE) Mrs Kepple (King's Best (USA))
2114a^{9}

Dancing Years (IRE) *Richard Fahey* a53 81
3 ch f Iffraaj Daganya (IRE) (Danehill Dancer (IRE))
(1487) 2693^{10}

Dandilion (IRE) *Alex Hales* a56 55
3 b f Dandy Man(IRE) Free Angel (USA) (Mystery Storm (USA))
6317^{4} ◆ *8290^{3} 8496^{5}*

Dandy Bird (IRE) *James Given* a67 51
2 b f Dandy Man(IRE) Labba (Tiger Hill (IRE))
6641^{5} *6925^{2} 7380^{6}*

Dandy Flame (IRE) *William Haggas* a79 19
2 ch g Dandy Man(IRE) Nouveau Riche (IRE) (Entrepreneur)
4205^{8} *(4713) 6124^{7} 6507^{7} 7258^{4} 7966^{2} 8136^{6} 8444^{3}*

Dandy Highwayman (IRE) *Ollie Pears* 78
2 ch g Dandy Man(IRE) Paradise Blue (IRE) (Bluebird (USA))
3707^{2} (4227) 4891^{3} 5352^{3} 6536^{4} 7120^{17}

Dandyleekie (IRE) *David O'Meara* a83 91
4 b g Dandy Man(IRE) Cockaleekie (USA) (Alphabet Soup (USA))
(1444) 1817^{3} 2016^{2} 2238^{10} 3414^{6} (3892) 4443^{6} 6382a^{16} 7094^{4} *7433^{5}* 7590^{4}

Dandy Maid *Michael Appleby* a41 48
5 b m Dandy Man(IRE) Cut Back (Factual (USA))
1435^{6} 1709^{6}

Dandyman Port (IRE) *E J O'Neill* 87
2 b f Dandy Man(IRE) Fillthegobletagain (IRE) (Byron)
(3507a)

Dandy Place (IRE) *Tim Easterby* a58 80
2 b c Dandy Man(IRE) Etta Place (Hawk Wing (USA))
4297^{6} *4642^{8}* 5271^{5} 5728^{6} 6222^{3} 6563^{2} 6954^{7} 7091^{3}

Dandy Roll (IRE) *Ralph Beckett* a60 49
2 b c Dandy Man(IRE) Soranna (IRE) (Compton Place)
1736^{6} *6673^{5} 7381^{8} 7981^{10}*

Dandys Perier (IRE) *Ronald Harris* a66 66
5 br g Dandy Man(IRE) Casual Remark (IRE) (Trans Island)
144^{11} 587a^{3} 663a^{7} 951^{6} 1544^{10} 2542^{11} *3474^{4} 3987^{9}* 4289^{11} 4992^{4} 5954^{12}

Dandy Star (IRE) *Marco Botti* a7
3 b g Dandy Man(IRE) Mount Street (IRE) (Pennekamp (USA))
639^{11}

Dandysteps (IRE) *Tracey Collins* a54 59
5 ch m Dandy Man(IRE) Peggys Rose (IRE) (Shalford (IRE))
7800a^{3}

Dandy Walk *Chris Wall* a59 54
2 b f Dandy Man(IRE) Amatara (IRE) (Indian Haven)
6454^{8} *6696^{7} 8151^{6}*

Danecase *David Dennis* a81 77
3 ch g Showcasing Yding (IRE) (Danehill (USA))
1288^{5} 1992^{9} 2239^{9} 2650^{11} 4058^{5} (4557) *4881^{2}* 5075^{9} 5960^{4} 6878^{4} 7301^{6} *7902^{12}*

Danehill Kodiac (IRE) *Richard Hannon* a82 101
3 b c Kodiac Meadow (Green Desert (USA))
2244^{4} 2889^{3} 3300^{5} 4396^{4} (5147) 6110^{2} 7117^{3}

Dangerous Ends *Brett Johnson* a38 52
2 b g Monsieur Bond(IRE) Stolen Glance (Mujahid (USA))
3254^{5} 4075^{9} 7414^{7} *7777^{4} 8046^{6}*

Dangerous Secret *Dr Jon Scargill* a61
3 gr f Medicean Holamo (IRE) (Montjeu (IRE))
814^{5} ◆ *1160^{3} 1800^{3}* ◆

Dangerous Thought (USA) *Doug Watson* a71
3 ch g Super Saver(USA) Trepidation (USA) (Seeking The Gold (USA))
466^{4} 834^{2} 952^{4} 1703^{5} 8576a^{6}

Danglydontask *David Arbuthnot* a63 64
5 b g Lucky Story(USA) Strat's Quest (Nicholas (USA))
882^{2} ◆ 1244^{9} 2338^{5} *3302^{8} 4019^{8}* (5573) 7270^{7}

Danielsflyer (IRE) *David Barron* a64 94
2 b c Dandy Man(IRE) Warm Welcome (Motivator)
1706^{2} (2358) 2865^{2} 5583^{14}

Daniel Thomas (IRE) *Heather Dalton* a45 45
14 b g Dansili Last Look (Rainbow Quest (USA))
175^{8}

Danileo (IRE) *F Rossi* a75 87
5 gr h Danehill Dancer(IRE) Saturnine (IRE) (Galileo (IRE))
5501a^{6}

Danilovna (IRE) *H Graham Motion* a76 97
3 bb f Dansili Hoity Toity (Darshaan)
2415^{5} 4356^{4} 7724a^{2}

Danish Duke (IRE) *Ruth Carr* a68 76
5 ch g Duke Of Marmalade(IRE) Bridge Note (USA) (Stravinsky (USA))
25^{2} 246^{6} 449^{3} 893^{3} 1030^{5} 1254^{3} 1525^{5} 2202^{4} 2571^{6} 3070^{3} (3776) (3940) 4544^{7} (4970)

Danish Dynaformer (CAN) *Roger L Attfield* a95 112
4 b h Dynaformer(USA) Danish Wildcat (USA) (Danehill (USA))
5431a^{5} 6600a^{5} 7405a^{6}

Dannyday *Sir Michael Stoute* a101 91
4 b h Dansili Dayrose (Daylami (IRE))
(1802) ◆ *(3657)*

Danot (IRE) *Jedd O'Keeffe* a42 75
4 ch g Zebedee Hapipi (Bertolini (USA))
1124^{9} 1596^{3} 1884^{6} *2918^{11}* 3327^{11} 5386^{2} *5845^{11}* 6226^{11} 7333^{9}

Danse Rouge (IRE) *Patrick J Flynn* a36 52
4 b m Archipenko(USA) Flapper (IRE) (Selkirk (USA))
5096a^{3}

Dan Troop *Richard Fahey* a69 66
2 b g Lawman(FR) Full Mandate (IRE) (Acclamation)
6159^{7} 6731^{5} *7748^{2} 8033^{5}*

Danzeb (IRE) *Ann Duffield* a67 65
3 gr g Zebedee Daneville (IRE) (Danetime (IRE))
1789^{4} 2049^{7} 2418^{5} 3211^{11} 4256^{3} 4874^{8} *5839^{3}* 6341^{9} *7145^{2}*

Danzella *Chris Fairhurst* a46 45
4 b m Desideratum Danzatrice (Tamure (IRE))
3418^{7} 3704^{5} 4430^{8} *4645^{8}* 5522^{7} 6097^{5}

Danzeno *Michael Appleby* 115
5 b g Denounce Danzanora (Groom Dancer (USA))
2159^{3} 3195^{2} 4151^{9} 4916^{2} 5614^{10} 6161^{2} 6837^{2}

Danzing Candy (USA) *Clifford Sise Jr* a114
3 bb c Twirling Candy(USA) Talkin And Singing (USA) (Songandaprayer (USA))
2063a^{15}

Danzoe (IRE) *Christine Dunnett* a64 15
9 br g Kheleyf(USA) Fiaba (Precocious)
341^{11}

Daphne *William Haggas* 90
3 b f Duke Of Marmalade(IRE) Daring Aim (Daylami (IRE))
1626^{3} (2215) 3341^{14} 4351^{6} 4859^{2} (6667)

Daqeeq (IRE) *Simon Crisford* a77 89
3 b c New Approach(IRE) Asawer (IRE) (Darshaan)
1426^{2} 2175^{4} (Dead)

Darabad (FR) *A De Royer-Dupre* 97
3 b c Dansili Daryakana (FR) (Selkirk (USA))
6392a^{4}

Darcey Lou *John Best* a45
2 b f Mullionmileanhour(IRE) Balletlou (IRE) (Peintre Celebre (USA))
6414^{12} 6866^{9}

Darebin (GER) *Gary Moore* a74 72
4 ch g It's Gino(GER) Delightful Sofie (GER) (Grand Lodge (USA))
603^{9}

Daredevil Day (IRE) *Joseph G Murphy* 85
5 b g Holy Roman Emperor(IRE) Le Montrachet (Nashwan (USA))
4811a^{9} 6389a^{22}

Dariga *Roger Varian* 64
2 b f Medicean Danelissima (IRE) (Danehill (USA))
7056^{5} 7465^{4}

Daring Day *George Peckham* a71 75
3 b f Acclamation Silver Kestrel (USA) (Silver Hawk (USA))
2606^{2} 3406^{4} 4058^{11} *7985^{9}*

Daring Dragon *Derek Shaw* a65 60
6 gr g Intikhab(USA) The Manx Touch (IRE) (Petardia)
21^{8}

Daring Guest (IRE) *George Margarson* a62 62
2 b g Fast Company(IRE) Balm (Oasis Dream)
4270^{8} 5792^{6} 6071^{8} *6670^{4}*

Daring Indian *Roger Teal* a72 60
8 ch g Zamindar(USA) Anasazi (IRE) (Sadler's Wells (USA))
222^{9} 622^{7}

Daring Knight *Martin Smith* a67 56
3 b g Dick Turpin(IRE) Fairy Slipper (Singspiel (IRE))
557^{4} ◆ *778^{4} 1238^{8}* 1860^{9} *6510^{7}*

Daring Lion (GER) *J Hirschberger* 67
3 b c Areion(GER) Daring Action (Arazi (USA))
1311a^{10}

Daring Match (GER) *J Hirschberger* a88 109
5 ch h Call Me Big(GER) Daring Action (Arazi (USA))
2722a^{2} 3992a^{4} 5943a^{6} 7758a^{8}

Dariyan (FR) *A De Royer-Dupre* 118
4 b h Shamardal(USA) Daryakana (FR) (Selkirk (USA))
843a^{2} 1107a^{6} (1909a) 2568a^{2} 4441a^{5} 5558^{10}

Dark Alliance (IRE) *M Halford* a85 80
5 b g Dark Angel(IRE) Alinda (IRE) (Revoque (IRE))
6382a^{14} *7339a^{2}*

Dark Amber *Brendan Powell* a62 62
6 b m Sakhee(USA) Donna Vita (Vettori (IRE))
875^{7} 1387^{11} 1775^{6} 2127^{5} 3121^{3} 3673^{8} 4157^{9} 4593^{6} 5096a^{6} 6058^{4} 6827^{2} 7272^{5} ◆ 7628^{4} *8155^{4}*

Dark Avenue *William Knight* a69 64
3 b f Champs Elysees Dark Quest (Rainbow Quest (USA))
2652[14] 4025[8]

Dark Castle *Micky Hammond* a47 58
7 b g Dark Angel(IRE) True Magic (Magic Ring (IRE))
2856[11] 4691[6] 5278[9] 5535[8]

Dark Command *Michael Dods* a66 69
3 b g Kheleyf(USA) Desert Liaison (Dansili)
1126[4] 1667[2] 2306[4] 2864[4] 3224[8] 3877[2] ◆ 4444[2] 4701[3] 5151[7] 5843[3] 6347[2] 7059[8]

Dark Confidant (IRE) *Richard Fahey* a65 57
3 b g Royal Applause Sleek Gold (Dansili)
1112[7] 2106[6] 2854[6] 3604[3] 3941[8] 4410[11] 4973[9] (7463) (7751)

Dark Crescent (IRE) *Charles Hills* a74 82
3 b c Elnadim(USA) Zenella (Kyllachy)
2237[8]

Dark Crystal *Linda Perratt* a52 66
5 b m Multiplex Glitz (IRE) (Hawk Wing (USA))
1663[8] 2092[5] 2574[5] 2960[7] 3922[2] 4102[7] (4444) (4701) 4933[8] 5115[7] 5779[6] 6005[8] 6502[4] 6772[3] 6838[4] 7254[7]

Dark Defender *Keith Dalgleish* a71 93
3 b g Pastoral Pursuits Oh So Saucy (Imperial Ballet (IRE))
2251[7] 2650[6] 3394[4] 3753[4] ◆ (3944) 4643[9] 5153[3] 5643[4] (6164) 6539[20] 7315[15]

Dark Destroyer (IRE) *Joseph Tuite* 80
2 b c Helmet(AUS) Oeuvre D'Art (IRE) (Marju (IRE))
4837[3] ◆ 5583[8] 6288[10]

Dark Devil (IRE) *Richard Fahey* 90
3 gr g Dark Angel(IRE) Ride For Roses (IRE) (Barathea (IRE))
1975[3] ◆ 2892[11] 3887[5] 6225[4] ◆ 6736[3] (7189)

Dark Diamond (IRE) *Michael Chapman* a72 67
6 b g Dark Angel(IRE) Moon Diamond (Unfuwain (USA))
132[5] 506[3] (1043) 1296[7] 3118[4] 4234[14] 5726[7] 6165[6] (Dead)

Dark Emerald (IRE) *Brendan Powell* a88 112
6 gr g Dark Angel(IRE) Xema (Danehill (USA))
95a[8] 375a[2] 623a[4] 810a[9] 3664[6] 4395[2] 5404[3] 6056[6]

Dark Enemy (IRE) *Brendan Powell* 42
3 b g Dark Angel(IRE) Headborough Lass (IRE) (Invincible Spirit (IRE))
5438[9] 6805[8] 7219[6]

Darkening Night *Sarah-Jayne Davies* a28
4 b g Cape Cross(IRE) Garanciere (FR) (Anabaa (USA))
1762[8]

Dark Forest *Marjorie Fife* a61 54
3 b g Iffraaj Through The Forest (USA) (Forestry (USA))
2239[7] 2657[3] 3716[6] 4139[9] 4517[6] 4714[6] 4835[7] 6872[6] 7995[12]

Dark Hero (IRE) *Charles Hills* a60 53
2 b g Kodiac Mistress Marina (AUS) (Galileo (IRE))
1621[9] 2500[4] 2786[4] 5806[3] 6440[3] 6670[10]

Dark Illustrator *Alan Swinbank* a55 25
3 b f Dutch Art Xtrasensory (Royal Applause)
145[7] 443[9] 688[2] 794[4] 1551[10] 3020[12]

Dark Intention (IRE) *Lawrence Mullaney* a80 77
3 b f High Chaparral(IRE) Ajiaal (Cape Cross (IRE))
1998[2] 2490[5] (3634) 5115[3] 6005[2] ◆ 6811[4] 7857[3]

Dark Ocean (IRE) *Jedd O'Keeffe* a83 89
6 b g Dylan Thomas(IRE) Neutral (Beat Hollow)
1122[5] 1526[4] 3884[4] 4717[7] 5886[10] 7428[8]

Dark Phantom (IRE) *Geoffrey Deacon* a51 44
5 b g Dark Angel(IRE) Stoneware (Bigstone (IRE))
341[7] 4202[12] 4993[6] 6311[6] 6853[7] 7298[10]

Dark Power (IRE) *Clive Cox* 75
2 gr c Dark Angel(IRE) Sixfields Flyer (IRE) (Desert Style (IRE))
6543[2] (7072)

Dark Red (IRE) *Ed Dunlop* a85 103
4 gr g Dark Angel(IRE) Essexford (IRE) (Spinning World (USA))
(1161) (1569) (1972) 2866[4] 5651[2] 6389a[16] 6786[28]

Dark Redeemer *N Caullery* a80 37
3 b g Dark Angel(IRE) Lush (IRE) (Fasliyev (USA))
128a[8] 3546a[10]

Darkroom Angel *Clive Cox* a52 68
2 gr f Dark Angel(IRE) Framed (Elnadim (USA))
4558[8] 5559[3] 6034[2] 6630[4] 7185[8] 7768[4] 8153[10]

Dark Ruler (IRE) *Alan Swinbank* a69 94
7 b g Dark Angel(IRE) Gino Lady (IRE) (Perugino (USA))
337[10] 1250[4] 1880[2] 5837[13] 6561[13]

Dark Shot *Andrew Balding* a63 90
3 b g Acclamation Dark Missile (Night Shift (USA))
1894[2] 2251[4] 2698[2] 2980[2] (3669) 4223[4] 4911[4] (6114)

Dark Side Dream *Chris Dwyer* a84 49
4 b g Equiano(FR) Dream Day (Oasis Dream)
198[12] 938[8] 1175[7] 1528[11] 6589[3] 7325[2] 7660[2] 7959[2] 8389[5]

Dark Side Princess *Chris Dwyer* a78
3 b f Strategic Prince Brazilian Breeze (IRE) (Invincible Spirit (IRE))
(57) ◆ 322[2] ◆ 686[5] 954[7]

Darksiteofthemoon (IRE) *Marco Botti* a77 55
3 b g Dark Angel(IRE) Moon Club (IRE) (Red Clubs (IRE))
1137[2] 2545[10] 2981[12]

Dark Wonder (IRE) *Ivan Furtado* a79 77
4 b g Dark Angel(IRE) Wondrous Story (USA) (Royal Academy (USA))
3262[2] 5273[6] (5935) 6453[2] 7076[2] 7436[9] 7691[2]

Darma (IRE) *Martyn Meade* a79 86
4 b m Acclamation Dark Dancer (FR) (Danehill (USA))
1419[2] (2794) (4496) 4984[4]

Darrell Rivers *Giles Bravery* a57 68
4 b m Hellvelyn First Term (Acclamation)
1928[2] 2403[4] 2655[6] 5038[U] 5793[7] 7611[6] 7774[11]

Darrington *Kristin Stubbs* a78 88
4 b g Archipenko(USA) Rosablanca (IRE) (Sinndar (IRE))
1620[6] 2017[5] 2620[9] 3113[10] 5482[5] ◆ 6160[16] (6618) 7408[4]

Darshini *Sir Michael Stoute* a97 96
4 b g Sir Percy Fairy Flight (USA) (Fusaichi Pegasus (USA))
(1480) ◆ 1972[10] 2866[7] 3435[2] 4276[3] 5145[3]

Dartmouth *Sir Michael Stoute* a114 121
4 b h Dubawi(IRE) Galatee (FR) (Galileo (IRE))
(1475) ◆ (1995) (3384) 4626[3] 6571[2] 7405a[2]

Darvie *David Barron* 45
2 b g Stimulation(IRE) Timeless Elegance (IRE) (Invincible Spirit (IRE))
4601[7]

Darwasl *Brian Meehan* 65
2 b f Sepoy(AUS) Hakeeka (Cape Cross (IRE))
3556[5] 4298[13]

Daschas *Amanda Perrett* a77
2 b c Oasis Dream Canada Water (Dansili)
7975[3] (8354)

Dasheen *Mark Johnston* a54 71
3 b g Bahamian Bounty Caribbean Dancer (USA) (Theatrical (IRE))
2780[6] 2957[4] 3400[2] 3841[2] ◆ 4102[9] 4729[9] 5322[6] 6028[2] 6226[10] 6838[5]

Dashing Poet *Jeremy Gask* a56 59
2 b f Poet's Voice Millisecond (Royal Applause)
4558[5] 5077[7]

Dashing Star *David Elsworth* a90 106
6 b g Teofilo(IRE) Dashiba (Dashing Blade)
7575[5] 7824[13]

Dauphine De France (FR) *J Parize* a38 42
4 b m Air Chief Marshal(IRE) Un Petit Tour (FR) (Double Bed (FR))
8422a[14]

Davarde (IRE) *David Evans* a35 72
2 ch g Dragon Pulse(IRE) Global Tour (USA) (Tour D'Or (USA))
1082[8] 2180[2] 2457[2] 3196[6] 4083[6] 5543[8] 6652[9]

Davey Boy *Michael Bell* a75 4
3 ch g Paco Boy(IRE) She's So Pretty (IRE) (Grand Lodge (USA))
1155[6] 2900[12] 6629[14] 7078[13] 7889[9]

David's Beauty (IRE) *Brian Baugh* a61 64
3 b f Kodiac Thaisy (USA) (Tabasco Cat (USA))
242[12] 365[6] 635[3] 763[3] 1497[6] 1554[5] 2503[4] (3140) 3900[5] 4691[9] 5200[3] 5570 [2] (5920) 6832[3] 8535[11]

David's Duchess (IRE) *Richard Fahey* a64 83
3 b f Zebedee Blue Daze (Danzero (AUS))
2740[2] 3209[2] (3754) 4398[2] 4741[3] 5372[4] 6114[5] 6946[12] 7434[7]

Davinci Dawn *Ann Duffield* 26
2 b f Poet's Voice Bonnie Brae (Mujahid (USA))
4037[9]

Davy's Dilemma *Michael Dods* a75 79
2 b g Sixties Icon Wansdyke Lass (Josr Algarhoud (IRE))
4829[4] 5363[2] (5885) 6554[5] 6903[5]

Dawaa *Mark Johnston* a88 99
3 ch f Tamayuz Athreyaa (Singspiel (IRE))
1115[4] 1851[4] 2466[9] 3116[2] 3635[6] (4116) 4651[3] 5588[6] 6109[7] 6764[12] (7550) 7822[4] 7978[6]

Dawn Flight (IRE) *John Davies* 68
3 b g Cacique(IRE) Ommadawn (IRE) (Montjeu (IRE))
3362[4] 3981[6]

Dawn Goddess *Gary Moore* a39
2 b f Dick Turpin(IRE) Aurora Sky (IRE) (Hawk Wing (USA))
8591[11]

Dawn Horizons *William Haggas* 94
3 ch f New Approach(IRE) Hidden Hope (Daylami (IRE))
2183[5] (3190) (4501) 5927[3] 7669[4]

Dawn Mirage *Richard Fahey* 95
4 b g Oasis Dream Prima Luce (IRE) (Galileo (IRE))
1122[8] 1924[2] 3884[3] 4307[3] (4727) 5538[2] 5874[2] 6753[3] 6956[2]

Dawn Missile *William Haggas* a70 98
4 b g Nayef(USA) Ommadawn (IRE) (Montjeu (IRE))
3630a[13] 4077[8] 5116[6] 5611[7] 6526[3] 7158[3]

Dawn Of A New Era (IRE) *J S Bolger* 82
2 b f New Approach(IRE) Hymn Of The Dawn (USA) (Phone Trick (USA))
6385a[7] 6815a[6]

Dawn Of Hope (IRE) *Roger Varian* a96 99
3 ch f Mastercraftsman(IRE) Sweet Firebird (IRE) (Sadler's Wells (USA))
(1771) 7119[5] 7823[4] (8148a)

Dawoodi *Hugo Palmer* 79
2 ch g Exceed And Excel(AUS) Anna Amalia (IRE) (In The Wings)
4765[3] 6009[2] 6524[9] 6954[18]

Dawreya (IRE) *Marcus Tregoning* a53
3 b f Acclamation Darajaat (USA) (Elusive Quality (USA))
2606[6]

Dawwass (USA) *S Seemar* a58
2 ch c Speightstown(USA) Quaintly (USA) (Giant's Causeway (USA))
8391a[4] 8574a[5]

Daybreak Lady *Jo Hughes* a57
3 ch f Firebreak Musical Day (Singspiel (IRE))
40[11] 1725[10] 4500[8]

Daydream (IRE) *Jamie Osborne* a61
3 b f Dream Ahead(USA) Intricate Dance (USA) (Aptitude (USA))
42[6] 249[7] 610[5] 794[2] 948[3] 1141[6] 2107[7]

Dayim Benim (IRE) *Tahir Kurt* 105
3 ch c Lion Heart(USA) St Clair Ridge (IRE) (Indian Ridge)
6181a[3]

Daylight *Michael Easterby* a64 72
6 ch g Firebreak Dayville (USA) (Dayjur (USA))
1030[9] 1125[5] 1489[10] 1712[5] 2201[5] 2416[2] 2680[9] 3474[6] 3713[13] 3892[8]

Dayli Love Royale (FR) *P Capelle* a51 49
3 b f Early March Luthita (FR) (Always Fair (USA))
5385a[10]

Day Of The Eagle (IRE) *Michael Easterby* a48 75
10 b g Danehill Dancer(IRE) Puck's Castle (Shirley Heights)
1632[6] 2347[9]

Dazacam *Michael Herrington* a81 45
2 b f Camacho Dazakhee (Sakhee (USA))
5524[7] 6588[5] 6925[6] 7330[6] 7510[4] 7981[4] (8097) (8285) (8453)

Dazeekha *Michael Herrington* a50 18
3 b f Captain Gerrard(IRE) Dazakhee (Sakhee (USA))
48[5]

Dazzling Rose *John Gosden* a71 89
3 ch f Raven's Pass(USA) Darmiana (USA) (Lemon Drop Kid (USA))
654[2] ◆ (4361) 6939[7]

D'bai (IRE) *Charlie Appleby* 100
2 b c Dubawi(IRE) Savannah Belle (Green Desert (USA))
4103[2] ◆ (4649) 6326[3] (7409) 7722a[11]

Dberto (IRE) *M Delcher Sanchez* a70 63
3 b g Cape Cross(IRE) Narya (IRE) (Halling (USA))
5704a[6]

Dea Dia (IRE) *Adrian Paul Keatley* a47 45
4 b m Holy Roman Emperor(IRE) Non Ultra (USA) (Peintre Celebre (USA))
5228[3]

Deadline Day (IRE) *Michael Mullineaux* a62 31
5 b g Montjeu(IRE) Madame Cerito (USA) (Diesis)
673[8] 819[6] 1038[9] 1156[7]

De Aguilar (USA) *Roger Charlton* a74 61
3 b g Cape Blanco(IRE) Golden Aster (USA) (Seeking The Gold (USA))
1184[2] 1739[6] 3728[4]

Dealer's Choice (IRE) *Roger Varian* a77
2 gr f Exchange Rate(USA) Micaela's Moon (USA) (Malibu Moon (USA))
7380[2] ◆ 7689[3] 8140[4]

Deansgate (IRE) *Julie Camacho* a78 77
3 b g Dandy Man(IRE) Romarca (IRE) (Raise A Grand (IRE))
1400[2] 2532[3] 3252[6] 4241[2] ◆ 5063[3] 5845[5] 6220[2] 7111[3]

Dear Bruin (IRE) *David W Drinkwater* 76
4 b m Kodiac Namu (Mujahid (USA))
3807[10] 4043[8] 4485[4] 4990[8] (5259) 5797[6] 6649[5]

Deauville (IRE) *A P O'Brien* 117
3 b c Galileo(IRE) Walklikeanegyptian (IRE) (Danehill (USA))
2190[2] 2896[11] ◆ (4173a) 5431a[3]

Deauville Dancer (IRE) *David Dennis* a31 91
5 b g Tamayuz Mathool (IRE) (Alhaarth (IRE))
5381[9]

Deauville Prince (FR) *Tom Dascombe* a90 96
6 b g Holy Roman Emperor(IRE) Queen Of Deauville (FR) (Diableneyev (USA))
1218[16] 1522[12] 1997[6] 3133[3]

Deauville Shower (IRE) *E Libaud* a92 99
5 b m High Chaparral(IRE) Endless Night (GER) (Tiger Hill (IRE))
4696a[12] 6107a[8]

Deben *Kevin Ryan* a66 61
3 b g Lilbourne Lad(IRE) Mocca (IRE) (Sri Pekan (USA))
582[3] ◆ 824[6] 1183[6] 1313[3] 2107[4] 2306[7] 3224[S] 3579[4] (4006) 4490[3] 4973[2] 5355[2] 7062[10] 7261[8] 7604[7]

Debit *Simon Hodgson* a62 76
5 b g Pivotal Silver Kestrel (USA) (Silver Hawk (USA))
65[5] 297[7] 463[2] 701[3] 982[9] 1456[P] (Dead)

Debonaire David *Richard Hughes* a66 55
2 b c Sir Prancealot(IRE) Peyto Princess (Bold Arrangement)
2147[6] 4879[3] 5593[7] 8097[2] 8467[2]

De Boss Man (IRE) *M D O'Callaghan* 97
2 b c Dandy Man(IRE) Dame Hester (IRE) (Diktat)
5940a[3] 7155[4]

Decadent Times (IRE) *Marjorie Fife* a74 66
2 b g Art Connoisseur(IRE) Be Special (IRE) (Sri Pekan (USA))
1082[3] 1233[2] 1407[2] 1749[3] 2500[3] 4000[2] 5833[8] 6564[7]

Decale *K Borgel* 62
2 b f Mawatheeq(USA) Ligurian Sea (Medicean)
3006a[5]

Decapulse (IRE) *J-V Toux* 77
2 b f Dragon Pulse(IRE) Decadence (Singspiel (IRE))
1118a[6] 3006a[9] 7490a[9]

Decathlete (USA) *S bin Ghadayer* a61 78
5 b g Medaglia d'Oro(USA) Rahiyah (USA) (Rahy (USA))
810a[11]

Decibelle *Barry Brennan* a4 2
4 b m Indesatchel(IRE) Buffy Boo (Agnes World (USA))
5080[9] 6587[10]

Decisive (IRE) *Anthony Carson* a59 56
4 ch m Iffraaj Guarantia (Selkirk (USA))
3078[7] 3973[5] 5080[6] 5475[4] 5636[2] 6100[14] 7201[2] 7489[6]

Decked Out (USA) *J Keith Desormeaux* a88 106
3 ch f Street Boss(USA) Once Around (CAN) (You And I (USA))
4174a[9]

Declamation (IRE) *Alistair Whillans* a62 60
6 ch g Shamardal(USA) Dignify (IRE) (Rainbow Quest (USA))
3940[2] ◆ 8316[7]

Declined *David C Griffiths* 19
4 b g Authorized(IRE) Three Secrets (IRE) (Danehill (USA))
1622[12] 3856[10] 4258[10] 5368[12]

Decorated Knight *Roger Charlton* 112
4 ch h Galileo(IRE) Pearling (USA) (Storm Cat (USA))
1774[4] (2464) 2867[2] ◆ (4326a)

Decruz (IRE) *Richard Hannon* 20
2 gr f Dark Angel(IRE) Yazmin (IRE) (Green Desert (USA))
3770[6]

Deebaj (IRE) *Richard Price* 74
4 br g Authorized(IRE) Athreyaa (Singspiel (IRE))
6765[4]

Dee Dee D'Or (IRE) *Stefano Botti* 105
3 gr c Zebedee Goldendale (IRE) (Ali-Royal (IRE))
2517a[2]

Deeds Not Words (IRE) *J F Levins* a75 76
5 b g Royal Applause Wars (IRE) (Green Desert (USA))
1015a[13]

Deeley's Double (FR) *Tony Carroll* a60
3 ch g Makfi Habilea (FR) (Grand Lodge (USA))
7753[7] 8320[5]

Dee Majesty (JPN) *Yoshitaka Ninomiya* 122
3 b c Deep Impact(JPN) Hermes Tiara (JPN) (Brian's Time (USA))
8129a[13]

Deep Blue Diamond *Denis Quinn* 74
4 b m Sir Percy Apple Blossom (IRE) (Danehill Dancer (IRE))
2176[9] 3480[8]

Deep Blue Sea *Anthony Carson* a77 81
4 b m Rip Van Winkle(IRE) Semaphore (Zamindar (USA))
564[7] 1158[2] 1455[5]

Deep Dream *Andrew Balding* a51
3 b f Dream Ahead(USA) Jessica's Dream (IRE) (Desert Style (IRE))
516[4]

Deep Resolve (IRE) *Alan Swinbank* a72 69
5 b g Intense Focus(USA) I'll Be Waiting (Vettori (IRE))
6[6] 367[2] 429[4] 802[6] 1222[4] (1399) 1560[7] 7594[12] 7895[5] 8238[4]

Deepsand (IRE) *Ali Stronge* a10 68
7 br g Footstepsinthesand Sinamay (USA) (Saint Ballado (CAN))
1391[3] 2502[3] 3191[5] 3767[6] 4995[5] 5624[6]

Deer Song *John Bridger* a63 50
3 b g Piccolo Turkish Delight (Prince Sabo)
83[3] 1414[9] 1935[9] 2435[5] 3469[9] 4264[4] 4529[3] 5554[2] 8149[9] 8248[6] 8596[7]

Defiance (IRE) *James Tate* a54
2 b f Medicean Plucky (Kyllachy)
8362[6]

Defiant Choice *Derek Shaw* a6 46
3 b g Teofilo(IRE) Endorsement (Warning)
2563[8] 3190[7]

Defiant Honor (USA) *James J Toner* 93
2 b f Speightstown(USA) Honor Bestowed (USA) (Honor Grades (USA))
8127a[2]

Defi Chope (FR) *C Boutin* a21 53
2 b f Captain Chop(FR) Lady Jak (FR) (American Post)
3182a[8] 7927a[9]

Defining Moment *Rae Guest* a47 60
2 b f Camacho Elfine (IRE) (Invincible Spirit (IRE))
7576[7] 8229[10]

Defining Year (IRE) *Hugo Froud* a84 80
8 b g Hawk Wing(USA) Tajaathub (USA) (Aljabr (USA))
3721[6] 4208[8] 6128[11]

Defoe (IRE) *Roger Varian* 94
2 bg c Dalakhani(IRE) Dulkashe (IRE) (Pivotal)
(6376) 6801[2] ◆ 7151[11]

Defoe Street (USA) *Gregory DiPrima*
6 b m Street Sense(USA) Kris Pit (USA) (Kris S (USA))
89a[8]

Deftera Lad (IRE) *Natalie Lloyd-Beavis* a58 50
4 b g Fast Company(IRE) Speedbird (USA) (Sky Classic (CAN))
2969[8] 3522[5] 3953[7] 5080[4] 6020[4] 6243[5] 7070[12] 7282[2] 7463[3] 7910[3] 8125[4] (8499)

Degas (GER) *Markus Klug* 108
3 ch c Exceed And Excel(AUS) Diatribe (Tertullian (USA))
2315a[2] 3183a[3] 4185a[5] 6067a[2] 6992a[2]

Degas Bronze *Gary Moore* 30
3 b f Showcasing Local Fancy (Bahamian Bounty)
7011[9]

Deitee (FR) *Louis Baudron* a74 94
3 b f Shakespearean(IRE) Baroness Snouckart (USA) (Quest For Fame)
7862a[10]

Delagate This Lord *Bill Turner* a61
2 b g Delegator Lady Filly (Atraf)
7883[12] 8074[7] 8189[7] 8340[8]

Delagoa Bay (IRE) *Sylvester Kirk* a63 60
8 b m Encosta De Lago(AUS) Amory (GER) (Goofalik (USA))
195[4] 354[8] 498[4] 634[3] 695[5] 981[3] 1039[5] 1322[4] 1550[2] 2131[8] 2634[8] (3528) 4012[7] (4816) 5473[5] 5745[6] 6422[4] 6825[12] 7367[5] 7507[10] (7739) 8039[3] 8211[5] 8359[5]

Delahay *Michael Blanshard* 42
2 b f Delegator Harryana To (Compton Place)
5890[5]

Delaire *Martin Bosley* a61 61
4 b g Sakhee's Secret Moody Margaret (Bahamian Bounty)
2849[7]

Delannoy *Eve Johnson Houghton* 71
2 ch g Le Havre(IRE) Raving Monsun (Monsun (GER))
6297[6] 6881[8]

Delectation *Bryan Smart* 106
2 b f Delegator Chushka (Pivotal)
(5272) (6555)

De Lesseps (USA) *John David Riches* a63 20
8 ch g Selkirk(USA) Suez (Green Desert (USA))
(216) 532[2] 670[8] 904[3] 1632[8]

Deleyll *John Butler* a56 41
2 ch g Sepoy(AUS) Strings (Unfuwain (USA))
4762[8] 5084[5] 5377[7] 7423[2] 8235[11]

Delfie Lane *Richard Hughes* a67 37
2 b g Harbour Watch(IRE) Anneliina (Cadeaux Genereux)
4205^{7} 7867^{6} 8027^{8} 8174^{9}

Deliberator *William Knight* a54
2 b c Delegator Purest (Shamardal (USA))
8404^{3} ◆

Delightfulsurprise *Scott Dixon* a31
2 b f Delegator Surprise Statement (Proclamation (IRE))
7659^{10} 7891^{13} 8237^{11}

Delirium (IRE) *Ed de Giles* a52 47
2 b f Tamayuz Coeur De La Mer (IRE) (Caerleon (USA))
6413^{12} 7056^{7} 7647^{7}

De Little Engine (AUS) *Danny O'Brien* 99
5 b g Encosta De Lago(AUS) Arapaho Miss (AUS) (Danehill Dancer (IRE))
7378a^{9} 7712a^{4} 7826a^{4} 7947a^{5}

De Little Engine (IRE) *Jamie Osborne* a65
2 ch c Power Reveuse De Jour (IRE) (Sadler's Wells (USA))
7648^{9} 7883^{3}

Dellaguista (IRE) *William Haggas* a73 61
2 gr f Sea The Stars(IRE) Lady Springbank (IRE) (Choisir (AUS))
7494^{6} ◆ 8130^{4} (8443)

Dell' Arca (IRE) *David Pipe* 71
7 b g Sholokhov(IRE) Daisy Belle (GER) (Acatenango (GER))
3533^{6}

Della Valle (GER) *Mike Murphy* a72 83
3 b f Lando(GER) Denial (Sadler's Wells (USA))
2339^{6} 3071^{3} (3467) 4977^{4} 6417^{5} 6876^{14} 7504^{14}

Dellbuoy *Pat Phelan* a58 58
7 b g Acclamation Ruthie (Pursuit Of Love)
62^{7} 354^{7} 3492^{2} 3798^{4} 4303^{3} 4950^{5} 7039^{8} 7739^{6}

Delta Bluesman (USA) *Jorge Navarro* a110 53
6 rg g Wagon Limit(USA) Smoke Alarm (USA) (Darn That Alarm (USA))
7832a^{5}

Deluxe *Pat Phelan* a66 77
4 b g Acclamation Ainia (Alhaarth (IRE))
608^{8} 773^{6} 1949^{2} 2965^{6} 3959^{4} 4531^{10} 5021^{4} 5303^{7} 5993^{4} 7298^{3}

Delve (IRE) *Sir Michael Stoute* 89
3 b f Dansili Cool And Composed (USA) (Buddha (USA))
2177^{2} 2877^{3} (3850) 4582^{7} 6939^{6} 7861a^{9}

Delysdream *Christine Dunnett* a5 42
4 br g Dutch Art Goodbye Cash (IRE) (Danetime (IRE))
2542^{15} 3040^{12} 3822^{11} 4200^{10}

Demand Respect *Henry Spiller* a37 37
3 ch g Paco Boy(IRE) Brilliance (Cadeaux Genereux)
5608^{4} 6423^{6} 8459^{6}

Demi's Quest *Tony Carroll* a30
2 b f Roderic O'Connor(IRE) Demi Voix (Halling (USA))
5022^{7} 6062^{9} 6867^{11}

Demographic (USA) *Emma Lavelle* a62
7 b g Aptitude(USA) Private Line (USA) (Private Account (USA))
728^{3}

Demoiselledavignon (FR) *D Windrif* a57 62
5 b m Astronomer Royal(USA) O'Keefe (IRE) (Be My Guest (USA))
(1157a) 1846a^{6} 3733a^{3}

Demonstration (IRE) *William Jarvis* a91 86
4 b g Cape Cross(IRE) Quiet Protest (USA) (Kingmambo (USA))
1861^{14} 2328^{2} (3057) 3525^{3} 4276^{5} 5160^{5} 6048^{5} 7383^{9}

Demora *Michael Appleby* a87 106
7 b m Deportivo Danzanora (Groom Dancer (USA))
91a^{6} 280a^{8} 626a^{12} (1453) 6230^{4} 7358^{13} 7771^{8}

Denga (IRE) *S Wattel* a92 95
3 b f Invincible Spirit(IRE) Dalarua (IRE) (King's Best (USA))
2928a^{8} 5987a^{5} 8368a^{6}

Denham Sound *Henry Candy* a73 75
3 ch f Champs Elysees Presbyterian Nun (IRE) (Daylami (IRE))
2183^{6} 2735^{5} 4661^{6} 5267^{4} 6239^{2} 7060^{8}

Deningy *Charlie Appleby* 94
2 ch g Sepoy(AUS) Sky Wonder (Observatory (USA))
1770^{2} ◆ 4552^{2} (5600) 6059^{5}

Denmead *John Butler* a70 71
3 b g Champs Elysees Glorious Dreams (USA) (Honour And Glory (USA))
1484^{10} 1918^{2} 4210^{4} 4942^{2} 5079^{3} (6367) 6659^{3}

Denver Spirit (IRE) *Luca Cumani* a48 42
2 b f Invincible Spirit(IRE) Leavingonajetplane (IRE) (Danehill (USA))
7439^{6} 7939^{7}

Deodoro (USA) *Mark Johnston* 82
3 b f Medaglia d'Oro(USA) Anna Wi'Yaak (JPN) (Dubai Millennium)
1786^{4} 2236^{5} 2490^{6} 3291^{3}

Deor (IRE) *John E Kiely* 88
5 b g Galileo(IRE) Something Mon (USA) (Maria's Mon (USA))
2114a^{3}

Depth Charge (IRE) *Kristin Stubbs* a81 93
4 b g Fastnet Rock(AUS) Myrtle (Batshoof)
64^{8} (239) 387^{6} 546^{3} 788^{4} 944^{5} 1186^{6} 1596^{4} 2491^{2} 2918^{3} 3367^{4} ◆ 3599^{8} 4497^{3} 5151^{10} (5367) ◆ 5845^{7} (6027) 6280^{6} (6437)

Derek Duval (USA) *Stuart Williams* 50
2 b g Lope De Vega(IRE) Lady Raj (USA) (El Prado (IRE))
5395^{8}

Deremah (USA) *A De Royer-Dupre* a102 100
3 bb f More Than Ready(USA) Darma (FR) (Danehill Dancer (IRE))
5451a^{6} 6497a^{2} 7029a^{3}

Dervahel (FR) *Mme C Barande-Barbe* a71 73
3 b f Le Havre(IRE) So Gold (FR) (Gold Away (IRE))
6912a^{6}

Dervish *Luca Cumani* a37
2 b g Cacique(IRE) Doggerbank (IRE) (Oasis Dream)
8227^{9} 8486^{14}

Derwent (USA) *J-P Gallorini* a59 65
6 b g Mizzen Mast(USA) Skiable (IRE) (Niniski (USA))
4927a^{13}

Desafinado (IRE) *Miss Joey Ellis* a45
4 ch m Dutch Art Sweetsformysweet (USA) (Forest Wildcat (USA))
402^{8} 1151^{13}

Des Annees Folles (FR) *P Adda* a76 75
3 ch f Bernebeau(FR) Celere (FR) (Kabool)
3007a^{4} 4220a^{4} 5280a^{5} 6912a^{4}

Desdichado *Ralph Beckett* a66 85
4 ch g Pivotal Murrieta (Docksider (USA))
1760^{2} ◆ 3161^{3} 3862^{8} 5231^{2} 6128^{8} 7077^{9}

Desert Ace (IRE) *Iain Jardine* a82 86
5 ch g Kheleyf(USA) Champion Place (Compton Place)
1672^{8} 2364^{4} 2665^{6} 4032^{3} ◆ 4428^{9} 4514^{2} ◆ 4831^{9} 5153^{7} 6080^{6} 6537^{17} (6793) 6926^{4} 7112^{6}

Desert Chief *Michael Appleby* a49 53
4 b g Kheleyf(USA) African Breeze (Atraf)
4425^{11} 8146^{9} 8572^{9}

Desert Command *Robert Cowell* a88 92
6 b g Oasis Dream Speed Cop (Cadeaux Genereux)
4^{4} 250^{2} 484^{4} 894^{6} 1744^{4} 2426^{4} 3193^{4} 7303^{8}

Desert Cross *Jonjo O'Neill* 63
3 b g Arcano(IRE) Secret Happiness (Cape Cross (IRE))
2148^{5} (2851) 3997^{4} 4500^{2} 6256^{3} 7421^{6}

Desert Dream *Sir Michael Stoute* 65
2 b c Oasis Dream Rosika (Sakhee (USA))
7317^{7}

Desert Encounter (IRE) *David Simcock* 107
4 b g Halling(USA) La Chicana (IRE) (Invincible Spirit (IRE))
(1853) (2249) (3670) ◆ 3889^{3} 6321^{2}

Desert Force *Doug Watson* a114 100
4 b g Equiano(FR) Mail The Desert (IRE) (Desert Prince (IRE))
1394^{6} 1856^{13} 2206^{13} (8578a)

Desert Fox *Mike Murphy* a68 50
2 b g Foxwedge(AUS) Snow Moccasin (IRE) (Oasis Dream)
5890^{4} 6369^{4} 7184^{9}

Desert Gift (IRE) *Robert Cowell* a43 39
2 gr f Dark Angel(IRE) Mickleberry (IRE) (Desert Style (IRE))
5631^{9} 7040^{6}

Desert Grey (IRE) *Roger Varian* a74 37
2 bz g Mastercraftsman(IRE) Endure (IRE) (Green Desert (USA))
7225^{7} 7470^{8} 7649^{4} 8353^{2} 8486^{13}

Desert Haze *Ralph Beckett* a100 98
3 br f New Approach(IRE) Ensemble (FR) (Iron Mask (USA))
1714^{3} (2420) (3107) ◆ 4130^{3} (4737) 6070a^{4} 6746^{5} 7676a^{2}

Desert Law (IRE) *Paul Midgley* a88 109
8 b g Oasis Dream Speed Cop (Cadeaux Genereux)
835^{8} 1862^{14} 2188^{14} 3151^{5} 3696a^{3} 4126^{12} 4584^{8} 5268^{7} 6779^{15} 7124^{16} 7358^{10} 7537^{17}

Desert Mark (IRE) *John Butler* a68 72
2 b c Approve(IRE) Profound Emotion (Mark Of Esteem (IRE))
2847^{5} 7296^{2} 8118^{3}

Desert Morning (IRE) *Anthony Carson* a73 53
4 b m Pivotal Arabian Mirage (Oasis Dream)
324^{5} (667) 792^{4}

Desert Recluse (IRE) *Henry Oliver* a49 50
9 ch g Redback Desert Design (Desert King (IRE))
103^{8}

Desert River (IRE) *Mark H Tompkins* a66 64
3 b g Showcasing Kathy's Rocket (USA) (Gold Legend (USA))
3069^{10} (3280) 5336^{2} 7203^{9}

Desert Ruler *Jedd O'Keeffe* 86
3 b g Kheleyf(USA) Desert Royalty (IRE) (Alhaarth (IRE))
1243^{8} 1585^{4} 2161^{13} 7126^{6} 7540^{7} 7743^{6}

Desert Samurai (AUS) *Adam O'Neill* 83
4 b g Desert King(IRE) Lost Valley (AUS) (Fuji Kiseki (JPN))
7637a^{6}

Desert Sensation (IRE) *Tracy Waggott* 65
4 b g Authorized(IRE) Awwal Malika (USA) (Kingmambo (USA))
1873^{9} 2260^{8} 2853^{3}

Desert Skyline (IRE) *David Elsworth* a54 92
2 ch g Tamayuz Diamond Tango (FR) (Acatenango (GER))
6085^{7} (6523) (7471)

Desert Skywalker (IRE) *E Charpy* a3
5 ch g Raven's Pass(USA) Damiana (IRE) (Thatching)
8a^{14}

Desert Sport (USA) *Robert Cowell* a73 73
2 b c Hat Trick(JPN) Desert Sky (IRE) (Green Desert (USA))
4473^{8} 5377^{3} 6071^{5} 7142^{2} (7845)

Desert Strike *Conor Dore* a90 59
10 b g Bertolini(USA) Mary Jane (Tina's Pet)
236^{2} 439^{6} 655^{8} 782^{10} 903^{9} 1321^{3} 1838^{2} (2768) 3407^{3} 3780^{6} 4014^{6} 4714^{4} 5189^{9} 5679^{12} 6425^{7} 7644^{13} 7887^{10} 8078^{3} (8234) 8365^{8}

Desert Strom (IRE) *Mme Pia Brandt* a77 57
2 b f Iffraaj Desert Sprite (IRE) (Tagula (IRE))
8420a^{2}

Desert Tango *Michael Mullineaux* a51 52
3 ch f Paco Boy(IRE) Photographie (USA) (Trempolino (USA))
1259^{9} 1740^{11} 2590^{6} 3765^{6} (5575) 5883^{9} 6443^{2} 7256^{7} 7910^{6}

Desert Water (IRE) *Richard Hannon* 76
2 b f Sepoy(AUS) Desert Sunrise (Green Desert (USA))
(5995) 6548^{4}

Desert Way (IRE) *Ralph Beckett* 87
3 ch f Giant's Causeway(USA) Desert Sage (Selkirk (USA))
1989^{5} 2929^{4} (4657) 5382^{3}

Desidero (SPA) *Pat Phelan* a27 45
2 b f Sixties Icon Atasari (IRE) (Whipper (USA))
4270^{14} 4523^{8} 6264^{9} 7208^{6}

Designamento (IRE) *Ed de Giles* a33 27
2 b c Casamento(IRE) Designed (Zamindar (USA))
5505^{8} 6480^{10} 7283^{10}

Designs On Rome (IRE) *John Moore* 117
6 b g Holy Roman Emperor(IRE) Summer Trysting (USA) (Alleged (USA))
1690a^{5} 8333a^{8}

Desirable *Hughie Morrison* a59 46
3 b f Stimulation(IRE) Hot Pursuits (Pastoral Pursuits)
2185^{10} 3062^{12} 3513^{4} 4641^{5} 5013^{8}

Desire *Richard Fahey* a60 73
4 ch m Kyllachy Colonel's Daughter (Colonel Collins (USA))
2201^{6} 2906^{2} 3132^{6} 3708^{6} 4142^{4} 5276^{3} 5887^{2} (6568) 7334^{3} 7887^{8} 8135^{4}

Desktop *Antony Brittain* a64 64
4 b g Desideratum First Harmony (First Trump)
(946) 1136^{6} 1955^{7} (2558) 3067^{11} 4045^{8} 4645^{7} 6102^{11}

Desperados Destiny *Ed McMahon* a74 61
2 b g Delegator Muara (Wolfhound (USA))
5884^{15} 6682^{4} (7259)

Dessertoflife (IRE) *Mark Johnston* a72 101
3 gr f Mastercraftsman(IRE) Cranky Spanky (IRE) (Spectrum (IRE))
1966^{4} 2394^{8} 3297^{12} 3860^{4} 4131^{5} 4757^{6} 5956^{4} 6115^{4} 6948^{5} 7365^{8}

Destin (USA) *Todd Pletcher* a119
3 rg c Giant's Causeway(USA) Dream Of Summer (USA) (Siberian Summer (USA))
2063a^{6} 3181a^{2} 5913a^{9}

Destination Aim *Fred Watson* a50 58
9 b g Dubai Destination(USA) Tessa Reef (IRE) (Mark Of Esteem (IRE))
4684^{6} 5717^{6} 6453^{9} 7797^{8}

Destroyer *William Muir* a85 83
3 b g Royal Applause Good Girl (IRE) (College Chapel)
1181^{2} 1859^{2} 2375^{2} (3155) 3635^{7} 3908^{8} 4481^{6} 5412^{3} 5765^{4} 6490^{4} ◆ 6899^{3}

Devastar (GER) *Markus Klug* 108
4 b h Areion(GER) Deva (GER) (Platini (GER))
2723a^{4} 4253a^{5} 5904a^{4} (7028a) 7564a^{2} 7843a^{3}

De Veer Cliffs (IRE) *Martyn Meade* 87
3 b f Canford Cliffs(IRE) Mill Guineas (USA) (Salse (USA))
(3578) 4113^{14} 5089^{3} 6323^{2} 7077^{12}

De Vegas Kid (IRE) *Tony Carroll* a41 71
2 ch c Lope De Vega(IRE) Fravolina (USA) (Lemon Drop Kid (USA))
8526^{5}

Devilish Guest (IRE) *Mick Channon* 67
2 gr g Dark Angel(IRE) Leceile (USA) (Forest Camp (USA))
2437^{6} 3093^{9} 3813^{7} 4802^{13} 5251^{7} 6366^{6}

Devil's Bridge (IRE) *Richard Hannon* a85 90
2 b c Casamento(IRE) Cantaloupe (Priolo (USA))
3054^{3} ◆ 3661^{2} 4349^{2} 4914^{2} (5363) 6059^{3} 7075^{2} ◆ 7839a^{5}

Devil's Guard (IRE) *Keith Dalgleish* 51
2 br g Dark Angel(IRE) Visual Element (USA) (Distant View (USA))
6535^{9} 7578^{14} 7741^{11}

Devilution (IRE) *Derek Shaw* a44 17
4 b g Bluegrass Cat(USA) Meniatarra (USA) (Zilzal (USA))
22^{7} 168^{4} 252^{9} 430^{9}

Devious Spirit (IRE) *Iain Jardine* a61 62
4 br g Intikhab(USA) Unintentional (Dr Devious (IRE))
2345^{10} 5972^{5} 6434^{8} 6838^{7} 7581^{2} 7992^{7} 8400^{8} 8586^{11}

Devon Cove *Jane Chapple-Hyam* a34 31
2 b f Sixties Icon Where I Be (Dubawi (IRE))
7695^{13} 7885^{14}

Devon Drum *David Brown* a83 62
8 b g Beat Hollow West Devon (USA) (Gone West (USA))
6050^{4} 6854^{7} 7332^{11}

Devon River (FR) *Simon Waugh* a24
6 gr g Stormy River(FR) Devon House (USA) (Chester House (USA))
4648^{10}

Devonshire (IRE) *W McCreery* 110
4 b m Fast Company(IRE) Nova Tor (IRE) (Trans Island)
1016a^{2} (2497a) 3271^{10} 4435a^{5} 6352a^{8}

Devoran *Alan King* 62
2 ch f Harbour Watch(IRE) Triple Cee (IRE) (Cape Cross (IRE))
5387^{5} 6874^{5} 7494^{14}

Dewan (IRE) *Mick Channon* 68
2 b c Elzaam(AUS) So Blissful (IRE) (Cape Cross (IRE))
3529^{11} 3799^{6} 4125^{4} 4510^{2} 4982^{3}

Dew Line (IRE) *Michael Mulvany* a63 92
4 bb m Vale Of York(IRE) Begin The Beguine (IRE) (Peintre Celebre (USA))
7393a^{4}

Dew Pond *Tim Easterby* a47 81
4 b g Motivator Rutland Water (IRE) (Hawk Wing (USA))
2018^{10} (2745) (3191) 3602^{3} (4004) 4664^{5} 6083^{3} 6565^{2}

Dhaba (GER) *Markus Klug* 99
3 ch f Areion(GER) Darshana (Medicean)
1513a^{3} 2949a^{8} 4175a^{7} 5220a^{13} 6992a^{7}

Dhahmaan (IRE) *Marco Botti* a102 97
3 b c Kodiac Heroine Chic (IRE) (Big Bad Bob (IRE))
1773^{4} 2242^{4} 3158^{5} 4062^{14} 7068^{2} 7758a^{6} 7932^{9} 8489^{7}

Dhajeej (IRE) *Roger Varian* 80
2 b c Cape Cross(IRE) Nimboo (USA) (Lemon Drop Kid (USA))
7225^{2} 7621^{2}

Dharoos (IRE) *John Gosden* a85 76
3 ch c New Approach(IRE) Cailiocht (USA) (Elusive Quality (USA))
3359^{5} 7384^{2} 7627^{4}

Dhaular Dhar (IRE) *Jim Goldie* a68 81
14 b g Indian Ridge Pescara (IRE) (Common Grounds)
3162^{14} 4409^{7}

Dheban (IRE) *Richard Hannon* a81 81
3 gr g Exceed And Excel(AUS) Comeback Queen (Nayef (USA))
1599^{17} 2218^{4} 2982^{7}

Dhevanafushi *H-A Pantall* a101 101
3 gr c Kendargent(FR) Tejaara (USA) (Kingmambo (USA))
972a^{5} 1374a^{12} 2927a^{4} 7292a^{3}

Dheyaa (IRE) *Owen Burrows* a70 74
3 b f Dream Ahead(USA) Lady Livius (IRE) (Titus Livius (FR))
2294^{2} 4009^{3} ◆ 5038^{2} ◆ 5822^{4}

Diable D'Or (IRE) *Eve Johnson Houghton* 84
2 gr g Clodovil(IRE) Caherassdotcom (Compton Place)
2203^{4} 2583^{2} 3196^{4} 4394^{4} 4825^{11} (5569) 6388a^{12} 7073^{7}

Di Alta (IRE) *Ed Walker* 76
2 b f High Chaparral(IRE) Dibiya (IRE) (Caerleon (USA))
(7548)

Diamante (IRE) *Daniel Kubler* 35
2 b f Big Bad Bob(IRE) Miracle Steps (CAN) (Theatrical (IRE))
7466^{6}

Diamond Avalanche (IRE) *Patrick Holmes* a39 64
3 b g Alfred Nobel(IRE) Queens Flight (King's Best (USA))
1673^{6} 2422^{5} 2864^{11} 4870^{6} 6434^{7} 7253^{6} 7850^{8}

Diamond Bear (USA) *Sir Mark Prescott Bt* a63 74
2 bb f First Dude(USA) Lady Mariah (USA) (Giant's Causeway (USA))
6454^{5} 6897^{9} (7297)

Diamond Charlie (IRE) *Simon Dow* a84 62
8 br g Diamond Green(FR) Rosy Lydgate (Last Tycoon)
323^{7} 484^{5} 604^{2} 714^{5} 955^{10} 1175^{3} 1782^{3} 2088^{4} 2584^{5} 2768^{5} 3650^{4} 4264^{5} 5189^{6} 8228^{8} 8429^{8} 8535^{7}

Diamond Eagle (IRE) *Shaun Harris*
4 b g Moss Vale(IRE) Purify (Sinndar (IRE))
8290^{10} 8570^{9} 8585^{8}

Diamond Fields (IRE) *T Stack* a92 105
3 b f Fastnet Rock(AUS) Question Times (Shamardal (USA))
2272a^{2} 2923a^{4} 3274^{2}

Diamond Fragance (FR) *C Lotoux* a64
3 bb f Diamond Green(FR) Fleur Du Bonheur (FR) (Vaguely Pleasant (FR))
5349a^{9}

Diamond Geyser (IRE) *Luca Cumani* a89 84
3 b c Champs Elysees Triomphale (USA) (Nureyev (USA))
1701^{7} 2248^{8} 2541^{9} (3652) 4057^{2} 4859^{5} 5875^{2} 6456^{5} (7053) ◆

Diamond Indulgence *Derek Shaw* a50
3 b f Cockney Rebel(IRE) Shaws Diamond (USA) (Ecton Park (USA))
8290^{4} 8472^{4} 8570^{7}

Diamond Joel *Mick Channon* a70 84
4 b g Youmzain(IRE) Miss Lacroix (Picea)
3639^{2} 4752^{18} 5642^{11} 5963^{9} 6565^{9}

Diamond Kut *Andrew Balding* a73 67
3 gr g Rock Of Gibraltar(IRE) Diamond Line (FR) (Linamix (FR))
6634^{7} 8366^{4}

Diamond Lady *William Stone* a86 84
5 b m Multiplex Ellen Mooney (Efisio)
670^{2} 1065^{9} 1237^{2} 2253^{3} 4066^{5} 4984^{5} 7288^{5} 7773^{6} 8233^{7}

Diamond Princess *Michael Appleby* 33
2 b f Bahri(USA) Rainbow's Destiny (Dubai Destination (USA))
6732^{6} 7285^{9} 7576^{11} 8344^{12}

Diamond Rio (IRE) *Anthony Mullins* a66 77
4 b m Captain Rio Lesoto Diamond (IRE) (Darnay)
1279a^{10} 5313a^{14} 6389a^{23}

Diamond Runner (IRE) *John Norton* a57 45
4 b g Amadeus Wolf Hawk Eyed Lady (IRE) (Hawk Wing (USA))
(1654) 1791^{4} 2045^{6} 2448^{12} 5064^{3} 5604^{9} 7336^{13}

Diamonds A Dancing *Donald McCain* a63 66
6 ch g Delta Dancer Zing (Zilzal (USA))
1186^{7} 1416^{8} 1498^{3} 1834^{2} 1899^{4} 2566^{7} 3125^{6} (4088) (4589) 5252^{3} 6008^{3} 6636^{9}

Diamond Sam *Sylvester Kirk* a50 51
4 ch g Compton Place Kurtanella (Pastoral Pursuits)
168^{10} 341^{2} 431^{10} 547^{8}

Diamondsaretrumps (IRE) *Denis Quinn* a52
3 b f Dick Turpin(IRE) Serial Sinner (IRE) (High Chaparral (IRE))
265^{5} 700^{5} 789^{9}

Diamonds Pour Moi *Ralph Beckett* a77 103
3 b f Pour Moi(IRE) Diamond Light (USA) (Fantastic Light (USA))
1966^{3} 2869^{P} (8024a)

Diamond Vine (IRE) *Ronald Harris* a52 57
8 b g Diamond Green(FR) Glasnas Giant (Giant's Causeway (USA))
272^{5} 730^{3} 1005^{6} 1138^{6} (1320) 1794^{4} 2187^{7} (2584) 2964^{6} 3486^{8} 3743^{6} 5827^{7} 6312^{5} 6852^{11}

Diaspora (FR) *C Escuder* a77 59
3 b f American Post Douceur Nocturne (FR) (Zieten (USA))
3007a^{6}

Diatomic (IRE) *Tom Dascombe* a59 62
4 b g Bushranger(IRE) Gilded Truffle (IRE) (Peintre Celebre (USA))
(942) 1117^{6} 1341^{9} 1549^{5} 2416^{11} 3210^{9} 3726^{5}

Dibaba Traou Land (FR) *C Gourdain* a55 51
2 ch f Milanais(FR) Reason Traou Land (FR) (Secret Singer (FR))
5279a[6]

Diboy (FR) *Matthieu Palussiere* 39
2 ch c Kendargent(FR) Diva Island (FR) (Stormy River (FR))
3871a[13] 4471a[10]

Dickie Dickens (NOR) *Are Hyldmo*
6 b g Deceptor(USA) Sarina (SWE) (Diaghlyphard (USA))
1957a[12]

Dick Tracy (IRE) *Richard Hannon* a81 84
2 b c Lawman(FR) Modeeroch (IRE) (Mozart (IRE))
6159[2] 6663[3] 7283[4] *(7726)*

Dick Whittington (IRE) *A P O'Brien* 109
4 b h Rip Van Winkle(IRE) Sahara Sky (IRE) (Danehill (USA))
1226a[6] 2159[7] 2495a[3] (3332a) 4433a[7]

Dicton *Gianluca Bietolini* a94 117
3 b c Lawman(FR) Saying (USA) (Giant's Causeway (USA))
(1024a) (1580a) 2283a[3] 2946a[3] 5449a[5] 6975a[6]

Diego Valor (FR) *A Carrasco Sanchez* 105
5 b h Le Havre(IRE) Summer Sea (Bahhare (USA))
1231a[3]

Different Journey *Saeed bin Suroor* 74
3 b c Poet's Voice Vintage Gardenia (Selkirk (USA))
3981[3]

Different Scenario *Antony Brittain* a67 52
5 b m Araafa(IRE) Racina (Bluebird (USA))
150[8]

Different Views (USA) *Mick Channon* 41
2 b g Proud Citizen(USA) Elite (Invincible Spirit (IRE))
5377[8]

Digitalis (IRE) *Mario Hofer* 90
3 b c Manduro(GER) Prem Ramya (GER) (Big Shuffle (USA))
6151a[7]

Digital Revolution *Antony Brittain* 10
2 ch f Monsieur Bond(IRE) Lujiana (Lujain (USA))
2793[11]

Dikta Del Mar (SPA) *T Hogan* a80 105
4 b m Diktat Marmaria (SPA) (Limpid)
3201a[5] 3696a[7] *4246a[12]* 5816a[5] 6384a[11]

Dildiko (FR) *T Lemer*
3 ch c Evasive Nakamti (FR) (Lahint (USA))
1311a[13]

Diletta Tommasa (IRE) *Daniel Mark Loughnane* a69 65
6 ch m Dylan Thomas(IRE) Chronicle (Observatory (USA))
191[7] 676[8] 3363[6] (4225) *4716[8] 5397[5]* 6058[3] 6730[6] *6965[2] 7656[9] 7905[8] 8257[8]*

Dilgura *Stuart Kittow* a79 88
6 b m Ishiguru(USA) Dilys (Efisio)
146[5] 713[7] 1044[2] ◆ (1318) (1898) 2460[3] 3895[4] 6276[6] 6914[14]

Dilly Daydream (IRE) *Giles Bravery* a62 65
3 ch f Zoffany(IRE) Hendrina (IRE) (Daylami (IRE))
361[6] 706[6] 2212[8] 2829[6] 3256[10]

Dimaniya (FR) *A De Royer-Dupre* a83 82
3 ch f Dalakhani(IRE) Diampilina (FR) (Trempolino (USA))
1542a[4] 2115a[3] 4331a[6]

Diminutive (IRE) *Grace Harris* a46 53
4 ch m Fast Company(IRE) Take It Easee (IRE) (Noverre (USA))
937[8] 1180[7] 2537[3] 3811[2] 4484[6] 5826[2] (6381) *7276[5]* 7595[7] *7863[7]*

Dimitre *Henry Candy* 72
2 gr c Showcasing Devoted (IRE) (Dalakhani (IRE))
5304[4] 6543[4] 7574[3]

Ding Ding *Sheena West* a44 50
5 ch m Winker Watson Five Bells (IRE) (Rock Of Gibraltar (IRE))
3401[8]

Dinkum Diamond (IRE) *Henry Candy* 110
8 b h Aussie Rules(USA) Moving Diamonds (Lomitas)
1441[12] 2027[4] 2691[5] 3386[13] 4152[7] 4865[22] 5585[8] 6331[3] 7121[3] 7821[10]

Dinneratmidnight *Richard Guest* a82 88
5 b g Kyllachy The Terrier (Foxhound (USA))
1143[4] 1447[5] (1787) 1869[15] 2476[12] 6718[8] 7094[14]

Dino Velvet (FR) *Alan King* 86
3 b g Naaqoos Matgil (FR) (Grape Tree Road)
6767[4]

Dinsdale *Michael Scudamore* a66
3 b g Cape Cross(IRE) Emmy Award (IRE) (Sadler's Wells (USA))
7280[9] 7753[4]

Diodorus (IRE) *A P O'Brien* 100
2 b c Galileo(IRE) Divine Proportions (USA) (Kingmambo (USA))
7707a[2]

Diploma *Sir Michael Stoute* 113
3 b f Dubawi(IRE) Enticement (Montjeu (IRE))
(2490) 3274[5] (4610) 5652[8]

Diplomat (GER) *Mario Hofer* 110
5 b h Teofilo(IRE) Desidera (IRE) (Shaadi (USA))
1376a[3] (2073a) 3449a[5] 4438a[4] 4928a[10] 6181a[6] 6823a[5] 7400a[3] 7841a[8]

Diptych (USA) *Sir Mark Prescott Bt* a61 11
2 b f Hat Trick(JPN) Fork Lightning (USA) (Storm Cat (USA))
6867[12] 7278[7] 7576[13]

Directorship *Patrick Chamings* a80 99
10 br g Diktat Away To Me (Exit To Nowhere (USA))
2246[8] 2628[8] 4271[3] 4776[7] 6076[9] 6710[10] 7017[8] 7671[8]

Dirgam (IRE) *Y Durepaire* 105
4 ch g Galileo(IRE) Pieds De Plume (FR) (Seattle Slew (USA))
2516a[5]

Dirty Randy (IRE) *Keith Dalgleish* a56 47
2 b g Notnowcato Regal Fairy (IRE) (Desert King (IRE))
7247[7] *7431[6] 7659[11]*

Discay *Philip Kirby* a42 56
7 b g Distant Music(USA) Caysue (Cayman Kai (IRE))
2659[7]

Discipline *D K Weld* 97
3 b f Dansili Fame At Last (USA) (Quest For Fame)
(3539a) 6604a[9]

Disclosure *Les Eyre* a65 65
5 b g Indesatchel(IRE) Gemini Gold (IRE) (King's Best (USA))
2345[12] *3610[4]* 4321[4] 4544[10] 6569[13] 6685[12] *7261[F] 8306[9]*

Disco Flash (FR) *M Boutin* a72 64
2 b g Martillo(GER) Flash McQueen (SPA) (Dyhim Diamond (IRE))
5819a[2]

Discovered (IRE) *Roger Charlton* a51
2 ch g Bated Breath Sandglass (Zafonic (USA))
7812[11]

Discreet Hero (IRE) *Simon Crisford* a79 87
3 ch g Siyouni(FR) Alfaguara (USA) (Red Ransom (USA))
152[2] 559[4] 1112[2] (2218) ◆ 2751[4] 4612[6] 4803[6] ◆ 6793[18]

Di's Gift *Shaun Harris* 77
7 b g Generous(IRE) Di's Dilemma (Teenoso (USA))
2663[6] 3191[6] 5758[8]

Dishy Guru *Michael Blanshard* a55 63
7 ch g Ishiguru(USA) Pick A Nice Name (Polar Falcon (USA))
714[9] 5546[6] 6296[9] 6669[7] *8234[8]*

Dismantle (IRE) *Grace Harris* a40 71
3 b f Invincible Spirit(IRE) Dismay (Dubawi (IRE))
2184[7] 2537[8] 3719[6] 4292[13]

Disobedience (USA) *Charlie Appleby* a77 70
3 b g Street Cry(IRE) Rosa Parks (Sadler's Wells (USA))
1738[7] 2224[9]

Disquotational *David Simcock* a63 66
3 ch f Nayef(USA) Doggerbank (IRE) (Oasis Dream)
1609[8] 3194[8] 4001[3] *5245[4]* 6334[9] 7582[9]

Dissertation *Denis Gerard Hogan* a63 36
4 b m Champs Elysees Reel Style (Rainbow Quest (USA))
27[3] 521[5] 674[12] 7517a[8]

Distant High *Richard Price* a47 68
5 b m High Chaparral(IRE) Distant Dreamer (USA) (Rahy (USA))
(1825) 2127[3] 2461[2] 3095[2] 3636[7] 4158[8] 4294[4] 4913[6] 7078[10]

Distant Past *Kevin Ryan* a96 96
5 b g Pastoral Pursuits Faraway Lass (Distant Relative)
2188[12] 2658[5] 3150[12] 3638[7] 4415a[3] (6633) 6944[3] 7358[6] *7610[10] 7752[11] 7990[2]* ◆ *8407[4] (8484)*

Distill (USA) *William Haggas* a19
2 ch c Elusive Quality(USA) Dovie (USA) (Coronado's Quest (USA))
6368[8]

District Attorney (IRE) *Chris Fairhurst* a52 52
7 b g Lawman(FR) Mood Indigo (IRE) (Indian Ridge)
1626[9] 2746[2] 3067[9] 3417[9]

District Twelve (FR) *Tony Carroll* a11 27
4 b m Aqlaam Zanna (FR) (Soviet Star (USA))
1681[1]

Diva Bere (FR) *E Wianny* a74 68
3 b f Hurricane Cat(USA) Shadow Of The Day (FR) (Until Sundown (USA))
3764a[12]

Diva Power (IRE) *Marcus Tregoning* 36
2 b f Power Kotdiji (Mtoto)
3812[11]

Divasesque (IRE) *Derek Shaw* a28
3 ch f Poet's Voice Lily Again (American Post)
4855[8] *5636[11] 8085[10]*

Divertimenti (IRE) *Roy Bowring* a57 58
12 b g Green Desert(USA) Ballet Shoes (IRE) (Ela-Mana-Mou)
257 547 341[4]

Divine (IRE) *Mick Channon* a74 115
5 b m Dark Angel(IRE) Carallia (IRE) (Common Grounds)
91a[2] ◆ 370a[4] 723a[11] 2042[6] (2923a) 4114[4] 4393[2] ◆ 4824[17] 5943a[5] 7403a[6]

Divine Bere (FR) *E Leenders* a92 96
3 bb f Hurricane Cat(USA) Nofa Bere (FR) (Trempolino (USA))
7862a[4] *8148a[6]*

Divine Boy (AUS) *Y S Tsui* 106
4 b g Street Cry(IRE) La Guichet (AUS) (Al Hareb (USA))
1911a[7]

Divine Call *Milton Bradley* a66 66
9 b g Pivotal Pious (Bishop Of Cashel)
68[6] 1975[6] ◆ *271[4] 543[6] 856[3] 872[3]* 2846[13] 3743[7] 4155[11] 4291[10] 5169[8] 5797[13] 6000[4] 6269[4] 6668[8] 7267[2] *7694[4] 7817[8] (7912) 8094[3] 8315[5]*

Divine Joy *Marco Botti* a71 54
3 b f Rip Van Winkle(IRE) Joyeaux (Mark Of Esteem (IRE))
591[2] 1063[2] 1429[5] 2783[8] 3955[4]

Divine Prince (GR) *Amanda Perrett* a54
3 ch g Apotheosis(USA) Pringipessa's Way (Machiavellian (USA))
4265[9] 7904[5] 8366[7]

Divine Quickstep (IRE) *Sir Michael Stoute* a64 64
3 b f Dansili La Divina (IRE) (Sadler's Wells (USA))
3235[6] ◆ 4955[7]

Divine Touch *Robert Eddery* a50 46
3 b f Kheleyf(USA) Easy To Love (USA) (Diesis)
509[2] 794[9] 1705[7] 2609[4] 2969[5] 3490[2] 3896[10] 3973[8]

Divisionist *Sir Michael Stoute* a85 67
3 b c Oasis Dream Exemplify (Dansili)
1653[2] 2541[4] *5082[3] 6247[5]* 7009[8]

Dixie Peach *Eve Johnson Houghton* 55
2 b f Avonbridge Support Fund (IRE) (Intikhab (USA))
3485[3] ◆ 3770[4] 4054[15] 6252[5] ◆ 6652[5]

Dixie's Double *Daniel Kubler* 69
2 b f Multiplex Dress Design (IRE) (Brief Truce (USA))
4083[3] 4790[3] (5258) 5707[6]

Dizzey Heights (IRE) *Stuart Kittow* a53 76
4 b m Halling(USA) Extreme Pleasure (IRE) (High Chaparral (IRE))
1455[2] 2463[4]

Django James (IRE) *Mlle A Rosa* a69 66
5 ch g Stormy River(FR) Abime (USA) (Woodman (USA))
(5216a)

Djiguite (FR) *D Smaga* a86 111
4 b h Makfi Envoutement (FR) (Vettori (IRE))
(8117a)

Dltripleseven (IRE) *Richard Hughes* a66 63
3 gr g Dark Angel(IRE) Namu (Mujahid (USA))
2005[11] 2459[4] 2698[8] 3489[5] 3998[6] (4385) 6825[5] 7270[4] *7692[4] (8164)*

Dnaneer (IRE) *William Knight* a58 54
3 b f Invincible Spirit(IRE) Lulua (USA) (Bahri (USA))
1337[5] 1554[2] ◆ 2435[3]

D'Niro (IRE) *Harry Dunlop* a79 44
3 br c Big Bad Bob(IRE) Causeway Charm (USA) (Giant's Causeway (USA))
1750[3] 2818[10] 6628[12]

Doc Sportello (IRE) *Adam West* a95 74
4 b g Majestic Missile(IRE) Queen Of Silk (IRE) (Brief Truce (USA))
1014a[5] *(8402)*

Doctor Bartolo (IRE) *Charles Hills* a74 79
2 gr c Sir Prancealot(IRE) Operissimo (Singspiel (IRE))
6750[2] *8119[2] 8340[3]*

Doctor Bong *Grace Harris* a69 65
4 b g Sleeping Indian Vax Rapide (Sharpo)
2187[2] 3004[2] 3803[9] 5075[3] 5752[5] 7240[3] 7577[14] *8037[9] 8190[8]*

Doctor Cross (IRE) *Richard Fahey* a70 72
2 b g Cape Cross(IRE) Doctrine (Barathea (IRE))
5271[4] ◆ 5778[3] 6274[4] *6741[5]* ◆

Doctor Dynamite (IRE) *Tim Easterby* 56
2 b g Alfred Nobel(IRE) Alhaadh (USA) (Diesis)
2800[7] 3208[11] 3772[4]

Doctor Kehoe *David Evans* a65 62
4 b g Cockney Rebel(IRE) Ogre (USA) (Tale Of The Cat (USA))
1456[3] *2105[8]* 2397[5] 3072[8] 3747[4] 4225[2] 5232[6] 6022[8] *6424[9]*

Doctor Of Music (IRE) *Jo Davis*
10 ch g Dr Fong(USA) Sublime Beauty (USA) (Caerleon (USA))
27[P]

Doctor Parkes *Stuart Williams* a87 79
10 b g Diktat Lucky Parkes (Full Extent (USA))
142[7] 192[2] (416) 655[5] 727[7] 901[3] (974) 1427[1] 1634[11] 2028[6] 2253[11] 2309[6] *3780[7] 4211[6] 4714[5]* 5169[4] 5259[2] 5599[6] *6235[3]* 6479[6] *7430[4] (7811) 7899[7] 7983[2] 8495[4]*

Doctor Sardonicus *David Simcock* a102 99
5 ch g Medicean Never A Doubt (Night Shift (USA))
2188[5] 2488[13] (4741) 6112[8] *7610[2] 8050[5]*

Dodgy Bob *Kevin Ryan* a79 76
3 b g Royal Applause Rustam (Dansili)
1243[6] (2200) 2802[8] 3893[5] *4643[6]* 5161[4] 5978[6] 6437[7] 7360[14] 7572[2] *8206[7] 8287[3]*

Doeadeer (IRE) *Keith Dalgleish* a66 72
3 b f Dandy Man(IRE) Bloomsday Babe (USA) (Cherokee Run (USA))
(791) 3284[8] *6426[8] 6851[12] 7663[12]*

Doesyourdogbite (IRE) *Jonjo O'Neill* a43 77
4 b g Notnowcato Gilah (IRE) (Saddlers' Hall (IRE))
1391[4] 2699[10] 3636[2] 4057[5]

Dogma (FR) *S Wattel* a99 84
4 ch m Mount Nelson Penne (FR) (Sevres Rose (IRE))
7652[2] 8068[9]

Doha Dream (FR) *A Fabre* 113
3 b c Shamardal(USA) Crystal Reef (King's Best (USA))
6392a[3] (6971a)

Do It In Rio (FR) *E J O'Neill* 73
2 b f Rio De La Plata(USA) Double Dollar (Agnes World (USA))
7491a[8]

Do It Tomorrow (IRE) *J R Jenkins* a58
4 b m Daylami(IRE) Seminova (Cape Cross (IRE))
26[5] 161[4] 325[5] 569[6] 898[7]

Dolce Strega (IRE) *W McCreery* a82 103
3 b f Zoffany(IRE) New Plays (IRE) (Oratorio (IRE))
(1939a) 3274[11] 6983a[7]

Dollar Reward *Sir Michael Stoute* a85 85
3 b g Shamardal(USA) Cape Dollar (IRE) (Cape Cross (IRE))
2029[7] 2693[5] 3415[2] *4474[2]* 5403[8]

Dolly Dagger (SWE) *Fredrik Reuterskiold* a80
3 ch f Eishin Dunkirk(USA) Little Green Apple (SWE) (Funambule (USA))
184a[5] 534a[5] 808a[3]

Dolly Dimples *William Jarvis* a59 34
2 gr f Sir Percy Brave Mave (Daylami (IRE))
5876[6] *6624[12] 7278[8] 8276[11]*

Dolokhov *J S Moore* a84 78
2 b g Harbour Watch(IRE) Forest Prize (Charnwood Forest (IRE))
1118a[P] *1203[6]* 2536[2] 3243[12] *4124a[2]* 4394[11] 4924a[7] 5141a[3] *5447a[2]* 5701a[2] 5985a[4] 6270a[6] 7136a[3] *(7293a)*

Dolphin Rock *Richard Ford* a65 70
9 b g Mark Of Esteem(IRE) Lark In The Park (IRE) (Grand Lodge (USA))
1884[4] 3220[9] 3946[2] 4335[2] 5149[3] (5717) 6501[9] 6838[10]

Dolphin Village (IRE) *Jane Chapple-Hyam* a90 87
6 b g Cape Cross(IRE) Reform Act (USA) (Lemon Drop Kid (USA))
1531[7] 2176[3] 2663[5] *3525[4] 4013[3]* (4888) 5413[3] 6074[5] *6676[3]* 7666[5] *8249[3]*

Dolphin Vista (IRE) *Richard Fahey* a72 102
3 b c Zoffany(IRE) Fiordiligi (Mozart (IRE))
1080[10] (1446) 1867[2] (2407) 3157[8] 4448[6] (5865) 7154[5]

Dominada (IRE) *Brian Ellison* 87
4 b g Mastercraftsman(IRE) Red Blossom (USA) (Silver Hawk (USA))
2163[12] (2659) 4004[3] 4969[3] 5611[9] 6565[4]

Dominance *Rae Guest* a71 58
3 b f Lilbourne Lad(IRE) Christmas Tart (IRE) (Danetime (IRE))
(902) 1112[5] 2288[4] 5269[7] 6361[7]

Dominandros (FR) *Gay Kelleway* a96 71
5 b g Teofilo(IRE) Afya (Oasis Dream)
266[8] (427) 512a[2]

Dominannie (IRE) *Alan Swinbank* a43 68
3 b f Paco Boy(IRE) English Rose (USA) (Kafwain (USA))
1589[2] 2095[8] 3213[3] ◆ 3521[3] 3982[3] 4145[4] *8587[11]*

Dominate *George Scott* a71 89
6 b g Assertive Blue Goddess (IRE) (Blues Traveller (IRE))
1447[2] 1528[5] 2016[7] 3892[11] 7288[8]

Dominating (GER) *Mark Johnston* a67 63
2 ch c Jukebox Jury(IRE) Dominante (GER) (Monsun (GER))
5290[4] 5916[4] *6590[7] 6923[6] 7734[2] (7866)*

Domineer *C Fownes* a92 110
6 b g Shamardal(USA) Mania (IRE) (Danehill (USA))
1105a[8]

Dominium (USA) *Jeremy Gask* a86 74
9 b g E Dubai(USA) Sudenlylastsummer (USA) (Rinka Das (USA))
198[4] ◆ *1040[3]* 2028[8] 2846[14] *4014[3]* 5439[7] 6072[4] *7206[7] 8206[6] 8345[8]*

Dominor (FR) *C Plisson* 50
3 b c Linda's Lad Abandon (FR) (King's Best (USA))
2287a[4]

Dommersen (IRE) *John Gosden* a102 97
3 ch c Dutch Art Kelowna (IRE) (Pivotal)
(1339) ◆ *(2565)* 3156[2] 4396[2] ◆ *(5552) 6126[4]*

Dommyah *Roger Varian* a69
2 b f Exceed And Excel(AUS) Modeyra (Shamardal (USA))
6866[6] ◆

Don Aurelio (IRE) *G Di Chio* 49
3 gr c Frozen Power(IRE) Belclare (IRE) (Verglas (IRE))
1686a[15]

Doneraile (IRE) *Robert Eddery* 54
2 b g Requinto(IRE) Yaky Romani (IRE) (Victory Note (USA))
2747[6]

Donjuan Triumphant (IRE) *Richard Fahey* a107 115
3 b c Dream Ahead(USA) Mathuna (IRE) (Tagula (IRE))
2692[2] 3338[9] 5217a[2] 6120[11] 7350[13] *7868[3] 8029[3] 8489[2]*

Donna Doria (GER) *J Hirschberger* 89
3 b f Samum(GER) Dominanz (GER) (Lando (GER))
1513a[9] 5695a[4] 7027a[6]

Donna Graciosa (GER) *Mark Johnston* a72 82
4 b m Samum(GER) Donna Alicia (GER) (Highland Chieftain)
1177[3] 1586[5] 1880[7] 2671[5]

Doncha (IRE) *Robert Eddery* a80 106
5 br h Captain Marvelous(IRE) Seasonal Style (IRE) (Generous (IRE))
1195[2] 2191[5] ◆ 3273[15] 3910[2] 4823[3] ◆ 6942[8] 7354[9] 7701[4]

Donnelly's Rainbow (IRE) *Rebecca Bastiman* 72
3 b g Lilbourne Lad(IRE) Donnelly's Hollow (IRE) (Docksider (USA))
(3744) 4605[6] 6501[5] 7743[11]

Donnerhall (IRE) *Simon Crisford* a75 63
3 b g Kendargent(FR) Daidoo (IRE) (Shamardal (USA))
3411[8] *5023[5]* 5380[4]

Donnerschlag *Jean-Pierre Carvalho* 109
6 ch g Bahamian Bounty Dame Hester (IRE) (Diktat)
2722a[3] (5943a)

Don Padeja *Ronald Harris* a50 58
6 br g Dansili La Leuze (IRE) (Caerleon (USA))
62[11] 257[9]

Don't Blame Me *Clive Cox* a77 61
3 b g Captain Gerrard(IRE) Dragon Flyer (IRE) (Tagula (IRE))
77[4] 3743[4] *(5769) (6418)*

Dont Bother Me (IRE) *Niall Moran* a92 102
6 br h Dark Angel(IRE) Faleh (USA) (Silver Hawk (USA))
3332a[3] 4625[17] 5343a[8] 6355a[13] *7523a[14]*

Dontforgettocall *Joseph Tuite* a57 68
2 ch g Foxwedge(AUS) Shaken And Stirred (Cadeaux Genereux)
1384[3] 1454[3] *2104[4]* 6189[5] *7900[6]*

Dont Have It Then *Henry Spiller* a68 71
5 b g Myboycharlie(IRE) Mondovi (Kyllachy)
3554[11] *4014[7] 6418[4]* 7059[12]

Dont Tell Chris (FR) *David O'Meara* 57
4 b g Lawman(FR) Enigma (GER) (Sharp Victor (USA))
3253[8]

Don't Tell Jo Jo *Bill Turner* a28 34
3 b g Hellvelyn Shake Baby Shake (Reel Buddy (USA))
5020[5] 5628[6] *8472[10]*

Dont Tell Louise *Brian Baugh* a56 53
4 b m Medicean Lyra's Daemon (Singspiel (IRE))
8221[1]

Don't Tell Nik (IRE) *David Loughnane* a9 44
3 b f Lawman(FR) Karliysha (IRE) (Kalanisi (IRE))
768[7] 1562[8] *2327[10]* 2804[6]

Don't Touch *Richard Fahey* a101 116
4 b g Dutch Art Expressive (Falbrav (IRE))
(2031) 2495a[5] (3195) 4151[16] 6941[4] 7350[5]

Donttouchthechips (IRE) *Nikki Evans* a39 64
3 b g Lilbourne Lad(IRE) Trim (IRE) (Ela-Mana-Mou)
2459[2] ◆ 3591[6] 4588[3] 5953[11]

Don't You Think *Richard Hughes* a26 45
2 b g So You Think(NZ) Lukrecia (IRE) (Exceed And Excel (AUS))
3799[9] 4533[9] 4786[6] *8080[8]*

Donuts Reyor (FR) *Y Barberot* a82 77
3 gr g Cat Junior(USA) Elegante Lady (FR) (Verglas (IRE))
2948a[7] *3546a[3]* 7680a[6] (7999a)

Don Vincenzo (IRE) *Colin Bowe* a58 74
7 b g Vinnie Roe(IRE) Hakuna (IRE) (Saddlers' Hall (IRE))
3680a[13]

Doonard Prince (IRE) *Ross O'Sullivan* a47 70
7 b g Footstepsinthesand Fly Haia (IRE) (Flying Spur (AUS))
7474a[2]

Dora's Field (IRE) *Ed Dunlop* a49 76
3 b f Rip Van Winkle(IRE) Rydal Mount (IRE) (Cape Cross (IRE))
1392[5] ◆ *1798[10]* 2795[8] 3878[2] ◆ 4462[6] 7076[12] 7669[5]

Doreen *Sir Michael Stoute* 52
2 b f Dansili Hi Calypso (IRE) (In The Wings)
7285[6]

Do Re Mi Fa Sol (FR) *P Decouz* 102
3 b f Wootton Bassett Maitresse (FR) (Singspiel (IRE))
3935a[3] 5451a[4] 6497a[6] (8042a)

Doria Road (USA) *Kevin Ryan* a55 60
2 b f Quality Road(USA) Celestic (USA) (Sky Classic (CAN))
5272[7] 6223[4] *7988[8]*

Dormello (IRE) *D Selvaratnam* a102 106
8 b h Dansili Field Of Hope (IRE) (Selkirk (USA))
285a[4] 540a[2] (812a) *8396a[12]*

Dornoch (USA) *Doug Watson* a90 99
5 br g Mizzen Mast(USA) Gainful (USA) (Gone West (USA))
535a[2]

Dor's Law *Dean Ivory* a60 63
3 b f Lawman(FR) Law Of Chance (Pennekamp (USA))
402[4] ◆ *691[3] 945[5]* 1758[6] 2829[3] 4987[2]

Dortmund (USA) *Bob Baffert* a122
4 ch h Big Brown(USA) Our Josephina (USA) (Tale Of The Cat (USA))
7808a[4]

Dose *Richard Fahey* a67 61
3 b f Teofilo(IRE) Prescription (Pivotal)
296[2] 725[7] 7442[4] *7994[6] 8145[5] 8382[6]*

Dosnueveuno (IRE) *Alex Fracas* a54 54
3 b c Roderic O'Connor(IRE) Back To My Roots (USA) (Fusaichi Pegasus (USA))
7492a[11] 7999a[12]

Dostoyevsky (IRE) *David Lanigan* a74 70
3 b g Galileo(IRE) My Branch (Distant Relative)
2208[7] *2815[4] 6415[4] 7384[6]*

Dot Green (IRE) *Mark H Tompkins* a72 85
3 b f Lawman(FR) Katajan (Halling (USA))
1989[4] 2405[2] *(3281)* 3914[10] 5089[2] 5616[17] 6710[11]

Double Czech (IRE) *Patrick Chamings* a58 77
5 b g Bushranger(IRE) Night Of Joy (IRE) (King's Best (USA))
(1387) 2129[3] 3097[8] 3802[2] 7017[12]

Double Dealites *Jamie Poulton* a42 51
6 b m Double Trigger(IRE) Linden Grace (USA) (Mister Baileys)
1807[7] 4019[7] 4385[2] 4995[2] 5573 [2]

Double Dream (FR) *A Wohler* 97
3 bl f Lawman(FR) High Limits (IRE) (High Chaparral (IRE))
1513a[5] 2949a[6] 6693a[9] 7719a[9]

Double Dutch *John Quinn* 31
2 ch c Dutch Art Duchess Dora (IRE) (Tagula (IRE))
1783[5]

Double Lady (FR) *A Fabre* 97
2 b f Stormy River(FR) Montagne Magique (IRE) (King's Best (USA))
7114[5]

Double Spin *John Gosden* a66
2 b f Hard Spun(USA) Dear Lavinia (USA) (Grand Slam (USA))
3782[4]

Double Touch *Richard Fahey* 84
2 ch c Dutch Art Classical Dancer (Dr Fong (USA))
4040[3] ◆ 4765[4] (5637) 6499[5] 7185[6]

Double Up *Roger Varian* a100 110
5 b g Exceed And Excel(AUS) My Love Thomas (IRE) (Cadeaux Genereux)
2438[3] 3244[12] 6327[4] 6642[3] *7520a[8]* 7771[4]

Doubly Clever (IRE) *Michael Blake* a62 63
4 ch g Iffraaj Smartest (IRE) (Exceed And Excel (AUS))
2738[7]

Doubly Motivated (IRE) *Charles Hills* 90
3 ch f Iffraaj Chicane (Motivator)
1771[5] 1966[7] 3389[6] 4318[3] 4737[11]

Douceur D'Antan (FR) *P Adda* a77 82
2 ch f Never On Sunday(FR) Inassouvie (FR) (Lord Of Men)
5755a[3] 7136a[2] *7879a[4]*

Dougan *David Evans* a105 99
4 b g Dutch Art Vive Les Rouges (Acclamation)
546[2] (1205) ◆ 1887[3] ◆ 2206[3] 4126[9] 4862[19] 6112[12] *6627[7] (6962)* ◆ 7242[4] 7497[4] *(7803a) 8407[3] 8530[5]*

Douglas Bank (IRE) *Roy Bowring* 71
4 b g Dandy Man(IRE) Balance The Books (Elmaamul (USA))
1524[4] 2040[4] 3368[12] 4006[13] 4370[6]

Douglas Macarthur (IRE) *A P O'Brien* 110
2 b c Galileo(IRE) Alluring Park (IRE) (Green Desert (USA))
6349a[3] 6783[5] 7722a[4]

Dounyapour (FR) *A De Royer-Dupre* 102
3 ch g Lope De Vega(IRE) Diamond Tango (FR) (Acatenango (GER))
6176a[2]

Dourado (IRE) *Richard Hannon* 79
2 b c Dark Angel(IRE) Skehana (IRE) (Mukaddamah (USA))
3058[6] 4653[4] (5166) 5644[4] 6260[18] 7467[5]

Dourdana (FR) *A De Royer-Dupre* 100
3 gr f Exceed And Excel(AUS) Dardania (Dalakhani (IRE))
2455a[3]

Dove Mountain (IRE) *Gordon Elliott* a60 70
5 b g Danehill Dancer(IRE) Virginia Waters (USA) (Kingmambo (USA))
222[6] 676[3] 684[3] 1002[5] 6464a[9]

Dovils Date *Tim Vaughan* a77 82
7 gr g Clodovil(IRE) Lucky Date (IRE) (Halling (USA))
329[4] 922[6] 1550[4] 5131[2]

Dovil's Duel (IRE) *Tony Newcombe* a65 69
5 b g Clodovil(IRE) Duelling (Diesis)
429[9] 769[8] 1735[3] (2144) 3748[4] 4531[2] 5994[6] 7078[8] *8207[3]* ◆ *8528[8]*

Dowayla (IRE) *Saeed bin Suroor* 85
2 b f Sepoy(AUS) Baheeja (Dubawi (IRE))
(6874) 7409[8]

Downeva (FR) *F Vermeulen* a81
3 ch c Evasive Exit Down (IRE) (Exit To Nowhere (USA))
7492a[5]

Downforce (IRE) *W McCreery* a62 103
4 b g Fast Company(IRE) Spinning Ruby (Pivotal)
4415a[11] 4921a[12] 6382a[4] 6819a[5] (6984a) 7706a[3]

Down Time (USA) *Brian Ellison* a76 63
6 b g Harlan's Holiday(USA) Frappay (USA) (Deputy Minister (CAN))
(957) ◆ *1156[3] 1296[3]*

Do You Know (IRE) *Marco Botti* a67
2 b f So You Think(NZ) Queen Of Lyons (USA) (Dubai Destination (USA))
7883[7] 8082[2]

Dozule (FR) *E Lellouche* a76 92
3 b f Le Havre(IRE) Arromanches (Sadler's Wells (USA))
7862a[6]

Drafted (USA) *Eoin Harty* a88 52
2 rg r Field Commission(CAN) Keep The Profit (USA) (Darn That Alarm (USA))
3247[17]

Dragan Darnoult (FR) *P Loth*
3 gr g Sirzane(FR) Durbane Darnoult (FR) (Isfandiyar (IRE))
2287a[5]

Drago (IRE) *David O'Meara* a77 12
4 b g Cape Cross(IRE) Eden (USA) (Holy Bull (USA))
6095[8] *6907[11] 7368[7] (7514) (7911) 8101[5]*

Dragon Dream (IRE) *Roger Ingram* a61 41
2 b f Dragon Pulse(IRE) Night Scent (IRE) (Scenic)
3954[14] 4304[5] 5772[7] *(6412) (7047) 7423[3] 7941[11]*

Dragon Fei (IRE) *Dermot Anthony McLoughlin* a68 85
6 b m Jeremy(USA) Wallonia (IRE) (Barathea (IRE))
1227a[5] 1509a[8] 4811a[12]

Dragonite (IRE) *Daniel Mark Loughnane* a46
2 ch g Dragon Pulse(IRE) Glamorous (GER) (Red Ransom (USA))
7366[8] 7891[12] 8074[9]

Dragon King (IRE) *Michael Dods* a91 94
4 ch g Dylan Thomas(IRE) Alexander Queen (IRE) (King's Best (USA))
2259[9] 3393[2] 4373[3] 5417[14] 6114[11] 6537[18] *7858[2] 7990[13]*

Dragon Mall (USA) *David Simcock* a106 107
3 b g Blame(USA) Petition The Lady (USA) (Petionville (USA))
2250[2] 4395[7] 4822[4] ◆ 6482[5] *8489[3]* ◆

Dragons Voice *Philip Hide* a63
2 b g Poet's Voice China (Royal Academy (USA))
8557[6]

Dragoon Guard (IRE) *Anthony Honeyball* a76 81
5 b g Jeremy(USA) Elouges (IRE) (Dalakhani (IRE))
256[7]

Drake Passage (IRE) *John M Oxx* a84 89
2 ch g Dandy Man(IRE) Piece Unique (Barathea (IRE))
(7917a)

Dramatic Voice *Paul Cole* a19
3 ch f Poet's Voice Darwinia (GER) (Acatenango (GER))
2368[7] 4290[13]

Dravid *Rod Millman* 55
2 b g Famous Name Sweet Power (Pivotal)
1736[7] 4154[7] 4479[5] 5251[6]

Drawn To Be A Lady *Michael Attwater*
3 b f Avonbridge Lady Killer (IRE) (Daggers Drawn (USA))
4017[10]

Draw Swords *John Gosden* a80
2 br c Dansili Sacred Shield (Beat Hollow)
5505[3] 6623[3] 7511[2] 7909[3]

Dr Drey (IRE) *Jamie Osborne* a73 64
3 ch g Bahamian Bounty Mount Lavinia (IRE) (Montjeu (IRE))
40[5] 379[2] ◆ *593[3] (729)* 2644[4] 3063[12]

Dream Ally (IRE) *John Weymes* a61 60
6 b g Oasis Dream Alexander Alliance (IRE) (Danetime (IRE))
230[6] 418[6] 528[5] 1005[10] 1164[3] (1319) 1720[3] 1794[6] 3984[2] 4647[4] 5127[3] 6852[5] 7145[3] 7489[3] 8013[5] 8542[5]

Dreamarcher (USA) *Jerry Hollendorfer* 96
3 bb f Archarcharch(USA) Dream Luck (USA) (Chester House (USA))
7724a[6]

Dream Bounty *John Holt* 66
4 b m Bahamian Bounty Dream In Waiting (Oasis Dream)
1600[2]

Dream Dana (IRE) *Jamie Osborne* a71 60
3 b f Dream Ahead(USA) Lidanna (Nicholas (USA))
2294[7] 2848[4] *3280[2] 3725[10]* 5088[6] *5769[2] (6051)* ◆

Dream Destination (IRE) *Sylvester Kirk* a103 90
3 b c Showcasing Never Let You Down (IRE) (Barathea (IRE))
2242[8]

Dream Dubai *Sylvester Kirk* a88 103
3 b c Kyllachy Welsh Anthem (Singspiel (IRE))
(1337) ◆ 1773[2] ◆ 2242[7] 3338[8] 4733[8] 5613[6] 6547[6] 6942[9]

Dream Dy (FR) *C Ferland* a84 77
3 ch g Dream Ahead(USA) Diyakalanie (FR) (Ashkalani (IRE))
2456a[2]

Dream Factory (IRE) *Marco Botti* a68 73
3 ch g Manduro(GER) Istishaara (USA) (Kingmambo (USA))
1200[9] *1961[3]* 2774[3] *3306[4]* 4277[3] 4636[4]

Dream Farr (IRE) *Ed Walker* a75 67
3 b g Dream Ahead(USA) French Lady (NZ) (Entrepreneur)
1414[3] ◆ 1894[6] 2776[5] *3307[3] 8429[2]* ◆

Dreamfield *John Gosden* 99
2 b c Oasis Dream Izzi Top (Pivotal)
(7071) ◆ (7469)

Dream Free *David Lanigan* a68 64
3 b g Oasis Dream Freedonia (Selkirk (USA))
2207[12] 2999[9] 3769[11] *4942[5]*

Dreaming Again *Jimmy Fox* a55 45
6 b g Young Ern Maedance (Groom Dancer (USA))
252[4] 346[2] 690[5] 876[2] 1035[2] 1578[8] 2610[6] 3731[6]

Dreaming Lady (IRE) *James Tate* a70 58
3 b f Dream Ahead(USA) Ballymore Lady (USA) (War Chant (USA))
984[3] 4041[6]

Dreaming Of Paris *William Haggas* a70
2 b f Oasis Dream Parisi (Rahy (USA))
8443[3]

Dream Journey (IRE) *Daniel O'Brien* a19 43
3 ch f Dream Ahead(USA) Khibraat (Alhaarth (IRE))
3769[7] *8212[8] 8471[12]*

Dream Love *Simon Dow* a71
3 b f Rail Link Love Always (Piccolo)
(8366) ◆

Dream Machine (IRE) *Michael Bell* a53 59
2 ch g Dream Ahead(USA) Last Cry (FR) (Peintre Celebre (USA))
6777[10] 7621[9] 7770[8] *7976[8]*

Dream Magic (IRE) *Daniel Mark Loughnane* a54
2 b g Lord Shanakill(USA) Pursuit of Passion (Pastoral Pursuits)
8208[12] 8340[9]

Dream Mover (IRE) *Marco Botti* a87 97
3 ch c Dream Ahead(USA) Maramba (USA) (Hussonet (USA))
344[2] ◆ *(638)* 1851[3] 3155[7] 4886[2] 5616[11] 6232[2] 7719a[2]

Dreamofdiscovery (IRE) *Julie Camacho* a57
2 b g Henrythenavigator(USA) Dreamwriter (USA) (Tale Of The Cat (USA))
8089[6] 8384[10]

Dream Of Dreams (IRE) *Kevin Ryan* 105
2 ch c Dream Ahead(USA) Vasilia (Dansili)
1422[2] (2649) 3678a[3] 5654[P] 6228[2] 7155[2]

Dream Of Joy (IRE) *Roger Varian* a65 69
2 b f Dream Ahead(USA) Love And Laughter (IRE) (Theatrical (IRE))
7118[6] *7484[4]*

Dream Of Summer (IRE) *Andrew Balding* a86 79
3 b c Canford Cliffs(IRE) Danehill's Dream (IRE) (Danehill (USA))
2479[7] *3523[4]* 4048[5] 4562[2] *6657[4] (7457) 7903[7]*

Dream On Dreamer (IRE) *Michael Dods* a51 65
2 b f Dream Ahead(USA) Marula (IRE) (Sadler's Wells (USA))
3516[9] 3872[5] 4442[2] 5853[2] 6130[6] *6741[7]*

Dreamorchid (IRE) *Tim Easterby* 59
2 br f Dream Ahead(USA) Dark Orchid (Shamardal (USA))
4037[8] 4451[10] 5476[5] 7041[7] 7330[11]

Dream Reversion *Tom Dascombe* a61 64
2 b c Oasis Dream Last Second (IRE) (Alzao (USA))
7072[4] ◆ 7331[3] *7639[6] 8229[6] 8467[6]*

Dream Revival *James Unett* a61
3 br f Captain Gerrard(IRE) Passkey (Medicean)
202[2] 948[2] 1325[5] 1497[5] 2107[3]

Dream Ruler *Jeremy Gask* a72 66
5 b g Holy Roman Emperor(IRE) Whatcameoverme (USA) (Aldebaran (USA))
4531[11] *5471[2]* 5824[6] *7429[2] 8462[14]*

Dream Serenade *Michael Appleby* a51 51
3 b f Dream Eater(IRE) Lady Santana (IRE) (Doyoun)
4690[4] 5383[3] 5888[6] *6698[6]* 7045[2] 7592[8] *8039[5]*

Dreams Of Glory *Ron Hodges* a71 73
8 ch g Resplendent Glory(IRE) Pip's Dream (Glint Of Gold)
5546[2] 5928[7] 6017[7] 6363[10] 6832[7] (7420) *8040[6] 8429[4] 8535[2]*

Dream Spirit (IRE) *Jamie Osborne* a89 91
5 b g Invincible Spirit(IRE) Dream Valley (IRE) (Sadler's Wells (USA))
184 240[4] 360[2]

Dream Team *Michael Dods* a70 56
2 b g Captain Gerrard(IRE) Mimi Mouse (Diktat)
2830[7] *5067[4]* 5728[5] 6678[8] *7110[4] (8087) (8235)*

Dream Trader (IRE) *Roger Varian* a55 26
3 b c Oasis Dream Vakiyla (FR) (Galileo (IRE))
1397[10] *1800[7] 2005[6]* 2784[11]

Dream Tune *Mlle M Henry* a76 78
7 b g Oasis Dream Play Bouzouki (Halling (USA))
715a[RR]

Dream Voice (IRE) *John Holt* a67 30
3 b f Approve(IRE) Louve Sereine (FR) (Sadler's Wells (USA))
3145[5] *8075[5] 8195[3]*

Dream Walker (FR) *Brian Ellison* a48 99
7 gr g Gold Away(IRE) Minnie's Mystery (FR) (Highest Honor (FR))
2620[13] 3166[14] 3398[2] (3895) (4448) 4811a[3] (4921a) 5941a[5] 6495a[3] 7354[19]

Dream Waltz *John Gosden* a57
2 b f Oasis Dream Valentine Waltz (IRE) (Be My Guest (USA))
7763[13] 7939[5]

Dreese (IRE) *Marjorie Fife* a86 77
5 b g Dandy Man(IRE) Lucky Flirt (USA) (Gulch (USA))
1488[11] 1954[6] 2555[RR]

Drefong (USA) *Bob Baffert* a123
3 b c Gio Ponti(USA) Eltimaas (USA) (Ghostzapper (USA))
(7832a)

Dressed In Fur (IRE) *Mme Pia Brandt* 100
3 b f Excellent Art Little Empress (IRE) (Holy Roman Emperor (IRE))
1309a[9] 6070a[7]

Drifting Spirit (IRE) *Richard Fahey* 88
3 b f Clodovil(IRE) Laureldean Spirit (IRE) (Whipper (USA))
4105[10] 5437[3] 5878[7] 6811[7] 7505[8]

Drinks For Losers (IRE) *R Mike Smith* 50
5 b g Mastercraftsman(IRE) Heart's Desire (IRE) (Royal Applause)
2525[2] 3287[10] 3921[14] 4444[6] 4705[U] 5149[2] 5576[6]

Drive Faster *Hugo Palmer* a74
3 b c Invincible Spirit(IRE) Fowey (USA) (Gone West (USA))
1208[6]

Driver's Girl (USA) *Marco Botti* a47
2 bb f Candy Ride(ARG) Sharbat (USA) (Dynaformer (USA))
2764[7]

Dr Julius No *Ralph Beckett* a92 80
2 b g Dick Turpin(IRE) Royal Assent (Royal Applause)
1713[4] ◆ (2536) *(8405)*

Drochaid *Andrew Balding* a77 77
2 ch c Mastercraftsman(IRE) Avon Lady (Avonbridge)
2756[8] 4128[3] *4642[2]* (5107) 6330[6]

Drop Kick Murphi (IRE) *George Baker* 80
2 b g Sir Prancealot(IRE) Rindiseyda (IRE) (Arakan (USA))
4287[8] 4738[3] (4815) 5265[5] (5707) (6830) 7820[14]

Dr Red Eye *Scott Dixon* a49 69
8 ch g Dr Fong(USA) Camp Fire (IRE) (Lahib (USA))
1252[2] 1746[6] 1954[2] 2491[14] 2677[5] 3595[6] 4005[5] 5104[4] 6568[10] *7751[10] 7896[5] 8094[8] 8236[7] 8350[11]*

Druid's Diamond *Mark Walford* 37
3 b g Piccolo Faithful Beauty (IRE) (Last Tycoon)
1217[6]

Drumfad Bay (IRE) *Mrs John Harrington* 96
2 b f Acclamation Manieree (IRE) (Medicean)
4573a[4] 5686a[5] 6555[4]

Drumlin *Geoffrey Deacon* a9
3 gr g Hellvelyn Live To Tell (Primo Dominie)
314[9]

Drummer (GER) *P Schiergen* 107
4 b g Duke Of Marmalade(IRE) Douala (Dubawi (IRE))
1376a[6] 2074a[3] 2633a[6] 4438a[3] 6067a[3] 6397a[2]

Druot *Richard Hughes* a52 54
4 b g Champs Elysees Trick Of Ace (USA) (Clever Trick (USA))
1796[8] 4226[5] 4711[6] *5303[10]* 5777[5] *6422[11]*

Dry Your Eyes (IRE) *David O'Meara* a61 73
5 b m Shamardal(USA) Kindling (Dr Fong (USA))
1561[3] 1842[2] 2678[7] 5294[2] 5801[4] 6450[6] 6620[6]

Dry Your Eyes (ITY) *Stefano Botti* 99
3 b f Ramonti(FR) Tirsa (Benny The Dip (USA))
2730a[8] 6824a[10]

Dschingis Secret (GER) *Markus Klug* 112
3 b c Soldier Hollow Divya (GER) (Platini (GER))
3453a[3] 4186a[3] 6175a[9] (7555a)

Dubai Art *Richard Fahey* a75
2 b c Dutch Art Enact (Kyllachy)
8384[3] ◆

Dubai Dunes *Saeed bin Suroor* a77
2 ch f Nathaniel(IRE) Amallna (Green Desert (USA))
6413[2] 7050[7] 7885[2] 8131[4]

Dubai Dynamo *Ruth Carr* a46 96
11 b g Kyllachy Miss Mercy (IRE) (Law Society (USA))
960[9] 1195[13] 1445[5] 1643[10] 1924[7] 2268[6] 2734[3] (3286) 3518[8] 3923[6] 4408[2] 4727[4] 4933[2] 5376[5] 5976[7] 6320[8] 6957[4] 7159[13]

Dubai Elegance *Saeed bin Suroor* a80 74
2 ch f Sepoy(AUS) Some Sunny Day (Where Or When (IRE))
2885[3] *(7527) 7956[5]*

Dubai Empress (IRE) *William Haggas* a19 14
3 b f Dubawi(IRE) The World (Dubai Destination (USA))
2005[13]

Dubai Fashion (IRE) *Saeed bin Suroor* a104 104
3 b f Dubawi(IRE) Oriental Fashion (IRE) (Marju (IRE))
534a[4] 807a[5] 4654[3] (6803) *7383[2]* 7823[2] *8427[2]*

Dubai Hero (FR) *Saeed bin Suroor* 88
2 b c Dark Angel(IRE) Bugie D'Amore (Rail Link)
(4103) ◆ 4622[7]

Dubai Hills *David O'Meara* a88 91
10 b g Dubai Destination(USA) Hill Welcome (Most Welcome)
1347 599[8] 866[P] (Dead)

Dubai Horizon (IRE) *Saeed bin Suroor* a81 81
2 b g Poet's Voice Chibola (ARG) (Roy (USA))
7157[2] ◆ *7649[2]*

Dubai In Bloom (IRE) *Simon Crisford* a73 39
3 b f Kheleyf(USA) Weood (IRE) (Dubawi (IRE))
(1027)

Dubai Knights (IRE) *P Monfort* a61 74
2 b c Sir Prancealot(IRE) Dubai Princess (IRE) (Dubai Destination (USA))
2235[3] 2552[2] 3283[3] 3839[5] *7422a[2]*

Dubai Mission (IRE) *Steve Flook* a80 78
3 b g New Approach(IRE) Al Joza (Dubawi (IRE))
1577[2] 2005[2] 2298[3] 2999[4] 6634[8] *6899[12]* 7594[13]

Dubai One (IRE) *Saeed bin Suroor* a88 70
2 ch f Exceed And Excel(AUS) Dresden Doll (USA) (Elusive Quality (USA))
6086[2] (6867) 7305[2] 7668[5] *(8136) (8209)* ◆

Dubai Post (IRE) *Miss B Deutrom* a41
5 br h Dubawi(IRE) Storming Sioux (Storming Home)
8576a[16]

Dubai Sand (IRE) *J S Bolger* 101
2 ch c Teofilo(IRE) Bring Back Matron (IRE) (Rock Of Gibraltar (IRE))
(7707a)

Dubai's Secret *Richard Hannon* 90
3 ch g Paco Boy(IRE) Lilli Marlane (Sri Pekan (USA))
(2299) 2891[5] 3574[4] (4055) 4654[2]

Dubaitwentytwenty *Hugo Palmer* a70
2 b f Poet's Voice Cairncross (IRE) (Cape Cross (IRE))
8355[2]

Dubara *Luca Cumani* a78 81
2 b f Dubawi(IRE) Kibara (Sadler's Wells (USA))
3074[5] ◆ 4147[3] 5298[2] 5995[2] (6472)

Dubawi Fifty *Karen McLintock* a85
3 b g Dubawi(IRE) Plethora (Sadler's Wells (USA))
1479[6] 7384[5] 7661[2] 7847[2] (8143) 8399[4]

Dubawi Hundred (IRE) *James Tate* a72 72
3 b c Dubawi(IRE) Casanga (IRE) (Rainbow Quest (USA))
3362[3] 5634[3] 6423[5] 7229[9]

Dubawi King *Isa Bin Ismail Al Baloch* 69
9 b g Dubawi(IRE) Laughing Girl (USA) (Woodman (USA))
744a[16]

Dubawi Light *Gary Moore* a83 65
5 b g Dubawi(IRE) Shesadelight (Shirley Heights)
2872[8] 4302[6] 4956[7]

Dubawi Prince *Roger Varian* 69
2 b c Dubawi(IRE) Flawly (Old Vic)
7013[7] 7318[2]

Dubka *Sir Michael Stoute* 102
3 b f Dubawi(IRE) Rosika (Sakhee (USA))
2182[6] (3094) (3846) ◆ (5328) ◆ (6584) 7271[5]

Duca Di Mantova *Il Cavallo In Testa* 108
7 ch g Manduro(GER) Vale Mantovani (Wolfhound (USA))
7555a[P]

Duc De Seville (IRE) *Michael Chapman* a52 27
4 b g Duke Of Marmalade(IRE) Splendid (IRE) (Mujtahid (USA))
1047[P] 3230[8] 4024[4] 7895[9]

Duchess Andorra (IRE) *J P Murtagh* a71 106
5 b m Duke Of Marmalade(IRE) Andorra (Cadeaux Genereux)
665a[2] 1018a[6] 2924a[6] 4218a[3] 4435a[9] 5939a[6] (6604a)

Duchess Of Fife *William Knight* a63 42
2 ch f Dutch Art La Adelita (IRE) (Anabaa (USA))
7284[9] 7458[4] 7885[6]

Duchess Of Marmite (IRE) *Richard Hughes* a92 82
4 b m Duke Of Marmalade(IRE) Reprise (Darshaan)
208a[2] 440[4] 1092[3] 1273[6] 1893[11]

Duchy *Michael Bell* a51 73
3 b f Kyllachy Albavilla (Spectrum (IRE))
1289[6]

Ducissa *Daniel Kubler* a63 38
3 b f Exceed And Excel(AUS) Baize (Efisio)
5300[5] 5766[3] 6317[7] 6960[5]

Duck A L'Orange (IRE) *Michael Bell* a79 78
3 ch g Duke Of Marmalade(IRE) Incheni (IRE) (Nashwan (USA))
1718[5] 2300[2] 3063[6] 3715[5] 4372[3] (4836) 5413[2] 5596[6] 7618[5] 8162[3]

Ducky Mallon (IRE) *Donal Kinsella* 82
5 gr g Jeremy(USA) Indus Ridge (IRE) (Indian Ridge)
4899a[4] 7475a[6]

Dufay (IRE) *Charlie Appleby* a69 69
3 b f Dubawi(IRE) White Moonstone (USA) (Dynaformer (USA))
1392[8] 1998[4]

Duke Cosimo *Michael Herrington* a83 89
6 ch g Pivotal Nannina (Medicean)
1869[4] ◆ 2476[3] ◆ (2803) 3346[3] 4366[4] 4896[11] 6263[7] 6539[4] 6780[8] 7094[10] 7434[3] 7965[4]

Duke Of Clarence (IRE) *Richard Fahey* a73 105
7 gr g Verglas(IRE) Special Lady (FR) (Kaldoun (FR))
1967[14]

Duke Of Dance (IRE) *Denis Quinn* a17 17
6 b g Duke Of Marmalade(IRE) Dust Flicker (Suave Dancer (USA))
3973[12] 5132[11]

Duke Of Diamonds *Julia Feilden* a56 79
4 gr g Duke Of Marmalade(IRE) Diamond Line (FR) (Linamix (FR))
1413[7] 1955[4] (3067) ◆ (3844) ◆ 5334[2] 7006[4] 7624[7]

Duke Of Firenze *David C Griffiths* a97 107
7 ch g Pivotal Nannina (Medicean)
1197[11] 1566[3] 2003[2] ◆ (2188) 2895[3] 3151[3] ◆ 3909[11] 4126[14] 4865[5] 5555[2] 6990a[6] 7250[6]

Duke Of North (IRE) *Jim Boyle* a71 72
4 b g Danehill Dancer(IRE) Althea Rose (IRE) (Green Desert (USA))
167[7] 398[10] 482[9] 671[7] 1544[3] 1735[6] (2187) 2401[3] 2769[3] 3004[4] (3739) 4302[4] 5017[5]

Duke Of Sonning *Alan King* 77
4 ch g Duke Of Marmalade(IRE) Moonshadow (Diesis)
3798[7] 4483[9]

Duke Of Yorkshire *Tim Easterby* a72 72
6 b g Duke Of Marmalade(IRE) Dame Edith (FR) (Top Ville (IRE))
(2343) 2573[6] 3342[8] 3547[2] 3711[5] 3901[6] (4260) 4828[2] 4934[2] (5805) 7500[14]

Dukes Den *Mark Usher* a65 57
5 b g Duke Of Marmalade(IRE) Green Room (FR) (In The Wings)
946[6] 1322[5] 1550[5] 2326[7] 2501[4] 2916[7] 3528[8] 4478[6]

Duke's Girl *Michael Bell* a53 66
2 b f Poet's Voice Juniper Girl (IRE) (Revoque (IRE))
6776[6] 7761[13]

Dukes Meadow *Roger Ingram* a75 57
5 b g Pastoral Pursuits Figura (Rudimentary (USA))
58[4] 629[4] 888[5] 1430[7] 1775[12] 2374[7] 2769[12] 4008[5] 4302[7] 5362[6] 5635[8] 6046[3] 6512[3] 7310[5] 7943[4] 8179[8] 8462[10]

Duke Street (IRE) *Dr Richard Newland* a88 90
4 b g Duke Of Marmalade(IRE) Act Of The Pace (IRE) (King's Theatre (IRE))
619[3]

Dulciboy *Stefano Botti* 90
2 b c Paco Boy(IRE) Dulcify (IRE) (Dubawi (IRE))
7839a[4]

Du Moto (IRE) *Sir Michael Stoute* a69 88
3 b c Galileo(IRE) Mauralakana (FR) (Muhtathir)
(1242) (1636) ◆ (Dead)

Duncan Of Scotland (IRE) *Lee Smyth* a61 62
3 ch g Roderic O'Connor(IRE) Cantando (IRE) (Hamas (IRE))
2360[5] 4309[5] 5578[4]

Dundonnell (USA) *C Fownes* 113
6 b g First Defence(USA) Family (USA) (Danzig (USA))
1912a[10]

Dundunah (USA) *David O'Meara* 77
2 ch f Sidney's Candy(USA) Sealedwithapproval (USA) (With Approval (CAN))
3112[2] 4161[9] 6515[3]

Dune Dancer (IRE) *David Lanigan* a84 85
3 b g Footstepsinthesand Leonica (Lion Cavern (USA))
(2640) 3365[2] 5768[3] 6870[13]

Dungannon *Andrew Balding* a99 91
9 b g Monsieur Bond(IRE) May Light (Midyan (USA))
(4) 338[6] 492[8] 835[7] 3573[3] ◆ 6119[9] 6633[7] 6944[15] 7537[16]

Dunnscotia *Paul Webber* a76 70
4 b g Showcasing Black And Amber (Weldnaas (USA))
2765[9] 3349[7] (4008) 4528[2] 4881[5] 6337[8]

Dunquin (IRE) *John Mackie* a76 75
4 b g Cape Cross(IRE) Last Resort (Lahib (USA))
273[8] 766[3] 1586[3] 2051[8] 2672[7] 4455[11] 7911[7]

Duramente (JPN) *Noriyuki Hori* 122
4 b h King Kamehameha(JPN) Admire Groove (JPN) (Sunday Silence (USA))
1107a[2]

Duretto *Andrew Balding* a83 111
4 ch g Manduro(GER) Landinium (ITY) (Lando (GER))
2024[2] 2897[5] 3889[11] 5145[2] ◆ 5639[2] 6940[5] (7545)

Durlindana *Il Cavallo In Testa* 94
4 b m Mastercraftsman(IRE) Serafina's Flight (Fantastic Light (USA))
7555a[7]

Dusker (USA) *Mark Johnston* a71 68
2 b g Elusive Quality(USA) Danuta (USA) (Sunday Silence (USA))
1203[4] ◆ 1520[8] 3562[3] 4825[6] 7319[P] (Dead)

Dusky Dawn *Alan Swinbank* a81 47
4 b m Kheleyf(USA) Piddies Pride (IRE) (Indian Lodge (IRE))
1400[6] (1708) 2223[9] 2917[6] 3152[10] 8239[6] 8347[2]

Dusky Raider (IRE) *Michael Dods* 68
3 gr g Clodovil(IRE) Rahila (IRE) (Kalanisi (IRE))
1619[4] (2772) 3778[5] 4810[3] (5183) 6503[4]

Dusty Berry *Eve Johnson Houghton* 62
2 ch f Sixties Icon Hazelberry (Bertolini (USA))
3812[5] 4287[14] 5120[6]

Dusty Bin *Garry Moss* a68 65
2 b g Sepoy(AUS) Short Affair (Singspiel (IRE))
4227[10] 5433[7] 6712[7] (7579) 7690[3] 8398[2] 8568[7]

Dusty Blue *Tony Carroll* a66 74
4 ch m Medicean Jazz Jam (Pivotal)
462[8] 658[8] 1059[8] 1334[8] (3316) 3559[5] 3994[11] (5009) 6363[3] ◆ 6832[2] 7268[6] 7644[5] 7945[9] 8228[5] 8473[8]

Dusty Raven *Neil Mulholland* a55 35
3 ch g Raven's Pass(USA) Dust Dancer (Suave Dancer (USA))
2828[7] 3256[9] 7103[6] 7767[6] 7969[2] 8180[5]

Dutch Archer *Jeremy Gask* a72 60
3 b g Dutch Art Cecily (Oasis Dream)
765[6] ◆ 1111[5] 1849[9] (2785) 3471[2] 4039[5] 6091[9]

Dutchartcollector *Tim McCarthy* a43 19
5 b g Dutch Art Censored (Pivotal)
55[P] 7282[13]

Dutch Art Dealer *Paul Cole* a92 80
5 b g Dutch Art Lawyers Choice (Namid)
18[7] 1041[5] 1418[6] 2430[6] 2821[3] 3035[2] 3523[6] 4086[5] ◆

Dutch Artist (IRE) *David O'Meara* 85
4 ch g Dutch Art Baltic Princess (FR) (Peintre Celebre (USA))
(1953) 2491[13] 3011[4] ◆ 4232[4] 5482[3] 6055[9] 7126[19]

Dutch Barney *Mark Brisbourne* a17
6 b g Dutch Art Celeb Style (IRE) (Tagula (IRE))
863[11] 1653[10] 2448[11]

Dutch Breeze *Tim Easterby* 83
5 ch g Dutch Art Oasis Breeze (Oasis Dream)
1817[8] 2345[13] 2677[8] 3168[7] 3645[7]

Dutch Cat *Clive Cox* a49 32
2 ch f Dutch Art Crimson Cheer (USA) (Van Nistelrooy (USA))
6648[8] 7277[7] 7939[8] 8174[11]

Dutch Connection *Charles Hills* 119
4 ch h Dutch Art Endless Love (IRE) (Dubai Destination (USA))
1606[2] ◆ 2243[9] 4127[2] (4733) 5217a[5] 6394a[6] 7837a[12]

Dutch Destiny *William Haggas* a93 95
3 b f Dutch Art Danehill Destiny (Danehill Dancer (IRE))
3034[5] 3575[2] (4344) 4652[9] 6770[3] 8098[2]

Dutch Dream *Linda Perratt* a33 58
3 ch f Dutch Art Starry Sky (Oasis Dream)
1839[5] 5804[8] (6003) 7323[9] 7747[18]

Dutch Gallery *Tom Dascombe* a66 73
3 b g Dutch Art Luluti (IRE) (Kheleyf (USA))
2179[8] 2650[13] 3029[4] 4631[6] 5609[7]

Dutch Garden *David Brown* a82 65
4 b g Fastnet Rock(AUS) Swan Wings (Bahamian Bounty)
246[2] ◆ (387) ◆ (795) 965[7]

Dutch Golden Age (IRE) *Gary Moore* a85 43
4 b g Kodiac Magic Melody (Petong)
(67) 169[5] 4014[10] 4627[15] 5774[8] 6589[6] 7206[6] (7644) 8083[2] 8176[4]

Dutch Law *Hughie Morrison* a87 102
4 b g Dutch Art Lawyers Choice (Namid)
1775[2] 2378[5] 3061[5] 3358[2] 4132[2] (4402) (5174) 5376[3] (6109) 6942[11] 7542[8]

Dutch Masterpiece *Gary Moore* a102 110
6 b g Dutch Art The Terrier (Foxhound (USA))
1862[16] 1969[4] 2546[9] 3696a[11] 4735[11] ◆ 6119[6] 6779[10] 6944[2] 7537[6]

Dutch Mist *Kevin Ryan* 91
3 ch f Dutch Art Solstice (Dubawi (IRE))
1599[8] 2161[12] 2683[6] (2972) 3714[2] 5836[4] 6518[4] 6770[4] 7550[9]

Dutch Quality *Marco Botti* a73
2 b c Dutch Art Miss Quality (USA) (Elusive Quality (USA))
6671[3] 7307[6]

Dutch S *Clive Cox* a78 68
5 ch m Dutch Art Park Law (IRE) (Fasliyev (USA))
683[10]

Dutch Treaty *Richard Hannon* a52 13
3 ch f Dutch Art Entreat (Pivotal)
1312[4] 1723[7]

Dutch Uncle *Ed Dunlop* a89 90
4 b g Dutch Art Evasive Quality (FR) (Highest Honor (FR))
1089[2] 1336[3] 1716[2] (2037) 2868[11] 3950[6] 4399[10] 7869[8] 8249[4] ◆ 8446[3]

Dutiful Son (IRE) *Simon Dow* a93 66
6 b g Invincible Spirit(IRE) Grecian Dancer (Dansili)
433[2] 486[6] 816[8] 8069[12] 8356[7]

Duxbury *Richard Fahey* a24
2 b c Dutch Art Triskel (Hawk Wing (USA))
8556[9]

Dux Scholar *Doug Watson* a65 81
8 b h Oasis Dream Alumni (Selkirk (USA))
91a[11] 370a[14]

Dwight D *William Haggas* a84 90
3 b g Duke Of Marmalade(IRE) Almatinka (IRE) (Indian Ridge)
(202) 1605[5] 1974[6] 4108[3] ◆ 4797[5]

Dwynant *Kevin Frost* a61 54
3 gr f Multiplex Nant Y Mynydd (Piccolo)
945[10] 1132[5] 1798[5] ◆ 2506[7] 2864[15] 4718[6] 5248[9]

Dylan Dancing (IRE) *A Marcialis* a92 94
3 b c Dylan Thomas(IRE) Raindancing (IRE) (Tirol)
1686a[11] 6310a[6]

Dylan Mouth (IRE) *Marco Botti* 116
5 b h Dylan Thomas(IRE) Cottonmouth (IRE) (Noverre (USA))
(2728a) 3936a[10] 6175a[7] 7402a[7]

Dylan's Storm (IRE) *David Dennis* a65 71
4 b g Zebedee Storm Lady (IRE) (Alhaarth (IRE))
3002[10]

Dyllan (IRE) *Ruth Carr* a71 77
3 b g Zebedee Luvmedo (IRE) (One Cool Cat (USA))
2742[11] 3368[5] 3948[3] (4426) 4855[5] 5284[2] 5992[2]

Dynamic *William Haggas* 75
2 b f Teofilo(IRE) White Cay (Dalakhani (IRE))
7548[3] ◆

Dynamic Dash (USA) *Kim Byung Hak* a58
4 b h Pleasantly Perfect(USA) See Rock City (USA) (Tapit (USA))
6399a[7]

Dynamic Drive (IRE) *Maurice Barnes* a43 50
9 b g Motivator Biriyani (IRE) (Danehill (USA))
4971[3]

Dynamic Girl (IRE) *Brendan Powell* 75
3 b f Holy Roman Emperor(IRE) Boca Dancer (IRE) (Indian Ridge)
(2459) 3111[2] 3689[4] 4354[5] (5330) 6182[4] 7146[13] 7415[2]

Dynamic Jilju (USA) *Kim Jeom Oh* a24
5 bb h Forestry(USA) Beat Your Feet (USA) (Dixieland Band (USA))
6399a[14]

Dynamic Lips (IRE) *Andreas Lowe* 99
3 ch f Excellent Art Devilish Lips (GER) (Konigstiger (GER))
1513a[8] 2949a[3] (5695a) 6824a[9]

Dyna Might *Ollie Pears* a46 43
2 b f Foxwedge(AUS) Dyna Bowl (USA) (Dynaformer (USA))
3947[9] 4966[5] 5728[8] 6681[6] 6963[4]

Dynamis (FR) *G Elbaz* a54 60
8 b g Gentlewave(IRE) Daisy Town (Doyoun)
5700a[7]

Dynamo (IRE) *Richard Hughes* a54 63
5 b g Galileo(IRE) Trading Places (Dansili)
65[9] 245[11] 428[10] 653[4] 796[4] 1748[3] (1807) 2326[U] (2634) 2850[3] 5624[5] 6022[5]

Dynamo Walt (IRE) *Derek Shaw* a97 79
5 b g Acclamation Cambara (Dancing Brave (USA))
213[2] 338[7] 492[4] 677[11] 835[5] 966[7] 1650[7] 2003[4] 2787[5] 3277[4] 4198[6] (5189) 5679[2] 6080[4] 7202[4] 7643[5] (7864) 8150[4] (8308) 8484[4]

Eager Beaver *William Muir* a80 86
4 b m Duke Of Marmalade(IRE) Kahlua Kiss (Mister Baileys)
1919[4] 2564[3] 2994[3] 3352[3] (4520) (4994) 5328[7] 6584[2] 6951[6] 8068[12]

Eaglecraft (USA) *I Al Hadhrami*
3 b g Street Cry(IRE) First Blush (IRE) (Pivotal)
8576a[12]

Eagle Creek (IRE) *Simon Crisford* 67
2 b c Raven's Pass(USA) Blue Angel (IRE) (Oratorio (IRE))
7503[5]

Eagle Eyes (GER) *Jean-Pierre Carvalho* a77 82
3 ch f Adlerflug(GER) Evening Breeze (GER) (Surumu (GER))
7720a[9]

Eagle Spirit (IRE) *Joseph Patrick O'Brien* a81 86
2 b c Holy Roman Emperor(IRE) Romie's Kastett (GER) (Halling (USA))
4574a[6] 6817a[4]

Eagle's Stare (IRE) *Saeed bin Suroor* a75 57
2 b c Bernardini(USA) Sander Camillo (USA) (Dixie Union (USA))
7003[5] 7940[2]

Eagle Top *John Gosden* 123
5 ch h Pivotal Gull Wing (IRE) (In The Wings)
2241[4] 3936a[9]

Eagle Valley (IRE) *Tracey Collins* a75 64
4 gr m Mastercraftsman(IRE) Zaafran (Singspiel (IRE))
(665a)

Earl (FR) *J-C Rouget* 72
2 gr c Peer Gynt(JPN) Kanonette (FR) (Kaldoun (FR))
3871a[6]

Early Bird (IRE) *Richard Fahey* 75
3 ch f Exceed And Excel(AUS) Crossmolina (IRE) (Halling (USA))
1647[7] 2050[3] 3138[3]

Early Morning (GER) *Dr A Bolte* 101
7 b m Mamool(IRE) Evening Danzig (GER) (Danzig Connection (USA))
2075a[4] 2723a[5]

Early Morning (IRE) *Harry Dunlop* a103 107
5 gr g New Approach(IRE) Summer's Eve (Singspiel (IRE))
(1576) ◆ 3273[8] 4163[14] (5146) 6075[2] 6482[7]

Earnshaw (USA) *S bin Ghadayer* a75 105
5 gr h Medaglia d'Oro(USA) Emily Bronte (Machiavellian (USA))
93a[9] 372a[3] 625a[8] 845a[6] 8396a[8]

Earring (USA) *A P O'Brien* 104
3 bb f Dansili Together (IRE) (Galileo (IRE))
3539a[2] 4218a[7] 4435a[2]

Eartha Kitt *Tom Dascombe* 84
2 bb f Pivotal Ceiling Kitty (Red Clubs (IRE))
6078[3] (7314)

Earth Drummer (IRE) *David Loughnane* a103 104
6 b g Dylan Thomas(IRE) In Dubai (USA) (Giant's Causeway (USA))
1478[3] 1871[15] 2027[5] 3273[10] 4165[3]

Earthly (USA) *Ralph Beckett* 71
2 b c Spring At Last(USA) Geographic (USA) (Empire Maker (USA))
6577[5] 7013[5]

Earthwindorfire *Geoffrey Deacon* a64 67
5 br g High Chaparral(IRE) Elemental (Rudimentary (USA))
728[5] 1140[6] 1529[5] 2369[6] 4369[4] 5954[11] 7037[6] 7614[2] 7870[9]

East Coast Lady (IRE) *William Stone* a73 62
4 b m Kodiac Alexander Anapolis (IRE) (Spectrum (IRE))
2217[5] 2794[6] 3410[6] 3894[3] 4356[7] 6334[6] 6901[3] 7205[7] 7609[4] 7889[10] (8085) 8178[3] 8378[4]

East Coker (IRE) *Mrs John Harrington* 62
3 b g Pour Moi(IRE) Bounce (FR) (Trempolino (USA))
4813a[18]

Easter Mate (IRE) *Ralph Beckett* a87 87
3 b g Acclamation Greek Easter (IRE) (Namid)
(770) 2891[3] 4139[6] (4841) 5376[6] 6628[4] 6803[5]

Eastern Dragon (IRE) *Iain Jardine* a82 79
6 b g Elnadim(USA) Shulammite Woman (IRE) (Desert Sun)
(681) (776) 822[4] 1326[2] 1546[2] ◆ 2960[3] 3327[2] 3922[3] (4189) 4446[3] 4704[9] 5579[4] 6160[17] 6838[6] (7141) 7796[5] 8092[6]

Eastern Express (IRE) *J Size* 112
4 b g Fastnet Rock(AUS) Mohican Princess (Shirley Heights)
8329a[10]

Eastern Impact (IRE) *Richard Fahey* 116
5 b g Bahamian Bounty Kate The Great (Xaar)
2159[4] 4151[6] 4916[3] 5213a[2] 5880[5] 6642[5]

Eastern Lady (IND) *William Knight* a62 74
3 ch f Dancing Forever(USA) Oriental Lady (IRE) (King's Best (USA))
1608[7] 2182[4] 2816[7] 3570[5]

Eastern Magic *Sarah Hollinshead*
9 b g Observatory(USA) Inchtina (Inchinor)
2370[P]

Eastern Racer (IRE) *Brian Ellison* 89
4 b g Bushranger(IRE) Queen Cobra (IRE) (Indian Rocket)
1444[13] 1848[5] (3266) 3646[11] 4193[3] 4689[5] 6539[14]

Eastern Rules (IRE) *M Halford* a104 107
8 b g Golden Snake(USA) Eastern Ember (Indian King (USA))
95a[2] 282a[6] 373a[8] 4921a[8] 5941a[22] 6355a[10]

Eastern Shore (IRE) *K R Burke* 57
3 b g Kodiac High Inthe Sky (IRE) (High Chaparral (IRE))
3856[5] 4983[6] 6618[4] 7581[7]

East India *George Baker* 82
4 ch g Galileo(IRE) Field Of Hope (IRE) (Selkirk (USA))
1914[9] 6301[9] 6889[3] ◆ 7246[3] 7500[6]

East Indies *John Gosden* a86 70
3 b g Authorized(IRE) Elan (Dansili)
1636[6]

Easton Angel (IRE) *Michael Dods* 113
3 gr f Dark Angel(IRE) Staceymac (IRE) (Elnadim (USA))
(2192) (3158) 4166[2] 4824[4] 5614[15]

East Street Revue *Tim Easterby* 96
3 ch g Pastoral Pursuits Revue Princess (IRE) (Mull Of Kintyre (USA))
1448[8] 1847[10] 2777[2] (3017) (3360) 3893[4] 4612[2] 5409[4] (5657) 6779[2] 7124[8]

Easy Code *William Haggas* 71
3 b g Bahamian Bounty Skirrid (Halling (USA))
2029[10] 4116[9] 5512[8] 5881[7]

Easydoesit (IRE) *Tony Carroll* a60 62
8 b g Iffraaj Fawaayid (USA) (Vaguely Noble (IRE))
170[7] (378) 498[7] 731[6] 1182[6] 1343[2] 1748[9] 2110[3] 2738[RR]

Easy Easy *Alan King* 68
3 ch g Rip Van Winkle(IRE) Nizza (GER) (Acatenango (GER))
2208^{11}

Easy Gold (IRE) *Ed Walker* 77
3 ch g Mastercraftsman(IRE) Aiming Upwards (Blushing Flame (USA))
6192^{3} 6634^{4}

Easy Road *Cathrine Erichsen* a83 113
6 b g Compton Place Broughtons Revival (Pivotal)
3992a^{5} 5098a^{2} (6943)

Easy Tiger *William Muir* a88 89
4 b g Refuse To Bend(IRE) Extremely Rare (IRE) (Mark Of Esteem (IRE))
1335^{2} 1752^{5} 2247^{5} 2934^{2} 3101^{2} 3622^{2}

Easy Victory *Saeed bin Suroor* 87
2 b f Dubawi(IRE) Independence (Selkirk (USA))
(4064) ◆ 5172^{8} 7116^{8} 7667^{8}

Eaton Square *John Gosden* 94
2 b g Invincible Spirit(IRE) Loch Jipp (USA) (Belong To Me (USA))
(4805) ◆ 6481^{2} 7544^{7}

Eavesdrop (IRE) *A P O'Brien* 80
3 b f Galileo(IRE) Native Force (IRE) (Indian Ridge)
7393a^{7}

Eba Chope (FR) *Mme M-C Naim* a42 58
5 b m Deportivo Easy Rocket (FR) (Indian Rocket)
8421a^{14}

Ebbesbourne (IRE) *Sir Michael Stoute* a77
2 b f Teofilo(IRE) Ebble (Oasis Dream)
(6897) ◆

Ebbisham (IRE) *Jim Boyle* a69 69
3 b g Holy Roman Emperor(IRE) Balting Lass (IRE) (Orpen (USA))
(1734) 2212^{11} 4269^{5} 4641^{8} *(7736) 8154^{4} 8590^{5}*

Ebediyin (IRE) *D K Weld* 100
3 b c Raven's Pass(USA) Ebadiyla (IRE) (Sadler's Wells (USA))
3341^{5} 3679a^{9} 6354a^{12}

Eblouis Moi (FR) *A Giorgi* a38 67
2 b f Diamond Green(FR) Coldgirl (FR) (Verglas (IRE))
2724a^{5} *7455a^{14}* 7927a^{12}

Eblouissante (FR) *R Chotard* 67
2 b f Air Chief Marshal(IRE) Sugarlegs (IRE) (Bertolini (USA))
5698a^{11}

Ebony N Ivory *Archie Watson* a67 78
3 b g Equiano(FR) Ile Deserte (Green Desert (USA))
(1892) 3137^{4} 5978^{8} 6409^{5} 6831^{10} *7899^{6}*

Ebqaa (IRE) *Marcus Tregoning* a59
2 b f Cape Cross(IRE) Estedaama (IRE) (Marju (IRE))
8081^{7}

Ebtihaal (IRE) *Saeed bin Suroor* 96
3 ch g Teofilo(IRE) Dance Troupe (Rainbow Quest (USA))
1603^{5} 2244^{8}

Ebtkaar (IRE) *Roger Varian* a68
2 b g Cape Cross(IRE) Clare Glen (IRE) (Sakhee (USA))
8034^{5}

Eburaci (IRE) *Charlie Fellowes* 61
2 b c Vale Of York(IRE) Dubai Pearl (IRE) (Refuse To Bend (IRE))
7208^{4}

Eccleston *David O'Meara* 104
5 b g Acclamation Miss Meggy (Pivotal)
1644^{9} 2803^{10} 3188^{3} 4946^{6} 5857^{4} 6556^{4} 7315^{10}

Echapee Divine (FR) *T Lerner* 46
2 b f Amadeus Wolf Eight Stars (IRE) (Chineur (FR))
3006a^{6}

Echo Brava *Jim Best* a86 87
6 gr g Proclamation(IRE) Snake Skin (Golden Snake (USA))
2966^{4}

Echoism (IRE) *Mark Johnston* a49 67
2 ch f Casamento(IRE) Epic Similie (Lomitas)
7356^{4} *7527^{7}* 7695^{8} *7941^{7} 8046^{8}*

Echo Of Lightning *Brian Ellison* a66 83
6 b g Echo Of Light Classic Lass (Dr Fong (USA))
1924^{8} *2620^{11}* 3252^{7} (4089) 4627^{18} 5033^{3} 5866^{8} 6280^{2} 6772^{6}

Ecoeye *Augustine Leahy* a73 77
4 b g Echo Of Light Evening Tale (IRE) (Rock Of Gibraltar (IRE))
7391a^{2}

Economic Crisis (IRE) *John David Riches* a63 83
7 ch m Excellent Art Try The Air (IRE) (Foxhound (USA))
4142^{6} (4488) 4831^{10} 5153^{8} (5780) 6324^{8}

Ecoute (IRE) *Kenneth Slack* a60 61
3 b g Pour Moi(IRE) Elusive Legend (USA) (Elusive Quality (USA))
2804^{5} 6221^{7}

Ectot *Todd Pletcher* 119
5 b h Hurricane Run(IRE) Tonnara (IRE) (Linamix (FR))
7835a^{8}

Ecureuil (IRE) *Hugo Palmer* a91 77
3 b f Lope De Vega(IRE) Takizada (IRE) (Sendawar (IRE))
2182^{3} 3350^{3} *3990^{5} (4978) (6048)*

Ecureuil (USA) *C Ferland* a101 101
4 ch g Tapit(USA) Nutcase (USA) (Forest Wildcat (USA))
8165a^{3}

Edana (FR) *Henk Grewe* 75
2 b f Tai Chi(GER) Elli (Polar Falcon (USA))
1579a^{2}

Edas *Thomas Cuthbert* a40 52
14 b g Celtic Swing Eden (IRE) (Polish Precedent (USA))
2616^{8} 4038^{9}

Eddy Mercs *Michael Appleby* a5
4 bl g Striking Ambition Bella Tutrice (IRE) (Woodborough (USA))
600^{7} 1151^{11} 6703^{9}

Ede's E Rider *Pat Phelan* a54
2 b g Equiano(FR) Run For Ede's (Peintre Celebre (USA))
7733^{7} 8355^{10} 8556^{6}

Ede's The Business *Ken Wingrove*
5 ch m Halling(USA) My Amalie (IRE) (Galileo (IRE))
8500^{13}

Ede's The Mover *Pat Phelan* a58 60
3 b f Bahamian Bounty Run For Ede's (Peintre Celebre (USA))
633^{6} 1163^{6} 3236^{9}

Edgar (GER) *David Bridgwater* a77
6 b g Big Shuffle(USA) Estella (GER) (Acatenango (GER))
(251) ◆ *(425) 786^{7} 940^{3} 1043^{2}*

Edgar Balthazar *Keith Dalgleish* a88 92
4 b g Pastoral Pursuits Assistacat (IRE) (Lend A Hand)
1195^{11} 1627^{9} 2268^{5} 2679^{12} (3518) 4104^{P} 6225^{8} 6557^{9} 7095^{12} *7796^{4} 7958^{9}*

Edge (IRE) *Bernard Llewellyn* a45 61
5 b g Acclamation Chanter (Lomitas)
1948^{3} *2448^{5}* 3748^{6} 4504^{5} (4993) 5823^{3} 5957^{5} (6651) 7035^{2} 7299^{3}

Edged In Blue *K R Burke* 61
2 b f Acclamation Dutch Diamond (Dutch Art)
3597^{5} 4943^{3}

Edged Out *Christopher Mason* 80
6 b m Piccolo Edge Of Light (Xaar)
(1827) 2846^{8} 4911^{5} 5285^{3} 6017^{8}

Edge Of Heaven *Jonathan Portman* a89 72
4 b m Pastoral Pursuits Halfwaytoparadise (Observatory (USA))
1207^{6} 1757^{8} *2154^{4}* 3061^{12} *8077^{9} 8343^{5} 8487^{8}*

Edge Of Reason *Ed Walker* a75 79
3 b f Authorized(IRE) Forest Express (AUS) (Kaaptive Edition (NZ))
968^{6} 2260^{4} 2735^{8} *(3318)* ◆ 4400^{8} 5122^{5}

Edification *Martyn Meade* 82
3 b g Dream Ahead(USA) Elegant Pride (Beat Hollow)
2179^{10} 3415^{6}

Edith Weston *Robert Cowell* a48 50
3 b f Showcasing Twitch Hill (Piccolo)
328^{6} 509^{4} 688^{7} 3970^{7} 5041^{5} 5378^{2} *6865^{6} 7693^{5} 8013^{3} 8288^{9}*

Educate *Ismail Mohammed* a110 116
7 b g Echo Of Light Pasithea (IRE) (Celtic Swing)
2464^{2} ◆ 3383^{5} (4165) 5652^{5} 6786^{17} 7700^{2} *7934^{2} 8427^{6}* (Dead)

Edward Lewis *John Gosden* 94
3 b g Kyllachy Tahirah (Green Desert (USA))
2207^{3} 2686^{4} 3572^{3} (4041) ◆ 4889^{6} 6079^{2} 6780^{2} 7315^{7}

Edya *G Botti* 97
3 b f Makfi Eminencia (Sadler's Wells (USA))
2730a^{6} 6069a^{4} 6497a^{4} 7029a^{10} 7862a^{9}

Eeny Mac (IRE) *John Wainwright* a42 52
9 ch g Redback Sally Green (IRE) (Common Grounds)
21^{3} 388^{5} 602^{8} 876^{11} 3480^{5} 4724^{7} (4929) 5323^{9} 5980^{7}

Eez Eh (IRE) *Keith Dalgleish* 79
3 b g Jeremy(USA) Step With Style (USA) (Gulch (USA))
3019^{4} 3343^{5} 3550^{5} 5580^{5} 5718^{2} ◆ 6006^{2} (6221) 7594^{6}

Effinex (USA) *James Jerkens* a122
5 bb h Mineshaft(USA) What A Pear (USA) (E Dubai (USA))
7838a^{7}

Effusive *William Haggas* a79 79
4 ch m Starspangledbanner(AUS) Thrill (Pivotal)
(41) 146^{3}

Efichope (FR) *S Culin* a48 74
2 b f Deportivo Acroleine (FR) (Indian Rocket)
(2724a) 3006a^{3} *5755a^{11}*

E Fourteen *Robyn Brisland* a53 43
3 b f Nayef(USA) Pale Blue Eyes (IRE) (Peintre Celebre (USA))
81^{4} (174) 286^{2}

Egisto (FR) *P Schaerer*
8 ch g Night Tango(GER) Eleora (FR) (Highest Honor (FR))
586a^{3}

Egyptian (USA) *Jeremy Noseda* a87 69
3 bb g Eskendereya(USA) Street Talk (USA) (Street Cry (IRE))
2320^{4} ◆ 2861^{7} *(4477)*

Egyptian Warrior (IRE) *A P O'Brien* a64 69
7 bb g Galileo(IRE) Beltisaal (FR) (Belmez (USA))
208a^{11}

Ehtiraas *Owen Burrows* a88 83
3 b c Oasis Dream Kareemah (IRE) (Peintre Celebre (USA))
2248^{3} 2998^{2} 3245^{7} 4895^{2} (5731) *6628^{3}*

Eid Rose *Scott Dixon* a29 43
2 b f Medicean Show Flower (Shamardal (USA))
1087^{7} 1813^{3} 2266^{4} 3008^{6} *7528^{P} 8285^{10} 8344^{9}*

Eighteen Summers (USA) *Edward Lynam* a81 54
9 ch g Lion Heart(USA) Azarina (IRE) (Kenmare (FR))
7517a^{6}

Eightfold *Mrs A Corson* a51 55
7 b g Cadeaux Genereux Nirvana (Marju (IRE))
1518a^{5}

Eighth Circle (IRE) *Henry Spiller* a58 33
2 b g Street Boss(USA) Distorted Promise (USA) (Distorted Humor (USA))
7770^{11} *8089^{5}* (Dead)

Einstein *Mrs Ilka Gansera-Leveque* a63 51
3 b c Aqlaam Park Crystal (IRE) (Danehill (USA))
7327^{4} 7583^{5} *8491^{4}*

Einsteins Folly (IRE) *Jessica Long* a69 95
6 b g Whipper(USA) Azra (IRE) (Danehill (USA))
3449a^{11}

Eisha Baby *Richard Hannon* a49 45
3 ch f Dutch Art Ainia (Alhaarth (IRE))
1814^{11} 2470^{12} *2606^{7}* 3490^{5} *4021^{8}*

Eisha Flower (USA) *Richard Fahey* 63
3 b f Distorted Humor(USA) Two Trail Sioux (USA) (Indian Charlie (USA))
3293^{2} *3609^{12}*

Eium Mac *Neville Bycroft* a60 48
7 b g Presidium Efipetite (Efisio)
247^{3} (526) 956^{2}

Ejaaby *Roger Varian* a73 71
2 ch c Helmet(AUS) Vivid Blue (Haafhd)
7665^{4} *7883^{2}*

Ejaazah (IRE) *Richard Hannon* 90
3 b f Acclamation English Ballet (IRE) (Danehill Dancer (IRE))
2736^{7}

Ejabah (IRE) *Chris Wall* a54 64
2 b f Iffraaj Relinquished (Royal Applause)
4564^{4} ◆ 5395^{6} *6414^{6} 8159^{8}*

Ejayteekay *Hughie Morrison* a71 81
3 b f Big Bad Bob(IRE) Lovely Dream (IRE) (Elnadim (USA))
1859^{7} 2415^{2} 2701^{4} (3684) 3911^{8} 5123^{5} 6378^{4} 6893^{3} 7220^{4} ◆

Ejbaar *Robert Cowell* a83 83
4 b g Oasis Dream Habaayib (Royal Applause)
3159^{4} 3995^{6} 4889^{4} 5599^{2} 6072^{13}

Ekatea (FR) *C Laffon-Parias* a60 70
2 b f Power Galaktea (IRE) (Statue Of Liberty (USA))
7294a^{3} (7490a)

Ekhtiyaar *Roger Varian* 85
2 b c Bated Breath Bayja (IRE) (Giant's Causeway (USA))
6524^{2} ◆ (7224)

El Abandonado (SWE) *Maria Sandh* 96
5 b g Dustoori Tawny Eagle (SWE) (Eagle Eyed (USA))
3449a^{7} 6390a^{4}

Elabela (IRE) *J E Hammond* a73 93
6 ch m Tamayuz Benalmadena (FR) (Nashwan (USA))
3090a^{9}

Ela Goog La Mou *Peter Charalambous* a57 66
7 b m Tobougg(IRE) Real Flame (Cyrano De Bergerac)
32^{3} 216^{2} 324^{7} 527^{5} 707^{5}

Eland Ally *Anabel K Murphy* a65 50
8 b g Striking Ambition Dream Rose (IRE) (Anabaa (USA))
541^{10} 733^{8} 857^{4} (1133) 1481^{5} 2088^{6} *2785^{5}* 3260^{7} *4529^{7} 6587^{8} 6853^{8}* 7046^{13} *8409^{4}*

Elas Ruby *John Gosden* a78 82
2 b f Raven's Pass(USA) Elas Diamond (Danehill Dancer (IRE))
3782^{3} 5119^{6} 6782^{4} 7543^{2} *(7885)* ◆

El Astronaute (IRE) *John Quinn* 93
3 ch c Approve(IRE) Drumcliffe Dancer (IRE) (Footstepsinthesand)
1492^{4} 1996^{2} 2218^{2} 2658^{6} 3393^{4} 4112^{15} 4803^{10} 5657^{4} (5961) 6119^{11}

El Beau (IRE) *John Quinn* a38 91
5 ch g Camacho River Beau (IRE) (Galileo (IRE))
2017^{11} 2688^{9} *3660^{9}* 4300^{8} 5180^{10} (6006) 6160^{3} 6517^{6} 7408^{2}

Elbereth *Andrew Balding* a84 105
5 b m Mount Nelson Masandra (IRE) (Desert Prince (IRE))
1569^{5} 2363^{4} (2797) 4165^{2} 6179a^{3} 7402a^{3}

El Bravo *Shaun Harris* a63 60
10 ch g Falbrav(IRE) Alessandra (Generous (IRE))
62^{12} 150^{9}

El Camila (FR) *Y Gourraud* a51 74
2 b f Coastal Path Alize Des Parcs (FR) (Denham Red (FR))
5986a^{4} 6639a^{9}

El Campeon *Simon Dow* a81 59
4 bb g Multiplex Villabella (FR) (Hernando (FR))
2549^{10} *3525^{9} 8161^{8} (8339) 8558^{3}*

El Cap (USA) *Sir Michael Stoute* a74
2 b c Speightstown(USA) Divine Presence (USA) (A.P. Indy (USA))
6850^{2} 7812^{2}

El Colombiano (FR) *H-A Pantall* a77 71
3 ch c Way Of Light(USA) Belle Suisse (FR) (Hamas (IRE))
2456a^{4}

Eldelbar (SPA) *M Delcher Sanchez* a77
2 ch c Footstepsinthesand Malinche (Hernando (FR))
7971a^{6}

El Dem I (IRE) *Michael G Cleary* a44 54
5 b m Ad Valorem(USA) El Tina (Unfuwain (USA))
5900a^{17}

Eldorado Creek (IRE) *Richard Fahey* a48 78
2 b g High Chaparral(IRE) Trail Of Tears (IRE) (Exceed And Excel (AUS))
2649^{9} 3382^{9} 4188^{6} *7142^{7}*

Eldritch (IRE) *John Gosden* 71
2 b c Dark Angel(IRE) Henties Bay (IRE) (Cape Cross (IRE))
(7318)

El Duque *Bill Turner* a58 62
5 b g Byron Royal Tavira Girl (IRE) (Orpen (USA))
32^{6} 1832^{3} 2297^{2} *2448^{2}* 2741^{5} (3255)

Election Day *Mark Johnston* a79 74
2 b c Invincible Spirit(IRE) Missisipi Star (IRE) (Mujahid (USA))
4297^{4} 5150^{3} *6085^{2}* 6274^{5} (6771) *(7322)*

Electrify (IRE) *Jeremy Noseda* a65 66
3 b f Invincible Spirit(IRE) Elopa (GER) (Tiger Hill (IRE))
5504^{5} 6661^{4} 7219^{3} *7727^{B}*

Elegant Annie *Jonathan Portman* a53 64
3 b f Lawman(FR) An Ghalanta (IRE) (Holy Roman Emperor (IRE))
1388^{7} *1553^{4}* 2366^{13} *2784^{5}* (3198) *3319^{7}* 4596^{7} 5326^{4} 6066^{5} 6636^{3} 7062^{8}

Elegante Bere (FR) *D Guillemin* 98
2 b f Peer Gynt(JPN) Particuliere (Spectrum (IRE))
6986a^{9} 7757a^{4}

Elegantly Bound (IRE) *James Given* a69 36
2 b g Choisir(AUS) Boundless Joy (AUS) (Montjeu (IRE))
2617^{5} 4363^{7} *4713^{2} 6743^{3} 7938^{4} 8033^{2} 8244^{11}*

Elementary *Michael Bell* a63 71
2 b g Exceed And Excel(AUS) Humdrum (Dr Fong (USA))
3526^{6} ◆ 4097^{3} 5084^{4} 7467^{9} *8159^{11} 8560^{4}*

Elemento *Phil McEntee*
2 ch g Assertive Black Baccara (Superior Premium)
2295^{6}

Elements Legacy *K R Burke* a51 60
2 b g Kheleyf(USA) New Romantic (Singspiel (IRE))
3114^{9} 3361^{4} 3897^{3} 4738^{4} *5297^{5}* 6388a^{28}

Elennga (FR) *J-C Rouget* a83 94
3 ch f Exceed And Excel(AUS) Elva (IRE) (King's Best (USA))
5006a^{11} 6357a^{5}

El Estruendoso (ARG) *S Seemar* a62 70
6 ch g Giant's Causeway(USA) Estricta (ARG) (Roy (USA))
540a^{13}

Eleuthera *J F Levins* a86 67
4 ch g Bahamian Bounty Cha Cha Cha (Efisio)
177^{2} (363) (703) ◆ *1291^{4}* ◆ 3875^{11} 4345^{7} 6216^{4} *6425^{3}* ◆ *7112^{10}* 7413^{8} *8197a^{8}*

Elfy James (FR) *D Windrif* a65 67
2 b f Kendargent(FR) Policalle (FR) (Poliglote)
5279a^{3} 5447a^{5} 6015a^{7}

Elhaame (IRE) *Saeed bin Suroor* a29 112
6 b g Acclamation Gold Hush (USA) (Seeking The Gold (USA))
283a^{4}

El Hayem (IRE) *Sir Michael Stoute* a54 90
3 b g Invincible Spirit(IRE) Winning Sequence (FR) (Zafonic (USA))
1474^{4} ◆ (2861) 4271^{2} 4624^{9}

El Hombre *Keith Dalgleish* a76 34
2 ch c Camacho Nigella (Band On The Run)
4308^{5} *(7142)*

Elide (IRE) *P Bary* a64 78
3 b f Wootton Bassett Elodie (Dansili)
3120a^{6}

Elidor *Mick Channon* 114
6 br g Cape Cross(IRE) Honorine (IRE) (Mark Of Esteem (IRE))
1995^{3} 2486^{7} 3436^{9} (4734) 5655^{19} 6283^{7}

Elis Eliz (IRE) *Michael Wigham* a91 71
4 b m Lord Shanakill(USA) Suailce (IRE) (Singspiel (IRE))
351^{3} 529^{8} 780^{3} 1003^{3} 1959^{6}

Elishpour (IRE) *Alan Fleming* 104
6 b g Oasis Dream Elbasana (IRE) (Indian Ridge)
3630a^{11}

Elite Army *Saeed bin Suroor* a83 113
5 b g Authorized(IRE) White Rose (GER) (Platini (GER))
(2025) 3340^{2} 4061^{6} 4821^{7} 6822a^{6}

Elizabeth Browning (IRE) *A P O'Brien* a60 84
2 b f Galileo(IRE) Inca Princess (IRE) (Holy Roman Emperor (IRE))
2718a^{12} 5136a^{7} 6815a^{9}

Eljaddaaf (IRE) *Dean Ivory* a82 45
5 b g Shamardal(USA) Almansoora (USA) (Bahri (USA))
65^{8} 314^{7} 442^{2} ◆ *(543)* ◆ *(872)* ◆ *1159^{8}* 1928^{10} *(2379) 2821^{4} (3780) (4714) 5810^{5} 6123^{4} 8319^{6}*

Eljeemi (IRE) *William Haggas* 84
3 b g Shamardal(USA) Arthur's Girl (Hernando (FR))
3066^{4} (7218)

Ellaal *Ruth Carr* a65 81
7 b g Oasis Dream Capistrano Day (USA) (Diesis)
683^{7} 964^{2} (1064) 1323^{11} (1841) (2091) 2673^{12} 2811^{6} 3214^{9} 3922^{6} 4089^{5} 4490^{2} 4704^{6} (4833) (5374) 6280^{7} 6772^{11} *7108^{12}*

Ella Diva (FR) *N Caullery* a92 95
3 ch f Heliostatic(IRE) Ellary (FR) (Equerry (USA))
1581a^{8} (5946a) 6611a^{3} 7348a^{10} *8563a^{8}*

Ella's Delight (IRE) *Martin Todhunter* 69
6 b m Camacho Swift Alchemist (Fleetwood (IRE))
2773^{15} 3262^{12}

Elle Dorado *David Loughnane* a46 71
4 ch m Paco Boy(IRE) Clever Millie (USA) (Cape Canaveral (USA))
1696^{7} 2573^{4} 2799^{6} 3706^{12} 4456^{6} 4767^{5}

Elle Rebelle *Mark Brisbourne* a56 56
6 b m Cockney Rebel(IRE) Lille Ida (Hawk Wing (USA))
20^{5} 150^{3} ◆ *255^{2}* 4456^{12} 5016^{2} 5708^{4} 6020^{6} *6143^{8}* 6405^{4}

Ellerina *Chris Fairhurst* a53 48
4 b m Stimulation(IRE) Dream Quest (Rainbow Quest (USA))
27^{2} 521^{3} 1121^{4} 1665^{10} *7138^{4} 7367^{P}*

Ellerslie Joe *Tom Tate* 43
4 b g Captain Gerrard(IRE) Madam Bijou (Atraf)
2048^{13} 2557^{9}

Ellery Lane (IRE) *P J Prendergast* 93
2 b f Holy Roman Emperor(IRE) Plum Sugar (IRE) (Footstepsinthesand)
3694a^{4}

Elleval (IRE) *David Marnane* a111 107
6 b g Kodiac Penny Rouge (IRE) (Pennekamp (USA))
93a^{2} 283a^{3} 455a^{2} 812a^{7} 3084a^{5} 4326a^{6} 5343a^{6}

Elliptical *Robert Cowell* 79
2 ch f Foxwedge(AUS) Gyroscope (Spinning World (USA))
(5119) 6063^{8}

Elliptique (IRE) *A Fabre* a113 114
5 br h New Approach(IRE) Uryale (FR) (Kendor (FR))
3544a^{2} (4928a) 6395a^{3} 7841a^{3} 8333a^{7}

El Loco (GER) *Markus Klug* 104
3 b c Lope De Vega(IRE) Elora (GER) (Alkalde (GER))
1689a^{2} 2711a^{2} 3453a^{2} 4186a^{11} 5696a^{3} 6397a^{3}

El Massivo (IRE) *Harriet Bethell* a61 57
6 bb g Authorized(IRE) Umthoulah (IRE) (Unfuwain (USA))
941^{5} 1649^{3} 2558^{11} *4212^{4}*

Elmley Queen *Roy Brotherton* a25 46
2 b f Piccolo All Business (Entrepreneur)
4759^{10} *5128^{5}* 5542^{8} *8313^{10}*

Elmwood *Andrew Slattery* 57
2 b c Paco Boy(IRE) Style Award (Acclamation)
3749[7]

Elnaawi (USA) *Kiaran McLaughlin* a107 86
6 bb h Street Sense(USA) Pilfer (USA) (Deputy Minister (CAN))
452a[9]

Elocution *Denis Coakley* 64
3 b f Paco Boy(IRE) Speech (Red Ransom (USA))
(1918) ◆ 2366[6] 3063[9] 3998[8] 5012[3] 5204[4]

El Pampa King (FR) *J-V Toux* a12 40
2 b g Kingsalsa(USA) Pampera (IRE) (Alhaarth (IRE))
4183a[6] 5819a[8]

El Principe *Les Eyre* a62 68
3 b g Strategic Prince Shamrock Lady (IRE) (Orpen (USA))
2864[5] 3776[2] 4445[4] (4771)

Elraazy *John Gosden* a73 85
3 b f Dubawi(IRE) Eswarah (Unfuwain (USA))
2767[5] ◆ (6052) 6584[4]

Elronaq *Charles Hills* a88 102
3 b g Invincible Spirit(IRE) Cartimandua (Medicean)
2250[5] *2788[4]* 3165[16] 4741[2] 5409[12]

El Suizo (FR) *H-A Pantall* 103
4 b h Meshaheer(USA) Belle Suisse (FR) (Hamas (IRE))
1172a[4] 1618a[4]

Eltanin (IRE) *John Quinn* 73
2 ch g Dragon Pulse(IRE) Maigh Nuad (IRE) (Alhaarth (IRE))
3112[3] 4663[11]

El Tel *Roger Varian* a69 34
4 ch g Sixties Icon Chelsea (USA) (Miswaki (USA))
33[9] 263[7] 435[11]

Eltham *Robyn Brisland* a76
3 ch f Kheleyf(USA) Baddi Heights (FR) (Shirley Heights)
(6247) 7119[P] *7486[9] 8101[7]*

El Torito (IRE) *Jim Boyle* 77
2 ch c Tagula(IRE) April Green (FR) (Green Tune (USA))
1736[3] 2147[3] 2583[3] (3231) 3858[5] 4825[4] 5560[9] 6525[4]

El Tren (IRE) *Michael Attwater* a56 60
5 b g Danehill Dancer(IRE) Dhamma (USA) (Broad Brush (USA))
189a[10] 372a[13] *722a[8]* 1861[13] 2628[11] *3525[11]*

Elucidation (IRE) *Sir Michael Stoute* 85
2 b c Oasis Dream Mimalia (USA) (Silver Hawk (USA))
5848[3] (6211)

Elusiva (FR) *K Borgel* a69 68
2 b f Elusive City(USA) Ypomoni (Green Tune (USA))
1284a[3] 2280a[4] 3006a[4] *5755a[8]*

Elusive Approach (IRE) *J S Bolger* a41 76
4 b m New Approach(IRE) Soilse Na Cathrach (IRE) (Elusive City (USA))
1016a[7]

Elusive Beauty (IRE) *K J Condon* a82 95
2 b f Elusive Pimpernel(USA) Lost Icon (IRE) (Intikhab (USA))
3694a[3] 5136a[4] 5686a[8]

Elusive Cowboy (USA) *Stuart Edmunds* a76 72
3 ch g Elusive Quality(USA) Sarmad (USA) (Dynaformer (USA))
8084[5] (8524)

Elusive Ellen (IRE) *Brendan Powell* a79 85
6 b m Elusive City(USA) Ellen's Girl (IRE) (Desert Prince (IRE))
(319) (1237) 1929[2] 2469[4] 2903[4] ◆ 3815[5] (5018) 6299[8] *7054[6]*

Elusive Gent (IRE) *Miss Nicole McKenna* a54 59
9 b g Elusive City(USA) Satin Cape (IRE) (Cape Cross (IRE))
2528[8]

Elusive Guest (FR) *Harry Dunlop* a90 82
5 b g Elusive City(USA) Mansoura (IRE) (Kalanisi (IRE))
1034a[12]

Elusive Heights (IRE) *G M Lyons* a104 99
3 b g Elusive Pimpernel(USA) Berg Bahn (IRE) (Big Bad Bob (IRE))
6389a[24] *7342a[2]*

Elusive In Paris (IRE) *John James Feane* a76 79
7 b g Elusive City(USA) Bradwell (IRE) (Taufan (USA))
4811a[15] *7517a[2] 7801a[5]*

Elusive Million (IRE) *Chad C Brown* 85
3 b f Pour Moi(IRE) Million Spirits (IRE) (Invincible Spirit (IRE))
5430a[14]

Elusive Olivia (USA) *Joseph Tuite* a56
2 b f Elusive Quality(USA) Kenza (USA) (Menifee (USA))
7733[5]

Elusivity (IRE) *Conor Dore* a86 82
8 b g Elusive City(USA) Tough Chic (IRE) (Indian Ridge)
76[3] 133[3] 278[7] 426[3] 520[5] (579) 784[3] (868) (919) 1046[2] 1528[2] 1827[2] (1956) *2768[7]* 4345[8] *5189[2] 5679[5] 6927[5] 7202[8] 7772[6] 7892[9] 8099[3] 8349[10]*

El Viento (FR) *Richard Fahey* a96 85
8 ch g Compton Place Blue Sirocco (Bluebird (USA))
3188[8] *3606[5]* 4373[6] 4862[16] 5857[8] 6539[16] *7864[9] 8176[7] (8380) 8583[8]*

El Vip (IRE) *Luca Cumani* 98
3 b c Pivotal Elle Danzig (GER) (Roi Danzig (USA))
(4857) 6081[4] 6715[3] (7573) ◆

Ely Place (IRE) *Mrs John Harrington* a72 72
2 b g Elusive Pimpernel(USA) Anessia (Fantastic Light (USA))
7917a[6]

Elysees Palace *Sir Mark Prescott Bt* a56
2 b g Champs Elysees Ventura Highway (Machiavellian (USA))
6368[4]

Elysian Fields (GR) *Amanda Perrett* a96 101
5 ch m Champs Elysees Second Of May (Lion Cavern (USA))
2433[7] *(3785)* 4800[6] 5328[5] 6667[4] (6951) 7271[10] *8068[10]*

Elysian Flyer (IRE) *Richard Hughes* a58 100
4 b g Majestic Missile(IRE) Starisa (IRE) (College Chapel)
3857[8] 4461[7] 4862[22] 5648[11]

Elysian Prince *Neil King* a86 78
5 b g Champs Elysees Trinkila (USA) (Cat Thief (USA))
332[6] 595[4] (616) 1093[2] 1221[11] 1933[2] 6267[8]

Embankment *Michael Attwater* a76 76
7 b g Zamindar(USA) Esplanade (Danehill (USA))
141[9] 518[6] 777[4] 951[7] 1416[4] 2153[8] 3554[13] *4009[4] (4882) 5399[6] 6662[14]*

Embiran (IRE) *D K Weld* 94
3 b c Shamardal(USA) Emiyna (USA) (Maria's Mon (USA))
1938a[3] 2716a[8]

Emblaze *Bryan Smart* a60 68
4 b m Showcasing Chushka (Pivotal)
21[9] 176[6] (525) 936[5] 1845[2] 2528[9] 4444[3] (5355) 5717[2] *5973[7]*

Embleton *Charlie Wallis* a53
2 b f Cacique(IRE) Morzine (Miswaki (USA))
6897[12] 7099[8] 7639[4] 7884[9]

Embroidery (IRE) *Harry Dunlop* a43 58
3 gr f Mastercraftsman(IRE) Joyful (IRE) (Green Desert (USA))
2826[3] 3508[9] *5504[9] 6857[12]*

Emell *Richard Hannon* a96 108
6 ch g Medicean Londonnetdotcom (IRE) (Night Shift (USA))
833[8] 1196[6] 1637[8] 2027[18] 2391[2] 3273[18] 4152[10] 4625[18] 5146[2] 5926[4] 6364[3] 6547[5] 7354[8] *7868[7]*

Emenem *Simon Dow* a75 63
2 b c Sir Percy Kahalah (IRE) (Darshaan)
4775[5] *5764[2]* 6264[4] *8153[2] (8244) 8466[11] (8525)*

Emerald (ITY) *Marco Botti* a94 93
4 b g High Chaparral(IRE) Ekta (Danehill Dancer (IRE))
1195[8] *1480[2]* 1861[9] 2216[5] *3304[9]* 4026[3] 4650[3] 6261[4] 7287[7] 7535[14]

Emerald Asset (IRE) *Paul Midgley* a54 62
3 b g Frozen Power(IRE) Balance The Books (Elmaamul (USA))
1126[10] 1839[2] 2503[6] 3017[6] 3368[3] 3978[4] 4192[4] *5070[4] 5369[4] 6105[5]* 6436[11]

Emerald Bay *Ronald Thompson* a59 60
3 b f Kyllachy Bahia Emerald (IRE) (Bahamian Bounty)
3[9] 2302[4] *2919[12]* 3009[10] *5126[7]* 5378[6] 5920[2] 7596[10] *8137[12] 8408[11]*

Emerald Loch *Ralph Beckett* a55 83
3 ch f Danehill Dancer(IRE) Loch Verdi (Green Desert (USA))
1312[2] 2207[9] *2578[10]* (3218) 3512[2] (4034) 4984[3] 6946[9] 7590[7]

Emerald Petrina (IRE) *Heather Main* a27 61
4 b m Byron Ohshauna (IRE) (Statue Of Liberty (USA))
1179[9] 1529[10]

Emerald Secret (IRE) *Paul Midgley* 65
2 b f Arcano(IRE) Limit (IRE) (Barathea (IRE))
2235[6] ◆ 3112[5] 4110[5] 5433[5] 6162[10] 6807[3]

Emergent *D K Weld* 89
3 b f Oasis Dream Trojan Queen (USA) (Empire Maker (USA))
1507a[3] 2068a[3] 4218a[8] 4812a[6]

Emilie Bronte *Chris Fairhurst* a42 42
3 b f Mullionmileanhour(IRE) Yorke's Folly (USA) (Stravinsky (USA))
2302[8] 2740[9] 3009[11] *5370[7]* 6452[6] *7327[6]*

Emilio Largo *Mark Pitman* a52 64
8 b g Cadeaux Genereux Gloved Hand (Royal Applause)
234[10]

Emily Goldfinch *Phil McEntee* a60 59
3 ch f Prime Defender Lakelands Lady (IRE) (Woodborough (USA))
496[3] 791[4] 1183[7] 2586[5] 3038[9] *8457[3]*

Eminent (IRE) *Martyn Meade* 84
2 b c Frankel You'll Be Mine (USA) (Kingmambo (USA))
(6704) ◆

Emirates Airline *Saeed bin Suroor* a58 49
4 b g Dubawi(IRE) Moonlife (IRE) (Invincible Spirit (IRE))
1978[11] 3055[11]

Emirates Flight *Saeed bin Suroor* a67
2 ch f New Approach(IRE) Flying Cloud (IRE) (Storming Home)
8034[3]

Emirates Flyer *Saeed bin Suroor* a104 100
5 b g Acclamation Galapagar (USA) (Miswaki (USA))
94a[2]

Emirates Skycargo (IRE) *Charlie Appleby* a99 106
4 b g Iffraaj Catchline (USA) (Bertolini (USA))
189a[9] *374a[7]*

Emjayem *Ed McMahon* a69 83
6 ch g Needwood Blade Distant Stars (IRE) (Distant Music (USA))
1601[10] *1964[7]* 2931[2] 3995[7] *7112[11] 7660[11] 8495[6]*

Emmaus (IRE) *Roger Varian* 92
2 b c Invincible Spirit(IRE) Prima Luce (IRE) (Galileo (IRE))
(6632) 7491a[4]

Emmie (IRE) *Harry Dunlop* 81
2 b f High Chaparral(IRE) Precious Dream (USA) (Mr Greeley (USA))
(3556) 5703a[9] 7547[8]

Emotionless (IRE) *Charlie Appleby* a98 101
3 b c Shamardal(USA) Unbridled Elaine (USA) (Unbridled's Song (USA))
3245[5] 4822[7]

Emperor Bob (IRE) *Patrick J McKenna* a76 71
4 b g Big Bad Bob(IRE) Simonda (Singspiel (IRE))
(6464a) 7801a[8]

Emperor Napoleon *Andrew Balding* a64 93
3 b g Champs Elysees Amarullah (FR) (Daylami (IRE))
1140[4] 1739[3] 2209[2] 2471[3] (3768) 4863[5] 5653[6]

Emperors Warrior (IRE) *Gary Moore* a64 55
4 ch g Thewayyouare(USA) World Sprint (GER) (Waky Nao)
167[10] 442[5] 608[6] 1544[8]

Empire Of The Star (FR) *A Wohler* 92
2 b c Siyouni(FR) Etoile Nocturne (FR) (Medicean)
7399a[6]

Empoli (GER) *P Schiergen* 100
6 ch h Halling(USA) Estefania (GER) (Acatenango (GER))
4031a[6]

Empress Ali (IRE) *Tom Tate* 94
5 b m Holy Roman Emperor(IRE) Almansa (IRE) (Dr Devious (IRE))
1786[3] 2157[9] 3113[4] 3593[5] 6115[3] (7408)

Enable *John Gosden* a83
2 b f Nathaniel(IRE) Concentric (Sadler's Wells (USA))
(8130) ◆

Encantar *Ann Duffield* a72 72
3 b f Equiano(FR) Enrapture (USA) (Lear Fan (USA))
2534[4] 3439[6] 5582[8] 6476[3] 6790[2] ◆ *7325[7] 7663[10] 8010[7]*

Encapsulated *Roger Ingram* a67 52
6 b g Zamindar(USA) Star Cluster (Observatory (USA))
159[4] 398[3] 658[5] 873[9] 1928[7] *5194[2] 5475[2] 6051[6] 6509[5] 7654[5] 8026[9] 8181[6] 8555[3]*

Enchanted Dawn (USA) *David Wachman* 56
3 b f War Front(USA) Good Vibes (USA) (Unbridled's Song (USA))
1014a[10]

Enchanted Moment *Chris Wall* a62 61
4 b m Lawman(FR) Gentle Thoughts (Darshaan)
2564[7] 3903[5] *5303[9] 6593[8] 7256[2] 7754[3] 8125[8]*

Encipher (USA) *A R Al Rayhi* a98 101
7 b h Elusive Quality(USA) Secret Charm (IRE) (Green Desert (USA))
95a[6] *374a[3] 717a[5]*

Encore D'Or *Robert Cowell* a108 83
4 b g Oasis Dream Entente Cordiale (IRE) (Ela-Mana-Mou)
(1650) (2003) ◆ 2438[8] *3277[3] 3606[9] (8050) 8232[4]*

Encore L'Amour *Ralph Beckett* 98
4 b m Azamour(IRE) Centime (Royal Applause)
1219[4] 1855[12]

Encore Moi *Marco Botti* a73 62
3 b f Exceed And Excel(AUS) Di Moi Oui (Warning)
2312[8] 3059[11] 3684[4] *4718[2] 5720[3] 6592[3] (7203) (7725)* ◆ *7985[3] 8158[7] 8357[3]*

Endeavour (IRE) *Richard Hannon* a48 73
2 b g Acclamation Miss Hawai (FR) (Peintre Celebre (USA))
5484[3] ◆ 6183[3] *7649[8] 8159[9]*

Endio (FR) *T Castanheira* a27 61
6 b m Enrique Dionissima (FR) (Baillamont (USA))
1157a[5]

Endive *Robert Stephens* a64 67
4 b m Champs Elysees Plum Fairy (Sadler's Wells (USA))
2463[7] 2994[5] 4979[7] 7270[2] *7739[3] 7955[3]*

Endless Acres (IRE) *Charlie Fellowes* a80 86
3 b g Champs Elysees Eternity Ring (Alzao (USA))
3235[2] ◆ 3845[4] ◆ *4265[2]* 7215[3] ◆

Endless Charm *Charlie Appleby* a75
2 ch f Dubawi(IRE) Whazzis (Desert Prince (IRE))
(8151)

Endless Credit (IRE) *Micky Hammond* 84
6 b g High Chaparral(IRE) Pay The Bank (High Top)
2163[16] 2406[8] 2911[3] 3263[2]

Endless Drama (IRE) *G M Lyons* 118
4 b h Lope De Vega(IRE) Desert Drama (IRE) (Green Desert (USA))
2243[3] ◆ 3242[9] 5685a[5]

Endless Gold *Charlie Appleby* a52 69
2 b c Dubawi(IRE) Love Charm (Singspiel (IRE))
5121[3] *5764[8]*

Endless Seas *Pat Phelan* a39 36
5 ch m Refuse To Bend(IRE) Ocean Ballad (Bering)
252[11]

Endless Summer (ITY) *M Guarnieri* a94 98
3 ch f Pounced(USA) Arafura (IRE) (Barathea (IRE))
1685a[4] 6357a[2] *8148a[2]*

Endless Time (IRE) *Charlie Appleby* a76 112
4 b m Sea The Stars(IRE) Mamonta (Fantastic Light (USA))
(3888) 5586[9] 6393a[2] 7569a[2]

Endorser *Emmet Michael Butterly* a19
8 ch g Le Vie Dei Colori Cinciallegra (Royal Applause)
674[11]

Enduring Power (IRE) *Brendan Powell* a73 24
3 b g Approve(IRE) Our Dear Ruth (USA) (Baldski (USA))
4480[8] *(4939) 5765[10]*

Endzinano *Simon Hodgson*
3 ch f Compton Place Oriental Girl (Dr Fong (USA))
2999[14]

Energia Colonial (BRZ) *Niels Petersen* a93 73
8 b g Giant Gentleman(USA) Karla Dora (BRZ) (Nugget Point (IRE))
284a[6] 624a[9] 1957a[9]

Energia Davos (BRZ) *Jane Chapple-Hyam* a110 113
7 rg g Torrential(USA) Star Brisingamen (USA) (Maria's Mon (USA))
(7700) *7934[8] 8165a[11]*

Energia Flavio (BRZ) *Ian Williams* a79 78
5 gr g Agnes Gold(JPN) Lira Da Guanabara (BRZ) (Pitu Da Guanabara (BRZ))
920[11] 1245[9] 1978[5] 2256[5] 2677[6] 3364[4] 3717[5] 4348[4] 4704[8] 6644[3] *8206[3]* ◆

Energia Fox (BRZ) *Richard Fahey* a87 85
5 ch m Agnes Gold(JPN) Super Eletric (BRZ) (Choctaw Ridge (USA))
4095[4] 4920[5] 6775[4] 7359[9] *7765[4] 8123[6] 8249[10]*

Energie Green (IRE) *F Head* a84 80
3 b f Invincible Spirit(IRE) Extreme Green (Motivator)
5946a[4] 6912a[11]

Enery (IRE) *M Al Mheiri* a84 83
7 b h Teofilo(IRE) Annee Lumiere (IRE) (Giant's Causeway (USA))
279a[4] 718a[4]

Enfin Seuls (FR) *Yves de Nicolay* a75 64
5 ch m Gold Away(IRE) Sister Trouble (FR) (Spectrum (IRE))
5281a[10] 6938a[6]

Enfolding (IRE) *James Fanshawe* a66 61
2 b g Fastnet Rock(AUS) Althea Rose (IRE) (Green Desert (USA))
4805[4] *8066[3]* ◆ *8557[2]*

Engage (IRE) *Sir Michael Stoute* a60 95
3 b f Pour Moi(IRE) Brooklyn's Storm (USA) (Storm Cat (USA))
1786[2] 2687[4] 4351[2] 5381[4] 5927[4] 6667[3] *7365[9]*

Engaging Smile *J Moon* a46 60
4 b m Exceed And Excel(AUS) Bronze Star (Mark Of Esteem (IRE))
1518a[7] 2284a[10] 2954a[6] 3381a[4] 3917a[6] 5458a[7] 6668[5] *7738[10]*

Engai (GER) *David Bridgwater* a59 66
10 b g Noroit(GER) Enigma (GER) (Sharp Victor (USA))
222[7] 505[6] 701[2] (1165) 2899[2] 3901[4] 4234[9]

English Deer (IRE) *A R Al Rayhi*
6 b g Shamardal(USA) Ya Hajar (Lycius (USA))
8578a[10]

English Hero *John Mackie* a69 77
3 b g Royal Applause Merton Matriarch (Cadeaux Genereux)
1809[8] 2650[7] 3415[8] 3466[2] 4344[4] 7360[12] 7506[7] 7743[5] *7959[7]*

Englishman *Milton Bradley* 96
6 b g Royal Applause Tesary (Danehill (USA))
1218[7] (1530) (1887) 2206[9] 2434[5] 2898[5] 6119[8] 6539[24] 6780[4] 7186[14]

English Summer *Ian Williams* a35 89
9 b g Montjeu(IRE) Hunt The Sun (Rainbow Quest (USA))
1972[4] 2744[11] 3162[6] 3670[3] 4095[5] 5157[3] 5837[7] 6209[7] 6804[9] 7357[4] 7594[14] *8477[14]*

Englishwoman *David Evans* a78 77
3 b f Acclamation Tesary (Danehill (USA))
105[5] 365[2] (510) (578) (635) 726[6] 924[12] 4155[3] 4585[9] 4910[8] 6255[8] 6831[9] *8358[4]*

Enhancement (IRE) *Richard Hannon* a68 61
2 b c Invincible Spirit(IRE) Gazebo (Cadeaux Genereux)
7468[10] ◆ *7906[5] 8118[4]*

Enigmatic (IRE) *Jamie Osborne* a57
2 b c Elnadim(USA) Meanwhile (IRE) (Haafhd)
3301[4]

Enjoy Life (IRE) *Kevin Ryan* a82 82
3 b f Acclamation Jeu De Plume (IRE) (Montjeu (IRE))
1562[6] 2304[5] 3267[3] 3879[2] 4378[4] 4770[8] (5714) 6215[3] *6851[5]* (7334) (7743) ◆ *7798[2] 8158[10]*

Enjoy The Silence (FR) *C Boutin* a76 79
3 b c Elusive City(USA) Cerita (IRE) (Wolfhound (USA))
2948a[2]

Enjoy Vijay (GER) *P Schiergen* 96
2 b c Nathaniel(IRE) Enjoy The Life (Medicean)
7399a[9] 7842a[3]

Enki Girl (FR) *P Leblanc* a73 73
3 b f Youmzain(IRE) Holly Girl (IRE) (Testa Rossa (AUS))
1542a[5]

Enlace *Mark Johnston* a87 101
4 b m Shamardal(USA) Crossover (Cape Cross (IRE))
2247[14] 2391[14] *3566[10]* 4109[9]

Enlighten Me (IRE) *Philip Kirby* a42 42
2 b f Sir Prancealot(IRE) Tea Chest (IRE) (In The Wings)
7090[7] 7356[5] *7599[5] 7854[7] 8344[11]*

Enmeshing *James Fanshawe* a76 66
3 ch g Mastercraftsman(IRE) Yacht Club (USA) (Sea Hero (USA))
4056[7] 4840[6] *6104[2]* ◆ *6702[4] 7141[12] 7911[5]*

Ennaadd *Roger Varian* a117 75
3 b c King's Best(USA) Zayn Zen (Singspiel (IRE))
(705) ◆ *(1208)* ◆ *(7978)*

Ennistown *David Pipe* 70
6 b g Authorized(IRE) Saoirse Abu (USA) (Mr Greeley (USA))
7150[22]

Ennobled Friend (USA) *A bin Harmash* a102 82
6 b g Malibu Moon(USA) Seek To Soar (USA) (Seeking The Gold (USA))
309a[3] 372a[12] 628a[14]

Enough Is Enough (IRE) *P Meany* a39 73
9 br m Pyrus(USA) Kind Enough (IRE) (Desert King (IRE))
6984a[12]

Enriching (USA) *Robyn Brisland* a73 76
8 ch g Lemon Drop Kid(USA) Popozinha (USA) (Rahy (USA))
212[3] 438[5] 491[6] 708[5]

En Souplesse (FR) *E Lellouche* 85
3 b f Air Chief Marshal(IRE) Saroushka (FR) (Westerner)
(1542a)

Entertaining Ben *William Muir* a74 77
3 b g Equiano(FR) Fatal Attraction (Oasis Dream)
1753[7] 2288[7] (3000) *3471[4]* 4224[9] 4502[7] 6018[2] *6425[8]* 6879[12]

Enter The Red (IRE) *Aidan Anthony Howard* a51 73
7 b g Red Clubs(IRE) Inter Madera (IRE) (Toca Madera (IRE))
7474a[4]

Entifaadha *M Al Mheiri* a65 74
7 b g Dansili Model Queen (USA) (Kingmambo (USA))
407a[6]

Entrechat (USA) *Neil Drysdale* 87
4 bb m Giant's Causeway(USA) Ballet Pacifica (USA) (Minardi (USA))
7829a[10]

Entrench *Amanda Perrett* a65 73
3 b f Oasis Dream Silent Entrance (Beat Hollow)
2877[4] 3350[5] 5504[3] 6021[9]

Entsar (IRE) *William Haggas* a88 98
3 b f Fastnet Rock(AUS) Starfish (IRE) (Galileo (IRE))
3059[4] 3601[3] 4978[2] (6661) (7504) ◆ 7823[6]

Envisaging (IRE) *James Fanshawe* a70 67
2 b c Zoffany(IRE) Star Of Stars (IRE) (Soviet Star (USA))
4775[4] ◆ 5828[3] 8089[3]

Envoy *James Eustace* 67
2 gr g Delegator La Gessa (Largesse)
7226[7] 7622[5]

Enzani (IRE) *John C McConnell* a79 72
5 b g Cape Cross(IRE) Eytarna (IRE) (Dubai Destination (USA))
4721a[20]

Eolian *William Knight* 63
2 b g Poet's Voice Charlecote (IRE) (Caerleon (USA))
3529[5] ◆ 3971[7] 4659[9] 5594[7] 6377[3] 7286[4]

Eos Quercus (IRE) *N Leenders* a87 101
4 ch g Arcano(IRE) Khaizarana (Alhaarth (IRE))
7946a[4] 8336a[13]

Epeius (IRE) *Ben Haslam* a68 66
3 b g Arakan(USA) Gilda Lilly (USA) (War Chant (USA))
2864[7] 5732[9] 6569[4] 7111[6] 7663[3] 8012[2] 8346[3]

Epicurious (IRE) *Brian Meehan* 35
2 ch g Makfi Indolente (IRE) (Diesis)
6108[12]

Epicuris *Mme C Head-Maarek* 108
4 b g Rail Link Argumentative (Observatory (USA))
1910a[11]

Eponina (IRE) *Ben Haslam* a65
2 b f Zoffany(IRE) Dame Rochelle (IRE) (Danehill Dancer (IRE))
7659[6] 8009[3]

Epsom Day (IRE) *Laura Mongan* a76 47
3 b g Teofilo(IRE) Dubai Flower (Manduro (GER))
(96) 729[6] 1532[4] 2580[6] 3306[7] 8367[7]

Epsom Flyer *Pat Phelan* a49 51
6 ch g Haafhd River Cara (USA) (Irish River (FR))
233[6] 417[2] 695[8]

Epsom Icon *Mick Channon* 104
3 b f Sixties Icon Hairspray (Bahamian Bounty)
1396[7] 1888[11] 2245[5] (2893) 4435a[4] 5645[8] 5939a[2] 6666[4] 6949[8]

Epsom Secret *Pat Phelan* a47 50
2 ch f Sakhee's Secret My Amalie (IRE) (Galileo (IRE))
4128[9] 4524[3] 4938[6] 5719[5]

Eqleem *Mark Johnston* 96
3 b g Acclamation Blessing (Dubai Millennium)
2161[7] 3026[5] 3884[6]

Eqtiraan (IRE) *Richard Hannon* 99
2 b g Helmet(AUS) Miranda Frost (IRE) (Cape Cross (IRE))
(4580) 5646[3] 6882[2]

Equally Fast *Peter Hiatt* a89 86
4 b g Equiano(FR) Fabulously Fast (USA) (Deputy Minister (CAN))
(1175) ◆ 1427[5] (1836) 2504[7] 3056[4] 3956[6] 5285[5] 5669[3] 6080[15] 8314[11]

Equal Point *William Knight* a61 66
3 b g Equiano(FR) Point Perfect (Dansili)
2541[6] 3104[6] 3648[9] 3744[6] 4796[5] 5827[9] 6587[4] (6853)

Equal Rights *Eve Johnson Houghton* 59
2 b c Equiano(FR) Australia Fair (Pivotal)
4053[7] 5202[11] 6264[8]

Equiano Springs *Tom Tate* 44
2 b g Equiano(FR) Spring Clean (FR) (Danehill (USA))
5884[11] 6447[6]

Equijade *Robert Stephens* a68 63
3 b f Equiano(FR) Royal Jade (Last Tycoon)
(562) ◆ 726[3] ◆ 6669[6] 7534[3] 8040[4]

Equilicious *Ollie Pears* a50 41
4 b m Equiano(FR) Fabine (Danehill Dancer (IRE))
54[5] 340[6] 525[3] 867[6]

Equimou *Robert Eddery* a83 97
2 ch f Equiano(FR) Culture Queen (King's Best (USA))
3718[5] (4195) 4669[2] 5359[2] 6230[3] 6282[6]

Equinette (IRE) *Amanda Perrett* a73 47
3 b f Equiano(FR) Rougette (Red Ransom (USA))
3036[11] 7207[2] 7603[7] 7935[3] 8358[10]

Equinoxe (FR) *P-J Fertillet* a65 73
3 b g Equiano(FR) Porza (FR) (Septieme Ciel (USA))
7492a[13]

Equipe *Richard Whitaker* 40
2 b f Equiano(FR) Charlevoix (IRE) (King Charlemagne (USA))
5414[11] 6477[12] 6873[8] 7331[8]

Equistar *Jonathan Portman* a76 85
3 ch g Equiano(FR) Halfwaytoparadise (Observatory (USA))
1385[7] 2186[5] 2981[10] 3559[3] 4224[5] (4521) 6190[2] (6831) 7221[2]

Equity *David Brown* a58 63
2 ch g Equiano(FR) Trinny (Rainbow Quest (USA))
2535[6] ◆ 3208[8] 4663[5] 5265[4] 5806[5] 6092[2] 7041[8]

Equleus *Jeremy Gask* a72 66
4 b g Equiano(FR) Merle (Selkirk (USA))
64[2] 2441[10]

Ercolano (FR) *F-X De Chevigny* a61 71
4 b g Artiste Royal(IRE) Chandi Dasa (IRE) (Sadler's Wells (USA))
3733a[5]

Erhaaf (USA) *Charlie Fellowes* a91 85
4 b g Street Sense(USA) Saraama (USA) (Bahri (USA))
(968) 4838[4] 7779[3] 8210[7]

Eric (GER) *C Von Der Recke* 106
5 ch h Tertullian(USA) Ericarrow (IRE) (Bollin Eric)
2075a[5] 2723a[6] 3934a[5] 5502a[6]

Erica Bing *Jo Hughes* a29 93
2 b f Captain Gerrard(IRE) Monica Geller (Komaite (USA))
1719[6] (2147) 2637[8] (3006a) (3763a) 4902a[5] 5450a[5] 6555[8] 7655a[6]

Erik The Red (FR) *Kevin Ryan* 103
4 b g Kendargent(FR) Norwegian Princess (IRE) (Fairy King (USA))
1629[2] 2157[3] 2527[2] 4070a[4] 4731[9] 5651[3] 6786[7] 7824[2]

Erinyes (IRE) *Archie Watson* a65
2 gr f Dalakhani(IRE) Endearing (Selkirk (USA))
7050[6]

Erissimus Maximus (FR) *Chris Dwyer* a76 75
2 b c Holy Roman Emperor(IRE) Tegan (IRE) (Cape Cross (IRE))
4473[9] 5188[5] 5395[4] (5931) 6525[5] 7440[3] 7893[3] 8136[3] 8453[3] ◆

Ermontois (FR) *L Viel* 57
2 b c Air Chief Marshal(IRE) Merka (FR) (Jimble (FR))
3871a[10]

Ernststavroblofeld (USA) *Martyn Meade* 83
2 ch c Elusive Quality(USA) Minute Limit (IRE) (Pivotal)
(5084) 7155[10]

Ershaad (IRE) *Shaun Harris* a54 49
4 b g Acclamation Emerald Peace (IRE) (Green Desert (USA))
1326[6] 1625[12] 1926[11] 2491[15] 3069[8] 5126[4] 6249[6] 7144[11] 7509[4] 7896[6] 8120[3] 8146[4] 8470[4]

Ertidaad (IRE) *Emma Owen* a57 55
4 b g Kodiac Little Scotland (Acclamation)
47[2] 272[3] 356[3] 430[3] 3522[9] 4009[13] 7645[5] 7986[3] 8121[5] 8470[5]

Ertijaal (AUS) *M F De Kock* a58 114
4 ch h Hard Spun(USA) Alharir (AUS) (Jeune)
372a[2] 627a[12] 845a[3] 1106a[4] 1690a[9]

Ertijaal (IRE) *A R Al Rayhi* a105 121
5 b g Oasis Dream Shabiba (USA) (Seeking The Gold (USA))
(91a) (450a) ◆ 1104a[2]

Erupt (IRE) *F-H Graffard* 119
4 b h Dubawi(IRE) Mare Nostrum (Caerleon (USA))
2568a[9] 3936a[2] ◆ 4626[5] 5947a[3] (7405a) 8129a[14]

Ervedya (FR) *J-C Rouget* 118
4 b m Siyouni(FR) Elva (IRE) (King's Best (USA))
1910a[2] 3242[5] 5449a[3] 6949[3]

Erysimum (IRE) *W McCreery* a88 93
3 br f Arcano(IRE) Mathool (IRE) (Alhaarth (IRE))
2719a[4] (5564a) 6983a[6] 7676a[11]

Escalating *Michael Appleby* a83 89
4 ch g Three Valleys(USA) Pure Joy (Zamindar (USA))
2253[4] 2787[3] 3168[3] ◆ (3580) 3800[4] 4954[6] 5857[6] 6539[15] 7094[13] 7593[13] 7892[5] ◆

Escapade *Les Eyre*
3 b f Monsieur Bond(IRE) Heart Of Svetlana (IRE) (Linamix (FR))
5388[11]

Escape Clause (IRE) *Mrs John Harrington* 82
2 b g Lawman(FR) Discophilia (Teofilo (IRE))
6817a[6]

Escobar (IRE) *Hugo Palmer* 104
2 b c Famous Name Saying Grace (IRE) (Brief Truce (USA))
(4349) ◆ (5401) 6707[7]

Esculape D'Emra (FR) *C Plisson* 9
2 ch c Sinndar(IRE) Talka (FR) (Vettori (IRE))
1021a[10]

Eshtiaal (USA) *Gordon Elliott* a92 97
6 b g Dynaformer(USA) Enfiraaj (USA) (Kingmambo (USA))
3246[19] 5559[6] 7195a[17]

Eskandari (IRE) *Simon Crisford* a83
3 b c Kodiac Alexander Icequeen (IRE) (Soviet Star (USA))
145[2] ◆ 4477[5]

Eskimo Bay (IRE) *Clive Cox* 72
2 b c Kodiac Magilini (IRE) (Bertolini (USA))
6071[6] 6295[5]

Eskimo Point (IRE) *Mario Hofer* a70 94
4 ch g Lope De Vega(IRE) Diamond Star (IRE) (Daylami (IRE))
6990a[17]

Esloobaha (IRE) *Charles Hills* 60
2 ch f Intikhab(USA) Esloob (USA) (Diesis)
5593[6] 6250[5] 7297[6]

Esoterique (IRE) *A Fabre* 120
6 b m Danehill Dancer(IRE) Dievotchka (Dancing Brave (USA))
2927a[2] 3242[13] 4926a[4] 5449a[6]

Espoir *David Evans* a55 52
3 b f Cockney Rebel(IRE) Quiquillo (USA) (Cape Canaveral (USA))
104[4] 443[8] 1325[2] 1734[4] 2325[9] 3146[5] 3975[3] 4504[7]

Espresso Freddo (IRE) *Sir Mark Prescott Bt* a76 77
2 b c Fast Company(IRE) Spring Bouquet (IRE) (King's Best (USA))
2319[5] 2747[2] 3254[6] 8009[2] ◆ 8189[2]

Esprit De Corps *Roger Charlton* a73
2 b g Sepoy(AUS) Corps De Ballet (IRE) (Fasliyev (USA))
7065[6] 7976[2]

Esprit De Tauber (IRE) *Don Cantillon* 74
3 b f Zoffany(IRE) Trois Graces (USA) (Alysheba (USA))
(4027) ◆

Essaka (IRE) *Tony Carroll* a60 65
4 b g Equiano(FR) Dream Vision (USA) (Distant View (USA))
1648[9] 2380[11] 2964[7] 3486[3] 3735[2] 4202[2] 5007[2] 5827[8] 6363[5] (7038) 7912[10]

Essenaitch (IRE) *David Evans* a69 79
3 b g Zoffany(IRE) Karlisse (IRE) (Celtic Swing)
1080[11] 1610[10] 1992[17] 2479[5] 3600[3] 4080[7] 5206[3] ◆ 5892[6] 6576[6] 7189[5] 7743[12] 8190[6] 8343[7]

Esspeegee *Alan Bailey* a52 35
3 b g Paco Boy(IRE) Goldrenched (IRE) (Montjeu (IRE))
675[6] 1155[8] 1698[8] 5630[4] 6103[2]

Esteaming *David Barron* a50 61
6 b g Sir Percy Night Over Day (Most Welcome)
6559[13] 7077[13]

Esteemable *James Fanshawe* a80 92
4 ch m Nayef(USA) Ring Of Esteem (Mark Of Esteem (IRE))
(710) (977) 1624[4] 2154[2] (2636) (3438) 3979[4]

Estibdaad (IRE) *Paddy Butler* a74 60
6 b g Haatef(USA) Star Of Siligo (USA) (Saratoga Six (USA))
88[4] 875[2] 2872[13] 3492[8] 4013[9] 5471[6] 5805[4] 6241[5] 6662[4] 7613[2] 7870[6] 8257[4] 8462[9]

Estidhkaar (IRE) *Richard Hannon* 111
4 b h Dark Angel(IRE) Danetime Out (IRE) (Danetime (IRE))
7213[2] (7701)

Estidraak (IRE) *Sir Michael Stoute* a91 93
3 ch g Iffraaj Gold Hush (USA) (Seeking The Gold (USA))
4065[10] 4867[6]

Estikmaal (IRE) *F Head* a92 99
3 b g Oasis Dream Rosie's Posy (IRE) (Suave Dancer (USA))
1580a[7]

Estrella Eria (FR) *George Peckham* a68 42
3 gr f Mastercraftsman(IRE) Madrid Beauty (FR) (Sendawar (IRE))
5979[4] (6514) (7103) (7609)

Etaad (USA) *Gary Moore* a72 14
5 b g Intidab(USA) Red's Lucky Lady (USA) (Lucky Lionel (USA))
(190) 482[6] 1416[2] 2401[10] 3354[11] 7899[9] 8163[10]

Etched (IRE) *A P O'Brien* 81
3 b f Dansili Gagnoa (IRE) (Sadler's Wells (USA))
5313a[11]

Eternal *Declan Carroll* 95
4 ch h New Approach(IRE) Sharp Mode (USA) (Diesis)
2744[12]

Eternal Army (FR) *H-A Pantall* a92 89
3 ch c American Post Earth Affair (GER) (Acatenango (GER))
2948a[5]

Eternal Dream *William Knight* 47
2 ch g Dream Ahead(USA) Get Happy (IRE) (Zamindar (USA))
3463[6]

Eternalist *Jim Goldie* a61 59
3 ch f Equiano(FR) Eternal Instinct (Exceed And Excel (AUS))
5388[5] 6744[3] 7362[3] 7793[2] 8290[5]

Eternally *John Gosden* a75 107
3 b f Dutch Art Ardent (Pivotal)
(2795) 3519[3] 4105[2] ◆ (5396) ◆ (6939) ◆

Eternitys Gate *Ivan Furtado* a82 79
5 b g Dutch Art Regency Rose (Danehill (USA))
1447[7] 2238[11] 2531[9] (2975) 4452[4] 5032[11] 5439[8] 5679[6] 6425[2] 6699[10] 7386[2] 7660[9]

Eternity Star (IRE) *Giuseppe Cannarella* 93
3 b f Baltic King Bacchanalia (IRE) (Blues Traveller (IRE))
1685a[3]

Etienne Gerard *Nigel Tinkler* a71 80
4 b g Captain Gerrard(IRE) Alucica (Celtic Swing)
1596[10] 2217[9] 3070[4] (3953) 4763[3] 5060[7] 5320[2] (5797) 6072[7] 6579[8] 7324[7]

Etijaah (USA) *Doug Watson* a98 86
6 b g Daaher(CAN) Hasheema (IRE) (Darshaan)
279a[2] 718a[3]

Etikaal *Simon Crisford* a77 68
2 ch g Sepoy(AUS) Hezmah (Oasis Dream)
6086[3] 6673[2] 7157[6]

Etoile Bere (FR) *N Clement* a63 73
2 b f Hurricane Cat(USA) L'Ete (CHI) (Hussonet (USA))
7291a[3] 7996a[3] 8420a[7]

Etonnez Moi (IRE) *Mme Pia Brandt* a70 99
3 b f High Chaparral(IRE) Hot Fudge (SWE) (Lomitas)
6497a[8] 7029a[5]

Eton Rambler (USA) *George Baker* a93 92
6 bb g Hard Spun(USA) Brightbraveandgood (USA) (Smart Strike (CAN))
1417[3] ◆ 1893[3] 2468[10] 3657[16] 4752[13] 5963[3]

Etta (FR) *M Boutin* a65 57
2 bb f Hurricane Cat(USA) Centralienne (USA) (Dixie Union (USA))
4965a[3]

Ettie Hart (IRE) *Mick Channon* a42 58
3 b f Bushranger(IRE) Miss Megs (IRE) (Croco Rouge (IRE))
1562[5] 1806[6] 2293[5] (2969) 3146[2] 3725[7] 3975[4] 4289[3] 4600[5] 4992[5] 5338[7] 6105[10] 7298[9]

Ettihadi (IRE) *Hugo Palmer* 76
2 b c Rip Van Winkle(IRE) Bright And Clear (Danehill (USA))
5166[4] 5740[5] 6663[8] 7768[3] ◆

Et Toi Et Moi (FR) *J-C Rouget* a82
3 b f Footstepsinthesand En Vitesse (Peintre Celebre (USA))
1240a[7]

Ettu *Jeremy Noseda* a75 75
2 b f Excelebration(IRE) Tragic Moment (USA) (Pivotal)
7055[7] 7696[2] 8362[2]

Euchen Glen *Jim Goldie* 89
3 b g Authorized(IRE) Jabbara (IRE) (Kingmambo (USA))
1883[5] 2197[5] (2859) (3347) 4108[12] 6110[6]

Eugenic *Rod Millman* a56 57
5 br g Piccolo Craic Sa Ceili (IRE) (Danehill Dancer (IRE))
2323[7] (2814) 3560[4] 4950[7] (6020) 6411[3] 6827[4] 7426[3]

Eugenie Feather (USA) *Marco Botti* a52
2 b f Brilliant Speed(USA) Ascension (IRE) (Night Shift (USA))
8082[10] 8355[9] 8591[10]

Euginio (IRE) *Richard Hannon* a89 94
2 b c Fastnet Rock(AUS) Starstone (Diktat)
(3730) 5450a[4] 6868[2] 7151[7]

Eula Varner *Henry Candy* 63
2 b f Showcasing Tremelo Pointe (IRE) (Trempolino (USA))
5869[6] 6881[3] ◆

Eurato (FR) *Steve Gollings* a70 70
6 ch g Medicean Double Green (IRE) (Green Tune (USA))
(796) (1182) 1955[2] (2792) 3302[4]

Euro Charline *Marco Botti* a99 116
5 b m Myboycharlie(IRE) Eurolink Artemis (Common Grounds)
809a[2] 1106a[2] 2243[2]

Euro Mac *Neville Bycroft* a46 58
4 ch m Sir Percy Oomph (Shareef Dancer (USA))
2303[7] 2773[13] 3850[10] 5178[4] 5979[2] 6643[5] 7323[12] 7602[5]

Euro Nightmare (IRE) *Keith Dalgleish* 79
2 b f Kodiac Kilakey (IRE) (Key Of Luck (USA))
5834[2] (6223) ◆ 6554[2] 7409[6]

Euroquip Boy (IRE) *Michael Scudamore* a55 68
9 b g Antonius Pius(USA) La Shalak (IRE) (Shalford (IRE))
2542[14] 3743[13] 4290[5]

Eurystheus (IRE) *Michael Appleby* a82 86
7 b g Acclamation Dust Flicker (Suave Dancer (USA))
2043[5] 2556[3] 2832[5] 3166[2] (4138) 4808[6] 5886[9] 6516[6] 6876[6] 7159[8] 7671[5] 8077[2] 8249[6]

Eutropius (IRE) *Alan Swinbank* a86 82
7 b g Ad Valorem(USA) Peps (IRE) (Val Royal (FR))
23[6] 337[8] 427[2] 866[2] 1122[10] 1817[5] 2256[7] 2620[7] 3166[7] 3517[5] 4455[2] 4687[6] 5579[6] 6160[18] 6854[8]

Euxton *Lawrence Mullaney* a58 69
4 ch m Equiano(FR) Mystic Love (Pivotal)
2053[7] 4229[3] 4647[DSQ] 5069[6] (6506)

Evacusafe Lady *John Ryan* a71 58
5 ch m Avonbridge Snow Shoes (Sri Pekan (USA))
463[7] 701[7] 815[6] 1058[7] 1131[5] 1202[3] 1578[11] 1762[5]

Eva Gore *David O'Meara* a61 65
2 b f Paco Boy(IRE) Inagh River (Fasliyev (USA))
2404[6] 2970[2] 3282[5] (4000) 4526[U] 4915[8] 5128[2] (5177)

Evalya Senora (FR) *Y Barberot* 77
2 b f Youmzain(IRE) Nina Senora (FR) (My Risk (FR))
5005a[4] 5986a[5]

Evanescent (IRE) *Tony Carroll* a64 79
7 b g Elusive City(USA) Itsanothergirl (Reprimand)
(1251) (1818) 2460[7] 2754[14] 3414[7] 3638[11] 3892[9] 6879[10] (7301) 7415[5] 8206[8] 8473[9]

Evangelical *Richard Fahey* 78
3 b f Dutch Art Pious (Bishop Of Cashel)
(1761) ◆ 3218[4] 3847[7] 4689[9]

Evasion Absolue (FR) *E Lellouche* a62 67
2 gr f Rajsaman(FR) Aglaia (IRE) (Invincible Spirit (IRE))
6639a[3]

Evenchop (FR) *K Borgel* 82
3 ch g Deportivo Ember Eve (Tiger Hill (IRE))
6310a[2]

Evening Attire *William Stone* a86 78
5 b g Pastoral Pursuits Markova's Dance (Mark Of Esteem (IRE))
1634[9] 3144[6] 5169[7] 6269[6] 6580[2] (7059) 7506[10] (8036) 8319[4] (8531)

Evening Hill *Richard Hughes* a72
2 b c Harbour Watch(IRE) Al Hawa (USA) (Gulch (USA))
7733[2] ◆

Evening Hush (IRE) *Evan Williams* 78
3 b f Excellent Art Applause (IRE) (Danehill Dancer (IRE))
6121[5]

Evening Starlight *Ron Hodges* a70 67
3 rg f Kyllachy Night Haven (Night Shift (USA))
126[6] 352[7] (711) 979[6] 1176[6] (1574) 2373[3] 7420[9] 8233[2] 8358[7] 8561[9]

Evenlode (IRE) *David Barron* 79
3 b g Elnadim(USA) Escudo (IRE) (Indian Ridge)
1870[2] 2668[4] (2886) ◆ 4134[6]

Even Song (IRE) *A P O'Brien* a78 108
3 b f Mastercraftsman(IRE) Guantanamera (IRE) (Sadler's Wells (USA))
1890[3] ◆ (3297) 4416a[7] 5586[7] 7351[8]

Event Mum (GER) *Waldemar Hickst* 70
3 b f Samum(GER) Evening Set (GER) (Second Set (IRE))
8024a[12]

Everdina *Ed Walker* a56
2 b f Pour Moi(IRE) Silent Music (IRE) (Peintre Celebre (USA))
7762[12]

Evergate *Hugo Palmer* a88 86
2 b g Exceed And Excel(AUS) Lion Forest (USA) (Forestry (USA))
2478[2] 2756[3] 4103[6] (4707) 6697[2] ◆ 7120[15] 7541[11]

Everkyllachy (IRE) *J S Moore* a57 62
2 br f Kyllachy Superfonic (FR) (Zafonic (USA))
4706[5] 5869[5] 6250[8] 6652[4] 7047[7] 7615[6] 7750[5] 8284[8]

Everlasting Sea *Stuart Kittow* 23
2 b f Harbour Watch(IRE) Doliouchka (Saumarez)
7208[9]

Ever Strong (GER) *Dr A Bolte* a70 98
8 b g Lomitas Emy Coasting (USA) (El Gran Senor (USA))
7564a[8]

Evervescent (IRE) *Graeme McPherson* a67 77
7 b g Elnadim(USA) Purepleasureseeker (IRE) (Grand Lodge (USA))
464[5] 676[5] 862[4] 1057[4] 1500[5] 2566[6]

Every Instinct (IRE) *David Simcock* a77 77
4 b g Danehill Dancer(IRE) Phrase (Royal Anthem (USA))
3972[5]

Every Nice Girl (USA) *Marco Botti* a58 56
2 rg f Mizzen Mast(USA) Joop (USA) (Zilzal (USA))
5022[5] 5747[6] *6897[10]*

Everything For You (IRE) *Kevin Ryan* 70
2 b c Pivotal Miss Delila (USA) (Malibu Moon (USA))
7496[4] ◆

Everywish *Jonathan Portman* a35 53
5 b m Quatre Saisons Reine De Violette (Olden Times)
796[10]

Evidence (FR) *Harry Dunlop* a71 56
3 b f Excellent Art Peachmelba (USA) (Theatrical (IRE))
400[4] *716a[3]* 1542a[7] *4018[5]* 5254[3] 6827[10] *7931[2]*

Evidence Sarthoise (FR) *C Plisson* 52
2 b f Konig Shuffle(GER) Delfina One (FR) (Apple Tree (FR))
1021a[5] 2844a[6]

Evident (IRE) *Tony Carroll* a71 55
6 b g Excellent Art Vestavia (IRE) (Alhaarth (IRE))
254[4] *297[3]* *609[11]* *985[5]* *1042[4]* *1319[7]*

Evil Spell *Endo Botti* 98
4 b m Dutch Art Yajala (Fasliyev (USA))
2518a[9] 7840a[3]

Exaggerator (USA) *J Keith Desormeaux* a123
3 bb c Curlin(USA) Dawn Raid (CAN) (Vindication (USA))
2063a[2] *(2499a)* *3181a[11]* *5913a[11]*

Exalted (IRE) *William Knight* a76 58
5 b g Acclamation Eman's Joy (Lion Cavern (USA))
64[4] *(141)* *(264)* ◆ *403[2]* *1415[3]* 1928[12] *(2579)* *3035[4]* ◆ *3783[8]*

Examiner (IRE) *Stuart Williams* a98 100
5 ch g Excellent Art Therry Girl (IRE) (Lahib (USA))
1195[15] 1861[2] ◆ (2868) 6786[25] 7546[12] *8317[3]* *8529[5]*

Exceedingly Sweet *Richard Fahey*
2 b f Exceed And Excel(AUS) Sugar Free (IRE) (Oasis Dream)
7939[F] (Dead)

Exceeding Power *Martin Bosley* a81 81
5 b g Exceed And Excel(AUS) Extreme Beauty (USA) (Rahy (USA))
58[2] *360[6]* *518[8]* (2213) 3061[3] 4058[2] 4841[3] 5357[2] *7886[4]* *8178[6]* *8487[6]*

Exceed The Limit *Robert Cowell* 98
3 b g Exceed And Excel(AUS) Clinet (IRE) (Docksider (USA))
1374a[13] 3857[4] 4359[5] 4803[17] 5148[8]

Excellent Addition (IRE) *Lee James*
6 ch g Excellent Art Race The Wild Wind (USA) (Sunny's Halo (CAN))
867[12]

Excellent Aim *George Margarson* a69 49
9 b g Exceed And Excel(AUS) Snugfit Annie (Midyan (USA))
21[2] *196[2]* *1496[9]* 3741[7] *4980[6]* 7018[9] *8149[4]* *8242[2]*

Excellent Alibi *Andrew Balding* a37 30
3 ch c Exceed And Excel(AUS) Indian Love Bird (Efisio)
2780[7]

Excellent George *Stuart Williams* a82 89
4 b g Exceed And Excel(AUS) Princess Georgina (Royal Applause)
3618[6] (4360) 5124[7] 5882[2] 6583[6] *7643[8]* *8083[10]*

Excellent Guest *George Margarson* a82 86
9 b g Exceed And Excel(AUS) Princess Speedfit (FR) (Desert Prince (IRE))
82[5]

Excellent Puck (IRE) *Shaun Lycett* a83 73
6 b g Excellent Art Puck's Castle (Shirley Heights)
160[4] *619[4]* *983[2]* 1999[8] *8161[6]*

Excellent Result (IRE) *Richard Spencer* 107
6 b g Shamardal(USA) Line Ahead (IRE) (Sadler's Wells (USA))
6118[15]

Excellent Sounds *Hughie Morrison* a80 74
3 b f Exceed And Excel(AUS) Siren Sound (Singspiel (IRE))
2904[8] 3684[2] 4041[2] *(4528)* *5551[3]* *7687[7]*

Excellent Sunset (IRE) *David Lanigan* 54
2 b f Exceed And Excel(AUS) Sunset Avenue (USA) (Street Cry (IRE))
4147[8]

Excellent World (IRE) *Tony Coyle* 62
3 b f Excellent Art Granny Kelly (USA) (Irish River (FR))
1246[3] 2349[5] 2557[3] 3603[10] 4240[10] 6436[12]

Excelli (IRE) *Aidan Anthony Howard* a85 86
6 ch g Great Exhibition(USA) Elli Pyrelli (IRE) (Tenby)
4748a[11]

Excelling Oscar (IRE) *Conor Dore* a64 21
4 b g Excellent Art Three Pennies (Pennekamp (USA))
2[7] *247[4]* *336[7]* *445[5]*

Excel Quest *Ed Walker* a48
3 b c Exceed And Excel(AUS) Rayyana (IRE) (Rainbow Quest (USA))
1837[5]

Excessable *Tim Easterby* 95
3 ch g Sakhee's Secret Kummel Excess (IRE) (Exceed And Excel (AUS))
1492[5] 2218[7] 3420[4] 4112[16] (4947) 5657[8] 6012[12] 6793[11]

Excess Knowledge *Gai Waterhouse & Adrian Bott* 113
6 br h Monsun(GER) Quenched (Dansili)
7552a[4] 7756a[16]

Exchequer (IRE) *David Brown* a101 93
5 ch g Exceed And Excel(AUS) Tara's Force (IRE) (Acclamation)
(1335) ◆ 1856[12] 2910[4] *3656[11]* 5124[3] 6082[7] *7530[8]* *7968[2]*

Excilly *Tom Dascombe* a70 102
4 bb m Excellent Art Afra Tsitsi (FR) (Belong To Me (USA))
187a[7] 451a[2] 809a[3] 3271[8] 3916a[8] 5185a[7] 5914a[6]

Exciting Times *Tom Dascombe*
2 ch g Tamayuz Catwalk (IRE) (Pivotal)
2649[14]

Exclusive Contract (IRE) *Ollie Pears* a59 66
5 br m High Chaparral(IRE) Birthday (IRE) (Singspiel (IRE))
2089[2] 2745[6] 4239[4] 4971[4]

Exclusive Diamond *David O'Meara* a59 68
4 b m Iffraaj Poppets Sweetlove (Foxhound (USA))
2661[5] *2915[2]* *3564[4]* 4424[2] *5064[4]* (5513) (5800)

Exclusive Potion (FR) *A Giorgi* a71 53
3 b c Elusive City(USA) Magie Noire (IRE) (Marju (IRE))
1686a[14] *3546a[6]*

Exclusive Waters (IRE) *George Charlton* a58 52
6 b g Elusive City(USA) Pelican Waters (IRE) (Key Of Luck (USA))
2618[11] *3564[11]* 4768[8] *5972[6]* 6683[9] *7438[4]* *7656[10]* *8134[7]*

Executive Bay *Tom Dascombe* 65
3 b c Bushranger(IRE) Munaawashat (IRE) (Marju (IRE))
4347[7] 5201[6]

Executive Force *William Haggas* a101 80
2 b c Sepoy(AUS) Mazuna (IRE) (Cape Cross (IRE))
(6543) *7130a[2]* 7544[12]

Executive Order *Martin Smith* a37
7 b g Overbury(IRE) Maiden Aunt (IRE) (Distant Relative)
318[6] *487[5]* *675[9]* 1854[12]

Executor *Roger Charlton* a58 74
3 b g Cacique(IRE) Star Cluster (Observatory (USA))
1777[5] 3982[8] *4528[7]*

Exemplar (IRE) *A P O'Brien* 110
2 ro c Galileo(IRE) Miarixa (FR) (Linamix (FR))
6817a[3]

Exentricity *Mick Channon* a70 67
4 b m Paco Boy(IRE) Wansdyke Lass (Josr Algarhoud (IRE))
41[4]

Exist *John Gosden* a94 80
3 b f Exceed And Excel(AUS) Harryana (Efisio)
(1812) 2192[7]

Ex Lover *Roger Varian* 69
3 ch c Monsun(GER) Tu Eres Mi Amore (IRE) (Sadler's Wells (USA))
3235[9] 3736[9]

Exmouth *Sir Michael Stoute* 90
2 b f Elusive Quality(USA) Havant (Halling (USA))
(5930) 6748[8]

Exoplanet Blue *Henry Candy* a76 80
4 b m Exceed And Excel(AUS) Tut (IRE) (Intikhab (USA))
1334[2] *1838[3]* 2737[5] 3575[5] (5309) 5992[6] 6649[3] 7227[7]

Exospheric *Lee & Anthony Freedman* a82 120
4 b h Beat Hollow Bright And Clear (Danehill (USA))
(1863) 3384[8] 4061[3] 5558[5] 7378a[3] 7756a[8]

Exoteric *Charles Hills* a76 93
3 b g Champs Elysees Short Dance (USA) (Hennessy (USA))
1970[2] *2619[4]* (5287) (5849) (7418)

Exotic Guest *Ruth Carr* a65 68
6 ch g Bahamian Bounty Mamoura (IRE) (Lomond (USA))
1154[9] 1488[9] 1692[4] *2332[4]* 2680[5] 3069[2] 3210[2] 3777[5]

Expected Ruler (USA) *Liam D Benson* a35 91
3 bb c Leroidesanimaux(BRZ) Expected Pleasures (USA) (Allen's Prospect (USA))
7403a[8]

Expenditure (IRE) *Jedd O'Keeffe* a48 56
2 b g Lilbourne Lad(IRE) Brunch Bellini (FR) (Peintre Celebre (USA))
2830[5] *3562[5]* 4227[6]

Experimentalist *Leo Braem* a44 50
8 b g Monsieur Bond(IRE) Floppie (FR) (Law Society (USA))
3184a[14]

Experto Crede (IRE) *Ed Walker* a80 87
3 b g Exceed And Excel(AUS) Shepherdia (IRE) (Pivotal)
1809[6] 2891[10] 3415[3] (4132) ◆

Explain *Ruth Carr* 90
4 ch g Kyllachy Descriptive (IRE) (Desert King (IRE))
1444[2] 2016[4] (2259) 2613[6] 3068[9] 4428[2] 4689[6] 5161[3] 5512[7] 6079[15] 6766[2] 7094[12]

Explosive Power (IRE) *K R Burke* 89
3 gr g Alfred Nobel(IRE) My Girl Lisa (USA) (With Approval (CAN))
1243[7] 1851[6] 2473[7] 3130[6] (3885) 6560[4] 6918[11] 7540[11]

Express (IRE) *Richard Hannon* 60
2 b f Kodiac High Dasher (IRE) (High Chaparral (IRE))
3511[5] 4205[6] 5250[3] 6630[11]

Express Himself (IRE) *Ed McMahon* 107
5 b g Dylan Thomas(IRE) Lightwood Lady (IRE) (Anabaa (USA))
1196[7] 1629[4] ◆ 2191[9] 2796[3] 3390[2] ◆

Exspectation (IRE) *Michael Blanshard* 63
2 b g Excelebration(IRE) Emeralds Spirit (IRE) (Rock Of Gibraltar (IRE))
5600[11] 6632[6] 7208[3]

Extortion *Bryan Smart* a46 75
3 b g Kheleyf(USA) Virtuality (USA) (Elusive Quality (USA))
1788[2] 2200[7] 6215[11] *8345[10]*

Extrasolar *Amanda Perrett* a88 89
6 b g Exceed And Excel(AUS) Amicable Terms (Royal Applause)
4735[14] 4862[28] 5285[2] 5669[9]

Extremely Vintage (IRE) *Endo Botti*
3 ch f Dylan Thomas(IRE) Birthday (IRE) (Singspiel (IRE))
2730a[12]

Extreme Supreme *Derek Shaw* a69 53
5 b g Piccolo Kitty Kitty Cancan (Warrshan (USA))
293[7] *444[6]* *733[3]* *868[3]* *937[3]* *1133[9]*

Extremis (IRE) *Mohammed Jassim Ghazali* a80 105
4 b h Invincible Spirit(IRE) Fidelite (IRE) (In The Wings)
757a[7]

Extremity (IRE) *Hugo Palmer* a84 94
5 ch g Exceed And Excel(AUS) Chanterelle (IRE) (Indian Ridge)
3109[11] 4081[12]

Eye Glass (IRE) *T G McCourt* a52 45
4 b m Intense Focus(USA) Petite Arvine (USA) (Gulch (USA))
867[7] *7800a[10]*

Eye In The Sky (IRE) *Niels Petersen* a90 103
5 gr h Sinndar(IRE) Saudade (GER) (Linamix (FR))
453a[9] 811a[12] 4329a[5]

Eye Of The Storm (IRE) *Amanda Perrett* 109
6 ch g Galileo(IRE) Mohican Princess (Shirley Heights)
1273[9] 2465[4]

Eyeshine *John Gosden* a89 77
3 b f Dubawi(IRE) Casual Look (USA) (Red Ransom (USA))
1609[9] 3094[2] *5723[2]* *(6239)* *7652[10]*

Eynhallow *Roger Charlton* 74
2 b g Nathaniel(IRE) Ronaldsay (Kirkwall)
5600[4] ◆ 6159[4] 7243[7]

Eyreborn (IRE) *Tom Dascombe* 62
2 b f Born To Sea(IRE) Eyrecourt (IRE) (Efisio)
6250[4] ◆ 6776[7] 7284[10]

Ey Up *Paul Midgley* a26 41
2 b f Harbour Watch(IRE) Glittering Prize (UAE) (Cadeaux Genereux)
2617[9] 2830[10] 4000[4] 5177[5]

Eze *H-F Devin* a62 90
3 b f Manduro(GER) Arabian Spell (IRE) (Desert Prince (IRE))
6310a[8]

Eziyra (IRE) *D K Weld* 108
2 ch f Teofilo(IRE) Eytarna (IRE) (Dubai Destination (USA))
5937a[2] (6815a)

Fable Of Arachne *Stuart Williams* a62 57
3 b f Dick Turpin(IRE) Las Hilanderas (USA) (El Prado (IRE))
(140) *376[3]* 1777[4] 2506[8]

Fabric *Richard Hannon* 75
2 b f Acclamation Decorative (IRE) (Danehill Dancer (IRE))
3613[4] 4205[3] (4804) 6630[5] 7217[2]

Fabricate *Michael Bell* 104
4 b g Makfi Flight Of Fancy (Sadler's Wells (USA))
2199[2] 3340[5] 5639[3] 6283[8] (7058)

Fabrino (IRE) *M Weiss* 74
8 b h Elnadim(USA) Trullitti (IRE) (Bahri (USA))
2318a[3]

Fabulous Flyer *Jeremy Gask* a51 51
3 b f Equiano(FR) Lucky Flyer (Lucky Story (USA))
1753[5] 3260[5] *3650[5]* 3994[4] 4658[6] 5007[9] *8409[3]*

Face Of Glory (IRE) *Ismail Mohammed* 2
3 b c Big Bad Bob(IRE) Interchange (IRE) (Montjeu (IRE))
4806[7]

Face The Facts (IRE) *John Gosden* 75
2 ch c Nathaniel(IRE) Aricia (IRE) (Nashwan (USA))
7622[2]

Facia De Tola *Stefano Botti* 86
3 ch f New Approach(IRE) Rosa Del Dubai (IRE) (Dubai Destination (USA))
7840a[9]

Facilitate *D Smaga* 92
2 br f Bated Breath Emergency (Dr Fong (USA))
4924a[2] 6694a[6]

Faction *Andrew Balding* 67
3 b g Champs Elysees Belladera (IRE) (Alzao (USA))
2098[7] 3160[9] 4458[4] 6066[10]

Fact Or Folklore (IRE) *W McCreery* a71 93
4 ch m Lope De Vega(IRE) Iuturna (USA) (Intidab (USA))
1279a[5] 2881a[2] 5002a[8] 6200a[3] 6820a[4] 7393a[8]

Fadillah *William Haggas* 86
3 b f Monsun(GER) Sasuela (GER) (Dashing Blade)
(1628) ◆ (2339) 6665[2] ◆

Faineog (IRE) *Mrs A M O'Shea* a76 83
5 b m Rock Of Gibraltar(IRE) Lady Gregory (IRE) (In The Wings)
2716a[7] 3201a[3] *4246a[9]* 4540a[9] *6461a[10]*

Faintly (USA) *Ruth Carr* a82 68
5 b g Kitten's Joy(USA) Tinge (USA) (Kingmambo (USA))
(1832) 2402[3] (2537) 3168[17] 3394[9] 4102[8] 4454[2] 4729[4] 5179[8] 6280[10] 6644[6] 7010[5] *7368[8]* *(7602)* *7817[7]* *(7995)*

Fair Comment *Michael Blanshard* a65 64
6 b m Tamayuz Cliche (IRE) (Diktat)
164[4] *348[2]* *606[4]* *781[4]* *5261[2]* 6256[2] 6825[6] *7870[12]* *8155[8]* *8448[3]*

Fair Eva *Roger Charlton* 111
2 ch f Frankel African Rose (Observatory (USA))
(3024) (4623) ◆ 5584[3] 6748[2]

Fair Game (IRE) *E J O'Grady* a55 84
3 b f Lawman(FR) Ascendancy (Sadler's Wells (USA))
7475a[4]

Fair Mountain (GER) *A Wohler* 105
4 b h Tiger Hill(IRE) Fair Breeze (GER) (Silvano (GER))
2075a[3] 2723a[8] 3934a[7] (5219a) 6612a[2] 7564a[12] 7843a[5]

Fair Point (USA) *Claude McGaughey III* a55 104
4 b m Smart Strike(CAN) Fair Rose (USA) (Harlan's Holiday (USA))
(7829a)

Fair Power (IRE) *Sylvester Kirk* a73 80
2 b g Power Pitrizzia (Lando (GER))
2748[3] *3315[2]* (3485) 4394[20] 5989[2] 6388a[5] 7016[9] 7549[14]

Fair Selene *Heather Main* a61 62
2 b f Equiano(FR) Jane Jubilee (IRE) (Mister Baileys)
1895[3] 2410[6] 4951[12] 6060[5] 6830[4] *7047[3]* *7750[9]* *8467[5]*

Fair's Fair (IRE) *Ralph Beckett* a77
4 b m Lawman(FR) Winning Sequence (FR) (Zafonic (USA))
26[2]

Fair Skies (IRE) *Ivan Furtado* a5 21
2 b c Vale Of York(IRE) Fayr Sky (IRE) (Fayruz)
3008[7] *3472[9]* 3820[4]

Fair Trade *Wilf Storey* a59 93
9 ch g Trade Fair Ballet (Sharrood (USA))
5841[10] *6738[9]*

Fairway To Heaven (IRE) *Michael Wigham* a82 86
7 b g Jeremy(USA) Luggala (IRE) (Kahyasi)
4415a[17] 4862[15] (5896) 6263[14] 6883[6] *8402[4]*

Fairy Duchess (IRE) *John Butler* a51 55
4 b m Duke Of Marmalade(IRE) Fairybook (USA) (El Prado (IRE))
1725[9]

Fairy Foxglove (IRE) *P J F Murphy* a79 68
6 b m Albano(IRE) Aegean Magic (Wolfhound (USA))
(418) *542[3]* ◆ *590[7]* *6465a[4]* *7339a[3]*

Fairy Lights *Roger Varian* a74
2 b f Shamardal(USA) Suba (USA) (Seeking The Gold (USA))
7277[2]

Fairy Lock (IRE) *David Barron* a53 39
2 b f Sir Prancealot(IRE) Too Close (IRE) (Danehill Dancer (IRE))
7040[8] 7578[12] *7988[9]* *8344[4]*

Fairy Mist (IRE) *John Bridger* a56 59
9 b g Oratorio(IRE) Prealpina (IRE) (Indian Ridge)
87[4] *168[7]* *(252)* *609[8]* *870[10]* *1145[4]* 1544[5] (1742) *2155[8]* 3255[3] (3489) 4389[6] 4640[2] *6238[3]* 6894[5] 7036[7] 7299[6]

Fairy Pools *Les Eyre* a54 27
5 ch m Halling(USA) Maritima (Darshaan)
863[5] *1263[4]* *1834[9]* 2409[12] 2810[8] 4772[13]

Faiseur De Miracle *Micky Hammond* a82 101
4 b g Makfi Flawly (Old Vic)
500[2] *(675)* (1250) ◆ 2199[6] *7383[10]*

Faithful Creek (IRE) *Michael Appleby* a89 91
4 b g Bushranger(IRE) Open Verse (USA) (Black Minnaloushe (USA))
3340[18] 4129[8] 4776[5] 5156[4] 5933[5] 6753[7] *8122[4]* *8317[6]* *8539[7]*

Faithful Mount *Ian Williams* a76 95
7 b g Shirocco(GER) Lady Lindsay (IRE) (Danehill Dancer (IRE))
3192[2] 3862[4] 4311[5] 5358[5] (6209) (6781) 7058[7]

Faith In Me (IRE) *Simon Crisford* a54 10
2 b f Henrythenavigator(USA) Faithful One (IRE) (Dubawi (IRE))
4350[12] *5242[6]*

Falak (IRE) *Roger Varian* 39
3 b c Teofilo(IRE) Family (USA) (Danzig (USA))
3235[13]

Falbon *Marco Botti* a62
2 b g Mayson Eleodora (Dubawi (IRE))
7975[9] *8377[3]*

Falcao (IRE) *John Butler* a71 84
4 br g Majestic Missile(IRE) Cafe Lassere (USA) (Giant's Causeway (USA))
8083[12] *8239[11]*

Falco Junior (FR) *Charley Rossi* a15 18
6 b g Falco(USA) Badaling (FR) (Loup Solitaire (USA))
5452a[14]

Falconet (DEN) *Bent Olsen* 102
6 b h Falco(USA) Seattle's Wood (USA) (Woodman (USA))
5187a[11]

Falcon Rising *Sylvester Kirk* 52
2 b g Kyllachy Fly Free (Halling (USA))
5052[5]

Falcon's Fire (IRE) *Keith Dalgleish* a74 79
3 ch g Thewayyouare(USA) Matadora (IRE) (Kris)
145[5] *298[7]* *533[5]* *688[5]* *794[11]* *1551[13]* 2124[4] 2308[3] 2772[3] 3015[2] 4255[4] (4340) 4447[2] 4875[6] *(6103)* ◆ (6346) 6503[3] 6773[7] 7251[8]

Falcon's Reign (FR) *Michael Appleby* a60 41
7 ch g Haafhd Al Badeya (IRE) (Pivotal)
(25) *246[3]* *430[6]* *1047[7]*

Falcon's Song (USA) *Ismail Mohammed* a76
4 bb m US Ranger(USA) Saudia (USA) (Gone West (USA))
5245[3] *6128[9]* *6656[7]*

Falest (IRE) *D Crisanti* 102
7 ch h Refuse To Bend(IRE) Mandolin (IRE) (Sabrehill (USA))
2518a[6]

Fallen For A Star *Luca Cumani* a97 93
4 b g Sea The Stars(IRE) Fallen Star (Brief Truce (USA))
2377[6] *(3660)* 4276[4] 5651[15]

False Id *Robert Eddery* a68 71
3 b g Aqlaam Miss Dutee (Dubawi (IRE))
(885) 1431[5] *2770[7]* 3353[5] (3740) 4563[6]

Fame Game (JPN) *Yoshitada Munakata* 121
6 bb g Heart's Cry(JPN) Hall Of Fame (JPN) (Allez Milord (USA))
8129a[17]

Famous Dynasty (IRE) *Michael Blanshard* a67 70
2 b g Famous Name Daffodil Walk (IRE) (Captain Rio)
2997[12] *4523[5]* 5325[2] 5740[7] 6289[5] 7016[6]

Famous Kid (USA) *Saeed bin Suroor* a116 112
5 ch g Street Cry(IRE) Moyesii (USA) (Diesis)
453a[3]

Famous Mark (MOR) *P Bary* a96 51
4 ch h Mr. Sidney(USA) Empreinte Celebre (IRE) (Peintre Celebre (USA))
1957a[3] *6399a[5]*

Famous Milly (IRE) *Gavin Cromwell* 83
2 b f Famous Name Gilah (IRE) (Saddlers' Hall (IRE))
6815a[10]

Fanciful Angel (IRE) *Marco Botti* a105 108
4 gr g Dark Angel(IRE) Fanciful Dancer (Groom Dancer (USA))
(375a) ◆ 720a[7] 2867[7] 4625[8] 5585[7] 8489[4]
Fanci That (IRE) *Rae Guest* a54 44
3 b f Elnadim(USA) Featherlight (Fantastic Light (USA))
5748[3] 6317[13] 7276[3] ◆ 8408[6]
Fancy Day (IRE) *Mark Johnston* a64 72
2 b f Shamardal(USA) Tizdubai (USA) (Cee's Tizzy (USA))
(3433) 3782[6] 4364[5] 5066[4] 6898[7] 7570[4] 7854[2] 8080[6] 8466[13]
Fandango (GER) *Jeremy Gask* a55 88
3 b c Lord Of England(GER) Fitness (IRE) (Monsun (GER))
1714[12] 3033[8] 3998[3] 5232[2] (5548) (5993) 6804[5] 7123[5]
Fanfair *Richard Hannon* a48 57
2 b f Royal Applause Fugnina (Hurricane Run (IRE))
2696[8] 3555[5] 4054[9] 4937[5] 5528[8]
Fanfaron (FR) *D Prod'Homme* 94
3 gr c Falco(USA) Farwana (FR) (Sinndar (IRE))
1024a[8]
Fang *William Jarvis* a84 86
3 b g Lawman(FR) Desert Tigress (USA) (Storm Cat (USA))
3029[7] (3976) (4569) 4954[7] 6492[6] 7737[3] 8032[3]
Fankairos Ranger (USA) *Cedric Rossi* 73
2 b g US Ranger(USA) Dancin Up A Storm (USA) (Stormin Fever (USA))
5141a[2]
Fannaan (USA) *John Gosden* 105
4 ch g Speightstown(USA) Titian Time (USA) (Red Ransom (USA))
6547[2] 7542[2]
Fanoulpifer *Stefano Botti* 102
5 b g High Chaparral(IRE) Furbeseta (Danehill Dancer (IRE))
2516a[2]
Fantastic Way (FR) *Mme C Barande-Barbe* a50 48
7 b g Way Of Light(USA) Fantastic Fire (GER) (Platini (GER))
8422a[4]
Fantasy Gladiator *Michael Appleby* a85 83
10 b g Ishiguru(USA) Fancier Bit (Lion Cavern (USA))
58[5] 6323[3] 6899[10] 7229[8] 7691[9] 7886[12] 8178[9]
Fantasy Justifier (IRE) *Ronald Harris* a40 77
5 b g Arakan(USA) Grandel (Owington)
1489[5] (2130) 2680[4] 3771[3] 3892[6] 4990[5] 7415[6] 7590[9]
Fantasy Keeper *Michael Appleby* a66 45
2 b c Mayson Expressive (Falbrav (IRE))
7818[8] 8229[2]
Fantasy King *James Moffatt* a84 79
10 b g Acclamation Fantasy Ridge (Indian Ridge)
2439[5]
Fantasy Queen *Eve Johnson Houghton* 65
3 b f Aqlaam Regal Curtsy (Royal Applause)
4017[4] (4587) 5013[4] (5571) 5953[5] 6635[7]
Farandine *Luca Cumani* a87 72
3 ch f Rock Of Gibraltar(IRE) Rivara (Red Ransom (USA))
6246[3] 6947[9] 7901[6]
Farang Jai Dee (IRE) *Declan Carroll* a30 50
4 b g Approve(IRE) Fruit O'The Forest (IRE) (Shinko Forest (IRE))
1383[5] 1495[10] 2448[9] 2741[6] 3069[14]
Fareeq *William Haggas* a77 79
2 gr g Dark Angel(IRE) Spate (IRE) (Danehill Dancer (IRE))
5084[6] 5477[5] 6099[3] (6743) ◆ 7185[2]
Farham (USA) *Richard Fahey* a77 75
4 b g Smart Strike(CAN) Diamondrella (Rock Of Gibraltar (IRE))
863[2] 1290[4] (1632) 2121[7] 2743[5] 3435[6] 3905[7] 4455[5] 5028[4] 5994[5]
Farkle Minkus *Keith Dalgleish* a59 87
3 b g Kheleyf(USA) Majestic Diva (IRE) (Royal Applause)
1763[8] 2200[8] 2554[5] 4488[7] 5070[7] 6215[7] 6435[6] 6769[8]
Farleigh Mac *Andrew Balding* 79
2 ch g Equiano(FR) Le Badie (IRE) (Spectrum (IRE))
2847[6] (3196) 4352[8] 5560[8] 6260[17]
Farletti *Andrew Balding* a74 78
4 b m Royal Applause Le Badie (IRE) (Spectrum (IRE))
14[4] 141[8]
Farlow (IRE) *Richard Fahey* a82 108
8 ch g Exceed And Excel(AUS) Emly Express (IRE) (High Estate)
1196[8] 1441[7] 4152[6] 4665[8] 5174[7] 5389[11] 5871[8]
Farook (IRE) *Charles Hills* a73 73
2 ro g Raven's Pass(USA) Wrong Answer (Verglas (IRE))
3408[7] 6904[2] 7468[4]
Farraaj (IRE) *D Selvaratnam* a93 114
7 b g Dubai Destination(USA) Pastorale (Nureyev (USA))
187a[8] 375a[3] 721a[7]
Farrah's Choice *James Grassick* a47 50
4 b m Equiano(FR) Esplanade (Danehill (USA))
787[11] 876[9] 1005[11] 2086[5] 3067[12] 6278[5] 8157[4] 8383[12]
Farrier (USA) *S Seemar* a103 105
8 b g Tapit(USA) Wild Vision (USA) (Wild Again (USA))
188a[4] 845a[2] 1106a[13] 8396a[2]
Farshad (GER) *Henk Grewe* 95
2 rg c Kendargent(FR) Forever Midnight (IRE) (Night Shift (USA))
6174a[4]
Fas (IRE) *Mme Pia Brandt* 103
2 b c Fastnet Rock(AUS) Sotka (Dutch Art)
(5701a) 6694a[3] 7347a[4]
Fascinating Rock (IRE) *D K Weld* 125
5 b h Fastnet Rock(AUS) Miss Polaris (Polar Falcon (USA))
1940a[3] (2512a) 5685a[2]

Fashaak (IRE) *Richard Hannon* a77 87
3 b g Starspangledbanner(AUS) Szabo (IRE) (Anabaa (USA))
1750[5] (2239) 2477[4] 2818[7] 3574[2] 5409[11] 5892[7] 6339[6]
Fashionable Spirit (IRE) *Amanda Perrett* a71 65
3 b f Invincible Spirit(IRE) White And Red (IRE) (Orpen (USA))
5725[5] 6190[5] 6290[5] 6669[8] 7200[3] 7513[3]
Fashionata (IRE) *Kristin Stubbs* a68 73
3 ch f Fast Company(IRE) Red Red Rose (Piccolo)
344[5] 612[3] 1183[3] 1922[8] 6235[7]
Fashion Design (IRE) *Sir Michael Stoute* a72 72
3 b f Montjeu(IRE) Sense Of Style (USA) (Thunder Gulch (USA))
3235[7] 5129[2] 5742[4] 6049[4]
Fashion Parade *Charles Hills* a89 86
3 b f Fastnet Rock(AUS) Festivale (IRE) (Invincible Spirit (IRE))
2177[3] 2614[4] (3736) (4462) ◆ 5331[5] 5851[6] 7067[3] 7618[2]
Fashion Queen *David O'Meara* 91
2 ch f Aqlaam Pizzarra (Shamardal (USA))
4110[2] (4601) ◆ 5584[5]
Fashion Queen (GER) *Frau C Barsig* 93
2 ch f Santiago(GER) Fashion Tycoon (IRE) (Chineur (FR))
4620a[5]
Fashion Theory *Charlie Appleby* 71
2 b f Dubawi(IRE) Lady's Purse (Doyen (IRE))
7118[9] 7494[3] ◆
Fast Act (IRE) *Kevin Ryan* a90 87
4 ch g Fast Company(IRE) Nullarbor (Green Desert (USA))
2258[10] 2803[9] 3346[6] 4079[17] 4514[13] 5780[7] (6195) (7202)
Fast And Hot (IRE) *Richard Hannon* a71 69
3 gr g Fastnet Rock(AUS) Hotelgenie Dot Com (Selkirk (USA))
85[5] 4288[5] (4635) 5011[2] 6194[4] 6662[2] 6827[3] (7613)
Fast Approach (IRE) *Andrew Balding* a50
4 ch m New Approach(IRE) Exorcet (FR) (Selkirk (USA))
155[10]
Fastar (IRE) *Brian Meehan* 74
2 ch c Fast Company(IRE) Asterism (Motivator)
2748[2] 3100[4]
Fast Dancer (IRE) *Joseph Tuite* a85 88
4 b g Fast Company(IRE) Tereed Elhawa (Cadeaux Genereux)
1335[13] 1997[4] 3133[5] 3803[3] 4306[3] 4534[4] 4917[4] 5892[4] 6806[7] 7189[2] 7623[4]
Fast Enough (IRE) *Saeed bin Suroor* a100 78
3 b g Kodiac La Chicana (IRE) (Invincible Spirit (IRE))
(16)
Faster Company (IRE) *J S Moore* a52 75
3 b g Fast Company(IRE) Lily Rio (IRE) (Marju (IRE))
140[5] 345[3] 533[4] 700[6] 5572 [10] 5625[11]
Fast Freddie *Mrs A Corson* a39 30
12 b g Agnes World(USA) Bella Chica (IRE) (Bigstone (IRE))
1519a[5] 2285a[3] 2955a[9] 5457a[3] 6402a[4]
Fastidious *M D O'Callaghan* a71 71
7 b g Exceed And Excel(AUS) Felicitous (King's Best (USA))
4748a[12]
Fast In The Wind (IRE) *P D Deegan* a79 80
5 b g Footstepsinthesand Close Regards (IRE) (Danehill (USA))
4415a[8] 6461a[6]
Fast Kar (IRE) *Matthieu Palussiere* 64
2 b f Fast Company(IRE) Karlinha (IRE) (Desert Style (IRE))
1284a[8] 2724a[4] 3006a[8] 5142a[12]
Fast Landing *Saeed bin Suroor* a55
2 b g Raven's Pass(USA) Miss Lucifer (FR) (Noverre (USA))
7812[8]
Fast Lightning (GER) *Waldemar Hickst* 93
3 b c Monsun(GER) Flashing Colour (GER) (Pivotal)
7843a[11]
Fast Lily (IRE) *P J Prendergast* a51 76
2 b f Fastnet Rock(AUS) Lovely Blossom (FR) (Spinning World (USA))
5242[7]
Fastnet Blast (IRE) *Ed Walker* a73 71
3 b g Fastnet Rock(AUS) Bright Bank (IRE) (Sadler's Wells (USA))
1200[7] 2000[4] 3981[5] 4686[5] 5607[5] 6730[3] 7321[5] 8462[2] ◆
Fastnet Monsoon (IRE) *Luca Cumani* a50 47
3 b g Fastnet Rock(AUS) Mona Lisa (Giant's Causeway (USA))
5681[6] 6192[5]
Fastnet Prince (IRE) *Phil York* a51 40
3 b c Fastnet Rock(AUS) Lucky Spin (Pivotal)
376[7] 3224[13] 3724[5] 4202[11] 7645[11] 7969[11]
Fastnet Spin (IRE) *David Evans* a54 78
2 b f Fastnet Rock(AUS) Lucky Spin (Pivotal)
1086[8] (1527) 1895[2] ◆ 5594[5] (6289) 6575[2] 7147[16] 7416[4] 7764[7]
Fastnet Tempest (IRE) *William Haggas* 93
3 b g Fastnet Rock(AUS) Dame Blanche (IRE) (Be My Guest (USA))
2197[2] 2804[2] (4347) 5391[2] (6490) 6915[4]
Fast On (IRE) *Seamus Fahey* a53 52
7 gr g Verglas(IRE) Dream State (IRE) (Machiavellian (USA))
(7641) 8125[6]
Fast Operator (IRE) *Nigel Tinkler* 51
3 b f Fast Company(IRE) Dialing Tone (USA) (Distant View (USA))
2835[7] 4316[7] 4973[8]
Fast Pick (IRE) *Keith Dalgleish* a78 74
4 b m Fastnet Rock(AUS) Dream Time (Rainbow Quest (USA))
(1347) (1552) ◆ 2163[8] 3345[7]

Fast Play (IRE) *Richard Hughes* a71 66
4 b m Fast Company(IRE) Akariyda (IRE) (Salse (USA))
4458[7] 4939[10] 5529[5] 6143[2] ◆ 6335[5] 6659[5] (7421) 7628[5] 8124[2] 8363[5]
Fast Shot *Tim Easterby* a34 99
8 b g Fasliyev(USA) Final Pursuit (Pursuit Of Love)
1444[6] 1787[7] 3265[9]
Fast Sprite (IRE) *John Best* a76 65
4 b g Fast Company(IRE) Salty Air (IRE) (Singspiel (IRE))
3554[6] 4362[4] 5085[6] (5635) 6416[4] (7619)
Fast Tack (IRE) *John Quinn* a15
2 b c Fast Company(IRE) Green Vision (IRE) (Green Desert (USA))
8526[8]
Fast Track *David Barron* a100 101
5 b g Rail Link Silca Boo (Efisio)
677[2] 835[2] 2188[17] 3151[14] 3606[6] 4667[4] 4862[13] 5417[13] 5641[4] 6792[8]
Fast Watch *Jose Santos*
2 ch f Harbour Watch(IRE) Duelling (Diesis)
3075[3]
Fasuba (IRE) *T Stack* 79
2 b c Power Varmint Lady (IRE) (Orpen (USA))
4171a[5]
Fateh (IRE) *David Dennis* a51
3 b g Big Bad Bob(IRE) Passarelle (USA) (In The Wings)
139[4] 2700[13]
Father Bertie *Tim Easterby* a84 99
4 b g Firebreak Magical Music (Fraam)
920[9] 1195[9] 1643[3] 3565[4] 3923[5] 4299[5] 4644[10] 5180[3] 5976[4] 6225[3] 6500[2] (6956) 7316[4] 7573[3] 7699[3] 8049[13]
Father Christmas (IRE) *A P O'Brien* 111
4 b h Bernardini(USA) Christmas Kid (USA) (Lemon Drop Kid (USA))
1995[5]
Fatherly Friend (USA) *K R Burke* a63 73
3 bb c Scat Daddy(USA) Grimace (USA) (Vindication (USA))
1599[12] 2029[8] 4010[11]
Father McKenzie *Mick Channon* a71 78
2 b g Sixties Icon Queen Of Narnia (Hunting Lion (IRE))
3668[6] 3954[7] 4287[4] 4473[2] 4762[2] 5029[5] 5410[2] 5631[3] 6159[8] 6515[2] (6712) 7004[7] 7313[2]
Fattsota *David O'Meara* a88 113
8 b g Oasis Dream Gift Of The Night (USA) (Slewpy (USA))
2222[9] 2744[9] 4407[14] 6715[2] 7154[6] 7575[3] 7824[10]
Faufiler (IRE) *H Graham Motion* 111
5 b m Galileo(IRE) Six Perfections (FR) (Celtic Swing)
3178a[5] 5430a[5]
Fa Ul Cuncert *C Boutin* a60 66
2 b f Poet's Voice Viennese Whirl (Montjeu (IRE))
7490a[7]
Faulkner *Doug Watson* a110
6 ch h Pivotal Fibou (USA) (Seeking The Gold (USA))
92a[4] 452a[3] (627a) 844a[3] 1101a[2]
Faulkwood *K R Burke* 68
2 gr g Hellvelyn Sleep Dance (Sleeping Indian)
4371[9] 4663[4]
Fausto *Tom Dascombe* 52
2 b c Poet's Voice Luluti (IRE) (Kheleyf (USA))
4479[6] 5890[13]
Fauvism (USA) *R Bouresly* a68 82
7 b g Zamindar(USA) Chaffinch (USA) (Lear Fan (USA))
309a[10] 8396a[11]
Favorable Outcome (USA) *Chad C Brown* a100 92
2 ch c Flatter(USA) Shananies Song (USA) (Eltish (USA))
7807a[12]
Favorite Girl (GER) *Michael Appleby* a68 72
8 b m Shirocco(GER) Favorite (GER) (Montjeu (IRE))
199[4] 420[4] 1711[2] 2369[3] (7775)
Favourite Royal (IRE) *Eve Johnson Houghton* 67
2 b f Acclamation Affirmative (Pivotal)
5705[5] 6062[3] 6648[6]
Favourite Treat (USA) *Ruth Carr* a87 83
6 b g Hard Spun(USA) Truart (USA) (Yes It's True (USA))
1125[7] (1595) 1954[9] 2361[5] (2960) 3344[3] 3595[4] 3945[4] 4453[7] 5179[6] 5482[11] 6027[5] 6579[9]
Fawaareq (IRE) *Owen Burrows* 95
3 b c Invincible Spirit(IRE) Ghandoorah (USA) (Forestry (USA))
1397[2] (2122) (3571) (4104)
Fawree (USA) *M F De Kock* a81
2 b c Candy Ride(ARG) Keeper Hill (USA) (Deputy Minister (CAN))
8574a[2]
Faydhan (USA) *John Gosden* a94 99
4 bb h War Front(USA) Agreeable Miss (USA) (Speightstown (USA))
7651[7] 7868[9]
Fayez (IRE) *David O'Meara* 84
2 b g Zoffany(IRE) Gems (Haafhd)
(2830) 3247[14] 4167[7] 5109[3] 5519[3]
Fazza *Grant Tuer* a39 77
9 ch g Sulamani(IRE) Markievicz (IRE) (Doyoun)
2673[11] 3367[9] 3952[10]
Fearbuster (IRE) *Hugo Palmer* a60 12
3 b f Fastnet Rock(AUS) Jewel In The Sand (IRE) (Bluebird (USA))
102[5] 258[3] 507[3] 820[5] 970[2] 1249[5] (1554)
Fearless Hunter (GER) *Rune Haugen* 103
6 b g Alhaarth(IRE) Firedance (GER) (Lomitas)
283a[7] 540a[4] 721a[6] 5950a[6]
Fearless Lad (IRE) *John Best* a69 64
6 b g Excellent Art Souffle (Zafonic (USA))
164[8] (2996) 3402[6] 4050[4] ◆ 4774[4] 5397[2] (6335)
Fearless Poppy *Christine Dunnett* a25 30
3 ch f Kyllachy Cesseras (IRE) (Cape Cross (IRE))
1289[7] 3411[11] 4895[10] 5338[12] 7201[6] 7444[8] 7646[10] 7986[14] 8351[10]

Fear Or Favour (IRE) *George Scott* a84 85
5 b g Haatef(USA) Insaaf (Averti (IRE))
(1945) (2309) 2754[15] 3123[7] 3726[4]
Fear The Fury (USA) *K R Burke* a57
2 ch c Elusive Quality(USA) O Beautiful (USA) (Unbridled's Song (USA))
8384[7]
Feb Thirtyfirst *Sheena West* a64 51
7 ch g Shirocco(GER) My Mariam (Salse (USA))
195[P]
Federico *J-C Rouget* 94
3 b g Acclamation Frangy (Sadler's Wells (USA))
7456a[6]
Feed The Goater (FR) *Richard Hannon* a89 86
3 b g Fastnet Rock(AUS) Lumiere Astrale (FR) (Trempolino (USA))
(2294) ◆ 3357[2] 3745[4] (4288) 4709[2] 5965[6] 6580[3] (6899)
Fee Du Hazard (FR) *C Ferland* 100
3 bb f Dr Fong(USA) Xachusa (FR) (Xaar)
3935a[5]
Feel Alive (FR) *F Rohaut* a66 79
3 b f American Post Golden Lily (FR) (Dolphin Street (FR))
2948a[4] 5946a[8]
Feelin Dicky *James Given* a70
3 b g Dick Turpin(IRE) Feelin Foxy (Foxhound (USA))
515[8] 797[8] 1183[5] 1558[6]
Feeling Easy (IRE) *Anthony Mulholland* a53 85
4 b m Bushranger(IRE) Easy Feeling (IRE) (Night Shift (USA))
1432[6] 2028[19] 3349[5] 3974[3] 7391a[3]
Feeltherhythm (IRE) *Chris Grant* a49 52
5 b m Yeats(IRE) Queen Althea (IRE) (Bach (IRE))
232[2] ◆ 368[12] 5155[2]
Feel The Vibes *Richard Hannon* 69
2 b g Medicean Apple Dumpling (Haafhd)
4552[6] 5202[7] 5325[4] 5796[4] 6289[9]
Feel This Moment (IRE) *Marco Botti* a69
3 b g Tamayuz Rugged Up (IRE) (Marju (IRE))
331[6]
Feisty Girl *Michael Mullineaux*
6 ch m Erhaab(USA) Dolly Duff (Alflora (IRE))
5353[4]
Felice (IRE) *Scott Dixon* a54 52
6 b m Papal Bull Tarabaya (IRE) (Warning)
6731[1]
Felician (GER) *Ferdinand J Leve* 106
8 b g Motivator Felicity (GER) (Inchinor)
2074a[7] 2633a[4] 3455a[7] 4438a[6] 5904a[3] 7400a[4] 7843a[8]
Felicita (FR) *P De Chevigny* a63 77
3 b f Sunday Break(JPN) Elle Donne (FR) (Johann Quatz (FR))
1542a[2]
Felix De Vega (IRE) *Michael Easterby* a63 98
4 b g Lope De Vega(IRE) Lafite (Robellino (USA))
1221[4] (1445) 1972[2] 2866[5] 6559[8] 7383[8]
Felix Leiter *K R Burke* 106
4 ch g Monsieur Bond(IRE) Spiralling (Pivotal)
1441[4] 2247[3] (2587) (3163) 3688[3]
Felix Mendelssohn (IRE) *David Simcock* 107
5 b g Galileo(IRE) Ice Queen (IRE) (Danehill Dancer (IRE))
2482[7] 3340[10] 6057[3] 6333[4]
Fellowship (USA) *Mark Casse* a106
3 ch c Awesome Of Course(USA) Go Girlfriend Go (USA) (Demidoff (USA))
2499a[8]
Felstead Queen *Joseph Tuite* a39 58
2 ch f Bated Breath Today's The Day (Alhaarth (IRE))
2310[6] 2696[7] 5202[8] 6652[10] 7615[9]
Fendale *Michael Dods* 97
4 b g Exceed And Excel(AUS) Adorn (Kyllachy)
3188[9] 3980[6] 4299[10] 5417[5] 6263[13] 6539[2] 6718[3] 7315[3] 7497[7]
Fen Lady *John Berry* a51 28
4 b m Champs Elysees Query (USA) (Distant View (USA))
55[8] 368[14]
Fenner Hill Neasa (IRE) *Pat Phelan* a40 52
3 b f Alfred Nobel(IRE) A Woman In Love (Muhtarram (USA))
345[6] 3973[10] 5019[3] 5204[6] 5708[7]
Ferdy (IRE) *Paul Green* a51 63
7 b h Antonius Pius(USA) Trinity Fair (Polish Precedent (USA))
1165[3] 1632[4] 2773[3] 3214[2] 3883[6] 5273[4] 5715[6] 5868[4]
Fergall (IRE) *Seamus Mullins* a87
9 br g Norwich Gaybrook Girl (IRE) (Alderbrook)
6089[3]
Fern Owl *Hughie Morrison* a85 77
4 ch g Nayef(USA) Snow Goose (Polar Falcon (USA))
(38) 343[2] (693) 1717[7] 2582[8] 4266[5] (6090) 7320[5] 7732[6] 8250[5] (8565) ◆
Ferocity (IRE) *Robyn Brisland* a72 57
2 b g Poet's Voice Foreign Language (USA) (Distant View (USA))
7184[5] 8082[7] (8536)
Ferro Nero (NZ) *Nigel Blackiston* 90
4 b g Savabeel(AUS) Floscula (USA) (Theatrical (IRE))
7637a[9]
Ferryview Place *Ian Williams* a56 46
7 b g Compton Place Songsheet (Dominion)
362[4] ◆ 569[4] 602[2] 701[4] (822) 982[8] 2566[8] 2899[4] 3997[10] 5011[8] 6857[5] 7369[10] 7515[10] 7641[2] 8492[3] (8528)
Festive Fare *Charlie Appleby* a114 108
4 b g Teofilo(IRE) Al Joza (Dubawi (IRE))
485[2] 748[4]
Fethiye Boy *Ronald Harris* a60 74
2 br g Pastoral Pursuits Ocean Blaze (Polar Prince (IRE))
1635[7] 1915[8] 5283[3] 6016[5] 6252[2] 7269[3] 7966[8]

Fever Few *Chris Wall* a80 83
7 b m Pastoral Pursuits Prairie Oyster (Emperor Jones (USA))
433[7] 703[5] 969[5] 3575[6] 4355[U] 5039[5] 6072[6] 6487[6] 7059[17]

Fibonacci *Hugo Palmer* 71
2 ch c Galileo(IRE) Tereschenko (USA) (Giant's Causeway (USA))
7470[5]

Fica Comigo *M Delzangles* a42 38
3 ch g Pivotal Tudor Court (IRE) (Cape Cross (IRE))
5280a[14]

Fidaawy *Sir Michael Stoute* 99
3 ch g New Approach(IRE) Haymana (IRE) (Pivotal)
2861[3] (4035) 4808[4] ◆ (5391) 5924[4] 6884[5]

Fidelma Moon (IRE) *K R Burke* a56 80
4 b m Dylan Thomas(IRE) Ridiforza (FR) (Starborough)
1158[7] (1412) 1631[9] 2420[2] 3132[4] 3521[4] 4145[3] 4871[2] 5076[3] 5844[6] 7010[9]

Fidra Bay (IRE) *Alan Swinbank* 70
3 b f Roderic O'Connor(IRE) Halicardia (Halling (USA))
1381[2] 1671[2] 2422[6]

Field Game *Hughie Morrison* a79 94
4 b g Pastoral Pursuits Tarqua (IRE) (King Charlemagne (USA))
1887[7] 2206[10] 2754[12] 3358[13] 3803[10] (4355) 4608[9] 5744[8] 6583[7]

Fieldmouse *Eve Johnson Houghton* a56 52
4 b m Champs Elysees Intervene (Zafonic (USA))
84[5] 255[4] 348[8]

Field Of Dream *David Nicholls* a87 105
9 b g Oasis Dream Field Of Hope (IRE) (Selkirk (USA))
464[4] 860[6]

Field Officer *Tim Easterby*
3 ch g Major Cadeaux Its Another Gift (Primo Dominie)
1494[7]

Field Of Vision (IRE) *Joseph Tuite* a102 92
3 b g Pastoral Pursuits Grand Design (Danzero (AUS))
235[2] 493[2] 821[5] 1070[7] 2751[6] 5148[9] 5657[9] 5961[9] 6207[5] 6944[14] 7737[11]

Fieldsman (USA) *George Scott* a83 95
4 b g Hard Spun(USA) R Charlie's Angel (USA) (Indian Charlie (USA))
(2247) 2868[8] 4109[10] 4627[6] 6710[6]

Fields Of Athenry (IRE) *Flemming Velin* a71 118
4 b h Galileo(IRE) Last Love (IRE) (Danehill (USA))
5187a[7] 6390a[9]

Fields Of Fortune *Richard Hannon* 71
2 b g Champs Elysees Widescreen (USA) (Distant View (USA))
4270[2] ◆ 5740[4] 7074[6]

Fields Of Song (IRE) *Kevin Ryan* 80
2 br f Harbour Watch(IRE) Singing Field (IRE) (Singspiel (IRE))
(3873) 5756[3] 6630[2] 7185[4] (7549)

Fierce Impact (JPN) *David Simcock* 76
2 b c Deep Impact(JPN) Keiai Gerbera (JPN) (Smarty Jones (USA))
(7226)

Fiery Character (IRE) *Tom Dascombe* 79
2 br f Dragon Pulse(IRE) Intricate Dance (USA) (Aptitude (USA))
(1437) ◆ 1965[4] 4343[5] 5638[8] 6222[12]

Fiery Spice (IRE) *Robert Cowell* a49
2 ch g Dream Ahead(USA) High Spice (USA) (Songandaprayer (USA))
8406[9]

Fiesole *Eoin Doyle* a50 58
4 b g Montjeu(IRE) Forgotten Dreams (IRE) (Olden Times)
7801a[14]

Fiftyshadesfreed (IRE) *George Baker* a90 92
5 gr g Verglas(IRE) Vasilia (Dansili)
1480[6] 1797[5] 2377[8] 3109[2] 3861[4] 4868[9] 6301[8] 6870[7] 7418[8]

Fiftyshadesofgrey (IRE) *George Baker* a98 100
5 gr g Dark Angel(IRE) Wohaida (IRE) (Kheleyf (USA))
1335[6] 1856[11] 2862[12] 4758[10]

Fiftyshadesofpink (IRE) *Hugo Palmer* a45 61
3 b f Pour Moi(IRE) Maakrah (Dubai Destination (USA))
4367[6]

Fiftytintsofsilver (IRE) *Jeremy Gask* a46 34
3 gr f Clodovil(IRE) Marju Guest (IRE) (Marju (IRE))
181[6] 436[6] 2083[5] 2559[8] 3140[4] 3473[4] 5636[7]

Fighting Temeraire (IRE) *Dean Ivory* a82 98
3 b c Invincible Spirit(IRE) Hot Ticket (IRE) (Selkirk (USA))
2239[2] ◆ 2695[2] 3299[27] (4886) 6918[6] 7153[5] ◆

Figurante (IRE) *Jamie Osborne* a78 76
3 ch f Excellent Art Savignano (Polish Precedent (USA))
15[4] 77[2] ◆ (211) 1420[4] (1725) 2108[5] (2585) 2935[3] 5247[3] 5602[3] 6426[2]

Filament Of Gold (USA) *Roy Brotherton* a66 42
5 b g Street Cry(IRE) Raw Silk (USA) (Malibu Moon (USA))
295[9] 569[9] 2566[2] 3476[3] (3732) 4715[5] 5130[4] 5610[7] 6143[5] 8038[6] 8410[7] 8540[8]

Filatore (IRE) *Bernard Llewellyn* 4
7 ch g Teofilo(IRE) Dragnet (IRE) (Rainbow Quest (USA))
1523[8]

File Of Facts (IRE) *Tom Dascombe* a62 65
3 b g Iffraaj Clever Day (USA) (Action This Day (USA))
1276[11] 1486[9] 4233[7] (4987) 5256[2] 5548[7] 6593[5] 7516[5]

Filfil (USA) *S Seemar* a57 47
6 b g Hard Spun(USA) Dixietwostepper (USA) (More Than Ready (USA))
183a[8]

Fillydelphia (IRE) *Patrick Holmes* a60 63
5 b m Strategic Prince Lady Fonic (Zafonic (USA))
1952[5] 2656[3] 3154[4] (3774) 4934[3] 5980[2] 6738[4] 7045[8] 7438[8]

Fils Anges (IRE) *Ali Jan* a90 110
6 gr h Dark Angel(IRE) La Piaf (FR) (Fabulous Dancer (USA))
373a[5] ◆ (623a) 810a[12]

Fils De L'Air (FR) *P Sogorb* a89 75
2 ch c Areion(GER) Chica Loca (FR) (American Post)
(7454a)

Fils Prodigue (FR) *F-H Graffard* a76 70
3 b g Shakespearean(IRE) Ribadesella (Hernando (FR))
7680a[10]

Filudo (FR) *David O'Meara* 46
2 b c Linngari(IRE) First Light (GER) (Big Shuffle (USA))
3382[13] 5885[8] 7248[7]

Filzeto (FR) *E Lellouche* a69 56
3 b c Siyouni(FR) Filzeta (IRE) (Fasliyev (USA))
5280a[6]

Final *Mark Johnston* a78 87
4 b g Arabian Gleam Caysue (Cayman Kai (IRE))
278[2] ◆ 367[5] 802[3] 1248[7] 1707[7] 2256[4] 3011[5] (3481) ◆ (4232) ◆ 4727[2] 5520[3]

Final Chapter *Tim Easterby* 74
2 ch c Nathaniel(IRE) My First Romance (Danehill (USA))
4423[11] 6054[9] 6640[4]

Final Choice *Roger Charlton* a48 61
3 b g Makfi Anasazi (IRE) (Sadler's Wells (USA))
2590[4] 2851[2] 3509[2] (3765)

Final Countdown *Rebecca Menzies* a64 77
5 ch g Selkirk(USA) Culture Queen (King's Best (USA))
1620[13] 8007[11]

Final Frontier (IRE) *Mrs John Harrington* 106
3 b c Dream Ahead(USA) Polly Perkins (IRE) (Pivotal)
4065[9] 4433a[9] 7706a[8]

Finalize (FR) *T Lemer* a67 68
2 b f Vertigineux(FR) Fligane (FR) (Bering)
7490a[4]

Final Reckoning (IRE) *Charlie Appleby* 89
2 gr g Dark Angel(IRE) Lan Force (ITY) (Blu Air Force (IRE))
2648[4] 3167[2] (3619) (4825) 5656[5]

Final Spring (IRE) *Jim Goldie* 20
3 b f Zebedee Baileys Cream (Mister Baileys)
1383[6] 1691[10] 2302[13] 3153[11] 3940[8]

Final Stage *Saeed bin Suroor* a57 70
3 ch f Street Cry(IRE) Moyesii (USA) (Diesis)
1609[7]

Final Venture *Paul Midgley* a99 107
4 b g Equiano(FR) Sharplaw Venture (Polar Falcon (USA))
1124[3] ◆ 1489[8] 1879[2] (2202) (2531) (3021) ◆ 3980[4] (4373) 4584[2] 5863[4] ◆ 8530[4]

Fineasa Bee's Wing (IRE) *Adrian Brendan Joyce* a47 41
3 gr f Campaign Swing(IRE) Salgrev (IRE) (Verglas (IRE))
8120[10]

Fine Blend (IRE) *William Muir* a95 99
3 br f Sakhee's Secret Coffee Time (IRE) (Efisio)
2192[3] 2923a[6] 3392[2] 4905a[10] 6574[5] 6943[8] 7520a[9]

Fine Example *Kevin Ryan* a70 67
3 b g Showcasing Belle Reine (King Of Kings (IRE))
1564[4] 1927[5] 2553[5] 3946[4] 5222[6] (5803) (6106) 7203[4]

Finelcity (GER) *Harry Dunlop* a93 76
3 b g Elusive City(USA) Finity (USA) (Diesis)
1270[3] (1570) 2393[6] 2892[14] 3745[2] 4382[4] 5027[2] (5301) (6416) (7462)

Fine 'n Dandy (IRE) *J R Jenkins* a76 73
5 ch g Dandy Man(IRE) Pearly Brooks (Efisio)
75[4] (444) ◆ 541[6] 580[7] 894[3] 1046[3] 1803[3] 1964[5] 3407[4] 3650[6] (4590) 4952[9] 5751[5] 7420[4]

Fine Resolve *Alexandra Dunn* a63 68
7 b g Refuse To Bend(IRE) Papillon De Bronze (IRE) (Marju (IRE))
6619[2] (6825) (7044) 7361[4]

Fine Share (IRE) *John Bridger* a44 52
3 b g Art Connoisseur(IRE) Novel Fun (IRE) (Noverre (USA))
155[14] 6030[5]

Finest City (USA) *Ian Kruljac* a117 105
4 ch m City Zip(USA) Be Envied (USA) (Lemon Drop Kid (USA))
(7836a)

Fingal's Cave (IRE) *Iain Jardine* a82 89
4 ch g Fast Company(IRE) Indiannie Moon (Fraam)
532[4] ◆ (680) 795[5] (1545) 1997[3] ◆ 2476[10] 3233[4] (3803) 4306[4] 7593[3] 7825[9] 8122[8] 8385[9]

Finn Class (IRE) *Michael Dods* a85 96
5 b g Exceed And Excel(AUS) Finnmark (Halling (USA))
1195[5] (1871) 2331[10] 3055[10] 3923[8] 4448[8] 5226[6] 5976[10] 6500[3] 7573[9]

Finn McCool (IRE) *A P O'Brien* 101
2 b c Galileo(IRE) Mystical Lady (IRE) (Halling (USA))
6386a[7] 7539[7]

Finsbury Square (IRE) *F Chappet* a85 111
4 b g Siyouni(FR) Diamond Square (FR) (Dyhim Diamond (IRE))
1172a[2] (2317a) 2943a[3] 3796a[4] 4824[9] (5949a) 6990a[4] 7758a[4]

Fire And Passion *Adrian Paul Keatley* a74 75
4 b g Dutch Art Mary Goodnight (King's Best (USA))
65[4] 778[5] 1501[2] 1737[7] 6501[2] 7801a[10]

Fire Brigade *Michael Bell* a75 54
2 b g Firebreak Island Rhapsody (Bahamian Bounty)
3100[7] 4594[8] 6622[8] 7228[7] (7881) 7974[2]

Firedanser *Richard Fahey* a49 80
3 b g Firebreak Citron (Reel Buddy (USA))
2477[7] 3567[5] 4789[8] 5539[3] 6541[9] 7333[5]

Fire Diamond *Tom Dascombe* a69 57
3 b c Firebreak Diapason (IRE) (Mull Of Kintyre (USA))
2349[7] 3478[6] 4701[9] 5803[3] 6347[7] 7602[3] (7850) (8248) (8555)

Fire Empress *James Unett* a52 35
3 b f Firebreak Tedsmore Dame (Indesatchel (IRE))
3475[9] 4017[7] 8342[6] 8528[10]

Fire Fighting (IRE) *Mark Johnston* a109 116
5 b g Soldier Of Fortune(IRE) Savoie (FR) (Anabaa (USA))
748[6] 1069[2] ◆ 1973[7] 2222[5] 2626[7] 2866[6] 3383[7] 4165[6] (4731) 5159[6] (5411) 5647[11] 5894[5]

Firefright (IRE) *Jeremy Noseda* 92
2 b c Dragon Pulse(IRE) Emsiyah (USA) (Bernardini (USA))
5371[3] 5959[2] 6260[3] 7502[2]

Fireglow *Mark Johnston* 110
3 b f Teofilo(IRE) Fading Light (King's Best (USA))
1888[4] 2160[2] 3339[11] 4184a[5] 4610[2] (4883) 5586[12] 6917[2] 7123[7]

Fire Jet (IRE) *John Mackie* a55 82
3 ch f Ask Lightning Jet (Dutch Art)
2009[7] 2505[11] 3990[7] (5375) (6193) 7060[4] 7624[3]

Fire Palace *Robert Eddery* a76 80
2 b f Royal Applause Inflammable (Montjeu (IRE))
4756[7] (5022) 6257[3] 7147[4] ◆ 7668[4]

Fire Ship *William Knight* a78 111
7 b g Firebreak Mays Dream (Josr Algarhoud (IRE))
1196[13] 2246[7] 2819[10] 3534[6] 3910[11] 5234[4] 7017[4]

Firesnake (IRE) *Lisa Williamson* a74 73
3 b g Dandy Man(IRE) La Bataille (USA) (Out Of Place (USA))
1485[6] 2200[4] 2695[5] 3111[9] 3567[7] 3775[7] 5732[6] 6418[7] 7255[3] 7611[7] (7815) 8094[7] 8365[5]

Firestorm (GER) *Michael Attwater* a71 76
5 b g Dylan Thomas(IRE) Fitness (IRE) (Monsun (GER))
1569[8] 2037[6] 2324[10] 2827[3] ◆ 3403[7] 3801[2] 4050[7] 8477[8]

Firey Speech (USA) *D K Weld* 105
2 b c Street Cry(IRE) Firey Red (IRE) (Pivotal)
6349a[2]

Firgrove Bridge (IRE) *Kevin Frost* a49 58
4 ch g Dandy Man(IRE) Over Rating (Desert King (IRE))
1596[7] 2040[7] 3098[9] 3674[7] 4202[8] 4557[4] 5386[8] 5797[5] 6373[4] 6636[8] 8350[9] 8499[11]

Firmament *David O'Meara* a104 114
4 b g Cape Cross(IRE) Heaven Sent (Pivotal)
(2620) 3303[2] ◆ 4399[4] (4976) (5585) 6109[2] 6942[2] 7354[3] ◆

Firmdecisions (IRE) *Dean Ivory* a95 90
6 b g Captain Rio Luna Crescente (IRE) (Danehill (USA))
2247[15] 4163[12] 4534[7] 4954[5] 5403[11] 6529[8] (7308) (7781) 8177[13]

Firnas *Charlie Appleby* 96
3 b c Dubawi(IRE) Crystal Music (USA) (Nureyev (USA))
(2175)

First Avenue *Laura Mongan*
11 b g Montjeu(IRE) Marciala (IRE) (Machiavellian (USA))
3798[9]

First Bombardment *David O'Meara* a87 80
3 br g Pastoral Pursuits Magic Myth (IRE) (Revoque (IRE))
1761[2] (1922) 2426[2] 3420[8] 4093[5] 4612[12] 5070[2] 5295[3] 5679[8] 6927[4] (7112) 7358[7]

First Cat *K Kukk* a21 47
9 b g One Cool Cat(USA) Zina La Belle (Mark Of Esteem (IRE))
1518a[3] 2285a[5] 3380a[3] 5456a[2] 6401a[5]

First Conde (FR) *M Nigge* a63 63
3 ch g Turtle Bowl(IRE) Makadane (Danehill Dancer (IRE))
7265a[5]

First Dance (IRE) *James Tate* a73 80
2 b f Cape Cross(IRE) Happy Wedding (IRE) (Green Tune (USA))
6414[4] 7118[2]

First Excel *Roy Bowring* a62 59
4 ch g First Trump Exceedingly Good (IRE) (Exceed And Excel (AUS))
387[7] (596) 936[7] 2013[3] 2542[3] 3069[9] 4321[2] 5270[2]

First Experience *Lee Carter* a82 78
5 b m Tamayuz Lolla's Spirit (IRE) (Montjeu (IRE))
67[10] 349[7] 558[4] 1754[2] (2001) 3197[2] 3802[4] 4787[2] 5075[5] 5677[5] (6299) 6806[12] 8493[3]

First Mohican *Alan King* a108 106
8 ch g Tobougg(IRE) Mohican Girl (Dancing Brave (USA))
31[5] 99[2] 861[6] 1067[4] 1273[4] 1963[3] 2468[7] 3387[7] 4734[4] 5639[4] 6283[3] 7150[2] 7979[6] 8210[8] 8479[2]

First Nation *Charlie Appleby* a79 62
2 b c Dubawi(IRE) Moyesii (USA) (Diesis)
7239[6] (7907) ◆

First Of Never (IRE) *Lynn Siddall* a44
10 b g Systematic Never Promise (FR) (Cadeaux Genereux)
7106[7] 7597[4] 7991[5]

First Of Spring (IRE) *J-C Rouget* 100
2 ch f Galileo(IRE) Homecoming Queen (IRE) (Holy Roman Emperor (IRE))
6986a[6]

First Party *Mark Johnston* a61 71
3 gr f Royal Applause Third Party (Terimon)
148[3]

First Priority *Saeed bin Suroor* a79
2 b f Street Cry(IRE) First Blush (IRE) (Pivotal)
(7689)

First Quest (USA) *Ed Dunlop* 77
2 b c First Defence(USA) Dixie Quest (USA) (Coronado's Quest (USA))
4649[6] (5073) 7471[7]

First Rate *Roger Varian* a62 71
3 b g Kyllachy Hooray (Invincible Spirit (IRE))
2333[5] 2742[14]

First Rebellion *Tony Carroll* a63 57
7 ch g Cockney Rebel(IRE) First Dawn (Dr Fong (USA))
230[4] 264[2] 381[4] 696[4] 895[2] 1005[4] 1180[8] 1320[5]

First Sargeant *Lawrence Mullaney* a48 79
6 gr g Dutch Art Princess Raya (Act One)
212[8] 1588[10] 2507[12] 2773[16] 3253[5] 3804[7] 3842[2] ◆ 4143[3] 4493[5] 4875[5] 5117[3] 5580[6] 6029[2] 6450[2] 7045[9] 7078[9]

First Selection (SPA) *Simon Crisford* a84 109
3 b c Diktat Villa Sonata (Mozart (IRE))
807a[6] 1864[7] 2283a[2] 3245[6] 4185a[7] 6117[6] 7115[12]

First Sitting *Chris Wall* 109
5 b g Dansili Aspiring Diva (USA) (Distant View (USA))
1620[7] (2979) 3340[4] 3889[12] (5173) 6178a[2] 6786[27]

First Summer *Shaun Harris* a69 63
4 b g Cockney Rebel(IRE) Silken Dalliance (Rambo Dancer (CAN))
97[4] 316[11] 870[6] 1323[5] 2046[5] 3031[2] 3564[6] 5264[2] (5739) (6243) 6514[2] 7246[8] 7613[8] 8480[6]

First Up (IRE) *Jeremy Noseda* a86 83
2 b c Rip Van Winkle(IRE) Doregan (IRE) (Bahhare (USA))
5615[5] ◆ 6159[3] (6672)

First Victory (IRE) *Saeed bin Suroor* 105
3 b f Teofilo(IRE) Eastern Joy (Dubai Destination (USA))
1396[6] 1890[4]

First Voyage (IRE) *Charlie Appleby* 87
3 ch g Dubawi(IRE) Concordia (Pivotal)
7009[2] 7218[2] (7627)

First Wheat *Michael Easterby* a60 75
3 b g Monsieur Bond(IRE) Ballet Fame (USA) (Quest For Fame)
3609[7] (4007) 4985[5] 5539[7] 6220[6] 6502[6] 7076[3] ◆ 7999a[6] 8240[7]

Fishergate *Richard Rowe* a55 68
3 b g Pastoral Pursuits Miss Meggy (Pivotal)
152[8] 344[8] 612[6] 3141[5] 3493[2] 4303[4] 5720[12] 6629[13] 7310[13]

Fisher Green (IRE) *Michael Dods* 79
3 b g Rip Van Winkle(IRE) Prealpina (IRE) (Indian Ridge)
(1216) 1623[9] 2532[5] 3914[8] 5526[8]

Fit For The Job (IRE) *David Wachman* 93
4 b g Lawman(FR) Spesialta (Indian Ridge)
4747a[12] 4921a[14] 5941a[20]

Fit The Bill (IRE) *James Tate* a77 75
4 b g Iffraaj Najam (Singspiel (IRE))
605[2] 888[8]

Fityaan *M Al Mheiri* a105 110
8 b g Haafhd Welsh Diva (Selkirk (USA))
91a[8] 280a[6] 370a[5] 450a[2] 626a[8] 723a[4] (841a) 1104a[6]

Fitzgerald (USA) *A bin Harmash* a113
4 b g Elusive Quality(USA) Filarmonia (ARG) (Slew Gin Fizz (USA))
(8396a)

Fitzwilliam *Mick Channon* a61 61
4 ch g Sixties Icon Canadian Capers (Ballacashtal (CAN))
1236[5] 1548[2] 1742[5] 1948[9] 3031[8] 3401[6] 3737[3]

Fitzwilly *Mick Channon* a78 81
6 b g Sixties Icon Canadian Capers (Ballacashtal (CAN))
1914[3] 2392[9] 3161[4] 3746[2] 4266[4] 4912[8] 6362[8]

Five Fifteen (FR) *X Thomas-Demeaulte* a83 103
4 gr m Zafeen(FR) Fragrancia (FR) (Linamix (FR))
6273a[3] 7929a[5]

Fivehundredmiles (IRE) *John Patrick Shanahan* a55 70
3 b c The Carbon Unit(USA) There's A Light (IRE) (Fantastic Light (USA))
3550[3] 4870[3] 5581[3]

Five Star Frank *Eve Johnson Houghton* a73 55
2 b c Exceed And Excel(AUS) Anadolu (IRE) (Statue Of Liberty (USA))
4736[9] 5631[4] 8065[5] 8175[5] 8453[2]

Fivetwoeight *Peter Chapple-Hyam* a75
2 b c Kyllachy Super Midge (Royal Applause)
8065[3] ◆ (8352)

Fixed Rate *D Smaga* 74
3 b g Oasis Dream Pretty Face (Rainbow Quest (USA))
5448a[7] 7088a[10]

Fixette (IRE) *F-H Graffard* 101
2 b f Kodiac Fixed Gaze (USA) (Speightstown (USA))
3182a[3] 3937a[2] 4925a[2] 6068a[4]

Fix Up Look Sharp *Jamie Poulton* a47 67
5 b h Sakhee(USA) Featherlight (Fantastic Light (USA))
1826[8] 4057[4] 5267[3]

Flag Of Glory *Peter Hiatt* a53 54
9 b g Trade Fair Rainbow Sky (Rainbow Quest (USA))
2616[9] 2899[11] 3470[2] 3492[3] 3901[2] 5708[2] 5883[10] 7628[11] 7936[7]

Flag War (GER) *Saeed bin Suroor* a103 99
5 b g Dubawi(IRE) Fantastic Flame (IRE) (Generous (IRE))
188a[7]

Flambeuse *E Leenders* a94 80
5 b m Cape Cross(IRE) Flamenba (USA) (Kingmambo (USA))
329[5] 4158[4] ◆ (4661) 5872[7] 7652[9] 7934[7] 8336a[14]

Flamboyant (FR) *Patrick Gallagher* a82 115
5 b g Peer Gynt(JPN) Relicia Bere (FR) (Until Sundown (USA))
1106a[5]

Flame And Fortune (IRE) *Clive Mulhall*
2 ch g Dragon Pulse(IRE) Fame And Fortune (IRE) (In The Wings)
7819[11]

Flame Hero (NZ) *L Ho* 111
6 b g Savabeel(AUS) Rhysess (NZ) (Pins (AUS))
8329a[9]

Flame Of Hope (IRE) *David Barron* a34 56
2 ch f Dragon Pulse(IRE) Saabga (USA) (Woodman (USA))
7040[4] *7845[4]*
Flaming Marvel (IRE) *James Fanshawe* a77
2 b g Redoute's Choice(AUS) Flame Of Hestia (IRE) (Giant's Causeway (USA))
7908[2] ◆ *8208[3]*
Flaming Spear (IRE) *Kevin Ryan* a103 96
4 ch g Lope De Vega(IRE) Elshamms (Zafonic (USA))
1441[2] ◆ 2158[18] 6558[19] 7821[12] *(8478)*
Flanders Flame *Helder Pereira* a53 104
3 ch g Dutch Art Pink Flames (IRE) (Redback)
(5502a) 6973a[6]
Flash City (ITY) *Ruth Carr* a79 82
8 b g Elusive City(USA) Furnish (Green Desert (USA))
1601[8] 1874[2] 2040[3] 2261[9] 2658[4] 2863[2] 3326[3] 3709[2] (4039) 4514[4] 5032[9] 5479[7] 5864[8] 6476[5] 6958[3] 7252[7]
Flash Fire (IRE) *Charlie Appleby* 114
4 b g Shamardal(USA) Flamelet (USA) (Theatrical (IRE))
189a[2] 373a[4] 628a[4] 1441[5] (2027) 3386[28] 4152[5] 4625[4] 5613[8] 5871[17]
Flashing Light *Tim Easterby* a57 59
2 b f Compton Place Heliograph (Ishiguru (USA))
5884[17] 6214[4] 6641[2] *8097[8]* *8285[11]*
Flashman *Gary Moore* a94 88
7 ch g Doyen(IRE) Si Si Si (Lomitas)
(78) *317[7]* *1209[7]*
Flash Of White *Bryan Smart* a52 72
2 b g Excelebration(IRE) Aberdovey (Mister Baileys)
3548[6] 4227[4] 4678[3] 6007[4] ◆ *6743[10]*
Flashy Approach *P Bradik* 94
6 ch g New Approach(IRE) Flashy Wings (Zafonic (USA))
2722a[7] 3992a[7]
Flashy King (IRE) *Joseph Tuite* a16 33
3 b g Tagula(IRE) Trixiebelle (IRE) (Kheleyf (USA))
778[8] *874[5]* *1577[12]* 2750[7] *3317[7]* 4289[14]
Flashy Snapper *Simon Crisford* a53
2 ch c Raven's Pass(USA) Super Sleuth (IRE) (Selkirk (USA))
7812[9]
Flauto (IRE) *Marco Botti* a68
2 ch g Excelebration(IRE) Flandre (USA) (Elusive Quality (USA))
5676[8] *6590[5]* *7100[5]*
Flawed Diamond (FR) *K R Burke* 53
2 gr f Tin Horse(IRE) Anaphora (IRE) (Goofalik (USA))
2771[9] *3561[9]* 4298[11] 4869[4] 5165[4] 6026[7]
Flawlessly (FR) *James Bethell* 68
2 b f Exceed And Excel(AUS) Privalova (IRE) (Alhaarth (IRE))
2424[2] 2800[4]
Fleabiscuit (IRE) *Hugo Palmer* 81
2 b f High Chaparral(IRE) Bluebelle Dancer (IRE) (Danehill Dancer (IRE))
(6776) 7116[7]
Fleckerl (IRE) *Conor Dore* a95 82
6 b g Danehill Dancer(IRE) Spinola (FR) (Spinning World (USA))
(260) *433[9]* *546[6]* *620[6]* *(670)* *(771)* *879[3]* *1335[12]* *1650[10]* 2581[7] *4644[13]* *6371[6]* 6914[7] 7221[9] *7965[7]* *8314[9]*
Fledermaus (IRE) *Tina Jackson* a16 44
6 br g Jeremy(USA) Khayrat (IRE) (Polar Falcon (USA))
3294[8] 3844[9] 4456[10] 5383[5] 5980[6] *7105[10]*
Fleetfoot Jack (IRE) *David O'Meara* 62
2 b c Kyllachy Move (Observatory (USA))
6679[4] 7157[13] 7741[4]
Fleeting Dream (IRE) *William Haggas* a69 66
3 b f Dream Ahead(USA) Flanders (IRE) (Common Grounds)
3267[7] 4041[8] 5041[3] 5626[2] (6291) 6790[7] *7363[9]* *7611[3]*
Fleeting Francesca *Chris Gordon* a52 49
2 ch f Paco Boy(IRE) Fleeting Echo (Beat Hollow)
5722[9] 6250[7] *6624[11]* *7047[5]* 7570[8]
Fleeting Glimpse *Andrew Balding* a65
3 b f Passing Glance Perfect Act (Act One)
7616[4] *7894[4]* *8320[8]*
Fleeting Motion *Richard Hannon* 80
2 ch f Sepoy(AUS) Fleeting Image (Sir Percy)
3556[6] (7494)
Fleeting Visit *Eve Johnson Houghton* a89 89
3 b g Manduro(GER) Short Affair (Singspiel (IRE))
5601[2] ◆ 6301[3] *6675[4]* ◆ 7117[12]
Fleetwood Bella *Michael Attwater* a28
5 ch m Byron Royal Ivy (Mujtahid (USA))
87[10] *237[10]*
Fleetwood Poppy *Michael Attwater* a51 20
4 br m Kheleyf(USA) Steppin Out (First Trump)
84[7] *(653)* *1748[12]* *2326[5]* 3560[11] 4385[7] *(5261)* *8180[11]* *8448[9]*
Flemish Duchesse (FR) *Andreas Lowe* 93
3 b f Duke Of Marmalade(IRE) Fabiana (Ashkalani (IRE))
1357a[4] 5220a[14]
Flers (GER) *Ecurie Fievez* a55 45
7 gr g Verglas(IRE) Firedance (GER) (Lomitas)
3733a[10]
Fleurdelune (FR) *M Delaplace* a69 70
2 bl f Sunday Break(JPN) Flower Of Freedom (FR) (Sadler's Wells (USA))
7454a[4]
Fleur Forsyte *James Fanshawe* a59
2 b f Teofilo(IRE) Fleurissimo (Dr Fong (USA))
7761[10]
Fleurtille *Ray Craggs* a40 76
7 b m Tillerman Miss Fleurie (Alzao (USA))
1600[6] *2332[9]* 2855[5]
Flexible Flyer *Chris Dwyer* a76 91
7 b g Exceed And Excel(AUS) Windermere Island (Cadeaux Genereux)
1634[12] 2253[6] 2903[8]
Flicka's Boy *Tony Coyle* a79 77
4 b g Paco Boy(IRE) Selkirk Sky (Selkirk (USA))
1110[3] ◆ *1321[10]* 1666[3] *1803[4]* 2270[2] 2426[5] 2975[7] 4452[11] 4689[7] 4726[2] 5032[6] 5296[4] 5864[5] *6248[6]* 6475[8] 6793[10] *7386[5]*
Flick Of An Eye (USA) *Danny Gargan*
4 bb m Afleet Express(USA) Dignified Diva (USA) (Meadowlake (USA))
89a[4]
Flight Of Fantasy *Harry Dunlop* a70
2 b f Nathaniel(IRE) Luminda (IRE) (Danehill (USA))
8465[2]
Flight Officer *Saeed bin Suroor* 99
5 b g New Approach(IRE) Danuta (USA) (Sunday Silence (USA))
3666[2] 4858[4] 6559[11] 7188[9]
Flight Risk (IRE) *J S Bolger* a76 110
5 ch g Teofilo(IRE) Raghida (IRE) (Nordico (USA))
1127a[2] 1226a[2] 1509a[3] 1730a[4] 2495a[2] 3681a[2] 4433a[5] 5213a[5] 6353a[5] 6816a[2] 6983a[4] 7191a[9] 7706a[10]
Flighty Filia (IRE) *Amanda Perrett* a71 62
4 gr m Raven's Pass(USA) Coventina (IRE) (Daylami (IRE))
1389 *(698)* *1236[6]*
Flintshire *Chad C Brown* a108 124
6 b h Dansili Dance Routine (Sadler's Wells (USA))
7835a[2]
Flinty Fell (IRE) *Keith Dalgleish* a73 73
3 b f Rock Of Gibraltar(IRE) Manoeuvre (IRE) (Galileo (IRE))
814[3] ◆ *1063[8]* 1628[9] *5844[2]* *5973[8]* 6342[2] *6742[10]* 7743[P]
Flirt (IRE) *David Wachman* a80 88
3 ch f Duke Of Marmalade(IRE) Miss Intimate (USA) (War Chant (USA))
4218a[11] 5313a[6] 5564a[6] 6495a[8] 7392a[10] *7676a[13]*
Flood Defence (IRE) *Chris Wall* a66
2 b f Harbour Watch(IRE) Krynica (USA) (Danzig (USA))
5022[4] *5809[2]* *7107[4]* ◆ *7640[5]*
Floodlight (USA) *A Fabre* 109
3 b c Medaglia d'Oro(USA) Flashing (USA) (A.P. Indy (USA))
2140a[2] 2946a[13] 5004a[4] 6598a[3]
Flood Warning *Clive Cox* a56
2 ch f Pivotal Sabreon (Caerleon (USA))
8361[5]
Florencio *Marco Botti* a89 86
3 b g Equiano(FR) Mary Pekan (IRE) (Sri Pekan (USA))
(1168) ◆ 1442[7] 1977[7] 4223[5] 4268[5] 5896[2] 6492[8] *7206[5]* *7461[5]* *8380[6]*
Florenza *Chris Fairhurst* 84
3 b f Haafhd Danzatrice (Tamure (IRE))
1628[11] 2239[4] 3213[11] (3643) 4398[6] 5199[4] 5588[3] 6096[5]
Florida Dream (FR) *Y Gourraud* a77 75
2 b f Muhtathir Red America (FR) (Red Ransom (USA))
(6015a)
Flower Of Love *Simon Crisford* a85 78
3 br f Poet's Voice Fragrancy (IRE) (Singspiel (IRE))
5504[4] ◆ 6278[2] ◆ (6765) *7732[5]* *(8076)* ◆
Flower Power *Tony Coyle* 79
5 br m Bollin Eric Floral Rhapsody (Alflora (IRE))
6634[5] (6795) 7158[11] *8283[12]*
Flowers On Venus (IRE) *Tom Dascombe* a91 93
4 ch g Raven's Pass(USA) Chelsea Rose (IRE) (Desert King (IRE))
580[2] ◆ 1530[10] 1990[2] 2547[6] 3068[4] 4079[3] 4889[8] 5488[10] *(6140)* *6962[5]*
Flowing Clarets *John Bridger* a63 74
3 ch f Pastoral Pursuits Flying Clarets (IRE) (Titus Livius (FR))
1647[2] 2802[4] 3292[8] 4034[5] 5032[8] (5855) 6770[8] (7415) *7899[8]* *8154[6]* *8357[4]*
Fluff (IRE) *A P O'Brien* 98
4 b m Galileo(IRE) Sumora (IRE) (Danehill (USA))
1016a[5] 1279a[7] 2497a[5]
Fluorescent Rock (IRE) *Damian Joseph English* a66 62
2 b f Rock Of Gibraltar(IRE) Black Tornado (IRE) (Pivotal)
5077[5]
Flutterbee *George Baker* a67 70
4 b m Equiano(FR) Dunya (Unfuwain (USA))
1947[2] 2738[2] 2799[2] *2814[5]* 4082[3] 4482[2] (5458a) (6403a) *7614[14]*
Fly *James Fanshawe* a85 69
4 ch m Pastoral Pursuits Hannda (IRE) (Dr Devious (IRE))
5024[3] ◆ *6084[6]*
Fly At Dawn (USA) *Charlie Appleby* a97 95
2 ch c Discreet Cat(USA) Emirates Girl (USA) (Unbridled's Song (USA))
(4594) *(5506)* ◆ *6122[3]* (6705) 7151[5] *8575a[2]*
Flyball *Dianne Sayer* a44 53
4 gr g Proclamation(IRE) Bella Bertolini (Bertolini (USA))
1124[7] 1565[7] 2053[6] 5889[12] 6568[4] 7097[3] *7438[6]*
Flyboy (IRE) *David O'Meara* 86
3 b g Zoffany(IRE) In Dubai (USA) (Giant's Causeway (USA))
1216[2] 1449[3] (2654) 2891[8] 3389[4] 4113[9] 5886[3] 6877[4] 6957[5] 7505[5] 7671[11]
Fly By Me (TUR) *A Sivgin* 105
6 b h Karabey Han Lady Fi (TUR) (Among Men (USA))
6179a[2]
Fly First *Ferdinand J Leve* 105
7 bb g Big Shuffle(USA) Felicity (GER) (Inchinor)
2722a[8] 3992a[2]
Flying Bear (IRE) *Jeremy Gask* a83 74
5 b g Kodiac Marinebird (IRE) (Bad As I Wanna Be (IRE))
3650[3] 4295[3] 5162[3] *7202[6]* 7420[3] 7626[3] *8032[2]* *8463[9]*
Flying Empress *Jassim Al Ghazali* 95
3 b f Holy Roman Emperor(IRE) Fly Free (Halling (USA))
756a[2]
Flying Fairies (IRE) *Joseph G Murphy* 102
3 b f Holy Roman Emperor(IRE) Bright Birdie (IRE) (Sadler's Wells (USA))
6495a[4] 7392a[3] (7558a)
Flying Fantasy *Stuart Williams* a80 81
4 b g Oasis Dream Disco Volante (Sadler's Wells (USA))
64[3] *438[3]* *683[7]* *872[7]* *(1117)* *1269[6]* *(1555)* (2401) 3137[2] 3803[5] 4627[7] *8456[10]*
Flying Fleur (FR) *N Clement* a59 60
3 b f Lawman(FR) Fleur De Sel (Linamix (FR))
7999a[3]
Flying Foxy *Michael Wigham* a58
2 b f Foxwedge(AUS) Fauran (IRE) (Shamardal (USA))
7689[5]
Flying Fynn (IRE) *Jose Santos* a40
2 ch g Byron Can She Dance (IRE) (Danehill Dancer (IRE))
8536[7]
Flying Hope (IRE) *Nigel Tinkler* a38 49
2 ch f Tagula(IRE) Unknowndestination (IRE) (Authorized (IRE))
4227[13] 4451[8] 4725[5] ◆ *5364[8]* 6010[13] 6214[10] 6471[4]
Flying Lesson (IRE) *Mark Johnston* a59
3 ch c Roderic O'Connor(IRE) Acushladear (IRE) (Tagula (IRE))
331[7] *428[3]*
Flying North *Richard Hannon* 83
2 b f Raven's Pass(USA) Round The Cape (Cape Cross (IRE))
5356[8] 5846[4] (6111) 7147[2]
Flying Officer (USA) *John Gosden* 117
6 b g Dynaformer(USA) Vignette (USA) (Diesis)
1772[3] 3298[6]
Flying Onsite (FR) *Nigel Tinkler* 61
2 gr g Rajsaman(FR) Infinitely (Fantastic Light (USA))
7496[6] 7819[7]
Flying Power *John Norton* a79 49
8 b g Dubai Destination(USA) Rah Wa (USA) (Rahy (USA))
1997 2233[17] 3641[7] 4320[8] *6424[7]* 6730[10] *7367[7]* *8038[11]*
Flying Pursuit *Tim Easterby* 97
3 ch g Pastoral Pursuits Choisette (Choisir (AUS))
2693[6] (3292) 4062[8] 4652[3] 5148[2] ◆ 6164[2] 6556[9] 6792[5] 7315[6]
Flying Sakhee *John Bridger* a49 51
3 b f Sakhee's Secret Sister Moonshine (Averti (IRE))
3958[12] 4639[7] 5168[7] 6291[2] 7212[12] *7725[10]* *8030[9]* *8234[6]* *8358[9]*
Flymetothestars *Sir Mark Prescott Bt* a96
3 b g Sea The Stars(IRE) Precious Gem (IRE) (Sadler's Wells (USA))
(428) *6675[6]* *(7139)*
Fly Round The Bend (IRE) *John J Walsh* 49
5 ch m Refuse To Bend(IRE) Hunzy (IRE) (Desert King (IRE))
5620a[8]
Fly True *Jeremy Gask* a69 62
3 b f Raven's Pass(USA) Have Faith (IRE) (Machiavellian (USA))
1597[6] 2303[4] *2780[4]* 3898[7] 4861[7] 7334[10] *(8149)* *8430[6]*
Fly With Emirates (IRE) *Marjorie Fife* 72
4 b g Lawman(FR) Keriyka (IRE) (Indian Ridge)
2047[8]
Fly With Me (FR) *E Libaud* a77 112
6 gr h Beat Hollow Bird Of Paradise (FR) (Highest Honor (FR))
(1688a) 2725a[2] 5692a[7] 6974a[11]
Foible *Mike Sowersby* a4 52
3 b g Fastnet Rock(AUS) Nyarhini (Fantastic Light (USA))
4319[9] 4857[5] *7597[5]*
Foie Gras *Chris Dwyer* a70 56
6 b g Kyllachy Bint Zamayem (IRE) (Rainbow Quest (USA))
387[9] *608[5]* *939[3]* *1064[2]* *1262[5]* *(1805)* *2918[6]* *4474[6]* *5367[5]* 5935[5] *6700[13]* *(7310)* *8101[6]* *8178[15]* *8588[11]*
Foiled *Jan Coomer*
6 b g Dutch Art Isengard (USA) (Cobra King (USA))
2952a[8]
Folkswood *Charlie Appleby* 107
3 b g Exceed And Excel(AUS) Magic Nymph (IRE) (Galileo (IRE))
(1867) ◆ 3299[8] 4624[3] 5932[2]
Follow Me (IRE) *Hugo Palmer* a57 48
2 b f Zoffany(IRE) Flower Of Kent (USA) (Diesis)
6625[11] 7125[9]
Followmeifucan (IRE) *C Lerner* a77 83
2 b f Elusive City(USA) Russiana (IRE) (Red Ransom (USA))
6937a[2]
Follow The Faith *Mick Channon* a49 58
4 b m Piccolo Keeping The Faith (IRE) (Ajraas (USA))
326[7] *514[13]*
Follow The Rules *S Seemar* a51 50
3 b c Kheleyf(USA) It's The War (USA) (Consolidator (USA))
185a[8] 536a[9]
Folly Bergere (IRE) *James Eustace* 80
3 ch f Champs Elysees Rainbow Queen (FR) (Spectrum (IRE))
1242[4] 1608[4] 3468[4] 4778[3] 5745[2]
Fol O'Yasmine *William Haggas* a40 69
3 b f Dubawi(IRE) Sewards Folly (Rudimentary (USA))
2004[9] 2294[4] 3080[4] (4279) 4596[3]
Fondie (IRE) *Mark Johnston* 59
3 b f Oasis Dream Prima Luce (IRE) (Galileo (IRE))
1589[4] 2148[6]
Fongani (FR) *P Sogorb* 73
2 b f Siyouni(FR) Maggi Fong (Dr Fong (USA))
5142a[4]
Foolaad *Roy Bowring* a69 82
5 ch g Exceed And Excel(AUS) Zayn Zen (Singspiel (IRE))
49[3] *518[5]* 7623[14] *8473[11]* *8587[3]*
Fool's Dream *Bryan Smart* a33 52
3 ch f Showcasing Folly Lodge (Grand Lodge (USA))
1673[8] 2019[7] 3850[7] 4870[5] 5515[4] 5889[5] *7144[8]*
Fool To Cry (IRE) *Roger Varian* a74 78
3 ch f Fast Company(IRE) Islandagore (IRE) (Indian Ridge)
1411[5] 2291[4] ◆ (3955)
Footbridge (USA) *Charlie Appleby* a105
6 b g Street Cry(IRE) Thousand Islands (Dubai Millennium)
281a[6] *624a[5]* *8396a[5]*
Footlight *Richard Fahey* a77 72
3 br f Showcasing Wood Fairy (Haafhd)
47[3] *248[6]* *443[3]* *688[4]* *(896)* *1031[2]* (1564) 1819[7] *7886[2]* *8286[8]* *8590[2]*
Footman (GER) *Richard Hughes* a67
2 b c Cacique(IRE) Flames To Dust (GER) (Oasis Dream)
8245[10] *8354[2]* ◆
Footprintinthesand (IRE) *M Weiss* a58
6 bb g Footstepsinthesand Cha Cha (IRE) (Charnwood Forest (IRE))
588a[6] *663a[4]*
Footstepsintherain (IRE) *Lee Carter* a83 74
6 b g Footstepsinthesand Champagne Toni (IRE) (Second Empire (IRE))
(1416)
For Ayman *Joseph Tuite* a72 61
5 b g Bertolini(USA) Saharan Song (IRE) (Singspiel (IRE))
28[2] ◆ *159[5]* *387[4]* *1261[3]* 1533[4] 1899[8] 3674[6] *3780[3]* *4008[7]* *(5509)* *6091[2]* *6418[6]* 7267[7] *7430[2]* *8067[3]*
Force (IRE) *Charles Hills* a72 87
3 ch g Raven's Pass(USA) Holly's Kid (USA) (Pulpit (USA))
2693[9] 3130[5] 4051[6] 4534[6] 5234[2] (5545) *6084[9]* 6877[2] 7189[3]
Forced Family Fun *George Baker* a53 82
6 b g Refuse To Bend(IRE) Juniper Girl (IRE) (Revoque (IRE))
1717[4] 2399[5] 3533[9] *8554[7]*
Forceful Appeal (USA) *Simon Dow* a99 57
8 bb g Successful Appeal(USA) Kinetic Force (USA) (Holy Bull (USA))
(221) *401[5]* *833[6]* *920[5]* *1068[8]* *1335[11]* *1576[6]* 4048[6] 4788[8] *7651[11]* *7984[7]* ◆ *8177[6]* *(8251)* *8427[4]* *(8529)*
Forcefull (IRE) *Adrian Paul Keatley* 78
3 b f Thousand Words Littlepromisedland (IRE) (Titus Livius (FR))
5154[8] 6503[8]
Force Of Destiny (GER) *Mrs Ilka Gansera-Leveque* a75
4 b h Galileo(IRE) Four Roses (IRE) (Darshaan)
245[6] *500[5]* *728[2]* *1002[6]* *(1236)*
Forecast *Martin Keighley* a34 76
4 ch g Observatory(USA) New Orchid (USA) (Quest For Fame)
1256[5] 1824[3] 2397[4]
Forecaster *Michael Bell* a79 73
3 b f Fastnet Rock(AUS) Aurore (IRE) (Fasliyev (USA))
2152[6] 2576[3] 4098[3] 5010[2] 5288[3] 5891[6] *6901[2]* *7609[2]* *7942[5]*
Foreign Diplomat *David O'Meara* a88 86
4 b g Oasis Dream Longing To Dance (Danehill Dancer (IRE))
142[4] 2857[5] 3266[2]
Foresee (GER) *Tony Carroll* a74 85
3 b g Sea The Stars(IRE) Four Roses (IRE) (Darshaan)
8249[9]
Foresight (FR) *David Simcock* 83
3 b g Dream Ahead(USA) Madhya (USA) (Gone West (USA))
1849[2] 2544[4] 3892[4] (4870) 6883[9] 7593[6]
Forest Angel (IRE) *Richard Hannon* 60
2 gr f Dark Angel(IRE) Fruit O'The Forest (IRE) (Shinko Forest (IRE))
5170[5] 5846[6]
Forest Lakes (IRE) *George Scott* a59 68
3 b f Iffraaj Cala (FR) (Desert Prince (IRE))
2415[6] 3823[7] 4587[8] 5087[3] *6512[4]* 7230[3]
Forest Ranger (IRE) *Richard Fahey* 96
2 b c Lawman(FR) Alava (IRE) (Anabaa (USA))
(6682) 7409[3]
Forest Steps (IRE) *J S Moore* a51
2 b f Footstepsinthesand Zeena (Unfuwain (USA))
6867[9] *7733[6]* *8404[5]*
For Ever (FR) *Y Barberot* a87 79
5 gr h Literato(FR) Ever In Love (FR) (Neverneyev (USA))
3376a[2]
Forever A Lady (IRE) *Keith Dalgleish* 85
3 b f Dark Angel(IRE) Unicamp (Royal Academy (USA))
1446[6] 2420[8] 3152[7] 3885[2] 4034[2] (4443) 5115[6] 5836[6] 6005[7] 6342[5] 6811[11] 7743[13]
Forever D'Oro (USA) *Dallas Stewart* a97
3 b c Medaglia d'Oro(USA) Lemons Forever (USA) (Lemon Drop Kid (USA))
3181a[13] *5913a[10]*
Forever Excel (IRE) *Charles Hills* 6
2 b f Excelebration(IRE) Never A Doubt (Night Shift (USA))
6782[13]
Forever Gold (GER) *Andreas Lowe* 66
3 ch f Lord Of England(GER) Forever Nadine (GER) (Kornado)
7720a[10] 8024a[13]
Forever Popular (USA) *William Haggas* a85 105
4 bb m Dynaformer(USA) Pussycat Doll (USA) (Real Quiet (USA))
2024[7] (2487) *3278[4]* (4400) 5461a[6] 6259[4] 6708[5]

Forever Unbridled (USA) *Dallas Stewart* a120
4 b m Unbridled's Song(USA) Lemons Forever (USA) (Lemon Drop Kid (USA))
7810a[3]

Forever Yours (IRE) *Dean Ivory* a33 65
3 b g Canford Cliffs(IRE) Gilded (IRE) (Redback)
5850[5] 6459[3]

Forge *Sir Michael Stoute* 111
3 b c Dubawi(IRE) Heat Haze (Green Desert (USA))
(1622) 2627[3] 3269[3] 4822[2] 5613[6] (6056) 6749[6]

Forgino (GER) *T Potters* a94 110
5 b g It's Gino(GER) Forlea (GER) (Lead On Time (USA))
2722a[4] 5943a[3] 7027a[9]

Forgivethenforget *Ismail Mohammed* a57 70
2 br c Foxwedge(AUS) Search Party (Rainbow Quest (USA))
4128[5] 5371[6]

Forgiving Flower *K R Burke* a68 64
3 ch f New Approach(IRE) Dance Lively (USA) (Kingmambo (USA))
1346[6] 1758[5] 3053[4] 3991[7]

Forgiving Glance *Alan King* a62 63
4 gr m Passing Glance Giving (Generous (IRE))
1456[2]

For Goodness Sake (IRE) *Warren Greatrex* a73 72
4 b m Yeats(IRE) Muschana (Deploy)
4637[2] 5262[3] ◆ 7270[6]

Forgotten Hero (IRE) *Kim Bailey* a89 102
7 b g High Chaparral(IRE) Sundown (Polish Precedent (USA))
1885[5] 2484[4] 3113[2] 4115[2] 5381[8] 6781[10] 7538[12]

Forgotten Rules (IRE) *D K Weld* 117
6 b g Nayef(USA) Utterly Heaven (IRE) (Danehill (USA))
6820a[2] 7349[7] 7946a[2]

Forjatt (IRE) *D Selvaratnam* a108 108
8 b g Iffraaj Graceful Air (IRE) (Danzero (AUS))
309a[2] 720a[5] 1106a[9]

Forries Waltz (SAF) *M F De Kock* 114
4 b h Greys Inn(USA) Rose Of Tralee (SAF) (Rich Man's Gold (USA))
(189a) (372a) 1106a[14]

For Shia And Lula (IRE) *Daniel Mark Loughnane* a76 65
7 b g Majestic Missile(IRE) Jack-N-Jilly (IRE) (Anita's Prince)
482[8] 680[7] 1269[8] 1555[3] 1780[5] 2153[3] 2769[6] 3989[10] 5068[9] 5734[2] 7261[2] ◆ 7513[9] 7751[2] (7817) 8258[9]

Forster Square (IRE) *Richard Fahey* 62
2 b c Dandy Man(IRE) Massuci (IRE) (Montjeu (IRE))
2757[9] 3396[3] 4000[7] 5177[3] 5351[3] (5974)

Fort Bastion (IRE) *Brian Ellison* a97 97
7 b g Lawman(FR) French Fern (IRE) (Royal Applause)
1871[3] 2027[7] 2485[4] 2796[6] 3390[8] 4448[3] 4758[13] 5585[20] 5915[4] 6557[3] 6736[8] 7121[10] (7529) (7778) 8049[10] 8279[10] 8478[5]

Fort Del Oro (IRE) *Edward Lynam* 109
4 b m Lope De Vega(IRE) Gilded (IRE) (Redback)
(1730a) 2495a[7] 2923a[2] (4540a) 5213a[4] 6816a[4] 7191a[7]

Forte *David O'Meara* a64 98
4 ch m New Approach(IRE) Prowess (IRE) (Peintre Celebre (USA))
2797[9] 4078[10]

Forth Bridge *Michael Bell* 87
3 b g Bernardini(USA) Sally Forth (Dubai Destination (USA))
1483[3] 1897[2] (3028) 5653[12] 6735[4] 7625[7]

For The Roses *Ralph Beckett* 68
2 b f Nathaniel(IRE) Ivory Rose (Green Desert (USA))
5266[4] 5995[7]

For Three (IRE) *John Joseph Murphy* a43
2 b g Pour Moi(IRE) Asmaa (USA) (Canadian Frontier (USA))
7917a[9]

Fortia *William Haggas* a42 43
2 b f Nathaniel(IRE) Veenwouden (Desert Prince (IRE))
7441[11] 7885[10]

Fortinbrass (IRE) *John Balding* a66 64
6 b g Baltic King Greta D'Argent (IRE) (Great Commotion (USA))
(54) 130[2] 272[2] 543[9] 799[5] 1299[2] 1401[2] (1712) 3070[2] 3843[9] 7144[7] 7859[11] 8236[3]

Fort Jefferson *Andrew Balding* a53 82
3 br g Passing Glance Florida Heart (First Trump)
2674[3] 3224[2] ◆ (3499) (3816)

Fort Moville (FR) *Ahmed Kobeissi* a90 103
4 ch h Le Havre(IRE) Fancy Dance (Rainbow Quest (USA))
757a[3]

Fortuities (IRE) *Jedd O'Keeffe* 58
2 b f Soldier Of Fortune(IRE) Inez (Dai Jin)
5728[3]

Fortuna Do Brasil (FR) *W Delalande* a23
5 b m Enrique Mapistolbabe (FR) (Pistolet Bleu (IRE))
512a[14]

Fortune Of War *Jane Chapple-Hyam* a74 77
2 b c Sixties Icon Susie May (Hernando (FR))
3356[6] 3971[2] 5036[2] 6108[4] 6705[7] 7306[3] 7483[3]

Forty Foot (IRE) *T Castanheira* a31 68
2 b c Kodiac Kinnego (IRE) (Sri Pekan (USA))
(5141a) 7422a[6]

Forza Libranno (FR) *F Chappet* a68 86
3 b g Dick Turpin(IRE) Bella Vento (Shirocco (GER))
5946a[15]

Fossa *Mark Brisbourne* a62 40
6 b g Dubai Destination(USA) Gayanula (USA) (Yonaguska (USA))
1720[5] 2447[5] 2584[12] 2964[5] 3486[6] 3987[3] 4290[6] 5080[8] 5706[5] 5808[9] 6853[3] 7261[5] 8278[3] 8408[5] 8542[7]

Fosun (GER) *Markus Klug* 93
3 b f Soldier Hollow Flamingo Sky (USA) (Silver Hawk (USA))
5220a[16]

Found (IRE) *A P O'Brien* 124
4 b m Galileo(IRE) Red Evie (IRE) (Intikhab (USA))
1227a[3] (1940a) 2512a[2] 2894[2] 3272[2] 5586[2] 6354a[2] (6989a) 7353[2] 7835a[3]

Foundation (IRE) *John Gosden* 115
3 ch g Zoffany(IRE) Roystonea (Polish Precedent (USA))
1440[2] 2190[3] 2946a[16] 5159[5] 5893[3] 6321[3]

Founding Father (FR) *James Tate* 70
2 b c Sir Percy A Beautiful Mind (GER) (Winged Love (IRE))
7216[3] 7664[3] (Dead)

Four Candles (IRE) *Philip McBride* a57
2 b g Lilbourne Lad(IRE) Common Rumpus (IRE) (Common Grounds)
7259[6] 7776[7] 8065[10] 8276[14]

Four Carat (GER) *Chris Waller* 94
5 b g Montjeu(IRE) Four Roses (IRE) (Darshaan)
7947a[4]

Four Dragons *Tom Dascombe* a66 75
2 ch f Dragon Pulse(IRE) Mysterious Girl (IRE) (Teofilo (IRE))
1443[2] 1976[5] 3128[3] 4296[6] (4712) 5598[5] (6564) 6763[5] (7313)

Fourioso (FR) *M Al Yaqout* 105
3 b c Footstepsinthesand Moojeh (IRE) (King's Best (USA))
1024a[7] 5004a[7] 8573a[13]

Four Kingdoms (IRE) *K R Burke* 48
2 b g Lord Shanakill(USA) Four Poorer (IRE) (Oasis Dream)
7247[6] 7740[15]

Four Mile Beach *Mark Johnston* a70 74
3 gr g Dalakhani(IRE) Rappel (Royal Applause)
600[3] ◆ 735[2] 863[3] 1242[3] 2687[8]

Four Nations (USA) *George Baker* a78 66
8 ch g Langfuhr(CAN) Kiswahili (Selkirk (USA))
138[4] 386[4]

Fourni (IRE) *Mrs A Malzard* 46
7 ch m Rakti Eckbeag (USA) (Trempolino (USA))
2078a[2]

Four On Eight *Luca Cumani* a85 84
3 gr c Lawman(FR) Pocket Watch (Pivotal)
2179[4] 3617[3] 5074[2] 5768[2] 6474[4]

Four Poets *David Simcock* a79 77
3 ch g Poet's Voice O Fourlunda (Halling (USA))
1779[4] (2428) 3823[3] 4088[4] 4742[3] 5752[3] 6657[3] 7066[2]

Fourth Way (IRE) *Roger Varian* 94
3 b f Iffraaj Spiritual Air (Royal Applause)
1396[8] 6947[12] 7472[7]

Four Wishes *Tim Easterby* 58
2 b c Sepoy(AUS) Postage Stampe (Singspiel (IRE))
3516[7] 5477[6] 6009[8]

Foxcatcher *Clive Cox* 74
2 ch f Foxwedge(AUS) Copy-Cat (Lion Cavern (USA))
4350[9] 5400[10] 6078[4] 6830[2] ◆ (7414)

Foxcub (IRE) *Tom Symonds* 76
8 b g Bahri(USA) Foxglove (Hernando (FR))
7411[6]

Foxford *Patrick Chamings* a65 59
5 b m Clodovil(IRE) Pulau Pinang (IRE) (Dolphin Street (FR))
1533[3] 2697[4] 3469[4] 4525[5] 5509[2]

Foxinthehenhouse *J R Jenkins* a68 44
3 ch f Bahamian Bounty Pants (Pivotal)
459[6] 1257[11] 2585[6] 3527[9]

Fox King *Ralph Beckett* a42 55
2 b g Foxwedge(AUS) King's Siren (IRE) (King's Best (USA))
6672[8] 7157[10]

Fox Mint *Stuart Williams* 45
2 ch f Foxwedge(AUS) Unasuming (IRE) (Orpen (USA))
7032[4]

Foxtrot Charlie (USA) *D K Weld* 101
3 ch c English Channel(USA) Flashy Four (USA) (Storm Cat (USA))
2510a[3] (3084a) 3677a[6]

Foxtrot Knight *Ruth Carr* a85 87
4 b g Kyllachy Rustam (Dansili)
3133[9] 3552[4] ◆ 3956[2] 4198[2] ◆ 4461[5] 4946[2] 5488[6] 5991[8] 6449[10]

Fox Trotter (IRE) *Brian Meehan* a75 102
4 br g Bushranger(IRE) Miss Brief (IRE) (Brief Truce (USA))
284a[7] 628a[12] 2391[11] ◆ 2862[4] 3358[14] 6287[5] 7316[6] 7573[8]

Foxy Boy *Michael Dods* a47 64
2 ch g Foxwedge(AUS) Suzy Wong (Auction House (USA))
2913[9] 3416[4] 3939[5] 4679[2] (5712) 6343[4] 6768[3] 7143[10]

Foxy Forever (IRE) *Michael Wigham* a87 85
6 b g Kodiac Northern Tara (IRE) (Fayruz)
91a[13] 450a[9] 3250[5] 4126[18] 4584[12] 5648[12] 6114[6] 6793[8] 7202[9] 8403[2] ◆

Foylesideview (IRE) *Harry Chisman* a55 47
4 b g Dark Angel(IRE) Showerproof (Peintre Celebre (USA))
107[3] 334[7] 609[5] 787[2] 986[4] 1145[7] 1768[7] 2462[7] 2901[3] 7642[13] 7937[7] 8410[9] 8528[6]

Framley Garth (IRE) *Patrick Holmes* a71 79
4 b g Clodovil(IRE) Two Marks (USA) (Woodman (USA))
1632[10] 2555[7] 3212[2] 3582[6] 3883[4] (4335) 4930[5] 5883[2] 6160[9] 6876[11] 7359[10]

Franca Florio (IRE) *Kevin Ryan* 73
2 b f Acclamation Lyca Ballerina (Marju (IRE))
3112[7] (3707) (4167) 4884[11] 6322[3]

Francisco *Richard Hannon* a82 93
4 b g Paco Boy(IRE) Blue Goddess (IRE) (Blues Traveller (IRE))
2206[2] ◆ 2547[9] 3279[6] 4079[11] 4475[8] 4910[5] 5744[2] 6583[9]

Francis Of Assisi (IRE) *Charlie Appleby* 109
6 b g Danehill Dancer(IRE) Queen Cleopatra (IRE) (Kingmambo (USA))
4164[4] ◆ 4734[6] (7637a) (7826a)

Franco's Secret *Peter Hedger* a88 59
5 b g Sakhee's Secret Veronica Franco (Darshaan)
313[3] 518[2] (712) 965[3] 1576[4] 2378[4] 2819[4] 3523[2] 3783[5] 5650[7] 7428[6] 7902[9] 8077[10] 8356[2]

Frangarry (IRE) *Alan Bailey* a63 63
4 b g Lawman(FR) Divert (IRE) (Averti (IRE))
541[3] 733[9] 1133[5] 1720[4] 2697[11] 3016[9] 3735[8] 3822[2] 4606[5] 5335[6] 6100[3] 6586[9] (7018) 7533[9] 7774[14]

Frangipani (GER) *Andreas Lowe* 46
2 rg f Jukebox Jury(IRE) Firedance (GER) (Lomitas)
7563a[11]

Frank Bridge *Eve Johnson Houghton* a42 74
3 b g Avonbridge First Among Equals (Primo Valentino (IRE))
2969[3] (3490) (3975) 4279[4] (4789) 5104[7] 6266[P]

Frank Conversation (USA) *Doug O'Neill* a86 107
3 b c Quality Road(USA) Rushen Heat (USA) (Unusual Heat (USA))
1103a[7]

Frank Cool *Tony Carroll* a52 16
3 b g Royal Applause Queen Of Heaven (USA) (Mr Greeley (USA))
8570[6]

Franked *A Fabre* 77
2 ch c Frankel Tarocchi (USA) (Affirmed (USA))
6638a[3]

Frankie *Jimmy Fox* a27 20
5 gr g Firebreak Winterbourne (Cadeaux Genereux)
7426[10] 8070[11]

Frankki M *Mrs A Corson* 12
6 b g Denounce Natacha Rostow (Pursuit Of Love)
1519a[10] 2079a[4] 2284a[7] 2955a[8] 3917a[9] 5458a[6]

Franklin D (USA) *Michael Bell* a98 112
4 b h Medaglia d'Oro(USA) Kissed By A Star (USA) (Kingmambo (USA))
353[8] ◆ 656[5] 2484[3] 3157[2] (4399) (4823) (Dead)

Frank Lloyd Wright (SWE) *Niels Petersen* a101
5 b g Philomatheia(USA) Little Green Apple (SWE) (Funambule (USA))
90a[7] 374a[6]

Frank Sandatra *Peter Crate* a48 40
3 b g Equiano(FR) Alhufoof (USA) (Dayjur (USA))
750[4] 970[6] 2750[6] 3317[5]

Frankster (FR) *Micky Hammond* a15 72
3 b g Equiano(FR) Milwaukee (FR) (Desert King (IRE))
4235[8] 4895[8] 5731[6] 7009[4] 7780[5]

Frank The Barber (IRE) *Steph Hollinshead* a62 50
4 gr g Zebedee Red Rosanna (Bertolini (USA))
75[3] 241[4] 293[2] 504[3] 541[2] 733[6] (4529) 5162[8] 5269[5] 6374[2] 6660[5] 6909[2] 7860[11] 8474[6] 8596[4]

Frankuus (IRE) *Mark Johnston* 103
2 gr c Frankel Dookus (IRE) (Linamix (FR))
(3054) ◆ 3382[5] 4622[3] 5401[4] (6116) (7169a) 7722a[8]

Frankwithouthel (IRE) *Patrick Martin*
5 b g Majestic Missile(IRE) Carrie McCurry (IRE) (Fath (USA))
1014a[16]

Frankyfourfingers (FR) *S bin Ghadayer* a72 64
6 b h Sunday Break(JPN) Texaloula (FR) (Kendor (FR))
92a[11] 8396a[10]

Franny Nisbet *William Muir*
2 b f Mount Nelson Don't Stop Me Now (FR) (Zamindar (USA))
8227[11]

Frantical *Tony Carroll* a62 68
4 b g Observatory(USA) Quest For Freedom (Falbrav (IRE))
2[8] 1347[6] 1654[10] 1948[5] 2323[11] 3043[7] (3737) 3973[6] 5264[5]

Frap *Ian Williams* a62 60
3 b g Makfi Frizzante (Efisio)
243[5] 593[4] 794[5] 1141[4] 1486[6] 1816[4] ◆ (2422) 2674[4] 3130[8] 3710[5] 4382[6] 6646[7] 8457[12] 8595[11]

Fray *Jim Goldie* a55 78
5 b m Champs Elysees Short Dance (USA) (Hennessy (USA))
1624[5] 3394[8] 3645[4] 3922[4] 4446[2] 5223[8] 5844[5] 6504[5] 7435[12] 7791[8]

Freddy With A Y (IRE) *Paul Burgoyne* a78 80
6 b g Amadeus Wolf Mataji (IRE) (Desert Prince (IRE))
263[3] 616[9] 815[2] 1173[3] 1387[10] 1546[8] 3783[10] 5024[5] 5503[8] 6237[7] 8064[2]

Frederic *Micky Hammond* a79 77
5 b g Zamindar(USA) Frangy (Sadler's Wells (USA))
2051[2] 2912[3] 3294[5] (4101) 4491[3] 5856[4]

Frederic Chopin *James Moffatt* a78 75
5 ch g Tamayuz Eliza Gilbert (Noverre (USA))
2439[3] ◆

Fredricka *David Barron* a74 89
5 ch m Assertive Vintage Steps (IRE) (Bahamian Bounty)
1601[4] 2261[10] (2775) 3393[3] 4112[10] 4585[7] 5153[5] 5479[9] 6793[16] 7112[3] 8403[9]

Fred's Filly *Bill Turner* a52 41
3 ch f Avonbridge Regal Quest (IRE) (Marju (IRE))
6586[6] 6660[9] 7046[15] 8079[14]

Free At Last (IRE) *Richard Fahey* a52 57
2 ch f Iffraaj Fortress (Generous (IRE))
5511[5] ◆ 6447[3] 7328[4]

Free Bounty *Philip McBride* a70 55
3 b c Dick Turpin(IRE) Native Ring (FR) (Bering)
1619[6] 2563[3] 3615[3] 4836[6] (6245) 6508[2] 7104[2] 8084[9]

Free Code (IRE) *David Barron* a83 93
5 b g Kodiac Gerobies Girl (USA) (Deposit Ticket (USA))
1394[4] 2027[19] 2862[11] 3419[7] ◆ 3566[9] 4402[2] 4665[9] 5156[5] 5389[13] 5866[7] 6082[10] 6914[5] 7702[3] 7957[7] 8239[7] 8319[3]

Freediver *Sir Michael Stoute* a55 55
2 ch f Bated Breath Grand Coral (Grand Lodge (USA))
7055[9] 8081[9]

Freedom Beel (IRE) *Stefano Botti* 93
3 b c Pour Moi(IRE) Querida (Rainbow Quest (USA))
2517a[6]

Freedom Tales (FR) *L Cendra* a52 52
5 b g Tertullian(USA) Fridas World (Agnes World (USA))
8422a[2]

Free From Desire (FR) *G Botti*
3 ch c Iffraaj Balle De Match (IRE) (Peintre Celebre (USA))
1580a[10]

Free One (IRE) *Ivan Furtado* a67 69
4 b g Fast Company(IRE) Tatamagouche (IRE) (Sadler's Wells (USA))
2540[7] 2734[9] 3476[5] 4493[6] 5064[7] 5513[11] 6047[4] 7742[RR] 7850[RR]

Free Passage *Henry Candy* 74
3 ch g Medicean Free Offer (Generous (IRE))
2749[6] ◆ 3357[7] 4562[5] 5207[2] 5824[3] 6654[8] (7274)

Free Port Lux *F Head* 115
5 b h Oasis Dream Royal Highness (GER) (Monsun (GER))
1023a[4] 1375a[11] 3544a[7] 6973a[9]

Free Running (IRE) *John James Feane* a79 75
4 b m Iffraaj Street Star (USA) (Street Cry (IRE))
223[2] 456[2] 813[3] 2154[3] 2791[7] (6463a)

Freesia (IRE) *Marco Botti*
3 b f Dansili Field Of Hope (IRE) (Selkirk (USA))
3990[12]

Free To Dance (IRE) *K R Burke* 68
2 ch f Tamayuz Flurry Of Hands (IRE) (Acclamation)
5728[2] 6776[8]

Free To Love *Charles Hills* a73 84
4 br m Equiano(FR) All Quiet (Piccolo)
2768[8] 3123[2] 3995[2] 4222[4] 5882[4]

Free To Roam (IRE) *Philip McBride* a56 56
3 gr f Bushranger(IRE) Operissimo (Singspiel (IRE))
(1325) (1548) 1927[10] 2784[6] 7260[4] ◆ 7515[9]

Freewheel (IRE) *Garry Moss* a78 84
6 br g Galileo(IRE) La Chunga (USA) (More Than Ready (USA))
1152[5] (1785) 2324[8] 3347[5] 3905[2] 6160[5] 6753[11] 6957[3] 7108[10] 7535[13] 8286[11]

Free Wheeling (AUS) *Saeed bin Suroor* a109 104
7 b g Ad Valorem(USA) Miss Carefree (AUS) (Last Tycoon)
92a[12] 374a[5]

Freeze A Crowd (IRE) *Ben Haslam* a44 43
3 b f Frozen Power(IRE) Skies Are Blue (Unfuwain (USA))
81[2] 730[5] 1045[4] 1710[3] 4511[4] 8346[5]

Freeze Fly (IRE) *J-V Toux* a45 60
2 b f Frozen Power(IRE) Wong Again (Araafa (IRE))
1284a[6] 2844a[4] 3763a[11]

Free Zone *Lee Carter* a89 89
7 b g Kyllachy Aldora (Magic Ring (IRE))
1672[9] 1874[8] 2857[7] 3419[12] (3880) (4142) 4428[6] 4954[2] 5488[12] 5825[7] 6371[3] 6539[6] 7206[11] 7778[3] (7983) 8150[2] 8380[5]

Freight Train (IRE) *Adrian Wintle* a75 82
4 b g Manduro(GER) Sigonella (IRE) (Priolo (USA))
1161[5] 1418[11] 1664[7] 1923[4] 2529[2] 2888[6] 3077[6] 3883[2] (4038) 4406[5] 4868[2] 5017[9] 6516[3] 6753[13] 8356[12]

French *Antony Brittain* a52 65
3 ch f Monsieur Bond(IRE) Guadaloup (Loup Sauvage (USA))
2742[10] ◆ 3439[9] 3978[9] 6451[15] 7797[7]

French Blue *W McCreery* a84 87
3 b f Iffraaj Powder Blue (Daylami (IRE))
3202a[9]

French Encore *Debbie Mountain* 90
3 b g Showcasing French Connexion (IRE) (Chineur (FR))
756a[3] 8573a[10]

Frenchie *Shaun Harris*
4 b m Paris House Clumber Pursuits (Pastoral Pursuits)
1597[16] 2425[8] 3421[12]

French Legend *Andrew Balding* a50 61
3 b f Pour Moi(IRE) Fast Flow (IRE) (Fasliyev (USA))
1259[7] 1740[5] 2126[11] 2590[8] 2967[2] (3256) (3482)

Frenchman (FR) *Charles Hills* a84 82
3 b c Le Havre(IRE) Como (USA) (Cozzene (USA))
945[3] (2005) 2935[2] 3571[7] 4132[7] 5301[4] 5960[3] 6190[8] 6878[14] (7324) 7462[3]

French Pass *Stuart Williams* 50
2 gr f Aussie Rules(USA) Etroubles (FR) (Indian Ridge)
4981[8]

French Silver (FR) *Tony Carroll* a34
2 gr f Rajsaman(FR) Senanque (IRE) (Pivotal)
5524[8] 6850[7]

Fresh Fox *Jonathan Portman* 35
2 ch f Sakhee's Secret May Fox (Zilzal (USA))
6061[9]

Fresh Strike (IRE) *F Head* a93 94
3 ch f Smart Strike(CAN) Only Green (IRE) (Green Desert (USA))
5006a[2] 6069a[5] 7029a[7]

Freud (FR) *Ian Williams* a85 72
6 b g Dalakhani(IRE) Ailette (Second Set (IRE))
38[4] (212) ◆ (267) 353[7] 888[4] 967[3] 1089[12] 2806a[7] 4074a[4] 4927a[14]

Fridge Kid *Dr Jon Scargill* a48 59
4 b m Kheleyf(USA) Snow Shoes (Sri Pekan (USA))
252[12]

Frightened Rabbit (USA) *Susan Corbett* a59 64
4 b g Hard Spun(USA) Champagne Ending (USA) (Precise End (USA))
865[4] 1560[4] 1881[4] 2233[12] 4314[9] 5227[8]

Friliad (FR) *M Cesandri* a8
5 b g Sagacity(FR) Tsarskoya Selae (FR) (Loup Solitaire (USA))
512a[15]

Frivolous Lady (IRE) *David Evans* a58 76
3 b f Bushranger(IRE) Ufallya (IRE) (Statue Of Liberty (USA))
(147) (613) 3135[6] 4206[9] 5529[12]

Frivolous Prince (IRE) *David Evans* a51 55
3 b g Baltic King Sweet Reflection (IRE) (Victory Note (USA))
69[2] 148[5] 533[3] 688[3] 896[7] (1062) 1259[4] 1551[9] 2563[2] (3141) 4159[4] 4527[5] 5204[5] 5777[6] 5824[7] 6654[4] 6966[3] 7231[8] 7641[3] 7745[4] 7888[4] 8528[3]

From Frost *C Von Der Recke* a60 86
5 b g Nayef(USA) Salutare (IRE) (Sadler's Wells (USA))
665a[7]

Front Five (IRE) *Martin Bosley* a75 64
4 b g Teofilo(IRE) Samdaniya (Machiavellian (USA))
1434[P] 3302[5] 7382[5]

Frontiersman *Charlie Appleby* 106
3 br c Dubawi(IRE) Ouija Board (Cape Cross (IRE))
2929[3] (4056) ◆ 5074[4] (6709) ◆ 7545[6]

Frontispiece *Sir Michael Stoute* 79
2 b c Shamardal(USA) Free Verse (Danehill Dancer (IRE))
(6108)

Frosted (USA) *Kiaran McLaughlin* a130
4 rg h Tapit(USA) Fast Cookie (USA) (Deputy Minister (CAN))
(452a) ◆ 1108a[5] 7838a[6]

Frosty Berry *Ed de Giles* a86 105
7 gr m Proclamation(IRE) Star Entry (In The Wings)
6147 (1273) 3387[17] 7545[7]

Frosty De Winter *Chris Gordon* a50 39
3 gr g Hellvelyn Rebecca De Winter (Kyllachy)
1894[9] 2578[12] 3406[F] (Dead)

Frosty The Snowman (IRE) *Ruth Carr* a57 60
5 gr g Mastercraftsman(IRE) Sleeveless (USA) (Fusaichi Pegasus (USA))
801[3] (1048) 1399[7] (1842) 2558[12] 2746[3] 3067[4] 3903[4] 4499[6] 5183[7]

Frozen Force (IRE) *Amanda Perrett* a81 87
3 ch c Frozen Power(IRE) La Mere Germaine (IRE) (Indian Ridge)
253[5] 1238[2] (1777) 2545[6] (2900) 4476[5] 4818[2] (5102) 5964[8] 6032[3] 6484[7] 7428[5]

Frozen Kiss *Bryan Smart* 72
2 b f Exceed And Excel(AUS) Transfix (Pivotal)
2254[9] 4451[3] 6002[7] (6343)

Frozen Lake (USA) *Mary Hambro* a74 69
4 b g Elusive Quality(USA) Creative Design (USA) (Stravinsky (USA))
2213[6] 5386[5] 6237[3] 7203[6]

Frozen Princess *Jamie Osborne* a63 53
4 b m Showcasing Super Midge (Royal Applause)
98[6] 151[3] 292[6]

Frozen Queen (IRE) *D Windrif* a66 68
2 b f Frozen Power(IRE) Our Sheila (Bahamian Bounty)
2457[5] (2844a) 3763a[2] 4471a[4] 7879a[10]

Frozon *Marjorie Fife* a61 63
3 b g Kheleyf(USA) Crozon (Peintre Celebre (USA))
1849[8] 3856[7] 4370[2] 4498[13] 5369[11] 7515[4] 7943[8] 8038[5] 8194[8]

Fruit Salad *James Bethell* a74 80
3 ch f Monsieur Bond(IRE) Miss Apricot (Indian Ridge)
686[7] 2049[4] 2742[7] 3397[2] 3847[2] 5370[2] 5730[2] (6959) 7288[4]

Fuel Injection *Paul Midgley* a61 57
5 gr g Pastoral Pursuits Smart Hostess (Most Welcome)
21[7] 292[4] 444[5] 504[6] 542[9] 1026[7] 1133[2] 1319[8] 1525[7] 2423[7] (2676) 3022[2] 3755[6] 4492[7] 8137[7] 8242[12] 8485[6]

Fugitive Motel (IRE) *John Gerard Fitzgerald* a22 17
7 b g Holy Roman Emperor(IRE) Zing Ping (IRE) (Thatching)
6466a[8]

Fujaira Bridge (IRE) *Roger Varian* 75
2 b c Sea The Stars(IRE) Garanciere (FR) (Anabaa (USA))
4103[7] 6777[2] 7239[3]

Fujin *Shaun Harris* a76 67
5 b g Oasis Dream Phantom Wind (USA) (Storm Cat (USA))
197[2] (272) 426[7] 520[2] 703[2] 903[10] 1154[2] 1489[12] 5296[3] 5736[2] 6216[9] 7663[5] 7852[9] 8236[10] 8473[6]

Fujin Dancer (FR) *Harriet Bethell* a58 58
11 ch g Storming Home Badaayer (USA) (Silver Hawk (USA))
5805[7] 6907[13] 7257[10]

Full Court Press (IRE) *J P Murtagh* a65 89
3 b g Frozen Power(IRE) Share The Feeling (IRE) (Desert King (IRE))
5147[5]

Full Day *Brian Ellison* a84 84
5 ch m Champs Elysees Capistrano Day (USA) (Diesis)
1166[3] ◆ 2782[9] 3149[11] 3690[5] 4230[4] (4664) 4883[7] 5321[2]

Full Drago (ITY) *Stefano Botti* 114
3 b c Pounced(USA) Almata (IRE) (Almutawakel)
2517a[3] (6612a) 7402a[2]

Full Intention *Tom Dascombe* 90
2 b c Showcasing My Delirium (Haafhd)
1384[2] 1976[3] 3247[4] 4133[2] 4890[2] 7090[5]

Full Mast (USA) *William Mott* a84 116
4 b h Mizzen Mast(USA) Yashmak (USA) (Danzig (USA))
6601a[4] 7403a[4]

Full Of Promise *Richard Fahey* a63 66
3 b f Kyllachy Arculinge (Paris House)
2809[3] 3439[5] 3898[5] 4445[3] 4861[8] 6436[3] (6834) 7363[4] 8031[8]

Fullon Clarets *Richard Fahey* a68 84
4 ch g Equiano(FR) Palinisa (FR) (Night Shift (USA))
1215[5] 1563[7] 2331[4] 3595[7] 4193[8] 4700[3] 5752[4] 6437[6] 7360[8] 7606[3]

Full Pelt (USA) *L Van Cauwenberghe* a57 16
8 bb g Orientate(USA) Class (USA) (Thunder Gulch (USA))
2806a[11]

Fully Focussed (IRE) *Ann Duffield* 45
2 br f Intense Focus(USA) Folcungi (IRE) (Mukaddamah (USA))
3283[9] 6472[6] 6682[8]

Fulminato (GER) *Andreas Lowe* 99
2 b c Excelebration(IRE) Fulminante (GER) (Dashing Blade)
6174a[6] 7399a[2]

Fumbo Jumbo (IRE) *Garry Moss* a61 90
3 b f Zebedee Baraloti (IRE) (Barathea (IRE))
962[2] 1558[2] (1839) 2334[9] 2854[2] (3709) 4100[4] ◆ 4612[4] 4831[2] 6537[10] 7124[3] 7358[11]

Fun Chief (FR) *Caroline Auvray* 26
3 b f Air Chief Marshal(IRE) Fennel (Montjeu (IRE))
1542a[9]

Funding Deficit (IRE) *Jim Goldie* a74 87
6 ch g Rakti Bukat Timah (Inchinor)
(1694) 2361[4] 3518[15] 4132[8] 4428[13] 5182[6] 6072[3] 7433[4] 7958[10] 8389[9]

Fun For All *James Tate* a68 34
3 ch f Iffraaj Funday (Daylami (IRE))
40[3] 325[3] 675[2] 2968[9]

Funky Footsteps (IRE) *Eve Johnson Houghton* 73
2 ch f Footstepsinthesand Felin Gruvy (IRE) (Tagula (IRE))
(3555) 4296[4] 4884[10] 7416[3]

Funky Mary (GER) *C Plisson* a42 83
7 b m Soldier Hollow Fairy Flame (GER) (Law Society (USA))
1157a[2] 5700a[3] 6938a[8]

Fun Mac (GER) *Hughie Morrison* a83 107
5 ch g Shirocco(GER) Favorite (GER) (Montjeu (IRE))
3298[13] 3913[10] 4734[9] 5655[10] (6293) 6708[3] 7150[20] 7411[3]

Fun Money *Ed Dunlop* a53 39
3 b f Authorized(IRE) Grand Lucre (Grand Slam (USA))
59[7] 325[9] 413[4] 1551[4] 3141[9] 3722[7]

Funny Kid (USA) *C Ferland* a92 86
3 b c Lemon Drop Kid(USA) Pitamakan (USA) (Danzig (USA))
8165a[8]

Funny Oyster (IRE) *George Baker* a41 61
3 gr f Dark Angel(IRE) Carpet Lover (IRE) (Fayruz)
1388[2] 1734[2] 2366[4] 3724[3] 5235[4] 6407[10] 7211[4] 7628[8]

Furia Cruzada (CHI) *John Gosden* a107 111
4 b m Newfoundland(USA) Nuestra Machi (CHI) (Hussonet (USA))
748[3] ◆ 1886[5] 3271[2] 3888[2] 5586[6] 6752[5] 7568a[3]

Furiant *Mark Johnston* a87 74
3 b g Invincible Spirit(IRE) Save Me The Waltz (FR) (Halling (USA))
881[2] 1029[5] 1385[6] 1647[8] 2446[8] 3284[7] (3952) 4562[6] 4769[5] 5201[5] 5782[6] 7111[7] 7620[3]

Furiously Fast (IRE) *Richard Fahey* a69 72
4 b g Fast Company(IRE) Agouti (Pennekamp (USA))
261[4]

Futoon (IRE) *Kevin Ryan* a86 90
3 b f Kodiac Vermilliann (IRE) (Mujadil (USA))
(2886) 3397[4] 3847[3] 4398[5] (5070) 5409[2] 6518[7] 7146[7]

Future Icon *Edward Lynam* a52 73
4 b m Acclamation Midnight Fantasy (Oasis Dream)
7474a[8]

Fuwairt (IRE) *Roger Fell* a97 91
4 b g Arcano(IRE) Safiya Song (IRE) (Intikhab (USA))
1563[11] 2238[4] 2531[10] 3115[4] 3419[2] 3645[3] 3945[6] 4299[6] (4474) 4976[3] (5886) 6372[3] ◆ 6956[8] 7825[13] 8177[4] 8311[2] 8478[3] ◆

Fuzzy Logic (IRE) *Bernard Llewellyn* a53 57
7 b g Dylan Thomas(IRE) Gates Of Eden (USA) (Kingmambo (USA))
1831[2] 2131[2] 3099[8] 4591[4]

Fyrecracker (IRE) *Grant Tuer* a59 71
5 ch g Kheleyf(USA) Spirit of Hope (IRE) (Danehill Dancer (IRE))
2259[14] 2531[5] 3021[8] 3646[14] 4376[4] 4608[3] 4848[5] 5295[5] 5867[9] 6215[6] 6680[17] 7663[8]

Gabbys Lad (IRE) *Eric Alston* a33 45
3 b f Lilbourne Lad(IRE) Phantom Waters (Pharly (FR))
3209[7] 4310[2] 5515[14] 6218[5] 6631[7] 6852[12]

Gabrial (IRE) *Richard Fahey* a104 117
7 b g Dark Angel(IRE) Guajira (FR) (Mtoto)
1106a[11] 1606[5] 1973[4] 2243[6] 3164[5] (3672) 4127[3] 4754[5] 5159[4] 5652[4] 6117[7] 7353[9]

Gabrial's Hope (FR) *Tracy Waggott* a51 51
7 b g Teofilo(IRE) Wedding Night (FR) (Valanour (IRE))
2343[11] 2915[11] 3363[4] 3564[8] 3842[5] 4427[6] (4456) 4767[8] 6647[10] 6920[4] 7105[6] 7382[4] 7657[10]

Gabrial's Kaka (IRE) *Richard Fahey* a95 101
6 b g Jeremy(USA) Love In May (IRE) (City On A Hill (USA))
1018a[3] (1478) 1629[12] 1993[2] 2246[2] 2684[2] (3390) 4163[8] 4823[18] 5640[6]

Gabrial's King (IRE) *Richard Fahey* a90 98
7 b g Hurricane Run(IRE) Danella (IRE) (Platini (GER))
1642[3] 1967[5] 2472[8] 3657[11] 4162[8] 4664[4] 5157[2] 5611[6] 6057[6] 6279[3] 6781[8]

Gabrial's Star *Richard Fahey* a70 97
7 b g Hernando(FR) Grain Only (Machiavellian (USA))
1642[9] 2685[5] 3345[4] 3657[20] 4230[3] 4703[5] (5321) 5642[3] 6118[11] 6540[5] 7150[14] 7498[8]

Gabrial The Duke (IRE) *Richard Fahey* a86 89
6 ch g Duke Of Marmalade(IRE) Literacy (USA) (Diesis)
73[4] 399[3] (838) 1081[5] 1296[4] 1999[7] 3149[9] 3639[6] 4634[11] 5061[4] 6083[7]

Gabrial The Hero (USA) *Richard Fahey* a99 101
7 b g War Front(USA) Ball Gown (USA) (Silver Hawk (USA))
1967[4] 3658[6] 5116[2] 5639[8] 6118[14] 7150[21] 7498[9]

Gabrial The Terror (IRE) *Ian Williams* a76 67
6 b g Kheleyf(USA) Simla Bibi (Indian Ridge)
52[5] 330[7] 545[11] 922[7] (1085) 2194[14] 2836[7] 3129[9] 3706[5] 4194[6] 5117[5] 5801[3] 6346[4] 8447[8]

Gabrial The Thug (FR) *Ian Williams* a32 32
6 b g Azamour(IRE) Baliyna (USA) (Woodman (USA))
263[4] 437[7] 8458[10]

Gabrial The Tiger (IRE) *Richard Fahey* a66 94
4 b g Kodiac Invincible (Slip Anchor)
2259[15] 2491[11] 2680[8] (3153) (3595) (4094) 4917[6] 6276[10] 6764[6]

Gabridan (IRE) *Richard Fahey* a56 50
2 b f Kyllachy Maugwenna (Danehill (USA))
2424[B] 3024[7] 4227[7] 4804[7] 5833[7] 6343[8] 6678[6] 6896[2] (7528)

Gabrielle *Ed Dunlop* a43 73
3 b f Paco Boy(IRE) Bounty Box (Bahamian Bounty)
1063[9] 1436[5] 2177[11] 3625[2] (7335)

Gabriel's Lad (IRE) *Denis Coakley* a89 108
7 b g Dark Angel(IRE) Catherine Wheel (Primo Dominie)
7868[6] 8279[P]

Gabster (IRE) *Amanda Perrett* a70 65
3 ch f Iffraaj Mozie Cat (IRE) (Mozart (IRE))
376[2] 593[2] ◆ 729[9] 1860[5] 2126[7] 2766[2] 3348[5] 4267[13] (5303) 5923[2]

Gaelic Angel (IRE) *Michael Scudamore* a60 29
3 b f Pour Moi(IRE) Missionary Hymn (USA) (Giant's Causeway (USA))
2505[13] 3732[8]

Gaelic Master (IRE) *Michael Scudamore* 41
3 b g Mastercraftsman(IRE) Colomone Cross (IRE) (Xaar)
1826[12] 2440[6] 3434[5]

Gaelic Silver (FR) *Gary Moore* a91 55
10 b g Lando(GER) Galatza (FR) (Johann Quatz (FR))
266[2] 556[3] 779[9] 1716[10] 2150[6] 4784[4] 5056[2] (5485) 7508[5] 8161[10] 8554[2]

Gaelic Tiger *Mark Johnston* 84
3 b g Teofilo(IRE) Green Swallow (FR) (Green Tune (USA))
(5716)

Gaelic Wizard (IRE) *Karen Tutty* a60 68
8 b g Fasliyev(USA) Fife (IRE) (Lomond (USA))
1299[3] 1676[6] (2053) 2571[7] 3009[7] 3322[3] 4309[4] 4606[4] 4931[9] 5277[7] 5483[2] 6023[3] (6451) 7584[4] 7797[13]

Gagner Sa Vie (ITY) *G Botti* a82 74
3 ch c Desert Prince(IRE) Ellendellendoo (IRE) (Ela-Mana-Mou)
1686a[13] 7999a[2]

Gaia Princess (IRE) *Gary Moore* a65 64
2 gr f Dark Angel(IRE) Mount Eliza (IRE) (Danehill (USA))
3356[7] 4951[15] 6244[7] 6829[7] 7571[8]

Gailo Chop (FR) *A De Watrigant* a115 117
5 ch g Deportivo Grenoble (FR) (Marignan (USA))
1107a[7]

Gala *John Gosden* 78
3 gr f Galileo(IRE) Misk (FR) (Linamix (FR))
3601[5] ◆ (5353) 6584[6]

Gala Celebration (IRE) *John Gallagher* 61
2 b g Excelebration(IRE) Elusive Galaxy (IRE) (Elusive City (USA))
3954[13] 4707[6] 6189[7] 6829[5] 7570[3]

Galactic Prince *Andrew Balding* 80
2 ch g Dubawi(IRE) Opera Gal (IRE) (Galileo (IRE))
4580[5] (4989) 5556[7] 6546[3] 7075[4]

Galahad *Richard Fahey* a67 65
2 ch g Sir Prancealot(IRE) Miss Mediator (USA) (Consolidator (USA))
2090[5] 2530[2] 3548[3] 4315[3] 6007[6] 7750[6] (8008) 8153[7] 8560[8]

Galantes Ivresses (FR) *Yves de Nicolay* a97 84
3 ch f Nombre Premier Loyal Lass (USA) (Cadeaux Genereux)
8563a[5]

Galesburg (IRE) *Mark Johnston* a56 69
3 b g Shamardal(USA) Calista (Caerleon (USA))
(1409) 1817[4] 2466[12] 3155[9] 3591[7] 4003[6]

Gale Song *Ed Walker* a76 82
3 b f Invincible Spirit(IRE) Please Sing (Royal Applause)
3714[4] (4565) 5744[6] 6299[2] 6918[10] 7668[3]

Galilean (IRE) *A P O'Brien* 94
2 b c Galileo(IRE) Hawala (IRE) (Warning)
7707a[8]

Galilee Chapel (IRE) *Alistair Whillans* a72 62
7 b g Baltic King Triple Zero (IRE) (Raise A Grand (IRE))
1696[9] 2330[7] 3287[6] 3921[3] (4314) 4705[2] 4772[3] 5576[2] 5835[4] 6647[3] (7336) 7794[3] 7992[3] 8134[2] ◆ (8318) (8586)

Galileo Gold *Hugo Palmer* 124
3 ch c Paco Boy(IRE) Galicuix (Galileo (IRE))
(1864) 2496a[2] (3245) 4754[2] 5449a[8] 7352[5]

Galinthias *Simon Dow* a75
4 b g Sixties Icon Tidie France (USA) (Cape Town (USA))
8449[2] 8559[2]

Galipad *A Fabre* 64
2 b c Galileo(IRE) Never Green (IRE) (Halling (USA))
7345a[5]

Galiteo (FR) *Gianluca Bietolini* 86
3 b c Teofilo(IRE) Queen Of Poland (Halling (USA))
6176a[5]

Galizzi (USA) *Charlie Appleby* a89 99
5 b g Dansili Dancing Abbie (USA) (Theatrical (IRE))
(2932) 3246[9] 4162[5] 4581[5]

Gallante (IRE) *Robert Hickmott* 112
5 b g Montjeu(IRE) Crazy Volume (IRE) (Machiavellian (USA))
7552a[7] 7756a[20]

Gallifrey *Lucy Wadham* a78
2 b f Sir Percy Crystal Gal (IRE) (Galileo (IRE))
8130[2] ◆ (8464)

Gallipoli (IRE) *Richard Fahey* a90 91
3 b g Compton Place Altadena Lady (IRE) (Imperial Ballet (IRE))
1599[7] 2251[5] 2972[2] ◆ 3635[8] 8256[6]

Gallope (IRE) *Mrs Prunella Dobbs* 87
4 ch m Lope De Vega(IRE) Lanzana (IRE) (Kalanisi (IRE))
3202a[7] 6495a[13]

Galloping Anger *Matthew J Smith* a56 48
4 b m Makfi Whispering Blues (IRE) (Sadler's Wells (USA))
5900a[10]

Galpi (IRE) *H-A Pantall* a56 61
2 ch f Mastercraftsman(IRE) Manuka (USA) (Mr Greeley (USA))
8420a[12]

Galuppi *J R Jenkins* a64 56
5 b g Galileo(IRE) La Leuze (IRE) (Caerleon (USA))
417[6] 461[2] 634[4] 1004[9] 1201[6] 2507[13] 2792[3] 3041[5] 5261[8] 6406[2] 7464[6]

Galvanize *Noel Wilson* a63 68
5 b g Bahamian Bounty Xtrasensory (Royal Applause)
76[4] 799[11] 1676[10] 1790[6]

Galvanize (USA) *Sir Michael Stoute* a80 89
3 b c Medaglia d'Oro(USA) Enthused (USA) (Seeking The Gold (USA))
(1288) 1891[7] (3026) 5175[7] 6372[9]

Gambino (IRE) *John David Riches* a71 84
6 b g Red Clubs(IRE) Temptation Island (IRE) (Spectrum (IRE))
1380[10] 2198[11] 2960[10] 4729[7]

Gambissara (FR) *Lennart Hammer-Hansen* 100
3 b f Adlerflug(GER) Gaggia (GER) (Monsun (GER))
2730a[2] 3935a[6] 4904a[5] 6972a[6] 7720a[3] 7929a[9]

Gambit *Tom Dascombe* a93 79
3 b g New Approach(IRE) Sospel (Kendor (FR))
(1134) 1610[12] 2694[7] 4475[5] ◆ 5507[2] 6079[8] 7221[6]

Gambol (FR) *Ian Williams* a56 73
6 ch g New Approach(IRE) Guardia (GER) (Monsun (GER))
6965[6] 7755[10]

Game Mascot *Shaun Harris* a58 49
6 ch g Kheleyf(USA) Tolzey (USA) (Rahy (USA))
156[5] 326[6] 505[8]

Gamesome (FR) *Paul Midgley* 106
5 b g Rock Of Gibraltar(IRE) Hot Coal (USA) (Red Ransom (USA))
1394[11] 2158[13] 3346[4] 4112[2] 4373[2] 4862[17] 5390[3] 5648[8] 6779[4] 7250[3] 7537[9]

Game Starter (IRE) *Saeed bin Suroor* 77
2 b c Dubawi(IRE) Opera Cloak (IRE) (Cape Cross (IRE))
7740[2] ◆

Gamesters Boy *Mark Brisbourne* a22 55
3 b g Firebreak Gamesters Lady (Almushtarak (IRE))
1970[4] 2589[4] 3028[5] 3509[12] 4210[9] 4987[11]

Game Theory (IRE) *N Clement* a96 105
4 b m Aussie Rules(USA) Atullia (GER) (Tertullian (USA))
4696a[6] 5691a[6] 6693a[6] 7087a[2] 7861a[2] 8165a[12]

Gamgoom *Mario Hofer* a110 86
5 b g Exceed And Excel(AUS) Danidh Dubai (IRE) (Noverre (USA))
17[2] 483[2] 745[9] 1066[12] 2722a[10] 4905a[12] 5906a[2] 7525a[7]

Gammarth (FR) *Robert Collet* a47 110
8 ch h Layman(USA) Emouna Queen (IRE) (Indian Ridge)
3796a[8] 6391a[12]

Gamoudiya (FR) *T Castanheira* a70 66
3 b f Orpen(USA) Tall Perfection (USA) (Distorted Humor (USA))
6912a[13]

Gamrah (IRE) *James Tate* a69
3 ch f Exceed And Excel(AUS) Fashionable (Nashwan (USA))
5527[4] ◆ 8247[4]

Gang Warfare *Jamie Osborne* a108 100
5 b g Medicean Light Impact (IRE) (Fantastic Light (USA))
(337) (1081) 1967[9] 3658[12] 4734[8] 5999[5] 8479[7]

Gannicus *Brendan Powell* a70 79
5 b g Phoenix Reach(IRE) Rasmani (Medicean)
1317[2] ◆ 1775[7] 2460[6] 3061[11] 3514[2] 4157[6] 4383[4] 5374[5] 6889[2]

Ganymede *Eve Johnson Houghton* a83 69
5 b g Oasis Dream Gaze (Galileo (IRE))
1756[5] 2187[8] 2540[6]

Garbanzo (IRE) *Ed Walker* a74 60
2 gr c Mastercraftsman(IRE) Noble Fantasy (GER) (Big Shuffle (USA))
7621[6] 7963[3] 8486[3]

Garboesque (IRE) *Shaun Harris* a29 19
2 b f Elzaam(AUS) Princess Nicole (IRE) (Alhaarth (IRE))
7576[12] 7988[12]

Garcia *Richard Fahey* 101
3 b g Paco Boy(IRE) Birdie (Alhaarth (IRE))
(1585) (2473) ◆ 3299[16] 6557[4] ◆

Garden World (IRE) *Nigel Tinkler* 76
3 b f Canford Cliffs(IRE) Elizabeth Swann (Bahamian Bounty)
1599[10] 2161[19] 2693[11] 6583[12]

Gardol City (FR) *G Botti* a98 103
3 b c Elusive City(USA) Plume Rose (Marchand De Sable (USA))
2140a[3]

Gargotiere (FR) *H-F Devin* 101
3 ch f Kendargent(FR) Bonne Gargotte (FR) (Poliglote)
(2115a) 2726a[4] 4331a[3] 5461a[5]

Garinsha (FR) *T Lemarie* a34 41
9 b m Diktat L'Impalpable (IRE) (Fumo Di Londra (IRE))
3733a[2]

Garlingari (FR) *Mme C Barande-Barbe* a97 117
5 b g Linngari(IRE) Garlinote (FR) (Poliglote)
(1023a) (1375a) 1909a[3] 2947a[2] 3936a[5] 4783a[4] 5500a[3] 5947a[4] 8329a[7]

Garter (IRE) *Charles Hills* a71 52
3 b f Fastnet Rock(AUS) Princess Iris (IRE) (Desert Prince (IRE))
4361[9] 6135[7] 6650[5] (7070) 7282[7] 7817[4] (8026) 8248[2]

Garth Rockett *Brendan Powell* 42
2 b g Delegator Leelu (Largesse)
3243[18] 5890[10] 6481[6]

Gasalto (FR) *F-H Graffard* a63
2 ch g Medicean Sainte Colombe (IRE) (Danehill Dancer (IRE))
8420a[10]

Gateshead (USA) *Bryan Smart* 49
4 b g First Defence(USA) Tsar's Pride (Sadler's Wells (USA))
1123[7]

Gatillo *Philip McBride* a74 70
3 gr g Showcasing Crystal Gale (IRE) (Verglas (IRE))
1421[8] 3464[4] 4319[8] 8240[2]

Gaval *David Barron* 67
2 b g Major Cadeaux Bold Bidder (Indesatchel (IRE))
5727[10] 6447[2] 6950[19]

Gavarnie Encore *Michael Blanshard* a61 42
4 b h Intikhab(USA) Greeley Bright (USA) (Mr Greeley (USA))
346[3] 609[3] (777) 951[5] 1544[14] 3030[9] 3522[3] 4009[9] 5080[5] 5326[5] 5808[7] 7070[8] 7427[5] 7736[5]

Gavlar *William Knight* a97 97
5 b g Gentlewave(IRE) Shawhill (Dr Fong (USA))
1209[2] ◆ 1642[5] 2468[4] 3658[9] 7979[11] 8424[8]

Gawdawpalin (IRE) *Sylvester Kirk* a93 89
3 b c Holy Roman Emperor(IRE) Dirtybirdie (Diktat)
1276[2] 1738[2] 2244[10] (2892) 6110[8] 6544[3] 7117[10] 7512[5] 7980[2]

G'Day Aussie *Brian Ellison* a63 69
3 b g Aussie Rules(USA) Moi Aussi (USA) (Mt. Livermore (USA))
1400[5]

Geeaitch *Peter Hiatt* a54 50
7 ch g Cockney Rebel(IRE) Grand Rebecca (IRE) (Namid)
53[3] 251[4] 368[7] 445[3] 505[7]

Geego *Richard Fahey* a47 51
2 ch c Compton Place Valediction (Fantastic Light (USA))
2264[6] 2913[10] 3873[6] 4315[5] 5112[6] 5974[8]

Gemina (IRE) *Ralph Beckett* 89
2 b f Holy Roman Emperor(IRE) Gravitation (Galileo (IRE))
(4775) ◆ 5595[2]

General Alexander (IRE) *Brian Ellison* a57 81
3 gr g Zebedee Alexander Express (IRE) (Sri Pekan (USA))
1217[2] 1494[3] (2019) 2650[3] 4643[11] 5978[3] 6537[4]

General Allenby *Henry Tett* a50 43
2 b c Medicean Cat Hunter (One Cool Cat (USA))
2756[11] 3524[7] 4154[8] 6313[11]

General Brook (IRE) *John O'Shea* a57 65
6 b g Westerner Danse Grecque (IRE) (Sadler's Wells (USA))
4088[10] 6514[5] 7103[5] 7936[4] 8179[9]

General Gerrard *Michael Madgwick*
2 b g Captain Gerrard(IRE) Dockside Strike (Docksider (USA))
5668[7]

General Hazard (IRE) *Michael Bell* a81 57
3 gr g Cacique(IRE) In The Soup (USA) (Alphabet Soup (USA))
1036[3] 1287[7] 2207[15] 3080[5] ◆ (8194) (8257) ◆ 8367[2] 8498[4]

General Macarthur (USA) *A P O'Brien* a84 102
3 b c War Front(USA) Imagine (IRE) (Sadler's Wells (USA))
2924a[4] 4065[7] 4326a[4] 5343a[7] 5564a[8] 5941a[15]

Generalship (IRE) *John Gosden* a89 85
3 b c New Approach(IRE) Ahla Wasahl (Dubai Destination (USA))
1570[3] 2248[5] 3062[2] 3614[7] (4010) ◆

General Tufto *Charles Smith* a57 57
11 b g Fantastic Light(USA) Miss Pinkerton (Danehill (USA))
2[5] 247[5] 336[4] 448[6] 526[4] 1202[16] 1295[5] 1707[6] 3044[6] 3620[10] 4234[12] 5868[8] 6243[7] 7889[3] 8240[6] (8470)

Generalyse *Anabel K Murphy* a78 66
7 b g Cadeaux Genereux Dance To The Blues (IRE) (Danehill Dancer (IRE))
236[8] 561[11] 856[6] 872[6] 1180[2] 1720[2] 2380[7] 3259[5] 3970[6] (4321) 4570[2] 5236[4] 5483[5] 5797[12] 8316[5]

Generosidade (URU) *Paulo H Lobo* 104
6 b m Nedawi Xiang-Vi (BRZ) (Quinze Quilates (BRZ))
3088a[3]

Generous Kitten (USA) *Michael J Maker* 100
5 b g Kitten's Joy(USA) Philanthropy Lady (USA) (Desert Style (IRE))
5428a[7]

Generous Times *Chris Grant* 36
2 b f Bahri(USA) Gerardina (Generous (IRE))
2913[13] 3361[5] 4509[3]

Genetics (FR) *Andrew Balding* 80
2 b c Manduro(GER) Garmerita (FR) (Poliglote)
5203[3] (5740) 7151[9]

Geneva Convention (IRE) *Richard Hannon* 84
2 gr c Clodovil(IRE) Boucheron (Galileo (IRE))
3529[8] (4125) 4802[8] (7016)

Gengis (FR) *G Doleuze* a79 108
6 gr h King's Best(USA) Ashiyna (IRE) (Green Desert (USA))
1172a[6] 2317a[8] 3090a[6]

Geno (IRE) *Kevin Ryan* 82
3 b g Holy Roman Emperor(IRE) Abama Lady (CAN) (Mr Greeley (USA))
1691[2] 2336[2] (2668) 3360[4] 3716[3] 4007[4] 4612[5] 5295[2] 5643[2] 6133[4] 6537[14] 7289[3]

Genres *Alan Swinbank* a69 67
4 b g Champs Elysees Musical Horizon (USA) (Distant View (USA))
1380[8] 2017[10] 2439[8] 5841[7] 6346[7] 8241[10] 8586[4] ◆

Gentle Maine (IRE) *J-M Beguigne* a59 65
6 ch g Muhtathir Maine Rose (Red Ransom (USA))
8421a[4]

Gentleman Giles (IRE) *Jamie Osborne* a52 39
2 b c Dutch Art Sularina (IRE) (Alhaarth (IRE))
3472[4] 4203[9] 4503[5] 5484[8] 8072[8] 8276[5] 8344[5]

Gentlemen *Phil McEntee* a102 68
5 ch g Ad Valorem(USA) Stoney Cove (IRE) (Needwood Blade)
(82) (159) 494[5] (1143) 1801[RR] (1958) (3279) 4246a[4] 4741[7] 5678[4] 6371[8] 8069[3] 8407[2] 8530[3]

Gentleshaw (FR) *W Mongil* a82 73
7 b m Gentlewave(IRE) Grenshaw (IRE) (Persian Heights)
3184a[2]

Gentle Whisper *Charlie Fellowes* 49
2 b f Lawman(FR) Speak Softly To Me (USA) (Ogygian (USA))
3073[7]

Gentora (FR) *P Sogorb* a98 100
4 b m Gentlewave(IRE) Oranor (FR) (Starborough)
(4903a) 5384a[10]

Genuine Approval (IRE) *John Butler* a72 82
3 ch f Approve(IRE) Genuinely (IRE) (Entrepreneur)
44[3] (458) 1759[3] 2433[4] (3251) 4351[7] 4994[4] 5671[5] 6065[5] 6870[10] 8162[9]

Geoff Potts (IRE) *Jeremy Gask* a72 74
3 ch g Zebedee Our Sheila (Bahamian Bounty)
2156[4] 2974[6] 3604[2] (3786) 4612[8] 6190[6]

Geological (IRE) *Damian Joseph English* a89 83
4 b g Rock Of Gibraltar(IRE) Bean Uasal (IRE) (Oasis Dream)
1015a[11] 7475a[7]

Geophony (IRE) *Mark Johnston* a77 78
2 b g Canford Cliffs(IRE) Dawn Chorus (IRE) (Mukaddamah (USA))
4209[5] 4523[2] (4829) 5644[6] 6563[7]

George Bailey (IRE) *Suzzanne France* a53 41
4 b g Zebedee Zuzu (IRE) (Acclamation)
1026[11] 1709[9] 2052[9] 3009[12] 4229[4] 5277[10] 5889[14] 6100[6] 7602[7] 8013[10] 8146[5] 8401[4]

George Baker (IRE) *George Baker* a73 73
9 b g Camacho Petite Maxine (Sharpo)
1416[6] 2006[2] 2646[4] 4008[6] 4656[2]

George Bowen (IRE) *Richard Fahey* a93 104
4 gr g Dark Angel(IRE) Midnight Oasis (Oasis Dream)
2158[10] 2898[6] 3656[8] 4415a[14] 5417[7] 6382a[8] 6556[15] 7156[6] 7497[5] 7821[5]

George Cinq *George Scott* a89 99
6 b g Pastoral Pursuits Fairnilee (Selkirk (USA))
1335[5] ◆ 2216[3] ◆ 2587[2] 3188[2] (3848) ◆ 4893[2] 5146[9]

George Dryden (IRE) *Ann Duffield* a87 108
4 gr g Zebedee Key To Fortune (GER) (Big Shuffle (USA))
1644[2] 2158[12] 3655[9] 5418[5] 6161[5]

George Guru *John Bridger* a80
9 b g Ishiguru(USA) Waraqa (USA) (Red Ransom (USA))
6870[14]

George Patton (USA) *J-C Rouget* a81 108
3 rg c War Front(USA) Photograph (USA) (Unbridled's Song (USA))
2283a[4] 3543a[2]

George Ravenscar *Ed Vaughan* a36 55
2 b g Pastoral Pursuits Cosmic Destiny (IRE) (Soviet Star (USA))
2311[5] 2583[6] 3231[3] 4221[4] 5364[7]

George Reme (IRE) *John Quinn* a78 59
2 ch g Power My Sweet Georgia (IRE) (Royal Applause)
4040[6] (4642) 5967[3] 6554[9]

George William *Richard Hannon* a95 93
3 b g Paco Boy(IRE) Basque Beauty (Nayef (USA))
(1324) 2695[3] (3029) 4358[2] 4867[8] 5601[5] 6082[5] ◆ (7530)

Georgian Bay (IRE) *K R Burke* a103 93
6 b g Oratorio(IRE) Jazzie (FR) (Zilzal (USA))
1204[3] 1627[3] 2031[5] 2485[7] 3566[7] 5552[6] 6126[2] 6788[7] 7933[5] 8049[4] 8317[8] 8478[7] 8593[6]

Georgio (GER) *Andrew Balding* a51 60
2 b g Approve(IRE) Gillenia (GER) (Greinton)
3404[10] 3872[9] 4387[3] 4802[6]

Geraldine (GER) *Stuart Williams* a65 50
2 b f Royal Applause Golden Whip (GER) (Seattle Dancer (USA))
3216[4] 6295[10] ◆ 6867[7] 7275[5] (7615) 7981[3] (8071)

Gereon (GER) *C Zschache* 99
8 b g Next Desert(IRE) Golden Time (GER) (Surumu (GER))
6397a[6]

German Whip *Gary Moore* a74 63
3 b g Zoffany(IRE) Tan Tan (King's Best (USA))
3406[8] 3669[3] 4401[7] 5104[3] ◆ (5721) ◆ (6047) 6629[3] 8590[10]

Gerrard's Fur Coat *Tom Dascombe* a72 52
2 b f Captain Gerrard(IRE) All Fur Coat (Multiplex)
(1799) 2104[6] 2786[2] 3128[7] 4195[2] 4629[5] 7258[6] 7966[5] 8453[7]

Gerrard's Quest *Mohammed Hussain* a91 99
3 b c Captain Gerrard(IRE) Ryan's Quest (IRE) (Mukaddamah (USA))
756a[11] 8573a[2]

Gerrard's Return *Tom Dascombe* a61 52
2 ch c Captain Gerrard(IRE) Dawn Lightning (Dark Angel (IRE))
2264[4] 2611[3] 3093[6] 4713[6] 4915[6] 5543[5] 5974[5] 6588[3] 6961[3]

Gerry The Glover (IRE) *Brian Ellison* a89 94
4 b g Approve(IRE) Umlani (IRE) (Great Commotion (USA))
1563[9] 2331[5] 2689[8] 3605[8] 5419[11] 5886[11]

Gershwin *David Lanigan* 108
3 b c Shamardal(USA) Gradara (Montjeu (IRE))
1610[6] ◆ (2538) ◆ 4129[2] ◆ 5160[2]

Getgo *David Lanigan* a75 75
2 b g Excelebration(IRE) Hip (Pivotal)
4128[10] 5670[2] 6044[3] 6473[2] (7032)

Get Knotted (IRE) *Michael Dods* 106
4 ch g Windsor Knot(IRE) Genuinely (IRE) (Entrepreneur)
1274[11] (2256) 2833[3] 3115[2] 3390[6] (4665) 5389[3] 6287[3] 6556[2] 7156[10] 7497[2]

Getna (USA) *Richard Hannon* a75
2 b f Lonhro(AUS) Aquarius Star (IRE) (Danehill Dancer (IRE))
7647[2] 8208[4]

Get Prancer *J R Jenkins* 27
4 ch g Archipenko(USA) Clever Omneya (USA) (Toccet (USA))
3040[10]

Get Ready To Rock (IRE) *Matthieu Palussiere* a50 56
2 bb c Rock Of Gibraltar(IRE) Sheezalady (Zafonic (USA))
5985a[8]

Gettin' Lucky *John Balding* a49 28
3 ch g Bertolini(USA) Loose Caboose (IRE) (Tagula (IRE))
2667[10] 6744[8] 8288[2] 8572[8]

Gettysburg (USA) *Steven Asmussen* a105
3 rg c Pioneerof The Nile(USA) L. A. Devine (USA) (Pulpit (USA))
3181a[8]

Get Up And Dance *William Haggas* 73
3 b f Makfi Our Little Secret (IRE) (Rossini (USA))
2234[2] (2667) 3716[5]

G Force (IRE) *Adrian Paul Keatley* 107
5 b g Tamayuz Flanders (IRE) (Common Grounds)
3681a[5] 4413a[6] 4865[27] 6558[4] 7191a[4]

Ghaaly *J-C Rouget* a98 103
3 b c Tamayuz Ghizlaan (USA) (Seeking The Gold (USA))
1230a[3] 5004a[2]

Ghaamer (USA) *A R Al Rayhi* a66 111
6 b g Hard Spun(USA) Teeba (USA) (Seeking The Gold (USA))
(95a) 282a[8] 720a[2] 1106a[15]

Ghadaayer (IRE) *Sir Michael Stoute* a73 39
2 b f Shamardal(USA) Eldalil (Singspiel (IRE))
6413[3] ◆ 7056[8] 7763[3]

Ghalib (IRE) *Ed Walker* a94 101
4 ch g Lope De Vega(IRE) Gorband (USA) (Woodman (USA))
2247[2] ◆ 2898[12] 3623[2] 4163[15] 5174[5] 6109[13] 6560[9] 7530[5]

Ghand (IRE) *Sir Michael Stoute* a51
2 b f Galileo(IRE) Landmark (USA) (Arch (USA))
7761[14] 8073[8]

Ghaseedah *Simon Crisford* a59
2 b f Kyllachy Represent (IRE) (Exceed And Excel (AUS))
8152[8]

Ghayyar (IRE) *Richard Hannon* a75 85
2 b c Power Al Ihtithar (IRE) (Barathea (IRE))
4866[12] (5373) 6122[5] 7471[2]

Gheedaa (USA) *William Haggas* a86 86
2 b f Tamayuz Soohaad (USA) (Hard Spun (USA))
6454[2] (7279) ◆ 7820[2] 8209[2] ◆

Gherdaiya *A Fabre* 100
3 b f Shamardal(USA) First Fleet (USA) (Woodman (USA))
1581a[7] 5498a[14]

Ghinia (IRE) *Pam Sly* 90
5 b m Mastercraftsman(IRE) Jorghinia (FR) (Seattle Slew (USA))
1757[2] ◆ 2689[9] 3438[5] 3667[4] 4761[3] 5487[2] 6483[5] 7017[5] 7671[15]

Ghostly Arc (IRE) *Noel Wilson* a42 67
4 b g Arcano(IRE) Cheyenne's Spirit (IRE) (Sadler's Wells (USA))
1399[5] (2094) 2365[3] 3012[3] 4038[4] 5294[4] 5580[3] 6219[5] 6812[2] 7251[9]

Ghost Train (IRE) *Tim McCarthy* a69 66
7 b g Holy Roman Emperor(IRE) Adrastea (IRE) (Monsun (GER))
398[2] 615[3] 1159[5] 2380[5] 8031[7] 8234[11]

Ghostwriter (IRE) *Hugo Palmer* a68
3 b g High Chaparral(IRE) Diara Angel (IRE) (Hawk Wing (USA))
29[3] ◆

Giant Bradley *Michael Appleby* a36
3 ch g Monsieur Bond(IRE) Cut Back (Factual (USA))
363[6] 507[5]

Giant Redwood (IRE) *Michael Bell* a71 81
4 b g Galileo(IRE) Gwynn (IRE) (Darshaan)
1273[8] 2025[6] 2468[8] 2820[4] 3437[3] 4101[3] 4353[8] 6565[10] 7006[9] 7507[11]

Giant Sequoia (USA) *Des Donovan*
12 ch g Giant's Causeway(USA) Beware Of The Cat (USA) (Caveat (USA))
7739[12]

Giant Spark *Paul Midgley* a54 98
4 b g Orientor Annie Gee (Primo Valentino (IRE))
1154[5] 1488[4] 1692[6] 2053[5] (2778) 3016[2] (3907) (6136) 6539[8] (7475a)

Giantstepsahead (IRE) *Alan Bailey* a92 86
7 br g Footstepsinthesand Salty Air (IRE) (Singspiel (IRE))
(66) 399[2] 656[3] 1089[6] 6753[8] 7408[3] 7980[6]

Giant Treasure (USA) *Richard Gibson* a70 118
5 rg g Mizzen Mast(USA) Palisade (USA) (Gone West (USA))
1912a[8] 8332a[11]

Gianyar (FR) *E Lellouche* a77 101
3 b c Le Havre(IRE) Chandi Dasa (IRE) (Sadler's Wells (USA))
7137a[4]

Gibbs Hill (GER) *Roger Varian* a82 88
3 gr c Mastercraftsman(IRE) Gold Charm (GER) (Key Of Luck (USA))
2327[3] 2914[2] 3535[2] (3914)

Gibson Park *A Oliver* a58 65
3 b g Poet's Voice Fifty (IRE) (Fasliyev (USA))
5900a[13]

Giddy *Richard Fahey* 80
3 b f Kyllachy Light Hearted (Green Desert (USA))
2267[2] ◆ 2683[3] 3116[9] 5836[7] 6537[21]

Giennah (IRE) *Brian Meehan* a79 71
2 b f Tamayuz Jamaayel (Shamardal (USA))
2637[4] ◆ 3122[4] 4261[7] (6139) 6697[8]

Gift Box (USA) *Chad C Brown* a105
3 rg r Twirling Candy(USA) Special Me (USA) (Unbridled's Song (USA))
5913a[4]

Gifted Lady (IRE) *Michael Mulvany* a49 72
2 br f Bushranger(IRE) La Scala (USA) (Theatrical (IRE))
6388a[8]

Gifted Master (IRE) *Hugo Palmer* 114
3 b g Kodiac Shobobb (Shamardal (USA))
(1423) (1773) 2692[3] 3269[9] 4733[3] 5217a[12] 6749[2] 7115[9]

Gift From God *Hugo Froud* a54 71
3 b g Teofilo(IRE) Piffling (Pivotal)
3147[3] 4041[11] 4939[8] 6091[8] 7212[8] 7754[11]

Giftorm (USA) *Fredrik Reuterskiold* a101 97
6 b g War Pass(USA) High Cholesterol (USA) (Until Sundown (USA))
189a[12] 374a[2] 717a[4] 1957a[4] (4421a) 5098a[3]

Gild Master *C Von Der Recke* a75 61
4 b g Excellent Art Nirvana (Marju (IRE))
587a[4]

Gilgamesh *George Scott* 79
2 b g Foxwedge(AUS) Flaming Cliffs (USA) (Kingmambo (USA))
4103[8] (4981)

Gilmer (IRE) *Brian Ellison* a55 77
5 b g Exceed And Excel(AUS) Cherokee Rose (IRE) (Dancing Brave (USA))
197[9] 1165[4] 1556[3] 1768[4] 2045[5] (2458) (2697) (3098) 3674[4] (4084) 4291[3] 5253[5] 5955[8] 6769[2] (6836) 7443[6]

Gilt Edged (IRE) *Julie Camacho* a52 57
3 br f Big Bad Bob(IRE) Caona (USA) (Miswaki (USA))
2557[5] 3249[6] 4681[8] 5844[4] 6513[5] 7103[4] 7532[11]

Gimlet *Hugo Palmer* a70 71
3 b g Poet's Voice Poppo's Song (CAN) (Polish Navy (USA))
1835[2] ◆ 2348[3] 3652[6]

Ginger Charlie *Ruth Carr* a7 50
3 ch g Haafhd Mandarin Lady (Timeless Times (USA))
1123[11] 1400[8] 3919[3] 4567[10] 4844[4] 5322[7] 5732[3] 7096[14]

Ginger Fizz *Ben Case* a66 52
9 ch m Haafhd Valagalore (Generous (IRE))
3067[10] 3528[6]

Ginger Jack *Garry Moss* a87 94
9 ch g Refuse To Bend(IRE) Coretta (IRE) (Caerleon (USA))
1521[8] (2257) 3518[5] ◆ (4894) 5419[4] (5802) 6786[8] 7316[11]

Ginger Joe *David Brown* a67 58
3 ch r Medicean Susi Wong (IRE) (Selkirk (USA))
817[3] 978[3] 1788[7] 2770[6] 3786[11] 4600[7] 6592[10]

Ginger Love *Bryan Smart* 49
2 ch g Kheleyf(USA) La Peinture (GER) (Peintre Celebre (USA))
6682[6]

Ginger Truffle *Brett Johnson* a52 52
2 ch f Sixties Icon Whassup (FR) (Midyan (USA))
2990[4] 4951[8] 5099[4] 6887[4] 7528[5] 8152[10]

Gin In The Inn (IRE) *Richard Fahey* 85
3 b g Alfred Nobel(IRE) Nose One's Way (IRE) (Revoque (IRE))
2972[7] 3646[5] 4344[8] 4896[5] (5439) 5774[4] 6714[5] 7221[10] 7590[6]

Ginzan *Malcolm Saunders* a74 86
8 b m Desert Style(IRE) Zyzania (Zafonic (USA))
1321[7] 1528[8] 1945[3] 2146[2] 2846[4] (3123) 3487[3] 3815[3] 4291[8] 5305[2] 6114[10] (6318) 6946[6]

Giogiobbo *Francesco Santella* 91
3 b c Bahamian Bounty Legnani (Fasliyev (USA))
1686a[9]

Giovanni Battista (IRE) *Brian Meehan* 85
2 b g Clodovil(IRE) Aloisi (Kalanisi (IRE))
(7664) ◆

Giovanni Boldini (USA) *Flemming Velin* a87 64
5 bb h War Front(USA) Dancing Trieste (USA) (Old Trieste (USA))
1957a[10]

Giovanni Di Bicci *Jim Boyle* a77 76
4 b g Medicean Marula (IRE) (Sadler's Wells (USA))
(346) (437) (875) (951) 1699[3] 5674[2] 5965[9] 5992[3] ◆

Girling (IRE) *Ralph Beckett* 89
3 b f Rock Of Gibraltar(IRE) Gravitation (Galileo (IRE))
1826[2] (2368) 3341[8] 4351[5] 5653[13]

Girlofinkandstars (IRE) *Rae Guest* 54
2 b f Power Gaselee (USA) (Toccet (USA))
2536[11] 4187a[9] 5052[4]

Girl Squad *William Jarvis* a52
2 b f Intikhab(USA) Foxtrot Alpha (IRE) (Desert Prince (IRE))
8443[7]

Girl With A Pearl (IRE) *Ed Dunlop* a37 61
3 ch f Dutch Art Pointed Arch (IRE) (Rock Of Gibraltar (IRE))
1389[3] 1816[6] 2325[12]

Girolamo (GER) *P Schiergen* 107
7 ch h Dai Jin Golden Time (GER) (Surumu (GER))
7759a[9]

Giselle's Charm (IRE) *M D O'Callaghan* 91
2 ch f Casamento(IRE) Princess Kyka (IRE) (Namid)
5661a[8] 6860a[6]

Giuseppe Piazzi (IRE) *Flemming Velin* 97
4 b h Galileo(IRE) Belesta (Xaar)
5187a[4] 6390a[6]

Giveagirlachance (IRE) *Seamus Mullins* a61
7 b m Iffraaj Farewell To Love (IRE) (Darshaan)
342[7] 695[11]

Giveaway Glance *Alan King* 84
3 br f Passing Glance Giving (Generous (IRE))
3107[2] ◆ 4556[6] 7220[9]

Giveitsomeginger *Jo Hughes* 33
2 ch f Stimulation(IRE) Glaze (Kyllachy)
5772[8] 6534[9]

Give Us A Belle (IRE) *Christine Dunnett* a62 60
7 b g Kheleyf(USA) Bajan Belle (IRE) (Efisio)
75[7] 504[5] (733) ◆ *889[7] 1059[9] 1133[3] 1833[7]* 2040[5] 2342[3] 2423[3] *2785[4] 3307[9]* 3822[5] 4264[7] *4980[7]* 5335[2] *5470[6] 6587[11] 6865[8] 7863[4]*

G K Chesterton (IRE) *Charlie Appleby* 88
3 ch g Poet's Voice Neptune's Bride (USA) (Bering)
6581[5] 7499[7]

Glacial Drift *T J Taaffe* 51
5 b m Rail Link Moraine (Rainbow Quest (USA))
5900a[11]

Glacier Point *Clive Cox* 73
2 ch f Foxwedge(AUS) Ahwahnee (Compton Place)
5869[7] 6733[3] 7314[4]

Gladiator King (IRE) *A J Martin* 54
7 b g Dylan Thomas(IRE) Sheer Bliss (IRE) (Sadler's Wells (USA))
7251[6]

Gladsome *Charlie Wallis* a51 69
8 b m Resplendent Glory(IRE) Christening (IRE) (Lahib (USA))
168[9]

Gladys Cooper (IRE) *Ed Walker* a61 56
3 b f Arcano(IRE) Anthyllis (GER) (Lycius (USA))
1389[9] *2325[2]* 3080[9] *3731[2] 4214[4] 4936[5] 5610[4] 6046[4] 6966[2]* 7300[5]

Glamorous Approach (IRE) *J S Bolger* 102
3 ch f New Approach(IRE) Maria Lee (IRE) (Rock Of Gibraltar (IRE))
1016a[4] 1507a[2] 2167a[5] 5587[4] 6200a[5] 7392a[7]

Glamorous Dream (FR) *Mme M-C Chaalon* a42 50
7 b m Dream Well(FR) Glamsalsa (FR) (Kingsalsa (USA))
1846a[5]

Glamour Time *Roger Varian* a69
2 gr f Teofilo(IRE) Gossamer Seed (IRE) (Choisir (AUS))
8130[5]

Glam'Selle *Ronald Harris* a42 53
2 b f Elnadim(USA) Town And Gown (Oasis Dream)
5542[9] *6866[11] 7259[8]* 7414[4] *7884[8] 8071[6]*

Glance My Way (IRE) *Richard Hannon* a55 81
3 ch g Rock Of Gibraltar(IRE) Glympse (IRE) (Spectrum (IRE))
1386[8] 1828[8] 2145[3] 2652[2] 3736[6] (4342) 5603[7] *6128[13]*

Glan Y Gors (IRE) *David Simcock* a92 92
4 b g High Chaparral(IRE) Trading Places (Dansili)
78[2] ◆ *385[2] 3784[10] 6089[8]* 6379[7]

Glaring *Amanda Perrett* 109
5 b h Champs Elysees Brightest (Rainbow Quest (USA))
1772[7] 2221[5] 4799[9] 5411[8] 5872[6] 6293[5]

Glasgon *Ray Craggs* a63 41
6 gr g Verglas(IRE) Miss St Tropez (Danehill Dancer (IRE))
2329[9] 2915[8] 3564[5] 4260[8] *5841[8]* 6029[9] *7438[3] (7656) 7992[14]*

Glasgow Central *Phil McEntee* a72 77
5 b g Rail Link Musical Key (Key Of Luck (USA))
170[8] 463[4] 622[6] (1578) (2086) *2374[2]* 2397[2] (2645)

Glassalt *Michael Bell* a64
2 b f Medaglia d'Oro(USA) Abergeldie (USA) (Street Cry (IRE))
8245[13] 8464[3]

Glastonberry *Geoffrey Deacon* a86 81
8 gr m Piccolo Elderberry (Bin Ajwaad (IRE))
142[3] 351[5] 632[8] 1237[4] 2146[3] 3098[4] 4222[7]

Gleaming Girl *David Simcock* a82 76
4 b m Arabian Gleam Desert Liaison (Dansili)
1932[2] 2084[2] 2737[2] 3197[4] 4087[5] *5190[3] (5973) 8538[3]*

Gleese The Devil (IRE) *Richard Fahey* a74 86
5 br g Manduro(GER) Causeway Song (USA) (Giant's Causeway (USA))
5642[9] 6011[6] 6773[3] (7158) 7320[9] *8051[7] 8250[7] 8539[6]*

Glenalmond (IRE) *Daniel Steele* a78 82
4 b g Iffraaj Balladonia (Primo Dominie)
1871[9] 1993[8] 2833[5] 3518[7] 3945[9] 5017[6] 6300[10] *7051[3] 7457[10] 8282[4] 8378[7]*

Glenamoy (IRE) *Harry Dunlop* a36 66
2 b f Kodiac Tarbiyah (Singspiel (IRE))
8341[7]

Glenamoy Lad *K J Condon* a68 90
2 b c Royal Applause Suzy Alexander (Red Ransom (USA))
3678a[8]

Glenbuck Lass (IRE) *Alan Bailey* a50 46
4 gr m Dandy Man(IRE) Certainlei (IRE) (Definite Article)
143[7] 237[6] 513[4] 596[5] 970[5]

Glencadam Glory *John Gosden* 84
2 b c Nathaniel(IRE) Lady Grace (IRE) (Orpen (USA))
5373[2] (6262)

Glendun (USA) *Brian Meehan* a72 74
2 b g First Defence(USA) La Mina (USA) (Mineshaft (USA))
3859[7] 5073[3] 5670[3] *6924[3]* 7297[3]

Glengarry *Keith Dalgleish* 90
3 b g Monsieur Bond(IRE) Lady McBeth (IRE) (Avonbridge)
2657[4] 2957[2] 4870[4] (5782) 6027[3] 6560[10]

Glen Lea (IRE) *Kenny Johnson*
7 b g Indian Danehill(IRE) Masquerade Ball (IRE) (Presenting)
1378[7] *2329[14]*

Glenmayne (IRE) *Mrs John Harrington* a74 86
3 ch f Duke Of Marmalade(IRE) Green Castle (IRE) (Indian Ridge)
5313a[5]

Glen Moss (IRE) *Michael Dods* a93 109
7 b h Moss Vale(IRE) Sail With The Wind (Saddlers' Hall (IRE))
921[6] 1197[4] 2158[5] 2485[3] 3386[3] (3891) 5613[10] 6558[22]

Glenrowan Rose (IRE) *Keith Dalgleish* a74 100
3 b f Bushranger(IRE) Choice House (USA) (Chester House (USA))
821[6] 1599[4] (1882) (2267) 7250[2]

Glens Wobbly *Jonathan Geake* a63 79
8 ch g Kier Park(IRE) Wobbly (Atraf)
1810[5] 2399[4] 3560[3] 3817[3] 4711[3] (4913) 5574[8] 6445[2] 6804[11] 7508[4]

Glenville Gardens (USA) *Sid Attard* a74 106
4 bb g Street Cry(IRE) Navy Gardens (USA) (Storm Cat (USA))
6601a[7]

Glenys The Menace (FR) *John Best* a66 61
2 b f American Post Elle S'Voyait Deja (USA) (Carson City (USA))
1749[5] 2376[6] 2649[10] (5165) *6236[3] (6670)*

Glicourt (FR) *P Bary* 75
2 b c Rajsaman(FR) Fusee Francaise (FR) (Anabaa (USA))
5905a[3]

Glimmer Of Hope *Mark Hoad* a23
5 b g Tiger Hill(IRE) Fontaine House (Pyramus (USA))
259[6]

Glitter Girl *William Haggas* 103
2 b f Invincible Spirit(IRE) Glitterball (IRE) (Smart Strike (CAN))
4064[5] ◆ (4603) (4966) (6257) 6748[4] 7114[2] 7547[2]

Glittering *James Eustace* a6 60
3 ch f Firebreak Razzle (IRE) (Green Desert (USA))
1436[9] 2234[15] 3577[4] 5860[9] 6826[7] *7369[12]*

Global Applause *Ed Dunlop* 103
2 b c Mayson Crown (IRE) (Royal Applause)
(1889) 2240[2] (2624) 3295[5] 4755[3] 5654[4] 6260[8] 6572[3]

Global Avenger (IRE) *Ed Dunlop* a48
3 b c Kodiac Silent Serenade (Bertolini (USA))
147[4] 265[7]

Global Revival (IRE) *Ed Dunlop* a58 75
2 b g Kyllachy Soliza (IRE) (Intikhab (USA))
2173[9] 2535[4] *2913[7]* (4315) 4802[9]

Global Storm (GER) *R Dzubasz* 105
3 bb g Areion(GER) Goonda (Darshaan)
7028a[3]

Glorious Artist (IRE) *Charles Hills* a75 78
2 b g Zoffany(IRE) Queenie Keen (IRE) (Refuse To Bend (IRE))
3813[6] 4390[4] 5029[4] 6319[2] *6869[4]*

Glorious Asset *Ivan Furtado* a67
4 b g Aqlaam Regal Asset (USA) (Regal Classic (CAN))
8190[3] 8586[8]

Glorious Dancer *Lee Carter* a63 59
4 br g Royal Applause Provence (Averti (IRE))
1262[13] 3522[8] 4009[12] 7282[8] (7888)

Glorious Empire (IRE) *Ed Walker* a94 106
5 br g Holy Roman Emperor(IRE) Humble And Proud (IRE) (Pivotal)
4152[P] *6400a[5]*

Glorious Forever *Ed Walker* 78
2 ch c Archipenko(USA) Here To Eternity (USA) (Stormy Atlantic (USA))
5885[4] (7012)

Glorious Legend (IRE) *Ed Walker* 71
3 b g Pour Moi(IRE) Endearing (Selkirk (USA))
1715[7] 2208[10] 2861[12] 5375[4] 5888[4] 6335[3] (6886) 7332[5]

Glorious Poet *Ed Walker* a38 77
3 ch g Poet's Voice Sky Wonder (Observatory (USA))
6650[6] *7384[8]* (7583)

Glorious Politics *David Barron* a83 68
2 b c Delegator Pelican Key (IRE) (Mujadil (USA))
7122[6] *8140[2]* ◆

Glorious Power (IRE) *Charles Hills* 29
2 ch c Power Arpege (IRE) (Sadler's Wells (USA))
4552[8]

Glorious Rocket *Luca Cumani* a78 74
2 b g Bated Breath Up And About (Barathea (IRE))
3569[4] 4856[4] *(6673) 7305[3]*

Gloriux *Charles Hills* a49 78
2 b c Exceed And Excel(AUS) Najraan (Cadeaux Genereux)
7818[2] *8027[7]*

Glorvina (IRE) *David O'Meara* a68 62
2 b f Dragon Pulse(IRE) Hawk Dance (IRE) (Hawk Wing (USA))
6473[5] ◆ *6741[4]*

Glory Awaits (IRE) *David Simcock* a90 104
6 ch g Choisir(AUS) Sandbox Two (IRE) (Foxhound (USA))
95a[9] 373a[11] 623a[5] 2191[4] 3273[11] 4152[15] 5146[6] 5956[2] 6585[8]

Gloryette *Ed Dunlop* a64 73
3 b f Raven's Pass(USA) Cara Fantasy (IRE) (Sadler's Wells (USA))
1608[6] 2215[5] 2735[6] 3251[5] 4057[7] 4777[7] *7609[5] 7905[5] 8211[6] 8481[5]*

Glory Of Paris (IRE) *Rod Millman* 71
2 b c Sir Prancealot(IRE) Paris Glory (USA) (Honour And Glory (USA))
3463[10] 4053[4] 4659[3] 5229[4] 6289[7]

Gloryzapper (USA) *Philip D'Amato* a98 99
4 bb m Ghostzapper(USA) Grand Glory (USA) (Distorted Humor (USA))
7836a[11]

Glyder *John Holt* a57 57
2 b f Camacho Blades Princess (Needwood Blade)
5242[10] 5884[3] 6448[3] 6887[2] *7381[5]*

Gmaash *Saeed bin Suroor* a63 67
2 b f Dubawi(IRE) Maids Causeway (IRE) (Giant's Causeway (USA))
6850[4] (7296)

Gm Hopkins *John Gosden* 116
5 b g Dubawi(IRE) Varsity (Lomitas)
(1774) 2243[8] 3273[21] 3860[3] 4392[4] 6786[12] 7354[15]

Gnaad (IRE) *Robert Cowell* a55 54
2 b c Invincible Spirit(IRE) Areyaam (USA) (Elusive Quality (USA))
6731[6] *7900[4]*

Goadby *John Holt* a49 65
5 gr m Kodiac Gone Sailing (Mizzen Mast (USA))
1600[4] 2013[6] 2697[10] (3070) 3674[10] 4005[8] 4763[6] 5760[9] 6685[16] 6894[8] 7747[8] *7913[4]*

Goal (IRE) *Sally Randell* a61 61
8 b g Mujadil(USA) Classic Lin (FR) (Linamix (FR))
2899[6] 3470[2] (5016)

Go Amber Go *Rod Millman* a49 61
4 ch m Compton Place Lady Chef (Double Trigger (IRE))
(3994) 4292[2] (4484) 5009[5] 5282[3] 5826[3] 6363[4] 7018[7]

Go Charlie *Lisa Williamson* a51 51
5 b g Myboycharlie(IRE) Branston Gem (So Factual (USA))
98[4] 241[7] ◆ 3010[9] 3260[3] 3994[5] 4292[7] *4472[5]* 5105[8] 5378[10]

God Given *Luca Cumani* 72
2 b f Nathaniel(IRE) Ever Rigg (Dubai Destination (USA))
6578[3] ◆ 7441[3]

Go Dreaming (AUS) *Grant Kluske* 90
6 br g Beautiful Crown(USA) No Faking (AUS) (Telesto (NZ))
7378a[16] 7637a[7]

Godric *J Carayon* a61 63
4 ch g Winker Watson Bea Menace (USA) (Mizzen Mast (USA))
(8422a)

God's Speed (IRE) *H Al Shuwaib* a96 83
5 b g Oratorio(IRE) Guilia (Galileo (IRE))
1101a[9]

God Willing *Declan Carroll* a95 98
5 b g Arch(USA) Bourbon Ball (USA) (Peintre Celebre (USA))
1848[3] 2158[15] 2476[7] 2689[10] 6320[2] (6585) 7121[11] 7573[2] 7821[17] *8122[6]*

Go Far *Alan Bailey* a96 103
6 b g Dutch Art Carranita (IRE) (Anita's Prince) (2434) 4136[10] 4865[18] 5418[19]

Gog Elles (IRE) *J S Moore* a44 32
2 b f Helmet(AUS) Hear My Cry (USA) (Giant's Causeway (USA))
3730[10] 5166[6] *7098[6] 7734[7] 8080[3]*

Go George Go (IRE) *Alan Swinbank* a75 40
3 gr g Zebedee La Bella Grande (IRE) (Giant's Causeway (USA))
3856[9] 4682[9] 5716[4] *(8134) (8386)* ◆ *(8480)*

Go Go Green (IRE) *Jim Goldie* a60 69
10 b g Acclamation Preponderance (IRE) (Cyrano De Bergerac)
1378[4] 1693[3] 1843[2] 2524[2] 2658[7] 2961[6] 3150[8] 3924[6] 3944[6] 4488[8] 4873[6] *5368[8]* 6093[5] 6506[8] 6813[2] 7093[9]

Going Up (IRE) *Rae Guest* a88 82
3 ch c Duke Of Marmalade(IRE) Guilia (Galileo (IRE))
5438[6] 5716[2] *7487[3] (8096)*

Going Viral (IRE) *Matthieu Palussiere* a41 65
3 b g Kodiac Dark Indian (IRE) (Indian Ridge)
1286a[9] 7492a[15] 7999a[13]

Goji Berry (FR) *M Boutin* 70
2 ro c Dunkerque(FR) Et Pourtant (FR) (Linamix (FR))
5348a[4] 5985a[5]

Go Kart (IRE) *P J Prendergast* a86 85
3 b f Intense Focus(USA) Kartiste (IRE) (Kalanisi (IRE))
4246a[3] 7803a[7] 8197a[4]

Goken (FR) *Kevin Ryan* a105 113
4 b h Kendargent(FR) Gooseley Chope (FR) (Indian Rocket)
1066[3] 1862[15] 2159[9] 3244[3] ◆ 4151[10] 4824[11] 5614[12] 6120[12] 6816a[7]

Gokena (FR) *Kevin Ryan* 58
2 br f Kendargent(FR) Gooseley Chope (FR) (Indian Rocket)
4759[6] 6712[9] 7331[7]

Golconda King (IRE) *Richard Fahey* a42 58
2 gr g Dark Angel(IRE) Vanity's Girl (IRE) (Compton Place)
7090[6] 7741[5] *7988[11]*

Golconda Prince (IRE) *Richard Fahey* 65
2 b g Arcano(IRE) Mujarah (IRE) (Marju (IRE))
4966[3] 5916[3] 6771[4]

Gold Actor (JPN) *Tadashige Nakagawa* 121
5 bb h Screen Hero(JPN) Heilong Xing (JPN) (Kyowa Alysheba (USA))
8129a[4]

Goldan Jess (IRE) *Philip Kirby* a67 37
12 b g Golan(IRE) Bendis (GER) (Danehill (USA))
2916[11] 3704[10] 4935[10]

Gold Award (IRE) *Mick Channon* 73
2 br c Bushranger(IRE) Sandtail (IRE) (Verglas (IRE))
(7184) 7544[11]

Gold Beau (FR) *Kristin Stubbs* a71 65
6 b g Gold Away(IRE) Theorie (FR) (Anabaa (USA))
68[2] 167[3] 608[2] 703[6] 955[3] 1415[8] *2332[6]* 2812[5] 3211[5] 3880[9] 4454[13] *7144[2] 7602[2] 7852[6] 8483[7]*

Gold Bud *George Baker* a45 62
4 b g Kyllachy Fluttering Rose (Compton Place)
6317[11] 7011[6] ◆ *7362[7]* 7774[13]

Gold Chain (IRE) *Dianne Sayer* a44 65
6 b m Authorized(IRE) Mountain Chain (USA) (Royal Academy (USA))
3154[5] (4935)

Gold City (IRE) *S Seemar* a109 97
7 b g Pivotal Storm Lily (USA) (Storm Cat (USA))
92a[9] 452a[2] 844a[11] 1101a[8]

Gold Class *Robert Alan Hennessy* a49 46
5 ch g Firebreak Silken Dalliance (Rambo Dancer (CAN))
5900a[8]

Gold Club *Ed McMahon* a84 80
5 b g Multiplex Oceana Blue (Reel Buddy (USA))
1291[2] 2028[7] 2613[4] *8083[4]* ◆ *8176[5]*

Gold Eliza (IRE) *Richard Hannon* a41 35
3 ch f Pivotal Srda (USA) (Kingmambo (USA))
1792[8] 2148[2] 2590[11] 2851[5] 3256[7]

Golden Amber (IRE) *Dean Ivory* a103 102
5 b m Holy Roman Emperor(IRE) Time Of Gold (USA) (Banker's Gold (USA))
1394[12] 3616[2] 4114[7] *5472[4]* 6161[6] *7610[6] 7868[2] 8098[3] 8489[5]*

Golden Apollo *Tim Easterby* 81
2 ch g Pivotal Elan (Dansili)
3805[6] 5414[3] 6002[4] ◆ 6534[3] 7541[9] (7820)

Golden Bridge (FR) *C Gourdain* 107
3 gr c Montmartre(FR) Golden Memory (FR) (Kendor (FR))
2946a[6] 4439a[9]

Golden Buck (FR) *P Van De Poele* a58 54
6 ch g Gold Away(IRE) Khaylama (IRE) (Dr Devious (IRE))
8421a[2]

Golden Cape *Michael Mullineaux* a31 53
3 ch f Native Ruler Lake Sabina (Diktat)
145[9] 679[10] 3744[4] 4275[8]

Golden Chapter *Ralph Beckett* a70
3 b f Danehill Dancer(IRE) Farfala (FR) (Linamix (FR))
(699)

Golden Doyen (GER) *Philip Hobbs* 84
5 b g Doyen(IRE) Goldsamt (GER) (Rienzi (EG))
1598[3] 6919[3]

Golden Easter (USA) *Kevin Ryan* a74 74
2 ch f Distorted Humor(USA) Easterette (USA) (Hard Spun (USA))
4110[3] 4804[2] ◆ *5242[2]*

Golden Eye *Sylvester Kirk* a66 67
2 ch g Kheleyf(USA) Gennie Bond (Pivotal)
4053[3] *4209[3]* 7209[8] *7750[3] 7941[5]*

Goldenfield (IRE) *Gary Moore* a89 88
3 b g Footstepsinthesand Society Gal (IRE) (Galileo (IRE))
(1860) (2644) 3687[3] 4827[12] *5738[2] 6675[7]*

Golden Gazelle (IRE) *A Fabre* 83
3 ch f Galileo(IRE) Grey Lilas (IRE) (Danehill (USA))
4331a[5]

Golden Glimmer (IRE) *Tom Dascombe* 85
3 b f Danehill Dancer(IRE) Gilded Vanity (IRE) (Indian Ridge)
1628[3] ◆ (1998) 2695[11] 4130[4] 4630[4]

Golden Guepard (IRE) *A Fabre* a85 99
5 b h Hurricane Run(IRE) Grey Lilas (IRE) (Danehill (USA))
7946a[6]

Golden Guest *George Margarson* a67 64
2 ch g Bated Breath Si Belle (IRE) (Dalakhani (IRE))
2173[6] 2536[10] 2976[8] *4937[2]* 5239[4] 6191[5]

Golden Harbour (FR) *Brian Barr* a47
2 b c Harbour Watch(IRE) Make Up (Kyllachy)
8119[6] 8352[10]

Golden Highway (USA) *Michael Appleby* a73 34
4 ch g Elusive Quality(USA) Awesome Chic (USA) (Awesome Again (CAN))
24[8] 621[11] 1416[7] 1805[8]

Golden Isles (IRE) *J S Moore* a62 61
3 ch f Mastercraftsman(IRE) Aphorism (Halling (USA))
29[8] 2366[10] 3080[3] 4463[3] 4819[5] 5571[2] 6827[9] *7754[12]*

Golden Jubilee (USA) *Nigel Twiston-Davies* a85 84
7 bb g Zavata(USA) Love Play (USA) (Friendly Lover (USA))
330[2] 447[4] 8249[12]

Golden Muscade (USA) *Brian Barr* a58 56
3 b f Medaglia d'Oro(USA) Kinda Spicy (USA) (A.P. Indy (USA))
5023[9] 5504[6] 6073[4]

Golden Nectar *Laura Mongan* a78
2 ch f Sakhee's Secret Mildoura (FR) (Sendawar (IRE))
7278[2] ◆ *(7762) 8360[3]* ◆

Golden Nino (FR) *H-A Pantall* a87 96
3 b c Sageburg(IRE) Golden Clou (FR) (Kendor (FR))
3183a[8]

Golden Opportunity *James Tate* a68
2 ch c Kheleyf(USA) Golden Waters (Dubai Destination (USA))
7649[6] 7891[3] ◆ *8352[4] 8569[2]*

Golden Pearl *M Halford* a87 87
3 b f Oasis Dream Pearl Banks (Pivotal)
4246a[7] 5441a[2]

Golden Reign (IRE) *William Haggas* a65 76
3 ch f Champs Elysees Fleche D'Or (Dubai Destination (USA))
1392[3] ◆ 2395[5] *3305[3]* 4597[3] 5709[2] 6024[2] *7205[9]*

Golden Rosanna *Steph Hollinshead* a38 44
3 b f Equiano(FR) Goldeva (Makbul)
3669[4] 4590[4] 5200[4] 6312[7] *6587[5] 7509[7] 8289[8]*

Golden Slam *Roger Varian* 71
2 ch g Pastoral Pursuits Strawberry Leaf (Unfuwain (USA))
2536[6] (2822)

Golden Soul (USA) *M F De Kock* a34 101
6 ch h Perfect Soul(IRE) Hollywood Gold (USA) (Mr Prospector (USA))
540a[3] *844a[12]*

Golden Spear *A J Martin* 94
5 ch g Kyllachy Penmayne (Inchinor)
(4850a) 6350a[5] 7150[5] (7708a)

Golden Spun (USA) *Michael Dods* a65 69
4 b g Hard Spun(USA) Scarlet's Tara (USA) (Goodbye Doeny (USA))
278[5] 426[9] 943[5] 1125[3] 1565[15]

Golden Steps (FR) *Marco Botti* a94 108
5 b g Footstepsinthesand Kocooning (IRE) (King's Best (USA))
483[8] 755a[3] 1887[6] 2206[7] 2684[3] (4152)

Golden Stunner (IRE) *Ralph Beckett* a77 99
3 ch f Dream Ahead(USA) Pina Colada (Sabrehill (USA))
1392[2] (2505) (3410) (4391) ◆ 5158[8] 7397a[5] 7861a[6]

Golden Thread *Neil King* a66 65
6 ch g Singspiel(IRE) Alpenrot (IRE) (Barathea (IRE))
156[7] 637[4] 781[2] 1057[8] 2397[3] 5319[11]

Golden Valentine (FR) *F Head* 107
3 rg f Dalakhani(IRE) Gold Round (IRE) (Caerleon (USA))
3450a[2] (4331a) (5451a) 6393a[6]

Golden Wedding (IRE) *Eve Johnson Houghton* a85 83
4 b g Archipenko(USA) Peace Lily (Dansili)
429[3] 616[4] 801[4] (1262) 1546[3] 2324[2] 2579[2] 3097[3] 3554[3] (4058) 4557[2] 5832[4] (6254) 7017[3] 7461[2] 7903[5]

Golden Wolf (IRE) *Richard Hughes* a70
2 bb c Big Bad Bob(IRE) Jeunesse Doree (IRE) (Rock Of Gibraltar (IRE))
7865[3]

Golden Wood (FR) *Charley Rossi* a84 112
6 ch g Gold Away(IRE) Twisting (FR) (Pivotal)
2077a[5]

Gold Faith (IRE) *Ralph Beckett* a80 90
3 gr g Dark Angel(IRE) Livadream (IRE) (Dalakhani (IRE))
1571[5] 2580[2] ◆ (4153) 4863[8] 6065[3] 7117[6] ◆

Gold Flash *Keith Dalgleish* a78 78
4 b g Kheleyf(USA) My Golly (Mozart (IRE))
1663[2] ◆ 1844[2] 2238[9] 2421[5] 2677[4] 2960[4] 3344[2] 3517[3] 4193[9] 5082[2] 5246[2] 6140[7] 7051[9] 7662[10] 7985[2] 8240[11]

Gold-Fun (IRE) *Richard Gibson* 120
7 ch g Le Vie Dei Colori Goodwood March (Foxhound (USA))
1911a[4] 3385[2] 5217a[F] (Dead)

Gold Hunter (IRE) *Steve Flook* a52 82
6 b g Invincible Spirit(IRE) Goldthroat (IRE) (Zafonic (USA))
2345[5] 3097[2] 3554[4] 4306[2] 4362[5] 4908[4] (5253) 5955[4] 6255[7] 6914[15]

Gold Knight (FR) *J Chapel* a6 6
6 b g Hannouma(IRE) Gold Charm (GER) (Key Of Luck (USA))
512a[16]

Gold Locket (IRE) *P J Prendergast* a65 52
2 b f Kyllachy Gold Lace (IRE) (Invincible Spirit (IRE))
5243[3]

Gold Luck (FR) *F Head* 94
2 b f Redoute's Choice(AUS) Born Gold (USA) (Blushing Groom (FR))
7491a[2]

Goldmadchen (GER) *James Given* a66 61
8 b m Ivan Denisovich(IRE) Goldkatze (GER) (Czaravich (USA))
673[3] 981[7]

Goldmember *David Simcock* 106
3 ch g New Approach(IRE) Sister Act (Marju (IRE))
1426[9] (2260) 4059[6] 4753[7] 5872[5] 6708[4]

Gold Merlion (IRE) *Mark Johnston* 75
3 b f Alhaarth(IRE) Sea Of Time (USA) (Gilded Time (USA))
3766[7] 4967[4]

Gold Not Silver (IRE) *Adrian Brendan Joyce* a55 54
7 b g Celtic Swing Molly-O (IRE) (Dolphin Street (FR))
684[5]

Gold Patch (IRE) *Michael Easterby* 51
2 ch g Zoffany(IRE) Sycamores (FR) (Gold Away (IRE))
3874[6] 4508[5] 5271[8] 5974[6]

Gold Prince (IRE) *Sylvester Kirk* 107
4 b g Nayef(USA) Premier Prize (Selkirk (USA))
2214[2] 2866[2] 3666[4] 3889[2] 4734[5] 5144[4] 5611[12] 6118[8] 6573[7] 7349[10]

Goldream *Robert Cowell* a102 119
7 br g Oasis Dream Clizia (IRE) (Machiavellian (USA))
841a[7] ◆ 1104a[9] 4824[3] 5614[7] 6391a[3] 6990a[14] 7520a[6]

Gold Return (IRE) *John Ryan* a66
3 b f Gold Away(IRE) Ourika (IRE) (Danehill Dancer (IRE))
2375[12] 3475[6] 4213[7] 5132[2] 6514[3] (7516) 7870[5] 8411[7]

Gold Sands (IRE) *James Tate* a95 93
4 b m Cape Cross(IRE) Lil's Jessy (IRE) (Kris)
2978[8] (5082) 6076[4] 6611a[2] 7650[7]

Gold Show *Grant Tuer* a64 66
7 gr m Sir Percy Pearl Bright (FR) (Kaldoun (FR))
3363[9] 3706[6] (4648) 5228[2] 5415[3] 5841[8] 6620[4] 7043[2] 7321[7]

Gold Sister (FR) *F Chappet* 73
2 b f Canford Cliffs(IRE) Golden Digger (USA) (Mr Prospector (USA))
6937a[6]

Goldslinger (FR) *Dean Ivory* a74 77
4 b g Gold Away(IRE) Singaporette (FR) (Sagacity (FR))
1531[5] 2041[3] 3636[6] 4381[11] 8253[7] 8476[2] 8565[5]

Gold Trade (IRE) *Hugo Palmer* a77 81
3 b g Raven's Pass(USA) Trading Places (Dansili)
2179[11] 2998[3] 3595[10]

Gold Trail (IRE) *Charlie Appleby* a106 113
5 ch h Teofilo(IRE) Goldthroat (IRE) (Zafonic (USA))
4165[4] ◆ (6333)

Gold Vibe (IRE) *P Bary* 98
3 ch c Dream Ahead(USA) Whisper Dance (USA) (Stravinsky (USA))
6391a[7]

Golly Miss Molly *Jeremy Gask* a70 60
5 b m Exceed And Excel(AUS) Amicable Terms (Royal Applause)
195[2] 488[6] 950[2] 1039[2] 2233[10] 3099[10] 4012[8] 5319[5]

Gomez *Rae Guest* 62
3 b g Multiplex Elfine (IRE) (Invincible Spirit (IRE))
3412[9] 4027[5] 4401[10] 5088[10] 5773[7]

Go Milady (FR) *Matthieu Palussiere* a71 72
2 b f Evasive Go To Win (FR) (Coroner (IRE))
7927a[2]

Gomo (USA) *Doug O'Neill* a106 96
3 b f Uncle Mo(USA) Gentle Audrey (USA) (Elusive Quality (USA))
7836a[13]

Go Nani Go *Ed de Giles* a78 82
10 b g Kyllachy Go Between (Daggers Drawn (USA))
4224[2] 4817[5] ◆ 5284[8] 6017[5] 6479[2] 6669[9] 6878[12] 7303[9]

Gone With The Wind (GER) *Rebecca Bastiman* a69 64
5 b g Dutch Art Gallivant (Danehill (USA))
1247[4] 1696[3] 2091[8] 2526[6] 3367[8] 3750[6] (4705) 4929[4] 5750[7] 6347[4] 7662[6] 8011[10]

Goninodaethat *Jim Goldie* a48 69
8 b g Proclamation(IRE) Big Mystery (IRE) (Grand Lodge (USA))
1692[7] 2360[4] 2528[2] 2960[9] 3344[9] 3941[2] 4191[2] 4701[5] 5152[6] 5225[5] 5839[5] 6100[9] (7092) 7585[9]

Gontchar (FR) *A Savujev* 92
3 b c Champs Elysees Gontcharova (IRE) (Zafonic (USA))
6971a[5]

Good Boy Jasper *Linda Perratt* 55
2 ch g Doncaster Rover(USA) Mitchelland (Namaqualand (USA))
5778[7] 6535[8] 7247[4]

Goodby Inheritence *Seamus Durack* a70 77
4 b g Medicean Chili Dip (Alhaarth (IRE))
8257[2] ◆ 8448[4]

Good Contact (USA) *Saeed bin Suroor* a102 106
4 b g Teofilo(IRE) Mayoress (Machiavellian (USA))
188a[2] 722a[6]

Good Craic *John Gosden* 79
2 b c Invincible Spirit(IRE) Riotous Applause (Royal Applause)
3813[10] 6297[2]

Good Friend (GER) *Mme M-C Chaalon* a9 29
6 b g Big Shuffle(USA) Good Harmony (King's Best (USA))
3733a[11]

Good Judge (USA) *Saeed bin Suroor* a81
4 gr g Cape Cross(IRE) Summer Fete (IRE) (Pivotal)
165[8]

Goodknight Percy (IRE) *Kevin Ryan* 72
3 ch g Sir Percy Ekhraaj (USA) (El Prado (IRE))
2124[9] 3015[U]

Good Luck Charm *Gary Moore* a78 82
7 b g Doyen(IRE) Lucky Dice (Perugino (USA))
1173[6] 1545[3] (1746) 2430[2] 3803[12] 4354[2] 5017[7] 5992[6] 7301[8] 7738[8]

Goodlukin Lucy *Gemma Anderson*
9 ch m Supreme Sound Suka Ramai (Nashwan (USA))
5971[14] 6619[10]

Good Move (IRE) *Brian Rothwell* 40
4 b m Aussie Rules(USA) Lady Lafitte (USA) (Stravinsky (USA))
4006[10] 5278[12]

Good Of Luck *Warren Greatrex* a70 75
7 b g Authorized(IRE) Oops Pettie (Machiavellian (USA))
(3064)

Goodoldhockeygame (CAN) *Robert Tiller* a98
4 ch g Old Forester(USA) Domasca Bella (CAN) (Domasca Dan (CAN))
6400a[6]

Good Omen *William Haggas* a94 87
2 b c Holy Roman Emperor(IRE) Magic Nymph (IRE) (Galileo (IRE))
4128[2] 5952[2] (6314) 7409[4] (7930)

Good Run (FR) *Saeed bin Suroor* a101 71
3 ch g Iffraaj Tadawul (USA) (Diesis)
2244[13] (8133)

Good Samaritan (USA) *William Mott* 110
2 b c Harlan's Holiday(USA) Pull Dancer (USA) (Pulpit (USA))
7807a[3]

Good Time Ahead (IRE) *Philip Kirby* a57 74
2 b g Iffraaj Good Time Sue (IRE) (Commander Collins (IRE))
2570[2] ◆ 3495[3] 4394[18] 4869[2] 5271[3] 5967[8] 6473[9] 7003[8] 7406[9] 8398[4] 8568[4]

Goodwood Crusader (IRE) *Richard Hughes* a64 61
2 b g Sir Prancealot(IRE) Pale Orchid (IRE) (Invincible Spirit (IRE))
2732[7] 3647[4] 4713[3] 5707[4] 6440[8]

Goodwood Mirage (IRE) *Michael Bell* 95
6 b g Jeremy(USA) Phantom Waters (Pharly (FR))
1885[3] ◆ 2176[8] 3077[3] 4300[2] (4561) 5647[2] 6573[18] 6786[18]

Goodwood Moonlight *Ian Williams* a59 59
4 gr g Azamour(IRE) Corrine (IRE) (Spectrum (IRE))
(20) 107[12] 326[4] 702[5] 1547[7] 2323[6] 2872[2] 4784[6] 5513[8]

Goodwood Zodiac (IRE) *William Knight* 106
3 b g Kodiac Insieme (IRE) (Barathea (IRE))
1992[15] 2892[2] (3687) 4797[10] (5962) 6940[9]

Goolagong Girl (IRE) *Jane Chapple-Hyam* a66 62
4 b m Avonbridge Lady Berta (Bertolini (USA))
190[7]

Go On Gal (IRE) *Julia Feilden* a52 59
3 b f Approve(IRE) Jeritza (Rainbow Quest (USA))
1551[2] 1705[3] 2608[2] 4275[2] 5101[2] 5630[7] 7230[2] 8194[7]

Go On Go On Go On *Clive Cox* a78 101
3 b f Medicean Piranha (IRE) (Exceed And Excel (AUS))
344[3] 3105[5] (3995) (4461) ◆ (5285) 6230[7]

Go On Mayson *David Evans* 70
2 br c Mayson Red Tiara (USA) (Mr Prospector (USA))
4349[7] ◆ 5203[4]

Go Parti (FR) *Alex Fracas* a70
6 gr h Archange D'Or(IRE) Alharixa (FR) (Linamix (FR))
7295a[4]

Gordon Lord Byron (IRE) *T Hogan* a105 118
8 b g Byron Boa Estrela (IRE) (Intikhab (USA))
1226a[8] 2495a[6] 3332a[5] (4433a) 5217a[8] 5816a[4] 6120[13] 6353a[6] 6816a[8] 6955[6]

Gorgeous (FR) *Tony Carroll* a56 37
3 b f Assertive Agent Kensington (Mujahid (USA))
2980[10] 5168[8] 5766[8] 6036[5] (8472)

Gorgeous Geezer *Martin Smith* a73
3 b c Kheleyf(USA) Arctic High (Polar Falcon (USA))
515[3] 659[3]

Gorgeous Noora (IRE) *Luca Cumani* a85
2 b f Raven's Pass(USA) Aneedah (IRE) (Invincible Spirit (IRE))
7099[3] (7939)

Goring (GER) *Eve Johnson Houghton* a88 89
4 b g Areion(GER) Globuli (GER) (Surako (GER))
1752[2] 1993[9] 2934[12] 4081[8] (4954) 5488[5] 5991[11] 6539[5] 6883[5]

Gormley (USA) *John Shirreffs* a116
2 b c Malibu Moon(USA) Race To Urga (USA) (Bernstein (USA))
7834a[7]

Gorokai (IRE) *David Simcock* a80 80
3 b g Kodiac Damask (IRE) (Red Clubs (IRE))
(193) (322) ◆ 559[3] 686[3] 954[2] 4803[12] 6409[2] 6668[4] 7965[9]

Gossiping *Gary Moore* a72 86
4 b g Dubawi(IRE) Gossamer (Sadler's Wells (USA))
7671[17] 7903[9] 8101[8] 8206[9]

Gotasinggotadance *Philip Hide* a33 31
4 b m Royal Applause Water Gipsy (Piccolo)
3258[7] 3729[6]

Gothic Empire (IRE) *James Fanshawe* a79 94
4 b g Dark Angel(IRE) Box Of Frogs (IRE) (One Cool Cat (USA))
2238[12] 2579[4] (3821) ◆ 4263[6] 6529[5] (6914)

Governor Malibu (USA) *Christophe Clement* a113
3 ch c Malibu Moon(USA) Akilina (USA) (Langfuhr (CAN))
3181a[4] 5913a[5]

Gowanharry (IRE) *Michael Dods* 90
7 ch m Choisir(AUS) Aahgowangowan (IRE) (Tagula (IRE))
3638[12]

Gowanless *Michael Dods* a43 76
3 b g Monsieur Bond(IRE) Aahgowangowan (IRE) (Tagula (IRE))
1599[14] 2650[12] 3420[6] 3978[7] 5059[8] 5582[6] 6023[6] 6436[10] 6745[10] 6959[7]

Gower Princess *Miss Clare Louise Cannon* a58 41
5 ch m Footstepsinthesand Hollow Quaill (IRE) (Entrepreneur)
146[6] 542[12] 6464a[8] 7800a[7]

Goya Girl (IRE) *Ralph Beckett* a73
2 b f Paco Boy(IRE) First Exhibit (Machiavellian (USA))
(5524)

Graasten (GER) *Gary Moore* 98
4 ch g Sholokhov(IRE) Golden Time (GER) (Surumu (GER))
7150[30]

Graceful Act *Ron Barr* a49 56
8 b m Royal Applause Minnina (IRE) (In The Wings)
1382[3] 1676[11] 2330[9] 4260[3] 4772[9] 5350[7] 5481[6] (5980) 7361[9]

Graceful Favour *David Barron* a50
3 gr f Hellvelyn Pontressina (USA) (St Jovite (USA))
177[4] 765[7]

Graceful James (IRE) *Jimmy Fox* a80 58
3 ch g Rock Of Gibraltar(IRE) Little Miss Gracie (Efisio)
2818[9] 5765[8] 6300[9] 7691[3] 7886[3] (8282)

Graceful Lady *Robert Eddery* a58 55
3 b f Sixties Icon Leitzu (IRE) (Barathea (IRE))
29[5] 325[4] 4562[9] 5513[6] 6335[4] 6698[2] 7309[P] 8039[6] 8468[2]

Graceland (FR) *Michael Bell* a92 90
4 gr m Mastercraftsman(IRE) Jeunesse Lulu (IRE) (Montjeu (IRE))
1802[2] ◆ 1999[6] 2753[2] 3278[6] 4646[3] 4994[2] 5328[3] 6050[2] 6667[2] 7669[3]

Gracesome (IRE) *Michael Blanshard* a66 58
5 b m Shirocco(GER) Simonda (Singspiel (IRE))
2205[11] 4716[3] 5303[4] 5763[3] (6424) 6871[2] 7508[6]

Gracious Diana *John Gosden* 51
2 ch f Foxwedge(AUS) Generous Diana (Generous (IRE))
7769[10]

Gracious George (IRE) *Jimmy Fox* a76 78
6 b g Oratorio(IRE) Little Miss Gracie (Efisio)
141[2] (532) (792) 965[6] 8178[10] 8469[4]

Gracious John (IRE) *David Evans* a115 112
3 b c Baltic King Dorn Hill (Lujain (USA))
(45) (235) 493[3] 1070[6] 1197[9] 1773[3] 2192[2] 2692[7] 4413a[3] 5816a[6] 6384a[13] (7771) 7932[4] (8232) ◆ 8484[2]

Gracious Tom (IRE) *David Evans* a74 64
2 b c Roderic O'Connor(IRE) Bigalo's Laura B (IRE) (Needwood Blade)
5202[3] 5593[4] 5890[7] 7690[8] 8027[2] (8230) (8344) 8467[4]

Graf (FR) *N Bellanger* 57
2 b c Elusive City(USA) Party Lover (FR) (Tobougg (IRE))
6638a[11]

Graffiti (FR) *N Clement* a75 75
2 b c Halling(USA) Mystic Spirit (IRE) (Invincible Spirit (IRE))
7588a[8]

Grainne's Dream (IRE) *W McCreery* a66 73
3 b f Acclamation Cold Cold Woman (Machiavellian (USA))
8496[4]

Gramercy (IRE) *Richard Fahey* a73 97
9 b g Whipper(USA) Topiary (IRE) (Selkirk (USA))
5915[3]

Grams And Ounces *Grace Harris* a64 65
9 b g Royal Applause Ashdown Princess (IRE) (King's Theatre (IRE))
2850[5] 4294[2] 4592[5] 5232[5] 5958[2] 6256[4] 6825[9] 7508[9] 7628[9]

Gran Canaria Queen *Tim Easterby* a70 98
7 bb m Compton Place Ex Mill Lady (Bishop Of Cashel)
1644[11] 1848[12] 2267[6] 2621[6] 3116[8] (3714) 4398[10] 4689[8]

Grandad Chunk (IRE) *Colin Teague* a40 47
5 gr g Acclamation Silverdreammachine (IRE) (Marju (IRE))
177[5] 936[8] 4512[6] 5760[7] 6100[13]

Grandad's World (IRE) *Richard Fahey* 93
4 b g Kodiac Nose One's Way (IRE) (Revoque (IRE))
1394[10] 2258[9] 2803[11] 4366[2] 4862[11] 5417[18] 6539[22] 7186[7] 7772[9]

Grand Akbar (FR) *J Phelippon* a50 60
9 b g Muhtathir Grande Epoque (FR) (Valanour (IRE))
1157a[4]

Grand Arch (USA) *Brian A Lynch* 114
7 b g Arch(USA) Bacinella (USA) (El Gran Senor (USA))
7172a[9]

Grand Argentier (FR) *Doug Watson* a103 72
4 b h Palace Episode(USA) Ashkadima (IRE) (Ashkalani (IRE))
279a[3] (535a)

Grand Beauty (IRE) *Robert Cowell* a86 86
4 ch m Kheleyf(USA) Grand Zafeen (Zafeen (FR))
1964[3] 2305[8] 2863[8]

Grand Canyon (IRE) *David O'Meara* a54 79
4 b g High Chaparral(IRE) Cleide Da Silva (USA) (Monarchos (USA))
1884[5] 2362[2] (2743) 3294[4] 3563[7]

Grand Coalition (IRE) *J P Murtagh* a80 92
2 b c Kodiac Defined Feature (IRE) (Nabeel Dancer (USA))
3243[15] 3678a[7] 5212a[4] 5977[3] 7130a[7]

Grande Bleue (IRE) *C Laffon-Parias* a75 74
2 b f Oasis Dream Oceanique (USA) (Forest Wildcat (USA))
5460a[3] 6937a[3]

Grandest *Brian Ellison* a55 75
5 b g Dansili Angara (Alzao (USA))
36[9] 964[7] 2773[10] 2958[2] 4425[2] 4648[5]

Grand Facile *Gary Moore* a55 48
4 b g Henrythenavigator(USA) Santolina (USA) (Boundary (USA))
195[6] 634[8] 8164[5] 8359[12]

Grand Inquisitor *Sir Michael Stoute* 101
4 b g Dansili Dusty Answer (Zafonic (USA))
1441[6] 2027[5] 3688[2] 4399[9] 5156[7] 6075[7]

Grand Jete *D Smaga* a89 80
3 b f Dansili Modern Look (Zamindar (USA))
(5385a) 5987a[4] 7998a[8]

Grand Marshal *Chris Waller* 111
6 br g Dansili Margarula (IRE) (Doyoun)
(7552a) 7756a[11]

Grand Meister *John Quinn* a85 81
5 gr g Mastercraftsman(IRE) Wait It Out (USA) (Swain (IRE))
385[4] 704[2] 1135[5] 8133[6] 8399[9]

Grand Myla (IRE) *Gary Moore* a62 73
2 gr f Dark Angel(IRE) Selfara (Oasis Dream)
3511[11] 4064[3] 4756[15] 5359[8] 5705[6] 6658[5]

Grand Proposal *Mike Murphy* a50 43
4 gr g Exceed And Excel(AUS) Si Belle (IRE) (Dalakhani (IRE))
2610[8] 3401[5] 4320[7]

Grand Salute (BRZ) *D Selvaratnam* a82
5 b h Salute The Sarge(USA) Espetaculo (BRZ) (Soberbo (BRZ))
309a[9]

Grand Vintage (FR) *Carina Fey* a88 102
7 b h Marchand De Sable(USA) Fifty Niner (FR) (Fijar Tango (FR))
5449a[11] 5948a[6] 7292a[4]

Granita (USA) *George Scott* a63 65
3 b f Blame(USA) Youre So Sweet (USA) (Storm Cat (USA))
274[4] ◆ 597[2] ◆ 7941[0] 1551[5]

Granite City Doc *Lucy Normile* 16
3 b g Arabian Gleam Hansomis (IRE) (Titus Livius (FR))
1667[6] 7096[12]

Granit Man (FR) *J Moon*
10 b g Passing Sale(FR) Red Flower (USA) (Trempolino (USA))
6403a[P]

Granny May (IRE) *John James Feane* a52 76
4 b m Holy Roman Emperor(IRE) Pure Jazz (IRE) (Marju (IRE))
7392a[9]

Gran Paradiso (IRE) *Micky Hammond* 79
4 ch g Galileo(IRE) Looking Lovely (IRE) (Storm Cat (USA))
2260[9] 3437[12]

Grapevine (IRE) *Charles Hills* 92
3 b c Lilbourne Lad(IRE) High Vintage (IRE) (High Chaparral (IRE))
1602[3] (2099) 2538[3] (3801) 4092[4] 6081[7] 7505[2]

Graphite Storm *Clive Cox* 84
2 bg c Delegator Ice Haven (IRE) (Verglas (IRE))
4075[10] (5890) (6575)

Graton *K R Burke* a22 43
2 b g Camacho Deslaya (IRE) (Green Desert (USA))
1293[8] 2301[6] 2648[8] 3114[8]

Gratzie *Mick Channon* a62 103
5 b m Three Valleys(USA) La Gazzetta (IRE) (Rossini (USA))
2026[6] (3124) 3979[10] 4391[5] 4688[4] 5158[10] 5396[6] 6076[3] 6736[10] 6778[2] 6947[7] 7316[7] 7546[11]

Gravity Flow (IRE) *William Haggas* a84 108
3 ch f Exceed And Excel(AUS) Landela (Alhaarth (IRE))
(3406) (4547) (5205) ◆ (6064) 7146[2]

Gravity Wave (IRE) *Sylvester Kirk* a67 77
2 br c Rip Van Winkle(IRE) Phrase (Royal Anthem (USA))
4907[3] (5324) *6240[6]*

Greanta (IRE) *Thomas Cleary* a40 66
5 b m Intense Focus(USA) Greannmhar (USA) (Distorted Humor (USA))
4813a[7]

Great And Small *Andrew Balding* a54 92
3 b f Galileo(IRE) Gryada (Shirley Heights)
3535[9] (4633) 5851[2] 6917[4]

Great Colaci *Keith Reveley* a55 51
3 b g Sulamani(IRE) Fairlie (Halling (USA))
5322[9] 5888[8] 6683[8] 6953[7] *(7604) 7794[7] 8145[6] (8589)*

Great Court (IRE) *Luca Cumani* a76
2 gr f Mastercraftsman(IRE) Neat Shilling (IRE) (Bob Back (USA))
7049[3] ◆ *7483[5] 7885[3]*

Great Demeanor (USA) *Dianne Sayer* a49 30
6 b g Bernstein(USA) Hangin Withmy Buds (USA) (Roar (USA))
867[5] 1845[7]

Great Dora (FR) *S Wattel* a84 79
3 bl f Great Journey(JPN) Dora De Green (IRE) (Green Tune (USA))
2948a[14] *5280a[10]*

Greatest Hits (USA) *Y Al Blooshi* a83 57
4 b h Cape Cross(IRE) Northern Melody (IRE) (Singspiel (IRE))
535a[8]

Great Expectations *J R Jenkins* a64 70
8 b g Storming Home Fresh Fruit Daily (Reprimand)
178[3] 426[8] 1489[3] 2643[7] 3144[4] 3821[4] 4321[6] 5169[5] 5259[7] *7260[3]* 7442[8] *7694[7] 8234[4] 8457[5] 8541[7]*

Great Fighter *Jim Goldie* a83 81
6 b g Street Cry(IRE) Evil Empire (GER) (Acatenango (GER))
4162[10] 4703[4] ◆ 6083[10] 6540[4]

Great Fun *Michael Blake* a84 73
5 b g Kyllachy Have Fun (Indian Ridge)
2309[2] *3729[2]* ◆ 5075[10] *5810[6] 6416[9] 7687[6]*

Great Glen *Ralph Beckett* a101 97
4 b g High Chaparral(IRE) Grand Opening (IRE) (Desert King (IRE))
(4384) 5145[4] 5879[7] *7365[2]*

Great Hall *Mick Quinn* a105 108
6 b g Halling(USA) L'Affaire Monique (Machiavellian (USA))
5411[4] 5879[8] 6489[2] (6802) (7287) 7700[5] *7814[3]*

Great Minds (IRE) *T Stack* 109
6 ch g Bahamian Bounty Raja (IRE) (Pivotal)
1127a[5]

Great Order (USA) *Saeed bin Suroor* 108
3 bb c Distorted Humor(USA) Michita (USA) (Dynaformer (USA))
3412[3] (4319) ◆ (6076) 6710[2] 7154[2]

Great Page (IRE) *Jerry Hollendorfer* a87 103
3 b f Roderic O'Connor(IRE) Areeda (IRE) (Refuse To Bend (IRE))
836[7] 1424[3] 2042[7] 3274[10] 7724a[10]

Great Return *Saeed bin Suroor* a68 63
3 b g New Approach(IRE) Under The Rainbow (Fantastic Light (USA))
1479[4] 2008[9]

Great Thoughts (IRE) *David Simcock* a86 74
3 ch f Iffraaj Fascination (IRE) (Galileo (IRE))
2619[3] 3781[5] 4462[3] *(5245) (5508)*

Great Trip (USA) *F Head* a71 81
3 bb f Lemon Drop Kid(USA) Sweet Travel (IRE) (Danzig (USA))
511a[4]

Great Uncle (IRE) *J S Bolger* 6
2 ch c Intense Focus(USA) Abigail's Aunt (Efisio)
7387a[7]

Grecian Divine (IRE) *Denis Gerard Hogan* a78 83
2 b f Kodiac Grecian Glory (IRE) (Zafonic (USA))
4171a[7]

Grecian King *James Tate* a67
3 b g Kheleyf(USA) Grecian Air (FR) (King's Best (USA))
423[2] 639[5] 750[2] 885[5]

Grecian Light (IRE) *Charlie Appleby* 103
2 b f Shamardal(USA) Akrivi (IRE) (Tobougg (IRE))
(4357) 5172[2] 5870[7] 6258[2] 6815a[2] 7114[12]

Greek Islands (IRE) *Neil Mulholland* a69 59
8 b g Oasis Dream Serisia (FR) (Exit To Nowhere (USA))
37[4] 621[10]

Green Door (IRE) *Robert Cowell* a97 108
5 b g Camacho Inourhearts (IRE) (Pips Pride)
91a[7] 280a[4] 450a[10] 626a[11] 1644[10] 1968[10] 2258[6] 2895[11] 3151[7] (3573)

Green Du Ciel (FR) *Carroll Gray* a60 48
11 gr g Smadoun(FR) Sucre Blanc (FR) (Green Tune (USA))
634[9]

Greenfyre (IRE) *Richard Hannon* a48 64
3 b f Kodiac Miss Chaumiere (Selkirk (USA))
1829[2] 2178[7] 2337[6] 3197[3] 3720[3]

Greengairs *Keith Dalgleish* 62
2 b g Delegator Shore Light (USA) (Gulch (USA))
5885[7] 6025[4] 6499[6]

Greengrassofyoming (USA) *Michael J Maker* a69 112
6 ch g Quest(USA) Flick (USA) (Dehere (USA))
5431a[4]

Green Howard *Rebecca Bastiman* a81 78
8 ch g Bahamian Bounty Dash Of Lime (Bold Edge)
1563[8] 2679[5] 3115[14] 3945[7] 4408[7] 4687[4] 5520[5] 6160[15] 6684[4] 7010[2] ◆ 7227[11] *7436[2] 7857[6]*

Green Light *Ralph Beckett* 97
5 b g Authorized(IRE) May Light (Midyan (USA))
2313[2] (2897) 3889[14] 5144[9] 6118[12] 7215[11] 7546[8]

Green Mask (USA) *Brad H Cox* a81 115
5 bb g Mizzen Mast(USA) Bonsai Beauty (USA) (Forestry (USA))
7833a[5]

Greenshoe (IRE) *F-H Graffard* a68 81
3 b f Footstepsinthesand Nymfia (IRE) (Invincible Spirit (IRE))
6912a[2]

Greenside *Henry Candy* a81 97
5 b g Dubawi(IRE) Katrina (IRE) (Ela-Mana-Mou)
1274[4] (7699) ◆

Green Soldier (FR) *Ana Imaz Ceca* 88
5 ch h Soldier Of Fortune(IRE) Love Green (FR) (Green Tune (USA))
6356a[3]

Greenview Paradise (IRE) *Richard Fahey* 56
2 gr f Exchange Rate(USA) Senza Rete (IRE) (Barathea (IRE))
4765[7] 5516[6] 6162[8]

Gregarious (IRE) *Lucy Wadham* a71 75
3 gr g Big Bad Bob(IRE) Sense Of Greeting (IRE) (Key Of Luck (USA))
2375[7] ◆ 3187[8]

Greg Pass (IRE) *Il Cavallo In Testa* 106
4 b g Raven's Pass(USA) Baranja (USA) (St Jovite (USA))
1516a[3] 2729a[2] (3455a) 6823a[7] 7400a[6] (7565a)

Grenade *Patrick Holmes* a30 57
4 b g Paco Boy(IRE) Amira (Efisio)
1565[8] 1953[5] 2425[5] 4257[6] 4511[3] 5729[15]

Grendisar (IRE) *Marco Botti* a115 59
6 b h Invincible Spirit(IRE) Remarkable Story (Mark Of Esteem (IRE))
(485) (748) (1069) ◆ *7934[4] 8427[3]*

Gretzky *Matthew J Smith* a58 68
9 b g King's Best(USA) Estabilizada (ARG) (Halo Sunshine (USA))
5790a[8]

Grey Britain *John Ryan* 97
2 gr c Arcano(IRE) Reaching Ahead (USA) (Mizzen Mast (USA))
4016[2] 4564[2] (5395) 5654[5] 6326[5] 6572[4]

Grey Destiny *Antony Brittain* a64 60
6 gr g Desideratum Mother Corrigan (IRE) (Paris House)
25[6] 430[5] 936[2] 1047[5] 1131[3] ◆ *1502[7] 2330[2] 2918[7] 3988[3] 5132[5] 5808[6] 7794[6]*

Greyfriarschorista *David Evans* a85 70
9 ch g King's Best(USA) Misty Heights (Fasliyev (USA))
276[2] (523) 694[3] 938[5] 960[7] 1291[8] 3726[2] 8252[8] 8455[4]

Grey Galleon (USA) *Clive Cox* 75
2 gr g Mizzen Mast(USA) Floresta (USA) (Forest Camp (USA))
4205[4] (4706) 5510[6] 6734[11]

Greyjoy (IRE) *Sylvester Kirk* a56
2 gr c Mastercraftsman(IRE) American Jewel (USA) (Quiet American (USA))
8354[5] 8557[9]

Grey Lion (IRE) *Matt Cumani* a81 108
4 gr h Galileo(IRE) Grey Lilas (IRE) (Danehill (USA))
2077a[3] 2947a[7] 5692a[8] 7481a[2] 7756a[14]

Grey Mirage *Marco Botti* a101 92
7 b g Oasis Dream Grey Way (USA) (Cozzene (USA))
125[5] 486[5] 816[6] 1204[9] 1576[7] 7933[3] ◆ *8256[8] 8593[10]*

Grey Panel (FR) *T Le Brocq* 43
8 gr g Largesse Minnie's Mystery (FR) (Highest Honor (FR))
(1519a) 2285a[7] 2955a[3] (3917a) 5457a[7]

Grey's Angel *Philip McBride* a71 61
4 gr m Notnowcato Kryena (Kris)
1962[6] 2792[7]

Greyscape (IRE) *Ibrahim Al Malki* 85
3 gr g Dark Angel(IRE) Sugar Blossom (IRE) (Marju (IRE))
756a[7]

Grey Thou Art (IRE) *Henry Candy* a49 47
2 gr f Canford Cliffs(IRE) Roystonea (Polish Precedent (USA))
6078[3] *6625[12]*

Greyway (FR) *J-M Lefebvre* a90 98
2 gr c Myboycharlie(IRE) Aliyeska (IRE) (Fasliyev (USA))
7086a[4] *(7588a)*

Grinty (IRE) *Michael Dods* 75
2 b c Elnadim(USA) Fire Line (Firebreak)
4371[6] 5713[2] 6535[3] 7004[8]

Griraz (FR) *David Pipe* 84
11 gr g Nombre Premier Niraz (FR) (Nikos)
3298[17]

Grizzel (IRE) *Richard Hannon* 96
2 b f Kodiac Milana (FR) (Mark Of Esteem (IRE))
(2410) (2670) 3336[13] 4560[3] 5172[6] 5638[3] 6063[4] 6282[8] 7536[6]

Groovejet *Richard Spencer* a81 102
5 b m Cockney Rebel(IRE) Vino Veritas (USA) (Chief's Crown (USA))
19[7] 6951[2]

Grosmont *James Given* a71 67
4 br g Hellvelyn Aimee's Delight (Robellino (USA))
76[6]

Groundworker (IRE) *Paul Midgley* a68 70
5 b g Tagula(IRE) Notepad (King's Best (USA))
942[8] 1525[6] 1956[5] 2572[3] 2808[8] 3713[3] 4039[4] 4452[5] 4691[3] 5354[10] 5867[3] 6435[8] *6910[2]* 7290[5] *(7859)* ◆ *8137[10]*

Groupie *Richard Hannon* 88
2 b f Requinto(IRE) Amour Fou (IRE) (Piccolo)
(2747) 3122[2] (3531) 4091[2] 6292[6] 7114[8]

Growing Glory (FR) *F Rohaut* a95 102
4 b m Orpen(USA) Trois Rivieres (IRE) (Dr Fong (USA))
4826[8]

Growl *Richard Fahey* a81 118
4 b g Oasis Dream Desert Tigress (USA) (Storm Cat (USA))
1644[4] 1968[4] 2259[4] (3068) (3671) 4152[4] 4865[4] ◆ 6558[2] 6942[6] 7350[2] (7822) 8330a[13]

Grumeti *Alan King* a82 92
8 b g Sakhee(USA) Tetravella (IRE) (Groom Dancer (USA))
1642[7] 2194[5] 3387[14] *3657[14]* 7150[9] 7670[4]

Guanabara Bay (IRE) *Martyn Meade* a68 67
3 b g Clodovil(IRE) Sakaka (Tobougg (IRE))
3982[11] 4410[6] 5088[2] 5827[3] 6291[5] *6592[2]* 7442[10] *7611[8]*

Guantoshol (IRE) *Ian Williams* a57 70
5 ch g Sholokhov(IRE) Glicine (GER) (Tiger Hill (IRE))
4711[4] 5597[9] 6212[6] 6444[4] 7037[10]

Guapaza (CHI) *Chad C Brown* 107
4 b m Seeking The Dia(USA) Guampa (CHI) (Dushyantor (USA))
3119a[3] 7404a[4]

Guapo Bay *Richard Hannon* a53 63
3 b g Showcasing Cumana Bay (Dansili)
258[2] 365[3] 578[2] 711[3] 979[4] 1148[7] 1573[4] 1795[6] (2155) 2560[2] 3527[8] 4289[4] 5020[3] *5248[6]* 6290[10] *6902[5]* 7212[5]

Guardia Svizzera (IRE) *John M Oxx* a74 78
2 b g Holy Roman Emperor(IRE) Winged Harriet (IRE) (Hawk Wing (USA))
7387a[4]

Guard of Honour (IRE) *George Baker* a100 87
5 b g Galileo(IRE) Queen Of France (USA) (Danehill (USA))
7708a[4] *8479[6]*

Guards Chapel *Gary Moore* a69 72
8 b g Motivator Intaaj (IRE) (Machiavellian (USA))
138[3] (1450) 7183[5]

Guavia (GER) *P Schiergen* 89
4 b m Invincible Spirit(IRE) Goathemala (GER) (Black Sam Bellamy (IRE))
7027a[8]

Guiding Light (IRE) *Andrew Balding* a67 80
4 b g Acclamation Venus Rising (Observatory (USA))
4086[8] 4481[4] 6339[5] 6806[13] 7189[9]

Guiding Star *Henry Candy* a64 39
2 b f Iffraaj Still I'm A Star (IRE) (Lawman (FR))
5400[13] *7279[4]*

Guignol (GER) *Jean-Pierre Carvalho* 114
4 bb h Cape Cross(IRE) Guadalupe (GER) (Monsun (GER))
2947a[4] 3934a[3] 5454a[3] 7402a[6] (7759a)

Guilded Rock *Stuart Kittow* a49 56
3 gr g Hellvelyn Once Removed (Distant Relative)
2544[6] 2980[9] 3900[4] 4085[7] *5126[9]* 6290[6] 7211[6] *7642[16]*

Guiliani (IRE) *Jean-Pierre Carvalho* 115
5 br h Tertullian(USA) Guadalupe (GER) (Monsun (GER))
(1376a)

Guishan *Michael Appleby* a93 96
6 b m Ishiguru(USA) Fareham (Komaite (USA))
198[11] 508[6] (3397) (3575) 4398[3] 5124[5] 6878[5] *8050[6] 8192[10]*

Guizot (IRE) *Jean-Pierre Carvalho* 94
3 ch g Tertullian(USA) Guantana (GER) (Dynaformer (USA))
3699a[6] 5699a[7]

Gulf Of Poets *Michael Easterby* a54 81
4 b g Oasis Dream Sandglass (Zafonic (USA))
1122[12] (1588) 2296[4] 3324[3] 4406[6] 4945[2] 6160[11] 6645[8] 7412[8]

Gulland Rock *Anthony Carson* a73 67
5 b g Exceed And Excel(AUS) Sacre Coeur (Compton Place)
(35) 216[9] (542) 671[5] 889[4] 1116[3] 1544[6] 1949[11] 3044[3] 3624[3] *(3988)* 4289[2] 4640[9] 4841[7] 5374[7] *(6238)* 6637[3] *7617[6] 8490[9]*

Gulliver *Hugo Palmer* 84
2 b c Sayif(IRE) Sweet Coincidence (Mujahid (USA))
1889[4] ◆ 2193[3] (7157)

Gumpo Sky (KOR) *Sung-J Kwon* a61
5 b h Vicar(USA) Perfect Storm (KOR) (Didyme (USA))
6399a[6]

Gun Case *Alistair Whillans* a75 75
4 b g Showcasing Bassinet (USA) (Stravinsky (USA))
1884[9] 3286[8] 3922[10] 4189[6] 4683[2] *(5068) 5845[6]* 6231[5] *6907[3]* (7333) *7662[4]*

Gung Ho Jack *John Best* a79 73
7 b g Moss Vale(IRE) Bijan (IRE) (Mukaddamah (USA))
4014[2] ◆ *4881[4]* 6000[3] *7644[3] 7899[2] 8561[2]*

Gunman *Richard Hannon* a70 70
3 ch c Monsieur Bond(IRE) Honesty Pays (Dr Fong (USA))
(1917) 2341[8] 2749[12] *3648[2]*

Gunmetal (IRE) *Charles Hills* 92
3 gr c Clodovil(IRE) March Star (IRE) (Mac's Imp (USA))
1622[5] 2207[2] (2698) (3415) 4062[10] 5403[5] 5881[4]

Gunner Lindley (IRE) *Stuart Coltherd* a34 62
9 ch g Medicean Lasso (Indian Ridge)
2656[7] 3547[3] 3706[2] 5155[6] *5971[12]*

Gunner Moyne *Gary Moore* a67 53
4 b g Excellent Art Maramkova (IRE) (Danehill Dancer (IRE))
(79) (175) 709[2] 877[6] 2153[9] 2769[8] 3488[5] *4267[3] 5021[5] 6243[6]*

Gunnery (FR) *Peter Chapple-Hyam* 98
3 ch g Le Havre(IRE) Loup The Loup (FR) (Loup Solitaire (USA))
(1626) 2209[5] 2687[2] 3341[6] 4059[7]

Gun Pit (AUS) *C Fownes* a106 116
5 b g Dubawi(IRE) Magic Tori (AUS) (Ali-Royal (IRE))
844a[2] 1108a[12] 1912a[7] 8333a[11]

Gun Runner (USA) *Steven Asmussen* a120
3 ch c Candy Ride(ARG) Quiet Giant (USA) (Giant's Causeway (USA))
2063a[3] 5913a[3] 7808a[2]

Guns Of Leros (USA) *Gary Moore* a64 94
3 bb g Cape Blanco(IRE) Zappeuse (USA) (Kingmambo (USA))
2008[7] 3042[4] ◆ 3959[2] (5596) (5875) (6804) 7123[13]

Gurkha Friend *Karen McLintock* a80 94
4 b g Showcasing Parabola (Galileo (IRE))
944[8] 1694[3] 1954[3] *2331[8] 2917[10]* 3115[8] (3517) 3884[5] (4374) 5160[4] 6225[2] 6560[8] 7287[10]

Gussy Goose (IRE) *David Wachman* 93
4 b m Danehill Dancer(IRE) Noahs Ark (IRE) (Charnwood Forest (IRE))
1939a[6] 2716a[13] 4218a[6] 4747a[14] 4812a[5]

Gusty Rocky (IRE) *Patrick J Flynn* 85
7 b g King's Theatre(IRE) Liss A Paoraigh (IRE) (Husyan (USA))
4721a[18]

Guy Fawkes *William Haggas* a65 88
3 b g Big Bad Bob(IRE) Flight Of Fancy (Sadler's Wells (USA))
(2774) 3300[F] (Dead)

Gwafa (IRE) *Paul Webber* 97
5 gr g Tamayuz Atalina (FR) (Linamix (FR))
5502a[4]

Gwendolyn (GER) *Robert Cowell* a83 87
3 b f Invincible Spirit(IRE) Golden Whip (GER) (Seattle Dancer (USA))
(1647) 1872[3] 2751[3] 3413[3] 5730[7]

Gworn *R Mike Smith* a46 86
6 b g Aussie Rules(USA) Crochet (IRE) (Mark Of Esteem (IRE))
1221[12] 1694[5] 2527[7] 3347[2] 3391[4] 3920[3] 4448[4] 4704[4] 5226[8] 5802[7] 6561[9] *7141[11]*

Gwydir *H Albloushi* a43
5 b g Exceed And Excel(AUS) Glen Innes (IRE) (Selkirk (USA))
8a[7]

Gymkhana *D Smaga* 84
3 ch c Equiano(FR) Village Fete (Singspiel (IRE))
6911a[4]

Gymnaste (IRE) *John Gosden* a74
2 b f Shamardal(USA) Galipette (Green Desert (USA))
8131[2]

Gypsy Eyes (IRE) *Charles Hills* 94
3 b f High Chaparral(IRE) Brown Eyes (Danehill (USA))
2245[9] 3274[9] 4130[2]

Gypsy Major *Garry Moss* a68 58
4 ch g Major Cadeaux Romany Gypsy (Indesatchel (IRE))
2323[10] 3043[2] 3946[3] 4102[3] 4454[7] *5069[3] (5369) (5839)* 6347[6] 6451[12] *7324[10] 7663[9] (7994) 8287[10]*

Gypsy Rider *Henry Tett* a40 54
7 b g Ishiguru(USA) Spaniola (IRE) (Desert King (IRE))
6312[8] 7302[12]

Gysoave (FR) *Waldemar Hickst* 83
3 b f Soave(GER) Gyrena (FR) (Esprit Du Nord (USA))
3452a[10]

Haabis (USA) *George Peckham* a65
3 bb g Super Saver(USA) Raise Fee (USA) (Menifee (USA))
691[5] 1036[2] 1287[9] 8154[12] 8498[13]

Haadeeth *K Kukk* a27 31
9 b g Oasis Dream Musical Key (Key Of Luck (USA))
1517a[8]

Haafaguinea *Saeed bin Suroor* a107 112
6 ch g Haafhd Ha'penny Beacon (Erhaab (USA))
(285a) 625a[2] 843a[3] 1102a[3]

Haaf A Sixpence *Ralph Beckett* a94 53
7 b g Haafhd Melody Maker (Diktat)
6915[14] *7781[2] (7902)* ◆ *8177[10] 8475[5]*

Haaffa Sovereign *Kevin Morgan* a53 35
5 ch g Haafhd Royal Nashkova (Mujahid (USA))
7657[6] 8212[4] 8497[7]

Haafhder Thought *Tim Easterby* 27
2 b f Haafhd Sea Flower (IRE) (Acclamation)
6477[11] 6789[8]

Haalan *James Tate* a93 97
4 b m Sir Percy Fin (Groom Dancer (USA))
(1290) 1907a[5] 2363[6] 4026[4] 4650[4] (5382) 5932[3] *7608[8]*

Haalick (IRE) *Roger Varian* a103 108
3 ch c Roderic O'Connor(IRE) Lucky Pipit (Key Of Luck (USA))
(836) ◆ *1071[3]* ◆ 2466[2] 2870[4] 3269[7]

Haames (IRE) *Kevin Morgan* a57 63
9 b g Kheleyf(USA) Jumilla (USA) (El Gran Senor (USA))
252[7] 609[12] 3648[6] 5132[7]

Haatheq (USA) *A R Al Rayhi* a107 94
9 b h Seeking The Gold(USA) Alshadiyah (USA) (Danzig (USA))
92a[7] 844a[9]

Habbad (FR) *Richard Hannon* a74
2 ch c Choisir(AUS) Arikaria (IRE) (Sri Pekan (USA))
7065[4] 7639[3] 7882[4] (8153)

Habeshia *C Lerner* a64 60
6 ch g Muhtathir Lumiere Rouge (FR) (Indian Ridge)
4927a[2]

Hab Reeh *Ruth Carr* a56 62
8 gr g Diktat Asian Love (Petong)
22[5] 178[4] 340[4] 418[3] 596[3] 895[3] 1005[7] 1676[12] 2053[12] (2359) 3016[5] (3941) 4570[7] *5069[13]* 5483[7] 5889[3] 6835[6] 7092[10]

Hackney Road *Henry Spiller* a76
3 b f Aqlaam West Lorne (USA) (Gone West (USA))
(8093) (8358)

Hadaj *Michael Herrington* a61 50
7 b g Green Desert(USA) My Amalie (IRE) (Galileo (IRE))
36[10] 271[7] 543[10]

Haddajah (IRE) *Sir Michael Stoute* a92 90
3 b f Sea The Stars(IRE) Ardbrae Lady (Overbury (IRE))
1989[6] *(2767)* ◆ 3665[5] *(4977)* 6456[4]

Hadeeqa (IRE) *Simon Crisford* a66
2 b f Cape Cross(IRE) Khulood (USA) (Storm Cat (USA))
7976[4]

Hadley *Tracy Waggott* a53 53
3 b g Royal Applause Brush Strokes (Cadeaux Genereux)
935[8] 2425[3] 8288[5] 8472[5]

Haggle *Luca Cumani* 99
3 ch f Pivotal Barter (Daylami (IRE))
4737[2] 6298[6] ◆ 6948[3]

Hagree (IRE) *Jose Santos* a69 49
5 b g Haatef(USA) Zuniga's Date (USA) (Diesis)
32[4] 252[2] ◆ 388[2] 609[6]

Haidees Reflection *Jim Goldie* a46 67
6 b m Byron Exchanging Glances (Diktat)
(1695) 2574[7] 2960[8] 4189[4] 4449[7] 5149[8] 6742[8] 7097[6] 7601[9] 7850[10] 8306[14]

Hail Clodius (IRE) *Richard Hannon* a93 90
4 gr g Clodovil(IRE) Dhairkana (IRE) (Soviet Star (USA))
1274[3] 2037[3] 2246[11] 3534[9] 3783[2] 4048[3] 4532[2]

Haines *Andrew Balding* a96 93
5 ch g Shirocco(GER) Spring Dream (IRE) (Kalanisi (IRE))
(234) 499[2] ◆ (1209) 1802[4] 2472[5] 3657[2] 5144[6] 6582[8] 7814[4]

Hairdryer *Andrew Balding* a77 64
3 b c Motivator Londonnetdotcom (IRE) (Night Shift (USA))
1185[3] 7214[8] (8048)

Hajaj (IRE) *Charlie Fellowes* a78 57
2 b c Dark Angel(IRE) And Again (USA) (In The Wings)
5410[8] (5676) 7460[4] 8360[2]

Hajjam *William Knight* a73 64
2 b g Paco Boy(IRE) Amanda Carter (Tobougg (IRE))
6881[4] ◆ 7649[3]

Hakam (USA) *Michael Appleby* a95 74
4 bb g War Front(USA) Lauren Byrd (USA) (Arch (USA))
1287[3] (1765) 2361[3] 2862[10] 4199[3] (6371) ◆ 6792[6] 7610[11] 8069[6]

Hakeem (FR) *J Smart* 89
2 b g Wootton Bassett Diamond Star (IRE) (Daylami (IRE))
1889[2] (2335) 2717a[5] 4732[9] 8564a[9]

Haky (IRE) *J E Hammond* 77
2 ch c Muhtathir Marah Dubai (FR) (Dubawi (IRE))
7345a[4]

Hala Madrid *Andrew Balding* a82 80
4 ch m Nayef(USA) Ermine (IRE) (Cadeaux Genereux)
1932[3] 2636[2] (3030) 3257[4]

Halawain (USA) *John Quinn* a55 75
2 b g Congrats(USA) Screen Giant (USA) (Giant's Causeway (USA))
4097[6] 4765[5] (5377) 6536[11] 7305[6]

Halawate (FR) *H-F Devin* a71 70
3 b f King's Best(USA) Afaf (FR) (Spectrum (IRE))
1240a[6]

Haldaw *Mick Channon* a40 24
2 b f Halling(USA) Dawnus (IRE) (Night Shift (USA))
7107[7] 7548[9]

Hale Soriano *P Bary* 105
5 ch g Halling(USA) Sureyya (GER) (Monsun (GER))
1688a[6]

Haley Bop (IRE) *Mark Johnston* 100
3 ch f Dream Ahead(USA) Hallie's Comet (IRE) (One Cool Cat (USA))
1243[5] 2875[7] (3152) 3600[4] 4080[6] 4534[3] 4737[7] 5396[2] 5588[13] (6320) 6557[2] 6947[8]

Halinka (IRE) *Roger Varian* a64 64
2 gr f Dark Angel(IRE) Mahaazen (IRE) (Cape Cross (IRE))
2817[7] 3122[5] 4558[4] 6630[8] 7073[12] 7884[10] 8072[2] ◆

Hallelujah *James Fanshawe* a106 104
8 b m Avonbridge My Golly (Mozart (IRE))
166[5] 486[13]

Halli Galli (GER) *U Stech* 82
3 ch f Areion(GER) Humaita (GER) (Surumu (GER))
5695a[6]

Hallingham *Chris Gordon* a63 71
6 b g Halling(USA) In Luck (In The Wings)
2911[6] 3560[7] 3999[9]

Halling River (IRE) *M Weiss* a36 66
9 ch g Halling(USA) Cunas (USA) (Irish River (FR))
2318a[8]

Hallings Comet *Shaun Lycett* a66 87
7 ch g Halling(USA) Landinium (ITY) (Lando (GER))
(7936)

Halling's Wish *Gary Moore* a69 70
6 br g Halling(USA) Fair View (GER) (Dashing Blade)
6659[8] (7614) 7739[4] 8084[10] 8367[5]

Hall Of Beauty *Shaun Harris* a28 24
4 ch m Halling(USA) Victorian Era (Cape Cross (IRE))
27[4] 170[5] 3067[14] 3528[13] 8180[14]

Hall Of Fame (IRE) *M Al Attiya* 101
4 ch h Teofilo(IRE) Halla Siamsa (IRE) (Montjeu (IRE))
757a[5]

Hall Of Fame (SWE) *Dina Danekilde* a71
4 bb h Gloria De Campeao(BRZ) Costumier (USA) (Mr Greeley (USA))
4421a[5]

Hallstatt (IRE) *John Mackie* a71 72
10 ch g Halling(USA) Last Resort (Lahib (USA))
386[3] 786[5] 1598[8] (2041) 2338[2] 2805[2] 3437[9] 4550[6] 5183[11] 8211[2]

Hallux *David Barron* 48
3 ch g Sakhee(USA) Jaconet (USA) (Hussonet (USA))
2557[7] 2835[9] 3422[8]

Hamada *Charlie Appleby* 83
2 b c Cape Cross(IRE) Sahraah (USA) (Kingmambo (USA))
5373[3] 6480[2] (7003)

Hamadryade *F Chappet* a54 62
2 b f Raven's Pass(USA) Blue Parade (IRE) (Singspiel (IRE))
7170a[11]

Hamba Kashe (IRE) *Tim Easterby* 62
2 gr g Clodovil(IRE) Final Favour (IRE) (Unblest)
5414[10] 5884[4] 6448[5]

Hamelin (IRE) *George Scott* a107 104
6 b g Cape Cross(IRE) Love Divine (Diesis)
317[6] 1209[3] 3340[19] 7766[6] 8123[8] 8424[4]

Hamidans Girl (IRE) *Keith Dalgleish* a68 72
2 ch f Bahamian Bounty Moynsha Lady (IRE) (Namid)
2090[2] 5516[3] 7381[3] 7938[7] 8118[10]

Hamilton Terrace *Henry Candy* a32 52
3 gb f Mount Nelson Striking Pose (IRE) (Darshaan)
2098[8] 2700[8] 5286[4] 6661[7]

Hamis Al Bin (IRE) *Milton Bradley* a62 49
7 b g Acclamation Paimpolaise (IRE) (Priolo (USA))
197[10] 271[3] 398[4] 542[5] 889[5] 1042[5]

Hamish McGonagain *Jeremy Gask* a57 65
3 b g Kyllachy Inya Lake (Whittingham (IRE))
1721[4] 2302[7] 3069[5] (3513) 4262[4] 5059[4] 5954[6] 6408[5]

Hammer Gun (USA) *Derek Shaw* a59 73
3 b g Smart Strike(CAN) Caraboss (Cape Cross (IRE))
1784[4] 2859[4] 3728[7] 6231[14] 7246[7] 7985[13]

Hammerindown (USA) *D Selvaratnam* a57
5 br g Put It Back(USA) Baba's Mandate (USA) (Full Mandate (USA))
8a[5]

Hammurabi (IRE) *S Seemar* a73
6 b g Exceed And Excel(AUS) Hashimiya (USA) (Gone West (USA))
407a[7]

Handful (IRE) *Roger Charlton* 17
2 b f Dark Angel(IRE) Delia Eria (IRE) (Zamindar (USA))
4261[11]

Handheld *Julia Feilden* a63 68
9 ch g Observatory(USA) Kid Gloves (In The Wings)
1241[9] 1498[6] 2174[10] 3582[2] 4493[2] 5729[7] 7078[11]

Handiwork *Steve Gollings* a88 88
6 ch g Motivator Spinning Top (Alzao (USA))
1209[6]

Handsome Dan (IRE) *Sarah Hollinshead* a74
10 b g Busy Flight Beautiful City (IRE) (Jurado (USA))
318[2] 567[2] 1067[12]

Handsome Dude *David Barron* a85 94
4 b g Showcasing Dee Dee Girl (IRE) (Primo Dominie)
1644[13] 1848[6] 2259[2] 2480[6] 3188[5] 3980[10] 4079[10] 4862[10] 5417[8] 5857[16] (6263) 6556[21] 7610[12] 7858[6] 8385[6] 8583[10]

Handytalk (IRE) *Rod Millman* 92
3 b g Lilbourne Lad(IRE) Dancing With Stars (IRE) (Where Or When (IRE))
1385[2] 1607[4] 2736[10] 3466[3] 4157[4] 4709[3]

Hangman Jury *Richard Hughes* a50
3 gr g Indian Haven Non Disclosure (IRE) (Clodovil (IRE))
5608[3] 5811[6] 7935[5] 8155[10] 8428[5]

Hank Williams *Kristin Stubbs* a47
4 b g Schiaparelli(GER) Jezadil (IRE) (Mujadil (USA))
259[5]

Hannah Just Hannah *Matthew Salaman* 66
7 gr m Proclamation(IRE) Evaporate (Insan (USA))
4792[4] 5623[7]

Hannahs Lad *Ronald Thompson* a21 24
3 b g Assertive Beyond The Rainbow (Mind Games)
3643[10]

Hannington *Barry Brennan* a85 64
5 ch g Firebreak Manderina (Mind Games)
23[2] 260[7] 518[9] 900[7] 2733[5] 2977[3] 8469[8]

Hanseatic *Michael Easterby* a64 83
7 b g Galileo(IRE) Insinuate (USA) (Mr Prospector (USA))
2257[5] 2651[6] (3185) 3717[3] 4113[7] 5482[2] 6055[8] 6517[3] 7077[6] 7408[6]

Happisburgh Man *Dr Jon Scargill* 47
4 br g Footstepsinthesand Contemplate (Compton Place)
3572[12] 4401[15]

Happy Approach (FR) *M Nigge* a90 97
3 ch f New Approach(IRE) Eire (Medicean)
3452a[12] 5006a[6] 7456a[4] 7862a[3] 8024a[5]

Happy Call *Simon Crisford* a91 75
3 b g Kodiac Munaa's Dream (Oasis Dream)
(2002) 2871[6] 4475[2] 5991[9]

Happy Cause (USA) *S Cerulis* a80 75
3 ch g Giant's Causeway(USA) Happy Week (USA) (Distorted Humor (USA))
7492a[3]

Happy Clapper (AUS) *Patrick Webster* 112
5 b g Teofilo(IRE) Busking (AUS) (Encosta De Lago (AUS))
7553a[6]

Happy Girl *Dr Jon Scargill* a52
3 b f Aqlaam Gwyneth (Zafonic (USA))
1149[4] 1575[8]

Happy Jack (IRE) *Dai Burchell* a58 44
5 b g Elusive City(USA) Miss Pelling (IRE) (Danehill Dancer (IRE))
155[4] 362[2] 514[5] 702[3] (981) 1170[2] 1578[5] 2781[4] 8318[10] 8338[4]

Happy Mesa (USA) *H Graham Motion* a80 94
2 bb f Sky Mesa(USA) Happy Choice (USA) (Broken Vow (USA))
7809a[12] 8127a[7]

Happy Queen *George Margarson* a66 67
2 ch f Mayson Rhal (IRE) (Rahy (USA))
4022[10] 4938[2] 5202[2] 5931[4] 6630[6]

Happy Tidings *Tom Dascombe* a71 65
3 b f Exceed And Excel(AUS) Helena Molony (IRE) (Sadler's Wells (USA))
2177[9] 2783[7]

Happy Trails (AUS) *Paul Beshara* 117
8 ch g Good Journey(USA) Madame Flurry (AUS) (Perugino (USA))
7553a[10]

Haqeeba (IRE) *Liam Lennon* a72 76
3 b f Haatef(USA) Katoom (IRE) (Soviet Star (USA))
4191[4]

Haraka (IRE) *Ralph Beckett* a70 65
2 b f Fastnet Rock(AUS) Luna Wells (IRE) (Sadler's Wells (USA))
6624[10] 7210[4] 7548[8] 8244[12] (8568) ◆

Haraz (IRE) *David O'Meara* 84
3 b g Acclamation Hanakiyya (IRE) (Danehill Dancer (IRE))
2122[3] 2349[2] 2657[2] 3389[3] 4313[2] 5063[2] 5579[2] 5865[5] 6217[11] 6567[4]

Harba (IRE) *William Haggas* a63 58
2 ch f Frankel Kirinda (IRE) (Tiger Hill (IRE))
6078[7] 7939[U]

Harbour Belle *Michael Dods* 54
2 b f Harbour Watch(IRE) Sans Reward (IRE) (Barathea (IRE))
3208[6] ◆

Harbour Grey (IRE) *Richard Hannon* a71
2 b f Zoffany(IRE) Caterina Di Cesi (Cape Town (IRE))
8361[2] ◆

Harbour Law *Laura Mongan* a80 116
3 b c Lawman(FR) Abunai (Pivotal)
980[2] ◆ (1897) (2411) 3341[2] 4059[4] (6329)

Harbour Lightning *Ann Duffield* a67 64
2 ch f Harbour Watch(IRE) Divine Power (Kyllachy)
3261[4] 3749[4] 4227[3] 4679[6] 5289[2] 5917[2] ◆ 6420[2] 6641[8]

Harbour Master *Jamie Osborne* a69 97
2 bb c Harbour Watch(IRE) Roodeye (Inchinor)
2976[5] 3730[4] 4594[2] (4877) ◆ (5644) 6330[2] 7266a[4]

Harbour Patrol (IRE) *Rebecca Bastiman* a37 57
4 b g Acclamation Traou Mad (IRE) (Barathea (IRE))
1489[11] 2347[11] 3078[10] 6685[15]

Harbour Rock *David Simcock* a69 74
2 b c Harbour Watch(IRE) Rock Lily (Rock Of Gibraltar (IRE))
6085[4] 7034[2]

Harbour Star *Laura Mongan* a41
3 b f Iffraaj Speak Softly To Me (USA) (Ogygian (USA))
5766[5]

Harbour Town *Harry Dunlop* 61
2 ch g Harbour Watch(IRE) Dress Code (IRE) (Barathea (IRE))
4270[12] 6480[6] 7209[9]

Hard Baby (TUR) *Ibrahim Bekirogullari* 98
5 b m Unaccounted For(USA) Uni Baby (IRE) (Flying Spur (AUS))
6158a[4]

Hardington *Alan King* a53 90
3 b g Fastnet Rock(AUS) La Cucina (IRE) (Last Tycoon)
2545[4] ◆ 3236[4] 4288[3] 5193[3] (6737) (7500)

Hardstone (USA) *Michael Dods* a92 97
5 bb h Birdstone(USA) Songerie (Hernando (FR))
1336[7] 2249[3] 2897[17] 3658[14] 4077[11] 5031[3] 5541[4] 6561[15] 7365[7] 7847[12]

Hard Toffee (IRE) *Conrad Allen* a75 77
5 b g Teofilo(IRE) Speciale (USA) (War Chant (USA))
(2588) 3641[3] 3844[5] (6001) 7653[4] 7993[8]

Hard To Handel *Clare Ellam* a91 85
4 b g Stimulation(IRE) Melody Maker (Diktat)
2121[3] 2620[2] 2917[3] 3518[16] 4408[4] 4894[2] 5180[7] 5886[7] 6500[8] 6753[9] 7108[11] (7745) 8035[8] (8338) 8524[8] 8584[7]

Hardy Black (IRE) *Kevin Frost* a72 53
5 b g Pastoral Pursuits Wondrous Story (USA) (Royal Academy (USA))
1117[7] 1555[4] 2229a[3] 3648[4] (3987) 5068[3] 5808[3] (6872)

Harebell (IRE) *Ralph Beckett* a64 69
2 ch f Halling(USA) Prairie Flower (IRE) (Zieten (USA))
7494[4] ◆ 8034[4]

Hargeisa (USA) *Mario Hofer* 103
2 ch f Speightstown(USA) Hasay (Lomitas)
(3701a) 4694a[3] 6068a[2]

Harikiri (IRE) *Charles Hills* a61 62
3 ch f Teofilo(IRE) Queen Of Lyons (USA) (Dubai Destination (USA))
654[4] 2312[6] 4978[9] 6444[8] 6893[4] 7048[8] 7272[8]

Harlech *Saeed bin Suroor* 49
3 ch f Pivotal Zoowraa (Azamour (IRE))
1892[5]

Harlem *A Fabre* 112
4 b h Champs Elysees Casual (Nayef (USA))
1375a[9] 2077a[2] 2947a[3] 3936a[8] 5692a[4]

Harlem Shake (IRE) *Marco Gasparini* 101
5 b g Moss Vale(IRE) Ladylishandra (IRE) (Mujadil (USA))
2518a[4] 7719a[10] 7840a[5]

Harlequeen *Mick Channon* 108
3 b f Canford Cliffs(IRE) Aurelia (Rainbow Quest (USA))
1438[2] ◆ 2160[4] 2869[3] 4416a[3] 5002a[3] 5586[11]

Harlequin Rock *Mick Quinn* a65 65
3 bl g Rock Of Gibraltar(IRE) Berry Baby (IRE) (Rainbow Quest (USA))
1163[4] 1486[3] 2212[6] 3042[8] 3615[7] 4279[3] 4764[4] 5775[2] 6265[12]

Harlequin Rose (IRE) *Mick Channon* a43 54
2 ch f Dutch Art Miss Chaussini (IRE) (Rossini (USA))
4951[14] 5400[12] 5820[7] 6652[3] (6887) 7041[3] 7423[7] 7690[5]

Harlequin Striker (IRE) *Dean Ivory* 90
4 b g Bahamian Bounty Air Maze (Dansili)
1215[12] 1545[5] 2430[5] (3234) 3803[2] 3957[5] 4953[2] 6442[3] 7017[7] ◆

Harlestone Hopes *Ed Dunlop* a70 65
4 b g Olden Times Harlestone Lady (Shaamit (IRE))
261[5] 1810[2] 2374[6] 3191[9]

Harly Forest *Brian Ellison*
3 b g Holy Roman Emperor(IRE) Goslar (In The Wings)
2327[11]

Harmonic Wave (IRE) *Rebecca Menzies* a64 43
3 b f Zebedee Pure Folly (IRE) (Machiavellian (USA))
2742[6] 3326[6] 6809[7] 7437[8] 7798[11] 8078[5] 8390[4]

Harmonika (FR) *F Vermeulen*
2 b f Bushranger(IRE) Hieroglyph (Green Desert (USA))
4187a[10]

Harmonise *Mick Channon* a70 74
2 b f Sakhee's Secret Composing (IRE) (Noverre (USA))
4154[2] 4877[3] 5524[3] 6787[2] 7147[8]

Harmonize (USA) *William Mott* 106
3 b f Scat Daddy(USA) Mesa Fresca (USA) (Sky Mesa (USA))
4174a[5] 7379a[2]

Harmony Bay (IRE) *Sylvester Kirk* a68 75
3 b f Fast Company(IRE) Consensus (IRE) (Common Grounds)
1572[6] 2108[11] 2585[4] 3003[4] 3975[2] 4269[3] 5248[2] 5954[8] (6290) 6592[9] 7725[8] 8031[9]

Harold Lloyd *Henry Candy* a45 83
4 b g Cape Cross(IRE) Silent Act (USA) (Theatrical (IRE))
1933[8] 3109[6]

Harome (IRE) *Roger Fell* a82 80
2 ch c Bahamian Bounty Clytha (Mark Of Esteem (IRE))
1868[3] 2193[6] 2570[3] (2807) 3515[7] 5352[2] (6007) 6322[4] 7600[2] 7820[6]

Harpers Ruby *Lynn Siddall* a59 38
6 b m Byron La Belle Katherine (USA) (Lyphard (USA))
174[10] 241[5] 543[12] (732) 1133[8] 1720[10] 3484[14] 3776[7] 4647[3] 6023[11] (6587) 6745[12] 7276[9] 7913[2] 8409[10]

Harps Of Bretagne *Lisa Williamson* a23 38
4 b m Monsieur Bond(IRE) Lavernock Lady (Don't Forget Me)
71[9]

Harri Bizia (FR) *F Sanchez* a52 42
5 b m Le Triton(USA) Grioun (FR) (Kaldoun (FR))
4927a[8]

Harrison *Mick Channon* 106
3 b g Sixties Icon Excellent Day (IRE) (Invincible Spirit (IRE))
1610[3] 2190[8] 3300[3] 4059[3] 4753[9] 5557[4] 6329[6]

Harrison Stickle *John Gallagher* 71
4 gr g Hellvelyn Hollybell (Beveled (USA))
1928[11]

Harristown *Charlie Longsdon* a42
6 ch g Bering New Abbey (Sadler's Wells (USA))
3528[7]

Harry Angel (IRE) *Clive Cox* 112
2 b c Dark Angel(IRE) Beatrix Potter (IRE) (Cadeaux Genereux)
2023[2] (6572)

Harry Beau *Richard Hannon* 63
2 ch c Kheleyf(USA) Lovellian (Machiavellian (USA))
5820[8] 6288[4] 7012[6] 7571[2]

Harry Bosch *Julia Feilden* a18 62
6 b g Kyllachy Fen Guest (Woodborough (USA))
1735[8] 2087[2] 2647[8] 3043[8] 5051[5]

Harry Champion *Hugo Palmer* a70 78
3 b g Cockney Rebel(IRE) Nine Red (Royal Applause)
2871[7] 4028[4] 4593[4] ◆ 5412[7] 6123[8] 6684[6] (7008) 7332[10]

Harry George (IRE) *Brian Ellison* a51
2 br g Big Bad Bob(IRE) Somva Of Liberty (IRE) (Statue Of Liberty (USA))
3561[5]

Harry Holland *Tom Dascombe* a86 47
4 b g Dutch Art Common Consent (IRE) (Common Grounds)
639[9] (746) ◆ (1142) 1797[8] 2378[7] 3061[13] 3783[12] 6055[11] 7051[10] 8036[7] 8154[9] 8531[9]

Harry Hunt *Graeme McPherson* a81 86
9 b g Bertolini(USA) Qasirah (IRE) (Machiavellian (USA))
922[4] 7183[2] 8250[11]

Harry Hurricane *George Baker* a98 105
4 b g Kodiac Eolith (Pastoral Pursuits)
1205[4] ◆ 1857[2] 2206[6] (2488) 2895[15] 4126[16] 4735[5] 5555[5] 6327[3] (6779) 6990a[13]

Harry's Endeavour *Daniel Kubler* a58 65
3 b g Paco Boy(IRE) Crabapple (Alhaarth (IRE))
122[4] 400[6] 1259[6] (1740) 2126[9] 2700[3] 3998[4] 4226[4] 5079[4] 5548[3] 5923[4] 6405[2]

Harry's Son (AUS) *C Alonso Pena* a80 111
4 b h Haradasun(AUS) Dash On Ruby (AUS) (Anabaa (USA))
282a[2] 720a[4] 845a[4] 1106a[12] 6991a[7] 8431a[10]

Hartford Starts (IRE) *Brian Ellison* a53 51
6 b g Chineur(FR) Desert Design (Desert King (IRE))
941[4] 1085[8]

Hart Hills Road (USA) *Michael B Campbell* 86
5 rg g Tapit(USA) Glimmering (IRE) (Sadler's Wells (USA))
5428a[8]

Hartnell *J O'Shea* 121
5 b g Authorized(IRE) Debonnaire (Anabaa (USA))
7553a[2] 7756a[3]

Hartside (GER) *Peter Winks* 65
7 b g Montjeu(IRE) Helvellyn (USA) (Gone West (USA))
1253[7] 2971[6] 3437[6]

Hart Stopper *Michael Bell* 61
2 b g Compton Place Angel Song (Dansili)
2437[3]
Hartswell *John Gosden* 81
2 b c Nathaniel(IRE) Bahama Spirit (IRE) (Invincible Spirit (IRE))
3661[4] 4649[3] 5036[3] 5637[6] 6130[10]
Harvest Moon *Richard Fahey* a48 66
2 b f Mayson Hamsat Elqamar (Nayef (USA))
7072[3] ◆ 7578[3] 8139[6]
Harvest Ranger *Michael Appleby* a40 44
2 b g Bushranger(IRE) Time Of Gold (USA) (Banker's Gold (USA))
7574[11] 7891[10] 8034[10]
Harvest Wind (IRE) *Clive Cox* 78
2 b c Elzaam(AUS) Harvest Joy (IRE) (Daggers Drawn (USA))
7071[7] 7818[3]
Harwood *David O'Meara* 41
2 b c Dutch Art Amicable Terms (Royal Applause)
6129[7]
Harwoods Star (IRE) *John Butler* a79 64
6 br g Danehill Dancer(IRE) Showbiz (IRE) (Sadler's Wells (USA))
49[4] 176[4] (869) ◆ 963[4] (1154) 1403[4] 2028[16] 2396[7] 4155[10] 7059[15] 7444[7] 8036[10] 8345[2] 8473[2]
Harwoods Volante (IRE) *David O'Meara* a95 95
5 ch g Kheleyf(USA) Semiquaver (IRE) (Mark Of Esteem (IRE))
2476[8] 3133[10] 4627[11] 4896[7] 5179[4] 5793[2] 6072[2] 6449[11] 6718[2] 7054[2] (7443) 7702[4] 7858[11]
Harzand (IRE) *D K Weld* 124
3 br c Sea The Stars(IRE) Hazariya (IRE) (Xaar) (1370a) (2896) (3679a) 6354a[8] 6989a[9]
Hasanour (USA) *M Halford* 106
6 b g Giant's Causeway(USA) Hasanka (IRE) (Kalanisi (IRE))
93a[16] 455a[12] 2716a[2] 3273[14] 4747a[7] 5941a[4] 6389a[25]
Hashtag Frenzy *Rebecca Menzies* a20 48
3 ch g Compton Place One Night In May (IRE) (Choisir (AUS))
1251[9] 1768[9] 2428[7] 3289[5] 3776[6] 4228[5] 4512[9] 4944[2] 5378[7]
Hassle (IRE) *Dr Richard Newland* 103
7 b g Montjeu(IRE) Canterbury Lace (USA) (Danehill (USA))
3246[20]
Hat Alnasar (IRE) *M Halford* a93 87
4 b g Moss Vale(IRE) Dream State (IRE) (Machiavellian (USA))
4250a[4] 4747a[11]
Hathal (USA) *William Haggas* 117
4 ch h Speightstown(USA) Sleepytime (IRE) (Royal Academy (USA))
(6117) 7352[8]
Hathfa (FR) *Richard Hughes* a70 71
2 gr f Dark Angel(IRE) Nepali Princess (IRE) (Mr Greeley (USA))
4951[4] ◆ 5400[6] 6086[4] 6762[7] 8313[5] 8454[3]
Hathiq (IRE) *Owen Burrows* a79 84
2 b c Exceed And Excel(AUS) Madany (IRE) (Acclamation)
3356[2] 4390[2] (7867)
Hatsaway (IRE) *Pat Phelan* a61 85
5 b g Dubawi(IRE) Scotch Bonnet (IRE) (Montjeu (IRE))
1413[5] (1947) (3533) (3798) 5553[8] 6582[6] 6919[12]
Hatton Cross (IRE) *T J O'Mara* a71 74
7 b g Moss Vale(IRE) Last Gasp (Barathea (IRE))
4899a[11]
Haulani (USA) *Philip Hide* a80 82
2 ch g Algorithms(USA) License To Speed (USA) (Thunder Gulch (USA))
2822[2] ◆ 3315[4] (5015) ◆ (5594) ◆ 6705[4] 7322[3]
Haunted (IRE) *Milton Bradley* a49 20
3 b f Invincible Spirit(IRE) Convention (Encosta De Lago (AUS))
325[8] 413[5] 770[6] 1141[8] 1829[10] 2148[10]
Hauraki (AUS) *J O'Shea* 115
4 b g Reset(AUS) Youthful Presence (AUS) (Dehere (USA))
7553a[8]
Havana Beat (IRE) *Tony Carroll* a81 99
6 b g Teofilo(IRE) Sweet Home Alabama (IRE) (Desert Prince (IRE))
3662[4] 3889[10] 4734[13] 5559[7] 5655[15] 6379[2] 7150[27] 8594[9]
Havana Moon (USA) *M Delzangles* a92 98
4 b m Malibu Moon(USA) Sobinka (IRE) (Sadler's Wells (USA))
1232a[3] 2077a[7] 3119a[7]
Have A Nice Day *Sabrina J Harty* a97 98
6 b g Oratorio(IRE) Centrepiece (Pivotal)
290[6] 4921a[7] 6355a[16] 7523a[10]
Havelock (IRE) *Mark Johnston* 78
2 ch c Helmet(AUS) Pearl Grey (Gone West (USA))
1736[2] 2682[2]
Haveyougoneaway (USA) *Thomas Morley* a113
5 ch m Congrats(USA) One Wise Cowgirl (USA) (Wiseman's Ferry (USA))
7836a[7]
Havisham *Andrew Balding* a74 92
4 b g Mount Nelson Ile Deserte (Green Desert (USA))
1037[2] (1914) 2486[9] 3387[18]
Havre De Paix (FR) *David Menuisier* a89 99
4 b m Le Havre(IRE) Bridge Of Peace (Anabaa (USA))
(1160) 2026[9] 6107a[6] 7397a[4] 7978[5] 8563a[11]
Hawaiian Freeze *J Moon* a39 45
7 b m Avonbridge Autumn Affair (Lugana Beach)
1517a[4] (2955a)
Hawana (USA) *John Gosden* a71 79
2 b f War Front(USA) Tare Green (USA) (Giant's Causeway (USA))
2817[6] (4063) 6525[2]
Hawatif (IRE) *Mark Johnston* a81 89
3 b f Royal Applause Excellerator (IRE) (Exceed And Excel (AUS))
1812[2] 2161[6] 2855[3] 3521[6] 4094[5] 4318[2] (4548) (4867) 5588[12] 6096[3] 6276[8] 6810[3]
Hawkbill (USA) *Charlie Appleby* a96 123
3 ch c Kitten's Joy(USA) Trensa (USA) (Giant's Causeway (USA))
(1866) (3296) (3912) 5558[8] 6354a[9] 7759a[3]
Hawke (IRE) *J P Murtagh* a106 87
4 b g Oratorio(IRE) Australie (IRE) (Sadler's Wells (USA))
3377a[3] 6389a[15] 6932a[3] (7342a)
Hawkeyethenoo (IRE) *Jim Goldie* a68 91
10 b g Hawk Wing(USA) Stardance (USA) (Rahy (USA))
2158[7] 2862[13] 3346[7] 4299[8] (4627) 6109[17] 6449[7] 6780[14] 7126[3] 7858[12]
Hawk Gold (IRE) *Paddy Butler* a20 24
12 ch g Tendulkar(USA) Heiress Of Meath (IRE) (Imperial Frontier (USA))
634[11]
Hawk Moth (IRE) *John Spearing* a64 67
8 b g Hawk Wing(USA) Sasimoto (USA) (Saratoga Six (USA))
190[4] 297[2] ◆ 590[5] 681[3] 877[4] 1064[5] 1147[5] 1781[3] (1949) 2542[5] (2647) 3258[5] 3739[6] 4388[7] 4715[7] 6188[5] 6407[6] 7036[5] 7299[2] 7642[7] 8026[11]
Hawksmoor (IRE) *Hugo Palmer* a84 106
3 b f Azamour(IRE) Bridal Dance (IRE) (Danehill Dancer (IRE))
2316a[3] (2949a) 4435a[3] 6352a[5] 7379a[3]
Haworth *James Bethell* a71 68
2 b g Showcasing Some Diva (Dr Fong (USA))
5476[9] (6099) 6536[6] 7120[11]
Hawridge Flyer *Stuart Kittow* 74
2 b c Sir Percy Strictly Lambada (Red Ransom (USA))
7503[3] ◆
Hawridge Glory (IRE) *Rod Millman* 60
2 b g Royal Applause Saint Lucia (IRE) (Whipper (USA))
1713[7] 2997[11] 3529[7] 4982[6] 5594[6]
Hay Chewed (IRE) *Conrad Allen* a84 101
5 b m Camacho Titian Saga (IRE) (Titus Livius (FR))
1862[8] 2895[14] 3244[17] 4359[2] 4735[10] 5268[6] 5555[7] ◆ 5961[4] (6207) 6642[9] 7242[8] 7520a[12]
Haymarket *R Mike Smith* a53 69
7 b g Singspiel(IRE) Quickstyx (Night Shift (USA))
1697[7] 3212[7] 3286[10] 3922[5] 4446[7] 4702[4] 5154[6] 5227[5] 6621[10] 7249[4] 7657[8] 8309[12]
Hayward Field (IRE) *Roger Varian* a76 70
3 b g Cape Blanco(IRE) Keepers Hill (IRE) (Danehill (USA))
1653[5] 2048[8] 2321[5] 3033[2] ◆ 3323[3]
Hazariban (IRE) *Seamus Fahey* a62 75
7 b g Kahyasi Hazarista (IRE) (Barathea (IRE))
5620a[5] 5900a[14]
Hazel Blue (IRE) *David Loughnane* a61 33
5 b m Kodiac Pure Folly (IRE) (Machiavellian (USA))
526[6] 822[5] ◆ (986) 1131[2] 1674[10]
Hazell Berry (IRE) *David Evans* a49 49
2 b f Big Bad Bob(IRE) Mudalalah (IRE) (Singspiel (IRE))
1793[6] 2612[7] 3472[7] 5528[3] 5719[3] 6412[8] 6963[12] 7571[12] 7881[5]
Hazel's Song *Steph Hollinshead* 21
4 b m Orpen(USA) Songbook (Singspiel (IRE))
1765[7] 2886[10]
Hazely *James Bethell* a60 55
3 b f Cape Cross(IRE) Sentimental Value (USA) (Diesis)
1698[6] 2772[4] (4450) 5888[7] (7138)
Hazy Manor (IRE) *Tom Dascombe* 58
2 b f Tagula(IRE) Hazarama (IRE) (Kahyasi)
3024[9] 4298[9] 5266[8] 6681[8] 7244[7]
Head Coach *Jane Chapple-Hyam* a66 57
4 ch g Medicean Lilli Marlane (Sri Pekan (USA))
964[3] 1340[2] 2205[10] 2781[5]
Head East (IRE) *Ivan Furtado* 80
3 ch g Showcasing Seeking Dubai (Dubawi (IRE))
4845[4] 5388[7]
Head High (IRE) *Kevin Ryan* a73 66
3 gr g Mastercraftsman(IRE) Elisium (Proclamation (IRE))
1406[5] 2224[U] 2687[7]
Head Space (IRE) *David Evans* a76 69
8 b g Invincible Spirit(IRE) Danzelline (Danzero (AUS))
319[2] 416[2] 782[4] 1143[6] 1827[4] 2469[8] 2765[11] 3510[2] 3985[3] 4355[4] 4590[2] 5230[3] 5773[4] 6653[5] 7018[2] 7092[8] 7533[3] 7800a[6] (8031) 8094[4] 8531[10]
Heads You Win *Jamie Osborne* a70 67
3 ch f Compton Place Miss Rimex (IRE) (Ezzoud (IRE))
400[3] ◆ 633[5] 1146[4] (2293) 2968[P] 7890[5] 8257[11] 8411[2]
Hearmenow (IRE) *J S Moore* a70
3 b g Kodiac Crystalline Stream (FR) (Polish Precedent (USA))
16[4] 6140[9] 7778[6]
Heartbreak City (FR) *A J Martin* a82 118
6 b g Lando(GER) Moscow Nights (FR) (Peintre Celebre (USA))
1967[16] (5655) 7756a[2]
Heartless *Andrew Balding* 85
4 ch m New Approach(IRE) Honorine (IRE) (Mark Of Esteem (IRE))
1919[6]
Heart Locket *Michael Easterby* a77 55
4 b m Champs Elysees Zante (Zafonic (USA))
103[7] 545[4] (772) 1135[2] 1552[3] 2782[10] 3278[3] 3711[8] 6504[9] 6922[4] 7205[4] (7993) 8283[4] 8524[3]
Heart Of An Angel *Philip McBride* a35 51
3 ro f Dark Angel(IRE) How High The Sky (IRE) (Danehill Dancer (IRE))
2177[5] 2653[6] 4563[5] 6426[11] 6631[10]
Heart Of Gold *William Muir* 62
2 b f Kyllachy Secret Era (Cape Cross (IRE))
4558[7] 5400[7]
Heart Of Lions (USA) *John Gosden* a59 55
3 b c Elusive Quality(USA) Ansong (USA) (Mizzen Mast (USA))
1421[4] 1653[4] (2321) 2891[14] 4358[7]
Heart Of Oak *George Peckham* a64 66
3 b f Oasis Dream Gakalina (IRE) (Galileo (IRE))
3066[5] 3412[7] 3958[4] 6194[10] 7257[7]
Hearts Of Stone (IRE) *Ahmed Kobeissi* 87
6 b h Acclamation Daqtora (Dr Devious (IRE))
744a[9]
Heartsong (IRE) *John Gallagher* a76 77
7 b m Kheleyf(USA) Semiquaver (IRE) (Mark Of Esteem (IRE))
(713) 969[6] 1178[5] 1530[6] 2238[14] 2903[6] 3580[3] 4355[8] 5103[6] 7430[5] 8052[14]
Heartstone (IRE) *Charles Hills* a73 77
3 b f Fastnet Rock(AUS) Eva's Request (IRE) (Soviet Star (USA))
2321[3] ◆ 4356[3] 4955[2] 5634[2] 5996[4] 6635[5] 7326[2] 7691[11]
Hearty (IRE) *Jeremy Noseda* a65 67
3 b g Big Bad Bob(IRE) Ulanova (IRE) (Noverre (USA))
1718[3] 2300[5] (2829) (3570) 6885[8] 7425[5] ◆
Heathfield Park (IRE) *William Stone* a54 13
3 b f Bushranger(IRE) Alexander Anapolis (IRE) (Spectrum (IRE))
611[3] 9521[0] 3735[11] 7442[11] 7641[12]
Heatongrad (IRE) *Richard Fahey* a64 73
2 b c Kodiac Best Mother (IRE) (King's Theatre (IRE))
2617[4] 3283[4] 3705[3] 5171[5] 6007[2] 6536[3] 7004[3] 7319[9]
Heat Storm (IRE) *James Unett* a46 47
5 b g Lawman(FR) Coconut Show (Linamix (FR))
383[6] 498[10] 2110[12] 2814[8] 3732[5] 5085[4] 5739[4] 6143[7] 7103[7] 7231[12]
Heatstroke (IRE) *Charles Hills* a86 89
4 b g Galileo(IRE) Walklikeanegyptian (IRE) (Danehill (USA))
2628[4] 4026[7]
Heave Ho (FR) *N Caullery* a90 49
4 b h Siyouni(FR) Shavya (Shavian)
7806a[8]
Heavenly Angel *Richard Hannon* 72
2 gr f Dark Angel(IRE) Ballyalla (Mind Games)
4350[6] 5119[4] 7118[3]
Heavenly Cry *Phil McEntee* a62 45
2 b g Dick Turpin(IRE) Acclamatory (Royal Applause)
1199[9] 1422[6] 2756[12] 3248[7] 6045[5] 6412[5] 6895[3] 7528[2] 7690[4] 7884[3] 8027[3] 8229[4] 8494[4]
Heaven Scent *Ann Duffield* a46 59
3 ch f Phoenix Reach(IRE) Hel's Angel (IRE) (Pyrus (USA))
2348[6] 3215[8] 3983[8] 4233[8] 5718[5] 6424[11]
Heavensfield *Mark H Tompkins* a65 71
3 b f Motivator Astrodiva (Where Or When (IRE))
1704[6] 2215[4] 2735[7] 3306[6] 3949[3] 5749[6] 7582[3] 8143[6] 8565[6]
Heaven's Guest (IRE) *Richard Fahey* 114
6 b g Dark Angel(IRE) Bakewell Tart (IRE) (Tagula (IRE))
1196[16] 1441[9] 2027[21] 2485[2] 4152[2] 4625[16] 5871[12] 6109[14] 6942[13]
Heaven's Rock (IRE) *Tom Dascombe* a68 69
2 b g Requinto(IRE) Rockfleet Castle (Rock Of Gibraltar (IRE))
3805[8] 4545[5] 5029[9] 6213[6] 8033[6] 8244[3] 8405[4]
Heavens Stream (FR) *Y Gourraud* a58 69
2 b f Scalo Taking Haven (FR) (Septieme Ciel (USA))
2724a[3] 4471a[11]
Heavy Metal *S bin Ghadayer* a99 83
6 b g Exceed And Excel(AUS) Rock Opera (SAF) (Lecture (USA))
95a[14] 189a[14] 717a[2] 8578a[2]
Heavy Weight (IRE) *J S Bolger* a78 57
7 b h Teofilo(IRE) Sister Angelina (USA) (Saint Ballado (CAN))
7391a[7]
Hebah (IRE) *J-C Rouget* 93
2 b f Sea The Stars(IRE) Lia (IRE) (Desert King (IRE))
7491a[3]
Hedging (IRE) *Eve Johnson Houghton* 74
2 rg g Mastercraftsman(IRE) Privet (IRE) (Cape Cross (IRE))
3093[3] (3742) 4315[2] 4553[9] 5821[4] 7033[8]
Hediddodinthe (IRE) *Richard Guest* a56
2 gr g Kendargent(FR) Damoiselle (USA) (Sky Classic (CAN))
7283[12] 7659[8] 7792[5]
Hee Haw (IRE) *Keith Dalgleish* 69
2 b g Sleeping Indian My American Beauty (Wolfhound (USA))
5577[2] 6833[2] 7248[6]
Heezararity *Jonathan Geake* a77 68
8 b g Librettist(USA) Extremely Rare (IRE) (Mark Of Esteem (IRE))
382[4] (773) 1390[9] 1751[3] 2151[7]
Heiba (IRE) *Robert Cowell* a76 72
4 ch h Starspangledbanner(AUS) Pina Colada (Sabrehill (USA))
952[5] 2234[10] 2999[7] 6744[2] 7362[2] (7793) (8228) 8495[3]
Heir Of Excitement (IRE) *Kevin Ryan* 77
2 b g Tagula(IRE) Gimli's Treasure (IRE) (King's Best (USA))
2301[5] 2956[2] (4188) 4699[5] 5583[15]
Heir To A Throne (FR) *Kevin Ryan* 91
3 ch g Siyouni(FR) Boaka (FR) (Kahyasi)
1622[2] 2122[2] (2686) 3885[4] 4917[3] 5616[7] (6217)
Heisman (IRE) *George Baker* a95 92
5 b g Teofilo(IRE) Luminata (IRE) (Indian Ridge)
3055[9] (4026) 4868[10]
Helene Charisma (FR) *Mme Pia Brandt* 116
3 b c Air Chief Marshal(IRE) Lidana (IRE) (King's Best (USA))
1024a[3] 1580a[6] (4332a)
Helene Happy Star (IRE) *John Moore* a107 113
5 b g Zamindar(USA) Harvest Queen (IRE) (Spinning World (USA))
1690a[7] 8329a[13]
Helene Paragon (FR) *John Moore* 118
4 b h Polan(FR) High Zaff (High Chaparral (IRE))
8332a[2]
Helene Super Star (USA) *A S Cruz* a102 113
6 bb g War Front(USA) Black Speck (USA) (Arch (USA))
1690a[13] 8333a[12]
Helfire *Hughie Morrison* a73 68
3 b f Archipenko(USA) Relkida (Bertolini (USA))
3464[10] 3684[6] (4202) 4525[3] (4881) 6091[4] 6237[4] 6851[8]
Helium (FR) *Alexandra Dunn* a68 56
11 b g Dream Well(FR) Sure Harbour (SWI) (Surumu (GER))
1450[3] 7039[3]
Hellarious *Geoffrey Deacon* 33
3 gr g Hellvelyn Yarrita (Tragic Role (USA))
4660[7] 6317[10] 7011[11]
Hellavashock *Alistair Whillans* a67 72
3 gr g Hellvelyn Surprise Statement (Proclamation (IRE))
2459[3] 3359[6] 3653[5] 5486[8] 6268[9] 8286[13] 8587[8]
Hell Boy (FR) *F-M Cottin* 44
2 bb c Martaline Queen Margot (FR) (Muhtathir)
6638a[12]
Hello Beautiful (IRE) *Brian Ellison* a39 57
5 ch m Captain Rio Tekhania (IRE) (Dalakhani (IRE))
961[3] 1119[4] 1490[6]
Hellofahaste *Rod Millman* 85
2 b f Hellvelyn Hasten (USA) (Lear Fan (USA))
2467[4] (2997) 3663[2] 4560[6] 5595[7]
Hellomoto *Kevin Ryan* 56
2 b g Firebreak Dayville (USA) (Dayjur (USA))
4423[8] 5290[6] 6682[10]
Hello My Love (FR) *Carina Fey* a97 109
5 gr g Literato(FR) Ciao My Love (FR) (Touch Down (GER))
3451a[6] 6975a[2]
Hello Traou Land (FR) *C Baillet* a66 73
2 b f Hello Sunday(FR) Risk Of Traou Land (FR) (Take Risks (FR))
1021a[6]
Hellracer *Bryan Smart* 48
3 b g Hellvelyn Racina (Bluebird (USA))
3362[7] 4035[4] 4870[7]
Hells Babe *Jonjo O'Neill* a45 82
3 gr f Hellvelyn Blues In Cee (IRE) (Sinndar (IRE))
7017[10] 7505[6]
Helm Reef (IRE) *Michael Dods* 35
2 ch f Helmet(AUS) Ekhraaj (USA) (El Prado (IRE))
6534[8]
Helmsdale *Richard Hannon* a74 65
2 b f Nathaniel(IRE) Sky Boat (IRE) (Dansili)
4154[3] 4801[7] 5722[3] 6077[5]
Helmsman (IRE) *J S Moore* a62 63
4 b g Alhaarth(IRE) La Cuvee (Mark Of Esteem (IRE))
195[3] 946[3] 1450[5] 1846a[2] 2850[8] 3733a[6]
Helovaplan (IRE) *Bryan Smart* 75
2 b g Helmet(AUS) Watsdaplan (IRE) (Verglas (IRE))
6262[7] 7329[8]
Helvic (IRE) *John Joseph Murphy* a71 64
3 b c Zoffany(IRE) Mystiara (IRE) (Orpen (USA))
828a[3]
Hemingway (IRE) *Kevin Ryan* 80
2 ch g Dragon Pulse(IRE) Degree Of Honor (FR) (Highest Honor (FR))
4161[5] (4685) 5583[9]
Henley *Tracy Waggott* a71 74
4 b g Royal Applause Making Waves (IRE) (Danehill (USA))
1046[5] ◆ 1525[3] ◆ (1843) 1956[2] 3326[4] 3713[2] 4100[2] 4691[5] 5762[6] 6506[9] 7386[3]
Henpecked *Alistair Whillans* a75 75
6 b m Footstepsinthesand Poule De Luxe (IRE) (Cadeaux Genereux)
1202[5] 1881[2] 2526[2] 3642[2] 3920[8] (4341) 5154[2] 6432[8] 7435[3] 7594[9] 7853[6] 7993[2] 8283[6] 8480[2]
Henrietta's Dream *John Wainwright* a13
2 b f Henrythenavigator(USA) Timeless Dream (Oasis Dream)
4451[11] 5242[12] 5974[9] 6678[18]
Henry Croft *Tony Carroll* a75 85
3 b c Dubawi(IRE) Karen's Caper (USA) (War Chant (USA))
1626[6] 3160[6] 3736[2] 5742[2] 8310[2]
Henry Did It (IRE) *Tony Carroll* a59 41
2 b g Henrythenavigator(USA) The Fairies Did It (USA) (Elusive Quality (USA))
4390[8] 4988[7] 5764[5] 6412[9] 7047[8] 7244[9]
Henry Grace (IRE) *Jimmy Fox* a55 39
5 b g Oratorio(IRE) Little Miss Gracie (Efisio)
1262[3] 2609[8] 3732[6] 5823[6] 7427[2] 8070[2]
Henryhudsonbridge (USA) *Edward Bevan* a47 68
4 b g Henrythenavigator(USA) Harlan Ash (USA) (Harlan (USA))
2442[8] (2542) 3097[6] 4088[11] 4763[7]
Henry Morgan *David Brown* 59
9 ch g Bahamian Bounty Hill Welcome (Most Welcome)
1525[8] 3022[5] 3484[6] 3709[8] 4309[6]
Henry Smith *Garry Moss* a66 90
4 b g Firebreak So Discreet (Tragic Role (USA))
505[2] 819[3] (941) 1048[3] 1405[6] (2110) 2326[2] 3288[2] (3706) (4099) 6346[3] 6719[3] (7043) 7359[3] 7594[7]
Henrytheaeroplane (USA) *Z Koplik* 91
4 b g Henrythenavigator(USA) April Pride (Falbrav (IRE))
7997a[5]
Henry The Explorer (CAN) *Jo Hughes* a57 80
3 b g Henrythenavigator(USA) Game (FR) (Montjeu (IRE))
1027[4] 1411[6] 2412[8] 3357[6] 3906[3] 4459[2] 5849[3] 6073[2] 6505[8] 6805[2] 7245[8]
Henrytheghost (USA) *Fawzi Abdulla Nass* a24
4 gr g Henrythenavigator(USA) Fonce De (FR) (Smadoun (FR))
8576a[14]
Henshaw *Charles Hills* 78
3 b g Archipenko(USA) Memory Lane (With Approval (CAN))
1946[7] 2545[9] 3612[2] 3957[6] 6323[10]

Hepburn *Ali Stronge* 56
3 b f Sixties Icon Mighty Splash (Cape Cross (IRE))
2183[10] 3508[8] 3958[11] 5958[8]
Hepplewhite *Robert Eddery* a80 85
3 b g Rail Link Millistar (Galileo (IRE))
968[2] 1636[2] 2548[2] 3736[3] 4153[7] 5849[6] 6528[3] *8048[5] (8554)*
Hepworth Marble (IRE) *Gary Moore* a69 71
3 b f Lilbourne Lad(IRE) Angel Nights (IRE) (Night Shift (USA))
2156[5] (3320) 3741[3] 4222[6] *4525[P]* (Dead)
Heraldic (USA) *Mark Johnston* a72 62
3 br c Discreet Cat(USA) Chilukki's Song (USA) (Elusive Quality (USA))
954[3] 1977[11] 2466[14] *2917[13]* 3716[8]
Herald The Dawn (IRE) *J S Bolger* 112
3 b c New Approach(IRE) Hymn Of The Dawn (USA) (Phone Trick (USA))
1864[8] 3269[17]
Hercullian Prince *Conor Dore* a62 58
4 b g Royal Applause Thara'A (IRE) (Desert Prince (IRE))
67[9] 239[2] 349[5] 502[6] 680[6] 792[6]
Hereawi *Ralph Beckett* a79 88
3 b f Dubawi(IRE) Look Here (Hernando (FR))
(1200) ◆ 1636[5] 2687[3] (4137) 4994[3] 6325[3] *7652[11]*
Here Comes When (IRE) *Andrew Balding* a104 111
6 b g Danehill Dancer(IRE) Quad's Melody (IRE) (Spinning World (USA))
1637[3] 2691[7] 3664[3] 4135[6] *5472[5]* (6364) 7354[10] *7978[4]*
Here For The Craic (IRE) *David Kenneth Budds* a80 84
9 br g Millenary Tongabezi (IRE) (Shernazar)
6389a[20]
Here I Go Again (IRE) *Christine Dunnett*
2 b g Fast Company(IRE) Jaldini (IRE) (Darshaan)
7225[9]
Here's Two *Ron Hodges* a73 78
3 b f Hellvelyn There's Two (IRE) (Ashkalani (IRE))
(1141) 2108[4] (2586) 3558[2] 4534[8]
Hereward The Wake *Sylvester Kirk* a59 69
3 gr g Fastnet Rock(AUS) Miss Universe (IRE) (Warning)
4156[4] 4660[5] 5288[5] 6408[10] 7036[6] *7606[5]*
Herm (IRE) *David Evans* 68
2 b c Bushranger(IRE) School Holidays (USA) (Harlan's Holiday (USA))
3100[5] 4154[4] 4866[9] 6275[2] 7185[12]
Hermann *Richard Hannon* a83 75
3 b c Authorized(IRE) Alamanni (USA) (Elusive Quality (USA))
1200[3] ◆ *(7942) 8447[7]*
Hermarna (IRE) *Harry Dunlop* a57 65
3 br f Heliostatic(IRE) Louverissa (IRE) (Verglas (IRE))
2701[7] 3496[3] 4794[4] 6654[3] *7425[10]*
Hermeneutics (USA) *Ed Walker* a55
2 b g Scat Daddy(USA) Rosangela (USA) (El Prado (IRE))
8119[7]
Hermitage Bay (USA) *John Gosden* a84 83
3 b c War Front(USA) City Sister (USA) (Carson City (USA))
428[2] 1091[5] 1287[6] 2039[2]
Hermosa Vaquera (IRE) *Gary Moore* a30 53
6 b m High Chaparral(IRE) Sundown (Polish Precedent (USA))
4225[7] 5100[3] 5777[3] 6891[6] *8468[12]*
Hernandes (FR) *Ed Walker* a71 67
2 gr g Clodovil(IRE) Gontcharova (IRE) (Zafonic (USA))
5081[4] 6439[4] 6881[5]
Hernandoshideaway *Michael Dods* 99
4 b g Hernando(FR) Alba Stella (Nashwan (USA))
1493[9] 2157[13] 4095[7] 5031[5] 6561[14]
Hernando Torres *Michael Easterby* a78 72
8 b g Iffraaj Espana (Hernando (FR))
33[3] 332[4] 360[3] 3605[9] 4113[13] 4930[3] 5540[5] *5841[4]* 6226[3] ◆ *7141[9] 7662[8] 8588[7]*
Heroes (FR) *R Chotard* a61 62
2 bb c Stormy River(FR) Windy (FR) (Rock Of Gibraltar (IRE))
6638a[8]
Heroine Queen *Robert Cowell* a70
2 ch f Mayson Resistance Heroine (Dr Fong (USA))
6244[8] 6696[3]
Hero's Story *Jim Goldie* a57 60
6 b g Mount Nelson Red Roses Story (FR) (Pink I (FR))
1697[3] 2813[4] 3288[3] 4194[5] *4645[3]* 5118[5] 5155[3] 5726[2]
Herridge (IRE) *Richard Hannon* a64 56
3 ch f Bahamian Bounty Quickstyx (Night Shift (USA))
148[4]
Hersigh *Saeed bin Suroor* a79 74
2 ch f Poet's Voice Zayn Zen (Singspiel (IRE))
4663[6] *6625[2] (7100)* 7471[4] *(7898)*
Her Terms *William Haggas* a67 77
2 ch f Pivotal Best Terms (Exceed And Excel (AUS))
1988[7] 2990[2] 4558[2] 6162[2] 6873[5] 7122[4] *8175[4] 8313[2] 8453[5]*
Hertford Dancer *John Gosden* a72 57
2 ch f Foxwedge(AUS) Tebee (Selkirk (USA))
7441[6] *8063[4] (8340)*
He's A Dreamer (IRE) *David O'Meara* a81 79
3 ch g Dream Ahead(USA) Illuminise (IRE) (Grand Lodge (USA))
(352) 1168[4] 1409[5] 2532[8] 2972[6] 3775[8]
He's A Lad (IRE) *Andrew Balding* 63
2 b c Lilbourne Lad(IRE) Make Amends (IRE) (Indian Ridge)
3954[5]
He's A Toff (IRE) *Tim Easterby* 63
2 br g Dandy Man(IRE) Prevarication (IRE) (In The Wings)
2344[3] 3208[9] 3872[8] 6213[5] 6681[10]
Heshem (IRE) *C Ferland* a102 114
3 b c Footstepsinthesand Doohulla (USA) (Stravinsky (USA))
(1240a) (4439a) 5499a[7] 6973a[2]

Heska (IRE) *Michael Appleby* a72 66
5 b g Rock Of Gibraltar(IRE) Sweet Sioux (Halling (USA))
61[5] 336[8]
He's Magic *Tim Fitzgerald* a35 34
5 b g Court Masterpiece Lady Magician (Lord Bud)
6052[13] 6520[7] *7106[6]*
He's My Boy (IRE) *James Fanshawe* a74 74
5 gr g Dark Angel(IRE) Rose Of Battle (Averti (IRE))
1415[10] (2045) 2646[2] 3823[5] 4362[3] 4839[6] 5337[3] 5750[5] *(7069) 7430[11]*
He's My Cracker *Clive Cox* a81 85
3 ch g Captain Gerrard(IRE) Dalmunzie (IRE) (Choisir (AUS))
1892[3] 2544[2] (3147) 3689[7] 4908[2] *6123[5]* 6255[3] 7540[4] *7965[8] 8239[3]*
He's No Saint *David O'Meara* a99 92
5 b g Dutch Art Stellar Brilliant (USA) (Kris S (USA))
2268[7] 3055[6] 4893[8] 5514[6] 6082[4] (6339) 6764[11] 7121[19] *7530[2] 7984[2] (8256) 8489[8]*
Hes Our Music (IRE) *Patrick J Flynn* a99 88
7 b g Oratorio(IRE) Matibibi (ITY) (Barathea (IRE))
(7517a) (7801a)
Hestina (FR) *Peter Chapple-Hyam* 91
3 b f Soldier Of Fortune(IRE) Diagora (FR) (Highest Honor (FR))
1608[3] ◆ (1920) 2433[6] 6747[6] 7060[2] ◆ (7669)
Heurtevent (FR) *Tony Carroll* a54
7 bb g Hold That Tiger(USA) Sybilia (GER) (Spectrum (IRE))
232[4] 417[3] 592[7]
Hey Ben *Ronald Thompson* a57
3 ch g Sakhee's Secret Gib (IRE) (Rock Of Gibraltar (IRE))
42[4] 291[6]
Hey Joe (FR) *J-Y Artu* a63 52
4 b g Redback Manon (Alzao (USA))
7295a[3]
Hiawassee (USA) *Mark Johnston* a40 31
2 b f Bernardini(USA) Marietta (USA) (Machiavellian (USA))
6223[5] *6590[10] 7050[10]*
Hibiscus (IRE) *A P O'Brien* a90 95
3 b f Galileo(IRE) Jacqueline Quest (IRE) (Rock Of Gibraltar (IRE))
7196a[2] 7393a[6] 7558a[6] *7676a[8]*
Hibou *Iain Jardine* a80 95
3 ch g Street Cry(IRE) Arlette (IRE) (King Of Kings (IRE))
4704[7] 5226[7] 5802[3] 6344[2] (6957) 7159[3] ◆
Hickster (IRE) *Roy Bowring* a82 83
5 br g Intense Focus(USA) Surrender To Me (USA) (Royal Anthem (USA))
1526[7] 2043[3] 2734[8]
Hidden Gem *Stuart Williams* a66 58
3 b f Shamardal(USA) Hidden Brief (Barathea (IRE))
1339[4] 1723[5] 2578[13] 4375[7] *4718[11]* 5252[4] *6373[2] 6512[2] 6908[9] 7642[4] 7986[7] 8320[2] 8449[6]*
Hidden Journey (USA) *D Selvaratnam* a33
2 ch c Broken Vow(USA) Shawklit Delight (USA) (Pine Bluff (USA))
8574a[8]
Hidden Justice (IRE) *John Quinn* a78 92
7 b g Lawman(FR) Uncharted Haven (Turtle Island (IRE))
(1598) 3680a[12] 6540[7]
Hidden Oasis (IRE) *David Wachman* 87
5 b g Lawman(FR) Spesialta (Indian Ridge)
4811a[7]
Hidden Rebel *Alistair Whillans* 93
4 b m Cockney Rebel(IRE) Medicea Sidera (Medicean)
1664[2] 2236[6] 3152[6] (3551) 4391[4] 4894[11] (5538) 6113[2] 7472[9] 7825[11]
Hidden Stash *Andrew Balding* 75
2 b g Sakhee's Secret Marajuana (Robellino (USA))
4552[7] (5099) ◆ 5543[7] 6664[7]
Hidden Steps *Andrew Balding* 87
2 b f Footstepsinthesand Hidden Valley (Haafhd)
(5771) 6258[7]
Hidden Treasures *Richard Fahey* a76 72
3 ch f Zoffany(IRE) Swynford Pleasure (Reprimand)
1960[8] 2420[7] (3137) 3803[4] 4299[14] 6437[10] *6742[12]*
Hide Your Fires (IRE) *Marco Botti* a75 46
3 b f Frozen Power(IRE) Omanah (USA) (Kayrawan (USA))
296[4]
Hi Emperor (IRE) *David Marnane* a56 73
7 b g Choisir(AUS) Musthav (IRE) (Fasliyev (USA))
6465a[8]
Hierarch (IRE) *David Simcock* a67 66
9 b g Dansili Danse Classique (IRE) (Night Shift (USA))
(158) 264[4] 532[3]
Hier Encore (FR) *David Menuisier* a60 60
4 ch g Kentucky Dynamite(USA) Hierarchie (FR) (Sillery (USA))
1575[9] 2370[7] 3221[2] *4019[2]* 5216a[9] *6090[8] 8039[2]* ◆ *8211[12]*
High Acclaim (USA) *Roger Teal* a82 89
2 b c Elusive Quality(USA) La Reine Lionne (USA) (Leroidesanimaux (BRZ))
2747[3] *(3315)* 4148[6] 4553[3] 4825[12] *6697[3]* (7004)
High Admiral *Andrew Balding* a83 87
4 ch g New Approach(IRE) Wosaita (Generous (IRE))
7365[5] ◆
High Alpha (FR) *Mario Hofer* 109
2 b g Fuisse(FR) Kikinda (FR) (Daliapour (IRE))
6270a[2] 7169a[4]
High And Flighty (IRE) *David O'Meara* a79 78
4 b m High Chaparral(IRE) Missionary Hymn (USA) (Giant's Causeway (USA))
30[8]
High Baroque (USA) *Richard Fahey* a90 77
4 b g Lookin At Lucky(USA) Yesterday (IRE) (Sadler's Wells (USA))
2484[7] *8231[4] 8529[6]*

High Bridge *Charlie Appleby* 81
5 b g Monsun(GER) Ameerat (Mark Of Esteem (IRE))
1873[2]
Highburgh Road (IRE) *Mark Johnston* a33 33
3 b f Pour Moi(IRE) Alta Lena (FR) (Alzao (USA))
29[9] 413[6]
High Command (IRE) *Roger Varian* a94 63
3 b g High Chaparral(IRE) Plaza (USA) (Chester House (USA))
1200[6] 6052[7] *6415[7] 7321[3] (7895)* ◆ *(8238) 8339[2]*
High Commander *Andrew Balding* 74
2 b c Teofilo(IRE) Pellinore (USA) (Giant's Causeway (USA))
7013[3] 7317[3]
High Draw (FR) *K R Burke* 86
3 ch g Falco(USA) Augusta Lucilla (USA) (Mr Greeley (USA))
1270[4] 1755[2] ◆ (2557) 3156[9] 3914[4] 6132[5] 6803[4] 7408[10]
High Duty *Karin Suter-Weber* 108
5 b g Oratorio(IRE) Heart Of Ice (IRE) (Montjeu (IRE))
(663a)
Higher Court (USA) *Emma Owen* a75 59
8 b g Shamardal(USA) Nawaiet (USA) (Zilzal (USA))
7644[11] 8150[6] 8280[5] 8490[2] ◆
Higher Power *James Fanshawe* a106 99
4 b g Rip Van Winkle(IRE) Lady Stardust (Spinning World (USA))
1633[2] *2377[3] (3525)* ◆ 7188[2] 7498[2] *(7979)*
Highest Quality (IRE) *Stuart Williams* a70 73
4 b m Invincible Spirit(IRE) Princess Taise (USA) (Cozzene (USA))
413[3] (516)
High Excitement (USA) *Charles Hills* 64
2 b f Blame(USA) Excelente (IRE) (Exceed And Excel (AUS))
2885[9] 4756[10] (Dead)
Highfield Lass *Michael Dods* a48 52
5 b m Cayman Kai(IRE) Jendorcet (Grey Ghost I)
3921[2] ◆ 4314[6] 5228[6] *5971[9]* 6953[3] *8142[7]*
Highgate (FR) *F-X De Chevigny* 62
2 b f Stormy River(FR) Heavenly Music (IRE) (Oratorio (IRE))
1579a[9] 2844a[5]
High Grounds (IRE) *Charles Hills* a91 99
3 b g High Chaparral(IRE) Civility Cat (USA) (Tale Of The Cat (USA))
(377) ◆ 1605[3] 1974[5] 2892[3] ◆ 4108[8] 6333[5]
High Honcho *John Quinn* a76 66
3 b f High Chaparral(IRE) Chieftess (IRE) (Mr Greeley (USA))
6742[9] 7111[11]
High Hopes *David Simcock* 92
3 b f Zamindar(USA) Dixielake (IRE) (Lake Coniston (IRE))
1609[4] 2395[3] ◆ (5233) (6378) ◆
High Intensity *Scott Dixon* a57 66
4 b g Sir Percy Woodbeck (Terimon)
675[7] 766[7] 3498[12]
Highland Acclaim (IRE) *David O'Meara* a96 96
5 b g Acclamation Emma's Star (ITY) (Darshaan)
2158[16] 2480[7] 2803[12] 2862[6] 3188[10] 4428[5] ◆ 4896[3] ◆ 5182[2] (5991) 6263[18] 6327[7] *6627[9] 7530[7] 7610[3] 7752[3] 7990[12] 8192[5] 8314[7]*
Highland Boy *Clive Cox* 25
2 b g Bated Breath Highland Jewel (IRE) (Azamour (IRE))
7502[15]
Highland Castle *David Elsworth* a90 99
8 b g Halling(USA) Reciprocal (IRE) (Night Shift (USA))
1209[8] 1417[6] 5879[3] 6293[3]
Highland Clearance (FR) *Giles Bravery* a50 26
2 b f Kyllachy Let My People Go (FR) (Country Reel (USA))
7439[10] *7733[8]* 7972a[11] *8243[10]*
Highland Colori (IRE) *Andrew Balding* a105 108
8 b g Le Vie Dei Colori Emma's Star (ITY) (Darshaan)
1153[4] 1856[15] 2628[5] 3358[5] 3910[3] 4887[2] 5146[3] 5956[5] 6557[7] (7121) 7354[6] 7573[5]
Highland Cradle *Sir Michael Stoute* 62
2 b c Bated Breath Orford Ness (Selkirk (USA))
6486[7]
Highland Dragon *William Haggas* a72
3 ch g Dutch Art Tiger Mist (IRE) (Galileo (IRE))
(2578) 3546a[5]
Highland Dream (IRE) *Clive Cox* 58
2 gr f Zebedee Red Blanche (IRE) (Red Clubs (IRE))
3143[5] 4261[4] 4951[11] 6289[6] 6652[8]
Highland Lotus *William Haggas* a73 67
2 b f Foxwedge(AUS) Tiger Mist (IRE) (Galileo (IRE))
4022[8] 4586[3] 4907 [2] *5549[8] (6421) 7140[3]* 7467[12]
Highland Pass *Andrew Balding* a72 83
2 bb f Passing Glance Lady Brora (Dashing Blade)
6088[4] 6706[3] ◆ 7118[7]
Highland Reel (IRE) *A P O'Brien* 124
4 b h Galileo(IRE) Hveger (AUS) (Danehill (USA))
1107a[4] 1690a[8] 3384[2] (4626) 5558[2] 6354a[7] 6989a[2] (7835a) 8329a[2]
Highland Sky (USA) *Barclay Tagg* 110
3 bb c Sky Mesa(USA) Kristi With A K (USA) (Petionville (USA))
4173a[2]
Highlands Queen (FR) *Y Gourraud* 111
3 b f Mount Nelson Queen Of Poland (FR) (Polish Precedent (USA))
(2726a) 3452a[DSQ] (5461a) 6393a[4]
High Laugh (IRE) *Marco Botti* a70
2 b f High Chaparral(IRE) Last Laugh (USA) (Smart Strike (CAN))
7050[3]
Highlife Dancer *Mick Channon* a49 71
8 br g Imperial Dancer Wrong Bride (Reprimand)
1947[5] 2507[3] 2645[7] 3072[9] 3620[2] 3748[3] 3997[7] 4294[5] 4784[5] (5383) 5575 [4] 5776[4] 6188[4] 6891[2] 7039[4] 7231[6] 7628[7]

Highly Focussed (IRE) *Ann Duffield* a59
2 b c Intense Focus(USA) Mood Indigo (IRE) (Indian Ridge)
8406[5]
Highly Sprung (IRE) *Mark Johnston* a80 93
3 b g Zebedee Miss Donovan (Royal Applause)
1258[5] 2642[2] 2981[5] 3265[2] 3439[2] (3716) 4803[19] 5199[2] (5372) 5991[3] (6492) 6718[7] 6916[10] 7186[13] *7610[4]* 7821[13]
Highly Toxic (IRE) *Patrick J Flynn* a23 97
5 gr g Dalakhani(IRE) Chiang Mai (IRE) (Sadler's Wells (USA))
3630a[3] 4417a[8] *7342a[8]*
High Mark (IRE) *Saeed bin Suroor* a68
2 ch c Pivotal Arlette (IRE) (King Of Kings (IRE))
7963[4] ◆
High On Light *David Barron* a76 73
3 b f Makfi Estephe (IRE) (Sadler's Wells (USA))
1123[5] 1562[7] 1814[10] 3015[8] 3482[4] (3921) 4233[3] 4522[6] (4847) (5117) 5481[2] 5888[2] 6345[2] *6922[3] (8387)*
High On Love (IRE) *Charlie Fellowes* 87
2 br f Requinto(IRE) Cant Hurry Love (Desert Prince (IRE))
2211[5] (2748) 3336[10] 4560[5] 5407[2] 6388a[21] 7147[13]
High Quality (IRE) *A Fabre* a78 97
3 gr f Invincible Spirit(IRE) High Maintenance (FR) (Highest Honor (FR))
2945a[6]
High Ridge Road (USA) *Chad C Brown* a101
4 b m Quality Road(USA) Detect (USA) (Devil's Bag (USA))
89a[3]
High Shields (IRE) *Roger Charlton* a70 93
3 b g Shamardal(USA) Marine City (JPN) (Carnegie (IRE))
2414[3] (2929) 4131[4] 4797[9]
High Star (FR) *Y Barberot* a87 71
9 ch g High Yield(USA) Etoile D'Or (FR) (Midyan (USA))
(4927a)
High Start (USA) *Doug Watson* a44 3
3 b f Distorted Humor(USA) High Change (USA) (Jump Start (USA))
184a[8] 536a[14]
High Strung (IRE) *J D Hillis* a75 90
5 ch m Mastercraftsman(IRE) High Fidelity (GER) (Peintre Celebre (USA))
664a[8]
Hightime Girl *Roger Fell* a61 58
3 ch f Pivotal Hightime Heroine (IRE) (Danetime (IRE))
2835[8] 3951[6] 4235[7] 4833[5] *8145[2] 8400[5]* ◆
High Waves (IRE) *Saeed bin Suroor* a75
2 br c Dream Ahead(USA) Lake Moon (Tiger Hill (IRE))
(7883)
Highway Code (USA) *David Evans* a35 75
10 b g Street Cry(IRE) Fairy Heights (IRE) (Fairy King (USA))
6737[12]
Highwayman *David Thompson* a73 65
3 b g Dick Turpin(IRE) Right Rave (IRE) (Soviet Star (USA))
519[4] 725[6] 959[2] 1400[4] 5845[10] 7745[2] *8585[6]*
Highway Robber *Wilf Storey* a50 53
3 b g Dick Turpin(IRE) Lawyers Choice (Namid)
1383[4] 1673[5] 2834[5] 3366[5] 4424[6] (5227) 6004[5] 7336[11] *7795[7] 8143[4] 8386[8]*
Hijran (IRE) *Michael Appleby* a68 74
3 ch f Mastercraftsman(IRE) Sunny Slope (Mujtahid (USA))
1275[3] 1759[5] *3033[11]* (5273) 5759[3] (5860) 6231[11] 6877[6] 7227[5] 7577[11] *7985[4] 8347[7]*
Hilario *Charles Hills* a83 93
2 b c Sepoy(AUS) Persario (Bishop Of Cashel)
3106[7] *(6086)* 7536[5] ◆
Hilary J *Ann Duffield* a79 89
3 b f Mount Nelson The Terrier (Foxhound (USA))
2740[3] 3422[2] 4035[3] (4604) *5070[3]* (5867) ◆ 7288[3] 7537[4]
Hillbilly Boy (IRE) *Tom Dascombe* a94 107
6 b g Haafhd Erreur (IRE) (Desert King (IRE))
503[4] 1274[9] ◆ (1993) (3594) (4916) 6558[16] 7997a[3]
Hilldale *Michael Dods* 74
3 b f Exceed And Excel(AUS) Miss Meltemi (IRE) (Miswaki Tern (USA))
3850[2] ◆ 4546[3] (5438)
Hillgrove Angel (IRE) *Iain Jardine* a69 79
4 gr g Dark Angel(IRE) Theben (GER) (Monsun (GER))
2362[6] (2911) 3149[5] 3751[2] (4491) 5837[8] 6540[9]
Hills And Dales (IRE) *Hans-Inge Larsen* a78 57
4 b g Acclamation Soul Mountain (IRE) (Rock Of Gibraltar (IRE))
4421a[7]
Hillside Dream (IRE) *James Tate* 78
3 b f Dream Ahead(USA) Knapton Hill (Zamindar (USA))
1423[5] 3038[2] 3899[2]
Hills Of Rome (IRE) *Richard Hannon* 66
3 b c Holy Roman Emperor(IRE) Fancy Intense (Peintre Celebre (USA))
1826[5] ◆ 2929[8]
Hilltop Ranger (IRE) *Daniel Kubler* a51 68
3 b f Bushranger(IRE) Beatrix Potter (IRE) (Cadeaux Genereux)
1859[4] 3145[3] 3996[5] 4844[10] *5808[8]*
Himalayan Queen *William Jarvis* a68 69
3 b f Poet's Voice Annapurna (IRE) (Brief Truce (USA))
1572[4] 2586[7] (5088) *5525[3]* 6190[9] *6872[11] 7255[6] (7612) 7887[14] 8233[6]*
Hi Milady (IRE) *Dominic Ffrench Davis* a60 68
2 b f Sir Prancealot(IRE) Hi Katriona (IRE) (Second Empire (IRE))
1342[5] 1793[3] 1915[3] 2885[6] (3592) 4090[4] *4974[4]* 5796[8] *7110[11]*
Himself *Richard Hannon* a76 74
2 b c High Chaparral(IRE) Self Centred (Medicean)
2976[4] 4154[5] (5237) 7541[8] *7764[3]*

Hint Of A Smile (USA) *Richard Fahey* 50
2 b f Elusive Quality(USA) Sign Off (USA) (Distorted Humor (USA))
5414[7]

Hint Of A Tint (IRE) *David Wachman* a92 105
6 b m Danehill Dancer(IRE) Mine Excavation (FR) (Galileo (IRE))
2497a[3] 3677a[3]

Hint Of Frost (IRE) *Mrs John Harrington* a57 79
3 ch g Excellent Art Glamorous (GER) (Red Ransom (USA))
5790a[2]

Hint Of Grey (IRE) *Don Cantillon* a62 67
3 gr f Mastercraftsman(IRE) Anamarka (Mark Of Esteem (IRE))
(1948) 2126[2] (2590) 2829[2] 3318[6] 3738[4] 7628[6] 7746[7] 8567[8]

Hiorne Tower (FR) *John Best* a68 58
5 b g Poliglote Hierarchie (FR) (Sillery (USA))
261[6] 461[6] 949[6] 1236[2] (5473) 6245[3] 7739[5] 8084[11]

Hiort (IRE) *P Bary* a73 98
3 b f Rip Van Winkle(IRE) Gifts Galore (IRE) (Darshaan)
2455a[5] 5987a[7]

Hippopus (NZ) *Gai Waterhouse & Adrian Bott* 79
6 b g High Chaparral(IRE) Straight Eight (NZ) (Danske (NZ))
7712a[12]

Hipz (IRE) *Laura Mongan* a65 63
5 br m Intense Focus(USA) Radha (Bishop Of Cashel)
1269[9] 1549[3] 1928[15] 2765[7] 3953[3] 4355[7] 4787[6] 5236[8] 6269[7] 6894[6] 7302[15] (7645) 8026[3] 8252[5] 8555[5]

Hisar (IRE) *Ronald Harris* 40
2 ch g Dragon Pulse(IRE) Delphie Queen (IRE) (Desert Sun)
4053[14]

His Kyllachy (IRE) *William Haggas* a86 85
3 ch g Kyllachy Thousandkissesdeep (IRE) (Night Shift (USA))
3723[3] (4682) 5198[2] 5865[7] (6626)

Hi There Silver (IRE) *Michael Madgwick* a45 59
2 gr g Clodovil(IRE) Elaborate (Sadler's Wells (USA))
2583[8] 3231[5] 4775[6] 5297[6] 5770[12] 6887[7] 7423[10] 7866[11]

Hit It A Bomb (USA) *A P O'Brien* a110 114
3 b c War Front(USA) Liscanna (IRE) (Sadler's Wells (USA))
5343a[3] 6353a[3] 7352[9] 7837a[9]

Hit List (IRE) *Andrew Balding* a76 72
4 ch g Makfi Kassiopeia (IRE) (Galileo (IRE))
1201[10] (1699)

Hitman *William Muir* 80
3 b g Canford Cliffs(IRE) Ballymore Celebre (IRE) (Peintre Celebre (USA))
2185[3] 2981[4] (4354) 4841[9] 5743[7]

Hit The Bid *D J Bunyan* 101
2 b c Exceed And Excel(AUS) Selinka (Selkirk (USA))
2494a[7] (5661a) 6282[11]

Hit The Jackpot (IRE) *David O'Meara* a55 103
7 ch g Pivotal Token Gesture (IRE) (Alzao (USA))
1245[6] (1620) 2157[6] 2744[7] 3436[7] 4115[7] 4858[5] 6081[5] 6802[8] 7287[6] 7535[8]

Hit The Lights (IRE) *David Nicholls* a63 72
6 b g Lawman(FR) Dawn Chorus (IRE) (Mukaddamah (USA))
868[2] ◆ 937[5] (1255) 1495[4] (1559) 1790[4] 1956[3] 2270[3] 3322[2] 3713[10] 3851[2] 4295[7] 4608[14] 4931[2] 5439[10] 6680[15] 6958[6] 7290[8] 7595[8] 8137[9] 8242[13]

Hit The Target (JPN) *Keiji Kato* 116
8 ch h King Kamehameha(JPN) Latir (JPN) (Tamamo Cross (JPN))
8129a[15]

Hoarding (USA) *S bin Ghadayer* a79 85
6 b g Elusive Quality(USA) What A Treasure (IRE) (Cadeaux Genereux)
229a[4]

Hochfeld (IRE) *Mark Johnston* a78
2 b c Cape Cross(IRE) What A Charm (IRE) (Key Of Luck (USA))
7908[11] 8034[2] (8208) 8525[4]

Hodgkins Trust (IRE) *Julia Feilden* a44 37
3 br g Key Of Luck(USA) Rumuz (IRE) (Marju (IRE))
2234[13] 2698[10] 3127[4] 3513[7] 3975[9] 5197[6] 6140[5] 7427[12] 7692[7]

Hoist The Colours (IRE) *Chris Grant*
5 b g Sea The Stars(IRE) Multicolour Wave (IRE) (Rainbow Quest (USA))
4949[U] (Dead)

Hokko Tarumae (JPN) *Katsuichi Nishiura* a115
7 b h King Kamehameha(JPN) Madam Cherokee (JPN) (Cherokee Run (USA))
1108a[9]

Hoku (IRE) *Bent Olsen* a48 90
5 b m Holy Roman Emperor(IRE) Scylla Cadeaux (IRE) (Cadeaux Genereux)
3448a[3]

Hokulaya (FR) *A Kleinkorres* a58 64
5 b m Konigstiger(GER) Hokulea (GER) (Lando (GER))
5452a[9]

Hold Firm *Mark H Tompkins* a60 57
4 b h Refuse To Bend(IRE) Four Miracles (Vettori (IRE))
216[3] (707) 7642[11] 7937[8] 8207[5] 8258[4] 8500[5]

Hold Hands *Brendan Powell* a63 67
5 b m Lawman(FR) Tiponi (IRE) (Traditionally (USA))
1140[3] 1529[2] 2182[8] 3497[5] 6137[6] 6426[9] 7257[8] 7614[5] 8038[3] 8155[3]

Hold Me Tight (IRE) *J S Moore* a56 52
2 b c Zoffany(IRE) All Embracing (IRE) (Night Shift (USA))
6085[9] 6655[6] 7273[5] 7941[4] 8284[4]

Hold On Magnolia *Richard Fahey* a67 44
3 ch g Monsieur Bond(IRE) Mawjoodah (Cadeaux Genereux)
242[3] 519[11] 1120[6] 1448[9] 7994[4] (8483)

Holdthasigreen (FR) *C Le Lay* a90 112
4 ch g Hold That Tiger(USA) Greentathir (FR) (Muhtathir)
8336a[3]

Hold Tight *Saeed bin Suroor* a103 97
4 ch g Exceed And Excel(AUS) Kangra Valley (Indian Ridge)
(220) ◆ 2027[26] 3566[2] 4109[6] 4865[16]

Holiday Henry (USA) *Richard Fahey* a63
3 b g Lookin At Lucky(USA) Lady Ilsley (USA) (Trempolino (USA))
70[5] 376[4]

Holiday Magic (IRE) *Michael Easterby* a102 76
5 gr g Dark Angel(IRE) Win Cash (IRE) (Alhaarth (IRE))
4374[7] 4644[4] 4868[7] 5417[9] 5857[11] 6263[12] 6539[21] 6914[9] 7593[9] 7957[2] (8319) (8455)

Holistic Approach (IRE) *J S Bolger* 82
2 b c New Approach(IRE) Sway Me Now (USA) (Speightstown (USA))
7559a[7]

Holland Park *Conor Dore* a75 79
4 b g More Than Ready(USA) B Berry Brandy (USA) (Event Of The Year (USA))
703[11] 868[6]

Holler (AUS) *J O'Shea* 114
3 b c Commands(AUS) Shouts (AUS) (Strategic (AUS))
3385[7]

Hollie Point *Sylvester Kirk* a80 78
4 b m Dubawi(IRE) Camlet (Green Desert (USA))
324[3] 415[2] ◆ 564[5]

Hollow Crown *Denis Coakley* a45 48
2 gr f Beat Hollow Lady Friend (Environment Friend)
4154[9] 4659[7] 5304[13] 6963[11] 7734[10] 8025[4]

Hollybrowne (IRE) *John James Feane* a64 63
3 b f Holy Roman Emperor(IRE) Jazz Up (Cadeaux Genereux)
7339a[6]

Hollywood All Star (IRE) *Graeme McPherson* a41 42
7 b g Kheleyf(USA) Camassina (IRE) (Taufan (USA))
701[6]

Hollywood Harry (IRE) *Keith Dalgleish* a54 51
2 ch g Dandy Man(IRE) Alifandango (IRE) (Alzao (USA))
1921[8] 2956[6] 4829[5] 5840[4]

Hollywood Ken (IRE) *Keith Dalgleish* a55 68
3 b g Arcano(IRE) Third Dimension (FR) (Suave Dancer (USA))
1155[7]

Hollywood Road (IRE) *Don Cantillon* a82 87
3 b g Kodiac Rinneen (IRE) (Bien Bien (USA))
3823[2] 4288[2] 4743[2] (5122) (5603) 6301[6] 6870[6]

Hollywood Style *William Knight* a44 45
2 b f Royal Applause Brazilian Style (Exit To Nowhere (USA))
6732[5] 7465[10] 8230[6] 8467[10]

Holmeswood *Michael Dods* a85
2 b c Mayson Anglezarke (IRE) (Acclamation)
7599[2] (7988) ◆

Holy Cat (IRE) *M D O'Callaghan* 95
2 ch f Kitten's Joy(USA) Holy Freud (USA) (Freud (USA))
5940a[2] 6784[6]

Holy Grail (IRE) *Simon West* 88
3 b f Canford Cliffs(IRE) Dashing Beauty (IRE) (Daggers Drawn (USA))
1882[5] 2267[7] 3187[4] 3885[6] 4358[3] 4841[2] 5616[13] 6217[9] 6778[6] 6956[15]

Holy Lute (USA) *James Cassidy* a107 109
6 rg h Midnight Lute(USA) Holy Christmas (USA) (Holy Bull (USA))
7833a[6]

Holy Makfi *J-Y Artu* a78 87
2 b f Makfi Holy Moly (USA) (Rock Of Gibraltar (IRE))
4330a[6] (5142a) 6271a[6] 7086a[6] 7480a[8] 7879a[5]

Holy Roma *William Haggas* a59 54
2 b f Holy Roman Emperor(IRE) Tamalain (USA) (Royal Academy (USA))
6696[6] ◆ 7208[5] 7510[9]

Holy Romane (FR) *H-A Pantall* a8
2 b f Holy Roman Emperor(IRE) Careless Charlie (USA) (Johannesburg (USA))
7970a[12]

Holyroman Princess *Rod Millman* 55
2 b f Holy Roman Emperor(IRE) Princess Ellen (Tirol)
5250[5] 6062[7] 6648[5]

Holy Water (FR) *Stefano Botti* 93
2 b c Falco(USA) Miss Bikini (IRE) (Titus Livius (FR))
7839a[2]

Hombre Rojo (IRE) *Simon Dow* a92 68
3 b c Intikhab(USA) Sidney Girl (Azamour (IRE))
(123) (154) 539a[3] 839a[4]

Home Again *Lee Carter* a54 62
3 b g Bahamian Bounty Celestial Welcome (Most Welcome)
376[6] 610[10] 1238[7] 3319[11] 5721[7] 7463[6] 8121[10]

Home Cummins (IRE) *Richard Fahey* a98 99
4 b m Rip Van Winkle(IRE) Alava (IRE) (Anabaa (USA))
1871[12] 2089[6] 3152[1] 3585[3] (4183) 4737[3] 5976[6] 6372[5] 7121[2] 7650[3]

Homeland (IRE) *Brian Rothwell* 80
4 b g Galileo(IRE) Withorwithoutyou (IRE) (Danehill (USA))
1221[9] 1526[9] 3517[9] 4232[3] 4727[6] 6516[8] 6645[7] 7334[11]

Home Of The Brave (IRE) *Hugo Palmer* a101 118
4 ch h Starspangledbanner(AUS) Blissful Beat (Beat Hollow)
(1637) (2691) 4733[2] 5404[2] 7833a[11]

Honcho (IRE) *John Ryan* a71 68
4 gr g Dark Angel(IRE) Disco Lights (Spectrum (IRE))
782[6] 1040[11] 1150[6] 1838[4] 2217[6] 3153[5] 3674[3] 3907[5] 4100[9] 4741[8] 5039[7] 5408[4] 6269[8] 6418[5] 7817[3] 8156[12]

Honey Badger *Eugene Stanford* a60 62
5 bb g Pastoral Pursuits Taminoula (IRE) (Tagula (IRE))
1201[3] 1547[6] (3043) 3612[4] 4743[6] 5929[RR]

Honeymoon Cocktail (FR) *David Pipe* a73 70
5 gr g Martaline Caipirinia (FR) (Hawk Wing (USA))
273[3] 1391[7]

Honey Required *Alan Bailey* a38 23
4 b m Makfi Tiger Mist (IRE) (Galileo (IRE))
334[10] 939[9] 1145[8] 2365[9]

Honeysuckle Lil (IRE) *Tim Easterby* a47 84
4 b m Alfred Nobel(IRE) Twinberry (IRE) (Tagula (IRE))
2016[10] 2421[2] 3132[3] 3708[4] 4318[3] 4932[2] 5379[4] 6501[4] (6770) 7126[17] 7434[9]

Hongkong Adventure *Rae Guest* a68 49
3 b g Roderic O'Connor(IRE) Queen Margrethe (Grand Lodge (USA))
818[3] ◆ 1134[3] 2260[6] 2766[3]

Honiara *Paul Cole* a87 78
3 b c Rock Of Gibraltar(IRE) Indian Maiden (IRE) (Indian Ridge)
(2456a) 2948a[16] 4271[5] 5878[5]

Honiton Lace *Phil McEntee* a58 45
5 ch m Tobougg(IRE) Mellifluous (IRE) (Noverre (USA))
(356) 904[6] 1158[5] 1544[13]

Honorina *Sir Michael Stoute* a84 56
3 ch f Sea The Stars(IRE) Honorine (IRE) (Mark Of Esteem (IRE))
4367[8] (5504) 6246[2]

Honourable *Richard Fahey* a60 72
2 b f Rip Van Winkle(IRE) Honour (Dansili)
4609[4] 5221[2] 5885[3] 6791[2] 7147[7] 7658[4]

Honourable Knight (IRE) *Mark Usher* a41 36
8 b g Celtic Swing Deemeh (IRE) (Brief Truce (USA))
138[8] 348[9]

Honour Promise (IRE) *Bernard Llewellyn* a30 63
4 b m Jeremy(USA) Karenaragon (Aragon)
3747[7] 4082[10] 4482[4]

Hoofalong *Michael Easterby* a99 105
6 b g Pastoral Pursuits Baymist (Mind Games)
106[2] 288[11] (580) 677[4] 771[4] 1205[5] (1801) (3151) ◆ 4126[12] 4865[14] 5555[8] 6327[6] 6556[5] 7156[7]

Hoof It *Michael Easterby* a91 105
9 b g Monsieur Bond(IRE) Forever Bond (Danetime (IRE))
1218[5] 2158[6] 2485[12] 3188[7] (3890) 4338[2] (4862) 6558[3] 7156[3]

Hoofithully *Michael Easterby* a46 44
4 ch g Stimulation(IRE) Splicing (Sharpo)
252[5] ◆ 294[5]

Hooks Lane *Shaun Harris* a47 50
4 ch g Bertolini(USA) Zaville (Zafonic (USA))
1027[6] 1622[11] 2307[9] 6478[4] ◆ 7262[6] 8180[8] 8497[11]

Hoonose *Emma Owen*
7 ch g Cadeaux Genereux Roodeye (Inchinor)
796[11] 1043[4]

Hoover Fever *David Evans* 53
2 b f Compton Place Aswaaq (IRE) (Peintre Celebre (USA))
4907[10] 5951[4] 6376[4]

Hope Against Hope (IRE) *Mark Johnston* a45 66
2 b f Dark Angel(IRE) Hope Of An Angel (IRE) (Intikhab (USA))
2173[8] 2417[2] 2739[2] 4002[5] 5707[7] 6420[9] (7228) ◆

Hope Cove *Ed Walker* a82 86
3 b g Shamardal(USA) Deveron (USA) (Cozzene (USA))
1442[4] 1865[4] 3571[6] 4086[2] 4569[5] 6883[4] 7443[5]

Hope Is High *John Berry* a55 58
3 b f Sir Percy Altitude (Green Desert (USA))
4567[2] ◆ (5011) 5625[3] 6738[3]

Hope Solo (IRE) *Tim Easterby* 79
2 ch f Dutch Art In Safe Hands (IRE) (Intikhab (USA))
3261[6] ◆ 3597[2] (4133) 4394[17]

Hope You Dance (FR) *David Simcock* a72 64
4 ch m Mastercraftsman(IRE) Anna Of Dubai (GER) (Dubai Destination (USA))
44[5] 342[4] 636[2] 838[3] 2149[5] 2564[2] 3302[3] 3825[3]

Hoppertunity (USA) *Bob Baffert* a118
5 b h Any Given Saturday(USA) Refugee (USA) (Unaccounted For (USA))
1108a[3] 7838a[4]

Horatia The Fleet *Willie Musson* a47
3 ch f Bahamian Bounty Countermarch (Selkirk (USA))
402[6] 3033[12]

Hornsby *Charlie Appleby* 98
3 b g Dubawi(IRE) Moonlife (IRE) (Invincible Spirit (IRE))
(3600) 4149[3] 4867[4] ◆ 6918[7]

Horrah *Roger Charlton* a14 82
3 b g Royal Applause Aegean Shadow (Sakhee (USA))
1622[4] 2999[5] (3572) 4271[4] 5743[6]

Horroob *Roger Varian* 80
2 b c Showcasing Funny Enough (Dansili)
4161[3]

Hors De Combat *James Fanshawe* a84 111
5 ch g Mount Nelson Maid For Winning (USA) (Gone West (USA))
1774[5] 2191[10] 3273[24] 4399[2] 4823[14] 6075[5]

Horseguardsparade *Nigel Twiston-Davies* a76 71
5 b g Montjeu(IRE) Honorlina (FR) (Linamix (FR))
200[5] 273[6] 864[2] 2445[8] 3221[3] 3746[4]

Horse Of Fortune (SAF) *A T Millard* 115
5 b g Stronghold Sweet Virginia (SAF) (Casey Tibbs (IRE))
1690a[11] 8333a[6]

Horseplay *Andrew Balding* 95
2 b f Cape Cross(IRE) Mischief Making (USA) (Lemon Drop Kid (USA))
4579[4] (7285) ◆

Horsforth *Richard Guest* a71 71
4 b m Kyllachy Lady McBeth (IRE) (Avonbridge)
2856[9] 4228[7] 4968[3] 6341[14] 6451[11] (6910) 6958[7] 7290[3] (7534) (7774) 8010[4] 8137[3] 8390[2]

Horsted Keynes (FR) *David Simcock* a103 96
6 ch g Giant's Causeway(USA) Viking's Cove (USA) (Miswaki (USA))
166[6] 290[13] 503[9]

Hortense Mancini *Mark Bradstock* 32
7 ch m King's Best(USA) Have Fun (Indian Ridge)
3094[9]

Hot Beat (IRE) *David Simcock* a94 97
4 b g Dylan Thomas(IRE) Hungry Heart (IRE) (Hawk Wing (USA))
8123[5]

Hotfill *David Barron* a70 65
2 b g Showcasing Reel Cool (Reel Buddy (USA))
2417[7] 4765[12] 6099[2] ◆ 6534[5] 7319[7] 8008[5] 8398[3]

Hot Gossip (IRE) *Dianne Sayer*
2 b f Fast Company(IRE) On The Make (IRE) (Entrepreneur)
2570[10]

Hot Hannah *Michael Dods* a63 70
2 gr f Hellvelyn Toy Top (USA) (Tactical Cat (USA))
4601[12] 5067[3] 5756[5] 6564[4] (6807) 7313[4]

Hot Lick *Andrew Balding* a53
2 b g Phoenix Reach(IRE) Sweet Mandolin (Soviet Star (USA))
7865[14] 7977[10] 8340[10]

Hot Mustard *William Muir* a73 81
6 b g Pastoral Pursuits Lihou Island (Beveled (USA))
1916[4] 2577[3] 3124[5] 3957[4] 4317[4] 4776[11] 5627[3] 6021[6] 7417[5]

Hot N Sassy (IRE) *J S Moore* a33 49
2 ch f Arcano(IRE) Cheeky Weeky (Cadeaux Genereux)
1086[4] 1233[6] 2125[6] 2724a[9] 3232[7] 4524[6] 4937[6] 6313[9] 6366[5]

Hototo *Fawzi Abdulla Nass* a55 110
6 ch g Sleeping Indian Harlem Dancer (Dr Devious (IRE))
450a[15] 626a[14]

Hot Sauce (IRE) *John Joseph Murphy* a89 97
4 ch m Peintre Celebre(USA) Heat (King's Best (USA))
1940a[4] 2512a[5]

Hot Spice *Michael Easterby* a17 84
8 b g Kodiac Harlestone Lady (Shaamit (IRE))
3659[11] 4311[6] 4892[6]

Hot Stuff *Tony Carroll* a66 63
3 b g Assertive Even Hotter (Desert Style (IRE))
286[4] 460[2] 883[2] 1167[2] 1761[3] 2503[5] 3994[17] 7793[3] 8290[7]

Hound Music *Jonathan Portman* a60 79
4 ch m Ashkalani(IRE) Saffron Fox (Safawan)
(1455) 1919[3] 2753[5] 3690[6] 4356[6]

Houndstooth (IRE) *Luca Cumani* a73 73
2 b c Dream Ahead(USA) Baileys Gleam (Compton Place)
5371[9] 6053[3] 7071[3] 7527[3]

House Of Commons (IRE) *Michael Appleby* a84 48
3 b g Sea The Stars(IRE) Reality (FR) (Slickly (FR))
(2835) 3465[6] 5765[7] 7462[7] 8343[3]

House Of Dixie (USA) *J-C Rouget* a90 87
3 b f War Front(USA) Homebound (USA) (Dixie Union (USA))
2141a[3]

House Of Frauds (IRE) *Tony Newcombe* a35
8 b g Storming Home Bogus Penny (IRE) (Pennekamp (USA))
8212[6]

Housesofparliament (IRE) *A P O'Brien* a90 115
3 ch g Galileo(IRE) Sharp Lisa (USA) (Dixieland Band (USA))
1994[3] 2510a[4] 3337[4] (4059) 5557[2] 6329[3]

Hout Bay (FR) *Mario Hofer* a72 83
3 bb c Whipper(USA) Iocaste (GER) (Acatenango (GER))
5385a[2]

How (IRE) *A P O'Brien* 87
2 b f Galileo(IRE) Lillie Langtry (IRE) (Danehill Dancer (IRE))
4623[6]

How About Zero (USA) *Doug O'Neill* 63
2 ch f Square Eddie(CAN) Too Much Excess (USA) (Inexcess (IRE))
8127a[10]

Howard Be Thy Name (AUS) *Darren Weir* 103
3 b c Redoute's Choice(AUS) Bellini Rose (NZ) (Faltaat (USA))
7637a[5] 7826a[6]

Howardian Hills (IRE) *Richard Hannon* a69 61
3 b g Vale Of York(IRE) Handsome Anna (IRE) (Bigstone (IRE))
691[6] 880[4] 1037[3] 1532[5] 2126[6] 2700[6]

How High The Moon (IRE) *A P O'Brien* a97 94
3 b f Fastnet Rock(AUS) Quarter Moon (IRE) (Sadler's Wells (USA))
2167a[4] 3202a[8] 3539a[3] 6200a[9] 6604a[6] 7196a[6] 7392a[5] 7676a[3]

Howliat (USA) *Charlie Appleby* a71 60
3 b f Cape Cross(IRE) Vine Street (IRE) (Singspiel (IRE))
4840[5] 6239[3] 6661[6]

How's Lucy *Jane Chapple-Hyam* a51 50
2 b f Approve(IRE) Murielle (Diktat)
2793[9] 6782[8] 7696[11] 8046[2] 8276[8]

Hoyamy *David O'Meara* 74
2 b f Dark Angel(IRE) Viola D'Amour (IRE) (Teofilo (IRE))
(1621)

Hubal (POL) *George Charlton*
4 b g Safety Wire(IRE) Hebra (POL) (Who Knows I (IRE))
3706[13]

Hubertas *John Quinn* a54 94
4 b g Lord Of England(GER) Western Eyes (IRE) (Rock Of Gibraltar (IRE))
1250[2] ◆ 1852[5] 2439[2] 2897[6] 3602[2] (5963) 6566[3]

Huda (FR) *M Le Forestier* a66 69
3 b f Equiano(FR) Leni Riefenstahl (IRE) (Mull Of Kintyre (USA))
2282a[13] 5907a[5]

Huddersfilly Town *Ivan Furtado* a48
2 b f Major Cadeaux Mortitia (Dansili)
7792[6]

Hueston *Conor O'Dwyer* a71 67
2 b c Frozen Power(IRE) Break Of Dawn (USA) (Mt. Livermore (USA))
5798[4]

Huge Future *Saeed bin Suroor* a89 103
3 b c Shamardal(USA) Time Honoured (Sadler's Wells (USA))
2248[4] ◆ (2914) (3557) 6581[2] 7538[5]

Hugging The Rails (IRE) *Tim Easterby* a44 63
2 b g Royal Applause Aqraan (In The Wings)
2649[12] 3854[5] 4423[5] ◆ 6130[7] 6791[7] 8071[8]

Hugie Boy (IRE) *Scott Dixon* 68
4 ch g Art Connoisseur(IRE) Piece Unique (Barathea (IRE))
4544[12]

Hulcolt (IRE) *Ivan Furtado* a44 85
5 b g Acclamation Fusili (IRE) (Silvano (GER))
1924[4] (2121) 2628[7] 3518[13] 4453[5] 5514[8] 5866[10] 6521[6] 7108[13]

Human Nature (IRE) *Saeed bin Suroor* 83
3 b g Kodiac Sundown (Polish Precedent (USA))
5881[6]

Humbert (IRE) *Hugo Palmer* 82
2 b c Kodiac Fee Eria (FR) (Always Fair (USA))
5477[2] 6388a[6]

Humidor (IRE) *George Baker* a86 105
9 b g Camacho Miss Indigo (Indian Ridge)
1862[17] 2546[10] 2895[13] 3386[17] 3909[9] 4735[4] 5961[2] 6327[2] 6779[9] 7242[3] 7537[11] 7771[5]

Humour (IRE) *Christine Dunnett* a71 59
5 b g Invincible Spirit(IRE) Hucking Hot (Desert Prince (IRE))
271[5] 541[8] 775[6] 1676[3] 2013[5] 7062[13] 7445[U] (7488) 7774[9] 7912[7] 8181[8] 8457[4]

Humphrey Bogart (IRE) *Richard Hannon* a99 107
3 b g Tagula(IRE) Hazarama (IRE) (Kahyasi)
1208[4] 1567[2] (2036) 2896[5] 3337[6] 4173a[9] 5402[4]

Humphry Repton *Mark H Tompkins* a25 53
4 b g Virtual Qilin (IRE) (Second Set (IRE))
277[6]

Hundred Acre Wood *Sandy Thomson* a39 37
6 b g Modigliani(USA) Bom Chicka Wah Wah (USA) (Dynaformer (USA))
5227[10] 5783[7] 6102[9]

Hungerford *Eve Johnson Houghton* a68 74
4 b g Pastoral Pursuits Truly Pink (Mr Greeley (USA))
5649[7] 6645[4] 7653[5] 8100[9] 8254[4] 8462[13]

Hunters Point (IRE) *John C McConnell* 52
3 b c Holy Roman Emperor(IRE) Fairy Dance (IRE) (Zafonic (USA))
1014a[14]

Hunting Ground (USA) *S bin Ghadayer* a103 80
6 b g Street Cry(IRE) Panty Raid (USA) (Include (USA))
94a[3] 188a[5] 722a[4]

Huntlaw *Mark Johnston* a95 99
3 b g Oasis Dream Attraction (Efisio)
(1662) 2654[11] 2907[8] (4408) 4654[7] (5437) 6372[2] (6710)

Huntsmans Close *Robert Cowell* a97 103
6 b g Elusive Quality(USA) Badminton (Zieten (USA))
1887[11] 2434[2] 3386[21] 5961[5] 6207[U] 7068[7] 7537[19] 8050[3] ◆ 8192[12] 8484[8]

Hurricane (FR) *J-C Rouget* a103 102
3 bb g Hurricane Cat(USA) Monatora (FR) (Hector Protector (USA))
972a[2] 3183a[4]

Hurricane Alert *Mark Hoad* a47 49
4 b g Showcasing Raggle Taggle (IRE) (Tagula (IRE))
1913[10] 2953a[6] 3970[13] 4264[8] 4658[4] 5335[4] 6865[5] 7863[8] 8409[9]

Hurricane Cass (IRE) *T Stack* a96 86
4 b g Hurricane Run(IRE) Rahya Cass (IRE) (Rahy (USA))
3084a[8]

Hurricane Red (IRE) *Lennart Reuterskiold Jr* a105 104
6 ch h Hurricane Run(IRE) Bounce (FR) (Trempolino (USA))
(1957a) (4329a) 5187a[5] 5950a[2] 6390a[2]

Hurricane Rock *Simon Dow* a56 66
3 ch g Rock Of Gibraltar(IRE) Seasonal Cross (Cape Cross (IRE))
7011[3] ◆ 7616[7]

Hurricane Rush (IRE) *Charles Hills* a76 88
2 b c Helmet(AUS) Without Precedent (FR) (Polish Precedent (USA))
3058[8] 3730[2] 4304[2] (5959) 6455[3]

Hurricane Volta (IRE) *Peter Hedger* a68 71
5 ch g Hurricane Run(IRE) Haute Volta (FR) (Grape Tree Road)
(1169) 1413[2] (1778) 2501[2] 2887[2] 4012[6] 4637[3] 5597[2] 6356a[11] 7274[11]

Hurry Home Poppa (IRE) *John Mackie* a71 74
6 b g Holy Roman Emperor(IRE) My Renee (USA) (Kris S (USA))
1760[3] 2502[2] (2887) 3602[4] 3903[6] 6565[8] 7332[3] ◆ 7592[5]

Hushood (IRE) *Richard Hannon* 83
2 b c Champs Elysees Cochin (USA) (Swain (IRE))
5356[6] ◆ (5952) 6499[4]

Hussar Ballad (USA) *Antony Brittain* a73 55
7 b g Hard Spun(USA) Country Melody (USA) (Gone West (USA))
38[9] 890[9] 1399[9] 2343[10] 2618[3] ◆ 3342[5] 5130[2] 5841[11] 7435[9]

Hutton (IRE) *Richard Fahey* a75 68
3 b g Lawman(FR) Moynsha Lady (IRE) (Namid)
(600) 1080[12] 1381[5]

Hyde Park *John Gosden* 94
2 b g Oasis Dream Deliberate (King's Best (USA))
2756[6] 3408[2] 4103[3] 6486[6] (7495)

Hydrangea (IRE) *A P O'Brien* 112
2 b f Galileo(IRE) Beauty Is Truth (IRE) (Pivotal)
5686a[2] 6385a[2] 7116[2] 7809a[14]

Hydrant *Richard Guest* a67 67
10 b g Haafhd Spring (Sadler's Wells (USA))
446[7] 569[9] 940[4] 1201[13] 1248[5] 1697[6] 2365[4] 2958[3] (3253) 3498[5] (3620) 3901[5] 5293[7] 7078[4] 7614[11] 8142[9] 8410[2] 8567[7] 8586[10]

Hydroxide *Hugo Palmer* a73 84
2 b c Lope De Vega(IRE) Craighall (Dubawi (IRE))
4649[2] ◆ 6262[2] ◆ 6655[2] 7074[3]

Hygrove Percy *Neil Mulholland* 73
3 ch g Sir Percy Hygrove Welshlady (IRE) (Langfuhr (CAN))
1738[10] 2749[9]

Hyland Heather (IRE) *Richard Fahey* a73 83
3 b f Lilbourne Lad(IRE) Maidservant (USA) (Seeking The Gold (USA))
2681[2] 3643[2] 3879[4] 4547[3] 5748[2] (6218) 8233[4] 8561[7]

Hymn For The Dudes *John Berry* a52 50
3 br g Sakhee's Secret Hermione's Dream (Oasis Dream)
2784[3] ◆

Hyper Dream (IRE) *Hugo Palmer* a76
2 b f Oasis Dream Virginia Waters (USA) (Kingmambo (USA))
6897[2] ◆ 7277[4]

Hyperfocus (IRE) *Hugo Palmer* a87 86
2 bb c Intense Focus(USA) Jouel (FR) (Machiavellian (USA))
(1635) ◆ 2865[4] (3562) 4150[9]

Hyper Hyper *Mario Hofer* a76 95
2 b c Fastnet Rock(AUS) Guerande (IRE) (Diesis)
4925a[5] 7170a[2] 8564a[8]

Hyperlink (IRE) *Heather Dalton* a66 6
7 b g Cape Cross(IRE) Surf The Web (IRE) (Ela-Mana-Mou)
786[4] 1136[7] 2338[9]

Hyzenthlay (IRE) *Joseph Patrick O'Brien* a70 74
2 b f Henrythenavigator(USA) Anka Britannia (USA) (Irish River (FR))
2494a[8] 2718a[10] 4171a[11]

I Am (IRE) *John Gosden* 65
3 b f Galileo(IRE) Nausicaa (USA) (Diesis)
2312[5]

I Am Charlie (FR) *J-P Gauvin* a99 74
3 bb f Great Journey(JPN) Freedom Sweet (FR) (Sicyos (USA))
8148a[5] 8563a[4]

I Am Not Here (IRE) *Brian Ellison* a89 88
5 b g Amadeus Wolf Newgate Lodge (IRE) (Namid)
1202[2] 1561[2] 2043[2] 3118[2] (3345) 4940[6] (5157) 6566[2] 6876[4] 7869[3] (8283)

Ian's Memory (USA) *Jeremy Noseda* a101 50
5 b h Smart Strike(CAN) Rite Moment (USA) (Vicar (USA))
599[2] 960[6] 4976[8]

Iballisticvin *Gary Moore* a70 66
3 b g Rail Link Guntakal (IRE) (Night Shift (USA))
1930[13] 2294[6] 3765[4] (5019) 5625[7] 6411[2] (6871) (7039) 7692[2] 7969[3]

Ibazz *G Botti* a92 89
3 b f Kyllachy Quite Elusive (USA) (Elusive Quality (USA))
8148a[10]

Ibergman (IRE) *Ms Sheila Lavery* 94
4 b m Big Bad Bob(IRE) Casablanca Jewel (IRE) (Kalanisi (IRE))
1018a[10] 1509a[6] 4812a[3] 6604a[8] 7392a[4] 7558a[4]

Iberica Road (USA) *Andrew Balding* a82 75
3 bb g Quality Road(USA) Field Of Clover (CAN) (Bluegrass Cat (USA))
3572[9] 4156[6] 4840[4] 5336[4] 6084[3] (6703) 8077[6] 8177[15]

Ibiza Empress (IRE) *C Von Der Recke*
3 b f Tertullian(USA) Ibiza Dream (Night Shift (USA))
1357a[6]

Ibn Malik (IRE) *Charles Hills* 112
3 ch g Raven's Pass(USA) Moon's Whisper (USA) (Storm Cat (USA))
(1424) 3269[4] 4393[9]

I Call The Shots *Ollie Pears* 25
2 b g Delegator Nellie Ellis (IRE) (Compton Place)
2301[9] 3772[11] 6446[14]

Icalo (FR) *H-A Pantall* 90
2 b c Scalo Indyca (GER) (Panis (USA))
(4330a) 5186a[6]

I Can't Stop *Milton Bradley* a62
3 gr f Kyllachy Vellena (Lucky Story (USA))
691[2] 1036[4] 8320[9]

Ice Age (IRE) *Eve Johnson Houghton* a78 88
3 b g Frozen Power(IRE) Incendio (Siberian Express (USA))
(1091) 1809[4] 2002[3] 2650[5] 3466[4] 4116[4] (4460) 4910[3] 5488[3] 5825[3] 6583[2] 7186[3]

Ice Alert (IRE) *John Ryan* a71 55
3 b g Frozen Power(IRE) Karenka (IRE) (Arakan (USA))
40[6] 1816[5] 5720[5] 6241[11] 6662[9] (6857) 7048[P]

Iceaxe *John Holt* a58 71
3 b f Stimulation(IRE) Laser Crystal (IRE) (King's Theatre (IRE))
1319[2] (1670) 2049[5] 2373[5] 2856[4] 3353[3] 4365[3] 5195[4] (5732) 6453[6] 7111[9]

Icebuster *Rod Millman* a81 86
8 ch g Iceman Radiate (Sadler's Wells (USA))
172[9] 566[2] 766[2] 899[4] 1737[2] 2296[7] 2699[2] (3766) 4208[7] 4793[3] 5650[8]

Icecapada (IRE) *Niels Petersen* a82 95
4 gr m Mastercraftsman(IRE) Bounce (FR) (Trempolino (USA))
451a[5] 809a[4] 1907a[4] 3449a[3] 6390a[3] 7395a[2]

Ice Cristal (IRE) *Sylvester Kirk* a26
3 ch f Frozen Power(IRE) Cristalita (IRE) (Entrepreneur)
122[7] 591[8]

Icefall (IRE) *Tim Easterby* 91
3 b g Frozen Power(IRE) Silvertine (IRE) (Alzao (USA))
1411[4] 2224[11] (4372) (4949) 5420[2] 5653[7] 6134[2] (6474) 7123[14]

Ice Galley (IRE) *Kevin Ryan* a70 76
3 br g Galileo(IRE) Ice Queen (IRE) (Danehill Dancer (IRE))
1784[3] 2260[3] 2858[2] 3607[4] 6474[5] 7043[11]

Ice Konig (FR) *Jimmy Frost* a46 48
7 gr g Epalo(GER) Isarwelle (GER) (Sternkoenig (IRE))
4226[7]

Ice Lord (IRE) *Clive Cox* 96
4 gr g Verglas(IRE) Special Lady (FR) (Kaldoun (FR))
1530[2] 1990[5] (2547) 3671[14] 6556[20] 7186[15]

Ice Royal (IRE) *Jamie Osborne* a90 90
3 b g Frozen Power(IRE) Salford Princess (IRE) (Titus Livius (FR))
171[2] ◆ 366[2] 495[2] 705[2] 887[2] 2818[2] 3523[7] 4132[4] ◆ (4532) 4976[7]

Ice Slice (IRE) *James Eustace* a81 98
5 b g Dark Angel(IRE) Ice Rock (IRE) (Rock Of Gibraltar (IRE))
1241[4] (1546) (1946) (2010) (2689) 3855[3] (4917) 5640[4] 6109[11] 7121[4]

Icespire *John Gosden* 83
2 b f Frankel Quest To Peak (USA) (Distant View (USA))
(7210) ◆

Ickymasho *Jonathan Portman* a85 89
4 b m Multiplex Icky Woo (Mark Of Esteem (IRE))
1825[3] (2564) 3257[2] (4383) (5489) 5963[10]

Iconic (IRE) *Henry Candy* a74 90
4 b m Kodiac Christa Maria (Alhaarth (IRE))
2378[9] (3061) 5866[11] 6710[5] 7550[3]

Iconic Belle *Mick Channon* 78
2 ch f Sixties Icon Five Bells (IRE) (Rock Of Gibraltar (IRE))
3812[7] 4603[2] 5036[5] 5266[5]

Iconic Figure (IRE) *Steve Gollings* a72 69
3 b g Approve(IRE) Tough Chic (IRE) (Indian Ridge)
177[3] 1151[4] 1829[3] 2255[2]

Iconic Sky *Lucy Wadham* a61 65
3 gr f Sixties Icon Kentucky Sky (Cloudings (IRE))
4367[12] 5163[3] 6239[4] 6659[6]

Icons Image *Alan Bailey* a43 40
3 ch g Sixties Icon Marrimeclaire (IRE) (Spartacus (IRE))
1140[11] 1426[10] 2008[12] 5263[6] 6966[7]

Icy Blue *Adam West* a45 57
8 b g Iceman Bridal Path (Groom Dancer (USA))
4444[8] 6140[4] 6512[14] 7529[10]

Idaho (IRE) *A P O'Brien* 120
3 b c Galileo(IRE) Hveger (AUS) (Danehill (USA))
1370a[2] 2069a[3] 2896[3] 3679a[2] (5557) 6329[U] 7405a[5]

I Dare To Dream *Lisa Williamson* a52 54
2 b f Mullionmileanhour(IRE) Shaymee's Girl (Wizard King)
5242[11] 5722[11] 6413[8] 6762[6] 7275[9] 7749[10]

Ideal Bounty (IRE) *Andrew Crook* a54 64
2 ch c Bahamian Bounty Dance Company (Aussie Rules (USA))
5029[8] 6789[2] 7381[7] 7578[13]

Idealist *Roger Varian* 75
3 b f Rip Van Winkle(IRE) Illusion (Anabaa (USA))
2312[4] 2653[5] (3264)

Identity Run Fast (IRE) *A Marcialis* a91 91
3 b f Footstepsinthesand Tipperary Boutique (IRE) (Danehill Dancer (IRE))
5006a[5] 7492a[6]

Idler (IRE) *A bin Harmash* a85 91
7 b g Exceed And Excel(AUS) Dilly Dally (AUS) (Rubiton (AUS))
229a[7]

Idle Talker (IRE) *Nick Gifford* a66 56
4 b g Dandy Man(IRE) Special Pearl (IRE) (Alhaarth (IRE))
8257[12]

Idol Deputy (FR) *James Bennett* a82 47
10 gr g Silver Deputy(CAN) Runaway Venus (USA) (Runaway Groom (CAN))
73[3] 465[8] (595) 788[5] 1001[9] 1166[6] 5082[7] 5246[5] 6138[7] 7911[12] 8101[4] 8343[6]

I Don't Believe It *Micky Hammond* a26 47
2 ch g Choisir(AUS) Special Destiny (Tobougg (IRE))
4508[6] 6009[7] 6682[7] 7777[6]

Idyllic (IRE) *Sir Michael Stoute* 58
3 b f Rip Van Winkle(IRE) Cilium (IRE) (War Chant (USA))
1931[7] 4983[3]

Ifan (IRE) *Tim Vaughan* a58 71
8 b g Ivan Denisovich(IRE) Montana Miss (IRE) (Earl Of Barking (IRE))
438[6] 566[12] 766[8] 982[11] (1747) 2086[2] 3738[5] 5264[4]

Ifandbutwhynot (IRE) *Tim Easterby* 60
10 b g Raise A Grand(IRE) Cockney Ground (IRE) (Common Grounds)
2858[3]

Iffranesia (FR) *Robert Cowell* a77 105
6 ch m Iffraaj Farnesina (FR) (Anabaa (USA))
1453[12] 1862[20] 2943a[4] 3909[6] 5614[16] 6384a[3] 6943[6]

I Fight For Kisses (GER) *Carina Fey* a84 59
8 ch g Ransom O'War(USA) Ice Lodge (GER) (Grand Lodge (USA))
7295a[5]

If I Say So *J S Moore* a73 77
2 b g Sayif(IRE) Glen Molly (IRE) (Danetime (IRE))
2822[11] 3404[5] 3986[4] 4270[16] 5120[2] 5279a[2] 5568a[2] 5988a[5] 7293a[2] (7422a)

Iftikaar (IRE) *Philip Kirby* a52 71
6 b g Cape Cross(IRE) Anbella (FR) (Common Grounds)
1565[4] ◆ 2046[4] 2555[9]

Iftiraaq (IRE) *Seamus Durack* a81 85
5 b g Muhtathir Alzaroof (USA) (Kingmambo (USA))
(1737) 2897[4] 4752[17]

Iftitah (IRE) *George Peckham* a65 46
2 b g Harbour Watch(IRE) Solstice (Dubawi (IRE))
1384[6] 2295[4] 2543[6] 5675[5] 6222[8] (6895) (7109) 7688[8]

Ifubelieveindreams (IRE) *Ismail Mohammed* a66
2 b f Iffraaj Oratrix (IRE) (Oratorio (IRE))
8362[4]

Ifwecan *Martin Smith* a95 97
5 b g Exceed And Excel(AUS) Kirk (Selkirk (USA))
2628[10] 3358[4] 4104[2] 4399[3] 5174[3] 5934[3]

Iggy Chop (FR) *C Boutin* 70
2 b c Captain Chop(FR) Via Appia (FR) (Exit To Nowhere (USA))
5568a[4] 5985a[6]

Ignacio Zuloaga (IRE) *Jo Hughes* a42
2 ch c Lope De Vega(IRE) Indian Express (Indian Ridge)
8305[8]

Ignight *Matthew Salaman* a38 42
5 ch g Compton Place Time Clash (Timeless Times (USA))
4484[7] 5282[6] 5605[8] 5953[12] 6444[10]

Iguacu *Richard Price* a49 45
12 b g Desert Prince(IRE) Gay Gallanta (USA) (Woodman (USA))
592[3] ◆ 946[8]

Iguazu Falls (USA) *A bin Harmash* a88 108
11 ch g Pivotal Anna Palariva (IRE) (Caerleon (USA))
375a[10]

Ihaveadream (POL) *W Mongil* a48 61
3 ch f October(USA) Irkucja (POL) (Royal Court (IRE))
4220a[3] 5280a[13]

Ijmaaly (IRE) *Saeed bin Suroor* a104 93
4 ch g Makfi Wedding Gown (Dubai Destination (USA))
(7779)

Ikc Moneypenny (USA) *Cathrine Erichsen* 78
4 b m Henrythenavigator(USA) Money Madam (USA) (A.P. Indy (USA))
3448a[5]

Ikerrin Road (IRE) *John Quinn* a87 93
3 b c Iffraaj Fantastic Spring (USA) (Fantastic Light (USA))
(639) 924[2] ◆ (1115) (1865) 3165[3]

Illaunmore (USA) *John Gosden* a79 59
2 bb f Shamardal(USA) Illaunglass (IRE) (Red Clubs (IRE))
2885[7] (7049) 7698[9]

I'll Be Good *Brian Ellison* a72 86
7 b g Red Clubs(IRE) Willisa (Polar Falcon (USA))
4100[11] 5296[2] (6324) ◆ 6537[13] 7358[5] 7413[2] ◆ 7892[10] 8561[10]

I'll Be Your Clown (IRE) *A Oliver* 92
5 b g Aqlaam Lady Avenger (IRE) (Namid)
4070a[7]

Illegally Blonde (IRE) *Jamie Osborne* a92 67
3 b f Lawman(FR) Kayak (Singspiel (IRE))
185a[5] 536a[5] 881[4] 1070[9] 8314[12]

Illuminate (IRE) *Richard Hannon* 113
3 b f Zoffany(IRE) Queen Of Stars (USA) (Green Desert (USA))
1888[14] 3338[5] 4393[10]

Illusive (IRE) *George Scott* a91 94
5 b g Galileo(IRE) Looking Back (IRE) (Stravinsky (USA))
749[5] ◆ 2017[6] 2752[9] 4300[6] (4868) 5874[7] 6489[5]

Illusive Force (IRE) *Derek Shaw* a65 60
4 ch g Iffraaj Geesala (IRE) (Barathea (IRE))
866[8] 959[5] 1152[9] 1416[9] 1654[5] 2330[3] 2610[2] 3220[10] (3474) 3987[2] 4715[3] 5503[10] 6047[9]

Illustration (IRE) *George Margarson* a56 71
8 b g Pivotal In Anticipation (IRE) (Sadler's Wells (USA))
5261[7]

Illustrious Prince (IRE) *Julie Camacho* a69 72
9 b g Acclamation Sacred Love (IRE) (Barathea (IRE))
1047[8] 1317[3] 1925[8] 2330[4] 3327[8] 3564[10]

Illustrissime (USA) *Roger Fell* a90 94
3 b g Mizzen Mast(USA) Ghost Friendly (USA) (Ghostzapper (USA))
(5349a) 6675[8] 7005[3] 7699[5]

Illyrio (IRE) *J Phelippon* 58
3 ch g Rip Van Winkle(IRE) Intarsia (GER) (Pentire)
7265a[6]

Ilovetoboogie (FR) *S Wattel* a61 34
2 ch f Kendargent(FR) Mark Of Brazil (FR) (Mark Of Esteem (IRE))
3763a[10]

Il Piccolo Grande (IRE) *James Tate* a79 79
3 ch c Iffraaj Soxy Doxy (IRE) (Hawk Wing (USA))
2412[6] 6580[8]

Il Sassicaia *Marco Botti* a66
3 b g Dick Turpin(IRE) Step Fast (USA) (Giant's Causeway (USA))
458[5] 613[4] 789[7] 1234[3]

Il Segreto (FR) *C Delcher-Sanchez* a93 101
4 ch h Turtle Bowl(IRE) Camille's Secret (FR) (Oasis Dream)
660a[3]

Il Sicario (IRE) *Mark Johnston* 63
2 b g Zebedee Starring (FR) (Ashkalani (IRE))
1635[6] 2648[11] 3248[4]

Ilzam (IRE) *Marco Botti* a84 74
3 b g Holy Roman Emperor(IRE) Let's Pretend (Rainbow Quest (USA))
171[5] 557[3] (924) 1267[4] ◆ 1750[2] 2099[8] 3824[9] (4717) 5246[6] 7204[4]

I'm A Chatterbox (USA) *J Larry Jones* a116
4 ch m Munnings(USA) Chit Chatter (USA) (Lost Soldier (USA))
7810a[5]

Imaginary *Heather Main* 32
3 ch f Mount Nelson Follow My Dream (Kyllachy)
1609[10] 2182[11] 6239[7]

Imagine If (IRE) *G M Lyons* 83
2 br g Dream Ahead(USA) Bogini (IRE) (Holy Roman Emperor (IRE))
7387a[2]

Imago Live (IRE) *N Minner* a53
8 b g Docksider(USA) Secret Live (IRE) (Mukaddamah (USA))
5452a[12]

Imari Kid (IRE) *Gary Moore* 78
3 b g Pour Moi(IRE) Breathe (FR) (Ocean Of Wisdom (USA))
2414[12] 3104[4] 3914[3] ◆ 4628[5] (6665)

Imasumaq (IRE) *Marco Botti* a49
3 b f Teofilo(IRE) Miss Dela (IRE) (King's Best (USA))
7727[5] 8048[6]

Imdancinwithurwife (IRE) *Tom Dascombe* a69 41
2 b f Sir Prancealot(IRE) Bishop's Lake (Lake Coniston (IRE))
1118a[10] (1342)

Im Dapper Too *John Davies* a62 66
5 b g Dapper Lonely One (Perryston View)
1047[4] ◆ 1631[3] 5887[5] (6226) 7007[7] 7601[5]

I'm Harry *George Baker* a75 83
7 b g Haafhd First Approval (Royal Applause)
164[3] ◆ 491[7] 773[2] 832[2] 1751[2] 2374[4] 3064[5] 4383[7]

Imjin River (IRE) *William Stone* a54 43
9 b g Namid Lady Nasrana (FR) (Al Nasr (FR))
339[2] 513[2] 579[2] 937[2] 1026[2] 1709[4] 3260[6] 3822[9] 8383[9]

Immediate *Robert Cowell* a75 89
4 b m Oasis Dream Emergency (Dr Fong (USA))
2787[8] 4585[8] 5205[4] 6699[4] 7030a[5]

Impassable (IRE) *C Laffon-Parias* a81 118
4 b m Invincible Spirit(IRE) Gwenseb (FR) (Green Tune (USA))
3451a[2] 4926a[7]

Impassioned *Sir Mark Prescott Bt* a63
2 ch f Bahamian Bounty Ardent (Pivotal)
3881[10] 5242[5] 7259[7] 7749[2] 7981[8]

Impeccability *John Mackie* a46 51
6 b m Lucky Story(USA) Impeccable Guest (IRE) (Orpen (USA))
1136[4] 3067[2] 4499[7] 4724[2] 5319[4] 6102[7] 6422[7]

Impediment (IRE) *Sir Michael Stoute* a63 69
3 ch g Pivotal Pediment (Desert Prince (IRE))
1602[8] 2545[2]

Imperial Aviator *Roger Charlton* a81 105
3 b c Paco Boy(IRE) Telescopic (Galileo (IRE))
(1639) (2244) ◆ 2946a[15] 5557[5] 6573[3] 7546[4]

Imperial City (USA) *Charles Hills* a61 65
2 ch f City Zip(USA) Imperial Pippin (USA) (Empire Maker (USA))
4011[5] ◆ 4762[6] 6016[3] 7570[2] 7974[6]

Imperial Focus (IRE) *Simon Waugh* 78
3 b g Intense Focus(USA) Mrs Cee (IRE) (Orpen (USA))
2835[2] 3264[3] 3951[2] 4611[10] 6014[2]

Imperialista *Tracy Waggott* 35
4 ch m Halling(USA) Empress Maud (USA) (Kingmambo (USA))
941[8]

Imperial Legend (IRE) *David Nicholls* a71 82
7 b g Mujadil(USA) Titian Saga (IRE) (Titus Livius (FR))
1956[6] 2261[5] (2572) 3552[2] 3875[7] 4100[6] 6537[20] 7252[10] 7660[8] 8010[6] ◆ 8403[13]

Imperial Link *John O'Shea* a54 41
4 b m Rail Link Imperia (GER) (Tertullian (USA))
2045[8] 2542[13] 2733[4] 3135[5] 3401[4] (3496) (3896) 4087[3] 4335[4] 7240[10] 7619[9] 7943[9] 8457[10]

Imperial State *George Scott* a87 85
3 b g Holy Roman Emperor(IRE) Seldemosa (Selkirk (USA))
2375[11] 2790[5] 3412[6] (4656) (4844) 5179[10] 7108[5] 7540[5]

Imperial Tango (FR) *G Botti* a80 66
2 b f Sageburg(IRE) Driving Miswaki (USA) (Miswaki (USA))
3507a[5] 4124a[3] 5755a[4]

Imphal *Marcus Tregoning* a42 62
2 b g Nathaniel(IRE) Navajo Rainbow (Rainbow Quest (USA))
4866[10] 5600[12] 7726[7]

Implausible *Jonathan Portman* 37
2 b f Royal Applause Tease (IRE) (Green Desert (USA))
6035[8]

Important Message *Saeed bin Suroor* a79 101
4 bb g New Approach(IRE) Plaza (USA) (Chester House (USA))
6057[9] 6781[7]

Important Point (USA) *Saeed bin Suroor* a84 35
4 br g Street Cry(IRE) Zofzig (USA) (Danzig (USA))
2378[10] 2689[13]

Impressionist (IRE) *A Fabre* 102
3 b f Montjeu(IRE) Charroux (IRE) (Darshaan)
1541a[4] 3935a[2] 5451a[7] 6972a[5]

Imprimatur (IRE) *John C McConnell* a31 33
4 b m Approve(IRE) Zingeeyah (Singspiel (IRE))
7800a[11]

Improver (IRE) *A J Martin* 59
5 b g Ad Valorem(USA) Titus Wonder (IRE) (Titus Livius (FR))
4813a[4]

Impulsive (TUR) *S Demiral* 103
3 ch c Mizzen Mast(USA) Good Evening (USA) (Dixieland Heat (USA))
6181a[4]

Impulsive American *David Pipe* a70 84
4 b g American Post Impulsive Decision (IRE) (Nomination)
(2912) 3149[4] (6540)

I'm Ready (IRE) *Richard Fahey* a54 38
3 ch f Iffraaj Ready When You Are (IRE) (Royal Applause)
1484[8] 2308[11]

Imshi's Little Bro (IRE) *Ivan Furtado* a47 45
3 b g Lilbourne Lad(IRE) Subtle Affair (IRE) (Barathea (IRE))
1031[7] 1551[6]

Imshivalla (IRE) *Richard Fahey* a61 97
5 b m Acclamation Subtle Affair (IRE) (Barathea (IRE))
(1380) 1643[8] 2026[8] (2866) 3608[10] 4163[4] 4731[12] 5651[9] 6115[8] 6505[5] 6559[3] 7744[4] 7823[11]

I'm Super Too (IRE) *Karen Tutty* a60 62
9 b g Fasliyev(USA) Congress (IRE) (Dancing Brave (USA))
936[3] 1596[8] 1925[5] 2810[6] 3479[9] 4234[3] 4456[9] (4730) 5323[2] 5868[6] 6647[11] 7795[6]

Imtiyaaz (IRE) *Roger Varian* a73 96
4 b m Starspangledbanner(AUS) Endure (IRE) (Green Desert (USA))
2042[4] 2474[6] 5436[5] 6012[7] 6449[3] 6939[10] 7146[6]

Inaam (IRE) *Richard Fahey* a81 61
3 b g Camacho Duckmore Bay (IRE) (Titus Livius (FR))
(105) 291[5] (610) 817[2] 1137[3] 1809[5] 7111[4] 7687[4] 8037[2] (8287) 8487[3] ◆

Inaya *Jessica Long* 99
5 b m High Chaparral(IRE) Vigelegere (SWE) (Be My Chief (USA))
5187a[2] 6390a[12]

Incahoots *F Head* a98 99
4 b m Oasis Dream In Clover (Inchinor)
(660a) 1231a[5] 1910a[7] 3451a[7] 5384a[3] 6693a[8] 7861a[4]

Incampo (FR) *H-A Pantall* a85 85
2 b c Campanologist(USA) Indian Cat (IRE) (One Cool Cat (USA))
6177a[6]

Incandescent *James Fanshawe* a64 54
2 b f Pivotal Bedazzled (Authorized (IRE))
7769[7] 8088[5]

Incantator (GER) *A Wohler* 108
4 ch h Areion(GER) Independent Miss (GER) (Polar Falcon (USA))
4253a[3] 4928a[11] 6598a[5] 7564a[11]

Incantu (IRE) *F Chappet* a73 66
2 b f Kheleyf(USA) Ice On Fire (Iceman)
5279a[4] 7294a[2] 7996a[4]

Ince Moss *Richard Fahey* a42 40
4 br m Invincible Spirit(IRE) Royal Grace (Royal Applause)
668[4]

Incentive *Stuart Kittow* 67
2 b f Stimulation(IRE) Folly Drove (Bahri (USA))
3511[9] 4287[5] 5869[4] 6830[5] 7571[13]

Inception (IRE) *Richard Hannon* a55 59
2 bb c Elusive Pimpernel(USA) Spiritville (IRE) (Invincible Spirit (IRE))
6054[8] 6480[7] 7424[9]

Inchikhan *James Fanshawe* a66 42
2 br f Dalakhani(IRE) Inchiri (Sadler's Wells (USA))
7285[7] 8131[5]

Incitator (FR) *Mme M Bollack-Badel* a80 85
3 b c Motivator Summer Wave (IRE) (King's Best (USA))
2281a[7]

Inclination (IRE) *Clive Cox* a72 81
3 b f Acclamation Interaction (Oasis Dream)
1451[3] (2373) (3126) (4155) 4708[2] 5896[3] 6340[7]

Incomparable *Scott Dixon* a44 59
11 ch g Compton Place Indian Silk (IRE) (Dolphin Street (FR))
136[8] 444[7] 2120[11] 2423[4] 2676[11] 3010[7]

Inconceivable (IRE) *Ralph Beckett* a70
2 b f Galileo(IRE) Mohican Princess (Shirley Heights)
7885[4] ◆

Incurs Four Faults *Keith Dalgleish* a60 60
5 b g Halling(USA) Rapsgate (IRE) (Mozart (IRE))
149[4] 247[7] 368[4] 1695[6] 2330[6] 2810[4] 3018[4] 3287[4] 3750[3] 4341[2] 4486[6] 4872[7] 5149[5] 5835[3]

Incus *Ed de Giles* a45 45
3 b g Bertolini(USA) Cloudchaser (IRE) (Red Ransom (USA))
2557[8] 4233[9] 6654[5] 7532[3]

Indastar *Michael Herrington* a63 63
6 b g Indesatchel(IRE) Charcoal (Primo Valentino (IRE))
2423[13] 2919[3] 3549[2] (4647) 5368[5] 5838[3] 6745[6] 6910[6]

Indecence Choisie (FR) *C Ferland* a93 94
3 bb f Kendargent(FR) The Jostler (Dansili)
1541a[6] 2726a[5]

Indego Blues *David Nicholls* 70
7 b g Indesatchel(IRE) Yanomami (USA) (Slew O'Gold (USA))
1676[13] 2053[13] 3776[3] 3940[7] 5222[8] 5760[4] 5889[10] 6616[8]

Independence Day (IRE) *David Wachman* 103
3 b c Dansili Damson (IRE) (Entrepreneur)
1730a[9] 2272a[12]

Independent Rose *Michael Bell* a63
4 ch m Mount Nelson Red Roses Story (FR) (Pink I (FR))
26[3] 180[5]

Indiana Dawn *Robert Stephens* a57 59
3 b f Sleeping Indian Street Diva (USA) (Street Cry (IRE))
6317[6] 7011[5] 7362[9] 8234[7] 8457[6]

Indian Affair *Milton Bradley* a75 69
6 b h Sleeping Indian Rare Fling (USA) (Kris S (USA))
236[9] 426[5] 680[3] (857) 1186[5] 1496[2] 1928[3] 2130[5] 2491[8] 3098[5] 3510[4] 4155[4] 4291[7] 4485[3] 4714[3] 5284[4] 7268[4] 8181[5] 8595[4]

Indiana Jones (ARG) *M Al Mheiri* a33 60
6 b h Emperor Jones(USA) Suntuosa Fitz (ARG) (Fitzcarraldo (ARG))
718a[8]

Indianapolis (USA) *S Seemar* a83
5 br h Medaglia d'Oro(USA) Pretty N Smart (USA) (Beau Genius (CAN))
186a[6] 454a[7]

Indian Blessing *Ed Walker* a75
2 ch f Sepoy(AUS) Alpen Glen (Halling (USA))
7484[2] ◆ (7855)

Indian Chief (IRE) *Rebecca Bastiman* a59 83
6 b g Montjeu(IRE) Buck Aspen (USA) (Seeking The Gold (USA))
1250[9] 1588[9] 2093[12] 2836[8] (3748) ◆ (3901) 4038[8] 4919[7] 5837[10] 7408[8] 7775[7]

Indian Giver *John David Riches* a52 64
8 b m Indesatchel(IRE) Bint Baddi (FR) (Shareef Dancer (USA))
1382[4] 2365[5] 2573[2] 2958[4] 3287[5] 4456[2] 4872[2] 6029[8] 6621[12] 6839[7]

Indian Gold *Milton Bradley*
3 b g Sleeping Indian Hiraeth (Petong)
6631[9]

Indian Landing (IRE) *Tracey Collins* a69 61
8 ch g Barathea(IRE) Lindissima (IRE) (Green Desert (USA))
6461a[3] 7339a[14]

Indian Pursuit (IRE) *John Quinn* a66 65
3 b g Compton Place Church Melody (Oasis Dream)
1448[6] 2049[14] 3948[7] 4517[5] 4972[2] 5537[8] 6451[6] 6685[7] 7324[4] 7585[6] 7859[3] 7961[6]

Indian Scout *Anabel K Murphy* a53 53
8 b g Indesatchel(IRE) Manderina (Mind Games)
233[5] 378[2] 592[9]

Indian's Lad (FR) *J-M Capitte* 47
2 ch f Linda's Lad Gone South (IRE) (Zamindar (USA))
5905a[8]

Indian Sly (FR) *P Capelle* 10
11 b g Indian Rocket Slyders (IRE) (Hector Protector (USA))
1172a[9]

Indian Tim *Milton Bradley* a24 43
4 b g Sleeping Indian River City Moon (USA) (Riverman (USA))
2845[11] 4292[14] 4484[4] 5127[7]

Indian Tinker *Robert Cowell* a71 81
7 b g Sleeping Indian Breakfast Creek (Hallgate)
1447[4] 1945[5] 3217[7] 3618[2] 4809[2] 5751[3] 6410[4] 6879[8]

Indian Vision (IRE) *Micky Hammond* 53
2 ch g Iffraaj Sweet Fairnando (Hernando (FR))
7578[8] 7819[9]

India's Song *David Simcock* a86 69
6 b m Zamindar(USA) Sea Chorus (Singspiel (IRE))
(14) (254) 422[2] 774[4] 967[4]

Indibeau *Garry Moss* a28 64
4 b m Indesatchel(IRE) Neardown Beauty (IRE) (Bahhare (USA))
428[9] 2303[5] 3014[8]

Indie Music *Sylvester Kirk* a61 68
3 ch f Sakhee's Secret Indiana Blues (Indian Ridge)
1345[5] 1572[8] 2108[10] 3003[6] 3970[3]

Indie Rock *Mark Johnston* 66
2 b f Exceed And Excel(AUS) Rock Opera (SAF) (Lecture (USA))
3839[6] 4110[4] 4494[3] 6768[4] 7820[12]

Indigo *Mark Usher* a67 62
3 gr f Medicean Jessica Ennis (USA) (English Channel (USA))
1960[3] 2795[10] 4206[8] 4641[6] 5010[3] 5602[2] 6066[6] 6826[8]

Indigo Beat *Ann Duffield* 62
2 b f Tamayuz Silver Kestrel (USA) (Silver Hawk (USA))
2254[4] ◆ 2670[6] 3548[5]

Indigo Princess *Michael Appleby* a70
3 b f Native Ruler Red To Violet (Spectrum (IRE))
352[6] ◆ 524[5] 679[7] 7912[5] 7986[2] 8188[2] 8381[6]

Indira *John Berry* a81 95
5 ch m Sleeping Indian Forever Loved (Deploy)
30[5] 420[3] 506[4] (1002) 1552[2] (1919) (1999) (2176) 2685[2] 4078[4]

Indiscrete (FR) *C Laffon-Parias* a56
2 b f Siyouni(FR) Ecoute (USA) (Manila (USA))
7783a[5]

Indomitable Spirit *Martin Smith* a62 30
4 b g Zebedee Gayala (IRE) (Iron Mask (USA))
2[9] 1047[11] 1596[11] 3624[9]

Indrahar (IRE) *M Halford* a93 88
3 b f Raven's Pass(USA) Viz (IRE) (Darshaan)
7676a[10]

Indrapura (IRE) *Paul Cole* a48 78
3 ch g Cape Blanco(IRE) A Mind Of Her Own (IRE) (Danehill Dancer (IRE))
1485[7] 1777[6] 5201[3] 5627[5] 6066[7]

Indulged *James Fanshawe* a88 88
3 b f Teofilo(IRE) Fondled (Selkirk (USA))
2008[4] (2804) 3467[2] 4827[6] ◆ 6286[6] 6870[4] (7901)

Indulgent *Tony Coyle* a42 66
3 b g Makfi Santa Agata (FR) (Anabaa (USA))
2408[2] 3015[9] 3482[7] 4375[6] 5517[2] 5921[5]

Indus Valley (IRE) *Lee Carter* a54 47
9 ch g Indian Ridge Gloriously Bright (USA) (Nureyev (USA))
97[8] 1949[7] (3970) 5051[2] 5706[6] 6269[10] 6677[7] 7048[7] 8595[9]

Indy (IRE) *David Barron* 99
5 b g Indian Haven Maddie's Pearl (IRE) (Clodovil (IRE))
1491[5] 1871[10] 3324[4] 3855[5] 5886[13] 5976[11] 7077[5] 7408[5] 7744[6]

Inexes *Marjorie Fife* a82 83
4 gr g Exceed And Excel(AUS) Likeable (Dalakhani (IRE))
1186[3] 1555[8] 2345[9] (2812) 3284[3] (3924) ◆ 4142[2] 4608[17] 5810[3] 6136[3] 6437[2] 7066[11]

Infantry (NZ) *Hai Wang Tan* a34
3 b g Tavistock(NZ) The Nightingale (NZ) (Stravinsky (USA))
6399a[12]

Infatuated *Tim Easterby* a24 65
2 b c Indesatchel(IRE) Citron (Reel Buddy (USA))
2648[13] 5058[4] 5477[3] 6053[8] 7688[12]

Infiniti (IRE) *Rae Guest* a59 60
3 b f Arcano(IRE) Seraphina (IRE) (Pips Pride)
2177[15] 2483[10] 3411[10] 4388[3] 4993[8] 5338[2] 6046[6] 6631[2] 7062[2] 7240[2] 7513[6] (7572)

In First Place *Richard Fahey* 80
2 b g Bated Breath Carved Emerald (Pivotal)
1621[3] 2162[5] 3223[2] 4167[2] 4394[16] 4915[5] 6002[2] 6536[5] (7042)

Inflexiball *John Mackie* a61 64
4 b m Refuse To Bend(IRE) Sphere (IRE) (Daylami (IRE))
1640[4] 2507[2] 4375[5] 6212[2] 6737[10] 7257[4] 7516[4]

Influent (IRE) *Hugo Palmer* a58
2 b f Shamardal(USA) Kaabari (USA) (Seeking The Gold (USA))
8443[6]

In Focus (IRE) *Alan Swinbank* a45 83
5 ch g Intense Focus(USA) Reine De Neige (Kris)
1403[6] 2345[15] 4684[8] 4933[9] 5538[6] 6432[10]

Ingen Brave *David Evans* a52
3 gr f Mastercraftsman(IRE) Antrim Rose (Giant's Causeway (USA))
44[6] 245[8] 517[7]

Ingleby Angel (IRE) *Colin Teague* a74 103
7 br g Dark Angel(IRE) Mistress Twister (Pivotal)
1196[20] 1871[14] 2191[18] 2862[15] 3364[5] 3923[7] 4611[6] 4894[8] 5180[8] 5886[8] 6217[6] 6956[13] 7436[6]

Ingleby Erin *Michael Easterby* a23 52
3 b f Medicean Mistress Twister (Pivotal)
3482[11] 3710[9] 4987[10]

Ingleby Hollow *David O'Meara* a41 84
4 ch g Beat Hollow Mistress Twister (Pivotal)
2745[2] 2813[3] (3942) (4239) 4430[2] 4969[6] 6163[6] 6565[5] 7320[11] 7594[3] 7846[9]

Ingleby Mackenzie *Mick Channon* 69
2 b g Sixties Icon Natalie Jay (Ballacashtal (CAN))
2489[6] 2822[12] 3108[4] 4148[7] 7319[5]

Ingleby Spring (IRE) *Richard Fahey* 67
4 br m Zebedee Jouel (FR) (Machiavellian (USA))
1841[4] 2091[4] 2555[2] 2810[3] 4145[5] (4784) 5392[3] 5868[2] 6684[9]

Ingleby Valley *Richard Fahey* a55 72
3 ch g Sakhee's Secret Ingleby Lady (Captain Rio)
5070[6] 5537[P]

Inglorious *Keith Dalgleish* a60 64
2 bl g Kheleyf(USA) Impulsive Decision (IRE) (Nomination)
2807[5] 5271[6] 5713[7] 7140[6]

In Haste (IRE) *Eve Johnson Houghton* a72 78
3 gr g Clodovil(IRE) Hasty Katie (IRE) (Whipper (USA))
4990[7] 5774[3] 6190[7] 7301[4]

Inis Meain (USA) *Denis Gerard Hogan* a23 95
9 b g Bernstein(USA) Runaway Fields (USA) (Runaway Groom (CAN))
4850a[12]

Initially *Charles Hills* a69
3 b f Dansili Emplane (USA) (Irish River (FR))
7661[3] 8093[5]

Injam (IRE) *Jedd O'Keeffe* 87
3 b g Pour Moi(IRE) Sniffle (IRE) (Shernazar)
1200[2] 1636[3] ◆ 3323[2] (3809) 5653[11] 7320[10]

Injun Sands *Jane Chapple-Hyam* a87 84
5 b g Halling(USA) Serriera (FR) (Highest Honor (FR))
1092[2]

Inke (IRE) *Jim Boyle* a81 85
4 br m Intikhab(USA) Chifney Rush (IRE) (Grand Lodge (USA))
(2827) ◆ 3467[3] 4307[2] 4737[9] 7504[8] 7902[6]

In Ken's Memory *John Butler* a69 70
3 b f Sakhee(USA) Suzi Spends (IRE) (Royal Applause)
2823[3] 4640[7] 5013[3] 5635[2] (6241) 6629[7] 7272[10]

Inland Sea (USA) *Richard Hannon* a88 80
3 b g Scat Daddy(USA) Cat's Eye Witness (USA) (Elusive Quality (USA))
1267[3] (2446) ◆ 2788[6] 4599[4]

Inlawed *Ed Walker* 65
2 b c Bahamian Bounty Regent's Park (Green Desert (USA))
4161[12] 4707[3] 5377[4] 6213[7]

In My Place *Richard Fahey* a65 75
3 b g Compton Place Luxuria (IRE) (Kheleyf (USA))
1431[6] 1847[6] ◆ 2336[4] (2776) (3211) 3924[3] 4643[7] 5224[10] 5960[8] 6435[9] 6836[2] 7240[5]

In My Pocket (IRE) *John M Oxx* 107
4 ch h Dubawi(IRE) Hidden Silver (Anabaa (USA))
2067a[3] 2716a[9] 3692a[3] 6495a[2]

Inner Circle (IRE) *Richard Hannon* 77
2 b c Choisir(AUS) Eternity Ring (Alzao (USA))
1770[6] 4989[9] 5304[5] (5796) 6060[2] 7033[2]

Inner Knowing (IRE) *K R Burke* a69 63
3 b f Raven's Pass(USA) Paint The Town (IRE) (Sadler's Wells (USA))
858[6] 2657[5] 3210[3] 3786[9] 4587[3] 5523[2] 6426[12]

Inniscastle Lad *Stuart Williams* a72 86
4 b g Kyllachy Glencal (Compton Place)
1502[10] (1808) (2085) (2623) 3057[3] 3520[6] 5650[6] (7419) 8249[8]

Innish Man (IRE) *John Mackie* a74 70
4 b g Fastnet Rock(AUS) Super Gift (IRE) (Darshaan)
329[2]

Innocently (IRE) *David O'Meara* a78 74
5 ch g Kheleyf(USA) Innocency (USA) (Diesis)
2622[6] 2975[8] 4452[6] 4726[6] 5162[2] 5354[4] 5762[2] ◆ 6248[3] 6959[4] 7660[6] 7945[10]

Innocent Touch (IRE) *Richard Fahey* 99
5 bl g Intense Focus(USA) Guajira (FR) (Mtoto)
1880[6] 2222[6] 2556[2] 3347[4] (3920) 4650[2] 5173[5] (5964) 6559[10]

Innocuous *M Al Mheiri* a63 55
9 b g Zafeen(FR) Talah (Danehill (USA))
535a[5]

Innoko (FR) *Tony Carroll* a67 66
6 gr g Carlotamix(FR) Chalana (Ashkalani (IRE))
381[0] 295[3] 435[5] 684[2] 781[3] 1057[3] 1547[2] 1778[3] (2461) 2814[2] 3095[2] 3748[5] 5102[4]

Innstigator *Ralph J Smith* a59
2 b c Delegator Page (Elmaamul (USA))
8246[12] 8352[6] 8591[7]

Inn The Bull (GER) *Alan King* 78
3 ch g Lope De Vega(IRE) Ile Rousse (Danehill (USA))
4055[12] 4662[4] 5306[4] 7076[10]

In Salutem *K J Condon* a85 107
6 ch g Sakhee's Secret Irish Light (USA) (Irish River (FR))
4415a[4] (5143) 6384a[5] 6816a[6] 7191a[8]

Inscribe (USA) *Sir Michael Stoute* a20
2 b c Harlan's Holiday(USA) Reflections (Sadler's Wells (USA))
6368[7]

Inshaa *Michael Herrington* a70 70
4 b g Dansili Hidden Brief (Barathea (IRE))
901[11] 2347[7] 2773[9] 3212[8] 3946[9] 5068[2] 5367[4] 5972[2]

Insight (IRE) *Lucinda Egerton* a31 53
5 b m Bushranger(IRE) Ribbon Glade (UAE) (Zafonic (USA))
1295[10] 1675[7] 2462[2] 7657[13]

Insolenceofoffice (IRE) *Richard Ford* a60 64
8 b g Kodiac Sharp Diversion (USA) (Diesis)
197[11] 340[8] (1138) 1320[4] 2360[2]

Insolito (FR) *A Bonin* a64 61
3 b g Diamond Green(FR) Chandrayaan (FR) (One Cool Cat (USA))
3764a[8] 4220a[7]

Inspector (IRE) *Hugo Palmer* a35
2 b c Lawman(FR) Helter Helter (USA) (Seeking The Gold (USA))
8063[10]

Inspector Norse *Tim Easterby* a41 71
5 b g Norse Dancer(IRE) Indiana Blues (Indian Ridge)
2121[11] 2673[10] 3563[9] 6647[8] 7500[10]

Instant Attraction (IRE) *Jedd O'Keeffe* a89 106
5 b g Tagula(IRE) Coup De Coeur (IRE) (Kahyasi)
1195[3] 1629[8] 1871[2] 2868[2] 3273[7] 5941a[19]

Instant Karma (IRE) *Michael Bell* a73 84
5 b g Peintre Celebre(USA) Kotdiji (Mtoto)
1717[5] 4634[8]

Instigation *Ed Dunlop* a63 52
2 b f Bated Breath Rainbow's Edge (Rainbow Quest (USA))
4063[10] 6625[5] 7099[9]

Insurplus (IRE) *Jim Goldie* a42 70
3 b g Bushranger(IRE) Emly Express (IRE) (High Estate)
1691[3] 2234[7] 2657[7] 4643[12] 5386[6] 5928[3] ◆ 6215[8]

Inswing (IRE) *Ralph Beckett* a77
3 b f Intikhab(USA) Vampire Blues (IRE) (Azamour (IRE))
40[7] (376) ◆ 495[4]

Intaglio (POR) *Ana Imaz Ceca*
3 ch c Bugatti(GER) Debony (POR) (Sorcerous)
5502a[13]

Intalza (IRE) *Michael Herrington* a33 65
3 b f Intikhab(USA) Talzaqueen (SWI) (Zilzal Zamaan (USA))
(1819) 2553[6] 2831[5] 3287[8] 5181[3] 5540[7] (5715) (6004) 6221[6]

Intelligence Cross (USA) *A P O'Brien* 111
2 b c War Front(USA) Good Vibes (USA) (Unbridled's Song (USA))
4060[2] 4798[3] (5940a) 6785[4] 7807a[9]

Intense Life (IRE) *Endo Botti* 98
4 ch h Intense Focus(USA) Miswadah (IRE) (Machiavellian (USA))
7840a[4]

Intense Starlet (IRE) *Marjorie Fife* a67 61
5 ch m Intense Focus(USA) Glady Starlet (GER) (Big Shuffle (USA))
858[2] 1111[4] 1524[10] 1925[10] 2428[4] 2778[3] 3262[10] 4513[5] 5126[2] 5368[4] (6100) (6745) 6909[5] 7255[10] 8095[8] 8390[10]

Intense Style (IRE) *Les Eyre* a75 97
4 ch g Intense Focus(USA) Style Queen (IRE) (Galileo (IRE))
920[12] 1408[2] 1857[4] 2158[11] 2803[4] (3188) 3890[3] 4338[3] 5124[6] 5857[5] 6263[2] 6556[10] 7315[13] 7610[9]

Intense Tango *K R Burke* a93 103
5 b m Mastercraftsman(IRE) Cover Look (SAF) (Fort Wood (USA))
19[2] 194[3] 2249[7] 3162[9] 4078[9] 4646[2] (5116) 5381[2] (6118) 6350a[3] 7271[13]

Intensical (IRE) *Ivan Furtado* a68 81
5 b g Intense Focus(USA) Christinas Letter (IRE) (Galileo (IRE))
3398[4] ◆ 4094[6] 8251[9]

Intensified (IRE) *Ruth Carr* a53 60
5 bb g Intense Focus(USA) Sway Me Now (USA) (Speightstown (USA))
1674[8] 2365[10] 2958[6] 3750[2] 4144[4] 4456[7] 4772[4] 5227[11] 5323[4] ◆ 5800[3] 6647[5]

Intercepted *David Lanigan* a82 69
3 b c Raven's Pass(USA) Cape Rocker (Cape Cross (IRE))
2929[7] 3736[5] 4792[9] (5471) ◆ 5824[8]

Interception (IRE) *David Lanigan* a92 113
6 ch m Raven's Pass(USA) Badee'A (IRE) (Marju (IRE))
2474[3] 3386[22]

Interchoice Star *Ray Peacock* a46 38
11 b g Josr Algarhoud(IRE) Blakeshall Girl (Piccolo)
3320[8] 3735[7] 5194[7]

Interconnection *Ed Vaughan* a65 96
5 ch g Mount Nelson Lacework (Pivotal)
1569[7] (2214) 5964[3] 6786[10]

Interior Minister *C Von Der Recke* a27 81
6 b g Nayef(USA) Sister Maria (USA) (Kingmambo (USA))
664a[4]

Interlink (USA) *Tony Coyle* a78 72
3 b g Kitten's Joy(USA) Seattle Tac (USA) (Seattle Slew (USA))
5480[4] 5716[3] 6567[3] (7207) 7737[6] 8176[11] 8349[4] 8473[5]

Intermittent *Roger Charlton* a76 81
3 b f Cacique(IRE) Innocent Air (Galileo (IRE))
925[2] (1063) 2181[4] 2795[6] 4206[3] 4761[4]

Intermodal *Amanda Perrett* a76
2 b g Rail Link Rule Of Nature (Oasis Dream)
7962[5] (8246) ◆

Intern (IRE) *David Wachman* 89
2 b c Rip Van Winkle(IRE) Uliana (USA) (Darshaan)
5136a[3]

International Law *Brian Meehan* 80
2 gr c Exceed And Excel(AUS) Cruel Sea (USA) (Mizzen Mast (USA))
6570[5] 7501[2]

Interpret (USA) *M Al Mheiri* a101 29
8 b g Distorted Humor(USA) Quendom (ARG) (Interprete (ARG))
309a[4]

Interweave *Sir Michael Stoute* 77
2 ch f Dutch Art Interlace (Pivotal)
6062[2] 6578[2] 7494[2]

In The City *William Haggas* 82
3 ch c Exceed And Excel(AUS) Soft Morning (Pivotal)
4401[2] (4840) ◆ 6132[U] (Dead)

In The Red (IRE) *Richard Hannon* a85 91
3 b g Elusive Pimpernel(USA) Roses From Ridey (IRE) (Petorius (IRE))
6210[2] 6915[6] 7005[4] 7699[7] 7902[7] 8446[9]

In The Spotlight (IRE) *Richard Hughes* a62 57
2 b f Exceed And Excel(AUS) Naruko (USA) (Street Cry (IRE))
3812[8] 4387[6] 4988[5] 5806[7] 6252[4]

Intibaah *George Baker* a84 102
6 b g Elnadim(USA) Mawaared (Machiavellian (USA))
186a[9] 370a[15] 923[9] 1272[2] 1618a[5] 6556[25] 7806a[3] 8402[2] 8583[9]

Intilaaq (USA) *Roger Varian* 122
4 b h Dynaformer(USA) Torrestrella (IRE) (Orpen (USA))
1106a[8] 2626[6]

Intimate Art (IRE) *Andrew Balding* a80 80
2 ch g Dutch Art Intimacy (IRE) (Teofilo (IRE))
4390[7] 4790[2] 6439[5] (7065)

Intimately *Jonathan Portman* a56 60
3 b g Intense Focus(USA) Midnight Fling (Groom Dancer (USA))
105[6] 327[6] 436[2] 711[6] 1148[2] 1574[4] 3146[13] 4202[4] (5338) 6290[3] (6637) 7062[4]

Intimation *Sir Michael Stoute* a91 110
4 b m Dubawi(IRE) Infallible (Pivotal)
1861[7] 3608[7] 4757[3] 6604a[3] (7392a)

Intimidator (IRE) *Miss Joey Ellis* a59 51
5 b g Intikhab(USA) Zither (Zafonic (USA))
2098[11] 2398[7] 3041[4] 3528[2] 4197[3]

Intisaab *David O'Meara* 110
5 b g Elnadim(USA) Katoom (IRE) (Soviet Star (USA))
1215[9] 1444[8] 2028[2] (2961) 3168[2] (3346) 4667[2] 5418[2] 6382a[2] 6556[11] 6942[4] (7156)

Intisari (IRE) *G M Lyons* a100 103
4 b g Intikhab(USA) Golden Rose (GER) (Winged Love (IRE))
3630a[2] 6350a[13]

Intisha (IRE) *Jonathan Portman* 67
2 b f Intikhab(USA) Shawaaty (IRE) (Monsun (GER))
3556[10] 4350[7] 5202[4] ◆ 6060[7]

Intiwin (IRE) *Richard Fahey* a79 91
4 b g Intikhab(USA) Muluk (IRE) (Rainbow Quest (USA))
1576[8] 2527[5] 3055[5] 4113[11] 4687[2] 5292[5] 6160[10] 6684[5] 7159[11]

Into The Wild (IRE) *A Peraino* 69
2 b c Mastercraftsman(IRE) Miss Tiptoes (USA) (Mr Greeley (USA))
3701a[6]

Intransigent *Andrew Balding* a110 101
7 b g Trans Island Mara River (Efisio)
166[2] 483[11] 1066[7] 1204[10] 4625[22] 4916[6] 5640[5] 5871[11] 6764[2] 7241[2] 7651[5] 7984[6]

Intrepidly (USA) *Jeremy Noseda* a82 62
2 b g Medaglia d'Oro(USA) Trepidation (USA) (Seeking The Gold (USA))
5332[4] (7064)

Intricately (IRE) *Joseph Patrick O'Brien* 113
2 b f Fastnet Rock(AUS) Inner Realm (IRE) (Galileo (IRE))
4573a[3] 5686a[3] (6385a) 7809a[11]

Intrigue *Daniel Kubler* a67 69
4 b m Fastnet Rock(AUS) Riberac (Efisio)
(4375) 5065[2] 6444[5] 6921[10]

Introductory (IRE) *Keith Dalgleish* a79 79
3 b f Roderic O'Connor(IRE) Pleasure Place (IRE) (Compton Place)
1346[2] 1553[2] 1961[4] (5083) (5801) 6345[5]

Intrude *Stuart Williams* a99 85
4 b g Intikhab(USA) Don't Tell Mum (IRE) (Dansili)
221[6] 401[6] (594) ◆ 920[3] ◆ 3113[7] 3304[6] 4368[5] 5514[9] 5752[2] 6580[6]

Invade (IRE) *Stuart Williams* a73 70
4 ch m Intense Focus(USA) Spinning Well (IRE) (Pivotal)
(77) 324[6] 564[4] 713[2] (969) 1237[3] 1811[2] 5379[2] 6269[9] 6851[2] 7985[12]

Invectus Hero *Derek Shaw* a63 18
4 b g Paco Boy(IRE) Blur (Oasis Dream)
(143) 257[6] 1676[16]

Invermere *Richard Fahey* 83
3 b f Kyllachy Kootenay (IRE) (Selkirk (USA))
1623[8] (2855) 3775[2] 4453[3] 5123[3] 5802[4] 6811[5] (7220) 7671[4]

Invernata (FR) *John James Feane* a50 71
3 b f Holy Roman Emperor(IRE) Idle Tears (Selkirk (USA))
(6094)

Investissement *Paddy Butler* a74 78
10 b g Singspiel(IRE) Underwater (USA) (Theatrical (IRE))
233[8] 382[10] 653[6] 1174[4] 1748[5] 2792[4] 4019[12]

Invictus (GER) *Micky Hammond* 90
4 b g Exceed And Excel(AUS) Ivowen (USA) (Theatrical (IRE))
1245[2] 2017[12] 2832[7] 3435[7]

Invigorate *Harry Dunlop* a69 68
3 b c Stimulation(IRE) Pesse (IRE) (Eagle Eyed (USA))
1806[2] 2459[9] 3554[10]

Invincible Bond *Simon Waugh* a24 55
3 b g Monsieur Bond(IRE) Royal Pardon (Royal Applause)
2835[10] 3475[10] 4001[5] 4340[6] 4971[11]

Invincible Diamond (IRE) *J S Moore* a82 72
4 ch g Arakan(USA) Invincible Woman (IRE) (Invincible Spirit (IRE))
944[3] ◆ 1090[8] 1724[8] 3233[8]

Invincible Missile (IRE) *T G McCourt* a39 22
4 b m Majestic Missile(IRE) Intimate Secret (IRE) (Invincible Spirit (IRE))
2229a[6]

Invincible Queen (FR) *F Head* 97
2 b f Invincible Spirit(IRE) Rhythm Queen (IRE) (Danehill Dancer (IRE))
6271a[4] 7480a[4]

Invincible Ridge (IRE) *Eric Alston* a77 89
8 b g Invincible Spirit(IRE) Dani Ridge (IRE) (Indian Ridge)
3638[9] 4366[9] (5153) 6080[11] 6263[9] 7289[9] 8403[11] 8571[7]

Invincible Ryker (IRE) *M Halford* 82
2 b c Invincible Spirit(IRE) Cabaret (IRE) (Galileo (IRE))
7387a[3]

Invincible Strike (IRE) *S Seemar* a74 89
5 gr g Invincible Spirit(IRE) Lazaretta (IRE) (Dalakhani (IRE))
279a[8]

Invincible Wish (IRE) *Trevor Wall* a66 64
4 b g Vale Of York(IRE) Moonlight Wish (IRE) (Peintre Celebre (USA))
1047[10] 1413[6] 1500[2] 2144[6] 2781[10] 3747[3] 4082[6] 5513[9] (5958) 6256[5]

In Vino Veritas (IRE) *Lynn Siddall* a64 68
5 b g Art Connoisseur(IRE) Robin (Slip Anchor)
3191[10] 3844[8]

Invocation (FR) *Alan King* a78 54
3 bb g Intense Focus(USA) Fabiola (GER) (Medicean)
2443[2] 2826[4] 3475[4]

Invoke (IRE) *Keith Dalgleish* a91 95
5 b m Kodiac Tides (Bahamian Bounty)
2223[8] 3923[9] 4443[5] 4700[2] ◆ 5419[15] (6096)

Inwithachance (IRE) *Daniel Mark Loughnane* a34 44
3 b g Thousand Words Sombreffe (Polish Precedent (USA))
3731[10] 4225[5] 4987[7] 6367[9]

Iona Island *Peter Hiatt* a64 69
3 b f Dutch Art Still Small Voice (Polish Precedent (USA))
1608[9] 4367[5] 4836[3] 5207[4] 5672[2] 6698[5] 7425[6] 8318[7] 8448[8]

Ionization (IRE) *John Patrick Shanahan* a71 89
3 ch f The Carbon Unit(USA) The Mighty Atom (USA) (Sky Mesa (USA))
1339[5] (3284) 3551[4] (4630)

Ipanemo (FR) *P Sogorb* a82
3 b c Iffraaj Faviva (USA) (Storm Cat (USA))
5349a[4] 7492a[2]

Iquitos (GER) *H-J Groschel* 116
4 b h Adlerflug(GER) Irika (GER) (Areion (GER))
(2723a) 3934a[2] 4928a[4] (6175a) 6822a[5] 7759a[4] 8129a[7]

Iraklion (GER) *Christian Sprengel* 100
4 ch h Areion(GER) Ircanda (GER) (Nebos (GER))
2286a[7] 4031a[5] 6151a[6] 6610a[5] 7088a[3]

Irish Cailin (IRE) *Paul Midgley* 61
3 b f Desert Millennium(IRE) Shone Island (IRE) (Desert Sun)
2302[15] 2854[7] 4426[8]

Irish Eclare (IRE) *Charles Hills* a81 66
3 br c Equiano(FR) Delitme (IRE) (Val Royal (FR))
(1431) 2002[6] 2818[3] 4086[9] 5412[8] 7206[8] 7308[12]

Irish Jasper (USA) *Chad C Brown* a110 84
4 bb m First Defence(USA) Irish Connection (USA) (Mr Greeley (USA))
7836a[8]

Irishman Mark (IRE) *Agostino Affe'* 85
3 b c Vocalised(USA) Zelloof (IRE) (Kheleyf (USA))
1686a[10]

Irish Melody (IRE) *Bill Turner*
2 ch g Haatef(USA) Rainbow Melody (IRE) (Rainbows For Life (CAN))
2739[8] 2963[3] 3770[2] 4221[7] 4842[5] 8494[7] 8569[8]

Irish Optimism (IRE) *John Quinn* a88 83
3 b g Approve(IRE) Miznapp (Pennekamp (USA))
1383[2] (1691) 2695[8] 3591[3] 3945[3] 5782[3] 6265[2] (6521) (7486)

Irish Rookie (IRE) *Martyn Meade* 113
4 b m Azamour(IRE) Bold Assumption (Observatory (USA))
1886[4] 2497a[2] 3178a[12] 4107[4] 4582[2] 6693a[3] 6949[5]

Irish Thistle (IRE) *Dai Williams* 54
9 b g Luso Which Thistle (IRE) (Saddlers' Hall (IRE))
2368[5] 3067[8] 3498[7]

Irish Valley (GER) *K Demme* 83
3 ch f Three Valleys(USA) Irish Eagle (GER) (Eagle Eyed (USA))
5695a[10]

Irondale Express *Barry Brennan* a49 71
5 b m Myboycharlie(IRE) Olindera (GER) (Lomitas)
950[9]

Ironicus (USA) *Claude McGaughey III* 115
5 rg h Distorted Humor(USA) Meghan's Joy (USA) (A.P. Indy (USA))
7172a[2] 7837a[4]

Iron Islands *K R Burke* 72
2 b g Dutch Art Night Premiere (IRE) (Night Shift (USA))
6129[4] 6535[4] 7741[6]

Iron Lady (IRE) *William Muir* a46 21
2 b f Exceed And Excel(AUS) Kahlua Kiss (Mister Baileys)
5722[10] 6223[6] 7279[6]

Irrevocable (IRE) *Roger Charlton* a42 73
3 br f Big Bad Bob(IRE) Out Of Time (IRE) (Anabaa (USA))
2312[3] ◆ 2877[8] 4480[6] 5603[5] 6128[15]

Irvine Lady (IRE) *Gay Kelleway* a36 39
3 ch f Footstepsinthesand Ascot Lady (IRE) (Spinning World (USA))
8320[10]

Isaak (FR) *Donald McCain* a59 52
3 b g Dalghar(FR) Ela's Giant (Giant's Causeway (USA))
1806[5] 4792[10] 5716[5] 6738[2]

Isabel De Urbina (IRE) *Ralph Beckett* 75
2 b f Lope De Vega(IRE) Roscoff (IRE) (Daylami (IRE))
(6648)

Isabella (IRE) *David O'Meara* 60
2 ch f Galileo(IRE) Song Of My Heart (IRE) (Footstepsinthesand)
7740[4]

Isabella Liberty (FR) *Gordon Elliott* a19 33
5 b m Soldier Of Fortune(IRE) Samsa (FR) (Zafonic (USA))
218[4]

Isabel's On It *William Haggas* a74 63
2 ch f Dubawi(IRE) Check The Label (USA) (Stormin Fever (USA))
7695[5] ◆ 7855[2] ◆

Iseemist (IRE) *John Gallagher* a89 102
5 gr m Verglas(IRE) Krasivaya (IRE) (Soviet Star (USA))
771[8] 1453[2] ◆ 2042[5] 2898[7] 3800[2] 4862[21] 6064[3] 6518[5] 6943[10] 7497[20]

Isfahan (GER) *A Wohler* 113
3 ch c Lord Of England(GER) Independent Miss (GER) (Polar Falcon (USA))
(1908a) 2517a[5] (4186a)

Isharah (USA) *Mark Johnston* a87 83
3 b g Kitten's Joy(USA) Menekineko (USA) (Kingmambo (USA))
603[3] ◆ (768) 3323[5] 3991[2] 4143[2] 4827[10] 5231[3] 6565[6] 7618[3] 8162[2] 8283[2] (8584)

Ishebayorgrey (IRE) *Patrick Martin* a92 84
4 gr g Clodovil(IRE) Superjet (IRE) (Soviet Star (USA))
7523a[7]

Ishikawa (IRE) *Ali Stronge* a28 59
8 b g Chineur(FR) Nautical Light (Slip Anchor)
6241[14] 7577[12]

Isis Blue *Rod Millman* a78 73
6 b g Cockney Rebel(IRE) Bramaputra (IRE) (Choisir (AUS))
(64) 518[U] 1142[7] 1418[10] 2174[5] 2623[6] 3192[4] 4081[13] 6365[12] (6827)

Island Cloud *Heather Main* a71
2 b f Harbour Watch(IRE) Cloud Illusions (USA) (Smarty Jones (USA))
6866[8] 7277[3] 7647[5] 8352[3]

Island Express (IRE) *Ann Stokell* a44 30
9 b g Chineur(FR) Cayman Expresso (IRE) (Fayruz)
834[6] 902[6] 2778[10]

Island Flame (IRE) *Richard Fahey* a80 76
3 b f Kodiac Noble Flame (IRE) (Doyoun)
(1671) 2532[4] ◆ (3189) 3593[7] 4549[3] 5415[4] 6504[7] (6922) 7901[4] 8584[3]

Island In The Sky (IRE) *David Simcock* a75 72
2 b f Kodiac When Not Iff (IRE) (Iffraaj)
4064[4] 5119[3] 5542[4] 7099[2]

Island Remede *Henry De Bromhead* a65 100
5 b m Medicean Island Odyssey (Dansili)
1279a[3] 6495a[12] 7393a[5]

Island Vision (IRE) *David Simcock* a79 92
2 ch f Arcano(IRE) Boo Boo Bear (IRE) (Almutawakel)
2771[5] (3275) 5066[3] 6257[4] (7147) 7698[3]

Ismane (FR) *L Cendra* a60 57
7 b m Layman(USA) Island Lady (FR) (Cardoun (FR))
5281a[3]

Isntshesomething *Richard Guest* a53 56
4 br m Assertive Princess Almora (Pivotal)
1754[4] 2778[4] 3479[11] 4240[7] 4498[9] 4861[2] 5276[5] 6908[4] 7144[6] 8289[10] 8401[6]

Isomer (USA) *Andrew Balding* 99
2 ch c Cape Blanco(IRE) Nimue (USA) (Speightstown (USA))
2204[2] ◆ 3382[2] (4154) 4732[6]

Isostatic *Rae Guest* a24 42
3 b f Champs Elysees Valencia (Kenmare (FR))
2177[16] 2790[12] 3577[6] 4225[9]

Israfel *Jamie Osborne* a57 45
3 b f Dark Angel(IRE) Border Minstral (IRE) (Sri Pekan (USA))
104[2] (328) 785[2] ◆ 820[3] 947[3] 2969[6] 4289[7] 4505[6]

Issue *James Fanshawe* a73
3 ch f Nayef(USA) Isis (USA) (Royal Academy (USA))
6674[3] 7727[4] 7991[2]

Isswara *Marco Botti* a47
2 b f Tamayuz Qilaada (USA) (Bernardini (USA))
2376[7]

Istan *A P O'Brien* 94
2 b c Excelebration(IRE) Something Exciting (Halling (USA))
6860a[3]

Istanbul Bey *William Haggas* a66 95
3 ro g Exceed And Excel(AUS) Starfala (Galileo (IRE))
1800[4] 2541[2] ◆ (3362) (4113)

Istimraar (IRE) *Alexandra Dunn* a66 65
5 b g Dansili Manayer (IRE) (Sadler's Wells (USA))
5957[3] 6618[5] 8459[4]

Istinfaar (USA) *A bin Harmash* a82 52
4 b g Street Cry(IRE) Yaqeen (Green Desert (USA))
12a[9]

Istiqlaal *Charlie Appleby* a34 35
3 b c Oasis Dream Independence (Selkirk (USA))
3412[11]

Italian Beauty (IRE) *John Wainwright* a72 40
4 b m Thewayyouare(USA) Edelfa (IRE) (Fasliyev (USA))
1122[3] 1702[6] 2015[5] (4348) 6028[4] 6772[10] 7581[4] 8035[3] 8190[9] 8538[7]

Italian Heiress *Clive Cox* 65
2 ch f Medicean Regal Heiress (Pivotal)
7055[3]

Italian Riviera *Kenneth Slack* a71 64
7 b g Galileo(IRE) Miss Corniche (Hernando (FR))
(7592)

I T Guru *Noel Wilson* a44 60
3 b c Bahamian Bounty Never Say Deya (Dansili)
105[9] 2302[10] (2425) 2741[7] 4007[6] 4236[5] 4944[6]

Itlaaq *Michael Easterby* a84 87
10 b g Alhaarth(IRE) Hathrah (IRE) (Linamix (FR))
1952[3] 3118[6] (3602) 4381[7] 4634[6] (4892) 6011[4] 6740[4] 7158[5]

It Must Be Faith *Michael Appleby* a92 78
6 b g Mount Nelson Purple Rain (IRE) (Celtic Swing)
213[10] 2903[7] 3068[7] 3618[3] 4496[8] 5679[11]

Ito (GER) *Jean-Pierre Carvalho* 117
5 b h Adlerflug(GER) Iota (GER) (Tiger Hill (IRE))
(2075a) 2723a[3] 4928a[8] 6395a[2]

Itorio (IRE) *Jassim Al Ghazali* 102
4 b h Oratorio(IRE) Image Of (IRE) (Close Conflict (USA))
744a[5]

Itsakindamagic *Andrew Balding* 74
2 b c Mount Nelson Carsulae (IRE) (Marju (IRE))
7622[3]

It's All A Game *Nigel Tinkler* a63 50
5 ch g Sleeping Indian St Edith (IRE) (Desert King (IRE))
20[4] ◆ 294[12]

It's A Mans World *Brian Ellison* a18 34
10 b g Kyllachy Exhibitor (USA) (Royal Academy (USA))
1222[10] 3470[11]

It's A Privilege *Mme J Hendriks* a69 56
7 gr g Verglas(IRE) No Rehearsal (FR) (Baillamont (USA))
4903a[8]

Its A Sheila Thing *Linda Jewell* a51 54
3 ch f Sir Percy Sefemm (Alhaarth (IRE))
2590[3] 3489[3] 4267[9] 5019[6] 5100[5] 5923[8]

It's A Stitch Up *Brian Meehan* a50
3 b f Kheleyf(USA) Colourflash (IRE) (College Chapel)
148[8]

It's How We Roll (IRE) *Charles Hills* a45 63
2 b c Fastnet Rock(AUS) Clodora (FR) (Linamix (FR))
6439[6] 7013[9] 7975[11]

Its Only Mossy (IRE) *Jennie Candlish* a72 64
3 b g Moss Vale(IRE) Bound To Glitter (USA) (Boundary (USA))
(1795) ◆ (2106) 2201[3] 3603[7]

It's Time For Bed *Linda Perratt* 58
4 gr m Zebedee Mystical Ayr (IRE) (Namid)
1878[8] 2360[9] 2523[7] 2808[10] 3022[7] 3755[9] 4096[7]

Ivan Grozny (FR) *W P Mullins* a88 100
6 b g Turtle Bowl(IRE) Behnesa (IRE) (Suave Dancer (USA))
3340[9]

Ivanhoe *Michael Blanshard* a65 71
6 b g Haafhd Marysienka (Primo Dominie)
2338[6] 2887[3] 3533[4] 3903[3] 4483[3] 5267[2] (5597) 6083[5] 6519[4] 6885[5] 7625[5]

I'Vegotthepower (IRE) *Brian Meehan* 68
2 b g Power Waterways (IRE) (Alhaarth (IRE))
4349[12] 4775[8] 6314[3]

Ivors Involvement (IRE) *Tina Jackson* a74 46
4 b g Amadeus Wolf Summer Spice (IRE) (Key Of Luck (USA))
2662[11] 3327[12] 3717[8] 7333[7] 7747[17] 7994[7] 8307[8]

Ivor's Magic (IRE) *David Elsworth* a61 64
2 ch f Zebedee Rinneen (IRE) (Bien Bien (USA))
3576[3] 4022[3] 4298[7] 4802[12] (5120) 5989[5] 6236[5]

Ivory Choice (FR) *F Chappet* 94
2 b f Choisir(AUS) Ivory Style (Desert Style (IRE))
4750a[3] 5497a[2] 6068a[8]

I Wouldn't Bother *Daniel Kubler* a61 50
2 b g Captain Gerrard(IRE) Dalmunzie (IRE) (Choisir (AUS))
6375[5] 7072[6] 7424[7] 7974[12]

Ixchell *Richard Fahey* 22
3 b f Equiano(FR) Amanda Carter (Tobougg (IRE))
6452[7] 7096[8]

Ixelles Diamond (IRE) *Andrew Reid* a72 61
5 br m Diamond Green(FR) Silk Point (IRE) (Barathea (IRE))
80[3] 223[3] 415[7] 667[2] 813[2] 977[5] 1171[4] 1266[4] 2127[4] 2646[7] 5132[8] 5891[7] 6662[13]

Iyouna (FR) *H-A Pantall* a52 66
2 ch f Siyouni(FR) Indianapolis (GER) (Tiger Hill (IRE))
1579a[3]

Izmir (IRE) *William Haggas* a75 85
3 b f Sir Percy Limit (IRE) (Barathea (IRE))
1630[5] 3062[5] 3649[2] 4087[2] (4909) 5545[3] 6576[2] 6964[7]

Izzo (GER) *Mario Hofer* 91
3 b c Tertullian(USA) Ioannina (Rainbow Quest (USA))
1908a[5]

Izzthatright (IRE) *Jassim Al Ghazali* 106
4 b g Moss Vale(IRE) Miss Adelaide (IRE) (Alzao (USA))
(755a)

Jaameh (IRE) *Mark Johnston* a61 87
3 b g Iffraaj Miss Gibraltar (Rock Of Gibraltar (IRE))
3343[3] (3853) 4409[2] 4863[4] 5653[8]

Jaaref (IRE) *J E Hammond* a62 85
3 ch g Sea The Stars(IRE) Tabassum (IRE) (Nayef (USA))
2948a[11] 5946a[9]

Jaarih (IRE) *Conor Dore* a81 81
4 ch g Starspangledbanner(AUS) Bridge Note (USA) (Stravinsky (USA))
(176) 319[3] ◆ (364) 462[7] 580[8] 764[3] 903[4] 1030[4] 1110[2] 1528[4] 1874[5] 2622[3] 3407[8] (4236) 5189[5] 5855[2] 6296[2] 6475[10] 6879[2] 7202[11] 7626[13]

Jabbaar *Owen Burrows* a69 79
3 ch g Medicean Echelon (Danehill (USA))
2320[5] ◆ 2790[9] (3483) 4549[6] 6254[2] 7051[11]

Jabbarockie *Paul Green* a56 70
3 b g Showcasing Canina (Foxhound (USA))
2333[7] 5862[2] 6218[7]

Jacbequick *David O'Meara* a91 95
5 b g Calcutta Toking N' Joken (IRE) (Mukaddamah (USA))
1588[2] 1923[2] 2198[2] 2677[2] (3011) 3166[5] 3518[10] 4312[2] (4453) 4727[3] 5419[7] 5802[6] 6076[2] 6225[S] 6775[3] 7121[16] 7535[5] 7744[10] 7967[3] 8123[3] 8231[5]

Jackapies Bay (IRE) *Thomas P O'Connor* a53 44
8 b g Hilton Head(USA) Minnie Tomina (IRE) (Oscar (IRE))
6463a[7]

Jack Bear *Harry Whittington* a68 85
5 b g Joe Bear(IRE) Colins Lady (FR) (Colonel Collins (USA))
(3221) 4381[2] 5381[5] 7215[9]

Jackblack *Patrick Chamings* a59
4 b g Crosspeace(IRE) Saharan Royal (Val Royal (FR))
7052[12] 7753[6] 7942[9] 8085[8]

Jack Blane *Daniel Kubler* 51
2 b g Kheleyf(USA) Blane Water (USA) (Lomond (USA))
5569 [4] 6515[7]

Jack Dexter *Jim Goldie* 113
7 bb g Orientor Glenhurich (IRE) (Sri Pekan (USA))
1197[12] 1439[8] 2159[12] 3386[9] 4126[4] ◆ 4625[11] 6558[12] 7350[8]

Jackhammer (IRE) *William Knight* a78 97
2 b c Thewayyouare(USA) Ask Annie (IRE) (Danehill (USA))
(3529) ◆ 4732[7] 5595[10] 6801[4] 6868[3]

Jack Hobbs *John Gosden* a114 125
4 br h Halling(USA) Swain's Gold (USA) (Swain (IRE))
1863[P] 7353[3]

Jack Luey *Lawrence Mullaney* a71 82
9 b g Danbird(AUS) Icenaslice (IRE) (Fayruz)
2491[12] 2665[10] 3552[7] 3875[9] (4691) 6324[5] 6766[10] 7252[8] 7660[14] 8349[5] 8473[4]

Jackman *Tony Carroll* a8 45
2 gr g Aussie Rules(USA) Fit To Burst (Pastoral Pursuits)
2757[12] 3897[4] 4524[7] 6208[8]

Jack Nevison *Henry Candy* a69 77
3 b g Dick Turpin(IRE) Creative Mind (IRE) (Danehill Dancer (IRE))
1414[2] 3036[5] 4155[2] ◆ 5305[4] 7268[7]

Jack Of Diamonds (IRE) *Roger Teal* a95 83
7 b g Red Clubs(IRE) Sakkara Star (IRE) (Mozart (IRE))
401[7] 594[6] (788) 1001[7] (1797) 3061[10] 4055[5] 4532[6] 5552[9] 6126[10] 6300[3] 6736[14] 8122[11] 8475[10]

Jackpot *Brendan Powell* a46 46
6 b m Avonbridge Strat's Quest (Nicholas (USA))
1263[2] 1742[4] 2609[10] 3380a[5] 3917a[4] 4635[6] 5630[9] 6020[5] 6890[8] 7426[11] 7944[8] 8252[9]

Jacksonfire *Michael Mullineaux* a7 56
4 ch g Firebreak Fitolini (Bertolini (USA))
2442[11] 3743[3] 5270[8] 6522[7] 7240[4] 7572[11] 7960[7]

Jack's Revenge (IRE) *George Baker* a84 93
8 br g Footstepsinthesand Spirit Of Age (IRE) (Indian Ridge)
1274[6] 2216[2] 2868[10] 3848[3] 4109[5] 4758[16] 6109[16] (6806) 7316[8] 7699[6] 7821[9] 8177[8] 8475[6] ◆

Jack The Laird (IRE) *Dean Ivory* a71 67
3 b g Acclamation Pretty Demanding (IRE) (Night Shift (USA))
1162[4] 1794[2] (2447) ◆ 3725[2] 3994[2] 4280[2] 5200[6] 5470[2] 5807[2] 6248[5] 8228[9] 8535[8]

Jacob Black *Keith Dalgleish* a67 67
5 b g Amadeus Wolf First Eclipse (IRE) (Fayruz)
2628[14] 3565[7] 7933[11] 8122[12]

Jacob Cats *William Knight* a88 90
7 b g Dutch Art Ballet (Sharrood (USA))
1093[8] 1717[8] 2176[6] (2930) (3409) 3862[2] 5553[4] 6074[3] 7188[8]

Jacob's Dream *Gary Moore* 22
2 b g Teofilo(IRE) Jessica's Dream (IRE) (Desert Style (IRE))
4075[12]

Jacob's Pillow *Rebecca Bastiman* a79 78
5 b g Oasis Dream Enticing (IRE) (Pivotal)
28[3] (135) 426[2] 703[3] 938[4] 1879[5] 2680[7] 3326[5] 4291[11] 4848[9] 5354[6] 5714[2] 6451[8] 6616[2] 6835[2] 7093[2] 7595[2] 7774[3]

Jacobs Son *John Balding* a84 41
8 ch g Refuse To Bend(IRE) Woodwin (IRE) (Woodman (USA))
273[7] 766[9] 1404[5]

Jacquard (IRE) *Mark Johnston* a87 85
2 b c Pivotal Camlet (Green Desert (USA))
2830[2] ◆ 3167[4] (3472) 3818[4] (4508) 6228[5]

Jacquotte Delahaye *David Brown* a85 81
5 ch m Kyllachy Mary Read (Bahamian Bounty)
7958[8] 8135[2] 8287[5]

Jadaayil *Charles Hills* 89
3 b f Oasis Dream Muthabara (IRE) (Red Ransom (USA))
(1436) ◆ 5588[2]

Jadhaba (IRE) *J-C Rouget* 98
3 b f Galileo(IRE) Naissance Royale (IRE) (Giant's Causeway (USA))
1541a[3]

Jaganory (IRE) *Christopher Mason* a61 67
4 b g Dylan Thomas(IRE) Jacquelin Jag (IRE) (Fayruz)
2130[12] 2845[2] 3098[2] 3510[12] 4084[5] 4484[5] 5007[8] 5546[5] 5954[9] 6311[2] 6832[8] 7268[11]

Jai Hanuman (IRE) *Seamus Durack* a50
2 b c Requinto(IRE) Almost Blue (USA) (Mr Greeley (USA))
8352[9]

Jailawi (IRE) *Ismail Mohammed* a97 103
5 b g Iffraaj Tortue (IRE) (Turtle Island (IRE))
(2033) 2628[2] 4823[13] 5585[12] 6585[6]

Jakastar (IRE) *Richard Hannon* 52
2 ch f Zebedee Sportsticketing (IRE) (Spectrum (IRE))
3902[6] 4261[8]

Jake's Hill *Eve Johnson Houghton* a46 78
2 b c Mount Nelson Flower Market (Cadeaux Genereux)
7074[4] ◆ 7726[6]

Jallota *Charles Hills* a90 115
5 b g Rock Of Gibraltar(IRE) Lady Lahar (Fraam)
373a[9] 623a[7] 1993[7] (2485) 3164[4] 3938a[2] (4380) 5404[5] 5613[3] 5926[3] (6272a) 6823a[2] 7115[3]

Jamacho *Brian Ellison* a69 71
2 ch g Camacho Obsessive Secret (IRE) (Grand Lodge (USA))
2301[3] 3562[4] 4379[4] 5833[4] 6554[10] 6954[16]

Jamaica Inn (IRE) *John Gosden* a55 54
3 b f Fastnet Rock(AUS) Vintage Tipple (IRE) (Entrepreneur)
818[7]

Jamaican Bolt (IRE) *David O'Meara* a59 95
8 b g Pivotal Chiming (IRE) (Danehill (USA))
6780[13] 7825[12]

Jameerah *James Tate* a87 72
3 b f Dansili Jira (Medicean)
3568[4] (5078) 6072[9] ◆ 6699[3] (7206)

Jameka (AUS) *Ciaron Maher* 115
3 b f Myboycharlie(IRE) Mine Game (AUS) (General Nediym (AUS))
(7378a) 7756a[15]

James Bond Girl (USA) *Robert Cowell* a72 68
4 b m Giant's Causeway(USA) Swan Nebula (USA) (Seeking The Gold (USA))
(177) 462[5] 713[6]

Jamesie (IRE) *David Marnane* a103 105
8 b g Kodiac Pretty Woman (IRE) (Night Shift (USA))
370a[3] 723a[3] 810a[3] 3681a[3] 4135[3] 4865[9] 5213a[6] 6355a[4]

James The Elder (IRE) *Seamus Durack* a73 64
3 b g Zebedee Annaofcompton (IRE) (Call Me Big (GER))
4939[2] 7061[3] 7459[4]

Jamhoori *Jim Best* a82 47
8 b h Tiger Hill(IRE) Tanasie (Cadeaux Genereux)
66[9] (330) 556[4] (1174) 4020[5] 4459[9]

Jamindeh *Ian Williams*
3 b c Zamindar(USA) Missy Wassie Gal (USA) (High Chaparral (IRE))
2340[9] 6192[6] 7009[9]

Jammy Guest (IRE) *George Margarson* a95 70
6 b g Duke Of Marmalade(IRE) Ardbrae Lady (Overbury (IRE))
36[2] (100) (231) 433[4] 486[4] (944) 1068[11] 1418[5] ◆ 2032[4] 3622[6] 4474[5] 4627[13] 6628[9] 7066[4] 7308[9] 7462[5]

Jammy Moment *Iain Jardine* a62 76
5 ch m Duke Of Marmalade(IRE) Special Moment (IRE) (Sadler's Wells (USA))
1842[5] 2093[11] 2575[2] 2656[P] 2813[RR] 6812[7]

Jam Session (IRE) *Ian Williams* 87
4 ch g Duke Of Marmalade(IRE) Night Dhu (Montjeu (IRE))
(2398) 3092a[4] 3602[5] 5031[6]

Jamyson 'n Ginger (USA) *Rudy Rodriguez* a105
2 b f Bernardini(USA) Ginger Brew (CAN) (Milwaukee Brew (USA))
7830a[5]

Janaab (IRE) *Tim Easterby* a72 79
6 ch g Nayef(USA) Mood Indigo (IRE) (Indian Ridge)
1247[8] 1631[5] 2662[8] 3327[6] (3807) 4232[6] 5033[7] 5521[6] 6055[7] 6231[2] 6907[4] ◆ 7577[8]

Jan De Heem *Tina Jackson* a59 65
6 ch g Dutch Art Shasta (Shareef Dancer (USA))
3363[11] 3876[6] 4455[3] 4768[4] 5294[3] 5718[4] 5918[2] 6346[6] 6738[5] 7044[2] 7361[2] 7746[4] 7955[4]

Jane's Memory (IRE) *Rae Guest* a91 106
4 ch m Captain Rio Dancing Jest (IRE) (Averti (IRE))
1969[7] (2474) 3909[3] 6120[6] 6816a[9] 7932[8]

Jannia *Eve Johnson Houghton* a51
2 b f Iffraaj Fairy Moss (IRE) (Amadeus Wolf)
8066[9] 8362[7]

Jan Smuts (IRE) *Wilf Storey* a63 74
8 b g Johannesburg(USA) Choice House (USA) (Chester House (USA))
1253[10] 1665[5] (2018) 2406[4] 3149[10] 4004[4] 4101[5] 4491[4] 4935[3] 5541[2] 5856[5] 6227[3] 6812[4] 6906[4] 7138[3] 7382[3] 7846[6] 8091[2] 8309[5]

Jan Steen (IRE) *Denis Coakley* a70 70
3 b g Footstepsinthesand Mi Rubina (IRE) (Rock Of Gibraltar (IRE))
2846[12] 4058[7] 4557[3] 5711[6] 6238[2] 7203[7] 7461[10]

Jantina *Sir Michael Stoute* 73
3 ch f Dutch Art Zykina (Pivotal)
2009[11] 3958[2] (5380)

Jantine (FR) *Mme M Bollack-Badel* a43 55
2 b f Medecis Jabberwocky (Catcher In The Rye (IRE))
3763a[6] 5279a[8]

Jan Van Eyck (USA) *Gerard O'Leary* a76 67
6 ch g Raven's Pass(USA) Layounne (USA) (Mt. Livermore (USA))
208a[5]

Jan Van Hoof (IRE) *Richard Fahey* a89 94
5 b g Dutch Art Cosenza (Bahri (USA))
1215[2] 7968[8]

Jarahi (IRE) *Andreas Lowe* 89
3 b c Lope De Vega(IRE) Jebel Musa (IRE) (Rock Of Gibraltar (IRE))
1689a[7]

Jarir *Richard Hannon* a78 79
3 b g Oasis Dream Generous Lady (Generous (IRE))
182[2] (379) ◆ 729[4] 1185[2] 1738[4] 2644[2] 2900[5] 3570[2]

Jashma (IRE) *Richard Hughes* 40
2 b c Power Daganya (IRE) (Danehill Dancer (IRE))
3231[6]

Jasmincita (IRE) *George Baker* 59
2 b f Dark Angel(IRE) Jasmine Flower (Kyllachy)
2467[9] 3024[4] 3556[9] 5796[6]

Jasmiralda (FR) *S Wattel* a90 70
3 b f Desert Style(IRE) Maid Of Dawkins (IRE) (Kendor (FR))
5006a[10]

Jason Bournes (FR) *E Lellouche* a69 56
9 b g Westerner Doucelisa (FR) (Cardoun (FR))
3184a[9]

Jasper Jay *Tony Coyle* 61
3 b g Haafhd Jenise (IRE) (Orpen (USA))
1379[3] 2271[6] 3362[8] 7581[6]

J'Aspire *Stuart Williams* a60 65
4 b m Zamindar(USA) Ipsa Loquitur (Unfuwain (USA))
14[7] 161[2] 259[3]

Jassur *Marco Botti* a63 44
3 b g Canford Cliffs(IRE) Child Bride (USA) (Coronado's Quest (USA))
253[3] 1804[4] 2212[7]

Jaunty Joh (IRE) *Henry Candy* 42
3 b f Zoffany(IRE) Don't Care (IRE) (Nordico (USA))
2698[9] 2999[11] 7219[7]

Jawaayiz *Simon Crisford* a85 82
3 b f Kodiac Silkenveil (IRE) (Indian Ridge)
2505[2] (3249) 4042[3] 4743[4] (5671) 7504[5] 7901[2]

Jayed Jidan (IRE) *R Bouresly* a95 99
6 gr h Teofilo(IRE) Cassandra Go (IRE) (Indian Ridge)
309a[7]

Jayjinski (IRE) *Richard Hughes* a74 60
3 gr g Zebedee Prime Time Girl (Primo Dominie)
1256[4] 1892[2] 2544[3] 2750[4] 4155[9] 5609[5] 5811[3] 6629[10]

Jay Kay *K R Burke* a58 81
7 b g Librettist(USA) Turn Back (Pivotal)
1954[7] 3571[5] 3895[8] 4189[2] 5151[2] 6502[7] 7360[7]

Jaywalker (IRE) *Rebecca Bastiman* a90 85
5 b g Footstepsinthesand Nipping (IRE) (Night Shift (USA))
1945[2] 2290[4] ◆ 2754[5] (3159) 3618[4] 3995[3] 4536[2] 6793[12] (7433) 7858[3] 7990[7]

Jazaalah (USA) *Owen Burrows* 26
2 ch f Hard Spun(USA) Teeba (USA) (Seeking The Gold (USA))
6336[8]

Jazri *Milton Bradley* a67 64
5 b g Myboycharlie(IRE) Read Federica (Fusaichi Pegasus (USA))
55[5] 173[4] 316[9] 606[7] 773[7] 2645[4] 2872[6] 3064[7] 3488[3] 4293[6] 4656[5] 8382[4] ◆ 8500[6]

Jazz Cat (IRE) *Paul Cole* a60 61
3 ch f Tamayuz Chelsea Rose (IRE) (Desert King (IRE))
6251[3] ◆ 6441[7] 7311[5] 7654[7]

Jazz Et Salsa (FR) *J-L Mace* a48 52
5 b g Kingsalsa(USA) Jazz Protegee (USA) (Della Francesca (USA))
8422a[6]

Jazzi Top *John Gosden* a85 113
4 b m Danehill Dancer(IRE) Zee Zee Top (Zafonic (USA))
1886[7] 3271[5]

Jazz Legend (USA) *Robert Cowell* a79 65
3 b g Scat Daddy(USA) Champion Ride (USA) (Candy Ride (ARG))
954[6] 1271[5] 1922[10] 2742[16] 4365[8] 4944[4] 5769[9] 6098[3]

Jazzy (IRE) *Martin Keighley* a77 78
3 b g Roderic O'Connor(IRE) Lucayan Beauty (IRE) (Marju (IRE))
(139) (253) 1260[5] 1828[3] 6300[8]

Jazzy Lady (IRE) *Jim Best* a50 26
5 b m Intikhab(USA) Lock's Heath (CAN) (Topsider (USA))
3470[5] 4018[7]

Jeanie's Place *Richard Fahey* a72 73
3 ch f Compton Place Good Again (Dubai Destination (USA))
419[4]

Jeans Lady *John Gallagher* a7
7 b m Milan Indian Miss (Idiots Delight)
318[7] 487[7]

Jeany (IRE) *Bryan Smart* 67
2 b f Kodiac Flower Bowl (IRE) (Noverre (USA))
3874[3] 4254[2] 4725[2] 6214[2] 6641[3]

Jebediah Shine *David O'Meara* a94 95
4 ch m Kyllachy Ardessie (Bahamian Bounty)
106[3] (323) ◆ 359[5] 966[4] 1650[6] 2305[2] 2658[9] 3392[9]

Jebel Tara *Alistair Whillans* a60 54
11 b g Diktat Chantilly (FR) (Sanglamore (USA))
1488[7] 1692[8] 2442[6] 3069[3] 3211[3] 4005[12] 4771[8] 5714[7] 6100[4] 6451[7] 6909[6] 7093[11] 7323[10] 7850[11] 8013[4] 8288[6] 8589[11]

Jeeraan (USA) *Doug Watson* a100 71
6 b g Distorted Humor(USA) Jaish (USA) (Seeking The Gold (USA))
453a[12]

Jelly Monger (IRE) *Dominic Ffrench Davis* a93 93
4 b m Strategic Prince Royal Jelly (King's Best (USA))
3860^{5} 4391^{6} 5240^{4}

Jemayel (IRE) *J-C Rouget* 110
3 ch f Lope De Vega(IRE) Nawal (FR) (Homme De Loi (IRE))
(2316a) 3452a^{9} ◆ 4864^{3} 5754a^{2} 6988a^{4}

Jembatt (IRE) *Michael Mulvany* a48 69
9 ch g Captain Rio Silly Imp (IRE) (Imperial Frontier (USA))
4899a^{13} 6464a^{5}

Jenji (IRE) *David Evans* a19 24
2 b f Pour Moi(IRE) Distant Symphony (FR) (Dalakhani (IRE))
1086^{9} 5637^{9} 6035^{10}

Jenniechild (IRE) *Peter Fahey* a73 77
3 b f Tagula(IRE) Belle Child (IRE) (Bijou D'Inde)
5730^{8}

Jennies Jewel (IRE) *Jarlath P Fahey* 104
9 b m Flemensfirth(USA) Fishin Joella (IRE) (Gone Fishin)
(3246) 6820a^{8} 7195a^{5} 7708a^{14}

Jenny Sparks *Sheena West* a45 43
5 b m Winker Watson Stephanie's Mind (Mind Games)
5710^{9} 6891^{5}

Jenychope (FR) *D Windrif* a37 70
2 ch f Soave(GER) Jennhill (FR) (Sabrehill (USA))
3763a^{3} 4471a^{2} 5279a^{9} 5568a^{6} 6015a^{5}

Jeremys Joy (IRE) *Emmet Michael Butterly* a49 93
4 b m Jeremy(USA) Desert's Queen (IRE) (Desert Prince (IRE))
1509a^{9}

Jersey Bull (IRE) *Michael Madgwick* a68 74
4 b g Clodovil(IRE) Chaguaramas (IRE) (Mujadil (USA))
6241^{10} 6827^{12} 7614^{10} 7937^{5} (8155) 8448^{5}

Jersey Heartbeat *Richard Hannon* a43 47
2 b f Bated Breath Selkirk Sky (Selkirk (USA))
7819^{6} 7976^{11} 8151^{11}

Jersey Jewel (FR) *Tom Dascombe* a74 75
4 b m Naaqoos Nikolenka (IRE) (Indian Ridge)
1825^{6} 2616^{6} 3642^{4} 4234^{4} 4730^{5} (4950) 5208^{U} 5805^{2} 7508^{2} 7732^{4}

Jersey Roy *Richard Fahey* a65 58
3 b g Major Cadeaux Charlie Girl (Puissance)
1146^{8} 1573^{5} 2733^{7} 3421^{8} 3838^{6}

Jess *Kevin Ryan* a69 53
3 b f Equiano(FR) Poyle Meg (Dansili)
(286) 612^{4} 797^{4} 2050^{7} 3017^{4} 3777^{8} 3985^{5} 8389^{10}

Jessiboo (IRE) *Tom Dascombe* a52
2 b f Approve(IRE) Mar Sin De (IRE) (Danetime (IRE))
7259^{5} 7510^{5}

Jessica Jo (IRE) *Mark Johnston* a58 64
3 ch f Mastercraftsman(IRE) Naomh Geileis (USA) (Grand Slam (USA))
1798^{13} 2197^{4} 3019^{3} 7043^{12} 7385^{10} 7735^{4} 7944^{3} 8194^{4} 8307^{5} 8471^{3}

Jessie Allan (IRE) *Jim Goldie* a52 42
5 b m Bushranger(IRE) Ishimagic (Ishiguru (USA))
3016^{10} 3946^{8} 4486^{8} 4771^{12} 7092^{11} 7603^{5} 7860^{13} 8288^{11} 8588^{4}

Jester Spirit (IRE) *Tom Dascombe* 55
2 b g Dragon Pulse(IRE) Gala Spirit (IRE) (Invincible Spirit (IRE))
1422^{8} 2417^{3} 3396^{4} 4404^{4}

Je Suis Charlie *Michael Bell* 73
2 b g High Chaparral(IRE) Fin (Groom Dancer (USA))
5740^{6} (6473) 7471^{3}

Je T'Aime Encore *Gay Kelleway* a65 60
4 b g Acclamation Mimisel (Selkirk (USA))
32^{5} 216^{4} 362^{6} 526^{5} 787^{3} 876^{5} 2899^{12}

Jethou Island *David Menuisier* a61 66
5 ch m Virtual Lihou Island (Beveled (USA))
(55) 232^{8} 438^{7} 1170^{4}

Jethro (IRE) *Brian Ellison* 49
5 b g Craigsteel Wee Mo (IRE) (Zaffaran (USA))
1662^{5} 2260^{7}

Jet Setter (IRE) *Brian Meehan* a67 70
2 ch g Fast Company(IRE) Raven One (IRE) (Titus Livius (FR))
1713^{6} 2732^{8} 6873^{4} 7440^{9} 7549^{3} 7898^{4} 8159^{7}

Jet Setting (IRE) *Adrian Paul Keatley* 120
3 b f Fast Company(IRE) Mean Lae (IRE) (Johannesburg (USA))
(1369a) 1888^{9} (2509a) 3339^{6} 6352a^{6} (6983a) 7352^{11}

Jetstream Express (IRE) *Simon Crisford* a58 68
3 b c New Approach(IRE) Airline (USA) (Woodman (USA))
2327^{7} 3723^{5}

Jewel House *John Gosden* a56 77
2 b c Dubawi(IRE) Arizona Jewel (Dansili)
4349^{10} 6368^{5} 7012^{2}

Jezza *Victor Dartnall* a63 67
10 br g Pentire Lara (GER) (Sharpo)
138^{5} 695^{2} 1038^{2} (1831) 3528^{10} 3746^{9}

Jim Dandy *Alan King* 79
3 ch g Dandy Man(IRE) Noctilucent (JPN) (Lammtarra (USA))
2393^{8} 3110^{8} 4055^{6} 4554^{4} 5391^{4}

Jimenez (IRE) *Brian Meehan* a86 86
3 b c Acclamation Fritta Mista (IRE) (Linamix (FR))
1714^{9} 2479^{3} 3066^{3} 4055^{7} (4562) 5603^{3} 6549^{6} 7153^{9} 7506^{6}

Jimmy's Hall *J S Moore* a80 79
4 b g Kyllachy Up At Dawn (Inchinor)
239^{3} 457^{4} 670^{4} 1545^{9} 1746^{5}

Jimmy Two Times (FR) *A Fabre* 114
3 gr c Kendargent(FR) Steel Woman (IRE) (Anabaa (USA))
1374a^{2} 2283a^{10} (3938a) 5217a^{3} 6991a^{4}

Jim's Journey (AUS) *Peter F Blanch* 97
4 ch g Good Journey(USA) Mandarina (AUS) (Jeune)
7826a^{7}

Jingle Jangle *Adrian Paul Keatley* 64
3 b f Monsieur Bond(IRE) Assuage (Wolfhound (USA))
5225^{7}

Jinky *Linda Perratt* a65 77
8 b g Noverre(USA) Aries (GER) (Big Shuffle (USA))
1692^{5} 2364^{5} 2524^{7} 2961^{7}

Jintshi *Mark Johnston* a78 73
3 b c Poet's Voice Ivory Gala (FR) (Galileo (IRE))
314^{4} (466) 705^{5} 1411^{3} 2145^{5} 2565^{3} 3252^{5} 3876^{2} 4046^{7}

Jive Factor (USA) *Ed Dunlop* a58 58
2 b g The Factor(USA) Jive Talk (USA) (Kingmambo (USA))
6945^{6} 7226^{9} 7483^{7}

Jive Talking (IRE) *Michael Bell* a71 73
2 ch f Zoffany(IRE) Inis Boffin (Danehill Dancer (IRE))
4397^{3} 4642^{5} 6828^{2} 8074^{2}

Jive Time *James Tate* a74 78
3 b c Motivator Lindy Hop (IRE) (Danehill Dancer (IRE))
(331) 2145^{4} 3042^{3} 3728^{5} 4568^{3} 6684^{7}

Joailliere (IRE) *D K Weld* 104
4 b m Dubawi(IRE) Majestic Silver (IRE) (Linamix (FR))
1016a^{3} 1226a^{3} 1509a^{7} 6983a^{2}

Joaldo *Antony Brittain* a43 36
4 b g Monsieur Bond(IRE) Labba (Tiger Hill (IRE))
892^{6} 1164^{5} 1556^{5}

Joanne Park *Clive Cox* 61
3 b f Kheleyf(USA) Sarah Park (IRE) (Redback)
4639^{6} 5388^{4} 6036^{7} 7038^{12}

Jocks Wa Hae (IRE) *John Patrick Shanahan* 65
3 b c High Chaparral(IRE) Queen Jock (USA) (Repent (USA))
3020^{3} ◆ (3287) 3750^{4} 4314^{7} (4872) 5580^{8} 7057^{3}

Jock Talk (IRE) *John Patrick Shanahan* a53 55
2 b c Famous Name Katdogawn (Bahhare (USA))
2570^{9} 4336^{6} 5834^{5}

Jocular *Edward U Hales* a34 79
5 b g Champs Elysees Heart Stopping (USA) (Chester House (USA))
4721a^{16} 6465a^{9}

Jodies Jem *William Jarvis* a91 93
6 br g Kheleyf(USA) First Approval (Royal Applause)
240^{3} 620^{4} 886^{3} (1418) 1959^{4} 2819^{6}

Joe Packet *Jonathan Portman* a64 81
9 ch g Joe Bear(IRE) Costa Packet (IRE) (Hussonet (USA))
2469^{2} 3233^{2} 5896^{4} 7221^{4}

Joe Palooka (IRE) *Alan Coogan*
6 b g Galileo(IRE) Glinting Desert (IRE) (Desert Prince (IRE))
5023^{11}

Joey's Destiny (IRE) *George Baker* a91 94
6 ch g Kheleyf(USA) Maid Of Ailsa (USA) (Pivotal)
1218^{9} 1856^{8} 2547^{5} 2898^{17} 7186^{5} 8256^{4}

Johannes Vermeer (IRE) *A P O'Brien* 115
3 b c Galileo(IRE) Inca Princess (IRE) (Holy Roman Emperor (IRE))
7152^{3} ◆

Johann Strauss *M F De Kock* a86 93
5 br h High Chaparral(IRE) Inchmina (Cape Cross (IRE))
720a^{8} 845a^{7}

Johara (IRE) *H-F Devin* a95 100
5 b m Iffraaj Hurricane Irene (IRE) (Green Desert (USA))
4696a^{2} 5384a^{4} 7087a^{5} 7312a^{4} 7650^{10}

John Biscuit (IRE) *Jo Davis*
8 ch g Hawk Wing(USA) Princess Magdalena (Pennekamp (USA))
4303^{6}

John Caesar (IRE) *Rebecca Bastiman* a69 68
5 b g Bushranger(IRE) Polish Belle (Polish Precedent (USA))
(1323) 1785^{6} 2673^{5} 3253^{2} 3876^{3} 4486^{7} 5030^{3} 5323^{3} 5715^{9} 6645^{3} 7007^{4} 7336^{4}

John Coffey (IRE) *Michael Appleby* a63 60
7 b g Acclamation Appleblossom Pearl (IRE) (Peintre Celebre (USA))
197^{6} 297^{6} 857^{P}

John Joiner *Peter Hedger* a49 68
4 b g Captain Gerrard(IRE) Nigella (Band On The Run)
1181^{3} 1913^{2} 2447^{8} 2845^{3} (3469) (4264) 4952^{2} 6296^{3} ◆ 7626^{6} 7774^{2}

John Milton (IRE) *Karen McLintock* a58
3 b g Poet's Voice Kelly Nicole (IRE) (Rainbow Quest (USA))
8481^{3} ◆ 8585^{7}

Johnny Barnes (IRE) *John Gosden* 110
4 b h Acclamation Mahalia (IRE) (Danehill (USA))
1637^{4} ◆ 2243^{10} 3672^{7} 6558^{8} 7497^{15}

Johnny B Goode (IRE) *Chris Dwyer* a73 71
4 b g Approve(IRE) Musica E Magia (IRE) (King's Theatre (IRE))
670^{7} 944^{9} 1178^{10} 1525^{4} 1878^{4} (2047) 2425^{2} 2537^{2} (3078) 3821^{3} 4360^{6} 4742^{5} 5369^{4} 5635^{5} (6510)

Johnny Cavagin *Ronald Thompson* a80 93
7 b g Superior Premium Beyond The Rainbow (Mind Games)
1215^{6} 3645^{2} (3980) 4299^{12} 4946^{7} 6539^{11} 6962^{10} 7702^{10}

Johnnys Legacy (IRE) *Ken Wingrove* a18 8
9 b g Ecton Park(USA) Lexy May (USA) (Lear Fan (USA))
563^{12} 673^{10}

Johnny Splash (IRE) *Roger Teal* a66 9
7 b g Dark Angel(IRE) Ja Ganhou (Midyan (USA))
319^{6} 604^{8} 775^{9} 1269^{4} 2697^{14} 3474^{10} 4264^{13}

John Potts *Brian Baugh* a60 43
11 b g Josr Algarhoud(IRE) Crown City (USA) (Coronado's Quest (USA))
334^{9} 563^{4} 787^{5} 1654^{6} 2566^{10}

John Reel (FR) *David Evans* a104 104
7 b g Country Reel(USA) John Quatz (FR) (Johann Quatz (FR))
614^{2} ◆ 793^{2} 871^{3} 1067^{9} 1967^{13} (2482) 3340^{17} 3662^{3} 5639^{9} 5894^{7} 6321^{4} 7575^{2} 8529^{3}

John T Chance (IRE) *Brian Meehan* a60 52
2 b g Lawman(FR) Classic Legend (Galileo (IRE))
4790^{7} 5304^{11} 5820^{6} 6681^{4} (6963) 7482^{4}

Jolievitesse (FR) *K R Burke* a81 83
4 b g Elusive City(USA) Volvoreta (Suave Dancer (USA))
66^{2} ◆ 1093^{6} 2163^{4} 3057^{2} 3520^{8} 4013^{5}

Jollify (IRE) *A Fabre* 100
3 b f Manduro(GER) Jomana (IRE) (Darshaan)
2944a^{4} 3935a^{7} 8024a^{2}

Jollydee (IRE) *Paul Midgley* a40 59
2 b f Frozen Power(IRE) Spinning Maid (USA) (Forestry (USA))
1199^{4} ◆ 1407^{3} 2344^{2} 3223^{6} 4725^{9} 5364^{9} 6388a^{29} 7091^{7}

Jolly Red Jeanz (IRE) *Anabel K Murphy* a58 53
5 ch m Intense Focus(USA) Sovienne (IRE) (Soviet Star (USA))
143^{5} 543^{8} 733^{2} 837^{6} 919^{7} 3970^{11}

Jona Black (FR) *W Delalande* a65 49
3 bb c Fine Grain(JPN) Jona Gold (FR) (Cricket Ball (USA))
2456a^{7}

Jon H The Lawman (IRE) *Ronald Thompson* a35 49
3 b g Lawman(FR) Lan Pham Ti (IRE) (Librettist (USA))
1217^{7} 1551^{7} 2308^{4} 3015^{11} 4233^{5} 4847^{6} 5319^{9} 5921^{7}

Jonnie Skull (IRE) *Phil McEntee* a63 70
10 b g Pyrus(USA) Sovereign Touch (IRE) (Pennine Walk)
158^{6} 264^{5} 617^{7} 707^{4} 1781^{6} 2609^{9} 2899^{5} 3043^{3} 3255^{5} 3354^{5} 4504^{8} 5090^{5}

Jonny Delta *Jim Goldie* 79
9 ch g Sulamani(IRE) Send Me An Angel (IRE) (Lycius (USA))
3942^{8} 4491^{6} 6812^{6} 7251^{7}

Jonofark (IRE) *Brian Rothwell* a49 63
3 b g Arcano(IRE) Dream Valley (IRE) (Sadler's Wells (USA))
4347^{6} 4983^{2} ◆ 6052^{9} 6520^{4} 7601^{11} 8145^{10}

Jordan James (IRE) *Brian Ellison* a27 73
3 b g Equiano(FR) Deira (USA) (Green Desert (USA))
1216^{8} 3366^{8} 3567^{8} 5539^{2} (6434) 7333^{2}

Jordan Sport *David Simcock* a91 75
3 b g Dubawi(IRE) Wonder Why (GER) (Tiger Hill (IRE))
1079^{4} (1817) 2239^{3} 3414^{9} 7462^{8} 7958^{6} (8407)

Jordaura *John Murray* a35 43
10 br g Primo Valentino(IRE) Christina's Dream (Spectrum (IRE))
8400^{12}

Jorvick (USA) *D Smaga* a94 95
3 gr c Mizzen Mast(USA) Deep Feeling (USA) (Empire Maker (USA))
5699a^{5} 7137a^{7}

Jorvik Prince *Karen Tutty* a61 53
2 br g Kheleyf(USA) Wotatomboy (Captain Rio)
4508^{4} 5477^{9} 6009^{5} 7579^{3} (7884) 8097^{6}

Joshlee (IRE) *Richard Hughes* 57
2 b f Dark Angel(IRE) Kay Es Jay (FR) (Xaar)
2097^{5} 3122^{7} 6543^{8} 7571^{10}

Josh Perry *Rod Millman* a48 41
3 b g Hellvelyn Emma Peel (Emarati (USA))
5544^{5} 6036^{6} 6967^{6} 7937^{9} 8247^{3} 8492^{10}

Joshua Reynolds *John Gosden* 66
2 b c Nathaniel(IRE) Dash To The Front (Diktat)
7226^{5} ◆

Josiane (IRE) *Richard Hannon* a41 42
2 gr f Zebedee High Society Girl (IRE) (Key Of Luck (USA))
1793^{7} 2097^{7} 6624^{13}

Joules *Natalie Lloyd-Beavis* a73 78
3 b c Oasis Dream Frappe (IRE) (Inchinor)
1423^{4} 2141a^{11} (4085) 4365^{9} 5336^{5} 6280^{11}

Journey *John Gosden* a70 121
4 b m Dubawi(IRE) Montare (IRE) (Montjeu (IRE))
2189^{3} (2690) (6747) (7351)

Journey Home (USA) *H Graham Motion* 96
2 bb f War Front(USA) Soul Search (USA) (A.P. Indy (USA))
(8127a)

Joyful Day (IRE) *Robert Cowell* a71 52
3 b c Lilbourne Lad(IRE) Blondie's Esteem (IRE) (Mark Of Esteem (IRE))
145^{4} 3267^{5} 4003^{8}

Joyful Dream (IRE) *J S Moore* a66 67
2 ch f Dream Ahead(USA) Tearsforjoy (USA) (Street Cry (IRE))
4350^{8} 4586^{6} 5142a^{10} 6035^{3} 6421^{4} 6875^{9} 7098^{3} 7294a^{5} 7688^{10} 8025^{3} 8230^{4}

Joyful Star *Fred Watson* a42 59
6 b g Teofilo(IRE) Extreme Beauty (USA) (Rahy (USA))
2096^{5} ◆ (2528) ◆ 3013^{4} 3344^{4} 4144^{8} 6478^{11}

Joyful Trinity (IRE) *John Moore* a93 118
4 b g Zanzibari(USA) Bargouzine (USA) (Stravinsky (USA))
8332a^{3}

Joyroo (IRE) *Brian Ellison*
2 b c Tagula(IRE) Memphis Belle (Linamix (FR))
3516^{11}

Joys Delight *Daniel Mark Loughnane* a61
2 b f Stimulation(IRE) Lambadora (Suave Dancer (USA))
8189^{3}

Joysunny *Michael Easterby* 38
2 b f Camacho Alustar (Emarati (USA))
3654^{10} 4000^{5}

J. S. Choice (USA) *Todd Pletcher* 95
2 bb c Congrats(USA) Oil Empress (USA) (Empire Maker (USA))
7807a^{13}

Juan Horsepower *Richard Hannon* a77 75
2 b g Foxwedge(AUS) Elysee (IRE) (Fantastic Light (USA))
2147^{2} 2756^{5} 3315^{3} 4076^{7} 4128^{8} 7319^{2} 8243^{4} (8494) 8582^{2}

Juanito Chico (IRE) *William Jarvis* a77 75
2 br g Pour Moi(IRE) Miss Kittyhawk (IRE) (Hawk Wing (USA))
2648^{9} 3819^{8} 4075^{5} 4553^{4} ◆ 6800^{2} (7033) 7460^{2}

Jubilance (IRE) *Bent Olsen* a87 98
7 b g Oratorio(IRE) Literacy (USA) (Diesis)
3449a^{8} 4329a^{8} 5187a^{8} 6390a^{8}

Jubilee Brig *Alan Swinbank* a80 73
6 b g Kheleyf(USA) Voile (IRE) (Barathea (IRE))
2677^{7} 7591^{9} 8287^{6}

Jubilee Song *Richard Whitaker* 55
4 b m Royal Applause Cosmic Song (Cosmonaut)
2015^{6} 2525^{6} 3921^{11} 4445^{7}

Judicial (IRE) *Julie Camacho* a101 105
4 b g Iffraaj Marlinka (Marju (IRE))
213^{4} 677^{9} (2258) ◆ 3151^{13} 4667^{12} (5641) 6327^{18} 6779^{3}

Judicial Enquiry *Mike Sowersby* a49 62
3 b g Lawman(FR) Koniya (IRE) (Doyoun)
1163^{5} 1835^{4} 2652^{8} 3732^{7} 4527^{11} 5319^{12}

Judicious *Geoffrey Harker* 61
9 ch g Pivotal Virtuous (Exit To Nowhere (USA))
2555^{11} 3212^{4} 3883^{5} 4456^{4} 5293^{2}

Judith Gardenier *Iain Jardine* a50 53
4 b m Rip Van Winkle(IRE) Millagros (IRE) (Pennekamp (USA))
2419^{6} 2958^{5} 3921^{13} 4314^{5} 4872^{5} 5227^{6} 5783^{5} 6102^{2} 6422^{8} (6619)

Judy Woods (IRE) *Bryan Smart* a59 51
2 b f Excelebration(IRE) Snowpalm (Halling (USA))
6477^{9} 7142^{5} 7855^{9} ◆ 8071^{5}

Jufn *Saeed bin Suroor* a82 76
3 b g Nayef(USA) Deyaar (USA) (Storm Cat (USA))
1398^{4}

Jukebox Jive (FR) *Anthony Honeyball* 79
2 b g Jukebox Jury(IRE) Sweetheart (Sinndar (IRE))
6663^{7} 7273^{3} 7580^{6}

Jule In The Crown *Mick Channon* 84
2 b f Harbour Watch(IRE) Jules (IRE) (Danehill (USA))
1988^{6} (2310) 2624^{4} 3270^{13}

Jules N Rome (USA) *Danny Gargan*
4 rg m Dunkirk(USA) Pretty Honoree (USA) (Double Honor (USA))
(89a)

Julia Dream *William Haggas* a81 81
3 b f Montjeu(IRE) Winds Of Time (IRE) (Danehill (USA))
2182^{2} 2767^{2} ◆ (4955)

Juliette Fair (IRE) *D K Weld* 101
3 gr f Dark Angel(IRE) Capulet Monteque (IRE) (Camacho)
1369a^{9} 2272a^{11} 4540a^{8}

Jumbo Prado (USA) *Daniel Mark Loughnane* a74 49
7 gr g El Prado(IRE) Sant Elena (Efisio)
(467) (860) 1502^{4} 3514^{9} (8190) 8343^{4}

Jumbo Vee (IRE) *Declan Carroll* 8
2 ch g Casamento(IRE) Marla (GER) (Pentire)
6716^{7} 7074^{9}

Jumeirah (DEN) *Lone Bager* 91
8 b g Black Sam Bellamy(IRE) Sypha (FR) (Saumarez)
4329a^{4}

Jumeirah Star (USA) *Robert Cowell* a64 70
3 b f Street Boss(USA) Cosmic Wing (USA) (Halo (USA))
1497^{2} (2560) (4262) 5523^{6} 6479^{7} 7811^{5} 8358^{5} 8595^{10}

Jumira Bridge *Roger Varian* 89
2 b c Invincible Spirit(IRE) Zykina (Pivotal)
3819^{2} ◆ 4274^{2} 6260^{6}

Jumira Prince (IRE) *Roger Varian* 39
2 ch c Exceed And Excel(AUS) Aoife Alainn (IRE) (Dr Fong (USA))
2756^{10}

Jumping Around (IRE) *William Haggas* 82
2 b f Dark Angel(IRE) Box Of Frogs (IRE) (One Cool Cat (USA))
3074^{4} (4261) 4884^{13} 5931^{2} 6292^{2}

Jumping Jack (IRE) *Richard Hughes* a73 72
2 b g Sir Prancealot(IRE) She's A Character (Invincible Spirit (IRE))
1233^{8} 1944^{3} 3531^{5} (4937) 5297^{2} (5528) 6191^{3} 6705^{3} 6898^{3}

Jungle Bay *Jane Chapple-Hyam* a74 81
9 b g Oasis Dream Dominica (Alhaarth (IRE))
1419^{8} 1945^{6} 2765^{8} ◆ 3144^{5}

Jungleboogie (GER) *C Von Der Recke*
4 b h Nicaron(GER) Jive (GER) (Montjeu (IRE))
(664a)

Jungle Cat (IRE) *Charlie Appleby* 114
4 b h Iffraaj Mike's Wildcat (USA) (Forest Wildcat (USA))
(370a) 841a^{2} 1104a^{4} 1862^{2} 3244^{4} ◆ 4151^{15} 4824^{14}

Jungle George *Scott Dixon* a38
2 b g Kheleyf(USA) Amouage Royale (IRE) (Mr Greeley (USA))
8569^{4}

Juno (BRZ) *Richard E Mandella* a88 102
3 ch f Setembro Chove(BRZ) Irmadohomemra (USA) (Candy Stripes (USA))
7829a^{11}

Junoesque *John Gallagher* 64
2 b f Virtual Snake Skin (Golden Snake (USA))
3859^{11} 4579^{5} 5387^{6} 6535^{7}

Junoob *Chris Waller* a97 112
8 ch g Haafhd Faydah (USA) (Bahri (USA))
7712a^{9}

Jununee (IRE) *M F De Kock* a16
4 b h Galileo(IRE) Kentucky Warbler (IRE) (Spinning World (USA))
8a^{10}

Jupiter Ascending *Michael Appleby*
2 b c Excelebration(IRE) Habita (IRE) (Montjeu (IRE))
6632[10] 7100[7] 7306[9]

Jupiter Custos (FR) *Michael Scudamore* a81 81
4 bb g Le Havre(IRE) Angel Rose (IRE) (Definite Article)
4785[4] 5413[5] 5963[2] 6267[2] 6804[3]

Jupiter Light *John Gosden* 52
2 b c Lonhro(AUS) Fantasia (Sadler's Wells (USA))
6211[6]

Just A Groove (IRE) *Ann Duffield* a57 71
3 b g Kodiac Callanish (Inchinor)
659[6]

Just An Idea (IRE) *Harry Dunlop* 86
2 b c Lilbourne Lad(IRE) Emreliya (IRE) (Danehill Dancer (IRE))
2125[3] 3247[8] 3858[3] 4755[7] 5497a[4] 6538[11] 7819[4]

Justanotherbottle (IRE) *Declan Carroll* 74
2 ch g Intense Focus(USA) Duchess K (IRE) (Bachelor Duke (USA))
4725[6] 5433[6] 5884[2] (6214) 6564[3]

Just Be Lucky (IRE) *Conor Dore* a47 45
4 ch g Intense Focus(USA) Anda (Selkirk (USA))
1387[3] 1785[3] 2010[4] (2441) (2555) 3517[10] (4511) 5191[5] 5972[8] 7017[13] 7240[11] 7644[12]

Juste Pour Nous *Mark Johnston* a69 76
3 b g Pour Moi(IRE) Steam Cuisine (Mark Of Esteem (IRE))
1220[2] 1636[4] 2252[2] 2909[5] 3300[10] 3814[4] 4406[2] 4561[8] 5147[10] 6110[12] 7060[11] 7535[16] 7791[7] 8161[9] (8364)

Just Fab (IRE) *Ali Stronge* a68 49
3 b f Canford Cliffs(IRE) Unlock (IRE) (Key Of Luck (USA))
1638[6] 2405[4] 4087[6] 4760[3] 5263[5] 6187[5] 6631[3] 7070[6] 7463[2] 8146[10]

Just Five (IRE) *John Weymes* a48 43
10 b g Olmodavor(USA) Wildsplash (USA) (Deputy Minister (CAN))
1165[7] 1791[3] 4214[11]

Just For Show (IRE) *Shaun Lycett* a58 50
3 b f Poet's Voice Starchy (Cadeaux Genereux)
3350[6] 3958[8] 5504[7] 8411[10]

Just For You *James Fanshawe* a81 69
3 b f Fastnet Rock(AUS) Quiet Protest (USA) (Kingmambo (USA))
5023[2] 7627[5] 7942[2] (8090)

Just Fred (IRE) *Denis Coakley* a54 46
3 br g Excellent Art Consignia (IRE) (Definite Article)
2325[11] 3975[5] 4290[12] 4993[5] 5604[4] 6513[2] 6967[2] 7464[4]

Just Glamorous (IRE) *Ronald Harris* a74 114
3 ch g Arcano(IRE) Glamorous Air (IRE) (Air Express (IRE))
2106[2] 2288[3] 2750[2] 3407[2] (3893) (4268) ◆ (4612) 4803[8] 5657[3] (6391a) 6990a[16]

Just Heather (IRE) *John Wainwright* 31
2 gr f Zebedee Miss Sundance (IRE) (Desert Sun)
2885[8] 3640[6] 4663[10]

Just Hiss *Tim Easterby* 94
3 b g Lawman(FR) Feather Boa (IRE) (Sri Pekan (USA))
1217[5] 1589[3] 1953[3] 3853[4] 4342[2] 4948[4] 5438[2] (5919) (6344) 7153[3]

Justice (IRE) *Jose Santos* a44 42
3 b f Lawman(FR) Sheboygan (IRE) (Grand Lodge (USA))
87[9] 174[7] 436[10] 763[8] 902[4] 1164[9] 7302[5] 8542[12]

Justice Angel (IRE) *David Elsworth* a71 88
3 gr f Dark Angel(IRE) Malaica (FR) (Roi Gironde (IRE))
1385[3] (1977) 2683[7] 3575[7]

Justice Belle (IRE) *Ed Walker* a98 102
4 b m Montjeu(IRE) Metaphor (USA) (Woodman (USA))
6118[5] (6708) 7569a[14]

Justice Ears (IRE) *David Elsworth* a55 56
3 b g Dylan Thomas(IRE) Shanghai Visit (IRE) (Peintre Celebre (USA))
314[6]

Justice First *Ed Dunlop* a84 86
4 b g Zebedee Nelly's Glen (Efisio)
169[3] 349[6] (518) 712[4] 900[2] 1041[6] ◆ (1724) 2579[10] 2903[2] 3414[12] 4644[9]

Justice Focused (IRE) *David Elsworth* a72
3 b g Intense Focus(USA) Moon Shine (FR) (Groom Dancer (USA))
1573[2]

Justice Frederick (IRE) *Paul D'Arcy* 81
2 br g Lawman(FR) Sheer Spirit (IRE) (Caerleon (USA))
3382[10] 5108[4] 7469[5]

Justice Good (IRE) *David Elsworth* a106 100
4 b g Acclamation Qui Moi (CAN) (Swain (IRE))
288[6] 483[6] 677[10] 1394[8] 1887[13] 7771[3] (8069)

Justice Grace (IRE) *Ralph Beckett* a75 86
3 b g Kodiac Right After Moyne (IRE) (Imperial Ballet (IRE))
639[4] 1091[2] 1577[4] 2694[4] (3596) 4092[2] 4920[7] 6445[4]

Justice Lady (IRE) *David Elsworth* a64 81
3 br f Dream Ahead(USA) Celestial Dream (IRE) (Oasis Dream)
(460) ◆ 783[4] 1935[2] 3000[3] 3360[2] (4280) (4658) 4861[3] 5882[5] 6195[4]

Justice Lass (IRE) *David Elsworth* a78 80
3 b f Canford Cliffs(IRE) Dibiya (IRE) (Caerleon (USA))
1898[3] 2239[10] 3001[6] 3410[5] 4157[5] 5649[4] 6742[2] 7227[8]

Justice Law (IRE) *David Elsworth* a92 92
3 gr c Acclamation Inishtearaght (IRE) (Verglas (IRE))
1603[7] ◆ 2161[15] 2870[6]

Justice Lucky (USA) *David Elsworth* 46
3 b g Scat Daddy(USA) Lucky Be Me (CAN) (Peaks And Valleys (USA))
2248[10] 2614[9]

Justice Pleasing *Roger Fell* a57 61
3 b g Kodiac Spangle (Galileo (IRE))
3023[6] 3400[5] 3643[7] 4256[6] 4701[8] 5068[11] 6905[5] 7850[4] 8013[2] 8146[6] (8401)

Justice Rock *Phil McEntee* a63 50
3 b g Acclamation Fashion Rocks (IRE) (Rock Of Gibraltar (IRE))
242[7] 286[3] 531[4] 883[3] 902[2] 1435[3] 1745[6] 3140[6] 3473[7] 4280[5] 4570[5] 5041[4] 5470[5] 5636[6] 8383[7]

Justice Smart (IRE) *Sir Michael Stoute* 85
3 ch c Kyllachy Laurentina (Cadeaux Genereux)
2039[4] (3996) ◆ 4886[6] 5892[5] 6736[12]

Justice Well *Luciano Vitabile* a94 88
4 b g Halling(USA) Porthcawl (Singspiel (IRE))
486[11] 7719a[7]

Justineo *Robert Cowell* a91 110
7 b h Oasis Dream Loulwa (IRE) (Montjeu (IRE))
1862[9] 2475[10] (3090a)

Just In Time *Alan King* a55 58
2 b g Excelebration(IRE) Flying Finish (FR) (Priolo (USA))
7283[7] 7622[8] 7976[7]

Just Isla *John Flint* a57 60
6 ch m Halling(USA) Island Rapture (Royal Applause)
3314[7] 3739[8] 4504[3] 5235[5] 5953[6] 6826[2] 7070[2] 7943[5]

Just Joan (IRE) *T Stack* 89
3 b f Pour Moi(IRE) Wanna (IRE) (Danehill Dancer (IRE))
3539a[8] 4218a[10] 4812a[4] 5564a[10] 6495a[9] 7372a[5]

Just Marion (IRE) *Clare Ellam* a25 22
4 b m Bushranger(IRE) Dolphin Stamp (IRE) (Dolphin Street (FR))
257[10] 431[13] 1742[10] 1781[5] 1949[5] 2647[7] 8383[8]

Just Maybe *Mike Murphy* a68 50
2 b c Mayson Phantasmagoria (Fraam)
3463[5] (4938) 6139[3]

Just Over *Robert Cowell* a55
3 b f Bahamian Bounty Kassuta (Kyllachy)
791[7] 1256[6] 2039[8]

Just Paul (IRE) *Micky Hammond* a47 75
6 b g Clodovil(IRE) Tatamagouche (IRE) (Sadler's Wells (USA))
1926[8] 2091[9] 2906[5] 3262[5] 5068[7] 5355[10]

Just Pretend (USA) *S Seemar* a56
3 ch g Drosselmeyer(USA) Cateress (USA) (Tabasco Cat (USA))
8576a[5]

Just That Lord *Bill Turner* a91 90
3 ch g Avonbridge Lady Filly (Atraf)
935[5] (1112) ◆ (1935) 2218[11] 2751[2] 6633[6] 7752[6] 7864[3] 8032[5]

Just Us Two (IRE) *Robert Cowell* a88 87
4 b g Royal Applause Sarah's First (Cadeaux Genereux)
1836[4] 2261[3] 2775[8] 6114[7] 6926[3] 7202[3] 8150[5]

Jutland *Doug Watson* a103 99
9 b g Halling(USA) Dramatique (Darshaan)
188a[8]

Kaaber (USA) *Roy Brotherton* a57 54
5 b g Daaher(CAN) Taseel (USA) (Danzig (USA))
2309[8] 2849[9] 3748[9] (5270) 5953[4] 6311[4] (6853) 8316[9] 8541[5]

Kaatskill Nap (FR) *David Menuisier* 92
3 ch g Rip Van Winkle(IRE) Last Cast (FR) (Marju (IRE))
1626[5] 2440[2] 3809[3] (6528) 7117[11]

Kabaw (IRE) *S Seemar* a76 71
3 b f Elusive Pimpernel(USA) Holly Hawk (IRE) (Dubai Destination (USA))
184a[4] 534a[3]

Kachess *Tom Dascombe* 80
2 b f Kyllachy Fibou (USA) (Seeking The Gold (USA))
(2874) ◆ 3270[10] 4623[12] 5638[5] 6734[7]

Kachy *Tom Dascombe* 113
3 b c Kyllachy Dubai Bounty (Dubai Destination (USA))
1424[6] (1996) 2475[6] 3338[2] 4166[6] 4824[10] 6120[10]

Kadi (IRE) *Joseph Tuite* 34
2 ch f Dandy Man(IRE) Roskeen (IRE) (Grand Lodge (USA))
3122[8] 3718[6]

Kadooment Day (IRE) *K R Burke* a63 72
3 ch g Lord Shanakill(USA) Four Poorer (IRE) (Oasis Dream)
275[5] 423[3] 1286a[6] 1764[4] 3262[11] 4003[7]

Kadra (IRE) *M Halford* a102 88
3 b f Holy Roman Emperor(IRE) Kadayna (IRE) (Dalakhani (IRE))
(7676a)

Kadrizzi (FR) *Dean Ivory* a104 107
3 ch g Hurricane Cat(USA) Kadiania (FR) (Indian Rocket)
(262) ◆ (493) 821[2] 1070[3] 3165[5] 4062[18] (5148) 6112[6] 6916[5]

Kaeso *Nigel Tinkler* 46
2 b g Excelebration(IRE) Bahia Breeze (Mister Baileys)
7495[9] 7818[9]

Kafeel (USA) *Linda Jewell* a63 71
5 b g First Samurai(USA) Ishraak (USA) (Sahm (USA))
7816[8] 8249[11] 8498[8]

Kafoo *Ed Dunlop* a71 47
3 b g Dansili Nidhaal (IRE) (Observatory (USA))
1141[2] 1917[6] (2770) 3568[10]

Kahrab (IRE) *R Bouresly* a66 64
2 gr c Dark Angel(IRE) Dance Club (IRE) (Fasliyev (USA))
1840[4] 2196[5] 2800[5] 4602[4] 8391a[5]

Kaisan *Michael Bell* a69 73
3 b g Rip Van Winkle(IRE) Orinoco (IRE) (Darshaan)
275[3] 687[3] 4566[2]

Kajaki (IRE) *Kevin Ryan* a69 76
3 gr g Mastercraftsman(IRE) No Quest (IRE) (Rainbow Quest (USA))
2123[3] 2615[2] 3025[3] 3715[3] 4346[3] (5111) 6011[3]

Kakapuka *Anabel K Murphy* a59 56
9 br g Shinko Forest(IRE) No Rehearsal (FR) (Baillamont (USA))
588a[8] 663a[8] 1147[7] 1556[P]

Kakatosi *Mike Murphy* a89 94
9 br g Pastoral Pursuits Ladywell Blaise (IRE) (Turtle Island (IRE))
3895[7]

Kalahari (IRE) *Henry Spiller* a72 64
7 b g Halling(USA) Semaphore (Zamindar (USA))
(435) 693[6] 1222[7]

Kalahari Soldier (GER) *Mario Hofer* a79
5 rg g Soldier Hollow Kaziyma (FR) (Daylami (IRE))
2806a[12]

Kalamata *Roger Varian* a69 71
3 b f Sir Percy Kalamkas (USA) (Kingmambo (USA))
(148) ◆ (517) 729[2] ◆ 2348[4] 2798[3]

Kalann (IRE) *Denis Gerard Hogan* a80 96
9 b g Barathea(IRE) Karkiyla (IRE) (Darshaan)
4721a[17] 6350a[12] 6582[17]

Kalinda (SPA) *A Carrasco Sanchez* a78
3 b f Caradak(IRE) Sonrisillas (Best Of The Bests (IRE))
8148a[9]

Kalinka (FR) *C Ferland* 28
2 b f Rip Van Winkle(IRE) Ecume Du Jour (FR) (Hawk Wing (USA))
5142a[P]

Kalisma (IRE) *D K Weld* 84
3 b f Cape Cross(IRE) Kalarouna (IRE) (Selkirk (USA))
7372a[7]

Kalk Bay (IRE) *Michael Easterby* a87 91
9 b g Hawk Wing(USA) Politesse (USA) (Barathea (IRE))
1380[3] (1625) 1997[5] 2679[7] (2910) 3518[9] 4893[9] 5389[4] 6082[11] 6500[12] 7126[15] 7593[10] (7958) 8052[10]

Kalkrand (IRE) *John Gosden* a74 17
3 b c Dubawi(IRE) Kiltubber (IRE) (Sadler's Wells (USA))
(85) 379[3]

Kallipso (FR) *A Junk* a61 59
2 b f Zanzibari(USA) Kriska (FR) (Kaldou Star)
7346a[9]

Kallisha *Brendan Powell* 100
5 b m Whipper(USA) Shallika (IRE) (Alhaarth (IRE))
3662[2] 5002a[5]

Kallisto Freedom (IRE) *Philip Kirby* 28
2 b f Equiano(FR) Still Small Voice (Polish Precedent (USA))
5966[14] 6446[13] 7355[7]

Kalon Brama (IRE) *Peter Charalambous* a81 60
5 b m Kodiac Gilded Truffle (IRE) (Peintre Celebre (USA))
72[5] (324) 494[6]

Kambura (FR) *K Borgel* 102
2 gr f Literato(FR) Tambura (FR) (Kaldoun (FR))
(4471a) 7757a[2]

Kamra (USA) *Jeremy Noseda* a64 80
2 b g Stay Thirsty(USA) Milliondollarbill (USA) (Speightstown (USA))
2786[5] 3818[2] (4494) 5560[14] 6697[10] 8444[6]

Kanaf (IRE) *M Al Mheiri* a94 102
9 b g Elnadim(USA) Catcher Applause (Royal Applause)
370a[10] 623a[2] 810a[6]

Kananee (USA) *Saeed bin Suroor* a101 89
2 b c Exceed And Excel(AUS) Zoowraa (Azamour (IRE))
(1749) (2162) 3247[22] (7764) (7989)

Kantara Castle (IRE) *John Mackie* a58 63
5 b g Baltic King Arbitration (IRE) (Bigstone (IRE))
3072[14] 4214[7] 4456[8] 4767[7] 5513[5] 6953[6]

Kapstadt (FR) *Ian Williams* a81 91
6 bb g Country Reel(USA) King's Parody (IRE) (King's Best (USA))
1001[8] 2556[5] 3057[4] (3219)

Karajol (GER) *Jean-Pierre Carvalho* 96
3 b c Wiener Walzer(GER) Karavel (GER) (Monsun (GER))
1908a[3]

Karaktar (IRE) *A De Royer-Dupre* 114
4 b h High Chaparral(IRE) Karawana (IRE) (King's Best (USA))
1375a[8]

Karalara (IRE) *D K Weld* 95
3 b f Shamardal(USA) Karasiyra (IRE) (Alhaarth (IRE))
4747a[3] 6389a[13]

Karam Albaari (IRE) *J R Jenkins* a76 63
8 b h King's Best(USA) Lilakiya (IRE) (Dr Fong (USA))
800[3] 1177[4] 1824[6] 2151[4] 2623[10] 3403[3] 5929[4] 6965[10] 8459[3]

Karar *F-H Graffard* 117
4 b g Invincible Spirit(IRE) In The Light (Inchinor)
5949a[7] 6272a[3] 6991a[2] 7833a[14]

Karawaan (IRE) *Sir Michael Stoute* 76
2 b c Sea The Stars(IRE) Magic Sister (Cadeaux Genereux)
6486[5]

Karbayane (FR) *J-M Beguigne* a53 77
3 b f Air Chief Marshal(IRE) Karbayouna (FR) (Kouroun (FR))
1357a[2]

Karens Star *Steph Hollinshead* a58 54
3 b f Piccolo Maarees (Groom Dancer (USA))
3998[10] 4522[7] 4987[9]

Karisma (IRE) *Roger Varian* a80 71
3 gr f Lawman(FR) Lucky Clio (IRE) (Key Of Luck (USA))
2877[5] (8449)

Karl Marx (IRE) *Mark Gillard* a33 42
6 b g Red Clubs(IRE) Brillano (FR) (Desert King (IRE))
2370[8] 2850[9] 4507[6]

Karnage (IRE) *Daniel Kubler* a79 66
4 b g Lawman(FR) Kazinoki (UAE) (Timber Country (USA))
164[2] (318) 899[3] 1144[6] 2930[7] 4288[11] 7051[7] 7436[8]

Karraar *William Haggas* 94
5 b g Dubawi(IRE) Maghya (IRE) (Mujahid (USA))
2897[7] 3670[5] 4858[7]

Karyfanny (FR) *S Labate* 85
2 ch f Milanais(FR) Freedom Sweet (FR) (Sicyos (USA))
4750a[8] 5698a[7] 7490a[8]

Kasalla (GER) *Markus Klug* 108
3 b f Soldier Hollow Kastila (GER) (Sternkoenig (IRE))
3207a[3] 4175a[5] 5220a[4] 6152a[2] 6822a[3] 7720a[4]

Kasaqui (ARG) *Ignacio Correas IV* a35 114
5 rg h Lasting Approval(USA) Kemosheba (USA) (Alysheba (USA))
5431a[2] 7172a[5]

Kasb (IRE) *A R Al Rayhi* a94 94
4 ch g Arcano(IRE) Cape Columbine (Diktat)
719a[3]

Kasbah (IRE) *Amanda Perrett* a99 95
4 b g Acclamation Dance Hall Girl (IRE) (Dansili)
3696a[9] 7242[7] 8069[8] 8232[3] 8407[10]

Kashgar *Bernard Llewellyn* a69 92
7 b g Hernando(FR) Miss Katmandu (IRE) (Rainbow Quest (USA))
2392[13] 2782[11] 4012[10] 4483[4] 4912[6]

Kashmar (GER) *Henk Grewe*
3 ch f Samum(GER) Kapitol (GER) (Winged Love (IRE))
4175a[8]

Kashmiri Sunset *Gordon Elliott* 58
5 b g Tiger Hill(IRE) Sagamartha (Rainbow Quest (USA))
7195a[15]

Kashmir Peak (IRE) *John Quinn* a87 85
7 b g Tiger Hill(IRE) Elhareer (IRE) (Selkirk (USA))
244[7] 447[3]

Kashtan *Harry Dunlop* a80 74
3 ch f Sakhee's Secret Gitane (FR) (Grand Lodge (USA))
5305[9] (7364)

Kasperenko *David Lanigan* 73
2 b g Archipenko(USA) Jardin (Sinndar (IRE))
6108[7] ◆ 6777[6] 7012[3]

Kaspersky (IRE) *Endo Botti* 113
5 b h Footstepsinthesand Croanda (IRE) (Grand Lodge (USA))
2073a[5] (2729a) (4438a) 6823a[3] 7565a[7]

Kassandra (IRE) *Richard Hannon* 51
2 b f Dandy Man(IRE) Gala Style (IRE) (Elnadim (USA))
7465[6]

Kassia (IRE) *Mick Channon* 109
3 b f Acclamation Speedy Sonata (USA) (Stravinsky (USA))
2875[6] (3512) (4223) 4803[2] (6518) (7146)

Kassim (IRE) *J-M Lefebvre* a75 80
4 b g Shamardal(USA) Kastoria (IRE) (Selkirk (USA))
5501a[8]

Kastano (GER) *Markus Klug* 96
2 b c Nathaniel(IRE) Kastila (GER) (Sternkoenig (IRE))
7842a[2]

Kastela Stari *Tim Fitzgerald* a51 31
9 b m Beat Hollow Campaspe (Dominion)
6508[8] 7367[11]

Katabatika *Hughie Morrison* a27 56
2 b f Shirocco(GER) Landinium (ITY) (Lando (GER))
7543[7] 8063[11]

Katalan (GER) *John Butler* a29
3 b g Adlerflug(GER) Kalla (Monsun (GER))
958[8] 1079[12] 1235[8] 1653[9]

Katebird (IRE) *Mark Johnston* a70 65
2 gr f Dark Angel(IRE) She Basic (IRE) (Desert Prince (IRE))
2235[4] 2852[2] 3148[4] 3977[3] 4679[5] 5364[3] 6419[4] 7047[4] ◆ (7286) (7482) 7697[5]

Kath's Boy (IRE) *Tony Carroll* a52 59
2 b g Bushranger(IRE) Elayoon (USA) (Danzig (USA))
2997[13] 3576[2] 4938[7] 5598[8] 6252[9] 7047[11]

Kath's Legacy *Ben De Haan* a67 76
3 ch f Cockney Rebel(IRE) It's Dubai Dolly (Dubai Destination (USA))
(2415) 2666[2] 3894[2] 4777[2] 5671[3] 6527[5]

Kath's Legend *Ben De Haan* a58
2 b f Dick Turpin(IRE) It's Dubai Dolly (Dubai Destination (USA))
6867[8]

Kathy Dream (IRE) *Luigi Biagetti* 108
4 ch m Arcano(IRE) Katy Guest (IRE) (Be My Guest (USA))
(7840a)

Kathy's Humor (USA) *Richard Violette Jr* a72
4 b m Justenuffhumor(USA) Top That (USA) (Top Account (USA))
89a[7]

Katie Canford *John Bridger* a58 70
3 b f Canford Cliffs(IRE) Serafina's Flight (Fantastic Light (USA))
344[7] 515[9] 814[4] 1148[5] 1420[10] 2585[9] 3000[7] 3256[8]

Katie Gale *Michael Appleby* a75 72
6 b m Shirocco(GER) Karla June (Unfuwain (USA))
2194[13] 8250[9] 8476[3] 8565[2]

Katie's Diamond (FR) *K R Burke* a92 107
3 b f Turtle Bowl(IRE) Aaliyah (GER) (Anabaa (USA))
1476[5]

Katie's Surprise (IRE) *John Butler* a33 38
2 b f Famous Name Lamh Eile (IRE) (Lend A Hand)
7072[9] 7576[10] 8465[9]

Katimavik (IRE) *D K Weld* 90
5 b g Invincible Spirit(IRE) Nunavik (IRE) (Indian Ridge)
1015a[12]

Katiymann (IRE) *M Halford* 86
4 b g Shamardal(USA) Katiyra (IRE) (Peintre Celebre (USA))
5941a^{9} 6389a^{11}

Katmandoo (USA) *Tom Dascombe* 62
2 b c Kitten's Joy(USA) Granny Franny (USA) (Grand Slam (USA))
6054^{6}

Katrine (IRE) *William Knight* a68 73
2 b f Kodiac Falcolnry (IRE) (Hawk Wing (USA)) (2014) 3270^{17} 4111^{7} 4869^{7} 5707^{2} 6033^{3} 6658^{3} ◆ 6829^{4}

Kawaii *Martin Smith* a65 67
4 b m Myboycharlie(IRE) Aliena (IRE) (Grand Lodge (USA))
2769^{11} 3612^{8}

Kawartha *Robert Stephens* a72 66
4 gr m Royal Applause Zarkavean (Medicean)
(728) 1236^{3} 1824^{5} 2995^{5} 4294^{6}

Kayenne (FR) *P Khozian* a94 94
4 ch m Air Chief Marshal(IRE) Victorian Dancer (IRE) (Groom Dancer (USA))
5384a^{7}

Kay Sera *Tony Newcombe* a68 56
8 b g Kayf Tara Inflation (Primo Dominie)
51^{3} 425^{6} 766^{4} 1057^{9} 1456^{11} 3002^{8} 3997^{8} 4567^{5} 6424^{3} 7910^{5} (8410) 8527^{2}

Kazanan (IRE) *Michael Dods* 42
2 b f Tamayuz Bosphorus Queen (IRE) (Sri Pekan (USA))
1621^{8} 3223^{7} 3749^{6}

Kazimiera *Charlie Appleby* 93
2 b f Dubawi(IRE) Kailani (Monsun (GER))
(4579) ◆ 7193a^{4} 7698^{2}

Kazoey *Chris Fairhurst* a30 53
3 b f Stimulation(IRE) Dubawi's Spirit (IRE) (Dubawi (IRE))
1698^{3} 2308^{14} 4255^{8} 5079^{5} (5888) 6698^{11}

Keene's Pointe *Kristin Stubbs* a66 69
6 br g Avonbridge Belle's Edge (Danehill Dancer (IRE))
1269^{5} 1496^{11} 1692^{3} 2201^{2} 2571^{2} 2812^{2} 3210^{4} 3924^{4} 4142^{5} 4544^{8} 5069^{12} 5535^{11} (6615) 6835^{3} 7444^{2}

Keen Glance (IRE) *Y Gourraud* a85 94
6 ch m Sakhee(USA) Glint Of Green (USA) (Jade Hunter (USA))
1688a^{11}

Keen Ice (USA) *Todd Pletcher* a123
4 b h Curlin(USA) Medomak (USA) (Awesome Again (CAN))
844a^{7} 1108a^{8} 7838a^{3}

Keep In Line (GER) *Saeed bin Suroor* a69 106
4 b g Soldier Hollow Kastila (GER) (Sternkoenig (IRE))
285a^{13} 453a^{10}

Keep It Dark *William Knight* a86 71
7 b g Invincible Spirit(IRE) Tarneem (USA) (Zilzal (USA))
4^{7} 1528^{12} 1929^{10} 2469^{9} 3159^{12} 3530^{4} 5599^{7} 5928^{9} 6669^{10} 7290^{6} 7811^{8} 8030^{2} 8234^{9}

Keep Quiet (FR) *Mark Casse* 102
2 b c Elusive City(USA) Luminosity (Sillery (USA))
7807a^{8}

Keep The Silence (IRE) *James Tate* a58
3 b f Iffraaj Lysandra (IRE) (Danehill (USA))
145^{8} 298^{4} 441^{6} 794^{6} 1031^{8}

Keep Up (GER) *Philip Kirby* a49 40
4 b g Monsun(GER) Katy Carr (Machiavellian (USA))
3418^{8} 4515^{5} 4971^{8}

Keepup Kevin *Pam Sly* a69 71
2 b g Haafhd Black Salix (USA) (More Than Ready (USA))
5764^{6} 6085^{5} 6480^{3} 6898^{6} 7640^{4}

Keiba (IRE) *Gary Moore* a62 60
3 gr g Dark Angel(IRE) True Magic (Magic Ring (IRE))
2186^{10} 2642^{7} 3786^{8} 5554^{3} 6677^{4} 7038^{11}

Kekko (IRE) *Gianluca Bietolini* a71
3 b c Lilbourne Lad(IRE) Perils Of Joy (IRE) (Rainbow Quest (USA))
511a^{5}

Kelinni (IRE) *Kevin Ryan* a105 113
8 b g Refuse To Bend(IRE) Orinoco (IRE) (Darshaan)
921^{4} (1491) 2030^{7} 3332a^{4} 4135^{4} 4921a^{10} 5585^{6} 6355a^{15}

Kellstorm (IRE) *A P O'Brien* 93
3 ch f Galileo(IRE) Another Storm (USA) (Gone West (USA))
5653^{9}

Kelly's Finest (IRE) *Michael Appleby* a68 72
4 ch m Intense Focus(USA) Priory Rock (IRE) (Rock Of Gibraltar (IRE))
30^{2} 583^{4} 884^{2} 1144^{5} 1434^{6} 1796^{9}

Kelpie Spirit (IRE) *John Weymes* a24
2 b c Born To Sea(IRE) Lady Of Kildare (IRE) (Mujadil (USA))
4642^{10}

Keltetu *E Large*
2 b c Kheleyf(USA) Diplomats Daughter (Unfuwain (USA))
1021a^{7} 5701a^{6}

Kelvingrove (IRE) *Jonjo O'Neill* a65 83
6 b g Hurricane Run(IRE) Silversword (FR) (Highest Honor (FR))
3639^{DSQ} 6163^{7}

Kelvin Hall *Mark Johnston* a73 68
3 ch f Halling(USA) Barawin (IRE) (Hawk Wing (USA))
29^{4} 275^{6} 413^{2} 699^{3} 814^{7} (1553) 2300^{8} 2766^{4} 3215^{7} (4013) 4447^{6} 5012^{2} 6840^{2} 7008^{2} 7249^{2} 7385^{11}

Kemsing (IRE) *Julia Feilden* a73 63
3 ch g Footstepsinthesand St Edith (IRE) (Desert King (IRE))
248^{3} (274) (597) 725^{9} 1155^{5} (1297) 2012^{9} 2644^{5}

Kendamara (FR) *Charles Hills* a45 52
2 b f Kendargent(FR) Damdam Freeze (FR) (Indian Rocket)
4804^{6} 6622^{5}

Kendy Bay (FR) *Gay Kelleway* a34
2 bb f Kendargent(FR) Lovna (USA) (Tale Of The Cat (USA))
7783a^{6} 7970a^{11}

Kenfay (FR) *Y Gourraud* a80 80
3 ch c Kendargent(FR) Daisy Fay (FR) (Dubawi (IRE))
2948a^{8}

Kennady (IRE) *Paul Nolan* 71
6 b g Kalanisi(IRE) Zafilly (Zafonic (USA))
4813a^{12}

Kenny The Captain (IRE) *Tim Easterby* a94 90
5 ch g Captain Rio Kelso Magic (USA) (Distant View (USA))
1489^{4} 1869^{5} (2416) 3021^{5} 3610^{3} 3892^{12} 4191^{8} 4932^{3} 5968^{2} 6131^{4} (6215) (6435) 7094^{3} ◆ 7443^{2} (7858)

Kenobe Star (IRE) *David Dennis* a15 58
4 b g Clodovil(IRE) Maimana (IRE) (Desert King (IRE))
1826^{7} 2370^{10} 3470^{9}

Kenouska (FR) *P Sogorb* a98 99
4 ch m Kendargent(FR) Dame Anouska (IRE) (Exceed And Excel (AUS))
5906a^{5} 6272a^{13} 7525a^{2}

Ken Party (FR) *Matthieu Palussiere* a24 58
2 b c Kendargent(FR) Summer Exhibition (Royal Academy (USA))
7588a^{10} 7927a^{11}

Kenrivash (FR) *Henk Grewe* 97
3 ch f Kendargent(FR) Cayetana's Raid (USA) (Rahy (USA))
2949a^{11} 6992a^{4} 7292a^{7}

Kenriya (FR) *C Ferland* a103 106
3 b f Kendargent(FR) Cherriya (FR) (Montjeu (IRE))
1581a^{2} 2282a^{11} 5498a^{7}

Kenshaba (FR) *M Boutin* a79 80
3 b f Kendargent(FR) Sabasha (FR) (Xaar)
3764a^{6} 5946a^{12} 6912a^{15}

Kensington Star *Simon Crisford* a75
3 b g Pivotal Wild Silk (Dansili)
2914^{3}

Ken's Ridge *Ronald Harris* 6
2 ch c Stimulation(IRE) Immortelle (Arazi (USA))
6439^{14}

Kenstone (FR) *Adrian Wintle* a65 40
3 gr g Kendargent(FR) Little Stone (FR) (One Cool Cat (USA))
1126^{13} 1420^{8} 1792^{6} 2293^{8} 2537^{4} 3146^{6} 3473^{3} 3735^{5} 3987^{10} 5554^{4} 6249^{3} 6853^{11} 7200^{2} 7489^{5} (8120) (8457)

Kent Ragstone (USA) *Daniel Steele* a37
7 ch g Stonesider(USA) Sweet Charity (USA) (A.P. Indy (USA))
1807^{10}

Kentuckyconnection (USA) *Bryan Smart* a78 108
3 b g Include(USA) Youcanringmybell (USA) (Street Cry (IRE))
1208^{5} 1864^{5} 2190^{10} 4065^{4} 4688^{5} 6328^{8}

Kenwana (FR) *P Sogorb* a66 73
3 b f Kendargent(FR) Matwan (FR) (Indian Rocket)
5907a^{6}

Kenyan (FR) *Seamus Durack* a43 27
2 b g Kendargent(FR) Landora (FR) (Lando (GER))
7273^{6} 8355^{12} 8556^{7}

Keravnos (FR) *C Gourdain* a96 71
6 b g Elusive City(USA) Kypriano's Angel (FR) (Kendor (FR))
8431a^{9}

Kerrera *Paul Webber* a62
3 ch f Champs Elysees Questa Nova (Rainbow Quest (USA))
7052^{6} 7607^{4} 8075^{7}

Kerry Icon *Iain Jardine* a49 47
3 b f Sixties Icon La Gifted (Fraam)
2308^{8} 2772^{7} 3015^{7} 3921^{4} 4098^{4} 4648^{3} 4872^{4} 5064^{6} 5576^{9} 6920^{3} 7438^{5} 8410^{6}

Kersivay *Mrs A Malzard* a24 24
10 b g Royal Applause Lochmaddy (Selkirk (USA))
2953a^{5}

Keshiro (IRE) *Michaella Augelli* 93
6 ch h Shirocco(GER) Kesh Kumay (IRE) (Danehill (USA))
2516a^{4} 5502a^{12}

Kesselring *Richard Hannon* a70 85
3 ch c New Approach(IRE) Anna Oleanda (IRE) (Old Vic)
1897^{5} 2208^{5} 2816^{6} (3348) 3914^{5} 4628^{2} 5147^{6} 6445^{6}

Kestila *J-C Rouget* a80 85
2 b f Siyouni(FR) Kerasha (FR) (Daylami (IRE))
(5460a)

Kestrel Call (IRE) *Michael Appleby* a80 80
3 b g Acclamation Winged Harriet (IRE) (Hawk Wing (USA))
126^{5} (365) 797^{6} 1061^{3} 1448^{11} 1789^{5} (3644) 5372^{5} 5730^{9} 6425^{9} 7798^{12}

Kestrel Dot Com *Chris Dwyer* a72 85
4 br g Oasis Dream Tanfidh (Marju (IRE))
1151^{10} 1529^{9} 1765^{5} (2540) 4599^{5} 5037^{2} 6490^{3} 6899^{13}

Keukenhof (IRE) *J P Murtagh* a71 62
3 ch f Dutch Art Clytha (Mark Of Esteem (IRE))
5096a^{14}

Keyman (IRE) *Jeremy Gask* a45 42
3 ch g Manduro(GER) Kesh Kumay (IRE) (Danehill (USA))
2320^{9} 3066^{8} 3577^{7} 4794^{3} 5958^{7} 7039^{10}

Keyser Soze (IRE) *Richard Spencer* 85
2 ch g Arcano(IRE) Causeway Queen (IRE) (Giant's Causeway (USA))
3818^{3} ◆ 4594^{4} 6260^{5} 6950^{7}

Keystroke *Jeremy Noseda* a101 82
4 b h Pivotal Fondled (Selkirk (USA))
(920) ◆ 1195^{12} 4448^{10} 7121^{13} 7933^{4} ◆ (8122) 8478^{4}

Key Success (IRE) *Y Barberot* a63 58
2 br f Kodiac Key Girl (IRE) (Key Of Luck (USA))
5460a^{4} 6015a^{11} 7455a^{8}

K'Gari Spirit *Jeremy Gask* a65 41
3 b f Major Cadeaux Ivory Silk (Diktat)
83^{2} 3669^{5} 4238^{9} 4980^{3} 5470^{4}

Khabaray (IRE) *David O'Meara* a47 72
3 b g Intikhab(USA) Rainbowskia (FR) (Rainbow Quest (USA))
4607^{4} 5154^{5}

Khafoo Shememi (IRE) *Richard Hannon* 94
2 b c Dark Angel(IRE) Appleblossom Pearl (IRE) (Peintre Celebre (USA))
(5876) 6481^{3} 7536^{4}

Khairaat (IRE) *Sir Michael Stoute* 97
3 b c Shamardal(USA) Mumayeza (Indian Ridge)
4156^{2} ◆ (4690) (6286)

Khajaaly (IRE) *Daniel Mark Loughnane* a64 57
9 b g Kheleyf(USA) Joyfullness (USA) (Dixieland Band (USA))
523^{6} 680^{8} 1044^{5} 1120^{9} 1498^{4} 1742^{7}

Khaleesy (IRE) *F Rohaut* a74 98
3 b f Galileo(IRE) Fleeting Spirit (IRE) (Invincible Spirit (IRE))
5451a^{9} 7312a^{7}

Khalidi *John Gosden* 90
2 br c High Chaparral(IRE) Bezique (Cape Cross (IRE))
3661^{3} 4103^{4} (5828) (6330)

Khamaary (IRE) *Mark Johnston* 69
2 br f Tamayuz Nufoos (Zafonic (USA))
(7331)

Khameela *David Simcock* a75
3 b f Equiano(FR) Mina (Selkirk (USA))
(42) 235^{4}

Kharbetation (IRE) *David O'Meara* 95
3 b g Dream Ahead(USA) Anna's Rock (IRE) (Rock Of Gibraltar (IRE))
(4895) ◆

Khattar *Hugo Palmer* a64 51
2 b g Frankel Danceabout (Shareef Dancer (USA))
6314^{5} 7034^{6} 8208^{8}

Khelly's Edge *Scott Dixon* a54 44
2 b f Kheleyf(USA) Edge Of Light (Xaar)
1082^{5} 2219^{11} 4713^{4} 6807^{4} 8285^{7}

Khelman (IRE) *Richard Fahey* 91
6 b g Kheleyf(USA) Mandolin (IRE) (Sabrehill (USA))
(1997) 2679^{8} 3419^{11} 3800^{3} 5417^{19} 5857^{10} 6263^{5} 6539^{3} 7126^{9} 7593^{7}

Kheskianto (IRE) *Michael Chapman* a5 25
10 b m Kheleyf(USA) Gently (IRE) (Darshaan)
3325^{11} 5522^{9}

Khien Shan (FR) *J Phelippon* a89 87
3 b c Medecis Lucky Game (FR) (Montjeu (IRE))
3546a^{11}

Khismet *Rae Guest* a70 50
3 b f Kheleyf(USA) Bisaat (USA) (Bahri (USA))
70^{6} 182^{4} 613^{3} 817^{5} 978^{7} (1234)

Khor Al Udaid *John Gosden* a18 75
3 b g Invincible Spirit(IRE) Brusca (USA) (Grindstone (USA))
1931^{10} 2999^{3} 3643^{6}

Khozabad (FR) *J-M Lefebvre* 88
4 b g Sinndar(IRE) Kozaka (FR) (Mark Of Esteem (IRE))
3092a^{3}

Khusoosy (USA) *A R Al Rayhi* a102 103
4 b g Hard Spun(USA) Elmaleeha (Galileo (IRE))
812a^{6}

Khyber (FR) *Wido Neuroth* 87
4 bb g Sinndar(IRE) Kill The Crab (IRE) (Petorius (IRE))
4329a^{6}

Kibaar *Kevin Ryan* 93
4 b g Pastoral Pursuits Ashes (IRE) (General Monash (USA))
1408^{3} ◆ 1848^{14} 2305^{4} 2665^{8} 3150^{3} 4415a^{13} (4831) 5641^{10} 6114^{12} 7124^{2} 7537^{18}

Kickboxer (IRE) *Saeed bin Suroor* 103
5 gr g Clodovil(IRE) Ajig Dancer (Niniski (USA))
2206^{5} 3671^{8} 6556^{23}

Kicking The Can (IRE) *David Thompson* a67 43
5 gr g Aussie Rules(USA) Silk Meadow (IRE) (Barathea (IRE))
463^{6} 769^{2} 1117^{4} 1323^{4} 2329^{4} 2660^{7} 3564^{2} 4648^{2} 5064^{10} 5971^{2} 6739^{3} 7382^{6} (7991) 8387^{3}

Kicky Blue (GER) *T Clout* a74 107
6 b m Dashing Blade Karina Du Commeaux (FR) (Law Society (USA))
1688a^{4} 3298^{9} 6396a^{4} 6974a^{9}

Kidane Traou Land (FR) *C Plisson* 58
2 b f Intrepid Jack China Silk (FR) (Fantastic Light (USA))
1021a^{9} 2724a^{8}

Kidmenever (IRE) *F Vermeulen* a74 107
3 b c Baltic King Pepys Tillergirl (IRE) (Tillerman)
2076a^{3} 4439a^{6}

Kifaah *A R Al Rayhi* a104 88
5 b g Dubawi(IRE) Mokaraba (Unfuwain (USA))
90a^{2} (371a) 537a^{6} 719a^{2} 840a^{2} 1105a^{P}

Ki Ki *Bryan Smart* a61 64
4 ch m Kheleyf(USA) Peryllys (Warning)
41^{5} 146^{7} 2416^{7} 6451^{3} 7747^{3} ◆

Kilbaha Lady (IRE) *Nigel Tinkler* 66
2 b f Elnadim(USA) Sidney Girl (Azamour (IRE))
1583^{8} 1921^{7} 2489^{8} 4364^{2} 4602^{2} 5112^{4} 5318^{3} 5799^{2} (6026)

Kilim *John Berry* a64 64
3 b f Dansili Kibara (Sadler's Wells (USA))
2011^{6} 2666^{6} 4740^{4} 5548^{5} 8194^{10}

Killermont Street (IRE) *Mark Johnston* a71
2 b f Dream Ahead(USA) Leopard Creek (Weldnaas (USA))
7099^{6} (8009) 8582^{5}

Kill Or Cure (IRE) *Gavin Cromwell* a71 46
4 b g Acclamation Welsh Mist (Damister (USA))
6464a^{4}

Kilmah *Mark Johnston* 105
2 b f Sepoy(AUS) Perfect Star (Act One)
(2211) 3336^{6} 4106^{4} ◆ 4623^{2} 5584^{7} (5870) 6258^{9}

Kiltara (IRE) *Mark Johnston* a93 99
4 b m Lawman(FR) Kiltubber (IRE) (Sadler's Wells (USA))
4757^{7} 5382^{5} 5851^{3} 6332^{2} (6526) 7271^{11} 7652^{7} 7766^{7}

Kimbelle *Mark Usher* a46
3 b f Compton Place Engaging (Oasis Dream)
400^{7} 562^{3} 947^{8} 1320^{8} 1918^{5}

Kimberella *David Nicholls* a106 113
6 b g Kyllachy Gleam Of Light (IRE) (Danehill (USA))
1644^{5} (1968) 2258^{4} 2488^{3} 2895^{2} 3151^{4} 3696a^{2} 4136^{2} ◆ (4667) 4865^{13} 5418^{10} 6558^{5} (6792) ◆ 6943^{7} 7250^{4} 7542^{5} 7822^{3} 7932^{3} 8050^{6}

Kindled *Ed McMahon* a43
3 b f Passing Glance Fireburst (Spectrum (IRE))
5129^{9} 6634^{9} 7106^{5}

Kindly *Simon Crisford* a87 52
3 b f Kyllachy Touching (IRE) (Kheleyf (USA))
2004^{3} (2606) 3439^{7} 6589^{2} ◆ 7363^{2} (7899) ◆

Kind Of Beauty (IRE) *Hugo Palmer* 77
2 ch f Helmet(AUS) Extreme Beauty (USA) (Rahy (USA))
(5747) 6713^{5}

Kind Of Magic (IRE) *A P O'Brien* 101
3 ch f Galileo(IRE) Look At Me (IRE) (Danehill Dancer (IRE))
1507a^{6} 2068a^{6} 4435a^{8}

Kinema (IRE) *Chris Waller* a79 109
5 b g Galileo(IRE) Bon Nuit (IRE) (Night Shift (USA))
1493^{13} (2468) (3340) 4799^{7} 5655^{11} 7481a^{4}

King Bolete (IRE) *Roger Varian* 107
4 b g Cape Cross(IRE) Chanterelle (FR) (Trempolino (USA))
(2024) (3027) 4734^{10} 5558^{12}

Kingbowl Menantie (FR) *C Bauer* a20
3 b c Turtle Bowl(IRE) Queen Menantie (FR) (Kingsalsa (USA))
511a^{8}

King Calypso *Denis Coakley* a90 87
5 ch g Sir Percy Rosa De Mi Corazon (USA) (Cozzene (USA))
1893^{7} 2932^{3} 3784^{8} 4661^{4} 5553^{3} 6362^{9} 7670^{6}

King Cole (USA) *Robert Cowell* a84 75
3 ch c Scat Daddy(USA) Volver (IRE) (Danehill Dancer (IRE))
1763^{2} ◆ 4662^{5} 8083^{5} ◆

King Crimson *John Butler* a86 88
4 ch g Captain Gerrard(IRE) Elegant Lady (Selkirk (USA))
714^{4} 903^{2} ◆ (1084) 1427^{8} (1744) 2253^{2} 2504^{5} 3193^{2} 3638^{10} 4032^{5} 4514^{12} 4911^{3} 5360^{5} (5669) 5961^{10} 7206^{9} 7643^{11} 7892^{13} 8150^{9} 8571^{12}

King David (FR) *M Boutin* a70 82
8 b g Iffraaj Azucar (IRE) (Desert Prince (IRE))
(7398a)

King Electric (IRE) *G M Lyons* a84 99
2 b g Elzaam(AUS) Kind Regards (IRE) (Unfuwain (USA))
3678a^{4} 4574a^{4} 7130a^{8}

Kingfisher Girl *Michael Appleby* a37 49
3 gr f Hellvelyn Caribbean Star (Soviet Star (USA))
2255^{13} 3268^{10} 3484^{13} 3777^{4} 4973^{4} 6569^{6} 7046^{5} 7584^{12} 8383^{6}

King Julien (IRE) *John Ryan* 51
3 b g Canford Cliffs(IRE) Western Sky (Barathea (IRE))
1715^{8} 2522^{5} 2686^{7} 3341^{17} 4597^{6} 6094^{3} 7230^{12}

King Kenny *Mrs A Corson* a34 35
11 ch g Lomitas Salanka (IRE) (Persian Heights)
2078a^{3} 2952a^{3} 3381a^{2} 3918a^{5} 5459a^{3}

Kinglami *John O'Shea* a80 84
7 b g Kingsalsa(USA) Red Japonica (Daylami (IRE))
1218^{12} 1530^{5} 1929^{12} 2754^{8} 3534^{11} 4086^{7} 6091^{3} 6418^{3} 6668^{6} 7430^{6}

King Malpic (FR) *T Lemer* a103 103
3 gr g King's Best(USA) Sablonniere (FR) (Verglas (IRE))
8431a^{3}

King Muro *Fergal O'Brien* a57 56
6 b g Halling(USA) Ushindi (IRE) (Montjeu (IRE))
4711^{7} 6267^{7}

King Of Arts (IRE) *David Simcock* a44 37
3 ch g Excellent Art Start The Music (IRE) (King's Best (USA))
1132^{7} 2109^{8} 3411^{9}

King Of Castilla *John Murray* a66 58
2 br g Sayif(IRE) Thicket (Wolfhound (USA))
1118a^{7} 1233^{3} 1482^{6} (2104) 2963^{7} 3472^{5} 5243^{2} 6033^{9} 6471^{6} 6588^{7} 8285^{9}

King Of Cornwall (IRE) *David Lanigan* a48 51
3 b g Duke Of Marmalade(IRE) Course De Diamante (IRE) (Galileo (IRE))
5610^{8} 7103^{11} 7532^{8}

King Of Dreams *David Simcock* a79 78
3 ch g Dream Ahead(USA) Complexion (Hurricane Run (IRE))
(153) 2099^{6} 5147^{9} 5875^{6}

Kingofmerrows (IRE) *Jamie Osborne* a79 81
2 br c Kodiac Tamara Gervasoni (IRE) (Namid)
6673^{9} 7122^{2} 7527^{2} 8089^{10} 8243^{3} 8454^{4}

King Of Naples *James Fanshawe* a79 91
3 b g Excellent Art Avon Lady (Avonbridge)
1256^{3} (1815) 2477^{5} 3466^{5} 5507^{4} 6123^{9} 6806^{9} (7540)

King Of Nepal *Henry Candy* a78 63
2 b c Sepoy(AUS) Empress Anna (IRE) (Imperial Ballet (IRE))
3569^{5} 4349^{11} 7224^{3} (7974)

King Of Paradise (IRE) *Eric Alston* a36 77
7 b g Hurricane Run(IRE) Silly Game (IRE) (Bigstone (IRE))
1633^{13} 1881^{6} 2616^{4} 3018^{3} 3903^{7} 4875^{7} 5106^{2} 5718^{6}

King Of Paris *Richard Hughes* 71
2 b c Exceed And Excel(AUS) Dubai Queen (USA) (Kingmambo (USA))
5377^{6} 5820^{3}

King Of Rooks *Richard Hannon* a79 107
3 b c Acclamation Slap Shot (IRE) (Lycius (USA))
2242^{5} 2546^{5} 3413^{6} 4062^{20} 5268^{8}

King Of Scotland (FR) *Hughie Morrison* a62
2 b c Rip Van Winkle(IRE) Water Fountain (Mark Of Esteem (IRE))
8063[8] 8423[4]

King Of Spades (FR) *F Vermeulen* 105
2 b c Foxwedge(AUS) And I (Inchinor)
2536[5] ◆ 3100[2] 3871a[2] 4622[8] 5325[6] (5905a) 6694a[2] 6987a[5] 7347a[5] 7721a[7]

King Of Spin *William Muir* a70 80
3 b g Pivotal Regina (Green Desert (USA))
352[8] 1183[2] 1414[5] 1847[8] (4485) (4985) ◆ 6339[3]

King Of Swing *James Given* a70 83
3 b g Dutch Art Mystic Spirit (IRE) (Invincible Spirit (IRE))
1061[5] 2049[2] 2337[5] 3716[7] 4605[2] 5482[14] 5859[2] 6437[3] 7540[9]

King Of The Celts (IRE) *Tim Easterby* 73
8 b g Celtic Swing Flamands (IRE) (Sadler's Wells (USA))
1923[6] (2672) 3012[6] 4455[4] 5293[6] 5883[7]

King Olav (UAE) *Tony Carroll* a67 62
11 ch g Halling(USA) Karamzin (USA) (Nureyev (USA))
234[5] (386) 619[8] 3528[9] 4478[3] 4979[5] 8038[8] (8488)

King Oswald (USA) *James Unett* a66 58
3 b g Street Cry(IRE) Northern Melody (IRE) (Singspiel (IRE))
735[6] 2341[9] 3877[8] 4214[5] 4718[4] (5132) ◆ 5529[6] 6646[13] 6737[9]

King Otto *Phil McEntee* a47
2 b g Holy Roman Emperor(IRE) Que Puntual (ARG) (Contested Bid (USA))
7812[12]

King Robert *Bryan Smart* a100 67
3 b g Royal Applause Generously Gifted (Sakhee (USA))
1442[8] 7858[5] 8192[4] ◆ 8583[7]

Kings Academy *Paul Cole* a72 67
2 ch c Mayson Intrusion (Indesatchel (IRE))
7291a[5] 7748[3] 8065[2] 8175[3]

Kings Bayonet *Alan King* a94 79
9 ch g Needwood Blade Retaliator (Rudimentary (USA))
556[2]

King's Coinage (IRE) *Ed Walker* a65 56
2 b g Holy Roman Emperor(IRE) Seducing (IRE) (Galileo (IRE))
4707[9] 5593[5] 6044[5] 6455[5] 6963[9] (7640)

Kingscombe (USA) *Linda Jewell* a81 50
7 rg g Mizzen Mast(USA) Gombeen (USA) (Private Account (USA))
273[2] 446[6]

Kingscroft (IRE) *Tom Dascombe* a88 69
8 b g Antonius Pius(USA) Handsome Anna (IRE) (Bigstone (IRE))
198[6]

King's Currency *Jedd O'Keeffe* 62
3 b g Kheleyf(USA) Mint Royale (IRE) (Cadeaux Genereux)
1669[5] 2255[10] 2776[4] (3604) 4365[7] 5277[11] 5920[9] 6105[14]

Kings Fete *Sir Michael Stoute* 114
5 b g King's Best(USA) Village Fete (Singspiel (IRE))
2464[5] 3340[3] (4821) (5402) 6940[3] 7545[3]

Kingsgate Native (IRE) *Robert Cowell* a73 113
11 b g Mujadil(USA) Native Force (IRE) (Indian Ridge)
1862[7] 2438[5] 3195[11] 4359[8] (5268) 5863[9]

Kings Gift (IRE) *Michael Dods* 100
2 ch c Casamento(IRE) Jawaaneb (USA) (Kingmambo (USA))
4423[2] ◆ (5150) (6213) 6783[7] 7544[2]

Kings Gold (IRE) *Michael Dods* a81 77
3 ch g Excellent Art Party Feet (IRE) (Noverre (USA))
1123[2] 1589[5] 2327[2] 2774[4] 3607[2] 3904[3] 4342[3] 5420[3]

Kings Heart (IRE) *Mark Usher* a65 69
2 b c Zoffany(IRE) Queens Flight (King's Best (USA))
2173[3] 2748[7] 4053[8] 4712[4] 4974[5] 5598[4] 5989[7] (6652) 7004[6] 7228[9] 7549[7] 7938[6] 8071[2]

Kingsley Klarion (IRE) *Mark Johnston* a93 78
3 b c Arcano(IRE) May Day Queen (IRE) (Danetime (IRE))
16[2] 131[4] 262[2] (344) 559[2] 1168[2] 1442[5] 1977[6] 2554[7] 3277[8] 4519[3] 8311[9]

King's Pavilion (IRE) *Mark Johnston* 96
3 b g King's Best(USA) Embassy (Cadeaux Genereux)
1446[3] 1585[5] 1975[4] (2871) 3157[3] 3299[26] 3910[5] 4163[10] 4625[23] 6331[7] 6803[6] 7153[11]

Kingspone (FR) *Mme P Butel* a83 71
5 gr h Vespone(IRE) Shaking (Linamix (FR))
1034a[5] (2806a) 3184a[7] 5501a[7]

King's Shadow (USA) *Saeed bin Suroor* 18
2 b c Distorted Humor(USA) Love Theway Youare (USA) (Arch (USA))
7239[8]

Kingston Kurrajong *Andrew Balding* 93
3 b c Authorized(IRE) Kingston Acacia (King Of Roses (AUS))
1994[6] 2473[6] (3688) 4624[4]

Kingston Sassafras *Phil McEntee* a53 54
4 b g Halling(USA) Kingston Acacia (King Of Roses (AUS))
79[4] 175[7] 346[5]

Kingston Tasmania *Andrew Balding* a29 41
2 b g Kheleyf(USA) Derartu (AUS) (Last Tycoon)
6439[10] 6888[9] 7297[8] 7866[8] 8080[10]

Kingstreet Lady *Richard Price* a60 61
3 b f Royal Applause Intellibet One (Compton Place)
1761[6] 2372[4] 3000[5] 3725[8] 4262[8]

Kingthistle *Ian Williams* a73 70
3 ch g Monsieur Bond(IRE) Chez Cherie (Wolfhound (USA))
1345[3] 1630[7] 2095[5] 2668[2] 3017[3] ◆ 3368[2] 3948[4] 4612[9] 7059[13] 7577[7] 8064[5] (8411)

King To Be (IRE) *David O'Meara* a57 99
4 b g Myboycharlie(IRE) Becuille (IRE) (Redback)
1871[7] ◆

King Torus (IRE) *Lee Carter* a87 52
8 b g Oratorio(IRE) Dipterous (IRE) (Mujadil (USA))
2378[11] 2977[6] 3729[4] 4020[4]

Kinloch Pride *Noel Wilson* a55 57
4 ch m Kyllachy Pride Of Kinloch (Dr Devious (IRE))
3010[2] 3368[8] 3843[8] 4410[3] 4874[2] 5582[3]

Kip *David O'Meara* a66 77
4 b m Rip Van Winkle(IRE) Catopuma (USA) (Elusive Quality (USA))
2427[2] (2836) 3118[7] 3251[3] 4143[4] 4455[8] 4949[5]

Kiribati *Mark Johnston* a53 76
2 b c Poet's Voice Oasis Jade (Oasis Dream)
5283[2] 6002[3] 6319[5] 7248[2] 7589[3] 8229[9]

Kiringa *Robert Cowell* a67 60
3 ch f Kyllachy Good Health (Magic Ring (IRE))
193[4] 436[5] 962[3] 1554[3] 2302[2] 2503[3] 2905[4] 3994[8] 4426[3] 5928[2] (6586) 6958[4] 7533[2]

Kirkby's Phantom *John David Riches* 25
2 gr f Sayif(IRE) Demolition Jo (Petong)
4140[6] 4678[9] 6025[5]

Kirkham *Julie Camacho* a70 68
3 b g Pastoral Pursuits Royal Grace (Royal Applause)
1584[3] 3224[7] 3567[9] 5732[4] 6436[9] 7333[3] 7743[2] 7994[2]

Kirkman (IRE) *Peter Hiatt* a51 68
5 ch g Virtual Validate (Alhaarth (IRE))
234[9] 521[6] 1322[9] 1550[6] 4478[4] 5726[11] 6422[9] 7270[10]

Kirtling *Andi Brown* a71 63
5 gr g Araafa(IRE) Cape Maya (Cape Cross (IRE))
4566[5] 5375[8] 5795[5] (6739) 7105[3] (7657) 8253[8]

Kiruna Peak (IRE) *Mick Channon* 71
2 ch f Arcano(IRE) Kirunavaara (IRE) (Galileo (IRE))
4054[4] (4397) 6713[8] 7075[5]

Kismet Hardy *Richard Hannon* a65 79
3 ch c Mount Nelson Quinzey's Best (IRE) (King's Best (USA))
1738[9] 1946[4] 3348[2] 5122[2] (5362) 5875[5] 6665[8]

Kissinger *Michael Bell* a57
2 b g Henrythenavigator(USA) Station House (IRE) (Galileo (IRE))
4907[12] 7977[8] 8340[11]

Kissoffire (IRE) *Marco Botti* a65
2 b c Elusive Quality(USA) Readyandaway (USA) (More Than Ready (USA))
5764[3] 7483[8]

Kiss The Stars (IRE) *T G McCourt* a70 56
6 b m Thousand Words Lady Piste (IRE) (Ali-Royal (IRE))
2229a[2] 6462a[5]

Kissy Suzuki *Hughie Morrison* a66 52
4 b m Sakhee's Secret Yonder (And Beyond (IRE))
30[6] 2872[11] 3470[U] 4716[6] 5805[6] 7507[7]

Kisumu *Micky Hammond* a61 72
4 b g High Chaparral(IRE) Arum Lily (USA) (Woodman (USA))
3118[9] 3711[P] 4237[7] 4971[6] 5522[2] 5758[5]

Kitaaby (IRE) *Brian Meehan* 95
3 b g Acclamation Flower Of Kent (USA) (Diesis)
3062[6] (3554) (4519) ◆ (5878)

Kitasan Black (JPN) *Hisashi Shimizu* 122
4 b h Black Tide(JPN) Sugar Heart (JPN) (Sakura Bakushin O (JPN))
(8129a)

Kitcat (CHI) *Juan C Silva* 99
3 bb f Scat Daddy(USA) Kossanova (USA) (Fly So Free (USA))
7831a[12]

Kite Davis (FR) *C Plisson* 62
2 ch f Doctor Dino(FR) Pink Davis (FR) (Chichicastenango (FR))
2844a[3]

Kitgame (FR) *D Prod'Homme* 76
2 b f Muhaymin(USA) Ultime Moment (IRE) (Anabaa (USA))
2280a[5] 5142a[13]

Kitsey (IRE) *Richard Hannon* 68
2 b f High Chaparral(IRE) Thistlestar (USA) (Lion Heart (USA))
5170[6] 6206[5] 6762[5]

Kitten's Johnstown (USA) *Kevin Ryan* 84
2 ch c Kitten's Joy(USA) Cellars Shiraz (USA) (Kissin Kris (USA))
(6535) ◆

Kitty Boo *Luca Cumani* a78
2 b f Invincible Spirit(IRE) Kitty Wells (Sadler's Wells (USA))
6414[2] 7761[3]

Kitty For Me *William Muir* a57
3 b f Pour Moi(IRE) Purring (USA) (Mountain Cat (USA))
3781[11]

Kiwayu *Philip Kirby* a70 83
7 b g Medicean Kibara (Sadler's Wells (USA))
103[3] 2406[7] (2746) 3118[3] 3417[2] 4101[6] 4430[4]

Kiwi Bay *Michael Dods* a78 81
11 b g Mujahid(USA) Bay Of Plenty (FR) (Octagonal (NZ))
1122[13] 1526[6] 1924[6] 2362[5] 2743[2] 2959[5] 3717[7] 4427[2] 4768[3] 5033[4] 5291[3] (5972) 6521[2] 6683[5] 7796[12] 8011[11] 8286[7]

Kizomba (FR) *N Caullery* a72 69
3 gr f Youmzain(IRE) Crusch Alva (FR) (Unfuwain (USA))
5280a[2]

Klaremount (IRE) *K R Burke* 71
2 b c Kodiac Hannah Greeley (USA) (Mr Greeley (USA))
3283[7] 3808[3]

Kleitomachos (IRE) *Stuart Kittow* 76
8 b g Barathea(IRE) Theben (GER) (Monsun (GER))
3746[6] 4795[2] (5745) 6362[4]

Klimt (USA) *Bob Baffert* a115
2 b c Quality Road(USA) Inventive (USA) (Dixie Union (USA))
7834a[8]

Kloud Gate (FR) *Gianluca Bietolini* 104
4 ch g Astronomer Royal(USA) Talkata (IRE) (Suave Dancer (USA))
1688a[7] 4578a[6] 6612a[4] 7402a[5] 7946a[3]

Knife Edge (IRE) *Marco Botti* a106 108
3 ch c Zoffany(IRE) Attalea (IRE) (Monsun (GER))
1208[3] 1477[2] (2315a)

Knight Commander *William Knight* a65 79
3 br g Sir Percy Jardin (Sinndar (IRE))
1260[6] 1828[7] 2900[11] 3468[2] 4277[5] 5596[3] 6380[5] 6885[6] 7421[5]

Knight Destroyer (IRE) *Jonjo O'Neill* 60
2 b g Dark Angel(IRE) Do The Deal (IRE) (Halling (USA))
4040[9] 6054[7] 6777[9]

Knight Music *Michael Attwater* a87 89
4 b g Sir Percy Lyric Art (USA) (Red Ransom (USA))
(1144) ◆ 1568[5] 2176[2] (2966) 4077[9] 4888[5] 5633[6] 6074[6]

Knight Of The Air *Joseph Tuite* a60 69
4 b g Bushranger(IRE) Picolette (Piccolo)
1546[5] 1735[2] 2187[3] 2635[5] 3125[2] 3258[4] 3739[4] 4388[4] 4683[8] 5326[12] 5627[2] (5953) 6066[8] 7508[8] 7732[8]

Knight Owl *James Fanshawe* a93 100
6 b g Rock Of Gibraltar(IRE) Miss Ivanhoe (IRE) (Selkirk (USA))
(1861) 3623[3] 5976[2] 6786[26] 7573[4]

Knightsbridge Liam (IRE) *Michael Easterby* a26
2 b g Lilbourne Lad(IRE) Carmona (Rainbow Quest (USA))
8237[9]

Knight's Parade (IRE) *Sarah Humphrey* a83 76
6 b g Dark Angel(IRE) Toy Show (IRE) (Danehill (USA))
(704) 1417[4] 2820[2] 2971[10] 3533[10] 4023[4] 5334[4] 8250[10]

Knights Table *James Tate* a78 98
3 b c Sir Percy Whole Grain (Polish Precedent (USA))
945[4] 1132[2] 1426[5] 1767[3] 2640[2] (3343) (3949) ◆ (4409) ◆ 4863[9] 5411[2] 5879[6]

Knockamany Bends (IRE) *John Wainwright* a52 55
6 b g Majestic Missile(IRE) Sweet Compliance (Safawan)
3010[6] 3984[12] 4691[8] 4931[13] (5838) 6774[3] 7596[7] 7860[10] 8409[11]

Knockmaole Boy (IRE) *J H Culloty* 79
4 b g Echo Of Light Kashmir Lady (FR) (Rock Of Gibraltar (IRE))
4811a[6]

Knotty Jack (IRE) *Iain Jardine* a52 35
4 b g Zebedee Half-Hitch (USA) (Diesis)
6003[U]

Know Your Limit (IRE) *Ed Walker* a63
2 ch c Tamayuz Rapid Ransom (USA) (Red Ransom (USA))
7649[5] 7883[4] 8354[3]

Know Your Name *Eric Alston* a81 80
5 ch g Halling(USA) Lady Agnes (Singspiel (IRE))
1785[10] 2198[4] 2441[3] 3286[5] 4094[9] 5367[9] 6055[10] 6737[15]

Kocollada (IRE) *Richard Fahey* 87
2 b f Kodiac Collada (IRE) (Desert Prince (IRE))
(2254) (2908) 3270[4] 4623[9] 5977[5] 6538[4] 7120[10] 7972a[8]

Kodiac Khan (IRE) *Mark Johnston* a82 79
2 b c Kodiac Mirwara (IRE) (Darshaan)
2604[3] 3819[5] 4601[2] 5265[6] (5989) ◆ 6800[4] 7764[5] (8360)

Kodiac Lady (IRE) *Simon West* a58 41
4 b m Kodiac Weeping Willow (IRE) (Kheleyf (USA))
1[8] 144[6] 387[10] 563[5] 769[11] 859[2] 943[4] 1116[9] 1171[2] 1501[6] 1725[8] 1762[6] 7852[10] 7995[6] 8146[8] 8307[13] 8499[7]

Kodiac Moment (IRE) *Brian Meehan* 52
2 b f Kodiac Empress Charlotte (Holy Roman Emperor (IRE))
1988[8] 2371[8] 2793[8]

Kodi Bear (IRE) *Clive Cox* 121
4 br h Kodiac Hawattef (IRE) (Mujtahid (USA))
2243[7] 3242[7] 4127[6] 4754[9]

Kodicat (IRE) *Kevin Ryan* a69 68
2 b f Kodiac Mimiteh (USA) (Maria's Mon (USA))
2617[3] ◆ 3024[5] 6162[4] 7122[5]

Kodicil (IRE) *Mark Walford* 76
3 b g Kodiac Miss Caoimhe (IRE) (Barathea (IRE))
1760[10]

Kodi Da Capo (IRE) *Keith Dalgleish* a72 79
2 b f Kodiac Red Trance (IRE) (Soviet Star (USA))
1342[3] 1793[2] 2254[3] 2908[5] (3282) 4679[8] (4832) (5113)

Kodiline (IRE) *Clive Cox* 93
2 b c Kodiac Kris Spring (Kris S (USA))
2847[2] (3954) 4352[3] 5977[4]

Kodimoor (IRE) *Christopher Kellett* a57 57
3 b g Kodiac Victoria Lodge (IRE) (Grand Lodge (USA))
1638[13] 2049[10] 3211[8] 3725[6] 4228[8] 5270[6] 6790[11] 7046[4] 7596[2] 8409[2] 8485[8]

Kody Ridge (IRE) *David Dennis* a61 78
2 b g Kodiac Top Of The Ridge (IRE) (Celtic Swing)
2104[3] 2289[2] 2902[2] 4022[4] 5884[10]

Koeman *Mick Channon* 76
2 b c Dutch Art Angelic Note (IRE) (Excellent Art)
6108[8] 6585[10] 6881[11] 7502[16]

Kohinoor Diamond (IRE) *Sir Mark Prescott Bt* a61 39
2 b f Excelebration(IRE) Gems Of Araby (Zafonic (USA))
6369[5] 6696[9] 7184[7]

Kokanee Creek *Mark Usher* a40 25
2 ch f Bated Breath Kootenay (IRE) (Selkirk (USA))
4054[10] 7279[7]

Kokoni (IRE) *Sir Michael Stoute* a69 60
3 b g Acclamation Belgique (IRE) (Compton Place)
1257[3] 1703[3]

Kommander Kirkup *John Davies* a61 87
5 ch g Assertive Bikini (Trans Island)
(1869) 2613[12] 5479[12] 5857[12] 6131[6] 6714[4] 7094[11] 7433[8]

Kontrastat (FR) *S Wattel* 108
2 ch c My Risk(FR) Sikkim (FR) (Linamix (FR))
(5348a) (6177a) 6987a[4]

Kool And The Gang (IRE) *J Albrecht* a83 80
6 b g Elusive City(USA) Knightsbridge (BRZ) (Yagli (USA))
7525a[9] 7806a[2]

Kool Kompany (IRE) *Richard Hannon* 110
4 br h Jeremy(USA) Absolutely Cool (IRE) (Indian Ridge)
7213[4] 7701[2]

Koora *Luca Cumani* 111
4 b m Pivotal Kithanga (IRE) (Darshaan)
2189[2] ◆ 3695a[4] 5586[10] 7545[10]

Koothrappali *David Barron* a58 64
3 b g Sakhee's Secret Grandmas Dream (Kyllachy)
5[2] 181[4] ◆

Kopassus (IRE) *Lawrence Mullaney* a49 57
4 b g Holy Roman Emperor(IRE) Couverture (USA) (Lear Fan (USA))
1696[8] 1926[9] 2234[9] 2676[7] 2974[12] 4424[4] 5065[5] 7850[6] 8146[12]

Koptoon *Jo Hughes* a84 84
4 b g Rip Van Winkle(IRE) Mania (IRE) (Danehill (USA))
1693[2] 2028[13] 2531[6] (2846) 2974[3] 3552[5] 4534[2] 5075[7] 5852[4] 6072[8] 6878[6] 7206[10]

Korbous (IRE) *Richard Brabazon* a76 76
7 ch g Choisir(AUS) Puppet Play (IRE) (Broken Hearted)
(6465a)

Koreen (IRE) *John Berry* a67 96
5 b g Samum(GER) Pony Girl (IRE) (Darshaan)
173[7] 425[10]

Koropick (IRE) *Hugo Palmer* a94 106
2 b c Kodiac Kathoe (IRE) (Fayruz)
(5476) 6124[2] 6785[5] 7347a[7]

Koskoroba (FR) *M Boutin* a84 83
3 b c Kingsalsa(USA) Sikkim (FR) (Linamix (FR))
2172a[8]

Kourkan (FR) *J-M Beguigne* 110
3 bb g American Post Kourka (FR) (Keos (USA))
3183a[6] (7137a) 7723a[3]

Kowaiyess (IRE) *Owen Burrows* a77 77
2 b g Exceed And Excel(AUS) Nidhaal (IRE) (Observatory (USA))
6622[3] 7269[2]

Kozier (GER) *Alan King* 57
2 ch g Muhtathir Kasumi (GER) (Poliglote)
4270[11] 4988[6] 5740[10] 6875[4]

Krafty One *Michael Scudamore* a61 60
4 ch m Mastercraftsman(IRE) Wonderful Desert (Green Desert (USA))
8318[6]

Krazy Paving *Anabel K Murphy* a58 54
4 b g Kyllachy Critical Path (IRE) (Noverre (USA))
542[5] 985[7] 1138[2] 1320[2] 1913[3] 3070[13] 4389[7] 6852[3] 7509[2] 8030[5] 8315[12]

Kreacher (TUR) *S Bilgic* 102
3 b c Dehere(USA) Aces Dancing (GER) (Big Shuffle (USA))
6181a[5]

Kreb's Cycle (IRE) *Richard Hannon* a85 83
2 ch g Helmet(AUS) La Noe (Nayef (USA))
1454[2] ◆ (1736) 2038[3] 2604[2] (3495) 4148[4] 5416[4] 7004[5] 7305[7]

Kristal Hart *Neil Mulholland* a61 58
7 b m Lucky Story(USA) Moly (FR) (Anabaa (USA))
55[2] (898) 2144[7] 8527[3]

Kristjano (GER) *Chris Wall* a74 73
4 b g Nayef(USA) Kalahari Dancer (Dalakhani (IRE))
2233[4] 3409[4] 4023[6] 5262[2] 6090[2]

Kristoff (IRE) *Jim Boyle* a54 31
3 b g Frozen Power(IRE) Easter Girl (Efisio)
87[2] 328[2] 436[4] 610[3] 4528[8] 5167[9] 5721[P] 6373[7] 6891[8] 8590[9]

Kroy *Ollie Pears* a57 60
2 b g Sleeping Indian Valley Of The Moon (IRE) (Monashee Mountain (USA))
1407[5] 2014[2] 3208[5] 4869[3] 5840[3]

Kruger Park (IRE) *Richard Fahey* 84
2 br c Requinto(IRE) Definite Opinion (IRE) (Kheleyf (USA))
4685[5] (6162)

Krypton Factor *Fawzi Abdulla Nass* a104 100
8 br g Kyllachy Cool Question (Polar Falcon (USA))
186[4] 371a[3] 537a[5] 624a[8] 719a[5] 841a[5]

Krystallite *Scott Dixon* a88 52
3 ch f Kheleyf(USA) Chrystal Venture (IRE) (Barathea (IRE))
57[2] 686[2] ◆ 821[4] 1070[5] 4112[18] 4198[4] 5296[7] 6699[6] 7864[8] 7892[11] 8280[9] 8495[5]

Ksenia (IRE) *Nigel Tinkler* a40 38
3 b f Dandy Man(IRE) Golden Chica (IRE) (Imperial Ballet (IRE))
824[5] 945[8] 1494[5] 2118[6] 3014[7] 4764[14]

Kuantan *Roger Charlton* 70
3 b g Acclamation Gay Mirage (GER) (Highest Honor (FR))
1714[7] 2340[4] 3558[7] 7214[6]

Kuanyao (IRE) *Ann Stokell* a59 59
10 b g American Post Nullarbor (Green Desert (USA))
46[2] 151[5] (381) 528[4] 837[2] (970) 1264[4] 2447[10] 2676[5] 3022[4]

Kubali (IRE) *G M Lyons* a82 90
3 b g Approve(IRE) Violet Flame (IRE) (Kalanisi (IRE))
5096a[2]

Kubeba (IRE) *Paul Cole* a73 63
5 b g Kodiac Brillano (FR) (Desert King (IRE))
7944[2] 8207[7]

Kuda Huraa (IRE) *Harriet Bethell* a51 76
8 b g Montjeu(IRE) Healing Music (FR) (Bering)
1586[8] 3470[4]

Kudu Country (IRE) *Evan Williams* a45 77
10 gr g Captain Rio Nirvavita (FR) (Highest Honor (FR))
701[9]

Kuiper Belt (USA) *David Lanigan* a58 50
2 b c Elusive Quality(USA) Youre So Sweet (USA) (Storm Cat (USA))
7665[7] 7908[10]

Kulgri *Kevin Ryan* 31
2 ch f Monsieur Bond(IRE) Jord (IRE) (Trans Island)
5272[12] 7314[12]

Kullu (IRE) *Charlie Fellowes* 75
3 b f Oasis Dream Mussoorie (FR) (Linamix (FR))
6650[2] (7009) 7504[4]

Kummiya *Roger Charlton* a76 92
3 bb g Dansili Balisada (Kris)
1992[13] 3574[6] (4497) (5234) 5603[6] 6581[4] 6915[8]

Kung Hei Fat Choy (USA) *Lucinda Egerton*
7 b g Elusive Quality(USA) Lady Succeed (JPN) (Brian's Time (USA))
23[3] 276[6] 3479[F] (Dead)

Kuraka *K R Burke* 76
2 b g Cacique(IRE) Puzzling (Peintre Celebre (USA))
6224[2] ◆ 6771[3] 7329[9]

Kurino Star O (JPN) *Yoshitada Takahashi* a110
6 bl h Admire Boss(JPN) Mayano Starlight (JPN) (Jade Robbery (USA))
6399a[2]

Kuriosa (IRE) *Marco Botti* a82 76
4 ch m Rip Van Winkle(IRE) Kite Mark (Mark Of Esteem (IRE))
(26) 1919[5] 2582[5] 3602[9] 4462[4]

Kuwait Star *Charlie Wallis* a65 51
7 ch g Resplendent Glory(IRE) Mofeyda (IRE) (Mtoto)
55[7]

Kwanto *Ken Wingrove* a18 29
6 b m Piccolo Craic Sa Ceili (IRE) (Danehill Dancer (IRE))
867[10]

Kylea (IRE) *Richard Hannon* a42 46
3 b f Iffraaj Pitrizza (IRE) (Machiavellian (USA))
5327[5] 6066[9] 7211[7] 7516[10]

Kylie's Kenny *Derek Shaw* a8
6 b g Deportivo Haunt The Zoo (Komaite (USA))
958[7]

Kylies Wild Card *Simon Hodgson* a32 45
4 b m Aussie Rules(USA) Jemiliah (Dubai Destination (USA))
3953[13] 6894[11] 7038[10]

Kylla *Shaun Harris* a26 23
3 b f Kyllachy Mamounia (IRE) (Green Desert (USA))
1597[13] 2107[11] 2559[10] 3423[10] 3941[9] 5270[10]

Kyllach Me (IRE) *Bryan Smart* a66 58
4 b g Kyllachy Good For Her (Rock Of Gibraltar (IRE))
(197) 320[5] 1116[5] 1496[12] 2332[10] 2856[6] 4512[3] 5760[6]

Kyllachykov (IRE) *Rebecca Bastiman* a55 34
8 ch g Kyllachy Dance On (Caerleon (USA))
368[13]

Kyllachy Queen (IRE) *Marco Botti* a104 102
4 bb m Kyllachy Queen Sensazione (IRE) (King Charlemagne (USA))
(1207) 1886[6] 3119a[5] 4435a[12]

Kyllachys Tale (IRE) *Roger Teal* a40 59
2 b f Kyllachy Betray (King's Best (USA))
6336[6] 7055[8] 7647[9]

Kylla Instinct *Philip McBride* a85 84
3 b f Kyllachy Craighall (Dubawi (IRE))
(1312) 1623[7] 3614[5] (4215) (5089) 5743[4] 6246[4] 7701[7]

Kyllang Rock (IRE) *James Tate* 91
2 b c Kyllachy Megec Blis (IRE) (Soviet Star (USA))
3037[4] ◆ (4205) 4755[6] 5656[7] (5756) ◆ 6734[2]

Kyllini *Marjorie Fife* 42
3 b f Kyllachy Chickini (IRE) (Rossini (USA))
1562[9] 1814[9] 2019[5] 3478[13]

Kyllukey *Charles Hills* a83 78
3 b g Kyllachy Money Note (Librettist (USA))
363[2] (668) (1060) 1763[6] 2446[2] 3394[3] 4211[3] ◆ 4662[3] 5034[7]

La Asomada *David Barron* a63 62
3 b f Arabian Gleam Morristown Music (IRE) (Distant Music (USA))
635[2] 763[2] 1839[6] 2118[2] 2559[5] 3773[5] 4512[5] (4944) 5523[7]

La Bacouetteuse (FR) *Iain Jardine* a56 72
11 b g Miesque's Son(USA) Toryka (Vettori (IRE))
1665[8] 2805[7] 3547[8] 4101[9] 4935[6] 5155[4] 5522[3] 5781[2] 6219[4] 6438[5] 7138[10] (7251)

Labaik (FR) *Gordon Elliott*
5 gr g Montmartre(FR) Avanguardia (GER) (Choisir (AUS))
2151[RR] 6463a[RR]

La Barata *Kevin Ryan* a20
3 b f Piccolo Peggy Spencer (Formidable I (USA))
958[6]

La Berlioz (FR) *P De Chevigny* a56 70
2 b f Kentucky Dynamite(USA) Baileys Applause (Royal Applause)
5698a[9] 5986a[7]

La Berma (IRE) *James Cassidy* a71 109
4 bb m Lawman(FR) Full Snow Moon (USA) (Vindication (USA))
3178a[9]

La Breviere *F Chappet* a70 74
2 b f Fastnet Rock(AUS) Zibeling (IRE) (Cape Cross (IRE))
6937a[5] 7970a[5]

Labyrinth (IRE) *Sir Michael Stoute* a73 80
3 b f Lawman(FR) Kerry Gal (IRE) (Galileo (IRE))
2578[4] 4361[2] (4991) 6113[6] 6947[10]

Lacan (IRE) *Ralph Beckett* a100 97
5 b h New Approach(IRE) Invincible Isle (IRE) (Invincible Spirit (IRE))
588a[5] 665a[5] 833[4]

La Casa Tarifa (IRE) *Mark Johnston* a76 83
2 b f Casamento(IRE) Cool Tarifa (IRE) (One Cool Cat (USA))
2530[4] 2807[3] 3947[2] (4725) 4974[2] 5560[2] 6007[3] 6257[12] 6787[8] 7820[10]

La Celebs Ville (IRE) *Tom Dascombe* a51 75
3 b f Sea The Stars(IRE) Bryanstown (IRE) (Galileo (IRE))
1758[8] 2666[7] 3399[2] 3856[3] 4139[5] 4382[2] 4986[5] 6278[4] 6742[11] 7609[8]

Lacey *Sarah Hollinshead* a63 48
7 b g Rail Link Shamana (USA) (Woodman (USA))
1649[6] 2105[7] 7367[12] 8039[11] 8211[8]

Lacey's Lane *Saeed bin Suroor* 79
3 b f Street Cry(IRE) Hibaayeb (Singspiel (IRE))
1392[11] 1920[2]

Lackaday *Mark Walford* a77 76
4 gr g Kyllachy Day Creek (Daylami (IRE))
856[2] 1030[6] (1254) 1489[6] 1869[14] 2416[12] 2680[6] 3262[7] 5386[12] 7255[11] 7584[8]

Lac Leman (GER) *Pauline Robson* a66 82
5 b g Doyen(IRE) Learned Lady (JPN) (Fuji Kiseki (JPN))
8584[6]

La Contessa (IRE) *Richard Fahey* a75 68
3 gr f Fastnet Rock(AUS) Cleide Da Silva (USA) (Monarchos (USA))
4235[3] ◆ 4682[4] 5811[2] 6344[6] 7008[4] 7853[3] 7993[7]

La Coronel (USA) *Mark Casse* a78 110
2 bb f Colonel John(USA) Listen (USA) (Chester House (USA))
7809a[6] ◆

La Cressonniere (FR) *J-C Rouget* 115
3 b f Le Havre(IRE) Absolute Lady (IRE) (Galileo (IRE))
(2282a) (3452a) (5754a)

La Cumparsita (FR) *C Lerner* a69 75
2 ch f American Post Tenepia (FR) (Keltos (FR))
5698a[6]

La Dame En Rouge (FR) *M Pimbonnet* 75
2 b f Requinto(IRE) Philosophers Guest (IRE) (Desert Prince (IRE))
1118a[8] 2280a[3] 7136a[4]

Ladofash *K R Burke* a66 71
2 b g Canford Cliffs(IRE) Curras Spirit (Invincible Spirit (IRE))
3516[5] 5966[6] 6319[4] ◆ 7140[5] 7406[10]

Ladurelli (IRE) *Paul Cole* a91 85
4 b g Mastercraftsman(IRE) Chanter (Lomitas)
2897[11] 3304[8] 4396[3] 4808[3] 5026[4] 6870[9]

Ladweb *John Gallagher* a55 87
6 ch g Bertolini(USA) Adweb (Muhtarram (USA))
(1447) (1601) 2504[6] 3193[3] (3857) 5153[4] 6537[16] 7358[8]

Lady Argentum (IRE) *Thomas Gibney* a45 66
3 b f Kodiac Silver Dip (Gulch (USA))
5900a[15]

Lady Aurelia (USA) *Wesley A Ward* a98 123
2 b f Scat Daddy(USA) D'Wildcat Speed (USA) (Forest Wildcat (USA))
(3270) (5690a) 6784[3]

Lady Bacchus *Richard Guest* a54 46
3 b f Compton Place Beauty (IRE) (Alzao (USA))
948[8] 6478[13] 7488[2] 7693[4] (7860) 8013[7] 8312[2] 8572[12]

Lady Bayside *Malcolm Saunders* a64 73
8 ch m Ishiguru(USA) Seldemosa (Selkirk (USA))
1735[15] (2129) 2783[4] (3096) 3514[3] 4087[4] 5571[4]

Lady Bergamot (FR) *James Fanshawe* a66
2 gr f Mastercraftsman(IRE) Mahima (FR) (Linamix (FR))
7762[6]

Lady Blanco (USA) *Andrew Balding* a63 73
3 bb f Cape Blanco(IRE) War Clan (USA) (War Front (USA))
1063[6] 1289[4] 3042[7] 3493[10] 3997[3] (4500) 4818[5] 5548[2] 6334[7] 7274[10]

Lady Broome *John David Riches*
5 ch m Erhaab(USA) Minnesinger (Fraam)
2858[5]

Lady Canford (IRE) *James Bethell* a62 54
3 b f Canford Cliffs(IRE) Soul Mountain (IRE) (Rock Of Gibraltar (IRE))
925[3] 1671[8] 3366[10] 3949[6] 4847[5] 5322[3] 5921[3] 7256[3] ◆ 7516[11]

Lady Capucine (FR) *Harry Dunlop* a67 64
2 b f Spirit One(FR) Run On Ruby (FR) (Muhtathir)
6087[3] 6937a[9]

Lady Cavallo *Neil Mulholland* 46
6 b m Tiger Hill(IRE) Cavallo Da Corsa (Galileo (IRE))
4505[3]

Lady Chara *Ann Duffield* 42
3 b f Stimulation(IRE) Noble Nova (Fraam)
3249[7] 4235[13]

Lady Clair (IRE) *K R Burke* a79 87
3 b f Canford Cliffs(IRE) Queen Of Carthage (USA) (Cape Cross (IRE))
1453[13] 2683[4] 3116[5] 3714[9] 4652[7] 4947[5] (5643) 6164[8] 7965[11]

Lady Cleo (IRE) *Stuart Williams* a68 65
2 b f Holy Roman Emperor(IRE) Miss Mariduff (USA) (Hussonet (USA))
5377[5] 6034[8] 6244[3] 6658[6] 7217[6] 7900[5] 7966[4]

Lady Clitico (IRE) *Rebecca Menzies* a75 77
5 b m Bushranger(IRE) Villa Nova (IRE) (Petardia)
330[4] 2564[8] 3118[11]

Lady Cordie *Jim Goldie* 52
4 b m Monsieur Bond(IRE) Lady Benjamin (Spinning World (USA))
1668[6] (2360) 4445[8] 5152[7] 5222[7] 5714[8]

Lady Cristal (IRE) *K R Burke* a72 73
2 b f Footstepsinthesand Scarborough Lily (Dansili)
2254[5] 2771[7] 3654[2] 4602[3] 5712[6] 6139[11] 6743[7]

Lady Dari (IRE) *Alfonso Nunez* 67
3 b f Montjeu(IRE) Double Green (IRE) (Green Tune (USA))
5249a[7]

Lady D's Rock (IRE) *Clive Cox* a54 50
4 gr m Aussie Rules(USA) Za Za (Barathea (IRE))
232[9] 4225[8]

Lady Eli (USA) *Chad C Brown* 114
4 bb m Divine Park(USA) Sacre Coeur (USA) (Saint Ballado (CAN))
5914a[2] 7831a[2]

Lady Elizabeth (IRE) *Scott Dixon* a55 58
3 b f Dandy Man(IRE) Disarm (IRE) (Bahamian Bounty)
181[8] 3423[9] 4141[2] 4647[13] 6774[7] 8242[14] 8290[6] 8472[9]

Lady Emma *Steph Hollinshead* 51
3 b f Mount Nelson Songbook (Singspiel (IRE))
2395[9] 3194[12]

Lady Fandango (IRE) *Gordon Elliott* a67 72
4 b m Holy Roman Emperor(IRE) Alifandango (IRE) (Alzao (USA))
200[3] 420[7] 4146[2]

Lady Fontenail *Neil King* a45 60
3 gr f Compton Place Nina Fontenail (FR) (Kaldounevees (FR))
63[5] 443[11] 700[3] 1062[10] 1734[11] 2184[4] 2825[2] 3651[5]

Lady Freyja *John Ryan* a49 54
2 b f Mayson Third Party (Terimon)
7107[5] 7695[6]

Lady Gemini *Jo Hughes* a71 69
4 b m Myboycharlie(IRE) Gemini Gold (IRE) (King's Best (USA))
146[2]

Lady Giselle (IRE) *John J Walsh* 91
6 ch m Indian Haven Makena (GER) (Acambaro (GER))
1018a[12] 4850a[14]

Lady Gwhinnyvere (IRE) *John Spearing* a16 22
2 b f Sir Prancealot(IRE) Johar Jamal (IRE) (Chevalier (IRE))
4981[10] 5668[6] 6873[9] 7748[10]

Lady Hare (IRE) *Ken Cunningham-Brown* a60 60
4 b m Approve(IRE) Peaceful Kingdom (USA) (King Of Kings (IRE))
2646[6] 3737[4] 4226[2] 5597[6] 6022[2] 6315[8] 6825[7]

Lady Hester (USA) *John Gosden* a55
2 b f Bernardini(USA) Questing (Hard Spun (USA))
6414[7] 8361[6]

Lady In Question (IRE) *Richard Fahey* 79
2 b f Elzaam(AUS) Black Meyeden (FR) (Black Minnaloushe (USA))
(3261) 4394[12] 4802[4] 5407[4] 6388a[7] 6787[7] 6954[5]

Lady Joanna Vassa (IRE) *Richard Guest* a63 65
3 ch f Equiano(FR) Lady Natilda (First Trump)
2302[5] (2503) 2834[2] 3423[4] 3581[2] 3806[3] (3900) 4855[6] 6745[9] 7093[8] 7533[8] 7859[5] (7961) 8149[10] 8242[4] 8485[12]

Lady Kaviar (IRE) *George Margarson* a61 52
2 b f Lope De Vega(IRE) Maoin Dor (IRE) (Manduro (GER))
3074[8] 5298[5] 6655[7]

Lady Kheleyf *George Margarson* a63 58
3 bl f Kheleyf(USA) Mosa Mine (Exceed And Excel (AUS))
1935[11]

Lady Kitty *John Davies* a54
2 b f Harbour Watch(IRE) Elidore (Danetime (IRE))
7659[7]

Lady Knight (IRE) *Sally Randell* a32 18
5 b m Champs Elysees Knight's Place (IRE) (Hamas (IRE))
251[9] 378[8]

Lady Kyllar *George Margarson* a70 90
4 b m Kyllachy Miss Otis (Danetime (IRE))
1744[3] 1929[9] 4585[12]

Lady Lara (IRE) *William Mott* 108
5 b m Excellent Art Shanty (Selkirk (USA))
3178a[4] (5185a)

Lady Lekki (IRE) *Ben Haslam* 77
4 b m Champs Elysees One Zero (USA) (Theatrical (IRE))
(1382) 2051[6] 3263[3]

Lady Linn (FR) *P Monfort* a69 72
3 ch f Linngari(IRE) Amerissage (USA) (Rahy (USA))
5946a[11]

Lady Lloyd *Phil McEntee* a64 57
3 b f Paco Boy(IRE) Carafe (Selkirk (USA))
611[2] 750[3] 834[3] 885[3] 1292[7] 1574[7] 4835[9] 5192[5]

Lady Lunchalot (USA) *Laura Mongan* a72 63
6 b m More Than Ready(USA) Betty Johanne (USA) (Johannesburg (USA))
631[5] 2374[5] (2607) 3142[6] 4201[5] 4880[4] 5397[6] 5776[3] 6334[8] 6662[7] 7609[7] 7936[6]

Lady Lydia (IRE) *Gay Kelleway* a91 70
5 b m Kheleyf(USA) Piece Unique (Barathea (IRE))
41[2] 558[3] 632[7] 1207[4] 1932[5] 2034[7] 8158[6]

Lady Macapa *William Knight* a71 104
3 b f Equiano(FR) Brazilian Style (Exit To Nowhere (USA))
1607[2] 2192[8] 3413[4] (3685) 5657[7] 6119[5] (7186) 7822[7]

Lady Madiba (FR) *Alfonso Nunez* 64
3 bb f Lawman(FR) Reform Act (USA) (Lemon Drop Kid (USA))
5249a[9]

Lady Maesmor *D J Bunyan* a60 61
4 b m Kyllachy Pulsate (Inchinor)
482[10]

Lady Makfi (IRE) *Johnny Farrelly* a84 73
4 b m Makfi Dulcet Tones (IRE) (Singspiel (IRE))
(2781) 3560[10] (4197) (4478) (5131) 5851[5] 6591[5]

Lady Mandeville (IRE) *Adrian McGuinness* a56 41
4 b m Strategic Prince My Causeway Dream (IRE) (Giant's Causeway (USA))
543[11]

Lady Marl *Gary Moore* a89 88
5 b m Duke Of Marmalade(IRE) Empress Anna (IRE) (Imperial Ballet (IRE))
254[5] 422[6] 967[2] 1093[7] 3979[6] 4501[5] 5054[3] 5384a[11]

Lady McGuffy (IRE) *David Evans* a56 62
3 b f Holy Roman Emperor(IRE) Fountain Of Honour (IRE) (Sadler's Wells (USA))
3[3] 502[5] 783[7] 1389[7] 2184[2] 3198[4] 3513[2] 3786[2] 3811[5] 4484[3] 5554[6] 6381[2]

Lady Mega (IRE) *Edward Lynam* a87 91
5 br m Kodiac Naias (IRE) (Namid)
4540a[4] 6819a[17]

Lady Molly (IRE) *Keith Dalgleish* a34 62
2 b f Kodiac Beth (Deportivo)
5798[3] 6214[3] 7040[3] 7748[8]

Lady Nahema (IRE) *Ann Duffield* a54 67
3 b f Zoffany(IRE) Jamary (IRE) (Grand Reward (USA))
1420[6] 2777[3] 3838[3] 4257[3]

La Dynamite (IRE) *Markus Klug* 99
3 br f Dylan Thomas(IRE) La Blue (GER) (Bluebird (USA))
3207a[8] 5220a[8] 7720a[12]

Lady Natasha (IRE) *K R Burke* 62
3 b f Alfred Nobel(IRE) Hot To Rock (IRE) (Kalanisi (IRE))
4806[4] 5361[6] 6052[10] 7582[2]

Lady Nayef *John Butler* a78 69
3 b f Nayef(USA) Luck Will Come (IRE) (Desert Style (IRE))
1847[9] 2742[12] 3581[3] 4280[4] 5078[8] 6248[4] 6680[3] 7420[8] 8078[2] (8390)

Lady Of Camelot (IRE) *John Gosden* a87 108
4 b m Montjeu(IRE) Marquesa (USA) (Kingmambo (USA))
(2735) 3888[5] 4883[5] 6747[2] 7119[2] 7545[8] 7823[3] 8068[11]

Lady Of Dubai *Roger Varian* 111
4 b m Dubawi(IRE) Lady Of Everest (IRE) (Montjeu (IRE))
2189[5] 4435a[10]

Lady Of Kyushu (USA) *F-H Graffard* 103
4 b m Smart Strike(CAN) Lady Aquitaine (USA) (El Prado (IRE))
2077a[6]

Lady Of York *Alan Bailey* a30 31
2 b f Sir Percy Parsonagehotelyork (IRE) (Danehill (USA))
7466[8] 7883[11] 8246[13]

Lady Of Yue *Eugene Stanford* a65 72
6 b m Manduro(GER) Desert Royalty (IRE) (Alhaarth (IRE))
1987[6] 2501[5] 3161[5] 4739[2] 6267[4] 8084[3]

Lady Parker (IRE) *J S Moore* a18 5
2 gr f Zebedee Westering Home (IRE) (Mull Of Kintyre (USA))
2748[9] 8361[10]

Lady Perignon *Andrew Balding* a42 83
3 b f Poet's Voice Amallna (Green Desert (USA))
5300[9] (5822) 6483[2]

Lady Petrus *K Kukk* a23 24
11 b m Oasis Dream Odalisque (IRE) (Machiavellian (USA))
1519a[6] 2955a[2] 3918a[9] 5458a[3]

Lady Poppy *Jedd O'Keeffe* a28 64
6 b m Kyllachy Poppets Sweetlove (Foxhound (USA))
(1668) 2052[11] 2676[4] 3484[12] 4492[6]

Lady President (IRE) *J S Moore* a46
3 b f Fast Company(IRE) Lovere (St Jovite (USA))
69[3]

Lady Ranger (IRE) *Peter McCreery* a61 73
5 b m Bushranger(IRE) Annus Iucundus (IRE) (Desert King (IRE))
7391a[15]

Lady Rocka *Amanda Perrett* a40 63
3 ch f Rock Of Gibraltar(IRE) Tap Dance Way (IRE) (Azamour (IRE))
1734[10] 2366[9] (2967) 3256[5] 4021[7]

Lady Rowena *Mark Johnston* a40
2 ch f Sepoy(AUS) Miss Ivanhoe (IRE) (Selkirk (USA))
8089[12] 8277[9] 8536[9]

Lady Shipman (USA) *Kiaran McLaughlin* 113
4 ch m Midshipman(USA) Sumthingtotalkabt (USA) (Mutakddim (USA))
1104a[7] 7829a[4]

Lady Sidney (FR) *R Le Dren Doleuze* a76 66
2 b f Mr. Sidney(USA) Marechale (FR) (Anabaa (USA))
5142a[9]

Lady's Spring (FR) *Mlle G Gadbled* a51 49
5 b m My Risk(FR) Doud's Lady (FR) (Balleroy (USA))
8421a[8]

Lady Turpin (IRE) *Richard Fahey* a32 55
3 gr f Arakan(USA) Proficiency (El Prado (IRE))
3015[5] 3493[7] (4146) 4522[4] ◆

Lady Valdean *Jose Santos* 72
2 ch f Helmet(AUS) Symphonic Dancer (USA) (Smart Strike (CAN))
4801[8] 5995[5] 6776[5] 7286[2] ◆

Lady Valeur (IRE) *Patrick Gallagher* 99
3 b f Multiplex Hawk Eyed Lady (IRE) (Hawk Wing (USA))
7724a[4]

Lady Vellyn *Matthew Salaman*
4 gr m Hellvelyn Alvarinho Lady (Royal Applause)
7509[9] 8346[7]

Lady Volante (IRE) *David Evans* a57 71
2 b f Teofilo(IRE) Empress Of Rome (IRE) (Holy Roman Emperor (IRE))
8237[3]

Lady Wootton *Keith Dalgleish* 67
3 b f Wootton Bassett Killer Class (Kyllachy)
1558[4] 2255[7] 2534[2] 2776[3] 3017[2] 3755[7] 3882[6] 5152[3] 5225[9] 6615[3] 6774[4]

Lady Zinaad (GER) *E Lellouche* a93 62
6 b m Areion(GER) Lady Lips (GER) (Zinaad)
(6938a)

Lady Zodiac (IRE) *Philip McBride* a31 55
4 br m Kodiac Treacle Noir (IRE) (Raise A Grand (IRE))
1795[5] 2087[5]

La Fibre (FR) *M Pimbonnet* a81
2 b c Whipper(USA) Eva Kant (Medicean)
(5755a) 7971a[5]

La Fibrossi (FR) *H-A Pantall* a72 52
2 b f Myboycharlie(IRE) Tamada (Lucky Story (USA))
7490a[11] 7879a[3]

La Force (GER) *Patrick Gallagher* 101
2 bb f Power La Miraculeuse (GER) (Samum (GER))
7809a[7] 8127a[12]

La Fortuna *Charlie Wallis* a55
3 b f Zamindar(USA) Hyperspace (Dansili)
7207[3] 7935[2] 8472[2]

La Fritillaire *James Given* a56 65
4 b m Champs Elysees Generous Diana (Generous (IRE))
1405[5] 2745[10] 3067[3] *4478[5]* (4739) (5522) 5781[3] 6519[2] (7006) 7592[7]

Laganore (IRE) *A J Martin* 111
4 b m Fastnet Rock(AUS) Lady Bones (IRE) (Royal Applause)
1015a[8] 2690[4] 6604a[2] (7119) 7566a[3]

Lagenda *Kevin Ryan* a65 92
3 b g Dick Turpin(IRE) Whirly Dancer (Danehill Dancer (IRE))
1446[8] 2161[4] 2477[2] 3029[2] 3635[5] 6164[3] 7668[6]

Lagertha (IRE) *Hugo Palmer* 37
2 b f Oasis Dream Tafiya (Bahri (USA))
7441[13]

Lagostovegas (IRE) *David Harry Kelly* 75
4 b m Footstepsinthesand Reine De Coeur (IRE) (Montjeu (IRE))
4721a[7]

La Guapita *Hugo Palmer* a69
2 ch f Bahamian Bounty Somersault (Pivotal)
7988[5] 8139[2]

Laguna Sun (FR) *L Cendra* a55 34
7 b m Speedmaster(GER) Loving Away (FR) (Gold Away (IRE))
5281a[7]

La Haule Lady *Paul Midgley* a51 65
2 ch f Helmet(AUS) Sea Of Leaves (USA) (Stormy Atlantic (USA))
2162[9] 2552[3] 3388[6] 5317[7] 6222[6] ◆ 6536[10] *7109[9]*

La Havrese (FR) *Lynn Siddall* a67 68
5 ch m Le Havre(IRE) La Buena (IRE) (Big Shuffle (USA))
334[4] ◆ (568) 769[3] ◆ (982) 1501[7] 2436[2] 2860[5] 3642[4] (4486) 5062[6] 6521[4] *6922[6] 7326[5] 7601[6] 8207[2] 8527[5]*

Laidback Romeo (IRE) *Clive Cox* 97
4 b g Kodiac Belmora (USA) (Scrimshaw (USA))
3157[7] 4055[2] ◆ (4776) (5206)

Laila Honiwillow *Jedd O'Keeffe* a77 79
3 b f Bahamian Bounty Anatase (Danehill (USA))
1670[11] 2255[3] ◆ (2777) (3603) ◆ 4376[2] (4861) *5969[5] 7325[5]*

La Isla Bonita *Richard Spencer* a30
2 b f Foxwedge(AUS) Excello (Exceed And Excel (AUS))
8377[8]

Lajatico *Ed Vaughan* a85 91
3 b f Equiano(FR) Italian Connection (Cadeaux Genereux)
1146[2] 1815[3] 3038[3] *(4525)* (4835)

Lakalas (FR) *J-C Rouget* 106
3 b f Turtle Bowl(IRE) Nazlia (FR) (Polish Precedent (USA))
4904a[2] 5754a[3]

Lake Hawk (IRE) *A R Al Rayhi* a63
7 b h Hawk Wing(USA) Princess Electra (IRE) (Lake Coniston (IRE))
8a[12]

Lake Placid *Charles Hills* 65
3 b g Champs Elysees Phantom Wind (USA) (Storm Cat (USA))
1639[10]

La Manga (IRE) *Jamie Osborne* a57
3 b f Kodiac Good Shot Noreen (IRE) (Sleeping Indian)
105[2] ◆ 140[7] 6826[14]

Lamar (IRE) *James Tate* a108 103
5 b m Cape Cross(IRE) Deveron (USA) (Cozzene (USA))
(125) 214[3] 485[3]

Lamarck *M G Mintchev* 97
3 b c Soldier Hollow Laronja (GER) (Areion (GER))
4439a[7] 5499a[9]

La Merced (GER) *P Schiergen* 100
3 b f Tiger Hill(IRE) La Pilaya (GER) (Pivotal)
1513a[2] 2949a[16] 3916a[9]

La Mere Beaude (FR) *S Jesus* a30 41
5 b m Royal Assault(USA) Blaina (FR) (Caerwent)
3733a[9]

La Messalina (FR) *M Aubry* a83 61
6 b m Apsis Mariyati (FR) (Marignan (USA))
1157a[9]

L'Ami Cagnois (FR) *S Jesus* 91
2 b g Doctor Dino(FR) Arthurs Princess (IRE) (Monashee Mountain (USA))
3871a[3]

La Milva (FR) *Alex Fracas* a77 67
3 b f Early March La Macchia (FR) (Lord Of Men)
5385a[6]

L'Amiral David (FR) *Alan King* a72
6 b g My Risk(FR) Mme La Vicomtesse (FR) (Baroud D'Honneur (FR))
245[5] 318[5]

Lamloom (IRE) *David O'Meara* 64
2 b c Cape Cross(IRE) Lulua (USA) (Bahri (USA))
6535[6] 7247[5]

La Mortola *John Gosden* 66
3 b f Dubawi(IRE) Claba Di San Jore (IRE) (Barathea (IRE))
1759[8]

L'Amour Du Risk (FR) *J-P Gallorini* 26
2 b c No Risk At All(FR) Lamaya (FR) (Azamour (IRE))
7345a[8]

Lancaster Bomber (USA) *A P O'Brien* 115
2 b c War Front(USA) Sun Shower (IRE) (Indian Ridge)
5683a[4] 6386a[5] 7149[2] 7807a[2]

Lancelot Du Lac (ITY) *Dean Ivory* a115 76
6 b g Shamardal(USA) Dodie Mae (USA) (Capote (USA))
(17) 1066[2] ◆ 1862[21] 3244[15] 3909[12]

Landfall (FR) *K J Condon* 110
2 b g Myboycharlie(IRE) Lana Girl (USA) (Arch (USA))
(6349a)

Landin (GER) *P Schiergen* a82 89
3 b c Sir Percy Lupita (GER) (Niniski (USA))
4186a[16]

Landing Night (IRE) *Rebecca Menzies* a84 75
4 b g Kodiac Night Delight (IRE) (Night Shift (USA))
2261[11] (2426) 2775[5] 3150[10] 6324[10] *6927[8]* 7252[3] ◆ *8099[4]* ◆ *(8349)* ◆ *8403[4]*

Land Of Dubai (IRE) *Clive Cox* 63
3 b f Dubai Destination(USA) Land Army (IRE) (Desert Style (IRE))
2848[3] 4156[5] 5327[3] 5832[8]

Landofhopeandglory (IRE) *A P O'Brien* 103
3 b g High Chaparral(IRE) Wurfklinge (GER) (Acatenango (GER))
1438[4] 2036[4] 2510a[5] 3341[4] 3697a[2] 4186a[18]

Land Over Sea (USA) *Doug O'Neill* a107 77
3 ch f Bellamy Road(USA) Belle Watling (USA) (Pulpit (USA))
4174a[12] *7810a[7]*

Landsman (IRE) *A J Martin* a61 89
3 b g Canford Cliffs(IRE) Mowaadah (IRE) (Alzao (USA))
7123[8]

Landwade Lad *James Fanshawe* a93 99
4 b g Dansili Sell Out (Act One)
(5240) 6233[2] 6884[2]

Landym (FR) *H-A Pantall* a51 104
5 b h Lando(GER) Ymlaen (IRE) (Desert Prince (IRE))
4783a[7]

Langham *Martyn Meade* a71 59
3 b f Royal Applause Three Ducks (Diktat)
1859[8] *2375[5] 3527[3]* 4280[6] *5725[6]*

Langley Vale *Roger Teal* a70 63
7 b g Piccolo Running Glimpse (IRE) (Runnett)
1178[7] 2396[10] 3349[6] *(3984) (5605) 6589[5]* 7267[5] 7774[8]

Langtang (GER) *A Wohler* 104
2 b c Campanologist(USA) La Vinchina (GER) (Oasis Dream)
(7399a)

Lani (USA) *Mikio Matsunaga* a117
3 rg c Tapit(USA) Heavenly Romance (JPN) (Sunday Silence (USA))
(1103a) 2063a[9] 2499a[5] 3181a[3]

Lanjano *Kevin Ryan* 79
2 ch c Foxwedge(AUS) Hot Property (USA) (Thunder Gulch (USA))
4363[6] (4765) 5510[3] 7120[7]

Laoban (USA) *Eric J Guillot* a116
3 bb c Uncle Mo(USA) Chattertown (USA) (Speightstown (USA))
2499a[6] 5913a[12]

La Patria *A Fabre* 91
3 ch f Dubawi(IRE) Evil Empire (GER) (Acatenango (GER))
7397a[8]

La Perle Doloise (FR) *A Bonin* a60 69
3 gr f Kingsalsa(USA) Claire Des Fieffes (FR) (Adieu Au Roi (IRE))
5907a[4]

Lapilli *William Haggas* a81 91
3 b g Bahamian Bounty Blue Lyric (Refuse To Bend (IRE))
(1167) 1935[8] (5751) (6018)

L'Apogee *Richard Fahey* 65
3 ch g Rip Van Winkle(IRE) Pappas Ruby (USA) (Red Ransom (USA))
1849[6] 2506[6] 2831[3] 3287[3] 3921[10] 4424[3] 4872[8] 5481[4] (5921)

Laqab (IRE) *Roger Varian* a86
3 b c Teofilo(IRE) Ghaidaa (IRE) (Cape Cross (IRE))
6703[2] (7384)

Laquyood *Werner Glanz* 53
3 ch g Medicean Elmaam (Nayef (USA))
5385a[9]

Lara Carbonara (IRE) *John Patrick Shanahan* 76
4 b m The Carbon Unit(USA) Janna's Jewel (IRE) (Traditionally (USA))
1884[3] 2198[13] 2575[3] 3018[2] (3547) 3751[7] 4311[3] 4875[3] 5580[2] 6011[5] 6773[5] 7251[3]

Lara Karay (FR) *Gianluca Bietolini*
5 b m Le Fou(IRE) La Latitude (FR) (Scribe I (IRE))
2806a[13]

Larch (IRE) *Mrs A Malzard* 29
4 b m Acclamation Shady Nook (IRE) (Key Of Luck (USA))
1519a[9] 3917a[8] 5457a[6]

Larchmont Lad (IRE) *Richard Hannon* 109
2 b c Footstepsinthesand Fotini (IRE) (King's Best (USA))
(3859) ◆ 6285[3] ◆ (6707)

L'Ardent (FR) *J-C Rouget* a82 66
5 ch g Soldier Of Fortune(IRE) Princesse De Viane (FR) (Kaldoun (FR))
4927a[5] (5452a)

Largent Du Bonheur (FR) *M Delzangles* 102
3 b c Kendargent(FR) La Joie (FR) (Montjeu (IRE))
2232a[8] 4905a[4] 6391a[10] 7030a[6]

La Rioja *Henry Candy* 111
3 b f Hellvelyn Talampaya (USA) (Elusive Quality (USA))
2692[5] 3338[4] 4114[3] 5436[3] 6281[5] 6816a[3] 7758a[3]

Laris (FR) *T Lemer* a77 84
3 ch g Literato(FR) Miss Lena (Medicean)
2141a[8]

Larno (FR) *D Prod'Homme* a76 77
2 gr c Milanais(FR) Honorable Sister (FR) (Highest Honor (FR))
(5279a) 6015a[3]

Larox (GER) *C Von Der Recke* 58
3 b f Tertullian(USA) Lajana (GER) (Goofalik (USA))
7265a[3]

Larry (FR) *U Stech* 52
3 b c Literato(FR) Sakkara Star (IRE) (Mozart (IRE))
4186a[15]

La Salesse (FR) *Mark Johnston* 63
3 b f Manduro(GER) Ailette (Second Set (IRE))
4001[4] 4372[7] 6014[5]

La Sarenne (FR) *P Bary* a55
2 gr f Rajsaman(FR) Aviane (GER) (Winged Love (IRE))
4187a[4] *5988a[9]*

Laseen (IRE) *J-P Gauvin* a89 95
5 b m Dylan Thomas(IRE) La Seine (USA) (Rahy (USA))
8042a[14]

Laser Blazer *Alan King* a74 69
8 b g Zafeen(FR) Sashay (Bishop Of Cashel)
78[4] 5745[4]

Lassana Angel *Roger Charlton* 64
2 b f High Chaparral(IRE) Diara Angel (IRE) (Hawk Wing (USA))
7285[3]

Last Impact (JPN) *Katsuhiko Sumii* 119
6 bb h Deep Impact(JPN) Superior Pearl (JPN) (Timber Country (USA))
1107a[3] 8129a[10]

Lastmanlastround (IRE) *Rae Guest* a69 77
3 b g Azamour(IRE) Lastroseofsummer (IRE) (Haafhd)
557[2] ◆ 3723[2] 4682[5] (5480) *6084[11]*

Last Paradise (IRE) *Harry Dunlop* 54
2 b f Caradak(IRE) Exotic Beauty (Barathea (IRE))
2417[5] 3361[3] 3763a[9]

L'Astrolabe (FR) *J Baudron* a51 77
2 b f Sageburg(IRE) Lavetoria (FR) (Danehill Dancer (IRE))
8420a[13]

Last Star Falling (IRE) *Henry Spiller* a68 62
3 b f Acclamation Star Port (Observatory (USA))
1294[3] 1725[2] 2306[8] 2968[6] 4316[4] *5248[5] 5973[10] (6509) 7255[9] 8365[9]*

Last Summer *Grace Harris* a51 57
5 ch g New Approach(IRE) Evil Empire (GER) (Acatenango (GER))
1499[6] 1722[5] 4792[8] *5303[13]* 5958[10] *7739[8]*

Last Tango (FR) *Alain Couetil* a37 64
3 b f Peintre Celebre(USA) L'Etoile De Mer (FR) (Caerleon (USA))
7265a[2]

Last Tango Inparis *Hughie Morrison* a93 93
3 ch f Aqlaam Strictly Lambada (Red Ransom (USA))
2245[8] 4331a[2] *7652[6]* 8024a[9]

Last Waltz (IRE) *Chad C Brown* 104
3 b f Danehill Dancer(IRE) Vivacity (Trempolino (USA))
4174a[7]

Last Wish (IRE) *Richard Guest* a58 61
5 b g Raven's Pass(USA) Quiet Dream (USA) (Seattle Slew (USA))
1131[8] 1841[6] *2329[12]* 2507[7] 2849[2] 3072[13] 3876[9]

Last Word *David Lanigan* a46 52
2 b f Bated Breath Intermission (IRE) (Royal Applause)
6733[7] 7055[11] *7647[8]*

La Superba (IRE) *David Elsworth* a60 83
4 ch m Medicean La Spezia (IRE) (Danehill Dancer (IRE))
1757[7] 2236[2] 2671[3] 3352[4] 4160[7]

La Surfeuse (FR) *T Lemer* a53 49
2 b f Bertolini(USA) Kialoskar (IRE) (Refuse To Bend (IRE))
7455a[9]

Lateran Accord (IRE) *G Arizkorreta Elosegui* a87 91
7 ch h Rock Of Gibraltar(IRE) La Ina (GER) (Monsun (GER))
5502a[10] 6356a[7]

Late Shipment *Nikki Evans* a59 87
5 b g Authorized(IRE) Time Over (Mark Of Esteem (IRE))
4634[10] 6380[8]

Late Starter (IRE) *Hugo Palmer*
3 ch g Compton Place Setting Forth (IRE) (Daggers Drawn (USA))
4017[11] 4806[8]

La Testerine (FR) *F Chappet* 44
2 b f Deportivo Mishkina (FR) (Vettori (IRE))
4965a[7]

Latest Quest (IRE) *Sylvester Kirk* a74 70
2 b g Zebedee Fancy Theory (USA) (Quest For Fame)
2204[5] 2429[4] 3668[3] *(4524)* 4802[15] 5560[19] 6060[6] 6950[23] 7217[15] *7974[5] 8276[6]*

Latharnach (USA) *Charlie Appleby* 116
4 b g Iffraaj Firth Of Lorne (IRE) (Danehill (USA))
(6955) ◆ 7701[3]

Lat Hawill (IRE) *Keith Dalgleish* a100 104
5 b g Invincible Spirit(IRE) Arbella (Primo Dominie)
501[3] 767[7] 1196[21] *2331[3]* 2833[2] 3390[9] 4448[11] 5156[2] 5585[18] *6126[7]* 6786[20]

Lathom *David O'Meara* 101
3 b g Compton Place Wigan Lane (Kheleyf (USA))
2895[8] 3165[7] 3413[5] 4112[5] 4803[5] ◆ 5390[6] 5657[10]

Latin Beat (IRE) *A P O'Brien* 83
2 b c Galileo(IRE) Breeze Hill (IRE) (Danehill (USA))
6817a[5]

Latin Charm (IRE) *Gay Kelleway* a74 57
5 b g Cape Cross(IRE) Di Moi Oui (Warning)
530[7] 747[9] 4927a[10] 5501a[10] 5700a[9]

Latin Rebel (IRE) *Jim Goldie* a25 63
9 b g Spartacus(IRE) Dance To The Beat (Batshoof)
3921[8] 4447[5] 4934[4] 5580[4] *5971[11]* 6619[9]

La Trinacria (USA) *Agostino Affe'* 96
3 b f Harlan's Holiday(USA) Almeria Gal (USA) (El Prado (IRE))
1685a[2]

Laugh Aloud *John Gosden* a63 111
3 ch f Dubawi(IRE) Opera Comique (FR) (Singspiel (IRE))
2653[2] 3412[2] (3958) 5831[2] ◆ (6746)

Laughton *Kevin Ryan* 87
3 b g Acclamation Peach Pearl (Invincible Spirit (IRE))
1922[7] 2337[3] (2742) 3644[2] 4093[2] ◆ (4803) 5657[5] 6164[6]

Launched (IRE) *P Bary* a92 113
4 b h Galileo(IRE) Apsara (FR) (Darshaan)
4333a[2] 5692a[6]

Lauraman *Martin Smith* a42
2 ch f Bated Breath Dance Away (Pivotal)
6696[11]

Laureate *Mark Johnston* 73
2 b f Poet's Voice Step This Way (USA) (Giant's Causeway (USA))
3597[6] 4037[2] 4728[3] 5266[2] 5518[3]

Laurence *Luca Cumani* 96
4 b g Dubawi(IRE) Victoire Celebre (USA) (Stravinsky (USA))
2484[8] 3113[9] 4026[4] ◆ 4858[3] 6286[2] 6753[5] 7535[2]

Lava Light *Henry Candy* a69 73
2 b f Sixties Icon May Light (Midyan (USA))
6086[5] 6866[4] 7576[2] *7966[7]*

La Valkyrie *P Van De Poele* a81 59
3 gr f Elusive City(USA) Symba's Dream (USA) (Vindication (USA))
716a[7]

Lavender Skye (IRE) *K R Burke* a31 34
2 b f Sir Prancealot(IRE) Pandoras Secret (IRE) (Monashee Mountain (USA))
1086[6] 1407[6] 2266[5] 5799[6] 5974[7]

Lavetta *Alan Swinbank* a73 91
4 b m Peintre Celebre(USA) Card Games (First Trump)
1125[2] (1563) ◆ 1757[6] 2223[10] (2890) *4644[8]* 7095[3] (7472)

La Vie En Rose *Mark Johnston* a59 55
2 b f Henrythenavigator(USA) Lady Jane Digby (Oasis Dream)
6924[6] 7284[7] *7647[6] 7954[2]*

Law And Order (IRE) *James Tate* 100
2 b c Lawman(FR) Catbells (IRE) (Rakti)
5332[3] (5848) 6707[5] 7148[8] 7544[3]

Lawfilly *Richard Hughes* a61 44
2 b f Lawman(FR) Red Boots (IRE) (Verglas (IRE))
5722[6] 6071[11] *6625[6]* 7185[13] *7777[3] 8071[9] 8153[12] 8425[4]*

Law Girl (FR) *N Clement* a65 96
3 b f Lawman(FR) Lamarsa (FR) (Chichicastenango (FR))
7897a[4]

Lawless Louis *David O'Meara* a69 81
2 ch g Equiano(FR) Peace And Love (IRE) (Fantastic Light (USA))
1868[5] (2235) (2675) 2908[4] 4111[5] 4832[4] 5510[5] *6507[5]* 6954[6]

Lawmaking *Henry Spiller* a80 107
3 b g Zamindar(USA) Canada Water (Dansili)
8069[9]

Lawman's Justice (IRE) *Michael Dods* 62
3 b g Lawman(FR) Brazilian Bride (IRE) (Pivotal)
4313[6]

Law Power *Sir Mark Prescott Bt* a69 76
2 b c Lawman(FR) Clarietta (Shamardal (USA))
3619[4] 3954[4] *4473[3]* 5171[4] *5840[2] 6240[5]* (6563) 6800[3] 7033[9]

Laws Of Spin (IRE) *W P Mullins* 97
3 b g Lawman(FR) Spinning Well (IRE) (Pivotal)
(7195a)

Lawyer (IRE) *David Barron* a84 85
5 b g Acclamation Charaig (Rainbow Quest (USA))
73[5] 581[5] 802[5] 1152[8] 1841[3] 2673[2] 2773[4] (3327) 4408[5] 4841[5] (4986) 5223[4] 5419[8] 6217[8] (6516) 6956[9] *7796[3]*

Layali Al Andalus *S Seemar* a76 90
9 b g Halling(USA) Lafite (Robellino (USA))
453a[8]

Layl (USA) *Doug Watson* a111 77
6 br h Street Cry(IRE) Cymbal (IRE) (Singspiel (IRE))
92a[2] ◆ *452a[7] 842a[5]*

Layla's Hero (IRE) *Roger Teal* a80 80
9 b g One Cool Cat(USA) Capua (USA) (Private Terms (USA))
1251[6] *(1401)* 1818[2] (3421) *3726[3]* 4291[6] *4881[10]* 5915[2] *(6235)* 6644[9] *8252[10] 8473[13]*

Layman Junior (FR) *S Bossert* a61 51
8 ch g Layman(USA) Summer Rain (Cadeaux Genereux)
8422a[12]

La Zamtoff (FR) *C Le Lay* a79 87
4 b m Zambezi Sun Tirtoff (FR) (Anabaa (USA))
7564a[13]

Lazizah *Marcus Tregoning* a47 59
3 b f Medicean Atyaab (Green Desert (USA))
2325[8] 2828[5] 3256[2] 4159[9]

Lazzam *Marco Botti* a94 91
3 ch c Archipenko(USA) Empire Rose (ARG) (Sunray Spirit (USA))
154[2] 539a[2] 839a[2] 1103a[6] 4624[10] *4976[4]* 7005[6]

Lbretha (FR) *F-H Graffard* a84 85
3 b f Exceed And Excel(AUS) Actrice Francaise (USA) (Dynaformer (USA))
8368a[2]

L C Saloon *David C Griffiths* 78
3 ch g Equiano(FR) Aberdovey (Mister Baileys)
3643[4] (4238) ◆ 4947[6] 5730[5] 6234[10]

Leader Queen *Francesco Pisano* 57
3 br f Strategic Prince Thumpers Dream (Cape Cross (IRE))
1685a[9]

Leader's Legacy (USA) *Saeed bin Suroor* 63
2 bb c War Front(USA) Bauble Queen (USA) (Arch (USA))
4533[6]

Leader Writer (FR) *H-A Pantall* 104
4 b h Pivotal Miss Emma May (IRE) (Hawk Wing (USA))
1910a[6] 5948a[5]

Leading Actress (IRE) *M Delcher Sanchez* a53 86
4 b m Makfi Emmy Award (IRE) (Sadler's Wells (USA))
1172a[8]

Leah Freya (IRE) *Pat Phelan* a55 94
5 b m Aussie Rules(USA) A Woman In Love (Muhtarram (USA))
1568[4] 4353[6] 5145[8] 5927[5] (6544) 7150[P] (Dead)

Lean Burn (USA) *Barry Leavy* a42 51
10 b g Johannesburg(USA) Anthelion (USA) (Stop The Music (USA))
1450[7] 1831[5]

Lean On Pete (IRE) *Ollie Pears* a73 64
7 b g Oasis Dream Superfonic (FR) (Zafonic (USA))
38[11] 179[4] 446[4] 640[3] 864[5] 1114[3] 1347[4] 1501[5] 1762[4] 2618[6] 2915[7] 3253[U] (3480) 3842[8] 4730[3] 5028[5] 5481[12] 6029[10] (6647) 7336[8]

Leaping *Roger Charlton* a60 68
3 b f Oasis Dream Avoidance (USA) (Cryptoclearance (USA))
2183[8] 2815[6]

Leapt *Roger Charlton* 63
2 b g Nathaniel(IRE) Liel (Pivotal)
5600[8] 7013[8] 7621[7]

Le Bernardin (USA) *A R Al Rayhi* a114
7 br h Bernardini(USA) La Rosa (USA) (Wild Again (USA))
(92a) 454a[4] 842a[3] 8396a[4]

Le Brivido (FR) *A Fabre* a78
2 b c Siyouni(FR) La Bugatty (IRE) (Dr Fong (USA))
(7783a)

Le Candidat (FR) *J-C Rouget* a64
2 ch c Literato(FR) Creamcake (USA) (Mr Greeley (USA))
7422a[3]

Le Chat D'Or *Michael Dods* 93
8 b g One Cool Cat(USA) Oh So Well (IRE) (Sadler's Wells (USA))
1122[14] (2527) 3923[10] 4448[2] 6225[5] 6557[5] 7316[9]

Le Colonel (GER) *A Schaerer* 102
4 ch h Sabiango(GER) La Hermana (Hernando (FR))
(2318a) 6151a[2]

Ledbury (IRE) *Lee Carter* a69 31
4 b g Lawman(FR) Truly Magnificent (USA) (Elusive Quality (USA))
138[7] 4197[7] 4784[8] 5399[8] 5777[11]

Le Deluge (FR) *Micky Hammond* a67 73
6 b g Oratorio(IRE) Princess Sofia (UAE) (Pennekamp (USA))
173[5] 3363[7] 3481[4] (4424) 4687[3] 4833[2] 6684[3] 7321[6]

Lee Bay *John Gosden* a58 63
3 b c Cacique(IRE) Bantu (Cape Cross (IRE))
3190[6] 3578[4] 4718[7]

Leedora *Karen Tutty* 39
3 b f Sir Percy Alizadora (Zilzal (USA))
1120[12]

Lee's Hall (IRE) *Murty McGrath* a66 64
3 b g Invincible Spirit(IRE) Russian Roubles (IRE) (Sadler's Wells (USA))
1388[9] 1860[13] 4279[7] 5167[7]

Lefortovo (FR) *Jo Hughes* a88 84
3 b c Arcano(IRE) Lorientaise (IRE) (Xaar)
1311a[4] (2287a) (3120a) 6911a[5] 8311[5]

Left Hand *C Laffon-Parias* 113
3 ch f Dubawi(IRE) Balladeuse (FR) (Singspiel (IRE))
2316a[4] 3452a[2] (4904a) (6393a) 6989a[12]

Legal Art *Brian Ellison* a63 57
4 ch m Dutch Art Sosumi (Be My Chief (USA))
1254[4] 1600[9] (2330) 3314[3]

Legalized *James Given* a29 42
2 bb f Authorized(IRE) Laurena (GER) (Acatenango (GER))
7285[8] 7769[15] 8130[9]

Legato (IRE) *Tom Dascombe* 30
2 ch g Power Lisa Gherardini (IRE) (Barathea (IRE))
7317[8]

Legendary Lunch (IRE) *Richard Hannon* 105
2 ch c Dragon Pulse(IRE) Taalluf (USA) (Hansel (USA))
(1713) 2311[2] (2865) 3295[6] 4352[7] 6282[2] 6572[6]

Legendoire (IRE) *John Gallagher* a60 32
2 b g Fast Company(IRE) Last Shaambles (IRE) (Shaamit (IRE))
2873[9] 3770[5] 7648[5] 7898[7] 8153[9]

Legitimus (IRE) *J S Bolger* 92
2 b f Lawman(FR) Imeall Na Speire (USA) (Galileo (IRE))
5937a[4] 6815a[3]

Leith Bridge *Mark Usher* a53
4 b g Avonbridge Ishibee (IRE) (Ishiguru (USA))
130[6] 320[6] 8149[5] 8409[8]

Leitrim Traveller (USA) *Jamie Osborne* a55 50
3 b g Henrythenavigator(USA) Purple (USA) (Royal Academy (USA))
248[5] (436) 578[3] 711[5]

Le Juge (IRE) *A Fabre* a101 106
3 b c Dansili Mambo Light (USA) (Kingmambo (USA))
2076a[5] 7137a[6] 7897a[3]

Le Laitier (FR) *Scott Dixon* a55 67
5 b g Milk It Mick La Brigitte (Tobougg (IRE))
1785[4] 2662[6] 3013[12]

Le Maitre Chat (USA) *Ian Williams* a93 97
5 b g Tale Of The Cat(USA) Bedside Story (Mtoto)
1967[10] 3246[17]

Le Manege Enchante (IRE) *Derek Shaw* a67 65
3 gr g Zebedee Beth (Deportivo)
1060[5] 1183[4] 1487[7] 2106[5] 2864[12] 3280[6] ◆ 3786[5] (4365) 5059[6] 5408[10] 6249[8] 7694[3] 8095[11] 8483[2]

Lemon Drop *Jim Boyle* a18 57
2 b f Paco Boy(IRE) Zia (GER) (Grand Lodge (USA))
4457[9] 4786[5] 5771[4] 6412[13]

Lemon Thyme *Mike Murphy* a57 45
3 b f Sakhee's Secret Limonia (GER) (Perugino (USA))
814[8] 1132[4] 1755[8]

Lendal Bridge *Tony Coyle* a54 60
5 ch g Avonbridge Dunloe (IRE) (Shaadi (USA))
563[3] 769[9] 1845[3] 2329[11] 3582[7] 6568[5] 7096[13] 7642[9]

Lenoire *John Gosden* a57 55
2 b f Galileo(IRE) Latice (IRE) (Inchinor)
7285[5] 7761[12] 8130[6]

Le Notre *Jeremy Noseda* a81 68
4 b g Champs Elysees Millistar (Galileo (IRE))
1144[7] 1717[10]

Leo Le Lion *S Cerulis* a61
3 ch g Zamindar(USA) Labour Of Love (USA) (Silver Deputy (CAN))
5704a[9]

Leomar (GER) *M Figge* 91
3 ch g Adlerflug(GER) Lovana (IRE) (Darshaan)
7088a[8]

Leo Minor (USA) *A P O'Brien* a93 92
2 b c War Front(USA) Kissed (IRE) (Galileo (IRE))
5661a[10] 7130a[3]

Leonard Thomas *Tony Carroll* a70 61
6 b g Singspiel(IRE) Monawara (IRE) (Namaqualand (USA))
38[7] 316[5] 606[5] 773[5] 6637[4] 7062[5] 7442[2] 7795[4] (8307)

Leoncavallo (IRE) *Charlie Appleby* a71 78
4 b g Cape Cross(IRE) Nafura (Dubawi (IRE))
(4637) 7006[2]

Leonida (FR) *C Boutin* a89 77
4 b g Lawman(FR) Avventura (USA) (Johannesburg (USA))
4901a[10]

Leonidas (IRE) *Marcus Tregoning* a59 64
2 b c Dalakhani(IRE) Marque Royale (Royal Academy (USA))
6183[5] 7243[6] 7648[6]

Leontes *Andrew Balding* 94
2 ch g Paco Boy(IRE) Robema (Cadeaux Genereux)
2371[2] 2696[4] 3247[10] 3805[2] (4336) (4918) 6260[9]

Leopard (IRE) *Paul Cole* a70
2 b g Iffraaj Appletreemagic (IRE) (Indian Danehill (IRE))
7930[5] 8073[7]

Le Phantom *E J O'Neill* 60
2 ch c Showcasing Musical Twist (USA) (Woodman (USA))
4471a[5]

Le Pinchy (GER) *Tom Dascombe* 13
2 ch g Adlerflug(GER) Lady Manners (USA) (Montbrook (USA))
7318[8]

Le Rebel (FR) *K Borgel* a91 99
4 b h Linngari(IRE) Slitana (FR) (Dansili)
7525a[10]

Le Rock (IRE) *J S Moore* a77 75
4 b g Rock Of Gibraltar(IRE) Reine Violette (FR) (Fly To The Stars)
975[3] ◆ 1852[9] 4057[10] (4266) 4941[3] 5334[3] 6362[6] 6938a[2]

Le Roi Du Temps (USA) *Ivan Furtado* a55 80
3 ch g Leroidesanimaux(BRZ) Minute Limit (IRE) (Pivotal)
2891[7] 4519[2] ◆ 5482[7] 7486[8]

Lesanti *Ed McMahon* a48 52
2 b g Royal Applause Kammaan (Diktat)
6679[7] 7496[9] 8118[7]

Les Darcy *Ken Cunningham-Brown* a34 38
5 b g Haatef(USA) Overcome (Belmez (USA))
5628[10] 5915[6] 7200[8]

L'Es Fremantle (FR) *Michael Chapman* a22 44
5 b g Orpen(USA) Grand Design (Danzero (AUS))
2[14] 2537[6] 3896[5] 4234[6] 5323[8] 6212[10]

Les Gar Gan (IRE) *Daniel Mark Loughnane* a64 61
5 b m Iffraaj Story (Observatory (USA))
107[2] (334) 563[7] 769[7] 862[3] 1058[2] 1323[3] 1654[3] 1747[3] 2397[6]

Leshlaa (USA) *Saeed bin Suroor* a88 83
2 ch c Street Cry(IRE) Vine Street (IRE) (Singspiel (IRE))
7664[2] ◆ (7975)

Les Pradeaux (FR) *H-A Pantall* a72 68
3 b c Acclamation Pennegale (IRE) (Pennekamp (USA))
1311a[12]

Lester Kris (IRE) *Richard Hannon* a51 70
2 b c Fame And Glory Wood Sprite (Mister Baileys)
3808[4] 4379[5] 5363[3]

Letbygonesbeicons *John Balding* a63 62
3 b g Sixties Icon Composing (IRE) (Noverre (USA))
2049[9] 2425[6] 2741[3] 3896[9] 5368[2] ◆ 5760[3] 6522[4] 6836[3] 7585[5] 8482[4]

Lethal Impact (JPN) *David Simcock* a75
2 b c Deep Impact(JPN) Musical Way (FR) (Gold Away (IRE))
7849[4]

Le Tissier *Michael Attwater* a63 66
3 ch g Sir Percy Incarnation (IRE) (Samum (GER))
1429[6] 1779[2] 2411[6] 3998[9] 4942[6] 5672[3] 5993[3] 6698[4] 7309[4] 7760[5] 7969[7] 8155[5] 8459[5]

Let It Go *Tony Carroll* a31 14
4 b m Halling(USA) Kisses (Sakhee (USA))
79[5] 346[9] 1035[10] 7645[12] 8491[6]

Let Me In (IRE) *Bernard Llewellyn* a64 50
6 ch g Pivotal I Hearyou Knocking (IRE) (Danehill Dancer (IRE))
39[7] 156[8] 568[2] 862[2] 1343[4] 2144[4]

Letmestopyouthere (IRE) *David Evans* a89 84
2 b g Sir Prancealot(IRE) Romanylei (IRE) (Blues Traveller (IRE))
1082[11] (1482) ◆ 1965[6] 3852[2] 4394[7] 5560[5] 6388a[9] 6734[4] 7120[12] 7549[2] 8405[2] 8525[5]

Le Torrent *Simon Dow* a75 67
4 ch g Sir Percy Cinnas Ransom (Red Ransom (USA))
2105[6]

Let Right Be Done *Linda Perratt* a40 62
4 gr g Lawman(FR) Cheerfully (Sadler's Wells (USA))
1695[5] 2091[6] 2661[9] 2906[8] 3943[9] 5114[3] 8307[11] 8588[8]

Let Rip (IRE) *Henry Candy* a68
2 b c Rip Van Winkle(IRE) Al Ihsas (IRE) (Danehill (USA))
8355[4]

Let's Be Happy (IRE) *Richard Hughes* a63 61
2 gr f Mastercraftsman(IRE) Corrozal (GER) (Cape Cross (IRE))
4523[7] 5052[3] (5809) 6289[4] 7640[8]

Let's Confer *Michael Attwater* a44 45
7 ch m Doyen(IRE) Vrennan (Suave Dancer (USA))
1807[11] 2398[8]

Let's Go (USA) *Saeed bin Suroor* a114 93
4 br g Street Cry(IRE) Lady Darshaan (IRE) (High Chaparral (IRE))
281a[5] 627a[3] ◆

Let'sgoforit (IRE) *Bodil Hallencreutz* a109 88
8 gr g Verglas(IRE) Slewcie (USA) (Seattle Slew (USA))
186a[3] 537a[7] 719a[8] 4421a[2]

Let's Sway *Martyn Meade* a51 47
2 b f Authorized(IRE) Let's Dance (IRE) (Danehill Dancer (IRE))
5298[7] 7284[8]

Let's Twist *Kristin Stubbs* a80 71
4 ch g Piccolo Takes Two To Tango (Groom Dancer (USA))
5367[8] 5845[2] (6237) 6899[2] 7141[5] 7738[6] 7958[4] 8052[15] 8287[2]

Letter Focus (IRE) *Brendan W Duke* 74
4 b g Intense Focus(USA) Christinas Letter (IRE) (Galileo (IRE))
4813a[6]

Let There Be Light *Gay Kelleway* a55 46
3 ch g Phoenix Reach(IRE) Pink Supreme (Night Shift (USA))
275[9] 361[7] (2083) 2293[7] 3975[8] 4262[9] 5041[9] 7230[5] 7641[6] 7742[6] 7910[4] 8180[9]

Lettuce Snow (IRE) *Geoffrey Deacon* a47 44
4 b m Clodovil(IRE) Lola Rosa (IRE) (Peintre Celebre (USA))
3401[12] 3997[13] 4504[9]

Le Vagabond (FR) *E J O'Grady* 97
4 b g Footstepsinthesand Miryale (FR) (Anabaa (USA))
4070a[5] 4850a[5] 6350a[7]

Level Of Intensity (IRE) *J S Bolger* 54
2 b c Intense Focus(USA) Teofolina (IRE) (Teofilo (IRE))
6388a[24]

Levelyne (FR) *J Bourgeais* a51
4 b m Hannouma(IRE) Marlene Alba (FR) (Tot Ou Tard (IRE))
8422a[3]

Lewisham *J R Jenkins* a66 78
6 b g Sleeping Indian Almunia (IRE) (Mujadil (USA))
543[2] (1481) 1827[3] 2396[5]

Lewis Valentine (IRE) *James Given* 74
4 b g Rip Van Winkle(IRE) Full Of Love (IRE) (Hawk Wing (USA))
1756[7]

Lexie Lou (CAN) *Mark Casse* a102 106
5 b m Sligo Bay(IRE) Oneexcessivenite (USA) (In Excess I (IRE))
3178a[10]

Lexington Abbey *Kevin Ryan* 103
5 b g Sleeping Indian Silvereine (FR) (Bering)
(1272) 2504[3] 4126[3] 4667[5] 5555[10] 6327[10] 6556[17] 7156[2]

Lexington Bay (IRE) *Philip Kirby* a61 74
8 b g High Chaparral(IRE) Schust Madame (IRE) (Second Set (IRE))
864[6] 1404[4] 2018[11]

Lexington Law (IRE) *Richard Hannon* a76 81
3 b g Lawman(FR) Tus Nua (IRE) (Galileo (IRE))
1200[8] 1931[3] 2175[2] 3359[3] 4265[4]

Lexington Place *Ruth Carr* a80 94
6 ch g Compton Place Elidore (Danetime (IRE))
1408[4] 1968[9] 2258[7] 2775[2] 3056[2] ◆ (3393) 3944[7] 4373[4] 4831[5] 5390[7] 6012[10]

Lexington Sky (IRE) *Richard Hannon* a78 79
2 b f Iffraaj Hurricane Lily (IRE) (Ali-Royal (IRE))
1437[4] ◆ 2211[3] (2764) 3511[2] 4843[5] 5407[8] 6954[U] 7185[9]

Lexington Times (IRE) *Ruth Carr* a99 87
4 b g Paco Boy(IRE) Fuaigh Mor (IRE) (Dubai Destination (USA))
816[5] 1153[3] ◆ 1441[11] 2033[9] 6287[6] 6764[4] 7095[9] 7593[5] ◆ 7825[15] 7990[10] 8122[9] 8385[5]

Lexi's Boy (IRE) *Donald McCain* a87 90
8 gr g Verglas(IRE) Jazan (IRE) (Danehill (USA))
1598[6] 2971[7] (4381) 4703[3] 5541[6] 6740[2] 8133[5]

Lexi's Hero (IRE) *Richard Fahey* a73 100
8 b g Invincible Spirit(IRE) Christel Flame (Darshaan)
1968[8] 2364[3] (3133) 3637[3] 4632[8] 5182[4] 6079[12] 6539[17] 6793[9]

Lexi's Red Devil (IRE) *Philip M Byrne* a23 52
4 b m Danehill Dancer(IRE) Challow Hills (USA) (Woodman (USA))
5900a[P]

Lex Talionis (IRE) *J F Levins* a78 85
3 b g Thewayyouare(USA) Dawn Air (USA) (Diesis)
644a[4] 3428a[8]

Leyburn *Mark Johnston* 29
3 ch f Shamardal(USA) Lurina (IRE) (Lure (USA))
1449[5]

Leyland (IRE) *Natalie Lloyd-Beavis* a25 51
7 b g Peintre Celebre(USA) Lasting Chance (USA) (American Chance (USA))
5708[5] 5963[7] 6245[4] 7421[4] 8164[7]

L'Heritier (FR) *M Seror* 10
5 b g Muhtathir La Grande Dame (FR) (Daliapour (IRE))
5700a[12]

L'Homme Du Lys (FR) *J-L Guillochon* a49 69
6 b g Kingsalsa(USA) Saca (FR) (Smadoun (FR))
8422a[10]

Liber *Bent Olsen* 100
6 b g Ishiguru(USA) Startori (Vettori (IRE))
370a[6] 450a[11]

Liberale (FR) *J-P Gauvin* 92
2 b f Literato(FR) Libre Lady (Librettist (USA))
6271a[5]

Liberality *Miss Evanna McCutcheon* a67 78
4 b m Shamardal(USA) Charity Belle (USA) (Empire Maker (USA))
5096a[7]

Liberatum *Ruth Carr* a51 66
2 b g Paco Boy(IRE) Fine Lady (Selkirk (USA))
2748[6] ◆ 7184[3] 7527[8] 7820[15]

Liberty Jack (IRE) *Adrian Paul Keatley* a87 90
6 b g Sakhee(USA) Azeema (IRE) (Averti (IRE))
4748a[10]

Librisa Breeze *Dean Ivory* a104 117
4 gr g Mount Nelson Bruxcalina (FR) (Linamix (FR))
(1344) ◆ 3273[2] (4625) 5613[4] (6942) ◆ 7350[6]

License To Thrill (USA) *Simon Dow* a62 18
2 b c Mizzen Mast(USA) Mystic Miracle (Dalakhani (IRE))
4988[9] 6655[7] 7962[9] 8560[5]

Licinius (GER) *Yasmin Almenrader* a67 91
3 b c Halling(USA) La Vinchina (GER) (Oasis Dream)
1908a[7] 4186a[17]

Liddle Dwiggs *Peter Hiatt*
5 b m Bertolini(USA) Slims Lady (Theatrical Charmer)
5572 [11] 6311[8]

Lido Lady (IRE) *Mark Johnston* a61 75
3 b f Danehill Dancer(IRE) Showbiz (IRE) (Sadler's Wells (USA))
1314[3] ◆ 3593[6] 3983[10] (4429) 5063[4] 6437[9] 6811[9] 7205[8]

Lie High (FR) *Eric Saint-Martin* 68
2 b c Rip Van Winkle(IRE) Sandy Light (IRE) (Footstepsinthesand)
5985a[7]

Lieutenant General (IRE) *A P O'Brien* 99
3 b c Fastnet Rock(AUS) Lady Lupus (IRE) (High Chaparral (IRE))
2069a[6] 2883a[3] 3428a[3]

Life Happens *Jonathan Portman* a50
2 b f Pastoral Pursuits Halfwaytoparadise (Observatory (USA))
7885[11] 8465[8]

Life Imitates Art (USA) *J Smart* 102
3 b c More Than Ready(USA) Habiboo (USA) (Unbridled's Song (USA))
8573a[9]

Life Knowledge (IRE) *Patrick Holmes* a60 64
4 ch g Thewayyouare(USA) Rosa Bellini (IRE) (Rossini (USA))
2330[5] 2915[6] 3287[12] 8400[7]

Life Less Ordinary (IRE) *Jamie Osborne* a89 96
4 b g Thewayyouare(USA) Dont Cross Tina (IRE) (Cape Cross (IRE))
1290[2] ◆ 1737[4] 2163[2] 2888[2] 3525[2] (4535) 5559[8] 6279[4] (6919)

Life Of Fame *Mark Walford* a62 65
3 b f Equiano(FR) Fame Is The Spur (Motivator)
5839[4] 6509[6] 6909[4] 7860[12] 8095[3] 8483[8]

Life Of Luxury *Mark Brisbourne* a59
3 b g Shamardal(USA) Champagnelifestyle (Montjeu (IRE))
8320[7]

Life On Mars *William Haggas* a65 65
2 b f Henrythenavigator(USA) Dilag (IRE) (Almutawakel)
4759[5] 5772[5] 6244[6] 7228[4] 7749[6] 7974[10]

Life Story *John Davies*
4 b g New Approach(IRE) Storyland (USA) (Menifee (USA))
1873[10]

Life Won't Wait *John Quinn* a60
2 b g Showcasing Manbaa (USA) (Jazil (USA))
8089[7]

Lifting Me Higher (IRE) *W P Browne* a68 59
4 b m Sea The Stars(IRE) Centreofattention (AUS) (Danehill (USA))
(601) 865[2] 957[3]

Light And Shade *James Tate* a92 103
4 b m Aqlaam Tara Moon (Pivotal)
1207[3] (2026) (3623) 4582[4] ◆ 5158[7] 6113[3] 6488[7]

Lightening Stricks (IRE) *Liam Roche* a53 54
9 b g King's Best(USA) Opera Comique (FR) (Singspiel (IRE))
5096a[10]

Lightfeet (USA) *Jeremy Gask* a67 64
3 b g Lonhro(AUS) Southern Protocol (USA) (Dixieland Band (USA))
1414[4] 2886[5]

Light From Mars *Ronald Harris* a82 73
11 gr g Fantastic Light(USA) Hylandra (USA) (Bering)
(67) 142[5] 953[2] 2028[9] 2579[8] 3989[4] 4910[6] 5408[8] 6235[4] 7066[6] 8037[8]

Light Gunner (IRE) *Henry Tett* a37 34
2 b g Lawman(FR) Neve Lieve (IRE) (Dubai Destination (USA))
7501[11] 8088[11]

Lightly Squeeze *Philip Hide* a45 50
2 b g Poet's Voice Zuleika Dobson (Cadeaux Genereux)
6085[8] 6480[8]

Light Music *William Haggas* a98 96
3 b f Elusive Quality(USA) Medley (Danehill Dancer (IRE))
2034[2] 3269[11] 4062[17] 5588[11]

Lightning Charlie *Amanda Perrett* a91 94
4 b g Myboycharlie(IRE) Lighted Way (Kris)
1143[5] 1419[3] (1838) 3144[2] (4014) ◆ 4460[3] 4862[12] 5744[5] 6123[2] 6883[2] 7186[2]

Lightning North *James Tate* 66
2 b f Mayson Purple Tiger (IRE) (Rainbow Quest (USA))
4022^{2} ◆ 4494^{4}
Lightning Spear *David Simcock* a98 122
5 ch h Pivotal Atlantic Destiny (IRE) (Royal Academy (USA))
3242^{3} ◆ 4754^{6} 5449a^{9} (5873) 7352^{3}
Lightning Spree (IRE) *Kevin Ryan* a72 73
4 gr g Jeremy(USA) Spree (IRE) (Dansili)
1202^{12} 1695^{4} 1884^{2} 2198^{3} 2555^{5}
Lightning Steps *Declan Carroll* a47 53
4 b g Champs Elysees Fairy Steps (Rainbow Quest (USA))
1674^{9} 3288^{7} 4194^{9} 4456^{13} (4971) 5522^{6} 6102^{8} 6438^{10} 6812^{5} 7044^{11}
Light Of Air (FR) *Gary Moore* 78
3 b g Youmzain(IRE) Height Of Vanity (IRE) (Erhaab (USA))
3453a^{8} 7223^{6}
Light Of Love *Brendan Powell* a52 63
4 b m Dylan Thomas(IRE) May Light (Midyan (USA))
7936^{RR}
Light Of The Moon (IRE) *David Evans* 34
5 b g Echo Of Light Song Of Sixpence (IRE) (Among Men (USA))
6890^{7}
Lightoller (IRE) *Mick Channon* 68
2 ch c Harbour Watch(IRE) April (IRE) (Rock Of Gibraltar (IRE))
4053^{12} 4405^{9} 4659^{5} 5014^{2} 5433^{3}
Light Rose (IRE) *Jeremy Gask* a74 50
6 b m Cape Cross(IRE) Laureldean Lady (IRE) (Statue Of Liberty (USA))
414^{4} 1139^{4} 1340^{9} 1811^{4}
Lights *Declan Carroll* a46 24
2 b f Delegator Sirenuse (IRE) (Exceed And Excel (AUS))
4804^{8} 5727^{11} 6141^{6} 6420^{8} 6807^{11}
Lightscameraction (IRE) *Gay Kelleway* a112 103
4 ch g Pastoral Pursuits Silca Boo (Efisio)
17^{3} 483^{4} (745) 1066^{8} 5641^{2} 6779^{5} 7242^{2} 8530^{6}
Lightsome *Harry Dunlop* a76 55
3 b f Makfi Aunty Mary (Common Grounds)
152^{5} 8248^{4} ◆
Light Up Our World (IRE) *Richard Hannon* a99 103
3 b f Zoffany(IRE) Shine Like A Star (Fantastic Light (USA))
1476^{2} 1771^{3} 2160^{6} 3274^{8} (3911) 4822^{3} 5498a^{12} 7152^{5}
Like A Diamond (IRE) *Brian Ellison* a85 48
6 b g Antonius Pius(USA) Silk Law (IRE) (Barathea (IRE))
3660^{3} 5033^{8}
Like A Prayer *Garvan Donnelly* a50 53
5 b g Compton Place Floating (Oasis Dream)
6462a^{6}
Like A Star (IRE) *A P O'Brien* 75
3 b f Galileo(IRE) Anna Karenina (IRE) (Green Desert (USA))
3539a^{10}
Likely (GER) *David Barron* a32 73
4 ch m Exceed And Excel(AUS) La Pilaya (GER) (Pivotal)
17^{7}
Like Minds *David Brown* a36 46
2 b f Royal Applause Creative Mind (IRE) (Danehill Dancer (IRE))
4981^{9} 6712^{6} 7269^{6} 7690^{7} 8046^{10}
Like No Other *Les Eyre* a85 77
3 b g Approve(IRE) Blue Beacon (Fantastic Light (USA))
2123^{7} 2774^{6} 2973^{6} (3568) 3807^{3} 4231^{5} 5759^{2} 6027^{6} 6810^{2} 7308^{7} 7903^{11} 8385^{2}
Lila Mahyana (FR) *C Boutin* 75
3 b f Muhaymin(USA) Lila Rose (IRE) (Kendor (FR))
2172a^{2} 3007a^{8}
Lilbourne Prince (IRE) *David Evans* a76 76
3 b g Lilbourne Lad(IRE) Defensive Boast (USA) (El Gran Senor (USA))
366^{3} 434^{5} 1485^{3} 2099^{7} ◆ 2538^{4} 3102^{5} 3687^{4} 4157^{7} 4589^{2} 4909^{3} 5234^{5} 6365^{4} 6576^{3} 6885^{7} 7415^{4} 7572^{4} 7801a^{7} 7931^{4} 8035^{6}
Lili Moon (GER) *Werner Glanz* 97
7 bb m Desert Prince(IRE) Lisibila (GER) (Acatenango (GER))
4783a^{8}
Lilliard (IRE) *John Patrick Shanahan* a72 52
3 b f Shamardal(USA) Idilic Calm (IRE) (Indian Ridge)
1337^{6} 2200^{5} 3017^{9}
Lilly Ballerina (IRE) *Tony Carroll* 9
2 b f Lilbourne Lad(IRE) Entrechat (Green Desert (USA))
1915^{10} 2822^{14} 3511^{12} 3820^{5}
Lilly Bonbon (IRE) *Gary Moore* a47 60
3 ch f Zoffany(IRE) Simonda (Singspiel (IRE))
3765^{5} 5101^{3} 5708^{3} 6185^{6} 6871^{13}
Lillyput (IRE) *Mick Channon* a20 63
3 b f Lilbourne Lad(IRE) Bellacoola (GER) (Lomitas)
102^{9} 2207^{6} 2470^{13} 3062^{8} 3513^{11} 3993^{6} 4641^{4} 5087^{4} 5335^{8}
Lilly Vega (IRE) *K R Burke* a73 55
3 ch f Lope De Vega(IRE) Salpiglossis (GER) (Monsun (GER))
1960^{5}
Lilozza (IRE) *Tim Easterby* 57
3 ro f Lilbourne Lad(IRE) Vanozza (FR) (Dylan Thomas (IRE))
4429^{6} 4972^{4} 5576^{12}
Lil's Affair (IRE) *Bryan Smart* a49 48
2 b f Lilbourne Lad(IRE) Subtle Affair (IRE) (Barathea (IRE))
2771^{11} 4037^{6} 5067^{5} 5799^{3} ◆ 6681^{9} 7109^{5} 8087^{3} 8284^{9}
Lil's Joy (IRE) *Giles Bravery* a61 103
3 b f Lilbourne Lad(IRE) Eman's Joy (Lion Cavern (USA))
1315^{2} 2232a^{5} 3158^{6} 4905a^{9}
Lil Sophella (IRE) *Patrick Holmes* a87 92
7 ch m Indian Haven Discotheque (USA) (Not For Love (USA))
(2223) 3152^{3} 3595^{5} 3979^{3} 5588^{5} 6113^{7} 7316^{12} 7472^{8} 7958^{5} 8177^{9} 8385^{7}
Lilvanita (IRE) *Brian Ellison* a68 24
3 b f Lilbourne Lad(IRE) Miss Vanita (IRE) (Refuse To Bend (IRE))
5295^{10} 6101^{4} 7145^{10} 7793^{4}
Lily Cliff *Paul D'Arcy* a25
2 b f Canford Cliffs(IRE) Night Lily (IRE) (Night Shift (USA))
7099^{12} 7441^{14} 8065^{9}
Lily Edge *John Bridger* a54 49
7 b m Byron Flaming Spirt (Blushing Flame (USA))
255^{6} 412^{7} 2977^{5} 3402^{8} (4019) 4527^{7} 5021^{10} 5208^{7} 6659^{10} 8359^{4} 8468^{4}
Lily Fontana (IRE) *Richard Fahey* a37
2 b f Dandy Man(IRE) Lily's Dream (IRE) (Celtic Swing)
7599^{3} 8118^{8} 8526^{9}
Lily Paramount (FR) *J C Napoli* a70 62
3 bb f Hurricane Cat(USA) Pink Candie (FR) (Fath (USA))
3764a^{5}
Lily Passion *P Bary* a62 102
3 ch f Sea The Stars(IRE) Alix Road (FR) (Linamix (FR))
7029a^{4} (7897a) 8336a^{5}
Lily's Rainbow (IRE) *Mrs Denise Foster* a88 103
4 b m Intikhab(USA) Fly By Magic (IRE) (Indian Rocket)
1018a^{4} (1509a) 2716a^{14} 3677a^{4} 4747a^{17} 5939a^{7} 7392a^{11}
Lily Trotter *Ralph Beckett* a64 73
3 b f New Approach(IRE) Hobby (Robellino (USA))
2183^{9} 3094^{7} 3781^{9} 4661^{3} 5286^{2} 5597^{5} 6730^{2} 7270^{5}
Limario (GER) *Doug Watson* a111 112
6 br h Areion(GER) Limaga (Lagunas)
187a^{4} 372a^{6} 812a^{13}
Limato (IRE) *Henry Candy* a100 126
4 b g Tagula(IRE) Come April (Singspiel (IRE))
2243^{4} (4151) 5614^{2} (6991a) 7837a^{6}
Limbrick *Ann Duffield* 46
2 ch f Equiano(FR) Haigh Hall (Kyllachy)
1951^{5} 2235^{8} 3290^{6} (Dead)
Lime And Lemon (IRE) *Clive Cox* a59 79
3 b f Makfi Nimboo (USA) (Lemon Drop Kid (USA))
1436^{6} 1798^{6} 2615^{5} (3878) 6549^{2} 7419^{3}
Limelight Lady *Harry Dunlop* a41 40
2 b f Sakhee's Secret Green Room (FR) (In The Wings)
1895^{4} 3529^{10} 4287^{16} 6236^{6} 6875^{11}
Limelite (IRE) *Richard Hannon* 74
2 b f Dark Angel(IRE) Light It Up (IRE) (Elusive City (USA))
2467^{3} 2990^{7} 4756^{16} 7549^{9}
Limerick Lord (IRE) *Julia Feilden* a67 64
4 b g Lord Shanakill(USA) Hollow Green (IRE) (Beat Hollow)
277^{4} 448^{7} 621^{6} 939^{2} 1044^{4} 1707^{5} 2646^{5} 3739^{5} 4389^{2} 4876^{2} 5090^{3} 5393^{3} 5734^{6} 7018^{13} 7200^{7} 7889^{2} 8241^{6}
Limeta (FR) *D De Waele* a72
3 bb f Le Havre(IRE) Elusive Queen (FR) (Elusive City (USA))
128a^{10}
Limitless (IRE) *Jamie Osborne* a54 110
3 b g Lope De Vega(IRE) Portelet (Night Shift (USA))
(1714) 2412^{4} (2891) (3299)
Limonata (IRE) *Harry Whittington* a67 69
3 b f Bushranger(IRE) Come April (Singspiel (IRE))
3059^{8} 3958^{6} 6485^{4} 8193^{5} 8428^{6}
Limousine Liberal (USA) *Ben Colebrook* a113
4 bb g Successful Appeal(USA) Gift Of Gab (USA) (In Excess I (IRE))
7832a^{4}
Lina De Vega (IRE) *P J Prendergast* a94 84
3 b f Lope De Vega(IRE) Caerlina (IRE) (Caerleon (USA))
5814a^{3} 7676a^{5}
Lincoln (IRE) *Mick Channon* a75 109
5 b g Clodovil(IRE) Gilt Linked (Compton Place)
1627^{11} ◆ 1856^{3} 2485^{5} 3163^{5} 3671^{11} 4263^{5} 4625^{6} 5389^{8} 6109^{12} (6537) (6714) 6779^{6} 7186^{9} 7497^{9}
Lincoln Day *Phil McEntee* a10
2 b g Doncaster Rover(USA) Enjoyment (Dansili)
6368^{10} 6750^{10} 7259^{10}
Lincoln Rocks *David O'Meara* 92
3 b f Rock Of Gibraltar(IRE) Redskin Dancer (IRE) (Namid)
2419^{2} (3014) 3438^{7} 4145^{6} (5062) 5415^{2} (6005) 6342^{3} (6811) 6947^{5}
Lindblad (GER) *Waldemar Hickst* a92 92
4 ch h Lando(GER) Lilia (GER) (Dashing Blade)
(3092a)
Lineman *Sarah Hollinshead* a61 61
6 b g Rail Link Shamana (USA) (Woodman (USA))
1057^{11} 3067^{5} 3999^{12} 4499^{3} 5267^{6} 8039^{7} 8540^{2}
Line Of Reason (IRE) *Paul Midgley* a110 116
6 br g Kheleyf(USA) Miss Party Line (USA) (Phone Trick (USA))
745^{4} ◆ 1083^{4} 1862^{13} 2438^{4} (3250) 3752^{3} 4359^{7} 4824^{15} 5143^{2} 5555^{4} 5863^{6} 6230^{9} 6642^{4} 6990a^{8} 8484^{3}
Line Sport (IRE) *Richard Fahey* a56 54
3 ch c Exceed And Excel(AUS) Majestic Dubawi (Dubawi (IRE))
2019^{3} 2561^{3}
L'Inganno Felice (FR) *Iain Jardine* a78 77
6 br g Librettist(USA) Final Overture (FR) (Rossini (USA))
332^{5} 446^{2} 734^{5} 6516^{7} 6907^{9} 7321^{9} 7791^{2} 8141^{3}
Linguine (FR) *Seamus Durack* a81 68
6 ch g Linngari(IRE) Amerissage (USA) (Rahy (USA))
1914^{5}
Linguist (FR) *Harry Dunlop* a74 52
3 ch g Linngari(IRE) Western Bowl (USA) (Gone West (USA))
1429^{7} 2545^{13}
Linguistic (IRE) *John Gosden* 104
3 b c Lope De Vega(IRE) Dazzle Dancer (IRE) (Montjeu (IRE))
(1438) ◆ 1994^{2} 2481^{2} 3337^{8}
Links Bar Marbella (IRE) *Eric Wheeler* a16 47
3 ch g Intense Focus(USA) Silesian (IRE) (Singspiel (IRE))
400^{8} 2148^{9} 3146^{8} 4156^{12} 4316^{6} 5775^{5}
Links Drive Lady *Dean Ivory* a85 94
8 br m Striking Ambition Miskina (Mark Of Esteem (IRE))
1530^{3} 1929^{13} 2875^{5} (3233) 4954^{10} 6263^{11} 7186^{10} 7550^{2} 7983^{6}
L'Invincible (FR) *A Fabre* a39
2 b f Invincible Spirit(IRE) Brasileira (Dubai Destination (USA))
7970a^{8}
Lions Charge (USA) *Seamus Mullins* a67 59
9 ch g Lion Heart(USA) Fellwaati (USA) (Alydar (USA))
295^{2} 949^{3} 1057^{5} 1796^{3} 2445^{5} 4527^{9} 6143^{6} 6411^{7} 8155^{7}
Lipsie (FR) *Gianluca Bietolini* a32 32
3 bb f Slickly(FR) Miss Talma (FR) (Orpen (USA))
128a^{7}
Lips Planet (GER) *Andreas Lowe* 93
3 ch f Mamool(IRE) Lips Plane (IRE) (Ashkalani (IRE))
2949a^{13} 5695a^{3}
Lipstickandpowder (IRE) *Dianne Sayer* a40 45
4 gr m Mastercraftsman(IRE) Raphimix (FR) (Linamix (FR))
3706^{14} 5149^{4} 5729^{12} 5800^{4}
Liquid (IRE) *David Barron* 73
2 ch c Zoffany(IRE) Playful Promises (IRE) (Elnadim (USA))
3148^{2} ◆ 3873^{5}
Liquid Mercury (SAF) *M F De Kock* 102
4 gr g Trippi(USA) Skip Poker (USA) (Skip Away (USA))
375a^{5} (538a)
Lisala (FR) *George Peckham* a60 60
3 b f Siyouni(FR) Lilac Charm (IRE) (Marju (IRE))
3359^{9} 3958^{9} 5529^{11} 6047^{3} 6512^{9}
Lisp (IRE) *Charles Hills* 68
2 ch g Poet's Voice Hora (Hernando (FR))
6777^{8} 7318^{4}
Litigant *Joseph Tuite* a104 117
8 b g Sinndar(IRE) Jomana (IRE) (Darshaan)
7349^{6} 7569a^{9} 8042a^{13}
Litterature (FR) *C Ferland* a86 92
4 ch m Alexandros Candidata (FR) (Kendor (FR))
5948a^{9}
Little *Steph Hollinshead* a67 43
4 b m Paco Boy(IRE) Wafeira (Dansili)
130^{8} 257^{8} 381^{3} 543^{5} 682^{7} 895^{5} 1005^{9} 1026^{10}
Little Avon *Ralph Beckett* 75
3 b f Makfi Bahamamia (Vettori (IRE))
(2011)
Little Belter (IRE) *Keith Dalgleish* a58 60
4 gr g Dandy Man(IRE) On Thin Ice (IRE) (Verglas (IRE))
1319^{3} 2202^{2} 2523^{8} 2808^{2} 3484^{7} 3755^{4} 4096^{6} 4410^{12} 4647^{5}
Little Big Man *Clare Ellam* a58 45
5 b g Sleeping Indian Doris Souter (IRE) (Desert Story (IRE))
60^{5} 222^{12} 347^{2} (412) 609^{4} 985^{8}
Little Buxted (USA) *Jim Best* a57 68
6 bb g Mr Greeley(USA) Mo Cheoil Thu (IRE) (In The Wings)
4383^{5} 4880^{9} 5397^{9}
Little Choosey *Roy Bowring* a65 60
6 ch m Cadeaux Genereux Little Nymph (Emperor Fountain)
149^{6} 383^{3} 514^{8} 981^{4} 1295^{2} 1768^{3} (2448) (2799) 3072^{3} 3582^{5} 4456^{3} 5264^{6} 6424^{10} (7642) 7890^{7}
Little Cupcake *Paul W Flynn* a57 36
5 b m Myboycharlie(IRE) Imco Cracking (IRE) (Piccolo)
7474a^{14}
Little Flo *William Stone* a57 15
5 ch m Midnight Legend Sweet Robinia (IRE) (Bob Back (USA))
84^{2} 368^{9} 461^{7} 796^{7} 981^{6} 1239^{6} 1748^{11} 3737^{10} 4567^{9}
Little Ghetto Boy *J-C Rouget* a80
3 b g Lawman(FR) Ahea (USA) (Giant's Causeway (USA))
(1286a) 3546a^{8} 5349a^{2}
Little Indian *J R Jenkins* a64 52
6 b g Sleeping Indian Once Removed (Distant Relative)
79^{6} 252^{3} 412^{3} 431^{2} (547) 696^{3} 985^{3} (1042) 1949^{9} 2155^{3} 2442^{2} 3146^{4} 3522^{4} 4008^{9} 5509^{7} 5808^{5} 7048^{6} 7261^{9} 7427^{6} 7850^{3} 8026^{6} 8120^{5} 8278^{10}
Little Kingdom (IRE) *Tracy Waggott* a47 36
2 b f Royal Applause Hadba (IRE) (Cape Cross (IRE))
6924^{9} 7330^{7} 8089^{9}
Little Kipling *Stuart Williams* a64 69
3 b f Royal Applause Victoria Sponge (IRE) (Marju (IRE))
2178^{3} 2795^{7}
Little Lady Katie (IRE) *K R Burke* 91
4 b m Lord Shanakill(USA) Akarita (IRE) (Akarad (FR))
1274^{7} (3667) 5419^{10} 6225^{9} 6736^{11} 7472^{2} 7744^{5}
Little Lizzie *Paddy Butler* a21
3 ch f Sleeping Indian Quality Street (Fraam)
7011^{15} 7616^{12} 7935^{8}
Little Lord Nelson *Stuart Williams* a70 74
4 b g Mount Nelson Cactus Curtsey (Royal Applause)
437^{6} 621^{2} 1502^{6} 1805^{4} 2769^{4} 3354^{4} 3802^{7}
Little Lotte (IRE) *Tom Gretton* a19 34
3 b f Kodiac Dancing Steps (Zafonic (USA))
1759^{7} 2300^{9} 7230^{8}
Little Miss Daisy *William Muir* a62 61
2 b f Arabian Gleam Desert Liaison (Dansili)
7576^{5} 7900^{8} (8229) 8453^{6}
Little Miss Kodi (IRE) *Daniel Mark Loughnane* a78 78
3 b f Kodiac Sensasse (IRE) (Imperial Ballet (IRE))
352^{9} 679^{2} 1079^{3} 3568^{2} 4215^{4} 4899a^{6} (5832) 6299^{4} 7281^{4}
Little Miss Lola *Alan Swinbank* 66
2 ch f Dandy Man(IRE) Purepleasureseeker (IRE) (Grand Lodge (USA))
3208^{10} 3515^{2} ◆ 3881^{8} 5289^{8}
Little Miss Nelly *Fred Watson* 14
6 b m Misu Bond(IRE) Shardda (Barathea (IRE))
2094^{6} 2419^{9}
Little Nosegay (IRE) *David Evans* a65 64
2 gr f Clodovil(IRE) Bank On Black (IRE) (Big Bad Bob (IRE))
1086^{5} 2535^{12} 2933^{3} 4015^{2} (4221) 4791^{2} (5243) 5638^{6} 6388a^{23} 6830^{6} 7313^{10} 7884^{4} 8097^{10}
Little Orchid *Julia Feilden* a55 56
3 b f Observatory(USA) Bushy Dell (IRE) (King Charlemagne (USA))
1149^{5} 1962^{5} 4212^{3} 5016^{3} 7039^{2} 7767^{9} 8193^{9} 8468^{11}
Little Palaver *Clive Cox* a85 94
4 b g Showcasing Little Nymph (Emperor Fountain)
2206^{12} 3068^{3} ◆ 4079^{13} (4910) 6263^{19} 7186^{12}
Little Pebbles *Jamie Osborne* a33 48
3 ch f Compton Place Pain Perdu (IRE) (Waajib (IRE))
286^{5}
Little Pippin *Tony Coyle* a47 55
3 b f Sir Percy Lady Le Quesne (IRE) (Alhaarth (IRE))
1276^{6} 1564^{2} 1927^{11} 2308^{5} 6621^{2} 6839^{3} 7581^{5} 8143^{5} 8386^{9}
Little Salamanca *Clive Cox* a54 50
3 ch g Sakhee's Secret Little Nymph (Emperor Fountain)
122^{6} 3765^{7}
Little Stampy (IRE) *D Broad* a69 69
5 ch m Artan(IRE) Gold Stamp (Golden Act (USA))
(150) (592) 1244^{7}
Little Sweetheart (IRE) *Patrick J Flynn* a67 79
5 b m Lawman(FR) Lady Gin (USA) (Saint Ballado (CAN))
3201a^{4}
Little Voice (USA) *Charles Hills* 88
3 b f Scat Daddy(USA) Excelente (IRE) (Exceed And Excel (AUS))
3815^{6} 4536^{3} (5040) 5360^{2}
Live Dangerously *John Bridger* a55 66
6 b g Zamindar(USA) Desert Lynx (IRE) (Green Desert (USA))
1546^{11} 1946^{6} 2430^{7} 2827^{2} 3234^{7} 3802^{9} 4058^{9} 4788^{3} 5241^{3} 5832^{5} 6266^{6} 6662^{10} 7037^{4} 7613^{14}
Livella Fella (IRE) *Keith Dalgleish* a76 80
3 b f Strategic Prince Ardent Lady (Alhaarth (IRE))
1619^{5} (2123) 2408^{3} 3286^{4} 3878^{4} (4098) 4768^{2} 6005^{4} 6504^{3} 6856^{4} 7853^{5} 8090^{5}
Lively Lily *Ann Duffield* a27 42
2 b f Excelebration(IRE) Hasty (IRE) (Invincible Spirit (IRE))
6679^{6} 6952^{11} 7380^{11}
Live Miracle (USA) *P Monfort* a57 60
4 b m Falco(USA) Zaragoza Girl (BRZ) (Trempolino (USA))
1250^{12} 8421a^{12}
Livinginafantasy (FR) *S Wattel* a88 88
3 ch f Monsun(GER) All Is Vanity (FR) (Gold Away (IRE))
(2948a) 5987a^{3} 7998a^{6}
Living Leader *Grace Harris* a58 78
7 b g Oasis Dream Royal Jade (Last Tycoon)
1269^{10} 1928^{8} 2540^{8} 3097^{10} 4293^{4} 5592^{4} 5958^{11} 7212^{7} 7577^{10}
Liwa Palace *Rod Collet* a65 95
3 b f Oasis Dream Ladeena (IRE) (Dubai Millennium)
6357a^{4}
Lizzy's Dream *Rebecca Bastiman* a56 59
8 ch g Choisir(AUS) Flyingit (USA) (Lear Fan (USA))
(341) (513) 589^{6} 1299^{7} 1668^{2} 2052^{5} 2423^{5} 3040^{6} 3843^{10} 4292^{3} 4492^{5} 4968^{8} 5335^{5}
Llewellyn *Declan Carroll* a76 74
8 b g Shamardal(USA) Ffestiniog (IRE) (Efisio)
179^{6} (278) 449^{4} 598^{5} 1251^{5} 1488^{3} 1818^{4} 2332^{14} 2680^{11} 3580^{2} 3880^{8} 4848^{10} 8094^{11} 8236^{5} 8350^{5}
Lloydminster (FR) *Mlle C Cardenne* a68 68
6 b g Elusive Quality(USA) Lady Aquitaine (USA) (El Prado (IRE))
7806a^{6}
Lmntrix *George Margarson* a62 32
4 b g Mount Nelson Big Mystery (IRE) (Grand Lodge (USA))
500^{7} 603^{11} 710^{4} 5380^{7} 6900^{2} 7103^{9} 7896^{2} 8207^{10}
Loaded (IRE) *Andrew Balding* a95 95
3 b g Kodiac Fikrah (Medicean)
2156^{2} ◆ 2686^{3} 4055^{8} (4480) (5507) (6225) ◆
Loading (IRE) *Richard Hannon* a77 79
3 b c Arcano(IRE) Sally Wood (CAN) (Woodman (USA))
1896^{4} 2099^{5} 2291^{7} 3355^{5} 3766^{2} 4272^{5} 4807^{7}
Loaves And Fishes *David O'Meara* a77 98
4 b m Oasis Dream Miracle Seeker (Rainbow Quest (USA))
1757^{4} 2363^{10} (2671) 2893^{6} 3979^{7} 4696a^{3} 5384a^{8} 6107a^{10}
Lobster Cocktail (IRE) *Ed Walker* a59 59
3 b c Footstepsinthesand Sanpala (Sanglamore (USA))
2005^{8} 2614^{7} 3412^{10} 4424^{11} 5080^{3} 6651^{3} 7256^{5} 7464^{3} 8212^{2} 8566^{4}

Local Artist (IRE) *John Quinn* a27 67
2 b f Requinto(IRE) A L'Aube (IRE) (Selkirk (USA))
2771[4] 3208[2] 3947[4] 4678[5] 5511[2] 6214[8] 6471[2] 7143[12]

Lockheed *William Haggas* 108
2 gr c Exceed And Excel(AUS) Clinical (Motivator)
4075[2] ◆ (4866) 5556[3] 6386a[3] 7148[5]

Locommotion *Matthew Salaman* a71 54
4 gr g Proclamation(IRE) Miss Madame (IRE) (Cape Cross (IRE))
4656[4] 5233[3] 7212[10] 7514[12] 7751[7] 8121[11] 8350[10]

Lodovico Il Moro (IRE) *Endo Botti* 99
6 b h Shamardal(USA) Kykuit (IRE) (Green Desert (USA))
2073a[P]

Logans Lad (IRE) *Daniel Mark Loughnane* a80 47
6 b g Baltic King Lulu Island (Zafonic (USA))
239[5] (424) 944[7]

Logarithm (USA) *John Gosden* a62
3 br f Lonhro(AUS) Lophorina (King's Best (USA))
384[3] 516[5]

Logi (IRE) *Richard Hannon* a30 82
2 b g Kodiac Feet Of Flame (USA) (Theatrical)
2162[3] 2669[5] 3093[2] 3668[4] 4802[10] 7305[11]

Log Off (IRE) *David Evans* a43 52
2 b f Sir Prancealot(IRE) Dolphin Stamp (IRE) (Dolphin Street (FR))
4203[7] 7501[9] 7885[9]

Logotype (JPN) *Tsuyoshi Tanaka* a104 119
6 bb h Lohengrin(JPN) Stereotype (JPN) (Sunday Silence (USA))
8332a[5]

Log Out Island (IRE) *Richard Hannon* a85 112
3 b g Dark Angel(IRE) White Daffodil (IRE) (Footstepsinthesand)
1477[3] (2242) 3338[10] 3909[8]

Lolita *J R Jenkins* a74 63
4 ch m Sir Percy Miss Ippolita (Diktat)
2217[8] 2794[5] 3038[8] 3974[5] 4587[7] 5725[2] 6487[8] 8358[2]

Lolwah *Sir Michael Stoute* 71
3 ch f Pivotal Palace Affair (Pursuit Of Love)
2505[7] ◆ (3464) 6265[10]

Lomu (IRE) *Keith Dalgleish* a81 85
2 ch c Dandy Man(IRE) Miss Me (Marju (IRE))
(1840) (2196) 7600[4]

Londinium *Mark Johnston* 82
2 b g New Approach(IRE) Historian (IRE) (Pennekamp (USA))
3408[4] (3854) 4379[3] (5109)

London (FR) *Phil McEntee* a86 83
3 b g Galileo(IRE) Altana (USA) (Mountain Cat (USA))
7779[5] 7903[4] ◆

London Citizen (USA) *Chris Wall* a86 91
6 ch h Proud Citizen(USA) Sally Bowles (SAF) (London News (SAF))
2377[7] 3785[6] 5026[7] 5724[11]

London Glory *Chris Wall* a73 74
3 b c Archipenko(USA) Reflected Image (IRE) (Refuse To Bend (IRE))
1036[5] (1806) 2545[3]

London Grammar (IRE) *John Quinn* 64
2 b f Sir Prancealot(IRE) Emmas Princess (IRE) (Bahhare (USA))
2970[6] 3416[2] 3772[8] 4442[3] 4509[2] 4842[2] (5853) 6253[2] 6446[4] 6681[5] 7330[9]

Londonia *Graeme McPherson* a51 65
4 gr g Paco Boy(IRE) Snowdrops (Gulch (USA))
6335[2] ◆ 7739[7]

London Master *Chris Wall* a57 55
2 ch c Mastercraftsman(IRE) Reflected Image (IRE) (Refuse To Bend (IRE))
7503[9] 7907[8] 8073[9]

London Prize *Ian Williams* 85
5 b g Teofilo(IRE) Zibet (Kris)
3190[3] 3508[5] 3845[6] 7320[2] (7507) (7624)

London Protocol (FR) *K R Burke* a87 99
3 ch g Muhtathir Troiecat (FR) (One Cool Cat (USA))
1080[5] 1585[3] 2161[11] 3155[2] 3908[3] 4116[6] 5004a[3] 5946a[5] 6560[3] 7821[16]

London Rebel (IRE) *Richard Spencer* a43
3 ch f Arcano(IRE) Piccadilly Filly (IRE) (Exceed And Excel (AUS))
8496[8]

Lonely The Brave (IRE) *Mark Johnston* a83 80
2 b g Lawman(FR) Luckbealadytonight (IRE) (Mr Greeley (USA))
3874[2] ◆ (4196) 4918[2] 5560[18] 6507[3] 7073[11]

Long Awaited (IRE) *Conor Dore* a78 83
8 b g Pivotal Desertion (IRE) (Danehill (USA))
1408[5] 1874[11] 2305[5] 2562[2] 2931[4] 3233[7] 3322[4] 3956[4] 4345[6] 4536[4] 5032[12] 5189[3] 5599[10] 5864[9] 6248[8] 6589[9] 8390[11] 8535[10]

Long Call *Charlie Appleby* 78
3 b g Authorized(IRE) Gacequita (URU) (Ride The Rails (USA))
3042[2] 3751[3]

Long Island *Mark Brisbourne* a21 64
3 b f Firebreak Fakhuur (Dansili)
1553[6] 2652[10] 2968[7] 3490[8] 4316[5] 4505[5] 4764[13] 5051[7]

Long Island Sound (USA) *A P O'Brien* a108 106
3 b c War Front(USA) Treasure Trail (USA) (Pulpit (USA))
3296[3] 4173a[6] 5429a[2] (6932a)

Long River (USA) *S bin Ghadayer* a109
6 ch h A.P. Indy(USA) Round Pond (USA) (Awesome Again (CAN))
92a[13] 454a[6] 627a[4] 842a[4]

Longroom *Noel Wilson* a54 64
4 b g Oasis Dream Phantom Wind (USA) (Storm Cat (USA))
1111[8] 1524[9] 2906[4] 4006[6] 4770[3] (6813) 7046[3] 7584[10]

Longshadow *Brian Ellison* a91 88
6 ch g Monsun(GER) La Felicita (Shareef Dancer (USA))
1250[7]

Longside *James Eustace* a68 70
4 b g Oasis Dream Hypoteneuse (IRE) (Sadler's Wells (USA))
1778[2] 2233[2] (3041) 3972[7] 5267[7] 6892[3] 7429[8]

Long Water (USA) *H Al Alawi* a90 77
5 b g Elusive Quality(USA) Round Pond (USA) (Awesome Again (CAN))
369a[5] 535a[6] 8396a[6]

Look Closer (IRE) *D K Weld* a71 75
3 ch g Danehill Dancer(IRE) Key Secure (IRE) (Sadler's Wells (USA))
6820a[10]

Look Here's Al *Karen Tutty* a47 54
5 gr g Alhaarth(IRE) Look Here's Dee (Dansili)
1165[9] 1404[6] 1676[18]

Lookin At Lee (USA) *Steven Asmussen* a109
2 b c Lookin At Lucky(USA) Langara Lass (USA) (Langfuhr (CAN))
7834a[4]

Looking On *Edward Bevan* a64 85
8 b g Observatory(USA) Dove Tree (FR) (Charnwood Forest (IRE))
200[8] 329[8]

Look My Way *Andrew Balding* a58
2 b g Pour Moi(IRE) Casual Glance (Sinndar (IRE))
7963[9] 8073[6] 8245[11]

Lookout Sister (USA) *Jerry Hollendorfer* a75 86
3 ch f Giant's Causeway(USA) Traveling Alone (USA) (Mt. Livermore (USA))
7724a[8]

Look Who's There *Sarah Hollinshead* a29
5 ch g Kyllachy Look Here's Carol (IRE) (Safawan)
6140[8] 7753[9] 8212[7]

Loose Ends *David Simcock* a63 54
3 b f Authorized(IRE) Crooked Wood (USA) (Woodman (USA))
968[8] 1289[5] 1962[4] 3722[5] 7105[7] 7438[9]

Looting *David Brown* 87
2 b c Bahamian Bounty Alice Alleyne (IRE) (Oasis Dream)
2489[5] 3054[5] 4765[2] 5265[2] (5598) ◆ (5821) 6734[5]

Lopera (GER) *P Schiergen* 96
3 bb f Monsun(GER) Larella (GER) (Anabaa (USA))
3207a[7] 5220a[15]

Lopes Dancer (IRE) *Alan Swinbank* 80
4 b g Lope De Vega(IRE) Ballet Dancer (IRE) (Refuse To Bend (IRE))
1241[2] 1664[9] 2662[3]

Lopito De Vega (IRE) *David C Griffiths* a56 70
4 ch g Lope De Vega(IRE) Athenian Way (IRE) (Barathea (IRE))
2672[5] 3011[9] 3804[2] (4377) 4919[4]

Lord Aratan (GER) *Patrick Holmes* a45 18
9 b g Tiger Hill(IRE) Luce (IRE) (Sadler's Wells (USA))
71[6]

Lord Aslan (IRE) *Andrew Balding* a39 43
3 b g Thewayyouare(USA) Lunar Lustre (IRE) (Desert Prince (IRE))
4001[6] 4384[5] 7532[7]

Lord Ben Stack (IRE) *K R Burke* a91 106
4 b g Dylan Thomas(IRE) Beringold (Bering)
1245[5] 4448[13] 5419[13] (6081) (6775) 7546[10] 7779[6]

Lord Bopper (IRE) *Ben Haslam* 36
3 b g Frozen Power(IRE) Lady Bracknell (IRE) (Definite Article)
2809[7] 3267[8] 4238[10] 4944[7]

Lord Clenaghcastle (IRE) *Gary Moore* a71 69
2 b c Big Bad Bob(IRE) Clenaghcastle Lady (IRE) (Acclamation)
(5668) (6236) 7033[3] 8153[11]

Lord Commander *Richard Fahey* 72
2 b c Nayef(USA) Kashoof (Green Desert (USA))
7125[3] ◆

Lord Cooper *Jose Santos* a68 59
2 b g Sir Percy Zooming (IRE) (Indian Ridge)
4053[10] 5325[8] 6071[9] 6678[5] 7275[6] 7776[2] (8467)

Lord Franklin *Eric Alston* a59 88
7 ch g Iceman Zell (IRE) (Lend A Hand)
1633[12] 1978[4] 2688[3] 3057[6] (3905) 4919[3] (5579) 6876[13] 7287[12]

Lord George (IRE) *James Fanshawe* a97 94
3 gr g Sir Percy Mahima (FR) (Linamix (FR))
1260[2] (3077) 4153[4] (6089) 7456a[9]

Lord Huntingdon *Andrew Balding* a74 86
3 b g Lord Of England(GER) Marajuana (Robellino (USA))
122[2] 379[4] 458[4] (892) 1828[2] 2099[4] 2393[9] 3557[2]

Lord Kelvin (IRE) *Charles Hills* 79
3 br g Iffraaj Eastern Appeal (IRE) (Shinko Forest (IRE))
2749[4] (3252) 3824[6] 4307[6]

Lord Marmaduke *Simon Crisford* 62
3 ch g Duke Of Marmalade(IRE) Maid To Treasure (IRE) (Rainbow Quest (USA))
6073[3]

Lord Murphy (IRE) *Daniel Mark Loughnane* a41 30
3 b c Holy Roman Emperor(IRE) Tralanza (IRE) (Traditionally (USA))
1132[8] 1339[8] 2008[13]

Lord Napier (IRE) *John Ryan* a80 77
3 b g Galileo(IRE) Jacqueline (IND) (King Charlemagne (USA))
1626[7] 2000[6] 3845[2] 8051[5]

Lord Of The Land (IRE) *David O'Meara* a114 104
5 b h Shamardal(USA) Lady Vettori (Vettori (IRE))
1196[19] 1627[5] 2191[19] 3566[4] 4393[5] 5213a[3] 5949a[3] 6272a[9] (7068) (7651) (7932)

Lord Of The North (IRE) *Gay Kelleway* a86 79
3 b g Roderic O'Connor(IRE) Kay Es Jay (FR) (Xaar)
3723[6] 4401[3] 5385a[3] 5850[3] (6104) (7492a)

Lord Of The Rock (IRE) *Michael Dods* a42 98
4 b g Rock Of Gibraltar(IRE) La Sylphide (Rudimentary (USA))
(1195) 2191[15] 3566[11]

Lord Of The Storm *Michael Attwater* a70 68
8 b g Avonbridge Just Run (IRE) (Runnett)
(769) 1064[3] 1340[7] 1747[2] 2085[4] 2635[3] 3514[4] (4200) 7417[4] 8101[9] 8282[7]

Lord Of The Valley *Mark Johnston* a68 25
3 b c Sir Percy Marakabei (Hernando (FR))
4001[8] 7487[6] 7848[5]

Lord Reason *John Butler* a76 81
4 b g Sixties Icon Luck Will Come (IRE) (Desert Style (IRE))
2046[2] (2646) 2965[2] (3612) 4307[5] 4940[5] 6186[2] 6889[8]

Lord Rob *David Thompson* a44 49
5 b g Rob Roy(USA) First Grey (Environment Friend)
4005[3] 4425[5] 5355[6] 5715[7] 6106[8] 6568[7] 7602[4] 7794[5]

Lord Shuffle (GER) *Stal Gastarui* a55 61
8 ch g Big Shuffle(USA) Legata (GER) (Sternkoenig (IRE))
1618a[7]

Lord Topper *Charles Hills* a80
3 b g Sir Percy Fugnina (Hurricane Run (IRE))
6674[7] 7063[3] (7487)

Lord Yeats *Jedd O'Keeffe* 93
3 b g Yeats(IRE) Bogside Theatre (IRE) (Fruits Of Love (USA))
1242[2] 1784[5] (3323) ◆ 4311[2] 5147[7] 5837[2] 7117[16]

Lorelei *William Muir* a64 59
4 b m Excellent Art Light Dreams (Fantastic Light (USA))
796[3] (1322) 1807[2] 2502[7] 4197[4] 8039[9] 8211[7] 8459[7]

Lorelina *Andrew Balding* a56 82
3 b f Passing Glance Diktalina (Diktat)
3062[11] (3745) (4788) 5965[4] 6803[3] 7504[2]

Lorenzetta (IRE) *Riccardo Santini* 90
4 ch m Mastercraftsman(IRE) Louise Aron (IRE) (Intikhab (USA))
6824a[6]

Lorikeet (USA) *Mark Johnston* a73 39
2 ch c Street Cry(IRE) Ishitaki (ARG) (Interprete (ARG))
7769[14] 7907[3] 8088[4] 8245[5]

Lorimer's Lot (IRE) *Mark Walford* a43 59
5 ch m Camacho Alwiyda (USA) (Trempolino (USA))
2423[6] 2676[2] 2919[8] 3268[8] 3779[4] 4492[3] 6098[8] 6341[11]

Loritania (IRE) *Il Cavallo In Testa* 104
4 gr m Teofilo(IRE) Sopran Lori (USA) (Irish River (FR))
1516a[4]

Los Cerritos (SWI) *Oliver Greenall* a55 103
4 ch g Dr Fong(USA) La Coruna (SWI) (Arazi (USA))
6286[9] 6628[13] 7301[12] 7612[8] 8040[10] 8527[10] 8586[7]

Los Olivos (USA) *William Haggas*
3 b c Lemon Drop Kid(USA) Lynnwood Chase (USA) (Horse Chestnut (SAF))
2008[14]

Lost At Sea *K R Burke* 99
2 b c Dutch Art Tahlia Ree (IRE) (Acclamation)
(6228) ◆ 7155[6] 7544[9]

Lostforwords (IRE) *Michael McCullagh* 60
5 b m Thousand Words Matadora (IRE) (Kris)
1014a[11]

Lostock *Richard Fahey* 59
2 b c Kodiac Green Silk (IRE) (Namid)
1976[6] ◆

Lostock Hall (IRE) *K R Burke* a81 70
4 b g Lord Shanakill(USA) Cannikin (IRE) (Lahib (USA))
73[6] 1633[10] 2043[4] 3012[5] 3883[3]

Lost The Moon *Mark H Tompkins* a73 60
3 b f Authorized(IRE) Missouri (Charnwood Forest (IRE))
3160[10] 6703[5] 7102[7] 8193[6] (8459)

Lotara *Jim Goldie* a65 44
4 b m Monsieur Bond(IRE) Cheviot Heights (Intikhab (USA))
(6101) 6506[14] 7852[7] 7995[10] 8390[5] 8485[4]

Lothair (IRE) *Alan Swinbank* a30 78
7 b g Holy Roman Emperor(IRE) Crafty Example (USA) (Crafty Prospector (USA))
2918[14] 3214[5] 3553[10] 4704[10] 6435[12] 7747[15]

Lots O' Lex (USA) *Gerald Russel Aschinger* 93
5 bb m Kitalpha(USA) Via Lactea (CAN) (Capote (USA))
5430a[13]

Lotus (FR) *Waldemar Hickst* a69 81
4 b g Elusive City(USA) Basse Besogne (IRE) (Pursuit Of Love)
4901a[8]

Loud *Denis Quinn* a53
6 ch g Dutch Art Applauding (IRE) (Royal Applause)
22[8] 175[5] 270[2] 431[11] 525[8] 617[4] 1162[5] 1781[7] 7646[RR] 8278[RR]

Loudly (USA) *George Peckham* a56 31
4 gr m War Front(USA) T.K.O. Lady (USA) (Two Punch (USA))
(46) 230[3]

Louis Leroy (IRE) *Edward Lynam* a67 74
4 b g Art Connoisseur(IRE) Chelsy (IRE) (Statue Of Liberty (USA))
7475a[8]

Louis The Pious *David O'Meara* 101
8 bb g Holy Roman Emperor(IRE) Whole Grain (Polish Precedent (USA))
2691[9] 4667[9] 5418[16] 6112[17] 6556[22] 7497[19]

Louis Vee (IRE) *John O'Shea* a65 48
8 bb g Captain Rio Mrs Evans (IRE) (College Chapel)
60[2] 197[7] (320) 356[4] 671[6] 856[5] 1180[6] 1533[5] 1721[6] 1827[6] 2458[10] 7533[10] 8316[11] 8541[4]

Loujain (IRE) *John Gosden* 72
2 ch c Dubawi(IRE) Eshaadeh (USA) (Storm Cat (USA))
7665[3]

Loumarin (IRE) *Michael Appleby* a71 56
4 b m Bushranger(IRE) Masela (IRE) (Medicean)
146[4] 4039[7] 4495[3] 4968[6] 5270[5] 7255[8] 7612[6] 8094[2] 8316[10]

Lou's Diamond *Michael Easterby* a66 64
2 br f Camacho Martha's Way (Tiger Hill (IRE))
2193[9] 4601[4] 5289[7] 6010[7] (7143)

Louvain (FR) *G Nicot* a78 75
7 b g Vatori(FR) Loupy Glitters (FR) (Loup Solitaire (USA))
3376a[5]

Louve Dancer (FR) *W Walton* 66
2 gr f Loup Breton(IRE) Funambula Dancer (FR) (Funambule (USA))
6639a[5]

Louvencourt (FR) *Mark Johnston* a58
3 bb g Halling(USA) Lungwa (IRE) (One Cool Cat (USA))
1184[5] 1406[8]

Louve Reine (FR) *Daniel Mark Loughnane* a47 50
3 b f King's Best(USA) Louve Solitaire (USA) (Our Emblem (USA))
6278[6]

Louversey *P Sogorb* 69
2 b f Arcano(IRE) Albisola (IRE) (Montjeu (IRE))
6937a[8]

Lovato (GER) *P Schiergen* 99
4 b h Lauro(GER) Larella (GER) (Anabaa (USA))
2286a[6] 2728a[6]

Loveable Helen (IRE) *Richard Fahey* a80 75
3 b f Dylan Thomas(IRE) Most-Saucy (Most Welcome)
4806[2] ◆ (5366) 5927[6] 7618[7] 8007[8] 8381[9]

Love And Be Loved *Peter Chapple-Hyam* a57 39
2 b f Lawman(FR) Rightside (High Chaparral (IRE))
7695[10] 8151[7] 8536[6]

Loveatfirstsight *Michael Attwater* a67
3 b f Bertolini(USA) Starbeck (IRE) (Spectrum (IRE))
6674[4] 7311[3] 7616[5] 8233[5] 8570[3]

Love Dreams (IRE) *Mark Johnston* 93
2 b c Dream Ahead(USA) Kimola (IRE) (King's Theatre (IRE))
(3283) (3712)

Love In The Dark *Nikki Evans* 39
3 b f Sleeping Indian Love In The Park (Pivotal)
3996[11] 5544[8] 6251[6] 6651[13]

Love Is All Around (IRE) *Dermot Anthony McLoughlin* a65 65
3 gr f Zebedee Shauna's Princess (IRE) (Soviet Star (USA))
1554[8] 7474a[13]

Love Island *Richard Whitaker* a88 98
7 b m Acclamation Sally Traffic (River Falls)
2158[9] 2267[4] 3116[6] 3566[13] 4428[11] 4946[4] 5390[14] (6013) 6518[3] ◆ 6793[6]

Loveisreckless (IRE) *William Muir* a66 65
3 b f Mount Nelson Sassari (IRE) (Darshaan)
1798[3] ◆ 2443[5] 3001[5] 3305[4]

Lovell *Charlie Appleby* 96
3 b g Dubawi(IRE) Cosmodrome (USA) (Bahri (USA))
1610[2] ◆ 3300[11]

Lovely Acclamation (IRE) *Ismail Mohammed* 67
2 b f Acclamation Titova (Halling (USA))
5237[2] ◆

Lovely Day (JPN) *Yasutoshi Ikee* 123
6 bb h King Kamehameha(JPN) Popcorn Jazz (JPN) (Dance In The Dark (JPN))
1690a[4] 8333a[4]

Lovely Memory (IRE) *Saeed bin Suroor* a94 95
4 b m Shamardal(USA) Folk Opera (IRE) (Singspiel (IRE))
1576[2] 2236[3] 3352[6]

Lovely Story (IRE) *Seamus Durack* a74 96
5 b m Cape Cross(IRE) Hush Money (CHI) (Hussonet (USA))
4078[3] 5025[3] 6634[3] 7015[12] 7280[6] 7669[6]

Love Marmalade (IRE) *David O'Meara* a65 82
6 ch g Duke Of Marmalade(IRE) Green Castle (IRE) (Indian Ridge)
1665[7] 2093[7] 2362[9] 2912[4] 3345[5] 3942[2] 4686[2] ◆ 4828[3] 5580[7] 6227[5] 7249[3]

Love Me Again *Charlie Fellowes* a45
2 b f Kheleyf(USA) Midnight Allure (Aragon)
7763[11]

Lovemedo (FR) *H-A Pantall* a83 96
4 ch m Zafeen(FR) Suvretta Queen (IRE) (Polish Precedent (USA))
7027a[12]

Lovemie (FR) *M Baudy* 7
4 ch m Air Chief Marshal(IRE) Lovoceane (Ocean Of Wisdom (USA))
7398a[12]

Love Moon (FR) *J Phelippon* a29 67
3 b g Spanish Moon(USA) Montana Moon (FR) (Hernando (FR))
7265a[4]

Love Oasis *Mark Johnston* a54 72
2 b f Oasis Dream Pickle (Piccolo)
1437[5] 1793[5] 2219[6] 2611[4] 3633[6] 4221[5] 4832[3] 7381[6]

Love On The Rocks (IRE) *Charles Hills* 89
3 ch f Exceed And Excel(AUS) My Love Thomas (IRE) (Cadeaux Genereux)
5205[5] 5657[2] 7124[9]

Love Power (IRE) *Mark Johnston* a65 59
2 b c Power Royal Fizz (IRE) (Royal Academy (USA))
6833[5] ◆ 7355[3] ◆ 7882[6]

Love Spirit *Louis Baudron* a81 111
6 b g Elusive City(USA) Indian Maiden (IRE) (Indian Ridge)
1172a[5] 2927a[5] 3796a[2] 5217a[13] 7758a[7]

Love Street (USA) *J-C Rouget* a91 88
3 ch f Kitten's Joy(USA) Bold World (USA) (Fortunate Prospect (USA))
5987a[6]

Loving *William Haggas* 76
2 gr f Mayson Courting (Pursuit Of Love)
6733[2] (7439) 7667[9]

Loving Clarets (IRE) *Richard Fahey* 35
2 b f Mayson Flying Clarets (IRE) (Titus Livius (FR))
4759[9] 5317[8]

Loving Things *Luca Cumani* 109
4 b m Pivotal Fallen In Love (Galileo (IRE))
(3436) 3888[3] 4821[4] 5586[8] (7568a)

Loving Your Work *Ken Cunningham-Brown* a68 72
5 b g Royal Applause Time Crystal (IRE) (Sadler's Wells (USA))
1340[5] ◆ 1834[4] (2205) 2645[5] (3817) 5405[6] 6737[14] 7429[9] 7911[8] 8462[12]

Lovin' Spoonful *Bryan Smart* a65 65
3 b f Kodiac Dispol Veleta (Makbul)
2667[7] 3879[5] 4766[3] 5887[10] 7253[4] (7603)

Low Key (IRE) *David Pipe* a69 92
9 b g Pentire La Capilla (Machiavellian (USA))
6582[16]

Low Latency *D J Bunyan* a47 65
2 b c Exceed And Excel(AUS) Ivory Gala (FR) (Galileo (IRE))
7130a[9]

Lowrie *John David Riches* a10 54
3 b f Assertive Miacarla (Forzando)
544[8] 2303[9] 2740[8] 3423[11] 4834[7] 5110[3] 5804[6] 5920[12] 6910[8]

Loyalty *Derek Shaw* a91 45
9 b g Medicean Ecoutila (USA) (Rahy (USA))
(58) 433[5] (620) 749[3] 886[5] 965[2] 7530[14] 7984[5] 8177[2] 8279[6]

Lozah *Roger Fell* a68 58
3 b f Lawman(FR) Princess Luna (GER) (Grand Lodge (USA))
2123[10] 2576[10] 3478[5] ◆ 4240[4] 4600[2] 4844[6] 5276[2] 5921[4] 6646[10] 7097[5] 7794[2] (8145) 8307[2] 8588[5]

L Stig *John O'Shea* a28 63
6 b g Striking Ambition Look Here's May (Revoque (IRE))
5255[4] 5623[6] 6415[12]

Lualiwa *Kevin Ryan* 77
2 b g Foxwedge(AUS) Sunpearl (Compton Place)
4336[3] 5476[7] 6632[3] 7541[4]

Luang Prabang (IRE) *Chris Wall* a75 59
3 b f Invincible Spirit(IRE) Sauvage (FR) (Sri Pekan (USA))
2483[9] 3572[7] 4401[6] 5088[7] 5769[4] (6592) 6851[3] ◆

Luath *Jeremy Gask* a65 56
3 ch g Archipenko(USA) Delaware Dancer (IRE) (Danehill Dancer (IRE))
182[5] 4528[6] 6238[7]

Lucan Sweet (ITY) *Il Cavallo In Testa* 96
3 gr c Dark Angel(IRE) Risera (IRE) (Royal Academy (USA))
1686a[4]

Lucata (IRE) *Tom Dascombe* a66 67
2 b c Sir Prancealot(IRE) Toy Show (IRE) (Danehill (USA))
1203[5] ◆ 1316[2] 1482[5] 1776[3]

Lucia Sciarra *Giles Bravery* a42 53
3 ch f Monsieur Bond(IRE) Oke Bay (Tobougg (IRE))
1045[6] 3003[7] 6373[5] 6902[7]

Lucia Valentina (NZ) *Kris Lees* 114
5 br m Savabeel(AUS) Staryn Glenn (NZ) (Montjeu (IRE))
7553a[7]

Lucida (IRE) *J S Bolger* 116
4 b m Shamardal(USA) Lura (USA) (Street Cry (IRE))
2497a[4] 3271[6] 3695a[3]

Lucie Rie (IRE) *K R Burke* a55 63
4 b m Excellent Art Farthingale (IRE) (Nashwan (USA))
27[7]

Lucifers Shadow (IRE) *Mrs C Gilbert* a62 50
7 gr g Dark Angel(IRE) Marianne's Dancer (IRE) (Bold Fact (USA))
1519a[3] 2285a[2] 2954a[5]

Lucky Beggar (IRE) *David C Griffiths* a68 86
6 gr g Verglas(IRE) Lucky Clio (IRE) (Key Of Luck (USA))
1205[6] 1394[9] 2188[8] 2787[10] 3573[2] 5857[7] 6263[16] 7289[7] 7593[14]

Lucky Bubbles (AUS) *K W Lui* 120
4 ch g Sebring(AUS) Bubble Below (AUS) (Hussonet (USA))
1911a[2] 8330a[2]

Lucky Clover *Malcolm Saunders* a61 68
5 ch m Lucky Story(USA) Willisa (Polar Falcon (USA))
1059[2] ◆ (1913) 2785[8] 3994[6] 4658[8]

Lucky Di *Peter Hedger* a55 65
6 br m Araafa(IRE) Lucky Date (IRE) (Halling (USA))
236[11] 558[2] 713[3] 2469[10] 4014[9] 4708[5] 5330[7] 5827[6] 7364[6] 7738[11] 8163[9] 8252[7]

Lucky Diva *Bill Turner* a52 59
9 ch m Lucky Story(USA) Cosmic Countess (IRE) (Lahib (USA))
2634[10] 3099[5] 4019[4] 4507[5] 5016[5] 5726[5]

Lucky Dottie *Pat Phelan* a61 51
5 bb m Lucky Story(USA) Auntie Dot Com (Tagula (IRE))
84[4] 461[3] 2645[6] 4019[11]

Lucky Esteem *Mark Johnston* a49 71
2 b f Yorgunnabelucky(USA) Dream Esteem (Mark Of Esteem (IRE))
3640[3] 4097[2] 4829[2] 5840[8]

Lucky Jim *David Dennis* a75 70
5 b g Lucky Story(USA) Lateralle (IRE) (Unfuwain (USA))
103[2] 234[2] 488[3]

Lucky Leyf *Philip Hide* a50 48
4 b m Kheleyf(USA) Lucky Dice (Perugino (USA))
777[12] 1139[6] 3146[3] 3490[4] 4388[11]

Lucky Lion *Andreas Lowe* a108 111
5 b h High Chaparral(IRE) Lips Arrow (GER) (Big Shuffle (USA))
1376a[2] 2074a[2] 3699a[7]

Lucky Lodge *Antony Brittain* a74 71
6 b g Lucky Story(USA) Melandre (Lujain (USA))
36[8] 943[2] 1116[10] (1496) 2332[2] 3153[10] 4714[2] 5845[9] 6453[4] 7325[9] 7798[8]

Lucky Louie *Roger Teal* a67 63
3 ch g Dutch Art Ardessie (Bahamian Bounty)
352[4] 639[6] 1451[2] 2186[4] 3062[9] 5088[5] 5769[5] 6290[4] 7059[5] 7654[8]

Lucky Mark (IRE) *John Balding* a63 62
7 b g Moss Vale(IRE) Vracca (Vettori (IRE))
22[2] 130[5] 178[6] 340[3] 869[3] 963[5] 1026[6] 1299[5] 3843[12]

Lucky Mistake (IRE) *J Reynier* a71 87
2 b c Fast Company(IRE) Torrmana (IRE) (Ela-Mana-Mou)
4161[2] 4394[15] 5067[2] 5798[2] 6448[2] 6950[21] (7407) 8062a[8]

Lucky Return *Des Donovan* a48 53
2 ch f Fast Company(IRE) Olindera (GER) (Lomitas)
2817[10] 3143[7] 3640[5] 7510[11]

Lucky Team (FR) *J Boisnard* a87 75
4 gr h Namid Kestria (IRE) (Keltos (FR))
(7525a)

Lucky Violet (IRE) *Iain Jardine* 77
4 b m Dandy Man(IRE) Rashida (King's Best (USA))
2419[4] 2809[5] 3264[5] ◆ 3754[2] 4486[2] (5115)

Lucques (AUS) *Mathew Ellerton & Simon Zahra* 98
4 bb g High Chaparral(IRE) Picholine (AUS) (Dehere (USA))
7481a[7]

Lucrezia *Sir Michael Stoute* a67 52
2 b f Nathaniel(IRE) Nannina (Medicean)
3433[6] 7885[7] 8208[5] ◆

Lucymai *Dean Ivory* a76 59
3 b f Multiplex Miss Lesley (Needwood Blade)
171[6] 519[3] 924[7] 8357[5]

Lucy's Law (IRE) *Tom Tate* a67 58
2 b f Lawman(FR) Lucy Limelites (Medicean)
3321[8] 3947[3] 4943[5] 6026[5] (6923)

Lucy The Painter (IRE) *Ed de Giles* a93 105
4 b m Excellent Art Royal Bounty (IRE) (Generous (IRE))
1139[DSQ] (1326) ◆ (1624) (2154) ◆ 2789[6] 3667[2] 3979[5] 5158[5] 5645[3] 6107a[5] 6746[9]

Luduamf (IRE) *Richard Hannon* a64 61
2 ch c Tamayuz Aphorism (Halling (USA))
3232[8] (3897) 4595[2] 5251[4] 5528[2] 6366[3] 7510[10]

Lugana (GER) *Mme Pia Brandt* a86 79
4 ch h Areion(GER) Lasuna (GER) (Monsun (GER))
4074a[3]

Lugano *Sir Mark Prescott Bt* a65 53
3 b c Galileo(IRE) Swiss Lake (USA) (Indian Ridge)
(7105)

Luis Vaz De Torres (IRE) *Richard Fahey* a86 88
4 b g Tagula(IRE) Tekhania (IRE) (Dalakhani (IRE))
220[3] 433[14] 771[7] 1040[10] 1291[7] 1844[4] (2857)

Lukoutoldmakezebak *James Bethell* a32 44
3 b g Arabian Gleam Angelofthenorth (Tomba)
4258[8] 5178[6] 5843[6] 6436[6]

Lulani (IRE) *Harry Dunlop* 83
4 b m Royal Applause Louverissa (IRE) (Verglas (IRE))
1756[3] ◆ 3673[6] (4777) 5357[8] 6316[6]

Lull (USA) *Christophe Clement* 105
2 b f War Front(USA) Quiet Now (USA) (Tiznow (USA))
7809a[4]

Lulu The Rocket *Peter Chapple-Hyam* a57 47
2 b f Authorized(IRE) Sagina (Shernazar)
6782[11] 7441[8] 7891[6] 8284[2]

Lulu The Zulu (IRE) *Michael Appleby* 106
8 ch m Danroad(AUS) Timbervati (USA) (Woodman (USA))
2684[11] 3163[6] (3616) 4338[4] 6056[4] 6558[21]

Lulworth (IRE) *William Jarvis* a61
3 b g Canford Cliffs(IRE) Aitch (IRE) (Alhaarth (IRE))
243[7]

Lumiere *Mark Johnston* 114
3 gr f Shamardal(USA) Screen Star (IRE) (Tobougg (IRE))
1888[16] (4065) 4926a[9] 6281[3] 7115[2]

Luminous *Simon Crisford* a35
2 b f Champs Elysees Tamzin (Hernando (FR))
6414[10]

Luna Mare (IRE) *Richard Fahey* a68 82
3 b f Galileo(IRE) Pale Moon Rising (IRE) (Kingmambo (USA))
(6024) 6504[2] 6951[9]

Lunar Deity *Stuart Williams* a103 68
7 b g Medicean Luminda (IRE) (Danehill (USA))
(18) 290[9] 486[9] (560) 833[3] 1068[12] 4654[8] 5374[4] 5965[8] 6636[2] 7301[9] 7933[9] 8049[11] 8279[7] 8593[12]

Lunar Jet *John Mackie* a64 57
2 ch g Ask Lightning Jet (Dutch Art)
7769[9] 8073[4]

Lunastorta (USA) *Agostino Affe'* 86
2 bb f Brilliant Speed(USA) Limerick (USA) (Black Minnaloushe (USA))
7839a[3]

Lundy *Joseph Patrick O'Brien* a87 99
2 b c Fastnet Rock(AUS) Princess Janie (USA) (Elusive Quality (USA))
2717a[2] 3243[14]

Lungarno Palace (USA) *John Gallagher* a76 93
5 b g Henrythenavigator(USA) Good Time Sally (USA) (Forestry (USA))
1568[7] 2024[10] 2699[7] 3117[5] 3972[3] 4550[5] 4912[3]

Lupie (IRE) *Mohammed Jassim Ghazali* a71 90
4 b h Lope De Vega(IRE) Valeriocia (IRE) (Invincible Spirit (IRE))
755a[8]

Lupo D'Oro (IRE) *John Best* a73 89
7 b g Amadeus Wolf Vital Laser (USA) (Seeking The Gold (USA))
231[2] 321[4]

Luqyaa *John Gosden* 72
2 b f Smart Strike(CAN) Maqaasid (Green Desert (USA))
7696[3]

Lusis Naturea *Noel C Kelly* a93 93
5 b g Multiplex Kenny's Dream (Karinga Bay)
6559[6]

Lusory *Charlie Appleby* a93 100
3 b g Shamardal(USA) Playful Act (IRE) (Sadler's Wells (USA))
(2614) ◆ 4403[2] 6261[3] 7608[6]

Lustrous *David O'Meara* 106
5 b m Champs Elysees Tamzin (Hernando (FR))
2690[6] 3436[8] 4610[6] 6332[3] 6951[3] 7271[9]

Lustrous Light (IRE) *G M Lyons* 104
3 ch c Galileo(IRE) Glinting Desert (IRE) (Desert Prince (IRE))
3337[7] 5095a[5]

Lutine Charlie (IRE) *Emma Owen* a54 54
9 b g Kheleyf(USA) Silvery Halo (USA) (Silver Ghost (USA))
168[3] 237[5] 341[3] 412[2] (690) 787[7] 985[6] 1262[10] 1556[4] 1742[3] 2087[4] 2442[7] 3489[2] 3973[9] 4505[2] 5055[4] 5710[7] 7070[10] 7298[5] 7427[4] 8070[13] 8278[6] 8492[6]

Luvly *Brian Baugh* a61
3 b g Multiplex Luv U Too (Needwood Blade)
765[12]

Luvlylynnthomas *Micky Hammond* 26
4 gr m Equiano(FR) Dansa Queen (Dansili)
3366[13] 4005[P]

Luv U Always *Iain Jardine* a51 47
2 b f Captain Gerrard(IRE) Lady Suesanne (IRE) (Cape Cross (IRE))
1799[3] 2097[6] 4638[4] 5125[4] 5606[3] 6678[13] 7740[16] 8285[2]

Luv U Lucky *Jo Hughes* a52
4 b g Multiplex Lady Suesanne (IRE) (Cape Cross (IRE))
2[6] 179[5] 527[8] 941[6] 1049[3] 1295[4] 1768[6] 2448[4] 8471[11]

Luv U Whatever *Michael Attwater* a102 48
6 b g Needwood Blade Lady Suesanne (IRE) (Cape Cross (IRE))
(19) 215[5] 499[5] 614[6] 1081[6] 1336[5] 7765[8] 8424[7]

Luxford *John Best* a43 51
2 b f Mullionmileanhour(IRE) Dolly Parton (IRE) (Tagula (IRE))
5258[3] 6295[U] 6673[11] 7099[10] 7528[4] 7884[11]

Lycidas (GER) *James Ewart* a99 98
7 b g Zamindar(USA) La Felicita (Shareef Dancer (USA))
1081[11] 1645[2] 1880[9]

Lydia's Place *Richard Guest* a61 90
3 ch f Equiano(FR) Peace And Love (IRE) (Fantastic Light (USA))
2218[12] 2554[4] 3420[7] 4488[3] 5040[7] 5274[6] 5657[14] 6476[4]

Lydiate Lady *Paul Green* a46 62
4 b m Piccolo Hiraeth (Petong)
784[8] 1255[7] 1676[9] 2423[8] 3211[4] (3882) 4378[2] 5110[6] 5162[4] 5714[9] 7596[4] 7913[5] 8541[9]

Lyfka *Paul Cole* a88 91
4 ch m Kheleyf(USA) Tarkamara (IRE) (Medicean)
(2084) 2890[5] 3405[7] (4086) 4737[6] 5396[5] 6914[6] 7281[7] 7781[6] 8098[6] 8158[4]

Lyin Eyes *Charles O'Brien* a53 71
2 b f Equiano(FR) Christmas Tart (IRE) (Danetime (IRE))
4171a[10]

Lykastos (IRE) *Mlle K Hoste* a82 53
6 b g Holy Roman Emperor(IRE) Granadilla (Zafonic (USA))
715a[2] 1034a[3] 2806a[3] 5452a[13]

Lynngale *Kristin Stubbs* a65 56
5 b m Myboycharlie(IRE) Belle Annie (USA) (Aptitude (USA))
39[6] 334[2] 982[6] 1263[6] 1791[2] 7256[12]

Lyrica's Lion (IRE) *Mark Hoad* a26
2 b g Dragon Pulse(IRE) Shishangaan (IRE) (Mujadil (USA))
8355[13]

Lytham St Annes (IRE) *Doug Watson* a88 89
3 b g Bahamian Bounty Kerrys Requiem (IRE) (King's Best (USA))
536a[4]

Maakaasib *Simon Crisford* a82 74
2 b c Equiano(FR) Majoune (FR) (Take Risks (FR))
3037[3] (4473) 7305[4]

Maarek *Miss Evanna McCutcheon* a49 106
9 b g Pivotal Ruby Rocket (IRE) (Indian Rocket)
1197[3] 1439[5] 1730a[7] 2495a[4] 2943a[5] 3681a[7] 5863[8] 6384a[4] 6990a[12] 7771[7]

Maarit (IRE) *Denis Coakley*
2 b f Harbour Watch(IRE) Atamana (IRE) (Lahib (USA))
8591[12]

Maazel (IRE) *Roger Varian* 77
2 b c Elzaam(AUS) Laylati (IRE) (Green Desert (USA))
2489[9] 2757[8] 3065[4] (4015) 6564[2] 6829[2] 7120[8]

Mabrokah *William Haggas* a44
3 b f Lonhro(AUS) Dubai Sea (USA) (Street Sense (USA))
2606[9]

Macalla (IRE) *R Mike Smith* a14 30
4 b g Echo Of Light Rum Raisin (Invincible Spirit (IRE))
2525[8] 5155[8]

Machiavelian Storm (IRE) *Richard Mitchell* a44 53
4 gr m Dark Angel(IRE) Terri's Charmer (USA) (Silver Charm (USA))
525[7] 860[3] 1578[10] 2326[6] 3230[F] 4019[5] 5021[11] 7299[7]

Machine Learner *Michael Bell* a76 86
3 b g Sir Percy My First Romance (Danehill (USA))
1571[3] 1891[6] 2580[5] 3607[3] 4303[2] 5083[2] 5397[3] 5607[3] (6450) 6730[3] (7359)

Macho Falcon (FR) *J-P Lopez* 51
2 b g Falco(USA) Macho Tempo (USA) (Macho Uno (USA))
3763a[8]

Macho Mac *Hughie Morrison* a79 62
3 ch g Pastoral Pursuits Clarice Orsini (Common Grounds)
1829[9] 7585[4] ◆ 8095[9] (8350) ◆

Mach One *Clive Cox* 64
2 b c Makfi Perfect Spirit (IRE) (Invincible Spirit (IRE))
6059[4] 7187[5] 7770[7]

Mack Attack *G M Lyons* 83
2 b c Mayson Faciascura (Oratorio (IRE))
6860a[5]

Mackiri (IRE) *Michael Appleby* a48 28
3 b g Makfi Inchiri (Sadler's Wells (USA))
6567[7] 7410[5] 8096[5] 8488[4]

Macksville (IRE) *Jeremy Gask* a67 63
3 gr g Mastercraftsman(IRE) Fairest Of All (IRE) (Sadler's Wells (USA))
4983[5] 5486[5] 7753[5] ◆ 8193[7] 8318[5]

Macmidnight *Donald Whillans* 14
4 b m Mawatheeq(USA) Rehlaat (USA) (Swain (IRE))
1883[6] 3287[14]

Mac's Kyllachy *James Fanshawe* a58 54
2 ch g Kyllachy Folly Lodge (Grand Lodge (USA))
6671[9] 7495[7] 7975[7]

Mac's Power (IRE) *Willie Musson* a68 65
10 b g Exceed And Excel(AUS) Easter Girl (Efisio)
67[7] 387[5] 590[10] 1533[14]

Mac Tiernan (IRE) *Philip Kirby* a50 51
9 b g Minashki(IRE) Softly Softly (IRE) (Lucky Guest)
247[11] 1169[7] 1343[8]

Madakheel (USA) *Simon West* a50 50
5 b m Mr Greeley(USA) Manaal (USA) (Bahri (USA))
2[12] 130[7] 388[9] 525[4] 867[9]

Madam Bounska (IRE) *Mrs Denise Foster* a58 72
2 b f Zebedee Lucky Apple (IRE) (Key Of Luck (USA))
4171a[9] 6388a[4]

Madam Dancealot (IRE) *Richard Baltas* 100
2 ch f Sir Prancealot(IRE) Sisal (IRE) (Danehill (USA))
1976[2] ◆ 3270[9] (4054) 4623[7] 5416[2] (6063) 7809a[13]

Madame Barker (IRE) *Bryan Smart* a68 46
3 ch f Frozen Power(IRE) Shadow Mountain (Selkirk (USA))
(104)

Madame Bond *Sally Hall* a35
4 ch m Monsieur Bond(IRE) Pigment (Zamindar (USA))
5843[7] 8388[5]

Madame Bounty (IRE) *Ed Walker* 73
2 b f Bahamian Bounty Madame Boulangere (Royal Applause)
2410[7] 2793[3] 3511[3] 4405[2]

Madame Butterfly (IRE) *David O'Meara* a82 61
4 b m Rip Van Winkle(IRE) Messias Da Silva (USA) (Tale Of The Cat (USA))
1765[2] 2094[2] (7727)

Madame Cherie (USA) *Mrs John Harrington* 78
2 b f First Samurai(USA) Antinous (USA) (Street Cry (IRE))
5937a[6]

Madame Chow (IRE) *Ralph Beckett* 64
3 b f Galileo(IRE) Landmark (USA) (Arch (USA))
2414[6] 3160[13] 3736[7] 4385[4] ◆ 5680[7] 6256[6]

Madame Claud *Hughie Morrison* a63 62
3 ch f Champs Elysees Change Partners (IRE) (Hernando (FR))
2829[7] (3509) 7309[3]

Madame Lafite *Jonathan Portman* a65 66
4 b m Dutch Art Poppo's Song (CAN) (Polish Navy (USA))
1039[4] ◆ 1831[4] 3099[3] 3528[4] 4637[5]

Madame Mistral (FR) *Matthieu Palussiere* 73
2 b f Exchange Rate(USA) Chinook Wind (IRE) (Encosta De Lago (AUS))
4620a[6]

Madame Thunder (IRE) *D J Bunyan* a81 85
3 gr f Zebedee Cuca Vela (USA) (Devil's Bag (USA))
1730a[10]

Madam Lilibet (IRE) *Sharon Watt* 71
7 b m Authorized(IRE) Foxilla (IRE) (Foxhound (USA))
1244[3] 1523[2] 1955[12] 2971[9] 3437[5] 5435[6] 6029[5] 6438[12] 7006[8]

Madam Mai Tai *Rebecca Bastiman* 52
4 ch m Compton Place Dash Of Lime (Bold Edge)
3044[7] (3946) 4369[7] 5222[4] 6621[11] 7097[8]

Madam Prancealot (IRE) *David Evans* a57 63
2 b f Sir Prancealot(IRE) Delia (IRE) (Darshaan)
1086[3] 1233[7] 2536[7] 5251[3] (5770) (6253) 6388a[14] 7286[10] 7570[9] 8087[4] 8341[4]

Maddys Dream *Lydia Pearce* a55 72
3 b g Arabian Gleam Group Force (IRE) (Montjeu (IRE))
1217[4] 1701[8] 2375[10] 2749[P]

Madeleine Bond *Henry Candy* 60
2 ch f Monsieur Bond(IRE) Spin A Wish (Captain Rio)
4054[7]

Mad Endeavour *Stuart Kittow* a60 71
5 b g Muhtathir Capefly (Cape Cross (IRE))
1533[8] 2130[8] 2697[2] (3349) 4155[7] 5060[8] 5797[3] (6269) 7059[16]

Madernia (IRE) *C Laffon-Parias* a93 96
4 ch m Duke Of Marmalade(IRE) Gali Gal (IRE) (Galileo (IRE))
4696a[11] 6273a[9] 7087a[3] 8042a[6]

Made You Look (USA) *Todd Pletcher* 101
2 bb c More Than Ready(USA) Night And Day (USA) (Unbridled's Song (USA))
7807a[6]

Madiva (FR) *Mme M Bollack-Badel* a74 71
4 gr m Aussie Rules(USA) Mahradeva (GER) (Medicean)
5501a[3]
Madness Light (FR) *Daniel Steele* 39
7 b g Satri(IRE) Majestic Lady (FR) (Octagonal (NZ))
4950[8] 7039[6]
Madrasa (IRE) *Tony Forbes* a55 57
8 b g High Chaparral(IRE) Shir Dar (FR) (Lead On Time (USA))
71[8] 4045[11]
Madrileno *G Arizkorreta Elosegui* 103
4 b h Sir Percy Alizadora (Zilzal (USA))
5502a[2]
Madrinho (IRE) *Richard Hannon* 97
3 ch g Frozen Power(IRE) Perfectly Clear (USA) (Woodman (USA))
1991[4] 2736[2] ◆ 3165[10] 4062[16] 5199[7] 5601[6] 6338[4]
Mad Rose (IRE) *J Reynier* a64
2 b f Royal Applause Na Zdorovie (Cockney Rebel (IRE))
7455a[2]
Maer Rocks (IRE) *Marcus Tregoning* a51 49
3 br f Dream Ahead(USA) Dream Of The Hill (IRE) (Tiger Hill (IRE))
2851[7] 6890[10] 7212[9]
Maestro Mac (IRE) *Hughie Morrison* a78 83
3 b g Roderic O'Connor(IRE) Union City Blues (IRE) (Encosta De Lago (AUS))
5405[5] 5849[4] 6474[2] ◆ 7060[10] *7618[6]*
Mafaaheem (IRE) *Owen Burrows* a70 68
2 b c Shamardal(USA) Hammiya (IRE) (Darshaan)
6577[7] *7726[4]*
Maftool (USA) *M Al Mheiri* a111 106
4 br g Hard Spun(USA) With Intention (USA) (Mr Greeley (USA))
(624a) 1101a[7] 8396a[9]
Magari (FR) *H-A Pantall* a93 95
3 b c Denon(USA) Shakila (Cadeaux Genereux)
1230a[4]
Magdalene Fox *Ed Dunlop* a60
2 ch c Foxwedge(AUS) Malelane (IRE) (Prince Sabo)
6671[8] 7307[7] 7649[7] 7881[6] 8276[12]
Magellan (GER) *Jean-Pierre Carvalho* 51
2 ch c Tertullian(USA) Miramare (GER) (Rainbow Quest (USA))
6174a[8]
Maggie Pink *Michael Appleby* a89 101
7 b m Beat All(USA) Top Notch (Alderbrook)
2145 351[4] 5190[6] 6281[6] 6764[5] 7241[5] 7825[19]
Maggi May (IRE) *David Brown* 28
2 b f Kodiac Virevolle (FR) (Kahyasi)
3112[11] 5029[10]
Maghfoor *Saeed bin Suroor* 82
2 b c Cape Cross(IRE) Thaahira (USA) (Dynaformer (USA))
7329[2] ◆
Magical Daze *John Mackie* a75 73
4 b m Showcasing Poulaine Bleue (Bertolini (USA))
2028[10] 2846[5] (3719) 4496[4] *5247[4] 6426[10] 7798[3]*
Magical Dreamer (IRE) *James Fanshawe* a76 66
2 b f Acclamation Double Fantasy (GER) (Indian Ridge)
4063[4] *(6866)*
Magical Effect (IRE) *Ruth Carr* a76 84
4 ch g New Approach(IRE) Purple Glow (IRE) (Orientate (USA))
3907[2] 4496[2] ◆ (4845) 5857[3] ◆ 6131[2]
Magical Fire (IRE) *M D O'Callaghan* 103
2 b f Dragon Pulse(IRE) Bridal Dance (IRE) (Danehill Dancer (IRE))
2718a[5] 3694a[5] 4106[2] 5584[8]
Magical Forest (IRE) *Marco Botti* a75 75
2 b f Casamento(IRE) Hurry Home Hydee (USA) (Came Home (USA))
2007[3] *2376[2]* 2885[4] 4877[2] *5549[3] 6044[2] 8464[2]*
Magical Lasso (IRE) *Keith Dalgleish* a47 50
3 ch g Monsieur Bond(IRE) How Sweet It Is (IRE) (Kodiac)
1027[5] 1671[10] 2533[7] 4337[4] 4705[3] 4872[10] 5355[13] 5800[5] 6004[4] 6094[4] *6739[4] 6920[9] 7256[11]*
Magical Memory (IRE) *Charles Hills* 118
4 gr g Zebedee Marasem (Cadeaux Genereux)
(1439) (2159) 3385[4] 4151[7] 6120[14]
Magical Molly Joe *David Barron* a26
2 b f Arabian Gleam Magical Music (Fraam)
8009[8]
Magical Path (IRE) *Hugo Palmer* a74
3 gb f Zebedee Road To Reality (IRE) (Indian Danehill (IRE))
824[2] (984) 1345[2]
Magical Peak *John O'Shea* a12 27
4 gr m Hellvelyn Enjoy The Magic (Namaqualand (USA))
1451[9] 1892[8] *6512[13]* 7240[14]
Magical Thomas *Neil Mulholland* a78 76
4 ch g Dylan Thomas(IRE) Magical Cliche (USA) (Affirmed (USA))
1717[11] 2399[9]
Magic Beans *Hughie Morrison* a53 13
2 br g Pastoral Pursuits Jasmeno (Catcher In The Rye (IRE))
7187[10] *7458[7] 7963[6]*
Magic Circle (IRE) *Ralph Beckett* 102
4 b g Makfi Minkova (IRE) (Sadler's Wells (USA))
1893[2] ◆ 3387[11] (4162) 6118[4] 7708a[3]
Magic City (IRE) *Michael Easterby* a78 83
7 b g Elusive City(USA) Annmarie's Magic (IRE) (Flying Spur (AUS))
4644[12] 4917[10] 5417[12] 5857[9] 6539[18] 7126[10] *7436[4] 7857[4] 8205[3]* ◆
Magic Empress (IRE) *Tony Coyle* a6
4 b m Baltic King Red Trance (IRE) (Soviet Star (USA))
251[13]
Magic Garden (IRE) *Jonathan Portman* a64 66
3 b f Zebedee Sisal (IRE) (Danehill (USA))
42[2] 291[8] 443[10] 711[4] 5628[7] *6852[10]*
Magician Coutinho *David O'Meara* a54 52
4 b g Misu Bond(IRE) Chez Cherie (Wolfhound (USA))
3474[7] ◆ *3731[12] 5080[7]*
Magic Ice *John Berry*
6 b m Royal Applause Winter Ice (Wolfhound (USA))
3043[10] *5734[8]*
Magicinthemaking (USA) *Jeremy Noseda* 52
2 br f Wildcat Heir(USA) Love In Bloom (USA) (More Than Ready (USA))
5400[9] 6034[10]
Magic Journey (IRE) *John Quinn* a55 55
2 gr g Zebedee Journey's End (IRE) (In The Wings)
3874[7] 4371[11] 4765[9] 6678[9] *7749[3]*
Magic Mirror *Mark Rimell* a41 45
3 b f Dutch Art Balatoma (IRE) (Mr Greeley (USA))
5544[6] 6135[5] 6441[8] *6966[6] 8492[14]*
Magic Moments *Alan King* a61
3 b f Kheleyf(USA) Magic Rhythm (Librettist (USA))
7616[10] 8075[8] 8559[6]
Magic Music Man *Alan King* a69 77
5 b g Authorized(IRE) Magic Music (IRE) (Magic Ring (IRE))
43[6] 5451[0]
Magic Strike (IRE) *Clive Cox* a59 66
3 b c Zebedee Artemis Culture (USA) (Smart Strike (CAN))
2642[4] 4269[14] *5027[6]* 5515[11] *6051[7]* 6290[7] 6894[9]
Magillen (IRE) *Charles Hills* 79
2 ch c Lope De Vega(IRE) Lady Natilda (First Trump)
2757[2] ◆ 3382[11]
Magique Touch *Roger Charlton* a73 58
2 b f Equiano(FR) Lavinia's Grace (USA) (Green Desert (USA))
6866[7] 7216[4] *7748[5] 7981[2] (8174)*
Magna Cartor *Ronald Thompson* a46
6 b g Motivator Hora (Hernando (FR))
567[9]
Magnanime *F Chappet* a92 102
3 b f Elusive City(USA) Mujabaha (Redoute's Choice (AUS))
2316a[5] 4174a[10] 5498a[10] 6693a[10]
Magnentius (FR) *Rod Collet* 94
3 b g Tiberius Caesar(FR) Miss Eva (Xaar)
5448a[5]
Magneticjim (IRE) *P Bary* a88 98
4 gr h Galileo(IRE) Dibenoise (FR) (Kendor (FR))
3377a[4]
Magnificent Madiba *George Baker* 68
3 b g Mount Nelson Mrs Penny (AUS) (Planchet (AUS))
1714[11] 2098[6] 2640[6] 5207[7] (5708) 6737[11] 7421[9]
Magnolea (IRE) *J-C Rouget* a94 102
3 b f Acclamation Carcassonne (IRE) (Montjeu (IRE))
2928a[3] 4184a[3] 6357a[6] 7397a[2] *8148a[3]*
Magnolia Ridge (IRE) *Mark Walford* a51 46
6 b g Galileo(IRE) Treasure The Lady (IRE) (Indian Ridge)
5054 673[4] 4499[5] *7656[2] 8091[4]*
Magnolia Rose (IRE) *D K Weld* 81
3 b f Fastnet Rock(AUS) Magnolia Lane (IRE) (Sadler's Wells (USA))
7195a[19] (Dead)
Magnum (IRE) *Brian Meehan* a77 82
3 gr g Lawman(FR) Coventina (IRE) (Daylami (IRE))
1715[5] 2291[3] *2816[3]* 3341[18] 3814[6] 4272[6] 5287[3]
Magnus Maximus *Robyn Brisland* a110 111
5 b g Holy Roman Emperor(IRE) Chanrossa (IRE) (Galileo (IRE))
17[4] 288[10] 529[3] 657[4] (2581) 3279[4] 3656[4] 4758[4] *(5678)* (6112)
Magnus Romeo *Johnny Farrelly* a46 50
5 b g Manduro(GER) Chili Dip (Alhaarth (IRE))
3402[9] 3999[8] *5473[6]*
Mahajanga (FR) *B Legros* a48 36
6 b m Amadeus Wolf Kota Kinabalu (Ashkalani (IRE))
7295a[8]
Mahari (IRE) *A Fabre* 92
3 b c Duke Of Marmalade(IRE) Mission Secrete (IRE) (Galileo (IRE))
3450a[5]
Mahfooz (IRE) *Charles Hills* a82 75
3 b c Teofilo(IRE) Itqaan (USA) (Danzig (USA))
1200[5] *1651[2]* 2368[2] 4384[4] *7280[3]*
Mahsoob *John Gosden* a91 118
5 b h Dansili Mooakada (IRE) (Montjeu (IRE))
(1425) 2243[11] 4666[5]
Maiandra (FR) *T Lemer* a52 77
2 b f Evasive Star Val (FR) (Enrique)
1118a[4] *4124a[5]*
Maiden Approach *Richard Fahey* a87 83
5 b m New Approach(IRE) Ivowen (USA) (Theatrical (IRE))
72[4] 254[3] 267[5]
Maid Of The Glens (IRE) *John Patrick Shanahan* a69 96
5 b m The Carbon Unit(USA) There's A Light (IRE) (Fantastic Light (USA))
187a[6] 1880[10] 2199[7]
Maid Of Tuscany (IRE) *Alexandra Dunn* a52 56
5 b m Manduro(GER) Tuscania (USA) (Woodman (USA))
6424[4] 6825[3] (7045) *7367[10]*
Maifalki (FR) *Mark Walford* a85
3 b g Falco(USA) Makila (IRE) (Entrepreneur)
7991[4] (8195) (8498)
Mailshot (USA) *Mark Johnston* a92 89
2 ch c Hard Spun(USA) Newsreel (IRE) (A.P. Indy (USA))
1293[2] (1783) 2240[4] 2669[4] *(3526)* 4825[5] 6180a[5] *8525[2]*
Maimara (FR) *M Delzangles* 113
4 b m Makfi Hideaway Heroine (IRE) (Hernando (FR))
(1231a) 1910a[9] 3271[9]
Mainstream *Sir Michael Stoute* 101
3 b g Dansili Golden Stream (IRE) (Sadler's Wells (USA))
(1896) 2471[4] 3532[5] 4403[3] 5434[2] 5865[2] 6545[2]
Maison Brillet (IRE) *Clive Drew* a71 72
9 b g Pyrus(USA) Stormchaser (IRE) (Titus Livius (FR))
138[6] 832[5] 950[10] 7739[9] 8359[7]
Maisons (FR) *E Lellouche* a81 89
3 ch f Le Havre(IRE) Malegganda (FR) (Divine Light (JPN))
7397a[9] 7998a[11]
Majdool (IRE) *Roger Varian* a92 89
3 b g Acclamation Maany (USA) (Mr Greeley (USA))
2477[8] 3155[8] 3980[13]
Majeed *David Simcock* a103 110
6 b g Mount Nelson Clever Millie (USA) (Cape Canaveral (USA))
94a[9] 285a[9] 455a[8] (4276) 4821[3] 5894[2] 6600a[4]
Majeste *Richard Hannon* 100
2 b c Acclamation Winged Valkyrie (IRE) (Hawk Wing (USA))
3954[2] (4390) 6326[4]
Majestic Girl (IRE) *Steve Flook* a54 53
3 b f Royal Applause Pretty Majestic (IRE) (Invincible Spirit (IRE))
1435[4] 3471[5] 4256[7] 5088[11] 6381[6] 6651[8] *6900[3] 7641[15]*
Majestic Hero (IRE) *Ronald Harris* a79 96
4 b g Majestic Missile(IRE) Xena (IRE) (Mull Of Kintyre (USA))
1528[3] (2253) 2665[2] 2863[3] 3618[5] 4461[3] (4911) 5360[3] 6114[2] 6633[12] 6944[10] 7124[13]
Majestic Manannan (IRE) *David Nicholls* a42 68
7 b g Majestic Missile(IRE) Miraculous (IRE) (Marju (IRE))
1956[7] 2120[12] 2676[8] 3010[8] 4492[10] *4647[8] 5069[10]* 5889[8] *6745[11]*
Majestic Moon (IRE) *Julia Feilden* a107 96
6 b g Majestic Missile(IRE) Gala Style (IRE) (Elnadim (USA))
816[2] ◆ 1627[13] 2027[9] 3386[23] 4152[12] 4625[21] 5146[10] 5871[16] 6210[4] 6764[9] 7542[7] *8279[8] 8593[11]*
Majestic Mount *S Seemar* a102 103
6 b h Exceed And Excel(AUS) Our Poppet (IRE) (Warning)
95a[3] 373a[7] 723a[9]
Majestic Myles (IRE) *Lee Carter* a93 58
8 b g Majestic Missile(IRE) Gala Style (IRE) (Elnadim (USA))
192[4] (457) 727[6] 878[3] 1041[12] 2033[6] 2579[9] 3803[6] 4627[10] *4881[8]* 5773[3] *6235[6]* 6806[11] *7529[3] 7887[12] 8258[10]*
Majestic Stone (IRE) *Robert Cowell* 46
2 b g Casamento(IRE) Pretty Majestic (IRE) (Invincible Spirit (IRE))
6873[7] 7414[6]
Majesto (USA) *Gustavo Delgado* a108
3 b r Tiznow(USA) Unacloud (USA) (Unaccounted For (USA))
2063a[18]
Major Assault *Clive Cox* a70 74
3 b c Kyllachy Night Premiere (IRE) (Night Shift (USA))
770[3] 1931[6] 3464[2] 4157[8] 4953[3] 7076[9]
Major Attitude *Patrick Chamings* a22 39
4 b g Major Cadeaux Alexander Ballet (Mind Games)
1162[11]
Major Ben *David Evans* a68 61
3 ch g Major Cadeaux La Jwaab (Alhaarth (IRE))
3723[7] 4792[7] 5486[6] *(8193) 8428[4]*
Major Cornwallis (IRE) *Richard Fahey* a74 70
2 ch g Dandy Man(IRE) Macnas (USA) (Orientate (USA))
2611[5] ◆ 3114[5] *3561[2]* 3872[2] *5081[3] 5967[4] 6903[2]*
Major Crispies *Jeremy Gask* a92 88
5 b g Pastoral Pursuits Nellie Melba (Hurricane Sky (AUS))
1990[9] *2378[3] 2819[3] 3303[5] 3783[4]* 5744[3] *6371[5]* 6780[10] *7617[2] 7902[11] 8356[10]*
Major Franko *Sarah-Jayne Davies* a47 41
4 ch g Major Cadeaux Royal Future (IRE) (Royal Academy (USA))
1038[8] 1174[6] 8540[9]
Majoris (IRE) *Hugo Palmer* 95
2 b c Frankel Drops (IRE) (Kingmambo (USA))
2649[6] ◆ (3971) (5171) 5646[5] 6285[4]
Major Jumbo *Kevin Ryan* 69
2 gr g Zebedee Gone Sailing (Mizzen Mast (USA))
2119[4] 2530[3] 3772[7] (4891) 5352[5] 6010[3]
Major Mac *Hughie Morrison* a53 78
4 ch g Shirocco(GER) Spring Fashion (IRE) (Galileo (IRE))
6561[2] 7183[3] 7498[11]
Major Maximus *Mrs C Gilbert* a72 49
9 br g Domedriver(IRE) Madame Maxine (USA) (Dayjur (USA))
3918a[7]
Major Muscari (IRE) *Shaun Harris* a61 42
8 ch g Exceed And Excel(AUS) Muscari (Indian Ridge)
75[2] ◆ *319[4] 444[3] 608[9] 799[9] 2442[5]* 3484[11] *3988[4] 5080[2] 5475[5] 6373[8] 8541[2]*
Major Pusey *John Gallagher* 92
4 ch g Major Cadeaux Pusey Street Lady (Averti (IRE))
1744[2] 2290[6] (3056) 3159[2] (3618) 3956[9] 5882[8] 6207[6] 6944[8] 7289[6]
Major Rowan *John Davies* a76 59
5 b g Captain Gerrard(IRE) Julie's Gift (Presidium)
(368) 2558[7] 3480[3] *(5065)* 6219[7]
Major Tom *Michael Appleby* a30
2 b g Native Ruler Top Level (IRE) (Fasliyev (USA))
8537[11]
Major Valentine *John O'Shea* a74 59
4 b g Major Cadeaux Under My Spell (Wizard King)
782[5] 955[7] 1419[9] 2201[7] *3780[4]* 4355[5] 4506[5] *6091[6] 6510[6] 7617[8] 8095[4] (8316)*
Majrooh (IRE) *George Peckham* a83 83
4 b g Acclamation Neve Lieve (IRE) (Dubai Destination (USA))
7053[2]
Makaarim *Marco Botti* a75
2 b c Tamayuz Dubawi Cheetah (IRE) (Dubawi (IRE))
8246[5] (8537) ◆
Makahiki (JPN) *Yasuo Tomomichi* 123
3 b c Deep Impact(JPN) Wikiwiki (JPN) (French Deputy (USA))
(6392a) 6989a[14]
Makday *Robert Stephens* a16
4 b g Makfi Flag Day (Pivotal)
728[7]
Make Fast *Andrew Balding* a93 98
3 b f Makfi Raymi Coya (CAN) (Van Nistelrooy (USA))
2034[5] 2870[2] 3274[7] 3911[5] 6939[8]
Make Memories (USA) *John Gosden* a37
2 ch c Street Cry(IRE) Winter Memories (USA) (El Prado (IRE))
8088[12] 8227[8]
Makemerichjohn (IRE) *David Evans* a40 43
2 b g Baltic King Golden Strands (Primo Dominie)
3813[13] 4349[13] 5484[6] 6033[8] 6388a[27] *6961[8]*
Make Music *Andrew Balding* a82 81
3 b f Acclamation Come What May (Selkirk (USA))
1246[5] 1898[4] 2585[2] (2824) (3649) 4139[4]
Make On Madam (IRE) *Les Eyre* a64 70
4 b m Captain Rio Rye (IRE) (Charnwood Forest (IRE))
598[4] ◆ *667[3] 859[8]* 1252[4] 1412[4] (1926) 2491[9] 3013[10] 3478[3] 4240[3] 4454[5] 5276[4] 5868[7] 6644[4]
Make Time (IRE) *David Menuisier* 95
2 ch c Makfi Poppet's Lovein (Lomitas)
6108[2] ◆ (6880) ◆
Makhfar (IRE) *Kevin Morgan* a61 41
5 b g Bushranger(IRE) Let Me Shine (USA) (Dixie Union (USA))
875[4] 1180[4] 1415[7] 3078[8] 3821[8] *7070[7] 7646[4] (7986) 8179[10] 8528[7]*
Making Light (IRE) *D K Weld* a64 102
2 b f Tamayuz Instant Sparkle (IRE) (Danehill (USA))
(7559a)
Making Trouble (GER) *D Moser* 97
4 bb g Paco Boy(IRE) Making Hay (Dr Fong (USA))
2722a[5] 5943a[10] 7027a[5]
Makkaar (IRE) *Mark Johnston* 81
2 b c Raven's Pass(USA) Beneventa (Most Welcome)
6640[3] 7243[3] (7665)
Makkadangdang *Andrew Balding* a67 68
2 ro g Mastercraftsman(IRE) Penny Cross (Efisio)
4524[5] 5324[5] *7605[2]*
Makman (IRE) *Ed Dunlop* a71 40
2 b g Kodiac Sheila Blige (Zamindar (USA))
1203[3] ◆ 1422[7] *4196[3] 4712[2] 6658[9]* 7073[9] *7510[2]*
Maknificent (IRE) *M D O'Callaghan* a72 81
4 b m Makfi Sally Wood (CAN) (Woodman (USA))
4811a[5]
Makzeem *Roger Charlton* 94
3 b g Makfi Kazeem (Darshaan)
1714[10] 2008[5] 3160[2] 4056[2] (4458) 7535[17] 7699[2]
Malagueta (FR) *A De Watrigant* 61
2 b f Henrythenavigator(USA) Dajariyda (FR) (Cape Cross (IRE))
5142a[11]
Malakky (IRE) *Brian Meehan* a81 77
3 b c Tamayuz Safiya Song (IRE) (Intikhab (USA))
2698[3] ◆ 3267[2] *4215[9]* (Dead)
Malaysian Boleh *Brian Ellison* a76 67
6 ch g Compton Place Orlena (USA) (Gone West (USA))
159[7] 349[3] ◆ *414[5] 629[6] 764[4] 901[4] 1159[4] 1291[3] 1700[3]* (1781) ◆ *2332[11]* 3040[2] 3491[3] *3985[7]* 5051[4] 5838[2] 6506[2] *6699[11]* 6958[10] *7325[4] 7852[3] 8037[3] 8389[6] 8531[2]*
Malcolm The Pug (IRE) *Richard Hannon* 74
2 b c Acclamation La Zona (IRE) (Singspiel (IRE))
4075[3] 4390[6]
Maldon (IRE) *Patrice Quinton* 62
4 b g Dark Angel(IRE) Mary Spring Rice (IRE) (Saffron Walden (FR))
5216a[11]
Maldonado (FR) *Charlie Appleby* 85
2 ch c Rio De La Plata(USA) Spanish Winner (IRE) (Choisir (AUS))
4877[4] 5371[2] 5916[2] (6264) 6791[6]
Maleficent Queen *Keith Dalgleish* 108
4 b m Mount Nelson Manila Selection (USA) (Manila (USA))
(1786) (2363) 3383[9] 6505[4] 7351[9] 7823[8]
Malefique (FR) *H-A Pantall* a58
2 b f Kendargent(FR) Magie Noire (FR) (Marju (IRE))
8420a[11]
Malhama *Roger Varian* a61 71
3 br f New Approach(IRE) Mahaatheer (IRE) (Daylami (IRE))
699[7] 1628[2] 2505[3] 3042[5] *6922[7]*
Malih *Eric Wheeler* a59 59
7 b g Echo Of Light Sultry Lass (USA) (Private Account (USA))
222[8] 653[8] 986[9] 1742[6] 2647[6] 3043[9]
Malinka (IRE) *D K Weld* 83
4 b m Pivotal Mad About You (IRE) (Indian Ridge)
4748a[14]
Maljaa *Roger Varian* 112
4 ch g Paco Boy(IRE) Kerry's Dream (Tobougg (IRE))
1969[2] 2895[17] 4126[7] 4735[7] 5268[4]
Malka (FR) *Mme Pia Brandt* a91 101
5 ch m Green Tune(USA) Quadrupa (GER) (Big Shuffle (USA))
451a[5] 809a[6]
Mallymkun *K R Burke* a76 67
4 b m Kheleyf(USA) Harriet's Girl (Choisir (AUS))
859[3] 1003[8] 2345[14] 3211[2] 3880[4] *(5247) 6426[7]* 7253[7] *8036[8] 8206[10]*

Malmoosa (IRE) *Brian Meehan* 94
3 b f Shamardal(USA) Mohafazaat (IRE) (Sadler's Wells (USA))
2183^{2} 2638^{3} 4160^{4} 5361^{3} (6032) ◆ 6948^{2} ◆ 7535^{9}

Malmostosa *Marco Botti* a81 78
3 b f Intikhab(USA) Tell Mum (Marju (IRE))
(1723) 2789^{7} 5089^{4} 5551^{6} 7220^{8} 8028^{8}

Malos Pelos (SPA) *J Lopez Sanchez* 72
5 b g Pyrus(USA) Harasueva (GER) (Tertullian (USA))
6356a^{6}

Malt Teaser (FR) *John Best* a51
2 ch g Muhtathir Abondante (USA) (Thunder Gulch (USA))
8486^{12} 8591^{8}

Maluhia (IRE) *Kieran P Cotter* a24 6
4 br g Captain Rio Daftiyna (IRE) (Darshaan)
6463a^{8}

Malvesi *Daniel Mark Loughnane* a38 39
7 b g Iceman Madam Valentine (Primo Valentino (IRE))
201^{6} 334^{3} 547^{6} 707^{7} 986^{8} 5235^{7} 6408^{8}

Malvia *Ian Williams* a46 61
4 b g Exceed And Excel(AUS) Always On My Mind (Distant Relative)
2380^{10} 3136^{3} 3953^{2} 4337^{3} 5088^{8}

Mama Africa (IRE) *David Barron* 68
2 br f Big Bad Bob(IRE) Colourpoint (USA) (Forest Wildcat (USA))
1641^{2} 4601^{3} 5289^{6} 5712^{4} 6388a^{11} 6787^{10}

Mamadysh (FR) *A Savujev* 62
2 b c Pivotal Verba (FR) (Anabaa (USA))
5701a^{5}

Mambo Dancer *Mark Johnston* a63
2 b c So You Think(NZ) Mambo Halo (USA) (Southern Halo (USA))
8246^{11} 8537^{10}

Mambo Fever *David C Griffiths* a66 65
5 b m Footstepsinthesand Mambo's Melody (Kingmambo (USA))
22^{3} (80) 269^{4} 415^{4} 558^{6}

Mambomiss (FR) *D De Watrigant* 106
5 ch m Mastercraftsman(IRE) Mambo Mistress (USA) (Kingmambo (USA))
1232a^{8} 5461a^{4} (6273a) 7569a^{15}

Mambo Paradise *Mark Johnston* a91 95
4 b m Makfi Mambo Halo (USA) (Southern Halo (USA))
1441^{10} 2223^{11}

Mambo Spirit (IRE) *Tony Newcombe* a68 66
12 b g Invincible Spirit(IRE) Mambodorga (USA) (Kingmambo (USA))
387^{8} 542^{2} 904^{4} 2130^{13} 2697^{9} 3510^{10} 4570^{4} (5628) 6312^{4} (7693) 8315^{11}

Mamdood (IRE) *Richard Hannon* a77 67
2 gr c Clodovil(IRE) Fact (American Post)
6850^{5} 7297^{4} (7812)

Mamillius *George Baker* 89
3 b g Exceed And Excel(AUS) Laika Lane (USA) (Street Cry (IRE))
2207^{8} (2999) 4867^{14} 6529^{10}

Mamnoon (IRE) *Roy Brotherton* a34
3 b g Cape Cross(IRE) Masaafat (Act One)
7942^{11}

Mamoo *Mike Murphy* a63 63
3 ch g Sir Percy Meredith (Medicean)
3357^{5} 4046^{4} 4836^{2} 5795^{2} 7008^{6} 7614^{3} 7969^{4} 8445^{7}

Manaboo (USA) *Charlie Appleby* a74 96
3 b f Hard Spun(USA) Pico Duarte (USA) (Storm Cat (USA))
2470^{5} (2877) 4065^{3} 5158^{13} 6746^{12}

Man About Town (IRE) *K R Burke* 71
2 ch g Dandy Man(IRE) Zanida (IRE) (Mujadil (USA))
2358 ^{4} 4161^{7} 5583^{18}

Manahir (FR) *H-A Pantall* 82
2 ch c Naaqoos Lerina (FR) (Priolo (USA))
5985a^{2} 6638a^{2}

Manama (IRE) *Charlie Appleby* a40 70
2 b f Cape Cross(IRE) Alareen (USA) (Selkirk (USA))
4063^{2} 4801^{12} 5722^{7}

Manangatang (IRE) *Luca Cumani* a68
2 b c Fastnet Rock(AUS) Mona Lisa (Giant's Causeway (USA))
(7962)

Manatee *A Fabre* a113 120
5 b h Monsun(GER) Galatee (FR) (Galileo (IRE))
1102a^{6} 2725a^{3} 3936a^{4}

Manatee Bay *David Nicholls* a85 83
6 b g Royal Applause Dash Of Lime (Bold Edge)
1787^{4} 2259^{7} 2531^{2} 2680^{2} ◆ 2857^{3} 3266^{4} 3892^{3} 4259^{6} 5858^{6} 6215^{4} 7324^{2} 7433^{3} (7798) 8083^{9} 8402^{6}

Manchego *Hugo Palmer* 77
2 b c Lope De Vega(IRE) Gooseberry Pie (Green Desert (USA))
7468^{2}

Mancinello (IRE) *Brian Meehan* a57 62
3 b g Bushranger(IRE) Queen Cobra (IRE) (Indian Rocket)
2864^{16} 3126^{7}

Mandalay King (IRE) *Marjorie Fife* a3 47
11 b g King's Best(USA) Mahamuni (IRE) (Sadler's Wells (USA))
3549^{11} 4228^{9}

Mandamus (IRE) *Ms Sheila Lavery* 99
4 b g Lawman(FR) Stefanella (IRE) (Alzao (USA))
1018a^{13} 6389a^{8}

Mandarin (GER) *Marco Botti* a85 64
2 ch c Lope De Vega(IRE) Margarita (GER) (Lomitas)
5848^{6} (6924)

Mandarin Monarch (IRE) *J S Bolger* a72 84
3 ch g Manduro(GER) Abigail Pett (Medicean)
7517a^{4}

Mandatario *J S Bolger* a97 99
5 br h Manduro(GER) Crystal Mountain (USA) (Monashee Mountain (USA))
829a^{3} 3680a^{11} 7342a^{5} 7708a^{19}

Mandela (IRE) *Seamus Mullins*
3 ch g Peintre Celebre(USA) For Freedom (IRE) (King Of Kings (IRE))
3736^{12}

Maneen *D K Weld* 99
3 b g Paco Boy(IRE) Tereshkina (IRE) (Sadler's Wells (USA))
5685a^{6} 6495a^{7} 7558a^{10}

Mange All *Charlie Wallis* a91 92
5 b g Zamindar(USA) Blancmange (Montjeu (IRE))
503^{3} ◆ 886^{6}

Mango Chutney *John Davies* a60 68
3 b g Sleeping Indian Crimson Topaz (Hernando (FR))
1671^{3} 2271^{3} 2553^{3} 3224^{5} 3952^{8} (4600) 4972^{3} 5732^{2} (6569) 7334^{6}

Mango Tango (FR) *P Bary* a76 106
3 b f Siyouni(FR) Alexandrina (GER) (Monsun (GER))
2726a^{2} 3935a^{4} 5461a^{2} 6972a^{4}

Mangusto (FR) *M Delcher Sanchez* 105
3 b c Roderic O'Connor(IRE) Mantadive (FR) (Okawango (USA))
1374a^{5} 2232a^{7}

Manhattan Skyline (IRE) *J S Moore* a78 91
3 gr f Clodovil(IRE) Rainbow Above You (IRE) (Mujadil (USA))
123^{4} 315^{5}

Maniaco *A Fabre* 112
3 b c Galileo(IRE) Plumania (Anabaa (USA))
4332a^{6} ◆ (7456a)

Manipura *Derek Shaw* a64 58
3 gr f Sleeping Indian Ming Meng (IRE) (Intikhab (USA))
2785^{9} 3307^{7} 3581^{5} 3900^{2} 4472^{6} 4861^{4} (5636) 6051^{4} ◆ 6509^{7}

Manisa (FR) *Steffen Schwarz* 60
7 b m Okawango(USA) Miss Neoki (IRE) (Alhaarth (IRE))
5695a^{9}

Manjaam (IRE) *Ed Dunlop* a85 98
3 ch c Tamayuz Priory Rock (IRE) (Rock Of Gibraltar (IRE))
678^{2} (887) (1185) ◆ 2209^{9} (2638) ◆ 3428a^{2} (4131) 7117^{15}

Mankib *F Head* 78
2 ch c Tamayuz Natagora (FR) (Divine Light (JPN))
(7345a)

Man Look *Andrew Balding* a74 94
4 b g Nayef(USA) Charlecote (IRE) (Caerleon (USA))
2367^{2} (3121) (3636) ◆ 4095^{8} 5650^{2} 6709^{5}

Manners Please *Ralph Beckett* a72 73
2 b g Sixties Icon Humility (Polar Falcon (USA))
5325^{5} ◆ (5728) 6377^{7} 7016^{10} 8174^{2} ◆

Manny Owens (IRE) *Jonjo O'Neill* a67 72
4 bb g Manduro(GER) Arabian Coral (IRE) (Intikhab (USA))
4208^{9} 4920^{P} 6445^{5} 7077^{11} 7500^{7} 7775^{6}

Man Of Harlech *Andrew Balding* a107 98
5 b g Dansili Ffestiniog (IRE) (Efisio)
333^{4} 1069^{4} ◆ 1196^{5} 3273^{16}

Man Of La Mancha (IRE) *Ben Haslam* a37 44
3 b g Zoffany(IRE) Sarella Loren (USA) (Theatrical)
1449^{6} 2667^{6} 5578^{6} 6105^{6}

Man Of Music *Tony Carroll* a50 50
5 b g Piccolo Blue Goddess (IRE) (Blues Traveller (IRE))
2013^{10} 2542^{9}

Man Of Plenty *Sophie Leech*
7 ch g Manduro(GER) Credit-A-Plenty (Generous (IRE))
7980^{12}

Man Of Verve (IRE) *John Quinn* 78
2 b g Dandy Man(IRE) She's Our Rock (IRE) (Rock Of Gibraltar (IRE))
5884^{12} 6477^{3} (7355)

Manolito *Hughie Morrison* a76 65
4 b g High Chaparral(IRE) Break Time (Dansili)
6899^{11} 7968^{4} 8100^{7}

Manolito De Madrid (GER) *Andrew Balding* 73
2 b c Soldier Hollow Molly Maxima (GER) (Big Shuffle (USA))
3108^{5} ◆ 3799^{2} 4866^{6} 6159^{5}

Manorov *T G McCourt* a69 52
6 b g Sholokhov(IRE) Mandel Set (GER) (Second Set (IRE))
7801a^{9}

Manshood (IRE) *William Haggas* 73
3 b g Iffraaj Thawrah (IRE) (Green Desert (USA))
4401^{8} 5168^{3} 5480^{2} 6218^{2}

Manson *Dominic Ffrench Davis* a101 98
3 ch g Equiano(FR) Swain's Gold (USA) (Swain (IRE))
(2412) 3299^{19} 4149^{4} 4624^{13} 5616^{8} 6298^{4} 7779^{2} 8160^{4}

Manton Grange *George Baker* a56 78
3 b g Siyouni(FR) Emulate (Alhaarth (IRE))
4766^{2} ◆ 6442^{7}

Many A Tale *Ismail Mohammed* a76 78
2 br f Poet's Voice Rustam (Dansili)
(5242) 5794^{4} ◆ 6292^{3}

Many Dreams (IRE) *Mark Usher* a69 68
3 b f Kodiac Deeday Bay (IRE) (Brave Act)
3974^{6} 4563^{4} 6091^{5} 6649^{2} 7725^{5} 8064^{13}

Maoi Chinn Tire (IRE) *Jennie Candlish* a74 79
9 b g Mull Of Kintyre(USA) Primrose And Rose (Primo Dominie)
(1760) 2338^{8} 3221^{5} 4101^{2} 5061^{6}

Maori Bob (IRE) *Michael Bell* a59 44
2 b c Big Bad Bob(IRE) Tekhania (IRE) (Dalakhani (IRE))
7297^{7} 7865^{8} 8377^{6}

Ma Peek (USA) *Brian Meehan* 69
3 bb c Arch(USA) Downtown Drifter (USA) (Devil His Due (USA))
1739^{9} 2414^{7} 3160^{8} 7223^{7}

Maple Stirrup (IRE) *Patrick Holmes* a61 60
4 b m Duke Of Marmalade(IRE) Street Shaana (FR) (Darshaan)
71^{3} ◆ 3842^{3} 4645^{2} 5155^{7} 8309^{2}

Maply (FR) *Y Barberot* a67 64
4 b h Slickly(FR) Mapow (FR) (Kendor (FR))
4901a^{6} 5501a^{9}

Mappin Time (IRE) *Tim Easterby* a97 81
8 b g Orientate(USA) Different Story (USA) (Stravinsky (USA))
338^{4} 923^{6} 1650^{3} 2476^{13} 2803^{7} 3168^{12} 3875^{2} ◆ 4428^{7} 4896^{13} (5296) 5780^{9} 6324^{6} 7752^{4} 7990^{8} 8308^{5}

Maqam (IRE) *Richard Hannon* 64
3 br f Dansili Thai Haku (IRE) (Oasis Dream)
4367^{7} 4792^{6} 5623^{4} 8381^{11}

Maqueda (USA) *Amanda Perrett* a63 63
3 b f Rock Hard Ten(USA) Proud Fact (USA) (Known Fact (USA))
2395^{6}

Maquette (USA) *A Fabre* 101
3 gr f Tapit(USA) Announce (Selkirk (USA))
4184a^{6} 4904a^{6} 7862a^{2}

Maraakib (IRE) *David O'Meara* a70 94
4 b g Dark Angel(IRE) Mrs Cee (IRE) (Orpen (USA))
1195^{18} 1445^{8} 2017^{4} 2487^{6} 3113^{3} 3435^{8}

Maraweh (IRE) *Lucinda Russell* 61
6 b g Muhtathir Itqaan (USA) (Danzig (USA))
6097^{4}

Marbooh (IRE) *David O'Meara* a82 82
3 b g Dark Angel(IRE) Muluk (IRE) (Rainbow Quest (USA))
2578^{5} 2999^{2} (3609) 4055^{4} 4654^{6} 6055^{12} 7486^{5} 7813^{2} 7957^{10}

Marcano (IRE) *Rod Millman* 80
4 b g Arcano(IRE) Aquatint (Dansili)
1387^{8} 1735^{4} 2187^{4} (2635) (3514) 4055^{9} 4368^{2} 5075^{4} 5357^{5}

Marcel (IRE) *Peter Chapple-Hyam* 118
3 b c Lawman(FR) Mauresmo (IRE) (Marju (IRE))
1864^{13}

Marchantie (FR) *Y Gourraud* 70
2 b f Chichi Creasy(FR) Marola (FR) (Kendor (FR))
7346a^{6}

Marchia Rosay (FR) *P Monfort* a54 62
3 ch f King's Best(USA) Marshvite (FR) (Anabaa (USA))
3764a^{11} 4220a^{6}

Marching Time *Doug Watson* a81 80
10 b g Sadler's Wells(USA) Marching West (USA) (Gone West (USA))
229a^{5} 407a^{5}

Marcle (IRE) *Ed de Giles* a66 69
3 b g Kodiac Mark One (Mark Of Esteem (IRE))
1703^{4} 2749^{11} 3740^{2} 4269^{12} 4641^{2} 5104^{5} 5515^{2} 6021^{5} 6592^{4} 6872^{8} 7203^{12} 7601^{13}

Marcmywords (IRE) *Christine Dunnett*
3 ch g Thousand Words Last Shaambles (IRE) (Shaamit (IRE))
5163^{4}

Marcret (ITY) *James Unett* a78 85
9 b g Martino Alonso(IRE) Love Secret (USA) (Secreto (USA))
4917^{11} 5640^{8} 6331^{8} 7903^{6} 8077^{7} 8498^{12}

Marcus Antonius *Lucinda Russell* a56 55
9 b g Mark Of Esteem(IRE) Star Of The Course (USA) (Theatrical (IRE))
6438^{4} 7361^{5}

Marendinio (FR) *D De Waele* a42 48
11 b g Trempolino(USA) Marende (FR) (Panoramic)
3733a^{8}

Marengo *Bernard Llewellyn* a60 84
5 gr g Verglas(IRE) Cloudchaser (IRE) (Red Ransom (USA))
2463^{6} (3129) 3636^{4} 4095^{6} (4634)

Marenko *Richard Hannon* a103 105
3 b f Exceed And Excel(AUS) Safina (Pivotal)
(1206) (1476) ◆ 3339^{12} 4826^{9}

Marettimo (IRE) *Charles Hills* a64
2 b c Harbour Watch(IRE) Renowned (IRE) (Darshaan)
7962^{7}

Margaret's Mission (IRE) *Jim Goldie* a82 91
5 b m Shamardal(USA) Wimple (USA) (Kingmambo (USA))
2026^{3} 3390^{3} 4130^{5} 4644^{5} 6915^{9} 7472^{4}

Margherita *Roger Varian* a74
2 b f Mayson Phillipina (Medicean)
6414^{3} ◆

Margoesque *William Muir* a50
3 br f Pivotal Showcall (USA) (Kingmambo (USA))
384^{6} ◆ 925^{5}

Margot Rose *Alan Berry* a52 46
4 b m Kheleyf(USA) Sanjuna (Tiger Hill (IRE))
5^{6}

Margrets Gift *Tim Easterby* a53 80
5 ch m Major Cadeaux Its Another Gift (Primo Dominie)
1402^{6} 1872^{4} 2794^{7} 3056^{8}

Maria's Choice (IRE) *Jim Best* a65 67
7 b g Oratorio(IRE) Amathusia (Selkirk (USA))
616^{10} 712^{7} 1028^{7} 1135^{6} 1434^{8} 1751^{5} 1810^{7} (5672) 6659^{7} 7037^{2} 7614^{12} 7905^{2} 8240^{10}

Mariee *Mark Johnston* a83 84
3 b f Archipenko(USA) Maria Di Scozia (Selkirk (USA))
(15) (296) 495^{3} 1946^{2} 2179^{3} 2473^{4} 3102^{3} 3364^{2}

Marie Of Lyon *Richard Fahey* 88
2 b f Royal Applause Virginia Hall (Medicean)
(3167) 3663^{3} 4623^{5} 6260^{12}

Marilyn *Chris Wall* 72
2 ch f Sixties Icon Donatia (Shamardal (USA))
3819^{4} ◆ (4738)

Mariners Moon (IRE) *Patrick Holmes* a53 58
5 ch g Mount Nelson Dusty Moon (Dr Fong (USA))
347^{6} 609^{10} 4424^{8} 4498^{10} 5293^{8}

Maritime Law (IRE) *Garvan Donnelly* a27 47
4 br g Lawman(FR) Dapple Dawn (IRE) (Celtic Swing)
5228^{7}

Markaz (IRE) *Owen Burrows* a116 113
4 gr h Dark Angel(IRE) Folga (Atraf)
1637^{5} 2030^{3} (3655) 4733^{5} 5404^{4} 5943a^{2}

Market Choice (IRE) *Michael Dods* a58 79
3 b g Majestic Missile(IRE) Ron's Secret (Efisio)
2802^{7} 3420^{9} 3978^{3} 4547^{6} 5439^{9} (6133) 6717^{3} 7325^{11}

Market Rally (USA) *D Selvaratnam* a106
3 ch c Unbridled's Song(USA) Boodles (USA) (Mr Greeley (USA))
185a^{4} (539a) (839a)

Markhan (USA) *David Marnane* a70 91
3 b c Birdstone(USA) Royal Flush (USA) (Smart Strike (CAN))
5616^{9} 6355a^{12}

Mark Hopkins *David Elsworth* 93
4 b g Mount Nelson Halska (Unfuwain (USA))
1893^{10} 3351^{6}

Marking (USA) *Kiaran McLaughlin* a114
4 b h Bernardini(USA) Seventh Street (USA) (Street Cry (IRE))
537a^{U} (719a) 1101a^{4}

Marlonne (FR) *H-F Devin* 61
2 gr f Martaline Loulane (FR) (Commands (AUS))
5986a^{9}

Marmajuke Bay *Mark Usher* a87 83
3 b g Duke Of Marmalade(IRE) Shimoni (Mark Of Esteem (IRE))
1113^{6} 1718^{2} (2615) (3532) 6121^{3} 7215^{7} (7618)

Marmalad (IRE) *Shaun Lycett* a79 44
4 b g Duke Of Marmalade(IRE) Primissima (GER) (Second Set (IRE))
212^{6} 332^{7} 683^{4} 1502^{11} 2441^{9} 3078^{9} 4200^{9}

Marmalady (IRE) *Robert Cowell* a83 92
6 ch m Duke Of Marmalade(IRE) Grecian Glory (IRE) (Zafonic (USA))
(1857) 2875^{8} 3956^{11} 4585^{10}

Marmaris (FR) *C Lerner* a60 44
7 b m Divine Light(JPN) Margaret (TUR) (Octagonal (NZ))
2806a^{10}

Marmarus *David Nicholls* a56 64
5 b g Duke Of Marmalade(IRE) Polly Perkins (IRE) (Pivotal)
424^{8} 520^{9} 1595^{13} 2409^{14} 3040^{11} 4102^{10}

Marmelo *Hughie Morrison* a85 98
3 b c Duke Of Marmalade(IRE) Capriolla (In The Wings)
2208^{6} 2815^{2} ◆ (3845) ◆ 5448a^{2} 6971a^{3} 7456a^{2}

Marmooz *Michael Appleby* a39 41
4 ch m Piccolo Aegean Mystery (Dr Fong (USA))
216^{10} 525^{9} 596^{8}

Maroc *Paul Cole* a65 77
3 b g Rock Of Gibraltar(IRE) Zietory (Zieten (USA))
3235^{4} 3959^{3} 4530^{6} 7078^{3} 7214^{2} 7492a^{9} 8254^{6} 8364^{2}

Maroosh *A Schennach* a75 78
7 br g Kyllachy Madamoiselle Jones (Emperor Jones (USA))
2318a^{6}

Marquee Club *Jamie Osborne* a78 74
2 b c Sixties Icon Rose Cheval (USA) (Johannesburg (USA))
2902^{5} 3770^{3} 4022^{5} (4638) ◆ 5014^{3} 5543^{2} 6139^{5} (6829) 7217^{7} 7938^{2} 8033^{9} 8453^{4}

Marseille (IRE) *Julie Camacho* a64
2 b f Excelebration(IRE) Marlinka (Marju (IRE))
6925^{7} 7845^{2}

Marsha (IRE) *Sir Mark Prescott Bt* a100 114
3 b f Acclamation Marlinka (Marju (IRE))
2251^{2} 2923a^{5} (3392) ◆ (4166) 4824^{5} 6391a^{2} (6990a)

Marshal Dan Troop (IRE) *Robyn Brisland* a57 73
3 b c Lawman(FR) Corrozal (GER) (Cape Cross (IRE))
1571^{8} 2695^{9} 3079^{7} 4272^{4} 5122^{11} 8124^{7} 8241^{11}

Marshall Aid (IRE) *Mark Usher* a74 69
3 b g Lawman(FR) Dievotchkina (IRE) (Bluebird (USA))
2175^{7} 2815^{5} 3190^{5} 3991^{3} 5398^{4} 5724^{10} 6854^{2} 7625^{8} 7987^{2} 8238^{3} 8558^{6}

Marshall Jennings (IRE) *Mrs John Harrington* 99
4 b g Lawman(FR) Zuniga's Date (USA) (Diesis)
4811a^{2} 5564a^{2}

Marshgate Lane (USA) *Neil Mulholland* a89 82
7 b g Medaglia d'Oro(USA) Louvain (IRE) (Sinndar (IRE))
(1404) 1722^{3} (2150) (2444) 8231^{9}

Marsh Hawk *Richard Hannon* 102
4 b m Invincible Spirit(IRE) Asaawir (Royal Applause)
1197^{10} 1453^{4} 2042^{2} 2474^{4} 4916^{7} 6161^{4} 7758a^{10}

Marsh Pride *K R Burke* a78 92
4 b m Stimulation(IRE) Peneia (USA) (Nureyev (USA))
1521^{7} 2121^{9} 5831^{4} (6342) 6811^{3} 7159^{2} 7823^{13}

Martha McCandles *Alan King* a66 76
5 b m Tobougg(IRE) Tabulate (Dansili)
3094^{6} 3578^{2} 4347^{5} 5245^{5}

Martini Gin (IRE) *J-P Perruchot* a71 67
2 b f Dragon Pulse(IRE) Lady Gin (USA) (Saint Ballado (CAN))
5755a^{5}

Martyna *John Spearing* 4
3 b f Paco Boy(IRE) Pintle (Pivotal)
2312^{12} 7218^{10}

Marwa *Ed Dunlop* a61 26
2 b f Exceed And Excel(AUS) La Cucina (IRE) (Last Tycoon)
4064^{9} 8362^{5}

Mary Ann Bugg (IRE) *Phil McEntee* a58 47
4 b m Bushranger(IRE) Shobobb (Shamardal (USA))
320^{8}

Mary Anne Evans *John Gosden* 73
2 b f Oasis Dream Gertrude Bell (Sinndar (IRE))
4147^{10} 5266^{7} (6077)

Mary Arden (FR) *P Bary* a53
2 bb f Fast Company(IRE) Mirandola's Dream (FR) (Dalakhani (IRE))
5460a^{6}

Mary Beale (IRE) *Mark Johnston* a65 64
3 ch f Shamardal(USA) What A Picture (FR) (Peintre Celebre (USA))
1063^{7} 1235^{6} 4477^{3} 6432^{5}

Mary Brady *David O'Meara* a52 62
2 b f Camacho Dot Hill (Refuse To Bend (IRE))
2739[6] 3223[3] 4227[8] 5257[8] 7143[6]

Mary E *Brian Ellison* 43
3 b f Monsieur Bond(IRE) Lily Lenor (IRE) (Bertolini (USA))
1490[3] 1814[8] 2118[8]

Marylebone *Ed Walker* a81 64
3 b g Shamardal(USA) Mary Boleyn (IRE) (King's Best (USA))
1992[10]

Mary Le Bow *Victor Dartnall* a68 47
5 b m Sir Percy Bermondsey Girl (Bertolini (USA))
101[6] 295[6] (676) 2367[7] 2783[6] 3476[4] 7755[2] 8124[3]

Marypop (FR) *Michael Stidham* 106
4 ch m Layman(USA) Sampaguita (FR) (Muhtathir)
(1232a) (1822a) 5430a[11]

Mary Sun (FR) *Henk Grewe* 93
3 b f Soldier Hollow Mary James (Ransom O'War (USA))
2115a[5] 3207a[5]

Marzouq (USA) *Jeremy Noseda* a78
2 bb c Spring At Last(USA) Smart 'n Special (USA) (Smart Strike (CAN))
6087[2] (6369)

Masamah (IRE) *Ian Williams* a50 83
10 gr g Exceed And Excel(AUS) Bethesda (Distant Relative)
1408[9] 1968[13] 3188[12] 3637[8] 4632[10] 5867[2] 6080[2] 6324[4] 6766[8] 8463[10]

Masarzain (IRE) *James Given* a81 80
3 br g Kodiac Cache Creek (IRE) (Marju (IRE))
4401[4] (6567) 7066[5] 8456[8]

Mashaaref *M Al Mheiri* a106 87
8 b g Cape Cross(IRE) Etizaaz (USA) (Diesis)
95a[13]

Mashadie Boy *David Simcock* a63 68
2 b c Rip Van Winkle(IRE) Happy Holly (IRE) (Holy Roman Emperor (IRE))
4975[4] 5952[3]

Masham Star (IRE) *Mark Johnston* a100 93
2 b c Lawman(FR) Croisiere (USA) (Capote (USA))
2193[2] ◆ 2489[3] (2956) 3382[12] 4669[6] 5560[4] 6180a[4] 7042[2] (7541) 7909[2] (8132) 8564a[10]

Mashhad (FR) *Mlle Y Vollmer* 58
2 b f Matrix(GER) Manapouri (GER) (Pentire)
7927a[3]

Masina City (FR) *H-A Pantall* a69 64
2 b f Soul City(IRE) Toamasina (FR) (Marju (IRE))
1284a[5]

Masked Bandit *Simon Dow*
3 b g Dick Turpin(IRE) Plaisterer (Best Of The Bests (IRE))
7219[10]

Mask Of Time (IRE) *A Fabre* a79 82
2 b c Holy Roman Emperor(IRE) Mission Secrete (IRE) (Galileo (IRE))
7971a[4]

Maskoon *Philip Kirby* a77 74
5 ch g Aqlaam Tamazug (Machiavellian (USA))
7517a[12] 7886[9] 8141[8] 8387[6]

Masochistic (USA) *Ronald W Ellis* a121
6 b g Sought After(USA) Trotinette (USA) (Unusual Heat (USA))
7832a[DSQ]

Masonic (IRE) *Robyn Brisland* a71 71
2 b g Intense Focus(USA) Green Tambourine (Green Desert (USA))
4738[2] 5549[9] 6264[6] 6898[2] 6950[14] 7304[2]

Masquerade Bling (IRE) *Simon Hodgson* a59 60
2 b f Approve(IRE) Mataji (IRE) (Desert Prince (IRE))
1741[2] 2535[11] 2847[7] 3485[6] 6829[8] 6950[25] 7423[4] 7734[4] 7941[8]

Masqueraded (USA) *Gay Kelleway* a71 45
3 ch g Drosselmeyer(USA) Maudie May (USA) (Gilded Time (USA))
182[3] 522[4] 613[2] 2506[13] 2733[6] 2825[3] 4204[6] 4518[3] (5087) 5775[4] 7606[7] 7931[6] 8190[4]

Massaat (IRE) *Owen Burrows* 117
3 b c Teofilo(IRE) Madany (IRE) (Acclamation)
1864[2] 2896[9] 5329[7]

Mass Rally (IRE) *Michael Dods* a70 100
9 b g Kheleyf(USA) Reunion (IRE) (Be My Guest (USA))
1218[10] 1848[9] 2613[2] 3265[3] 3646[15] 3945[8] 4608[4] 5182[10] 6714[6] 7094[8]

Master Archer (IRE) *James Fanshawe* a68
2 gr g Mastercraftsman(IRE) Kinigi (IRE) (Verglas (IRE))
7976[9] 8245[4]

Master Billie (IRE) *William Muir* a51 52
2 ro g Mastercraftsman(IRE) Billie Jean (Bertolini (USA))
5792[7] 6044[7] 7622[10]

Masterblaster (FR) *C Lotoux* a69
4 ch g Sunday Break(JPN) Monatora (FR) (Hector Protector (USA))
4901a[3]

Master Blueyes (IRE) *Alan King* a69 93
3 gr g Mastercraftsman(IRE) Miss Blueyes (IRE) (Dushyantor (USA))
(2224) (2687) 3532[3] 4137[3] 4863[6] 5653[4] 7123[2]

Master Bond *John C McConnell* a84 80
7 b g Misu Bond(IRE) Bond Royale (Piccolo)
1848[11] 2261[6] 2665[7] 3056[7] 3875[12] 4495[2] (5969) 6093[4] 6537[19] 7434[4] 8197a[12]

Master Burbidge *Neil Mulholland* a64
5 b g Pasternak Silver Sequel (Silver Patriarch (IRE))
62[3] 354[3] 634[2] (695) 8164[2]

Master Carpenter (IRE) *Rod Millman* 114
5 ch h Mastercraftsman(IRE) Fringe (In The Wings)
1198[4] 1604[4] 1973[3] 2464[4] 2894[6] 4392[6] 4688[3] 5329[5] 6364[4] 6884[6]

Master Choice (IRE) *Paul Green*
4 b g Mastercraftsman(IRE) No Quest (IRE) (Rainbow Quest (USA))
5513[12]

Master Dancer *Tim Vaughan* a56 68
5 gr g Mastercraftsman(IRE) Isabella Glyn (IRE) (Sadler's Wells (USA))
62[9] 3737[7] (4995) (6256)

Master Degree (IRE) *Debbie Mountain* a45 15
2 b c Masterofthehorse(IRE) Rioja Reserva (Haafhd)
5834[6] 7003[9] 7366[7] 8564a[13]

Masterfilly (IRE) *Ed Walker* a51 49
2 gr f Mastercraftsman(IRE) Waldena (USA) (Storm Cat (USA))
2467[11] 4357[5] 5036[7] 8284[6]

Masterful Act (USA) *David O'Meara* a83 50
9 ch g Pleasantly Perfect(USA) Catnip (USA) (Flying Paster (USA))
6[2]

Masterful Man (IRE) *K R Burke* a40
3 gr g Mastercraftsman(IRE) Lamanka Lass (USA) (Woodman (USA))
600[6]

Master Gunner (USA) *Sir Michael Stoute* a87 83
3 b c War Front(USA) Queen Of The Night (Sadler's Wells (USA))
2175[6] 3066[6] 5086[2] 5308[2] (6138) 6877[9]

Master Kochanwong (AUS) *D J Hall* a102 95
6 br g Commands(AUS) Elmira (AUS) (Timber Country (USA))
1105a[9]

Mastermind (SAF) *M F De Kock* 108
4 b g Var(USA) Model I.Q. (SAF) (Jallad (USA))
282a[3] 623a[3] 810a[8]

Master Mirasol (IRE) *Kevin Ryan* 77
3 b g Arcano(IRE) Hidden Meaning (Cadeaux Genereux)
1448[2] 2049[12] 3924[10] 5224[9]

Masterofdiscovery *Clive Cox* 73
2 b c Henrythenavigator(USA) Wonderful Desert (Green Desert (USA))
4125[5] 4856[11] 5600[13] (6313) 6875[6]

Master Of Finance (IRE) *Mark Johnston* a77 102
5 ch g Mastercraftsman(IRE) Cheal Rose (IRE) (Dr Devious (IRE))
1089[11] (1245) 1493[10] 1972[9] 2157[10] 2484[2] 2866[10] 3666[6]

Master Of Heaven *Jim Boyle* a69 59
3 b g Makfi Maid In Heaven (IRE) (Clodovil (IRE))
1235[3] 2545[7] 2749[13] 3236[7] 6046[5] 6513[7] 6890[9] 7309[6] 7464[10] 7767[4] 8281[5] (8492)

Master Of Irony (IRE) *Ralph Beckett* a74 96
4 b g Makfi Mother Of Pearl (IRE) (Sadler's Wells (USA))
1195[14] 1643[6] (2752) 3109[10] 5651[7] 6379[4] 7015[5]

Master Of Song *Roy Bowring* a62 56
9 ch g Ballet Master(USA) Ocean Song (Savahra Sound)
(247) 346[6] 3072[5] 3825[5] 5319[3] 6212[4] 7642[10] 7888[8] 8306[13] 8471[5] 8567[5]

Masterpaver *Richard Fahey* a93 88
5 gr g Mastercraftsman(IRE) Most-Saucy (Most Welcome)
99[6] 353[5] 499[7] 747[5] 861[3] 975[6] 1802[3] (2436) (2651) 3162[2] ◆ 3520[3] ◆ 4077[4] 4583[2] 5879[4] 6715[5] 7967[7] 8210[4] 8584[2]

Master Pekan *Roy Brotherton* a46 41
3 b g Piccolo Lady Pekan (Sri Pekan (USA))
419[5] 763[5] 4085[8] 4590[5] 5570 [5] 6317[8]

Master Singer (USA) *John Gosden* 73
2 br c Giant's Causeway(USA) Ring Of Music (Sadler's Wells (USA))
7769[4] ◆

Masterson (IRE) *Mick Channon* a68 70
3 gr g Lawman(FR) Indian Dumaani (Indian Ridge)
2126[4] 2700[5] 3141[2] 3256[3] 4500[4] 4764[6] 5101[5] 5420[4] (5777) (6102) 6185[2] 6325[2] 6767[3] 7223[4]

Master Speaker (IRE) *Martin Hassett* a98 102
6 b g Danehill Dancer(IRE) First Breeze (USA) (Woodman (USA))
1015a[6] 4415a[2] 6382a[6] 6819a[9] 6984a[2] 7191a[2] 7520a[10] 7706a[7]

Master's Spirit (IRE) *J Reynier* a95 106
5 gr h Mastercraftsman(IRE) Lavayssiere (FR) (Sicyos (USA))
7312a[2] 8336a[6]

Master The World (IRE) *David Elsworth* a109 114
5 gr g Mastercraftsman(IRE) Zadalla (Zaha (CAN))
1861[5] 2191[8] 4823[2] 5329[2] 5647[9] 6786[30] 7354[12] 7700[3] 7934[3] 8160[2]

Master Zephyr *Darren Weir* a54 89
4 b g Shirocco(GER) Missy Dancer (Shareef Dancer (USA))
7552a[8]

Matador De Toros (SAF) *M Al Mheiri* a57 69
7 b g Toreador(IRE) Western Smoke (SAF) (Among Men (USA))
8a[6]

Matara (FR) *H-A Pantall* a83 84
3 bb f Rip Van Winkle(IRE) My Girl Charlie (IRE) (Kodiac)
3120a[5] 5695a[11]

Matauri (IRE) *Niels Petersen* 95
5 b g Soldier Of Fortune(IRE) Moonrise (GER) (Grand Lodge (USA))
4329a[7] 5187a[6]

Matauri Jewel (IRE) *M Delzangles* 89
3 b f Authorized(IRE) Moonrise (GER) (Grand Lodge (USA))
8024a[11]

Match My Fire (IRE) *Ralph Beckett* 71
3 ch g Makfi High Lite (Observatory (USA))
1276[4] 6665[7] 7214[3] 7500[5]

Matchwinner (GER) *A Kleinkorres* 98
5 ch h Sternkoenig(IRE) Mahamuni (IRE) (Sadler's Wells (USA))
6612a[5] 7843a[4]

Material *Mme C Head-Maarek* a59 54
3 b c Cacique(IRE) Talkative (Oasis Dream)
1311a[9]

Materialist *Roger Varian* 78
2 b c Dansili Mundana (IRE) (King's Best (USA))
7317[2]

Materialistic *Luca Cumani* 99
3 b f Oasis Dream Pongee (Barathea (IRE))
(5487) 6488[4] 7119[7] 7823[5]

Mate Story (IRE) *D Smaga* 109
2 b c Makfi Tierra Luna (IRE) (Giant's Causeway (USA))
6177a[2] (7086a) 7721a[6]

Mateur (FR) *Meret Kaderli* a80 80
7 b g Echo Of Light Joy Of Life (FR) (Exit To Nowhere (USA))
(586a)

Matey (FR) *Mme Pia Brandt* a95 98
3 b c Slickly(FR) Madeleine's Blush (USA) (Rahy (USA))
5946a[16]

Mathison (FR) *D De Waele* a66 71
3 b f Elusive City(USA) Pierre Bleue (FR) (Poliglote)
128a[6]

Mathix (FR) *William Haggas* 75
2 b c Kendargent(FR) Matwan (FR) (Indian Rocket)
6751[7] 7503[2]

Maths Prize *Roger Charlton* 89
2 b g Royal Applause Hypoteneuse (IRE) (Sadler's Wells (USA))
3859[2] ◆ (4479) ◆ (5518) 6330[3]

Matidia *Ralph Beckett* a67 74
3 ch f Manduro(GER) Caesarea (GER) (Generous (IRE))
1410[2] 3318[3] (3722)

Matilda Gleam *Lisa Williamson* a56 14
3 b f Arabian Gleam Matilda Peace (Namaqualand (USA))
104[6] 783[6] 883[5] 1292[3] 1554[4] 7362[10]

Matilda's Law *Chris Wall* a67 65
3 b f Aussie Rules(USA) Oatey (Master Willie)
2152[3] ◆ 3724[8] 5525[5] 6241[9]

Matorico (IRE) *Jonjo O'Neill* a47 88
5 gr g Mastercraftsman(IRE) Hashbrown (GER) (Big Shuffle (USA))
2194[6] ◆ 2472[4]

Matraash (USA) *Daniel Mark Loughnane* a69 68
10 b h Elusive Quality(USA) Min Alhawa (USA) (Riverman (USA))
38[5] 316[6] 464[2] 676[12] (815) 1058[6]

Matthioli (FR) *Michael Attwater* a59 56
2 b c Sepoy(AUS) Ossun (FR) (Anabaa (USA))
4775[9] 5394[2] 6741[6] 7482[11]

Mattmu *Tim Easterby* 115
4 b h Indesatchel(IRE) Katie Boo (IRE) (Namid)
1439[3] 2159[8] 3385[9]

Maua (IRE) *Waldemar Hickst* 27
3 b f Rock Of Gibraltar(IRE) Macara (GER) (Acatenango (GER))
4220a[11]

Maudlin Magdalen (IRE) *Donal Kinsella* a87 87
6 b m Dylan Thomas(IRE) Carolines Secret (Inchinor)
4070a[9] 4811a[14] (6389a) 6604a[12]

Maulesden May (IRE) *Keith Dalgleish* a74 72
3 b f Dark Angel(IRE) Jemima's Art (Fantastic Light (USA))
(1816) 2652[5] 3285[6] 6541[6] 7435[4] 7853[2] 7993[10] 8480[5]

Maureb (IRE) *Tony Coyle* a74 79
4 br m Excellent Art Almost Blue (USA) (Mr Greeley (USA))
1158[3] 1334[3] 1663[4] 2223[6] 2491[16] 3132[8] (3521) 4452[3] 4689[2] 5034[6] 5190[5] 5867[8] 6908[10]

Maurice (JPN) *Noriyuki Hori* 124
5 b h Screen Hero(JPN) Mejiro Frances (JPN) (Carnegie (IRE))
(1912a) (8333a)

Maverick Wave (USA) *John Gosden* a113 113
5 ch h Elusive Quality(USA) Misty Ocean (USA) (Stormy Atlantic (USA))
748[2] 871[4] 1069[5] 3383[12] 5962[2] 7353[10] 7934[10]

Maverik *Ali Stronge* a70 62
8 ch g Iceman Nouvelle Lune (Fantastic Light (USA))
260[8] 414[7] 616[7] 1501[4] 1699[5] 2369[5] 2849[3] 5929[3] 6405[3] 6857[8] (7300) 7515[3] 7754[4]

Mawaany (IRE) *Sir Michael Stoute* a64 79
3 gr g Teofilo(IRE) Middle Persia (Dalakhani (IRE))
1499[2] 1739[2] 2638[6]

Mawhub *S Seemar* a102 89
7 b g Singspiel(IRE) Native Blue (Seeking The Gold (USA))
94a[5] 309a[5]

Mawqed (IRE) *Sir Michael Stoute* a59
2 b f Invincible Spirit(IRE) Mumayeza (Indian Ridge)
6624[7]

Max Beddow (IRE) *Geoffrey Deacon* a55
3 b g Tagula(IRE) Copper Harbour (IRE) (Foxhound (USA))
544[6]

Max Dynamite (FR) *W P Mullins* a77 118
6 b g Great Journey(JPN) Mascara (GER) (Monsun (GER))
2625[3] 3298[10]

Maximian (IRE) *Charlie Appleby* a87 86
3 ch c Shamardal(USA) Via Milano (FR) (Singspiel (IRE))
1337[2] ◆ (1849) 2695[4] (Dead)

Maximum Aurelius (FR) *F-H Graffard* 108
3 b c Showcasing Feld Marechale (FR) (Deputy Minister (CAN))
3543a[3] 5948a[4] 6823a[4] 7723a[5] 8117a[3]

Max Zorin (IRE) *Andrew Balding* 95
2 b g Cape Cross(IRE) My (King's Best (USA))
4775[2] 5615[10] (6274) 6801[3]

Mayasa (IRE) *James Tate* a83
3 ch f Iffraaj Lanzana (IRE) (Kalanisi (IRE))
85[2] 2900[3] (3991) 5526[4] 7512[11]

Maybelater *Jonathan Portman* a95 103
4 b m Mount Nelson Muscovado (USA) (Mr Greeley (USA))
1088[3] 5307[3] 6488[8]

May Be Some Time *Stuart Kittow* a63 73
8 ch g Iceman Let Alone (Warning)
1824[F]

Maydale *Colin Teague*
3 ch f Monsieur Bond(IRE) Jaldarshaan (IRE) (Fath (USA))
6744[10]

Mayfair Lady *Richard Fahey* 111
3 b f Holy Roman Emperor(IRE) Lady Luachmhar (IRE) (Galileo (IRE))
(3116) 4114[6] 5436[6] 5880[7] 6792[4] 7156[11]

Mayfield Boy *Antony Brittain* a42 63
5 b g Authorized(IRE) Big Pink (IRE) (Bigstone (IRE))
893[10] 5323[5] ◆ 7514[10] 7642[14]

Mayfield Girl (IRE) *Antony Brittain* a48 44
6 br m One Cool Cat(USA) Rose Of Mooncoin (IRE) (Brief Truce (USA))
2334[5]

Mayflair *Jonathan Portman* a58
2 b f Zamindar(USA) Madhaaq (IRE) (Medicean)
8464[7]

Mayla (USA) *W Bret Calhoun* a98 91
4 b m Sharp Humor(USA) Fifteen Moons (USA) (Malibu Moon (USA))
5185a[9]

Mayleaf Shine (IRE) *Joseph G Murphy* 91
2 b f Mayson Let Me Shine (USA) (Dixie Union (USA))
5661a[6] 5940a[9]

Mayleen (IRE) *Ann Duffield* 66
2 br f Big Bad Bob(IRE) Miss Megs (IRE) (Croco Rouge (IRE))
3248[3] 6716[3] 7003[6]

May Mist *Trevor Wall* a64
4 b m Nayef(USA) Midnight Mist (IRE) (Green Desert (USA))
8075[6] 8195[5] 8342[2]

Maymyo (IRE) *Sylvester Kirk* a74 67
5 b g Invincible Spirit(IRE) Lady Windermere (IRE) (Lake Coniston (IRE))
561[8] 1545[8] 4910[9] 5797[8] 6653[4] 7069[4] 7612[5]

May Rose (IRE) *Charles Hills* a81 83
3 b f Lawman(FR) Rose De France (IRE) (Diktat)
2004[4] 2606[3] 4763[2] (5238) (5523) 6195[5] 6926[9]

May's Boy *James Moffatt* a16 52
8 gr g Proclamation(IRE) Sweet Portia (IRE) (Pennekamp (USA))
2436[6] 3564[13]

Maysonri *Mark Hoad* a44 51
2 b g Mayson Roshina (IRE) (Chevalier (IRE))
4016[9] 5166[7] 6288[7] 7244[5] 7734[8]

Mazaaher *Owen Burrows* a38 37
6 b g Elnadim(USA) Elutrah (Darshaan)
3030[11]

Mazaaji (FR) *George Peckham* a68
2 b g Motivator Zalia (FR) (Oasis Dream)
7976[10] 8119[4] 8423[3]

Mazalto (IRE) *Pat Phelan* a75 77
3 b f Teofilo(IRE) Mazaaya (USA) (Cozzene (USA))
2767[4] ◆ 3781[3] 4597[2] 5405[8] 6242[5] 6886[4]

Mazaz (IRE) *John Gosden* a89 74
3 b c Galileo(IRE) Ice Mint (USA) (Awesome Again (CAN))
1406[3] 1739[4] 2816[2] (7052)

Mazeed (USA) *M F De Kock* a74
2 ch c Street Cry(IRE) Speed Succeeds (USA) (Gone West (USA))
8391a[3] 8576a[2]

Mazovian (USA) *Neil Mulholland* a60 51
8 b g E Dubai(USA) Polish Style (USA) (Danzig (USA))
577[2]

Mazyoun *Hugo Palmer* a85 91
2 br g Mayson Hypnotize (Machiavellian (USA))
4736[6] 5876[2] 6260[2] 6954[3] (7599)

Mazzini *James Fanshawe* a97 87
3 ch g Exceed And Excel(AUS) Firenze (Efisio)
1849[3] 2298[8] 3036[3] 4835[2] (5968) 6492[4] 6916[3] (7737)

McCarthy Mor (IRE) *Mandy Rowland* a43 52
5 b g Bushranger(IRE) Alexander Anapolis (IRE) (Spectrum (IRE))
7260[6] 7910[8] 8146[13]

McCools Gold *Eve Johnson Houghton* a61 67
3 b g Yeats(IRE) Gold Reef (Double Trigger (IRE))
4265[8] 4955[5] 5548[4] 6127[5] 6367[5] (7270)

McDelta *Ian Williams* a64 67
6 b g Delta Dancer Mcnairobi (Josr Algarhoud (IRE))
347[4] ◆ 609[2] 769[10] 1735[9] (3214) 5753[3] 6028[7] 6737[13] 7336[5] 7613[13]

Mc Diamond (IRE) *Michael Mullineaux* a61 71
4 b g Windsor Knot(IRE) Vinesgrove (IRE) (Danetime (IRE))
1913[8] 2845[4] 4278[7]

Mcelligott (IRE) *Richard Price* 10
3 b g Dark Angel(IRE) Nina Blini (Bertolini (USA))
2999[13]

Mcguigan (IRE) *J S Bolger* a80 85
4 ch g Teofilo(IRE) Scribonia (IRE) (Danehill (USA))
(5096a) 7523a[8]

McKinley *W P Mullins* a66 83
6 b g Kheleyf(USA) Priera Menta (IRE) (Montjeu (IRE))
3680a[6]

Mclovin Riverdance *T G McCourt* a37 47
4 b g Lawman(FR) Electric Dream (Royal Applause)
869[5]

Mc Queen (FR) *Yasmin Almenrader* a72 99
4 gr h Silver Frost(IRE) Misdirect (Darshaan)
2633a[5] 3992a[3] 5943a[9] 7027a[7] 7525a[12]

Mcvicar *John Davies* a59 66
7 b g Tobougg(IRE) Aries (GER) (Big Shuffle (USA))
251[12] 368[3] 601[4] 1048[2] (1675) 2093[5] 2836[6] 5481[10] 5971[6] 6103[4]

Meadow Creek *Doug Watson* a98 110
5 b h Dansili Gentle On My Mind (IRE) (Sadler's Wells (USA))
455a[5] ◆ 625a[3] 811a[4] 1102a[5]

Meadow Cross (IRE) *Denis Gerard Hogan* a70 54
4 b m Cape Cross(IRE) Hovering (IRE) (In The Wings)
5900a[12]

Meadow View Girl *David Flood* 17
2 b f Sir Percy Bruma (IRE) (Footstepsinthesand)
5250[6] 5853[6]

Meadow View Madam *David Flood* a18
2 ch f Piccolo Crochet (IRE) (Mark Of Esteem (IRE))
5243[5]

Meadra (FR) *E Caroux* a61 61
3 gr f Gris De Gris(IRE) Ge Decoiffe (FR) (The Mask (FR))
1357a[7]

Meadway *Bryan Smart* a99 100
5 b g Captain Gerrard(IRE) Tibesti (Machiavellian (USA))
17[6] 2188[16] (3150) *3606[11]* 5555[20] 7537[21] *8308[9]*

Meandmyshadow *Alan Brown* a81 79
8 ch m Tobougg(IRE) Queen Jean (Pivotal)
1625[15] 2050[8] 2531[7] 2794[2] 3168[14] 3553[4] 4034[3] 4608[5] 5379[3] 6013[4] 6435[11] *6908[7] 7324[3] (7663) 7798[4] 7959[12]*

Meandre (FR) *A Savujev* a92 110
8 gr h Slickly(FR) Penne (FR) (Sevres Rose (IRE))
4333a[4] 6175a[6] 6973a[8]

Meccabah (FR) *Andrew Balding* 35
2 gr f Makfi Mintly Fresh (USA) (Rubiano (USA))
7695[11]

Mecca's Angel (IRE) *Michael Dods* a97 125
5 gr m Dark Angel(IRE) Folga (Atraf)
2475[2] 3244[16] (4413a) (5614) 6990a[3] 7350[12]

Mecca's Missus (IRE) *Michael Wigham* 72
3 b f Lilbourne Lad(IRE) Silk Dress (IRE) (Gulch (USA))
1126[6] 2049[8] 2306[3] 2801[4] 3285[8] 4316[2] 4600[4] 4760[2] (5197) 5515[12] 6631[4] 7572[9]

Medahim (IRE) *Richard Hannon* a87
2 b c Kodiac Novel Fun (IRE) (Noverre (USA))
(8243) ◆

Medaillon (FR) *Mario Hofer* a48 48
5 b g Medicean Raisonnable (Common Grounds)
5281a[15]

Medalla De Oro *Peter Chapple-Hyam* a68 62
2 b c Teofilo(IRE) Nyarhini (Fantastic Light (USA))
7468[9] *7940[4] 8486[6]*

Medal Of Valour (JPN) *Roy Brotherton* a21 31
8 b g Medaglia d'Oro(USA) Tres Tres Joli (USA) (Gone West (USA))
149[8] 383[8]

Medburn Cutler *Paul Henderson* a62 82
6 ch g Zafeen(FR) Tiegs (IRE) (Desert Prince (IRE))
1854[5] 2392[6] (3498) (3746) 4795[5] 6267[3] 6445[3] 6804[7] 7507[2]

Medburn Dream *Paul Henderson* a58 90
3 b c Showcasing Tiegs (IRE) (Desert Prince (IRE))
(1388) (1571) (1828) 2892[9] 3465[5] 5601[9] (5956) 6298[9] 6803[9] 7213[7] 7505[10]

Meddlesome *Sir Mark Prescott Bt* a44 61
3 b g Medicean Meddle (Diktat)
7037[3] 7249[5]

Mediate *Richard Rowe* a49 74
5 ch g New Approach(IRE) Miss Prim (Case Law)
88[7] 438[8]

Mediation *Roger Varian* a82 80
4 b m Azamour(IRE) Macleya (GER) (Winged Love (IRE))
1933[6] *3278[5]* 3846[3]

Medicean Ballet (IRE) *Henry Candy* a37 75
2 b f Medicean Ballet Dancer (IRE) (Refuse To Bend (IRE))
6414[9] 6880[6] (7466)

Medicean Dream (IRE) *Luca Cumani* a28 53
2 br g Medicean Oasis Fire (IRE) (Oasis Dream)
7225[5] 7769[13] *7882[12]*

Medicean El Diablo *Jimmy Fox* a74 53
3 b g Medicean Al Joudha (FR) (Green Desert (USA))
2002[8] 3036[12] 5896[7] *(8156) (8490)* ◆

Medicean Man *Jeremy Gask* a113 110
10 ch g Medicean Kalindi (Efisio)
626a[7] 841a[6] 3244[6] 4584[6] 5143[5] 5555[6] 6943[2] *7520a[3] 7932[5]*

Medicean Queen (IRE) *Phil McEntee* a58 39
5 b m Medicean Qui Moi (CAN) (Swain (IRE))
487[2] 4978[8] 5737[5] 6901[5] 7515[5] 7609[6] 7905[3] 8554[4]

Medici Banchiere *K R Burke* 99
2 ch c Medicean Fairy Shoes (Kyllachy)
2162[2] (2530) 4060[5] 5654[6] 6954[12]

Mediciman *Henry Candy* 78
3 b g Medicean Quintrell (Royal Applause)
2412[7] 4104[5] 4654[4] 5849[5] 6877[8] 7229[6]

Medici Moon *Scott Dixon* a46
2 ch c Medicean Cockney Fire (Cockney Rebel (IRE))
7658[7] 8237[5]

Medicine Hat *Marjorie Fife* a77 71
5 b g Multiplex Blushing Heart (Observatory (USA))
(8211) 8565[4]

Medicine Jack *G M Lyons* 107
2 ch c Equiano(FR) Agony Aunt (Formidable I (USA))
2240[6] (3678a) 5212a[3] 6388a[3] 6785[7]

Medieval (IRE) *Paul Cole* 101
2 b c Kodiac Quickstyx (Night Shift (USA))
(2203) 3243[4] 4732[8] 5450a[2] (6801) 7491a[5]

Medieval Bishop (IRE) *Tony Forbes* a65 66
7 b g Bachelor Duke(USA) On The Backfoot (IRE) (Bob Back (USA))
199[3] 498[2] 592[8] 946[9] 1170[8] 1649[2] 2502[5] 3139[3] 4045[4]

Medina Sidonia (IRE) *Tim Easterby* 78
4 b g Montjeu(IRE) Valdara (Darshaan)
1586[4] 1852[6] 2663[2] 2911[5] 3118[5] 4237[6] 4634[2] 4935[2] 5321[3] 5642[5] 6163[2] (6519) 7006[7] 7670[9]

Meergorl (GER) *R Dzubasz* 100
3 ch f Adlerflug(GER) Mouette (GER) (Tertullian (USA))
(3207a) 5220a[10]

Meetings Man (IRE) *Ali Stronge* a69 78
9 gr g Footstepsinthesand Missella (IRE) (Danehill (USA))
4057[6] 5035[3] *6090[6]* 6892[5]

Megalala (IRE) *John Bridger* a58 53
15 b g Petardia Avionne (Derrylin)
1547[5] 1747[6] 2901[5] *(3401)* 3737[6] *4267[2] 4882[4] 5399[3]* 5895[4] 6406[4] 6891[4] *7464[11]*

Megan Lily (IRE) *Richard Fahey* a73 91
2 b f Dragon Pulse(IRE) Nebraas (Green Desert (USA))
2489[2] 2718a[11] 3633[10] 4586[4] *(5188)* 5656[6] 6763[2] 7170a[3] 7655a[4] 7972a[5]

Megara *Sir Mark Prescott Bt* a79 52
4 ch g Medicean Alicante (Pivotal)
61[2] ◆ *(195) 358[2] (488) 583[3] 5970[5] 6740[3]* 7183[11]

Mehdi (IRE) *Richard Fahey* a76 76
7 b g Holy Roman Emperor(IRE) College Fund Girl (IRE) (Kahyasi)
7591[4] *7798[6] 8150[3]*

Mehmas (IRE) *Richard Hannon* 114
2 b c Acclamation Lucina (Machiavellian (USA))
(1976) ◆ (2240) ◆ 2624[2] 3243[2] (4060) (4798) 6386a[2] 6785[3]

Mehronissa *Ed Vaughan* a62 111
4 ch m Iffraaj Miss University (USA) (Beau Genius (CAN))
(2476) 3116[3] 3616[4] (5124) (5436) 6120[4] 6941[2] ◆ 7829a[9]

Mekhtaal *J-C Rouget* 112
3 ch c Sea The Stars(IRE) Aiglonne (USA) (Silver Hawk (USA))
(2281a) 2946a[8] 4332a[4] 6597a[2]

Melabi (IRE) *Richard Ford* a61 81
3 b g Oasis Dream Briolette (IRE) (Sadler's Wells (USA))
3079[3] 3824[4] 4272[3] 5102[2] 7222[7] *7857[13] 8498[10]*

Melaniemillie *Ollie Pears* 63
2 gr f Hellvelyn Real Diamond (Bertolini (USA))
1583[5] ◆ 2404[2] (3114) 3290[4] 4364[4] 4915[7] 6010[12] 7041[11]

Melatonin (USA) *David Hofmans* a118 96
5 b g Kodiak Kowboy(USA) Yanquee Reign (USA) (Yankee Victor (USA))
7838a[5]

Melcano *Shaun Harris* 51
2 b f Arcano(IRE) Sablonne (USA) (Silver Hawk (USA))
2757[11] 5387[7] 5885[6] 6253[5] 6681[12]

Melendez (USA) *Jamie Osborne* a82 77
3 b g Point Given(USA) Miss Mockingbird (USA) (Birdstone (USA))
633[7] 789[8] 1027[2] 1294[2] (1400) 3801[3] *4476[3]* 4818[3]

Melesina (IRE) *Richard Fahey* 103
2 b f Dark Angel(IRE) Lastroseofsummer (IRE) (Haafhd)
1407[4] 1976[7] ◆ 2718a[9] 3336[8] 4037[3] (4728) 6554[6] (7480a)

Melgate Melody *Michael Easterby* a57 55
3 b g Royal Applause Maeander (FR) (Nashwan (USA))
2308[2] *2608[10] 6739[6]* 7336[7] *7604[3] (7795)*

Melinoe *Sir Mark Prescott Bt* a53
2 b f Sea The Stars(IRE) Persefona (IRE) (Montjeu (IRE))
6413[7]

Meliora (IRE) *M G Mintchev* 98
4 b m Starspangledbanner(AUS) Messelina (Noverre (USA))
(6107a)

Melissa Jane *Henry Spiller* a70 50
2 b f Foxwedge(AUS) Queensgate (Compton Place)
2173[7] *(6696) 7305[9] 8560[6]*

Mellow *Hughie Morrison* a53 28
2 ch f Bahamian Bounty Tarqua (IRE) (King Charlemagne (USA))
7502[12] *7763[9] 8066[5]*

Melodic Motion (IRE) *Ralph Beckett* a64 78
2 b f Nathaniel(IRE) Quad's Melody (IRE) (Spinning World (USA))
6085[6] 7284[2] 7770[2]

Melodya (IRE) *Brian Ellison* a37 18
3 b f Arcano(IRE) Fall Habit (IRE) (Hamas (IRE))
6218[9] 6452[P] *6905[4]* 7583[7] *8134[10]*

Melo Magic *J R Jenkins* 10
2 b f Dick Turpin(IRE) Sakhacity (Sakhee (USA))
4951[16]

Melting Dew *Sir Michael Stoute* a70 61
2 b c Cacique(IRE) Winter Sunrise (Pivotal)
7065[7] 7621[5] *(7963)*

Melvin The Grate (IRE) *Andrew Balding* a97 101
6 b g Danehill Dancer(IRE) Hawala (IRE) (Warning)
221[4] 2868[9] 3910[4]

Memorial Day (IRE) *Saeed bin Suroor* a67 110
5 b g Cape Cross(IRE) Reunite (IRE) (Kingmambo (USA))
(6715) 7545[12]

Memories Galore (IRE) *Harry Dunlop* a95 86
4 b g Invincible Spirit(IRE) Persian Memories (IRE) (Indian Ridge)
2581[2] 3606[3] 6780[9] *7054[3] 7752[10] (8150) 8308[3]* ◆

Memory Cloth *Micky Hammond* a58 79
9 b g Cape Cross(IRE) Gossamer (Sadler's Wells (USA))
1445[6] 1521[4] 1785[7] 2556[10] *5842[4]*

Memyselfie (IRE) *Derek Shaw* a53 41
3 b f Kodiac Cool Tarifa (IRE) (One Cool Cat (USA))
81[5] 181[2] 510[3] 732[7] 820[7]

Menai (IRE) *Charles Hills* a78 92
3 b g Dark Angel(IRE) Glisten (Oasis Dream)
1397[8] *1837[3]* 4156[3] 4660[3] (5168) 6210[5] 6583[4] (7221) 7443[3]

Menardais (FR) *T Castanheira* a104 76
7 b g Canyon Creek(IRE) Madeleine's Blush (USA) (Rahy (USA))
(1034a) 1910a[8] *3376a[4]* 4074a[6] *4927a[4]*

Mendacious Harpy (IRE) *George Baker* a42 61
5 b m Dark Angel(IRE) Idesia (IRE) (Green Desert (USA))
1147[8] 3734[4] 3993[3] 4290[3] 4516[4] (5457a) (6401a) 6826[10] *7426[7]*

Menelik (IRE) *Des Donovan* a62 52
7 b g Oasis Dream Chica Roca (USA) (Woodman (USA))
60[6] 216[6] 8278[2]

Mengli Khan (IRE) *Hugo Palmer* a102 98
3 b g Lope De Vega(IRE) Danielli (IRE) (Danehill (USA))
1395[4] 1891[8] *(6675)* 7188[4]

Men United (FR) *Garry Moss* a54 57
3 b g Acclamation Moore's Melody (IRE) (Marju (IRE))
57[4] 322[6] 797[7] 2255[8] 2506[14] 3070[9] 3423[5] 3581[7] 4007[3] 4365[4] 4968[5] 5270[4] *7860[5] 8137[8] 8351[5] 8572[4]*

Mercers *Peter Crate* 63
2 b f Piccolo Ivory's Joy (Tina's Pet)
5258[5] 6034[7] 7414[2]

Mercers Row *Michael Herrington* a63 70
9 b g Bahamian Bounty Invincible (Slip Anchor)
1869[11] 2259[13] 2531[12] 3284[6] *3610[10]* 4376[7] 4970[3] 5714[6] *5969[4]* 6215[5] 6453[7] 6685[9] *6909[7]* 7093[7] 7595[11] *7860[4]*

Merchant Of Dubai *Jim Goldie* a45 75
11 b g Dubai Destination(USA) Chameleon (Green Desert (USA))
1842[4] 2362[8] 2962[5] 4099[12] 4489[2] 4828[5] 5392[2] 5783[6] 6503[6] *6920[8]*

Merchant Of Medici *Micky Hammond* a71 64
9 b g Medicean Regal Rose (Danehill (USA))
2436[5] 2616[3] 3052[4] 3325[6] 4260[5] 4515[3] 5028[3] 5106[4] 6730[11] 7336[9] 7628[13] *7992[12]*

Mercifilly (FR) *Ed Walker* a69 64
3 b f Whipper(USA) Coco (USA) (Storm Bird (CAN))
2375[8] 3357[4] 4087[7] *5302[5] (7368)*

Merci Patron (FR) *N Caullery* a66 90
2 b c Literato(FR) Magic Roses (FR) (Indian Danehill (IRE))
3182a[5] 4330a[7] *8420a[9]*

Mercury *Kevin Ryan* a62 65
4 ch g Showcasing Miss Rimex (IRE) (Ezzoud (IRE))
(60) 264[3] 482[5] 590[9] 1926[3] 2525[9] 2673[7] 3013[5] (3479) 4314[13] 4729[3] 5273[8] 6028[11]

Mercy Me *John Ryan* a76 67
4 b m Mawatheeq(USA) Fantastic Santanyi (Fantastic Light (USA))
1810[6] (3076) *3402[3] 6901[6] (7205) 7531[7] 8253[3] 8381[3] 8427[7]*

Merdon Castle (IRE) *Ruth Carr* a88 86
4 b g Acclamation Siren's Gift (Cadeaux Genereux)
6449[4] ◆ *6962[9]* 7443[9] 7773[7] *8192[9] 8475[13]*

Mere Anarchy (IRE) *Robert Stephens* a71
5 b g Yeats(IRE) Maracana (IRE) (Glacial Storm (USA))
5723[7] 6415[6]

Mere Brow *Bryan Smart* 64
2 b f Clodovil(IRE) Saunta (Invincible Spirit (IRE))
4451[4] 5713[6] 6214[7] 7740[9]

Merhee (AUS) *S Seemar* a79 102
7 b h Elusive Quality(USA) Dizzy De Lago (AUS) (Encosta De Lago (AUS))
95a[7]

Merhoob (IRE) *John Ryan* a89 91
4 b g Cape Cross(IRE) Lady Slippers (IRE) (Royal Academy (USA))
518[7] 697[2] (834) (1291) ◆ *1958[4]* 2028[3] *2581[4]* ◆ 2903[5] 3150[11] *(3405)* 4079[2] 5124[4] *7206[4]*

Meri Devie (FR) *N Clement* a83 98
3 ch f Spirit One(FR) Folle Biche (FR) (Take Risks (FR))
2316a[7]

Merlin *Michael Bell* 78
2 b c Oasis Dream Momentary (Nayef (USA))
5332[8] 6523[2]

Meroula (FR) *Harry Dunlop* a42 66
3 b f Vision D'Etat(FR) Laureldean Desert (Green Desert (USA))
2004[8] 4058[10] 5309[6]

Merriment *Peter Niven* a68 58
3 ch f Makfi Trianon (Nayef (USA))
5731[4] 6135[6] 6450[7] *7992[6] (8091) 8143[2] 8387[5]*

Merry Banter *Paul Midgley* a70 85
2 b f Bated Breath Merry Diva (Bahamian Bounty)
1082[4] 1377[2] 1951[3] (2424) 2807[2] 4111[3] 4669[3] *5125[2]* (6010) (6734)

Merry Dancer (IRE) *Patrick Chamings* a59 65
4 ch m Duke Of Marmalade(IRE) Starlit Sky (Galileo (IRE))
2210[8] (3230) 3722[4] *4880[8] 6508[7]*

Merry Me (IRE) *Andrew Balding* a89 101
5 b m Invincible Spirit(IRE) Thought Is Free (Cadeaux Genereux)
1207[7] 2893[5] 3672[5] 3979[9]

Meshardal (GER) *Ruth Carr* a59 96
6 b g Shamardal(USA) Melody Fair (IRE) (Montjeu (IRE))
1997[8] 2476[9] 2803[5] 3188[4] 3646[10] 4259[8] 4873[5] 5182[7] 5858[7] 6769[7]

Meshaykh (IRE) *Sir Michael Stoute* a68 50
2 b f Lope De Vega(IRE) French Lady (NZ) (Entrepreneur)
6782[7] *7763[6]*

Mesmeric Moment *Shaun Harris* a57 57
2 b f Showcasing Shared Moment (IRE) (Tagula (IRE))
1087[4] 1342[6] 2793[7] (3232) *4937[8] 5675[8]*

Mesonera (FR) *J Parize* a56 87
3 b f Sunday Break(JPN) Niska (USA) (Smart Strike (CAN))
3764a[9] 6310a[9] 6912a[10]

Mesophere *John Gosden* a61
2 ch c Exceed And Excel(AUS) Monturani (IRE) (Indian Ridge)
8089[4]

Met By Moonlight *Ron Hodges* 58
2 b f Sakhee's Secret Starlight Walk (Galileo (IRE))
2180[8] 2822[5] 3556[7]

Meteoric Riser (USA) *Richard Hughes* a65
2 b c More Than Ready(USA) Silimiss (Dansili)
7065[5]

Meteorite (FR) *G Doleuze* a61 53
2 ch f Medecis Amber Two (Cadeaux Genereux)
5905a[6] *7455a[4]*

Meteor Light (IRE) *Ed Vaughan* 61
2 b g Clodovil(IRE) Nordkappe (GER) (High Chaparral (IRE))
5600[7]

Metisian *Jedd O'Keeffe* a37 63
2 b c Sleeping Indian Blushing Heart (Observatory (USA))
5067[9] 5713[5]

Me Too Nagasaki (IRE) *Jeremy Noseda* a76 76
2 b c Iffraaj Distinguish (IRE) (Refuse To Bend (IRE))
7502[4] ◆ *(8353)*

Metronomic (IRE) *Richard Hannon* a56 62
2 b c Roderic O'Connor(IRE) Meon Mix (Kayf Tara)
3408[5] 3799[5] 4336[7] 6440[4] 7286[7] *7941[9] 8276[4] 8582[4]*

Metropol (IRE) *Mme Pia Brandt* a109 93
5 b h Holy Roman Emperor(IRE) Monetary (GER) (Winged Love (IRE))
1069[3] 7524a[8] 7934[5]

Mette *Rod Millman* 49
3 b f Virtual Regal Gallery (IRE) (Royal Academy (USA))
4991[5] 5822[6]

Mexican Mick *Peter Hiatt* a41 58
7 ch g Atraf Artic Bliss (Fraam)
2462[6] 3498[2] 3747[5] 4294[3] *5680[6]* 6256[7] 7044[10]

Meyandi *Andrew Balding* 59
2 ch c Mount Nelson Susi Wong (IRE) (Selkirk (USA))
7125[10] 7769[8]

Meyrick *William Haggas* 63
2 b g Helmet(AUS) Esteemed Lady (IRE) (Mark Of Esteem (IRE))
5356[9]

Mezah (IRE) *Richard Hannon* 38
2 b f Invincible Spirit(IRE) Countess Ferrama (Authorized (IRE))
6162[9] 6732[7]

Mezajy (IRE) *Ed Walker* a80 87
4 b g Makfi Maidin Maith (IRE) (Montjeu (IRE))
7287[9]

Mezmaar *Kevin Morgan* a84 69
7 b g Teofilo(IRE) Bay Tree (IRE) (Daylami (IRE))
236[5] ◆ *(433) 694[4] 1418[8] (3035)* 3622[5] *5301[7]*

Mezyan (IRE) *David Evans* a28 53
2 b f Acclamation Queen Of Carthage (USA) (Cape Cross (IRE))
4951[7] 5820[10] *6421[7]*

Mezzotint (IRE) *Lee Carter* a86 77
7 b g Diamond Green(FR) Aquatint (Dansili)
1702[2] 1946[3] 3234[6] 4081[7] 5017[8] *5677[3]* 6266[4] *6899[5] 7486[2] 7813[6] 8052[6] 8455[3]*

Mfiftythreedotcom (IRE) *Richard Fahey* a57 73
5 ch g Tamayuz Pearl Trader (IRE) (Dubai Destination (USA))
149[2] 316[3] 463[9]

Mia Cara *David Evans* a47 71
2 b f Camacho Vita Mia (Central Park (IRE))
2612[3] 3024[6] 5951[2] 6377[4] 7016[8] 7440[7] *7688[9]*

Mia Tesoro (IRE) *Charlie Fellowes* a84 81
3 b f Danehill Dancer(IRE) Souter's Sister (IRE) (Desert Style (IRE))
(3080) (4301) (5326) (6021) *6964[2]* ◆ *7816[3]*

Mia Tia *James Given* a53
2 ch f Equiano(FR) Tia Mia (Dr Fong (USA))
8569[3]

Mica Mika (IRE) *Richard Fahey* a87 91
8 ch g Needwood Blade Happy Talk (IRE) (Hamas (IRE))
4650[5] 5226[3] 5790a[7] 6802[5] *8539[3]*

Michaels Boots *Des Donovan* a20
2 ch g Paco Boy(IRE) Miss Excel (Exceed And Excel (AUS))
7387a[8] *7917a[11]*

Michael's Mount *Ed Dunlop* a61 83
3 ch g Mount Nelson Dumnoni (Titus Livius (FR))
1091[8] (1718) 2291[6] 3103[6] 3949[2] 4859[3] 6083[2] *6626[7]* (7594)

Michele Strogoff *Roger Fell* a94 96
3 b g Aqlaam Maschera D'Oro (Mtoto)
1686a[5] *(5280a)* 6132[3] 6710[4] *7383[5]* 7744[3] *8122[5] 8279[5] 8478[9]*

Mick Duggan *Michael Blake* a87 64
6 ch g Pivotal Poppy Carew (IRE) (Danehill (USA))
78[5]

Mickey (IRE) *Tom Dascombe* a83 96
3 b g Zoffany(IRE) Enchantment (Compton Place)
(2780) ◆ 4338[14] 5161[2] 5881[2] *6371[7]*

Mickey Haller (IRE) *Brian Meehan* a79 76
4 b g Approve(IRE) Miss Assertive (Zafonic (USA))
1765[3] 2579[5]

Micolys (FR) *K R Burke* a67 73
2 b f Myboycharlie(IRE) Lady Sadowa (Nayef (USA))
3872[6] (4442) *5066[2]* 6015a[2]

Midaawi (IRE) *Kevin Ryan* a69 73
2 b g Kodiac Cuca Vela (USA) (Devil's Bag (USA))
3939[2] ◆ 4762[3] 7090[2] *7432[3]*

Middle Kingdom (USA) *John Gosden* a86
2 b c War Front(USA) River Belle (Lahib (USA))
(8088)

Midge Hall (IRE) *Ann Duffield* 38
2 ch f Helmet(AUS) Allegrissimo (IRE) (Redback)
4699[6]

Midhmaar *Owen Burrows* a80 95
3 b g Iffraaj Merayaat (IRE) (Darshaan)
1603[2] 2413[2] 3300[8] 4108[11]

Midlight *Richard Whitaker* a72 75
4 b g Elusive City(USA) My Heart's Deelite (USA) (Afternoon Deelites (USA))
1925[9] 2409[5] 3952[2] ◆ 5273[3] 5521[3]

Midnight Crossing (IRE) *Edward Lynam* a90 93
3 b f Dark Angel(IRE) Line Ahead (IRE) (Sadler's Wells (USA))
4218a[4] 5313a[9] *7676a[7]*

Midnight Destiny (IRE) *Derek Shaw* a54 49
4 ro m Dark Angel(IRE) Cappella (IRE) (College Chapel)
46[3] 217[9]
Midnight Macchiato (IRE) *David Brown* 83
3 b g Dark Angel(IRE) Lathaat (Dubai Destination (USA))
1630[3] ◆ 2179[2] 2907[7] 5601[3] 5878[10]
Midnight Malibu (IRE) *Tim Easterby* 89
3 b f Poet's Voice Midnight Martini (Night Shift (USA))
1492[6] 2218[5] 2554[3] 3420[2] (4093) (4585) 6133[2] 6518[6] 6793[5] 7124[18]
Midnight Man (FR) *K R Burke* a21 65
2 ch g Evasive Moon Tree (FR) (Groom Dancer (USA))
3054[7] 5203[5] 5728[4] 6130[4] 6791[4] 7482[13]
Midnight Mood *Dominic Ffrench Davis* a49 63
3 b f Aqlaam Inflammable (Montjeu (IRE))
1179[7] 2182[9] 2877[6] 3509[6] (4159) 4987[4] 7223[5]
Midnight Mystic *Michael Bell* a24
3 b f Fastnet Rock(AUS) In The Mist (Pivotal)
2816[8]
Midnight Rider (IRE) *Rod Millman* a74 90
8 b g Red Ransom(USA) Foreplay (IRE) (Lujain (USA))
879[6] 1041[10] 1318[4] 1528[6] 2491[4] 3123[5] 3771[4] 4086[3] 4481[3] 4909[4] 5253[4]
Midnight Robbery *Bryan Smart* a28 58
3 br g Dick Turpin(IRE) Zietunzeen (IRE) (Zieten (USA))
3010[5] 3423[7] 4229[6] 5920[4]
Midnight Storm (USA) *Philip D'Amato* a116 116
5 bb h Pioneerof The Nile(USA) My Tina (USA) (Bertrando (USA))
7837a[3]
Midnight Vixen *Sir Michael Stoute* a63 71
2 b f Foxwedge(AUS) Midnight Ransom (Red Ransom (USA))
4357[4] 5298[4] 6336[2]
Midnight Warrior *Ron Barr* a45 62
6 b g Teofilo(IRE) Mauri Moon (Green Desert (USA))
1674[7] 2233[9] 2558[4] 3191[8] (4430) 4828[4] 5183[3] 5758[4] 6097[3] 6738[8]
Midnight Whistler (USA) *Martyn Meade* a76 71
4 b g Henrythenavigator(USA) Ball Gown (USA) (Silver Hawk (USA))
(487) 6165[7] 7245[5]
Midnite Ride (IRE) *Patrick Martin* a52 40
4 b m Footstepsinthesand Takaliyda (IRE) (Azamour (IRE))
6463a[6]
Midtech Star (IRE) *Ian Williams* a88 55
4 b g Kodiac Royal Rival (IRE) (Marju (IRE))
343[4] 640[2] (832) (922) ◆ 1092[4] 1914[4] 2887[7] 8558[5]
Midterm *Sir Michael Stoute* 117
3 b c Galileo(IRE) Midday (Oasis Dream)
(1605) ◆ 2190[5] 6392a[2] 7353[7]
Midweek *Mme C Head-Maarek* 108
3 b f Motivator Contiguous (USA) (Danzig (USA))
1309a[2] 1888[8] 5498a[4] 6070a[2] 7348a[12]
Mightaswellsmile *James Given* a68 71
2 b f Elnadim(USA) Intishaar (IRE) (Dubai Millennium)
1799[4] ◆ 2219[8] 2771[2] 3261[7] (3902) 4712[3] 5712[9] 6564[6] 7313[6]
Mighty Bond *Tracy Waggott* a41 52
4 b g Misu Bond(IRE) Mighty Flyer (IRE) (Mujtahid (USA))
1776 1378[3] 1490[2] 3268[14]
Mighty Lady *Robyn Brisland* a77 83
3 ch f Mighty Spia (USA) (Diesis)
(325) 2339[5] 2900[2] ◆ 3593[3] 4919[2]
Mighty Minks *Michael Appleby* a19
4 b m Denounce Ivy Bridge (IRE) (Namid)
7410[7] 7607[7]
Mighty Mouse (GER) *Annika Fust* 100
8 b g King's Best(USA) Megaperls (GER) (Zinaad)
5219a[2] 6610a[6]
Mighty Thor *Lydia Richards* a62
6 b g Norse Dancer(IRE) Leyaaly (Night Shift (USA))
195[5] 354[9] 695[3] 1039[7]
Mighty Zip (USA) *Lisa Williamson* a84 52
4 ch g City Zip(USA) Incredulous (FR) (Indian Ridge)
198[13] 484[6] 694[12] 879[5] 974[4] 1251[8] 1490[5] 2120[9] 2571[5] 7255[7] 7612[3] 7945[8] 8535[9]
Migwar (IRE) *F Head* 115
4 b h Sea The Stars(IRE) Katyusha (USA) (Kingmambo (USA))
6989a[15]
Migyaas (USA) *Saeed bin Suroor* 63
2 b g Lonhro(AUS) Nasmatt (Danehill (USA))
4387[2]
Mijhaar *David O'Meara* a95 97
8 b g Shirocco(GER) Jathaabeh (Nashwan (USA))
4165[15] 5116[4] 5611[15] 6142[5] 6540[2] 6919[6] 7411[5]
Mikey Ready (USA) *Ed Walker* a59
2 b c Frankel Reaching (IRE) (Dansili)
8245[7] 8537[7]
Mikmak *William Muir* a89 92
3 b c Makfi Rakata (USA) (Quiet American (USA))
1603[6] 3299[22] 3600[2] 4448[5] 6132[7] 7699[9] 7903[2] ◆ 8177[12] 8356[3]
Mikro Polemistis (IRE) *Brian Ellison* a48 59
3 b f Big Bad Bob(IRE) Kristal Xenia (IRE) (Xaar)
1051[10] 335[4] 1259[8] 1484[7] 1819[2] 2124[3] 2772[2] 3318[9] 3722[6] 6438[2] ◆ 6698[10] 7045[4] 7582[4]
Milaya (USA) *Michael Dilger* a87
4 bb m Eskendereya(USA) Trendy Lady (USA) (Unbridled's Song (USA))
89a[6]
Milburn Jack *Clive Cox* a57
2 br c Foxwedge(AUS) Tintac (Intikhab (USA))
8243[7]
Mildmay Arms *Simon Hodgson* a54 17
4 b g Kheleyf(USA) Akathea (Barathea (IRE))
701[8] 8761[2]
Milenia (GER) *Markus Klug* 97
3 b f Soldier Hollow Milana (GER) (Highest Honor (FR))
2949a[5] 5220a[9] 6611a[7]
Military Angel (USA) *M D O'Callaghan* 102
4 b m Big Brown(USA) Hannabarbera (FR) (Darshaan)
1016a[6] 1858[6] 5564a[7] 6984a[5] 7392a[8]
Military Attack (IRE) *C Fownes* a97 121
8 b g Oratorio(IRE) Almaaseh (IRE) (Dancing Brave (USA))
1690a[2]
Millady Percy *Roy Brotherton* a36 27
3 b f Sir Percy Steady Rain (Zafonic (USA))
1451[1] 331[9] 7218[8] 8075[9]
Mille Et Mille *C Lerner* a84 112
6 b g Muhtathir Quezon Sun (GER) (Monsun (GER))
1688a[10] 3298[4] 4333a[6] 6396a[6] 6974a[5] 7569a[4]
Millefiori (IRE) *Adrian Paul Keatley* a48 77
4 ch m Mastercraftsman(IRE) La Lunete (Halling (USA))
(2365) (2525) (2573) 2959[3] 6505[7] 7392a[14]
Millfield (FR) *D Smaga* a83 102
3 b c Whipper(USA) Victoria College (FR) (Rock Of Gibraltar (IRE))
1024a[4] 1580a[8]
Millie May *Jimmy Fox*
2 b f Sixties Icon Maydream (Sea Freedom)
8354[12]
Millie's Kiss *Philip McBride* a76 70
2 b f Aussie Rules(USA) Aliena (IRE) (Grand Lodge (USA))
5084[3] 5722[5] 7689[2] 8047[3]
Millowitsch (GER) *Markus Klug* 103
3 bb c Sehrezad(IRE) Muriel (IRE) (Fath (USA))
(1689a) 2315a[4]
Mill Springs *John Gosden* a67 104
4 b m Shirocco(GER) Mezzogiorno (Unfuwain (USA))
2690[7] 3246[3] ◆ 4800[4] 6259[12] 7150[24]
Millybond *David Brown* a5 26
2 b f Misu Bond(IRE) Noble Attitude (Best Of The Bests (IRE))
6129[8] 6712[12] 7142[11]
Milly Royale *Michael Blanshard* a39 10
4 b m Royal Applause Milly Fleur (Primo Dominie)
7426[12]
Milrow (IRE) *Martyn Meade* a77
3 b g Tamayuz Cannikin (IRE) (Lahib (USA))
29[2] 287[3] 331[3] 557[5] 729[3]
Milu Mac *Neville Bycroft* 23
5 b m Milk It Mick Efipetite (Efisio)
4236[6] 4766[6] 5319[10] 5868[9]
Milyaar (IRE) *Roger Teal* a49
3 b c Vale Of York(IRE) Central Force (Pivotal)
219[8] 400[9] 533[6]
Mime Dance *David O'Meara* a58 92
5 b g Notnowcato Encore My Love (Royal Applause)
1444[16] 1787[6] 2259[16] 3168[13] 3646[12] 5030[2] 5151[9] 6220[10]
Mimic's Memory *Ann Duffield* a48
2 b f Sayif(IRE) Blue Crest (FR) (Verglas (IRE))
7988[10]
Minabest (FR) *Robert Collet* 29
3 gr f King's Best(USA) Welimina (IRE) (Sadler's Wells (USA))
7265a[13]
Min Alemarat (IRE) *Tim Easterby* a80 86
5 ch g Galileo(IRE) Baraka (IRE) (Danehill (USA))
1642[10] 1967[15] 3117[7] 3657[15] 5275[5] 6163[8]
Minamya (FR) *A De Royer-Dupre* a84 84
3 gr f Makfi Minatlya (FR) (Linamix (FR))
6069a[9] 6971a[6]
Minding (IRE) *A P O'Brien* 123
3 b f Galileo(IRE) Lillie Langtry (IRE) (Danehill Dancer (IRE))
(1888) ◆ 2509a[2] (2869) ◆ (3695a) (4864) 6354a[3] (7352)
Mind That Boy (IRE) *S bin Ghadayer* a100 105
4 b h Acclamation Pegase Hurry (USA) (Fusaichi Pegasus (USA))
284a[4] 452a[8] 624a[11] 842a[7]
Mindurownbusiness (IRE) *Roger Varian* a117 95
5 b h Cape Cross(IRE) Whos Mindin Who (IRE) (Danehill Dancer (IRE))
(501) 1068[3]
Mind Your Biscuits (USA) *Robert N Falcone Jr* a118
3 ch c Posse(USA) Jazzmane (USA) (Toccet (USA))
7832a[2]
Mindy Pendance (IRE) *John Patrick Shanahan* 24
3 b f The Carbon Unit(USA) Kristal Komet (IRE) (High Chaparral (IRE))
7061[6]
Ming Dynasty (FR) *M Delzangles* 117
4 b h King's Best(USA) Memoire (FR) (Sadler's Wells (USA))
1375a[5] 1909a[10] 2947a[8]
Ming Jung (FR) *Markus Klug* 93
2 b c Kallisto(GER) Muriel (IRE) (Fath (USA))
7399a[4]
Miniaturist (FR) *Mark Johnston* a79 59
3 b g Shamardal(USA) Herboriste (Hernando (FR))
2299[4] 2907[4] 3079[6] 3523[3] 4199[7]
Mini Minstrel *Colin Teague* 43
4 br m Pastoral Pursuits Bruma (IRE) (Footstepsinthesand)
2052[12] 2304[9]
Mininggold *Tim Easterby* a48 75
3 b f Piccolo Rosein (Komaite (USA))
1789[9] 2334[6] 2742[3] 3210[5] 3611[5] 4834[5] (5320) 5864[7] 6476[6] (6790) 7252[6]
Miningrocks (FR) *Declan Carroll* a17 75
4 b g Lawman(FR) Fashion School (Shamardal (USA))
1120[8] 2799[3] 3072[7] (3497) 3921[5] 4875[4] (5228) (5868) 6103[8] 6953[2] 7581[3] 7973[13]
Minminwin (IRE) *Gay Kelleway* a59 72
3 ch f Art Connoisseur(IRE) Anne-Lise (Inchinor)
2560[3] 3735[3] 5280a[11] 5907a[2] 6182[2] (6317) 6946[5] 7743[7] 8490[6]
Minority Interest *Daniel O'Brien* a11 1
7 ch g Galileo(IRE) Minority (Generous (IRE))
5208[8]
Minotaur (IRE) *N Clement* a93 105
4 b g Azamour(IRE) Mycenae (Inchinor)
4578a[2]
Minstrels Gallery (IRE) *Lucy Wadham* a80 73
7 ch g Refuse To Bend(IRE) Lilakiya (IRE) (Dr Fong (USA))
(1649) (2105) 2782[3] 3221[4]
Mint Julep (FR) *F-H Graffard* a80 96
3 gr f Mastercraftsman(IRE) Minted (USA) (Mineshaft (USA))
5448a[4] 6273a[8]
Minty Jones *Michael Mullineaux* a43 56
7 b g Primo Valentino(IRE) Reveur (Rossini (USA))
2013[2] 2523[2] 3070[10] 3484[8] 4228[3] 4968[10] 5535[12] 7595[4] 7860[9] 8482[8]
Miracle Garden *Roy Brotherton* a86 49
4 ch g Exceed And Excel(AUS) Sharp Terms (Kris)
106[5] 462[2] (604) 1321[2] 1650[4] 6195[10] 8463[8]
Miracle Ninetynine (IRE) *John James Feane* a81 62
4 b g Big Bad Bob(IRE) Scrumptious (Sakhee (USA))
4899a[8]
Miracle Of Medinah *Mark Usher* a91 104
5 ch g Milk It Mick Smart Ass (IRE) (Shinko Forest (IRE))
2027[10] 2684[7] 4399[6] 5174[4] 5934[5] 6287[2] 6764[8]
Mirae Yeongung (KOR) *M G Song* a32
5 ch h Aragorn(IRE) Willing Miss (USA) (More Than Ready (USA))
6399a[13]
Mirage Dancer *Sir Michael Stoute* 87
2 b c Frankel Heat Haze (Green Desert (USA))
(7496)
Miramonte Dancer (IRE) *David C Griffiths* a4 62
3 b f Fast Company(IRE) Bonne (Namid)
1671[4] 2095[3] 2553[8] 3479[5] 5732[12] 6105[12] 8347[8]
Mirdif *M D O'Callaghan* 102
2 b c Kodiac Irina Princess (Selkirk (USA))
3678a[6] 4171a[3] 4414a[3]
Miriam Violet *Paul Henderson* a39 20
2 b f Dick Turpin(IRE) Velvet Band (Verglas (IRE))
6071[12] 6622[7] 7210[10] 8467[8]
Mirimar (IRE) *Ed Vaughan* a53
2 br g Kalanisi(IRE) Peratus (IRE) (Mujadil (USA))
8486[9]
Miro (IRE) *Gordon Elliott* a76
4 b g Rock Of Gibraltar(IRE) Mission Secrete (IRE) (Galileo (IRE))
245[7] 6466a[6]
Mirror City *Charlie Appleby* a83 78
3 b f Street Cry(IRE) Ama (USA) (Storm Cat (USA))
5089[5]
Mirrorsonthewall (FR) *Gianluca Bietolini* a46 67
3 b c Aussie Rules(USA) Diotima (High Estate)
128a[11]
Mirsaalah *James Tate* 88
3 b f Sir Percy Lyric Art (USA) (Red Ransom (USA))
(1758) 1966[8] 2394[7] 3846[4] 5333[2]
Mirsaale *Keith Dalgleish* a74 103
6 ch g Sir Percy String Quartet (IRE) (Sadler's Wells (USA))
704[3] 890[7] (1253) (1642) 1880[3] 3246[12] 3913[8]
Mirza *Rae Guest* a67 112
9 b g Oasis Dream Millyant (Primo Dominie)
626a[9] 841a[9] 1172a[7] 1862[19] 2317a[4] 2943a[8] 4905a[5] 6391a[6] 6943[3] ◆ (7242) 7537[15]
Mirzam (IRE) *Mick Channon* 53
2 gr f Mastercraftsman(IRE) Luxie (IRE) (Acclamation)
7125[6]
Mischief Maisy (IRE) *Gordon Elliott* a62 53
3 gr f Clodovil(IRE) Maise And Blue (USA) (Distant View (USA))
219[6] 1779[3] 2126[10] 2967[6] (4018) 4813a[8]
Mise En Rose (USA) *Charlie Appleby* a98 108
3 bb f War Front(USA) Buy The Barrel (USA) (E Dubai (USA))
(1960) 2789[3] 3274[15] (4105) 4826[2] 5498a[8] 6281[2] 7146[3] 7650[9]
Mishaal (IRE) *Michael Herrington* a94 93
6 ch g Kheleyf(USA) My Dubai (IRE) (Dubai Millennium)
1090[5] 1672[7] 2581[3] 3133[4] 3646[6] 4259[4] (4689) 5417[2] 6082[3]
Mishari *Tom Dascombe* 48
2 b c Oasis Dream Nessina (USA) (Hennessy (USA))
6731[7]
Mishrif (USA) *J R Jenkins* a71 67
10 bb g Arch(USA) Peppy Priscilla (USA) (Latin American (USA))
1145[6]
Mishwaar *Charles Hills* a68
3 b g Arcano(IRE) Misdaqeya (Red Ransom (USA))
976[2]
Misleading *Lee Carter* a31 29
4 ch g Footstepsinthesand Danny's Choice (Compton Place)
974[5] 1832[6] 3726[6]
Missandei *Steph Hollinshead* a56 61
4 b m Red Rocks(IRE) Onda Chiara (ITY) (Dane Friendly)
150[4] 255[7] (498) 731[5] 946[5] 1004[5] 1182[7] 4226[8]
Miss Anticipation (IRE) *Roger Charlton* 72
2 br f Bated Breath Dusting (IRE) (Acclamation)
4054[12] 4951[3] 5516[4] 7467[11]
Miss Bates *Ann Duffield* 73
2 b f Holy Roman Emperor(IRE) Jane Austen (IRE) (Galileo (IRE))
3248[5] 3705[5] 4728[2] 5318[6] 6026[2] 6563[5] 7406[4]
Miss Blondell *Marcus Tregoning* a70 66
3 ch f Compton Place Where's Broughton (Cadeaux Genereux)
8163[4] ◆
Miss Bombay (IRE) *A Giorgi* 57
2 br f Famous Name Sunblush (UAE) (Timber Country (USA))
3763a[12] 5905a[9]
Miss Buckaroo (IRE) *Peter Hedger* a54 42
4 b m Acclamation Pearl Trader (IRE) (Dubai Destination (USA))
163[6] 525[6] (787) 1165[10] 1791[5] 2409[7] 3072[11] 3620[7] 4992[8] 5055[6] 5326[7]
Miss Carbonia (IRE) *Ismail Mohammed* 89
3 b f Lilbourne Lad(IRE) Carbonia (IRE) (Alhaarth (IRE))
(3145) (4317) 4886[4] (6113) ◆
Miss Charlotte (IRE) *F Vermeulen* a58 71
2 b f Kheleyf(USA) Miss Penelope (FR) (Kendor (FR))
5142a[7] 5905a[5] 7455a[5]
Miss Cogent (IRE) *J P Murtagh* a88 90
2 b f Clodovil(IRE) Onomatomania (USA) (Mr Greeley (USA))
3694a[7] 4171a[8] 5661a[7] 6388a[19]
Miss Danby (IRE) *Mark Johnston* a67 62
2 gr f Mastercraftsman(IRE) Dunbrody (FR) (Jeune Homme (USA))
3592[4] 4603[10] 4966[2] 8087[2]
Miss Double D'Oro (USA) *Neil Drysdale* 101
4 bb m Medaglia d'Oro(USA) Lost Gold (USA) (Dynaformer (USA))
7829a[2]
Miss Dusky Diva (IRE) *David W Drinkwater* a56 47
4 gr m Verglas(IRE) Dispol Veleta (Makbul)
6020[8] 6651[9] 7463[13] 7614[6] 8497[4]
Missed Call (IRE) *James Fanshawe* a99 101
6 b m Authorized(IRE) Incoming Call (USA) (Red Ransom (USA))
2025[3] 3340[13] 5411[6] 6332[6] 7188[7]
Missed The Cut *Michael Wigham* a37
3 b g Zebedee Nairobi (FR) (Anabaa (USA))
1701[10] 2175[13] 2790[15]
Miss Elizabeth (IRE) *Edward Lynam* 99
3 b f Intense Focus(USA) Passaggio (Pivotal)
1369a[6] 1939a[4] 2272a[8] 7191a[14]
Miss Fay (IRE) *Michael Bell* 68
2 br f Sayif(IRE) Lough Mewin (IRE) (Woodman (USA))
5771[3] 6888[3]
Miss Florence *David Barron* 32
2 gr f Zebedee Scented Garden (Zamindar (USA))
3216[5]
Miss Fortune *Mark Usher* a43 52
3 ch f Notnowcato Rowan Flower (IRE) (Ashkalani (IRE))
140[4] 345[5] 688[8] 5610[10] 6485[11] 6855[5]
Miss Galidora (IRE) *David O'Meara* 68
3 b f Galileo(IRE) Clodora (FR) (Linamix (FR))
3362[2] ◆ 4682[8]
Miss Geronimo *Ken Cunningham-Brown* a37
4 b m Hellvelyn Churn Dat Butter (USA) (Unbridled (USA))
5766[9] 6674[9] 7727[8]
Miss Giler *John Gosden* a75 93
4 b m High Chaparral(IRE) Funday (Daylami (IRE))
127[2] 325[2] 487[4] (630)
Miss Goldsmith (IRE) *Richard Fahey* a66
3 gr f Mastercraftsman(IRE) Golden Legacy (IRE) (Rossini (USA))
102[3] 249[5] 7995[9] 8188[3] 8493[4]
Miss Gregarious *Chris Dwyer* 47
2 b f Kheleyf(USA) Symphony Star (IRE) (Amadeus Wolf)
2583[5] (Dead)
Miss Icon *Patrick Chamings* a68 69
2 b f Sixties Icon Pretty Miss (Averti (IRE))
4523[3] 5395[2] (6035) 6630[10] 7688[5]
Missile Command (IRE) *Jane M Foley* a56 52
8 b g Majestic Missile(IRE) Blusienka (IRE) (Blues Traveller (IRE))
2229a[4] 7800a[8]
Miss Infinity (IRE) *Mark Johnston* 105
3 b f Rock Of Gibraltar(IRE) Muravka (IRE) (High Chaparral (IRE))
3024[3] ◆ (3388) ◆ (3805) 4352[5] (5186a) 5583[5] 6174a[2] 6748[3] 7114[7]
Miss Inga Sock (IRE) *Eve Johnson Houghton* a68 72
4 ch m Tagula(IRE) Support Fund (IRE) (Intikhab (USA))
1268[4] 1735[5] 2379[7] 2636[4] 3514[6] 4389[4] 5051[8] 6237[6] 6826[3] 7062[6] 7212[3]
Mission Authorized (IRE) *Adrian Paul Keatley* a33 66
2 b f Bushranger(IRE) Witnessed (Authorized (IRE))
4287[9]
Mission Mars *Patrick Holmes* 59
3 b g Kyllachy Ashraakat (USA) (Danzig (USA))
1670[14] 2553[14] 4973[10]
Miss Island Ruler *Shaun Harris* a45 40
2 b f Elzaam(AUS) Kodiac Island (Kodiac)
2771[13] 3561[10] 3947[13] 5364[11] 5606[4] 6252[8] 6588[8] 6950[22]
Mississippi *Paul Midgley* a86 93
7 b g Exceed And Excel(AUS) Ruby Rocket (IRE) (Indian Rocket)
944[4] 1444[5] 1848[10] 2803[3] 3115[15] 4428[3] ◆ 5512[9] 5852[5] 6131[5]
Mississippi Delta (USA) *Mark Casse* a97 102
4 b m Giant's Causeway(USA) Texas To A Tee (USA) (Purge (USA))
7171a[10]
Mississippi Miss *Dr Jon Scargill* a69 75
2 ch f Equiano(FR) Junket (Medicean)
6295[4] 7099[4] (7576)
Miss Katie Mae (IRE) *H Graham Motion* 102
3 b f Dark Angel(IRE) Kate The Great (Xaar)
7829a[5]

Miss Laila (IRE) *Richard Hughes* a68 72
2 b f Dark Angel(IRE) Sister Red (IRE) (Diamond Green (FR))
4457[4] *5524[5]* (6250)

Miss Lillie *Roger Teal* a65 60
5 b m Exceed And Excel(AUS) Never Lose (Diktat)
2[4] 277[2] 336[5] 563[2] (701) 813[5] 1266[5] 1735[14] 2087[3] *2566[3] (3731)* 4589[4] 5085[8] 6826[9] *7514[7]*

Miss Macchiato (IRE) *Keith Dalgleish* a48 36
3 b f Holy Roman Emperor(IRE) Cafe Lassere (USA) (Giant's Causeway (USA))
1662[6] 2741[10] *7991[7] 8386[4]*

Miss Marina Bay *Sir Mark Prescott Bt* a61 59
3 ch f Galileo(IRE) Miss Corniche (Hernando (FR))
2124[10] 2772[9] *4210[8]* 4591[2] *(5079)* 5573 [5]

Miss Marjurie (IRE) *Denis Coakley* a89 110
6 b m Marju(IRE) Kazatzka (Groom Dancer (USA))
1855[6] 2690[3] 4400[3] *6125[6]*

Miss Mayson *Roger Teal* a59 34
2 b f Mayson High Class Girl (Royal Applause)
4054[13] 4586[7] *6141[4] 7275[2] 7528[8] 8097[7]*

Miss Minuty *Alexandra Dunn* a86 82
4 gr m Verglas(IRE) Miss Provence (Hernando (FR))
330[5] 595[5] 3001[9] 4501[3] 5406[6] 6019[2] *7512[7] 8076[4]*

Miss Mittens *Geoffrey Deacon* 17
4 b m Shirocco(GER) River Of Silence (IRE) (Sadler's Wells (USA))
2368[6] 2901[7] 3747[10] 5016[6]

Miss Monro (IRE) *Brian Ellison* 59
2 br f Intense Focus(USA) Runway Girl (IRE) (Dansili)
1951[6] 2536[8] 3222[5]

Miss Montana (IRE) *Mrs John Harrington* 61
3 b f High Chaparral(IRE) Miletrian (IRE) (Marju (IRE))
4813a[17]

Miss Montes *Bryan Smart* a57 33
2 ch f Monsieur Bond(IRE) Preference (Efisio)
6009[6] *8140[5]*

Miss Mozaico *Richard Whitaker* 34
3 b f Pastoral Pursuits Grin (Key Of Luck (USA))
2741[11] 4001[9] 5197[7]

Miss Osier *Rae Guest* a63 33
2 ch f Mastercraftsman(IRE) Lacy Sunday (USA) (King's Best (USA))
7695[12] *8082[3]*

Miss Patience *Peter Chapple-Hyam* 56
2 b f Excelebration(IRE) Connote (Oasis Dream)
7696[8]

Miss Pepper (IRE) *Paul Midgley* 42
2 b f Acclamation Somerset Falls (UAE) (Red Ransom (USA))
5727[8] 6214[11] 6641[9]

Miss Phillyjinks (IRE) *Paul D'Arcy* a67 65
3 b f Zoffany(IRE) Smoken Rosa (USA) (Smoke Glacken (USA))
515[5] 726[2] 1060[8] 1761[4] 2435[6] *3280[5] 3725[4] 4009[6] 5302[7] 6051[5]*

Miss Popov *Noel Wilson* a37 40
3 b f Monsieur Bond(IRE) Priti Fabulous (IRE) (Invincible Spirit (IRE))
1564[9] 2359 [6] 5277[12]

Miss Quick *Ann Duffield* a40
2 b f Equiano(FR) Quixada (GER) (Konigstiger (GER))
6925[13]

Miss Ranger (IRE) *Brian Ellison* a68 75
4 gr m Bushranger(IRE) Remiss (IRE) (Indian Ridge)
1412[2] 1825[2] *2618[5]* 3251[7] (3642) 3983[2] 4293[2] 4687[8] 5392[6]

Miss Reignier *Michael Blanshard* a54 29
2 b f Paco Boy(IRE) Arculinge (Paris House)
2764[5] 4261[10] 6189[4] *7423[9]*

Miss Rosina (IRE) *George Margarson* a64 69
2 ch f Choisir(AUS) Vera Lilley (IRE) (Verglas (IRE))
2310[7] (2552) 3037[5] 3686[3] 4843[2] 6010[8] *7966[6] 8174[10]*

Miss Salt *Dominic Ffrench Davis* a41 35
2 b f Delegator Miss Firefly (Compton Place)
4054[14] *5244[5] 5606[7]* 6652[7] 6887[8]

Miss Sayif *George Margarson* 54
2 b f Sayif(IRE) Delma (IRE) (Authorized (IRE))
4877[7] 5846[8]

Miss Sheridan (IRE) *Michael Easterby* a65 67
2 br f Lilbourne Lad(IRE) Sues Surprise (IRE) (Montjeu (IRE))
3433[2] 4037[4] 4603[4] 7541[5] *7688[4] 7956[4] 8405[6]*

Miss Steff (IRE) *Stefano Botti* a70 69
3 b f Dark Angel(IRE) Stefanella (IRE) (Alzao (USA))
2730a[7]

Miss Sugars *Jeff Mullins* a72 89
2 ch f Harbour Watch(IRE) Three Sugars (AUS) (Starcraft (NZ))
(3222) *3782[2]* 4296[2] 4884[3] 5998[2] 8127a[4]

Miss Temple (IRE) *Gavin Cromwell* a62 67
4 b m Acclamation Movie Queen (Danehill (USA))
6462a[8]

Miss Temple City (USA) *H Graham Motion* 113
4 bb m Temple City(USA) Glittering Tax (USA) (Artax (USA))
3271[4] 5914a[5] (7172a) 7837a[5]

Miss Terre (FR) *F-X De Chevigny* a72
3 b f Heliostatic(IRE) Multimedia (FR) (Exit To Nowhere (USA))
7168a[5]

Miss Tiger Lily *Harry Dunlop* a73 73
6 b m Tiger Hill(IRE) Waitingonacloud (In The Wings)
4950[2] ◆ 5208[2] (6058) 6885[3] 7507[8] *8363[2]*

Miss Tree *John Quinn* a59 57
5 b m Literato(FR) Tunguska (Silver Patriarch (IRE))
7044[4] (7361) *7656[5] 7992[5] 8309[9]*

Miss Understood (IRE) *David Simcock* a82 57
4 b m Excellent Art Puck's Castle (Shirley Heights)
72[7]

Miss Uppity *Ivan Furtado* a52 40
3 ch f Notnowcato Instructress (Diktat)
2255[9] *7642[12] 8471[10]*

Miss Van Gogh *Richard Fahey* a68 94
4 b m Dutch Art Accede (Acclamation)
1380[6] (1757) ◆ 2236[4] 2868[3] 4163[9] 4757[9] 6115[9] 6500[4] *7796[8] 8122[10]*

Miss Victory (IRE) *Mark Usher* a39 39
3 b f Mount Nelson Wars (IRE) (Green Desert (USA))
328[8]

Mistaken Lady *Jo Hughes* a26 25
3 b f Multiplex Sharoura (Inchinor)
328[9]

Mister Art (IRE) *Matthieu Palussiere* a81 88
2 b c Art Connoisseur(IRE) Miss Chaumiere (Selkirk (USA))
3871a[11] 5905a[2] 7170a[7]

Mister Belvedere *Michael Dods* a60 84
2 b g Archipenko(USA) Diablerette (Green Desert (USA))
3561[3] 4188[2] (6025) 6499[2]

Mister Blue Sky (IRE) *Sylvester Kirk* 79
2 gr c Royal Applause Mujdeya (Linamix (FR))
2535[5] 3065[3] (3576) 4076[2] 5644[2] 6191[4] 6664[2]

Mister Bob (GER) *James Bethell* a79 32
7 ch g Black Sam Bellamy(IRE) Mosquera (GER) (Acatenango (GER))
2105[9] 2782[4] (4012) (4941) 5553[6] (6740) 8399[6]

Mister Fizz *Miss Imogen Pickard* a80 82
8 b g Sulamani(IRE) Court Champagne (Batshoof)
838[4]

Mister Freeze (IRE) *Clive Cox* a53
2 ch c Frozen Power(IRE) Beacon Of Hope (IRE) (Barathea (IRE))
8066[10] 8354[6]

Misterioso (IRE) *Jamie Osborne* a91 96
4 b h Iffraaj Roystonea (Polish Precedent (USA))
2247[6] 2587[6] 3101[4] 3414[3] (4079) *4475[4]* ◆ 4862[25] *5678[9]* 6263[4] 6780[6]

Mister Manduro (FR) *Mark Johnston* a77 74
2 ch c Manduro(GER) Semenova (FR) (Green Tune (USA))
6297[3] ◆ *7431[2] (7605)*

Mister Marcasite *Antony Brittain* a47 56
6 gr g Verglas(IRE) No Rehearsal (FR) (Baillamont (USA))
1169[9] 1500[12] 2507[10] 5383[2] 5980[3] 6647[9] *7369[11] 7641[7]*

Mister Martini (IRE) *Edward Lynam* 69
4 b g Lope De Vega(IRE) Slip Dance (IRE) (Celtic Swing)
4748a[8]

Mister Mischief *Paul Midgley* a70 72
3 b g Makfi Bluebelle Dancer (IRE) (Danehill Dancer (IRE))
1111[2] ◆ 2049[13] 2667[3] 3603[6] 3754[3] 4701[6]

Mister Moosah (IRE) *Micky Hammond* 73
2 gr c Clodovil(IRE) Hendrina (IRE) (Daylami (IRE))
3167[5] 3661[5] 4423[6] 5290[5] 6130[9] 6791[5]

Mister Music *Tony Carroll* a84 88
7 b g Singspiel(IRE) Sierra (Dr Fong (USA))
1318[7] 2734[7] 4841[4] ◆ *6084[2]* 6300[2] 7189[6] 7671[3]

Mister Musicmaster *Ron Hodges* a83 89
7 b g Amadeus Wolf Misty Eyed (IRE) (Paris House)
1041[9] 1418[9] 1724[2] 1933[3] 2549[11] 3124[4] 3766[5] 4157[11] 4908[5] 5357[7] 6021[4] 6365[13] 6889[7]

Mister Royal (IRE) *Brian Ellison* a4 72
5 ch g Mister Fotis(USA) Jardin Royal (IRE) (Royal Academy (USA))
(4005) 4369[2] (4683) *5068[P]* (Dead)

Mister Showman *Jonathan Portman* a27 63
3 b g Showcasing Theatre Royal (Royal Applause)
1897[6] *2816[10]* 3508[6] 4385[9] 5204[2] ◆ 5548[6] 6367[2]

Mister Strong (TUR) *C Filiksac* a94
4 b h Dilum(USA) Helloimustbegoing (USA) (Red Ransom (USA))
6157a[5]

Mister Sunshine (IRE) *Clive Cox* 80
2 ch g Fast Company(IRE) Second Omen (Rainbow Quest (USA))
1915[2] ◆ (2289) 3196[9] 4394[23] 6800[5]

Mister Trader *D J Bunyan* 97
2 br c Hellvelyn Rehlaat (USA) (Swain (IRE))
2494a[2] 3247[20]

Mister Universe *Mark Johnston* a112 104
4 br h Cape Cross(IRE) Miss Ivanhoe (IRE) (Selkirk (USA))
(833) (921) 1068[6] 2027[25] 5585[19] 5871[15]

Mister York *Antony Brittain* 42
4 b g Monsieur Bond(IRE) Knavesmire (IRE) (One Cool Cat (USA))
2428[9]

Mistime (IRE) *Mark Johnston* a74 84
2 b f Acclamation Out Of Time (IRE) (Anabaa (USA))
2162[6] 2371[3] *(2786)* (3100) 3531[2] ◆ 4148[3]

Mistiroc *John Quinn* 100
5 br g Rocamadour Mistinguett (IRE) (Doyoun)
1620[8] 2199[8] 3162[7] (4095) (5145) 5639[11] 7150[18] 7824[6]

Mistress Marinrio (IRE) *Kevin Frost* a45 37
5 b m Captain Rio Dafalia (IRE) (Mark Of Esteem (IRE))
2610[7]

Mistress Quickly (IRE) *Ralph Beckett* 73
2 b f Mastercraftsman(IRE) In My Life (IRE) (Rainbow Quest (USA))
6874[4]

Mistress Viz (IRE) *John Mackie* 66
2 gr f Mastercraftsman(IRE) Vizean (IRE) (Medicean)
4603[6] 5221[3] 5861[4] 6713[7]

Mistry *Mark Usher* a47
3 b f Mullionmileanhour(IRE) Smart Ass (IRE) (Shinko Forest (IRE))
7935[7] 8496[6]

Misty Lord (IRE) *Marco Botti* a85 87
3 b c Lilbourne Lad(IRE) Misty Night (IRE) (Galileo (IRE))
(298) 4593[2] *5191[3] (5677)* 6490[2] 6918[5] ◆

Misty Love (FR) *F Vermeulen* a94 78
4 b g Duke Of Marmalade(IRE) Misty Heights (Fasliyev (USA))
4901a[7] 5501a[11]

Misty Millie (IRE) *P Cluskey* 85
3 b f Dylan Thomas(IRE) Mystic Mile (IRE) (Sadler's Wells (USA))
2068a[5] 6495a[10]

Mistymoistymorning (IRE) *John Ryan* a70 38
3 gr f Alhaarth(IRE) Bermuxa (FR) (Linamix (FR))
1758[7] 2178[11] 3080[7]

Misty Moo *Michael Appleby* a48 55
2 b f Piccolo Siryena (Oasis Dream)
2007[10] 2335[4] 2732[4] *6139[10] 6895[4]* 7244[4] 7571[11] *8284[5]*

Misu Mac *Neville Bycroft* a76 57
6 b m Misu Bond(IRE) Umbrian Gold (IRE) (Perugino (USA))
3610[13] 3847[6] *4714[11]* 6136[6] 6685[20] *7437[7] 7961[9]*

Misu Moneypenny *Scott Dixon* a59 70
3 b f Misu Bond(IRE) Watersilk (IRE) (Fasliyev (USA))
1647[5] 1872[2] *2334[10]* 3218[5] 3581[6] 4378[7]

Misu Pete *Mark Usher* a66
4 b g Misu Bond(IRE) Smart Ass (IRE) (Shinko Forest (IRE))
321[2] (943) (1116) 1415[6] *1700[6]* ◆ *2379[3] 2918[5] 5605[11] 6051[9] 6677[5] 7260[5] 7751[4] 8095[7] 8490[5]*

Mitchum *Ron Barr* a79 77
7 b g Elnadim(USA) Maid To Matter (Pivotal)
1120[3] (1378) (1495) (1878) 2572[8] 3494[2] 4089[11] 4932[U] 5867[4] 6216[8]

Mitchum Swagger *David Lanigan* a109 116
4 b g Paco Boy(IRE) Dont Dili Dali (Dansili)
1637[9] 3273[3] ◆ *5472[2]* 6117[2] 7352[12] *7868[5]*

Mithqaal (USA) *Michael Appleby* a94 85
3 ch g Speightstown(USA) Bestowal (USA) (Unbridled's Song (USA))
979[2] 2322[6] 2864[3] (3823) 4593[3] (6753) 7153[7] *7608[3] 7779[7] (8475)*

Mitigate *David Elsworth* a71
2 b f Lawman(FR) Marika (Marju (IRE))
8152[4] ◆ *8362[3]*

Mitre Peak *Richard Fahey* a83 70
4 ch m Shamardal(USA) Milford Sound (Barathea (IRE))
(245) 422[4] 485[7] 734[6]

Mittens *Sir Michael Stoute* a76 54
2 b f New Approach(IRE) Warm Hands (Oasis Dream)
7118[10] *(7647)* ◆

Mix And Mingle (IRE) *Chris Wall* 106
3 ch f Exceed And Excel(AUS) Mango Lady (Dalakhani (IRE))
1396[4] 1888[7] 4582[5] 5158[2] 5645[4] 6939[11]

Mixed Message (IRE) *Mandy Rowland* a36 56
6 b m Kodiac Berenica (IRE) (College Chapel)
2566[11]

Mizaah (IRE) *Kevin Prendergast* 96
3 b c Invincible Spirit(IRE) Miss Beabea (IRE) (Catrail (USA))
6355a[3] 6984a[3]

Mizzou (IRE) *Luca Cumani* 117
5 b h Galileo(IRE) Moments Of Joy (Darshaan)
(1772) ◆ 3298[2]

Mjjack (IRE) *K R Burke* 80
2 gr c Elzaam(AUS) Docklands Grace (USA) (Honour And Glory (USA))
3805[3] ◆ 4343[4] (6731)

Moamar *Ed Dunlop* a52
2 ch g Sepoy(AUS) Palitana (USA) (Giant's Causeway (USA))
8486[10]

Moans Cross (USA) *Alan King* 50
2 ch g Spring At Last(USA) Playful Wink (USA) (Orientate (USA))
7769[12]

Moayadd (USA) *Neil Mulholland* a38 38
4 b g Street Cry(IRE) Aryaamm (IRE) (Galileo (IRE))
3996[12] 4458[9] *5023[7]* 5486[10]

Mobsta (IRE) *Mick Channon* 111
4 b h Bushranger(IRE) Sweet Nicole (Okawango (USA))
(1197) 1439[9] (2495a) 6941[6] 7771[6]

Moccasin (FR) *Geoffrey Harker* a64 53
7 b g Green Tune(USA) Museum Piece (Rainbow Quest (USA))
1057[10] 1561[7] 2555[10] 2958[8] 4038[7] 4425[12] *8497[9]*

Mockery (IRE) *Mark Johnston* a40
2 ch f Tamayuz Storm Lily (USA) (Storm Cat (USA))
7639[7]

Mockinbird (IRE) *Sir Mark Prescott Bt* a69 72
3 b f Makfi Littlefeather (IRE) (Indian Ridge)
59[5] 5717[7] 6265[3] ◆ *6742[5]* 7301[3] *7725[11]*

Modello (IRE) *Giles Bravery* a59 64
3 b f Intikhab(USA) Precious Citizen (USA) (Proud Citizen (USA))
265[6] 335[6]

Modem *Mrs John Harrington* a77 96
6 b g Motivator Alashaan (Darshaan)
208a[9] 2881a[3] 3680a[2] 4417a[3] 5559[11] 6350a[15] 7150[26]

Moderah *James Fanshawe* 98
4 b m Makfi Meetyouthere (IRE) (Sadler's Wells (USA))
1855[9] 6259[8] 7575[7]

Modern History (IRE) *M Al Mheiri* a86 78
8 b g Shamardal(USA) Fatefully (USA) (Private Account (USA))
369a[7]

Modernism *Ian Williams* a90 89
7 b g Monsun(GER) La Nuit Rose (FR) (Rainbow Quest (USA))
1214[4] 1978[10] 2688[6] 3129[2] 3520[2] ◆ 4095[3] 4407[7] 5434[4] 6081[3] 6794[6] *8446[10]*

Modern Life (IRE) *David Elsworth* a65
2 gr c Roderic O'Connor(IRE) Missliyna (IRE) (Rainbow Quest (USA))
7424[5] 7865[4]

Modern Palace (FR) *M Nigge* 23
4 b g Palace Episode(USA) Princesse Stesa (FR) (Nikos)
5700a[10]

Modern Tutor *Miss Nicole McKenna* a77 62
7 b g Selkirk(USA) Magical Romance (IRE) (Barathea (IRE))
2525[5]

Modest *Michael Bell* a78 69
3 b f Kyllachy Coy (IRE) (Danehill (USA))
3[2] ◆ *(131) 322[5]*

Modh Coinniolach (IRE) *Dermot Anthony McLoughlin* a50
3 b g Frozen Power(IRE) Just One Look (Barathea (IRE))
828a[4]

Modhilah (IRE) *S Seemar* a60 6
2 ch f Helmet(AUS) Deira Dubai (Green Desert (USA))
5593[8] *6413[6] 7647[10] 8574a[12]*

Mohaayed *Kevin Prendergast* 106
4 b g Intikhab(USA) Reyaada (Daylami (IRE))
1018a[9] 1509a[5] 4747a[16]

Mohab *Kevin Ryan* a84 91
3 b c Sir Percy Princess Aurora (USA) (Mr Greeley (USA))
1393[4] 4065[6] 4624[12] 5651[13] 6557[12] *7984[8]*

Mohadjer (FR) *Waldemar Hickst* 90
4 ch h Lord Of England(GER) Nicara (GER) (Nebos (GER))
5216a[2]

Mohallela (USA) *Owen Burrows* a65
2 b f Teofilo(IRE) Zaroof (USA) (Street Cry (IRE))
7761[8]

Mohatem (USA) *Owen Burrows* a89 83
4 ch g Distorted Humor(USA) Soul Search (USA) (A.P. Indy (USA))
6870[2] ◆ *7512[6]*

Mohaymen (USA) *Kiaran McLaughlin* a116
3 rg c Tapit(USA) Justwhistledixie (USA) (Dixie Union (USA))
2063a[4]

Moheet (IRE) *Richard Hannon* 104
4 b g High Chaparral(IRE) Abunai (Pivotal)
744a[3] 1774[8]

Mo Henry *Adrian Paul Keatley* a77 68
4 b g Monsieur Bond(IRE) Mo Mhuirnin (IRE) (Danetime (IRE))
(1692) 2524[5] 2961[2] 4291[4] 5224[4] 6502[8] 7474a[3] 7774[6]

Moi Aussie *Ed McMahon* a61 62
3 gr f Aussie Rules(USA) Oceana Blue (Reel Buddy (USA))
1564[5] *(2107)* 3003[2] *3988[11]* 5515[7] *6106[4] 7261[6] 7751[9]*

Moi Moi Moi (IRE) *Ibrahim Al Malki* 87
2 b c Acclamation I'm Sensational (Selkirk (USA))
4053[6] 4707[4] 5072[2] (6679) 7263a[3] 8564a[6]

Mojito (IRE) *William Haggas* a80 76
2 b c Requinto(IRE) Narva (USA) (Grand Slam (USA))
7157[3] ◆ *(7658)*

Mokarris (USA) *Simon Crisford* 106
2 b c More Than Ready(USA) Limonar (IRE) (Street Cry (IRE))
(2648) 3243[16] (4352) 5654[2] 6785[6]

Mokat (USA) *Richard Baltas* a95 106
3 bb f Uncle Mo(USA) Flashy Frolic (USA) (Premiership (USA))
7379a[5]

Mokhalad *Sir Michael Stoute* 56
3 ch g Dubawi(IRE) Model Queen (USA) (Kingmambo (USA))
2340[8]

Molans Mare (IRE) *Jason Cairns* a36 37
6 ch m Shirocco(GER) Devious Diva (IRE) (Dr Devious (IRE))
6731[2] 7800a[12]

Molivias Gem *David Thompson* a3 41
3 b f Baltic King Mississippi Millie (IRE) (Tagula (IRE))
5278[7] *5843[9]* 5889[7] 7097[13]

Moll Anthony (IRE) *Peter Chapple-Hyam* 15
2 b f Kheleyf(USA) Kalinova (IRE) (Red Ransom (USA))
7439[11]

Mollasses *Harry Whittington* a73 61
5 b m Authorized(IRE) Muscovado (USA) (Mr Greeley (USA))
1640[7]

Mollie's Girl (IRE) *Michael Appleby* a68 51
3 b f Elusive Pimpernel(USA) Ebony Star (Desert Prince (IRE))
1719[9] 1759[6] 3135[4]

Molly Approve (IRE) *Tony Coyle* a54 51
4 b m Approve(IRE) Kathleen Rafferty (IRE) (Marju (IRE))
135[3] 247[10] 297[4] 418[5] 547[5] 787[12]

Molly Dolly (IRE) *W T Farrell* a76 99
4 b m Exceed And Excel(AUS) Garra Molly (IRE) (Nayef (USA))
1939a[5] 5313a[4] 5939a[4] 6746[6] 7706a[11]

Molly Jones *Matthew Salaman* a36 55
7 b m Three Valleys(USA) And Toto Too (Averti (IRE))
3004[7] 3994[15] 4658[5] 5007[11] (5282) 5628[11] 5826[6] *6586[8]*

Molly King (GER) *J Hirschberger* a89 89
3 rg c Lando(GER) Molly Maxima (GER) (Big Shuffle (USA))
1689a[6] 2315a[7]

Molly Le Clou (GER) *J Hirschberger* a81 102
4 rg h Doyen(IRE) Molly Maxima (GER) (Big Shuffle (USA))
1376a[7] 2633a[9]

Mollyow (IRE) *Dai Burchell* a31 35
8 ch m Iceman Corryvreckan (IRE) (Night Shift (USA))
4591[5]

Molten Gold *Andrew Balding* a69 71
3 b c New Approach(IRE) Flash Of Gold (Darshaan)
1479[5] 2000[5] 2615[3] 3063[7] 3468[5]

Molten Lava (IRE) *Paul Cole* a75 78
4 b g Rock Of Gibraltar(IRE) Skehana (IRE) (Mukaddamah (USA))
1387[6] 1916[2] 2174[4] 2827[7] 4288[8] 4807[3] 5750[6] 6365[7] *6656[6] 7529[5]*

Momentori *Scott Dixon* 24
3 ch f Observatory(USA) True Melody (IRE) (Grand Lodge (USA))
2505[14] 2861[13]

Moment To Dream *Ken Wingrove* a13
4 b m Halling(USA) Pretty Majestic (IRE) (Invincible Spirit (IRE))
1762[7] 2292[6] 8499[12]

Monaco Rose *Richard Fahey* a68 70
3 b f Sir Percy Pallas (Statue Of Liberty (USA))
1970[3] 2300[6] 2687[5] *3306[3]* 4137[5] 5111[2] 5718[3] 6767[5]

Monaco Show (FR) *A Wohler* 102
3 b f Kheleyf(USA) Good Lady (IRE) (Barathea (IRE))
2949a[4] 4184a[7]

Monaleen (IRE) *Ian Williams* a96 96
5 bb m High Chaparral(IRE) Dawn Air (USA) (Diesis)
614[4] 1067[13] 1855[8] 3436[6] 4581[3]

Monarch (IRE) *A P O'Brien* 83
3 b c Galileo(IRE) Secret Garden (IRE) (Danehill (USA))
3299[20]

Monarch Maid *Peter Hiatt* a75 81
5 b m Captain Gerrard(IRE) Orange Lily (Royal Applause)
2290[8] (3004) 3980[9] 4291[2] 5253[3] 5774[7] 6255[5] 6487[3] 6831[12] 7267[12]

Monarchs Glen *John Gosden* 85
2 b c Frankel Mirabilis (USA) (Lear Fan (USA))
6663[2] ◆ (7187)

Mon Beau Visage (IRE) *David O'Meara* a86 79
3 br g Footstepsinthesand Hurricane Lily (IRE) (Ali-Royal (IRE))
1599[9] 2650[10] 2802[9] *3568[7]* 5439[4] 5860[2] 6231[7] (6644) *6907[2] (7111)* 7360[9] *7958[7] 8052[8]*

Mon Bisou (IRE) *G Botti* a65 80
3 b c Pour Moi(IRE) Blessed Luck (IRE) (Rock Of Gibraltar (IRE))
2948a[9] 7999a[8]

Mon Brav *Brian Ellison* a53 85
9 b g Sampower Star Danehill Princess (IRE) (Danehill (USA))
1298[4] 1787[8] 2238[3] ◆ 3168[11] 4608[11] 5439[5] ◆ 6136[7] 6522[3] 6714[10]

Moncarno *John Best* a58 54
6 b g Lucarno(USA) Sparkling Jewel (Bijou D'Inde)
2205[6] 3041[3] *3528[12]*

Monday Club *Dominic Ffrench Davis* a59 65
3 ch g Strategic Prince Support Fund (IRE) (Intikhab (USA))
1734[5] *2325[10]* 2851[6] 3997[2] ◆ 4500[5] *5303[5]* (6443) 7057[2] 7628[2]

Mondial (IRE) *Charlie Appleby* a73
3 b f Shamardal(USA) Mannington (AUS) (Danehill (USA))
102[4]

Mondialiste (IRE) *David O'Meara* a84 118
6 b h Galileo(IRE) Occupandiste (IRE) (Kaldoun (FR))
2568a[7] 3242[11] 4666[2] (5431a) 7172a[4] 7835a[12]

Mondrian Jones *Charles Hills*
3 b g Dutch Art Akhira (Emperor Jones (USA))
1653[12]

Monet's Sky (IRE) *Lucy Wadham* a32
3 ch g Roderic O'Connor(IRE) La Sibilla (Fantastic Light (USA))
96[7]

Money In My Pocket (IRE) *Richard Hannon* a35 72
2 b f Acclamation Azabara (Pivotal)
4706[6] 5705[3] 5869[2] 6257[10] *7640[9]*

Money Multiplier (USA) *Chad C Brown* 110
4 bb r Lookin At Lucky(USA) Intensify (USA) (Unbridled's Song (USA))
7835a[6]

Moneyoryourlife *Richard Hannon* a54 62
2 b c Dick Turpin(IRE) Truly Pink (Mr Greeley (USA))
2822[6] 2997[9] 3668[5] 4982[5] 5239[3] 6313[3] 7244[3] *7866[3]*

Money Team (IRE) *David Barron* a86 86
5 b g Kodiac Coral Dawn (IRE) (Trempolino (USA))
(28) 159[3] 901[10] 4514[7] 5274[7] (6131) 6449[6] 6714[7] *7434[6]* 7590[2] 7773[8] *8083[11]*

Mongolian Saturday (USA) *Enebish Ganbat* a107 118
6 b g Any Given Saturday(USA) Miss Hot Salsa (USA) (Houston (USA))
1911a[9] 3244[9] 4151[11] 7833a[9]

Monique Rosa (FR) *George Baker*
3 b f Naaqoos Apulia (USA) (Street Cry (IRE))
3145[8]

Monjeni *Sir Mark Prescott Bt* a65 67
3 b g Montjeu(IRE) Polly's Mark (IRE) (Mark Of Esteem (IRE))
3493[11] *3991[5]* 4450[2] 4971[12] *5473[2]* 6219[6] 6519[5] 7006[5]

Monks Stand (USA) *Jeremy Noseda* a87 85
2 b g More Than Ready(USA) Return The Jewel (USA) (Broken Vow (USA))
1749[2] ◆ 2082[3] *(2319)* ◆ (2641) 3243[7] 4150[6] 4825[7] *5299[2]*

Monna Valley *Stuart Williams* a68 62
4 ch g Exceed And Excel(AUS) Monnavanna (IRE) (Machiavellian (USA))
1838[8] 2379[11] 3078[6] *3522[6]* 4278[8] 4740[2] *(5399) 6662[12] 7257[6] 8179[2] 8410[4]*

Monologue (IRE) *Simon Hodgson* a53 48
3 ch g Manduro(GER) Homily (Singspiel (IRE))
3464[8] 3769[12] 4156[9] *6967[3]*

Monopoli *Ivan Furtado* a58 54
7 ch m Cadeaux Genereux Jump Ship (Night Shift (USA))
1048[8] 1202[7] 3896[6] 4456[5] 4724[3] 5513[4] 5868[5] 6212[9] *7262[5]*

Monoshka (IRE) *Richard Hannon* a63 78
2 b g Kodiac Coastal Waters (Halling (USA))
3813[4] 4075[8] (4837) 5644[5] 6800[7]

Monotype (IRE) *Roger Varian* 101
4 b g Makfi Mill Guineas (USA) (Salse (USA))
2468[2] 3351[2] 4162[6] (6379) ◆ 7058[P]

Monpazier (IRE) *K R Burke* a30 44
3 gr g Tamayuz Wicked Maria (IRE) (Daylami (IRE))
423[7] 858[7] 959[7] 2308[12] 2829[5] 3493[12] 4024[6]

Mon Petite Etoile (FR) *David Elsworth* a53
3 b f What A Caper(IRE) Arundhati (IRE) (Royal Academy (USA))
814[9] 6415[10] 7607[5]

Mon Petit Fleur *Lydia Pearce* a58
4 b m Arabian Gleam Mon Petit Diamant (Hector Protector (USA))
143[10] 381[7]

Monsea (IRE) *Mlle M Henry* a68 62
5 gr g Manduro(GER) Sea Drift (FR) (Warning)
7295a[12]

Monsieur Bernard (FR) *G Botti* 69
3 gr c Siyouni(FR) Delvita (FR) (Pinmix (FR))
2172a[8]

Monsieur Chevalier (IRE) *Nikki Evans* a65 88
9 b g Chevalier(IRE) Blue Holly (IRE) (Blues Traveller (IRE))
266[7] 2328[9] 5357[6] *6138[13]* 7076[16]

Monsieur Glory *Tom Dascombe* a52 76
3 ch g Monsieur Bond(IRE) Chushka (Pivotal)
1275[8] 1667[3] (2308) 2652[6] 3482[2] 3751[4] ◆ (4455) 4892[5] 6767[8] 7274[2]

Monsieur Jamie *J R Jenkins* a71 76
8 b g Monsieur Bond(IRE) Primula Bairn (Bairn (USA))
21[5] 176[3] 579[5] 869[6] (937) 1026[5] 1298[7] 4389[8] 6410[6] 7444[10]

Monsieur Jimmy *Declan Carroll* a73 50
4 ch g Monsieur Bond(IRE) Artistic License (IRE) (Chevalier (IRE))
246[5] 276[3] 448[3] 523[5] (799) 1154[10] 1254[11] *(1298)* 1495[12] *1712[3]* 2053[2] *2332[12]* 3070[11] 3484[5] *3610[12] 7663[13] 8094[9]*

Monsieur Joe (IRE) *Paul Midgley* a100 113
9 b g Choisir(AUS) Pascali (Compton Place)
1730a[2] 2317a[7] 2895[10] 3151[8] (3752) 3909[2] 4166[4] (4359) 4905a[2]

Monsieur Opera (FR) *Barbara Valenti* a55 81
7 b h Lando(GER) Mensa Sonne (FR) (Monsun (GER))
5216a[13]

Monsieur Paddy *Tony Carroll* a68 14
3 ch g Monsieur Bond(IRE) Minnina (IRE) (In The Wings)
7011[13] *(8290)*

Monsieur Valentine *Tony Carroll* a55 66
4 ch g Monsieur Bond(IRE) Minnina (IRE) (In The Wings)
247[9] 2542[10] 3745[7] (5051) 5711[5] 6408[7] 7572[5] *8121[2]*

Montague Way (IRE) *Andrew Balding* 27
3 b g Rock Of Gibraltar(IRE) Shanghai Lily (IRE) (King's Best (USA))
1146[9] 1829[11]

Montaly *Andrew Balding* a93 104
5 b g Yeats(IRE) Le Badie (IRE) (Spectrum (IRE))
2468[9] 3246[5] 4353[3] 6118[2] 7569a[12] 7824[15]

Montataire (IRE) *Mark Johnston* 105
2 b c Cape Cross(IRE) Chantilly Pearl (USA) (Smart Strike (CAN))
2264[2] ◆ 2873[4] (3548) (4076) (4595) 4802[2] (5595) 6783[6] 7148[4]

Montclair (IRE) *Roger Brueggemann* 98
6 b g Montjeu(IRE) Minaccia (GER) (Platini (GER))
5428a[4]

Monteamiata (IRE) *Ed Walker* a66
2 b f Dream Ahead(USA) Tiger Spice (Royal Applause)
8151[3] 8443[5]

Monte Cinq (IRE) *Jason Ward* a87 66
2 b c Bushranger(IRE) Invincible Me (IRE) (Invincible Spirit (IRE))
1199[3] 1377[4] 4678[7] *5244[3]* 6010[9] 6807[7] *7381[2] (7748) 8209[4]*

Monte Fanum (ITY) *Gianluca Bietolini* a72 76
6 ch h Blu Air Force(IRE) Arsulvela (IRE) (Wixim (USA))
4074a[9]

Monte Napoleone (FR) *G Pannier* a63 71
7 ch g Fol Parade(ARG) Kyria (Grand Lodge (USA))
512a[13]

Monteverdi (FR) *Jamie Osborne* 94
3 b g Kyllachy West Of Saturn (USA) (Gone West (USA))
1442[2] ◆ 2161[3] 3299[25] 3908[6] 4867[12]

Monticello (IRE) *Mark Johnston* a66 96
2 b c Teofilo(IRE) Towards (USA) (Fusaichi Pegasus (USA))
(3108) (3705) 4622[2] 5646[6] 7409[5]

Mont Kiara (FR) *Kevin Ryan* 99
3 b g Kendargent(FR) Xaarienne (Xaar)
1996[6] 2736[8] 3413[2] ◆ 4062[5] (4652) 5409[9] 6327[14] 6916[8] 7537[14]

Mont Ras (IRE) *Roger Fell* a99 88
9 ch g Indian Ridge Khayrat (IRE) (Polar Falcon (USA))
594[3] 767[6] 1001[2] 1344[3] 3565[5] 3855[6] 4163[11] 4611[8] 5156[10] ◆ 5802[8] *7108[3] 7796[9] 7957[8] 8478[11]*

Mont Royal (FR) *Ollie Pears* 75
2 gr c Naaqoos Take Blood (FR) (Take Risks (FR))
5029[2] ◆ 5713[3] ◆ 6712[8]

Montsarrat (IRE) *Mark Johnston* a95 99
3 br c Poet's Voice Flying Flag (IRE) (Entrepreneur)
1080[2] 1867[6] 2407[2] 2889[2] 3688[5] (3950) ◆ 4339[3] 4797[11] 5651[8] 5932[5] 6715[7] *7608[10]*

Montycristo *Philip Hide* a27
3 br g Motivator Water Gipsy (Piccolo)
691[10]

Montys Angel (IRE) *John C McConnell* a37 25
6 b m Definite Article Montys Bank (IRE) (Montelimar (USA))
5900a[21]

Monumental Man *Michael Attwater* a83 83
7 b g Vital Equine(IRE) Spark Up (Lahib (USA))
1566[5] 1857[9] 2290[3] 2643[4] 3123[6] 3487[4] *4198[3] 4475[6]* 5050[5] 5928[6] *6248[2] 6699[2] (8280) 8571[8]*

Monzino (USA) *Michael Chapman* a53 33
8 bb g More Than Ready(USA) Tasso's Magic Roo (USA) (Tasso (USA))
6[5] 891[4] 1156[4] 1405[8] 1952[8] 2853[4] *7895[7] 8180[7]*

Moohaarib (IRE) *Marco Botti* a75 115
5 b g Oasis Dream Evita (Selkirk (USA))
372a[10] 540a[12] 628a[15]

Mooizo (IRE) *Peter Chapple-Hyam* a38 49
3 b f Rock Of Gibraltar(IRE) Skid (IRE) (Montjeu (IRE))
96[6] 4367[11] 5101[8]

Moojaned (IRE) *David Evans* a67 79
5 b g Raven's Pass(USA) Mufradat (IRE) (Desert Prince (IRE))
890[5] 1002[8] 1236[7] (1531) 1717[6] 2399[2] 3192[5] 4417a[9] 4795[7] 5231[5] 5406[7] *6128[14]* 6380[3] 6889[10] *6965[9]* 7418[9] *7515[11] 7992[9] (8567)*

Moonadee (IRE) *Daniel Mark Loughnane* 75
4 gr g Haatef(USA) Again Royale (IRE) (Royal Academy (USA))
2441[8] 4348[6]

Moon Arc (IRE) *Keith Dalgleish* a52 60
4 b g Arcano(IRE) Moon Unit (IRE) (Intikhab (USA))
506[6] 1697[8] 2558[13] 2836[4] 3288[5] 3547[5]

Moon Arrow (IRE) *Michael Blake* a58 34
3 b g Authorized(IRE) Moon Sister (IRE) (Cadeaux Genereux)
5811[4] 6411[5] 6871[6] 7767[10] 8194[2]

Moonbi Creek (IRE) *Richard Ford* a61 54
9 b g Fasliyev(USA) Moonbi Range (IRE) (Nordico (USA))
201[2] ◆ *297[5] 1117[5]*

Moonday Sun (USA) *John Butler* a81 81
7 gr g Mizzen Mast(USA) Storm Dove (USA) (Storm Bird (CAN))
(173) 773[3] (1114) 1652[2] 2296[3] 2743[8]

Moondust (IRE) *John Gosden* a33 67
2 b f Exceed And Excel(AUS) Lady Hawkfield (IRE) (Hawk Wing (USA))
2467[10] 7056[3] *7380[9]*

Moondyne Joe (IRE) *K R Burke* 84
3 b g Bushranger(IRE) Golden Shine (Royal Applause)
(2982)

Moone Dancer (IRE) *Mrs John Harrington* a37 65
4 b m Rip Van Winkle(IRE) Celeste (FR) (Muhtathir)
5620a[9]

Moon Idol *Richard Hannon* 41
2 ch c Pivotal Moon Goddess (Rainbow Quest (USA))
6945[7]

Moonlight Blue (IRE) *Michael Dods* a68 43
2 b g Approve(IRE) Nouvelle Reve (GER) (Acatenango (GER))
4642[4] 5966[10] 6534[7]

Moonlight Dream (FR) *A Marcialis* a7 77
2 gr g Myboycharlie(IRE) Moonlight Kiss (IRE) (Verglas (IRE))
1579a[8]

Moonlight Magic *J S Bolger* 115
3 b c Cape Cross(IRE) Melikah (IRE) (Lammtarra (USA))
1370a[5] (2069a) 2896[16] 3679a[6] 5685a[3] 6354a[6] 6975a[3]

Moonlightnavigator (USA) *John Quinn* a86 93
4 bb g Henrythenavigator(USA) Victorica (USA) (Exbourne (USA))
749[6] 1215[4] 1924[12] 2257[6] 2743[9] 3398[3] 4193[2] 4443[2] 4704[2] (4933) 5538[5] 6500[6] (7095) 7825[18]

Moonlight Silver *William Muir* a63
2 gr f Makfi Moon Empress (FR) (Rainbow Quest (USA))
6413[10] 8355[6]

Moonlight Venture *Conor Dore* a79 79
5 ch g Tobougg(IRE) Evening (Mark Of Esteem (IRE))
(37) (276) 424[6] 448[4] 581[7] (598) 683[13] 974[3] 1251[2] *1403[3]* 1625[3] 1818[6] 2402[5] *2821[10]* 3421[7] *5810[10] 6235[8]*

Moonlit Show *Charlie Fellowes* a66 98
2 b f Showcasing Shona (USA) (Lyphard (USA))
4457[3] *5242[4]* (6078) (6860a) 7757a[6]

Moonmeister (IRE) *A J Martin* a88 90
5 b g Mastercraftsman(IRE) Moon Unit (IRE) (Intikhab (USA))
4417a[7] 4850a[6] 5611[3] 7150[10] 7708a[7]

Moon Over Mobay *Michael Blanshard* a61 61
3 b f Archipenko(USA) Slew The Moon (ARG) (Kitwood (USA))
1755[7] *2108[6]* 3198[2] 3509[9] 6194[7] *7760[4] 8445[6]*

Moon Over Rio (IRE) *Ben Haslam* 69
5 b m Captain Rio Moonchild (GER) (Acatenango (GER))
1560[3] 2836[11] 3498[8] 5481[3] ◆ 6029[3]

Moonraker *Mick Channon* a107 109
4 ch g Starspangledbanner(AUS) Licence To Thrill (Wolfhound (USA))
2159[10] 2438[9] 3195[8] *3656[2]* 4126[11] 4865[21] 5418[13] 6112[15]

Moonrise Landing (IRE) *Ralph Beckett* a107 110
5 gr m Dalakhani(IRE) Celtic Slipper (IRE) (Anabaa (USA))
(1067) ◆ (2486)

Moon River (IRE) *Michael Appleby* a99 87
4 b m Exceed And Excel(AUS) Dame Blanche (IRE) (Be My Guest (USA))
(1) 254[7] (581) ◆ *(960) (1153)* 1757[5] 2026[5] 2890[2]

Moonshine Dancer *David Simcock* a70
2 b f Dark Angel(IRE) Raggle Taggle (IRE) (Tagula (IRE))
7855[4] 8443[4]

Moonshiner (GER) *Jean-Pierre Carvalho* 108
3 ch c Adlerflug(GER) Montezuma (GER) (Monsun (GER))
5218a[2] (6176a) 6971a[2]

Moonshine Ridge (IRE) *Alan Swinbank* a76 62
5 b m Duke Of Marmalade(IRE) Dreams Come True (FR) (Zafonic (USA))
26[4] 180[3] 428[8] 957[2] ◆ *(1049)* ◆ *(1156) (1296) 1711[3]* 4239[5]

Moonstone Rock *Jim Boyle* a51 63
2 ch f Rock Of Gibraltar(IRE) Komena (Komaite (USA))
4951[6] *6673[8]* 7216[5] 7571[3] *7974[11]*

Moon Sun Star (IRE) *David O'Meara* 25
2 b c Teofilo(IRE) Twice The Ease (Green Desert (USA))
7580[8]

Moon Trip *Geoffrey Deacon* a27 52
7 b g Cape Cross(IRE) Fading Light (King's Best (USA))
3999[6] 4995[3] 6315[9]

Moon Trouble (IRE) *F Head* a83 109
3 ch c Lope De Vega(IRE) Shake The Moon (GER) (Loup Solitaire (USA))
1308a[3] 2283a[8] 3183a[2] 3938a[6] 5004a[5] 6991a[11]

Moonwalk Step (FR) *T Castanheira* a77 80
3 b c Whipper(USA) Egypt Moon (Zieten (USA))
1311a[6]

Moorside *Charles Hills* a82 98
3 b f Champs Elysees Marching West (USA) (Gone West (USA))
1966[2] 2735[4] *(5025)* 6332[4] 7271[6]

Moorstone *Giles Bravery* a37
4 b m Manduro(GER) Pan Galactic (USA) (Lear Fan (USA))
8281[6]

Mops Angel *Michael Appleby* a64 61
5 b m Piccolo Tanning (Atraf)
173[9] 676[9] 859[5] 1241[5] 1595[4] 2403[7] 2542[6] *3474[9]* 4025[7] *5604[3]* 5753[5] *7850[9]*

Morache Music *Patrick Chamings* a87 92
8 b g Sleeping Indian Enchanted Princess (Royal Applause)
2581[8] 3358[11] 4051[2] ◆ 4954[8] *5507[6]* 5991[5] ◆ 6806[4] *7461[8]*

Morando (FR) *Roger Varian* 109
3 b g Kendargent(FR) Moranda (FR) (Indian Rocket)
1714[4] (1930) (3130) (6557) 7354[7]

Morawij *D Selvaratnam* a106 80
6 ch g Exceed And Excel(AUS) Sister Moonshine (FR) (Piccolo)
91a[9] *1105a[3]*

Mordoree (IRE) *Clive Cox* 38
2 ch f Mayson Lisieux Orchid (IRE) (Sadler's Wells (USA))
7056[9] 7696[10]

More Aspen (USA) *S Seemar* a86 103
5 ch m More Than Ready(USA) Jade Aspen (USA) (Jade Hunter (USA))
(187a) 451a[3] 809a[5]

More Beau (USA) *David Nicholls* a74 73
5 bb g More Than Ready(USA) Frontier Beauty (USA) (Gone West (USA))
3610[2] 4337[2] 4970[5] 5439[3] *5969[3]* 6136[5] 7059[4] *7663[11] (7851) 8067[4] 8389[7]*

More Kudos (USA) *John Quinn* a59 55
3 ch g Exchange Rate(USA) Marquise Quest (USA) (Coronado's Quest (USA))
328[3] 610[6] 794[7]

Morello (IRE) *Henry Candy* 40
2 b f Medicean Mullein (Oasis Dream)
6880[12] 7210[9]

More Mischief *Jedd O'Keeffe* a101 103
4 b m Azamour(IRE) Mischief Making (USA) (Lemon Drop Kid (USA))
(1221) 1855[4] 2363[2] *3608[2]* 5002a[6] 6200a[7]

More Spice (IRE) *Robert Cowell* a73 76
4 b g Exceed And Excel(AUS) High Spice (USA) (Songandaprayer (USA))
(151) 504[8] (775) 1433[2] 2088[2] 2342[10] *3307[2]*

More Than A Dream (IRE) *H Al Jehani* a91 104
3 b c Halling(USA) Chabelle (Shirocco (GER))
1582a[2] 8573a[16]

More Than Munny (USA) *J P Murtagh* a83 73
3 ch g Munnings(USA) Winner's Ticket (USA) (Jolie's Halo (USA))
644a[3] 7339a[9]

More Than This (FR) *Y Barberot* a75 75
3 b c Authorized(IRE) Magic Date (FR) (Sagamix (FR))
1286a[7] 5704a[4]

Morga (IRE) *Desmond McDonogh* a69 97
6 b m Whipper(USA) Langfuhrina (USA) (Langfuhr (CAN))
6200a[2] 6820a[6]

Morgan Blond (IRE) *A Giorgi* a45 74
2 ch c Intense Focus(USA) Siansa (IRE) (Teofilo (IRE))
5755a[12]

Morigane Forlonge (FR) *A Giorgi* 87
2 b f American Post Wonderful Life (GER) (Tiger Hill (IRE))
1118a[2] 4694a[4] 5703a[8] 7170a[10]

Moritzburg *M Halford* 92
2 ch c Dutch Art Providencia (Oasis Dream)
2717a[3]

Morning Suit (USA) *Mark Johnston* a81 65
2 rg c Street Boss(USA) Blue Dress (USA) (Danzig (USA))
1621[5] *(3032) 5299[3]* 6275[7] *7956[2] 8132[2]*

Mornington *Marcus Tregoning* a71 59
3 b g Aussie Rules(USA) Giusina Mia (USA) (Diesis)
8157[2] 8255[3]

Morocco *Karen Tutty* a41 68
7 b g Rock Of Gibraltar(IRE) Shanghai Lily (IRE) (King's Best (USA))
1201[14] *2329[13]* 3253[3] 4489[5]

Mor Spirit (USA) *Bob Baffert* a114
3 bb r Eskendereya(USA) I'm A Dixie Girl (USA) (Dixie Union (USA))
2063a[10]

Moscato *Sir Mark Prescott Bt* a99 100
5 gr g Hernando(FR) Alba Stella (Nashwan (USA))
2472[2] 3246[4] 3658[4] 4752[8]

Moshe (IRE) *Philip Kirby* a85 85
5 b g Dansili Rosinka (IRE) (Soviet Star (USA))
6[7] 3520[12] 4004[2] 4381[4] 5061[5] 5856[3]

Mossgo (IRE) *John Best* a79 74
6 b g Moss Vale(IRE) Perovskia (USA) (Stravinsky (USA))
56[7] 604[3] 714[6] 1173[10] 1433[3] 2342[2] 2768[2] 2931[7] 3159[11] 7420[7] 8010[10] 8228[7] 8430[2]

Moss Street *Conor Dore* a45 60
6 b g Moss Vale(IRE) Street Style (IRE) (Rock Of Gibraltar (IRE))
2849[8] 5011[4] 5624[3] 6315[6] (6890) 7300[2] 7421[3] 7888[9]

Mossy's Lodge *Anthony Carson* a68
3 b f Royal Applause Tee Cee (Lion Cavern (USA))
275[8] 441[2] (611) 978[5] 7069[5] 7612[2] 7817[2] 7985[10]

Mostahel *Richard Hannon* 27
2 b c Acclamation Entente Cordiale (IRE) (Ela-Mana-Mou)
7502[14]

Mostashreqah *Milton Bradley* a44 47
3 ch f Equiano(FR) China Cherub (Inchinor)
296[5] 924[11] 1061[8] 2186[11] 3126[5] 3513[9] 3987[11] 4796[5] 5167[4] 5721[6] 5954[14] 6631[8]

Most Beautiful *Thomas F Proctor* a92 106
3 b f Canford Cliffs(IRE) Saphira's Fire (IRE) (Cape Cross (IRE))
2272a[4] 2923a[9] 4540a[3] 7829a[3]

Most Celebrated (IRE) *Saeed bin Suroor* 89
3 b c New Approach(IRE) Pietra Santa (FR) (Acclamation)
3023[2] (3723) 4396[5] 6209[3]

Motabaary (IRE) *Mme Pia Brandt* a99 98
6 b g Tamayuz Truly Yours (IRE) (Barathea (IRE))
4074a[2] 7524a[3]

Motdaw *Mick Channon* 103
3 b f Motivator Dawnus (IRE) (Night Shift (USA))
(1275) 1409[3] 1828[5] 2244[12] 3060[4] 3352[2] (3894) 4078[5] 4757[5] (6115) 6505[2]

Mothers Finest (IRE) *Adrian Paul Keatley* a102 99
4 ch m Tamayuz Sheer Glamour (IRE) (Peintre Celebre (USA))
1858[7] 2191[14] 2890[3] (3565) 3979[8] 4812a[7] 5313a[13]

Motivate *Sir Mark Prescott Bt* a57
3 b g Motivator Hispalis (IRE) (Barathea (IRE))
1000[5] 1160[5] 1653[7] 6698[8] 7138[6]

Mo Tom (USA) *Thomas Amoss* a110
3 bb c Uncle Mo(USA) Caroni (USA) (Rubiano (USA))
2063a[8]

Motorbike (IRE) *G Botti* a40 54
3 ch c Manduro(GER) Ars Nova (IRE) (Barathea (IRE))
7999a[14]

Moueenn *Roger Varian* a76 76
3 ch g Lope De Vega(IRE) Quesada (IRE) (Peintre Celebre (USA))
958[3] 1324[2] 1630[4] 2012[3] 2580[3] 3607[5]

Mouille Point *Richard Hannon* 72
2 b f Motivator Turning Leaf (IRE) (Last Tycoon)
6336[3] ◆ 7210[2]

Moulin Rouge (DEN) *Kevin Frost* a63 46
5 ch m Zambezi Sun Embattle (FR) (Dernier Empereur (USA))
199[2]

Mountain Angel (IRE) *Roger Varian* a61
2 b c Dark Angel(IRE) Fanciful Dancer (Groom Dancer (USA))
8384[5]

Mountain Bell *Ralph Beckett* 107
3 b f Mount Nelson Shenir (Mark Of Esteem (IRE))
(1386) 2035[3] (6321) 7545[2]

Mountain Man *Michael Easterby* a59 48
4 b g Hellvelyn Jane Jubilee (IRE) (Mister Baileys)
320[3] 504[4] 733[10]

Mountain Rescue (IRE) *Chris Wall* a92 86
4 b g High Chaparral(IRE) Amber Queen (IRE) (Cadeaux Genereux)
267[2] ◆ 1737[3] (2296) 3660[4] 4300[4] 5082[6] (6628) 7428[2]

Mount Cheiron (USA) *Richard Ford* a60 53
5 b g Henrythenavigator(USA) Chalamont (IRE) (Kris)
986[6] 1035[3] 1165[2] (1791) 2448[6] 4214[8] 4648[7] 4929[3] (5064) (5604) 6137[11] 6857[9] 7300[6] 7944[4] 8499[9]

Mount Isa (IRE) *Mme Pia Brandt* a90 78
4 b g Bushranger(IRE) Fee Eria (FR) (Always Fair (USA))
4074a[7]

Mount Logan (IRE) *Roger Varian* 114
5 ch g New Approach(IRE) Vistaria (USA) (Distant View (USA))
(2465) 3384[4] 4821[6] (6233) 6666[3]

Mount Moriah *Ralph Beckett* a73 80
2 b g Mount Nelson Rule Britannia (Night Shift (USA))
5073[5] (5764) 6330[4] 6875[2] (7406)

Mount Rock *Michael Easterby* a63
2 b g Mount Nelson Holamo (IRE) (Montjeu (IRE))
8384[4]

Mount Shamsan *Gary Moore* a54 66
6 b g Danehill Dancer(IRE) Shamaiel (IRE) (Lycius (USA))
2977[2] 5485[2]

Mount Tahan (IRE) *Kevin Ryan* a83 96
4 b g Lope De Vega(IRE) Sorpresa (USA) (Pleasant Tap (USA))
1694[5] 2689[4] 3115[17] 3645[12] (5866) 6560[2] 7095[5] 7821[4]

Mount Vesuvius (IRE) *Paul Henderson* a55
8 b g Spartacus(IRE) Parker's Cove (USA) (Woodman (USA))
8559[9]

Moveable Asset (IRE) *Henry Tett* a56 64
8 b g Trans Island Mica Male (ITY) (Law Society (USA))
8164[8]

Move In Time *David O'Meara* a111 113
8 ch g Monsieur Bond(IRE) Tibesti (Machiavellian (USA))
745[5] 1197[7] 1862[10] 2475[7] 3244[8] 3752[2] 4824[12] 5555[17] 6327[19]

Mo'Vette (USA) *Richard Baltas* 71
2 bb f Uncle Mo(USA) Apple Strudel (USA) (More Than Ready (USA))
8127a[9]

Move Up *Saeed bin Suroor* a59 116
3 b c Dubawi(IRE) Rosinka (IRE) (Soviet Star (USA))
(4129) 4863[3] (6179a) (6940)

Movie Magic *Mark Hoad* a51 48
5 b m Multiplex Alucica (Celtic Swing)
155[12] 378[6] 417[5] 724[6]

Moviesta (USA) *Edward Lynam* a112 97
6 b g Hard Spun(USA) Miss Brickyard (USA) (A.P. Indy (USA))
1730a[8] 2159[11] 3681a[8] 4415a[18] 7520a[2]

Moving Robe (IRE) *Conrad Allen* a47 48
3 b f Iffraaj Emma Dora (IRE) (Medaglia d'Oro (USA))
2177[10] 3473[6] 7240[13] 7645[3] 7931[8] 8379[5] 8492[7]

Mowhoob *Brian Barr* a50 49
6 b g Medicean Pappas Ruby (USA) (Red Ransom (USA))
2409[3] 3043[4] 3363[8] 4454[8] 6512[12] 7817[5] 8070[12] 8278[13]

Mo Wonder *Adrian Paul Keatley* a30 50
3 b f Monsieur Bond(IRE) Mo Mhuirnin (IRE) (Danetime (IRE))
2360[3] 4292[12]

Moxey *Christopher Kellett*
5 ch g Nayef(USA) Emily Blake (IRE) (Lend A Hand)
2297[5]

Mozimba *Antony Brittain* a12 29
3 ch f Monsieur Bond(IRE) Mozayada (USA) (Street Cry (IRE))
896[8]

Mr Andros *Andrew Balding* a68 70
3 b g Phoenix Reach(IRE) Chocolada (Namid)
1421[10] 1859[5] 2375[6]

Mr Black *George Scott* a84 58
2 b g Showcasing Fuschia (Averti (IRE))
5727[7] (6622) 7258[5]

Mr Boomer (USA) *Jeremy Noseda* a76
4 ch g Giant's Causeway(USA) Element Of Truth (USA) (Atticus (USA))
600[4]

Mr Boss Man (IRE) *Adrian McGuinness* a76 56
8 b g Beneficial Sarah Massini (IRE) (Dr Massini (IRE))
(71) 545[2]

Mr Bossy Boots (IRE) *Amanda Perrett* a100 81
5 b g Teofilo(IRE) Zelding (IRE) (Warning)
50[P] 290[4] 599[7] 1204[6] (1752) 2027[15] 3157[5] (3566) 4758[12] 8256[3] 8593[3]

Mr Bounty *M D O'Callaghan* a63 67
6 b g Bahamian Bounty Zamindari (Zamindar (USA))
6461a[4]

Mr C (IRE) *Ollie Pears* 47
2 b g Fast Company(IRE) Vanitycase (IRE) (Editor's Note (USA))
2264[7] 3477[7]

Mr Caffrey *John Flint* a62 74
4 b g Duke Of Marmalade(IRE) Quest For Eternity (IRE) (Sadler's Wells (USA))
567[7] 728[4] 1253[5]

Mr Chocolate Drop (IRE) *Mandy Rowland* a53 43
12 b g Danetime(IRE) Forest Blade (IRE) (Charnwood Forest (IRE))
32[7] 334[5]

Mr Christopher (IRE) *Tom Dascombe* a82 47
4 b g Bahamian Bounty Embassy Pearl (IRE) (Invincible Spirit (IRE))
590[3] (682) 777[5] 1186[2] 1496[7] (1648) 2028[20] 3595[9] 3989[7] 7457[14] (8037) 8251[4] 8531[3]

Mr Chuckles (IRE) *Daniel Mark Loughnane* a52 50
3 b g Arcano(IRE) Caribbean Escape (Pivotal)
1448[5] 1789[7] 3478[11] 4007[7] 5968[9] 6646[12] 7096[6] 7896[9] 8145[11] 8542[2]

Mr Coco Bean (USA) *Ann Duffield* a74 69
2 b g Gio Ponti(USA) Ing Ing (FR) (Bering)
6741[3] ◆ 7247[3]

Mr Conundrum *Lynn Siddall* a54 46
3 b g Paco Boy(IRE) Folly Drove (Bahri (USA))
4382[7] 5178[8] 5578[3] 6436[7] 6835[7] (7509) 8288[3] 8542[10]

Mr Cool Cash *Richard Guest* a51 74
4 b g Firebreak Cashleen (USA) (Lemon Drop Kid (USA))
1125[6] 1488[8] 2045[2] (2673) 2918[10] 3478[8] 3952[7] 4102[4] 4729[6] 5151[8] 5887[11] 6568[8] (7010) 7253[5] 7671[7]

Mr Davies *David Brown* a68
2 ch g Shirocco(GER) Pasithea (IRE) (Celtic Swing)
7940[6] 7982[4]

Mr Enthusiastic *Noel Wilson* a13 56
2 b g Assertive Selkirk Rose (IRE) (Pips Pride)
1641[7] 2552[6] 3839[7] 6214[12] 7690[10]

Mr Fickle (IRE) *Gary Moore* a78 77
7 b g Jeremy(USA) Mamara Reef (Salse (USA))
3798[3] 6193[6] 6886[10] 7183[6]

Mr Frankie *Richard Phillips* a74 79
5 b g Sleeping Indian Shes Minnie (Bertolini (USA))
73[8] 893[8] 1501[10] 1652[7] 2153[12] 3476[6] (7369) ◆

Mr Globetrotter (USA) *Iain Jardine* a47 68
3 b g Henrythenavigator(USA) Sunshine For Life (USA) (Giant's Causeway (USA))
1671[9] 8411[8]

Mr Grumpy *Keith Dalgleish* a24 79
3 b g Sir Percy Panna (Polish Precedent (USA))
768[6] 1242[5] (2831) 3285[2]

Mr Hill *Rebecca Bastiman* a9
2 b g Misu Bond(IRE) Smiddy Hill (Factual (USA))
7122[13] 7331[10] 7845[7]

Mr Hobbs *Sylvester Kirk* a80 80
2 b c Harbour Watch(IRE) Stoneacre Sarah (Cadeaux Genereux)
2536[3] ◆ 2997[2] 3472[2] (4053) 5583[11] 6229[6] 6664[3] 7185[7] 7549[11]

Mr Lando *Johnny Farrelly* a62 60
7 b g Shirocco(GER) Capitana (GER) (Lando (GER))
877[10] (4716) 5303[3] 5680[3]

Mr Lucas (IRE) *Peter Niven* a47 53
3 b g Le Cadre Noir(IRE) Maripova (IRE) (Marju (IRE))
1031[3] 1564[7] 1819[6] 2741[4] 3838[9] 4844[3] 5181[5] 5732[13]

Mr Lupton (IRE) *Richard Fahey* a100 115
3 ch g Elnadim(USA) Chiloe Wigeon (IRE) (Docksider (USA))
1882[3] 2251[3] (3165) ◆ 3655[5] 4393[11] 5863[5] ◆ 6120[5] 7350[9]

Mr Mac *Peter Hedger* a56 24
2 b g Makfi Veronica Franco (Darshaan)
6880[11] 7458[6] 8354[9]

Mr Marchwood *Sylvester Kirk* a69 51
3 gr g Medicean Crocus Rose (Royal Applause)
2186[8] 2770[9] 3558[8] 4794[8] 6593[9] 7035[8] 7282[3] 7463[5] (7767) 7969[6] 8155[6] 8193[4] 8540[7]

Mr Maximum (USA) *Harry Dunlop* a66 54
2 bb g Creative Cause(USA) Allegro Lady (USA) (Souvenir Copy (USA))
5505[5] 6632[7] 7424[4] 7898[12]

Mr Minerals *Richard Hughes* a79
2 ch g Poet's Voice River Song (USA) (Siphon (BRZ))
(8404)

Mr Morocco *Giles Bravery* a48 55
4 b g Shirocco(GER) Moxby (Efisio)
20[7]

Mr Morse *Brian Ellison* a66 67
3 ro g Hellvelyn Songsheet (Dominion)
(8346)

Mr Opulence *T Le Brocq* a39 51
7 ch g Generous(IRE) Miss Opulence (IRE) (Kylian (USA))
2952a[2] (3381a) (3918a) 5459a[5]

Mr Orange (IRE) *Paul Midgley* a64 75
3 b g Paco Boy(IRE) Shirley Blake (IRE) (Acclamation)
1126[3] 1564[3] (2255) 2777[5] 3439[3] ◆ 3978[2] (4376) 5032[5] 6215[2] 6522[2] 7059[2] 7663[6]

Mr Owen (USA) *F Rohaut* a109 111
4 b h Invincible Spirit(IRE) Mrs Lindsay (USA) (Theatrical (IRE))
1910a[3] 3273[13] 4441a[2] 6601a[6] (8165a)

Mr Pickwick *James Fanshawe* a70 78
4 b g Mount Nelson Never Lose (Diktat)
1756[2] ◆

Mr Piglet *William Jarvis* 44
3 ch g Haafhd Pigment (Zamindar (USA))
3572[11] 4401[14]

Mr Pocket (IRE) *Paul Cole* a77 80
2 b c Acclamation Midnight Martini (Night Shift (USA))
4205[2] 4707[2] 5188[2] 5876[5] 7748[6] (7938)

Mr Potter *Richard Guest* a60 52
3 ch g Assertive Enclave (USA) (Woodman (USA))
1126[12] 1448[13] 1927[6] 2422[8] 2553[2] 2801[2] 3080[13] 4600[10] 5355[8] 6569[11] 6646[3] 7641[9] 7795[2] 7850[2] (8146) 8288[4] 8589[4]

Mr Quicksilver *Ed Walker* a73 86
4 gr g Dansili Last Second (IRE) (Alzao (USA))
3571[9] 4081[2] 4868[16] 5333[3] 6055[5] 6316[5] 7245[7]

Mr Red Clubs (IRE) *Michael Appleby* a77 83
7 b g Red Clubs(IRE) Queen Cobra (IRE) (Indian Rocket)
38[3] 256[10] 437[4] 491[2] 683[3] 734[3] 899[5] (1498) (1762) 2444[2] 2791[8] 4497[4] 4774[5]

Mr Right (IRE) *J F Levins* a75 93
4 b g Echo Of Light Danetime Lily (IRE) (Danetime (IRE))
4250a[2] 5941a[18]

Mr Rock (IRE) *George Baker* a69 62
5 b g Galileo(IRE) Kitza (IRE) (Danehill (USA))
4459[4] ◆ 7037[5]

Mrs Biggs *Declan Carroll* a61 68
4 ch m Paco Boy(IRE) Hoh Chi Min (Efisio)
1254[9] 1565[12] 2050[2] 2794[3] 3214[4] 3776[4] 4240[6] 4770[4] 5887[12] 6568[6] 7062[3] 7261[4] 7513[4] 7943[7] 8306[4] 8351[6]

Mrs Bubbles (IRE) *J S Moore* a68
4 b m Lord Shanakill(USA) Champagne Blitz (IRE) (Viking Ruler (AUS))
80[7] 192[6]

Mrs Burbidge *Neil Mulholland* a54 49
6 b m Pasternak Twin Time (Syrtos)
233[3] 348[3] 981[5] 1322[2] 7262[2] ◆

Mr Scaff (IRE) *Paul Henderson* 66
2 br c Vocalised(USA) Nancy Rock (IRE) (Rock Of Gibraltar (IRE))
5890[14] 6542[6] 7502[11]

Mr Scaramanga *Simon Dow* a78 101
2 b c Sir Percy Lulla (Oasis Dream)
1384[4] (2082) 2786[3] 3382[4] 4150[3] 5401[2] 5595[5] 6388a[22] (8423)

Mrs Conn (IRE) *Thomas Cleary* a43 47
5 b m Grandera(IRE) Judge Lily (FR) (Nikos)
5900a[19]

Mrs Danvers *Jonathan Portman* 106
2 gr f Hellvelyn Rebecca De Winter (Kyllachy)
(3143) (3686) (4394) (5359) (7113)

Mrs Eve (IRE) *Alan Bailey* a58 53
4 ch m Bahamian Bounty Catbells (IRE) (Rakti)
3599[U] (Dead)

Mrs Frosty (IRE) *Clive Mulhall* 21
3 b f Frozen Power(IRE) Petticoat Hill (UAE) (Timber Country (USA))
4041[13] 5388[9] 6567[8]

Mr Shekells *Philip McBride* a68 67
4 b g Three Valleys(USA) Quip (Green Desert (USA))
321[3] 437[9] 680[10] 1064[4]

Mr Singh *John Gosden* a55 112
4 b g High Chaparral(IRE) Sundari (IRE) (Danehill (USA))
2465[6] 4164[8] 5872[3] 6293[4]

Mr Skinnylegs *Brian Ellison* 50
2 b g Dream Win Impeccable Guest (IRE) (Orpen (USA))
3114[6]

Mrs McDougal (USA) *Chad C Brown* a97 107
4 b m Medaglia d'Oro(USA) Distorted Passion (USA) (Distorted Humor (USA))
3178a[3]

Mr Snoozy *Mark Walford* a62 74
7 b g Pursuit Of Love Hard To Follow (Dilum (USA))
132[6] 957[P] 1523[10] 2887[5]

Mr Standfast *Alan Phillips* a44 52
3 b g Mullionmileanhour(IRE) Phantom Ridge (IRE) (Indian Ridge)
1859[9] 2553[13]

Mr Strutter (IRE) *John Quinn* 58
2 ch g Sir Prancealot(IRE) Khajool (IRE) (Haafhd)
4161[10] 4423[9] 4966[6] 6010[4] 6222[9]

Mr Sundowner (USA) *Wilf Storey* a62 67
4 bb g Scat Daddy(USA) Bold Answer (USA) (Dynaformer (USA))
1252[11] 2092[8] 2618[4] 3363[5] 4144[6] 4486[4] 4930[7] 5068[13] 5729[5] 8307[3] 8589[6]

Mrs Warren *George Baker* a57 65
6 b m Kyllachy Bold Bunny (Piccolo)
1262[12] 1949[4] 2403[2] ◆ 3258[3] ◆ 3743[9] 4640[6]

Mr Turner *Mark H Tompkins* a18 58
3 b g Nayef(USA) Seasonal Blossom (IRE) (Fairy King (USA))
1784[8] 3080[8] 5085[10] 5636[8]

Mr Tyrrell (IRE) *Richard Hannon* 78
2 b c Helmet(AUS) Rocking (Oasis Dream)
4103[5] 4349[6] 5196[2] 6881[10]

Mr Vendman (IRE) *Ian Williams*
6 b g Whipper(USA) So Precious (IRE) (Batshoof)
199[10]

Ms Arsenal *Giles Bravery* 58
4 b m Mount Nelson Magical Dancer (IRE) (Magical Wonder (USA))
2904[10] 3572[8] 4565[7]

Ms Eboracum (IRE) *Michael Appleby* a46 48
4 b m Vale Of York(IRE) Ms Victoria (IRE) (Fasliyev (USA))
22[6] 130[3] 442[8] 617[6]

Ms Gillard *David Simcock* a64
3 b f Aussie Rules(USA) Oval Office (Pursuit Of Love)
458[7] 706[3] 1346[3] 5192[3] 5763[6]

Mshawish (USA) *Todd Pletcher* a114 115
6 b h Medaglia d'Oro(USA) Thunder Bayou (USA) (Thunder Gulch (USA))
1108a[6]

Muaanid *Doug Watson* a103 101
6 ch g Kheleyf(USA) Rifqah (USA) (Elusive Quality (USA))
374a[P]

Muaither (IRE) *John Gosden* a67 74
3 b g Poet's Voice Past The Post (USA) (Danzig (USA))
153[3] ◆ 287[4] 603[7] 2615[4] (3063) 3615[5]

Muarrab *M Al Mheiri* a118 87
7 b g Oasis Dream Licence To Thrill (Wolfhound (USA))
186a[5] 537a[2] (840a) (1105a)

Muatadel *Ed Dunlop* a62 63
3 b g Exceed And Excel(AUS) Rose Blossom (Pastoral Pursuits)
1337[8] 2156[6] 7782[4]

Mubajal *Owen Burrows* a91 83
3 br g Dubawi(IRE) Jadhwah (Nayef (USA))
3411[3] 3996[4] 4657[2] (5634) 6517[11]

Mubhirah *John Gosden* 66
2 br f Raven's Pass(USA) Ezima (IRE) (Sadler's Wells (USA))
7284[5]

Mubtaahij (IRE) *M F De Kock* a117 77
4 b h Dubawi(IRE) Pennegale (IRE) (Pennekamp (USA))
454a[5] 844a[4] 1108a[2]

Mubtaghaa (IRE) *M Al Mheiri* a88 109
4 b g Acclamation Mabalane (IRE) (Danehill (USA))
450a[7] ◆ 626a[13]

Mubtasim (IRE) *William Haggas* 102
2 b c Arcano(IRE) Start The Music (IRE) (King's Best (USA))
(3819) ◆ (5058) ◆ 5654[8] (6260) 6785[9]

Mucho Applause (IRE) *Andrew Balding* 81
2 b c Acclamation Pediment (Desert Prince (IRE))
3569[3] ◆ 4203[4] (6881)

Mudallel (IRE) *Ed Dunlop* 82
2 b c Invincible Spirit(IRE) Lixirova (FR) (Slickly (FR))
6751[2] ◆

Mufeed (USA) *S Seemar* a74
2 ch c Gemologist(USA) Hannah's Dowery (USA) (Stephen Got Even (USA))
8575a[5]

Muffri'Ha (IRE) *William Haggas* a111 112
4 b m Iffraaj Grecian Dancer (Dansili)
4582[8] 5158[4] 5647[7] 6746[3] (6947) (7152) (7650) ◆

Muhaafiz (IRE) *David Brown* a81 89
4 br g Lord Shanakill(USA) Yasmin Satine (IRE) (Key Of Luck (USA))
1633[3] ◆ 2163[14] 2620[3] (2811) 3113[8] 5180[12] 6753[18]

Muhadathat *Mark Johnston* 101
3 b f Showcasing Cavallo Da Corsa (Galileo (IRE))
3752[4] 4803[3] ◆ 5148[3] ◆ 5409[7] 6109[15]

Muhajjal *Owen Burrows* 79
2 b c Cape Cross(IRE) Muqantara (USA) (First Samurai (USA))
5356[3] 6108[3] 6777[4]

Muharaaj (IRE) *Mlle M-L Mortier* a90 105
5 b h Iffraaj Desert Sprite (IRE) (Tagula (IRE))
371a[6] 450a[13] 810a[13] 3090a[5] 5949a[9]

Muhazwara (IRE) *George Peckham* a54 20
4 b m Fastnet Rock(AUS) Carn Lady (IRE) (Woodman (USA))
325[6]

Muhtadim (IRE) *Charles Smith* a49 49
4 b g Dubawi(IRE) Dhelaal (Green Desert (USA))
582[6] 959[6] 1676[14] *2609[7]* 3040[8] 3634[7] 3879[3]

Muhtaram *M Al Mheiri* a91 86
6 b g Shamardal(USA) Neshla (Singspiel (IRE))
12a[2] 183a[4]

Muhtaris (IRE) *James Evans* a87 87
6 b g Teofilo(IRE) Fann (USA) (Diesis)
(132)

Muir Lodge *George Baker* a80 97
5 ch g Exceed And Excel(AUS) Miss Chaussini (IRE) (Rossini (USA))
(1990) 2547[3] 4109[8] 4862[23] 5825[5] *6627[12]*

Muirsheen Durkin *Tom Dascombe* 80
2 b g Fastnet Rock(AUS) Be My Queen (IRE) (Sadler's Wells (USA))
2873[8] 3477[3] (3872) (5318) 5829[3] 7416[2]

Mujaamil *William Haggas* 79
3 b c Dansili Muwakleh (Machiavellian (USA))
2614[3] 4657[3] 5380[2] (5979) 6344[10]

Mujaarib (AUS) *M F De Kock* 107
7 br h Nadeem(AUS) Mihnah (IRE) (Lahib (USA))
187a[3] 372a[4] 538a[9]

Mujassam *David O'Meara* 103
4 ch g Kyllachy Naizak (Medicean)
1441[14] 1856[14] 2480[3] 3163[10] 3622[3] 5418[11] 6556[24]

Mujazif (IRE) *Michael Appleby* a66 85
6 br g Shamardal(USA) Red Bandanna (IRE) (Montjeu (IRE))
239[6] 2441[6] (3220) 3395[2] 4446[4]

Mujeeb *F Head* a65 76
2 b c Dubawi(IRE) Naahedh (Medicean)
7588a[7]

Mukaabra *F Chappet* a94 84
3 b f Iffraaj Peace Signal (USA) (Time For A Change (USA))
(697) (2178) 3410[3] 4028[2] 4556[4] *(5765) (6964) 7676a[6] 8563a[14]*

Mukalal *Marcus Tregoning* a76
2 b g Mawatheeq(USA) Misdaqeya (Red Ransom (USA))
8088[2] ◆

Mukallaf (IRE) *Roger Varian* a57 64
2 b c Zoffany(IRE) Dashing Beauty (IRE) (Daggers Drawn (USA))
3730[9] 7226[8] *7975[8] 8398[5]*

Mukaynis (IRE) *Kevin Ryan* a97 96
5 b g Tamayuz Wild Ways (Green Desert (USA))
1205[2] 1968[5] 2895[4] 4862[24] 5641[12] (Dead)

Mukhayyam *Tim Easterby* a86 96
4 b g Dark Angel(IRE) Caster Sugar (USA) (Cozzene (USA))
1522[6] 1871[13] 2268[4] *2620[6]* 3113[4] 3520[7] ◆ 3950[4] 4520[2] 4680[2] 5031[2] 5837[3] 6165[3] 6561[4] (6794) 7538[8] 7824[7]

Mulk *Sir Michael Stoute* 88
3 ch g New Approach(IRE) Nannina (Medicean)
1421[2] (1970) 3296[9]

Mullarkey *John Best* a70 71
2 b c Mullionmileanhour(IRE) Hannah's Dream (IRE) (King's Best (USA))
6264[3] ◆ *6655[5] 6672[6]* 7185[3] 7467[7] *8153[8] 8466[12] 8592[3]*

Mulled Wine *John Best* a58 45
3 b g Mullionmileanhour(IRE) Numanthia (IRE) (Barathea (IRE))
400[5] 976[5] 1389[6] *7986[10] 8382[8]*

Mullionheir *John Best* a79 69
4 b g Mullionmileanhour(IRE) Peyto Princess (Bold Arrangement)
2206[11] 4625[20] *7990[11] 8069[11]*

Mullover *John Best* a47
3 b f Mullionmileanhour(IRE) Daughters World (Agnes World (USA))
140[10]

Multellie *Tim Easterby* 89
4 b g Multiplex Bollin Nellie (Rock Hopper)
1493[5] 2163[13] 3520[10] 4044[3] 4703[2] 5157[4] (5837) 6781[2] 7498[12]

Multicultural (IRE) *James Tate* 69
2 b f Fastnet Rock(AUS) Cochabamba (IRE) (Hurricane Run (IRE))
7695[4] ◆

Multiculture (IRE) *John Joseph Murphy* a72 80
4 b g Mount Nelson Gracious Melange (Medicean)
3630a[7]

Multigifted *Michael Madgwick* a63 62
3 b f Multiplex Attlongglast (Groom Dancer (USA))
610[9] 725[5] 1141[3] 2083[4] *3033[3] 3318[5]* 4159[2] 4562[7] 5891[5] 6194[3] *6871[12]* 7300[4] *7614[7] (7760) 8359[8]*

Multi Grain *Micky Hammond* 72
4 b m Sir Percy Grain Only (Machiavellian (USA))
2427[4] 3018[6] 3480[4] 4489[8]

Multi Quest *John E Long* a54 56
4 b m Multiplex Ryan's Quest (IRE) (Mukaddamah (USA))
174[4] 381[5] 528[2] (790) 1005[2] 1319[10] 1794[8] 2584[4] 3040[5] 3993[11] 4278[3] 4878[3] *5475[8] 6249[9] 6902[10]* 7445[2] *7694[2] 8474[8]*

Multitask *Gary Moore* a80 72
6 b g Multiplex Attlongglast (Groom Dancer (USA))
433[10] 561[6] 953[5] 1143[7] 1544[12] 2584[8] *4014[11] (4715)* (5710) *(6657)* (7036) *7457[7] 8178[4]*

Mulwith (IRE) *David Barron* 65
2 b g Kodiac Crying Aloud (USA) (Street Cry (IRE))
1377[5] 1850[9] 2830[3] 4602[9] 5112[2] 5799[7]

Mulzamm (IRE) *James McAuley* a106 55
4 b g Cape Cross(IRE) Vine Street (IRE) (Singspiel (IRE))
8197a[14]

Mulzim *Ed Dunlop* 66
2 b c Exceed And Excel(AUS) Samaah (IRE) (Cape Cross (IRE))
7157[7] 7574[6]

Mumbles Magic (IRE) *Jo Hughes* a41 16
3 b f Thousand Words Chaguaramas (IRE) (Mujadil (USA))
274[8]

Mumford *Geoffrey Harker* a42 62
4 b g Stimulation(IRE) Noble Nova (Fraam)
2307[5] *3563[8]*

Mumgala (FR) *F Vermeulen* a49 66
6 b m Samum(GER) Stamingala (IRE) (Alzao (USA))
6938a[7]

Mums The Word *Richard Fahey* a75 85
2 b f Mayson Tell Mum (Marju (IRE))
2732[6] *3647[8]* 4457[2] *5506[3]* 5794[9] 6289[2] 8062a[6] *8397[2]*

Munaaser *A R Al Rayhi* a104 103
5 b g New Approach(IRE) Safwa (IRE) (Green Desert (USA))
(188a) 452a[4] 624a[5] 844a[5]

Munaashid (USA) *D K Weld* 89
3 bb c Lonhro(AUS) Freefourracing (USA) (French Deputy (USA))
6389a[9]

Munaawib *Ray Peacock* a69 41
8 b g Haafhd Mouwadh (USA) (Nureyev (USA))
144[12] 449[6] 1202[15] *8337[4]*

Munawer *Hugo Palmer* a73 73
2 ch g Dutch Art Cantal (Pivotal)
7013[2] *(7366)*

Munfallet (IRE) *David Brown* a63 96
5 b g Royal Applause Princess Mood (GER) (Muhtarram (USA))
(1634) *1958[8]* 4338[9] 4946[3] 5417[15] (5955) (7315)

Mungo Madness *Julia Feilden* a50 72
2 gr g Sir Percy Emma's Gift (IRE) (Aussie Rules (USA))
4103[10] 5036[4] 7074[8] 7471[8] *8560[11]*

Munjally *Patrick Holmes* a61 66
5 b g Acclamation Parabola (Galileo (IRE))
1254[7] 1676[4] 2053[9] 3478[10] 3941[5] 4005[4] 4314[3] 4872[6] 5835[8] *6105[2]* 6569[5]

Munro *Ralph Beckett* a83
2 b c Kyllachy Meddle (Diktat)
7867[10] (8065) (8444)

Munsarim (IRE) *Lee Carter* a62 40
9 b g Shamardal(USA) Etizaaz (USA) (Diesis)
101[5] 289[4] 435[6] 949[10] 1834[10] 2326[9] (3031) 5021[8] 5393[7] 5547[4] *6411[11] 7103[8] (7464)*

Munstead Star *Andrew Balding* 49
2 ch f Sir Percy Royal Patron (Royal Academy (USA))
7543[8]

Muntadab (IRE) *Roger Fell* a89 99
4 b g Invincible Spirit(IRE) Chibola (ARG) (Roy (USA))
(1215) *1480[3]* ◆ 1924[3] *2328[3]* 3518[12] 4081[4] 4611[2] (4893) 5403[6] 6276[4] 6556[12] 7095[13] (7497)

Muntahaa (IRE) *John Gosden* a97 116
3 gr c Dansili Qertaas (IRE) (Linamix (FR))
1421[3] 2008[2] *(2815)* 3337[3] ◆ (5639) 6329[4]

Muntazah *Owen Burrows* 106
3 b c Dubawi(IRE) Rumoush (USA) (Rahy (USA))
2190[4] 4061[7]

Muqaatil (USA) *Richard Hannon* a69 69
2 bb c Lonhro(AUS) Lightning Lydia (USA) (Broad Brush (USA))
7317[5] *7963[2]*

Muqarred (USA) *Roger Fell* a73 76
4 bb g Speightstown(USA) Bawaara (FR) (Quiet American (USA))
1817[7] 2296[6] 2743[6] 2959[2] 3252[4] 5028[7] 5579[9] 5883[3] 6323[8] 6684[13] *8011[8] 8286[4]*

Muraabit *Ismail Mohammed* a65 95
4 ch g Makfi Ho Hi The Moon (IRE) (Be My Guest (USA))
(6160) (6549)

Murad Khan (FR) *Hugo Palmer* a86 104
3 b c Raven's Pass(USA) Lady Elgar (IRE) (Sadler's Wells (USA))
(1287) (2237) (6132) ◆ 7701[8]

Murdanova (IRE) *Karen McLintock* a73 50
3 gr g Zebedee Agnista (IRE) (Iffraaj)
171[8] 3036[10] 4714[7] 5714[10] *5969[9] 8287[11]*

Murgan *Peter Chapple-Hyam* 95
4 b g Galileo(IRE) Approach (Darshaan)
2484[10]

Mur Hiba (IRE) *M D O'Callaghan* 97
2 b f Helmet(AUS) Miss Brief (IRE) (Brief Truce (USA))
5661a[2]

Murillo (FR) *M Boutin* a57 57
6 b h Anabaa Blue Materialiste (IRE) (Zafonic (USA))
1157a[3]

Murmuration (IRE) *Brendan W Duke* a65 59
3 b f Vocalised(USA) Lily Marette (IRE) (Lil's Boy (USA))
7339a[4]

Muroor *David O'Meara* 60
3 ch g Nayef(USA) Raaya (USA) (Giant's Causeway (USA))
1815[4] 2532[7] 3224[14] 4036[2] 4681[3] 4871[8] 6838[8] (7057)

Murphy's Delight (IRE) *Chris Waller* a76 88
6 b g Hurricane Run(IRE) Akoya (IRE) (Anabaa (USA))
7947a[6]

Murraqib (USA) *Brett Johnson* a48
3 ch g Summer Bird(USA) Golden Party (USA) (Seeking The Gold (USA))
6247[7] 6703[8] 7052[10] 7532[4] 7760[9] 8468[9] 8566[8]

Musaaid (IRE) *Michael Easterby* a73 83
4 br g Lawman(FR) Fonda (USA) (Quiet American (USA))
1215[11] 1563[U] 1954[8] *2917[5]* 3327[5] 3807[8] 4932[7] 6521[5] *7324[8] 7662[12]*

Musaanada *William Haggas* a84
3 b f Sea The Stars(IRE) Gaze (Galileo (IRE))
(6415) (7853)

Musaddas *Saeed bin Suroor* a94 107
6 b g Exceed And Excel(AUS) Zuleika Dobson (Cadeaux Genereux)
189a[3] (540a) 812a[12]

Musawaat *Charles Hills* 83
2 b c Equiano(FR) Starry Sky (Oasis Dream)
(6542) 7544[10]

Muscika *Richard Hannon* a74 61
2 b g Kyllachy Miss Villefranche (Danehill Dancer (IRE))
6543[6] *7307[5]*

Musdam (USA) *Sir Michael Stoute* a77 95
3 b c Exchange Rate(USA) Valid Lilly (USA) (Valid Expectations (USA))
1339[3] ◆ 1953[2] (2298) ◆ *2788[5]* 4662[2] 5934[2] 6210[8] (6918)

Mushaireb *Richard Fahey* a82
2 b c Invincible Spirit(IRE) Hidden Brief (Barathea (IRE))
(5966)

Musharrif *Declan Carroll* a82 85
4 b g Arcano(IRE) Cefira (USA) (Distant View (USA))
198[9] 1444[14] 2217[3] 3217[4] 3851[5] *4211[7]* (4809) 5274[3] 5857[14] 6234[3] (6475) 6766[6]

Musical Comedy *Mike Murphy* a73 101
5 b g Royal Applause Spinning Top (Alzao (USA))
3671[13] 3956[8] 4584[11] 4954[4] *5678[10] 7530[9]* 7825[16]

Musical Taste *Pat Phelan* a75 48
3 b f Makfi Blas Ceoil (USA) (Mr Greeley (USA))
1258[6] 1571[7] 3803[13] 4563[8] *7430[10] 7931[7] 8163[12] 8358[3] 8595[5]*

Music Hall (FR) *Shaun Harris* a58 40
6 gr g Stormy River(FR) Aaliyah (GER) (Anabaa (USA))
388[3] 526[3] 674[4] 822[3] 981[10] 3943[5] *5630[5]* 6405[6] *6900[8] 7103[12]*

Music Lesson *Hughie Morrison* a73 69
2 ch f Dutch Art Triple Sharp (Selkirk (USA))
7548[6] *7761[2]*

Music Major *Michael Attwater* a71 51
3 br g Bertolini(USA) Music Maid (IRE) (Inzar (USA))
126[7] 268[6] 496[4] 711[2] (1148) ◆ *1420[3]* ◆ *1792[2] 2325[3] 2770[3] (4936) 6629[4]* 7035[5] *(7735) 8154[2] 8248[3] 8590[6]*

Music Man (IRE) *Laura Mongan* a85 80
6 b g Oratorio(IRE) Chanter (Lomitas)
66[3] 779[2] 975[4] 1934[4] 3533[5] *4012[3]* (5035)

Musico (IRE) *Patrick Holmes* a56
2 b g Lilbourne Lad(IRE) Viola Da Gamba (IRE) (Alhaarth (IRE))
7328[6] 7792[7]

Music Seeker (IRE) *James Eustace* 53
2 b g Henrythenavigator(USA) Danehill Music (IRE) (Danehill Dancer (IRE))
7283[6]

Musique Sacree (FR) *J C Rosell* 80
4 ch m Doctor Dino(FR) Peinture Celeste (IRE) (Peintre Celebre (USA))
5249a[3]

Mustaaqeem (USA) *Sir Michael Stoute* a95 90
4 b g Dynaformer(USA) Wasseema (USA) (Danzig (USA))
1629[6] 2246[5] ◆ 4129[4] *4976[2] 5552[4]*

Mustadeem (IRE) *A R Al Rayhi* a11 103
4 b g Arcano(IRE) Hureya (USA) (Woodman (USA))
189a[15] *284a[14]* 455a[9]

Mustahdaf (USA) *M Al Mheiri* a70 91
5 b g Dynaformer(USA) Tabrir (IRE) (Unfuwain (USA))
718a[5]

Mustajeer *Owen Burrows* a101 99
3 b g Medicean Qelaan (USA) (Dynaformer (USA))
1395[2] ◆ *7101[3]*

Mustallib (IRE) *Charles Hills* a106 101
3 b g Iffraaj Rocking (Oasis Dream)
(2039) 2693[4] 4079[6] *(4643)* (5199) ◆ 6112[11] *6627[2]*

Mustaqbal (IRE) *Michael Dods* a56 79
4 b g Invincible Spirit(IRE) Alshamatry (USA) (Seeking The Gold (USA))
1124[2] 1625[10] 2347[10] 2960[5] (3366) 3711[4] 3922[7] 4933[3] 5223[3]

Mustaqqil (IRE) *David O'Meara* a84 46
4 b g Invincible Spirit(IRE) Cast In Gold (USA) (Elusive Quality (USA))
1978[12] *2917[9] 3605[4] 4199[6] 5082[5] 5609[3] 5845[4]* 6643[9] *7051[4] 7141[8]*

Mustarrid (IRE) *Richard Hannon* a85
2 br g Elzaam(AUS) Symbol Of Peace (IRE) (Desert Sun)
7977[3] (8189)

Mustashry *Sir Michael Stoute* a89 109
3 bb c Tamayuz Safwa (IRE) (Green Desert (USA))
1474[2] (2048) 3299[12] (4624) 5585[2] ◆ 6482[4]

Must Be Amazing *Jeremy Gask* a50 51
2 b f Foxwedge(AUS) Be Amazing (IRE) (Refuse To Bend (IRE))
7259[4] 7818[6]

Mustique (IRE) *Richard Fahey* a75 82
3 b f Danehill Dancer(IRE) Blessing (USA) (Pulpit (USA))
2802[3] 3266[5] 4398[7] 5115[2] 5588[7] *6964[6] 7326[6]* 7743[9]

Mustn't Grumble (IRE) *David Loughnane* a66 65
3 ch g Intense Focus(USA) Lough Mist (IRE) (Captain Rio)
1126[5] 1558[3] *1721[5]* 2834[3] 3140[2] 3604[10] 5515[9] 5732[11] 6451[10] 6685[3] *7069[6]* 7572[7] *8315[7] 8474[5]*

Mutadaffeq (IRE) *David O'Meara* a79 74
3 b g New Approach(IRE) Saajidah (USA) (Dynaformer (USA))
7384[4] 7597[2] 7847[8]

Mutafaakir (IRE) *Ruth Carr* a73 75
7 b g Oasis Dream Moon's Whisper (USA) (Storm Cat (USA))
764[5] 942[7] 1159[9]

Mutahaady (IRE) *K R Burke* a91 84
2 b g Elzaam(AUS) Midnight Oasis (Oasis Dream)
1915[6] 3971[3] 4609[8] (6222) ◆ (6614) ◆ (6800) *7764[2] 7809[4]*

Mutakayyef *William Haggas* 122
5 ch g Sea The Stars(IRE) Infallible (Pivotal)
(3164) (4127) ◆ 5558[3] 6601a[3]

Mutamakkin (AUS) *M F De Kock* 95
4 b h Redoute's Choice(AUS) Quiet Maggy (USA) (Quiet American (USA))
375a[11] 810a[14]

Mutamakkin (USA) *Sir Michael Stoute* 102
4 bb g War Front(USA) La Laja (USA) (El Prado (IRE))
1441[3] ◆ 1861[8] (3157) 3910[14] 4731[7]

Mutamid *Ismail Mohammed* a88 65
4 b g Medicean Inchberry (Barathea (IRE))
1707[2] (2821) 3605[2] 4474[4]

Mutarabby (IRE) *Saeed bin Suroor* a76
2 ch c Tamayuz Shaarfa (USA) (Dynaformer (USA))
7849[3] ◆

Mutarajjil (IRE) *Roger Varian* a77 73
3 b g Acclamation Rouge Noir (USA) (Saint Ballado (CAN))
1894[5] *2446[3]* ◆ (Dead)

Mutarakez (IRE) *Brian Meehan* a75 90
4 ch g Fast Company(IRE) Nightswimmer (IRE) (Noverre (USA))
1196[11] 7354[17] *7933[10]*

Mutawaaly (IRE) *Roger Varian* a85 79
3 b c Cape Cross(IRE) Sana Abel (IRE) (Alhaarth (IRE))
1398[5] 2538[8]

Mutawakked (IRE) *Brian Meehan* 84
2 b c Kodiac Your Opinion (IRE) (Xaar)
3106[3] 3813[9] (4552) 6260[16]

Mutawathea *Simon Crisford* a104 107
5 b g Exceed And Excel(AUS) Esteemed Lady (IRE) (Mark Of Esteem (IRE))
221[2] ◆ *560[5] 816[3]* ◆ 2027[2] 3386[11] 4152[3] 4625[8]

Mutawatheb (IRE) *Richard Hannon* 95
2 gr c Dark Angel(IRE) Queen Myrine (IRE) (Oratorio (IRE))
2873[2] (3813) 4622[4] 5560[6] 6229[3] (7493)

Muthmir (IRE) *William Haggas* a116 120
6 b g Invincible Spirit(IRE) Fairy Of The Night (IRE) (Danehill (USA))
745[3] ◆ 1104a[5] 2475[8] 4166[3] 4824[6] 5863[3]

Muthmira *Simon Crisford* a75 84
2 ch f Arcano(IRE) Carding (USA) (Street Cry (IRE))
5469[3] ◆ 6071[10] (6454)

Muthraab Aldaar (IRE) *Jim Boyle* a75 56
3 b g Baltic King Vertigo On Course (IRE) (Anabaa (USA))
(1113) 1636[7] *7204[6] 7617[9] 7887[13] 8086[7]*

Mutineer *Daniel Kubler* a69 43
2 ch g Sepoy(AUS) Violet (IRE) (Mukaddamah (USA))
2649[11] *7906[7] 8353[4]*

Mutinne (IRE) *Y Gourraud* a80 83
5 gr m Verglas(IRE) Trip To Glory (FR) (Where Or When (IRE))
715a[9]

Mutoondresdashorse *Paul Cole* 75
2 ch c Harbour Watch(IRE) Mutoon (IRE) (Erhaab (USA))
2173[2]

Muwaary *John Gosden* 110
5 b h Oasis Dream Wissal (USA) (Woodman (USA))
3164[3] ◆ 3664[5] 6056[2] 6482[3]

Muzaahim (IRE) *Kevin Morgan* a66 80
5 ch g Tamayuz Elizabeth Swann (Bahamian Bounty)
231[5] 607[7] *8085[3] 8469[3]*

Muzdawaj *William Haggas* a86 100
3 b g Dansili Shabiba (USA) (Seeking The Gold (USA))
(1653) (3365) ◆ 4403[4] (5405) 6081[2] 6573[9]

Muzeel (IRE) *Sir Michael Stoute* a74 81
2 b g Dark Angel(IRE) Kondakova (IRE) (Soviet Star (USA))
3598[3] 4274[5] *6672[2]*

My Amigo *Ann Duffield* 91
3 gr g Stimulation(IRE) Blue Crest (FR) (Verglas (IRE))
1599[3] 2200[3] (2554) 3292[3]

My Anchor *Charlie Mann* a60 44
5 b g Mount Nelson War Shanty (Warrshan (USA))
4019[10]

My Approach (IRE) *Robert Collet* a63 66
6 b g New Approach(IRE) Zelding (IRE) (Warning)
1034a[10]

My Aussie Rules *Clive Cox* a56
2 b c Aussie Rules(USA) Robe Chinoise (Robellino (USA))
7906[9] 8237[8] 8353[10]

Mybee Davis (IRE) *G Botti* a76 63
2 b c Myboycharlie(IRE) Majesty Davis (IRE) (Dansili)
6638a[7]

My Bo Chop (FR) *A Chopard* 93
2 b c Myboycharlie(IRE) Hoosick Falls (USA) (Precise End (USA))
5186a[4]

Myboydaniel *Derek Shaw* a54 49
4 b g Myboycharlie(IRE) Priti Fabulous (IRE) (Invincible Spirit (IRE))
1[7] 5677[9] 6238[6] 6685[18] 7062[14] 7240[9] *7515[8] 7641[10]*

My Brother (IRE) *Lee Smyth* 89
3 b c Roderic O'Connor(IRE) Victory Peak (Shirley Heights)
6505[6] 7558a[9]

Mybrotherjohnny *Jamie Poulton* 47
5 b g Tiger Hill(IRE) Montjeu's Melody (IRE) (Montjeu (IRE))
2929[11] 3464[11] 4156[8]

My Brother Mike (IRE) *Daniel Mark Loughnane* a61
2 b g Bated Breath Coming Back (Fantastic Light (USA))
7908[9] 8305[6]

My Brown Eyed Girl *Susan Corbett* 33
3 b f Ferrule(IRE) Chalosse (Doyoun)
1246[7] *2327[9]* 3886[8] *7656[13]*

My Bubba *John Flint* a52 55
4 b g Dutch Art Moyoko (IRE) (Mozart (IRE))
201^{10} 431^{9} 7645^{10} 7910^{7} (8070) 8500^{11}

My Call *Saeed bin Suroor* a103 91
4 b m Shamardal(USA) Hush Money (CHI) (Hussonet (USA))
214^{2} 483^{9} 1207^{8}

My Catch (IRE) *Doug Watson* a110 102
5 b g Camacho Catch The Sea (IRE) (Barathea (IRE))
90a^{3} 371a^{2} 537a^{4}

My Cherry Blossom *Tim Easterby* a21 62
2 b f Kyllachy Echo River (USA) (Irish River (FR))
3290^{3} *3654^{9}* 4890^{6} 6010^{6} 6343^{5} 6807^{2} ◆ 7313^{7}

My Dad Syd (USA) *Ian Williams* a80 77
4 bb g Acclamation Weekend Fling (USA) (Forest Wildcat (USA))
960^{10} 1143^{9} 2547^{8} 4362^{6} 5386^{11} 6027^{4} 6790^{3} 7333^{4} (7506) *7662^{2} 8052^{3} 8389^{2}*

My Darling Memory (FR) *Rod Collet* a57 46
5 b m Elusive City(USA) Noble Presence (FR) (Fasliyev (USA))
8421a^{9}

My Dear Baby (IRE) *Robert Cowell* a78 52
2 gr f Arcano(IRE) Daliana (Verglas (IRE))
3143^{8} *(4209)* ◆ 5416^{6} 6525^{8}

My Delight (FR) *A Sagot* a41 50
9 b g Maille Pistol(FR) Green House (FR) (Houston (FR))
715a^{6}

My Dream Boat (IRE) *Clive Cox* 123
4 b h Lord Shanakill(USA) Betty Burke (Choisir (AUS))
(1604) 2568a^{5} (3272) 3912^{5} 6354a^{5} 7353^{4}

My Escapade (IRE) *Simon Waugh* 30
5 ch m Tamayuz Highly Respected (IRE) (High Estate)
4935^{8}

My Fantasea (IRE) *David Evans* a81 25
3 b g Sea The Stars(IRE) Speed Song (Fasliyev (USA))
8251^{8} 8539^{8}

My Favourite Thing *Roger Varian* a72 75
3 b f Oasis Dream The Sound Of Music (IRE) (Galileo (IRE))
1392^{4} *2783^{5}* 6893^{7}

My Girl Maisie (IRE) *Richard Guest* a10 47
2 b f Fast Company(IRE) Queen Al Andalous (IRE) (King's Best (USA))
2193^{7} 3167^{9} *3561^{8}*

My Girl Market (FR) *J Reynier* a67 67
3 b f Myboycharlie(IRE) Silver Market (FR) (Marchand De Sable (USA))
6912a^{14}

My Good Brother (IRE) *T G McCourt* a84 65
7 b g Elusive City(USA) Final Favour (IRE) (Unblest)
4246a^{10} (6461a)

Myhorsewithnoname (IRE) *Natalie Lloyd-Beavis* 5
2 gr c Lilbourne Lad(IRE) Colleville (Pharly (FR))
6404^{9} 6828^{6}

My Isla *James Tate* a66 29
3 b f Makfi Islandia (USA) (Johar (USA))
687^{2} 980^{5}

My Jamaican Guy (IRE) *James Given* 24
3 b g Duke Of Marmalade(IRE) Mustique Dream (Don't Forget Me)
4682^{10}

My Lady Marie *Amanda Perrett* a69
2 b f Bated Breath Poppo's Song (CAN) (Polish Navy (USA))
7763^{5} 8081^{10} 8355^{7}

Myllachy *Tim Easterby* a37 53
2 b f Kyllachy Enchanted Princess (Royal Applause)
3947^{7} 4227^{9} 4601^{8} 5712^{2} ◆ 5833^{5} 7579^{4} *8072^{9}*

My Lord *Paddy Butler* a70 71
8 br g Ishiguru(USA) Lady Smith (Greensmith)
101^{8} 862^{9} 1002^{2} (1057) 1201^{2} (2078a) 2210^{2} 2436^{3} (2977) 4049^{5} 4383^{6} 5056^{3} 5406^{8}

My Lucille (IRE) *Tim Easterby* 81
3 b f Lawman(FR) Stroke Of Six (IRE) (Woodborough (USA))
1123^{10} 1597^{3} 2304^{2} 2681^{3} 3209^{5} (3810) (4145) 4668^{4} 5437^{2} 6005^{6} 6504^{11}

My Man Charlie (FR) *N Caullery* a74 70
3 bb c Myboycharlie(IRE) Queen Of Wands (Sakhee (USA))
1286a^{8}

My Man Sam (USA) *Chad C Brown* a109
3 b c Trappe Shot(USA) Lauren Byrd (USA) (Arch (USA))
2063a^{11} 5913a^{8}

My Matador (IRE) *Victor Dartnall* a72 44
5 b g Kandahar Run My Special (IRE) (Peintre Celebre (USA))
8448^{2}

Mymatechris (IRE) *Andrew Balding* a99 86
5 br g High Chaparral(IRE) Splendeur (FR) (Desert King (IRE))
1963^{4}

My Miss Sophia (USA) *William Mott* a113 107
5 ch m Unbridled's Song(USA) Wildwood Flower (USA) (Langfuhr (CAN))
3178a^{13}

My Mistress (IRE) *Phil McEntee* a54 53
4 ch m Mastercraftsman(IRE) Majestic Eviction (IRE) (King's Theatre (IRE))
3737^{9} 4024^{3} 4567^{4} 5085^{2} 5375^{7} 5753^{6} *7641^{8} 7936^{5} (8527)*

My Mo (FR) *David Dennis* a77 65
4 b g Silver Frost(IRE) Anna Ivanovna (FR) (Fasliyev (USA))
899^{2} 1002^{10} 1652^{6} 2205^{9} 2507^{11} 5392^{8}

My Name Is Rio (IRE) *Michael Dods* a68 96
6 ch g Captain Rio Walk In My Shadow (IRE) (Orpen (USA))
1218^{4} 1522^{11} 3419^{8} (3875) 3944^{4} 4338^{6} 4831^{3} 5857^{15} 6556^{7} 6944^{4} 7124^{6} 7537^{8}

Myopic *Luca Cumani* 92
3 b f Teofilo(IRE) Blinking (Marju (IRE))
(5361) 5927^{2} 6528^{2}

Myredbush (IRE) *Simon Dow* a45 38
2 b f Bushranger(IRE) Damask (IRE) (Red Clubs (IRE))
2376^{8} 2963^{8} 3799^{8} 5165^{7}

My Renaissance *Sam England* a57 50
6 bb g Medicean Lebenstanz (Singspiel (IRE))
3031^{13} 8386^{2} (8497)

My Reward *Tim Easterby* a96 100
4 b g Rail Link Tarot Card (Fasliyev (USA))
1642^{2} (2472) *3658^{11}* 4734^{7} 5559^{9} 6118^{7} 7150^{29} 7538^{9}

My Rosie (IRE) *John Gosden* a47
2 b f Redoute's Choice(AUS) My Branch (Distant Relative)
7762^{14} 8081^{11}

My Scat Daddy (USA) *Nikki Evans* a19 13
7 b g Scat Daddy(USA) Will Be A Bates (USA) (Bates Motel (USA))
237^{8}

My Sharona *Jassim Al Ghazali* a74 94
7 gr m Dark Angel(IRE) Tanda Tula (IRE) (Alhaarth (IRE))
755a^{5}

My Shootin Star *Peter Hedger*
3 bg f Winker Watson Miss Venice (IRE) (Fasliyev (USA))
432^{7} 770^{7}

My Son Max *Nikki Evans* a83 71
8 b g Avonbridge Pendulum (Pursuit Of Love)
518^{10}

Mysterial *Declan Carroll* a53 84
6 b g Invincible Spirit(IRE) Diamond Dilemma (IRE) (Sinndar (IRE))
1250^{8} 1633^{14} 2233^{15} 2672^{3} (3012) 3481^{2} 3641^{6} 4455^{10} (4768) 4920^{4} 5434^{5} (6517) 6957^{8} 7535^{15} *7980^{10}*

Mysterious Boy (FR) *Y Gourraud* 77
2 gr g Myboycharlie(IRE) Mysterious Lina (FR) (Linamix (FR))
5348a^{3}

Mysterious Glance *Ed McMahon* a70 78
3 b f Cacique(IRE) Largo (IRE) (Selkirk (USA))
3471^{3} (6879)

Mysterious Look *Ed McMahon* a78 82
3 ch f Sakhee's Secret Look Here's Carol (IRE) (Safawan)
242^{6} ◆ *515^{4} (797) 1029^{2}* 1271^{2} 1935^{3} (7626) *8099^{5} 8349^{7}*

Mystery Code *Alan King* a79 83
4 b m Tobougg(IRE) Mystery Lot (IRE) (Revoque (IRE))
2296^{12}

Mystery Drama *Alexandra Dunn* a48 85
6 b m Hernando(FR) Mystery Lot (IRE) (Revoque (IRE))
1893^{12}

Mystery Sky (FR) *J Parize* a39 58
2 b f Naaqoos Water Feature (Dansili)
1118a^{14} 7927a^{4}

Mystical King *Linda Perratt* 52
6 b g Notnowcato Mystical Ayr (IRE) (Namid)
1668^{7} 1878^{5} 2359 ^{5} 2523^{6} 3755^{8} 3925^{8} 4192^{6} 5838^{4} 6003^{3} 6098^{6} 6615^{6} (6774) 6835^{9} 7093^{12}

Mystical Maze *Mark Brisbourne* a51 47
5 b m Multiplex Musical Maze (Distant Music (USA))
3492^{5} 4493^{4} 5019^{5} 5264^{7} 5708^{6} 6406^{7}

Mystical Nelly *Jonathan Portman* 50
2 b f Sakhee's Secret Dancing Nelly (Shareef Dancer (USA))
4885^{6} 6062^{6}

Mystical Sapphire *Laura Mongan* a84 79
6 b m Sakhee's Secret Nadyma (IRE) (Daylami (IRE))
433^{3} 780^{2} 2579^{7} 3035^{6}

Mystical Spirit (FR) *Martyn Meade* a88 82
4 ch g Spirit One(FR) Miss Maguilove (FR) (Dyhim Diamond (IRE))
518^{3} (965) 1161^{4}

Mystic Blaze (IRE) *Andrew Balding* a77 61
3 ch c Arcano(IRE) Star Approval (IRE) (Hawk Wing (USA))
524^{2} 691^{4}

Mystic Dawn (IRE) *David Simcock* 96
2 b f Oasis Dream Frivolity (Pivotal)
(5705) 6063^{2} 7114^{6} 7667^{3}

Mystic Jade *Richard Hannon* a76 60
4 ch m Raven's Pass(USA) Mauri Moon (Green Desert (USA))
2001^{3} 2401^{8} 3097^{7}

Mystic Maeve (IRE) *Roger Fell* a51 58
2 b f Tagula(IRE) Celtic Lynn (IRE) (Celtic Swing)
1921^{11} 6632^{5} 6874^{8} 7244^{6} *7431^{7} 7854^{6} 8087^{7}*

Mystic Miraaj *Tim Easterby* 86
4 ch g Iffraaj Salsa Brava (IRE) (Almutawakel)
1380^{4} 1625^{4} (2491) 2910^{5} 3115^{16} 3945^{5} 4611^{9} 4933^{4} 5482^{13} 6772^{5} 7360^{2}

Mystikana *Marcus Tregoning* a72 73
3 ch f Sir Percy Peintre D'Argent (IRE) (Peintre Celebre (USA))
2700^{9} 3063^{8} 3878^{3} *(4530)* 4778^{5} 7274^{4} *7429^{4} 8253^{6}*

Mystique Heights *Sir Mark Prescott Bt* a73 72
3 b g High Chaparral(IRE) Musique Magique (IRE) (Mozart (IRE))
2563^{5} 3033^{5} 4033^{2} (4273) ◆ 4810^{2} ◆ (5012) *6245^{2}*

My Sweet Girl (USA) *Barclay Tagg* 100
4 b m Bernardini(USA) Bit Of Whimsy (USA) (Distorted Humor (USA))
5185a^{5}

My Target (IRE) *Michael Wigham* a97 87
5 b g Cape Cross(IRE) Chercheuse (USA) (Seeking The Gold (USA))
546^{7} 620^{5} 712^{2} 2213^{3} 3595^{3} 4094^{3} (6579) 6914^{8} 7702^{8} *(7933) 8049^{8} 8177^{14} (8593)* ◆

Myth *Waldemar Hickst* a84 92
3 ch f Soldier Of Fortune(IRE) Dareen (IRE) (Rahy (USA))
5006a^{8} 6497a^{7} 7720a^{11}

Mythical Madness *David O'Meara* a103 97
5 b g Dubawi(IRE) Miss Delila (USA) (Malibu Moon (USA))
(8035) 8122^{2} (8317) 8529^{10}

Mythical Spirit (IRE) *James Tate* 48
2 b f Dragon Pulse(IRE) Call This Cat (IRE) (One Cool Cat (USA))
4064^{8}

Mythmaker *Bryan Smart* a111 104
4 b g Major Cadeaux Mythicism (Oasis Dream)
(86) ◆ *529^{U}* 2158^{2} *3656^{10}* 5418^{7} (6449) 7156^{13} *7932^{2} 8530^{2}*

My Time *Michael Mullineaux* a51 51
7 b g Mind Games Tick Tock (Timeless Times (USA))
237^{11} 542^{11} 730^{9} (867) 1035^{4} 1295^{8} 4516^{10} *5127^{8} 6105^{13}*

Mytimehascome *Roger Varian* a75 80
3 b f Montjeu(IRE) Vital Statistics (Indian Ridge)
2183^{3} 4207^{3}

My Tringaling (IRE) *Stuart Williams* a61 51
4 ch m Summer Bird(USA) Lady Amira (USA) (Langfuhr (CAN))
20^{2} 61^{3} 180^{2} 254^{8} 422^{8} 527^{6} 622^{5} 1049^{4} 1405^{2} 2292^{5} *2792^{6}*

My Two Scoops *Ann Duffield* 71
3 ch g Showcasing Miss Beaudacious (IRE) (Antonius Pius (USA))
3153^{3} 3877^{7}

My Valentino (IRE) *Dianne Sayer* 70
3 ch g Duke Of Marmalade(IRE) Nadwah (USA) (Shadeed (USA))
2422^{4} 2576^{7} 3215^{6}

Mywayistheonlyway (IRE) *Grant Tuer* a73 82
3 b c Tamayuz Soul Custody (CAN) (Perfect Soul (IRE))
(1847) 2654^{10} 3079^{4} 3614^{8} (5336) 5759^{7} 6164^{7}

Mzuri (IRE) *Ms Sheila Lavery* a77 77
4 b m Tagula(IRE) Meadow (Green Desert (USA))
4748a^{9} 7391a^{8}

Naadirr (IRE) *Marco Botti* a98 113
5 b g Oasis Dream Beach Bunny (IRE) (High Chaparral (IRE))
450a^{4} ◆ 723a^{2} 1104a^{13} 2546^{3} 3195^{10} *3655^{6}* (4860) 5880^{4} 6941^{8}

Naafer *William Haggas* a77 88
2 br f Oasis Dream Shabiba (USA) (Seeking The Gold (USA))
2410^{2} *2764^{2}* (4110) 4825^{9} 5560^{10} 6734^{14}

Nabhan *Bernard Llewellyn* 89
4 b g Youmzain(IRE) Danidh Dubai (IRE) (Noverre (USA))
2313^{5} 2685^{7} 3129^{5} 3639^{9} 4634^{5} 4920^{8}

Nacar (GER) *Mario Hofer* 99
3 bb c Tertullian(USA) Nacella (GER) (Banyumanik (IRE))
1908a^{2} 2711a^{6} 3699a^{3} 4928a^{9}

Nacida (GER) *Yasmin Almenrader* a58
2 b f Wiener Walzer(GER) Nacella (GER) (Banyumanik (IRE))
7970a^{7}

Nadeschda (FR) *Mario Hofer* 67
2 b f Soldier Hollow Nadin (GER) (Alkalde (GER))
4187a^{6} 5142a^{8}

Nafaath (IRE) *Donald McCain* a47 68
10 ch g Nayef(USA) Alshakr (Bahri (USA))
4045^{6} 4551^{3} 4950^{3} 5726^{8}

Nafaqa (IRE) *E Charpy* 107
4 b g Sir Percy Maghya (IRE) (Mujahid (USA))
628a^{10} 812a^{14}

Naggers (IRE) *Paul Midgley* 91
5 ch g Excellent Art Trika (First Trump)
3168^{9} 3646^{9} (4191) (4873) 6382a^{10} (7094)

Nag's Wag (IRE) *George Baker* a78 75
3 b f Approve(IRE) Street Kitty (IRE) (Tiger Hill (IRE))
(1745) ◆ 2314^{3} 2642^{3} 4222^{2} 5284^{6} *(5725) 8493^{6}*

Nahual (FR) *J Bertran De Balanda* a82 111
5 b g American Post Nahuala (FR) (Chichicastenango (FR))
6396a^{2} 6974a^{6} (7946a)

Naifah (IRE) *John Gosden* 77
2 b f Kodiac Windy Lane (Dubai Destination (USA))
2467^{6} 2885^{2} ◆ 3556^{2} 4298^{2}

Najd *Richard Hannon* 76
3 b c Dick Turpin(IRE) Mookhlesa (Marju (IRE))
1570^{2} ◆ 2234^{4} 2614^{8} (3259)

Nakeeta *Iain Jardine* a96 105
5 b g Sixties Icon Easy Red (IRE) (Hunting Lion (IRE))
1967^{2} *3658^{10}* 4162^{4} 4581^{2} 5559^{2} ◆ 7150^{16} *7708a^{2}*

Naldina (IRE) *Riccardo Santini* 86
3 b f Mujahid(USA) Nicole Dillon (Inchinor)
1685a^{10}

Nalon *J-M Lefebvre* a76 60
5 b g Holy Roman Emperor(IRE) Drama Playout (Kendor (FR))
2806a^{8}

Nalout (USA) *S Seemar* a57
2 br f Afleet Alex(USA) Glory Glory (USA) (Honour And Glory (USA))
8575a^{6}

Named Asset *Martin Bosley* a52 63
4 b g Invincible Spirit(IRE) Sabria (USA) (Miswaki (USA))
3953^{10} *7693^{7} 7913^{9} 8079^{3}*

Nameitwhatyoulike *Bryan Smart* 111
7 b g Trade Fair Emma Peel (Emarati (USA))
1644^{3} 4338^{7} (5418) (6161) 6558^{7} 7191a^{6}

Name That Toon *Derek Shaw* a48 16
3 b f Paco Boy(IRE) Saktoon (USA) (El Prado (IRE))
763^{6} 962^{5} 1045^{5} 1420^{9}

Nam Hai (IRE) *Kim Bailey* a73 77
5 b g Fastnet Rock(AUS) Bowstring (IRE) (Sadler's Wells (USA))
1222^{6} 1854^{3} (2501) ◆ 3221^{7}

Namhroodah (IRE) *James Tate* a72 107
4 gr m Sea The Stars(IRE) Independant (Medicean)
2363^{3} 2690^{5} (3358) 4582^{3} 4826^{3} 6939^{12}

Nancy Hart *Tom Dascombe* 69
2 b f Sepoy(AUS) Lucky Token (IRE) (Key Of Luck (USA))
6548^{3} 7157^{4}

Nanny Makfi *Stuart Kittow* a42 57
3 b f Makfi Pan Galactic (USA) (Lear Fan (USA))
1740^{8} 2590^{2} 3493^{3} 4794^{2} 5625^{5} 6654^{2}

Naousa (FR) *R Schoof* a72 69
3 bb f Loup Breton(IRE) Baklava (IRE) (Cape Cross (IRE))
5704a^{8}

Napadac (GER) *P Schiergen* 32
3 b c Lando(GER) Nouvelle Fortune (IRE) (Alzao (USA))
7999a^{15}

Naples Bay *John Quinn* 76
2 b g Kodiac Trombe (FR) (Bering)
(3839) ◆ 4343^{3} 4825^{13} 6562^{2} 7820^{8}

Napoleon Solo *David Barron* a69 68
4 b g Cockney Rebel(IRE) Trump Street (First Trump)
141^{3} 246^{7} 621^{5} 6008^{5} 6568^{3} 7253^{2} *7797^{12} 7960^{2} (8570)*

Naqdy *William Haggas* a73 63
3 b g Aqlaam Shuhra (IRE) (Marju (IRE))
1755^{6} *2109^{3} 3475^{7}*

Nareia (GER) *Mario Hofer* 75
2 b f Areion(GER) Navicella (FR) (Beat Hollow)
(7927a)

Nargiza (USA) *Chris Wall* a60
2 ch f Elusive Quality(USA) Any For Love (ARG) (Southern Halo (USA))
7278^{9} 7762^{8} 8074^{5}

Narjes *James Fanshawe* a62 64
2 b f Sepoy(AUS) Dubai Sea (USA) (Street Sense (USA))
6624^{6} 7209^{3}

Narnia Dawn (IRE) *F-H Graffard* 96
3 b f Roderic O'Connor(IRE) Nordkappe (GER) (High Chaparral (IRE))
(7998a)

Naseem (IRE) *John Gosden* a90
2 br g Sea The Stars(IRE) Chiosina (IRE) (Danehill Dancer (IRE))
8227^{3} (8486)

Nashville (IRE) *Andrew Crook* a49 63
7 b g Galileo(IRE) Brown Eyes (Danehill (USA))
1121^{6} 1955^{9} 2678^{2} 2971^{8} 4045^{5}

Nasimi *Charlie Appleby* a82 86
2 b f Shamardal(USA) Gamilati (Bernardini (USA))
(2612) ◆ 4106^{9} 4623^{8} *6088^{3}* 7547^{11}

Nasive De Cerisy (FR) *G Elbaz* 65
2 b f Evasive Nagha (FR) (Enrique)
5698a^{10}

Nasri *Emma Owen* a72 104
10 b g Kyllachy Triple Sharp (Selkirk (USA))
68^{4} (167) 607^{3} 799^{10} 872^{4} 955^{2} 1159^{2} 1496^{10} 1700^{2} 2577^{11} 2821^{7} 3035^{8} 4008^{10} 4715^{10} 8156^{8} 8457^{13}

Nassuvian Pearl *Ralph Beckett* a74 42
3 br f Bahamian Bounty Melody Maker (Diktat)
1476^{P} 3034^{3} ◆ *3649^{3}* 4043^{7} *5027^{4}*

Nastenka *Ed Walker* a61 69
2 b f Aussie Rules(USA) Nezhenka (With Approval (CAN))
6111^{6} 6874^{6} 7741^{2} *8131^{6}*

Natajack *Tom Dascombe* 82
2 ch c Showcasing Douro (Manduro (GER))
6542^{2}

Natalia *Sarah Hollinshead* a47 47
7 ch m Dutch Art Pintle (Pivotal)
730^{6} 986^{3} 1165^{5} 1768^{5} 2778^{7} *3731^{4}* 4260^{7} 4516^{6} 5383^{6} 7211^{5}

Nathania *Richard Hughes* 78
2 ch f Nathaniel(IRE) Glen Rosie (IRE) (Mujtahid (USA))
5170^{3} 5995^{4}

Nathan Mayer *Sir Michael Stoute* a56 63
2 b c Nathaniel(IRE) Rosacara (Green Desert (USA))
7318^{6} *7907^{10}*

Nathr (USA) *Doug Watson* a97 80
5 br h Dixie Union(USA) Sweet Rider (USA) (Seeking The Gold (USA))
183a^{2}

Nathra (IRE) *John Gosden* 111
3 b f Iffraaj Rada (IRE) (Danehill (USA))
(1396) 1888^{5} 2282a^{2} 3339^{9} 6749^{3}

National Defense *Mme C Head-Maarek* 119
2 b c Invincible Spirit(IRE) Angel Falls (Kingmambo (USA))
6270a^{3} (6987a)

National Service (USA) *Richard Ford* a75 59
5 b g War Chant(USA) Cotton Club Ballet (USA) (Street Cry (IRE))
(201) (230) 424^{2} 680^{4} (685) 942^{4} 1159^{3} 1496^{4} 1925^{7} *2332^{5}* 2416^{6} 2571^{8} *3985^{9}* 5760^{8} 7302^{2} ◆ *7751^{12} 7994^{10} 8542^{9}*

Nations Alexander (IRE) *Richard Hannon* 104
2 gr f Dark Angel(IRE) Party Whip (IRE) (Whipper (USA))
2612^{2} ◆ 3024^{2} (3663) 4106^{3} (5172) ◆ 5584^{4} 6748^{5} 7347a^{3}

Native Falls (IRE) *Alan Swinbank* a52 69
5 ch g Elnadim(USA) Sagrada (GER) (Primo Dominie)
2426^{7} 2665^{11} 2857^{11} 3265^{10} 3552^{6} 3882^{3} 4691^{2} 5060^{12} 5535^{4} 6341^{12} 7596^{11}

Native Prospect *Andrew Balding* 78
2 ch c Bated Breath Jakarta Jade (IRE) (Royal Abjar (USA))
2478^{4} 3529^{3} 4533^{7} 6377^{2} ◆ 7125^{2}

Native Soldier (IRE) *William Haggas* a72
2 b g Sepoy(AUS) Electra Star (Shamardal (USA))
7648^{7} (8089) (Dead)

Natsume (FR) *S Kobayashi* 67
3 ch f Monsun(GER) Primo Ordine (JPN) (Afleet (CAN))
1542a^{6}

Natural Beauty *John Gosden* a75 77
3 b f Oasis Dream Maskunah (IRE) (Sadler's Wells (USA))
2035^{5} 3001^{4}

Natural Scenery *Saeed bin Suroor* a97 86
3 b f Dubawi(IRE) Argentina (IRE) (Sadler's Wells (USA))
(3359) 3914[6] 4561[3] (7512) 8231[2] 8594[3] ◆

Natural Wonder *Richard Hannon* 74
3 ro f Paco Boy(IRE) Galapagar (USA) (Miswaki (USA))
1436[7] 2181[6]

Nature Boy (IRE) *Peter Chapple-Hyam* a71 57
2 ch c Intikhab(USA) Miss Latina (IRE) (Mozart (IRE))
3495[5] ◆ 7328[2]

Naupaka *Brian Ellison* a68
2 b f Haafhd Lily Lenor (IRE) (Bertolini (USA))
8034[6] 8397[3] ◆

Nautical Haven *Kevin Ryan* 84
2 b g Harbour Watch(IRE) Mania (IRE) (Danehill (USA))
3167[6] 4133[3] (4663) 5560[17] 6734[12]

Navajo Storm (IRE) *Michael Appleby* a59 67
3 gr f Dark Angel(IRE) Strike Lightly (Rainbow Quest (USA))
63[7] 243[8]

Navajo Thunder (IRE) *Michael Appleby* a53 42
2 b f High Chaparral(IRE) Evening Dress (Medicean)
5272[9] 5747[8] 6421[6]

Navajo War Dance *K R Burke* 90
3 bb g Makfi Navajo Rainbow (Rainbow Quest (USA))
(2522) 3300[14] 3887[4] 5226[2] 6802[7] 7287[8] 7505[7]

Naval Warfare (IRE) *Andrew Balding* 84
2 b c Born To Sea(IRE) Three Days In May (Cadeaux Genereux)
3859[4] 4479[2] (6534)

Navarone (IRE) *Richard Fahey* 78
2 b g Casamento(IRE) Flash And Dazzle (IRE) (Bertolini (USA))
3854[3] ◆ 4304[3] 4914[4] 5713[9] 6535[5]

Navarra King (IRE) *P Schiergen* 105
2 ch c Lope De Vega(IRE) Navarra Queen (Singspiel (IRE))
(6174a) (Dead)

Navigate (IRE) *Martyn Meade* 93
4 b g Iffraaj Dorothy Dene (Red Ransom (USA))
1218[6] 1530[9] 2613[10]

Nawkhatha (USA) *Brian Meehan* a64 72
3 ch f Tapit(USA) Lear's Princess (USA) (Lear Fan (USA))
4361[5] 4978[4] 6485[10]

Nawwaar (USA) *A R Al Rayhi* a105 97
7 ch h Distorted Humor(USA) Mostaqeleh (USA) (Rahy (USA))
(90a)

Nayel (IRE) *Richard Hannon* 95
4 b h Acclamation Soliza (IRE) (Intikhab (USA))
1716[4] (2157) 3162[5] 4129[5] 4598[3] 6081[8]

Nay Secret *Jim Goldie* a34 38
8 b g Nayef(USA) Nouveau Cheval (Picea)
6102[12]

Nayyar *Charles Hills* 86
2 ch c Exceed And Excel(AUS) Miss Queen (USA) (Miswaki (USA))
(4083) 4755[8] (5741) 6322[8]

Nazbanou (IRE) *P Schiergen* 99
3 b f High Chaparral(IRE) Neele (IRE) (Peintre Celebre (USA))
7720a[2]

Naziba (IRE) *David Menuisier* a66 65
3 gr f Zebedee Nashaat (Redoute's Choice (AUS))
783[3] 1061[2] 2106[7] 3740[5] 5330[3] 5935[6] 6408[3]

Nazik *J Reynier* 71
2 b c Delegator Rockburst (Xaar)
1736[4] (2125) 2429[6] 3114[4] 3576[4] 3742[3] 4750a[10]

Ndesha (FR) *D Guillemin* a65
2 gr f Tin Horse(IRE) Barsha (USA) (Cherokee Run (USA))
5988a[3]

Near England (IRE) *Markus Klug* 107
3 br f Lord Of England(GER) Near Galante (GER) (Galileo (IRE))
2949a[14] (4175a) 5220a[12] (6610a)

Nearly Caught (IRE) *Hughie Morrison* a107 115
6 b g New Approach(IRE) Katch Me Katie (Danehill (USA))
1273[5] 1963[2] 3658[3] 3913[3] (4578a) (5692a) 6974a[3] 7349[5]

Nebula Storm (IRE) *Michael Blake* a60 62
9 b g Galileo(IRE) Epping (Charnwood Forest (IRE))
5958[3] 7870[14]

Nebulla *John M Oxx* 93
4 ch g Iffraaj Kelowna (IRE) (Pivotal)
1018a[21]

Need To Know (SAF) *A R Al Rayhi* a104 99
7 b g Western Winter(USA) Promisefrommyheart (SAF) (Elliodor (FR))
229a[2] 6399a[16] 8396a[7]

Neelanjali (FR) *N Caullery* a79 91
2 b f Elusive City(USA) Rubies (Inchinor)
5186a[7] 7086a[8] 7879a[6]

Nefetari *Alan Brown* a49 41
3 b f Kodiac Town And Gown (Oasis Dream)
2302[14] 2561[5] 3009[4] 4229[8] 5370[5] 7603[2] 7793[5] 8289[2] 8589[12]

Neguev (IRE) *J-C Rouget* 83
2 b c So You Think(NZ) Lady Bering (Bering)
(5985a)

Neigh Kid *Keith Dalgleish* 50
2 b f Dandy Man(IRE) Italian Affair (Fumo Di Londra (IRE))
2424[4] 2675[7] 2807[6] 6026[9]

Nella Di Roma (GER) *J Hirschberger* a70 68
3 b f Dashing Blade Nella Di Monsone (Monsun (GER))
1357a[8]

Nellie Deen (IRE) *David Elsworth* a63 64
3 b f Dream Ahead(USA) Dorothy Dene (Red Ransom (USA))
3572[5] ◆ 5023[6] 5766[4] 6237[8] 6629[6] 7611[5] 7727[F] 8559[7]

Nellie's Dancer *Scott Dixon* a63 56
2 b f Mount Nelson Xaphania (Sakhee (USA))
6808[3] 7107[3] 7494[9] 7891[8]

Nelson's Bay *Wilf Storey* a60 61
7 b g Needwood Blade In Good Faith (USA) (Dynaformer (USA))
2329[5] 2661[4] 3262[8] 3327[4] 3564[9] 4768[5] 5068[5] 5355[7] 5800[2] 5883[5] 6346[8] 6921[13] 8142[6]

Nelson's Pride *Roger Ingram* a41 41
5 b m Mount Nelson Bandanna (Bandmaster (USA))
837[5] 2294[5] 3320[9] 3486[5] 3735[6] 7489[9]

Nelson's Victory *Gary Moore*
6 b g Green Horizon First Class Girl (Charmer (IRE))
3572[14]

Nemoralia (USA) *Jeremy Noseda* a96 114
3 bb f More Than Ready(USA) Alina (USA) (Came Home (USA))
(2220) ◆ 3339[2] ◆ 4185a[4] (5613) 6281[7] 7171a[4]

Nemqueteba (FR) *J-M Osorio* 97
3 b c Pour Moi(IRE) Beyond The Dream (USA) (Fusaichi Pegasus (USA))
5502a[5]

Neo Black Dia (JPN) *Yuichi Shikato* 111
8 bb h Zenno Rob Roy(JPN) Orange Paradise (JPN) (Helissio (FR))
1102a[8]

Neoclassical *John Gosden*
3 ch g Dubawi(IRE) Teeky (Daylami (IRE))
1200[10]

Neorealism (JPN) *Noriyuki Hori* 118
5 ch h Neo Universe(JPN) Tokio Reality (USA) (Meadowlake (USA))
8332a[9]

Nepal (GER) *Dr A Bolte* 105
3 b f Kallisto(GER) Nassau (GER) (Soldier Hollow)
(2730a)

Nepeta (USA) *Mark Johnston* a71 71
2 ch f Kitten's Joy(USA) La Coruna (USA) (Thunder Gulch (USA))
4756[8] 5221[4] (5778) 6713[4] 7140[2] 7598[4]

Neptunes Secret *Sylvester Kirk* 69
2 ch g Sakhee's Secret Lochangel (Night Shift (USA))
4047[4] 4659[4] 5670[4] 6289[8] 7217[10]

Neruda (IRE) *Waldemar Hickst* 63
3 b c Rock Of Gibraltar(IRE) Nicea (GER) (Lando (GER))
1686a[12]

Neshmeya *Charles Hills* 80
2 b f Lawman(FR) High Heeled (IRE) (High Chaparral (IRE))
6782[2] ◆ 7441[4]

Nessita *Hugo Palmer* a76 73
3 ch f Shamardal(USA) Neshla (Singspiel (IRE))
1602[9] 3355[8]

Netley Abbey *Harry Dunlop* a58 51
2 b g Myboycharlie(IRE) Ana Style (FR) (Anabaa Blue)
4533[10] 6288[8] 6623[6]

Netsuke (IRE) *Mlle L-L Rohn-Pelvin* a86 82
5 b m Aragorn(IRE) Notting Hill (BRZ) (Jules (USA))
660a[7]

Neuf Des Coeurs *Iain Jardine* a47 74
5 b m Champs Elysees Intervene (Zafonic (USA))
2656[5] 3154[3] 3564[7] 3706[7] 4099[3] 4489[3] 5117[2] (5350) (5580) 5783[4] 6097[2] 6346[2]

Never A Word (USA) *Charlie Appleby* a73 60
2 br g Lonhro(AUS) Janetstickettocats (USA) (Storm Cat (USA))
3054[6] 7906[3]

Never Caught (USA) *A Fabre* a90 82
3 bb c Tapit(USA) Honest Pursuit (USA) (Storm Cat (USA))
1240a[5] 7168a[3]

Never Compromise (FR) *Henk Grewe* a85 86
3 b g Astronomer Royal(USA) Noor Forever (FR) (Highest Honor (FR))
511a[2] (1311a) 2141a[5] 2722a[9]

Never Give In *K R Burke* a44 72
3 b g Alfred Nobel(IRE) Mad Annie (USA) (Anabaa (USA))
3609[9] 7246[9]

Never In Doubt *Richard Whitaker* a33 70
3 b g Royal Applause African Breeze (Atraf)
1669[4] 2802[10] 5034[5] 5759[4] 6790[6] 7111[10] 7335[2] 7851[8]

Never Never (IRE) *Iain Jardine* a63
6 b g Jeremy(USA) Argus Gal (IRE) (Alzao (USA))
567[6]

Never Say (IRE) *Jason Ward* a49 53
3 b f Monsieur Bond(IRE) Wong Again (Araafa (IRE))
48[2] 274[2] 509[3] 688[6] 896[2] 1031[5] 2015[3] 2608[6]

Never Surrender (IRE) *Charles Hills* 83
2 b c High Chaparral(IRE) Meiosis (USA) (Danzig (USA))
4349[8] 4988[4] 6262[4] 6945[2]

Never To Be (USA) *Nikki Evans* a65 60
5 b g Thewayyouare(USA) Kitty Foille (USA) (Black Minnaloushe (USA))
37[2] 239[7] 457[3] 3097[5] 3594[4] 4589[7] 6254[7] 6651[6] 7274[12] 8500[12]

New Abbey Angel (IRE) *Keith Dalgleish* a60 62
3 gr g Dark Angel(IRE) Alinda (IRE) (Revoque (IRE))
(700) 1698[2] 3482[6] 4267[10] 4936[7] 5222[2] 5539[4] 5803[4] 6106[3] 6621[8] 7096[7]

New Agenda *Paul Webber* a84 73
4 b g New Approach(IRE) Prove (Danehill (USA))
945[2] 2577[4] 8101[3] (8337) 8498[5]

New Bay *A Fabre* a77 122
4 ch h Dubawi(IRE) Cinnamon Bay (Zamindar (USA))
2568a[6] (5500a) 6354a[4] 6989a[7]

New Bidder *David Barron* 100
5 bb g Auction House(USA) Noble Nova (Fraam)
1218[2] 1887[9] 3671[7] 3890[2] 4338[13] 5390[12] (6382a) 7497[17]

New Caledonia (IRE) *Mark Johnston* 101
3 b c Cape Cross(IRE) Tessa Reef (IRE) (Mark Of Esteem (IRE))
1891[3] 2413[4] 5924[2] (6110) 6545[3] 7117[2]

New Colours *Linda Perratt* a41 70
5 gr g Verglas(IRE) Briery (IRE) (Salse (USA))
1881[9] 2089[5] 2575[9] 2656[6] 2912[6] 3154[6] 4099[5] 4489[9] 4875[9]

Newera *Tom Dascombe* 90
4 ch g Makfi Coming Home (Vettori (IRE))
1620[9] (1978) 1999[10] 2439[4] 3129[6] 3639[4] 4095[2]

Newgate Sioux *Tony Coyle* 60
2 b f Sleeping Indian Rio's Girl (Captain Rio)
2301[11] 2800[6] 3128[9] 5317[9] 5756[8] (6471)

New Lease Of Life *Keith Dalgleish* a62 71
7 b g Orientor Primo Heights (Primo Valentino (IRE))
799[4] 1120[10] 1378[2] 1559[2] 1878[3] 2201[U] 2418[7]

New Legend (IRE) *Robert Cowell* a65
3 b c Lilbourne Lad(IRE) Next To The Top (Hurricane Run (IRE))
466[5] 735[3]

New Leyf (IRE) *Jeremy Gask* a70 68
10 bb g Kheleyf(USA) Society Fair (FR) (Always Fair (USA))
76[7] 236[7]

New Look (IRE) *Ralph J Smith* a57
6 b g New Approach(IRE) Lady Miletrian (IRE) (Barathea (IRE))
7282[12]

Newmarket Warrior (IRE) *Iain Jardine* a72 74
5 b g Dalakhani(IRE) Heavens Peak (Pivotal)
1785[2] 2529[5] 2773[6] 3366[3] 3952[4] ◆ 4335[5] 8588[2]

New Money Honey (USA) *Chad C Brown* 110
2 b f Medaglia d'Oro(USA) Weekend Whim (USA) (Distorted Humor (USA))
(7809a)

New Outlook (USA) *F Chappet* a91 92
8 b g Awesome Again(CAN) Tikkanita (USA) (Cozzene (USA))
2806a[4]

Newport Place (IRE) *Jamie Osborne* a43 44
2 ch c Dragon Pulse(IRE) Mokama (Motivator)
4387[5] 4815[7] 5243[4] 5675[6]

New Reaction *Alexandra Dunn* a45
5 b g New Approach(IRE) Intaaj (IRE) (Machiavellian (USA))
7870[13]

New Record (IRE) *James Eustace* a75 75
4 br g Dansili Precocious Star (IRE) (Bold Fact (USA))
6510[5] 6701[3] (7531)

New Revive *Patrick Chamings* a45 30
4 b g New Approach(IRE) Dance Lively (USA) (Kingmambo (USA))
1826[13] 4477[6]

New Rich *Eve Johnson Houghton* a69 70
6 b g Bahamian Bounty Bling Bling (IRE) (Indian Ridge)
167[5] (615) 873[2] 1159[7] 2380[2] 2697[5] 3258[2] 3530[2] 4763[5] 7654[9] 8064[8] 8181[7] 8365[3]

New Road Side *Richard Guest* a82 84
3 b f Paco Boy(IRE) Spring Green (Bahamian Bounty)
1647[4] 2218[9] 3420[10] 3978[5] (4256) 4947[7] 5730[6] 7112[2] (7288) 7772[8] 7892[6]

Newrock (IRE) *X Thomas-Demeaulte* a91 90
3 b f Rock Of Gibraltar(IRE) Newyearresolution (USA) (Arch (USA))
8148a[12]

New Signal *David O'Meara* a69 70
3 b g New Approach(IRE) Davie's Lure (USA) (Lure (USA))
5480[3] 6905[3] (8320)

New Society (IRE) *James Bethell* a23 40
2 b g Rock Of Gibraltar(IRE) Ajiaal (Cape Cross (IRE))
6054[11] 6924[10]

Newspeak (IRE) *Fred Watson* a24 53
4 b g New Approach(IRE) Horatia (IRE) (Machiavellian (USA))
5716[8] 6452[4] 7323[13]

Newstead Abbey *David Barron* a68 105
6 b g Byron Oatcake (Selkirk (USA))
5389[12] 5976[12] 6560[12] 6764[3] 7095[11] 7593[11]

New Strategy (IRE) *Saeed bin Suroor* a57 55
4 b g Lawman(FR) Kate The Great (Xaar)
172[7] 2017[7] 2549[6]

New Street (IRE) *Jim Best* a77 70
5 gr g Acclamation New Deal (Rainbow Quest (USA))
1480[7] 2043[10] 2965[4] 3403[2] 3991[6] 4459[3] 7486[12] 7653[9] 7973[8] 8282[8] 8458[11]

Newt *Sir Mark Prescott Bt* a64 51
2 b f Sixties Icon Froglet (Shaamit (IRE))
6414[11] 7049[8] 7494[12]

New Tarabela *Tony Carroll* a60 64
5 ch g New Approach(IRE) Tarabela (CHI) (Hussonet (USA))
8125[9] 8499[13]

Newton's Law (IRE) *Brian Meehan* a86 91
5 b g Lawman(FR) Royal Alchemist (Kingsinger (IRE))
3193[5] 3857[5] 4536[6] (4817) ◆ 5050[3] 5360[6] 5669[4] 6699[8] 7301[10]

Newtown Cross (IRE) *Jimmy Fox* a57 54
6 ch g Kheleyf(USA) Sacred Pearl (IRE) (Daylami (IRE))
695[4] 7739[10] 8359[9]

New Trier (IRE) *Wesley A Ward* a23 45
2 b f Holy Roman Emperor(IRE) Clicquot (USA) (Elusive Quality (USA))
1203[8] 1736[5]

New World Power (JPN) *Roger Varian* 83
3 b c Deep Impact(JPN) Listen (IRE) (Sadler's Wells (USA))
2208[2] 3160[3] 6294[4]

New Year's Night (IRE) *Charlie Appleby* a92 99
5 ch g Raven's Pass(USA) Nightime (IRE) (Galileo (IRE))
4276[2] (Dead)

Newz Watch *Mick Quinn* a53 55
2 ch f Harbour Watch(IRE) Angus Newz (Compton Place)
3074[6] 4558[9] 5469[7] 6033[11] 7777[7]

Next Challenge (GER) *Saeed bin Suroor* a79
2 ch g Shamardal(USA) Next Holy (IRE) (Holy Roman Emperor (IRE))
7726[3] ◆

Next Edition (IRE) *Philip Kirby* a67 67
8 b g Antonius Pius(USA) Starfish (IRE) (Galileo (IRE))
329[6] 498[5] 731[7] (786) 1253[2] 1560[6] 2018[6] 3118[8] 4430[5] 5183[2] 5522[4] 5970[2] 6566[6] 7138[7]

Next Life *Saeed bin Suroor* a83 50
3 b f Oasis Dream Silkwood (Singspiel (IRE))
3029[8]

Next Stage *Saeed bin Suroor* a79 94
3 ch c Dubawi(IRE) Dash To The Front (Diktat)
2891[2] 3534[13]

Next Stop *David Nicholls* a72 77
5 b m Rail Link Reaching Ahead (USA) (Mizzen Mast (USA))
6504[10] 7007[11]

Next Train's Gone *James Eustace* a71 59
3 b g Rail Link Coh Sho No (Old Vic)
1575[6] 2774[5] 6626[6] (7104)

Nezar (IRE) *John Quinn* a86 88
5 ch g Mastercraftsman(IRE) Teddy Bears Picnic (Oasis Dream)
2238[5] 2857[9] (3322)

Nezwaah *Roger Varian* a108 111
3 b f Dubawi(IRE) Ferdoos (Dansili)
(59) (421) ◆ 2245[3] (3608) 5754a[5] 6488[2] ◆ 7404a[7]

Ngendha (FR) *N Caullery* a65 62
2 gr f Evasive Non Resolu (FR) (Nombre Premier)
5755a[7] 7455a[12]

Niblawi (IRE) *Ismail Mohammed* a95 93
4 b g Vale Of York(IRE) Finnmark (Halling (USA))
1390[3] 1652[5] (6365) (6684) 7015[4] 7365[3]

Nibras Again *Ismail Mohammed* a73 76
2 b c Kyllachy Regina (Green Desert (USA))
4363[5] 6524[3] 6950[9] 7424[2]

Nibras Bounty (IRE) *Richard Hannon* a68 80
2 ch c Bahamian Bounty Oh Sedulous (IRE) (Lawman (FR))
2180[4] (2478) 3243[17] 4076[6] 5239[5] 7460[3]

Nicarra (IRE) *Henry Candy* 79
3 b f Kodiac Nassma (IRE) (Sadler's Wells (USA))
2009[6] 2483[6] 2795[4] (5891) 6483[3] 7220[2]

Nice Name (IRE) *Marco Gasparini* 93
3 b c Royal Applause Grand Zafeen (Zafeen (FR))
1686a[6]

Niceofyoutotellme *Ralph Beckett* a105 101
7 b g Hernando(FR) Swain's Gold (USA) (Swain (IRE))
1861[10] 2626[5] 4276[6] 5411[5] 6261[9] 7779[8] 7967[4] 8356[8]

Niceonecenturion *William Knight* a70 83
3 ch g Teofilo(IRE) Turn Of A Century (Halling (USA))
1429[3] 1930[5] 2414[13] 3063[3] (4057) 5358[6]

Nice To See You (FR) *Robert Collet* a100 94
3 b c Siyouni(FR) Around Me (IRE) (Johannesburg (USA))
8165a[5] 8431a[8]

Nice Vintage (IRE) *Adrian Paul Keatley* a37 78
4 bb m Big Bad Bob(IRE) High Vintage (IRE) (High Chaparral (IRE))
(1697) (2362)

Nicholas T *Jim Goldie* 85
4 b g Rail Link Thorntoun Piccolo (Groom Dancer (USA))
(2957) 3391[2] 3923[3] ◆ 4448[9] 5226[5] 6500[14]

Nick Vedder *K R Burke* a62 13
2 b c Rip Van Winkle(IRE) Devotion (IRE) (Dylan Thomas (IRE))
7318[9] 8305[3]

Nicky Baby (IRE) *Dean Ivory* a57 59
2 gr g Dark Angel(IRE) Moon Club (IRE) (Red Clubs (IRE))
2543[4] ◆ 3526[7] 5848[8]

Nidnod *John Bridger* a65 51
3 b f Myboycharlie(IRE) Littlemisstutti (IRE) (Noverre (USA))
151[4] 380[3] 725[4] 1234[4] 1548[8] 3198[3] 3740[7] 4262[12] 5720[7] 6290[2] 6865[4] 8070[14]

Nietzsche *Brian Ellison* a60 89
3 ch g Poet's Voice Ganga (IRE) (Generous (IRE))
1062[5] (1484) ◆ (1587) 2224[5] 3162[4] 3300[7] 5226[4] (5761) (6561)

Nifty Kier *Phil McEntee* a52 54
7 b g Kier Park(IRE) Yeldham Lady (Mujahid (USA))
79[7] 1742[9] 3044[4] 3354[10] (4505) 4876[5] 5708[8]

Nifty Niece (IRE) *Ann Duffield* 62
2 gr f Zebedee Hasty Harriet (IRE) (Choisir (AUS))
3515[3] 4254[4] 4725[7] 5712[11] 6678[17]

Nigel *Richard Hughes* a91 91
4 b g New Approach(IRE) Deirdre (Dubawi (IRE))
1987[8] 2699[5] (2965) (3972) 4838[5] 6142[2] (6711)

Nigh Or Never (IRE) *Tom Dascombe* 48
2 b c Excelebration(IRE) Nigh (IRE) (Galileo (IRE))
6211[8]

Night Adventure (GER) *Jean-Pierre Carvalho* 18
2 ch f Poseidon Adventure(IRE) Nachtigall (GER) (Danehill (USA))
7563a[12]

Nightflower (IRE) *P Schiergen* 113
4 ch m Dylan Thomas(IRE) Night Of Magic (IRE) (Peintre Celebre (USA))
2723a[7] 3888[4] 5454a[2] 6175a[2] (6822a) 8129a[12]

Night Generation (GER) *Chris Gordon* a79 47
4 ch g Sholokhov(IRE) Night Woman (GER) (Monsun (GER))
7183[12] 7732[10] 8084[8]

Nightingale Valley *Stuart Kittow* 78
3 ch f Compton Place Dancing Storm (Trans Island)
1894[3] 2470[6] 2998[11] (3720) 4291[12] 6883[8]

Night Law *Andrew Balding* 76
2 b f Lawman(FR) Night Carnation (Sleeping Indian)
2410^{5} 4083^{4} (4558) 5638^{4} 7147^{9}

Nightmare (IRE) *Jamie Osborne* a63
3 b g Dream Ahead(USA) Chantilly Pearl (USA) (Smart Strike (CAN))
687^{5} 818^{5}

Night Music (GER) *A Wohler* 95
3 rg f Sea The Stars(IRE) Night Woman (GER) (Monsun (GER))
3207a^{4} 4175a^{4} 5220a^{11} 6152a^{8}

Night Of Paris (FR) *S Morineau* a40 40
7 b m Sandwaki(USA) Night Symphony (GER) (Big Shuffle (USA))
512a^{6}

Night Run (FR) *Y Al Blooshi* 104
4 gr h Martaline Spring Morning (FR) (Ashkalani (IRE))
812a^{9}

Night Shadow *Scott Dixon* 48
2 ch c Haafhd Totally Trusted (Oasis Dream)
2265^{6}

Nightswift *James Evans* a56 45
4 b g Midnight Legend Sharbasia (IRE) (King's Best (USA))
1140^{12} 1639^{8} *5023^{8} 7280^{11} 8039^{12}*

Night To Remember (IRE) *Ralph Beckett* a62 72
3 b g Dark Angel(IRE) Night Club (Mozart (IRE))
63^{4}

Night Wish (GER) *Frau S Steinberg* a93 105
6 b h Sholokhov(IRE) Night Woman (GER) (Monsun (GER))
1516a^{2} 2075a^{7} 3544a^{3} (4783a)

Nil Dream (FR) *J-P Gallorini* 75
2 b c Dream Well(FR) Nova Cristina (FR) (Dalakhani (IRE))
5348a^{9}

Nile Desire *D Smaga* 73
2 b f Makfi Arrow Of Desire (Danehill Dancer (IRE))
6639a^{4} 7346a^{8}

Nile Empress *Hugo Palmer* a50 77
2 b f Holy Roman Emperor(IRE) Temple Of Thebes (IRE) (Bahri (USA))
1741^{6} (4022) 4843^{6} 5931^{6} *7305^{8}*

Nile Paris (FR) *J-P Gallorini* 73
2 b c Apsis Nini De Paris (FR) (Lord Of Men)
5985a^{3} 6638a^{10} 7345a^{6}

Nimo (FR) *E Caroux* a73 68
3 ch g Muhtathir Nimohe (FR) (Excellent Art)
8368a^{7}

Nimr *Richard Fahey* a98 91
3 b g Shamardal(USA) Riberac (Efisio)
2237^{2} 3600^{5} *(8192)* ◆

Nimrod (IRE) *P Schiergen* 92
3 b c High Chaparral(IRE) Night Of Magic (IRE) (Peintre Celebre (USA))
2711a^{5} 4186a^{10}

Nine Carat (IRE) *Keith Henry Clarke* a36 37
5 b g Diamond Green(FR) Bonkers (Efisio)
765^{11}

Ninedarter *Antony Brittain*
2 b g Monsieur Bond(IRE) Carambola (Lucky Story (USA))
7818^{12}

Ninepointsixthree *John O'Shea* a67 72
6 b g Bertolini(USA) Armada Grove (Fleetwood (IRE))
640^{8} 704^{4} 838^{5} 1002^{9} 3498^{4} *4197^{6}*

Nineteenth Hole (IRE) *Michael Wigham* a64
4 b g Dark Angel(IRE) Kingpin Delight (Emarati (USA))
51^{4}

Ninetta (IRE) *Ann Duffield* 84
3 b f New Approach(IRE) Pine Chip (USA) (Nureyev (USA))
1438^{7} 2407^{3} 3291^{5} 4042^{4} 4631^{4} 5180^{9} 5919^{2} 6811^{10} 7360^{13}

Ninety Years Young *David Elsworth* a68 64
2 b c Paco Boy(IRE) Lady Of Windsor (IRE) (Woods Of Windsor (USA))
3954^{11} *6087^{7}* 6712^{3} 7041^{5} 7313^{9} *(7777) 7884^{2} 8159^{6} 8560^{7}*

Ningaloo (GER) *Simon Crisford* a64
2 b g Siyouni(FR) Notre Dame (GER) (Acatenango (GER))
5676^{5}

Ningara *Jassim Al Ghazali* a98 98
6 b g Singspiel(IRE) Garanciere (FR) (Anabaa (USA))
757a^{10}

Ninian Des Aigles (FR) *Mme C Barande-Barbe* a54 43
2 b g Le Houssais(FR) Boum Des Aigles (FR) (Slickly (FR))
6015a^{13}

Ninjago *Paul Midgley* a88 108
6 b g Mount Nelson Fidelio's Miracle (USA) (Mountain Cat (USA))
2488^{4} 3386^{24} 3891^{3} 4667^{7} 4865^{20} 5143^{9} 5555^{15} 6556^{6} 6837^{3} 7156^{9} 7497^{6}

Nip Down The Jug *Adam West* 52
2 b g Piccolo The City Kid (IRE) (Danetime (IRE))
5922^{3} 6264^{10} 6663^{10}

Niqnaaqpaadiwaaq *Eric Alston* a62 70
4 b g Aqlaam Aswaaq (IRE) (Peintre Celebre (USA))
1596^{6} 2345^{7} 3807^{4} 4369^{3} 4445^{2} 5151^{3} 6226^{2} 7010^{4} *7889^{6} 8188^{6}*

Niseko *William Muir* 10
2 b g Cacique(IRE) Snow Crystal (IRE) (Kingmambo (USA))
7770^{13}

Nisser *Robert Cowell* a67 85
3 b c Dream Ahead(USA) Poppy Seed (Bold Edge)
2251^{6} 2693^{3} ◆ 3105^{3} 3415^{4} 5955^{9} *7054^{7} 7461^{12}*

Noah Amor (IRE) *David Nicholls* a52 72
3 b g Kodiac Jumbo Romance (IRE) (Tagula (IRE))
1669^{7} 2019^{6} 3293^{3} 3773^{4} (4229) 4855^{2} *8390^{7}*

Nobel Duke (IRE) *William Haggas* a68
3 ch g Duke Of Marmalade(IRE) Dowager (Groom Dancer (USA))
2443^{3}

Nobility (IRE) *Tim Easterby* a48 57
2 b c Alfred Nobel(IRE) Structura (USA) (Stormin Fever (USA))
1641^{8} 5476^{8} *5809^{7}* 6214^{9} 6678^{11}

Noble Act *Rae Guest* a74 74
3 b f Kyllachy Noble Desert (FR) (Green Desert (USA))
2561^{4} 4041^{4} ◆ 4521^{3} (5200) 5751^{4} (6410) 6946^{11} *8010^{11} 8228^{4} 8430^{3}*

Noble Asset *Milton Bradley* a71 78
5 ch g Compton Place Chance For Romance (Entrepreneur)
1964^{6} 3193^{7} 4461^{6} 4817^{4} *5189^{7}* 5285^{7} 6195^{6} *6425^{5}* 6669^{3} 7303^{6} *7811^{6} 7945^{4} 8078^{7} 8535^{5}*

Noble Attitude (FR) *John Best* a52 50
2 b c Dunkerque(FR) Silent Flight (FR) (Sicyos (USA))
2822^{8} *3315^{8} 8377^{7}*

Noble Aussie (IRE) *Damian Joseph English* a41 41
5 gr g Aussie Rules(USA) Nobilissima (IRE) (Orpen (USA))
6466a^{4}

Noble Ballad *Ralph Beckett* a60 46
2 b g Royal Applause Melody Maker (Diktat)
6671^{6} 7209^{6} *7883^{6} 8560^{9}*

Noble Beauty (USA) *Chad C Brown* 99
3 b f Kitten's Joy(USA) Money Huntress (USA) (Mineshaft (USA))
4174a^{8}

Noble Behest *Marcus Tregoning* a47
2 b c Sir Percy Lady Hestia (USA) (Belong To Me (USA))
8088^{9} 8246^{10}

Noble Dancer (IRE) *Doug O'Neill* 84
2 b f Alfred Nobel(IRE) Marianne's Dancer (IRE) (Bold Fact (USA))
8127a^{11}

Noble Deed *Michael Attwater* a80 65
6 ch g Kyllachy Noble One (Primo Dominie)
(236) (561) 901^{9} 1178^{8} 1419^{4} 2028^{12} 2469^{11} 3259^{3} 3953^{11} 5827^{10} *8561^{11}*

Noble Gift *William Knight* a104 104
6 ch g Cadeaux Genereux Noble Penny (Pennekamp (USA))
1088^{2} (1645) 2465^{3} 3383^{8} 3913^{12} 4731^{13} *6125^{5}* 7058^{6} *7765^{3}*

Noble House (GER) *Mario Hofer* 94
3 b c Lando(GER) Noble Lady (GER) (Sholokhov (IRE))
2711a^{3} 4186a^{14} 5696a^{4} 8573a^{12}

Noble Intention (IRE) *G M Lyons* a77 79
2 gb g Zebedee Lear's Crown (USA) (Lear Fan (USA))
7917a^{4}

Noble Kind *David Evans*
2 b f Cockney Rebel(IRE) Ogre (USA) (Tale Of The Cat (USA))
3093^{P}

Nobleman (GER) *Hughie Morrison* a56 57
2 b g Lord Of England(GER) Naomia (GER) (Monsun (GER))
7187^{6} *7865^{9} 7977^{9}*

Noble Peace *Henry Candy* a81 88
3 b g Kyllachy Peace Concluded (Bertolini (USA))
(1837) 2466^{10} 3105^{4} 5403^{16} (6210) 6918^{8}

Noble Reach *Lawrence Mullaney* a49 49
5 b m Phoenix Reach(IRE) Comtesse Noire (CAN) (Woodman (USA))
368^{8} 2745^{4} 3067^{13} 3417^{5} *4645^{5}*

Noble Silk *Lucy Wadham* a92 101
7 gr g Sir Percy Tussah (Daylami (IRE))
4077^{6} 4581^{6} ◆ 5144^{5} 6526^{5} 6919^{2} 7498^{13}

Noble Star (IRE) *James Fanshawe* a79 73
3 b g Acclamation Wrong Answer (Verglas (IRE))
1397^{4} *(7960)*

Noble Storm (USA) *Ed McMahon* a84 88
10 b g Yankee Gentleman(USA) Changed Tune (USA) (Tunerup (USA))
1408^{8} 1968^{12} 6234^{8} 6633^{5} *6926^{6}* ◆ 7288^{10} *7892^{2}*

Noblewoman *Roger Charlton* a30
3 b f Showcasing Rare Virtue (USA) (Empire Maker (USA))
7207^{5}

Nobly Born *John Gosden* 94
2 ch c Mayson Noble One (Primo Dominie)
3356^{3} (3818) ◆ 4352^{2}

No Body's Fool *Michael Madgwick* a35 42
3 ch f Sixties Icon Leleyf (IRE) (Kheleyf (USA))
978^{8} 1574^{5} 2288^{6} *3317^{6}* 3975^{11}

Noce (FR) *C Baillet* 100
3 ch f Le Havre(IRE) Simple Solution (USA) (Dynaformer (USA))
1374a^{11}

No Contest (FR) *G Doleuze* a24 44
5 ch g Dylan Thomas(IRE) Babola (IRE) (Grand Lodge (USA))
1157a^{8}

Nocturn *Ronald Harris* a55 76
7 b g Oasis Dream Pizzicato (Statoblest)
2754^{11} 3956^{7} 4461^{9} 5285^{6} 5774^{6} 6195^{9} 6653^{2} 7267^{6} 7415^{7} 7626^{5} *8280^{10} 8430^{8}*

Nodachi (IRE) *Andrew Balding* 80
3 b g Rip Van Winkle(IRE) Jabroot (IRE) (Alhaarth (IRE))
2440^{4} 3103^{2}

Nodiac (IRE) *Philip D'Amato* 94
3 b f Kodiac No Way (IRE) (Rainbows For Life (CAN))
7724a^{7}

No Education *Jo Hughes* 107
3 b c Showcasing Ceilidh Band (Celtic Swing)
1024a^{9} 4380^{3} 5004a^{8}

No Fault Of Mine (USA) *Chris Block* a101 102
4 b m Blame(USA) Single Solution (USA) (Flatter (USA))
5430a^{6}

Nofizzophobia *Derek Shaw* a34
3 ch f Bahamian Bounty Croeso Cusan (Diktat)
7311^{14} 7603^{6} 7859^{8}

Nofoemaypass (FR) *H-F Devin* 84
2 b c Myboycharlie(IRE) Sundancer (Hernando (FR))
4330a^{5} 7170a^{12} 7655a^{9}

Noguchi (IRE) *Chris Dwyer* a78 75
11 ch g Pivotal Tuscania (USA) (Woodman (USA))
382^{3} 833^{7}

No Heretic *Nicky Henderson* a84 101
8 b g Galileo(IRE) Intrigued (Darshaan) (1967) 3246^{14} *3658^{17}* 4752^{P} (Dead)

Noholdingback Bear (USA) *Michael P De Paulo* a110
3 b c Put It Back(USA) Pleasant Quality (CAN) (Elusive Quality (USA))
7832a^{6}

Nokhada (IRE) *David Simcock* a86 78
3 b c Lilbourne Lad(IRE) Silverdreammachine (IRE) (Marju (IRE))
434^{2}

Nolecce *Tony Forbes* a64 62
9 ch g Reset(AUS) Ghassanah (Pas De Seul)
295^{4} 731^{4} 1085^{4} 1347^{7} 2110^{5} 2738^{4} 3903^{2} (4499)

Nolohay (IRE) *M Al Mheiri* a95 94
5 ch h Dubawi(IRE) Antioquia (Singspiel (IRE))
455a^{13} *717a^{6}* 812a^{4}

No Luck Penny *Noel Wilson* 41
2 b f Delegator Rutba (Act One)
3939^{6} 4943^{10} 6446^{12}

Nomadic (FR) *P Bary* 97
3 b f Duke Of Marmalade(IRE) Teepee (JPN) (Deep Impact (JPN))
1309a^{10}

No Mood *C Laffon-Parias* a85 66
5 ch h Monsun(GER) Impressionnante (Danehill (USA))
4903a^{2}

Nomorerichblondes (USA) *A bin Harmash* a75
2 b f Hard Spun(USA) Miss Luann (USA) (Unbridled's Song (USA))
8575a^{4}

Nona Blu *Michael Wigham* a54 70
4 b g Diktat Shivering (Royal Applause)
2734^{11} 3997^{5} 5055^{2} 5326^{2} 5592^{2} 6645^{2} *7339a^{13}*

Nonagon *Wilf Storey* a66 65
5 b g Pastoral Pursuits Nine Red (Royal Applause)
1561^{6} (1881) *2916^{2}* 3418^{6} *5065^{4} 6103^{5}* 6438^{6} (Dead)

Nonchalant *Hugo Froud* a67 45
5 gr g Oasis Dream Comeback Queen (Nayef (USA))
1664^{4} 2093^{3} 2651^{5} 2888^{3} 3166^{18} 3481^{5} 4455^{7} 4768^{6} 6953^{4} *7385^{4} 7656^{6} 7870^{11} 8124^{4} 8528^{2}*

Noneedtotellme (IRE) *James Unett* a39 45
3 gr f Fast Company(IRE) Gemma's Delight (IRE) (Clodovil (IRE))
4017^{6} 4806^{6} 5338^{10} *6902^{8} 7646^{5} 8499^{8}*

Nonios (IRE) *David Simcock* a89 78
4 b g Oasis Dream Young And Daring (USA) (Woodman (USA))
4458^{3} 5231^{4} *6128^{3} 6676^{4} 7911^{2} (8077)* ◆ *8317^{13}*

Nonno Giulio (IRE) *Roger Fell* a79 83
5 ch g Halling(USA) Contrary (IRE) (Mark Of Esteem (IRE))
1954^{5} (2347) 3011^{7} 3419^{5} 4408^{8} 5179^{5} 5482^{12} *5972^{4}* (6220) 6683^{2} 7126^{13} 7623^{10} (7742) *7857^{8}*

No No Cardinal (IRE) *Mark Gillard* a30 51
7 ch g Touch Of Land(FR) Four Moons (IRE) (Cardinal Flower)
3996^{8} (4504) 5572 ^{4} 6405^{5}

No Not Again (IRE) *Richard Hannon* a65 73
2 b c Roderic O'Connor(IRE) Bella Bella (IRE) (Sri Pekan (USA))
6542^{3} 6750^{4} 7184^{4} 7574^{9} *7776^{6} 8174^{7} 8466^{3}*

No Not Yet *Michael Dods* a45 50
4 b m Notnowcato True Vision (IRE) (Pulpit (USA))
1628^{10} 2048^{14} 2745^{5} 3417^{6} 3704^{3} 5155^{5} *6102^{6}*

Noodles Blue Boy *Ollie Pears* a57 82
10 b g Makbul Dee Dee Girl (IRE) (Primo Dominie)
1447^{3} 1666^{2} 2270^{5} *2622^{9}* 3494^{3} 4295^{5} 4726^{5} 5295^{6} 6023^{7} 6774^{6}

Noor Al Hawa (FR) *A Wohler* 110
3 ch c Makfi Majestic Roi (USA) (Street Cry (IRE))
1689a^{3} 2315a^{3} 3699a^{2} (5004a) (6397a) (6992a) (8573a)

Noor Al Haya (IRE) *Laura Mongan* a60 63
6 b m Tamayuz Hariya (IRE) (Shernazar)
1575 695^{9} 1450^{10}

Noozhoh Canarias (SPA) *J A Remolina Diez* 107
5 b h Caradak(IRE) Noozhah (Singspiel (IRE))
6272a^{8}

No Pleasing You (IRE) *Bill Turner* 22
3 b f Frozen Power(IRE) Villafranca (IRE) (In The Wings)
5731^{7} 6443^{4}

Norab (GER) *Bernard Llewellyn* a83 95
5 b g Galileo(IRE) Night Woman (GER) (Monsun (GER))
2468^{11} 2685^{10} 3351^{7} 3639^{8} 4912^{2} 6279^{7}

Nora Batt (IRE) *David Evans* a59 72
3 ch f Art Connoisseur(IRE) Mrs Batt (IRE) (Medecis)
4820^{2} 6018^{5} *8430^{9}*

Noray (FR) *Enrique Leon Penate* a87 78
4 b h Naaqoos Stadore (FR) (Kendor (FR))
4903a^{3}

Norberina (FR) *G Cherel* 35
4 b m Konig Turf(GER) Blue Sky Du Mont (FR) (Muhtathir)
1157a^{7}

Nordenfelt (IRE) *Ed Dunlop* a8
3 b g Lilbourne Lad(IRE) There With Me (USA) (Distant View (USA))
6751^{11} 1184^{8}

Nordic Combined (IRE) *Brian Ellison* 68
2 b g Haafhd Chilly Filly (IRE) (Montjeu (IRE))
2335^{5} 2682^{5} 3223^{5} 5414^{9} (6130)

Nordic Dream (IRE) *A Fabre* a90 99
3 b c Dream Ahead(USA) Nyramba (Night Shift (USA))
1374a^{8}

Nordico (GER) *Mario Hofer* a73 105
5 ch h Medicean Norwegian Pride (FR) (Diktat)
1376a^{4} *1957a^{7}* 6397a^{7} 6992a^{3} 7564a^{6} 7843a^{7} 8117a^{9}

Nordwienerin (IRE) *P Schiergen* 90
3 ch f Wiener Walzer(GER) North Queen (IRE) (Desert King (IRE))
5219a^{7}

Noreena *Paul D'Arcy* 14
2 b f Medicean Nurai (Danehill Dancer (IRE))
6874^{9}

No Refund (IRE) *David Loughnane* a52 57
5 b g Invincible Spirit(IRE) Evangeline (Sadler's Wells (USA))
4005^{7} 4516^{2} 5576^{11} 5887^{13} 6636^{4} (7212) *7751^{8} 7912^{12} 8288^{10}*

Norfolk Sound *Stuart Coltherd* a42 43
5 b m Pastoral Pursuits Cayman Sound (Turtle Island (IRE))
2093^{10} 2573^{9} *7438^{11}*

Normal Equilibrium *Robert Cowell* a90 94
6 b g Elnadim(USA) Acicula (IRE) (Night Shift (USA))
86^{5} 220^{4} 492^{5} (1566) 1857^{7} 2188^{9} 2488^{5} 2895^{9} *3277^{7}* 4066^{8} *8463^{6}*

Normandel (FR) *Mme Pia Brandt* 102
2 b f Le Havre(IRE) Lidana (IRE) (King's Best (USA))
(5698a) 6271a^{2} 6986a^{7}

Normandie (GER) *Mme Pia Brandt* 80
2 b f Redoute's Choice(AUS) Ninas Rainbow (Rainbow Quest (USA))
6639a^{2} (7346a)

Normandie Lady *Richard Fahey* a80 81
3 b f Kheleyf(USA) Normandie Art (Rainbow Quest (USA))
984^{4} (1562) ◆ 3029^{5} 3521^{8} (4871) 5919^{4} 7419^{4} *8028^{3}* ◆

Normandy Barriere (IRE) *Nigel Tinkler* 103
4 b g Rock Of Gibraltar(IRE) Ma Paloma (FR) (Highest Honor (FR))
1787^{3} (2028) 3115^{3} 3645^{15} 4079^{9} 4627^{2} (5161) 6112^{4} (6287) 7156^{16}

Normandy Kitten (USA) *Gianluca Bietolini* a84 84
3 ch c Kitten's Joy(USA) Keeping Watch (IRE) (Danehill (USA))
2948a^{6}

Normandy Knight *Richard Fahey* a79 81
4 b g Acclamation Prayer (IRE) (Rainbow Quest (USA))
1785^{9} 2198^{6} (2734) 3166^{16} 4113^{8} 4593^{7} (5180) 5866^{4} 6516^{2} 6956^{6} *7436^{3}*

Norphin *Simon Hodgson* a23 24
6 b g Norse Dancer(IRE) Orphina (IRE) (Orpen (USA))
233^{10} 1742^{8} 2086^{4}

Norse Castle *Martin Bosley* a65 5
3 b g Norse Dancer(IRE) Hursley Hope (IRE) (Barathea (IRE))
287^{7} 377^{4} 7775^{13} *8257^{9} 8448^{7}*

Norse King (FR) *Mme M Bollack-Badel* a55 98
7 ch g Norse Dancer(IRE) Angel Wing (Barathea (IRE))
1909a^{9} 8042a^{10}

Norse Magic *Sylvester Kirk* 76
3 b f Norse Dancer(IRE) Gift Of Love (IRE) (Azamour (IRE))
1312^{3} 1758^{3} 2431^{5} 3673^{7}

North Bay Lady (IRE) *John Wainwright* a38 39
4 b m Fast Company(IRE) Straight Sets (IRE) (Pivotal)
26^{9} 170^{9} 602^{10} 8195^{8}

North Creek *Chris Wall* a85 65
3 b g Iffraaj Maine Rose (Red Ransom (USA))
(979) ◆ *1267^{2}* 4010^{2} 4742^{6} *5765^{3} 7108^{8}*

Northdown *David Lanigan* a78 20
2 b g Paco Boy(IRE) Hazita (Singspiel (IRE))
4125^{7} *(4523) 5506^{2} 6240^{7}*

Northern Bay (GER) *Keith Reveley*
6 b g Desert Prince(IRE) Nova Scotia (GER) (Sholokhov (IRE))
6900^{14}

Northern Beau (IRE) *Miss Clare Louise Cannon* a21 40
3 b f Canford Cliffs(IRE) View (IRE) (Galileo (IRE))
2360^{8}

Northern Eclipse *David O'Meara* 57
2 b g Kyllachy Quadrophenia (College Chapel)
4161^{11} 4765^{13}

Northern Meeting (IRE) *Robert Stephens* a76 77
6 b m Dylan Thomas(IRE) Scottish Stage (IRE) (Selkirk (USA))
2753^{4} 4501^{6} *6090^{4}* 7507^{3} *8161^{7}*

Northern Sky (IRE) *Adrian Paul Keatley* 63
3 b g Danehill Dancer(IRE) Moon Flower (IRE) (Sadler's Wells (USA))
2576^{2} 4813a^{5}

Northern Surprise (IRE) *Timothy Doyle* a91 69
5 b g Azamour(IRE) Surprise Treat (IRE) (Shalford (IRE))
7523a^{12}

Northern Thunder (IRE) *Richard Hannon* a80 77
2 b c Dragon Pulse(IRE) Miss Gibraltar (Rock Of Gibraltar (IRE))
1850^{3} 2358 ^{2} 2611^{2} 4053^{5} (4629) *(5299)* 6538^{9} 7549^{4}

Northgate Lad (IRE) *Brian Ellison* a96 100
4 gr g Dark Angel(IRE) Canosa (IRE) (Catrail (USA))
2488^{14} 2862^{8} *3566^{3} 4644^{2}* 6287^{8} 6560^{11}

Northlands *H-A Pantall* 67
3 ch g Aqlaam From This Day On (USA) (El Prado (IRE))
2287a^{2}

Northman (IRE) *Jim Boyle* a45 31
3 b g Frozen Power(IRE) Chifney Rush (IRE) (Grand Lodge (USA))
1259^{5} 1740^{10} *2000^{7}*

Northside Prince (IRE) *Alan Swinbank* a76 72
10 b g Desert Prince(IRE) Spartan Girl (IRE) (Ela-Mana-Mou)
132[4] 425[2] 583[2] 891[2] 1405[4] 2018[4] 2805[5] 3547[6] 4934[5] *5842[2] 6103[6] 7138[2]* 7592[6]

North Spirit (IRE) *David O'Meara* a59 59
3 b g Zebedee Zara's Girl (IRE) (Tillerman)
2534[5] 2854[5] 4141[4]

North Thunder (FR) *A Fabre* 105
2 b c Invincible Spirit(IRE) Precocious Star (IRE) (Bold Fact (USA))
4925a[3] 7086a[3]

Nortron (IRE) *Andrew Balding* a85 85
4 b h Makfi Nessa (FR) (Marchand De Sable (USA))
82[3] 260[3]

Norville (IRE) *Lee Smyth* a65 61
9 b g Elusive City(USA) Saraposa (IRE) (Ahonoora)
2365[7] (5222) 5576[7]

Norwegian Highness (FR) *Kevin Ryan* a76 77
2 ch f Kendargent(FR) Norwegian Princess (IRE) (Fairy King (USA))
1850[6] 2254[6] (5727) 6257[9] *6743[2]* ◆ 7120[14] *7956[3]*

Nosey Barker (IRE) *Richard Hannon* a72 79
4 b h Rip Van Winkle(IRE) Cold Cold Woman (Machiavellian (USA))
448[5] 2996[5] 3802[8] *4201[3]* 4531[6] 4774[2]

Nostalgie *Rae Guest* a73 73
2 gr f Archipenko(USA) Neige D'Antan (Aussie Rules (USA))
6897[4] ◆ 7465[3] *7882[2] 8139[5] 8340[6]*

Not A Bad Oul Day (IRE) *Mrs D A Love* a56 61
4 ch g Captain Rio Woodville (Deploy)
6464a[6]

No Taboo (FR) *Robert Collet* a59 71
3 b f Whipper(USA) Taboo (GER) (Pivotal)
716a[9]

Not A Given (USA) *A R Al Rayhi* a94 28
7 b g Any Given Saturday(USA) Any For Love (ARG) (Southern Halo (USA))
229a[9] *8578a[9]*

Notaire (IRE) *J Bourgeais* a1 13
6 b h Nayef(USA) Aiglonne (USA) (Silver Hawk (USA))
5216a[14]

Notalot (IRE) *Hilal Kobeissi* 83
2 b g Sir Prancealot(IRE) Hapipi (Bertolini (USA))
2535[8] 3216[2] 3772[2] ◆ 4825[8] (5251) (5543) 6229[4] 6563[4] 7120[9] 8564a[5]

Not Another Bill *Chris Wall* a60 40
5 ch g Notnowcato Composing (IRE) (Noverre (USA))
1873[8] 3845[12] *5129[8]*

Notarised *Mark Johnston* a106 107
5 b g Authorized(IRE) Caribbean Dancer (USA) (Theatrical (IRE))
614[3] (793) 1067[10] 1645[5] 2468[3] 3340[16] *3658[15]* 3889[9] 4734[3] 5144[P] (Dead)

Notary *Roger Varian* a64 83
3 b f Lawman(FR) Purity (Pivotal)
5765[12]

Noted And Quoted (USA) *Bob Baffert* a108
2 rg f The Factor(USA) Silver Cub (USA) (City Zip (USA))
7830a[7]

Nothing Compares *Mark Johnston* a29
2 b f Harbour Watch(IRE) Endorsement (Warning)
7940[8] 8227[10]

Notice (IRE) *David Simcock* a65 80
3 ch f New Approach(IRE) Classic Remark (IRE) (Dr Fong (USA))
3094[5] *3781[7] 5025[5]* (5749) (6527)

Notion Of Beauty (USA) *K R Burke* a62 65
3 b f Harlan's Holiday(USA) Gypsy Monarch (USA) (Wavering Monarch (USA))
3601[7] 4857[4] 5353[3] *7385[6] 7853[9] 8193[10] 8339[4]*

Not Listenin'tome (AUS) *John Moore* 121
5 b g Dylan Thomas(IRE) Flame Of Sydney (AUS) (Encosta De Lago (AUS))
1104a[8] 1911a[6] 8330a[7]

Not My Way (IRE) *John O'Shea*
3 b f Acclamation Wildsplash (USA) (Deputy Minister (CAN))
4480[9] 6311[9]

Not Never *Hugo Palmer* 103
4 ch g Notnowcato Watchoverme (Haafhd)
6544[2] 7215[2] 7498[5]

Not Now Mum *Dean Ivory* a43 49
2 ch g Dutch Art Fisadara (Nayef (USA))
6086[8] 6524[7] *7776[9] 7975[13]*

Not Now Nadia (IRE) *Michael Dods* 59
2 b f Footstepsinthesand Lake Wanaka (IRE) (Fasliyev (USA))
2970[8] 3873[4] 5727[5] 6807[6] 7579[5]

Notnowsam *Dan Skelton* a10 1
5 ch g Notnowcato First Fantasy (Be My Chief (USA))
1914[8]

Not Only Florina (IRE) *C Ferland* a91 100
3 b f Makfi Nightdance Sun (GER) (Monsun (GER))
(6357a) 7568a[5]

Notoursortdear *John Gallagher* a60 49
4 b m Monsieur Bond(IRE) Jasmine Breeze (Saddlers' Hall (IRE))
4521[7] 7011[8] *7459[5]*

Notre Sage (FR) *P Decouz* a65 77
2 b f Sageburg(IRE) Numerieus (FR) (Numerous (USA))
(1284a) 4750a[7] 7490a[3] *7879a[7]*

Not So Sleepy *Hughie Morrison* a97 105
4 ch g Beat Hollow Papillon De Bronze (IRE) (Marju (IRE))
2626[4] 3383[11] 4253a[4] 5893[6] 6321[5] 7546[3] *8068[8]*

Notte A Roma (IRE) *C Lerner* 91
2 b c Holy Roman Emperor(IRE) Japan (GER) (Key Royal (GER))
3507a[2]

Notte D'Oro (IRE) *Mme Pia Brandt* 95
4 b m Montjeu(IRE) Notting Hill (BRZ) (Jules (USA))
3092a[2] 6273a[6] 8024a[8]

Notte Illuminata (IRE) *K R Burke* a76 75
3 b f Acclamation Sogno Verde (IRE) (Green Desert (USA))
(8388)

Not This Time (USA) *Dale Romans* a122
2 bb c Giant's Causeway(USA) Miss Macy Sue (USA) (Trippi (USA))
7834a[2]

Not Touch *Richard Hannon* a42 75
3 ch c Dream Ahead(USA) Umlilo (Mtoto)
1397[9] 2185[4] 2654[12] 4554[6] 5287[2] 5895[2] 6186[3] *7529[8]*

Notts So Blue *Shaun Harris* a47 44
5 b m Pastoral Pursuits Blue Nile (IRE) (Bluebird (USA))
822[9] 1049[8] 1548[9]

Not Your Call (IRE) *Lee Carter* a73
5 b g Balmont(USA) Cafe Lassere (USA) (Giant's Causeway (USA))
190[8] 346[7] 617[5] 1042[2] (1147) 1834[3] 2155[2] (2610) 3474[3] (5194) (5475) 6510[9]

Nouvelle Ere *Tony Carroll* a66 59
5 b g Archipenko(USA) Sinister Ruckus (USA) (Trippi (USA))
173[10] 701[U] 898[2] 1340[10] 1796[6] 3560[12] 3997[15] *8500[9]*

Nouvelle Vision (FR) *E Libaud* a17
2 b f Vision D'Etat(FR) Nakiya (FR) (Kendor (FR))
8420a[16]

Nouvelli Dancer (IRE) *David C Griffiths* a86 84
3 b f Lilbourne Lad(IRE) Kiralik (Efisio)
(327) (345) 947[2] (1137) 2239[17] 4139[3] 4429[2] *(5191)* (5992) *6964[5] 7781[7]*

Novabridge *Karen Tutty* a62 57
8 ch g Avonbridge Petrovna (IRE) (Petardia)
418[10] (589) 837[3] 7747[12] 7860[2] (8312) (8485)

Novalina (IRE) *William Haggas* a70 92
3 b f Galileo(IRE) Baraka (IRE) (Danehill (USA))
3601[6] 4056[5] (4948) 5596[5] (6345) 6917[5] *7652[12]*

Novancia (IRE) *Mark Johnston* 87
4 b m Fastnet Rock(AUS) Ceoil An Aith (IRE) (Accordion)
2433[9] 3027[4] 3263[6]

Nova Negrita (FR) *Henk Grewe* 42
2 b f Linngari(IRE) Nova Scotia (GER) (Sholokhov (IRE))
4187a[7]

Novano (GER) *Waldemar Hickst* 105
4 ch g Samum(GER) Nicella (GER) (Lando (GER))
2728a[3] 4578a[7] 5219a[4] 6151a[8]

Novela (IRE) *Rod Collet* 55
2 b f Showcasing Isolde's Return (Avonbridge)
7996a[7]

Novelty Seeker (USA) *Michael Easterby* a86 93
7 b g Street Sense(USA) Nawaiet (USA) (Zilzal (USA))
1620[10] 1972[7] 2688[10] 3113[6] 4113[2] (7159)

Noverre To Go (IRE) *Ronald Harris* a59 67
10 ch g Noverre(USA) Ukraine Venture (Slip Anchor)
872[8] 919[5] 1261[8] 1549[4] *1720[8]* 2130[4] *2765[4]* 3098[10] 3510[7] (3741) 4485[7] 5103[8] 5546[4] 6894[7]

Novinophobia *Richard Fahey* 78
3 ch g Showcasing Malelane (IRE) (Prince Sabo)
2029[12] 2407[5] 2891[12] 3344[5] 4003[2] (4490) 6501[8]

Novis Adventus (IRE) *Jeremy Noseda* a96 100
4 b h New Approach(IRE) Tiffed (USA) (Seattle Slew (USA))
8210[9] 8424[5]

Novoman (IRE) *William Haggas* 92
2 ch g Sir Prancealot(IRE) Rublevka Star (USA) (Elusive Quality (USA))
3799[3] ◆ 5332[2] (5670) 6575[5] 7004[2] ◆ 7541[3] ◆

Now Children (IRE) *Iain Jardine* 89
2 ch c Dragon Pulse(IRE) Toberanthawn (IRE) (Danehill Dancer (IRE))
4678[2] (5834) (6554)

Now Or Never (IRE) *M D O'Callaghan* 108
3 b f Bushranger(IRE) Queenofthefairies (Pivotal)
1369a[2] (2068a) 2509a[3] 3339[4] 6352a[4] 7171a[8]

Now We Can *N Clement* a96 113
7 b g Martillo(GER) Notre Dame (GER) (Acatenango (GER))
4333a[3] 6178a[3] 6598a[4] 7396a[3]

Nuala Tagula (IRE) *John Quinn* a68 63
3 b f Tagula(IRE) Dangle (IRE) (Desert Style (IRE))
(6744) ◆ *8403[10] 8535[4]*

Nubar Boy *Daniel Mark Loughnane* a69 40
9 ch g Compton Place Out Like Magic (Magic Ring (IRE))
190[9] 951[3] 2153[10] 2635[7] *3476[8]*

Nucky Thompson *Richard Spencer* a78 78
3 b g Cockney Rebel(IRE) Vino Veritas (USA) (Chief's Crown (USA))
2291[5] 2859[2] *3728[2]* 5111[5] *6242[3]*

Nuclear Power *William Muir* a85 99
2 b g Equiano(FR) Miss Rimex (IRE) (Ezzoud (IRE))
2371[4] 2649[5] 3295[8] *5631[2]* (6016) 7113[5] ◆ 7536[3] *7989[5]*

Nudge Nudge *D Windrif* a54 52
2 ch g Winker Watson Silca Key (Inchinor)
2535[10] 3075[2] *4183a[2]* 5819a[7]

Nuee Ardente (FR) *M Boutin* 81
2 b f Soave(GER) Country Jane (FR) (Country Reel (USA))
(1021a)

Nuit De Mai (FR) *B De Montzey* a67 75
2 b f Evasive Pixy (Pivotal)
4925a[6] *5755a[9]*

Numeration (FR) *B De Montzey* a80 87
2 b f Shakespearean(IRE) Addition (FR) (Numerous (USA))
7263a[5]

Nuncio *Roger Charlton* a71 41
2 b g Authorized(IRE) Sweet Pilgrim (Talkin Man (CAN))
6570[10] *7867[8] 8065[4] 8560[2]*

Nuno Tristan (USA) *Richard Fahey* a96 101
4 b g Henrythenavigator(USA) Saintly Speech (USA) (Southern Halo (USA))
(198) ◆ *529[2] 657[5] 960[5]* 3115[6] (3419) 4625[5] 4862[3] ◆ 5418[9] 5871[4] 6287[4] 6556[3]

Nuovo Record (JPN) *Makoto Saito* 114
5 ch m Heart's Cry(JPN) Omega Spirit (JPN) (Spinning World (USA))
1690a[6] 7831a[11] 8329a[4]

Nuptials (USA) *Eve Johnson Houghton* a26 52
2 b f Broken Vow(USA) European Union (USA) (Successful Appeal (USA))
2637[10] 4756[18] 5400[11] 5770[4] ◆

Nurse Nightingale *Hugo Palmer* a70
2 b f Nathaniel(IRE) Whazzat (Daylami (IRE))
8465[3]

Nutbourne Lad (IRE) *Amanda Perrett* a62 64
3 b g Lilbourne Lad(IRE) Cape Sydney (IRE) (Cape Cross (IRE))
1275[2] 1860[12] 2366[12] *(3651)*

Nutcracker Suite (IRE) *A P O'Brien* a58 69
2 b f Fastnet Rock(AUS) Dietrich (USA) (Storm Cat (USA))
6815a[8]

Nutzma *Mike Murphy* a47 38
3 b f Multiplex Nut (IRE) (Fasliyev (USA))
1705[6] 2608[7] 4987[8] *6513[8]* 7230[4] *7532[9] 8567[6]*

Nuzha *David Evans* a72 26
2 ch f Mayson Always On My Mind (Distant Relative)
7314[11] *7689[6] 7939[2] 8174[3] 8453[9] (8569)*

Nymeria (GER) *Waldemar Hickst* 108
4 b m Soldier Hollow Narooma (GER) (Silver Hawk (USA))
1822a[2] 2633a[2] 3916a[2] 4928a[6] 6397a[5] 6992a[5]

Nyquist (USA) *Doug O'Neill* a124
3 b c Uncle Mo(USA) Seeking Gabrielle (USA) (Forestry (USA))
(2063a) 2499a[3]

Nyx *Richard Guest* 35
2 ch f Harbour Watch(IRE) Fantastic Santanyi (Fantastic Light (USA))
3167[11] 3576[5] 5433[9] 6807[9]

Oak Bluffs (IRE) *Richard Fahey* a68 70
5 b g Royal Applause Key Stage (IRE) (King's Best (USA))
37[3] 276[4] 482[2] 795[3] 1116[7] 1326[4] 1596[2] 1925[4] 7254[2] *7985[6] 8156[5] 8588[3]*

Oak Forest *Michael Attwater* a46
3 b g Mullionmileanhour(IRE) Lady Royal Oak (IRE) (Exceed And Excel (AUS))
193[5] 436[9] 635[6]

Oakledge (IRE) *W McCreery* a81 76
2 b g Sir Prancealot(IRE) Cinarosa (IRE) (Kodiac)
6388a[26]

Oakley Girl *Stuart Williams* a102 101
4 b m Sir Percy Pivotting (Pivotal)
(72) ◆ *254[2] 422[3]* 1858[2] 2893[4] *3608[3]* 4610[5]

Oakley Pride (IRE) *Gay Kelleway* a51 45
2 b g Lilbourne Lad(IRE) There With Me (USA) (Distant View (USA))
4564[6] *5244[4] 8569[5]*

Oakley Star *Gay Kelleway* a59 60
4 b m Multiplex Star Welcome (Most Welcome)
527[3] 819[5]

Oasis Fantasy (IRE) *Ed Dunlop* 109
5 br g Oasis Dream Cara Fantasy (IRE) (Sadler's Wells (USA))
1568[6] (1885) 2222[2] 4165[8] 4731[2] 5647[5] 6233[4] 6786[16] 7154[9]

Oasis Moon *William Haggas* a56 60
3 b f Oasis Dream Quan Yin (IRE) (Sadler's Wells (USA))
2904[9] *3406[6]* 3643[8] 4275[10] (5020) *5554[5] 5725[3]* 6436[2]

Oasis Rose (FR) *Jeremy Gask* a37
4 b m Naaqoos Dream Rose (IRE) (Anabaa (USA))
202[6] 431[12]

Oasis Spear *Chris Wall* a84 92
4 b g Oasis Dream Sunspear (IRE) (Montjeu (IRE))
1777[5] (2978) 3861[8] 6298[8] 7287[11]

Oat Couture *Henry Candy* a66 68
4 b m Kyllachy Oat Cuisine (Mujahid (USA))
1419[5] 2396[9] 3070[7] 4058[3] 4557[6] 5326[11] 5953[8] 6317[2] *6677[3]* 7038[9]

Obboorr *Tim Fitzgerald* a78 79
7 b g Cape Cross(IRE) Felawnah (USA) (Mr Prospector (USA))
156[3] (382) 640[4] 1796[2] 2616[2] 3711[2] (4934) 5350[4] 6083[6] *7139[3]*

Obedient *P Bary* 99
2 ch f Motivator Namaskar (Dansili)
4902a[3] 5703a[4]

Oberyn (IRE) *Sylvester Kirk* a51
2 b f Holy Roman Emperor(IRE) Daraliya (IRE) (Kahyasi)
7792[8] 8313[8] 8536[5]

Obviously (IRE) *Philip D'Amato* a89 115
8 b g Choisir(AUS) Leala (IRE) (Montjeu (IRE))
(7833a)

Occasional Dream (IRE) *Joseph Tuite* a4 53
3 b f Dream Ahead(USA) Almaviva (IRE) (Grand Lodge (USA))
3958[7] 4480[7] 4991[4] *6513[9]* 7057[5] 7628[12]

Occult *Simon Dow* a64 74
4 b g Oasis Dream Trojan Queen (USA) (Empire Maker (USA))
256[8] 606[6] 815[7] 950[7] 1413[10] 3737[11]

Ocean Air (FR) *James Tate* 73
2 b c Rio De La Plata(USA) Silver Miss (FR) (Numerous (USA))
(5792)

Ocean Bentley (IRE) *Tony Carroll* a47 40
4 b g Amadeus Wolf Bentley's Bush (IRE) (Barathea (IRE))
233[9] 653[7] 796[9] 1038[7] 2448[3] 3043[6] 3489[6] 4024[5] 4290[10] 5051[3] 6030[3]

Ocean Crystal *Mrs A Malzard* a39 61
4 b m Stimulation(IRE) Crystal Gale (IRE) (Verglas (IRE))
1519a[4] 5457a[5] 6401a[4]

Oceane (FR) *Alan King* 96
4 b g Kentucky Dynamite(USA) Zahrana (FR) (Zamindar (USA))
2699[4] 3162[13] (4077) 4752[3] ◆ (5559) 6582[9]

Ocean Eleven *John Ryan* a80 83
3 b g Equiano(FR) Fittonia (FR) (Ashkalani (IRE))
3079[9] 3269[18] 4709[4] 4840[2] 5362[2] *5765[6]* 6265[5] *(6702)* (7229) *7816[6]*

Oceanella (IRE) *K R Burke* 62
3 b f Canford Cliffs(IRE) Mundus Novus (USA) (Unbridled's Song (USA))
2422[7] 2801[8] 3499[4] 4275[7] 4425[8]

Ocean Gale *Richard Price* 49
3 b f Shirocco(GER) Ocean Transit (IRE) (Trans Island)
1628[12] 2368[3] 3509[14] 4159[10] 4794[9] 5252[7]

Oceanic (IRE) *John Quinn* a56 61
2 b c Born To Sea(IRE) Shanghai Lily (IRE) (King's Best (USA))
3388[5] 4371[8] 4609[5] *6139[4] 6743[9] 7143[9]*

Ocean Jive *Brian Meehan* 87
3 b g Norse Dancer(IRE) Kaylianni (Kalanisi (IRE))
756a[16] 3300[9] 4559[4]

Ocean Kave *Tony Newcombe*
6 b g Silca Blanka(IRE) Fiery Angel (IRE) (Machiavellian (USA))
8320[12]

Ocean Legend (IRE) *Tony Carroll* a75 69
11 b g Night Shift(USA) Rose Of Mooncoin (IRE) (Brief Truce (USA))
(76) 231[9] 502[3] 671[3] 875[5] 1044[7] 1261[5] 1928[5] *2379[4] 2821[5]* 3719[2] 5090[6] *6237[5] 7048[4]*

Ocean Of Love *Saeed bin Suroor* a70
2 ch f Distorted Humor(USA) Michita (USA) (Dynaformer (USA))
7761[4]

Oceanographer *Charlie Appleby* a106 109
4 b g Sea The Stars(IRE) Que Puntual (ARG) (Contested Bid (USA))
1885[4] 3383[15] (4858) 5655[7] 7481a[3] (7712a) 7756a[12]

Ocean Princess (IRE) *Michael Dods* a61 61
2 b f Acclamation Fathoming (USA) (Gulch (USA))
3321[4] ◆ *6925[3] 7380[4]*

Ocean Promise (USA) *Richard Hughes* a65
2 b f Quality Road(USA) I'm From Dixie (USA) (Dixieland Band (USA))
8065[7] 8151[4] 8423[2]

Ocean Ready (USA) *Sir Mark Prescott Bt* a84 83
3 b g More Than Ready(USA) Tjinouska (USA) (Cozzene (USA))
958[2] 2907[10] *4010[6]* (6066) (6186) 6665[6] *(7067)*

Ocean Sheridan (IRE) *Michael Dods* 95
4 b g Starspangledbanner(AUS) Endless Night (GER) (Tiger Hill (IRE))
1218[3] 1522[2] 2476[5] 2679[11] 3595[2] 3980[7] 4893[3] (5857) 6539[7] ◆ (7358) 7497[12]

Ocean Tempest *John Ryan* a65 93
7 gr g Act One Ipsa Loquitur (Unfuwain (USA))
1196[14] 2684[8] 3672[8] *4644[11] 8231[10] 8539[12]*

Ocean Temptress *John Ryan* a65 65
2 b f Equiano(FR) Ipsa Loquitur (Unfuwain (USA))
1527[3] 2211[6] 4397[5] 5266[6] 5747[5] *6240[4]* 7697[4] *8080[9]*

Oceanus (IRE) *Ed Dunlop* a54 75
2 b g Born To Sea(IRE) Alkhawarah (USA) (Intidab (USA))
2204[3] 2682[6] 3859[6] 5990[3] 6716[2] 7319[10] *8153[13] 8560[13]*

Ocelot *Tim Easterby* 69
2 b f Poet's Voice Desert Lynx (IRE) (Green Desert (USA))
3290[11] 5727[3] 6162[3] 6477[7] 7004[9] 7356[3]

Ochos Rios *David Evans* 61
3 b g Shirocco(GER) Society Rose (Saddlers' Hall (IRE))
1484[6] 2851[3] 3063[10] 3509[10] 4500[3] 5204[3]

O'Connor's Girl *Sir Mark Prescott Bt* a64 66
3 b f Roderic O'Connor(IRE) Dollar Bird (IRE) (Kris)
44[2] ◆ *139[2] 5763[5]* 6565[7] *7104[6]*

Ocotillo (IRE) *Kevin Frost* a53 47
3 ch g Raven's Pass(USA) Meiosis (USA) (Danzig (USA))
8191[6] 8470[7] (8541)

Octavia (FR) *H-A Pantall* a82 68
3 ch f Aqlaam Orlena (USA) (Gone West (USA))
2141a[6] 5280a[4]

October Storm *Mick Channon* a76 80
3 br g Shirocco(GER) Cyber Star (King's Best (USA))
(1037) 1532[3] 2411[3] 3025[2] 4559[5] 6121[7] 7332[4] 7670[3]

Oddsocks (IRE) *Tony Carroll* a27 41
4 b m Tagula(IRE) Datura (Darshaan)
7302[6] *8288[8]*

O Dee *Jose Santos* a63
4 ch g Iffraaj Queen's Grace (Bahamian Bounty)
952[6] 1533[16] *(5734) 6046[7]*

Odelouca (IRE) *Brendan Powell* a68 43
2 b f Elusive City(USA) Church Road (IRE) (Danehill Dancer (IRE))
5846[9] *6867[6] 7278[4] (7776)*

Oden *Roger Varian*
2 ch c Lope De Vega(IRE) Dashing (IRE) (Sadler's Wells (USA))
8305[10]

Odeon *James Given* 85
5 b g Galileo(IRE) Kite Mark (Mark Of Esteem (IRE))
2163[17] (2888) 3345[6] 4407[6] 4892[3] 5275[2] 5611[11] 6163[13] 6457[3] 7158[6] 7412[5]

Ode To Evening *Mark Johnston* a102 107
3 ch c Poet's Voice Ever Love (BRZ) (Nedawi)
1338[2] ◆ 1605[6] 1975[5] 2473[12] 3157[6] (4108) 4797[2] 5160[3] 5651[14] 5865[3] 6261[5] 6786[9]

Ode To Glory *Rae Guest* a68 64
2 b f Poet's Voice Blue Lyric (Refuse To Bend (IRE))
5990[4] *(6590)* 7471[5]

Ode To Paris *Ed Dunlop* a64 66
2 b g Poet's Voice Dream Belle (Oasis Dream)
6086[6] 6750[6] 7072[8]

Oeil De Tigre (FR) *Tony Carroll* a43 76
5 b g Footstepsinthesand Suerte (Halling (USA))
2253[12] 3004[5] (3510) 6831[7] 7772[5] *8236[9]*

Off Art *Tim Easterby* 99
6 ch g Dutch Art Off Camera (Efisio)
1620^3 2157^7 2796^2 3390^{10} 4163^{13} 5156^9 5976^{13} 6517^7 6957^9 7159^{10}

Officer Drivel (IRE) *Jim Best* a71 73
5 b g Captain Rio Spiritville (IRE) (Invincible Spirit (IRE))
2085^2 2205^5 3817^6 4711^2 *5397^4* (5895) *8254^8 8455^5*

Officer In Command (USA) *Alan Bailey* a55 36
10 bb g Officer(USA) Luv To Stay N Chat (USA) (Candi's Gold (USA))
20^3 294^{10} 4516^8 *6900^9 7986^{12} 8190^{10}*

Offshore (USA) *Neil Drysdale* 96
2 bb c Exchange Rate(USA) Mattie Camp (USA) (Forest Camp (USA))
7266a^6

Off The Pulse *John Mackie* a86 64
6 b g Araafa(IRE) Off By Heart (Royal Applause)
73^2 465^3 734^4 823^2 (1652) 2328^8

Off The Road (BRZ) *Richard E Mandella* a90 90
4 bb m Quick Road(BRZ) Intuicao Direta (BRZ) (Roi Normand (USA))
7829a^7

Off The Scale (IRE) *Brian Ellison* a33 77
4 b g Strategic Prince Vanilla Delight (IRE) (Orpen (USA))
(1488) 1869^{16} 3394^5 4191^6

Ogwen Valley Girl *Michael Mullineaux* 24
5 b m Indian Danehill(IRE) Lucky Find (IRE) (Key Of Luck (USA))
1708^6 3019^5

Oh Geno *Richard Spencer* a63 63
2 b g Paco Boy(IRE) Key Light (IRE) (Acclamation)
5229^5 7414^3 7578^5 *8344^3*

Oh Grace (IRE) *J S Bolger* a88 93
2 b f Lawman(FR) Flea Cheoil (IRE) (Galileo (IRE))
2718a^6 3336^{11} 4573a^6 5686a^9 *7130a^4*

Oh It's Saucepot *Chris Wall* a60 41
2 b f Sir Percy Oh So Saucy (Imperial Ballet (IRE))
4594^{10} *6625^7* 7695^9

Oh James *Tim Easterby* 74
3 b g Monsieur Bond(IRE) Sea Flower (IRE) (Acclamation)
(1494)

Oh So Dandy (IRE) *Derek Shaw* a58 59
2 ch g Dandy Man(IRE) Kelso Magic (USA) (Distant View (USA))
5077^8 6099^7 6641^4 7073^{10} *8097^4 8285^8*

Oh So Sassy *Chris Wall* a97 96
6 b m Pastoral Pursuits Almasi (IRE) (Petorius (IRE))
1427^6 2253^{10} (2863) 3573^4 4461^2

Ohsosecret *Stuart Williams* a67 63
4 ch m Sakhee's Secret Warden Rose (Compton Place)
(75) 269^5 398^8

Oh This Is Us (IRE) *Richard Hannon* a104 109
3 b c Acclamation Shamwari Lodge (IRE) (Hawk Wing (USA))
(1804) ◆ (2179) (2466) 3299^{18} 4624^8 (4887) 5956^8 6788^8 *7651^3* ◆ (7821)

Oh What A Species (IRE) *Alan Berry* a61
3 b f Captain Rio Aspired (IRE) (Mark Of Esteem (IRE))
363^5

Oil Strike *Michael Easterby* a71 67
9 b g Lucky Story(USA) Willisa (Polar Falcon (USA))
293^4

Okana *C Laffon-Parias* a104 100
3 b f Zamindar(USA) Oceanique (USA) (Forest Wildcat (USA))
1309a^8 3938a^4 6824a^2

Ok By Me (IRE) *David Evans* 67
2 ch f Arcano(IRE) Kindest (Cadeaux Genereux)
2648^6 3854^4 4579^7 5951^3 6366^4

Okool (FR) *Owen Burrows* 84
2 b c Cape Cross(IRE) Seschat (IRE) (Sinndar (IRE))
6262^5 6704^6

Olala (GER) *M Figge* 96
3 b f Tertullian(USA) Ostdogin (GER) (Doyen (IRE))
3297^{10} 4175a^6 7029a^8

Old China *John Davies* 62
3 b g Archipenko(USA) Porcelain (IRE) (Peintre Celebre (USA))
4546^9 4895^4 5438^8

Old Town Boy *Philip McBride* a90 99
5 b g Myboycharlie(IRE) Native Ring (FR) (Bering)
1219^3

Olive Branch (IRE) *Sir Michael Stoute* a43
2 b f Arcano(IRE) Athene (IRE) (Rousillon (USA))
8486^{11}

Oliver's Gold *Mark Walford* a47 52
8 b g Danehill Dancer(IRE) Gemini Gold (IRE) (King's Best (USA))
3325^4 4239^6

Olivia Fallow (IRE) *Paul Midgley* 94
4 b m Vale Of York(IRE) Spinning Maid (USA) (Forestry (USA))
2305^7 2658^2 ◆ 3150^2 3392^6 4831^8 5390^8 ◆ 5780^2 5961^6 6327^{11}

Olympic Duel (IRE) *Peter Hiatt* 62
3 b g Acclamation Olympic Medal (Nayef (USA))
1673^3 2349^6 2980^5 3877^5 4370^5 4764^{11} 5309^5

Olympic Runner *William Haggas* a79 85
3 ch f Exceed And Excel(AUS) Lochridge (Indian Ridge)
3038^5 (3625) 4585^6 4803^{15} *7202^5*

Olympus Mons (FR) *Jo Hughes* a45 36
3 b g Multiplex Shemrana (USA) (Woodman (USA))
3483^7 4001^{10} 5181^6 *6967^7 7256^8*

Om (USA) *Dan L Hendricks* a104 115
4 ch h Munnings(USA) Rare Cat (USA) (Tabasco Cat (USA))
7833a^2

Omar Bradley (USA) *Flemming Velin* 107
3 b c War Front(USA) Louve Des Reves (IRE) (Sadler's Wells (USA))
2315a^8

Omeros *Hugo Palmer* a77
2 ch c Poet's Voice Caribbean Pearl (USA) (Silver Hawk (USA))
(7483)

Omid *Kenneth Slack* a52 58
8 b g Dubawi(IRE) Mille Couleurs (FR) (Spectrum (IRE))
1523^3 2089^8 *7138^5*

Ominotago *Michael Appleby* a71 71
4 ch m Aqlaam Sharp Dresser (USA) (Diesis)
7942^7 8076^2

Omotesando *Mark Brisbourne* a76 78
6 b g Street Cry(IRE) Punctilious (Danehill (USA))
1762^2 ◆ 2296^{13} 2651^4 3129^8 3395^5 3636^5 4138^4 4377^5

Omran *Marco Botti* a84 80
2 ch c Choisir(AUS) Ruff Shod (USA) (Storm Boot (USA))
7819^2 *(8377)*

On A Whim *Daniel Mark Loughnane* a74 21
4 b m Tamayuz Love Me Tender (Green Desert (USA))
39^5 (294) (383) 822^2 982^5 (1170) (1500) (1796) 2105^2

On Budget (IRE) *Anthony Carson* a42
3 b g Duke Of Marmalade(IRE) Henties Bay (IRE) (Cape Cross (IRE))
2175^{12} *3281^5*

Oncle Fernand (FR) *C Bauer* 74
2 bb c Aqlaam Mixfeeling (IRE) (Red Ransom (USA))
(4965a) 5819a^3

Onda District (IRE) *Richard Ford* a64 79
4 b g Oasis Dream Leocorno (IRE) (Pivotal)
1999^9 2876^4 3942^6 4377^3 5154^3

Ondamoura (IRE) *T Hogan* a61 61
4 b g Intense Focus(USA) Corking (IRE) (Montjeu (IRE))
4813a^2

One And Only (JPN) *Shinsuke Hashiguchi* 115
5 bb h Heart's Cry(JPN) Virtue (JPN) (Taiki Shuttle (USA))
1107a^5 8129a^8

One Big Surprise *Richard Hughes* a70 78
4 b m Kier Park(IRE) Cloridja (Indian Ridge)
531^3 791^5 1167^3 1781^2 ◆ 1899^2 (2403) ◆ 2697^7 3510^5 3974^2 (4389) 4787^3 5169^3 *5725^4* 7303^3 *7644^8*

One Boy (IRE) *Paul Midgley* 84
5 ch g Captain Gerrard(IRE) Paris Song (IRE) (Peintre Celebre (USA))
1488^2 1869^7 2346^4 3217^3 3875^8 4428^8 5296^5 5780^3 5864^4 6506^3 (6809) 7252^4 (7474a)

One Foot In Heaven (IRE) *A De Royer-Dupre* a85 117
4 b h Fastnet Rock(AUS) Pride (FR) (Peintre Celebre (USA))
(2077a) (2947a) 3936a^6 6395a^4 6989a^6 (7396a) 8329a^3

One For Jodie (IRE) *Michael Appleby* a41 28
5 ch g Majestic Missile(IRE) Tough Chic (IRE) (Indian Ridge)
1622^{10} *1800^8*

Onehelluvatouch *Philip Hide* a63 61
3 gr f Hellvelyn Soft Touch (IRE) (Petorius (IRE))
1608^{10} 2395^{10} 3141^8 5101^4 *5630^3* 6185^5 (6891) *7103^2*

One Last Dream *Ron Hodges* a56 49
7 ch g Resplendent Glory(IRE) Pip's Dream (Glint Of Gold)
155^3 252^8 569^5

One Man Army *Julia Brooke* a75 33
4 b g Mount Nelson Hms Pinafore (IRE) (Singspiel (IRE))
2918^9

One Man Band (IRE) *Doug Watson* a117 77
5 b h Pivotal Musicanna (Cape Cross (IRE))
(94a) 454a^2 (717a) (1101a)

One Mean Man (USA) *Bernard Flint* 103
3 rg c Mizzen Mast(USA) Abbeyville Miss (USA) (Grand Slam (USA))
5429a^4

Onenightidreamed (IRE) *T Stack* 114
5 ch g Footstepsinthesand Pivotalia (IRE) (Pivotal)
1018a^7 (1226a) 1509a^4

Oneoveryou (IRE) *S J Mahon* a82 61
5 b m Tagula(IRE) Sun Slash (IRE) (Entrepreneur)
(8197a)

One Pekan (IRE) *Roger Varian* a91 79
6 b g Hard Spun(USA) Stormy Blessing (USA) (Storm Cat (USA))
267^3 494^2 620^7 2620^{10} 3324^5

Onesie (IRE) *Marco Botti* a57 60
3 b g Dandy Man(IRE) Easee On (IRE) (Hawk Wing (USA))
4017^9 4639^4 5178^7 *5721^4 6373^3 6700^{10}*

One Too Many (IRE) *David Brown* a59 71
2 gr f Zebedee Speckled Hen (IRE) (Titus Livius (FR))
4494^5 4981^2 ◆ 5317^4 6033^7 *6658^4*

One Word More (IRE) *Tim Easterby* a96 110
6 b g Thousand Words Somoushe (IRE) (Black Minnaloushe (USA))
1627^6 2191^3 4163^3 4823^7 5585^{13} 6056^3 6331^4 6557^6 7121^6

On Fire *James Bethell* a57 61
3 b g Olden Times La Notte (Factual (USA))
1646^3 2306^6 *8585^3*

On Her Toes (IRE) *William Haggas* 98
2 b f Kodiac Dancing Jest (IRE) (Averti (IRE))
3073^3 (3668) (3977) (4560) 5172^3

Onirique (IRE) *D Windrif* a87 65
5 b m Teofilo(IRE) Blue Blue Sky (IRE) (Anabaa (USA))
3376a^8

On Leave (USA) *Claude McGaughey III* 106
3 rg f War Front(USA) Meghan's Joy (USA) (A.P. Indy (USA))
7379a^4

Onlyjim (FR) *P Bary* a88 85
3 b c Manduro(GER) Dansilady (IRE) (Dansili)
7168a^4

Only Mine (IRE) *Joseph G Murphy* 111
3 b f Pour Moi(IRE) Truly Mine (IRE) (Rock Of Gibraltar (IRE))
1396^9 2272a^3 (2719a) 2923a^3 6120^7 6384a^{10}

Only Orsenfoolsies *Micky Hammond* 92
7 b g Trade Fair Desert Gold (IRE) (Desert Prince (IRE))
1493^{12} 4680^7 5275^6 6165^9 6565^{11} 6773^2 *7321^{11}*

Only Ten Per Cent (IRE) *J R Jenkins* a69 65
8 b g Kheleyf(USA) Cory Everson (IRE) (Brief Truce (USA))
68^5 167^4 607^4 873^6 1261^2 2380^4 3780^4 4658^2 *5368^3 5807^4 6374^4 7069^3 7611^2 8064^{12}*

Onomatopoeia *Roger Ingram* a49 61
2 b f Raven's Pass(USA) Manoeuvre (IRE) (Galileo (IRE))
3859^9 *5022^6*

Onorina (IRE) *Jim Boyle* a66 74
4 b m Arcano(IRE) Miss Honorine (IRE) (Highest Honor (FR))
1456^4 ◆ 1854^2 (2400) 3798^8 (4551) 5406^5 6885^4

On Show (IRE) *David Brown* a37 33
2 b g Iffraaj Effige (IRE) (Oratorio (IRE))
2648^{12} 4363^{10} 4601^{11} 5770^7 6313^{10} *6923^8*

On The Bill (IRE) *Ed Dunlop* a81 85
3 b g Kyllachy Secret Flame (Machiavellian (USA))
1931^4 *(2578)* 4317^2

On The Clock *Denis Quinn* a37 11
3 b f Aqlaam Azzoom (IRE) (Cadeaux Genereux)
77^6 423^6 4361^{14} *5132^{10}* 5795^6

On The High Tops (IRE) *Colin Teague* a4 43
8 b g Kheleyf(USA) Diplomats Daughter (Unfuwain (USA))
6910^9

On The Huh *Derek Shaw*
4 b g Avonbridge Red Sovereign (Danzig Connection (USA))
5509^{11}

Onthemoonagain (FR) *J-C Rouget* 96
2 b f Cape Cross(IRE) Ma Preference (FR) (American Post)
7480a^3

On The Rocks (JPN) *Hideyuki Mori* a101 98
3 b c Samurai Heart(JPN) Belmont Hermes (JPN) (Timber Country (USA))
1103a^5

On The Sea *Mme C Head-Maarek* 75
2 b c Oasis Dream Quenched (Dansili)
6638a^5

On To Victory *Eve Johnson Houghton* 79
2 b g Rock Of Gibraltar(IRE) Clouds Of Magellan (USA) (Dynaformer (USA))
4866^{11} 6054^3 6577^3 7125^7

Onus (USA) *Claude McGaughey III* 105
4 rg m Blame(USA) Silviculture (USA) (Forestry (USA))
5914a^4 7171a^7

Oopper Wallah (USA) *Peter Miller* a83 97
2 ch c Congrats(USA) Miss Singhsix (IRE) (Singspiel (IRE))
7266a^5

Opal Tiara (IRE) *Mick Channon* a82 109
3 b f Thousand Words Zarafa (Fraam)
2539^2 3274^{17} (3519) 4826^7 (5588) (5926) 7115^7

Opening Time *Richard Hannon* 60
2 b g Harbour Watch(IRE) Dozy (IRE) (Exceed And Excel (AUS))
3408^6 4154^6 4981^7

Open 'n Shut *Ibrahim Al Malki* 93
3 ch g Kyllachy Our Faye (College Chapel)
(2998) 8573a^5

Open The Red *Amanda Perrett* a81 83
4 b g Lawman(FR) Acquainted (Shamardal (USA))
4868^{14} *6128^7* 6892^2 *7512^8*

Open Wide (USA) *Amanda Perrett* 77
2 bb c Invincible Spirit(IRE) Nunavik (IRE) (Indian Ridge)
6543^7 6880^7 (7216)

Opera Baron *Mohammed Jassim Ghazali* a70 94
3 b g Equiano(FR) Opera Dancer (Norse Dancer (IRE))
(756a) 8573a^4

Opera Buff *Rae Guest* a65 51
7 b g Oratorio(IRE) Opera Glass (Barathea (IRE))
156^4 461^4 698^7 1038^6 1413^4 1450^{12} *2326^{10} 2814^6* 3409^8

Opera Buffa (IRE) *Steve Flook* a58 49
3 b f Exceed And Excel(AUS) Dubai Opera (USA) (Dubai Millennium)
105^3 242^{10} 443^{12} 1148^8 1551^{11} 3509^{13} 4504^4 5011^3 5572 ^{7} 5625^{10}

Opera Lad (IRE) *Andrew Balding* a77 79
4 b g Teofilo(IRE) Opera Glass (Barathea (IRE))
1824^2 3533^{11}

Operateur (IRE) *Ben Haslam* a49 61
8 b g Oratorio(IRE) Kassariya (IRE) (Be My Guest (USA))
1561^{10} 3901^3 *5971^4* 6619^7

Operational *Jedd O'Keeffe* a23 39
2 b c Royal Applause Oatcake (Selkirk (USA))
2913^{12} 3516^8 4405^{10}

Operative *Ed de Giles* 83
3 ch g Pastoral Pursuits Gilt Linked (Compton Place)
1894^8 2234^3 (3422) 4134^5 4496^{10} 5253^6 5832^7

Opinionate *Amanda Perrett* a72
2 b g Cacique(IRE) Comment (Sadler's Wells (USA))
8245^2

Opposition *Ed Dunlop* 86
3 gr g Dalakhani(IRE) Censored (Pivotal)
(1619) (2252) 3341^{13} 4628^3

O'Prado Ole (USA) *Dale Romans* 107
6 ch h English Channel(USA) Mexican Moonlight (USA) (El Prado (IRE))
5428a^9

Optima Petamus *Patrick Holmes* a75 80
4 gr g Mastercraftsman(IRE) In A Silent Way (IRE) (Desert Prince (IRE))
2328^7 3219^4 4113^4 4704^{11} 5579^7 6517^9 7010^6 *8142^2*

Opt Out *David O'Meara* a50 63
6 ch g Pivotal Easy Option (IRE) (Prince Sabo)
1663^3 2091^5 2661^6 2906^9 3344^6 3750^9 3943^4 4772^5 5114^5 5835^2 7096^4 (7253)

Opulent D'Oroux (FR) *S Smrczek* a71 90
3 ch c Monos(GER) Opportunistic (IRE) (Mukaddamah (USA))
7897a^7

Opus Too (IRE) *John Ryan* a46 40
5 b g Lawman(FR) Jerez (IRE) (Lake Coniston (IRE))
505^{13} 634^6 796^{12} 1039^8 1322^{10} 1807^8 2502^8

Oracle Boy *Michael Chapman* a26 26
5 b g Mount Nelson Snow Princess (IRE) (Ela-Mana-Mou)
601^7 865^P

Oracolo (IRE) *David Simcock* a96 96
4 b g Cape Cross(IRE) Illuminise (IRE) (Grand Lodge (USA))
1797^4 ◆ 2191^6 ◆ 3164^9

Orangecherie (IRE) *Mike Murphy* a49
3 b f Duke Of Marmalade(IRE) Ochre (IRE) (Diktat)
325^7 1163^9

Orange Gin (IRE) *Roger Charlton* a46 52
2 b g Bushranger(IRE) Gin Twist (Invincible Spirit (IRE))
5890^{11} 6295^9 6543^9 *7047^{10}*

Oratorio's Joy (IRE) *Jamie Osborne* a83 73
6 b m Oratorio(IRE) Seeking The Fun (USA) (Alhaarth (IRE))
(30) 385^6 440^2 1092^5 2149^3 3002^4 4023^8 4507^2 4816^3 5624^4 6315^3 *8524^9*

Orbit The Moon (IRE) *Grace Harris* a55 52
8 b g Oratorio(IRE) Catch The Moon (IRE) (Peintre Celebre (USA))
2130^{10} 2849^{10} 3743^{14}

Orcia (IRE) *H-F Devin* a90 97
4 b m Shamardal(USA) Amathia (IRE) (Darshaan)
2716a^4 3084a^3 4218a^9 5313a^{12} *8431a^7*

Ordensritter (GER) *Chris Down* a68 72
8 ch g Samum(GER) Dramraire Mist (Darshaan)
234^7

Order Of Service *Shaun Harris* a76 85
6 ch g Medicean Choir Gallery (Pivotal)
2010^6 2491^7 3185^5 4089^8 5291^6

Order Of St George (IRE) *A P O'Brien* 125
4 b h Galileo(IRE) Another Storm (USA) (Gone West (USA))
(2881a) (3298) (5660a) 6387a^2 6989a^3 7349^4

Order Of The Sun (AUS) *Koh Chor Yung* a20 105
5 br g Encosta De Lago(AUS) Sequin (AUS) (Lure (USA))
6399a^{15}

Ordinal *Mark Johnston* a86 75
3 b c Shamardal(USA) Mille (Dubai Millennium)
1151^7 (1497) (1574) 2422^3 (2906) 3292^5 3775^3 *4211^2*

Oregon Gift *Brian Ellison* a67 60
4 b g Major Cadeaux Dayville (USA) (Dayjur (USA))
7368^2 8100^3

Orewa (IRE) *Brian Ellison* 89
2 ch g Helmet(AUS) Lucky (IRE) (Sadler's Wells (USA))
(1407) ◆ (2119) 2664^3 4669^5 (5917) ◆ (6388a) 6954^9

Organza *Mick Channon* 77
3 b f Pour Moi(IRE) Cephalonie (USA) (Kris S (USA))
3634^3 4035^2 4682^3 4991^2 5438^3 6135^2 (6452) 6746^{14} 7220^6

Oriental Fox (GER) *Mark Johnston* a100 107
8 ch g Lomitas Oriental Pearl (GER) (Big Shuffle (USA))
2025^4 3387^4 3913^6 4799^{13} 5655^6 5999^2 6283^{10} 7150^{28} (7411) *7979^9 8479^5*

Oriental Relation (IRE) *James Given* a90 76
5 gr g Tagula(IRE) Rofan (USA) (Cozzene (USA))
4^8 198^3 250^5 529^{10} 694^8 (901) 1040^6 1447^{11} *1650^8* 2120^3 2418^3 2975^6 *4198^8* (4495) 4809^4 5274^8 *(6425) 6927^7 7643^3 7752^9 7892^8 (8314)*

Oriental Splendour (IRE) *Ruth Carr* a37 78
4 br g Strategic Prince Asian Lady (Kyllachy)
1559^5 ◆ 2120^6 2572^5 2975^2 3217^2 (3713) 4452^2 4726^7 5295^9 *5968^{10}* 6475^5

Oriental Tiger *Iain Jardine* 81
5 b g Tiger Hill(IRE) Cal Norma's Lady (IRE) (Lyphard's Special (USA))
1633^{11} 2198^5 2651^3 (3052) 3363^{10} (4143)

Orient Class *Paul Midgley* a72 89
5 ch g Orientor Killer Class (Kyllachy)
784^6 1110^5 ◆ 1559^3 *2622^2 2919^4* 3326^2 (3851) 4345^2 ◆ (5269) (6080) 6537^9 7288^2 7773^9

Orientelle *Richard Whitaker* a39 12
2 ch f Compton Place Oriental Girl (Dr Fong (USA))
6447^7 *7107^6* 7407^6

Original Choice (IRE) *William Haggas* 81
2 ch g Dragon Pulse(IRE) Belle Watling (IRE) (Street Cry (IRE))
5848^7 6542^4 (7740)

Orion's Bow *David Nicholls* a104 111
5 ch g Pivotal Heavenly Ray (USA) (Rahy (USA))
1252^7 1625^{11} 1869^8 *(2332)* (2680) (3265) *(3606)* (4338) 4865^2 5418^8 6558^{15}

Orithia (USA) *Seamus Durack* a61 52
2 b f More Than Ready(USA) Tiz My Time (USA) (Sharp Humor (USA))
6622^9 7216^8 7502^7 *7881^2 8072^3*

Orlando Rogue (IRE) *Keith Dalgleish* a57 64
4 b g Bushranger(IRE) Boston Ivy (USA) (Mark Of Esteem (IRE))
64^6 424^3 629^7 857^7 943^7 1120^{11} *2380^6 3474^2 3732^9 3989^{11} 4528^9 5127^4 5734^4 8499^4*

Ormanumps (IRE) *Daniel Mark Loughnane* a49 17
3 b g Elnadim(USA) Tawjeeh (Haafhd)
104^7 327^3 820^4 1162^8 1325^6

Ormering *Roger Teal* a43 48
3 b f Kyllachy Lihou Island (Beveled (USA))
2083^{3} 3198^{8} 4262^{10} 5380^{6} 6311^{7} 6646^{11} 6857^{6}

Ormindo (USA) *A bin Harmash* a84 59
6 ch g Discreet Cat(USA) Dearly (Rahy (USA))
279a^{6} 535a^{3}

Ormito (GER) *Andrew Balding* 104
3 b c Mamool(IRE) Ormita (GER) (Acatenango (GER))
1974^{3} 2432^{3} 3341^{11} 4339^{2} 5402^{2} 6329^{7}

Ormskirk *Brian Ellison* 78
3 gr g Hellvelyn River Song (USA) (Siphon (BRZ))
2200^{6} 2891^{11} 3580^{4}

Ornate *William Haggas* a93 109
3 b g Bahamian Bounty Adorn (Kyllachy)
45^{2} 3158^{3} 4359^{6} 5268^{5} 6207^{2} 6642^{2} 6916^{2}

Orobas (IRE) *Ron Barr* a4 45
4 b g Dark Angel(IRE) Miss Mujadil (IRE) (Mujadil (USA))
3367^{13} 4766^{5}

Oromo (IRE) *T Stack* a68 68
3 b g High Chaparral(IRE) Miss Beatrix (IRE) (Danehill Dancer (IRE))
5096a^{11}

Orpello (IRE) *Mme G Rarick* a54 80
7 b h Orpen(USA) Princess Angelina (IRE) (Almutawakel)
8421a^{6}

Orphic (FR) *J Phelippon* a84 53
7 b g Orpen(USA) Villemanzie (FR) (Villez (USA))
1034a^{4} 2806a^{5}

Or So (USA) *Derek Shaw* a34
4 ch g Rock Slide(USA) Miss Santa Anita (CAN) (Ide (USA))
7889^{11} 8156^{13} 8408^{10}

Ortano (USA) *Mark Johnston* a42 60
2 b c Elusive Quality(USA) Dear Bela (ARG) (Indygo Shiner (USA))
1749^{6} 2265^{4} 2641^{4}

Orvar (IRE) *Robert Cowell* 100
3 b c Dandy Man(IRE) Roskeen (IRE) (Grand Lodge (USA))
1773^{6} 2192^{6} 7156^{17} 7537^{12}

Osaruveetil (IRE) *David O'Meara* a84 82
5 b g Teofilo(IRE) Caraiyma (IRE) (Shahrastani (USA))
2051^{4} 2659^{4} 3659^{3} 4409^{4}

Oscar Hill (IRE) *David Bridgwater* a54
10 b g Oscar(IRE) Elizabeth Tudor (IRE) (Supreme Leader)
630^{4} 728^{8}

Oscar Hughes (IRE) *Julie Camacho* a61 36
3 br g Frozen Power(IRE) Pedra Ona (IRE) (Mark Of Esteem (IRE))
1324^{3} 1815^{5} 2533^{5} 3568^{8}

Oscar Nominated (USA) *Michael J Maker* a100 105
3 ch r Kitten's Joy(USA) Devine Actress (USA) (Theatrical (IRE))
2063a^{17} 5429a^{5}

Oscar Performance (USA) *Brian A Lynch* 114
2 b c Kitten's Joy(USA) Devine Actress (USA) (Theatrical (IRE))
(7807a)

Oscars Journey *J R Jenkins* a71 71
6 ch g Dubai Destination(USA) Fruit Of Glory (Glory Of Dancer)
28^{8} 176^{2} 364^{4} 579^{3} 868^{4} (1299) 3469^{2} 5369^{9} 7018^{14} 7774^{12} 8242^{7} 8474^{13}

Ostatnia (IRE) *W McCreery* a97 94
4 b m Amadeus Wolf Ostrusa (AUT) (Rustan (HUN))
3696a^{8} 4246a^{6} 5816a^{3}

Osteopathic Remedy (IRE) *Michael Dods* a53 92
12 ch g Inchinor Dolce Vita (IRE) (Ela-Mana-Mou)
1380^{5} 2256^{9} 2662^{10} 3327^{9} 4683^{6} 6226^{7} ◆ 6434^{2} ◆ 7010^{7}

Ost Wind *Michael Attwater* a69 73
4 b g Oasis Dream Maroussies Wings (IRE) (In The Wings)
2577^{12} 3402^{2} 4773^{6} 6657^{10} 7613^{10}

Otomo *Philip Hide* a68 68
2 b g Equiano(FR) Akhira (Emperor Jones (USA))
3404^{11} 6404^{2} 7032^{2} 7605^{4} 7891^{2}

Oud Metha Bridge (IRE) *Ed Dunlop* a78
2 ch c Helmet(AUS) Central Force (Pivotal)
6673^{7} 7307^{3}

Oudwood *David O'Meara* a61 70
2 ch f New Approach(IRE) Jumeirah Palm Star (Invincible Spirit (IRE))
5469^{9} 5930^{3} 6624^{4} 7228^{5} 8174^{8}

Ouezy (IRE) *J-C Rouget* a79 98
3 br f Le Havre(IRE) Merville (FR) (Montjeu (IRE))
5754a^{4}

Ouja *John Gosden* 55
2 b f Sea The Stars(IRE) Royale Danehill (IRE) (Danehill (USA))
7494^{10} ◆

Our Boy (IRE) *David Evans* 78
2 ch g Raven's Pass(USA) Burren Rose (USA) (Storm Cat (USA))
2203^{3} 2649^{4} 3598^{4} (5820) 6554^{4} 7075^{6}

Our Boy Jack (IRE) *Conor Dore* a69 87
7 b g Camacho Jina (IRE) (Petardia)
1251^{3} 1643^{9} 2679^{13} 3421^{5} 3849^{2} 4427^{3} (4767) 5291^{2} (5915) 6500^{5} 7436^{10} 7606^{4} 7886^{10} 8036^{11} 8240^{12}

Our Boy John (IRE) *Richard Fahey* a53 62
2 b c Dandy Man(IRE) Jina (IRE) (Petardia)
3208^{7} 3749^{5} 4140^{3} 5109^{5} 6213^{9} 7109^{8} 7570^{7} 7866^{4} 8046^{7} 8284^{3} 8568^{6}

Our Century (IRE) *Robert Hickmott* 92
5 b g Montjeu(IRE) Mixed Blessing (Lujain (USA))
7637a^{3}

Our Channel (USA) *Jamie Osborne* a108 77
5 ch g English Channel(USA) Raw Gold (USA) (Rahy (USA))
(215) 767^{3} (871) (1088) 1604^{7} 4165^{18} 4731^{17} 8529^{4}

Our Charlie Brown *Tim Easterby* a67 76
2 b g American Post Cordoba (Oasis Dream)
1407^{7} 2264^{5} 3872^{7} (5799) 6229^{7} 6903^{4}

Our Cilla *Julia Feilden* 27
2 gr f Sixties Icon Kinetix (Linamix (FR))
7470^{9} 7696^{12}

Our Folly *Stuart Kittow* a37 70
8 b g Sakhee(USA) Regent's Folly (IRE) (Touching Wood (USA))
1450^{4} 2338^{3} 3746^{5}

Our Greta (IRE) *Michael Appleby* 75
2 gr f Exchange Rate(USA) Academicienne (USA) (Royal Academy (USA))
1965^{3} ◆ 2670^{7} (4890) 5583^{10} 6322^{5} 7004^{10}

Our Ivanhowe (GER) *Lee & Anthony Freedman* 116
6 b h Soldier Hollow Indigo Girl (GER) (Sternkoenig (IRE))
7378a^{6} 7756a^{17}

Our Joy (IRE) *Clive Cox* a80 80
3 b f Kodiac Great Joy I (IRE) (Grand Lodge (USA))
2220^{7} 3519^{6}

Our Kylie (IRE) *Brian Ellison* a61 67
4 b m Jeremy(USA) Prakara (IRE) (Indian Ridge)
3564^{3} (4489)

Our Last Summer (IRE) *Niels Petersen* 91
3 br c Zamindar(USA) Hoh My Darling (Dansili)
4186a^{6}

Our Little Sister (IRE) *Hughie Morrison* a66
3 b f Big Bad Bob(IRE) Rehearsed (IRE) (In The Wings)
287^{6} 384^{2} 591^{6} 789^{6} 7755^{7} 7969^{8}

Our Lois (IRE) *Keith Dalgleish* 52
2 b f Bushranger(IRE) Atishoo (IRE) (Revoque (IRE))
4037^{7} 4442^{4} 4943^{8} 5799^{4}

Our Lord *Bill Turner* a65 67
4 gr g Proclamation(IRE) Lady Filly (Atraf)
1110^{4} ◆ 1451^{10} 1833^{3} 2342^{5} (3260) 4529^{5} 5105^{4}

Our Manekineko *J A Nash* a74 48
6 b g Kyllachy Gallivant (Danehill (USA))
6462a^{4}

Ourmullion *John Best* a59 62
2 b g Mullionmileanhour(IRE) Queen Ranavola (USA) (Medaglia d'Oro (USA))
5237^{4} 5959^{7} 7064^{10} 8008^{3}

Our Place In Loule *Noel Wilson* a53 58
3 ch g Compton Place Show Off (Efisio)
2302^{12} 3940^{6} 4238^{7} 5370^{4} 6100^{11}

Outback Blue *David Evans* a79 79
3 gr g Aussie Rules(USA) Beautiful Lady (IRE) (Peintre Celebre (USA))
296^{3} 638^{5} 1977^{8} (2545) 2749^{2} 3130^{4} 3591^{4} 4139^{8} 5545^{4} 6323^{5} 7159^{9} 7204^{7} 8077^{8}

Outback Guy (IRE) *Kevin Frost* a52
3 b g Bushranger(IRE) Little Doll (Gulch (USA))
1767^{6} 2443^{9} 2780^{8} 5604^{10} 5971^{13}

Outback Princess *Gary Moore* a30 50
3 gr f Aussie Rules(USA) Royal Assent (Royal Applause)
1734^{7} 1948^{8} 2828^{3} 7936^{8}

Outback Ruler (IRE) *Clive Cox* 88
4 gr g Aussie Rules(USA) My American Beauty (Wolfhound (USA))
1545^{2} 2246^{10} 2934^{3} 3645^{10} 4306^{6} 5075^{8} 5649^{2} 6300^{4} 7017^{2}

Outback Traveller (IRE) *Robert Cowell* a84 112
5 b g Bushranger(IRE) Blue Holly (IRE) (Blues Traveller (IRE))
1627^{7} ◆ 2027^{13} ◆ (3386) 4166^{9} 6941^{5} 7932^{12}

Outcrop (IRE) *Hughie Morrison* a68 50
2 b c Rock Of Gibraltar(IRE) Desert Sage (Selkirk (USA))
7622^{11} 7962^{8} 8245^{3}

Out Do *David O'Meara* a95 114
7 ch g Exceed And Excel(AUS) Ludynosa (USA) (Cadeaux Genereux)
2438^{7} 3244^{7} 4166^{8} 4860^{2} 5143^{3} 5614^{18} 6112^{7} 6327^{17} 6792^{7}

Outer Space *Jamie Osborne* a98 94
5 b g Acclamation Venoge (IRE) (Green Desert (USA))
1797^{3} ◆ 2033^{5} 3055^{8} 4109^{7} (4534) 5174^{9}

Outfox *Bryan Smart* 64
2 b f Foxwedge(AUS) Spontaneity (IRE) (Holy Roman Emperor (IRE))
4805^{5} 5713^{4} 6078^{5} 6614^{5} 6954^{19}

Outlaw Country (IRE) *Charlie Appleby* 90
4 br h Teofilo(IRE) Neverletme Go (IRE) (Green Desert (USA))
4823^{15}

Outlaw Kate (IRE) *Michael Mullineaux* a33 53
4 b m Bushranger(IRE) Diosper (USA) (Diesis)
1631^{10} 2528^{5} 2810^{9} 4289^{10} 5235^{6} 5953^{14} 6106^{13}

Outlaw Torn (IRE) *Richard Guest* a62 59
7 ch g Iffraaj Touch And Love (IRE) (Green Desert (USA))
683^{9} 862^{12} 939^{6} 1202^{9} 1654^{4} 2330^{10} 2409^{4} 2566^{9} 2915^{5} 3564^{12} 3943^{6} 4146^{4} 4425^{9} 4929^{5} 5064^{9} (5323) 7369^{8} 7794^{11} 8070^{8} 8125^{3} 8141^{9} 8307^{7} 8492^{2} 8527^{9}

Out Of Ideas (FR) *Andrew Hollinshead* 40
2 b c Sinndar(IRE) Out Of Honour (IRE) (Highest Honor (FR))
5348a^{10}

Out Of Order (IRE) *Tim Easterby* a60 45
2 b g Holy Roman Emperor(IRE) Barring Order (IRE) (Barathea (IRE))
4040^{11} 6162^{11} 7988^{7}

Out Of The Ashes *Mohamed Moubarak* a82 10
3 ch g Phoenix Reach(IRE) Shrewd Decision (Motivator)
3066^{9} 4319^{10} (7782) 8456^{3}

Out Of The Dark (IRE) *Richard Hannon* a76 88
3 b f Kyllachy Assumption (IRE) (Beckett (IRE))
(2470) 3107^{4} 7281^{8} 7462^{10}

Outrage *Daniel Kubler* a100 87
4 ch g Exceed And Excel(AUS) Ludynosa (USA) (Cadeaux Genereux)
2040^{8} 3713^{7} 3989^{5} 4485^{2} (4744) (5162) 6234^{11} 6878^{17} 7643^{4} ◆ 7864^{5} 8083^{8} 8308^{8} (8403) (8463) 8583^{3}

Outrath (IRE) *Jim Best* a49 45
6 b g Captain Rio Silver Grouse (IRE) (Zagreb (USA))
5544^{4} 5850^{4} 6247^{6} 7943^{10} 8458^{8}

Outre Mer (IRE) *John Gosden* a71 90
2 b c Raven's Pass(USA) Sea Chanter (USA) (War Chant (USA))
2757^{6} 3524^{4} 4649^{4} (6875) (7075)

Outwork (USA) *Todd Pletcher* a112
3 b c Uncle Mo(USA) Nonna Mia (USA) (Empire Maker (USA))
2063a^{14}

Overhaugh Street *Keith Dalgleish* 73
3 b g Bahri(USA) Bom Chicka Wah Wah (USA) (Dynaformer (USA))
1691^{6} 2532^{9} 2741^{9}

Overlord *Mark Rimell* a62 60
4 b g Lawman(FR) Hip (Pivotal)
1502^{3} 1796^{4} ◆ 4214^{6} 4567^{3} 4986^{7} 5625^{9} 6143^{3} (6411) 6871^{4} 7516^{13} 7614^{4}

Overrider *Shaun Lycett* a57 58
6 b g Cockney Rebel(IRE) Fustaan (IRE) (Royal Applause)
294^{2} (388) 986^{10} 1323^{7} 1556^{9}

Overstone Lass (IRE) *John Spearing* a5 42
4 b m Excellent Art Clinging Vine (USA) (Fusaichi Pegasus (USA))
2969^{10} 3735^{9} 4290^{14} 5051^{9}

Over The Ocean (USA) *Niels Petersen* a92 92
6 rg h Rockport Harbor(USA) Endless Sea (CAN) (Mt. Livermore (USA))
450a^{14} 717a^{3} 842a^{8} 4421a^{3} 5098a^{4}

Overview *A Fabre* 65
2 b f Frankel Take The Hint (Montjeu (IRE))
7346a^{4}

Owaseyf (USA) *Roger Varian* a83 81
3 b f Medaglia d'Oro(USA) Nasmatt (Danehill (USA))
(2303) 2855^{4} ◆ 5551^{2} 5891^{4} 7281^{5} 7617^{4} 8028^{4}

Ower Fly *Richard Hannon* a92 87
3 b g Pastoral Pursuits Contrary Mary (Mujadil (USA))
(1385) 1452^{2} 3105^{8} 3689^{5} (4662) 5403^{14} 6916^{4} (7461)

Owners Day *Neil Mulholland* a66 72
6 gr m Fair Mix(IRE) Charmeille (FR) (Exit To Nowhere (USA))
1140^{9} 1324^{5} 1529^{4} (2127) 2292^{4} 2996^{5}

Oxford Blu *Sir Mark Prescott Bt* a63 33
2 b g Aqlaam Blue Zealot (IRE) (Galileo (IRE))
3730^{7} 4287^{12} 5081^{7} 7640^{7} (7954) 8080^{4}

Oxford Thinking (IRE) *John Gosden* a67
2 b c Holy Roman Emperor(IRE) Larceny (IRE) (Cape Cross (IRE))
8074^{4} 8305^{2}

Oyster Card *Michael Appleby* a53 51
3 b g Rail Link Perle D'Or (IRE) (Entrepreneur)
1953^{6} 2667^{5} 3483^{8} 4498^{5} 4987^{5} 6444^{7} 6900^{7} 7103^{3} 7464^{9} 7987^{3} 8359^{6}

Oyster Pearl (IRE) *Carroll Gray* a17 63
3 gr f Thousand Words Rectify (IRE) (Mujadil (USA))
4992^{10} 5263^{7} 6367^{8}

Pabouche (IRE) *H-A Pantall* 95
3 ch f Dubawi(IRE) High Heeled (IRE) (High Chaparral (IRE))
5695a^{5} (6611a) 7565a^{5}

Pabusar *Micky Hammond* a76 48
8 b g Oasis Dream Autumn Pearl (Orpen (USA))
1790^{7} 2052^{7} 2270^{6} 2812^{4} 3022^{3} 3289^{8} 3549^{6} 3776^{10} 4512^{7} 6008^{4} 7046^{12} 7145^{8}

Pacabag *Peter Hedger* a42
3 b f Paco Boy(IRE) Veronica Franco (Darshaan)
516^{6} 7459^{8} 8383^{10}

Paca Punch *Michael Blanshard* a25 4
3 b f Paco Boy(IRE) Plumage (Royal Applause)
3744^{7} 4213^{8} 4939^{12}

Pacches (IRE) *Mick Channon* a58 74
3 b f Clodovil(IRE) Ringarooma (Erhaab (USA))
726^{5}

Pacelli Road (IRE) *J P Broderick* a57 75
7 b g Oratorio(IRE) Lexy May (USA) (Lear Fan (USA))
208a^{10}

Pacharana *Luca Cumani* a78 84
3 b f Oasis Dream Cascata (IRE) (Montjeu (IRE))
2653^{8} 3509^{5} (4567) (5086) (5763) (6380) ◆ 6719^{2}

Pacific Angel (IRE) *M Delzangles* 105
4 b m Dalakhani(IRE) Perstrovka (IRE) (Sadler's Wells (USA))
1232a^{4} (4696a) 5218a^{4}

Pacific Salt (IRE) *Pam Sly* a72 67
3 gr g Zebedee Villa Nova (IRE) (Petardia)
1337^{7} ◆ 2544^{8} 3319^{3} 3732^{2} (4764) 5322^{8} 6241^{2} 6700^{4} 7613^{6} (8086)

Pacify *Ralph Beckett* a73 108
4 b g Paco Boy(IRE) Supereva (IRE) (Sadler's Wells (USA))
1569^{2} 2157^{2} 3383^{14}

Packing (IRE) *Jamie Osborne* a70
3 b c Lilbourne Lad(IRE) Elegant Ridge (IRE) (Indian Ridge)
443^{6} 610^{4} (1792) 2770^{4} (3648)

Packing Empire (IRE) *Jamie Osborne* a41
3 b g Holy Roman Emperor(IRE) Ceoil An Aith (IRE) (Accordion)
794^{8} 1062^{9}

Packing Pins (NZ) *P F Yiu* 115
5 b g Pins(AUS) Splashing Out (NZ) (O'Reilly (NZ))
1912a^{3} 8332a^{14}

Pack It In (IRE) *Brian Meehan* 76
3 br g Big Bad Bob(IRE) Evening Dress (Medicean)
1738^{6} (2145) 2366^{11} 4046^{3} 4554^{5} (5164) 6268^{3}

Pacodali (IRE) *J P Murtagh* 93
3 br g Paco Boy(IRE) Dont Dili Dali (Dansili)
1938a^{4} 3299^{15} 6983a^{8}

Paco Dawn *Philip Hide* a44
2 ch f Paco Boy(IRE) First Dawn (Dr Fong (USA))
6881^{14} 7277^{8} 7963^{10}

Pacofilha *Paul Cole* a74 74
2 b f Paco Boy(IRE) Seradim (Elnadim (USA))
1793^{4} 3782^{5} 5722^{4} 5995^{3} 6240^{3} 6875^{5} 7286^{3}

Pacohontas *John E Long* a58 51
3 bb f Paco Boy(IRE) Balliasta (IRE) (Grand Lodge (USA))
984^{7} 1339^{7} 1577^{9} 3319^{9} 3734^{5} 5167^{2} 8559^{P}

Paco Lady *Ivan Furtado* a16
2 b f Paco Boy(IRE) Rosa Luxemburg (Needwood Blade)
7269^{9} 7845^{5}

Pacolita (IRE) *Sylvester Kirk* a72 79
4 ch m Paco Boy(IRE) Clara (IRE) (In The Wings)
(144) 191^{2} ◆ 2655^{8} 3554^{5} (3974) 4206^{2} 4737^{8} 5017^{3} 6266^{2}

Pacommand *Marco Botti* a70 51
3 b g Paco Boy(IRE) Indian Story (IRE) (Indian Ridge)
1992^{11} 3357^{8}

Paco Pat *Richard Hannon* a63 59
3 b c Paco Boy(IRE) Tanwir (Unfuwain (USA))
2152^{7} 3745^{6} (4204)

Paco's Angel *Richard Hughes* 98
2 b f Paco Boy(IRE) Papabile (USA) (Chief's Crown (USA))
2637^{2} ◆ 3143^{2} (3718) 4884^{2} ◆ (5998) 7114^{4}

Pactolus (IRE) *Stuart Williams* a97 92
5 b g Footstepsinthesand Gold Marie (IRE) (Green Desert (USA))
31^{4} 160^{2} 530^{2} 656^{2} 767^{5} (888) 1089^{5} 4399^{5} 4868^{4} 5874^{4} 7608^{5} (8049) 8279^{4}

Paddy A (IRE) *Philip McBride* a68
2 bb g Holy Roman Emperor(IRE) Lilting (IRE) (Montjeu (IRE))
3954^{F} 4975^{3} 6590^{4} 7306^{8} 7898^{11}

Paddy Power (IRE) *Richard Fahey* a75 90
3 ch g Pivotal Rag Top (IRE) (Barathea (IRE))
1014a^{2} (1435) 2218^{3} ◆ 2658^{3} ◆ 3292^{4} 4112^{17} 4652^{4} 4803^{11} 5409^{6} 6164^{5} 6793^{15} 7289^{4}

Paddys Motorbike (IRE) *David Evans* a95 95
4 ch g Fast Company(IRE) Saffa Garden (IRE) (King's Best (USA))
19^{3} (244) ◆ 499^{6} 747^{3} 861^{7} 1081^{8} 1885^{2} 3889^{17} 4407^{11} 5879^{9}

Paddy's Rock (IRE) *Lynn Siddall* a61 64
5 b g Whipper(USA) Hedera (USA) (Woodman (USA))
2618^{13} 3563^{6} 4038^{5} 4377^{2} 5841^{6} 5868^{3} 6432^{9} 6839^{5} 7515^{6} 8038^{4} 8410^{11}

Paddys Runner *Alan King* a77 81
4 gr g Sir Percy Frosty Welcome (USA) (With Approval (CAN))
566^{5} 1760^{8}

Padleyourowncanoe *Daniel Mark Loughnane* a51 64
2 b g Nayef(USA) Pooka's Daughter (IRE) (Eagle Eyed (USA))
2335^{3} 3032^{6} 5203^{6} 5840^{5} 6253^{4}

Padrinho (IRE) *John Best* 63
2 b g High Chaparral(IRE) Belanoiva (IRE) (Motivator)
5356^{11} 6108^{9}

Paene Magnus (IRE) *A bin Harmash* a86 105
7 ch g Teofilo(IRE) Luminaria (IRE) (Danehill (USA))
93a^{11} 285a^{5} 453a^{2} 811a^{10}

Pagella (GER) *J Hirschberger* 103
3 b f Soldier Hollow Princess Lala (GER) (Royal Dragon (USA))
3207a^{2} 5220a^{7} 6175a^{3} 6988a^{7}

Page Of Wands *Karen McLintock* a57 64
3 b f Multiplex No Page (IRE) (Statue Of Liberty (USA))
40^{10} 3550^{4} 4098^{2} 4681^{5} 5365^{6} 5844^{3} 6344^{4} 7992^{8} 8386^{10} 8400^{6}

Page One (FR) *M Arienti* 96
3 ro f Stormy River(FR) Stadenanz (Rainbow Quest (USA))
2730a^{9}

Pagino (GER) *Waldemar Hickst* 95
3 b c Sholokhov(IRE) Peace Flower (IRE) (Dashing Blade)
1908a^{4} 3699a^{4}

Paisible Et Sage (FR) *F Chappet* 70
2 b f Sageburg(IRE) Peace Fonic (FR) (Zafonic (USA))
5005a^{5}

Paisley Abbey *Paul Midgley* 12
2 b g Orientor Killer Class (Kyllachy)
1199^{10} 1813^{6}

Pakora (FR) *P Sogorb* a74 101
3 gr f Gentlewave(IRE) Panthesilea (FR) (Kendor (FR))
(716a) 2944a^{6} 5451a^{5}

Palace Moon *Michael Attwater* a61 56
11 b g Fantastic Light(USA) Palace Street (USA) (Secreto (USA))
190^{5} 403^{4} 709^{U} (877) 1262^{8} 1834^{6} 3255^{4} 5055^{8} 5832^{9}

Palace Prince (GER) *Andreas Lowe* 111
4 bb h Areion(GER) Palace Princess (GER) (Tiger Hill (IRE))
1231a^{6} 5904a^{7} 7028a^{6} (7564a) 7843a^{2}

Paladin (IRE) *Michael Blake* a72 72
7 b g Dubawi(IRE) Palwina (FR) (Unfuwain (USA))
875^{8} 1403^{5} 2153^{7} (3522) 3731^{3} 4009^{5} 6241^{13} 6872^{14} 8350^{4} (8566)

Palang (USA) *Andreas Lowe* 100
4 bb h Hat Trick(JPN) Pavlova (USA) (Stravinsky (USA))
4253a^{6} 7028a^{7} 7564a^{5} 7843a^{6}

Palavicini Run (IRE) *J F Levins* a70 76
3 ch f Palavicini(USA) Dawn's Sharp Shot (IRE) (Son Of Sharp Shot (IRE))
7801a^{6}

Palawan *Richard Hannon* a92 105
3 b g Mount Nelson Apple Sauce (Prince Sabo)
1338^{5} 1605^{4} 3299^{17} 3534^{4} 4149^{6} 5403^{13} 6918^{3}

Pale Enchantment (IRE) *Tom Dascombe* 59
2 b f Sir Prancealot(IRE) Bronze Queen (IRE) (Invincible Spirit (IRE))
6477^{5} ◆ 7269^{5}

Palenville (IRE) *Simon Crisford* a79 77
3 ch f Rip Van Winkle(IRE) Faithful Duchess (IRE) (Bachelor Duke (USA))
3111[4] 3821[2] *5027[3] 8357[2]*

Palindrome (USA) *Ronald Thompson* a68 42
3 b g Poet's Voice Hi Dubai (Rahy (USA))
7627[12] *7991[6] 8310[3]*

Paling *Roger Charlton* a77 94
3 b c Zamindar(USA) Solar Pursuit (Galileo (IRE))
1238[3] 1602[4] (2291) 3102[2] 4561[2] (5198)

Palinodie (FR) *E Leenders* a81 105
3 b f Doctor Dino(FR) Palmeriade (FR) (Kouroun (FR))
6069a[3] (7029a)

Palisade *Sir Mark Prescott Bt* a96 85
3 b g Fastnet Rock(AUS) Portal (Hernando (FR))
2366[8] 2798[4] 3215[2] 3738[2] *(4021)* 4277[2] (5071) *(5365)* 5603[4] 6528[4] *(7383)*

Pallasator *Sir Mark Prescott Bt* a96 116
7 b g Motivator Ela Athena (Ezzoud (IRE))
(2625) 3298[12] 3913[4] 4799[2] 5612[2] ◆ 7569a[8]

Palmerston *Michael Appleby* a71 83
3 b g Oasis Dream Marywell (Selkirk (USA))
1276[12] 1587[3] 2123[4] ◆ (3224) 3983[11] (4654) 5376[2] 5933[7] 6753[10] *7796[13]*

Palmina *Dean Ivory* a54
3 ch f Bahamian Bounty Starfleet (Inchinor)
350[6] 885[4] 7444[9] 7913[11]

Pal Of The Cat *Michael Attwater* 7
6 ch g Choisir(AUS) Evenstorm (USA) (Stephen Got Even (USA))
4461[P]

Palpitation (IRE) *David Brown* a74 58
3 b g Fast Company(IRE) Sensation (Soviet Star (USA))
(947) ◆ *(1031) 1137[4]* 2123[6] *2900[10]* 5030[6] *5609[4] 7203[8] 7486[4] 7691[10]*

Pamona (IRE) *Ralph Beckett* 104
4 b m Duke Of Marmalade(IRE) Palanca (Inchinor)
1855[13] 2797[7] (4164) 4800[5] 5639[6] 6259[6]

Panama (FR) *D Windrif* a53 63
6 b g Sholokhov(IRE) Prophecie (FR) (Dansili)
512a[12]

Panameras (FR) *T Castanheira* a71 60
2 ch f Medecis So Long Girl (Selkirk (USA))
6937a[10]

Pancake Day *David C Griffiths* a63 54
4 b g Mullionmileanhour(IRE) Fangfoss Girls (Monsieur Bond (IRE))
224 130[4] 418[2] 589[3] 732[5] 1255[4] 1495[13] *(1709)* 2052[14] *7859[10] 8031[5] 8242[6] 8312[12]*

Pandar *Michael Attwater* a70 80
7 b g Zamindar(USA) Pagnottella (IRE) (Dansili)
(2013) (2088) 4355[3] *4714[9]* (5773) 6409[4] 7221[7] *7737[7]*

Pandora (IRE) *David O'Meara* 103
4 ch m Galileo(IRE) Song Of My Heart (IRE) (Footstepsinthesand)
2026[7] (3113) 4610[3] 5587[3] 6273a[7] 6747[4]

Pandora's Pyx *Gary Moore* a44 17
4 b m Indesatchel(IRE) Hope Chest (Kris)
603[10] 697[7] 1748[13]

Panko (IRE) *Ed de Giles* a82 85
3 b g Iffraaj Engraving (Sadler's Wells (USA))
1826[4] 2012[2] (2701) 3189[4] 4046[2] (4293) 6365[2] 6665[3] ◆ *7067[4]* 7418[3]

Panova *Sir Michael Stoute* a80
2 b f Invincible Spirit(IRE) Safina (Pivotal)
6244[5] 6867[2] ◆ *(7380)*

Pantera Negra (IRE) *Ed Dunlop* 68
2 b f Champs Elysees Penchee (Grand Lodge (USA))
3186[3] 4125[3] 4856[5] 6130[8]

Panther In Pink (IRE) *Ann Duffield* a50 51
2 b f Zebedee Annus Iucundus (IRE) (Desert King (IRE))
6009[4] *8118[9] 8406[6]*

Panther Patrol (IRE) *Eve Johnson Houghton* a80 78
6 b g Tagula(IRE) Quivala (USA) (Thunder Gulch (USA))
5744[10] 6255[2] 6668[3] 7267[4] *7617[3] 8052[7] 8176[13]*

Pao De Acuca (IRE) *Jose Santos* a71 36
4 b g Rip Van Winkle(IRE) Splendeur (FR) (Desert King (IRE))
1551[3] 255[9] (634) (673) 819[8] 1347[9] 1405[7] 2400[8] *3470[8] 4212[5]* 5016[8] *5261[4]*

Paola Queen (USA) *Gustavo Delgado* a106
3 b f Flatter(USA) Kadira (USA) (Kafwain (USA))
7836a[12]

Papa Delta *Tony Carroll* 46
2 b c Makfi Step Softly (Golan (IRE))
2295[5] 2902[4]

Papagayo (IRE) *Barry Murtagh* a40 47
4 b g Shirocco(GER) Jomana (IRE) (Darshaan)
2916[8] 4194[8] *4648[8]*

Papal Parade (IRE) *Eamonn O'Connell* 71
5 br m Papal Bull Easter Parade (Entrepreneur)
5096a[18]

Papa Luigi (IRE) *Richard Hannon* a92 93
3 b c Zoffany(IRE) Namaadhej (USA) (Swain (IRE))
2186[3] *(2561)* (2981) *(3036)* 4223[2] 4652[11] 4911[7] 5148[6] 5991[7]

Papa's Way (IRE) *P D Deegan* a78 90
6 b g Rakti Clew Bay Coral (IRE) (Spectrum (IRE))
(3680a) 7195a[P]

Paper Faces (USA) *Roger Varian* a67 65
3 ch f Lemon Drop Kid(USA) Liffey Dancer (IRE) (Sadler's Wells (USA))
4361[4] *6511[5] 6960[4] 7326[4] 7613[7] 7870[3] 8193[2] 8459[8]*

Papou Tony *George Baker* a72 60
3 b g Raven's Pass(USA) Lukrecia (IRE) (Exceed And Excel (AUS))
(691) 924[6] 2299[8] *4010[12] 5302[3]* 5824[9] *6416[8]*

Paques Island (FR) *J Phelippon* a72 72
3 b f Slickly Royal(FR) Isula Di Isula (FR) (Anabaa (USA))
6310a[10]

Paquita Bailarina *James Given* a57 40
2 ch f Paco Boy(IRE) Prima Ballerina (Pivotal)
7099[7] 7407[4] *7776[3]*

Paradise (GER) *Waldemar Hickst* a104 105
4 b m Samum(GER) La Parabol (FR) (Trempolino (USA))
1102a[11]

Paradise Cove *William Haggas* 54
2 ch f Harbour Watch(IRE) Peace Signal (USA) (Time For A Change (USA))
7465[5]

Paradise Lake (IRE) *Sir Michael Stoute* a61 65
2 b c Siyouni(FR) Kalandara (IRE) (Rainbow Quest (USA))
7468[8] *7812[6]*

Paradise Palm *Philip McBride* a59
3 ch f Sakhee's Secret Akathea (Barathea (IRE))
441[3] 565[5] 7514[3] 7755[9] 7986[9]

Paradise Spectre *Zoe Davison* a59 40
9 b g Firebreak Amber's Bluff (Mind Games)
876 230[8]

Paradwys (IRE) *Charles Hills* 71
2 b f Exceed And Excel(AUS) First Of Many (Darshaan)
4756[17] 5846[5] 7118[5] 7439[4]

Parauari (FR) *A De Royer-Dupre* a74
2 b c Lawman(FR) Parade Militaire (IRE) (Peintre Celebre (USA))
7971a[9]

Parfait (IRE) *John Gosden* a82 84
2 b g Invincible Spirit(IRE) Rakiza (IRE) (Elnadim (USA))
4363[3] *6122[4]* 6880[8] (7502)

Parinacota (FR) *Mlle V Dissaux* a59
2 b f Dobby Road(FR) Surtsey (FR) (Anabaa Blue)
7970a[9] 8420a[14]

Parish Boy *J S Bolger* 89
4 gr g New Approach(IRE) Requesting (Rainbow Quest (USA))
5941a[16]

Parisian Chic (IRE) *Lee Carter* a62
2 b f Kodiac Divine Design (IRE) (Barathea (IRE))
7279[5] 8361[3]

Parisianna *Richard Fahey* a46
3 b f Champs Elysees Simianna (Bluegrass Prince (IRE))
48[6]

Parisian Pyramid (IRE) *Lee Carter* a50 53
10 gr g Verglas(IRE) Sharadja (IRE) (Doyoun)
2584[10]

Parisienne Rose (IRE) *Simon Crisford* 62
2 br f Big Bad Bob(IRE) Daidoo (IRE) (Shamardal (USA))
7055[5]

Paris Magic *Hugo Palmer* a82 85
3 b g Champs Elysees Belgooree (Haafhd)
2098[2] *7106[3]* 7499[5] *(8310) 8584[4]*

Paris Protocol *Richard Hannon* 95
3 b g Champs Elysees Island Vista (Montjeu (IRE))
1610[5] 3300[6] 4131[6] 6110[11]

Parkour (IRE) *Marco Botti* a87 46
3 b g Holy Roman Emperor(IRE) School Holidays (USA) (Harlan's Holiday (USA))
1763[5] 4460[6] *7965[5] 8176[2] 8380[10]*

Park Square (FR) *H-A Pantall* a69 59
3 b g Myboycharlie(IRE) Adeje Park (IRE) (Night Shift (USA))
2172a[6]

Parkwarden (IRE) *Chris Grant* a54 34
2 b g Bushranger(IRE) Honour And Obey (IRE) (Hurricane Run (IRE))
2301[7] *3561[4] 4642[9] 5840[9]*

Parlance (IRE) *Sir Michael Stoute* a82 50
2 b f Invincible Spirit(IRE) Pleasantry (Johannesburg (USA))
2793[10] *6866[2] (7484)* ◆

Parliamentarian (IRE) *Charlie Appleby* 95
3 b g Dubawi(IRE) Forum Floozie (NZ) (Danasinga (AUS))
(3550) (4559) 6735[2] 7215[6]

Parnassian (IRE) *K R Burke* a90 88
2 b c Elzaam(AUS) Adaptation (Spectrum (IRE))
(5067) ◆ (5713) ◆ 6388a[10] 7469[4] *7893[2] 7989[3]*

Parnell's Dream *Ralph Beckett* a79 82
4 b m Oasis Dream Kitty O'Shea (Sadler's Wells (USA))
1853[3] 2433[5] *(2994)* 3409[2] 7625[9]

Parsnip (IRE) *Michael Bell* 83
2 ch f Zebedee Hawattef (IRE) (Mujtahid (USA))
(4287) 4884[8] 5794[2] ◆ 7147[10]

Parthenius (GER) *Mario Hofer* 101
3 b c Soldier Hollow Princess Li (GER) (Monsun (GER))
1689a[5] 4186a[19] 4928a[12]

Par Three (IRE) *Tony Carroll* a64 53
5 bb g Azamour(IRE) Little Whisper (IRE) (Be My Guest (USA))
3488[7] 3997[14] 4493[8] *5680[5] 6422[6] 8084[6] 8309[7] 8497[2]*

Partitia *Sir Michael Stoute* 93
2 br f Bated Breath Palmette (Oasis Dream)
4350[10] (5400) (5638) 6555[5]

Partyinthepaddock (USA) *Carla Gaines* 88
2 rg f Harlan's Holiday(USA) All About Anna (USA) (Maria's Mon (USA))
8127a[13]

Party Nights *Luca Cumani* a73 71
2 b f Lawman(FR) Funseeker (UAE) (Halling (USA))
3073[5] 3947[5] 4707[11] 5324[3] (6377) *6898[4]* 7406[5]

Party Royal *Nick Gifford* a63 44
6 b g Royal Applause Voliere (Zafonic (USA))
1387[9] 2491[17] 2872[14] 7775[11] *8458[5]*

Party Thyme *Chris Wall* 67
3 ch f Medicean Thymesthree (IRE) (Galileo (IRE))
2212[12] 3823[6] 4279[2] 5038[3] *5720[11]* 6646[4] 7035[6]

Party Tiger *Richard Fahey* a76 76
2 b g Excelebration(IRE) Poly Pomona (Green Desert (USA))
3416[8] 4685[4] 5377[2] (6833) 7440[2] 7820[11] *8244[4]*

Parvaneh (IRE) *Waldemar Hickst* 106
3 b f Holy Roman Emperor(IRE) College Fund Girl (IRE) (Kahyasi)
(1513a) 2315a[5] 2949a[12] 5220a[5] (6152a) 6822a[4] 7404a[8]

Parys Mountain (IRE) *Charles Hills* 80
2 gr g Dark Angel(IRE) Muzdaan (IRE) (Exceed And Excel (AUS))
2756[2] ◆ 3243[10] 4736[5] 5560[13] 6162[7] 7217[4] 7467[4]

Pasaka Boy *Jonathan Portman* a68 84
6 ch g Haafhd Shesha Bear (Tobougg (IRE))
2024[9] 2866[9] 3861[10] 5963[6] 6549[3] *7053[7]* 7666[9]

Pas D'Action *Mrs A Malzard* 54
8 ch g Noverre(USA) Bright Vision (Indian Ridge)
(1518a) 2079a[3] (2284a) 2954a[2] (3380a) 5456a[3]

Pas De Deux (GER) *Yasmin Almenrader* a100 117
6 b g Saddex Palucca (GER) (Big Shuffle (USA))
(3451a) 4438a[2] (6067a)

Pas De Soucis (IRE) *Robert Collet* a91 100
3 b f Footstepsinthesand Whip And Win (FR) (Whipper (USA))
(7348a) 7723a[10]

Passcode *Andrew Balding* 70
2 b f Camacho Passata (FR) (Polar Falcon (USA))
7466[3]

Passeport (IRE) *S Jesus* a67 69
3 b c Heliostatic(IRE) Fearless Flyer (IRE) (Brave Act)
3764a[2] *5280a[8]*

Passing Dream *Hughie Morrison* a50
3 b f Passing Glance Violet's Walk (Dr Fong (USA))
2321[8] 4882[8] 6046[8]

Passing Star *Charles Hills* a88 90
5 b g Royal Applause Passing Hour (USA) (Red Ransom (USA))
1441[P] 2247[9] 2587[3] ◆ *3303[9]* 4104[P] *7530[3] 7903[10] 8593[8]*

Passionateprincess (IRE) *Ann Duffield* a46 52
3 b f Elnadim(USA) Romany Princess (IRE) (Viking Ruler (AUS))
635[7] 7301[0]

Passion For Action (CAN) *Michael P De Paulo* a108 110
4 b h Speightstown(USA) Maritime Passion (CAN) (Stormy Atlantic (USA))
6601a[8] 7403a[7]

Pass Muster *Philip Kirby* a75 80
9 b g Theatrical(IRE) Morning Pride (IRE) (Machiavellian (USA))
1665[4] 2659[5] 3149[12]

Passover *Andrew Balding* a55 102
5 b g Passing Glance Floriana (Selkirk (USA))
1088[8] 1245[8] 2037[5] 2752[3] 2979[3] 3670[2] 5173[2] 5411[3] 5894[6] 6573[10] 7058[2]

Pass The Cristal (IRE) *William Muir* a42 53
2 b g Raven's Pass(USA) Crystal Melody (Nureyev (USA))
4125[6] 4659[8] *7064[9]*

Pass The Moon (IRE) *Lydia Pearce* a30 33
3 ch f Raven's Pass(USA) Dubai Moon (USA) (Malibu Moon (USA))
3822[8]

Pass The Time *Neil Mulholland* a66 57
7 b m Passing Glance Twin Time (Syrtos)
71[2] (521) 592[5]

Pastfact *Malcolm Saunders* 63
2 b g Pastoral Pursuits Matterofact (IRE) (Bold Fact (USA))
4659[10] 5304[7] 5569 [2] 6440[6] 7217[12]

Pastoral Music *Hughie Morrison* a81 78
3 b g Pastoral Pursuits Jasmeno (Catcher In The Rye (IRE))
2098[9] 2548[4] ◆ 3434[2] *3653[3] 4530[3]* 6193[2] *(7063)* 7624[4] *8161[5] 8254[5]*

Pastoral Player *Hughie Morrison* a74 94
9 b g Pastoral Pursuits Copy-Cat (Lion Cavern (USA))
1959[8] 2391[9] (3101) 3848[2] 4758[8] 5403[7] 6076[5] 6915[11] 7825[6]

Pastoral Star *Jim Boyle* a61 67
3 ch f Pastoral Pursuits Movie Star (IRE) (Barathea (IRE))
1388[3] *2152[8]* 3496[4] 3955[3] (4482) 5254[2] 5923[7] 7037[9]

Patanjali (IRE) *Eve Johnson Houghton* a53 61
3 b f Poet's Voice Penang (IRE) (Xaar)
1734[6] 2148[4] 2851[8] 3973[3] (4275) 4764[7] 4819[2] 6485[5]

Patching *Giles Bravery* a65 55
2 b f Foxwedge(AUS) Crinolette (IRE) (Sadler's Wells (USA))
5861[5] 6578[10] *7484[3] 7885[8]*

Patent *Peter Niven* a48 69
3 b g Paco Boy(IRE) Film Script (Unfuwain (USA))
1714[6] 2340[5] *2790[11]* 3906[2] 4522[3] 5011[5] 5308[4] *7993[9]*

Path Of Silver (IRE) *Richard Brabazon* 61
3 b f Strategic Prince Silver Tide (USA) (Silver Hawk (USA))
5096a[8]

Pathway To Freedom *Charlie Appleby* a68
2 b c Cape Cross(IRE) Emancipation (Kingmambo (USA))
6590[6] 6924[4]

Patience A Plenty (IRE) *Adrian Paul Keatley* 66
3 b f Kodiac Suffer Her (IRE) (Whipper (USA))
1014a[8] 1691[5]

Patrick (IRE) *Richard Fahey* a96 93
4 b g Acclamation Red Liason (IRE) (Selkirk (USA))
7713 ◆ *9233* 1015a[10] *1958[2]* 2488[11] *3606[8]* 4126[15] 4667[13] 5417[16] 6079[10] 7413[9]

Patriotic (IRE) *Chris Dwyer* a92 72
8 b g Pivotal Pescara (IRE) (Common Grounds)
(49) 427[3] 581[9] 866[3] 1152[6] 1404[2] 1722[2] 2791[6] 5526[5]

Patron Of Explores (USA) *Patrick Holmes* a52 33
5 b g Henrythenavigator(USA) India Halo (ARG) (Halo Sunshine (USA))
35[5] 690[4] 707[U] 1323[9] 1556[8] 8306[11]

Patrouille De Nuit (IRE) *J S Moore* a39 52
2 b g Bushranger(IRE) Kyanight (IRE) (Kodiac)
1082[7] 1965[7] 2933[4] 3232[6] 4015[9] 4221[6] 5165[6]

Pattie *Mick Channon* a71 71
2 ch f Sixties Icon Excellent Day (IRE) (Invincible Spirit (IRE))
6776[4] *8139[3] 8340[2]*

Paulassilverlining (USA) *Michelle Nevin* a112
4 b m Ghostzapper(USA) Seeking The Silver (USA) (Grindstone (USA))
7836a[3]

Paulownia (IRE) *Richard Hannon* 78
2 ch f Nathaniel(IRE) Petite Nymphe (Golan (IRE))
3613[2] (4128)

Pause For Applause *Jonathan Portman*
3 b g Royal Applause Zarkavean (Medicean)
1897[7] 2398[9]

Pavela (IRE) *Scott Dixon* a54 60
2 b f Approve(IRE) Passage To India (IRE) (Indian Ridge)
2637[12] 6319[7] 6648[4] *6961[5]* 7330[2] *7510[3] 7893[9]*

Pavers Pride *Noel Wilson* 54
2 ch g Bahamian Bounty Pride Of Kinloch (Dr Devious (IRE))
5477[7] 7122[10]

Pavers Star *Noel Wilson* a49 56
7 ch g Pastoral Pursuits Pride Of Kinloch (Dr Devious (IRE))
2676[3] 3268[12] 3709[4] 4968[4] 5225[4] 5354[7] 5804[7] 6680[13] 6813[7] *7144[9]*

Pavillon *Clive Cox* a73
2 b f Showcasing Park Law (IRE) (Fasliyev (USA))
(8152)

Payitaht (TUR) *Mehmet Tekcan* a96
5 ch h Red Bishop(USA) Marica (TUR) (Marlin (USA))
6157a[4]

Pazeer (FR) *Ibrahim Al Malki* 90
2 b c Siyouni(FR) Parandeh (FR) (Kahyasi)
(3871a) (5568a) 6270a[5] (8564a)

Pc Dixon *Mick Channon* a64 73
3 ch g Sixties Icon Lakaam (Danzero (AUS))
4213[6] 4657[4] 4955[4] 5623[5] 6031[3] 6294[11] *8590[7]*

Peace And Plenty *William Muir* a69 60
2 ch c Exceed And Excel(AUS) Putois Peace (Pivotal)
4479[4] 5073[6] 7496[7] *7941[3] (8080)*

Peace Dreamer (IRE) *Robert Cowell* a30 60
2 b f Sir Prancealot(IRE) See Nuala (IRE) (Kyllachy)
6515[5] 7296[3] *7867[11]*

Peace Envoy (FR) *A P O'Brien* a83 113
2 b c Power Hoh My Darling (Dansili)
(2717a) 3295[4] 3678a[2] (4414a) 5690a[3] 6785[8]

Peaceful Journey *Marco Botti* a72
3 ch f Exceed And Excel(AUS) Dove (IRE) (Sadler's Wells (USA))
6960[2]

Peaceful Passage (USA) *John Gosden* a71 55
2 b f War Front(USA) Flying Passage (USA) (A.P. Indy (USA))
7740[6] *7982[2] 8227[6]*

Peacehaven (IRE) *J P Murtagh* a72 81
4 b m Rip Van Winkle(IRE) Crystal Gaze (IRE) (Rainbow Quest (USA))
7191a[12]

Peace Seeker *Ronald Harris* a93 74
8 b g Oasis Dream Mina (Selkirk (USA))
192[5] 339[4]

Peace Telegram *Michael Bell* 44
2 b g Henrythenavigator(USA) Princess Danah (IRE) (Danehill (USA))
6288[9]

Peachey Carnehan *Michael Attwater* a67 62
2 ch g Foxwedge(AUS) Zubova (Dubawi (IRE))
2429[2] 2675[3] 2963[4] 3485[5] 4638[6] 6033[4] *6743[4] 7109[10] 8591[2]*

Peach Pavlova (IRE) *Ann Duffield* 74
2 b f Elzaam(AUS) Zvezda (USA) (Nureyev (USA))
3261[2] ◆ 3772[9] 4685[2] ◆ 5477[4] 6162[6] 7248[3]

Peadar Miguel *Michael Mullineaux* a54 29
9 b g Danroad(AUS) La Corujera (Case Law)
2616[10]

Peak Hill *David Evans* a73 61
3 ch g Bahamian Bounty River Naiad (Nayef (USA))
434[4] 705[4] 2044[10] 3029[6] 3807[9] 4354[7] 6190[11]

Peak Princess (IRE) *Richard Hannon* 83
2 b f Foxwedge(AUS) Foot Of Pride (IRE) (Footstepsinthesand)
4885[2] ◆ (5861) 7547[6] 7698[8]

Peak Storm *John O'Shea* a69 86
7 b g Sleeping Indian Jitterbug (IRE) (Marju (IRE))
823[6] 1221[14] *1724[5]* 2460[2] 2734[5] 3124[3] 3766[4] 4086[4] 4909[2] 5545[5] 5956[3] 6316[4] 6442[2]

Pealer (GER) *John Gosden* 83
2 b c Campanologist(USA) Praia (GER) (Big Shuffle (USA))
7187[2]

Pearl Acclaim (IRE) *David Nicholls* a87 83
6 b g Acclamation With Colour (Rainbow Quest (USA))
213[3] ◆ *323[2]* ◆ *359[6]* 1672[6] 1874[3] 2261[4] 2488[10] 2863[5] 3150[4] 4100[3] 4514[3] 4831[11] 5780[4] 6080[5] 6537[7] *7206[2] 7434[8] 8010[2] 8280[8] 8403[12]*

Pearl Bridge *Zuhair Mohsen* a82 81
6 b g Avonbridge Our Little Secret (IRE) (Rossini (USA))
744a[13]

Pearl Castle (IRE) *K R Burke* a98 98
6 b g Montjeu(IRE) Ghurra (USA) (War Chant (USA))
317[5] 793[3] 1067[6] 1645[3] 2222[10]

Pearl Dragon (FR) *M Delzangles* a84 97
5 b h Nicobar La Marlia (FR) (Kaldounevees (FR))
7946a[7]

Pearl Nation (USA) *Michael Appleby* a108 95
7 b g Speightstown(USA) Happy Nation (USA) (Lear Fan (USA))
92a[10] 624a[12] 1153[5] 1478[7]

Pearl Noir *Scott Dixon* a63 72
6 b g Milk It Mick Cora Pearl (IRE) (Montjeu (IRE))
106[9] 364[8] 764[9] 784[5] (2270) 2863[6] *8078[10] 8236[11] 8474[9]*

Pearl Phoenix (FR) *John Quinn* 58
6 ch h Kendargent(FR) La Marlia (FR) (Kaldounevees (FR))
2858^{4}

Pearl Secret *David Barron* 114
7 ch h Compton Place Our Little Secret (IRE) (Rossini (USA))
2475^{4} 3244^{14} 4824^{7} 5614^{11} 6230^{6}

Pearl Spectre (USA) *Phil McEntee* a93 79
5 ch g Street Cry(IRE) Dark Sky (USA) (Storm Cat (USA))
18^{3} 215^{6} (1152) 1775^{13} 7781^{10} 7965^{6} (8052) (8083) 8176^{9} 8256^{5} 8475^{8}

Pearly Prince *Peter Hedger* a72 49
4 b g Cockney Rebel(IRE) Princess Raya (Act One)
314^{5} 710^{2} ◆ 899^{7} 2151^{3} 2996^{2} 3817^{8}

Pearly Queen *Dean Ivory* a63 57
3 b f Dutch Art Surprise (IRE) (Anabaa Blue)
4565^{4} 4939^{4} 5300^{6} 7255^{12} 7442^{12} 8026^{7} 8457^{8}

Pea Shooter *Brian Ellison* a77 87
7 b g Piccolo Sparkling Eyes (Lujain (USA))
1601^{6} 2261^{2} (2346) 4488^{2} 4896^{2} 5417^{4} 6234^{12}

Pechora (IRE) *John Gosden* a66
3 b f Sea The Stars(IRE) Bitooh (Diktat)
(818)

Pecking Order (IRE) *James Fanshawe* a94 98
4 b m Fastnet Rock(AUS) Shemaya (IRE) (Darshaan)
3785^{7} (4646) ◆ 6273a^{2} 8024a^{6}

Pedestal (IRE) *A P O'Brien* 92
2 b c Invincible Spirit(IRE) Ashley Hall (USA) (Maria's Mon (USA))
3247^{3}

Pedro Serrano (IRE) *Henry Candy* a78 51
6 b g Footstepsinthesand Shaiyadima (IRE) (Zamindar (USA))
5862^{4}

Peeps *Mark H Tompkins* a65 60
4 ch m Halling(USA) Twelfth Night (IRE) (Namid)
261^{2} 445^{6} 630^{3} 772^{2} 949^{4} 1170^{9} 1807^{5} 2995^{4} 5261^{3} 5680^{4} 6335^{8} 7905^{9} 8155^{P}

Peggy Joyce *David Barron* a37 41
3 b f Aussie Rules(USA) Ashtaroute (USA) (Holy Bull (USA))
768^{5} 892^{5} 1123^{6}

Peking Flyer (IRE) *Ed Walker* a43
2 b c Zoffany(IRE) Wing Diva (IRE) (Hawk Wing (USA))
7648^{8} 7976^{12}

Pelham Crescent (IRE) *Matthew Salaman*
13 ch g Giant's Causeway(USA) Sweet Times (Riverman (USA))
6444^{RR}

Pellucid *David Simcock* 93
2 b f Excelebration(IRE) Sky Crystal (GER) (Galileo (IRE))
(3223) 6063^{3} 6784^{5} 7667^{6}

Peloponnese (FR) *Sir Michael Stoute* 101
3 b f Montjeu(IRE) Mimalia (USA) (Silver Hawk (USA))
1860^{2} (2666) (3352) ◆ 4078^{2}

Peloton *Pat Phelan* 67
2 b f Mount Nelson Les Verguettes (IRE) (Iffraaj)
5922^{2} 6404^{3} 7209^{2} 7697^{7}

Pelvoux (FR) *W Mongil* a47 67
11 b g Diktat Thiva (USA) (Concern (USA))
5700a^{13}

Pemberley (NZ) *Ciaron Maher* 102
4 b g Darci Brahma(NZ) Upstaged (AUS) (In The Wings)
7378a^{14}

Pemberley House (IRE) *Paul D'Arcy* a50 51
2 b f Paco Boy(IRE) Geordie Iris (IRE) (Elusive City (USA))
3613^{7} 5298^{9} 5930^{6} 6420^{5} 7734^{11}

Pemina (GER) *J Hirschberger* 103
2 b f Soldier Hollow Princess Lala (GER) (Royal Dragon (USA))
6797a^{5} 7563a^{2}

Penalty (ITY) *Stefano Botti* 95
2 b c Mujahid(USA) Fidate Correnti (IRE) (Noverre (USA))
3701a^{3}

Penardini (USA) *Y Gourraud* a57 62
7 b g Bernardini(USA) Peinture Rose (USA) (Storm Cat (USA))
6938a^{3}

Pencaitland *Noel Wilson* a29 49
4 b m Champs Elysees Anthea (Tobougg (IRE))
2746^{4} 3325^{8} 3704^{6} 4724^{5} 5319^{7} 5781^{4}

Pendo *John Best* a80 80
5 b g Denounce Abundant (Zafonic (USA))
437^{5} 4956^{4} 5503^{2} 6657^{2} (7227) 7671^{10} 8011^{5} (8378)

Penelope Pitstop *Lee Smyth* a46 50
4 b m Captain Gerrard(IRE) Obsessive Secret (IRE) (Grand Lodge (USA))
2365^{2} 4314^{4} 5227^{2} 5576^{8} 6839^{2}

Penglai Pavilion (USA) *Charlie Appleby* 104
6 bb g Monsun(GER) Maiden Tower (Groom Dancer (USA))
3246^{8} 3889^{5} (6582) 7569a^{11}

Peniaphobia (IRE) *A S Cruz* 119
5 b g Dandy Man(IRE) Umlani (IRE) (Great Commotion (USA))
1104a^{3} 1911a^{13} 8330a^{3}

Penjack (FR) *G Botti* a81 59
3 b c Orpen(USA) A Ma Yen (ITY) (Doyen (IRE))
7492a^{7}

Pennerley *James Eustace* a67 69
3 b f Aqlaam Penelewey (Groom Dancer (USA))
1639^{6} 1989^{8} 2666^{3} 3318^{7} 4836^{5} 6485^{8} 7214^{5}

Pennine Warrior *Scott Dixon* a73 62
5 b g Lucky Story(USA) Discoed (Distinctly North (USA))
426^{10} 1488^{5} 1787^{10} 2047^{5} 6769^{4} 7577^{13} 7896^{10}

Pennington *Mark Johnston* a42 68
2 b c Poet's Voice Pryka (ARG) (Southern Halo (USA))
6368^{6} 6682^{5} 7318^{5} 7688^{11}

Pennsylvania Dutch *William Haggas* 81
2 b g Dutch Art Map Of Heaven (Pivotal)
(6053)

Penny Dreadful *Scott Dixon* a79 77
4 b m Piccolo Trina's Pet (Efisio)
901^{7} 969^{2} 1291^{6} 1958^{7} 2267^{3} 2875^{9} 4548^{4} 4787^{5} 7363^{6} 7644^{2} 7851^{10} 8233^{8} 8347^{6} 8571^{9}

Penny Green *James Eustace* a63 51
2 b f Halling(USA) Penelewey (Groom Dancer (USA))
2817^{8} 6874^{7} 7441^{12} 7974^{8} 8341^{6}

Penny Lane Forever *Roger Varian* 67
3 b f Pivotal Ventura Highway (Machiavellian (USA))
1392^{10} 1628^{5} 2419^{5}

Penny Pepper (IRE) *Kevin Prendergast* a84 91
4 b m Fast Company(IRE) Evening Time (IRE) (Keltos (FR))
1015a^{5} 4415a^{7} 6819a^{6} 7392a^{6} 7706a^{6}

Penny Pot Lane *Richard Whitaker* a69 75
3 b f Misu Bond(IRE) Velvet Band (Verglas (IRE))
1922^{3} 2336^{3} 2777^{P} 3603^{9} 5320^{10} 5714^{3} (5978) 6435^{2} 6878^{7} 7364^{4}

Penny Red *William Knight* a67
2 ch f Medicean Peintre D'Argent (IRE) (Peintre Celebre (USA))
7050^{5} 7761^{9}

Penny Royale *Tim Easterby* a67 75
4 b m Monsieur Bond(IRE) Royal Punch (Royal Applause)
1119^{3} 2120^{8} 2622^{5} 2974^{5} 3268^{11} 3925^{3} (4606) 4931^{6} 5535^{5} 6023^{9}

Pensax Boy *Ian Williams* a86 85
4 b g Rail Link Cyclone Connie (Dr Devious (IRE))
1775^{10} 2345^{11} (3605) 4104^{4} 4776^{4}

Pensax Lad (IRE) *Ronald Harris* a93 83
5 gr g Verglas(IRE) Betelgeuse (Kalaglow)
(106) 492^{7} 1601^{2} 2581^{5} 2787^{7} 3956^{5} 4345^{5} 4817^{3} 5408^{9} (6296) 6653^{3} 7268^{3} (7626) 7772^{11}

Pensax Lady (IRE) *Daniel Mark Loughnane* a59 48
3 b f Fast Company(IRE) Aljafliyah (Halling (USA))
145^{6} 384^{4} 675^{5} 3732^{10} 5572 ^{5} 6478^{5} 6857^{4} (6967) 7256^{6} (7910) 8125^{2} 8527^{8}

Pensierieparole *Il Cavallo In Testa* 102
4 ch g Exceed And Excel(AUS) Pursuit Of Charge (Pursuit Of Love)
2518a^{2}

Pension Madness (IRE) *Mark Usher* a58 61
3 b g Vocalised(USA) Grinneas (IRE) (Barathea (IRE))
6411^{6} 6871^{9} 7231^{4} 7767^{7}

Pentathlon (NZ) *John Wheeler* 103
4 ch g Pentire Pinders Prize (NZ) (Prized (USA))
7552a^{3} 7712a^{7} 7756a^{9}

Pentito Rap (USA) *Rod Millman* a46 50
2 b g Smart Strike(CAN) Sing Like a Bird (USA) (Lawyer Ron (USA))
4083^{7} 4363^{9} 4975^{6} 6253^{3} ◆

Penuche *Derek Shaw*
2 ch f Paco Boy(IRE) Fenella Fudge (Rock Hard Ten (USA))
4195^{8} 4759^{11} 5125^{6} 6471^{7}

Penwortham (IRE) *Richard Fahey* a79 94
3 b g Dandy Man(IRE) Portofino Bay (IRE) (Montjeu (IRE))
2095^{4} (2935) 3635^{2} 4306^{7} 5878^{8} (6276)

Peny Arcade *Alistair Whillans* a57 53
2 b f Misu Bond(IRE) Bond Royale (Piccolo)
4097^{4} 5067^{6} 5798^{5} 6678^{7} (7792)

Pepita (IRE) *Richard Hannon* a78 85
2 ch f Sir Prancealot(IRE) Esterlina (IRE) (Highest Honor (FR))
2467^{2} 2718a^{7} 3275^{2}

Pepite Noire (FR) *K Borgel* a52 74
3 ch f Redback Baileys Applause (Royal Applause)
3007a^{7}

Peppard *Charles Hills* 60
3 b f Dansili Arum Lily (USA) (Woodman (USA))
2182^{7} 4633^{4} 5308^{5} 5823^{5}

Pepparone (IRE) *Silvia Casati*
6 ch g Stormy River(FR) Lady Dettoria (FR) (Vettori (IRE))
7400a^{9}

Pepper (IRE) *Derek Shaw* a46
3 b f Elusive City(USA) Rocky Mistress (Rock Of Gibraltar (IRE))
2375^{14} 2578^{11} 3406^{7}

Peppy Miller *George Margarson* a43 30
3 b f Cockney Rebel(IRE) Solar Crystal (IRE) (Alzao (USA))
1553^{5}

Pepys *Bryan Smart* a65 68
2 b c Aqlaam Generously Gifted (Sakhee (USA))
3516^{6} 6473^{3} 6771^{5} 7286^{8} 8009^{4}

Perardua *David Evans* a63 78
4 ch m Cockney Rebel(IRE) Quiquillo (USA) (Cape Canaveral (USA))
1110^{6} 1402^{3} 1929^{7} 2146^{5}

Perceived *Henry Candy* a72 81
4 ch m Sir Percy New Light (Generous (IRE))
1825^{5} 2296^{2} 3001^{3} 3721^{2} 5650^{4} 7504^{13}

Percella *Ian Williams* a72 68
4 b m Sir Percy Temple Of Thebes (IRE) (Bahri (USA))
101^{3} ◆ (156) (261) 636^{5} 884^{3} 1552^{5}

Perceus *James Eustace* a71 89
4 b g Sir Percy Lady Hestia (USA) (Belong To Me (USA))
1598^{2} 6582^{11}

Perceysvivace *Richard Fahey* a56 66
3 b f Sir Percy Calico Moon (USA) (Seeking The Gold (USA))
1927^{4} 2269^{3} 2652^{7} 3365^{4} 3853^{5} 4375^{4} 7385^{5}

Percy (IRE) *G M Lyons* 99
2 gb c Kodiac Bysshe (Linamix (FR))
6349a^{4} 7707a^{4}

Percy B Shelley *John Gosden* a72
2 ch c Archipenko(USA) Oshiponga (Barathea (IRE))
8340^{5} ◆

Percy's Endeavour *Mark Walford* a28 33
3 b f Sir Percy Bruma (IRE) (Footstepsinthesand)
2327^{8} 2914^{8} 4235^{12} 4724^{9}

Percy's Gal *Karen Tutty* a81 81
5 ch m Sir Percy Galette (Caerleon (USA))
1030^{8} 1402^{4} 2332^{8} 3211^{9} 3553^{6} 4006^{7} 4604^{5} 4932^{4} 6216^{7} 7742^{4}

Percy's Lass *Brian Ellison* a51 60
4 gr m Sir Percy Brave Mave (Daylami (IRE))
7326^{7} 8306^{7} 8528^{9}

Percys Princess *Michael Appleby* a73 65
5 b m Sir Percy Enford Princess (Pivotal)
132^{3} 273^{5} 636^{4} 766^{6} 1002^{7} 1085^{6} 1455^{3} 2149^{2} 2564^{5} 2738^{3} 3774^{3} 4320^{5} 5795^{3} 6212^{11} 6424^{8}

Percy's Romance *Sir Michael Stoute* a76 78
3 ch f Sir Percy Top Romance (IRE) (Entrepreneur)
1750^{6} 2178^{9} 3355^{2} 5508^{2} ◆ 6193^{4}

Percy Street *K R Burke* 104
3 br c Sir Percy Star Of Gibraltar (Rock Of Gibraltar (IRE))
1567^{5} 1866^{7} 2892^{5} (3666) 4339^{6} 5699a^{9} 6559^{5} 7538^{2}

Percy's Word *Simon Crisford* a77
2 b g Sir Percy Laverre (IRE) (Noverre (USA))
(6623)

Percy Thrower (IRE) *Charles Hills* a65 63
2 ch g Sir Percy Dayrose (Daylami (IRE))
4989^{7} 5505^{4} ◆ 5952^{5} 6875^{10}

Percy Toplis *Kevin Ryan* a63 72
2 b g Kheleyf(USA) West Lorne (USA) (Gone West (USA))
1293^{3} ◆ 1520^{3} 1976^{10} 4602^{5} (4869) 5712^{10} 6007^{8} 6536^{15} 7688^{7}

Percy Veer *Sylvester Kirk* a94 91
4 ch g Sir Percy Fandangerina (Hernando (FR))
19^{5} 1987^{10} 2932^{4} 3784^{2} 4353^{5} 4752^{2} 5999^{4} 6919^{5} 7670^{5} 7979^{5} 8250^{4}

Percy Verence *K R Burke* a61 65
3 b g Sir Percy Bermondsey Girl (Bertolini (USA))
4235^{6} 4895^{3} 5178^{5} 6221^{10} 7336^{12} 7754^{5} 7937^{4} 8134^{4} 8387^{7}

Peremptory (IRE) *M A Gunn* 64
4 b m Lawman(FR) Hasty Katie (IRE) (Whipper (USA))
7391a^{16}

Perennial *Philip Kirby* a65 57
7 ch g Motivator Arum Lily (USA) (Woodman (USA))
2558^{15} 2853^{P} 3418^{4} 3704^{4} 4045^{7} 5183^{6} 6739^{5} 7044^{6} 7138^{9} 7746^{3} 7955^{6}

Perestroika *Henry Candy* 95
4 b m Sir Percy Lekka Ding (IRE) (Raise A Grand (IRE))
2024^{4} 3027^{3} 4078^{6} 5328^{2} ◆ 5851^{4}

Perfect Alchemy (IRE) *Patrick Chamings* a82 62
5 b m Clodovil(IRE) Desert Alchemy (IRE) (Green Desert (USA))
124^{2} (415) (558) 1545^{10} 2001^{2} 2821^{11} 3815^{7} 5190^{4} 5551^{8} 6426^{5} 7485^{6} 8037^{10}

Perfect Angel (IRE) *Andrew Balding* 101
2 br f Dark Angel(IRE) The Hermitage (IRE) (Kheleyf (USA))
3555^{2} (4756) 6063^{5} 6572^{2} 7155^{3} 7667^{4}

Perfect Bounty *Patrick Chamings* a63 65
4 ch m Bahamian Bounty Perfect Cover (IRE) (Royal Applause)
615^{4} 872^{10} 1139^{2}

Perfect Cracker *Clive Cox* a97 93
8 ch g Dubai Destination(USA) Perfect Story (IRE) (Desert Story (IRE))
(73) 465^{2} 767^{2} (1001) ◆ 1972^{3} 2752^{4} 3304^{7} 8317^{5} 8529^{2}

Perfect Fit (IRE) *Tony Coyle* a70 73
4 ch m Teofilo(IRE) Queen Of Lyons (USA) (Dubai Destination (USA))
133^{8} 223^{5} 591^{5}

Perfect In Pink *Mick Channon* 66
2 ch f Raven's Pass(USA) Fashion Rocks (IRE) (Rock Of Gibraltar (IRE))
6578^{5}

Perfectly Fair *Simon West* a60 50
3 b f Invincible Spirit(IRE) She Storm (IRE) (Rainbow Quest (USA))
2886^{9} 3776^{8} 4231^{9} 4517^{4} 4835^{5}

Perfectly Spirited *John Gosden* a82 50
3 b f Invincible Spirit(IRE) Design Perfection (USA) (Diesis)
6135^{4} (6960) 7550^{7}

Perfect Madge (IRE) *Kevin Ryan* 93
2 b f Acclamation Soul Mountain (IRE) (Rock Of Gibraltar (IRE))
1437^{2} ◆ 2219^{3} ◆ 3336^{14} 4394^{13} (5029) 5583^{6} 6748^{6}

Perfect Orange *Lucy Wadham* a40 69
4 ch m Sir Percy La Peinture (GER) (Peintre Celebre (USA))
3739^{9} 5090^{4}

Perfect Pastime *Jim Boyle* a65 75
8 ch g Pastoral Pursuits Puritanical (IRE) (Desert King (IRE))
1150^{7} 1549^{2} 1928^{14} 2469^{5} 3530^{5} 3953^{6} (5236) 5599^{4} 6269^{11}

Perfect Pasture *Michael Easterby* a95 112
6 b g Pastoral Pursuits Word Perfect (Diktat)
1218^{14} (1522) ◆ 1856^{7} 1993^{10} 2898^{3} (4415a) 5418^{20} 6558^{10} 7771^{2} 7997a^{9}

Perfect Peak *Michael Easterby* a61 66
4 ch m Distant Peak(IRE) Word Perfect (Diktat)
22^{11} 869^{2} 1026^{9} (1119) 1255^{3}

Perfect Quest *Clive Cox* 76
3 br f Bushranger(IRE) Love Quest (Pursuit Of Love)
1388^{4} ◆ 2011^{2} 2795^{3} 3236^{5} 4635^{5} (5254) 6485^{3}

Perfect Rhythm *Patrick Chamings* a69 60
5 b m Halling(USA) Bassinet (USA) (Stravinsky (USA))
2399^{8} 2850^{6} 3403^{6} 4880^{3} 5895^{5} 7429^{12} 7905^{4} 8448^{6}

Perfect Storm (IRE) *Ibrahim Al Malki* 87
2 b c Excelebration(IRE) Lady Miletrian (IRE) (Barathea (IRE))
8564a^{2}

Perfect Summer (IRE) *Ian Williams* a80 81
6 b m High Chaparral(IRE) Power Of Future (GER) (Definite Article)
1760^{6} 4664^{8} 4752^{12} 5642^{2}

Perfect Symphony (IRE) *Kevin Ryan* a73 76
2 b g Dandy Man(IRE) Fields Of Joy (GER) (Waky Nao)
3881^{2} 4227^{2} 4890^{3} 5583^{13} 6833^{3} (7381)

Perfect Words (IRE) *Marjorie Fife* a63 68
6 ch g Thousand Words Zilayah (USA) (Zilzal (USA))
(2052) 2523^{5} 2808^{5} 3268^{4} 3779^{3} (3925) 4257^{4} 4931^{4} 5354^{5} 5762^{4} 6216^{5} 6685^{8} 7386^{9}

Performer *Richard Hannon* a67 53
3 b f New Approach(IRE) Annalina (USA) (Cozzene (USA))
814^{2} 1392^{9} 4593^{8} 7485^{9}

Performing (IRE) *John Quinn* a48 64
2 ch g Showcasing Mansiya (Vettori (IRE))
5778^{6} 6319^{6} 6789^{3} 7228^{11} 7510^{7}

Peribsen (IRE) *F Head* 95
3 b c Lonhro(AUS) Pepiniere (IRE) (Sadler's Wells (USA))
5448a^{3} 6971a^{4}

Pericles (IRE) *Peter Chapple-Hyam* a51 54
3 ch g Danehill Dancer(IRE) Althea Rose (IRE) (Green Desert (USA))
1710^{5}

Perigee *John Gosden* 85
3 b c Cacique(IRE) Purissima (USA) (Fusaichi Pegasus (USA))
2175^{3} 2614^{2} 3066^{2} (3577)

Peril *Simon Crisford* a103 97
5 ch g Pivotal Portodora (USA) (Kingmambo (USA))
(503) 2331^{2} 7651^{14}

Periwig (IRE) *Edward Lynam* 65
3 b f Monsieur Bond(IRE) Suntory (IRE) (Royal Applause)
1014a^{13} 7474a^{P}

Perkunas (IRE) *Brian Meehan* 100
3 b g Baltic King Zafine (Zafonic (USA))
756a^{5} 4149^{5} 4624^{6}

Perla Blanca (USA) *Marcus Tregoning* a49 50
2 gr f Dalakhani(IRE) Trend Line (IRE) (Holy Roman Emperor (IRE))
6061^{8} 6570^{6} 7726^{5}

Perle De La Mer (IRE) *W McCreery* 89
2 b f Born To Sea(IRE) Law Review (IRE) (Case Law)
6815a^{5}

Permaisuri (IRE) *Kevin Ryan* a46
3 b f Sea The Stars(IRE) Puteri Wentworth (Sadler's Wells (USA))
3990^{9}

Permanent *Daniel Kubler* a50 69
2 b c Invincible Spirit(IRE) Love Everlasting (Pursuit Of Love)
3058^{11} 3808^{6} 4829^{3} 5670^{6} 6632^{8} 7749^{8}

Permera *Mark H Tompkins* a55 59
3 b f Sir Percy Four Miracles (Vettori (IRE))
2124^{5} 3318^{8} 4273^{5} 6185^{4} 6508^{4} 7309^{7} 7692^{6} 8179^{12}

Permian (IRE) *Mark Johnston* a80 99
2 b c Teofilo(IRE) Tessa Reef (IRE) (Mark Of Esteem (IRE))
(3524) 4699^{2} (5239) ◆ (5519) 5967^{5} 7151^{3}

Permission *James Fanshawe* 91
3 b f Authorized(IRE) Continua (USA) (Elusive Quality (USA))
(3411) ◆ 4105^{5} ◆ 6070a^{9} 6746^{11}

Pernickety *Lucy Wadham* a71 71
3 b f Sir Percy Nicola Bella (IRE) (Sadler's Wells (USA))
1289^{2} 4633^{3} 5089^{6} 6485^{6} 6901^{10}

Perpetual Change (IRE) *Clive Cox* 70
3 b c Pour Moi(IRE) Sallanches (USA) (Gone West (USA))
1930^{8} 2541^{8} 3769^{4} 4459^{5} 6194^{6} 7214^{10}

Perrault (IRE) *Richard Fahey* 90
4 gr g Rip Van Winkle(IRE) La Persiana (Daylami (IRE))
1972^{11} 2406^{9} 3149^{8} 3636^{9}

Persaverance *Gary Moore* a62 65
3 b g Sir Percy Marliana (IRE) (Mtoto)
1529^{6} 1931^{9} 2640^{4} 3033^{6} 4942^{7} 6654^{7}

Persephone (IRE) *Paul Cole* a51
2 b f Kodiac Demeter (USA) (Diesis)
7277^{6}

Persian Breeze *Lucy Wadham* a71 82
4 b m Pivotal Persian Jasmine (Dynaformer (USA))
2965^{5} 3641^{4}

Persian Steel (IRE) *Brian Ellison* a56
4 ch g Lucarno(USA) Persian Walk (FR) (Persian Bold)
8481^{7} 8585^{4}

Persona Grata *Ed Walker* a98 103
5 b m Sir Percy Kaldounya (Kaldoun (FR))
1886^{8} 2363^{9} 2893^{P} 5384a^{5} 6107a^{2} 6693a^{4} 7566a^{5} 7929a^{6}

Personal Diary (USA) *Victoria H Oliver* a97 102
5 ch m City Zip(USA) Latest Scoop (USA) (Tiznow (USA))
5430a^{9}

Personal Touch *Michael Appleby* a84 84
7 ch g Pivotal Validate (Alhaarth (IRE))
1848^{7} 2247^{12} 3133^{6} 3646^{3} ◆ 3980^{8} 5301^{5} 5858^{5} 7112^{12} 7434^{5} 8037^{5} 8205^{6} 8239^{4} 8345^{4}

Perspicace *David Pipe* a69 62
5 b g Sir Percy Cassique Lady (IRE) (Langfuhr (CAN))
3639^{10}

Persuasive (IRE) *John Gosden* a98 113
3 gr f Dark Angel(IRE) Choose Me (IRE) (Choisir (AUS))
(2431) (2789) ◆ (3274) (5645) 6352a^{2}

Persun *Mick Channon* 89
4 ch m Sir Percy Sunley Shines (Komaite (USA))
2868^{7} 3438^{3} 5956^{7} 6549^{4} 6948^{4} 7222^{5} 7669^{2}

Pertuis (IRE) *Micky Hammond* a70 70
10 gr g Verglas(IRE) Lady Killeen (IRE) (Marju (IRE))
1560^{9} 1955^{6} 2558^{3} (3325) 4409^{8}

Peru *Hugo Palmer* a76 90
3 b f Motivator Bolsena (USA) (Red Ransom (USA))
1890^{6} 2220^{6} (4556) 5158^{12}

Perusal (IRE) *Jonathan Portman* a49
3 b f Sir Percy Overlook (Generous (IRE))
44^{7} 1149^{6}

Petanca (FR) *Yannick Fouin* a30 46
2 b f Trajano(USA) Minerva (FR) (Muhtathir)
7970a^{10}

Petard (FR) *F Doumen* a41 27
2 b c Kentucky Dynamite(USA) Pretty As Can Be (Giant's Causeway (USA))
3871a^{16}

Peter Anders *Zuhair Mohsen* a57 81
7 b h Pivotal Astorg (USA) (Lear Fan (USA))
757a^{16}

Peterhouse (USA) *Jason Ward* a76 87
4 ch g Elusive Quality(USA) Dynaire (USA) (Dynaformer (USA))
465^{9} 779^{7} 1633^{6} 1923^{9} *2328^{6}* 2743^{3} 3252^{2} 3481^{3} 5292^{4} 6165^{2} 6794^{2} 7498^{7}

Peter Park *Clive Cox* a69 75
3 b g Kheleyf(USA) Go Go Girl (Pivotal)
3111^{8} 3976^{4} (4517) 4985^{6} 6190^{3} 6831^{8}

Pete So High (GER) *Richard Hannon* a76 43
2 b g High Chaparral(IRE) Paulaya (GER) (Peintre Celebre (USA))
7501^{10} *7908^{4} 8246^{2}* ◆ *8537^{2}*

Peticoatgovernment (IRE) *W McCreery* a69 86
3 b f Holy Roman Emperor(IRE) Fotini (IRE) (King's Best (USA))
4415a^{6} 6819a^{8} 7191a^{10}

Petit Ecuyer (FR) *Dai Williams* 3
10 b g Equerry(USA) Petite Majeste (FR) (Riverquest (FR))
3747^{9}

Petite Jack *Neil King* a95 47
3 ch g Champs Elysees Pilcomayo (IRE) (Rahy (USA))
2826^{5} *(3653) 4013^{6}* 6268^{8} *(7653) (8162)*

Petit Filous *Giles Bravery* a62 59
2 b g Equiano(FR) Haiti Dancer (Josr Algarhoud (IRE))
7495^{6} *8277^{3} 8404^{2}*

Petit Prince (FR) *Charley Rossi* 68
3 bb g Silver Frost(IRE) Parisella (IRE) (Key Of Luck (USA))
2287a^{3}

Petrify *Bernard Llewellyn* a62 60
6 b g Rock Of Gibraltar(IRE) Frigid (Indian Ridge)
2370^{3} 2634^{7} 2850^{7} (4082) (4294) 4592^{2} 4913^{4} 6001^{5}

Petrucci (IRE) *Derek Shaw* a67 71
4 b g Azamour(IRE) Spring Symphony (IRE) (Darshaan)
2377^{4} 7535^{19} *7869^{13} 8077^{11} 8286^{10} 8476^{5}*

Pettochside *John Bridger* a68 83
7 b g Refuse To Bend(IRE) Clear Impression (IRE) (Danehill (USA))
1928^{4} 2396^{2} (2469) 2931^{3} 4051^{3} 4355^{2} 6195^{3} 6668^{2} (6883)

Petunia (IRE) *C Laffon-Parias* a56 59
3 b f Pivotal Esneh (IRE) (Sadler's Wells (USA))
8024a^{15}

Pevensey (IRE) *Jacqueline Coward* a51 59
14 b g Danehill(USA) Champaka (IRE) (Caerleon (USA))
4234^{5} 4730^{8} 4934^{9}

Phalaborwa *Ed Vaughan* a80 60
2 b f Poet's Voice Sigurwana (USA) (Arch (USA))
5371^{5} *(6414)*

Phantom Dancer (IRE) *Alan Swinbank* a31 62
4 gr m Arakan(USA) Zibaline (FR) (Linamix (FR))
1379^{2} *1708^{3}* 2048^{9}

Phantom Flipper *David Nicholls* a72 76
3 ch c Bahamian Bounty Artistic License (IRE) (Chevalier (IRE))
126^{4} 268^{2} 496^{2} 507^{2} 582^{2} 668^{2} 798^{2} 935^{6} 1788^{10}

Phantomine (IRE) *Brendan Powell*
4 br m Jeremy(USA) Phantom Waters (Pharly (FR))
6661^{8}

Phantom River *Alan King* a69 69
4 b m Observatory(USA) Madam'X (Xaar)
1825^{4} 2369^{4} 2860^{4} 3498^{3} 4294^{7}

Pharmaceutical (IRE) *Stuart Williams* a85 88
4 b g Invincible Spirit(IRE) Pharmacist (IRE) (Machiavellian (USA))
1887^{16} 2430^{3} 2934^{4} 3414^{4}

Pharoh Jake *John Bridger* a67 67
8 ch g Piccolo Rose Amber (Double Trigger (IRE))
658^{2} 669^{3} 873^{5} 1150^{5} 1533^{9} *(1833)* 2584^{2} *3316^{5}* (3559) 3811^{3} *4529^{2}* 5827^{5} 6269^{5} 7018^{11} *7964^{4} 8365^{4} 8430^{4} 8596^{3}*

Phedre *S Wattel* 85
3 b f Rock Of Gibraltar(IRE) Piping (IRE) (Montjeu (IRE))
7456a^{10}

Phijee *William Muir* 95
2 bg c Sepoy(AUS) Likeable (Dalakhani (IRE))
4053^{2} ◆ (4678) (5416)

Philadelphia (IRE) *Roger Varian* a70 83
3 b g Roderic O'Connor(IRE) Harvest Joy (IRE) (Daggers Drawn (USA))
824^{4} (1217) 2179^{9} 3957^{3} 4953^{4} 5649^{8} *6416^{10}*

Philba *Michael Appleby* a99 68
4 b g Cockney Rebel(IRE) Hisaronu (IRE) (Stravinsky (USA))
(50) ◆ *134^{2} (599) 960^{4} 1153^{6} 7530^{10} 8049^{7} 8475^{2}*

Phileas Fogg (IRE) *Martyn Meade* a66
3 b g Arcano(IRE) Ava's World (IRE) (Desert Prince (IRE))
6511^{4} 7102^{8} 7942^{6} 8085^{7}

Philosopher (IRE) *S bin Ghadayer* a92 98
4 ch g Shamardal(USA) Philae (USA) (Seeking The Gold (USA))
8578a^{6}

Phoceen (FR) *F Chappet* 89
2 b c Myboycharlie(IRE) Atlantic Slew (FR) (Helissio (FR))
3871a^{4} 5450a^{6}

Phoenix Beat *Gay Kelleway* a50 71
3 b f Phoenix Reach(IRE) Beat Seven (Beat Hollow)
984^{5} $1357a^{3}$ 1859^{6} 2586^{2} 2824^{2} 3496^{2} 4025^{4} 4596^{4}

Phoenix Dawn *Brendan Powell* 71
2 b g Phoenix Reach(IRE) Comtesse Noire (CAN) (Woodman (USA))
2478^{5} 3058^{12} 3495^{2} 4595^{5} 6875^{8} (7416) 7768^{2}

Phosphorescence (IRE) *George Scott* a66 77
6 b g Sakhee(USA) Eccentricity (USA) (Kingmambo (USA))
(6231)

Photo Call (IRE) *Todd Pletcher* a79 115
5 b m Galileo(IRE) Theann (Rock Of Gibraltar (IRE))
3119a^{6} (7171a) 7837a^{13}

Phu Hai (FR) *V Luka Jr* a96 90
7 b g Elusive City(USA) Piste Sauvage (IRE) (Brief Truce (USA))
7525a^{6}

Phyllis Maud (IRE) *Simon Crisford* a81 81
4 ch m Halling(USA) Debonnaire (Anabaa (USA))
165^{5}

Physicist (IRE) *Paul Cole* 70
2 b g Galileo(IRE) Impressionist Art (USA) (Giant's Causeway (USA))
7003^{3}

Piaffe (USA) *Ralph Beckett* a13
2 b f Successful Appeal(USA) Palisade (USA) (Gone West (USA))
8464^{9}

Piazon *John Butler* a82 91
5 br g Striking Ambition Colonel's Daughter (Colonel Collins (USA))
1444^{12} 2016^{14} 2531^{8} 3137^{5} 3892^{7} *4714^{8} 6235^{5}* 7584^{5} *8030^{3} (8242) (8474) 8571^{2}*

Piazza San Pietro *Zoe Davison* a46 47
10 ch g Compton Place Rainbow Spectrum (FR) (Spectrum (IRE))
1549^{6} 1945^{7} 2584^{9} 3822^{10}

Picansort *Peter Crate* a74 62
9 b g Piccolo Running Glimpse (IRE) (Runnett)
56^{5} 319^{9} 775^{7} (1150) 1950^{5} 2584^{15} *2768^{3}* 3260^{2} *3317^{2}* 5105^{6} 6269^{12} 7302^{9} *7964^{6} (8429)*

Piccacard *Michael Appleby* a49 51
3 b f Piccolo All Business (Entrepreneur)
48^{4} 3473^{8} 3838^{8} 4258^{6}

Piccardo *Richard Fahey* a28 64
3 ch g Piccolo Billiard (Kirkwall)
1789^{8} 2571^{10} 3069^{13}

Piccola Poppy *John Bridger* a33 40
3 br f Piccolo Waraqa (USA) (Red Ransom (USA))
7219^{5} *7616^{11}*

Piccolilly *Derek Shaw* a4
3 b f Piccolo Dancing Duo (Groom Dancer (USA))
7782^{6} 7856^{5}

Piccolino *John David Riches*
2 b f Piccolo Miacarla (Forzando)
4451^{12} 5536^{7}

Pichola Dance (IRE) *Roger Varian* a77 93
2 ch f Distorted Humor(USA) Liffey Dancer (IRE) (Sadler's Wells (USA))
4147^{4} *(6413)* (6787) 7114^{10} 7547^{3}

Pick A Little *Michael Blake* a72 75
8 b g Piccolo Little Caroline (IRE) (Great Commotion (USA))
788^{9} 1041^{11} 1545^{7} 1916^{8} *2378^{8}* 2734^{4} 3491^{2} *4008^{3}* 5017^{2} 5674^{5} (6184) 7301^{13} *7691^{6} 8037^{7} 8240^{5}*

Pickapocket (IRE) *Andrew Balding* a71 68
3 b c Fast Company(IRE) Ann's Annie (IRE) (Alzao (USA))
400^{2} 1027^{3}

Pickering *Denis Quinn* a49
3 b g Kheleyf(USA) Bella Chica (IRE) (Bigstone (IRE))
350^{5} 765^{8} 880^{6}

Picket Line *Geoffrey Deacon* a80 77
4 b g Multiplex Dockside Strike (Dockside (USA))
561^{5} 955^{5} (1419) 1648^{2} 2028^{5} 2846^{9} *3780^{2}* 4990^{9} *7738^{7}*

Pickett's Charge *Richard Guest* a71 72
3 b g Clodovil(IRE) Chelsea Morning (USA) (Giant's Causeway (USA))
2269^{4} 3224^{4} 5478^{3} 5860^{8} 6643^{8} *7435^{6} 8092^{11} 8586^{2}*

Pick Of Any (IRE) *Tony Carroll* a43 67
3 b g Zoffany(IRE) Choice Pickings (IRE) (Among Men (USA))
8149^{8} 8474^{10}

Picks Pinta *John David Riches* a55 70
5 b g Piccolo Past 'N' Present (Cadeaux Genereux)
424^{9} 680^{9} 1595^{3} 2092^{3} 2416^{3} 2660^{3} 3210^{8} 4544^{5} 5535^{2} (6008) 6836^{5}

Pick Your Battle *Iain Jardine* a71 72
4 b g Makfi Saphira's Fire (IRE) (Cape Cross (IRE))
1502^{2} (1696) 1805^{7}

Pick Your Choice *William Haggas* a91 97
4 b g Elusive Quality(USA) Enticement (Montjeu (IRE))
(3622)

Pictograph (USA) *Charlie Appleby* a74 19
3 b g Lonhro(AUS) Puppet Queen (USA) (Kingmambo (USA))
314^{3}

Picture Dealer *Lydia Pearce* a99 75
7 b g Royal Applause Tychy (Suave Dancer (USA))
5678^{8} 6627^{10} 7737^{9} 8176^{10} 8380^{8}

Picture Painter (IRE) *Jim Goldie* 73
3 gr g Zoffany(IRE) Sisceal (Dalakhani (IRE))
1381^{3} 1992^{12} 2909^{12} 3920^{5} 4769^{4} 5227^{7} 5923^{5}

Piedita (IRE) *Sir Mark Prescott Bt* a53 66
2 b f Authorized(IRE) Archina (IRE) (Arch (USA))
6336^{5} *7050^{8}* 7441^{7}

Pierre Precieuse (FR) *E Caroux* a54 66
4 b m Vertigineux(FR) Poca De Gracia (IRE) (Royal Applause)
7806a^{7}

Pieta (FR) *J-P Gallorini* 54
2 ch f No Risk At All(FR) Princesse Gallo (FR) (Bering)
6639a^{12}

Pietrafiore (IRE) *H-A Pantall* a89 96
3 ch f Dubawi(IRE) Porto Roca (AUS) (Barathea (IRE))
2009^{4} 2483^{3} *(2783)* ◆ 7348a^{5} 7998a^{5} *8563a^{10}*

Pike Corner Cross (IRE) *Ed de Giles* a89 72
4 b g Cape Cross(IRE) Smart Coco (USA) (Smarty Jones (USA))
607^{9} 777^{2} 951^{2} 1340^{4} 2153^{5} (2577) 3817^{2} 4377^{7} 4774^{3} 5057^{3} *(5503)* 6231^{6} *6657^{7} 7457^{5} (8011)* ◆ *(8101) 8478^{12}*

Pilgrims Path *Scott Dixon* a60 55
3 b g Sakhee(USA) Scrooby Baby (Mind Games)
1670^{7} 2118^{3} *2559^{4}* 3549^{5} 4006^{9}

Pilgrims Rest (IRE) *George Baker* a17 88
7 ch g Rock Of Gibraltar(IRE) Holly Blue (Bluebird (USA))
1531^{6}

Pillard (FR) *Jonjo O'Neill* 67
4 b g Muhaymin(USA) Ultime Moment (IRE) (Anabaa (USA))
1830^{3}

Pillar Of Society (IRE) *Richard Hannon* 75
2 b g Roderic O'Connor(IRE) Specific (IRE) (Dubawi (IRE))
3058^{7} 3598^{6} 6439^{2} 7072^{2}

Pilote (IRE) *S bin Ghadayer* 108
6 ch h Pivotal Legerete (USA) (Rahy (USA))
93a^{13} 283a^{5} 538a^{4} 812a^{10}

Pina *Roger Charlton* a50 77
3 b f Dansili Bourbonella (Rainbow Quest (USA))
1622^{6} 2545^{5} 4279^{5} (4794) 5629^{3} (6485)

Pinch A Kiss *Jonathan Portman* a40 66
3 ch f Sakhee's Secret Pin Cushion (Pivotal)
1257^{9} 2968^{8}

Pincheck (IRE) *Luca Cumani* 71
2 b c Invincible Spirit(IRE) Arty Crafty (USA) (Arch (USA))
6777^{5} 7283^{8} 7740^{5}

Pindaric *Alan Lockwood* 68
2 ch g Poet's Voice Hunter's Fortune (USA) (Charismatic (USA))
6952^{7} 7331^{6} 7740^{7}

Pine Ridge *Clive Cox* 82
3 b f Elusive City(USA) Fisadara (Nayef (USA))
1935^{5} 2981^{7} 3512^{3} (4502) (5305) 6114^{8} 6318^{3}

Pink Courageous (FR) *B Legros* a43 42
5 gr m Kouroun(FR) Pink Cloud (FR) (Octagonal (NZ))
6938a^{12}

Pinkie Brown (FR) *Neil Mulholland* a74 36
4 gr g Gentlewave(IRE) Natt Musik (FR) (Kendor (FR))
5023^{10} 5486^{11} *8366^{3}*

Pink Lips *Neil Mulholland* a59 67
8 b m Noverre(USA) Primrose Queen (Lear Fan (USA))
62^{8}

Pink Martini (IRE) *Joseph Tuite* a76 78
3 b f Tagula(IRE) Ohwhatalady (IRE) (Invincible Spirit (IRE))
(83) 515^{6} (726) 881^{3} 3815^{8} 4093^{4} 4502^{8} (4952) 5103^{3} 5379^{6} 5960^{5} 6340^{5} *6699^{7}* 7303^{5} *7485^{8}*

Pink Paint (FR) *M Delcher Sanchez* 75
2 b f Redoute's Choice(AUS) Peinture Rose (USA) (Storm Cat (USA))
6937a^{4} 7346a^{2}

Pink Ribbon (IRE) *Sylvester Kirk* a72 74
4 b g Dark Angel(IRE) My Funny Valentine (IRE) (Mukaddamah (USA))
212^{5} 1947^{6} 2645^{2} (2872) 3230^{5} 3817^{7} 4383^{3} (5207) 5650^{5} (5925) 6549^{5} 7418^{7} *7973^{4}*

Pinotage *Peter Niven* a67 53
8 br g Danbird(AUS) Keen Melody (USA) (Sharpen Up)
150^{2} (199) ◆ *329^{3} 637^{5} 786^{6}*

Pinstripe *Luca Cumani* a70 68
3 br c Dansili Paisley (Pivotal)
2012^{6} 2652^{4} 3348^{4} *3991^{8} 4942^{3}*

Pintle's Image *John Spearing* a40 51
4 b m Paco Boy(IRE) Pintle (Pivotal)
3720^{6} 4289^{15} *7427^{7}*

Pintura *Alistair Whillans* a85 98
9 ch g Efisio Picolette (Piccolo)
2527^{3} (3923) 4448^{12} 4921a^{13} 6225^{10} 7573^{10}

Pinwood (IRE) *Adam West* a70 80
3 b g Bushranger(IRE) Anne Bonney (Jade Robbery (USA))
5765^{11} 6242^{4} 6665^{10} *6965^{7}*

Pinzolo *Ismail Mohammed* a108 98
5 b g Monsun(GER) Pongee (Barathea (IRE))
317^{3} 793^{4} 3387^{10} 4115^{5} 4583^{3} 7188^{3} *8160^{5} (8424)*

Pioneering (IRE) *Charlie Appleby* 64
2 b g Shamardal(USA) Oregon Trail (USA) (Gone West (USA))
5990^{5} 6523^{6}

Pipe Dreamer *Kevin Ryan* a33 47
2 ch g Piccolo Card Games (First Trump)
7741^{10} *7988^{13}*

Piper Bill *Jim Goldie* 16
5 b g Halling(USA) Murielle (Diktat)
3919^{4} 4935^{11} *6103^{7}* 6839^{6} 7096^{9}

Pipers Note *Ruth Carr* a100 108
6 ch g Piccolo Madam Valentine (Primo Valentino (IRE))
1644^{12} 3250^{3} 4667^{10} 4860^{4} 5418^{4} (6012) 6327^{9} 7156^{4} 7358^{9}

Pipers Piping (IRE) *Mandy Rowland* a57 48
10 b g Noverre(USA) Monarchy (IRE) (Common Grounds)
328^{3} 334^{6} 590^{6} 985^{2} 1556^{6} 2448^{8} 3731^{8} 4234^{13} 4369^{8} *(8500)*

Pipes Of Peace (IRE) *A P O'Brien* 96
2 b c Galileo(IRE) Coachella (Danehill (USA))
7559a^{5}

Pique Sous (FR) *W P Mullins* a71 98
9 gr g Martaline Six Fois Sept (FR) (Epervier Bleu)
3246^{7}

Pirandello *A Fabre* a69 77
2 b c Invincible Spirit(IRE) Taranto (Machiavellian (USA))
7588a^{5}

Pirate Look (IRE) *Marco Botti* a78 76
2 b c Canford Cliffs(IRE) Gerika (FR) (Galileo (IRE))
(7741) *8132^{3}*

Pirate's Cove (IRE) *A Fabre* a86 88
3 b g Dubawi(IRE) Dunnes River (USA) (Danzig (USA))
(6911a)

Pirate's Treasure *James Tate* a86 49
3 b c Iffraaj Musical Sands (Green Desert (USA))
145^{3} (522) (678) (1155) ◆ 1602^{10} *2565^{4} 3605^{3}*

Pirouette *Hughie Morrison* a69 105
3 ch f Pivotal Passiflora (Night Shift (USA))
(2341) (4042) ◆ 4624^{2} 5158^{3} 5645^{5} 6746^{2}

Piscar D'Olhos (FR) *N Caullery* a58 69
2 ch c Naaqoos Direction Home (USA) (Gone West (USA))
7588a^{11}

Pistoletto (SPA) *N Caullery* a72 72
5 b h Green Tune(USA) Ishi Adiva (Ishiguru (USA))
5501a^{5}

Pitch High (IRE) *Julia Feilden* 65
2 br g Requinto(IRE) Distant Skies (Tiger Hill (IRE))
4270^{4} 4738^{7} 6404^{7} 7286^{13}

Pit Stop (IRE) *S bin Ghadayer* a89 86
5 b h Iffraaj Journey's End (IRE) (In The Wings)
188a^{6} 722a^{5}

Pivoine (IRE) *Sir Michael Stoute* a79 64
2 b c Redoute's Choice(AUS) Fleur De Cactus (IRE) (Montjeu (IRE))
6945^{3} *(7458)* ◆

Pivotal Dream (IRE) *Mark Brisbourne* a53 52
3 br f Excellent Art Oasis Fire (IRE) (Oasis Dream)
274^{6} 1551^{8} 2590^{12} 3906^{6} 4764^{3} 5019^{4} 5101^{6} *5604^{5}* 5710^{3} 6407^{8} *6966^{4} 8194^{6} 8411^{5} 8500^{4}*

Pivotal Flame (IRE) *James Tate* a67 74
3 b f Pivotal Saadiah (IRE) (Dubai Destination (USA))
(863) 1185^{7} 3652^{5} (5010) 5629^{4} *6901^{12}*

Pivotal Rio (IRE) *F Boccardelli* 69
4 ch g Captain Rio Luvmedo (IRE) (One Cool Cat (USA))
7840a^{7}

Pivot Bridge *Adrian McGuinness* a77 76
8 ch g Pivotal Specifically (USA) (Sky Classic (CAN))
208a^{4}

Pivotman *Michael Easterby* a85 74
8 ch g Pivotal Grandalea (Grand Lodge (USA))
1247^{2} 1785^{8} 2662^{9} 3166^{17} *3605^{6}* 4113^{12} *4717^{5}* 4933^{7} *5810^{7}* 6434^{4} (7078) *7886^{7} 8100^{2}*

Pixel (IRE) *Denis Quinn* a46 55
3 b f Rip Van Winkle(IRE) Hadarama (IRE) (Sinndar (IRE))
2312^{7} 3194^{10} *7529^{11} 7760^{7} 7987^{7} 8359^{10} 8488^{6}*

Pixeleen *Malcolm Saunders* a78 92
4 b m Pastoral Pursuits Ballyalla (Mind Games)
1237^{5} 2754^{2} 3068^{2} 3575^{3} 4460^{2} 4910^{2} 5955^{3} 6946^{2} 7146^{8}

Placedela Concorde *Anthony Carson* 58
3 b g Champs Elysees Kasakiya (IRE) (Zafonic (USA))
1639^{9} 2008^{11} 2548^{8} *5079^{P}*

Place Des Ternes (FR) *M Boutin* a63 65
3 ch f Evasive Vocatine (IRE) (Royal Applause)
128a^{5}

Placere (IRE) *Richard Brabazon* a31 69
8 ch m Noverre(USA) Puppet Play (IRE) (Broken Hearted)
5900a^{9}

Plage Depampelonne *James Bethell* a50 41
2 gr f Redoute's Choice(AUS) Arabescatta (Monsun (GER))
5966^{9} 7494^{13}

Plagiarism (USA) *Mark Johnston* 91
3 b f Lonhro(AUS) Journalist (IRE) (Night Shift (USA))
1865^{9} 2267^{9} 2683^{5} 3056^{3} 3573^{7} 4051^{7}

Plain Ambition *Dr Jeremy Naylor*
5 b m Striking Ambition Sweet Request (Best Of The Bests (IRE))
1256^{8}

Planchart (USA) *Andrew Slattery* a76 98
3 b f Gio Ponti(USA) Tarrip (USA) (Green Desert (USA))
3539a^{5} (4812a) 5939a^{8} 6383a^{5} 7392a^{13}

Plane Song (IRE) *Alan Swinbank* 84
4 ch g Nayef(USA) Kitty Hawk (Danehill Dancer (IRE))
1221^{10} 2556^{8} (3263) 3520^{11} 5434^{3} 6517^{8}

Planetaria (IRE) *Garry Moss* a84 84
3 b g Lilbourne Lad(IRE) Red Planet (Pivotal)
1155^{3} ◆ 1671^{6} (2306) 2674^{2} (3285) 4232^{2} 4769^{2} 6344^{9} 6956^{3} 7623^{8} *7796^{2}* ◆

Planetoid (IRE) *Jim Best* a86 85
8 b g Galileo(IRE) Palmeraie (USA) (Lear Fan (USA))
(1177) 2782^{5} *3784^{6}* 4077^{13} 4752^{5} 5176^{2} 6582^{10} 7158^{10}

Plantagenet (SPA) *Niels Petersen* a96 96
9 ch h Trade Fair Crafty Buzz (USA) (Crafty Prospector (USA))
281a^{2} 627a^{7} 722a^{7}

Plantation (IRE) *Robert Cowell* a46 53
3 b g Invincible Spirit(IRE) Matula (IRE) (Halling (USA))
4278^{12} 5335^{3} ◆ 5920^{6} *6587^{9} 7463^{10}*

Plant Pot Power (IRE) *Richard Hannon* a85 84
2 b c Lawman(FR) Featherweight (IRE) (Fantastic Light (USA))
3859^{3} 4989^{8} 5356^{7} (5847) 6575^{8} *(7460) 7909^{5}*

Plata O Plomo *Tony Coyle* 86
2 ch g Paco Boy(IRE) Branston Gem (So Factual (USA))
(2611) 3295^{11} 4091^{3}

Platitude *Sir Michael Stoute* a74 110
3 b g Dansili Modesta (IRE) (Sadler's Wells (USA))
1994^{4} 3300^{2} 4059^{2} 4753^{8} (5872) 6917^{3}

Platon *G E Mikhalides* 82
2 ch c Zamindar(USA) Sanada (IRE) (Priolo (USA))
4620a^{4}

Plato's Kode (IRE) *Seamus Durack* a62 65
2 b g Kodiac Speedy Sonata (USA) (Stravinsky (USA))
3463[3] 3971[6] 7071[5] 7467[8] 7750[8]

Plauseabella *Stuart Kittow* a32 65
5 b m Royal Applause Ellablue (Bahamian Bounty)
2401[4] 3096[2] 3974[7] 4589[6] 5627[7] (6337) 6893[8]

Playboy Bay *Ron Barr* 43
4 b g Indesatchel(IRE) Dim Ofan (Petong)
1953[7] 2307[6] 3013[11] 3366[11] 4424[12] 4724[11] 5517[7]

Playful Dude (USA) *Phil McEntee* a63 50
3 b g Drosselmeyer(USA) Choice Play (USA) (Vindication (USA))
139[3] 428[4] 2640[7] 3896[8] 6700[11] 7057[6] 8500[2] 8570[2]

Playful Sound *Sir Michael Stoute* 98
3 b f Street Cry(IRE) Giants Play (USA) (Giant's Causeway (USA))
(3194) (4668) (6277) ◆ 7119[8]

Playful Trickster (IRE) *Tom Dascombe* a58 51
2 br f Intikhab(USA) Anyaas (IRE) (Green Desert (USA))
1086[2] 1719[7] 2612[5] 4404[3]

Play Gal *David Evans* 88
3 b f Multiplex Plead (FR) (Bering)
1966[5] 2394[3] 3060[6]

Play It Again Tom (FR) *Mlle K Hoste* 63
3 b g Panis(USA) Kestria (IRE) (Keltos (FR))
4220a[9]

Play Nicely *David Barron* a96 83
4 ch g Naaqoos Aalya (IRE) (Peintre Celebre (USA))
(53) 132[2] (447) ◆ (800) 1250[11] 1633[9] (1923) 6134[5] 6517[2] 7229[4] 7535[12]

Play The Blues (IRE) *Henry Tett* a55 67
9 gr m Refuse To Bend(IRE) Paldouna (IRE) (Kaldoun (FR))
876[4] 1145[5] 1263[7] 4505[8] 7427[11] 8070[9]

Play The Game (IRE) *John C McConnell* 104
3 b c Lawman(FR) Neutral (Beat Hollow)
1370a[7]

Playtothewhistle *Bryan Smart* a74 68
5 b g Sakhee's Secret Prima Ballerina (Pivotal)
5114[2] 6095[2]

Plead *Archie Watson* a72 66
2 ch f Dutch Art Entreat (Pivotal)
6624[8] 6897[8] 7285[2] 8131[3] (8227)

Pleadings (USA) *Charlie Wallis* a44
3 ch g Street Cry(IRE) Say No Now (IRE) (Refuse To Bend (IRE))
7311[11] 7782[5] 7815[6] 8457[9] 8572[11]

Pleasant Flight (FR) *D Windrif* a70 62
5 ch g Redback Silent Flight (FR) (Sicyos (USA))
512a[3]

Pleascach (IRE) *J S Bolger* 116
4 b m Teofilo(IRE) Toirneach (USA) (Thunder Gulch (USA))
6988a[2] ◆

Pleaseletmewin (IRE) *Ralph Beckett* a82 106
2 b g Power Jacaranda Ridge (Indian Ridge)
2390[4] ◆ (2779) 3408[3] (4148) 4732[4] 7148[7] (7544)

Pleasemetoo (IRE) *A Fabre* 100
3 b f Vale Of York(IRE) Shakeyourbody (USA) (Giant's Causeway (USA))
1581a[6]

Pleasure Dome *Peter Chapple-Hyam* a75 90
3 b f Makfi Nouvelle Lune (Fantastic Light (USA))
1609[6] 2395[2] ◆ 3060[7] 3578[3] 4633[2] 5353[2] (6049) (6457) (6767) 7215[4]

Pleasure Requested (IRE) *Eve Johnson Houghton* a46
2 b c Acclamation Ribot's Guest (IRE) (Be My Guest (USA))
7733[13] 8082[11] 8237[10]

Plein Air (IRE) *Stefano Botti* 102
3 b f Manduro(GER) Too In Love (IRE) (Galileo (IRE))
7566a[4]

Plenary (USA) *Jeremy Noseda* a75 73
3 ch g Kitten's Joy(USA) Southern Alibi (USA) (Elusive Quality (USA))
2414[2] 3028[2] 3359[4] 5366[2] 6192[4] 7280[8]

Plethon (GER) *S Smrczek*
2 b g It's Gino(GER) Pakama (GER) (Kalatos (GER))
4187a[8]

Pleuven (FR) *Philip A Sims* 110
5 bb g Turtle Bowl(IRE) Under Estimated (FR) (Singspiel (IRE))
7172a[6]

Plougastel (ITY) *A Marcialis* a82 87
3 b c Pounced(USA) Piazzetta (ITY) (Zamindar (USA))
(3546a)

Plough Boy (IRE) *Garvan Donnelly* a85 88
5 b g Dandy Man(IRE) Ribald (Alhaarth (IRE))
4748a[5] 5941a[10] 6320[5]

Plover *Michael Attwater* a64 45
6 b m Oasis Dream Short Dance (USA) (Hennessy (USA))
155[6] 602[5] 898[8]

Plucky Dip *John Ryan* a89 90
5 b g Nayef(USA) Plucky (Kyllachy)
694[6] 923[11] 1090[2] 1205[DSQ] 1929[5] 1990[8] (2677) 2862[2] 4109[4] 4402[8] 4599[3] 4758[7] 5174[10] 6529[3] 7308[5] 7462[2] 7530[4] 7825[14] 8083[3] 8311[4] 8380[2]

Plunder *Alan Berry* a44 36
6 ch g Zamindar(USA) Reaching Ahead (USA) (Mizzen Mast (USA))
135[6] 418[11]

Plus Night (FR) *Stuart Williams* a76
3 b c Exceed And Excel(AUS) Two Pass (IRE) (Mtoto)
7725[3] ◆ 8163[3] 8378[3] 8490[4]

Plusquemavie (IRE) *V Fazio* 106
5 b h Kheleyf(USA) Kathy Pekan (IRE) (Sri Pekan (USA))
(2518a) 3796a[6]

Plutocracy (IRE) *Gary Moore* a97 95
6 b g Dansili Private Life (FR) (Bering)
194[5] 530[4] 747[4] 2024[3] ◆ 2482[3] 4583[4] 5145[6] 5964[7] 6854[4] 7980[3] (8447)

Plymouth Mo *Rod Millman* a49
3 b g Hellvelyn Welcome Home (Most Welcome)
219[10] 423[5] 697[5] 3003[12]

Plymouth Sound *Eve Johnson Houghton* a84 84
4 b g Fastnet Rock(AUS) Shardette (IRE) (Darshaan)
1716[8] 2214[6] 4055[11] 4940[4] 5724[3] 6065[2] 6676[5] 7869[9]

Pobbles *Roger Charlton* a68
2 b f Medicean Oystermouth (Averti (IRE))
6625[9] 7762[7] 8081[5] 8244[6] 8466[9]

Pocket *James Eustace* a48 36
3 b f Paco Boy(IRE) Take The Plunge (Benny The Dip (USA))
1484[9] 1705[8]

Pocketfullofdreams (FR) *David Wachman* 88
2 b f Invincible Spirit(IRE) Dubai Rose (Dubai Destination (USA))
5937a[5]

Poeta Diletto *Stefano Botti* 102
3 ch c Poet's Voice Mia Diletta (Selkirk (USA))
(1686a) 2517a[7] 3455a[6]

Poetic Force (IRE) *Tony Carroll* a75 69
2 ch g Lope De Vega(IRE) Obligada (IRE) (Beat Hollow)
3058[13] 4128[6] 4907 [6] 7406[6] (7941) 8153[5] (8341) 8525[3]

Poetic Guest *George Margarson* a49 51
3 ch g Poet's Voice Diamond Run (Hurricane Run (IRE))
3572[10] 4401[13] 4477[4] 4936[12] 6900[10]

Poetic License (IRE) *James Grassick* a39 14
4 b g Dylan Thomas(IRE) Bright Bank (IRE) (Sadler's Wells (USA))
1830[9] 2087[8]

Poetic Lord *Rebecca Menzies* a59 68
7 b g Byron Jumairah Sun (IRE) (Scenic)
1131[7] 1399[6] 2110[9]

Poetic Principle (IRE) *J S Moore* 73
2 b g Royal Applause Lady Links (Bahamian Bounty)
4736[10] 5008[4] 5890[3]

Poetic Queen (IRE) *Eric Alston* a59
3 b f Dylan Thomas(IRE) Jubilant Lady (USA) (Aptitude (USA))
6855[6] 7410[8] 7856[2] 8093[6] 8290[2]

Poetic Verse *John Quinn* a76 87
6 gr m Byron Nina Fontenail (FR) (Kaldounevees (FR))
2051[3] 2663[8] 3263[5]

Poetic Voice *Ralph Beckett* 45
2 b g Poet's Voice Perfect Flight (Hawk Wing (USA))
4270[10]

Poetique (IRE) *John Gosden* a86
2 ch c Halling(USA) Lyrique (IRE) (Iffraaj)
(8305)

Poet's Beauty (IRE) *Ismail Mohammed* 87
3 ch g Poet's Voice Extreme Beauty (USA) (Rahy (USA))
(1638) 2654[2] (4368)

Poet's Charm (IRE) *Simon Crisford* a61
2 b g Poet's Voice Antillia (Red Ransom (USA))
4533[11] 6183[6] 8034[7]

Poet's Princess *Hughie Morrison* 85
2 ch f Poet's Voice Palace Affair (Pursuit Of Love)
3196[5] (3812) 4623[11] 6536[2] 7547[9]

Poet's Society *Mark Johnston* a91 87
2 ch c Poet's Voice Rahiyah (USA) (Rahy (USA))
1384[7] ◆ 2038[2] 2319[2] (2617) 2908[2] (3654) 4629[4] 4891[4] 5113[3] 5917[4] (6697) ◆ 7600[3]

Poet's Song (IRE) *Marcus Tregoning* a76 78
3 b g Poet's Voice Bee Eater (IRE) (Green Desert (USA))
2698[5] 4557[5] 5301[3] 5765[5] 6423[3] 7219[2]

Poet's Time *Tim Easterby* 13
2 ch f Poet's Voice Sandtime (IRE) (Green Desert (USA))
1583[9]

Poet's Vanity *Andrew Balding* 106
2 b f Poet's Voice Vanity (IRE) (Thatching)
5170[4] (6061) (7114)

Poet's Wish *George Margarson* 50
2 b c Poet's Voice Winner's Wish (Clodovil (IRE))
6297[8] 7012[10]

Poet's Word (IRE) *Sir Michael Stoute* a84 111
3 b c Poet's Voice Whirly Bird (Nashwan (USA))
1474[3] ◆ (2008) 2892[4] (4827) ◆ 6261[2]

Pointel (FR) *James Fanshawe* a89 90
3 b g Le Havre(IRE) Polysheba (FR) (Poliglote)
1715[3] ◆ 2208[8] 3235[3] (3904) 5724[2] 6804[8] 7060[3] (7625)

Pointillism *Iain Jardine* a59 75
4 b g Manduro(GER) Impressionism (IRE) (Elusive Quality (USA))
(5178) (5540) ◆ 5925[2] 6165[4]

Point North (IRE) *John Balding* a81 62
9 b g Danehill Dancer(IRE) Briolette (IRE) (Sadler's Wells (USA))
293[6] (541) (784) (1110) 2613[8] 4211[8] 7324[12] 7660[10] 8389[8]

Point Of View (IRE) *Roger Varian* a90 92
3 b g New Approach(IRE) Artisti (Cape Cross (IRE))
1426[4] 2175[5] (2816) 3300[13] 6456[3] 7015[11]

Point Of Woods *Ralph Beckett* a76 85
3 b g Showcasing Romantic Myth (Mind Games)
2751[5] 3131[4] 3689[9] 4268[3] 5305[5] 6018[3] 6479[5] 7267[3]

Point Piper (USA) *Jerry Hollendorfer* a111 89
6 b h Giant's Causeway(USA) Imagine (IRE) (Sadler's Wells (USA))
7808a[6]

Poitin *Keith Henry Clarke* a92 72
6 b m Kheleyf(USA) Port Providence (Red Ransom (USA))
2194[15] 4721a[19] 6932a[5]

Poker Alice *Peter Chapple-Hyam*
2 b f Holy Roman Emperor(IRE) Grain Only (Machiavellian (USA))
2970[P]

Polar Eyes *Mme Pia Brandt* a85 97
5 b m Dubawi(IRE) Everlasting Love (Pursuit Of Love)
4578a[3]

Polar Forest *Richard Guest* a78 83
6 br g Kyllachy Woodbeck (Terimon)
1445[2] 1643[11] 2017[8] 2328[13] 2832[4] 3364[7] 3721[4] 3905[6] 6517[5] 6876[12] 7246[5] 7500[4] 7775[8] (8142) 8337[2] 8498[7] 8584[5]

Polarisation *Charlie Appleby* a75 106
4 b g Echo Of Light Concordia (Pivotal)
2897[2] 3658[20] 6283[4]

Polar Kite (IRE) *Michael Attwater* a69 77
8 b g Marju(IRE) Irina (IRE) (Polar Falcon (USA))
482[3] 607[10] 953[9] (1269) 1945[8] 2153[2] ◆ 7310[4] 8163[4] 8458[6] 8555[6]

Polar River (USA) *Doug Watson* a112
3 b f Congrats(USA) Bayou Tortuga (USA) (Empire Maker (USA))
(184a) ◆ (534a) ◆ (808a) 1103a[2]

Pole Celeste (FR) *Robert Collet* 21
2 b c Zizany(IRE) Petite Ourse (Green Desert (USA))
7927a[7]

Polish Empress *William Muir* a49
3 b f Equiano(FR) Polish Belle (Polish Precedent (USA))
6960[8] 7603[3] 7856[4]

Politbureau *Micky Hammond* a65 71
9 b g Red Ransom(USA) Tereshkova (USA) (Mr Prospector (USA))
2916[3] 3417[8] 7592[9]

Political Policy (IRE) *Gavin Cromwell* a103 72
5 b g Bushranger(IRE) Alexander Express (IRE) (Sri Pekan (USA))
829a[2] 1069[6] 5790a[5]

Politico *Marjorie Fife*
4 ch m Medicean Tafawut (Nayef (USA))
2573[10]

Polkadot Princess (IRE) *Nikki Evans* 53
2 b f Sir Prancealot(IRE) Miriam's Song (Royal Applause)
5542[7] 6375[3] 6648[7] 7210[6]

Polkarena (FR) *J-P Gauvin* a76
4 b m Policy Maker(IRE) Arena (FR) (Marchand De Sable (USA))
5501a[4]

Polly Glide (IRE) *Luca Cumani* 64
2 ch f Nathaniel(IRE) Majestic Dancer (IRE) (Danehill Dancer (IRE))
7696[6]

Polly's Angels (IRE) *Richard Hughes* 61
2 b f Choisir(AUS) Angel Stevens (IRE) (Hawk Wing (USA))
2310[5] 6016[6] 6295[6] 7217[14]

Polly's Serenade *Richard Hughes* a54
3 b f Kyllachy Flamenco Dancer (Mark Of Esteem (IRE))
834[4] 1111[6]

Polybius *David Lanigan* a87 111
5 b g Oasis Dream Freedonia (Selkirk (USA))
3195[9] 3655[10] 6943[9]

Polymnia *Richard Hannon* a72 73
3 br f Poet's Voice Lucky Token (IRE) (Key Of Luck (USA))
4587[2] 5309[2] 5711[3] 6851[4] 7272[2] 7619[3] 8048[2] 8381[7] 8590[8]

Pomme De Terre (IRE) *Michael Dods* 90
4 ch g Sakhee's Secret Suzie Quw (Bahamian Bounty)
(1489) 1869[13] (3168) 3646[13] 4896[12] 6079[7] 6263[17] 7094[9]

Pondering *Eve Johnson Houghton* 70
2 b f So You Think(NZ) Lebenstanz (Singspiel (IRE))
7548[5]

Ponfeigh (IRE) *Debbie Mountain* 102
5 gr h Teofilo(IRE) Water Fountain (Mark Of Esteem (IRE))
757a[9]

Pongo Twistleton *Jonjo O'Neill* 66
3 b g Champs Elysees Pretty Girl (IRE) (Polish Precedent (USA))
1826[9] 2700[2] 3998[2]

Pontecarlo Boy *Richard Whitaker* a46 61
2 ch g Piccolo Dahshah (Mujtahid (USA))
3223[10] 3562[7] 4609[6] 5318[7] 6473[6] 6678[10] 7110[6]

Ponty Royale (IRE) *Tim Easterby* a61 67
3 b f Royal Applause Sodashy (IRE) (Noverre (USA))
1584[4] (2533) 3567[6] 3885[7] 4604[3] 5059[3] 5525[4] 5978[5] 6685[4]

Poole Belle (IRE) *Henry Candy* 83
3 b f Canford Cliffs(IRE) Anbella (FR) (Common Grounds)
2177[4] 2877[7] 3720[2] (4990) 5744[P]

Pool House *Mike Murphy* a75 55
5 b g Sakhee's Secret Gitane (FR) (Grand Lodge (USA))
349[5] 8077[12] 8364[6]

Poolstock *Michael Dods* a55 60
4 b g Equiano(FR) Pure Speculation (Salse (USA))
1495[9] 2359 [2] 2778[2] 3368[10] 4770[11] (5278) 5483[13] 5535[7] 6685[11] 7097[2] 7323[2]

Poor Duke (IRE) *Michael Mullineaux* a52 61
6 b g Bachelor Duke(USA) Graze On Too (IRE) (Rainbow Quest (USA))
388[7] 3342[4] 4290[2] 5149[9] 5572 [3] (5954) 6637[2] 7577[3] 8588[10]

Pop By (USA) *F-H Graffard* a82 95
3 bb f City Zip(USA) Seven Moons (JPN) (Sunday Silence (USA))
2141a[4] 7348a[11]

Pop Culture *Jonathan Portman* a57 68
3 ch f Equiano(FR) Naizak (Medicean)
1630[9] 2586[8] 3786[7] 4262[7] 5236[7]

Popeswood (IRE) *Lee Carter* a55 89
4 b g Haatef(USA) Binfield (IRE) (Officer (USA))
1929[8] 2460[9] 2587[9] 3234[5] 3721[8] 4557[7] 5197[5] 5773[6] 6656[10] 8064[11] 8458[12]

Poplar *Robyn Brisland* a66 42
3 b g Hellvelyn Amelie Pouliche (FR) (Desert Prince (IRE))
3280[3] 3822[6] 4835[6] 4980[2] 5474[4] 6249[2] 6509[3] 7201[5]

Poppet Rocket (IRE) *Seamus Mullins* a54 45
4 b m Myboycharlie(IRE) Zacchera (Zamindar (USA))
124[6] 277[7] 1323[10]

Poppy In The Wind *Alan Brown* a76 69
4 b m Piccolo Vintage Steps (IRE) (Bahamian Bounty)
1525[9] 2053[4] 2334[2] 3010[3] 3484[2] (3843) 4544[6] 5320[4] 7852[4] (8137) 8403[5] ◆

Poppy May (IRE) *James Given* a53 53
2 b f Zoffany(IRE) Lara Amelia (IRE) (Ishiguru (USA))
4603[7] 5272[6] 6732[4] 7881[3] 8344[8]

Poppy Pivot (IRE) *Ann Duffield* a18 63
2 b f Pivotal Havin' A Good Time (IRE) (Jeremy (USA))
1293[7] 1951[2] 2424[5] 3208[12] 3707[5]

Poppy Time *James Eustace* a10 68
3 b f Pour Moi(IRE) Shamandar (FR) (Exceed And Excel (AUS))
1931[13] 5361[4] 5742[6] 6901[11] 7627[8]

Popsies Joy (IRE) *Tim Easterby* a63 71
3 b f Alfred Nobel(IRE) Senzate (Lujain (USA))
1381[7] 2428[3] (2674) 3213[2] 3521[5] 3877[4] 4769[3] 5115[5] 5478[2] ◆ 5732[5] 6220[4] ◆ 6908[6]

Popsilca *Mick Quinn* a48 44
2 b f Captain Gerrard(IRE) Silca Destination (Dubai Destination (USA))
5930[8] 6696[10] 7414[5]

Porcupine Creek (IRE) *Daniel Mark Loughnane* a49 60
3 b g Zebedee Daanaat (IRE) (Kheleyf (USA))
432[5] 785[6] 1292[5]

Porsenna (IRE) *Stefano Botti* a85 89
6 b h Dylan Thomas(IRE) Miss Mariduff (USA) (Hussonet (USA))
2073a[4] 2729a[5] 6612a[7]

Port *Jimmy Fox* 65
4 b g Hurricane Run(IRE) Captain's Paradise (IRE) (Rock Of Gibraltar (IRE))
1456[10]

Portage (IRE) *M Halford* 115
4 b h Teofilo(IRE) Galley (Zamindar (USA))
(2924a) (3273) 4326a[2]

Portalay (FR) *Rod Collet* a62 68
5 ch h Layman(USA) Portella (GER) (Protektor (GER))
3184a[6]

Port Douglas (IRE) *A P O'Brien* 112
3 b c Galileo(IRE) Walzerkoenigin (USA) (Kingmambo (USA))
1974[2] 2896[14] 3679a[5]

Porte Joie (GER) *E Lellouche* 57
3 b f Soldier Hollow Pretty Su (IRE) (Surumu (GER))
7265a[8]

Port Gaverne (IRE) *Marcus Tregoning* a62 69
3 b g Lord Shanakill(USA) Jillian (USA) (Royal Academy (USA))
152[7] 350[4] 519[12] 5027[5] 5509[6]

Porthilly (FR) *J E Hammond* a87 104
6 ch m Pivotal Ricine (IRE) (Titus Livius (FR))
3090a[3] 4905a[7] 6391a[5] 6990a[11] 7758a[2]

Port Isaac (IRE) *Marcus Tregoning* a74 78
3 b g Sakhee's Secret Dombeya (IRE) (Danehill (USA))
5327[2] ◆ 6459[2] 7459[2] 7782[2]

Port Lairge *Michael Chapman* a62 67
6 b g Pastoral Pursuits Stylish Clare (IRE) (Desert Style (IRE))
1546[10] 1746[4] 3097[4] 3491[4] 4354[3] 5104[6] 5711[8] 6408[4] 7442[3] 7968[7] 8242[9] 8350[7] 8477[6] 8567[2]

Portland Belle (IRE) *Jeremy Gask*
3 b f Fastnet Rock(AUS) Square Pants (USA) (King Of Kings (IRE))
8157[7]

Portland Street (IRE) *Bryan Smart* a65 73
3 b g Dream Ahead(USA) Danaskaya (IRE) (Danehill (USA))
1691[8] 2122[6] 2667[4] 3603[2] ◆ (3948) ◆ (5537) ◆ 6435[3] 6769[5] 7852[8]

Portledge (IRE) *James Bethell* a70 77
2 b c Acclamation Off Chance (Olden Times)
4545[3] 5615[6] 6129[5] 7541[7] 8405[5]

Port Master *Ann Duffield* a58 50
2 b g Harbour Watch(IRE) Gentle Guru (Ishiguru (USA))
6952[9] 8425[5]

Porto Ferro (IRE) *Dr Jon Scargill* a83 85
2 b f Arcano(IRE) Sassari (IRE) (Darshaan)
8152[3]

Port Paradise *William Jarvis* a72 65
3 gr g Paco Boy(IRE) Yacht Woman (USA) (Mizzen Mast (USA))
242[9] 3080[2] 3823[10] (4518) 5085[5] 5720[2] 6194[8] 7653[3]

Portrush Storm *Ray Peacock* a10 28
11 ch m Observatory(USA) Overcast (IRE) (Caerleon (USA))
4202[10] 5628[9] 6381[5]

Poseidon (IRE) *Ed Walker* a64 72
2 ch g Born To Sea(IRE) Maskaya (IRE) (Machiavellian (USA))
6054[5] 6704[5] 7658[5]

Posh Bounty *Joseph Tuite* a56 79
5 ch m Bahamian Bounty Fission (Efisio)
873[8] 1533[2] (1600) 1928[6] 2130[2] (2146) 3771[6] (6649) 6770[5] 7506[4] 7738[12]

Positive Vibration (IRE) *J-C Rouget* a58 69
3 br f Canford Cliffs(IRE) Midnight Partner (IRE) (Marju (IRE))
1581a[9] 2282a[14] 4185a[9] 4926a[10]

Possible Future *Ismail Mohammed* a79 72
3 b g Compton Place Lalectra (King Charlemagne (USA))
1185^{4} 4522^{5} (5193) 6265^{8}

Postbag *Henry Candy* a64 88
4 b m Three Valleys(USA) Postage Stampe (Singspiel (IRE))
2628^{6} 3410^{8} 5514^{5} 6300^{7}

Poster Girl *Jonathan Portman* 75
3 b f Excellent Art Accede (Acclamation)
1758^{9} 2431^{4} 5891^{2} 6635^{4} 7220^{7}

Postponed (IRE) *Roger Varian* 126
5 b h Dubawi(IRE) Ever Rigg (Dubai Destination (USA))
(843a) (1107a) (2894) (5558) 6989a^{5}

Post Var (FR) *S Wattel* a92 107
3 b c American Post Life Of Risks (FR) (Take Risks (FR))
972a^{4} 1374a^{3} 2232a^{4} 6911a^{2}

Potemkin (GER) *A Wohler* 113
5 bb g New Approach(IRE) Praia (GER) (Big Shuffle (USA))
(3699a) 4928a^{3} 5904a^{2} (6973a) (7841a)

Poti (SPA) *R Avial Lopez* 70
5 b m Pyrus(USA) Double Mix (FR) (Sagamix (FR))
5249a^{8} 7929a^{12}

Potternello (IRE) *Mick Channon* a68 71
4 b m Captain Marvelous(IRE) Purepleasureseeker (IRE) (Grand Lodge (USA))
713^{4} 859^{6} 1334^{6} 1533^{6} 3070^{8} 3469^{6} 3674^{2} 3898^{2} 3953^{9} 4378^{5}

Potters Lady Jane *Lucy Wadham* a74
4 b m Sir Percy Arabescato (UAE) (Gone West (USA))
3305^{2} 4265^{7} 7487^{2}

Pouliche *Harry Dunlop* a68 56
3 b f Monsieur Bond(IRE) Tarneem (USA) (Zilzal (USA))
611^{5}

Pour Deux (IRE) *John M Oxx* a89 85
4 b m Dansili Gagnoa (IRE) (Sadler's Wells (USA))
3084a^{7}

Pour La Victoire (IRE) *Tony Carroll* a85 81
6 b g Antonius Pius(USA) Lady Lucia (IRE) (Royal Applause)
236^{4} 414^{2} ◆ 433^{8} (727) 879^{4} 1041^{4} 1946^{5} (2396) (2643) 3159^{7} 5017^{4} 5103^{5} 6000^{5} 6878^{3} 7267^{10}

Pour Pavot (IRE) *Gary Moore* a35 60
3 b f Pour Moi(IRE) Lake Windermere (IRE) (Oasis Dream)
140^{9} 376^{10} 700^{7} 2967^{7}

Pourquoi Non (IRE) *Denis Coakley* a67 61
3 b g Pour Moi(IRE) Anyuta (Singspiel (IRE))
1860^{8} 2900^{4} 3652^{P}

Powderhorn (IRE) *Mark Johnston* a75 84
3 b g Raven's Pass(USA) Innclassic (IRE) (Stravinsky (USA))
1288^{6} 2161^{20} 3523^{8} 4048^{7}

Powderonthebonnet (IRE) *Richard Phillips* a51 62
8 b g Definite Article Zuhal (Busted)
802^{8} 1028^{5} 1399^{8} 5805^{8} 7367^{4}

Powder Snow (USA) *H-A Pantall* 105
3 ch f Dubawi(IRE) Snow Ballerina (Sadler's Wells (USA))
2945a^{5} 7566a^{6} (7929a)

Powerallied (IRE) *Richard Fahey* 93
3 b g Camacho Kaplinsky (IRE) (Fath (USA))
1996^{3} 2693^{7} 3131^{3} (3637) 4632^{2} 5641^{11} 6779^{13}

Power Blade (KOR) *Kim Young Kwan* a75
3 b c Menifee(USA) Cheonmachong (KOR) (Lost Mountain (USA))
6399a^{4}

Powered (IRE) *David Evans* a59 45
3 b g Frozen Power(IRE) Confirm (IRE) (In The Wings)
275^{4} 8457^{7}

Powerful Dream (IRE) *Ronald Harris* a73 73
3 b f Frozen Power(IRE) Noble View (USA) (Distant View (USA))
(763) (883) ◆ 1060^{6} 2373^{8} 4502^{2} 6018^{4} 7945^{5} 8040^{3} 8429^{7}

Powerful Love (IRE) *Mark Johnston* a64 71
2 b c Clodovil(IRE) Ruby Ridge (IRE) (Acatenango (GER))
6952^{5} 7247^{2} 7511^{6}

Powerfulstorm *Michael Appleby* a63 57
4 b m Bertolini(USA) Frisson (Slip Anchor)
776^{4} (904) 985^{4}

Powerful Wind (IRE) *Charlie Wallis* a82 82
7 ch g Titus Livius(FR) Queen Of Fools (IRE) (Xaar)
56^{8} 364^{3} 604^{5} 764^{7} (2342) 2931^{5} 3995^{9} 4809^{6} 5189^{10} 8349^{6}

Power Game *Saeed bin Suroor* a98 90
4 ch g Shamardal(USA) Counterclaim (Pivotal)
(31) ◆ 1478^{4} 6089^{4} 6802^{4} 7765^{7}

Power Grid (IRE) *John James Feane* a88 59
3 b g Frozen Power(IRE) Springfort (IRE) (Captain Rio)
7517a^{3}

Power Home (IRE) *Denis Coakley* a58 62
2 ch f Power Ascendancy (Sadler's Wells (USA))
6035^{4} 6421^{5} 7733^{4} 8082^{8}

Powerless (IRE) *Tim Easterby* 46
2 b g Frozen Power(IRE) Hallucination (IRE) (Last Tycoon)
1641^{6} 2014^{4} 3477^{8} 5796^{9}

Power Of The Cross *D Guillemin* a65
2 b f Cape Cross(IRE) Portmeirion (Polish Precedent (USA))
5279a^{5}

Power Power (IRE) *Marco Botti* a55 53
2 ch g Power Charmingly (USA) (King Of Kings (IRE))
7740^{8} 8088^{7}

Power Struggle (IRE) *A Oliver* a81 85
3 b c Turtle Bowl(IRE) Anestasia (IRE) (Anabaa (USA))
3428a^{4}

Power Up *Roger Ingram* a65 58
5 b m Rail Link Melpomene (Peintre Celebre (USA))
88^{8} 316^{10} 2607^{5} 3402^{5} 4267^{7} 4882^{2} 5399^{2} 6243^{4} 6871^{3} 7613^{4} 8381^{12}

Pow Wow *Roger Charlton* a49 62
2 b g Medicean Ship's Biscuit (Tiger Hill (IRE))
6664^{6} ◆ 7622^{9} 7883^{10}

Poyle Emily *Ralph Beckett* a55 63
3 b f Compton Place Poyle Dee Dee (Oasis Dream)
3958^{3} 4939^{7}

Poyle Thomas *Ralph Beckett* a98 98
7 b g Rail Link Lost In Lucca (Inchinor)
2249^{2} 3657^{3} 4752^{4} 5559^{10}

Poyle Vinnie *Michael Appleby* a103 106
6 b g Piccolo Poyle Dee Dee (Oasis Dream)
1272^{3} 1887^{5} 2546^{6} 3386^{14} 4136^{3} 4865^{24} 5143^{7} 5641^{3} 6558^{18} 7156^{15} 7242^{5} 7497^{13} 8232^{6} 8308^{6} ◆ 8583^{2} ◆

Practical Joke (USA) *Chad C Brown* a115
2 b c Into Mischief(USA) Halo Humor (USA) (Distorted Humor (USA))
7834a^{3}

Pradesh (IRE) *M Ibrahim* a70 69
3 b c Elusive Quality(USA) Pleione (FR) (Sadler's Wells (USA))
1311a^{5} 8576a^{9}

Prairie Hawk (USA) *Adrian Wintle* a46 50
11 b g Hawk Wing(USA) Lady Carla (Caerleon (USA))
673^{9}

Prairie Impulse *Ann Duffield* 59
3 b f Major Cadeaux Prairie Sun (GER) (Law Society (USA))
2809^{4} 3289^{7} 4314^{8}

Prairie Light *Sylvester Kirk* a51 47
2 b f High Chaparral(IRE) Dimelight (Fantastic Light (USA))
5298^{8} 5995^{8} 7484^{8}

Prairie Pearl (FR) *H-A Pantall* 95
3 ch f Le Havre(IRE) Prairie Scilla (GER) (Dashing Blade)
2945a^{8} 6070a^{6} 6611a^{4}

Prairie Town (IRE) *Tony Carroll* a44 67
5 b g High Chaparral(IRE) Lake Baino (Highest Honor (FR))
1391^{10} 1873^{6} 7053^{8}

Praise N Glory *Linda Jewell* 8
5 ch m Resplendent Glory(IRE) Tapsalteerie (Tipsy Creek (USA))
3490^{7} 3970^{12} 5485^{4}

Pranceleya (IRE) *Marco Botti* a68 75
2 b f Sir Prancealot(IRE) Good For Her (Rock Of Gibraltar (IRE))
3301^{5} 3902^{3} (4564) 4884^{12} 5794^{8} (7098)

Prancelina (IRE) *Phil McEntee* a62 54
2 ch f Sir Prancealot(IRE) Fingal Nights (IRE) (Night Shift (USA))
4022^{9} 5188^{4} 5705^{8} (6420) 7258^{10}

Prancing Oscar (IRE) *Ben Haslam* 53
2 b c Sir Prancealot(IRE) Beguiler (Refuse To Bend (IRE))
5885^{5}

Praskovia (IRE) *A Fabre* a61 82
3 ch f Manduro(GER) Petrushka (IRE) (Unfuwain (USA))
4331a^{7}

Praticks (IRE) *J-F Doucet* 58
5 gr m Bertolini(USA) Plique A Jour (FR) (Hernando (FR))
1846a^{4}

Prayer For Relief (USA) *M F De Kock* a110 53
8 bb h Jump Start(USA) Sparklin Lil (USA) (Mr Sparkles (USA))
92a^{3} 452a^{5} 624a^{3} 845a^{8} 1101a^{6}

Prayer Time *Mark H Tompkins* a71 55
4 ch g Pastoral Pursuits Nice Time (IRE) (Tagula (IRE))
429^{8} 801^{2} 890^{3} (1028) 1675^{8} 3798^{6}

Pray For Paris *Martyn Meade* a73 50
3 ch f Champs Elysees Port Providence (Red Ransom (USA))
2735^{9} 3845^{13} 5723^{4} 6856^{3} 7846^{8}

Prazeres *William Haggas* 75
2 b g Sepoy(AUS) Sewards Folly (Rudimentary (USA))
4552^{3} ◆ 5476^{2} 6129^{6} 7296^{5}

Precast *David Simcock* a64 57
4 ch m Halling(USA) Preceder (Polish Precedent (USA))
456^{7} 964^{5}

Precieuse (IRE) *F Chappet* 93
2 ch f Tamayuz Zut Alors (IRE) (Pivotal)
7291a^{2} 7655a^{2} 7972a^{2}

Precious Angel (IRE) *Richard Hannon* 49
2 b f Excelebration(IRE) Evangeline (Sadler's Wells (USA))
7543^{9}

Precious Equity (FR) *David Menuisier* a41 11
2 b f Equiano(FR) Anasy (USA) (Gone West (USA))
4287^{15} 7977^{12}

Precious Plum *Chris Dwyer* a77 27
2 b f Equiano(FR) Miss Polly Plum (Doyen (IRE))
2786^{6} 4473^{6} 5188^{3} (6419) 6830^{7} (7258)

Precious Ramotswe *John Gosden* a76
2 b f Nathaniel(IRE) Miss Pinkerton (Danehill (USA))
(8465)

Precious Skye (IRE) *David O'Meara* 51
2 b f Born To Sea(IRE) Secret Flame (Machiavellian (USA))
3112^{9} 3515^{6} 4000^{3} 4404^{7}

Precision Five *Alan King* a91 88
7 b m Proclamation(IRE) Sashay (Bishop Of Cashel)
19^{4} 244^{4} 440^{5} 1092^{6}

Precision Strike *Richard Whitaker* a55 67
6 b g Multiplex Dockside Strike (Docksider (USA))
7385^{8} 7846^{P} (Dead)

Predetermined (IRE) *H-F Devin* a77 82
3 b g Lope De Vega(IRE) Queen Bodicea (IRE) (Revoque (IRE))
2207^{4} 2790^{4} 3634^{2} 4344^{5} 4803^{18} 7680a^{8} 8368a^{8}

Predilection (USA) *John Gosden* a101 102
3 b c First Defence(USA) Summer Shower (Sadler's Wells (USA))
1338^{3} 3299^{28} 4665^{7} (5376)

Predominance (IRE) *William Haggas* 101
4 b g Danehill Dancer(IRE) Gilded Vanity (IRE) (Indian Ridge)
1195^{10} (1627) ◆ 2027^{12} 2684^{5}

Preferment (NZ) *Chris Waller* 114
4 b h Zabeel(NZ) Better Alternative (AUS) (Flying Spur (AUS))
7378a^{11}

Premier Currency (IRE) *Mike Murphy* a42 72
3 b g Elusive Pimpernel(USA) Zeena (Unfuwain (USA))
1485^{2} 2099^{9} 2749^{8} 3579^{5} 4269^{11} 5302^{10} 7895^{12} 8458^{7}

Premier Jack's *Nikki Evans*
5 b g Tobougg(IRE) Arabellas Homer (Mark Of Esteem (IRE))
505^{12}

Prendergast Hill (IRE) *Ed de Giles* a88 90
4 b g Raven's Pass(USA) Daraliya (IRE) (Kahyasi)
1093^{4} 1568^{3} 2163^{19} 2556^{7} 2978^{2} 3525^{8} (4208) 4710^{3} 5240^{3} 5574^{5} 6048^{6} 6628^{6} 7671^{12}

Preobrajenska *Michael Bell* a60 69
2 b f Paco Boy(IRE) Unex Mona Lisa (Shamardal (USA))
3074^{3} 3592^{2} 8377^{5}

Prepared *A R Al Rayhi* a86 57
7 ch g More Than Ready(USA) Mannington (AUS) (Danehill (USA))
12a^{7} 183a^{5}

Prerogative (IRE) *Richard Hannon* a79 81
2 b g Rock Of Gibraltar(IRE) Tedarshana (Darshaan)
2023^{5} 2757^{3} 3526^{2} 3977^{2} 4479^{3} 5171^{3} 5959^{4} 6288^{2} 7100^{2}

Presence Process *Pat Phelan* a66 70
2 b c Dansili Loulwa (IRE) (Montjeu (IRE))
5332^{6} 6211^{3} 6632^{4} 7467^{13} 7898^{8} 8360^{4} 8560^{12}

Presley (ITY) *Stefano Botti* 58
3 b c Gladiatorus(USA) Pasionaria (IRE) (Celtic Swing)
2517a^{8}

Press Gang *James Eustace* a78 74
3 b g Mount Nelson Rutba (Act One)
1619^{3} 2300^{3} 6370^{2}

Prestige Vendome (FR) *N Clement* 104
5 gr g Orpen(USA) Place Vendome (FR) (Dr Fong (USA))
4783a^{3}

Presto Boy *Richard Hughes* a58 51
4 b g Compton Place Presto Levanter (Rock Of Gibraltar (IRE))
381^{2} 528^{7} 790^{4} 1005^{5} 1164^{2} 1795^{3} 2458^{6} 2845^{9} 3146^{7} 3719^{5} 6312^{2} 7863^{5} 8079^{2} 8121^{4} 8408^{7}

Presumido (IRE) *Simon Dow* a90 62
6 b g Iffraaj Miss Megs (IRE) (Croco Rouge (IRE))
313^{4} 494^{3} (1041) 1335^{3} 1752^{4} 2378^{12} 7461^{6} 7902^{5} 8256^{7} (8356) 8593^{9}

Pretend (IRE) *Charlie Appleby* a113 99
5 b g Invincible Spirit(IRE) Fafinta (IRE) (Indian Ridge)
3655^{2} 4166^{7} 4916^{5}

Pretorius (FR) *G Taupin* a61 27
10 b g Lomitas Jabirou (FR) (Slip Anchor)
3184a^{13}

Pretty Bubbles *J R Jenkins* a92 90
7 b m Sleeping Indian Willmar (IRE) (Zafonic (USA))
254^{6} 422^{7} 581^{11} 1003^{5} ◆ 1158^{4} (1432) 2084^{4} 2469^{3} 2621^{5} (4708) 5488^{2} 6340^{4} 7054^{9} 8158^{11} (8233)

Pretty Girl (ARG) *M Delzangles* a81 96
4 b m Harlan's Holiday(USA) Piba Como Vos (ARG) (Candy Stripes (USA))
3544a^{6} 5430a^{7}

Pretty Jewel *James Tate* a64 63
3 b f Aqlaam Highland Jewel (IRE) (Azamour (IRE))
2152^{5} 3236^{8}

Pretty Perfect (IRE) *A P O'Brien* 113
3 b f Galileo(IRE) Milanova (AUS) (Danehill (USA))
(1507a) 2167a^{2} 2509a^{9} (3202a) 4416a^{10} 5586^{4} 6259^{2} 7351^{4} 7831a^{13}

Pretty Vacant *Roger Varian* a85 87
2 gr c Elzaam(AUS) Jillolini (Bertolini (USA))
2437^{2} ◆ (2732) ◆ 3247^{6} (3647) 3858^{4}

Pricedtoperfection (USA) *Chad C Brown* 101
3 b f Temple City(USA) Glittering Tax (USA) (Artax (USA))
4174a^{4}

Price Is Truth (USA) *S Seemar* a103 47
6 ch g Distorted Humor(USA) Secret Thyme (USA) (Storm Cat (USA))
186a^{8}

Priceless *Clive Cox* 107
3 b f Exceed And Excel(AUS) Molly Brown (Rudimentary (USA))
1773^{9} 2474^{5} 4062^{2} 4652^{2} ◆ 5436^{4} (6230)

Prickly (IRE) *E J O'Grady* 81
6 ch g Definite Article Connemara Rose (IRE) (Desert King (IRE))
(5620a) 7195a^{12}

Prigsnov Dancer (IRE) *John Balding* a53 57
11 ch g Namid Brave Dance (IRE) (Kris)
197^{8} 320^{7} 542^{4} 730^{7} 1481^{6} 1956^{4} 2856^{3} 4513^{7} 5378^{3} 7290^{10} 7961^{2} 8312^{8} 8541^{10}

Primadonia *Richard Hannon* 4
2 b f Dated Breath Pretty Primo (IRE) (Kyllachy)
6189^{8}

Primal Snow (USA) *James M Ryan* a67 68
4 b m Langfuhr(CAN) Lotta Rhythm (USA) (Rhythm (USA))
5096a^{15}

Prim And Proper *John Flint* a63 65
5 b m Sleeping Indian Quite Fantastic (IRE) (Fantastic Light (USA))
3748^{10} 4288^{10} 4876^{6} (5252) 6021^{7} 6872^{4} 7620^{5} 7735^{6} 8156^{7} 8252^{6} 8555^{9}

Primanora *Michael Appleby* 67
3 ch f First Trump Danzanora (Groom Dancer (USA))
2886^{4} ◆

Primitivo *Alan King* a74 108
3 b g Excellent Art Dolcetto (IRE) (Danehill Dancer (IRE))
(2209) ◆ (2413) (3300)

Primitorio (IRE) *O Al Dhafa* a60 78
5 b g Oratorio(IRE) Primissima (GER) (Second Set (IRE))
744a^{14}

Primobella *Ed McMahon* a51 67
3 ch f Duke Of Marmalade(IRE) Arbella (Primo Dominie)
3015^{6} 3509^{3} 3998^{7} 4987^{3} 6541^{5} (7230)

Primogeniture (IRE) *Mary Hambro* a93 93
5 b g Glory Of Dancer Jacqueline (IND) (King Charlemagne (USA))
(3304) ◆ 3861^{5} 5552^{10} 6298^{7} 6711^{3}

Primo Uomo (IRE) *Gerard O'Leary* a90 95
4 b g Strategic Prince Mooching Along (IRE) (Mujahid (USA))
4246a^{2} (5441a) 6819a^{3}

Primrose Brown *Conrad Allen* a69 50
5 b m Indian Danehill(IRE) Royal Tango (Petoski)
59^{4} 324^{2} ◆ 532^{9} 1158^{6} 4596^{10} 4950^{6}

Primrose Place *Richard Hannon* a56 66
2 ch f Compton Place Pretty Girl (IRE) (Polish Precedent (USA))
1635^{4} 2007^{4} 2637^{7} 3254^{4} 5543^{4} ◆ 6670^{7} 7047^{6} 7734^{9}

Primrose Valley *Ed Vaughan* a95 94
4 b m Pastoral Pursuits Cosmic Destiny (IRE) (Soviet Star (USA))
290^{11} 657^{6} 780^{7} 1065^{7} ◆ 4066^{2} 4584^{15} 5390^{10} 6371^{4} 6780^{7} 8083^{7} 8233^{3}

Prince Alzain (USA) *Doug Watson* a75 63
7 b h Street Sense(USA) Monaassabaat (USA) (Zilzal (USA))
627a^{8}

Prince Apache *Andreas Lowe* a84 75
3 b c Royal Applause Park Melody (IRE) (Refuse To Bend (IRE))
5907a^{11}

Prince Connoisseur (IRE) *John James Feane* a82 60
5 ch g Art Connoisseur(IRE) Brewing Storm (IRE) (King Charlemagne (USA))
4246a^{13} 7800a^{14}

Prince Jai *S Seemar* a53 49
3 ch g Showcasing Play Around (IRE) (Niniski (USA))
185a^{6}

Prince Nomad (FR) *Eric Saint-Martin* 104
5 b h Galileo(IRE) En Public (FR) (Rainbow Quest (USA))
1688a^{9} 8042a^{2} 8336a^{7}

Prince Of Arran *Charlie Fellowes* a104 79
3 b g Shirocco(GER) Storming Sioux (Storming Home)
(1260) 2244^{6} 2892^{8} 3574^{7} (7765) 8068^{4}

Prince Of Baden (IRE) *Matthieu Palussiere* a46
2 b c Dark Angel(IRE) Leopoldine (Desert Prince (IRE))
5988a^{11}

Prince Of Cardamom (IRE) *Jonathan Geake* a64 68
4 b g Nayef(USA) Tiger Spice (Royal Applause)
2205^{7} 2634^{14} 3125^{7} (4290) (4876) 4993^{4} 5954^{13} 7035^{9}

Prince Of Clappers *Tim Easterby* 56
2 b g Royal Applause Blodwen (USA) (Mister Baileys)
4856^{12} 5792^{5} 6473^{8}

Prince Of Cool *James Given* a80 80
2 b c Royal Applause Methayel (IRE) (Araafa (IRE))
(2437) 3295^{10} 4196^{2} 4825^{17} 5510^{2} 5931^{5} 6507^{2} 7600^{8}

Prince Of Islay (IRE) *Amanda Perrett* a53 56
5 ch g Nayef(USA) Feolin (Dr Fong (USA))
950^{3} 1748^{6} 2131^{3} 3099^{2} 3528^{3} 4385^{3}

Prince Of Johanne (IRE) *Tom Tate* a14 82
10 gr g Johannesburg(USA) Paiute Princess (FR) (Darshaan)
6710^{8} 7316^{13}

Prince Of Lir (IRE) *Robert Cowell* 107
2 b c Kodiac Esuvia (IRE) (Whipper (USA))
(2669) (3295) 4694a^{5} 5614^{13} 6282^{7}

Prince Of Paris *Roger Ingram* a72 67
4 b g Champs Elysees Cool Kitten (IRE) (One Cool Cat (USA))
1934^{5} 2399^{6} 2623^{7} 3002^{7} 4307^{8} 6050^{7} 6628^{11} 7428^{7}

Princeofthequeen (USA) *David O'Meara* a54 73
2 br c Lonhro(AUS) Catch The Queen (USA) (Miswaki (USA))
3222^{2} 3749^{2} 4209^{7} 5265^{8} 6743^{11}

Prince Of Time *Richard Ford* a50 69
4 ch g Bahamian Bounty Touching (IRE) (Kheleyf (USA))
1926^{12} 2365^{11} 3987^{6} 4516^{9} 6106^{5} 7427^{9}

Prince Orpen (FR) *Helena Blazkova* 97
5 b h Orpen(USA) Indian Princess (IRE) (Mujadil (USA))
2722a^{6}

Princess Aloof (IRE) *Mrs John Harrington* a69 93
5 b m Big Bad Bob(IRE) Little Miss Diva (IRE) (Diktat)
1018a^{20} 1279a^{8} 3630a^{5} 4747a^{18}

Princess Asta (FR) *Mario Hofer* a78 97
3 b f Canford Cliffs(IRE) Lune Rouge (IRE) (Unfuwain (USA))
2949a^{7} 7027a^{10} (7719a)

Princess Cookie *Philip McBride* a79
3 b f Sakhee's Secret Rouge Dancer (Elusive City (USA))
(268) (515) 954^{8}

Princesse Ava (FR) *Mlle S Delaroche* a53
3 b f King's Best(USA) Calyx (FR) (Irish River (FR))
7999a^{16}

Princesse Eva (FR) *James Fanshawe* a59 70
3 b f Manduro(GER) Wing Stealth (IRE) (Hawk Wing (USA))
2774^7 3475^5 4025^3 4956^5 5749^2

Princess Emma (FR) *S Jesus* a66 71
3 b f Ski Chief(USA) Arthurs Princess (IRE) (Monashee Mountain (USA))
128a^4

Princess Holly *Robert Cowell* a54 63
2 b f Compton Place Khyber Knight (IRE) (Night Shift (USA))
1706^3 2097^3 2641^2 2874^4 4712^6 5258^6 5606^6

Princess Kay (IRE) *B Grizzetti & L Riccardi* 43
3 b f Strategic Prince Keyoura (IRE) (Intikhab (USA))
2518a^{15}

Princess Kodia (IRE) *Brian Meehan* a58 88
3 b f Kodiac Pixie's Blue (IRE) (Hawk Wing (USA))
6079^{13} 6409^7 7221^{12}

Princess Momoka *Roger Varian* a54 68
3 b f Exceed And Excel(AUS) Impressionism (IRE) (Elusive Quality (USA))
2298^6 2886^3 4238^5 6487^5 7437^5

Princess Nearco (IRE) *Patrick Holmes* 44
2 b f Elzaam(AUS) Royal Jubilee (IRE) (King's Theatre (IRE))
4943^7 5414^6

Princess Nia (IRE) *Brian Meehan* a77 49
3 b f Acclamation Shirley A Star (USA) (Cozzene (USA))
6703^6 7218^6 7616^2 (8075)

Princess Of Snow (IRE) *H De Nicolay* a58 67
2 gr f Rajsaman(FR) Mahendra (GER) (Next Desert (IRE))
5005a^7

Princess Peaches *James Bethell* a62 66
4 ch m Notnowcato Miss Apricot (Indian Ridge)
49^7 430^2 682^3 1047^6 1695^3 2096^2 2655^2 3210^6 6568^{11} 7889^4 7995^5 8587^{10}

Princess Raihana *Marco Botti* a75 72
3 br f Cape Cross(IRE) Raihana (AUS) (Elusive Quality (USA))
2183^{11} 3601^4 4206^6 4777^5 5749^4 6334^4 (6901) 8090^6 8381^5

Princess Roania (IRE) *Peter Bowen* a62 77
5 b m Dubai Destination(USA) Lady Roania (IRE) (Saddlers' Hall (IRE))
1140^5 1346^4 1499^4 (3767) 4023^3

Princess Tansy *Gay Kelleway* a80 81
4 b m Equiano(FR) Tanasie (Cadeaux Genereux)
2253^{13} 2794^4 3407^5 4585^5 5040^2 (5882) 6318^2 6793^{13} 7398a^5 7864^4 8032^6

Princess Way (IRE) *David Evans* a62 60
2 gr f Zebedee Stef's Girl (IRE) (Petardia)
1087^6 1454^4 1741^4 3122^6 4315^4 5606^2 6033^2 (6060) 6388a^{16} 6670^{12} 7228^8 7750^2 7974^7 8072^4

Princess Zoffany (IRE) *Jimmy Fox* a33 54
3 b f Zoffany(IRE) Tara Gold (IRE) (Royal Academy (USA))
2005^{10} 2967^3 4159^3 5824^5 6406^5

Prinz Hlodowig (FR) *M Delzangles* 104
2 b c Rajsaman(FR) Princess Cheri (GER) (Mondrian (GER))
7169a^2 7722a^6

Priore Philip (ITY) *Stefano Botti* 103
5 ch g Dane Friendly Lan Force (ITY) (Blu Air Force (IRE))
7565a^4

Priors Brook *Andrew Balding* a81 83
5 b g Champs Elysees Dyanita (Singspiel (IRE))
1934^2 2549^5 3690^4 4138^8 7222^2 (8161)

Priory *Martin Smith* a65 42
3 b f Mullionmileanhour(IRE) Alectrona (FR) (Invincible Spirit (IRE))
3^7

Prisom (IRE) *Gay Kelleway* a71 57
3 b f Zebedee Crystal Theatre (IRE) (King's Theatre (IRE))
2372^7 3496^5 6851^{11} 7261^3 ◆ 7896^3 8145^7

Private Dancer *Ron Barr* 32
5 b g Halling(USA) Anamilina (IRE) (Anabaa (USA))
2048^{15} 2307^{10} 2746^7 3774^{11} 4146^5

Private Donald *Robert Cowell* a64
3 ch g Sakhee's Secret Excello (Exceed And Excel (AUS))
8290^9 8472^3

Private Jet *Charles Hills* a60 34
3 b c Paco Boy(IRE) Sheer Indulgence (FR) (Pivotal)
1421^{11} 1714^{13} 3475^8

Private Lesson's (FR) *P Bigot* a63 57
8 b g Crillon(FR) High Fright (FR) (Croco Rouge (IRE))
5281a^{13}

Private Matter *Richard Fahey* 100
2 b g Mayson Privacy Order (Azamour (IRE))
2552^8 (3216) 5058^3 5977^2 6538^{10} (7655a)

Private Mission *Hughie Morrison* a71
2 ch g Sepoy(AUS) Pivotal Drive (IRE) (Pivotal)
8243^6 (8557) ◆

Private Money (FR) *J-M Lefebvre* 63
2 gr c Kendargent(FR) Private Riviera (Stormy River (FR))
7136a^5

Prize Diva *David Elsworth* a66 57
2 b f Motivator Premier Prize (Selkirk (USA))
6088^5 7494^8

Prize Exhibit *James Cassidy* a70 110
4 b m Showcasing Roodeye (Inchinor)
3178a^6

Prize Money *Saeed bin Suroor* 116
3 b g Authorized(IRE) Dresden Doll (USA) (Elusive Quality (USA))
1891^2 ◆ 2432^2 3296^2 4059^8 4753^5 (7824)

Probably (IRE) *Rune Haugen* 97
6 b h Danehill Dancer(IRE) Wedding Morn (IRE) (Sadler's Wells (USA))
188a^{10} 3449a^9

Proctor *Stuart Kittow* 87
3 b g Makfi Super Motiva (Motivator)
1426^7 2614^5 3577^3 (4272) ◆ (5074) 6735^5

Procurator (IRE) *Richard Hannon* 82
2 b c Canford Cliffs(IRE) Lulawin (Kyllachy)
4533^4 5107^3 ◆ 5356^5 (5829) 7185^5 7549^8 7820^5

Profitable (IRE) *Clive Cox* 120
4 b h Invincible Spirit(IRE) Dani Ridge (IRE) (Indian Ridge)
(1862) (2475) (3244) ◆ 4151^4 5614^6 6990a^7

Profusion *Sir Michael Stoute* 64
4 b g Dansili Red Bloom (Selkirk (USA))
2414^8

Project Bluebook (FR) *John Quinn* a72 85
3 bl g Sinndar(IRE) Apperella (Rainbow Quest (USA))
245^3 ◆ 458^3 ◆ (789) ◆ (1410) 2224^4 2909^7 3809^2 4137^4 (4969) 6561^{12}

Projection *Roger Charlton* 110
3 b g Acclamation Spotlight (Dr Fong (USA))
4062^4 4862^5 ◆ 5409^3

Prominna *Tony Carroll* a64 58
6 ch g Proclamation(IRE) Minnina (IRE) (In The Wings)
292^5 (669) 1059^3

Promised Money (IRE) *Edward Lynam* 92
3 b f Dark Angel(IRE) Hartstown House (IRE) (Primo Dominie)
2272a^9

Promise To Be True (IRE) *A P O'Brien* 111
2 b f Galileo(IRE) Sumora (IRE) (Danehill (USA))
(4573a) 6385a^5 6986a^2 7721a^3

Promising (IRE) *Richard Hannon* 104
2 b f Invincible Spirit(IRE) Lethal Quality (USA) (Elusive Quality (USA))
4756^2 5400^3 5870^2

Promising Run (USA) *Saeed bin Suroor* a96 110
3 b f Hard Spun(USA) Aviacion (BRZ) (Know Heights (IRE))
184a^2 534a^2 2160^3 3339^5 4822^6 (6158a) 6746^4 7351^{11}

Properus (IRE) *Keith Dalgleish* 87
4 b g Lord Shanakill(USA) Amistad (GER) (Winged Love (IRE))
1215^7 (Dead)

Prophetess *Giles Bravery* a22
3 b f Equiano(FR) Bible Box (IRE) (Bin Ajwaad (IRE))
791^6

Prophets Pride *F Vermeulen* a82 55
6 b h Sakhee(USA) Winner's Call (Indian Ridge)
(3184a)

Prosecute (FR) *David Simcock* a50 84
3 b g Lawman(FR) Dissitation (IRE) (Spectrum (IRE))
2212^2 (3042) ◆ 3557^8 4358^6 6055^2 6803^8 7153^{10} 7486^{11}

Prosecution *Hughie Morrison* a63
2 b c Lawman(FR) Convention (Encosta De Lago (AUS))
7733^{12} 7976^6 8246^7

Prospectus *Hughie Morrison* a63 70
3 b g Sakhee(USA) Some Sunny Day (Where Or When (IRE))
1235^5 2126^5 (6654) 7321^8

Prosper *Roger Varian* a74
2 gr f Exceed And Excel(AUS) Ela Athena (Ezzoud (IRE))
(7761)

Prost (GER) *Ed Vaughan* a78 57
2 b g Tin Horse(IRE) Plebeya (IRE) (Dubawi (IRE))
7665^5 (8420a)

Protectionist (GER) *A Wohler* 119
6 b h Monsun(GER) Patineuse (IRE) (Peintre Celebre (USA))
(3934a) (5454a) 7405a^9

Protest (IRE) *Sylvester Kirk* a64 55
3 b g Fastnet Rock(AUS) Phrase (Royal Anthem (USA))
1345^4 1917^5 3558^9 3988^6 4269^{10} 4882^6 5167^5 5554^8 6651^4 (6966) (7256) (7754)

Proud Archi (IRE) *Michael Dods* a53 80
2 b g Archipenko(USA) Baharah (USA) (Elusive Quality (USA))
(3477) ◆ 4699^4 5518^2 5967^9 6791^3

Proud Kate *Christine Dunnett* 30
2 b f Proud Citizen(USA) Oceans Apart (Desert Prince (IRE))
7224^7 7439^9 8081^{12}

Proudofyou (USA) *Gianluca Bietolini* a65 76
3 b f Tizway(USA) Proudeyes (GER) (Dashing Blade)
3120a^2

Proud Show *David Dennis* 49
2 b g Showcasing Fakhuur (Dansili)
4805^6 5820^5 6439^{12} 7244^{10}

Proud Sky *J S Bolger* a76 89
3 b g Acclamation Claiomh Solais (IRE) (Galileo (IRE))
828a^2

Proud Times (USA) *Ali Stronge* a5 4
10 bb g Proud Citizen(USA) Laura's Pistolette (USA) (Big Pistol (USA))
2131^9

Proven Point (IRE) *Tony Coyle* a73 63
3 b g Fastnet Rock(AUS) Speciale (USA) (War Chant (USA))
768^3 ◆ 1113^4 2835^4 3281^4 4372^4 5028^6 5322^5

Provident Spirit *David O'Meara* 91
5 b g Invincible Spirit(IRE) Port Providence (Red Ransom (USA))
1215^P (Dead)

Provoking (USA) *David Evans* a43 69
3 bb g Any Given Saturday(USA) Fair And Lively (USA) (Lively One (USA))
1532^6 2798^5 3998^{13} 4794^7 5720^8

Prufrock (IRE) *David Simcock* a62 73
2 ch f Roderic O'Connor(IRE) Indaba (IRE) (Indian Ridge)
4759^2 ◆ 5469^4 ◆ 5772^2 ◆ 6292^8

Pryers Princess *David C Griffiths* a63 61
4 ch m Medicean Opening Ceremony (USA) (Quest For Fame)
1334^5 2332^{13} 2655^9 3069^4 3553^7 3984^{11}

Prying Pandora (FR) *Richard Fahey* 84
3 b f Dark Angel(IRE) Leniency (IRE) (Cape Cross (IRE))
2419^3 (3899) 4318^5 6810^4 7540^8

Psychedelic Funk *G M Lyons* 104
2 ch c Choisir(AUS) Parabola (Galileo (IRE))
3243^3 4414a^2 6386a^6

Psychology *Kenny Johnson* a53
3 b g Shamardal(USA) Emotion Parade (ARG) (Parade Marshal (USA))
8310^5 8481^4

Publilia *Mark Johnston* a82 90
4 b m Makfi Terentia (Diktat)
360^5 712^6

Pucon *Roger Teal* a68 79
7 b m Kyllachy The Fugative (Nicholas (USA))
714^8 903^8 1150^2 1811^5 (2905) 4224^3 5669^7

Pudding Chare (IRE) *Richard Fahey* a63 71
2 b c Arcano(IRE) Rosy Dudley (IRE) (Grand Lodge (USA))
5029^3 6002^6 7381^4

Puelo (FR) *A De Royer-Dupre* 65
2 b c Sinndar(IRE) Premiere Danseuse (Gold Away (IRE))
3871a^9

Pullman Brown (USA) *David Marnane* a81 88
4 b g Big Brown(USA) Touch Too Much (USA) (Holy Bull (USA))
4070a^5

Pull The Pin (IRE) *Heather Dalton* a53 63
7 b g Kheleyf(USA) Inscribed (IRE) (Fasliyev (USA))
22^{10} 135^4 340^2 418^{12} 442^6 895^8

Pull The Plug (IRE) *Declan Carroll* a86 85
5 b m Sleeping Indian Babylonian (Shamardal (USA))
1447^9 (1872)

Pulsating (IRE) *Ali Stronge* a69 66
2 b f Dragon Pulse(IRE) Safqa (Singspiel (IRE))
2014^3 2675^2 3282^3 3654^3 4209^2 ◆ 4508^3 5265^7 5840^6 6588^2 7143^3 (7510) 7893^5 8230^2

Pumaflor (IRE) *Richard Whitaker* a48 87
4 b g Aussie Rules(USA) Krasotka (IRE) (Soviet Star (USA))
2121^5 2347^2 2662^7 3185^2 3517^7 4611^3 4893^{10} 5886^2 6217^3 (6736) 6956^4 7796^{10}

Pumblechook *Lucy Wadham* a71 83
3 b c Dalakhani(IRE) Chiang Mai (IRE) (Sadler's Wells (USA))
1651^3 (3434) 4859^4 7060^{13}

Pumpkin Rumble (USA) *Gary Scherer* 108
5 ch g English Channel(USA) Clarins (USA) (Storm Cat (USA))
5431a^9

Punkawallah *Tom Dascombe* a65
2 b g Sepoy(AUS) Max One Two Three (IRE) (Princely Heir (IRE))
7065^9 7366^4

Puntrooskie (USA) *Donald C MacRae* a106 92
5 bb g In Summation(USA) Siren Cove (USA) (Montbrook (USA))
6400a^2

Pupa Di Saronno (FR) *H-A Pantall* 99
5 b m Orpen(USA) Olonella (Selkirk (USA))
2317a^{10} 3090a^4 3796a^3 4905a^{11} 7030a^{10} 7758a^{11}

Pupil (IRE) *S Seemar* a88 92
5 b g Mastercraftsman(IRE) Blue Iris (Petong)
229a^3 718a^7

Purana *Mrs Ilka Gansera-Leveque* a40 32
5 ch m Pastoral Pursuits Arruhan (IRE) (Mujtahid (USA))
985^{11} 1162^7

Pure Art *Ralph Beckett* a77 101
3 b f Dutch Art Pure Song (Singspiel (IRE))
(1577) ◆ 2795^2 4042^2 4737^4 (5650) 6357a^7 7119^3

Pure Diamond *Saeed bin Suroor* a90 103
3 b f Street Cry(IRE) White Rose (GER) (Platini (GER))
184a^3 ◆ 536a^2 (807a) ◆ 1858^5 3274^{21} 4395^6

Pure Fantasy *Roger Charlton* a70 90
3 b f Fastnet Rock(AUS) Fictitious (Machiavellian (USA))
(3071) 4160^5 4793^2 5520^4 (6301) 6948^6

Pure Innocence (IRE) *Ralph Beckett* a61 58
3 b f Montjeu(IRE) Festoso (IRE) (Diesis)
3535^8 4319^6 4978^6

Pure Sensation (USA) *Christophe Clement* a94 114
5 rg g Zensational(USA) Pure Disco (USA) (Disco Rico (USA))
7833a^3

Pure Shores *Charlie Appleby* a66
2 b f Dubawi(IRE) Polly's Mark (IRE) (Mark Of Esteem (IRE))
8081^4

Pure Soul *Ismail Mohammed* a68 59
3 b g Iffraaj Spiritual Healing (IRE) (Invincible Spirit (IRE))
1270^8 1701^6 3491^5

Pure Vanity *Roger Charlton* a65 62
3 b f New Approach(IRE) Miss Pinkerton (Danehill (USA))
1577^{10} 5122^8 5508^3 6367^7

Purford Green *Michael Attwater* a48 20
7 ch m Kyllachy Mo Stopher (Sharpo)
168^6 431^8 696^7

Purley Queen (IRE) *Mrs C Gilbert* a51 58
7 b m Piccolo Queenie (Indian Ridge)
1517a^7 2284a^9 2953a^3

Purple Belle *Jimmy Fox* a48 22
3 br f Assertive Stunning In Purple (IRE) (Kheleyf (USA))
4264^{10} 5766^6 7282^4 8179^5 8492^{13}

Purple Lane (IRE) *Luke Dace* a65 66
5 ch g Danehill Dancer(IRE) Big Heart (Mr Greeley (USA))
3648^{10} 4267^8 5021^2

Purple Magic *Michael Bell* a71 98
3 b f Rip Van Winkle(IRE) Discerning (Darshaan)
2181^3 3251^4 (3778) (4351) (5851) 7271^4

Purple 'n Gold (IRE) *David Pipe* a65 60
7 b g Strategic Prince Golden Dew (IRE) (Montjeu (IRE))
773^8

Purple Party (IRE) *Gary Moore* a55 56
3 b f Cockney Rebel(IRE) Lille Ida (Hawk Wing (USA))
2009^{14} 2483^{11} 2980^8 3973^4 (6187) 6890^2 7427^3

Purple Raven *Michael Bell* a68 71
3 b f Poet's Voice Juniper Girl (IRE) (Revoque (IRE))
1276^3 1619^7 3318^{10} 6698^3 7104^4 7425^{11}

Purple Rock (IRE) *Michael Easterby* a86 84
4 b g Fastnet Rock(AUS) Amethyst (IRE) (Sadler's Wells (USA))
1215^{10} 1521^5 1797^7 3115^{12} 3840^3 ◆ 4129^9 4611^4 5292^3 (5392) 6160^6 7159^{12} (8007) 8231^7

Pursuing Steed *John Gallagher* 56
2 b g Pastoral Pursuits Emma Peel (Emarati (USA))
2847^9 4805^7

Pursuitofthestars (IRE) *John Gosden* a81 80
3 b f Sea The Stars(IRE) Pursuit Of Life (Pursuit Of Love)
1179^2 (1704) 1966^6

Pursuit Of Time *Neil Mulholland* a48 50
3 br f Pastoral Pursuits Pressed For Time (IRE) (Traditionally (USA))
735^5 896^6 948^6 1548^7 2107^9 2373^4 3993^8 4993^9 5706^8

Pusey's Secret *John Gallagher* a76 78
3 b f Sakhee's Secret Pusey Street Lady (Averti (IRE))
(1451) 1812^5 2554^6 2981^3

Pushaq (IRE) *Marco Botti* a81 53
3 b g Roderic O'Connor(IRE) Et Dona Ferentes (Green Desert (USA))
1000^2 (1132) 2412^{10} 3187^{10} 5082^3 5810^8 7529^6

Pushjockeypush *Stuart Williams* 16
2 gr g Silver Frost(IRE) Daraiyna (FR) (Refuse To Bend (IRE))
7468^{13}

Pushkin Museum (IRE) *Richard Fahey* a51 65
5 gr g Soviet Star(USA) Chaste (Groom Dancer (USA))
1084^3 1433^4 1843^3 2572^7 3307^4 3709^7 4452^9 5162^5 5714^4 ◆ 6008^6 6660^6

Push Me (IRE) *Iain Jardine* a85 81
9 gr m Verglas(IRE) Gilda Lilly (USA) (War Chant (USA))
(2198) 2347^6 ◆ 2917^2 3152^9 4042^5

Pushy Lady *Rod Millman* 63
3 b f Piccolo Jane's Payoff (IRE) (Danetime (IRE))
1892^7 2544^9

Pussy Galore (IRE) *Richard Hannon* a66 57
2 b f Harbour Watch(IRE) Green Chorus (IRE) (Oratorio (IRE))
6062^5 6578^8 6897^7 7098^4 7482^3

Putaringonit (IRE) *Jeremy Gask* a75 74
4 ch m Peintre Celebre(USA) Virginias Best (King's Best (USA))
2860^2 3560^6 4383^8 5397^7

Puteminthebootn (IRE) *David Evans* a48 47
3 b f Medicean Tiger Royale (Tiger Hill (IRE))
3^8 2458^5 3000^4 3140^3 3811^7

Put The Boot In (IRE) *Barry Brennan* a60 65
4 ch g Duke Of Marmalade(IRE) Mubkera (IRE) (Nashwan (USA))
164^9 435^7 695^{12} 8469^7

Pyjamarama *Roger Varian* a69
2 b f Exceed And Excel(AUS) Dylanesque (Royal Applause)
6625^8 6897^4 7527^6

Pyla (IRE) *Amy Murphy* a71 74
4 b m Footstepsinthesand Beautiful Hill (IRE) (Danehill (USA))
437^2 621^4 777^6 1725^6 1926^7 3078^2 3974^4 (4388) 6453^{12} 7485^2

Pylon (SAF) *M F De Kock* a88
7 b g Fort Wood(USA) Golden Cell (SAF) (Goldkeeper (USA))
624a^{10} 844a^{10}

Pyroclastic (IRE) *Nick Kent* a69 42
4 b g Tagula(IRE) Gypsy Royal (IRE) (Desert Prince (IRE))
97^3 190^3 482^{11} 696^2 955^8 1261^9 4005^{11} 4715^6 6636^8 7260^{11}

Pyromaniac (IRE) *A J Martin* a69 91
6 b g Invincible Spirit(IRE) Silly Goose (IRE) (Sadler's Wells (USA))
6350a^2 7195a^7

Python *Andrew Crook* 24
4 b g Dansili Imbabala (Zafonic (USA))
5353^5 5979^5 6452^9

Qaffaal (USA) *Michael Easterby* a93 79
5 b g Street Cry(IRE) Wasseema (USA) (Danzig (USA))
(1502) 1652^3 (2660) 3517^2 ◆ 4231^6 5017^{11} 5886^6 6217^{12} (6907) (7691) (8177) 8279^2 8593^2

Qamarain (USA) *Brian Meehan* 80
3 ch f Hard Spun(USA) Emtyazat (Gone West (USA))
(5850) 6483^6 6947^3 7504^{15}

Qassem (IRE) *Hugo Palmer* a75 97
3 b g Lope De Vega(IRE) Biswa (USA) (Kafwain (USA))
7824^8

Qasser (IRE) *Harry Whittington* a79 69
7 b g Intikhab(USA) Surrender To Me (USA) (Royal Anthem (USA))
465^7 708^2 1652^4

Qatar Dream (IRE) *F Rohaut* 102
3 b c Makfi Baine (FR) (Country Reel (USA))
1686a^2

Qatari Gold (USA) *M Delzangles* 102
3 b c Lemon Drop Kid(USA) Forest Valentine (USA) (Forestry (USA))
6597a^6

Qatari Hunter (IRE) *J S Bolger* a106 107
3 b c Footstepsinthesand Inis Boffin (Danehill Dancer (IRE))
(4070a) 4753^4 6932a^4

Qatari Riyals (IRE) *Richard Hannon* a64
2 b f Kodiac Mary Frith (Acclamation)
7279^3

Qatar Light (IRE) *Majed Seifeddine* a59 90
4 bb g Zebedee Belle Child (IRE) (Bijou D'Inde)
755a^7

Qatar Lion (IRE) *Conrad Allen* 12
2 b g Tamayuz Tonle Sap (IRE) (Manduro (GER))
6751^9

Qatar Man (IRE) *Marco Botti* a81
2 b c Archarcharch(USA) Dough On The Go (USA) (Bernardini (USA))
5676^2 6368^2 (7977)

Qatar Power (FR) *F Head* 101
3 b f Le Havre(IRE) Brave Power (USA) (Aldebaran (USA))
2928a^7 6272a^10 7348a^3

Qatea (IRE) *Donald McCain* 36
4 ch g Duke Of Marmalade(IRE) Taking Liberties (IRE) (Royal Academy (USA))
1560^12 4772^12 5383^9

Q Cee *Eugene Stanford* a66 66
3 b g Denounce Gibraltar Lass (USA) (Concerto (USA))
4840^8 7011^4 7362^5 8496^3

Qemah (IRE) *J-C Rouget* 117
3 b f Danehill Dancer(IRE) Kartica (Rainbow Quest (USA))
(1581a) 2282a^3 (3339) ◆ (4926a) 6352a^3

Qewy (IRE) *Charlie Appleby* 112
6 b g Street Cry(IRE) Princess Nada (Barathea (IRE))
3246^2 ◆ 4734^2 (7481a) 7756a^4 (7947a)

Qeyaadah (IRE) *Ed Dunlop* 92
3 b g Acclamation Effervesce (IRE) (Galileo (IRE))
2871^3 6210^6

Qibtee (FR) *Les Eyre* a44 61
6 b g Antonius Pius(USA) Embers Of Fame (IRE) (Sadler's Wells (USA))
2343^3 2799^4 3052^6 3711^6 3983^5 4340^3 5028^2 5343^4 6029^4 6840^4

Qortaaj *David Loughnane* a71 71
3 b g Kyllachy Cardrona (Selkirk (USA))
3267^6 3609^6 3948^9 4238^8 4517^2 4771^10 5386^9 7738^3 8037^6 8067^9 8287^8 8411^3

Q Ten Girl (IRE) *James Unett* a61 47
3 ch f Zebedee Regresa A Mi (IRE) (Spartacus (IRE))
147^6 7240^12 8191^5

Quadriga (IRE) *Chris Grant* a41 30
6 b g Acclamation Turning Light (GER) (Fantastic Light (USA))
2^10 867^3 1064^10 1156^2 (1295) 3342^7 7795^12 8350^8 8471^4

Quality Art (USA) *Simon Hodgson* a71 64
8 b g Elusive Quality(USA) Katherine Seymour (Green Desert (USA))
106^8 293^5 462^3 714^7 856^7 1059^4 1721^2 2785^U 3316^3 3469^5 4529^6 7018^6 7913^7 7945^6 8040^8 8408^4

Quality Moment (IRE) *Saeed bin Suroor* a64
2 ch f Casamento(IRE) Ashirah (USA) (Housebuster (USA))
8063^3

Quality Song (USA) *Richard Hughes* a86 67
4 b g Elusive Quality(USA) Run In (USA) (Dynaformer (USA))
779^3 ◆ 1144^2 2399^7 3783^9

Quality Time (IRE) *Saeed bin Suroor* a94 74
3 b f Exceed And Excel(AUS) Crinoline (USA) (Street Cry (IRE))
1206^3 2034^4 3274^16 4105^12

Quandary Peak *J S Moore* a64 88
2 b f Mount Nelson Sahariri (IRE) (Red Ransom (USA))
2822^13 (3404) 4148^8 4902a^6 5447a^6

Quantum Dot (IRE) *Ed de Giles* a61 68
5 ch g Exceed And Excel(AUS) Jeed (IRE) (Mujtahid (USA))
(241) 504^10 889^6 1133^6 1913^4 2458^4 3136^5 3316^6 (4292) 4590^3 5105^5 (5546)

Quantum Field (USA) *David Brown* a17 65
2 b f Distorted Humor(USA) Bootery (USA) (Storm Boot (USA))
1437^10 2885^5 4423^3 5109^6 6026^10 7143^14

Quarterback (GER) *Rune Haugen* a54 108
4 b h American Post Quebra (GER) (Surumu (GER))
285a^3 538a^5 811a^7 3340^14 4329a^3 (5187a) 5950a^9 (6390a) 7545^13

Quasillo (GER) *A Wohler* 106
4 ch h Sea The Stars(IRE) Quetena (GER) (Acatenango (GER))
4253a^2

Quatorze (FR) *A De Mieulle* a97 108
6 b g Elusive City(USA) Queseraisjesanstoi (FR) (Rainbow Quest (USA))
744a^10

Quatrieme Ami *Philip McBride* a97 87
3 b g Equiano(FR) Hundred Year Flood (USA) (Giant's Causeway (USA))
1070^4 5657^13 7315^8 7610^5 8050^8

Quebee *Clive Cox* a69 106
3 b f Sir Percy Tintac (Intikhab (USA))
1256^2 2009^3 (2749) (3957) 4737^5 ◆ (5874) (6482) 7119^4

Quechua (ARG) *Patrick Shaw* 108
5 b g Pure Prize(USA) Queen Cabaret (BRZ) (Wild Event (USA))
8329a^8

Queen Agdal (IRE) *M Delcher Sanchez* a66 66
3 b f Mastercraftsman(IRE) Street Romance (USA) (Street Cry (IRE))
716a^8

Queen Aggie (IRE) *Tony Carroll* a81 72
6 b m Elnadim(USA) Catfoot Lane (Batshoof)
24^4 (269) 415^5 ◆ (564) 632^3 670^6 3132^7 3398^6 4094^4 4630^6 5190^7

Queen Alpha (IRE) *Denis Gerard Hogan* a24 49
3 b f Thewayyouare(USA) Liturgy (IRE) (Catcher In The Rye (IRE))
5096a^17

Queen Alphabet (IRE) *Peter Fahey* a63 87
7 b m King's Theatre(IRE) A-To-Z (IRE) (Ahonoora)
4850a^8 6350a^4 7708a^21

Queen Anne's Lace (USA) *D K Weld* 96
2 gr f Lonhro(AUS) Harpeth (USA) (Sadler's Wells (USA))
7193a^3 7707a^9

Queen Blossom (IRE) *P J Prendergast* 95
3 b f Jeremy(USA) Mark Of An Angel (IRE) (Mark Of Esteem (IRE))
(1016a) 1507a^5 2167a^6

Queen Caroline (USA) *Michael Matz* 95
3 bb f Blame(USA) Queen's Plaza (USA) (Forestry (USA))
7379a^8

Queen Catrine (IRE) *G M Lyons* a89 106
5 b m Acclamation Kahira (IRE) (King's Best (USA))
1016a^10 2067a^7 2497a^6 4826^6

Queen Celeste (IRE) *Mark Johnston* 60
2 b f Acclamation Wiltshire Life (IRE) (Camacho)
2254^7 (3396) 3686^5 6807^10 7041^10 7528^10

Queen Elsa (IRE) *K R Burke*
3 b f Frozen Power(IRE) Spring Surprise (Hector Protector (USA))
2009^16

Queen In Waiting (IRE) *Mark Johnston* a77 72
2 rg f Exceed And Excel(AUS) Princess Taise (USA) (Cozzene (USA))
5317^2 (5631)

Queen Kindly *Richard Fahey* 112
2 ch f Frankel Lady Of The Desert (USA) (Rahy (USA))
(2852) ◆ 3336^3 ◆ (4254) ◆ (5584) 6784^4

Queen Of Norway (IRE) *Paddy Butler*
5 b m Papal Bull Fanacanta (IRE) (Olden Times)
5056^4 5710^10 5925^8

Queen Of Sicily (USA) *J S Bolger* 94
3 b f Cape Cross(IRE) Jealous Again (USA) (Trippi (USA))
1369a^8

Queen Of The Stars *William Haggas* a72 83
3 b f Sea The Stars(IRE) Queen Of Pentacles (IRE) (Selkirk (USA))
2215^7 3028^3 3781^4 6052^2 (6520)

Queen Of Time *Henry Candy* 79
2 b f Harbour Watch(IRE) Black Belt Shopper (IRE) (Desert Prince (IRE))
6782^6 ◆ 7314^6 7695^2 ◆

Queensbrydge *Robyn Brisland* a89 86
2 ch f Dutch Art Meydan Princess (IRE) (Choisir (AUS))
4011^3 4951^10 5469^2 (5632) 6124^4 6555^7 7155^9

Queen's Code (IRE) *Charles Hills* 59
3 b f Shamardal(USA) Dehbanu (IRE) (King's Best (USA))
1392^12 1998^3 3634^5

Queen's Novel *James Tate* a76 74
4 b m King's Best(USA) Jane Austen (IRE) (Galileo (IRE))
1633^8 5037^8 6128^4

Queens Parade (IRE) *Sharon Watt* 21
2 b f Sir Prancealot(IRE) Straight Sets (IRE) (Pivotal)
1520^6 2771^12 3433^8 5364^12 6026^12

Queen's Pearl (IRE) *Roger Varian* a77 89
4 b m Exceed And Excel(AUS) Gimasha (Cadeaux Genereux)
2042^9 3116^P 4398^14 6627^11

Queens Ring (JPN) *Keiji Yoshimura* 112
4 bb m Manhattan Cafe(JPN) Aqua Ring (JPN) (Anabaa (USA))
8333a^9

Queens Royale *Michael Appleby* a56 64
2 b f Stimulation(IRE) Sofia Royale (Royal Applause)
7071^4 7819^8 8065^6

Queen Starbond *Ben Haslam* 15
2 b f Monsieur Bond(IRE) Presidium Star (Presidium)
7741^13

Queen's Trust *Sir Michael Stoute* a85 115
3 b f Dansili Queen's Best (King's Best (USA))
2245^4 ◆ 3297^4 ◆ 4864^2 5586^3 7351^3 (7831a)

Queen Zain (IRE) *Charlie Fellowes* a58 55
4 b m Lawman(FR) Tropical Lady (IRE) (Sri Pekan (USA))
326^3 ◆ 383^5

Quelindo (GER) *Gabor Maronka* 97
4 rg h Aussie Rules(USA) Quintana (GER) (Fantastic Light (USA))
5904a^6

Quenby (USA) *A Wohler* 97
4 b m Ambassador(GER) Quintela (Giant's Causeway (USA))
2633a^8

Quench Dolly *John Gallagher* 77
2 gr f Hellvelyn Hollybell (Beveled (USA))
(2429) 3270^11 4503^4 (5014) 5741^4 6763^7

Querido (GER) *Paddy Butler* a41 30
12 b g Acatenango(GER) Quest Of Fire (FR) (Rainbow Quest (USA))
155^11

Quest For More (IRE) *Roger Charlton* a85 117
6 b g Teofilo(IRE) No Quest (IRE) (Rainbow Quest (USA))
2486^2 4164^3 4799^6 (5612) 6284^2 (6974a) 7349^2

Question Of Faith *Martin Todhunter* a56 55
5 b m Yeats(IRE) Anastasia Storm (Mozart (IRE))
1626^8 1873^7 2094^4 2573^5 ◆ 2962^3 3921^6 4194^3 (5726) 6102^4

Questo *Tracy Waggott* a60 73
4 ch g Monsieur Bond(IRE) Ex Gracia (Efisio)
2346^7 3422^4 4428^14 5069^7 5968^8 6215^9 6744^6 6910^3 7584^2 (7747)

Quest Of Colour (IRE) *Richard Fahey* a74 70
5 b m Iffraaj With Colour (Rainbow Quest (USA))
(266)

Quetzaltenango (FR) *J S Moore* 58
3 b g Evasive Grande Fiore (GER) (Lando (GER))
6443^3 7014^3 7265a^9

Queveda De Lopa *Yasmin Almenrader* a53
3 ch c Lope De Vega(IRE) Hot Property (USA) (Thunder Gulch (USA))
128a^12

Quevillon (FR) *C Lerner* a72 78
2 ch c Siyouni(FR) Princess Roseburg (USA) (Johannesburg (USA))
6638a^4

Quick Artist (IRE) *Simon Crisford* a44 62
2 ch f Dutch Art Excellerator (IRE) (Exceed And Excel (AUS))
4586^2 ◆ 7484^9

Quickaswecan *Milton Bradley* a73 81
5 b g Shamardal(USA) Arctic Air (Polar Falcon (USA))
955^9 1341^7 2643^8 3259^6 3559^2 (3811) 4084^4 5762^8 6255^10 7268^12

Quick Jack (IRE) *A J Martin* a67 110
7 ch g Footstepsinthesand Miss Polaris (Polar Falcon (USA))
1967^6 5655^3 (6350a) 7569a^6

Quick Look *William Jarvis* a53 85
3 b g Kheleyf(USA) Weqaar (USA) (Red Ransom (USA))
4889^3 ◆ 5372^3 5881^3 6371^11 7443^4

Quick March *Roger Charlton* a57 81
3 b f Lawman(FR) Strut (Danehill Dancer (IRE))
1599^16 2002^9 3105^6 4222^3 4990^3 6296^6

Quick N Quirky (IRE) *Tim Easterby* 85
3 b f Lilbourne Lad(IRE) Beseech (IRE) (Danehill (USA))
1599^5 (2095) 2532^2 2907^6 3519^5 3775^4 4116^3 4548^3 5180^2 5588^8 6342^6 6811^8 6956^12

Quick Thought (IRE) *Dr Jon Scargill* a64 62
2 b f Sir Percy Contemplate (Compton Place)
3301^2 4016^3 4397^6 6630^9 7147^11 7866^6

Quick Witted *Harry Dunlop* a54
3 b f Poet's Voice Fastback (IRE) (Singspiel (IRE))
29^6 163^5 517^6 818^8

Quidura *A Wohler* 104
3 b f Dubawi(IRE) Quetena (GER) (Acatenango (GER))
1513a^10

Quiet Approach *John Davies* 8
3 b g Makfi Silent Act (USA) (Theatrical (IRE))
3578^6

Quiet Moment (IRE) *Ben Haslam* 68
2 br f Dandy Man(IRE) Easee On (IRE) (Hawk Wing (USA))
3902^2 4725^3 5414^5 7091^6

Quiet Reflection *K R Burke* 120
3 b f Showcasing My Delirium (Haafhd)
(1374a) (2692) (3338) 4151^3 (6120) 7350^7

Quiet Warrior (IRE) *Tony Carroll* a67 44
5 b g Kodiac Pretty Woman (IRE) (Night Shift (USA))
3510^8 (5080) (6249) 8483^5

Quiet Weekend *James Bethell* 49
2 b g Mawatheeq(USA) Maid Of Perth (Mark Of Esteem (IRE))
5150^6 6535^10

Quiliano (FR) *C Aubert* 89
3 ch c Dylan Thomas(IRE) Queen Of Fire (Dr Fong (USA))
8336a^11

Quina Brook (IRE) *Daniel Mark Loughnane* a64 34
3 b f Peintre Celebre(USA) Barconey (IRE) (Danehill Dancer (IRE))
4718^10 5130^7 6514^8 7896^8

Quindiana (FR) *H-A Pantall* 88
2 ch f Linngari(IRE) Belle Suisse (FR) (Hamas (IRE))
(7996a)

Quinteo (IRE) *Jo Hughes* a71 48
2 b g Requinto(IRE) Haraplata (GER) (Platini (GER))
6211^7 (6850)

Quintessential *Richard Fahey* a23
2 b f Dick Turpin(IRE) Quiquillo (USA) (Cape Canaveral (USA))
7939^11 8313^9 8526^7

Quintus Cerialis (IRE) *Karen George* a61 47
4 b g Vale Of York(IRE) Red Fox (IRE) (Spectrum (IRE))
236^3 561^3 782^2 1040^7 2290^7 2846^11 5301^8 6138^12 7738^13 8064^9 8382^12

Quite A Story *Patrick Chamings* a74 69
4 ch m Equiano(FR) Perfect Story (IRE) (Desert Story (IRE))
41^3 424^4 2846^10 4460^5 5330^6 (5827) 7203^5 8181^3

Quite Smart (IRE) *Robert Cowell* a76 78
4 b m Arcano(IRE) Lyca Ballerina (Marju (IRE))
80^2 (223)

Quite Sparky *Lucinda Egerton* a52 89
9 b g Lucky Story(USA) Imperialistic (IRE) (Imperial Ballet (IRE))
107^8 294^7 822^10

Quixote (GER) *Tony Carroll* a93 96
6 b h Pivotal Quebrada (IRE) (Devil's Bag (USA))
3910^9 4395^5 6298^10 7573^7 7868^8 8478^8

Quloob *Owen Burrows* a70 64
2 b c New Approach(IRE) Jadhwah (Nayef (USA))
6751^5 7239^5 7907^4

Quoteline Direct *Micky Hammond* a69 66
3 ch g Sir Percy Queen's Pudding (IRE) (Royal Applause)
2239^16 2695^12 3224^9 4241^7 4844^2 5539^6 5860^3 6646^5 7010^10 7755^3

Quothquan (FR) *Michael Madgwick* a74 68
2 b c Myboycharlie(IRE) Lonestar Spirit (IRE) (Invincible Spirit (IRE))
3463^8 3971^8 4989^5 5594^2 (6191) 7016^3 7697^6 8153^3 8466^2

Qurbaan (USA) *F Rohaut* a106 104
3 ch c Speightstown(USA) Flip Flop (FR) (Zieten (USA))
539a^5 7292a^2 (8431a)

Raaqy (IRE) *Owen Burrows* 93
3 gr f Dubawi(IRE) Natagora (FR) (Divine Light (JPN))
1771^2 3911^9 4582^9 5436^7

Raashdy (IRE) *Peter Hiatt* a69
3 b g Intikhab(USA) Maghya (IRE) (Mujahid (USA))
8195^7 (8342)

Race Day (IRE) *Saeed bin Suroor* a102 100
3 ch g Dubawi(IRE) Nadia (Nashwan (USA))
836^4 1071^2 2250^4 3296^6 4059^9 7651^4

Racemaker *Andrew Crook* 72
2 b g Stimulation(IRE) Sophies Heart (Hurricane Run (IRE))
2873^6 3254^3 3668^2 3971^5 (4404) (4509) 5536^2 5833^6 5977^6 6563^3 7319^11

Race Time (USA) *Seamus Durack* a43 31
3 bb f Street Sense(USA) Well At The Top (IRE) (Sadler's Wells (USA))
3996^7 6960^9 8157^6

Rachel's Temper (USA) *David Cannizzo* a95
5 bb m Flatter(USA) Fergie's Folly (USA) (Down The Aisle (USA))
89a^2

Racing Angel (IRE) *Mick Quinn* a71 76
4 b m Dark Angel(IRE) Roclette (USA) (Rock Of Gibraltar (IRE))
1119^6 2217^2 2403^6 (3136) 3559^6 4744^2 5040^8 6487^2 6946^7 7811^3

Racing History (IRE) *Saeed bin Suroor* 118
4 b h Pivotal Gonbarda (GER) (Lando (GER))
7353^6 7759a^2

Racing Knight (IRE) *David Evans* a59 69
4 b g Sir Percy Salydora (FR) (Peintre Celebre (USA))
1796^7 2233^13 3142^5 4226^3 5473^3

Racing Spirit *Kevin Frost* a39 47
4 ch g Sir Percy Suertuda (Domedriver (IRE))
981^9 1322^11

Raconteur *W McCreery* a72 61
3 b c Acclamation Red Bloom (Selkirk (USA))
3428a^7

Racquet *Richard Hannon* 86
3 br g Pastoral Pursuits Billie Jean (Bertolini (USA))
1442^9 2239^11 4079^12 4662^6 5284^3 6017^3 6363^13 7268^9 7415^3

Radanpour (IRE) *D K Weld* 102
4 b h Sea The Stars(IRE) Rose Quartz (Lammtarra (USA))
6350a^9

Radar Love (IRE) *J S Moore* a62 18
2 b f Sir Prancealot(IRE) Sonic Night (IRE) (Night Shift (USA))
3093^10 6189^6 6696^4 7455a^6 7690^9

Radiantly *W McCreery* 103
3 gr f Aussie Rules(USA) Eccentricity (USA) (Kingmambo (USA))
1369a^4 2068a^2 2509a^6 3274^4 5939a^5 6604a^11

Radio Silence (USA) *J S Bolger* 105
2 b c War Front(USA) Maryfield (CAN) (Elusive Quality (USA))
4414a^4 5683a^2 6349a^5

Radjash *Charlie Appleby* a77 77
2 b c Shamardal(USA) White Moonstone (USA) (Dynaformer (USA))
7065^2 ◆ 7495^3

Rafaaf (IRE) *Richard Phillips* a64 77
8 b g Royal Applause Sciunfona (IRE) (Danehill (USA))
1648^5 3474^11 5604^6 6280^9 7369^3

Rafeej *M Al Mheiri* a106 98
7 b h Iffraaj Muffled (USA) (Mizaaya)
90a^6 371a^4

Raffinee (FR) *D Smaga* a54 63
5 b m Air Eminem(IRE) Gioconda Umbra (ITY) (Sicyos (USA))
8422a^11

Raffle King (IRE) *Mick Channon* 71
2 b g Kodiac Tap The Dot (IRE) (Sharp Humor (USA))
1543^3 2023^6

Ragazzo (NOR) *Annike Bye Hansen* a105 102
7 b g Academy Award(IRE) Private Property (IRE) (Pips Pride)
5098a^5 5950a^12

Ragdollianna *Mark Hoad* a61 56
12 b m Kayf Tara Jupiters Princess (Jupiter Island)
2149^4 2634^9 4385^8

Ragner *David Simcock* a73
3 ch g New Approach(IRE) Frivolity (Pivotal)
219^2 377^3 746^3 1134^2

Rag Tatter *Kevin Ryan* 77
2 b g Kheleyf(USA) Golden Nun (Bishop Of Cashel)
4371^10 4805^2 5289^3 7355^2

Raheen House (IRE) *Brian Meehan* 111
2 b c Sea The Stars(IRE) Jumooh (Monsun (GER))
5740^2 6546^2 (7125) 7539^4

Rahmah (IRE) *Geoffrey Deacon* a74 76
4 b g Vale Of York(IRE) Sweet Home Alabama (IRE) (Desert Prince (IRE))
4208^6 4953^5 5547^2 6254^4 7076^6 7429^3 7895^8

Rah Rah *Mark Johnston* a100 100
3 b f Lonhro(AUS) Rahiyah (USA) (Rahy (USA))
(1083) 2034^9 4652^10

Rahyah *Adrian Paul Keatley* a82 77
3 b f Acclamation Kahlua Kiss (Mister Baileys)
59^2 253^6 (6504) 7823^12 7901^3

Rail Dancer *Richard Rowe* a59 57
4 b g Rail Link Mara Dancer (Shareef Dancer (USA))
401^8 620^8 788^10 1173^11 3230^6 3498^6 7421^10 8566^6

Rainbow Black *A Giorgi* a52 71
2 b c Kheleyf(USA) Highly Spiced (Cadeaux Genereux)
(2280a) 3006a^11

Rainbow Charlie *Mrs A Corson* 12
5 b g Rainbow High Natacha Rostow (Pursuit Of Love)
2285a^10 3917a^7

Rainbow Chimes (IRE) *Ann Duffield* a41 59
2 b f Galileo(IRE) Chiming (IRE) (Danehill (USA))
3433^5 8089^11

Rainbow Dreamer *Alan King* 92
3 b g Aqlaam Zamhrear (Singspiel (IRE))
1610^8 2209^3 2471^2 3768^4 4346^2 5331^2

Rainbow Lad (IRE) *Michael Appleby* a58 60
3 b g Lilbourne Lad(IRE) Carmona (Rainbow Quest (USA))
248[8] 509[6] 818[6] 1062[2] (1163) 1297[4] 2124[6] (3015) 3509[8] 4255[5] 4847[3] 8193[8] 8410[5]

Rainbow Legacy (IRE) *Sir Michael Stoute* 30
2 b c Frankel Gift Range (IRE) (Spectrum (IRE))
6632[9]

Rainbow Line (JPN) *Hidekazu Asami* 118
3 b c Stay Gold(JPN) Regenbogen (JPN) (French Deputy (USA))
8129a[6]

Rainbow Majesty (FR) *J-M Beguigne* 49
3 gr f Denon(USA) Rainbow Pointe (ITY) (Linamix (FR))
1542a[8]

Rainbow Mist (IRE) *Ann Duffield* 100
2 b c Lilbourne Lad(IRE) Misty Night (IRE) (Galileo (IRE))
(1868) 2264[3] 2669[3] (4111) 5583[7] 6282[5] 6954[8] 7170a[4]

Rainbow Orse *Robert Cowell* a56 79
4 b g Zebedee Khafayif (USA) (Swain (IRE))
2270[4] (3217) 4039[6] 5050[6] 6879[5] 7413[12]

Rainbow Pride (IRE) *Sir Mark Prescott Bt* a72 80
4 gr g Clodovil(IRE) Rahila (IRE) (Kalanisi (IRE))
4266[3] 4816[2] 5131[4] 5597[4] 6090[7] 6886[2]

Rainbow Rebel (IRE) *Mark Johnston* a68 94
3 b g Acclamation Imperial Quest (Rainbow Quest (USA))
(5539) (5779) (6323) (6772) 7005[2] 7287[2] 7499[6]

Rainfall Radar (USA) *Joseph G Murphy* a68 76
4 b m Rebuttal(USA) Sun Shower (IRE) (Indian Ridge)
6495a[6]

Rainford Glory (IRE) *Tim Fitzgerald* a50 51
6 ch g Rock Of Gibraltar(IRE) My Dolly Madison (In The Wings)
222[11] 1085[2] 1343[9] 2343[9] 3325[9] 4234[10] 6647[6] 7369[4] 7888[7] 8180[10] 8497[10]

Rainha Da Bateria (USA) *Chad C Brown* a92 106
4 ch m Broken Vow(USA) Amelia (USA) (Dixieland Band (USA))
3178a[7] 7404a[5]

Rain In The Face *Karen Tutty* a75 3
3 b g Naaqoos Makaaseb (USA) (Pulpit (USA))
275[2] 600[2] 892[2] 2640[8] 3653[9] 7857[14]

Rainmaker (FR) *R Rohne* a57 61
3 bb c Myboycharlie(IRE) Nikolenka (IRE) (Indian Ridge)
4220a[8]

Raise A Billion *John David Riches* 55
5 b g Major Cadeaux Romantic Destiny (Dubai Destination (USA))
4874[4] 5152[5] 5535[6]

Raise The Game (IRE) *Bill Turner* a64
3 b g Bushranger(IRE) Fancy Feathers (IRE) (Redback)
8320[3] 8559[8]

Raising Sand *Jamie Osborne* a94 100
4 b g Oasis Dream Balalaika (Sadler's Wells (USA))
2544[5] (2980) 3645[5] (4481) 5206[2] (6915) (7316) 7608[7]

Rajadamri *Rod Millman* a61 67
3 gr g Hellvelyn Crofters Ceilidh (Scottish Reel I (IRE))
3724[4] 4288[4] 5288[2] (5629) 6194[5] 6626[5] 6827[8]

Rajapur *Philip Kirby* a56 69
3 rg g Dalakhani(IRE) A Beautiful Mind (GER) (Winged Love (IRE))
69[4] 1062[8] 1484[3] 2308[7]

Rajar *Richard Fahey* a77 94
2 b f Archipenko(USA) Barnezet (GR) (Invincible Spirit (IRE))
1342[2] ◆ 3315[6] (4011) ◆ (4553) (4884) 5359[5] 5998[3] 7547[7] 7972a[3]

Raj Balaraaj (GER) *George Baker* 66
2 b g Kyllachy Ragazza Mio (IRE) (Generous (IRE))
3463[9] 5304[10] 6314[4] (7570) ◆

Rajeline (FR) *M Nigge* 79
2 gr f Rajsaman(FR) Tengeline (FR) (Cardoun (FR))
5142a[2]

Rakaan (IRE) *Brendan Powell* a74 66
9 ch g Bahamian Bounty Petite Spectre (Spectrum (IRE))
191[3] 457[6]

Rakematiz *Brett Johnson* 59
2 ch g Pivotal Regal Velvet (Halling (USA))
3859[12] 4707[8] 5202[5]

Rake's Progress *Heather Main* a63 51
2 b g Sir Percy Cartoon (Danehill Dancer (IRE))
3404[6] 6828[5] 7012[6] (7734)

Ralis (USA) *Doug O'Neill* a106 111
3 b c Square Eddie(CAN) Silar Rules (USA) (Ten Most Wanted (USA))
4173a[8] 7835a[9]

Ralphy Boy (IRE) *Alistair Whillans* a32 79
7 b g Acclamation Silcasue (Selkirk (USA))
1844[6] 2421[3] 2910[7] 3344[8] 3708[5] 4094[7] 4830[2] (5033) 5482[15] 5779[2] 6280[4] 6644[2] 7007[9] 7436[12]

Ralphy Lad (IRE) *Alan Swinbank* a82 57
5 b g Iffraaj Hawattef (IRE) (Mujtahid (USA))
7[2] 52[2] 337[2] 800[5] 1445[7] 2051[10] 4143[7] 4702[7] 6438[9] 8477[9]

Ramblow *Michael Appleby* a62 52
3 b f Notnowcato Nsx (Roi Danzig (USA))
1063[5] ◆ 1383[3] 4401[11] 4764[8] 5263[2] 6405[7] 7230[7] 8566[9]

Rampers (IRE) *Jamie Osborne* a64 65
3 b g Thewayyouare(USA) Korresia (IRE) (Elnadim (USA))
363[3] 510[2] 635[4] (750) 962[U] 1721[8] 4820[6] 5570[8]

Ramya (IRE) *Sir Michael Stoute* a54
2 ch f Pivotal Ebtisama (USA) (Kingmambo (USA))
7762[13]

Randall's Alannah (IRE) *Seamus Fahey* a49 45
6 b m High Chaparral(IRE) Randall's Diana (IRE) (Monashee Mountain (USA))
7646[2] 8121[7]

Randall Stevens (IRE) *M D O'Callaghan* 86
2 b c Tamayuz Sweet Surprise (IRE) (Danetime (IRE))
6388a[18]

Rangali *D Guillemin* 98
5 ch h Namid Tejaara (USA) (Kingmambo (USA))
7997a[4]

Range Of Knowledge (IRE) *E J O'Neill* a78 87
3 b g Bushranger(IRE) Pearls Of Wisdom (Kyllachy)
511a[3] 1311a[8]

Rantan (IRE) *David Barron* a66 87
3 b g Kodiac Peace Talks (Pivotal)
131[3] 2802[2] 3893[2] 4344[2]

Rapacity Alexander (IRE) *David Evans* a59 97
2 b f Dandy Man(IRE) Umlani (IRE) (Great Commotion (USA))
1087[3] 2007[2] (2583) (3182a) 3937a[5] 4755[9]

Rapid Ranger *Gary Moore* a79 54
2 b c Kyllachy Director's Dream (IRE) (Act One)
2543[3] 6622[2] 7748[4]

Rapid Rise (IRE) *David Brown* a77 65
2 b c Fast Company(IRE) French Doll (IRE) (Titus Livius (FR))
1635[3] 2196[3] 2913[2] 8140[3]

Rappelle Moi (FR) *D Prod'Homme* a81 81
3 b c Slickly(FR) Rafale Bere (FR) (Verglas (IRE))
2948a[10]

Rare Rhythm *Charlie Appleby* 101
4 b g Dubawi(IRE) Demisemiquaver (Singspiel (IRE))
3340[8]

Ras Al Qimmah (FR) *Mohammed Jassim Ghazali* 72
2 b f Falco(USA) Dynalosca (USA) (Dynaformer (USA))
8564a[12]

Rasaman (IRE) *Jim Goldie* a62 82
12 b g Namid Rasana (Royal Academy (USA))
1378[5] 1625[6] 2660[5] 2906[7] 3708[8] (4102) 4830[4] ◆ 5151[4] 5779[3] 6220[9]

Rasasee (IRE) *Marco Botti* a74 81
3 gr g Rip Van Winkle(IRE) Gleaming Silver (IRE) (Dalakhani (IRE))
1184[3] 1479[3] 2411[2] 3025[4] 5111[3] 6049[5]

Raseed *F Head* a97 110
3 b c Dubawi(IRE) Sudoor (Fantastic Light (USA))
(1582a) 2946a[9] 4439a[4]

Rashaan (IRE) *Colin Kidd* a45 87
4 ch g Manduro(GER) Rayyana (IRE) (Rainbow Quest (USA))
7195a[6] 7708a[9]

Rashawn (FR) *H-A Pantall* a81 85
3 b c Siyouni(FR) Retina (GER) (Dashing Blade)
2948a[12] 6310a[4]

Rashford's Double (IRE) *Richard Fahey* a79 82
2 b c Zoffany(IRE) Ardent Lady (Alhaarth (IRE))
2648[7] 4786[4] 5778[4] (7140) (7598) (7768) ◆

Rasikh (IRE) *Zuhair Mohsen* a70 86
3 b c Thewayyouare(USA) Ann Kastan (Red Ransom (USA))
756a[6]

Rasmee *Marco Botti* a87 54
3 b c Fastnet Rock(AUS) Reem (AUS) (Galileo (IRE))
3578[5] 5129[3] 5681[3] 6626[2] (7106)

Rasmiya (IRE) *William Haggas* a82 82
3 b f Galileo(IRE) Crystal Valkyrie (IRE) (Danehill (USA))
1704[2] ◆ (3508) 4655[2] 5768[4]

Raspberry Princess *Stuart Williams* a23
2 b f Royal Applause Eraadaat (IRE) (Intikhab (USA))
7466[9] 7696[13] 8354[10]

Rat Catcher (IRE) *Lisa Williamson* a59 48
6 b g One Cool Cat(USA) Molly Marie (IRE) (Fasliyev (USA))
98[7] 241[2] 504[7] 589[5] 732[8] 1319[5] 1720[9] 2447[6] 2856[5]

Rathbride Raven *Kevin Prendergast* a61 73
3 b f Raven's Pass(USA) Broadway Hit (Sadler's Wells (USA))
5096a[13]

Rathvale *Linda Perratt* a50 34
3 b f Prime Defender Frabrofen (Mind Games)
6617[6] 7097[12] 7253[10] 7603[4]

Rationality (USA) *John Gosden* a64 35
3 b f Dansili Real Sense (IRE) (Galileo (IRE))
1289[3] 1989[12]

Rattle On *Jim Boyle* a64 61
3 ch g Pivotal Sabreon (Caerleon (USA))
5996[6] 6294[9] 6805[5] 7214[11] 7642[2] 8085[5]

Rattling Jewel *Miss Nicole McKenna* a84 84
4 b g Royal Applause Mutoon (IRE) (Erhaab (USA))
1015a[3] 6819a[2] 7475a[2]

Raucous *William Haggas* 109
3 b g Dream Ahead(USA) Shyrl (Acclamation)
1424[5] 2870[3] 3269[8] 4393[3] 4865[3] 5880[6] 6941[3]

Ravelin (USA) *Charles Hills* 35
3 ch f Congrats(USA) Rouwaki (USA) (Miswaki (USA))
3856[8]

Raven Banner (IRE) *Daniel Mark Loughnane* a71 73
3 b f Raven's Pass(USA) Ask Annie (IRE) (Danehill (USA))
984[6] 1798[7] 2304[3] 3053[3] ◆ (3804) 4098[5] (5057) 6378[6] 7853[6] 8090[4]

Ravenhoe (IRE) *Mark Johnston* a78 79
3 ch g Bahamian Bounty Breathless Kiss (USA) (Roman Ruler (USA))
1112[4] 1492[3] 1922[9] 3266[7] (3877) 4358[4] 4717[2] 5017[10] 5677[7] 6220[3] (6645) 7051[8] 7687[2] 7813[5] 8011[13] 8205[4] 8379[2] 8531[7]

Ravenoak (IRE) *Tom Dascombe* a42 32
2 ch g Raven's Pass(USA) Fantastic Account (Fantastic Light (USA))
4125[8] 5107[5] 6009[9] 7482[8]

Ravenous *Luke Dace* a77 86
5 b g Raven's Pass(USA) Supereva (IRE) (Sadler's Wells (USA))
457[7] 616[5] 815[5] 1387[2] 1546[6] 2549[7] 3403[4] 3817[5] (4711) 5053[4] (5381) 6582[14] 7015[7]

Raven's Corner (IRE) *John Gosden* a85 87
3 ch c Raven's Pass(USA) Beautiful Filly (Oasis Dream)
1397[5] 1701[2] 2320[2] 2861[9] 3411[2] (4546)

Ravens Heart (IRE) *Dean Ivory* a39 49
4 b g Dansili Hymn Of Love (IRE) (Barathea (IRE))
1930[10] 3235[14] 3464[9] 8070[6] 8492[12]

Ravens Hill (IRE) *P J Prendergast* a51 56
3 ch g Raven's Pass(USA) Sister Red (IRE) (Diamond Green (FR))
7517a[11]

Raven's Lady *Marco Botti* a83 78
2 ch f Raven's Pass(USA) Pivotal Lady (Pivotal)
4885[4] 5722[2] ◆ (6624) ◆ 7114[9]

Ravens Quest *John Ryan* a71 84
3 ch g Raven's Pass(USA) Seradim (Elnadim (USA))
2209[7] (3906) ◆ 4793[5] 6416[12] 8363[6]

Ravenswood *Jonathan Portman* a53 55
3 b g Lawman(FR) Whatami (Daylami (IRE))
7052[9] 7627[9] 7904[6]

Ray *Jessica Long* 90
4 b m Rock Of Gibraltar(IRE) Mondschein (Rainbow Quest (USA))
(3448a)

Rayaa *John Butler* 78
3 b f Virtual Winsa (USA) (Riverman (USA))
1890[9] 5975[3] ◆ 6380[4] 7500[16]

Rayadour (IRE) *Micky Hammond* a62 62
7 b g Azamour(IRE) Rayyana (IRE) (Rainbow Quest (USA))
4239[7] 5726[10]

Rayanne *Sarah Hollinshead* a28 26
3 b f Sir Percy Wulfrida (IRE) (King's Best (USA))
5129[7] 5811[5] 7014[6] 7532[P]

Ray Donovan (IRE) *David O'Meara* 66
2 b g Acclamation Always The Lady (Halling (USA))
2119[7] 2344[8] 4227[12] (5112) 6045[6]

Rayisa (IRE) *M Halford* 97
3 b f Holy Roman Emperor(IRE) Rayka (IRE) (Selkirk (USA))
4812a[2]

Ray Of Light (IRE) *Richard Hannon* a49 60
3 b f Canford Cliffs(IRE) Elusive Galaxy (IRE) (Elusive City (USA))
1723[9] 2653[7]

Rayon Vert (FR) *H-A Pantall* 77
2 b c Harbour Watch(IRE) Mansoura (IRE) (Kalanisi (IRE))
7345a[2]

Ray's The Money (IRE) *Michael Bell* 83
2 b c Dragon Pulse(IRE) Riymaisa (IRE) (Traditionally (USA))
4125[2] ◆ 4866[2] 5637[5] 6682[2]

Rayvin Black *Oliver Sherwood* a68 85
7 b g Halling(USA) Optimistic (Reprimand)
(1854) 2392[2] ◆

Raze Aqlaam *Giles Bravery* 40
2 b f Aqlaam White Turf (GER) (Tiger Hill (IRE))
4054[11] 4524[8] 5853[4] 7098[7]

Razin' Hell *John Balding* a91 75
5 b g Byron Loose Caboose (IRE) (Tagula (IRE))
21[4] ◆ (426) 520[7] (938) 2416[13] 4039[3] 4544[2] 5060[4] 5867[5] 6680[9] 7643[10] 7892[3] 8308[4]

Razor Wind (IRE) *Charlie Appleby* a107 105
5 b g Dubawi(IRE) Tender Is Thenight (IRE) (Barathea (IRE))
594[2] ◆ 871[7]

R Bar Open (FR) *Dean Ivory* a61 59
3 bb g Orpen(USA) Bahama Love (USA) (Hennessy (USA))
2106[8] (3003) 3740[10] 4641[3] 5013[5] 5515[13] 6337[7] 7230[9] 7529[7]

Reach For Glory *Bill Turner*
2 ch g Phoenix Reach(IRE) Calgary (Pivotal)
5484[9] 5676[9]

Reachforthestars (IRE) *David O'Meara* 93
2 b f Sea The Stars(IRE) Behkiyra (IRE) (Entrepreneur)
(3640) ◆ 6130[2] 6258[4] 7409[7]

Reach High *Saeed bin Suroor* 85
2 ch c Distorted Humor(USA) Silent Moment (USA) (Giant's Causeway (USA))
1621[2] (2023)

Ready (IRE) *Clare Ellam* a95 82
6 ch g Elnadim(USA) Fusili (IRE) (Silvano (GER))
7[3] 1001[5] 1344[7] 2444[4] 7535[11] (7791) 7967[2] 8035[2] 8160[6] 8317[11] 8529[9]

Ready Steady (USA) *Kenneth Slack* a53 41
3 b f More Than Ready(USA) Medal Winner (USA) (Medaglia d'Oro (USA))
258[4] 402[5] 578[5] 597[6] 1134[5] 1698[7] 2772[8] 3015[10] 5222[9]

Ready To Roc (IRE) *J P Murtagh* a86 95
2 b c Roderic O'Connor(IRE) Acushladear (IRE) (Tagula (IRE))
2494a[5] 3678a[5] 4414a[5] 4574a[5]

Real Art *Kevin Ryan* a44 45
3 ch f Dutch Art Castaway Queen (IRE) (Selkirk (USA))
959[4] 1246[6]

Real Dominion (USA) *Andrew Balding* a83 100
3 bb c Cape Blanco(IRE) Real Doll (USA) (Known Fact (USA))
1260[3] 1897[3] (2580) 4092[3] (4628) 5147[3] ◆ 5879[2] 6110[10] 7117[5] ◆

Realize *Stuart Williams* a109 87
6 b g Zafeen(FR) Relkida (Bertolini (USA))
(290) (486) 921[3] ◆ 1066[5] 4889[6] 6276[5] 6914[3] ◆ 7702[9] 7932[7] (8489)

Real Love (AUS) *Darren Weir* 111
5 ch m Desert King(IRE) Flaming Heart (AUS) (Salieri (USA))
7378a[5] 7712a[6]

Really Special *Saeed bin Suroor* a84 100
2 b f Shamardal(USA) Rumh (GER) (Monsun (GER))
(7099) (7698) ◆

Really Super *Ralph Beckett* 68
2 b f Cacique(IRE) Sensationally (Montjeu (IRE))
7187[4]

Real Steel (JPN) *Yoshito Yahagi* 120
4 b h Deep Impact(JPN) Loves Only Me (USA) (Storm Cat (USA))
(1106a) 8129a[5]

Realtra (IRE) *Roger Varian* a107 111
4 gr m Dark Angel(IRE) Devious Diva (IRE) (Dr Devious (IRE))
(8563a)

Real Value (FR) *Mario Hofer* 99
2 b c Rip Van Winkle(IRE) Rosey De Megeve (Efisio)
3871a[5] 4620a[3] 6174a[3] 7399a[3] 7842a[8]

Reaver (IRE) *Eve Johnson Houghton* a85 78
3 b g Sabiango(GER) Mattinata (Tiger Hill (IRE))
2128[4] 3111[6] 3483[4] (4009) 4269[6] (5241) 5765[2] 6416[2] ◆ 6628[5] 7189[7]

Rebecca Rocks *Henry Candy* 69
2 b f Exceed And Excel(AUS) Rebecca Rolfe (Pivotal)
2990[5] 7216[2]

Rebel Cause (IRE) *Richard Spencer* a82 87
3 b g Cockney Rebel(IRE) Happy Go Lily (In The Wings)
1767[2] (2443) 3187[2]

Rebel Collins (IRE) *David Evans* a76
5 gr g Jeremy(USA) Million All Day (IRE) (Daylami (IRE))
43[3] 234[4]

Rebel Dane (AUS) *Gary Portelli* 117
6 bb h California Dane(AUS) Texarcana (AUS) (More Than Ready (USA))
8330a[11]

Rebel De Lope *Charles Hills* a87 94
2 b c Lope De Vega(IRE) Rivabella (FR) (Iron Mask (USA))
2873[3] 3388[4] (4387) 5595[6] (6481) 7130a[6]

Rebel Flame *Jedd O'Keeffe* a41 24
2 b c Firebreak Spirit Of Dixie (Kheleyf (USA))
6214[13] 7142[8]

Rebel Heart *Bill Turner* a51 57
2 b f Kyllachy Just Like A Woman (Observatory (USA))
1203[7] 4133[6] 5099[2] 5675[7] (6252) 6887[3] 7615[5]

Rebel Lightning (IRE) *Richard Spencer* a78 73
3 gr g Zebedee Bellechance (Acclamation)
1409[4] 2099[2] 2694[5] 4010[5] 4841[6] 5374[3] 6702[6] (7240) 7577[4] 7985[5] 8163[2] 8378[2]

Rebel Raiser *Richard Spencer* a55 69
3 b g Kheleyf(USA) Trump Street (First Trump)
1806[4] 2864[9] 3604[5]

Rebel Sky *J R Jenkins* a64 45
3 b f Cockney Rebel(IRE) Sakhacity (Sakhee (USA))
2606[8] 4565[5] (5192)

Rebel State (IRE) *Richard Spencer* a78 65
3 b g Zoffany(IRE) Stately Princess (Robellino (USA))
1917[3] 5248[3] 5515[10] 6241[3] 6700[2] 7257[5] 7735[2] 8086[6] 8248[8] 8382[3]

Rebel Surge (IRE) *Richard Spencer* a91 89
3 b f Kodiac Face The Storm (IRE) (Barathea (IRE))
1476[6] 2220[5] 2949a[9] 3274[12] 4105[4] 4651[5] 5396[4] 6340[3] ◆ 7550[4] 7702[2] 7958[3] 8158[5]

Rebel Woman *Mrs A Corson*
10 b m Royal Applause Wild Woman (Polar Falcon (USA))
3917a[10] 5458a[8] 6402a[5]

Rebel Woods (FR) *Geoffrey Deacon* 44
3 b g Cockney Rebel(IRE) In The Woods (You And I (USA))
4458[12] 6441[6] 6650[7]

Rebel Yell *Richard Price* a48 54
4 b g Shamardal(USA) Solaia (USA) (Miswaki (USA))
1131[9] 1343[11] 2462[12]

Rebounded *Declan Carroll* 61
2 ch g Mayson Winter Dress (Haafhd)
3873[8] 4725[4] ◆ 5727[6]

Recently Acquired *David Loder* a66 87
4 b g Beat Hollow Acquisition (Dansili)
6217[14]

Recepta (USA) *James J Toner* a77 107
5 bb m Speightstown(USA) Honor Bestowed (USA) (Honor Grades (USA))
3178a[2]

Reckless Endeavour (IRE) *G M Lyons* a102 101
3 b g Kodiac Red Fanfare (First Trump)
4921a[2] 6355a[5] 7523a[3]

Reckless Lad (IRE) *Patrick Martin* a90 83
6 b g Chevalier(IRE) Zingeeyah (Singspiel (IRE))
1018a[14] 4250a[3] 7801a[3]

Reckless Serenade (IRE) *Keith Dalgleish* a48 69
2 b f Bushranger(IRE) Tomintoul Singer (IRE) (Johannesburg (USA))
3881[4] (4140) 4832[5] 5712[7] 6007[5] (6768) 7091[2] 7938[10]

Reckless Wave (IRE) *Ed Walker* a65 59
3 b f Cape Cross(IRE) Fairybook (USA) (El Prado (IRE))
3482[3] ◆ (4267) 5064[2] 8428[3] ◆

Recognition (IRE) *Roger Varian* a74 54
3 gr c Rip Van Winkle(IRE) Bali Breeze (IRE) (Common Grounds)
1062[DSQ] (1835) ◆ 2411[8] 3306[5] 3728[6]

Reconcilliation *Ed Vaughan* a69 82
3 b g Aqlaam Gretna (Groom Dancer (USA))
3653[4] 4372[2] (6031)

Rectitude *Henry Tett* a50 22
5 b m Virtual Evasive Quality (FR) (Highest Honor (FR))
347[7] 609[13] 7879[13] 1547[12]

Redalani (IRE) *Alan Brown* a53 54
6 b m Redback Zafaraya (IRE) (Ashkalani (IRE))
46[4] 5320[11] 6101[5] 6586[4] 7863[2] 8079[12]

Red Alert *Joseph Tuite* a61 73
2 b g Sleeping Indian Red Sovereign (Danzig Connection (USA))
5237[6] 6086[7] 6189[2] 6873[2] 7269[4]
Red All Star (IRE) *Gerard Keane* a56 42
6 b g Haatef(USA) Star Of Russia (IRE) (Soviet Star (USA))
(7800a)
Redarna *Dianne Sayer*
2 ch g Aqlaam Curtains (Dubawi (IRE))
2014[6]
Red Artist *Simon Crisford* a87 85
3 b g Archipenko(USA) Danceatdusk (Desert Prince (IRE))
(1763) 2695[7] 3600[6] 4534[5] 4867[10] 6492[3] 7054[4] 7506[17]
Red Avenger (USA) *Gary Moore* a90 80
6 bb g War Front(USA) Emotional Rescue (USA) (Smart Strike (CAN))
2391[13] 4823[17] 5552[8] 6076[8] 6628[8] 7189[11]
Red Baron (IRE) *Eric Alston* a97 107
7 b g Moss Vale(IRE) Twinberry (IRE) (Tagula (IRE))
1083[2] 1969[6] 2188[4] 2258[2] 3151[15] 3606[13] 4584[14] 4735[15] 6119[12]
Red Bordeaux (FR) *Tony Carroll* 15
2 b g Myboycharlie(IRE) Blue Sail (USA) (Kingmambo (USA))
7239[9]
Red Box *Sir Mark Prescott Bt* a98 105
3 b f Exceed And Excel(AUS) Confidential Lady (Singspiel (IRE))
2294[3] (3209) 3519[2] (4263) (4582) ◆ 5158[6] 5645[7] 7676a[4]
Redbrook (IRE) *Doug Watson* a73 105
5 b h Raven's Pass(USA) Nawal (FR) (Homme De Loi (IRE))
623a[9] 810a[10]
Red Caravel (IRE) *Richard Hughes* a62 59
2 b c Henrythenavigator(USA) Red Fantasy (IRE) (High Chaparral (IRE))
5959[9] 6288[5] 6655[4]
Red Cardinal (IRE) *A Wohler* a82 111
4 b g Montjeu(IRE) Notable (Zafonic (USA))
(1739) (3192) (3621) 5402[3] 6822a[2]
Red Charmer (IRE) *Ann Duffield* a58 81
6 b g Red Clubs(IRE) Golden Charm (IRE) (Common Grounds)
1252[8] 1596[9] 1926[10] (2529) (2810) 3478[9] 3983[4] 6231[3] 6907[8]
Red Chatterbox (IRE) *Scott Dixon* a51 17
3 b f Thousand Words Red Empress (Nashwan (USA))
5[4] 249[4] 428[7] 578[4] 2834[9] 3988[5]
Redcold (FR) *C Laffon-Parias* 84
3 b f Nayef(USA) Russiana (IRE) (Red Ransom (USA))
4904a[7]
Red Cossack (CAN) *Paul Webber* a75 75
5 ch g Rebellion Locata (USA) (Stravinsky (USA))
1838[7] 2129[2] 2821[9] 3612[7] 7076[15] 7620[2] 8154[3] 8462[4]
Red Douglas *Scott Dixon* a40 21
2 ch c Sakhee(USA) Chrystal Venture (IRE) (Barathea (IRE))
7142[9] 7599[4] 7819[10]
Red Dragon (IRE) *Michael Blanshard* a63 58
6 b g Acclamation Delphie Queen (IRE) (Desert Sun)
62[2] 435[3]
Red Emperor (IRE) *Amanda Perrett* 50
2 b g Holy Roman Emperor(IRE) Rougette (Red Ransom (USA))
6750[9]
Redenca (GER) *A Wohler* 92
3 b f Lope De Vega(IRE) Rosa Di Brema (ITY) (Lomitas)
2949a[15] 6611a[5]
Red Ensign (IRE) *Simon Crisford* a84 82
2 b g Dark Angel(IRE) Rayon Rouge (IRE) (Manduro (GER))
4349[3] ◆ (5505) ◆ 6116[6] 6705[5]
Redera (IRE) *A J Martin* a75 70
10 b g Chevalier(IRE) Lady Redera (IRE) (Inzar (USA))
2114a[14]
Red Falx (JPN) *Tomohito Ozeki* a86 118
5 gr h Swept Overboard(USA) Vermouth (JPN) (Sunday Silence (USA))
8330a[12]
Red Flute *Denis Quinn* a56 53
4 ch g Piccolo Fee Faw Fum (IRE) (Great Commotion (USA))
136[6] (217) 513[5] 970[3] 1709[3] 1833[2] 2447[4] 3316[2] (3650) 4264[12] 6660[2] 7276[7] 7534[4] 7811[7]
Red Forever *Thomas Cuthbert* a35 47
5 ch g Major Cadeaux Spindara (IRE) (Spinning World (USA))
136[9] 3925[5] 4931[14] 5483[11] 7046[7]
Red Four *George Baker* a18 38
6 ch m Singspiel(IRE) Protectorate (Hector Protector (USA))
1391[9]
Redgrave (IRE) *Charles Hills* 76
2 b g Lope De Vega(IRE) Olympic Medal (Nayef (USA))
3954[6] 6881[2] 7243[5]
Red Guana (IRE) *William Jarvis* a69 44
2 ch f Famous Name Guana (IRE) (Dark Angel (IRE))
6696[12] 7407[3] (7891)
Red Gunner *William Haggas* a78 70
2 b c Oasis Dream Blue Maiden (Medicean)
7818[4] (8119) 8405[7] 8592[6]
Red Harry (IRE) *David C Griffiths* a76 61
4 ch g Manduro(GER) Iktidar (Green Desert (USA))
2974[15] 3645[16]
Red Hot Chilly (IRE) *Joseph Tuite* a74 72
3 ch g Frozen Power(IRE) She's Got The Look (Sulamani (IRE))
557[6] 874[2] 1113[5] 1429[2] 1961[2] 4046[5] 4818[4] 5746[3] 5895[3]
Red House Hill (IRE) *C Byrnes* 73
6 b g Ad Valorem(USA) Laetitia (IRE) (Priolo (USA))
2114a[5]
Redicean *Peter Chapple-Hyam* a70 85
2 b c Medicean Red Halo (IRE) (Galileo (IRE))
6071[4] 6850[3] 7151[8] ◆
Red Invader (IRE) *Paul D'Arcy* a71 75
6 b g Red Clubs(IRE) Tifariti (USA) (Elusive Quality (USA))
795[8] 1496[13] 3494[7] (5470)
Red Label (IRE) *Luca Cumani* 78
2 b c Dubawi(IRE) Born Something (IRE) (Caerleon (USA))
6750[3] (7239)
Red Legacy *Sean Regan*
8 ch m Distant Music(USA) Emma May (Nicholas Bill)
8401[7]
Red Lodge (USA) *Wesley A Ward* 95
2 ch f Midshipman(USA) Star Silver (USA) (Aldebaran (USA))
3295[9]
Redmane *Jamie Osborne* a68
3 b c Bahamian Bounty Miss Villefranche (Danehill Dancer (IRE))
253[2] 421[5]
Red Mohican *Phil McEntee* a54
2 ch f Harbour Watch(IRE) Magical Cliche (USA) (Affirmed (USA))
1082[6] 1293[4] 8140[8] 8404[4] 8536[2]
Red Napoleon (USA) *Ralph Beckett* 101
4 b g War Chant(USA) Rose Red (USA) (Fashion Find (USA))
3164[7] (4555) 5585[3] ◆
Red Onion *C Lerner* 96
2 b c Fast Company(IRE) Capsicum (Holy Roman Emperor (IRE))
(1579a) 4620a[2] 5450a[3] (8062a)
Red Orator *Jim Best* a62 66
7 ch g Osorio(GER) Red Roses Story (FR) (Pink I (FR))
7980[9]
Red Paladin (IRE) *Kristin Stubbs* a88 83
6 b g Red Clubs(IRE) Alexander Goldmine (Dansili)
1142[3] 1884[7] 3185[4] 3517[4] 3884[8] 4768[9] (5386) (5793) 6914[10] (7108)
Red Pike (IRE) *Bryan Smart* a99 102
5 ch g Kheleyf(USA) Fancy Feathers (IRE) (Redback)
1522[10] 2158[3] 2803[2] 3250[2] 4865[8] 6327[16] 6642[6] 7156[5] 7497[8] 7990[4]
Red Rannagh (IRE) *David Simcock* a92 89
3 b c Teofilo(IRE) Red Top (IRE) (Fasliyev (USA))
154[4] 4797[6] 5874[3] 6675[3] 7618[4] 7869[12]
Red Refraction (IRE) *Richard Hannon* a85 96
6 b h Red Clubs(IRE) Dreamalot (Falbrav (IRE))
1818[3]
Red Rose Riot (IRE) *David Menuisier* a54 61
3 b f Tamayuz Red Bandanna (IRE) (Montjeu (IRE))
697[3] 885[6] 1146[7] 1792[5] 2586[4] 3141[4] 4159[6] (5824)
Redrosezorro *Eric Alston* 60
2 b g Foxwedge(AUS) Garter Star (Mark Of Esteem (IRE))
1976[9] 2530[5] 3128[6] 4133[8] 5712[3] 6734[15] 7313[8]
Red Royalist *Marcus Tregoning* 81
2 b c Royal Applause Scarlet Royal (Red Ransom (USA))
6071[2] 6950[3]
Red Ruffian (IRE) *Dean Ivory* a60
3 ch g Tamayuz Hatria (IRE) (Royal Applause)
42[5] 291[9] 979[5] 7048[9] 7754[13]
Red Savina *Kevin Ryan* a41 29
2 b f Exceed And Excel(AUS) Chili Dip (Alhaarth (IRE))
2424[6] 3148[6] 4678[8] 5364[4] 6420[7] 7528[6]
Red Shadow *Alan Brown* a54 44
7 b m Royal Applause Just A Glimmer (Bishop Of Cashel)
35[8] 230[5] 341[6]
Red Shanghai (IRE) *Charles Smith* a24 36
2 ch f Tamayuz Rouge Noir (USA) (Saint Ballado (CAN))
1583[7] 1951[7] 2970[9] 4712[7] 6368[9] 6896[6] 7589[5] 8569[6]
Red Skipper (IRE) *John O'Shea* a23 40
11 ch g Captain Rio Speed To Lead (IRE) (Darshaan)
1343[12]
Red Sniper (IRE) *Peter Chapple-Hyam* a49 48
2 ch f Casamento(IRE) Lady Caprice (Kyllachy)
6404[5] 7209[7] 7776[8]
Redstarovervchina (IRE) *M Halford* a80 88
3 b f Starspangledbanner(AUS) Fragrant Air (CAN) (El Prado (IRE))
536a[12]
Red Stars (IRE) *John M Oxx* 97
3 ch f Manduro(GER) Magen's Star (IRE) (Galileo (IRE))
1369a[5] 3539a[4] 4416a[8]
Redstart *Ralph Beckett* a86 105
4 b m Cockney Rebel(IRE) Ecstasy (Pursuit Of Love)
1207[9]
Red Stripes (USA) *Lisa Williamson* a91 83
4 b g Leroidesanimaux(BRZ) Kaleidoscopic (USA) (Fortunate Prospect (USA))
213[9] 3637[7] 4198[7] 4632[11] 4735[8] 5360[7] 5774[5] 6080[10] 6425[6] 6879[7] 7202[7] 7811[2] 7945[3] 8495[7] 8571[4]
Red Tea *Peter Hiatt* a86 89
3 ch f Sakhee(USA) Maimoona (IRE) (Pivotal)
3062[3] 3673[2] (4593) (4819) ◆ 5487[3] 6300[5] (6580) 6914[11] 7505[3] 7903[3]
Red Touch (USA) *Michael Appleby* a88 75
4 bb g Bluegrass Cat(USA) Touchnow (CAN) (Pleasant Tap (USA))
427[4] (893) ◆ (956) ◆ 1152[2] 1797[6] 2620[8]
Red Trooper (FR) *George Baker* a81
3 ch g Shamardal(USA) Solar Midnight (USA) (Lemon Drop Kid (USA))
2005[3] ◆ (7616) 8251[5]
Red Tycoon (IRE) *David Barron* a79 88
4 b g Acclamation Rugged Up (IRE) (Marju (IRE))
1215[13] 2259[6] 2677[3] 3168[15] (4428) 6079[5] 6780[15]
Red Unico (IRE) *Brian Barr* a67 60
4 b g Vale Of York(IRE) Testa Unica (ITY) (Nordance (USA))
367[3] 598[2] 862[5] 1064[6] 1124[5] 2769[7] 3514[10] 3988[2] 4715[2] 5393[5] 6637[6] (7260)
Red Verdon (USA) *Ed Dunlop* a78 114
3 ch c Lemon Drop Kid(USA) Porto Marmay (IRE) (Choisir (AUS))
1602[2] (1971) ◆ (2471) ◆ 2896[6] 3679a[4] 4332a[2]
Redvers (IRE) *Noel Wilson* a52 91
8 br g Ishiguru(USA) Cradle Brief (IRE) (Brief Truce (USA))
1522[5] 1990[11] 2910[10] 4132[6] 4627[9]
Reedanjas (IRE) *Gay Kelleway* 77
2 b f Sir Prancealot(IRE) Blue Holly (IRE) (Blues Traveller (IRE))
(6641) 7972a[10]
Reeh (IRE) *John Gosden* 80
2 ro f Invincible Spirit(IRE) Vanishing Grey (IRE) (Verglas (IRE))
1988[5] 2793[2] 3270[12]
Reflation *Michael Dods* a58 67
4 b g Stimulation(IRE) Miss Poppy (Averti (IRE))
1254[8] 1692[10] 2329[6] 3016[5] 3925[2] 4192[3] 4931[12] 5483[8] 5535[9] 6008[7] 6100[2] (6616) 6769[6] (6835) 7092[4] 7334[8]
Reflektor (IRE) *Tom Dascombe* a51 100
3 ch g Bahamian Bounty Baby Bunting (Wolfhound (USA))
1243[3] (1492) 1977[2] 3131[2] 3671[5] 3890[8]
Refulgence (FR) *Marco Botti* a64 61
3 b f Azamour(IRE) Ares Flight (IRE) (Hernando (FR))
291[3] 443[7] 725[3] 1388[5] 2108[2] 4025[5]
Refuse Colette (IRE) *Mick Quinn* a65 81
7 ch m Refuse To Bend(IRE) Roclette (USA) (Rock Of Gibraltar (IRE))
1159[6] 1811[3] 2380[8] 3038[7] 3898[4] 5038[4] 7059[14] 7442[9]
Refuse To Bobbin (IRE) *M Narduzzi* 94
6 ch g Refuse To Bend(IRE) Super Bobbina (IRE) (Daggers Drawn (USA))
2516a[3]
Regal Dan (IRE) *David O'Meara* a88 93
6 b g Dark Angel(IRE) Charlene Lacy (IRE) (Pips Pride)
1848[13] 2679[6] 3115[10] 4299[2] 4644[7] 5678[3] 6263[15] 6714[3] 7126[14] 7702[7] 7778[2] 7983[4]
Regal Decree *Jedd O'Keeffe* a51 49
2 b g Lawman(FR) Regal Riband (Fantastic Light (USA))
2830[9] 3516[4] 4227[5] 5364[5] 6222[11]
Regal Gait (IRE) *Harry Whittington* a65 19
3 b g Tagula(IRE) Babylonian (Shamardal (USA))
2790[6] 3727[5] (7692)
Regal Galaxy *Mark H Tompkins* a55 36
3 b f Royal Applause Astromancer (USA) (Silver Hawk (USA))
274[5] 1149[3] 1553[3] 4210[5] 4810[4] 5398[5] 6698[7] 7532[2] 7767[3]
Regal Mirage (IRE) *Tim Easterby* 45
2 ch g Aqlaam Alzaroof (USA) (Kingmambo (USA))
7125[11] 7496[10]
Regal Miss *Patrick Chamings* a69 63
4 b m Royal Applause Pretty Miss (Averti (IRE))
2403[8] 3527[4] 4222[5] 5009[3] 5474[2] 6374[3] 8078[9]
Regal Missile (IRE) *Mark Walford* a9 68
4 b g Royal Applause Leenane (IRE) (Grand Lodge (USA))
1202[14] 2330[13]
Regal Monarch *Mark Johnston* a51 100
3 b g Notnowcato Regal Fairy (IRE) (Desert King (IRE))
1619[2] (2126) (2408) 2909[3] (3615) ◆ 4598[2] (5434) 5653[2]
Regal Parade *Charlie Wallis* a78 75
12 ch g Pivotal Model Queen (USA) (Kingmambo (USA))
1419[6] 2028[14] 2396[3] 3349[2] 3907[3] 5039[2] 5797[7] 6237[9] 6583[8] 7059[10] 7442[6]
Regal Power *Marcus Callaghan* a52 57
7 b g Royal Applause Be My Charm (Polish Precedent (USA))
2229a[9]
Regal Response (IRE) *Michael Dods* a77 72
3 b g Acclamation Qalahari (IRE) (Bahri (USA))
3609[4] 4605[3] 5782[7] 6502[12] 7111[5] 7333[12]
Regal Ways (IRE) *Brian Ellison* a72 60
4 bb m Royal Applause Step This Way (USA) (Giant's Causeway (USA))
2121[13] 3660[6] 4300[6]
Regent's Rock *Peter Niven* a49
4 b m Shirocco(GER) Tiger's Gene (GER) (Perugino (USA))
384[9] 591[7] 639[8] 7871[10]
Regicide (IRE) *James Fanshawe* a83 83
3 b g Archipenko(USA) Armoise (Sadler's Wells (USA))
1575[2] ◆ 2414[4] 7063[2]
Regina Cordium (IRE) *John Gosden* a48
3 ch f Raven's Pass(USA) Sugar Mill (FR) (Polar Falcon (USA))
96[4]
Reginald Claude *Mark Usher* a67 59
8 b g Monsieur Bond(IRE) Miller's Melody (Chief Singer)
197[4] ◆ 542[7] 682[6]
Regulation (IRE) *Neil King* a93 95
7 br g Danehill Dancer(IRE) Source Of Life (IRE) (Fasliyev (USA))
3109[5]
Rehana (IRE) *M Halford* 107
2 b f Dark Angel(IRE) Rayka (IRE) (Selkirk (USA))
5686a[4] 6385a[4]
Rehearse (IRE) *Andrew Balding* a77 72
3 b c Big Bad Bob(IRE) And Again (USA) (In The Wings)
2640[9] 3535[4] 5026[3] 5724[6] 6380[7] 7063[4]
Reign On *Ralph Beckett* a80 73
2 ch g Equiano(FR) Queens Jubilee (Cayman Kai (IRE))
2038[4] (2295) 3100[6] 4076[8] 7549[10] 8033[4] (8159) ◆ (8592)
Reine Gianna (FR) *G Botti* a68 55
3 b f Orpen(USA) Reine Sirocco (IRE) (Shirocco (GER))
1357a[5]
Reinforced *Michael Dods* a49 68
3 ch g Equiano(FR) Fonnie (IRE) (Barathea (IRE))
2776[2] ◆ 4278[5] 5537[4] (5887) 6541[3] (7096) 7323[8]
Reinstorm *Richard Fahey* a45 57
2 b g Canford Cliffs(IRE) Bridle Belle (Dansili)
3054[8] 4040[10] 4609[9] 5528[5] 6130[3] 6681[2]
Rekindling *David Wachman* 88
2 b c High Chaparral(IRE) Sitara (Salse (USA))
7722a[13]
Related *Paul Midgley* a101 101
6 b g Kheleyf(USA) Balladonia (Primo Dominie)
1090[4] 1522[8] 2027[22] 2488[12] 4112[12] 4667[3] 4862[2] 5418[15] 5678[2] 6327[13] 6627[3] 8069[7] 8407[5] 8583[11]
Relaxed Boy (FR) *P Sogorb* a83 86
3 b c Le Havre(IRE) Joyce (GER) (Chato (USA))
5946a[2]
Relight My Fire *Tim Easterby* a77 78
6 ch g Firebreak Making Music (Makbul)
1925[6] 2347[4] ◆ 2673[6] 3478[2] 3840[2] 4231[3] 4453[3] 4729[5] 4930[4] 5521[2] 6027[9] 6643[6] 7010[13]
Rely On Me (IRE) *Andrew Balding* 77
2 br f Kyllachy Life Rely (USA) (Maria's Mon (USA))
7314[9] (7818)
Remal Dubai (USA) *Saeed bin Suroor* a42
2 b f Hard Spun(USA) Chilukki's Song (USA) (Elusive Quality (USA))
6925[11]
Remarkable *John Gosden* a82 110
3 b g Pivotal Irresistible (Cadeaux Genereux)
(959) (1599) 2242[2] ◆ 3269[5] 6942[12] 7354[2]
Remarkable Lady (IRE) *H Rogers* a44 87
3 b f Zoffany(IRE) Casual Remark (IRE) (Trans Island)
5790a[6] 6200a[8] 6932a[8]
Remember Me *Hughie Morrison* a77 70
3 b f Acclamation Forgotten Me (IRE) (Holy Roman Emperor (IRE))
1257[8] 2372[3] 2905[3] 3126[4] (4640) 5309[3] 5935[7] 7203[2] 7985[7] 8490[7]
Remember Rocky *Lucy Normile* a45 71
7 ch g Haafhd Flower Market (Cadeaux Genereux)
1697[4] 2959[7] 4038[6] 4449[3] 5227[4] 5715[3] 6221[4]
Rene Mathis (GER) *Richard Fahey* a79 111
6 ch g Monsieur Bond(IRE) Remina (GER) (Erminius (GER))
1196[15] 1491[2] 1969[5] 2027[17] 2684[4]
Renewing *Roy Brotherton* a48 40
5 b g Halling(USA) Electric Society (IRE) (Law Society (USA))
150[7] 1170[7] 1322[6] 1830[7] 2462[9]
Renfrew Street *Mark Johnston* a62 88
3 br f Iffraaj Malpas Missile (IRE) (Elusive City (USA))
2420[4] (2973) 3251[2] 3347[7] 5837[4] 6074[2] 6332[8] 6667[5] 7139[8]
Renneti (FR) *W P Mullins* 105
7 b g Irish Wells(FR) Caprice Meill (FR) (French Glory)
3630a[9] 4721a[4] 5559[13] 6350a[11] 7708a[10]
Rennie Mackintosh (IRE) *John Bridger* a68 55
4 b g Excellent Art Mac Melody (IRE) (Entrepreneur)
62[4] 222[5] 348[6] 6411[13] 6890[5] 7282[11] 7464[14]
Renny Storm (CZE) *C Von Der Recke* a93 93
6 b g Stormy Jail(IRE) Renaissance (CZE) (High Extreme (IRE))
588a[4] 663a[5]
Renounce (FR) *D De Waele* a51 53
5 b g Peer Gynt(JPN) Former Probe (USA) (Dynaformer (USA))
7398a[10]
Renounce (IRE) *Charlie Wallis* a74 63
4 b g Elnadim(USA) Relinquished (Royal Applause)
198[8] 433[13] 1838[6] 2309[5] 2821[8] 3674[9] 3994[10] 4744[7]
Repeater *Miss Amanda Mooney* a43 87
7 b g Montjeu(IRE) Time Over (Mark Of Esteem (IRE))
1999[2] 2897[3] 4850a[4] 5559[14]
Repeat Offender (IRE) *J S Moore* a75 80
3 b g Thewayyouare(USA) Dame Rochelle (IRE) (Danehill Dancer (IRE))
70[2] 243[3] 379[6]
Replenish (FR) *James Fanshawe* a101 62
3 ch g Le Havre(IRE) Brambleberry (Cape Cross (IRE))
(1267) 2161[18] (2917) 5552[7] 6126[3] 7383[3]
Repton (IRE) *Richard Hannon* 103
2 b c Zebedee African Moonlight (UAE) (Halling (USA))
2390[2] ◆ (2696) 4732[5] 5646[8] 6954[15]
Reputation (IRE) *John Quinn* 98
3 b g Royal Applause Semaphore (Zamindar (USA))
2161[8] 2871[4] 3885[3] 4402[7] 4689[3] ◆ 4867[5] ◆ (5512) 5852[2] 6556[19]
Re Run (IRE) *Richard Fahey* a74 69
2 b c Harbour Watch(IRE) Encore View (Oasis Dream)
6534[4] 7432[2] 8062a[10] 8557[4]
Resiliency (IRE) *Michael Appleby* a82 90
5 ch g Mastercraftsman(IRE) Euroceleb (IRE) (Peintre Celebre (USA))
1893[4] 2249[5] 3117[9]
Resolute Response (IRE) *M Al Mheiri* a87 87
6 b h Dansili Lady Luck (IRE) (Kris)
369a[8]
Respectability *Ivan Furtado* 29
4 b m Echo Of Light Respectfilly (Mark Of Esteem (IRE))
2735[10] 3066[10] 3643[9] 3987[12]

Respect Me *Ismail Mohammed* a98 86
6 b g Street Cry(IRE) Secret Charm (IRE) (Green Desert (USA))
(279a) 627a^{9} 811a^{14}

Response *Michael Appleby* a65 72
6 ch g New Approach(IRE) Spotlight (Dr Fong (USA))
429^{6} 939^{7} 1546^{12}

Responsibleforlove (IRE) *Endo Botti* 100
3 ch f Duke Of Marmalade(IRE) Vee Gita (IRE) (Vettori (IRE))
2730a^{10}

Ressurreto (IRE) *Keith Dalgleish* a26 53
3 b f Frozen Power(IRE) Silver Whale (FR) (Highest Honor (FR))
593^{5} 785^{10}

Rest Easy *Seamus Mullins* 52
4 b m Rip Van Winkle(IRE) Early Evening (Daylami (IRE))
5958^{12}

Restiana (FR) *P Sogorb* 99
3 b f Kendargent(FR) Restia (FR) (Montjeu (IRE))
2316a^{8} 7029a^{9} 7568a^{7} 7929a^{2}

Restive (IRE) *Iain Jardine* a82 86
3 b g Rip Van Winkle(IRE) I Hearyou Knocking (IRE) (Danehill Dancer (IRE))
8539^{11}

Restore (IRE) *Richard Hannon* a60 63
2 b c Dark Angel(IRE) Attracted To You (IRE) (Hurricane Run (IRE))
2319^{4} 2847^{10} 3742^{4} 4315^{6} 5265^{9} 6236^{3} 6963^{5} 7423^{5}

Restorer *William Muir* a105 108
4 gr g Mastercraftsman(IRE) Moon Empress (FR) (Rainbow Quest (USA))
1088^{4} 1475^{3} 1863^{4} 7766^{3} 7934^{6}

Restraint Of Trade (IRE) *Jennie Candlish* 82
6 br g Authorized(IRE) Zivania (IRE) (Shernazar)
5611^{10} 6134^{7} 6775^{7}

Rethra (IRE) *J-P Gauvin* a59 38
4 b m Elusive City(USA) Relight's Best (Grand Lodge (USA))
5452a^{6}

Retour Gagnant (IRE) *Yves de Nicolay* a48 61
2 b f US Ranger(USA) On Point (USA) (Pulpit (USA))
5986a^{8} 7455a^{13}

Retribution *David Lanigan* a52 51
2 b g Iffraaj The Giving Tree (IRE) (Rock Of Gibraltar (IRE))
7664^{8} 7906^{11} 8074^{8}

Return Ace *James Fanshawe* a86 97
4 b m Zamindar(USA) Match Point (Unfuwain (USA))
(3665) 7946a^{5}

Return To Grace (USA) *Mark Casse* 97
4 ch m English Channel(USA) Golden Attraction (USA) (Mr Prospector (USA))
3088a^{6}

Revel *Stuart Williams* a67 68
2 b g Makfi Cecily (Oasis Dream)
7468^{7} 7867^{7}

Reverend Jacobs *William Haggas* 67
2 b c Nathaniel(IRE) Light Impact (IRE) (Fantastic Light (USA))
5600^{6} ◆ 6777^{7}

Reverent (IRE) *James Tate* a56
4 b m Teofilo(IRE) Wadaat (Diktat)
325^{10}

Revision (FR) *John Best* a92 85
4 bb g Vision D'Etat(FR) Karmibola (FR) (Persian Bold)
3889^{8} 4752^{9}

Revolutionist (IRE) *Mark Johnston* a99 112
4 b h Pivotal Mysterial (USA) (Alleged (USA))
(886) ◆ 1344^{4} 1629^{9} 1861^{3} 2157^{5} (2484) (2744) 3383^{3} 4165^{13} 4731^{15} 5647^{12} 6233^{5}

Rewarding Hero *John Moore* 115
7 b g Exceed And Excel(AUS) Caldy Dancer (IRE) (Soviet Star (USA))
1912a^{9}

Rex Bell (IRE) *John Gosden* 97
3 b c Dubawi(IRE) Clara Bow (IRE) (Sadler's Wells (USA))
1386^{2} 1715^{2} (3235) 3532^{2} 6775^{2} 7188^{6}

Rex Imperator *David O'Meara* a83 99
7 b g Royal Applause Elidore (Danetime (IRE))
3115^{18} 4299^{3} 4758^{3} 5417^{3} 5871^{10} 6792^{3} 7610^{7}

Rey Loopy (IRE) *Ben Haslam* a51 35
2 b g Lope De Vega(IRE) Al Basar (USA) (Sahm (USA))
7496^{11} 8089^{13} 8384^{9}

Reynaldothewizard (USA) *S Seemar* a114
10 b g Speightstown(USA) Holiday Runner (USA) (Meadowlake (USA))
(186a) 537a^{3} 1105a^{4}

Reynardo De Silver *Gary Moore* a57 56
2 gr g Foxwedge(AUS) Sakhee's Pearl (Sakhee (USA))
5600^{14} 5990^{6} 7187^{7} 8046^{3} 8080^{7}

Rezwaan *Murty McGrath* a68 58
9 b g Alhaarth(IRE) Nasij (USA) (Elusive Quality (USA))
97^{7} 346^{8} 707^{6} 870^{2} 2323^{14} 3031^{10} 3401^{7}

Rhenius (FR) *M Nigge* a68 39
2 ch g Soldier Of Fortune(IRE) Rhenania (IRE) (Shamardal (USA))
6638a^{13}

Rhododendron (IRE) *A P O'Brien* 117
2 b f Galileo(IRE) Halfway To Heaven (IRE) (Pivotal)
(4801) ◆ (5686a) 6385a^{3} (7116)

Rhombus (IRE) *John Butler* a57 103
6 b g Authorized(IRE) Mathool (IRE) (Alhaarth (IRE))
8338^{5} 8348^{5}

Rhythm And Blues *Clive Cox* a73 72
3 b g Poet's Voice Golden Nun (Bishop Of Cashel)
352^{5} (765) 1452^{4} 1847^{7} 2935^{6} 5284^{7} 6091^{10}

Rhythmical *Mark Johnston* a76 91
4 b m Halling(USA) Caribbean Dancer (USA) (Theatrical (IRE))
1642^{13} 2176^{4} 2556^{6} 2911^{2} 2994^{7}

Rhythm Of Life (GER) *G Bernaud* a57 54
7 b h Auenadler(GER) Rosomachia (GER) (Machiavellian (USA))
7398a^{7}

Rhythm Star *Jamie Snowden* a55
6 b m Beat All(USA) Star Award (IRE) (Oscar (IRE))
259^{4}

Rial (IRE) *Phil McEntee* a71 42
3 b f Dark Angel(IRE) Coin Box (Dubai Destination (USA))
1442^{10} 1673^{9} 2337^{9} 3649^{6} 6051^{11} 6513^{10}

Rialto Magic *Jamie Osborne* a65
4 b m Monsieur Bond(IRE) Discover Roma (IRE) (Rock Of Gibraltar (IRE))
68^{7} 201^{3} 321^{5} 543^{4} (889) 1139^{3} 1264^{3} 6464a^{2}

Rianna Star *Gary Moore* a59
3 b f Haafhd Sayrianna (Sayaarr (USA))
5735^{5} 6661^{5} 7727^{7} 8179^{4}

Ribbing (USA) *David Simcock* a65 67
3 ch f Distorted Humor(USA) Contentious (USA) (Giant's Causeway (USA))
8388^{3}

Ribchester (IRE) *Richard Fahey* 124
3 b c Iffraaj Mujarah (IRE) (Marju (IRE))
1308a^{5} 1864^{3} (3269) 4754^{3} (5449a) 7352^{2}

Rich Again (IRE) *James Bethell* a85 82
7 b g Amadeus Wolf Fully Fashioned (IRE) (Brief Truce (USA))
198^{7} (462) 694^{2} 1040^{4} 1321^{5} ◆ 1601^{3} 2016^{5} 2346^{5} 3168^{5} (4211) 5679^{7} 6425^{4} (6926) 7112^{4} 8583^{6}

Rich And Famous (USA) *Mark Johnston* 83
2 b g Bernardini(USA) Enrichment (USA) (Ghostzapper (USA))
4736^{2} ◆ (5410) ◆ 7155^{12}

Richard Pankhurst *John Gosden* a92 117
4 ch h Raven's Pass(USA) Mainstay (Elmaamul (USA))
4127^{5} 4754^{10} (5404) 6328^{5} 7115^{6}

Rich Harvest (USA) *Ray Peacock* a23 36
11 bb g High Yield(USA) Mangano (USA) (Quiet American (USA))
3469^{10} 3953^{12} 4484^{9}

Richie McCaw *Ian Williams* a78 84
3 b g Zamindar(USA) Cochin (USA) (Swain (IRE))
5391^{3} ◆ 6484^{4} 7159^{4} ◆

Rich Legacy (IRE) *Ralph Beckett* 105
2 b f Holy Roman Emperor(IRE) Borghesa (GER) (Galileo (IRE))
(5371) 5870^{4} ◆ (6258) 7116^{4} 7722a^{12}

Rich Pursuit *James Bethell* 39
3 ch g Pastoral Pursuits Salvia (Pivotal)
1646^{5} 2048^{12} 2271^{4} 3482^{13}

Rich Tapestry (IRE) *C W Chang* a119 113
8 b g Holy Roman Emperor(IRE) Genuine Charm (IRE) (Sadler's Wells (USA))
(537a) 840a^{3} 1105a^{7}

Richter Scale (IRE) *Iain Jardine* a74 60
3 gr f Lilbourne Lad(IRE) Danamight (IRE) (Danetime (IRE))
4643^{8} 5274^{10} 7437^{9} 8403^{7} (8535)

Rickrack (IRE) *Luca Cumani* 73
2 b f Teofilo(IRE) Arazena (USA) (Woodman (USA))
4885^{7} 5747^{3} 6776^{3}

Ride Like The Wind (IRE) *F Head* a96 111
4 b g Lope De Vega(IRE) Biswa (USA) (Kafwain (USA))
2317a^{3} 2943a^{7}

Rideonastar (IRE) *Brendan Powell* a76 89
5 b g Manduro(GER) Capestar (IRE) (Cape Cross (IRE))
1391^{2} (1893) 2699^{3} 3161^{2} 3670^{7} 6919^{7} 7215^{10} 7625^{11} 7814^{5}

Ride The Lightning *Archie Watson* a86 73
3 b g Dalakhani(IRE) Bright Halo (IRE) (Bigstone (IRE))
1438^{6} 2209^{6} 2900^{8} 3728^{3} 5975^{5} 6365^{5} 6965^{3} (7429) 7732^{2} (8253) 8447^{2} 8594^{8}

Ridge Pride (IRE) *Rebecca Menzies*
3 gr f Zebedee Alexander Ridge (IRE) (Indian Ridge)
2561^{7}

Ridge Ranger (IRE) *Eric Alston* 113
5 b m Bushranger(IRE) Dani Ridge (IRE) (Indian Ridge)
1453^{6} (2042) 2474^{2} 3392^{4} (4114) 4865^{7} 5436^{2} 6574^{3} 6941^{7}

Ridgeway Storm (IRE) *Alan King* a95 95
6 b g Hurricane Run(IRE) Hesperia (Slip Anchor)
747^{7}

Rien Que Pour Toi (FR) *T Castanheira* a72 99
3 b f Orpen(USA) Ilinka (FR) (Gentlewave (IRE))
6070a^{5} 7998a^{9}

Riflescope (IRE) *S Seemar* a73 79
3 b g Raven's Pass(USA) Red Intrigue (IRE) (Selkirk (USA))
1607^{8} 1996^{4} 3165^{17} 4062^{15} 4399^{12} 8578a^{4}

Rigel Star (IRE) *M Delzangles* 77
3 ch c Danehill Dancer(IRE) Rosa Bonheur (USA) (Mr Greeley (USA))
3764a^{13}

Right Action *Richard Fahey* 81
2 b g Dandy Man(IRE) Rockaby Baby (IRE) (Beckett (IRE))
3881^{9} 4371^{2} 4856^{10} 5414^{4} 5884^{5}

Right Charlie (FR) *J E Hammond* a76
3 bb g Myboycharlie(IRE) Hoosick Falls (USA) (Precise End (USA))
2456a^{5}

Rightdownthemiddle (IRE) *Michael Mulvany* a40 64
8 b g Oscar(IRE) Alternative Route (IRE) (Needle Gun (IRE))
5900a^{18}

Right Honourable (IRE) *D K Weld* 87
2 b g Famous Name Agnetha (GER) (Big Shuffle (USA))
5136a^{6}

Right Madam (IRE) *Sarah Hollinshead* a55 53
4 b m Jeremy(USA) Mawaared (Machiavellian (USA))
294^{9} 568^{4} 6593^{4} 7262^{4} 8497^{5}

Right Rebel *Alan Bailey* a76
4 b m Cockney Rebel(IRE) Right Rave (IRE) (Soviet Star (USA))
5300^{3} 6674^{2} (7327)

Right To Dream (IRE) *Ibrahim Al Malki* a82 100
7 b g Oasis Dream Granny Kelly (USA) (Irish River (FR))
757a^{11}

Right Touch *Richard Fahey* a104 106
6 b g Royal Applause Amira (Efisio)
1195^{7} 1627^{10} 1856^{4} (4136) 5640^{2} 6942^{10} 7542^{6} 7821^{7} 7984^{10} 8311^{3}

Rightway (IRE) *Tony Carroll* a79 72
5 b g Cockney Rebel(IRE) Caeribland (IRE) (Namaqualand (USA))
67^{3} 256^{9} 1390^{10} 2577^{10} 3030^{8} 3395^{6} (4773) 8154^{11}

Rigid Rock (IRE) *Adrian McGuinness* a55 59
9 b g Refuse To Bend(IRE) Delia (IRE) (Darshaan)
6464a^{3}

Rigolleto (IRE) *Anabel K Murphy* a77 72
8 b g Ad Valorem(USA) Jallaissine (IRE) (College Chapel)
167^{8} (658) (873) 955^{4} 1419^{11} 2217^{7} 5797^{2} 6461a^{8} 6831^{5} 7430^{9} 7964^{2}

Rigsby *Zoe Davison* a51
3 b g Mullionmileanhour(IRE) Naemi (GER) (Tannenkonig (IRE))
7459^{10} 7935^{4} 8472^{6}

Rimraam *John Gosden* 78
3 b f Dutch Art Sinduda (Anabaa (USA))
2470^{3}

Ring Eye (IRE) *John O'Shea* a58 66
8 b g Definite Article Erins Lass (IRE) (Erins Isle)
640^{6} 819^{4} 1004^{4} 1169^{3} 1500^{6} 2462^{4} 3052^{2} 3747^{2} 4082^{4} (4591) 4913^{5} 5573 ^{3} 5958^{4} 6508^{6} 7270^{8}

Ring Of Art *Gemma Anderson* a49 55
3 b g Dutch Art Katimont (IRE) (Montjeu (IRE))
3014^{5} 3499^{2} 6004^{7}

Ringside Humour (IRE) *J S Bolger* a100 98
4 b m Teofilo(IRE) Intriguing Humor (CAN) (Distorted Humor (USA))
3630a^{8} 4747a^{6} 4850a^{3} 6389a^{3} 6604a^{7}

Ring Weekend (USA) *H Graham Motion* a103 112
5 ch g Tapit(USA) Free The Magic (USA) (Cryptoclearance (USA))
7172a^{7} 7837a^{7}

Rinky Dink Dawn (IRE) *R Schoof* a50 57
2 ch c Born To Sea(IRE) Saffa Garden (IRE) (King's Best (USA))
1316^{5} ◆ 3404^{9} 4183a^{3} 4471a^{6} 5141a^{6} 5819a^{4} 6015a^{9} 7293a^{7}

Rio Amare (FR) *Matthieu Palussiere* 37
2 ch c Rio De La Plata(USA) Rosalita (FR) (Nashamaa)
4924a^{8}

Rioca (IRE) *Sir Mark Prescott Bt* 92
3 b f Jeremy(USA) Rising Wind (IRE) (Shirocco (GER))
4757^{8}

Rio Deva (IRE) *Keith Dalgleish* a51 66
3 b f Captain Rio Kenema (IRE) (Petardia)
(3773) (4141) 4834^{3} 5152^{9} 5225^{10}

Rio Falls (IRE) *Jennie Candlish* a75
4 b g Captain Rio Swallow Falls (IRE) (Lake Coniston (IRE))
464^{6} 1498^{5} 1722^{4}

Rio Glamorous *Roy Bowring* a58 22
3 b g Aussie Rules(USA) Glamorous Spirit (IRE) (Invincible Spirit (IRE))
2503^{8}

Rioja Day (IRE) *Jim Goldie* a43 57
6 b g Red Clubs(IRE) Dai E Dai (USA) (Seattle Dancer (USA))
1201^{9} 2365^{8} 2810^{7} 3287^{11} 6621^{6} (7097) 7602^{8}

Rio Ronaldo (IRE) *Mike Murphy* a80 92
4 b g Footstepsinthesand Flanders (IRE) (Common Grounds)
1143^{8} 1634^{10} (2754) 3671^{2} 4079^{5} 4584^{5} 5488^{9} 6112^{13} 6944^{9} 7443^{12} 7737^{5}

Rio's Cliffs *Martyn Meade* a84 80
3 b f Canford Cliffs(IRE) What's Up Pussycat (IRE) (Danehill Dancer (IRE))
2239^{8} 3213^{12} 4360^{5} 6182^{3} 6635^{3} 7301^{2} 8036^{3} (8357)

Rio Tigre (IRE) *S bin Ghadayer* a84 104
5 b h Teofilo(IRE) Braziliz (USA) (Kingmambo (USA))
285a^{14} 453a^{4} 811a^{8}

Rip (FR) *F Rossi* a87
2 bb c Rip Van Winkle(IRE) Kylayne (Kyllachy)
7454a^{2}

Ripinto (IRE) *Jim Boyle* a80 80
4 ch g Rip Van Winkle(IRE) For Evva Silca (Piccolo)
1178^{3} 1419^{10} 2213^{10} 2765^{5} 3780^{9}

Ripoll (IRE) *Sylvester Kirk* a86 78
3 b g Alfred Nobel(IRE) Lahu Lady (Red Ransom (USA))
1860^{6} 2366^{3} 2652^{12} 4764^{2} 5013^{2} (5525) 5965^{2} 6265^{4} (7066) ◆ 7462^{9} 7902^{3} 8319^{2} 8456^{6}

Riponian *Susan Corbett* a6 58
6 ch g Trade Fair Dispol Katie (Komaite (USA))
2330^{12} 2525^{3} 3020^{4} 3750^{7} 4444^{4} 6105^{11} (6347) 6621^{3} 7253^{8} 7333^{11}

Ripon Rose *Paul Midgley* a44 47
4 br m Ferrule(IRE) Dispol Isle (IRE) (Trans Island)
596^{7} 867^{4} 1120^{5} 1495^{5} 1696^{6}

Ripper Street (IRE) *Ed Dunlop* a59 63
2 b g Big Bad Bob(IRE) Caster Sugar (USA) (Cozzene (USA))
3818^{9} 4473^{5} 4837^{7} 5796^{7} 8072^{6}

Ripp Orf (IRE) *David Elsworth* a72
2 b g Rip Van Winkle(IRE) Barzah (IRE) (Darshaan)
7424^{3} ◆ 7867^{4} 8352^{2}

Riptide *Michael Scudamore* 72
10 b g Val Royal(FR) Glittering Image (IRE) (Sadler's Wells (USA))
1244^{5} 1523^{6} 2338^{4} 2971^{4} 3437^{2} 3746^{7} 5435^{2} 6519^{7} 7006^{3} 7411^{7}

Rip Van Suzy (IRE) *Jo Hughes* a69 72
3 b f Rip Van Winkle(IRE) Suzy Bliss (Spinning World (USA))
102^{7} 785^{7} 948^{4} 2172a^{4} 3007a^{3} (3764a) 4220a^{2} 5280a^{3} 6310a^{7} 6912a^{12}

Rise Hit (FR) *H-A Pantall* a66
2 b c American Post Rose The One (FR) (Meshaheer (USA))
7588a^{6}

Rise Of Phoenix *John Spearing* 27
2 b f Approve(IRE) Emerald Fire (Pivotal)
3485^{8} 3897^{6} 4713^{9} 5008^{5}

Riser (USA) *Blaine Wright* 86
2 rg c Mizzen Mast(USA) Goodbye Cat (USA) (Tale Of The Cat (USA))
7266a^{9}

Rise Up Singing *Colin Teague* 39
3 b f Showcasing Sambarina (IRE) (Victory Note (USA))
2118^{4} 2302^{11} 3010^{10} 4005^{10} 5839^{8}

Rising (IRE) *Brian Meehan* 70
2 b c Rip Van Winkle(IRE) Cause Celebre (IRE) (Peintre Celebre (USA))
7502^{5} ◆

Rising Breeze (FR) *Tony Carroll* a70 56
5 b g Shirocco(GER) Moon Tree (FR) (Groom Dancer (USA))
101^{4} ◆ 343^{3} 566^{7} 832^{4} 1202^{6}

Rising Eagle *Charles Hills* 66
2 b g Royal Applause The Clan Macdonald (Intikhab (USA))
2543^{5} 3065^{5} 3485^{2} 4015^{3} ◆ 4553^{7} 6033^{5} 6888^{6}

Rising Rainbow *Ivan Furtado* 10
5 b g Rainbow High Lord Conyers (IRE) (Inzar (USA))
1952^{9} 2297^{4} 3012^{9} 3823^{15}

Rising Romance (NZ) *David A Hayes & Tom Dabernig* 104
5 b m Ekraar(USA) Post Romance (NZ) (Postponed (USA))
1690a^{10}

Rising Sunshine (IRE) *Richard Hannon* a55 59
3 b g Dark Angel(IRE) Little Audio (IRE) (Shamardal (USA))
1079^{10} 1287^{8} 2207^{10} 2828^{6} 3319^{6} 3988^{7} 4159^{7}

Risk Major (FR) *J Phelippon* a94 99
3 b c My Risk(FR) Major's Love (FR) (Majorien)
1374a^{9} 6310a^{11} 6911a^{6}

Rita's Boy (IRE) *K R Burke* a90 87
4 b g Captain Rio The Oldladysays No (IRE) (Perugino (USA))
4^{9} 1444^{9} 1672^{2} 1874^{10} 3638^{8} 3944^{5} 4873^{11} 6012^{8} 6537^{3} 7289^{8}

Rita's Girl *K R Burke* a33 56
2 b f Harbour Watch(IRE) Brazilian Breeze (IRE) (Invincible Spirit (IRE))
3282^{6} 4586^{5} 6025^{3} 7974^{9} 8235^{10}

Rita's Man (IRE) *Richard Hannon* a66 62
2 b c Lawman(FR) French Fern (IRE) (Royal Applause)
3526^{5} 4203^{8} 4790^{5} 6898^{5} 8560^{10}

Ritasun (FR) *Richard Hannon* a77 71
3 bb g Monsun(GER) Baselga (GER) (Second Set (IRE))
(366) 421^{2} 6899^{7} ◆ 7419^{5} 7816^{7} 7931^{3} 8379^{3}

Rite To Reign *Philip McBride* a88 95
5 b g Tiger Hill(IRE) Magical Cliche (USA) (Affirmed (USA))
2194^{3} 3117^{2}

Rivellino *K R Burke* a108 105
6 b g Invincible Spirit(IRE) Brazilian Bride (IRE) (Pivotal)
(483) 755a^{6} 1066^{9} 2027^{11} 3655^{8} 4865^{6} 5871^{9} 6558^{14} 7068^{6} 7932^{10}

River Dart (IRE) *Tony Carroll* a86 81
4 ch g Dutch Art Sky Galaxy (USA) (Sky Classic (CAN))
3109^{8} 4208^{5} 5071^{5} 7067^{6} 8254^{2}

River Du Nord (FR) *Sue Gardner* a42 40
9 b m Voix Du Nord(FR) Palala River (Colmore Row)
1830^{8} (5459a)

Riverlynx (IRE) *Ben Haslam* a43 37
4 b m Holy Roman Emperor(IRE) Banba (IRE) (Docksider (USA))
294^{6} 590^{11} 1708^{5}

River Prince (FR) *P Adda* a69 71
6 b g Stormy River(FR) Princess Liu (IRE) (Desert Style (IRE))
512a^{4}

Rivers Of Asia *Philip McBride* a76 71
3 ch g Medicean Aliena (IRE) (Grand Lodge (USA))
466^{3} 618^{3} 968^{4} 7687^{8} 8178^{5} 8590^{3}

Rivers Of Babylon (IRE) *W McCreery* 95
4 b m Holy Roman Emperor(IRE) Sweet Times (Riverman (USA))
1018a^{19}

Rivers Run (IRE) *Ralph Beckett* a72 68
4 b m High Chaparral(IRE) Quiet Waters (USA) (Quiet American (USA))
44^{4} (342) 636^{6} 2400^{5}

River Thames *Mark Johnston* a72 40
3 b c Bernardini(USA) River Street (Machiavellian (USA))
778^{3} (Dead)

Rivet (IRE) *William Haggas* 116
2 b c Fastnet Rock(AUS) Starship (IRE) (Galileo (IRE))
4580^{2} ◆ (5615) (6326) 7149^{5} (7539)

Riviere Argentee (FR) *K R Burke* a65 84
2 gr f Hurricane Cat(USA) River Trebor (USA) (Myrakalu (FR))
3024^{8} (4037) 5005a^{3} 5967^{7} 7493^{7}

Rivolochop (FR) *C Boutin* a64 61
4 ch h American Post Bouboulina (Grand Lodge (USA))
4901a^{5}

Rizal Park (IRE) *James Evans* a81 56
5 b g Amadeus Wolf Imelda (USA) (Manila (USA))
149[9] 336[6] 5021[6]

Road To Dubai (IRE) *George Scott* a68 66
2 ch c Aqlaam Fragrancy (IRE) (Singspiel (IRE))
7503[7] 8119[5]

Roar (IRE) *Brian Ellison* a61 70
2 b g Pour Moi(IRE) Evening Rushour (IRE) (Mull Of Kintyre (USA))
2335[2] (3248) 5967[6]

Roaring Character (IRE) *Tom Dascombe* a69 79
2 b c Arcano(IRE) Dolce Dovo (Medicean)
3730[5] 3986[5] 4914[3] 6053[2] 6274[2] 7328[3]

Roaring Rory *Ollie Pears* a69 69
3 ch g Sakhee's Secret Barbieri (IRE) (Encosta De Lago (AUS))
962[4] (2118) 2785[2] 3009[5] 4236[2] 4426[6] 5070[5] 5855[3] 8078[8] 8390[9]

Robanne *William Knight* 101
3 b f Paco Boy(IRE) Arctic Song (Charnwood Forest (IRE))
1396[3] 1888[12] 2928a[4] 6939[2] ◆ 7348a[4]

Robben *John Mackie* a50 50
4 b g Dutch Art Little Greenbird (Ardkinglass)
295[5] 637[3] 731[2] 1004[3] 1182[3] 1649[5]

Robben Rainbow *David Barron* 79
2 b c Delegator Sally Can Wait (Sakhee (USA))
4336[4] (5414) 6536[9]

Robbian *Charles Smith* a40 57
5 b g Bertolini(USA) Crathes (Zilzal (USA))
1026[12] 1490[4] 2013[8] 2537[9] 6478[12] (7444) (7596)

Robbie Roo Roo *Mrs Ilka Gansera-Leveque* a63 60
3 br f Kheleyf(USA) Haiti Dancer (Josr Algarhoud (IRE))
5167[8] 5554[7] (5889) (6852) 7290[12] 7445[5]

Robero *Brian Ellison* a78 83
4 b g Piccolo Ceilidh Band (Celtic Swing)
67[5] 561[4] 703[8] 2773[11] (2918) (3262) (4362) 4627[8] 5858[2]

Robert Le Diable (FR) *J E Hammond* a94 111
7 ch g Dutch Art Red Begonia (Pivotal)
7806a[5]

Robert The Painter (IRE) *Lee Carter* a88 95
8 b g Whipper(USA) Lidanna (Nicholas (USA))
221[5] 313[2] 599[5] 727[5] 860[5] 1775[11] 2150[5] 2297[3] 3405[8] 3719[4]

Robillard (USA) *Kiaran McLaughlin* 100
4 ch m Distorted Humor(USA) Magnificience (USA) (Stormy Atlantic (USA))
5185a[6]

Robinnielly (IRE) *Keith Dalgleish* 95
3 b g Approve(IRE) Beauty And Style (AUS) (King Of Kings (IRE))
1220[3] 1623[4] 2269[2] (4312) (5226) ◆

Robin Of Navan (FR) *Harry Dunlop* a112 112
3 ch c American Post Cloghran (FR) (Muhtathir)
2076a[2] 2946a[11] 6125[2] 6571[5] 7137a[2] 7841a[2]

Robin Park *Richard Fahey* 83
4 b m Invincible Spirit(IRE) Haigh Hall (Kyllachy)
1197[13]

Robins Pearl (FR) *Harry Dunlop* a80 70
4 ch m Linngari(IRE) Fire Sale (ARG) (Not For Sale (ARG))
66[5] 332[2] 1808[2] 2415[8] 3721[7]

Robin's Purse *Charles Hills* 68
2 b f Sir Percy Morant Bay (IRE) (Montjeu (IRE))
4885[9] 5772[3] 6111[8]

Robot Boy (IRE) *David Barron* 110
6 ch g Shamardal(USA) Pivotal's Princess (IRE) (Pivotal)
3151[6] ◆ 4126[2] ◆ 4584[7] 5555[11] 6119[4] 6779[11] (7124) 7537[10]

Rob's Legacy *Shaun Harris* a33 43
3 ch g Phoenix Reach(IRE) Clumber Pursuits (Pastoral Pursuits)
3951[7] 4450[4] 5079[7] 5888[5] 7532[10]

Roca Rojo (IRE) *Chad C Brown* 107
4 b m Strategic Prince Lucy Diamonds (IRE) (Orpen (USA))
5185a[4]

Rocaverde (IRE) *Ralph Beckett* 93
3 b f Rock Of Gibraltar(IRE) Green Room (FR) (In The Wings)
(1609) 3297[14]

Roccor *Tim Vaughan* a66 62
3 b f Rock Of Gibraltar(IRE) Corinium (IRE) (Turtle Island (IRE))
2004[7] 2578[7] 2999[8] 3558[11] 4085[4] 4596[5] 6367[10] 6857[10] 7282[10]

Rocco's Delight *Shane Kieran Ryder* a78 83
4 b g Multiplex No Page (IRE) (Statue Of Liberty (USA))
(1252) ◆ 1403[2] 1521[6] 3517[12] 4443[8] 7801a[13]

Roc De Prince *Keith Dalgleish* a53 69
7 b g Shirocco(GER) Louella (USA) (El Gran Senor (USA))
946[7] 1523[4] 2089[3] (2678) 3417[3] 3704[2] (4194) 4491[5]

Rochelle (IRE) *Roy Brotherton* a67 7
5 b m Duke Of Marmalade(IRE) Emilion (Fantastic Light (USA))
683[12]

Roche Rose (IRE) *E Lellouche* a84 90
3 gr f Rock Of Gibraltar(IRE) Roche Ambeau (FR) (Chichicastenango (FR))
5006a[9] 7897a[6]

Rockabilly Riot (IRE) *Martin Todhunter* a62 65
6 br g Footstepsinthesand Zawariq (IRE) (Marju (IRE))
1674[5] 2558[6] 4515[2] 5758[7] 6103[3] 7044[8] 7321[10] 8134[8]

Rockalater *Sylvester Kirk* a25
2 b f Delegator Rock Candy (IRE) (Rock Of Gibraltar (IRE))
8536[8]

Rockaria *Philip Hide* a38 15
2 br c Pivotal Vassaria (IRE) (Rock Of Gibraltar (IRE))
3315[10] 4786[7] 6480[11] 6895[6]

Rock Canyon (IRE) *Linda Perratt* a19 69
7 b g Rock Of Gibraltar(IRE) Tuesday Morning (Sadler's Wells (USA))
4191[7] 4488[11] 4932[10] 5152[2] 5224[6] 5582[2] 5838[5] 6347[8] 6506[12] 6615[4] 6774[5] 6809[4] 7092[3] 7851[9]

Rock Cocktail (AUS) *M F De Kock* 103
6 br g Rock Of Gibraltar(IRE) Brandy Cocktail (AUS) (Hennessy (USA))
189a[13] 375a[P]

Rockery (IRE) *Ed Dunlop* a49 71
3 b f Fastnet Rock(AUS) Rain Flower (IRE) (Indian Ridge)
603[8] 2914[5] 3411[4]

Rocket Power *James Tate* a81
3 ch g Kyllachy Rhal (IRE) (Rahy (USA))
298[3] (582) ◆ 924[3] ◆ 2818[5] 4211[5] 5810[4]

Rocket Rob (IRE) *Willie Musson* a66 71
10 b g Danetime(IRE) Queen Of Fibres (IRE) (Scenic (IRE))
(98) 398[5] 541[7] 775[5] 873[7] 1833[6] 2785[7] 3159[8] 3559[4] 3843[5] 5194[4]

Rocket Ronnie (IRE) *Ed McMahon* a77 78
6 b g Antonius Pius(USA) Ctesiphon (USA) (Arch (USA))
3011[2] 3612[6] 4232[7] 4807[6] 5273[9] 6028[6] 6643[4] 7227[6] 7755[11] 8035[7] 8191[3]

Rock Eyes *G Arizkorreta Elosegui* 91
4 ch m Rock Of Gibraltar(IRE) Art Eyes (USA) (Halling (USA))
(5249a)

Rock Icon *Patrick Chamings* a61 69
3 b g Sixties Icon Monashee Rock (IRE) (Monashee Mountain (USA))
2184[6] 4021[6] 4504[2] (5167) 7310[8] 7755[5] 8207[8]

Rocking Rudolph (USA) *Robert Cowell* a75 13
3 b f Discreetly Mine(USA) Empire Spring (USA) (Empire Maker (USA))
7112[13]

Rockley Point *Paul D'Arcy* a81 76
3 b g Canford Cliffs(IRE) Statua (IRE) (Statoblest)
7061[2] (7311) 8052[8] 8456[7]

Rockliffe *Micky Hammond* a49 72
3 b g Notnowcato Hope Island (IRE) (Titus Livius (FR))
274[9] 533[2] 1062[7] 1484[5] 1740[6] (2366) 2590[7] 3509[4] 4033[7] 4635[2] 5086[3] 5288[4] 5957[2] 7582[6]

Rock Lobster *Gordon Elliott* a83 16
4 ch g Bahamian Bounty Reeling N' Rocking (IRE) (Mr Greeley (USA))
6466a[DSQ]

Rock Montjeu (IRE) *Adrian Paul Keatley* a58 46
4 b g Rock Of Gibraltar(IRE) Leala (IRE) (Montjeu (IRE))
1696[4]

Rockmount River (IRE) *David Bridgwater* a85 58
7 b g Rock Of Gibraltar(IRE) Littlefeather (IRE) (Indian Ridge)
2507[5]

Rock'n Gold *Luca Cumani* a76 81
3 b g Fastnet Rock(AUS) La Concorde (FR) (Sadler's Wells (USA))
6294[2] 7102[4] 7487[5]

Rock 'n Red (IRE) *Ed Dunlop* a69 63
3 b f Fastnet Rock(AUS) Red Fantasy (IRE) (High Chaparral (IRE))
591[3] 746[6] 1163[3] ◆ (1346) 1860[10] 2574[6] 3318[4]

Rock N Rolla (IRE) *Keith Dalgleish* 83
2 ch c Intikhab(USA) Fantastic Opinion (IRE) (Fantastic Light (USA))
5834[4] (6129) 6536[14]

Rock N Roll Global (IRE) *Richard Hughes* a68
2 ch c Power Laughter (IRE) (Sadler's Wells (USA))
8353[5]

Rock Of Ages *Steve Flook* a68 20
7 ch g Pivotal Magic Peak (IRE) (Danehill (USA))
27[6]

Rock Of Max *Michael Bell* a74 73
4 b g Royal Applause Poldhu (Cape Cross (IRE))
1434[2] 2605[8] 3560[9]

Rock Of Monaco *Antony Brittain* a56 20
3 b f Monsieur Bond(IRE) Melandre (Lujain (USA))
5525[9] 6106[9] 7323[14]

Rock Of Romance (IRE) *A Wohler* a75 104
6 br h Rock Of Gibraltar(IRE) Romantic Venture (IRE) (Indian Ridge)
2286a[4] (4031a) 6610a[4] 7555a[4] 7946a[9]

Rock On Bollinski *Brian Ellison* 77
6 b g Bollin Eric Bred For Pleasure (Niniski (USA))
1222[3] 1852[2] 2805[3] 3602[7] 4381[5] (5856) 6540[8] 7332[9] ◆

Rock On Dandy (FR) *Harry Dunlop* a66 65
2 gr c Rajsaman(FR) Minnie's Mystery (FR) (Highest Honor (FR))
2180[6] 3093[11] 5166[3] 6888[5] 7454a[6]

Rock On Rosie (IRE) *Adrian Brendan Joyce* a67 68
7 b m Gamut(IRE) Macs Goose (Kayf Tara)
1279a[9] 2114a[6]

Rock Palm (IRE) *Brendan Powell* a59 64
3 b f Rock Of Gibraltar(IRE) Palm Pilot (IRE) (Oasis Dream)
1628[8] 2009[15] 2459[7] 3059[7] 4009[7] ◆ 4317[3] 4777[4] 5503[7] 6194[9]

Rockshine *Richard Hannon* 66
2 b f Fastnet Rock(AUS) Shine Like A Star (Fantastic Light (USA))
6111[4] ◆ 6776[9] 7284[4]

Rock Song *John Mackie* a72 79
7 b g Rock Of Gibraltar(IRE) Jackie's Opera (FR) (Indian Ridge)
1114[4] (1501) (1633) 2043[9] 2556[9]

Rockspirit (IRE) *Marco Botti* a107 100
3 b g Fastnet Rock(AUS) Phillippa (IRE) (Galileo (IRE))
(2548) 3687[2] 4153[2] (5932) (7101)

Rock Steady (IRE) *Roger Charlton* a103 94
3 ch g Intikhab(USA) Mannsara (IRE) (Royal Academy (USA))
3465[3] 4010[4] (4710) 5240[2] 6209[2] 7067[2] 7869[2] (8123) 8210[2]

Rocktherunway (IRE) *Michael Dods* a61 77
7 ch g Nayef(USA) Femme Fatale (Fairy King (USA))
1665[6] 4239[3] 5435[3] 5970[4] 6503[2] (6840) 7251[2] 7993[11]

Rockview Emperor (IRE) *N Dooly* a57 63
6 b g Holy Roman Emperor(IRE) River Fairy (USA) (Irish River (FR))
4813a[11]

Rock Warbler (IRE) *Oliver Greenall* a75 70
3 ch g Raven's Pass(USA) Rare Tern (IRE) (Pivotal)
4631[8] 5246[7] 6592[11] 6852[2] ◆ (7145) ◆ 7611[4] ◆ (7797) 8052[5] 8531[6]

Rockweiller *Shaun Harris* a46 63
9 b g Rock Of Gibraltar(IRE) Ballerina Suprema (IRE) (Sadler's Wells (USA))
505[11] 1222[9] 1547[9]

Rockwood *Karen McLintock* a79 78
5 b g Rock Of Gibraltar(IRE) Hannah Frank (IRE) (High Chaparral (IRE))
(39) 336[2] ◆ (569) (683) 1114[2] 1664[5] 2618[2] 3166[4] 3605[5] 4190[2] 4930[8] 6838[3] 7408[12] 8007[3]

Rocky Hill Ridge *John Balding* a50
5 b g Auction House(USA) Amwell Star (USA) (Silver Buck (USA))
334[11]

Rocky Two (IRE) *Philip Kirby* a22 45
6 ch g Rock Of Gibraltar(IRE) Toorah Laura La (USA) (Black Minnaloushe (USA))
2745[7] 4971[10]

Rococoa (IRE) *Ed Walker* a67 86
3 b f Zebedee Nightbird (IRE) (Night Shift (USA))
126[3] 211[2] 2428[2] (3069) ◆ 3716[2] 4360[3] 4984[2] (5881)

Roconga (IRE) *E J O'Grady* a65 92
6 b g Rakti Nafzira (IRE) (Darshaan)
4721a[12] 7708a[12]

Rodaini (USA) *Simon Crisford* 104
2 ch c Exchange Rate(USA) Blessings Count (USA) (Pulpit (USA))
(2757) (5394) (5877) (6285) 7148[9] 7807a[14]

Roderic Queen (IRE) *Simone Brogi* a64 80
3 b f Roderic O'Connor(IRE) Vampire Queen (IRE) (General Monash (USA))
1685a[7] 5349a[7]

Roderic's Secret (IRE) *David Menuisier* a66 73
3 ch g Roderic O'Connor(IRE) Midris (IRE) (Namid)
1386[4] 2411[4] 3025[5] 6380[2] 6886[6] 7408[9]

Rod Of Iron *Michael Madgwick* a41 46
3 br g Alkaased(USA) Leading Star (Motivator)
3160[12] 3765[9] 5777[8] 6406[11]

Rodrigo De Torres *Garry Moss* a87 89
9 ch g Bahamian Bounty Leonica (Lion Cavern (USA))
2677[12]

Roger Thorpe *Deborah Sanderson* a64 62
7 b g Firebreak Nunthorpe (Mystiko (USA))
2[3] 247[2] 336[3] 936[6] 1654[7] 1925[3] 2046[3] 2409[2] 3013[6]

Rogue Runner (GER) *P Schiergen* a78 103
4 b g King's Best(USA) Rosa Di Brema (ITY) (Lomitas)
540a[8] 757a[15] 3455a[4] 4253a[7] 5950a[7] 7400a[8]

Roibeard (IRE) *G M Lyons* 87
3 b g Big Bad Bob(IRE) Queen Myrine (IRE) (Oratorio (IRE))
1938a[7]

Roicead (USA) *D Selvaratnam* a78 108
9 b g Giant's Causeway(USA) Coachella (Danehill (USA))
(280a) 371a[5] 626a[2]

Roi De Vitesse (IRE) *Ali Jan* a102 102
9 ch h Chineur(FR) Face The Storm (IRE) (Barathea (IRE))
91a[4] 370a[7] 450a[3] 626a[3] 755a[2]

Roja Dove (IRE) *David Thompson* a15 21
7 b m Jeremy(USA) Knight's Place (IRE) (Hamas (IRE))
1121[5]

Rojina (IRE) *Lisa Williamson* a55
3 ch f Intense Focus(USA) Hurricane Havoc (IRE) (Hurricane Run (IRE))
42[3] 177[7] 432[4] 562[2] 635[8] 1249[7] 1574[8] 7509[6]

Rokerby Hall *Tim Easterby* 57
3 b f Dutch Art Royal Punch (Royal Applause)
1819[9]

Rolando (IRE) *A Wohler* 79
2 b c Campanologist(USA) Rosa Di Brema (ITY) (Lomitas)
7842a[7]

Rolanna (IRE) *W J Martin* a47 57
4 b m Strategic Prince Dalaika (CAN) (Rhythm (USA))
2462[3]

Rolen Sly *Neville Bycroft* a45 47
7 b g Tillerman Feiticeira (USA) (Deposit Ticket (USA))
2[11] 251[7] 2836[RR] 6450[8] 7045[13] 7604[8]

Roller *Michael Easterby* a82 77
3 b g Rail Link Buffering (Beat Hollow)
(8481) ◆

Roll On Rory *Jason Ward* 95
3 b g Mullionmileanhour(IRE) Fangfoss Girls (Monsieur Bond (IRE))
1599[11] 1922[6] 2742[8] (3439) (4134) 4547[2] (5412) 6232[6] (6810) 7668[2]

Roly Poly (USA) *A P O'Brien* 112
2 b f War Front(USA) Misty For Me (IRE) (Galileo (IRE))
2494a[4] 3270[8] (3694a) (4106) 5584[2] 6784[2] 7809a[9]

Roly Tricks *Natalie Lloyd-Beavis* a45 71
5 b m Pastoral Pursuits Freya Tricks (Noverre (USA))
1390[7] 1743[4] 2205[8] 3488[4] 4370[3] (5776) 6212[7]

Roman Beauty (FR) *D Prod'Homme* a64 45
2 b f Holy Roman Emperor(IRE) Golden Wings (USA) (Devil's Bag (USA))
7346a[7]

Romancingthestone *Karen George* a44 48
3 b f Bertolini(USA) Diamond Vanessa (IRE) (Distinctly North (USA))
81[3] 242[5] 327[9] 5330[8] 5721[8] 6902[11] 7212[11]

Roman De Brut (IRE) *Daniel Mark Loughnane* a72 49
4 ch g Rock Of Gibraltar(IRE) Nesmeh (USA) (More Than Ready (USA))
149[5] 568[7] 3563[3] 4214[9] 4527[2] 5529[3] 5841[2] 6662[5] 6921[3] (7755) 8141[4]

Roman Flight (IRE) *David Dennis* a69 77
8 b g Antonius Pius(USA) Flight Sequence (Polar Falcon (USA))
5381[6]

Roman Holiday (IRE) *Ed Vaughan* a81 71
3 b f Holy Roman Emperor(IRE) Burn The Breeze (IRE) (Beat Hollow)
4639[2] 5192[2] (6459) (7430)

Roman Impero *M Halford* a85 71
3 b g Holy Roman Emperor(IRE) Diksie Dancer (Diktat)
(644a)

Roman Legend (IRE) *Jassim Al Ghazali* a70 102
5 b h Holy Roman Emperor(IRE) Taking Liberties (IRE) (Royal Academy (USA))
744a[2]

Roman Legion (IRE) *Dean Ivory* 59
2 b g Holy Roman Emperor(IRE) Kibini (Galileo (IRE))
2641[5] ◆ 2963[5] 4016[5]

Roman Navigator (IRE) *Marco Botti* a42
2 b c Henrythenavigator(USA) Lollina Paulina (Holy Roman Emperor (IRE))
8065[8]

Romanor *Ed Walker* 72
2 b g Holy Roman Emperor(IRE) Salinia (IRE) (Rainbow Quest (USA))
5959[5] 6523[3] 7034[4]

Romansh (USA) *S bin Ghadayer* a100 82
6 br h Bernardini(USA) Cologny (USA) (Go For Gin (USA))
94a[6] 281a[3]

Romantic Angel (USA) *Ismail Mohammed* a55 51
3 b f Macho Uno(USA) Non Sibi (USA) (Wild Deputy (USA))
2298[7] 2848[8] 5475[7]

Romantic Comedy (IRE) *James Tate* a60 43
3 ch f Equiano(FR) Gay Romance (Singspiel (IRE))
140[3] 248[4]

Romantic Touch (AUS) *A S Cruz* 115
5 br g Northern Meteor(AUS) Dearness (AUS) (Snippets (AUS))
8332a[8]

Romantic View *Charlie Appleby* 88
2 b f Shamardal(USA) Mondalay (Monsun (GER))
1988[2] (2467) 3336[16] 6787[5] 7147[15] 7667[10]

Roman Times (IRE) *John David Riches* a53 61
3 b f Holy Roman Emperor(IRE) Timeless Dream (Oasis Dream)
365[8] (5578) 6436[5]

Roman Urn *Brett Johnson* a51 18
3 ch g Major Cadeaux Symphonic Dancer (USA) (Smart Strike (CAN))
1256[7] 1577[11] 3653[8] 4267[12] 4760[6] 5721[9] 6187[10]

Romiac (IRE) *Ms Sheila Lavery* 61
4 b g Kodiac Romanylei (IRE) (Blues Traveller (IRE))
1018a[18]

Romosh (IRE) *R Bouresly* a34 74
4 b m Yeats(IRE) River Patrol (Rousillon (USA))
8a[11]

Ronald Gee (IRE) *Jim Goldie* a50 73
9 ch g Garuda(IRE) Panache Lady (IRE) (Cyrano De Bergerac)
1853[5] 2618[10] 2911[7] 3706[11] 6503[7] 6920[11] 7438[10]

Ronaldinho (IRE) *Dianne Sayer* a45 57
6 b g Jeremy(USA) Spring Glory (Dr Fong (USA))
4099[6] 4935[9] 5801[2]

Ronaldjamessach (IRE) *James Bethell* a48
3 ch g Lord Shanakill(USA) Boschendal (IRE) (Zamindar (USA))
428[6]

Ronald R (IRE) *Michael Bell* 85
2 ch c Nathaniel(IRE) Amazon Beauty (IRE) (Wolfhound (USA))
3058[3] (4274) ◆ 5595[8]

Ronnie Baird *Kristin Stubbs* a64 79
3 ch g Poet's Voice Fleur De Lis (Nayef (USA))
945[6] (1449) 1971[5] 2654[9] 3286[9] 3567[4] 4241[5] 4549[5] 5365[4] 5975[4] 6541[8]

Ronnie The Rooster *David Barron* a66 54
2 b c Captain Gerrard(IRE) Piranha (IRE) (Exceed And Excel (AUS))
4765[11] 5713[8] 6515[8] (7110) (7854)

Ronni Layne *Conrad Allen* a65 50
2 b f Native Ruler Cindy Incidentally (Shinko Forest (IRE))
6782[12] 7465[7] 7930[4]

Ron's Ballad *Michael Madgwick* a41 49
3 ch g Sakhee's Secret Nom De La Rosa (IRE) (Oratorio (IRE))
610[8] 979[7] 1548[3] 2967[9] 3973[11] 7298[11] 7735[7]

Ron Waverly (IRE) *Paddy Butler* a37 45
6 ch g Haatef(USA) Mermaid Beach (Slew O'Gold (USA))
84[8] 505[10] 602[7] 673[5] 1748[8] 2899[10] 3492[6]

Ronya (IRE) *Tracy Waggott* a43 65
5 b m Bushranger(IRE) Beenablaw (IRE) (Alzao (USA))
2555[6] 2860[3] 3363[3] (4425) 5273[5] 5800[6] 6953[5] (7581)

Rooke *D Henderson* 102
6 b g Pastoral Pursuits Gibraltar Bay (IRE) (Cape Cross (IRE))
1023a[7] 5502a[3] 6356a[5]

Room Key *Eve Johnson Houghton* a89 94
4 ch g Mount Nelson Saturday Girl (Peintre Celebre (USA))
1856[10] 2485[8] 2796[4] 4395[9] 4625[15] 4823[16] 5874[8] (6466a) 7308[4]

Rooney O'Mara *W M Roper* 64
2 ch f Dragon Pulse(IRE) Date Mate (USA) (Thorn Dance (USA))
7193a[7]

Roryslittlesister (IRE) *S M Duffy* a44 41
6 ch m Captain Rio Teacher Preacher (IRE) (Taufan (USA))
7474a[5] 7800a[5]

Rosabelle *Alan Bailey* a74 89
2 b f Mayson Kirk (Selkirk (USA))
3074[2] (3633) ◆ 4195[3] 5638[2] 6257[5] (6763)

Rosairlie (IRE) *Micky Hammond* a68 84
8 ch m Halling(USA) Mrs Mason (IRE) (Turtle Island (IRE))
1253[11]

Rosamaria (FR) *H-A Pantall* a54 71
3 b f Literato(FR) Rampoldina (Montjeu (IRE))
5349a[10]

Rosamaria (IRE) *Michael Dods* 72
3 gr f Rip Van Winkle(IRE) Rosa Grace (Lomitas)
2574[4] 2973[4] 3399[3] 3551[2] 3885[5] 6541[7]

Rosarios (FR) *Rebecca Menzies* a64 16
3 b g Alexandros Rose Of Logis (FR) (Slickly (FR))
7955[5]

Rosarno (IRE) *Charles Hills* a64 81
2 b c Fastnet Rock(AUS) Jouet (Reprimand)
6924[5] (7501)

Rosay (IRE) *J-C Rouget* 102
3 b f Raven's Pass(USA) Petit Calva (FR) (Desert King (IRE))
1309a[3] 2945a[4] 5498a[9]

Rose Above *Andrew Balding* a76 85
4 b m Yeats(IRE) Sabah (Nashwan (USA))
161[3] 487[3] (781) (882) ◆ 1092[9] 2876[2] 3409[9] 3972[2] ◆ 5053[5] 5574[2]

Rosealee (IRE) *Jeremy Gask* a78 82
3 gr f Zebedee Why Now (Dansili)
57[3] 344[4] 515[2] (1061) 1452[8] 2002[4] 3036[4] (3407) (4224) 4585[4] 4831[6]

Rosebay (GER) *Markus Klug* a85 104
5 b m It's Gino(GER) Royal Fong (GER) (Dr Fong (USA))
2633a[2] 3916a[6] 6067a[4] 6824a[8] 7723a[9]

Rose Berry *Chris Dwyer* a77 66
2 b f Archipenko(USA) Desert Berry (Green Desert (USA))
1889[7] 3037[6] 3597[7] (5257) 6139[2] (6658) 7113[9]

Rosebride *Richard Fahey* 98
2 b f Mayson Wedding Party (Groom Dancer (USA))
2732[2] ◆ (3290) 4111[6] 4915[2] (5794) 6555[2] 7155[11]

Roseburg (IRE) *Roger Varian* 115
5 ch g Tamayuz Raydaniya (IRE) (In The Wings)
2894[3] (Dead)

Rosecomb (IRE) *Michael Bell* a39 60
3 b f Rip Van Winkle(IRE) Malyana (Mtoto)
148[7] 4275[4] 4987[6] 5548[8]

Rose De Pierre (IRE) *D K Weld* 105
3 b f Dubawi(IRE) Profound Beauty (IRE) (Danehill (USA))
7392a[2] 7706a[5]

Rose Eclair *Tim Easterby* a75 77
3 b f Major Cadeaux Katie Boo (IRE) (Namid)
2428[8] 2776[8] (3368) 3806[2] 4007[2] 4378[3] (5110) 5836[3] 6133[3] 6717[5] 7363[3] 7591[7]

Rose Fantaisie (FR) *J-P Gauvin* a47
2 b f Amadeus Wolf Divine Fantaisie (FR) (Lando (GER))
5988a[12]

Roseland (USA) *Hugo Palmer* a53
2 b f First Defence(USA) Aviate (Dansili)
1719[3]

Rose Marmara *Brian Rothwell* a70 84
3 ch f Exceed And Excel(AUS) Show Rainbow (Haafhd)
2334[3] 2777[4] (3394) ◆ 3893[3] 4612[7] 4947[2] 5730[3] ◆ 6096[4] 6793[14]

Rosemay (FR) *Simon Crisford* a68
2 b f Mayson Maine Rose (Red Ransom (USA))
6897[6] 7882[7]

Rosenborg Rider (IRE) *Ralph Beckett* a79 63
3 b g Kodiac Miss Sundance (IRE) (Desert Sun)
639[3] ◆ (952) 2477[10] 3187[7] 4010[8] 4881[3] 5810[2] 6899[8]

Rosenhill (IRE) *Gerald Geisler* 69
3 b c Tiger Hill(IRE) Rosengeste (IRE) (Be My Guest (USA))
4186a[13]

Rosental *Luca Cumani* a99 108
4 b m Pivotal Rose Trail (USA) (Kingmambo (USA))
2671[2] 3608[4] 4610[7] 6115[2] (7087a) 7929a[3]

Rose Of Virginia (NZ) *Lee & Shannon Hope* 95
6 b m Thorn Park(AUS) Centapin (NZ) (Pins (AUS))
7712a[11] 7756a[24]

Rose Rized (GER) *P Schiergen* 96
4 b m Authorized(IRE) Rosenreihe (IRE) (Catcher In The Rye (IRE))
1907a[6] 5219a[3] 6107a[3] 7720a[7]

Rosette *Alan Swinbank* a30 64
4 b m Archipenko(USA) Roses (Muhtarram (USA))
51[6] 1873[4] 2260[5] 3190[4] (4045) 5118[4]

Roshanara (FR) *A De Royer-Dupre* a88 95
3 b f Sea The Stars(IRE) Rosawa (FR) (Linamix (FR))
7998a[2]

Rosie Briar *Andrew Balding* 95
2 ch f Mayson Lighted Way (Kris)
3718[4] (6733) (7536)

Rosie Cotton (IRE) *Mme Pia Brandt* a75 100
4 b m King's Best(USA) Luce (IRE) (Sadler's Wells (USA))
1232a[6] 2893[3]

Rosie Crowe (IRE) *Shaun Harris* a55 52
4 b m Approve(IRE) Tolzey (USA) (Rahy (USA))
35[6] 270[3] 430[8] 730[11] 3044[2] 4498[3] 5604[7] 6047[2] 6512[5] (7646) 8278[4] 8589[8]

Rosie Hall (IRE) *John Wainwright* a47 52
6 ch m Lion Heart(USA) Baltic Dip (IRE) (Benny The Dip (USA))
26[7] 175[3] 4240[12] 4772[11] 5323[10] 5800[7] 5868[10]

Rosie Royale (IRE) *Roger Teal* a58 76
4 gr m Verglas(IRE) Fearn Royal (IRE) (Ali-Royal (IRE))
801[8] 1547[4] 2210[5] 2634[11] 3002[2] 3409[5] 4019[6] (5256) (5624) (6315) 7183[14]

Rosie Royce *Henry Candy* a49 70
3 b f Acclamation Rebecca Rolfe (Pivotal)
5330[4] 6190[4] 6879[6] 7420[5] 7964[7]

Rosie's Premiere (IRE) *Dean Ivory* 93
4 b m Showcasing Golden Rosie (IRE) (Exceed And Excel (AUS))
2875[4] ◆ 3714[5] 4066[7] 4461[4] 4911[2] 5488[6] 6263[8] 7186[8]

Rosie's Vision *Mark Usher* a53 50
3 b f Passing Glance Bold Rose (Bold Edge)
1734[8] 2325[7] 2851[9] 3141[3] 3493[5] 4159[5] 4794[5] 5572[9] 6243[9]

Rosina *Ann Duffield* a86 86
3 b f Showcasing Mondovi (Kyllachy)
1453[9] 2192[5] 2658[8] 3292[7] 4947[3] 5780[5] 6927[2] 7772[3]

Roskilly (IRE) *P Monfort* a72 79
5 ch g Hurricane Run(IRE) Party Feet (IRE) (Noverre (USA))
1846a[3] (3733a)

Ross (IRE) *P Schiergen* a106 100
4 b h Acclamation Ronja (USA) (El Corredor (USA))
374a[4] ◆ 624a[7] 842a[2] 1231a[4] 6067a[5] 8431a[4]

Ross Castle (IRE) *Matthieu Palussiere* a77 105
3 b c Bushranger(IRE) Bulrushes (Byron)
(2232a) 3269[12] 3796a[5] 5217a[14] 6391a[13] 7758a[12]

Rossington *John Wainwright* a49 20
7 b g Gentleman's Deal(IRE) Ettrbee (IRE) (Lujain (USA))
569[7] 865[7]

Ross Raith Rover *Robert Eddery* a62 40
3 b g Oasis Dream Baqah (IRE) (Bahhare (USA))
7061[4] 7311[7] 7616[8] 8156[3] ◆

Rossvoss *T M Walsh* 69
8 b g Medicean Dixielake (IRE) (Lake Coniston (IRE))
4417a[4]

Rostova (USA) *Sir Michael Stoute* 102
3 b f Arch(USA) Tsar's Pride (Sadler's Wells (USA))
1992[6] 3410[2] (4358) (5831) 6488[5] (7397a) 7929a[4]

Rosvana (FR) *A De Royer-Dupre* 100
3 b f Dansili Rosanara (FR) (Sinndar (IRE))
2316a[6]

Rosy Blush *Mme Pia Brandt* a50 93
4 b m Youmzain(IRE) Sweet Lilly (Tobougg (IRE))
6107a[4] 7087a[6] 8024a[14]

Rosy Morning (IRE) *Mark Johnston* a74 77
3 b f Exceed And Excel(AUS) Bright Morning (Dubai Millennium)
1432[3] 1872[6] 2305[10] 3152[2] 3438[2] 3717[9] 4145[2] 4306[8]

Rosy Ryan (IRE) *Tina Jackson* a59 48
6 b m Tagula(IRE) Khaydariya (IRE) (Akarad (FR))
6569[9] 6742[3] ◆ 7794[8] 8146[2] 8306[6] 8401[3]

Roter Baron (IRE) *Eamonn O'Connell* a52 45
7 bb g Red Clubs(IRE) Ghibli Gal (IRE) (Desert Style (IRE))
5096a[19]

Rotherwick (IRE) *Paul Cole* a91 96
4 ch g Starspangledbanner(AUS) Pivotalia (IRE) (Pivotal)
2216[4] 2832[3] 3660[2] 4208[2] 4710[4] 6286[3] 6802[2] 7067[5] 7419[2] 7666[2]

Rothesay Chancer *Jim Goldie* a33 86
8 ch g Monsieur Bond(IRE) Rhinefield Beauty (IRE) (Shalford (IRE))
1378[6] 1666[7] 2364[8]

Roudee *Tom Dascombe* a81 107
4 b g Kodiac Eau Rouge (Grand Lodge (USA))
(1218) 1566[2] 1968[2] 2895[12] 3671[9] 4136[7] (5417) (6556) 7156[8]

Rouge Buck (JPN) *Masahiro Otake* 112
4 b m Manhattan Cafe(JPN) Ginger Punch (USA) (Awesome Again (CAN))
8129a[9]

Rouge Noir *Jeremy Noseda* a43
3 b f Showcasing Vive Les Rouges (Acclamation)
5300[8] 6187[11] 7509[8]

Rouge Nuage (IRE) *Conrad Allen* a88 79
6 ch g Indian Haven Nom Francais (First Trump)
2213[2] 2862[5]

Rougeoyant (FR) *B De Montzey* a72 98
3 b g Air Chief Marshal(IRE) Red Vixen (IRE) (Agnes World (USA))
5349a[5]

Roughlyn *Lisa Williamson* a3 2
7 ch g Haafhd Dime Bag (High Line)
7955[7] 8180[13]

Rouleau *Charlie Appleby* a102 101
3 b c Exceed And Excel(AUS) Rachelle (IRE) (Mark Of Esteem (IRE))
185a[2] 539a[6] 6788[11]

Roundabout Magic (IRE) *Simon Dow* a62 62
2 b c Zebedee Cayo Largo (IRE) (Captain Rio)
3315[9] 3647[7] 4205[5] 5257[3] 6420[6] 6830[8] 7217[8] 7900[2] 7981[6] (8027) 8444[5]

Round The Island *Richard Whitaker* a65 66
3 b g Royal Applause Luanshya (First Trump)
1673[4] ◆ 2302[9] (2834) 4376[6] 5059[5] 5864[11] 6451[14] 6685[5] (7144) ◆ 7386[10]

Round Two (IRE) *J S Bolger* 104
3 b c Teofilo(IRE) Khazina (USA) (Kingmambo (USA))
1938a[6] 3677a[10] 7558a[3]

Rousayan (IRE) *David O'Meara* a86 94
5 b g Invincible Spirit(IRE) Rose Quartz (Lammtarra (USA))
(1924) ◆ 2689[3] 3364[6] 4894[3] 5419[3] 5976[5] ◆ 6736[4] 6915[5] 7316[2] 8049[9] 8122[7]

Rowlestonerendezvu *Tony Carroll* a53 57
3 b f Rail Link Charmante Femme (Bin Ajwaad (IRE))
2008[10] 2414[11] 2998[8] 4025[6] 6654[6] 7369[5]

Roxie Lot *Pam Sly* a71 67
4 b m Exceed And Excel(AUS) Orlena (USA) (Gone West (USA))
(1262) 2577[6] 3354[3] 3823[8] 4596[8] 5635[7] 6137[2] 6901[7]

Royal Acclaim (IRE) *Rebecca Bastiman* 56
4 b g Acclamation Top Row (Observatory (USA))
3264[7] 4895[9] 5835[5] 6478[8] 7299[8]

Royal Acquisition *Ivan Furtado* a83 79
6 b g Royal Applause Flavian (Catrail (USA))
2863[9] 3637[9] 4495[6]

Royal Alstroemeria *Stuart Kittow* a50 56
3 b f Intikhab(USA) Delta Diva (USA) (Victory Gallop (CAN))
5504[8]

Royal Artillery (USA) *John Gosden* 117
3 bb c War Front(USA) Masseuse (USA) (Dynaformer (USA))
2627[4] 3296[5] (5159) 5499a[3]

Royal Avatar (IRE) *Donal Kinsella* a40 31
5 br g Arakan(USA) Perfect Order (USA) (Red Ransom (USA))
2229a[10]

Royal Bajan (USA) *Robert Cowell* a93 75
8 rg g Speightstown(USA) Crown You (USA) (Two Punch (USA))
4[11] 1782[2] 1950[6] 2342[6] 2931[8] 5269[6]

Royal Battalion *Gary Moore* a77 59
5 b g Sea The Stars(IRE) Yummy Mummy (Montjeu (IRE))
1854[8] 3767[7]

Royal Beekeeper *George Scott* a46
3 ch g Champs Elysees Lasso (Indian Ridge)
96[5]

Royal Birth *Stuart Williams* a107 100
5 b g Exceed And Excel(AUS) Princess Georgina (Royal Applause)
106[7] (213) ◆ 492[3] ◆ 677[3] (835) 2188[6] 2488[6] 3151[10] (3277) (4126) 4584[3] 5555[12] 6112[2]

Royal Blessing *Peter Fahey* a67 66
4 b g Royal Applause Zuleika Dobson (Cadeaux Genereux)
5096a[5]

Royal Blossom (IRE) *Michael Wigham* a14
3 b f Royal Applause Dynacam (USA) (Dynaformer (USA))
1181[4]

Royal Brave (IRE) *Rebecca Bastiman* a78 78
5 b g Acclamation Daqtora (Dr Devious (IRE))
1444[10] 2016[12] 2426[3] 2975[4] 3552[3] 4488[5] 5032[2] 5284[5] 6093[3] 6476[2] 6809[3] 7660[3] (8010)

Royal Caper *Miss Joey Ellis* a64 53
6 b g Royal Applause Ukraine (IRE) (Cape Cross (IRE))
3078[5] 4388[9] 5734[7]

Royal Celebration *Bryan Smart* a53 55
2 b g Excelebration(IRE) Auntie Kathryn (IRE) (Acclamation)
2417[8] 6447[5] 6789[5] 8285[3]

Royal Connoisseur (IRE) *Richard Fahey* a75 86
5 b g Art Connoisseur(IRE) Valferno (IRE) (Val Royal (FR))
1869[9] 2238[13] (3289) 3553[8] (4337) 4873[8] 6136[4] (6769) (7590) 7798[7]

Royal Cosmic *Richard Fahey* a57 57
2 b f Wootton Bassett Cosmic Case (Casteddu)
4336[5] 4943[6] 5727[12] 7110[5] 7571[7] 7941[10]

Royal Display *Kevin Ryan* a49 69
3 ch g Showcasing Amouage Royale (IRE) (Mr Greeley (USA))
104[9]

Royal Dolois (FR) *J-M Lefebvre* a88 106
4 gr h Silver Frost(IRE) Mixture (Linamix (FR))
4783a[6] 5500a[5]

Royal Duchess *Lucy Normile* 79
6 b m Dutch Art Royal Citadel (IRE) (City On A Hill (USA))
1663[5] (4193) 4443[7] 6027[8] 6501[7]

Royal Etiquette (IRE) *Lawney Hill* a63 64
9 b g Royal Applause Alpine Gold (IRE) (Montjeu (IRE))
2814[7] 3072[12] 4052[6] 4551[4] 4950[10]

Royale Wave (FR) *Mario Hofer* a44
2 b f Elusive City(USA) Rocky Mixa (FR) (Rock Of Gibraltar (IRE))
7455a[11]

Royal Flag *Brian Ellison* a63 70
6 b g New Approach(IRE) Gonbarda (GER) (Lando (GER))
6323[9] 6957[7] 7106[4] 7627[7] 7847[9] 8586[12]

Royal Flute *Mark Walford* a50
2 b f Piccolo Princess Almora (Pivotal)
8305[5]

Royal Hero *Amanda Perrett* 66
3 b c Royal Applause Heronetta (Halling (USA))
2207[13] 3464[5] 4017[P]

Royal Holiday (IRE) *Marjorie Fife* a78 76
9 ch g Captain Rio Sunny Slope (Mujtahid (USA))
523[3] (1124) 1252[3] 1707[3] 2051[7] 2198[7] 2918[8] 3479[2] 3922[9] 4930[6] 6838[2] 8241[4] 8477[4]

Royal Icon *Kevin Ryan* a63 34
2 b f Sixties Icon Gillstown Great (Royal Applause)
3223[9] 7380[5] ◆ 7659[2] 7891[4]

Royal Irish Hussar (IRE) *Nicky Henderson* 79
6 b g Galileo(IRE) Adjalisa (IRE) (Darshaan)
4353[7]

Royal Julius (IRE) *A De Watrigant* 106
3 b c Royal Applause Hflah (IRE) (Dubawi (IRE))
1580a[5] 2281a[3] 2946a[7] 7723a[8]

Royal Mahogany (IRE) *Luca Cumani* a61 60
3 b c Kodiac Chiba (UAE) (Timber Country (USA))
1800[5] 2248[9] 3042[6] 3998[11]

Royal Marskell *Gay Kelleway* a96 89
7 b g Multiplex Socialise (Groom Dancer (USA))
(52) 337[6] (556) 747[2] 975[2] 1067[7] 2194[8] 3657[6] 4520[3] 8133[3] 8210[11] 8594[6]

Royal Melody *Heather Main* a65 56
2 b f Royal Applause Wannabe Free (Red Ransom (USA))
1988[9] 2376[5] 2990[3] 4350[11] 5257[7] 5770[10] 6236[8] 7366[2] 7543[6] 7974[13]

Royal Mezyan (IRE) *Henry Spiller* a86 81
5 b g Royal Applause Rice Mother (IRE) (Indian Ridge)
2253[5] 2754[9] 4360[11] 5969[6] (7386) (8099) 8403[3]

Royal Mighty *Jane Chapple-Hyam* a47 40
3 b f Mighty Royal Hush (Royal Applause)
2829[8] 4567[6] 5338[9] 5630[8] 6900[12] 8048[7]

Royal Navy Ship (USA) *P V Lafferty* a103 103
4 b h War Front(USA) Indy Punch (USA) (Pulling Punches (USA))
284a[11] 540a[9] 721a[5]

Royal Normandy *Roger Fell* a53 64
4 b g Royal Applause Border Minstral (IRE) (Sri Pekan (USA))
142[2] 236[6] 2217[10] 3101[5] 4089[9] 4970[8] 5386[4] 5717[10] 6569[14] 7141[10] 7435[13] 7797[14] 7994[9] 8188[9]

Royal Occassion *Jim Boyle* 68
4 b h Royal Applause Stagecoach Jade (IRE) (Peintre Celebre (USA))
2414[9] 3535[6] 4458[8] 5362[5]

Royal Opera House (IRE) *Jamie Osborne* a84
2 b c Royal Applause Jackie's Opera (FR) (Indian Ridge)
7891[7] (8277)

Royal Peace (IRE) *Richard Hannon* a65
2 b f Royal Applause Trianon (Nayef (USA))
7763[7]

Royal Pearl *Tom Gretton* a57 52
3 gr f Aussie Rules(USA) Gower Diva (Sakhee (USA))
2123[8] 2666[8]

Royal Peculiar *Michael Appleby*
8 b g Galileo(IRE) Distinctive Look (IRE) (Danehill (USA))
6719[6]

Royal Performer *David Brown* a97 89
3 ch c Medicean Quadri (Polish Precedent (USA))
(1080)

Royal Phoenix *Gary Moore*
3 b f Royal Applause Ashes (IRE) (General Monash (USA))
4639[P] 6674[12] 7011[14]

Royal Prize *Mme M Bollack-Badel* a93 97
6 ch g Nayef(USA) Spot Prize (USA) (Seattle Dancer (USA))
3090a[7] 7030a[9] 7525a[8] 7997a[7]

Royal Reef (IRE) *William Knight* a87 66
4 b g Duke Of Marmalade(IRE) Bintalreef (USA) (Diesis)
2210[7] (2582) 2820[3] (3784) 4795[6] 5767[3] (6591) ◆ (6854)

Royal Regent *Lucy Normile* a33 81
4 b g Urgent Request(IRE) Royal Citadel (IRE) (City On A Hill (USA))
1664[8] 2362[3] ◆ (4190) 4680[5] 5226[9] 8007[14]

Royal Reserve *William Muir* a87 84
3 b g Duke Of Marmalade(IRE) Lady Hawkfield (IRE) (Hawk Wing (USA))
(1750) 1992[16] 2889[4] 4827[7] 5198[6] 6048[4] 6675[5] 7189[10]

Royal Rettie *Paddy Butler* a64 29
4 b m Royal Applause Bended Knee (Refuse To Bend (IRE))
25[3] 249[3] 269[3] ◆ 356[2] 442[3] 7069[8]

Royal Ridge (SAF) *M F De Kock* a93 100
7 ch g Tiger Ridge(USA) Princess Faberge (SAF) (Jallad (USA))
90a[4] 282a[5] 373a[3]

Royal Roman *Kevin Frost* a55 15
4 b m Holy Roman Emperor(IRE) Noble Penny (Pennekamp (USA))
163[4] 423[10] 681[7] 1049[10]

Royal Sentiment (IRE) *Mark Usher* a49
2 b g So You Think(NZ) Rose Parade (Machiavellian (USA))
7733[11] 8025[5] 8355[11]

Royal Shaheen (FR) *Alistair Whillans* 91
3 b c Myboycharlie(IRE) Viola Royale (IRE) (Royal Academy (USA))
2315a[9] 6320[7] 6877[3] 7540[10] 7744[11]

Royal Solitaire (IRE) *P Schiergen* a89 110
4 b m Shamardal(USA) Reverie Solitaire (IRE) (Nashwan (USA))
(1907a) (2633a) 4928a[2] 5691a[7] 6988a[5] 7759a[7]

Royal Sunday (FR) *Alan King* 65
2 gr g Never On Sunday(FR) Royale Malaisie (FR) (Villez (USA))
7770[6]

Royal Toast (IRE) *Richard Hannon* a81 91
4 b g Duke Of Marmalade(IRE) Ripalong (IRE) (Revoque (IRE))
3861[9] 4520[4]

Royal Trooper (IRE) *Mark Brisbourne*
10 b g Hawk Wing(USA) Strawberry Roan (IRE) (Sadler's Wells (USA))
2738[RR]

Royal Warranty *Andrew Balding* a88 88
5 ch m Sir Percy Royal Patron (Royal Academy (USA))
66[7]

Royboy *Ollie Pears* a45
3 b g Equiano(FR) Pretty Bonnie (Kyllachy)
8012[7] 8290[8] 8496[9]

Roy Rocket (FR) *John Berry* a53 79
6 gr g Layman(USA) Minnie's Mystery (FR) (Highest Honor (FR))
1747[4] 2645[3] (3492) (3738) 3972[6] 4785[6] 5963[5] 6892[6] 7429[13]

Roys Dream *Kristin Stubbs* a69 70
2 b f Monsieur Bond(IRE) Velvet Jaguar (Hurricane Run (IRE))
1342[7] 2007[8] 2771[6] 3881[3] 4296[5] (5675) (6033) 6614[3] 7440[4]

Roy's Legacy *Shaun Harris* a71 41
7 b h Phoenix Reach(IRE) Chocolada (Namid)
196^{3} 293^{9} 604^{9} 775^{8} 1481^{3} 1668^{3} 2052^{4} (2523) (2808) (2919) 3307^{6} 3713^{12} 4295^{11} 6879^{14} 7290^{14} 8181^{12} 8409^{5} 8485^{5} 8596^{2}

Rozy Boys *David Barron* a85
2 b g Kyllachy Responsive (Dutch Art)
(8118) 8209^{6}

Ruban (IRE) *Stuart Williams* a85 74
7 ch g Dubawi(IRE) Piece Unique (Barathea (IRE))
2378^{6} 2819^{7} 3358^{8} 6123^{10} 6579^{10} 7066^{9} 7457^{6} 7886^{11}

Rubensian *David Simcock* a86 67
3 ch g Medicean Hymnsheet (Pivotal)
3235^{11} 3904^{5} 5193^{2} ◆ (5607) ◆ (6242) 6417^{3} 7499^{9}

Rubheira *Paul Burgoyne* a15 30
4 ch m Arkadian Hero(USA) Devon Ruby (Zilzal (USA))
2635^{11} 2964^{9} 3811^{8} 4264^{9} 4658^{7} 8430^{10}

Rubiesnpearls *Richard Fahey* a48 65
2 b f Kyllachy Piece Of Cake (Exceed And Excel (AUS))
3112^{4} 4110^{6} 4663^{8} 6026^{8} 7110^{10}

Rubis *Richard Fahey* a63 60
3 ch f Monsieur Bond(IRE) Princess Cocoa (IRE) (Desert Sun)
253^{4} ◆ 335^{3} 678^{6} 1031^{4} 1275^{4} 1667^{5} 2576^{6} 4233^{6} 4730^{2} 6004^{2} 6647^{2} 7692^{5} (7937) 8194^{3} 8586^{6}

Ruby's Day *David Brown* a50 72
7 ch m Vital Equine(IRE) Isabella's Best (IRE) (King's Best (USA))
2050^{4} 2572^{2} ◆ 3056^{6} 3713^{8} 4295^{6} 4495^{4} 4809^{5} 5110^{5} 6476^{8} 6680^{12} 7817^{9} 7961^{8}

Ruby Wednesday *John Best* a71 65
3 b f Mullionmileanhour(IRE) Cheap N Chic (Primo Valentino (IRE))
516^{2} 706^{2} ◆ (978) 1267^{5} 1572^{5} 2341^{5} 3558^{5} 5302^{8} 6246^{6} 6629^{9} 7531^{6} 7870^{4} 8459^{2}

Ruby Woo *Stuart Williams* 63
2 b f Bated Breath Annapurna (IRE) (Brief Truce (USA))
3073^{4} 5395^{7}

Rue Balzac (IRE) *Neil King* a27 58
3 b g Champs Elysees Rondo Alla Turca (IRE) (Noverre (USA))
2368^{4} 3508^{7} 5255^{6} 6659^{9}

Ruggero *Roy Brotherton* a35 101
6 b g Tiger Hill(IRE) Bergamask (USA) (Kingmambo (USA))
1169^{10}

Ruler Of Course (IRE) *Niels Petersen* 56
3 b c Roderic O'Connor(IRE) Scarpe Rosse (IRE) (Sadler's Wells (USA))
$536a^{10}$ $807a^{9}$

Ruler Of France *P Twomey* a76 86
5 b g Holy Roman Emperor(IRE) Syvilla (Nayef (USA))
(4250a) $4811a^{8}$

Ruler Of The Nile *Robert Stephens* a79 27
4 b g Exceed And Excel(AUS) Dinka Raja (USA) (Woodman (USA))
354^{2} (583) ◆ 698^{4} 1296^{5}

Rummani *Charlie Appleby* 81
2 gr c Dubawi(IRE) Claba Di San Jore (IRE) (Barathea (IRE))
5848^{2} 7468^{3}

Rum Swizzle *Harry Dunlop* a65 73
4 b m Mawatheeq(USA) Port Providence (Red Ransom (USA))
2210^{10} 2564^{6} 3064^{8} (4507) 4913^{2} 5624^{2} 6315^{13}

Runaiocht (IRE) *Paul Burgoyne* a65 58
6 ch g Teofilo(IRE) Julie Girl (USA) (Jules (USA))
222^{2} 316^{2} 491^{3} 724^{5} 898^{5} 1340^{8} (1834) 2769^{9} 3030^{4} 3522^{2} 4009^{11} 8462^{7}

Runaway (GER) *Frau M Muller* 91
9 b g Slickly(FR) Rain Lily (IRE) (Red Ransom (USA))
$664a^{7}$ $2318a^{5}$

Run For The Roses (IRE) *Augustine Leahy* a3
2 b f Elusive Pimpernel(USA) Gra Geal Mo Chroi (IRE) (Imperial Ballet (IRE))
$7917a^{12}$

Runhappy (USA) *Laura Wohlers* a124
4 b h Super Saver(USA) Bella Jolie (USA) (Broken Vow (USA))
$7808a^{8}$

Runmhar (IRE) *J S Bolger* a62 78
3 b f Discreetly Mine(USA) Excuse Me (USA) (Distorted Humor (USA))
$5620a^{10}$

Running Wolf (IRE) *Alex Hales* a53 71
5 b g Amadeus Wolf Monet's Lady (IRE) (Daylami (IRE))
261^{8}

Run Rio Run (IRE) *Michael Dods* a67 70
3 ch g Captain Rio Anklesocks (IRE) (Night Shift (USA))
1494^{2} 2049^{16} 3422^{7} 4310^{3} 4771^{5} (5370) 6341^{10} 6680^{2} 6958^{8} 7386^{8}

Run To The Hills (USA) *George Peckham* a88 88
3 b g Quality Road(USA) Masada (USA) (Pleasant Tap (USA))
2578^{3} 3609^{3} 4477^{2} (5859) 7095^{10} 7902^{4} ◆

Run With Pride (IRE) *Derek Shaw* a91 86
6 b g Invincible Spirit(IRE) Zibilene (Rainbow Quest (USA))
82^{7} 2577^{5} 3035^{9} 3303^{11} 5736^{6}

Rupert Boy (IRE) *Scott Dixon* a47 34
3 ch g Frozen Power(IRE) Curious Lashes (IRE) (Footstepsinthesand)
104^{5} 248^{2} 365^{4} (509) 1031^{6} 1486^{7} 3357^{11} 5386^{10} 5808^{10} 7261^{10} 7463^{9} 8470^{9}

Rupertcambellblack (IRE) *Ronald Harris*
2 b g Canford Cliffs(IRE) Negotiate (Red Ransom (USA))
5828^{4}

Rural Celebration *David O'Meara* a91 81
5 b m Pastoral Pursuits Queens Jubilee (Cayman Kai (IRE))
1408^{10} 1848^{15} 2621^{3} 3116^{4} 3575^{4} 4034^{4} 6013^{3} 6537^{7} 6793^{4} 7364^{3} (7437) (7660) 7892^{7}

Ruscombe *Sir Michael Stoute* a95 95
3 b f Dansili Eva Luna (USA) (Alleged (USA))
2735^{3} ◆ (3601) 4351^{3} 7498^{3} 7652^{4}

Russian Bolero (GER) *David Dennis* a72 47
5 ch g Tertullian(USA) Russian Samba (IRE) (Laroche (GER))
78^{7} 259^{2} 342^{5} 6193^{5}

Russian Finale *William Haggas* a76 72
3 b f Dansili Russian Rhythm (USA) (Kingmambo (USA))
4690^{3} ◆ 5438^{5} (6251) ◆ 6742^{4}

Russian Radiance *Jonathan Portman* a89 71
4 ch m Paco Boy(IRE) Russian Ruby (FR) (Vettori (IRE))
351^{2} 780^{5} 1003^{4} 6299^{5} 7506^{14} 7781^{3} ◆ 8028^{2} 8158^{9}

Russian Ranger (IRE) *Jonathan Portman* a66 64
3 b g Bushranger(IRE) Pink Sovietstaia (FR) (Soviet Star (USA))
874^{4} 1184^{4} 1386^{7} 1917^{4} 2293^{3} 4269^{15} 4764^{10} 6826^{4} 7516^{6} (7944)

Russian Rascal *Clive Drew* 39
3 b g Kyllachy Russian Ruby (FR) (Vettori (IRE))
1826^{11} 2851^{10} 3765^{8} 4210^{10} 7230^{10}

Russian Realm *Paul Midgley* a87 102
6 b g Dansili Russian Rhythm (USA) (Kingmambo (USA))
86^{3} ◆ 290^{8} 486^{7} 656^{4} 871^{6} (1856) 2391^{8} 5825^{8} 6140^{3} 6792^{10} 7095^{8}

Russian Regard (IRE) *Jonathan Portman* a61 54
2 ch g Intense Focus(USA) Russian Rave (Danehill Dancer (IRE))
7503^{10} 7865^{11} 8074^{6}

Russian Remarque *Jonathan Portman* a70 72
5 b g Archipenko(USA) Accede (Acclamation)
1391^{11} 2210^{9}

Russian Reward (IRE) *Amanda Perrett* a80 84
4 b g Iffraaj Forever Times (So Factual (USA))
670^{5} 901^{5} 1041^{8} 7506^{16} 7738^{2} (7886) 8052^{9} 8356^{9}

Russian Royale *Micky Hammond* a73 79
6 b m Royal Applause Russian Ruby (FR) (Vettori (IRE))
1248^{3} (1561) 2663^{3} 3117^{8} 4409^{6} 4969^{4} 5350^{9} 6083^{11}

Russian Soul (IRE) *M Halford* a109 96
8 b g Invincible Spirit(IRE) Russian Hill (Indian Ridge)
745^{10} 1066^{6} $4246a^{5}$ $6355a^{11}$ $7523a^{6}$ $7803a^{3}$ $8197a^{2}$

Rustique *Ed Walker* a66 68
4 ch m Pastoral Pursuits Nihal (IRE) (Singspiel (IRE))
2151^{5} 2607^{2} (3044) ◆ 3367^{6} 4200^{3} (5085) 5750^{3} 6485^{7}

Rusty Rocket (IRE) *Paul Green* a86 88
7 ch h Majestic Missile(IRE) Sweet Compliance (Safawan)
894^{2} 1084^{8} 1672^{5} (2305) 2426^{6} 2775^{6} 3638^{6} 4032^{4} 4514^{6} 5274^{11} 6080^{13} 7593^{15}

Rusumaat (IRE) *Mark Johnston* a43 94
2 b c Arcano(IRE) Queen Wasp (IRE) (Shamardal (USA))
1233^{5} 1850^{2} (2301) 3243^{13} (3772) 4825^{2} 5583^{2} 6260^{13}

Rutherford (IRE) *Kevin Ryan* 73
2 ch f Dutch Art Carraigoona (IRE) (Rock Of Gibraltar (IRE))
5272^{13} 6472^{4} 7055^{2}

Ruth Melody (IRE) *Lee Smyth* a64 11
4 b m Intikhab(USA) Mermaid Melody (Machiavellian (USA))
$7393a^{15}$

Rutterkin (USA) *John David Riches* a47 43
8 gr g Maria's Mon(USA) Chilukki Cat (USA) (Storm Cat (USA))
217^{3} 528^{6} 787^{8} 1165^{8} 1320^{6}

Ruwaiyan (USA) *James Tate* a97 99
7 bb g Cape Cross(IRE) Maskunah (IRE) (Sadler's Wells (USA))
2434^{6} 3656^{7} 4395^{8}

Ruwasi *James Tate* a57 97
5 b g Authorized(IRE) Circle Of Love (Sakhee (USA))
2979^{2} 3621^{2} (4044) ◆ (4598) 5145^{7} 6057^{8} 7538^{7}

Ruzeiz (USA) *Peter Hedger* a66 74
7 b g Muhtathir Saraama (USA) (Bahri (USA))
156^{2} 382^{7} 724^{7} 1747^{7} 7508^{10} 7628^{14} 8359^{11}

Ryans Charm (USA) *Patrick Gallagher* 105
6 b m Heatseeker(IRE) Lemon Fresh Tide (USA) (Lemon Drop Kid (USA))
$7831a^{6}$

Ryan Style (IRE) *Lisa Williamson* a58 48
10 b g Desert Style(IRE) Westlife (IRE) (Mind Games)
4472^{4} 4980^{5} 5060^{6} 5826^{5} 6660^{7} 6902^{4} 7200^{6} 7489^{2} 7694^{5} 8013^{8} 8079^{4} 8383^{11}

Ryan The Giant *Keith Dalgleish* a54 55
3 b g Fastnet Rock(AUS) Comeraincomeshine (IRE) (Night Shift (USA))
328^{5} 509^{5} 3020^{8} 3287^{13} 3921^{9} 4210^{3} 5079^{2} 5319^{2} 5783^{2} 6029^{7} 6094^{2} 7262^{7} 7746^{10} 8309^{3} 8488^{3} 8540^{5}

Rydan (IRE) *Gary Moore* a101 89
5 ch g Intense Focus(USA) Lough Mewin (IRE) (Woodman (USA))
2549^{8} 2966^{3} 4888^{3} 5650^{3} (6065) 6775^{5} 8424^{3} 8594^{5}

Ryedale Rio (IRE) *Tim Easterby* a67 63
3 b g Captain Rio Hallucination (IRE) (Last Tycoon)
1216^{5} 2333^{3} 2668^{5} 3293^{6} 3882^{2} ◆ 4096^{8} 4512^{10}

Rymska (FR) *Chad C Brown* 107
2 bl f Le Havre(IRE) Foreign Raider (IRE) (Lend A Hand)
$7809a^{5}$

Saafarr *J S Bolger* 104
3 b c Teofilo(IRE) Hall Hee (IRE) (Invincible Spirit (IRE))
$2069a^{5}$

Saane (FR) *G Taupin* a77 98
5 b g Le Havre(IRE) Salamon (Montjeu (IRE))
$4903a^{6}$ (5501a) $7088a^{6}$ $8336a^{9}$

Saayerr *D Selvaratnam* a65 100
5 b g Acclamation Adorn (Kyllachy)
$280a^{2}$ $450a^{12}$ $719a^{7}$

Sabaani *James Tate* a76
3 b c Aqlaam Sabaweeya (Street Cry (IRE))
458^{2} (618) 1080^{8}

Sabador (FR) *Ed Walker* a60
2 gr g Kendargent(FR) Sabadora (FR) (Anabaa (USA))
7431^{4}

Sabato (IRE) *Fergal O'Brien* a46 59
3 ch g Shamardal(USA) Mondalay (Monsun (GER))
1829^{4} 2143^{4} 3994^{16} 4321^{10} 4718^{8} 5958^{13}

Sabawa (FR) *R Rohne* a59 63
2 bb f Air Chief Marshal(IRE) Star Of Pompey (Hernando (FR))
$5142a^{5}$

Sabegg (USA) *A bin Harmash* a17
2 ch c Girolamo(USA) Lady Dora (USA) (Lord At War (ARG))
$8391a^{6}$

Sabha (IRE) *K R Burke* a42 46
4 b m Thewayyouare(USA) Genipabu (IRE) (Danetime (IRE))
8386^{11}

Sable Island (IRE) *Sir Michael Stoute* a70 54
2 b c New Approach(IRE) Ratukidul (FR) (Danehill (USA))
6881^{6} 7908^{6}

Saborido (USA) *Amanda Perrett* a85 83
10 gr g Dixie Union(USA) Alexine (ARG) (Runaway Groom (CAN))
1417^{7} 1914^{7} (2995) 3784^{9} 4941^{2} 5553^{2} 5767^{2} 8558^{6}

Sabre Rock *Julia Feilden* a81 46
6 b g Dubawi(IRE) Retainage (USA) (Polish Numbers (USA))
1775^{15} 2163^{18} 3659^{4} 5724^{8}

Sabre Squadron (IRE) *Peter Chapple-Hyam* 82
3 b g Lope De Vega(IRE) Caravan Of Dreams (IRE) (Anabaa (USA))
2048^{5} (2541) ◆ 7412^{9}

Sabrewing (IRE) *Robert Cowell* 79
3 b f Fast Company(IRE) Tawaafur (Fantastic Light (USA))
(2681) 4651^{6}

Sabrina Brazzo *Michael Dods* 36
3 br f Showcasing Sabrina Brown (Polar Falcon (USA))
1691^{7} 2304^{7}

Sacrament (IRE) *David Evans* a59 69
3 b f Acclamation Alstemeria (IRE) (Danehill (USA))
253^{10}

Sacred Act *John Gosden* a94 103
5 b g Oasis Dream Stage Presence (IRE) (Selkirk (USA))
(6298) ◆

Sacred Harp *Stuart Williams* a61 63
3 b f Oasis Dream Zabeel Park (USA) (Medicean)
2503^{2} 3000^{8} 3360^{3} 4521^{4} 5041^{7} 5475^{3} 5721^{3} 6249^{10} 6660^{3} 7200^{5}

Sacred Master (NZ) *Chris Waller* 106
4 b g Mastercraftsman(IRE) Trickle (NZ) (Storm Creek (USA))
$7378a^{15}$

Sacred Square (GER) *Conor Dore* a67 80
6 ch g Peintre Celebre(USA) Square The Circle (Second Empire (IRE))
218^{5} 438^{4} 708^{7} 862^{13}

Sacred Trust *Hugo Palmer* a83 79
3 b g Acclamation Paracel (USA) (Gone West (USA))
1653^{3} 2538^{5} 3156^{8} 5677^{2} 6703^{7}

Sacrifice My Soul (IRE) *Mme Pia Brandt* 97
4 b m Nayef(USA) Via Saleria (IRE) (Arazi (USA))
$6273a^{5}$ $7088a^{2}$ $7396a^{4}$

Sadalmelik (ITY) *R Biondi* 94
3 gr f Aussie Rules(USA) Lanka (Medicean)
$7719a^{3}$

Sadeek's Song (USA) *M Al Subouse* a3 37
8 ch h Kingmambo(USA) New Morning (IRE) (Sadler's Wells (USA))
$229a^{8}$

Sadhbh (IRE) *Richard Hannon* a68
2 b f Lilbourne Lad(IRE) Stoney Cove (IRE) (Needwood Blade)
7939^{6} (8082) 8244^{8}

Sadie Babes (IRE) *Richard Fahey* a65 66
3 b f Iffraaj Daffodil Walk (IRE) (Captain Rio)
659^{2} (961) 1249^{3} 1670^{5}

Sadieroseclifford (IRE) *Denis Quinn* a57 48
2 b f Poet's Voice Voltairine (Selkirk (USA))
3947^{6} 4564^{7} 4943^{9} 5631^{5} 5876^{7} 6412^{4} 6670^{8} 6895^{7} 7040^{7} 7275^{8} 7528^{9}

Saeedan (IRE) *Marco Botti* a78 35
3 b c Tagula(IRE) Sharadja (IRE) (Doyoun)
885^{2} (1414) 2239^{13} 2818^{11}

Saengil Gippeum (USA) *Kim Gil Jung* a42
3 b c Parading(USA) Minny's Niece (USA) (Quiet American (USA))
$0399a^{0}$

Safepac Lad *Des Donovan* a8
2 b g Dick Turpin(IRE) Sciantusa (Barathea (IRE))
$7917a^{13}$

Safety Check (IRE) *Charlie Appleby* a100 119
5 ch h Dubawi(IRE) Doors To Manual (USA) (Royal Academy (USA))
(282a) (720a) $1912a^{5}$

Safe Voyage (IRE) *John Quinn* a66 77
3 b g Fast Company(IRE) Shishangaan (IRE) (Mujadil (USA))
3609^{5} 4041^{7} (4848) 6502^{U} 6810^{5}

Safira Menina *Martin Smith* a78 74
4 b m Paco Boy(IRE) Isla Azul (IRE) (Machiavellian (USA))
1947^{3} 2233^{14} 2313^{4} (2738) ◆ 3139^{4} 4023^{2} 4462^{2} 5176^{5} 6457^{5} 6892^{7} (7732) 7895^{2} 8162^{6} 8253^{5} 8476^{6}

Safwah (IRE) *John Quinn* 31
2 b f Dark Angel(IRE) Lisa's Strong (IRE) (Kalanisi (IRE))
7356^{6}

Saga Bolton (IRE) *Anthony Mullins* a81 66
4 b g Intense Focus(USA) Emlach Star (IRE) (Cape Cross (IRE))
(208a)

Sagaciously (IRE) *Ed Dunlop* a95 107
4 b m Lawman(FR) Saga Celebre (FR) (Peintre Celebre (USA))
1336^{2} 1855^{5} (2236) 2797^{5} 3662^{5} (4757) 5307^{2} $6107a^{9}$ 6948^{9}

Sagaroi (FR) *D Guillemin* 98
3 gr c King's Best(USA) Saga D'Ouilly (FR) (Linamix (FR))
$6176a^{4}$ $7456a^{11}$ $7897a^{5}$

Saga Sprint (IRE) *J R Jenkins* a74 73
3 b f Excellent Art Queen Of Malta (IRE) (Exceed And Excel (AUS))
3341^{15} 3904^{4} 5245^{2} 6370^{5} 7214^{12}

Sagely (IRE) *Ed Dunlop* a79 100
3 b f Frozen Power(IRE) Saga Celebre (FR) (Peintre Celebre (USA))
(925) (2269) ◆ 2490^{2} 3608^{11} 4757^{2} 5587^{5} $6069a^{7}$

Sahaafy (USA) *M Al Mheiri* a105 106
4 br h Kitten's Joy(USA) Queen's Causeway (USA) (Giant's Causeway (USA))
$628a^{8}$

Sahalin *Marco Botti* a66
3 b f Red Rocks(IRE) Tamathea (IRE) (Barathea (IRE))
243^{6} 565^{2}

Sahara (IRE) *Chris Wall* a76 82
4 b m Clodovil(IRE) Celtic Lynn (IRE) (Celtic Swing)
1624^{6} 2978^{4} 3721^{5} 4568^{2} 5489^{2} 6504^{4} 7077^{8}

Sahreej (IRE) *Adrian Paul Keatley* a92 82
3 gr g Zebedee Petite Boulangere (IRE) (Namid)
2251^{11} 3393^{7} 3857^{3} $6819a^{16}$ $7520a^{14}$ $8197a^{11}$

Saigon City *Declan Carroll* a96 98
6 b g Mount Nelson Hoh Chi Min (Efisio)
1642^{8} (2194) 3658^{5} 5144^{3} ◆

Sai Kung Star *Nigel Tinkler* 33
2 ch f Harbour Watch(IRE) Warden Rose (Compton Place)
3597^{8} 4298^{14}

Sailana (GER) *Christina Bucher* 80
2 ch f Call Me Big(GER) Still Standing (FR) (Martillo (GER))
$7757a^{8}$

Sailor Malan *Gay Kelleway* a62 57
4 b g Mount Nelson Flying Hi (Kyllachy)
2634^{13} 3041^{6}

Sailors Warn (IRE) *Daniel Mark Loughnane* a43 64
9 b g Redback Coral Dawn (IRE) (Trempolino (USA))
8477^{12}

Sail With Sultana *Mark Rimell* a56 55
5 ch m Black Sam Bellamy(IRE) Strathtay (Pivotal)
71^{4} 695^{13} 946^{11}

Saimaa (IRE) *H-F Devin* 99
3 b f Zoffany(IRE) Serisia (FR) (Exit To Nowhere (USA))
$2928a^{6}$ $7397a^{5}$ $7861a^{3}$

Saint Bernard *Simone Langiano* a64 98
7 b h Three Valleys(USA) Savignano (Polish Precedent (USA))
$2073a^{3}$ $2729a^{7}$ $7565a^{8}$

Saint Contest (FR) *Alan King* a80
3 b c Air Chief Marshal(IRE) Sainte Adresse (Elusive City (USA))
7512^{4}

Saint Cuthberts *David Brown* 7
2 b c Shirocco(GER) Gladys' Gal (Tobougg (IRE))
6262^{8} 7329^{10}

Sainte Amarante (FR) *Yves de Nicolay* a98 96
4 ch m Le Havre(IRE) Loyal Lass (USA) (Cadeaux Genereux)
$1822a^{9}$ $3377a^{2}$ $5384a^{6}$ $7524a^{2}$ $8165a^{6}$ $8563a^{16}$

Sainted *William Haggas* 90
3 ch f Dutch Art Blithe (Pivotal)
3138^{2} (3614) ◆

Sainte Helene (IRE) *C Lerner* a40 48
3 b f Lawman(FR) Atullia (GER) (Tertullian (USA))
$1357a^{11}$

Saint Equiano *Keith Dalgleish* 83
2 b c Equiano(FR) St Athan (Authorized (IRE))
3516^{10} 6534^{2} ◆ (7090) ◆

Saint Helena (IRE) *Mark Gillard* a65 75
8 b m Holy Roman Emperor(IRE) Tafseer (IRE) (Grand Lodge (USA))
348^{11} (1735) 2367^{5} 2635^{2} (2849) ◆ 4288^{7} 5627^{6} 7272^{7} 8144^{4}

Saint Honore *Pat Phelan* a76 72
4 b m Champs Elysees Gwyneth (Zafonic (USA))
(101) 488^{2} 693^{4} 1390^{8} 2623^{8} 3560^{2} 4049^{7} 8446^{4}

Saint Joseph (FR) *E Lellouche* a74 75
3 b c Kheleyf(USA) Bon Escient (Montjeu (IRE))
$7492a^{4}$

Saint Pois (FR) *Tony Carroll* a77 77
5 b g Le Havre(IRE) Our Dream Queen (Oasis Dream)
159^{2} 416^{6} 439^{5} 782^{9} 1632^{9} 1916^{3} 2347^{15} 3514^{8} 4200^{2} 5076^{5}

Saint Thomas (IRE) *John Mackie* a56 73
9 b g Alhaarth(IRE) Aguilas Perla (IRE) (Indian Ridge)
1057^{12} 1347^{5} 1796^{5} 2738^{5} 3012^{4} 3480^{2} (3842) (4320) 4686^{3} 5294^{5} 5795^{4} 7045^{3} 7361^{6}

Sajah (IRE) *Harry Dunlop* a8
2 ch f Approve(IRE) Forget Me Not (IRE) (Danehill Dancer (IRE))
7733^{14}

Sakhalin Star (IRE) *Richard Guest* a73 71
5 ch g Footstepsinthesand Quela (GER) (Acatenango (GER))
823^{3} 1241^{3} 1596^{5} 2091^{7} 2526^{4} 2555^{8} 3220^{2} 3497^{3} 3599^{2} 4234^{8} 4702^{2} 6231^{9} 6620^{3} 6737^{5} 7007^{5} 7500^{8} 7775^{5} 8142^{8} 8400^{4} 8528^{4} 8566^{7}

Sakhastic *John Mackie* a41 23
3 b g Sakhee's Secret Rutland Water (IRE) (Hawk Wing (USA))
1162^{9} 1670^{10} 3080^{14} 3970^{9} 4316^{9} 6967^{8}

Sakhee's Jem *Gay Kelleway* a68 70
3 ch f Sakhee's Secret Amandian (IRE) (Indian Ridge)
(5748) 6487^{4} 7364^{7} 7725^{7} 8064^{3}

Sakhee's Return *Tim Easterby* a80 93
4 b g Sakhee's Secret Sofia Royale (Royal Applause)
3848^{5} 4627^{3} 4893^{6} 5389^{9} 6263^{3}

Sakhee's Rose *Ed McMahon* a67 54
6 b m Sakhee's Secret Isobel Rose (IRE) (Royal Applause)
68^{10} 239^{9} 543^{3} 2794^{9} 3527^{7} 3984^{8} 5605^{5} 5706^{3} 6100^{8} 6853^{10} 8120^{2}

Sakhra *Mark Brisbourne* a50 45
5 b g Nayef(USA) Noble Desert (FR) (Green Desert (USA))
2110^{8} 3221^{8} 3999^{11} 4320^{6} 4739^{5} 5100^{4} 5805^{5} 6406^{6} 7367^{3} 8039^{4} 8211^{4}

Sakurajima (IRE) *Charles Hills* 72
2 ch c Helmet(AUS) Park Approach (IRE) (Indian Ridge)
2976^{2} 4837^{5} 5890^{9} 7286^{9}

Salamah (IRE) *Simon Crisford* a75 64
2 b f Shamardal(USA) Spirit Of Dubai (IRE) (Cape Cross (IRE))
(6244) 6787^{11}

Salar Glorious *A Marcialis* a61 64
7 b h Singspiel(IRE) Salar Violet (IRE) (Orpen (USA))
$7295a^{11}$

Salateen *David O'Meara* 111
4 ch h Dutch Art Amanda Carter (Tobougg (IRE))
2030^{6} 2485^{6} 3386^{27} 5389^{5} (6338) (6788)

Saleh (IRE) *Lee Carter* a72 57
3 b g Iffraaj Pellinore (USA) (Giant's Causeway (USA))
4939^{6} 5544^{7} 7218^{5} 7736^{4} (8163) 8555^{2}

Salford Dream *Pauline Robson* a56 44
7 ch g Halling(USA) Spitting Image (IRE) (Spectrum (IRE))
2916^{4} (4645)

Salient *Michael Attwater* a62 60
12 b g Fasliyev(USA) Savannah Belle (Green Desert (USA))
101^{7} 1239^{2} 1854^{14} 2397^{7} (5021) 5672^{5} 6411^{10} 7039^{9} 7464^{12} 7905^{U}

Salieri (FR) *Alan King* a68
2 b g Paco Boy(IRE) Ticklestone (IRE) (Mark Of Esteem (IRE))
3986^{3} 4524^{2} 7865^{10}

Salieris Mass *Mark Johnston* 100
4 b g Mount Nelson Sunley Gift (Cadeaux Genereux)
2017^{3} (3324) ◆

Salla *Ismail Mohammed* 76
2 b f Foxwedge(AUS) Sahara Sunshine (Hernando (FR))
3073^{2}

Sallee *Adrian Wintle* a42 29
2 b f Sakhee's Secret Rabshih (IRE) (Green Desert (USA))
7012^{11} 7548^{10} 7906^{10}

Salmon Sushi *Tim Easterby* a92 88
5 ch g Dalakhani(IRE) Salsa Steps (USA) (Giant's Causeway (USA))
1122^{6} 1445^{3} 2017^{2} 2487^{12} 3950^{2} 4300^{3} 4945^{3} (5526) 5837^{6} 6775^{6} 7365^{6} 8007^{9} 8283^{9}

Saloon Sold (GER) *Markus Klug* 94
2 b f Soldier Hollow Saloon Rum (GER) (Spectrum (IRE))
$6797a^{3}$ $7563a^{9}$

Salouen (IRE) *Sylvester Kirk* 111
2 b c Canford Cliffs(IRE) Gali Gal (IRE) (Galileo (IRE))
3196^{2} 3813^{3} 4349^{9} 4736^{4} (5203) 5646^{2} (6059) $6987a^{2}$ 7539^{3}

Salsabeel (IRE) *Charlie Appleby* 104
2 b c Exceed And Excel(AUS) Tokyo Rose (UAE) (Jade Robbery (USA))
(5332) ◆ 6285^{2} ◆

Saltarello (IRE) *Marjorie Fife* a57 46
4 b g Fast Company(IRE) Step Dancing (Distant Music (USA))
1116^{8} 1495^{3} 3016^{4} 3367^{5} 4006^{5} 4144^{5} 4771^{9} 4932^{5} 5355^{12} 5729^{8} 5887^{9} 6569^{10} 7369^{9}

Saltonstall *M Halford* 95
2 ch c Pivotal Macleya (GER) (Winged Love (IRE))
$7707a^{6}$

Salt Whistle Bay (IRE) *Rae Guest* 52
2 b c Royal Applause Quantum (IRE) (Alhaarth (IRE))
7664^{7}

Salut Fripouille (FR) *S Jesus* 49
2 bb g Zizany(IRE) Salut Lisa (FR) (Sagacity (FR))
$4183a^{7}$

Saluti (IRE) *Amanda Perrett* a80
2 b c Acclamation Greek Easter (IRE) (Namid)
7867^{3} 8066^{2} 8243^{2}

Salvado (IRE) *Tony Carroll* a53 48
6 b g Invincible Spirit(IRE) Easter Fairy (USA) (Fusaichi Pegasus (USA))
174^{5} 270^{5} 669^{4} 1164^{6} 3469^{8} 3729^{5} 3970^{8}

Salvatore Fury (IRE) *Keith Dalgleish* a89 77
6 b g Strategic Prince Nocturnal (FR) (Night Shift (USA))
1663^{6} 2028^{11} 2202^{3} 2812^{6} 3021^{6} 4100^{7} 5060^{2} ◆ 5295^{4} (5354) (5582) 6475^{7} 7054^{8} 7965^{2} 8314^{8}

Salve Estelle (GER) *Waldemar Hickst* 98
4 b m Dansili Salve Regina (GER) (Monsun (GER))
$1907a^{10}$ $4696a^{10}$

Salve Sicilia (FR) *Waldemar Hickst* 85
3 b f Soldier Hollow Salve Aurora (GER) (King's Best (USA))
$7862a^{8}$

Salve Venezia (GER) *Andreas Lowe* 86
4 b m Areion(GER) Salve Aurora (GER) (King's Best (USA))
$7929a^{7}$

Salvo *Charlie Fellowes* 81
3 b f Acclamation Passe Passe (USA) (Lear Fan (USA))
2179^{5} 2795^{11} 4028^{5} 5089^{7} 5487^{4}

Samara Belle *Christine Dunnett*
3 gr f Black Sam Bellamy(IRE) Scrupulous (Dansili)
7487^{8}

Samarie *Mme Pia Brandt* a33 70
3 bb f Acclamation Saturnine (IRE) (Galileo (IRE))
$2172a^{5}$

Samba Pa Ti (IRE) *J-C Rouget* 79
2 b f Hat Trick(JPN) Amourette (FR) (Halling (USA))
$4924a^{6}$ $5698a^{3}$

Same Jurisdiction (SAF) *Ed Dunlop* 102
4 b m Mambo In Seattle(USA) Diana De Carlo (SAF) (Captain Al (SAF))
6281^{4} $6991a^{9}$

Samharry *John Gosden* 81
2 b c Exceed And Excel(AUS) Ballymore Celebre (IRE) (Peintre Celebre (USA))
(4545)

Sam Missile (IRE) *James Fanshawe* a98 90
3 b g Smart Strike(CAN) Kitty Matcham (IRE) (Rock Of Gibraltar (IRE))
(65) 1891^{5} 3102^{4} 4044^{2} 6065^{4} (6417) ◆ 6675^{2} 7869^{4}

Sammy's Choice *Paul Burgoyne* a53
4 ch g Pastoral Pursuits Diane's Choice (Komaite (USA))
341^{10}

Samphire Coast *Derek Shaw* a59 38
3 b g Fastnet Rock(AUS) Faslen (USA) (Fasliyev (USA))
7061^{5} 7894^{5} 8481^{6}

Samran Says (IRE) *P Monfort* a58 53
2 b f Dark Angel(IRE) Chachalacas (IRE) (Hawk Wing (USA))
2612^{8} 3148^{5} 3707^{3} 4843^{3} $5905a^{6}$ $7455a^{3}$

Samson *Hughie Morrison* a36
5 ch g Black Sam Bellamy(IRE) Riverine (Risk Me (FR))
342^{9}

Samsonite (IRE) *Tony Coyle* a44 79
4 ch g Pivotal Silca's Sister (Inchinor)
523^{7} 823^{8} 1058^{8} 1785^{5} (2015) 2672^{8} 3327^{10} 3849^{4} 4424^{5} 4724^{10}

Sams R Man *Linda Jewell* 20
4 b g Mullionmileanhour(IRE) Santiburi Girl (Casteddu)
4939^{14} 5238^{5} 6036^{8} 7063^{7}

Sam The Rebel *Mike Hammond* 32
2 b g Cockney Rebel(IRE) Casablanca Minx (IRE) (Desert Story (IRE))
5952^{6} 6314^{8} 7259^{11}

Samtu (IRE) *Marjorie Fife* a63 86
5 b g Teofilo(IRE) Samdaniya (Machiavellian (USA))
5406^{2}

Samuna (FR) *C Ferland* 91
2 ch f Samum(GER) Ordargent (FR) (Kendargent (FR))
(5986a) $7263a^{2}$

Sanaadh *Richard Fahey* 78
3 ch c Exceed And Excel(AUS) Queen's Logic (IRE) (Grand Lodge (USA))
(1669) ◆

San Cassiano (IRE) *Ruth Carr* a49 74
9 b g Bertolini(USA) Celtic Silhouette (FR) (Celtic Swing)
1201^{12} 1560^{8} 2093^{2} 2362^{4} 2656^{4} 3325^{5} 3774^{5} (4234) 4730^{4} 5293^{5} (5883) 6221^{11} 6684^{14}

Sandacres *Laura Mongan* a69 60
3 b g Frozen Power(IRE) Lady Golan (IRE) (Golan (IRE))
402^{3} 544^{2} 2185^{7} 4789^{7} 5605^{6} 5769^{6}

Sandara (FR) *H-F Devin* a69 65
2 b f Siyouni(FR) Sandy Winner (FR) (Priolo (USA))
$8420a^{5}$

Sandbetweenourtoes (IRE) *Jassim Al Ghazali* a76 95
7 b g Footstepsinthesand Callanish (Inchinor)
$755a^{4}$

Sand By Me *Peter Crate* a44 27
3 b g Piccolo Marysienka (Primo Dominie)
562^{4} 659^{5} 883^{4} 1574^{6}

Sandfrankskipsgo *Peter Crate* a93 91
7 ch g Piccolo Alhufoof (USA) (Dayjur (USA))
220^{6} (655) 835^{4} 2003^{3} 2895^{16} 4066^{9} (5360) 5961^{8} 6114^{4} 8232^{10} 8463^{7}

Sandra's Secret (IRE) *Les Eyre* a59 84
3 gr f Zebedee Good For Her (Rock Of Gibraltar (IRE))
2742^{4} 3713^{5} 4256^{2} ◆ 4612^{3} (5032) ◆ 5643^{3} (5864) 6234^{9} 6926^{12}

Sandro Botticelli (IRE) *John Ryan* a107 110
4 b g Galileo(IRE) Ask For The Moon (FR) (Dr Fong (USA))
(1219) ◆ 1475^{2} 1772^{6} 3387^{5} (3913) 4799^{11} 7349^{9} $7946a^{10}$

Sands Chorus *James Given* a83 83
4 b g Footstepsinthesand Wood Chorus (Singspiel (IRE))
595^{2} 823^{4} (1241) 1526^{2} 1924^{5} 2257^{3} 2620^{3} 2917^{4} 3324^{2} 3717^{6} 5333^{4} 6048^{7} 7007^{2} 7227^{2} 7623^{9} 7911^{6} 8101^{2} (8343)

Sandstream *Tracy Waggott* a25 31
3 ch g Paco Boy(IRE) Descriptive (IRE) (Desert King (IRE))
7583^{6} 7960^{4} 8402^{7}

Sandwood Bay *Mark H Tompkins* a51 68
2 b f Footstepsinthesand Diverting (Nayef (USA))
3073^{6} 5469^{8} 5747^{4} 6713^{6} 7286^{12}

Sandy Cove *James Eustace* a75 74
5 br g Oasis Dream Maganda (IRE) (Sadler's Wells (USA))
606^{2} 766^{5} (949) 1810^{4} (2605) 3121^{2} (4023) 5035^{2} 5724^{9} 6457^{6}

Sandy Shores *Brian Meehan* a52
2 b f Sixties Icon Salim Toto (Mtoto)
8361^{8}

Sangria (SPA) *F Chappet* 105
3 b g American Post Noozhah (Singspiel (IRE))
$1374a^{4}$ $2232a^{2}$

Sanjita (IRE) *C Laffon-Parias* 83
2 ch f Zamindar(USA) Barbayam (Stormy River (FR))
$8062a^{7}$

San Quentin (IRE) *Roger Fell* a78 79
5 gr g Lawman(FR) In The Soup (USA) (Alphabet Soup (USA))
(62) (170) ◆ 357^{3} 545^{5} 1144^{3} 1391^{5} 1854^{10} (2575) 2813^{2} 3751^{6} 3983^{6} 4892^{4} (5293) 5392^{4} 6684^{2} 7139^{7} $7517a^{7}$ 7993^{12} 8282^{2}

San Salvador (GER) *Andreas Lowe* 96
3 ch g Lord Of England(GER) Saratina (IRE) (Monsun (GER))
$2711a^{4}$ $3453a^{6}$ $7456a^{3}$

San Sebastiana *K R Burke* 85
2 b f Power Spanish Quest (Rainbow Quest (USA))
(4298) 5172^{9}

Sans Equivoque (GER) *D Guillemin* 108
2 gr f Stormy River(FR) Suissesse (USA) (Malibu Moon (USA))
$3182a^{2}$ $3937a^{3}$ (5497a) (6694a) (7347a)

Sanshaawes (SAF) *M F De Kock* a113 110
6 b g Ashaawes(USA) Vicario (SAF) (Northern Guest (USA))
$93a^{3}$ (283a) $455a^{4}$ $625a^{4}$ $843a^{5}$

Sans Souci Bay *Richard Hannon* a78 70
2 b c Medicean Cumana Bay (Dansili)
2371^{7} 3106^{6} 4203^{3} (7688) 7898^{2} 8360^{5} 8592^{4}

Santadelacruze *Mark Hoad* a55 53
7 b g Pastoral Pursuits Jupiters Princess (Jupiter Island)
3402^{7} 4527^{3} 5019^{8} 7282^{5} 7641^{4} 8070^{3} 8500^{3}

Santafiora *Roger Charlton* 76
2 b f Poet's Voice Acquifer (Oasis Dream)
(3511) 6292^{7} 7185^{11}

Sant'Alberto (ITY) *D Teixeira* 102
8 b h Colossus(IRE) Adya (FR) (Sillery (USA))
$5502a^{11}$ $6356a^{8}$

Sant'Amanza (FR) *R Le Dren Doleuze* a94 94
5 bl m American Post Davia (IRE) (Marchand De Sable (USA))
$7861a^{7}$

Santa Monica *Charles O'Brien* a79 99
3 b f Mastercraftsman(IRE) Zacchera (Zamindar (USA))
$2510a^{2}$ $2883a^{6}$ $3539a^{6}$ $4435a^{7}$ $5313a^{2}$ $6383a^{3}$ $7558a^{5}$

Sant Angelo (GER) *Henk Grewe* 87
2 b c Areion(GER) St Aye (USA) (Nureyev (USA))
$7399a^{7}$

Sante (IRE) *Charles Hills* 86
3 b f Dream Ahead(USA) Zeiting (IRE) (Zieten (USA))
1436^{10} 2470^{15} 3951^{5} 4777^{3} (5544) ◆

Santefisio *Keith Dalgleish* a96 93
10 b g Efisio Impulsive Decision (IRE) (Nomination)
1797^{9} 2910^{9} 3518^{14}

Sant'Elia *Mark H Tompkins* a63 12
4 b m Authorized(IRE) Trew Class (Inchinor)
1711^{4} 6719^{5} 7104^{8}

Santiburi Spring *John Best* a72 69
3 b f Mullionmileanhour(IRE) Santiburi Girl (Casteddu)
268^{3} ◆ 519^{2} 725^{2} 2152^{2} 2652^{3} 5471^{3} ◆ 5720^{4} 6662^{8} (7425) 7993^{5} 8253^{2} 8445^{5}

Santorina (FR) *Mlle M-L Mortier* a82 52
3 b f Trajano(USA) Madinella (FR) (Anabaa (USA))
$3546a^{9}$ $5280a^{12}$

Santorini (IRE) *Henry Candy* 72
3 b g Tagula(IRE) Rags (IRE) (Whipper (USA))
(7011) 7443^{U}

Santo Spirito *F Rohaut* a102 90
5 ch g Monsun(GER) San Sicharia (IRE) (Daggers Drawn (USA))
$5502a^{9}$

Sanus Per Aquam (IRE) *J S Bolger* 109
3 b c Teofilo(IRE) Fainne (IRE) (Peintre Celebre (USA))
$2496a^{8}$ $3692a^{4}$

Saoi (USA) *William Knight* a94 96
9 ch g Wiseman's Ferry(USA) Careyes (IRE) (Sadler's Wells (USA))
1089^{10} 1568^{12} 2176^{7} 3525^{10}

Saon Secret (FR) *T Castanheira* a87 97
6 ch g Medecis Secret Formula (So Factual (USA))
$5949a^{6}$ $7030a^{4}$ $7525a^{5}$ $7997a^{6}$

Sao Tome (FR) *C Lerner* a43 77
3 b f Stormy River(FR) Love Liu (FR) (Librettist (USA))
$1374a^{10}$

Sarabi *Scott Dixon* a69 73
3 b f Rip Van Winkle(IRE) Xaphania (Sakhee (USA))
3^{6} 181^{3} 2834^{7} 3268^{2} 3581^{4} (3847) 4874^{9} 6506^{16} 7437^{3} 7626^{11} 8040^{9} 8474^{2}

Sarafina *David Thompson* a38 44
4 b m Mullionmileanhour(IRE) Nala (USA) (Lion Heart (USA))
1550^{7} 3421^{11}

Sarakova (IRE) *Kevin Frost* a57 55
3 b g Iffraaj Mary Pickford (USA) (Speightstown (USA))
8190^{5} 8471^{6}

Sarandia (GER) *P Schiergen* 105
3 b f Dansili Salontasche (GER) (Dashing Blade)
$5220a^{2}$ $6152a^{5}$ $7566a^{11}$

Sarangoo *Malcolm Saunders* a45 87
8 b m Piccolo Craic Sa Ceili (IRE) (Danehill Dancer (IRE))
2460^{8} 3571^{8} 4086^{10} 4563^{3} 4908^{3} 5075^{2} 5507^{9} 6184^{4} (6266)

Saranne My Love (FR) *P Monfort* a69
2 b f Footstepsinthesand Agapimou (IRE) (Spectrum (IRE))
$7454a^{7}$

Sark (IRE) *David Evans* a69 80
3 b g Zoffany(IRE) Breezeway (IRE) (Grand Lodge (USA))
70^{4} 379^{5} 729^{7} (1602) 2393^{5} 3103^{4} 4158^{2} 4827^{9} 6277^{4} 6665^{9} 8100^{8}

Sarmadee (IRE) *Mick Channon* a80 79
4 b g Fast Company(IRE) Veronica Cooper (IRE) (Kahyasi)
500^{3} 710^{3} 1140^{10} 1746^{2} ◆ 2010^{7} 2441^{4} 3097^{9} 3554^{7} 3907^{6} 4155^{8} 4640^{4} (5104) 5393^{2} 5711^{7}

Sarsted *Hughie Morrison* a88 81
4 b g Paco Boy(IRE) Red Blooded Woman (USA) (Red Ransom (USA))
1480^{4} 1978^{9} 2377^{2} 3525^{7} 5026^{2} 6050^{5} 6676^{6} 7077^{7}

Sartori *Marjorie Fife* a40 69
5 b g Elnadim(USA) Little Caroline (IRE) (Great Commotion (USA))
(178) 520^{4} 1298^{6} (1490)

Saryshagann (FR) *J-C Rouget* 98
3 gr g Iffraaj Serasana (Red Ransom (USA))
$1374a^{6}$

Sas (IRE) *Denis W Cullen* a75 81
3 b f Zebedee Sarah Stokes (IRE) (Brief Truce (USA))
$5946a^{10}$ $7372a^{6}$ $7517a^{10}$

Sasini *Charles Hills* 60
2 b f Fastnet Rock(AUS) Eva's Request (IRE) (Soviet Star (USA))
4147^{6}

Sasparella (FR) *C Laffon-Parias* 108
3 b f Shamardal(USA) Desertiste (Green Desert (USA))
$1374a^{7}$ $2282a^{6}$ $2945a^{9}$ $6272a^{5}$ $6975a^{7}$ $7348a^{2}$

Sassella (IRE) *A Fabre* 103
4 b m Lope De Vega(IRE) Sevenna (FR) (Galileo (IRE))
$1822a^{8}$ $2727a^{5}$ $4578a^{4}$

Sassoferrato (IRE) *Jo Hughes* a69 67
2 b g Zoffany(IRE) Jacquotte (IRE) (Alhaarth (IRE))
5166^{5} 5332^{10} 5848^{9} 6751^{6} 7228^{3} 7768^{6} 7974^{3} 8159^{2}

Satanic Beat (IRE) *Phil Middleton* a30 80
7 br g Dark Angel(IRE) Slow Jazz (USA) (Chief's Crown (USA))
2296^{11} 3409^{7}

Satanicjim (IRE) *Alain Couetil* a93 108
7 ch h Pivotal Infinity (FR) (Bering)
(8336a)

Satchville Flyer *David Evans* a75 82
5 ch g Compton Place Palinisa (FR) (Night Shift (USA))
124^{7} 271^{8} 502^{7} 857^{8} 1064^{11} 1502^{9} 1720^{6} (2081a) 2442^{3} 3255^{6} (3743) 4084^{3} 4321^{3} 4389^{9} (5235) 5475^{6} (5826) 5953^{2} 6255^{4} (6653) 7288^{9} 8205^{7} 8345^{11}

Satin And Lace (IRE) *Michael Madgwick* 69
4 b m Mawatheeq(USA) Katayeb (IRE) (Machiavellian (USA))
3161^{13} 6405^{9}

Satish *John Gosden* a79 79
3 b g Dansili Maycocks Bay (Muhtarram (USA))
1426^{8} 4597^{4} 5623^{3} 6049^{2} 6415^{2} 6711^{2} 7487^{4}

Satis House *Susan Corbett* a37
2 b f Bahri(USA) Ex Mill Lady (Bishop Of Cashel)
8009^{7} 8305^{9}

Satono Aladdin (JPN) *Yasutoshi Ikee* 116
5 b h Deep Impact(JPN) Magic Storm (USA) (Storm Cat (USA))
$8332a^{7}$

Satono Crown (JPN) *Noriyuki Hori* 122
4 bb h Marju(IRE) Jioconda (IRE) (Rossini (USA))
$1690a^{12}$ (8329a)

Satpura *Mick Channon* a44 72
2 b f Indian Haven Selinda (Piccolo)
4885^{8} 5387^{4} 6336^{7}

Sattar (IRE) *Martin Smith* a60
2 b c Zebedee Patroller (USA) (Grand Slam (USA))
7776^{5} 7891^{9}

Sattelac *Keith Dalgleish* a65 70
3 b f Kodiac Sattelight (Fraam)
(1698) 2666^{U} 3215^{4} 4033^{5} (4702) 6504^{6} 8347^{5}

Saucy Minx (IRE) *Amanda Perrett* a98 99
6 b m Dylan Thomas(IRE) Market Day (Tobougg (IRE))
(632) 1065^{4} 1207^{5} 2034^{6}

Saucy Spirit *Hughie Morrison* a81 37
3 b f Invincible Spirit(IRE) Salsa Steps (USA) (Giant's Causeway (USA))
7443^{11}

Saumur *Denis Coakley* a81 79
4 b m Mawatheeq(USA) Sparkling Montjeu (IRE) (Montjeu (IRE))
1919^{2} (2399) 2994^{2} 4078^{7} 6667^{6} 7067^{7}

Saunter (FR) *David Menuisier* a87 104
3 b g Myboycharlie(IRE) Marie Des Fleurs (FR) (Smart Strike (CAN))
$1240a^{2}$ (5996) (6581) 7117^{8} $7897a^{2}$

Sautter *Peter Chapple-Hyam* 71
3 b c Kyllachy Regency Rose (Danehill (USA))
2861^{10} 3981^{4} 5164^{3}

Savannah Beau *Iain Jardine* a74 70
4 b m Major Cadeaux Mancunian Way (Green Desert (USA))
2621^{7} 3397^{6} 4428^{12} 5295^{7} 5479^{10} 6680^{6} 6809^{5} (7959) 8135^{6}

Savannah Moon (IRE) *Kevin Ryan* 62
2 b f Canford Cliffs(IRE) Tennessee Moon (Darshaan)
4298^{12} 5221^{5} 6477^{2} ◆

Savannah's Dream *David O'Meara* 87
2 b f Showcasing Grandmas Dream (Kyllachy)
2800^{3} 3247^{2} 4685^{3} 5359^{7} 5583^{3} 6538^{8}

Savannah Slew *James Given* 81
2 b f Kheleyf(USA) Saratoga Slew (IRE) (Footstepsinthesand)
1437^{9} 2007^{6} 3433^{3} (4843) 5794^{7} (7440) 7820^{4}

Savannah Star *Nick Kent* 38
3 b f Haafhd Mitsuki (Puissance)
2234[14] 4006[12] 4369[6] 5383[7]

Savannah Storm *G M Lyons* 80
3 b c Dubawi(IRE) Savannah Belle (Green Desert (USA))
6389a[18]

Savea (IRE) *David O'Meara* 49
2 b g Dream Ahead(USA) Poussiere d'Or (IRE) (Grape Tree Road)
2489[7] 6129[9] 6446[8]

Saved By The Bell (IRE) *David O'Meara* a81 97
6 b g Teofilo(IRE) Eyrecourt (IRE) (Efisio)
1642[4] 2472[7] 3246[11] 4664[3] 5559[15] 6540[6]

Saved My Bacon (IRE) *Chris Dwyer* a83 78
5 b m Camacho Sally Green (IRE) (Common Grounds)
56[2] 269[6] 359[2] 439[2] 903[5] 969[2] 1237[6] (1402) (1803) 2787[6] 3847[4] 5040[6]

Save The Bees *Declan Carroll* a83 86
8 b g Royal Applause Rock Concert (Bishop Of Cashel)
1317[5] 1526[5] 2233[7] 2673[3] 2743[4] 3212[3] (3883) 4138[7] (4687) 4919[6] 5292[2] 5579[8] 6323[6] (6876) 7159[15]

Savile Row (FR) *Frau Erika Mader* 89
2 b c Ransom O'War(USA) Shikoku (Green Desert (USA))
7086a[7] 7842a[4]

Saving Kenny (IRE) *Roy Arne Kvisla* a97 93
6 b h Footstepsinthesand Cycle Of Life (USA) (Spinning World (USA))
4421a[5]

Savoir Vivre (IRE) *Jean-Pierre Carvalho* 117
3 ch c Adlerflug(GER) Soudaine (GER) (Monsun (GER))
3453a[5] 4186a[2] (5947a) 6989a[8] 7759a[5]

Sawwala *J R Jenkins* a40 26
6 b m Sakhee(USA) Jawwala (USA) (Green Dancer (USA))
378[5] 673[2] 5208[6]

Saxagogo *George Scott* a66 56
2 ch f Dutch Art Injaaz (Sheikh Albadou)
3074[7] 4203[6] 4707[5] *(5364) 5675[3] 6419[3] 7143[4]*

Saxo Jack (FR) *Sophie Leech* a50 62
6 b g King's Best(USA) Gamma (FR) (Sadler's Wells (USA))
7535[20] *8035[11] 8319[9]*

Saxon Gold (IRE) *John Davies* a30 54
3 ch f Zoffany(IRE) Apple Brandy (USA) (Cox's Ridge (USA))
1819[3] 2308[6] 2801[3] 3479[8] 4844[9] *6106[10]*

Saxony *Matthew Salaman* a45 32
5 b m Bertolini(USA) Just Down The Road (IRE) (Night Shift (USA))
4290[11] 5009[6] *8346[4]*

Saxum (FR) *Edward Lynam* 63
3 b f Whipper(USA) Spy Eye (USA) (Tale Of The Cat (USA))
7391a[12]

Sayana (FR) *A De Royer-Dupre* a88 105
4 b m Galileo(IRE) Sichilla (IRE) (Danehill (USA))
2893[2] 5691a[8] 6693a[2]

Sayedaati Saadati (IRE) *John Butler* a41 41
3 b g Montjeu(IRE) Guessing (USA) (Kingmambo (USA))
1662[4] *2619[7]* 3841[5] 7223[8] *8337[8] 8459[9]*

Sayem *Ed Walker* a78
2 b f Sayif(IRE) Usem (Bahamian Bounty)
8152[6] (8362) ◆

Sayesse *Mick Channon* 86
2 b g Sayif(IRE) Pesse (IRE) (Eagle Eyed (USA))
1316[4] (1741) (2173) 2865[6] 3531[3] 4076[4] 4553[8] 4825[15] (5510) 5741[5] (6322) 6950[17] 7113[8] 7549[13]

Sayeuri *David Evans* a43 13
4 b m Siyouni(FR) Nalear (FR) (Lear Fan (USA))
74[4] 618[7]

Sayif Magic *George Scott* 55
2 br c Sayif(IRE) Pearl Magic (USA) (Speightstown (USA))
6473[7] 7032[6]

Say It Loud (FR) *R Rohne*
2 b c Sageburg(IRE) Simple Act (USA) (Kingmambo (USA))
4187a[5]

Sbraase *James Tate* a91 90
5 ch h Sir Percy Hermanita (Hernando (FR))
465[6] 861[5] 1166[2] 2549[4] 3077[2] *3785[2]* 4153[5] *5026[5] 5633[3] 6142[3] 6854[6]*

Scales Of Justice (IRE) *Charles Hills* 65
2 b c Galileo(IRE) Half Queen (USA) (Deputy Minister (CAN))
7622[6]

Scamper *Roger Charlton* 57
3 b f Oasis Dream Wince (Selkirk (USA))
1597[9] 2298[4]

Scandaleux (FR) *E Lellouche* a70 81
3 b c On Est Bien(IRE) Goldance (FR) (Goldneyev (USA))
5704a[7]

Scannermandango *Jim Goldie* a32
3 b f Bahamian Bounty Regal Asset (USA) (Regal Classic (CAN))
8388[6]

Scapina (GER) *Henk Grewe* 79
2 bb f Tai Chi(GER) Sunshine Story (IRE) (Desert Story (IRE))
7563a[6]

Scarborough (IRE) *Paul Midgley* a93 83
5 ch m Dandy Man(IRE) Alchimie (IRE) (Sri Pekan (USA))
4[10] 1084[9]

Scarlet Bounty (IRE) *Richard Fahey* a65 70
4 b m Bahamian Bounty Red Kyte (Hawk Wing (USA))
246[10]

Scarlet Dragon *Eve Johnson Houghton* 112
3 gr g Sir Percy Welsh Angel (Dubai Destination (USA))
1571[2] ◆ 2029[3] 2393[4] 2892[6] (3814) (4554) ◆ 4797[4] (5651) 6573[2] (7117) 8573a[14]

Scarlet Minstrel *Andrew Balding* a87 76
4 b g Sir Percy Sweet Mandolin (Soviet Star (USA))
78[3] 440[3] 922[2] 1135[3] 1893[5] 3351[5]

Scarlet Not Blue *Matthew Salaman* 3
4 b g Clodovil(IRE) Blue Bamboo (Green Desert (USA))
4156[13] 5233[4] 6441[10]

Scarlet Pimpernel *Hughie Morrison* a72 67
3 b f Sir Percy Sweet Pea (Persian Bold)
1235[4] 2700[4] *3652[7]*

Scarlet Thrush (IRE) *Marco Botti* a61 70
2 b f Kodiac Reveal The Star (USA) (Aptitude (USA))
7056[2] 7494[5] *8465[5]*

Scarlet Wings *K R Burke*
3 ch f Sir Percy Wendylina (IRE) (In The Wings)
3264[9]

Scarpeta (FR) *Mark Johnston* a72 79
3 b g Soldier Of Fortune(IRE) Sanada (IRE) (Priolo (USA))
1740[2] (2124) *(2563)* 2798[2] *3306[2]* 3778[3] 4137[2] (4636) 5176[4]

Scattered Stars *Charlie Appleby* a83 81
3 b f Dubawi(IRE) Midnight Angel (GER) (Acatenango (GER))
5361[2] (5742) *6417[4]*

Scenic Star (IRE) *Gavin Cromwell* a63 61
6 b g Erewhon(USA) African Scene (IRE) (Scenic (IRE))
946[2]

Scent Of Power *Barry Leavy* a53 60
4 b m Authorized(IRE) Aromatherapy (Oasis Dream)
1640[9] 2015[4] 2462[8] (2733) 3135[2] 3497[4] 4498[7] 5957[4] 6212[3] 6827[6] 7628[10] *7754[6]*

Schamberg (FR) *J Bertran De Balanda* 67
2 b c Sunday Break(JPN) Ahdaaf (USA) (Bahri (USA))
6638a[14]

Schang (GER) *P Vovcenko* 112
3 b c Contat(GER) Shaheen (GER) (Tertullian (USA))
(3992a) 5217a[10] 5943a[8] 7027a[4] 7719a[5]

Schindlers Ark (USA) *Charles O'Brien* a59
2 gr c Exchange Rate(USA) Sweet Science (USA) (Diesis)
7917a[10]

Schmooze (IRE) *Linda Perratt* a56 64
7 b m One Cool Cat(USA) If Dubai (USA) (Stephen Got Even (USA))
1881[3] 2575[7] 2813[7] 3018[5]

Schoolboy Error (IRE) *Jamie Osborne* a68 65
3 ch g Roderic O'Connor(IRE) La Grande Zoa (IRE) (Fantastic Light (USA))
148[2] 265[3] 376[5] 517[2] 729[8] 1062[4] 1551[3] (1705) 2366[5] 3053[2] *3652[3] 4942[8]*

School Fete (IRE) *Michael Bell* a80 81
3 b g Authorized(IRE) Local Spirit (USA) (Lion Cavern (USA))
976[3] ◆ 1406[2] *2000[2]* 2858[7] (Dead)

School Run (IRE) *David O'Meara* a64
2 b f Invincible Spirit(IRE) By Invitation (USA) (Van Nistelrooy (USA))
8406[3]

Schottische *Alan Bailey* a61 56
6 ch m Pastoral Pursuits Calligraphy (Kris)
158[2] 216[5] (563) 769[13] 1695[8] *2609[6]* 3354[2] *3731[9] 5132[3] 5635[3] 6512[8] 7529[4] 7642[5] 8337[5] 8471[2]*

Schutzenpost (GER) *J Hirschberger* 98
4 b m American Post Schutzenprinzess (GER) (Dashing Blade)
3916a[3] 5695a[7] 7027a[11]

Sciarra *Michael Bell* a66 71
3 ch f Monsieur Bond(IRE) Tibesti (Machiavellian (USA))
1246[4] 1673[2] 2459[5] *3280[4]* 4262[2] 4517[8] (6036) *6908[3]*

Scissors And Tape (USA) *Michael J Maker* 55
3 ch c Curlin(USA) One Lucky Storm (USA) (Tale Of The Cat (USA))
5429a[9]

Scofflaw *Richard Fahey* 79
2 b g Foxwedge(AUS) Belle Des Airs (IRE) (Dr Fong (USA))
(2682) 3712[3] 4825[10] 6260[10] 7120[13]

Scoones *James Fanshawe* 35
2 ch c Sepoy(AUS) Hannda (IRE) (Dr Devious (IRE))
7283[9]

Scorching Heat *Andrew Balding* a65 75
2 b c Acclamation Pink Flames (IRE) (Redback)
4938[4] 5325[3] (6375) 7549[5]

Scotch Myst *Richard Fahey* a59 55
2 ch c Sepoy(AUS) Shena's Dream (IRE) (Oasis Dream)
2830[8] 3388[7] 4685[6] ◆ 5712[5] 7579[6] *7884[5] 8097[3] 8344[2]*

Scot Daddy (USA) *Denis Quinn* a45 42
4 ch g Scat Daddy(USA) Flor De Oro (USA) (Out Of Place (USA))
97[5] 158[3] 568[8] 682[5] 951[9] 5264[8] *6512[6]*

Scotland (GER) *Andrew Balding* 111
5 b g Monsun(GER) Sqillo (IRE) (Bachelor Duke (USA))
2025[2] 3298[15]

Scotland Forever (IRE) *S Seemar* a76 90
6 b g Rock Of Gibraltar(IRE) Wee Mad Snout (IRE) (Soviet Star (USA))
189a[11] *537a[9]*

Scots Piper *Mark Johnston* 69
2 b c Shamardal(USA) Miss Jean Brodie (USA) (Maria's Mon (USA))
(6808)

Scottish (IRE) *Charlie Appleby* 119
4 b g Teofilo(IRE) Zeiting (IRE) (Zieten (USA))
2626[3] (4392) 5159[2] (5652) 7378a[2]

Scottish Command *Richard Hannon* a59 67
3 b g Kyllachy Angel Song (Dansili)
181[5]

Scottish Glen *Patrick Chamings* a96 101
10 ch g Kyllachy Dance For Fun (Anabaa (USA))
2033[3] 2391[10] 3358[3] 4625[3] 5174[6] 6109[5] 6788[6] *7933[7]*

Scottish Summit (IRE) *Sir Michael Stoute* a71 75
3 b g Shamardal(USA) Scottish Stage (IRE) (Selkirk (USA))
1483[4] *2816[5]* 4272[2] ◆

Scrafton *Tony Carroll* a74 69
5 b g Leporello(IRE) Some Diva (Dr Fong (USA))
357[2] 772[3] 1222[8] 1854[7] 2501[3] 3052[3] *8477[10]*

Screaming Gemini (IRE) *Roger Varian* a69 56
2 b c Shamardal(USA) Littlefeather (IRE) (Indian Ridge)
7665[6] *7908[7] 8354[4]*

Screen Angel (IRE) *Richard Fahey* 64
2 gr f Dark Angel(IRE) Silverscreen Queen (IRE) (Saffron Walden (FR))
3261[3]

Scribner Creek (IRE) *Daniel Mark Loughnane* a65
3 b g Roderic O'Connor(IRE) Nebraska Lady (IRE) (Lujain (USA))
7459[9] 7616[9] 7960[3] (8207) 8411[4]

Scruffy McGuffy *Ann Duffield* 67
3 b g Firebreak Eloquent Isle (IRE) (Mull Of Kintyre (USA))
4314[11] (5181) (5729)

Scrutineer (IRE) *Mick Channon* 106
3 b c Intense Focus(USA) Royal Esteem (Mark Of Esteem (IRE))
1424[2] 2250[3] 2870[5] 3269[13] 4062[9] 4916[4] 6161[3] (6837)

Scrutinise *Ed Dunlop* a97 104
4 b g Intense Focus(USA) Tetravella (IRE) (Groom Dancer (USA))
1568[11] 2468[6] 3861[2] 4858[2] 5647[6] 6573[16] *7365[4]*

Scrutiny *Barry Murtagh* a5 80
5 b g Aqlaam Aunty Mary (Common Grounds)
1221[15]

Scudding (USA) *Mohammed Jassim Ghazali* a67
2 b f Mizzen Mast(USA) Pearl In The Sand (IRE) (Footstepsinthesand)
2764[4] ◆ *(3301)* 8564a[11]

Scuzeme *David Barron* 30
2 ch g Kheleyf(USA) Barbieri (IRE) (Encosta De Lago (AUS))
1840[5] 4110[8]

Seaborn (IRE) *Simon Hodgson* a55
2 b c Born To Sea(IRE) Next To The Top (Hurricane Run (IRE))
8246[9] 8557[10]

Sea Calisi (FR) *Chad C Brown* 112
4 b m Youmzain(IRE) Triclaria (GER) (Surumu (GER))
3119a[2] (5430a) 7831a[7]

Sea Dweller *Anthony Carson* a72
3 b f High Chaparral(IRE) Langoustine (AUS) (Danehill (USA))
8195[2] 8491[2]

Seaesta *Laura Mongan* a51
2 b f Harbour Watch(IRE) Lady Golan (IRE) (Golan (IRE))
6413[9]

Seafarer (IRE) *Marcus Tregoning* 76
2 br g Henrythenavigator(USA) Rose Of Petra (IRE) (Golan (IRE))
4287[7] (5325) 5829[4]

Seaforth (IRE) *John Joseph Murphy* a64 80
4 b g Acclamation Hendrina (IRE) (Daylami (IRE))
4899a[10] 7391a[9]

Sea Fox (IRE) *David Evans* 107
2 b c Kodiac City Maiden (USA) (Carson City (USA))
3058[2] 3529[2] (4016) 5595[3] ◆ 6059[2] 6270a[4] 6783[3] 7148[6] 7544[4]

Sea Front (FR) *E Libaud* a103 106
5 b m Le Havre(IRE) Freedom Herself (FR) (Freedom Cry)
3451a[3] 5691a[4] 6988a[6] *8165a[4]*

Seafront *James Tate* 97
2 b f Foxwedge(AUS) Locharia (Wolfhound (USA))
1437[6] (1583) 2211[2] 2718a[3] 3694a[2] 4106[5]

Seagull Star *Keith Dalgleish* a77 67
5 b g Sea The Stars(IRE) Dash To The Top (Montjeu (IRE))
5579[10] 7359[7] *7911[11] 8477[2]*

Seamoor Secret *Alex Hales* a44 49
4 b m Sakhee's Secret Labaqa (USA) (Rahy (USA))
174[6] 513[6] 8499[10]

Seamour (IRE) *Brian Ellison* a107 110
5 b g Azamour(IRE) Chifney Rush (IRE) (Grand Lodge (USA))
2486[6] *3658[2]* 4164[9] 5655[5] 6283[2] 6708[2]

Seamster *David Loughnane* a61 88
9 ch g Pivotal Needles And Pins (IRE) (Fasliyev (USA))
21[6] 271[2] (398) 561[2] 703[7] 901[12] 1178[2] 1401[6] 1668[5] *2622[8]* 3268[3] (3484) 3709[3] (3779) 3843[2] 4039[2] (4295) 4544[3] 4831[4] (5274) 5479[3] (5762) 5864[2] 6131[8] 6234[7]

Sea My Diamond (IRE) *Mark Hoad* a10 24
2 b f Born To Sea(IRE) She's My Rock (IRE) (Rock Of Gibraltar (IRE))
5771[7] *6622[10]*

Seanie (IRE) *David Marnane* a103 90
7 b g Kodiac Cakestown Lady (IRE) (Petorius (IRE))
370a[9] *921[5] 1068[9]* 4921a[15] 6984a[13] *7523a[13]*

Sea Of Flames *David Elsworth* a105 94
3 ch g Aqlaam Hidden Fire (Alhaarth (IRE))
(314) (459) ◆ *836[8] (1071) (1338)* 2190[11] 2867[6] 3299[10] 4065[8] *7651[12] 7933[6]* ◆

Sea Of Grace (IRE) *John M Oxx* 104
2 ch f Born To Sea(IRE) Lady Dettoria (FR) (Vettori (IRE))
(5937a)

Sea Of Green *Jim Goldie* a51 51
4 b m Iffraaj Sea Of Leaves (USA) (Stormy Atlantic (USA))
2359[7] *2919[6]* 4410[10] *4647[9]* 4770[7] 5277[4] 5804[2] 6098[4] 6341[8] *8289[7] 8483[4] 8589[13]*

Sea Of Heaven (IRE) *Sir Mark Prescott Bt* a82 101
4 b g Sea The Stars(IRE) Maid Of Killeen (IRE) (Darshaan)
3657[12] 4353[2] (4581) 5144[2] ◆ 5639[5] 7150[3]

Sea Of Hope (IRE) *Adrian Paul Keatley* a61 60
3 b f Rock Of Gibraltar(IRE) Labrusca (Grand Lodge (USA))
2234[5] 7747[11]

Sea Of Lights (GER) *N Clement* a56
2 b f Areion(GER) Senaida (IRE) (Danehill Dancer (IRE))
7294a[4]

Sea Of Snow (USA) *Mark Johnston* 86
2 ch f Distorted Humor(USA) Snow Ballerina (Sadler's Wells (USA))
(2097) (2311) 2865[3] 3336[9] 4884[7] 5998[8]

Sea Of Uncertainty *James Evans* a67 45
3 b g Kyllachy Moving Sea (IRE) (Rock Of Gibraltar (IRE))
3[4] 242[4] 335[2] 597[5] 1120[2] 1486[5] *1764[2]* 3499[7] *5808[12] 7260[8]*

Seaperle *Tim Easterby* a51 61
3 b f Firebreak Ocean Grove (IRE) (Fairy King (USA))
1670[2] 1927[9] 2255[6] *2559[6]*

Searanger (USA) *Rebecca Menzies* a70 69
3 b g US Ranger(USA) Baby Lets Cruise (USA) (Tale Of The Cat (USA))
1487[5] 1922[5] 2742[9] (3423) 3709[6] *5370[3] 5969[8]* 6506[18] 6959[5] *7533[5] 8137[5] 8390[3]*

Searchlight *Jim Boyle* a93 84
5 b g Kyllachy Baralinka (IRE) (Barathea (IRE))
(142) 323[6] 529[7] 771[2] 1090[7] 1929[11]

Sea's Aria (IRE) *Denis Gerard Hogan* a57 59
5 b g Sea The Stars(IRE) Speed Song (Fasliyev (USA))
5620a[6]

Sea Shack *William Knight* 77
2 b c Equiano(FR) Folly Bridge (Avonbridge)
4075[7] 4736[3] 5890[2] (6664) 6950[8]

Sea Shanty (USA) *M Al Subouse* a79 86
6 b g Elusive Quality(USA) Medley (Danehill Dancer (IRE))
229a[DSQ]

Seaside Sizzler *William Knight* a91 93
9 ch g Rahy(USA) Via Borghese (USA) (Seattle Dancer (USA))
(1092) 1987[2] 2932[6] 3387[9] 4581[10] 4752[P]

Sea Silk *Dean Ivory* a15
4 b g Shamardal(USA) Ocean Silk (USA) (Dynaformer (USA))
245[12]

Sea Skimmer *Saeed bin Suroor* 69
2 ch c Dubawi(IRE) Portmanteau (Barathea (IRE))
7501[5]

Sea Swift (IRE) *D K Weld* 96
3 b f High Chaparral(IRE) Agnetha (GER) (Big Shuffle (USA))
6604a[5] 7393a[3]

Sea Tea Dea *Anthony Carson* a67
2 b f Archipenko(USA) Half Sister (IRE) (Oratorio (IRE))
6696[2] 7484[5] 8277[4]

Sea The Waves *Emma Owen* 68
3 b c Canford Cliffs(IRE) April (IRE) (Rock Of Gibraltar (IRE))
3572[13] 4041[5]

Sea Tide *Hugo Palmer* a74 77
2 b f Champs Elysees Change Course (Sadler's Wells (USA))
7284[3] ◆ *7762[2]*

Sea Urchin (IRE) *R Bouresly* a49
4 b m Fastnet Rock(AUS) Fand (USA) (Kingmambo (USA))
8576a[8]

Seaview *Dean Ivory* 53
2 b f Harbour Watch(IRE) Welanga (Dansili)
3954[8] 5511[7] 5869[10] 6208[3]

Sea Wolf (IRE) *G M Lyons* 106
4 b g Amadeus Wolf Rose De France (IRE) (Diktat)
1694[2] 4747a[13] (5941a) 7354[11]

Sebastian's Wish (IRE) *Richard Whitaker* a55 47
3 b g Aqlaam Swish (GER) (Monsun (GER))
1449[7] 2408[4] 6029[6] *7105[9] 7438[2] 7992[10]*

Seb's Choice (IRE) *Lady Jane Gillespie* a25 51
7 br g Hurricane Run(IRE) Sevi's Choice (USA) (Sir Ivor (USA))
5900a[7]

Secly (IRE) *F Chappet* a53 72
5 b g Marju(IRE) Zaya (GER) (Diktat)
7398a[3]

Second Bullet (AUS) *Danny O'Brien* 93
5 b g Encosta De Lago(AUS) Private Steer (AUS) (Danehill Dancer (IRE))
7637a[2] 7826a[5]

Second Nature *James Tate* a65 80
2 bl c Bated Breath Frabjous (Pivotal)
2847[3] ◆ *3647[3]* (4363) 5877[3] *6697[9]*

Second Page *Richard Hannon* a73 53
2 b c Harbour Watch(IRE) Almunia (IRE) (Mujadil (USA))
7495[8] *7812[3] 8377[4]*

Second Serve (IRE) *Mark Johnston* a85 84
3 b c Cape Cross(IRE) Aguinaga (IRE) (Machiavellian (USA))
1113[3] ◆ *1265[2] (1429)* 2224[2] 2687[6] 3103[3] 3300[12] 4131[7] 4628[4] 5053[3] 5761[6] 6345[3] *7512[2]*

Second Step (IRE) *Luca Cumani* 119
5 b g Dalakhani(IRE) My Dark Rosaleen (Sadler's Wells (USA))
2221[3] 2894[5] 4061[5] 4626[7] 5894[3] 6752[4]

Second Thought (IRE) *William Haggas* a82 82
2 b c Kodiac Bobby Jane (Diktat)
2696[2] ◆ *(8406)*

Second Wave (IRE) *Charlie Appleby* a109 112
4 b g New Approach(IRE) Tessa Reef (IRE) (Mark Of Esteem (IRE))
3383[2] 4731[4] 7552a[9]

Secret Agent *William Muir* a58 75
2 b c Equiano(FR) Varnish (Choisir (AUS))
3954[12] 6731[3] 7224[2] 7574[7] *8033[10] 8352[7] 8494[3]*

Secretariatus (FR) *V Luka Jr* 60
3 ch c Medicean Shagadellic (USA) (Devil's Bag (USA))
3764a[10]

Secret Art (IRE) *William Knight* a94 100
6 ch g Excellent Art Ivy Queen (IRE) (Green Desert (USA))
1344[5] 2216[7] 2628[3] 3157[4] (3910) *5552[5] 6126[13]* 7121[17]

Secret Asset (IRE) *Lisa Williamson* a83 86
11 gr g Clodovil(IRE) Skerray (Soviet Star (USA))
162[3] 439[3] (714) 1084[2] 1321[6] 1836[3] 2003[5] 3123[3] 3638[4] (4536) 4632[3] 5360[4] 5648[10]

Secret Ballerina *Julia Feilden* a53 30
2 ch f Sakhee's Secret Ballyea (IRE) (Acclamation)
1799[5] 2104[7] 2289[3] 4564[8] *6896[7] 7866[12]*

Secret Bird (IRE) *Dean Ivory* a61 48
4 br g Arcano(IRE) Asfurah (USA) (Dayjur (USA))
1533[13] 2130[11] 3469[7] 6408[12] *7912[6] (8079) (8408)*

Secret Brief (IRE) *Charlie Appleby* a73 109
4 b g Shamardal(USA) Discreet Brief (IRE) (Darshaan)
284a[9] 628a[3] (1196) 3273[17] 3910[10]

Secret City (IRE) *Rebecca Bastiman* 68
10 b g City On A Hill(USA) Secret Combe (IRE) (Mujadil (USA))
1120[4] 1565[14] 3289[3] 3940[4] 4513[3] 5278[8] 5889[13]

Secret Clause *Michael Appleby* a51 68
3 b c Sakhee's Secret Claws (Marju (IRE))
1487[6] (2337) 2834[4] *8473[12] 8571[11]*

Secret Coin (IRE) *Jamie Osborne* a45 44
2 b f Approve(IRE) Coin Box (Dubai Destination (USA))
1915[5] 2125[5] 2933[5] *5128[4] 5606[5]*

Secret Dancer (IRE) *John Flint* a31 93
11 b g Sadler's Wells(USA) Discreet Brief (IRE) (Darshaan)
498[9]

Secret Dragon (IRE) *Jamie Osborne* 13
2 ch f Dragon Pulse(IRE) Ra Hydee (USA) (Rahy (USA))
2173[11]

Secret Dreamer *Kevin Morgan* a69 20
4 b g Arcano(IRE) Badweia (USA) (Kingmambo (USA))
5178[10] *5843[2] 6674[6] 7661[5]*

Secret Existence (IRE) *F Chappet* a87 93
3 b f Sakhee's Secret Mad Existence (IRE) (Val Royal (FR))
5006a[3] 7168a[2]

Secretfact *Malcolm Saunders* 77
3 br g Sakhee's Secret Matterofact (IRE) (Bold Fact (USA))
2143[5] 2458[12] 4262[6] 4506[2] 4796[3] (5570) 5628[8] (6361) (6832)

Secret Glance *Richard Rowe* a71 84
4 b g Sakhee's Secret Look Here's Dee (Dansili)
484[7] 771[10] 1040[9] 2577[9] (3097) 3571[4] 4627[12] *5507[7] 6416[11]* 7189[13] *8350[6]*

Secret Hint *Andrew Balding* a95 97
5 b m Oasis Dream Teeky (Daylami (IRE))
2144[4] 1065[8] 2223[2] (2683) 3163[7] 4136[8] 5098a[7] 6064[5] 7146[12]

Secret House (USA) *Doug O'Neill* a67 84
2 bb c Tiznow(USA) Mega Dream (USA) (Medaglia d'Oro (USA))
7266a[11]

Secret Icon *Jamie Osborne* a37 45
2 b f Sixties Icon Stan's Smarty Girl (USA) (Smarty Jones (USA))
4938[9] 5202[6] 5395[10]

Secret Insider (USA) *Hugo Palmer* a81 70
3 b f Elusive Quality(USA) Fashion Insider (USA) (Indian Charlie (USA))
(171) ◆ *519[10] 924[4]* ◆ *1155[2]* 3197[5]

Secret Interlude (IRE) *Roger Fell* a58 33
3 b f Clodovil(IRE) Elouges (IRE) (Dalakhani (IRE))
327[2] 3513[3] 3970[10] *5554[9] 6853[9] 8070[7] 8589[7]*

Secretinthepark *Robert Cowell* a92 100
6 ch g Sakhee's Secret Lark In The Park (IRE) (Grand Lodge (USA))
3151[12] 4126[17]

Secretjim (FR) *P Bary* a69 87
3 b c Equiano(FR) Hometown (Storming Home)
2141a[7]

Secret Lady *Mme M Bollack-Badel* a81 77
2 b f Arcano(IRE) Lady McBeth (IRE) (Avonbridge)
1021a[2] 5142a[6]

Secret Lightning (FR) *Michael Appleby* a56 62
4 ch m Sakhee's Secret Dimelight (Fantastic Light (USA))
3096[7] 3291[6] 3642[9] 5264[9] 5415[5] 5729[6] *6900[4] (7261) 7943[6] 8179[13] 8351[8]*

Secret Look *Richard Phillips* a73 75
6 ch g Sakhee's Secret Look Here's Carol (IRE) (Safawan)
36[6] 963[3] 1299[6] (1533) 2130[7] 2697[3] 3069[6] (3674) *(3985)* 5896[6] 6269[13] 7059[18]

Secret Millionaire (IRE) *Shaun Harris* a52 66
9 b g Kyllachy Mithl Al Hawa (Salse (USA))
98[3] 151[2] 292[2] 339[3] (504) 685[3] 775[4] 872[9] (1549) 1950[2] 2088[5] 3741[4] 3925[6] 4931[8] 5295[8] *7747[9] 7913[6]* ◆ *8312[3] 8542[6]*

Secret Missile *Gary Moore* a98 87
6 b g Sakhee's Secret Malelane (IRE) (Prince Sabo)
1090[9] 2547[10] 2898[15] 4862[26] *6371[9] 6962[11]*

Secret Number *Saeed bin Suroor* a108 112
6 b g Raven's Pass(USA) Mysterial (USA) (Alleged (USA))
(6505) 7756a[21] 7948a[7]

Secret Poet (IRE) *Jamie Osborne* a40
2 b f Poet's Voice Nawaashi (Green Desert (USA))
7885[12] 8245[12] 8353[11]

Secret Potion *Ronald Harris* a41 72
2 b g Stimulation(IRE) Fiancee (IRE) (Pivotal)
3485[4] 4287[10] (5008) 5656[8] *7258[9]* 7589[4]

Secret Sense (USA) *H-A Pantall* a84 81
3 b f Shamardal(USA) Shastye (IRE) (Danehill (USA))
(1289) ◆ 2490[4] *3608[8]* 6357a[8]

Secret Shot *David Dennis* a37
4 b g Sakhee's Secret Vodka Shot (USA) (Holy Bull (USA))
544[7] 778[7] 3028[6]

Secret Sinner (IRE) *Jamie Osborne* a49
3 b f Lawman(FR) Mamela (GER) (Protektor (GER))
148[6] 517[4] 700[2]

Secret Someone (USA) *Michael Stidham* 105
5 ch m A.P. Indy(USA) Private Gift (USA) (Unbridled (USA))
5430a[8] 7171a[9]

Secret Sonnet *Stuart Williams* a50 35
3 ch f Sakhee's Secret Warden Rose (Compton Place)
834[5] 1181[5] 1597[12] 2905[6] 3975[10] 4321[11] 5013[10]

Secret Soul *Ralph Beckett* a68 66
2 b f Street Cry(IRE) Shastye (IRE) (Danehill (USA))
6061[5] *7050[4]*

Secret Storm *J R Jenkins*
2 ch c Sakhee's Secret Sally Southill (Byron)
7414[10]

Secret Striker *Ken Cunningham-Brown* a39 30
4 ch m Sakhee's Secret Silver Purse (Interrex (CAN))
7011[10] *7935[6]*

Secret Tale (IRE) *Ahmed Kobeissi* 61
3 b f Zoffany(IRE) Intimate Secret (IRE) (Invincible Spirit (IRE))
756a[12]

Secret Weapon *C H Yip* 118
6 b g Choisir(AUS) Just Devine (IRE) (Montjeu (IRE))
1912a[11] 8333a[2]

Secret Willow *John E Long* a40
2 ch c Sakhee's Secret Willow Beauty (Val Royal (FR))
7977[13] 8377[9]

Secret Witness *Ronald Harris* a66 62
10 ch g Pivotal It's A Secret (Polish Precedent (USA))
319[5] 398[7] 873[3] 1147[3] 1261[4] 1495[6] 2584[3] *3320[6]* 3510[3] 3743[8] 5827[2] 6311[3] *7912[8]*

Secular Society *George Baker* a76 77
6 b g Royal Applause Fantastic Santanyi (Fantastic Light (USA))
165[9] 6365[11] 6889[4]

Secure Access (USA) *Claude McGaughey III* 91
3 ch f Kitten's Joy(USA) Code Book (USA) (Giant's Causeway (USA))
4174a[11]

Secure Cloud (IRE) *Lawney Hill* a74 59
5 b g High Chaparral(IRE) Cabo (FR) (Sagamix (FR))
2582[6] 4012[9]

Seduce Me *K R Burke* 84
2 b f Dutch Art Deep Bleu (Kyllachy)
3261[5] (3947) ◆ 4623[10] 5416[3] 6257[8] 6950[4] 7147[6]

See And Be Seen *Sylvester Kirk* a77 85
6 b g Sakhee's Secret Anthea (Tobougg (IRE))
1987[7] 2392[12] 3437[7] 4353[9] 4581[4] 5176[6] 6362[10]

Seebeedee *Harry Dunlop* a65 78
4 b m Multiplex Border Ballet (IRE) (Noverre (USA))
1455[4]

Seebring (IRE) *Brian Ellison* a42 66
2 b g Tagula(IRE) Sunlit Romance (IRE) (Hernando (FR))
2552[4] *3654[7]*

Seed Corn *William Haggas* 75
2 b f Exceed And Excel(AUS) Scarlet Runner (Night Shift (USA))
3037[2] 3511[10]

See Dex (GER) *D Windrif* a76
6 ch g Saddex See Me Well (IRE) (Common Grounds)
715a[8]

Seeing Things (IRE) *Philip McBride* a27
2 b c Poet's Voice Sonning Rose (IRE) (Hawk Wing (USA))
8066[11] 8353[12]

Seeking Magic *Clive Cox* a101 101
8 b g Haafhd Atnab (USA) (Riverman (USA))
1887[2] 2434[3] 2895[6] 4862[8] 5648[3] 6633[8] *6962[3] 7752[2]*

Seeking The Soul (USA) *Dallas Stewart* a94
3 b c Perfect Soul(IRE) Seeking The Title (USA) (Seeking The Gold (USA))
3181a[12]

Seek The Fair Land *Lee Carter* a77 60
10 b g Noverre(USA) Duchcov (Caerleon (USA))
629[8] 671[4] 857[6] (1264) 1415[4] 1832[5] 2006[4] 6510[4] 6872[13] 7654[3] 7964[5] (8258) 8469[6]

See Of Rome *Richard Hughes* 78
2 gr c Pour Moi(IRE) Balandra (Medicean)
6288[3] 6663[4] ◆ 7501[4]

See The City (IRE) *Mark Johnston* a66 76
2 b g Lawman(FR) Cedar Sea (IRE) (Persian Bold)
2478[3] 3598[7] *4642[6]* ◆ (4982) ◆ 5318[4]

See The Master (IRE) *Clive Cox* 51
2 b c Dutch Art See Emily Play (IRE) (Galileo (IRE))
6108[11]

See The Rock (IRE) *Jonjo O'Neill* 87
6 b g Shirocco(GER) Samara (IRE) (Polish Patriot (USA))
4208[4] 6736[7]

See The Sea (IRE) *Richard Hannon* a36 74
2 b f Born To Sea(IRE) Shahmina (IRE) (Danehill (USA))
3640[2] ◆ 4298[6] *4975[7]*

See The Storm *Ann Duffield* a46 80
8 bb g Statue Of Liberty(USA) Khafayif (USA) (Swain (IRE))
1869[17] *5845[13]* 6644[7] 7590[8]

See The Sun *Tim Easterby* a93 97
5 ch g Assertive Cocabana (Captain Rio)
(1848) (2158) 3151[17] *3656[6]* 4136[5] 4667[16] 5417[20] 6449[12]

See Vermont *Rebecca Bastiman* a64 70
8 b g Kyllachy Orange Lily (Royal Applause)
1059[5] 1721[3] 2120[2] 2808[3] 3009[6] 3779[5] 4295[9] 4691[4] 5282[5] (5804) 6098[2] 6341[4] 6680[11] 6813[4]

See You After (IRE) *Sir Mark Prescott Bt*
2 b c Siyouni(FR) Zaziyra (IRE) (Dalakhani (IRE))
6850[8] 7064[11]

See You Mush *Chris Dwyer* a58 4
2 b g Archipenko(USA) Snow Shoes (Sri Pekan (USA))
5631[7] 6141[7] 6524[10] *6895[9]*

See Your Starr (FR) *Y Gourraud* a78 76
3 b g Siyouni(FR) Bright Style (FR) (Fasliyev (USA))
972a[6]

See You Soon (FR) *N Caullery* a83 60
5 b h Zafeen(FR) Summer Dance (FR) (Machiavellian (USA))
1034a[2]

See You When (IRE) *Richard Hannon* a68 76
3 b g Acclamation Lighthouse (Warning)
2998[5] 3411[5] *4010[13]* 4519[4] 4908[9] 6576[4] 7076[4] *7529[12]*

Seffeara (CAN) *Steve Owens* a78
4 b g Old Forester(USA) Town Dance (CAN) (Dance Brightly (CAN))
6400a[7]

Sefri (USA) *E Charpy* a105 85
6 b g Jazil(USA) Taseel (USA) (Danzig (USA))
(309a) 845a[9]

Sehail (USA) *George Peckham* a3
3 b g Giant's Causeway(USA) Persist (USA) (Tiznow (USA))
7753[10]

Sehayli (IRE) *Lee Carter* a75 70
3 b g Iffraaj Quaich (Danehill (USA))
1577[3] ◆ 2686[2] 3014[3] 4235[4] *4939[3]* 6265[11] *6629[12] 8163[11] 8365[7] 8555[12]*

Seismos (IRE) *Marco Botti* a106 103
8 ch g Dalakhani(IRE) Sasuela (GER) (Dashing Blade)
1273[3] 1772[8] *3658[7]* 5655[9] 7150[U]

Sekuras Girl (IRE) *Clive Mulhall* a52 56
4 b m Approve(IRE) Alinda (IRE) (Revoque (IRE))
2053[15] 4729[8]

Selection (FR) *William Haggas* a69 72
3 ch g Siyouni(FR) Perspective (FR) (Funambule (USA))
6104[4] 7009[3] *7384[7]*

Selena Rose *Ronald Harris* a30 35
3 b f Stimulation(IRE) Dot Hill (Refuse To Bend (IRE))
735[7] 947[7] 1141[11]

Sellingallthetime (IRE) *Michael Appleby* a75 87
5 ch g Tamayuz Anthyllis (GER) (Lycius (USA))
2163[9] 2688[4] 3129[10] 4115[8] 4687[5] 5381[7] 6165[5] 6794[7]

Semana Santa *David Barron* a78 77
3 b f Arabian Gleam La Zamora (Lujain (USA))
935[3] ◆ *(1181)* 2742[5] *3611[3]* 3978[6] 4985[2] 5478[7] *5969[2]* 6216[3]

Semeen *Fawzi Abdulla Nass* a30 92
7 b g Dubawi(IRE) Zeeba (IRE) (Barathea (IRE))
453a[7] *627a[13]*

Semilla (FR) *A Schaerer* 93
5 b m Dunkerque(FR) Rose Rose (USA) (Cozzene (USA))
665a[3]

Semille Obon *Jamie Poulton* a53
4 rg g Royal Applause Starparty (USA) (Cozzene (USA))
1837[4] 2647[9]

Seminole Dream (IRE) *Philip Kirby* a41 40
2 ch f Arcano(IRE) Seminole Lass (USA) (Indian Charlie (USA))
2637[11] 2956[5] 3290[9] 5165[8] *5528[4]* 6026[11]

Sempre Medici (FR) *W P Mullins* 94
6 b g Medicean Sambala (IRE) (Danehill Dancer (IRE))
3246[13]

Semra (USA) *Marco Botti* a76 53
3 b f Candy Ride(ARG) Smara (USA) (Storm Cat (USA))
102[2] (441) 1432[2] ◆ *3034[4]* 3821[7]

Senator *Richard Fahey* 90
2 ch g Frankel Red Bloom (Selkirk (USA))
(4762) (5536) ◆ 6285[7]

Send Up (IRE) *Sir Mark Prescott Bt* a49 50
2 b f Fastnet Rock(AUS) Briolette (IRE) (Sadler's Wells (USA))
6472[5] *6624[9]*

Senga (USA) *P Bary* 109
2 b f Blame(USA) Beta Leo (USA) (A.P. Indy (USA))
6986a[4]

Seniority *William Haggas* 86
2 ch c Dubawi(IRE) Anna Palariva (IRE) (Caerleon (USA))
(5121) ◆ 5646[10]

Sennockian Song *Mark Johnston* a70 67
3 ch g New Approach(IRE) Chorist (Pivotal)
3348[3] 3636[10] 7223[9] *7531[2] 7732[7] 8134[5] 8318[4]*

Sennockian Star *Mark Johnston* a90 90
6 ch g Rock Of Gibraltar(IRE) Chorist (Pivotal)
1569[10] 1972[6] 2482[6] 2866[8] *3304[4] 3785[8]* 4129[3] 4300[5] 4680[4] 5173[3] 5651[4] 5964[2] *6089[2]* 6301[4] 6573[8] 6794[3] 7222[3] 7535[4] *7869[5] 8317[2] 8539[5] 8594[4]*

Senor Firecracker (IRE) *Brett Johnson* a54 52
4 b g Acclamation Miss Eze (Danehill Dancer (IRE))
790[5]

Senor George (IRE) *Simon Hodgson* a70 62
9 b g Traditionally(USA) Mrs St George (IRE) (Orpen (USA))
862[7] 1057[2] ◆ *1236[4]* 1747[8] *2605[9]* 3002[5] 3121[4] 5326[8] 6022[6] *6871[7] 7464[5] 8038[9]*

Senrima (IRE) *Brian Meehan* a59 49
4 b g High Chaparral(IRE) Alexander Divine (Halling (USA))
2897[15] 4396[6] *6050[9] 6591[6]*

Sense Of Snow (IRE) *William Muir* 15
3 ch c Kyllachy Miss Smilla (Red Ransom (USA))
5388[10] 6317[14] 7572[10] *7778[7]*

Sense Of Victory (IRE) *J P Murtagh* 78
4 b m Montjeu(IRE) Shaanara (IRE) (Darshaan)
2114a[4]

Senses Of Dubai *Jamie Osborne* a74 75
3 b g Royal Applause Umseyat (USA) (Arch (USA))
1577[5] 2321[4] 7616[3] 7894[2] (8247)

Sensible Girl (IRE) *Tracey Collins* a52 16
4 b m Moss Vale(IRE) Sensible Lady (Tobougg (IRE))
5900a[20]

Sentiero Italia (USA) *Kiaran McLaughlin* 114
4 b m Medaglia d'Oro(USA) Golden Way (IRE) (Cadeaux Genereux)
5914a[3] 7831a[10]

Sentinel *Charlie Fellowes* a57 32
2 b c Sepoy(AUS) Baralinka (IRE) (Barathea (IRE))
7818[10] *8066[6] 8243[9]*

Senza Una Donna *Hughie Morrison* a61 86
3 b g Sir Percy Sensationally (Montjeu (IRE))
2615[7] (3135) 4293[3] (4956) (5574) 6804[6]

Sepal (USA) *Charles Hills* a67 79
3 b f Afleet Alex(USA) Faraway Flower (USA) (Distant View (USA))
1960[4] 2973[3] 4207[4] 4761[5] *6922[5]*

Seprani *Marco Botti* a62 61
2 b f Sepoy(AUS) King's Guest (IRE) (King's Best (USA))
3037[7] *3647[6] 4195[6]* 5257[2] *5806[4] 7143[11] 7615[2] 8174[5]*

September Issue *Gay Kelleway* a83 76
3 b g Dutch Art Alexander Ballet (Mind Games)
(935) 1115[5] 2002[5] 2981[2] *(3611)* 4803[9] *7892[4] 8176[12]*

September Stars (IRE) *Ralph Beckett* a85 100
3 ch f Sea The Stars(IRE) Altesse Imperiale (IRE) (Rock Of Gibraltar (IRE))
1483[2] 2394[5] *3990[2]* (4709) (4953) 5645[9] 6746[8]

Septimius (IRE) *E J O'Neill* a29
2 b f Requinto(IRE) Beenablaw (IRE) (Alzao (USA))
8420a[15]

Seraffimo *Sharon Watt* 52
4 ch g Monsieur Bond(IRE) Hula Ballew (Weldnaas (USA))
1121[9]

Serangoon *Michael Appleby* a48 30
3 b f Authorized(IRE) Sharp Dresser (USA) (Diesis)
5300[7] 5527[7] 6520[6]

Seraphima *Lisa Williamson* a49 59
6 b m Fusaichi Pegasus(USA) Millestan (IRE) (Invincible Spirit (IRE))
75[6] 217[4] 504[2] 732[6] 919[4] 970[9] 1164[8] 5110[8] *5807[9] 6586[7]*

Serenada *Roger Varian* 80
2 b f Azamour(IRE) Serres (IRE) (Daylami (IRE))
7543[3] ◆

Serenade The Stars (IRE) *James Tate* a56
2 b c Sea The Stars(IRE) Silent Serenade (Bertolini (USA))
7907[9] 8073[10] 8227[7]

Serena Grae *Marcus Tregoning* a90 94
5 gr m Arakan(USA) Success Story (Sharrood (USA))
66[11] (2685) *3278[2]* 5144[7]

Serendib's Glory (IRE) *Julia Feilden* a60 38
3 b f Holy Roman Emperor(IRE) Rose Of Mooncoin (IRE) (Brief Truce (USA))
441[4] 618[5] ◆ *817[6] 1148[3]* 1670[9] *2107[8]* 3080[12] *4525[7]* 5338[11] *7256[10]*

Serengeti Sky (USA) *Charlie Appleby* 79
2 b c Lonhro(AUS) Wild Idle (USA) (Seeking The Gold (USA))
4390[3] (4786) 5644[3] 6525[3]

Serenity Dove *K R Burke* 52
2 b f Harbour Watch(IRE) Khumba Mela (IRE) (Hero's Honor (USA))
2404[5] 2970[4] 3477[5] 4442[5]

Serenity Now (IRE) *Brian Ellison* a80 76
8 b g Key Of Luck(USA) Imdina (IRE) (Soviet Star (USA))
8476[4] ◆

Serenu (FR) *D Retif* a69 82
6 gr g Walk In The Park(IRE) Doraflor (FR) (Kendor (FR))
6178a[8]

Serez (IRE) *Charley Rossi* a83 83
6 b h Shamardal(USA) Afya (Oasis Dream)
3376a[3]

Serienholde (GER) *A Wohler* 106
3 b f Soldier Hollow Saldenehre (GER) (Highest Honor (FR))
(5220a) 6175a[5] 6822a[8]

Serradura (IRE) *Charles Hills* a71 63
3 b f Acclamation Days Of Summer (IRE) (Bachelor Duke (USA))
1812[6] 3649[5] 4556[5] *6418[2]* 6790[10] *7364[8]*

Sersar *Ismail Mohammed* 81
2 b c Dream Ahead(USA) Libys Dream (IRE) (Invincible Spirit (IRE))
6486[4] ◆ 6952[3] ◆ 7495[2]

Servantes (IRE) *B Legros* a29 26
5 b g Invincible Spirit(IRE) Sail (IRE) (Sadler's Wells (USA))
1034a[11]

Servo (IRE) *Alan Swinbank* a52 61
2 b c Power Parade Scene (USA) (Parade Ground (USA))
2301[4] 3223[8] 3854[7] *5840[7]*

Set In Stone (IRE) *John Patrick Shanahan* 80
2 b f Famous Name Storminateacup (IRE) (Galileo (IRE))
7056[6]

Settle For Red (IRE) *David Marnane* a73 74
6 ch g Redback Balmy Choice (IRE) (Balla Cove)
5096a[4]

Settle Petal *Pat Phelan* a64
2 b f Peintre Celebre(USA) Shall We Dance (Rambo Dancer (CAN))
7733[10] 8355[3] 8591[3]

Settler's Son (IRE) *J Michal* 105
5 b g Whipper(USA) Settler (Darshaan)
6396a[3] 7088a[7] 7569a[10]

Seve *Tom Dascombe* a96 96
4 ch g Exceed And Excel(AUS) Flamenco Dancer (Mark Of Esteem (IRE))
2138 677[8] 1968[11] 2504[2] 4112[9] 4373[7] 4632[4] 5641[8] 6234[6] ◆ 6793[17] 7752[7] (8032) 8232[8] 8463[4]

Seven Clans (IRE) *Neil Mulholland* a64 51
4 b g Cape Cross(IRE) Cherokee Rose (IRE) (Dancing Brave (USA))
4088[7] 4463[7] 5207[6] 8035[10] 8190[2]

Seven Heavens *John Gosden* 104
2 b c Frankel Heaven Sent (Pivotal)
(4075) (5997) 7149[7]

Sevenleft (IRE) *Ms Sheila Lavery* a98 97
3 br c Manduro(GER) Fleeting Affair (USA) (Gone West (USA))
2716a[3] 3299[21] 6355a[9] (7523a)

Seven Summits (IRE) *Sophie Leech* a41 42
9 b g Danehill Dancer(IRE) Mandavilla (IRE) (Sadler's Wells (USA))
514[6] 870[11] 2462[5] 4716[7]

Seventh Heaven (IRE) *A P O'Brien* a95 121
3 b f Galileo(IRE) La Traviata (USA) (Johannesburg (USA))
(2035) 2869[6] (4416a) (5586) 7351[5] 7831a[4] ◆

Seventii *Robert Eddery* 43
2 b f Medicean Lowndes (Rail Link)
7441[10]

Several (USA) *Kevin Frost* a72
4 b g Rock Hard Ten(USA) Proud Fact (USA) (Known Fact (USA))
164[7] 435[9] 862[11] 1182[8] 6411[12]

Severus (GER) *Des Donovan* a83 80
6 b g Shirocco(GER) Shikoku (Green Desert (USA))
2401[9] 2821[2] 3612[5] 4748a[2] 6984a[8] 7391a[4] 7738[5] (8206)

Sewn Up *Keith Dalgleish* a72 56
6 ch g Compton Place Broughton Bounty (Bahamian Bounty)
36[4] 144[2] 239[4] 703[9] 857[2]

Sexton Blake (IRE) *Gary Moore* a69 56
3 b g Rip Van Winkle(IRE) Soviet Treat (IRE) (Ashkalani (IRE))
2005[4] 3406[5] 4269[8] 5259[6] 6592[6] 7725[6] 8064[4] 8248[5]

Sexy Secret *Lydia Pearce* a62 60
5 b g Sakhee's Secret Orange Walk (IRE) (Alzao (USA))
107[10] (326) 1578[2] 3072[4] 3620[4] (4566) 5739[3] 6406[8] 7231[2] 8155[9]

Seyadah *Marco Botti* a73 64
2 ch f Raven's Pass(USA) Festivale (IRE) (Invincible Spirit (IRE))
5036[6] 7049[5] 7855[7]

Seyasah (IRE) *Chris Wall* a66 65
2 b f Casamento(IRE) Defensive Boast (USA) (El Gran Senor (USA))
3818[7] 4759[7] 6413[5] ◆ 7071[8]

Seychelloise *Sir Mark Prescott Bt* a101 59
4 b m Pivotal Starlit Sands (Oasis Dream)
86[2] 503[5] 5441a[7] 6371[2] (6627) 7520a[13] 8029[2] 8563a[7]

Sfumato *Roger Charlton* 81
2 br g Bated Breath Modern Look (Zamindar (USA))
3058[10] 4552[5] ◆ 5304[2] (6034)

Shaan (IRE) *Richard Hannon* a86 97
3 b f Iffraaj Evening Time (IRE) (Keltos (FR))
(163) 1960[2] 2412[3] (4403) 4757[4] ◆

Shaaqaaf (IRE) *John Gosden* a70
2 b f Sepoy(AUS) Burke's Rock (Cape Cross (IRE))
7278[3] ◆ 7647[4]

Shabbab (FR) *H-F Devin* a81 89
3 b g Siyouni(FR) Floride (IRE) (Sadler's Wells (USA))
6911a[3]

Shabbah (IRE) *Sir Michael Stoute* a54 94
3 br c Sea The Stars(IRE) Alizaya (IRE) (Highest Honor (FR))
(1738) (2012) (3110) 4131[2] 4863[11] 6715[4]

Shabeeb (USA) *Roger Varian* 103
3 b c Smart Strike(CAN) Sortita (GER) (Monsun (GER))
(2414) (2889) ◆ 4059[5] 6715[6]

Shabeeh (IRE) *Mark Johnston* a71 78
2 b g Raven's Pass(USA) Mid Mon Lady (IRE) (Danetime (IRE))
5593[2] 5997[2] 6562[4] 7812[4] 8175[6] 8353[9]

Shackled N Drawn (USA) *Peter Hedger* a83 84
4 b g Candy Ride(ARG) Cajun Flash (USA) (Bertrando (USA))
1803[2] (2040) ◆ 2768[4] 4198[9] 5305[7] 5669[8] 8032[4] 8280[12]

Shackles *Alistair Whillans* a45 48
2 b g Equiano(FR) Silent Waters (Polish Precedent (USA))
6904[7] 7432[9] 7741[9]

Shadad (IRE) *Ralph Beckett* a78 56
3 b g Zamindar(USA) Tender Morn (USA) (Dayjur (USA))
2375[4] 2780[2] (3475) 4157[10]

Shadagann (IRE) *M Halford* a84 89
6 b g Invincible Spirit(IRE) Shamadara (IRE) (Kahyasi)
3630a[4]

Shadele (IRE) *Jeremy Noseda* a65 44
3 b f Rip Van Winkle(IRE) Zadalla (Zaha (CAN))
8388[4]

Shaden (IRE) *George Scott* 105
3 b f Kodiac Lady Avenger (IRE) (Namid)
3158[7]

Shades Of Silver *Ed de Giles* a94 94
6 b g Dansili Silver Pivotal (IRE) (Pivotal)
1417[2] 1987[11] 2932[8] 3387[16] 3784[7]

Shadow Beauty *Marco Botti* a63
2 b c Pivotal Rivara (Red Ransom (USA))
8277[2]

Shadow Game *Mark Johnston* a72 81
3 b c Shamardal(USA) Victoria Star (IRE) (Danehill (USA))
1176[3] 2322[4] 3062[4] 3286[3] (3478) 3945[10]

Shadow Hunter (IRE) *Hugo Palmer* a82 97
3 b f Arcano(IRE) Sweet Irish (Shamardal (USA))
821[3] 1453[3] 2192[4] 3392[5] 6056[5] 6939[9]

Shadow Of Hercules (IRE) *Michael Mullineaux* a26 39
2 ch c Roderic O'Connor(IRE) Baltic Princess (FR) (Peintre Celebre (USA))
3805[9] 4545[10] 5637[10] 6681[14] 7954[7]

Shadow Of The Day *Lee James* 42
9 b g Sugarfoot She Who Dares Wins (Atraf)
4228[10] 4772[14]

Shadow Rock (IRE) *Richard Hannon* a51 84
4 gr g Verglas(IRE) Ice Rock (IRE) (Rock Of Gibraltar (IRE))
261[10]

Shadow Sadness (GER) *C Von Der Recke* 104
4 b h Soldier Hollow Shadow Queen (GER) (Lando (GER))
2075a[6]

Shadow Spirit *Iain Jardine* a76 73
3 b f Makfi Highland Shot (Selkirk (USA))
2012[7] 2339[3] 3071[4] 3853[6] 5527[3] 5822[2] 6856[5] 7435[2] 7853[8] 8090[3] 8524[5]

Shadowtime *Tracy Waggott* a46 61
11 b g Singspiel(IRE) Massomah (USA) (Seeking The Gold (USA))
3011[8] 3838[4] 4454[4] 5030[7]

Shadow Warrior *Paul D'Arcy* a70 54
2 b g Born To Sea(IRE) Dolcetto (IRE) (Danehill Dancer (IRE))
3524[6] 5332[9] 6034[9] 7688[2]

Shadow Wing (IRE) *Ann Stokell* a51 41
2 ch f Sakhee's Secret Go Maggie Go (IRE) (Kheleyf (USA))
1641[5] 2007[9] 3290[5] 4002[4] 4842[4] 6141[5] 6419[8] 6887[5] 7296[6] 7845[6]

Shady McCoy (USA) *Ian Williams* a33 96
6 b g English Channel(USA) Raw Gold (USA) (Rahy (USA))
3890[5] (4758) 5871[6] 6788[2] 7121[9] 7699[4] 7821[11]

Shafafya *Ed Dunlop* a73 90
3 b f Shamardal(USA) Tanaghum (Darshaan)
1630[2] 2654[3] (3291) 3846[2] 5123[8] 6115[5] 6948[7]

Shagaf (USA) *Chad C Brown* a105
3 b c Bernardini(USA) Muhaawara (USA) (Unbridled's Song (USA))
2063a[P]

Shahaama *Jane Chapple-Hyam* a59 69
3 br f Showcasing Oystermouth (Averti (IRE))
1414[7] ◆ 1814[7] 2039[3] 3038[4] 3126[2] (3353) 4878[6] 5330[11] 6291[4] 6835[4] 7364[5] 7912[9] 8457[11]

Shahabad *Roger Varian* a73
3 b f Shamardal(USA) Gulbarg (Dubawi (IRE))
8075[2]

Shahbar *Marco Botti* 92
3 b g Champs Elysees Dahama (Green Desert (USA))
1220[4] 2244[11] 3077[4] (3824) 5074[5]

Shah Of Armaan (IRE) *Kevin Ryan* a75 73
3 b g Fastnet Rock(AUS) Queen Of Tara (IRE) (Sadler's Wells (USA))
6617[2] ◆ 7009[5] 7583[3] 7942[4] 8286[6]

Shahroze (IRE) *M Halford* a78 57
2 b c Holy Roman Emperor(IRE) Shareen (IRE) (Bahri (USA))
7917a[2]

Shaishee (USA) *M Al Mheiri* a105 78
6 br g Indian Charlie(USA) Hatpin (USA) (Smart Strike (CAN))
719a[4] 840a[4]

Shaiyem (IRE) *Richard Hannon* a80 88
3 b c Starspangledbanner(AUS) Shaanbar (IRE) (Darshaan)
1809[2] ◆ (2029) 2473[10]

Shakabula (IRE) *Brian Ellison* a57
2 b g Kheleyf(USA) Tinaar (USA) (Giant's Causeway (USA))
3654[8] 5067[7] 5966[8] 7109[11]

Shaka Zulu (IRE) *Ibrahim Al Malki* a74 81
3 b g Holy Roman Emperor(IRE) High Figurine (IRE) (High Chaparral (IRE))
756a[14]

Shake And Bakes *Marjorie Fife* 37
2 b g Major Cadeaux Mancunian Way (Green Desert (USA))
3283[10] 3939[8] 4890[7]

Shake The Bucket (IRE) *Niall Madden* a64 55
9 b g Ashkalani(IRE) San Diego (IRE) (Leading Counsel (USA))
5900a[4]

Shakko (FR) *Charley Rossi* a66 65
6 b h Sulamani(IRE) Shakkirah (FR) (Octagonal (NZ))
5452a[11]

Shakopee *Luca Cumani* a102 100
4 b g High Chaparral(IRE) Tentpole (USA) (Rainbow Quest (USA))
2214[4] 2752[5] (4300) 4731[14] 5611[2] 6118[17] 6709[7] (7365)

Shakshuka (IRE) *Seamus Mullins* a45 38
4 b m Dark Angel(IRE) Tropical Moment (IRE) (Cape Cross (IRE))
7627[11] 7904[7] 8247[6]

Shalaa (IRE) *John Gosden* 120
3 b c Invincible Spirit(IRE) Ghurra (USA) (War Chant (USA))
(6941) 7350[10]

Shalakar (FR) *M Delzangles* 97
3 b g Cape Cross(IRE) Shalanaya (IRE) (Lomitas)
5448a[6] 7456a[12] 7946a[8]

Shalalee (SWE) *Wido Neuroth* 93
4 ch m Strategic Prince The Stick (Singspiel (IRE))
7395a[3]

Shalaman (IRE) *David Marnane* a100 99
7 b g Oratorio(IRE) Shalama (IRE) (Kahyasi)
829a[4] 1067[8]

Shalambar (IRE) *Tony Carroll* a73 62
10 gr g Dalakhani(IRE) Shalama (IRE) (Kahyasi)
138[2] (289) 1177[2] 1854[11] 2370[4] 3099[9]

Shalamzar (FR) *Micky Hammond* a47 83
7 ch g Selkirk(USA) Shamalana (IRE) (Sinndar (IRE))
1248[4] 2093[9] (2616) 3117[10] 7043[8]

Shalianzi (IRE) *Gary Moore* a51 56
6 b g Azamour(IRE) Shalama (IRE) (Kahyasi)
4637[4]

Shalimah (IRE) *Clive Cox* a68 77
4 br g Dark Angel(IRE) Jemima's Art (Fantastic Light (USA))
(3095) 4158[5] 4785[5] 6065[6] 7274[6] 7507[6] 7987[4]

Shall We (IRE) *Sir Michael Stoute* a68 102
3 b f Dansili Insight (FR) (Sadler's Wells (USA))
1609[2] (2183) 3297[5] 4400[7] 6747[8] 7393a[2]

Shamaal Nibras (USA) *Doug Watson* a101 104
7 b g First Samurai(USA) Sashay Away (USA) (Farma Way (USA))
309a[6] 540a[5] 812a[8]

Shamaheart (IRE) *Geoffrey Harker* a74 89
6 b g Shamardal(USA) Encouragement (Royal Applause)
1124[6] 1488[10] 2092[2] ◆ 2345[6] (2773) 3327[3] 3708[2] 4231[2] 4497[2] (4807) (5179) 5866[6] 6217[4] 6956[5] 7702[5] 7796[7]

Shamal *A bin Harmash* a51
6 b g Exceed And Excel(AUS) Miss Meltemi (IRE) (Miswaki Tern (USA))
8a[8]

Shamalgan (FR) *Artut Resulov* a62 75
9 ch h Footstepsinthesand Genevale (FR) (Unfuwain (USA))
7565a[6]

Shamar (FR) *R K Watson* a74 85
8 br g Dr Fong(USA) Shamalana (IRE) (Sinndar (IRE))
2114a[13] 5620a[11]

Shambra (IRE) *James Tate* a59 48
2 b f Clodovil(IRE) Shambodia (IRE) (Petardia)
6625[10] 7297[5] 7977[6]

Shamlan (IRE) *Johnny Farrelly* a77 45
4 br g Shamardal(USA) Atamana (IRE) (Lahib (USA))
67[8] 683[11] (1186) 1652[8] 3989[9] 5810[9] 6138[11] 6510[8] 6872[10] 7368[12]

Shamreen (IRE) *D K Weld* 106
3 b f Dubawi(IRE) Shareen (IRE) (Bahri (USA))
3202a[2] 5002a[4] (6383a)

Shamrokh (IRE) *John Gosden* a63
2 b c Invincible Spirit(IRE) Alshakr (Bahri (USA))
8486[7]

Shamsaya (IRE) *Simon Crisford* a83 93
2 b f Shamardal(USA) Masaya (Dansili)
(2800) 3663[4] 4297[2] 5510[4] (6292) ◆ 6555[12] 7893[7]

Shamshon (IRE) *Jamie Osborne* a102 101
5 b g Invincible Spirit(IRE) Greenisland (IRE) (Fasliyev (USA))
1083[6] 2188[10] 3277[5] 3800[5] (4198) 4584[4] 4862[14] 5648[4] 6112[10] 6327[8] 6627[5] (6944)

Shan Dun na nGall (IRE) *Amy Murphy* a59 55
5 b g Shantou(USA) Omanah (USA) (Kayrawan (USA))
(8180) (8309) 8540[4]

Shanghai Beauty (IRE) *K J Condon* a76 86
4 b m Jeremy(USA) Shanghai Visit (IRE) (Peintre Celebre (USA))
1015a[9] 5441a[6] 6819a[13] 7475a[3]

Shanghai Glory (IRE) *Charles Hills* a72 105
3 ch g Exceed And Excel(AUS) Hecuba (Hector Protector (USA))
2186[2] (3144) 3414[2] (3800) 5389[14] 6232[4] (7191a)

Shannah Bint Eric *Kevin Ryan* 35
2 ch f Poet's Voice Crystal Mountain (USA) (Monashee Mountain (USA))
4603[11] 6679[9]

Shannon *Robyn Brisland* 54
2 b f Big Bad Bob(IRE) Morena Park (Pivotal)
6214[5] 6524[6] 6950[16]

Shaqoos (FR) *Jo Hughes* a40 22
2 ch f Naaqoos Shemrana (USA) (Woodman (USA))
4965a[8] 6208[7] 7927a[6] 8237[6]

Sharaakah (IRE) *Ed Dunlop* 100
3 b f Roderic O'Connor(IRE) Lanark Belle (Selkirk (USA))
3274[3] 3911[3] 4651[4] 5158[9] 5588[9] 6947[4] ◆ 7472[3]

Shared Equity *Jedd O'Keeffe* 109
5 b g Elnadim(USA) Pelican Key (IRE) (Mujadil (USA))
1197[5] ◆ 1627[8] 2898[2] 3386[10] 4136[6] 7497[10]

Shareni (IRE) *Zoe Davison* 51
7 b g Azamour(IRE) Sharesha (IRE) (Ashkalani (IRE))
1854[13] 2588[3] 3498[11]

Shargiah (IRE) *Roger Varian* 80
3 ch g New Approach(IRE) Zacheta (Polish Precedent (USA))
2541[7] 3412[5] (3951) ◆

Sharjah (IRE) *Andrew Slattery* a80 78
6 b g Shamardal(USA) Lunar Lustre (IRE) (Desert Prince (IRE))
(2369) (3751)

Sharja Queen *Roger Varian* 112
3 b f Pivotal Dubai Queen (USA) (Kingmambo (USA))
1888[15] 3593[2] (4160) ◆ 5307[5] (6948) 7568a[6]

Sharpalo (FR) *Y Durepaire* a95 80
4 b g Shamardal(USA) Pony Girl (IRE) (Darshaan)
660a[4]

Sharp Boy (IRE) *Stuart Williams* a58 45
3 b g Arcano(IRE) Melanesia (IRE) (Chevalier (IRE))
5168[9] 5474[5] 5748[4] 7201[4]

Sharp Defence (USA) *S Seemar* a82 78
2 br c First Defence(USA) Jazz Drummer (USA) (Dixieland Band (USA))
8574a[7]

Sharp Jack *Tom Dascombe* a45 29
3 ch g Pivotal Sharp Terms (Kris)
1451[0] 4546[10] 5529[10]

Sharp Sword (IRE) *Neil Mulholland* a78 57
5 ch g King's Best(USA) Pictavia (IRE) (Sinndar (IRE))
330[6] 693[8] 899[6] 2369[7] 3125[8]

Shavaughn *Alexandra Dunn*
4 b m Kheleyf(USA) Shannon Falls (FR) (Turgeon (USA))
4516[P] 4730[10]

Shawaahid (IRE) *Richard Hannon* a91 99
3 b g Elnadim(USA) Vexatious (IRE) (Shamardal (USA))
(5246) 5878[2] 6298[2] 7153[8]

Shawami (IRE) *Mick Channon* 65
2 b f Acclamation Valeur (Rock Of Gibraltar (IRE))
2467[7] 6548[2] 6882[4] 7228[10]

Shawkantango *Derek Shaw* a73 58
9 b g Piccolo Kitty Kitty Cancan (Warrshan (USA))
21[3] 176[7]

Shaw Ting *Michael Appleby* a60 75
4 b m Winker Watson Shawhill (Dr Fong (USA))
802[4] 1201[5] 2045[4] 2507[6]

Shearian *Declan Carroll* a69 49
6 b g Royal Applause Regal Asset (USA) (Regal Classic (CAN))
179[3] 429[10] 939[8] 1120[13] 1845[9] 3421[9] 5729[13] 5887[7] (8471)

Shebebi (USA) *Doug Watson* a70 91
6 b g Mr Greeley(USA) Tashawak (IRE) (Night Shift (USA))
229a[6]

Sheepscar Lad (IRE) *Nigel Tinkler* 72
2 b g Arcano(IRE) Piccadilly Filly (IRE) (Exceed And Excel (AUS))
3222[8] 3873[2] 4405[5] 5433[2] 5727[4] 6010[10] 6515[4] 7122[7] 7407[5]

Sheer Honesty *Anabel K Murphy* a66 76
4 b m Hellvelyn Honesty Pays (Dr Fong (USA))
6675 1387[12] 5010[7] 5503[12]

Sheer Intensity (IRE) *David Evans* a63 59
3 ch f Dutch Art Sheer Elegance (IRE) (Pivotal)
8258[3]

Shee's Lucky *Mark Johnston* a67
2 b f Yorgunnabelucky(USA) She's The Lady (Unfuwain (USA))
8073[3] 8237[7] 8397[4] 8537[6]

Sheikh The Reins (IRE) *John Best* a58 53
7 b g Iffraaj Wychwood Wanderer (IRE) (Barathea (IRE))
1262[6] 1413[11] 2323[5] 2901[8]

Sheikhzayedroad *David Simcock* 117
7 b g Dubawi(IRE) Royal Secrets (IRE) (Highest Honor (FR))
(811a) 1107a[8] 3298[3] 4799[3] (6284) (7349)

Sheikspear *Joseph Tuite* a77 64
2 b c Bahamian Bounty Crinkle (IRE) (Distant Relative)
4981[4] 7064[2] 7578[4]

Sheila's Buddy *J S Moore* a89 83
7 ch g Reel Buddy(USA) Loreto Rose (Lahib (USA))
121[2] (656) 1001[3] 1716[9] 3557[9] 7295a[6]

Sheila's Fancy (IRE) *J S Moore* a50
2 ch g Casamento(IRE) Fancy Vivid (IRE) (Galileo (IRE))
7962[11]

Sheila's Lad (IRE) *D Windrif* 72
2 b g Lilbourne Lad(IRE) Lady Dottie (IRE) (Motivator)
1316[3] 1543[2] 1741[3] 2724a[2] 3006a[2]

Sheila's Palace *J S Moore* a57 66
2 ch f Sakhee's Secret Loreto Rose (Lahib (USA))
3231[4] 4083[2] 4706[3] 5542[6] 5569 [5] 7258[3] 8027[4]

Sheila's Return *Bryan Smart* a56 55
2 ch f Bated Breath Deora De (Night Shift (USA))
1621[6] 2119[6] 3805[7] 4679[7] 5364[2] 6419[6] 6678[4] 7110[2] 7750[4]

Sheila's Treat (IRE) *Denis Coakley* a71 65
3 b g Frozen Power(IRE) Bonny Rose (Zaha (CAN))
1992[7] 3110[6] 3558[4] 4463[6] 5013[9] 5503[11]

She Is No Lady *Ralph Beckett* a98 105
4 b m Lope De Vega(IRE) Capestar (IRE) (Cape Cross (IRE))
2433[2] (3278) 3913[2] 5655[14] (7088a)

Shell Bay (USA) *Richard Hannon* a93 94
4 b g Hard Spun(USA) Rebel Account (USA) (Dixieland Band (USA))
2752[8] 2897[14] 3785[3] 4838[6] 5647[8] 5874[5] 6209[5] 6573[13]

Shelneverwalkalone *Ivan Furtado*
2 b f Captain Gerrard(IRE) Rabarama (Xaar)
2970[10]

She Loves You *Roger Charlton* a73 84
5 b m Lawman(FR) On Fair Stage (IRE) (Sadler's Wells (USA))
58[6]

Sheltered Waters *Eve Johnson Houghton* a43
2 b f Aqlaam Velvet Waters (Unfuwain (USA))
7458[8]

Shenanigans (IRE) *Roger Varian* a80
2 b f Arcano(IRE) Ladylishandra (IRE) (Mujadil (USA))
7762[4] 7977[2] (8139)

Sheng Chi Dragon (IRE) *K R Burke* a31 5
2 ch c Dragon Pulse(IRE) Shin Feign (USA) (El Prado (IRE))
6053[10] 6515[11] 6741[8]

Shepherd's Purse *Joseph G Murphy* a94 96
4 b g Pastoral Pursuits Neyraan (Lujain (USA))
3696a[10] 4415a[15] 7523a[9] 7803a[4]

Sheppard's Gift *Tim Easterby* 51
2 b f Dick Turpin(IRE) Sheppard's Watch (Night Shift (USA))
2265[5] 2612[6] 2970[7] 3114[11] 4509[5] 5853[5] 6446[11]

Sherbert *Richard Hannon* 33
2 b f Power Original (Caerleon (USA))
7314[10]

Sherdat (IRE) *Roger Varian* a73 45
3 b f Shirocco(GER) Jathaabeh (Nashwan (USA))
1704[3] 2398[5] *2767[11]*

Shere Calm (FR) *G Doleuze* a75 62
3 gr g Peer Gynt(JPN) Blowaway (FR) (Linamix (FR))
5385a[7]

Sheriff Garrett (IRE) *Tim Easterby* 64
2 b g Lawman(FR) Few Are Chosen (IRE) (Sulamani (IRE))
4371[13] 4966[4] 5778[5] 6213[8] 6681[11]

Sherman McCoy *Marjorie Fife* a57 71
10 ch g Reset(AUS) Naomi Wildman (USA) (Kingmambo (USA))
1253[3] 1561[5] 2678[3] 3547[7] 3774[2] 4004[5] 4934[7] 6058[2] 6566[4] 7043[4] 7508[3] *8134[9]*

She's All Mine *Richard Hannon* a61 68
3 b f Sakhee's Secret I'm All Yours (IRE) (High Chaparral (IRE))
1431[4] 1917[2] 2212[9] 2824[6] *3527[6]*

Shes An Art (IRE) *James M Barrett* a80 80
3 br f Excellent Art Ballyronan Girl (IRE) (Elbio)
6200a[10]

She's Electric (IRE) *Keith Dalgleish* a58 70
3 b f Roderic O'Connor(IRE) Maundays Bay (IRE) (Invincible Spirit (IRE))
2422[2] 2533[9] 2906[12] 5273[7] 5539[5] 6501[12] *6921[6] 7601[8] 7795[13]*

She's Gina (GER) *Markus Klug* 100
3 bb f It's Gino(GER) Song Of Night (GER) (Tiger Hill (IRE))
4175a[3] 5220a[6] 6610a[7] 7720a[8]

She's Golden *Ann Duffield* 56
3 br f Sakhee's Secret Action Platinum (IRE) (Act One)
3710[6] 4370[7] 4701[7] 5087[5]

Shesnotforturning (IRE) *Ben Haslam* a34 56
6 b m Refuse To Bend(IRE) Diplomats Daughter (Unfuwain (USA))
5483[14] 6615[2] 6834[6] 7584[11]

She's Not Here (USA) *Victoria H Oliver* a84 104
5 b m Street Cry(IRE) Where's Bailey (USA) (Aljabr (USA))
7171a[5]

She's Rosanna *Steph Hollinshead* 47
2 b f Poet's Voice She Storm (IRE) (Rainbow Quest (USA))
1527[5] 1976[8] 2371[U] 2611[8] *6236[11] 6588[10]* 7768[12]

Shesthedream (IRE) *David O'Meara* a49 67
3 b f Dream Ahead(USA) Tatiana Romanova (USA) (Mr Greeley (USA))
2886[8] 4238[3] 4521[2] 5110[7] *6744[5]* 7335[3]

She's Zoff (IRE) *John Quinn* a45 29
2 b f Zoffany(IRE) Vindication People (USA) (Vindication (USA))
6534[10] *6925[10] 7380[7]*

Shifting Star (IRE) *John Bridger* a77 77
11 ch g Night Shift(USA) Ahshado (Bin Ajwaad (IRE))
1173[7] 1387[5] 1780[4] 3234[2] (3724) 4463[5] *5024[6]* 5965[7] *6656[4]* 7417[3] *7620[4] 7973[5] 8154[13] 8462[8]*

Shift On Sheila *Pam Sly* a60 54
3 b f Aussie Rules(USA) Black Salix (USA) (More Than Ready (USA))
3781[10] 4319[7] *5527[6] 6513[4] 6857[2] 7516[12]*

Shift The Blame *Jimmy Fox* a9
3 b f Bertolini(USA) Michelle Shift (Night Shift (USA))
516[8]

Shikari *Rebecca Bastiman* a15 57
5 ch g Sakhee's Secret Hickleton Lady (IRE) (Kala Shikari)
341[9]

Shillbourne Lad (IRE) *Bill Turner* a29
2 bb g Lilbourne Lad(IRE) Gemma's Delight (IRE) (Clodovil (IRE))
7882[13] 8230[8] 8425[9]

Shillong *H Al Alawi* a68
3 b c Dubawi(IRE) Rainfall (IRE) (Oasis Dream)
8576a[4]

Shiloh *Simon Crisford* a51 23
2 b f Poet's Voice Loveable (Oasis Dream)
7056[10] *8361[9]*

Shimba Hills *Lawney Hill* a78 77
5 b g Sixties Icon Search Party (Rainbow Quest (USA))
256[12] 414[6] 616[3] (2151)

Shimrano (GER) *M Delzangles* 102
4 bb h Monsun(GER) Shimrana (IRE) (Daylami (IRE))
1688a[12]

Shine *Jonathan Portman* a61 61
3 ch f Exceed And Excel(AUS) Sensational Mover (USA) (Theatrical (IRE))
1962[3] 3094[8] 3878[6] 5286[3] 5597[8] 6825[4]

Shine Likeadiamond *Mick Channon* a69 46
3 ch f Atlantic Sport(USA) Solmorin (Fraam)
1167[4] 5826[7] *6101[2]* 6361[8] 6832[10] *7362[4] 7534[6] 7693[6]*

Shingwedzi (SAF) *Ed Dunlop* a52 79
5 b m Trippi(USA) Buffalo Dance (IRE) (Sadler's Wells (USA))
1802[7] 2671[6] 3438[6]

Shining Emerald *A Wohler* 112
5 b g Clodovil(IRE) Janayen (USA) (Zafonic (USA))
(2722a) 7027a[3] 7719a[8]

Shining Romeo *Denis Quinn* a72 71
4 b g Royal Applause Silver Pivotal (IRE) (Pivotal)
618[4] 697[4] 885[7] 1501[9] (1640) 2174[9] *2445[2] 2996[4]* 3354[7] 3823[14] *5130[5] 5529[8]* 7628[U] *7937[2] 8038[2] 8257[7] 8477[7]*

Shiny *Jamie Osborne* a57
2 b c Kyllachy Maysarah (IRE) (Green Desert (USA))
5809[6]

Shiny Line (IRE) *John Butler* a31 54
2 b f Famous Name Faithful Duchess (IRE) (Bachelor Duke (USA))
5809[8] 6208[2] 6733[6]

Ship Canal *Jacqueline Coward* a50 39
4 ch g Major Cadeaux Smooth As Silk (IRE) (Danehill Dancer (IRE))
7848[4] 7960[5] 8134[3] 8386[7] 8497[6]

Shipping Forecast *Brian Meehan* a57 77
2 b g Harbour Watch(IRE) Early Morning Rain (IRE) (Rock Of Gibraltar (IRE))
4128[4] ◆ (5250) 6575[3] *7460[7]*

Shipshape Myfoot *Andrew Reid* a52
3 b f Bahamian Bounty Rise (Polar Falcon (USA))
976[6] 1292[6] 8121[8]

Shipyard (USA) *Michael Appleby* a89 97
7 ch g Pivotal Nadia (Nashwan (USA))
1990[3] 2476[2] 3150[9] 4366[5] 5417[6] 5648[2] 6012[4] 6263[6] 6556[16] 6944[5] 7124[5] 7537[13] ◆

Shirataki (IRE) *Peter Hiatt* a61 59
8 b g Cape Cross(IRE) Noodle Soup (USA) (Alphabet Soup (USA))
84[3] (233) 261[7] ◆ *378[4] 606[3] 653[5] 781[7] 949[7] 1343[7] 2110[6]* 2901[4] *3470[10]* (5208) 5350[3] 5575 [2] 6256[8]

Shirls Son Sam *Chris Fairhurst* a52 53
8 b g Rambling Bear Shirl (Shirley Heights)
199[6] 368[5] 637[7]

Shirocco Cloud *Mrs Ilka Gansera-Leveque* a30
4 b m Shirocco(GER) Cloud Hill (Danehill (USA))
268[7] 384[10] 487[6]

Shivajia (GER) *U Stech* 101
4 ch m Adlerflug(GER) Shivara (GER) (Monsun (GER))
2075a[9] 5454a[4]

Shiver In The River (FR) *G Botti* a72 74
3 b f Orpen(USA) Shiver Stream (IRE) (Cape Cross (IRE))
511a[6] 3546a[4] 5946a[13] 7680a[2]

Shocking Blu *Stefano Botti* 94
4 b h Champs Elysees Princess Angelina (IRE) (Almutawakel)
1516a[5] 2516a[7]

Shogun (IRE) *A P O'Brien* 109
3 b g Fastnet Rock(AUS) Perihelion (IRE) (Galileo (IRE))
1440[3] 2069a[2] 2496a[5] 2896[15] 3679a[7] 4753[3] 5095a[4]

Sholaan (IRE) *D Selvaratnam* a89 78
7 b g Invincible Spirit(IRE) Jazz Up (Cadeaux Genereux)
723a[8]

Shongololo (IRE) *Andrew Balding* 62
3 b g Manduro(GER) Nipping (IRE) (Night Shift (USA))
2459[6] 3464[6] 4017[3] 5013[6] ◆ 5823[4] 7212[6]

Shoofly (IRE) *Martyn Meade* a77 55
3 b f Azamour(IRE) Natural Flair (USA) (Giant's Causeway (USA))
603[5] 880[2] (980) 2224[8] 3615[6] *3991[4]*

Shootingsta (IRE) *Bryan Smart* a87 84
4 b g Fast Company(IRE) Kiva (Indian Ridge)
24[5] 2421[4] 4893[11] *7433[11]*

Shore Step (IRE) *Mick Channon* 98
6 br g Footstepsinthesand Chatham Islands (USA) (Elusive Quality (USA))
1990[4] 4735[13] 5390[11] 5825[6] 6287[9] 6780[5]

Short Work *Ralph Beckett* 84
3 ch g Kyllachy Agony Aunt (Formidable I (USA))
(1894) 2871[9] 3155[4] 3635[3] 5206[4] 6442[5] 6806[2] 7506[13]

Shotgun (FR) *C Boutin* a73 50
4 ch g Muhtathir Bouffeylight (FR) (Sevres Rose (IRE))
3733a[7]

Shot In The Dark (FR) *F Chappet* a100 102
3 b g Dark Angel(IRE) Velvet Revolver (IRE) (Mujahid (USA))
2232a[10]

Shouldertoshoulder *Stuart Williams* a54
2 ch g Paco Boy(IRE) Miss Bond (IRE) (Danehill Dancer (IRE))
8353[8]

Shouranour (IRE) *Alan Brown* a79 91
6 b g Lawman(FR) Sharesha (IRE) (Ashkalani (IRE))
1380[7] 1643[5] *2331[9] 2620[12]* 3166[13] (3717) 3840[5] 4408[6] 4611[7] 5482[9] 6160[14] (7007) (7360) (7593) 7825[7] *8475[14]*

Showbizzy *Richard Fahey* a40 72
3 ch f Showcasing Nellie Ellis (IRE) (Compton Place)
2622[11] 3136[4] *3725[11]* 4229[9] (4855) 5320[3] (5626) 6363[6] 6959[6] 7252[14]

Show Boat *Ann Duffield* a57 59
4 b g Showcasing Bluegrass Gal (USA) (Cape Canaveral (USA))
130[10] 1254[12]

Showboating (IRE) *John Balding* a95 79
8 b g Shamardal(USA) Sadinga (IRE) (Sadler's Wells (USA))
50[4] 134[3] 960[3] ◆ *1153[8]* 3414[10] 3645[13] 4299[11] 7360[4] *7858[10] 8475[9]*

Showdaisy *Keith Dalgleish* a94 85
3 ch f Showcasing Darling Daisy (Komaite (USA))
460[4] 4202[3] (4874) 5110[2] 5320[6] (6093) (7252) *7437[2] (7892) 8308[2]* ◆

Showdance Kid *K R Burke* 75
2 b g Showcasing Maid To Dance (Pyramus (USA))
2344[U] 2570[5] (3208)

Show Day (IRE) *H-A Pantall* 100
3 b f Shamardal(USA) Monday Show (USA) (Maria's Mon (USA))
6824a[3] 7723a[6]

Showing Off (IRE) *Michael Wigham* a77 85
3 ch g Notnowcato Walk On Water (Exceed And Excel (AUS))
(1859) 2695[6] 5412[5] *7066[10] 7781[9] 8052[13] 8319[10] 8456[9]*

Show Legend *Michael Bell* 57
3 ch g Showcasing Dubai Legend (Cadeaux Genereux)
1623[11] 2299[7] 3062[10] 3604[8] 4835[8] 6291[7]

Show Me Again *David Dennis* a86 70
3 ch g Showcasing Broughtons Revival (Pivotal)
2412[11] 2891[13] 4908[6] 5793[5] *6123[11] 6899[9] 7486[10] 7606[6]*

Show Me Baileys (FR) *James Given* a33 30
4 b g Naaqoos Exhibitor (USA) (Royal Academy (USA))
526[7]

Show Me The Music *Richard Fahey* 74
2 b f Dubawi(IRE) Music Show (IRE) (Noverre (USA))
5387[3] 5861[3]

Showmethewayavrilo *Malcolm Saunders* a74 77
3 ch g Showcasing Avrilo (Piccolo)
1060[3] ◆ *(1420) 2106[4]* 3000[2] 3126[3] (3771) 4224[6] 4502[5] 4990[6] 5626[4] 6363[2] 6831[2] 7268[2]

Show Palace *Jennie Candlish* 71
3 ch g Showcasing Palais Polaire (Polar Falcon (USA))
(2302) 2854[3] 3268[5] (3806) 4495[8] 6506[10] 7626[9]

Showreel *Amanda Perrett* a63 83
3 b f Showcasing Reel Style (Rainbow Quest (USA))
2470[2] *5300[4]*

Show Stealer *Rae Guest* 98
3 ch f Showcasing Winifred Jo (Bahamian Bounty)
(2251) 4062[7] 4652[5] 5588[4] 6064[2] 6518[8]

Showtime Blues *Jim Boyle* a75 15
4 b g Showcasing Night Symphonie (Cloudings (IRE))
607[8] 943[10] (7654) 7751[3] 8064[7] 8258[7]

Showtime Lady (IRE) *Mark Johnston* 69
2 ch f Mastercraftsman(IRE) Fig Tree Drive (USA) (Miswaki (USA))
4487[4] 5052[2] 5854[3]

Showtime Star *Gay Kelleway* a63 67
6 b g Byron Piddies Pride (IRE) (Indian Lodge (IRE))
192[3] 338[3] 508[4] 655[9] 894[8] 3259[4] 3741[5] 4389[3] 4741[6]

Shozita *Ralph Beckett* 73
2 b f Showcasing Azita (Tiger Hill (IRE))
(4659) ◆ 5407[3]

Shraaoh (IRE) *Sir Michael Stoute* a97 99
3 b c Sea The Stars(IRE) Jumooh (Monsun (GER))
1421[6] 2008[3] *(2619)* ◆ 3300[15] 4863[2] 5653[5]

Shrewd *Iain Jardine* a93 106
6 b g Street Sense(USA) Cala (FR) (Desert Prince (IRE))
(1135) 2487[5] (3117) 4164[5] 5655[2] 6118[13] 6582[3] 7150[12]

Shrill *W McCreery* a71 92
3 b f Shamardal(USA) Wood Vine (USA) (Woodman (USA))
1730a[5] 2272a[5] 3392[7]

Shrubland *Ed Walker* a57 61
3 b g High Chaparral(IRE) Ratukidul (FR) (Danehill (USA))
1930[6] 2541[10] 3066[7] 3804[5] 4342[5] *4942[9] 7104[3] 7309[2]*

Shudbeme *Neville Bycroft* 40
3 ch g Monsieur Bond(IRE) Oomph (Shareef Dancer (USA))
2740[7] 3224[15]

Shufoog *William Haggas* a73 85
3 b f Mawatheeq(USA) Hamloola (Red Ransom (USA))
2011[3] *2900[6]* ◆ 4607[2] 5975[2] (6268) 7504[12]

Shukhov (IRE) *Gerard O'Leary* a70 60
7 b g Ivan Denisovich(IRE) Just One Smile (IRE) (Desert Prince (IRE))
5096a[9]

Shulammite Man (IRE) *Alan Swinbank* a33 52
3 ch g Arcano(IRE) Shulammite Woman (IRE) (Desert Sun)
524[6] 1294[5] 1406[7] 2348[5] 3886[5] 4255[6]

Shumaker (IRE) *Noel C Kelly* 45
4 ch g Whitmore's Conn(USA) Blazing Love (IRE) (Fruits Of Love (USA))
2522[6] 3343[8] 4447[4]

Shutterbug (FR) *M Figge* 110
4 ch h Soldier Of Fortune(IRE) Nazlia (FR) (Polish Precedent (USA))
4441a[4] 7564a[4] 8336a[8]

Shutter Speed *John Gosden* 80
2 br f Dansili Photographic (Oasis Dream)
(7441)

Shwaiman (IRE) *William Jarvis* a83 87
6 br g Authorized(IRE) Blue Lightning (Machiavellian (USA))
244[8]

Shwaimsa (IRE) *Richard Hannon* 92
3 b f Canford Cliffs(IRE) Sharp Point (IRE) (Royal Academy (USA))
3358[9] 4080[3] 4391[3] 4737[10]

Shymkent *Roger Varian* 12
2 b g Pivotal Shabyt (Sadler's Wells (USA))
7770[12]

Shypen *Richard Fahey* a85 81
3 b f Archipenko(USA) Coconut Shy (Bahamian Bounty)
123[5] 1638[8] 2585[5] (3038) 3625[3] 4708[4] 5039[6] (6487) *(7363) 7485[7] 7965[10] 8158[2] 8380[4]*

Shyron *George Margarson* a97 72
5 b g Byron Coconut Shy (Bahamian Bounty)
290[2] 486[2] (816) 1204[5] 1752[3] 2033[8] 2587[7] 3163[8] 6914[16] *7651[10] 8256[2]*

Shy Witch (GER) *H-J Groschel* 106
3 b f Areion(GER) Shyla (GER) (Monsagem (USA))
2949a[2] (3916a) 6067a[6]

Siamsaiocht (IRE) *J S Bolger* a90 92
3 b f Teofilo(IRE) Halla Siamsa (IRE) (Montjeu (IRE))
2068a[4] 2883a[4] 3202a[5] 3539a[7] 5313a[10] 6389a[17]

Siberian Height's (USA) *Doug Watson* a25
3 ch c Cape Blanco(IRE) Run For Joy (USA) (Geiger Counter (USA))
8a[9]

Siberian Power (IRE) *Jennie Candlish* 36
3 b g Frozen Power(IRE) Novosibirsk (USA) (Distant View (USA))
2308[13] ◆

Sibilance *Ralph Beckett* a79
2 gr f Bated Breath Santa Sophia (IRE) (Linamix (FR))
(2817)

Side Hill (USA) *John Gosden* a88 81
3 b f Speightstown(USA) Hidden Face (USA) (Empire Maker (USA))
2483[4] ◆ 3059[2] *(5527)*

Sidewinder (IRE) *Tom Dascombe* a73 71
2 b g Majestic Missile(IRE) Ron's Secret (Efisio)
1520[2] ◆ *2779[4]* 3054[4] 3852[4] 5792[3] *8556[2]*

Sid Sweeney *Gay Kelleway* a38
3 b g Phoenix Reach(IRE) Rainbows Guest (IRE) (Indian Lodge (IRE))
2109[6] 2790[14]

Siege Of Boston (IRE) *Gordon Elliott* a61 72
3 ch g Starspangledbanner(AUS) Milton Of Campsie (Medicean)
1216[4] 4143[5] 4899a[14]

Sightline *Ralph Beckett* 93
3 b f Rock Of Gibraltar(IRE) Look So (Efisio)
(1406) 3001[2] (3593) 4668[5] 6948[10]

Signal Hill (IRE) *Andrew Balding* a60 45
3 b g Rock Of Gibraltar(IRE) Izzy Lou (IRE) (Spinning World (USA))
2320[8] 2999[12] 3996[10] 7298[8]

Signed And Sealed *Mark Johnston* a49 70
3 b g Authorized(IRE) Broken Peace (USA) (Devil's Bag (USA))
3189[2] *3652[9]* 4233[2] 4375[2]

Signed Sealed (USA) *John Gosden* a81 86
4 ch h Giant's Causeway(USA) Latice (IRE) (Inchinor)
(51) ◆

Sign Manual *Donald McCain* a59 81
7 b g Motivator New Assembly (IRE) (Machiavellian (USA))
1523[7] (2439) 3162[P] (Dead)

Sign Of A Victory (IRE) *Nicky Henderson* a89 91
7 b g Kayf Tara Irish Wedding (IRE) (Bob Back (USA))
2024[5] 3117[3]

Sign Of The Kodiac (IRE) *James Given* a103 97
3 b c Kodiac Summer Magic (IRE) (Desert Sun)
1070[2] ◆ 1607[5] 1996[7] *(2788)* 3165[8] (3413) 4062[12] 4803[7] 5390[15] 5657[11] *8232[7] 8484[7]*

Sign Of The Times *J R Jenkins* a41
4 b m Medicean Still Small Voice (Polish Precedent (USA))
27[8]

Signora Queen (FR) *A Wohler* 99
3 b f Exceed And Excel(AUS) Queen's Rose (Street Cry (IRE))
6824a[4]

Signore Piccolo *David O'Meara* 91
5 b g Piccolo Piccolo Cativo (Komaite (USA))
2259[10] 2613[7] 3265[6] 4608[8] 4873[2] 5512[3] 5858[3] 6131[3] 6437[5] 6766[7] 7360[10]

Signs Of Blessing (IRE) *F Rohaut* a109 119
5 b g Invincible Spirit(IRE) Sun Bittern (USA) (Seeking The Gold (USA))
(1172a) 2317a[5] 3385[3] (5217a) 7350[4] 8330a[5]

Signs Of Success (IRE) *M Delcher Sanchez* a81 78
3 b g Elusive City(USA) Quartz (FR) (Muhtathir)
1308a[7] *2141a[10]*

Sigurd (GER) *Kevin Ryan* 54
4 ch g Sholokhov(IRE) Sky News (GER) (Highest Honor (FR))
2558[14] 3842[6] 5183[10]

Sikandar (IRE) *Brian Ellison* 85
4 ch g Medicean Siniyya (IRE) (Grand Lodge (USA))
2199[5] 3162[11]

Sikandarabad (IRE) *D K Weld* 105
3 b g Dr Fong(USA) Sindiyma (IRE) (Kalanisi (IRE))
5941a[2] 6355a[6]

Silca Star *Mick Channon* 78
3 ch g Medicean Silca Chiave (Pivotal)
1570[5]

Silca Wings *James Fanshawe* a69
3 b f Multiplex Silca Destination (Dubai Destination (USA))
153[4]

Silent Approach *William Haggas* 61
2 b f New Approach(IRE) Firth Of Lorne (IRE) (Danehill (USA))
7543[5]

Silent Assassin (IRE) *Ed Walker* 74
2 b c Shamardal(USA) La Belle Dane (Danetime (IRE))
4203[2] (5477) 6525[7]

Silent Attack *Saeed bin Suroor* a88 105
3 b g Dream Ahead(USA) Chanterelle (FR) (Trempolino (USA))
2298[2] ◆ *(2790)* (3574) ◆ 4149[2] 6181a[2] 7542[4]

Silent Cat (TUR) *S Ozolke* 80
3 b f Mountain Cat(USA) Silent Bull (USA) (Holy Bull (USA))
6158a[5]

Silent Dreamer *Mark Johnston* a49 69
3 b f Dream Ahead(USA) In A Silent Way (IRE) (Desert Prince (IRE))
1388[8]

Silent Echo *Roger Charlton* 56
2 b g Oasis Dream Quiet (Observatory (USA))
2976[7]

Silently *Daniel Kubler* a49
3 b f Zamindar(USA) Quiet Elegance (Fantastic Light (USA))
7815[4]

Silent Romance (FR) *J E Hammond* a60 70
3 b f Dream Ahead(USA) Silent Sunday (IRE) (Testa Rossa (AUS))
5907a[3]

Silhouette (IRE) *Daniel Kubler* a74 76
3 ch g Frozen Power(IRE) Missalonghi (IRE) (In The Wings)
2207[5] ◆ 2749[5] *3653[6]* 4088[3] 4562[4] 5362[4] 5996[5] *6629[5] (6855)*

Silhuette (IRE) *Colin Teague* 87
3 b f Canford Cliffs(IRE) Lisfannon (Bahamian Bounty)
3519[8] 6164[9] 6810[7] 7126[18] 7591[5] 7743[15]

Siljan's Saga (FR) *J-P Gauvin* 118
6 bl m Sagamix(FR) Humoriste (FR) (Saint Cyrien (FR))
1375a[4] 1909a[8] 2727a[2] 3936a[3] 5947a[2] 6989a[4] 7569a[3]
Silk Bow *James Given* a76 82
3 b f Elusive City(USA) Ishraaqat (Singspiel (IRE))
686[4] 821[9] 3392[10]
Silk Cravat *Simon Crisford* 88
3 ch g Kyllachy Polly Floyer (Halling (USA))
1931[2] 2861[4] 3908[2] 4886[5]
Silken Skies (IRE) *Clive Cox* 90
3 ch f Zoffany(IRE) Sky Red (Night Shift (USA))
2314[2] 2982[2] 3685[3] 4223[6] 5040[4] 6195[2] 7289[2] 7772[7]
Silk Gem (IRE) *James Tate* a75
3 b c Roderic O'Connor(IRE) Fine Silk (USA) (Rahy (USA))
123[6] 1258[4]
Silk Mill Blue *Richard Whitaker* a60 66
2 b g Piccolo Marysienka (Primo Dominie)
3515[5] 4371[7] 5029[6] 5884[13] 6789[4] *7109[6] 7749[7]*
Silk Of Rio (FR) *Y Gourraud* a69
2 b f Rio De La Plata(USA) Silk Gallery (USA) (Kingmambo (USA))
7454a[8]
Silk Suit (FR) *Luca Cumani* 39
3 b g Rip Van Winkle(IRE) Silk Gallery (USA) (Kingmambo (USA))
3535[10]
Silk Words *H-A Pantall* a70 85
3 b f Dubawi(IRE) Gossamer (Sadler's Wells (USA))
6912a[3]
Si Luna (GER) *W Mongil* a87 107
7 ch m Kallisto(GER) Signorita (GER) (Generous (IRE))
451a[4] 809a[7] 1822a[11]
Silva Eclipse *Jedd O'Keeffe* a64 83
3 gr g Multiplex Linen Line (Double Eclipse (IRE))
2327[4] (3215) (4033) (6011)
Silvanus (IRE) *Paul Midgley* a97 89
11 b g Danehill Dancer(IRE) Mala Mala (IRE) (Brief Truce (USA))
1083[3] 1272[4] 2258[3] 2504[4] 3151[16] 3393[5] 4112[13] 4373[9] 5479[4] ◆ 6012[9] 6793[7] 7413[10] *(7643)*
Silva Samourai *Susan Corbett* a45 47
7 gr g Proclamation(IRE) Ladykirk (Slip Anchor)
23[7] 2094[5] 2522[4] 3706[9] 4099[8] *4648[6]* 5227[3]
Silver Alliance *Julia Feilden* a74 78
8 gr g Proclamation(IRE) Aimee Vibert (Zilzal (USA))
1114[7] 2085[5] 3064[3] (4052) (5028) 6753[19] 7500[17] 7775[9]
Silver Asset (IRE) *Michael Wigham* 28
2 rg g Zebedee Tipperary Boutique (IRE) (Danehill Dancer (IRE))
1635[8] 2543[7] 3231[7]
Silver Bid (USA) *Alan Bailey* a75 63
4 gr g Exchange Rate(USA) Micaela's Moon (USA) (Malibu Moon (USA))
1079[6] 1151[2] 1435[2] 2253[9] *3035[10]* 3669[2] 4360[10]
Silver Cape (FR) *T Clout* 84
2 b f Silver Frost(IRE) Cape Talks (IRE) (Cape Cross (IRE))
7491a[6]
Silver Chimes *William Knight* a48 52
2 gr f Campanologist(USA) Nolas Lolly (IRE) (Lomitas)
4397[8] 5324[6] 5951[5] *6963[7] 7423[8]*
Silver City (FR) *A Giorgi* a31 67
2 b c Silver Frost(IRE) Tanea (FR) (Exit To Nowhere (USA))
4183a[5]
Silver Cloud (GER) *S Smrczek* 89
2 b f Soldier Hollow Sassicaia (GER) (Doyen (IRE))
6797a[4]
Silver Concorde *D K Weld* 102
8 b g Dansili Sacred Pearl (IRE) (Daylami (IRE))
1967[3] ◆ 3246[16] 6350a[8]
Silver Dixie (USA) *Peter Hedger* a72 83
6 br g Dixie Union(USA) More Silver (USA) (Silver Hawk (USA))
1916[9] 2296[8] 3109[9]
Silver Duke (IRE) *Jim Goldie* a47 67
5 gr g Papal Bull Dumaani's Dream (USA) (Dumaani (USA))
1841[2] 2091[3] 2661[10] 2811[3] 2959[4]
Silver Galaxy *M Al Mheiri* a104
5 b h Galileo(IRE) Silver Pivotal (IRE) (Pivotal)
309a[8]
Silver Ghost (IRE) *Geoffrey Deacon* 76
3 gr g Dark Angel(IRE) Aqualina (IRE) (King's Theatre (IRE))
4657[8] ◆ 6294[3] 7419[6]
Silver Gleam (IRE) *Chris Fairhurst* a36 59
2 gr f Zoffany(IRE) Gleaming Silver (IRE) (Dalakhani (IRE))
4298[8] 5387[9] 5854[5] 7041[6] *8087[8]*
Silverheels (IRE) *Paul Cole* a91 89
7 gr g Verglas(IRE) Vasilia (Dansili)
(715a) 1576[9] 3376a[7]
Silver Line (IRE) *Saeed bin Suroor* 106
2 gr c Dark Angel(IRE) Admire The View (IRE) (Dubawi (IRE))
(2500) 3295[3] ◆ 4060[4] 6785[10] 7155[5] 7544[5]
Silver Lining (IRE) *Mark Hoad* a62 49
4 gr g Dark Angel(IRE) Out Of Woods (USA) (Woodman (USA))
62[10] 568[3] 898[9] 1778[6] *2323[12]* 7421[11] *8468[10]*
Silver Link (IRE) *Marcus Tregoning* 79
2 b f Arcano(IRE) Miss Bellbird (IRE) (Danehill (USA))
4801[9] 5600[10] 6250[3] 6713[3] ◆ 7016[5] 7406[2]
Silver Mist *Richard Hannon* 37
2 gr f Kyllachy Mundus Novus (USA) (Unbridled's Song (USA))
5869[11] 6570[9] 7502[13]
Silver Mountain *J R Jenkins* a80 72
5 gr g Sir Percy Pearl Bright (FR) (Kaldoun (FR))
1716[11]

Silver Ocean (USA) *Niels Petersen* a99 103
8 br g Silver Train(USA) Endless Sea (CAN) (Mt. Livermore (USA))
284a[8] 628a[16] *1957a[2]* 3449a[12]
Silver Penny *Jim Boyle* 69
2 gr f Hellvelyn Pennyspider (IRE) (Redback)
5258[7] (6189) 6829[3]
Silver Poker (FR) *D Chenu* a50 51
2 b c Policy Maker(IRE) Silver Diane (FR) (Silver Rainbow)
5186a[9] *7293a[6]*
Silver Quay (IRE) *Jamie Osborne* a101 89
4 gr g Dark Angel(IRE) She Runs (FR) (Sheyrann (IRE))
(975) 1081[2] 1336[8] 1885[7] 4731[10] 5145[5] 6544[4] 7015[9] *8594[7]*
Silver Rainbow (IRE) *Charles Hills* a85 110
4 gr m Starspangledbanner(AUS) Enchanting Way (Linamix (FR))
2903[3] (3815) (4398) (4905a) 5614[14] 5949a[4]
Silverrica (IRE) *Malcolm Saunders* 81
6 gr m Ad Valorem(USA) Allegorica (IRE) (Alzao (USA))
3123[4] (3530) 3995[8] 4911[6] 5305[8] (6017) 6296[7] 6831[4]
Silver Sands (IRE) *Tim Easterby* 69
3 gr g Zebedee Eloquent Rose (IRE) (Elnadim (USA))
1126[9] 2742[2] 3010[4] 3422[5] 3948[5] 4410[2]
Silver Shuffle (IRE) *Dianne Sayer* a57 66
9 ch g Big Shuffle(USA) Silvetta (Lando (GER))
1955[8] 2558[2] 5758[3]
Silver Springs (IRE) *David Evans* a69 49
3 gr f Zebedee Charming Vista (Josr Algarhoud (IRE))
171[3] 443[2] 610[2] 978[2] 1061[6] 1176[4] 1812[4] 2322[7] 3473[2] 3974[8] *4525[8]* 5570 [4] 6291[8] *(7201) 7513[8] 7693[9]*
Silver Step (FR) *Mme Pia Brandt* a73 101
3 gr f Silver Frost(IRE) Negra Del Oro (GER) (Danehill Dancer (IRE))
5498a[13] (6824a)
Silver Streak (IRE) *Ann Duffield* 76
3 gr g Dark Angel(IRE) Happy Talk (IRE) (Hamas (IRE))
1409[6] 2019[2] 2524[8]
Silvertoni (USA) *Wesley A Ward* a90 70
2 rg f Tapit(USA) Somasach (USA) (Johannesburg (USA))
3243[9]
Silver Top (FR) *N Caullery* 58
2 gr c Silver Frost(IRE) Lamora (Sinndar (IRE))
3006a[12] 5568a[7] 5819a[5]
Silverwave (FR) *P Bary* a83 118
4 b h Silver Frost(IRE) Miss Bio (FR) (River Mist (USA))
1375a[7] 1909a[2] 2568a[3] (3936a) (6395a) 6989a[13] 8329a[12]
Silver Wings (IRE) *Roger Ingram* a78 89
3 gr g Zebedee Daisy Hill (Indian Ridge)
344[6] 515[7] 979[9] 2435[9]
Silvery Moon (IRE) *Tim Easterby* 96
9 gr g Verglas(IRE) Starry Night (Sheikh Albadou)
1245[3] 1871[4] 2157[12] 2689[7] 3055[7] (3855) 4374[4] 4894[4] 5156[11] 5520[6] 6081[6] (6500) 6778[4]
Silwana (IRE) *Takashi Kodama* 108
5 b m Peintre Celebre(USA) Simawa (IRE) (Anabaa (USA))
2275a[3] 2881a[5] 6387a[4] 6820a[9]
Simannka (IRE) *D K Weld* a66 100
3 gr f Mastercraftsman(IRE) Simkana (IRE) (Kalanisi (IRE))
6389a[7]
Simba (FR) *C Lerner* a87 92
8 gr h Anabaa Blue Saiga (FR) (Baryshnikov (AUS))
3377a[5] 4903a[5]
Simba *C Von Der Recke* 106
5 ch h Teofilo(IRE) Sarabia (GER) (One Cool Cat (USA))
664a[5]
Simbel (IRE) *F Doumen* 53
4 b m Alfred Nobel(IRE) Simla Bibi (Indian Ridge)
3092a[8]
Simenon (IRE) *W P Mullins* 108
9 b g Marju(IRE) Epistoliere (IRE) (Alzao (USA))
3387[15]
Simmie (IRE) *Sylvester Kirk* a81 97
2 b f Fast Company(IRE) Kathy Sun (IRE) (Intikhab (USA))
2457[3] (2902) 3270[5] 3663[5] 4394[8] ◆ *(5125)* 6063[7] 6950[2] 7536[7] (7972a)
Simmy's Temple *Doug O'Neill* 86
2 b f Royal Applause Samasana (IRE) (Redback)
1199[2] ◆ 8127a[5]
Simoon (IRE) *Andrew Balding* a74 64
2 b c Sixties Icon Astragal (Shamardal (USA))
7501[8] *(7865)*
Simple Verse (IRE) *Ralph Beckett* a77 118
4 b m Duke Of Marmalade(IRE) Guantanamera (IRE) (Sadler's Wells (USA))
1863[2] ◆ 2894[4] 3384[7] (6259) 7349[3]
Simplon *P Vovcenko* a74 91
7 b m Rail Link Neath (Rainbow Quest (USA))
1907a[11]
Simply Black (IRE) *Ann Stokell* a46 49
5 br m Kheleyf(USA) Tashyra (IRE) (Tagula (IRE))
1133[10] 1913[6] 2537[7] 2845[8] 3260[4] 3486[10] 4931[15] *6587[7] 6902[3]* 7302[8] *7488[6] 7859[12] 8079[11] 8288[7]*
Simply Clever *David Brown* a58 60
3 ch f Stimulation(IRE) Well Of Echoes (Diktat)
509[7] 794[3] 1163[2] 1705[2] (2553) 3285[7] 5201[7] *7609[9] 8499[2]*
Simply Me *Tom Dascombe* a70 57
3 b f New Approach(IRE) Ego (Green Desert (USA))
1438[8] 3023[5] 4206[5] 5062[3] *5721[2] (7513) 7725[2]*
Simply Shining (IRE) *Richard Fahey* a71 88
6 ch m Rock Of Gibraltar(IRE) Bright Smile (IRE) (Caerleon (USA))
1274[5] 1624[3] 2216[6] 3011[3] 3438[4] 4408[3]

Sinakar (IRE) *David O'Meara* a70 77
5 br g Manduro(GER) Siniyya (IRE) (Grand Lodge (USA))
1244[6] 1665[3] 2018[5] 2853[2]
Sinamas (IRE) *Eric Alston* a6
3 b f Dylan Thomas(IRE) Sinamay (USA) (Saint Ballado (CAN))
5581[5] *6423[8]*
Sinbad The Sailor *George Baker* a67 67
11 b g Cape Cross(IRE) Sinead (USA) (Irish River (FR))
1038[4] 1450[2] 4045[2]
Sincil Bank (USA) *David Simcock* a82 94
2 b c Hat Trick(JPN) Asuncion (USA) (Powerscourt)
5966[2] (6904) ◆ 7469[3]
Sindaco (GER) *H Blume* a74 75
8 b g Sakhee(USA) Sly (GER) (Monsun (GER))
4927a[6]
Sindarban (IRE) *Keith Dalgleish* a71 96
5 ch g Teofilo(IRE) Sinndiya (IRE) (Pharly (FR))
(2197) (3520) ◆ 4407[8] 5611[14] 6561[3] *7383[6]*
Sinema *Christine Dunnett* a71 32
4 gr g Compton Place Dictatrix (Diktat)
168[8] 547[10] 867[10]
Sinfonietta (FR) *David Menuisier* a71 100
4 b g Sinndar(IRE) Final Whistle (IRE) (Rossini (USA))
(1274) 1856[2] 2246[4] 3534[2] 5956[6]
Singapore Sling *James Fanshawe* a69 73
3 b g Paco Boy(IRE) Buena Notte (IRE) (Halling (USA))
3464[3] 7218[4] *8481[2]*
Singaraja (FR) *K Borgel* 62
3 ch f Turtle Bowl(IRE) Hello Sindarella (FR) (Sinndar (IRE))
3007a[2]
Singeur (IRE) *Rebecca Bastiman* a86 91
9 b g Chineur(FR) Singitta (Singspiel (IRE))
1408[6] 1874[9] 2346[3] 2665[5] 3168[16] 3875[4] (4514) 4817[2] 5479[8] (6234) 7124[6]
Singing Sands (IRE) *Ralph Beckett* a71 73
2 b f Harbour Watch(IRE) Elektra Marino (Mount Nelson)
3511[4] *4011[2]* ◆ 4981[3] 5594[3] 6289[3] 6762[9]
Single Estate *Sir Mark Prescott Bt* 45
2 b g Tamayuz Duo De Choc (IRE) (Manduro (GER))
3819[9] 4274[7] 5120[5]
Single Summit *J R Jenkins* a46 30
4 b g Hellvelyn Once Removed (Distant Relative)
5[3] 217[6] 432[6] 513[8] 3822[12] 4278[10] *7489[7] 8472[8]*
Sing Something *P Monfort* a71 68
3 gr c Paco Boy(IRE) Rock Ace (IRE) (Verglas (IRE))
128a[3] 3764a[4]
Singula *Alan King* a51 65
2 b g Mayson Tagula Sunrise (IRE) (Tagula (IRE))
3813[8] 4287[6] *7424[10]*
Singular Quest *Kevin Frost* a73 74
4 ch g Dalakhani(IRE) Singuliere (IRE) (Singspiel (IRE))
567[5] 922[3] 1550[3] 2678[6] *3470[7] 3651[4]*
Sing With Bess (IRE) *M Weiss* 72
5 gr m Clodovil(IRE) Five Of Wands (Caerleon (USA))
2318a[4]
Singyoursong (IRE) *David Simcock* a75 90
3 b f Aqlaam Dhan Dhana (IRE) (Dubawi (IRE))
(122) 2108[3] (3039) ◆ (4130) ◆ 4391[7] 5054[2] 5382[4]
Singzak *David C Griffiths* a68 45
8 ch g Singspiel(IRE) Zakuska (Zafonic (USA))
425[5] 637[6]
Siouxperhero (IRE) *William Muir* a66 68
7 b g Sleeping Indian Tintern (Diktat)
7514[8] (7943) 8154[10]
Sirajiah (IRE) *William Haggas* a79 78
3 ch f Exceed And Excel(AUS) Miss Honorine (IRE) (Highest Honor (FR))
2848[2] 4238[2] 5238[2] (6190) 6492[5] *7364[2]*
Sir Billy Wright (IRE) *David Evans* a89 92
5 b g High Chaparral(IRE) Lure Of The Moon (USA) (Lure (USA))
338[2] 508[3] 894[5] 938[7] 1634[6] (2460) 2613[3] 2862[3] 3671[3] 3956[10] 4366[3] 4954[9] 5825[2] 5955[2] 6320[6] 6539[9] 6780[3] 7095[2] 7825[5] *7990[9] 8192[8]*
Sir Chauvelin *Jim Goldie* a96 100
4 b g Authorized(IRE) Jabbara (IRE) (Kingmambo (USA))
(1880) (2199) 2685[3] *3657[4]* 4164[6] 5655[20] 7824[12]
Sir Compton *Stuart Kittow* a63 56
3 b g Compton Place Dilys (Efisio)
1892[6] *4939[5]* 5327[4] *6238[4]*
Sirdaab (USA) *Ann Stokell* a49 64
4 b g City Zip(USA) Stormy Union (USA) (Dixie Union (USA))
531[6] 798[5]
Sirdaal (USA) *Owen Burrows* 61
3 b c Medaglia d'Oro(USA) Sarayir (USA) (Mr Prospector (USA))
3160[14] 4056[9] 4498[15]
Sir Dancealot (IRE) *David Elsworth* a92 107
2 b c Sir Prancealot(IRE) Majesty's Dancer (IRE) (Danehill Dancer (IRE))
3954[9] *(5549) (6122)* 6707[3] ◆ (7155) 7539[6]
Sir Domino (FR) *Patrick Holmes* a77 79
4 b g Evasive Domino Queen I (IRE) (Primo Dominie)
1488[6] (1879) 2524[6] 3284[2] 3580[5] 4032[2] 4873[9] *5679[4] 6699[12] 6927[3] 7386[6] 7660[7] 7959[13]*
Sir Dudley (IRE) *James Given* a86 74
3 b c Arcano(IRE) Rosy Dudley (IRE) (Grand Lodge (USA))
16[3] 171[4] 519[7] 612[2] 821[8] 1060[2] (1176) 1647[3] *2002[2] 2446[5]* 2736[4] 3420[5] 4547[5] 4947[4] *6962[8]*
Sir Dylan *Polly Gundry* a55 48
7 b g Dylan Thomas(IRE) Monteleone (IRE) (Montjeu (IRE))
684[9]

Sir Ector (USA) *Miss Nicole McKenna* 103
9 br g Dynaformer(USA) Beyond The Waves (USA) (Ocean Crest (USA))
7708a[16]
Siren's Cove *Kenneth Slack* a84 79
4 b m Sir Percy Siren Sound (Singspiel (IRE))
4113[5] 4668[2] 6504[8] *7139[6] 7853[4] 8283[3] 8399[5]*
Sir Fever (URU) *Charlie Appleby* a110 38
4 b g Texas Fever(USA) Sirina (ARG) (Rainbow Corner)
6708[6]
Sir Geoffrey (IRE) *Scott Dixon* a66 59
10 b g Captain Rio Disarm (IRE) (Bahamian Bounty)
136[2] (340) 444[4] 520[8] 799[3] 869[4] (963) (1030) 1255[6] 1481[8] 3326[8] 3811[4] 4295[8] 4512[2] 5277[8] *5807[10] 6509[8]* 7018[12] 7046[6] 7595[10] *7859[2] 7961[7] 8094[12] 8242[11] 8474[12]*
Sir George Somers (USA) *Sir Michael Stoute* 76
3 ch g Cape Blanco(IRE) Sense Of Class (USA) (Fusaichi Pegasus (USA))
1715[6] 2098[4] 2557[4]
Sir Harry Collins (IRE) *Richard Spencer* a47 16
2 gr g Zebedee Unreal (Dansili)
4494[6] *5077[6]* 5410[9]
Siri *Mick Channon* a59 74
3 br f Atlantic Sport(USA) Search Party (Rainbow Quest (USA))
1149[2] (1755) 2178[8] 2749[10] 3111[7] 3521[7] 4058[6] 4587[6] 6501[10] 7036[8]
Sir Isaac Newton *A P O'Brien* a88 117
4 b h Galileo(IRE) Shastye (IRE) (Danehill (USA))
2924a[3] (3383) (3692a) 4626[4] 5558[4] 6354a[10] 7378a[7]
Sirius (GER) *Andreas Lowe* 113
5 ch h Dashing Blade Saratina (IRE) (Monsun (GER))
2075a[2] 3934a[6] 6822a[7] 7759a[8]
Sirius Move *David O'Meara* a45 54
3 b g Monsieur Bond(IRE) Lady Paris (IRE) (Invincible Spirit (IRE))
1554[7] 1764[6]
Sirius Prospect (USA) *Dean Ivory* a104 102
8 bb g Gone West(USA) Stella Blue (FR) (Anabaa (USA))
215[4] 501[2] 692[3] 1196[22] 1856[6] 2391[7] 4380[2] *5552[3] 6126[14]*
Sir Jack *Tony Carroll* a40 62
3 b g Sir Percy Play Bouzouki (Halling (USA))
5811[7] 6423[7] 7240[7] 7572[3] 7794[9] 8471[7] 8566[3]
Sir Jamie *Tony Carroll* 41
3 ch g Monsieur Bond(IRE) First Dawn (Dr Fong (USA))
6317[9] 7299[5] ◆
Sir John Hawkwood (IRE) *John P Thompson* 110
7 b g Sir Percy Athene (IRE) (Rousillon (USA))
7378a[10] 7756a[18]
Sir Lancelott *David O'Meara* a68 73
4 b g Piccolo Selkirk Rose (IRE) (Pips Pride)
8085[9] 8588[9]
Sirma Traou Land (FR) *B De Montzey* a35 80
2 bl f Soul City(IRE) Peldrine (FR) (Pelder (IRE))
4750a[9] *5755a[14] 7294a[9]* 7490a[5]
Sir Maximilian (IRE) *Ian Williams* a109 114
7 b g Royal Applause Nebraska Lady (IRE) (Lujain (USA))
166[4] 450a[6] (626a) 841a[4] 1104a[11] (1969) 2317a[6] 2475[9] 3244[13] *8050[10] 8232[9]*
Sir Nigel Gresley (USA) *Alan King* 72
2 b g Bullet Train Poule D'Eau (USA) (Orientate (USA))
4533[3] ◆ 6663[6] 7273[4]
Sir Pass I Am *Andrew Balding* 67
3 b g Passing Glance Orbital Orchid (Mujahid (USA))
2541[5] 3235[7] 6444[6] 7222[3]
Sirpertan *Marjorie Fife* a50 56
5 b g Sir Percy Tanwir (Unfuwain (USA))
1048[6] 1675[2] 2656[2]
Sir Pitt *David Bridgwater*
9 b g Tiger Hill(IRE) Rebecca Sharp (Machiavellian (USA))
506[7]
Sir Plato (IRE) *Rod Millman* 57
2 b g Sir Prancealot(IRE) Dessert Flower (IRE) (Intikhab (USA))
3529[12] 4907 [8] 5324[7] 6060[3] 6313[2]
Sir Renos Santi *Ian Williams* a30 24
3 b g Observatory(USA) Diamond Reef (Alzao (USA))
1835[6] 3998[12]
Sir Robert Cheval *Robert Cowell* a102 103
5 b g Green Desert(USA) Aunt Ruby (USA) (Rubiano (USA))
2480[2] *3656[3]* 4865[17] 6112[3] 6558[11] 7156[14]
Sir Roderic (IRE) *Rod Millman* 101
3 b g Roderic O'Connor(IRE) Begin The Beguine (IRE) (Peintre Celebre (USA))
(1389) (1630) 1896[3] 2299[2] (3465) (3908) (4271) 5175[2] 6075[9] 6573[12]
Sir Roger Moore (IRE) *John Butler* a75 70
3 b g Kodiac Truly Magnificent (USA) (Elusive Quality (USA))
2981[6] 3625[5] *4215[2]*
Sir Runs A Lot *David Barron* a75
4 b g Sir Percy Monjouet (IRE) (Montjeu (IRE))
600[5]
Sir Theodore (IRE) *Richard Spencer* a57 78
3 b g Arcano(IRE) Key Rose (IRE) (Key Of Luck (USA))
1448[4] 2288[2] 2435[2] 2834[8] (3581) 3806[5] 4985[3] 5230[5] 7626[16] *8349[12]*
Sir Titan *Marcus Tregoning* 70
2 b g Aqlaam Femme De Fer (Hamas (IRE))
5890[8] 6577[6]
Sir Valentine (GER) *Alan King* a88 82
3 b c Cacique(IRE) Singuna (GER) (Black Sam Bellamy (IRE))
3160[5] 4319[3] 4792[2] *(5723)* 7117[14]

Sir Veillance *Ivan Furtado*
4 b g Authorized(IRE) Caught You Looking (Observatory (USA))
5178[11]

Sir Viktor (IRE) *K R Burke* 74
2 b c Sir Prancealot(IRE) Wild Academy (IRE) (Royal Academy (USA))
1520[7] 3872[4] 4564[3] (5289) 5917[5] 6562[3] 7042[5]

Sisania (IRE) *Gary Moore* a51 64
3 rg f Mastercraftsman(IRE) Avril Rose (IRE) (Xaar)
1704[5] 2215[6] *2815[8]* 3722[3] 6367[6]

Si Senor (IRE) *Ed Vaughan* a103 85
5 b g Dansili Kotsi (IRE) (Nayef (USA))
(401) 560[2] 749[2] 920[7] 1068[6] 1195[20] *3565[2]*

Sissi Doloise (FR) *A Bonin* a66 62
2 b f Motivator Sirene Doloise (FR) (Marchand De Sable (USA))
7970a[6]

Sister Blandina (IRE) *J P Murtagh* a53 88
3 rg f Mastercraftsman(IRE) Tara's Wells (IRE) (Sadler's Wells (USA))
(2148)

Sister Dude *K R Burke* 70
3 ch f Notnowcato Inaminute (IRE) (Spectrum (IRE))
1628[7] 2653[4] 3213[10] 5062[5] 5718[8] (6501) 7743[10]

Sisterleon Davis (FR) *C Plisson* 60
2 b f Myboycharlie(IRE) Aldovea (Nashwan (USA))
2724a[7] 5905a[10]

Sister Slew (IRE) *Shane Nolan* a66 71
6 br m Kheleyf(USA) Capote West (USA) (Capote (USA))
4899a[7] *6461a[5]*

Sistine Chapel *Brian Meehan* 40
3 b f Cape Cross(IRE) Ambria (GER) (Monsun (GER))
4361[10]

Sisyphus *Ollie Pears* 84
4 b g Halling(USA) Cape Dancer (IRE) (Cape Cross (IRE))
(1665) 2194[12] 2659[2] 4581[9] 5321[4] 6457[7]

Sitaarah *Simon Crisford* 53
2 b f Sea The Stars(IRE) Edaraat (USA) (Rahy (USA))
4579[6]

Sitar *James Fanshawe* a63 67
2 b f Aqlaam Soundwave (Prince Sabo)
7071[2] ◆ 7576[3] *7939[3]*

Six Strings *Richard Fahey* a83 81
2 b g Requinto(IRE) Island Music (IRE) (Mujahid (USA))
3562[2] ◆ 4394[9] *(8140)*

Sixth Of June *Rod Millman* a25 54
2 b f Crosspeace(IRE) Eccentricity (Emarati (USA))
6061[7] *6673[12]* 6880[10]

Sixth Sense (IRE) *Mark Johnston* 100
3 ch c Shamardal(USA) Shinko Hermes (IRE) (Sadler's Wells (USA))
6287[10] 6778[7] 7546[9]

Sixties Groove (IRE) *Jeremy Noseda* a102 96
3 b g Sixties Icon Gift Dancer (Imperial Dancer)
1653[6] 2005[9] (3033) 3468[3] (4046) ◆ 4827[2] 7117[4] *(7869)*

Sixties Habana *Pat Phelan* a57 66
2 b g Sixties Icon Vilnius (Imperial Dancer)
2822[3] ◆ (3075) 6800[8] *7460[8] 7974[4] 8244[7]*

Sixties Idol *Mick Channon* a42 54
3 b f Sixties Icon Fading Away (Fraam)
2207[11] 2470[11] 2589[3] 3063[11] 3765[3] *4210[7]* 4636[5] *7367[8]*

Sixties Love *Simon Dow* a78 73
5 b m Sixties Icon Love Always (Piccolo)
2623[9] *2994[8]* 3738[3] 4303[7] 6334[5] 6892[9]

Sixties Queen *Lisa Williamson* a51 42
6 b m Sixties Icon Lily Of Tagula (IRE) (Tagula (IRE))
155[9] 362[5] 527[7] 776[5] 1035[5]

Sixties Sheila *Mick Channon* 53
2 ch f Sixties Icon Quinzey's Best (IRE) (King's Best (USA))
5356[12]

Sixties Sue *Mick Channon* a81 90
3 gr f Sixties Icon Rose Cheval (USA) (Johannesburg (USA))
1315[3] 1453[5] 1607[3] 1882[4] 3165[15] 4803[13] 5409[8] 5643[7] 6064[6] 6340[2] ◆ 6883[7] 6946[8] 7221[11]

Sixties Symphony *Michael Blanshard*
2 b f Sixties Icon Moyoko (IRE) (Mozart (IRE))
4349[14] 5771[8]

Siyahamba (IRE) *Bryan Smart* a59 13
2 ch g Helmet(AUS) Kalabunga (IRE) (Val Royal (FR))
6679[10] *6924[8] 7431[5] 7954[6]*

Siyaka (FR) *F Rohaut* a83 79
3 bb f Siyouni(FR) Kutika (FR) (Kutub (IRE))
5946a[7]

Siyounor (FR) *F-H Graffard* a83 102
3 gr c Siyouni(FR) Oranor (FR) (Starborough)
2551a[3] 3183a[5]

Siyoushake (IRE) *F Head* a74 115
4 b m Siyouni(FR) Shakeyourbody (USA) (Giant's Causeway (USA))
1910a[4] 4926a[5] (5948a) 6949[4] (7723a)

Size Matters *Mark Walford* a48 44
2 b g Captain Gerrard(IRE) Icky Woo (Mark Of Esteem (IRE))
7578[11] *7845[8] 8305[7]*

Sizzler *Ralph Beckett* a92 105
6 ch g Hernando(FR) Gino's Spirits (Perugino (USA))
244[6] 747[8]

Skadi *Garry Moss* a37 56
4 b m Kheleyf(USA) Just Joey (Averti (IRE))
5843[5] 6218[4] *6744[9]* 7747[5]

Skara Mae (IRE) *Charles Hills* a64
3 b f Canford Cliffs(IRE) Winged Valkyrie (IRE) (Hawk Wing (USA))
7354 2790[10] 7727[8] 7780[3] 8124[10]

Skarino Gold (GER) *Jean-Pierre Carvalho* 109
2 b c Wiener Walzer(GER) Saaleland (GER) (Lando (GER))
(7401a)

Skaters Waltz (IRE) *D Prod'Homme* a90 90
5 gr g Verglas(IRE) Xarzee (IRE) (Xaar)
660a[2] 4074a[5]

Skeaping *Richard Hannon* a69 83
3 b g Excellent Art Gale Green (Galileo (IRE))
1314[2] *1575[5]* 2548[3] 2826[2] 3465[2] 3814[5] 5874[9] 6294[6] (7014)

Skellig Michael *Ben Haslam* a56 59
2 b g Arakan(USA) Ambonnay (Ashkalani (IRE))
5884[19] 6448[4] 7040[5] *7615[4]*

Ski Blast *Ivan Furtado* 80
5 ch g Three Valleys(USA) Chasing Stars (Observatory (USA))
1954[4] 2256[3]

Skidby Mill (IRE) *Laura Mongan* a77 68
6 b m Ramonti(FR) Glasnas Giant (Giant's Causeway (USA))
190[2] 456[3] (709) (813) 1065[10] 1268[2] 1546[7] *2001[4] 2324[3] 2577[8] 3314[6] 7691[7] 7887[4] 7985[11] 8163[8] (8382) 8458[2]*

Skiddaw Valleys *Alan Swinbank* a73 78
4 ch g Three Valleys(USA) Skiddaw Wolf (Wolfhound (USA))
1923[8] 2406[5] 2911[4] (3294) 3520[9] 3942[4] 4680[6] 5918[6] 7332[6] *7847[5]*

Skiff *Brendan Powell* a10 51
4 b g Indian Danehill(IRE) Dongola (IRE) (Xaar)
3464[7] 3996[6] 4384[6] *6900[13]* 7300[7]

Skiffle *Charlie Appleby* 104
3 b f Dubawi(IRE) Princesse Dansante (IRE) (King's Best (USA))
1989[3] (2394) 2869[5] 5939a[3]

Skilful Lord (IRE) *Stuart Kittow* 47
2 ch g Lord Shanakill(USA) Monsusu (IRE) (Montjeu (IRE))
2147[4] 2997[14] 6439[9] 7570[5]

Skilled *Anabel K Murphy* a42 68
5 b g Mastercraftsman(IRE) Treacle (USA) (Seeking The Gold (USA))
8339[5]

Skinnydipper *A Wohler* a70 67
2 br c Harbour Watch(IRE) Blas Ceoil (USA) (Mr Greeley (USA))
6638a[9]

Sky Ballerina *Simon Crisford* a69 66
2 b f Makfi Maid In Heaven (IRE) (Clodovil (IRE))
3812[4] 4756[12] *5524[4]*

Sky Ferry *J S Moore* a58 58
3 br g Captain Gerrard(IRE) Ellovamul (Elmaamul (USA))
63[2] 147[2] 328[4] 345[4]

Skygazer (IRE) *A R Al Rayhi* a72 63
4 b h Echo Of Light Calando (USA) (Storm Cat (USA))
8a[4]

Sky Gypsy *David Brown* 70
2 gr f Dandy Man(IRE) Gypsy Style (Desert Style (IRE))
4308[3] 4804[5] (5433)

Sky Hunter *Saeed bin Suroor* a112 119
6 b g Motivator Pearl Kite (USA) (Silver Hawk (USA))
6125[3] (6666) 7569a[5]

Sky Kingdom (IRE) *William Haggas* 112
3 b c Montjeu(IRE) We Can Say It Now (AUS) (Starcraft (NZ))
(1421) 1866[3] 5499a[8] (6597a)

Skylark Lady (IRE) *Michael Wigham* a61 64
3 ch f Tamayuz Allegrissimo (IRE) (Redback)
96[3] (265) 517[5] 729[5] 1062[6] 1297[2] 3998[5] (6030) 6367[3] *7309[5]*

Sky Of Stars (IRE) *William Knight* a66 71
3 b g Frozen Power(IRE) So So Lucky (IRE) (Danehill (USA))
1140[2] 1738[8] 3570[3] *4530[4] 5471[4]*

Skyron (FR) *D Guillemin* 83
2 gr f Rock Of Gibraltar(IRE) Epatha (IRE) (Highest Honor (FR))
7263a[4]

Sky Ship *Sir Michael Stoute* a88 84
3 ch c Raven's Pass(USA) Angara (Alzao (USA))
2412[5] 3130[3] ◆ 3635[4] 4776[8] *6628[2]* 7017[11] *7108[4]*

Skywards Miles (IRE) *Tim Fitzgerald* a71 42
4 b m New Approach(IRE) Park Twilight (IRE) (Bertolini (USA))
5053 673[7] 801[9]

Slatina (IRE) *S Wattel* a78 106
4 gr m Mastercraftsman(IRE) Saudade (GER) (Linamix (FR))
4578a[5] 7569a[7] 8024a[10]

Slave To Freedom *Ann Duffield* a50
2 b f Equiano(FR) Fontegiusta (IRE) (Desert Prince (IRE))
7355[8] *8140[7] 8406[8]*

Sleeper King (IRE) *David O'Meara* a47 54
5 b g Holy Roman Emperor(IRE) Catherine Palace (Grand Lodge (USA))
2016[13]

Sleeplessinseattle *James Fanshawe* a72 66
3 b f Rip Van Winkle(IRE) Caught On Camera (Red Ransom (USA))
2008[8] 3350[4] *3990[6] 7205[6]*

Sleepy Blue Ocean *John Balding* a82 76
10 b g Oasis Dream Esteemed Lady (IRE) (Mark Of Esteem (IRE))
250[8] 364[2] 580[6] 894[7] (1046) 4495[5] 4809[7]

Sleepy Haven (IRE) *Jennie Candlish* a42 59
6 b g Indian Haven High Society Girl (IRE) (Key Of Luck (USA))
3288[4] 4499[4]

Sleet (IRE) *Michael Appleby* a60 50
5 b g Amadeus Wolf Secret Justice (USA) (Lit De Justice (USA))
60[3] 175[4] 412[5] 431[7]

Slemy (IRE) *Ruth Carr* a83 85
5 b g Raven's Pass(USA) Wolf Cleugh (IRE) (Last Tycoon)
1817[2] (2345) 2862[14] 3419[9] (3708) 4299[9] 4893[7] 5538[4] 5866[3] 6437[8]

Sliceoflife *Marco Botti* a66 29
2 b g Sayif(IRE) Cherrego (USA) (Borrego (USA))
1850[8] *7306[6] 7659[4] 8033[7] 8159[12] 8467[12]*

Slim Chance (IRE) *Simon West* a62 63
7 b m Clodovil(IRE) Valluga (IRE) (Ashkalani (IRE))
2773[17] 3211[7] 3755[5] 3843[3] ◆ 4228[4] 4309[3] *4647[2]* 4931[5] 6008[2] 6023[5] 6616[3] 6834[2] 7093[3] 7747[16] *7961[4] 8485[9] 8542[4]*

Slingsby *Michael Easterby* a77 79
5 b g Dutch Art Ballet Fame (USA) (Quest For Fame)
1124[10] *1555[7]* 2016[16] 2974[13] *(3610)* 4608[18] *5367[10] 5968[4] (7325) 7798[10] 7959[10] 8389[3]*

Slipper Satin (IRE) *Simon West* a63 72
6 b m Excellent Art In The Ribbons (In The Wings)
2912[5] 4381[12] 5183[8] 5522[5] 6219[11]

Sloane Avenue (USA) *Jeremy Noseda* a112 86
5 ch h Candy Ride(ARG) Apt (USA) (A.P. Indy (USA))
692[2] 1101a[5]

Slovak (IRE) *James Tate* a81 61
4 ch m Iffraaj Bratislava (Dr Fong (USA))
(456) 632[2] 965[5] 2001[5] 7486[3]

Slowfoot (GER) *Jim Best* a69 52
8 b h Hernando(FR) Simply Red (GER) (Dashing Blade)
1569[11] 2037[7] 3913[11] *6142[7]* 7546[13] *7765[9] 7967[8] 8249[13] 8447[9]*

Slumdogmillionaire (SAF) *Doug Watson* 103
7 b h Strike Smartly(CAN) Make A Million (AUS) (Last Tycoon)
540a[6] 721a[4]

Slunovrat (FR) *David Menuisier* a39 92
5 bb g Astronomer Royal(USA) Slewmamba (FR) (Kingsalsa (USA))
(1391) 1885[10] 4888[2] (6163) 7195a[14]

Smaih (GER) *Jamie Osborne* a70 89
4 b h Paco Boy(IRE) Solola (GER) (Black Sam Bellamy (IRE))
2247[11] 2628[9] 2978[3] 3557[11] *4199[5]* 4710[8]

Smalljohn *Bryan Smart* a61 69
10 ch g Needwood Blade My Bonus (Cyrano De Bergerac)
201[5] 681[4] (985) 2096[4]

Smart Daisy K *Sarah Hollinshead* a77 76
6 b m Pastoral Pursuits Katy-Q (IRE) (Taufan (USA))
3637[5] 4632[9]

Smart Dj *Sarah Hollinshead* a60 56
5 ch g Major Cadeaux Katy-Q (IRE) (Taufan (USA))
1971[3] 504[11] 1481[7] *1794[3] 7534[8] 8315[13]*

Smart Layer (JPN) *Ryuji Okubo* 111
6 gr m Deep Impact(JPN) Snow Style (JPN) (White Muzzle)
8329a[5]

Smart Mover (IRE) *Nikki Evans* a51 69
3 b f Fast Company(IRE) Alltherightmoves (IRE) (Namid)
1381[6] (1789) 3421[6] 4257[2] 4511[2] 5197[2] 5571[3] 6019[6] 6442[6] 7272[9]

Smart Together (USA) *John Gosden* 33
2 b f Smart Strike(CAN) Forever Together (USA) (Belong To Me (USA))
6782[9]

Smashed (IRE) *William Haggas* 77
3 b g Beat Hollow Sel (Salse (USA))
6052[4]

Smash Williams (IRE) *J S Bolger* 112
3 ch c Fracas(IRE) Take Flight (IRE) (Pivotal)
2719a[5]

Smile Of Approval (IRE) *Jonathan Portman* a61 28
3 b f Approve(IRE) Min Asl Wafi (IRE) (Octagonal (NZ))
1725[11] 2184[5] 3003[9]

Smile That Smile *Mark H Tompkins* a56 66
4 b m Champs Elysees Tenpence (Bob Back (USA))
1253[12] 2645[8] 3620[8] 3896[3]

Smiley Bagel (IRE) *Ed Walker* a48 56
3 b g Kyllachy Epistoliere (IRE) (Alzao (USA))
1259[3] 1740[3] 6890[3] *7425[8]*

Smiley Riley (IRE) *Tony Coyle* 67
2 b c Fast Company(IRE) Betty Fontaine (IRE) (Mujadil (USA))
2090[4] 2552[7] 3114[2] 3712[4] 4364[6] 4728[4] 5351[4] 5974[4]

Smirnova (IRE) *Kenny Johnson* a55 50
3 b f Dylan Thomas(IRE) Seminova (Cape Cross (IRE))
122[5] 384[7] 706[4] 1725[5] 4316[3] *5365[8] 5843[8] 5973[6]* 6617[5] 7045[12]

Smokethatthunders (IRE) *James Unett* a82 81
6 gr g Elusive City(USA) Zinstar (IRE) (Sinndar (IRE))
795[2] 965[4] 1625[5] 2213[8] 2540[3] 3137[3] *3605[7]* 4627[14] *8531[5]*

Smokey Lane (IRE) *David Evans* a79 94
2 ch c Zebedee Masela (IRE) (Medicean)
3388[2] ◆ 3858[2] ◆ 4352[6] (5484) 5656[3] *6124[6]* 6538[3] (6882) 7155[8]

Smoky Hill (IRE) *Tony Carroll* a60 68
7 gr g Galileo(IRE) Danaskaya (IRE) (Danehill (USA))
2616[5] 3641[2] ◆ (3825) 4052[3] 5053[8] 6058[7] 7274[9] *7614[8] 8039[10] 8468[8]*

Smoothtalkinrascal (IRE) *Peter Crate* a92 66
6 b g Kodiac Cool Tarifa (IRE) (One Cool Cat (USA))
1175[6] 1566[7] 2469[7] 3159[10] 3491[6] 3953[5] 4640[10] 4952[7] *5509[5]*

Smugglers Lane (IRE) *David Evans* a56 47
4 b g Bushranger(IRE) Finty (IRE) (Entrepreneur)
(84) 170[6] 378[3] 622[3] 684[6] 865[5] 1004[8] 1239[7]

Smuggler's Moon *Brian Meehan* 109
3 b g Danehill Dancer(IRE) Alchemilla (Dubai Destination (USA))
(2207) ◆ (2870) ◆

Snan (IRE) *Richard Hannon* 87
3 b c High Chaparral(IRE) Slow Sand (USA) (Dixieland Band (USA))
(1826) 2209[8] 2638[2] (3025) 3768[5] (4346) 5413[6]

Snap Call *C Lotoux* a73 59
6 ch g Tamayuz Sister Agnes (IRE) (Dr Fong (USA))
4927a[9]

Snappydresser *Tracy Waggott* 55
3 b f Medicean Dand Nee (USA) (Kabool)
3362[6] 3981[7] 4766[4] 5803[8]

Snappy Guest *George Margarson* a78 76
4 b g Kodiac Golden Shadow (IRE) (Selkirk (USA))
1415[2] 1746[3] 2217[4] *2577[2]* 3821[9] 4463[4] 5037[3] 6453[11] 7076[13] 7417[11]

Snap Shots (IRE) *Tony Coyle* a89 98
4 b g Kodiac Refuse To Give Up (IRE) (Refuse To Bend (IRE))
1650[5] 1968[14] 2476[4] (2613) 3637[6] 4066[4] (4946) 5418[6] 6792[9] 7156[11]

Sneakin'Pete *Linda Perratt* 24
3 b c Frozen Power(IRE) Jillolini (Bertolini (USA))
1691[9] 2360[10] 3017[8]

Sniper Viper *Daniel Kubler* 9
2 ch f Paco Boy(IRE) Brilliance (Cadeaux Genereux)
7184[10]

Snoano *Tim Easterby* a85 101
4 b g Nayef(USA) White Dress (IRE) (Pivotal)
920[10] 1245[4] ◆ 1493[2] ◆ 1885[6] 2744[4] (3162) 3889[4] 4407[2] 4731[6] 5651[10] 6057[5] (6559) 7154[8]

Snobbery (IRE) *Roger Charlton* a77
3 b g Duke Of Marmalade(IRE) Boast (Most Welcome)
5723[3] (8212)

Snookered (IRE) *Richard Fahey* a57 60
2 b g Born To Sea(IRE) Secret Quest (Pivotal)
3416[5] 4227[11] 4890[8] 5796[2] *6923[2]* (7244)

Snoozing Indian *T J O'Mara* a52 74
4 ch g Sleeping Indian Balnaha (Lomond (USA))
6463a[3] (7391a)

Snoozy Sioux (IRE) *Martin Smith* a58 64
2 b f Sleeping Indian Castalian Spring (IRE) (Oasis Dream)
1233[4] 2007[5] 2410[4] 5598[7] 5931[9] *7275[4] 7881[12]*

Snow Cloud (IRE) *James Cassidy* a93 85
4 b m Kodiac Thistlestar (USA) (Lion Heart (USA))
7829a[12]

Snow Conditions *Philip Hide* a73 67
5 b m Aussie Rules(USA) Snow Gonal (FR) (Octagonal (NZ))
(1039) 2582[4] 3302[6]

Snow Falcon (IRE) *Noel Meade* 92
6 b g Presenting Flocon De Neige (IRE) (Kahyasi)
7708a[5]

Snow King (USA) *Ted Powell* a59 62
6 ch g Elusive Quality(USA) Cloudspin (USA) (Storm Cat (USA))
2584[16]

Snowmaster (FR) *H-A Pantall* a75 99
3 ch c Linngari(IRE) Indochine (BRZ) (Special Nash (IRE))
1024a[6]

Snow Moon *John Gosden* 93
3 b f Oasis Dream Sariska (Pivotal)
(2009) 3060[3] 3911[4]

Snow Pixie (USA) *Ed Dunlop* 35
3 b f Flower Alley(USA) Woodland Dream (IRE) (Charnwood Forest (IRE))
2312[11]

Snow Prince *Steve Gollings* a59 77
5 gr g Royal Applause Snowdrops (Gulch (USA))
(2858) 4044[5] 4949[3]

Snow Squall *A bin Harmash* a74 86
5 b g Dansili Snow Ballerina (Sadler's Wells (USA))
538a[7] 812a[11]

Snow Squaw *David Elsworth* a75 71
2 ch f Excelebration(IRE) Snoqualmie Girl (IRE) (Montjeu (IRE))
4063[9] 4579[3] *5022[2] 5722[8] 8464[8]*

Snow Tigress (FR) *Mme J Proietti* a71
5 b m Tertullian(USA) Snow Ballet (IRE) (Sadler's Wells (USA))
512a[5]

Snowy Dawn *Steph Hollinshead* a71 75
6 gr g Notnowcato Tereyna (Terimon)
1914[2] 2392[8] 3767[5] 5061[2] 5642[7] 6083[4] *6906[3]* 7507[4] *7846[5] 8339[3]*

Snug *Jane Chapple-Hyam* a43 52
3 b f Sixties Icon Susie May (Hernando (FR))
3736[11] *3990[11]*

Snuggy (IRE) *David Barron* a64 67
2 b f Elzaam(AUS) Mandhooma (Oasis Dream)
2970[3] ◆ 3261[9] 4371[4] (5511) 6343[9] *8097[5] 8285[4] 8467[3]*

Soapy Aitken *Clive Cox* 96
3 b c Pastoral Pursuits Littlemisssunshine (IRE) (Oasis Dream)
3158[4] 3909[10] 5148[10] 5555[19]

Soaring Spirits (IRE) *Dean Ivory* a68 79
6 ch g Tamayuz Follow My Lead (Night Shift (USA))
231[6] 398[9] 621[8] 1544[7] *2155[6]* 2647[2] ◆ (2964) (3491) (4763) 5673[2] 6184[3] 6409[3] *7644[6] 8036[6] 8205[8]*

So Beloved *David O'Meara* a96 117
6 b g Dansili Valencia (Kenmare (FR))
(2030) 2691[3] 3664[4] 4754[7] 5613[2] 5926[5] 6547[4] 6955[3] 7115[10]

Sober Up *Ivan Furtado* a64 61
4 b m Kheleyf(USA) Morning After (Emperor Jones (USA))
251[11] (2609) 3078[3] *6700[12]* 7260[7] *7890[9] 8236[8] 8470[8]*

Sobetsu *Charlie Appleby* 99
2 b f Dubawi(IRE) Lake Toya (USA) (Darshaan)
5846[3] (6578) ◆ 7116[5]

So Celebre (GER) *Ian Williams* a73 83
3 ch g Peintre Celebre(USA) Saldennahe (GER) (Next Desert (IRE))
1971[4] *2900[7]* 3323[6] 4341[3] 4956[2] ◆ (5308) 6268[4] 7229[2]

Social Climber (IRE) *Ronald Harris* a60 68
4 b g Strategic Prince Ivy Queen (IRE) (Green Desert (USA))
53[6] 316[12]

Socialites Red *Scott Dixon* a65 75
3 ch f Sakhee's Secret Tipsy Girl (Haafhd)
1029[3] 1432[4] 1922[2] 2863[4] 3131[6] 4256[4] *4643[13]* 5320[8] 5864[3] 6475[2] *7255[5] 7534[7]*

Social Media *Ed Dunlop* a58 55
3 b f New Approach(IRE) Mischief Making (USA) (Lemon Drop Kid (USA))
2914[7] 3601[9] *3990[10] 6424[5]* 7746[6] *(8039)*

Society Red *Richard Fahey* 80
2 ch c Arcano(IRE) Idonea (CAN) (Swain (IRE))
(5271) ◆ 6025[2] 6950[6] 7493[2]

Socrates *Daniel Kubler* a63
2 b g Dick Turpin(IRE) Lisathedaddy (Darnay)
6108[13] *7975[6] 8066[8]*

Sofias Number One (USA) *Roy Bowring* a56 43
8 bb g Silver Deputy(CAN) Storidawn (USA) (Hennessy (USA))
368[11] 1048[4] 3498[10]

Sofia's Rock (FR) *Mark Johnston* 84
2 b c Rock Of Gibraltar(IRE) Princess Sofia (UAE) (Pennekamp (USA))
4423[4] ◆ 5107[2] 5834[3] (7580)

So Funny (USA) *F Head* a69 67
3 b f Distorted Humor(USA) Colony Band (USA) (Dixieland Band (USA))
716a[4] 3120a[7]

Soghan (IRE) *John Gosden* a49
2 br c Cape Cross(IRE) Quiet Dream (USA) (Seattle Slew (USA))
8063[7]

Sognando La Cometa (IRE) *P L Giannotti* 89
5 gr m Clodovil(IRE) Shamaness (USA) (Darshaan)
6824a[11]

Sogno D'Amore (USA) *Mark Johnston* a62 30
3 b g Bernardini(USA) Love Dancing (ARG) (Salt Lake (USA))
1134[4] 1406[6]

Sohcahtoa (IRE) *Julia Brooke* a54 50
10 b g Val Royal(FR) Stroke Of Six (IRE) (Woodborough (USA))
4489[4]

So Hoity Toity *E J O'Neill* a45 75
2 ch f Harbour Watch(IRE) Dignify (IRE) (Rainbow Quest (USA))
1284a[4] *4124a[7]* 4924a[9]

Soho Starlight *H-A Pantall* 67
3 ch c Pivotal Soho Star (Smarty Jones (USA))
5004a[9]

Soho Universe (FR) *H-A Pantall* 74
2 ch c Exceed And Excel(AUS) Soho Star (Smarty Jones (USA))
1118a[3]

Soie D'Leau *Kristin Stubbs* a91 105
4 b g Monsieur Bond(IRE) Silky Silence (High Chaparral (IRE))
1427[2] 1848[2] 2364[6] *3606[4]* (4066) 4862[7] 5390[5] 5648[5] (6119) 6327[5] 6819a[7] (7537)

Soiree *Eve Johnson Houghton* a34 50
3 b f Piccolo Nightunderthestars (Observatory (USA))
1497[11] 3146[12]

So It's War (FR) *Keith Dalgleish* a79 75
5 b g Orpen(USA) Impulsive Decision (IRE) (Nomination)
1555[9] 2198[9] 2673[4] 3013[2] *7141[2]* ◆ *7436[5] 8011[12]*

Solar Cross *Roger Charlton* 73
2 b g Sea The Stars(IRE) Nantyglo (Mark Of Esteem (IRE))
7503[4] 7769[6]

Solar Deity (IRE) *Jane Chapple-Hyam* a111 95
7 b h Exceed And Excel(AUS) Dawn Raid (IRE) (Docksider (USA))
31[3] (333) ◆ *594[4] 692[4] 920[6]* 3273[27] 4399[11] 4823[8] 5585[17] *6399a[10] 7524a[7] 8049[6] 8317[4] 8529[7]*

Solar Flair *William Knight* a98 106
4 b g Equiano(FR) Air Biscuit (IRE) (Galileo (IRE))
1204[2] 1856[5] 2480[4] 3358[7] (4366) 5124[2] 6112[16] 7497[3]

Solar Halo (USA) *W McCreery* 87
2 b f Harlan's Holiday(USA) Dreams Of Fire (USA) (Dynaformer (USA))
5940a[7]

Solarmaite *Roy Bowring* a70 61
7 b m Needwood Blade Marinaite (Komaite (USA))
367[7] 802[7] 939[4] 1399[3] ◆ *(1711) 2445[9] 8477[13]*

Solar Spirit (IRE) *Tracy Waggott* a46 77
11 b g Invincible Spirit(IRE) Misaayef (USA) (Swain (IRE))
1252[13] 2680[12] 3777[7] *7850[12]*

Sol Car (FR) *A Sagot* a13 41
5 b m Solon(GER) River Tune (FR) (Green Tune (USA))
512a[17]

Soldier Black (FR) *A Giorgi* 19
2 b c Soldier Of Fortune(IRE) Kensita (FR) (Soviet Star (USA))
5819a[9]

Soldier In Action (FR) *Mark Johnston* a81 108
3 ch g Soldier Of Fortune(IRE) Ripley (GER) (Platini (GER))
(1220) ◆ 1610[4] 1971[2] 2244[15] 2892[7] 3341[10] (4407) 4863[12] (7188) 7824[11]

Soldier's Girl (IRE) *Richard Hannon* a84 85
2 br f Sepoy(AUS) Crystal Bull (USA) (Holy Bull (USA))
4579[2] *(5298) 5632[3]* 6713[2] 7493[4]

Solent Meads (IRE) *Daniel Kubler* a73
2 ch g Intense Focus(USA) No Trimmings (IRE) (Medecis)
6672[7] 7659[3] 8082[4] 8340[4]

Sole Power *Edward Lynam* a91 119
9 br g Kyllachy Demerger (USA) (Distant View (USA))
841a[3] 1104a[10] 1862[11] 4151[8] 4413a[4] 5614[8] 6384a[7] 6943[5]

Soliana *John O'Shea* a60 39
4 ch m Dutch Art Pink Stone (FR) (Bigstone (IRE))
362[7] 412[9] 1548[12]

Solid Justice (IRE) *Tim Vaughan* a47 64
5 b g Rock Of Gibraltar(IRE) Burnin' Memories (USA) (Lit De Justice (USA))
247[12] (1674) 2558[10] 2813[5] 3547[4] *4645[12]* 5319[6] *5971[5] 6739[7] 8180[3]*

Solitary Sister (IRE) *Richard Spencer* 56
2 br f Cockney Rebel(IRE) Sweet Afton (IRE) (Mujadil (USA))
4261[5]

Solmen (FR) *M Krebs* a57 81
8 b g Solon(GER) Amen (GER) (Dashing Blade)
(1846a) 3733a[4]

Solo Hunter *Martyn Meade* a95 95
5 b g Sleeping Indian Night Owl (Night Shift (USA))
401[2] 1195[4] 1978[13] 3109[3] 4026[6] 5964[5]

Solo Mission *William Haggas* 61
2 b g Sea The Stars(IRE) Lonely Ahead (USA) (Rahy (USA))
6704[9] 7225[6] 7622[7]

Solomon's Bay (IRE) *Roger Varian* 83
2 ch c Exceed And Excel(AUS) Gentle On My Mind (IRE) (Sadler's Wells (USA))
4075[6] (6486) ◆ 7148[10]

Solveig's Song *Steve Woodman* a77 73
4 b m Norse Dancer(IRE) Ivory Lace (Atraf)
155[7] 514[4] 602[3] 728[6] (870) 1948[6] 2086[3] (2292) 2930[4] (3488) 3737[2] 4302[3] 4531[4] 5054[5] 5489[5] 6001[3] 6485[2] 6889[6] *(7973) 8462[11]*

Somebody To Love (IRE) *Richard Hannon* 90
2 b f Power Starchy (Cadeaux Genereux)
(3106) ◆ 3663[7] 4106[8] 5407[5]

Somehow (IRE) *A P O'Brien* 114
3 b f Fastnet Rock(AUS) Alexandrova (IRE) (Sadler's Wells (USA))
(1966) 2869[4] 4416a[5] 5002a[2] (5939a)

Someone Exciting *David Thompson* a42 70
3 b f Notnowcato Quite Something (Footstepsinthesand)
2304[4] 2801[7] 3367[10] 3773[2] *4647[6]* (5277) 5889[2] *6100[10]* 6834[3] 7334[2] 7747[2]

Somepink (IRE) *Daniel Mark Loughnane* a41
3 b f Lilbourne Lad(IRE) Cloonkeary (In The Wings)
298[8] 984[8] 1324[6] 6966[8] 8194[11]

Somerset House (USA) *Charlie Appleby*
2 br c
(8576a)

Something Brewing (FR) *Matthieu Palussiere* 82
2 gr c Clodovil(IRE) Talwin (IRE) (Alhaarth (IRE))
3871a[8] 4187a[2]

Something Lucky (IRE) *Kristin Stubbs* a84 84
4 gr g Clodovil(IRE) Lucky Leigh (Piccolo)
(764) 1084[6] 1666[4] 3875[3] 4608[16] 5153[10] *7112[5]* ◆ *7959[8] 8349[13] 8403[8]*

Somethingthrilling *David Elsworth* a95 83
4 b m Makfi Something Exciting (Halling (USA))
1932[4] 4160[6] *6416[5]* 6914[4] ◆ 7504[3] *(8028)* ◆ *8160[3] (8426)* ◆

Somewhere Secret *Robert Cowell* 74
2 ch c Sakhee's Secret Lark In The Park (IRE) (Grand Lodge (USA))
6053[6] 7331[4] 7819[3]

So Mi Dar *John Gosden* 118
3 b f Dubawi(IRE) Dar Re Mi (Singspiel (IRE))
(1567) (2160) (6488) 6988a[3]

Somnambulist *Keith Dalgleish* a75 53
2 b g Rip Van Winkle(IRE) Sister Moonshine (Averti (IRE))
4188[8] *7431[3] 7658[2]*

So Much Fun (IRE) *Ismail Mohammed* a70 73
3 b f Iffraaj Seminole Lass (USA) (Indian Charlie (USA))
2795[12] 3357[9] *4215[3] 5525[8] 6856[7] 7619[4] 7887[7]*

So Much Water (FR) *John Berry* 55
4 gr m Le Havre(IRE) Minnie's Mystery (FR) (Highest Honor (FR))
1931[11]

Sonata *Mick Channon* 46
2 b f Acclamation Serenada (FR) (Anabaa (USA))
6542[7] 7072[5] 7296[4]

Son Castello (IRE) *Brian Meehan* a24 45
2 b g Lilbourne Lad(IRE) Dancing Lauren (IRE) (Oratorio (IRE))
1713[5] 2390[5] 4815[6] 5770[11] *6236[9]*

Son Cesio (FR) *H-A Pantall* 115
5 b h Zafeen(FR) Slitana (FR) (Dansili)
2317a[2] (2943a) 5943a[7] 6990a[5]

Song And Dance Man *Jane Chapple-Hyam* a64 73
6 b g Danehill Dancer(IRE) Song (IRE) (Sadler's Wells (USA))
(3142) *4201[8] 4880[7]*

Songbird (USA) *Jerry Hollendorfer* a124
3 bb f Medaglia d'Oro(USA) Ivanavinalot (USA) (West Acre (USA))
7810a[2]

Song Lark *David Simcock* a55
3 b f Dick Turpin(IRE) Sovereign Abbey (IRE) (Royal Academy (USA))
202[3] 458[6]

Song Light *Seamus Mullins* a59 83
6 b g Echo Of Light Blue Lullaby (IRE) (Fasliyev (USA))
6870[11] 7625[3]

Song Maker *Charlie Appleby* a77 79
2 b f Oasis Dream Please Sing (Royal Applause)
6472[3] *7049[2]* 7441[2]

Song Of Namibia (IRE) *Sir Michael Stoute* a84 82
5 br g Cape Cross(IRE) Spring Symphony (IRE) (Darshaan)
3023[3] 4401[9] *7106[2]*

Song Of Norway *Chris Wall* a82 78
5 b m Halling(USA) Amarullah (FR) (Daylami (IRE))
2213[5] 4519[6] *5301[2]* 6580[5]

Song Of Paradise *Chris Wall* a69 44
3 ch f Kyllachy Merry Diva (Bahamian Bounty)
2337[10] *3786[3]* 4517[9] *5027[8]*

Song Of Shadows *Michael Wigham* a76 82
3 b g Invincible Spirit(IRE) Lyrique (IRE) (Iffraaj)
(8496)

Sonic Boom (USA) *Ian Wilkes* 99
2 ch c More Than Ready(USA) Silent Circle (USA) (Indian Charlie (USA))
7266a[2]

Son Macia (GER) *Andreas Lowe* 100
3 b f Soldier Hollow Sinaada (GER) (Zinaad)
2730a[3] 4175a[2] 5451a[8] 6152a[6] (7720a)

Sonnentanz (IRE) *Daniel Kubler* a17 51
3 b f Vale Of York(IRE) Irish Fountain (USA) (Irish River (FR))
1063[11] 6251[5] *7311[10] 7910[11]*

Sonnet (IRE) *David Evans* a68 68
3 b f Kyllachy Poetical (IRE) (Croco Rouge (IRE))
679[5] 2303[3] 3249[2] 3810[2] 4789[2] *5247[7] 7725[9] 7995[2] 8093[3]*

Sonnythenavigator (USA) *David Simcock* a69 58
4 bb g Henrythenavigator(USA) Lady Simpson (Yankee Victor (USA))
55[4] (218) (354) (417) ◆

Son Of Africa *Henry Candy* a54 103
4 b g Equiano(FR) Generously Gifted (Sakhee (USA))
1439[11] 2188[13] 3573[5] ◆ 4366[6] 5418[18] (5648) 5863[7] 6327[15] 6642[7]

Son Of Rest *T Stack* 104
2 b c Pivotal Hightime Heroine (IRE) (Danetime (IRE))
6386a[4]

Son Of The Stars *Richard Hannon* a80
2 b c Delegator Michelle Shift (Night Shift (USA))
(8245) ◆

Sooqaan *Antony Brittain* a68 53
5 bl g Naaqoos Dream Day (FR) (Spectrum (IRE))
448[2] 956[5] 2409[8] 3344[7] *4715[4] 7368[6]*

Sophie P *R Mike Smith* 87
3 b f Bushranger(IRE) Fountains Abbey (USA) (Giant's Causeway (USA))
1216[3] 1691[4] 3343[7] 3945[2] 4193[4] 4700[6] 5151[6] 5782[2] (6541) 6811[2] ◆ 7126[4]

Sophie's World (IRE) *Alan Fleming* a40 89
5 b m Captain Rio Nirvavita (FR) (Highest Honor (FR))
4811a[10]

Sophistica (IRE) *Iain Jardine* a59 49
3 b f Thousand Words Texas Queen (Shamardal (USA))
2571[11] *2919[9]* 3423[8] 4141[5]

Sophisticated Heir (IRE) *Michael Herrington* a85 77
6 b g New Approach(IRE) My Girl Sophie (USA) (Danzig (USA))
1152[3] ◆ 1521[9] 2960[6] ◆ 3807[7] 4231[4] 4427[4] 6231[8] *(6589)* 6766[4] *7433[6] 7983[3] 8176[3] 8314[3] 8561[3]*

Sopran Secreter (ITY) *Carina Fey* a69 81
3 b c Johnny Red Kerr(USA) Northern Secret (Sinndar (IRE))
5280a[9]

Sorry Erik (USA) *Doug O'Neill* 71
2 b c Wilburn(USA) Tiz The Day (USA) (Tiznow (USA))
7266a[12]

Sors (IRE) *Andrew Slattery* a84 101
4 b g Acclamation Maid Of Ailsa (USA) (Pivotal)
(3696a) 4415a[10] 6382a[3] 6819a[11]

Sory *Tina Jackson* 25
9 b g Sakhee(USA) Rule Britannia (Night Shift (USA))
1955[10]

So Si Bon (AUS) *Robbie Laing* 109
2 bk c So You Think(NZ) Black Minx (NZ) (Lonhro (AUS))
7948a[4]

So Sleek *Luca Cumani* a70 61
2 b f Lawman(FR) So Silk (Rainbow Quest (USA))
7285[4] *7762[3]*

Sotteville (FR) *J-C Rouget* 103
3 b f Le Havre(IRE) Sandsnow (IRE) (Verglas (IRE))
5451a[3] 6972a[3]

Soul Brother (IRE) *Tim Easterby* a83 84
5 b g Captain Rio Goodwood March (Foxhound (USA))
1447[8] (1874) 2305[6] 2665[9] 3944[3] 5153[9] 5479[11] *7112[8] 7433[2]*

Soul Intent (IRE) *Brian Ellison* a82 79
6 b g Galileo(IRE) Flamingo Guitar (USA) (Storm Cat (USA))
3659[9] 4550[2] *4940[2]* 5406[4]

Soul Searcher (IRE) *J P Murtagh* a89 94
4 b m Motivator Israar (Machiavellian (USA))
6200a[6] 6820a[5] 7196a[3] 7393a[10]

Soul Silver (IRE) *David Simcock* a89 87
2 ch f Dragon Pulse(IRE) Free Lance (IRE) (Grand Lodge (USA))
(3073) 4106[10] *5632[2] (6088)* 7547[5]

Sound Advice *Keith Dalgleish* a100 108
7 b g Echo Of Light Flylowflylong (IRE) (Danetime (IRE))
920[8] 1153[9] 1629[7] 1993[4] (2684) 3390[4] 4688[6] 4846[2] 5640[9] 6557[14] 7121[14]

Sound Bar *Ralph Beckett* 81
2 b c Oasis Dream Milford Sound (Barathea (IRE))
5600[9] 6632[2] (7503) ◆

Soundbyte *John Gallagher* a36 36
11 b g Beat All(USA) Gloaming (Celtic Swing)
6825[10]

Sound Check (GER) *P Schiergen* 89
3 bb c Lando(GER) Sky Dancing (IRE) (Exit To Nowhere (USA))
6612a[6]

Sound Of Freedom (IRE) *Stefano Botti* a92 107
4 ch m Duke Of Marmalade(IRE) Paint In Green (IRE) (Invincible Spirit (IRE))
1475[6] 2797[4] *3608[6]* 4400[6] (7566a)

Sounds Of Earth (JPN) *Kenichi Fujioka* 118
5 bb h Neo Universe(JPN) First Violin (USA) (Dixieland Band (USA))
8129a[2]

Soundstrings *William Haggas* a81 80
3 b f Oasis Dream Straight Lass (IRE) (Machiavellian (USA))
3850[6] 4565[2] 5388[2] (5757) 6342[4] *(6908)* ◆

Soundtrack (IRE) *P Schaerer* a72 83
5 br g Excellent Art Umthoulah (IRE) (Unfuwain (USA))
588a[2] 664a[2]

Souter *Keith Dalgleish* 81
2 br c Poet's Voice Storming Sioux (Storming Home)
5150[4] 5778[2] (6499)

Southdown Lad (IRE) *William Knight* a72 98
3 b g Lilbourne Lad(IRE) Elizabelle (IRE) (Westerner)
1398[3] 2244[3] ◆ (6545) 7188[5]

Southern Belle (IRE) *Robert Cowell* a51 94
3 b f Aqlaam Areyaam (USA) (Elusive Quality (USA))
4223[3] ◆ (4984) ◆ 6207[4] 6518[9]

Southern Gailes (IRE) *K R Burke* a83 79
3 ch g Frozen Power(IRE) Pardoned (IRE) (Mujadil (USA))
1080[9] 1602[5] 3687[5] *5365[2] 5738[4]* 6344[3] *(7436)*

Southern Seas *Ann Duffield* a62 60
3 ch f Archipenko(USA) Sourire (Domedriver (IRE))
147[5] 335[5]

Southern Stars *John Gosden* a7 84
3 b f Smart Strike(CAN) Stacelita (FR) (Monsun (GER))
(1608) 2245[10] *7980[11]*

Southern States *Lydia Richards* a67 52
3 b g Medaglia d'Oro(USA) Little Belle (USA) (A.P. Indy (USA))
6294[10] *7425[7] 7760[2] 8445[3]*

Southern Storm (IRE) *Ralph Beckett* a89 88
4 b m Cape Cross(IRE) Stormy Blessing (USA) (Storm Cat (USA))
163[3] ◆ *(413) 788[6] (1171) (1266)* 1743[3] *4646[5]* 4883[6]

Southern Strife *Tim Easterby* a55 73
5 b g Dubawi(IRE) Savannah Belle (Green Desert (USA))
3845[11] 4546[5] 4895[7] 5480[6] (6432) 7043[7] 7359[6] *7775[4] 8011[7]*

South Sea Belle (IRE) *David Menuisier* 66
2 ch f New Approach(IRE) South Atlantic (USA) (Stormy Atlantic (USA))
6061[4]

South Seas (IRE) *Andrew Balding* 107
2 ch c Lope De Vega(IRE) Let It Be Me (USA) (Mizzen Mast (USA))
(3463) (4343) (5646) 7149[6] 7721a[2]

Southview Lady *Sean Regan* a36 57
4 b m Misu Bond(IRE) Salalah (Lion Cavern (USA))
7795[8]

Souville *Chris Wall* a77 96
5 b m Dalakhani(IRE) Royale Danehill (IRE) (Danehill (USA))
1453[11] 2042[8] 2474[7] 4398[13] 5744[4] ◆ 6340[6] 6583[11]

Sov (IRE) *James Given* a51 71
5 gr g Duke Of Marmalade(IRE) Exotic Mix (FR) (Linamix (FR))
273[9] 5737[4]

Sovereign Bounty *Jedd O'Keeffe* a76 86
4 ch g Bahamian Bounty Sovereign Abbey (IRE) (Royal Academy (USA))
1844[3] ◆ 2345[2] *2579[3]* 3517[14] (4231) (5482) 5866[9]

Sovereign Debt (IRE) *David Nicholls* a115 115
7 br g Dark Angel(IRE) Kelsey Rose (Most Welcome)
921[2] 1068[2] ◆ 1425[6] 1910a[5] 2867[4] 3164[2] 3677a[2] 4135[2] 4433a[2] 6955[4] (7542) (7706a) *7978[3] 8431a[2]*

Sovereign Parade (IRE) *John Gosden* 99
3 b f Galileo(IRE) Dialafara (FR) (Anabaa (USA))
(2182) ◆ 3297[7]

Sovrano Dolce (IRE) *Mike Murphy* a50 65
3 b f Roderic O'Connor(IRE) Tartufo Dolce (IRE) (Key Of Luck (USA))
6674[5] 7219[4] *7727[U] 8075[10]*

Sowgay (FR) *C Plisson* 62
2 ch g Air Chief Marshal(IRE) Kitty Yield (FR) (High Yield (USA))
1021a[8] 2724a[6] 3871a[14] 5819a[6]

So You Go (IRE) *Mme C Head-Maarek* a67
2 b f So You Think(NZ) Seal Bay (IRE) (Hernando (FR))
5460a[5]

Space Artist (IRE) *Nigel Tinkler* a79 66
6 b g Captain Marvelous(IRE) Dame Laura (IRE) (Royal Academy (USA))
1433[7] 1874[12] 5274[12] 5864[10] 6475[3] 6879[11] 6958[5]

Space Cowboy (GER) *Markus Klug* 100
4 ch h Adlerflug(GER) St Aye (USA) (Nureyev (USA))
2286a[9]

Space Mountain *Mark Johnston* a79 79
3 b g Sea The Stars(IRE) Ripples Maid (Dansili)
(593) 3621[4] 4949[2] (5294) *5633[2]* 6121[8] 6345[4] *6591[3] 7512[10]*

Space War *Michael Easterby* a72 69
9 b g Elusive City(USA) Princess Luna (GER) (Grand Lodge (USA))
1252[9] *(2006)* 2872[7] 4848[3] 5034[3] ◆ 5859[3] 6220[7] 7334[9] *7797[2] 7887[3] 7994[5] 8315[2]*

Spader (IRE) *G M Lyons* a73 87
3 b g Jeremy(USA) Poulkovo (IRE) (Sadler's Wells (USA))
2244[14] 3428a[9]

Spain Burg (FR) *Kathy Ritvo* 100
2 b f Sageburg(IRE) Spain Blues (FR) (Anabaa Blue)
(6748) 7809a[10]

Spangled *Roger Varian* 111
4 ch m Starspangledbanner(AUS) Zykina (Pivotal)
(2539) ◆ 3271[13] 4114[5] (4651) (6281)

Spanish Beauty *Ollie Pears* a47 48
2 b f Paco Boy(IRE) Basque Beauty (Nayef (USA))
3321[5] 3947[10] 5271[10] *6923[7]*

Spanish Bounty *Mrs A Malzard* a36 58
11 b g Bahamian Bounty Spanish Gold (Vettori (IRE))
2284a^{11} 3380a^{7} 5456a^{5}

Spanish City *Roger Varian* a90 78
3 ch c Exceed And Excel(AUS) Annabelle's Charm (IRE) (Indian Ridge)
(2750) ◆ 3644^{4} *(7434)* ◆ *7990^{6}*

Spanish Fly (IRE) *M Delcher Sanchez* 98
2 b f Iffraaj Hundredsnthousands (IRE) (Thousand Words)
5703a^{6} 6694a^{4}

Spanish History (USA) *A Fabre* 58
2 bb c Street Cry(IRE) Infanta (IRE) (Cape Cross (IRE))
7291a^{6}

Spanish Queen *Mark Gillard* 41
3 b f Fantastic Spain(USA) Smart Cassie (Allied Forces (USA))
6441^{5} 7219^{9}

Spanish Romance (IRE) *E J O'Neill* 97
3 b f Rip Van Winkle(IRE) Utr (USA) (Mr Prospector (USA))
3090a^{8}

Spanish Squeeze (IRE) *Hugo Palmer* a104 95
4 ch g Lope De Vega(IRE) Appetina (Perugino (USA))
2157^{8} 4276^{7} 5173^{7}

Spanish Tenor (IRE) *Timothy Doyle* 100
2 ch c Lope De Vega(IRE) Devious Soprano (IRE) (Orpen (USA))
7559a^{4}

Sparkle *Ed Dunlop* a72 69
2 b f Oasis Dream Gemstone (IRE) (Galileo (IRE))
4350^{5} ◆ 5119^{8} 7314^{5} ◆ *7898^{3} 8244^{5}*

Sparkle Jack (FR) *Mlle A Rosa* a61 55
3 b f Cat Junior(USA) Hoian (FR) (Nombre Premier)
5704a^{5}

Sparkling Cossack *Jeremy Gask* a45
2 ch f Famous Name Eleanor Eloise (USA) (Minardi (USA))
8151^{10}

Spark Plug (IRE) *Brian Meehan* 115
5 b g Dylan Thomas(IRE) Kournikova (SAF) (Sportsworld (USA))
2246^{6} ◆ 2796^{5} 3273^{12} 3860^{2} 4392^{5} 5585^{4} ◆ (6786)

Sparks (IRE) *Sarah-Jayne Davies*
4 br m Elusive City(USA) Hambye (Distant Relative)
1708^{7}

Sparring (IRE) *Charlie Appleby* a96 97
4 b g Teofilo(IRE) Henties Bay (IRE) (Cape Cross (IRE))
2979^{4}

Sparring Queen (USA) *Ralph Beckett* a62 49
3 b f War Front(USA) Spa Break (USA) (Giant's Causeway (USA))
2470^{9} *3319^{2} 4214^{2} 4936^{9}*

Spa's Dancer (IRE) *James Eustace* a82 94
9 b g Danehill Dancer(IRE) Spa (Sadler's Wells (USA))
1274^{2} 1978^{6} 2556^{4} 3621^{3} 6301^{11}

Spatial *Sir Michael Stoute* 83
2 b f New Approach(IRE) Spacious (Nayef (USA))
5170^{2} ◆ (5846) 7116^{6}

Special Code (IRE) *Heather Dalton* a67 59
4 b g Iffraaj Najmati (Green Desert (USA))
579^{4}

Speciale Di Giorno (IRE) *Marco Botti* a50 55
2 b f High Chaparral(IRE) Special Assignment (USA) (Lemon Drop Kid (USA))
3640^{4} 4397^{10} 5747^{7} *7482^{10}*

Special Fighter (IRE) *M Al Mheiri* a115 91
5 ch h Teofilo(IRE) Susu (Machiavellian (USA))
92a^{6} (281a) 452a^{6} (844a) 1108a^{4}

Special Relation (IRE) *Hughie Morrison* a69 66
2 b c Casamento(IRE) Sindiyma (IRE) (Kalanisi (IRE))
7239^{4} *8377^{2}*

Special Request (FR) *N Caullery* a96 80
9 gr g Kaldounevees(FR) Radio Mesnil (FR) (Nashamaa)
3184a^{8}

Special Season *Jamie Osborne* a100 93
3 ch g Lope De Vega(IRE) Keep Dancing (IRE) (Distant Music (USA))
154^{3} 1071^{5} 2473^{11} 7546^{7} *7967^{5}* ◆ *8177^{5}*

Specialv (IRE) *Brian Ellison* a70 80
3 br f Big Bad Bob(IRE) Montbretia (Montjeu (IRE))
(248) ◆ 1381^{4} 1816^{3} 2095^{7} 2506^{4} 3224^{12} (3673) 4382^{5} 4873^{3} (5224) ◆ 5836^{5} 6537^{12} 6770^{7} 7743^{3} *8036^{9}*

Specific Gravity (FR) *Adrian McGuinness* a83 68
8 b g Dansili Colza (USA) (Alleged (USA))
6465a^{5} 7801a^{4}

Spectre (FR) *M Munch* 115
3 ch f Siyouni(FR) Inez (Dai Jin)
(1309a) 2282a^{5} 4185a^{3} 5449a^{4} 6394a^{2} 7837a^{11}

Spectroscope (USA) *A Fabre* a82 106
3 bb c Medaglia d'Oro(USA) Diamondrella (Rock Of Gibraltar (IRE))
4439a^{3} 5699a^{4} 6597a^{3} 7137a^{3}

Speculator *John Butler* a74 74
4 gr h Bahamian Bounty Swift Dispersal (Shareef Dancer (USA))
1340^{3} (1810) 2623^{4} 3002^{3} 4158^{3} 4785^{2} 6001^{2} *8124^{11} 8282^{10}*

Speed Company (IRE) *John Quinn* 104
3 b g Fast Company(IRE) Trentini (IRE) (Singspiel (IRE))
(1398) ◆ 1866^{4} 2432^{4} 3299^{24} 5173^{4} 5865^{6} 6559^{4} (7499)

Speed Freak *Ralph Beckett* a69 72
2 b f Fastnet Rock(AUS) The Thrill Is Gone (Bahamian Bounty)
2310^{4} 2637^{3} 3261^{8} 4386^{3} 4879^{2} *8313^{4} 8526^{3}*

Speed Hawk (USA) *Robert Cowell* a109 109
5 br g Henny Hughes(USA) Cosmic Wing (USA) (Halo (USA))
91a^{3} *186a^{7}* 450a^{5} 626a^{10}

Speedo Boy (FR) *Ian Williams* a79
2 ch c Vision D'Etat(FR) Shamardanse (IRE) (Shamardal (USA))
7865^{7} 8074^{3}

Speedy Boarding *James Fanshawe* 116
4 b m Shamardal(USA) Dash To The Front (Diktat)
2189^{4} (2727a) 3695a^{5} (5691a) (6988a) 7351^{2}

Speightowns Kid (USA) *Ann Stokell* a73 33
8 rg g Speightstown(USA) Seize The Wind (USA) (Maria's Mon (USA))
(22) (130) 246^{8} 520^{6} 1030^{7} 1298^{5} 1712^{7} 4484^{8} 4932^{9} *5736^{9}*

Spelling Again (USA) *Brad H Cox* a108
5 b m Awesome Again(CAN) Spelling (USA) (Alphabet Soup (USA))
7836a^{6}

Spellmaker *Tony Newcombe* a81 63
7 b g Kheleyf(USA) Midnight Spell (Night Shift (USA))
398^{11} (1180) 1496^{8} 2697^{13} 3510^{11} *6589^{4}*

Spello (IRE) *John Ryan* a36
2 br g Born To Sea(IRE) Carina Ari (IRE) (Imperial Ballet (IRE))
6850^{6}

Spend The Cash (IRE) *W Mongil* 105
5 ch h Adlerflug(GER) Splash Mountain (IRE) (Peintre Celebre (USA))
285a^{11} 538a^{8}

Spes Nostra *Iain Jardine* a93 78
8 b g Ad Valorem(USA) Millagros (IRE) (Pennekamp (USA))
465^{10} (734) 861^{2} 975^{7} 1445^{11} 3391^{7} 4312^{6} *5082^{8} 8007^{6}* ◆ *8283^{10}*

Spey Secret (IRE) *Tom Dascombe* 13
3 br g Kyllachy Chiarezza (AUS) (Fantastic Light (USA))
1421^{12}

Spiaggia (IRE) *F Chappet* 80
2 b f Makfi Spectacular Show (IRE) (Spectrum (IRE))
3270^{16}

Spice Boat *Paddy Butler* a47 38
4 ch g Shamardal(USA) Frizzante (Efisio)
7010^{10} 3401^{13} 6891^{10}

Spice Fair *Mark Usher* a83 84
9 ch g Trade Fair Focosa (ITY) (In The Wings)
2699^{6} 3351^{4} 3862^{6} 4795^{3} *7732^{11}*

Spice Mill (IRE) *Michael Appleby* a69 62
3 b g Dream Ahead(USA) High Spice (USA) (Songandaprayer (USA))
798^{3} ◆ *935^{2} 1151^{3} 1435^{5}* 2974^{4} 3604^{4} 3907^{7} 4985^{7} 5760^{10} *8181^{2} 8473^{7}*

Spice Trail *A Fabre* 89
3 ch f Champs Elysees Cinnamon Bay (Zamindar (USA))
7568a^{9}

Spicy Jam *Marco Botti* a97 96
4 bb m Holy Roman Emperor(IRE) Jalys (IRE) (Sri Pekan (USA))
214^{6} 529^{4}

Spifer (IRE) *Julia Brooke* 83
8 gr g Motivator Zarawa (IRE) (Kahyasi)
7043^{13}

Spiga (IRE) *A Fabre* a73 93
3 ch f Lope De Vega(IRE) Spesialta (Indian Ridge)
7348a^{8}

Spike (IRE) *David Barron* 77
3 b g Lilbourne Lad(IRE) Vintage Allure (IRE) (Barathea (IRE))
2218^{10} 2802^{6} 5439^{6} 5978^{7} 6717^{6}

Spin A Disc (GER) *Mark Johnston* a49 40
2 gr c Jukebox Jury(IRE) Sun Society (GER) (Law Society (USA))
5728^{9} 6092^{3} *6623^{7}*

Spinart *Pam Sly* a68 68
3 ch g Dutch Art Spinneret (Pivotal)
5438^{7} 7009^{6} *7753^{3}*

Spin Doctor *Richard Fahey* a84 84
2 gr f Mayson Doctor's Glory (USA) (Elmaamul (USA))
(2007) 2670^{3} 3336^{15} 5560^{16} 6536^{8} 7073^{6} *(7600) (7893)*

Spinnaka (IRE) *Luca Cumani* 72
2 b f Invincible Spirit(IRE) Spinning Well (IRE) (Pivotal)
5705^{2}

Spinnaker Bay (IRE) *William Jarvis* a70 73
2 b f Lawman(FR) Wizz Kid (IRE) (Whipper (USA))
4350^{2} ◆ 4804^{3} 6162^{12} 7217^{3} *7689^{4} 7966^{9}*

Spinners Ball (IRE) *Sylvester Kirk* a80 69
3 b g Excellent Art Meek Appeal (USA) (Woodman (USA))
3744^{2} ◆ *4213^{4}* 4639^{3} *(5397)* 6121^{6} *7993^{4} 8161^{4}* ◆

Spinning Cobblers *Stuart Williams* a71 55
5 b g Royal Applause Tychy (Suave Dancer (USA))
28^{5} 782^{8} 1159^{P} (Dead)

Spinning Pearl (IRE) *Phil Middleton* a64 67
3 b f Dylan Thomas(IRE) Spinning Gold (Spinning World (USA))
699^{6} (1149) 1835^{3} 2700^{11} 4522^{2} *5529^{4}* (5923) 6827^{11}

Spinning Rose *Dean Ivory* a62 53
4 ch m Pivotal Aqua Rose (USA) (Redoute's Choice (AUS))
65^{7} 245^{9} 445^{7} 2901^{2} 3624^{5} *4267^{4} (4527) 4882^{7} 5635^{4} 6513^{3} 7257^{3} 7515^{2}*

Spin Point (IRE) *Ian Williams* a69 84
4 b g Pivotal Daneleta (IRE) (Danehill (USA))
8446^{7}

Spin Top *Joseph Tuite* a64 62
2 b g Acclamation Miss Work Of Art (Dutch Art)
1203^{P} 1543^{6} 2180^{5} 2847^{8} 4553^{6} 5257^{4} 5543^{3} 6033^{10} *6588^{4} 7275^{3} 7615^{7} 8230^{3} (8425)*

Spinwheel *Mark Johnston* a67
2 ch f Pivotal Angel's Tears (Seeking The Gold (USA))
8557^{5}

Spiraea *Ivan Furtado* a21 72
6 ch m Bahamian Bounty Salvia (Pivotal)
4398^{8} 4708^{7} *8571^{13}*

Spirit Be With You (IRE) *Miss Natalia Lupini* a45 60
3 b f Dandy Man(IRE) Mar Sin De (IRE) (Danetime (IRE))
6615^{5} *7339a^{12}*

Spirit De Cerisy (FR) *Matthieu Palussiere* 82
2 ch c Tagula(IRE) Child Bride (Invincible Spirit (IRE))
4330a^{4}

Spirit Doll (HOL) *Prof Dr R P Dollevoet* 73
9 b g Alkalde(GER) Second D (Atraf)
5943a^{11}

Spiritfix *A Fabre* a97 97
3 b f Invincible Spirit(IRE) Beautifix (GER) (Bering)
2141a^{2} 4905a^{6} 6391a^{4} 7030a^{3}

Spirit Glance *Tim Easterby* a67 47
3 b f Invincible Spirit(IRE) Gonfilia (GER) (Big Shuffle (USA))
679^{4} 765^{2} 858^{3} 3806^{6} 4517^{11}

Spiriting (IRE) *Roger Varian* 91
4 b g Invincible Spirit(IRE) Gold Bubbles (USA) (Street Cry (IRE))
2587^{5}

Spirit In Time (IRE) *Malcolm Saunders* a43 49
4 b m Vale Of York(IRE) Star Port (Observatory (USA))
1320^{7}

Spirit Of Belle *Pat Phelan* a70 66
2 b c Sir Percy Yensi (Doyen (IRE))
6264^{7} 7013^{6} *7458^{3} 8466^{10}*

Spiritofedinburgh (IRE) *Brendan Powell* a71 73
2 b g Lilbourne Lad(IRE) Xema (Danehill (USA))
1384^{5} 2535^{3} 5395^{9} 5989^{4} *6672^{3}*

Spirit Of Gondree (IRE) *Milton Bradley* a68 61
8 b g Invincible Spirit(IRE) Kristal's Paradise (IRE) (Bluebird (USA))
141^{6} 621^{3} 792^{3} 1064^{9} 1502^{8} 6700^{8} 7048^{2} 7368^{9} 7514^{6} 7735^{5} 7944^{5}

Spirit Of India *John Gosden* 65
2 ch f Galileo(IRE) Sundari (IRE) (Danehill (USA))
6111^{7} 6578^{6}

Spirit Of Rome (IRE) *James Bethell* a56 41
2 ch f Mastercraftsman(IRE) Zagreb Flyer (Old Vic)
7157^{12} 7855^{6} 8130^{7}

Spirit Of Rosanna *Steph Hollinshead* a46 64
4 gr m Hellvelyn Tharwa (IRE) (Last Tycoon)
22^{9} 54^{10} 1600^{3} 2458^{2} 3486^{4} (3898) (4378)

Spirit Of Sarwan (IRE) *Julia Feilden* a74 77
2 b c Elzaam(AUS) Hidden Heart (USA) (Kingmambo (USA))
2173^{5} (2963) 3477^{2} 4150^{8} 4595^{3} *5506^{4}*

Spirit Of Teofilo (FR) *D De Waele* a70 49
6 b g Teofilo(IRE) Spirit Of Pearl (IRE) (Invincible Spirit (IRE))
7398a^{9}

Spirit Of The Sea (IRE) *Richard Whitaker* a35 61
4 b m Invincible Spirit(IRE) Cedar Sea (IRE) (Persian Bold)
26^{6} 251^{10} 4446^{8} 4833^{4}

Spirit Of The Vale (IRE) *Oliver Greenall* a49 64
3 b f Royal Applause Nesmeh (USA) (More Than Ready (USA))
7888^{6} 8194^{12} 8492^{4}

Spiritoftomintoul *Tony Carroll* a86 80
7 gr g Authorized(IRE) Diamond Line (FR) (Linamix (FR))
66^{6} 337^{5} (545) 983^{3} 1598^{7} 2392^{4} *2782^{8}* 3639^{7} *8476^{7}*

Spirit Of Valor (USA) *A P O'Brien* 102
2 b c War Front(USA) Stone Hope (USA) (Grindstone (USA))
(7387a) 7559a^{2}

Spirit Of Wedza (IRE) *Julie Camacho* a66 73
4 b g Footstepsinthesand Sampers (IRE) (Exceed And Excel (AUS))
1116^{4} 1555^{6} 2571^{3} (3210) 3880^{5} 4496^{6} 5060^{3} *5368^{6}* 5864^{6}

Spirit Of Zeb (IRE) *Richard Fahey* a91 85
4 ch g Zebedee Miss Glitters (IRE) (Chevalier (IRE))
2680^{3} 3021^{3} (3753) 4259^{2} 5161^{5} 5991^{6} 7094^{7} 7572^{8}

Spirit Of Zebedee (IRE) *John Quinn* a63 67
3 gr g Zebedee Sampers (IRE) (Exceed And Excel (AUS))
1670^{12} 3940^{3} (4410) (4513) ◆ 4770^{10} 6506^{11} 6790^{4} 7092^{5} 7584^{6} *7852^{5}*

Spiritous (USA) *John Gosden* 88
2 b c Invincible Spirit(IRE) Andina (IRE) (Singspiel (IRE))
2203^{2} ◆ 2649^{3} (3356) 4148^{5} 4553^{2} 6734^{8} 7073^{5}

Spirit Quartz (IRE) *N Caullery* a93 112
8 b g Invincible Spirit(IRE) Crystal Gaze (IRE) (Rainbow Quest (USA))
1862^{4} 2317a^{9} (3201a) 3909^{5} ◆ 4824^{13} (5816a) 6384a^{8} 6574^{4} 7030a^{2} (7997a)

Spirit Raiser (IRE) *James Fanshawe* a103 105
5 b m Invincible Spirit(IRE) Macadamia (IRE) (Classic Cliche (IRE))
(2796) 3273^{23} (3979) 5645^{6}

Spirit's Revench (FR) *P Demercastel* a76 103
6 ch h Spirit One(FR) European Style (FR) (Ezzoud (IRE))
8042a^{11} 8336a^{10}

Spiritual Lady *Philip McBride* a94 101
2 b f Pastoral Pursuits Rouge Dancer (Elusive City (USA))
(3613) 4394^{5} ◆ *(4974)* (7667)

Spiritual Star (IRE) *Lee Carter* a90 61
7 b g Soviet Star(USA) Million Spirits (IRE) (Invincible Spirit (IRE))
172^{6} 266^{4} 401^{4} 494^{7} 2150^{4} 2402^{6} 2977^{4} *3405^{P}* 4784^{7} 5994^{7} *6656^{5}* ◆ *7051^{5} 7457^{2} 7886^{6} 8178^{12}*

Spiritueux (IRE) *C Laffon-Parias* a60 77
5 b g Invincible Spirit(IRE) Stormina (USA) (Gulch (USA))
(5281a)

Spitfire *J R Jenkins* a74 70
11 b g Mujahid(USA) Fresh Fruit Daily (Reprimand)
135^{2} 799^{6} 963^{2} 1401^{3}

Splash Around *Sir Michael Stoute* 73
2 ch c Nathaniel(IRE) Splashdown (Falbrav (IRE))
5848^{5} ◆ 6523^{4}

Splash Of Verve (IRE) *Philip Kirby* a66 67
4 b g Fast Company(IRE) Ellistown Lady (IRE) (Red Sunset)
1057^{6} 1253^{8} 1561^{8} 3711^{11} 4143^{6} 4515^{4}

Split The Atom (IRE) *David Marnane* a92 81
4 ch g The Carbon Unit(USA) The Mighty Atom (USA) (Sky Mesa (USA))
1335^{4} 5441a^{4} 6382a^{9} *7523a^{5} 8197a^{5}*

Spoil The Fun (FR) *C Ferland* a100 108
7 ch h Rock Of Gibraltar(IRE) Avezia (FR) (Night Shift (USA))
5948a^{7}

Spoken Words *John David Riches* a46 53
7 b m Fruits Of Love(USA) Jerre Jo Glanville (USA) (Skywalker (USA))
547^{9} 2359 ^{3} 2571^{9} 4492^{2} 4931^{11} 5278^{2} 6023^{12} 6615^{10}

Spokesperson (USA) *Fred Watson* a42 55
8 b g Henny Hughes(USA) Verbal (USA) (Kingmambo (USA))
2526^{8} *3564^{14} 5842^{7}*

Spongy (IRE) *Mohammed Jassim Ghazali* a67 85
3 b c Zoffany(IRE) Eminence Gift (Cadeaux Genereux)
756a^{13}

Sporting Times *Ed Dunlop* 80
2 ch c Sir Percy Queen Of Iceni (Erhaab (USA))
6211^{2}

Sports Barrow (IRE) *Ms Sandra Hughes* 63
4 b g Windsor Knot(IRE) Liberty Grace (IRE) (Statue Of Liberty (USA))
(5900a)

Sportsmanship (USA) *A P O'Brien* 96
2 b c War Front(USA) Wild Poppy (USA) (El Prado (IRE))
4755^{4} 5661a^{5} 5940a^{6}

Sporty Yankee (USA) *K R Burke* 81
3 gr g Paddy O'Prado(USA) I Insist (USA) (Green Dancer (USA))
1410^{3} 2224^{10} 2576^{8} 3236^{2} ◆ (3468) 3959^{6} 5420^{5} (6503) 7332^{2}

Spowarticus *Scott Dixon* a70 54
7 ch g Shamardal(USA) Helen Bradley (IRE) (Indian Ridge)
133^{4} 178^{2} 426^{6} 680^{11} 799^{2} 942^{3} 1030^{3} 1154^{7} 1712^{4} 3553^{9} 4142^{3} *8095^{12} 8234^{10}*

Spray Tan *Tony Carroll* a55 55
6 b m Assertive Even Hotter (Desert Style (IRE))
217^{2} 513^{7} 732^{3} (1164) 1721^{9} 1913^{7} *2447^{3}* 2845^{6} 3741^{6} 3993^{13}

Spring Bird *Alan Swinbank* a42 75
7 b m Danbird(AUS) Dolphin Dancer (Dolphin Street (FR))
1119^{5} *1402^{8}* 3211^{12} 3549^{10} 4931^{3} ◆ 5889^{9} 7093^{10}

Springbourne *Sylvester Kirk* 79
2 b g Hellvelyn Musical Key (Key Of Luck (USA)) (3770)

Spring Dixie (IRE) *Mrs A Malzard* a23 73
4 gr m Zebedee Dixie Jazz (Mtoto)
14^{6} 1518a^{6} 2952a^{6} 5458a^{4}

Spring Eternal *Charles Hills* 14
2 b f Oasis Dream Short Dance (USA) (Hennessy (USA))
6078^{11}

Spring Fling *Henry Candy* a101 99
5 b m Assertive Twilight Mistress (Bin Ajwaad (IRE))
1453^{7} 2754^{3} 3188^{6} 3815^{2} (6780) 7146^{4} *7990^{3}*

Springforth *Richard Fahey* 68
2 ch g Mayson Spirit Na Heireann (IRE) (Dubawi (IRE))
1783^{3} 2266^{2} 3008^{3} 3361^{2} (4002) 4602^{7} 7330^{3}

Springhouse (CAN) *Michael Keogh* 102
3 rg g Limehouse(USA) Silver Spring (CAN) (Langfuhr (CAN))
7403a^{5}

Spring In Kentucky *Daniel Kubler* a49 32
4 b m Nayef(USA) Red Blossom (Green Desert (USA))
1930^{11} *2443^{8}* 2901^{6}

Spring Jig (USA) *Hugo Palmer* a77 80
2 b g Spring At Last(USA) Make A Dance (USA) (Empire Maker (USA))
4775^{3} 5373^{4} *6623^{2}* (6828) 7471^{6} *7982^{3}*

Spring Leaf (FR) *A De Royer-Dupre* a104 97
4 bb m Footstepsinthesand Spring Wave (IRE) (Dr Fong (USA))
3544a^{5} 4696a^{9} 7087a^{4} 7397a^{7}

Spring Loaded (IRE) *Paul D'Arcy* a113 100
4 gr g Zebedee Nisriyna (IRE) (Intikhab (USA))
(288) ◆ *(657)* ◆ *(1090)* 3386^{7} 4415a^{12} 4865^{19} ◆ 5389^{6} 6112^{14} *8069^{2} (8530)*

Spring Master *P Bary* a68 104
3 b c Mastercraftsman(IRE) Cracovie (Caerleon (USA))
(3450a) 4332a^{7}

Spring Offensive (IRE) *Richard Fahey* 99
4 b g Iffraaj Night Sphere (IRE) (Night Shift (USA))
1018a^{8} (1521) 1861^{11} (2268) 2868^{6} 3923^{4} 4374^{2} 5156^{3} ◆

Spring Of Hope *Simon Crisford* a45
3 ch g Dutch Art Puzzling (Peintre Celebre (USA))
7311^{8}

Spring Overture *Brendan Powell* 31
4 ch m Pastoral Pursuits April Stock (Beveled (USA))
1739^{11} 3381a^{3} 3918a^{8} 4204^{5} 5016^{7}

Springtime Winnie *Eric Alston* 46
4 b m Multiplex Springtime Parkes (Medicean)
1870^{3}

Springwater (FR) *S Wattel* a72 54
3 bb g Siyouni(FR) Spring Wave (IRE) (Dr Fong (USA))
5907a^{7}

Springwood (IRE) *Richard Fahey* a77 72
2 ch c Zebedee Nasharaat (IRE) (Green Desert (USA))
1199^{6} (1520) 2173^{4} 2669^{6} 3977^{4} 5109^{4} *(5840) 6903^{6}*

Spruce Lodge *David Barron* 62
2 b g Compton Place Beautiful Lady (IRE) (Peintre Celebre (USA))
6477^6 6789^7

Spruce Meadows (IRE) *John James Feane* a95 88
3 b g Intikhab(USA) Taziria (SWI) (Zilzal Zamaan (USA))
5616^10 7342a^7

Spryt (IRE) *Conor Dore* a87 65
4 b g Invincible Spirit(IRE) Out Of Thanks (IRE) (Sadler's Wells (USA))
1724^7 2345^3 3185^3 (3840) 4453^6 5419^12 5866^12 6465a^7 6683^4 7066^14 7436^11 7778^5 8037^11 8181^11 8351^7

Spun Gold *Luca Cumani* 66
2 ch c Exceed And Excel(AUS) Victoire Celebre (USA) (Stravinsky (USA))
3065^6 3819^6

Spunky Heart (IRE) *S Kobayashi* a64 73
2 ch f Iffraaj Own Gift (Rahy (USA))
6639a^11

Spykes Bay (USA) *Vanja Sandrup* a80 89
7 ch g Speightstown(USA) She's A Rich Girl (USA) (Affirmed (USA))
4421a^4

Spy Ring (IRE) *M D O'Callaghan* 97
2 b f Bushranger(IRE) Refuse To Give Up (IRE) (Refuse To Bend (IRE))
2718a^8 3694a^6 7667^2

Squash *Philip McBride* a98 103
3 b f Pastoral Pursuits Super Midge (Royal Applause)
836^9 1396^2 2034^3 7650^8 7998a^7 8098^P 8538^4

Squats (IRE) *William Haggas* a96 109
4 b g Dandy Man(IRE) Light Sea (IRE) (King's Best (USA))
2027^23 4625^2 4887^4 6109^4 ◆ 6942^3

Squiggley *Henry Candy* a37 74
3 b f Sir Percy Oat Cuisine (Mujahid (USA))
(6805) 7653^12

Squire *Michael Attwater* a81 82
5 b g Teofilo(IRE) Most Charming (FR) (Darshaan)
1142^2 1633^4 3061^7 3557^5 4307^4 6753^14 7457^3 7813^4 (8178) 8487^5

Squire Hockey *Gary Moore* 45
3 b g Green Horizon Luisa Miller (IRE) (Entrepreneur)
3406^8 4401^12 5260^5 5996^7

Sretaw (IRE) *Gavin Cromwell* a64 81
7 b m Kalanisi(IRE) Thats The Lot (IRE) (Flemensfirth (USA))
4721a^15 5790a^3

Sr Swing *Peter Niven* a16 52
5 b m Passing Glance Wigman Lady (IRE) (Tenby)
7746^F 8309^13

Sruthan (IRE) *P D Deegan* a83 114
6 b g Arakan(USA) Giveupyeraulsins (IRE) (Mark Of Esteem (IRE))
(1018a) 1226a^4 2067a^6 (3677a) 6353a^4 6983a^3 7372a^4

Ss Vega *James Bethell* 54
3 b f Kheleyf(USA) Annie Gee (Primo Valentino (IRE))
1524^6 3293^4 3941^3 ◆ 4444^5 5578^8 6436^8

Stacked Deck (USA) *Barbara J Minshall* a111 111
5 bb g First Samurai(USA) Bel Air Beauty (USA) (Smart Strike (CAN))
(6400a) 7403a^2

Staffa (IRE) *Denis Coakley* 51
3 b f Rock Of Gibraltar(IRE) Gabriellina Klon (IRE) (Ashkalani (IRE))
1894^7 2848^6 4156^7

Staff College (FR) *Henry Spiller* 76
2 b g Slickly(FR) School Of Music (FR) (Green Tune (USA))
6376^3 7345a^3

Stag Party (IRE) *Andrew Balding* a50 59
2 b g Thewayyouare(USA) Betrothed (IRE) (Oratorio (IRE))
3742^8 4270^7 4907 ^9 8072^7 8235^8

Stags Leap (IRE) *Julia Brooke* a44 64
9 b g Refuse To Bend(IRE) Swingsky (IRE) (Indian Ridge)
6739^9

Staintondale Lass (IRE) *Ed Vaughan* a76 91
3 b f Bushranger(IRE) Siphon Melody (USA) (Siphon (BRZ))
(1572) 2322^3 2935^7 (4222) (5774) ◆ 6072^10

Staisenzapenzieri (IRE) *Francesco Santella* a72 87
3 b c Royal Applause Emreliya (IRE) (Danehill Dancer (IRE))
1686a^16

Stake Acclaim (IRE) *Dean Ivory* a84 97
4 b g Acclamation Golden Legacy (IRE) (Rossini (USA))
213^7 492^6 694^11 (1528) 1857^6 3857^7 4954^3 6114^9

Stamford Raffles *Jane Chapple-Hyam* a84 67
3 b g Champs Elysees Romantic Retreat (Rainbow Quest (USA))
3411^7 4319^5 4458^10 5193^5 6242^2 (6698) (7846) 8051^4 (8399)

Stamp Duty (IRE) *Suzzanne France* a45 52
8 b g Ad Valorem(USA) Lothian Lass (IRE) (Daylami (IRE))
5064^12 5971^7 6857^7 8400^9 8527^6

Stamp Hill (IRE) *Richard Fahey* 96
3 b g Zoffany(IRE) Edelfa (IRE) (Fasliyev (USA))
(1243) 1865^5 2466^5 2871^2 4867^9 (6232) 6556^13

Stamp Of Approval (IRE) *Chris Wall* a53 31
4 b m Approve(IRE) Wassendale (Erhaab (USA))
257^7 528^8 (730) 1005^8 1138^10

Stamp Of Authority (IRE) *T G McCourt* a72 63
4 b g Invincible Spirit(IRE) Silver Bracelet (Machiavellian (USA))
7391a^13

Stanarley Pic *Alan Swinbank* 78
5 b g Piccolo Harlestone Lady (Shaamit (IRE))
1253^4 1852^7 2502^4 3191^3 3437^8 4703^6

Stand Guard *John Butler* a63 37
12 b g Danehill(USA) Protectress (Hector Protector (USA))
693^9 864^8 1085^7 1796^10 (8468) 8567^4

Standing Strong (IRE) *Zoe Davison* a51 23
8 b g Green Desert(USA) Alexander Three D (IRE) (Pennekamp (USA))
233^7 602^4 672^6 3401^11 3737^8

St Andrews (IRE) *Ian Williams* a42 74
3 ch g Rip Van Winkle(IRE) Stellavera (FR) (Anabaa (USA))
1079^11 1151^9 3579^6

Stanghow *Antony Brittain* a89 90
4 b g Monsieur Bond(IRE) Melandre (Lujain (USA))
1601^7 1874^6 2346^2 (2665) 3150^5 4373^10 (5479) 6012^3 6633^10 7643^2

Stanhope *Mick Quinn* 79
2 b g Equiano(FR) Nicoise (IRE) (Lear Spear (USA))
3619^2 4594^3 5084^2 5931^3 6295^3 7574^2

Stanley *Luca Cumani* a81 79
3 ch g Sea The Stars(IRE) Deirdre (Dubawi (IRE))
3160^4 3845^9 7384^3 7753^2

Stanley (GER) *Jonjo O'Neill* 81
5 bl g Pivotal Sky Dancing (IRE) (Exit To Nowhere (USA))
4561^7 5925^3 6516^5 (7076) 7623^5

Stanlow *Michael Mullineaux* a54 54
6 b g Invincible Spirit(IRE) Ghazal (USA) (Gone West (USA))
35^4 149^3 294^11 383^7 563^6 1742^2 2525^7 3020^6 4516^5 5252^2 5835^7 6434^6 7262^10 7795^5 8471^9 8589^5

Staphanos (JPN) *Hideaki Fujiwara* 117
5 b h Deep Impact(JPN) Kokoshnik (JPN) (Kurofune (USA))
8333a^3

Staplehurst (IRE) *Geoffrey Deacon* a54 53
3 b f Beat Hollow Kelpie (IRE) (Kahyasi)
3194^11 3684^7 4056^11 7767^11 8468^3 ◆ 8540^6 ◆

Star Anise (FR) *Paddy Butler* a72 42
5 b m Astronomer Royal(USA) Sasicha (IRE) (Montjeu (IRE))
261^9 461^8 684^10 949^5 1500^11 1778^4 2400^6 6335^9 7732^12

Star Archer *Hugo Palmer* 89
2 b c Champs Elysees Postale (Zamindar (USA))
4609^2 5203^2 (6054) 7151^6

Star Ascending (IRE) *Jennie Candlish* a69 65
4 ch g Thousand Words Sakaka (Tobougg (IRE))
445^2 601^2 (684) 865^3 1399^2 1824^4 2445^4 7657^9 7895^10 8318^9 8527^4

Star Blaze *Mick Channon* 86
3 b g Shamardal(USA) Gallic Star (IRE) (Galileo (IRE))
1714^8 (2248) 3156^7 6803^7 7666^7

Starboard *David Simcock* a91 86
7 b g Zamindar(USA) Summer Shower (Sadler's Wells (USA))
333^5 560^7 1274^12 3623^4 5191^4 6084^5 7813^7 8487^4

Star Catch *Charles Hills* 76
2 b f Cacique(IRE) Jolie Etoile (USA) (Diesis)
2637^6 6732^2

Starchitect (IRE) *David Pipe* 91
5 b g Sea The Stars(IRE) Humilis (IRE) (Sadler's Wells (USA))
(2699) 7150^23

Star Citizen *Fred Watson* 67
4 b g New Approach(IRE) Faslen (USA) (Fasliyev (USA))
3346^8 4032^6

Star Cracker (IRE) *Jim Goldie* a46 74
4 ch g Starspangledbanner(AUS) Champagne Cracker (Up And At 'Em)
1692^9 2332^7 2812^3 ◆ 2961^4 3150^13 (4192) 4874^3 5479^5 6506^15 7094^6 7252^12

Starcrossed *Eve Johnson Houghton* a73 70
4 b g Cape Cross(IRE) Gretna (Groom Dancer (USA))
43^4 1854^6 2400^3 2850^2 4012^5 7183^10

Stardrifter *Richard Fahey* 80
4 b g Rock Of Gibraltar(IRE) Alchemilla (Dubai Destination (USA))
2010^5 2662^2 3057^5 3983^3 4611^11 5965^3 6521^3 7159^5 7500^9

Star Empire *Wesley A Ward* a95
2 b c Foxwedge(AUS) Celestial Empire (USA) (Empire Maker (USA))
7834a^11

Star Empire (SAF) *M F De Kock* a99 113
9 b g Second Empire(IRE) Lady Maroof (NZ) (Maroof (USA))
(93a) 453a^5 811a^3 1102a^9

Starfield *Mandy Rowland* a74 65
7 b g Marju(IRE) Sister Moonshine (FR) (Piccolo)
7308^13 7623^13 8077^13 8239^5 8343^8

Star Focus (IRE) *Mark Johnston*
3 b f Intense Focus(USA) Star Of Siligo (USA) (Saratoga Six (USA))
7141^13

Stargazer (IRE) *Sir Michael Stoute* 104
3 b c Canford Cliffs(IRE) Star Ruby (IRE) (Rock Of Gibraltar (IRE))
(1610) ◆ 4797^3 6110^5

Star Glimmer (IRE) *Henry Spiller* a68 63
3 b f Kodiac Skyscape (Zafonic (USA))
1298^8 1573^6

Star Jeanie *Richard Hannon* 72
3 b f Kyllachy Floating (Oasis Dream)
1452^7 2185^8 3000^6 3740^6

Starlight Circus (IRE) *Marco Botti* a66 54
2 b f High Chaparral(IRE) Mountain Law (USA) (Mountain Cat (USA))
7494^11 7885^5 8464^6

Starlight Genie *Richard Phillips* a65 5
4 b m Hellvelyn Anneliina (Cadeaux Genereux)
39^11

Starlight Romance (IRE) *Richard Fahey* 77
2 b f Excelebration(IRE) Takizada (IRE) (Sendawar (IRE))
3167^3 ◆ 4161^4 4603^3 6433^2 7356^2

Star Links (USA) *S Donohoe* a50 42
10 b g Bernstein(USA) Startarette (USA) (Dixieland Band (USA))
149^7 388^4 (514) 602^6 870^5 986^11 7339a^5 8500^8

Starlit Cantata *Eve Johnson Houghton* a86 82
5 b m Oratorio(IRE) Starlit Sky (Galileo (IRE))
18^6 353^9 5489^3 5831^3 6482^8 6947^6 7222^4 8077^3 8381^2

Starlite Sienna (IRE) *Richard Fahey* a65 70
2 b f Elusive Pimpernel(USA) Devious Diva (IRE) (Dr Devious (IRE))
4397^4 5524^6 6388a^25 6904^4

Star Maker *Sylvester Kirk* 72
2 ch g Mastercraftsman(IRE) Snoqualmie Star (Galileo (IRE))
3108^6 3529^4 4988^3 5594^9 6060^4 6377^8 7467^3 7768^7

Star Of Bristol (USA) *Richard Hughes* a70
2 ch f Speightstown(USA) Starlight Dreams (USA) (Black Tie Affair)
6413^4 ◆ 6897^11

Star Of Broadway *H Albloushi*
6 b g Echo Of Light Susie May (Hernando (FR))
8a^13

Star Of Doha *Ralph Beckett* a67 32
2 b f Lawman(FR) Smart Step (Montjeu (IRE))
7239^7 7761^6

Star Of Kheleyf *Michael Appleby* a55 44
3 b g Kheleyf(USA) Semplicita (IRE) (In The Wings)
892^4 1000^7 2039^6 2610^4

Star Of Lombardy (IRE) *Mark Johnston* a69 48
3 b f Cape Cross(IRE) Million Waves (IRE) (Mull Of Kintyre (USA))
8212^5

Star Of Namibia (IRE) *Michael Mullineaux* a37 39
6 b g Cape Cross(IRE) Sparkle Of Stones (FR) (Sadler's Wells (USA))
7410^6 7775^10

Star Of Rory (IRE) *Tom Dascombe* 98
2 b c Born To Sea(IRE) Dame Alicia (IRE) (Sadler's Wells (USA))
(4379) ◆ 6116^2 6801^5

Star Of Spring (IRE) *Iain Jardine* a70 75
4 b m Iffraaj Gift Of Spring (USA) (Gilded Time (USA))
1663^7 2574^2 3660^7 3920^6 4684^7 5223^9 7995^8 (8306)

Star Of The East (IRE) *Mark Johnston* 84
2 b c Cape Cross(IRE) Serenity Star (Monsun (GER))
4580^6 5015^2 (5990) 6455^6 (6791)

Star Of The Stage *John Butler* a75 66
4 b g Invincible Spirit(IRE) Enact (Kyllachy)
893^4 ◆ (1047) 1735^11 (2153) ◆ 3479^6 4528^4 5503^3 7203^10 7619^6 8490^11

Star Pursuits *Jimmy Fox* a53 56
4 b m Pastoral Pursuits Garter Star (Mark Of Esteem (IRE))
97^6 237^3 347^3 707^2 904^7

Star Rider *Hughie Morrison* a72 103
4 gr m Cape Cross(IRE) Starfala (Galileo (IRE))
2433^3 ◆ 3351^3 (4752) 6259^11 7150^8 (7670)

Star Rock *Hughie Morrison* a66 66
2 b f Fastnet Rock(AUS) Starfala (Galileo (IRE))
7543^4 7762^5

Stars At Night (IRE) *John Gosden* a70
3 b f Galileo(IRE) Miarixa (FR) (Linamix (FR))
(44)

Starshell (IRE) *Sir Mark Prescott Bt* a58
2 b g Sea The Stars(IRE) Aquarelle Bleue (Sadler's Wells (USA))
6590^8 6924^7 7366^5

Stars N Angels (IRE) *Michael Appleby* 76
3 gr f Dark Angel(IRE) Passage To India (IRE) (Indian Ridge)
1275^5 1638^2 ◆ 1927^3 2506^2 (3197) 3614^2

Stars Over The Sea (USA) *Mark Johnston* 109
5 b g Sea The Stars(IRE) Exciting Times (FR) (Jeune Homme (USA))
2897^12 3889^7 (4396) 4731^3 ◆ (5031) 5611^4 ◆ 6057^2 6333^2 6573^5 7058^4

Star Storm (IRE) *James Fanshawe* a111 104
4 b h Sea The Stars(IRE) Sayyedati Storm (USA) (Storm Cat (USA))
1863^5 2241^5 2894^8 6752^3 6940^8 7766^2 8068^7 8479^4

Star Story *Ralph Beckett* 56
2 b f Sea The Stars(IRE) Stylish One (IRE) (Invincible Spirit (IRE))
7074^7

Star Stream *Marcus Tregoning* 81
2 b g Acclamation Ellen (IRE) (Machiavellian (USA))
4866^4 5615^11 7216^6

Star System (IRE) *M Rulec* a82 89
6 b h Danehill Dancer(IRE) Silver Rain (FR) (Rainbow Quest (USA))
2074a^5

Start Right *S Seemar* a92 98
9 b g Footstepsinthesand Time Crystal (IRE) (Sadler's Wells (USA))
93a^4 283a^8

Start Seven *Joseph Tuite* a71 60
4 br g Dilum(USA) Dancingintheclouds (IRE) (Rainbow Quest (USA))
342^2 630^2 ◆ 3002^9 4082^9

Start Time (IRE) *Saeed bin Suroor* 99
3 b g Invincible Spirit(IRE) Silca's Sister (Inchinor)
536a^8

Star Victory (FR) *J-L Dubord* a88 105
5 b h Tot Ou Tard(IRE) Tadrou (FR) (Kadrou (FR))
7564a^3 8336a^4

Starving Faithful *Ralph Beckett* a63
4 ch m Makfi Sensational Mover (USA) (Theatrical (IRE))
51^5

Star Washwasha (IRE) *E J O'Neill* 74
2 b f Sea The Stars(IRE) Derivatives (IRE) (Dansili)
7170a^9

Starwatch *John Bridger* a86 91
9 b g Observatory(USA) Trinity Reef (Bustino)
1531^4 1716^7 3557^6

State Law (IRE) *Doug Watson* a93 47
5 b g Invincible Spirit(IRE) Mayoress (Machiavellian (USA))
12a^5 369a^2

Stateofthenation (IRE) *Matthieu Palussiere* a65 69
3 b c Intikhab(USA) Razana (IRE) (Kahyasi)
4220a^5

State Of The Union (IRE) *Henry Spiller* a52 72
4 ch g Approve(IRE) First Lady (IRE) (Indian Ridge)
162^5 561^10 856^9 5236^5 5807^7 6374^6 7445^6

Statuesque *Sir Michael Stoute* a81 81
3 b f Sea The Stars(IRE) Kahara (Sadler's Wells (USA))
3194^2 3990^4 7102^3 7904^3 8090^2 8310^4

Statu Quo (FR) *E Schepens* a37 44
7 b g American Post Porza (FR) (Septieme Ciel (USA))
715a^7

Status Quo (IRE) *Sir Mark Prescott Bt* a74 77
3 br g Thewayyouare(USA) Again Royale (IRE) (Royal Academy (USA))
2565^6 3355^9 7043^3 7251^4

Staunch *Clive Cox* 92
3 bl c Pivotal Striving (IRE) (Danehill Dancer (IRE))
2340^7 (3066) ◆ 4403^5 5306^2 6298^3

Stays In Vegas (USA) *Jerry Hollendorfer* a100 105
3 ch f City Zip(USA) Double Jackpot (USA) (Broken Vow (USA))
7379a^6

St Brelades Bay (IRE) *Mrs John Harrington* a89 89
4 b g Camacho Tides (Bahamian Bounty)
1015a^7

St Dunstan (IRE) *John Quinn* 55
3 b g Zoffany(IRE) Box Of Frogs (IRE) (One Cool Cat (USA))
2864^17 4764^5

Steady Major (IRE) *Mark Brisbourne* a61 56
4 b g Invincible Spirit(IRE) Combust (USA) (Aptitude (USA))
6464a^7 8498^11

Steady Pace *Saeed bin Suroor* a100 111
3 b g Dark Angel(IRE) Cool Kitten (IRE) (One Cool Cat (USA))
(185a) 539a^4 3269^16 4359^4 6458^3

Steal The Scene (IRE) *Richard Hannon* a91 82
4 b h Lord Shanakill(USA) Namoos (USA) (Sahm (USA))
172^4 260^2 ◆ 1775^4 2247^8 2460^5 3101^3 3645^11 4474^3 4839^4 5357^3 6501^11

Steam Ahead *Ralph Beckett* a78
3 b g Dream Ahead(USA) Tropical Treat (Bahamian Bounty)
352^2 668^3

Steaming (IRE) *Ralph Beckett* 72
2 ch g Rail Link Dazzling Day (Hernando (FR))
7622^4

Steccando (IRE) *Alan Swinbank* a63 77
3 b g Lawman(FR) Second Act (Sadler's Wells (USA))
1123^3 1449^2 1883^3 2327^5 2907^9 5063^5 5919^6

Steel Blade (GER) *H Blume* a90 67
7 b h Dashing Blade Selva Nera (GER) (Valanour (IRE))
5452a^4

Steel City Boy (IRE) *Shaun Harris* a45 46
13 b g Bold Fact(USA) Balgren (IRE) (Ballad Rock)
1827^7 2052^15 2676^9 3734^8 4229^5 4647^12 5636^5

Steel Helmet (IRE) *Brian Ellison* a63 64
2 ch g Helmet(AUS) Marine City (JPN) (Carnegie (IRE))
3477^4 ◆ 4188^5 4642^7 6535^11

Steel Of Madrid (IRE) *Richard Hannon* a96 110
3 b c Lope De Vega(IRE) Bibury (Royal Applause)
1440^5 2029^2 (2481) 3296^4 4753^6 5499a^5 6179a^5 7117^7

Steel Rain *Nikki Evans* a34 57
8 b g Striking Ambition Concentration (IRE) (Mind Games)
241^9 732^9 985^9 1827^8 2458^7 3743^12

Steelriver (IRE) *David Barron* a101 77
6 b g Iffraaj Numerus Clausus (FR) (Numerous (USA))
288^5 677^7 923^2 1090^6 3606^12 4259^9 5182^8 5882^7 6371^10 7610^8 7858^8 8314^4 ◆ 8463^5

Steel Stockholder *Antony Brittain* a59 67
10 b g Mark Of Esteem(IRE) Pompey Blue (Abou Zouz (USA))
939^5 2329^7 3987^5 4715^9 6105^9 7646^8

Steel Train (FR) *David O'Meara* a104 99
5 b g Zafeen(FR) Silent Sunday (IRE) (Testa Rossa (AUS))
1563^10 2268^2 2689^12 3324^6 4893^5 5514^3 6320^10 6914^2 (7825) 8049^3 (8311)

Steely *K Kukk* a42 52
8 b g Librettist(USA) No Comebacks (Last Tycoon)
2955a^7

Steely Rock *Mark Johnston* a65 68
3 gr g Rock Of Gibraltar(IRE) La Gandilie (FR) (Highest Honor (FR))
2619^6 3362^5 3886^3

Steip Amach (IRE) *D Smaga* 109
4 b m Vocalised(USA) Ceist Eile (IRE) (Noverre (USA))
1016a^9 1939a^2 (2067a) 3938a^5 4926a^3 5691a^3 7723a^4

Stella Pyla (FR) *C Baillet* 15
2 b f Bertolini(USA) Desert City (FR) (Simon Du Desert (FR))
1021a^3

Stellar Mass (IRE) *J S Bolger* 114
3 b c Sea The Stars(IRE) Juno Marlowe (IRE) (Danehill (USA))
(3428a) 3679a^3 (5095a) 6351a^5 7196a^7

Stellar Surprise *Stuart Williams* 74
2 b f Notnowcato Crystal Etoile (Dansili)
(5951) 6575[7] 7016[4]
Stellarta *Michael Blanshard* a85 98
5 b m Sakhee's Secret Torgau (IRE) (Zieten (USA))
142[6] (879) (1040) 1929[4] 2547[2] ◆ 2875[3] 3671[12]
4398[4] 4862[4] (5488) 6064[7] 6518[2] 6946[4] ◆ 7146[9]
Stellar Wind (USA) *John W Sadler* a119
4 ch m Curlin(USA) Evening Star (USA) (Malibu Moon (USA))
7810a[4]
Stencive *Charlie Wallis* a85 104
7 b g Dansili Madeira Mist (IRE) (Grand Lodge (USA))
244[5] 7791[0] 1001[10]
Stenographer (USA) *J S Bolger* 99
3 ch c Distorted Humor(USA) Sadler's Secretary (IRE) (Sadler's Wells (USA))
(1014a) 5816a[8] 6495a[11]
Stephill (FR) *J Phelippon* a74 60
5 ch g Footstepsinthesand Magic Hill (FR) (Danehill Dancer (IRE))
1034a[7]
Step In Late (FR) *Mme C Head-Maarek* a76 72
3 b f Footstepsinthesand Titillate (IRE) (Barathea (IRE))
5385a[4]
Step On It (IRE) *Daniel Mark Loughnane* a76 57
4 b g Footstepsinthesand Woodyousmileforme (USA) (Woodman (USA))
(180) 295[P] (Dead)
Steppe Daughter (IRE) *Denis Coakley* a85 87
5 b m Steppe Dancer(IRE) Carmencita (Rock Of Gibraltar (IRE))
1568[9] 2549[3] ◆ 2966[2] 3785[5] 4501[2]
Stepper Point *William Muir* a101 115
7 b g Kyllachy Sacre Coeur (Compton Place)
280a[5] 626a[6] 841a[11] 1439[10] 3386[20] 4126[8]
4584[10] 5143[6] 5648[9] 6119[10] 6633[11]
Steps (IRE) *Roger Varian* a84 118
8 gr g Verglas(IRE) Killinallan (Vettori (IRE))
1862[18] 2475[11] (Dead)
Stereo (FR) *E Lellouche* a94 93
3 b c Soul City(IRE) Solitudine (Inchinor)
1286a[3]
Sterling Silva (IRE) *Richard Hannon* 83
2 ch c Sakhee's Secret Silicon Star (FR) (Starborough)
(1316) ◆ 1770[4] (3093)
Stetchworth (IRE) *Mark Johnston* a88 93
5 ch g New Approach(IRE) Hallowed Park (IRE) (Barathea (IRE))
18[5] 240[6] 888[2] 1290[6] 2150[7]
Stetchworth Park *Michael Bell* a78 83
3 b g Duke Of Marmalade(IRE) Perseida (IRE) (Galileo (IRE))
1000[4] 1575[3] 2224[6] 3727[2] (4001) 4559[3] 5176[3]
Steve Rogers (IRE) *Roger Varian* a105 101
5 b g Montjeu(IRE) Three Owls (IRE) (Warning)
(1417) ◆ 1967[12] 3658[8] 4077[2] 5116[5] 7979[2]
8479[3]
Stevie Brown *David Brown* a41 65
2 b g Bushranger(IRE) Oriental Romance (IRE) (Elusive City (USA))
4545[6] 5271[2] 7208[8] 7659[9]
St Gallen (IRE) *John Joseph Murphy* a92 92
3 b c Majestic Missile(IRE) Fly With Me (IRE) (Montjeu (IRE))
2924a[5] 7342a[4]
Sthenic (FR) *Micky Hammond* a47 72
4 b g Fastnet Rock(AUS) Ela's Giant (Giant's Causeway (USA))
1881[8] 2678[5] 5435[7]
Sticks McKenzie *Michael Bell* 52
2 b c Sepoy(AUS) Bended Knee (Refuse To Bend (IRE))
6486[9] 7225[8]
Still Kicking (IRE) *Phil McEntee* a15 28
3 b g Bahamian Bounty Sister Clement (IRE) (Oasis Dream)
42[7] 380[4] 2039[7]
Stillman (FR) *P Khozian* a51 109
5 b h Vespone(IRE) Kikinda (FR) (Daliapour (IRE))
1231a[2] 1910a[10] 3451a[4] 7292a[9]
Still On Top *Tim Easterby* 82
3 b g Royal Applause Poulaine Bleue (Bertolini (USA))
1975[7] 2473[13] 3165[12] 4631[7] 5409[13] 6079[14]
Still Waiting *William Jarvis* a61 54
2 b g Kheleyf(USA) First Approval (Royal Applause)
4594[7] 5244[7] 7574[10] 7866[2] 8235[4]
Stimulator *Chris Gordon* a19 5
3 b g Motivator Fleeting Echo (Beat Hollow)
7052[13] 7572[12]
Stinger (DEN) *Hanne Bechmann* 72
4 b g Academy Award(IRE) Embattle (FR) (Dernier Empereur (USA))
5187a[12]
Sting Jet (IRE) *Seamus Mullins* a41
7 b g Ashkalani(IRE) Pharrambling (IRE) (Phardante (FR))
6415[11]
Stipulate *Brian Ellison* 101
7 b g Dansili Indication (Sadler's Wells (USA))
1196[17] 4747a[4] 4921a[9] 5651[6] 6283[6] 6786[21]
St Malo (USA) *Roger Varian* a89
3 b g Street Cry(IRE) Arkadina (IRE) (Danehill (USA))
7102[5] 7280[2] ◆ (7597)
St Mary'S *Andrew Balding* a82 82
3 b f Siyouni(FR) Once Over (Sakhee (USA))
2470[14] 3684[3] (4235) 5024[4] 5738[5] 6378[2] 6951[4]
St Michel *Sir Mark Prescott Bt* a79 113
3 b c Sea The Stars(IRE) Miss Provence (Hernando (FR))
2300[4] 2909[2] (3306) 3768[2] (4230) 4559[2] (5176)
(5999) 6284[3] 7150[17] ◆
Stock Exchange (FR) *J-F Doucet* a65 63
9 b m American Post Chop And Change (FR) (Double Bed (FR))
5700a[2] 6938a[4]
Stockhill Diva *Brendan Powell* a61 98
6 ch m Haafhd April Stock (Beveled (USA))
1717[2] (2753) 3665[2] 4400[4] 6057[7] 6584[5] 7575[6]
Stocking *Bryan Smart* a92 64
4 gr m Acclamation Red Boots (IRE) (Verglas (IRE))
106[6] 1650[9] 2267[8] 2787[9] 7112[9] 7798[9]
Stoked (IRE) *Chris Dwyer* a19 77
4 b g Fast Company(IRE) Es Que (Inchinor)
2402[2] ◆ 3612[3] 4362[9] 4841[8] 5337[5] 6231[12]
6702[11] (7442)
Stomachion (IRE) *John Butler* 86
6 b g Duke Of Marmalade(IRE) Insight (FR) (Sadler's Wells (USA))
4399[13]
Stoneboat Bill *Declan Carroll* a76 68
4 ch g Virtual Applauding (IRE) (Royal Applause)
1317[4] 1632[7] 2555[12] 3220[3] 3804[4] 4320[3] 4686[4]
4892[8] 5715[2] (6212) 6432[4] ◆ 6737[7] 7078[2]
7257[2] ◆ 7656[7]
Stonecoldsoba *David Evans* a66 63
3 b g Aqlaam Aswaaq (IRE) (Peintre Celebre (USA))
2451[0] 778[6] 2126[3] 4385[5] 5607[2] 6143[9] 7692[3]
(8038) 8318[8]
Stonecutter (IRE) *James Unett* a93 74
5 gr g Mastercraftsman(IRE) Sparkle Of Stones (FR) (Sadler's Wells (USA))
(983) 1642[12] (2782) 3657[5]
Stoneham *Iain Jardine* a40 70
5 b m Sixties Icon Cibenze (Owington)
498[8] 2813[6] (3418) (3704) (5118) 5758[9] 6812[3]
7251[5]
Stone Quercus (IRE) *Donald McCain* a57 66
3 b g Rock Of Gibraltar(IRE) Redglow (IRE) (Fasliyev (USA))
519[6] 725[8] 947[5] 1484[2] 1819[8] 2015[2] 5783[3]
Stone Roses (FR) *F Head* 101
4 b m Rip Van Winkle(IRE) Sailor Moon (IRE) (Tiger Hill (IRE))
2727a[11] 7087a[7] 8024a[4]
Stone The Crows *Roger Charlton* a69 70
2 b g Cape Cross(IRE) Stars In Your Eyes (Galileo (IRE))
7770[4] ◆ 8063[2]
Stoney Broke *James Fanshawe* 75
3 b f Dansili Alvee (IRE) (Key Of Luck (USA))
5415[6]
Stoneyford Lane (IRE) *Steph Hollinshead* 81
2 b g Bushranger(IRE) Peace Talks (Pivotal)
(1454) 1965[2] ◆ 3243[11] 6275[3] 7004[11]
Stopdworldnletmeof *David Flood* 27
2 b c Piccolo Dilli Dancer (Dansili)
5283[5]
Stop The Wages (IRE) *Brian Meehan* a85 98
2 b f Acclamation Agustapower (IRE) (Hawk Wing (USA))
2817[2] ◆ 3555[4] 4054[6] 4494[2] (4879) 5359[6]
5583[4] 6124[5] 7347a[6]
Storm Ahead (IRE) *Marcus Tregoning* a80 95
3 b g Iffraaj Loose Julie (IRE) (Cape Cross (IRE))
2891[4] ◆ (3534) ◆ 6585[2] 7153[4]
Stormardal (IRE) *Ismail Mohammed* a108 100
5 b g Shamardal(USA) Dievotchkina (IRE) (Bluebird (USA))
(12a) 183a[6]
Storm Belt (USA) *Doug Watson* a106 93
7 b h More Than Ready(USA) Mari's Thunder (USA) (Thunder Gulch (USA))
281a[4] 722a[2] 844a[8]
Stormberg (IRE) *N Caullery* a66 48
2 b g Invincible Spirit(IRE) Toolentidhaar (USA) (Swain (IRE))
6015a[12]
Stormbound (IRE) *Paul Cole* a75 71
7 b g Galileo(IRE) A Footstep Away (USA) (Giant's Causeway (USA))
141[4] 683[2] 875[3] (1780) 4589[5] 5592[3] 7619[5]
8154[5] 8469[5]
Storm Check *Andrew Crook* a37 61
4 b g New Approach(IRE) Lunda (IRE) (Soviet Star (USA))
1247[6] 1631[8] 2507[4] 3844[3] 4499[P] (Dead)
Storm Cry *Mark Johnston* a54 86
2 b f Poet's Voice Street Fire (IRE) (Street Cry (IRE))
4011[7] 4663[2] (4943) 5560[3] 5794[3] 6257[2] 6706[4]
Stormflower *John Bridger* a73 73
3 gr f Arcano(IRE) Someone's Angel (USA) (Runaway Groom (CAN))
1385[5] 1935[4] 2435[4] 3353[4] (3650) 4268[4] 4952[3]
5928[5] (6669) 7420[2] 7899[3] 8228[2] 8429[6]
Storm Hawk (IRE) *Emma Owen* a58 40
9 b g Hawk Wing(USA) Stormy Larissa (IRE) (Royal Applause)
786[8] 946[13] 1043[3]
Storming Ambition *Conrad Allen* a45
3 b g Captain Gerrard(IRE) Lady Roxanne (Cyrano De Bergerac)
902[5] 1414[8] 5554[10] 8382[11]
Stormin Tom (IRE) *Tim Easterby* a51 82
4 b g Dylan Thomas(IRE) She Storm (IRE) (Rainbow Quest (USA))
1253[6] 1675[4] ◆ 2018[2] 2406[2] (2805) 3149[3]
6540[10] 7158[4] 8051[9]
Storm King *David C Griffiths* a79 83
7 b g Shamardal(USA) Tarandot (IRE) (Singspiel (IRE))
1959[7] 2819[12] 5180[4] 5866[5] 7308[10] 7791[4] 8007[5]
◆ 8282[5]
Storm Lightning *Mark Brisbourne* a73 83
7 b g Exceed And Excel(AUS) All For Laura (Cadeaux Genereux)
3217[8] 3487[6] 3907[9] 4606[6] (5050) 5105[7] 5605[7]
5807[5] 6410[7]
Storm Melody *Jonjo O'Neill* 81
3 b g Royal Applause Plume (Pastoral Pursuits)
1935[7] 2982[5] 4155[6] 4517[3] 5259[4] 5626[3] (6363)
7626[7] 7772[4]
Stormont Bridge *Maurice Barnes*
8 b g Avonbridge Stormont Castle (USA) (Irish River (FR))
7794[13]
Storm Over (IRE) *Robert Cowell* a72
2 b c Elnadim(USA) Stormy View (USA) (Cozzene (USA))
(5244)
Storm Rider (IRE) *David Nicholls* 19
5 b g Fastnet Rock(AUS) On The Nile (IRE) (Sadler's Wells (USA))
6719[7]
Storm Rising (IRE) *Richard Hannon* 94
3 b c Canford Cliffs(IRE) Before The Storm (Sadler's Wells (USA))
1975[6] 2237[3] 2479[4] 2871[8] 3600[7]
Storm Rock *Harry Dunlop* a99 106
4 b h Rock Of Gibraltar(IRE) Seasonal Cross (Cape Cross (IRE))
1196[9] 1871[11] 3688[6] 4731[16] 6089[7] (6884) 7546[5]
7869[11]
Storm Runner (IRE) *George Margarson* a64 46
8 b g Rakti Saibhreas (IRE) (Last Tycoon)
701[5] 877[7] 1131[4] 2153[6] 3522[7]
Storm Trooper (IRE) *David Nicholls* a57 72
5 b g Acclamation Maid To Order (IRE) (Zafonic (USA))
4100[8] 5032[10] (6341) 6680[5] 6959[2] 7252[9] 7959[14]
8137[11] 8390[6]
Stormy (FR) *S Cerulis* a74 28
2 ch g Stormy River(FR) Compulsive Quality (USA) (Elusive Quality (USA))
6638a[15]
Stormy Angel (FR) *Andrew Hollinshead* 42
3 ro g Stormy River(FR) Angel's Camp (USA) (Honour And Glory (USA))
4220a[10] 7265a[10]
Stormy Antarctic *Ed Walker* 116
3 ch c Stormy Atlantic(USA) Bea Remembered (Doyen (IRE))
(1440) ◆ 1864[11] 4185a[2] 5449a[7] 7352[6]
Stormy Art (IRE) *Michael Dods* a27 53
3 br g Excellent Art Maybe Grace (IRE) (Hawk Wing (USA))
1849[5] 2533[4] 3224[11] 3946[6] 4600[8] 5197[4] 5803[7]
6100[12]
Stormy Clouds (IRE) *Richard Hannon* a73 98
2 b f Sir Prancealot(IRE) Singingintherain (IRE) (Kyllachy)
1087[2] ◆ (1233) (1895) ◆ 2219[10] 3270[7] 3858[7]
4394[2] 5359[3] (5583) 6260[7] 6555[11]
Stormy Dance (FR) *A Giorgi* a71 57
3 b c Stormy River(FR) Danzigs Grandchild (USA) (Anabaa (USA))
4220a[12]
Stormy Ride (IRE) *E Libaud* a81 85
5 gr g Verglas(IRE) Fontcia (FR) (Enrique)
3376a[6]
Stormy Star (FR) *J-V Toux* a50 22
7 b g Stormy River(FR) Ladygoon (FR) (Rangoon I (FR))
8422a[15]
Stormy Victoria (FR) *Christophe Clement* a84 101
4 rg m Stormy River(FR) Dakota Go (Anabaa (USA))
5185a[2]
Storytale *Dave Roberts* a56 51
4 ch g Rip Van Winkle(IRE) Night Haven (Night Shift (USA))
505[5] (674) 981[2] 2110[11]
Stosur (IRE) *Gay Kelleway* a85 83
5 b m Mount Nelson Jules (IRE) (Danehill (USA))
72[2] 160[5] 313[5] 595[3] 774[5] 967[6] 2636[3] 3257[3]
4206[4] 4819[3] (5190) 5831[5] 6316[2] 6899[4] 7671[6]
8028[5] (8347) 8538[5]
St Patrick's Day (IRE) *J R Jenkins* a88 65
4 b g Fastnet Rock(AUS) Race For The Stars (USA) (Fusaichi Pegasus (USA))
33[6] (367) (448) 5811[0] 1775[14] 2313[7] 3783[11]
4497[5] 4717[10] 7076[14] 7457[11] 8101[11] 8241[3]
Strada Di Carsoli *G M Lyons* a84
3 br g Showcasing Carsulae (IRE) (Marju (IRE))
1014a[18]
Stradater (IRE) *Sandy Thomson* a74 29
7 b g Catcher In The Rye(IRE) Starring Role (IRE) (Glenstal (USA))
2089[6] 2915[13]
Stradivari (USA) *Todd Pletcher* a114
3 bb c Medaglia d'Oro(USA) Bending Strings (USA) (American Chance (USA))
2499a[4] 3181a[5]
Stradivarius (IRE) *John Gosden* a77 77
2 ch c Sea The Stars(IRE) Private Life (FR) (Bering)
7074[5] 7470[4] (7849)
Straduff (IRE) *J S Moore* a54 49
3 b g Kodiac She's A Minx (IRE) (Linamix (FR))
557[7] 770[4] 1148[9] 1497[10] 3003[13]
Straight Arrow *Noel C Kelly* a32 67
4 b g Refuse To Bend(IRE) Spring Goddess (IRE) (Daggers Drawn (USA))
4444[7]
Straightothepoint *Bryan Smart* a66 88
4 b g Kyllachy Choisette (Choisir (AUS))
(2016) 2613[5] 3133[7] 5512[2] 6080[3] 6633[4] 7772[2]
Strait Of Zanzibar (USA) *K J Condon* a86 85
7 b g Arch(USA) Royal Opportunity (USA) (Kingmambo (USA))
4748a[3] 6465a[3]
Straits Of Malacca *Simon Dow* a74 76
5 ch g Compton Place Cultural Role (Night Shift (USA))
457[5] 1178[9] 1419[7] 1838[5] 2379[2] 2643[2] 2765[2]
3405[2] 3803[11] 4051[4] 5236[2] 5599[8] 6269[2] 6668[7]
7430[3] 7462[6]
Stranger In Paris (FR) *N Caullery* a92 69
9 b g Oasis Dream Isalou (FR) (Unfuwain (USA))
4903a[4]
Strategic Blue (FR) *T Clout* a65 74
3 b f Strategic Prince Halcyon Lodge (FR) (Grand Lodge (USA))
6912a[7]
Strategic Force (IRE) *Gerard O'Leary* a87 70
5 b g Strategic Prince Mooching Along (IRE) (Mujahid (USA))
7800a[2]
Strategic Heights (IRE) *John James Feane* a73 59
7 b g Strategic Prince Shot Of Redemption (Shirley Heights)
5225[6]
Strategic Way (FR) *G E Mikhalides* a69
3 b c Strategic Prince Polyegos (IRE) (Hawk Wing (USA))
511a[7]
Strath Burn *Robert Cowell* 118
4 b h Equiano(FR) Irish Light (USA) (Irish River (FR))
2546[4] 3195[6] 4860[3] 5268[3] ◆ 6120[8] 6941[9]
Strathearn (IRE) *Michael Bell* a66 71
3 b g Halling(USA) Polska (USA) (Danzig (USA))
1671[7] 2538[6] 3482[5] 3896[2]
Strathmore (AUS) *A T Millard* 115
4 b g Fastnet Rock(AUS) Egyptian Raine (NZ) (Desert Sun)
1911a[3] 8330a[9]
Stratton Street (USA) *A Fabre* 92
2 b c Street Cry(IRE) Ihtifal (Dansili)
1284a[7] 3937a[6]
Stratum *John Gosden* a94 97
3 b c Dansili Lunar Phase (IRE) (Galileo (IRE))
1270[2] 2929[2] 4319[2] 4857[3] (5486) 6417[2] 7015[2]
Strawberryfields *Des Donovan* a49 15
4 ch m Three Valleys(USA) Crossed Wire (Lycius (USA))
20[9] 8701[3] 1547[13] 2781[11]
Strawberry Martini *H-A Pantall* a86 91
5 ch m Mount Nelson Strawberry Lolly (Lomitas)
6273a[11]
Strawberry Sorbet *Clive Cox* a70 53
3 b f Street Cry(IRE) Strawberrydaiquiri (Dansili)
123[2] 421[3] 654[3] (814)
Straw Hat (IRE) *William Haggas* 76
3 b f Galileo(IRE) Velouette (Darshaan)
1989[7] 4367[4] (4983)
Streele (USA) *Ken Wingrove*
6 gr m Thunder Gulch(USA) Crown Capers (USA) (Chief's Crown (USA))
505[14]
Street Act (USA) *A R Al Rayhi* a80 51
9 br g Street Cry(IRE) Cannons Crown (USA) (Best Of Luck (USA))
279a[7]
Street Art (IRE) *Mike Murphy* a56
4 ch g Excellent Art Via Aurelia (IRE) (Antonius Pius (USA))
841[0] ◆ 1239[4] 2781[8] 5303[12] 7262[8] 8180[12]
8540[12]
Street Artist (IRE) *David Nicholls* a89 49
6 ch g Street Cry(IRE) Portrayal (USA) (Saint Ballado (CAN))
2150[2] 3304[3] 3660[8] 4230[7] 5633[5] 6050[8] 7732[3]
7847[P]
Street Duel (USA) *Ismail Mohammed* a87 72
3 b c Street Cry(IRE) Fifth Avenue Doll (USA) (Marquetry (USA))
(958) ◆ 1260[4] 3949[5] 4476[2] 4687[7] 8487[2] ◆
Street Force (USA) *Michael Appleby* a88 72
5 b h Street Cry(IRE) Maskunah (IRE) (Sadler's Wells (USA))
172[7] 240[5] 433[6] 900[4] (1403) 2213[11] 3303[8]
4474[8]
Street Jazz *James Given* a70 70
2 b f Acclamation Wake Up Call (Noverre (USA))
4451[5] 4943[2] 5317[3] 6733[4] 7313[3] 7966[3] 8118[5]
8229[5] 8453[8] (8526)
Street Jester *Robert Stephens* a36
2 b g Avonbridge Street Diva (USA) (Street Cry (IRE))
8556[8]
Street Of Dreams *Saeed bin Suroor* 69
3 b g Shamardal(USA) Express Way (ARG) (Ahmad (ARG))
3919[2] ◆
Street Outlaw (IRE) *Daniel Mark Loughnane* a67 56
3 b g Haatef(USA) Helen Wells (IRE) (Sadler's Wells (USA))
1113[9] 1651[5] 2563[6] (4210) 5232[4] 5398[P] 8338[2]
Street Poet (IRE) *Sir Michael Stoute* a56 82
3 b c Poet's Voice Street Star (USA) (Street Cry (IRE))
1397[7] 1800[6] 3723[4] 6268[2] ◆ 6665[5] 7408[13]
Stretewise (IRE) *Jason Ward*
2 b f Tagula(IRE) Leglen Wood (IRE) (High Chaparral (IRE))
7142[12]
Strictly Art (IRE) *Alan Bailey* a63 62
3 b g Excellent Art Sadinga (IRE) (Sadler's Wells (USA))
1711[0] 522[3] 2341[6] 3596[2] 4942[11] 6541[4] 7577[5]
7986[6] 8337[6] 8382[5] 8490[8]
Strictly Carter *Alan Bailey* a63 49
3 b g Multiplex Compolina (Compton Place)
531[2] 1176[5] 1431[3] 1745[2] 2337[7] 2503[7] 3017[5]
3360[5] 3970[5] 5470[3]
Strictly Glitz (IRE) *Clare Ellam* a21 18
5 b m Kodiac Dancing Steps (Zafonic (USA))
822[12] 981[12] 1120[15] 1323[12]
Stright Way (ITY) *Endo Botti* 89
4 b m Distant Way(USA) Kathy Ridge (IRE) (Indian Ridge)
2518a[7]
Strike Charmer (USA) *Mark Hennig* 110
6 b m Smart Strike(CAN) Cat Charmer (USA) (Storm Cat (USA))
3178a[8] (5914a)
Strikemaster (IRE) *Lee James* a33 53
10 b g Xaar Mas A Fuera (IRE) (Alzao (USA))
2746[8] 3704[9]
Striking Nigella *Michael Chapman*
6 b m Striking Ambition Fiona Fox (Foxhound (USA))
1597[17] 1953[8] 2539[5] 3322[5] 5729[11] 8348[6]
Stringybark Creek *Mick Channon* a78 80
2 b g Bushranger(IRE) Money Note (Librettist (USA))
1082[2] (1203) 2240[7] 2696[5] 3247[11] 6950[20] 7258[8]
7549[15]

Striving (GER) *F Rohaut* 87
5 b h Konigstiger(GER) Stravina (GER) (Platini (GER))
5502a[8]

Strobe *Lucy Normile* a44 49
12 ch g Fantastic Light(USA) Sadaka (USA) (Kingmambo (USA))
5118[2] 7138[12]

Stroll Patrol *Ralph Beckett* a85 104
4 b m Mount Nelson Maid For Winning (USA) (Gone West (USA))
3616[3] 4135[8]

Strong Challenge (IRE) *Saeed bin Suroor* a88 83
3 ch g Exceed And Excel(AUS) Miss Brief (IRE) (Brief Truce (USA))
2466[11] 4062[13] 4889[11]

Stronger Than Me (IRE) *W T Farrell* a96 94
8 b g Marju(IRE) Easter Song (USA) (Rubiano (USA))
4070a[8] 6389a[6] 7558a[7]

Strong Force *Saeed bin Suroor* a90 79
3 b g Sea The Stars(IRE) Rhadegunda (Pivotal)
6567[2] (7102) 7967[6]

Strong Man *Michael Easterby* a76 81
8 b g Gentleman's Deal(IRE) Strong Hand (First Trump)
3884[7] 4894[12] 5419[6] 6027[7] 6500[7] 7141[P]

Strong Steps *Hugo Palmer* a98 95
4 br g Aqlaam Wunders Dream (IRE) (Averti (IRE))
1861[4] 2246[3] 2689[5] (3303) 4976[6]

Struck By The Moon *Charles Hills* 45
2 b f Fastnet Rock(AUS) Ho Hi The Moon (IRE) (Be My Guest (USA))
6206[6]

Strummer (IRE) *Kevin Ryan* a66 66
3 b g Frozen Power(IRE) Question (USA) (Coronado's Quest (USA))
2095[6] 2533[2] 3568[3] 4036[3] 4684[5] 4972[5] 5537[7] 6023[8] 6432[7] (7515) 7656[4]

Strut The Course (CAN) *Barbara J Minshall* a101 106
6 b m Strut The Stage(USA) Bold Course (CAN) (Trajectory (USA))
7404a[10]

St Saviour *Philip Hobbs* a60 83
4 b g Danehill Dancer(IRE) Titivation (Montjeu (IRE))
7053[9]

Stubytuesday *Michael Easterby* a54 49
2 b g Dick Turpin(IRE) Just Dreams (Salse (USA))
2344[5] 7142[6] 7741[8]

Studio Star *Wilf Storey* a30 45
4 ch g Showcasing Forrest Star (Fraam)
2528[4] 3549[9] 3941[4] 4228[6] 4449[6] 5369[10]

Stun Gun *Derek Shaw* a72 59
6 b g Medicean Tapas En Bal (FR) (Mille Balles (FR))
(2) 277[3] 429[2] 598[6] 956[4] 1047[2] 3185[6] 3876[5] 4498[14] (6046) 6700[9] 7310[6] (7890) 8240[8]

Stunned *Doug Watson* a101 86
5 b g Shamardal(USA) Amazed (Clantime)
369a[3]

Style And Grace (IRE) *John Gosden* a27 65
2 b f So You Think(NZ) Sense Of Style (USA) (Thunder Gulch (USA))
7741[3] ◆ 8063[12]

Stylish Minerva *Richard Hannon* a33 68
3 b f Paco Boy(IRE) Lady In The Bath (Forzando)
2585[8] 3003[10] 3735[12]

Stylish Queen *Lydia Pearce*
3 b f Arabian Gleam Stylish Clare (IRE) (Desert Style (IRE))
352[10] 7311[13]

Stylistik *Luke Dace* a73 66
3 ch f Sakhee's Secret Passing Hour (USA) (Red Ransom (USA))
1258[2] 1750[4] 3107[7] 6580[7] 7220[11] 7428[10]

Stynes (IRE) *Graeme McPherson* a52 61
6 b g Aussie Rules(USA) Magic Princess (Bahhare (USA))
674[5] 1170[3] 1578[7] (2370) 2634[4] (6406)

Subatomic *Ralph Beckett* a60 79
2 b f Makfi Miss Universe (IRE) (Warning)
5298[6] 6250[6] (7056)

Subjective *David Simcock* a73 73
2 ch g Equiano(FR) Hope Island (IRE) (Titus Livius (FR))
5885[2] 6375[2] 7259[2]

Sublimation (IRE) *Steve Gollings* a57 74
6 ch g Manduro(GER) Meon Mix (Kayf Tara)
2343[6] 3582[3] 3901[7] 5753[8]

Sublime *Rod Millman* a44
2 b f Exceed And Excel(AUS) Singuliere (IRE) (Singspiel (IRE))
8556[4]

Subordinate (GER) *Emma Lavelle* a63 63
7 b g Echo Of Light Suborneuse (USA) (Diesis)
1499[3] 1739[7] 2398[4] 2996[7] 3748[7]

Subtle Knife *Giles Bravery* a89 94
7 ch m Needwood Blade Northern Bows (Bertolini (USA))
23[4] 254[4] (351) 632[5] 780[6] 1003[7] 1065[6] 1318[2] 1478[5] 2084[3] 2789[5] 3448a[2] (4318) 5396[3] 5695a[2]

Suburban Sky (IRE) *H Rogers* a34 55
5 b m Dandy Man(IRE) Amorous Pursuits (Pursuit Of Love)
6462a[7] 7474a[6]

Subway Dancer (IRE) *Z Koplik* 106
4 b g Shamardal(USA) Sub Rose (IRE) (Galileo (IRE))
(7312a)

Success Days (IRE) *K J Condon* 116
4 gr h Jeremy(USA) Malaica (FR) (Roi Gironde (IRE))
1227a[2] 1940a[2] 2512a[3] (5685a) 6354a[11]

Success Story (KOR) *Jang G Min* a100
5 b h Peace Rules(USA) Power Pack (USA) (Lil's Lad (USA))
284a[3] 722a[3]

Suddenbreakingnews (USA) *Donnie K Von Hemel* a114
3 b r Mineshaft(USA) Uchitel (USA) (Afleet Alex (USA))
2063a[5] 3181a[9]

Sudden Wish (IRE) *Michael Attwater* a57 56
7 b m Jeremy(USA) Fun Time (Fraam)
155[8] 514[11] 653[2] 796[2] 1039[3] 1413[8] 1748[2] 2326[4]

Suedois (FR) *David O'Meara* a104 118
5 b g Le Havre(IRE) Cup Cake (IRE) (Singspiel (IRE))
1197[2] 2159[2] 3385[5] 4151[2] 5217a[4] 6120[3] 6991a[3]

Suegioo (FR) *Richard Fahey* a87 111
7 ch g Manduro(GER) Mantesera (IRE) (In The Wings)
1102a[4] 1772[4] 2221[4] 2625[2] 3298[8] 4164[7] 4799[8] 5612[6] 6118[6] 7349[8]

Sue's Angel (IRE) *Richard Fahey* 61
2 gr f Dark Angel(IRE) La Chassotte (FR) (Until Sundown (USA))
5290[2] 5854[4]

Suetonius *Ed McMahon* a38 62
2 b c Royal Applause Vespasia (Medicean)
1719[5] 2536[9] (3008)

Suffragette City (IRE) *Richard Hannon* a71 71
2 b f Dragon Pulse(IRE) Queen Of Stars (USA) (Green Desert (USA))
3718[3] 4064[6] 4756[4] 5524[2] 5989[3] 6439[3] 6787[12] 7467[6] 8466[7] 8591[4]

Suffused *William Mott* 108
4 ch m Champs Elysees Scuffle (Daylami (IRE))
(3088a) 7404a[2]

Sufi *Richard Hannon* a75 71
2 ch c Pivotal Basanti (USA) (Galileo (IRE))
6751[4] ◆ 7483[2]

Sufoof (IRE) *Kevin Prendergast* a79 79
3 b f Acclamation Walayef (USA) (Danzig (USA))
1014a[3]

Sufrah (USA) *Brian Meehan* a67 68
2 b c War Chant(USA) Arion (USA) (High Yield (USA))
3058[9] 3730[5] 4877[5] 5594[4] 6377[6]

Sugar Beach (FR) *Ann Duffield* a59 72
2 b f Canford Cliffs(IRE) Aktia (IRE) (Danehill Dancer (IRE))
5516[2] 5966[5] 6712[5]

Sugar Boy (IRE) *S Seemar* a90 103
6 b h Authorized(IRE) Steel Princess (IRE) (Danehill (USA))
285a[7] 538a[3]

Sugar Lump *Eric Alston* 81
4 b g Sakhee's Secret Icing (Polar Falcon (USA))
(1125) (1247)

Sugar Plum (IRE) *Bill Turner* a38
2 b f Dandy Man(IRE) Monet's Lady (IRE) (Daylami (IRE))
8152[12] 8313[7] 8536[10]

Sugar Strand (USA) *Saeed bin Suroor* a57
3 bb f Hard Spun(USA) Siyaadah (Shamardal (USA))
1704[4]

Sugar Town *Peter Niven* a62 58
6 b m Elusive City(USA) Sweetsformysweet (USA) (Forest Wildcat (USA))
4240[9] (4770) (5069) 5483[3] 5839[2] 6745[3]

Suitcase 'N' Taxi *Tim Easterby* 67
2 br g Major Cadeaux Finalize (Firebreak)
2611[6] 3222[3] 3772[3] 4602[6]

Suited *Tim Easterby* a61
2 b f Paco Boy(IRE) Birthday Suit (IRE) (Daylami (IRE))
7988[4] ◆

Suitor *Brian Ellison* a85 75
4 ch g Dutch Art Entreat (Pivotal)
1775[9] (3563) 4417a[6]

Suitsus *Geoffrey Deacon* a58 57
5 b g Virtual Point Perfect (Dansili)
3320[7] 4202[13] 7736[3]

Sukiwarrior (IRE) *Charles Hills* 61
2 ch f Power Umniya (IRE) (Bluebird (USA))
2467[12] 3812[6] 5400[14] 5794[10]

Sulafah (IRE) *Roger Varian* a46 72
2 b f Mawatheeq(USA) Maany (USA) (Mr Greeley (USA))
7055[10] 7466[2] 7855[8]

Sultan Baybars *Roger Varian* a82 95
2 b g Invincible Spirit(IRE) Rock Salt (Selkirk (USA))
(6671) 7544[6] 7930[3]

Sumbal (IRE) *David Simcock* 116
4 gr h Danehill Dancer(IRE) Alix Road (FR) (Linamix (FR))
1023a[2] 1375a[2] 1909a[6] 2947a[5] 6940[6] 7545[4]

Summer Chorus *Andrew Balding* a80 92
3 b f Exceed And Excel(AUS) Soviet Terms (Soviet Star (USA))
(152) 559[5] 3995[4] 4496[5] 5103[2] (5409) 5878[3] 6583[3] (6946)

Summer Collection (IRE) *K R Burke* a68 69
3 b f Teofilo(IRE) Towards (USA) (Fusaichi Pegasus (USA))
59[6] 1179[3] 1739[5] 2644[3] 3673[3] 8241[9] 8480[3]

Summer Falls (IRE) *Rae Guest* a66
3 b f Iffraaj Encouragement (Royal Applause)
8157[5] 8559[5]

Summer Icon *Mick Channon* a91 91
3 b f Sixties Icon Summer Cry (USA) (Street Cry (IRE))
1436[2] 1771[4] (2177) 2466[13] 8158[3] ◆ 8426[2]

Summerinthecity (IRE) *Richard Fahey* a75 80
9 ch g Indian Ridge Miss Assertive (Zafonic (USA))
36[7] (271) 398[6] 671[2] 919[2]

Summer Isles *Paul Midgley* a72 64
6 b m Exceed And Excel(AUS) Summer's Lease (Pivotal)
293[3] 903[3] 1433[5] 1872[5] 2050[6] 4834[6] 5296[9]

Summerlea (IRE) *Micky Hammond* a57 61
10 ch g Alhaarth(IRE) Verbania (IRE) (In The Wings)
1121[3] (1955)

Summerling (IRE) *Phil McEntee* a47 58
5 br m Excellent Art Sun Seasons (IRE) (Salse (USA))
3401[10] 4267[11]

Summer Music (IRE) *Robert Cowell* a61
3 b f Elnadim(USA) Startori (Vettori (IRE))
268[5] 432[3] 791[3]

Summersault (IRE) *Jamie Osborne* a71 73
5 b g Footstepsinthesand Sumingasefa (Danehill (USA))
236[10] 424[10] (1928) 2396[8] 2846[6] 4058[4] 4485[5] 5259[3] 6461a[2] 7612[4] (8064)

Summershine (IRE) *Frau Anna Schleusner-Fruhriep* 91
5 ch m Three Valleys(USA) Sulamith (GER) (Acatenango (GER))
4031a[2] 6610a[9]

Summertime Lucy (IRE) *Giles Bravery* a53 38
3 ch f Frozen Power(IRE) Sanfrancullinan (IRE) (Bluebird (USA))
984[9] 5192[4] 6036[4] 6900[11] 7230[11]

Sumner Beach *Brian Ellison* a72
2 ch g Aqlaam Cosmic Song (Cosmonaut)
(1706) ◆

Sumou (IRE) *Marcus Tregoning* 82
3 b g Arcano(IRE) Three Times (Bahamian Bounty)
3572[4] 4347[2]

Sun Angel (IRE) *Henry Candy* a73 77
2 ch f Sir Prancealot(IRE) Fuerta Ventura (IRE) (Desert Sun)
4063[11] 4801[5] 5484[2] ◆ 6244[10] 6733[5] 8152[4] 8560[3]

Sun'Aq (IRE) *Sir Mark Prescott Bt* a83 70
3 b f Kodiac Zingeeyah (Singspiel (IRE))
5825[10]

Sunbaked (IRE) *Eve Johnson Houghton* a64 35
3 b f Kodiac Bronze Baby (USA) (Silver Charm (USA))
443[4] 610[7] (785) 978[6] 1257[6] 1764[3] 4588[4] 5087[6] 5721[5]

Sunblazer (IRE) *Kim Bailey* a102 94
6 gr g Dark Angel(IRE) Damask Rose (IRE) (Dr Devious (IRE))
(165) (499) (747) ◆ 1067[11] 3246[18] 3658[19] 5358[3] 6074[4] 6919[10] 7765[2] 8210[10] 8424[6]

Sunday Prospect (FR) *K R Burke* 57
2 ch g Sunday Break(JPN) Green Shadow (FR) (Green Tune (USA))
4423[7]

Sunday Royal (FR) *Harry Dunlop* a72 80
4 b g Sunday Break(JPN) Princess D'Orange (FR) (Anabaa (USA))
1737[6] 2463[3] 4049[3] 4785[3] 5256[4] 6090[3] 6362[3] 7270[9]

Sunday Winner (FR) *Y Gourraud* a67 67
2 b c Sunday Break(JPN) Lisztomania (FR) (Halling (USA))
1579a[7] 4124a[9] 4471a[9] 4965a[4] (5819a) 7293a[3] 7879a[8]

Sund City (FR) *Harry Dunlop* a55 61
3 b f Turtle Bowl(IRE) Calithea (IRE) (Marju (IRE))
1930[4] 2312[10] 4939[9] 5746[6] 6444[3] 7421[8] 7464[7] 8164[3] 8359[2] 8468[6]

Sunderia (FR) *Mme S Allouche* 77
2 b f Hannouma(IRE) Aldoussa (FR) (Numerous (USA))
4330a[3] 5568a[3] 6937a[7]

Sun Devil (ITY) *Stefano Botti* 99
2 b c Desert Prince(IRE) Dondup (IRE) (Hurricane Run (IRE))
7401a[4]

Sunflower *Andrew Balding* 95
3 ch f Dutch Art Swan Wings (Bahamian Bounty)
2242[10] 5148[5] 6230[8] 6916[9]

Sunglider (IRE) *David O'Meara* a82 78
3 br g High Chaparral(IRE) Desert Ease (IRE) (Green Desert (USA))
2048[2] 2271[2] 2909[9] 6795[2] 7159[14] 7594[4] 7791[3] 7991[3] (8100) 8283[5] 8524[7]

Suni Dancer *Tony Carroll* a56 54
5 b m Captain Gerrard(IRE) Sunisa (IRE) (Daggers Drawn (USA))
175[6] 4493[7] 5019[7] 5055[5] 5954[3] 6651[11] (7302) (8289) 8542[8]

Sun In His Eyes *Ed de Giles* a42 33
4 ch g Compton Place Sunset Lady (IRE) (Red Sunset)
423[8] 4156[11] 4546[11] 5126[8] 5605[10]

Sun Jewellery (AUS) *J Size* 115
4 ch g Snitzel(AUS) Tan Tat Star (AUS) (Umatilla (NZ))
8332a[12]

Sunlit Forest (USA) *Saeed bin Suroor* a47
2 b f Bernardini(USA) Game Face (USA) (Menifee (USA))
7639[5]

Sunlit Waters *Eve Johnson Houghton* a63 61
3 ch f New Approach(IRE) Faraway Waters (Pharly (FR))
1989[11] 3482[8] 4018[8] 5011[7]

Sun Lover *Roger Varian* a86 75
3 b g Oasis Dream Come Touch The Sun (IRE) (Fusaichi Pegasus (USA))
6452[2] (6905)

Sunnua (IRE) *Richard Fahey* a79 83
3 gr f Dark Angel(IRE) Island Sunset (IRE) (Trans Island)
3026[3] 3551[3] (4139) 4630[5] 6246[5] 7360[6] 7623[11] 8028[9]

Sunny Belle (IRE) *P Schiergen* 82
2 b f Exceed And Excel(AUS) Survey (GER) (Big Shuffle (USA))
6797a[6]

Sunny Future (IRE) *Malcolm Saunders* a67 83
10 b g Masterful(USA) Be Magic (Persian Bold)
1914[6] 2699[11] (4158) 4661[5] 6065[7] (6362)

Sunnyhills Belford *Noel Wilson* 52
3 ch f Monsieur Bond(IRE) Zamindari (Zamindar (USA))
3014[9] 4238[11] 5069[14] 6218[8] 6478[10] 6953[8]

Sunny Monday *Emma Owen* a42
4 br g Manduro(GER) Sunray Superstar (Nashwan (USA))
1529[8] 2443[10]

Sunny Sahara *G Guillermo* a39 18
8 b m Hernando(FR) Sahara Sonnet (USA) (Stravinsky (USA))
1618a[8]

Sunnyside Bob (IRE) *Neville Bycroft* a77 69
3 b g Big Bad Bob(IRE) Jinxy Jill (Royal Applause)
1870[4] 2668[3] 3439[8] 4426[4] 4521[6] 6680[14] 8287[7] 8490[10]

Sunovarebel *Alan Bailey* a62
2 b g Cockney Rebel(IRE) Atacama Sunrise (Desert Sun)
7882[11] 8245[6] 8354[8]

Sunraider (IRE) *Paul Midgley* a80 87
9 b g Namid Doctrine (Barathea (IRE))
901[8] 1251[7] 1787[5] 2028[18] 2531[4] 3021[7] 3753[6] 3980[12] (4544) 5034[4] 5291[5] 5852[6]

Sunrise Dance *Kenny Johnson* a44 51
7 ch m Monsieur Bond(IRE) Wachiwi (IRE) (Namid)
2052[8] 2423[12] 2676[6] 3549[8] 3940[5] 4192[7] 4604[6] 5277[13] 5368[11]

Sunscape (IRE) *Hughie Morrison* a71 78
3 ch f Roderic O'Connor(IRE) Opatja (Nashwan (USA))
2339[4] 3001[8] 4549[7] 4986[2] 5302[6] (6019) 6702[10] 7504[7]

Sunset Dream (IRE) *Richard Hannon* a89
3 b f Acclamation Oasis Sunset (IRE) (Oasis Dream)
2578[6] 5300[2] (5735) 7550[10] (7687) 7813[3]

Sunset Sail (IRE) *Gerald Geisler* a69 87
4 b g Arcano(IRE) Mythologie (FR) (Bering)
7398a[2] 7806a[4]

Sunset Sally (IRE) *John Quinn* a35 50
2 b f Clodovil(IRE) Trentini (IRE) (Singspiel (IRE))
6952[8] 7658[8]

Sunshine Always (IRE) *Michael Attwater* a50 6
10 gr g Verglas(IRE) Easy Sunshine (IRE) (Sadler's Wells (USA))
1147[6] 1834[7] 2155[10] 3489[8]

Sunshineandbubbles *Daniel Mark Loughnane* a63 62
3 b f Multiplex Dockside Strike (Docksider (USA))
1998[8] 2405[3] 3878[5] 4267[5] 4882[3] 5263[3] 5399[5] 6143[4] 6593[7] 6920[7] 7614[9] 7937[3] 8125[7] (8255) 8524[10]

Sunshine Quest *Lucinda Egerton* a32 10
4 b m Bahamian Bounty Intermission (IRE) (Royal Applause)
824[7] 959[8] 1597[15]

Supa Seeker (USA) *Emma Owen* a38
10 bb g Petionville(USA) Supamova (USA) (Seattle Slew (USA))
294[8] 412[6] 690[8] 8179[P]

Super Chic (IRE) *Il Cavallo In Testa* 105
3 gr c Strategic Prince Eroica (GER) (Highest Honor (FR))
1686a[3] (2517a)

Super City (FR) *S Wattel* a88 88
5 b m Elusive City(USA) Super Anna (FR) (Anabaa (USA))
5906a[4]

Supercopa (SPA) *C Laffon-Parias* a29 53
2 b f Caradak(IRE) La Copa (IRE) (Pivotal)
5279a[10] 5905a[12]

Super Dream (FR) *Louis Baudron*
3 b g Creachadoir(IRE) Super Nana (FR) (Anabaa (USA))
7265a[14]

Super Duplex *David Arbuthnot* a22 24
9 b g Footstepsinthesand Penelope Tree (IRE) (Desert Prince (IRE))
6405[8]

Super Icon *Malcolm Saunders* a60 54
4 b g Sixties Icon Brigadiers Bird (IRE) (Mujadil (USA))
2187[11] 2635[6] 2781[9]

Super Jockey (NZ) *A T Millard* a114 114
7 b g Sandtrap(USA) Pennies In Heaven (NZ) (Pompeii Court (USA))
1105a[5] 1891a[12] 8330a[8]

Super Julius *Eve Johnson Houghton* 88
2 ch g Bated Breath Paradise Isle (Bahamian Bounty)
2023[4] 2543[2] (3128) 4394[6] ◆ 4918[3] 5560[15] 6763[6]

Super Kid *Saeed bin Suroor* a103 92
4 b g Exceed And Excel(AUS) Crimson Year (USA) (Dubai Millennium)
194[2]

Super Mac (FR) *Gianluca Bietolini* a79 78
3 b c Makfi Super Pie (USA) (Pivotal)
1286a[2] 2551a[5] 3546a[2] 7999a[4]

Super Seer *Philip Hide* a45
3 b g Pivotal Entre Nous (IRE) (Sadler's Wells (USA))
675[8] 980[P] 5129[6]

Supersonic Dreamer (IRE) *Matthieu Palussiere* 73
3 b c Dream Ahead(USA) Birmanie (USA) (Aldebaran (USA))
(4220a)

Supersta *Michael Appleby* a100 90
5 ch g Pivotal Resort (Oasis Dream)
(494) (546) 620[3] 920[2] 1441[8] (1959) 2027[20] 3055[3] 7984[4] 8279[9]

Superyacht (IRE) *Sir Michael Stoute* 83
3 b g Fastnet Rock(AUS) Olympienne (IRE) (Sadler's Wells (USA))
1626[2] 2440[3]

Supreme Power (IRE) *Philip McBride* a64
2 bb g Power Supreme Spirit (IRE) (Invincible Spirit (IRE))
5631[6] 6622[6] 7748[7] 7981[5]

Suprise Vendor (IRE) *Stuart Coltherd* a70 69
10 ch g Fath(USA) Dispol Jazz (Alhijaz)
1244[8]

Suqoor *Chris Dwyer* a96 86
3 b g Equiano(FR) Ukraine (IRE) (Cape Cross (IRE))
1091^{4} (1258) ◆ 1442^{6} (1809) 2251^{9} 2788^{2} 3466^{6} 5148^{4} 5657^{12} 6962^{12}

Suraat (IRE) *George Scott* a49 40
2 b f Kodiac Baltic Belle (IRE) (Redback)
2612^{9} 6413^{11}

Surava *C Ferland* a72 78
3 b f Big Bad Bob(IRE) Irish Flower (IRE) (Zieten (USA))
5498a^{15}

Sureness (IRE) *Charlie Mann* a79 85
6 ch m Hurricane Run(IRE) Silk Dress (IRE) (Gulch (USA))
(2374) 2791^{4} (2876) 3352^{5} 4049^{2} 5249a^{2} 6356a^{9}

Surety (IRE) *James Tate* a76 76
5 b h Cape Cross(IRE) Guarantia (Selkirk (USA))
1648^{4} 5169^{6} 5935^{2} 6337^{2} 7066^{7}

Surewecan *Mark Johnston* a77 87
4 b g Royal Applause Edge Of Light (Xaar)
877^{5} 1044^{3} 1269^{2} 1416^{5} 1555^{2} (1663) 2091^{2} ◆ (2421) 2960^{2} 3405^{3} 3708^{7} 4089^{6} 4402^{3} 4830^{5} 5538^{3}

Sureyoutoldme (IRE) *Richard Hannon* a73
2 ch g Tamayuz Place De Moscou (IRE) (Rock Of Gibraltar (IRE))
7306^{7} 7648^{2}

Surfer (USA) *S Seemar* a111 83
7 ch g Distorted Humor(USA) Surf Club (USA) (Ocean Crest (USA))
92a^{5}

Surfina *Dean Ivory* a42 51
2 b f Acclamation Drift And Dream (Exceed And Excel (AUS))
2764^{8} 3954^{10} 4706^{4} 5257^{5} 5668^{4} 6035^{9} 6895^{8} 7510^{8}

Surgical Strike (USA) *Ben Colebrook* a99 106
3 ch c Red Giant(USA) Preemptive Attack (CAN) (Smart Strike (CAN))
4173a^{5} 5429a^{7}

Surprise Us *Mark Gillard* a48 48
9 b g Indian Ridge Pingus (Polish Precedent (USA))
2634^{5} 3031^{12} 3999^{4} 4225^{6} 5575 ^{5} 7039^{5}

Surrey Hope (USA) *Joseph Tuite* 68
2 b c Lemon Drop Kid(USA) She Be Classy (USA) (Toccet (USA))
7501^{6}

Surround Sound *Tim Easterby* a69 70
6 b g Multiplex Tintera (IRE) (King's Theatre (IRE))
199^{9} 640^{7} 1169^{5} 1674^{6} 2738^{6} 3154^{2}

Suspect Package (USA) *James Fanshawe* a76
2 b g Lonhro(AUS) Pretty Meadow (USA) (Meadowlake (USA))
5966^{3} 6904^{5} 7907^{5} ◆ 8466^{6}

Sussex Girl *John Berry* 2
2 ch f Compton Place Palinisa (FR) (Night Shift (USA))
7407^{8}

Sussex Ranger (USA) *Gary Moore* a74 52
2 b g Hat Trick(JPN) Purple (USA) (Royal Academy (USA))
6663^{9} 7977^{4} 8246^{3} ◆

Sussudio (FR) *Frau Hella Sauer* a85 113
6 ch h Nayef(USA) Soudaine (GER) (Monsun (GER))
1023a^{6} 6598a^{6} 6992a^{6} 7723a^{7} 8117a^{7}

Susukino (FR) *S Kobayashi* a47 46
7 gr m Great Journey(JPN) Sapporo (FR) (Smadoun (FR))
8422a^{8}

Susurro *David Simcock* a49 50
3 ch f Rip Van Winkle(IRE) Heavenly Whisper (IRE) (Halling (USA))
1113^{10}

Sutter County *Mark Johnston* a103 92
2 b c Invincible Spirit(IRE) Rio Osa (AUS) (Canny Lad (AUS))
(1082) (1422) 5656^{4} 6572^{7} 7989^{2} 8209^{3}

Sutton Sid *Paddy Butler*
6 ch g Dutch Art Drastic Measure (Pivotal)
4020^{6}

Suuki *Adam West*
3 ch f Major Cadeaux Smooth As Silk (IRE) (Danehill Dancer (IRE))
5101^{9} 5355^{15}

Suvenna (IRE) *M Halford* a89 90
3 b f Arcano(IRE) Sovana (IRE) (Desert King (IRE))
7676a^{14}

Suzi Icon *John Butler* a13 69
4 ch m Sixties Icon Suzi Spends (IRE) (Royal Applause)
2127^{7} 2901^{9} 3624^{8} 4640^{11}

Suzi's Connoisseur *Stuart Williams* a94 105
5 b g Art Connoisseur(IRE) Suzi Spends (IRE) (Royal Applause)
3671^{10} 4109^{2} 4625^{13} 4865^{11} 5871^{2} 6109^{8} 6942^{15} 7156^{19} 8407^{9}

Suzu *Ivan Furtado* a32
3 ch f Monsieur Bond(IRE) Moorhouse Girl (Makbul)
384^{11} 507^{6} 639^{10}

Swacadelic (GER) *Aaron Purcell* 98
5 ch g Adlerflug(GER) Swish (GER) (Monsun (GER))
7481a^{5} 7947a^{2}

Swag (IRE) *Richard Hannon* 73
2 b c Bahamian Bounty Tahtheeb (IRE) (Muhtarram (USA))
4736^{8} 5410^{5} 6053^{4} 6575^{4} 7033^{5}

Swaheen *Julie Camacho* a75 92
4 b g Lawman(FR) Whole Grain (Polish Precedent (USA))
1493^{6} 1880^{5} 3117^{6} 3657^{17} 4664^{6} 6134^{3} ◆ 6781^{9} 7624^{9}

Swallow Street (IRE) *Jamie Osborne* a62 63
2 ch c Sir Prancealot(IRE) Fey Rouge (IRE) (Fayruz)
4209^{8} 4526^{3} 4815^{5} 5120^{4} (6678) 6895^{2}

Swamp Fox (IRE) *Joseph G Murphy* 91
4 br g Windsor Knot(IRE) Brogella (IRE) (King's Theatre (IRE))
(4721a) 7195a^{3} 7708a^{11}

Swanning Around (IRE) *Matthieu Palussiere* a72 77
2 ch f Dragon Pulse(IRE) Swan Sea (USA) (Sea Hero (USA))
4124a^{6} 4471a^{3}

Swan Serenade *Jonathan Portman* a48 59
2 b f Paco Boy(IRE) Accede (Acclamation)
2467^{7} 2902^{3} 4011^{9} 4815^{2} 5511^{8} 6412^{10}

Swansway *Michael Easterby* a66 53
3 ch g Showcasing Spring Stroll (USA) (Skywalker (USA))
1270^{6} 2212^{5} 2784^{9} 7585^{7} 7751^{6} 7890^{2} 8145^{3} 8350^{2} (8587) ◆

Swanton Blue (IRE) *Ed de Giles* a72 70
3 b g Kodiac Cabopino (IRE) (Captain Rio)
1176^{7} 1451^{8} 2185^{9} 4085^{3} 4502^{3} 4820^{5} 6296^{10} 7534^{9} 7964^{3} (8095) 8316^{6}

Swashbuckle *Andrew Balding* a66 90
3 b g Dashing Blade Inhibition (Nayef (USA))
2589^{2} 3727^{3} 4001^{2} (4793) (5231) 6163^{3}

Swashbuckling (IRE) *Michael Wigham* a73 92
4 b g Raven's Pass(USA) Hazarayna (Polish Precedent (USA))
(2556)

Sweeping Paddy (USA) *Dale Romans* a76 100
2 b f Paddy O'Prado(USA) C. S. Royce (USA) (Unbridled's Song (USA))
7809a^{8}

Sweeping Rock (IRE) *John Spearing* a43 47
6 b g Rock Of Gibraltar(IRE) Sweeping Story (USA) (End Sweep (USA))
8410^{10}

Sweeping Up *Hughie Morrison* a101 106
5 b m Sea The Stars(IRE) Farfala (FR) (Linamix (FR))
2465^{2} 2690^{2} 3436^{4} 4883^{4} 6273a^{4}

Sweet Amazement *Mark Usher* 36
2 ch f Kheleyf(USA) Sweetest Revenge (IRE) (Daggers Drawn (USA))
3143^{6}

Sweet Charity (FR) *N Clement* 100
3 bb f Myboycharlie(IRE) Sapfo (FR) (Peintre Celebre (USA))
3120a^{3} (6069a)

Sweet Cherry (IRE) *E D Delany* a68 76
5 b m Mastercraftsman(IRE) Dear Gracie (IRE) (In The Wings)
2114a^{2}

Sweet Dragon Fly *Paul Cole* a80 93
3 b f Oasis Dream Sweet Cecily (IRE) (Kodiac)
1079^{2} 2470^{4} (2848) 5551^{4} (6340) ◆ 6946^{3} 7146^{10} 7738^{4}

Sweet Dream Lady (IRE) *Gary Moore* a52 58
3 b f Rip Van Winkle(IRE) Visite Royale (USA) (Danehill Dancer (IRE))
4936^{8} 5923^{3} 6407^{5} (Dead)

Sweet Electra (FR) *P Bary* a73 88
3 gr f Sea The Stars(IRE) Ysoldina (FR) (Kendor (FR))
1541a^{8}

Sweet Grass Creek (CAN) *Michael Keogh* a96
4 ch g Wando(CAN) Sweet Bama Breeze (USA) (City Zip (USA))
6400a^{3}

Sweetie Jar (IRE) *John Joseph Murphy* a70 47
3 br f Alfred Nobel(IRE) Rum Raisin (Invincible Spirit (IRE))
7800a^{9}

Sweet Loretta (USA) *Todd Pletcher* a107
2 b f Tapit(USA) Ithinkisawapudycat (USA) (Bluegrass Cat (USA))
7830a^{11}

Sweet P *Marcus Tregoning* a91 89
5 b m Sir Percy Desert Run (IRE) (Desert Prince (IRE))
3670^{8} 6332^{7}

Sweet Piccolo *Paddy Butler* a43 12
6 ch g Piccolo Quality Street (Fraam)
3734^{11}

Sweet Pursuit *Rod Millman* a44 48
2 b f Pastoral Pursuits Sugar Beet (Beat Hollow)
4457^{7} 5304^{12} 6414^{8}

Sweet Selection *Hughie Morrison* a73 103
4 b m Stimulation(IRE) Sweet Coincidence (Mujahid (USA))
1854^{4} (2338) (3149) ◆ (4353) 5559^{4} 6284^{5} (7150)

Sweet Sienna *Dean Ivory* a47 13
2 ch f Harbour Watch(IRE) Look Busy (IRE) (Danetime (IRE))
2376^{9} 6244^{9} 6873^{11} 7528^{3} 7884^{6}

Sweet Swap (USA) *K Al Subaie* a76 117
7 ch h Candy Ride(ARG) Fair Exchange (USA) (Storm Cat (USA))
840a^{5}

Sweet Temptation (IRE) *Stuart Williams* a72 64
3 b f Amadeus Wolf Summer Spice (IRE) (Key Of Luck (USA))
296^{6} 1960^{7} 2322^{9} 2824^{8} 3976^{3}

Sweet Thomas (GER) *Christian Sprengel* a72 96
4 b h Dylan Thomas(IRE) Sworn Pro (GER) (Protektor (GER))
4903a^{9}

Sweet World *Bernard Llewellyn* a42 55
12 b g Agnes World(USA) Douce Maison (IRE) (Fools Holme (USA))
4082^{8}

Sweet Zain (IRE) *Charlie Fellowes* a44 61
2 b f Requinto(IRE) Pillars Of Society (IRE) (Caerleon (USA))
6183^{2} 6388a^{20} 7050^{9}

Swell Hill *Richard Hannon* 63
2 b f Foxwedge(AUS) Sea Fret (Nayef (USA))
1543^{5} 6016^{4} 6648^{3} 7286^{6}

Swendab (IRE) *John O'Shea* a63 74
8 b g Trans Island Lavish Spirit (USA) (Southern Halo (USA))
889^{3} ◆ 1180^{3} 1720^{7} 1827^{5} 2202^{5} 3098^{3} 3530^{6} 4084^{2} 4590^{6} 5236^{6} 6677^{6} 7267^{9} 7913^{3} 8315^{3} 8542^{3}

Swift Approval (IRE) *Kevin Ryan* a104 102
4 ch g Approve(IRE) Tiltili (IRE) (Spectrum (IRE))
(1844) (2679) 2910^{6} (4109) 4665^{6} 4865^{25} (5906a) (7027a)

Swift Cedar (IRE) *David Evans* a83 82
6 ch g Excellent Art Ravish (Efisio)
52^{3} 337^{4} 566^{10} (890) 1250^{3} 5231^{6} 5642^{10}

Swiftee (IRE) *Ivan Furtado* a44 52
3 ch g Camacho Algaira (USA) (Irish River (FR))
1421^{9} 1930^{3} 2443^{6} 3236^{11} 7775^{12} 8458^{9}

Swift Emperor (IRE) *David Barron* 96
4 b g Holy Roman Emperor(IRE) Big Swifty (IRE) (Intikhab (USA))
1445^{10} 1643^{2} 2268^{3} 2744^{3} 3390^{11} 4163^{6} 4858^{6}

Swift Mover (IRE) *Richard Hannon* a55 70
2 b f Sir Prancealot(IRE) Ajla (IRE) (Exceed And Excel (AUS))
5395^{5} (5593) 6139^{9} 7217^{9}

Swiftsure (IRE) *Sir Michael Stoute* 83
2 b c Dubawi(IRE) La Sylphide (SWI) (Barathea (IRE))
6880^{2} 7495^{4}

Swing Easy *Gary Moore* a84 95
6 b g Zamindar(USA) Shahmina (IRE) (Danehill (USA))
121^{5}

Swinging Hawk (GER) *Ian Williams* a61 70
10 ch g Hawk Wing(USA) Saldenschwinge (GER) (In The Wings)
891^{3}

Swirral Edge *David Brown* 83
3 b f Hellvelyn Pizzarra (Shamardal (USA))
1847^{3} ◆ 2373^{2} 3284^{5} 5040^{5} (5730) 6133^{7} 6653^{6} 7773^{5}

Swish (IRE) *John James Feane* a77 91
2 gr f Lilbourne Lad(IRE) Maidservant (USA) (Seeking The Gold (USA))
4171a^{2} 5661a^{9} 5940a^{4} 6555^{9}

Swiss Affair *Robert Cowell* 51
4 b m Pivotal Swiss Lake (USA) (Indian Ridge)
2042^{12} 7289^{10} 7643^{12}

Swiss Cross *Phil McEntee* a85 70
9 b g Cape Cross(IRE) Swiss Lake (USA) (Indian Ridge)
76^{2} 169^{4} 795^{7} 1186^{8} 1746^{7} 2765^{6} ◆ 3078^{4} 3320^{4} 4051^{9} 4362^{2} 4593^{5} (5456a) 5992^{5} 6051^{3} 6509^{4} 6872^{7} 7255^{2} (7654) (7964) (8030) 8197a^{6} (8561)

Swiss Lait *Patrick Holmes* a56 61
5 b m Milk It Mick Matilda Peace (Namaqualand (USA))
4258^{5} (4930) 5715^{10} 6221^{8} 6839^{4} 7336^{10} 8144^{5} 8400^{3} 8586^{9}

Swiss Range *John Gosden* 105
3 b f Zamindar(USA) Spanish Sun (USA) (El Prado (IRE))
(1392) (1890) 3452a^{8} 4864^{4} 7404a^{6}

Swiss Storm *David Elsworth* 86
2 b c Frankel Swiss Lake (USA) (Indian Ridge)
6053^{7} (6570) ◆

Switching (USA) *A Fabre* 104
3 b f Street Cry(IRE) Wavering (IRE) (Refuse To Bend (IRE))
5498a^{5} 6069a^{2} 7029a^{2} 7568a^{2} 7862a^{5}

Swnymor (IRE) *Kevin Frost* 85
7 b g Dylan Thomas(IRE) Propaganda (IRE) (Sadler's Wells (USA))
1586^{9} 1852^{8}

Sword Exceed (GER) *Charlie Appleby* 71
2 b g Exceed And Excel(AUS) Sword Roche (GER) (Laroche (GER))
2038^{5} 6034^{3} 6477^{4}

Sword Fighter (IRE) *A P O'Brien* 114
3 bb g Galileo(IRE) Tarbela (IRE) (Grand Lodge (USA))
(3341) ◆ (3697a) 4799^{5} 6329^{5}

Sword Of The Lord *Nigel Twiston-Davies* a59 76
6 b g Kheleyf(USA) Blue Echo (Kyllachy)
586a^{2} 665a^{4} 2174^{8} 5620a^{2}

Swordshire (GER) *Werner Glanz* 98
5 b h Shirocco(GER) Sword Roche (GER) (Laroche (GER))
7088a^{9}

Swot *Roger Teal* a69 50
4 b g Exceed And Excel(AUS) House Point (Pivotal)
953^{7} 1178^{6} 1928^{9} 2379^{9} 3030^{3} 6241^{8} 8258^{2} 8555^{4}

Sycara (IRE) *Jeremy Noseda* 61
3 b f Canford Cliffs(IRE) Sentimental (IRE) (Galileo (IRE))
3059^{10} 3736^{8}

Sydney Ruffdiamond *Richard Hughes* a87 83
4 b g Equiano(FR) Pirouetting (Pivotal)
1857^{5} 2754^{13} 3233^{5} (4291) 4911^{8} 5488^{14} 5955^{7} 6339^{4} 7017^{6} 7461^{3}

Sylvanes (IRE) *A De Royer-Dupre* a64 81
4 b m Teofilo(IRE) Sierra Slew (Fantastic Light (USA))
8042a^{15}

Sylvette *Roger Varian* a61 47
4 ch m Selkirk(USA) Souvenance (Hernando (FR))
170^{3} 463^{8} 569^{3} 877^{3} 1047^{13} 3739^{7} 4200^{7}

Symbolic *John Gosden* a92 86
3 b c Shamardal(USA) Resort (Oasis Dream)
(1800) 2237^{5} 4080^{8} 5191^{2} 5878^{4}

Symbolic Star (IRE) *Barry Murtagh* a72 71
4 b g New Approach(IRE) Epitome (IRE) (Nashwan (USA))
2917^{12} 3659^{7} ◆ 4190^{5} 4377^{8} 6138^{10} 6921^{12} 8141^{7} 8400^{13} 8589^{10}

Symbolist (IRE) *John Norton* a59 63
4 b m Yeats(IRE) Pescia (IRE) (Darshaan)
329^{7} 592^{6} 1121^{2} 1523^{9} 2746^{6} 7138^{11} 7592^{10}

Sympathy (USA) *Chad C Brown* 44
4 bb m Henrythenavigator(USA) Sweet Temper (USA) (Stormy Atlantic (USA))
5914a^{7}

Symposium *William Haggas* a78 94
3 ch f Exceed And Excel(AUS) Soodad (King's Best (USA))
2446^{4} 4134^{3} 4708^{3} 5115^{4} (6182) (6668) (6916) ◆ 7146^{5}

Syncopate *Pam Sly* a76 86
7 b g Oratorio(IRE) Millistar (Galileo (IRE))
4049^{6} 5724^{7} (7508) 7980^{8}

Syncopation (IRE) *Sylvester Kirk* a55 73
2 b c Dark Angel(IRE) Cross Section (USA) (Cape Cross (IRE))
4128^{7} 4866^{7} 4989^{2} 5796^{3} 6071^{7} 6658^{8}

Syndergaard (USA) *Todd Pletcher* a115
2 ch c Majesticperfection(USA) Magic Belle (USA) (Gold Case (USA))
7834a^{5}

Syndicate *Ralph Beckett* a81 74
2 b f Dansili Indication (Sadler's Wells (USA))
5356^{2} 6088^{2} 7049^{4} (8237)

Synodic (USA) *Seamus Durack* a62 46
4 br g Henrythenavigator(USA) Seven Moons (JPN) (Sunday Silence (USA))
2579^{13} 3234^{10} 3724^{6} 7260^{10} 7641^{5} 7986^{11} (8179) ◆

Synopsis *G M Lyons* 84
4 b m Azamour(IRE) Censored (Pivotal)
(2114a) 3680a^{10} 4721a^{11} 7195a^{10}

Synoptic Dream (USA) *Derek Shaw* a43 41
4 b m Medicean Specific Dream (Danehill Dancer (IRE))
941^{7} 1048^{10} 1139^{7}

Syphax (USA) *Kevin Ryan* 109
2 b c Arch(USA) Much Obliged (USA) (Kingmambo (USA))
(4097) (5556)

Syrian Pearl *Chris Wall* a77 92
5 gr m Clodovil(IRE) Syrian Queen (Slip Anchor)
1634^{8} 2247^{7} 2754^{7} (3414) 4360^{9} (5408) (6878)

Syrita (FR) *M Nigge* a87 103
3 ch f Siyouni(FR) Garmerita (FR) (Poliglote)
2282a^{9} 5987a^{2} 7348a^{6} 7998a^{12}

Szoff (GER) *A Wohler* a101 102
6 b h Shirocco(GER) Slawomira (GER) (Dashing Blade)
(7524a)

Taajub (IRE) *Peter Crate* a89 79
9 b g Exceed And Excel(AUS) Purple Tiger (IRE) (Rainbow Quest (USA))
86^{7} (484) 655^{4} 835^{6} 3193^{6} 4584^{9} 4954^{11} 5669^{5} 6195^{8} 6669^{5} 7303^{2} 8099^{7}

Taamol (IRE) *Sir Michael Stoute* 93
2 b c Helmet(AUS) Supreme Seductress (IRE) (Montjeu (IRE))
(3661) 6285^{5}

Taareef (USA) *J-C Rouget* a95 113
3 ch c Kitten's Joy(USA) Sacred Feather (USA) (Carson City (USA))
1580a^{2} 2283a^{7} (3543a) 5499a^{4} (6975a)

Taayel (IRE) *M Al Mheiri* a82 92
6 b g Tamayuz Sakhee's Song (IRE) (Sakhee (USA))
719a^{10} 841a^{8}

Tabarrak (IRE) *Richard Hannon* 108
3 b g Acclamation Bahati (IRE) (Intikhab (USA))
1393^{2} (1991)

Tabla *Lee Carter* a73 54
4 b m Rail Link Questa Nova (Rainbow Quest (USA))
349^{4} 631^{4} 667^{6} 3314^{2} 4773^{5} 8381^{4}

Table Manners *Wilf Storey* a58 56
4 b m Dutch Art Nine Red (Royal Applause)
1814^{4} 2419^{7} 3609^{10} 4425^{6} 5064^{5} 6739^{10} (7794) 8144^{3} 8306^{2} 8589^{2}

Taboule *Carla O'Halloran* a61 56
6 b h Mount Nelson Zia (GER) (Grand Lodge (USA))
(8421a)

Tadaany (IRE) *David O'Meara* a85 87
4 b g Acclamation Park Haven (IRE) (Marju (IRE))
1526^{8} 2257^{9} 3166^{6} ◆ 3286^{7} 4704^{5} ◆ (5223) 5521^{5} 6217^{2} 6500^{9} 7095^{6} 7593^{4} 8092^{9} 8456^{2}

Tadaawol *Roger Fell* a71 73
3 b g Kyllachy Bright Edge (Danehill Dancer (IRE))
(8012) ◆ 8287^{9}

Tadkhirah *William Haggas* 72
2 b f Acclamation Pin Cushion (Pivotal)
4261^{3} (5072) 5543^{6}

Tael O' Gold *Iain Jardine* a58 45
2 ch f Zoffany(IRE) Wedding Dream (Oasis Dream)
3290^{7} 3947^{11} 5809^{4} 6950^{26} 7110^{9} 7854^{3} 8046^{11} 8284^{7}

Taexali (IRE) *John Patrick Shanahan* 101
3 ch g Raven's Pass(USA) Enchanted Evening (IRE) (High Chaparral (IRE))
536a^{7} 807a^{3} 1882^{2} 2272a^{10} 3165^{13} 3909^{4} 4338^{10} 6012^{13} 6230^{5} 6837^{4} 7250^{5}

Tafaakhor (IRE) *Richard Hannon* a82 86
2 gr g Dark Angel(IRE) Tellelle (IRE) (Trans Island)
2193^{4} 2648^{2} 3065^{2} 4363^{4} 5077^{3} 6869^{3} 7496^{2}

Tafahom (IRE) *Michael Easterby* a59 77
4 b g Acclamation Dance Set (Selkirk (USA))
1241^{7} 1588^{11} 2347^{14} 2673^{6} 3983^{7} 5529^{7} 6226^{4} 6569^{3} 7254^{4}

Taffeta Lady *Lucy Wadham* a79 85
3 ch f Sir Percy Bombazine (IRE) (Generous (IRE))
1609^{3} ◆ 2215^{3} 3194^{6} 3894^{4} (5550) (6527)

Taffetta *Tony Coyle* a57 68
4 ch m Paco Boy(IRE) Tarneem (USA) (Zilzal (USA))
1119^{2} 1402^{5} 1525^{2} 1790^{3} 2120^{7} 4378^{6} 4691^{7} 6616^{5} (7093) 7290^{2} ◆ 7437^{4} 7595^{5}

Tafteesh (IRE) *Michael Easterby* a70 57
3 b g Kodiac Mudalalah (IRE) (Singspiel (IRE))
7126^{16} 7857^{11}

Taghleeb (USA) *Michael J Maker* 111
5 ch h Hard Spun(USA) Judhoor (Alhaarth (IRE))
7405a^{7}

Taglietelle *Gordon Elliott* a85 86
7 b g Tagula(IRE) Averami (Averti (IRE))
208a^6

Tagula Night (IRE) *Dean Ivory* a94 74
10 ch g Tagula(IRE) Carpet Lady (IRE) (Night Shift (USA))
1528^10 2309^4 3159^9 3414^8 4990^4 6091^7 7887^11 8067^6

Tagur (IRE) *Kevin Ryan* a68 65
2 ch g Tagula(IRE) Westcote (USA) (Gone West (USA))
1921^4 ◆ 2196^4 3283^5 3852^3 6130^5 7109^2 7640^2 7898^5

Tahiti *David Brown* 50
2 b f Royal Applause Dubai Bounty (Dubai Destination (USA))
7576^8

Tahiti One *Tony Carroll* a61 58
3 b f Bertolini(USA) Club Tahiti (Hernando (FR))
783^8 947^9 1325^3 1670^15 2148^7 3353^6 (3725) 5020^2 5523^4 6361^4 7276^6 8248^7 8541^6

Tahoo (IRE) *K R Burke* 88
2 b f Zebedee Suffer Her (IRE) (Whipper (USA))
(2417) 2908^7 4111^2 (4669) 5359^9 6322^7 7972a^9

Tai Hang Dragon (IRE) *Richard Hannon* a34
2 b f Tamayuz Give A Whistle (IRE) (Mujadil (USA))
7939^10

Tailor's Row (USA) *Mark Johnston* a79 80
2 ch c Street Cry(IRE) Raw Silk (USA) (Malibu Moon (USA))
(2604) 2913^6 4167^3 4915^3 6563^6 7893^8 8405^3 8592^2

Tailwind *Roger Varian* a81 60
3 b c Dubawi(IRE) Time Saved (Green Desert (USA))
7443^8 7737^4 8385^10

Taisce Naisiunta (IRE) *J S Bolger* 101
3 b f Lawman(FR) Ciste Naisiunta (IRE) (Galileo (IRE))
2716a^11

Tai Sing Yeh (IRE) *Charles Hills* a74 70
2 b c Exceed And Excel(AUS) Cherry Orchard (IRE) (King's Best (USA))
7157^5 ◆ (7648)

Taj Mahal (IRE) *A P O'Brien* a90 108
2 b c Galileo(IRE) You'resothrilling (USA) (Storm Cat (USA))
6704^7 7559a^3 7722a^5

Takahiro *Linda Perratt* a60 39
4 b g Kyllachy Marliana (IRE) (Mtoto)
1663^9 2096^10 2528^7 2812^8 2906^11 3925^7 3941^6 4192^5 4445^9

Takatul (USA) *Charles Hills* 90
3 b c Smart Strike(CAN) Torrestrella (IRE) (Orpen (USA))
(3267) (4742) (5306) 6076^6 6778^5

Takbeer (IRE) *Nikki Evans* a65 50
4 b g Aqlaam Precious Secret (IRE) (Fusaichi Pegasus (USA))
6870^12

Take A Deep Breath *M D O'Callaghan* 102
2 b f Bated Breath Fatal Attraction (Oasis Dream)
4573a^2

Take A Look (FR) *Gianluca Bietolini* 88
3 b g Siyouni(FR) Glint Of Green (USA) (Jade Hunter (USA))
3764a^7

Take A Note *Patrick Chamings* a95 81
7 b g Singspiel(IRE) Ela Paparouna (Vettori (IRE))
4305^4 4758^14 5301^9 5992^4 6579^6 7301^11 7738^9

Take A Turn (IRE) *David Lanigan* a60 44
2 b g Henrythenavigator(USA) Satwa Pearl (Rock Of Gibraltar (IRE))
7665^9 7865^6 8353^7

Take Charge *David Brown* a63 68
3 b g Showcasing Be Decisive (Diesis)
1079^5 1599^15 2049^6 2809^2 3293^7 4517^7 5195^5 6685^13

Take Cover *David C Griffiths* a114 117
9 b g Singspiel(IRE) Enchanted (Magic Ring (IRE))
745^2 1862^5 (2438) 3244^11 (4824) 5614^3 6384a^6 6990a^15

Takedown (AUS) *G W Moore* 114
3 bb g Stratum(AUS) Apamea (Zafonic (USA))
8330a^6

Take In Time *Michael Easterby* 26
3 b g Hellvelyn Barnacla (IRE) (Bluebird (USA))
2835^13 3293^8

Takeitfromalady (IRE) *Lee Carter* a72 66
7 b g Intikhab(USA) Pinheiros (IRE) (Rock Of Gibraltar (IRE))
698^5 1038^3 1854^9 2210^4

Take Note (IRE) *Seamus Mullins* a67 50
4 b m Azamour(IRE) Lolla's Spirit (IRE) (Montjeu (IRE))
62^14

Take The Helm *Brian Meehan* a96 89
3 ch g Monsieur Bond(IRE) Oasis Breeze (Oasis Dream)
315^2 459^2 836^5 1865^7 2251^10 3890^7 4886^3 6232^5 6918^8 7505^9 7902^8 8251^6

Take The Stand (ARG) *William Mott* 110
4 bb h Not For Sale(ARG) Taken Away (BRZ) (Wild Event (USA))
5431a^11

Take This Waltz *Bill Turner* a28 41
2 b f Royal Applause Constant Craving (Pastoral Pursuits)
4011^11 5099^5 6888^8 8276^15

Take Two *Alex Hales* a76 84
7 b g Act One Lac Marmot (FR) (Marju (IRE))
7043^10 7653^2 8161^3

Taking Libertys *Kevin Ryan* 88
3 b g Makfi Liberty Chery (Statue Of Liberty (USA))
1446^5 1975^9 2538^7 2973^5 3841^3 4446^5 6432^2 (6838)

Talaayeb *Owen Burrows* 90
2 b f Dansili Rumoush (USA) (Rahy (USA))
(6782)

Talent Scout (IRE) *Karen Tutty* a69 81
10 b g Exceed And Excel(AUS) Taalluf (USA) (Hansel (USA))
1124^8 1595^11 1926^4 2662^4 3013^3 3214^8 3838^2 4231^8 4729^2 (5291) 6028^10 6643^2 6907^7

Talent To Amuse (IRE) *Roger Varian* a49 86
3 b f Manduro(GER) Burn Baby Burn (IRE) (King's Theatre (IRE))
29^7 2215^2 (2826) 3665^4 4351^4 ◆ 6584^3 6767^2 7320^8

Talisa (IRE) *David Simcock* 56
3 b f Pour Moi(IRE) Onereuse (Sanglamore (USA))
2395^8

Talismanic *A Fabre* 112
3 bb c Medaglia d'Oro(USA) Magic Mission (Machiavellian (USA))
2946a^4 4332a^5 6989a^11

Tallinski (IRE) *Brian Ellison* a76 76
2 ch g Mayson Estonia (Exceed And Excel (AUS))
1199^7 1840^2 2617^2

Tallulah Fleur *Ann Duffield* 47
3 b f Royal Applause Topflightcoolracer (Lujain (USA))
1953^4 2234^12 3070^12 3777^9

Tallulah Rocks *Jonathan Portman* a35 4
2 b f Tagula(IRE) Daunt Rock (IRE) (Rock Of Gibraltar (IRE))
4011^10 6062^8

Tallulah Rose *George Baker* 92
2 b f Exceed And Excel(AUS) Blinking (Marju (IRE))
2696^3 ◆ (3122) 4623^4 5359^11

Tally (AUS) *J O'Shea* 111
3 b g Street Cry(IRE) Itemise (USA) (Kris S (USA))
7378a^12 7712a^3

Tally's Son *Grace Harris* 31
2 b g Assertive Talamahana (Kyllachy)
6439^15 7269^8

Tally's Song *Grace Harris* a39 42
3 b f Piccolo Talamahana (Kyllachy)
1451^6 1795^7 2848^7 3994^13 4084^6 4292^6 5007^7 5378^5 5628^4 6361^5 7362^8 7694^9

Tamara Love (IRE) *Stuart Williams* a56 56
3 b f Tamayuz Lovers Peace (IRE) (Oratorio (IRE))
402^7 706^5 1703^7 2824^5 4279^6

Tamarillo Grove (IRE) *Sophie Leech* a57 62
9 b g Cape Cross(IRE) Tamarillo (Daylami (IRE))
4082^5 4592^3 7367^6

Tamarin *Lisa Williamson* a64 35
4 ch m Paco Boy(IRE) Les Hurlants (IRE) (Barathea (IRE))
270^6 381^6 542^8 682^9

Tamarind Cove (IRE) *Josef Vana* 104
4 b h Galileo(IRE) Saoire (Pivotal)
2729a^3 3544a^4

Tamarkuz (USA) *Kiaran McLaughlin* a121 80
6 ch h Speightstown(USA) Without You Babe (USA) (Lemon Drop Kid (USA))
(7808a)

Tamayef (IRE) *Hugo Palmer* a76
2 b c Sir Prancealot(IRE) Miss Glitters (IRE) (Chevalier (IRE))
(6741) ◆ 7322^4

Tamayuz Magic (IRE) *Michael Easterby* a62 87
5 b g Tamayuz Anne Tudor (IRE) (Anabaa (USA))
1248^2 (2051) 3118^13 4044^4 4680^3 5275^3 (6134) 6773^4 7359^2 7594^2

Tamil Nadu *Andrea Renzi* a99 88
4 ch h Beat Hollow Taurakina (Selkirk (USA))
2518a^14 8431a^5

Tamleek (USA) *Saeed bin Suroor* 71
2 bb c Hard Spun(USA) Tafaneen (USA) (Dynaformer (USA))
7226^3

Tam O'Shanter (IRE) *Charlie Appleby* 69
3 b g Poet's Voice River Mountain (Reset (AUS))
3235^10

Tamujin (IRE) *Ken Cunningham-Brown* a53 54
8 b g Elusive City(USA) Arabian Princess (Taufan (USA))
294^4 1948^2 2323^9 3997^9 4225^3 5481^11 5625^4 6020^2

Tanaasub (IRE) *Robert Cowell* 75
3 ch f Lope De Vega(IRE) Corryvreckan (IRE) (Night Shift (USA))
(3293) (5059) 6013^5

Tan Arabiq *Michael Appleby* a71 66
3 b g Arabian Gleam Tanning (Atraf)
2674^11 3776^9 (4241) 4844^7 7691^5 ◆ 7911^3 8100^5

Tanasoq (IRE) *Owen Burrows* a70 83
3 b g Acclamation Alexander Youth (IRE) (Exceed And Excel (AUS))
4041^3 (4660) 5512^4 6492^2 7433^7

Tanau (IRE) *M Delcher Sanchez* 32
2 b f Holy Roman Emperor(IRE) La Llanura (CAN) (El Prado (IRE))
5905a^11

Tanawar (IRE) *Ruth Carr* a64 70
6 b g Elusive City(USA) Parakopi (IRE) (Green Desert (USA))
1785^11 2198^8 2529^4 2918^4 3262^4 ◆ 4005^2 4231^7 4701^4 5223^6 5717^5 6226^12 7097^4

Tanaza (IRE) *D K Weld* 110
3 b f Dubawi(IRE) Tanoura (IRE) (Dalakhani (IRE))
2509a^7 3339^8 4435a^11 (5814a)

Tancred (IRE) *Conor Dore* a51 68
5 b g Oratorio(IRE) Mythologie (FR) (Bering)
1254^10 1565^2 1595^7 2047^4 2342^8 2741^2 2856^7 3258^6 3674^5

Tandem *D K Weld* a88 102
7 b g Dansili Light Ballet (Sadler's Wells (USA))
540a^11

Taneen (USA) *Roger Varian* a95 106
3 bb g Speightstown(USA) Moon And Sun (USA) (Malibu Moon (USA))
2242^6 (2736) ◆ 4062^6 7068^5

Tanera Mor (IRE) *Alan Bailey* a27 46
3 ch f Teofilo(IRE) Zavaala (IRE) (Rock Of Gibraltar (IRE))
3601^10 5527^8

Tanfeeth *M Al Mheiri* a92 86
8 ch h Singspiel(IRE) Nasij (USA) (Elusive Quality (USA))
718a^6

Tangba *Roger Varian* a65 72
3 b f Dansili Tamarind (IRE) (Sadler's Wells (USA))
2182^5 3194^7 3781^8 7205^P 7624^11

Tangerine Trees *Michael Appleby* a77 97
11 b g Mind Games Easy To Imagine (USA) (Cozzene (USA))
(2504) 3151^11 4366^7 6119^7 6642^8 7413^13

Tang Fleming *Andrew Balding* a78 97
3 b g Makfi High Cross (IRE) (Cape Cross (IRE))
(1079) (1975) 2466^3

Tango Sky (IRE) *Paul Midgley* a64 47
7 b g Namid Sky Galaxy (USA) (Sky Classic (CAN))
680^5 1252^5 1489^9 8483^3 ◆

Tangramm *Dean Ivory* a88
4 bb g Sakhee's Secret Tripti (IRE) (Sesaro (USA))
38^2 (343) (640) (823) (899) 2377^5 8249^7

Taniya (FR) *J-C Rouget* 103
4 b m High Chaparral(IRE) Takaniya (IRE) (Rainbow Quest (USA))
5384a^9 5904a^5

Tanksalot (IRE) *Harry Dunlop* a48 52
2 b f Sir Prancealot(IRE) Pearly Brooks (Efisio)
8425^6

Tannaaf (IRE) *M F De Kock* 104
4 b h High Chaparral(IRE) Wanna (IRE) (Danehill Dancer (IRE))
285a^6 ◆ 455a^11 757a^6

Tansholpan *Roger Varian* 92
2 b f Dansili Tamarind (IRE) (Sadler's Wells (USA))
(7284) ◆ 7698^3 ◆

Tanzania Road (USA) *James Tate* a58
3 b f Arch(USA) Banyan Street (USA) (Gone West (USA))
5735^3 7727^3

Tanzeel (IRE) *Charles Hills* 110
5 b g Elusive City(USA) Royal Fizz (IRE) (Royal Academy (USA))
4152^13 4667^6 ◆ 5174^8

Tanzina *Laura Mongan* a54 40
4 b m Equiano(FR) Pilcomayo (IRE) (Rahy (USA))
5710^6 8121^3 8499^3

Taopix *Karen McLintock* a69 57
4 bb g Rip Van Winkle(IRE) Sinister Ruckus (USA) (Trippi (USA))
3750^5 4375^8 5540^3 (5841) 6920^2 7105^5 7657^4 (7992) 8141^2 8586^3

Taper Tantrum (IRE) *Michael Bell* a87 89
4 b g Azamour(IRE) Maramba (USA) (Hussonet (USA))
967^5 1702^3 2121^2 2791^3 3276^2 3525^5 4208^3

Tap Focus (IRE) *J S Bolger* a65 62
4 ch m Intense Focus(USA) Gilded Butterfly (USA) (Tapit (USA))
5900a^2

Tapis Libre *Jacqueline Coward* a63 88
8 b g Librettist(USA) Stella Manuela (FR) (Galileo (IRE))
2163^10 3162^3 (4049) ◆ 4407^3 5157^5 6134^8 6517^10 7159^16 7594^8

Tapitry (USA) *Claude McGaughey III* 103
4 rg m Tapit(USA) My Trusty Cat (USA) (Tale Of The Cat (USA))
3178a^11

Tap Tap Boom *George Baker* 77
2 ro g Foxwedge(AUS) Exclusive Approval (USA) (With Approval (CAN))
1776^2 2125^2 3100^3 (3799) 4802^5 7033^4 (7467) 7768^13

Tap The Honey *K R Burke* a84 77
3 b g Fastnet Rock(AUS) Balladonia (Primo Dominie)
2048^4 (2327) 2889^5 3365^5 3904^2

Taqaareed (IRE) *John Gosden* a88 78
3 ch f Sea The Stars(IRE) Ezima (IRE) (Sadler's Wells (USA))
1609^5 (3781) 4400^9

Taqdeer (IRE) *John Gosden* a96 98
3 ch c Fast Company(IRE) Brigantia (Pivotal)
(1474) ◆ (1891)

Taqdees (IRE) *John Gosden* a69 69
3 ch f Sea The Stars(IRE) Aquarelle Bleue (Sadler's Wells (USA))
1608^5 (1962)

Taqneen (IRE) *A R Al Rayhi* a87 82
5 b g Cape Cross(IRE) Badee'A (IRE) (Marju (IRE))
407a^3

Taqwaa (IRE) *Richard Hannon* a78 46
3 ch c Iffraaj Hallowed Park (IRE) (Barathea (IRE))
4776^10 5507^5

Taraabut (IRE) *Richard Hannon* a81
3 b c Lilbourne Lad(IRE) Cuilaphuca (IRE) (Danetime (IRE))
1235^2 ◆

Tara Celeb *Mick Channon* 81
2 b f Excelebration(IRE) Tara Moon (Pivotal)
(5869) (6630) 7147^14

Tara Dylan (IRE) *Thomas Mullins* a82 85
4 b m Dylan Thomas(IRE) Tara's Wells (IRE) (Sadler's Wells (USA))
(4813a) 6389a^19 7393a^12 7708a^20

Tarakkom (FR) *Peter Hiatt* a59 64
4 ch g Naaqoos Sahabah (USA) (Swain (IRE))
(138) 354^10 498^6 1831^3 (2131) 2501^8 3528^14 8039^13 8164^4 8359^13 8565^3

Tara's Tango (USA) *Jerry Hollendorfer* a110
4 rg m Unbridled's Song(USA) Scarlet Tango (USA) (French Deputy (USA))
7836a^4

Taratchi (FR) *J Parize* a90 93
4 b h Chichi Creasy(FR) Al Tottara (FR) (Tot Ou Tard (IRE))
2728a^5 8165a^9

Taraz *David O'Meara* 85
4 b g Oasis Dream Tamarind (IRE) (Sadler's Wells (USA))
2743^10 5292^7 6160^7 6521^8 7245^4

Tarazani (IRE) *D K Weld* a77 89
3 ch g Dutch Art Tarakala (IRE) (Dr Fong (USA))
5790a^4

Tarbawi (IRE) *A bin Harmash* a65 90
6 b g Anabaa(USA) Born Something (IRE) (Caerleon (USA))
189a^16 372a^9

Tarboosh *William Haggas* a79 88
3 b g Bahamian Bounty Mullein (Oasis Dream)
(2375) 3029^3 4134^2 4569^6 6079^9 6699^9

Targaryen (IRE) *Luciano Vitabile* 100
6 b g Red Clubs(IRE) Beenablaw (IRE) (Alzao (USA))
2516a^6

Tarnend Lass *Tim Easterby* 53
3 b f Equiano(FR) Valjarv (IRE) (Bluebird (USA))
2303^8 2740^5 3368^4 3773^3 4141^3 4968^7 5578^10 5920^3

Taroneesh *Derek Shaw* a33
3 b g Canford Cliffs(IRE) Blur (Oasis Dream)
763^7 1045^8 1141^10 1497^7

Tarseekh *Roger Varian* a70 64
3 b g Kyllachy Constitute (USA) (Gone West (USA))
3023^4 8157^3 8342^5

Tartan Bute *Mark Johnston* a63 81
3 b g Azamour(IRE) On A Soapbox (USA) (Mi Cielo (USA))
96^2 245^4 1297^5 (2348) 2909^8 3025^6 4969^2 5111^4

Tartan Trip *Michael Appleby* a76 60
9 b g Selkirk(USA) Marajuana (Robellino (USA))
23^8 49^5 239^8 424^11

Tartini (USA) *John Gosden* 82
2 ch c Giant's Causeway(USA) Vignette (USA) (Diesis)
(7621)

Tasaaboq *Phil McEntee* a62 57
5 b g Aqlaam Seldemosa (Selkirk (USA))
35^2 60^4 174^3 321^8 355^7 790^3 867^2 936^9 1162^2 1556^2 (1720) 2447^2 2584^14 3040^3 3735^4 3984^3 4278^4 4472^3 8149^6 8316^4 8408^3 8541^3 8572^3

Tashaar (IRE) *Richard Hannon* 109
4 b g Sea The Stars(IRE) Three Moons (IRE) (Montjeu (IRE))
757a^13 5894^4 6571^3 7545^11

Taskeen (IRE) *Richard Hannon* 80
3 b c Lilbourne Lad(IRE) Lola Rosa (IRE) (Peintre Celebre (USA))
6209^8

Tasleet *William Haggas* a107 109
3 b c Showcasing Bird Key (Cadeaux Genereux)
(1477) 7115^8

Tasteofexcellence (IRE) *Roger Ingram* a51 61
3 b f Excellent Art Scrumptious (Sakhee (USA))
2005^7 2999^10 3958^5 4789^3 5720^10 6265^6 7037^8 7931^5 8428^8

Taste The Wine (IRE) *Bernard Llewellyn* a66 68
10 gr g Verglas(IRE) Azia (IRE) (Desert Story (IRE))
1830^6 2131^6 3099^6 4591^3

Tasty Ginger (IRE) *J R Jenkins* a60 62
3 ch g Tamayuz Secret Fashion (King's Best (USA))
(5204) 6367^4

Tatawu (IRE) *Peter Hiatt* a67 70
4 b g Mawatheeq(USA) Mooteeah (IRE) (Sakhee (USA))
202^4 467^3 640^10 1340^6 1640^3 (2174) 4158^7 4531^3 4956^6 5392^10 5629^5 6212^8

Tathqeef (USA) *John Gosden* a84 101
3 b c Tapit(USA) Foxy Danseur (USA) (Mr Greeley (USA))
1395^3 ◆ 1866^6 2481^3

Tatlisu (IRE) *Richard Fahey* a96 100
6 b g Red Clubs(IRE) Zwadi (IRE) (Docksider (USA))
1644^7 2158^17 3890^4 4338^8 4667^11 5418^17 5934^7 6560^7 7315^9 7990^5 ◆ 8583^5

Tatting *Lawrence Mullaney* a84 79
7 ch g Street Cry(IRE) Needlecraft (IRE) (Mark Of Esteem (IRE))
33^5 464^3 595^7 683^5 (801) (865) 1058^4 1404^3 1952^2 (8348)

Tatvan Incisi (TUR) *Ibrahim Bekirogullari* 100
4 b m Scarface(TUR) Hanimkiz (TUR) (Always A Classic (CAN))
6158a^3

Taurean Star (IRE) *Michael Bell* 92
3 b g Elnadim(USA) Marhaba (Nayef (USA))
(1992) 3299^9 4263^3 4624^5 ◆ 5175^5

Taurian *Ian Williams* a72 73
5 b m Central Park(IRE) Emma-Lyne (Emarati (USA))
30^7 2374^8 2994^6 3722^2 4018^3 4082^7 5294^6 6334^2 7274^3

Tavener *David C Griffiths* a65 69
4 b g Exceed And Excel(AUS) Sea Chorus (Singspiel (IRE))
1648^7 2974^7 3610^7 4606^3 4770^9 4848^7 5269^4 7798^5 7961^3 8078^4 8137^6

Tawaafoq *Richard Hannon* 68
2 b g Showcasing Gilt Linked (Compton Place)
4659^6 5410^4 7157^8

Tawakkol *Mark Johnston* a88 85
3 b g Firebreak Dayville (USA) (Dayjur (USA))
(1000) 1867^5 2407^4 3130^2

Tawan *Brian Rothwell*
5 b g Tiger Hill(IRE) Lady Netbetsports (IRE) (In The Wings)
4425^13

Tawaret (FR) *Mme M-C Naim* a72 75
2 b f Mr. Sidney(USA) Divinatrice (FR) (Numerous (USA))
1118a^9 2280a^6 5142a^3 5755a^2 7294a^8

Tawayna (IRE) *David O'Meara* 70
3 b f Invincible Spirit(IRE) Bratislava (Dr Fong (USA))
2742^15

Tawdeea *David O'Meara* a94 109
4 b g Intikhab(USA) Sharedah (IRE) (Pivotal)
1662^3 (1883) (2328) ◆ 2744^5 3027^2 (3889) 4165^9 4734^12 5655^13 7058^3 (7575) ◆ 7824^5

Tawdheef (IRE) *Simon Crisford* 95
3 gr g Zebedee Duchess Of Foxland (IRE) (Medecis)
2736[5] 3165[14] 4116[7] 6132[6]

Tawfik (IRE) *Harry Dunlop* a72 57
2 b c Bushranger(IRE) Tree House (USA) (Woodman (USA))
5250[4] 6590[2]

Tawny Port *James Given* a64 85
2 ch c Arcano(IRE) Tawaasul (Haafhd)
1621[7] 2301[2] 2913[4] (3852) (4364) (5833) 6275[6] (6536) 6954[17]

Tawseef (IRE) *Colin Bowe* a66 73
8 b g Monsun(GER) Sahool (Unfuwain (USA))
358[5]

Taxmeifyoucan (IRE) *Keith Dalgleish* 71
2 b g Beat Hollow Accounting (Sillery (USA))
6771[2] ◆ 7329[7] 7580[5]

Tax Reform (IRE) *Natalie Lloyd-Beavis* a47 60
6 b g Namid Happy Flight (IRE) (Titus Livius (FR))
46[5] 143[4] 230[7] 514[7] 690[3] 876[6] 1035[7] 1518a[2] 2079a[2] 2284a[2] 2954a[4] 3973[7] 4289[8]

Tayaar (IRE) *John Ryan* a65 42
3 b g High Chaparral(IRE) Ursula Minor (IRE) (Footstepsinthesand)
6765[6] 8096[4] 8366[8]

Tayarat (IRE) *Michael Chapman* a5 13
11 b g Noverre(USA) Sincere (IRE) (Bahhare (USA))
1674[11]

Taysh (USA) *Michael Appleby* a56 89
4 bb g Bernstein(USA) Normandy's Nell (USA) (Mt. Livermore (USA))
7[5] 1274[8] 1563[2] ◆ (1954) 2256[6] 2833[6] 3419[4] 3645[14]

Tazmania (IRE) *Clive Cox* a53 53
2 b f Helmet(AUS) Red Fuschia (Polish Precedent (USA))
6062[4] 7763[10]

Tea El Tee (IRE) *Gay Kelleway* a49 55
2 b g Holy Roman Emperor(IRE) Mayenne (USA) (Nureyev (USA))
4837[6] 5371[11] 7224[4] 7615[8] 8344[6]

Teagan Angel (IRE) *Ms M Dowdall Blake* a63 69
4 b m Dark Angel(IRE) Good Time Sue (IRE) (Commander Collins (IRE))
6463a[4] 7391a[5]

Tea Gown (IRE) *Ed de Giles* a58 83
5 ch m Iffraaj Dignify (IRE) (Rainbow Quest (USA))
127[7] 256[13] 4777[6] 5822[5]

Teajan (IRE) *James Tate* a72 19
3 gr c Dandy Man(IRE) Red Riddle (IRE) (Verglas (IRE))
1753[3] 7386[12]

Teak (IRE) *Ian Williams* a70 87
9 b g Barathea(IRE) Szabo (IRE) (Anabaa (USA))
4752[10] 5559[12] 6582[7] 6919[8] 7150[13] 8051[6]

Team Meeting (USA) *Saeed bin Suroor* a66
2 b c Exceed And Excel(AUS) Sylvan Song (USA) (Street Cry (IRE))
(7900)

Team Of Teams (USA) *J-C Rouget* a80 97
2 rg f Elusive Quality(USA) Teammate (USA) (A.P. Indy (USA))
(4124a) 6177a[5]

Team Talk *Saeed bin Suroor* a111 94
3 b g Teofilo(IRE) Native Blue (Seeking The Gold (USA))
(7061) 7701[5] (7934)

Tears Of The Sun *Clive Cox* a91 101
5 b m Mastercraftsman(IRE) Perfect Star (Act One)
(1743) 2797[2] 3608[9] 5307[7]

Techno Queen (IRE) *T Potters* 104
5 b m Manduro(GER) Tryphaena (FR) (Priolo (USA))
1907a[7] 3934a[4] 5218a[5] 6152a[3] 6610a[3] 7720a[6]

Tectonic (IRE) *Keith Dalgleish* a70 67
7 b g Dylan Thomas(IRE) Pine Chip (USA) (Nureyev (USA))
2198[12] 2575[6] 2811[8] 3212[6] 3883[7] 4038[3] 4146[3] 4314[2] 4341[4] 4871[4] (5154) 5540[9] 5715[4] 6028[8] 6502[3] 6620[2] 6838[12] 7385[3] 7657[2] 7847[10] 8142[3] 8387[4]

Teddy Edward *Richard Whitaker* a54 50
2 ch g Medicean Pinkai (IRE) (Caerleon (USA))
5885[9] 6679[5] 7328[5]

Ted's Brother (IRE) *Richard Guest* a61 51
8 b g Fath(USA) Estertide (IRE) (Tagula (IRE))
682[4] 982[4] 1323[8] 1595[10] 1696[2] 2046[6] 2096[9] 3043[5] 3287[7] 3624[7] 4144[7] 4424[9] 4929[2] (5149) 5576[5] 6621[4] 7097[7] 7426[5]

Ted Veale (IRE) *A J Martin* 95
9 b g Revoque(IRE) Rose Tanner (IRE) (Roselier (FR))
4721a[2]

Tee It Up Tommo (IRE) *Daniel Steele* a70 69
7 gr g Clodovil(IRE) Lamh Eile (IRE) (Lend A Hand)
73[7] 1546[13] 5674[4] 6186[4] 6241[7] 7035[7] 7613[12] 7817[6]

Teenage Dream (IRE) *Brian Ellison* a55 57
8 b g Antonius Pius(USA) Lucayan Star (IRE) (First Trump)
1201[7] 1405[3]

Teepee Time *Brian Baugh* a24 55
3 b f Compton Place Deora De (Night Shift (USA))
785[8] 5197[8]

Teetotal (IRE) *Nigel Tinkler* a54 70
6 ch g Footstepsinthesand Tea Service (USA) (Atticus (USA))
943[11] 1154[4] 1254[5] 1676[7] 2053[14] 2974[2] 3289[RR] 4321[5] 4376[5] 4770[6] 4848[6] 5278[3] (5483) ◆ 5889[4] 6522[10] 6685[2] 7059[11] 7584[9]

Tegara *James Fanshawe* a76 67
3 ch f Hard Spun(USA) Damaniyat Girl (USA) (Elusive Quality (USA))
3951[4] ◆ (5766) 8135[3] 8493[2]

Teide Peak (IRE) *Grace Harris* a51 58
7 b g Cape Cross(IRE) Teide Lady (Nashwan (USA))
378[7] 463[5] 674[7] 981[8] 2462[10]

Telegram *Richard Hannon* a84 78
3 b g Dream Ahead(USA) Miss Chaussini (IRE) (Rossini (USA))
(219) 1992[14] 2393[7] 3783[7]

Teletext (USA) *S Al Harabi* a95 116
5 b h Empire Maker(USA) Conference Call (Anabaa (USA))
1108a[10]

Tell A Story *David Simcock* a59
3 b f Dutch Art Ghenwah (FR) (Selkirk (USA))
8320[6] 8449[4]

Tellina (SAF) *A Wohler* 107
6 b g Silvano(GER) Tachina (IRE) (Spectrum (IRE))
282a[9] 455a[6] 625a[7] 811a[6] ◆ 1102a[7] 6610a[2] 7555a[6]

Tell Me When *Tony Coyle* a25 57
5 b m Monsieur Bond(IRE) Giffoine (Timeless Times (USA))
54[8]

Tellovoi (IRE) *Richard Guest* a79 77
8 b g Indian Haven Kloonlara (IRE) (Green Desert (USA))
178[7] 1565[5] 1695[2] 1925[2] (2092) 2677[10] 3166[11] 5374[2] 6521[9] 6643[7] 7141[6] 7457[9] 7662[5] 7959[5] 8239[8] 8385[4] (8487)

Tell The Stars *Ollie Pears* a55 52
3 ch f Monsieur Bond(IRE) Valley Of The Moon (IRE) (Monashee Mountain (USA))
2740[6] 3209[6] 3483[5] 5248[7] 6100[5] 6745[4] 7144[5]

Temerity (IRE) *Richard Fahey* a84 82
2 b f Zoffany(IRE) Gamra (IRE) (Green Desert (USA))
3597[4] (4699) ◆ 5967[2] 6554[7] 7322[2]

Tempete Nocturne (FR) *J-P Gauvin* a104 97
5 ro g Stormy River(FR) Princess Liu (IRE) (Desert Style (IRE))
7524a[10]

Temple Church (IRE) *Hughie Morrison* 92
2 b c Lawman(FR) All Hallows (IRE) (Dalakhani (IRE))
5740[3] (6546)

Temple Road (IRE) *Milton Bradley* a79 56
8 b g Street Cry(IRE) Sugarhoneybaby (IRE) (Docksider (USA))
604[6] 655[7] 714[2] 903[7] 1341[8] 2768[6] 3307[5] 3780[11] 4292[10] 4529[4] 8430[5] ◆ 8535[3] (8596)

Templier (IRE) *Gary Moore* a77 69
3 b g Mastercraftsman(IRE) Tigertail (FR) (Priolo (USA))
880[3] 980[4] 2859[6] 4312[5] 4833[3] 5293[4] (5783) 7760[6]

Tempuran *David Bridgwater* a78 72
7 gr g Unbridled's Song(USA) Tenderly (IRE) (Danehill (USA))
(43) 358[3] 1947[4] 2995[2] 3302[7] 4266[2] 4816[4] 5208[4]

Tempus Temporis (USA) *John Gosden* a71 68
4 b g Dynaformer(USA) Tempus Fugit (USA) (Alphabet Soup (USA))
767[4]

Temujins Quest (IRE) *Derek Shaw* a7 22
3 b g Dream Ahead(USA) Chinese Wall (IRE) (Aussie Rules (USA))
798[7] 1217[8] 1669[8] 2333[9] 2561[6]

Tendresse (GER) *Henk Grewe* 83
5 ch m Croco Rouge(IRE) Traumwolke (GER) (Irish Stew (GER))
6611a[6]

Tenerezza (IRE) *David Lanigan* a69 59
3 b f Shamardal(USA) Geminiani (IRE) (King Of Kings (IRE))
2767[8] 3194[9] 4361[7] 5130[3] 6901[4] 7531[5]

Ten In The Hat (IRE) *Shaun Harris* a28 42
2 b g Sir Prancealot(IRE) Vampire Queen (IRE) (General Monash (USA))
6044[9] 6682[9] 7142[10] 7570[6]

Tennessee Rose (IRE) *Tom Dascombe* a62 54
2 b f Tagula(IRE) Bonny Rose (Zaha (CAN))
1793[8] 3301[6] 3633[8] 4457[5] (5128) 6236[2] 6670[6] 6963[2]

Tennessee Wildcat (IRE) *G M Lyons* a100 107
6 b g Kheleyf(USA) Windbeneathmywings (IRE) (In The Wings)
2716a[6] 3084a[2] 4070a[2] 4326a[5] 6932a[6] 7342a[3]

Tennesse Waltz (IRE) *David Marnane* a58 46
5 b g Footstepsinthesand Shellin (IRE) (Sinndar (IRE))
7339a[10]

Tenor Des Neiges (FR) *A Schaerer*
9 b g Nononito(FR) Ludiana Des Neiges (FR) (Lute Antique (FR))
586a[4]

Ten Rocks *Lisa Williamson* a66 69
3 b g Kheleyf(USA) Exultate Jubilate (USA) (With Approval (CAN))
152[4] 211[3] 350[3] 2686[6] 3634[6] 3985[6] 5162[7] 5769[8] 6036[2] 6855[3] 7654[6] 7815[7] 8012[5] 8096[7] 8236[6] 8346[U]

Tenzing Norgay *Sir Mark Prescott Bt* a88 76
3 gr g Aussie Rules(USA) Miss Katmandu (IRE) (Rainbow Quest (USA))
2126[8] (2589) (2766) ◆ 2859[5] (5633) 6050[3]

Teodoro (IRE) *Tom Dascombe* a67 65
2 ch c Teofilo(IRE) Altesse Imperiale (IRE) (Rock Of Gibraltar (IRE))
6480[5] 7849[5]

Teofilo Wolf *Ismail Mohammed* 58
3 b f Teofilo(IRE) She Wolf (Medicean)
3359[10]

Teofonic (IRE) *Mark Johnston* a82 91
2 b f Teofilo(IRE) Dusty Answer (Zafonic (USA))
2570[4] (2970) 3275[3] (4510) 4802[3] 7698[5]

Teo's Music (IRE) *J S Bolger* a56 81
2 b f Intense Focus(USA) Teo's Sister (IRE) (Galileo (IRE))
5940a[8]

Teosroyal (IRE) *Simon Crisford* a30 81
4 br m Teofilo(IRE) Fille De Joie (IRE) (Royal Academy (USA))
1757[9]

Tepin (USA) *Mark Casse* a96 121
5 b m Bernstein(USA) Life Happened (USA) (Stravinsky (USA))
(3242) (6601a) 7171a[2] 7837a[2]

Teputina *Julia Feilden* a50
4 ch m Teofilo(IRE) West Lorne (USA) (Gone West (USA))
325[11]

Teqany (IRE) *Owen Burrows* a70 72
2 gr c Dark Angel(IRE) Capulet Monteque (IRE) (Camacho)
7065[3] 7468[5]

Teresar (IRE) *Richard Hannon* a75 82
3 ch f Dandy Man(IRE) High Chart (Robellino (USA))
2218[8] 3685[4]

Terhaal (IRE) *David O'Meara* 83
4 b g Raven's Pass(USA) Silk Trail (Dubai Destination (USA))
1521[2] 2734[6] 3166[9] 4312[3] ◆ 4704[3] 5482[10] 5915[5]

Term Of Art (USA) *Doug O'Neill* a93
2 b c Tiznow(USA) Miles Of Style (USA) (Storm Cat (USA))
7834a[9]

Termsnconditions (IRE) *Tim Vaughan* a51
2 b c Kodiac Sweet'n Sassy (IRE) (Grand Lodge (USA))
8027[6] 8454[6] 8537[12]

Terra Fina *J-F Doucet* a64 66
4 b m American Post Pink Topaz (USA) (Tiznow (USA))
4901a[2]

Terrific Feeling (IRE) *Matthieu Palussiere* a62 47
2 b c Sir Prancealot(IRE) Easy Feeling (IRE) (Night Shift (USA))
6068a[10]

Territories (IRE) *A Fabre* 119
4 b h Invincible Spirit(IRE) Taranto (Machiavellian (USA))
2927a[3] 3451a[5] 4441a[3] 6272a[6]

Teruntum Star (FR) *Kevin Ryan* a74 105
4 ch g Dutch Art Seralia (Royal Academy (USA))
(1394) 1887[8] 6558[23] 7156[18]

Tesko Fella (IRE) *Richard Hannon* 72
2 b c Myboycharlie(IRE) Foundation Filly (Lando (GER))
4736[7] 6053[5] 6731[4] 6888[4] 7319[8]

Tesoro (IRE) *Dean Ivory* a69 58
3 b f Galileo(IRE) Theann (Rock Of Gibraltar (IRE))
3036[8] 4269[13]

Tessellate (IRE) *Sylvester Kirk* a56 43
3 b f Acclamation Sterope (FR) (Hernando (FR))
1148[6] 1234[2] 1918[4]

Tess Graham *Sarah Hollinshead* 16
2 b f Pastoral Pursuits Zartwyda (IRE) (Mozart (IRE))
4133[7] 4713[8] 6129[10]

Testa Rossa (IRE) *Jim Goldie* a85 67
6 b g Oratorio(IRE) Red Rita (IRE) (Kefaah (USA))
1697[2] 2093[8] 2526[3] (2958) 3342[3] 4190[6] 4702[6] 5228[5] 5841[5] 6921[2] (7601) (7857) 8092[3] (8286)

Testarossa (POL) *P Sobry* a66 66
5 b m Kornel(POL) Toga (POL) (Dixieland (POL))
5281a[9] 5700a[4] 7568a[8]

Testimonio *Luca Cumani* a31 79
3 b c Cacique(IRE) Witness (Efisio)
(5709) 6804[10] 7512[12]

Testing (FR) *David Thompson* a43 58
5 gr m New Approach(IRE) Testama (FR) (Testa Rossa (AUS))
1952[7]

Tetradrachm *David Lanigan* a82 68
3 b g Holy Roman Emperor(IRE) Dahlia's Krissy (USA) (Kris S (USA))
(2000) ◆ 2638[7]

Teversham *Martin Smith* a55 65
3 b g Kheleyf(USA) Snow Shoes (Sri Pekan (USA))
242[11] (443) (783) 1061[4] ◆ 1257[7] 1638[11] 2642[5] 3280[8] 3603[11] 6509[10] 7062[7] (7577)

Tewafeedj *Kevin Ryan* 64
2 b c Mawatheeq(USA) It's The War (USA) (Consolidator (USA))
7580[4]

Texada *F-H Graffard* a73 61
3 b f Cacique(IRE) Spacecraft (USA) (Distant View (USA))
2948a[15] (7265a)

Texas Chrome (USA) *J R Caldwell* a110
3 b c Grasshopper(USA) Margarita Mistress (USA) (Naevus (USA))
7808a[9]

Texas Holdem (FR) *Mlle S Delaroche* a57 49
3 bl g Vasywait(FR) Hourloupe (IRE) (Damister (USA))
128a[13]

Texas Katie *Archie Watson* a70 73
2 b f Clodovil(IRE) Nadinska (Doyen (IRE))
3556[3] 4063[2] 4350[4] 4659[2] 4756[5] (5081) 5407[7] 5794[5] 5998[7] 6292[4] 6446[2] 7228[2] 7467[2] 7688[6] 7898[6] 8159[5] 8467[7]

Texas Rock (IRE) *M C Grassick* a87 101
5 b g Rock Of Gibraltar(IRE) Vestavia (IRE) (Alhaarth (IRE))
5941a[6]

Texas Ryano (USA) *Carla Gaines* 110
5 ch h Curlin(USA) Blending Element (IRE) (Great Commotion (USA))
7835a[6]

Texas Scramble *Michael Wigham* a52 42
4 b g Nayef(USA) Footlight Fantasy (USA) (Nureyev (USA))
191[6]

Textured (IRE) *Sir Michael Stoute* a81 80
2 b f Dark Angel(IRE) Timbre (Dubai Destination (USA))
2817[9] 5930[2] 6454[7] 7147[12] (7956)

Tez *M Ramadan* a2 15
5 b h Exceed And Excel(AUS) Gwyneth (Zafonic (USA))
8a[15]

Thaaqib *Charles Hills* a77 77
2 gr c Invincible Spirit(IRE) Light Shine (Dansili)
3356[5] 4349[5] 6368[3] (7306)

Thackeray *Chris Fairhurst* a46 52
9 b g Fasliyev(USA) Chinon (IRE) (Entrepreneur)
(4447) 5842[5] 6438[14] 6840[3]

Thafeera (USA) *Charles Hills* a74
2 b f War Front(USA) Aqsaam (USA) (Dynaformer (USA))
7763[2]

Thahab Ifraj (IRE) *Ismail Mohammed* a73 71
3 ch g Frozen Power(IRE) Penny Rouge (IRE) (Pennekamp (USA))
2701[3] 5375[3] 6702[9] 8282[3] 8477[3]

Tha'ir (IRE) *Saeed bin Suroor* a109 109
6 b h New Approach(IRE) Flashing Green (Green Desert (USA))
283a[9]

Thais (FR) *P Bary* 101
2 b f Rio De La Plata(USA) Tianshan (FR) (Lahint (USA))
5005a[2] (6639a) 6987a[6] 7757a[3]

Thames Knight *Marcus Tregoning* a64 85
4 b g Sir Percy Bermondsey Girl (Bertolini (USA))
2978[5] 3557[7] (4050) 4710[5] 5053[2] 5574 [6] 6804[2] 7015[6]

Thammin *Owen Burrows* a83 81
2 gr c Dark Angel(IRE) Gimme Some Lovin (IRE) (Desert Style (IRE))
2757[4] ◆ 4075[4] (4790) (6507) ◆

Thane Of Cawdor (IRE) *Joseph Tuite* a65 55
7 b g Danehill Dancer(IRE) Holy Nola (USA) (Silver Deputy (CAN))
164[10] 491[5] 676[4] 949[9] 1413[12] 5739[2] 6243[8] 6411[9] 6871[8] (7257) 7754[7] 8179[11] 8337[9]

Thank You Bye Bye (FR) *J-P Gauvin* a94 101
4 b m Zanzibari(USA) Puritanical (IRE) (Desert King (IRE))
1822a[5] 2727a[9] 4783a[5] 5384a[2] 6693a[11] 7566a[9]

Thankyou Stars *K R Burke* 77
3 b f Exceed And Excel(AUS) Magic Music (IRE) (Magic Ring (IRE))
1597[2] 5388[3] 6003[2]

Thankyou Very Much *James Bethell* a59 62
6 b m Lucky Story(USA) Maid Of Perth (Mark Of Esteem (IRE))
601[3] 801[5] 1697[5] 2093[4] 2558[8] 3417[4] 3706[8]

Thaqaffa (IRE) *Marcus Tregoning* a86 84
3 b g Kodiac Incense (Unfuwain (USA))
1804[2] ◆ 2393[2] ◆ 2935[5] (3841) ◆ 4374[3] 5024[2] 5601[7] 6877[7]

Thataboy (IRE) *Tom Dascombe* a82 67
5 b g Green Desert(USA) Hawas (Mujtahid (USA))
76[5] 462[4] 784[7] 919[3]

That Be Grand *Shaun Harris* a9 50
5 b m Firebreak Manila Selection (USA) (Manila (USA))
1121[8] 1560[10] 2233[16] 2745[9] 3325[10] 3641[8] 4934[12]

That Is The Spirit *David O'Meara* a89 101
5 b g Invincible Spirit(IRE) Fraulein (Acatenango (GER))
2485[11] 3163[9] 4665[10] 5585[10] 5871[7] (6560) 7241[6] 7984[9]

Thatsallimsaying (IRE) *David Evans* a80 97
3 br f Dandy Man(IRE) Model Looks (IRE) (Majestic Missile (IRE))
235[3] 493[4] 686[6] 1029[4] 1315[4] 1977[10]

Thats Notall Folks (IRE) *J-P Sauvage* a46 66
6 b g Kheleyf(USA) Turkana Girl (Hernando (FR))
8422a[9]

That's Ours (USA) *E Sheehy* a39 34
8 b g Giant's Causeway(USA) Magnificent Honour (USA) (A.P. Indy (USA))
819[7]

Thatsthewaytodoit (IRE) *Daniel Mark Loughnane* a56
3 ch f Lord Shanakill(USA) Van De Cappelle (IRE) (Pivotal)
544[4] 765[9] 858[5] 4718[13] 6967[4] 7515[7] 7910[2] 8194[5] 8471[8]

That Which Is Not (USA) *F-H Graffard* a93 99
3 bb f Elusive Quality(USA) Shiva (JPN) (Hector Protector (USA))
(5006a) 6069a[6] 7397a[3]

The Amber Fort (USA) *John Gosden* a81 40
2 b c Elusive Quality(USA) Unreachable (USA) (Giant's Causeway (USA))
3730[3] ◆ (5077) 6697[7] 7549[12]

The Anvil (IRE) *A P O'Brien* 109
2 b c Galileo(IRE) Brightest (Rainbow Quest (USA))
6262[3] 6783[2] 7148[3] 7539[10]

The Armed Man *Chris Fairhurst* a59 62
3 b g Misu Bond(IRE) Accamelia (Shinko Forest (IRE))
1849[4] 2776[9] 3368[6] 3843[4] 4771[4] 5069[4] 5367[6] 7096[10] 7585[3]

The Bandit (JPN) *John D Sadler* 86
4 br h Empire Maker(USA) Ravi's Lovin (USA) (Giant's Causeway (USA))
7552a[6] 7712a[10]

The Bard's Advice *Keith Dalgleish* a57
2 ch f Poet's Voice Flylowflylong (IRE) (Danetime (IRE))
6099[5]

The Batham Boy (IRE) *Daniel Mark Loughnane* 44
2 b g Thewayyouare(USA) Margaux Dancer (IRE) (Danehill Dancer (IRE))
3576[7] 5290[7] 6314[6]

The Bay Bandit *Neil Mulholland* a58 43
9 b g Highest Honor(FR) Pescara (IRE) (Common Grounds)
2110[2] 2323[2] 3997[11] 6825[8]

The Begum *Ralph Beckett* a80 81
3 b f Zamindar(USA) Sacred Shield (Beat Hollow)
2208[4] (3919) 4977[3] 6378[3] 6951[8]

The Big Day (IRE) *Nigel Tinkler* a9 55
3 gr f Le Cadre Noir(IRE) Grey Galava (Generous (IRE))
4546[6] 5178[3] 5578[5] 5887[6] 6478[6] 6631[5] 8589[14]

The Big Guy *Mick Channon* a57
3 br g Atlantic Sport(USA) Linda Green (Victory Note (USA))
105[4] 291[4] 376[11]

The Big Lad *Richard Hughes* a85 73
4 ch g Kheleyf(USA) Cultured Pride (IRE) (King's Best (USA))
(782) 2028[17] *2581[10]* 3101[6] *4014[8]* 4563[7] *7899[5] 8067[5] (8430)*

The Big Short *Charles Hills* a61 59
2 ch g Bahamian Bounty Royal Punch (Royal Applause)
2648[10] 3196[7] 4047[3] ◆ 6252[3] *6896[5] 7615[3]*

The Black Cygnet *David Menuisier*
3 br f Pastoral Pursuits The Dark Eider (Superlative)
2098[12] 4367[14] *5550[7]*

The Black Princess (FR) *John Gosden* a73 103
3 b f Iffraaj Larceny (IRE) (Cape Cross (IRE))
1758[2] ◆ 2394[2] 3297[3] (7862a)

The Blue Banana (IRE) *Grant Tuer* a37 57
7 b g Red Clubs(IRE) Rinneen (IRE) (Bien Bien (USA))
(3018) 3842[7]

The Blue Eye *Jassim Al Ghazali* 109
4 b h Dubawi(IRE) Soneva (USA) (Cherokee Run (USA))
(757a) 1107a[9]

The Blues Master (IRE) *Mark Johnston* a73 67
2 gr c Mastercraftsman(IRE) Catch The Blues (IRE) (Bluebird (USA))
6224[4] 6473[4] 7003[7] *7640[3] 8008[4] 8227[2]*

The Boys So Sharp *Oliver Greenall* a13
2 b g Captain Gerrard(IRE) Villa Del Sol (Tagula (IRE))
6588[9] 6961[10]

The Burnham Mare (IRE) *J S Moore* a69 68
3 b f Kodiac Courte Paille (IRE) (Common Grounds)
2314[7] *3036[9]* 3976[6] *4525[6] (4980)* 5230[2] 6361[6] 6879[9]

The Burning Man *Charlie Fellowes* a59
3 b c Desert Party(USA) Ras Shaikh (USA) (Sheikh Albadou)
2375[9]

The Captain (FR) *P Van De Poele* a94 84
5 b g Kingsalsa(USA) Storma (FR) (Starborough)
(3377a)

The Cashel Man (IRE) *David Simcock* a92 97
4 b g High Chaparral(IRE) Hadarama (IRE) (Sinndar (IRE))
2194[2] *3657[8]* 4752[14] 5559[3] 6582[2] 7150[4]

The Character (IRE) *Tom Dascombe* a84 88
5 b g Bushranger(IRE) Operissimo (Singspiel (IRE))
1221[13] 1978[8] 1999[11] 2651[7] 3057[7] 3636[3] 4138[5] 4377[6]

The Cheese Gang *Susan Corbett* a51 45
4 b g Bahri(USA) Aahgowangowan (IRE) (Tagula (IRE))
4035[5] 4766[7] 5178[9] *6101[6]* 6341[7] 6616[9] *8012[3] 8390[P]*

The Coffee Hunter (FR) *Nick Williams* a49
4 gr g Doctor Dino(FR) Mama Mia (FR) (Linamix (FR))
1651[7]

The Commendatore *David Barron* a53 84
3 b c Starspangledbanner(AUS) Donna Giovanna (Mozart (IRE))
15[3] (126) 1763[7] (2336) 3266[3] 4652[8] 5179[2] 5878[9]

Thecornishbarron (IRE) *John Ryan* a80 80
4 b g Bushranger(IRE) Tripudium (IRE) (Night Shift (USA))
1201[15] *1805[2]* 2174[2] *2577[7]* 3077[5] 4052[2] 4302[9] (4568) 4807[4] 5037[4] 5874[6] 6490[5] *6701[2] 7457[12]* 7671[14]

Thecornishcavalier (IRE) *John Ryan* 37
3 b g Frozen Power(IRE) Structura (USA) (Stormin Fever (USA))
4017[8] 4555[3]

The Corsican (IRE) *David Simcock* a83 118
5 b h Galileo(IRE) Walklikeanegyptian (IRE) (Danehill (USA))
1106a[7] 1909a[5] (Dead)

The Daley Express (IRE) *Ed McMahon* a74 71
2 b c Elzaam(AUS) Seraphina (IRE) (Pips Pride)
2732[3] 8118[2] ◆ *8313[3]* ◆ *8494[5]*

The Dancing Lord *Adam West* a79 66
7 br g Imperial Dancer Miss Brookie (The West (USA))
5965[10] 6300[6] 6637[7] *7457[13]*

The Detainee *Jeremy Gask* a61 64
3 b g Aqlaam Jakarta Jade (IRE) (Royal Abjar (USA))
1714[14] 2398[3] *2815[7]* 3715[7] 4794[10] *5303[11]*

The Ducking Stool *Julia Feilden* a64 75
9 ch m Where Or When(IRE) Dance Sequel (Selkirk (USA))
1156[8] 2501[7] 3191[2] 4023[5] 4551[2] 5035[4] 7507[12]

The Dukkerer (IRE) *James Given* a64 66
5 bb m Footstepsinthesand Saffron Crocus (Shareef Dancer (USA))
564[6] 898[4] 982[3] 1500[7] 2343[2] 2666[4] 3072[2] 3642[7] 4493[3] 5085[3] *6137[8]*

Thee And Me (IRE) *Mike Murphy* a72 66
3 b g Canford Cliffs(IRE) Lake Ladoga (Green Desert (USA))
(1183) 1452[6] *1763[4]* 2336[5] *3036[6] 3473[5] 3985[8]*

The Excel Queen (IRE) *Tony Coyle* a51 58
3 br f Excellent Art Gypsie Queen (IRE) (Xaar)
1379[4] 1819[4] 3249[3] 3982[5] 6646[6] 7336[6] *7646[9] 7890[8] 8146[7] 8401[5]*

The Feathered Nest (IRE) *Richard Fahey* a79 69
2 b f Dragon Pulse(IRE) Jorum (Dansili)
7122[3] *(7639) 7893[6]*

The Fenland Man *James Unett* a57
5 b g Rob Roy(USA) Spark Up (Lahib (USA))
144[9]

The Firm (IRE) *Daniel Mark Loughnane* a71 70
7 b g Acclamation Aspen Falls (IRE) (Elnadim (USA))
37[5] (277) (429) 598[8] 956[3] 1152[7] 1632[3] *1707[4]* 2673[9] 3599[6] 3876[8] 4348[3]

The Fossil *Tom Dascombe* a28 40
2 b g Bushranger(IRE) Sweet Wind Music (Zamindar (USA))
1293[6] 1454[7] 1813[4] 3361[6]

The Fox Tully (IRE) *Gerard Keane* a57 77
11 b g Monashee Mountain(USA) Then Came Bronson (IRE) (Up And At 'Em)
2114a[7]

The Gay Cavalier *John Ryan* a82 82
5 b g Henrythenavigator(USA) Dear Daughter (Polish Precedent (USA))
1933[10] 2965[3] 3582[4] 4050[2] (4307) 4555[2] 4838[3] 5122[3] 5750[2] 5925[6] 6489[4]

The Ginger Berry *Dr Jon Scargill* a70 47
6 ch g First Trump Dolly Coughdrop (IRE) (Titus Livius (FR))
256[3] 5929[5] *7429[6] 7870[2]*

The Graduate (IRE) *Andrew Balding* 96
3 gr c Mastercraftsman(IRE) Ballyvarra (IRE) (Sadler's Wells (USA))
1270[5] 2145[2] (2700) 3532[4] (3862) ◆ 4137[6] (5358) (6121) 7123[9]

The Grape Escape (IRE) *Richard Hannon* 87
2 b c Arakan(USA) Bessichka (Exceed And Excel (AUS))
(6297) 7544[8]

The Greedy Boy *Mick Channon* a47 50
3 b g Atlantic Sport(USA) Indian Girl (Erhaab (USA))
3816[4] 4505[7] 5326[6] 5710[4] 6187[4] 6407[7] 6651[5] *6967[5] 7532[12]*

The Grey Gatsby (IRE) *Kevin Ryan* 125
5 gr h Mastercraftsman(IRE) Marie Vison (IRE) (Entrepreneur)
3272[4] 4061[2] 5558[6] 6989a[16] 7353[5]

The Grey Hobbit *Ed de Giles* a32
3 gr f Shirocco(GER) Princess Pivotal (Pivotal)
8096[6]

The Grey Warrior (IRE) *Kevin Ryan* 72
2 gr c Mastercraftsman(IRE) Cranky Spanky (IRE) (Spectrum (IRE))
7329[4]

The Gurkha (IRE) *A P O'Brien* 124
3 b c Galileo(IRE) Chintz (IRE) (Danehill Dancer (IRE))
(2283a) ◆ 3245[2] 3912[2] (4754)

The Happy Hammer (IRE) *Eugene Stanford* a71 48
10 b g Acclamation Emma's Star (ITY) (Darshaan)
124[3] ◆ *(321) 532[8] 1117[8] (1700)* 2542[4] 4388[12] *7310[10]*

The Happy Prince (IRE) *A P O'Brien* a110 114
4 b h Rip Van Winkle(IRE) Maid To Dream (Oasis Dream)
1226a[5] 1730a[6] 2716a[5] 3386[15] 3681a[4] 4415a[9] 4921a[11] 5816a[2] 6328[2] (6816a) 6983a[9] *7520a[4]*

The Hooded Claw (IRE) *Tim Easterby* a79 79
5 ch g Dandy Man(IRE) Changari (USA) (Gulch (USA))
1522[3] 1997[10] 2613[11] 3133[8] 4259[10] 7590[5] *7959[4]*

The Invisible Dog (IRE) *Richard Hannon* 82
3 b g Canford Cliffs(IRE) Aljumar (IRE) (Marju (IRE))
2698[6] 2998[4] 3769[6] 4480[2] 4788[6]

The Islander (IRE) *Patrick Griffin*
5 b g Fastnet Rock(AUS) Blue Cloud (IRE) (Nashwan (USA))
6466a[7]

The Jean Genie *Clive Cox* 79
2 bb f Lawman(FR) Miracle Seeker (Rainbow Quest (USA))
6776[2]

The Juggler *William Knight* a58 58
3 b g Archipenko(USA) Oblige (Robellino (USA))
1484[4] *1835[5]* 2366[7] 2828[8] *3653[7]* 6335[6] 7231[3] *7767[2]*

The Juliet Rose (FR) *N Clement* 113
3 bb f Monsun(GER) Dubai Rose (Dubai Destination (USA))
1541a[2] (2944a) 3452a[13] 5451a[2] 6393a[3] (6972a)

The Kid *John Quinn* a79 79
5 b g High Chaparral(IRE) Shine Like A Star (Fantastic Light (USA))
200[2] 545[7] 1028[6] (2853) 3751[5] 4237[4] 4550[4] 4967[2] 5350[5] 6450[3] 7274[7]

The King's Steed *Micky Hammond* a67 53
3 b g Equiano(FR) King's Siren (IRE) (King's Best (USA))
1339[6] ◆ 1828[6] 2506[3] 3236[6] 3876[3] ◆ 4607[9] 5030[5] 5521[8] 5975[9] 6432[12] 7096[11] *7513[10]*

The Knave (IRE) *Scott Dixon* a55 62
3 b g Dick Turpin(IRE) Bayswater (Caerleon (USA))
1486[2] 2506[9] 3499[3] 5386[13] *6512[7] 7323[6] 7604[4]*

The Lacemaker *Ed Dunlop* 72
2 b f Dutch Art Sospel (Kendor (FR))
4063[5] 4756[9] 6782[3]

The Lady Hysteria (IRE) *Phil McEntee* a29
2 b f Sir Prancealot(IRE) Sand N Sea (IRE) (Desert Story (IRE))
4196[4] 5188[6] 5631[11] 6419[9] 7689[9]

The Lampo Genie *Johnny Farrelly* a53 62
4 b g Champs Elysees Samar Qand (Selkirk (USA))
381[3] 3528[5] 5573[4]

The Last Debutante *Mark Johnston* a67
2 b f Henrythenavigator(USA) Lady Eclair (IRE) (Danehill Dancer (IRE))
7977[7] 8082[5] 8340[7] ◆

The Last Lion (IRE) *Mark Johnston* a106 118
2 b c Choisir(AUS) Mala Mala (IRE) (Brief Truce (USA))
(1199) 1770[3] 2669[2] 3295[2] (3858) 4755[2] 5654[3] *(6124)* 6282[2] (6785)

The Lillster *Tony Carroll* a62 66
3 b f Kodiac Wind Surf (USA) (Lil's Lad (USA))
242[8] 1558[5] 2255[11] *2559[2]* 3513[10] *3725[9]* (4257) 5051[6]

Thello *Garry Moss* a67 65
4 b g Arcano(IRE) Silca Destination (Dubai Destination (USA))
(32) 247[8] 2329[8] 2773[12] 3013[7] 4424[7] ◆ 4767[3] 5264[3] (5517) 5980[4] 6647[7] (6953) *7794[4] (8400) 8586[5]*

The Lock Master (IRE) *Michael Appleby* a86 68
9 b g Key Of Luck(USA) Pitrizza (IRE) (Machiavellian (USA))
(7) 337[3] 447[5] 704[5] 800[4] 1250[5] 1640[8] 2233[3] 2663[9] *8477[11]*

The Lynch Man *John Quinn* a69 71
3 b g Sakhee's Secret Diliza (Dilum (USA))
1788[5] 2533[6] 3224[10] 4003[5] (4449) 4871[9] 6221[3] *7435[5] 8092[7] 8240[9]*

The Magic Pencil (IRE) *Kevin Ryan* a71 61
3 b g Dream Ahead(USA) Kylemore (IRE) (Sadler's Wells (USA))
287[5] 603[5] 818[4] 2327[6] 3952[6] 4768[7] *6701[7] (8588)*

The Major *Michael Bell* a69 76
3 b g Major Cadeaux Ballerina Suprema (IRE) (Sadler's Wells (USA))
1587[2] 2123[2] 2341[4] *3653[2] 5193[4]* 6268[5]

The Major General (IRE) *A P O'Brien* 110
3 b g Galileo(IRE) Scribonia (IRE) (Danehill (USA))
(2883a) 3300[4] 4753[2] 5557[6]

The Mcgregornator (IRE) *Adrian Paul Keatley* 81
2 bz g Bushranger(IRE) Bridal Path (Groom Dancer (USA))
2494a[9]

The Minch (IRE) *Jim Goldie* 93
5 b g Flemensfirth(USA) Akayid (Old Vic)
2486[5] 3387[8] 4164[10] 7150[P]

The Moore Factor (IRE) *D K Weld* 97
3 b g Baltic King Belleinga (IRE) (Orpen (USA))
1014a[4]

The Name's Bond *Richard Fahey* a48 48
4 ch g Monsieur Bond(IRE) Fairlie (Halling (USA))
2365[6] 2958[7] *4648[4]* 4929[6] 5715[5] 6621[7] *6900[5] 7604[9] 8179[6]*

The Name's Paver *Noel Wilson* 68
3 ch g Monsieur Bond(IRE) Pride Of Kinloch (Dr Devious (IRE))
1448[3] 1788[4] 2533[3] 2864[13] 4036[4] 4873[7] 5478[4] 5782[5] 6737[8] 7254[6]

The Nazca Lines (IRE) *John Quinn* a72 80
2 ch g Fast Company(IRE) Princess Banu (Oasis Dream)
1840[3] 2162[4] 2371[5] 3633[4] 4002[2] (4405) 4629[3] 4891[5] 5113[5] *6507[4]* 7120[4]

The New Master *David Elsworth* a73
3 br g New Approach(IRE) Maziona (Dansili)
377[5] 746[2] ◆ *980[3]*

The New Pharaoh (IRE) *Chris Wall* a68 80
5 b g Montjeu(IRE) Out West (USA) (Gone West (USA))
(2210) (3139) 3862[3] *7053[6]* 7507[9]

Thenewsfromspain (IRE) *Ollie Pears* a14 31
2 b g Holy Roman Emperor(IRE) Always Attractive (IRE) (King's Best (USA))
4363[8] *6924[11]*

The Night Before *Robert Cowell* 56
2 b c Equiano(FR) Morning After (Emperor Jones (USA))
6034[6] 7122[11]

The Night Is Ours (IRE) *J S Moore* a50 57
2 b f Bushranger(IRE) Yashila (IRE) (Indian Haven)
1988[10] 2933[2] 3507a[4] 6543[5] 6829[6] *7455a[10] 7749[9]*

Thenobleprankster (IRE) *Emma Owen*
7 b g Dynaformer(USA) Aqaarid (USA) (Nashwan (USA))
3464[12] *4477[7] 8366[9]*

Theocratic *Charlie Fellowes* a52 24
3 b g Teofilo(IRE) Centime (Royal Applause)
6452[8] 6805[6] *7052[7] 7760[8]*

Theo Danon (GER) *Mario Hofer* a83 72
8 ch g Lord Of England(GER) Ticinella (GER) (Hernando (FR))
2806a[2] 4927a[3]

Theodorico (IRE) *J S Bolger* 88
3 b g Teofilo(IRE) Yes Oh Yes (USA) (Gone West (USA))
1370a[6]

Theomour (FR) *Mlle B Renk* 97
4 b g Azamour(IRE) Theola (IRE) (Kalanisi (IRE))
3092a[6]

Theophilus (IRE) *J S Bolger* 95
5 br g Teofilo(IRE) Simonetta (IRE) (Lil's Boy (USA))
7708a[6]

Theory (USA) *Todd Pletcher* a104
2 b c Gemologist(USA) Gem Sleuth (USA) (Officer (USA))
7834a[10]

Theos Lolly (IRE) *Richard Fahey* a76 83
3 b g Kodiac Aluana (IRE) (Alzao (USA))
459[3] (633) 887[5] 1080[6] 1288[2] 2239[14] 3591[5] (3982) 4409[3] ◆ 4827[8] (5420) 5653[10] 6561[5] 6957[6] 7359[12] *8007[7]*

The Osteopath (IRE) *John Davies* 69
13 ch g Danehill Dancer(IRE) Miss Margate (IRE) (Don't Forget Me)
6684[12]

Theos Well *Michael Winters* 85
8 b g Tamure(IRE) Singing Cottage (Greensmith)
7195a[16]

The Otmoor Poet *Alan King* a79 80
3 b g Yeats(IRE) Kristalette (IRE) (Leporello (IRE))
3235[5] 3736[4] ◆ *4530[2]* 6665[4] 7215[8]

The Perfect Show *Ed Walker* a58 73
3 ch g Showcasing Nizhoni (USA) (Mineshaft (USA))
5169[9] *5843[4] 7362[6]*

The Pizza Man (USA) *Roger Brueggemann* 113
7 b g English Channel(USA) I Can Fan Fan (USA) (Lear Fan (USA))
5431a[6] (6600a) 7405a[4]

The Plough (IRE) *Martyn Meade* a65 65
3 gr g Sea The Stars(IRE) Chinese White (IRE) (Dalakhani (IRE))
85[4]

The Quarterjack *Ron Hodges* a59 62
7 b g Haafhd Caressed (Medicean)
1760[9] 2210[6] *2605[5] 3302[P]* 4950[4] 5958[5] 6335[7]

The Rectifier (USA) *Seamus Durack* a102 107
9 bb g Langfuhr(CAN) Western Vision (USA) (Gone West (USA))
3157[9] 4129[10]

The Reel Way (GR) *Patrick Chamings* a41 49
5 br m Reel Buddy(USA) Nephetriti Way (IRE) (Docksider (USA))
2969[4] 4289[9] 5572[6] 6312[6] 6894[2] 7302[4]

Theresas Candyrose (USA) *Robert Barbara*
5 ch m Candy Ride(ARG) Kelliher (USA) (Forestry (USA))
89a[5]

The Resdev Way *Richard Whitaker* a83 52
3 b g Multiplex Lady Duxyana (Most Welcome)
2308[10] 2801[9] *3987[4]* 4410[4] 5480[5] *(5971) 6739[2]* ◆ *(6920) (7385) 7847[3]*

The Right Man *D Guillemin* 110
4 br g Lope De Vega(IRE) Three Owls (IRE) (Warning)
(1618a) 3090a[2] 5217a[11] (7030a) (7758a)

Thermal Column (IRE) *Michael Appleby* a68
4 b g Vale Of York(IRE) Swiss Roll (IRE) (Entrepreneur)
6700[7] 6921[7] 7435[8] 7754[9]

Therthaar *Ismail Mohammed* a71 47
3 b c Kyllachy Red Tiara (USA) (Mr Prospector (USA))
(1551) (1768) ◆ *(2784)* ◆ 4341[6]

The Salmon Man *Brendan Powell* a79 81
4 b g Showcasing Donna Vita (Vettori (IRE))
1632[5] 2540[2] 3234[3] 4048[2] ◆ 4788[5] 6021[3] 7007[6] *7653[6] 7973[2] 8255[2]*

The Scourge (IRE) *Sarah Humphrey* a58 68
5 b g Whipper(USA) House Rebel (IRE) (Spartacus (IRE))
698[8]

These Are The Days (USA) *George Baker*
2 b g Elusive Quality(USA) Sovereign Crisis (USA) (Congrats (USA))
2649[13]

The Secrets Out *Luke Dace* a63 57
2 bl c Sakhee's Secret Brooksby (Diktat)
4866[13] *6087[8] 6868[4] 7460[5]*

The Skipper's Cat *Michael Appleby* a15 20
4 ch m Captain Gerrard(IRE) Bond Cat (IRE) (Raise A Grand (IRE))
1400[7] 1597[14] 2557[10] 3498[13]

Thesme *Nigel Tinkler* 109
4 b m Exceed And Excel(AUS) Final Dynasty (Komaite (USA))
1453[10] 2188[3] 3151[2] ◆ 4112[3] 4735[2] 5268[2] 5614[5] 6230[2]

The Special House (IRE) *Brian Ellison* a39 40
4 ro g Dalakhani(IRE) Noble Galileo (IRE) (Galileo (IRE))
8309[10]

The Special One (IRE) *Clive Cox* 61
3 br f Cape Cross(IRE) Capote West (USA) (Capote (USA))
2288[5] 3994[9] 5088[4] 6408[6]

The Stalking Moon (IRE) *John Quinn* 72
2 b f Arcano(IRE) Cornakill (USA) (Stormin Fever (USA))
4508[2] ◆ 4801[6] 5414[2] (5884) 6257[6] 6630[7]

The Statesman *Jamie Osborne* a75 72
2 b g Zoffany(IRE) Chelsey Jayne (IRE) (Galileo (IRE))
8088[3] 8227[4]

The Steward (USA) *D K Weld* a100 87
5 b g Street Cry(IRE) Candlelight (USA) (Kingmambo (USA))
99[4] (385) 1940a[5] 2512a[6] 5685a[7]

The Supreme (FR) *Mick Channon* a99 83
3 b g Holy Roman Emperor(IRE) Reine Violette (FR) (Fly To The Stars)
638[2] ◆ *836[3]* ◆

The Taj (USA) *Doug Watson* a70 68
6 ch g Street Cry(IRE) India (USA) (Hennessy (USA))
719a[6] ◆

The Tartan Spartan (IRE) *John Patrick Shanahan* 96
3 ch c The Carbon Unit(USA) The Real Thing (IRE) (Traditionally (USA))
(1873) 3341[7] 6329[8] 6917[6]

The Third Man *Henry Spiller* a82 47
5 gr g Dalakhani(IRE) Spinning Queen (Spinning World (USA))
1430[4] 1702[5] 2651[8] *3563[5] 5609[2]* 6138[8] *8100[4] 8498[9]*

The Tichborne (IRE) *Patrick Morris* a75 42
8 b g Shinko Forest(IRE) Brunswick (Warning)
141[5] 457[2] (629) 879[7] 1173[9] 1832[2] 2849[6] *(3729) 8036[5] 8191[2] 8447[6]*

The Tin Man *James Fanshawe* 121
4 b g Equiano(FR) Persario (Bishop Of Cashel)
(2546) ◆ 3385[8] (4393) ◆ 6120[2] (7350)

Thetis (IRE) *Sir Michael Stoute* 105
3 b f Invincible Spirit(IRE) Serres (IRE) (Daylami (IRE))
2220[3] 2539[4] 4652[6] ◆

Thetrioandme (IRE) *John Best* a65 43
2 b g Tagula(IRE) Peninsula Girl (IRE) (Cape Cross (IRE))
5371[10] *8557[3]*

The Turning Point (FR) *J-C Rouget* 107
3 b c Hurricane Cat(USA) L'Ete (CHI) (Hussonet (USA))
1308a[6]

The Twisler *Roger Ingram* a88 89
4 b g Motivator Panna (Polish Precedent (USA))
2286a[8] 3298[16] 4799[12] 5655[17] 6118[16] 7150[19] 7498[10] *7979[12] 8447[6]*

The Wagon Wheel (IRE) *Richard Fahey* 90
2 b f Acclamation Bahati (IRE) (Intikhab (USA))
(4451) (5560) 5998[5] 6954[3]

The Warrior (IRE) *Amanda Perrett* a97 97
4 b g Exceed And Excel(AUS) Aymara (Darshaan)
1335[7] ◆ 2027[8] 2391[6] ◆ 2796[8] 3534[7] 4104[8] 4263[4] 4532[4] 4758[5]

The Way You Dance (IRE) *Neil Mulholland* a71 63
4 b g Thewayyouare(USA) Beautiful Dancer (IRE) (Danehill Dancer (IRE))
(862) 1456[9]

Thewayyouwish (IRE) *Mohammed Jassim Ghazali* a94 104
3 b c Thewayyouare(USA) Faby Douglas (IRE) (Danetime (IRE))
2281a[2] 8573a[11]

The Wee Barra (IRE) *Kevin Ryan* a65 72
4 b m Rock Of Gibraltar(IRE) Gamra (IRE) (Green Desert (USA))
1412[3] 1697[9] 2233[8] (2574) 3012[8] 3342[2] 3876[7] 4486[3] 4871[5] 5540[2] 6005[5] (6621) 7336[2]

The Wee Chief (IRE) *Jimmy Fox* a44 59
10 ch g King Charlemagne(USA) La Belle Clare (IRE) (Paris House)
1261[7] 3993[5] 4264[3] 4658[3]

The Winningtipster *Susan Corbett* 9
3 ch g Kheleyf(USA) Freedom Song (Singspiel (IRE))
2858[6]

Thewizardofoz (AUS) *J Size* 106
4 b g Redoute's Choice(AUS) Princess Coup (AUS) (Encosta De Lago (AUS))
1911a[10]

The Yank *David Bridgwater* a71 52
7 b g Trade Fair Silver Gyre (IRE) (Silver Hawk (USA))
2616[7]

Theydon Bois *Peter Charalambous* a59 68
4 b m Three Valleys(USA) Velvet Waters (Unfuwain (USA))
437[8] 1699[4] 2607[4] 3076[5] 3825[2] 4320[2] 4739[4] 5737[3] 6411[4]

Theydon Girls *Peter Charalambous* a43 4
3 b f Poet's Voice Match Point (Unfuwain (USA))
1392[14] 1704[7] 2483[12]

Theydon Grey *Peter Charalambous* a90 89
3 gr g Champs Elysees Cheerfully (Sadler's Wells (USA))
(495) ◆ 705[3] 887[4] 1080[4] 2244[9] 6456[2] 7067[8]

Theydon Thunder *Peter Charalambous* a66 66
4 b g Virtual Lady Agnes (Singspiel (IRE))
(1035) 1145[2] 1165[6] (3354) (3624) 3896[4] 4362[10] 5734[5] (6512)

They Seek Him Here (IRE) *Hugo Palmer* a66 99
3 bb c Elusive Pimpernel(USA) Spiritville (IRE) (Invincible Spirit (IRE))
5956[9] 6559[14]

Thief Of Hearts *Bill Turner* a51 11
3 br f Dick Turpin(IRE) Constant Craving (Pastoral Pursuits)
47[5] 436[7] 689[9] 1764[5] 3198[10]

Thiepval *Jason Ward* a43 44
4 ch g Kyllachy Lady Broughton (IRE) (Grand Lodge (USA))
500[6] 863[7] 1123[8] 4260[13] 6105[4]

Thikriyaat (IRE) *Sir Michael Stoute* a78 109
3 b g Azamour(IRE) Malaspina (IRE) (Whipper (USA))
(1393) (2250) 3269[2] ◆ (4822) ◆ 5873[5]

Thimaar (USA) *Sarah Hollinshead* a70 58
8 bb g Dynaformer(USA) Jinaan (USA) (Mr Prospector (USA))
200[7] 386[5] 506[5] 865[6] 1038[5] 1450[6] 1830[2] 2131[5] 2502[6] 3099[7]

Things Happen *David Evans* a70 62
2 ch g Captain Gerrard(IRE) Aquasulis (IRE) (Titus Livius (FR))
6375[4] 7090[3] 7502[9] 8033[3] 8244[2]

Think *Clive Mulhall* a35 34
9 ch g Sulamani(IRE) Natalie Jay (Ballacashtal (CAN))
3253[6]

Think Ahead *Saeed bin Suroor* a103 107
5 b g Shamardal(USA) Moonshadow (Diesis)
188a[3] (455a) 721a[2]

Think Fashion (IRE) *Brian Meehan* 73
2 b f So You Think(NZ) Passionforfashion (IRE) (Fasliyev (USA))
5400[8] 6078[2]

Think So (IRE) *Mark Johnston* 38
2 b c So You Think(NZ) Mabalane (IRE) (Danehill (USA))
6808[5] 7649[9]

Third Dimension *Jassim Al Ghazali* a56 103
5 b g Dubawi(IRE) Round The Cape (Cape Cross (IRE))
744a[7]

Third Order (IRE) *K R Burke* a70 75
2 b c Hat Trick(JPN) Fifth Commandment (IRE) (Holy Roman Emperor (IRE))
4040[5] 4642[3] (5916) 6554[8]

Third Rock (IRE) *Sir Michael Stoute* a60 78
3 b g Hat Trick(JPN) Rochitta (USA) (Arch (USA))
2044[6] 2701[2] (3721)

Third Time Lucky (IRE) *Richard Fahey* a104 106
4 gr g Clodovil(IRE) Speckled Hen (IRE) (Titus Livius (FR))
2191[11] 4823[19] 5585[5] ◆ 6786[4] 7354[5] ◆ 8049[5] 8317[9] 8593[5]

This Is For You *Andrew Balding* 80
3 b g Paco Boy(IRE) Waypoint (Cadeaux Genereux)
2982[3] 3685[2] 4093[3] 4803[14]

Thisvi *E Lellouche* 78
3 b f High Chaparral(IRE) Axioniki (IRE) (Holy Roman Emperor (IRE))
3120a[4]

Thomas Blossom (IRE) *Ali Stronge* a70 66
6 b g Dylan Thomas(IRE) Woman Secret (IRE) (Sadler's Wells (USA))
261[3] 698[2] 882[3] 4478[2] 4979[4] 6825[2]

Thomas Cranmer (USA) *Mark Johnston* a68 82
2 b c Hard Spun(USA) House Of Grace (USA) (Limehouse (USA))
3315[5] ◆ 4473[4] (4914) 6275[F]

Thomas Crown (IRE) *James Tate* 12
2 b c Helmet(AUS) Picture Of Lily (Medicean)
6288[11]

Thomas Girtin (IRE) *Gary Moore* a38 38
2 b g Canford Cliffs(IRE) Spiritual Air (Royal Applause)
4706[7] 5484[7] 6086[9]

Thora Barber *David Evans* a78 88
2 b f Rip Van Winkle(IRE) How High The Sky (IRE) (Danehill Dancer (IRE))
1087[8] (1719) 2240[3] 3382[6]

Thornaby Nash *Colin Teague* a36 89
5 br g Kheleyf(USA) Mistress Twister (Pivotal)
3011[10] 3605[13] 4830[7] 5482[16] 6434[3] 6618[3] 6921[11] 7253[9]

Thornaby Princess *Colin Teague* a25 65
5 b m Camacho Ingleby Princess (Bold Edge)
2423[U] 3009[8] 3484[10] 3777[6] 4096[2] 4492[4] (4834) 5277[2] 5804[3] (6098) 6341[5] 6813[8]

Thorndyke *Kevin Ryan* a68 79
2 b g Bahamian Bounty Nurse Gladys (Dr Fong (USA))
4297[5] 5150[2] 6274[3] 7322[5]

Thornton *Richard Fahey* 62
2 b c Mayson Cardrona (Selkirk (USA))
2193[5]

Thornton Frank *Brian Rothwell*
2 b g Misu Bond(IRE) Byton (Byron)
5067[10] 8237[13]

Thornton Mary *Brian Rothwell* a42
2 b f Mawatheeq(USA) Bezant (IRE) (Zamindar (USA))
8139[7] 8397[7]

Thorntoun Lady (USA) *Jim Goldie* a66 71
6 b m Henrythenavigator(USA) Valery Lady (ARG) (Roy (USA))
5390[13] 5780[10] 6080[7] 6234[13] 6809[9] 7437[6] 7797[3] 7994[3] 8482[3]

Thorpe Bay *P G Van Kempen* a57 61
7 b g Piccolo My Valentina (Royal Academy (USA))
7398a[4]

Thou Swell (IRE) *Shaun Harris* a68 61
4 b g Tiznow(USA) Kamarinskaya (USA) (Storm Cat (USA))
173[8] 425[3] 583[6] 801[6] 957[5] 8540[10]

Threat Assessed (IRE) *Clive Cox* 90
3 b g Holy Roman Emperor(IRE) High Reserve (Dr Fong (USA))
(2128) 2654[8] (3156) 3887[2]

Threave *Laura Mongan* a31 75
8 b m Diktat Bianca Sforza (Anabaa (USA))
3857[6] 5825[11]

Threebagsue (IRE) *J S Moore* a74 72
3 ch f Lord Shanakill(USA) Feet Of Flame (USA) (Theatrical)
123[3] 315[6] 459[4] 678[4] 1286a[4] (1573) 6140[2] 7492a[12] (7931) 8158[8] (8379)

Three Brothers (FR) *Harry Dunlop* a40 49
3 gr c Slickly(FR) Vivartic (FR) (Verglas (IRE))
1767[7] 2398[6]

Three Colours Red (IRE) *Warren Greatrex* a31 72
4 b g Camacho Colour's Red (IRE) (Red Ransom (USA))
3064[6]

Three C'S (IRE) *David Dennis* 77
2 b g Kodiac Ms Mary C (IRE) (Dolphin Street (FR))
2437[5] 3633[2] 4047[2] 4679[4] 5099[3]

Threediamondrings *Brendan Powell* a69 58
3 ch c Geordieland(FR) Five Gold Rings (IRE) (Captain Rio)
6073[5] 6294[8] 6805[7] 7905[8] (7969) 8318[3] 8428[2] 8524[2]

Three Duchesses *Michael Bell* a71 70
2 b f Dutch Art Three Ducks (Diktat)
3555[7] 4054[3] 4442[6] 5549[4] 6421[2] (7107)

Three Gracez *George Scott* a89 82
4 b m Kyllachy Three Ducks (Diktat)
(780) 1003[6] 1441[13] 2223[5] 2621[8] 8028[7]

Threeinoneday (IRE) *Nigel Tinkler* a41 61
3 b g Bushranger(IRE) Star Studded (Cadeaux Genereux)
896[9]

Three Jacks (IRE) *Martin Hassett* 82
2 b c Iffraaj Burn Baby Burn (IRE) (King's Theatre (IRE))
7707a[10]

Three Kingdoms (IRE) *D K Weld* 83
7 ch g Street Cry(IRE) Chan Tong (BRZ) (Hampstead (URU))
3680a[7]

Three Loves (IRE) *Andrew Balding* a56 48
3 b f Duke Of Marmalade(IRE) Three Moons (IRE) (Montjeu (IRE))
2182[12] 3781[12] 4657[6] 5012[4]

Three Rules (USA) *Jose Pinchin* a112
2 bb c Gone Astray(USA) Joy Rules (USA) (Full Mandate (USA))
7834a[6]

Three Star General *A P O'Brien* 78
3 b g Montjeu(IRE) Honorlina (FR) (Linamix (FR))
5620a[3]

Three Times A Lord *Ivan Furtado* a53 64
4 gr h Three Valleys(USA) Sesmen (Inchinor)
3400[4] 6104[7] 6569[12]

Thrilled (IRE) *David Lanigan*
3 b f Kodiac Fuerta Ventura (IRE) (Desert Sun)
5797[15]

Throckley *John Davies* 84
5 b g Passing Glance Porcelain (IRE) (Peintre Celebre (USA))
2048[3] 2804[3] (3856) 4933[5] 5482[6] 6160[4] 7412[7]

Thrtypointstothree (IRE) *Nikki Evans* a48 50
5 b g Kodiac Miss Taken (IRE) (Dubai Destination (USA))
107[7] 294[3] 822[8] 870[9] 5383[8] 8499[5]

Thrust Home (IRE) *Y Durepaire* a62 97
2 b f Fastnet Rock(AUS) Garden City (FR) (Majorien)
4124a[4] 7757a[5] 8062a[5]

Thunderbell *Scott Dixon* a52
2 ch f Haafhd Trustthunder (Selkirk (USA))
8139[4]

Thunderbird *Scott Dixon* a55
4 b m Sakhee(USA) Trustthunder (Selkirk (USA))
54[4]

Thundering Blue (USA) *David Menuisier* a74 77
3 gr g Exchange Rate(USA) Relampago Azul (USA) (Forestry (USA))
1421[5] 5260[2] 6247[2] 7102[6] 7461[11]

Thundering Home *Richard Mitchell* a50 37
9 gr g Storming Home Citrine Spirit (IRE) (Soviet Star (USA))
3747[8] 4057[11]

Thunder Pass (IRE) *David Pipe* a67 82
5 b g High Chaparral(IRE) Hadarama (IRE) (Sinndar (IRE))
2820[6]

Thunder Snow (IRE) *Saeed bin Suroor* 119
2 b c Helmet(AUS) Eastern Joy (Dubai Destination (USA))
(2756) ◆ 3243[6] 4732[2] 6326[2] 7149[4] (7721a)

Thunder Speed *T Stack* a80
2 b c Dylan Thomas(IRE) Insoumise (IRE) (Galileo (IRE))
7917a[7]

Tiberian (FR) *Alain Couetil* 110
4 b h Tiberius Caesar(FR) Toamasina (FR) (Marju (IRE))
2077a[4] 3298[14] 6175a[4] 7396a[2]

Tibibit *Henry Tett* a58
3 b f Kyllachy Cat Hunter (One Cool Cat (USA))
8093[4]

Tibr (USA) *Ed Dunlop* a74 91
2 b c Distorted Humor(USA) Spare Change (USA) (Bernardini (USA))
(2038) 2865[5] 3526[4] 4352[4] (6562) 7155[6]

Tiburtina (IRE) *Sylvester Kirk* a72 98
2 bb f Holy Roman Emperor(IRE) Interchange (IRE) (Montjeu (IRE))
2817[5] (4350) 5172[5] 5870[5] 6258[5] 6797a[2] 8127a[8]

Ticking Away *David Brown* a90 67
3 gr g Monsieur Bond(IRE) Pendulum (Pursuit Of Love)
(962) ◆ (1029) 1607[6] 2788[8] 4643[10] 5274[13] 5552[13]

Tickle Me Blue (GER) *Markus Klug* 102
3 b f Iffraaj Tickle Me Pink (Groom Dancer (USA))
1513a[4] 4184a[4] 5696a[5] 6397a[4]

Ticks The Boxes (IRE) *Michael Herrington* a90 82
4 ch g Fast Company(IRE) Swan Sea (USA) (Sea Hero (USA))
966[9] 1205[7] 1787[11] 8099[10] 8236[2] (8473) ◆ 8571[10]

Ticonderoga (USA) *Chad C Brown* 103
2 b c Tapit(USA) Keertana (USA) (Johar (USA))
7807a[4]

Tidal's Baby *Lee Carter* a62 64
7 b g Dutch Art Tidal (Bin Ajwaad (IRE))
196[4] 403[3] 696[5] 2647[4] 3349[4]

Tidal Way (IRE) *Shaun Lycett* a71 50
7 gr g Red Clubs(IRE) Taatof (IRE) (Lahib (USA))
199[5] 786[3] 1039[6] 1434[5] (Dead)

Tiercel *Roger Varian* a91 93
3 b c Olden Times Sharp Mode (USA) (Diesis)
1474[5] (6674) (7017)

Tierra Del Fuego (FR) *G E Mikhalides* 100
3 ch f Champs Elysees Marella (Desert Prince (IRE))
1541a[5] 2316a[9] 3452a[P]

Tifl *Heather Main* a71
3 ch g Approve(IRE) Isobel Rose (IRE) (Royal Applause)
8247[2] 8559[4]

Tiga Tuan (FR) *Kevin Ryan* a56 66
3 b f Le Havre(IRE) Ramita (Fasliyev (USA))
1628[6] 2108[8] 3878[8] 4429[3] 5057[2] 5975[8] 6742[6] 7435[10]

Tigerfish (IRE) *William Stone* a43 49
2 b f Lilbourne Lad(IRE) Nisriyna (IRE) (Intikhab (USA))
2535[9] 4397[11] 4638[5] 5165[3] 5770[3] 7286[5] 7571[4] 7866[7] 8072[5] 8276[9]

Tiger Jim *Jim Goldie* a82 92
6 b g Tiger Hill(IRE) Quintrell (Royal Applause)
1218[11] 1848[4] 2331[6] 3646[8] 4193[6] 4443[3] 4896[8] 5857[2] 6079[4] 7094[2] 7957[9] 8311[8]

Tiger's Home *Iain Jardine* a71 57
6 b m Tiger Hill(IRE) Homeward (IRE) (Kris)
1[6] 24[7] 246[9] 2661[8] 3020[7] 3946[5] 4314[12] 5835[10]

Tiger's Nest (ITY) *Simone Brogi* a73
2 b f Blu Air Force(IRE) Cryadora (IRE) (Street Cry (IRE))
(7455a)

Tiger Twenty Two *Brian Rothwell* 68
5 b g Authorized(IRE) Collette's Choice (Royal Applause)
1588[8] 3294[6]

Tigerwolf (IRE) *Mick Channon* a76 90
3 br g Dream Ahead(USA) Singing Field (IRE) (Singspiel (IRE))
1423[3] 1701[4] 4867[3] ◆ (5327) 5878[6]

Tiggaliscious (IRE) *Richard Hannon* a51 74
2 b f Acclamation Mea Parvitas (IRE) (Oasis Dream)
1749[4] 2097[2] 2310[3] 2637[5] 4015[4]

Tigserin (IRE) *Giles Bravery* a73 53
3 ch f Approve(IRE) Mairead Anne (USA) (Elusive Quality (USA))
(1292) 1572[3] 2585[7] 2824[4] 3527[2] ◆ 4525[2] 5078[2] 7363[7]

Tijuca (IRE) *Ed de Giles* a68 52
7 b m Captain Rio Some Forest (IRE) (Charnwood Forest (IRE))
39[2] (149) 420[6] 676[7] 862[8]

Tikiouine (FR) *J-M Lefebvre* a76 75
4 gr m Mastercraftsman(IRE) Mislix (FR) (Linamix (FR))
3184a[5]

Tikitiki (FR) *N Clement* a77 62
2 b f Fastnet Rock(AUS) Green Diamond Lady (USA) (Johannesburg (USA))
(7970a)

Tikthebox (IRE) *David Brown* a62 80
3 b g Approve(IRE) Nicene (USA) (Pulpit (USA))
954[5] 2200[2] 3753[7] 4547[8] 5182[5] 5274[9] 5881[5] 5960[7] 7268[10]

Tilly Devine *Scott Dixon* a42
2 gr f Aussie Rules(USA) Cora Pearl (IRE) (Montjeu (IRE))
5469[10] 6925[14] 7855[10]

Tilly Trotter (IRE) *D K Weld* a91 79
2 b f Kodiac Inourthoughts (IRE) (Desert Style (IRE))
2718a[13]

Tilstarr (IRE) *Roger Teal* a70 71
6 b m Shamardal(USA) Vampire Queen (IRE) (General Monash (USA))
62[13]

Tilsworth Micky *J R Jenkins* a65 56
4 br g Kheleyf(USA) Tilsworth Charlie (Dansili)
77[5] 211[5] 460[5] 5259[5] 6249[11] 6745[7] 7445[4] 7747[7] 8026[10] 8346[6] (8383)

Tilsworth Phyllis *J R Jenkins* 8
4 b m Schiaparelli(GER) Subtle One (IRE) (Polish Patriot (USA))
1037[5] 1400[9] 2589[6] 5473[8]

Time Again *David Brown* a49
3 b f Kyllachy Record Time (Clantime)
2560[4] 4766[8]

Time And Motion (USA) *James J Toner* 111
3 b f Tapit(USA) Ellie's Moment (USA) (Kris S (USA))
4174a[2] (7379a)

Time Chant *Stefano Botti* 105
4 b h War Chant(USA) Snowfield (USA) (Tale Of The Cat (USA))
(2516a)

Time Check (USA) *Saeed bin Suroor* a40 84
4 ch m Shamardal(USA) Alizes (NZ) (Rory's Jester (AUS))
(1597) 2016[6] 2621[9]

Time Down Under *Mark H Tompkins* 46
2 b g Aussie Rules(USA) Nice Time (IRE) (Tagula (IRE))
3619[5] 4047[6] 4762[9]

Time Dream (IRE) *M Boutin* a67 67
5 b m Bushranger(IRE) Softlanding (IRE) (Nashwan (USA))
4927a[7]

Timekeeping (IRE) *Saeed bin Suroor* a90 90
3 ch c New Approach(IRE) Midnight Line (USA) (Kris S (USA))
1784[2] (7410) 7980[4] 8250[3]

Timeless Art (IRE) *K R Burke* a63 91
3 b g Medicean Bellona (IRE) (Bering)
1160[4] 2239[6] (3389) 6877[5] (7671)

Timeless Flight *Charlie Appleby* a86 84
2 b c Helmet(AUS) Kathy's Rocket (USA) (Gold Legend (USA))
3598[2] (4161) (6869) 7536[9]

Time Medicean *Tony Carroll* a57 67
10 gr g Medicean Ribbons And Bows (IRE) (Dr Devious (IRE))
100[3] 418[4] 589[4] ◆ 1782[5] 3719[3] 3970[2] 5050[4] 5408[7] 5706[2] 6410[2] 7018[4] 7301[7]

Time Of My Life (GER) *Patrick Holmes* 91
5 ch g Nayef(USA) Tamaja (GER) (Tiger Hill (IRE))
1880[4] 2487[8] 3602[6] (4311) 5837[9] 6561[11]

Time Shanakill (IRE) *G Botti* a80 80
3 b c Lord Shanakill(USA) Cherry Creek (IRE) (Montjeu (IRE))
2518a[12] 6310a[3] 7680a[5]

Times In Anatefka (IRE) *Adrian Brendan Joyce* a58 43
6 b m Pyrus(USA) Brooklands Time (IRE) (Danetime (IRE))
7800a[4]

Time Sky (ITY) *G Botti* a65
2 b g Mujahid(USA) Trans Gold (IRE) (Dushyantor (USA))
5988a[4]

Times Legacy *Peter Chapple-Hyam* 78
3 b c Cape Cross(IRE) Simply Times (USA) (Dodge (USA))
2650[9] 3580[7] 6190[10] (Dead)

Time Square (FR) *Tony Carroll* a60 59
9 b g Westerner Sainte Parfaite (FR) (Septieme Ciel (USA))
39[8] 362[3] 514[10] (602) 672[5] 870[4] 1201[4]

Time Test *Roger Charlton* 124
4 b h Dubawi(IRE) Passage Of Time (Dansili)
(2626) 3912[3] (4666)

Time To Blossom *Simon Crisford* a77 74
3 b f Cape Cross(IRE) Time Over (Mark Of Esteem (IRE))
5996[2] 6661[3] 7410[3]

Time To Exceed (IRE) *Henry Candy* 81
3 b f Exceed And Excel(AUS) In Your Time (Dalakhani (IRE))
2470[8] 2904[4] (5388) 6064[4]

Time To Inspire (IRE) *D K Weld* 93
4 ch g Galileo(IRE) Utterly Heaven (IRE) (Danehill (USA))
3630a[12] 4721a[8]

Time To Reason (IRE) *J P Murtagh* a87 102
3 b g Kyllachy Danehurst (Danehill (USA))
6355a[17] 7191a[11]

Time To Sea (IRE) *John Butler* 38
2 b c Born To Sea(IRE) Eastern Glow (Cape Cross (IRE))
6211[10]

Time To Study (FR) *Mark Johnston* a85 83
2 ch c Motivator Dissertation (FR) (Sillery (USA))
(6224) ◆ 7930[2] (7982)

Time To Tango (IRE) *Joseph Tuite* a48
5 b g Tiger Hill(IRE) Bravo Dancer (Acatenango (GER))
945[7] 1767[5] 8281[4]

Time Warp *Sir Mark Prescott Bt* a86 108
3 ch g Archipenko(USA) Here To Eternity (USA) (Stormy Atlantic (USA))
(2551a)

Time Zone *Peter Chapple-Hyam* 83
2 b c Kheleyf(USA) Be Joyful (IRE) (Teofilo (IRE))
(6750)

Timia *Ed Dunlop* a69 48
3 b f Cape Cross(IRE) Cinerama (IRE) (Machiavellian (USA))
(47) 495^{7} 1238^{6} 1745^{4} 2585^{10}

Timoneer (USA) *Tim Easterby* a65 46
6 bb g Elusive Quality(USA) Gentle Gale (USA) (Storm Cat (USA))
1124^{12}

Tim The Taxi *David Evans* 53
3 b g Compton Place Polar Dawn (Polar Falcon (USA))
1251^{4} 1829^{5} 2107^{10} 3126^{6} 4085^{9} 4796^{7}

Tindaro (FR) *Paul Webber* a76 83
9 gr g Kingsalsa(USA) Star's Mixa (FR) (Linamix (FR))
1987^{5} 6356a^{10} 8558^{7}

Tinder (IRE) *Mrs John Harrington* 94
2 gr f Fast Company(IRE) Platinum Darling (IRE) (Iffraaj)
6815a^{4}

Tingo In The Tale (IRE) *Sophie Leech* a63 65
7 b g Oratorio(IRE) Sunlit Skies (Selkirk (USA))
949^{2} 5303^{2} 6871^{10} 8410^{8}

Tink *Mark Brisbourne* a51
2 ch f Captain Gerrard(IRE) Ensign's Trick (Cayman Kai (IRE))
8494^{6}

Tinseltown *Harriet Bethell* a29 62
10 b g Sadler's Wells(USA) Peony (Lion Cavern (USA))
674^{10} 4648^{11} 5607^{7} 6102^{13}

Tinsill *Nigel Tinkler* a48 55
5 ch g Firebreak Concentration (IRE) (Mind Games)
1481^{2} 1790^{5} 2120^{10} 3009^{9} 3484^{3} 3843^{6} 4228^{2} 4309^{2} 4606^{2} 4931^{7} 5320^{5} 5582^{7} 6023^{2} 6680^{10} 6774^{2} 7860^{7}

Tioga Pass *Paul Cole* a80 102
5 b m High Chaparral(IRE) Seren Devious (Dr Devious (IRE))
1569^{9} 1855^{11} (2433) 4400^{5} 4800^{2} 6259^{7} 7271^{7}

Tipstaff *J S Bolger* 96
3 b c Street Cry(IRE) Firth Of Lorne (IRE) (Danehill (USA))
7372a^{3}

Tiptree (IRE) *Luca Cumani* 103
3 b f Duke Of Marmalade(IRE) Taking Liberties (IRE) (Royal Academy (USA))
1890^{5} 3060^{5} 4883^{3} ◆ 5587^{8} 7271^{8} 8024a^{16}

Tirmizi (FR) *D K Weld* 94
3 b c Sea The Stars(IRE) Timabiyra (IRE) (Linamix (FR))
2069a^{7}

Tisbutadream (IRE) *David Elsworth* a65 27
2 ch f Dream Ahead(USA) Choose Me (IRE) (Choisir (AUS))
3613^{6} 8151^{2} ◆ 8557^{7}

Tis Marvellous *Clive Cox* 110
2 b c Harbour Watch(IRE) Mythicism (Oasis Dream)
3813^{2} (4203) (4694a) 5690a^{5} 6282^{9}

Tisnowornever (IRE) *J S Moore* a2
2 b f Bushranger(IRE) Lipsia (IRE) (Dubai Destination (USA))
4526^{7} 5606^{8}

Tis Wonderful (IRE) *Clive Cox* a57 61
2 b g Casamento(IRE) Cosenza (Bahri (USA))
4877^{6} 5356^{10} 7065^{8}

Titan Goddess *Mike Murphy* a78 78
4 b m Equiano(FR) Phoebe Woodstock (IRE) (Grand Lodge (USA))
1805^{5} 2607^{6} 3624^{4} 4498^{8} (5753) (6373) (7062) 7298^{2} 7671^{2} 8052^{4} 8178^{11}

Tithonus (IRE) *Denis Gerard Hogan* a85 95
5 b g Glory Of Dancer Aurora Aurealis (IND) (Indictment (IND))
(4899a) (6819a) 7537^{2}

Titi Makfi *Mark Johnston* a69 70
2 b f Makfi Titivation (Montjeu (IRE))
7432^{7} 7740^{3} ◆ 7975^{2} 8159^{3} 8465^{4}

Titus Secret *Malcolm Saunders* a48 66
4 ch g Sakhee's Secret Crimson Fern (IRE) (Titus Livius (FR))
1319^{9} 1794^{7} 1949^{10} (3486) 3734^{2} (3993) ◆

Tivra (IRE) *Bryan Smart* 56
2 b f Kodiac Bokhara Silk (IRE) (Barathea (IRE))
5317^{5}

Tiz Herself (IRE) *Jonathan Portman* a56 59
3 gr f Dandy Man(IRE) Pitullie (USA) (Rockport Harbor (USA))
1091^{7} 1414^{11}

Tiz Now Tiz Then (USA) *S Seemar* a100
11 b g Tiznow(USA) Trepidation (USA) (Seeking The Gold (USA))
(183a) 284a^{5} 627a^{2}

Toad Corner *Mary Hambro* a59 11
4 b g Shirocco(GER) Didbrook (Alzao (USA))
62^{6}

Tobacco (ARG) *Doug Watson* a80
3 b g Roman Ruler(USA) Tacanuya (ARG) (Southern Halo (USA))
8a^{2}

To Be Wild (IRE) *Hugo Palmer* 106
3 br c Big Bad Bob(IRE) Fire Up (Motivator)
(4792) (7538) ◆

Tobias (USA) *Rafael A Fernandez* 98
7 bb g Arch(USA) Listen Well (USA) (Secretariat (USA))
5428a^{6}

Toboggan's Fire *Ann Duffield* a82 85
3 b f Firebreak Toboggan Lady (Tobougg (IRE))
(1381) 1446^{7} 3252^{3} 3895^{3} ◆ 4871^{3} (5609) 6277^{5} 6772^{2} 7360^{3} 7623^{7}

Toboggan's Gift *Ann Duffield* a55 52
4 b m Major Cadeaux Toboggan Lady (Tobougg (IRE))
150^{5} 368^{2} (577) 674^{3} 941^{2} 1399^{4} 4260^{4}

Tobouggaloo *Stuart Kittow* a57 74
5 ch m Tobougg(IRE) Let Alone (Warning)
3094^{3} 3845^{8} 4792^{5} ◆ 5597^{7} 6090^{9}

Tobrave (IRE) *Roger Varian* a73 17
2 b g Invincible Spirit(IRE) Qasirah (IRE) (Machiavellian (USA))
3524^{3} 6439^{11} 7648^{4}

Toccata Blue (IRE) *G M Lyons* a88 87
6 gr g Verglas(IRE) Jinxy Jill (Royal Applause)
7801a^{2}

Todd *Anabel K Murphy* a76 69
6 b g Gentlewave(IRE) Voice (Zamindar (USA))
43^{2} 234^{3} 545^{6} 838^{2} 1092^{7} 2995^{6}

To Dibba *Roger Varian* 74
2 gr c Dubawi(IRE) Rose Diamond (IRE) (Daylami (IRE))
7495^{5}

To Eternity *John Gosden* a77 104
3 b f Galileo(IRE) All's Forgotten (USA) (Darshaan)
3601^{2} ◆ 4367^{2} (5129) 5587^{2} ◆

Toe The Line (IRE) *John E Kiely* 106
7 b m Shantou(USA) Bluebell Line (IRE) (Charnwood Forest (IRE))
2275a^{2} 6495a^{5} 6820a^{3} (7393a)

Toffee Apple (IRE) *Keith Dalgleish* a50 61
3 b f Zoffany(IRE) Myrtle Beach (IRE) (Kenmare (FR))
40^{8} 509^{8} 1162^{10} 1548^{4} 1734^{12} 3710^{2} 3943^{2} ◆ (4144) (4233) 4449^{4} 4681^{6} 6004^{3} 6407^{12} 7097^{P} 7385^{7} 7754^{10}

Toga Tiger (IRE) *Kevin Frost* a84 81
9 b g Antonius Pius(USA) Minerwa (GER) (Protektor (GER))
332^{3} 595^{8} 2662^{5} 4568^{6} (4919) 5287^{4} 6517^{4} 8539^{2} ◆

Togetherness (IRE) *Harry Dunlop* 81
3 b g Pour Moi(IRE) Madeira Mist (IRE) (Grand Lodge (USA))
4857^{6} 5255^{2} 5742^{5} 6121^{4} 7060^{12}

Togetherwecan (IRE) *Mark Johnston* a58 61
4 b m Danehill Dancer(IRE) Crystal Bull (USA) (Holy Bull (USA))
59^{8} 500^{4} 859^{7} 1145^{3} 1263^{3} 1654^{9} 1948^{7} 2087^{6} 3020^{5} (3342) 3620^{3} 3901^{8} 4260^{10} 4635^{8} 5010^{4} 5228^{10} 5980^{5}

Togoville (IRE) *Georgios Pakidis* a105 91
6 gr g Verglas(IRE) Road Harbour (USA) (Rodrigo De Triano (USA))
4246a^{11} 7523a^{11} 7803a^{2}

To Have A Dream (IRE) *J S Moore* a37 35
2 b f Zoffany(IRE) Tessa Romana (IRE) (Holy Roman Emperor (IRE))
1087^{5} 1527^{6} 1813^{5}

Toinette (IRE) *H-A Pantall* a90 97
3 gr f Makfi Trip To Glory (FR) (Where Or When (IRE))
(1357a) 3916a^{4} 7397a^{12}

Toledo *Marjorie Fife* a71 57
3 b g Exceed And Excel(AUS) Alovera (IRE) (King's Best (USA))
152^{6} (419) 2200^{10} 2524^{10} 3326^{9} 4970^{6} 5760^{5} 6685^{19}

Toliman *A & G Botti* a102 102
3 b c Hat Trick(JPN) Tell It As It Is (USA) (Chester House (USA))
(972a) 3269^{19}

Tomahawk Kid *Ian Williams* 84
3 b c Major Cadeaux Say A Prayer (Indesatchel (IRE))
(3400) 4382^{3} 5201^{2} ◆ 5849^{2} (6877) 7671^{18}

Tombe Girl *Keith Dalgleish* a59 56
3 b f Royal Applause Tahfeez (IRE) (Alhaarth (IRE))
384^{5} ◆ 597^{3} 785^{4} 947^{4} 1045^{2} 1497^{9} 1667^{4}

Tom Dooley (IRE) *John James Feane* a62 58
5 b g Dylan Thomas(IRE) Shizao (IRE) (Alzao (USA))
547^{4}

Tomily (IRE) *Richard Hannon* a74 99
2 b c Canford Cliffs(IRE) Cake (IRE) (Acclamation)
1203^{2} ◆ 1422^{3} (1944) (2457) 3247^{15} 6763^{4} 7120^{3} 7536^{2}

Tom Melbourne (IRE) *Lee & Anthony Freedman* a79 105
5 b g Dylan Thomas(IRE) Roshanak (IRE) (Spinning World (USA))
7712a^{2} 7826a^{3}

Tommy Docc (IRE) *Keith Dalgleish* a90 98
4 b g Thewayyouare(USA) Liturgy (IRE) (Catcher In The Rye (IRE))
793^{5} 3387^{12} 3658^{13}

Tommy G *Jim Goldie* a63 76
3 ch g Makfi Primo Heights (Primo Valentino (IRE))
1217^{3} ◆ 1622^{3} 2333^{4} 3643^{3} 4334^{7} 6218^{6}

Tommys Geal *Michael Madgwick* a66 69
4 b m Halling(USA) Steel Free (IRE) (Danehill Dancer (IRE))
222^{4} (631) ◆ 777^{3} 977^{3} (1547) 2292^{3} 3230^{3} 4531^{5} 4784^{3} 5776^{2} 6485^{9} 7272^{11} 7870^{8} 8257^{5} 8462^{6}

Tommy's Secret *Jane Chapple-Hyam* a79 68
6 gr g Sakhee's Secret La Gessa (Largesse)
1173^{8} 1430^{6} 2010^{8} 3354^{6} 3823^{11} 5033^{5} 5677^{8} 6700^{5} 7310^{2} 8086^{5} 8458^{4}

Tommy Taylor (USA) *Kevin Ryan* 100
2 b c Mizzen Mast(USA) Sharp Apple (USA) (Diesis)
3854^{2} ◆ (4609) 5109^{2} 5556^{4} 6326^{6}

Tomorrowcomes (IRE) *Richard Fahey* 83
2 b f Oasis Dream Yesterday (IRE) (Sadler's Wells (USA))
4603^{9} 5266^{3} 5747^{2} (6713) 7075^{3}

Tomorrow Mystery *Jamie Osborne* a56
2 b f Nathaniel(IRE) Retake (Reset (AUS))
8465^{6}

Tomsamcharlie *Gary Moore* a60 54
2 b c Nathaniel(IRE) Windy Britain (Mark Of Esteem (IRE))
7187^{8} 7503^{11} 8063^{5}

Tom's Anna (IRE) *Sean Regan* a23 47
6 b m Antonius Pius(USA) Vanilla Delight (IRE) (Orpen (USA))
4772^{6} 5355^{9} 6106^{11} 6478^{9} 8307^{12}

Tom Sawyer *Julie Camacho* a65 81
8 b g Dansili Cayman Sunset (IRE) (Night Shift (USA))
1321^{11} 1601^{9} 2572^{6} 2975^{9} 3882^{5} 4770^{5} 5369^{2} 5968^{6} 6522^{9}

Tom's Ready (USA) *Dallas Stewart* a110
3 bb c More Than Ready(USA) Goodbye Stranger (USA) (Broad Brush (USA))
2063a^{12} 7808a^{5}

Tom's Rock (IRE) *John Butler* a68 79
3 gr g Rock Of Gibraltar(IRE) Asheyana (IRE) (Soviet Star (USA))
2414^{14} 2780^{3} ◆ 3411^{6} 4530^{5} (6194) 7227^{3}

Tomyris *Roger Varian* a70
2 b f Invincible Spirit(IRE) Totally Devoted (USA) (Seeking The Gold (USA))
7763^{4}

Tonahutu (IRE) *Ed Vaughan* a71 63
2 b f Sir Prancealot(IRE) Really Polish (USA) (Polish Numbers (USA))
4759^{4} 5549^{2} (6044) 6787^{9} 8008^{2}

Toni's A Star *Tony Carroll* a67 69
4 b m Avonbridge Canina (Foxhound (USA))
1648^{8} 2380^{9} 2785^{3} ◆ 3397^{3} 3851^{3} 4952^{4} (6311) 6831^{6} 7774^{10}

Tonkinese *M Halford* a94 96
3 b g Authorized(IRE) Honky Tonk Sally (Dansili)
3428a^{6}

Tonto's Spirit *Kenneth Slack* 52
4 b g Authorized(IRE) Desert Royalty (IRE) (Alhaarth (IRE))
(3154) 3706^{10} 5227^{9}

Tony Curtis *Richard Hannon* a92 106
3 b c Rock Of Gibraltar(IRE) Strawberry Lolly (Lomitas)
756a^{4} 1440^{4} 4822^{5} ◆ 5329^{4} 5893^{4} 7101^{4}

Tony's Power *A Marcialis* a58 67
9 b g Mujahid(USA) Cuba Lady (IRE) (Bluebird (USA))
6938a^{5}

Tony The Gent (IRE) *G M Lyons* 97
3 b g Kodiac Becuille (IRE) (Redback)
6355a^{14}

Toocoolforschool (IRE) *K R Burke* a47 97
4 b g Showcasing Spring Surprise (Hector Protector (USA))
1491^{4} 3566^{14}

Toofi (FR) *Robert Cowell* 109
5 b g Henrythenavigator(USA) Silver Bark (Royal Applause)
2188^{11} 3386^{8} 4865^{23} 5418^{14} 6112^{18} 7497^{16}

Toola Boola *Jedd O'Keeffe* a57 68
6 b m Tobougg(IRE) Forsythia (Most Welcome)
3845^{5} 4682^{6} 5842^{3} 6219^{8} 7332^{7} 7656^{14}

Too Many Diamonds (IRE) *Clare Ellam* a54 44
5 br g Diamond Green(FR) Too Much Color (USA) (Spectrum (IRE))
5457a^{2} 6406^{12} 7262^{11}

Too Many Shots *John Best* a56 68
2 b g Mullionmileanhour(IRE) Neissa (USA) (Three Wonders (USA))
3799^{7} 5166^{2} 6297^{7} 7228^{6} 7640^{6} 7954^{5}

Toormore (IRE) *Richard Hannon* 120
5 b h Arakan(USA) Danetime Out (IRE) (Danetime (IRE))
(1606) 2243^{5} 3242^{4} 4127^{8} 4754^{4} 5873^{4} 6328^{7}

Topaling *Mark H Tompkins* a70 55
5 ch m Halling(USA) Topatori (IRE) (Topanoora)
43^{5} 234^{6} 425^{9} 698^{6} 882^{7} (1136) 1766^{3} 2971^{11} 3221^{6} 8076^{6} 8162^{5} 8254^{3} 8488^{5}

Topalova *Mark H Tompkins* a58 54
3 ch f Champs Elysees Topatori (IRE) (Topanoora)
654^{5} 880^{5} 1235^{7} 1705^{U} 2123^{5} 2563^{7} 5630^{10} 7231^{5} 7592^{4}

Topamichi *Mark H Tompkins* a80 73
6 b g Beat Hollow Topatori (IRE) (Topanoora)
212^{9} 3802^{5} 4050^{3} 6701^{6} 7531^{8}

Top Beak (IRE) *Hughie Morrison* 96
3 b g Lawman(FR) Tree Tops (Grand Lodge (USA))
1567^{7} 2190^{12} 4797^{15} 5514^{2} 5933^{2} 6736^{2} 7287^{4}

Top Boy *Derek Shaw* a91 89
6 b g Exceed And Excel(AUS) Injaaz (Sheikh Albadou)
1084^{4} 1321^{4} 1601^{5} (1964) 2253^{7} 2787^{4} 4066^{3} 4345^{4} 5189^{4} (5679) 6234^{5} 6633^{3} 6944^{13} 7202^{2} 7752^{8} ◆ 8232^{5} 8484^{5}

Topclas (FR) *A bin Harmash* a86 92
10 b g Kutub(IRE) Noble Presence (FR) (Fasliyev (USA))
453a^{6}

Top Clearance (USA) *D Selvaratnam* a101
4 b g Majestic Warrior(USA) Sweet Beat (USA) (Tiznow (USA))
92a^{8} (284a) 627a^{5} 842a^{6}

Top Cop *Ronald Harris* a61 62
7 b g Acclamation Speed Cop (Cadeaux Genereux)
197^{3} 543^{7} 942^{6} 1138^{7} 1319^{6} 2458^{8} 2845^{7} 3993^{12} 4290^{9} 6853^{6} 6865^{7} 7302^{7}

Top Diktat *Gary Moore* a80 82
8 b g Diktat Top Romance (IRE) (Entrepreneur)
165^{7} 605^{3} 1390^{4} 1716^{5} 2623^{5} 4459^{7} 6889^{5} 7429^{5} 7973^{11}

Top Face (USA) *M Al Ramzani* a86 89
3 bb c Tiznow(USA) Toppisme (USA) (Saint Ballado (CAN))
8573a^{8}

Top Hatter *Jamie Osborne* 59
2 ch f Helmet(AUS) Miss Marvellous (USA) (Diesis)
2536^{4} 2874^{6}

Topmeup *Stuart Edmunds* a53 51
2 ch f Mayson Ambrix (IRE) (Xaar)
4457^{6} 4759^{8} 5242^{9} 6412^{7} 7244^{8} 7482^{6} 7734^{3}

Top Mission *Saeed bin Suroor* 76
2 b c Dubawi(IRE) Ever Love (BRZ) (Nedawi)
7665^{2}

Top Notch Tonto (IRE) *Brian Ellison* 116
6 ch g Thousand Words Elite Hope (USA) (Moment Of Hope (USA))
1604^{6} 1973^{6} 3164^{10} 4165^{14} 4747a^{2}

Top Offer *Patrick Morris* a74 63
7 b g Dansili Zante (Zafonic (USA))
144^{7} 387^{3} (502) 680^{2} 856^{4} 1555^{5} 1845^{5} 2096^{3} ◆ 2542^{2} 2906^{6} 3366^{9} 3729^{3} 3989^{2} 5114^{8}

Top Of The Bank *Kristin Stubbs* a65 73
3 b g Piccolo America Lontana (FR) (King's Theatre (IRE))
(1673) 4547^{7} 5657^{15} 6476^{7} 8010^{8} 8205^{9} 8482^{6} 8555^{11}

Top Of The Glas (IRE) *Brian Ellison* a85 92
5 gr g Verglas(IRE) Fury Dance (USA) (Cryptoclearance (USA))
1122^{4} 1221^{5} 1978^{7} 2328^{4} 3520^{4} 3659^{2} (4680) 5837^{11}

Top Of The Rocks (FR) *Tom Dascombe* a24 60
3 b g Rock Of Gibraltar(IRE) Runaway Top (Rainbow Quest (USA))
1276^{10} 1484^{11} 4255^{7} 4847^{4} (5319) 5830^{3} 6730^{5} 7309^{8}

Topology *Joseph Tuite* a79 78
3 br g Passing Glance Bold Byzantium (Bold Arrangement)
1894^{4} 3689^{3} 4481^{5} 7204^{2} 7506^{3} 7813^{9}

Topolski (IRE) *David Arbuthnot* a44 48
10 b g Peintre Celebre(USA) Witching Hour (IRE) (Alzao (USA))
7739^{13} 8164^{6}

Top Pocket *Michael Madgwick* a58 49
4 b g Royal Applause Movie Mogul (Sakhee (USA))
252^{13} 347^{5} 514^{2} 870^{3} 1578^{3} 3031^{4} 4773^{4} 4992^{7} 6891^{3} 7464^{2} (Dead)

Top Score *Saeed bin Suroor* 99
2 b c Hard Spun(USA) Windsor County (USA) (Elusive Quality (USA))
1889^{3} (2264) 3247^{9} 4825^{3} 6180a^{2} 7042^{3} 7469^{2}

Top Sensation (FR) *T Castanheira* a70 90
3 gr f Kouroun(FR) Top Wave (FR) (Medaaly)
1240a^{8} 2172a^{3} 5349a^{11}

Top Set (IRE) *Richard Phillips* a50 47
6 ch g Tamayuz Pray (IRE) (Priolo (USA))
5261^{6} 5777^{4} 6422^{3} 7262^{3} 8180^{2} 8497^{3}

Topsoil *Ronald Harris* a53 53
3 b g Kheleyf(USA) Edge Of Gold (Choisir (AUS))
2459^{8} 4820^{3} ◆ (5007) 5570 ^{6} 6363^{15} 6852^{7} 7863^{6} 8278^{5} 8383^{4}

Toptempo *Ralph J Smith* a74 55
7 ch m Halling(USA) Topatoo (Bahamian Bounty)
27^{5} 461^{9}

Top Tug (IRE) *Alan King* a103 105
5 ch g Halling(USA) Top Romance (IRE) (Entrepreneur)
(1336) 2222^{3} 3340^{7} 4115^{3} 5655^{12}

Tor *Keith Dalgleish* a53 79
2 b g Orientor Dance In The Sun (Halling (USA))
6833^{4} (7247) 7956^{8}

Torcedor (IRE) *David Wachman* a92 102
4 b g Fastnet Rock(AUS) Magnolia Lane (IRE) (Sadler's Wells (USA))
2025^{5} 4850a^{7}

Torch *John Butler* a80 84
3 b g Paco Boy(IRE) Singed (Zamindar (USA))
1859^{3} 2248^{2} 2557^{2} 3355^{4} 4055^{3} (4806) 5306^{3} 6628^{7} 7418^{6} 8251^{11} 8455^{7}

Toretto (IRE) *Jan Coomer* a57 47
8 ch g Peintre Celebre(USA) Petite-D-Argent (Noalto)
695^{6} 946^{12} 1450^{13} 2080a^{3}

Toriano *James Eustace* a86 80
3 ch g Equiano(FR) Ticki Tori (IRE) (Vettori (IRE))
(1256) (2322) ◆ 5199^{5}

Torment *Richard Hannon* a74 79
3 rg g Dark Angel(IRE) Selkirk Sky (Selkirk (USA))
7903^{8} 8356^{5} 8590^{4}

Tornibush (IRE) *P Decouz* 92
2 b c Dream Ahead(USA) Celenza (FR) (Dansili)
3871a^{7} 5186a^{5}

Torqit (IRE) *John Ryan* a39
2 b g Myboycharlie(IRE) Traou Mad (IRE) (Barathea (IRE))
7307^{8}

Torquay *Harry Dunlop* a71 75
3 b f Aqlaam Torcross (Vettori (IRE))
2000^{3} ◆ 4056^{4} 4265^{5} 4636^{2} ◆ 5164^{2} 5550^{3} 6031^{2} 6886^{9}

Torremar (FR) *Kevin Ryan* a68 76
3 br g Excellent Art Sabela (IRE) (Sinndar (IRE))
1630^{6} 2522^{2} 3365^{3} 3853^{3} 4342^{4} 5365^{5} 6737^{3} 7008^{5} (7582) 7846^{7}

Torreon (IRE) *John Ryan* a91 76
5 b g High Chaparral(IRE) Teide Lady (Nashwan (USA))
423^{4} ◆ 639^{2} (858) 1041^{2} ◆ 1143^{2} 1929^{6}

Torrid *Michael Easterby* a71 83
5 ch g Three Valleys(USA) Western Appeal (USA) (Gone West (USA))
1122^{11} 1526^{3} ◆ 2256^{8} 3166^{8} 3517^{6} 5246^{4} 6644^{5} ◆ 7010^{8} 7623^{2}

Tortueuse (IRE) *David Peter Dunne* a39 32
9 b m Indian Danehill(IRE) Taffety (Last Tycoon)
8211^{11}

Toscanini (IRE) *M Halford* a96 114
4 b g Shamardal(USA) Tuzla (FR) (Panoramic)
626a^{5} ◆ 841a^{10} (3681a) 4433a^{3} (5213a) 6384a^{12}

Tosen Basil (JPN) *Hideaki Fujiwara* 111
4 bb h Harbinger Careless Whisper (JPN) (Fuji Kiseki (JPN))
8129a^{11}

Tostaky Blue (FR) *A Spanu* a67 63
7 b g Anabaa Blue Jane Eria (IRE) (King's Best (USA))
715a^{4} 1034a^{9} 7295a^{10}

Total Demolition (IRE) *J Larkin* a54 82
4 ch g Thewayyouare(USA) Margaux Dancer (IRE) (Danehill Dancer (IRE))
(4811a)

Totalize *Brian Ellison* a96 103
7 b g Authorized(IRE) You Too (Monsun (GER))
1081^{9} 1967^{7} 3246^{6}

Totally Committed *Clive Cox* 78
3 b g Invincible Spirit(IRE) Zanzibar (IRE) (In The Wings)
3816^{7} (5288) 6365^{3} 6484^{5} 7246^{4}

Totally Magic (IRE) *Richard Whitaker* a71 65
4 b m Captain Rio Hypocrisy (Bertolini (USA))
1565[10] 2655[3] 3479[3] 4006[3] 4449[5] *5247[6]* 5887[16] *(6742)* 7007[8] *(7326)* *7601[2]*

Total Obsession *Mark Hoad* a45 30
9 b m Mujahid(USA) Buon Amici (Pivotal)
2397[9] 2588[4] *2899[13]*

Total Power *Brian Ellison* 70
3 b g Sleeping Indian House Of Frills (Paris House)
1271[4] 1487[4] 1847[5] 2545[14] *3568[9]*

Total Star *Luca Cumani* a91 89
2 gr c Pivotal Millennium Star (IRE) (High Chaparral (IRE))
4545[2] (5290) 5646[9] *(6868)*

Totzo (IRE) *Paul D'Arcy* a46 56
3 b f Lilbourne Lad(IRE) Later (IRE) (Marju (IRE))
345[7]

Touchdown Banwell (USA) *Andrew Balding* a69 60
3 br g Fairbanks(USA) Friendly Thunder (USA) (Friends Lake (USA))
1294[4] 2548[6] *3281[3]* 4342[6] 6365[10]

Touched By Love (USA) *Ismail Mohammed* a60 45
3 b c Street Sense(USA) Love Of Dubai (USA) (More Than Ready (USA))
8366[6]

Touching The Sky (IRE) *Alex Fracas* a82 75
2 b f Rip Van Winkle(IRE) Kyniska (IRE) (Choisir (AUS))
(7294a) 7490a[6] *7971a[2]*

Touch Me (IRE) *K R Burke* a63
2 b f Masterofthehorse(IRE) User Name (USA) (Mr Greeley (USA))
8130[8] 8397[6] (8591)

Touch Of Color *Jane Chapple-Hyam* a51 62
3 b f Sixties Icon Shesells Seashells (Tiger Hill (IRE))
1638[10] 2701[6] 3906[8] 5515[6] 6187[2] 6826[6] 7298[6] *7642[3]*

Touch Of Genius (IRE) *Josef Vana* 97
4 b h Galileo(IRE) Festoso (IRE) (Diesis)
2728a[4]

Touch Of Real (FR) *M Boutin* a66 76
3 b f Soldier Hollow Topkapi Diamond (IRE) (Acclamation)
6912a[8]

Touch The Clouds *William Stone* a50 54
5 b g Sleeping Indian Aptina (USA) (Aptitude (USA))
4264[11] *6374[7] 6865[9]* 7445[7] *7646[7]*

Touch The Sky *David Elsworth* 93
5 br g Sea The Stars(IRE) Love Divine (Diesis)
1826[3] 2174[6] (2663) (3161) 3533[3] 4535[4] 5358[4] 6163[11]

Toughest 'Ombre (USA) *Thomas Albertrani* 98
3 b c Tale Of The Cat(USA) True Sensation (USA) (Itaka (USA))
4173a[12]

Tough To Bear *Ollie Pears* 57
2 b g Hellvelyn Mix It Up (Linamix (FR))
1921[5] 2675[6] 3008[5] 4000[6]

Toulifaut (IRE) *J-C Rouget* a85 104
2 b f Frankel Cassydora (Darshaan)
(5447a) (6271a) 6986a[8]

Toulson *Eve Johnson Houghton* a80 85
3 b g Champs Elysees Flower Market (Cadeaux Genereux)
3769[2] 4347[3] *5023[3]* (6484) 7077[4]

Toumar *Roger Varian* a75
3 ch f Sea The Stars(IRE) Tingling (USA) (Storm Cat (USA))
(384) 887[3]

Toungi (IRE) *F Rossi* a93 105
4 ch m Rock Of Gibraltar(IRE) Tounsi (FR) (Sendawar (IRE))
660a[5]

Tourist (USA) *William Mott* 120
5 bb h Tiznow(USA) Unbridled Melody (USA) (Unbridled's Song (USA))
7172a[3] (7837a)

Tournament *Seamus Durack* a86 94
5 b g Oasis Dream Concentric (Sadler's Wells (USA))
1122[15] *2579[6]* 4368[3] *(5024) 6084[7] 6628[10]*

Tourtiere *Andrew Crook* 73
8 b g Act One Kindle (Selkirk (USA))
1674[3] (2656) 3294[3] 4237[5]

Towerlands Park (IRE) *Michael Bell* a97 78
3 b c Danehill Dancer(IRE) Strategy (Machiavellian (USA))
(8249) ◆

Tower Of Texas (CAN) *Roger L Attfield* a97 117
5 b g Street Sense(USA) Rare Opportunity (USA) (Danzig Connection (USA))
6601a[2] 7172a[10]

Tower Power *Phil McEntee* a83 84
5 b g Nayef(USA) Voile (IRE) (Barathea (IRE))
88[2] (200) 399[5]

Town Charter (USA) *Mark Johnston* 87
2 gr c Lonhro(AUS) Summer Fete (IRE) (Pivotal)
3516[2] ◆ (3939) ◆ 5058[2]

Town Ranger (IRE) *Peter Casey* 9
4 b m Bushranger(IRE) Tubbertown Rose (IRE) (Elbio)
1014a[15]

Town's History (USA) *Saeed bin Suroor* a86 89
3 ch g Hard Spun(USA) Smooth Charmer (USA) (Easy Goer (USA))
15[2] (496) 2654[5] 3079[2] 3853[2] ◆ (4406)

Townsville *Keith Dalgleish* a87 49
4 b g Zamindar(USA) Rule Of Nature (Oasis Dream)
50[3] ◆ 1694[7] 2531[11] 5224[7] *7737[10]*

Toxaris (IRE) *Mlle M Henry* a68 72
4 ch m Teofilo(IRE) Right Key (IRE) (Key Of Luck (USA))
1266[6] 2292[8] 5216a[10]

Toymaker *Phil McEntee* a70 65
9 b g Starcraft(NZ) Eurolink Raindance (IRE) (Alzao (USA))
39[9] 467[2] 532[5] 769[4] 986[2] (1131) 1323[2] 1654[12] 1805[3]

Toy Theatre *Mark Johnston* a57 54
2 b f Lonhro(AUS) Puppet Queen (USA) (Kingmambo (USA))
1889[6] 2990[8] *7049[9]* 7571[9]

Tractive Effort *Michael Attwater* a48 37
3 b g Rail Link Anastasia Venture (Lion Cavern (USA))
2815[9] 3535[11] *7904[8] 8428[7] 8468[7]*

Trading Point (FR) *John Quinn* 80
2 b c Siyouni(FR) Zita Blues (IRE) (Zieten (USA))
6535[2] ◆ (7317)

Trading Punches (IRE) *David Brown* 81
2 b g Elzaam(AUS) Kiralik (Efisio)
4856[9] 5196[4] 5484[5] (6439) 6800[9]

Traditional Dancer (IRE) *Iain Jardine* 41
4 b g Danehill Dancer(IRE) Cote Quest (USA) (Green Desert (USA))
5581[4]

Trail Blaze (IRE) *Kevin Ryan* 85
7 b g Tagula(IRE) Kingpin Delight (Emarati (USA))
1625[7] 1924[11] 2677[9] 3327[7]

Trainnah *William Haggas* 91
3 b f Pivotal Whazzat (Daylami (IRE))
2009[2] 3194[3] (3981) (5054) 6115[7]

Tranquil Daze (IRE) *David Brown* a57 61
2 ch g Sir Prancealot(IRE) Endless Peace (IRE) (Russian Revival (USA))
4601[6] 5484[4] 6034[11] *8071[4]*

Tranquil Time *James Tate* a69 43
3 b f Poet's Voice Peaceful Soul (USA) (Dynaformer (USA))
4361[8] *5527[5] 6242[6] 6856[6]*

Tranquil Tracy *John Norton* a10 51
2 b f Stimulation(IRE) Tranquil Flight (Oasis Dream)
1868[4] 2265[7] 2771[10] 7579[7] *8344[10]*

Transfer Allowance (AUS) *Peter Roche* 100
6 bb g Danzero(AUS) Banishing (AUS) (Red Ransom (USA))
7712a[8] 7948a[6]

Transmitting *Sir Michael Stoute* a71 70
3 b g Cacique(IRE) Shuttle Mission (Sadler's Wells (USA))
5486[4] ◆ 6294[7] 6520[2] 7214[4] *7531[3]*

Transpennine Star *Michael Dods* 80
3 ch g Mount Nelson Brave Mave (Daylami (IRE))
1873[3] 4033[3] 4447[3] (6219) (6438) 7624[8]

Trautmann (IRE) *Daniel Mark Loughnane* a35
2 ch g Casamento(IRE) Klang (IRE) (Night Shift (USA))
8404[9]

Traveller (FR) *Charles Hills* a60
2 b c Henrythenavigator(USA) Nantes (GER) (Night Shift (USA))
7883[5]

Traveltalk (IRE) *Brian Ellison* 67
2 b g Fast Company(IRE) Laheen (IRE) (Bluebird (USA))
2344[6] 2675[4] 3515[4] 5271[7] 5796[5] 6681[7] (7041)

Travertine (IRE) *Niall Madden* a90 107
6 b g Danehill Dancer(IRE) Mer De Corail (IRE) (Sadler's Wells (USA))
4850a[9] 6350a[10] 7708a[23]

Tread Lightly *Tim Easterby* 54
2 b g Canford Cliffs(IRE) Step Lightly (IRE) (Danehill Dancer (IRE))
3598[5]

Treagus *Charlie Fellowes* a51 52
2 b c Mayson Danceatdusk (Desert Prince (IRE))
7468[11] *7812[10] 7883[9]*

Treasure The Ridge (IRE) *Andrew Reid* a88 91
7 b g Galileo(IRE) Treasure The Lady (IRE) (Indian Ridge)
440[7]

Treasury Notes (IRE) *David O'Meara* a72 106
4 b g Lope De Vega(IRE) Elegant As Well (IRE) (Sadler's Wells (USA))
1122[2] ◆ 1221[6] (1643) 2527[4] (2833) 3390[5] (5156) (5976) 6786[13]

Treaty Of Rome (USA) *Derek Shaw* a66 54
4 bb g War Front(USA) Blading Gold Ring (USA) (During (USA))
8570[4]

Tred Softly (IRE) *John Quinn* a57 55
3 b g Yeats(IRE) Elayoon (USA) (Danzig (USA))
863[4] ◆ *945[9]* 2124[11] 2772[5] *8386[3] 8567[3]*

Tree Of Grace (FR) *Andrew Hollinshead* a59 69
5 ch g Gold Away(IRE) Three Times (SWE) (Domynsky)
1034a[8]

Tree Of Knowledge (IRE) *A P O'Brien* 110
3 b g Oasis Dream Wonder Of Wonders (USA) (Kingmambo (USA))
6351a[4]

Tremendous (IRE) *Richard Hannon* a56
2 b f Kodiac Clockwise (Pivotal)
6414[5]

Trenches (USA) *Charlie Appleby* a81 83
3 b g War Front(USA) Sangrita (USA) (Mr Greeley (USA))
3609[2] (4401) 4886[7]

Trending (IRE) *Jeremy Gask* a73 66
7 gr g Dark Angel(IRE) Call Later (USA) (Gone West (USA))
97[2] (316) (461) 640[5] 832[3] 5823[7] *7429[7] 7905[7] 8211[10]*

Trendsetter (IRE) *Micky Hammond* a88 91
5 b g Mastercraftsman(IRE) Fashion Trade (Dansili)
1999[3] 2685[9] 3129[4] (5541) 6561[6] (7357) 7538[4] 7824[9] *8317[10]*

Trento (FR) *L A Urbano-Grajales* a83 74
3 ch c Zoffany(IRE) Going For Gold (ITY) (Gold Away (IRE))
5280a[7]

Tres Coronas (IRE) *David Barron* a66 104
9 b g Key Of Luck(USA) Almansa (IRE) (Dr Devious (IRE))
5976[14] 6261[10] 6559[12] 7077[10] 7408[6] 7744[8]

Tresor (IRE) *F Head* 73
2 b c Henrythenavigator(USA) Sapphire Pendant (IRE) (Danehill Dancer (IRE))
5348a[6]

Tresorier *Mme C Head-Maarek* 96
2 b c Dunkerque(FR) Treasure (FR) (Anabaa (USA))
7721a[4]

Trespassed (IRE) *Gordon Elliott* a67 68
3 b g Thewayyouare(USA) Trespass (Entrepreneur)
70[3] 85[3] 7653[10]

Tres Rock Glory (IRE) *F Head* 97
3 b f Fastnet Rock(AUS) Tres Ravi (GER) (Monsun (GER))
2944a[4]

Trevisani (IRE) *David Lanigan* a91 86
4 b g Dubawi(IRE) Geminiani (IRE) (King Of Kings (IRE))
3263[4] *4013[4]* (5061) *(5767)* 7670[8]

Triassic (IRE) *Mark Johnston* a56 50
3 b g Vale Of York(IRE) Livadiya (IRE) (Shernazar)
3711[9] 4258[7] 4872[9] 5921[6] *6508[3] 6698[9] 7104[7] 7532[5]*

Triathlon (USA) *Sir Michael Stoute* 74
3 bb f Hat Trick(JPN) Relaxed (USA) (Royal Academy (USA))
2505[5] 3810[5]

Tribal Beat (IRE) *J S Bolger* 114
3 b c Street Cry(IRE) Tashelka (FR) (Mujahid (USA))
(5343a) 6353a[7]

Tribal Dance (IRE) *John O'Shea*
10 br g Flemensfirth(USA) Native Sparkle (IRE) (Be My Native (USA))
6765[7]

Tribalism (USA) *A Al Shamsi* a82 38
3 gr g Tapit(USA) Well Related (USA) (Quiet American (USA))
8576a[13]

Tribal Path (IRE) *Damian Joseph English* a83 92
6 b g Giant's Causeway(USA) Navajo Moon (IRE) (Danehill (USA))
4921a[3] 6382a[5] 6984a[7] 7191a[13]

Tribesman *Marjorie Fife* a74 63
3 ch g Equiano(FR) Millsini (Rossini (USA))
1448[10] 1922[11] 2418[4] 2854[4] 3265[5] 3755[3] 4192[2] 4612[10] 4770[2] 5277[6] 5483[4] 6023[10] *7323[7] 7961[5] 8242[3] 8312[9] 8572[2]*

Tribute Act *James Fanshawe* a72
2 b f Exceed And Excel(AUS) Sister Act (Marju (IRE))
(7278)

Trick Of The Light (IRE) *Roger Varian* 75
2 ch g Dragon Pulse(IRE) Galistic (IRE) (Galileo (IRE))
6542[5] ◆ (6873) 7217[5]

Trick Of The Lyte (IRE) *John Quinn* a51 67
2 b c Kodiac Alpine River (IRE) (Redback)
2852[6] *3654[6]* 3874[4] 4679[3] 4915[4] (5352) 5833[2] 6614[6]

Tricky Dicky *Olly Williams* 69
3 b g Holy Roman Emperor(IRE) Tricky Situation (Mark Of Esteem (IRE))
(1126) 1670[4] 2553[7] 3579[3] 4003[4] (4512) 4970[2] (5152) 5960[2] 6451[4] (7585)

Tricky Issue (IRE) *Seamus Mullins* a19 57
4 b m Manduro(GER) Tricky Situation (Mark Of Esteem (IRE))
1048[9]

Trident Tested *John Best* a40 63
3 gr g Arabian Gleam Neptune's Girl (IRE) (Verglas (IRE))
1163[8] 2589[5] (2825) 3493[6] 4273[4] 4636[6]

Trigger Flash (FR) *F Cheyer* a55 57
5 b m Librettist(USA) Trigger Shot (IRE) (High Chaparral (IRE))
5216a[3]

Trigger Park (IRE) *Ronald Harris* a56 56
5 ch g Tagula(IRE) Raazi (My Generation)
107[5] 252[10] 388[6] 867[8]

Trikingdom *Alan Swinbank* a8 65
3 b g Showcasing Spritzeria (Bigstone (IRE))
1667[7] 2533[8]

Trilliant (IRE) *David Lanigan* 62
2 b f Dansili Priceless Jewel (Selkirk (USA))
7548[7]

Trimoulet *Daniel Kubler* a89 84
7 b g Teofilo(IRE) Riberac (Efisio)
1933[5]

Trinity House (IRE) *Michael Smith*
4 b g Shamardal(USA) Love Style (USA) (Mr Prospector (USA))
2858[F]

Trinity Star (IRE) *Michael Dods* 87
5 gr g Kheleyf(USA) Zamiyla (IRE) (Daylami (IRE))
1521[3] 2257[4] 3166[10] 3717[2] 4374[6] 5482[8] ◆ 6055[4] 7623[15]

Tripartite (IRE) *Jeremy Gask* a70 78
3 b g Zebedee Baltic Belle (IRE) (Redback)
(2864) 3554[2] 4563[2] *6416[7]* 7506[11]

Triple Dream *Milton Bradley* a72 50
11 ch g Vision Of Night Triple Joy (Most Welcome)
68[9] 1496[3] (2380) (2765) 4292[8] 5270[9] *5736[7]* 6311[5] 6894[4] *8181[9] 8365[6] 8595[3]*

Triple Eight (IRE) *Philip Kirby* a67 68
8 b g Royal Applause Hidden Charm (IRE) (Big Shuffle (USA))
1253[9] 1561[4] 1955[3] 2659[3] 2962[4] 4934[6] 5522[8] 6219[3] 6438[11] 7044[5] 7746[2]

Triple Nine (KOR) *Kim Young Kwan* a82
4 ch h Ecton Park(USA) A Little Poke (USA) (Pleasant Tap (USA))
6399a[3]

Triple Threat (FR) *William Mott* 107
6 b h Monsun(GER) Drei (USA) (Lyphard (USA))
7172a[11]

Trip To Paris (IRE) *Ed Dunlop* a95 116
5 b g Champs Elysees La Grande Zoa (IRE) (Fantastic Light (USA))
4392[3] 5612[4] 6387a[3]

Trip To Rhodos (FR) *Pavel Tuma* 111
7 b g Rail Link Tropical Mark (Mark Of Esteem (IRE))
1688a[3] 5692a[3] 6974a[4]

Trishuli Rock (IRE) *Marco Botti* a75
3 b f Fastnet Rock(AUS) Trishuli (Indian Ridge)
5504[2] ◆ *5735[2] 7607[2] 8075[3] 8195[4]*

Tristram's Sun (NZ) *Robbie Laing* 93
7 b g Yamanin Vital(NZ) Second Edition (AUS) (Desert Sun)
7948a[8]

Triticum Vulgare (IRE) *F Saggiomo* 79
2 br c Frozen Power(IRE) Tatamagouche (IRE) (Sadler's Wells (USA))
3701a[4]

Trixia (FR) *A De Royer-Dupre* 109
3 b f Siyouni(FR) Tianshan (FR) (Lahint (USA))
1581a[4] (5498a) ◆ 6394a[5] 6991a[10]

Trodero *Dr Jon Scargill* a69 54
3 b f Mastercraftsman(IRE) Jules (IRE) (Danehill (USA))
(350) 519[5] 817[4] 1804[8] 4743[5]

Trois Bon Amis (IRE) *Tim Easterby* 64
2 b g Lilbourne Lad(IRE) Vanozza (FR) (Dylan Thomas (IRE))
1520[5] 2739[3] 3223[4] 3852[6]

Trois Points (FR) *Gay Kelleway* a51 62
4 b g Motivator Trading (FR) (Anabaa (USA))
8422a[5]

Trojan Nation (USA) *Patrick Gallagher* a108 97
3 b c Street Cry(IRE) Storm Song (USA) (Summer Squall (USA))
2063a[16] 3181a[10]

Trojan Rocket (IRE) *Michael Wigham* a102 76
8 b g Elusive City(USA) Tagula Bay (IRE) (Tagula (IRE))
86[6] 290[12] (694) 960[2] 1153[10]

Trooper's Gold *Kevin Ryan* a79 79
2 ch c Sepoy(AUS) Samira Gold (FR) (Gold Away (IRE))
4545[8] 4856[2] ◆ 6129[3] *6741[2]* ◆ *(7328)*

Troopingthecolour *Steve Gollings* a89 82
10 b g Nayef(USA) Hyperspectra (Rainbow Quest (USA))
66[8]

Trophee (FR) *Christophe Clement* a92 102
5 bb m Mr. Sidney(USA) Trevise (FR) (Anabaa (USA))
3119a[4]

Tropical Rock *Ralph Beckett* 85
2 b f Fastnet Rock(AUS) Tropical Treat (Bahamian Bounty)
1988[3] 4064[2] (4457) (6525)

Trotter *Stuart Kittow* 41
2 b g Piccolo Vintage Steps (IRE) (Bahamian Bounty)
4083[5]

Troublemaker (ITY) *Stefano Botti* 96
3 b c Vita Rosa(JPN) Mooney Ridge (IRE) (Indian Ridge)
7555a[2]

Trouble Of Course (FR) *Niels Petersen*
2 gr c Rajsaman(FR) Sister Trouble (FR) (Spectrum (IRE))
8564a[2]

Troy Boy *Rebecca Bastiman* a50 52
6 b g Choisir(AUS) Love Thing (Phountzi (USA))
1697[10] 2089[7] 2853[5] 3041[2] 3620[9] 4724[8] 5155[9] 6620[5] 7231[9] 7300[3]

True Companion (IRE) *Adrian Brendan Joyce* a66 71
3 b g Fast Company(IRE) Panglossian (IRE) (Barathea (IRE))
4899a[12]

True Romance (IRE) *James Given* 69
2 gr c Mastercraftsman(IRE) Full Of Love (IRE) (Hawk Wing (USA))
6952[6] 7318[7] 7580[7]

True Solitaire (IRE) *D K Weld* 108
3 b c Oasis Dream Majestic Silver (IRE) (Linamix (FR))
2517a[9]

Truffles (IRE) *Ms Sheila Lavery* a43 83
3 b f Canford Cliffs(IRE) Parlour (Dansili)
7706a[9]

Trulee Scrumptious *Peter Charalambous* a61 74
7 b m Strategic Prince Morning Rise (GER) (Acatenango (GER))
3132[5] 3894[5] 4356[2] (4596) 5037[5] 5122[4] 5375[2] 5671[6] 6876[10]

Trulove *John David Riches* a23 20
3 b f Piccolo Snow Dancer (IRE) (Desert Style (IRE))
102[8] 785[9] 2308[15] 2657[6] 5803[9]

Truly *Colin Teague* a63 67
5 b m Archipenko(USA) Sincerely (Singspiel (IRE))
2048[11] 2307[4] 3012[7] *5068[6]* 5223[10]

Trump Card (IRE) *Conor O'Dwyer* a47 48
3 b g Lilbourne Lad(IRE) Breach Of Peace (USA) (Royal Academy (USA))
5803[6] *8194[9]*

Trump's Magic (USA) *David Evans* 65
2 br c Lonhro(AUS) Bright Magic (USA) (Prized (USA))
6016[2] ◆ 7216[9]

Trust Me Boy *John E Long* a69 43
8 gr g Avonbridge Eastern Lyric (Petong)
(430) 893[6] 1544[11] 3624[6] 7212[4] 7442[5] *8351[9] 8555[13]*

Trust The Indian *Bill Turner* a46 45
2 ch c Sleeping Indian Trust Fund Babe (IRE) (Captain Rio)
1813[2] 2933[6] 3232[5] 4015[5] *4526[4]*

Trust The Man (IRE) *Simon Dow* a54 63
3 br c Manduro(GER) Saree (Barathea (IRE))
1265[4] 3652[10] 7464[8] 7767[5] 8180[6] 8445[4] 8540[3]

Trust You *Endo Botti* 97
4 ch g Kheleyf(USA) Evening Guest (FR) (Be My Guest (USA))
2518a[8] 7840a[6]

Truth Or Dare *William Muir* a97 94
5 b g Invincible Spirit(IRE) Unreachable Star (Halling (USA))
221^{3} 560^{4} 871^{2} 1088^{5} 1959^{3} 2484^{6} 6075^{4} 6915^{7}

Try Again (IRE) *Paul W Flynn* a60 45
3 b g Dubai Destination(USA) Diamond Katie (IRE) (Night Shift (USA))
7943^{2}

Try Please (FR) *Louis Baudron* a44 71
2 bb g Sageburg(IRE) Petite Elite (USA) (Fusaichi Pegasus (USA))
4620a^{7}

Tryster (IRE) *Charlie Appleby* a114 117
5 b g Shamardal(USA) Min Alhawa (USA) (Riverman (USA))
(625a) (845a) 1106a^{3} 3272^{5} 5431a^{8}

Tsarglas *Colin Teague* a59 3
5 gr g Verglas(IRE) Russian Empress (IRE) (Trans Island)
2047^{7} *3988^{10} 4214^{10}*

Tsar Paul (IRE) *J A Nash* a52 56
11 b g Xaar Jelba (Pursuit Of Love)
431^{6}

Tschierschen (IRE) *William Haggas* a73 74
2 b f Acclamation Roo (Rudimentary (USA))
4706^{2} 5272^{2} 5542^{2} (7269) 7589^{2} *7938^{5}*

Tseo *David Brown* a62
4 ch g Mount Nelson Pasithea (IRE) (Celtic Swing)
161^{6} 2899^{9} 3750^{10}

Ttainted Love *Chris Wall* a79 84
4 b m Mastercraftsman(IRE) Eve (Rainbow Quest (USA))
1390^{2} 2174^{3} 2734^{2} 3234^{4} 4081^{10} 6650^{3} 7220^{5} *8075^{4}*

Tudor Icon *Rae Guest* a62 27
3 b g Sixties Icon Boleyna (USA) (Officer (USA))
618^{6} 789^{4} 2589^{7} 2825^{5}

Tuff Rock (USA) *Ed Walker* 55
2 b c Fastnet Rock(AUS) Wonder Of Wonders (USA) (Kingmambo (USA))
7769^{11}

Tukhoom (IRE) *Marcus Tregoning* 85
3 b g Acclamation Carioca (IRE) (Rakti)
(3104) 3574^{3} ◆ 4080^{4} 6277^{6} 7005^{5}

Tukitinyasok (IRE) *Clive Mulhall* a47 54
9 b g Fath(USA) Mevlana (IRE) (Red Sunset)
2573^{8}

Tulip Dress *Anthony Carson* a62 65
3 ch f Dutch Art White Dress (IRE) (Pivotal)
(2559) 3080^{10} *3987^{8}* 4278^{6} 4570^{3} *5127^{6}* (5515) *6592^{7} 8555^{10}*

Tullinahoo (IRE) *Denis Coakley* a61 62
2 b g Elzaam(AUS) Pitullie (USA) (Rockport Harbor (USA))
2747^{7} 4016^{6} 4815^{4} 5668^{5} *6420^{4} 7690^{6}*

Tullius (IRE) *Andrew Balding* a111 117
8 ch g Le Vie Dei Colori Whipped Queen (USA) (Kingmambo (USA))
748^{5} 1023a^{5} 1425^{3} 1604^{5} (2867) 5652^{9} 6666^{2} 7354^{14}

Tumblewind *Richard Whitaker* 91
6 ch m Captain Rio African Breeze (Atraf)
(1672) 2258^{11} 2803^{6} 3116^{7}

Tundra *Roger Varian* a69
2 b f Bated Breath Tanouma (USA) (Mr Greeley (USA))
6867^{4} 7279^{2}

Tunes (AUS) *Grant Young* 99
7 br g Viscount(AUS) Tin Pan (AUS) (Commands (AUS))
7947a^{8}

Tunnel Creek *T J O'Mara* a29 45
4 b g Tobougg(IRE) Free Offer (Generous (IRE))
4748a^{16}

Tuolumne Meadows *Paul Cole* a79 44
3 b f High Chaparral(IRE) Seren Devious (Dr Devious (IRE))
3781^{2} 5025^{2} 5723^{5}

Tupi (IRE) *Richard Hannon* 114
4 b h Tamayuz Carioca (IRE) (Rakti)
1439^{2} 2159^{6} 2691^{6} 3386^{18} 4135^{7} 4733^{6} 5329^{3} 6117^{8}

Turaathy (IRE) *Tony Newcombe* a56 41
3 b f Lilbourne Lad(IRE) Key Girl (IRE) (Key Of Luck (USA))
2372^{8} 3003^{8} 4500^{7} 6651^{14} *(8278)*

Turanga Leela *Ian Williams* a73 80
2 ch f Paco Boy(IRE) Sunday Bess (JPN) (Deep Impact (JPN))
2764^{3} ◆ 3122^{3} 3597^{3} 3902^{4} *(4526)* (4915) 5560^{11} 6292^{5} 7073^{2} 7820^{9}

Turbine (IRE) *Mark Johnston* a93 93
3 b c Cape Cross(IRE) Chiquita Linda (IRE) (Mujadil (USA))
644a^{2} 1991^{3} *(2331)* 2466^{7}

Turf Laurel (IRE) *S Kobayashi* 100
2 ch f Footstepsinthesand Dame D'Honneur (IRE) (Teofilo (IRE))
7480a^{2}

Turnbury *Nikki Evans* a66 68
5 b g Azamour(IRE) Scottish Heights (IRE) (Selkirk (USA))
218^{3} 731^{8} (1239) 1456^{6} 1747^{5} 3230^{2} (3560) 4057^{8}

Turning Gold *Sir Mark Prescott Bt* 50
2 ch g Pivotal Illusion (Anabaa (USA))
6439^{13} 6952^{10} 7495^{10}

Turning The Table (IRE) *David Simcock* 88
3 gr f Mastercraftsman(IRE) Duchess Dee (IRE) (Bachelor Duke (USA))
1890^{7} 2490^{3} ◆ 6332^{5} 6951^{5}

Turret Rocks (IRE) *J S Bolger* 110
3 b f Fastnet Rock(AUS) Beyond Compare (IRE) (Galileo (IRE))
1888^{6} 2869^{7} 4416a^{4} 5586^{5}

Tuscan Gold *Micky Hammond* a79 80
9 ch g Medicean Louella (USA) (El Gran Senor (USA))
1244^{2} 1523^{5} 2018^{8} 2971^{5} 5435^{4} 6083^{8} 6519^{8} 7006^{6}

Tuscany (IRE) *Paul Cole* a71
2 ch c Poet's Voice Avril Rose (IRE) (Xaar)
5676^{4}

Tusked Wings (IRE) *Jean-Pierre Carvalho* 88
2 ch f Adlerflug(GER) Tucana (GER) (Acatenango (GER))
7563a^{4}

Tuttipaesi (IRE) *William Mott* a99 105
6 rg m Clodovil(IRE) Ruby Ridge (IRE) (Acatenango (GER))
5430a^{4} 7404a^{9}

Tutu Nguru (USA) *William Haggas* a97 98
3 b f Blame(USA) Haka Girl (USA) (War Chant (USA))
836^{2} 1206^{2} 1338^{4} 2026^{2}

Tuvalu *J-M Osorio* 94
4 b h Shirocco(GER) Light Impact (IRE) (Fantastic Light (USA))
6356a^{2}

Twaddle *Alan Coogan* a3 26
2 b f Paco Boy(IRE) Blue Dream (IRE) (Cadeaux Genereux)
3073^{10} 3408^{8} 5930^{7} *6412^{14}*

Tweetheart *Ron Barr* a55 56
3 ch f Dutch Art Strictly (USA) (Fusaichi Pegasus (USA))
1814^{5} 2302^{16} 5276^{7} 5889^{6}

Tweet Lady *Bernhard J Friesdorf* a71 69
7 b m Royal Applause Fuschia (Averti (IRE))
588a^{7} 665a^{6}

Twentysvnthlancers *Paul Midgley* a62 74
3 b g Hellvelyn Subtle Move (USA) (Known Fact (USA))
797^{5} 1112^{6} (2534) 3420^{3} 3806^{4} 4256^{8} 4855^{3} (6023) 6341^{2} 6958^{2} *7660^{13}*

Twenty Times (IRE) *Richard Hughes* 69
2 b f Dream Ahead(USA) Mad Existence (IRE) (Val Royal (FR))
6061^{3} 6577^{4}

Twiggy *Jane Chapple-Hyam* a66 67
2 b f Sixties Icon Queen's Pudding (IRE) (Royal Applause)
3818^{8} 4759^{3} 5410^{6} *6244^{4}* 6762^{3} *7898^{10}*

Twilight Angel *Emma Owen* a52 34
8 ch m Compton Place Leaping Flame (USA) (Trempolino (USA))
8048^{4} 8491^{5}

Twilight Eclipse (USA) *Thomas Albertrani* a103 114
7 b g Purim(USA) My Twilight Dancer (USA) (Twilight Agenda (USA))
7835a^{10}

Twilight Payment (IRE) *J S Bolger* 109
3 b c Teofilo(IRE) Dream On Buddy (IRE) (Oasis Dream)
3341^{3} ◆ 5660a^{2} (6820a)

Twilight Pursuits *Natalie Lloyd-Beavis*
3 b f Pastoral Pursuits Exexel (Dansili)
2998^{12} *5504^{10}* 6031^{5}

Twilight Son *Henry Candy* 120
4 b h Kyllachy Twilight Mistress (Bin Ajwaad (IRE))
2159^{5} (3385) 4151^{14} 7350^{11}

Twilight Spirit *Tony Carroll* 62
2 b f Assertive Twilight Mistress (Bin Ajwaad (IRE))
5229^{3} 5869^{8} 6732^{3}

Twin Appeal (IRE) *David Barron* a92 93
5 b g Oratorio(IRE) Velvet Appeal (IRE) (Petorius (IRE))
5417^{11} 6449^{8} 6539^{19} 7126^{2} ◆ 7825^{3}

Twin Point *Charlie Fellowes* a83 82
5 br g Invincible Spirit(IRE) Gemini Joan (Montjeu (IRE))
(124) 231^{3} 4742^{2} (5337) 5793^{3} 6529^{4} *7308^{8} 7902^{2}*

Twin Sails *Dean Ivory* 105
3 b c Sir Percy Atwirl (Pivotal)
1991^{5} 2242^{9} 3165^{11} 4116^{2} 4758^{2} 5175^{3} 5616^{12} 6109^{9}

Twisting Hay *Mark Johnston* a51 72
3 b c Cape Cross(IRE) Blaugrana (IRE) (Exceed And Excel (AUS))
952^{7}

Twiston Shout (IRE) *Richard Spencer* a39
2 b g Lawman(FR) Minkova (IRE) (Sadler's Wells (USA))
7769^{17} *7907^{11} 8063^{9}*

Twitch (IRE) *Hugo Palmer* a90 104
4 b m Azamour(IRE) Blinking (Marju (IRE))
1855^{3} 2486^{4} 3202a^{4} 4400^{2} 4800^{3} 5587^{7} (7271) 7545^{9}

Twizzell *K R Burke* 79
2 b f Equiano(FR) Greensand (Green Desert (USA))
(1921) 2219^{4} 5998^{6} 6734^{9}

Twobeelucky *Mark Johnston* a80 86
3 b g Tobougg(IRE) She's The Lady (Unfuwain (USA))
4857^{2} 5163^{2} 5581^{2}

Two Dollars (IRE) *William Jarvis* 14
2 ch g Casamento(IRE) Two Marks (USA) (Woodman (USA))
7769^{16}

Two For Two (IRE) *Roger Fell* a83 99
8 b g Danehill Dancer(IRE) D'Articleshore (IRE) (Definite Article)
1871^{6} 2191^{12} 2796^{7} 3390^{7} 3923^{2} ◆ 4917^{2} ◆ 5156^{8} 5976^{3} 6557^{11} 7121^{5} 7316^{10} 7699^{8} *8177^{11} 8478^{10}*

Two In The Pink (IRE) *Ralph J Smith* a70 62
6 rg m Clodovil(IRE) Secret Circle (Magic Ring (IRE))
456^{5} 1334^{4} 2006^{3} 2403^{5} *2769^{10} 3314^{4} 4201^{6}* 5393^{4} ◆ *7754^{2}* ◆ *7936^{2} 8848^{11}*

Two Jabs *Michael Appleby* a90 91
6 b g Teofilo(IRE) Red Bravo (USA) (Red Ransom (USA))
(779) 1081^{4} 2163^{3} 3117^{4} 3520^{5} 4162^{2} 5144^{8}

Two Many Words (IRE) *Bill Turner* a48
4 b g Thousand Words Three Days In May (Cadeaux Genereux)
402^{9} 500^{8}

Two Moons *Daniel Mark Loughnane* a86 86
6 b g Echo Of Light Forever Loved (Deploy)
23^{5}

Two No Bids (IRE) *Phil McEntee* a41 20
6 bb g Footstepsinthesand Milwaukee (FR) (Desert King (IRE))
5677^{10} 7691^{13}

Two Shades Of Grey (IRE) *M Guarnieri* a73 91
5 gr g Oratorio(IRE) Elitista (FR) (Linamix (FR))
2518a^{10}

Two Turtle Doves (IRE) *Michael Mullineaux* a40 60
10 b m Night Shift(USA) Purple Rain (IRE) (Celtic Swing)
230^{9} 2794^{8} 3016^{7} 3494^{6} 4378^{8}

Tylery Wonder (IRE) *Paul Midgley* a80 92
6 ch g Choisir(AUS) Over The Tylery (IRE) (Swallow Flight (IRE))
3696a^{6} *5441a^{3}* 6234^{2} 6819a^{4} 7124^{14} 7358^{12} 7413^{11}

Tynecastle Park *Robert Eddery* a40 67
3 b g Sea The Stars(IRE) So Silk (Rainbow Quest (USA))
2548^{7} 3359^{8} 3723^{8} *6702^{8}*

Tyrannical *Sir Mark Prescott Bt* a58 54
3 br g Dansili Queen Of Mean (Pivotal)
1948^{4} *(2608)* 2967^{5} 3715^{6} *6102^{3} 6659^{4}* 7045^{10}

Tyrell (IRE) *Alan King* a58 77
3 b g Teofilo(IRE) Sleeveless (USA) (Fusaichi Pegasus (USA))
3033^{4} 3493^{8} (3998) 4273^{3} (4810) 5830^{2} 7223^{2}

Tyrsal (IRE) *Clifford Lines* a70 69
5 b g Jeremy(USA) Blanchelande (IRE) (Subotica (FR))
33^{4} 212^{4} 3276^{7} 3617^{4} *4013^{8} 5471^{5}* (5929) 6212^{5} 7078^{4} ◆ *7613^{3} 7870^{7} 8085^{4} 8257^{10}*

Uae King *Roger Varian* 67
2 b c Frankel Zomaradah (Deploy)
7501^{7}

Uae Prince (IRE) *Roger Varian* 95
3 b c Sea The Stars(IRE) By Request (Giant's Causeway (USA))
1639^{3} (6634) 7538^{6}

Ubla (IRE) *Gay Kelleway* a73 58
3 ch g Arcano(IRE) Manuelita Rose (ITY) (Desert Style (IRE))
65^{3} 253^{8} 502^{4} 1832^{4} (2152) 2506^{11} 5086^{4} *(5302)* 5860^{7} *6629^{8} 8191^{4}*

Ucel (IRE) *F Chappet* a77 71
2 b g Kyllachy Umthoulah (IRE) (Unfuwain (USA))
5701a^{3}

Udododontu (IRE) *Saeed bin Suroor* 107
4 b g Lope De Vega(IRE) Fifer (IRE) (Soviet Star (USA))
(229a) 628a^{2} 1196^{18}

Udogo *Joseph Patrick O'Brien* a82 82
5 b g Lucky Story(USA) Welanga (Dansili)
4417a^{2} 7195a^{18}

Udontdodou *Richard Guest* a86 94
3 b g Fastnet Rock(AUS) Forever Times (So Factual (USA))
(1870) (2314) ◆ 3165^{9} 5409^{10} 6449^{5} 7358^{4} 7537^{7} *7858^{4}*

Ulfah Dream *Marco Botti* a66 22
3 b f Oasis Dream Ulfah (USA) (Danzig (USA))
2004^{10} 2333^{4} 2905^{7}

Ullswater (IRE) *Philip Kirby* a55 58
8 b g Singspiel(IRE) Uluwatu (IRE) (Unfuwain (USA))
1399^{10} 1955^{13} 2558^{5} 3067^{6} 3288^{6} 3774^{8} *6422^{10}*

Ultimate Avenue (IRE) *Ed Walker* 97
2 b c Excelebration(IRE) Dance Avenue (IRE) (Sadler's Wells (USA))
4274^{3} (5356) 6707^{6}

Ultimate Fight (FR) *F Monnier* a83 73
2 ch c Muhaymin(USA) Fantastica (GER) (Big Shuffle (USA))
5141a^{5} 5905a^{4}

Ultimate Star *David Simcock* a77 79
3 gr g Starspangledbanner(AUS) Ultimate Best (King's Best (USA))
(735) 2237^{4} 3399^{5}

Ultimat Power (IRE) *Mark Hoad* a46 16
2 ch c Power Trumbaka (IRE) (In The Wings)
4270^{15} *5549^{11}* 5922^{4} *6412^{3}* 7570^{11} *7734^{6} 7881^{4} 8046^{P}*

Ultra (IRE) *A Fabre* 112
3 ch c Manduro(GER) Epitome (IRE) (Nashwan (USA))
4439a^{2} 5499a^{6}

Ultra Thef (IRE) *Ms Sheila Lavery* a35 67
3 ch g Haatef(USA) Non Ultra (USA) (Peintre Celebre (USA))
7517a^{14}

Ulysses (IRE) *Sir Michael Stoute* 118
3 ch c Galileo(IRE) Light Shift (USA) (Kingmambo (USA))
1639^{2} ◆ (2208) ◆ 2896^{12} (4753) 5893^{2} 7835a^{4}

Unabated (IRE) *Marco Botti* a93 93
2 b c Bated Breath Elhareer (IRE) (Selkirk (USA))
(3569) 4653^{2} 5654^{9} *6124^{3}* 6572^{5}

Unblinking *Nigel Twiston-Davies* 67
3 b g Cacique(IRE) Deliberate (King's Best (USA))
7627^{10}

Uncle Charlie (IRE) *Ann Duffield* a56 70
2 b c Vale Of York(IRE) Velvet Kiss (IRE) (Danehill Dancer (IRE))
2570^{7} (6789) 7467^{10} *8174^{6}*

Uncle Dermot (IRE) *Brendan Powell* a18 75
8 b g Arakan(USA) Cappadoce (IRE) (General Monash (USA))
1125^{8} 1387^{4} 1546^{9} 1916^{7} 2367^{6} 2460^{4} (3582) 3802^{3} 7010^{12} 7417^{10} *7986^{13}*

Uncle Lino (USA) *Gary Sherlock* a104
3 b c Uncle Mo(USA) Haysee (USA) (Orientate (USA))
2499a^{7}

Uncle Rufus (IRE) *Patrick Chamings* 36
5 ch g Iffraaj Astuti (IRE) (Waajib (IRE))
4202^{6}

Under Approval *Karen Tutty* a45 55
5 b g Captain Gerrard(IRE) Dockside Strike (Dockside (USA))
869^{8} 1026^{8} 1495^{14} 1676^{17} 2052^{9} (2423) 2676^{12} 2808^{9} 3549^{4} 3843^{14} (4492) 4968^{11} *6910^{7}* 7046^{14} *7859^{13}*

Under Attack (IRE) *Sir Michael Stoute* a79 83
3 b g Dubawi(IRE) Ship's Biscuit (Tiger Hill (IRE))
1287^{2} 1646^{2}

Under Control (IRE) *William Haggas* a75 70
2 b g Power High Figurine (IRE) (High Chaparral (IRE))
4594^{9} (6092) *(6898)* ◆

Underdressed *Keith Dalgleish* a66 66
3 b f Elnadim(USA) Bijan (IRE) (Mukaddamah (USA))
3^{5}

Under Siege (IRE) *Stuart Williams* a85 88
4 b g Invincible Spirit(IRE) Interpose (Indian Ridge)
901^{2} 1040^{5} 1958^{6} 4014^{4} (4475) 5103^{4} 5991^{4} (6583)

Understory (USA) *Tim McCarthy* a55 55
9 b g Forestry(USA) Sha Tha (USA) (Mr Prospector (USA))
222^{10} 326^{5} 672^{4} 870^{8} 2323^{3} 3401^{2} 7103^{10} 7937^{6} 8492^{5}

Undertow (IRE) *K R Burke* a64 50
3 b f Arcano(IRE) Tides (Bahamian Bounty)
(249) ◆ *519^{9}* 2834^{6} 3603^{8} 3898^{8}

Undiscovered Angel (FR) *K R Burke* 72
2 b f Wootton Bassett Angel Voices (IRE) (Tagula (IRE))
6223^{2} ◆ 6762^{4}

Undrafted (USA) *Wesley A Ward* a98 123
6 ch g Purim(USA) French Jeannette (USA) (French Deputy (USA))
3385^{6} 7833a^{8}

Unex El Greco *Martin Smith* a87 89
8 b g Holy Roman Emperor(IRE) Friendlier (Zafonic (USA))
31^{7}

Unex Modigliani (IRE) *Derek Shaw* a67 55
7 ch g Hurricane Run(IRE) Chronicle (Observatory (USA))
435^{8} 592^{2} 695^{10} 1136^{3} 1675^{3} *2605^{3} 2792^{5} 3302^{2}*

Unforeseen *Daniel Kubler* a12
3 b f Sky Mesa(USA) Distinctive (Tobougg (IRE))
4939^{13}

Unforgetable Filly *Hugo Palmer* 100
2 b f Sepoy(AUS) Beautiful Filly (Oasis Dream)
5846^{2} (6336) 6706^{2} 7114^{3}

Unforgiving Minute *John Butler* a96 46
5 b g Cape Cross(IRE) Ada River (Dansili)
90a^{8} 284a^{13} 833^{2} 1335^{10} 1576^{3} 1959^{2} 2033^{4} 2628^{13} *5552^{12} 6372^{10} (7606) 8122^{3} 8279^{11}*

Uni *F Chappet* a78
2 ch f More Than Ready(USA) Unaided (Dansili)
7783a^{2}

Unicorn (IRE) *A P O'Brien* 103
3 b g Galileo(IRE) One Moment In Time (IRE) (Danehill (USA))
5653^{3}

Unilit (IRE) *David Evans* a69 66
3 b f Approve(IRE) Riymaisa (IRE) (Traditionally (USA))
1599^{13} 2042^{11} *3034^{6}*

Uninhibited (IRE) *Charles O'Brien* 85
3 b f High Chaparral(IRE) Irish Style (IRE) (Mujadil (USA))
5313a^{7} 7393a^{11}

Union Rose *Ronald Harris* 102
4 b g Stimulation(IRE) Dot Hill (Refuse To Bend (IRE))
3857^{2} 4126^{5} 5143^{8} 5555^{16} 5961^{7} 6944^{16}

Union Strike (USA) *Craig Dollase* a104
2 bb f Union Rags(USA) Classic Strike (USA) (Smart Strike (CAN))
7830a^{6}

Unison (IRE) *Jeremy Scott* a67 83
6 b g Jeremy(USA) Easter Song (USA) (Rubiano (USA))
4052^{5} (5076) (5649) 7189^{8}

United Color (USA) *D Selvaratnam* a104 81
7 b h Ghostzapper(USA) Silk Candy (CAN) (Langfuhr (CAN))
95a^{15}

Universal Mind (IRE) *R McGlinchey* a50 34
9 b g Chevalier(IRE) Professional Mom (USA) (Spinning World (USA))
674^{6}

Unnoticed *Ollie Pears* a70 72
4 b g Observatory(USA) Celestial Empire (USA) (Empire Maker (USA))
2540^{4} 3554^{9} 4878^{2} *5736^{4}* 6408^{2} 7059^{6} *7890^{3} 8188^{5} 8351^{2} 8482^{9}*

Unonothinjonsnow *Richard Guest* a18 17
2 b g Arakan(USA) Kleio (Sadler's Wells (USA))
7125^{13} 7407^{7} *7659^{12}*

Unsuspected Girl (IRE) *David Simcock* a74 56
3 b f Rip Van Winkle(IRE) Sweet Sioux (Halling (USA))
3198^{9} *4018^{6}* 4275^{3} 4566^{3} *(5630) 5763^{2} (6370) 6626^{3} 7205^{2} 7609^{3}*

Untapped Spectrum (IRE) *W J Martin* a52 50
4 b m Aqlaam Romea (Muhtarram (USA))
3096^{5}

Until Midnight (IRE) *Eugene Stanford* a85 77
6 b g Moss Vale(IRE) Emma's Star (ITY) (Darshaan)
(169) 727^{2} 2028^{4} 4360^{8} 5372^{7} 6072^{5} 6579^{11}

Unzipped *Stuart Edmunds* a32 66
2 ch f Captain Gerrard(IRE) Justazippy (Where Or When (IRE))
6319^{3} 7056^{4} *7484^{10} 7898^{13}*

Upavon *Stuart Williams* a100 83
6 b g Avonbridge Blaina (Compton Place)
288^{9} (2217) (2290) ◆ 3068^{6} 4362^{7} (5039) (5673) 7221^{8} *8050^{9} 8192^{2}* ◆ *8407^{8}*

Upendi (FR) *Robert Collet* 91
2 b f Siyouni(FR) Courchevel (IRE) (Whipper (USA))
5698a^{2} 5986a^{2} 7169a^{5} 7757a^{7}

Upgrade *K R Burke* a73 75
2 gr c Excelebration(IRE) Pinch Of Posh (IRE) (Pivotal)
5615^{13} 6054^{2} 6499^{7} *7366^{3} 7598^{2} 7909^{4} 8008^{6} 8466^{8}*

Uphold *Gay Kelleway* a67 69
9 b g Oasis Dream Allegro Viva (USA) (Distant View (USA))
4903a^{7} 5281a^{11} 8421a^{5}

Up In Lights (IRE) *James Fanshawe* a90 95
4 ch m Makfi Spotlight (Dr Fong (USA))
2819^{5} (5123) 6331^{6} 7472^{5}

Up North (IRE) *Micky Hammond* a40
4 b g Dylan Thomas(IRE) Difiya (IRE) (Cadeaux Genereux)
863^{8} 1037^{4}

Upper Lambourn (IRE) *John Holt* a41 22
8 b g Exceed And Excel(AUS) In The Fashion (IRE) (In The Wings)
418^{8} 596^{6} 8288^{12} 8383^{5}

Upstaging *Paul Cole* a100 87
4 b g Mount Nelson Corndavon (USA) (Sheikh Albadou)
1040^{2} 1724^{3} 2290^{2} 2754^{6} 3233^{3} (4051) 4910^{4} 6000^{2} (6409) (7054) (7752)

Up Ten Down Two (IRE) *Michael Easterby* a60 55
7 b g Hurricane Run(IRE) Darabela (IRE) (Desert King (IRE))
7105^{4}

Uptight (FR) *Kevin Ryan* a85 80
4 b g Zamindar(USA) Terre D'Espoir (FR) (Oasis Dream)
(250) ◆ 364^{6} 901^{13} 1444^{17} 3168^{18} 3713^{11}

Up Todate Du Casse (FR) *F Plouganou* 98
8 b g Tonitruant(USA) Ordalie Du Casse (FR) (Seurat)
8042a^{9}

Uptown Funk (IRE) *John Gosden* 26
2 b c Galileo(IRE) All's Forgotten (USA) (Darshaan)
7501^{13}

Up To You (USA) *John Gosden* a72 64
3 ch f Giant's Causeway(USA) Vignette (USA) (Diesis)
2767^{6} 3673^{5}

Urban Fox *James Tate* a79 98
2 b f Foxwedge(AUS) Lomapamar (Nashwan (USA))
(3074) (3782) ◆ 4560^{4} 5172^{4} 5870^{3} 6258^{3} (6706) 7116^{3}

Urban Space *John Flint* a67 73
10 ch g Sulamani(IRE) Rasmalai (Sadler's Wells (USA))
1456^{7} 2370^{2} (2462) 2850^{4} (3099) 3746^{3} 3999^{3} (4483) (4592) 4816^{5} 6315^{12} 6886^{7} 7270^{11}

Urban Spirit (IRE) *David O'Meara* a44 43
2 b c Born To Sea(IRE) Rose Of Mooncoin (IRE) (Brief Truce (USA))
2913^{11} 4765^{10} 7740^{10}

Usa (IRE) *S J Mahon* a58
9 b g Bertolini(USA) Varnay (Machiavellian (USA))
6466a^{5}

US Army Ranger (IRE) *A P O'Brien* 122
3 b c Galileo(IRE) Moonstone (Dalakhani (IRE))
(1974) 2896^{2} 5685a^{4} 6351a^{2} 7353^{8}

Used To Be *K R Burke* 75
2 ch g Kyllachy Polly Floyer (Halling (USA))
3112^{8} 4040^{2} 4609^{3} 5371^{4} 6229^{5}

Usherette (IRE) *A Fabre* a106 119
4 b m Shamardal(USA) Monday Show (USA) (Maria's Mon (USA))
(1886) ◆ (3271) ◆ 4107^{6}

U S Navy Seal (USA) *J R Jenkins* a88 67
4 br g War Front(USA) Questress (USA) (Seeking The Gold (USA))
66^{10} 267^{4} 447^{2} 619^{6} 1620^{12} 2214^{7} 2791^{9} 3276^{5} 4568^{7} 5607^{6} 5935^{8}

Ustinov *David O'Meara* a93 96
4 b g Exceed And Excel(AUS) Tamzin (Hernando (FR))
4259^{5} ◆ 5161^{7} (6079) 6792^{11} 6962^{7} 7315^{14}

Utah (IRE) *A P O'Brien* 92
2 b c Galileo(IRE) Healing Music (FR) (Bering)
6987a^{7}

Utmost (USA) *John Gosden* 83
2 ch c Giant's Causeway(USA) Fugitive Angel (USA) (Alphabet Soup (USA))
(7243)

Vaasa (IRE) *A bin Harmash* a59 94
5 ch h Dalakhani(IRE) La Sylphide (SWI) (Barathea (IRE))
93a^{15}

Va Bank (IRE) *M Janikowski* 113
4 b h Archipenko(USA) Vinales (IRE) (Dilshaan)
(5904a)

Vadamos (FR) *A Fabre* a113 122
5 b h Monsun(GER) Celebre Vadala (FR) (Peintre Celebre (USA))
1108a^{11} (1910a) 2568a^{4} (4441a) 5449a^{2} (6394a) 7553a^{4}

Vadsariya (FR) *A De Royer-Dupre* 91
2 b f Exceed And Excel(AUS) Valasyra (FR) (Sinndar (IRE))
7480a^{6}

Vagabonde (IRE) *C Laffon-Parias* 68
2 b f Acclamation Desertiste (Green Desert (USA))
3507a^{6}

Valadorna (USA) *Mark Casse* a110
2 b f Curlin(USA) Goldfield (USA) (Yes It's True (USA))
7830a^{2}

Valaynna (FR) *G Derat* 75
5 gr m Al Namix(FR) Dayna (Tobougg (IRE))
7946a^{11}

Valbchek (IRE) *Jane Chapple-Hyam* a98 85
7 b g Acclamation Spectacular Show (IRE) (Spectrum (IRE))
4889^{7} 5678^{5} 7525a^{4} 7868^{4} 8311^{7} 8489^{9}

Valcartier (IRE) *John Gosden* 53
2 b c Redoute's Choice(AUS) Vadawina (IRE) (Unfuwain (USA))
7496^{8}

Valdaya (FR) *J-C Rouget* a78 81
3 b f Acclamation Valima (FR) (Linamix (FR))
5946a^{6}

Vale Dori (ARG) *M F De Kock* a111
3 b f Asiatic Boy(ARG) Valerina (ARG) (Halo Sunshine (USA))
808a^{2} 1103a^{4}

Vale Do Sol (IRE) *Fawzi Abdulla Nass* a94 101
4 b g Vale Of York(IRE) Condilessa (IRE) (Key Of Luck (USA))
625a^{9}

Valenka (GER) *M Munch* a67 90
3 b f Sholokhov(IRE) Vera Longa (GER) (Lando (GER))
716a^{2} 1541a^{7} 2455a^{6}

Valentine Conde (FR) *R Chotard* a65 63
3 b f King's Best(USA) Sintra (IRE) (Kris)
1357a^{10}

Valentine Mist (IRE) *Seamus Mullins* a62
4 b m Vale Of York(IRE) Silvertine (IRE) (Alzao (USA))
964^{6}

Valentino Boy (IRE) *Brian Ellison* 79
2 b g Bated Breath Capistrano Day (USA) (Diesis)
1482^{2} ◆ 1783^{2} 2090^{3}

Vale Of Flight (IRE) *Rae Guest* a67 54
3 b f Vale Of York(IRE) Barbera (GER) (Night Shift (USA))
2886^{7} 4238^{6} 5474^{3} 6051^{8} (6374) 6660^{4} 7303^{10}

Vale Of Iron (IRE) *John Best* a77 73
4 b h Vale Of York(IRE) Lady Van Gogh (Dubai Destination (USA))
256^{4} (587a) 663a^{6} 2401^{7} 2930^{2} (3403) 3798^{5}

Vale Of Rock (IRE) *Michael Appleby* a36 64
3 b f Vale Of York(IRE) Pirans Rock (IRE) (Rock Of Gibraltar (IRE))
4764^{12} 5085^{9} 5610^{9} 6052^{11} 6634^{6} 7231^{7}

Valkena (FR) *C Boutin* a75 100
3 ch f Kendargent(FR) Vaillante (IRE) (Zilzal (USA))
1582a^{3}

Vallance Road *Robyn Brisland* a61 61
3 b f Kheleyf(USA) Last Romance (IRE) (Last Tycoon)
171^{7} 495^{6} 2770^{8} 3496^{6}

Vallante (GER) *J Hirschberger* 91
3 b f Soldier Hollow Vive La Reine (GER) (Big Shuffle (USA))
7720a^{5}

Vallarta (IRE) *Ruth Carr* a83 86
6 b g Footstepsinthesand Mexican Miss (IRE) (Tagula (IRE))
894^{4} 1291^{5} 1879^{4} 2524^{4} 2961^{5} 3394^{2} 3924^{2} 4376^{3} (4700) 5224^{5} 5845^{3} 6216^{2} 6502^{2} 6718^{5} 7126^{11}

Valley Kid (FR) *N Caullery* a77 82
3 gr c Kendargent(FR) Valera (GER) (Acatenango (GER))
7999a^{9}

Valley Lodge *Julia Feilden* a40 64
2 ch c Mayson Beat As One (Medicean)
2311^{4} 2779^{6} 3396^{2} 4015^{8} 6440^{10} 8235^{7} 8568^{10}

Valley Of Fire *Les Eyre* a91 97
4 b g Firebreak Charlie Girl (Puissance)
2027^{24} 2485^{10} 2684^{10} 2898^{11} 3163^{2} ◆ 4079^{7} 4402^{4} 5403^{4} (6082) 6529^{6} 7530^{5} 7825^{10}

Valley Of Rocks (IRE) *Mark Johnston* a73 70
2 b g Big Bad Bob(IRE) Arctic Hunt (IRE) (Bering)
6904^{3} 7243^{4}

Valmina *Philip Hide* a68 69
9 b g Val Royal(FR) Minnina (IRE) (In The Wings)
(1517a) 2284a^{3} 2953a^{2} 3380a^{4} 7038^{8} 7899^{3} ◆ 8163^{7} 8365^{10}

Valtashyra (IRE) *Ann Stokell* a28 39
3 br f Vale Of York(IRE) Tashyra (IRE) (Tagula (IRE))
5862^{6} 6317^{12} 7793^{6}

Valuta Pregiata *Stefano Botti* 98
3 b f Holy Roman Emperor(IRE) Veronica Franco (ITY) (Lomitas)
1685a^{5} 2730a^{5} 7566a^{7}

Vanbijou (GER) *Eva Fabianova* 71
4 bb m Pomellato(GER) Vancovia (FR) (Dream Well (FR))
6611a^{9}

Vanderbilt (IRE) *Martyn Meade* a75 77
2 ch g Intense Focus(USA) Star Of The West (Galileo (IRE))
5081^{5} 5959^{3} 7034^{3} 7882^{3} 8189^{4}

Van Der Decken *Charlie Appleby* a99 99
2 b c Dutch Art Celeste (Green Desert (USA))
3243^{5} 4653^{3} 5646^{7} (8575a)

Van Dyke *Hughie Morrison* a83 73
3 b c Excellent Art Respectfilly (Mark Of Esteem (IRE))
1575^{4} 3104^{2} 3475^{2} 4213^{5} 5349a^{3} (5608) 6138^{3} 7051^{2}

Van Gerwen *Les Eyre* a5 83
3 ch g Bahamian Bounty Disco Ball (Fantastic Light (USA))
1922^{4} (2049) 2802^{5} 2972^{4} 3716^{4} 5439^{2} 6079^{6} (6717) 7413^{14} 7892^{14}

Van Huysen (IRE) *Dominic Ffrench Davis* a86 82
4 br g Excellent Art Tara Too (IRE) (Danetime (IRE))
360^{4} 629^{2} 795^{4} 1173^{4} 1699^{2} 2085^{3} 3124^{2} (3276) 4081^{5} (4774) 4868^{11} 5526^{6} (7245) 7666^{3} (8231) (8446)

Vanishing Point *Andrew Balding* a72 78
3 b c Pivotal Hyperspectra (Rainbow Quest (USA))
2208^{9} 2816^{4} ◆ 3508^{2} (3886) 6083^{12} 6767^{7}

Vanity Queen *Luca Cumani* 78
2 b f Fastnet Rock(AUS) Victoire Finale (Peintre Celebre (USA))
4298^{3} (5266) 5847^{2} 6455^{4}

Van Mildert (IRE) *Kenneth Slack* 52
7 b m Observatory(USA) Vanilla Delight (IRE) (Orpen (USA))
(2962) 3325^{7} 3704^{8} 4934^{11}

Vantage Point (IRE) *John Gosden* a65 82
2 b c Galileo(IRE) Adoration (USA) (Honor Grades (USA))
6704^{2} ◆ 7273^{2} 7940^{7}

Vaporetto Capri (IRE) *F Doumen* a72 80
3 ch c Manduro(GER) Anacapri (FR) (Anabaa (USA))
7680a^{9}

Vardaris (IRE) *J Bertin* a42 58
6 b g Beat Hollow Drosia (IRE) (King's Best (USA))
5216a^{8}

Varlo (SAF) *Lars Kelp*
4 b g Var(USA) I`m Like Hello (SAF) (Dominion Royale)
4421a^{8}

Varsovian *Dean Ivory* a89 74
6 ch g Refuse To Bend(IRE) Queen Of Poland (Halling (USA))
529^{5} 771^{6} 1040^{8} 1634^{7} 2581^{9} 3035^{7} 4839^{5} 8176^{8} 8378^{5} 8561^{6}

Varun's Bride (IRE) *Richard Hannon* a52 56
2 b f Lawman(FR) Belgique (IRE) (Compton Place)
3556^{8} 4147^{9} 5015^{3} 6236^{7} 6412^{11} 6896^{3}

Vastly (USA) *Sophie Leech* a76 58
7 rg g Mizzen Mast(USA) Valentine Band (USA) (Dixieland Band (USA))
53^{5} (464) 676^{11} 1058^{3} 2444^{5} (3072) (3476) (4201) 4717^{3} 5149^{7} 5724^{5} 6138^{2} 6702^{2}

Vastonea (IRE) *Kevin Prendergast* a84 91
8 gr g Verglas(IRE) Roystonea (Polish Precedent (USA))
5941a^{11} 6389a^{4}

Vatican Hill (IRE) *Jamie Osborne* a76 69
2 b c Canford Cliffs(IRE) Empress Ella (IRE) (Holy Roman Emperor (IRE))
2417^{4} 2913^{8} 4371^{12} 5318^{2} 5770^{9} (6446) (8560)

Vaulted *Richard Fahey* 72
2 b f Kyllachy Palatial (Green Desert (USA))
4805^{3} ◆ 5272^{3} 5876^{4} 7040^{2} 7355^{5}

Vaux (IRE) *Ben Haslam* a60 75
2 b g Sir Prancealot(IRE) Greenflash (Green Desert (USA))
1706^{4} 2265^{2} ◆ 2552^{5} 3881^{7} 4510^{4} 6010^{11} 6743^{6} 7143^{8}

Vazirabad (FR) *A De Royer-Dupre* 120
4 bb g Manduro(GER) Visorama (IRE) (Linamix (FR))
(1102a) (2725a) 3936a^{7} (6396a) 6974a^{2} (7569a)

Vecheka (IRE) *Micky Hammond* 71
5 b g Lawman(FR) Lidanski (IRE) (Soviet Star (USA))
1565^{11} 1845^{4} 2409^{9} 2778^{6}

Vedani (IRE) *Tony Carroll* a58 60
7 b g Dalakhani(IRE) Velandia (IRE) (Sadler's Wells (USA))
164^{12} 417^{4} 634^{5} 1322^{3} 2110^{4} 3325^{3} 4023^{7} 7039^{7}

Vedevani (FR) *A De Royer-Dupre* 107
3 b c Dubawi(IRE) Vadawina (IRE) (Unfuwain (USA))
1308a^{4} 1580a^{4} 2551a^{4} 5699a^{6} 6989a^{10}

Veena (FR) *David Simcock* a84 62
3 b f Elusive City(USA) Kensita (FR) (Soviet Star (USA))
1476^{7} 2789^{9} 4398^{9} 4708^{8}

Veeraya *Julia Feilden* a72 66
6 b g Rail Link Follow Flanders (Pursuit Of Love)
482^{4} 943^{3} 1116^{2} 1415^{9} 2643^{5} 4715^{8} 5337^{2} 6872^{3} (7738) 8555^{7}

Vega Sicilia (FR) *Y Barberot* 95
2 b f Elusive City(USA) Volvoreta (Suave Dancer (USA))
1284a^{2} 3937a^{4}

Veiled Secret (IRE) *Sir Mark Prescott Bt* a61 57
2 b c Teofilo(IRE) Seven Veils (IRE) (Danehill Dancer (IRE))
6486^{8} 6904^{6} 7306^{5} 7812^{7}

Veldargent (FR) *H-A Pantall* a50 61
2 b f Kendargent(FR) Velvet Revolver (IRE) (Mujahid (USA))
7996a^{6}

Velveteen *G M Lyons* 92
2 b f Exceed And Excel(AUS) Ermine And Velvet (Nayef (USA))
5661a^{4} 5940a^{5}

Velvet Revolution *Marco Botti* a88 77
3 ch g Pivotal Gino's Spirits (Perugino (USA))
1113^{8} 2012^{8} (7223) 7625^{4} (8051)

Velvet Voice *Mark H Tompkins* a59
2 b f Azamour(IRE) Battery Power (Royal Applause)
7761^{11} 8131^{7} 8486^{8}

Venecia Style (FR) *P Sogorb* a100 101
3 b f Desert Style(IRE) Verone (USA) (Dixie Union (USA))
1309a^{4} 5949a^{8} 6272a^{12}

Venerable (FR) *H-A Pantall* a73 77
3 b f Way Of Light(USA) Verzasca (IRE) (Sadler's Wells (USA))
1542a^{3}

Venetian Proposal (IRE) *Zoe Davison* a60 40
2 b f Fast Company(IRE) Ide Say (IRE) (Grand Lodge (USA))
4951^{13} 6867^{10} 7277^{9} 7866^{13} 8361^{4}

Veneto (GER) *Andreas Lowe* 86
3 b c New Approach(IRE) Venia Legendi (GER) (Zinaad)
2315a^{10}

Venezia (SWI) *H-A Pantall* 69
2 b f Blue Canari(FR) Vertana (IRE) (Sinndar (IRE))
6639a^{7}

Veneziano (FR) *Robert Collet* a54 51
7 ch g Peintre Celebre(USA) Venetian Beauty (USA) (Lear Fan (USA))
5281a^{5}

Vengeur Masque (IRE) *Michael Moroney* 104
4 b g Monsun(GER) Venetian Beauty (USA) (Lear Fan (USA))
7378a^{8} 7826a^{2}

Ventaron (FR) *V Luka Jr* a100 51
5 ch h Le Havre(IRE) Piemontaise (FR) (Ultimately Lucky (IRE))
7524a^{4}

Vent De Force *Hughie Morrison* a56 110
5 b g Hurricane Run(IRE) Capriolla (In The Wings)
3913^{7} 5655^{16}

Vent Du Large (FR) *R Chotard* a43 71
3 b c Shakespearean(IRE) Traicy (FR) (Neverneyev (USA))
5907a^{10}

Ventry Bay (USA) *Wesley A Ward* 97
2 ch c Scat Daddy(USA) Raffishing Look (USA) (Kingmambo (USA))
7266a^{3}

Ventura Blues (IRE) *Richard Hannon* a79 83
2 bb f Bated Breath Salmon Rose (IRE) (Iffraaj)
1482^{4} (2376) (3134)

Ventura Castle *Jamie Snowden* a59 56
4 b g Paco Boy(IRE) Bisaat (USA) (Bahri (USA))
3470^{6}

Ventura Falcon (IRE) *Richard Hannon* a59 36
3 b f Excellent Art Danish Gem (Danehill (USA))
516^{3} 611^{4} 679^{8} 1325^{4} ◆ 2148^{8} 2609^{5} (3319) 3731^{7} 4936^{6} 5254^{4} 6513^{P}

Ventura Jazz *Richard Fahey* a48
2 b f Dandy Man(IRE) Aljafliyah (Halling (USA))
8119^{8} 8406^{7}

Ventura Secret (IRE) *Tim Easterby* a67 78
2 ch g Roderic O'Connor(IRE) Bajan Belle (IRE) (Efisio)
2119^{5} 2617^{8} (3148) 3839^{4} 4394^{22} 5756^{2} ◆ 6322^{6} 6954^{14} 7600^{6} 7820^{13}

Ventura Storm (IRE) *Richard Hannon* 115
3 b c Zoffany(IRE) Sarawati (IRE) (Haafhd)
(1395) 2069a^{8} 2281a^{6} 2946a^{12} (4339) (5218a) 6329^{2} (7402a)

Venturous (IRE) *Charlie Appleby* 101
3 ch g Raven's Pass(USA) Bold Desire (Cadeaux Genereux)
1865^{3} 2251^{8} 3165^{4} 4062^{11} 4867^{7}

Venue *Donald McCain* a38 88
6 b g Beat Hollow Shirley Valentine (Shirley Heights)
1967^{11} 2472^{6} 2685^{12}

Venus Grace *Michael Appleby* a70 69
5 b m Royal Applause Basque Beauty (Nayef (USA))
14^{3} 169^{6} 532^{6} 564^{8} 769^{6} 813^{4} 977^{4} (1145) 1334^{7}

Venutius *Ed McMahon* a75 82
9 b g Doyen(IRE) Boadicea's Chariot (Commanche Run)
2347^{12} 4807^{2} (5521)

Verbal Link (FR) *M Delzangles* a68 82
3 gr c King's Best(USA) Verba (FR) (Anabaa (USA))
1311a^{2}

Vercingetorix (IRE) *Harriet Bethell* a79 83
5 b g Dylan Thomas(IRE) Great Artist (FR) (Desert Prince (IRE))
2484^{9} 2752^{7} 3391^{5} 3688^{7} 4129^{6} 4793^{4} (5547) 8348^{3}

Verdi (IRE) *John Ryan* a17 40
2 b g Invincible Spirit(IRE) Leopard Hunt (USA) (Diesis)
7224^{6} 7527^{10}

Vermeulen *John Gosden* a85 78
3 b g Fastnet Rock(AUS) Crystal Maze (Gone West (USA))
4458^{6} 5681^{2} 6192^{2} 6703^{3} (7280)

Vermilion *Ed Walker* 32
2 ch f Dutch Art Makara (Lion Cavern (USA))
6078^{10}

Vermont (IRE) *A Schaerer* a96 85
6 b g Muhtathir Venetian Beauty (USA) (Lear Fan (USA))
664a^{10}

Vermuyden *Pam Sly*
7 b g Oasis Dream Speciosa (IRE) (Danehill Dancer (IRE))
39^{12}

Vernatti *Pam Sly* a31 65
3 b f Teofilo(IRE) Speciosa (IRE) (Danehill Dancer (IRE))
4319^{4} ◆ 7384^{9}

Verne Castle *Andrew Balding* a85 70
3 ch g Sakhee's Secret Lochangel (Night Shift (USA))
1753^{2} 2186^{7} 2750^{3} 3127^{3} 3976^{5} 4224^{4} 4502^{6} 5305^{3} (5474) (6248) (6699)

Vero (GER) *Jean-Pierre Carvalho* a66 57
4 b h Youmzain(IRE) Viscaya (GER) (Peintre Celebre (USA))
5216a^{7}

Versant *Lee Carter* a72 69
4 b g Authorized(IRE) Tanzania (USA) (Darshaan)
5129^{4} 6052^{6} 6415^{5} 6886^{5} 7053^{5} 7429^{14} 8281^{3}

Vertueux (FR) *Tony Carroll* a41 41
11 gr g Verglas(IRE) Shahrazad (FR) (Bering)
289^{5}

Verus Delicia (IRE) *Daniel Mark Loughnane* a64 74
7 b m Chineur(FR) Ribbon Glade (UAE) (Zafonic (USA))
2442^{10} 3098^{6} 3474^{5} 3984^{10} 4506^{6}

Very Dashing *Luca Cumani* 98
3 br f Dansili Dash To The Top (Montjeu (IRE))
(4367) 5307^{4} 7029a^{6} 7862a^{7}

Very First Blade *Michael Mullineaux* a41 55
7 b g Needwood Blade Dispol Verity (Averti (IRE))
(136) 340^{5} 504^{9} 868^{5} 961^{2} 1026^{4} 1299^{4} 1709^{5} 2447^{9} (3022) 3549^{3} 4292^{4} 5200^{5} 5483^{9} (7046) 7859^{7} 8485^{11}

Very Honest (IRE) *Brett Johnson* a83 87
3 b f Poet's Voice Cercle D'Amour (USA) (Storm Cat (USA))
952^{2} (2004) (3105) 3815^{4} 5205^{6}

Very Special (IRE) *Saeed bin Suroor* a103 113
4 ch m Lope De Vega(IRE) Danielli (IRE) (Danehill (USA))
(451a) (809a) 1106a^{6} ◆ 4107^{2}

Very Talented (IRE) *Saeed bin Suroor* 102
3 b c Invincible Spirit(IRE) Crystal House (CHI) (Golden Voyager (USA))
1440^{6} 6075^{3} 6786^{3}

Via Egnatia (USA) *John Gosden* 95
2 b c Distorted Humor(USA) Honest Lady (USA) (Seattle Slew (USA))
3619^{3} ◆ 4390^{5} (6945) ◆

Via Firenze (IRE) *Mme Pia Brandt* a100 88
3 b f Dansili Via Medici (IRE) (Medicean)
8563a[3]

Via Serendipity *Hugo Palmer* 84
2 b c Invincible Spirit(IRE) Mambo Light (USA) (Kingmambo (USA))
5615[3] ◆ 6486[3] (6751)

Via Via (IRE) *James Tate* 89
4 b h Lope De Vega(IRE) Atalina (FR) (Linamix (FR))
6579[3] (7702) ◆

Vibes (IRE) *Jamie Osborne* a65 72
2 ch g Helmet(AUS) Smoken Rosa (USA) (Smoke Glacken (USA))
5324[4] ◆ 7216[7] *7424[8] 8175[7] 8352[8]*

Vibrant Chords *Henry Candy* a73 97
3 b g Poet's Voice Lovely Thought (Dubai Destination (USA))
1442[3] *2788[7]* ◆ 4079[4] 5199[3] 6449[2] 6916[7]

Vicarage Gold *Shaun Lycett* a6
4 b m Kheleyf(USA) Kyleene (Kyllachy)
822[13]

Vice Versa *Sir Michael Stoute* 54
2 b f Oasis Dream Mascarene (USA) (Empire Maker (USA))
7696[9]

Vicky Park *Dean Ivory* a28 34
2 b f Compton Place Sonko (IRE) (Red Clubs (IRE))
7414[9] *7748[9]*

Vicomte Alco (FR) *A Schaerer*
7 ch g Dom Alco(FR) First Wool (FR) (Matahawk)
586a[5]

Victim Of Love (ITY) *Stefano Botti* 95
3 b f Ramonti(FR) Imco Imagination (IRE) (Darshaan)
1685a[11] 2730a[14]

Victoire De Lyphar (IRE) *Ruth Carr* a7 85
9 b g Bertolini(USA) Victory Peak (Shirley Heights)
1818[5] (2297) 3011[6] 3421[4] (3599) 3840[6] (4704) 5886[12] 6500[11]

Victoria Pollard *Andrew Balding* a82 88
4 b m Sir Percy Victoria Montoya (High Chaparral (IRE))
1290[5] 1743[2] 2313[6] 2671[4] *2994[4] 3659[5]*

Victorious Laugh (IRE) *Marco Botti* a25
3 b c High Chaparral(IRE) Last Laugh (USA) (Smart Strike (CAN))
2790[13]

Victoriously *Andi Brown* a60 70
4 b g Azamour(IRE) Ambria (GER) (Monsun (GER))
2397[10] 4567[8] *6046[2] 6900[6] 7369[2] 7888[3] (8125)*

Victor's Beach (IRE) *Mark Michael McNiff* a65 26
6 b g Footstepsinthesand Your Village (IRE) (Be My Guest (USA))
388[11]

Victor's Bet (SPA) *Ralph J Smith* a67 77
7 b g Leadership Marmaria (SPA) (Limpid)
1415[5] (1899) 2872[9] 3064[9] *4008[8]* 4302[5] 4531[9] 5592[5] 5925[7] 7037[7]

Victory Angel (IRE) *Roger Varian* 82
2 b c Acclamation Golden Shadow (IRE) (Selkirk (USA))
3818[10] 7496[3] ◆ (7819)

Victory Bond *William Haggas* 99
3 b g Medicean Antebellum (FR) (Anabaa (USA))
(1646) 2190[6] 3543a[4]

Victory Laurel (IRE) *Ibrahim Al Malki* 88
6 b g Holy Roman Emperor(IRE) Special Cause (IRE) (Fasliyev (USA))
755a[9]

Victory Song (IRE) *Frau S Steinberg* a81 83
6 b h Dansili All Too Beautiful (IRE) (Sadler's Wells (USA))
6612a[8]

Viewpoint (IRE) *Michael Appleby* a91 85
7 b g Exceed And Excel(AUS) Lady's View (USA) (Distant View (USA))
860[4] 1001[4] 1089[9] (1722) 2214[3] *2917[11] 3304[5] 3525[6]* 4919[8]

Vif Monsieur (GER) *Mario Hofer* 110
6 bb h Doyen(IRE) Vive Madame (GER) (Big Shuffle (USA))
2075a[8] 3934a[8] 4253a[8] 5219a[8] 7564a[10] 7843a[9]

Vigee Le Brun (IRE) *Brian Meehan* 67
2 gr f Dark Angel(IRE) Wonderful Town (USA) (Bernstein (USA))
6543[3] 7118[8] 7547[10]

Viking Hoard (IRE) *Harry Dunlop* a58 81
2 b c Vale Of York(IRE) Tibouchina (IRE) (Daylami (IRE))
4270[9] *5549[5]* (6288) 7075[7]

Villa Royale *Michael Appleby* a88 94
7 b m Val Royal(FR) Villa Carlotta (Rainbow Quest (USA))
78[6] 385[5]

Villa Salaria (FR) *G Doleuze* a47 38
2 ch f Footstepsinthesand Viking's Cove (USA) (Miswaki (USA))
6937a[12]

Villebaudon (FR) *C Ferland* a95 92
3 b f Le Havre(IRE) Vidiyna (FR) (Danehill Dancer (IRE))
1309a[7] 7348a[13] *8563a[6]*

Vilman (IRE) *Simon West* a75 87
4 b g Mastercraftsman(IRE) Velandia (IRE) (Sadler's Wells (USA))
1598[5] 1852[4] 3117[P] (Dead)

Vimy Ridge *Alan Bailey* a95 79
4 ch g American Post Fairy Shoes (Kyllachy)
17[5] 213[5] 288[8] 529[9] 655[2] 966[8] 1084[7] 1427[3] 3414[11] 3638[5] 4066[6] 5039[3] *5679[9]* 5852[3] 6537[5] 6809[2] 7443[7] *7644[4] 8280[2] 8561[4]*

Vincent's Forever *John Gosden* a87 85
3 b g Pour Moi(IRE) Glen Rosie (IRE) (Mujtahid (USA))
1393[5] 4080[5] 4554[3] 5405[4] *(5768)*

Vincentti (IRE) *Ronald Harris* a60 82
6 b g Invincible Spirit(IRE) Bint Al Balad (IRE) (Ahonoora)
2028[21] 2290[5] 3771[2] 4291[13] 4990[2] (5103) 5673[3] 5774[2] 5955[6] (6255) 6363[7] 6766[5] 7221[5] 7591[6]

Vincenzo Coccotti (USA) *Ken Cunningham-Brown* a76 66
4 rg g Speightstown(USA) Ocean Colors (USA) (Orientate (USA))
2697[12] (4278) 4878[4] 6017[4] 7018[8] *(7255) (7887) 8206[5] 8456[5]*

Vin Chaud (FR) *F Rohaut* 113
4 b g Teofilo(IRE) Mulled Wine (FR) (Night Shift (USA))
375a[8] 810a[5]

Vinnievanbaileys *Chris Dwyer* a61 72
2 ch g Excelebration(IRE) Lady's Art (FR) (Verglas (IRE))
1422[5] *1719[4]* 2082[2] *2604[5]* 4315[7] 5015[4] *5806[8] 6045[4]* 6681[3] *6923[3] 7482[5]*

Vintage Dream (IRE) *Noel Wilson* a61 67
2 b g Dream Ahead(USA) Stella Del Mattino (USA) (Golden Gear (USA))
2617[6] 3222[4] 4678[4]

Vintage Folly *Hugo Palmer* a75
2 b f Makfi Katimont (IRE) (Montjeu (IRE))
(8131) ◆

Viola Park *Ronald Harris* a49 36
2 b g Aqlaam Violette (Observatory (USA))
3742[9] 4907 [11] 5283[4] 5770[P] 6060[8] *7881[8] (8072) 8276[2] 8568[11]*

Violet Mist (IRE) *Ben Haslam* a25 14
2 b f Clodovil(IRE) Vision Of Peace (IRE) (Invincible Spirit (IRE))
4254[5] 6515[9] *7381[10]*

Viren's Army (IRE) *Richard Hannon* a83 104
3 b c Twirling Candy(USA) Blue Angel (IRE) (Oratorio (IRE))
1567[3] (1994)

Virgil Earp *Ian Williams* a42 44
9 b g Fasliyev(USA) Karakorum (IRE) (Fairy King (USA))
1035[9] 1343[10] 1456[5] 1831[7]

Virginie (FR) *T Clout* a84 86
3 b f Silver Frost(IRE) Hallen (FR) (Midyan (USA))
7680a[3]

Virile (IRE) *Sylvester Kirk* a66 70
5 ch g Exceed And Excel(AUS) Winding (USA) (Irish River (FR))
2229a[7] 3993[4] 4292[5] 5007[3] *(5127)* 5282[4] *5605[3] 6137[9]* 6363[11] (6894) 7038[2] *7255[4] 8030[8] 8064[6] 8188[7] 8555[8]*

Virnon *Alan Swinbank* a78 73
5 b g Virtual Freedom Song (Singspiel (IRE))
43[7] (273) 447[6] 864[4]

Virtual Song *Barry Leavy* a36 36
3 b f Virtual Song Of The Desert (Desert Sun)
3135[7] 3499[6] 4518[5] 5957[6]

Virtuous Belle *Daniel Kubler* a25
3 b f Virtual Petong's Pet (Petong)
298[6]

Visage Blanc *Mick Channon* 80
3 b f Champs Elysees Russian Empress (IRE) (Trans Island)
1276[5] (2181) 2394[4] 2638[5] 3914[7] 4160[2] 5054[4] 5596[2] 5875[3]

Viscount Barfield *Andrew Balding* a78 98
3 b g Raven's Pass(USA) Madonna Dell'Orto (Montjeu (IRE))
952[3] (1257) 2477[6] *2818[4]* (3591) 3840[4] (4631) 5616[6] 6276[2]

Viserano (FR) *D Prod'Homme* a96 101
3 b c Rock Of Gibraltar(IRE) Visinada (IRE) (Sinndar (IRE))
1230a[2] 4439a[10]

Viserion *David Simcock* a72 83
4 ch g Tamayuz Frivolity (Pivotal)
64[5] 491[4] 616[8] 1640[5] *2374[3]* (3118) (3363) (3641) 3905[4] 6165[8]

Visionary (IRE) *Robert Cowell* a83 85
2 b c Dream Ahead(USA) Avodale (IRE) (Lawman (FR))
(1543) 2023[3] *8209[5]*

Vision Of Beauty (FR) *Keith Dalgleish* a59
3 b f Vision D'Etat(FR) Belle Dame (GER) (Pilsudski (IRE))
7848[3] 8212[3]

Visitant *David Thompson* a68 64
3 ch g Pivotal Invitee (Medicean)
(5843) 7743[4] ◆ *8011[4] 8286[3]*

Vista Steppe *David Simcock* a59 62
2 b f Dutch Art Rare Ransom (Oasis Dream)
4298[10] *5022[3]* 6078[6] 7440[8]

Vitello *M Halford* a93 89
3 b f Raven's Pass(USA) Vitoria (IRE) (Exceed And Excel (AUS))
4540a[5] *7523a[4] 7803a[5]*

Vivacissimo (IRE) *Ivan Furtado* a65
9 ch g Muhtathir Valley Orchard (FR) (Zilzal (USA))
(27) 157[4] 521[5] (Dead)

Vivardia (IRE) *Ben Haslam* a48 56
2 ch f Rip Van Winkle(IRE) Raggiante (IRE) (Rock Of Gibraltar (IRE))
6447[4] 7090[4] 7578[10] *8087[6]*

Vivat Rex (IRE) *John James Feane* a83 81
5 b g Fastnet Rock(AUS) Strawberry Roan (IRE) (Sadler's Wells (USA))
829a[5] 1018a[16]

Viva Verglas (IRE) *Daniel Mark Loughnane* a70 69
5 gr g Verglas(IRE) Yellow Trumpet (Petong)
520[3] 784[4] 1030[2] 1264[5] 3211[6] 3807[6] 4640[8] *5069[2] 5605[2]* ◆ 6451[16]

Vive Ma Fille (GER) *Mark Johnston* a72 105
4 b m Doyen(IRE) Vive Madame (GER) (Big Shuffle (USA))
2249[6] 2472[3] 4162[3] 4353[10] 5116[3] 5328[6] 5639[7] 5872[2] 6293[2] 7271[2]

Vivernus (USA) *M Al Mheiri* a79 79
3 br c Street Cry(IRE) Lady Pegasus (USA) (Fusaichi Pegasus (USA))
8576a[7]

Vivian Ward *John Gosden* a48
2 b f Kyllachy Al Joudha (FR) (Green Desert (USA))
8362[8]

Vivo Per Lei (IRE) *Dr Jon Scargill* a58 53
4 gr m Mastercraftsman(IRE) Sabancaya (Nayef (USA))
631[6] 781[5] 1547[3] *(2323) 3031[9]*

Vivre La Reve *James Unett* a64 48
4 b m Assertive Noor El Houdah (IRE) (Fayruz)
39[10] 201[12] 563[11] 1735[7] 2799[5] 3973[13] 5088[3] 5335[7] *8346[2] 8572[6]*

Vivre Pour Vivre (IRE) *Ed Dunlop* a88 90
3 b g Pour Moi(IRE) Miss Quality (USA) (Elusive Quality (USA))
(945) (1314) 2244[7] *6142[6]* 6781[12] 7408[11]

Vixenta (FR) *Eric Saint-Martin* a67 71
2 b f Milanais(FR) Red Vixen (IRE) (Agnes World (USA))
5005a[8] *5755a[15] 7294a[7]*

Vizcaya (IRE) *G Arizkorreta Elosegui* 67
4 b m Intikhab(USA) Thoroughly (IRE) (Woodman (USA))
5502a[16]

Vizier *David O'Meara* a77 79
3 b g Pivotal Rare Ransom (Oasis Dream)
1777[3] (6617) *8007[13]*

Vocal Activity (IRE) *J S Bolger* 61
2 br c Vocalised(USA) Rachida (IRE) (Hurricane Run (IRE))
7707a[11]

Vocal Experience (IRE) *J S Bolger* a48 69
3 b g Vocalised(USA) Cloigin Gorm (IRE) (Lil's Boy (USA))
7801a[12]

Vocalisation (IRE) *John Weymes* a39 46
2 ch f Poet's Voice Mi Rubina (IRE) (Rock Of Gibraltar (IRE))
4601[5] 4890[4] *5966[11]* 6678[12] 6807[8]

Vocalise *Charles Smith* a16 26
3 gr f Hellvelyn Church Hill Queen (Monsieur Bond (IRE))
935[9] 1249[4] 1670[13] 2118[7] 3140[5] 6567[9] 7445[9] *7894[7]*

Vocaliser (IRE) *Robin Dickin* a46 80
4 b g Vocalised(USA) Bring Back Matron (IRE) (Rock Of Gibraltar (IRE))
2819[11] 3570[6] 4057[9]

Vodkato (FR) *S Wattel* a104 96
8 b g Russian Blue(IRE) Perfidie (IRE) (Monsun (GER))
7524a[5] 8165a[10]

Vogueatti (USA) *Marco Botti* a73
3 b f Arch(USA) Not Here (USA) (Gone West (USA))
8048[3] (8491)

Voice Control (IRE) *Laura Mongan* a76 70
4 gr g Dalakhani(IRE) Scottish Stage (IRE) (Selkirk (USA))
2400[7] *(3302) 4012[4] 4941[4]* 5745[5] 7183[6] *8084[2]*

Voice From Above (IRE) *Patrick Holmes* a47 59
7 b m Strategic Prince Basin Street Blues (IRE) (Dolphin Street (FR))
950[8] 1674[4] ◆ 1881[7] 5718[7] 6619[3] *7105[8]* 7361[7] *8134[11]*

Voice Of A Leader (IRE) *Andi Brown* a72 101
5 b g Danehill Dancer(IRE) Thewaytosanjose (IRE) (Fasliyev (USA))
438[9] 621[9]

Voice Of Love (IRE) *Stefano Botti* 108
3 ch c Poet's Voice Snowfield (USA) (Tale Of The Cat (USA))
1686a[8] 3455a[2] (7400a) 7841a[7]

Voice Of The North (USA) *S Seemar* a65
2 b c Biondetti(USA) Rebooted (USA) (Mr Greeley (USA))
8574a[9]

Voice Of Truth (IRE) *Saeed bin Suroor* a76 79
2 ch f Dubawi(IRE) Express Way (ARG) (Ahmad (ARG))
4357[2] ◆ *6099[4] (7307)*

Voices Of Kings *William Muir* a50 37
3 b c Poet's Voice Khubza (Green Desert (USA))
15[5] 3535[12] *4021[9]* 4500[6]

Volare Alto *Miss V Haigh* a49 40
2 ch c Haafhd Bailadeira (Intikhab (USA))
3871a[12]

Volatile *James Tate* a87 72
2 b c Poet's Voice Neshla (Singspiel (IRE))
7468[6] *(7882)*

Volatile (SWE) *Jessica Long* a56 104
4 b g Strategic Prince Look That Chick (USA) (Souvenir Copy (USA))
3992a[9]

Volcancito (SWI) *A Wohler* 86
3 b c Myboycharlie(IRE) Vertana (IRE) (Sinndar (IRE))
1689a[8] 2711a[7]

Vol Dolois (FR) *A Bonin* a66 60
6 gr g Stormy River(FR) Vol Sauvage (FR) (Always Fair (USA))
8421a[11]

Volition (IRE) *Sir Michael Stoute* a83 80
3 gr f Dark Angel(IRE) Warshah (IRE) (Shamardal (USA))
2483[2] ◆ 3059[3] 4042[6] 5018[2] (6135) *6964[3] (7617) 7957[5]*

Volpe Fiona (GER) *M Munch* a52 43
5 ch m Tertullian(USA) Vera Longa (GER) (Lando (GER))
5452a[7]

Volstora (FR) *T Castanheira* a51 41
2 ch f Yellowstone(IRE) Volsora (FR) (Volochine (IRE))
5698a[14] *5988a[8]*

Volta (FR) *F-H Graffard* a69 113
3 b f Siyouni(FR) Persian Belle (Machiavellian (USA))
(2945a) 3452a[3] ◆ 4926a[2] 6949[7]

Volta Do Mar (IRE) *Richard Fahey* a60 62
2 b f Henrythenavigator(USA) Feeling Wonderful (IRE) (Fruits Of Love (USA))
1921[6] 5272[11] 5756[7] 6222[2] ◆ 6614[4] (7330) *7854[4]*

Volunteer Point (IRE) *Mick Channon* a103 100
4 b m Footstepsinthesand Piffling (Pivotal)
(214) ◆ *(774) (1065)* ◆ *1207[2]* 1858[4] *2034[8]* 3271[14] 6547[8] 6939[13] *7650[5] 7984[3] (8098) 8563a[9]*

Volzapone (FR) *Y Fertillet* a60 64
6 ch g Vespone(IRE) Liberte De Penser (FR) (Pennekamp (USA))
5281a[2]

Vona (IRE) *Richard Fahey* a10 89
2 b f Dark Angel(IRE) Trading Places (Dansili)
1293[9] 1976[4] (2219) 3270[15] 4111[4] 4669[4] 6388a[15] 7170a[5] 7655a[3]

Von Blucher (IRE) *John Gosden* a88 103
3 ch c Zoffany(IRE) Tropical Lady (IRE) (Sri Pekan (USA))
1603[4] (4149) 4624[7] 5403[2] 6109[3] ◆ 6788[3]

Vortex (NOR) *Rune Haugen* a68 93
7 br g Deceptor(USA) Norella (IRE) (Common Grounds)
284a[12] 375a[6] *627a[10]* 5950a[13]

Vote *James Eustace* 69
2 b f Aqlaam Bidding Time (Rock Of Gibraltar (IRE))
3106[4] ◆ 5511[3] 6950[11] 7440[6]

Voyageofdiscovery (USA) *T J O'Mara* a73 62
5 b g Henrythenavigator(USA) Look Out Lorie (USA) (Orientate (USA))
4811a[11]

Vrika Bay *Robert Eddery* a61 41
2 b f Mastercraftsman(IRE) Fascination Street (IRE) (Mujadil (USA))
4801[11] *8464[4]*

Vroom (IRE) *Gay Kelleway* a78 57
3 ch g Poet's Voice Shivaree (Rahy (USA))
924[10] 1060[7] 7386[11] *7644[10] 8067[7] (8236) 8345[3] 8473[3]*

Vue Du Ciel (FR) *J-C Rouget* a70 72
2 b f Canford Cliffs(IRE) Al Ribh (USA) (A.P. Indy (USA))
5698a[8] *7454a[3]*

Vuela *Luca Cumani* a76 61
3 ch f Duke Of Marmalade(IRE) Victoire Finale (Peintre Celebre (USA))
6520[3] ◆ *(7848)*

Vyjack (USA) *Philip D'Amato* a108 113
6 b g Into Mischief(USA) Life Happened (USA) (Stravinsky (USA))
7808a[7]

Waady (IRE) *John Gosden* 114
4 b g Approve(IRE) Anne Bonney (Jade Robbery (USA))
1862[3] 2475[3] ◆ 3244[5] 4151[17]

Wacaria (GER) *A Wohler* a71 92
3 b f Makfi Wurfspiel (GER) (Lomitas)
8117a[6] *8563a[13]*

Wadia (GER) *A Wohler* 54
2 b f Campanologist(USA) Walayta (GER) (Oasis Dream)
7563a[10]

Wadigor *Roger Varian* a81 100
3 b c Champs Elysees Haven's Wave (IRE) (Whipper (USA))
(6423) ◆ (7666)

Wadood (IRE) *Robert Cowell* a28 76
2 b c Kodiac Cakestown Lady (IRE) (Petorius (IRE))
4713[7] (7040)

Wafi Star (IRE) *Simon Crisford* a69 69
3 b g Showcasing Ophelia's Song (Halling (USA))
1800[2] 2749[7] 3824[8]

Waggle (IRE) *Michael Wigham* a41
3 b g Acclamation Week End (Selkirk (USA))
8320[11] 8570[5]

Wagoner *Tony Carroll* a26
2 b c Bushranger(IRE) Artistry (Night Shift (USA))
5244[6]

Wahaab (IRE) *Iain Jardine* a72 69
5 ch g Tamayuz Indian Ink (IRE) (Indian Ridge)
100[4] 442[7] 2635[4] 3004[3] 3486[2] 3743[11] 5236[3] 5309[4] (5706) 6616[4] 6834[4] 7092[2] 7254[3] 7585[2] *7797[11] (7851) 7959[9] 8287[4] 8389[4]*

Wahash (IRE) *Richard Hannon* a85 75
2 gr c Dark Angel(IRE) Delira (IRE) (Namid)
2203[5] 3569[2] 4533[2] *4974[3]* 5637[4] *6240[2] (6655)*

Wahiba (GER) *Marco Botti* a68
3 b f Poet's Voice Walayta (GER) (Oasis Dream)
8559[3]

Wai Key Star (GER) *A Wohler* 109
3 b c Soldier Hollow Wakytara (GER) (Danehill (USA))
(2711a) 4186a[4] (5696a) 7028a[5]

Waikika (FR) *Y Barberot* a88 110
5 b m Whipper(USA) Fruhling Feuer (FR) (Green Tune (USA))
3377a[6] 5948a[3] (6823a)

Waitaki (IRE) *D K Weld* a77 77
3 b f Invincible Spirit(IRE) Bluebell Park (USA) (Gulch (USA))
1939a[7]

Wait And Win (FR) *Mlle S Delaroche* 58
2 b f Vasywait(FR) Smoothie (FR) (Berkoutchi (FR))
1118a[13] 2280a[7]

Waiting For Richie *Tom Tate* 72
3 b g Rail Link Heart Of Hearts (Oasis Dream)
3434[3] ◆ 4372[5] 6052[5] 6795[5]

Wajeez (IRE) *John Gosden* 95
3 ch c Lope De Vega(IRE) Chanter (Lomitas)
4339[7]

Wakame (IRE) *Ed de Giles* a81 75
3 b g Kodiac Awwal Malika (USA) (Kingmambo (USA))
2770[2] 3478[4] 4088[2] (4369) 4789[6] (5627) *6138[4] (6656) (7204)*

Wakeas (USA) *Karl Thornton* a83 103
5 b g Cape Cross(IRE) Imiloa (USA) (Kingmambo (USA))
7708a[22]

Wake Forest (GER) *Chad C Brown* 114
6 b h Sir Percy Wurfspiel (GER) (Lomitas)
5431a[10] 6600a[2] 7405a[3]

Wakened (IRE) *Tom Dascombe* a53 58
2 b f Rip Van Winkle(IRE) Goldamour (IRE) (Fasliyev (USA))
2771[8] 3134[4] *4011[8] 5297[3]* 5770[8]

Waki Delight (FR) *A Sagot* a54 56
3 b f Sandwaki(USA) Green House (FR) (Houston (FR))
716a^{12}

Waldenon (FR) *S Jesus* a68 56
3 b g Denon(USA) Waldouma (FR) (Ajdayt (USA))
7265a^{7}

Waldgeist *A Fabre* 113
2 ch c Galileo(IRE) Waldlerche (Monsun (GER))
7169a^{3} (7722a) ◆

Walec *P Sogorb* a96 102
4 b g Shamardal(USA) Sail (IRE) (Sadler's Wells (USA))
5949a^{2} 7030a^{8}

Walking In Rhythm (IRE) *Richard Hannon* 62
3 b f Lord Shanakill(USA) So Sweet (IRE) (Cape Cross (IRE))
3572^{6} 4017^{5} 4361^{6} 4794^{11} 5330^{5} 6187^{6} (6631)

Walking Primrose (FR) *Kevin Ryan* 55
3 ch f Raven's Pass(USA) Celebre Fragance (FR) (Peintre Celebre (USA))
2298^{5}

Walk Like A Giant *Julia Brooke* a75 78
5 b g Sir Percy Temple Of Thebes (IRE) (Bahri (USA))
33^{8} 3294^{7} 3849^{8}

Wallangarra *Jeremy Gask* a72 69
3 b g Teofilo(IRE) Whos Mindin Who (IRE) (Danehill Dancer (IRE))
2048^{7} 2614^{6} 3577^{5} 4301^{2} 4794^{6} 5308^{3} 5824^{4} 6593^{2}

Wall Of Fire (IRE) *Hugo Palmer* a87 110
3 b c Canford Cliffs(IRE) Bright Sapphire (IRE) (Galileo (IRE))
2331^{7} 3299^{13} (3887) 4863^{10} (5653) (6283) ◆

Wall Of Light *Tom Dascombe* a57 72
3 b f Zamindar(USA) Veiled Beauty (USA) (Royal Academy (USA))
2653^{3} 3107^{5} 5602^{4}

Wally's Wisdom *Lee Carter* a67 57
4 b g Dutch Art Faldal (Falbrav (IRE))
3402^{11} 3724^{7}

Walpole (IRE) *Hugo Palmer* a79 90
4 b g Rock Of Gibraltar(IRE) Serena's Storm (IRE) (Statue Of Liberty (USA))
(567) (1934) 2487^{3} (5275) ◆ 6118^{10}

Walsingham Grange (USA) *Pam Sly* 79
3 b g Paddy O'Prado(USA) Mambo Queen (USA) (Kingmambo (USA))
(1276) 1602^{6} 2224^{7} 7060^{9}

Walter Raleigh (IRE) *John Ryan* a83 28
2 b c Nathaniel(IRE) Regrette Rien (USA) (Unbridled's Song (USA))
1889^{9} (4975)

Walter White (IRE) *Philip Hobbs* a67 67
6 b g Dark Angel(IRE) Fun Time (Fraam)
4912^{5} 5597^{3} (Dead)

Waltz Darling (IRE) *Keith Reveley* a50 54
8 b g Iffraaj Aljafliyah (Halling (USA))
2558^{9} 2745^{8} 3191^{7} 4645^{6} 8091^{3} 8309^{6}

Walun (GER) *P Schiergen* 92
3 b f Areion(GER) Winterthur (GER) (Alkalde (GER))
2949a^{10} 3916a^{7}

Walzertakt (GER) *Jean-Pierre Carvalho* 114
7 b h Montjeu(IRE) Walzerkoenigin (USA) (Kingmambo (USA))
1688a^{5} 2286a^{5} 2725a^{4} 4333a^{5} 5692a^{5} 6396a^{5}

Wanderina (IRE) *F Head* a75 97
3 b f Manduro(GER) Wandering Spirit (GER) (Dashing Blade)
6070a^{3} 7723a^{11}

Waneen (IRE) *Joseph Tuite* a80 63
3 b g Approve(IRE) Million All Day (IRE) (Daylami (IRE))
1487^{3} 2185^{5} 2561^{2} 2776^{7} 5626^{5} 5954^{10} 6509^{2} 7069^{2} (7362) (7533) 8099^{6} 8280^{6}

Waneta (TUR) *Z Firat* 90
2 b f Mountain Cat(USA) Blushing Doe (USA) (Running Stag (USA))
(6180a)

Wannabe Friends *Luca Cumani* 79
3 ch g Dubawi(IRE) Wannabe Posh (IRE) (Grand Lodge (USA))
2175^{8} 2861^{5}

Want The Fairytale *Clive Cox* a64 57
3 b f Mount Nelson Tattercoats (FR) (Whywhywhy (USA))
4056^{8} 4367^{9} 5550^{5} (6143) 6593^{6}

Wapping (USA) *David Lanigan* a58 88
3 b g Smart Strike(CAN) Exciting Times (FR) (Jeune Homme (USA))
5405^{3} 6032^{2} ◆

Waqaas *Charles Hills* 94
2 b c Showcasing Red Mischief (IRE) (Red Clubs (IRE))
2203^{6} 2649^{2} (4040) ◆ 4798^{4}

Waqt (IRE) *Marcus Tregoning* 74
2 b g Acclamation Needles And Pins (IRE) (Fasliyev (USA))
2874^{2}

War At Sea (IRE) *David Simcock* a67
2 ch c Mastercraftsman(IRE) Swirling (IRE) (Galileo (IRE))
7908^{8}

Warba (IRE) *Mohamed Moubarak* a59 34
2 ch f Intense Focus(USA) Have A Heart (IRE) (Daggers Drawn (USA))
3555^{10} 8151^{5} 8425^{2}

War Chief *Alan King* a71 80
2 ch c Aqlaam My Colleen (USA) (Discreet Cat (USA))
6590^{3} (7208) ◆

Warcraft (FR) *Mlle V Dissaux*
2 b c Dobby Road(FR) Sweet Fortune (FR) (Slickly (FR))
7291a^{8}

War Decree (USA) *A P O'Brien* 113
2 b c War Front(USA) Royal Decree (USA) (Street Cry (IRE))
4150^{2} (4732)

Warden Bond *William Stone* a63 45
8 ch g Monsieur Bond(IRE) Warden Rose (Compton Place)
107^{6} 346^{4}

War Department (IRE) *Keith Dalgleish* a88 71
3 b g Frozen Power(IRE) On My Kness (FR) (Fasliyev (USA))
315^{4} 612^{5} 2650^{8} 3079^{5} 4684^{4} 5223^{5} (5845) 5968^{3} 6810^{8} 7433^{9} 7957^{6} 8092^{2} 8385^{3}

Warfare *Tim Fitzgerald* a83 83
7 b g Soviet Star(USA) Fluffy (Efisio)
121^{3} 267^{7} 656^{7} 1923^{5} 2163^{15} 4113^{6} 4930^{2} 5883^{8}

War Flag (USA) *J-C Rouget* a102 107
3 b f War Front(USA) Black Speck (USA) (Arch (USA))
2115a^{2} (4184a)

War Girl (USA) *David Barron* a44 42
4 bb m War Front(USA) Valarchos Destiny (USA) (Monarchos (USA))
4425^{7} 4772^{10}

War Glory (IRE) *Richard Hannon* a91 94
3 b c Canford Cliffs(IRE) Attracted To You (IRE) (Hurricane Run (IRE))
(145) (4199) 4631^{2} 6232^{3} 6710^{9}

Warleggan (FR) *Linda Perratt* a47 16
2 gr g Rajsaman(FR) Nostalchia (FR) (Genereux Genie)
1454^{6} 3986^{7} 4526^{2} 6343^{11} 6534^{11}

Warm Love *David O'Meara* 72
2 ch f Dutch Art Irish Song (FR) (Singspiel (IRE))
5854^{2} 6640^{2}

Warm Order *Tony Carroll* a60 54
5 b m Assertive Even Hotter (Desert Style (IRE))
292^{8} 418^{7} 589^{7} 669^{2} 837^{8}

Warm Words *Ralph Beckett* a70 64
2 b f Poet's Voice Limber Up (IRE) (Dansili)
6087^{5} 7210^{5} 7882^{5} 8235^{2}

Warofindependence (USA) *Alan Bailey* a80 63
4 bb g War Front(USA) My Dear Annie (USA) (Smart Strike (CAN))
1287^{4} 2213^{9} 3030^{2} 3617^{5} 4476^{7} 4940^{8}

War Of Succession *Andrew Balding* a84 79
2 b c Casamento(IRE) Rohlindi (Red Ransom (USA))
2203^{9} 5108^{2} 6122^{2}

Warp Factor (IRE) *John Patrick Shanahan* 88
3 b c The Carbon Unit(USA) Storminateacup (IRE) (Galileo (IRE))
1883^{2} 2197^{3} 3550^{2} 4339^{5} 5579^{3} (6014) 6286^{7} 7060^{7}

Warranted *Michael Attwater* a56
3 b c Authorized(IRE) Steppin Out (First Trump)
6415^{9} 7052^{5}

Warrant Officer *Sheena West* a43 40
6 gr g Misu Bond(IRE) Kilmovee (Inchinor)
1807^{6}

War Reporter (FR) *F Rossi* 80
3 gr c Kendargent(FR) Freeze Frame (FR) (In The Wings)
2948a^{13}

Warrigal (IRE) *Leo Braem* a57 46
6 ch g Mount Nelson Waldblume (GER) (Halling (USA))
2806a^{9}

Warring States (JPN) *A Wohler* 91
2 ch c Victoire Pisa(JPN) Ciliege (JPN) (Sakura Bakushin O (JPN))
7722a^{10}

Warrior Chant (USA) *Norman Cassidy* a24
10 b g War Chant(USA) Toocloseto Comfort (USA) (Mt. Livermore (USA))
7800a^{13}

Warrior Prince *Ed Dunlop* 79
3 ch g Sakhee(USA) Queen Of Iceni (Erhaab (USA))
1714^{5} 2248^{6} 3264^{2} 4027^{4}

Warrior's Spirit (IRE) *Richard Hannon* 80
2 b c Requinto(IRE) Sandbox Two (IRE) (Foxhound (USA))
4552^{4} (6577)

War Room (IRE) *S M Duffy* a71 45
7 b g Holy Roman Emperor(IRE) Shot At Love (IRE) (Last Tycoon)
6462a^{2}

War Singer (USA) *Johnny Farrelly* a71 69
9 b g War Chant(USA) Sister Marilyn (USA) (Saint Ballado (CAN))
1620^{11} 8239^{10}

War Story (IRE) *Luca Cumani* a88 93
3 gr c Myboycharlie(IRE) America Nova (FR) (Verglas (IRE))
(1701) 2479^{6} 3155^{3} 4080^{2} 4776^{9} 5601^{4}

War Story (USA) *Mario Serey Jr* a103
4 ch g Northern Afleet(USA) Belle Watling (USA) (Pulpit (USA))
7838a^{8}

War Whisper (IRE) *Richard Hannon* a71 83
3 b c Royal Applause Featherweight (IRE) (Fantastic Light (USA))
6263^{10} 6788^{9} 6916^{6} 7781^{8}

Wasatch Range *John Gosden* 75
2 b c High Chaparral(IRE) Pearl City (IRE) (Zamindar (USA))
7770^{3}

Waseefa *John Butler* 67
3 b f Showcasing Tobaranama (IRE) (Sadler's Wells (USA))
2980^{3} 3603^{4} 4365^{5}

Waseem Faris (IRE) *Joseph Tuite* a95 95
7 b g Exceed And Excel(AUS) Kissing Time (Lugana Beach)
338^{5} 966^{6} 1427^{4} 1857^{3} 2898^{4} 3573^{8} 5669^{2} 5961^{3} 6779^{8} 6944^{11} 7124^{10}

Washington Blue *Clive Cox* a72 72
2 b f Rip Van Winkle(IRE) Powder Blue (Daylami (IRE))
4907^{4} 5772^{6} 6250^{2} ◆ 7494^{7} 7891^{5} 8159^{4} (8466)

Washington DC (IRE) *A P O'Brien* a110 115
3 b c Zoffany(IRE) How's She Cuttin' (IRE) (Shinko Forest (IRE))
1773^{7} (2272a) 2719a^{2} 3338^{3} 4151^{5} 4824^{2} ◆ 5614^{17} 6384a^{2} 6990a^{2} 7833a^{7}

Washington Winkle *Donald McCain* 27
4 b g Rip Van Winkle(IRE) Bluebelle Dancer (IRE) (Danehill Dancer (IRE))
2015^{8}

Wasir (GER) *A Wohler* 105
4 b h Rail Link Wellola (IRE) (Lomitas)
811a^{9} (2286a) 3298^{11} 5428a^{3} 6175a^{8}

Wassail *Ed de Giles* a41 34
3 b f Shamardal(USA) Gower Song (Singspiel (IRE))
1704^{8} 2183^{13} 2929^{10} 4505^{4} ◆ 5263^{8} 5625^{8} 7767^{8}

Wasseem (IRE) *Simon Crisford* a66 67
3 ch g Approve(IRE) Vintage Escape (IRE) (Cyrano De Bergerac)
1806^{3} 2790^{6} 3264^{4} 3982^{10} 7035^{3} 7514^{4} 8382^{10}

Watchable *David O'Meara* a109 115
6 ch g Pivotal Irresistible (Cadeaux Genereux)
2031^{3} 2546^{2} 3195^{3} 3655^{3} 4393^{12} 5943a^{4} 6558^{13} 6942^{18}

Waterclock (IRE) *Micky Hammond* a68 83
7 ch g Notnowcato Waterfall One (Nashwan (USA))
2194^{7} 2971^{2} 3437^{10} 6163^{9} 7158^{9}

Water For Life *Martin Smith* a23 28
5 ch m Mount Nelson Echo River (USA) (Irish River (FR))
1035^{11}

Waterloo Bridge (IRE) *A P O'Brien* a102 105
3 b c Zoffany(IRE) Miss Childrey (IRE) (Dr Fong (USA))
1423^{2} 2272a^{7} 2719a^{6} 3338^{7}

Waterloo Dock *James Unett* a62 8
11 b g Hunting Lion(IRE) Scenic Air (Hadeer)
35^{9} 216^{8} 388^{12}

Watershed (USA) *Kiaran McLaughlin* a104
4 b h Bernardini(USA) Thousand Islands (Dubai Millennium)
454a^{3} 844a^{6}

Watersmeet *Mark Johnston* a107 103
5 gr g Dansili Under The Rainbow (Fantastic Light (USA))
485^{5} (829a) 1069^{9} 1885^{8} 2482^{2} 3889^{15} 4731^{11} 5411^{7} (6142) ◆ 6573^{17} 7814^{2} (8210)

Water Sprite (IRE) *Gordon Elliott* a62 81
5 b m Papal Bull Wish Upon A Star (IRE) (Russian Revival (USA))
7195a^{11}

Wattaboutsteve *Ralph J Smith* a52 21
5 b g Araafa(IRE) Angel Kate (IRE) (Invincible Spirit (IRE))
136^{5} 1709^{2} 3320^{2} 3674^{8} 4472^{7} 5194^{3} 5509^{3} 5636^{4}

Wavelet *David Simcock* a77 78
4 b m Archipenko(USA) Weather Report (Rainbow Quest (USA))
(127) 420^{2} 2433^{8} (2860) 3076^{4}

Wavell Avenue (CAN) *Chad C Brown* a120
5 bb m Harlington(USA) Lucas Street (CAN) (Silver Deputy (CAN))
7836a^{2}

Wave Power (FR) *D Windrif* a57 70
4 b g Motivator Wave Goodbye (FR) (Linamix (FR))
5700a^{8}

Wave Reviews *William Haggas* a85 89
3 b c Fastnet Rock(AUS) Critical Acclaim (Peintre Celebre (USA))
1714^{2} 2619^{2} (3535) 4131^{8} 5074^{3} 6581^{7}

Waves (IRE) *Eve Johnson Houghton* a43 63
2 b f Born To Sea(IRE) Johannesburg Cat (USA) (Johannesburg (USA))
1736^{8} 2997^{5} 4022^{7} 5165^{2} 6033^{6} 6670^{9}

Wayside Flower *G M Lyons* 90
2 b f Shamardal(USA) Umseyat (USA) (Arch (USA))
2718a^{4}

Wayside Magic *Michael Dods* 55
3 b g Thewayyouare(USA) Poppy's Rose (Diktat)
1698^{4} 2615^{8} 3482^{9} 4275^{5} 4449^{2} 5576^{10} 6646^{2} 7096^{5}

Wayward Hoof *K R Burke* 86
3 b g Equiano(FR) Mystical Spirit (IRE) (Xaar)
1977^{9} (2650) 2972^{5} 3689^{2}

Weald Of Kent (USA) *Michael Appleby* a82
4 b g Successful Appeal(USA) Apple Of Kent (USA) (Kris S (USA))
(445) (506) 800^{2} 864^{3} 2549^{12} 3659^{12} 3991^{10} 4476^{8} 7847^{11}

Wealth Tax *Ed Dunlop* a73
3 gr g Canford Cliffs(IRE) Firoza (FR) (King's Best (USA))
6511^{2} 7311^{2} 7780^{2}

Weapon Of Choice (IRE) *Dianne Sayer* a55 72
8 b g Iffraaj Tullawadgeen (IRE) (Sinndar (IRE))
864^{7} 1633^{5} 2526^{5} 4038^{2}

Weardiditallgorong *Des Donovan* a61 65
4 b m Fast Company(IRE) Little Oz (IRE) (Red Ransom (USA))
84^{6} 2144^{2} 2781^{2} 3142^{3} 4201^{6} 7515^{12}

We Are (IRE) *F Head* 114
5 b m Dansili In Clover (Inchinor)
1822a^{10}

We Are Ninety (IRE) *Hugo Palmer* a85 104
3 b f Thewayyouare(USA) Brigids Cross (IRE) (Sadler's Wells (USA))
(1703) ◆ 1804^{3} (2245) 3297^{6} 4416a^{9} 6488^{6}

Wearethepeople *William Muir* a63 63
2 b c Poet's Voice Electric Feel (Firebreak)
3813^{11} 5125^{3} 5569^{3} 6420^{3} 6652^{2} 7143^{5} (Dead)

Weather Front (USA) *Karen McLintock* a79 77
3 ch g Stormy Atlantic(USA) Kiswahili (Selkirk (USA))
2212^{4} (3367) 3745^{5} 4199^{2} 6344^{5} 7141^{3} 7436^{7} 7857^{7} 8092^{12}

Weather Watch (IRE) *Mrs John Harrington* 88
6 b g Hurricane Run(IRE) Caravan Of Dreams (IRE) (Anabaa (USA))
3680a^{3} 4721a^{14}

Website *Robert Cowell* a64 70
4 b g Oasis Dream Homepage (Dansili)
2667^{8} 4238^{4} 5238^{3}

Wedding Dress *David Brown* a75 77
2 b f Tamayuz Dream Day (Oasis Dream)
(1793) ◆ 2664^{2} 3186^{5} 5583^{17} 6563^{8}

Wedgewood Estates *Tony Carroll* a59 63
5 ch m Assertive Heaven (Reel Buddy (USA))
237^{4} 790^{2} 1005^{3} 1795^{2} (3040) 3984^{4} 5194^{5} 6853^{5}

Wedgewood Wonder *Tony Carroll* 20
2 b f Medicean Katya Kabanova (Sadler's Wells (USA))
7216^{10}

Wediddodontwe *Richard Guest* 68
2 b g Equiano(FR) Vodka Shot (USA) (Holy Bull (USA))
(6447)

Weekender *John Gosden* 73
2 b c Frankel Very Good News (USA) (Empire Maker (USA))
7317^{4}

Weekend Offender (FR) *Kevin Ryan* 94
3 ch g Lope De Vega(IRE) Huroof (IRE) (Pivotal)
1883^{4} (2657) ◆ 2907^{3} (4769) 5616^{4} 6778^{3} (7153) ◆

Weetles *Clive Cox* 97
4 b m High Chaparral(IRE) Millestan (IRE) (Invincible Spirit (IRE))
(1716) 2797^{3} 4696a^{5} 5894^{8} 7087a^{8}

Wefait (IRE) *Richard Hannon* a65 70
2 br c Harbour Watch(IRE) Night Club (Mozart (IRE))
3108^{3} 7975^{5}

We Have A Dream *Heather Dalton* a48 50
11 bb g Oasis Dream Final Shot (Dalsaan)
341^{8}

Weld Al Emarat *Simon Crisford* a82 95
4 b g Dubawi(IRE) Spirit Of Dubai (IRE) (Cape Cross (IRE))
3061^{2} 4104^{7}

Weld Al Khawaneej (IRE) *Kevin Ryan* a62 66
3 ch g Fast Company(IRE) Law Review (IRE) (Case Law)
63^{6} 376^{9} 565^{3} 2576^{4} 3020^{2} ◆ 3285^{4} 3877^{6} 3982^{4} 4454^{3} 4730^{9} 4844^{5} 5478^{5}

Weld Arab (IRE) *Michael Blake* a73 60
5 b g Shamardal(USA) Itqaan (USA) (Danzig (USA))
173^{3} 435^{2} (606) 2605^{6}

Welease Bwian (IRE) *Stuart Williams* a82 73
7 b g Kheleyf(USA) Urbanize (USA) (Chester House (USA))
68^{3} (162) 439^{4} 703^{4} (903) (1433) 1964^{2} 2469^{6} 2787^{2} 4198^{5} 4475^{3} 5189^{8} 5679^{10} 6410^{3} 7303^{4} 8176^{14}

Welford *Mark Johnston* a87 94
3 b c Dubawi(IRE) Avongrove (Tiger Hill (IRE))
3534^{10} 4108^{6} 4407^{9} 4827^{13} 5738^{3} 6474^{3} 6767^{6}

Wellabled (USA) *Larry Rivelli* a108 99
2 b c Shackleford(USA) Expressive Diva (USA) (In Excess I (IRE))
7807a^{10}

Well Done (IRE) *Simon Crisford* a84 77
2 b g Lawman(FR) Quixotic (Pivotal)
4580^{4} (6141) 6734^{13}

Welliesinthewater (IRE) *Derek Shaw* a85 86
6 b g Footstepsinthesand Shadow Ash (IRE) (Ashkalani (IRE))
82^{2} 169^{2} (449) 532^{7} (1702) 2378^{2} (2862) 3895^{5} 4976^{5} 6126^{6} 7308^{6} 8052^{12} 8239^{9}

Well Owd Mon *Sarah Hollinshead* a62 44
6 b g Vitus Farina (IRE) (Golan (IRE))
255^{8} 819^{2} 1170^{6} 2110^{10} 2781^{7}

Wells (AUS) *Kathryn Durden* 85
8 b g Galileo(IRE) Embraceable You (NZ) (Rodrigo De Triano (USA))
7481a^{8}

We'll Shake Hands (FR) *K R Burke* a30 79
5 b g Excellent Art Amou Daria (FR) (Kendor (FR))
1633^{15} 2051^{9} 2526^{7} 3804^{6} (4493) (4740) 5392^{9} 5929^{2}

Well Spoken (GER) *Markus Klug* 103
2 b f Soldier Hollow Well American (USA) (Bertrando (USA))
(7563a)

Weloof (FR) *Ed Dunlop* 20
2 b c Redoute's Choice(AUS) Peinted Song (USA) (Unbridled's Song (USA))
7501^{14}

Welsh Gem *Clive Cox* a75 65
4 b m Dylan Thomas(IRE) Gemini Joan (Montjeu (IRE))
1898^{6} 2636^{5} 4055^{10} 4777^{8}

Welsh Inlet (IRE) *John Bridger* a64 73
8 br m Kheleyf(USA) Ervedya (IRE) (Doyoun)
1915^{5} 2187^{9} 3101^{7} 3648^{7} 4302^{8} 5503^{9} 7070^{9} 7426^{4} 7736^{7}

Welsh Rebel *Nikki Evans* a55 46
4 ch g Cockney Rebel(IRE) Lasting Image (Zilzal (USA))
3747^{6} 4483^{8} 6422^{5}

Welsh Rose *Ed de Giles* a76 44
3 b f Exceed And Excel(AUS) Nantyglo (Mark Of Esteem (IRE))
4398^{11} 5078^{3} 5551^{5} 6960^{6}

Weltmacht *Markus Klug* 104
5 b m Mount Nelson Wild Side (GER) (Sternkoenig (IRE))
1376a^{5} 1822a^{12} (6151a) 6610a^{10}

Weltmeister (GER) *P Schiergen* 84
3 b c Areion(GER) Wonderful World (GER) (Dashing Blade)
1908a^{8}

Wensara Dream *Andrew Balding* a39 54
3 b f Lilbourne Lad(IRE) Emerald Fire (Pivotal)
4660^{4} 5238^{4} 5748^{5} 6290^{8} 7463^{12} 8079^{10}

Wentwell Yesterday (IRE) *Jamie Osborne* a72 58
2 b c Kodiac Roisin's Star (IRE) (Accordion)
2180^{7} 3742^{5} 3971^{9} 4386^{5} 4712^{8} 5675^{2} 6412^{2} ◆ 6670^{2} 6963^{10} 7690^{2} 7777^{2} (7981) 8071^{3} 8174^{4}

Wentworth Falls *Geoffrey Harker* a99 93
4 gr g Dansili Strawberry Morn (CAN) (Travelling Victor (CAN))
7315[11] (7772) ◆

Wernotfamusanymore (IRE) *Kevin Ryan* 74
3 b g Oasis Dream Dhanyata (IRE) (Danetime (IRE))
4845[2] 5582[11]

Werther (NZ) *John Moore* 123
4 b g Tavistock(NZ) Bagalollies (AUS) (Zabeel (NZ))
(1690a)

Westbourne Grove (USA) *John Butler* a61 48
3 b g Munnings(USA) Catch Me Later (USA) (Posse (USA))
1753[4] 2750[5] 3822[4] 4278[9] 5041[6] 5338[8] (6865) 6902[6] 7276[4]

West Coast Flyer *David Simcock* a94 76
3 b c Cape Cross(IRE) La Felicita (Shareef Dancer (USA))
361[5] (687) 2859[3] (3607) 4346[4] (5026) (6050) 7123[12]

West Drive (IRE) *Roger Varian* 85
3 ch g Sea The Stars(IRE) Fair Sailing (IRE) (Docksider (USA))
2224[3] 2909[6] 3508[3] (6192) 6581[6]

Westerly *Luke Dace* a66 62
5 b m Rail Link Humility (Polar Falcon (USA))
882[4] 3528[11] 4052[4] 4950[9]

Western Duke (IRE) *Ralph Beckett* 87
2 b c High Chaparral(IRE) Witch Of Fife (USA) (Lear Fan (USA))
3859[5] (4856) 5519[2] ◆

Western Hymn *John Gosden* a112 118
5 b g High Chaparral(IRE) Blue Rhapsody (Cape Cross (IRE))
1604[2] 1973[2] 2626[2] 3272[3] 3912[6] 4626[6] 6940[4] 7545[5] (7766)

Western Presence *Richard Fahey* a65 62
2 ch c Sleeping Indian Mawjoodah (Cadeaux Genereux)
4140[4] 4725[8] 5289[5] 6007[7] 6641[6] 7143[2] 7749[4] 7981[7]

Western Prince *Michael Appleby* a83 74
3 b g Cape Cross(IRE) Vigee Le Brun (USA) (Pulpit (USA))
1421[7] 1930[12] 2248[7] 3042[9] 3355[6] 3824[7] (6812) ◆ (8476) ◆

Western Way (IRE) *Don Cantillon* 75
7 b g Westerner Faucon (Polar Falcon (USA))
3264[8] 3577[2] ◆ 4235[9] 4841[10] 5482[17] 6490[7]

Westit *C Laffon-Parias* 78
2 gr f Tapit(USA) West Ocean (USA) (Elusive Quality (USA))
6068a[9]

West Leake (IRE) *Paul Burgoyne* a60 52
10 b g Acclamation Kilshanny (Groom Dancer (USA))
124[8] 403[6] 607[5] 709[3] 877[2] 1064[8] 1416[3] 1834[5] 3030[10] 7427[8]

Westward Ho (IRE) *James Bethell* a81 50
3 b g Fastnet Rock(AUS) Thought Is Free (Cadeaux Genereux)
4895[5] 6104[3] ◆ (7661) 8092[10]

Westwood Hoe *Tony Coyle* a98 77
5 b g Oasis Dream Disco Volante (Sadler's Wells (USA))
50[5] 221[7] 599[4] 960[8] 6320[9] 7095[7] 7593[8] 8385[13]

Wexford Opera (IRE) *J S Bolger* a78 87
6 bb g New Approach(IRE) Sister Angelina (USA) (Saint Ballado (CAN))
1018a[5]

Weybridge Light *David Thompson* a48 58
11 b g Fantastic Light(USA) Nuryana (Nureyev (USA))
1156[5]

Whacking Bullock (IRE) *Daniel Mark Loughnane* a55
3 b g Lovelace Carracove (IRE) (Key Of Luck (USA))
1000[6] 1653[8] 2109[7] 7992[13]

Whaleweigh Station *J R Jenkins* a71 49
5 b g Zamindar(USA) Looby Loo (Kyllachy)
124[4] 319[7] 658[3] 877[9] 1262[10] 2087[7] 3320[3] 3648[5] 4278[13] 4388[5] 4876[4] 6677[9] 7516[9] 7888[5] 8125[11] 8492[9]

Wharane (FR) *Ian Williams* a60 60
3 br g Diktat Nova Lady (USA) (Mr Greeley (USA))
1389[5] 1740[4] 1918[3] 4212[6]

What About Carlo (FR) *Eve Johnson Houghton* a98 106
5 b g Creachadoir(IRE) Boccatenera (GER) (Artan (IRE))
1569[3] 1972[8] 2866[3] 3383[13] 3910[8] 4165[10] 5647[10] 5962[3] 6573[4] (7546)

What A Boy *Ralph Beckett* a64 63
2 b g Paco Boy(IRE) Kurtanella (Pastoral Pursuits)
2747[5] 4016[4] 4938[5]

What A Dandy (IRE) *Jim Boyle* a67 56
5 b g Dandy Man(IRE) Ibtihal (IRE) (Hamas (IRE))
173[2] 316[7] 2996[3] 3651[3] 4527[4] 6662[6]

Whatalove *Martin Keighley* 29
2 ch f Arcano(IRE) Secret Happiness (Cape Cross (IRE))
3718[7] 4457[10] 5072[5]

What A Party (IRE) *Gay Kelleway* a61 61
4 ch m Windsor Knot(IRE) Tarziyma (IRE) (Kalanisi (IRE))
218[2] 631[3] 815[3] 1174[2] 1807[4] 2292[2] 2792[2] 3076[3] 3825[4] 4739[3]

What A Scorcher *Nikki Evans* 73
5 b m Authorized(IRE) Street Fire (IRE) (Street Cry (IRE))
2463[2] 3094[4] 5574 [3]

What A Surprise (IRE) *Ibrahim Al Malki* 50
2 b g Rip Van Winkle(IRE) Superstitious (USA) (Kingmambo (USA))
6750[8] 8564a[7]

What A View (USA) *Kenneth D Black* 116
5 bb g Vronsky(USA) Oceans N Mountains (USA) (Manila (USA))
7172a[8] 7837a[14]

What Could She Be (IRE) *Michael Dods* a75 71
4 b m Dark Angel(IRE) Halliwell House (Selkirk (USA))
1[5] 273[4]

Whatelseaboutyou (IRE) *Richard Fahey* a60 60
2 b f Canford Cliffs(IRE) Brigids Cross (IRE) (Sadler's Wells (USA))
8208[7] 8384[8]

What Say You (IRE) *K R Burke* a71 94
4 b m Galileo(IRE) Alta Anna (FR) (Anabaa (USA))
1088[7] 1757[3] 3055[4] 4026[8]

What's In A Kiss (IRE) *J-C Rouget* 93
2 ch f Fast Company(IRE) Sir Cecil's Girl (IRE) (Thunder Gulch (USA))
4902a[4]

Whatsthemessage (IRE) *Keith Dalgleish* a47 78
2 b f Bushranger(IRE) Fatwa (IRE) (Lahib (USA))
(5221) ◆ 6554[3] 7042[4]

Whats The Plot (IRE) *A L T Moore* a59 68
4 b g Alfred Nobel(IRE) Hazarama (IRE) (Kahyasi)
4417a[5] 5620a[7]

What's The Story *Keith Dalgleish* 83
2 b c Harbour Watch(IRE) Spring Fashion (IRE) (Galileo (IRE))
3283[2] 3548[2] 4336[2]

What Usain *Michael Appleby* a67 43
4 b g Misu Bond(IRE) Bond Shakira (Daggers Drawn (USA))
3476[2] 4715[11] 8587[4]

Wheneverwecan (IRE) *Mark Johnston* 73
2 ch f Power Jallaissine (IRE) (College Chapel)
1868[2] (2090) 2424[F] (Dead)

Where Next *Henry Candy* 70
3 b g Compton Place Neqaawi (Alhaarth (IRE))
2698[7] 2998[10] 4401[5] 5284[9] 6036[3] 6441[3] 7036[4] 7290[4]

Where's Stewart *Nigel Tinkler* 30
2 ch g Firebreak Sukuma (IRE) (Highest Honor (FR))
5271[11] 5536[5] 5884[16] 6678[15]

Where's Tiger *Lucinda Russell* 73
5 b g Tiger Hill(IRE) Where's Broughton (Cadeaux Genereux)
2575[8]

Whigwham *Richard Fahey* a57 67
2 ch f Sleeping Indian Normandy Maid (American Post)
3772[5] 4405[3] ◆ 4804[4] ◆ 6139[7] 6471[5]

Whinging Willie (IRE) *Gary Moore* a86 86
7 b g Cape Cross(IRE) Pacific Grove (Persian Bold)
(256) 382[2] 1568[2] 2897[13] 3861[7] 5053[6] 5406[3] 5963[4] 6267[6] (6892)

Whip Nae Nae (IRE) *Richard Hannon* a80 80
2 ch c Dragon Pulse(IRE) Love In May (IRE) (City On A Hill (USA))
4594[5] 5073[2] 5600[3] 6314[2] 6705[2] (7511)

Whippa D'Or (FR) *S Wattel* a78 94
4 bl m Whipper(USA) Fedora (FR) (Kendor (FR))
8117a[5] 8563a[12]

Whipphound *Ruth Carr* a58 61
8 b g Whipper(USA) Golden Symbol (Wolfhound (USA))
2052[2] 2342[9] 2919[10] 3211[10] 3984[5] 4513[4] 5127[2] ◆ 5368[9] (5807) 6509[9] 6852[3] 7046[2] 7444[4] (7595) 7860[6] 8315[10]

Whip Up A Frenzy (IRE) *Richard Rowe* a45 59
4 b g Vale Of York(IRE) Answer Do (Groom Dancer (USA))
100[6] 615[8] 2573[3] 3142[2] 3488[2] 3737[5] 6411[14] 7310[14] 8070[5] 8497[8]

Whirl Me Round *Kevin Ryan* 86
2 ch g Piccolo Give Her A Whirl (Pursuit Of Love)
3839[2] ◆ (4308) 5113[4] ◆ 5536[3] 6538[6] 6954[2] 7536[8]

Whiskey Sour (IRE) *Edward Lynam* a82 89
3 b c Jeremy(USA) Swizzle Stick (IRE) (Sadler's Wells (USA))
4747a[10] 5941a[21] 6389a[14]

Whisky Marmalade (IRE) *Ben Haslam* a59 59
4 b m Duke Of Marmalade(IRE) Nashatara (USA) (Nashwan (USA))
(295) 684[7] 1169[6] 7657[12] 8386[5]

Whisper A Word (IRE) *Tim Easterby* 46
2 ch f Bated Breath Affability (IRE) (Dalakhani (IRE))
2739[7] 3947[12]

Whispered Kiss *Mike Murphy* a55 47
3 b f Medicean Desert Kiss (Cape Cross (IRE))
5735[4] 6511[6] 7218[7] 7986[4]

Whispered Promise (IRE) *Charles Hills* 59
2 b f Lawman(FR) Whisp (GER) (Rainbow Quest (USA))
4147[7]

Whispering Bell (IRE) *John Gosden* 79
2 b f Galileo(IRE) Red Avis (Exceed And Excel (AUS))
6874[3]

Whispering Soul (IRE) *Brian Baugh* a56 43
3 b f Majestic Missile(IRE) Belle Of The Blues (IRE) (Blues Traveller (IRE))
1839[4] 2302[6] 2919[2] 3289[2] (3549) 4513[8] 5378[8] 6586[2] 6852[6] 8409[6]

Whispering Warrior (IRE) *David Simcock* a100 99
7 b g Oasis Dream Varenka (IRE) (Fasliyev (USA))
31[6] ◆ 215[3] 353[2] 530[6] 594[7] 1089[8]

Whispering Wolf *Suzzanne France* a47 51
3 b f Amadeus Wolf Ashover Amber (Green Desert (USA))
1670[3] 2559[3] 3289[4] 4513[9] 5069[9] 6105[8] 6852[9] 7509[3] 8013[12] 8485[2]

Whistle (IRE) *Martyn Meade* a68 42
3 b f Holy Roman Emperor(IRE) Multaka (USA) (Gone West (USA))
402[2] ◆ 639[7]

Whistler Mountain *Brian Barr* a45 34
4 b g Oasis Dream Canda (USA) (Storm Cat (USA))
2635[9] 3973[14]

Whistle Stop (SAF) *M F De Kock* 103
5 b g Silvano(GER) Gap Year (SAF) (Rich Man's Gold (USA))
95a[11] 283a[2]

Whitby Bay *Michael Easterby* a45 45
2 b f Camacho Whitby (IRE) (Dubawi (IRE))
3562[6] 4601[9] 5177[4] 6446[3] 7109[7] 7881[7]

Whitchurch *Philip Kirby* a68 58
4 b g Mawatheeq(USA) Silvereine (FR) (Bering)
1201[16] 1560[11] 2045[7] 3342[6] 3774[4] 4340[5] (4515) 5065[2] 5481[7] 5971[10] 6738[7] 7369[6] (7628) 7888[2] 8125[10] 8400[11]

Whiteandgold *Bryan Smart* 72
2 b f Major Cadeaux Irrational (Kyllachy)
1583[4] 2196[2] (2739) 3290[8] 6222[7]

White Bullet *Sir Mark Prescott Bt* a68 87
3 b f Exceed And Excel(AUS) Chili Dip (Alhaarth (IRE))
(507)

White Chin (IRE) *Tom Dascombe* a83 61
2 ch g Mayson Coachhouse Lady (USA) (Rahy (USA))
2757[10] 3106[8] 4203[5] (5806) 6697[4] (7305)

White Chocolate (IRE) *David Simcock* a70 77
2 gr f Mastercraftsman(IRE) Coco Demure (IRE) (Titus Livius (FR))
7107[2] (7465)

Whitecliff Park (IRE) *Brian Ellison* a64 65
3 b g Canford Cliffs(IRE) Venetian Rhapsody (IRE) (Galileo (IRE))
(69) 517[3] 1062[3] 1619[8]

Whitecliffsofdover (USA) *A P O'Brien* 108
2 b c War Front(USA) Orate (USA) (A.P. Indy (USA))
6707[2] 6987a[3]

Whitecrest *John Spearing* a55 82
8 ch m Ishiguru(USA) Risky Valentine (Risk Me (FR))
1782[4] (1950) 2931[6] 3487[5] 4039[9] 4495[7] 4952[6] 5050[2] 5669[6] 6017[6] 6410[5] 6831[11] 7303[7]

White Dog (IRE) *Sarah Humphrey* a52 43
4 b g Le Cadre Noir(IRE) Little Annie (Compton Place)
60[8] 514[3] 622[2] 8492[8] 8540[11]

White Dollar Sign (AUS) *John Thom* 89
4 b g Dash For Cash(AUS) Shining Impression (AUS) (Dangerous (AUS))
7552a[5]

White Flag *Tim Easterby* a26 68
5 b m Sakhee's Secret Rainbow Spectrum (FR) (Spectrum (IRE))
1495[8] 2053[8] 3013[8] 4006[U] (4516) 5276[6] 5887[3] 6568[9]

White Lake *Roger Varian* 105
4 b g Pivotal White Palace (Shirley Heights)
1637[6] 3910[6]

Whiteley (IRE) *Mick Channon* 67
2 b f Dark Angel(IRE) Carallia (IRE) (Common Grounds)
2097[4] 2410[8] 3686[4] (4386) 4884[9] 5598[6] 7185[10]

White Mischief (IRE) *Richard Hannon* 40
2 gr f Dark Angel(IRE) Galileo's Star (IRE) (Galileo (IRE))
7210[8]

White Poppy (IRE) *Andrew Balding* a77 98
3 b f Frozen Power(IRE) Symbol Of Peace (IRE) (Desert Sun)
(1767) 2412[2] (3001)

White Royale (USA) *Kevin Ryan* a75 44
2 b f Speightstown(USA) Sweet Hope (USA) (Lemon Drop Kid (USA))
1783[4] (2913) 7600[5] 7893[4] 8444[4] 8582[3]

White Shaheen *William Muir* a87 91
3 b g Makfi Likeable (Dalakhani (IRE))
(1294) 1623[6] 3110[3] (3728) ◆ 3914[2] 5147[8]

White Tower (IRE) *Mark Johnston* 92
2 b c Cape Cross(IRE) Star Blossom (USA) (Good Reward (USA))
(3321) ◆ 4150[5] 5108[3] 5536[6] 6481[5]

White Witch (USA) *H-A Pantall* 87
3 b f Invincible Spirit(IRE) Ishitaki (ARG) (Interprete (ARG))
(5907a) 7997a[8]

Whitkirk *Jedd O'Keeffe* a46 69
3 b g Iffraaj Bedouin Bride (USA) (Chester House (USA))
2122[5] 2864[10] 3224[3] (3750) 3982[7] 5273[2] 6095[6] 7601[14]

Whitman *Mark Johnston* 99
3 bb c Poet's Voice Sundrop (JPN) (Sunday Silence (USA))
1865[10] 2480[5] 3389[2] 3910[15] 4149[7] 4625[12] 4867[13] 5802[5] 6585[3] 7005[7]

Whitmore (USA) *Ronald Moquett* a110
3 ch g Pleasantly Perfect(USA) Melody's Spirit (USA) (Scat Daddy (USA))
2063a[19]

Whitstable Native *Sophie Leech* a37 44
8 b g Bertolini(USA) Break Of Dawn (USA) (Mt. Livermore (USA))
2448[7] 4088[8] 5529[9]

Whitstable Pearl (IRE) *Sophie Leech* a56 58
3 b f Kodiac Amber's Bluff (Mind Games)
(794) 4021[4] 4942[4] 5399[7] 5777[2] 6508[4] ◆ 6871[5] 7987[6]

Who Dares Wins (IRE) *Alan King* a81 98
4 b g Jeremy(USA) Savignano (Polish Precedent (USA))
(4920) 5381[3] 6545[5]

Whole Lotta Rosie (GER) *M Rulec* 95
3 b f Tiger Hill(IRE) Wonderful Day (GER) (Kahyasi)
1513a[7] 3207a[10]

Wholesome (USA) *K R Burke* 85
3 b f Lemon Drop Kid(USA) Nite In Rome (CAN) (Harlan's Holiday (USA))
(2419) 3107[6] 3593[4] 4757[10] 5761[4] 6345[6]

Whoopsy Daisy *Jane Chapple-Hyam* a80 75
4 b m Champs Elysees Humility (Polar Falcon (USA))
(967) ◆ 1161[3] 1290[3] ◆ 1999[5] (2791) 3276[3]

Whosasking (IRE) *A J Martin* a27
2 b g Ask Winning Indian (IRE) (Indian Danehill (IRE))
7387a[9]

Who Shot Thebarman (NZ) *Chris Waller* 115
7 b g Yamanin Vital(NZ) Ears Carol (NZ) (Carolingian (AUS))
7552a[2] 7756a[5] 7948a[5]

Who's Shirl *Chris Fairhurst* a60 61
10 b m Shinko Forest(IRE) Shirl (Shirley Heights)
2330[8] 3479[10] 4043[3] 6908[5] ◆ 7323[3] 7795[3] 8144[2] 8588[6]

Who'sthedaddy *Daniel Kubler* a62 72
4 br g Avonbridge Lisathedaddy (Darnay)
295[7] 463[10] 4293[5] 4635[9]

Who Told Jo Jo (IRE) *Bill Turner* a76 76
2 b c Bushranger(IRE) Shenkara (IRE) (Night Shift (USA))
1082[9] 1293[5] (1641) 2014[DSQ] 2779[3] 3128[5] 7440[10]

Whozthecat (IRE) *Declan Carroll* a53 71
9 b g One Cool Cat(USA) Intaglia (GER) (Lomitas)
1408[7] 1672[4] 1997[7] 2259[11] 3168[8] 3394[6] ◆ 3646[16] 3875[6] 4191[5] 4452[10] 4608[7] 4896[4] 5060[10] 5296[8] 5753[2] (5858) 6137[7] 6453[3] 6579[5] 6684[11] 7851[7] 8095[10] 8241[7]

Wickedly Smart (USA) *Jeremy Noseda* a71 70
4 rg m Smart Strike(CAN) Wickedly Wise (USA) (Tactical Cat (USA))
89a[9]

Wicked Tara *Natalie Lloyd-Beavis* a16 30
6 b m Assertive Tara King (Deploy)
1519a[8] 2080a[2] 2952a[5]

Wicked Woo *Jo Hughes* a41 53
3 b f Multiplex Icky Woo (Mark Of Esteem (IRE))
711[7] 1234[5] 1970[5]

Wicklow Brave *W P Mullins* 115
7 b g Beat Hollow Moraine (Rainbow Quest (USA))
1995[2] 3384[6] 4799[4] 5612[3] (6387a) 7756a[22]

Wick Powell *David Barron* a80 84
2 b c Sakhee's Secret London Welsh (Cape Cross (IRE))
(1293) 4891[2] ◆ 5113[2] 5560[7] 6388a[2] (6954)

Widnes *Alan Bailey* a72 69
2 b g Showcasing Largo (IRE) (Selkirk (USA))
7468[12] 7818[5] 7976[3] 8244[10]

Wigan Warrior *David Brown* a43 75
2 b g Doncaster Rover(USA) Rattleyurjewellery (Royal Applause)
2649[7] 2956[3] 3705[2] 4379[2] 5150[8] 7496[5] 7768[5] 7956[7]

Wikileaks (GER) *Waldemar Hickst*
3 b c Toylsome Wabrimida (GER) (Monsun (GER))
7999a[17]

Wikita (FR) *T Lemer* a82 81
5 b m Desert Style(IRE) Vagabonde (FR) (Valanour (IRE))
7525a[3]

Wilamina (IRE) *Martyn Meade* 99
3 b f Zoffany(IRE) Tropical Lake (IRE) (Lomond (USA))
2877[2] (3412) ◆ 3911[2] 5158[11] 6746[15]

Wild Acclaim (IRE) *Ann Duffield* a50 64
2 b c Acclamation Anam Allta (IRE) (Invincible Spirit (IRE))
4308[2] 8140[9]

Wild Approach (GER) *Melanie Sauer* 88
3 ch f New Approach(IRE) Wildfahrte (GER) (Mark Of Esteem (IRE))
3207a[6]

Wild Approach (IRE) *Robert Cowell* a54 54
2 b g Approve(IRE) Mike's Wildcat (USA) (Forest Wildcat (USA))
2852[5] 5631[8] 6295[8]

Wild At Heart (USA) *Richard E Mandella* a97 89
4 b m Indian Charlie(USA) Lady Cerise (USA) (Honor Grades (USA))
7829a[8]

Wild Bloom *Ed Vaughan* a52
3 b f Exceed And Excel(AUS) Wild Gardenia (Alhaarth (IRE))
1337[11] 7311[9] 7910[9]

Wild Chief (GER) *J Hirschberger* 116
5 ch h Doyen(IRE) Wild Angel (IRE) (Acatenango (GER))
1375a[6] 1909a[4] 2568a[8] 3699a[5] 5904a[8]

Wild Dancer *Patrick Chamings* 79
3 b f Mawatheeq(USA) Pretty Miss (Averti (IRE))
(4017) 4588[2] 5960[6] 6576[5] (7267)

Wilde Extravagance (IRE) *Julie Camacho* a45 74
3 ch g Dandy Man(IRE) Castanetta (IRE) (Dancing Dissident (USA))
1167[5] 1788[3] 2534[3] (3978) 5978[9] 6717[4]

Wilde Inspiration (IRE) *Julie Camacho* a82 97
5 ch g Dandy Man(IRE) Wishing Chair (USA) (Giant's Causeway (USA))
1195[6] 1629[3] 1871[5] 2833[4] 3566[8] 4894[13] 5976[9] 6736[6] 7623[3]

Wilderswood (IRE) *Ann Duffield* 64
2 b c Invincible Spirit(IRE) Putyball (USA) (Silver Deputy (CAN))
4405[6] 4765[6] 5727[9] 6343[7]

Wild Flower (IRE) *Jimmy Fox* a40 55
4 b m Approve(IRE) Midsummernitedream (GER) (Thatching)
321[6] 431[4] 547[7] 964[4] 1162[3] 1544[2] 1949[3] 2647[3] 2969[U] 4289[5] 4993[2] 5710[2] 5954[2] 6407[11] 7240[8] 7641[11]

Wild Hacked (USA) *Marco Botti* a94 101
3 b c Lemon Drop Kid(USA) Dance Pass (IRE) (Sadler's Wells (USA))
(1931) 2473[5] 3156[3] 4108[4] 4838[2] (5738) 6110[4] (7015)

Wild Hill Boy *David C Griffiths*
6 b g Tiger Hill(IRE) Kalamansi (IRE) (Sadler's Wells (USA))
2330[14] 2746[9]

Wild Irish Rose (IRE) *A P O'Brien* 78
2 b f Galileo(IRE) Sea Picture (IRE) (Royal Academy (USA))
6815a[7]

Wild Motion (GER) *Markus Klug* 78
4 rg m Motivator Wild Side (GER) (Sternkoenig (IRE))
1907a[9]

Wildomar *Peter Hiatt* a66 49
7 b g Kyllachy Murrieta (Docksider (USA))
103[6] 545[9] 693[2] 1347[8] 2445[7] 5607[8]

Wildpark (GER) *D Moser* 103
5 b g Shamardal(USA) Wildfahrte (GER) (Mark Of Esteem (IRE))
(2074a) 2633a[7] 4438a[5] 5904a[9] 6992a[8]

Wild Shot *James Eustace* a71 65
2 br g So You Think(NZ) Highland Shot (Selkirk (USA))
6716[6] 7100[4] 7907[2] 8208[9]

Wild Tempest *Charlie Appleby* 88
2 ch c Raven's Pass(USA) Sayyedati Storm (USA) (Storm Cat (USA))
7470[2] ◆

Wild Tobacco *Richard Hannon* a58 75
4 br h More Than Ready(USA) Princess Janie (USA) (Elusive Quality (USA))
(339)

Wiley Post *Richard Hannon* 83
3 b g Kyllachy Orange Pip (Bold Edge)
1847[4] 2185[6] (2435) 2982[4] 4910[7] 6000[6]

Willbeme *Neville Bycroft* a65 101
8 b m Kyllachy Befriend (USA) (Allied Forces (USA))
4366[11] 4946[5] 6080[9] 7112[7] 7433[10]

Willem (FR) *David Pipe* a44 63
6 b g Turtle Bowl(IRE) Zita Blues (IRE) (Zieten (USA))
3746[8]

William Ashford (IRE) *J C Hayden* a38 71
4 ch g Art Connoisseur(IRE) Song Of Sixpence (IRE) (Among Men (USA))
5096a[12] 7391a[6]

William Booth (IRE) *Daniel Mark Loughnane* a64
2 b g Born To Sea(IRE) Chaguaramas (IRE) (Mujadil (USA))
8208[10] 8537[5]

William Hunter *Alan King* a66 90
4 b g Mawatheeq(USA) Cosmea (Compton Place)
1400[3] 2098[5] 2414[5] 3139[2] (3690) 4535[3] (5053) (6074) 6709[6] 7824[4] ◆

William Of Orange *Donald McCain* a8 102
5 b g Duke Of Marmalade(IRE) Critical Acclaim (Peintre Celebre (USA))
1967[17] 6781[11]

Willie's Anne (IRE) *Daniel Mark Loughnane* a53 48
2 b f Lilbourne Lad(IRE) Cape Sydney (IRE) (Cape Cross (IRE))
5951[6] 6590[9] 7366[6]

Will Mac *Neville Bycroft* a52 63
5 b g Misu Bond(IRE) Zacinta (USA) (Hawkster (USA))
6220[8] 6645[5] 7078[12] 7327[5]

Willow Spring *Denis Quinn* a54 55
4 b m Compton Place Upstream (Prince Sabo)
217[7] 513[9] 1709[7] 2052[13] 2447[7] 3040[9] (3822) 4264[6] (5335) 5628[3] 6587[3] 7276[2] 7533[6] 8408[8]

Willpower (TUR) *Ibrahim Bekirogullari* 107
6 b m Victory Gallop(CAN) Free Trade (TUR) (Shareef Dancer (USA))
6158a[2]

Willshebetrying *Jim Best* a49
5 b m Act One Precedence (IRE) (Polish Precedent (USA))
1748[7] 4019[3] 7262[9]

Willsy *Karen Tutty* a73 69
3 b g Sakhee's Secret Blakeshall Rose (Tobougg (IRE))
(519) 924[5] (1452) 1847[2] 2477[9] 3155[6] 3465[7] 3771[5] 4354[6] 4789[4] 5336[3] 7886[5] 8101[10]

Willyegolassiego *Neil Mulholland* a35 17
3 br f Kheleyf(USA) Kryena (Kris)
2321[7] 2750[8] 3769[10]

Willytheconqueror (IRE) *William Muir* a99 107
3 b g Kodiac Jazzie (FR) (Zilzal (USA))
(1271) (1607) 2232a[6] 2788[3] 3158[2] 3909[7] 4359[3] 5143[4] 5863[2] 6943[4]

Wilsons Ruby (IRE) *Marjorie Fife* a66 52
3 b g Lilbourne Lad(IRE) Atlas Silk (Dansili)
2200[9] 2622[10] 3568[6] 5069[8] 5354[11] 7324[11] 7694[6]

Wilspa's Magic (IRE) *Ron Hodges* 60
3 gr f Zebedee Triple Zero (IRE) (Raise A Grand (IRE))
1451[7] 2128[3] 2823[4] 3198[5] 3513[8]

Wily Rumpus (IRE) *Ed Walker* a44 65
2 b g Intense Focus(USA) Supercat (IRE) (Indian Rocket)
5067[8] 6034[5] 6712[10] (7571)

Wimboldsley *Scott Dixon* a55 52
5 ch g Milk It Mick Chrystal Venture (IRE) (Barathea (IRE))
5470[7] 6587[2] 7144[3] 7488[5] 7850[7] 7896[4] 8079[6] 8288[13]

Wimple's Lad (IRE) *N Milliere* 19
3 b f Lilbourne Lad(IRE) Wimple's Girl (IRE) (Cape Cross (IRE))
2172a[11]

Wimpole Hall *William Jarvis* a88 91
3 b g Canford Cliffs(IRE) Sparkling Eyes (Lujain (USA))
1385[4] 2239[5] (2818) 3415[7] 4010[3] ◆ 4776[2] (5601) 6126[5] ◆ 6710[7]

Wind Cries Mary (GER) *M Rulec* 79
2 b f Campanologist(USA) Wonderful Day (GER) (Kahyasi)
7563a[7]

Windfast (IRE) *Brian Meehan* 114
5 b g Exceed And Excel(AUS) Fair Sailing (IRE) (Docksider (USA))
3664[8] 4395[3] 4887[3] (5880)

Windforpower (IRE) *Tracy Waggott* a67 61
6 b g Red Clubs(IRE) Dubai Princess (IRE) (Dubai Destination (USA))
1046[7] 1255[8] 1559[4] 2052[3] 2120[4] (2418) 2622[4] 2919[5] 3010[11] 3779[6] 4452[7] 4968[9] 5354[8] 5760[2] 6098[7] 6451[13] 6685[14] 6745[5] 6909[3] 7595[9] 7663[7] 7859[4] 8485[3]

Wind In Her Sails (IRE) *Giles Bravery* a63 70
2 b f Lilbourne Lad(IRE) Sail With The Wind (Saddlers' Hall (IRE))
4054[5] 5395[3] 6369[3] 7184[6] 7820[16] 8569[7]

Wind In My Sails *Ed de Giles* a72 91
4 b g Footstepsinthesand Dylanesque (Royal Applause)
1173[5] 2401[6] (3125) 4157[3] 4788[4] (5357) (5892) 6585[7]

Wind In The Trees (FR) *George Baker* a31 10
2 b f Sunday Break(JPN) Swift Winged (Motivator)
5460a[7] 6639a[14] 7304[4]

Windjammer (GER) *A Wohler* 71
2 ch f Campanologist(USA) Warrior Czarina (USA) (Pleasantly Perfect (USA))
7563a[8]

Windmills Girl *Jeremy Gask* a54 50
3 b f Sir Percy Cosmic Countess (IRE) (Lahib (USA))
2559[7] 3987[7] 4640[5] 5235[3] 5710[5]

Wind Of Change (GER) *Jean-Pierre Carvalho* 101
3 bb c Monsun(GER) Wells Present (GER) (Cadeaux Genereux)
7456a[8]

Wind Of Heaven (IRE) *Henry Candy* 15
2 b f Kodiac Aluana (IRE) (Alzao (USA))
6873[10] 7209[10]

Window Shopping (IRE) *Mark Usher* a38 37
3 b f Lilbourne Lad(IRE) Stained Glass (Dansili)
274[7] 327[7]

Wind Place And Sho *James Eustace* 95
4 br g Shirocco(GER) Coh Sho No (Old Vic)
1568[10] 2194[9] (3437) 4752[7] 6582[15] 7150[25]

Windshear *Richard Hannon* a92 110
5 b g Hurricane Run(IRE) Portal (Hernando (FR))
1088[6] 1219[5] 3340[11] 3889[13] 6233[3] 6884[7]

Windstoss (GER) *Markus Klug* 82
2 bb c Shirocco(GER) Wellenspiel (GER) (Sternkoenig (IRE))
7842a[6]

Windy York (IRE) *Frank Turner* 73
3 br f Vale Of York(IRE) Jumeirah Palm (USA) (Distorted Humor (USA))
6824a[12]

Wine List *Andrew Balding* 66
2 ch g Champs Elysees Masandra (IRE) (Desert Prince (IRE))
7503[6]

Winged Dancer *Sylvester Kirk* a77 66
3 b g Norse Dancer(IRE) Winged Diva (IRE) (Hawk Wing (USA))
(63) 243[2] 434[3] 1267[6] 2565[7] 3591[9] 3914[9]

Wings of Desire *John Gosden* a79 119
3 ch c Pivotal Gull Wing (IRE) (In The Wings)
1426[3] (1651) (2190) 2896[4] 4626[2] 5558[9]

Wings Of Eagles (FR) *A P O'Brien* 100
2 b c Pour Moi(IRE) Ysoldina (FR) (Kendor (FR))
7151[4] 7722a[9]

Wings Of Esteem (IRE) *Martin Smith* a79 73
3 b f Sir Percy Wings Of Fame (IRE) (Namid)
(524) 2011[5] 2795[9] 4025[2] 5122[6] 6656[2] 6856[2] 7671[9]

Winitall *J-M Baudrelle* a68 41
5 b g Invincible Spirit(IRE) Rapid Ransom (USA) (Red Ransom (USA))
715a[3]

Wink And Win (IRE) *Charles Hills* a43 59
3 b f Rip Van Winkle(IRE) Windmill (Ezzoud (IRE))
5361[5] 6239[6] 6795[6]

Winklemann (IRE) *Marco Botti* a85 95
4 br g Rip Van Winkle(IRE) Kykuit (IRE) (Green Desert (USA))
370a[13] 723a[10] 5640[10] 6372[7] 7825[8]

Wink Oliver *Jo Hughes* a79 40
4 b g Winker Watson Nadinska (Doyen (IRE))
263[6] 518[U] 629[5] 795[6] 953[8] 1416[10] 1700[7] 2635[8] 7203[11] 7611[9] 7817[10] 8156[6]

Win Lose Draw (IRE) *Michael Appleby* a67 23
4 b g Dark Angel(IRE) Caherassdotcom (Compton Place)
298[5] 582[8] 1079[8] 7010[11] 7516[7] 7780[4] 7890[4] (8121) 8207[9]

Winning Bid *Harry Dunlop* a68 52
2 b c Captain Gerrard(IRE) Best Bidder (USA) (Mr Greeley (USA))
2822[9] 3404[4] 4523[6] 6404[6] 7304[3]

Winning Return (IRE) *Saeed bin Suroor* 66
2 b f Exceed And Excel(AUS) Vincennes (King's Best (USA))
4762[4] 6524[8]

Winning Story *Saeed bin Suroor* a109 93
3 b g New Approach(IRE) Tanzania (USA) (Darshaan)
(1426) 2036[5] 7814[U] 7979[3] 8210[6] (8479)

Winning Ways (IRE) *William Haggas* 71
2 b c Lope De Vega(IRE) Sahara Sky (IRE) (Danehill (USA))
3463[2] ◆ 3805[4]

Winshine (FR) *V Luka Jr* a68 93
5 b m Chineur(FR) Fusee Francaise (FR) (Anabaa (USA))
(7806a)

Winslow (USA) *Doug Watson* a97 65
4 b g Distorted Humor(USA) Justwhistledixie (USA) (Dixie Union (USA))
8578a[5]

Winston C (IRE) *Michael Bell* 77
2 b c Rip Van Winkle(IRE) Pitrizza (IRE) (Machiavellian (USA))
(5036) 5847[3]

Winter House *Saeed bin Suroor* a94 93
4 b g Cape Cross(IRE) Villarrica (USA) (Selkirk (USA))
2037[2] ◆ 2744[10] 3785[4]

Winterlude (IRE) *Jennie Candlish* a102 90
6 b g Street Cry(IRE) New Morning (IRE) (Sadler's Wells (USA))
99[5] 244[2] ◆ (353) 530[5] (861) 1069[8] 1336[4] 1893[8] 2685[6] 3435[5] 8317[7] 8529[8]

Winter Rose (IRE) *Richard Hannon* a89 83
3 b f Dark Angel(IRE) Rose Of Battle (Averti (IRE))
2565[2] 3034[2] 3410[7] 4630[7]

Winter Spice (IRE) *Clive Cox* a85 79
5 gr g Verglas(IRE) Summer Spice (IRE) (Key Of Luck (USA))
385[3] 2582[9] 8363[4]

Winterton *Christine Dunnett* 24
3 b f Oasis Dream Quenched (Dansili)
3958[13] 4361[12]

Winterval *Roger Varian* 89
4 b g Dubawi(IRE) Festivale (IRE) (Invincible Spirit (IRE))
2010[2] 6286[8]

Win The Space (USA) *George Papaprodromou* a110 69
4 rg h Pulpit(USA) Teamgeist (ARG) (Mutakddim (USA))
7838a[9]

Winx (AUS) *Chris Waller* 130
4 b m Street Cry(IRE) Vegas Showgirl (NZ) (Al Akbar (AUS))
(7553a)

Wireless (FR) *V Luka Jr* a73 108
5 ch h Kentucky Dynamite(USA) Sachet (USA) (Royal Academy (USA))
(4074a) 6975a[4] 7841a[4]

Wishing Time (IRE) *David O'Meara* a28
2 b f Frankel Beyond Desire (Invincible Spirit (IRE))
8526[6]

Wishing Tree *Brian Ellison* a54 50
3 ch f Haafhd Ananda Kanda (USA) (Hero's Tribute (USA))
1669[6] 2333[6] 2681[4] 3423[6] 4289[13] 5578[9] 7097[11]

Wishing Well *Micky Hammond* a63 76
4 b m Bahri(USA) Amourallis (IRE) (Dushyantor (USA))
789[3] 1674[2] 2018[7] 2836[2] 3294[2] 4239[2] 4949[4] 5856[2] 6011[2] 6565[3] (7332)

Wishpoint (USA) *Michael Bell* 58
3 b g Street Cry(IRE) Key Point (IRE) (Galileo (IRE))
1639[7]

Wishsong *David Nicholls* a71 70
3 b f Dansili Princess Janie (USA) (Elusive Quality (USA))
(242) 365[5] 1060[4] ◆ 1789[3] 2106[3] 2336[8] 2834[10]

Wisteria *Susan Corbett* a25 44
4 br m Winker Watson Begonia (IRE) (Selkirk (USA))
3421[10] 4001[7] 4489[10] 5228[8]

Witchcraft (FR) *J-M Beguigne* a73 83
3 b c Elusive City(USA) Latinia (FR) (Barathea (IRE))
5385a[5]

Witch From Rome *Nick Lampard* a28
5 b g Holy Roman Emperor(IRE) Spangle (Galileo (IRE))
84[9] 673[6] 981[11]

With Approval (IRE) *Laura Mongan* a72 71
4 b g Approve(IRE) Kelsey Rose (Most Welcome)
2151[6] 3030[5] 3554[12] 4008[2] ◆ 4881[6] (5711) 6184[6] 7985[8]

Wither Hills (IRE) *Dermot Anthony McLoughlin* a81 72
10 b g Karinga Bay Bonnie Article (IRE) (Definite Article)
208a[7]

Withernsea (IRE) *Richard Fahey* 103
5 b g Dark Angel(IRE) Charlene Lacy (IRE) (Pips Pride)
1018a[11] 1627[2] 3163[4] 4109[3] 4625[7] 4865[11] 5871[14] 6355a[2] 7821[8]

With Hindsight (IRE) *Steve Gollings* a75 79
8 b g Ad Valorem(USA) Lady From Limerick (IRE) (Rainbows For Life (CAN))
103[5] 425[4] 506[2] 772[4]

Withhold *Charles Hills* a83 88
3 b c Champs Elysees Coming Back (Fantastic Light (USA))
1626[4] ◆ 2260[2] 3190[2] 3845[7] 4948[2] (5623) 6127[2] (7320)

With Honors (USA) *J Keith Desormeaux* a107 96
2 b f War Front(USA) All Her Class (USA) (Street Cry (IRE))
7830a[9] 8127a[3]

With Intent *Ollie Pears* a7 24
2 gr g Monsieur Bond(IRE) Dim Ofan (Petong)
5966[13] 6446[9]

Withnell *Brian Ellison* 61
2 b g Iffraaj Chalet Girl (Oasis Dream)
3854[6] 4423[10]

With One Accord *Richard Hannon* a14
2 b f Acclamation Raymi Coya (CAN) (Van Nistelrooy (USA))
6141[8]

With Pleasure *David O'Meara* a70 70
3 b g Poet's Voice With Fascination (USA) (Dayjur (USA))
(40) 366[5] 3187[6] 7486[6] 7857[10] 8101[12] 8178[2] 8282[6] 8379[4]

Wolfcatcher (IRE) *Charlie Appleby* a62 98
4 b g King's Best(USA) Miss Particular (IRE) (Sadler's Wells (USA))
2249[4] 3246[10]

Wolf Country *Charlie Appleby* 88
2 b c Dubawi(IRE) Goathemala (GER) (Black Sam Bellamy (IRE))
6262[6] (7225)

Wolf Heart (IRE) *Lucy Normile* a76 53
8 b g Dalakhani(IRE) Lisieux Orchid (IRE) (Sadler's Wells (USA))
4038[10]

Wolf Of Windlesham (IRE) *Stuart Edmunds* a79 75
4 ch g Mastercraftsman(IRE) Al Amlah (USA) (Riverman (USA))
(1038) 2392[3] 8250[2]

Wolowitz (IRE) *David Barron* a97 71
3 b g Intense Focus(USA) Tranquil Sky (Intikhab (USA))
(686) ◆ (821) ◆ (1070)

Wolverine (FR) *H Billot* 68
9 b g Take Risks(FR) Sevres (USA) (Lyphard's Wish (FR))
5216a[4] 6938a[10]

Womble *Laura Young*
3 b c Equiano(FR) Little Caroline (IRE) (Great Commotion (USA))
74[5] 145[12] 507[7]

Wonder Bolt (USA) *Ji Young Hun* a58
6 rg h Desert Warrior(USA) Little Champ (CAN) (Great Gladiator (USA))
6399a[7]

Wonderful Life (IRE) *Richard Spencer* a63 69
3 b f Canford Cliffs(IRE) Feeling Wonderful (IRE) (Fruits Of Love (USA))
2177[7] 3850[3] 4546[7] 8449[3]

Wonder Gal (USA) *Leah Gyarmati* a102
4 bb m Tiz Wonderful(USA) Passe (USA) (Dixie Union (USA))
7836a[10]

Wonder Of Dubai (IRE) *Jamie Osborne* a55
2 b c So You Think(NZ) Ruby Suesday (Refuse To Bend (IRE))
7882[8]

Woodacre *Richard Whitaker* a72 74
9 b g Pyrus(USA) Fairy Ring (IRE) (Fairy King (USA))
1221[7] 1445[4] 2017[9] 7412[3] 7500[3] 7791[5] 7993[6] ◆

Woodukheleyfit *Sylvester Kirk* a70 44
2 b g Kheleyf(USA) Wood Chorus (Singspiel (IRE))
2997[10] (3986) 4523[4] 8525[6]

Woody Bay *Mark Walford* a40 87
6 b g New Approach(IRE) Dublino (USA) (Lear Fan (USA))
1122[9] 1643[12] 2257[8] 2679[9] (3166) 3518[4] 4113[3] 4611[12] 5482[4] 6160[8] 7796[11]

Woofie (IRE) *Laura Mongan* a79 79
4 b g Duke Of Marmalade(IRE) Violet Ballerina (IRE) (Namid)
82[6] 1775[17] 2150[3] 2827[5] 4463[8] 5607[4]

Wootton Vale (IRE) *Richard Fahey* a57 54
3 b g Wootton Bassett Shining Vale (USA) (Twilight Agenda (USA))
3946[7] (4370) 4681[7] 5228[4] 6478[2] 7256[4] 7516[2]

Wootyhoot (FR) *James Fanshawe* a65
2 b g Wootton Bassett Orlena (USA) (Gone West (USA))
6672[5]

Wordiness *David Evans* a93 88
8 br g Dansili Verbose (USA) (Storm Bird (CAN))
861[6] 1081[7] 1987[3] 2932[7] 3657[9] 4077[10] 4752[11] 5642[4] 6279[5] 6591[4] 6919[9] 7158[8] 7507[13] 7993[13] 8250[8] 8480[4] ◆

Wordismybond *Richard Hughes* a63 76
7 b g Monsieur Bond(IRE) La Gessa (Largesse)
1735[10] (2087) 2646[3] 3142[4] (4302) 4589[3] 4656[3] (5393) 5674[3] 5925[4] 6184[2] 6656[9]

Wordless (IRE) *Stefano Botti* 99
4 bb m Rock Of Gibraltar(IRE) Holy Moon (IRE) (Hernando (FR))
7566a[8]

Wordsearch (USA) *Hugo Palmer* a73 63
2 b c Pleasantly Perfect(USA) Jibe (USA) (Danzig (USA))
7329[5] 7658[3] 7865[2] 8153[6]

Work (IRE) *David Simcock* a60 49
3 b f Mastercraftsman(IRE) Abbeyleix Lady (IRE) (Montjeu (IRE))
2653[9] 4740[7] 5958[6] 6185[3] (7309) (7532)

Working Class *Peter Chapple-Hyam* 60
2 b g Bahri(USA) Louise D'Arzens (Anabaa (USA))
7283[5] ◆

Wor Lass *Susan Corbett* a79 88
8 br m And Beyond(IRE) Patience Please (King Of Spain)
2659[6] 3149[7] 3659[6] 4101[7] 4646[7] 5541[5] (5970) (6097) 6227[2] 6561[8] 6740[5]

World Approval (USA) *Mark Casse* 114
4 rg g Northern Afleet(USA) Win Approval (USA) (With Approval (CAN))
5431a[7] 6600a[3] 7405a[8]

World Of Good *John Joseph Murphy* a73 64
3 ch f Danehill Dancer(IRE) Edaraat (USA) (Rahy (USA))
5814a[4]

World Record (IRE) *Mick Quinn* a51 65
6 b g Choisir(AUS) Dancing Debut (Polar Falcon (USA))
1247[5] 1780[3] 2213[7] 2827[4] 3354[8] 3823[9] 5085[7] (6188) 7298[4] 7986[5]

World's Greatest (USA) *Stuart Williams* a69 75
3 ch f Discreet Cat(USA) Say You Will (IRE) (A.P. Indy (USA))
(291) 678[7] 979[3] (2212) 3039[5] 4788[7] 5412[9] 7485[5] 7887[6]

Worlds His Oyster *John Quinn* a69 87
3 b g Pivotal Regal Salute (Medicean)
2161[14] 2907[5] 3415[5] 4139[2] 4631[3] (5063) 5886[4] 6585[4] 6778[9]

Worth Avenue (IRE) *W T Farrell* a44 47
5 ch m Rock Of Gibraltar(IRE) Hayworth (IRE) (Night Shift (USA))
6651[7]

Wotabond *Richard Whitaker* a27 36
3 ch g Monsieur Bond(IRE) Wotatomboy (Captain Rio)
1564[6] 7602[10]

Wotabreeze (IRE) *John Quinn* 86
3 ch g Excellent Art Sparkling Crystal (IRE) (Danehill Dancer (IRE))
1449[8] 1927[2] (2576) ◆ 2831[2] 3711[3] (4255) 4340[4] 4892[2] 5761[2] 6566[5] 6794[9]

Wotadoll *Dean Ivory* a50
2 b f Harbour Watch(IRE) Rhapsilian (Dansili)
7689[7] 7939[9] 8152[11]

Wotnot (IRE) *Bryan Smart* a65 61
4 gr m Exceed And Excel(AUS) Whatami (Daylami (IRE))
1402[7] 2201[8] 4770[13] 5200[2] 6098[9] 6909[10]

Wouldntitbelovely (IRE) *Richard Hughes* a51 36
2 b f Kodiac Geht Fasteur (IRE) (Chineur (FR))
6696[8] 7032[5]

Wowcha (IRE) *John Quinn* a78 82
3 b f Zoffany(IRE) Muravka (IRE) (High Chaparral (IRE))
(1246) 1638[4] 2336[6] 3567[2] 4043[2] 4643[4] 5367[2] 5836[2] 6770[6]

Wowee *Tony Carroll* a66 48
5 b g Archipenko(USA) Katya Kabanova (Sadler's Wells (USA))
602[11] 690[7]

Wrangler *William Haggas* a92 91
5 b g High Chaparral(IRE) Tipsy Me (Selkirk (USA))
7015[10] 7538[3] 7979[4] 8210[3] ◆ 8594[10]

Wrapped *William Haggas* a65 83
3 ch f Iffraaj Muffled (USA) (Mizaaya)
3951[3] ◆ (4766) 5743[5] 6635[2] (6893)

Wright Patterson (IRE) *John Quinn* 55
3 b g Dream Ahead(USA) Anam Allta (IRE) (Invincible Spirit (IRE))
3609[13] 4041[12] 5835[9]

Wuheida *Charlie Appleby* 113
2 ch f Dubawi(IRE) Hibaayeb (Singspiel (IRE))
(5170) ◆ (6986a)

Wun Destination *John Panvert* 14
7 b m Dubai Destination(USA) Mourir D'Aimer (USA) (Trempolino (USA))
2929[12]

Wurood *William Haggas* 71
2 gr f Dark Angel(IRE) Key Rose (IRE) (Key Of Luck (USA))
7439[3] 7819[5]

Wychwood Warrior (IRE) *M Halford* a99 101
4 b g Lope De Vega(IRE) Pearlitas Passion (IRE) (High Chaparral (IRE))
189a[7] 375a[7] 5564a[9] 5941a[17]

Wynford (IRE) *Andrew Balding* a70 79
3 ch g Dylan Thomas(IRE) Wishing Chair (USA) (Giant's Causeway (USA))
4372[6] 5746[4] (6227) ◆ 6886[3] 7320[4]

Xaarino (FR) *A Fabre* 103
2 gr c Kendargent(FR) Xaarienne (Xaar)
(5450a)

Xceedingly Xcited (IRE) *Marco Botti* a37
3 b f Exceed And Excel(AUS) Alamouna (IRE) (Indian Ridge)
249[6]

Xceleration *Ed Vaughan* a66 49
3 b g Acclamation Hijab (King's Best (USA))
1420[11]

Xclusive *Ronald Harris* a34 37
6 b g Pivotal Dance A Daydream (Daylami (IRE))
7910[10]

Xebec (USA) *John M Oxx* a87 95
4 gr g Mizzen Mast(USA) Xinji (IRE) (Xaar)
(5790a) 7196a[5]

Xenon *Sir Mark Prescott Bt* a59 38
2 b f Kyllachy Cool Question (Polar Falcon (USA))
3290[10] 3647[5] 4195[5] 5299[4] 5806[6] 6419[7] 6564[11]

Xenophanes (IRE) *M Boutin* a63 68
6 b g Shamardal(USA) Nipping (IRE) (Night Shift (USA))
7398a[6]

Xo (FR) *Mme Pia Brandt* a89 85
2 b c Holy Roman Emperor(IRE) Xstase (SWE) (Trempolino (USA))
(7971a)

X Raise (IRE) *David Brown* a55 58
4 gr m Aussie Rules(USA) Raise (USA) (Seattle Slew (USA))
368[6] 568[9]

X Rated (IRE) *Mark Johnston* a78 76
2 gr g Exceed And Excel(AUS) Screen Star (IRE) (Tobougg (IRE))
5577[3] 6002[5] 7239[2] 7483[4] 7917a[3] (8074)

X Y Jet (USA) *Jorge Navarro* a120
4 rg g Kantharos(USA) Soldiersingsblues (USA) (Lost Soldier (USA))
1105a[2]

Yaa Wayl (IRE) *D Selvaratnam* a91 98
9 b g Whipper(USA) Lidanna (Nicholas (USA))
373a[6] 628a[9] 810a[4]

Ya Boy Sir (IRE) *Iain Jardine* a27 53
9 ch g Alhaarth(IRE) Champs Elysees (USA) (Distant Relative)
3022[6] 3549[7] 4096[5] 4834[8]

Yair Hill (IRE) *Thomas Cuthbert* a46 54
8 b g Selkirk(USA) Conspiracy (Rudimentary (USA))
1845[6] 2096[6] 3016[8] 4683[4] 5149[6] 5323[7] 5717[4] 6226[6] 6434[5] 7254[5] ◆ 7850[5]

Ya Jammeel *Richard Fahey* 68
3 b g Dubawi(IRE) Silver Touch (IRE) (Dansili)
2861[8] 3343[6] 3886[4]

Yakaba (FR) *F Head* 107
3 ch f Medicean Kayaba (Anabaa (USA))
4905a[3] 5949a[5] 7030a[11]

Yalawin (IRE) *Roger Varian* a80 79
2 b c Lawman(FR) Urgele (FR) (Zafonic (USA))
7502[3] ◆ 7726[2]

Yalta (IRE) *Mark Johnston* 111
2 b c Exceed And Excel(AUS) Lacily (USA) (Elusive Quality (USA))
(2390) ◆ (2664) 3243[8] 4060[8] (4755) 5614[19] 6282[10] 7113[6]

Yamato (IRE) *M Halford* a79 70
3 b g Big Bad Bob(IRE) Himiko (IRE) (Aussie Rules (USA))
7339a[8]

Yamllik *Brian Barr* a86 63
4 b g King's Best(USA) Anaamil (IRE) (Darshaan)
2819[9] 3234[9] 4158[9] 5234[6] 5824[10] 7257[11]

Yangtze *Sir Michael Stoute* a82 98
3 b g Dansili Hi Calypso (IRE) (In The Wings)
1639[5] ◆ 2413[3] 2909[4] 3814[3] (4778) 5633[4] (6735) 7123[3]

Yankee Mail (FR) *Gay Kelleway* a67 74
4 b m American Post Mercredi (FR) (Groom Dancer (USA))
1157a[6] 2733[2] 3076[2] (3257) 3972[4] 4356[5] 4901a[4] 5452a[3]

Yankee Rose (AUS) *David Vandyke* 113
2 bb f All American(AUS) Condesaar (AUS) (Xaar)
7553a[3]

Yard Of Ale *Martin Smith* a70 43
5 ch g Compton Place Highly Liquid (Entrepreneur)
(431)

Yarmouk (FR) *Richard Fahey* a69 70
2 ch g Siyouni(FR) Tassara (FR) (Sendawar (IRE))
4545[7] 5150[5] 5966[4] 6614[2] 7004[4] 7820[7]

Yarrow (IRE) *Sir Michael Stoute* a76 101
4 b m Sea The Stars(IRE) Highland Gift (IRE) (Generous (IRE))
1855[10] 3436[2] 4800[7] 5879[5]

Yasir (USA) *Conor Dore* a66 66
8 b g Dynaformer(USA) Khazayin (USA) (Bahri (USA))
(819) 898[3] 1002[3] (1343) 1500[3] 2445[3] (3470) (4212) 4716[4] (4979) 5473[4] (5737) 6701[8] 6965[4] 7321[4] 7656[8] 7746[5] ◆ 7987[5] 8124[5] 8211[3] 8359[3] 8488[2]

Yasood (IRE) *Phil McEntee* a56 61
3 b g Acclamation Lucina (Machiavellian (USA))
5122[10] 5635[6] 6051[10] 7310[7] 7514[5] 7969[10] 8411[6]

Yattwee (USA) *Saeed bin Suroor* a90 104
3 bb g Hard Spun(USA) Alzerra (UAE) (Pivotal)
1865[2] ◆ (2480) 3299[5] 4135[5] 6109[10]

Yawail *Brian Rothwell* a62 58
5 bb m Medicean Al Tamooh (IRE) (Dalakhani (IRE))
4456[14] 4730[7]

Yeah Baby Yeah (IRE) *Gay Kelleway* a90 96
3 b f Art Connoisseur(IRE) Royal Interlude (IRE) (King's Theatre (IRE))
193[2] 350[2] (511a) 1071[4] 1396[10] 2115a[7] 2539[3] 3039[2] 3274[13] 4263[7] 5123[2] (5987a) 6939[4] 7348a[9] 8098[4] 8426[6] 8538[6]

Yeats Magic (IRE) *Ronald Harris* a55 77
4 b g Yeats(IRE) Orinoco (IRE) (Darshaan)
661[2] 313[7] 2129[5] 2367[8]

Yeeoow (IRE) *K R Burke* a90 87
7 b g Holy Roman Emperor(IRE) Taraya (IRE) (Doyoun)
142[9] (192) 416[3] 1090[3] 1205[3] 1394[3] 1887[4] 1990[6] 2581[6] 4079[8] 4366[10] 4689[4] 4741[5] 5034[2] (6000) 6382a[12] 6714[8] 7968[5] 8314[5] 8402[5]

Yellow Agate (USA) *Christophe Clement* a105
2 b f Gemologist(USA) Lemon Sorbet (USA) (Lemon Drop Kid (USA))
7830a[10]

Yellowhammer *Roger Charlton* 78
2 b f Raven's Pass(USA) Magical Romance (IRE) (Barathea (IRE))
7055[4] (7696) ◆

Yelow Bird *Chris Grant* a34 24
2 b g Power Aiaam Al Wafa (IRE) (Authorized (IRE))
5433[8] 6099[9] 6789[9]

Yensir *Pat Phelan* a58 78
3 ch g Sir Percy Yensi (Doyen (IRE))
1570[4] 3801[4] 4307[7] 5027[7]

Yes Daddy (IRE) *Robert Stephens* a76 78
8 b g Golan(IRE) Hollygrove Samba (IRE) (Accordion)
8051[3] 8363[3]

Yes You (IRE) *James Given* 54
2 ch f Choisir(AUS) Mexican Milly (IRE) (Noverre (USA))
1443[5] 2007[7] 2830[6] 4002[3]

Yisty *Derek Shaw* a49 34
3 ch f Compton Place Meditation (Inchinor)
(81) 510[4] 635[9] 970[4]

Yonna (FR) *E Lellouche* a85 99
5 bb m Le Havre(IRE) Folie Danse (FR) (Petit Loup (USA))
660a[8]

Yooroppa (FR) *Y Gourraud* a71 79
3 b f Dunkerque(FR) Orzie (FR) (Solicitor I (FR))
7999a[7]

Yorkee Mo Sabee (IRE) *Mark Johnston* a70 83
3 ch g Teofilo(IRE) Pivotal's Princess (IRE) (Pivotal)
(4036) 4481[7] 4946[8]

Yorker (SAF) *William Haggas* 116
6 b g Jet Master(SAF) Little Indian (SAF) (Al Mufti (USA))
5652[2] ◆ 6482[2] 6973a[5]

York Glory (USA) *Ruth Carr* a60 82
8 rg h Five Star Day(USA) Minicolony (USA) (Pleasant Colony (USA))
1787[9] 3265[4] ◆

Yorkidding *Mark Johnston* a94 103
4 b m Dalakhani(IRE) Claxon (Caerleon (USA))
1642[P] 2163[6] 2487[2] 2685[4] 2897[16] 3162[12] (4115) (4583) 5219a[6] 5611[5] (5879) 6151a[3] 7150[7] 7652[5] 7766[4]

Yorkindred Spirit *Mark Johnston* a76 77
4 b m Sea The Stars(IRE) Paracel (USA) (Gone West (USA))
1085[5] 1434[7] 1766[2] 2379[12] (2915) 3012[2] 3276[6] 3593[8] (4025) 4455[6] 4646[4] 4919[5] 5489[4] 5671[4] 5918[5] 6323[7] 6702[7] 6965[5]

Yorkshire Bounty *Richard Fahey* 50
2 ch c Bahamian Bounty Nicola's Dream (Alhaarth (IRE))
2301[8] 4110[7] 4663[9]

Yorkshiredebut (IRE) *Paul Midgley* 70
2 ch f Sir Prancealot(IRE) Yasmeena (USA) (Mr Greeley (USA))
2739[4] 3112[10] 4254[3] 4832[2] (5798) 6343[3] 6564[8]

Yorkshireman (IRE) *Lynn Siddall* a63 47
6 b g Red Clubs(IRE) Ossiana (IRE) (Polish Precedent (USA))
71[5] 592[4] 946[10] 1136[5] 1955[11] 2916[6] 3417[7] 4645[9] 4971[5] 5435[5] 6102[10]

Yorkshire Star (IRE) *Bill Turner* a31 48
2 ch g Fast Company(IRE) March Star (IRE) (Mac's Imp (USA))
3897[2] 4404[8] 6208[6] 6588[6] 6828[4] 7571[14]

Yosemite *Richard Fahey* a72 79
3 gr f Makfi Dansa Queen (Dansili)
4496[7] 5858[4] 6435[10] 7325[8] 7540[6]

Youarewonder (IRE) *John James Feane* a33 97
2 b c Thewayyouare(USA) Vera Mont (GER) (Danehill Dancer (IRE))
7707a[3]

Youceeyouceecee (IRE) *Miss Susan A Finn* 80
4 br g Rock Of Gibraltar(IRE) Tonique (Lujain (USA))
1014a[6] 4811a[13]

You'll Do *Maurice Barnes* a61 64
3 b g Approve(IRE) Tentears (Cadeaux Genereux)
331[8] 3343[4] 3886[7] 7601[7] 7797[10] 7995[11] 8387[8]

You Look Different *Antony Brittain* a41
2 ch f Sleeping Indian First Harmony (First Trump)
7432[8] 7855[11]

Youm Jamil (USA) *Tony Carroll* a64 55
9 gr g Mizzen Mast(USA) Millie's Choice (IRE) (Taufan (USA))
231[7] 621[7] 777[9]

Youmkin (USA) *Saeed bin Suroor* 78
2 ch c Street Cry(IRE) Aryaamm (IRE) (Galileo (IRE))
(7622)

Young Christian *Tom Tate* a70 70
3 b g Captain Gerrard(IRE) Shallow Ground (IRE) (Common Grounds)
40[4] 331[4] 1646[6] 2307[3] 2891[6] 4241[9] 5273[11] 6220[11]

Young John (IRE) *Richard Fahey* a90 89
3 b g Acclamation Carpet Lady (IRE) (Night Shift (USA))
1851[5] 2477[3] 2934[5] (3466) 4079[18] 5488[11] 7540[3] (7957) 8314[6] 8475[7]

Young Officer (IRE) *Brian Meehan* a49 49
2 b g Fast Company(IRE) Sara Mana Mou (Medicean)
5356[13] 5792[8] 8243[8]

Young Tiger *Tom Tate* a60 65
3 b g Captain Gerrard(IRE) Blades Princess (Needwood Blade)
5388[6] 5862[3] 6744[7] 7626[14] 7860[3] 8137[4]

Young Tom *Michael Appleby* 66
3 b g Sir Percy Enford Princess (Pivotal)
3215[3] (3493) 4033[6] 5761[5] 6840[5] 7582[7]

Young Windsor (IRE) *Ann Duffield* a58 64
3 ch g Windsor Knot(IRE) Invincible Woman (IRE) (Invincible Spirit (IRE))
181[7] 1045[7]

Yourartisonfire *Lisa Williamson* a78 86
6 ch g Dutch Art Queens Jubilee (Cayman Kai (IRE))
1629[11] 2216[8] 3518[6] (3849) 4917[8] 5419[16] 7461[13] 7781[4] 8356[11]

You're A Goat *Gary Moore* a84 81
3 b f Notnowcato Three Wrens (IRE) (Second Empire (IRE))
140[6] 265[2] (533) 4269[4] (5013) (5994) (6856)

Youre Always Right (IRE) *Clive Cox* 82
3 b f Pour Moi(IRE) Zaraba (IRE) (Sakhee (USA))
(2312) 3574[5] 4710[7] 6301[10]

You're Back (USA) *H-A Pantall* a90 97
3 b f Street Cry(IRE) Nawaiet (USA) (Zilzal (USA))
8431a[6] 8563a[15]

You're Cool *John Balding* a76 76
4 b g Exceed And Excel(AUS) Ja One (IRE) (Acclamation)
56[3] 162[2] 323[4] 764[8] 3713[6] 4295[2] 4744[4] 5269[2] 6215[10] 8349[8]

You're Fired (IRE) *K R Burke* a111 111
5 b g Firebreak My Sweet Georgia (IRE) (Royal Applause)
1196[10] (1629) 2030[2] 3164[8] 3910[7] 4823[11] 5585[11] 7978[2]

You're Hired *Amanda Perrett* 95
3 b c Dalakhani(IRE) Heaven Sent (Pivotal)
(4156) (4797) 5924[3] ◆ (6456)

Your Gifted (IRE) *Lisa Williamson* a72 55
9 b m Trans Island Dame Laura (IRE) (Royal Academy (USA))
75[5] (293) 541[5] 733[5] 1059[6] (1721) 2334[7] 2785[6] 3994[7] 4378[9]

Yourholidayisover (IRE) *Patrick Holmes* a54 48
9 ch g Sulamani(IRE) Whitehaven (Top Ville (IRE))
796[5] 949[8] 1343[3]

Your Lucky Day *Chris Dwyer* a59
4 b g Cockney Rebel(IRE) Fontaine House (Pyramus (USA))
54[3] 241[8]

Your Pal Tal *J F Levins* a81 78
6 b g Dark Angel(IRE) Good Health (Magic Ring (IRE))
4415a[19] 8197a[13]

Yours Forever *Kevin Ryan* a58 57
3 ch f Peintre Celebre(USA) Sincerely (Singspiel (IRE))
925[4] 1798[8] 2557[6] 3710[4] 3955[5]

Ypres *Jason Ward* a60 74
7 b g Byron Esligier (IRE) (Sabrehill (USA))
278[8] 541[9] 856[8] 2120[5] 2680[10] 4544[4] 5060[11] 5354[3] 6685[10] 6910[4]

Ythan Waters *Bryan Smart* a70 76
4 b g Hellvelyn Primrose Queen (Lear Fan (USA))
1[3] 49[6]

Yucatan (IRE) *A P O'Brien* 112
2 b c Galileo(IRE) Six Perfections (FR) (Celtic Swing)
6817a[2] 7539[2]

Yu Change (JPN) *Hideyuki Mori* a104 108
3 bb c Swift Current(JPN) Yu Carat (JPN) (Winning Ticket (JPN))
1103a[3]

Yuften *Roger Charlton* a103 110
5 b g Invincible Spirit(IRE) Majestic Sakeena (IRE) (King's Best (USA))
2716a[10] 3084a[4] 3681a[9] 6788[4] (7354)

Yul Finegold (IRE) *Conor Dore* a63 79
6 b g Invincible Spirit(IRE) Mascara (Mtoto)
(6) 337[9] 734[8] 888[7] 1166[5] 1391[6] (1824) 2463[5] 2930[6] 6048[9] 7816[9] 8007[12] 8238[7] 8364[7]

Yulong Baobei (IRE) *M Halford* a88 104
2 ch f Choisir(AUS) Bless You (Bahamian Bounty)
2718a[2] 3247[7] (4171a) 5661a[3]

Yulong Xiongba (IRE) *Julie Camacho* a69 72
4 b g Kodiac Moon Legend (USA) (Gulch (USA))
53[2] 676[2] 823[5] 2555[4] 2915[4] 3367[2] 3952[3] 4335[3] (4684) 6437[4] 7334[7]

Zaakhir (IRE) *Charles Hills* a81 83
3 b f Raven's Pass(USA) Zahoo (IRE) (Nayef (USA))
2394[6] 4160[3] 5596[4] 6019[4] 6948[8]

Zaatar (IRE) *Mick Channon* a32 61
2 b f Fast Company(IRE) Amazing Win (IRE) (Marju (IRE))
2429[3] 2583[4] 4304[6] 4815[3] 8467[11]

Zabdi *Lee Carter* a55 52
3 b c Zebedee Musical Moonlight (Observatory (USA))
978[4] 2935[4] 3558[10] 4085[6] 4518[4] 4760[4] 6237[10] 6677[8] 7070[5] 7463[11] 8457[2]

Zabeel Prince (IRE) *Roger Varian* 74
3 ch g Lope De Vega(IRE) Princess Serena (USA) (Unbridled's Song (USA))
7583[2]

Zabeel Princess *Roger Varian* 67
3 b f Dubawi(IRE) Mundana (IRE) (King's Best (USA))
1597[11] 2483[5]

Zabeel Star (IRE) *Graeme McPherson* a78 75
4 ch g Arcano(IRE) Deep Winter (Pivotal)
2620[5] 4406[4] 5392[5] 7141[7] 7911[4] 8141[6] (8462)

Zac Brown (IRE) *Charlie Wallis* a100 79
5 b g Kodiac Mildmay (USA) (Elusive Quality (USA))
529[6] 677[5] (923) 1857[8] 2480[8] 2903[9] 6371[12] 7288[7] 7752[5] 7983[5] 8192[7] 8407[6]

Zacchetto (USA) *Mark Johnston* a60
2 bb c Bernardini(USA) Minister's Melody (USA) (Deputy Minister (CAN))
5637[11]

Zac Courageous (IRE) *James Bennett* a37
4 b g Mastercraftsman(IRE) Thats Your Opinion (Last Tycoon)
675[10] 863[10] 1036[8] 1263[8] 1748[14]

Zacynthus (IRE) *Ivan Furtado* a66 73
8 ch g Iffraaj Ziria (IRE) (Danehill Dancer (IRE))
3419[10] 3645[9] 4299[13] 6266[8] 7702[14]

Zaeem *Ivan Furtado* a95 84
7 b g Echo Of Light Across (ARG) (Roy (USA))
(24) ◆ 134[5] 4299[15] 4917[7] 6276[9] 6806[5] 7126[5] 7529[2] 7968[6] 8251[7] 8475[4] ◆

Zafaranah (USA) *Roger Varian* 52
2 ch f Raven's Pass(USA) Jiwen (CAN) (Singspiel (IRE))
7695[7]

Zafayan (IRE) *D K Weld* 104
5 b g Acclamation Zafayra (IRE) (Nayef (USA))
4721a[13]

Zaffinah (IRE) *A Wohler* 90
2 ch f Casamento(IRE) Grand Zafeen (Zafeen (FR))
6174a[5]

Zafraaj *Pat Murphy* 29
5 b g Iffraaj Woodbury (Woodborough (USA))
1899[7] 2542[12]

Zahee (NZ) *M F De Kock* a110 109
6 b g Dylan Thomas(IRE) Zaheeya (AUS) (Encosta De Lago (AUS))
95a[16] 720a[3] 845a[5]

Zahiria (FR) *P Adda* a66 48
2 b f Bertolini(USA) Remember Mix (FR) (Desert Style (IRE))
2844a[2] 3182a[9] 7454a[5]

Zahrat Narjis *Richard Fahey* a55 71
3 b f Exceed And Excel(AUS) Nijoom Dubai (Noverre (USA))
1409[2] 1816[7] 2178[10]

Zain Arion (IRE) *John Butler* a76 70
3 b f Danehill Dancer(IRE) Shaanara (IRE) (Darshaan)
2009[10] 2505[10] 2861[11] 3652[2] (4277) 5508[4] 5746[5] (8381)

Zaina Rizeena *Richard Fahey* 78
3 ch f Shamardal(USA) Sweet Lilly (Tobougg (IRE))
2179[7] 3213[6] 3714[6]

Zainat (IRE) *K R Burke* a75 75
3 b g Masterofthehorse(IRE) Think Fast (IRE) (Songandaprayer (USA))
(243)[2] ◆ 421[4] 1185[8] 2044[4] 2654[13] 6516[4]

Zain Emperor (IRE) *John Butler* a79 82
3 b c Holy Roman Emperor(IRE) Love Thirty (Mister Baileys)
1257[2] ◆ 1788[6] 2336[7] (3079) 4010[7] 6490[6] 8446[5]

Zainhom (USA) *Sir Michael Stoute* 106
2 ch c Street Cry(IRE) Kaseema (USA) (Storm Cat (USA))
5196[3] (6159) 7148[2] ◆

Zain Time *Charlie Fellowes* 59
4 b m Pivotal Hypnology (USA) (Gone West (USA))
3220[11]

Zakatal *Rebecca Menzies* a86 86
10 gr g Kalanisi(IRE) Zankara (FR) (Linamix (FR))
(103) 157[2] (329) 545[3] 619[2] 1135[4] (1766) 2782[2] 3784[5] 8399[2] ◆

Zalfana (IRE) *D K Weld* 94
3 ch f Dutch Art Zafayra (IRE) (Nayef (USA))
2883a[5] 3428a[5]

Zalkaya (FR) *Mlle S Sine* a46 43
4 b m Chichi Creasy(FR) Zalka (FR) (Indian Rocket)
7398a[11]

Zalvados (FR) *H-A Pantall* a83 83
3 ch c Soldier Of Fortune(IRE) Zariyana (IRE) (Desert Prince (IRE))
7680a[7]

Zamaam *E Charpy* a69 107
6 br h Muhtathir Nasheed (USA) (Riverman (USA))
187a[5] 372a[8] 455a[3] 625a[6] 721a[3]

Zamadance *Sylvester Kirk* a62 71
2 ch g Zamindar(USA) Opera Dancer (Norse Dancer (IRE))
2204[7] 3032[5] 3799[4] 4982[7] (5719) 6366[2] 6664[4] 6923[4] 7482[7]

Zamalight *Amanda Perrett* a59
2 ch c Zamindar(USA) Mountain Chain (USA) (Royal Academy (USA))
7064[6]

Zamastar Brendan Powell a54 62 5 b g Zamindar(USA) Kissogram (Caerleon (USA)) 3739[10] 4200[5] 5132[9] 5604[2] 6857[11]

Zambeasy Philip Hide a80 90 5 b g Zamindar(USA) Hanella (IRE) (Galileo (IRE)) 1093[9] (1717) 2549[2] 5358[8] 6089[6] 7015[8]

Zambezi Queen (IRE) Paul Cole a53 53 2 gr f Helmet(AUS) Lesotho (IRE) (Excellent Art) 2637[9] 8066[4] 8229[8]

Zambucca (SAF) S Seemar a103 104 7 ch h Lundy's Liability(BRZ) Jazz Champion (SAF) (Dancing Champ (USA)) 93a[5] 283a[6] 455a[7] 625a[10] 811a[11]

Zam I Am Christine Dunnett 3 b g Zamindar(USA) Prayer (IRE) (Rainbow Quest (USA)) 4027[7] 8048[8]

Zamindo Mark Johnston a51 56 3 ch g Zamindar(USA) Mosqueras Romance (Rock Of Gibraltar (IRE)) 4313[7] 4983[4] 5233[2] 6095[7] 6514[6]

Zamjar Ed Dunlop a83 80 2 b c Exceed And Excel(AUS) Cloud's End (Dubawi (IRE)) 2319[3] ◆ 2779[2] 3321[2] (4047) 7305[5] 7764[4] 8444[2] (8582)

Zamoyski Steve Gollings a87 81 6 ch g Dutch Art Speech (Red Ransom (USA)) 4049[4] (5106) 5350[8] 7624[6]

Zamperini (IRE) Mike Murphy a89 93 4 ch g Fast Company(IRE) Lucky Date (IRE) (Halling (USA)) 2377[9] 3109[7] (3861) 6884[8] 7538[11] 7869[10] 8447[5]

Zand (IRE) Mark Johnston a80 87 6 b g Zamindar(USA) Zanara (IRE) (Kahyasi) 2037[4] 2318a[2] 2685[11] 4583[5] 5116[7]

Zanetto John Quinn a83 100 6 b g Medicean Play Bouzouki (Halling (USA)) 2158[4] 2898[13] 3890[9] 5555[18] 6449[9] 7858[13]

Zangokari (FR) T Lemer a71 69 2 b c Alexandros Tequila Heat (IRE) (Clodovil (IRE)) 5701a[4] 5988a[2]

Zanini (GER) K Demme 86 3 b c Poseidon Adventure(IRE) Zuccarella (GER) (Banyumanik (IRE)) 4186a[12]

Zanjabeel Simon Crisford a81 59 3 b g Aussie Rules(USA) Grain Only (Machiavellian (USA)) 1767[4] 2774[2] 3727[4] 4661[8]

Zannda (IRE) D K Weld 103 4 b m Azamour(IRE) Zanoubiya (IRE) (Dalakhani (IRE)) 1279a[4]

Zanzari (FR) C Boutin a60 67 2 b g Kendargent(FR) Zaltana (USA) (Cherokee Run (USA)) 7293a[5] 7422a[5]

Zanzi Way (FR) Mlle T Puitg 80 3 ch g Zanzibari(USA) Pearl Away (FR) (Gold Away (IRE)) 7999a[10]

Zapel Stefano Botti 100 3 b c Kyllachy Viadeigiardini (Dubai Destination (USA)) 2518a[5] 7719a[6] 7840a[2]

Zapper Cass (FR) Roger Fell a85 85 3 bb g Elusive City(USA) Moonlight Cass (IRE) (Danehill Dancer (IRE)) 5946a[3] 8083[6] 8308[7]

Zappeuse (FR) Y Barberot a77 78 3 b f Zamindar(USA) Sans Chichi (FR) (Chichicastenango (FR)) 716a[6]

Zarak (FR) A De Royer-Dupre 116 3 b c Dubawi(IRE) Zarkava (IRE) (Zamindar (USA)) 2283a[5] 2946a[2] 5499a[2] ◆ 6394a[4] 6973a[3]

Zarawi (IRE) John Gallagher a45 62 5 b g Marju(IRE) Zarwala (IRE) (Polish Precedent (USA)) 4050[6] 5100[2] 6730[13] 7367[9]

Zaria Richard Price a52 67 5 b m Tomba Princess Zara (Reprimand) 1632[2] ◆ 2129[4] 2655[7] 3096[3] (3802) 4302[2] 5062[4] 5571 [6] 6635[6]

Zarkavon John Wainwright a17 2 b f Avonbridge Zarkavean (Medicean) 3167[10] 3561[7]

Zarliman (IRE) Neil Mulholland a59 45 6 ch g Zamindar(USA) Zarlana (IRE) (Darshaan) 79[3] 155[2] (255) (1413) 3918a[2] 5021[9]

Zarras (GER) P Schaerer a86 57 7 b g Big Shuffle(USA) Zanana (Zafonic (USA)) (588a) 663a[3]

Zarwaan Doug Watson 113 5 b g Dutch Art Develyn (Pivotal) 282a[7] 628a[13]

Zarzal (IRE) Evan Williams a62 60 8 b g Dr Fong(USA) Zarwala (IRE) (Polish Precedent (USA)) 4483[6]

Zarzis Beauty (FR) D Prod'Homme a20 70 3 b f Whipper(USA) Arabian Beauty (FR) (Dubawi (IRE)) 5280a[15]

Zarzuela (DEN) Niels Petersen 86 6 ch m Singspiel(IRE) Singita (DEN) (Diaghlyphard (USA)) 3448a[7] 7395a[5]

Zauffaly (FR) Ed Dunlop a73 65 3 ch g Zoffany(IRE) Lady Sadowa (Nayef (USA)) 1258[3] 1638[3] 2128[2]

Zavikon Richard Hughes a67 2 b c Compton Place Hakuraa (IRE) (Elnadim (USA)) 6087[6] 6622[4]

Zawraq (IRE) D K Weld 101 4 b h Shamardal(USA) Sundus (USA) (Sadler's Wells (USA)) 7558a[2]

Zaytoon (IRE) J E Hammond 25 3 b g Cape Cross(IRE) Megec Blis (IRE) (Soviet Star (USA)) 5907a[12]

Zayva (FR) A De Royer-Dupre 103 3 ch f Raven's Pass(USA) Zayanida (IRE) (King's Best (USA)) 2945a[7] (6070a) 6975a[5]

Zealous (IRE) Alan Swinbank 86 3 br g Intense Focus(USA) Velvet Kiss (IRE) (Danehill Dancer (IRE)) 2029[5] 2479[9] (3187) 3855[7] 5616[16] 7623[12]

Zebby Sizz (IRE) Richard Hannon 43 2 gr c Zebedee Derval (IRE) (One Cool Cat (USA)) 3196[8] 3742[6] 4287[11] 4791[3]

Zebedee Cat (IRE) Iain Jardine 67 2 b c Zebedee Kitty Softpaws (IRE) (Royal Applause) 2090[6] 2570[6] 3283[6] 3881[5] 4679[9] 6807[5] 7579[10]

Zebedee's Girl (IRE) David Evans a64 69 3 gr f Zebedee Rafelite (Fraam) 74[3] 211[4] 291[2] 858[4] 979[8] 4587[4] 5571 [5] 6290[9] 6651[10] 7057[7] 7444[5]

Zebedee's Son (IRE) Phil York a51 58 3 gr g Zebedee Lady Ginevra (IRE) (Touch Of The Blues (FR)) 1259[10] (1486) 2325[6] 2545[12] 2828[4] 3509[11] 5399[10] 5830[6]

Zebedee Star Keith Dalgleish 60 2 b f Zebedee Sonna Star (IRE) (Red Clubs (IRE)) 3772[6] 4890[9] 5272[4] 6010[14] 6614[7]

Zebelini (IRE) Roy Bowring a53 53 4 gr m Zebedee Ma Nikitia (IRE) (Camacho) 2423[9] 3484[4] 4229[7] 4968[2] 5378[4] 6098[5] 6586[3] 6865[2] 7046[11] 8312[6] 8572[7]

Zeb's Fantasy (IRE) Amy Murphy a55 76 3 b f Zebedee Fantastic Cee (IRE) (Noverre (USA)) 1998[5] 7694[8] 7983[7] 8312[11]

Zebs Lad (IRE) Nikki Evans a65 65 4 ro g Zebedee Dubai Princess (IRE) (Dubai Destination (USA)) 197[12] 1913[9] 2458[11] (3146) 4088[9] 7062[11] 7211[10]

Zebspear (IRE) Joseph Tuite a57 72 2 br c Zebedee Canary Bird (IRE) (Catrail (USA)) 1915[4] 2311[3] 2641[3] 3114[10] 4638[2] (4791) 5125[5] 6658[7] 7217[11]

Zebstar (IRE) James Unett 101 3 b g Zebedee Zinstar (IRE) (Sinndar (IRE)) 1773[8] 1996[5] 2736[9]

Zebulon (IRE) Richard Hannon a70 73 2 gr c Zebedee Novelina (IRE) (Fusaichi Pegasus (USA)) 2204[6] 6108[6] 6673[3]

Zed Candy Girl Daniel Mark Loughnane a59 58 6 ch m Sakhee's Secret Musical Twist (USA) (Woodman (USA)) 201[4] 430[7] 590[2] (609) 1064[7] 1116[6] 1565[6] 2566[5] 3474[8] 7944[6] 8120[8] 8207[11] 8499[6]

Zeebee (IRE) Conrad Allen a24 7 3 gr f Zebedee Etta Place (Hawk Wing (USA)) 948[7]

Zeehan Clive Cox a73 76 3 gr f Aussie Rules(USA) Cross Current (Sakhee (USA)) 122[3] 331[2] 1759[2] ◆ 2181[2] 2909[10] 3468[7] 8076[3] (8281)

Zeelander Roger Varian 59 2 b c Dubawi(IRE) Zeeba (IRE) (Barathea (IRE)) 7770[9]

Zeeoneandonly (IRE) David Evans a72 78 3 b f Zebedee Subtle Shimmer (Danehill Dancer (IRE)) 419[6] 1638[5] (2186) 2372[2] 2693[13]

Zeeyalater (IRE) Ms Sheila Lavery a81 75 2 b g Zebedee Later (IRE) (Marju (IRE)) 6388a[17]

Zefferino Roger Charlton a69 85 2 ch c Frankel Turama (Pivotal) 5121[2] ◆ 6481[4] 7906[4]

Zeftan (IRE) Adrian Paul Keatley a75 86 7 ch g Bachelor Duke(USA) Zarafsha (IRE) (Alzao (USA)) (4417a)

Zelzal (FR) J-C Rouget a112 122 3 b c Sea The Stars(IRE) Olga Prekrasa (USA) (Kingmambo (USA)) 2283a[11] (3183a) (4185a) 6394a[3]

Zemario (IRE) Joseph G Murphy a60 60 10 b g Dalakhani(IRE) Noushkey (Polish Precedent (USA)) 5620a[4]

Zemindari (FR) H-F Devin a87 103 4 b g Zanzibari(USA) Villa Joyeuse (FR) (Kahyasi) 4578a[8]

Zenafire Sarah Hollinshead a54 72 7 b g Firebreak Zen Garden (Alzao (USA)) 2439[6] 3129[3] 3602[8] 4381[9] 6058[6] 6438[7] (6730) 7274[5] 7625[6]

Zenani (FR) A Fabre a80 66 3 b f Rip Van Winkle(IRE) Zaltana (USA) (Cherokee Run (USA)) 6912a[9]

Zenon (IRE) John Gosden 73 2 b c Galileo(IRE) Jacqueline (IND) (King Charlemagne (USA)) 5073[4] ◆

Zenovia (IRE) David Simcock a63 2 b f Invincible Spirit(IRE) Zallerina (Zamindar (USA)) 8131[9] 8397[5]

Zen Zansai Zaid (SWE) Tommy Gustafsson a75 100 7 ch g Dubai Destination(USA) La Petite Chinoise (Dr Fong (USA)) 93a[10] 285a[8] 6390a[11]

Zephuros (IRE) Charlie Appleby a83 86 4 b g Invincible Spirit(IRE) West Wind (Machiavellian (USA)) 12a[4] 279a[5] (Dead)

Zephyr Breeze Noel Wilson a73 68 3 b g Piccolo Bold Love (Bold Edge) 77[7] 821[7] 1111[9] 2534[7]

Zephyros (GER) David Bridgwater a68 69 5 br g Areion(GER) Zandra (GER) (Lagunas) 1949[6] ◆ 3125[3] 3255[2] (3997) 4383[2] 5207[3] 5925[5] 8498[3] ◆

Zero Euro (IRE) H Rogers a49 56 8 b m Chineur(FR) Triple Zero (IRE) (Raise A Grand (IRE)) 4813a[14]

Zeshov (IRE) Rebecca Bastiman a73 80 5 b g Acclamation Fathoming (USA) (Gulch (USA)) 1521[10] 2121[10] 2773[7] 3922[8] 4454[10] 5090[2] 5753[4] (6095) (6643)

Zest (IRE) James Fanshawe a86 92 3 b f Duke Of Marmalade(IRE) Affinity (Sadler's Wells (USA)) 1206[4] 1992[5] 3410[4] (4808) ◆ 6115[6] 6581[8] 6915[3]

Zeteah Tony Carroll a57 52 6 b m Passing Glance Ajeebah (IRE) (Mujtahid (USA)) 1791[6] 2542[7] 3044[5] 3997[12] 4993[7] 5604[8] 6188[2] 7036[9] 7426[8] 7642[15]

Zghorta Dance (FR) J-C Rouget a97 105 3 ch f Le Havre(IRE) Ana Zghorta (Anabaa (USA)) (2455a) 3452a[7] 4904a[4] 7566a[2]

Zhayrem (FR) P Van De Poele a57 53 5 b m Montmartre(FR) Cortiguera (Oasis Dream) 5281a[14] 5700a[11]

Zhui Feng (IRE) Amanda Perrett a87 106 3 b c Invincible Spirit(IRE) Es Que (Inchinor) 1393[3] 1864[10] 2466[6] 3299[11] 4797[8] 5699a[3] (5924) 6573[6] 6786[5] 7137a[5] 7354[12]

Zhukova (IRE) D K Weld 117 4 b m Fastnet Rock(AUS) Nightime (IRE) (Galileo (IRE)) (1227a) (2167a) (6351a) 7351[7]

Ziga G Arizkorreta Elosegui 80 5 br m Authorized(IRE) Classic Remark (IRE) (Dr Fong (USA)) 6356a[4] 8336a[12]

Ziggy Lee Lawrence Mullaney a86 86 10 b g Lujain(USA) Mary O'Grady (USA) (Swain (IRE)) 2775[7] (4452) 5274[2] 5648[6] 5882[2] 6234[4] 6926[2]

Ziggys Star Michael Appleby a83 68 4 b g Compton Place Ziggy Zaggy (Diktat) (36) 278[6] (414) 1380[9]

Zig Zag Girl Scott Dixon a9 50 2 b f Sixties Icon Mistic Magic (IRE) (Orpen (USA)) 1527[2] 1583[6] 2125[4] (2266) 2404[4] 7820[17]

Zilza (IRE) Conrad Allen a66 2 b f Paco Boy(IRE) Helen Glaz (IRE) (Giant's Causeway (USA)) 8362[DSQ] 8591[9]

Zindaya (USA) Chad C Brown 104 5 bb m More Than Ready(USA) Aristocratic Lady (USA) (Kris S (USA)) 5185a[3]

Zing (FR) Robert Collet a31 69 2 ch c Zizany(IRE) Volhynie (FR) (Volochine (IRE)) 3763a[13] 4183a[4]

Zingiber Wilf Storey a41 30 4 ch g Manduro(GER) Titoli Di Coda (IRE) (Bertolini (USA)) 1565[9] 2409[10] 4645[11] 6619[8] 6920[5] 7438[7] 7656[11]

Zio Gianni (USA) Jamie Osborne a71 66 3 b c Lemon Drop Kid(USA) August Storm (USA) (Storm Creek (USA)) 687[4] 818[2] 1113[2] 1429[4]

Zip Code (FR) Robert Collet a81 81 3 b f American Post Rendorina (FR) (Kendor (FR)) 1286a[5] 3007a[5] 3546a[7]

Zipedee John Ryan a42 48 2 rg f Zebedee White Shift (IRE) (Night Shift (USA)) 5258[4] 5631[10] 6524[5] 6887[6] 7528[7] 7884[7] 8276[10] 8425[8]

Zipedeedodah (IRE) Joseph Tuite a79 63 4 gr g Zebedee Beverley Macca (Piccolo) 56[4] 162[4] 462[6] 1150[3] 1433[6] 1950[4] 2676[10] 3316[4] 5706[7] (6660) 7018[5] 7534[2] (7945) (8040) 8280[7] 8495[9]

Zipessa (USA) Michael Stidham 107 4 ch m City Zip(USA) Precious Princess (USA) (Horse Chestnut (SAF)) 5430a[3] 7831a[5]

Zippy Daniel Kubler a30 67 3 b f Hellvelyn Ziggy Zaggy (Diktat) 2470[10] 6317[3] 6677[11] 7038[4] ◆ (7445)

Zip Wire (IRE) Donald McCain a45 58 7 b g Oratorio(IRE) Jaya (USA) (Ela-Mana-Mou) 157[6] 1048[7]

Zitat (GER) Waldemar Hickst a41 4 ch m Wiesenpfad(FR) Zita (GER) (Tannenkonig (IRE)) 7295a[7]

Zlatan (IRE) Ed de Giles a79 78 3 b g Dark Angel(IRE) Guard Hill (USA) (Rahy (USA)) 4498[4] 4936[3] 5326[13] 5720[6] 6407[4] 6651[2] (6826) 7036[2] (7417) 7619[2]

Zodiakos (IRE) Hugo Palmer a73 93 3 b g Kodiac Zonic (Zafonic (USA)) 1867[3] ◆ 3299[7] 4108[9] 4624[11] 6084[10] 7222[9]

Zoffanist (IRE) Amanda Perrett a59 55 2 ch g Zoffany(IRE) Frynia (USA) (Cat Thief (USA)) 6570[11] 6945[4] ◆ 7458[5]

Zoffanys Pride (IRE) Andrew Balding 82 3 b g Zoffany(IRE) Lioness (Lion Cavern (USA)) 1398[6] 1896[5] 2694[6] 5071[4] 5824[2] 6737[2]

Zoffany's Way (IRE) James Fanshawe a68 43 3 gr g Zoffany(IRE) Enchanting Way (Linamix (FR)) 63[3] 253[9] 361[4]

Zonderland Clive Cox a91 114 3 ch c Dutch Art Barynya (Pivotal) 1864[6] ◆ (2627) 4185a[8] (5329) ◆ 5873[2]

Zophilly (IRE) Jeremy Gask a62 3 b f Zoffany(IRE) Extreme Pleasure (IRE) (High Chaparral (IRE)) 1725[12] 2560[6] 8408[9]

Zoravan (USA) Keith Dalgleish a70 3 ch g More Than Ready(USA) Zaralanta (IRE) (Danehill Dancer (IRE)) 7973[9]

Zoria Katiba (FR) Mlle A Voraz a66 56 4 bb m Silver Frost(IRE) Zoriana (FR) (Danehill Dancer (IRE)) 3184a[11]

Zorlu (IRE) John O'Shea a40 57 3 b g Invincible Spirit(IRE) Special Assignment (USA) (Lemon Drop Kid (USA)) 1646[4] 6511[8] 7219[8] 7937[10]

Zouk (FR) P Bary a72 66 2 b f Delegator Singapore Belle (FR) (Sagacity (FR)) 7346a[5] 7970a[4]

Zruda David Thompson 50 5 b m Observatory(USA) Pagan Princess (Mujtahid (USA)) 2419[8] 3774[9] 4430[7]

Zubaidah Heather Dalton a65 56 4 b m Exceed And Excel(AUS) Bedouin Bride (USA) (Chester House (USA)) 1071[1] 347[8]

Zubeida Ismail Mohammed 87 3 b f Authorized(IRE) Tegwen (USA) (Nijinsky (CAN)) 2395[4] ◆ 3063[4] 3715[2] 4340[2] 5872[4] 7271[12]

Zugzwang (IRE) Ed de Giles a85 93 5 b g Kodiac Kris's Bank (Inchinor) 2819[13] 3303[10]

Zulu Rod Millman 40 2 b c Cockney Rebel(IRE) Pantita (Polish Precedent (USA)) 5820[9]

Zumran Hugo Palmer 67 2 b f Rock Of Gibraltar(IRE) Maid For Winning (USA) (Gone West (USA)) 1437[7] 1783[7] 4558[6] 5598[3]

Zumurudee (USA) Marco Botti a87 76 2 b c Stormy Atlantic(USA) Voting Right (FR) (High Chaparral (IRE)) 7100[3] 7769[2] (8073) ◆

Zwayyan William Haggas 94 3 ch c Pivotal Mail The Desert (IRE) (Desert Prince (IRE)) 3412[8] 4546[2] (5260) (6055) 6585[5]

Zylan (IRE) David Marnane a75 68 4 ch g Kyllachy Belgique (IRE) (Compton Place) 6461a[7]

Zymyran David Simcock a84 84 2 b g Henrythenavigator(USA) Zimira (IRE) (Invincible Spirit (IRE)) 4287[13] 5081[2] 5990[2] (6455) (6903) ◆ 7493[5] 7909[6]

Zzoro (IRE) Amanda Perrett a80 90 3 b c Manduro(GER) Krynica (USA) (Danzig (USA)) 1398[2] 1971[3] 2479[8] 4827[11] 7077[2] 7505[4]

Season Statistics Trainers - GB Flat 2016 (Jan 1-Dec 31)

NAME	WINS–RUNS	%	2ND	3RD	4TH	WIN PRIZE	TOTAL PRIZE	£1 STAKE
A P O'Brien	28–133	21%	28	16	17	£5,059,170	£8,130,756	+22.67
John Gosden	141–613	23%	107	78	64	£1,957,729	£3,462,784	+2.14
Richard Fahey	198–1739	11%	195	225	217	£1,555,030	£3,162,108	-397.84
Richard Hannon	173–1357	13%	185	166	173	£1,602,588	£2,847,607	-203.92
Mark Johnston	195–1413	14%	206	176	169	£1,553,728	£2,724,681	-316.95
Sir Michael Stoute	111–505	22%	93	67	49	£1,491,548	£2,525,774	-25.48
Roger Varian	97–554	18%	73	66	61	£1,788,832	£2,393,915	-141.34
William Haggas	137–596	23%	107	89	48	£1,423,781	£2,126,782	-83.29
Hugo Palmer	71–344	21%	54	50	36	£1,277,308	£2,091,598	+13.28
Charlie Appleby	70–331	21%	62	44	36	£1,307,474	£1,979,286	-15.97
David O'Meara	103–975	11%	124	115	105	£767,372	£1,679,545	-336.62
Andrew Balding	107–731	15%	103	96	91	£1,038,999	£1,672,624	-102.74
David Simcock	85–457	19%	61	76	65	£955,353	£1,646,019	-29.73
Clive Cox	65–435	15%	54	52	43	£1,175,717	£1,524,464	-51.45
Kevin Ryan	94–733	13%	91	93	75	£769,403	£1,457,569	-106.12
Saeed bin Suroor	68–319	21%	62	33	36	£720,144	£1,385,648	-38.64
Ralph Beckett	101–506	20%	70	56	60	£834,320	£1,300,689	+7.83
K R Burke	68–587	12%	54	59	69	£883,227	£1,196,416	-16.74
Charles Hills	76–543	14%	74	74	58	£670,583	£1,172,073	-192.65
Roger Charlton	48–250	19%	38	27	36	£683,191	£1,137,712	-49.31
Mick Channon	71–625	11%	79	65	85	£695,033	£1,133,050	-139.15
J-C Rouget	2–5	40%	0	2	0	£964,070	£1,071,670	+4.38
Henry Candy	22–225	10%	21	29	31	£786,789	£1,020,717	-64.88
James Fanshawe	43–243	18%	35	32	35	£640,458	£974,381	-36.02
Marco Botti	51–397	13%	55	51	48	£580,516	£895,727	-126.45
D K Weld	1–8	13%	0	1	0	£876,170	£889,715	-0.50
Tom Dascombe	75–569	13%	62	58	62	£505,921	£796,517	+14.80
Tim Easterby	76–807	9%	82	84	81	£472,566	£781,669	-213.08
Michael Dods	50–487	10%	57	58	49	£525,112	£764,312	-148.88
Keith Dalgleish	81–664	12%	88	60	81	£496,197	£742,517	-103.56
Michael Bell	37–323	11%	51	56	33	£518,422	£684,699	-134.77
Sir Mark Prescott Bt	55–278	20%	45	23	23	£367,258	£655,882	-60.61
Ed Dunlop	51–385	13%	49	39	34	£366,753	£636,239	-111.01
Michael Appleby	70–787	9%	63	70	94	£376,253	£634,622	-200.78
Hughie Morrison	43–351	12%	47	31	36	£432,904	£627,943	-80.88
David Evans	70–720	10%	94	99	86	£287,452	£621,355	-241.98
Dean Ivory	35–318	11%	34	26	22	£440,727	£619,456	-111.63
Michael Easterby	61–476	13%	52	55	47	£426,954	£618,295	-6.29
Stuart Williams	51–369	14%	32	38	40	£423,098	£581,206	-50.01
Luca Cumani	38–255	15%	36	38	31	£252,606	£574,486	-82.38
David Barron	38–354	11%	42	32	27	£383,017	£559,051	-57.03
James Tate	54–302	18%	39	51	39	£286,630	£511,161	-33.10
Eve Johnson Houghton	41–329	12%	32	42	51	£354,124	£502,560	+9.19
Laura Mongan	13–120	11%	9	12	9	£439,698	£479,838	+13.75
Robert Cowell	34–340	10%	29	46	35	£342,506	£477,043	-114.42
Brian Ellison	60–471	13%	51	54	50	£278,091	£462,550	-88.70
Jamie Osborne	48–376	13%	60	44	52	£319,979	£457,385	-57.83
Jeremy Noseda	19–109	17%	20	11	13	£240,116	£445,246	-47.85
David Nicholls	24–241	10%	38	26	21	£195,947	£427,541	-59.42

Season Statistics Jockeys - GB Flat 2016 (Jan 1-Dec 31)

NAME	WINS–RUNS	%	2ND	3RD	4TH	WIN PRIZE	TOTAL PRIZE	£1 STAKE
Jim Crowley	189–1017	19%	137	113	103	£1,267,082	£1,920,275	-46.53
Silvestre De Sousa	165–928	18%	125	108	108	£1,285,813	£2,091,201	-116.95
Luke Morris	159–1391	11%	194	186	146	£1,005,430	£1,576,248	-509.69
Adam Kirby	152–932	16%	102	112	117	£1,886,587	£2,467,603	-118.48
Joe Fanning	129–1025	13%	129	118	129	£864,958	£1,330,176	-311.14
Pat Cosgrave	120–734	16%	113	105	63	£981,163	£1,361,277	+21.80
Andrea Atzeni	116–618	19%	99	68	61	£2,452,894	£3,538,446	-49.72
Oisin Murphy	114–869	13%	101	112	105	£984,010	£1,962,569	-101.61
George Baker	114–683	17%	91	79	90	£1,067,563	£1,702,706	-124.04
Richard Kingscote	113–703	16%	80	77	70	£729,072	£1,084,308	+97.79
Paul Mulrennan	106–932	11%	101	96	99	£836,546	£1,196,999	-308.14
Ryan Moore	103–462	22%	72	60	53	£5,849,891	£8,085,004	-113.21
James Doyle	99–541	18%	95	66	64	£1,075,672	£2,244,190	-70.11
Jamie Spencer	96–597	16%	72	86	72	£1,206,614	£1,958,964	-74.20
Graham Gibbons	93–657	14%	90	79	47	£677,621	£962,008	-33.42
Daniel Tudhope	90–595	15%	90	79	72	£603,185	£1,088,235	-46.59
Tony Hamilton	89–753	12%	78	92	87	£500,616	£802,199	-120.09
Josephine Gordon	87–834	10%	103	109	103	£467,565	£728,496	-250.39
Frankie Dettori	85–391	22%	65	44	45	£2,625,038	£4,132,945	-0.85
Robert Havlin	81–557	15%	77	65	63	£688,116	£1,138,190	+15.88
P J McDonald	79–812	10%	78	102	94	£469,208	£725,722	-103.30
William Buick	79–421	19%	60	57	41	£1,466,638	£2,711,325	-27.87
Martin Harley	76–602	13%	64	73	77	£795,652	£1,288,836	-133.46
Ben Curtis	74–620	12%	75	59	68	£332,769	£538,250	-132.14
Franny Norton	74–504	15%	83	64	59	£496,832	£832,372	-64.89
Paul Hanagan	73–519	14%	72	60	45	£586,225	£1,423,142	-146.96
Tom Eaves	71–837	8%	73	88	75	£536,490	£880,987	-148.16
Sean Levey	67–519	13%	73	73	67	£692,780	£1,080,861	-128.59
Tom Marquand	63–663	10%	57	76	57	£371,588	£604,244	-161.60
Phillip Makin	63–476	13%	63	57	60	£402,548	£703,565	-81.08
Robert Winston	63–475	13%	51	56	43	£567,173	£793,399	-14.79
Connor Beasley	61–603	10%	70	72	56	£427,736	£626,949	-183.25
David Allan	61–533	11%	63	57	58	£520,366	£802,686	-77.33
J F Egan	60–629	10%	83	66	82	£270,072	£508,206	-211.08
David Probert	60–468	13%	59	49	54	£498,929	£734,321	-71.45
Shane Kelly	59–671	9%	74	75	91	£312,048	£546,011	-318.16
Harry Bentley	59–344	17%	36	44	43	£678,614	£965,541	-5.27
Andrew Mullen	57–671	8%	58	62	73	£391,480	£614,533	-103.42
James Sullivan	57–655	9%	63	58	80	£262,007	£417,194	-186.52
Martin Dwyer	54–483	11%	42	54	37	£356,274	£587,257	-42.64
Graham Lee	53–644	8%	78	63	74	£386,740	£828,647	-281.35
Adam McNamara	53–424	13%	54	52	54	£406,361	£569,366	-126.37
Tom Queally	49–536	9%	44	46	43	£641,732	£851,744	-176.92
Nathan Evans	49–451	11%	46	59	46	£338,189	£523,965	-93.90
Liam Keniry	47–552	9%	53	53	46	£182,142	£294,242	-175.42
William Carson	46–665	7%	59	68	85	£289,129	£450,229	-279.47
Ted Durcan	46–354	13%	49	31	45	£400,745	£563,280	-88.34
Kieran O'Neill	43–607	7%	57	59	73	£207,981	£411,592	-248.93
Frederik Tylicki	42–405	10%	45	44	54	£256,170	£641,576	-183.32

Season Statistics Owners - GB Flat 2016 (Jan 1-Dec 31)

NAME	WINS–RUNS	%	2ND	3RD	4TH	WIN PRIZE	TOTAL PRIZE
Godolphin	165–805	20%	151	89	89	£2,872,273	£5,016,525
D Smith & Mrs J Magnier & M Tabor	11–44	25%	10	3	5	£3,147,400	£4,073,827
Hamdan Al Maktoum	117–660	18%	112	98	68	£923,908	£1,954,243
Al Shaqab Racing	52–250	21%	40	28	34	£1,300,115	£1,908,730
M Tabor & D Smith & Mrs J Magnier	6–30	20%	11	1	4	£550,087	£1,780,234
Mrs J Magnier & M Tabor & D Smith	8–46	17%	9	8	6	£740,293	£1,453,770
Cheveley Park Stud	78–300	26%	59	39	25	£746,838	£1,333,944
Sh M Obaid Al Maktoum	21–101	21%	22	11	4	£1,021,845	£1,204,005
K Abdullah	59–287	21%	50	43	30	£630,064	£1,140,922
Sh H bin Mohammed Al Maktoum	65–443	15%	54	54	48	£560,601	£951,575
H H Aga Khan	1–8	13%	1	1	0	£876,170	£936,681
Qatar Racing Limited	29–202	14%	29	33	29	£295,032	£872,503
Ecurie Antonio Caro	1–1	100%	0	0	0	£737,230	£737,230
Paul & Clare Rooney	21–113	19%	13	15	10	£570,797	£685,202
Lady Bamford	15–71	21%	19	13	10	£181,605	£626,651
A D Spence	19–95	20%	10	7	9	£475,426	£621,827
Dr Marwan Koukash	21–288	7%	21	31	40	£189,982	£596,016
J C Smith	25–198	13%	25	25	22	£442,418	£582,415
The Queen	23–122	19%	22	17	15	£325,744	£557,108
Ontoawinner, Strecker & Burke	3–5	60%	0	1	0	£457,083	£514,514
Saleh Al Homaizi & Imad Al Sagar	26–190	14%	16	21	23	£346,694	£499,847
Sh Juma Dalmook Al Maktoum	38–165	23%	18	25	20	£374,719	£478,882
George Strawbridge	9–38	24%	4	5	3	£426,553	£462,725
Fred Archer Racing - Ormonde	3–5	60%	1	0	0	£395,269	£456,759
Mrs Fitri Hay	23–164	14%	18	21	24	£232,305	£456,335
Mohammed Jaber	10–48	21%	4	8	7	£330,503	£450,230
Mrs Jackie Cornwell	4–34	12%	7	6	3	£408,776	£446,004
W J and T C O Gredley	13–60	22%	6	14	4	£395,805	£443,488
Paul G Jacobs	2–19	11%	2	2	4	£305,924	£421,124
Saeed Manana	38–243	16%	36	37	33	£217,702	£420,444
Abdulla Al Mansoori	27–155	17%	20	22	15	£269,396	£368,850
H R H Sultan Ahmad Shah	11–66	17%	13	11	7	£185,953	£357,882
Godolphin & Prince A A Faisal	2–4	50%	1	0	1	£219,468	£353,560
Mrs Angie Bailey	9–47	19%	8	6	3	£206,056	£347,842
G Wilson & Cheveley Park Stud	1–4	25%	0	0	0	£340,260	£343,488
Robert E Masterson	1–1	100%	0	0	0	£340,260	£340,260
Sh Rashid Dalmook Al Maktoum	14–109	13%	13	22	11	£212,324	£326,099
Saeed Suhail	14–54	26%	12	6	6	£226,176	£302,795
Tony Bloom	4–22	18%	4	0	2	£219,917	£278,553
Norcroft Park Stud	4–37	11%	2	4	5	£212,853	£276,159
David T J Metcalfe	2–14	14%	3	1	2	£239,210	£263,116
Sultan Ali	12–73	16%	14	11	6	£165,776	£262,684
Abdullah Saeed Al Naboodah	19–56	34%	9	2	5	£206,711	£258,072
George Turner	3–20	15%	3	5	1	£44,927	£251,241
L J Williams/Mrs J Magnie et al	1–1	100%	0	0	0	£226,840	£226,840
John Brown & Megan Dennis	4–13	31%	4	2	0	£147,110	£225,663
The Starship Partnership	4–7	57%	1	0	0	£198,801	£217,383
Chris Giles & Richard Webb	2–9	22%	1	1	0	£154,656	£217,055
The Cool Silk Partnership	13–152	9%	23	20	15	£140,222	£215,576

Season Statistics Sires - GB & Ire 2016 (Jan 1-Dec 31)

	WINNERS–RUNNNERS	%	WINS	RUNS	2ND	3RD	4TH	WIN PRIZE	TOTAL PRIZE
Galileo	104–273	38%	143	848	128	109	86	£6,543,947	£10,489,764
Dubawi	79–190	42%	115	529	81	70	45	£2,728,708	£3,610,709
Sea The Stars	61–133	46%	79	369	54	40	43	£2,338,517	£2,947,168
Dark Angel	109–346	32%	137	1235	119	116	151	£1,594,368	£2,421,768
Pivotal	75–202	37%	102	747	99	86	77	£1,005,526	£2,262,692
Kodiac	115–363	32%	161	1332	159	149	145	£1,288,701	£2,060,873
Acclamation	111–350	32%	160	1401	141	168	150	£1,394,443	£2,030,887
Invincible Spirit	81–248	33%	100	901	86	114	104	£1,315,714	£1,923,223
Exceed And Excel	101–329	31%	142	1116	137	138	113	£1,060,236	£1,814,875
Shamardal	68–207	33%	92	677	84	68	89	£975,393	£1,719,672
Cape Cross	71–227	31%	106	718	72	97	87	£1,047,227	£1,665,554
Fastnet Rock	79–229	34%	115	733	96	83	85	£1,167,714	£1,639,427
Teofilo	62–198	31%	84	626	81	69	74	£841,387	£1,594,690
Iffraaj	66–211	31%	88	749	78	82	71	£685,611	£1,470,343
Kyllachy	86–280	31%	113	1117	107	118	113	£988,071	£1,453,927
Dansili	70–172	41%	88	601	71	65	70	£648,409	£1,435,152
Paco Boy	41–175	23%	54	588	71	62	59	£822,605	£1,366,861
Wootton Bassett	5–15	33%	6	56	9	4	8	£1,271,276	£1,285,880
Lope De Vega	34–118	29%	50	345	44	35	40	£747,038	£1,279,173
Lawman	65–240	27%	87	840	92	92	87	£870,855	£1,232,870
War Front	29–71	41%	40	206	37	17	19	£663,983	£1,210,510
Dutch Art	68–230	30%	89	787	79	73	88	£809,063	£1,187,114
Zoffany	40–160	25%	51	548	66	72	48	£392,232	£1,179,731
Equiano	61–206	30%	82	740	82	79	84	£827,269	£1,168,824
Mastercraftsman	41–211	19%	63	654	66	88	83	£523,812	£1,115,805
Oasis Dream	71–224	32%	94	756	91	83	83	£529,111	£1,082,548
Showcasing	49–161	30%	63	583	58	61	55	£757,139	£1,017,764
Holy Roman Emperor	62–209	30%	81	710	76	67	81	£648,979	£965,628
Arcano	64–181	35%	90	694	90	60	93	£626,470	£954,830
Footstepsinthesand	48–130	37%	65	559	66	65	54	£681,375	£923,224
Champs Elysees	51–156	33%	79	540	73	56	73	£575,960	£884,259
Sir Percy	48–208	23%	68	682	84	88	71	£478,570	£797,886
Bushranger	55–206	27%	66	818	69	75	78	£512,325	£792,096
Duke Of Marmalade	36–136	26%	52	446	31	50	40	£547,166	£777,717
New Approach	46–179	26%	56	470	45	57	51	£482,126	£775,535
Mount Nelson	27–112	24%	36	330	38	51	31	£463,281	£764,429
Pastoral Pursuits	49–166	30%	66	730	69	71	79	£479,212	£753,121
Rock Of Gibraltar	40–156	26%	62	604	54	94	44	£461,557	£727,055
Zebedee	55–226	24%	78	849	93	75	95	£428,552	£699,955
High Chaparral	42–164	26%	52	475	63	51	51	£259,358	£696,878
Fast Company	41–170	24%	53	588	52	46	72	£478,056	£684,359
Tagula	18–90	20%	21	312	24	33	34	£434,552	£671,590
Rip Van Winkle	44–158	28%	57	479	54	66	54	£430,221	£670,776
Lord Shanakill	10–44	23%	15	168	14	21	20	£517,411	£662,436
Azamour	22–88	25%	29	280	36	24	30	£368,076	£655,652
Dylan Thomas	30–95	32%	39	352	43	39	39	£460,863	£630,940
Bahamian Bounty	41–183	22%	65	706	95	69	72	£348,191	£623,588
Canford Cliffs	37–164	23%	47	494	44	60	50	£311,824	£616,844
Aqlaam	26–97	27%	36	304	28	39	32	£508,861	£613,823

Raceform Ratings - British Flat 2016

Two-Year-Olds

123	Lady Aurelia	Wesley A Ward
120	Churchill	A P O'Brien
118	Caravaggio	A P O'Brien
118	The Last Lion	Mark Johnston
117	Rhododendron	A P O'Brien
116	Blue Point	Charlie Appleby
116	Rivet	William Haggas
115	Lancaster Bomber	A P O'Brien
114	Boynton	Charlie Appleby
114	Mehmas	Richard Hannon
113	Capri	A P O'Brien
113	Intricately	Joseph Patrick O'Brien
113	Thunder Snow	Saeed bin Suroor
113	War Decree	A P O'Brien
112	Brave Anna	A P O'Brien
112	Harry Angel	Clive Cox
112	Hydrangea	A P O'Brien
112	Queen Kindly	Richard Fahey
112	Roly Poly	A P O'Brien
112	Yucatan	A P O'Brien

Three-Year-Olds

129	Almanzor	J-C Rouget
124	Galileo Gold	Hugo Palmer
124	Harzand	D K Weld
124	Ribchester	Richard Fahey
124	The Gurkha	A P O'Brien
123	Hawkbill	Charlie Appleby
123	Makahiki	Yasuo Tomomichi
123	Minding	A P O'Brien
123	Satono Diamond	Yasutoshi Ikee
122	Awtaad	Kevin Prendergast
122	Dee Majesty	Yoshitaka Ninomiya
122	US Army Ranger	A P O'Brien
122	Zelzal	J-C Rouget
121	Seventh Heaven	A P O'Brien
120	Idaho	A P O'Brien
120	Jet Setting	Adrian Paul Keatley
120	Leontes	Katsuhiko Sumii
120	Quiet Reflection	K R Burke
119	Mikki Rocket	Hidetaka Otonashi
119	Wings of Desire	John Gosden

Older Horses

130	Winx	Chris Waller
126	A Shin Hikari	Masanori Sakaguchi
126	Limato	Henry Candy
126	Postponed	Roger Varian
125	Aerovelocity	P O'Sullivan
125	Fascinating Rock	D K Weld
125	Mecca's Angel	Michael Dods
124	Chautauqua	M W & J Hawkes
124	Found	A P O'Brien
124	Highland Reel	A P O'Brien
124	Maurice	Noriyuki Hori
124	Terravista	Joseph Pride
124	Time Test	Roger Charlton
123	My Dream Boat	Clive Cox
123	Werther	John Moore
122	Belardo	Roger Varian
122	Black Heart Bart	Darren Weir
122	Duramente	Noriyuki Hori
122	Jack Hobbs	John Gosden
122	Kitasan Black	Hisashi Shimizu

All-Weather

117	Ennaadd	Roger Varian
116	Muthmir	William Haggas
115	Gracious John	David Evans
115	Grendisar	Marco Botti
115	Sovereign Debt	David Nicholls
114	Lord Of The Land	David O'Meara
114	Alben Star	Richard Fahey
114	Take Cover	David C Griffiths
113	Curbyourenthusiasm	David Simcock
113	Spring Loaded	Paul D'Arcy
113	Maverick Wave	John Gosden
112	Western Hymn	John Gosden
112	Captain Cat	Roger Charlton
112	Lightscameraction	Gay Kelleway
112	Mister Universe	Mark Johnston
111	Muffri'Ha	William Haggas
111	Mythmaker	Bryan Smart
111	Sovereign Debt	David Nicholls
111	Star Storm	James Fanshawe
111	Team Talk	Saeed bin Suroor

Raceform Jumps Median Times 2016

Some distances have been omitted where insufficient data exists to establish a reliable median time

ASCOT

- **5f** 1m 0.5s
- **6f** 1m 14.5s
- **7f** 1m 27.6s
- **1m (Str)** 1m 40.8s
- **1m (Rnd)** 1m 40.7s
- **1m 2f** 2m 7.4s
- **1m 4f** 2m 32.5s
- **1m 6f** 3m 1.0s
- **2m** 3m 29.0s
- **2m 4f** 4m 24.8s
- **2m 5f 159y** 4m 49.4s

AYR

- **5f** 59.4s
- **6f** 1m 12.4s
- **7f 50y** 1m 33.4s
- **1m** 1m 43.8s
- **1m 1f 20y** 1m 57.5s
- **1m 2f** 2m 12.0s
- **1m 5f 13y** 2m 54.0s
- **1m 7f** 3m 20.4s
- **2m 1f 105y** 3m 55.0s

BATH

- **5f 11y** 1m 2.5s
- **5f 161y** 1m 11.2s
- **1m 5y** 1m 40.8s
- **1m 2f 46y** 2m 11.0s
- **1m 3f 144y** 2m 30.6s
- **1m 5f 22y** 2m 52.0s
- **1m 6f** 3m 3.8s
- **2m 1f 34y** 3m 51.9s

BEVERLEY

- **5f** 1m 3.5s
- **7f 100y** 1m 33.8s
- **1m 100y** 1m 47.6s
- **1m 1f 207y** 2m 7.0s
- **1m 4f 16y** 2m 39.8s
- **2m 35y** 3m 39.8s

BRIGHTON

- **5f 59y** 1m 2.3s
- **5f 213y** 1m 10.2s
- **6f 209y** 1m 23.1s
- **7f 214y** 1m 36.0s
- **1m 1f 209y** 2m 3.6s
- **1m 3f 196y** 2m 32.7s

CARLISLE

- **5f** 1m 0.8s
- **5f 193y** 1m 13.7s
- **6f 195y** 1m 27.1s
- **7f 173y** 1m 40.0s
- **1m 1f** 1m 57.6s
- **1m 3f 39y** 2m 23.1s
- **1m 6f 32y** 3m 7.5s
- **2m 1f 47y** 3m 53.0s

CATTERICK

- **5f** 59.8s
- **5f 212y** 1m 13.6s
- **7f** 1m 27.0s
- **1m 3f 214y** 2m 38.9s
- **1m 5f 175y** 3m 3.6s
- **1m 7f 177y** 3m 32.0s

CHELMSFORD (AW)

- **5f** 1m 0.2s
- **6f** 1m 13.7s
- **7f** 1m 27.2s
- **1m** 1m 39.9s
- **1m 2f** 2m 8.6s
- **1m 5f 66y** 2m 53.6s
- **1m 6f** 3m 3.2s
- **2m** 3m 30.0s

CHEPSTOW

- **5f 16y** 59.3s
- **6f 16y** 1m 12.0s
- **7f 16y** 1m 23.2s
- **1m 14y** 1m 36.2s
- **1m 2f 36y** 2m 10.6s
- **1m 4f 23y** 2m 39.0s
- **2m 49y** 3m 38.9s
- **2m 2f** 4m 3.6s

CHESTER

- **5f 16y** 1m 1.0s
- **5f 110y** 1m 6.2s
- **6f 18y** 1m 13.8s
- **7f 2y** 1m 26.5s
- **7f 122y** 1m 33.8s
- **1m 2f 75y** 2m 11.2s
- **1m 3f 79y** 2m 24.8s
- **1m 4f 66y** 2m 38.5s
- **1m 5f 89y** 2m 52.7s
- **1m 6f 91y** 3m 7.0s
- **1m 7f 195y** 3m 28.0s
- **2m 2f 147y** 4m 4.8s

DONCASTER

- **5f** 1m 0.5s
- **5f 140y** 1m 8.8s
- **6f** 1m 13.6s
- **6f 110y** 1m 19.9s
- **7f** 1m 26.3s
- **1m (Str)** 1m 39.3s
- **1m (Rnd)** 1m 39.7s
- **1m 2f 60y** 2m 9.4s
- **1m 4f** 2m 34.9s
- **1m 6f 132y** 3m 7.4s
- **2m 110y** 3m 40.4s
- **2m 2f** 3m 55.0s

EPSOM

- **5f** 55.7s
- **6f** 1m 9.4s
- **7f** 1m 23.3s
- **1m 114y** 1m 46.1s
- **1m 2f 18y** 2m 9.7s
- **1m 4f 10y** 2m 38.9s

FFOS LAS

- **5f** 58.3s
- **6f** 1m 10.0s
- **7f 80y** 1m 33.0s
- **1m** 1m 41.0s
- **1m 2f** 2m 9.4s
- **1m 4f** 2m 37.4s
- **1m 6f** 3m 3.8s
- **2m** 3m 30.0s

GOODWOOD

- **5f** 1m 0.2s
- **6f** 1m 12.2s
- **7f** 1m 27.0s
- **1m** 1m 39.9s
- **1m 1f** 1m 56.3s
- **1m 1f 192y** 2m 8.1s
- **1m 3f** 2m 26.5s
- **1m 4f** 2m 38.4s
- **1m 6f** 3m 3.6s
- **2m** 3m 29.0s
- **2m 5f** 4m 31.0s

HAMILTON

- **5f 7y** 1m
- **6f 6y** 1m 12.2s
- **1m 67y** 1m 48.4s
- **1m 3f 14y** 2m 25.6s
- **1m 5f 14y** 2m 53.9s

HAYDOCK

- **5f** 1m 0.8s
- **5f (Inner)** 1m 0.8s
- **6f** 1m 13.8s
- **6f (Inner)** 1m 13.8s
- **7f** 1m 30.7s
- **1m** 1m 43.7s
- **1m 2f 95y** 2m 15.5s
- **1m 3f 200y** 2m 33.8s
- **1m 6f** 3m 2.0s
- **2m 45y** 3m 34.3s

KEMPTON (AW)

- **5f** 1m 0.5s
- **6f** 1m 13.1s
- **7f** 1m 26.0s
- **1m** 1m 39.8s
- **1m 2f** 2m 8.0s
- **1m 3f** 2m 21.9s
- **1m 4f** 2m 34.5s
- **2m** 3m 30.1s

LEICESTER

- **5f** 1m
- **6f** 1m 13.0s
- **7f** 1m 26.2s
- **1m 60y** 1m 45.1s
- **1m 1f 218y** 2m 7.9s
- **1m 3f 183y** 2m 33.9s

LINGFIELD

- **5f** 58.2s
- **6f** 1m 11.2s
- **7f** 1m 23.3s
- **7f 140y** 1m 32.3s
- **1m 1f** 1m 56.6s
- **1m 2f** 2m 10.5s
- **1m 3f 106y** 2m 31.5s
- **1m 6f** 3m 10.0s
- **2m** 3m 34.8s

LINGFIELD (AW)

- **5f 6y** 58.8s
- **6f 1y** 1m 11.9s
- **7f 1y** 1m 24.8s
- **1m 1y** 1m 38.2s
- **1m 2f** 2m 6.6s
- **1m 4f** 2m 33.0s
- **1m 5f** 2m 46.0s
- **1m 7f 169y** 3m 25.7s

MUSSELBURGH

- **5f** 1m 0.4s
- **5f 1y** 1m 0.4s
- **7f 30y** 1m 29.0s
- **7f 33y** 1m 29.0s
- **1m** 1m 41.2s
- **1m 2y** 1m 41.2s
- **1m 208y** 1m 53.9s
- **1m 1f** 1m 53.9s
- **1m 4f 100y** 2m 42.0s
- **1m 5f** 2m 52.0s
- **1m 5f 164y** 3m 1.9s
- **1m 6f** 3m 5.3s
- **2m** 3m 33.5s

NEWBURY

- **5f 34y** 1m 1.4s
- **6f 8y** 1m 13.0s
- **6f 110y** 1m 19.3s
- **7f (Str)** 1m 25.7s
- **1m (Str)** 1m 39.7s
- **1m 7y (Rnd)** 1m 38.7s
- **1m 1f** 1m 55.5s
- **1m 2f 6y** 2m 8.8s
- **1m 3f 5y** 2m 21.2s
- **1m 4f 5y** 2m 35.5s
- **1m 5f 61y** 2m 52.0s
- **2m** 3m 32.0s

NEWCASTLE (AW)

- **5f** 59.5s
- **6f** 1m 12.5s
- **7f 14y** 1m 26.2s
- **1m 5y** 1m 38.6s
- **1m 2f 42y** 2m 10.4s
- **1m 4f 98y** 2m 41.1s
- **2m 56y** 3m 35.2s

NEWMARKET

- **5f (Row)** 59.1s
- **6f (Row)** 1m 12.2s
- **7f (Row)** 1m 25.4s
- **1m (Row)** 1m 38.6s
- **1m 1f (Row)** 1m 51.7s
- **1m 2f (Row)** 2m 5.8s
- **1m 4f (Row)** 2m 32.0s
- **1m 6f (Row)** 2m 57.0s
- **2m (Row)** 3m 30.5s
- **2m 2f (Row)** 3m 52.0s

NEWMARKET (JULY)

- **5f (July)** 59.1s
- **6f (July)** 1m 12.5s
- **7f (July)** 1m 25.7s
- **1m (July)** 1m 40.0s
- **1m 2f (July)** 2m 5.5s
- **1m 4f (July)** 2m 32.9s
- **1m 5f (July)** 2m 44.0s
- **2m 24y (July)** 3m 27.0s

NOTTINGHAM

- **5f 13y** 1m 1.5s
- **5f 13y (Inner)** 1m 1.5s
- **6f 15y** 1m 14.7s
- **1m 75y** 1m 49.0s
- **1m 75y (Inner)** 1m 49.0s
- **1m 1f** 1m 57.6s
- **1m 2f 50y** 2m 14.3s
- **1m 2f 50y (Inner)** 2m 14.3s
- **1m 6f 15y** 3m 7.0s
- **1m 6f 15y (Inner)** 3m 7.0s
- **2m 9y** 3m 34.5s

PONTEFRACT

- **5f** 1m 3.3s
- **6f** 1m 16.9s
- **1m 4y** 1m 45.9s
- **1m 2f 6y** 2m 13.7s
- **1m 4f 8y** 2m 40.8s
- **2m 1f 22y** 3m 44.6s
- **2m 1f 216y** 3m 56.2s
- **2m 5f 122y** 4m 51.0s

REDCAR

- **5f** 58.6s
- **6f** 1m 11.8s
- **7f** 1m 24.5s
- **1m** 1m 36.6s
- **1m 1f** 1m 53.0s
- **1m 2f** 2m 7.1s
- **1m 6f 19y** 3m 4.7s
- **2m 4y** 3m 31.4s

RIPON

- **5f** 1m
- **6f** 1m 13.0s
- **1m** 1m 41.4s
- **1m 1f** 1m 54.7s
- **1m 1f 170y** 2m 5.4s
- **1m 4f 10y** 2m 36.7s
- **2m** 3m 31.8s

SALISBURY

- **5f** 1m 1.0s
- **6f** 1m 14.8s
- **6f 212y** 1m 28.6s
- **1m** 1m 43.5s
- **1m 1f 198y** 2m 9.9s
- **1m 4f** 2m 38.0s
- **1m 6f 21y** 3m 7.4s

SANDOWN

- **5f 6y** 1m 1.6s
- **7f 16y** 1m 29.5s
- **1m 14y** 1m 43.3s
- **1m 1f** 1m 55.7s
- **1m 2f 7y** 2m 10.5s
- **1m 6f** 3m 4.5s
- **2m 78y** 3m 38.7s

SOUTHWELL (AW)

- **5f** 59.7s
- **6f** 1m 16.5s
- **7f** 1m 30.3s
- **1m** 1m 43.7s
- **1m 3f** 2m 28.0s
- **1m 4f** 2m 41.0s
- **1m 6f** 3m 8.3s
- **2m** 3m 45.5s

THIRSK

- **5f** 59.6s
- **6f** 1m 12.7s
- **7f** 1m 27.2s
- **1m** 1m 40.1s
- **1m 4f** 2m 36.2s
- **2m** 3m 28.3s

WETHERBY

- **5f 110y** 1m 6.0s
- **7f** 1m 27.0s
- **1m** 1m 41.0s
- **1m 1f** 1m 55.0s
- **1m 2f** 2m 9.0s
- **1m 6f** 3m 5.0s

WINDSOR

- **5f 10y** 1m 0.3s
- **6f** 1m 13.0s
- **1m 67y** 1m 44.7s
- **1m 2f 7y** 2m 8.7s
- **1m 3f 135y** 2m 29.5s

WOLVERHAMPTON (AW)

- **5f 20y** 1m 1.9s
- **5f 216y** 1m 14.5s
- **7f 32y** 1m 28.8s
- **1m 141y** 1m 50.1s
- **1m 1f 103y** 2m 0.8s
- **1m 4f 50y** 2m 40.8s
- **1m 5f 194y** 3m 4.8s
- **2m 119y** 3m 43.7s

YARMOUTH

- **5f 42y** 1m 2.7s
- **6f 3y** 1m 14.4s
- **7f 3y** 1m 26.6s
- **1m 3y** 1m 40.6s
- **1m 1f 21y** 1m 55.8s
- **1m 2f 23y** 2m 10.5s
- **1m 3f 104y** 2m 28.7s
- **1m 6f 17y** 3m 7.6s
- **2m** 3m 32.4s

YORK

- **5f** 59.3s
- **5f 89y** 1m 4.1s
- **6f** 1m 11.9s
- **7f** 1m 25.3s
- **1m** 1m 39.0s
- **1m 208y** 1m 52.0s
- **1m 2f 88y** 2m 12.5s
- **1m 4f** 2m 33.2s
- **1m 6f** 3m 0.2s
- **2m 88y** 3m 34.5s

Raceform Flat Record Times

ASCOT

Distance	Time	Age	Weight	Going	Horse	Date
5f	58.80	2	9-1	Good To Firm	No Nay Never	Jun 20 2013
5f	57.44	6	9-1	Good To Firm	Miss Andretti	Jun 19 2007
6f	1m 12.46	2	9-1	Good To Firm	Henrythenavigator	Jun 19 2007
6f	1m 11.50	3	9-10	Good To Firm	Mince	Aug 11 2012
7f	1m 26.55	2	9-0	Good To Firm	Malabar	Jly 25 2014
7f	1m 24.28	4	8-11	Good To Firm	Galician	Jly 27 2013
1m	1m 39.55	2	8-12	Good	Joshua Tree	Sep 26 2009
1m	1m 38.32	3	9-0	Good To Firm	Ghanaati	Jun 19 2009
1m	1m 37.09	4	9-0	Good To Firm	Integral	Jun 18 2014
1m 2f	2m 1.90	5	8-11	Good To Firm	The Fugue	Jun 18 2014
1m 4f	2m 24.60	4	9-7	Good To Firm	Novellist	Jly 27 2013
2m	3m 24.12	4	8-12	Good To Firm	Mizzou	Apr 29 2015
2m 4f	4m 16.92	6	9-2	Good To Firm	Rite of Passage	Jun 17 2010
2m 5f 159y	4m 45.67	7	9-2	Good To Firm	Oriental Fox	Jun 20 2015

AYR

Distance	Time	Age	Weight	Going	Horse	Date
5f	56.98	2	8-11	Good	Boogie Street	Sep 18 2003
5f	55.68	3	8-11	Good To Firm	Look Busy	Jun 21 2008
6f	1m 9.73	2	7-10	Firm	Sir Bert	Sep 17 1969
6f	1m 8.37	5	8-6	Good To Firm	Maison Dieu	Jun 21 2008
7f 50y	1m 28.99	2	9-0	Good	Tafaahum	Sep 19 2003
7f 50y	1m 28.07	5	9-0	Good To Firm	Ginger Jack	May 30 2012
1m	1m 39.18	2	9-7	Good	Moonlightnavigator	Sep 18 2014
1m	1m 36.00	4	7-13	Firm	Sufi	Sep 16 1959
1m 1f 20y	1m 50.30	4	9-3	Good	Retirement	Sep 19 2003
1m 2f	2m 4.02	4	9-9	Good To Firm	Endless Hall	Jly 17 2000
1m 5f 13y	2m 45.81	4	9-7	Good To Firm	Eden's Close	Sep 18 1993
1m 7f	3m 13.16	3	9-4	Good	Romany Rye	Sep 19 1991
2m 1f 105y	3m 45.20	4	6-13	Firm	Curry	Sep 16 1955

BATH

Distance	Time	Age	Weight	Going	Horse	Date
5f 11y	59.50	2	9-2	Firm	Amour Propre	Jly 24 2008
5f 11y	58.75	3	8-12	Firm	Enticing	May 1 2007
5f 161y	1m 8.70	2	8-12	Firm	Qalahari	Jly 24 2008
5f 161y	1m 8.10	6	9-0	Firm	Madraco	May 22 1989
1m 5y	1m 39.51	2	9-2	Firm	Natural Charm	Sep 14 2014
1m 5y	1m 37.20	5	8-12	Good To Firm	Adobe	Jun 17 2000
1m 5y	1m 37.20	3	8-7	Firm	Alasha	Aug 18 2002
1m 2f 46y	2m 5.80	3	9-0	Good To Firm	Connoisseur Bay	May 29 1998
1m 3f 144y	2m 25.74	3	9-0	Hard	Top The Charts	Sep 8 2005
1m 5f 22y	2m 47.20	4	10-0	Firm	Flown	Aug 13 1991
2m 1f 34y	3m 43.41	6	7-9	Firm	Yaheska	Jun 14 2003

BEVERLEY

Distance	Time	Age	Weight	Going	Horse	Date
5f	1m 0.89	2	8-12	Good To Firm	Langavat	Jun 8 2013
5f	1m 0.08	6	9-7	Good	Line Of Reason	Jun 14 2016
7f 100y	1m 31.10	2	9-7	Good To Firm	Champagne Prince	Aug 10 1995
7f 100y	1m 31.10	2	9-0	Firm	Majal	Jly 30 1991
7f 100y	1m 29.50	3	7-8	Firm	Who's Tef	Jly 30 1991
1m 100y	1m 43.30	2	9-0	Firm	Arden	Sep 24 1986
1m 100y	1m 42.20	3	8-4	Firm	Legal Case	Jun 14 1989
1m 1f 207y	2m 1.00	3	9-7	Good To Firm	Eastern Aria	Aug 29 2009
1m 4f 16y	2m 33.35	5	9-2	Good To Firm	Two Jabs	Apr 23 2015
2m 35y	3m 29.50	4	9-2	Good To Firm	Rushen Raider	Aug 14 1996

BRIGHTON

Distance	Time	Age	Weight	Going	Horse	Date
5f 59y	1m 0.10	2	9-0	Firm	Bid for Blue	May 6 1993
5f 59y	59.30	3	8-9	Firm	Play Hever Golf	May 26 1993
5f 213y	1m 8.10	2	8-9	Firm	Song Mist	Jly 16 1996
5f 213y	1m 7.30	5	9-1	Good To Firm	Blundell Lane	May 4 2000
5f 213y	1m 7.30	3	8-9	Firm	Third Party	Jun 3 1997
6f 209y	1m 19.90	2	8-11	Hard	Rain Burst	Sep 15 1988
6f 209y	1m 19.40	4	9-3	Good To Firm	Sawaki	Sep 3 1991
7f 214y	1m 32.80	2	9-7	Firm	Asian Pete	Oct 3 1989
7f 214y	1m 30.50	5	8-11	Firm	Mystic Ridge	May 27 1999
1m 1f 209y	2m 4.70	2	9-0	Good To Soft	Esteemed Master	Nov 2 2001
1m 1f 209y	1m 57.20	3	9-0	Firm	Get The Message	Apr 30 1984
1m 3f 196y	2m 25.80	4	8-2	Firm	New Zealand	Jly 4 1985

CARLISLE

Distance	Time	Age	Weight	Going	Horse	Date
5f	1m 0.10	2	8-5	Firm	La Tortuga	Aug 2 1999
5f	58.80	3	9-8	Good To Firm	Esatto	Aug 21 2002
5f 193y	1m 12.30	2	9-2	Good To Firm	Burrishoole Abbey	Jun 22 2016
5f 193y	1m 10.83	4	9-0	Good To Firm	Bo McGinty	Sep 11 2005
6f 195y	1m 24.30	3	8-9	Good To Firm	Marjurita	Aug 21 2002
7f 173y	1m 37.02	4	9-5	Good To Firm	Edgar Balthazar	Jun 22 2016
1m 1f	1m 53.84	3	9-0	Firm	Little Jimbob	Jun 14 2004
1m 3f 39y	2m 20.83	5	9-10	Good To Firm	Sindarban	Jun 22 2016
1m 6f 32y	3m 2.20	6	8-10	Firm	Explosive Speed	May 26 1994
2m 1f 47y	3m 46.20	3	7-10	Good To Firm	Warring Kingdom	Aug 25 1999

CATTERICK

Distance	Time	Age	Weight	Going	Horse	Date
5f	57.60	2	9-0	Firm	H Harrison	Oct 8 2002
5f	57.10	4	8-7	Firm	Kabcast	Jly 6 1989
5f 212y	1m 11.40	2	9-4	Firm	Captain Nick	Jly 11 1978
5f 212y	1m 9.86	9	8-13	Good To Firm	Sharp Hat	May 30 2003
7f	1m 24.10	2	8-11	Firm	Linda's Fantasy	Sep 18 1982
7f	1m 22.56	6	8-7	Firm	Differential	May 31 2003
1m 3f 214y	2m 30.50	3	8-8	Good To Firm	Rahaf	May 30 2003
1m 5f 175y	2m 54.80	3	8-5	Firm	Geryon	May 31 1984
1m 7f 177y	3m 20.80	4	7-11	Firm	Bean Boy I	Jly 8 1982

CHELMSFORD (A.W)

Distance	Time	Age	Weight	Going	Horse	Date
5f	58.72	2	9-7	Standard	Sun'Aq	Nov 19 2015
5f	57.30	7	8-13	Standard	Brother Tiger	Feb 7 2016
6f	1m 11.19	2	8-13	Standard	Florencio	Oct 15 2015
6f	1m 10.16	4	9-4	Standard	Golden Amber	Aug 18 2015
7f	1m 23.23	4	9-0	Standard	Volunteer Point	Jan 16 2016
1m	1m 37.15	2	9-3	Standard	Dragon Mall	Sep 26 2015
1m	1m 35.46	4	9-7	Standard	Mindurownbusiness	Nov 23 2015
1m 2f	2m 2.33	8	9-7	Standard	Bancnuanaheireann	Nov 5 2015
1m 5f 66y	2m 47.00	4	8-7	Standard	Coorg	Jan 6 2016
1m 6f	2m 55.65	4	10-0	Standard	Castle Combe	Sep 3 2015
2m	3m 22.37	5	9-3	Standard	Notarised	Mar 3 2016

CHEPSTOW

Distance	Time	Age	Weight	Going	Horse	Date
5f 16y	57.60	2	8-11	Firm	Micro Love	Jly 8 1986
5f 16y	56.80	3	8-4	Firm	Torbay Express	Sep 15 1979
6f 16y	1m 8.50	2	9-2	Firm	Ninjago	Jly 27 2012
6f 16y	1m 8.10	3	9-7	Firm	America Calling	Sep 18 2001
7f 16y	1m 20.80	2	9-0	Good To Firm	Royal Amaretto	Sep 12 1996
7f 16y	1m 19.30	3	9-0	Firm	Taranaki	Sep 18 2001
1m 14y	1m 33.10	2	8-11	Good To Firm	Ski Academy	Aug 28 1995
1m 14y	1m 31.60	3	8-13	Firm	Stoli	Sep 18 2001
1m 2f 36y	2m 4.10	3	8-5	Good To Firm	Ela Athena	Jly 23 1999
1m 2f 36y	2m 4.10	5	8-9	Hard	Leonidas	Jly 5 1983
1m 2f 36y	2m 4.10	5	7-8	Good To Firm	It's Varadan	Sep 9 1989
1m 4f 23y	2m 31.00	5	8-11	Hard	The Friend	Aug 29 1983
1m 4f 23y	2m 31.00	3	8-9	Good To Firm	Spritsail	Jly 13 1989
2m 49y	3m 27.70	4	9-0	Good To Firm	Wizzard Artist	Jly 1 1989
2m 2f	3m 56.40	5	8-7	Good To Firm	Laffah	Jly 8 2000

CHESTER

Distance	Time	Age	Weight	Going	Horse	Date
5f 16y	59.94	2	9-2	Good To Firm	Leiba Leiba	Jun 26 2010
5f 16y	58.88	3	8-7	Good To Firm	Peterkin	Jly 11 2014
5f 110y	1m 6.39	2	8-7	Good To Soft	Kinematic	Sep 27 2014
5f 110y	1m 5.02	6	8-9	Good	Ballesteros	Aug 22 2015
6f 18y	1m 12.85	2	8-10	Good To Firm	Flying Express	Aug 31 2002
6f 18y	1m 12.02	5	9-5	Good To Firm	Deauville Prince	Jun 13 2015
7f 2y	1m 25.29	2	9-0	Good To Firm	Due Respect	Sep 25 2002
7f 2y	1m 23.75	5	8-13	Good To Firm	Three Graces (GER)	Jly 9 2005
7f 122y	1m 32.29	2	9-0	Good To Firm	Big Bad Bob	Sep 25 2002
7f 122y	1m 30.91	3	8-12	Good To Firm	Cupid's Glory	Aug 18 2005
1m 2f 75y	2m 7.15	3	8-8	Good To Firm	Stotsfold	Sep 23 2006
1m 3f 79y	2m 22.17	3	8-12	Good To Firm	Perfect Truth	May 6 2009
1m 4f 66y	2m 33.70	3	8-10	Good To Firm	Fight Your Corner	May 7 2002
1m 5f 89y	2m 45.43	5	8-11	Firm	Rakaposhi King	May 7 1987
1m 7f 195y	3m 20.33	4	9-0	Good To Firm	Grand Fromage	Jly 13 2002
2m 2f 147y	3m 58.89	7	9-2	Good To Firm	Greenwich Meantime	May 9 2007

DONCASTER

Distance	Time	Age	Weight	Going	Horse	Date
5f	58.04	2	9-1	Good	Gutaifan	Sep 11 2015
5f	57.31	7	9-10	Good	Tabaret	Aug 14 2010
5f 140y	1m 5.38	4	9-7	Good	Muthmir	Sep 13 2014
6f	1m 10.65	2	9-7	Good To Firm	Blossomtime	Jly 16 2015
6f	1m 9.56	3	8-10	Good To Firm	Proclaim	May 30 2009
6f 110y	1m 17.19	2	8-9	Good	Mr Lupton	Sep 10 2015
7f	1m 22.78	2	9-5	Good	Basateen	Jly 24 2014
7f	1m 21.81	6	8-7	Good To Firm	Signor Peltro	May 30 2009
1m	1m 36.72	2	8-12	Good	Dance Of Fire	Sep 13 2014
1m	1m 38.37	2	8-6	Good To Soft	Antoniola	Oct 23 2009
1m	1m 34.46	4	8-12	Good To Firm	Staying On	Apr 18 2009
1m	1m 34.95	6	8-9	Firm	Quick Wit	Jly 18 2013
1m 2f 60y	2m 4.81	4	8-13	Good To Firm	Red Gala	Sep 12 2007
1m 4f	2m 27.48	3	8-4	Good To Firm	Swift Alhaarth	Sep 10 2011
1m 6f 132y	3m 0.44	3	9-0	Good To Firm	Masked Marvel	Sep 10 2011
2m 110y	3m 34.52	7	9-0	Good To Firm	Inchnadamph	Nov 10 2007
2m 2f	3m 48.41	4	9-4	Good To Firm	Septimus	Sep 14 2007

EPSOM

Distance	Time	Age	Weight	Going	Horse	Date
5f	55.02	2	8-9	Good To Firm	Prince Aslia	Jun 9 1995
5f	53.60	4	9-5	Firm	Indigenous	Jun 2 1960
6f	1m 7.85	2	8-11	Good To Firm	Showbrook	Jun 5 1991
6f	1m 7.21	5	9-13	Good To Firm	Mac Gille Eoin	Jly 2 2009
7f	1m 21.30	2	8-9	Good To Firm	Red Peony	Jly 29 2004
7f	1m 20.15	4	8-7	Firm	Capistrano I	Jun 7 1972
1m 114y	1m 42.80	2	8-5	Good To Firm	Nightstalker	Aug 30 1988
1m 114y	1m 40.75	3	8-6	Good To Firm	Sylva Honda	Jun 5 1991
1m 2f 18y	2m 3.50	5	7-11	Firm	Crossbow	Jun 7 1967
1m 4f 10y	2m 31.33	3	9-0	Good To Firm	Workforce	Jun 5 2010

FFOS LAS

Distance	Time	Age	Weight	Going	Horse	Date
5f	57.06	2	9-3	Good To Firm	Mr Majeika	May 5 2011
5f	56.35	5	8-8	Good	Haajes	Sep 12 2009
6f	1m 9.00	2	9-5	Good To Firm	Wonder Of Qatar	Sep 14 2014
6f	1m 7.80	8	8-4	Good To Firm	The Jailer	May 5 2011
1m	1m 39.36	2	9-2	Good To Firm	Hala Hala	Sep 2 2013
1m	1m 37.12	5	9-0	Good To Firm	Zebrano	May 5 2011
1m 2f	2m 4.85	8	8-12	Good To Firm	Pelham Crescent	May 5 2011
1m 4f	2m 31.58	4	8-9	Good To Firm	Men Don't Cry	Jly 23 2013
1m 6f	2m 58.61	4	9-7	Good To Firm	Lady Eclair	Jly 12 2010
2m	3m 29.58	4	8-9	Good To Firm	Annaluna	Jly 1 2013

GOODWOOD

Distance	Time	Age	Weight	Going	Horse	Date
5f	57.14	-			Yalta	Jly 27 2014
5f	56.01	5	9-0	Good To Firm	Rudi's Pet	Jly 27 1999
6f	1m 9.81	2	8-11	Good To Firm	Bachir	Jly 28 1999
6f	1m 9.10	6	9-0	Good To Firm	Tamagin	Sep 12 2009
7f	1m 24.99	2	8-11	Good To Firm	Ekraar	Jly 29 1999
7f	1m 23.88	3	8-7	Firm	Brief Glimpse	Jly 25 1995
1m	1m 37.21	2	9-0	Good	Caldra	Sep 9 2006
1m	1m 35.61	4	8-9	Good To Firm	Spectait	Aug 4 2006
1m 1f	1m 56.27	2	9-3	Good To Firm	Dordogne	Sep 22 2010
1m 1f	1m 52.81	3	9-6	Good	Vena	Jly 27 1995
1m 1f 192y	2m 2.81	3	9-3	Good To Firm	Road To Love	Aug 3 2006
1m 3f	2m 23.00	3	8-8	Good To Firm	Asian Heights	May 22 2001
1m 4f	2m 31.57	3	8-10	Firm	Presenting	Jly 25 1995
1m 6f	2m 57.61	4	9-6	Good To Firm	Meeznah	Jly 28 2011
2m	3m 21.55	5	9-10	Good To Firm	Yeats	Aug 3 2006

HAMILTON

Distance	Time	Age	Weight	Going	Horse	Date
5f 4y	57.95	2	8-8	Good To Firm	Rose Blossom	May 29 2009
5f 4y	57.95	2	8-8	Good To Firm	Rose Blossom	May 29 2009
6f 5y	1m 10.00	2	8-12	Good To Firm	Break The Code	Aug 24 1999
6f 5y	1m 9.30	4	8-7	Firm	Marcus Game	Jly 11 1974
1m 65y	1m 45.46	2	9-5	Good To Firm	Laafiraaq	Sep 20 2015
1m 65y	1m 42.70	6	7-7	Firm	Cranley	Sep 25 1972
1m 1f 36y	1m 53.60	5	9-6	Good To Firm	Regent's Secret	Aug 10 2005
1m 3f 16y	2m 18.66	3	9-3	Good To Firm	Postponed	Jly 18 2014
1m 4f 17y	2m 30.52	5	9-10	Good To Firm	Record Breaker	Jun 10 2009
1m 5f 9y	2m 45.10	6	9-6	Firm	Mentalasanythin	Jun 14 1995

HAYDOCK

Distance	Time	Age	Weight	Going	Horse	Date
5f	58.51	2	9-1	Good	Four Dragons	Oct 14 2016
5f	58.56	2	8-2	Good To Firm	Barracuda Boy	Aug 11 2012
5f	56.39	5	9-4	Firm	Bated Breath	May 26 2012
5f	57.67	4	9-4	Good To Firm	Sole Power	May 21 2011
6f	1m 10.98	4	9-9	Good To Firm	Wolfhound	Sep 4 1993
6f	1m 10.72	2	9-2	Good To Firm	Easy Ticket	Sep 4 2010
6f	1m 9.40	7	9-3	Good To Firm	Markab	Sep 4 2010
6f	1m 9.92	4	9-0	Good To Firm	Iktamal	Sep 7 1996
7f	1m 27.57	2	9-2	Good To Firm	Contrast	Aug 5 2016
7f	1m 25.50	3	8-11	Good	Forge	Sep 1 2016
1m	1m 38.50	4	8-11	Good To Firm	Express Himself	Jun 10 2015
1m 2f 95y	2m 7.71	3	8-8	Good To Firm	Royal Artillery	Aug 6 2016
1m 3f 200y	2m 25.53	4	8-12	Good To Firm	Number Theory	May 24 2012
1m 6f	2m 55.20	5	9-9	Good To Firm	Huff And Puff	Sep 7 2012
2m 45y	3m 26.98	5	8-13	Good To Firm	De Rigueur	Jun 8 2013

KEMPTON (A.W)

Distance	Time	Age	Weight	Going	Horse	Date
5f	58.96	2	8-6	Standard	Glamorous Spirit	Nov 28 2008
5f	58.33	3	9-1	Standard	Exceedance	May 7 2012
6f	1m 11.36	2	9-0	Standard	Tendu	Sep 3 2014
6f	1m 9.79	4	8-11	Standard	Trinityelitedotcom	Mar 29 2014
7f	1m 23.95	2	8-10	Standard	Tamarkuz	Oct 10 2012
7f	1m 23.10	6	9-9	Standard	Sirius Prospect	Nov 20 2014
1m	1m 37.50	2	9-4	Standard	I'm Back	Oct 3 2012
1m	1m 35.73	3	8-9	Standard	Western Aristocrat	Sep 15 2011
1m 2f	2m 2.97	5	9-0	Standard	Rebellious Guest	Mar 5 2014
1m 3f	2m 16.09	4	8-7	Standard	Salutation	Mar 29 2014
1m 4f	2m 28.99	6	9-3	Standard	Spring Of Fame	Nov 7 2012
2m	3m 21.50	4	8-12	Standard	Colour Vision	May 2 2012

LEICESTER

Distance	Time	Age	Weight	Going	Horse	Date
1m 60y	1m 44.05	2	8-11	Good To Firm	Congressional	Sep 6 2005
1m 60y	1m 41.89	5	9-7	Good To Firm	Vainglory	Jun 18 2009
1m 1f 218y	2m 5.30	2	9-1	Good To Firm	Windsor Castle	Oct 14 1996
1m 1f 218y	2m 2.40	4	9-6	Good To Firm	Lady Angharad	Jun 18 2000
1m 1f 218y	2m 2.40	3	8-11	Firm	Effigy I	Nov 4 1985
1m 3f 183y	2m 27.10	5	8-12	Good To Firm	Murghem	Jun 18 2000

LINGFIELD

Distance	Time	Age	Weight	Going	Horse	Date
5f	57.07	2	9-0	Good To Firm	Quite A Thing	Jun 11 2011
5f	56.09	3	9-4	Good To Firm	Whitecrest	Sep 16 2011
6f	1m 8.36	2	8-12	Good To Firm	Folly Bridge	Sep 8 2009
6f	1m 8.13	6	9-8	Firm	Clear Praise	Aug 10 2013
7f	1m 20.55	2	8-11	Good To Firm	Hiking	Aug 17 2013
7f	1m 20.05	3	8-5	Good To Firm	Perfect Tribute	May 7 2011
7f 140y	1m 29.32	2	9-3	Good To Firm	Dundonnell	Aug 4 2012
7f 140y	1m 26.73	3	8-6	Good To Firm	Hiaam	Jly 11 1987
1m 1f	1m 52.40	4	9-2	Good To Firm	Quandary	Jly 15 1995
1m 2f	2m 4.61	3	9-3	Firm	Usran	Jly 15 1989
1m 3f 106y	2m 23.95	3	8-5	Firm	Night-Shirt	Jly 14 1990
1m 6f	2m 59.10	5	9-5	Firm	Ibn Bey	Jly 1 1989
2m	3m 23.71	3	9-5	Good To Firm	Lauries Crusador	Aug 13 1988

LINGFIELD (A.W)

Distance	Time	Age	Weight	Going	Horse	Date
5f 6y	58.11	2	9-5	Standard	Ivors Rebel	Sep 23 2014
5f 6y	56.67	5	8-12	Standard	Ladies Are Forever	Mar 16 2013
6f 1y	1m 9.99	2	8-12	Standard	Swiss Diva	Nov 19 2008
6f 1y	1m 8.75	7	9-2	Standard	Tarooq	Dec 18 2013
7f 1y	1m 22.67	2	9-3	Standard	Complicit	Nov 23 2013
7f 1y	1m 21.92	5	9-6	Standard	Grey Mirage	Feb 22 2014
1m 1y	1m 35.84	2	9-5	Standard	Brave Hero	Nov 25 2015
1m 1y	1m 34.34	5	8-13	Standard	My Target	Dec 31 2016
1m 2f	2m 0.99	4	9-0	Standard	Farraaj	Mar 16 2013
1m 4f	2m 27.09	4	9-2	Standard	Burcan	Dec 31 2016
1m 5f	2m 39.70	3	8-10	Standard	Hidden Gold	Oct 30 2014
1m 7f 169y	3m 16.73	5	9-2	Standard	Arch Villain	Jan 22 2014

MUSSELBURGH

Distance	Time	Age	Weight	Going	Horse	Date
5f	57.70	2	8-2	Firm	Arasong	May 16 1994
5f	57.10	6	8-6	Good To Firm	Red Baron	Jun 13 2015
7f 30y	1m 27.46	2	8-8	Good	Durham Reflection	Sep 14 2009
7f 30y	1m 25.00	9	8-8	Good To Firm	Kalk Bay	Jun 4 2016
1m	1m 40.34	2	8-12	Good To Firm	Succession	Sep 26 2004
1m	1m 36.83	3	9-5	Good To Firm	Ginger Jack	Jly 13 2010
1m 1f	1m 50.42	8	8-11	Good To Firm	Dhaular Dhar	Sep 3 2010
1m 4f 100y	2m 36.80	3	8-3	Good To Firm	Harris Tweed	Jun 5 2010
1m 5f	2m 46.41	3	9-5	Good To Firm	Alcaeus	Sep 29 2013
1m 6f	2m 57.98	7	8-5	Good To Firm	Jonny Delta	Apr 18 2014
2m	3m 25.62	4	8-3	Good To Firm	Aldreth	Jun 13 2015

NEWBURY

Distance	Time	Age	Weight	Going	Horse	Date
5f 34y	59.19	2	8-6	Good To Firm	Superstar Leo	Jly 22 2000
5f 34y	58.44	5	9-1	Good To Firm	Robot Boy	Apr 17 2015
6f 8y	1m 11.07	2	8-4	Good To Firm	Bahati	May 30 2009
6f 8y	1m 9.42	3	8-11	Good To Firm	Nota Bene	May 13 2005
6f 110y	1m 18.06	2	9-5	Good To Firm	Twin Sails	Jun 11 2015
7f	1m 23.04	2	8-11	Good To Firm	Haafhd	Aug 15 2003
7f	1m 20.80	3	9-0	Good To Firm	Muhaarar	Apr 18 2015
1m	1m 37.50	2	9-1	Good To Firm	Winged Cupid	Sep 16 2005
1m	1m 33.59	6	9-0	Firm	Rakti	May 14 2005
1m 7y	1m 37.29	2	9-0	Good	Master Willie	Oct 1 1979
1m 7y	1m 34.90	3	8-9	Good To Firm	Philidor	May 16 1992
1m 1f	1m 49.65	3	8-0	Good To Firm	Holtye	May 21 1995
1m 2f 6y	2m 1.29		-		Wall Street I	Jly 20 1996
1m 3f 5y	2m 16.54	3	8-9	Good To Firm	Grandera	Sep 22 2001
1m 4f 5y	2m 28.26	4	9-7	Good To Firm	Azamour	Jly 23 2005
1m 5f 61y	2m 44.90	5	10-0	Good To Firm	Mystic Hill	Jly 20 1996
2m	3m 25.42	8	9-12	Good To Firm	Moonlight Quest	Jly 19 1996

NEWCASTLE (A.W)

Distance	Time	Age	Weight	Going	Horse	Date
5f	57.83	3	9-4	Standard	First Bombardment	Oct 7 2016
6f	1m 9.9	5	8-10	Standard	Kenny The Captain	Nov 8 2016
7f 14y	1m 24.48	4	9-7	Standard	Alice Thornton	Oct 14 2016
1m 5y	1m 36.54	6	9-3	Standard	Red Paladin	Oct 7 2016
1m 2f 42y	2m 4.88	3	8-6	Standard	Palisade	Oct 16 2016
1m 4f 98y	2m 36.76	3	8-7	Standard	Ajman Prince	Oct 14 2016
2m 56y	3m 29.87	4	9-8	Standard	Dannyday	Jun 25 2016

NEWMARKET

Distance	Time	Age	Weight	Going	Horse	Date
5f	58.69	2	8-12	Good To Firm	Mrs Danvers	Oct 7 2016
5f	56.81	6	9-2	Good To Firm	Lochsong	Apr 30 1994
6f	1m 9.56	2	8-12	Good To Firm	Bushranger	Oct 3 2008
6f	1m 9.55	3	9-1	Good To Firm	Captain Colby	May 16 2015
7f	1m 22.39	2	8-12	Good To Firm	Ashram	Oct 2 2008
7f	1m 21.98	3	9-0	Good To Firm	Tupi	May 16 2015
1m	1m 35.67	2	8-12	Good	Steeler	Sep 29 2012
1m	1m 34.07	4	9-0	Good To Firm	Eagle Mountain	Oct 3 2008
1m 1f	1m 47.26	5	8-12	Good To Firm	Manduro (GER)	Apr 19 2007
1m 2f	2m 2.89	2	8-11	Good	Coronet	Oct 8 2016
1m 2f	2m 0.13	3	8-12	Good	New Approach	Oct 18 2008
1m 4f	2m 26.07	3	8-9	Good To Firm	Mohedian Lady	Sep 22 2011
1m 6f	2m 51.59	3	8-7	Good	Art Eyes	Sep 29 2005
2m	3m 18.64	5	9-6	Good To Firm	Times Up	Sep 22 2011
2m 2f	3m 47.50	3	7-12	Hard	Whiteway	Oct 15 1947

NEWMARKET (JULY)

Distance	Time	Age	Weight	Going	Horse	Date
5f	58.52	2	8-10	Good	Seductress	Jly 10 1990
5f	56.09	6	9-11	Good	Borderlescott	Aug 22 2008
6f	1m 10.35	2	8-11	Good	Elnawin	Aug 22 2008
6f	1m 9.11	4	9-5	Good To Firm	Lethal Force	Jly 13 2013
7f	1m 23.33	2	9-1	Good To Firm	Birchwood	Jly 11 2015
7f	1m 22.59	3	9-7	Firm	Ho Leng	Jly 9 1998
1m	1m 37.47	2	8-13	Good	Whippers Love	Aug 28 2009
1m	1m 34.42	3	8-12	Good To Firm	Alice Springs	Jly 8 2016
1m 2f	2m 0.91	3	9-5	Good To Firm	Maputo	Jly 11 2013
1m 4f	2m 25.11	3	8-11	Good	Lush Lashes	Aug 22 2008
1m 5f	2m 40.75	5	9-10	Good	Wadi Al Hattawi	Aug 29 2015
2m 24y	3m 20.28	7	9-10	Good	Yorkshire I	Jly 11 2001

NOTTINGHAM

Distance	Time	Age	Weight	Going	Horse	Date
5f 13y	59.43	2	9-5	Good To Firm	Burtonwood	Apr 19 2014
5f 13y	57.90	2	8-9	Firm	Hoh Magic	May 13 1994
5f 13y	57.71	4	8-11	Good To Firm	Dinkum Diamond	Aug 14 2012
5f 13y	57.52	3	8-10	Good	Gracious John	Nov 2 2016
6f 15y	1m 11.40	2	8-11	Firm	Jameelapi	Aug 8 1983
6f 15y	1m 10.00	4	9-2	Firm	Ajanac	Aug 8 1988
1m 75y	1m 45.23	2	9-0	Good To Firm	Tactfully	Sep 28 2011
1m 75y	1m 45.14	2	9-6	Good	Rashford's Double	Nov 2 2016
1m 75y	1m 42.25	5	9-1	Good To Firm	Rio De La Plata	Jun 2 2010
1m 75y	1m 43.41	3	9-2	Good	Al Mukhdam	Apr 20 2013
1m 2f 50y	2m 16.66	2	9-3	Soft	Lethal Glaze	Oct 1 2008
1m 2f 50y	2m 7.13	5	9-8	Good To Firm	Vasily	Jly 19 2013
1m 2f 50y	2m 9.40	3	9-5	Good	Centurius	Apr 20 2013
1m 6f 15y	2m 57.80	3	8-10	Firm	Buster Jo	Oct 1 1985
2m 9y	3m 34.39	3	8-0	Good	Benozzo Gozzoli	Oct 28 2009
2m 9y	3m 25.25	3	9-5	Good	Bulwark	Sep 27 2005

PONTEFRACT

Distance	Time	Age	Weight	Going	Horse	Date
5f	1m 1.10	2	9-0	Firm	Golden Bounty	Sep 20 2001
5f	1m 0.84	4	8-9	Firm	Blue Maeve	Sep 23 2004
6f	1m 14.00	2	9-3	Firm	Fawzi	Sep 6 1983
6f	1m 12.60	3	7-13	Firm	Merry One	Aug 29 1970
1m 4y	1m 42.80	2	9-13	Firm	Star Spray	Sep 6 1983
1m 4y	1m 42.80	2	9-0	Firm	Alasil	Sep 26 2002
1m 4y	1m 40.60	4	9-10	Good To Firm	Island Light	Apr 13 2002
1m 2f 6y	2m 10.10	2	9-0	Firm	Shanty Star	Oct 7 2002
1m 2f 6y	2m 8.20	4	7-8	Hard	Happy Hector	Jly 9 1979
1m 2f 6y	2m 8.20	3	7-13	Hard	Tom Noddy	Aug 21 1972
1m 4f 8y	2m 33.72	3	8-7	Firm	Ajaan	Aug 8 2007
2m 1f 22y	3m 40.67	4	8-7	Good To Firm	Paradise Flight	Jun 6 2005
2m 1f 216y	3m 51.10	3	8-8	Good To Firm	Kudz	Sep 9 1986
2m 5f 122y	4m 47.80	4	8-4	Firm	Physical	May 14 1984

REDCAR

Distance	Time	Age	Weight	Going	Horse	Date
5f	56.88	2	9-7	Good To Soft	Wolfofwallstreet	Oct 27 2014
5f	56.01	10	9-3	Firm	Henry Hall	Sep 20 2006
6f	1m 8.84	2	8-3	Good To Firm	Obe Gold	Oct 2 2004
6f	1m 8.60	3	9-2	Good To Firm	Sizzling Saga	Jun 21 1991
7f	1m 21.28	2	9-3	Firm	Karoo Blue	Sep 20 2006
7f	1m 21.00	3	9-1	Firm	Empty Quarter	Oct 3 1995
1m	1m 34.37	2	9-0	Firm	Mastership	Sep 20 2006
1m	1m 32.42	4	10-0	Firm	Nanton	Sep 20 2006
1m 1f	1m 52.44	2	9-0	Firm	Spear	Sep 13 2004
1m 1f	1m 48.50	5	8-12	Firm	Mellottie	Jly 25 1990
1m 2f	2m 10.10	2	8-11	Good	Adding	Nov 10 1989
1m 2f	2m 1.40	5	9-2	Firm	Eradicate	May 28 1990
1m 6f 19y	2m 59.81	4	9-1	Good To Firm	Esprit de Corps	Sep 11 2006
2m 4y	3m 24.90	3	9-3	Good To Firm	Subsonic	Oct 8 1991

RIPON

Distance	Time	Age	Weight	Going	Horse	Date
5f	57.80	2	8-8	Firm	Super Rocky	Aug 5 1991
5f	57.28	5	8-12	Good	Desert Ace	Sep 24 2016
6f	1m 10.40	2	9-2	Good	Cumbrian Venture	Aug 17 2002
6f	1m 9.43	6	9-10	Good	Kimberella	Sep 24 2016
1m	1m 38.77	2	9-4	Good	Greed Is Good	Sep 28 2013
1m	1m 36.62	4	8-11	Good To Firm	Granston	Aug 29 2005
1m 1f	1m 49.97	6	9-3	Good To Firm	Ginger Jack	Jun 20 2013
1m 1f 170y	1m 59.12	5	8-9	Good To Firm	Wahoo Sam	Aug 30 2005
1m 4f 10y	2m 31.40	4	8-8	Good To Firm	Dandino	Apr 16 2011
2m	3m 27.07	5	9-12	Good To Firm	Greenwich Meantime	Aug 30 2005

SALISBURY

Distance	Time	Age	Weight	Going	Horse	Date
5f	59.30	2	9-0	Good To Firm	Ajigolo	May 12 2005
5f	59.30	2	9-0	Good To Firm	Ajigolo (when 2yo)	May 12 2005
6f	1m 12.10	2	8-0	Good To Firm	Parisian Lady	Jun 10 1997
6f	1m 11.09	3	9-0	Firm	L'Ami Louis	May 1 2011
6f 212y	1m 25.97	2	9-0	Firm	More Royal	Jun 29 1995
6f 212y	1m 24.91	3	9-4	Firm	Chilworth Lad	May 1 2011
1m	1m 40.48	2	8-13	Firm	Choir Master	Sep 17 2002
1m	1m 38.29	3	8-7	Good To Firm	Layman	Aug 11 2005
1m 1f 198y	2m 4.00	4	9-2	Good To Firm	Chain Of Daisies	Aug 10 2016
1m 4f	2m 31.69	3	9-5	Good To Firm	Arrive	Jun 27 2001
1m 6f 21y	3m 0.48	7	9-2	Good To Firm	Highland Castle	May 23 2015

SANDOWN

Distance	Time	Age	Weight	Going	Horse	Date
5f 6y	59.48	2	9-3	Firm	Times Time	Jly 22 1982
5f 6y	58.82	6	8-9	Good To Firm	Palacegate Touch	Sep 17 1996
7f 16y	1m 26.56	2	9-0	Good To Firm	Raven's Pass	Sep 1 2007
7f 16y	1m 26.36	3	9-0	Firm	Mawsuff	Jun 14 1986
1m 14y	1m 41.14	2	8-11	Good To Firm	Reference Point	Sep 23 1986
1m 14y	1m 38.87	7	9-10	Good To Firm	Prince Of Johanne	Jly 6 2013
1m 1f	1m 54.63	2	8-8	Good To Firm	French Pretender	Sep 20 1988
1m 1f	1m 52.40	7	9-3	Good To Firm	Bourgainville	Aug 11 2005
1m 2f 7y	2m 2.14	4	8-11	Good	Kalaglow	May 31 1982
1m 6f	2m 56.90	4	8-7	Good To Firm	Lady Rosanna	Jly 19 1989
2m 78y	3m 29.38	6	9-0	Good To Firm	Caucus	Jly 6 2013

SOUTHWELL (A.W)

Distance	Time	Age	Weight	Going	Horse	Date
5f	57.85	2	9-3	Standard	Arctic Feeling	Mar 31 2010
5f	56.80	5	9-7	Standard	Ghostwing	Jan 3 2012
6f	1m 14.00	2	8-5	Standard	Panalo	Nov 8 1989
6f	1m 13.50	4	10-0	Standard	Saladan Knight	Dec 30 1989
7f	1m 26.82	2	8-12	Standard	Winged Icarus	Aug 28 2012
7f	1m 26.38	4	8-6	Standard	Moon River	Mar 30 2016
1m	1m 38.00	2	8-10	Standard	Andrew's First	Dec 30 1989
1m	1m 38.00	2	8-9	Standard	Alpha Rascal	Nov 13 1990
1m	1m 37.25	3	8-6	Standard	Valira	Nov 3 1990
1m 3f	2m 21.50	4	9-7	Standard	Tempering	Dec 5 1990
1m 4f	2m 33.90	4	9-12	Standard	Fast Chick	Nov 8 1989
1m 6f	3m 1.60	3	7-8	Standard	Erevnon	Dec 29 1990
2m	3m 37.60	9	8-12	Standard	Old Hubert	Dec 5 1990

THIRSK

Distance	Time	Age	Weight	Going	Horse	Date
5f	57.20	2	9-7	Good To Firm	Proud Boast	Aug 5 2000
5f	56.92	5	9-6	Firm	Charlie Parkes	Apr 11 2003
6f	1m 9.20	2	9-6	Good To Firm	Westcourt Magic	Aug 25 1995
6f	1m 8.80	6	9-4	Firm	Johayro	Jly 23 1999
7f	1m 23.70	2	8-9	Firm	Courting	Jly 23 1999
7f	1m 22.80	4	8-5	Firm	Silver Haze I	May 21 1988
1m	1m 37.97	2	9-0	Firm	Sunday Symphony	Sep 4 2004
1m	1m 34.80	4	8-13	Firm	Yearsley	May 5 1990
1m 4f	2m 29.90	5	9-12	Firm	Gallery God	Jun 4 2001
2m	3m 22.30	3	9-0	Firm	Tomaschek	Jly 17 1981

WETHERBY

Distance	Time	Age	Weight	Going	Horse	Date
5f 110y	1m 4.85	4	9-4	Good	Hardy Black	Jly 21 2015
7f	1m 24.72	4	9-2	Good	Slemy	Jly 21 2015
1m	1m 39.28	5	9-1	Good	Rosy Ryan	Jly 21 2015
1m 2f	2m 5.13	5	9-5	Good	First Sargeant	Jly 21 2015
1m 6f	3m 4.03	5	9-6	Good	Slipper Satin	Jly 13 2015

WINDSOR

Distance	Time	Age	Weight	Going	Horse	Date
5f 10y	58.69	2	9-0	Good To Firm	Charles The Great	May 23 2011
5f 10y	58.08	5	8-13	Good To Firm	Taurus Twins	Apr 4 2011
6f	1m 10.50		-		Cubism	Aug 17 1998
6f	1m 9.58	7	9-0	Good To Firm	Tropics	Jun 1 2015
1m 67y	1m 41.73	2	9-5	Good To Firm	Salouen	Aug 7 2016
1m 67y	1m 39.81	5	9-7	Good	French Navy	Jun 29 2013
1m 2f 7y	2m 1.62	6	9-1	Good	Al Kazeem	Aug 23 2014
1m 3f 135y	2m 21.50	3	9-2	Firm	Double Florin	May 19 1980

WOLVERHAMPTON (A.W)

Distance	Time	Age	Weight	Going	Horse	Date
5f 20y	59.75	2	9-6	Standard	Quatrieme Ami	Nov 13 2015
5f 20y	59.39	5	9-8	Standard	Boom The Groom	Feb 22 2016
5f 216y	1m 12.67	2	9-6	Standard	Parkour (IRE)	Nov 14 2015
5f 216y	1m 11.84	3	8-6	Standard	Pretend	Dec 19 2014
7f 32y	1m 27.53	2	9-5	Standard	Always Welcome	Dec 22 2015
7f 32y	1m 25.35	4	9-3	Standard	Mister Universe	Mar 12 2016
1m 141y	1m 47.38	2	9-5	Standard	Jack Hobbs	Dec 27 2014
1m 141y	1m 45.43	4	9-4	Standard	Keystroke	Nov 26 2016
1m 1f 103y	1m 56.64	8	8-13	Standard	Perfect Cracker	Mar 19 2016
1m 4f 50y	2m 33.92	3	8-13	Standard	Natural Scenery	Oct 21 2016
1m 5f 194y	2m 57.55	6	9-7	Standard	Entihaa	Dec 6 2014
2m 119y	3m 33.34	4	9-0	Standard	Moonrise Landing	Dec 12 2015

YARMOUTH

Distance	Time	Age	Weight	Going	Horse	Date
5f 42y	1m 0.40	2	8-6	Good To Firm	Ebba	Jly 26 1999
5f 42y	59.80	4	8-13	Good To Firm	Roxanne Mill	Aug 25 2002
6f 3y	1m 10.40	2	9-0	Firm	Lanchester	Sep 15 1988
6f 3y	1m 9.82	3	8-6	Good To Firm	Shypen	Jun 8 2016
7f 3y	1m 22.20	2	9-0	Good To Firm	Warrshan	Sep 14 1988
7f 3y	1m 22.12	4	9-4	Good To Firm	Glenbuck	Apr 26 2007
1m 3y	1m 36.30	2	8-2	Firm	Out Run	Sep 15 1988
1m 3y	1m 33.90	3	8-8	Firm	Bonne Etoile	Jun 27 1995
1m 1f 21y	1m 52.00	3	9-5	Good To Firm	Touch Gold	Jly 5 2012
1m 2f 23y	2m 2.83	3	8-8	Firm	Reunite	Jly 18 2006
1m 3f 104y	2m 23.10	3	8-9	Firm	Rahil	Jly 1 1993
1m 6f 17y	2m 57.80	3	8-2	Good To Firm	Barakat	Jly 24 1990
2m	3m 26.70	4	8-2	Good To Firm	Alhesn	Jly 26 1999

YORK

Distance	Time	Age	Weight	Going	Horse	Date
5f	57.11	2	9-0	Good	Big Time Baby	Aug 20 2015
5f	56.16	3	9-3	Good To Firm	Dayjur	Aug 23 1990
5f 89y	1m 3.20	2	9-3	Good To Firm	The Art Of Racing	Sep 9 2012
5f 89y	1m 1.72	4	9-7	Good To Firm	Bogart	Aug 21 2013
6f	1m 8.90	2	9-0	Good	Tiggy Wiggy	Aug 21 2014
6f	1m 8.23	3	8-11	Good To Firm	Mince	Sep 9 2012
7f	1m 22.32	2	9-1	Good To Firm	Dutch Connection	Aug 20 2014
7f	1m 21.83	4	9-8	Good To Firm	Dimension	Jly 28 2012
1m	1m 39.20	2	8-1	Good To Firm	Missoula	Aug 31 2005
1m	1m 35.10	4	8-12	Good	Home Cummins	Jly 9 2016
1m 208y	1m 46.76	5	9-8	Good To Firm	Echo Of Light	Sep 5 2007
1m 2f 88y	2m 5.29	3	8-11	Good To Firm	Sea The Stars	Aug 18 2009
1m 4f	2m 26.28	6	8-9	Firm	Bandari	Jun 18 2005
1m 6f	2m 54.96	4	9-0	Good To Firm	Tactic	May 22 2010
2m 88y	3m 28.97	5	9-5	Good To Firm	Gabrial's King	Jly 12 2014

SPLIT SECOND SPEED RATINGS

The following lists the fastest performances of 3yo+ and 2yo horses which have recorded a speed figure of 105 or over during the 2016 season. Additional information in the parentheses following the speed figure shows the distance of the race in furlongs, course, state of going and the date on which the figure was achieved.

Turf

A Few Dollars More 105 *(5f,Cur,Y,Jun 26)*
A Momentofmadness 106 *(5f,Sal,G,Jun 12)*
A Shin Hikari 113 *(10f,Asc,S,Jun 15)*
A Soldier's Life 106 *(12f,Asc,GS,Jun 17)*
Aared 107 *(8f,Cur,G,Aug 28)*
Aasheq 107 *(10f,Cur,HY,Apr 3)*
Abdon 106 *(10f,Nmk,GS,Apr 30)*
Abe Lincoln 110 *(8f,Asc,S,Jun 16)*
Abingdon 110 *(14½f,Don,G,Sep 8)*
Above N Beyond 111 *(7½f,Chs,G,May 5)*
Above The Rest 116 *(7f,Chs,GS,Sep 24)*
Abraham 107 *(15f,Leo,GF,Jun 9)*
Absolute Zero 105 *(10f,Rip,G,Aug 1)*
Absolutely So 111 *(6f,Asc,GS,Jun 18)*
Abushamah 106 *(8f,Rip,G,Aug 13)*
Accalia 105 *(5f,Cur,GY,Oct 9)*
Accession 111 *(7f,Lei,GF,Oct 11)*
Ace Master 105 *(6f,Pon,GF,Aug 3)*
Aclaim 114 *(7f,Nmk,GF,Oct 7)*
Across The Stars 113 *(11½f,Lin,G,May 7)*
Adaay 115 *(7f,Nmk,HY,Jun 25)*
Adam's Ale 107 *(5f,Thi,GF,Aug 9)*
Admirable Art 106 *(8f,Bri,G,Oct 13)*
Admiral's Sunset 113 *(12f,Pon,S,Oct 17)*
Adventurous 108 *(7f,Nmk,GS,Apr 13)*
Aeolus 112 *(6f,Nmk,GS,Apr 14)*
Afjaan 109 *(8f,Asc,G,Oct 15)*
Agent Gibbs 106 *(12f,Chp,GF,Aug 18)*
Agree 106 *(6f,Pon,G,Jly 5)*
Aim To Please 114 *(8f,Cha,S,Jun 5)*
Ainippe 108 *(7f,Cur,S,May 2)*
Air Force Blue 108 *(6f,Nmk,GF,Jly 9)*
Air Of York 109 *(7½f,Ffo,G,Jly 19)*
Air Pilot 113 *(10½f,Yor,GF,Jly 23)*
Air Vice Marshal 113 *(8f,Nmk,GS,Apr 30)*
Ajman Princess 105 *(12f,Lei,GF,May 30)*
Ajwad 109 *(7f,Mey,G,Feb 11)*
Al Destoor 110 *(11f,Ham,G,Jly 30)*
Al Jazi 110 *(7f,Goo,GF,Jly 29)*
Al Khan 107 *(8f,Hay,G,Oct 14)*
Al Neksh 107 *(10f,Yar,GF,Sep 14)*
Al Shahaniya 106 *(10f,Bri,GF,Aug 21)*
Alben Star 106 *(6f,Goo,GF,Jly 30)*
Alcatraz 106 *(8½f,Eps,GS,Jun 3)*
Aldreth 105 *(16½f,Yor,G,Oct 8)*
Aleef 108 *(5f,Cat,S,Oct 15)*
Alejandro 106 *(7½f,Bev,G,Aug 27)*
Alexandrakollontai 105 *(8f,Crl,GF,Jun 22)*
Alfred Hutchinson 107 *(7f,Yor,GS,Jun 11)*
Alfredo 105 *(16f,Nmk,G,Oct 28)*
Algaith 108 *(8f,Pon,GF,Jly 24)*
Algometer 108 *(10f,San,GS,Apr 22)*
Alice Springs 119 *(8f,Leo,Y,Sep 10)*
Alignement 115 *(10f,Cha,G,Oct 1)*
Aljuljalah 109 *(7f,Lin,G,Sep 10)*
Allnecessaryforce 105 *(11½f,Wdr,S,Apr 18)*
Almanzor 121 *(10f,Leo,Y,Sep 10)*
Almela 112 *(12f,Cha,G,Oct 1)*
Almodovar 112 *(10½f,Yor,GF,Aug 17)*
Almuhalab 107 *(8f,Mus,G,Aug 5)*
Alnashama 111 *(7f,Nmk,GF,Jly 29)*
Alpha Delphini 119 *(5f,Asc,GF,Jly 22)*
Alpine Dream 106 *(6f,Not,G,Sep 28)*
Alqubbah 106 *(6f,Not,GF,May 7)*
Alquffaal 108 *(12f,Pon,GF,Jun 27)*
Alsvinder 105 *(5f,Thi,G,Apr 24)*
Altesse 108 *(12f,Leo,HY,Apr 6)*
Alveena 116 *(14f,Cur,Y,Jun 26)*
Always Resolute 106 *(16f,Mus,GF,Jly 19)*
Always Smile 115 *(8f,Nmk,GF,Jly 8)*
Alyaa 106 *(8f,Nmk,GS,Apr 30)*
Alyssa 109 *(14f,Asc,G,Sep 30)*
Amazing Maria 112 *(8f,Nmk,GF,Jly 8)*
American Artist 107 *(10f,Don,G,Apr 23)*
American Hope 109 *(7f,Mey,G,Mar 3)*
Amy Blair 105 *(9f,Ham,HY,Sep 26)*
An Cailin Orga 107 *(10f,Leo,GF,Jun 9)*
An Saighdiur 114 *(7f,Cur,G,Aug 20)*
Anaerobio 113 *(7f,Mey,G,Jan 21)*
Anastazia 108 *(7f,Yar,GF,Aug 4)*
Anonymous John 105 *(7½f,Chs,GS,Jun 24)*
Anonymous Lady 107 *(5f,Ayr,GS,May 18)*
Another Touch 106 *(8f,Ayr,GS,Sep 17)*
Another Wise Kid 105 *(6f,Hay,G,Oct 14)*
Anzhelika 108 *(14f,Bat,GF,Oct 12)*
Apilobar 109 *(10½f,Cha,S,Jun 5)*
Appleberry 106 *(5f,Not,S,Oct 12)*
Apricot Sky 106 *(5f,Rip,G,Jun 16)*
Arab Poet 107 *(7f,Goo,G,May 21)*
Arab Spring 109 *(12f,Asc,S,Oct 1)*
Arabian Queen 111 *(10f,Yar,GF,Sep 14)*
Arcanada 110 *(7f,Chs,G,Jun 25)*
Arcano Gold 107 *(8f,Pon,S,Apr 18)*
Arch Villain 106 *(16f,Asc,GF,Aug 6)*
Archie 105 *(8f,Hay,GF,Jun 9)*
Archippos 108 *(10f,Red,GS,Nov 1)*
Architecture 115 *(12f,Asc,G,Oct 15)*
Arctic Feeling 108 *(5f,Bev,S,Apr 13)*
Ardhoomey 115 *(5f,Cur,Y,Sep 11)*
Argaki 106 *(8f,Mus,GF,Aug 25)*
Argus 108 *(12f,Don,G,Sep 10)*
Aridity 108 *(8f,Cur,GF,Aug 7)*
Arlecchino's Leap 106 *(7f,Goo,G,May 20)*
Arnold Lane 107 *(7f,Goo,GF,Jun 5)*
Arod 116 *(8f,Goo,GF,Aug 27)*
Arrowzone 107 *(8f,Nmk,GF,May 13)*
Art Obsession 106 *(6f,Don,G,Jun 25)*
Artful Artist 107 *(15f,Leo,Y,Oct 29)*
Arthenus 113 *(10f,Cha,G,Oct 1)*
Arty Campbell 106 *(16f,Asc,G,Sep 30)*
Arya Tara 107 *(14f,Cur,G,Aug 20)*
Ashaadd 106 *(6f,Mey,G,Jan 28)*
Ashadihan 113 *(8f,Nmk,GF,Jly 8)*
Ashpan Sam 111 *(6f,Eps,G,Aug 30)*
Aspen Mountain 111 *(8f,Cur,GF,Aug 7)*
Ataman 105 *(8f,Nby,GF,Jun 9)*
Athlon 109 *(10f,Wdr,S,Jun 13)*
Atlantic Sun 106 *(7f,Yor,GF,Jly 23)*
Attendu 114 *(7f,Cha,G,Oct 2)*
Auspicion 105 *(9f,Yor,GS,Jun 11)*
Aussie Valentine 108 *(8f,Cur,YS,Mar 20)*
Autocratic 108 *(10f,San,GF,Jun 11)*
Available 106 *(6f,Yor,GF,Jly 22)*
Avenante 109 *(12f,Cur,GY,Jun 24)*
Avon Breeze 110 *(6f,Rip,GS,Apr 23)*
Avon Pearl 105 *(8f,Mey,G,Feb 18)*
Awake My Soul 114 *(10f,Red,GS,Nov 1)*
Awtaad 116 *(8f,Cur,Y,May 21)*
Ayrad 105 *(12f,Cha,S,Jun 5)*
Azaelia 107 *(10½f,Cha,S,Jun 19)*
Azizaan 105 *(8½f,Not,GF,May 17)*
Azraff 112 *(8f,Nby,G,May 14)*

B Fifty Two 108 *(7f,Mey,G,Jan 7)*
Baadi 105 *(11½f,Wdr,G,May 23)*
Baccarat 111 *(6f,Rip,G,Aug 13)*
Bahaarah 107 *(8f,Nby,GF,Jly 16)*
Bahamian Bird 106 *(7f,Ayr,GS,Aug 6)*
Bainne 105 *(8f,Cur,GY,Oct 9)*
Bakht A Rawan 105 *(10½f,Chs,G,May 28)*
Balios 110 *(12f,Mey,G,Mar 5)*
Ballesteros 106 *(6f,Cat,S,Oct 25)*
Ballet Concerto 105 *(8f,Thi,S,Sep 3)*
Ballybacka Queen 107 *(12f,Leo,HY,Apr 6)*
Ballydoyle 111 *(8f,Nmk,G,May 1)*
Ballymore Castle 106 *(7f,Hay,G,Sep 2)*
Balmoral Castle 110 *(10f,Goo,GF,Jly 26)*
Baltic Brave 106 *(7f,Nmk,GF,Jly 29)*
Balty Boys 105 *(7f,Thi,S,Apr 16)*
Banaadeer 110 *(7f,Mey,G,Jan 28)*
Banksea 107 *(10f,Pon,GF,Jun 19)*
Bapak Asmara 107 *(5f,Wdr,GF,Jly 4)*
Baraweez 107 *(8f,Yor,GF,May 12)*
Barkston Ash 105 *(6f,Rip,G,May 6)*
Barleysugar 108 *(8f,Nmk,GF,May 21)*
Barnet Fair 106 *(5f,Thi,GF,May 14)*
Baron Bolt 108 *(7f,Nmk,S,Jun 24)*
Barren Brook 105 *(8½f,Eps,GS,Jun 30)*
Barsanti 111 *(12f,Yor,GF,May 13)*
Barwick 108 *(12f,Eps,S,Apr 20)*
Barye 108 *(10f,Nmk,GF,Aug 6)*
Basateen 111 *(10f,Mey,G,Feb 25)*
Basem 108 *(10½f,Yor,G,Jly 9)*
Bashiba 109 *(5f,Don,GF,Aug 13)*
Basil Berry 108 *(6f,Yar,GF,Sep 13)*
Bastille Day 106 *(8½f,Eps,G,Jly 7)*
Bateel 105 *(12f,Nmk,S,Jun 25)*
Bathos 105 *(9f,Goo,G,May 19)*
Battalion 112 *(10½f,Chs,G,May 5)*
Battersea 116 *(14f,Mey,G,Feb 4)*
Battle Of Marathon 109 *(8f,Asc,S,Jun 15)*
Battlement 106 *(8f,Nmk,GF,May 12)*
Baydar 114 *(10f,Nmk,GF,Jly 23)*
Bayrir 105 *(10f,Mey,G,Feb 4)*
Be Kool 108 *(8½f,Eps,G,Sep 8)*
Beach Bar 110 *(8f,Mey,G,Jan 28)*
Beacon Rock 105 *(10f,Leo,HY,Apr 10)*
Beardwood 115 *(10f,Red,GS,Nov 1)*
Beau Satchel 108 *(8f,Leo,Y,Oct 23)*
Beauly 105 *(10f,Nby,GF,Jun 9)*
Beautiful Romance 112 *(10½f,Yor,GF,May 12)*
Bebhinn 106 *(7f,Leo,Y,Oct 29)*
Becca Campbell 105 *(10f,Bri,G,Oct 4)*
Bedrock 110 *(10f,San,G,Sep 14)*
Bel Canto 107 *(5f,Mey,G,Mar 26)*
Belardo 113 *(8f,Nby,G,May 14)*
Belgian Bill 108 *(8f,Goo,GF,Jly 29)*
Bell Heather 106 *(7½f,Chs,GS,Jun 24)*
Belledesert 106 *(6f,Don,GF,Jly 21)*
Benkei 107 *(14f,Leo,G,Sep 10)*
Berkeley Vale 105 *(10f,San,G,Jun 10)*
Berkshire 111 *(11½f,Wdr,GF,Aug 27)*
Berlusca 106 *(10½f,Chs,G,May 28)*
Bermondsey 112 *(10f,San,G,Jun 10)*
Bernie's Boy 107 *(8f,San,GF,Jly 20)*
Bertiewhittle 107 *(6f,Nmk,GS,Apr 12)*
Besharah 109 *(6f,Yor,G,Jly 8)*
Besotted 115 *(8f,Cha,S,Jun 5)*
Bess Of Hardwick 109 *(12f,Don,G,Sep 10)*
Best Of Times 112 *(10f,Goo,GF,Jly 26)*
Best Trip 105 *(6f,Cat,GF,Jly 13)*
Biff Johnson 106 *(10f,Ayr,G,Jun 17)*
Big Baz 109 *(8f,Mey,G,Feb 25)*
Big Orange 112 *(16f,Mey,G,Mar 26)*
Big Time 108 *(7f,Goo,GF,Aug 27)*
Big Time Dancer 108 *(8½f,Bev,GF,Aug 11)*
Bigger And Better 106 *(10f,Sal,GS,Oct 10)*
Bint Dandy 107 *(8f,Asc,GF,May 7)*
Biodynamic 107 *(10f,Nmk,GS,Apr 14)*
Birchwood 112 *(7f,Chs,S,Jly 9)*
Birdman 107 *(8f,Wdr,S,Jun 26)*
Black Cherry 112 *(8f,Pon,G,Jly 5)*
Black Sea 110 *(10½f,Yor,GF,May 12)*
Blacklister 105 *(8½f,Not,GF,May 17)*
Blackout 109 *(8f,Nmk,GS,Jun 17)*
Blaine 108 *(6f,Eps,GS,Jun 4)*
Blair House 108 *(8½f,Not,GF,May 17)*
Blakeney Point 105 *(14f,Yor,G,Oct 7)*
Blaze Of Hearts 105 *(10f,Wdr,GF,Jly 18)*
Blithe Spirit 109 *(5f,Chs,G,Jly 23)*
Blond Me 111 *(8f,Goo,G,Apr 30)*
Blossomtime 105 *(7f,Sal,GS,May 1)*
Blue De Vega 110 *(7f,Cur,S,May 2)*
Blue Hussar 109 *(12f,Pon,GF,Aug 3)*
Blue Rambler 108 *(14f,Hay,S,Sep 3)*
Blue Surf 111 *(10f,San,GS,Aug 20)*
Bob's Boy 105 *(10f,Bat,GF,Aug 20)*
Bobby Jean 106 *(8f,Cur,HY,Sep 25)*
Bobby Wheeler 109 *(7f,Goo,GF,Jly 30)*
Bocca Baciata 113 *(10½f,Cur,YS,May 22)*
Bocking End 106 *(10f,Rip,G,Aug 13)*
Bogart 110 *(5f,Don,G,Oct 22)*
Boite 108 *(14f,Goo,S,Jun 17)*
Bondi Beach Boy 107 *(5f,Thi,GF,May 14)*
Boom The Groom 111 *(5f,Goo,G,Jly 26)*
Boomerang Bob 106 *(6f,Asc,GF,Sep 3)*
Booming Delight 107 *(7f,Hay,G,May 28)*
Boomshackerlacker 108 *(8f,Goo,GF,Jly 29)*
Boots And Spurs 109 *(7f,Lei,S,Jly 2)*
Bop It 105 *(6f,Yor,GF,Jly 22)*
Bossipop 106 *(6f,Pon,GF,Jun 6)*
Bossy Guest 108 *(8f,Asc,S,Jun 15)*
Botany Bay 107 *(16½f,Yor,GF,Aug 17)*
Both Sides 110 *(10f,San,G,Sep 14)*
Bouclier 105 *(5f,Bri,GS,Jun 21)*
Bounce 105 *(6f,Lei,GF,May 30)*
Bowson Fred 109 *(5f,Asc,GF,Jly 9)*
Boy In The Bar 109 *(6f,Asc,GF,Sep 2)*
Boycie 106 *(7f,Nmk,S,Jun 24)*
Braes Of Lochalsh 105 *(14½f,Don,S,Apr 30)*
Brando 119 *(6f,Asc,G,Oct 15)*
Brave Hero 107 *(7f,Yar,GF,Sep 15)*
Bravery 108 *(12f,Cur,G,Oct 9)*
Bravo Zolo 105 *(8f,Don,S,Apr 2)*
Breakable 108 *(7½f,Chs,G,Aug 20)*
Breathe Easy 110 *(8f,Cur,GY,Jun 25)*
Breenainthemycra 106 *(10f,Leo,Y,Oct 29)*
Breton Rock 116 *(7f,Nmk,HY,Jun 25)*
Bridey's Lettuce 109 *(14f,Red,GF,Aug 6)*
Brief Visit 105 *(10f,Lei,GF,Jly 27)*
Bright Flash 105 *(9f,Mus,GF,Apr 24)*
Brigliadoro 105 *(8f,Yar,GF,Jly 6)*
Bring It On 105 *(8f,Leo,SH,Apr 6)*
Briyouni 106 *(8½f,Not,G,May 22)*
Brockholes 108 *(7f,Cat,S,Jun 29)*
Brontide 106 *(10f,Leo,G,Jly 7)*
Bronze Angel 106 *(9f,Nmk,GF,Sep 24)*
Brorocco 105 *(10f,Yar,GF,Aug 28)*
Brosnan 106 *(10f,Leo,GF,Jun 3)*
Bubbly Bellini 107 *(6f,Cur,YS,Mar 20)*
Buccaneers Vault 105 *(7f,Wet,GF,May 17)*
Buckstay 110 *(6f,Asc,GS,Jun 18)*
Buenos Y Bobos 108 *(10f,Cur,HY,Apr 3)*
Buffering 117 *(5f,Mey,G,Mar 26)*
Buonarroti 105 *(12f,Ffo,S,Sep 11)*
Burano 106 *(10f,Don,G,Apr 23)*
Buratino 108 *(6f,Hay,G,May 28)*
Burmese 112 *(20f,Asc,S,Jun 16)*
Burnt Sugar 110 *(6f,Asc,GS,Jun 18)*
Bush Beauty 113 *(7½f,Chs,S,Jun 11)*
Buying Trouble 106 *(6f,Nmk,GF,Aug 27)*

C Note 116 *(7f,Lei,GF,Oct 11)*
Cadmium 105 *(8f,Pon,HY,Apr 5)*
Calder Prince 107 *(7f,Yor,GF,Jly 23)*
California 112 *(14½f,Don,G,Sep 8)*
California Whip 108 *(8f,Asc,S,Jun 16)*
Calling Out 105 *(9f,Mey,G,Jan 28)*
Calvinist 108 *(14f,Yor,G,Oct 7)*
Can't Change It 109 *(7f,Goo,G,May 19)*
Canary Row 106 *(8f,Leo,Y,Oct 23)*
Candarliya 108 *(12f,Cha,G,Sep 11)*
Candelisa 105 *(6f,Pon,HY,Apr 5)*
Cannock Chase 116 *(10½f,Chs,G,May 5)*
Canny Kool 105 *(5f,Hay,GF,May 20)*
Cape Cova 110 *(12f,Don,GF,Nov 5)*
Cape Discovery 107 *(11½f,Wdr,G,May 16)*
Capo Rosso 108 *(8f,Hay,GF,Jun 9)*
Captain Cat 110 *(8f,Wdr,S,Jun 25)*
Captain Colby 110 *(6f,Don,G,Sep 10)*
Captain Dion 105 *(6f,Pon,GS,Sep 22)*
Captain Dunne 108 *(5f,Thi,GF,Aug 9)*
Captain Felix 108 *(10f,Red,GF,Jly 17)*
Captain Joy 106 *(8f,Leo,GF,Aug 11)*
Captain Morley 107 *(12f,Pon,GF,Jun 19)*
Carbon Dating 113 *(11f,Ham,G,Jly 30)*
Card High 107 *(12f,Cat,G,Sep 17)*
Carnachy 107 *(10f,Don,GF,Nov 5)*
Carnageo 106 *(8½f,Not,G,Oct 26)*
Carnival King 110 *(7f,Nmk,GF,Jly 29)*
Carntop 114 *(11½f,Lin,G,May 7)*
Carolinae 105 *(8f,Yar,GF,Aug 3)*
Carpe Diem Lady 107 *(8f,Bri,GF,Sep 29)*
Carrington 106 *(10f,Goo,GF,Jly 28)*
Carry On Deryck 113 *(9f,Nmk,GF,Sep 24)*
Cartmell Cleave 105 *(6f,Wdr,G,May 23)*
Cartwright 109 *(12f,Pon,GS,Sep 22)*
Casablanca 106 *(10½f,Chs,GS,Sep 24)*
Caspian Prince 111 *(5f,Eps,GS,Jun 4)*
Castle Guest 112 *(8f,Cur,GF,Aug 7)*
Catcall 112 *(5f,Cha,S,Jun 5)*
Cayirli 107 *(14f,Goo,GS,May 21)*
Celebration 111 *(5f,Thi,S,Apr 16)*
Celestial Path 109 *(9f,Nmk,GF,Sep 24)*
Celtic Power 109 *(14f,Red,GF,Aug 6)*
Celtic Sixpence 106 *(7½f,Chs,S,Jun 11)*
Central Square 109 *(10f,Red,GF,May 30)*
Ceol Na Nog 108 *(12f,Cur,Y,Aug 21)*
Certerach 109 *(14f,Mey,G,Mar 3)*
Certificate 111 *(7f,Nmk,GF,Oct 7)*
Chain Of Daisies 116 *(10f,Wdr,GF,Aug 27)*
Champagne Champ 106 *(14f,Sal,GS,Oct 10)*
Champagne Or Water 107 *(8f,Cur,YS,May 22)*
Championship 115 *(7f,Mey,G,Jan 30)*
Chancery 106 *(12f,Don,S,Apr 3)*
Chaplin Bay 106 *(7f,San,G,Aug 4)*
Charles Molson 107 *(7f,Nby,GF,Aug 13)*
Charlie Croker 109 *(7f,Mey,G,Jan 30)*
Charming Thought 108 *(6f,Sal,G,Jun 12)*
Cheikeljack 107 *(6f,Asc,GS,Jun 17)*
Chelsea Lad 109 *(8f,Nmk,GF,May 21)*
Chester Street 108 *(10f,Nmk,G,May 1)*
Chestnut Fire 107 *(7f,Cur,GY,Oct 10)*
Chevallier 108 *(8f,San,GF,May 26)*
Chez Vegas 105 *(6f,Don,G,May 14)*
Chil The Kite 108 *(8f,Wdr,S,Jun 25)*
Choreographer 110 *(10½f,Yor,GF,May 12)*
Chosen Character 110 *(8f,Hay,G,May 20)*
Cincuenta Pasos 106 *(7f,Chp,S,Sep 13)*
Cirin Toinne 107 *(12f,Cur,Y,Aug 21)*
Classic Seniority 107 *(7f,Yor,G,Jun 10)*
Classy Anne 106 *(5f,Ayr,GS,May 18)*
Claudio Monteverdi 110 *(8f,Leo,SH,Apr 6)*
Clayton 106 *(10f,Eps,S,Apr 20)*
Clear Spring 110 *(6f,Nby,GS,May 13)*
Clear Water 105 *(7f,Nmk,GF,May 21)*
Cleonte 108 *(15f,Dea,G,Aug 14)*
Clever Bob 107 *(8f,Wdr,S,Oct 17)*
Clever Cookie 112 *(20f,Asc,S,Jun 16)*
Cleverconversation 105 *(8½f,Not,GF,Jun 1)*
Clotilde 109 *(8f,Wdr,S,Jun 25)*
Cloudberry 106 *(8f,Nby,GS,Oct 21)*
Club Wexford 107 *(7f,Cur,GY,Jly 16)*
Code Of Honor 106 *(12f,Mey,G,Feb 11)*
Code Red 109 *(7f,Goo,G,Aug 28)*
Coeur De Lion 107 *(17f,Bat,GF,Oct 12)*
Cold Fusion 105 *(10f,Nmk,G,Jly 15)*
Collision Course 108 *(7f,Cur,S,May 2)*
Colour Blue 110 *(7f,Leo,Y,Sep 10)*
Colourfilly 106 *(7f,Hay,GS,May 27)*
Column 105 *(8f,San,GF,Jly 27)*
Combative 107 *(12f,Asc,GF,Aug 6)*
Comicas 113 *(7f,Mey,G,Feb 11)*
Compton Mill 107 *(10f,San,GF,Jly 21)*
Compton Park 105 *(6f,Don,G,Jun 25)*
Confessional 109 *(5f,Don,G,Oct 22)*
Constantino 106 *(8f,Don,GS,Jun 12)*
Continuum 106 *(13f,Nby,GF,Aug 12)*
Convey 113 *(8f,Hay,S,Sep 3)*
Cook Islands 108 *(10½f,Chs,G,May 6)*
Cool Bahamian 106 *(6f,Lin,G,Jun 4)*
Coolmore 106 *(10½f,Cha,S,Jun 19)*
Cordite 106 *(8½f,Eps,GS,Jun 3)*
Cornwallville 108 *(7f,Nby,GF,Aug 13)*
Corpus Chorister 105 *(14f,Not,G,Oct 26)*
Corridor Kid 109 *(5f,Thi,G,Apr 24)*
Corton Lad 105 *(10f,Rip,G,Jun 2)*
Cosmeapolitan 107 *(12f,Nby,GF,Aug 13)*
Cosmic Chatter 111 *(6f,Red,GF,Aug 6)*
Cosmopolitan Girl 108 *(5f,Bat,F,Jun 11)*

Cotai Glory 113 *(5f,Nby,GS,Sep 17)*
Cote D'Azur 108 *(10f,Bat,GF,Jly 29)*
Cougar Mountain 112 *(8f,Leo,GF,Aug 11)*
Could Should Would 110 *(8f,Cur,GF,Aug 7)*
Coulsty 111 *(7f,Lei,GS,Apr 23)*
Countermeasure 113 *(10½f,Yor,GF,Jly 23)*
Courier 106 *(6f,Thi,GF,Jly 22)*
Cradle Mountain 108 *(16f,Cur,G,Oct 9)*
Craftsmanship 105 *(9f,Goo,GF,Jly 30)*
Crazy Horse 112 *(7f,Sal,GS,Oct 10)*
Creggs Pipes 110 *(8f,Leo,Y,Sep 10)*
Crew Cut 106 *(6f,Wdr,G,May 2)*
Cricklewood Green 109 *(8f,Bri,GS,Aug 3)*
Crimean Tatar 108 *(12f,Nmk,GF,Jly 22)*
Croquembouche 107 *(12f,Yor,GF,May 13)*
Crowning Glory 107 *(8f,Nmk,GF,Oct 1)*
Curbyourenthusiasm 109 *(18f,Don,G,Sep 9)*
Curley Bill 106 *(12f,Cur,Y,May 21)*
Current State 105 *(8f,Leo,GF,Jun 9)*
Curtain Call 105 *(5f,Ham,G,Jun 23)*
Custom Cut 113 *(8½f,Eps,GS,Jun 3)*
Cymraeg Bounty 112 *(6f,Red,GF,Aug 6)*
Cymric 109 *(8f,Nmk,GF,Jly 7)*
Cymro 107 *(14f,Cur,Y,Jun 26)*

Daisy Bere 109 *(10f,Pon,GF,Jun 6)*
Daisy Boy 105 *(10f,San,GF,Jly 21)*
Dal Harraild 108 *(12f,Asc,G,Sep 3)*
Dame Judi 106 *(8f,Wdr,G,May 16)*
Damila 106 *(5f,Cha,S,Jun 5)*
Dance King 107 *(10f,Rip,G,May 6)*
Dance Of Fire 107 *(8f,Hay,HY,Jly 1)*
Dance The Dream 107 *(12f,Lei,GS,Oct 4)*
Dancing Star 113 *(6f,Yor,GS,Jun 11)*
Dandyleekie 107 *(6f,Hay,S,Jly 2)*
Danehill Kodiac 109 *(12f,Asc,GF,Aug 6)*
Danzeno 113 *(6f,Yor,G,May 11)*
Daphne 107 *(14f,Goo,GS,Sep 21)*
Dariyan 115 *(12f,Mey,G,Mar 5)*
Dark Defender 107 *(6f,Yor,GS,Sep 4)*
Dark Devil 109 *(7½f,Chs,G,May 5)*
Dark Emerald 111 *(8f,Mey,G,Jan 28)*
Dark Red 110 *(10f,Eps,S,Apr 20)*
Dark Ruler 106 *(13f,Ham,S,May 1)*
Dark Shot 108 *(6f,Sal,G,May 28)*
Darrington 105 *(10f,Don,G,Apr 23)*
Darshini 105 *(10f,Pon,GF,Jun 19)*
Dartmouth 113 *(12f,Asc,GS,Jun 18)*
David's Duchess 107 *(6f,Yar,GF,Jly 26)*
Dawaa 106 *(7f,Nmk,GF,Jly 23)*
Dawn Horizons 106 *(12f,Don,S,Jun 12)*
Dawn Mirage 109 *(8½f,Bev,G,May 2)*
Dawn Missile 107 *(12f,Yor,GF,Aug 19)*
Dawn Of Hope 106 *(10f,Nmk,GF,Oct 7)*
Day Of Conquest 106 *(8f,Mey,G,Feb 13)*
De Veer Cliffs 105 *(10½f,Chs,GS,Sep 10)*
Dear Bruin 106 *(6f,Lin,GF,Aug 9)*
Deauville 117 *(10½f,Yor,GF,May 12)*
Decorated Knight 113 *(8½f,Eps,GS,Jun 3)*
Delve 105 *(7f,Nmk,GF,May 12)*
Demora 110 *(5f,Bat,S,Apr 15)*
Depth Charge 105 *(7f,Crl,GS,Sep 13)*
Desdichado 109 *(12f,Ffo,G,Aug 8)*
Desert Ace 108 *(5f,Rip,G,Sep 24)*
Desert Cross 107 *(10f,Bat,F,Jly 20)*
Desert Encounter 107 *(12f,Hay,S,Jly 2)*
Desert Haze 107 *(8f,Nmk,GF,Sep 23)*
Desert Law 110 *(5f,Asc,GF,Jly 22)*
Dessertoflife 105 *(10f,Goo,GF,Jly 27)*
Devonshire 112 *(8f,Cur,Y,May 21)*
Dhahmaan 108 *(6f,Asc,GS,Apr 27)*
Diamond Fields 105 *(6f,Cur,GF,Jun 4)*
Diamond Rio 110 *(8f,Cur,G,Jly 17)*
Diamonds A Dancing 106 *(8f,Chp,GF,Jly 22)*
Dick Whittington 111 *(6f,Cur,YS,May 21)*
Dicton 112 *(8f,Cha,G,Oct 1)*
Dilgura 107 *(7f,Sal,GS,May 1)*
Dinkum Diamond 108 *(7f,Nmk,GF,Jly 9)*
Dinneratmidnight 106 *(6f,Pon,GS,Apr 27)*
Diploma 110 *(10½f,Yor,GF,Jly 22)*
Distant Past 108 *(5f,Lei,GS,Sep 19)*
Divine 111 *(6f,Cur,GF,Jun 4)*
Dltripleseven 106 *(17f,Bat,GF,Oct 12)*
Doctor Parkes 105 *(6f,Lin,GF,Aug 9)*
Doctor Sardonicus 108 *(6f,Yar,GF,Jly 26)*
Dodgybingo 107 *(10f,Cur,YS,May 22)*
Doha Dream 115 *(15f,Cha,G,Oct 1)*
Dolce Strega 110 *(7f,Cur,S,May 2)*
Dolphin Village 107 *(12f,Nmk,G,Jly 30)*
Dolphin Vista 108 *(8f,Nmk,GS,Apr 30)*
Dominada 109 *(14f,Cat,GF,Aug 2)*
Dominium 106 *(6f,Asc,GF,Sep 2)*
Dommersen 109 *(10f,Nby,GF,Jly 16)*
Don't Touch 118 *(6f,Asc,G,Oct 15)*
Donjuan Triumphant 109 *(6f,Hay,G,May 28)*
Donncha 109 *(8f,Goo,GF,Jly 29)*
Dont Bother Me 108 *(7f,Leo,G,May 8)*
Dormello 109 *(9f,Mey,G,Feb 11)*
Double Czech 110 *(8½f,Eps,GS,Jun 30)*
Double Up 110 *(5f,Not,G,Nov 2)*
Dougan 108 *(6f,Don,G,Oct 21)*
Downforce 112 *(6f,Cur,YS,May 21)*
Dragon King 107 *(5f,Ayr,GF,Jun 18)*
Dragon Mall 105 *(8f,Goo,GF,Jly 29)*
Dream Dubai 111 *(6f,Asc,GS,Apr 27)*
Dream Mover 105 *(7f,Nmk,G,Jly 30)*
Dream Walker 111 *(7f,Lei,S,Jly 2)*
Dubai Dynamo 106 *(8f,Rip,GS,Aug 29)*
Dubai Fashion 106 *(8½f,Eps,G,Sep 25)*
Dubai's Secret 105 *(8f,Lei,G,May 16)*
Dubka 108 *(12f,Sal,GF,Aug 11)*
Duchess Andorra 105 *(8f,Cur,GY,Jun 25)*
Duke Cosimo 108 *(6f,Rip,G,Jun 1)*
Duke Of Diamonds 105 *(12f,Don,S,Jly 1)*
Duke Of Firenze 112 *(5f,Cha,G,Oct 2)*
Duke Of North 107 *(8f,Bri,GS,Aug 3)*
Duramente 115 *(12f,Mey,G,Mar 26)*
Duretto 113 *(12f,Nby,GS,Oct 22)*
Dusky Raider 111 *(14f,Red,GF,Aug 6)*
Dusty Blue 106 *(6f,Bat,GS,Aug 3)*
Dutch Connection 113 *(8f,San,GS,Apr 22)*
Dutch Law 109 *(7f,Nmk,GF,Aug 6)*
Dutch Masterpiece 108 *(5f,Don,G,Oct 22)*
Dutch Mist 107 *(6f,Pon,GF,Jun 6)*
Dutch Uncle 109 *(10f,Lin,G,May 7)*
Dwight D 109 *(10f,Goo,GF,Jly 28)*

Eager Beaver 106 *(12f,Lei,GF,Jly 20)*
Early Morning 108 *(8f,Asc,S,Jun 15)*
Earnshaw 107 *(9f,Mey,G,Jan 28)*
Earth Drummer 110 *(10½f,Yor,G,Jly 9)*
East Street Revue 109 *(6f,Nmk,GF,Aug 13)*
Eastern Impact 112 *(6f,Nmk,GF,Jly 9)*
Eastern Racer 105 *(6f,Thi,G,Jun 14)*
Eastern Rules 108 *(7f,Mey,G,Jan 7)*
Easton Angel 114 *(5f,Goo,GF,Jly 29)*
Easy Road 109 *(5f,Asc,S,Oct 1)*
Easy Tiger 107 *(7f,Yar,G,Jun 24)*
Eccleston 106 *(6f,Thi,S,Aug 26)*
Economic Crisis 108 *(5f,Mus,GF,Jly 19)*
Eddystone Rock 109 *(10f,Cur,Y,Jun 26)*
Edgar Balthazar 107 *(8f,Crl,GF,Jun 22)*
Educate 111 *(10½f,Yor,G,Jly 9)*
Ejayteekay 106 *(8f,Bri,GF,Sep 29)*
El Astronaute 109 *(5f,Eps,G,Aug 29)*
El Beau 107 *(10½f,Yor,GS,Sep 4)*
El Vip 109 *(8f,Lei,G,Oct 24)*
Elbereth 110 *(10½f,Yor,G,Jly 9)*
Elidor 110 *(14f,Goo,GF,Jly 26)*
Elite Army 112 *(12f,Asc,GF,May 7)*
Elleval 111 *(10f,Mey,G,Jan 7)*
Elliptique 112 *(12f,Cha,G,Sep 11)*
Elocution 106 *(10f,Bat,G,May 2)*
Elronaq 107 *(6f,Yar,GF,Jly 26)*
Elusive Ellen 105 *(6f,Wdr,G,May 2)*
Elusive In Paris 105 *(10f,Cur,Y,Jun 26)*
Elysian Fields 107 *(12f,Nmk,GF,Oct 1)*
Elysian Prince 105 *(10f,Wdr,G,May 2)*
Embiran 109 *(7f,Cur,S,May 2)*
Emell 110 *(7f,Goo,G,Aug 28)*
Emerald 111 *(10f,Nmk,GF,Jly 23)*
Emerald Loch 105 *(6f,Crl,GS,Jly 7)*
Emjayem 105 *(5f,Goo,GF,Jun 5)*
Empress Ali 106 *(10f,Pon,S,Oct 17)*
Encipher 107 *(7f,Mey,G,Jan 7)*
Endive 107 *(17f,Bat,GF,Oct 12)*
Endless Drama 111 *(8f,Nby,G,May 14)*
Endless Time 110 *(12f,Cha,G,Sep 11)*
Energia Davos 105 *(10f,Nmk,GF,Oct 29)*
Engage 106 *(14f,Goo,GS,Sep 21)*
English Summer 105 *(11½f,Wdr,S,Jun 25)*
Englishman 109 *(6f,Nmk,G,May 1)*
Entertaining Ben 106 *(5f,Bat,F,Aug 31)*
Entsar 112 *(10f,Nby,GS,Oct 21)*
Epsom Icon 108 *(8½f,Eps,GS,Jun 4)*
Equally Fast 106 *(5f,Bri,GF,Aug 21)*
Erik The Red 110 *(12f,Don,GF,Nov 5)*
Ertijaal 115 *(5f,Mey,G,Mar 26)*
Erupt 110 *(12f,Asc,GF,Jly 23)*
Ervedya 111 *(8f,Dea,G,Aug 14)*
Eshtiaal 107 *(16½f,Yor,GF,Aug 17)*
Esoterique 113 *(8f,Dea,G,Jly 31)*
Esteemable 110 *(8f,Pon,G,Jly 5)*
Estidhkaar 112 *(8f,Nmk,GF,Oct 29)*
Estidraak 106 *(7f,Goo,GF,Jly 30)*
Eternally 112 *(8f,Lin,GF,Aug 13)*
Eton Rambler 105 *(14f,Sal,GS,May 1)*
Euchen Glen 107 *(10f,Ayr,G,Jun 17)*
Euro Charline 112 *(8f,Nby,G,May 14)*
Eurystheus 105 *(9f,Yor,GS,Jun 11)*
Evanescent 106 *(7f,Cat,S,Apr 6)*
Even Song 108 *(12f,Asc,G,Oct 15)*
Examiner 109 *(8½f,Eps,GS,Jun 3)*
Exceeding Power 107 *(7f,Nmk,GF,May 13)*
Excelli 112 *(7f,Cur,G,Aug 20)*
Exchequer 106 *(6f,Nmk,GF,Aug 5)*
Excilly 107 *(8f,Mey,G,Feb 4)*
Exospheric 117 *(10½f,Yor,GF,Aug 17)*
Exoteric 106 *(10f,Wdr,S,Oct 17)*
Explain 109 *(6f,Thi,GF,May 14)*
Express Himself 109 *(8f,Ayr,GF,Jun 18)*
Eye In The Sky 106 *(14f,Mey,G,Feb 4)*
Eyeshine 106 *(12f,Chp,GF,Jun 10)*

Fabricate 110 *(12f,Lei,GS,Oct 4)*
Face Value 105 *(15f,Leo,GF,Jun 9)*
Fact Or Folklore 108 *(16f,Cur,HY,Sep 25)*
Faiseur De Miracle 110 *(12f,Cat,S,Apr 6)*
Faithful Mount 106 *(12f,Lei,GS,Sep 6)*
Famous Kid 115 *(14f,Mey,G,Feb 4)*
Fanciful Angel 112 *(8f,Mey,G,Jan 28)*
Fandango 106 *(14f,Yor,G,Oct 7)*
Fannaan 109 *(7f,Nby,S,Sep 16)*
Fantasy Gladiator 105 *(10½f,Chs,GS,Sep 10)*
Farlow 108 *(7f,Nmk,GF,Jly 9)*
Farraaj 110 *(8f,Mey,G,Jan 28)*
Fascinating Rock 120 *(10½f,Cur,YS,May 22)*
Fast Act 105 *(5f,Wdr,GS,Sep 5)*
Fast Dancer 105 *(7½f,Chs,G,Jly 31)*
Fast Track 105 *(6f,Yor,GF,Jly 23)*
Fastnet Tempest 106 *(10f,Rip,G,Jun 1)*
Father Bertie 108 *(8f,Ayr,S,Sep 15)*
Fattsota 106 *(10f,Pon,GS,Sep 22)*
Fawaareq 107 *(8f,Nmk,GF,Jly 8)*
Fearless Hunter 108 *(9f,Mey,G,Feb 11)*
Feed The Goater 106 *(8f,Nmk,GS,Jun 17)*
Felix De Vega 107 *(10f,Rip,HY,Apr 14)*
Felix Leiter 109 *(7f,Yor,GS,Jun 11)*
Felix Mendelssohn 105 *(12f,Don,G,Sep 10)*
Fendale 107 *(6f,Hay,G,Oct 14)*
Fidaawy 106 *(10f,Sal,S,Sep 28)*
Fidelma Moon 105 *(8f,Crl,GF,May 20)*
Fieldsman 106 *(7f,Nmk,GF,May 14)*
Fiftyshadesfreed 108 *(10f,San,G,Jun 10)*
Fighting Temeraire 106 *(7f,Nmk,G,Jly 30)*
Fils Anges 108 *(7f,Mey,G,Jan 28)*
Final 105 *(8½f,Bev,GF,Jly 26)*
Final Venture 118 *(5f,Asc,GF,Jly 22)*
Fine Blend 107 *(5f,Ayr,GF,Jun 18)*
Fingal's Cave 106 *(7f,Eps,GS,Jun 30)*
Finn Class 109 *(8f,Thi,S,Apr 30)*
Finsbury Square 114 *(5f,Cha,G,Oct 2)*
Fire Fighting 116 *(10f,Goo,GF,Jly 26)*
Fire Ship 106 *(8f,San,S,Jly 2)*
Fireglow 110 *(8f,Nmk,G,May 1)*
Firmament 111 *(8f,Yor,GF,Aug 18)*
Firnas 108 *(10f,Nmk,GF,May 12)*
First Bombardment 105 *(5f,Cat,GF,May 20)*
First Experience 106 *(8½f,Eps,GS,Jun 30)*
First Mohican 108 *(18f,Nmk,G,Oct 8)*
First Selection 109 *(8f,Hay,S,Sep 3)*
First Sitting 112 *(10f,Nmk,GF,Aug 6)*
Fityaan 113 *(5f,Mey,G,Mar 5)*
Fitzwilly 105 *(17f,Bat,GF,May 2)*
Flamboyant 106 *(9f,Mey,G,Mar 26)*
Flanders Flame 113 *(10f,Cha,G,Oct 1)*
Flash Fire 111 *(7f,Asc,GF,May 7)*
Fleeting Visit 105 *(8f,San,GF,Aug 19)*
Flight Risk 115 *(7f,Cur,HY,Apr 3)*
Flinty Fell 105 *(8f,Mus,G,Sep 10)*
Florenza 106 *(7f,Yor,GF,Aug 18)*
Flower Of Love 107 *(10½f,Chs,GS,Sep 24)*
Flowers On Venus 107 *(6f,Asc,GF,May 6)*
Fluff 105 *(8f,Cur,Y,May 21)*
Flying Fairies 109 *(8f,Cur,Y,Aug 21)*
Flying Officer 112 *(20f,Asc,S,Jun 16)*
Flying Pursuit 111 *(6f,Nmk,GF,Jly 23)*
Folkswood 111 *(8f,Nmk,GS,Apr 30)*
Force 106 *(8½f,Not,G,Sep 28)*
Forecaster 109 *(9f,Mus,G,Jly 8)*
Forever Popular 110 *(14½f,Don,G,Sep 8)*
Forge 111 *(7f,Hay,G,Sep 1)*
Forgotten Hero 108 *(12f,Yor,G,Jly 8)*
Forgotten Rules 110 *(16f,Cur,HY,Sep 25)*
Forjatt 109 *(8f,Mey,G,Feb 25)*
Forries Waltz 111 *(9f,Mey,G,Jan 28)*
Fort Bastion 108 *(8f,Ayr,GS,Sep 17)*
Fort Del Oro 107 *(6f,Cur,YS,May 21)*
Fort Jefferson 105 *(8f,Nby,GS,Jun 30)*
Found 120 *(12f,Cha,G,Oct 2)*
Foundation 116 *(10½f,Yor,GF,May 12)*
Four On Eight 107 *(10f,San,G,Aug 4)*
Fox Trotter 106 *(8f,Hay,G,Oct 14)*
Foxtrot Charlie 109 *(8f,Leo,GF,Jun 9)*
Foxtrot Knight 107 *(5f,Wdr,GF,Jly 4)*
Framley Garth 105 *(10f,Red,GS,Aug 27)*
Francis Of Assisi 106 *(14f,Goo,GF,Jly 26)*
Francisco 108 *(6f,Nby,GS,May 13)*
Franklin D 114 *(8f,Nmk,GF,Jly 16)*
Frantical 105 *(10f,Bri,G,Jun 28)*
Frederic 105 *(16f,Mus,G,Jly 8)*
Fredricka 107 *(5f,Ayr,GF,Jun 18)*
Free Port Lux 106 *(10f,Cha,G,Oct 1)*
Free Zone 107 *(6f,Crl,GS,Jly 2)*
Freewheel 105 *(10½f,Yor,GS,Sep 4)*
Freight Train 106 *(9f,Goo,GF,Jly 30)*
French Legend 105 *(10f,Bri,GF,Jun 14)*
Frontiersman 108 *(12f,Nby,GS,Oct 22)*
Frosty Berry 106 *(12f,Nby,GS,Oct 22)*
Frosty The Snowman 105 *(14f,Red,GF,Aug 6)*
Frozen Force 106 *(10f,Bat,GF,Jly 29)*
Fumbo Jumbo 106 *(5f,Mus,G,Jly 29)*
Fun Mac 116 *(16f,Nmk,GF,Sep 22)*
Funding Deficit 107 *(6f,Red,GF,Aug 6)*
Furia Cruzada 108 *(8f,Asc,S,Jun 15)*
Furiant 105 *(8f,Rip,G,Jly 4)*
Futoon 109 *(6f,Nmk,GF,Aug 13)*
Fuwairt 106 *(8f,Red,GS,Aug 27)*

G Force 109 *(6f,Ayr,GS,Sep 17)*
Gabrial 113 *(10½f,Chs,G,May 5)*
Gabrial The Hero 114 *(14f,Mus,G,Aug 5)*
Gabrial's Kaka 110 *(8f,Nby,G,May 14)*
Gabrial's King 107 *(12f,Yor,GF,Aug 19)*
Gabrial's Star 105 *(16f,Bev,GF,Aug 11)*
Gaelic Wizard 106 *(6f,Thi,GF,Sep 13)*
Gailo Chop 112 *(12f,Mey,G,Mar 26)*
Galileo Gold 117 *(8f,Nmk,GS,Apr 30)*
Gallipoli 106 *(6f,Pon,GF,Jun 6)*
Gallope 107 *(10f,Cur,HY,Apr 3)*
Gamesome 107 *(5f,Yor,G,Jly 8)*
Gang Warfare 105 *(14f,Goo,GF,Jly 26)*
Garcia 107 *(8f,Ayr,GS,Sep 17)*
Garlingari 107 *(12f,Cha,S,Jun 5)*
Gavlar 107 *(14f,Goo,GS,May 21)*
Gawdawpalin 111 *(10f,Eps,GS,Jun 4)*
George Bowen 108 *(6f,Don,G,Oct 21)*
George Cinq 110 *(7f,Thi,GS,Jly 30)*
George Dryden 109 *(6f,Rip,G,Aug 13)*
George William 106 *(7f,Hay,GF,Jun 8)*
Georgetown 107 *(9f,Mey,G,Jan 30)*
Georgian Bay 107 *(7f,Hay,G,Apr 23)*
Gershwin 107 *(10f,Asc,GF,Jly 9)*
Get Knotted 109 *(6f,Don,G,Oct 21)*
Ghaamer 112 *(8f,Mey,G,Feb 25)*
Ghalib 105 *(7f,Nmk,GF,May 14)*
Ghinia 106 *(8½f,Not,GS,Apr 26)*
Ghostly Arc 106 *(9f,Mus,GF,May 9)*
Gifted Master 114 *(6f,Asc,GS,Apr 27)*
Ginger Jack 108 *(9f,Nmk,GF,Sep 24)*
Ginzan 106 *(5f,Bat,GS,Sep 10)*
Glaring 107 *(16f,Asc,GS,Apr 27)*
Gleese The Devil 106 *(16½f,Yor,G,Oct 8)*
Glen Moss 112 *(6f,Asc,GS,Jun 18)*
Glenrowan Rose 114 *(5f,Ham,S,May 1)*
Glens Wobbly 108 *(12f,Chp,GF,Jly 31)*
Glory Awaits 108 *(8f,Yor,GF,May 12)*
Gm Hopkins 109 *(8f,Asc,GS,Apr 27)*
Go Amber Go 105 *(5f,Ffo,G,Jly 19)*
Go On Go On Go On 107 *(5f,Wdr,GF,Jly 18)*
God Willing 107 *(8f,Lei,G,Oct 24)*
Goken 110 *(6f,Nmk,GF,Jly 9)*
Gold Faith 106 *(12f,Nmk,GF,Oct 7)*
Gold Hunter 106 *(6f,Chp,GF,Aug 9)*
Gold Prince 109 *(12f,Hay,S,Jly 2)*
Gold Sands 105 *(8f,Asc,GF,Sep 2)*
Gold Trail 115 *(12f,Don,G,Sep 10)*
Gold-Fun 115 *(6f,Asc,GS,Jun 18)*
Golden Bridge 109 *(10½f,Cha,S,Jun 5)*
Golden Doyen 106 *(16f,Asc,G,Sep 30)*
Golden Soul 108 *(9f,Mey,G,Feb 11)*
Golden Spear 111 *(15f,Leo,Y,Oct 29)*
Golden Steps 111 *(7f,Nmk,GF,Jly 9)*
Golden Stunner 109 *(8½f,Not,G,May 22)*
Golden Valentine 108 *(12f,Cha,G,Sep 11)*
Golden Wedding 105 *(8f,Wdr,GS,Oct 3)*
Goldmember 116 *(16f,Nmk,GF,Sep 22)*
Goldream 114 *(5f,Goo,GF,Jly 29)*
Gontchar 107 *(15f,Cha,G,Oct 1)*
Good Luck Charm 105 *(7f,Goo,G,May 20)*
Goodwood Mirage 111 *(10f,San,GS,Aug 20)*
Goodwood Zodiac 110 *(10f,Eps,G,Aug 29)*
Gordon Lord Byron 108 *(7f,Cur,G,Jly 17)*
Gothic Empire 106 *(7f,Asc,G,Sep 30)*
Graceland 107 *(12f,Sal,GF,Aug 11)*
Gracious John 114 *(5f,Not,G,Nov 2)*
Grand Inquisitor 109 *(8f,Wdr,S,Jun 26)*
Grandad's World 105 *(6f,Not,G,Jly 15)*
Gratzie 107 *(8f,Hay,G,Sep 24)*
Gravity Flow 110 *(6f,Don,GF,Jly 21)*
Great Hall 108 *(10f,Eps,G,Sep 25)*
Great Order 107 *(8f,Asc,GF,Sep 2)*
Great Page 108 *(7f,Nmk,GS,Apr 13)*
Great Wide Open 105 *(15f,Cur,GY,Oct 10)*
Greeb 108 *(7f,Mey,G,Jan 30)*
Green Door 108 *(5f,Nmk,S,Jun 23)*
Green Light 106 *(11½f,Wdr,G,May 16)*
Green Or Black 105 *(10f,Cur,YS,Sep 22)*
Greenside 106 *(8f,Nmk,GF,Oct 29)*
Groor 109 *(8f,Mey,G,Feb 13)*
Groovejet 106 *(12f,Nmk,GF,Oct 1)*
Growl 119 *(6f,Asc,G,Oct 15)*
Grumeti 105 *(18f,Nmk,G,Oct 8)*
Guard of Honour 109 *(15f,Leo,Y,Oct 29)*
Guignol 106 *(12f,Cha,S,Jun 5)*
Guishan 107 *(6f,Nmk,S,Jun 23)*
Gunmetal 109 *(6f,Sal,G,May 28)*
Guns Of Leros 105 *(12f,Sal,G,Aug 19)*
Gurkha Friend 107 *(8f,Crl,GF,Jun 22)*
Guy Fawkes 106 *(10f,Red,GF,May 31)*
Gwendolyn 106 *(5f,Rip,GS,Apr 23)*
Gworn 106 *(10f,Ayr,G,Jun 17)*

Haafaguinea 114 *(12f,Mey,G,Mar 5)*
Haalan 109 *(10f,Nmk,GF,Jly 23)*
Haalick 108 *(7f,Goo,G,May 21)*
Haggle 105 *(8f,San,G,Sep 9)*
Hail Clodius 108 *(8f,San,GF,Jly 20)*
Haley Bop 108 *(8f,Ayr,GS,Sep 17)*
Handsome Dude 108 *(6f,Thi,GF,May 14)*
Hanseatic 105 *(8f,Don,GS,Jun 12)*
Harbour Law 109 *(14½f,Don,G,Sep 10)*
Hardstone 111 *(12f,Pon,GF,Aug 3)*
Harlem 107 *(12f,Cha,S,Jun 5)*
Harlequeen 108 *(10f,Nmk,GS,Apr 14)*

Harlequin Striker 105 (7f,Eps,GS,Jun 30)
Harrison 110 (10½f,Yor,GF,May 12)
Harry Hurricane 110 (5f,Yor,G,May 21)
Harry's Son 115 (7f,Mey,G,Jan 21)
Harwoods Volante 108 (6f,Asc,GF,Sep 2)
Harzand 115 (10f,Leo,Y,Sep 10)
Hasanour 106 (8f,Asc,S,Jun 15)
Hathal 114 (8f,Hay,S,Sep 3)
Hatsaway 106 (14f,Sal,S,Jun 22)
Havana Beat 106 (16½f,Yor,GF,Aug 17)
Have A Nice Day 109 (7f,Cur,G,Aug 20)
Havisham 106 (17f,Bat,GF,May 2)
Hawatif 110 (7f,Goo,GF,Jly 30)
Hawk Moth 106 (7f,Bri,G,May 27)
Hawkbill 114 (10f,San,S,Jly 2)
Hawkeyethenoo 106 (6f,Yor,G,May 11)
Hawksmoor 113 (8f,Leo,Y,Sep 10)
Hay Chewed 110 (5f,Lei,GS,Sep 6)
He's No Saint 105 (7f,Hay,G,Sep 2)
Heaven's Guest 110 (7f,Nmk,GF,Jly 9)
Heir To A Throne 105 (7½f,Chs,G,Jly 31)
Hello My Love 114 (8f,Cha,G,Oct 1)
Henry The Explorer 105 (10f,Asc,G,Sep 2)
Henry's Girl 106 (12f,Cur,Y,May 21)
Herald The Dawn 108 (8f,Nmk,GS,Apr 30)
Here Comes When 113 (7f,Nmk,HY,Jun 25)
Hernandoshideaway 106 (12f,Pon,GF,Aug 3)
Hes Our Music 106 (7f,Cur,G,Aug 20)
Heshem 115 (10f,Cha,G,Oct 1)
Hibiscus 108 (12f,Cur,G,Oct 9)
Hibou 107 (10½f,Yor,G,Oct 8)
Hidden Justice 106 (16½f,Don,GS,Apr 22)
Hidden Rebel 106 (8f,Crl,GF,Aug 17)
Hidden Treasures 105 (7f,Lei,S,Jun 11)
High Grounds 107 (10f,Eps,GS,Jun 4)
High Quality 112 (8f,Cha,S,Jun 5)
High Shields 106 (10f,Goo,GF,Jly 28)
Higher Power 109 (10½f,Hay,G,Apr 23)
Highland Acclaim 112 (6f,Eps,G,Aug 30)
Highland Colori 109 (7f,Nmk,G,Jly 30)
Highland Reel 120 (10½f,Yor,GF,Aug 17)
Highlands Queen 109 (12f,Cha,G,Sep 11)
Highly Sprung 108 (6f,Lei,GF,Aug 7)
Highly Toxic 106 (12f,Cur,GY,Jun 24)
Hilary J 109 (5f,Don,G,Oct 22)
Hillbilly Boy 110 (7½f,Chs,G,May 6)
Hillgrove Angel 107 (16f,Mus,GF,Jly 19)
Hillside Dream 107 (6f,Yar,GF,Jun 8)
Hint Of A Tint 109 (8f,Cur,Y,May 21)
Hint Of Grey 107 (12f,Chp,S,May 10)
His Kyllachy 105 (9f,Crl,GS,Jly 24)
Hit It A Bomb 111 (8f,Leo,GF,Aug 11)
Hit The Jackpot 108 (10f,Don,G,Apr 23)
Holler 109 (6f,Asc,GS,Jun 18)
Holy Grail 106 (8f,Hay,G,Sep 24)
Home Cummins 110 (8f,Yor,G,Jly 9)
Home Of The Brave 114 (7f,Lei,GS,Apr 23)
Hoof It 110 (6f,Ayr,GS,Sep 17)
Hoofalong 115 (5f,Mus,G,Jun 11)
Hope Is High 106 (10f,Yar,GF,Jly 21)
Hornsby 111 (8f,Nmk,GF,Jly 9)
Hors De Combat 108 (8f,Nmk,GF,Jly 16)
Hot Sauce 108 (10½f,Cur,YS,May 22)
Housesofparliament 111 (10½f,Chs,G,May 6)
Hubertas 106 (12f,Cat,S,Apr 6)
Huge Future 106 (10f,Nby,S,Jun 23)
Hulcolt 107 (8½f,Bev,G,May 2)
Humidor 108 (5f,Goo,G,Jly 26)
Humphrey Bogart 115 (11½f,Lin,G,May 7)
Hunters Creek 105 (9f,Mey,G,Jan 30)
Huntlaw 108 (8f,Nmk,GF,Sep 22)
Huntsmans Close 106 (5f,Eps,G,Aug 29)
Hyland Heather 106 (6f,Don,GF,Jly 21)

I Am Not Here 106 (12f,Cat,G,Sep 17)
I'll Be Good 106 (5f,Chs,GS,Sep 10)
I'm Super Too 107 (10f,Bev,GF,Jly 26)
Ibn Malik 114 (7f,Nmk,GS,Apr 13)
Ice Age 108 (6f,Chp,GF,Jly 31)
Ice Lord 108 (6f,Wdr,G,May 23)
Ice Royal 109 (8f,San,GF,Jly 20)
Ice Slice 113 (8f,Bri,G,May 3)
Icebuster 105 (10f,Bat,S,Jun 29)
Iconic 106 (8f,Nby,GF,Jun 9)
Idaho 112 (12f,Cur,GY,Jun 25)
Iffranesia 111 (5f,Cur,Y,Sep 11)
Iftiraaq 105 (10f,Bat,G,Apr 26)
Ifwecan 106 (7f,Nmk,GS,Jun 17)
Ikerrin Road 107 (6f,Yor,GS,Jun 11)
Illuminate 107 (6f,Asc,GS,Jun 17)
Illusive 107 (9f,Goo,GF,Jly 30)
Illustrissime 105 (8f,Pon,GS,Oct 3)
Impassable 112 (8f,Cha,S,Jun 19)
Imperial Aviator 112 (10f,Nby,GS,Sep 17)
Impressionist 105 (12f,Cha,G,Oct 1)
Imshivalla 113 (10f,Red,GS,Nov 1)
Imtiyaaz 106 (6f,Thi,GF,Sep 13)
In Salutem 109 (5f,Cur,Y,Sep 11)
Incahoots 107 (8f,Cha,S,Jun 19)
Indira 106 (12f,Nmk,GF,May 12)
Indulged 107 (10f,Rip,G,Jun 1)
Indus Valley 105 (7f,Bri,G,Aug 4)
Indy 111 (10f,Red,GS,Nov 1)
Infiniti 107 (7f,Lei,GS,Sep 19)
Inke 105 (9f,Lin,S,Jun 2)
Innocent Touch 113 (10f,Nmk,GF,Jly 23)
Instant Attraction 108 (8½f,Eps,GS,Jun 3)
Intense Style 107 (6f,Don,S,Jun 12)
Intense Tango 115 (14f,Mus,G,Aug 5)
Interconnection 107 (10f,Nmk,GF,May 13)
Intermittent 105 (8½f,Not,GF,Jun 1)
Intibaah 106 (5f,Not,HY,Apr 6)
Intilaaq 105 (10f,San,GF,May 26)
Intimately 105 (7f,Yar,G,Aug 11)
Intimation 109 (10f,Goo,GF,Jly 27)
Intisaab 111 (6f,Rip,G,Aug 13)
Intisari 109 (12f,Leo,G,May 8)
Intiwin 105 (8f,Ayr,GS,May 23)
Intransigent 114 (7f,Lei,GF,Oct 11)
Invermere 105 (8f,Mus,GF,Aug 25)
Invincible Ridge 106 (5f,Ayr,GS,Aug 6)
Ionization 105 (7½f,Chs,G,Jly 23)
Irish Optimism 107 (8½f,Eps,G,Sep 8)
Irish Rookie 114 (8f,Nmk,GF,Jly 8)
Iseemist 109 (5f,Bat,S,Apr 15)
Isharah 109 (12f,Ffo,G,Aug 8)
Island Remede 105 (12f,Leo,HY,Apr 6)
Istanbul Bey 106 (10½f,Yor,G,Jly 8)
Ito 113 (12f,Cha,G,Sep 11)
Izmir 106 (8f,Chp,G,Jly 31)

Jaarih 105 (5f,Not,G,Sep 28)
Jacbequick 105 (8½f,Bev,GF,Jun 8)
Jack Dexter 114 (6f,Asc,G,Oct 15)
Jack Hobbs 108 (10f,Asc,G,Oct 15)
Jack's Revenge 106 (8f,Nmk,GF,May 13)
Jacob Cats 106 (12f,Asc,G,Sep 2)
Jacobs Well 107 (8f,Cur,HY,Sep 25)
Jadaayil 107 (7f,Yor,GF,Aug 18)
Jailawi 107 (8f,San,GF,May 26)
Jallota 112 (7f,Goo,G,Aug 28)
Jamesie 108 (7f,Chs,S,Jly 9)
Jane's Memory 109 (6f,Hay,S,Sep 3)
Jaqen H'Ghar 105 (10f,Leo,GF,Aug 11)
Jawaayiz 107 (10f,Bri,GF,Aug 21)
Jay Kay 105 (7f,Ayr,GS,Aug 6)
Jayed Jidan 106 (7f,Mey,G,Jan 30)
Jaywalker 105 (5f,San,GF,Jun 11)
Jazzi Top 107 (8f,Asc,S,Jun 15)
Jebediah Shine 106 (5f,Red,GF,May 16)
Jemayel 112 (10f,Goo,GF,Jly 30)
Jennies Jewel 109 (20f,Asc,S,Jun 14)
Jeremys Joy 110 (10f,Leo,HY,Apr 6)
Jet Setting 112 (8f,Cur,YS,May 22)
Jimenez 105 (8½f,Not,GF,Jun 9)
Jimmy Two Times 115 (7f,Cha,G,Oct 2)
Joailliere 114 (7f,Cur,HY,Apr 3)
Johann Strauss 105 (8f,Mey,G,Feb 25)
Johnny Barnes 110 (7f,Lei,GS,Apr 23)
Johnny Cavagin 107 (6f,Pon,G,Jly 5)
Journey 119 (12f,Asc,G,Oct 15)
Judicial 112 (5f,Thi,GF,May 14)
Jungle Cat 114 (5f,Mey,G,Mar 26)
Just Be Lucky 112 (8f,Hay,G,May 20)
Just Glamorous 113 (5f,Cha,G,Sep 11)
Just That Lord 110 (5f,Wdr,G,May 2)
Justice Belle 117 (16f,Nmk,GF,Sep 22)
Justice First 105 (6f,Lin,G,Jun 4)
Justice Good 113 (5f,Not,G,Nov 2)

Kachy 109 (6f,Asc,GS,Jun 17)
Kadrizzi 108 (6f,Asc,GF,Aug 6)
Kalann 106 (13f,Leo,G,Jly 7)
Kalk Bay 108 (7f,Mus,GF,Jun 4)
Kanaf 107 (7f,Mey,G,Feb 18)
Karar 116 (7f,Cha,G,Oct 2)
Kasb 108 (6f,Mey,G,Feb 13)
Kassia 107 (6f,Nmk,G,Oct 8)
Keep In Line 106 (14f,Mey,G,Feb 4)
Kelinni 112 (7f,Thi,S,Apr 16)
Kenny The Captain 106 (6f,Red,G,Sep 6)
Kentuckyconnection 111 (8f,Nmk,GS,Apr 30)
Kerry Icon 107 (9f,Mus,G,Jly 8)
Khairaat 106 (10f,Don,G,Sep 9)
Khelman 106 (6f,Eps,GS,Jun 30)
Kibaar 107 (5f,Mus,G,Jly 29)
Kickboxer 105 (6f,Nby,GS,May 13)
Kicky Blue 111 (20f,Asc,S,Jun 16)
Kiltara 107 (12f,Don,G,Sep 10)
Kimberella 110 (6f,Rip,G,Sep 24)
Kinema 110 (12f,Asc,GS,Jun 17)
King Bolete 108 (12f,Asc,GF,May 7)
King Crimson 108 (5f,Bri,GF,Aug 21)
King Of Rooks 111 (6f,Wdr,G,May 23)
King Of Swing 105 (7f,Thi,S,Aug 26)
King's Pavilion 108 (7½f,Chs,G,May 5)
Kings Fete 112 (12f,Nby,GS,Oct 22)
Kingsgate Native 110 (5f,Not,GF,Aug 9)
Kingston Kurrajong 110 (8f,Wdr,S,Jun 26)
Kip 106 (12f,Rip,G,Jun 2)
Kitaaby 105 (7f,Lei,GF,Jly 20)
Kiwi Bay 107 (10f,Red,GF,Jly 17)
Knavery 106 (7f,Mey,G,Jan 30)
Knight Music 105 (12f,Nmk,GF,May 12)
Knight Owl 108 (8f,Rip,GS,Aug 29)
Knights Table 108 (12f,Nmk,GF,Aug 13)
Kodi Bear 107 (8f,Goo,GF,Jly 27)
Kommander Kirkup 106 (6f,Thi,S,Apr 30)
Kool Kompany 111 (8f,Nmk,GF,Oct 29)
Koora 111 (10½f,Yor,GF,May 12)
Kourkan 111 (8f,Sai,S,Oct 30)
Krypton Factor 108 (5f,Mey,G,Mar 5)
Kullu 106 (10f,Nby,GS,Oct 21)
Kummiya 107 (8½f,Not,GF,Jly 19)
Kylla Instinct 105 (7f,Nmk,S,Jun 24)

La Cressonniere 109 (10½f,Cha,S,Jun 19)
La Rioja 108 (6f,Yor,G,Jly 8)
Ladurelli 108 (10f,Nby,GF,Jly 16)
Ladweb 108 (5f,San,S,Jly 1)
Lady Blanco 109 (10f,Bat,F,Jly 20)
Lady Clair 106 (6f,Nmk,GF,Jly 23)
Lady Macapa 108 (6f,Goo,G,Oct 9)
Lady Marl 105 (8f,Pon,G,Jly 5)
Lady Of Camelot 107 (12f,Lei,GF,May 30)
Lady Shipman 112 (5f,Mey,G,Mar 26)
Laganore 111 (10f,Nmk,GF,Oct 7)
Lagenda 105 (7f,Hay,GF,Jun 8)
Laidback Romeo 107 (8f,Wdr,GF,Aug 7)
Laila Honiwillow 108 (6f,Don,GS,Jun 24)
Landing Night 106 (5f,Cat,GF,May 20)
Landofhopeandglory 117 (14f,Cur,Y,Jun 26)
Landwade Lad 108 (10f,Sal,S,Sep 28)
Lapilli 107 (5f,Bat,F,Aug 31)
Lara Carbonara 106 (11f,Ham,G,Jly 30)
Last Impact 114 (12f,Mey,G,Mar 26)
Lat Hawill 107 (8f,Rip,G,Jun 2)
Latharnach 108 (8f,Nmk,GF,Oct 29)
Laugh Aloud 113 (8f,Nmk,GF,Sep 23)
Laughton 105 (5f,Goo,GF,Jly 28)
Laurence 105 (10f,Don,G,Sep 9)
Lavetta 107 (7f,Cat,GS,Apr 20)
Laws Of Spin 109 (16f,Cur,G,Oct 9)
Layali Al Andalus 108 (14f,Mey,G,Feb 4)
Layla's Hero 105 (6f,Red,S,Apr 28)
Le Chat D'Or 109 (8f,Ayr,GS,Jly 18)
Le Vagabond 107 (14f,Leo,G,Sep 10)
Leah Freya 109 (12f,Nby,S,Jun 23)
Lean On Pete 105 (12f,Bev,G,Jun 21)
Left Hand 111 (12f,Cha,G,Sep 11)
Let Right Be Done 105 (8f,Mus,G,Aug 5)
Lexi's Hero 108 (6f,Red,GF,Aug 6)
Lexington Abbey 110 (5f,Asc,GF,Jly 9)
Lexington Place 108 (5f,Ayr,GF,Jun 18)
Librisa Breeze 116 (6f,Asc,G,Oct 15)
Life Less Ordinary 108 (16f,Asc,G,Sep 30)
Light And Shade 110 (8f,Asc,GF,May 7)
Light Up Our World 105 (8f,Goo,GF,Jly 29)
Lightning Charlie 107 (6f,Goo,G,Oct 9)
Lightning Spear 118 (8f,Goo,GF,Aug 27)
Lightscameraction 108 (5f,Lei,GF,Oct 11)
Lil Sophella 111 (8f,Pon,G,Jly 5)
Lilbourne Prince 105 (8f,Chp,GF,Jly 22)
Lily Trotter 106 (17f,Bat,GF,Oct 12)
Lily's Rainbow 106 (8f,Cur,YS,Mar 20)
Limario 105 (9f,Mey,G,Jan 28)
Limato 120 (7f,Cha,G,Oct 2)
Lime And Lemon 106 (10f,Nby,S,Sep 16)
Limitless 111 (8f,Asc,S,Jun 16)
Lina De Vega 110 (8f,Cur,G,Jly 17)
Lincoln 106 (6f,Don,G,Oct 21)
Lincoln Rocks 108 (8f,Hay,GF,Aug 4)
Line Of Reason 110 (5f,Bev,G,Jun 14)
Linguistic 111 (10½f,Chs,G,May 6)
Links Drive Lady 106 (6f,Wdr,S,Jun 13)
Liquid Mercury 109 (8f,Mey,G,Jan 28)
Little Kipling 106 (8f,Nmk,GF,May 12)
Little Lady Katie 111 (10f,Red,GS,Nov 1)
Little Lord Nelson 105 (8½f,Eps,GS,Jun 30)
Little Palaver 110 (6f,Chp,GF,Jly 31)
Live Twice 105 (8f,Cur,G,Jly 17)
Livella Fella 110 (9f,Mus,G,Jly 8)
Loaded 108 (8f,Crl,GS,Sep 7)
Loaves And Fishes 107 (10f,Bev,GF,May 28)
Log Out Island 111 (6f,Nby,G,May 14)
Long Awaited 106 (5f,Wdr,GF,Jly 4)
Long Island Sound 107 (10f,Asc,S,Jun 16)
Lord Franklin 105 (10f,Not,S,Jly 2)
Lord George 106 (11½f,Yar,GF,Jun 9)
Lord Of The Land 106 (7f,Hay,G,Apr 23)
Lord Of The Rock 108 (8f,Don,S,Apr 2)
Lord Reason 105 (8f,Bri,G,May 27)
Lorelina 110 (10f,Nby,GS,Oct 21)
Love On The Rocks 106 (5f,Yor,G,Aug 20)
Loveable Helen 105 (8½f,Not,GF,Jly 28)
Lovely Story 106 (12f,Asc,GF,Jly 8)
Loving Things 111 (12f,Pon,GF,Jun 19)
Lucida 107 (8f,Cur,Y,May 21)
Lucky Violet 105 (7f,Mus,G,Aug 5)
Lucy The Painter 110 (8f,Pon,G,Jly 5)
Luis Vaz De Torres 106 (6f,Cat,GF,Jun 3)
Lulu The Zulu 106 (7f,Hay,G,Sep 1)
Lumiere 115 (8f,Nmk,GF,Jly 7)
Lustrous 107 (12f,Don,G,Sep 10)
Lydia's Place 106 (5f,Thi,GF,Aug 9)
Lytham St Annes 108 (7f,Mey,G,Feb 11)

Maarek 111 (6f,Nmk,GS,Apr 14)
Madame Butterfly 105 (9f,Mus,GF,May 9)
Madrinho 106 (6f,Lei,GF,May 30)
Magic Circle 109 (15f,Leo,Y,Oct 29)
Magical Effect 108 (6f,Thi,S,Aug 26)
Magical Memory 115 (6f,Yor,G,May 11)
Magnentius 106 (15f,Dea,G,Aug 14)
Magnus Maximus 110 (6f,Asc,GF,Sep 3)
Mahsoob 110 (9f,Nmk,GS,Apr 13)
Maid Of The Glens 106 (10f,Cur,HY,Apr 3)
Mainstream 106 (12f,Pon,G,Aug 14)
Majeed 110 (11½f,Wdr,GF,Aug 27)
Majestic Hero 107 (5f,Chp,GF,Jly 31)
Majestic Moon 106 (7f,Asc,GF,May 7)
Majestic Mount 108 (7f,Mey,G,Jan 7)
Major Pusey 106 (5f,Hay,GF,Jun 9)
Maknificent 109 (10f,Leo,GF,Jun 3)
Makzeem 107 (10f,Wdr,GF,Jly 18)
Maleficent Queen 109 (10f,Ayr,GS,May 18)
Maljaa 109 (5f,Asc,GF,Jly 9)
Malmoosa 106 (10f,Nmk,GF,Oct 1)
Man Of Harlech 105 (8f,Asc,S,Jun 15)
Manaboo 108 (8f,Nmk,GF,Jly 7)
Manatee 107 (16f,Mey,G,Mar 26)
Mandamus 106 (12f,Leo,G,May 8)
Mandatario 108 (15f,Leo,GF,Jun 9)
Maneen 113 (10f,Cur,YS,May 22)
Mango Tango 108 (12f,Cha,G,Oct 1)
Manjaam 105 (12f,Bat,GF,May 27)
Manson 110 (8f,Nmk,GF,Jly 9)
Maraakib 107 (10½f,Yor,G,Jun 10)
Margaret's Mission 109 (8f,Asc,GF,May 7)
Mariee 109 (8f,Bri,G,May 3)
Markaz 109 (7f,Nby,GF,Aug 13)
Marmalady 108 (5f,Goo,GS,Apr 30)
Marmelo 110 (15f,Cha,G,Oct 1)
Maroc 105 (10f,Sal,GS,Oct 10)
Marsh Hawk 108 (6f,Not,GF,May 7)
Marsh Pride 108 (10½f,Yor,G,Oct 8)
Marsha 117 (5f,Cha,G,Oct 2)
Massaat 115 (8f,Nmk,GS,Apr 30)
Master Blueyes 107 (14f,Yor,G,Oct 7)
Master Carpenter 115 (10½f,Chs,G,May 5)
Master Of Finance 106 (10f,Nmk,GF,May 21)
Master Of Irony 108 (10f,Wdr,GF,May 30)
Master Speaker 106 (6f,Cur,HY,Apr 3)
Master The World 116 (8f,Sal,GF,Aug 11)
Mastermind 113 (7f,Mey,G,Jan 21)
Masterpaver 110 (12f,Asc,GF,Jly 22)
Materialistic 108 (10f,Yar,GF,Sep 14)
Mattmu 112 (6f,Nmk,GS,Apr 14)
Maverick Wave 109 (10f,Eps,G,Aug 29)
Max Dynamite 109 (20f,Asc,S,Jun 16)
Maximum Aurelius 108 (8f,Sai,S,Oct 30)
May Rose 105 (5f,Wdr,GF,Aug 8)
Maybelater 109 (10f,Sal,GF,Aug 10)
Mayfair Lady 109 (6f,Yor,G,Jun 10)
Mazzini 107 (6f,Asc,G,Sep 30)
McCools Gold 108 (17f,Bat,GF,Oct 12)
Mcguigan 107 (7f,Cur,G,Aug 20)
Meadow Creek 109 (14f,Mey,G,Mar 3)
Meadway 107 (5f,Mus,G,Jun 11)
Meandre 113 (10f,Cha,G,Oct 1)
Mecca's Angel 117 (5f,Yor,G,Aug 19)
Medburn Cutler 107 (12f,Lei,HY,Jun 21)
Medburn Dream 106 (8½f,Eps,S,Apr 20)
Medicean Man 111 (5f,Asc,GF,Jly 22)
Medina Sidonia 108 (12f,Pon,G,May 27)
Mega Fortune 109 (10f,Cur,YS,May 22)
Mehronissa 113 (6f,Asc,S,Oct 1)
Mekhtaal 107 (10½f,Cha,S,Jun 5)
Melvin The Grate 108 (8f,San,S,Jly 2)
Memorial Day 113 (10f,Pon,GS,Sep 22)
Memory Cloth 107 (8f,Pon,S,Apr 18)
Menai 105 (6f,Wdr,GF,Oct 10)
Merhee 107 (7f,Mey,G,Jan 7)
Merhoob 106 (6f,Asc,GF,Jly 8)
Merry Me 106 (8f,Wdr,S,Jun 25)
Meshardal 106 (6f,Red,GF,Aug 6)
Mexican Mick 106 (12f,Lei,HY,Jun 21)
Mezzotint 107 (8f,Bri,G,May 3)
Mica Mika 107 (10f,Ayr,GS,May 23)
Michael's Mount 106 (12f,Cat,S,Oct 25)
Michele Strogoff 113 (10f,Red,GS,Nov 1)
Midnight Macchiato 107 (8f,Nmk,GF,May 12)
Midnight Rider 108 (7½f,Ffo,G,Jly 19)
Midnight Warrior 110 (14f,Red,GF,Aug 6)
Midterm 111 (10½f,Yor,GF,May 12)
Midweek 107 (8f,Nmk,G,May 1)
Mighty Lady 105 (10½f,Chs,G,Jly 31)
Mijhaar 112 (14f,Mus,G,Aug 5)
Mikmak 105 (8f,Ayr,GS,Jly 18)
Mill Springs 108 (20f,Asc,S,Jun 14)
Mille Et Mille 113 (20f,Asc,S,Jun 16)
Millefiori 112 (8f,Ayr,GS,May 23)
Minding 118 (10f,Leo,Y,Sep 10)
Miningrocks 106 (11f,Ham,G,Jly 30)
Mint Julep 106 (15f,Dea,G,Aug 14)
Miracle Of Medinah 109 (6½f,Don,G,Sep 9)
Mirsaale 108 (16f,Rip,GS,Apr 23)
Mirza 109 (5f,Lei,GF,Oct 11)
Mise En Rose 108 (7f,Goo,GF,Jly 29)
Mishaal 106 (7f,Hay,G,Sep 2)
Miss Carbonia 105 (7f,Lin,S,Jun 11)
Miss Elizabeth 105 (7f,Cur,S,May 2)
Miss Temple City 107 (8f,Asc,S,Jun 15)
Miss Van Gogh 110 (8½f,Not,GS,Apr 26)
Missed Call 109 (12f,Asc,GF,May 7)

Mister Music **105** *(8f,San,G,Sep 9)*
Mister Musicmaster **105** *(10f,Wdr,G,May 2)*
Misterioso **107** *(6f,Asc,GF,Jly 8)*
Mistiroc **107** *(12f,Don,GF,Nov 5)*
Mitchum Swagger **113** *(8f,Hay,S,Sep 3)*
Mithqaal **108** *(9f,Nmk,GF,Sep 23)*
Mix And Mingle **107** *(8f,Nmk,G,May 1)*
Mizaah **105** *(7f,Leo,Y,Sep 10)*
Mizzou **115** *(20f,Asc,S,Jun 16)*
Mobsta **112** *(6f,Cur,YS,May 21)*
Molly Dolly **106** *(8f,Nmk,GF,Sep 23)*
Monaleen **107** *(12f,Pon,GF,Jun 19)*
Mondialiste **116** *(10½f,Yor,GF,Jly 23)*
Money Team **106** *(6f,Thi,S,Sep 3)*
Mongolian Saturday **109** *(6f,Nmk,GF,Jly 9)*
Monotype **108** *(14f,Goo,GS,May 21)*
Monsieur Joe **112** *(5f,San,S,Jly 2)*
Monsieur Valentine **106** *(7f,Bri,G,Aug 4)*
Mont Kiara **114** *(6f,Nmk,GF,Jly 23)*
Montaly **109** *(14f,Hay,S,Sep 3)*
Montsarrat **107** *(10f,Rip,G,Jly 4)*
Moojaned **107** *(12f,Ffo,G,Aug 8)*
Moon River **106** *(8f,Asc,GF,May 7)*
Moonlight Magic **116** *(10f,Leo,Y,Sep 10)*
Moonlight Venture **105** *(7f,Cat,S,Apr 6)*
Moonlightnavigator **108** *(7f,Ayr,S,Oct 6)*
Moonmeister **109** *(12f,Yor,GF,Aug 19)*
Moonraker **105** *(5f,Asc,GF,Jly 9)*
Moonrise Landing **107** *(14f,Yor,G,May 21)*
Moonshiner **114** *(15f,Cha,G,Oct 1)*
Moorside **107** *(14f,Bat,GF,Oct 12)*
Morache Music **105** *(6f,Eps,G,Aug 30)*
Morando **111** *(8f,Ayr,GS,Sep 17)*
More Aspen **106** *(8f,Mey,G,Feb 4)*
More Mischief **106** *(10f,Ayr,GS,May 18)*
Morga **111** *(12f,Cur,Y,Aug 21)*
Moscato **107** *(20f,Asc,S,Jun 14)*
Most Celebrated **107** *(8f,Wdr,GS,Jun 27)*
Motdaw **111** *(10f,Lei,S,Jly 2)*
Mount Logan **110** *(10f,Goo,GS,Sep 21)*
Mount Tahan **108** *(7½f,Bev,G,Aug 27)*
Mountain Bell **112** *(12f,Nby,GS,Oct 22)*
Mountain Rescue **105** *(10f,Lei,G,May 16)*
Move In Time **107** *(5f,Hay,GS,May 21)*
Move Up **110** *(12f,Asc,S,Oct 1)*
Mr Cool Cash **105** *(8½f,Bev,GF,May 28)*
Mr Lupton **114** *(6f,Yor,GS,Jun 11)*
Mr Owen **106** *(8f,Asc,S,Jun 15)*
Mr Right **107** *(6f,Cur,HY,Apr 3)*
Muffri'Ha **109** *(10f,San,GS,Aug 20)*
Muhaafiz **107** *(10½f,Hay,G,Apr 23)*
Muhtaram **107** *(7f,Mey,G,Jan 30)*
Muir Lodge **108** *(6f,Asc,GF,May 6)*
Mujaarib **107** *(9f,Mey,G,Jan 28)*
Mujassam **105** *(7f,Yar,G,Jun 24)*
Mukaabra **108** *(8f,Nmk,GF,May 12)*
Mukaynis **107** *(5f,Eps,GS,Jun 4)*
Mukhayyam **113** *(12f,Pon,GF,Aug 3)*
Multitask **105** *(8f,Bri,G,Aug 22)*
Munfallet **108** *(6f,Hay,G,Oct 14)*
Muntadab **111** *(7f,Thi,GS,Jly 30)*
Muntahaa **110** *(13½f,Chs,G,Aug 20)*
Muntazah **114** *(10½f,Yor,GF,May 12)*
Muqarred **105** *(10f,Red,GS,Aug 27)*
Muraabit **109** *(10½f,Yor,GS,Sep 4)*
Murad Khan **106** *(8f,Thi,S,Sep 3)*
Musaddas **111** *(9f,Mey,G,Feb 11)*
Musdam **106** *(7f,Yar,GF,Aug 28)*
Musharrif **110** *(5f,Thi,GF,Aug 9)*
Mustaaqeem **107** *(8f,Nby,G,May 14)*
Mustadeem **106** *(10f,Mey,G,Feb 4)*
Mustallib **109** *(6f,Lei,GF,Aug 7)*
Mustashry **110** *(8f,Yor,GF,Aug 18)*
Mutakayyef **119** *(10½f,Yor,GF,Aug 17)*
Mutamakkin **110** *(10f,Goo,GF,Jly 26)*
Mutasayyid **108** *(8f,Mey,G,Feb 13)*
Mutawathea **110** *(7f,Asc,GF,May 7)*
Muthmir **113** *(5f,Mey,G,Mar 26)*
Muwaary **109** *(7f,Hay,G,Sep 1)*
Muzdawaj **107** *(10f,Nby,GS,Sep 17)*
My Dad Syd **105** *(7f,Nby,GS,Oct 21)*
My Dream Boat **117** *(10f,Asc,S,Jun 15)*
My Mistress **105** *(10f,Yar,GF,Jly 21)*
My Name Is Rio **107** *(5f,Don,G,Oct 22)*
My Reward **106** *(16f,Rip,GS,Apr 23)*
My Target **105** *(7f,Nmk,GF,May 13)*
Myopic **107** *(10f,Nby,GF,Aug 12)*
Mysterial **106** *(10f,Pon,GF,Sep 15)*
Mysterious Glance **106** *(5f,Not,G,Sep 28)*
Mythmaker **109** *(6f,Yor,G,May 11)*

Naadirr **114** *(6f,Wdr,G,May 23)*
Naggers **107** *(6f,Ayr,S,Oct 6)*
Nahual **113** *(15f,Cha,G,Sep 11)*
Nakeeta **110** *(15f,Leo,Y,Oct 29)*
Nameitwhatyoulike **112** *(6f,Rip,G,Aug 13)*
Namhroodah **111** *(8f,Asc,GF,Jly 22)*
Nathra **108** *(8f,Nmk,G,May 1)*
Natural Scenery **107** *(10f,San,GF,Jly 21)*
Navajo War Dance **108** *(10f,Ayr,GS,Aug 8)*
Nayel **109** *(10½f,Yor,G,May 11)*
Need To Know **108** *(9f,Mey,G,Jan 30)*
Nemoralia **113** *(7f,Yor,G,Aug 19)*
Neo Black Dia **106** *(16f,Mey,G,Mar 26)*
New Bay **116** *(10f,Leo,Y,Sep 10)*
New Bidder **108** *(6f,Hay,S,Jly 2)*
New Caledonia **112** *(10f,Nmk,G,May 1)*
New Road Side **106** *(5f,Not,S,Oct 12)*
Newera **107** *(10½f,Chs,G,May 5)*
Newsman **111** *(10f,Cur,YS,May 22)*
Newstead Abbey **105** *(7f,Chs,GS,Sep 24)*
Newton's Law **106** *(5f,Bat,GF,Jly 29)*
Next Edition **110** *(14f,Red,GF,Aug 6)*
Nezwaah **111** *(10f,Yar,GF,Sep 14)*
Nicarra **106** *(8½f,Not,GF,Jun 1)*
Niceofyoutotellme **108** *(10f,San,GF,May 26)*
Nicholas T **106** *(10f,Ayr,GS,Aug 8)*
Nietzsche **107** *(10f,Ayr,GS,Aug 8)*
Ninjago **108** *(5f,Yor,G,May 21)*
Noble Gift **106** *(10f,Asc,GS,Jun 18)*
Noble Silk **107** *(16f,Asc,G,Sep 30)*
Nonetheless **106** *(12f,Cur,Y,Aug 21)*
Nonios **108** *(12f,Ffo,G,Aug 8)*
Nonno Giulio **105** *(8f,Wet,GF,May 17)*
Normal Equilibrium **108** *(5f,Eps,S,Apr 20)*
Normandy Barriere **110** *(6½f,Don,G,Sep 9)*
Normandy Knight **105** *(8f,Lei,GF,May 30)*
Not Listenin'tome **111** *(5f,Mey,G,Mar 26)*
Not Never **107** *(12f,Nby,S,Sep 16)*
Not So Sleepy **109** *(10f,San,GF,May 26)*
Notarised **109** *(14f,Goo,GF,Jly 26)*
Notice **105** *(11½f,Yar,GF,Sep 15)*
Nouvelli Dancer **105** *(7f,Eps,G,Aug 30)*
Novelty Seeker **110** *(10½f,Yor,G,Oct 8)*
Now Or Never **114** *(8f,Leo,Y,Sep 10)*
Nuno Tristan **108** *(6f,Ayr,GS,Sep 17)*

Oakley Girl **107** *(8f,Goo,G,Apr 30)*
Oasis Fantasy **115** *(10f,Goo,GF,Jly 26)*
Ocean Eleven **105** *(10f,Yar,S,Oct 10)*
Ocean Sheridan **111** *(6f,Thi,S,Aug 26)*
Ocean Tempest **105** *(7½f,Chs,G,May 28)*
Oceane **109** *(16½f,Yor,GF,Aug 17)*
Ode To Evening **110** *(10f,Goo,GF,Jly 28)*
Odeon **106** *(12f,Don,GF,Jun 4)*
Off Art **108** *(8½f,Not,GF,Jun 1)*
Oh So Sassy **106** *(5f,Don,GF,Jun 3)*
Oh This Is Us **110** *(7f,Nmk,G,Jly 30)*
Olivia Fallow **106** *(5f,Mus,G,May 27)*
One And Only **113** *(12f,Mey,G,Mar 26)*
One Foot In Heaven **115** *(12f,Cha,G,Oct 2)*
One In All In **105** *(10f,Leo,Y,Oct 29)*
One Word More **109** *(8f,Yor,GF,May 12)*
Onenightidreamed **116** *(7f,Cur,HY,Apr 3)*
Only Mine **108** *(6f,Hay,S,Sep 3)*
Opal Tiara **113** *(7f,Goo,G,Aug 28)*
Operative **107** *(6f,Red,GS,Jun 18)*
Oracolo **107** *(8f,Yor,GF,May 12)*
Orcia **107** *(8f,Leo,GF,Jun 9)*
Order Of St George **117** *(20f,Asc,S,Jun 16)*
Orient Class **106** *(5f,Hay,G,Sep 2)*
Oriental Fox **108** *(12f,Asc,GF,May 7)*
Oriental Relation **105** *(5f,Not,GF,Jly 19)*
Oriental Splendour **105** *(5f,Pon,GF,Jun 27)*
Orion's Bow **110** *(6f,Goo,GF,Jly 30)*
Ormito **107** *(11f,Ham,S,Jly 15)*
Ornate **109** *(6f,Asc,G,Sep 30)*
Orvar **105** *(6f,Asc,GS,Apr 27)*
Ottilie **106** *(8f,Cur,Y,May 2)*
Our Boy Jack **105** *(10f,Red,GF,Jly 17)*
Out Do **109** *(6f,Don,G,Jly 30)*
Out Of The Dark **110** *(7f,Goo,GS,May 21)*
Outback Blue **105** *(7½f,Chs,GS,Jun 24)*
Outback Ruler **105** *(8f,Wdr,GS,Oct 3)*
Outback Traveller **115** *(6f,Asc,GS,Jun 18)*
Overlord **105** *(10f,Yar,GF,Jly 21)*
Ower Fly **106** *(6f,Wdr,S,Apr 11)*

Pacharana **108** *(10f,Yar,GF,Jly 21)*
Pacify **109** *(10f,Eps,S,Apr 20)*
Pacodali **109** *(7f,Cur,S,May 2)*
Pacolita **108** *(8f,Bri,GS,Aug 3)*
Pactolus **106** *(8f,Nmk,GF,Jly 16)*
Paddy Power **108** *(6f,Nmk,GF,Jly 23)*
Paene Magnus **115** *(14f,Mey,G,Feb 4)*
Page Of Wands **109** *(9f,Mus,G,Jly 8)*
Palavicini Run **105** *(7f,Cur,S,Sep 22)*
Paling **108** *(10f,San,GF,Jly 21)*
Pallasator **110** *(16f,Goo,GF,Jly 28)*
Pamona **109** *(14½f,Don,G,Sep 8)*
Pandora **108** *(10½f,Yor,G,Jun 10)*
Panther Patrol **105** *(6f,Chp,GS,Sep 8)*
Papa's Way **107** *(10f,Cur,HY,Apr 3)*
Paris Protocol **106** *(12f,Asc,S,Jun 16)*
Parliamentarian **107** *(14f,San,GF,Jly 21)*
Pas De Deux **113** *(8f,Cha,S,Jun 19)*
Passover **110** *(10f,Nmk,GF,Aug 6)*
Pastoral Player **105** *(7f,Goo,GF,Jly 27)*
Pea Shooter **105** *(6f,Thi,G,Jly 30)*
Peak Storm **105** *(7f,Chp,S,Sep 13)*
Pearl Secret **110** *(5f,Hay,GS,May 21)*
Peloponnese **107** *(12f,Asc,GF,Jly 8)*
Penglai Pavilion **106** *(12f,Hay,S,Jly 2)*
Peniaphobia **115** *(5f,Mey,G,Mar 26)*
Penny Pepper **107** *(6f,Cur,YS,May 21)*
Penny Pot Lane **105** *(6f,Rip,GS,Aug 29)*
Pensax Boy **105** *(8f,Nmk,GF,Jly 8)*
Pensax Lad **105** *(5f,Wdr,GF,Jly 4)*
Penwortham **109** *(7f,Chs,G,Jun 25)*
Perceus **105** *(16½f,Don,GS,Apr 22)*
Percy Street **106** *(12f,Don,G,Oct 22)*
Percy Veer **105** *(16f,Asc,G,Sep 30)*
Perennial **108** *(14f,Red,GF,Aug 6)*
Perestroika **107** *(12f,Sal,GF,Aug 11)*
Perfect Pasture **113** *(5f,Not,G,Nov 2)*
Perfect Quest **106** *(8½f,Not,GF,Jun 1)*
Peribsen **109** *(15f,Cha,G,Oct 1)*
Perigee **106** *(8½f,Not,GF,Jun 9)*
Perkunas **109** *(8f,Nmk,GF,Jly 9)*
Personal Touch **107** *(7f,Thi,S,Aug 26)*
Persuasive **115** *(8f,Leo,Y,Sep 10)*
Persun **107** *(8f,Pon,GF,Jun 19)*
Pettochside **109** *(6f,Goo,GS,May 21)*
Pharmaceutical **105** *(7f,Goo,G,May 20)*
Pick A Little **108** *(8f,Bri,GS,Aug 3)*
Pick Your Choice **108** *(7f,Yar,G,Jun 24)*
Pina **106** *(10f,Ffo,GS,Jly 28)*
Pine Ridge **105** *(5f,Bat,F,Jly 20)*
Pink Martini **105** *(6f,Bri,G,Aug 5)*
Pintura **105** *(8f,Ayr,GS,May 23)*
Pinzolo **107** *(12f,Asc,GF,Jly 22)*
Pipers Note **110** *(6f,Rip,G,Aug 13)*
Pirouette **110** *(8f,Nmk,GF,Sep 23)*
Pivotman **106** *(8f,Pon,HY,Apr 5)*
Pixeleen **109** *(6f,Chp,GF,Jly 31)*
Platitude **110** *(12f,Asc,S,Jun 16)*
Play Gal **105** *(10f,Goo,G,May 19)*
Play Nicely **105** *(10f,Bev,G,May 2)*
Playtothewhistle **105** *(8f,Mus,G,Aug 5)*
Pleascach **106** *(10f,Cha,G,Oct 2)*
Plenary **105** *(10f,San,GF,May 19)*
Plough Boy **108** *(7f,Cur,G,Aug 20)*
Plucky Dip **107** *(7f,Don,GF,Jun 3)*
Plutocracy **106** *(12f,Asc,GF,Jly 22)*
Pocket Of Stars **107** *(8f,Cur,G,Jly 17)*
Poet's Word **107** *(10f,Eps,GS,Jun 4)*
Pointel **106** *(14f,Not,G,Oct 26)*
Pomme De Terre **106** *(6f,Yor,GS,Jun 11)*
Ponty Royale **105** *(6f,Thi,GF,Jly 22)*
Poole Belle **108** *(6f,Sal,S,Aug 2)*
Port Douglas **108** *(12f,Cur,GY,Jun 25)*
Portage **112** *(8f,Asc,S,Jun 15)*
Porthilly **109** *(5f,Cha,G,Oct 2)*
Portland Street **107** *(6f,Don,GS,Jun 24)*
Postponed **121** *(10½f,Yor,GF,Aug 17)*
Potemkin **117** *(10f,Cha,G,Oct 1)*
Pour Deux **105** *(8f,Cur,G,Jly 17)*
Pour La Victoire **107** *(8f,Bri,GS,Aug 3)*
Powder Snow **113** *(8f,Cha,S,Jun 5)*
Power Struggle **105** *(10f,Leo,G,Jly 7)*
Powerallied **107** *(5f,Chs,G,Jun 25)*
Powerful Wind **108** *(5f,Not,GF,May 17)*
Poyle Thomas **105** *(16½f,Yor,GF,Aug 17)*
Poyle Vinnie **109** *(6f,Wdr,G,May 23)*
Prairie Pearl **111** *(8f,Cha,S,Jun 5)*
Predominance **110** *(7f,Hay,G,Apr 23)*
Prendergast Hill **105** *(12f,Eps,S,Apr 20)*
Pretty Bubbles **105** *(6f,Wdr,GF,Jly 25)*
Pretty Perfect **115** *(12f,Asc,G,Oct 15)*
Priceless **113** *(6f,Nmk,GF,Jly 23)*
Primitivo **113** *(12f,Asc,S,Jun 16)*
Primo Uomo **107** *(5f,Cur,HY,Sep 25)*
Princess Aloof **107** *(12f,Cur,Y,May 21)*
Princess Tansy **105** *(5f,Bat,GS,Sep 10)*
Priors Brook **105** *(10f,Wdr,GF,Oct 10)*
Prize Money **113** *(10f,Nmk,G,May 1)*
Proctor **108** *(10f,San,G,Aug 4)*
Profitable **115** *(5f,Hay,GS,May 21)*
Project Bluebook **112** *(14f,Cat,GF,Aug 2)*
Projection **109** *(6f,Nmk,GF,Aug 13)*
Promising Run **107** *(12f,Asc,G,Oct 15)*
Pucon **109** *(5f,Lin,G,Jun 4)*
Pumaflor **107** *(8f,Hay,G,Sep 23)*
Pumblechook **105** *(12f,Don,G,Jly 30)*
Pupil **105** *(8f,Mey,G,Jan 16)*
Pure Art **107** *(8½f,Not,GF,Jun 1)*
Pure Diamond **112** *(7f,Mey,G,Feb 11)*
Purple Magic **108** *(14f,Bat,GF,Oct 12)*
Purple Rock **107** *(8f,Pon,S,Apr 18)*
Pyromaniac **109** *(14f,Leo,G,Sep 10)*

Qaffaal **105** *(8f,Crl,GF,Jun 22)*
Qamarain **105** *(8f,Nmk,GF,Oct 1)*
Qassem **106** *(12f,Don,GF,Nov 5)*
Qatari Hunter **105** *(10f,Cur,GY,Jun 24)*
Qemah **117** *(8f,Dea,G,Jly 31)*
Qewy **109** *(14f,Goo,GF,Jly 26)*
Quarterback **108** *(14f,Mey,G,Mar 3)*
Quebee **109** *(8f,San,G,Sep 14)*
Queen Alphabet **108** *(14f,Leo,G,Sep 10)*
Queen Blossom **109** *(8f,Cur,YS,Mar 20)*
Queen's Trust **116** *(12f,Asc,G,Oct 15)*
Quest For More **114** *(18f,Don,G,Sep 9)*
Quick Jack **110** *(14f,Leo,G,Sep 10)*
Quick March **105** *(6f,Sal,S,Aug 2)*
Quiet Reflection **117** *(6f,Hay,S,Sep 3)*
Quixote **106** *(8f,San,S,Jly 2)*

Race Day **105** *(10f,Asc,S,Jun 16)*
Racing History **106** *(10f,Asc,G,Oct 15)*
Rainbow Dreamer **105** *(14f,Sal,GF,Aug 11)*
Rainbow Rebel **106** *(10½f,Chs,GS,Sep 10)*
Rainfall Radar **105** *(10f,Cur,YS,Sep 22)*
Raising Sand **111** *(7½f,Ffo,G,Jly 19)*
Rantan **105** *(5f,Hay,S,Jly 2)*
Raseed **106** *(10½f,Cha,S,Jun 5)*
Rashaan **106** *(16f,Cur,G,Oct 9)*
Rasmiya **107** *(12f,Bat,S,Jun 22)*
Rattling Jewel **108** *(6f,Cur,GY,Jun 24)*
Raucous **111** *(6f,Asc,S,Oct 1)*
Ravenhoe **105** *(5f,Thi,S,Apr 16)*
Ravenous **108** *(14f,Not,GF,Aug 12)*
Rayisa **108** *(8f,Cur,G,Jly 17)*
Razin' Hell **106** *(6f,Don,GF,Jly 21)*
Real Dominion **106** *(12f,Nmk,GF,Oct 7)*
Real Steel **109** *(9f,Mey,G,Mar 26)*
Rebel Cause **107** *(8f,Don,GS,Jun 12)*
Reckless Gold **109** *(8f,Cur,GY,Jun 24)*
Red Baron **109** *(5f,Thi,GF,May 14)*
Red Box **110** *(8f,Asc,GF,Jly 22)*
Red Cardinal **106** *(12f,Sal,GF,Jun 12)*
Red Napoleon **109** *(8f,Yor,GF,Aug 18)*
Red Paladin **107** *(7f,Lei,G,Aug 25)*
Red Pike **109** *(6f,Yor,G,May 11)*
Red Rannagh **108** *(10f,Goo,GF,Jly 28)*
Red Stripes **105** *(5f,Goo,G,Jly 26)*
Red Tea **109** *(8f,Wdr,S,Jun 25)*
Red Tycoon **107** *(6f,Red,GF,Jly 17)*
Red Verdon **110** *(12f,Cur,GY,Jun 25)*
Reflektor **113** *(5f,Thi,S,Apr 16)*
Regal Monarch **108** *(12f,Chp,S,May 10)*
Related **108** *(6f,Goo,GF,Jly 30)*
Remarkable **110** *(8f,Asc,G,Oct 15)*
Rene Mathis **108** *(7f,Thi,S,Apr 16)*
Renfrew Street **111** *(10f,Pon,GF,Jun 6)*
Renneti **106** *(15f,Leo,Y,Oct 29)*
Repeater **109** *(12f,Cur,Y,May 21)*
Reputation **108** *(7f,Goo,GF,Jly 30)*
Resolute Response **107** *(6f,Mey,G,Feb 13)*
Revolutionist **110** *(10f,Red,GF,May 30)*
Rex Imperator **107** *(7f,Goo,GF,Jly 27)*
Ribchester **116** *(8f,Asc,G,Oct 15)*
Richard Pankhurst **112** *(7f,Nby,GF,Aug 13)*
Richie McCaw **110** *(10f,San,G,Sep 14)*
Rideonastar **108** *(14f,Sal,GS,May 1)*
Ridge Ranger **112** *(6f,Yor,G,Jly 8)*
Right Touch **107** *(7½f,Chs,G,Aug 20)*
Rimraam **107** *(7f,Goo,GS,May 21)*
Ringside Humour **110** *(10f,Cur,Y,Jun 26)*
Rio Ronaldo **112** *(5f,Asc,GF,Jly 22)*
Rio Tigre **114** *(14f,Mey,G,Feb 4)*
Rivellino **109** *(6f,Goo,GF,Jly 30)*
Roaring Rory **109** *(5f,Bev,GF,May 10)*
Robanne **105** *(7f,Asc,GS,Oct 1)*
Robero **110** *(7f,Thi,S,Aug 26)*
Robinnielly **109** *(10f,Ayr,GS,Aug 8)*
Robot Boy **111** *(5f,Asc,GF,Jly 22)*
Rock Song **111** *(10½f,Hay,G,Apr 23)*
Rock Steady **107** *(8f,Wdr,S,Jun 20)*
Rockspirit **109** *(10f,Yar,GF,Aug 28)*
Rococoa **105** *(6f,Nmk,GF,Aug 27)*
Roconga **105** *(15f,Leo,Y,Oct 29)*
Roi De Vitesse **108** *(5f,Mey,G,Feb 18)*
Roicead **111** *(5f,Mey,G,Jan 21)*
Roll On Rory **108** *(6f,Don,GF,Jly 21)*
Room Key **106** *(8½f,Not,GF,Jun 1)*
Roossey **107** *(6f,Mey,G,Feb 13)*
Rosamaria **105** *(10f,Pon,GF,Jun 6)*
Rosay **114** *(8f,Cha,S,Jun 5)*
Rose Above **109** *(12f,Chp,GF,Aug 18)*
Rose De Pierre **112** *(8f,Cur,G,Jly 17)*
Rosental **106** *(10½f,Hay,GS,Sep 3)*
Rosie Royale **105** *(12f,Chp,GF,Aug 9)*
Rosie's Premiere **105** *(5f,Chp,GF,Jly 31)*
Rostova **110** *(8f,Goo,G,Aug 26)*
Rosy Morning **107** *(8f,Pon,GF,Jun 19)*
Rotherwick **106** *(10f,Eps,G,Sep 25)*
Roudee **109** *(6f,Ayr,GS,Sep 17)*
Rouge Nuage **105** *(7f,Nmk,GF,May 13)*
Rousayan **112** *(8½f,Bev,G,May 2)*
Royal Artillery **108** *(10½f,Hay,GF,Aug 6)*
Royal Birth **113** *(5f,Asc,GF,Jly 22)*
Royal Connoisseur **106** *(6f,Cat,S,Oct 25)*
Royal Duchess **105** *(7f,Ayr,S,Jly 11)*
Royal Julius **108** *(10½f,Cha,S,Jun 5)*
Royal Revival **105** *(8f,Mey,G,Feb 13)*
Royal Ridge **110** *(7f,Mey,G,Jan 28)*
Rubis **106** *(10f,Bev,GF,Jly 26)*
Run To The Hills **107** *(7f,Thi,S,Aug 26)*
Ruscombe **105** *(12f,Lei,GF,May 30)*
Russian Royale **108** *(12f,Pon,G,May 27)*
Rusty Rocket **107** *(5f,Red,GF,May 16)*
Rydan **106** *(12f,Sal,GF,Sep 1)*

Saayerr **107** *(5f,Mey,G,Jan 21)*
Sacred Act **108** *(8f,San,G,Sep 9)*
Safety Check **117** *(7f,Mey,G,Jan 21)*
Safira Menina **105** *(11½f,Wdr,G,May 16)*
Sagaciously **112** *(10f,Goo,GF,Jly 27)*
Sagely **109** *(10f,Goo,GF,Jly 27)*
Saigon City **105** *(16f,Asc,GF,Aug 6)*
Sainted **112** *(7f,Nmk,S,Jun 24)*
Sakhee's Return **105** *(6f,Don,G,Sep 8)*
Salateen **110** *(7f,Lin,G,Sep 10)*

Salieris Mass 105 (10f,Rip,G,May 6)
Salmon Sushi 106 (10f,Rip,G,May 6)
Sam Missile 106 (10f,Nmk,G,May 1)
San Cassiano 106 (10f,Red,GS,Aug 27)
Sanaadh 110 (5f,Thi,G,Apr 24)
Sandro Botticelli 109 (12f,Don,S,Apr 3)
Sands Chorus 105 (8½f,Bev,G,May 2)
Sanshaawes 109 (12f,Mey,G,Mar 5)
Sante 106 (7f,Chp,GF,Aug 17)
Sarabi 105 (5f,Don,S,Jly 1)
Sarangoo 105 (7f,San,G,Aug 4)
Sasparella 110 (8f,Cha,G,Oct 1)
Satchville Flyer 106 (6f,Chp,S,Jun 28)
Saumur 105 (11½f,Lin,G,May 19)
Saunter 107 (10f,Nmk,G,Sep 17)
Save The Bees 106 (10f,Not,G,Sep 28)
Saved By The Bell 105 (16f,Rip,GS,Apr 23)
Savoir Vivre 114 (12f,Cha,G,Oct 2)
Sbraase 105 (11½f,Yar,GF,Jun 9)
Scarlet Dragon 113 (10f,Nby,GS,Sep 17)
Scattered Stars 106 (10f,Nby,GF,Aug 12)
Scotland 111 (12f,Asc,GF,May 7)
Scotland Forever 106 (7f,Mey,G,Jan 30)
Scottish 114 (9f,Yor,G,Aug 20)
Scottish Glen 107 (7f,Nmk,GS,Jun 17)
Scrutineer 112 (6f,Ham,HY,Sep 26)
Scrutinise 109 (10f,San,GS,Aug 20)
Sea Front 112 (8f,Cha,S,Jun 19)
Sea Of Flames 105 (10½f,Yor,GF,May 12)
Sea Of Heaven 108 (18f,Nmk,G,Oct 8)
Sea Wolf 109 (8f,Cur,G,Aug 28)
Seamour 116 (16f,Nmk,GF,Sep 22)
Seamster 113 (5f,Thi,GF,Aug 9)
Second Step 109 (12f,Asc,GF,Jly 23)
Second Wave 114 (10f,Goo,GF,Jly 26)
Secret Art 111 (8f,San,S,Jly 2)
Secret Asset 105 (5f,San,GF,Jly 20)
Secret Brief 109 (8f,Mey,G,Feb 18)
Secret Glance 108 (7f,Chp,GS,Jun 10)
Secret Hint 106 (7f,Yor,GF,May 13)
Secret Look 105 (6f,Wdr,S,Jun 25)
Secret Number 110 (10f,Ayr,S,Sep 15)
Secret Splendour 107 (10f,Cur,Y,Jun 26)
Secretfact 107 (5f,Bat,GS,Sep 11)
See The Sun 110 (6f,Yor,G,May 11)
Seeking Magic 108 (6f,Nmk,G,May 1)
Semeen 111 (14f,Mey,G,Feb 4)
Sennockian Star 109 (10f,Nmk,GF,Aug 6)
Senza Una Donna 111 (12f,Chp,GF,Aug 18)
Sepal 107 (10f,Pon,GF,Jun 6)
September Stars 108 (8f,Wdr,GF,Jly 25)
Settler's Son 112 (15f,Cha,G,Sep 11)
Seve 107 (5f,Not,G,May 22)
Seventh Heaven 115 (12f,Yor,GF,Aug 18)
Shaakis 106 (9f,Mey,G,Jan 30)
Shaan 107 (10f,Goo,GF,Jly 27)
Shabeeb 106 (10f,San,GF,May 19)
Shadagann 108 (12f,Leo,G,May 8)
Shadow Hunter 106 (7f,Hay,G,Sep 1)
Shady McCoy 108 (7f,Goo,GF,Jly 27)
Shafafya 106 (10f,Rip,G,Jun 15)
Shakopee 109 (12f,Yor,GF,Aug 19)
Shalaa 114 (6f,Asc,S,Oct 1)
Shamaal Nibras 107 (9f,Mey,G,Feb 11)
Shamaheart 105 (8½f,Not,GF,Jly 19)
Shamshon 113 (5f,Asc,GF,Jly 22)
Shanghai Glory 112 (6f,Lin,S,Jun 11)
Shared Equity 108 (6f,Asc,GS,Jun 18)
Sharja Queen 111 (10f,Sal,GF,Jly 9)
Shawaahid 107 (8f,San,G,Sep 9)
Sheikhzayedroad 115 (18f,Don,G,Sep 9)
Shell Bay 108 (10f,San,GS,Aug 20)
Shipyard 106 (6f,Asc,GF,May 6)
Shogun 105 (12f,Cur,GY,Jun 25)
Shore Step 106 (6f,Asc,GF,May 6)
Short Work 107 (7f,Chs,G,Jun 25)
Shouranour 106 (7f,Cat,S,Oct 25)
Show Day 107 (8f,Sai,S,Oct 30)
Show Stealer 108 (6f,Nmk,GF,May 14)
Showbizzy 107 (5f,Don,G,Jly 30)
Showdaisy 106 (5f,Mus,GF,Sep 2)
Showreel 109 (7f,Goo,GS,May 21)
Shwaimsa 105 (8f,Nby,GF,Jly 16)
Shypen 109 (6f,Yar,GF,Jun 8)
Siamsaiocht 109 (8f,Cur,G,Jly 17)
Sign Of A Victory 105 (12f,Asc,GF,May 7)
Signore Piccolo 110 (7f,Thi,S,Aug 26)
Signs Of Blessing 118 (6f,Asc,G,Oct 15)
Sikandarabad 108 (8f,Cur,G,Aug 28)
Silent Attack 111 (8f,Nmk,GF,Jly 9)
Siljan's Saga 117 (12f,Cha,G,Oct 2)
Silken Skies 105 (5f,Not,S,Oct 12)
Silvanus 108 (5f,Thi,GF,May 14)
Silver Concorde 106 (14f,Leo,G,Sep 10)
Silver Quay 107 (10f,Goo,GF,Jly 26)
Silver Rainbow 108 (6f,Nmk,GF,Jly 16)
Silverwave 114 (12f,Cha,G,Sep 11)
Silvery Moon 109 (8f,Ayr,S,Sep 15)
Silwana 107 (14f,Cur,Y,Sep 11)
Simple Verse 115 (14½f,Don,G,Sep 8)
Simply Shining 107 (8f,Pon,GF,Jun 19)
Sindarban 107 (9f,Ham,GF,May 13)
Sinfonietta 113 (8½f,Not,HY,Apr 6)
Singeur 108 (5f,Don,GS,Sep 7)
Sir Billy Wright 106 (7f,Don,GF,Jun 3)
Sir Chauvelin 108 (12f,Ham,GF,May 13)
Sir Domino 105 (6f,Ham,S,May 1)
Sir Isaac Newton 117 (10½f,Yor,GF,Aug 17)
Sir Maximilian 113 (5f,Chs,G,May 4)
Sir Robert Cheval 108 (6f,Nmk,GF,May 21)
Sir Roderic 109 (8f,Wdr,S,Jun 20)
Sister Blandina 108 (12f,Cur,Y,Aug 21)
Sixties Groove 107 (10f,Eps,G,Jly 7)
Siyoushake 113 (8f,Sai,S,Oct 30)
Skeaping 107 (8f,Wdr,S,Jun 20)
Skiffle 112 (10f,Goo,G,May 19)
Sky Hunter 114 (10f,Goo,GS,Sep 21)
Sky Kingdom 105 (10f,Nmk,GS,Apr 30)
Sky Ship 105 (7f,Chs,G,Jun 25)
Slemy 108 (7f,Wet,GF,May 17)
Slipper Satin 105 (14f,Red,GF,Aug 6)
Slumdogmillionaire 106 (9f,Mey,G,Feb 11)
Slunovrat 106 (11½f,Wdr,S,Apr 11)
Snap Shots 108 (6f,Rip,G,Aug 13)
Snoano 110 (10f,Goo,GF,Jly 26)
Snow Falcon 108 (15f,Leo,Y,Oct 29)
Snowy Dawn 105 (17f,Bat,GF,May 2)
So Beloved 112 (7f,Hay,G,May 7)
So Mi Dar 112 (10f,Yar,GF,Sep 14)
Soie D'Leau 111 (5f,Don,G,Oct 22)
Solar Deity 107 (8f,Goo,GF,Jly 29)
Solar Flair 109 (6f,Nmk,GF,Aug 5)
Soldier In Action 108 (12f,Goo,G,Oct 9)
Sole Power 112 (5f,Mey,G,Mar 5)
Solo Hunter 106 (10f,San,G,Jun 10)
Somehow 113 (9f,Cur,G,Aug 28)
Somethingthrilling 107 (10f,Nby,GS,Oct 21)
Son Cesio 113 (5f,Cha,S,Jun 5)
Son Of Africa 107 (5f,San,G,Aug 20)
Sophie P 107 (8f,Mus,G,Sep 25)
Sors 110 (5f,Cur,Y,Jun 26)
Sotteville 109 (12f,Cha,G,Oct 1)
Soul Brother 106 (5f,Thi,S,Apr 30)
Soul Searcher 108 (12f,Cur,G,Oct 9)
Sound Advice 110 (7½f,Chs,G,May 28)
Southdown Lad 105 (12f,Nby,S,Sep 16)
Southern Strife 106 (9f,Crl,GS,Sep 13)
Sovereign Bounty 106 (7f,Wet,GF,May 17)
Sovereign Debt 112 (7f,Leo,Y,Oct 29)
Spa's Dancer 107 (8½f,Not,HY,Apr 6)
Spangled 107 (7f,Lei,GF,May 23)
Spark Plug 115 (9f,Nmk,GF,Sep 24)
Special Focus 107 (8f,Leo,Y,Oct 23)
Special Season 105 (10f,Nby,GS,Oct 22)
Specialv 110 (8f,Wdr,S,Jun 25)
Spectre 115 (8f,Cha,G,Sep 11)
Speed Company 109 (10f,Nmk,GF,Aug 6)
Speedy Boarding 116 (12f,Asc,G,Oct 15)
Spirit Of Zeb 105 (6f,Eps,G,Aug 30)
Spirit Of Zebedee 105 (6f,Rip,G,Jly 16)
Spirit Quartz 108 (5f,Nby,GS,Sep 17)
Spirit Raiser 113 (8f,Pon,G,Jly 5)
Sporty Yankee 108 (10f,Wdr,S,Jun 13)
Spring Loaded 109 (6f,Asc,GS,Jun 18)
Spring Offensive 110 (8f,Pon,S,Apr 18)
Spryt 105 (7f,Wet,GF,May 17)
Squats 108 (7f,Asc,GF,Jly 23)
Squire 106 (10½f,Hay,G,Apr 23)
Sruthan 113 (7f,Cur,HY,Apr 3)
St Brelades Bay 105 (6f,Cur,GY,Jun 24)
St Michel 113 (18f,Don,G,Sep 9)
Stake Acclaim 106 (5f,Wdr,S,Apr 18)
Stamp Hill 107 (7f,Goo,G,May 21)
Stanghow 106 (5f,Pon,G,May 27)
Stanley 105 (10f,San,GF,Jly 21)
Star Empire 114 (14f,Mey,G,Feb 4)
Star Rider 107 (16f,Nmk,G,Oct 28)
Starchitect 106 (14f,Sal,G,May 28)
Stardrifter 105 (10½f,Yor,G,Oct 8)
Stargazer 110 (10f,Goo,GF,Jly 28)
Starlit Cantata 105 (8f,Goo,G,Aug 26)
Stars N Angels 108 (7f,Nmk,S,Jun 24)
Stars Over The Sea 117 (12f,Pon,GF,Aug 3)
Start Right 107 (10f,Mey,G,Jan 7)
Staunch 110 (8½f,Not,GF,Jun 9)
Steal The Scene 106 (7f,Nmk,GF,Jly 29)
Steel Of Madrid 106 (10f,Asc,S,Jun 16)
Steel Train 107 (7f,Don,GF,Nov 5)
Steelriver 106 (6f,Red,GF,Aug 6)
Steip Amach 113 (8f,Dea,G,Jly 31)
Stellar Mass 110 (12f,Cur,GY,Jun 25)
Stellarta 110 (6f,Wdr,GF,Aug 15)
Stepper Point 108 (5f,Asc,GF,Jly 9)
Stetchworth Park 105 (14f,San,GF,Jly 21)
Steve Rogers 106 (14f,Mus,G,Aug 5)
Stillman 111 (8f,Cha,S,Jun 19)
Stonecoldsoba 105 (12f,Chp,S,May 10)
Storm Ahead 108 (8f,Sal,S,Jun 22)
Storm Lightning 106 (5f,Bri,G,Aug 4)
Storm Melody 106 (6f,Bat,GS,Sep 11)
Storm Rising 107 (7½f,Chs,G,May 5)
Storm Rock 110 (10f,Sal,S,Sep 28)
Stormy Antarctic 111 (8f,Dea,G,Aug 14)
Straightothepoint 106 (6f,Rip,G,May 6)
Strath Burn 113 (6f,Wdr,G,May 23)
Stratum 106 (11½f,Wdr,GS,Oct 3)
Strong Steps 110 (8f,Nby,G,May 14)
Subtle Knife 105 (7f,Lei,G,Jly 14)
Success Days 116 (10½f,Cur,YS,May 22)
Suedois 116 (7f,Cha,G,Oct 2)
Suegioo 112 (20f,Asc,S,Jun 16)
Sugar Lump 107 (8f,Pon,HY,Apr 5)
Sumbal 110 (12f,Nby,GS,Oct 22)
Summer Chorus 110 (6f,Nmk,GF,Aug 13)
Summer Collection 105 (8f,Wdr,S,Jun 25)
Summer Icon 106 (7f,Nmk,GF,May 12)
Summersault 105 (6f,Wdr,G,May 2)
Sunblazer 105 (12f,Asc,G,Sep 2)
Sunnua 105 (7½f,Chs,S,Jly 9)
Sunny Future 105 (17f,Bat,GS,Sep 11)
Sunraider 107 (6f,Don,GF,Jly 21)
Supersta 105 (8f,Hay,GF,Jun 9)
Surewecan 105 (7f,Mus,GF,Apr 24)
Sussudio 105 (8f,Sai,S,Oct 30)
Suzi's Connoisseur 108 (7f,Goo,GF,Aug 27)
Swamp Fox 108 (16f,Cur,G,Oct 9)
Swashbuckle 111 (12f,Ffo,G,Aug 8)
Sweeping Up 107 (12f,Pon,GF,Jun 19)
Sweet Dragon Fly 107 (7f,Goo,GS,May 21)
Sweet Selection 111 (18f,Don,G,Sep 9)
Swift Approval 107 (7f,Cat,G,May 28)
Swift Cedar 107 (12f,Ffo,G,Aug 8)
Swift Emperor 108 (10f,Red,GF,May 30)
Swiss Range 107 (10f,Goo,GF,Jly 30)
Sword Fighter 119 (14f,Cur,Y,Jun 26)
Sydney Ruffdiamond 105 (6f,Chp,GF,Jly 14)
Symposium 110 (6f,Asc,G,Sep 30)
Syrian Pearl 107 (6f,Not,G,Sep 28)

Taajub 105 (5f,Asc,GF,Jly 22)
Taareef 116 (8f,Cha,G,Oct 1)
Taayel 105 (5f,Mey,G,Mar 5)
Tabarrak 107 (7f,Asc,GF,May 6)
Taexali 112 (5f,Ham,S,May 1)
Taffeta Lady 105 (11½f,Yar,GF,Sep 15)
Takatul 106 (8f,Hay,G,Sep 24)
Take Cover 115 (5f,Goo,GF,Jly 29)
Taking Libertys 105 (9f,Crl,GS,Sep 13)
Talismanic 109 (10½f,Cha,S,Jun 5)
Tamayuz Magic 105 (12f,Thi,G,May 7)
Taneen 112 (6f,Lei,GF,May 30)
Tanfeeth 105 (9f,Mey,G,Jan 30)
Tang Fleming 112 (7½f,Chs,G,May 5)
Tangerine Trees 108 (5f,Not,G,May 22)
Tannaaf 105 (10f,Mey,G,Feb 4)
Tanzeel 105 (7f,Nmk,GF,Jly 9)
Taqdeer 114 (10f,Nmk,G,May 1)
Tartan Bute 111 (14f,Cat,GF,Aug 2)
Tashaar 108 (11½f,Wdr,GF,Aug 27)
Tasleet 107 (7f,Nmk,GF,Oct 7)
Tatawu 105 (10f,Nmk,GF,May 12)
Tatlisu 105 (6f,Hay,S,Jly 2)
Taurean Star 106 (8f,Lin,GF,Jly 13)
Tawdeea 110 (12f,Hay,S,Jly 2)
Taysh 105 (7f,Cat,GS,May 3)
Team Talk 108 (7f,Lei,GS,Oct 4)
Tears Of The Sun 106 (10f,Not,GF,Jun 1)
Tellina 108 (14f,Mey,G,Mar 3)
Tellovoi 105 (8f,Mus,GF,May 9)
Tennessee Wildcat 108 (8f,Leo,GF,Jun 9)
Tenzing Norgay 110 (11½f,Lin,G,May 25)
Tepin 109 (8f,Asc,S,Jun 14)
Terhaal 108 (8f,Pon,S,Apr 18)
Territories 111 (8f,Cha,S,Jun 19)
Teruntum Star 109 (6f,Nmk,GS,Apr 12)
Texas Rock 108 (7f,Cur,GY,Oct 10)
That Is The Spirit 105 (7f,Ayr,GS,Sep 17)
The Black Princess 111 (10f,Goo,G,May 19)
The Blue Eye 105 (12f,Mey,G,Mar 26)
The Cashel Man 107 (16½f,Yor,GF,Aug 17)
The Commendatore 106 (6f,Nmk,GF,Jly 23)
The Corsican 105 (9f,Mey,G,Mar 26)
The Graduate 108 (14f,Hay,S,Sep 3)
The Grey Gatsby 113 (10f,Asc,S,Jun 15)
The Gurkha 113 (10f,San,S,Jly 2)
The Happy Prince 112 (7f,Cur,HY,Apr 3)
The Invisible Dog 106 (7½f,Ffo,G,Jly 19)
The Juliet Rose 114 (12f,Cha,G,Oct 1)
The King's Steed 105 (8½f,Not,G,May 22)
The Major General 107 (12f,Asc,S,Jun 16)
The Salmon Man 105 (8½f,Eps,G,Jly 7)
The Tin Man 121 (6f,Asc,G,Oct 15)
The Tulip 107 (8f,Cur,G,Jly 17)
The Warrior 107 (7f,Asc,GF,May 7)
Theophilus 108 (15f,Leo,Y,Oct 29)
Thesme 113 (5f,Mus,G,Jun 11)
Thetis 107 (6f,Nmk,GF,Jly 23)
Theydon Thunder 107 (8f,Nmk,GS,Jun 17)
Thikriyaat 112 (8f,Goo,GF,Aug 27)
Think Ahead 111 (10f,Mey,G,Feb 4)
Third Rock 105 (10f,Wdr,GS,Jun 27)
Third Time Lucky 111 (9f,Nmk,GF,Sep 24)
Threat Assessed 107 (8f,Chp,S,May 10)
Throckley 106 (10½f,Yor,GS,Sep 4)
Tiercel 106 (8f,Wdr,GS,Oct 3)
Tiger Jim 108 (6f,Thi,S,Aug 26)
Tigerwolf 109 (7f,Goo,GF,Jly 30)
Tikthebox 107 (6f,Red,GF,Aug 6)
Time For Mabel 108 (12f,Leo,G,May 8)
Time Of My Life 105 (13f,Ham,G,Jly 14)
Time Test 117 (10f,San,GF,May 26)
Time To Exceed 105 (6f,Don,GF,Aug 13)
Time To Reason 111 (7f,Cur,G,Aug 20)
Timekeeping 116 (12f,Pon,S,Oct 17)
Tioga Pass 106 (14½f,Don,G,Sep 8)
Titan Goddess 107 (7f,Lei,GS,Oct 4)
Tithonus 110 (5f,Don,G,Oct 22)
To Be Wild 109 (12f,Don,G,Oct 22)
Toboggan's Fire 107 (7f,Lei,S,Jly 2)
Tobouggaloo 105 (12f,Chp,GF,Jun 10)
Toe The Line 108 (16f,Cur,HY,Sep 25)
Toffee Apple 105 (8f,Ham,GS,Jly 9)
Toga Tiger 107 (10½f,Chs,G,Jly 31)
Tomahawk Kid 108 (8½f,Not,G,Sep 28)
Tony Curtis 114 (8f,Sal,GF,Aug 11)
Toofi 109 (6f,Asc,GS,Jun 18)
Toormore 114 (8f,San,GS,Apr 22)
Top Beak 106 (8f,Hay,G,Sep 23)
Top Boy 105 (5f,Lei,GS,Sep 19)
Top Notch Tonto 110 (10½f,Chs,G,May 5)
Top Tug 108 (12f,Yor,GF,May 13)
Topamichi 105 (8½f,Eps,GS,Jun 30)
Topclas 112 (14f,Mey,G,Feb 4)
Torcedor 107 (12f,Asc,GF,May 7)
Torch 108 (8½f,Not,GF,Jly 28)
Torchlighter 109 (9f,Mey,G,Jan 30)
Torrid 105 (8½f,Not,G,Oct 26)
Toscanini 111 (6f,Cur,GY,Jun 25)
Total Demolition 108 (8f,Leo,GF,Jun 9)
Totalize 105 (20f,Asc,S,Jun 14)
Totally Committed 107 (10f,San,G,Sep 14)
Touch The Sky 111 (12f,Pon,G,May 27)
Toulson 111 (10f,San,G,Sep 14)
Travertine 107 (10f,Cur,Y,Jun 26)
Treasure Chest 105 (10f,Leo,GF,Jun 9)
Treasury Notes 109 (8f,Rip,GS,Aug 29)
Trendsetter 105 (12f,Don,G,Oct 22)
Tres Coronas 108 (10f,Red,GS,Nov 1)
Tribal Beat 114 (8f,Leo,GF,Aug 11)
Trinity Star 108 (8f,Pon,S,Apr 18)
Trip To Paris 107 (14f,Cur,Y,Sep 11)
Trixia 110 (8f,Cha,G,Sep 11)
Trulee Scrumptious 106 (8f,Nmk,GF,Jly 22)
Truth Or Dare 106 (8f,Asc,GF,Sep 2)
Tryster 113 (10f,Asc,S,Jun 15)
Tukhoom 105 (8f,Goo,G,Jun 10)
Tullius 114 (8½f,Eps,GS,Jun 3)
Tumblewind 106 (5f,Thi,G,Apr 24)
Tupi 114 (8f,Sal,GF,Aug 11)
Turbine 105 (7f,Goo,G,May 21)
Turning The Table 105 (12f,Don,G,Sep 10)
Turret Rocks 108 (12f,Yor,GF,Aug 18)
Tutu Nguru 109 (8f,Asc,GF,May 7)
Twilight Payment 112 (14f,Cur,G,Aug 20)
Twilight Son 116 (6f,Asc,GS,Jun 18)
Twin Sails 107 (7f,Goo,GF,Jly 27)
Twitch 109 (14f,Bat,GF,Oct 12)
Two For Two 108 (8f,Rip,GS,Aug 29)
Tylery Wonder 107 (5f,Don,GS,Sep 7)

US Army Ranger 109 (12f,Eps,GS,Jun 4)
Udododontu 110 (8f,Mey,G,Feb 18)
Udogo 106 (10f,Leo,GF,Aug 11)
Udontdodou 107 (5f,Don,G,Oct 22)
Ulysses 115 (10f,Wdr,GF,Aug 27)
Uncle Dermot 108 (8½f,Eps,GS,Jun 30)
Under Siege 105 (6f,Bri,G,Aug 5)
Undrafted 112 (6f,Asc,GS,Jun 18)
Union Rose 109 (5f,Asc,GF,Jly 9)
Unison 105 (8f,San,G,Aug 4)
Until Midnight 105 (6f,Asc,GF,Sep 2)
Upavon 105 (6f,Bri,GF,May 16)
Usherette 112 (8f,Nmk,GF,Jly 8)

Vadamos 117 (8f,Cha,G,Sep 11)
Vale Do Sol 107 (8f,Mey,G,Feb 13)
Valley Of Fire 107 (7f,Yor,GS,Jun 11)
Van Gerwen 106 (6f,Pon,GF,Jun 6)
Vanishing Point 105 (12f,Bat,S,Jun 22)
Vastonea 107 (10f,Leo,Y,Oct 29)
Vazirabad 114 (15f,Cha,G,Sep 11)
Vedevani 112 (12f,Cha,G,Oct 2)
Ventura Storm 108 (11f,Ham,S,Jly 15)
Venturous 106 (6f,Yor,GS,Jun 11)
Venutius 105 (8f,Rip,G,Aug 16)
Very Dashing 107 (10f,Sal,GF,Aug 10)
Very Special 115 (8f,Nmk,GF,Jly 8)
Very Talented 111 (9f,Nmk,GF,Sep 24)
Vibrant Chords 107 (6f,Thi,GF,Sep 13)
Victoire De Lyphar 107 (8f,Ayr,S,Jly 25)
Victory Bond 110 (10½f,Yor,GF,May 12)
Vin Chaud 105 (8f,Mey,G,Jan 28)
Vincentti 107 (6f,Bri,G,Aug 5)
Vintage Charm 105 (10f,Cur,HY,Apr 3)
Viren's Army 112 (10½f,Chs,G,May 6)
Visage Blanc 106 (10f,Sal,GF,Jly 9)
Viscount Barfield 111 (7½f,Chs,GS,Jun 24)
Viserion 105 (12f,Yor,G,Jun 10)
Vive Ma Fille 113 (14f,Mus,G,Aug 5)
Volta 119 (8f,Cha,S,Jun 5)
Volunteer Point 106 (8f,Goo,G,Apr 30)
Von Blucher 113 (8f,Nmk,GF,Jly 9)
Vortex 108 (8f,Mey,G,Jan 28)

Waady 110 (5f,Hay,GS,May 21)
Wadigor 109 (10f,Nmk,G,Oct 28)

Walking In Rhythm 108 *(7f,Lei,GS,Sep 19)*
Wall Of Fire 106 *(14½f,Don,G,Sep 9)*
Walzertakt 111 *(15f,Cha,G,Sep 11)*
Wapping 105 *(10f,Nby,GF,Aug 13)*
Waseem Faris 107 *(5f,Eps,G,Aug 29)*
Washington DC 115 *(5f,Cha,G,Oct 2)*
Wasir 107 *(14f,Mey,G,Mar 3)*
Watchable 115 *(6f,Wdr,G,May 23)*
Waterloo Bridge 107 *(6f,Nmk,GS,Apr 13)*
Watersmeet 107 *(10f,Goo,GF,Jly 26)*
Wave Reviews 107 *(10f,San,G,Aug 4)*
Wayward Hoof 105 *(6f,Pon,GF,Jun 6)*
We Are Ninety 106 *(10f,Yar,GF,Sep 14)*
Weapon Of Choice 106 *(10½f,Hay,G,Apr 23)*
Weekend Offender 107 *(7f,Mus,G,May 27)*
Weetles 105 *(10f,Not,GF,Jun 1)*
Wekeyll 105 *(7f,Mey,G,Jan 30)*
Weld Al Emarat 105 *(8f,Nby,GF,Jun 9)*
Welliesinthewater 108 *(7f,Don,GF,Jun 3)*
Wentworth Falls 106 *(5f,Not,G,Nov 2)*
Western Hymn 116 *(10f,San,GF,May 26)*
Wexford Opera 105 *(8f,Cur,YS,Mar 20)*
What A Scorcher 106 *(12f,Chp,GF,Aug 18)*
What About Carlo 112 *(10f,Nby,GS,Sep 17)*
Whinging Willie 107 *(12f,Eps,S,Apr 20)*
White Lake 107 *(7f,Lei,GS,Apr 23)*
White Poppy 106 *(10f,Sal,GF,Jun 7)*
Whitecrest 105 *(5f,Bri,G,Aug 4)*
Who Dares Wins 106 *(14f,Not,GF,Aug 12)*
Whozthecat 111 *(7f,Thi,S,Aug 26)*
Wicklow Brave 117 *(14f,Cur,Y,Sep 11)*
Wilamina 110 *(8f,Nmk,GS,Jun 18)*
Wild Hacked 107 *(12f,Asc,G,Sep 3)*
Wilde Inspiration 109 *(8f,Hay,G,Apr 23)*
Wiley Post 108 *(5f,Goo,G,May 20)*
William Hunter 107 *(12f,Asc,G,Sep 2)*
Willytheconqueror 110 *(5f,Bev,G,Aug 27)*
Wimpole Hall 107 *(8f,San,GF,Aug 19)*
Wind In My Sails 105 *(8f,Nby,GF,Aug 12)*
Windfast 107 *(7f,Nmk,G,Jly 30)*
Windsor Beach 106 *(8f,Leo,GF,Jun 9)*
Wings of Desire 118 *(10½f,Yor,GF,May 12)*
Winning Story 107 *(11½f,Lin,G,May 7)*
Winter House 108 *(10f,Lin,G,May 7)*
Winterval 105 *(8½f,Not,GF,May 6)*
Wireless 113 *(8f,Cha,G,Oct 1)*
Withernsea 108 *(7f,Hay,G,Apr 23)*
Woody Bay 106 *(9f,Yor,GS,Jun 11)*
Wowcha 105 *(6f,Pon,HY,Apr 5)*
Wrangler 106 *(12f,Don,G,Oct 22)*
Wrapped 108 *(8f,Bri,GF,Sep 29)*
Wychwood Warrior 107 *(8f,Mey,G,Jan 28)*

Xebec 108 *(12f,Leo,G,May 8)*

Yaa Wayl 106 *(7f,Mey,G,Jan 28)*
Yangtze 107 *(14f,Yor,G,Oct 7)*
Yarrow 109 *(12f,Pon,GF,Jun 19)*
Yattwee 109 *(6f,Nmk,GF,May 21)*
Yeeoow 106 *(6f,Nmk,GS,Apr 12)*
Yorker 115 *(10f,Cha,G,Oct 1)*
Yorkidding 111 *(12f,Asc,GF,Jly 22)*
Yosemite 109 *(7f,Thi,S,Aug 26)*
You're Fired 110 *(8f,Hay,G,Apr 23)*
You're Hired 111 *(10f,Goo,GF,Jly 28)*
Young John 108 *(6f,Wdr,S,Jun 20)*
Your Pal Tal 105 *(6f,Cur,GF,Jun 4)*
Youre Always Right 108 *(8f,Wdr,G,May 16)*
Yuften 111 *(8f,Asc,G,Oct 15)*

Zaakhir 105 *(10f,Sal,GF,Jly 9)*
Zahee 111 *(8f,Mey,G,Feb 25)*
Zamaam 110 *(10f,Mey,G,Feb 4)*
Zambeasy 105 *(11½f,Wdr,GS,Apr 25)*
Zambucca 108 *(10f,Mey,G,Feb 4)*
Zamperini 105 *(10f,San,GS,Jly 1)*
Zand 106 *(10f,Lin,G,May 7)*
Zanetto 108 *(6f,Yor,G,May 11)*
Zarak 115 *(10f,Cha,G,Oct 1)*
Zaria 111 *(8½f,Eps,GS,Jun 30)*
Zarwaan 105 *(7f,Mey,G,Jan 21)*
Zayva 112 *(8f,Cha,G,Oct 1)*
Zealous 108 *(8f,Don,GS,Jun 12)*
Zeeoneandonly 107 *(6f,Sal,GS,May 12)*
Zelzal 114 *(8f,Cha,G,Sep 11)*
Zeshov 105 *(7f,Yar,GF,Aug 4)*
Zghorta Dance 106 *(10½f,Cha,S,Jun 19)*
Zhui Feng 110 *(9f,Nmk,GF,Sep 24)*
Zhukova 117 *(10f,Cur,HY,Apr 3)*
Ziggy Lee 112 *(5f,Thi,GF,Aug 9)*
Zlatan 108 *(8f,Wdr,S,Oct 17)*
Zodiakos 107 *(8f,Nmk,GS,Apr 30)*
Zonderland 118 *(8f,Sal,GF,Aug 11)*
Zubeida 105 *(12f,Pon,GF,Jun 27)*
Zwayyan 105 *(8f,Hay,G,Sep 1)*

THREE YEAR-OLDS AND UPWARDS -AW

A Momentofmadness 112 *(6f,Kem,SD,Mar 16)*
Abareeq 108 *(10f,Cfd,SD,Oct 26)*
Abbey Angel 111 *(9f,Wol,SD,Feb 1)*
Above N Beyond 108 *(7f,Lin,SD,Mar 5)*
Abrahams Blessing 109 *(16½f,Wol,SD,Sep 12)*
Acclio 105 *(7f,Lin,SD,Jun 18)*
Active Spirit 110 *(8f,Mey,FT,Jan 30)*
Ada Lovelace 105 *(5f,Cfd,SD,Jun 16)*
Addictive Dream 108 *(6f,Sth,SD,Feb 9)*
Adventurous 107 *(8f,Kem,SD,Apr 2)*
Aeolus 106 *(6f,Lin,SD,Nov 12)*
Afjaan 112 *(8f,Kem,SS,Sep 3)*
Afkar 106 *(7f,Sth,SD,Feb 4)*
Afonso De Sousa 110 *(10f,Cfd,SD,Jan 16)*
Agent Gibbs 105 *(14f,Wol,SD,Mar 25)*
Aguerooo 106 *(6f,Wol,SD,Dec 2)*
Air Of Astana 105 *(10f,Cfd,SD,Mar 17)*
Air Of York 107 *(6f,Kem,SD,Feb 24)*
Airton 107 *(12½f,Ncs,SD,Oct 14)*
Ajman Prince 109 *(12½f,Ncs,SD,Oct 14)*
Ajraam 112 *(6f,Mey,FT,Nov 3)*
Al 111 *(14f,Wol,SD,Sep 27)*
Al Khan 107 *(7f,Lin,SD,Jan 22)*
Al's Memory 105 *(10f,Lin,SD,Feb 17)*
Alareef 108 *(7f,Mey,FT,Jan 28)*
Albahar 107 *(16f,Ncs,SD,Jun 25)*
Alben Star 109 *(6f,Lin,SD,Mar 25)*
Aleator 111 *(10f,Lin,SD,Jan 9)*
Aleef 110 *(5f,Cfd,SD,Nov 21)*
Alejandro 105 *(7f,Cfd,SD,Oct 13)*
Alexandrakollontai 109 *(8f,Ncs,SD,Nov 4)*
Alfred Hutchinson 114 *(8f,Lin,SD,Nov 12)*
Alfredo 111 *(16f,Lin,SD,Dec 14)*
Alinstante 111 *(10f,Lin,SD,Dec 5)*
Aljuljalah 106 *(8f,Lin,SD,Oct 27)*
All About Time 106 *(12½f,Ncs,SD,Oct 8)*
All My Love 108 *(12f,Wol,SD,Aug 16)*
All The Rage 105 *(12f,Lin,SD,Jun 25)*
Almodovar 111 *(11f,Kem,SD,May 18)*
Alpha Tauri 106 *(7f,Sth,SD,Jan 21)*
Alraased 105 *(8f,Mey,FT,Nov 3)*
Alshan Fajer 108 *(12f,Lin,SD,Jan 30)*
Alyssa 107 *(12f,Wol,SD,Jun 27)*
Amantius 107 *(16½f,Wol,SD,Sep 12)*
Amazement 105 *(8f,Ncs,SD,Nov 25)*
Amazour 110 *(6f,Kem,SS,Oct 5)*
Ambitious Icarus 106 *(6f,Ncs,SD,Nov 7)*
Amood 107 *(7f,Ncs,SD,Oct 28)*
Angelic Lord 105 *(6f,Wol,SD,Dec 16)*
Anglophile 111 *(16f,Lin,SD,Mar 25)*
Angrywhitepyjamas 107 *(11f,Kem,SS,Aug 3)*
Anonymous John 109 *(5f,Sth,SD,Jan 1)*
Another Wise Kid 106 *(6f,Ncs,SD,Nov 8)*
Ansaab 110 *(10f,Lin,SD,Jan 27)*
Antiquarium 110 *(16f,Ncs,SD,Jun 25)*
Apache Glory 105 *(12f,Lin,SD,Feb 26)*
Apache Storm 108 *(5f,Cfd,SD,Jan 28)*
Appeared 105 *(10f,Cfd,SD,Apr 14)*
Aprovado 105 *(5f,Ncs,SD,Sep 30)*
Aqua Ardens 109 *(9f,Wol,SD,Apr 9)*
Arab Spring 107 *(12f,Kem,SS,Sep 3)*
Aramist 108 *(16f,Ncs,SD,Jun 25)*
Arcanada 106 *(7f,Wol,SD,Mar 27)*
Arch Villain 114 *(16f,Lin,SD,Feb 17)*
Archipeligo 110 *(9½f,Wol,SD,Jan 25)*
Ardamir 110 *(12f,Wol,SD,Oct 21)*
Arnold Lane 111 *(7f,Lin,SD,Jan 22)*
Artful Rogue 107 *(12f,Lin,SD,Dec 7)*
Artigiano 107 *(9½f,Mey,FT,Jan 7)*
Ashadihan 105 *(7f,Lin,SD,May 7)*
Ask The Guru 105 *(5f,Kem,SD,Feb 17)*
Assault On Rome 105 *(7f,Sth,SD,Jan 2)*
Athlon 110 *(10f,Cfd,SD,Sep 1)*
Athollblair Boy 106 *(7f,Ncs,SD,Oct 28)*
Atreus 105 *(9f,Wol,SD,Apr 8)*
Attain 108 *(10f,Lin,SD,Feb 22)*
Attenzione 105 *(12f,Wol,SD,Apr 16)*
Atwix 107 *(12f,Lin,SD,Mar 30)*
Aurora Gray 110 *(16f,Lin,SD,Dec 18)*
Available 107 *(6f,Wol,SD,Apr 9)*
Awesome Quality 105 *(7f,Ncs,SD,Jun 23)*
Azilian 107 *(12f,Wol,SD,May 20)*
Azrur 106 *(7f,Sth,SD,Mar 23)*

Baby Ballerina 107 *(7f,Cfd,SD,Oct 20)*
Baddilini 108 *(7f,Lin,SD,Jan 22)*
Bag Of Diamonds 109 *(8f,Kem,SS,Sep 2)*
Baileys Mirage 107 *(6f,Cfd,SD,Jun 15)*
Ballista 106 *(6f,Lin,SD,Jan 7)*
Ballynanty 111 *(16f,Lin,SD,Mar 25)*
Bamako Du Chatelet 105 *(12f,Lin,SD,Apr 26)*
Ban Shoof 107 *(11f,Kem,SS,Sep 28)*
Bancnuanaheireann 106 *(10f,Lin,SD,Nov 30)*
Banditry 110 *(10f,Cfd,SD,Oct 26)*
Banish 115 *(11f,Kem,SS,Sep 28)*
Bargain Buy 111 *(7f,Lin,SD,Nov 30)*
Barleysugar 109 *(8f,Cfd,SD,Jun 1)*
Barnmore 108 *(8f,Kem,SD,Apr 13)*
Baroot 105 *(9½f,Mey,FT,Jan 16)*
Barracuda Boy 107 *(7f,Ncs,SD,Jly 23)*
Barsanti 116 *(11f,Kem,SD,Mar 26)*
Barwah 107 *(8f,Ncs,SD,Aug 26)*
Barye 112 *(12f,Lin,SD,Dec 17)*
Basem 112 *(10f,Cfd,SD,Oct 6)*
Basil Berry 109 *(6f,Kem,SS,Oct 5)*
Basingstoke 109 *(7f,Sth,SD,Mar 15)*
Bastille Day 107 *(8f,Kem,SD,Jun 2)*
Battalion 115 *(10f,Lin,SD,Nov 30)*
Battle Of Marathon 108 *(10f,Lin,SD,Feb 27)*
Battlement 105 *(8f,Lin,SD,Oct 27)*
Bay Mirage 109 *(6f,Ncs,SD,Oct 28)*
Bayan Kasirga 110 *(12f,Wol,SD,Mar 31)*
Be My Sea 107 *(16f,Sth,SD,Apr 7)*
Be Perfect 108 *(14f,Wol,SD,Sep 27)*
Be Royale 107 *(6f,Ncs,SD,Nov 7)*
Beardwood 113 *(10f,Lin,SD,Nov 15)*
Beauty Sleep 105 *(10f,Cfd,SD,Aug 21)*
Berkshire 110 *(10f,Lin,SD,Nov 12)*
Berlusca 109 *(9½f,Wol,SD,Feb 5)*
Bermondsey 112 *(10f,Ncs,SD,Oct 16)*
Bertie Blu Boy 106 *(5f,Lin,SD,Apr 1)*
Bertiewhittle 109 *(7f,Lin,SD,Jan 22)*
Besharah 105 *(7f,Cfd,SD,Apr 16)*
Best Example 106 *(9f,Wol,SD,Jan 18)*
Big Amigo 106 *(6f,Kem,SD,Mar 16)*
Big Baz 105 *(8f,Lin,SD,Mar 25)*
Big Time 110 *(8f,Lin,SD,Feb 27)*
Bint Dandy 107 *(8f,Cfd,SD,Jun 1)*
Biotic 109 *(11f,Kem,SS,Sep 3)*
Blue Creek 108 *(8f,Mey,FT,Jan 30)*
Blue Surf 109 *(16½f,Wol,SD,Feb 8)*
Bluegrass Blues 109 *(10f,Lin,SD,Dec 5)*
Bold Prediction 112 *(8f,Lin,SD,Feb 27)*
Bollihope 108 *(10f,Ncs,SD,Nov 29)*
Boom The Groom 118 *(5f,Wol,SD,Feb 22)*
Boomerang Bob 110 *(6f,Cfd,SD,Oct 26)*
Boonga Roogeta 106 *(10f,Cfd,SD,Jan 3)*
Boots And Spurs 106 *(8f,Sth,SD,Jan 10)*
Borough Boy 110 *(6f,Kem,SD,Feb 24)*
Bosham 115 *(5f,Wol,SD,Feb 22)*
Both Sides 105 *(10f,Cfd,SD,May 4)*
Bouclier 107 *(6f,Kem,SD,Mar 16)*
Bowson Fred 110 *(5f,Ncs,SD,Jun 24)*
Brabbham 108 *(10f,Mey,FT,Feb 25)*
Brandybend 105 *(10f,Lin,SD,Dec 17)*
Brasted 108 *(10f,Lin,SD,Feb 17)*
Bravo Zolo 111 *(9½f,Wol,SD,Feb 29)*
Brazen Spirit 109 *(6f,Kem,SS,Sep 7)*
Bridey's Lettuce 107 *(10f,Ncs,SD,Dec 16)*
Brigliadoro 110 *(10f,Cfd,SD,Nov 3)*
Brilliant Vanguard 107 *(6f,Kem,SS,Nov 1)*
Brocklebank 108 *(10f,Lin,SD,Jan 27)*
Brother Tiger 109 *(5f,Cfd,SD,Feb 7)*
Buccaneers Vault 106 *(6f,Ncs,SD,Oct 18)*
Buckland Beau 107 *(10f,Cfd,SD,Jan 3)*
Buckstay 106 *(7f,Cfd,SD,Aug 15)*
Bunbury 109 *(10f,Lin,SD,Dec 18)*
Buratino 105 *(6f,Ncs,SD,Jun 25)*
Burcan 110 *(12f,Lin,SD,Dec 31)*
Burning Blaze 106 *(7f,Sth,SD,Jan 21)*
Burning Thread 107 *(5f,Wol,SD,Jan 8)*
Burnside 109 *(16f,Lin,SD,Dec 18)*
Bush Warrior 111 *(5f,Wol,SD,Mar 2)*
Busy Street 108 *(11f,Sth,SD,Mar 10)*
Buying Trouble 106 *(7f,Wol,SD,Mar 27)*
Byronegetonefree 106 *(16f,Ncs,SD,Jun 4)*

C Note 105 *(7f,Cfd,SD,Dec 22)*
Cacica 110 *(12f,Wol,SD,Oct 1)*
Cadeau Magnifique 108 *(9f,Wol,SD,Dec 12)*
Cadeaux Pearl 105 *(7f,Sth,SD,Mar 15)*
Caeser The Gaeser 108 *(6f,Ncs,SD,Oct 28)*
Cahar Fad 107 *(9½f,Wol,SD,Mar 7)*
California Chrome 117 *(10f,Mey,FT,Mar 26)*
California Lad 105 *(9½f,Wol,SD,Jly 11)*
Callendula 107 *(12f,Wol,SD,Oct 21)*
Calypso Choir 107 *(5f,Kem,SS,Nov 9)*
Candy Boy 112 *(10f,Mey,FT,Mar 26)*
Cantankerous 106 *(16½f,Wol,SD,Apr 8)*
Cape Cova 106 *(12f,Lin,SD,Jly 13)*
Cape Crystal 106 *(10f,Cfd,SD,Sep 22)*
Cape Icon 105 *(8f,Kem,SD,May 18)*
Cape Of Glory 109 *(10f,Cfd,SD,Jan 3)*
Capelita 108 *(8f,Kem,SD,Apr 13)*
Capo Rosso 112 *(9f,Wol,SD,Apr 9)*
Captain Cat 111 *(10f,Lin,SD,Feb 6)*
Captain Dion 109 *(6f,Cfd,SD,Dec 1)*
Captain Joy 110 *(8f,Lin,SD,Mar 25)*
Captain Lars 107 *(5f,Wol,SD,Dec 22)*
Captain Navarre 108 *(11f,Kem,SD,Mar 26)*
Captain Revelation 109 *(7f,Sth,SD,Dec 20)*
Cardinal Walter 110 *(16f,Ncs,SD,Jun 25)*
Carolinae 105 *(8f,Lin,SD,Nov 11)*
Carry Me Home 106 *(10f,Lin,SD,Mar 9)*
Case Key 105 *(5f,Wol,SD,Mar 27)*
Caspian Prince 110 *(5f,Ncs,SD,Dec 21)*
Castilo Del Diablo 112 *(11f,Kem,SD,Mar 26)*
Castle Harbour 107 *(8f,Lin,SD,Nov 12)*
Cat Royale 110 *(11f,Kem,SS,Sep 3)*
Cayirli 112 *(11f,Kem,SD,Mar 26)*
Celtic Ava 109 *(10f,Lin,SD,Feb 22)*
Certificate 106 *(7f,Sth,SD,Jan 5)*
Chain Of Daisies 107 *(10f,Ncs,SD,Jun 24)*
Charismatic Man 107 *(12f,Wol,SD,Nov 26)*
Charles Molson 108 *(7f,Cfd,SD,Nov 17)*
Charlie Bear 116 *(11f,Kem,SS,Sep 3)*
Charlies Mate 115 *(11f,Kem,SS,Sep 3)*
Chester Street 107 *(8f,Cfd,SD,Dec 8)*
Chetan 107 *(6f,Cfd,SD,Aug 23)*
Chevallier 106 *(8f,Cfd,SD,Nov 21)*
Chookie Royale 110 *(6f,Kem,SD,Jan 13)*
Choral Clan 105 *(10f,Lin,SD,Nov 16)*
City Chic 106 *(9f,Wol,SD,Oct 1)*
City Dreams 112 *(16½f,Wol,SD,Mar 29)*
City Of Angkor Wat 105 *(6f,Wol,SD,Mar 7)*
Claim The Roses 109 *(7f,Sth,SD,Mar 30)*
Classical Rose 105 *(8f,Lin,SD,May 17)*
Clear Water 107 *(6f,Wol,SD,Oct 1)*
Clement 107 *(7f,Lin,SD,Feb 6)*
Cliff Face 109 *(12f,Kem,SD,Nov 16)*
Cloud Seven 105 *(8f,Kem,SD,Apr 13)*
Cloudberry 111 *(8f,Kem,SS,Sep 2)*
Clovelly Bay 105 *(12f,Lin,SD,Dec 14)*
Clubland 109 *(6f,Sth,SD,Feb 9)*
Coarse Cut 107 *(12f,Kem,SS,Aug 1)*
Cocoa Beach 107 *(6f,Ncs,SD,Jly 23)*
Coillte Cailin 113 *(9½f,Wol,SD,Feb 5)*
Cold As Ice 106 *(6f,Lin,SD,Feb 6)*
Colourbearer 106 *(6f,Cfd,SD,Mar 31)*
Column 105 *(8f,Kem,SS,Oct 18)*
Combative 113 *(10f,Lin,SD,Apr 20)*
Come Back King 108 *(11f,Sth,SD,Dec 20)*
Come On Dave 108 *(5f,Cfd,SD,Jan 28)*
Commodore 109 *(8f,Kem,SD,Apr 13)*
Communicator 107 *(12f,Wol,SD,Jan 18)*
Compas Scoobie 107 *(6f,Ncs,SD,Nov 14)*
Complicit 113 *(10f,Lin,SD,Feb 27)*
Confrontation 107 *(8f,Mey,FT,Feb 4)*
Consulting 115 *(6f,Ncs,SD,Dec 15)*
Cool Cowboy 112 *(8f,Mey,FT,Mar 26)*
Cool Strutter 106 *(7f,Ncs,SD,Sep 2)*
Coorg 107 *(13f,Cfd,SD,Jan 6)*
Coronation Day 105 *(7f,Kem,SS,Oct 12)*
Corporal Maddox 106 *(7f,Lin,SD,Jan 20)*
Corton Lad 108 *(9½f,Wol,SD,Feb 5)*
Cosmic Chatter 105 *(6f,Ncs,SD,Nov 8)*
Cosmic Halo 108 *(10f,Lin,SD,Feb 22)*
Cote D'Azur 107 *(10f,Cfd,SD,Jly 19)*
Coto 107 *(5f,Ncs,SD,May 17)*
Countermeasure 106 *(8f,Kem,SD,Jun 2)*
Craftsmanship 109 *(10f,Cfd,SD,Sep 1)*
Crazy Chic 107 *(7f,Kem,SD,Apr 2)*
Crew Cut 106 *(6f,Cfd,SD,Jun 15)*
Crimean Tatar 105 *(12f,Kem,SS,Nov 23)*
Criminalistic 112 *(7f,Mey,FT,Nov 3)*
Crosse Fire 107 *(5f,Sth,SD,Jan 26)*
Cryptic 107 *(8f,Kem,SS,Oct 18)*
Curbyourenthusiasm 105 *(14f,Cfd,SD,Nov 5)*
Curious Fox 106 *(6f,Kem,SS,Sep 2)*

Daily Bulletin 108 *(8f,Cfd,SD,Sep 11)*
Daisy Bere 107 *(8f,Sth,SD,Feb 10)*
Daisy Boy 107 *(13f,Cfd,SD,Apr 28)*
Dakota City 106 *(12f,Lin,SD,Jan 30)*
Dana's Present 106 *(8f,Kem,SS,Oct 26)*
Dance Of Fire 107 *(10f,Kem,SD,Mar 9)*
Danglydontask 106 *(16f,Lin,SD,Mar 9)*
Dannyday 118 *(13f,Cfd,SD,Apr 28)*
Dark Side Dream 107 *(6f,Ncs,SD,Nov 14)*
Darma 105 *(6f,Kem,SD,Apr 13)*
Dartmouth 108 *(13f,Cfd,SD,Apr 16)*
Decisive 106 *(6f,Cfd,SD,Aug 20)*
Dehbashi 105 *(10f,Mey,FT,Dec 15)*
Delagoa Bay 107 *(16½f,Wol,SD,Dec 3)*
Demonstration 112 *(11f,Kem,SD,Jun 22)*
Denmead 105 *(12f,Kem,SS,Aug 1)*
Desdichado 105 *(11f,Kem,SS,Sep 3)*
Desert Force 107 *(7f,Mey,FT,Dec 1)*
Desert Morning 107 *(8f,Lin,SD,Feb 22)*
Desert Strike 107 *(6f,Kem,SD,Jan 17)*
Desktop 105 *(16½f,Wol,SD,Mar 15)*
Destroyer 106 *(8f,Kem,SS,Aug 24)*
Devon Drum 106 *(14f,Wol,SD,Sep 27)*
Dhahmaan 111 *(6f,Kem,SS,Oct 5)*
Diamond Charlie 108 *(5f,Kem,SD,Feb 17)*
Diamond Geyser 107 *(12f,Lin,SD,Jun 25)*
Diletta Tommasa 109 *(12f,Wol,SD,Oct 1)*
Dilgura 105 *(7f,Sth,SD,Mar 23)*
Discreet Hero 107 *(5f,Wol,SD,Mar 27)*
Distant Past 117 *(5f,Ncs,SD,Dec 21)*
Divisionist 108 *(9f,Wol,SD,Aug 4)*
Doc Sportello 107 *(6f,Ncs,SD,Dec 16)*
Docket 109 *(7f,Mey,FT,Nov 3)*
Doctor Parkes 108 *(6f,Kem,SD,Feb 1)*
Doctor Sardonicus 109 *(6f,Cfd,SD,Oct 26)*
Dolphin Village 112 *(11f,Kem,SD,Jun 22)*
Dominium 112 *(6f,Kem,SD,Mar 23)*
Dommersen 109 *(8f,Kem,SS,Aug 17)*
Donjuan Triumphant 109 *(7f,Cfd,SD,Dec 22)*
Dornoch 106 *(7f,Mey,FT,Jan 1)*
Dougan 110 *(6f,Wol,SD,Oct 1)*
Dovils Date 105 *(16½f,Wol,SD,Aug 5)*
Down Time 107 *(16f,Sth,SD,Apr 7)*
Dr Drey 105 *(10f,Lin,SD,Jan 29)*
Drago 110 *(9½f,Wol,SD,Nov 11)*
Dragon King 113 *(6f,Ncs,SD,Nov 8)*
Dragon Mall 109 *(7f,Cfd,SD,Dec 22)*

Dream Dubai 108 *(6f,Lin,SD,Apr 9)*
Dream Of Summer 109 *(8f,Kem,SS,Oct 19)*
Dream Spirit 105 *(9f,Wol,SD,Jan 18)*
Dubai Fashion 113 *(10f,Ncs,SD,Oct 16)*
Duck A L'Orange 105 *(12f,Kem,SS,Oct 26)*
Dukes Den 107 *(16½f,Wol,SD,Apr 8)*
Dukes Meadow 106 *(10f,Cfd,SD,Mar 10)*
Dune Dancer 106 *(11f,Kem,SS,Aug 24)*
Dungannon 110 *(5f,Sth,SD,Jan 1)*
Dunquin 106 *(9½f,Wol,SD,Nov 11)*
Dutch Art Dealer 106 *(8f,Kem,SD,Apr 13)*
Dutch Golden Age 106 *(6f,Cfd,SD,Oct 27)*
Dutch Uncle 113 *(11f,Kem,SD,Mar 26)*
Dutiful Son 108 *(7f,Kem,SD,Feb 3)*
Dynamo Walt 113 *(5f,Ncs,SD,Dec 10)*

Early Morning 110 *(8f,Lin,SD,Apr 20)*
East Coast Lady 105 *(10f,Cfd,SD,Sep 29)*
Easy Tiger 106 *(7f,Lin,SD,Apr 9)*
Ecureuil 111 *(10f,Cfd,SD,Sep 1)*
Edgar Balthazar 105 *(8f,Ncs,SD,Nov 4)*
Educate 115 *(10f,Lin,SD,Nov 12)*
Egyptian 109 *(8f,Cfd,SD,Jly 19)*
El Campeon 105 *(16f,Lin,SD,Dec 28)*
El Viento 107 *(6f,Cfd,SD,Dec 15)*
Eleuthera 109 *(6f,Cfd,SD,Feb 25)*
Eljaddaaf 106 *(6f,Kem,SD,Jun 29)*
Elusive Cowboy 105 *(12f,Wol,SD,Dec 26)*
Elusivity 110 *(5f,Wol,SD,Mar 2)*
Elysian Fields 107 *(12f,Kem,SD,Jun 29)*
Elysian Prince 110 *(10f,Lin,SD,Feb 17)*
Emell 106 *(8f,Lin,SD,Mar 5)*
Emirates Flyer 108 *(9½f,Mey,FT,Jan 7)*
Encapsulated 110 *(6f,Cfd,SD,Jan 13)*
Encipher 108 *(7f,Mey,FT,Jan 28)*
Encore D'Or 112 *(5f,Cfd,SD,Nov 21)*
Encore Moi 106 *(7f,Lin,SD,Nov 30)*
Endless Acres 105 *(12f,Lin,SD,Jly 13)*
Energia Davos 110 *(10f,Lin,SD,Nov 12)*
Enery 105 *(10f,Mey,FT,Jan 30)*
Enjoy Life 109 *(6f,Ncs,SD,Nov 4)*
Enmeshing 107 *(9½f,Wol,SD,Nov 11)*
Ennaadd 114 *(8f,Kem,SD,Nov 16)*
Entsar 105 *(10f,Cfd,SD,Aug 2)*
Epeius 109 *(6f,Ncs,SD,Oct 28)*
Epsilon 110 *(7f,Mey,FT,Nov 3)*
Equally Fast 107 *(5f,Lin,SD,Apr 1)*
Erhaaf 112 *(10f,Cfd,SD,Nov 3)*
Estrella Eria 105 *(10f,Cfd,SD,Oct 26)*
Etijaah 114 *(10f,Mey,FT,Nov 3)*
Evervescent 107 *(9½f,Wol,SD,Mar 7)*
Exalted 109 *(7f,Kem,SD,May 25)*
Exchequer 108 *(7f,Lin,SD,Apr 9)*
Eyeshine 107 *(12f,Kem,SS,Aug 22)*

Faithful Creek 113 *(9f,Wol,SD,Nov 26)*
Falcon's Song 105 *(11f,Kem,SS,Sep 3)*
Fanciful Angel 108 *(7f,Cfd,SD,Dec 22)*
Farrier 107 *(8f,Mey,FT,Dec 15)*
Fashion Design 108 *(12f,Wol,SD,Aug 5)*
Fashion Parade 106 *(12f,Kem,SS,Oct 26)*
Fast Play 106 *(16f,Lin,SD,Dec 14)*
Fast Track 117 *(5f,Wol,SD,Feb 22)*
Fastnet Blast 105 *(10f,Kem,SD,Dec 20)*
Faulkner 112 *(8f,Mey,FT,Mar 26)*
Fearless Lad 110 *(10f,Lin,SD,Jun 7)*
Fergall 111 *(11f,Kem,SS,Sep 2)*
Festive Fare 118 *(10f,Lin,SD,Feb 27)*
Fever Few 105 *(6f,Cfd,SD,Feb 25)*
Field Of Vision 108 *(6f,Kem,SD,Jan 17)*
Fiftyshadesfreed 108 *(11f,Kem,SS,Sep 28)*
Final 108 *(7f,Sth,SD,Jan 21)*
Final Venture 107 *(6f,Wol,SD,Dec 26)*
Fine 'n Dandy 105 *(5f,Cfd,SD,May 4)*
Fine Example 105 *(7f,Ncs,SD,Sep 2)*
Finelcity 107 *(8f,Kem,SS,Sep 12)*
Fingal's Cave 110 *(9f,Wol,SD,Nov 26)*
Finn Class 105 *(7f,Ncs,SD,May 17)*
Fire Fighting 117 *(10f,Lin,SD,Feb 27)*
Firmament 110 *(8f,Cfd,SD,Aug 2)*
Firmdecisions 106 *(7f,Cfd,SD,Oct 13)*
First Bombardment 106 *(5f,Ncs,SD,Oct 7)*
First Mohican 116 *(16f,Ncs,SD,Dec 21)*
First Summer 106 *(9f,Wol,SD,Apr 8)*
Fitzgerald 113 *(8f,Mey,FT,Dec 15)*
Flambeuse 111 *(10f,Lin,SD,Nov 12)*
Flashman 105 *(16f,Lin,SD,Jan 23)*
Fleckerl 109 *(6f,Lin,SD,Mar 1)*
Fleeting Visit 110 *(11f,Kem,SS,Sep 21)*
Flinty Fell 106 *(8f,Ncs,SD,Aug 26)*
Flowers On Venus 105 *(6f,Wol,SD,Oct 1)*
Fly 106 *(8f,Kem,SS,Sep 2)*
Flymetothestars 109 *(8f,Sth,SD,Feb 2)*
For Ayman 107 *(6f,Cfd,SD,Jan 13)*
Force Of Destiny 105 *(16f,Lin,SD,Apr 4)*
Forceful Appeal 110 *(8f,Lin,SD,Jan 16)*
Forecaster 107 *(10f,Cfd,SD,Sep 29)*
Four On Eight 107 *(11f,Kem,SS,Aug 24)*
Foxtrot Knight 105 *(5f,Cfd,SD,Jly 11)*
Franco's Secret 108 *(8f,Kem,SD,Feb 10)*
Franklin D 107 *(10f,Lin,SD,Feb 20)*
Free Zone 111 *(6f,Cfd,SD,Sep 11)*
Freud 108 *(10f,Cfd,SD,Mar 10)*

Frosted 115 *(9½f,Mey,FT,Feb 4)*
Frosty Berry 108 *(16f,Lin,SD,Feb 17)*
Frozen Force 105 *(8f,Kem,SS,Oct 18)*
Fujin 107 *(6f,Ncs,SD,Oct 28)*
Full Day 109 *(12f,Wol,SD,Mar 31)*
Fullon Clarets 109 *(7f,Ncs,SD,May 17)*
Furia Cruzada 119 *(10f,Lin,SD,Feb 27)*
Futoon 105 *(5f,Ncs,SD,Aug 4)*
Fuwairt 107 *(7f,Ncs,SD,Dec 10)*

Gabrial The Duke 106 *(12f,Lin,SD,Jan 30)*
Gabrial The Hero 107 *(16f,Ncs,SD,Jun 25)*
Gabrial's Kaka 106 *(8f,Cfd,SD,Apr 16)*
Gabrial's King 108 *(16f,Ncs,SD,Jun 25)*
Gallipoli 106 *(7f,Lin,SD,Dec 7)*
Gamgoom 108 *(6f,Lin,SD,Feb 6)*
Gang Warfare 111 *(16f,Ncs,SD,Dec 21)*
Gavlar 106 *(16f,Ncs,SD,Jun 25)*
Gawdawpalin 109 *(12f,Wol,SD,Oct 21)*
Generalship 107 *(8f,Kem,SD,Jly 6)*
Gentlemen 112 *(6f,Cfd,SD,Jan 13)*
George William 106 *(7f,Cfd,SD,Oct 22)*
Georgian Bay 111 *(8f,Kem,SS,Sep 3)*
Gerry The Glover 108 *(7f,Ncs,SD,May 17)*
Giantstepsahead 110 *(11f,Kem,SD,Mar 26)*
Giftorm 109 *(7f,Mey,FT,Jan 28)*
Giovanni Di Bicci 106 *(8f,Kem,SD,Jan 27)*
Glan Y Gors 106 *(16½f,Wol,SD,Jan 29)*
Glasgon 105 *(12½f,Ncs,SD,Oct 28)*
Glastonberry 105 *(6f,Kem,SD,Jan 11)*
Gloryette 106 *(16½f,Wol,SD,Dec 3)*
God Willing 111 *(9f,Wol,SD,Nov 26)*
Going Up 105 *(14f,Wol,SD,Nov 25)*
Goken 105 *(6f,Lin,SD,Mar 25)*
Gold Beau 106 *(6f,Kem,SD,Mar 16)*
Gold City 111 *(9½f,Mey,FT,Feb 4)*
Gold Club 109 *(6f,Cfd,SD,Apr 7)*
Gold Flash 109 *(9f,Wol,SD,Aug 4)*
Gold Sands 111 *(9f,Wol,SD,Aug 4)*
Golden Amber 107 *(7f,Cfd,SD,Dec 22)*
Golden Wedding 108 *(7f,Kem,SD,May 25)*
Goldenfield 110 *(10f,Cfd,SD,Aug 23)*
Good Contact 105 *(10f,Mey,FT,Jan 14)*
Good Run 107 *(16f,Ncs,SD,Nov 28)*
Gorokai 111 *(6f,Kem,SD,Mar 16)*
Gothic Empire 106 *(7f,Kem,SD,May 25)*
Graceland 115 *(13f,Cfd,SD,Apr 28)*
Gracious John 114 *(5f,Ncs,SD,Dec 21)*
Grand Argentier 108 *(8f,Mey,FT,Feb 11)*
Grand Beauty 109 *(5f,Cfd,SD,May 4)*
Grand Meister 105 *(16½f,Wol,SD,Jan 29)*
Great Glen 110 *(12f,Wol,SD,Oct 15)*
Great Page 108 *(7f,Lin,SD,Mar 5)*
Grendisar 121 *(10f,Lin,SD,Feb 27)*
Grey Destiny 108 *(7f,Sth,SD,Mar 15)*
Grey Mirage 113 *(8f,Lin,SD,Nov 12)*
Greyfriarschorista 111 *(6f,Kem,SD,Feb 24)*
Groundworker 109 *(5f,Ncs,SD,Sep 29)*
Grumeti 106 *(16f,Ncs,SD,Jun 25)*
Guard of Honour 113 *(16f,Ncs,SD,Dec 21)*
Guishan 107 *(5f,Cfd,SD,Nov 21)*
Gun Case 106 *(7f,Ncs,SD,Oct 28)*
Gun Pit 106 *(10f,Mey,FT,Mar 5)*
Gurkha Friend 107 *(7f,Ncs,SD,May 17)*

Haaf A Sixpence 105 *(7f,Sth,SD,Dec 20)*
Haalan 106 *(10f,Cfd,SD,Oct 26)*
Haalick 113 *(7f,Lin,SD,Mar 5)*
Hackney Road 106 *(6f,Ncs,SD,Nov 25)*
Haines 112 *(16f,Ncs,SD,Jun 25)*
Hakam 114 *(6f,Cfd,SD,Sep 11)*
Hallelujah 105 *(6f,Kem,SD,Jan 13)*
Hallstatt 108 *(16½f,Wol,SD,Dec 3)*
Hamelin 110 *(12f,Lin,SD,Dec 17)*
Handsome Dude 108 *(6f,Ncs,SD,Nov 8)*
Handsome Man 109 *(10f,Mey,FT,Nov 3)*
Happy Call 107 *(6f,Lin,SD,May 6)*
Happy Jack 106 *(12f,Wol,SD,Mar 31)*
Hard Toffee 105 *(10f,Lin,SD,Oct 27)*
Harmonic Wave 105 *(5f,Ncs,SD,Dec 15)*
Harwoods Volante 109 *(6f,Kem,SS,Oct 4)*
Have A Nice Day 109 *(7f,Lin,SD,Jan 22)*
Hayward Field 107 *(11f,Kem,SD,Jun 8)*
Hazel Blue 105 *(9f,Wol,SD,Mar 18)*
He's No Saint 108 *(7f,Lin,SD,Dec 7)*
Head Space 107 *(6f,Kem,SD,Feb 1)*
Heart Locket 106 *(14f,Wol,SD,Feb 12)*
Heavy Metal 108 *(7f,Mey,FT,Feb 25)*
Helfire 105 *(7f,Lin,SD,Jly 30)*
Hepplewhite 106 *(10f,Cfd,SD,Mar 17)*
Heraldic 110 *(6f,Kem,SD,Mar 16)*
Here Comes When 107 *(8f,Kem,SD,Nov 16)*
Hermitage Bay 108 *(8f,Sth,SD,Feb 2)*
Hernando Torres 108 *(9½f,Wol,SD,Jan 25)*
High Admiral 106 *(12f,Wol,SD,Oct 15)*
High Baroque 112 *(10f,Lin,SD,Dec 5)*
High Command 106 *(12½f,Ncs,SD,Oct 14)*
High On Light 106 *(12½f,Ncs,SD,Dec 15)*
Higher Power 114 *(11f,Kem,SD,Jun 22)*
Highland Acclaim 108 *(6f,Cfd,SD,Oct 26)*
Hightime Girl 105 *(10f,Ncs,SD,Dec 16)*
His Kyllachy 105 *(12f,Kem,SS,Sep 19)*
Hokko Tarumae 108 *(10f,Mey,FT,Mar 26)*

Hold Tight 108 *(6f,Lin,SD,Jan 16)*
Hollywood Road 109 *(11f,Kem,SS,Sep 28)*
Hombre Rojo 110 *(8f,Lin,SD,Jan 9)*
Home Cummins 105 *(6f,Lin,SD,Oct 27)*
Hoofalong 116 *(5f,Wol,SD,Feb 22)*
Hoppertunity 113 *(10f,Mey,FT,Mar 26)*
Horsforth 110 *(5f,Ncs,SD,Sep 29)*
House Of Commons 107 *(9f,Wol,SD,Dec 12)*
Humphrey Bogart 105 *(8f,Kem,SD,Apr 2)*
Hunting Ground 108 *(9½f,Mey,FT,Jan 7)*
Huntlaw 105 *(8f,Cfd,SD,Sep 11)*
Huntsmans Close 108 *(5f,Cfd,SD,Nov 21)*

I Am Not Here 105 *(12½f,Ncs,SD,Dec 9)*
I'm Harry 107 *(12f,Lin,SD,Mar 5)*
I'm Super Too 106 *(7f,Sth,SD,Mar 15)*
Ian's Memory 106 *(7f,Sth,SD,Feb 16)*
Iberica Road 109 *(8f,Kem,SS,Sep 2)*
Idol Deputy 107 *(9½f,Wol,SD,Feb 15)*
Iguacu 109 *(16½f,Wol,SD,Feb 15)*
Ijmaaly 113 *(10f,Cfd,SD,Nov 3)*
Ikerrin Road 107 *(7f,Wol,SD,Mar 27)*
Illusive 109 *(8f,Lin,SD,Feb 27)*
Ilzam 105 *(9f,Wol,SD,Jly 25)*
Impeccability 106 *(16½f,Wol,SD,Mar 29)*
India's Song 110 *(9f,Wol,SD,Feb 1)*
Indira 106 *(12f,Wol,SD,Mar 19)*
Indulged 110 *(11f,Kem,SS,Sep 28)*
Intense Tango 109 *(12½f,Ncs,SD,Jly 23)*
Interpret 107 *(10f,Mey,FT,Nov 3)*
Intransigent 109 *(6f,Kem,SD,Jan 13)*
Intrude 107 *(9f,Wol,SD,Mar 12)*
Invincible Diamond 105 *(6f,Kem,SD,Mar 26)*
Invincible Wish 106 *(12f,Wol,SD,Apr 16)*
Irish Optimism 105 *(8f,Cfd,SD,Oct 20)*
Iseemist 105 *(6f,Lin,SD,Mar 1)*
Isharah 109 *(12f,Wol,SD,Jly 5)*
Island Flame 108 *(12½f,Ncs,SD,Dec 30)*

Jacbequick 112 *(10f,Lin,SD,Dec 5)*
Jack Of Diamonds 105 *(8f,Kem,SS,Sep 3)*
Jack's Revenge 105 *(7f,Sth,SD,Dec 20)*
Jacob's Pillow 106 *(6f,Cfd,SD,Feb 25)*
Jailawi 111 *(8f,Lin,SD,May 7)*
Jameerah 107 *(6f,Wol,SD,Aug 4)*
Jammy Guest 107 *(8f,Kem,SD,Apr 13)*
Jarir 109 *(10f,Lin,SD,Jan 29)*
Jaywalker 113 *(6f,Ncs,SD,Nov 8)*
Jebediah Shine 109 *(5f,Cfd,SD,Jan 24)*
Jodies Jem 110 *(8f,Kem,SD,Apr 13)*
Joey's Destiny 107 *(7f,Lin,SD,Dec 7)*
John Caesar 108 *(9f,Wol,SD,Apr 8)*
John Reel 113 *(16f,Lin,SD,Feb 17)*
Johnny B Goode 105 *(7f,Cfd,SD,Sep 15)*
Jolievitesse 105 *(12f,Kem,SD,Jan 6)*
Jordan Sport 109 *(6f,Wol,SD,Dec 16)*
Judicial 111 *(5f,Wol,SD,Feb 22)*
Jumbo Prado 106 *(9f,Wol,SD,Dec 12)*
Just That Lord 112 *(5f,Wol,SD,Mar 27)*
Justice First 109 *(8f,Kem,SD,Feb 10)*
Justice Good 112 *(6f,Kem,SS,Nov 23)*

Kadrizzi 108 *(5f,Wol,SD,Mar 4)*
Kalkrand 106 *(10f,Lin,SD,Jan 7)*
Kashmir Peak 105 *(12f,Wol,SD,Jan 18)*
Keen Ice 111 *(10f,Mey,FT,Mar 26)*
Kelinni 108 *(7f,Wol,SD,Mar 12)*
Kenny The Captain 114 *(6f,Ncs,SD,Nov 8)*
Keystroke 115 *(9f,Wol,SD,Nov 26)*
Kicking The Can 106 *(9f,Wol,SD,Apr 8)*
Kifaah 108 *(6f,Mey,FT,Jan 28)*
Kilt Rock 108 *(7f,Mey,FT,Jan 1)*
Kimberella 109 *(6f,Lin,SD,Nov 12)*
King Robert 110 *(6f,Ncs,SD,Nov 8)*
Kinglami 105 *(6f,Kem,SS,Sep 2)*
Kirkman 105 *(16½f,Wol,SD,Apr 8)*
Knife Edge 108 *(7f,Cfd,SD,Apr 16)*
Knight Music 111 *(12f,Lin,SD,Mar 30)*

L'Inganno Felice 108 *(9½f,Wol,SD,Jan 25)*
Lacan 108 *(8f,Lin,SD,Mar 5)*
Ladurelli 108 *(11f,Kem,SS,Aug 3)*
Lady Lydia 107 *(7f,Lin,SD,Nov 30)*
Lady Makfi 106 *(16½f,Wol,SD,Aug 5)*
Lady Nayef 110 *(5f,Ncs,SD,Dec 15)*
Lamar 111 *(10f,Lin,SD,Feb 6)*
Lancelot Du Lac 111 *(5f,Cfd,SD,Jan 2)*
Lani 107 *(9½f,Mey,FT,Mar 26)*
Laqab 105 *(10f,Ncs,SD,Oct 16)*
Lat Hawill 110 *(7f,Ncs,SD,May 17)*
Lawyer 105 *(8f,Ncs,SD,Nov 4)*
Layl 107 *(8f,Mey,FT,Jan 7)*
Layla's Hero 110 *(6f,Kem,SS,Sep 7)*
Lazzam 105 *(8f,Cfd,SD,Aug 2)*
Le Bernardin 108 *(8f,Mey,FT,Jan 7)*
Lean On Pete 107 *(12f,Wol,SD,Feb 19)*
Les Gar Gan 108 *(9½f,Wol,SD,Mar 7)*
Let Me In 108 *(9½f,Wol,SD,Mar 7)*
Let's Twist 105 *(7f,Ncs,SD,Aug 26)*
Let'sgoforit 105 *(6f,Mey,FT,Jan 14)*
Lexington Times 109 *(7f,Lin,SD,Mar 4)*

Librisa Breeze 113 *(9f,Wol,SD,Apr 9)*
Life Knowledge 105 *(10f,Ncs,SD,Dec 16)*
Life Less Ordinary 113 *(11f,Kem,SD,Jun 22)*
Light From Mars 105 *(7f,Kem,SD,May 25)*
Light Up Our World 105 *(7f,Cfd,SD,Apr 16)*
Lightning Charlie 106 *(6f,Lin,SD,Apr 29)*
Lightscameraction 108 *(5f,Cfd,SD,Jan 2)*
Line Of Reason 114 *(5f,Ncs,SD,Dec 21)*
Little Stampy 111 *(16½f,Wol,SD,Feb 15)*
Llewellyn 110 *(7f,Sth,SD,Jan 21)*
Loaded 107 *(7f,Kem,SS,Aug 16)*
Logans Lad 107 *(7f,Wol,SD,Feb 1)*
London 105 *(10f,Cfd,SD,Nov 3)*
Long Water 116 *(7f,Mey,FT,Nov 3)*
Lord Ben Stack 105 *(10f,Cfd,SD,Nov 3)*
Lord George 113 *(11f,Kem,SS,Sep 2)*
Lord Of The Land 113 *(6f,Kem,SS,Oct 5)*
Lorelei 111 *(16½f,Wol,SD,Apr 8)*
Lovely Memory 109 *(8f,Lin,SD,Apr 20)*
Loyalty 110 *(8f,Lin,SD,Feb 27)*
Luis Vaz De Torres 106 *(6f,Lin,SD,Mar 1)*
Lunar Deity 111 *(8f,Lin,SD,Feb 13)*
Lusory 107 *(10f,Cfd,SD,Oct 26)*
Luv U Whatever 109 *(16f,Lin,SD,Feb 17)*
Lyfka 107 *(7f,Lin,SD,Nov 30)*

Macho Mac 107 *(7f,Sth,SD,Dec 13)*
Magical Daze 106 *(6f,Ncs,SD,Nov 4)*
Magnus Maximus 111 *(6f,Cfd,SD,Aug 21)*
Majestic Moon 110 *(7f,Lin,SD,Mar 4)*
Major Crispies 106 *(8f,Kem,SD,Jun 2)*
Major Rowan 108 *(12½f,Ncs,SD,Aug 4)*
Makzon 107 *(11f,Mey,FT,Mar 5)*
Malaysian Boleh 108 *(6f,Cfd,SD,Apr 7)*
Man Of Harlech 106 *(10f,Lin,SD,Mar 25)*
Manatee Bay 110 *(6f,Ncs,SD,Nov 4)*
Mange All 106 *(8f,Cfd,SD,Mar 10)*
Manipura 108 *(6f,Cfd,SD,Aug 20)*
Manjaam 108 *(9½f,Wol,SD,Apr 1)*
Manson 112 *(10f,Cfd,SD,Nov 3)*
Mappin Time 111 *(5f,Ncs,SD,Dec 10)*
Marenko 108 *(8f,Kem,SD,Apr 2)*
Markaz 113 *(6f,Ncs,SD,Jun 25)*
Market Rally 105 *(9½f,Mey,FT,Mar 5)*
Marking 111 *(6f,Mey,FT,Feb 25)*
Marmajuke Bay 107 *(12f,Kem,SS,Oct 26)*
Marmalad 105 *(9½f,Wol,SD,Jan 25)*
Marmelo 106 *(12f,Kem,SD,Jun 2)*
Marshall Aid 111 *(14f,Wol,SD,Sep 27)*
Marshgate Lane 110 *(11f,Sth,SD,Apr 12)*
Master Gunner 106 *(9f,Wol,SD,Sep 3)*
Master The World 115 *(10f,Lin,SD,Nov 12)*
Masterpaver 111 *(13f,Cfd,SD,Apr 28)*
Maverick Wave 120 *(10f,Lin,SD,Feb 27)*
Maverik 105 *(10f,Lin,SD,Feb 17)*
Maximian 107 *(6f,Lin,SD,Apr 9)*
Mayasa 110 *(12f,Wol,SD,Jly 5)*
Mazaz 106 *(12f,Kem,SD,Jun 2)*
Mazzini 112 *(6f,Ncs,SD,Aug 29)*
Meadway 107 *(5f,Ncs,SD,Dec 10)*
Meandmyshadow 110 *(6f,Ncs,SD,Oct 28)*
Medicean Man 106 *(6f,Lin,SD,Nov 12)*
Medicine Hat 112 *(16½f,Wol,SD,Dec 3)*
Megara 105 *(16f,Lin,SD,Jan 15)*
Melvin The Grate 108 *(8f,Lin,SD,Jan 16)*
Memories Galore 112 *(5f,Ncs,SD,Dec 10)*
Mengli Khan 113 *(11f,Kem,SS,Sep 21)*
Merhoob 110 *(6f,Cfd,SD,Apr 7)*
Metropol 114 *(10f,Lin,SD,Nov 12)*
Mezmaar 110 *(6f,Kem,SD,Feb 24)*
Mia Tesoro 107 *(9f,Wol,SD,Oct 1)*
Michele Strogoff 111 *(9f,Wol,SD,Nov 26)*
Mickey Haller 106 *(7f,Kem,SD,May 25)*
Midtech Star 111 *(12f,Lin,SD,Mar 5)*
Milrow 106 *(10f,Cfd,SD,Jan 3)*
Min Alemarat 106 *(16f,Ncs,SD,Jun 25)*
Mindurownbusiness 111 *(9f,Wol,SD,Feb 8)*
Minstrels Gallery 106 *(14f,Wol,SD,May 9)*
Miracle Garden 110 *(5f,Kem,SD,Feb 17)*
Mise En Rose 108 *(8f,Cfd,SD,Jun 1)*
Mishaal 108 *(6f,Kem,SD,Mar 26)*
Miss Giler 107 *(12f,Lin,SD,Feb 19)*
Miss Minuty 107 *(12f,Wol,SD,Oct 21)*
Miss Tiger Lily 109 *(16f,Lin,SD,Dec 14)*
Miss Van Gogh 105 *(9f,Wol,SD,Nov 26)*
Mister Bob 105 *(16f,Ncs,SD,Sep 23)*
Mister Music 109 *(8f,Kem,SS,Sep 2)*
Mister Parma 106 *(8f,Mey,FT,Nov 3)*
Mister Universe 112 *(8f,Lin,SD,Mar 5)*
Mitchum Swagger 105 *(7f,Cfd,SD,Aug 15)*
Mithqaal 112 *(7f,Sth,SD,Dec 20)*
Mitre Peak 109 *(9f,Wol,SD,Feb 1)*
Mizbah 108 *(11f,Mey,FT,Jan 1)*
Modernism 109 *(10f,Lin,SD,Jan 9)*
Mohatem 114 *(11f,Kem,SS,Sep 28)*
Monaleen 112 *(16f,Lin,SD,Feb 17)*
Money Team 110 *(6f,Cfd,SD,Jan 3)*
Mont Ras 111 *(9f,Wol,SD,Apr 9)*
Montsarrat 105 *(9f,Wol,SD,Mar 25)*
Monumental Man 106 *(5f,Cfd,SD,Sep 8)*
Moon Over Mobay 105 *(16f,Lin,SD,Dec 18)*
Moon River 111 *(7f,Sth,SD,Mar 16)*
Moonlight Venture 111 *(7f,Sth,SD,Feb 16)*
Moonlightnavigator 108 *(8f,Lin,SD,Feb 27)*

Moonraker 107 (6f,Ncs,SD,Jun 25)
Moonrise Landing 112 (16f,Lin,SD,Mar 25)
Moonshine Ridge 108 (16f,Sth,SD,Apr 7)
Moosir 106 (8f,Mey,FT,Dec 15)
Morawij 109 (6f,Mey,FT,Dec 15)
More Beau 108 (6f,Ncs,SD,Nov 7)
More Mischief 108 (10f,Ncs,SD,Jun 24)
More Spice 107 (5f,Lin,SD,Mar 1)
Moscato 108 (16f,Ncs,SD,Jun 25)
Mossgo 107 (5f,Kem,SD,Feb 17)
Mothers Finest 106 (8f,Ncs,SD,Jun 23)
Mountain Rescue 108 (8f,Kem,SS,Oct 18)
Mr Boss Man 108 (14f,Wol,SD,Feb 12)
Mr Bossy Boots 110 (7f,Lin,SD,Jan 22)
Mr Lupton 107 (6f,Ncs,SD,Jun 25)
Mr Red Clubs 107 (9½f,Wol,SD,Feb 26)
Mrs Burbidge 108 (16½f,Wol,SD,Apr 8)
Mshawish 112 (10f,Mey,FT,Mar 26)
Muarrab 113 (6f,Mey,FT,Mar 5)
Mubtaahij 114 (10f,Mey,FT,Mar 26)
Muffri'Ha 108 (8f,Lin,SD,Oct 27)
Muhtaram 111 (7f,Mey,FT,Nov 3)
Muhtaris 106 (12f,Sth,SD,Jan 10)
Mukaabra 109 (9f,Wol,SD,Oct 1)
Mukaynis 107 (6f,Kem,SD,Apr 2)
Munaaser 108 (9½f,Mey,FT,Feb 4)
Munjally 105 (7f,Ncs,SD,Sep 2)
Muntahaa 110 (12f,Kem,SD,Jun 2)
Music Man 108 (11f,Kem,SD,Mar 2)
Mustaaqeem 108 (8f,Cfd,SD,Aug 2)
Mustajeer 110 (10f,Cfd,SD,Oct 6)
Mustallib 108 (6f,Ncs,SD,Jly 23)
Mustaqqil 107 (9f,Wol,SD,Aug 4)
Mustique 105 (9f,Wol,SD,Oct 1)
Mutahaddith 109 (6f,Mey,FT,Nov 3)
Mutamid 105 (7f,Kem,SD,Jun 2)
Mutawathea 110 (7f,Lin,SD,Mar 4)
My Call 109 (7f,Cfd,SD,Jan 16)
My Catch 119 (6f,Mey,FT,Dec 15)
My Dad Syd 112 (6f,Ncs,SD,Dec 15)
My Reward 106 (16f,Ncs,SD,Jun 25)
My Target 115 (8f,Lin,SD,Nov 12)
Mystical Sapphire 106 (7f,Kem,SD,May 25)
Mystical Spirit 108 (8f,Kem,SD,Feb 10)
Mythical Madness 114 (9f,Wol,SD,Nov 26)
Mythmaker 111 (6f,Lin,SD,Nov 12)

Naadirr 105 (6f,Ncs,SD,Jun 25)
Nakeeta 106 (16f,Ncs,SD,Jun 25)
Nasri 106 (6f,Kem,SD,Jan 13)
Nathr 111 (8f,Mey,FT,Nov 3)
Natural Scenery 113 (12f,Wol,SD,Oct 21)
Nawwaar 106 (6f,Mey,FT,Jan 7)
Nearly Caught 108 (16f,Ncs,SD,Jun 25)
New Agenda 105 (9f,Wol,SD,Mar 15)
Next Train's Gone 105 (10f,Lin,SD,Apr 20)
Nezwaah 111 (10f,Ncs,SD,Jun 24)
Niblawi 109 (12f,Wol,SD,Oct 15)
Niceofyoutotellme 110 (10f,Lin,SD,Nov 15)
Nimr 109 (6f,Wol,SD,Dec 2)
Noble Deed 108 (6f,Kem,SD,Jan 17)
Noble Gift 106 (10f,Kem,SD,Mar 26)
Nonios 110 (11f,Kem,SS,Sep 3)
Normal Equilibrium 105 (6f,Lin,SD,Jan 7)
North Creek 107 (8f,Kem,SS,Aug 24)
Northgate Lad 106 (7f,Ncs,SD,Jun 23)
Nortron 107 (7f,Lin,SD,Jan 20)
Notarised 113 (16f,Lin,SD,Feb 17)
Nouvelli Dancer 106 (9f,Wol,SD,Oct 1)
Novis Adventus 109 (12f,Lin,SD,Dec 17)
Nuno Tristan 113 (6f,Cfd,SD,Feb 11)

Oakley Girl 110 (9f,Wol,SD,Feb 1)
Obboorr 107 (12f,Wol,SD,Feb 19)
Ocean Eleven 106 (10f,Cfd,SD,Sep 22)
Ocean Legend 105 (6f,Lin,SD,Feb 22)
Ocean Telegraph 105 (6f,Mey,FT,Nov 3)
Ode To Fortune 110 (8f,Lin,SD,Apr 9)
Off The Pulse 111 (9½f,Wol,SD,Feb 5)
On A Whim 107 (12f,Wol,SD,Mar 31)
One Man Band 117 (8f,Mey,FT,Mar 26)
Open The Red 108 (11f,Kem,SS,Sep 3)
Orient Class 107 (5f,Wol,SD,Mar 2)
Oriental Fox 113 (16f,Ncs,SD,Dec 21)
Oriental Relation 108 (6f,Wol,SD,Dec 10)
Orion's Bow 112 (5f,Ncs,SD,Jun 24)
Ornate 106 (5f,Lin,SD,Jan 5)
Our Channel 112 (10f,Cfd,SD,Jan 16)
Outer Space 107 (8f,Lin,SD,May 7)
Outrage 109 (5f,Kem,SD,Dec 20)
Over The Ocean 107 (7f,Mey,FT,Feb 25)
Ower Fly 106 (7f,Kem,SS,Oct 19)
Owners Day 106 (10f,Lin,SD,Jun 7)

Pactolus 110 (11f,Kem,SD,Mar 26)
Paddys Motorbike 110 (12f,Wol,SD,Jan 18)
Padlock 106 (7f,Mey,FT,Jan 16)
Page Of Wands 105 (10f,Ncs,SD,Dec 16)
Palawan 106 (8f,Lin,SD,Apr 9)
Palisade 114 (10f,Ncs,SD,Oct 16)
Papa Luigi 105 (6f,Kem,SD,Jun 8)
Papou Tony 106 (8f,Kem,SD,Feb 24)
Paris Magic 105 (12½f,Ncs,SD,Dec 30)
Parkour 106 (6f,Cfd,SD,Dec 1)
Parnell's Dream 105 (12f,Lin,SD,Jun 7)
Pass The Time 107 (16½f,Wol,SD,Feb 15)
Passing Star 106 (8f,Lin,SD,Dec 31)
Patent 106 (8f,Mey,FT,Nov 3)
Patrick 109 (6f,Cfd,SD,May 4)
Patriotic 105 (11f,Sth,SD,Apr 12)
Pearl Acclaim 107 (5f,Cfd,SD,Jan 24)
Pearl Castle 108 (16f,Lin,SD,Jan 23)
Pearl Noir 109 (5f,Wol,SD,Mar 2)
Pearl Spectre 107 (7f,Cfd,SD,Nov 21)
Pearly Prince 108 (10f,Lin,SD,Jun 7)
Pecking Order 111 (12½f,Ncs,SD,Jly 23)
Peeps 105 (12f,Lin,SD,Feb 19)
Pensax Lad 110 (5f,Wol,SD,Jan 8)
Perfect Cracker 112 (9½f,Wol,SD,Feb 5)
Peril 111 (7f,Ncs,SD,May 17)
Persuasive 111 (8f,Cfd,SD,Jun 1)
Petite Jack 107 (10f,Lin,SD,Oct 27)
Philba 109 (7f,Sth,SD,Dec 20)
Philosopher 111 (8f,Mey,FT,Nov 3)
Piazon 105 (5f,Sth,SD,Dec 20)
Picket Line 106 (6f,Kem,SD,Apr 13)
Pike Corner Cross 105 (8f,Kem,SS,Aug 16)
Pinzolo 114 (12f,Lin,SD,Dec 17)
Pirate's Treasure 108 (8f,Sth,SD,Feb 10)
Planetaria 105 (8f,Ncs,SD,Nov 4)
Planetoid 105 (16f,Lin,SD,Apr 1)
Plantagenet 107 (9½f,Mey,FT,Jan 21)
Play Nicely 105 (12f,Sth,SD,Jan 10)
Plucky Dip 111 (6f,Kem,SD,Mar 26)
Plutocracy 111 (14f,Wol,SD,Sep 27)
Point North 114 (5f,Wol,SD,Mar 2)
Point Of View 107 (12f,Kem,SD,Jun 2)
Polar Forest 105 (12½f,Ncs,SD,Dec 30)
Polar River 110 (7f,Mey,FT,Jan 14)
Port Paradise 105 (10f,Lin,SD,Oct 27)
Possible Future 108 (10f,Cfd,SD,Aug 7)
Pour La Victoire 107 (6f,Kem,SD,Jan 17)
Power Game 111 (11f,Kem,SS,Sep 2)
Poyle Thomas 112 (16f,Ncs,SD,Jun 25)
Poyle Vinnie 111 (5f,Ncs,SD,Dec 10)
Prayer For Relief 108 (9½f,Mey,FT,Feb 4)
Prayer Time 106 (11f,Sth,SD,Mar 10)
Precision Five 106 (12f,Wol,SD,Jan 18)
Predilection 110 (8f,Lin,SD,Apr 9)
Prendergast Hill 107 (10f,Cfd,SD,Sep 1)
Presumido 109 (7f,Kem,SD,Mar 23)
Pretend 111 (6f,Ncs,SD,Jun 25)
Pretty Bubbles 106 (6f,Cfd,SD,Apr 14)
Primogeniture 106 (10f,Cfd,SD,Jun 16)
Primrose Valley 107 (7f,Lin,SD,Jan 22)
Prince Of Arran 109 (12f,Kem,SS,Nov 2)
Princess Cookie 108 (6f,Cfd,SD,Jan 21)
Princess Raihana 108 (10f,Cfd,SD,Sep 29)
Princess Tansy 106 (5f,Kem,SS,Nov 9)
Purple Rock 111 (10f,Lin,SD,Dec 5)
Pushaq 108 (9f,Wol,SD,Aug 4)

Qaffaal 109 (8f,Lin,SD,Dec 31)
Quality Song 110 (12f,Lin,SD,Mar 30)
Quality Time 106 (8f,Kem,SD,Apr 2)
Quatrieme Ami 106 (5f,Cfd,SD,Nov 21)
Queen's Novel 110 (11f,Kem,SS,Sep 3)
Questo 106 (5f,Ncs,SD,Sep 29)
Quiet Warrior 106 (6f,Cfd,SD,Sep 8)
Quintus Cerialis 108 (6f,Kem,SD,Mar 23)

Race Day 110 (7f,Lin,SD,Mar 5)
Rah Rah 105 (5f,Wol,SD,Mar 25)
Raising Sand 107 (10f,Cfd,SD,Oct 26)
Ralphy Lad 108 (12f,Sth,SD,Jan 26)
Rasmee 107 (12f,Wol,SD,Aug 5)
Rasmiya 106 (11f,Kem,SS,Aug 24)
Ravenous 106 (10f,Lin,SD,Feb 17)
Ravens Quest 105 (16f,Lin,SD,Dec 14)
Razin' Hell 112 (5f,Ncs,SD,Dec 10)
Razor Wind 106 (10f,Kem,SD,Mar 9)
Ready 112 (10f,Lin,SD,Nov 15)
Realize 112 (7f,Lin,SD,Jan 22)
Reaver 107 (8f,Kem,SS,Aug 24)
Rebel Surge 107 (7f,Lin,SD,Nov 30)
Red Cossack 105 (8f,Kem,SS,Oct 26)
Red Rannagh 110 (11f,Kem,SS,Sep 21)
Red Touch 107 (7f,Sth,SD,Mar 10)
Red Unico 107 (9½f,Wol,SD,Mar 7)
Regicide 111 (10f,Lin,SD,Apr 20)
Rehearse 108 (11f,Kem,SS,Aug 3)
Related 108 (6f,Kem,SD,Mar 26)
Renewing 107 (16½f,Wol,SD,Apr 8)
Replenish 112 (10f,Ncs,SD,Oct 16)
Respect Me 107 (9½f,Mey,FT,Jan 21)
Restorer 114 (12f,Kem,SS,Nov 2)
Revolutionist 111 (8f,Cfd,SD,Mar 10)
Reynaldothewizard 110 (6f,Mey,FT,Jan 14)
Rich Again 111 (6f,Kem,SD,Feb 24)
Rich Tapestry 112 (6f,Mey,FT,Feb 11)
Ride The Lightning 108 (12f,Wol,SD,Oct 1)
Right Touch 106 (7f,Ncs,SD,Dec 10)
Rigolleto 106 (6f,Kem,SD,Mar 16)
Rivellino 109 (6f,Lin,SD,Feb 6)
River Dart 105 (12f,Lin,SD,Dec 7)
Robert The Painter 107 (8f,Lin,SD,Jan 16)
Robin Of Navan 105 (12f,Kem,SS,Sep 3)
Robins Pearl 109 (9½f,Wol,SD,Jan 25)
Rockley Point 105 (7f,Cfd,SD,Oct 13)
Rockspirit 113 (10f,Cfd,SD,Oct 6)
Roman De Brut 105 (10f,Ncs,SD,Nov 29)
Romansh 105 (9½f,Mey,FT,Jan 21)
Room Key 105 (7f,Cfd,SD,Oct 13)
Rose Above 107 (16f,Lin,SD,Mar 9)
Rosenborg Rider 107 (6f,Kem,SD,Mar 16)
Rosental 107 (10f,Ncs,SD,Jun 24)
Ross 108 (7f,Mey,FT,Jan 28)
Rousayan 110 (9f,Wol,SD,Nov 26)
Royal Birth 116 (5f,Wol,SD,Feb 22)
Royal Marskell 110 (16f,Ncs,SD,Jun 25)
Royal Normandy 106 (6f,Kem,SD,Jan 11)
Royal Performer 106 (9f,Wol,SD,Mar 25)
Royal Reef 112 (14f,Wol,SD,Sep 27)
Royal Reserve 109 (10f,Cfd,SD,Sep 1)
Rubensian 107 (10f,Cfd,SD,Aug 7)
Rural Celebration 106 (5f,Ncs,SD,Oct 18)
Russian Realm 108 (7f,Lin,SD,Jan 22)
Rydan 111 (12f,Lin,SD,Dec 17)

Saigon City 107 (16f,Ncs,SD,Jun 25)
Saint Contest 110 (12f,Wol,SD,Oct 21)
Saint Honore 108 (10f,Lin,SD,Dec 18)
Saint Pois 111 (6f,Cfd,SD,Jan 13)
Sakhalin Star 105 (10f,Ncs,SD,Dec 16)
Sakhra 107 (16½f,Wol,SD,Dec 3)
Salmon Sushi 112 (12f,Wol,SD,Aug 16)
Sam Missile 110 (11f,Kem,SS,Sep 21)
San Quentin 107 (12f,Lin,SD,Mar 30)
Sandfrankskipsgo 108 (5f,Lin,SD,Feb 20)
Sandro Botticelli 105 (13f,Cfd,SD,Apr 16)
Sands Chorus 109 (9f,Wol,SD,Dec 12)
Santiburi Spring 106 (16f,Lin,SD,Dec 18)
Sarsted 109 (11f,Kem,SD,Jun 22)
Saucy Minx 106 (7f,Lin,SD,Feb 19)
Savannah Beau 108 (6f,Ncs,SD,Nov 14)
Saved My Bacon 110 (5f,Cfd,SD,Jan 28)
Sbraase 109 (12f,Wol,SD,Mar 31)
Scandicci 109 (7f,Mey,FT,Nov 3)
Scarlet Minstrel 106 (14f,Wol,SD,Mar 12)
Schoolboy Error 105 (12f,Lin,SD,Jun 25)
Scottish Glen 108 (8f,Lin,SD,May 7)
Scrutinise 107 (12f,Wol,SD,Oct 15)
Sea Of Flames 111 (8f,Lin,SD,Apr 9)
Sea Of Heaven 107 (16f,Ncs,SD,Jun 25)
Seagull Star 106 (11f,Sth,SD,Dec 20)
Seamour 109 (16f,Ncs,SD,Jun 25)
Seamster 105 (6f,Lin,SD,Feb 13)
Seanie 107 (7f,Wol,SD,Mar 12)
Searanger 106 (5f,Ncs,SD,Dec 15)
Searchlight 108 (6f,Lin,SD,Mar 1)
Second Serve 111 (12f,Wol,SD,Oct 21)
Secret Art 110 (9f,Wol,SD,Apr 9)
Secret Asset 105 (5f,Lin,SD,Feb 25)
Seek The Fair Land 105 (6f,Lin,SD,Apr 6)
Seeking Magic 108 (5f,Wol,SD,Nov 1)
Seismos 107 (16f,Ncs,SD,Jun 25)
Semra 105 (6f,Cfd,SD,Apr 14)
Sennockian Star 112 (11f,Kem,SS,Sep 2)
Senor George 106 (9½f,Wol,SD,Mar 7)
Serena Grae 105 (14f,Cfd,SD,Jun 15)
Seve 112 (5f,Wol,SD,Feb 22)
Seychelloise 113 (6f,Cfd,SD,Sep 11)
Shackled N Drawn 105 (5f,Cfd,SD,Apr 28)
Shakopee 111 (12f,Wol,SD,Oct 15)
Shalaman 105 (16f,Lin,SD,Mar 25)
Shamlan 105 (7f,Wol,SD,Apr 1)
Shamshon 107 (5f,Cfd,SD,Jly 11)
Sharpalo 105 (10f,Mey,FT,Nov 3)
Shawaahid 105 (9f,Wol,SD,Aug 8)
She Is No Lady 107 (14f,Cfd,SD,Jun 15)
Sheila's Buddy 110 (10f,Lin,SD,Jan 9)
Shell Bay 106 (12f,Kem,SD,Jun 29)
Shimba Hills 107 (10f,Lin,SD,Feb 17)
Shining Romeo 107 (10f,Lin,SD,Jun 7)
Shoofly 106 (12f,Wol,SD,Jly 5)
Shouranour 107 (7f,Ncs,SD,May 17)
Showboating 109 (7f,Sth,SD,Mar 16)
Showdaisy 112 (5f,Ncs,SD,Dec 10)
Showtime Star 105 (6f,Sth,SD,Feb 9)
Shypen 109 (7f,Lin,SD,Nov 30)
Shyron 111 (7f,Lin,SD,Jan 22)
Si Senor 111 (8f,Lin,SD,Feb 27)
Sign Of The Kodiac 110 (6f,Cfd,SD,Jun 1)
Silvanus 105 (5f,Cfd,SD,Oct 27)
Silver Quay 108 (14f,Wol,SD,Mar 25)
Sir Billy Wright 107 (6f,Sth,SD,Feb 9)
Sir Chauvelin 111 (16f,Ncs,SD,Jun 25)
Sir Dudley 106 (6f,Lin,SD,May 6)
Sir Maximilian 106 (6f,Kem,SD,Jan 13)
Sir Robert Cheval 105 (6f,Ncs,SD,Jun 25)
Sir Valentine 108 (12f,Kem,SS,Aug 22)
Sirius Prospect 108 (9f,Wol,SD,Feb 8)
Sixties Groove 108 (11f,Kem,SD,Jun 8)
Sizzler 105 (12f,Wol,SD,Jan 18)
Skeaping 106 (10f,Lin,SD,Apr 20)
Sky Hunter 105 (12f,Kem,SS,Sep 3)
Sky Jockey 105 (9½f,Mey,FT,Jan 16)
Sleepy Blue Ocean 105 (5f,Sth,SD,Mar 23)
Slingsby 112 (6f,Ncs,SD,Dec 15)
Sloane Avenue 106 (8f,Kem,SD,Feb 24)
Soie D'Leau 107 (5f,Ncs,SD,Jun 24)
Solar Deity 107 (9½f,Wol,SD,Jan 25)
Solar Flair 106 (7f,Kem,SD,Apr 2)
Solveig's Song 107 (10f,Kem,SD,Nov 16)
Somethingthrilling 111 (10f,Lin,SD,Nov 30)
Sophisticated Heir 107 (6f,Wol,SD,Sep 17)
Sound Of Freedom 105 (10f,Ncs,SD,Jun 24)
Soundstrings 105 (7f,Ncs,SD,Sep 29)
Southern Gailes 108 (10f,Cfd,SD,Aug 23)
Southern States 108 (16f,Lin,SD,Dec 18)
Southern Storm 106 (12½f,Ncs,SD,Jly 23)
Sovereign Bounty 107 (7f,Kem,SD,May 25)
Sovereign Debt 110 (7f,Wol,SD,Mar 12)
Spanish City 107 (6f,Ncs,SD,Oct 18)
Special Fighter 112 (10f,Mey,FT,Mar 26)
Special Season 109 (10f,Lin,SD,Nov 15)
Speedy Move 111 (6f,Mey,FT,Nov 3)
Spes Nostra 110 (9½f,Wol,SD,Feb 26)
Spicy Jam 110 (6f,Cfd,SD,Feb 11)
Spin Point 105 (10f,Lin,SD,Dec 18)
Spiritoftomintoul 109 (14f,Wol,SD,Feb 12)
Spiritual Star 107 (8f,Kem,SS,Oct 19)
Spring Loaded 113 (6f,Wol,SD,Dec 26)
Squire 105 (8f,Kem,SS,Oct 19)
St Mary'S 108 (10f,Cfd,SD,Aug 23)
Star Ascending 105 (12f,Wol,SD,Feb 23)
Star Storm 116 (12f,Kem,SS,Nov 2)
Starboard 108 (8f,Kem,SS,Sep 2)
Start Seven 105 (12f,Lin,SD,Feb 19)
State Law 107 (7f,Mey,FT,Jan 16)
Steal The Scene 107 (7f,Lin,SD,Jan 20)
Steel Train 108 (7f,Ncs,SD,Dec 10)
Steelriver 114 (5f,Wol,SD,Feb 22)
Stellarta 113 (6f,Kem,SD,Mar 23)
Stencive 106 (12f,Wol,SD,Jan 18)
Stetchworth 109 (10f,Cfd,SD,Mar 10)
Stetchworth Park 109 (10f,Lin,SD,Apr 20)
Steve Rogers 114 (16f,Ncs,SD,Dec 21)
Stocking 105 (5f,Wol,SD,Jan 8)
Stonecutter 111 (16f,Ncs,SD,Jun 25)
Storm Belt 113 (10f,Mey,FT,Dec 15)
Storm Rock 107 (11f,Kem,SS,Sep 2)
Stormardal 117 (8f,Mey,FT,Nov 3)
Stosur 105 (7f,Cfd,SD,Aug 7)
Straits Of Malacca 106 (7f,Lin,SD,Jun 18)
Street Act 106 (11f,Mey,FT,Jan 1)
Street Artist 105 (10f,Lin,SD,May 11)
Street Force 106 (7f,Sth,SD,Apr 12)
Strong Force 108 (10f,Lin,SD,Nov 15)
Stynes 105 (12f,Wol,SD,Mar 31)
Summer Chorus 106 (6f,Lin,SD,Jan 12)
Summer Icon 108 (7f,Lin,SD,Nov 30)
Summerinthecity 106 (6f,Lin,SD,Feb 22)
Sunblazer 111 (16½f,Wol,SD,Feb 8)
Sunset Dream 107 (8f,Cfd,SD,Aug 23)
Super Kid 108 (12f,Lin,SD,Jan 15)
Supersta 107 (9f,Wol,SD,Mar 12)
Suqoor 108 (6f,Cfd,SD,Jun 1)
Surewecan 105 (7f,Lin,SD,Jun 18)
Swift Cedar 110 (11f,Sth,SD,Mar 10)
Swing Easy 108 (10f,Lin,SD,Jan 9)
Swiss Cross 105 (6f,Lin,SD,Dec 28)
Swiss Lait 106 (10f,Ncs,SD,Dec 16)
Sydney Ruffdiamond 105 (7f,Kem,SS,Oct 19)

Taajub 107 (5f,Lin,SD,Feb 6)
Tadaawol 106 (6f,Ncs,SD,Nov 18)
Tadmir 106 (11f,Mey,FT,Jan 1)
Take Cover 105 (5f,Lin,SD,Feb 27)
Take The Helm 110 (7f,Lin,SD,Mar 5)
Take Two 106 (10f,Lin,SD,Oct 27)
Tan Arabiq 108 (9½f,Wol,SD,Nov 11)
Taneen 108 (6f,Kem,SS,Oct 5)
Tangramm 108 (12f,Wol,SD,Feb 19)
Taopix 107 (10f,Ncs,SD,Nov 29)
Taper Tantrum 110 (11f,Kem,SD,Jun 22)
Taqaareed 105 (12f,Kem,SD,Jun 29)
Taqdeer 107 (8f,Cfd,SD,Apr 16)
Taqneen 106 (8f,Mey,FT,Jan 30)
Tasleet 109 (7f,Cfd,SD,Apr 16)
Tatting 105 (11f,Sth,SD,Mar 3)
Tawdeea 105 (10f,Ncs,SD,May 17)
Team Talk 116 (10f,Lin,SD,Nov 12)
Telegram 106 (8f,Lin,SD,Jan 16)
Tellovoi 107 (6f,Ncs,SD,Nov 14)
Tempus Temporis 110 (9½f,Wol,SD,Feb 29)
Tenerezza 105 (10f,Cfd,SD,Sep 29)
Tenzing Norgay 106 (14f,Cfd,SD,Sep 1)
Tetradrachm 105 (12f,Lin,SD,May 6)
Thahab Ifraj 105 (11f,Sth,SD,Dec 20)
Thataboy 106 (5f,Wol,SD,Mar 2)
The Cashel Man 110 (16f,Ncs,SD,Jun 25)
The Hooded Claw 107 (6f,Ncs,SD,Nov 14)
The Lock Master 108 (12f,Sth,SD,Jan 26)
The Salmon Man 106 (10f,Kem,SD,Nov 16)
The Steward 107 (16½f,Wol,SD,Jan 29)
The Supreme 110 (7f,Lin,SD,Mar 5)
The Way You Dance 109 (9½f,Wol,SD,Mar 7)
Thello 108 (10f,Ncs,SD,Dec 16)
Third Time Lucky 108 (8f,Lin,SD,Dec 31)
Thomas Blossom 106 (16f,Lin,SD,Mar 9)
Tiger Jim 108 (7f,Ncs,SD,May 17)
Tigserin 105 (6f,Wol,SD,Aug 4)

Time Square 106 *(10f,Lin,SD,Feb 22)*
Timekeeping 106 *(12f,Kem,SD,Nov 16)*
Tiz Now Tiz Then 110 *(9½f,Mey,FT,Feb 18)*
To Eternity 110 *(12f,Wol,SD,Aug 5)*
Toboggan's Fire 105 *(9f,Wol,SD,Aug 19)*
Toga Tiger 108 *(9½f,Wol,SD,Jan 25)*
Tony Curtis 106 *(10f,Cfd,SD,Oct 6)*
Top Boy 113 *(5f,Cfd,SD,May 4)*
Top Clearance 107 *(10f,Mey,FT,Dec 15)*
Top Offer 105 *(7f,Wol,SD,Feb 22)*
Topaling 113 *(16½f,Wol,SD,Mar 29)*
Torreon 108 *(7f,Kem,SD,Mar 23)*
Tournament 106 *(7f,Kem,SD,May 25)*
Towerlands Park 106 *(11f,Kem,SS,Dec 7)*
Toymaker 107 *(9f,Wol,SD,Apr 8)*
Trending 107 *(12f,Wol,SD,Feb 19)*
Trinity Force 110 *(7f,Mey,FT,Nov 3)*
Trojan Rocket 113 *(6f,Kem,SD,Feb 24)*
Trust The Man 107 *(16f,Lin,SD,Dec 18)*
Truth Or Dare 109 *(10f,Kem,SD,Mar 9)*
Tullius 117 *(10f,Lin,SD,Feb 27)*
Turbine 113 *(7f,Ncs,SD,May 17)*
Tutu Nguru 111 *(7f,Lin,SD,Mar 5)*
Two Jabs 109 *(11f,Kem,SD,Mar 2)*

Ubla 106 *(8f,Kem,SS,Aug 10)*
Udontdodou 110 *(6f,Ncs,SD,Nov 8)*
Under Siege 110 *(6f,Kem,SD,Mar 23)*
Understory 107 *(10f,Lin,SD,Feb 22)*
Unex Modigliani 109 *(16½f,Wol,SD,Feb 15)*
Unforgiving Minute 113 *(9f,Wol,SD,Nov 26)*
Until Midnight 105 *(7f,Cfd,SD,Jan 14)*
Upavon 108 *(6f,Wol,SD,Dec 2)*
Upstaging 112 *(6f,Kem,SD,Mar 23)*
Uptight 105 *(5f,Sth,SD,Jan 19)*

Vale Dori 105 *(9½f,Mey,FT,Mar 26)*
Vallarta 105 *(7f,Ncs,SD,Aug 26)*
Van Dyke 107 *(10f,Lin,SD,Apr 20)*
Van Huysen 114 *(10f,Lin,SD,Dec 5)*
Varsovian 109 *(6f,Cfd,SD,Feb 11)*
Vastly 105 *(10f,Cfd,SD,Sep 22)*
Vedani 108 *(16½f,Wol,SD,Apr 8)*
Verne Castle 109 *(5f,Cfd,SD,Sep 8)*
Viewpoint 109 *(11f,Kem,SD,Jun 22)*
Vimy Ridge 106 *(5f,Lin,SD,Feb 20)*
Vincent's Forever 108 *(11f,Kem,SS,Aug 24)*
Vincenzo Coccotti 105 *(7f,Cfd,SD,Nov 10)*
Viserion 105 *(10f,Lin,SD,Feb 17)*
Viva Verglas 110 *(5f,Wol,SD,Mar 2)*
Vivre Pour Vivre 106 *(9f,Wol,SD,Mar 15)*
Volition 107 *(9f,Wol,SD,Oct 1)*
Volunteer Point 110 *(7f,Cfd,SD,Jan 16)*

Wahaab 110 *(6f,Ncs,SD,Dec 15)*
Wall Of Fire 107 *(7f,Ncs,SD,May 17)*
War Department 110 *(6f,Ncs,SD,Aug 29)*
War Story 105 *(7f,Cfd,SD,Apr 25)*
Warfare 109 *(10f,Lin,SD,Jan 9)*
Watchable 110 *(6f,Ncs,SD,Jun 25)*
Watersmeet 108 *(10f,Lin,SD,Feb 6)*
We Are Ninety 105 *(8f,Cfd,SD,Apr 25)*
Weald Of Kent 105 *(12f,Sth,SD,Feb 9)*
Welease Bwian 111 *(5f,Cfd,SD,May 4)*
Welford 109 *(10f,Cfd,SD,Aug 23)*
Welliesinthewater 107 *(7f,Sth,SD,Feb 4)*
Welsh Rose 105 *(6f,Wol,SD,Aug 4)*
West Coast Flyer 110 *(11f,Kem,SS,Aug 3)*
Western Hymn 117 *(12f,Kem,SS,Nov 2)*
What A Dandy 108 *(10f,Lin,SD,Jun 7)*
Whispering Warrior 110 *(10f,Lin,SD,Jan 27)*
White Shaheen 106 *(12f,Wol,SD,Jun 27)*
Whoopsy Daisy 105 *(10f,Cfd,SD,Mar 17)*
Wild Hacked 112 *(10f,Cfd,SD,Aug 23)*
Willytheconqueror 107 *(6f,Cfd,SD,Jun 1)*
Wimpole Hall 107 *(8f,Kem,SS,Sep 3)*
Wings of Desire 107 *(12f,Wol,SD,Apr 23)*
Winning Story 117 *(16f,Ncs,SD,Dec 21)*
Winter House 105 *(12f,Kem,SD,Jun 29)*
Winter Spice 106 *(16f,Lin,SD,Dec 14)*
Winterlude 111 *(10f,Lin,SD,Jan 27)*
Wolowitz 109 *(5f,Wol,SD,Mar 4)*
Wordiness 109 *(16f,Ncs,SD,Jun 25)*

X Y Jet 111 *(6f,Mey,FT,Mar 26)*

Yasir 107 *(16½f,Wol,SD,Dec 3)*
Yeeoow 110 *(6f,Kem,SD,Mar 26)*
Yes Daddy 107 *(16f,Lin,SD,Dec 14)*
Yorkidding 110 *(12f,Kem,SS,Nov 2)*
Yorkindred Spirit 108 *(12½f,Ncs,SD,Jly 23)*
Yorkshireman 108 *(16½f,Wol,SD,Feb 15)*
You're Fired 111 *(8f,Kem,SD,Nov 16)*
Yu Change 106 *(9½f,Mey,FT,Mar 26)*
Yul Finegold 105 *(10f,Cfd,SD,Mar 10)*

Zabeel Star 107 *(9½f,Wol,SD,Nov 11)*
Zac Brown 116 *(5f,Wol,SD,Feb 22)*
Zaeem 112 *(7f,Sth,SD,Jan 2)*
Zain Arion 106 *(12f,Lin,SD,Jun 25)*
Zain Emperor 108 *(10f,Lin,SD,Dec 18)*
Zakatal 107 *(14f,Wol,SD,Feb 12)*
Zambeasy 107 *(11f,Kem,SS,Sep 2)*
Zapper Cass 110 *(5f,Ncs,SD,Dec 10)*
Ziggys Star 106 *(8f,Kem,SD,Feb 1)*

TWO YEAR-OLDS - AW

Addicted To You 109 *(10f,Lin,SD,Dec 5)*
Al Boraq 109 *(7f,Mey,FT,Nov 3)*

Capezzano 110 *(7f,Mey,FT,Dec 15)*
Cosmo Charlie 114 *(7f,Mey,FT,Dec 15)*

Don't Lie Kitten 110 *(7f,Mey,FT,Nov 3)*

Equimou 105 *(5f,Cfd,SD,Jly 11)*
Erissimus Maximus 106 *(6f,Sth,SD,Nov 10)*

Holmeswood 108 *(6f,Ncs,SD,Oct 25)*

Intrepidly 105 *(7f,Kem,SS,Oct 5)*

Kananee 112 *(6f,Ncs,SD,Nov 17)*

Leap Of Hope 109 *(7f,Mey,FT,Nov 3)*

Mazeed 107 *(7f,Mey,FT,Dec 15)*
Mazyoun 109 *(6f,Ncs,SD,Oct 25)*
Monte Cinq 105 *(5f,Wol,SD,Nov 1)*
Mr Black 105 *(5f,Kem,SS,Sep 19)*
Mutahaady 107 *(6f,Ncs,SD,Nov 17)*

Naseem 110 *(10f,Lin,SD,Dec 5)*
Nuclear Power 107 *(6f,Ncs,SD,Nov 17)*

Parlance 106 *(7f,Cfd,SD,Oct 20)*
Parnassian 108 *(6f,Sth,SD,Nov 10)*
Peaceful Passage 108 *(10f,Lin,SD,Dec 5)*
Plead 112 *(10f,Lin,SD,Dec 5)*
Pulsating 105 *(6f,Sth,SD,Nov 10)*

Simmie 105 *(5f,Wol,SD,Aug 5)*
Spin Doctor 109 *(6f,Sth,SD,Nov 10)*
Spiritual Lady 107 *(6f,Cfd,SD,Aug 2)*
Sutter County 111 *(6f,Ncs,SD,Nov 17)*

The Blues Master 110 *(10f,Lin,SD,Dec 5)*
The Last Lion 105 *(6f,Kem,SS,Sep 3)*
The Statesman 110 *(10f,Lin,SD,Dec 5)*

White Royale 105 *(6f,Sth,SD,Nov 10)*

TWO YEAR-OLDS - Turf

Afandem 107 *(5f,Yor,G,Aug 20)*
Al Hamdany 105 *(8f,Pon,S,Oct 17)*
Aneen 107 *(7f,Cur,GY,Oct 10)*
Anfaass 105 *(6f,Don,GF,Nov 5)*
Apamurra 105 *(5f,Goo,G,Jun 3)*
Arcada 106 *(7f,Cur,YS,Aug 21)*
Ardad 110 *(5f,Cha,G,Oct 2)*

Battaash 105 *(5f,Nmk,GF,Oct 7)*
Battered 105 *(6f,Yar,GF,Sep 15)*
Best Of Days 105 *(7f,San,GF,Jly 20)*
Best Solution 107 *(8f,Nmk,G,Oct 8)*
Big Time Baby 108 *(5f,Yor,G,Aug 20)*
Billesdon Bess 106 *(7f,Sal,GS,Oct 10)*
Bletchley 105 *(6f,Asc,GS,Jun 17)*
Blue Point 110 *(6f,Yor,G,Aug 20)*
Bound 109 *(8f,Cur,G,Aug 20)*
Boynton 106 *(7f,Nmk,GF,Jly 9)*
Brave Anna 106 *(6f,Asc,GS,Jun 17)*
Butterflies 105 *(8f,Cur,G,Aug 28)*

Capri 106 *(8f,Cur,HY,Sep 25)*
Caravaggio 112 *(6f,Asc,S,Jun 14)*
Churchill 110 *(7f,Cur,YS,Aug 21)*
Clem Fandango 106 *(5f,Ayr,GS,Sep 16)*
Cliffs Of Moher 116 *(7f,Leo,Y,Oct 29)*
Colibri 105 *(7f,Bri,GS,Sep 5)*
Coronet 111 *(10f,Nmk,G,Oct 8)*
Cunco 110 *(10f,Nmk,G,Oct 8)*

D'bai 106 *(8f,Pon,S,Oct 17)*
Dabyah 105 *(8f,Cha,G,Oct 2)*
Dainty Dandy 106 *(6f,Asc,GF,Jly 23)*
Delectation 105 *(6f,Ayr,GS,Sep 17)*
Devil's Bridge 105 *(7f,Nmk,S,Jun 25)*
Diamond Bear 105 *(8f,Bri,G,Oct 13)*
Drumfad Bay 106 *(7f,Cur,YS,Aug 21)*

Eartha Kitt 105 *(6f,Hay,G,Oct 14)*
Elizabeth Browning 105 *(7f,Leo,Y,Oct 29)*
Equimou 109 *(5f,Don,GS,Sep 7)*
Euginio 105 *(10f,Nmk,G,Oct 8)*
Eziyra 108 *(8f,Cur,G,Aug 28)*

Fair Eva 113 *(6f,Asc,GF,Jly 23)*
Firefright 106 *(6½f,Nby,GS,Oct 21)*
Fly At Dawn 106 *(10f,Nmk,G,Oct 8)*

Gheedaa 106 *(6f,Don,GF,Nov 5)*
Golden Apollo 107 *(6f,Don,GF,Nov 5)*

Harbour Master 106 *(8f,Lin,GF,Jly 30)*
Harry Angel 108 *(6f,Nby,GS,Sep 17)*
Hawana 105 *(6f,Yar,GF,Sep 15)*
Hydrangea 111 *(7f,Cur,YS,Aug 21)*

I'm So Fancy 107 *(8f,Cur,G,Aug 20)*
Intelligence Cross 108 *(6f,Cur,G,Aug 28)*
Intricately 110 *(7f,Cur,YS,Aug 21)*

Kachess 111 *(5f,Goo,G,Jun 3)*
Key To My Heart 109 *(8f,Cur,G,Aug 20)*
Kilmah 107 *(6f,Asc,GF,Jly 23)*

Lady Aurelia 116 *(5f,Asc,S,Jun 15)*
Lady Clinch 105 *(8f,Cur,G,Aug 20)*
Lady Lambada 105 *(8f,Cur,G,Aug 20)*
Lancaster Bomber 107 *(7f,Nmk,G,Oct 8)*
Larchmont Lad 105 *(7f,Nmk,GF,Sep 22)*
Law And Order 106 *(7f,Nmk,GF,Aug 26)*
Legendary Lunch 106 *(5f,Don,G,Sep 9)*
Looting 105 *(5f,San,GF,Aug 19)*

Majoris 105 *(7f,Nmk,GF,Aug 6)*
Make Time 107 *(7f,Sal,S,Sep 28)*
Making Light 105 *(7f,Leo,Y,Oct 23)*
Medieval 105 *(6f,Asc,S,Jun 14)*
Mehmas 109 *(6f,Asc,S,Jun 14)*
Merry Banter 105 *(5f,Cat,GF,May 20)*
Miss Sugars 107 *(6f,Goo,G,Aug 30)*
Mister Trader 107 *(5f,Cur,YS,Mar 20)*
Mokarris 108 *(6f,Nby,GF,Jly 15)*
Montataire 109 *(8f,Sal,G,Aug 19)*
Mrs Danvers 109 *(5f,Nmk,GF,Oct 7)*
Mubtasim 105 *(6f,Yar,GF,Jun 30)*
Mujaazy 110 *(8f,Cur,G,Aug 20)*

National Defense 108 *(8f,Cha,G,Oct 2)*

Oh Grace 108 *(7f,Leo,GF,Jun 9)*
Orderofthegarter 109 *(7f,Leo,Y,Oct 29)*
Outre Mer 105 *(10f,Not,G,Sep 28)*

Paco's Angel 109 *(6f,Goo,G,Aug 30)*
Parfait 108 *(6½f,Nby,GS,Oct 21)*
Permian 110 *(10f,Nmk,G,Oct 8)*
Poet's Vanity 105 *(7f,Nmk,GF,Oct 7)*
Promise To Be True 106 *(7f,Sai,S,Oct 30)*
Psychedelic Funk 105 *(6f,Asc,S,Jun 14)*

Queen Kindly 107 *(6f,Yor,GF,Aug 18)*

Radio Silence 107 *(7f,Cur,YS,Aug 21)*
Rajar 105 *(6f,Goo,G,Aug 30)*
Really Special 107 *(8f,Nmk,GF,Oct 29)*
Rehana 109 *(7f,Cur,YS,Aug 21)*
Rhododendron 112 *(7f,Cur,YS,Aug 21)*
Roly Poly 106 *(6f,Yor,GF,Aug 18)*
Rosie Briar 106 *(6f,Don,G,Oct 22)*
Rusumaat 106 *(6f,Red,GF,May 16)*

Salouen 105 *(8f,Wdr,GF,Aug 7)*
Sea Of Grace 109 *(8f,Cur,G,Aug 28)*
Serengeti Sky 105 *(6f,Yar,GF,Sep 15)*
Silver Line 107 *(5f,Not,G,May 22)*
Sobetsu 107 *(8f,Nmk,G,Sep 17)*
Sofia's Rock 106 *(9f,Red,S,Oct 24)*
South Seas 108 *(7f,Sai,S,Oct 30)*
Spatial 105 *(7f,Nmk,GF,Aug 26)*
Spiritual Lady 107 *(6f,Nmk,S,Jun 24)*
Star Archer 105 *(10f,Nmk,G,Oct 8)*

Taamol 107 *(7f,Nmk,S,Jun 25)*
Tallulah Rose 105 *(6f,Asc,GF,Jly 23)*
The Last Lion 106 *(5f,Don,G,Sep 9)*
Thunder Snow 114 *(7f,Sai,S,Oct 30)*
Tomily 105 *(6f,Don,G,Oct 22)*
Tropical Rock 109 *(6f,Yar,GF,Sep 15)*

Van Der Decken 105 *(6f,Asc,S,Jun 14)*
Via Egnatia 108 *(8f,Nmk,GF,Oct 1)*
Victory Angel 105 *(6f,Don,GF,Nov 5)*

Waldgeist 105 *(10f,Sai,S,Oct 30)*
Waqt 106 *(5f,Goo,G,Jun 3)*
War Decree 105 *(7f,Nmk,GF,Jly 9)*
White Satin Dancer 112 *(8f,Leo,Y,Oct 23)*
Wild Irish Rose 107 *(8f,Cur,G,Aug 20)*
Wings Of Eagles 107 *(10f,Nmk,G,Oct 8)*
Wolf Country 105 *(8f,Yar,GS,Oct 10)*
Wuheida 106 *(8f,Cha,G,Oct 2)*

Xenobia 107 *(8f,Leo,Y,Oct 23)*

Yalawin 106 *(6½f,Nby,GS,Oct 21)*
Yalta 109 *(5f,Goo,G,Jly 27)*
Yucatan 105 *(8f,Cur,HY,Sep 25)*

Zainhom 105 *(8f,Nmk,G,Oct 8)*